A COMMENTARY ON THE
HOLY BIBLE

by
Matthew Poole

VOLUME III: MATTHEW-REVELATION

HENDRICKSON PUBLISHERS

ISBN 0-917006-28-3

ANNOTATIONS

ON THE

GOSPEL ACCORDING TO S. MATTHEW

THE ARGUMENT

THE whole revelation of the will of God to the children of men is usually called The Bible, that is, The book, (for the word Bible derives from the Greek Βίβλος or Βιβλίον,) with a note of eminency, being indeed the Book of books, so as Luther said well that he should wish all his books burned if he could know that men by them would be kept from reading the Scriptures. And to distinguish this from other books, we have (in the ordinary titles of our Bibles) added Holy, with respect to the authority, the matter, and end of it. This sacred book, with us Christians, is usually divided into the Old and New Testament: indeed the term Testament doth not so properly belong to the law and the prophets, as to the books of the evangelists, the Acts, and Epistles, &c. The title of New Testament in Greek is, ΤΗΣ ΚΑΙΝΗΣ ΔΙΑΘΗΚΗΣ ΑΠΑΝΤΑ; that is, the whole of the new disposition, or new law, or new covenant, or new testament. The word originally and primarily signifieth a disposition of things. In regard that, amongst men, things are ordered, or disposed, by a law, or by contract, or covenant, or by will and testament, the word hath been used to signify any of these. But in regard that until a testator be dead a testament is of no force, Christ having not come nor died before all the law and the prophets were finished, (I mean the writings containing the law, and what other holy men wrote by inspiration from God, which the Jews call the prophets, or the holy writings,) it is not so proper (but that use hath now obtained) to call those writings by the name of a Testament; especially considering, that a part of them (which contained the ceremonial law) was abolished by the Testator's death, and another great part of them fulfilled in his coming and dying. The name therefore of Testament doth most properly belong to the books of the evangelists, the Acts, and Epistles, which do not only contain the new law, (so far as it is new, either in respect of the full interpretation of the moral law, or in respect of the law concerning the worship of God under the gospel, and the government of the church,) but also the new covenant, which though made with Adam, first revealed to him, Gen. iii. 15, yet is more fully revealed in those books, and they are indeed the last will and testament of our blessed Lord and Saviour. These books do obviously divide themselves into the Gospels, the Acts of the apostles, the Epistles of the apostles, and the Revelation. The evangelists, or Gospels, are four, Matthew, Mark, Luke, John, whose books are called the Gospels, that is. books containing the good tidings (for so the word εὐαγγέλιον signifies) which was brought to all people, by the coming, life, and death of Christ, the history of which, as also his resurrection and ascension into heaven, they relate. So as they are not called evangelists, as the term signifieth such an extraordinary officer as is mentioned Eph. iv. 11, such a one as Philip was, Acts xxi. 8, and Timothy, 2 Tim. iv. 5; but as they were evangelical historiographers, writing the history, as well as publishing the mystery, of the gospel. Of these, Matthew and John were apostles, the other two only disciples to the apostles. In the account they give us of Christ, what he did, and what he said, we are not to expect either a full account of all he did or spake, (we are assured of the contrary, John xxi. 25,) nor yet an exact account of every speech in any one sermon, or all the circumstances of any of his actions: we must conceive of them, not as exact notaries, but such who wrote from their memories (not without the inspiration of the Holy Spirit). Hence it is manifest, that although they do not contradict one another, (that indeed were incompetent with the Spirit of truth, their common guide,) yet one evangelist hath what another hath not, and in the same piece of his history one hath more circumstances than another: and hardly any of them relate all things in the same order of time in which they were spoke or done, but set them down as their memory did serve them, keeping to the substance, and being less careful as to circumstances; so as where more evangelists relate the same history or sermon, what all say must be taken in to complete the history or discourse, so far as the Holy Spirit thought fit Christians should be acquainted with it; which is the method I have taken in my notes upon the Gospel according to St. Matthew. Matthew was the son of Alpheus, Mark ii. 14, called also Levi: by his employment he was a publican, that is, one who gathered custom for the Romans (which sort of people were generally hated, and perhaps none of the honestest men). Christ called him from the receipt of custom to be his disciple, Matt. ix. 9, 10; Mark ii. 14, 15. He was sent out as one of the twelve apostles, Matt. x. 3, so as he was both an eye and ear-witness of what he wrote. What became of him after Christ's ascension I cannot tell, not knowing what credit is to be given to what ecclesiastical historians say in the case who wrote three or four hundred years after. The time of his writing this Gospel is as uncertain; some say eight, some nine, some fifteen years after Christ's ascension. It hath been a question, also, whether he wrote in Hebrew or Greek: it is most probable that he (as the other evangelists) wrote it in Greek, though it hath been once or twice translated into Hebrew. Those who as to that question have a curiosity to know what is written on both sides, (not to mention other books,) may read enough in Mr. Pool's Prolegomena to this Gospel in his Synopsis Criticorum. The matter of his Gospel is principally the history of the birth, life, death, and resurrection of our Saviour. The passages after his resurrection and before his ascension are most fully related by St. John. Luke more fully relates the history of his birth, and what went before it. The history of the wise men coming from the east to inquire for Christ is related by Matthew alone; so are some parables, as that of the virgins, chap. xxv. &c.

CHAP. I

The genealogy of Christ from Abraham to Joseph, 1—17. *The miraculous conception of Mary: Joseph's doubts are satisfied by an angel, who declareth the name and office of Christ: Jesus is born,* 18—25.

THE book of the *generation of Jesus Christ, ᵇthe Son of David, ᶜthe son of Abraham.

ᵃ Luke 3. 23.
ᵇ Ps. 132. 11.
Is. 11. 1.
Jer. 23. 5.
ch. 22. 42.
John 7. 42.
Acts 2. 30. & 13. 23. Rom. 1. 3. ᶜ Gen. 12. 3. & 22. 18. Gal. 3. 16.

The book of the generation signifieth no more than the writing containing the genealogy or pedigree; for the Jews called all writings books. Thus, Jer. xxxii. 10,11, *the evidences of a purchase* are called the *book*. So Isa. l. 1, and Mark x. 4, the writings called a *bill of divorce* are both in the Hebrew and the Greek called a *book of divorce*. Thus in ecclesiastical courts still, the term libel (which signifieth a little book) is used. So as these words are not to be looked upon as the title to the whole Gospel according to St. Matthew, but only to the following pedigree of our Saviour's ancestors. *Of Jesus Christ;* of that person to whom the name of Jesus was given by the angel, as we shall hear further, ver. 20, 21, because he should *save his people from their sins* (for Jesus, as also Joshua, signifies a saviour or deliverer); and who also was the Christ, or the Messiah, prophesied of by Daniel, chap. ix. 25, 26, expected by the Jews, as doth appear from John i. 41 (for Messiah and Christ denoted the same person, John iv. 25); only Messiah was a Hebrew word, and Christ of Greek extraction, both signifying Anointed, and so God's designation of a person to the office of a priest, a prophet, or a king. *The Christ* signifieth a designation to all three. *The Son of David, the son of Abraham :* not the immediate Son of either, but, by a long traduction, lineally descended from both. Abraham was long before David, but is here put after him, either because he was a king, or because the Jews expected Messiah was to be *the Son of David;* or because the evangelist's design was to begin the pedigree from Abraham, whom he therefore last mentioneth. Both are named, because both were concerned in the promise of Christ. It was made to Abraham, Gen. xii. 3; xxii. 18: and to David renewed and enlarged, Psal. lxxxix. 36, 37. Hence it appeareth that the Jews looked that Christ should be *the Son of David*, Matt. xxii. 42; Mark xii. 35. Hence the evangelist puts David in the front. From Abraham the Jews derived themselves, they usually gloried they had Abraham to their father. The evangelist, by proving Christ to have descended from Abraham by Isaac, proveth him an Hebrew of the Hebrews, and to be descended from the seed to whom the promise was made; and by proving him the Son of David, he proves him *David's righteous Branch*, or *Branch of righteousness*, mentioned Jer. xxiii. 5, 6 ; xxxiii. 15, and so to have descended from the royal family.

2 ^dAbraham begat Isaac; and ^eIsaac begat Jacob; and ^fJacob begat Judas and his brethren ;

<small>d Gen. 21. 2, 3.
e Gen. 25.26.
f Gen. 29. 35.</small>

The evangelist reckoneth the genealogy of our Saviour by three periods, reckoning thrice fourteen descents. The first period began in Abraham, and ended in David. The second began in Solomon, and ended in Jehoiachin. The third began with Jehoiachin, and ended in Christ. Luke (as we shall see in its place) fetcheth our Saviour's line from Adam. From Abraham to David there is no difference betwixt Matthew and Luke, they both reckoned up the same fourteen persons, Luke iii. 32—34. But Luke repeating our Saviour's pedigree by his mother's side, and Matthew by his supposed father's side, Joseph, after David they must differ, Mary descending from David's family by his son Nathan, Joseph descending from him by Solomon. All interpreters agree that there are great difficulties about the genealogy of Christ, especially in reconciling Matthew and Luke; and the enemies of Christianity have in all times made their advantage of them, to weaken our faith as to the gospel: but Christians ought to consider, 1. That the Jews had without doubt perfect genealogies, and were more especially exact in keeping them as to the royal tribe of David, which was Judah, and the priestly tribe of Levi, that they might have a right king and high priest; and it cannot be expected that after seventeen hundred years almost we should make out genealogies as they could. 2. That they were very apt to make strifes about words and endless genealogies; as appears by the apostle's cautioning both Timothy and Titus against it, 1 Tim. i. 4; vi. 4; Tit. iii. 9. 3. That it had been a sufficient exception against Christ if they could have proved he had not lineally descended from David. 4. That though they cavilled at Christ for many things, yet they never made any such cavil. 5. That we are forbidden strife and endless labour about genealogy. And therefore it is the most unreasonable thing imaginable for us to make such little dissatisfactions grounds for us to question or disbelieve the gospel, because we cannot untie every knot we meet with in a pedigree. But in this first period no such difficulties occur; both the evangelists are agreed, and the Old Testament agrees with both. That Abraham begat Isaac (when he was an hundred years old) we are assured by Moses, Gen. xxi. 2, 5; that Isaac begat Jacob he also telleth us, Gen. xxv. 26. So also that Jacob begat Judah and his brethren, Gen. xxix. 35. Judah was Jacob's third son by Leah, and that son of whom dying Jacob prophesied, That *him should his brethren praise, and to him should his father's children bow down*. That the *sceptre should not depart from Judah, nor the lawgiver from between his feet, until Shiloh came; and unto him should the gathering of the people be*, Gen. xlix. 8—10. Though Saul, who was the first king of Israel, (given them in wrath,) was of the tribe of Benjamin, 1 Sam. ix. 21 ; yet David was of the tribe of Judah, in whose line the kingdom held unto the captivity. *And his brethren :* the brethren of Judah are here mentioned, being the heads of the Jewish nation : Christ descended from Judah.

3 And ^gJudas begat Phares and Zara of Thamar; and ^hPhares begat Esrom ; and Esrom begat Aram ;

<small>g Gen. 38. 27.
h Ruth 4.18, &c. 1 Chron. 2. 5, 9, &c.</small>

That *Judas begat Phares and Zara* (they were twins begot of Thamar his daughter-in-law, the relict of his son Er whom God slew, Gen. xxxviii. 7) appeareth from Gen xxxviii. 27—30. That *Phares begat Ezrom* appeareth from Ruth iv. 18; 1 Chron. ii. 5 ; and from the same texts appears also that *Ezrom begat Aram*, Ruth iv. 19; 1 Chron. ii. 9, where he is called *Ram*. Some may possibly be offended that amongst all the ancestors of Christ there are but three women named, and all of them such as had a great stain and blot upon their reputation. This *Thamar*, the mother of Phares and Zara, was blotted with incest, and Phares was one of the children begot in that incest. Rahab also is mentioned, ver. 5, whom the Scripture calleth an *harlot*, Josh. ii. 1 ; and Bathsheba was stained with adultery. But we ought to consider, 1. That (abating original corruption, which we indeed all derive from our parents) no man deriveth any intrinsic badness from the vice of his parents, though he may derive a blot upon his honour and reputation from it. 2. That this was one degree of our Saviour's humiliation. 3. That it was no way incongruous, that He who came into the world to die for great sinners, should be born of some that were such.

4 And Aram begat Aminadab ; and Aminadab begat Naasson ; and Naasson begat Salmon ;

This exactly agreeth with the Old Testament, Ruth iv. 19, 20; 1 Chron. ii. 10, 11; only it is there said that *Naasson* was *prince of the children of Judah*, Numb. i. 7; ii. 3, and *Salmon* is there called *Salma*.

5 And Salmon begat Booz of Rachab ; and Booz begat Obed of Ruth ; and Obed begat Jesse ;

6 And ⁱJesse begat David the king ;

<small>i 1 Sam. 16. 1. & 17. 12.</small>

This agreeth with Ruth iv. 22, and 1 Sam. xvi. 1, 13. Here now ariseth the first difficulty we meet with in this genealogy, and it is rather an appearance of a difficulty than a real one. *Salmon* being the son of Aminadab, who was the prince of the children of Judah in Moses's time, Salmon cannot be imagined to have lived later than in the times of Joshua. *Booz* seemeth to have lived in Eli's time, which (if chronologers count right) was three hundred years after : here are but four men wanted to take up these years, Salmon, Booz, Obed, Jesse. *Answ.* The world, according to chronologers, wanted but five of two thousand five hundred years old, when the Israelites (under the conduct of Joshua) entered into Canaan : we will suppose Salmon to have then been a young man. Eli is by them said to have lived about the two thousand eight hundred and tenth. So that the distance is three hundred and fifteen years. David is said to have been born in the two thousand eight hundred and sixtieth. So as from Salmon to David are three hundred and sixty-five years. Admit Salmon. Boaz, Obed, and Jesse to have each of them lived a hundred years, or upward, and this is no difficulty; nor can there be any absurdity in admitting this, if we consider the age and vigour of persons in that age of the world. Moses (though a man spent with travels and battles) lived one hundred and twenty years, Deut. xxxiv. 7. Caleb at eighty-five years was strong, and as fit for war as ever, Josh. iv. 11, 12. If we allow these four men the life of Moses they might live four hundred and eighty years, which might allow to each of them fifteen or sixteen years apiece for the concurrency of their lives with their parents, yet three hundred and sixty-five years might be well allowed for all their time : nor is it unreasonable for us to suppose, that God might allow those whom he intended thus to dignify a something longer life than the ordinary sort of men lived in that age of the world. So as the thing being neither naturally impossible (for in our age we see particular persons live upward of a hundred years) nor morally improbable, and directly affirmed in three or four texts, they must have a great mind to quarrel with a Divine revelation who question the truth of it upon such a pretence; especially considering that the lives of men in our declining and debauched age of the world, are no measures by which we can guess at the lives of extraordinary persons who lived near three thousand years ago. *David the king:* possibly that term is added to distinguish the David here intended from others of the same name; or because he was the first king of the tribe of Judah, to whom the sceptre of Israel was promised, Gen. xlix. 10; or the first king not given to the Israelites in wrath, as Saul was upon their murmuring against Samuel; or to show that Christ descended from that family, to whom the promise of the Messias was made, Jer. xxiii. 5, and a kingdom established for ever, Psal. lxxxix. 36, 37. Thus our evangelist hath given us the names in his first period of fourteen generations : Abraham, Isaac, Jacob, Judas, Phares, Esrom, Aram, Aminadab, Naasson, Salmon, Booz, Obed, Jesse, David.

k 2 Sam. 12. 24. —And ᵏDavid the king begat Solomon of her *that had been the wife* of Urias;

Solomon was not the eldest child of David by Bathsheba; that died, 2 Sam. xii. 22, 23. He was born after David had taken Bathsheba (who had been the wife of Uriah) for his wife, ver. 25, compared with 2 Sam. xi. 27.

l 1 Chron. 3 10, &c. 7 And ¹Solomon begat Roboam; and Roboam begat Abia; and Abia begat Asa;

This exactly agrees with the history of the Old Testament, 1 Kings xi. 43 (where he is called *Rehoboam*); he reigned but seventeen years, and died, 1 Kings xiv. 21, 31. Abijam his son reigned in his stead; he is here called *Abia;* but we shall observe frequent alteration of names, both as to the final terminations, and where the quiescent letters in Hebrew fall into the name. Abia, or Abijam, reigned but three years, and was succeeded by Asa his son, 1 Kings xv. 2, 8. Asa reigned forty-one years, 2 Chron. xvi. 13. So as these three princes reigned sixty years.

8 And Asa begat Josaphat; and Josaphat begat Joram; and Joram begat Ozias;

Jehoshaphat, here called *Josaphat,* in the Greek, (they having no letter to express the Hebrew ה by,) was the son of Asa, a good son of a good father, 2 Chron. xvii. 1, 2; he reigned twenty-five years, 1 Kings xxii. 42. Jehoram, here called *Joram,* succeeded him in his kingdom : he *slew his brethren; he walked in the ways of Ahab,* 2 Chron. xxi. 4, 6; he reigned but eight years, lived and died wickedly, and was buried infamously, 2 Chron. xxi. 19, 20. But here ariseth another difficulty from what is said, *Joram begat Ozias.* It is certain that he did not beget him immediately, for Uzziah was the fourth from Joram. Jehoram or Joram begat Ahaziah, he was his youngest son; he lived but one year as king, 2 Chron. xxii. 1, 2; then Athaliah usurped the kingdom for six years, not counting her usurpation. Joash the son of Ahaziah reigned forty years, 2 Chron. xxiv. 1. He dies, and Amaziah his son reigned in his stead, 2 Kings xii. 21. He was the father of Uzziah, 2 Chron. xxvi. 1, called *Azariah,* 2 Kings xiv. 21. So that when it is said, that *Joram begat Ozias,* we must only understand that Uzziah lineally descended from Joram : thus, ver. 1, Christ is called the *Son of David, the son of Abraham.* Thus the Jews said, *We have Abraham to our father;* and Elisabeth is said to be *of the daughters of Aaron,* Luke i. 5. But it is a greater question why the evangelist leaves out Ahaziah, Joash, and Amaziah, who were all three lawful princes, and rightly descended from the family of David. To pass by various conjectures, the best account I find given of it is this. 1. It is manifest the evangelist had a design to divide all the generations from Abraham to Christ into three periods. The first of which should contain the *growing state* of the Jewish commonwealth, till it came at the height, which was in David's time. The second should contain its *flourishing state;* which was from David's time till the first carrying into captivity. The third should contain its *declining state,* from the first carrying them into captivity to the coming of Christ. 2. He designed to reduce all the generations in each period to fourteen; this appeareth from ver. 17. Now although the first period contained exactly fourteen descents or generations, yet in the second there was manifestly seventeen, so as the evangelist was obliged to leave out three to bring them to the number of fourteen : now though it be a little too curious to inquire why the evangelist chose to leave out these three, Ahaziah, Joash, and Amaziah, rather than any other three, yet there is a probable good account of it given by learned men, who have waded into these speculations. Ahaziah was the son of Jehoram by Athaliah the daughter of Ahab, 2 Chron. xxi. 6; Joash her grandchild; Amaziah her great-grandchild. Now God had cursed the house of Ahab, and threatened to root out all his house, 1 Kings xxi. 21. This (as is supposed) made the evangelist, who was necessitated to leave out three to bring the generations to fourteen, rather to choose to leave out these princes, who were of Ahab's half blood, than any others. If any say, Why then did he not leave out more? Besides that he was not obliged any other way, (than as he would keep to his number to leave out these,) he knew God's threatenings of children for the sins of parents usually terminate in the third and fourth generation.

9 And Ozias begat Joatham; and Joatham begat Achaz; and Achaz begat Ezekias;

That Jotham succeeded his father Uzziah, and reigned sixteen years, agreeth with 2 Chron. xxvi. 23, and that Ahaz his son succeeded him, agreeth with 2 Chron. xxvii. 9; he also reigned sixteen years, and Hezekiah his son reigned in his stead, 2 Chron. xxviii. 27. Some here have cavilled at the truth of the history of holy writ, because it appeareth from 2 Kings xvi. 2 that Ahaz died at thirty-six years of age, and that Hezekiah began to reign at twenty-five years of age doth also appear from 2 Chron. xxix. 1, whence it appeareth that Hezekiah must be born when his father was but eleven years of age, which they think improbable : but those who will question the truth of what we have so good a proof of as the revelation of holy writ is, are obliged not only to tell us of things in it that are improbable to their apprehensions, but either in nature impossible, or at least inconsistent with some other piece of Divine revelation. Of the latter sort, we hear of nothing objected in this case. Now though with us it be not ordinary for persons at that age to beget children, yet that it is not impossible in nature, nor more than hath happened in the world sometimes, Spanhemius hath largely proved in his Dubia Evangelica, Dub. 5, and that by no less authorities than those of Hierome amongst the ancients, and the learned Scaliger amongst the more modern writers. It is what may be. The Scripture telleth us it was so; that is enough for us, though it be not a thing very ordinary.

10 And ᵐEzekias begat Manasses; and Manasses begat Amon; and Amon begat Josias; m 2 Kings 20. 21. 1 Chro. 3. 13.

All this exactly agreeth with the Scriptures of the Old Testament. These three princes in a lineal descent immediately succeeded each other, Manasseh reigning fifty-five, Amon two, and Josiah thirty-one years, altogether eighty-eight years.

11 And ‖ ⁿJosias begat Jechonias and his brethren, about the time they were °carried away to Babylon : |Some read, *Josias begat Jakim, and Jakim begat Jechonias.* n See 1 Chro. 3. 15, 16. o 2 Kings 24. 14, 15, 16. & 25. 11. 2 Chron. 36. 10, 20. Jer. 27. 20. & 39. 9. & 52. 11, 15, 28, 29, 30. Dan. 1. 2.

In this *Jechonias* (whoever he was) determined the evangelist's second period of fourteen generations. But there is much dispute, both about the Jechonias who is here mentioned, and the sons of Josiah as they are reckoned up 1 Chron. iii. 15, where it is said, *The sons of Josiah were, the first-born Johanan, the second Jehoiakim, the third Zedekiah, the fourth Shallum.* It is plain that Jehoahaz succeeded Josiah his father, 2 Kings xxiii. 31; 2 Chron. xxxvi. 1. It is certain that amongst the Jews it was very ordinary for persons to have two names; thus king Uzziah in the

Book of Kings is called *Azariah*, 2 Kings xiv. 21. Most if not all of Josiah's sons had two names: it is plain that Jehoahaz his eldest son is the same who in 1 Chron. iii. 15 is called *Johanan*; but he reigned but three months, probably set up by the people, and put down by Pharaoh-necho, in a battle against whom Josiah was slain; he pursuing his victory put him down and set up Eliakim his next brother, calling him Jehoiakim, as he is called 1 Chron. iii. 15. He reigned eleven years, 2 Chron. xxxvi. 5. The king of Babylon puts him down, and setteth up Jehoiachin his son, who is also called Jeconiah, and Coniah. He reigned but three months and ten days, 2 Chron. xxxvi. 9; and the king of Babylon fetcheth him away, and sets up his uncle Zedekiah, called also Mattaniah. He reigned eleven years, as appeareth by 2 Chron. xxxvi. 11; then the whole body of the Jews were carried away captive into Babylon. We do not read, either in the Book of Kings or Chronicles, that Shallum (Josiah's fourth son) ever reigned, yet it should seem that he did, by Jer. xxii. 11. Some think that he was set up instead of Jehoahaz, when he was carried away. But the Scripture saith nothing of it, nor is it very probable that the conqueror should skip over the second and third son, and set up the fourth. But it is not my present concern to inquire after Shallum, but only after Jechonias mentioned in this verse, and the other Jechonias mentioned in the 12th verse, as the head of those generations which make up the last period. As to this Jechonias, the most probable opinion is, that it was Jehoiakim, who was also called Jeconiah, and that the Jechonias mentioned ver. 12 was Jehoiachin, the son of Jehoiakim. In this I find some of the best interpreters acquiescing, nor indeed is there any great difficulty in allowing Jehoiakim the father, as well as Jehoiachin the son, to be called Jeconiah (so near are the names akin, and the signification of both the same); but then the question is, how Josiah could be said to *beget Jehoiakim about the time of the carrying into the captivity of Babylon;* for it appeareth by 2 Chron. xxxvi. 5, that *Jehoiakim was twenty-five years old when he began to reign, and he reigned eleven years;* and in his time was the first carrying into Babylon; so that there must be thirty-seven years betwixt the begetting of Jehoiakim and the first transportation into Babylon. The margin of our Bibles tells us of another reading, *Josias begat Jakim,* (Jakim and Jehoiakim are the same,) *and Jakim begat Jechonias* (that is, Jehoiachin). Beza thinks this the truest reading, taken out of an old copy of R. Stephens, magnified by Stapulensis and Bucer. But he thinks it should be thus, *Josias begat Jakim and his brethren,* (for we know that Josiah had four sons,) *and Jakim begat Jechonias* (that is, Jehoiachin) *about the time of the carrying into the captivity of Babylon.* For Jehoiachin or Jeconiah was not nine years old when himself was carried away, and his father was carried away before. *About the carrying away into Babylon:* the Greek preposition ἐπὶ doth not signify any determinate certain time, but doth include sometimes many and distinct times, as it must do here; for Josiah began to reign at eight years old, and reigned thirty-one years, so that he died at thirty-nine years of age, 2 Chron. xxxiv. 1. Jehoahaz (or Johanan) his eldest son succeeded him at twenty-three years old, so he must be born when Josiah was sixteen years of age; Jehoiakim began to reign at twenty-five years of age; Zedekiah at one and twenty; as appeareth from 2 Chron. xxxvi. 2, 5, 11. So that Zedekiah must be but about nine years old when his father died, which was not twelve years before Jehoiakim was carried into Babylon, as appeareth by the history, 2 Chron. xxxvi. Thus the persons in this period (which was the flourishing time of the kingdom of Judah) are fourteen: Solomon, Rehoboam, Abia, Asa, Jehoshaphat, Joram, Uzziah, Jotham, Ahaz, Hezekiah, Manasseh, Amon, Josiah. Jehoiakim; only here is no mention made of Jehoahaz's reign, who was Josiah's eldest son, who, it may be, is not mentioned by the evangelist, either because Jehoiakim (here called Jechonias) was a second son of the same father, or in regard of his short reign (for it was but three months and odd days); or, it may be, because in all probability he was tumultuously set up by the people, and not fixed in his throne before he was turned out by the conqueror Pharaoh-necho; nor do we read of any sons he left; to be sure he left none who could succeed him in the throne, for Jehoiakim was set up, and his son Jehoiachin succeeded him, as the history telleth us.

12 And after they were brought to Babylon, ᵖJechonias begat Salathiel; and Salathiel begat ᵠZorobabel;

p 1 Chron. 3. 17. 19.
q Ezra 3. 2. & 5. 2.
Neh. 12. 1.
Hag. 1. 1.

This *Jechonias* is generally thought to be Jehoiachin the son of Jehoiakim; he is called *Jeconiah*, 1 Chron. iii. 16, as well as *Jehoiachin*, 2 Chron. xxxvi. 8; so also he is called *Jeconiah the son of Jehoiakim*, Jer. xxiv. 1. That this *Jechonias begat Salathiel* appeareth from 1 Chron. iii. 17. It is here objected that God said concerning this Jeconiah, called also Coniah, *Write ye this man childless*, Jer. xxii. 30; how then did he beget Salathiel? But it is easily answered, for that verse. Jer. xxii. 30, will expound itself: *Write ye this man childless, a man that shall not prosper in his days; for no man of his seed shall prosper, sitting upon the throne of David, and ruling any more in Judah:* so as that text is plainly to be understood, without a child that shall actually succeed in the crown; for the text itself supposeth that he should have *seed*, but none that should *prosper, sitting upon the throne of David, and ruling in Judah*, which the Scripture, 2 Chron. xxxvi., justifieth, for the king of Babylon set up Zedekiah his uncle in his stead, who was the last king in Judah, in the eleventh year of whose reign the Jews were all carried captive. This Jeconiah had eight sons, as we read, 1 Chron. iii. 17, 18. Salathiel is there reckoned as his second son; possibly Assir died young, or at least childless, so as the right of the crown was in Salathiel, who is the person alone here named. But how *Salathiel* is here said to have *begat Zorobabel* is yet a greater difficulty; for, 1 Chron. iii. 19, it is said, *The sons of Pedaiah* (not of Salathiel) *were, Zerubbabel, and Shimei*. If Zorobabel were the son of Pedaiah, how could he be the son of Salathiel? Several answers are given to this. Some think that Zorobabel, because he descended lineally from Salathiel, is called his son, which were a sufficient answer if the supposition were true, that Zorobabel were lineally descended from Salathiel: but that it is not, for according to 1 Chron. iii. 18 Pedaiah was not the son, but the brother of Salathiel. Others think that Salathiel is here said to have begot Zorobabel, because Zorobabel succeeded him in the kingdom; but as that is a strange interpretation of the word *begat*, so neither was Salathiel a king, though possibly the title of the crown was in him as the great-grandchild of Josiah, nor did ever Zorobabel assume the crown that we read of. Whereas others say, that there were two Zorobabels, and that this son was the adopted son of Salathiel: both these things are suggested without proof. The most probable opinion, which I perceive the best interpreters acquiesce in, is, that Salathiel dying without issue, Pedaiah his brother married his wife, according to the law of God, Deut. xxv. 5, and begat Zorobabel of her that had been the wife of Salathiel; and thence it is said Salathiel begat him, Pedaiah so raising up seed to his brother according to the law aforesaid. To this it is objected by some, that the law was, that the child should succeed in the name of the brother that was dead: so that if this were the sense, it should not have been, *Salathiel begat Zorobabel*, but Salathiel begat Salathiel. The answer to this is not difficult; for, to succeed in the name of the brother that is dead, doth not signify, to be called by the very name with which he was called, but to be denominated his son, as if begotten by him. And this is evident from Ruth iv. 10, where Boaz hath these words, *Ruth the Moabitess, the wife of Mahlon, have I purchased to be my wife, to raise up the name of the dead upon his inheritance, that the name of the dead be not cut off from among his brethren.* Yet, ver. 21, Boaz, having a son by Ruth, did not call his name Mahlon, by the name of his father, but Obed.

13 And Zorobabel begat Abiud; and Abiud begat Eliakim; and Eliakim begat Azor;

14 And Azor begat Sadoc; and Sadoc begat Achim; and Achim begat Eliud;

15 And Eliud begat Eleazar; and Eleazar begat Matthan; and Matthan begat Jacob;

Here are divers objections made to this last part of the genealogy, and in a great measure caused from the difference between Matthew and Luke; but I shall not attempt any reconciliation of those differences till I come to Luke, chap. iii. There is no *Abiud* reckoned amongst the sons of Zorobabel, 1 Chron. iii. 19, 20; and for the others named, we have no certain account of them in any part of the holy writ. From the time of Jehoiakim were above five hundred years to the birth of Christ, of which seventy were spent in the captivity of Babylon. Zorobabel was alive at the end of the captivity, Ezra v. 2, and, as it appears, the ruler of the Jews, though not under the title and style of king. For *Eliakim, Azor, Sadoc, Achim, Eliud, Eleazar, Matthan,* and *Jacob,* though we have no mention of them in any canonical books of holy writ but only this, yet Matthew's credit in the church of God ought to outweigh any other writings, pretending any thing contrary to what he saith; we are therefore obliged to believe they all lineally descended from David, but, living in a private state and condition, and holy writ not extending its history beyond Zorobabel's time, (the time when the Jews came out of Babylon,) it is no wonder that we have no better means than we have from holy writ to know their lineal descent from the royal family. That Matthew in what he wrote was guided by the unerring Spirit, and that he had rolls of pedigrees which we want, we have reason to believe. This is enough for us Christians, who own the books of the New as well as the Old Testament to be wrote by persons Divinely inspired; so, as to them, we have nothing to do but to reconcile Matthew and Luke, both whom we own to have had the same infallible inspiration and direction. If Jews or pagans argue from any other topic than this, it is enough to tell them, that the Jews kept exact genealogies, and more especially as to the descents in the tribes of Judah and Levi, that they might never be at loss as to the Messiah, whom they expected as the Son of David, nor yet as to the true high priest. Though these records and rolls of genealogy be now lost, yet we have no reason to believe they were so in Matthew's time; of which genealogies (as to this part) doubtless what Matthew saith was but a copy, directed by that Holy Spirit by which he was inspired.

16 And Jacob begat Joseph the husband of Mary, of whom was born Jesus, who is called Christ.

How Luke cometh to make Joseph the son of Heli we shall inquire (if God please) when we come to his third chapter: but from this verse ariseth a very grave question, viz. How, or wherefore, the evangelist, in deriving the pedigree of Christ, bringeth the line down to Joseph, from whom our Saviour did not descend, being no flesh of his flesh. Christ being the promised Messias, the prophecy, Isa. vii. 14, must be and was fulfilled in him, *A virgin shall conceive, and bear a Son, and shall call his name Immanuel.* Now if Joseph were not the true, but only the legal or supposed, father of Christ, what had the evangelist to do with his genealogy? Many answers are given to this. Some think that the evangelist accommodateth himself to the vulgar opinion; they took him generally for the true and natural son of Joseph; they said, *Is not this the carpenter's son?* But then the Holy Spirit must have attempted to have proved a conclusion true from a medium that was false, which must by no means be allowed. Besides, neither could this be Matthew's design, who afterwards relateth the mystery of our Saviour's incarnation plain enough; and tells us, ver. 18, that Mary was *found with child before Joseph and she came together.* Others therefore say that amongst the Jews the genealogies of women use not to be reckoned. How universally true that is I cannot tell; generally it is, (very probably,) it being usual almost with all nations to reckon descents from the males. It is granted by most that Luke deriveth the descent of Mary. In the present case, it seemeth of high concern that the genealogy both of Joseph and Mary should be counted. Though our Saviour's being the Messias could not have been proved from his being the Son of Joseph, for then he could not have been the Son of a virgin, yet (admitting the Jewish error in that case, not knowing the mystery of Christ's incarnation) Christ, by their own confession, was confirmed to be the Son of David because Joseph was so. On the other side, Luke deriving Mary's genealogy from David, and affirming Christ to be born of *a virgin espoused,* confirmed him to all the world to be both the Son of David, descending from Mary a virgin, that was a daughter to one who was the son of David, and also the true Messiah, in whom the prophecy was fulfilled, of a virgin's conceiving and bearing a Son. So that by the reckoning of the generation of two persons, both of which were lineally descended from David, he was proved to be the Son of David, both to the generality of the Jews, who could not deny but Joseph was so, and to all believers, both Jews and Gentiles, to whom God should give to believe the mystery of the incarnation by the conception of the Holy Ghost. This to me seems a sufficient reason for the reckoning up our Saviour's descent from David both by father and mother. Which is advantaged by considering that Joseph was not only the *reputed* father, but the *legal* father of Christ; and although his being not the natural but the legal father of Christ will not prove him the Son of David, further than to the Jews who would have him to be the natural son of Joseph, yet the genealogy reckoned from Abraham to Joseph will prove Joseph the son of David, (whom they judged Christ's natural father,) so as they had nothing to say against that and the other parts of this Gospel; and this chapter indeed, with the genealogy of Mary, will prove that he was both the Son of David, and the true Messias, as a Son born of a virgin. Whereas some say that Mary was of the tribe of Levi, and think to prove it by her being cousin to Elisabeth, who is expressly called a daughter of Aaron, Luke i. 5; besides that Luke iii. plainly proveth her of the tribe of Judah, and of the family of David, the proof is by no means sufficient; for although the law, Numb. xxxvi. 8, 9, for the avoiding of a confusion of inheritances, commanded them to marry within their tribes, yet this law concerned not the daughters of the tribe of Levi, for that tribe had no inheritance as the rest. So as that kindred might easily be, though Mary was not of the tribe of Levi, but of Judah, as indeed she was. But leaving this question, let us come to the words of the verse. *And Jacob begat Joseph the husband of Mary;* that is, the espoused husband of Mary. Espousals make a marriage before God: the angel afterward saith to Joseph, (but yet espoused,) *Fear not to take unto thee Mary thy wife.* And he was soon after the legal, actual husband of Mary. *Of whom was born Jesus, who is called Christ;* that person who was called Jesus by the direction of the angel, as we shall by and by see, who was also called Christ, which, as we said, signifieth Anointed, and the same with Messiah. It is observed by some that the name Christ was given to kings of Judah (because of their anointing) before the captivity, but to none after, till he came who was *the Christ;* God by that providence (if the Jews would have understood it) pointing out to them, that the person was now come who was promised them under the notion of the Messiah, Dan. ix. 25, 26, and whom they expected, as appeareth from John i. 41; iv. 25, and no longer to be expected.

17 So all the generations from Abraham to David *are* fourteen generations; and from David until the carrying away into Babylon *are* fourteen generations; and from the carrying away into Babylon unto Christ *are* fourteen generations.

The evangelist, for reasons which we cannot fathom, reduceth our Saviour's progenitors to *fourteen* in each period of the Jewish state; and in the first period, determining with David, there were no more. In the second, he leaveth out three kings descended from the daughter of Ahab. In the third, which was from the captivity to Christ, there were doubtless more; Luke reckoneth up twenty-four, (taking in Christ for one,) and agreeth in very few with Matthew, who was forced to leave out some to keep to his number of fourteen. Nor doth Matthew speak any thing false, or contradictious to Luke, in saying there were fourteen though there were more. Besides, there might be many more progenitors of Mary than of Joseph, whose pedigree Matthew deriveth.

18 ¶ Now the ʳbirth of Jesus Christ was on this wise: When as his mother Mary was espoused to Joseph, before they came together, she was found with child ˢ of the Holy Ghost.

The Fifth Year before theCommon Account called Anno Domini.
r Luke 1. 27.
s Luke 1. 35.

The evangelist prefaceth this extraordinary birth of our Saviour in this manner. *Now the birth of Jesus Christ was on this wise;* not in the ordinary course and manner in which children are conceived and brought forth into the world, but in this wonderful manner. *When as his mother Mary was espoused to Joseph.* Betrothing, or espousing, was nothing else but a solemn promise of marriage made by two persons each to other, at such a distance of time as they agreed upon. It was a decent usage, approved of (if not ordained) by God, as appears by Deut. xx. 7. That we are obliged still to use it I dare not say; it might be a prudential order and constitution of that state. There was nothing in it typical, nothing to bring it under the notion of a carnal ordinance, as the apostle calls some of their ordinances relating to the worship of God. It seemeth equitable, that the parties to be married might have some convenient time to think seriously of the great change they are soon to make in their lives, and more solemnly seek unto God for his blessing upon them; as also that they might more freely discourse together about their household affairs, and the settlement of their families, than the modesty of the virgins of that age would otherwise have allowed them. It made them man and wife before God, though they came not together for some time after. The distance of time seemeth to have been left to the agreement of parties and parents. In this case we cannot certainly assert the distance, but it appeareth to have been such, as that she was *found with child* before they came together. Mary knew what the evangelist here asserteth, that it was by *the Holy Ghost;* for as she must know that she had not known man, as she told the angel. Luke i. 34; so the angel had satisfied her, saying, ver. 35, *The Holy Ghost shall come upon thee, and the power of the Highest shall overshadow thee. Therefore also that holy thing which shall be born of thee shall be called the Son of God.* It cannot be doubted but that she revealed this to some of her friends, but how it came to be found, or who found it, we are not told. Joseph as yet had no such revelation. God would have his Son to be born of a virgin, 1. For the fulfilling of the promise, Isa. vii. 14. 2. Of the Holy Ghost, that the womb of the virgin being sanctified by the Spirit of holiness, there might be no traduction of original sin. Of a betrothed virgin, 1. That he might not be under the reproach of illegitimacy. 2. Nor his mother subjected to the punishment of the Judaical law. 3. That Mary's stock might be by her betrothed husband. 4. That Christ might have a guard in his infancy.

19 Then Joseph her husband, being a t Deut. 24.1. **just *man*, and not willing ᵗto make her a publick example, was minded to put her away privily.**

It was found she was with child, possibly herself or some of her friends told it to Joseph her espoused husband; it is plain from this text he came to the knowledge of it, for upon it, the evangelist saith, he *was minded to put her away privily.* Had Joseph at this time heard and believed that the Holy Ghost had come upon her, and the power of the Most High overshadowed her, being a good man, he would not have entertained thoughts of putting her away. But though she had before received this revelation, and might possibly have communicated it to some of her friends, yet it is manifest that her husband Joseph had not heard it, or at least was not easy to believe a thing of so unusual and extraordinary a nature. That she was with child was evident, how she came to be so was as yet hidden from him in nature, and so incredible a thing, as it had argued too much of easiness of belief for him to have believed, had not Joseph had (as afterward he had) a Divine revelation for it: he therefore receiving such a report, and finding it to be true, resolves to put her away in the privatest manner he could, rather than to expose her to a public shame, or to be made a public example. Their being betrothed was a thing publicly taken notice of, and he could not put her away so privately but there must be witnesses of it; the meaning therefore must be, as privately as the nature of the thing would bear. Joseph in this case had the choice of three things: 1. He might, notwithstanding this, have taken her to his house as his wife, for the law of divorce, or putting away, was but a law giving a liberty in case of a discerned uncleanness to put away the wife, it did not lay any under an obligation so to do. 2. He might give her a bill of divorce, and leave her with her friends. Now those skilled in the Jewish writings tell us this might be done, either more privately before two or three witnesses, putting a writing of that import into her bosom; or more openly and publicly before the magistrate. 3. He might, according to the law, Deut. xxii. 23, 24, &c., have brought her forth to be examined, whether she had only suffered a rape, or had herself consented. If it was done with her consent, she was by the law to be stoned. Of these Joseph, in his first thoughts upon the matter, and before he rightly did understand the thing, chooseth the second and the milder part, and resolves to put her away, but in the most private manner the law would in that case allow him. He did this (saith the evangelist) because he was *a just man,* where the term δίκαιος signifieth equitable, in opposition to severity and rigour; nor ought any to say Joseph in this showed himself an unjust man, because by the law she ought to have been stoned to death; for that is a mistake. Supposing she had been with child by man, yet if she had been forced the man only was to die, Deut. xxii. 25, 26; or she might have been with child before her betrothing, in which case she was only obliged to marry him that had so abused her. A kind and equitable man always presumeth the best, especially in a case where life is concerned; besides that, no doubt Mary had by this time told Joseph the truth, and what the angel had said to her, to which (it being so incredible a thing as not to be believed but upon a Divine revelation) though Joseph was not obliged, having as yet no such revelation, to give a present easy faith, yet he might reasonably give so much credit as to resolve upon the mildest course he could take, though he was willing also to avoid the blot upon himself by taking her to him for his wife according to his contract. God will not leave so good a man long unresolved what to do.

20 But while he thought on these things, behold, the angel of the Lord appeared unto him in a dream, saying, Joseph, thou son of David, fear not to take unto thee Mary thy wife: ᵘfor that which is † conceived in her is of the Holy Ghost. u Luke 1.35. † Gr. *begotten.*

What we have in this verse assureth us, that Joseph was not only inclined, by the kindness and benignity of his own natural temper, and by his charity, to that moderate resolution he had taken up, but also more immediately influenced by God, who was now sending a messenger to him to tell him what he would have him to do in this case. Whether this angel was the angel Gabriel, who Luke tells us, chap. i. 26, was sent to Mary, to tell her that the power of the Most High should overshadow her, or some other angel, none can assert; an angel it was. He appeareth to Joseph while he was asleep, in and by a dream. By dreams was one way by which God revealed his mind to people formerly, Heb. i. 1; one of those ways by which God made himself known to prophets, Numb. xii. 6; and not to prophets only, but to pagan princes sometimes, as appeareth by the instances we have in Scripture of the dreams which Pharaoh and Nebuchadnezzar both had. Dreams are either natural, or supernatural, or preternatural. How to distinguish the former from the two latter is not my work in this place, and possibly a difficult task, especially in our times, when God, having spoken to us by his Son, and given us his word as a perfect rule, hath left off ordinary speaking to his prophets by dreams and visions, though not limited himself but that he may sometimes so speak. We are assured of the truth of a Divine revelation to Joseph by this way of dreams, while his head was full of thoughts what he was to do in this case. God thinks of us when we sleep, and one way or other will not be wanting to our inquisition in sincerity to know his will, in the difficult cases of our lives. The angel saith unto Joseph, *Joseph, thou son of David;* by which compellation he lets him know he was to be the supposed and legal, though not the natural, father of the Messias, who was by the confession of all men to be the Son of David. *Fear not to take unto thee Mary thy wife;* she that is thy betrothed wife, and so thy wife in my sight; thou hast espoused her, and called me to witness that thou wilt consummate this marriage with her in a due time, and take her to thine house. I see what hath happened which troubleth thy thoughts; possibly thou art afraid lest thou shouldst offend me, marrying one who appeareth unto thee to be defiled; or thou art afraid of bringing a blot upon thyself if thou shouldst consummate this marriage; but do not fear any of these things, but go on, and consummate thy marriage. She is not, as thou supposest, or mayst fear, defiled by man, *for that which is conceived in her is of the Holy Ghost. That holy thing*, (as Luke speaks,) that human body which is in her womb, is created in her, and is of the Holy Ghost. The Holy Ghost, by his almighty creating power, hath supplied what is wanting from the help of the creature, as to ordinary productions of this nature.

x Luke 1. 31.
∥ That is, *Saviour*, Heb.
y Acts 4. 12. & 5. 31. & 13. 23, 38.

21 ˣAnd she shall bring forth a son, and thou shalt call his name ∥JESUS: for ʸhe shall save his people from their sins.

When the usual time of women is accomplished, *she shall bring forth a Son, and thou shalt call his name Jesus*. He shall not be thy natural son, but he shall be her son, not begot by thee, but brought forth by her, so flesh of her flesh. His name shall be called Jesus by thee, or by his mother. It is the will of God thou shouldst give him that name. *For he shall save his people from their sins.* It was the custom of the Jews (God's ancient people) to give names to their children, either expressive of the mercy which God had showed them in giving them their children, or of the duty which their children did owe unto God. This name was given by God, expressing the mercy of God to his people in giving them this child; *for he shall save his people from their sins*, saith the angel. Jesus comes from a Hebrew word, which signifies salvation. Joshua had his name from the same word, because he was to be a temporal saviour to save the Jews, the whole body of the Jews, from the Canaanites their enemies. This Jesus was to save his people, all that should believe in his name, whether Jews or Gentiles, from their sins. Hereby the angel hints the mistake of the Jews, in thinking the Messias should be a temporal saviour, who should save the Jews from their enemies, minding them that he was to save them, not from their bodily, but spiritual enemies, from their sins; the guilt of them, and the power of them, and from the eternal danger of them: and he alone should do it; *There is none other name under heaven given among men, neither is there salvation in any other*, Acts iv. 12.

22 Now all this was done, that it might be fulfilled which was spoken of the Lord by the prophet, saying,

z Is. 7. 14.
∥ Or, *his name shall be called*.

23 ᶻBehold, a virgin shall be with child, and shall bring forth a son, and ∥they shall call his name Emmanuel, which being interpreted is, God with us.

By these great acts of Divine Providence, that which was spoken and prophesied of by Isaiah, chap. vii. 14, speaking by inspiration from God, was fulfilled. Though things are said in the evangelists to be fulfilled when the types have had their accomplishment in the antitype, and when something cometh to pass much like, or bearing some proportion to, something which before happened in the world, (as I shall show hereafter,) yet I take the sense of being fulfilled here to be literally fulfilled; believing so much of that prophecy as is here quoted did literally concern Christ, and none but him. But we must take heed of interpreting the particle *that* as signifying the end of God's action in this great work of Providence; for the end for which God sent his Son into the world was before expressed, to *save his people from their sins*, not to fulfil a prophecy. *That* here only signifies the consequent of that act of Divine Providence, and the sense is but only this, By all this which was done, was fulfilled that which was spoken of the Lord by the prophet, &c. But the Jews so much clamouring against the application of that text (Isa. vii. 14) to Christ, and some learned interpreters thinking the fulfilling mentioned to be no more than the fulfilling of a type in the antitype, it will be necessary that we make it appear that it was literally fulfilled. To which I know of but two prejudices: 1. That it could be no relief to Ahaz, nor to the Jews, against their sense and fear of their present danger, to tell them that Christ should be born of a virgin eight hundred years after. 2. That whereas it is added, ver. 16, *Before the child shall know to refuse the evil, and choose the good, the land that thou abhorrest shall be forsaken of both her kings.* Supposing those two kings to be Pekah king of Israel and Rezin king of Syria, who were at that time joined in a siege against Jerusalem, or at least preparing for it, and the child mentioned ver. 16 to be the son of a virgin promised ver. 14, it could be no relief to Ahaz, nor any great news for the prophet to have told Ahaz, that they should both leave the country before eight hundred years were elapsed. Let us therefore first consider the history to which that prophecy related. Isa. vii. 1, 2, we are told, that in the time of Ahaz, *Rezin the king of Syria, and Pekah the son of Remaliah, king of Israel, went up toward Jerusalem to war against it. And it was told the house of David*, (that is, Ahaz,) *saying, Syria is confederate with Ephraim. And his heart was moved, and the heart of his people, as the trees of the wood are moved with the wind.* The expedient which Ahaz thought upon in this distress, was to get Tiglath-pileser, the king of Assyria, to join with and help him; which he afterward did, hiring him with *the silver and gold found in the house of the Lord, and in the treasures of the king's house*, as we find 2 Kings xvi. 7, 8. This conjunction with idolaters was what the Lord had forbidden, and had often declared his abhorrence of. To prevent it, he sends his prophet Isaiah to him: Isa. vii. 3, 4, *Go forth now to meet Ahaz, thou, and Shear-jashub thy son, at the end of the upper pool in the highway of the fuller's field; and say unto him, Fear not, neither be faint-hearted, &c.* In short, he assureth him in the name of the Lord, that the counsel of these two kings should *not stand*, nor *come to pass*, that *within threescore and five years* Israel should *not be a people*, &c., ver. 7, 8. Ahaz knew not how to believe this. Isaiah offereth him from God to ask a sign for the confirmation of his word, either *in the depth, or in the height.* Ahaz refuseth it under pretence that he would not *tempt the Lord*, as if it had been a tempting God to have asked a sign at his command. At this the Lord was angry, as appeareth by the prophet's reply, ver. 13; *And he said, Hear ye now, O house of David; Is it a small thing for you to weary men, but will you weary my God also?* Then he goeth on, *Therefore the Lord himself shall give you a sign; Behold, a virgin, &c.* There was nothing more ordinary in the prophets than to comfort the people of God amongst the Jews in their distresses with the promise of the Messias; this we find they often did with reference to the captivity of Babylon, and in other causes of distress and trouble. And certainly that is the design of the prophet here, in these words: *Behold, a virgin shall conceive, and bear a Son, and shall call his name Emmanuel.* Ahaz had refused to believe the promise God gave him, to defeat the counsel of these two kings; he had refused to ask a sign, for the confirmation of God's word. Well, (saith the prophet,) God shall give you that fear him a sign, he shall in his own time send you the Messias, whose name shall be called Emmanuel, and he shall be born of a virgin. Nor yet doth he leave Ahaz and his people comfortless, as to their present distress, for saith he, ver. 16, *Before the child shall know to refuse the evil, and choose the good, the land that thou abhorrest shall be forsaken of both her kings.* The Hebrew is הכער which I think were better translated *this child*, than *the child*, for ה seems not to be a relative, (referring to the child, mentioned in ver. 14,) but a demonstrative, referring to the son of Isaiah, Shear-jashub, whom God, ver. 3, commanded the prophet, going to meet Ahaz, to carry with him, who probably was a very young child. Saith the prophet, Here is a little child whom God hath commanded me to bring with me; before this child be much older, this land which thou art so much afraid of shall be quitted of both those kings who have now some possession of it; for at this time Rezin had taken Elath, a city of Judah, 2 Kings xvi. 6; and doubtless he and Pekah had taken divers places, for they were come up to Jerusalem itself. And indeed, if this be not the sense, it is very hard to conceive to what purpose God commanded Isaiah to take Shear-jashub with him when he went upon this errand, Isa. vii. 3. So that ver. 14 remains as a prophecy respecting the Messiah only, and given not for any relief of unbelieving Ahaz as to his present distress, but for some relief to God's people among the Jews, with reference to their posterity. This will appear a much more probable sense than theirs, who think that Maher-shalal-hash-baz is the son mentioned ver. 14, whom we read of Isa. viii. 3, who was born to Isaiah of the prophetess, (who some think was at this time a virgin,) and was a type of Christ; for the Scripture doth not tell us whether that prophetess was a virgin or a widow, neither was it any great wonder that a virgin being married should conceive, and bear a son. Nor had this been any relief to Ahaz, as to his present distress, for this virgin (if she were such) was yet to be married, to conceive, and bear a son; so that, according to that notion, we must allow three or four years before Ahaz could have expected relief. This is further advantaged by that passage, Isa. viii. 18, *Behold, I and the children which the Lord hath given me are for signs:* not the child, but *the children.* Shear-jashub was for a sign of God's deliverance of the Jews from those two kings; Maher-shalal-hash-baz was for a sign of the destruction of the Israelites within five years, and also of Syria, which fell out afterward. Thus ver. 14 remains a literal prophecy of Christ. For the Jewish interpretation of it concerning Hezekiah, (born fifteen years after,) it is too ridiculous to be mentioned.

24 Then Joseph being raised from sleep did as the angel of the Lord had bidden him, and took unto him his wife:

25 And knew her not till she had ᵃ Ex. 13. 2. brought forth ᵃher firstborn son: and he Luke 2. 7, 21. called his name JESUS.

The will of God (as we heard) was revealed to Joseph in a dream. It is God that giveth a power to sleep, and a power to awake; therefore it is said, *being raised from sleep,* he showed both his faith and obedience; his faith in the Divine revelation, a certainty of which he had doubtless by some extraordinary Divine impression, and his obedience to the Divine precept. He *took unto him his wife,* that is, he took her unto his house, (for betrothed virgins used to abide at their own friends' houses till the consummation of the marriage,) and owned her as his wife, yet not fully using her as such, for the text saith he *knew her not* (a modest phrase used from the beginning of the world, as appears from Gen. iv. 1, to express the conjugal act) *till she had brought forth her first-born Son.* Some make a great stir in determining whether he knew her afterwards, yea or no. Some of the ancients were stiff in their opinion that he did not, so are the popish writers, and many protestant interpreters. Mr. Calvin I think determines best, that none will move such a question, but such as are unwarrantably curious; nor contend for either part, but such as are unreasonably quarrelsome. For as, on the one side, none can conclude that she had more children from the word *till,* further than they can conclude, from Psal. cx. 1, that Christ shall not for ever sit at his Father's right hand, (the word *until* being a particle only exclusive of a preceding time, not affirming the thing in future time,) nor doth the term *first-born* conclude any born afterward; so, on the other side, there are no cogent arguments to prove that Mary had no more children by Joseph. We read of the brother of our Lord, Gal. i. 19, and of his mother and his brethren, Matt. xii. 47; and though it be true *brethren* may signify kinsmen, according to the Hebrew dialect, yet that it doth so in these texts cannot be proved. The Holy Ghost had made use of the virgin for the production of the Messias; why after this her womb should be shut up, and Joseph take her home to be his wife, and not use her as such, I cannot tell, nor yet what reproach it could be to Mary or to our Saviour, marriage being God's ordinance, and the undefiled bed honourable: and those who think our Saviour would have been dishonoured in any others lying in the same bed after him, seem to forget how much he humbled himself in lying in that bed first, and then in a stable and a manger. We know he knew her not till Christ was born, whether he did afterward or no we are willingly ignorant because God hath not told us. *And he called his name Jesus:* this is added to declare his obedience to the command received by the angel. We shall meet with more circumstances relating to the birth of Christ when we come to the two first chapters of Luke.

CHAP. II

Wise men from the east come to Jerusalem to inquire after Christ, 1, 2. *Herod is alarmed,* 3—8. *The wise men are directed by a star to Christ, and worship him, offering gifts,* 9—12. *Joseph, warned by an angel, fleeth with the young child and his mother into Egypt,* 13—15. *Herod's massacre of the children in Bethlehem and round about,* 16—18. *Upon the death of Herod Christ is brought out of Egypt, and dwelleth at Nazareth,* 19—23.

NOW when ᵃJesus was born in Bethlehem of Judæa in the days of Herod the king, behold, there came wise men ᵇfrom the east to Jerusalem,
The Fourth Year before theCommon Account called Anno Domini. ᵃ Luke 2. 4, 6, 7. ᵇ Gen. 10. 30. & 25. 6. 1 Kings 4. 30.

That Joseph, the legal father of Jesus, was of Nazareth in Galilee, appears from Luke ii. 4, where we are told that he went from thence *unto the city of David, which is called Bethlehem; (because he was of the house and lineage of David;) to be taxed with Mary his espoused wife:* for, it seems, so was the emperor's decree, ver. 1, and Cyrenius the governor of Syria had ordered that every one should go to be taxed in his own tribe and city. Those words, *of Judea,* were added to distinguish the place from another Bethlehem, which was in the territories of Zebulun, Josh. xix. 15. The verse further tells us, that this was *in the days of Herod the king:* these words, *the king,* are added to distinguish him from Herod the tetrarch, Matt. xiv. 1, or other Herods. This was that Herod the Great, commonly called the Ascalonite, the son of Antipater. There are three opinions of learned men concerning him. Some think that he was by birth an Idumean, and that his mother was an Arabian, and say he was the first foreigner that ever reigned in Judea; and that in him the prophecy was fulfilled, Gen. xlix. 10, that *the sceptre should not depart from Judah till Shiloh came.* Others contend that he was a native Jew. A third sort say he was originally an Idumean, but that his predecessors had for some ages been proselyted to the Jewish religion: which last opinion is judged the most probable. Judea was at that time subject to the Romans, whose senate made him king over it. Christ being born at this time, it is said, *there came wise men from the east to Jerusalem.* How long it was after he was born that they came the Scriptures tell us not. Some think they came presently; some think within thirteen days; some think it was two years after. It is certain they were directed to find Christ at Bethlehem, ver. 8, 9. There he was born, and circumcised the eighth day. There his mother accomplished the days of her purification, according to the law; which days were thirty-three, as may be seen Lev. xii. 2, 3, &c. Luke tells us, chap. ii. 22, that after the accomplishment of those days, *they brought him to Jerusalem, to present him* (as their first-born) *to the Lord,* Exod. xiii. 2, *and to offer a sacrifice;* and he tells us there of his meeting with Simeon and Anna, and of their prophecies, ver. 25, &c.; and it is said, ver. 39, *When they had performed all things according to the law of the Lord, they returned into Galilee, to their own city Nazareth.* It is not probable that these wise men came before our Lord was carried to Jerusalem, (which was about six weeks after he was born,) for besides that they had a long journey to come, after such a noise made by the wise men's coming, it is no way probable that Joseph and Mary would have carried him to Jerusalem, where the inquiry was first made; especially considering Herod's trouble about it, and his sending messengers presently to slay *all the children in Bethlehem, and in all the coasts thereof,* ver. 16. It is therefore most probable that it was near two years after the birth of Christ before they came; for though no such thing can be concluded from Herod's decree, which was for the slaying those that were *two years old and under,* yet one would think the following words signify some such thing, *according to the time which he had diligently nquired of the wise men.* He had then made inquiry about what time this child should be born; possibly they could not tell him the exact time, but if they said a year or a year and half before, Herod (to make sure) might make his decree for all to be slain from *two years old and under;* but had they said a month or six weeks, it is not probable Herod would have been so barbarous as to have slain all of two years old: so as, if we wisely consider the history of Scripture, it is no way probable that they came before Mary's purification was over, and their offering him to the Lord, &c. mentioned Luke ii. But then how should they find him at Bethlehem? for he went to Nazareth, Luke ii. 39. *Answ.* God might order some motion of Joseph to Bethlehem (of which the

Scripture is silent); it was a city within the tribe to which he related, where probably he had kindred. So as, though it were a year or more after the birth of Christ before these wise men came, yet it is possible they might find him at Bethlehem, his parents being as guests there, though inhabitants at Nazareth. This is enough to have spoken of the time when these wise men came, viz. at what distance from the birth of Christ, considering that nothing can be in the case certainly determined. It is yet a greater question who these wise men were, and from what part of the world (here called *the east*) they came. The uncertainties of men's conclusions in their points of curiosity, rather than profit, let us know how vainly men search for satisfaction when God hath hidden a thing from them. They cannot agree in the number of these men, some will have them twelve, some but three; and they undertake to tell us their names, though neither can they agree in it. Some will have them to be kings; and the papists make us believe they have their sepulchres with them to this day at Cologne; and by the number of the tombs they know their number; and that Church hath a festival for them, which is our Twelfthday. These and a hundred more fables there are about them. The Scripture saith no more than *wise men*, and telleth us nothing of their number. Whether they were mere astrologers, or such as were skilled in magical arts, or more generally philosophers, is vainly disputed; only we have their observation of this extraordinary star, together with what the Scripture tells us of the use those Eastern nations made of astrologers, to guide us to think they were such as were famous in their country for astrology: though others think them persons skilled in Divine and human laws. The Scripture only calls them *wise men*. Whether they came from the eastern parts of the world, or that part of the world which lay eastward to the city of Jerusalem, is another unprofitable question: pagans they were, without doubt; whether Persians or Arabians, or of some other country, is of no great concern for us to know, and almost impossible to determine. These were the firstfruits of the Gentiles owning Christ as King of the Jews, whilst he came amongst his own, and they received him not; nor do I know any thing more worthy of our observation concerning them. Those that think it worth the while to read what more is said concerning them, may read enough in Spanhem. his Dub. Evang., Heinsius, his Exercitat. Sac. and Poli Critica, which I rather choose to name than the popish writers, because in some of these he will find the antidote together with the poison of those fabulous discourses, and be taught a pious wariness of obtruding old wives' fables into canonical history, and lightly imposing upon the faith of ignorant people.

c Luke 2. 11.
d Num. 24. 17. Is. 60. 3.

2 Saying, ᶜWhere is he that is born King of the Jews? for we have seen ᵈhis star in the east, and are come to worship him.

Jerusalem was the metropolis of Judea; thither they come, as to the most likely place where to receive satisfaction. Of whom they inquired the Scripture saith not, but it is observable that they took notice that there was a person born who was to be an illustrious King of the Jewish nation, they speak not at all doubtfully as to that. This information they doubtless had from a Divine revelation, for although there was an extraordinary star appeared, which might let them know that God had produced, or was producing, so extraordinary a work of providence in the world, yet without a supernatural interpreter they could not have made so true and particular interpretation of it, as upon the sight of it to have come with such a confidence to Jerusalem, affirming that there was a King of the Jews born, and that this was his star, a light which God had put forth to direct that part of the world to the true Messiah. All guesses at the nature of this star, and the means how the wise men came to know that the King of the Jews was born upon the sight of it, and its motion, are great uncertainties; God undoubtedly revealed the thing unto them, and caused this extraordinary star, as at first to appear to confirm what he told them, so at last to appear directing them to the very house in which the young Child with his mother were. *And are come to worship him*: whether worshipping here signifieth only a civil honour, which those Eastern nations ordinarily gave unto great princes, or that religious homage and adoration which was due unto the Messias, is variously opened by interpreters. It is said, ver. 11, they *fell down and worshipped him: and when they had opened their treasures, they presented unto him gifts; gold, frankincense, and myrrh*. This might be upon a civil or upon a religious account; and doubtless was according to the revelation which they had, concerning which nothing can be certainly determined.

3 When Herod the king had heard *these things*, he was troubled, and all Jerusalem with him.

Herod was hardly warm in his kingdom, and had taken Jerusalem by force, and was therefore much concerned to hear that there was a new King born; and supposing him to have been all his life acquainted with the Jewish writings and records, where were prophecies of the Messias under the notion of a King, and not knowing that the kingdom of the Messias was not to be of this world, but being possessed of the ordinary notion of the Jews, that the Messias should restore a temporal kingdom to Israel, he could not but be troubled at the news of one born who was to be the *King of the Jews*, especially having a confirmation of it by such an extraordinary means, as persons coming from a far country, and being directed to their journey by some extraordinary impulse, upon the sight of a new star, which pointed to Judea, as the place to which it related: Herod upon this might justly think that his newly acquired kingdom would not last long. And though most people are quickly weary of conquerors, yet their former miseries being fresh in their minds, and the renewing of them likely upon a change in the government, it is no wonder if the generality of the people were also troubled.

4 And when he had gathered all ᵉthe Chief Priests and ᶠScribes of the people together, ᵍhe demanded of them where Christ should be born.

e 2 Chron. 36. 14.
f 2 Chron. 34. 13. 1 Mac. 5. 42. & 7. 12.
g Mal. 2. 7.

In this perplexity the king Herod calleth a synod or convocation, which was made up of the chief priests and scribes; the single question which he propoundeth to them was to resolve him *where Christ should be born*. It is most likely this was an extraordinary convention of such of these persons as the king thought fit, who were best skilled in the law, and other revelations of holy writ, not any orderly meeting of the sanhedrim; for the question propounded to them was of mere ecclesiastical concern, and to be resolved from the prophecies and writings of the Old Testament. The stating of the question to them, not where the King of the Jews, but where Christ should be born, makes it manifest, that although (that we read of) the wise men said nothing of Christ, yet Herod presently conceived that this King of the Jews, that was born, must be the Messiah prophesied of Psal. ii., and in Dan. ix.; he therefore desired to know of them the place in which, according to their received tradition, and sense of the prophecies of holy writ, the Messiah whom they expected (that is, Christ) should be born.

5 And they said unto him, In Bethlehem of Judæa: for thus it is written by the prophet,

6 ʰAnd thou Bethlehem, *in* the land of Juda, art not the least among the princes of Juda: for out of thee shall come a Governor, ⁱthat shall ‖ rule my people Israel.

h Mic. 5. 2. John 7. 42.
i Rev. 2. 27.
‖ Or, *feed*.

It was (as it seems) so received a tradition, and interpretation of Micah v. 2, that they gave him an answer without any hesitation, telling him he was to be born *in Bethlehem of Judea*; this they confirm by the prophecy of the prophet Micah, chap. v. 2; so confirming the Son of the virgin Mary (at unawares) to be the Messiah from the testimony of the prophet Micah. The words in Micah something vary from those here mentioned; they are thus: *But thou, Bethlehem Ephratah, though thou be little among the thousands of Judah, yet out of thee shall he come forth unto me that is to be Ruler in Israel; whose goings forth have been from of old, from everlasting.* We must know, 1. That the writers of the New Testament, in their quotations out of the Old Testament, ordinarily quote only so much of them as makes to their purpose, and not always in the very terms in which they are found in the Old Testament, but keeping to the sense. 2. That it is more than probable that the evanlist keeps to the words in which the priests and scribes delivered in their answer to the king, for in this relation he is but reciting their answer. The sole question propounded to them was, What the place was, where the Messiah, according to their records, was to be born? They answer, In Bethlehem Judah: they prove their answer from the testimony of the prophet. If any object that the prophet calls it Bethlehem Ephratah, not Bethlehem Judah, the answer is, that it is in sense the same, for Bethlehem Ephratah was within the tribe of Judah. It should seem by Gen. xxxv. 19, and xlviii. 7, that it was formerly in Jacob's time called Ephrath. Some think that it was a town within Caleb's portion, and called Ephratah from his second wife, whose name was Ephrath, or Ephratah, 1 Chron. ii. 19, 50, if it were not the same place, only fortified anew. We read of another Bethlehem in Judah builded by Rehoboam, 2 Chron. xi. 6; whether it had this addition from its old name in Jacob's time, or from Caleb's wife, or to distinguish it from Bethlehem belonging to the tribe of Zebulun, is hard to say: it is plain that that Bethlehem is meant, both by Micah and Matthew, which was in Judah; possibly in tract of time the addition Ephratah was lost. But, say some, there is a contradiction betwixt Micah and Matthew; Micah saith it was *the least*, Matthew saith it was *not the least*. *Answ*. Here is no contradiction; consider Bethlehem itself, it was but a small city, (if it were in Caleb's lot it is not named,) but in other respects it was not the least. It was of old famous for Ibzan, one of the judges, for Elimelech, Boaz, Jesse, David; and now last of all for the birth of Christ, with respect to which the evangelist calls it *not the least;* or if he reciteth the scribes' and priests' words, they might call it *not the least* upon the account of Boaz, Jesse, and David, all which were born or dwelt there; and particularly with respect to Christ, who was born there. The prophet calls it *the least* with respect to its state in his time, the evangelist *not the least* with respect to its state then, its state being magnified by the birth of Christ. Micah saith *among the thousands*, Matthew, *among the princes*. It is the same thing, for, Numb. i. 16, their princes were *heads of thousands in Israel*. The Jews would by no means have this text interpreted of Christ, but either of Zerubbabel or David: but as to Zerubbabel, he was born in Babylon, not in Bethlehem, and David was dead long before this prophecy; neither could the following words, *whose goings forth have been from of old, from everlasting*, agree to Zerubbabel or David: Zerubbabel's name tells us where he was born, and we never read that Bethlehem was thus celebrated with reference to David, though he was born there, 1 Sam. xvi. 1; xvii. 58, upon which account it is called *the city of David*, Luke ii. 4. The prophecy certainly related to Christ, and him only, and so is interpreted by the Chaldee paraphrast, who some think was one of this council called by Herod in this cause.

7 Then Herod, when he had privily called the wise men, enquired of them diligently what time the star appeared.

Herod having heard the answer of the priests and scribes, did not think fit to make any noise of it amongst the people; he knew the Jews were apt enough to rebel, and being so late a conqueror had no reason to presume much of their good-will towards him; he therefore calls the wise men privily, and takes no notice of any King they talked of, but only inquireth the time when this new star first appeared. To what end he made this inquiry may be learned from ver. 16; only that he might be able to govern himself in his bloody decree, that he might neither destroy more children than would serve his present design, nor yet leave this Child behind.

8 And he sent them to Bethlehem, and said, Go and search diligently for the young child; and when ye have found *him*, bring me word again, that I may come and worship him also.

He tells the wise men that Bethlehem was the place, wherein his wise men had informed him that the King of the Jews was to be born, and sends them thither with these instructions: That they should go, and *search diligently* there *for the young Child*, whom he doth not call King;

thereby dissembling his bloody mind, and making as if he had no jealousy of him; yet withal he suggests to them that he was like to be a great Prince, or else he would never have pretended that he had a design, when once he knew certainly where he was, to go and pay a homage to him. This text lets us see the malignity of Herod's heart, and indeed of all wicked men's hearts. Herod knew that the Messiah was born. The extraordinary star and the coming of the wise men, the priests' and scribes' answer to him, could not but confirm him that he was born, who was long since promised, as a King and Governor to Israel; yet could he not obtain of his wretched heart to comply with the counsels of God, but, contrary to his own convictions, shows the folly of his heart, in thinking it was in his power to frustrate the Divine counsels, and be too hard for God himself. Nor is his folly less remarkable, not sending any of his own courtiers with them, whom he might better have trusted than mere strangers to have come back and brought him an account; but whether it was that he durst not trust any of the Jews, or that he was over-credulous in trusting to the innocent simplicity of these wise men, being not made acquainted with his intentions, he suffereth them to go alone upon this errand, whom he might possibly think would be least suspected of Joseph and Mary, so as at their return he should have a more full account of all circumstances concerning him, than he could have expected from one who had been taken notice of as one that belonged to his court.

9 When they had heard the king, they departed; and, lo, the star, which they saw in the east, went before them, till it came and stood over where the young child was.

They departed toward Bethlehem Judah; how long their journey was we cannot tell: some wonder that none of the Jews did attend them in their journey, coming out of their own country upon such a discovery, and impute it either to the Jews' fear of the tyrant under which they were, or to the blindness and hardness of their hearts, for St. John tells us he came amongst his own, and they received him not; but it is possible that the wise men's immediate applications were to the court, as thinking that the most probable place to hear of one that should be born King of the Jews; and it may be questioned whether Herod, though he called the scribes and the priests together, told them that his summoning of them was occasioned by the coming of the wise men, for the only question he propounded to them was where Christ was to be born, which they might understand without any relation to the wise men's question. Nor is it probable that Herod should be more open than needed in publishing the coming of these wise men, or their errand. Yet the text saying that not only Herod, but all Jerusalem, was troubled, suggests to us that both their coming, and the occasion of it, was noised abroad, more than probably Herod could have wished; but it is like their dismission was so private, that if any of the Jews had had a heart and courage enough to have gone with them, yet they might not have had opportunity. It is more admirable that Herod sent none that he could securely trust with them. But the hand of God was in this thing. They shall be hid whom he will hide. The Lord had prepared them a better guide. *The star*, which probably had disappeared for a good time while they were upon their journey to Jerusalem, (for they needed no star to guide them to so famous a place,) as soon as they were out of Jerusalem appeared again, and *went before them, till it came and stood over where the young Child was*: probably the star appeared in the lower region, and though it could not point so directly that they should know the very house, yet it might point so near as by inquiry they might easily find it, especially by the influence of God upon their spirits, which doubtless they did not want. Whether these wise men were of the posterity of Balaam, who prophesied of *a sceptre that should rise out of Israel, that should smite the corners of Moab*, one that should *have dominion*, &c., Numb. xxiv. 17, 19, or this star had any relation to the star mentioned there, ver. 17, is very uncertain: it is more probable that these wise men came a much further journey, and that the star there mentioned was not to be understood in a literal sense, but better expounded by Simeon, Luke ii. 32, *A light to lighten the Gentiles, and* to be *the glory of* his *people Israel*.

S. MATTHEW II

10 When they saw the star, they rejoiced with exceeding great joy.

Joy is but the natural consequent of desire satisfied: they had in their own country seen an extraordinary star, which, according to the rules of their own art, they might guess to be an indication of a great Prince born, or, by a Divine revelation, they might know to be so. This kindled in them a strong desire to go and pay a homage to him; upon this they take a long journey to Jerusalem. When they come there they were more fully confirmed, from the answer of the priests and scribes, that there was a Christ to be born in Bethlehem Judah. Thither they go. In their journey the same star they had before seen appears to them again, confirming both their former apprehensions, and, by its standing over Bethlehem, and a particular house in it, (to their apprehensions,) they were fully confirmed that they had right instructions from Herod, and rejoiced in the satisfaction of their desires naturally, and possibly rejoiced spiritually in this matter of joy to all people, if they had (as is probable) a spiritual illumination, and believed that this Christ was also Jesus, one come to save both Jews and Gentiles from their sins.

11 ¶ And when they were come into the house, they saw the young child with Mary his mother, and fell down, and worshipped him: and when they had opened their treasures, [k] they ‖ presented unto him gifts; gold, and frankincense, and myrrh.

k Ps. 72. 10. Is 60. 6.
‖ Or, *offered*.

How long the virgin Mary and her holy Child had been there is not expressed; those that think these wise men came within six weeks or two months, judge that Joseph and Mary came thither from Jerusalem after that he had been there offered to the Lord, of which you read Luke ii.; but they are forced, to uphold this, to interpret Luke ii. 39, which saith that after *they had performed all things according to the law of the Lord, they returned into Galilee, to their own city Nazareth*, of a considerable time after they had performed these things, which seemeth something hard and needless, especially considering Nazareth was Joseph's own city, i. e. the city where his fixed habitation was. It is most probable that they, after so long absence, went right home, and if the wise men (which is said) found them in Bethlehem, they were gone thither again to visit some relations. *They saw the young Child with Mary his mother;* under what other circumstances the Scripture saith not, but questionless they were very poor and mean, which is a very strong inducement to us to believe that they had a spiritual Divine revelation, that this was a King whose kingdom was not of this world, the true Messiah and Saviour of the world; they would hardly else have treated a poor infant, in an ordinary house and no more attended, at the rate they did, for the text saith they *fell down and worshipped him;* a usual homage indeed which the Eastern nations paid to princes, but they used then to have better evidences of their royal state and dignity than these wise men seemed to have had, if they had not, besides the star, a Divine revelation what manner of King this was to be. We may therefore rather judge that their revelation extended not only to the birth of a King, but of such a King as indeed he was, the eternal Son of God clothed with human flesh; and that their falling down and worshipping him is to be understood of a Divine worship they paid to him, as the Saviour of the world: and so they were the first-fruits of the Gentiles, owning and believing in the Lord Jesus Christ. And that their following offerings to him were upon that account, for opening *their treasures, they presented to him gold, frankincense, and myrrh*. The guesses of those who think that they offered him gold as to a King, frankincense as a High Priest, and myrrh to sweeten the place where he was, I take to be but the product of luxuriant fancies. It is most certain that those Eastern people seldom came to their princes without some presents, and that their presents were usually of the most choice things their country afforded. This is plain from Gen. xliii. 11; and if what naturalists tell us be true, that myrrh was only to be found in Arabia, and frankincense in Sabea, (a part of Arabia,) and that country also had gold, which it is plain that it had from 2 Chron. ix. 14, it makes a very probable argument, that these wise men came from Arabia, which was full of men that were astrologers. The providence of God was wonderfully seen in these presents, by them providing for the sustenance of Joseph, and Mary, and Jesus in that exile which they were soon after to endure. For other allegorical and mystical significations of these presents, they are but conjectures, and the exuberancies of men's fancies.

12 And being warned of God [1]in a dream that they should not return to Herod, they departed into their own country another way.

1 ch. 1. 20.

Now the wise God beginneth to defeat the crafty counsels of Herod, whose bloody hand he had stayed till he should from the wise men have had a perfect intelligence concerning this new-born King. God in a dream appeareth to the wise men, and warneth them to go no more to Herod. The wise men came with no intention to serve Herod's bloody designs, but came in the simplicity of their hearts. This simplicity of theirs Herod would have abused, to have made them accessaries to his guilt. God will not suffer it: *He who walketh uprightly walketh safely.* Thus the integrity of Abimelech in taking Sarah protected him from guilt with reference to her, Gen. xx. 6. The word which we here translate *warned of God,* is used of persons whom God is pleased to honour, so far as to discourse with, either by himself or an angel, Luke ii. 26; Acts x. 22; Heb. viii. 5; xi. 7. Thus hath God honoured these wise men, whose hearts were inclined towards him and his Christ; 1. By giving them a star, to guide them. 2. Confirming their hearts by his word, from the mouth of the chief priests and scribes, that they were not mistaken concerning the star and its indication. 3. By speaking himself to them, to keep them from any guilt, or being so much as accessaries any way to that bloody tragedy, which upon their departure he knew would be acted. They take another way to go into their own country, so we hear of them no more.

13 And when they were departed, behold, the angel of the Lord appeareth to Joseph in a dream, saying, Arise, and take the young child and his mother, and flee into Egypt, and be thou there until I bring thee word: for Herod will seek the young child to destroy him.

How long it was before this apparition to Joseph the Scripture saith not, but admitting what is affirmed by some geographers, that Bethlehem Judah was but two days' journey from Jerusalem, it cannot be presumed long, for Herod had (doubtless) quick intelligence of the wise men's motions. Here was a second temptation upon Joseph, who was of no great quality, (a carpenter,) and might have anxious thoughts how he in Egypt should maintain himself, his wife, and child; but Joseph knew that *the earth was the Lord's, and the fulness thereof*: though Egypt therefore was a land of idolaters, and he had no visible way of subsistence there, yet we shall hear that none of these things made him hesitate. Egypt was near to Palestine, and the dominions of another prince, within which Herod had nothing to do. Jeroboam fled thither, 1 Kings xi. 40, and stayed there till the death of Solomon. God's precept here did not only indicate his care and special providence for and over this holy Child, but included a promise of sustenance and support for it and its parents; and the Lord further assured Joseph that he should not die in that exile, for he would likewise tell him the time when he should come back. Christ's time to die was not yet come, and therefore he would have him out of the way, for he who searcheth the heart and trieth the reins, and knoweth the thoughts of man afar off, did know that *Herod* would *seek the young child to destroy him:* he should but seek him, for God had resolved to preserve him, but he would show the malice of his heart in seeking of him, therefore God commands him to go away, and directeth him whither to go. The certainty of an issue, from the Divine counsels, or a Divine revelation, ought not to encourage us in the neglect of any rational and just means for the obtaining of it. Though God will provide for his church and people, yet it is his will they should use all just and lawful means for their own preservation.

14 When he arose, he took the young child and his mother by night, and departed into Egypt:

15 And was there until the death of Herod: that it might be fulfilled which was spoken of the Lord by the prophet, saying, [m]Out of Egypt have I called my son.

[m] Hos. 11. 1.

True faith, or assent to a Divine revelation, always produceth obedience to the precept of it. Thus it did in the wise men, thus in Joseph, thus every where in holy writ. By which we may learn, that they indeed believe not the Scriptures to be the word of God, who take no care to live up to the rule of life prescribed in them. Joseph not only obeyed, but readily and presently obeyed: *When he arose, he took the young Child and his mother.* The poverty of our Saviour's parents is not obscurely gathered from this hasty motion of Joseph. His motion was not delayed for the packing up of goods, gathering in of debts, &c.; if he lost any thing by his haste, yet he carried with him the promise and special care of God for him and his. Yet he moveth prudentially, and therefore he beginneth his journey *by night*, when least notice could be taken of his motion. We are not to put God upon working miracles for our preservation, though we have never so many sure promises, when it may be obtained in the use of means. They are God's security given to creatures, whom he hath endued with reason, and express that we should use it, while we yet trust in his word. We are not told into what part of Egypt Joseph went, nor how long he stayed there: some say six or seven years; others, but three or four months. The text saith he *was there until the death of Herod.* Some say that was before the paschal solemnity that year. But these things are great uncertainties. It is certain he stayed there till Herod died, but when that certainly was we know not, nor is it material for us to be curious in inquiring. *That it might be fulfilled which was spoken of the Lord by the prophet, Out of Egypt have I called my Son. That it might be fulfilled* is a phrase we often meet with in the New Testament, to declare the harmony of Scripture, and the faithfulness of God in fulfilling the prophecies or promises of the Old Testament. Spanhemius tells us, The Scripture is said to be fulfilled properly or improperly. Properly two ways, either literally or mystically. Improperly, secondarily, when some such-like thing happeneth as was before foretold or spoken of, or an example is brought parallel to some former example. Literally the Scripture is said to be fulfilled, 1. When a thing before prophesied of, or promised, cometh to pass. Thus the prophecy, Isa. vii. 14, was literally fulfilled chap. i. 23; so Micah v. 2 was literally fulfilled chap. ii. 6, by Christ's being born in Bethlehem; so Zech. ix. 9 was literally fulfilled chap. xxi. 5. Or else, 2. When the type is fulfilled in the antitype. Thus we read of many scriptures of the Old Testament fulfilled in Christ, several things about the paschal lamb, the brazen serpent, Solomon, David, Jonah, &c. Improperly the Scripture is said to be fulfilled, when any thing is reported as done, which bear a proportion to something before recorded in holy writ, as spoken or done: thus Christ applieth the same thing to the hypocrites which lived in his time, chap. xv. 7, 8, which Isaiah spake of those who lived in his time, Isa. xxix. 13: so chap. xiii. 14; Isa. vi. 9: this divines call a fulfilling *per accommodationem, aut transumptionem.* The question is, whether this scripture, which is Hos. xi. 1, was fulfilled in Christ's being carried into Egypt, properly or improperly. There is a great variety of opinions; those possibly judge best who think that the Israelites going into and coming out of Egypt, was a type of Christ's going into Egypt, being preserved there, and coming out again. Matthew saith the scripture was fulfilled, whether properly or improperly is not much material for us to know. I have only added thus much to shorten my discourse hereafter where we shall meet with this phrase.

16 ¶ Then Herod, when he saw that he was mocked of the wise men, was exceeding wroth, and sent forth, and slew all the children that were in Bethlehem, and in all the coasts thereof, from two years old and under, according to the time which he had diligently enquired of the wise men.

Herod now expounds what he meant by his coming and worshipping Christ also, which he talked of ver. 8. *When he saw that he was mocked, &c.;* really mocked by their coming no more to him; not that they used any mocking lauguage, or designed by their actions to deceive him, but probably intended to have gone back according to his desire, but that they were otherwise admonished by God in a dream. *He was exceeding wroth,* as great persons used to be when they see any great design they have frustrated by their inferiors, *and sent forth, and slew all the children in Bethlehem, and in the coasts thereof, from two years old and under:* he sent forth soldiers, or executioners, and slew all the children. There is a tradition that amongst them he slew his own son, and that Augustus Cæsar, hearing it, should say, It was better to be Herod's hog than his child, because the Jews will eat no swine's flesh. Others say this is but a fable, for his son died very few days before himself. *From two years old and under:* if we take these words as they seem to sound, they would incline us to think that Christ was near two years old before the wise men came; but some very learned men think they came within a year or little more, and that the term we translate *two years old,* signifieth persons that had never so little entered upon the second year of their age: so as if a child were but a year and a week old, he was properly enough called διετής, one of two years old, that is, who had began his second year. Hence they think that the star appeared some little matter above a year before they came to Bethlehem; and considering at how great distance some parts in Arabia were from Jerusalem, they think that a year might well be ran out in their deliberations about, and preparations for, and despatch of their journey. Thus they interpret the next words, *according to the time he had diligently inquired of the wise men,* that they had told them that it was something above a year since the star appeared first. This is now a middle way betwixt those who (very improbably) think that they came within thirteen days, too short a time doubtless for such a journey, and those that think they came not till near two years, which to some seemeth as much too long. I leave it to the reader's judgment.

17 Then was fulfilled that which was spoken by [n]Jeremy the prophet, saying,

[n] Jer. 31. 15.

18 In Rama was there a voice heard, lamentation, and weeping, and great mourning, Rachel weeping *for* her children, and would not be comforted, because they are not.

The text quoted is Jer. xxxi. 15. This prophecy was literally fulfilled when Judah was carried into captivity; there was then a great mourning in the tribes of Benjamin and Judah, for their children that were slain and carried into captivity. It was now fulfilled, that is, verified, a second time. There is no need that *Rama* here should be taken appellatively, as it signifieth a high place, from whence a noise is most loudly and dolefully heard. There were several places so named, one near Bethlehem, (formerly called Ephrath, Gen. xxxv. 16, 19,) Judg. iv. 5, a city in the lot of Benjamin, Josh. xviii. 25. The slaughter was in Bethlehem and the coasts thereof; the noise reached to Rama, which was close by. Both Benjamin and Judah made up the one kingdom of Judah. *Rachel* was the mother of Benjamin, a woman passionately desirous of children, therefore the fittest person to have her name used to express the sorrow of all those mothers who had lost their children in this slaughter. The slaughter of these children caused a lamentable mourning by tender mothers throughout Benjamin and Judah, such as the former captivity caused to be mentioned, Jer. xxxi. 15.

19 ¶ But when Herod was dead, behold, an angel of the Lord appeareth in a dream to Joseph in Egypt,

The Third Year before the Account called Anno Domini.

20 Saying, Arise, and take the young child and his mother, and go into the land of Israel: for they are dead which sought the young child's life.

That is, as some say, within three or four months, for

Herod, they say, no longer outlived this bloody act; and if we may believe historians, he was in his death made a dreadful example of Divine vengeance. But we cannot assert the just time how long he outlived this bloody act; when he was dead, God, who had promised Joseph, ver. 13, to tell him by an angel, (as before,) let Joseph know he might safely return. It is probable this apparition was not immediately upon the death of Herod, for Archelaus was reigning, who must be allowed some time to go to Rome, and to have this dignity conferred on him; but soon after he was dead this apparition was, with a command to him to return into the land of Israel, to which he soon yieldeth obedience.

21 And he arose, and took the young child and his mother, and came into the land of Israel.

22 But when he heard that Archelaus did reign in Judæa in the room of his father Herod, he was afraid to go thither: notwithstanding, being warned of God in a dream, he turned aside °into the parts of Galilee:

o ch. 3. 13. Luke 2. 39.

The true King of the Jews being born, the singular providence of God so ordered it, that there was no more constituted governors of Judea under the title of kings, though they are said to reign, because the tetrarchs in their provinces exercised a regal power; for though Archelaus was by his father's will declared his successor in the kingdom, yet the emperor and senate of Rome was to confirm him, who made Archelaus tetrarch of Judea, as appears by this verse; Antipas, another of his sons, called also by his father's name, tetrarch of Galilee; Philip, another of his sons, tetrarch of Iturea; and Lysanias tetrarch of Abylene; and set a governor over Judea, which was Pontius Pilate; as appeareth by Luke iii. 1. Of all the sons of Herod, Archelaus is said to be of the most fierce and bloody disposition, which made Joseph afraid to go thither. His brother Herod Antipas is reported of a much milder disposition, and more inactive temper. So Joseph, not without the direction of God, goeth into his own province, which was Galilee.

23 And he came and dwelt in a city called ᴾNazareth: that it might be fulfilled qwhich was spoken by the prophets, He shall be called a Nazarene.

p John 1. 45.
q Judg. 13.5.
1 Sam. 1. 11.

It appeareth by Luke ii. 4, that Joseph dwelt in Nazareth before our Saviour was born; and, Luke ii. 39, after Mary's purification it is said, *they returned into Galilee, to their own city Nazareth;* and, Luke iv. 16, he was there brought up. Hence, John i. 45, he is called by Philip, *Jesus of Nazareth*. But the following words of this verse afford as great difficulties as any other in holy writ. 1. How Christ could be called a Nazarene, who apparently was born at Bethlehem. 2. How the evangelist saith that was fulfilled which was spoken by the prophet, *He shall be called a Nazarene;* whereas there is no such saying in all the prophets. There is a strange variety of opinions as to these questions. Spanhemius acquiesceth in that which seemeth least liable to exception, viz. That Christ was to put a period to that order of Nazarites amongst the Jews, whose rules we have Numb. vi. 2, 3; of which order Samson was, as appears by Judg. xiii. 7, and Joseph was called נזיר Gen. xlix. 26, the very same word which is used Judg. xiii. 7. Both Joseph and Samson were eminent types of Christ. And it was spoken of Christ by the prophets, (the holy men of God who wrote the Scriptures,) that Christ should be called נזיר *Nezir*, as it is in the Hebrew, in that it was spoken of those that were his types; who are both expressly so called. The word signifieth a holy person, one separated to God, and from ordinary converse with men. Christ was to be such a Nazarite, separated to God, for the accomplishment of our redemption, and, like Joseph, separated from his brethren: Isa. liii. 3, he was *rejected of men:—we hid as it were our faces from him, and we esteemed him not*. God by his singular providence so ordered it, that he who was the antitype to all the Nazarites, and the true *Nezir*, or person separated, should be educated at Nazareth, a poor contemptible town: John i. 46, *Nathanael said, Can there any good come out of Nazareth?* That while his education there gave the Jews an occasion to reproach him, as a Nazarene, because born at Nazareth, believers amongst the Jews might understand him to be the true Nazarite, understood in Joseph and Samson called by this name, as types and figures of him who was to come, separated by God to a more excellent end, and from men in a more eminent manner. So that what the prophets spake of this nature concerning Christ, they spake of those who were the true types of Christ. Those who will read Spanhemius, and Poli Critica, will find large discourses about the difficulties of this text, but this seemeth to be Spanhemius's opinion, improving the notion of Mr. Calvin.

CHAP. III.

The preaching of John the Baptist; his office, and manner of living, 1—4. He baptizeth in Jordan, 5, 6, and rebuketh the Pharisees, 7—12. Christ is baptized, and receiveth a witness from heaven, 13—17.

IN those days came ᵃJohn the Baptist, preaching ᵇin the wilderness of Judæa,

A. D. 26.
a Mark 1. 4, 15. Luke 3. 2, 3. John 1. 28. b Josh. 14 10.

That is, in the 15th year of Tiberius Cæsar, (as Luke expounds it, Luke iii. 1,) when John the Baptist and Christ also were *about thirty years of age,* Luke iii. 23, for there was no great difference betwixt the age of Christ and John, as may be learned from Luke i. 31, 41, 57. *In those days,* while Joseph and Mary, and our blessed Lord, dwelt in Nazareth. See Exod. ii. 11. This phrase *in those days* is the same with *in those years.* It is an ordinary thing in the Hebrew to confound the words signifying a day and a year, and the Greeks did the same, as appears by the seventy interpreters, 1 Sam. i. 3, 7. The evangelists pass over with a great deal of silence our Saviour's minority, only mentioning his disputing with the doctors in the temple, Luke ii. 46. *Came John the Baptist; John the son of Zacharias,* Luke iii. 2, called the Baptist, either because he baptized Christ, or because by him God instituted the ordinance of baptism, which before that time the Jews used in the admission of their proselytes. *Preaching,* according to his commission, Luke iii. 2, where it is said the word of the Lord came to him. *In the wilderness of Judea;* some parts of Judea, where houses and inhabitants were very few. None must think that the history of the second chapter is continued in this, there was a distance of twenty-eight or twenty-nine years; the evangelist designing not to satisfy men's curiosity, but only to give us that part of Christ's story which might be profitable to us to know.

2 And saying, Repent ye: for ᶜthe kingdom of heaven is at hand.

c Dan. 2. 44. ch. 4. 17. & 10. 7.

The evangelist only gives us the sum and scope of the Baptist's doctrine, the other evangelists give us a more full account of his pressing also faith in Christ, John i. 29; iii. 29, 36: so Acts xix. 4. Repentance, faith, and new obedience ought to be the substance and scope of all our sermons. Repentance signifieth the change of the heart and reformation of the life, a turning from sin unto God. *For the kingdom of heaven is at hand;* that blessed state of the church (foretold by the prophets) under the Messias, wherein God will exhibit his Son as the King in Zion, and exert his power and kingdom, both extensively, subduing all nations to the obedience of his gospel, and intensively, in all the administrations of his government; for *the kingdom of heaven* is not to be understood here of the kingdom of glory, but of the kingdom of grace, in all the administrations of it. This passage containeth the argument upon which the Baptist in his sermons pressed, repentance and faith, and obedience to the will of God revealed.

3 For this is he that was spoken of by the prophet Esaias, saying, ᵈThe voice of one crying in the wilderness, ᵉPrepare ye the way of the Lord, make his paths straight.

d Is. 40. 3. Mark 1. 3. Luke 3. 4. John 1. 23. e Luke 1. 76.

It is not much material whether we understand these words as the words of the evangelist concerning John, as it should seem by Mark i. 3, and Luke iii. 4, or the words of John himself, for he thus spake, John i. 23. As the words of the prophet they are found Isa. xl. 3. The words are judged literally, but typically, to concern Cyrus and

Darius, and either these princes, who were instrumental in the restoring of the Jews to their liberty from the captivity of Babylon, or those prophets who encouraged them to their return, or upon their return to build the temple and city. But they are confirmed by all the four evangelists, Mark i. 3; Luke iii. 4; John i. 23, to have a special relation also to John the Baptist, who was to come more immediately before Christ, and with the fervency and in the spirit of Elias, Luke i. 17, crying, *Prepare ye the way of the Lord, make his paths straight.* As the harbingers of great princes are sent before them to call to persons to remove things out of the way which may hinder their free passage, so John was sent before this great King in Zion, now coming forth to show himself, and to set up his kingdom in the world; to cry fervently to all people, by a true and timely repentance, to cast off those sinful courses, and to reject those false opinions, of which they were possessed, the holding of and to which might hinder the progress of this spiritual kingdom.

f Mark 1. 6.
g 2 Kin. 1. 8.
Zech. 13. 4.
h Lev. 11. 22.
i 1 Sam. 14. 25, 26.

4 And ᶠthe same John ᵍhad his raiment of camel's hair, and a leathern girdle about his loins; and his meat was ʰlocusts and ⁱwild honey.

There are great and insignificant disputes about the habit and the diet of John the Baptist. The evangelists doubtless designed no more than to let us know, that John Baptist's habit was not of soft raiment, like those who are in princes' houses, but a plain country habit, suited to the place in which he lived; and his diet plain, such as the country afforded. In vain therefore do some contend that John wore watered stuff, fine and splendid, as art in our days hath improved camel's hair; and others as vainly contend that he went in a camel's skin raw and undressed: but lie was habited in a plain suit of camel's hair, such as ordinary persons of that country used, or else such a rough garment as is mentioned Zech. xiii. 4, used by the prophets. Elijah had much such a habit, 2 Kings i. 8. There is likewise a variety of opinions about these locusts which John did eat; the most probable is, that they were true locusts, for locusts might be eaten, Lev. xi. 22. Nor is it to be thought that John did eat nothing else; all that is intended is, to let us know that John was a man not at all curious as to his meat or clothes, but was habited plainly, and fared ordinarily, as the men of that country fared; if there were any difference in his habit, it was to proportion himself to Elijah, and the habit of prophets. In this the evangelist teacheth us what the ministers of the gospel should be and do. They should be men contemning the gaudery and delicacies of the world, and by their habit and diet, as well as other things, set an example of severity and gravity to others.

k Mark 1. 5.
Luke 3. 7.

5 ᵏThen went out to him Jerusalem, and all Judæa, and all the region round about Jordan,

The preacher being described, the evangelist proceedeth to tell us what auditors he had. The term *all* here twice repeated, is enough to let us know, that it is often in Scripture significative no further then *many*, for it cannot be imagined that every individual person in Jerusalem and the region about Jordan went to hear John the Baptist, but a great many did. It is not to be wondered that there went out such a concourse of people to hear John the Baptist, 1. If it be true, that from Ezra's time till now no prophet had appeared. Our Saviour speaking of John, *What went ye out for to see? A prophet?* seems to hint that a prophet was a great rarity amongst them. 2. If we consider the severity of his life. Our Saviour saith he *came neither eating nor drinking*, that is, as other men. 3. If we consider the new doctrine he brought, and his fervency in the pressing it: he came to preach the Messias, whom the Jews had long expected; to tell them his kingdom was at hand. 4. Especially if we consider the new rite of baptizing, which he brought in. For admit their washing of proselytes in use before, yet he baptized Jews. He was *sent to baptize with water*, John i. 33. So as from his time the institution of the sacrament of baptism must be dated, and he did baptize many.

l Acts 19. 4, 18.

6 ˡAnd were baptized of him in Jordan, confessing their sins.

A great part of those who went out to hear John were *baptized*, that is dipped, *in Jordan;* but from hence it will not follow that dipping is essential to baptism, the washing of the soul with the blood of Christ (the thing signified by baptism) being expressed by sprinkling or pouring water, as well as by dipping or being buried in water, Isa. xliv. 3; Ezek. xxxvi. 25; Col. ii. 12. Whether they confessed their sins, man by man, by word of mouth, or by submitting to the doctrine of the gospel declared their renunciation of the righteousness of the law, and their engagement to a holy life, is not expressed; but it is most certain, that a profession of faith and repentance was ordinarily required before the baptism of adult persons. It may be wondered that this new practice of John (if it were wholly new) made no more stir amongst the Jews. Either (as some think) baptism was in use before that time, as an appendix to circumcision, (though circumcision only be mentioned,) or they had some notion that Christ, Elias, and that prophet, when they came, should baptize; for, John i. 25, they asked John, *Why baptizest thou then, if thou be not that Christ, nor Elias, neither that prophet.* That which seemeth to me most probable is, that before that time there was a baptism in ordinary use amongst them after circumcising the child, beside the baptizing of proselytes. And as in the other sacrament Christ left out the typical part, and blessed the bread, used at last in that administration, and made use of that for the institution of the sacrament of the supper; so as to the ordinance of circumcision, he in the institution of that gospel ordinance left out circumcision, (which was typical also,) and retained only the washing of the person with water, and so instituted the other sacrament of the New Testament. But yet there was so much new in the Baptist's practice, (for he did not baptize proselytes only, but Jews, nor did he use it as an appendix to circumcision preceding, but baptized adult Jews,) that if the state of the Jewish church had not been declining, and their power of discipline very little, (if any,) they would more than have sent to John to know by whose authority he baptized: but they were under the Roman power, and their ecclesiastical officers were more pragmatical than mischievous, God in the wisdom of his providence having so ordered it, that the change of worship should be at such a time brought in when it should be least potently opposed.

7 ¶ But when he saw many of the Pharisees and Sadducees come to his baptism, he said unto them, ᵐO generation of vipers, who hath warned you to flee from ⁿthe wrath to come?

m ch. 12. 34.
& 23. 33.
Luke 3. 7, 8, 9.
n Rom. 5. 9.
1 Thes. 1. 10.

We shall often meet with the mention of these Pharisees and Sadducees; we will therefore inquire here a little more largely concerning them. There were three more eminent religious sects among the Jews. The Essenes, of whom we read nothing in holy writ: their main doctrine was fate, they ascribed all things to it. The two others are here mentioned, and often in other parts of the New Testament we read of the Pharisees and Sadducees: the latter were most acceptable to the great men amongst the Jews; the former were more popular, and acceptable to the people. The Sadducees were directly opposite to the Essenes; they ascribed nothing to fate, but maintained the liberty and power of man's will in the most extravagant height: they denied the immortality of the soul, the resurrection, angels, &c., all which the Pharisees owned: this we may learn from Acts xxiii. 8. where Paul wrought his own escape by setting these two factions on quarrelling about these points. In short, these were no better than atheists, for what must they be less that deny spirits and the resurrection? The Pharisees, as to their doctrine, were much more sober; they owned spirits and the resurrection; and though they held much of the freedom of, and a power in, man's will, yet they also ascribed much to the providence and grace of God. They were the interpreters of the law, and, as Mr. Calvin thinks, had their name from thence, not from their dividing and separating themselves from others, as some think. They spent much of their time in fasting and prayer; but, 1. They held a righteousness by the works of the law to be our righteousness for which we are accepted of God. 2. They made a very jejune interpretation of the law, as may appear from our Saviour's correcting it, chap. v. 3. They held many unwritten traditions of equal force with the law of God. 4. They were very hypocrites in their practice, neglecting the weighty things of the law, making long prayers for a pretence for their wickedness, and doing all they did but to be seen of men. Some of these Sadducees and Pharisees came to John's baptism, and no wonder, for, Mark vi. 20, *Herod observed him, heard him, did many things, and heard him gladly;* but, Luke vii. 30, it is said the Pharisees were *not baptized of him.* It is like they came out of curiosity. *He said unto them, O generation of vipers;* the very language which Christ used to them, chap. xii. 34; xxiii. 33. The viper, to which he compareth them, is the worst and most dangerous of serpents. We need give no account of the Baptist's treating them so roughly, because our Saviour justifieth the term by applying it to them. Corrupt teachers are the worst of men, and of all orders of sinners, fewest of them repent and have their hearts changed. *Who hath warned you to flee from the wrath to come?* what comes in your mind, who think there is no resurrection, no hell, or who think you are so righteous that you need fear none, to do any thing that might testify you are afraid of wrath to come?

‖ Or, *answerable to amendment of life.*

8 Bring forth therefore fruits ‖ meet for repentance :

You come here and thrust yourselves into a crowd of penitents, but this is not enough, true repentance is not a barren thing; neither are your leaves of external profession a sufficient indication of it, you must bring forth the fruits of holiness, fruits that may answer the nature of true repentance. The proper products of habits are called their fruits; thus we read of *the fruit of sin,* and *the fruit of righteousness. Fruits meet for repentance* are works that are the proper product of repentance, or justly answering an external profession of repentance. As faith, so repentance, without works is dead.

o John 8. 33, 39. Acts 13. 26. Rom. 4. 1, 11, 16.

9 And think not to say within yourselves, °We have Abraham to *our* father : for I say unto you, that God is able of these stones to raise up children unto Abraham.

All hypocrites bear up themselves upon something, upon which they promise good to themselves, and a freedom from the judgments of God. The Jews rested much upon their descent from Abraham, as appeareth also from John viii. 39, by which means they entitled themselves to the covenant, Gen. xvii., extended to his seed as well as to himself, as also to the name of the church, Abraham's posterity by Isaac being all the visible church which God had upon the earth at that time. It is the great work of ministers to drive hypocrites from their vain confidences. This John doth here; as if he should say, I know what you trust to, you think with yourselves that, because you are the only church of God upon the earth, judgment shall not come upon you, God would then have no seed of Abraham to show mercy to, and to keep his covenant with; but mistake not, God, of stones, if he please, can raise up Abraham a seed. To keep covenant with papists and formalists have much the same presumption, though with this difference, the Jews were the true, the only church of God, these do but arrogate the name to themselves.

p ch. 7. 19. Luke 13. 7. 9. John 15. 6.

10 And now also the ax is laid unto the root of the trees : ᵖtherefore every tree which bringeth not forth good fruit is hewn down, and cast into the fire.

A prediction, as some think, of that dreadful destruction which within a few years came by the Romans upon the whole Jewish nation. The sense is, The vengeance of God is very near to be revealed, men must repent now or never, for *every tree which bringeth not forth good fruit* shall be *hewn down, and cast into the fire;* judgment now is as nigh unto men, as the tree is to falling, to the root of which the axe is already applied : whether it be to be understood of the judgment common to all unbelievers, all that *know not God, and obey not the gospel of Christ,* as 2 Thess. i. 8, 9, or the particular destruction of this nation of the Jews, I shall not determine, though I rather judge the latter probable. The latter part of the text is made use of by our Saviour, chap. vii. 19, in the latter part of his sermon upon the mount. It letteth us know, that it is not improper, nor dissonant to the style of John Baptist, and Christ, and others the most eminent first gospel preachers, to press repentance, faith, and holiness of life, from arguments of terror.

q Mark 1. 8. Luke 3. 16. John 1. 15, 26, 33. Acts 1. 5. & 11. 16. & 19. 4. r Is. 4. 4. & 44. 3. Mal. 3. 2. Acts 2. 3, 4. 1 Cor. 12. 13.

11 ᵠI indeed baptize you with water unto repentance : but he that cometh after me is mightier than I, whose shoes I am not worthy to bear : ʳhe shall baptize you with the Holy Ghost, and *with* fire :

I am not the Christ, Mark i. 8; Luke iii. 15, 16; John i. 15, 26; I am but the messenger and forerunner of Christ, sent before him to baptize men with the baptism of water, in testimony of their repentance; but there is one immediately coming after me, who is infinitely to be preferred before me, so much, that I am not worthy to carry his shoes, or unloose his shoe-latchet. He shall baptize men with another kind of baptism, the baptism of the Holy Ghost and fire. *With the Holy Ghost,* inwardly washing away their sins with his blood, and sanctifying their hearts : the Holy Ghost working in their hearts like fire, purging out their lusts and corruptions, warming and inflaming their hearts with the sense of his love, and kindling in them all spiritual habits. Or, *with the Holy Ghost,* as in the days of Pentecost, there appearing to them *cloven tongues like as of fire,* as Acts ii. 3 : thus the term *fire* is made exegetical of the term *the Holy Ghost.* Or, *with the Holy Ghost, and with fire;* changing and renewing the hearts of those that believe in him, by the operation of the Holy Ghost, and consuming and destroying others, that will not believe, as with fire.

s Mal. 3. 3.

12 ˢWhose fan *is* in his hand, and he will throughly purge his floor, and gather his wheat into the garner; but he will ᵗburn up the chaff with unquenchable fire.

t Mal. 4. 1. ch. 10. 00.

Judea is at present God's floor, the only church he hath upon the earth; but there is chaff upon this floor, as well as wheat. Now he is come who will make a separation betwixt the chaff and the wheat; who by his preaching the gospel will distinguish betwixt Israel and those that are of Israel, Rom. ix. 6; betwixt those who, living in the true expectation of the Messias, shall receive him now he is come, and those who, by their not owning and receiving him, shall declare that they never had any true expectation of him : shall separate them into distinct heaps, raising up a gospel church, and shall at the last day make yet a stricter discrimination, and *throughly purge his floor,* taking true believers into heaven, and burning unbelievers *with unquenchable fire,* casting them into torments like unquenchable fire.

A. D. 27. u Mark 1. 9. Luke 3. 21. x ch. 2. 22.

13 ¶ ᵘThen cometh Jesus ˣfrom Galilee to Jordan unto John, to be baptized of him.

Christ, who now was about thirty years of age, Luke iii. 23, cometh from Nazareth, a city in Galilee, where Joseph lived, Luke ii. 4, and whither he went with Joseph and Mary, Luke ii. 39, and again after he had disputed with the doctors at twelve years of age, Luke ii. 46; cometh from thence to Jordan, the great river, where John was baptizing disciples, offering himself to be baptized of him. He showed his humility by going to him, and also made the action public. If any ask to what end Christ, who had no sin, was baptized, himself gives us an account, ver. 15, *to fulfil all righteousness* (of which more in its place). He thus owned John's ministry and mission to baptize, and confirmed the institution of baptism by water, and offered himself to that testimony which he knew his Father would give of him. He thus initiated himself in the Christian church, as by circumcision he had made himself of the Jewish church, and so was the Head both of the believing Jews and Gentiles. He was not (as others) baptized in testimony of his repentance, or for the remission of sins, for he was without sin.

14 But John forbad him, saying, I have need to be baptized of thee, and comest thou to me?

He did not absolutely repel him, but modestly excused himself for a time, knowing that Christ was already baptized with a more excellent baptism than he could administer to him, for God gave him the Spirit not by measure, John iii. 34.

15 And Jesus answering said unto him, Suffer *it to be so* now: for thus it becometh us to fulfil all righteousness. Then he suffered him.

Jesus said unto him, Suffer it to be so now. The question is not whether thou or I be more excellent. It is thy duty to baptize, for my Father hath sent thee to baptize. It is my pleasure and duty to be obedient to my Father, whose will I know, though it be hidden from thee. Baptism is a new law of the gospel church, of which though I be the Head, yet I must be conformed to the members of it, concerning which my Father's will is, that they should be baptized with water, as well as with the Holy Ghost. Besides that, I am to put an end to the Jewish typical circumcision, and to put a new face upon the church, by instituting another sacrament of initiation. It is therefore both just and equal that I should be baptized (though not for those ends for which others, that are my members, are baptized, not for remission of sins, but) for the fulfilling of all righteousness, in obeying my Father's will. *Then he suffered him*: he that erreth through ignorance will correct his error upon better information. We may learn from this example of Christ, that being baptized with the Holy Ghost will excuse none for contempt or neglect of baptism by water, because it is the revealed will of God, that all the members of his church should come under that ordinance; so as there is a fulfilling of righteousness in our case, as well as in Christ's, though in a different measure.

16 ʸAnd Jesus, when he was baptized, went up straightway out of the water: and, lo, the heavens were opened unto him, and he saw ᶻthe Spirit of God descending like a dove, and lighting upon him:

17 ᵃ And lo a voice from heaven, saying, ᵇThis is my beloved Son, in whom I am well pleased.

This story is also related Mark i. 10, 11, and Luke iii. 21. Luke saith that *Jesus praying, the heaven was opened*. Mark saith, cloven asunder. It is most probable that the opening of the heavens mentioned (though possibly far more glorious) bare a proportion to that opening of the heavens which we often see in a time of great lightning, when the air seemeth to divide to make the fuller and clearer way for the light. *Unto him*; that is, unto John. *And he saw the Spirit of God descending like a dove, and lighting upon him.* The Spirit of God is an invisible substance, and cannot be seen by human eyes, but the shape assumed by any person of the Trinity may be seen. Whether it was a real dove, or only the appearance of a dove, is little material for us to know. It was certainly one or the other; nor could any representation at this time be more fit, either to let the world know the dove-like nature of Christ, Isa. xlii. 2, or what should be the temper of all those who receive the same Spirit, though by measure, and are by it taught to be innocent as doves. Not that Christ had not received the Spirit before, but that his receiving of it might be notified to others. This dove, or appearance of a dove, lighted upon Christ, thereby showing for whose sake this apparition was. Christ was not confirmed only to be the Son of God by this appearance of the Holy Spirit in the form of a dove, and lighting upon him, but also by *a voice from the excellent glory*, saith Peter, 2 Pet. i. 17; God forming a voice in the air which spake, saying, *This is my beloved Son, in wnom I am well pleased*. The word signifieth, a dearly beloved Son. The same voice was repeated at Christ's transfiguration, Matt. xvii. 5. Peter from it concludes the certainty of the faith of the gospel, in the aforementioned text. *In whom I am well pleased*: the word signifieth a special and singular complacency and satisfaction: I am pleased in his person, according to that, Prov. viii. 30; I am well pleased in his undertaking, in all that he shall do and suffer in the accomplishment of the redemption of man. We are *made accepted in the Beloved*, Eph. i. 6. This text (as is generally observed) is a clear proof of the trinity of persons or subsistences in the one Divine Being: here was the Father speaking from heaven, the Son baptized and come out of the water, the Holy Ghost descending in the form or shape of a dove.

CHAP. IV

Christ fasteth forty days, is tempted of the devil, and ministered unto by angels, 1—11. *He dwelleth in Capernaum,* 12—16; *beginneth to preach,* 17; *calleth Peter and Andrew,* 18—20, *James and John,* 21, 22; *teacheth in the synagogues, and healeth the diseased,* 23—25.

THEN was ᵃJesus led up of ᵇthe spirit into the wilderness to be tempted of the devil.

This is mentioned by two of the other evangelists, Mark i. 12; Luke iv. 1. Luke saith that, *being full of the Holy Ghost, he returned from Jordan, and was led by the Spirit*, &c. Mark saith, *immediately the Spirit drove him*. Great manifestations of Divine love are commonly followed with great temptations. Others observe, that temptations usually follow baptism, the beginnings of spiritual life, and covenants made with God. He *was led up*: some think he was taken up; Mark useth the word ἐκβάλλει, the Spirit thrust him out: we must not understand an act of compulsion, doubtless he went voluntarily. *Of the Spirit*; the Holy Spirit, that lighted upon him as a dove. *Into the wilderness*. Mark's saying, chap. i .13, that he was there *with wild beasts*, lets us know that it was not such a wilderness as John began to preach in, chap. iii. 1; but a howling wilderness full of wild beasts. The end is expressed in the last words, *to be tempted of the devil*: thus his temptations are distinguished from Divine temptations, such as Abraham had, Gen. xxii. 1; and by *tempted* here is meant solicited, or moved to sin, in which sense God tempteth no man, James i. 13. The general notion of tempting is, making a trial; God makes a trial of his people for the proof and manifestation of their gracious habit. Satan, by moving to sin, makes a trial of corruption, which was the reason that, although Christ was tempted, that he might be *able to succour those that are tempted*, Heb. ii. 18, and that he might taste all those evils to which we are exposed, and might overcome the devil; yet when the Prince of this world came, he could effect nothing against him, because he found nothing in him to comply with his motions.

2 And when he had fasted forty days and forty nights, he was afterward an hungred.

He was in the wilderness, a place of solitude, and so fitter for Satan's purpose, and he was *an hungred*, which was another advantage Satan had. But he was not an hungred till *he had fasted forty days and forty nights*. Here was the Divine power miraculously seen, in upholding the human nature of Christ without any thing to eat: this was a miracle. The like did Moses before the law, Elijah under the law. Christ doth the same in the beginning of the gospel; nor did he fast as the Jews were wont, of whom we sometimes read that they kept fasts several days; they only fasted in the day time, but ate their food at night; or sometimes only forbare pleasant bread, as Daniel did, Dan. x. 2, 3, for three full weeks. But Christ fasted from all food, and that not only forty days, but forty nights also; from whence may easily be gathered, how idly, if not impiously, the papists found their fasting forty days in Lent. Here all Christ's acts (most certainly his miraculous works) are not recorded for our imitation; some of them are only for our adoration; all his miraculous acts are so. There can be nothing more sottish than for us to think, that because Christ (supported by the Divine nature) fasted forty days, therefore we are obliged to do it; and because we cannot fast forty days and forty nights, without eating something, therefore we may eat fish, though no flesh (when all know that to some palates there is no more delicate food than fish); or we are obliged to fast in the day time, though not at night. And because Christ once in his lifetime fasted forty days and forty nights, therefore we must do so every year; or that the church hath any power to enjoin any such thing. If papists think Christ's fast of forty days and forty nights obligeth them to imitation, let them keep them as he did, (with such a fasting I mean,) and try whether they be able to do it, or whether four days or nights, instead of forty, will not convince them of their folly. Christ fasted forty days and forty nights, and thereby showed he was God-man, the Divine nature supported the human; afterward he was hungry, to show that he was truly man, *touched with the feeling of our infirmities, in all points tempted as we are, yet without sin,* Heb. iv. 15.

3 And when the tempter came to him, he said, If thou be the Son of God, command that these stones be made bread.

And when the tempter, viz. Satan, the devil, as he is called, *came unto him,* probably in some visible shape, *he,* forming an audible voice of the air, *said, If thou be the Son of God,* (not that he doubted it, which showed his horrible impudence,) *command that these stones, (this stone,* saith Luke, chap. iv. 3) *be made bread.* The temptation plainly was to the use of means which God did not allow him, to relieve him in his distress of hunger, to distrust the providence of God in supporting of him. A temptation common to those who are the members of Christ, and enough to instruct us, that we ought to look upon all thoughts and motions to the use of means not allowed by God, in order to a lawful end, as temptations *vel a carne, vel hoste,* either from our own flesh, for *every man is tempted, when he is drawn away of his own lust and enticed,* James i. 14, or from our grand adversary the devil. It is not much material for us to know from which, they being both what we ought to resist, though those from Satan are usually more violent and impetuous.

4 But he answered and said, It is written, ^cMan shall not live by bread alone, but by every word that proceedeth out of the mouth of God.

c Deut. 8. 3.

So also Luke iv. 4. There is no better answering the tempter than by opposing the precepts of holy writ to his motions to sin. The word is called *the sword of the Spirit,* Eph. vi. 17. The papists, therefore, denying people the use of the word, disarm them as to the spiritual combat. *It is written* Deut. viii. 3. Though man ordinarily liveth by common bread, such food as men usually eat, yet God's power is not restrained, he can uphold the life of man when that is wanting, as he supported the Israelites by manna (to which that text relates); nor is God obliged to create any extraordinary means, for his power, which is seen in creating such means, can produce the same effect without such means if it pleaseth him. His power must be seen in creating the means, and in upholding the proper power and faculty of the means, in order to their end; why cannot he by the same power produce the effect without any such means?

d Neh. 11. 1, 18. Is. 48. 2. & 52. 1. ch. 27. 53. Rev. 11. 2.

5 Then the devil taketh him up ^dinto the holy city, and setteth him on a pinnacle of the temple,

By *the holy city* is meant Jerusalem, once a holy city, Dan. ix. 24; now, though a most impure and filthy city upon many accounts, yet, upon other accounts still a holy city, being the only city in the world which had then in it the true worship of the true God, and in which God doubtless, who in Ahab's time had seven thousand in Israel, had many holy people. How the devil took Christ into the holy city is variously argued and judged; the words used in the Greek are such as would incline us to think he was not carried by force, but followed the tempter willingly, and set upon a place on the top of the temple, higher than the other parts of it. The end of his being set there the next verse tells us.

6 And saith unto him, If thou be the Son of God, cast thyself down: for it is written, ^eHe shall give his angels charge concerning thee: and in *their* hands they shall bear thee up, lest at any time thou dash thy foot against a stone.

e Ps. 91. 11, 12.

Before the devil had tempted our Lord to diffidence or distrust in God's providence, and the use of means not allowed by God to supply himself; here he tempts him to an unwarrantable presumption, and confidence of and concerning the Divine protection. In the former temptation the devil used no Scripture, but having been repelled in that assault by *the sword of the Spirit, which is the word of God.* Eph. vi. 17, he here takes up the same weapon. The thing to which the tempter soliciteth our Saviour, was the throwing himself down from a precipice, a temptation, in effect, to destroy himself; which is one of those fiery darts which he commonly throweth at the people of God in their hours of melancholy, or under great pressures of affliction; but the usual argument which he useth to them, is deliverance from their terrors, the preventing of want, or avoiding shame. The argument he useth to our Lord is quite of another nature, the special protection of God promised to God's people, Psal. xci. 11, 12. Herein he transformeth himself *into an angel of light,* according to 2 Cor. xi. 14, and lets us know that truth may be abused to the patronage of lies; and that there is no hook more dangerous to the members of Christ, than that which is baited with Scripture misinterpreted and misapplied, which holy writ always is when it is so interpreted or so applied as to be made an argument to sin. This portion of holy writ is both, 1. Falsely cited; and, 2. As ill applied. 1. In the quotation the tempter leaves out those words, *in all thy ways.* This was none of our Saviour's ways, he had no call, no warrant from God to decline the stairs by which he might have gone down, and to throw himself down. God had never promised, nor ever given, any the protection of angels in sinful and forbidden ways. 2. He misapplieth this text, using it not to instruct, but to deceive; dividing betwixt man's duty and God's providence; making this word a promise to be fulfilled upon Christ's neglect of his duty; extending the promise of special providence as to dangers into which men voluntarily throw themselves; putting God upon working miracles to declare Christ to be his Son, where there was no need, and of which there was no use, mocking our Saviour's true use of Scripture, with Scripture abused, and many other ways: but he had to do with one not ignorant of his devices.

7 Jesus said unto him, It is written again, ^fThou shalt not tempt the Lord thy God.

f Deut. 6. 16.

This is written Deut. vi. 16. To make an undue and unwarrantable trial of God, is to tempt God, whether the trial respecteth his power or his goodness; thus the word is used, Numb. xiv. 22; Psal. lxxviii. 18; Isa. vii. 12; chap. xvi. 1. By this answer Christ lets the devil know that he abused Scripture in his quotation of it; such a casting of himself down, when he had a plain way to go down by the stairs, would not have been an act of faith, but presumption; not a trusting God upon his word, but a tempting of God, expressly contrary to his command, Deut. vi. 16.

8 Again, the devil taketh him up into an exceeding high mountain, and sheweth him all the kingdoms of the world, and the glory of them;

9 And saith unto him, All these things will I give thee, if thou wilt fall down and worship me.

This is the third temptation by which the tempter soliciteth our Saviour to sin, and of all other the most impudent. For what can be more impudent than for the creature to expect a homage to him from him who was his Creator. What mountain this was, and how our Saviour was taken up into it, are things not revealed, and of very little concern for us to know. The text tells us it was exceeding high, yet not high enough from whence one kingdom could be seen in the extent of it. It is therefore most probable that Dr. Lightfoot judgeth most truly, that "the devil, being the prince of the power of the air, formed an airy horizon before the eyes of Christ, carrying such pompous and glorious appearance of kingdoms, states, and royalties in the face of it, as if he had seen those very kingdoms and states indeed." Such things the devil can do, and doth do, by condensing the air first, then shaping and figuring, and lastly so colouring it, that it may represent what he intendeth. All these things he promised to give our Saviour, if he would fall down and worship him. The same eminent person well observes, that "what Luke calls worshipping before the devil, Matthew calls worshipping the devil;" and concludes solidly, "that if to worship before the devil be to worship the devil, worshipping before an image (as the papists do) must be worshipping the image." The devil here arrogates to himself what was God's alone to give, and such ordinarily are the devil's promises of things, as to which he hath no power to fulfil what he promiseth.

10 Then saith Jesus unto him, Get thee

hence, Satan: for it is written, ^gThou shalt worship the Lord thy God, and him only shalt thou serve.

^g Deut. 6. 13. & 10. 20. Josh. 24. 14. 1 Sam. 7. 3.

As this was of all the three the most impudent temptation, so our Lord receiveth it with the highest detestation, saying, *Get thee hence, Satan!* by which words he doth not only show his detestation of this temptation, but also chides him off from any further tempting him. The sense is, Satan, I know better things, viz. that a religious adoration is not to be given unto any but unto God alone. Thou art a creature; no worship is due unto thee: to worship before thee (so Luke phraseth it, Luke iv. 7) is to worship thee. This is expressly contrary to the command of God, Deut. vi. 13; x. 20. It is also observable, that our Saviour opposeth this to the devil's words, ἐὰν πεσὼν προσκυνήσῃς μοι, if thou falling down wilt worship me; and that Christ answers, Τὸν Θεόν σου προσκυνήσεις καὶ αὐτῷ μόνῳ λατρεύσεις; which shows the idleness of the papists' distinction of *doulia* and *latreia*; the first of which they say may be given to the creature, the second only unto God; by which they justify their veneration of images. The using a posture of adoration before the creature in an act of worship, Christ here interpreteth a worshipping the creature, if the creature either exacts it of us, or we purposely set it before us, or choose it as an object exciting or moving us to such an act of adoration, which the papists do. Not that all prostration before the creature is an act of Divine adoration; there is a civil as well as a Divine worship; and in Divine worship the position of the creature before us may be merely for conveniency, or accidental. But all prostration in an act of Divine worship is a posture of adoration, and where a creature is chosen and set before us in that act or posture, to excite or move us, it partaketh of the homage. There is some little difference betwixt the words, Deut. vi. 13; x. 20, and those of St. Matthew; but that is said to be written, which is written as to the substance and sense, though not in those terms. Moses saith, *Thou shalt fear*; as Matthew quotes it it is, *Thou shalt worship.* The term *fear* applied unto God, signifieth any act of religion, whether external or internal, and though the last words in Deuteronomy, *thou shalt swear by his name*, be not mentioned in Matthew, yet enough are quoted for our Saviour's purpose. Falling down and worshipping belongeth only to God, (saith our Saviour,) not to thee; let me therefore hear of thee no more.

11 Then the devil leaveth him, and, behold, ^hangels came and ministered unto him.

^h Heb. 1. 14.

Resist the devil, saith James, chap. iv. 7, *and he shall flee from you.* Thus he did from the Head, thus he shall do from the members: but as he did not flee from Christ till commanded away, so neither till commanded off by God doth he leave the people of God; but upon our resistance God will command him off, that we may not be tempted above our strength. The evil angels leaving him, the good *angels came and ministered unto him*, whether by bringing him food, or bringing him off the mount, or otherwise executing his commands, is not expressed, and it is too much curiosity to inquire. God by this teacheth us, that our lives are to have their vicissitudes of temptations and consolations, and that our temptations shall have a happy issue, and that when ordinary means fail we may expect extraordinary influences and assistances. Luke saith, *he departed from him for a season*, to let us know, that though here was an end of his more eminent temptations, yet he was not afterward without Satan's assaults.

12 ¶ ⁱNow when Jesus had heard that John was ‖cast into prison, he departed into Galilee;

A. D. 30. ⁱ Mark 1. 14. Luke 3. 20. & 4. 14, 31. John 4. 43. ‖ Or, *delivered up.*

John was some time after this cast into prison, for his free reproving Herod Antipas, the tetrarch of Galilee, for taking Herodias his brother Philip's wife, and other evils, chap. xiv. 3, 4; Mark vi. 17; Luke iii. 19, 20. Jesus heard of this accident, and *departed into Galilee.* There were many things happened betwixt Christ's temptations and this his motion into Galilee, which are omitted by all the evangelists except John, and by him recorded in his four first chapters. Neither by *Galilee* must we understand the Nether Galilee, which was within the jurisdiction of Herod, but the Upper Galilee, called *Galilee of the Gentiles*, ver. 15, in the borders of Zebulun and Naphtali, which was in the jurisdiction of Philip, a man of a less bloody disposition. Others make it under Herod's jurisdiction, but where the Pharisees had less to do than in Judea. Our Saviour doth not out of cowardice avoid danger, but he knew his time was not yet come. But some judicious interpreters think that our Saviour first went into the Lower Galilee, and from thence soon after into the Upper Galilee: that which makes this more probable is the next words, *And leaving Nazareth, he came and dwelt in Capernaum;* so as it should seem he first went to Nazareth, which was in the Lower Galilee.

13 And leaving Nazareth, he came and dwelt in Capernaum, which is upon the sea coast, in the borders of Zabulon and Nephthalim:

A. D. 31.

By this (as was said before) it should seem that our Lord first went into the Nether Galilee, where Nazareth was, which after a time he left, and went to Capernaum; which Capernaum was a city near the sea, in the borders of Zebulun and Naphtali, whose lots in the land of Canaan were contiguous, and by the sea-side, as appeareth by Josh. xix.

14 That it might be fulfilled which was spoken by Esaias the prophet, saying,

15 ^kThe land of Zabulon, and the land of Nephthalim, *by* the way of the sea, beyond Jordan, Galilee of the Gentiles;

^k Is. 9. 1, 2.

16 ^lThe people which sat in darkness saw great light; and to them which sat in the region and shadow of death light is sprung up.

^l Is. 42. 7. Luke 2. 32.

The text in Isa. ix. 1, 2, where the words are, *Nevertheless the dimness shall not be such as was in her vexation, when at the first he lightly afflicted the land of Zebulun and the land of Naphtali, and afterward did more grievously afflict her by the way of the sea, beyond Jordan, in Galilee of the nations. The people that walked in darkness have seen a great light: they that dwell in the land of the shadow of death, upon them hath the light shined.* The Jews make a great many objections against the application of this text unto Christ, as indeed they do against the application of all texts cited out of the Old Testament by the evangelists. Christians, believing that the evangelists being holy men, who wrote not from a private spirit private interpretations, have not any reason to regard what their interest leadeth them to object: but even Christian interpreters are divided in their sentiments whether these words are said to be fulfilled, in this motion of Christ unto Galilee, in a literal, or typical, or a more improper and analogical sense; nor is it any great matter with which of them we agree. For my own part, I see no reason why ver. 2 should not be literally understood of and applied unto Christ. There is nothing more ordinary in the prophets, than, after a threatening of judgment and captivity unto the people, to comfort such as feared God amongst them with promises of the Messiah, and the spiritual salvation which was to be brought in. The land of Zebulun and Naphtali suffered much by Benhadad, 1 Kings xv. 20, and more by Tiglath-pileser, 2 Kings xv. 29, before the general captivity of the ten tribes, 2 Kings xvii. 6. The Lord by the prophet, chap. viii., had been threatening this general captivity; possibly the prophet might say the affliction of those parts should not be so great as the second mentioned, 2 Kings xv. 29; because by the story it seems they were generally carried into captivity before the more general destruction of the other tribes there. Saith he, This darkness shall be abundantly hereafter compensated, by the coming of the Messiah, and preaching amongst this people; who living at a great distance from Jerusalem, never had such a light as some other parts of Judea, and first drank of the cup of God's wrath in their captivity. It was called *Galilee of the Gentiles*, because it was near to the men of Tyre, who were Gentiles, and had doubtless in it a greater mixture of Gentiles than any other part of Canaan, ever since Solomon gave Hiram twenty cities in this Galilee, 1 Kings ix. 11.

17 ¶ ^mFrom that time Jesus began to

^m Mark 1. 14, 15.

S. MATTHEW IV

preach, and to say, ⁿRepent: for the kingdom of heaven is at hand.

<small>n ch. 3. 2.
& 10. 7.</small>

From the time of Christ's baptism, or from the time that he heard that John was committed to prison, he, who before had preached and taught privately, and more rarely, began to preach more ordinarily and publicly, and the sum of his doctrine was the same with that of John the Baptist, confirming his doctrine, *Repent, for the kingdom of heaven is at hand.* See the sense of those words, chap. iii. 2. Mark hath the same, chap. i. 15.

18 ¶ °And Jesus, walking by the sea of Galilee, saw two brethren, Simon ^pcalled Peter, and Andrew his brother, casting a net into the sea: for they were fishers.

<small>o Mark 1.
16, 17, 18.
Luke 5. 2.
p John 1. 42.</small>

Whether *the sea* he here meant the lake of Gennesaret, or the ocean, is not worth the arguing, for the Jews called all great collections of waters the seas, according to Gen. i. 10. *He saw two brethren, Simon called Peter, and Andrew his brother,* whether natural brethren, or called so because of their joint employment, *casting a net into the sea,* either for the catching of fish, or for the washing of their nets: see Luke v. 2. *For they were fishers:* sea-men (as the word seems to signify) used to fish in the sea. Simon had a ship of his own, Luke v. 3. The evangelists' differing relation of the call of Simon and Andrew hath made a great deal of work for interpreters. The greatest difference seemeth to be betwixt Matthew, in this text, and John, chap. i. 35—38. But certainly John speaketh of one call in those verses, the other evangelists of another. According to John, they were called to the knowledge of and first acquaintance with Christ while John was in the public exercise of his ministry, for they were his disciples, John i. 35, 36, and, ver. 39, they are said at that time *to have abode with him that day.* Probably they again returned to their old employment, and when John was imprisoned, Christ, walking by the sea, saw them, and then called them to the apostleship. There are other differences in their call observed betwixt Matthew, Mark, and Luke, but such as may be easily answered by those who observe, that there is nothing more ordinary, than for the evangelists, in reporting the same history, one of them to supply more largely what the other had recorded more summarily.

19 And he saith unto them, Follow me, and ^qI will make you fishers of men.

<small>q Luke 5. 10, 11.</small>

Here was their call to the office of apostles. It is observable that God's calls of men to places of dignity and honour, and his appearances of favour to them, have ordinarily been when they have been busied in the honest employments of their callings. Saul was seeking his father's asses, David keeping his father's sheep, when the Lord called them to the kingdom. The shepherds were feeding their flocks when they had the revelation of Christ. He calleth four apostles from their fishery; Amos from amongst the herdmen of Tekoa; Matthew from the receipt of custom; Moses when keeping Jethro's flock, Exod. iii. 1, 2; Gideon from the threshing-floor, Judg. vi. 11. God never encourageth idleness, but despiseth not persons in meanest employments. *Follow me,* that is, to return no more to your employment. *I will make you fishers of men:* here is the work of ministers set out, to gain souls to God; they are not to fish merely for a livelihood, much less for honour and applause to themselves, but to win souls to God, and are to bait their hooks and order their nets to this end, which they will never serve, if either by general discourses they make the meshes so wide that all will dart through them, or if by their wit and learning they make their discourses so fine and curious that few or none of their hearers can understand them. Nor will all our art make us fishers of men: *I will make you,* saith Christ. Paul may plant, and Apollos may water, God must give the increase. But yet we must order our nets rationally and probably in order to our end, and without that cannot expect God's blessings. Nor were the apostles presently to enter upon the work of the ministry, but first to *follow* him. And indeed such should all gospel ministers be. In the choice of Matthias, Peter limited the people in their election to *those that had accompanied with them all the time the Lord Jesus went in and out amongst them,* Acts i. 21. Other ministers commonly prove fishers for something else, not for the souls of men.

20 ^rAnd they straightway left *their* nets, and followed him.

<small>r Mark 10. 28.
Luke 18. 28.</small>

When Christ calls, men shall obey; when he calls, he draweth. It is not of indispensable necessity that men who exercise the ministry should have nothing else to do, Paul's hands ministered to his necessities; but nothing but a providing for ourselves and households can excuse ministers in entangling themselves with the things of this life. Churches that are able ought better to provide for their ministers, and ministers so provided for sin if they do not wholly give up themselves to their work, 1 Tim. iv. 15.

21 ^sAnd going on from thence, he saw other two brethren, James *the son* of Zebedee, and John his brother, in a ship with Zebedee their father, mending their nets; and he called them.

<small>s Mark 1. 19, 20.
Luke 5. 10.</small>

22 And they immediately left the ship and their father, and followed him.

There was another James, Matt. x. 3, the son of Alpheus, called James the less, brother of Joses and Salome, Mark xv. 40. This was *James the son of Zebedee, and John,* who is thought to be the evangelist. Christ calleth them, not with his voice only, but by his Spirit, affecting their hearts, so as they immediately *left their ship and their father.* Elsewhere the disciples say, *Master, we have left all and followed thee;* probably their employment with their ship was their *all.* They left *their father* also, but it was upon Christ's call, in which case it is every man's duty, *and followed him,* to learn of him before they went out to preach him, and to be witnesses of his miracles, &c.

23 ¶ And Jesus went about all Galilee, ^tteaching in their synagogues, and preaching ^uthe Gospel of the kingdom, ^xand healing all manner of sickness and all manner of disease among the people.

<small>t ch. 9. 35.
Mark 1. 21, 39. Luke 4. 15, 44.
u ch. 24. 14.
Mark 1. 14.
x Mark 1. 34.</small>

Jesus Christ having now called four disciples, did not judge it sufficient to send them about, but himself *went about all* the places of that dark country of *Galilee, teaching in their synagogues;* the word signifieth both the congregation convened and the place. Here it signifieth both. Synagogues were of old time, Acts xv. 21; how ancient we know not. Some think that they were no older than the return out of the captivity of Babylon: but I am posed then in determining where the body of the Jews ordinarily worshipped God on the sabbath days, for it is certain they did not all go up to the temple at Jerusalem. In the Old Testament we read of them only, Psal. lxxiv. 8, as at that time *burnt up.* As to the order of them, we only read, that they had some rulers, Acts xiii. 15, who directed those who were to speak *words of exhortation.* The Scriptures were read in them, Acts xv. 21; the law and the prophets, Acts xiii. 15. They prayed in them, Matt. vi. 5; they expounded Scripture in them, Luke iv. 16—19. Christ preached in the synagogues; not only there, we shall find him preach on the mount in the next chapter, and in private houses; but he did not decline the synagogues, either as to preaching or hearing, not wholly separating from a church corrupt enough through traditions, but not idolatrous. But what did he preach? *The gospel of the kingdom;* the glad tidings for lost sinners, that was come into the world, by the revelation of him, who was the true Messias, and the true and only way by which men might come to the kingdom of God, and be eternally saved. This is what all his ministers should publish; not their own conceits, or dictates of men, or things impertinent to the salvation of souls, but *the gospel of the kingdom. And healing all manner of sickness and all manner of disease amongst the people:* the Greek is, *all diseases and sicknesses,* yet surely some died in Galilee in that time. This is another text, to prove that the term *all* in Scripture doth not always signify every individual, but some individuals of every species. Christ confirmed his doctrine, and Divine mission, by these miraculous operations.

24 And his fame went throughout all Syria: and they brought unto him all sick people that

were taken with divers diseases and torments, and those which were possessed with devils, and those which were lunatick, and those that had the palsy; and he healed them.

Syria is said to be bounded on the north by Cilicia, by Egypt on the south, on the west with the sea, and on the east with Euphrates, and to comprehend within it all Judea, Bethany, Galilee, Decapolis, Samaria, Idumea, Palestina, Syrophœnicia, Syria of Damascus, and Syria of Antioch. Christ's *fame* spread very far doubtless, because of the good he did, and the miracles he wrought, *and they brought unto him all sick people that were taken with divers diseases:* all here again can signify no more than very many that were indisposed and ill affected as to their bodily health, those that were sick of, or detained in their beds or houses by, divers diseases. Though Christ showed his power in curing some diseases which physicians judge incurable, yet he showed his kindness also in relieving others not so fatally sick. *And torments;* such as were troubled with great pains, as if they were upon racks, or in the hands of tormentors, that set themselves to torture them. *And those which were possessed with devils:* of these sorts of persons we shall read often in the gospel: this is the first time we meet with the term. It is observed that in the Old Testament we read little of any such persons; (we read only of Saul's being vexed with an evil spirit;) we read much of them in the New Testament, and in ecclesiastical history for some years after Christ: they called them *energumeni*. Some think God, in those first times of the gospel, permitted the devil to this degree, that the power of our Saviour might be the more seen in casting them out, and in giving authority to his disciples to cast them out, which was a great demonstration of his Divinity. Others think that God did it for a demonstration of the error of the Sadducees, who held there were no spirits. The gospel seemeth to hint two sorts of these persons: some upon whom the devil had power no further than to rack and torture them, Mark v. 3—5; Luke ix. 39; others in whom he dwelled bodily, and divined and prophesied in them, Acts xvi. 16. *And those which were lunatic;* affected with such diseases as use to increase in some times of the moon, or at such times to seize persons: of this nature we know divers, more particularly the falling sickness and dropsy. *And those that had the palsy,* a disease caused by the resolution of the nerves. Those diseases here mentioned which men account hardest to be cured, if capable of cure by men: Christ, to show his Divine power, healed them. Christ did not only cure these bodily distempers, but he also preached the gospel of the kingdom to heal their soul distempers. We read of many who came to him for bodily cure, but of none that said to him, *What shall we do to be saved?* How sensible are men and women of their bodily pains and diseases, more than of their soul's wants!

y Mark 3. 7.   25 ʸ And there followed him great multitudes of people from Galilee, and *from* Decapolis, and *from* Jerusalem, and *from* Judæa, and *from* beyond Jordan.

They followed for the loaves, for the benefit of the bodily cures, or out of curiosity, though some (probably) followed him out of love, and to learn of him. *Decapolis* hath its name from ten cities comprehended in it. Here was a mixture both of Jews and Gentiles following Christ, who came to be a Saviour of them both, and to pull down the partition wall betwixt both, to make them both one gospel church, Eph. ii. 14.

CHAP. V

Christ beginneth his sermon upon the mount, declaring who are blessed, 1—12. He calleth his disciples the salt of the earth, the light of the world; and by the similitudes of a city on a hill, and of a candle, he urgeth upon them the necessity of setting a good example, 13—16. He came not to destroy, but to fulfil, the law, 17—20. He extendeth the precepts against murder, 21—26, adultery, 27—32, and false swearing, 33—37: exhorteth to suffer wrong patiently, 38—42; to love our enemies, 43—47; and to aim at perfection, 48.

AND seeing the multitudes, ᵃhe went up into a mountain: and when he was set, his disciples came unto him:

a Mark 3. 13, 20.

2 And he opened his mouth, and taught them, saying,

The last chapter concluded with telling us that a great multitude followed Christ, which he observing, that he might with more conveniency to himself, and advantage to them, speak what he had to say, *he went up into a mountain;* and sitting down, after the manner of the Jewish doctors to show their authority, which our Saviour also at other times observed, Matt. xxvi. 55; Luke iv. 20; John viii. 2, *his disciples came unto him;* both those strictly so called, and others also, viz. the multitude, mentioned in the last chapter, or some of them; and he began to speak to them with freedom, so as the multitude might hear. Christ thought it as lawful to preach in the mountain as in the synagogues; nor did his disciples doubt the lawfulness of hearing him, wherever he thought fit to speak.

3 ᵇ Blessed *are* the poor in spirit: for their's is the kingdom of heaven.

b Luke 6. 20. See Ps. 51. 17. Prov. 16. 19. & 29. 23. Is. 57. 15. & 66. 2.

Happy are they, who, though they be not rich in this world's goods, yet have a spirit suited to their state and condition, not looking for their consolation here, but, having a poor and low opinion of the world and all that is therein, looking after more excellent riches; and, in order to it, are of broken and contrite spirits for their manifold sins, and cannot entertain any proud opinion of their own righteousness, but flee unto the free grace of God, and the righteousness of the Lord Jesus Christ. Not the great, and rich, and proud men of the world are happy, but these are the blessed men; for true happiness lieth not in worldly possessions, but in the favour of God, and a right to the kingdom of heaven, and that these men have, Psal. xxxiv. 18; li. 17; Isa. lxvi. 2.

4 ᶜ Blessed *are* they that mourn: for they shall be comforted.

c Is. 61. 2, 3. Luke 6. 21. John 16. 20. 2 Cor. 1. 7. Rev. 21. 4.

The world is mistaken in accounting the jocund and merry companions the only happy men; their mirth is madness, and their joy will be like crackling of thorns under a pot: but those are rather the happy men, who mourn; yea, such are most certainly happy, who mourn out of duty in the sense of their own sins, or of the sins of others, or who mourn out of choice rather to suffer afflictions and persecutions with the people of God, than to enjoy the pleasure of sin for a season. Though such sufferings do excite in them natural passions, yet it is a blessed mourning, for those are the blessed tears which God will wipe at last from his people's eyes, and such are these. *They shall be comforted,* either in this life, with the consolations of the Spirit, or with their Master's joy in the life that is to come, Isa. lxi. 3; John xvi. 20; James i. 12. So as this promise, and declaration of blessedness, is not to be extended to all mourners, but only to such as God hath made so, or who in duty have made themselves so, obeying some command of God, for sympathizing with God's glory, or with his afflicted people, Rom. xii. 15, or testifying their repentance for their sins; for there is a mourning which is a mere natural effect of passion, and a worldly sorrow which worketh unto death, as well as a godly sorrow working repentance to salvation, 2 Cor. vii. 10.

5 ᵈ Blessed *are* the meek: for ᵉthey shall inherit the earth.

d Ps. 37. 11. e See Rom. 4. 13.

Men count the hectors of the world happy, whom none can provoke but they must expect as good as they bring, *an eye for an eye, and a tooth for a tooth:* but I tell you these are not truly happy; they are tortured with their own passions; as their hand is against every one, so every man's hand is against them; besides that there is a God, who will revenge the wrongs they do. But *the meek,* who can be angry, but restrain their wrath in obedience to the will of God, and will not be angry unless they can be angry and not sin; nor will easily be provoked by others, but rather use soft words to pacify wrath, and give place to the passions of others; these are the blessed men. For though others may by their sword and their bow conquer a great deal of the earth to their will and power, yet they will never quietly and comfortably inherit or possess it; they are possessors *malæ fidei,* forcible possessors, and they will enjoy what they have, as rapacious birds enjoy theirs, unquietly, every one hath his gun ready charged and cocked against them: but those who are of meek and quiet spirits, though they may not take so deep root in the earth as others more boisterous, yet there will be no worm at the root of what they have, and they shall enjoy what God giveth them with more quiet and certainty; and God will provide for them, verily they shall be fed, Psal. xxxvii. 3, 11.

6 Blessed *are* they which do hunger and thirst after righteousness: ^ffor they shall be filled.

^f Is. 55. 1. & 65. 13.

You see many men and women hungering and thirsting after sensual satisfactions, or after sensible enjoyments; these are unhappy, miserable men, they often hunger and thirst, and are not satisfied: but I will show you a more excellent way. a more excellent object of your hunger and thirst, that is, *righteousness;* both a righteousness wherein you may stand before God, which is in me, Jer. xxiii. 6, and is *revealed from faith to faith,* Rom. i. 17. and the righteousness of a holy life. Those are blessed men, who *first seek the kingdom of heaven, and the righteousness thereof,* God will fill these men with what they desire, Isa. lv. 1, 2; Luke i. 53. There are some who understand this text of a hungering after the clearing of their innocency towards men, which is natural to just and innocent persons falsely accused and traduced, and they have a promise of being filled. Psal. xxxvii. 6; but I see no reason to conclude this the sense of this text.

^g Ps. 41. 1. ch. 6. 14. Mark 11. 25. 2 Tim. 1. 16. Heb. 6. 10. Jam. 2. 13.

7 Blessed *are* the merciful: ^gfor they shall obtain mercy.

The men of the world bless themselves if they can take care of themselves, let others do what they will, and as well as they can: but I tell you, that those alone are the blessed men, who are touched with a true sense and feeling of the wants and miseries of others, and that not out of a mere goodness and tenderness of nature, but out of a true obedience to the will of God, and a sense of his love to them, and faith in his promises; and, moved from these principles, do not only pity and compassionate them, and wish them well, but extend their helping hand to them, suitably to their miseries: for these men *shall obtain mercy,* and that not only from men, if they come into straits and distress, but from the hand of God, Psal. xxxvii. 26; cxii. 5, 6: he doth not say they shall merit mercy at God's hand, but they shall be mercified, they shall obtain mercy.

^h Ps. 15. 2. & 24. 4. Heb. 12. 14. i 1 Cor. 13. 12. 1 John 3. 2, 3.

8 ^hBlessed *are* the pure in heart: for ⁱthey shall see God.

The men of the world bless those who appear pure and holy to men, and put on a vizard and mask of purity, though they be but painted sepulchres, and their hearts be as cages of all unclean birds: but those alone are blessed, who, being washed from their filthiness by my blood, are of a sincere and upright heart; though they be not legally pure and free from all sin, yet are so pure as that God will accept them, the bent of their hearts being after holiness; who have not a heart and a heart, no doubleness of mind, who are persons in whom is no guile. For though no mortal eye can see and comprehend the essence of God, yet these men shall by an eye of faith *see* and enjoy *God* in this life, though in a glass more darkly, and in the life to come face to face, and as he is, 1 Cor. xiii. 12; Heb. xii. 14; 1 John iii. 2.

9 Blessed *are* the peacemakers: for they shall be called the children of God.

The world blesseth the boisterous, unquiet party of it, that can never be still, but are continually thinking of more worlds to conquer, and blowing up the coals of war, division, and sedition: but they are blessed indeed, who study to be quiet, seeking peace, and pursuing it; and are so far from sowing the seeds of discord, or blowing those coals, that their great study is to make peace between God and man, and betwixt a man and his neighbour, doing this in obedience to God, and out of a principle of love to God and men; for those that do so shall approve themselves like unto God, to be his children, and so they shall be called. *To be called* and *to be* is much the same: so what Moses said, Gen. xxi. 12, is interpreted by Paul, Rom. ix. 7, 8; so what is said by Matthew, chap. xxi. 13, is interpreted by Luke, chap. xix. 46; what was said by St. John, chap. i. 12, is interpreted 1 John iii. 1; for God is the God of peace, 1 Cor. xiv. 33.

10 ^kBlessed *are* they which are persecuted for righteousness' sake: for their's is the kingdom of heaven.

^k 2 Cor. 4. 17. 2 Tim. 2. 12. 1 Pet. 3. 14.

The men of the world judge those men very unhappy and miserable whom their rulers make the objects of their wrath and malice, and pursue violently to the loss of their estates, liberties, or lives, never considering the cause for which they are so pursued: but they are quite mistaken; for that man who is pursued by such violence, and hunted upon this account, because to please men he durst not sin against God, but labours to keep a *conscience void of offence toward God, and toward men,* Acts xxiv. 16, is a blessed man; and if he be hunted out of the kingdoms of the earth, yet he shall be hunted but to heaven, for to such men belongeth the kingdom of God in glory, James i. 12; 1 Pet. iii. 14; iv. 13.

11 ^lBlessed are ye, when *men* shall revile you, and persecute *you,* and shall say all manner of ^mevil against you †falsely, for my sake.

^l Luke 6. 22.
^m 1 Pet. 4. 14.
† Gr. *lying.*

Reviling and speaking evil of persons falsely, because of their profession of Christ, and because they dare not sin against God, is a species of persecution, Gen. xxi. 9; Gal. iv. 29, though the lowest degree of it. It hath been the constant lot of God's servants. David said, Psal. xxxv. 11, that *false witnesses did rise up,* and *laid to his charge things that he knew not.* Thus John and Christ were served, Matt. xi. 18, 19; Luke vii. 33, 34; nor is it to be wondered that those whose consciences are so seared that they cannot feel the guilt of persecuting others for righteousness' sake, should not feel the guilt of lying and false swearing. But, saith our Saviour, you are blessed when these things happen unto you, 1 Pet. iv. 13.

12 ⁿRejoice, and be exceeding glad: for great *is* your reward in heaven: for ^oso persecuted they the prophets which were before you.

ⁿ Luke 6. 23. Acts 5. 41. Rom. 5. 3. Jam. 1. 2. ^o 1 Pet. 4. 13. Neh. 9. 26. 2 Chron. 36. 16. ch. 23. 34, 37. Acts 7. 52. 1 Thess. 2. 15.

Be so far from being troubled, as to count it all joy, when you fall into these trials, James i. 2. Let it be music in your ears to hear that the drunkards make you their song. Rejoice in your hearts, express it in your lips and behaviour, *for great is your reward,* not of debt, but of grace; for our light and momentary afflictions are not worthy to be compared with an eternal and exceeding weight of glory; where there is no proportion, there can be no merit: especially, when it is given to us on the behalf of Christ to suffer, Phil. i. 29. Peter upon this argument saith, *The spirit of glory and of God resteth upon you,* 1 Pet. iv. 14. Our Saviour adds, *for so persecuted they the prophets before you.* The magistrates, and the rulers of the Jews, persecuted Elijah, Micaiah, Jeremiah, Amos, and the rest of the prophets, whom you succeed, not in time only, but in the same office of revealing the mind of God to the people.

13 ¶ Ye are the salt of the earth: ^pbut if the salt have lost his savour, wherewith shall it be salted? it is thenceforth good for nothing, but to be cast out, and to be trodden under foot of men.

^p Mark 9. 50. Luke 14. 34, 35.

In our Christian course we are not to trouble ourselves with what men say of us, and do unto us, but only to attend to our duty of holiness, and an exemplary life, which is what our Saviour presseth plainly, ver. 16, and leads his hearers to it by four comparisons, which he instituteth betwixt them and four other things. The first we have in this verse, *Ye are the salt of the earth:* the doctrine which you profess is so, a thing as opposite as can be to the putrefaction of the world, both in respect to corrupt doctrine and corrupt manners (therefore, by the way, it will be no wonder if they resist it by reviling and persecuting you). You are the salt of the earth, through the grace of God bestowed upon you, Mark ix. 50; Col. iv. 6. If it were not for the number of sound and painful ministers, and holy and gracious persons, the earth would be but a stinking dunghill of drunkards, unclean persons, thieves, murderers, unrighteous persons, that would be a stench in the nostrils of a pure and holy God. Look as it is in the world, *if the salt hath lost its savour,* its acrimony, by which it opposeth putrefaction in fish and flesh, not the fish or flesh only will be good for nothing, but the salt itself, so infatuated, (as it is in the Greek,) will be *good for nothing, but to be cast* upon a dunghill *and trodden under foot.* So it is with ministers of the gospel, so with the professors of it; if they have lost their soundness in the faith, and holiness of life, they are of no value, nay, they are worse than other men. Money, if it be clipped in pieces, and hath lost its usefulness as coin, yet is of use for a goldsmith; meat corrupted, if it will not serve for men, yet will feed dogs; salt is good for nothing. No more are pretended ministers or Christians; their excellency lies in their savour; if that be lost, wherewith shall they be salted? of what use are they, unless to cause the name of God and religion to be blasphemed? Such another similitude the prophet useth, Ezek. xv. 2, 3.

q Prov 4 18. Phil. 2. 15. 14 ᑫ Ye are the light of the world. A city that is set on an hill cannot be hid.

You that are to be my apostles are so eminently, but all you that are my disciples are so also. Christ is the Light of the world, John i. 4, 9; but though the sun be the light of the world, yet it doth not follow that the moon and the stars also are not so: he is the original Light, the great Light who hath light from and in himself. The ministers of the gospel are the lights of the world also; the angels of churches are stars, Rev. i. 20, and holy persons are *children of light,* 1 Thess. v. 5. *A city that is set on an hill cannot be hid.* The church is often called the city of God. Christ compares his people here not to a city, but to a city upon a hill; so that all for which our Saviour mentions a city here, is the conspicuity of a city so built. It is as much as if our Saviour should have said, You had need be holy, for your conversation cannot be hid, any more than a city can that is built upon a hill, which is obvious to every eye. All men's eyes will be upon you.

r Mark 4. 21. Luke 8. 16. & 11. 33. ‖ The word in the original signifieth a measure containing about a pint less than a peck. 15 Neither do men ʳlight a candle, and put it under ‖a bushel, but on a candlestick; and it giveth light unto all that are in the house.

You ought also to consider the end why I have communicated of my light unto you; it is in part the same with that of men: when they light up a candle in a room, which is to show light to all those that are in the room, they do not use to light it up to hide it under a vessel, or a bushel; so I have not communicated my truths or my grace unto you merely for your own use, but for others' use. It is said of John, (by our Saviour,) he was a *burning and shining light:* so is every true minister of the gospel, yea, and every true Christian; not only a burning light, burning with love to God, and zeal for God, and love to and zeal for the souls of others; but also a shining light, communicating his light to others, both by instruction and a holy conversation. Others' pretended candles were never of God's lighting.

s 1 Pet. 2. 12. t John 15. 8. 1 Cor. 14. 25. 16 Let your light so shine before men, ˢthat they may see your good works, and ᵗglorify your Father which is in heaven.

Our Saviour now plainly tells us what he intended by the comparisons before mentioned. Let the light of that doctrine which you receive from me, and the light of your holy conversation, (the latter by the following words seemeth to be here principally intended,) *so shine before men,* be so evident and apparent unto men, *that they may see your good works;* all sorts of good works, whatsoever I have commanded or shall command you; and as I command you, and in obedience to such commands, otherwise they are no good works; *and glorify your Father which is in heaven.* You are not in your good actions to aim at yourselves, to be seen of men, as Matt. vi. 1, nor merely at doing good to others; *good works* are to be maintained *for necessary uses,* Tit. iii. 14, but having a primary and principal respect to the glorifying of your Father; for, John xv. 8, *Herein is my Father glorified, if ye bear much fruit:* not that we can add any thing to God's essential glory, but we may predicate and manifest his glory; which how we can do by good works, if they proceed from mere power and liberty of our own wills, not from his special efficacious grace, is hard to understand. Our Father is said to be *in heaven,* because, though his essential presence filleth all places, yet he is pleased there, more than any where, to manifest his glory and majesty.

17 ¶ ᵘ"Think not that I am come to destroy the Law, or the Prophets: I am not come to destroy, but to fulfil. u Rom. 3.31. & 10. 4. Gal. 3. 24.

There are so many adversaries, Jews, papists, Socinians, Anabaptists, Antinomians, &c., that make their advantages of this text, for the establishing their several errors, that it would require a volume to vindicate it from their several exceptions; those who desire satisfaction may read Spanhemius Dub. Evang. 12. 3. The plain sense of the text is this: It would have been a great cavil, with the Jews especially, (who had a great reverence for the law,) if either our Saviour's enemies amongst them could have persuaded people that Christ came to destroy the law and the prophets, or his own hearers had entertained from his discourse any such apprehensions. Our Saviour designing, in his following discourse, to give a more full and strict interpretation of the law than had been given by the Pharisees and other Jewish doctors, prefaceth that discourse with a protestation against his coming *to destroy the law,* and averring that he came *to fulfil* it. It is manifest, by his following discourse, that he principally spake of the moral law, though he also fulfilled the ceremonial law, he being the Antitype in whom all the types of that had their complement, and real fulfilling and accomplishment. Saith he, I am not come to destroy and put an end to the moral law. I am come to fulfil it: not to fill it up, as papists and Socinians contend, adding any new precept to it; but by yielding myself a personal obedience to it, by giving a fuller and stricter interpretation of it than you have formerly had, and by taking the curse of it (so far as concerneth my disciples) upon myself, and giving a just satisfaction to Divine justice for it. The greatest objection urged against Christ destroying part of the law, and adding new precepts to the moral law, is that about the change of the sabbath; but this is none, if we consider that the moral law required no more than one day of seven to be kept as a day of holy rest, not this or that particular day; for the particular day, the Jews learned it from the ceremonial law, as Christians learn theirs from Christ's and the apostles' practice. Nor is it any objection against this, that the seventh day from the creation is mentioned in the law, to those who know how to distinguish betwixt the precept and the argument; the seventh from the creation is not in the precept, but in the argument, *For in six days,* &c. Now there is nothing more ordinary than to have arguments of a particular temporary concernment used to enforce precepts of an eternal obligation, where the precepts were first given to that particular people, as to whom those arguments were of force, an instance of which is in the first commandment, as well as in this: as, on the other side, arguments of universal force are oft annexed to precepts, which had but a particular obligation upon a particular people for a time. Thus in the ceremonial law, we often find it is an argument to enforce many ceremonial precepts, *For I am the Lord thy God.*

18. For verily I say unto you, ʷTill heaven and earth pass, one jot or one tittle shall in no wise pass from the law, till all be fulfilled. w Luke 16. 17.

Amen I say unto you, so it is in the Greek, a phrase, as some observe, never used but by God, and Christ himself, who is *the Amen, the faithful and true Witness,* Rev. iii. 14, though the servants of God have sometimes used it, as an adverb of wishing. It is by most concluded a form of an oath, God by it swearing by his truth and faithfulness. *Till heaven and earth pass, &c.;* that is, the law is the certain and unchangeable will of God concerning reasonable creatures, and it shall never be altered in the least tittle, nor ever be abolished; you may therefore be secure that I come into the world upon no such errand.

19 ˣWhosoever therefore shall break one of these least commandments, and x Jam. 2. 10

shall teach men so, he shall be called the least in the kingdom of heaven: but whosoever shall do and teach *them*, the same shall be called great in the kingdom of heaven.

Whosoever shall in his practice violate but one of the commandments of God, which the Pharisees judge of the least, and which possible are so compared with others, and shall teach men that they may do as he doth, making such false interpretations of the law as may warrant such a practice, he shall be accounted of the least value and esteem in the church of God, and shall never come into the kingdom of glory: but he who shall strictly and uniformly obey all the commandments, and teach others to do the like by his doctrine and example, that man shall have a great renown and reputation in the church. which is the kingdom of heaven upon earth, and shall have a great reward in the kingdom of glory hereafter.

y Rom. 9. 31. & 10. 3.

20 For I say unto you, That except your righteousness shall exceed ʸ *the righteousness* of the Scribes and Pharisees, ye shall in no case enter into the kingdom of heaven.

I am so far from giving a liberty to the violation of my Father's law, (as the scribes and Pharisees may possibly suggest,) that I assure you, that unless your obedience to it exceed that obedience which the scribes and Pharisees teach you, and themselves practise, you shall never come into heaven. What the righteousness of the scribes and Pharisees was we cannot better learn than from St. Paul, who was himself a Pharisee, and bred up at the feet of Gamaliel, a great doctor amongst them, Acts xxiii. 6; xxvi. 5; Phil. iii. 5. That it was a righteousness of works appeareth from Phil. iii., and the whole Epistles to the Romans and Galatians; and their not owning Christ as the Messiah, nor believing on him, John vii. 48, made it impossible that it should be any other. That they looked upon their mere obedience to the ceremonial law as their righteousness cannot be proved, yea, the contrary is enough evident by their obedience to the moral law, according to the interpretation they put upon it. But their interpretation of the moral law was so short and jejune, that it is manifest that their righteousness was not only a righteousness not of faith but of works, but works that were very imperfect and short of what the true sense of the law required, as our Saviour afterward proveth. That is to say, it was no righteousness, for he that keepeth the whole law, if he be guilty in one point, is guilty of all, James ii. 10.

∥ Or, *to them.*
z Ex. 20. 13. Deut. 5. 17.

21 ¶ Ye have heard that it was said ∥ by them of old time, ᶻ Thou shalt not kill; and whosoever shall kill shall be in danger of the judgment:

a 1 John 3. 15.

22 But I say unto you, That ᵃ whosoever is angry with his brother without a cause shall be in danger of the judgment: and whosoever shall say to his brother,

∥ That is, *vain fellow,*
2 Sam. 6. 20.
b Jam. 2. 20.

∥ ᵇ Raca, shall be in danger of the council: but whosoever shall say, Thou fool, shall be in danger of hell fire.

The Pharisees, in their lectures upon the law, usually thus prefaced, *It was said by them of old time;* this, saith Christ, *ye have heard. Thou shalt not kill:* this was spoken by God in Mount Sinai, it was the sixth of the ten words then spoke. *And whosoever shall kill shall be in danger of the judgment:* this now was the Pharisees' addition, for we read of no such addition to the law as delivered, Exod. xx. 13. Thus they mixed their traditions with the word of God, which possibly might be the reason of their saying rather, *It was said by them of old time,* than, It was said by Moses, or, It was said in the law of God; for under that phrase, It was said by the ancients, they both comprehended the law given by Moses to the ancient people of God, and also their own traditions and false glosses, which though not so ancient as the law, yet had obtained for some considerable time in the corrupt state of the Jews. *Shall be in danger of,* or obnoxious unto, *the judgment;* not to the wrath and vengeance of God, of that they said nothing, but to those courts of judgment which sat amongst them, to administer justice in criminal causes. As if this law of God had been only intended to uphold peace, and to preserve human society and civil order. *Thou shalt not kill;* that is, (as they interpreted,) Thou shalt not, without a warrant from God, or from the law, actually take away the life of another. It appears by what followeth, that they extended not this law to unjustifiable passions in the heart, such as rash anger, malice, revengeful thoughts; nor to any opprobrious or revengeful words. *But I say unto you;* I shall give you another sense of this law. The killing here forbidden is as well rash and causeless anger, and opprobrious, threatening speeches, as bloody actions. *Whosoever is angry with his brother without a cause shall be in danger of the judgment, &c.* Our Saviour (as most interpreters judge) speaks this with allusion to the three courts amongst the Jews. The one was the court of three men, which only judged of smaller and lighter causes, not in capital causes. Another was their court of twenty-three men, which much answered our courts at Westminster. The third was their sanhedrim, consisting of seventy men, which answered our parliament. Some think that by *the judgment* is meant the first or second of the courts; by *the council,* the superior courts amongst the Jews. But the judgment of our reverend Dr. Lightfoot seemeth much more probable, that by *the judgment* is meant the judgment of God; by *the council* and *hell fire,* not only the judgment and vengeance of God, but the judgments and punishments that are inflicted in the courts of men, that are magistrates, and bear not the sword in vain: so as the sense is this: I say unto you, that if a man doth but in his heart nourish wrath and anger against another without a just cause, and lets it grow up into malice, and thoughts and desires of private revenge, though he be not by it obnoxious to courts of justice, who can only determine upon overt acts, yet he is accountable to God, and liable to his judgment: but if men suffer their passions to break out into reviling terms and language, such as *Raca,* (signifying a vain person,) or, *Thou fool,* (speaking this from anger or malice,) they are not only liable to the eternal vengeance of God, compared to the fire of Gehenna, but ought to be subjected to the punishment of the civil magistrate. Every civil government being by the law of God, in order to the prevention of quarrels or bloodshed, (which often followeth revilings of each other,) obliged to punish such offences, as being the beginnings of murder, provocations to it, and indications of murderous hearts, hearts full of that which in the eye of God is murder.

c ch. 8. 4. & 23. 19.

23 Therefore ᶜ if thou bring thy gift to the altar, and there rememberest that thy brother hath ought against thee;

d See Job 42. 8. ch. 18. 19.
1 Tim. 2. 8.
1 Pet. 3. 7.

24 ᵈ Leave there thy gift before the altar, and go thy way; first be reconciled to thy brother, and then come and offer thy gift.

The Jews were to *offer gifts and sacrifices,* Heb. v. 1. Their gifts were their free-will offerings, they were the most frequent oblations amongst the Jews, as may appear from Leviticus, and what the priests pressed with the greatest importunity, as may appear from Mark vii. 11; therefore our Saviour instanceth in these, rather than in other parts of their worship. Bring unto God the best and most acceptable sacrifices (in your or the teacher's judgment) that you can, if there be found malice or rash anger in your hearts, God will not accept them. Therefore, how near soever you be come to a religious action, if you there remember that your brother hath a just reason to be offended with you, for any malice or rash anger showed or expressed by you, do not think this will discharge you of your obligation to pay your homage to God; but forbear a while, *leave your gift before the altar,* and do what in you lies to be reconciled to your brother, to have a placable spirit to him, to purge your heart of wrath and malice, and any desire of revenge, *and then come and offer your gift,* pay that homage which you owe, and it was in your heart to pay to God. It is a text usually applied with reference to communion with God in the Lord's supper, but equally extensive to any other part of worship, hearing the word, James i. 21, and prayer, 1 Tim. ii. 8. God accepteth no service, no homage, from an implacable, malicious heart.

S. MATTHEW V

e Prov. 25.
8. Luke 12.
58, 59.
f See Ps. 32.
6. Is. 55. 6.

25 *e Agree with thine adversary quickly, f whiles thou art in the way with him; lest at any time the adversary deliver thee to the judge, and the judge deliver thee to the officer, and thou be cast into prison.

26 Verily I say unto thee, Thou shalt by no means come out thence, till thou hast paid the uttermost farthing.

Forasmuch as the overt acts and expressions of unjust wrath and malice are iniquities punishable by the judge, let it be the care of those that will be my disciples, if by their passions they have provoked any, and made them their adversaries, quickly to agree with them; for you know the ordinary course of enraged adversaries amongst men, is to bring their actions, and to bring men before the civil judge; and when the judge upon inquiry hath found them guilty, he useth to deliver them to the gaoler to be carried to prison, until they have fully paid their fines for such offences. And forasmuch as not only the overt acts, but the passions which cause such acts, are culpable before God, and make men obnoxious to his righteous judgment, and God by them is made an adversary to the soul, as having violated his great command, *Thou shalt do no murder*; let all my disciples, who have been or may be overtaken with such faults, by repentance and faith in me make their peace with God in this life, lest dying in impenitency they be put under the eternal displeasure and wrath of God, from whence they shall never be delivered, chap. vi. 15; xviii. 35.

27 ¶ Ye have heard that it was said by them of old time, *g* Thou shalt not commit adultery:

g Ex. 20. 14.
Deut. 5. 18.

28 But I say unto you, That whosoever *h* looketh on a woman to lust after her hath committed adultery with her already in his heart.

h Job 31. 1.
Prov. 6. 25.
See Gen. 34.
2. 2 Sam. 11.
2.

The scope of our Saviour in these verses is the very same as in the verses immediately preceding, viz. to correct the jejune interpretation which the Pharisees had put upon the Divine law, and to show that he, instead of coming to destroy the law, came to fulfil it, as other ways, so by giving a more strict and true interpretation of it; and whereas they interpreted it only as to overt acts, which disturb human society and break civil order, he showeth that it reacheth to the inward thoughts, and unlawful desires of the heart, and any means that have a tendency to such prohibited acts. It was said by God to those fathers of the Jews, *Thou shalt not commit adultery*, Exod. xx. 14. This law (saith our Saviour) your doctors expound, You shall not carnally lie with a woman that is not your wife; but there is a great deal more in it than so, for he that but secretly in his heart desireth such a thing, or taketh pleasure in such thoughts, and casts his eyes upon a woman in order to such a thing, is in the sight of God an adulterer. Hence we read of *eyes full of adultery*, to avoid which Job *made a covenant with* his *eyes*, Job xxxi. 1, and would not suffer his heart to walk after his eyes, ver. 7. We must so interpret the commandments of God, as not to extend them only to forbid or command those acts which are plainly mentioned in them, but the inward pleasing of our hearts with such things as are forbidden, the desires of our hearts after them, or whatsoever is a probable means to give us that sinful pleasure of our thoughts, or further inflame such unlawful desires in our souls.

i ch. 18. 8, 9.
Mark 9. 43,
—47.
‖ Or, *do cause thee to offend.*
k See ch. 19.
12. Rom. 8.
13. 1 Cor. 9.
27. Col. 3. 5.

29 *i* And if thy right eye ‖ offend thee, *k* pluck it out, and cast *it* from thee: for it is profitable for thee that one of thy members should perish, and not *that* thy whole body should be cast into hell.

30 And if thy right hand offend thee, cut it off, and cast *it* from thee: for it is profitable for thee that one of thy members should perish, and not *that* thy whole body should be cast into hell.

The sum of these two verses is, that the salvation of our immortal souls is to be preferred before all things, be they never so dear and precious to us; and that if men's ordinary discretion teacheth them for the preservation of their bodies to cut off a particular member, which would necessarily endanger the whole body, it much more teacheth them to part with any thing which will prejudice the salvation of their souls. Not that any person is by this text obliged to cut off any bodily member, (as some have done,) because there can be no such necessity; but only to mortify their members, Col. iii. 5. the deeds of the body, Rom. viii. 13, their inward lusts, which being mortified there will be no need of mutilating ourselves; for the members of the body are but commanded and animated to their motions from the inward lusts of the heart: but if there could happen such a case, as that a man must voluntarily part with the most useful member of his body, or sin against God to the damnation of his soul, he ought rather to choose the former than the latter. How much more then ought Christians to mortify their inward lusts and unlawful desires, which can be of no profit nor advantage to them; but will certainly make them to offend God, and so run them upon the danger of hell fire!

31 It hath been said, *l* Whosoever shall put away his wife, let him give her a writing of divorcement:

l Deut. 24. 1.
Jer. 3. 1. See
ch. 19. 3, &c.
Mark 10. 2,
&c.

32 But I say unto you, That *m* whosoever shall put away his wife, saving for the cause of fornication, causeth her to commit adultery: and whosoever shall marry her that is divorced committeth adultery.

m ch. 19. 9.
Luke 16. 18.
Rom. 7. 3.
1 Cor. 7. 10,
11.

The law to which our Saviour referreth here, or rather the indulgence and toleration, (for none was obliged to put away their wives in case of uncleanness,) is that Deut. xxiv. 1, where we have it in these words: *When a man hath taken a wife, and married her, and it come to pass that she find no favour in his eyes, because he hath found some uncleanness in her; then let him write her a bill of divorcement, and give it her in her hand, and send her out of his house.* The Pharisees had extended this toleration which God gave husbands amongst the Jews to other cases, besides that of uncleanness or adultery; so as they put away their wives upon every slight occasion, interpreting those words, *that she find no favour in his eyes*, separately from the following words, *because he hath found some uncleanness in her*, and gave a liberty for men upon any dislike of their wives to put them away, provided that they first gave them a bill of divorcement; and that in these cases it was lawful for the parties, thus separated from each other, to marry to whom either of them pleased; and this is expressed in terms in their form of those writings of divorcement, in Josephus and other writers. This indeed is a case properly relating to the judicial law; but all the judicial laws are either appendices to the moral or to the ceremonial law. This particular indulgence was an appendix to the moral law, by the seventh commandment, to which our Saviour is now speaking, and giving the true sense of it. He here opposeth the Pharisees in two points. 1. Asserting that all divorces are unlawful except in case of adultery. 2. Asserting that whosoever married her that was put away committed adultery. It hath been a great question, not so much amongst divines as amongst lawyers, whether it be not lawful in any case to put away a wife, unless for adultery? The canonists have found out many cases in which they affirm it lawful. And the Council of Trent (from whom we may learn the sense of the popish divines) anathematize those who deny the church a power of determining other causes of divorce. But their blasphemous curse falleth upon him, who is above them, God over all blessed for ever, who in this text hath determined that point. Nor indeed did Moses give a toleration in any other cases. There may indeed be a parting betwixt man and wife upon other accounts, either wholly or in part: in case one of them will part from the other, which the apostle determineth, 1 Cor. vii. 11, 15; in which case the person departing is only guilty if he or she marry again. In case of an error, through ignorance or inadvertency, upon the marriage, that it appeareth that the persons married were such as by the law of nature and of God ought not to have married, &c. But if we take divorce for the voluntary act of the husband putting away of his wife, it is unlawful in any case but that of adultery, which dissolves the marriage knot and covenant. A second question is also here determined by our Saviour, viz. that it is unlawful for her, that is justly put away, to marry to any other, or for any other to marry her wittingly.

33 ¶ Again, ye have heard that [n]it hath been said by them of old time, [o]Thou shalt not forswear thyself, but [p]shalt perform unto the Lord thine oaths:

n ch. 23. 16.
o Ex. 20. 7.
Lev. 19. 12.
Num. 30. 2.
Deut. 5. 11.
p Deut. 23. 23.

This was said Exod. xx. 7, and more plainly Lev. xix. 12; the substance was there said, though the words be not *verbatim* recited.

q ch. 23. 16, 18, 22. Jam. 5. 12.
r Is. 66. 1.

34 But I say unto you, [q]Swear not at all; neither by heaven; for it is [r]God's throne:

35 Nor by the earth; for it is his footstool: neither by Jerusalem; for it is [s]the city of the great King.

s Ps. 48. 2. & 87. 3.

36 Neither shalt thou swear by thy head, because thou canst not make one hair white or black.

Doth our Saviour here oppose himself to the law of God, which saith, Deut. vi. 13; x. 20, *Thou shalt fear the Lord thy God, and swear by his name?* Doth he condemn Abraham, who sware his servant by the Lord God of heaven and earth? Gen. xxiv. 3. Doth he destroy such a useful means for the end of strife? Heb. vi. 16. None of all these. We must consider that our Saviour is here opposing himself to the corruptions of that age brought in by the Pharisees, who had taught people that swearing was nothing, if they did not forswear themselves; or at least swearing *by the heaven, by the earth, by Jerusalem, by their head,* or in such-like forms, was no sin, if they forbore the name of God; that they were only obliged to swear by the name of God in public courts of justice, but they were not tied up to it at other times. To these and such-like corruptions our Saviour opposeth these words, *I say unto you, Swear not at all;* not at all voluntarily, but where it is necessary for the end of strife; not at all in your common discourse, James v. 12: and so it is expounded in the next verse. The law doth not only forbid false swearing, but common and ordinary swearing, needless swearing, which speaks a great want of reverence in the heart of the name of God. And let not your teachers cheat you, in telling you God, or the name of God, is not concerned, in your swearing by heaven: is not heaven the throne of God? Or by earth: is not that the footstool of God? Or by Jerusalem: is not that the city of God? Or by your head: is it not God that hath given you your life and bodily members? Is it in your power to make a hair of your head white or black? So as the great thing here forbidden, is common and ordinary swearing, where God calleth us not unto it for the determination of strife. Do not only think that false swearing, but be assured that ordinary, common, needless swearing, is forbidden by God.

t Col. 4. 6.
Jam. 5. 12.

37 [t]But let your communication be, Yea, yea; Nay, nay: for whatsoever is more than these cometh of evil.

St. James saith much the same, James v. 12. Let your ordinary discourse in the world be mere affirmations or denials of things in terms or phrases of the same import with *yea* and *nay*, though you do not always use those terms. Let forms of swearing be preserved for special times, when the providence of God calls to you for them to determine strife, and make some weighty matters which you assert credible unto others who will not take your bare assertions. Have such a reverence for the name of God, as not to use it for every trifle; and let not my ordinance for the end of strife be made of no use by your common use of the name of God; for in ordinary discourse and common talk, whatsoever is more than bare affirmations and denials, cometh of an evil heart, or from the devil, or from the corruption of other men's hearts. Some would make the communication mentioned here to be understood as if it were conversation; Let your ways of dealing with men be plain, without fraud and guile; and so think our Saviour here strikes at the root and cause of so much idle and vain swearing, viz. the common falsehood, frauds, and cozenages of men in their dealings; but it seemeth hard so to interpret λόγος in this place, our Saviour especially being speaking concerning words and forms of speech.

38 ¶ Ye have heard that it hath been said, "An eye for an eye, and a tooth for a tooth:

u Ex. 21. 24.
Lev. 24. 20.
Deut. 19. 21.

This was the commandment of God to the magistrate, in case a woman with child were struck, and any mischief came of it, Exod. xxi. 24; in case of damage done to a neighbour, Lev. xxiv. 20; and in the case of false witness, Deut. xix. 21. But in the mean time God had said to private persons, Lev. xix. 18, *Thou shalt not avenge;* and it is said, Prov. xxiv. 29, *Say not, I will do to him as he hath done to me.* The Pharisees had interpreted this law of God into a liberty for every private person, who had been wronged by another, to exact a satisfaction upon him, provided that he did not exceed this proportion of taking an eye for an eye, and a tooth for a tooth, doing no more wrong to another than that other had done to him.

39 But I say unto you, [x]That ye resist not evil: [y]but whosoever shall smite thee on thy right cheek, turn to him the other also.

x Prov. 20. 22. & 24. 29.
Luke 6. 29.
Rom. 12.17, 1 Cor. 6. 7. 1 Thes. 5. 15. 1 Pet. 3. 9.
y Is. 50. 6.
Lam. 3. 30.

40 And if any man will sue thee at the law, and take away thy coat, let him have *thy* cloke also.

41 And whosoever [z]shall compel thee to go a mile, go with him twain.

z ch. 27. 32.
Mark 15. 21.

The apostle Paul giveth the best exposition upon this text, Rom. xii. 17—19, 21, *Recompense to no man evil for evil.—If it be possible, as much as lieth in you, live peaceably with all men. Dearly beloved, avenge not yourselves, but rather give place unto wrath: for it is written, Vengeance is mine; I will repay, saith the Lord.—Be not overcome of evil, but overcome evil with good.* The general scope of our Saviour is that which they must observe, who would understand the sense of these words; they must not think that the particular things mentioned are their duty, but, 1. That it is the will of their Lord that they should not take any private revenge, but leave the avenging of their injuries unto God, and to the public magistrate, who is God's vicegerent, before whom, notwithstanding any thing here said, they may seek a just satisfaction. 2. That in lighter cases we should rather remit the wrong done to us for peace' sake than stand upon a rigour of justice; rather overcome evil with good, than suffer ourselves to be overcome by the evil of others; rather suffer a blow on the other cheek, than with our own hands revenge the blow which is given thus on our cheek; rather lose our cloak also, than contend for our coat, taken away in judgment from us, though we be in that judgment oppressed. No injury can deserve a private revenge. Light injuries are not of that nature that we should contend for a public revenge of them.

42 Give to him that asketh thee, and [a]from him that would borrow of thee turn not thou away.

a Deu. 15. 8, 10. Luke 6. 30, 35.

In these words our Saviour presseth another piece of charity, viz. liberality to those who are poor; who are of two sorts: some such as are never able to repay us; to those he commandeth Christians *to give. To him that asketh,* who hath need to ask, and in that order too which God hath directed, who hath commanded us to provide for our own household, and to do good to all, but especially to the household of faith. The other sort are such as may have only a temporary want: to these he commandeth us to lend, and not to turn away from them, when they desire to borrow of us, and we can spare it. This was an ancient precept of God, Deut. xv. 7—9, confirmed by Christ, as a piece of his will under the gospel.

43 ¶ Ye have heard that it hath been said, [b]Thou shalt love thy neighbour, [c]and hate thine enemy.

b Lev. 19.18.
c Deu. 23. 6.
Ps. 41. 10.

Thou shalt love thy neighbour as thyself, was the old law of God, Lev. xix. 18; the other part, *and hate thine enemy,* was the Pharisees' addition, or rather their collection, because the law only commanded them to love their neighbour. ע signifies sometimes a friend, sometimes more largely any other person ; they took it in the strict sense, yet they could not be so blind as not to extend it to all those of their own nation, for ver. 17 there are two words used, one signifying *thy brother*, the other *thy countryman*, whom they are commanded in that verse not to hate in their hearts. But it appeareth by Luke x. 29, that they did not very well know their neighbour. The lawyer asked, *Who is my neighbour?* Christ instructs him by the parable of him that was *fallen among thieves*, that they ought not to look upon those of their own country only as neighbours, for a Samaritan might deserve the name better than a priest or Levite. But they generally looked upon all the uncircumcised as not their neighbours, but their enemies, whom the precept did not oblige them to love.

d Luke 6. 27, 35. Rom. 12. 14, 20.
e Luke 23. 34. Acts 7. 60. 1 Cor. 4. 12, 13. 1 Pet. 2. 23. & 3. 9.

44 But I say unto you, ^dLove your enemies, bless them that curse you, do good to them that hate you, and pray ^e for them which despitefully use you, and persecute you;

That this is no counsel of perfection, (as the papists would have it,) nor any new precept added to the law of God, (as the Socinians would have it,) is plain from Prov. xxv. 21, where we find it commanded under the Old Testament. Neither is it, I advise you, but, *I say unto you*, which argueth a command. *Love* here doth not signify the complacency of the heart in an object, which is love in the strict sense ; but, Be charitable unto, do good to your enemies : nor are we equally obliged to do good to our enemies as to our friends ; but it is expounded by the following words, and to be understood, 1. Of not seeking unlawful private revenge. *Bless them that curse you :* do not return reviling for reviling, while they curse do you bless. 2. Doing them common offices of kindness. *If thine enemy hunger, feed him; if he thirst, give him to drink,* Rom. xii. 20. This is a doing good to them that hate us, relieving them in their pressing necessities. 3. Doing them all the good we can for their souls. *Pray for them which despitefully use you, and persecute you.* So did our Saviour, Luke xxiii. 34, and Stephen, Acts vii. 60 ; so did David, Psal. xxxv. 13—15. In the mean time we may hate those who are God's enemies, as such, Psal. cxxxix. 21, 22 ; and for such we may seek a due revenge of God's honour upon them. And for our enemies, this precept prohibits not the seeking of a just satisfaction for wrongs done unto us in a way of public justice, yet not without a mixture of charity.

f Job 25. 3.

45 That ye may be the children of your Father which is in heaven: for ^fhe maketh his sun to rise on the evil and on the good, and sendeth rain on the just and on the unjust.

As your heavenly Father hath a common love, which he extendeth to all mankind, in supplying their necessities, with the light and warmth of the sun, and with the rain ; as well as a special love and favour, which he exerciseth only toward those that are good, and members of Christ ; so ought you to have : though you are not obliged to take your enemies into your bosom, yet you ought to love them in their order. And as your heavenly Father, though he will one day have a satisfaction from sinners, for the wrong done to his majesty, unless they repent ; yet, to heap coals of fire on their heads, gives them good things of common providence, that he might not leave them without witness, yea, and affords them the outward means of grace for their souls : so, although you are bound to seek some satisfaction for God's honour and glory from flagitious sinners, and though you may in an orderly course seek a moderate satisfaction for the wrong done to yourselves, yet you ought to love them with a love consistent with these things ; that so you may imitate your heavenly Father, and approve yourselves to be his children.

g Luke 6.32.

46 ^gFor if ye love them which love you, what reward have ye ? do not even the Publicans the same ?

47 And if ye salute your brethren only, what do ye more *than others ?* do not even the Publicans so ?

Reason obligeth you, who expect a reward from God for what you do, to do something more than those who know of no such reward, or at least live in no expectation of any such thing ; and you who condemn others as great sinners, and men not worthy of your converse, ought to do something by which you may outdo those whom you so condemn, both in offices of piety towards God and charity towards men. But if you only show kindness to your relations and to your countrymen, you do no more than those whom you look upon as heathens and the worst of men, who act only from the light and law of nature, and know of no reward God hath to give, nor live in any such expectation of it. By loving here is meant doing good offices, either for the souls or bodies of others. By saluting is meant common offices of kindness, such as inquiring of our neighbours' health, wishing them well, &c. The publicans were civil officers appointed by the Romans to gather up public taxes and revenues. The chief commissioners were knights and gentlemen of Rome, who either let out these revenues to others, or employed others under them in the collecting of them. These thus employed were some Jews, (such were Matthew and Zaccheus,) some Romans. These (as is ordinary) made their own markets, and exacted of the people, upon which accounts they were exceeding odious : and therefore ordinarily in Scripture we shall find *publicans and sinners* put together, chap. ix. 11 ; xi. 19 ; and they are joined with harlots, chap. xxi. 32 ; and the Pharisee in his justification gloried he was not as that publican, Luke xviii. 11. Those who condemn others ought to take care that they be better than others.

h Gen. 17. 1. Lev. 11. 44. & 19. 2. Luke 6. 36.

48 ^hBe ye therefore perfect, even as your Father which is in heaven is perfect.

Col. 1. 28. & 4. 12. iJam. 1. 4. 1 Pet. 1. 15, 16. i Eph. 5. 1.

Perfect here is not taken in that sense as it is taken in other texts of Scripture, where it signifieth sincerity and uprightness, as Job ii. 3, or where it signifieth a comparative perfection, as Paul saith he spake to those that were perfect ; but for an absolute perfection, such as is in our *Father which is in heaven,* and so much is signified by the proposing of our heavenly Father as our example. Nor will it therefore follow, either that this is a mere counsel, not a precept, or that an absolute perfection in holiness is a thing in this life attainable. But that it is our duty to labour for it, *forgetting what is behind, and reaching forth unto those things which are before, pressing towards the mark for the prize of the high calling of God in Christ Jesus,* as the apostle speaks, Phil. iii. 13, 14. *Pro perfecto est qui perfecto proximus.* God accounteth him perfect who is nearest to perfection.

CHAP. VI

Christ continuing his sermon, giveth directions about alms-giving, 1—4, *prayer,* 5—13, *forgiving our brethren,* 14, 15, *fasting,* 16—18, *laying up treasure in heaven,* 19—21, *keeping a single eye,* 22, 23 ; *and exhorteth not to be anxious about worldly things, but principally to seek God's kingdom and righteousness,* 24—34.

|| Or, *righteousness.* Deut. 24. 13. Ps. 112. 9. Dan. 4. 27. 2 Cor. 9. 9, 10. || Or, *with.*

TAKE heed that ye do not your ||alms before men, to be seen of them : otherwise ye have no reward || of your Father which is in heaven.

Alms are any acts of kindness freely done by us for the relief of any that are in distress and misery, which, when they are done from a principle of love to God, his precepts commanding them, obedience in faith to his promises made to the giving of them, and that he may be glorified, are truly good works, acts of religion, and acceptable to God, Acts x. 31, though meritorious of nothing from him ; otherwise they are merely acts of humanity and morality, to the reward of which God is by no promise obliged. Therefore Christ's disciples are obliged to take heed, that in the doing of their alms, though they may do them before men, God may be glorified, Phil. ii. 15 ; 1 Pet. ii. 12 ; yet they do them not before men on purpose that they should take notice of them, and applaud them for them, for God rewardeth no action of which he is not the end.

a Rom.12. 8

2 Therefore ^awhen thou doest *thine*

S. MATTHEW VI

¶ Or, cause not a trumpet to be sounded.

alms, ‖do not sound a trumpet before thee, as the hypocrites do in the synagogues and in the streets, that they may have glory of men. Verily I say unto you, They have their reward.

3 But when thou doest alms, let not thy left hand know what thy right hand doeth:

4 That thine alms may be in secret: and thy Father which seeth in secret himself [b] shall reward thee openly.

a Luke 14. 14.

There are some who think that our Saviour here reflects upon some practice of the Pharisees then in use for ostentation, who, under a pretence of a means to call people together, caused a trumpet to be sounded when they distributed their alms; but those learned in their writings assure us they could never find in them any foundation for such an opinion. The speech is rather metaphorical, prohibiting all ostentation in acts of charity, and inviting others to take notice of them, as Jehu invited Jonadab to come and see his zeal, 2 Kings x. 16; as the 3rd verse is but a proverbial expression expounded ver. 4, *That thine alms may be in secret.* Not that it is not lawful to give a poor body money, or bread, &c., in the sight of others; but only to do it for that end, that we might be seen of others. The thing forbidden under the metaphorical expression is ostentation, and seeking our own honour and applause. The thing commanded is sincerity with respect to our end. The apostle calls it a giving with simplicity, singly aiming at the glorifying of God, by an obedient performance of our duty. He tells us those who give their alms to be honoured of men *have their reward,* that is, all which they are like to have; men applaud and cry them up, there is their reward: others shall have their reward from God, *who seeth in secret,* and so needeth not such a publication of our good deeds; and he will reward them openly before men and angels at the last day, chap. xxv. 31, 32, 34, and ordinarily in this life, Psal. xxxvii. 25; xli. 1; cxii. 9, 10.

5 ¶ And when thou prayest, thou shalt not be as the hypocrites *are:* for they love to pray standing in the synagogues and in the corners of the streets, that they may be seen of men. Verily I say unto you, They have their reward.

Our Saviour here cautioneth them against the same thing in prayer, as he had done before in giving alms, viz. hypocrisy and ostentation, doing this duty upon that design, merely to be taken notice of and applauded by men; it was lawful to pray *standing in the synagogues,* but not to do it merely to be taken notice of by men for devout persons, nor yet to confine themselves to praying in the synagogues. If they chose to pray *standing,* that they might be more conspicuous, and *in the synagogues,* because those places were more holy, (as they might dream,) or, which seems rather to be here meant, because there most people would see them, for which purpose only they chose *corners of streets,* as was the old popish custom, upon which account they set up crosses at three-way leets, &c., these things were sinful: but to pray standing was usual, Mark xi. 25; and to pray in the synagogues and in the temple standing was usual, Luke xviii. 13. But those who do it merely for vain-glory *have their reward,* and must expect none from God.

c 2 Kings 4. 33.

6 But thou, when thou prayest, [c] enter into thy closet, and when thou hast shut thy door, pray to thy Father which is in secret; and thy Father which seeth in secret shall reward thee openly.

By this public prayer is not condemned, but secret prayer is established, and made every Christian's duty; and Christians are warned not to think that their duty of prayer is discharged by their going to places of public worship, and praying there: but that which our Saviour here cautioneth us against is ostentation, by which men may as much offend in their closets as elsewhere. Wherever we pray, we must take heed that our ends be right, that the glory of God be our principal end, and yielding obedience to his command; and there is no better means in order to this than the right setting of God before our eyes, as he that *seeth in secret,*

and knoweth the most secret designs, scopes, and intentions of our hearts, and who, if we thus perform our duty, will reward us of his free grace and mercy; not as persons who by our prayers have merited any thing at his hand, (for what merit can there be in our prayers?) but as having showed our obedience to his will, and in the fulfilling of those many promises which he hath made to those that seek his face for the hearing of their prayers.

7 But when ye pray, [d] use not vain repetitions, as the heathen *do:* [e] for they think that they shall be heard for their much speaking.

d Eccles. 5. 2. Ecclus. 7. 14.
e 1 Kings 18. 26, 29.

8 Be not ye therefore like unto them: for your Father knoweth what things ye have need of, before ye ask him.

It appeareth from hence, and from what followeth also, that the praying here spoken of is vocal prayer; not the mere homage which the heart payeth to God, by a recognition of him as the fountain of all good, and our secret desires that God would supply our wants, but the expression of those desires by the words of our mouths, which is that duty which the Scripture generally calleth prayer, and is most certainly a duty incumbent on every person. Nor are *repetitions* of the same requests in prayer, or *much speaking,* (that is, praying to some length of time,) here absolutely forbidden: our Saviour before his passion prayed thrice for the same thing within a short compass of time, (though he did not use the same words,) and, Luke vi. 12, he *continued all night in prayer to God.* But that which is here forbidden, is an opinion of being heard for over-long prayers, and using vain repetitions, as the priests of Baal continued from morning to night crying, *O Baal, hear us! O Baal, hear us!* as if their god had been asleep, or gone a journey, as the prophet mocketh them, 1 Kings xviii. 26, 27. Repetitions are then vain, when they are affected, and flow from some irreverent thoughts we have of God; not when they are as it were forced from the heat and intension of our affections. The like is to be said of much speaking in prayer. Long prayers are not to be condemned, but the affectation of them is, and long prayers upon pretences and designs are: but when the mind is attent, and the affections fervent, length of prayer is no fault, especially upon solemn occasions, when we come not to ask a particular mercy at the hand of God, nor for a particular person or family. But repetitions after the manner of heathens are condemned, as proceeding from irreverent thoughts of God, as if he did not know what things we have need of, or were, like a man, to be prevailed upon by a multitude of words.

9 After this manner therefore pray ye: [f] Our Father which art in heaven, Hallowed be thy name.

f Luke 11. 2, &c.

Not always in these words, but always to this sense, and in this manner. None ever thought Christians obliged to use no other words than these in prayer, though none must deny the lawfulness of using those words which Christ hath sanctified. *After this manner;* first seeking the kingdom of God, and begging those things which more immediately concern God's glory, and then those things which more immediately concern yourselves. Or, *After this manner,* praying only in particular for such things as are more generally couched in the following petitions. *Our Father which art in heaven:* a compellation speaking our faith both in the power and in the goodness of God; our eyeing him as in heaven speaketh his power, Psal. cxv. 3, our considering him as our Father speaks our faith in his goodness, Matt. vii. 11. *Hallowed be thy name.* God's name is whatsoever he hath made himself known by: Let the Lord be glorified in every thing whereby he hath made himself known.

10 Thy kingdom come. [g] Thy will be done in earth, [h] as *it is* in heaven.

g ch. 26. 39, 42.
Acts 21. 14.
h Ps. 103. 20, 21.

Let the Lord rule over all the nations of the earth, and let them be freely subject to his laws, and to his Son Jesus Christ; let the gospel of the kingdom be published, and prosper, by bringing all thoughts into a captivity to it. And let the kingdom of God come more within the hearts of all men, and hasten the revelation of the kingdom of glory. Let the will of the Lord be every where done, and that on earth, with as much freedom and cheerfulness, and with as little reluctancy, as it is done by the angels and saints in heaven. These three first petitions are of great cognation one to another; God is then glorified when his kingdom is advanced, and his kingdom is then promoted when there is most free and cheerful obedience yielded to his will: the sum is, Let God be glorified.

i See Job 23. 12.
Prov. 30. 8.

11 Give us this day our [i]daily bread.

And forasmuch as in thee we live, and move, and have our life, so the means for the upholding and the preserving of our lives, and the blessing upon them, must be from thee. We beseech thee to give us food convenient for us, that which thou hast ordained for our nourishment and preservation; and that thou wouldst preserve it to us, that we may have it from day to day whilst we live in the world, with thy blessing upon it; that we may not be tempted to take bread which is not ours, nor be over-solicitous and careful for to-morrow, but by daily prayer may obtain daily supplies from thee, so far as shall be necessary or convenient for us.

k ch. 18. 21, &c.

12 And [k]forgive us our debts, as we forgive our debtors.

Our Saviour here doth not teach us the order in which we should pray for good things for ourselves, only in three petitions comprehendeth whatsoever we should ask of God. For doubtless we are obliged, according to Matt. vi. 32, first to seek the kingdom of God, and the righteousness thereof. That by our *debts* are here meant our *sins* is plain from Luke xi. 4, as also from ver. 14 of this chapter, where they are called *trespasses*. The sense is, then, Discharge us from that obligation to death which our sins have laid us under; give us a pardon for our sins past and present; for who liveth, and sinneth not against thee? *As we forgive our debtors;* not as perfectly, but in like manner as we, according to the imperfect state of our natures, forgive those who have done us injury, not seeking any revenge upon them, nor bearing them any malice: so as indeed those who, retaining their malice in their hearts, put up this prayer unto God, do in effect pray down Divine vengeance upon their souls: well therefore doth the apostle command, that we should lift up pure hands unto God, *without wrath or doubting,* 1 Tim. ii. 8. So that not only faith, but charity also, is necessary to our praying acceptably.

l ch. 26. 41.
Luke 22. 40, 46. 1 Cor. 10. 13. 2 Pet. 2. 9. Rev. 3. 10.
m John 17. 15.
n 1 Chron. 29. 11.

13 [l]And lead us not into temptation, but [m]deliver us from evil: [n]For thine is the kingdom, and the power, and the glory, for ever. Amen.

The term *temptation* in the general signifieth a trial, and is sometimes used to express God's trials of his people's faith and obedience, but most ordinarily to express Satan's trials of us, by motions to sin; which may be from our own lusts, James i. 13, 14; or from the devil, who is therefore called the tempter; or from the world. These are the temptations which we are commanded to pray against: not that God leads any persons into such temptations, unless by the permission of his providence. *But deliver us from evil;* from the evil one, as some read it, because of the article prefixed; but others think it not material whether we understand the devil, who is the evil one, or the evil of temptations, which harm us not if we be not overcome by them. *For thine is the kingdom, and the power, and the glory, for ever. Amen.* These words are omitted by Luke, chap. xi. 4; but many think that Luke speaks of another time, when he dictated this prayer. The words both show us that the honour and glory of God ought to be the end and scope of all our prayers, and that we can expect no audience but upon the account of God's grace and mercy; and they likewise confirm our faith, that God is able to grant what we ask of him. *Amen:* this in the close of a sentence is a particle of wishing, and signifieth our desire to be heard; and as it is a term that signifies truth and certainty, it likewise signifieth our faith in God that we shall be heard.

o Ecclus. 28. 1, &c. Mark 11. 25, 26. Ephes. 4. 32. Col. 3. 13.
p ch. 18. 35.
Jam. 2. 13.

14 [o]For if ye forgive men their trespasses, your heavenly Father will also forgive you:

15 But [p]if ye forgive not men their trespasses, neither will your Father forgive your trespasses.

Not that our mere forgiving our brethren the injuries done unto us is all that God requireth of us in order to the forgiveness we expect from him, the contrary is plain from several other texts, John iii. 18, 36; Acts ii. 38; xvi. 31, &c.; but that without this forgiveness of our brethren, God will not forgive us, Matt. xviii. 35. It is one piece of that obedience which we owe to God, and also of our gratitude, without the performance of which it is vain for us to hope for forgiveness from God.

16 ¶ Moreover [q]when ye fast, be not, as the hypocrites, of a sad countenance: for they disfigure their faces, that they may appear unto men to fast. Verily I say unto you, They have their reward.

q Is. 58. 5.

17 But thou, when thou fastest, [r]anoint thine head, and wash thy face;

r Ruth 3. 3. Dan. 10. 3.

18 That thou appear not unto men to fast, but unto thy Father which is in secret: and thy Father, which seeth in secret, shall reward thee openly.

Our Saviour in these words returns to his former work, to caution his disciples against hypocrisy, vain-glory, and ostentation in their religious duties, the doing them to be seen of men. What he before said as to giving alms and prayer, he here again applieth as to private fasting, which is by this discourse of our Saviour confirmed, though not as a stated, yet as an occasional duty of Christians, in order to, and as an indication of, their humbling of their souls for their sins, or under the mighty hand of God; but he requireth that it should be in sincerity, not in hypocrisy, for the glory of God, not for ostentation and appearance unto men. Our Saviour probably in this discourse hath a respect to some hypocritical usages of the Pharisees, using to disfigure their countenances, and look demurely or sourly upon their fasting days. Not that he prohibiteth here habits or gestures suited to the duty, himself sometimes commanded the Jews to put off their ornaments, nor was any thing more ordinary for good men than to cover themselves with sackcloth, and put ashes on their heads. All that our Lord prohibiteth is the affecting of these things, to cover the hypocrisy of their hearts. Nor must we think that it is the will of God, that we on such days should indeed anoint our heads and wash our faces; or (which is the same thing with us) adorn, paint, or perfume ourselves, or use any habits or gestures unsuitable to mourning, and not indicative of afflicted souls; but that we should rather do this than the other, viz. put on a mask and vizard of sorrow for sin, when indeed we had no sense of it; for still we must appear to our heavenly Father to fast, which we cannot very well do, if our outward habit and demeanour be not something proportioned to the inward sorrow and affliction of our souls; for the putting on of fine dresses and ornaments must be an imperate act of the soul, and not like to be commanded by a soul in affliction, it being natural to such a soul to neglect the culture of the body, being wholly swallowed up with bitter thoughts relating to its own spiritual and eternal state. Our Saviour addeth the same argument to press sincere fasting, which he had before used concerning the duty of giving alms and secret prayer, where I have before spoken to those words.

19 ¶ [s]Lay not up for yourselves treasures upon earth, where moth and rust doth corrupt, and where thieves break through and steal:

s Prov. 23. 4. 1 Tim. 6. 17. Heb. 13. 5. Jam. 5. 1, &c.

20 [t]But lay up for yourselves treasures in heaven, where neither moth nor rust doth corrupt, and where thieves do not break through nor steal:

t Ecclus. 29. 11. ch. 19. 21. Luke 12. 33, 34. & 18. 22. 1 Tim. 6. 19. 1 Pet. 1. 4.

21 For where your treasure is, there will your heart be also.

A *treasure* (according to the notation of the word) signifieth something laid up for to-morrow, for future time; more largely it signifieth any riches, or what we judge a

S. MATTHEW VI

valuable portion. Make not the things of the earth your riches, or portion, with reference to future time ; for all the riches of the earth are perishing, contemptible things ; silver and gold is what rust will corrupt, clothes are what moths will spoil, any other things are subject to casualties, and, amongst others, to the violence of unreasonable men, who, though they have no right to them, will ordinarily take them from you. But let your riches. your treasure, be that which is heavenly, those habits of grace which will bring you to heaven, the *things which accompany salvation*, Heb. vi. 9, which make you *meet to be partakers of the saints in light*, Col. i. 12 : be *rich in good works, laying up in store for yourselves a good foundation against the time to come, that you may lay hold on eternal life*, 1 Tim. vi. 18, 19 ; chap. xix. 21 ; xxv. 34 ; Luke xviii. 22. Those treasures will not be liable to such accidents as all earthly treasures are. Wherever you fix your treasure, your heart will be there also, thinking upon it, delighting in it. &c.

u Luke 11. 34, 36.

22 "The light of the body is the eye : if therefore thine eye be single, thy whole body shall be full of light.

23 But if thine eye be evil, thy whole body shall be full of darkness. If therefore the light that is in thee be darkness, how great *is* that darkness !

You had need look to your hearts, your understanding, judgment, and affections ; for look what proportion there is betwixt your bodily eye and the rest of the bodily members, with regard to their guidance and conduct, the same proportion there is betwixt your heart and whole conversation, with reference to the guidance of it with relation to God. The eye is the window by which the soul looks out to guide the body ; if that be not impaired by the defluxion of humours, &c., but be single, it directs all the motions of the body right ; but if that be defective, or any way impaired, the whole body is at a loss how to move safely, and with advantage to it. So if your hearts be set right, if you have a right and sound judgment, a true and sanctified affection, they will influence and guide all your actions, your whole conversation will be regular and holy : but if that inward *eye be evil*, through covetousness, too much adherence to the earth, or through envy, (both which are called *evil eyes* in Scripture,) or through the prevalence of any other lusts or passions, your darkness will be exceeding great, you will not be able to set one step right ; for out of the abundance of the heart the mouth speaketh, and according to the dictates and affections of the heart the hand and the whole man acteth.

x Luke 16. 13.

24 ¶ ˣNo man can serve two masters : for either he will hate the one, and love the other ; or else he will hold to the one, and despise the other. ʸYe cannot serve God and mammon.

y Gal. 1. 10. 1 Tim. 6. 17. Jam. 4. 4. 1 John 2. 15.

No man can serve two masters, that is, two masters that command contrary things each to other, for that is the present case of God and mammon. Or, No man with the like diligence, and alacrity, and faithfulness, can serve two masters. It is a proverbial speech, and in reason to be understood of contrary masters. He will either hate the one, or the first, and love the second, or else he will cleave to the first, and contemn the other, that is, so in his actions behave himself, that he will appear a true servant but to one of them, and despise or slight the other. *Ye cannot serve God and mammon.* It is not improbable that some of the ancients have thought, that amongst some of the heathen they had an idol called Mammon, which they made the god of money ; thence mammon by a figure signifieth riches, as Luke xvi. 9. So as it is of an equivalent sense to, No man can serve God and Bacchus, or God and Venus ; that is, none can be a drunkard, or an unclean person, and a true servant of God. So no man can serve God, and yet make the getting of riches, right or wrong, his study ; hence the apostle calls *covetousness idolatry*, Col. iii. 5. So that by *serving* here must be understood a giving up of ourselves chiefly or wholly to the service of God, and to the business of getting the world ; or, serving the latter, in what it tempteth or commandeth us to, contrary to the will of God.

z Ps. 55. 22. Luke 12. 22, 23. Phil. 4. 6. 1 Pet. 5. 7.

25 Therefore I say unto you, ᶻTake no thought for your life, what ye shall eat, or what ye shall drink ; nor yet for your body, what ye shall put on. Is not the life more than meat, and the body than raiment ?

This text must not be interpreted in a sense contradictory to those many other texts, which forbid an idle life, and command us in the sweat of our face to eat our bread, or to provide for our families, 2 Thess. iii. 10, 11 ; 1 Tim. v. 8 : nor did Christ himself live such a life ; he went about doing good, finishing the work which his Father had given him to do. It must be therefore understood, 1. Of no such thoughts as are inconsistent with the service of God, mentioned in the last words. 2. Of no anxious and distracting thoughts. 3. Of no such thoughts as should show any distrust and diffidence in God's providing for us. God hath given us our lives and our bodies, without our care for the existence of them ; why should we, in a lawful and moderate use of means, distrust God for a subsistence for them ? He hath given us the greater, will he not (think you) give us the less ?

26 ᵃBehold the fowls of the air : for they sow not, neither do they reap, nor gather into barns ; yet your heavenly Father feedeth them. Are ye not much better than they ?

a Job 38. 41. Ps. 147. 9. Luke 12. 24, &c.

God takes care of all his creatures. For example, consider *the fowls*, and those not the tame fowls about your houses, but the fowls *of the air*, for whom the housewife's hand doth not provide, neither hath God fitted them for any labour by which they can procure their livelihood, nor doth he require any such thing of them, nor do they labour ; yet their Creator (who is *your heavenly Father*) *feedeth them*. You have much more reason to trust in God, if you could not labour, being hindered by his providence, for you are more excellent beings than sensitive creatures, and you have a further relation to God than that of creatures to the Creator, for God is your heavenly Father ; you are in the order of nature, and especially considering that God is your Father, much better than they.

27 Which of you by taking thought can add one cubit unto his stature ?

How vain a thing is it to distract yourselves with anxious thoughts about your body and your life ! all your thinking will not add a cubit to your stature : as your being and existence deriveth from God, so the increase of your stature dependeth upon him ; likewise he maketh the child to grow to the just proportion which he hath intended him, and beyond that he cannot pass. If God's blessing be necessary to this, and so necessary that no thoughts, no means, will add any thing without the Divine blessing, what reason have you to take any such thoughts, as you cannot expect he should bless to their desired effect and issue ?

28 And why take ye thought for raiment ? Consider the lilies of the field, how they grow ; they toil not, neither do they spin :

29 And yet I say unto you, That even Solomon in all his glory was not arrayed like one of these.

30 Wherefore, if God so clothe the grass of the field, which to day is, and to morrow is cast into the oven, *shall he* not much more *clothe* you, O ye of little faith ?

From sensitive creatures our Lord proceedeth to vegetables, an order of creatures which have more than mere being, they have also life, though no sense, but yet two degrees beneath man, wanting not only reason, but sense. He shows us from an instance in these, that we have no more reason to be troubled and anxious about clothing, than about meat or drink. Clothing is of no other use than for warmth or ornament : for such clothing as will serve us for warmth, a little care will serve the turn ; *Sudamus ad supervacanea*, our sweating thoughts are mostly for superfluities in clothing : if God see them fit for us, he will also give us them, without so many thoughts about them. Look upon *the lilies ;* (whether he means what we call tulips, or other flowers called lilies, which probably those countries had in greater variety and beauty, is not

VOL. III—2

worth the arguing;) God designing to glorify himself in those creatures, though of meanest orders, hath given them a greater beauty than Solomon had in all his rich array; to let us know that art must not contend with nature, and that beauty and glory in apparel is no more than is to be found in creatures much inferior to our order; which made Solon (though a heathen) prefer the sight of a peacock to that of Crœsus. And therefore this is a thing not worthy of any anxious thoughts, for if God seeth such things good for us, he that so clotheth *the grass of the field*, which is but of a few days' continuance, will much more clothe us; and if we distrust him for such provision, we show ourselves persons of little faith.

31 Therefore take no thought, saying, What shall we eat? or, What shall we drink? or, Wherewithal shall we be clothed?

32 (For after all these things do the Gentiles seek :) for your heavenly Father knoweth that ye have need of all these things.

Our Lord repeateth the precept before given, ver. 25, wherein he forbids not all moderate and provident thoughts for things necessary, but only such thoughts as shall argue our distrust in God, or perplex and distract our minds, or be inconsistent with our duty, and the employment of our thoughts about higher and better things. This he here presseth by two arguments. 1. Because these are the things which people spend all their thoughts upon, who are not aware that they have souls to take care for, or do not understand the providence of God, or have no such relation to God as Christians have, who call God Father. 2. You have (saith he) a heavenly Father, who, being the God of heaven, knoweth what you need, and, being your Father, will also supply your needs.

b See 1 Kin. 3. 13.
Ps. 37. 25.
Mark 10. 30.
Luke 12. 31.
1 Tim. 4. 8.

33 But [b]seek ye first the kingdom of God, and his righteousness; and all these things shall be added unto you.

The kingdom of God, and his righteousness, in this verse, are terms comprehensive of whatsoever appertaineth to the honour and glory of God, either as means, or as the end. Let your principal care and study be how to get to heaven, and how to promote the kingdom of God in the world; to bring your hearts into subjection to the will of God, that the kingdom of God may be within you, and how to bring others to the obedience of faith and of the will of God. And for the things of this life, it shall fare with you as it did with Solomon, 1 Kings iii. 12, who asked not riches and honour, but had them. You shall have for your necessities, Psal. xxxvii. 4; Mark x. 30; 1 Tim. iv. 8.

34 Take therefore no thought for the morrow: for the morrow shall take thought for the things of itself. Sufficient unto the day *is* the evil thereof.

No such thoughts as before mentioned, for God will provide for you to-morrow when to-morrow cometh. Besides, every new day will bring forth some new cares; you know not what to-morrow will bring forth, nor what you will have need of to-morrow; and if you did, why should you torment yourselves before the time? it will be time enough when you feel the evils of a succeeding time. You need not torment yourselves with prophesying against yourselves, what it may be shall never be; or if it be, you had not need weaken yourselves for the encountering such evils, by a previous disturbance of your thoughts about them.

CHAP. VII

Christ proceedeth in his sermon to condemn rash judgment, 1—5; forbiddeth the prostitution of holy things, 6; recommendeth prayer, 7—12; exhorteth to enter in at the strait gate, 13, 14; to beware of false prophets, who may be known by their fruits, 15—20; and not to be his disciples in profession only, but in practice, 21—23. He compareth the doers of the word to houses built on a rock, those that are hearers only to houses built on the sand, 24—27. Christ endeth his sermon; the people are astonished at his doctrine, 28, 29.

JUDGE [a]not, that ye be not judged.

2 For with what judgment ye judge, ye shall be judged: [b]and with what measure ye mete, it shall be measured to you again.

a Luke 6. 37.
Rom. 2. 1. &
14. 3, 4, 10, 13.
1 Cor. 4. 3, 5.
Jam. 4. 11, 12.
b Mark 4. 24.
Luke 6. 38.

Our Saviour must not be understood here prohibiting any judgment, which is elsewhere in holy writ allowed, for the Holy Spirit doth not command and prohibit the same thing; whence it is evident, that it is not to be understood of political or ecclesiastical judgments, nor was our Saviour here speaking to any such persons: it is therefore to be understood of private judgments, nor of them absolutely, for it is lawful for us to judge ourselves, yea, it is our duty, 1 Cor. xi. 31. Nor is that judgment of our neighbour's opinions or actions here forbidden which terminateth in ourselves, in our satisfaction as to the truth or falsehood of the former, or the goodness or badness of the latter; we ought so to prove all things in order to our holding fast that which is good. Nor is all judgment of our neighbour's actions with reference to him forbidden: how can we reprove him for his errors, or restore him that is fallen, without a previous judgment of his actions? But that which is here forbidden, is either, 1. A rash judgment of his state, or a judging him for doing his duty: such was Simon's judging the woman, or the disciples' judgment of that woman, Matt. xxvi. 8, 9. Or, 2. A judging of others for things which they judge to be indifferent, forbidden Rom. xiv. 1—3. Or, 3. A judging them for secret things, such as inward habits of grace, when no apparent fruits to the contrary are seen. Or, 4. Condemning others for single acts, or a public censuring and condemning others for private failings. Or, finally, Any open and public censuring the actions of others, when and where it cannot conduce either to God's glory or our brother's good. *That ye be not judged*: this is expounded in the next verse, telling us either the ordinary temper of men, or the just judgment of God, repaying such uncharitable actions *per legem talionis*, with suffering others to do the like to us, Luke vi. 37.

3 [c]And why beholdest thou the mote that is in thy brother's eye, but considerest not the beam that is in thine own eye?

c Luke 6. 41, 42.

4 Or how wilt thou say to thy brother, Let me pull out the mote out of thine eye; and, behold, a beam *is* in thine own eye?

5 Thou hypocrite, first cast out the beam out of thine own eye; and then shalt thou see clearly to cast out the mote out of thy brother's eye.

Whether the word translated *mote* signifieth a mote or a splinter, is of no great concern to know. Our Saviour expounded this text, when he said to the Pharisees, bringing him a woman taken in adultery, *Let him that is guiltless throw the first stone*. So doth the apostle Paul, Rom. ii. 1. The text teacheth us these lessons: 1. That those who are most censorious of others, are usually more notorious and culpable themselves, if not for the same sins, yet for others of equal if not greater magnitude. 2. That it is notorious hypocrisy to spy smaller faults in others, and not to see greater in ourselves. 3. That it is notorious impudence to pretend to censure and judge others for sins in which we live ourselves. 4. That there is no such way to teach us charity in not hastily, rashly, or too severely judging others, as to look first into our own hearts and ways, and seeing if we have not the same or greater failings. Our charity in this kind should begin at home.

6 ¶ [d]Give not that which is holy unto the dogs, neither cast ye your pearls before swine, lest they trample them under their feet, and turn again and rend you.

d Prov. 9. 7, 8. & 23. 9.
Acts 13. 45, 46.

By *swine* and *dogs*, our Saviour doubtless understandeth wicked men of several sorts, either such as are more tame sinners, trampling upon holy things, and with swine wallowing in the mire of lusts and corruptions, Prov. xxvi. 11; 2 Pet. ii. 22; or, by *dogs*, more malicious, revengeful, boisterous sinners may be meant, whose consciences will serve them to bark and grin at the word of God, to mock at holy things, to persecute those that bring them the gospel, and are their open enemies, because they tell them the truth. The gospel is to be preached *to every creature*, Mark xvi. 15. But when the Jews *were hardened*, and *spake evil of that way before the multitude*, &c., Acts xix. 9, the apostles left preaching to them. The precept doubtless is general, directing the ministers of Christ to administer the holy things, with which they are intrusted, only to such as have a right to them, and under prudent circumstances, so as the holy name of God may not be profaned, nor they run into needless danger.

e ch. 21. 22.
Mark 11. 24.
Luke 11. 9,
10. & 18. 1.
John 14. 13.
& 15. 7. &
16. 23, 24.
1 John 3. 22.
& 5. 14, 15.
f Prov. 8. 17.
Jer. 29. 12, 13.

7 ¶ ^eAsk, and it shall be given you; seek, and ye shall find; knock, and it shall be opened unto you:

8 For ^fevery one that asketh receiveth; and he that seeketh findeth; and to him that knocketh it shall be opened.

Here is a precept expressed by three words, *ask, seek, knock*; and a promise annexed in three distinct terms, *it shall be given you, ye shall find, it shall be opened unto you*. The thing commanded is prayer; the thing promised is an audience of prayer, or an answer to prayer. The multiplying of the terms in which the precept is expressed is not idle and superfluous, it lets us know our averseness to the duty, and that God in it requireth of us faith, diligence, constancy, and importunity. Christ had before told us of whom we should ask, *our Father*; it is not said what we should ask, both in regard we have a liberty to ask any thing we have need of, and he had, chap. vi., particularly directed the matter of our prayers. The promise, that we shall have, signifies an answer, either in kind or in value; the promise of giving lets us know that our prayers are not meritorious. *For every one that asketh* the things he needeth, and in faith, according to the will of God, and for a right end, *receiveth*, &c. See James iv. 3.

g Luke 11. 11, 12, 13.

9 ^gOr what man is there of you, whom if his son ask bread, will he give him a stone?

10 Or if he ask a fish, will he give him a serpent?

h Gen. 6. 5. & 8. 21.

11 If ye then, ^hbeing evil, know how to give good gifts unto your children, how much more shall your Father which is in heaven give good things to them that ask him?

Asking is but a verbal expression of an inward desire; no man desireth that which is evil, but that which he at least apprehendeth to be good, that is, suitable unto his wants. As earthly parents, knowing that their children, though through weakness of understanding they may ask that which is really evil for them, yet will not give them any such things, and gratify their ignorance; so neither will your heavenly Father, knowing what you truly need, and what is truly good for you, give you any thing which he knoweth is not suitable for you, but noxious to you: but if you ask any thing which is either absolutely good for you, and cannot be evil, or which your heavenly Father knoweth to be good for you under your present circumstances, you may be assured, considering he is your Father, and hath as great a kindness for you as an earthly father for his child, and that he is your heavenly Father, and therefore hath a sufficiency to give, will give good things to you asking them of him: and this you may be assured of from that good will and inclination which you, though you come infinitely short of the perfection and good inclinations of your heavenly Father, find in yourselves towards your children; for you derive from him, as his children, all that goodness and benignity which you have. If therefore we in prayer ask any thing of God, which may be good or evil under different circumstances, and receive it not, we may conclude, that though we thought what we asked bread, yet indeed it was a stone; though we thought it a fish, yet God saw it was a scorpion; and account that God answered our general desires, which were for some good, by denying our specifical request.

12 Therefore all things ⁱwhatsoever ye would that men should do to you, do ye even so to them: for ^kthis is the Law and the Prophets.

i Tob. 4. 15.
Luke 6. 31.
k Lev. 19. 18.
ch. 22. 40.
Rom. 13. 8, 9, 10. Gal. 5. 14.
1 Tim. 1. 5.

Most interpreters think the term *therefore* here redundant, as some such little particles often are in holy writ, for it is hard to make out this to be a proper inference from the premises. This precept containeth in it the substance of all that is to be found in the books of the law and the prophets which concerneth us in reference to others, the sum of the second table, which requireth only justice and charity. Christ doth not say, this is all the law and the prophets, but *this is the law and the prophets*. There is no man but would have others deal justly with him in giving him what is his own, whether honour, or tribute, or estate, &c., neither taking nor withholding his own from him. Nor is there any but, if he stood in need of it, would desire the charitable help of another, or a charitable remission from him of what he might in exact justice require. Do ye (saith our Saviour) the same unto them. And indeed this is but a confirmation of the light and law of nature, no more than what men would do if they would hearken to the light within them. And without this in vain do men pretend to religion, as our Saviour teacheth, Mark vii. 9—13; which makes some think that our Saviour by this reflects upon the Pharisees, who laid all their religion upon ceremonies, and some ritual performances in observance of their traditions, and omitted *the weightier things of the law, judgment, mercy, and faith*, Matt. xxiii. 23.

13 ¶ ^lEnter ye in at the strait gate: for wide *is* the gate, and broad *is* the way, that leadeth to destruction, and many there be which go in thereat:

l Luke 13. 24.

14 ‖ Because strait *is* the gate, and narrow *is* the way, which leadeth unto life, and few there be that find it.

| Or, *How*,

Our Saviour having in this sermon delivered many hard sayings to flesh and blood, here obviates a twofold temptation they might have to the neglect of them: 1. From their difficulty. 2. From the paucity of them who live according to these rules. He here compareth heaven to a house, a stately house, into which a *strait gate* leadeth to a city, the way to which is a *narrow way*. There is nothing more ordinary in holy writ, than to call a common course of men's actions a *way*. It is also compared to a *gate*. The sum of what our Saviour here saith is this: There are but two ultimate ends of all men, eternal destruction and eternal life. The course that leadeth to destruction is like a broad way that is obvious to all, and many walk in that. That course of life and actions which will bring a man to heaven is strait, unpleasing to flesh and blood, not at all gratifying men's sensitive appetites, and narrow, (the Greek is, afflicted,) a way wherein men will meet with many crosses and temptations; and there are but a few will find it. You must not therefore wonder if my precepts be hard to your carnal apprehensions, nor be scandalized though you see but few going in the right road to the kingdom of heaven.

15 ¶ ^mBeware of false prophets, ⁿwhich come to you in sheep's clothing, but inwardly they are ^oravening wolves.

m Deu. 13. 3.
Jer. 23. 16.
ch. 24. 4, 5, 11, 24. Mark 13. 22. Rom. 16. 17, 18.
Eph. 5. 6. Col. 2. 8. 2 Pet. 2. 1, 2, 3. 1 John 4. 1. n Mic. 3. 5. 2 Tim. 3. 5. o Acts 20. 29, 30.

The term *prophets* in holy writ is of larger extent than to signify only such as foretold things to come; others also who taught the people, pretending authority from God so to do, were called prophets. Thus *Bar-jesus*, Acts xiii. 6, is called *a false prophet*. A false prophet is of the same significancy with a false teacher. Against those our Saviour cautioneth his hearers, as being the most fatal and dangerous enemies to faith and holiness. Some of them indeed come *in sheep's clothing*, under very fair pretences, and a fair show of religion and strictness; but *they are ravening wolves*, as dangerous to your souls as ravenous wolves are to a flock of sheep.

16 ^pYe shall know them by their fruits. ^qDo men gather grapes of thorns, or figs of thistles?

p ver. 20.
ch. 12. 33.
q Luke 6. 43, 44.

S. MATTHEW VII

<small>Jer. 11. 19.
ch. 12. 33.</small> 17 Even so 'every good tree bringeth forth good fruit; but a corrupt tree bringeth forth evil fruit.

18 A good tree cannot bring forth evil fruit, neither *can* a corrupt tree bring forth good fruit.

<small>s ch. 3. 10.
Luke 3. 9.
John 15. 2, 6.</small> 19 ˢEvery tree that bringeth not forth good fruit is hewn down, and cast into the fire.

20 Wherefore by their fruits ye shall know them.

A proper effect discovereth the cause. Lest his disciples should ask, How shall we distinguish true from false teachers? our Saviour tells them, *By their fruits ye shall know them.* Our Saviour sends not his disciples to inquire into the truth of their mission, whether that more internal from God, of which they could not judge, or more external from men, who may err, and send out those whom God never sent; but you shall know them (saith our Saviour) by their faithful or unfaithful discharge of their duty: if they be true teachers, by their discharging the ministry in a faithful revelation of the mind and will of God, or by their holy life, living as ensamples to the flock; by their fruits of true doctrine and a holy life, by the discharge of their ministry in good conscience; for it is with men as it is with the trees, good trees bring forth good fruit, corrupt trees bring forth evil fruit. If men have the root of the matter, the seed of God abiding in them, they will in every relation bring forth the fruits of truth and holiness: if they have not, they will bring forth error and wickedness. From whence we may learn, that our Lord expecteth from his people such a knowledge of the Scriptures, as that they may be able to discern truth from falsehood; and such a diligence, as to search the Scriptures, whether those things which their teachers deliver to them be according to them or not, Acts xvii. 11; not taking divine truths upon trust, nor believing any thing because dictated by teachers, using their teachers not as dictators, but only as helpers of their faith.

<small>t Hos. 8. 2.
ch. 25. 11, 12.
Luke 6. 46.
& 13. 25.
Acts 19. 13.
Rom. 2. 13.
Jam. 1. 22.</small> 21 ¶ Not every one that saith unto me, ᵗLord, Lord, shall enter into the kingdom of heaven; but he that doeth the will of my Father which is in heaven.

Some that say unto Christ, *Lord, Lord,* shall be saved, being the true disciples of Christ; but every one that owneth Christ by an external profession as his Lord, every one that prayeth, though he doth it often, and with some appearing zeal and importunity, shall not be saved, nor doth by it approve himself a true disciple of Christ; but he alone who doth endeavour to fulfil the whole will of God, both by faith and holiness, Rom. ii. 13; 1 Thess. iv. 3; James i. 22, 23. True religion lies in obedience to the whole will of God.

<small>u Num. 24. 4.
John 11. 51.
1 Cor. 13. 2.</small> 22 Many will say to me in that day, Lord, Lord, have we ᵘnot prophesied in thy name? and in thy name have cast out devils? and in thy name done many wonderful works?

<small>x ch. 25. 12.
Luke 13. 25,
27. 2 Tim.
2. 19.
y Ps. 5. 5.
& 6. 8. ch.
25. 41.</small> 23 And ˣthen will I profess unto them, I never knew you: ʸdepart from me, ye that work iniquity.

That by *that day* is to be understood the day of judgment is generally agreed by interpreters. *We have prophesied in thy name;* that is, revealed thy will unto people; *and in thy name,* that is, by thy authority and power, *cast out devils, and done many wonderful works,* that is, wrought many miraculous operations. In the Old Testament we find Baalam and Saul prophesying, who were both wicked men. Judas was sent out (under the New Testament) both to preach and to work miracles. So as none from gifts, no, not the most eminent and extraordinary gifts, can conclude the goodness of his state, or any special favour with God. *I will profess,* that is, I will openly declare to them, *I never knew you,* that is, so as to approve you, or take pleasure in you. *Depart from me, ye that work iniquity*: see Matt. xxv. 41.

24 ¶ Therefore ᶻwhosoever heareth <small>z Luke 6. 47, &c.</small> these sayings of mine, and doeth them, I will liken him unto a wise man, which built his house upon a rock:

25 And the rain descended, and the floods came, and the winds blew, and beat upon that house; and it fell not: for it was founded upon a rock.

Our Saviour maketh frequent use of that ancient way of instructing people by similitudes and parables, which by their easy incurring into the senses give advantage to the memory: he here chooseth a similitude to conclude his excellent sermon upon the mount. The builder intended, who our Saviour dignifieth with the name of *a wise man,* is he that not only heareth Christ's sayings, but doeth them. Under the notion of hearing is comprehended understanding and believing them; by doing them, he understandeth a sincere desire and endeavour to do them, with a practice so far as human frailty will permit. The *house* intended seems to be a hope for eternal life and salvation: by the *rock* is meant Christ, 1 Cor. x. 4; Eph. ii. 20; 1 Pet. ii. 4. Every wise Christian, before he buildeth up to himself a hope of eternal life and salvation through Christ, must find that he is one who doth not only read and hear the word of God, but so hears as to understand and believe it, that has an operative faith, working upon his soul to the obedience of the will of God, or at least a sincere endeavour to it. And he who doth so, though his hope may be sometimes assaulted with fears, doubts, temptations, (which are like the assaults of a house builded on a rock, by winds, floods, and storms,) yet it shall not fail, because it is truly founded on Christ, according to the revelation of his will, Prov. x. 28; 1 John iii. 3.

26 And every one that heareth these sayings of mine, and doeth them not, shall be likened unto a foolish man, which built his house upon the sand:

27 And the rain descended, and the floods came, and the winds blew, and beat upon that house; and it fell: and great was the fall of it.

There are and will be others, that, as foolish builders, run up a house in haste, without looking to the goodness of the foundation, and happen to build it upon loose ground. So they flatter themselves with the hopes of the house in the heavens not made with hands, 2 Cor. v. 1, without looking to the bottom and foundation of these hopes, whether they be such as Christ hath warranted or no; but either build their hopes upon God's infinite mercy, or the sufficiency of Christ's merits, or their own works, hearing the word of God, and performing some other duties of religion, never regarding to live to the obedience of the will of God. And the same event will be to these men as to such foolish builders; their building may stand a while, but when a day of visitation, or death, or sharp afflictions, or temptation, comes, then their house, their hopes, all fail and perish in a moment, because they had no good foundation, Job viii. 13, 14; xi. 20; xxvii. 8; Prov. xi. 7. *And great was the fall of it:* their misery and calamity shall be the greater, by how much their hopes have been the stronger, the disappointment of their expectation adding to their misery.

28 And it came to pass, when Jesus had ended these sayings, ᵃthe people were astonished at his doctrine: <small>a ch. 13. 54.
Mark 1. 22.
& 6. 2.
Luke 4. 32.</small>

29 ᵇFor he taught them as *one* having authority, and not as the Scribes. <small>b John 7. 46.</small>

The same words also are repeated, Mark i. 22; Luke iv. 32. They declare the effect of this and other of our Saviour's sermons upon the hearts of those that heard him, and the reason of it. They *were astonished,* affected with an admiration at what they heard him in this and other sermons deliver: the Divine verities revealed in his discourses, the purity of his doctrine, the convincing power that attended it, his bold and free speech without respect of persons, the simplicity of his phrase, the gravity of his matter, the majesty he showed in his discourses, affected the people, and made him appear to them one sent of God, and clothed with his authority. He did not teach as the scribes, the ordinary teachers amongst the Jews, from whom they had the discourses about traditions, and rites, and ceremonies, cold and dull discourses, of little or no tendency to their eternal salvation.

CHAP. VIII

Christ cleanseth the leper, 2—4; healeth the centurion's servant, 5—13, Peter's mother-in-law, 14, 15, and many other diseased, 16, 17; showeth how he is to be followed, 18—22; stilleth the tempest on the sea, 23—27; driveth the devils out of two men possessed, and suffereth them to go into the swine, 28—34.

WHEN he was come down from the mountain, great multitudes followed him.

^a Mark 1. 40, &c. Luke 5. 12, &c.

2 ^aAnd, behold, there came a leper and worshipped him, saying, Lord, if thou wilt, thou canst make me clean.

We heard of Christ's going up into the mountain, Matt. v. 1; and of great multitudes that followed him from Decapolis, and from Judea, and from Jerusalem, and from beyond Jordan: whether the same multitude, or others, followed him upon his coming down, is not said. But *behold*, (saith the evangelist,) *there came a leper:* both Mark and Luke have the same story, or one very like to it, Mark i. 40; Luke v. 12. Of the plague, or leprosy, we read much in the books of Moses. It was a white scab in the flesh, which gradually consumed the body, and was contagious. The leper, and he who touched him, or any thing he came near, was legally unclean: thrice we read of it inflicted as a severe punishment; upon Gehazi, for lying and taking bribes, and upon king Uzziah, for offering sacrifice. It was a disease of very difficult cure. This leper comes and worshippeth Christ. Mark saith that he kneeled down to him: whether he only kneeled down, or prostrated himself, is not much material, for either of them might be done according to the fashion of those countries, in token either of a civil respect, paid to him as a great and eminent prophet, or a piece of religious homage (if he had so early a revelation that he was the Son of God, which some doubt). *Saying, Lord, if thou wilt, thou canst make me clean.* The term *Lord* will not conclude his recognising Christ as the Son of God, being a term used by Sarah to Abraham, and afterwards to Elijah. The words import his desire, though they be not a form of prayer, but an acknowledgment of the power of Christ. The leper acknowledging Christ's power, submits himself to his will, and so with the same breath declareth his faith and modesty He indeed declareth no faith in the will of God, nor can any person exercise any such faith as to any temporal mercy, any further than as God shall judge it for our good.

3 And Jesus put forth *his* hand, and touched him, saying, I will; be thou clean. And immediately his leprosy was cleansed.

By the law of God, Lev. v. 3, he that touched another who was unclean (as the leper was, Lev. xiii., xiv.) was unclean; how then doth Christ (who was subject to the law) touch the leper? Some say he did not touch the unclean leper, but him that was a leper, and by his touch made clean. But it is a better answer, that by what Christ did as he was God (such were his miraculous operations) he could not contract any ritual uncleanness; and possibly under the law the priest was exempted from that uncleanness, for he came very near the leper in his office about him, expressed Lev. xiii., xiv. Nor do we read of any uncleanness contracted by Aaron in his performance of his office to Miriam under her leprosy, nor by the priests, 2 Chron. xxvi. 20, though it be said they thrust out Uzziah. Christ, by putting forth his hand, showed his kindness to this miserable creature; by healing him with a touch, he showed his Divine power. *Saying, I will; be thou clean:* he answereth him in his own term, *I will*, and then commands the thing. How acceptable is faith to God! *And immediately his leprosy was cleansed*, that is, removed; the word *immediately* confirms the miracle, it was not only a thing done without ordinary means, but without the ordinary time requsite for such a cure.

^b ch. 9. 30. Mark 5. 43.

4 And Jesus saith unto him, ^bSee thou tell no man; but go thy way, shew thyself to the Priest, and offer the gift that ^cMoses commanded, for a testimony unto them.

^c Lev. 14. 3, 4, 10. Luke 5. 14.

Some think that our Saviour only commanded him silence until he had showed himself unto the priest, and he, according to the law, Lev. xiii., should have pronounced him clean, lest their envy upon hearing of it should have caused them to have obscured the miracle, by delaying to pronounce him clean; but it is observable that this was not the only time when Christ commanded those upon whom he had wrought miracles to say nothing of it: see chap. ix. 30; xii. 16; xvii. 9. It is therefore more probable, that this precept was not to be understood with that limitation, but that Christ did it, either that he might not be thought to seek his own glory, or rather, because Christ judged it not yet time to his miracles to be publicly made known: but he sends him to the priest, both to teach him obedience to the law, and that the truth of the miracle might by a public record be confirmed. He also commands him to *offer the gifts* appointed by the law, Lev. xiv., thereby both acknowledging his cure to be from God, and testifying his thankfulness. *That Moses commanded;* to show that he came not to oppose Moses. *For a testimony unto them;* that hereafter it may be a testimony unto them, that I am more than the Son of man, John v. 36.

5 ¶ ^dAnd when Jesus was entered into Capernaum, there came unto him a centurion, beseeching him,

^d Luke 7. 1, &c.

6 And saying, Lord, my servant lieth at home sick of the palsy, grievously tormented.

7 And Jesus saith unto him, I will come and heal him.

8 The centurion answered and said, Lord, ^eI am not worthy that thou shouldest come under my roof: but ^fspeak the word only, and my servant shall be healed.

^e Luke 15. 19, 21. ^f Ps. 107. 20.

9 For I am a man under authority, having soldiers under me: and I say to this *man*, Go, and he goeth; and to another, Come, and he cometh; and to my servant, Do this, and he doeth *it*.

10 When Jesus heard *it*, he marvelled, and said to them that followed, Verily I say unto you, I have not found so great faith, no, not in Israel.

Many think that this story was in order before the other. It is related by Luke, chap. vii., with some larger circumstances: there is only this difference betwixt the two evangelists; Matthew seems to speak as if the centurion at first came in person to him; Luke saith, that he first sent the elders of the Jews to him, then some friends. But we are accounted ourselves to do that which we set others on work to do. *There came unto him a centurion;* there came some elders of the Jews first, then some particular friends of one that was a Roman captain, to him, to tell him that the captain had a servant at his house that lay grievously sick of and tormented with the palsy; that which we usually call the dead palsy, in which a fit of the apoplexy usually issueth, when it doth not presently kill. Our Lord promiseth to come and heal him, therein showing both his kindness, and how acceptable to him the humanity of this centurion to his servant was. The centurion by his friends, as Luke tells us, sends to him, desiring him not to trouble himself to that degree, telling him. 1. That it was a favour of which he was not worthy. The best men have always the meanest thoughts of themselves. 2. That it was needless, for if he would only *speak the word*, commanding out the distemper, that was enough to effect the cure. For he tells him, that he believed diseases were as much at Christ's command as his servants were at his command. That they came at God's command, wrought according to their commission from God, and went off when God commanded them off; so that if he, though at a distance, would command off his servant's disease, it would be as effectual as his presence. Whether this captain were actually proselyted to the Jewish religion or no, is uncertain : it should seem by our Saviour's next words that he was not an Israelite ; but it is most certain that he had a right notion of the power of the true God, and it looks very probable that he had a revelation of Christ, as the true Messiah and Son of God. *When Jesus heard it, he marvelled ;* admiration agreed not to Christ as God, but as man it did ; *and said to them that followed him, Verily I say unto you, I have not found so great faith in Israel;* that is, in the generality of the Israelites, for if we speak of particular persons, both Joseph and Mary had showed a greater faith. This expression is enough to let us know, that the centurion was no native Israelite, and make it probable he was not of the Jewish church, which might be, though he was so kind to the Jewish nation as to build them a synagogue, upon which account, Luke vii. 3, &c., the elders of the Jews pleaded with Christ for him. This made our Saviour go on, prophesying of a further conversion of the Gentiles.

^g Gen. 12.3.
Is. 2. 2, 3.
& 11. 10.
Mal. 1. 11.
Luke 13. 29.
Acts 10. 45.
& 11. 18. &
14. 27. Rom.
15. 9, &c.
Eph. 3. 6.
^h ch. 21. 43.
i ch. 13. 42,
50. & 22. 13.
& 24. 51.
& 25. 30.
Luke 13. 28.
2 Pet. 2. 17. Jude 13.

11 And I say unto you, That ^g many shall come from the east and west, and shall sit down with Abraham, and Isaac, and Jacob, in the kingdom of heaven.

12 But ^h the children of the kingdom ⁱ shall be cast out into outer darkness : there shall be weeping and gnashing of teeth.

That is, in short, many of those who are now heathens shall be saved ; and many of the Jews shall be damned. *Many,* not all, *shall come from the east and west,* from all parts, from the remotest parts in the world. Luke saith, *east, west, north, and south,* Luke xiii. 29 : so Isa. xi. 12 ; xliii. 5, 6. *And sit down with Abraham, Isaac, and Jacob in the kingdom of God ;* in heaven, where Abraham, Isaac, and Jacob, the heads of the Jewish nation, are, to whom the promises were made ; or, in the church of God, for the church triumphant and militant are both but one church. They shall *sit down* with them, as men sit down at a banquet, an expression oft used to signify the rest and pleasure the saints shall have in heaven, Isa. xxv. 6—8 ; Luke xxii. 29, 30. *But the children of the kingdom,* the Jews, who boast much that they are the children of Abraham, and think themselves the only church, and the only heirs of glory, and who are indeed the only church of God as yet, *shall be cast out into outer darkness :* either the darkness of errors, ignorance, and superstition, the gospel light shall not shine upon them, they shall be no more the church of God ; or, the darkness of hell, where shall be nothing but pain and misery, and lamentations for the gospel, and the grace thereof, first offered to them, but unthankfully rejected by them, by which they judge themselves unworthy of the grace of God and of eternal life, Acts xiii. 46.

13 And Jesus said unto the centurion, Go thy way ; and as thou hast believed, *so* be it done unto thee. And his servant was healed in the selfsame hour.

Luke saith, *And they that were sent, returning to the house, found the servant whole that had been sick,* Luke vii. 10 ; so as it seemeth that what Christ *said unto the centurion,* must be interpreted, to those whom the centurion sent in his name. Go your way, your business is done, the centurion's faith hath obtained, it shall be done to him as he hath *believed ;* where believing must signify, a certain persuasion of the power of Christ, with a relying on his mercy and goodness. The proximate object of faith is some word of God. How far this centurion was acquainted with the oracles of the Old Testament (though he lived amongst the Jews, and, as appears by his building a synagogue for them, Luke vii., had a kindness for their religion) I cannot tell. It is most probable that he had some immediate revelation of God concerning Christ, which he is here said to have believed, and to have had a full persuasion of and trusted in. All revelations of God are the object of faith, though the Scriptures, being now written, are to us that have them the tests and touchstones to try such impressions by. *As thou believest,* not because thou believest. Our faith is not meritorious of the least mercies, but it is an exercise of grace which gives glory to God, and receiveth the reward not of debt but of grace. The miracle appeared in that the disease was of an incurable nature, and the cure was wrought without application of means, and in such a moment of time as means, though used, could not have wrought it.

14 ¶ ^k And when Jesus was come into Peter's house, he saw ^l his wife's mother laid, and sick of a fever.

k Mark 1.
29, 30, 31.
Luke 4. 38,
39.
l 1 Cor. 9. 5.

15 And he touched her hand, and the fever left her : and she arose, and ministered unto them.

This story is related, with some further circumstances, Mark i. 29—31 ; Luke iv. 38, 39. Mark tells us it was *the house of Simon and Andrew, with James and John ;* (it seems they lived there together ;) that they told him of her sickness, after he had been there some time ; that he *took her by the hand, and lifted her up.* Luke saith it was *a great fever ;* that *they besought him for her ;* that *he stood over her, and rebuked the fever.* Here is no contradiction, only some amplifications of the story. It is plain from this text, that Peter was a married man, and continued so though called to be an apostle, and that he had a family. Fevers are ordinary distempers, and often cured by ordinary means, but this was a great fever. The miracle here was not in the cure of an incurable disease, but in the way of the cure, by a touch of his hand, or a lifting her up ; and the suddenness of the cure, it immediately left her ; and her sudden recovery of strength, that she could presently arise and minister to them : that she could do it, argued her cure miraculous ; that she did do it, argues her sense of Christ's goodness, and thankfulness, and teacheth us the use we should make of all God's gracious providences to us, to make us fitter for the service of God, and to employ ourselves in it ; so taking *the cup of salvation,* and praising *the name of the Lord,* Psal. cxvi. 13.

16 ¶ ^m When the even was come, they brought unto him many that were possessed with devils : and he cast out the spirits with *his* word, and healed all that were sick :

m Mark 1.
32, &c.
Luke 4. 40,
41.

17 That it might be fulfilled which was spoken by Esaias the prophet, saying, ⁿ Himself took our infirmities, and bare *our* sicknesses.

n Is. 53. 4.
1 Pet. 2. 24.

Mark hath much the same chap. i. 32—34 ; and Luke, chap. iv. 40, 41. Luke adds, *he laid his hands upon them, and healed them.* We before, chap. iv. 24, showed who were meant by persons possessed by devils. It is only observable that it is said, *he cast out the spirits by his word,* by the same power by which he made the world and all things therein, Gen. i., his authoritative word. He *healed all that were sick,* that is, all that were brought to him. Laying on of his hands, was but an external symbol or rite used in blessing, in miraculous operations, and in ordination of ministers. The great question is, how that which the prophet Isaiah said, chap. liii. 4, was fulfilled by these miraculous operations. The words are, *Surely he hath borne our griefs, and carried our sorrows ;* and, ver. 5, *with his stripes we are healed :* and the apostle Peter, referring to that text, saith, *Who bare our sins in his own body on the tree,* 1 Pet. ii. 24. The words neither seem truly quoted, nor doth the sense appear the same, the evangelist applying what the prophet seems to speak of our sins, to our bodily infirmities, and his bearing them, to his curing them ; whereas Peter seemeth to apply it to his bearing our sins, that is, the punishment of our sins, in his stripes, and by his sufferings on the cross. What I observed here is here to be considered, that the evangelists, in their quotations out of the Old Testament, took themselves only concerned to keep to the sense, not exactly to the words (which is a liberty we ordinarily take in quotations). As to the sense, *grief* and *sorrows* are terms capable of an interpretation, as to whatsoever comes upon us as the fruit and demerit of our sins, so as the prophet designed to express Christ's suffering all the punishment due to us for sin, of which nature are all the afflictions of this life, and death itself, as well as the pains of hell. The only question is, how Matthew's saying, he healed the people's diseases, answered the prophet's expression, he bare our griefs and carried our sorrows. This scripture was twice fulfilled in Christ: as to their bodily griefs and sorrows, that is mentioned by Matthew, though he bare them not all in his own body, yet he had compassion on men with reference to them, and showed himself afflicted in their afflictions, by his putting forth his Divine power to heal them; and he bare the guilt that was the cause of these and other griefs and sorrows upon the tree, as is said by Peter; and he therefore healed them, that he might demonstrate himself to be the true Messias prophesied of by Isaiah, who was to come, who was to bear our griefs and to carry our sorrows.

18 ¶ Now when Jesus saw great multitudes about him, he gave commandment to depart unto the other side.

When Jesus did these things before mentioned, he was in Capernaum, ver. 5; but the multitudes pressing him, he gave order to pass over *the sea of Galilee*, otherwise called *the sea of Tiberias*, John vi. 1.

o Luke 9. 57, 58.   19 °And a certain Scribe came, and said unto him, Master, I will follow thee whithersoever thou goest.

20 And Jesus saith unto him, The foxes have holes, and the birds of the air *have* nests; but the Son of man hath not where to lay *his* head.

We have the same story Luke ix. 57, 58; only Luke saith it was *as they went in the way;* and saith, *a certain man* thus *said unto him.* Matthew more particularly describeth the man from his office, or ordinary employment. Both agree in what he said to our Saviour, *Master,* (so they usually called their teachers, to whose conduct they gave up themselves,) *I will follow thee,* that is, I am resolved or I am ready to follow thee, *whithersoever thou goest.* Thus men often take up sudden resolutions to walk with God, and to be his servants, upon sinister accounts, and before they have well considered what they are like to meet withal who own themselves the disciples of Christ. Our Saviour, knowing his heart, and that this resolution was either bottomed in his curiosity to see his miracles, or in a hope of some livelihood from him, fits him with an answer, letting him know what difficulties those that followed him must look to meet with. *The foxes have holes, &c.* Alas! thou dost not know what it is to follow me; my external condition is worse than that of *the birds of the air*, they have fixed nests, or the beasts of the earth, the worst of them have holes, but I have no fixed habitation on earth. He both here and in many other texts calls himself *the Son of man*, (a name never, that we read of, given to him but by himself,) to declare the truth of his human nature, and that he had a natural compassion for men; that he was *a child born, a son given* to us, Isa. ix. 6; the person prophesied of as the Messias. Dan. vii. 13; the person mentioned who was to have *all things put under his feet,* Psal. viii. 6; 1 Cor. xv. 27; Heb. ii. 8.

p Luke 9. 59, 60. q See 1 Kin. 19. 20.   21 ᵖAnd another of his disciples said unto him, Lord, ᑫsuffer me first to go and bury my father.

22 But Jesus said unto him, Follow me; and let the dead bury their dead.

Luke repeating the same history, chap. ix. 59, 60, saith that Christ said to this man, *Follow me.* He replieth, *Lord, suffer me first to go and bury my father;* to live at home with my father, who is an old man, till I have performed my last filial office to him in burying him. Others think that he was already dead, and that this disciple would not have begged leave for so uncertain a time. Christ saith unto him, *Follow me;* not that our Lord disapproved the decent manner of burying the dead, but by this let him know, that no office of love and duty to men must be preferred before our duty to God, to whom we owe our first obedience. It appeareth by Luke ix. 60, that this disciple was called to preach the gospel, a work not to be omitted or neglected for any offices to men. Of old, the high priests and the Nazarites were not to touch dead bodies, Numb. vi. 6, because of their separation to the more immediate service of God. Preachers of the gospel ought to keep themselves as free as they can from what may distract them. Saith our Saviour, *Let the dead bury their dead:* there are enough to bury the dead; persons that are spiritually dead, not alive to God, let them take care of those meaner offices; I have higher employment for thee than that is. Lawful and decent offices become sinful when they hinder greater duties.

23 ¶ And when he was entered into a ship, his disciples followed him.

24 ʳAnd, behold, there arose a great tempest in the sea, insomuch that the ship was covered with the waves: but he was asleep.   r Mark 4. 37, &c. Luke 8. 23, &c.

25 And his disciples came to *him,* and awoke him, saying, Lord, save us: we perish.

26 And he saith unto them, Why are ye fearful, O ye of little faith? Then ˢhe arose, and rebuked the winds and the sea; and there was a great calm.   s Ps. 65. 7. & 89. 9. & 107. 29.

27 But the men marvelled, saying, What manner of man is this, that even the winds and the sea obey him!

It is apparent that the evangelists did not set down all the motions and actions of our Saviour in order, as done by him: whether therefore this was the same motion, and over the same sea, of which mention was made before, is uncertain, nor much material for us to know. Nor yet whether the storm which here arose was in the ordinary course of providence, or raised on purpose for our Saviour to show his power in quieting it. It is enough for us to know that a great storm did arise. It is expressly said that our Saviour was *asleep;* hereby he showed himself to be truly man, subject to like infirmities with us, sin only excepted, Heb. iv. 15. That *the disciples came to him, and awoke him, saying, Lord, save us, we perish,* argued both their faith in his power, and their frailty in not considering who was with them in the ship, one who, though his humanity was asleep, yet was He who watcheth over Israel, who never slumbereth nor sleepeth. Our Saviour saith unto them, *Why are ye fearful, O ye of little faith?* The prevalence of fears in us upon imminent dangers will not argue no faith, but will argue a weak faith; which yet he that will not break a bruised reed, nor quench a smoking flax, will not discourage. He will therefore give them a proof of his Divinity; *he arose, and rebuked the winds and the sea,* let them know he was their Lord, and commanded them to cease, *and there was a calm.* It is he that rebuketh the waves of the sea when they roar, and stilleth the ragings of the people. *The men,* either the sea-men, or the passengers, or both, *marvelled, saying, What manner of man is this, that even the winds and the sea obey him?* surely this is more than a man, that can command winds and seas.

28 ¶ ᵗAnd when he was come to the other side into the country of the Gergesenes, there met him two possessed with devils, coming out of the tombs, exceeding fierce, so that no man might pass by that way.   t Mark 5. 1, &c. Luke 8. 26, &c.

This history is related by Mark, chap. v. 1, &c., and by Luke, chap. viii. 26, &c., more largely than by Matthew. The other two evangelists report it to be done in *the country of the Gadarenes;* Matthew, *in the country of the Gergesenes;* they were the same people, sometimes denominated from one great city in their territories, sometimes from another: whoso readeth the story in all three evangelists will easily conclude it the same, though related with different circumstances. Matthew saith there were two of these demoniacs. Mark and Luke mention but one. Luke saith, the man *had devils long time,* that he *wore no clothes, neither abode in any house, but in the tombs.* Mark saith, *there met him out of the tombs a man with an unclean spirit, who had his dwelling among the tombs; and no man could bind him, no, not with chains: because that he had been often bound with fetters and chains, and the chains had been plucked asunder by him, and the fetters broken in pieces: neither could any man tame him. And always, night and day, he was in the mountains, and in the tombs, crying, and cutting *himself with stones.* Matthew saith he came out of the tombs, was exceeding fierce, so as none could pass that way. Divines agree, that the power of the evil angels was not abated by their fall, they were only depraved in their will. That the power of an angel is much more than is here mentioned is out of question. That the evil angels do not exert this power upon us is from the restraining power of God; we live in the air in which the devil hath a principality, Eph. ii. 2. Why God at that time suffered the devil more to exercise this power over the bodies of men, we probably showed before, upon Matt. iv. 24. The world was grown very ignorant, and wicked, and sottishly superstitious. Besides, he was now come who was to destroy the works of the devil, and was to show his Divine power in casting him out. The Jews buried their dead out of their cities; the richer of them had tombs hewed out of rocks, &c., and those very large, as may be learned from Isa. lxv. 4; John xx. 6. The devil chose these places, partly to affright persons through the horror of the places, and torment the possessed with the noisomeness of them; partly to cheat men, with an opinion they were the souls of the persons deceased that were there buried.

29 And, behold, they cried out, saying, What have we to do with thee, Jesus, thou Son of God? art thou come hither to torment us before the time?

Mark saith, chap. v. 8, that Jesus first said to him, *Come out of the man;* and, ver. 6, 7, *when he saw Jesus afar off, he ran and worshipped him, and cried with a loud voice, What have I to do with thee, Jesus, thou Son of the most high God? I adjure thee, that thou torment me not.* Luke's relation, chap. viii. 28, 29, is much the same with Mark's. The devils possessing these poor creatures, hearing Christ, to whose power they knew they were subject, to command them out of this man, or these two men, said, *What have we to do with thee, Jesus, thou Son of God?* The devils knew Christ to be the Son of God, though the Jews would not believe it; they say unto him, *What have we to do with thee?* a usual phrase, made use of where men had no desire to be troubled with the company, converse, or importunity of others, Josh. xxii. 24; 2 Sam. xvi. 10; 2 Kings ix. 18; 2 Chron. xxxv. 21; Joel iii. 4; John ii. 4, when they came to them with some ungrateful motions, &c. *Art thou come hither to torment us before the time?* either they look upon their dispossession as a torment, for the devil is not at quiet but when he is doing evil; and as this is the temper of the old serpent, so we shall observe that he communicateth it to his seed, Prov. iv. 16: or else the devil was afraid lest Christ should have commanded him to his chains before the day of judgment.

30 And there was a good way off from them an herd of many swine feeding.

31 So the devils besought him, saying, If thou cast us out, suffer us to go away into the herd of swine.

Both Mark and Luke interpose here something more. Mark saith, *And he asked him, What is thy name? And he answered, saying, My name is Legion; for we are many.* Luke saith, *And Jesus asked him, saying, What is thy name? And he said, Legion: because many devils were entered into him.* A Roman legion consisted of twelve thousand five hundred soldiers. Not that there were precisely so many evil spirits which had a power over this poor man, but many had. A certain number is named for one uncertain. Christ knew his case well enough, but probably asked him the question for the further glorifying of his Divine power in casting them out. Luke adds, ver. 31, *And they besought him that he would not command them to go out into the deep.* I cannot think that the meaning of that is, into the sea, for surely the devil did not fear drowning: the word is ἄβυσσον, into the abyss, that is, into hell, into the bottomless pit, where he could do no more mischief. Mark says, chap. v. 10, the devil *besought him that he would not send them out of the country.* Still, upon the same grounds, the devil hath an insatiable thirst to do mischief, and would gladly be where he may do it. In the mean time he knoweth it is in the power of Christ to send him whither he pleaseth. Now comes in the 30th and 31st verses of Matthew. They saw *an herd of many swine feeding.* Mark saith, chap. v. 11, *nigh unto the mountains.* Luke saith, *on the mountain.* They beseech Christ to give them leave to enter into the swine, and the text saith, *he suffered them.* The devil cannot so much as trouble a swine without leave from God. The next verse tells us the consequent of it.

32 And he said unto them, Go. And when they were come out, they went into the herd of swine: and, behold, the whole herd of swine ran violently down a steep place into the sea, and perished in the waters.

Mark gives us much the same account, chap. v. 13, only adding, *they were about two thousand.* Luke differeth not, only what Matthew calls a *sea* Luke calls a *lake;* but the Jews called all great gatherings together of waters seas. The devil is naturally so fond of doing mischief, that he will rather play at a small game than stand out. This way of executing his malice, upon the beasts, we have often had experience of in the practice of witchcraft. And it may teach husbandmen, and those that trade in much cattle, to whom they are beholden for the preservation of their cattle, and how rightly God is styled, he that preserveth both man and beast; and what need they have to keep up daily prayer in their families, and to live so as they may not make God their enemy, who hath legions of devils, as well as many legions of less hurtful creatures, to revenge his quarrels.

33 And they that kept them fled, and went their ways into the city, and told every thing, and what was befallen to the possessed of the devils.

Mark and Luke in this differ not from Matthew, only they add, that they *told it in the city and country.* Those that most serve the devil are afraid of him when he cometh to show himself in his true colours. These men go and publish abroad the miracle, what had happened to the man that was so famous an object of the devil's malice, and what had happened to the swine.

34 And, behold, the whole city came out to meet Jesus: and when they saw him, "they besought *him* that he would depart out of their coasts. ^{u See Deu. 5. 25. 1 Kings 17. 18. Luke 5. 8. Acts 16. 39.}

Both Mark and Luke here add much. Mark saith, chap. v. 14—20, *And they went out to see what it was that was done. And they come to Jesus, and see him that was possessed with the devil, and had the Legion, sitting, and clothed, and in his right mind: and they were afraid. And they that saw it told them how it befell to him that was possessed with the devil, and also concerning the swine. And they began to pray him to depart out of their coasts. And when he was come into the ship, he that had been possessed with the devil prayed him that he might be with him. Howbeit Jesus suffered him not, but saith unto him, Go home to thy friends, and tell them how great things the Lord hath done for thee, and hath had compassion on thee. And he departed, and began to publish in Decapolis how great things Jesus had done for him: and all men did marvel.* Luke saith, chap. viii. 37—39, *Then the whole multitude of the country of the Gadarenes round about besought him to depart from them; for they were taken with great fear: and he went up into the ship, and returned back again. Now the man out of whom the devils were departed besought him that he might be with him: but Jesus sent him away, saying, Return to thine own house, and show how great things God hath done unto thee. And he went his way, and published throughout the whole city how great things Jesus had done unto him.* By *the whole city,* or the whole country, we must understand a very great part of it. *Came out to meet Jesus:* Mark expoundeth it, *to see what it was that was done,* and *to pray him to depart out of their coasts.* They saw him, and not him only, but him that had been possessed of the devils, sitting at his feet clothed, in his right mind. A great miracle wrought! They did not only see it, but they heard their servants, the swine-herds, attesting it; they had all the external means of faith imaginable. How are they affected? The text saith, *they were afraid.* An awe of this great person seized them, and possibly they were afraid lest he should have done them some further evil. What is the effect of this fear? Surely they will fall down at his feet beg his grace and favour, and that he would continue with them, and be the author of more good amongst them. Though they had lost two thousand swine, yet they were delivered from the fear of him that was possessed with the devil; and that poor creature was delivered from as great an affliction as we can imagine. Nothing of all this. They came, and prayed, and besought him to go out of their coasts. Certainly, our Saviour's knowledge of the nature of this people, and what was in their hearts, provoked him to give the devils such a liberty as he did to destroy their swine: we are ordinarily punished in the thing wherein we offend, we need no more than our ordinary wishes and prayers to ruin us: who shall hereafter tell us of a power in man's will to do that which is spiritually good upon a moral suasion? what higher moral suasion could these Gadarenes have had, than the sight of Christ, and what he had done, afforded? yet (for aught appears) they were unanimous in this desire, that Christ should be gone. They do not do what was in their power to do, desiring him to stay. But oh how dangerous a thing it is for men to reject Christ! he immediately departeth, and we do not read that he came here any more. But he out of whom the devils were cast abideth with him, sits at his feet, desires he may go along with him. How great a difference there is betwixt seeing and hearing of Christ, and tasting how good he is! The poor demoniac would have left his country, and gone with him. But Christ suffered him not; probably he saw it would be more for the glory of God for him to stay; he therefore commands him to return to his house, and show what God had done for him, and how he had compassion on him. We cannot more show our thankfulness to God, than by declaring his wonderful works, and what in particular he hath done for us. This poor man doth accordingly, and publisheth the name of Christ in Decapolis, which name comprehendeth a space of the country within which were ten cities, (as the word doth signify,) whereof Gadara (saith Pliny) was one; from which city these people had their denomination of Gadarenes, that is, citizens of Gadara; or, inhabitants of the country adjacent to that city.

CHAP. IX

Christ cureth one sick of the palsy, 1—8; calleth Matthew from the receipt of custom, 9; justifieth himself for eating with publicans and sinners, 10—13, and his disciples for not fasting, 14—17; is entreated by a ruler to go and heal his daughter, 18, 19; healeth by the way a woman of an inveterate issue of blood, 20—22; raiseth to life the ruler's daughter, 23—26; giveth sight to two blind men, 27—31; healeth a dumb man possessed of a devil, 32—35; hath compassion on the multitudes, and teacheth his disciples to pray that God would send forth labourers into his harvest, 36—38.

AND he entered into a ship, and passed over, ᵃand came into his own city.

<small>a ch. 4. 13.</small>

Whether the same ship he came in or no it is not material: he *passed over* the lake of Gennesaret, *and came into his own city;* not Bethlehem, in which he was born, but either Nazareth, where he was brought up, or (which most judge) Capernaum, whither, leaving Nazareth, he went formerly to dwell, chap. iv. 13, whither he is said to have entered, Mark ii. 1; this was upon the sea-coast of Zebulun and Naphtali, chap. iv. 13.

2 ᵇAnd, behold, they brought to him a man sick of the palsy, lying on a bed: ᶜand Jesus seeing their faith said unto the sick of the palsy; Son, be of good cheer; thy sins be forgiven thee.

<small>b Mark 2. 3. Luke 5. 18.
c ch. 8. 10.</small>

The history of this miracle is reported by Mark, chap. ii. ver. 3—12; by Luke, chap. v. ver. 18—26; by both with more circumstances than Matthew doth report it. Mark saith, *He entered into Capernaum after some days; and it was noised that he was in the house. And straightway many were gathered together, insomuch that there was not room to receive them, no, not so much as about the door: and he preached the word unto them. And they came unto him, bringing one sick of the palsy, which was borne of four. And when they could not come nigh unto him for the press, they uncovered the roof where he was; and when they had broken it up, they let down the bed wherein the sick of the palsy lay. When Jesus saw their faith, he said unto the sick of the palsy, Son, thy sins be forgiven thee,* ver. 1—5. Luke mentioneth not the place, nor our Saviour's being preaching, but saith, *And, behold, men brought in a bed a man which was taken with a palsy: and they sought means to bring him in, and to lay him before him. And when they could not find by what way they might bring him in, they went upon the house-top, and let him down through the tiling with his couch into the midst before Jesus. And when he saw their faith, he said unto him, Man, thy sins are forgiven thee,* ver. 18—20. All interpreters agree it to be the same history. Mark, in his preface to the report of the miracle, tells us where Christ was, viz. in Capernaum; what he was doing, preaching the word; the occasion of the people breaking up the roof of the house, viz. the press of the people, so as they could not come nigh to Christ. All three evangelists agree the sick man's disease to be the palsy, which being the resolution of the nerves, besides the pain that attends it, debilitates the person, and confineth him to his bed, or couch, which was the reason of his being brought in his bed, and by four men. All the evangelists mention Jesus seeing their faith, their inward persuasion of his Divine power, and their confidence in his goodness, both the faith of the sick person and of those who brought him. He saw it in their hearts, for the inward principles and habits are not visible to us, yet they are seen and known to him who searcheth the heart, and knoweth what is in the heart of man. He saw it in the fruits, their endeavouring to lay him before Christ. He *said unto the sick of the palsy, Son, be of good cheer, thy sins be forgiven thee.* But what was this to his palsy? Our Saviour by this lets him, and those who brought him, know, 1. That sin is the root from which our evils spring. 2. That being forgiven, bodily distempers (how fatal soever) can do a man no hurt. 3. That his primary end of coming into the world was to save his people from their sins. 4. That in the hour wherein remission of sins is granted to a soul, it becomes God's son, dear to Christ. 5. That remission of sins followeth the exercise of faith in Christ. 6. Possibly he begins with this to give the scribes and Pharisees occasion of some discourse.

3 And, behold, certain of the Scribes said within themselves, This *man* blasphemeth.

Mark saith, *There were certain of the scribes sitting there, and reasoning in their hearts, Why doth this man thus speak blasphemies? who can forgive sins but God only?* ver. 6, 7. Luke saith, *The scribes and the Pharisees began to reason, saying, Who is this which speaketh blasphemies? Who can forgive sins, but God alone?* ver. 21. It should seem they did not speak it out. Mark saith, they reasoned in their hearts. Matthew in the next verse saith, *Jesus, knowing their thoughts.* It seemeth that it was then agreed on all hands, that forgiving of sins was the prerogative of God alone; and that for man to arrogate to himself such a power as belonged to God alone was no less than blasphemy, as all ascribings of Divine perfections to creatures must be. It stands the pope and priests in hand to clear themselves from this guilt. It was also agreed by the scribes and Pharisees, that Christ spake blasphemy in pronouncing to the sick of the palsy, that his sins were forgiven. The reason was, because they did not believe him to be the Son of God, but looked on him as mere man.

4 And Jesus ᵈknowing their thoughts said, Wherefore think ye evil in your hearts?

<small>d Ps. 139. 2. ch. 12. 25. Mark 12. 15. Luke 5. 22. & 6. 8. & 9. 47. & 11. 17.</small>

5 For whether is easier, to say, *Thy* sins be forgiven thee; or to say, Arise, and walk?

6 But that ye may know that the Son of man hath power on earth to forgive sins, (then saith he to the sick of the palsy,) Arise, take up thy bed, and go unto thine house.

Mark repeats almost the same words, ver. 8—10. So doth Luke, ver. 22—24. Christ here giveth the scribes and Pharisees a demonstration of his Deity, by letting them know that he knew their thoughts. *Jesus knowing their thoughts said;* a thing not competible to angels, much less to one who is mere man; yet these blind scribes and

Pharisees take no notice of it. *Wherefore think ye evil in your hearts;* evil concerning me? I did this, saith he, on purpose to let you know, that I, who am indeed *the Son of man,* and whom you mistake in thinking to be no more than the Son of man, hath power, *while he is upon the earth,* and so conversing amongst you, *to forgive sins,* and you may make suitable applications to him for that end. It had been as easy for me every whit to have said to this sick man, *Arise and walk;* and that I will demonstrate to you. Then saith he to the sick of the palsy, Arise, take up thy bed, and go unto thine house. The same power is required to the one as to the other; God, by your confession, can forgive sins, and God alone can raise men from the grave. The end of my miraculous operations is to convince you that I am he who hath a power to forgive men their sins. I therefore chose first to pronounce this man's sins forgiven, that I might have the advantage to confirm to you by a subsequent miracle this great truth, that I am the Son of God, though you think me no more than the Son of man, and that I have a power to forgive sins upon men's exercise of their faith and coming unto me. Now therefore believe, not because of my word only, but because of the sign I show you confirmative of it.

7 And he arose, and departed to his house.

8 But when the multitudes saw *it*, they marvelled, and glorified God, which had given such power unto men.

Mark saith, *And immediately he arose, took up his bed, and went forth before them all; insomuch that they were all amazed, and glorified God, saying, We never saw it on this fashion,* ver. 12. Luke saith, *And immediately he rose up before them, and took up that whereon he lay, and departed to his own house, glorifying God. And they were all amazed, and they glorified God, and were filled with fear, saying, We have seen strange things to-day,* ver. 25, 26. They all agree in sense, though not in words. With Christ's word there went out a power, enabling him to do what he had commanded him. He immediately stands upon his feet, takes up his bed, or couch, *that whereon he lay,* (saith Luke,) and went home in the sight of them all, so as none could doubt concerning the cure. What effect hath this upon the people? *They marvelled,* saith Matthew; *they were amazed, and filled with fear,* saith Luke. Here is not a word of their believing and owning Christ as the Son of God, which was the great thing the miracle was wrought to bring them to; but blindness was happened to Israel, seeing they saw and could not perceive. The miracle wrought in them an awe and reverence of him as an extraordinary person, and put them into a kind of ecstasy and admiration; and the text saith they *glorified God;* but not aright: they praised God, not for sending his Son into the world to save sinners, but for giving *such power unto men;* they would still own Christ no more than a man, though a man to whom God had given great power. *No man can say that Jesus is the Lord, but by the Holy Ghost,* 1 Cor. xii. 3. Truly to believe, own, and receive Christ as our Lord, requireth the operation of the Spirit of grace, working such a faith and persuasion in us.

e Mark 2. 14. Luke 5. 27.

9 ¶ °And as Jesus passed forth from thence, he saw a man, named Matthew, sitting at the receipt of custom: and he saith unto him, Follow me. And he arose, and followed him.

Mark hath the same story, chap. ii. 14, only he calleth him *Levi,* and tells us he was *the son of Alpheus.* Luke also mentioneth it, chap. v. 27, 28, and calls him *Levi,* adding that he was *a publican,* and saith that *he left all, rose up, and followed him.* This Matthew might have also the name of Levi; all interpreters agree he was the same man. All three evangelists say, that when Christ called him, he was sitting in the custom-house *at the receipt of custom.* This Matthew was one of the twelve apostles, chap. x. 3, and the penman of this Gospel. His father Alpheus was honoured to have four of his sons apostles, James the less, and Thaddeus, (called Lebbeus,) Simon the Canaanite, and Matthew. He was a publican, an officer under the Romans to gather the public revenue; it was an odious name amongst the Jews, but Matthew, to magnify the grace of Christ in calling him, is not ashamed thus to describe himself, both here and chap. x. 3. *He saith unto him, Follow me. And he arose and followed him.* His word carried a secret power with it, which Matthew obeyed by leaving his employment and going after Christ.

10 ¶ ʳAnd it came to pass, as Jesus sat at meat in the house, behold, many Publicans and sinners came and sat down with him and his disciples.

f Mark 2. 15, &c. Luke 5. 29, &c.

Luke saith that *Levi made him a great feast in his own house: and there was a great company of publicans and of others that sat down with them,* chap. v. 29. Mark saith, *there were many, and they followed him,* chap. ii. 15. Matthew, touched with the sense of the free and infinite love of Christ to him, maketh Christ a feast: this speaketh him a man of some estate: he invites many to dine with him, some of them publicans, some noted sinners. He designs good undoubtedly to such as had been his former companions, that they might also see the Lord, and be brought to follow him. Grace teacheth a man to study the conversion of others, and never dwelleth in a narrow soul, nor studieth its concealment from others.

11 And when the Pharisees saw *it*, they said unto his disciples, Why eateth your Master with ᵍPublicans and ʰsinners?

g ch. 11. 19. Luke 5. 30. & 15. 2. h Gal. 2. 15.

Mark hath the same, chap. ii. 16; so hath Luke, chap. v. 30, only he saith they *murmured.* The Pharisees having a perfect malice to Christ, did not only seek all means to carp at him, but to bring him under a popular odium: this seemed a fair opportunity. The publicans being an order of persons who both for their employment, and perhaps also their ill management of it, were abominated by the Jews, and reckoned amongst the more notorious sort of sinners; they therefore come to his disciples clamouring against their Master, that he kept communion with publicans and sinners.

12 But when Jesus heard *that*, he said unto them, They that be whole need not a physician, but they that are sick.

13 But go ye and learn what *that* meaneth, ⁱI will have mercy, and not sacrifice: for I am not come to call the righteous, ᵏbut sinners to repentance.

i Hos. 6. 6. Mic. 6. 6, 7, 8. ch. 12. 7. k 1 Tim. 1. 15.

Mark and Luke, in the places before mentioned, have the same answer, only leaving out these words, *Go ye and learn what that meaneth, I will have mercy, and not sacrifice,* quoted from Hos. vi. 6. Our Saviour's reply to the Pharisees, to him that duly considers it, will appear very smart. 1. They were a generation that laid all religion upon rituals, sacrifices, and traditions. 2. That justified themselves, Luke xvi. 15, and thought they needed no repentance. Saith our Saviour, I am the spiritual Physician. With whom would they have the physician to converse, but with such as are sick? Those that are whole (as the Pharisees account themselves) think they have no need of my coming amongst them. By their peevishness at the acts of mercy which I do (and those of the highest mercy too, healing souls) they show that they do not understand what Hosea (a prophet acknowledged by themselves) long since taught them, that the Lord desired mercy before sacrifice; for that appeareth to be the sense of *not sacrifice* in that text, both by the next words, *and the knowledge of God more than burnt offerings,* and by the many precepts by which God declared that he did desire sacrifices. *For I am not come to call the righteous,* that is, those who are swelled in an opinion of their own righteousness, *but* sensible *sinners to repentance:* first to repentance, then to the receiving remission of sins through me, and eternal life.

14 ¶ Then came to him the disciples of John, saying, ˡWhy do we and the Pharisees fast oft, but thy disciples fast not?

l Mark 2. 18, &c. Luke 5. 33, &c. 18. 12.

15 And Jesus said unto them, Can ᵐthe children of the bridechamber mourn, as long as the bridegroom is with them? but the days will come, when the bride-

m John 3. 29.

groom shall be taken from them, and then shall they fast.

16 No man putteth a piece of ||new cloth unto an old garment, for that which is put in to fill it up taketh from the garment, and the rent is made worse.

17 Neither do men put new wine into old bottles: else the bottles break, and the wine runneth out, and the bottles perish: but they put new wine into new bottles, and both are preserved.

Mark hath this same history, almost in the same words, chap. ii. 18—22, only he saith that some of the disciples of the Pharisees came with the disciples of John. Luke also hath it varying little, chap. v. 33—38; only he saith, *fast often, and make prayers*, and, *the piece that was taken out of the new agreeth not with the old*. And he addeth at last, ver. 39, *No man also having drank old wine, straightway desireth new: for he saith, The old is better:* which I shall consider, it plainly belonging to this history. Mark beginneth his narration of this history with telling us, *And the disciples of John and of the Pharisees used to fast;* which is implied, though not expressed, by the two other evangelists. For the Pharisees, it is plain enough from the Pharisee's boast, Luke xviii. 12, that he fasted *twice in the week*. John also used his disciples to a severer discipline than Christ did (of which we shall afterward hear more). It should seem that the Pharisees had a mind to make a division betwixt the followers of John and the followers of Christ, and set on John's disciples to go and ask an account of this. Hypocrites are always hottest for ritual things, as things most fit to raise a division about. There was no precept of God for any fast, but once in a year, though indeed God left people a liberty to fast oftener, as their circumstances more fitted and called for the duty. The Pharisees had set up themselves a method, and would fain have imposed it on Christ's disciples; especially considering John's disciples complied with the practice of frequent fasts, and seemed to suggest as if Christ set up a new and more jovial religion. (As if religion lay only or principally in rituals, as to which God had set no rule.) The papists are at this day the Pharisees' true successors in these arts. Christ answereth them in two particulars: 1. He tells them that his disciples were not as yet under such a dispensation as called for fasting. 2. That his disciples were new converts, and to be brought on by degrees to the severer practices of external discipline and godliness. This is the sum of ver. 15—17. This he delivers in metaphorical expressions: *Can the children of the bride-chamber mourn, as long as the bridegroom is with them? but the days will come, when the bridegroom shall be taken from them, then shall they fast*. Your master John hath compared me to a bridegroom, John iii. 29. These my disciples are *the children of the bride-chamber*. It is as yet a festival time with them. Fasting is a duty fitted to a day of mourning and affliction. It is not yet a time of mourning for my disciples: yet do not envy them. There will shortly come a time when, as to my bodily presence, I shall be taken from them: then they shall mourn and fast. The second thing he saith he illustrateth by two similitudes. First, (saith he,) amongst men no discreet person will put in an old garment a new piece of cloth, for they will not agree together; the strength of the new cloth will bear no proportion to the strength of the old, which by wearing is made weak, so as if the garment comes to a stress the rent will be the greater. So as to wine, men do not use to put new wine into old bottles, that through much use are weakened, for fear of breaking the bottles and spilling the wines; but they use to put new wine into new bottles, to proportion the thing containing to the thing contained. My disciples are newly converted. Should I impose upon them the severer exercises of religion, it might discourage them, and be a temptation to them to go back; for, as Luke addeth, *No man having drank old wine desireth new; for he saith, The old is better*. Custom is a great tyrant, and men are not on the sudden brought off from their former practices, but by degrees. This is a portion of Scripture which much commendeth prudence to ministers, both teaching their people as they are able to bear, and also putting them upon duties with respect to their stature and proficiency in the ways of God; especially in such things as are but our free-will offerings to God.

18 ¶ While he spake these things unto them, behold, there came a certain ruler, and worshipped him, saying, My daughter is even now dead: but come and lay thy hand upon her, and she shall live.

19 And Jesus arose, and followed him, and *so did* his disciples.

Mark hath this history, chap. v. 22—24, *And, behold, there cometh one of the rulers of the synagogue, Jairus by name; and when he saw him, he fell at his feet, and besought him greatly, saying, My little daughter lieth at the point of death: I pray thee, come and lay thy hands on her, that she may be healed; and she shall live. And Jesus went with him; and much people followed him, and thronged him.* Luke hath it, chap. viii. 42, adding only that she was his *only daughter, twelve years of age.* Two evangelists say she was at the point of death, or dying: Matthew saith that he said she was dead; that might be according to his apprehension; she was so near death, that he concluded that by that time he was got to Christ she was dead. Others observe out of Greek authors, that the particle ἄρτι, here used, doth not always signify a time past, but sometimes a time near at hand. But the best answer is, that Matthew relates the story compendiously. It appears from Luke viii. 49, that the maid did die. Matthew reports that first, which the messenger brought them the news of afterwards, as we shall see ver. 23 of this chapter. By the *ruler* here both Mark and Luke tell us is to be understood *Jairus;* not a civil magistrate, but one who was the ruler of the synagogue in that place; for in their synagogues they had an order, there was one chief who ordered the affairs of it, and they say the interpretation of the law belonged to him. *And worshipped him,* with a civil worship, or respect, *saying, My daughter is even now dead,* or dying. One would judge the latter should be the evangelist's meaning of the particle, because of what the other evangelists say, *Come and lay thy hands on her, and she shall live*. His faith riseth not up to the centurion's faith, who declared his faith that if Christ would but speak the word his servant should live. Jairus desires him to come and lay his hands upon her. *And Jesus arose, and followed him, and his disciples*. The Jews thrust Christ's followers out of their synagogues; he is more kind to the ruler of their synagogue, he presently goeth, and his disciples followed him: they were to be witnesses of his miracles. Mark adds, *much people followed, and thronged him;* which gave occasion to another miracle, which Christ did in his way to Jairus's house, the relation of which Matthew giveth us before he perfecteth the history of this miracle.

20 ¶ And, behold, a woman, which was diseased with an issue of blood twelve years, came behind *him*, and touched the hem of his garment:

21 For she said within herself, If I may but touch his garment, I shall be whole.

Mark addeth, chap. v. 26, 27, that she *had suffered many things of many physicians, and had spent all that she had, and was nothing bettered, but rather grew worse; when she had heard of Jesus, she came in the press behind, and touched his garment, &c.* Luke saith, *the border of his garment*. In the crowd there cometh a woman that had a bloody flux twelve years. Inveterate diseases are hard to be cured. Nor had means been neglected, she had tried many physicians, and had spent all her estate upon them. She *came behind him,* out of modesty, and perhaps shame, desiring not to be taken notice of. That which induced her to come, was the fame she had heard of Jesus, and a persuasion wrought in her heart, (doubtless by the Spirit of God,) that if she could but come to touch the hem or border of his garment she should be cured. In this she judged rightly, that Christ was all virtue, and that his virtue was not restrained to his laying his hand upon her. She believed that the oil poured on his head was like that poured on the head of Aaron, which ran down to the skirts of his garment. But if she thought that she could thus steal a cure, and that Christ's cures flowed not from his grace and good-will, but a kind of necessity, herein she wonderfully erred, and Christ afterward let her know it, though he pardoned her mistake.

22. But Jesus turned him about, and when he saw her, he said, Daughter, be of good comfort; ᵠthy faith hath made thee whole. And the woman was made whole from that hour.

^q Luke 7. 50. & 8. 48. & 17. 19. & 18. 42.

Matthew relates this story shortly, as he doth many others, being only intent upon recording the miracle. We must here supply something out of Mark and Luke. Mark saith, chap. v. 29—34, *And straightway the fountain of her blood was dried up; and she felt in her body that she was healed of that plague. And Jesus, immediately knowing in himself that virtue had gone out of him, turned him about in the press, and said, Who touched my clothes? And his disciples said unto him, Thou seest the multitude thronging thee, and sayest thou, Who touched me? And he looked round about to see her that had done this thing. But the woman fearing and trembling, knowing what was done in her, came and fell down before him, and told him all the truth. And he said unto her, Daughter, thy faith hath made thee whole; go in peace, and be whole of thy plague.* Luke reports the same circumstances with little variation, chap. viii. 45—48. Christ was not ignorant of this woman's coming and touching his garment, he doubtless influenced her to the motion, his inquiry was therefore only that the miracle might be taken notice of: he knew that virtue was gone out of him, and had healed the woman, for he had commanded it so to go out, or she had not been healed; but he desired that the people might take notice that she was healed by his grace, not by any magical virtue in his clothes. The woman is brought openly to come and confess it, that she had touched his clothes, and that she was healed. She feared and trembled, lest she should have offended. Christ comforts her, by assuring her the cure, and telling her, that her faith in him, as an instrumental cause, had effected it. We have met with Christ often before, as well as in this text, and shall again often meet with him, ascribing much to the exercise of faith. And the faith to which he ascribeth so much seemeth not to be justifying faith, or that exercise of grace whereby a soul, in the sense of its lost estate by reason of sin, accepteth of him as its Saviour, and relieth upon his merits alone for salvation; for we read nothing of the persons' repentance for sin, nor reliance upon Christ for the salvation of their souls, or any profession of any such thing. Is it then so valuable an act of faith to believe that Christ is the Son of God? I answer, 1. Though faith in Christ be the only saving faith, yet a faith in God, being persuaded of his power and trusting in him, is an exercise of grace, which God (as appeareth in Scripture) much rewarded with blessings of this life; it giveth God the honour of his power, &c. 2. But, secondly, The great truth, That Christ was the eternal Son of God, was that which God more especially aimed at to give the world's assent unto and persuasion of at this time; and indeed preliminary and necessary to people's receiving of him as their Saviour, for, *Cursed is he that trusteth in man.* It was also the great truth which the Pharisees and the rest of the Jews did oppose. Hence our Saviour takes all occasions both to confirm and to encourage this faith; which was but a persuasion that he was clothed with a Divine power, and did that which no man could do; and that he had in him Divine goodness, ready to relieve man's infirmities, according to that power. 3. It is hardly possible that any should truly and seriously believe that Christ, being apparently man, and the Son of man, should also exercise a power which none but God could do; and that they should not believe in him as the Saviour of the world, and be quickened to the use of those means which he should reveal for their salvation. For these reasons, amongst others, we may conceive that Christ predicates this faith so much in those in whom he found it. This miracle being wrought by our Lord in his way to Jairus's house, after the first notice he had of the dangerous sickness of his daughter, the evangelist now goeth on to give us an account of his perfecting that good work.

23 ʳAnd when Jesus came into the ruler's house, and saw ˢthe minstrels and the people making a noise,

^r Mark 5. 38. Luke 8. 51. ^s See 2 Chro. 35. 25.

Neither Mark nor Luke speak any thing of the minstrels, but only of the people's wailing. Amongst the Jews we read not in any part of the Old Testament of musical instruments used at funerals, but amongst the pagans it was usual, as we read in their writers. Amongst the Jews, they had some songs sang, as some gather from Jer. ix. 17; xxii. 18; xxxiv. 5; Amos v. 16. It is very like that the Jews having long lived amongst the heathens, had learned this usage from them. Before this Mark addeth, chap. v. 35—40, that there came some from the ruler's house, *which said, Thy daughter is dead: why troublest thou the Master any further? But Jesus, as soon as he had heard the word that was spoken, said to the ruler of the synagogue, Be not afraid, only believe. And he suffered no man to follow him, save Peter, and James, and John the brother of James. And he cometh to the house of the ruler of the synagogue, and seeth the tumult, and them that wept and wailed greatly. And when he was come in, he saith unto them, Why make ye this ado, and weep? the damsel is not dead, but sleepeth. And they laughed him to scorn. But when he had put them all out, he taketh the father and the mother of the damsel, and them that were with him, and entereth in where the damsel was lying.* Matthew saith nothing of what happened in the way, neither the messengers' coming, and telling Jairus that his daughter was dead, nor our Saviour's comforting of him; but Luke mentioneth all, chap. viii. 49, 50. Matthew goes on with an account of what Christ did in the house, seeing the minstrels, and the tumult caused by the mourners there.

24 He said unto them, ᵗGive place for the maid is not dead, but sleepeth. And they laughed him to scorn.

^t Acts 20. 10.

Mark saith, chap. v. 39, 40, *When he was come in, he saith unto them, Why make ye this ado, and weep? the damsel is not dead, but sleepeth. And they laughed him to scorn. But when he had put them all out, he taketh the father and mother, and them that were with him, and entereth in where the damsel was lying.* Luke saith, chap. viii. 51—53, *When he came into the house, he suffered no man to go in,* (that is, into the chamber where the dead body lay,) *save Peter, James, and John, and the father and mother of the maiden. And all wept, and bewailed her: but he said, Weep not; she is not dead, but sleepeth. And they laughed him to scorn, knowing that she was dead.* The history is plain: when Christ came into the house, there was a mixed noise of fiddlers or pipers, and mourners. Christ coming in, with Peter, James, and John, asked them what they made such ado for? the maid was not dead, but asleep. They apprehending that she was dead, mocked him. He desires to go into the chamber where the corpse lay; but would suffer none but Peter, James, and John, and the father and mother of the maid, to go in with him; the reason appeareth afterward, because he did not desire that this miracle should be presently published. The only question is, in what sense our Saviour saith, *she is not dead, but sleepeth;* whenas they knew she was dead. 1. Some think our Saviour speaketh ambiguously, for death is in Scripture often called a sleep, (1 Kings xiv. 20; John xi. 11; Acts vii. 60; 1 Cor. xv. 6,) with respect to the resurrection. Others think that our Saviour speaks ironically, knowing that some of them would so diminish the miracle, to calumniate him, or abate his reputation. But it is a better answer to say that he speaks with reference to their opinion; *she is not dead* in that sense you judge her dead, so as she shall not come to life before the resurrection; she is not so dead but she shall come to life again; as he said to Mary concerning Lazarus, John xi. 23. Or, to me she is not dead. Or shall we say, as soon as Christ was come into the house, who is *the resurrection, and the life,* John xi. 25, her soul again returned into her body, which though to their appearance it was separated from her body, was not yet fixed in its eternal mansion? In what sense soever he spake it, they judged it ridiculous, and laughed him to scorn.

25 But when the people were put forth, he

went in, and took her by the hand, and the maid arose.

|| Or, this fame. 26 And || the fame hereof went abroad into all that land.

Mark saith, chap. v. 41—43, *And he took the damsel by the hand, and said unto her, Talitha cumi; which is, being interpreted, Damsel, I say unto thee, arise. And straightway the damsel arose, and walked; for she was of the age of twelve years. And they were astonished with a great astonishment. And he charged them straitly that no man should know it; and commanded that something should be given her to eat.* Luke saith, chap. viii. 54—56, *And he put them all out, and took her by the hand, and called, saying, Maid, arise. And her spirit came again, and she arose straightway: and he commanded to give her meat. And her parents were astonished: but he charged them that they should tell no man what was done.* It was the power and virtue that went out of Christ which wrought the miracles: he performeth them under a variety of circumstances; sometimes he used only his word, (as in the case of Lazarus,) sometimes he touched the persons, laying his hand upon them; here he takes the maid by the hand, and also saith, Daughter, or maid, arise. They were words of power and authority, she presently arose. Luke saith her spirit returned again. Luke by this lets us know, that the soul is not the crasis, or some accident to the body, but a distinct subsistence of itself. For the curious question of some, where the soul of this maiden was, as also the soul of Lazarus, of whom we read John xi., and others restored to life, when dead, were in the time whilst they were separated from their bodies; it is a matter of no great concern to us to know where: this we know, that God designed their return to their bodies again, they were not therefore fixed in their eternal mansions. Our Saviour hath taught us, that souls departed are under the conduct of angels to their stations. Lazarus's soul was carried by angels into Abraham's bosom. What can be opposed if we say, that it is probable the souls of these persons were under the guard of angels, about or near the dead bodies, waiting the pleasure of God with reference to them, until the Lord again commanded the restoring of them to their bodies? *He commanded to give her meat*, to confirm the truth of the miracle. Concerning our Lord's command that they should not publish what he had done, we spake before in the case of the leper. Our Lord's time was not yet come, and he was not willing his enemies should take too public a notice of him. But Matthew saith, *The fame thereof went abroad into all that land*, that is, Galilee, at some distance from Jerusalem, which was the great seat of his enemies, where probably our Saviour did least desire any public notice should as yet be taken of him.

u ch. 15. 22. & 20. 30, 31. Mark 10. 47, 48. Luke 18. 38, 39. 27 ¶ And when Jesus departed thence, two blind men followed him, crying, and saying, "*Thou* Son of David, have mercy on us.

28 And when he was come into the house, the blind men came to him: and Jesus saith unto them, Believe ye that I am able to do this? They said unto him, Yea, Lord.

29 Then touched he their eyes, saying, According to your faith be it unto you.

x ch. 8. 4. & 12. 16. & 17. 9. Luke 5. 14. 30 And their eyes were opened; and Jesus straitly charged them, saying, ˣSee *that* no man know *it*.

y Mark 7. 36. 31 ʸ But they, when they were departed, spread abroad his fame in all that country.

This miracle is reported only by St. Matthew, though the other evangelists tell us of some others of the same kind. They *followed him* in the way, *crying, and saying, Thou Son of David, have mercy on us*. These are the first we read of in this Gospel, that made their applications to Christ under the notion of the Messiah (for so much that compellation, *Thou Son of David*, importeth). He was to open the blind eyes, Isa. xxxv. 5; xlii. 7, and was to be the Son of David, according to the prophecies of him; nor can any reason be given, why they called him the Son of David, but this their belief that he was the true Messias. *Have mercy on us*: their petition is general, though without doubt they had a particular respect to their want of sight, and so our Saviour understood them. Others, that came to Christ for cure before, looked upon Christ as a man to whom God had given great power, and glorified God upon that account, as ver. 8. Their courage and boldness in the faith also appeared, in that they feared not the Pharisees' decree made, as appeareth from John ix. 22; for *the Christ* and *the Son of David* amongst the Jews at this time signified the same person, as appears by chap. xxii. 42. Christ listeneth not unto them till he came into the house; there he saith, *Believe ye that I am able to do this?* Christ forgetteth not the prayer of faith, though he doth not give a present answer according to our expectation, that he may continue us in our duty, and quicken us yet to further importunity. Our Lord puts the common test upon them, *Believe ye that I am able to do this?* There is no absolute particular promise for good things of a temporal concern; it is enough for us in those cases to believe that God is able to do the thing, and that he will do it if he seeth it be for our good; he only therefore questioneth their faith as to his power. In their former owning him as the Messiah, the Son of David, they had declared that they believed his kindness to the sons of men. *They said unto him, Yea, Lord*, we believe thou art able; and we believe thee the Messiah, come to do good, and we have a trust in thee thou wilt do it; for this cause we are come, we cry unto thee. *Then touched he their eyes, saying, According to your faith be it unto you.* See the mighty power of the prayer of faith. *Their eyes were opened*, that is, their visive faculty was restored, or given to them. *And Jesus straitly charged them, saying, See that no man know it.* It was known they were blind, and men must know that they now saw; but he chargeth them not to publish it as done by him. The word used signifieth to command with authority, and with a threatening annexed: we have met with several such commands to persons cured, and none of them observed, nor the persons blamed by Christ for not observing them. We must say the parties sinned in publishing the things, unless the command was with some limitations not mentioned by the evangelists; but we are not able, either to give a just account why or how Christ commanded them, nor how they published the things, or were excusable in doing of it.

z See ch. 12. 22. Luke 11. 14. 32 ¶ ᶻAs they went out, behold, they brought to him a dumb man possessed with a devil.

33 And when the devil was cast out, the dumb spake: and the multitudes marvelled, saying, It was never so seen in Israel.

Some think this the same mentioned Luke xi. 14, as shortly as it is here. The word in the Greek signifies deaf as well as dumb, for all persons who are deaf from their birth are also dumb. But it is probable this man was only accidentally dumb, from the power of the devil, that had possessed him, and suppressed his speech. It is observed that Christ cured, 1. Some that came on their own accord to him, as the woman with her bloody flux. 2. Others that could not come, but were brought to him, as the paralytic, before mentioned in this chapter, who was willingly brought. 3. Others who neither came nor were willingly brought, but he occasionally met, Luke vii. 12; John v. 5; ix. 1. 4. Others that were brought without their consent, as the demoniac before mentioned, and this in this verse. His design was, by these operations, to show himself the Son of God, and therefore did not always stay for people's voluntarily offering him occasions, but sometimes took them when they were not voluntarily offered, to show the freeness of his grace.

a ch. 12. 24. Mark 3. 22. Luke 11. 15. 34 But the Pharisees said, ᵃHe casteth out devils through the prince of the devils.

This was not the only time they said so: see chap. xii. 24; Mark iii. 22; Luke xi. 15. I shall in my notes on chap. xii. 24 speak more fully to this text, where we shall also meet with our Saviour's vindication of himself from this imputation. At present, I shall only observe the miserable effects of blindness and malice. The common people marvelled, and said there was never seen such things in Israel. The Jewish doctors are mad, and charge our Saviour to have made a contract with the devil, and to have derived this power from him. But how did this appear to them? Nothing appeared as to any thing which our Saviour had done that could conduct their reason to such a judgment; nothing but what led their more charitable neighbours to a quite contrary judgment. But something they must say to defame our Saviour's reputation amongst the people; having nothing else, but what the people would have judged false, they thus charge him. Nor are the children of the devil to learn his arts, who, when they cannot charge good and holy men with profaneness, charge them with hypocrisy, of which it is impossible they should be competent judges.

b Mark 6. 6.
Luke 13. 22.
c ch. 4. 23.

35 ᵇ And Jesus went about all the cities and villages, ᶜ teaching in their synagogues, and preaching the Gospel of the kingdom, and healing every sickness and every disease among the people.

We met with these words chap. iv. 23, only there it was *all Galilee*, by which probably this text ought to be expounded: see the notes there.

d Mark 6. 34.
∥ Or, were tired and lay down.
e Num. 27. 17. 1 Kings 22. 17. Ezek. 34. 5. Zech. 10. 2.

36 ¶ ᵈ But when he saw the multitudes, he was moved with compassion on them, because they ∥ fainted, and were scattered abroad, ᵉ as sheep having no shepherd.

Mark hath something of this, chap. vi. 34. It pitied him, who came down from heaven to earth to seek and to save lost souls, to see what a company of people followed him, willing to be instructed, because they were ἐκλελυμένοι, or, as some read it, ἐσκυλμένοι, tired and wearied with running after him to hear the gospel, and ἐρριμμένοι, scattered abroad, *as sheep having no shepherd*. Had then the Jews at this time no ministry? They had the temple at Jerusalem, scribes, and Pharisees, and priests; synagogues in other places, where the law was read and interpreted. Christ accounts those people to have no ministers who have no good ones; but either dumb dogs, that cannot bark, or lazy ones, that will not. Such was the generality of the Jewish ministry at this time. This moved the bowels of Christ (so the word signifies). It is a great misery when the congregation of the Lord are as sheep which have no shepherd, Numb. xxvii. 17; and so they are when they have no true prophets of the Lord to instruct them, 1 Kings xxii. 17.

37 Then saith he unto his disciples,

f Luke 10. 2.
John 4. 35.

ᶠ The harvest truly *is* plenteous, but the labourers *are* few;

g 2 Thess. 3. 1.

38 ᵍ Pray ye therefore the Lord of the harvest, that he will send forth labourers into his harvest.

The plain sense of these two verses is this: John the Baptist and Christ had now been preaching for some time, God inclined the hearts of great multitudes to follow both the one and the other; there was a great people prepared for the Lord: Matt. xi. 12, *From the days of John the Baptist, the kingdom of heaven had suffered violence, and the violent took it by force;* men were exceeding fond of hearing the gospel. *The fields were white to the harvest,* as our Saviour expresseth it, John iv. 35. But there were few that would faithfully deliver the mind of God; there were abundance of idle Pharisees, and scribes, and priests, that spent their time in teaching people their rites, and ceremonies, and traditions, but the labourers were few; such must be God's gift to the people, and they must be thrust out. No arguments will be sufficient to persuade men to the weighty work of the ministry, with an intention to fulfil it, but the power of God inclining their hearts to it. You had need therefore pray unto God that he would send, nay, that he would ἐκβάλῃ, thrust out, labourers into his harvest. 1. The inclination and desire of multitudes to hear Divine truth is God's harvest. 2. Ministers' work is a labour, Gal. iv. 11; Phil. iv. 3; 1 Tim. v. 17; if rightly discharged, it must be with labour. 3. God is the Lord of the harvest; ministers ought to look upon him as so. 4. None ought to thrust themselves into the work of the ministry, till God thrust them out, Heb. v. 4. 5. There always were but a few labourers in God's harvest. Hence Chrysostom thought that but a few ministers would be saved. Our Saviour in this chapter prefaceth his work of which we shall discourse in the next chapter, viz. his sending forth his twelve apostles.

CHAP. X

Christ sendeth out his twelve apostles with power to do miracles, 1—4. He instructeth them, 5—15; and forewarning them of persecutions, suggesteth motives of comfort and constancy, 16—39. He promiseth a blessing to those who should receive them, 40—42.

a Mark 3. 13, 14. & 6. 7.
Luke 6. 13. & 9. 1.
∥ Or, over.

AND ᵃ when he had called unto *him* his twelve disciples, he gave them power ∥ against unclean spirits, to cast them out, and to heal all manner of sickness and all manner of disease.

Mark saith, chap. iii. 14, 15, *And he ordained twelve, that they should be with him, and that he might send them forth to preach, and to have power to heal sicknesses, and to cast out devils.* Luke repeats almost the same words, chap. ix. 1, 2; only he saith he *gave them power and authority over devils, —and to preach the kingdom of God.* This was the first mission which the apostles had, much different from that given them after his resurrection; they were now sent only to the lost sheep of the house of Israel, then they were sent to all nations. They were not called *disciples* as that term signified only the common hearers of Christ, but in a more emphatical sense. He chooseth out *twelve,* that as the twelve patriarchs begat the Jewish church, so these twelve men might be the fathers to all the gospel church. The number of twelve seems a sacred number. The new Jerusalem, Rev. xxi. 12, is described as having *twelve gates,* and *at the gates twelve angels,* and to have *written* on the gates *the names of the twelve tribes;* and, ver. 14, *the wall of the city* is said to have *had twelve foundations, and in them the names of the twelve apostles;* the dimensions of it *twelve thousand furlongs,* ver. 16. The power he gave to the apostles was, 1. To preach the kingdom, that is, the gospel, which as it showeth the way to the kingdom of glory, so it was the means to gather the Christian church, which is the kingdom of grace, and to subdue men's hearts to the obedience of Christ. 2. To cast out devils, and heal all manner of sicknesses. By which they gained repute amongst people, confirming people that they were sent of God, doing (though not as Christ did them) things which none but God could do, by a derivation of power from him: Christ did the same things, but by a power inherent in himself. These twelve were ordinarily to be with Christ, and to go forth (as occasion served) clothed with his power to preach and to work miracles.

b John 1. 42.

2 Now the names of the twelve apostles are these; The first, Simon, ᵇ who is called Peter, and Andrew his brother; James *the son* of Zebedee, and John his brother;

3 Philip, and Bartholomew; Thomas, and Matthew the Publican; James *the son* of Alphæus, and Lebbæus whose surname was Thaddæus;

c Luke 6. 15.
Acts 1. 13.
d John 13. 26.

4 ᶜ Simon the Canaanite, and Judas ᵈ Iscariot, who also betrayed him.

Mark reckoneth up the same persons, chap. iii. 16—19, with some additions, which we shall consider as we come at the persons whom they concern. *Apostles* signifies persons sent; the term applied to Christ's disciples signifies the persons that were first sent by him to preach the gospel. It was reasonable for the evangelists to set down their names, because the whole Christian church was to be builded upon their doctrine, Eph. ii. 20. *The first, Simon, who is called Peter,* because the term signifies a rock, and the confession of faith which he made our Saviour declares to be a rock, on which he would build his church, Matt. xvi. 18. He is not here called *the first* because he was first called, or first believed, the contrary is plain from John i. 41; but when

S. MATTHEW X

many are named, one must be first named. He was *the son of Jonas*; Christ gave him the name of *Cephas, which is, by interpretation, a stone*. He was called Simon Peter to distinguish him from Simon the Canaanite, afterward mentioned. So that it seems the papists are put hard to it for arguments to prove Peter's primacy and superiority over the apostles, and headship over the church, when they are enforced to make use of this, because he is here called *the first*. Yet such another was brought at the disputation of Berne, 1528, when Alexius Grad, the nuns' confessor, would prove Peter's headship because he is called Cephas; and he had read in some dictionary, that Κίφας anciently signified a head; as if the evangelist had not interpreted it, John i. 41, *Peter*, or *a stone*. By the same argument they can from hence prove Peter the first, Gal. ii. 9 will prove him the second, for so he is there reckoned, *James, Cephas, and John*. *Andrew his brother;* Simon Peter's brother; by John directed to Christ, John i. 40; called by Christ together with his brother Peter, Mark i. 16, 17. *James the son of Zebedee*, so called to distinguish him from another of the apostles of the same name, who was the son of Alpheus. This is he of whose death we read, Acts xii. 2; he was slain by Herod. *And John his brother*, viz. the son of Zebedee: this is he who was called the beloved disciple, who also wrote the Gospel of John, John xxi. 20, 24. *Philip, and Bartholomew*. *Philip was of Bethsaida, the city of Andrew and Peter*, John i. 44, found and called by Christ, ver. 43. Of the call of Bartholomew we do not read; some think him the same with Nathanael, mentioned John i. 45, 46, &c. It is some inducement to believe it, that he is here named with Philip, who was the instrument to bring him to Christ, ver. 45; but there is nothing of this certain. *Thomas*, the same who was called Didymus, who was so unbelieving as to Christ's resurrection, John xx. 24, 27; *and Matthew the publican*, he that wrote this history of the Gospel: we heard before of his call from the receipt of custom; he was also called Levi. *James the son of Alpheus, and Lebbeus, whose surname was Thaddeus*. This James is called *James the less*, Mark xv. 40, and so distinguished from James the son of Zebedee. *The Lord's brother*, Gal. i. 19; that is, as some think, his kinsman, judging him not the son of Alpheus who was the father of Matthew, but another Alpheus, the husband of Mary the wife of Cleophas, John xix. 25. But this appeareth not from Scripture. Instead of *Lebbeus, whose surname was Thaddeus*, Luke saith, chap. vi. 16, *Judas the brother of James* (he that wrote the Epistle of Jude, as appeareth by Jude). Mark, chap. iii. 18, mentions not Lebbeus at all, which makes some think that the words are transposed, and should be Thaddeus the son of Lebbeus; for Thaddai in the Syriac is the same with Judas. *Simon the Cannanite;* Luke calls him *Simon Zelotes*, Luke vi. 15; Acts i. 13. We must not understand by *Canaanite* a pagan, (for Christ sent out none but Jews,) but one of Cana, which by interpretation is Zelus, from whence it is that Luke calleth him Zelotes. *And Judas Iscariot, who also betrayed him*. There are many guesses how Judas had the name of Iscariot, whether from Kerioth, supposed to be his town, or on some other account: the guesses of the best are but uncertainties, nor is it material for us to know. It here distinguisheth him from the other Judas. Of his betraying his Master we shall hear afterward. Christ altered the name of Simon, whom he called *Peter*, Mark iii. 16. He added to the names of James and John, calling them *Boanerges*, that is, *The sons of thunder*, ver. 17. Thaddeus is called Judas, and by Matthew also Lebbeus. These were the twelve first apostles, to which were added (after Christ's ascension) Matthias, (instead of Judas Iscariot,) Paul, and Barnabas; but these conversed with Christ, and were the first sent out by him. We shall now hear the instruction he gives them.

e ch. 4. 15.
f See 2 Kings 17. 24. John 4. 9, 20.
g ch. 15. 24. Acts 13. 46.
h Is. 53. 6. Jer. 50. 6. 17. Ezek. 34. 5, 6, 16. 1 Pet. 2. 25.

5 These twelve Jesus sent forth, and commanded them, saying, ᵉ Go not into the way of the Gentiles, and into *any* city of ᶠ the Samaritans enter ye not:

6 ᵍ But go rather to the ʰ lost sheep of the house of Israel.

Here Christ limiteth their ministry to the Jews. The apostle tells us, Rom. xv. 8, *Christ was a minister of the circumcision for the truth of God, to confirm the promises made unto the fathers;* and the apostle tells the Jews, Acts xiii. 46, *It was necessary that the word of God should first have been spoken to you*. Therefore in this his first mission, he restrains his apostles from going to the Gentiles, to whom they had afterwards a commission to go, Matt. xxviii. 19, and did go, but not before the Jews had judged themselves *unworthy of everlasting life*, Acts xiii. 46, by rejecting and blaspheming the gospel, and persecuting the ministers of it. They are also commanded not to go *into any city of the Samaritans*. The Samaritans were partly Jews apostatized, and partly heathens, descended from those whom the king of Syria sent thither, when the ten tribes were carried into captivity, 2 Kings xvii. 6, and from some Jews left in the land. You shall read of their religion there, ver. 31—41. They were perfectly hated by the Jews, and as perfect haters of them, as may be gathered from Luke ix. 52, 53; John iv. 9. Our Lord, partly in regard they also were no better than Gentiles, and so hated as they were of the Jews, would not suffer these his first ministers to go and preach amongst them. Not that they were forbidden (if some particular persons, whether Gentiles or Samaritans, came to them) to preach to them, but only not to make it their work to go into their country or cities; the time was not yet come for this great light to shine upon the Gentiles. *But go rather to the lost sheep of the house of Israel*. By *Israel* he here meaneth the two tribes that clave to the house of David, for the ten tribes ever since their captivity (2 Kings xvii. 6) had lost their share in that name. He calls them *lost sheep* in the sense that Jeremiah speaks, chap. l. 6, *My people hath been lost sheep: their shepherds have caused them to go astray*. So that *lost sheep* here signifies wandering sheep, for want of proper guides. The Jews at this time had miserable teachers, so as they wandered as lost sheep. And this comporteth with what we had in the last verses of the former chapter. There was a great harvest and but few labourers; he is therefore providing them labourers, shepherds that should gather those scattered sheep into one fold.

7 ⁱ And as ye go, preach, saying, ᵏ The kingdom of heaven is at hand.

i Luke 9. 2.
k ch. 3. 2. & 4. 17.
Luke 10. 9.

8 Heal the sick, cleanse the lepers, raise the dead, cast out devils: ˡ freely ye have received, freely give.

l Acts 8. 18, 20.

In these words he gives them power, 1. To preach the gospel. 2. To confirm the doctrine they preached to be of God by miraculous operations, healing the sick, cleansing lepers, raising the dead, casting out devils. He bids them *go preach*, Κηρύσσετε, Cry like heralds; something like Isaiah's commission, Isa. lviii. 1, *Cry aloud, spare not, lift up thy voice like a trumpet*. He teacheth them what should be the sum of their sermons, *The kingdom of heaven is at hand;* the same thing which John Baptist preached, chap. iii. 2, which Christ preached, Mark i. 15, and which he directed the seventy to preach, Luke x. 9: not that they were to use no other words, but that all the words they used were to have this tendency, to declare that the time was now come, when God had fulfilled his promise of the Messiah, who was setting up his kingdom in the world, and to whose laws they were to be obedient. This doctrine they were to confirm by miracles, which he gives them a charge they should work *freely*, without receiving any reward for them, that the miracles being used to their private profit, might not lose their end, which was the confirmation of their doctrine.

9 ᵐ ‖ Provide neither gold, nor silver, nor ⁿ brass in your purses,

m 1 Sam. 9. 7. Mark 6. 8. Luke 9. 3. & 10. 4. & 22. 35.
‖ Or, Get.
n See Mark 6. 8.

10 Nor scrip for *your* journey, neither two coats, neither shoes, nor yet †staves: ᵒ for the workman is worthy of his meat.

† Cr. a staff.
o Luke 10...
1 Cor. 9. 7, &c. 1 Tim. 5. 18.

Our Saviour having in the last verse commanded them to give freely, they might reasonably be thinking that they had need to provide well for their journey. No, saith our Saviour, *Provide neither gold, nor silver, nor brass,* &c. That this was but a temporary precept, the will of God concerning them for this short journey, appeareth from Luke xxii. 35, 36, *But now, he that hath a purse, let him take it, and likewise his scrip,* &c. They were to finish this journey in a short time, and much provision would have been a hinderance to their motion. Besides, our Saviour designed to give them an experience of the providence of God, and to teach them to trust in it; as also to teach people that *the labourer is worthy of his hire*, and that God expecteth that his ministers should not live of their own, but upon the altar which they served; so as at once he taught his apostles not to be covetous, nor overmuch solicitous, and people to provide for those who ministered to them in things spiritual. I pass over what others have critically observed concerning the words, that being not my proper work. Mark saith, chap. vi. 8, 9, that he *commanded them that they should take nothing for their journey, save a staff only; no scrip, no bread, no money in their purse: but be shod with sandals; and not put on two coats.* From whence is plain that the *staves* forbidden in Matthew were either staves for defence, or to bear burdens upon, not merely travellers' staves. The sum is, in this their first journey, which they were soon to despatch, he would have them trust God for protection and sustenance, and load themselves with nothing more than necessary.

p Luke 10. 8.   11 ᵖAnd into whatsoever city or town ye shall enter, enquire who in it is worthy; and there abide till ye go thence.

12 And when ye come into an house, salute it.

q Luke 10. 5.   13 ᵠAnd if the house be worthy, let
r Ps. 35. 13.   your peace come upon it: ʳbut if it be not worthy, let your peace return to you.

s Mark 6. 11.   14 ˢAnd whosoever shall not receive
Luke 9. 5.
& 10. 10, 11.   you, nor hear your words, when ye de-
t Neh. 5. 13.   part out of that house or city, ᵗshake off
Acts 13. 51.
& 18. 6.   the dust of your feet.

u ch. 11. 22, 24.   15 Verily I say unto you, ᵘIt shall be more tolerable for the land of Sodom and Gomorrha in the day of judgment, than for that city.

Our Lord had before set them their limits, and appointed them their work, and directed them as to their accoutrements for their journey; here he directeth them their methods. Luke hath much of the same instructions, chap. x. 4—6, but applied to the seventy, not to the twelve. Mark hath something of them applied to the twelve, chap. vi. 10, 11, *And he said unto them, In what place soever ye enter into an house, there abide till ye depart from that place. And whosoever shall not receive you, nor hear you, when ye depart thence, shake off the dust under your feet for a testimony against them. Verily I say unto you, It shall be more tolerable for Sodom and Gomorrha in the day of judgment, than for that city.* The method Christ set them was, when they came into any of the cities of Israel, to inquire if there were any worthy persons in it, and thither to go, and there to abide (if they did not find they were mistaken) until they left that place; and when they came into a house to salute it, wishing all peace and happiness to it; if they found themselves welcome, to preach to it the gospel of peace. But if they found themselves unwelcome, and discerned that the people of the city, or of that house, did not care for their company, and refused to hear them, they should not make themselves or the gospel a burden to them, but show their contempt of those who contemned the gospel, and the ministry of it, by shaking the dust off their feet as a testimony against them. Then he concludes, telling them, that the Lord would so grievously at last revenge such contempt, that the condition of the men of Sodom and Gomorrah, who were destroyed by fire and brimstone, Gen. xix. 24, would at the last day be more tolerable than theirs. This is the sum, by which our Saviour doth obviate the solicitous thoughts which might from his former words arise in their minds. How shall we live, going amongst strangers, if we carry nothing with us? Saith our Saviour, When you first come into a town or city, do not inquire for the inns that entertain strangers, but who is worthy, worthy of such guests; so Heb. xi. 38; a *son of peace*, Luke x. 6; who are accounted the most pious and religious persons in that town or city, or best affected to the gospel. (He hereby hints, that John the Baptist and his ministry had had such success, that in most places there were some such persons.) *Worthy* doth not in our ordinary discourse signify always a meritorious person, but a person excelling, either in religion or knowledge, or moral virtue. Such persons our Lord presumes would entertain those who came upon so kind an errand to their houses. He commands them to go, and when they came to a house to salute it, to say, Peace be to this house; which was the Jews' ordinary salutation; under the notion of peace they comprehended all good. But, *let your peace come upon it* (I conceive) comprehendeth more, viz. preach the gospel of peace unto it; or, my peace shall be upon it, I will bless that house. But if you find you are misinformed, or mistaken, your peace shall return unto you; you have done your work, and you shall have your reward. If they will *not receive you, nor hear your words;* if they declare any contempt of you, and will not hear the glad tidings of the gospel; *when ye depart out of that house or city, shake off the dust of your feet.* This was more than a sign of contempt of them; we read of Nehemiah, chap. v. 13, that he shook his lap, and said, *So God shake out every man from his house, and from his labour, that performeth not this promise.* We have but one instance of this practice of the apostles, Acts xiii. 51. Mark adds, *for a testimony against them:* a testimony of God's despising them who despised his grace, and of the vengeance of God that should come upon them for that contempt. For he adds, *it shall be more tolerable for Sodom and Gomorrha in the day of judgment,* the last judgment, *than for that city:* their condemnation will be more dreadful, as having sinned against greater light, and fairer offers of greater grace, than ever they had.

16 ¶ ˣBehold, I send you forth as   x Luke 10. 3.
sheep in the midst of wolves: ʸbe ye   y Rom. 16.
                                      19.
therefore wise as serpents, and ᶻ‖harmless   Eph. 5. 15.
                                      z 1 Cor. 14.
as doves.   20.
                                      Phil. 2. 15.
                                      ‖ Or, simple.

Our Lord having hitherto instructed his twelve apostles as to the places whither they were to go, the work they had to do, and the methods he would have them observe, now comes to arm them against their difficulties, and the temptations they were like to meet with. *I send you forth* (saith he) *as sheep in the midst of wolves.* It is most probable that our Saviour speaks this with reference to what they were like to meet with when he should be taken from them, for we do not read of any great opposition which they at present met with. *I send you,* saith he, *as sheep,* which are feeble creatures in themselves, and without any natural armour to defend themselves, *in the midst of wolves,* which are rapacious creatures, and have a particular enmity to sheep: amongst enemies who will have as great an inclination from their malice to devour you, as wolves have from their nature to devour sheep. *Be ye therefore wise as serpents.* It is said of the serpent, Gen. iii. 1, that he *was more subtle than any beast of the field.* Naturalists observe, yet, a great natural sagacity in the serpent, which they note in several particulars. It is hard to say that Christ aimed at this or that particular thing wherein the sagacity of serpents appeareth; he only proposeth the serpent as a pattern of subtlety, and commendeth prudence to them so far as it consisteth with innocency, for it followeth, *harmless as doves.* Amongst the beasts of the field there is none more innocent than a sheep; amongst the birds of the air none more innocent than a dove; to both these our Lord compareth his disciples. This text teacheth us, 1. That wisdom may dwell with prudence. 2. That all true prudence must be attended with innocency.

17 But beware of men: for ᵃthey will   a ch. 24. 9.
                                      Mark 13. 9.
deliver you up to the councils, and ᵇthey   Luke 12. 11.
                                      & 21. 12.
will scourge you in their synagogues;   b Acts 5. 40.

18 And ᶜye shall be brought before   c Acts 12. 1.
                                      & 24. 10.
governors and kings for my sake, for a   & 25. 7, 23.
                                      2 Tim. 4. 16.
testimony against them and the Gentiles.

The last word, *Gentiles,* maketh it plain, that our blessed Lord is not here arming his disciples so much against any opposition they were like to meet with upon this their first going out, for they were not to go to the Gentiles, as those they should meet with some years after his ascension; yet not excluding what they should meet with from the Jews, for what is said about delivering up to the councils and scourging in the synagogues seemeth to have a particular reference to the Jews. This scripture was most eminently fulfilled, as to the apostles, Acts iv. 1—3, &c.; v. 27; vi. 12: and as to being brought before governors and kings, there are instances enough in the Acts, more in ecclesiastical stories. Neither do I think our Saviour hath in these words any reference to the distinction of their councils amongst the Jews; he only designed to let them know the time would come, when, for their owning him, and preaching his gospel, they should be brought before all sorts of magistrates, and in all kinds of courts. That phrase, *and they will scourge you in their synagogues*, hath mightily perplexed some, especially such as have dreamed religious synagogues too holy places for such offices: but there is no need that we should take the term *synagogues* here for the places of their worship, it doth as well signify, in their conventions; and there are some that think that they had, adjoining to their synagogues, a place in which they punished offenders upon the account of religion; certain it is, 2 Cor. xi. 24, that Paul was five times scourged by the Jews according to their law, Deut. xxv. 3. *For a testimony against them and the Gentiles:* a testimony for me, that is expressed in those words, *for my sake;* and against them, whether Jews or Gentiles. A testimony against them in the day of judgment, εἰς μαρτύριον, hence our terms of martyr and martyrdom, the one signifies a witness, the other a testimony.

d Mark 13. 11, 12, 13. Luke 12. 11. & 21. 14, 15. e Ex. 4. 12. Jer. 1. 7.

19 ᵈ But when they deliver you up, take no thought how or what ye shall speak: for ᵉ it shall be given you in that same hour what ye shall speak.

f 2 Sam. 23. 2. Acts 4. 8. & 6. 10. 2 Tim. 4. 17.

20 ᶠ For it is not ye that speak, but the Spirit of your Father which speaketh in you.

Mark hath much the same, chap. xiii. 11; so hath Luke, chap. xi. 11, 12. The apostles being men but of an ordinary education before Christ called them, he might reasonably suppose that they would not appear before councils, and kings, and governors without some abashment, having not been accustomed to such presences; he therefore arms them in these words, wherein he doth not prohibit ordinary thoughts, which every man hath before he speaketh, but anxious thoughts beforehand, *for*, saith he, *it shall be given you in that same hour what ye shall speak*. The Lord seemeth to speak here as he did to Moses, Exod. iv. 12, complaining he was *slow of speech, and of a slow tongue:* ver. 11, *Who hath made man's mouth? It shall*, saith Christ, *be given you* from God. *For it is not ye that speak, but the Spirit of your Father which speaketh in you;* that is, not you from yourselves only: the Holy Spirit shall influence your thoughts as to the matter, and suggest that to you, and it shall influence your tongues, giving you a freedom of speech. This was verified in Stephen, Acts vi. 10, and hath been eminently verified in a multitude of martyrs. We may observe from hence, that the influence of the Spirit is not to be confined to the will and affections. It hath also an influence upon our words in the service of God: not that we can conclude, that whatsoever Christians so speak, either in their confessions or other duties, is from such immediate assistance; but there is such an influence, though the Spirit in this, as in other operations, like the wind, bloweth where and when it listeth.

g Mic. 7. 6. ver. 35, 36. Luke 21. 16.

21 ᵍ And the brother shall deliver up the brother to death, and the father the child: and the children shall rise up against *their* parents, and cause them to be put to death.

h Luke 21. 17. i Dan. 12. 12. 13. ch. 24. 13. Mark 13. 13.

22 And ʰ ye shall be hated of all *men* for my name's sake: ⁱ but he that endureth to the end shall be saved.

Luke speaketh much the same, chap. xxi. 16, 17, though as spoken upon another occasion. Our Saviour here tells them, that the persecutions would reach even to death itself, and that the malice of the world against him and his gospel should proceed so far, as to extinguish all natural affection, betwixt brethren, and parents, and children, and that they would meet with a multitude of enemies (for that is here meant by *all*, not every individual man, as in a multitude of other scriptures). The root of all persecution is hatred.

For my name's sake; for preaching or professing of my gospel, and living up to the rule of it, Acts iv. 18; v. 41. This is that which Peter calleth suffering *as a Christian*, 1 Pet. iv. 16. And by this phrase he doth not only admonish them of their duty, to see that they suffered for his name's sake, but also encourage them from the honourable cause of their suffering, it was for his name's sake. He also addeth another argument, *But he that endureth to the end shall be saved*. There shall be an end of these sufferings, if they end not in your lifetime they will end with your lives, and if you continue to the end you shall be saved. It is neither true patience, nor will it be profitable, if it holdeth not out to the end, Mark xiii. 13; 1 Cor. ix. 24; Heb. iii. 6.

23 But ᵏ when they persecute you in this city, flee ye into another: for verily I say unto you, Ye shall not ∥ have gone over the cities of Israel, ¹ till the Son of man be come.

k ch. 2. 13. & 4. 12. & 12. 15. Acts 8. 1. & 9. 25. & 14. 6. ∥ Or, end, or, finish. 1 ch. 16. 28.

Whether this text at all warranteth ministers' flight in a time of persecution I doubt; it seemeth to be a special command given to the apostles, that they might have a time before the coming of Christ, here spoken of, to preach the gospel over all the cities of Israel. But that in some cases it is lawful to flee I do not at all doubt, though I do question whether it be to be warranted from this text. What those cases are is largely discoursed, particularly by Mr. Torshell. Generally it is said, wherever the glory of God, or the good of others, calls to us for such a flight. But what may be judged such cases is a more particular question. Augustine to Honoratus speaketh well in the case. Ministers ought not to flee rashly, nor out of cowardice, nor that they might live elsewhere lazily, nor when their flight will betray the church of God: not where the persecution is general; but where the persecution is particular, against some of them, and there will be enough left for the care of the church in their absence, and with the consent of the church, they may flee. But this is too large a case to be spoken to here; especially considering (as I said) that I do not think that any flight is to be justified from this text, the precept being particular for special reasons. *Till the Son of man be come*. There is a wonderful variety of interpreters' senses of this text, founded upon the various comings of Christ mentioned in holy writ. He was already come in the flesh, so as it, speaking of a time to come, could not be meant of that: nor can it be understood of his second coming to judgment, for they have gone through the cities of Israel long ago. Christ is therefore said in Scripture to come, when he appeareth in some great work of providence, whether of judgment or mercy. This makes some interpret it of the destruction of Jerusalem; in which sense some think the coming of Christ is mentioned, Matt. xxiv. Some, of the resurrection of Christ, from whence they say Christ's epocha commenced. Others understand it of the effusion of the Spirit in the day of Pentecost; this they ground on John xiv. 17, 18, where they think Christ's coming, promised ver. 18, is the coming of the Spirit, promised ver. 17. Undoubtedly, in the general, our Saviour means, till the time be accomplished when you must leave preaching to the Jews and go to the Gentiles, and my kingdom shall be further extended than it is at present; which dispensation of God may for aught I know be called the coming of Christ, being an eminent act of God's providence, by which Christ was more showed to the world, and his kingdom further extended.

24 ᵐ The disciple is not above *his* master, nor the servant above his lord.

m Luke 6. 40. John 13. 16. & 15. 20.

25 It is enough for the disciple that he be as his master, and the servant as his lord. If ⁿ they have called the master of the house † Beelzebub, how much more *shall they call* them of his houshold?

n ch. 12. 24. Mark 3. 22. Luke 11. 15. John 8. 48, 52. † Gr. Beelzebul.

As much as if he had said, Think not much if you meet with persecutions: I am your Lord and Master, you are my servants and household; you have no reason to look for better measure from the world than I your Lord meet with; it is honour enough for you to be used as well as I am. You know they have persecuted me, they call me Beelzebub, saying that I cast out devils by Beelzebub, the prince of devils. Why should you expect better? Our Saviour used the same argument, Luke vi. 40. *Beelzebub* was the idol of Ekron, 2 Kings i. 2. The word signifies, the lord of flies; either because they invocated his help against the flies, or (as others say) the name was in derision to that idol given by the Jews to the prince of the devils, because the places wherein they sacrificed to it were infested with flies, which they say God's temple at Jerusalem never was, notwithstanding the multitude of sacrifices which were there killed. Certain it is they understood by it the prince of devils.

o Mark 4. 22.
Luke 8. 17. & 12. 2, 3.

26 Fear them not therefore: °for there is nothing covered, that shall not be revealed; and hid, that shall not be known. This is a proverbial speech, used by our Saviour upon more occasions than this, Mark iv. 22; Luke viii. 17; xii. 2. As to his present use of it, the sense is, Though my gospel be now covered and hid, yet it shall be revealed and made known. Or, Though your innocency be hid and covered, yet God shall bring forth your judgment as the light, and your righteousness as the noon-day. Or, Though your enemies' rage and malice be hid, and their vengeance seemeth to sleep, yet it shall be revealed. The first seemeth most probable, from what followeth in the next verse, which he seemeth to speak as a means to it.

27 What I tell you in darkness, *that* speak ye in light: and what ye hear in the ear, *that* preach ye upon the housetops.

The candle of the gospel, which God hath by John the Baptist and me lighted up, is not to be hid; though therefore you have it from me in private, yet do you publish it. I do as it were whisper it in your ear by private discourses, and in a private converse, but it shall be made as public as if it were published to the greatest advantage; and do you contribute what you can unto it, do you publish my gospel as it were upon the house-tops.

p Is. 8. 12, 13.
Luke 12. 4.
1 Pet. 3. 14.

28 ᵖAnd fear not them which kill the body, but are not able to kill the soul: but rather fear him which is able to destroy both soul and body in hell.

As I told you before, you will in the publication of my gospel meet with opposition from men. Now that it is preached as it were in darkness, and whispered in men's ears, there is no great noise made in the world; but the case will be otherwise when it cometh to be publicly revealed, and published upon the house-tops. But consider, the enemies can only kill the bodies of my disciples: you have souls as well as bodies; they have no power over your souls; but he that hath sent you to preach, and called you to the owning and profession of the gospel, hath a power over your souls as well as over your bodies, and to punish both in hell. We have the same Luke xii. 4, 5. There is nothing so effectual to drive out of our hearts a slavish fear of man in the doing of our duty, as a right apprehension of the power of God, begetting a fear of him in our souls.

‖ *It is in value half-penny farthing in the original, as being the tenth part of the Roman penny:* See on ch. 18. 28.

29 Are not two sparrows sold for a ‖ farthing? and one of them shall not fall on the ground without your Father.

q 1 Sam. 14. 45. 2 Sam. 14. 11.
Luke 21. 18. Acts 27. 34.

30 ᑫBut the very hairs of your head are all numbered.

31 Fear ye not therefore, ye are of more value than many sparrows.

Besides, consider, there is a God that governeth the world, and by his providence influenceth and watcheth over the most minute and invaluable beings in it, and preserveth and upholdeth them; it extendeth to the very hairs of your head, and to a sparrow (two of which are sold ordinarily for an assarion, the tenth part of a Roman penny): these little birds fall not when they are shot, without the notice of him who is your heavenly Father, and he will much more regard even your bodies, for you are of more value than many sparrows. Our Lord here, 1. Asserts the providence of God to extend to the most minute things, not to be restrained to things in heaven, or some greater and more noble creatures. 2. He teacheth his disciples to take courage from the consideration of it, as being assured that their greatest enemies should not be able to steal or wrest them out of God's hands. But if they should die in their testimony, it should be by God's ordering.

32 ʳWhosoever therefore shall confess me before men, ˢhim will I confess also before my Father which is in heaven.

r Luke 12. 8.
Rom. 10. 9, 10.
s Rev. 3. 5.

33 ᵗBut whosoever shall deny me before men, him will I also deny before my Father which is in heaven.

t Mark 8. 38.
Luke 9. 26.
2 Tim. 2. 12.

As this is a time for you publicly to own me, so there will be a time (in the day of judgment) for me to confess and publicly own you, *before the angels of God* (which Luke addeth to this sentence, chap. xii. 8): as men deal with me in this life, so I shall deal with them in that day. Our Saviour speaketh much the same thing, as repeated by Mark, chap. viii. 38, and Luke, chap. ix. 26; only there instead of *whosoever shall deny me*, it is, *whosoever shall be ashamed of me and my words*. Christ requireth of us not only a believing on him, but an external profession: nor that only, but a confession of him, which signifieth a profession of him and his gospel in the face of opposition and enemies: see Rom. x. 10; 2 Tim. ii. 12. It is dangerous, either through shame or fear, to withhold our public owning and acknowledgment of Christ, and his truths, when we are called to it; much more to deny them; but the guilt is greater when it is through shame, for where fear is the cause the temptation is more high. This text must be understood of those who persist in such denial, for Peter denied his Master, yet was graciously upon his repentance received by him.

34 ᵘThink not that I am come to send peace on earth: I came not to send peace, but a sword.

u Luke 12. 49, 51, 52, 53.

35 For I am come to set a man at variance ˣagainst his father, and the daughter against her mother, and the daughter in law against her mother in law.

x Mic. 7. 6.

Luke hath much the same with the 34th verse, chap. xii. 51. As the Jews were much mistaken in their notion of the Messiah, as if he were to be a temporal prince, to restore the kingdom to Israel, and as the kingdom, so a peaceful kingdom; so many persons think still that where true religion comes, there must be forthwith peace and union. And indeed so it should be, and so it would be if the gospel were cordially and universally received. It is impossible that a system of laws should be compiled better fitted to human society, or conducible to peace, the great end of it, than the laws of the gospel are: but eventually it is not so, nor was such a civil peace the end of Christ's coming. Accidentally, through the corruption of men's hearts, the consequent of Christ's coming into the world, and of his gospel coming into and prevailing in any part of the world, is (as Luke phraseth it) *rather division*, which is here called *a sword*. Through men's fondness of their idolatry, superstition, and lusts, and madness on them, their impatience of being outdone in religion and righteousness of conversation, the event of Christ's coming was division, wars, variances, like the times prophesied of by Micah, chap. vii. 6; God either stirring up wars to revenge the contempt of the gospel, (as it happened to the Jews,) or men taking up arms to compel all others to their idolatries and superstitions. And that natural antipathy which men have to holiness, setting them at variance with those who, embracing the gospel, live a life as becometh the gospel of the Lord Jesus Christ, worketh so far, that men will have no respect to their nearest relations.

36 And ʸa man's foes *shall be* they of his own houshold.

y Ps. 41. 9.
& 55. 13.
Mic. 7. 6.
John 13. 18.

Not of the household of faith, which showeth that it is not the gospel, but men's corruptions, which causeth division. Those who truly receive the gospel agree well enough, at least break not out into open feuds; but the tie of no natural or moral relations will hold together the seed of the woman and the seed of the serpent. This doth not always happen, but very ordinarily, and therefore there was need that Christ should forewarn his disciples of it.

37 ᶻHe that loveth father or mother

z Luke 14. 26.

more than me is not worthy of me: and he that loveth son or daughter more than me is not worthy of me.

Luke seemeth to speak higher, chap. xiv. 26, *If any man come to me, and hate not his father, and mother, and wife, and children, and brethren, and sisters, yea, and his own life also, he cannot be my disciple.* But the sense is the same, for by hatred there is only meant displacency, and a setting them in his esteem below Christ and his commands. Christ doth not command or encourage want of natural affection, but only by this saying he reduceth it to order, and showeth that our first love and homage is due to God; and where we cannot show what love and affections our father, or mother, or son, or daughter call for, without failing in that duty which we owe unto God, or violating some Divine precept, we must acknowledge our heavenly Father, even by disobeying our earthly parents. Instead of *is not worthy of me*, Luke saith, *cannot be my disciple*, which expoundeth this term. He is not worthy of my favour, of the name of my disciple, or the reward I intend my disciples.

n ch. 16. 24. Mark 8. 34. Luke 9. 23. & 14. 27.

38 ^a And he that taketh not his cross, and followeth after me, is not worthy of me.

We have much the same chap. xvi. 24; Mark viii. 34; Luke ix. 23. It is not he that maketh not, but *he that taketh not his cross;* that is, he that doth not willingly, and cheerfully, and patiently bear and undergo those trials, and afflictions, and persecutions, which God in the way of his providence shall lay upon him, and bring him into, for my sake and my gospel, is not worthy of the name or reward of my disciples. Our Saviour calls all such trials, *the cross*, either with reference to the Roman last punishment, by crucifying, or signifying what death he should die, and with reference to his own cross.

b ch. 16. 25. Luke 17. 33. John 12. 25.

39 ^bHe that findeth his life shall lose it: and he that loseth his life for my sake shall find it.

John, chap. xii. 25, giveth us a commentary upon these words thus, *He that loveth his life shall lose it; and he that hateth his life in this world shall keep it unto life eternal.* He in this text is said to find his life, who thinks that he hath found, that is, saved it, who is so much in love with his life that, rather than he will lose it, he will lose God's favour, deny the Lord that bought him, deny the most fundamental truths of the gospel. The man that doth thus (saith Christ) shall lose it; possibly he shall not obtain the end he aimeth at here, but if he doth he shall lose eternal life. When, on the contrary, he that is valiant for the truth shall sometimes be preserved, notwithstanding his enemies' rage; but if this happens not, yet he shall have life eternal, his mortality shall be swallowed up in life.

c ch. 18. 5. Luke 9. 48. & 10. 16. John 12. 44. & 13. 20. Gal. 4. 14.

40 ¶ ^cHe that receiveth you receiveth me, and he that receiveth me receiveth him that sent me.

d 1 Kings 17. 10. & 18. 4. 2 Kings 4. 8.

41 ^dHe that receiveth a prophet in the name of a prophet shall receive a prophet's reward; and he that receiveth a righteous man in the name of a righteous man shall receive a righteous man's reward.

e ch. 8. 5, 6. & 25. 40. Mark 9. 41. Heb. 6. 10.

42 ^eAnd whosoever shall give to drink unto one of these little ones a cup of cold *water* only in the name of a disciple, verily I say unto you, he shall in no wise lose his reward.

He that receiveth you receiveth me, &c.; we have the same Luke x. 16, only there it is, *He that heareth you heareth me;* and there is added, *and he that despiseth you despiseth me; and he that despiseth me despiseth him that sent me.* In John xiii. 20, it is, *Verily, verily, I say unto you, He that receiveth whomsoever I send receiveth me; and he that receiveth me receiveth him that sent me.* As great princes account what favour is shown to their ambassadors, who represent their persons, shown unto themselves, and whatsoever indignities or affronts are done unto them as done to themselves, so doth Christ. *Receiving* is a general term, and capable of a large interpretation. That *hearing* is one branch of it, Luke tells us. The scope of the context, and the words that follow, do manifest that a giving entertainment to them in their houses is another thing here meant. There is another more inward, receiving of their doctrine by faith and love, to which undoubtedly there will be a great reward. But whether it be here intended, I doubt. Our Saviour was sending the twelve out, he had commanded them to take with them no gold, silver, nor brass, no scrip, &c.; but when they came into any city, to inquire who there were in that city who were worthy men, favourers to the gospel, and ready to entertain strangers, and to go to their house or houses, saluting them, and to abide there till they left the place. He furnisheth them here as it were with a ticket, or bill of exchange. He gives them an assurance, that whatsoever kindness should be done to them, he would account it as done to himself. And further hath assured both them, and all the world, that if any should come to them to reveal the will of God, (for that the term *prophet* signifieth,) if they give him an entertainment upon that account, they should be rewarded. What is here meant by the term, *a prophet's reward*, is variously guessed, whether it be, 1. The reward which God hath appointed for such as entertain his prophets; or, 2. Such a reward as such a prophet shall himself receive; or, 3. The reward which the prophet will give him or them, viz. prayers and instruction. That which appears to me most probable is, that no more is meant than a liberal reward, for such shall be the reward of those who *turn many to righteousness*, Dan. xii. 3. Those words, *in the name of a prophet*, are both exclusive of those from the benefit of this promise who receive and entertain the ministers of the gospel upon any other account than this, that they are the Lord's prophets; and also encouraging to those who may discern they have been mistaken in their acts of charity of this nature; If they have been sincere in their designs and actions, they shall not lose their reward, though the pretended prophet so entertained prove but an impostor. *And whosoever shall give to drink unto one of these little ones a cup of cold water only in the name of a disciple, he shall in no wise lose his reward.* Christ will not only reward those who show love to his prophets, but those who show kindness to his members, whom the world counts contemptible, and calleth *little ones;* nor shall those only be rewarded who give them great entertainments, and make them great presents, but (if it be proportionable to what they are able to do) though it be a kindness of the most minute consideration, but *a cup of cold water*, they shall be rewarded. God rewards the love we show to him, and the good actions that flow from it. Here are three persons mentioned, for whose entertainment and reception God hath provided in this promise; *a prophet, a righteous man, a little one:* and a threefold reward promised; the reward of a prophet, the reward of a righteous man, and his reward. How to distinguish the righteous man and the little one I cannot tell, unless we understand by the righteous man one more perfect, more eminent in holiness; and by the little one, one that is sincere, though we cannot judge him so grown in grace and the knowledge of Christ. I should understand no more by the threefold rewards, than God's more particular value for his ministers, and for such as are more perfect in holiness; while in the mean time he will not *break the bruised reed, nor quench the smoking flax;* and that every one shall be rewarded according to his works; which shall not be measured by the quantity of the gift, but by the obedience, and affection, and ability of the giver, Luke xxi. 2, 3; Heb. vi. 10.

CHAP. XI

John sendeth his disciples to Christ, 2—6. *Christ's testimony concerning John,* 7—15. *The perverse judgments of the people concerning both John and Christ,* 16—19. *Christ upbraideth the cities of Chorazin, Bethsaida, and Capernaum with their long unfruitfulness and impenitency,* 20—24. *He thanketh the Father for revealing his gospel to the simple only,* 25—27; *and inviteth the weary to partake of his rest,* 28—30.

AND it came to pass, when Jesus had made an

end of commanding his twelve disciples, he departed thence to teach and to preach in their cities.

We never find our Saviour idle, but continually going up and down doing good, and we find him most intent upon preaching and teaching, which doubtless is the great work of the ministers of the gospel; of what quality soever they be, they can pretend to no higher than Christ's. Nor did our Saviour think it enough to send others in his stead, as his curates, he went himself. Luke noteth, chap. x. 1, that he sent the seventy, two by two, into every city whither himself was to follow; so as it seems he did not judge it enough that one proclamation of the gospel should be made to them. For those that think there is a distinction to be made betwixt preaching and teaching, κηρύσσειν and διδάσκειν, they may learn from this text, that they are both the work of Christ's ministers, if they be bound to take example from their Master, and not think the servant is above his Lord. Those that undervalue preaching, as the least part of the ministerial work, do both forget this text, and what Paul said, that Christ sent him not to baptize, but to preach the gospel; that is, not so much to baptize as to preach. If any think that people are now so instructed that there is no such need of preaching, they should do well to question their people a little, and they may discover their own great mistakes. Besides that experience teacheth us, that those who are best instructed are most desirous of that which deserveth the name of preaching; which lets us know that there is yet something further to be known, or that we had need have our remembrance stirred up, or at least our affections quickened.

a Luke 7. 18, 19, &c.
b ch. 14. 3.

2 ^aNow when John had ^bheard in the prison the works of Christ, he sent two of his disciples,

c Gen. 49.10.
Num. 24. 17.
Dan. 9. 24.
John 6. 14.

3 And said unto him, Art thou ^che that should come, or do we look for another?

The instance of this text alone is enough to convince the observing reader of holy writ, that the evangelists do not set down all things in that order as they were done. We have heard nothing before of John's being cast into prison in this gospel, nor do we hear any thing here of the story of it, till Matt. xiv. 6, when our evangelist occasionally relateth it something largely. He here tells us of something done during his imprisonment, viz. his sending two of his disciples to Christ, to be satisfied whether he was the promised Messias, or they must look for another. Luke reports the same thing, chap. vii. 19. Could he that was sent before Christ to prepare his way, and that had baptized him, and seen the Spirit descending on him, and heard the voice from heaven, saying, *This is my beloved Son, in whom I am well pleased*, and who had showed Christ to his disciples, John i. 29—31, &c., doubt whether he was the Messiah? Undoubtedly no; but John saw how some of his disciples, either envying for his sake, as John iii. 26, or else inclinable to the common error of the Jews about the Messiah, were something shaken with the clamours of the scribes and Pharisees (who were far more favourable to John than to Christ). That they might be satisfied from their own sight of the works of Christ, he a little before his death sendeth them to Christ on this errand, *Art thou he who should come* (in the Greek, *who is coming*)? which lets us know the full expectation the Jews generally had at that time of a Messias coming. They desire only to be satisfied whether Christ was he.

d Is. 29. 18.
& 35. 4, 5.
6. & 42. 7.
John 2. 23.
& 3. 2. & 5.
36. & 10. 25,
38. & 14. 11.
e Ps. 22. 26.
Is. 61. 1.
Luke 4. 18.
Jam. 2. 5.
f Is. 8. 14, 15.
ch. 13. 57.
& 24. 10.
& 26. 31.
Rom. 9. 32,
33. 1 Cor. 1.
23. & 2. 14.
Gal. 5. 11.
1 Pet. 2. 8.

4 Jesus answered and said unto them, Go and shew John again those things which ye do hear and see:

5 ^dThe blind receive their sight, and the lame walk, the lepers are cleansed, and the deaf hear, the dead are raised up, and ^ethe poor have the Gospel preached to them.

6 And blessed is *he*, whosoever shall not ^fbe offended in me.

We must imagine these disciples of John to have stayed with Christ some time, and to have seen him work some of these miracles, and to have heard him preach, and seen the great success of his ministry, and then to have left him with this answer. Luke therefore addeth, chap. vii. 21, *And in the same hour he cured many of their infirmities and plagues, and of evil spirits; and unto many that were blind he gave sight.* Then he repeateth the answer which we have here, in which our Saviour referreth unto his works as sufficiently testifying of him, John v. 36, 37; x. 25, 37, 38. We read not that these disciples saw any dead person raised whilst they were with Christ, but it appeareth from Luke vii. 18, &c. that the report of such a miracle was the occasion of their coming to Christ. The question is, how the sight of these things done by our Saviour could be a sufficient argument to confirm to them that he was the Messias, especially considering that his apostles did the same things? *Answ.* First, It was prophesied by Isaiah, chap. xxxv. 4—6, that when God should come to save them, the eyes of the blind should be opened, and the ears of the deaf unstopped; *then shall the lame man leap as an hart, and the tongue of the dumb sing:* and Isa. lxi. 1, that the Messiah should *preach good tidings to the meek*, that is, *the poor*, Luke iv. 18, which Christ, ver. 21, applied to himself. So that the fulfilling of these promises argued that the Messias was come, and no other was to be looked for, whether these things were done by him or by his disciples. Secondly, The disciples as yet had done no such things, so as his doing of them plainly evidenced his Divine power; the others did them but as his disciples, by his power and authority. Thirdly, It is more than probable, that when the disciples did them, they used some such form as Peter used, Acts iii. 6, *In the name of Jesus Christ of Nazareth rise up and walk.* We find Peter, ver. 12, very wary that the people should not mistake in thinking they did it by their own power or holiness. *And the poor have the gospel preached unto them.* Gr. πτωχοὶ εὐαγγελίζονται, which may be translated, the poor preach the gospel, in an active sense, as the word is used Luke ii. 10; or, the poor are gospelized, taking the word in a passive sense, as Heb. iv. 2; 1 Pet. i. 25; iv. 6. In the passive sense it may be understood either of a more external reception of the gospel upon preaching, or of a more internal reception of the gospel by faith. In all senses it was true of the times of the Messiah, 1. The poor preached the gospel; nor was this a mean evidence that the Messiah was come, to see a few poor fishermen at his call leaving their nets and their friends, and following one calling them to preach a new doctrine to the new world. 2. The poor had the gospel preached to them; nor was this a less evidence of Christ to be the Messiah, considering the prophecy, Isa. lxi. 1, and the contempt of the poor amongst the Jews, John vii. 49. But that the poor, who commonly are the more ignorant and rude sort of people, should vouchsafe to hear the gospel, and be turned into the likeness of the gospel upon Christ's preaching to them, this was yet a higher evidence. Many by *poor* understand the poor in spirit. The binding up of broken hearts, and bringing glad tidings to souls sadded on spiritual accounts, is a great effect of the Divine power. It followeth, *And blessed is he, whosoever shall not be offended in me.* It is not improbable that our Saviour here reflecteth on the disciples of John, who out of a great honour for their master took many occasions to be offended at Christ. One while because he and his disciples did not fast so often as they and the Pharisees, as chap. ix. 14; another while because so many followed him, John iii. 26. But the words spoken have a further reference than to John's disciples. The Lord Jesus and his doctrine are to many *a stone of stumbling and a rock of offence*, according to the prophecy, Isa. viii. 14; xxviii. 16; Luke ii. 34; Rom. ix. 33; 1 Cor. i. 23; 1 Pet. ii. 6. The Jews stumbled at the meanness of his person and parentage, and the meanness of his followers. The Gentiles, not at these things only, but his ignominious death. At this day many stumble at the sublimeness and strictness of his doctrine, &c. Christ speaks here with reference to all, and pronounceth that man a blessed man, who shall so take offence at nothing, whether respecting his person, his life, or his death, his doctrine, or his followers, as to deter or discourage him from embracing him, and believing in him as the Saviour of lost sinners, that shall by faith receive him.

7 ¶ ^gAnd as they departed, Jesus be- g Luke 7. 24.

gan to say unto the multitudes concerning John, What went ye out into the wilderness to see? ʰA reed shaken with the wind?

ʰ Eph. 4. 14.

8 But what went ye out for to see? A man clothed in soft raiment? behold, they that wear soft *clothing* are in kings' houses.

9 But what ye went out for to see? A prophet? yea, I say unto you, ⁱand more than a prophet.

ⁱ ch. 14. 5.
& 21. 26.
Luke 1. 76.
& 7. 26.

Luke repeating the same story, chap. vii. 24—26, instead of *they that wear soft clothing*, saith, *they that are gorgeously apparelled, and live delicately, are in kings' courts.* Our Saviour here doth tacitly imply, that the ministers of the gospel should neither be uncertain and inconstant men, nor yet delicate men, affecting splendid apparel or delicate diet, but minding their great work, viz. the revelation of the will of God. But the scope of his present speech here, was to confirm the multitude in their good opinion of John, and to keep them from being scandalized, or altering their opinion of him, because he was now in prison. All men held John as a prophet, chap. xiv. 5; xxi. 26. You went out (saith our Saviour) into the wilderness to hear John preach: you did not go out to see some idle, light man, such as a reed shaken with the wind, nor yet to see a man clothed gorgeously, (the wilderness is no place for such persons, they are to be found in the courts and palaces of princes,) you went out to hear one revealing the will of God to you. Nor did you mistake. He was a prophet. Not that Prophet of which Moses spake, Deut. xviii. 15. But *a prophet; yea, and more than a prophet*; one that hath taught you what none of the prophets ever could teach you, that I, the Messias, am come; they could only tell you that I should come.

10 For this is *he*, of whom it is written, ᵏBehold, I send my messenger before thy face, which shall prepare thy way before thee.

ᵏ Mal. 3. 1.
Mark 1. 2.
Luke 1. 76.
& 7. 27.

11 Verily I say unto you, Among them that are born of women there hath not risen a greater than John the Baptist: notwithstanding he that is least in the kingdom of heaven is greater than he.

St. Luke hath the same, chap. vii. 27, 28, only he saith, *there is not a greater prophet than John the Baptist*. It was written, Mal. iii. 1, *Behold, I will send my messenger, and he shall prepare the way before me: and the Lord, whom ye seek, shall suddenly come to his temple, even the messenger of the covenant, whom ye delight in: behold, he shall come, saith the Lord of hosts.* The latter part was a prophecy of Christ. The former part a prophecy of John the Baptist, and applied to him not in this text only, but Mark i. 2; Luke i. 76; vii. 27. Christ is set out as a great Prince, who sends his harbingers before him to prepare his way, and by John's preaching we may learn the ministers' duty, who are to prepare Christ's way to people's souls, viz. to preach repentance and faith in Christ. *Verily I say unto you, Among those that are born of women there hath not risen a greater*; that is, (as Luke expounds it,) *a greater prophet*; i. e. amongst all the prophets of the Old Testament, God raised up none greater than John. *Notwithstanding he that is least in the kingdom of heaven is greater than he.* Mr. Calvin and many others think that by this phrase is to be understood, the least of those who shall preach the gospel after my resurrection will be greater than he, that is, as to their doctrine. John could only declare me to be come. They shall preach me, as having died for my people's sins, and risen again for their justification, Rom. iv. 25. The death and the resurrection of Christ were indeed great points of the gospel, which John could only prophesy of, not preach of, and declare us things in his time accomplished.

12 ˡAnd from the days of John the Baptist until now the kingdom of heaven ‖suffereth violence, and the violent take it by force.

ˡ Luke 16. 16.
‖ Or, *is gotten by force, and they that thrust men.*

As John Baptist was a great man, so the Lord hath owned him as such, giving such a success to his ministry, that ever since he began the course of it, men have been carried on with a great ardour and heat, in hearing and receiving the gospel, which is the gospel of the kingdom, and bringeth men into the kingdom of Christ amongst men, and at last to the kingdom of glory. The hearts of men and women have been inflamed with a desire after the knowledge and obtaining of heaven, and heavenly things. They are great persons whom God thus owneth; and those whom the Lord thus owneth, are ordinarily such as have some measures of the spirit of this first gospel ministry, making the great things of God the matter of their discourse, and doing their work with a seriousness, zeal, and fervour fitted to it. *The violent take it by force:* they are not lazy wishes or cold endeavours that will bring men to heaven.

13 ᵐFor all the prophets and the law prophesied until John.

ᵐ Mal. 4. 6.

It is no wonder that there was such a heat kindled in the souls of people upon John the Baptist's coming, for they understood that Christ, typified in the law, and only foretold by the prophets, was now come. So as the ceremonial law from his time began to die, and all the prophecies of Christ in the prophets began then to have their complement. John showed them with his finger him who before had been only darkly revealed under types and figures, and in the prophecies of the prophets; men came to see that they had not hoped or waited in vain for the salvation of Israel. *Prophesied*, in this verse, signifies, made dark revelations of Christ and the kingdom of heaven.

14 And if ye will receive *it*, this is ⁿElias, which was for to come.

ⁿ Mal. 4 5.
ch. 17. 12.
Luke 1. 17.

God had told the Jews, Mal. iv. 5, 6, that he would send them *Elijah the prophet before the coming of the great and dreadful day of the Lord: and he shall turn the heart of the fathers to the children, and the heart of the children to the fathers, lest* (saith he) *I come and smite the earth with a curse.* This prophecy related to John the Baptist, as our Saviour here teacheth us; so, Luke i. 17, it is confirmed by the angel to Zacharias, and Mark ix. 11. From which last text it appeareth, that the scribes had a tradition, that Elias should come before the Messiah. Their mistake was that they looked for an Elias to come in person, whenas God meant no more (as the angel expoundeth it, Luke i. 17) than one *in the spirit and power of Elias*, as bold and free a preacher, who should no more fear the face of men in the discharge of his duty than Elias did. Saith our Saviour, if you will believe, this John was that Elias prophesied of by Malachi.

15 ᵒHe that hath ears to hear, let him hear.

ᵒ ch. 13. 9.
Luke 8. 8.
Rev. 2. 7, 11,
17, 29. & 3. 6, 13, 22.

It is an epiphonema or conclusion often used by our Saviour, (and by St. John in the Revelation,) quickening up the hearers to a just attention to and belief of what in the doctrine preceding he had revealed to them; intimating that he knew, that what he had said would not be entertained or believed of all, but only of such whose ears and hearts God had opened, or should open to receive spiritual mysteries. But it was a matter of great concernment, he therefore calls upon those whose ears God had opened to attend to it. So chap. xiii. 9, 43; Mark iv. 9; vii. 16; Luke viii. 8.

16 ¶ ᵖBut whereunto shall I liken this generation? It is like unto children sitting in the markets, and calling unto their fellows,

ᵖ Luke 7. 31.

17 And saying, We have piped unto you, and ye have not danced; we have mourned unto you, and ye have not lamented.

Luke, telling to us the same history, chap. vii. 31—35, prefaceth it thus. ver. 29, 30, *And all the people that heard him, and the publicans, justified God, being baptized with the baptism of John. But the Pharise and the lawyers rejected the counsel of God against themselves, being not baptized of him.* Which letteth us know that our Saviour by the term *this generation* here doth not mean all the people of that generation; but the Pharisees and the lawyers, whom nothing could allure or persuade to the receiving of Jesus

Christ, neither the ministry and example of John, nor yet his own preaching and example. For the people and the publicans justified the words of Christ, which he had spoken in commendation of John, and were baptized of him; but the Pharisees and lawyers did not believe, nor would be baptized of him. These our Saviour likens to a company of sullen children, whom their fellows could not persuade any way to a compliance with them: if they piped they would not dance; if they sang to them some mournful songs, neither would they be affected with them; so as no tune would please them. It is thought that our Saviour doth here allude to some sport used then amongst children, which we are not so well acquainted with, wherein children were wont to sing, sometimes more merry and pleasant, sometimes more sad and mournful songs one to another; and that he here likeneth the Pharisees and lawyers to a sullen set of children, that, let their companions sing what they would, would not answer them. Our Saviour's meaning is expounded plainly enough by the next words.

18 For John came neither eating nor drinking, and they say, He hath a devil.

19 The Son of man came eating and drinking, and they say, Behold a man gluttonous, and a winebibber, [q] a friend of Publicans and sinners. [r] But wisdom is justified of her children.

q ch. 9. 10.
r Luke 7. 35.

Luke hath the same words, chap. vii. 33—35. The sense of the words is this: God hath by his providence used all means to win this people to the gospel. The doctrine of John the Baptist and Christ was the same, but their temper and converse was very different: John was an austere and morose man, Christ was of a more free and familiar conversation; but these men would neither give the one nor the other a good word; they reviled both of them, and rejected them both, and the doctrine which they brought. *John came neither eating nor drinking,* that is, not as other men ordinarily do; he was a man that lived most in the wilderness, and fed upon very ordinary diet, not eating with publicans and sinners, not coming at any feasts, &c.; and they said of him, *He hath a devil;* he is a melancholic, hypochondriac fellow, a kind of a madman. *The Son of man came eating and drinking,* he was of a more affable, pleasant temper, of a more free and less reserved converse, eating and drinking as other men (though keeping to the law of temperance) such things as the country afforded, not refusing to be present at feasts, though publicans and sinners were there. They said of him, *Behold a man gluttonous, and a winebibber, a friend of publicans and sinners:* he displeased them with the two great freedom of his conversation; from whence, by the way, they may be better instructed, who place some perfection, or merit, in living like monks and hermits; by that rule John the Baptist was to be preferred before Christ. But Christ could please the Pharisees and lawyers, and their followers, no more than John did. They could not say he was melancholic or morose; but they blasphemed him to a higher degree, calling him a glutton and drunkard, and a friend of publicans and sinners. A godly man, let his temper and converse be what it will, pleaseth none who hateth the truth of the gospel, and the power of godliness. If he be reserved, then he is a morose, melancholic man; if he be of a more free and open converse, then he is a drunkard, or a glutton; something or other they must have to say against a man that will not run with them to the same excess of riot, though they lay to their charge things that they know not. The business is, they hate the power of godliness in them. This instance of these men's thus treating John the Baptist and Christ, is of mighty use to strengthen those who meet with the very same things. *But wisdom is justified of her children.* There is a great variety amongst interpreters in giving the sense of these words. Some think them spoken ironically, for the Pharisees went for the children of wisdom. Some think them spoken plainly, and think it should be, wisdom is judged, or condemned, of her children; but though the word δικαιοῦμαι, signifying to justice or do justice to another, which, according to the merit or demerit of the person, may be by justifying or condemning, upon which account it was true here that wisdom was condemned of those who pretended to be her children, and the word is so used in other authors, yet we have no such usage of it in Scripture. Not to reckon the various senses others put upon the words, the plain sense of them seems to be this. It is a proverbial speech, something like that, *Ars non habet inimicum præter ignorantem,* Learning hath no enemies but the ignorant. 1. I, who am the Wisdom of God, am justified by you, who truly believe on me: you know I am no glutton, no winebibber, no friend of publicans and sinners. Or, 2. Grace is justified of all that are partakers of it. Godly men that are wise will own the grace of God in all men, whether they be of John's temper or of mine, whether of more austere or more pleasant tempers. Or, 3. The wise counsel of God, making use of several instruments of several tempers to win these people unto his gospel, will be justified, that is, acquitted, defended, praised, adored of those who belong unto God, and are acquainted with his wisdom and counsels. Luke saith, *The people justified God,* chap. vii. 29. Some, by the children of wisdom, understand the scribes and Pharisees themselves, (who thought themselves the children of wisdom,) or the generality of the Jews, who were condemned in their own consciences, and could not but in heart justify Christ, though in their speeches they condemned him. But Christ never called them the children of wisdom. This interpretation therefore seemeth something strained. That which seemeth the most natural is what I before hinted. Though those that pretend to be the children of wisdom thus speak of John and of me, yet those who are truly wise will justify me, and also the counsels and wisdom of my Father in the use of all means to bring them to receive the glad tidings of salvation, brought to them both by my more austere and reserved forerunner, and by myself, who have chosen, though a holy and unblamable, yet a more free and pleasant way of converse with them.

20 ¶ [s] Then began he to upbraid the cities wherein most of his mighty works were done, because they repented not:

s Luke 10. 13, &c.

Our Lord had hitherto spent most of his time in Galilee, and the cities belonging to that province: there both John the Baptist and himself had preached the gospel, there he had wrought many miracles, by both aiming at their repentance; but there were multitudes that did not receive him, nor would be brought to any sight of their sins, or any acknowledgment of him as the Messias. He now begins to reprove them smartly, not that they did not applaud and commend him, but because they did not repent. This was Christ's end in all his preaching, and in all his miraculous operations, to bring men to repentance, and to receive him as the Messias; and this should be the great end pursued by all his ministers.

21 Woe unto thee, Chorazin! woe unto thee, Bethsaida! for if the mighty works, which were done in you, had been done in Tyre and Sidon, they would have repented long ago [t] in sackcloth and ashes.

t Jonah 3. 7, 8.

22 But I say unto you, "It shall be more tolerable for Tyre and Sidon at the day of judgment, than for you.

u ch. 10. 15. ver. 24.

Luke hath the same, chap. x. 13, 14. *Chorazin* and *Bethsaida* were two cities of Galilee not far from one another, only the lake of Gennesaret was betwixt them. Capernaum (by and by spoken of) was betwixt them both, on the same side of the lake as Bethsaida, which was the city of Philip, Andrew, and Peter, John i. 44. In these towns Christ had often preached, so probably had the apostles, and Christ had done many great works in them. *Tyre and Sidon* were habitations of heathens, their country joined to Galilee. They were places of great traffic, inhabited with Canaanitish idolaters, and exceedingly wicked; threatened by the prophet Isaiah, chap. xxiii., and by the prophet Ezekiel, chap. xxvi.—xxviii., and by Amos, chap. i. 9, 10; a people odious to the Jews upon many accounts. To these our Lord here compareth the Galileans, telling them that they were worse than that pagan people, who were so contemptible in their eyes, and that their plagues in the day of judgment would be greater. For (saith he) *if the mighty works, which were done in you, had been done in Tyre and Sidon, they would have repented long ago in sackcloth and ashes.* Some think this a strong proof, that where the gospel is preached God gives a sufficiency of grace ; so as if men will but use that power which they have in their own wills, they may, with the assistance only of that grace, truly repent and be saved. I shall not meddle with that dispute, but cannot see how that notion can derive any proof from this text, 1. Because the text only mentioneth Christ's miracles, not his preaching. 2. The text doth not say, they would long ago have repented unto life, but they would have *repented in sackcloth and ashes.* they would have been more affected than these Galileans were, who showed no sense at all of their sins. The king of Nineveh and his people repented, Jonah iii. 7, 8 ; so did Ahab, 1 Kings xxi. 27 ; yet none will say they repented unto life. None ever denied a power in man's will (his understanding being by the gospel enlightened to his duty) to perform acts of moral discipline. 3. Our Saviour might here speak after the manner of men, according to rational conjectures and probabilities. The scope of our Saviour in these words is to be attended, which was only to show, that the men of Chorazin and Bethsaida, showing no signs of remorse for sin, or conviction of the Messias upon the sight of his miracles, confirming his doctrine to be from heaven, had showed a greater stubbornness and hardness of heart than these heathens, who, though they were bad enough, yet had not had such means to reform and to convince them. Therefore he tells them their place in hell would be more dreadful than the place of the men of Tyre and Sidon. And so we are by this text taught, that as the sins of men who have the light of the gospel are much greater than the sins of the worst of men who have it not, so their condemnation in the day of judgment will be much heavier, John iii. 19.

a See Is. 14. 13. Lam. 2. 1. 23 And thou, Capernaum, ˣwhich art exalted unto heaven, shalt be brought down to hell : for if the mighty works, which have been done in thee, had been done in Sodom, it would have remained until this day.

y ch. 10. 15. 24 But I say unto you, ʸThat it shall be more tolerable for the land of Sodom in the day of judgment, than for thee.

This speech of our Saviour is much of the same import with the other. The scope and sense of it is the same, to let the Capernaites know that the hardness of their heart was greater in contempt of the gospel, confirmed by so many miraculous operations, and their guilt greater, than the guilt of Sodom, long since destroyed by fire and brimstone, Gen. xix.; for though they were guilty of prodigious sinning, yet they had not such means to convince, reclaim, and reform them. God had not sent his Son amongst them, nor given them such testimonies of that act of grace as he had given these, by vouchsafing to confirm the doctrine of his Son by miracles ; and therefore they must expect that God, in the day of judgment, should deal more severely with them than with the filthy and impure Sodomites. Our Saviour here speaketh not as an all-knowing God, but as the Son of man to the sons of men, who speak upon probabilities and rational conjectures. If we should say that Christ spake this as an all-knowing God, all that can be inferred is this, that an external reformation may be a lengthening out of persons' tranquillity. In the mean time God was just to both in not giving them such means, they sinning notoriously against the light of nature, which they had, and the light of Lot's holy example, whose righteous soul they vexed with their filthy conversation and unrighteous deeds, 2 Pet. ii. 7, 8 ; and he was also just in destroying of them. Capernaum is here said to have been *exalted to heaven,* either with respect to their trading and outward prosperity, or with respect to the means of grace they enjoyed in hearing Christ's sermons and seeing his miracles. The casting down to hell, seems to be meant of a temporal destruction, the word ᾅδης not signifying the place of the damned, but the state of the dead ; but ver. 24 must be understood of eternal condemnation, which shall be *in the day of judgment.*

z Luke 10. 21. 25 ¶ ᶻAt that time Jesus answered and said, I thank thee, O Father, Lord of heaven and earth, because ᵃthou hast hid these things from the wise and prudent, ᵇand hast revealed them unto babes. a See Ps. 8. 2. 1 Cor. 1. 19, 27. & 2. 8. 2 Cor. 3. 14. b ch. 16. 17.

26 Even so, Father : for so it seemed good in thy sight.

Luke, chap. x. 21, hath the same thing, only he thus prefaceth, *In that hour Jesus rejoiced in spirit, and said, I thank thee, O Father, Lord of heaven and earth,* &c. He rejoiced in spirit, his heart was inwardly affected with this grace of God his Father. Then he *answered and said.* Answering in Scripture doth not always signify replying to the words of others, but a speaking upon some fit occasion offered, a beginning of a speech. *I thank thee, O Father, Lord of heaven and earth.* In the Greek the same word is used which signifieth to confess. In all thanksgiving and praising there is a confession of the power, wisdom, or goodness of God, so as all praising is a confessing, though all confession be not praising. By calling his Father *Lord of heaven and earth,* he acknowledgeth his absolute power to have done otherwise, even as it pleased him. *Because thou hast hid these things from the wise and prudent.* By the *wise and prudent* he here plainly means the scribes and Pharisees, the learned doctors of that age, who should have been wise and prudent, and were so both in their own and in their followers' opinion. By *these things* he means the mysteries of the gospel, as chap. xiii. 11, *The mysteries of the kingdom of heaven.* God is said to have *hid* them, because he had not revealed them to them ; nor can it be understood of a mere external revelation by the preaching of the gospel, but of an internal revelation by his Spirit, so as they embraced and believed them, 1 Cor. ii. 10 ; in which sense Paul saith, *If our gospel be hid, it is hid to them that are lost,* 2 Cor. iv. 3. *And hast revealed them unto babes,* νηπίοις. It signifieth persons that are young in years, infants, and weak in understanding. He principally means his apostles, together with those ordinary persons that believed in him, for the Pharisees said, John vii. 48, 49, *Have any of the rulers or of the Pharisees believed on him? But this people who knoweth not the law are cursed.* O Father, (saith our Saviour,) thou hast all power in thine hand, thou art the Lord of heaven and earth, thou couldst by thy Spirit have caused these learned men to have received and embraced thy gospel, and followed me, as well as these poor fishermen, and other Jews of none of the highest quality ; in that thou hast not done it, thou hast declared thy justice, for their rejecting of thy counsel for their salvation, but in that thou hast revealed these things to any, especially to these persons, not under the same worldly advantages for reputation, wisdom, and wit, herein thou hast showed thy special and abounding grace, as well as the greatness of thy power. Lord, I rejoice in thy dispensations, and I give thee thanks that out of the mouths of babes and sucklings thou hast perfected thy praise. There can be no other reason given of this, but thy good pleasure ; *Even so, Father ; for so it pleased thee.* We may from hence observe, 1. That the further revelations of Christ some souls have more than others enjoying the same outward means, are not to be ascribed to the power or goodness of the will of man, but solely to the good pleasure of God. 2. That from the beginning of the gospel, the special and effectual revelations of the mysteries of the kingdom of heaven have, from the good pleasure of God, been made generally not to the most learned and wise men in men's account, but mostly to persons of a meaner rank. *Surgunt indocti, et cœlum rapiunt : Nos cum doctrina nostra in Gehennam trudimur.* 1 Cor. i. 26—28 ; James ii. 5. 3. That wheresoever God by his Spirit reveals the mysteries of the kingdom of God, it is matter of great joy and thanksgiving ; especially where God reveals these mysteries to persons most unlikely to have received them.

27 ᶜAll things are delivered unto me of my Father : and no man knoweth the Son, but the Father ; ᵈneither knoweth any man the Father, save the Son, and he to whomsoever the Son will reveal him. c ch. 28. 18. Luke 10. 22. John 3. 35. & 13. 3. & 17. 2. 1 Cor. 15. 27. d John 1. 18. & 6. 46. & 10. 15.

John saith, chap. iii. 35, *The Father loveth the Son, and hath given all things into his hand.* Matt. xxviii. 18, *All power is given unto me.* John xvii. 2, *Thou hast given him power over all flesh, that he should give eternal life to as many as thou hast given him.* God is the Fountain of power, Psal. lxii. 11. He hath committed also power to Christ as Mediator, Psal. ii. 7—9, more particularly the power of life and eternal salvation, as John xvii. 2; he hath *the keys of hell and death,* Rev. i. 18, and all the means that lead to eternal life are in his power and disposal. *And no man knoweth the Son but the Father;* no man knoweth his Divine essence, his eternal generation; and therefore men are not to listen to what the scribes and Pharisees say of him, but to attend to and to believe what the Father hath revealed from heaven concerning him, who best knoweth him. *Neither knoweth any man the Father, save the Son:* no man knoweth the essence of the Father, or the counsels of the Father, as to the dispensations of the gospel. *Save the Son, and he to whomsoever the Son will reveal him.* The prophets inquired and searched diligently concerning this salvation, *searching what, or what manner of time the Spirit of Christ which was in them did signify, when it testified beforehand the sufferings of Christ, and the glory that should follow,* 1 Pet. i. 10—12. Mr. Calvin saith, the Son is said to know the Father, as he is his lively image, the express image of his person, and the brightness of his glory. *And he to whomsoever the Son will reveal him,* John vi. 46. *He that hath seen me hath seen the Father,* John xiv. 9. All our saving knowledge of God is in and through Christ.

28 ¶ Come unto me, all *ye* that labour and are heavy laden, and I will give you rest.

29 Take my yoke upon you, ^eand learn of me; for I am meek and ^flowly in heart: ^gand ye shall find rest unto your souls.

e John 13. 15.
Phil. 2. 5.
f 1 et. 2. 21.
1 John 2. 6
f Zech. 9. 9.
Phil. 2. 7. 8.
g Jer. 6. 16.

h 1 John 5. 3.

30 ^hFor my yoke *is* easy, and my burden is light.

Our Lord having before showed, 1. That all power was given to him; 2. That none could know the Father but by and in him; closeth his discourse with an invitation of persons to him. By the weary and heavy laden, in the text, some understand those that are laden with the sense of their sins, and the feeling the guilt of them. Others understand, with the burden of the law, which the apostles called *a yoke,* Acts xv. 10. Mr. Calvin thinks this too strait an interpretation. Others understand heavy laden with trials and afflictions. Christ will give rest to all those of his people that are any ways weary and heavy laden, but in an order first to souls wearied and heavy laden with the burden of their sins, and their want of a righteousness wherein to stand before God. Then to such to whom he hath given this rest, he promiseth also rest from their troubles and persecutions in the world, John xvi. 33. It is very like he used this term, *Come,* with respect to that of Isaiah, chap. lv. 1, 2. That by coming is to be understood believing is plain from John vi. 44—46; Heb. xi. 6. The rest promised chiefly respecteth the soul, as appears from ver. 29. The promise may be understood both of that rest which believers have in this life, Rom. v. 2; xv. 13, and also of that rest which after this life *remaineth to the people of God,* Heb. iv. 9. Whatever the rest be, it must be of Christ's giving and our seeking; nor is it to be obtained without labour and suffering, for it followeth, *Take my yoke upon you.* The members of Christ are not without a yoke, a law and rule by which they are obliged to walk; and though the service of God be a perfect freedom, yet to flesh and blood it is a yoke, grating upon our sensitive appetite, and restraining our natural motions and inclinations. *For I am meek and lowly.* Humility and meekness are in themselves yokes, as they are contrary to our pride, and aptness to swell in a high opinion of ourselves; and to our wrath and danger, which sometimes boileth to a great height, without any due fuel: and as in themselves they are a great part of Christ's yoke, so they fit and dispose us to take Christ's further yoke upon us, and may be here considered as means directed for the better performance of the precept, *Take my yoke upon you.* Our Lord also by this precept lets us know there can be no true faith without obedience to the commands of Christ. Though true faith and obedience be two things, yet they are inseparable; *Show me thy faith* (saith James) *by thy works;* and the rest of the text is not

promised to either of them severally, but to both jointly. *For my yoke is easy, and my burden is light.* Our Saviour had before (chap. vii.) told us that the way to heaven is a strait way, how doth he now tell us his yoke is easy and his burden light? *Answ.* 1. Nothing makes it hard or burdensome but our corruption, which floweth from the depravation of human nature. 2. It is much easier than the yoke and burden of the law. 3. Though it be hard to beginners, yet it is easy when we have once accustomed ourselves to it. 4. It is easy, considering that we do it not in our own strength, but by assistance from God, Jer. xxxi. 33; Ezek. xxxvi. 25, 26; John xv. 3: we are delivered even from the moral law, considered as a covenant, and as merely commanding us, and affording no help and assistance. 5. It is also easy; as we are by the love of God constrained to our duty, so we are freed from the rigour of the law. It is easy and light, as it is a course of life highly consonant to our reason, once delivered from a bondage to our passions. Finally, it is much more easy and light than the service of our lusts is. There is no greater slavery than a subjection to our lusts, that if a drunkard saith Come, we must come, if an harlot saith Go, we must go. Or than our service to the world, &c. To say nothing of the exceeding easiness of it, from the prospect of the great reward proposed and promised to those who keep the commandments of Christ, the *exceeding and eternal weight of glory,* 2 Cor. iv. 17; as Jacob's hard service of fourteen years seemed to him but a few days.

CHAP. XII

Christ allegeth scripture in excuse of his disciples, whom the Pharisees charged with breaking the sabbath in plucking the ears of corn on the sabbath day, 1—8. *He appealeth to reason, and healeth the withered hand on the sabbath day,* 9—13. *The Pharisees seek to destroy him: a prophecy of Esaias fulfilled in him,* 14—21. *He healeth one possessed of a devil, who was blind and dumb,* 22, 23; *and confuting the absurd charge of his casting out devils by Beelzebub, he showeth that blasphemy against the Holy Ghost is an unpardonable sin, and that every idle word must be accounted for,* 24—37. *He rebuketh those that sought of him a sign,* 38—45; *and showeth whom he regardeth as his nearest relations,* 46—50.

AT that time ^aJesus went on the sabbath day through the corn; and his disciples were an hungred, and began to pluck the ears of corn, and to eat.

a Deut. 23. 25.
Mark 2. 23.
Luke 6. 1.

Mark relating this story, chap. ii. 23, varieth little. Luke relating it, chap. vi. 1, saith it was on *the second sabbath after the first, and his disciples did eat, rubbing them.* God in his law, Deut. xxiii. 25, had said, *When thou comest into the standing corn of thy neighbour, thou mayst pluck the ears with thine hand, but thou shalt not move a sickle unto thy neighbour's standing corn.* To take for our need so much of our neighbour's goods as we may reasonably think that, if he were present, and knew our circumstances, he would give us, is no theft. The Pharisees therefore do not accuse them of theft, but of violation of the sabbath. Luke saith this happened upon the second sabbath after the first. Whether that was the sabbath next following the feast of unleavened bread, (which was about the time of our Easter,) the first and last days of which were sabbaths in the Jewish sense, or the feast of tabernacles, or any other, is not much material for us to know. But on a sabbath day it was that our Saviour *went through the corn, and his disciples were an hungred:* this may teach us their low estate and condition in the world. He could quickly have supplied their hunger, but he chose to leave them to relieve themselves with plucking, rubbing, and eating of the corn, that he might have an opportunity to instruct them and the Pharisees in the true doctrine of the sabbath.

2 But when the Pharisees saw *it,* they said unto him, Behold, thy disciples do that which is not lawful to do upon the sabbath day.

So saith Mark, chap. ii. 24, only he puts it into the form of a question. Luke adds nothing, chap. vi. 2, but saith, *certain of the Pharisees.* They granted the thing lawful to be done another day, but not on the sabbath day. How blind is superstition, that they could think that it was contrary to the will of God, that his people should fit themselves for the service of the sabbath by a moderate refreshment! Some of the Pharisees ordinarily attended Christ's motions, not to be instructed by him, but (as is afterward said) that they might have something whereof to accuse him. What a little thing do they carp at! Wherein was the sin? the plucking of a few ears of corn, and rubbing them, could hardly be called servile labour, especially not in the sense of the commandment, which restrained not necessary labour, but such labour as took them off from the duties of the sabbath; but their tradition had made this unlawful, as it was a little reaping and a kind of threshing. Hypocrites and formalists are always most zealous for little things in the law, or for their own additaments to it.

3 But he said unto them, Have ye not read ^bwhat David did, when he was an hungred, and they that were with him;

4 How he entered into the house of God, and did eat ^cthe shewbread, which was not lawful for him to eat, neither for them which were with him, ^dbut only for the Priests?

b 1 Sam. 21. 6.

c Ex. 25. 30. Lev. 24. 5.

d Ex. 29. 32, 33. Lev. 8. 31. & 24. 9.

Mark and Luke add little, only Mark specifieth the time, *in the days of Abiathar the high priest*, and saith, *when he had need, and was an hungred.* We have the history, 1 Sam. xxi. David was upon his flight from Saul, upon the notice of his danger given him by Jonathan, chap. xx., and being hungry, he asks of the high priest five loaves of bread; the high priest tells him he had none but *hallowed bread*, which the high priest gave him, ver. 6. What the shewbread was may be read, Lev. xxiv. 5—9. It is expressly said, a stranger shall not eat thereof. Now (saith our Saviour) notwithstanding this, David and his followers, being an hungred, did eat thereof, though strictly, according to the letter of the law, none but the priests might eat it. But some may object, What was this to the purpose? It was not upon the sabbath day. *Answ.* 1. It was either upon the sabbath day, or immediately after, for it was to be set on every sabbath day, and to be eaten *in the holy place*, Lev. xxiv. 8, 9, and the high priest told David, 1 Sam. xxi. 6, that it was taken away to set hot bread in the room of it. 2. But secondly, that which our Saviour produceth this for, was to prove a more general proposition, which being proved, the lawfulness of his disciples' act would easily be inferred from it. That was this, That the letter of a ritual law is not to be insisted upon, where some eminent necessity urgeth the contrary, in the performance of some natural or moral duty. The law of nature commandeth every man to feed himself when he is hungry. The moral law confirms this, as it is a means to the observation of the sixth commandment, and especially on the sabbath day, so far as may fit us for the best sanctification of it. The law concerning the shew-bread was but a ritual law, and that part of it which restrained the use of it when taken off from the holy table was of lightest concern, as it commanded it should be eaten by the priests only, and by them in the holy place. Where the life, or necessary relief, of men was concerned, the obligation of the ritual law ceased, and that was lawful, both for David and the high priest, which in ordinary cases had not been lawful. Works necessary either for the upholding of our lives, or fitting us for sabbath services, are lawful upon the sabbath day. Though the law concerning the sabbath be a moral law, yet it is *jus positivum*, not a law natural, but positive, and must be so interpreted as not to destroy the law natural, which commands men to feed themselves; nor yet to destroy itself. The scope and end of it is to be considered, which is the keeping of a day as a day of holy and religious rest. What labour is necessary to such keeping of it is also lawful. The time of the sabbath is not more holy than the shew-bread; and as David in a case of necessity might make a common use of that holy bread, so the disciples in a case of like necessity might make use of a little of that holy time, in such necessary servile work as might fit them for their sabbath service. Thus it was lawful by the law of God, and if the Pharisees had not been ignorant, or had understood what they had read, they would never have disputed this, the instance of holy David might have satisfied. So that this little kind of labour could only be a breach of one of their by-laws, by which they pretended to expound the law of God, in which he showeth they had given a false interpretation.

5 Or have ye not read in the ^elaw, how that on the sabbath days the Priests in the temple profane the sabbath, and are blameless?

e Num. 28. 9. John 7. 22.

Neither Mark nor Luke have this argument of our Saviour's. The meaning is, all acts of servile labour are not unlawful on the sabbath day. The priests, according to the law, Numb. xxviii. 9, offer sacrifices, and do many other acts, such as circumcising, and many other things, which in your sense would be a profanation of the sabbath; yet you do not blame them, neither are they to be blamed, because God permitted and directed them. If any say, But how doth this agree to what our Saviour is speaking to? *Answ.* The disciples of Christ were employed with and by him in going about and preaching the gospel, and what they now did was but in order to fit them for his work, when they had not had such leisure as others beforehand to provide: and this establisheth a second rule, That works of piety, and tending to fit us for acts of piety, that cannot conveniently be done before, are lawful on the sabbath day.

6 But I say unto you, That in this place is ^fone greater than the temple.

f 2 Chr. 6. 18. Mal. 3. 1.

The Jews had very superstitious conceits concerning the temple, and might object, But the priests' works are done in the temple. The Jews had a saying, That in the temple there was no sabbath. They looked upon the temple as sanctifying all actions done there. To obviate this, (saith our Saviour,) *In this place is one* (that is, I am) *greater than the temple.* The temple was but a type of me, If the temple can sanctify so much labour, will not my authority and permission, think you, excuse this little labour of my disciples?

7 But if ye had known what *this* meaneth, ^gI will have mercy, and not sacrifice, ye would not have condemned the guiltless.

g Hos. 6. 6. Mic. 6. 6, 7, 8. ch. 9. 13.

Neither Mark nor Luke have this argument. Our Lord yet goeth on taxing these great doctors of ignorance. The text he quoteth is Hos. vi. 6; we met with it before quoted by our Saviour, chap. ix. 13. The meaning is, that God preferreth mercy before sacrifice. Where two laws in respect of some circumstance seem to clash one with another, so as we cannot obey both, our obedience is due to that which is the more excellent law. Now, saith our Saviour, the law of mercy is the more excellent law; God preferreth it before sacrifice; which had you well considered, you would never have accused my disciples, who in this point are guiltless.

8 For the Son of man is Lord even of the sabbath day.

This argument Luke hath, chap. vi. 5. Mark hath it thus, chap. ii. 27, 28, *And he said unto them, The sabbath was made for man, and not man for the sabbath: therefore the Son of man is Lord also of the sabbath.* Some interpreters make these two arguments: 1. The Son of man is Lord of the sabbath; therefore it is in my power to dispense with this action of my disciples, though it had been contrary to the letter of the law: or rather, therefore it is in my power to interpret the law, which I myself made. 2. The sabbath is made for man, not man for the sabbath. A law made for the good of another bindeth not, in such cases where the observation of it would be evidently for his harm and ruin. The law of the sabbath was made for the good of man, that he might have a solemn time, in which he should be under an obligation to pay his homage unto God; this must not be so interpreted as would tend to the destruction of a man. I find interpreters divided about that term *the Son of man.* Some think that it is not to be interpreted, as usually in the gospel, concerning Christ; but of ordinary men, and that man's lordship over the sabbath is proved by the subserviency of it to his good, to which end also it was ordained. But certainly that is both a dangerous and unscriptural interpretation: dangerous to give man a lordship over a moral law, for it is very improper to call any lord of a thing, because he hath the use of it, and it is for his advantage: I cannot see but we may as well make man lord of the whole ten commandments as of one of them. Unscriptural, for though our Saviour useth this term more than threescore times in the gospel, yet he always useth it with relation to himself, never with reference to any mere man; neither is there any necessity to understand it otherwise here. Christ affirming himself Lord of the sabbath, spake properly enough to the Pharisees' quarrel; for it must needs then follow, that he had power to dispense with the observation of it at particular times, and much more to give a true and right interpretation of the law concerning it.

h Mark 3. 1.
Luke 6. 6.

9 ʰ And when he was departed thence, he went into their synagogue:

Mark saith, chap. iii. 1, *he entered again into the synagogue* on the sabbath day. This our Saviour was often wont to do, to own there what was done according to his Father's institution, and himself to do what good he could; nor doth he now decline it because he had had so late a contest with them: it is therefore said that *he went into their synagogue*, as being neither ashamed of what he had delivered, nor afraid to own it in the face of his adversaries.

10 ¶ And, behold, there was a man which had *his* hand withered. And they asked him, saying, ¹Is it lawful to heal on the sabbath days? that they might accuse him.

i Luke 13. 14. & 14. 3. John 9. 16.

Mark, repeating the same history, saith, chap. iii. 1, 2, *There was a man which had a withered hand, and they watched him, whether he would heal him on the sabbath day, that they might accuse him.* So saith Luke, chap. vi. 6, 7, only he addeth that it was his *right hand*, which made his affliction greater. They asked him not that they might rightly inform themselves, but *that they might accuse him* to their magistrates, that had power in those cases, for the violation of the sabbath was, amongst the Jews, a capital crime.

11 And he said unto them, What man shall there be among you, that shall have one sheep, and ᵏ if it fall into a pit on the sabbath day, will he not lay hold on it, and lift *it* out?

k See Ex. 23. 4, 5.
Deut. 22. 4.

12 How much then is a man better than a sheep? Wherefore it is lawful to do well on the sabbath days.

Mark saith, chap. iii. 3—5, *And he saith unto the man which had the withered hand, Stand forth. And he saith unto them, Is it lawful to do good on the sabbath days, or to do evil? to save life, or to kill? But they held their peace.* Luke reports it thus, chap. vi. 8, 9, *But he knew their thoughts, and said to the man which had the withered hand, Rise up, and stand forth in the midst. And he arose and stood forth. Then said Jesus unto them, I will ask you one thing; Is it lawful on the sabbath days to do good, or to do evil? to save life, or to destroy it?* Christ knew their thoughts; he needed not that any man should tell him what was in the heart of men; he knew their design in coming, and propounding this question. He calls this man with the withered hand to stand forth, that all men might see, and take notice of him. Then he argueth the case with the Pharisees, telling them, that they themselves would grant, that if a man had a sheep fallen into a pit on the sabbath day, they might labour so far as to take it out; so, it seemeth, in Christ's time they did expound the law. They also knew that the life or good of a man was to be preferred before the life of a beast. In their reproving him, therefore, they condemned themselves in a thing which they allowed. Then he propounds a question to them, which Matthew hath not, but it is mentioned both by Mark and Luke. He asketh them whether it was *lawful on the sabbath days to do good, or to do evil? to save life, or to destroy it?* The argument is this, Whatsoever is good to save the life of man may be done on the sabbath day; but this is a good action; if I should not lend him my help when it is in my power, I should, in the sense of God's law, kill him.

13 Then saith he to the man, Stretch forth thine hand. And he stretched *it* forth; and it was restored whole, like as the other.

Mark saith, *they held their peace,* they made him no answer to his question, upon which he, looking round about him *with anger, being grieved for the hardness of their hearts, saith unto the man, Stretch forth thine hand.* Luke saith, *Looking round about upon them all, he said,* &c. Our Saviour looked about him to see if any of them would adventure to answer him, but he saw their mouths were shut. He was angry that these great doctors of the law should understand the law of God no better, and should yet be so hardy as to take upon them to instruct him. He was also grieved (saith Mark) at *the hardness of their hearts.* That which we call hardness, is a quality in a thing which resisteth the truth, a non-impressiveness, when a thing will receive no impression from things apt to make impressions: the hardness of the Pharisees' hearts lay in this, that whereas Christ's words and works might reasonably and ought to have made an impression upon them of faith, that they should have owned and received him as the Messiah, yet they had no such effect, nor made any such impressions upon them. He said to the man, *Stretch forth thine hand. And he stretched it forth,* &c. Christ sometimes used the ceremony of laying on his hand; here he doth not, to let us know that that was but a sign of what was done by his power. What little things malicious men will carp at! What was here of servile labour on the sabbath day? They did far more themselves, as often as they lifted a beast out of a pit. Our Saviour compounds or prepareth no medicaments, he only speaks the word, and he is healed. But Matthew tells us that

14 ¶ Then ¹the Pharisees went out, and ‖ held a council against him, how they might destroy him.

l ch. 27. 1.
Mark 3. 6.
Luke 6. 11.
John 5. 18.
& 10. 39. &
11. 53. ‖ Or, took counsel.

Luke saith, *they were filled with madness, and communed one with another what they might do to Jesus.* Mark saith, *they straightway took counsel with the Herodians against him, how they might destroy him.* What cause of their madness was here offered? A poor lame man was miraculously healed. They certainly were mad to see themselves confuted, who would not acknowledge him to be the Messiah, or to hear themselves nonplussed, or to find themselves contradicted (a thing proud men cannot bear). They take counsel with the Herodians (of whom we shall have occasion to say more when we come to chap. xxii.): all agree them and the Pharisees to have been steady enemies one to another, but Herod and Pilate can agree when Christ is to be crucified.

15 But when Jesus knew *it,* ᵐ he withdrew himself from thence: ⁿ and great multitudes followed him, and he healed them all;

m See ch.10. 23. Mark 3. 7.
n ch. 19. 2.

16 And ᵒ charged them that they should not make him known:

o ch. 9. 30.

Here is nothing in these two verses but what we have before met with: the multitudes have followed Christ in all his motions, from his first beginning to preach and to work his miraculous operations. *He healed them all,* must be understood of those that were sick. The charge he gives is the same which we have often met with, of which no satisfactory account can be given, further than that, knowing his time was not yet come, and he had much work to do before his death, he useth all prudent means to preserve his life, reserving himself for the further work which his Father left him to do. The publishing of his miracles would have made a great noise, and possibly have more enraged the Pharisees against him; neither did he seek his own glory, but the glory of him that sent him.

17 That it might be fulfilled which was spoken by Esaias the prophet, saying,

Christ did this, that is, he withdrew himself when he heard what counsels the Pharisees and Herodians had taken, he charged those whom he had cured that they should not publish it abroad, he did those good acts before spoken of, *That it might be fulfilled which was spoken by the prophet;* that he might show himself to be the very person whom the

S. MATTHEW XII

prophet Isaiah long since did foretell, Isa. xlii. 1—4. The words in the prophet are thus: *Behold my servant, whom I uphold; mine elect, in whom my soul delighteth; I have put my Spirit upon him: he shall bring forth judgment to the Gentiles. He shall not cry, nor lift up, nor cause his voice to be heard in the street. A bruised reed shall he not break, and the smoking flax shall he not quench: he shall bring forth judgment unto truth. He shall not fail nor be discouraged, till he have set judgment in the earth: and the isles shall wait for his law.* Thus far that prophet; let us now consider his words, or prophecy, as repeated by the evangelist.

p Is. 42. 1.
q ch. 3. 17. & 17. 5.

18 P Behold my servant, whom I have chosen; my beloved, q in whom my soul is well pleased: I will put my spirit upon him, and he shall shew judgment to the Gentiles.

The alteration is very little, and we must not expect to meet with quotations out of the Old Testament verbatim: it is enough that the sense is the same. *Behold my servant, whom I have chosen.* The word indifferently signifieth a child or a servant, Christ is called the Lord's servant, because he *took upon him the form of a servant, and became obedient even to death,* Phil. ii. 7, 8. *Whom I have chosen; my beloved, in whom my soul is well pleased:* in Isaiah it is, *whom I uphold; mine elect, in whom my soul delighteth.* Matthew seems to have left out *whom I uphold,* and to have taken the next words, *mine elect,* and to have translated them, *whom I have chosen,* which was all said by the prophet. God chose the Lord Jesus Christ to be our Redeemer, and the Head of the elect; hence we are said to be *chosen in him,* Eph. i. 4. Peter saith he was *foreordained,* 1 Pet. i. 20; and ii. 6, he is called *a chief Cornerstone, elect. My beloved, in whom my soul is well pleased:* in Isaiah it is, *in whom my soul delighteth:* the sense is the same. *He shall bring forth judgment to the Gentiles,* or to the nations. The words משפט, in the Hebrew, κρίσις in the Greek, and *judgment* in the English, are all so variously used, as gives interpreters a great latitude to abound in their senses. The most probable to me is this: *Judgment* signifies a thing adjudged: all judgment is either of approbation or condemnation. *He shall bring forth,* or he shall show, the things which God approveth and judgeth right, both in matters of doctrine, worship, and the government of the church of God, and in matters which concern the government of men's lives and conversations: and to this end God promiseth to put his Spirit upon him, so Isa. xi. 2; lxi. 1; and John tells us it was not given him by measure, chap. iii. 34, which is the same with being *anointed with the oil of gladness above* his *fellows,* Psal. xlv. 7, which the apostle applieth to Christ, Heb. i. 9.

19 He shall not strive, nor cry; neither shall any man hear his voice in the streets.

These words declare the meekness, and gentleness, and modesty of our blessed Saviour. His meekness, that he should not do his work in any passion or roughness, nor carry on his kingdom with any strife or violence. Therefore when the Pharisees took counsel against him, he made no opposition, but peaceably withdrew, until the time came when he was to be delivered; and then he as meekly yielded up himself, rebuking Peter for but drawing a sword for him, and healing his ear which he had wounded. His not crying, nor lifting up his voice, or suffering his voice to be heard in the streets, might either signify his meekness, not crying out to stir up any sedition; or not setting a trumpet to his mouth, when he had wrought a miracle, that people might take notice of it; instead of it he charged the persons healed not to publish it.

20 A bruised reed shall he not break, and smoking flax shall he not quench, till he send forth judgment unto victory.

He shall carry on his work with so little noise, that if he trod upon a bruised reed he should not break it. Or, he shall not despise the afflicted, that are as bruised reeds and smoking flax. But the best expositors interpret it of Christ's kindness to people's souls; he will not discourage those that are weak in faith, or weak in hope. *Smoking flax* signifieth flax in the kindling of which the fire had not pre-

vailed, and so is a very apt metaphor to express such as believe, but are full of doubts and fears, or such as have a truth of grace, but yet much corruption; Christ is prophesied of as one that will encourage, not discourage, such souls. *Until he hath brought forth judgment unto victory;* Isaiah saith, *unto truth.* Some think that *until* here only signifies the event of the thing, not a term of time, for there shall never be a time when Christ shall break a bruised reed, or quench a smoking flax, in the sense before mentioned. By *judgment* here may be meant, as before, what his Father hath judged right, until he hath caused the doctrine of the gospel, and the Messiah, to be believed and embraced of all the world. Or, until he shall have brought forth the judgment of those broken reeds and that smoking flax unto victory, until such souls be made perfect in faith and holiness, and shall have got a victory over all its unbelief and other corruptions. Or, until he hath brought forth condemnation unto victory, (for so the word signifieth,) till he hath conquered death and hell, so as there shall be no condemnation to any soul that is in Christ Jesus, Rom. viii. 1. Or, until the last judgment comes, which shall determine in a perfect absolution and acquittal of all his people, and in a perfect victory over all his enemies.

21 And in his name shall the Gentiles trust.

This makes some think, that the bringing of judgment unto victory referreth to the final destruction of the Jews by the Romans, after which the Gentiles came more universally to receive the gospel. Though Christ be meek and gentle with men a long time, while there is any hope of their reformation, yet he will not be so meek and patient always. Neither was he so with the Jews. But the falling of them proved the rising of the Gentiles. Christ is beholden to no people for bearing the name of his church; if the Jews fail in their duty, they shall be cast off, and *in his name shall the Gentiles trust.* God is able of stones to raise up children unto Abraham. Isaiah saith, *the isles shall wait for his law;* his law, both of faith and holiness, shall be acceptable to the Gentiles. The term *law* here seemeth to expound that phrase, ver. 18, *he shall show judgment to the Gentiles,* that is, right things, he shall give them his law.

22 ¶ r Then was brought unto him one possessed with a devil, blind, and dumb: and he healed him, insomuch that the blind and dumb both spake and saw.

r See ch. 9. 32. Mark 3. 11. Luke 11. 14.

Some think this person was the same mentioned Luke xi. 14, I presume, because the following discourse there is much the same with what followeth here; but others are of another mind; and it is certain Luke speaketh of no blindness in him. We heard before a discourse of such as were possessed by devils, so as this verse affords nothing new.

23 And all the people were amazed, and said, Is not this the Son of David?

This is the first conviction we meet with, from the miracles wrought by our Saviour, that he was the Messiah, unless that of the two blind men, mentioned chap. ix. 27; and their faith in it appears but weak, for they do not plainly affirm it, only ask the question, like the faith of those mentioned John vii. 31, *When Christ cometh, will he do more miracles than these which this man hath done?*

24 s But when the Pharisees heard *it,* they said, This *fellow* doth not cast out devils, but by † Beelzebub the prince of the devils.

s ch. 9. 34. Mark 3. 22. Luke 11. 15.
† Gr. Beelzebul: and so ver. 27.

We met with the same blasphemous calumny from the same persons, chap. ix. 34. The Pharisees, not acknowledging the Deity of Christ, nor that he was the Messiah, were for their interest concerned not to acknowledge, and as much as in them lay to keep others from believing, that he did that from his own power which God alone could do. But yet they might have allowed him to have by a power derived from God done these miraculous things, as Elijah and Elisha of old did. But they blaspheme at the highest rate imaginable, ascribing that to the devil which was proper to God alone. Christ's miracles were exceeding many, and it was a time when the Messiah was expected. The sceptre was departed from Judah, and, as it appears from John vii. 31, (whatever the Jews now say impudently,) they heard that when the Messiah did come he should work many miracles. These things put them into a rage. This remarkable piece of history is recorded by three evangelists: by Matthew in this place; by Mark, chap. iii. 22—30; and by Luke, chap. xi. 15—20.

t ch. 9. 4.
John 2. 25.
Rev. 2. 23.

25 And Jesus ᵗknew their thoughts, and said unto them, Every kingdom divided against itself is brought to desolation; and every city or house divided against itself shall not stand:

26 And if Satan cast out Satan, he is divided against himself; how shall then his kingdom stand?

This is our Lord's first argument. Mark relates it, chap. iii. 23—26, with little alteration in the phrase; so doth Luke, chap. xi. 17, 18. The sum of the argument is, The devil is so wise, that he will look to the upholding of his own kingdom in the world. This will require an agreement of the devils amongst themselves, for if they be divided they cannot uphold their kingdom, nor stand, any more than a house, city, or kingdom in the world so divided can stand; therefore the prince of devils will not forcibly cast out the inferior devils. There is but one imaginable objection to this: Do we not see the contrary to this in people's going to cunning men for help against those that are bewitched, to get help for them? and is there no truth in those many stories we have of persons that have found help against the devil for some that have traded with the devil? I answer, It is one thing for the devils to play one with another, another thing for them to cast out one another. One devil may yield and give place to another, to gain a greater advantage for the whole society, but one never quarrelleth with another. The first may be for the enlarging of Satan's kingdom. This must be to destroy it. When a poor wretched creature goeth to one who dealeth with the devil for help for one who is vexed with some effect of the devil, one devil here doth but yield and give place to another by compact, voluntarily, and for the devil's greater advantage; for it is more advantage to the devil (who seeks nothing so much as a divine homage) to gain the faith of one soul, than to exercise a power to afflict many bodies. In such cases as these, the devil, for the abatement of a little bodily pain, gains a power over the soul of him or her who cometh to implore his help, and exerciseth a faith in him. This is an establishing, promoting, and enlarging his kingdom. But Christ forced the devils out of persons; they did not yield voluntarily, for a greater advantage, but forcibly, for no advantage. He did not pray the devils to come out, nor make use of any of the devil's sacraments, upon the use of which, by some original compact, he was obliged to come out upon a soul's surrender of itself by faith to him; but they came out unwillingly, upon the authoritative words of Christ, without the use of any magical rites and ceremonies testifying the least homage done to him.

27 And if I by Beelzebub cast out devils, by whom do your children cast *them* out? therefore they shall be your judges.

Our Saviour's argument is this, Where the case is the same the judgment ought to be the same, and the contrary judgment speaketh malice, and hatred of the person. Do I cast out devils? so do your children. You say they do it by the power of God; why do you say that I do it by a prince of devils? What appeareth in their casting of them out more than in mine, which can argue that they do it by the power of God, and I by the power of the prince of devils? The only question is who our Saviour here meaneth by their *children*. Some think that he meaneth his own apostles, who were all of them Jews, and to whom they might be more favourable than to him, because of their relation to them. Others think that he means some exorcists amongst the Jews; such they had, Acts xix. 13. But concerning these there is a double opinion. Some think that they were such as themselves, acted by compact of the devil. Others think that they invocating the God of Abraham, Isaac, and Jacob, God might honour them so far, as upon that invocation to command the devil out of persons. Origen and Justin Martyr both tell us, that there were some that used that form with such success. But so they might do, and yet not obtain their effect from a Divine influence, nor so much cast as flatter out devils, upon a homage first paid to the devil. I find some difficulty to persuade myself that in those times, especially when God by this miraculous effect was demonstrating the Messias, God should so far concur with any but him, and those that did it by his express name and authority; and I observe, that when the seven sons of Sceva attempted such a thing, Acts xix. 13, they called *over them which had evil spirits the name of the Lord Jesus, saying, We adjure you by Jesus, whom Paul preacheth*, (which they, being the sons of the chief of the priests, would not have done if the more grateful form of, The God of Abraham, Isaac, and Jacob, would have done it,) yet could they not prevail, as you read there, ver. 14—16. Our Saviour's meaning therefore must certainly be either, 1. You do not say so of your children, my apostles, who do, and profess to do, what they do by a power derived from me; why do you say this of me, not of them? Or, 2. There are some of you who seem to cast out devils, whenas the devil only plays with them, and yields to their magical arts for his own advantage, and abates some more external effects on people's bodies, upon the surrender of their souls to him, by believing he is able to cure them, and imploring his help; yet you think these men endowed with the power of God: why are you so unequal to me? I observe, though we read of exorcists amongst the Jews, Acts xix. 13, yet they are called περιερχόμενοι, vagrants. They were an idle, vagabond sort of persons, (such probably as we call gipsies,) with whom, or by whom, it is not probable God would work such effects, especially at such a time, though they used the names of Abraham, Isaac, and Jacob. Nay, it is plain from the story of the Acts, that though they used the name Jesus, God would not work by them; ver. 16, the demoniac *leaped on them, overcame them, prevailed against them, so that they fled out of that house naked and wounded*.

28 But if I cast out devils by the Spirit of God, then ᵘ the kingdom of God is come unto you.

u Dan. 2. 44.
& 7. 14. Luke
1. 33. & 11.
20. & 17. 20,
21.

Luke hath the same, chap. xi. 20, only for *the Spirit of God* he hath *the finger of God*. By *the kingdom of God* he here meaneth the coming of the Messiah, which is so called, Dan. ii. 44. The time is come, when the Lord begins his kingdom of grace, setting up his King upon his *holy hill of Zion*, Psal. ii. 6; whence we may observe, that Christ giveth in his casting out of devils by a Divine power, as an argument to prove himself the Messiah; for saith he, By this you may know the kingdom of God is come amongst you, that there is one come among you who by the finger, power, or Spirit of God casts out devils. But where had the force of this argument been, if the Jews had had exorcists whom God had so honoured, though vagabonds, as to cast out devils, upon their calling upon the God of Abraham, Isaac, and Jacob, while in the mean time they derided and contemned Christ?

29 ˣOr else how can one enter into a strong man's house, and spoil his goods, except he first bind the strong man? and then he will spoil his house.

x Is. 49. 24.
Luke 11. 21,
22, 23.

Mark hath the same words, with little variation, chap. iii. 27; Luke saith, chap. xi. 21, 22, *When a strong man armed keepeth his palace, his goods are in peace: but when a stronger than he shall come upon him and overcome him, he taketh from him all his armour wherein he trusted, and divideth his spoil*. The sense is the same, though the words be multiplied. Our Saviour showeth how his casting out of devils by the Spirit and power of God argued that the Messiah was come, and the time come when God would set up his kingdom amongst men. The devil, (saith he,) who is the god of the world, and the prince of the power of the air, is very strong; there is none, save God only, who is stronger than he. If I were not God, I could never cast out this strong man, who reigns in the world as in his house; as you see amongst men, the strong man is not overcome but by one stronger. He by this also lets them know, that he was so far from any covenant or compact with Beelzebub, that he came into the world a professed enemy to him, to dispossess him of that tyrannical power he exercised amongst men, by his keeping them in darkness, blinding them with error and superstition, and seducing them to sinful practices, till God, for their prodigious sins, had also given him a power over their bodies, variously to vex, afflict, and torment them. Christ took from this strong man all his armour: by scattering the darkness which was in the world by the full revelation of gospel truth: by expelling error and superstition, teaching people the truths of God, and the right way of his worship: by taking away the guilt, and destroying the power of sin and death, ignorance, error, profaneness; the sense of the guilt of sin, and the power of lusts within us, being the devil's armour, by which he kept up his power, and doth yet keep up what dominion he hath in the world.

30 He that is not with me is against me; and he that gathereth not with me scattereth abroad.

Luke hath the same, chap. xi. 23. Some understand this concerning the devil, whom he was so far from favouring, that his work was quite opposite. Some understand it concerning some neuters, that would neither show themselves for Christ nor against him. Our Saviour tells them, that this cause would bear no neutrality, they must be either for him or against him. But possibly it is best understood concerning the scribes and Pharisees, whom he lets know, that he was one who showed men the true way of life and salvation, and those that complied not with him were his enemies, and instead of gathering, scattered the sheep of God.

y Mark 3. 28.
Luke 12. 10.
Heb. 6. 4,
&c. & 10. 26,
29. 1 John
5 16.
z Acts 7. 51.

31 ¶ Wherefore I say unto you, ^yAll manner of sin and blasphemy shall be forgiven unto men: ^zbut the blasphemy *against* the *Holy* Ghost shall not be forgiven unto men.

a ch 11. 19.
& 13. 55.
John 7. 12,
52.
b 1 Tim. 1.
13.

32 And whosoever ^aspeaketh a word against the Son of man, ^b it shall be forgiven him: but whosoever speaketh against the Holy Ghost, it shall not be forgiven him, neither in this world, neither in the *world* to come.

Mark repeateth the same, chap. iii. 28, 29, with no alteration as to the sense, and instead of *neither in this world, neither in the world to come,* he saith, *but is in danger of eternal damnation.* Luke hath something of it, chap. xii. 10, *And whosoever shall speak a word against the Son of man, it shall be forgiven him: but unto him that blasphemeth against the Holy Ghost it shall not be forgiven.* It is a text hath very much exercised great divines, and much more perplexed poor Christians in their fits of melancholy and under temptations. There is in it something asserted, that is, that *all manner of sin and blasphemy shall be forgiven,* ver. 32. *Whosoever speaketh a word against the Son of man, it shall be forgiven;* that is, upon the terms other sins are forgiven, repentance and faith in Jesus Christ. By *the Son of man* here some would understand any ordinary man; but, 1. Christ never spake of any under the notion but himself. 2. It had been no great news for Christ to have told them, that ordinary evil-speaking against men should be forgiven. Doubtless by *the Son of man* here Christ meaneth himself. He declareth that sins of ignorance should be forgiven; though a man should blaspheme Christ, yet if he did it ignorantly, verily thinking he was no more than the son of man, it should, upon his repentance and faith in him, be forgiven: a text yielding exceeding great relief to souls labouring under the burden of their sins, and reflecting upon their aggravation. But the difficulty lieth in the latter part of the text, which denieth forgiveness to any who blaspheme the Holy Ghost. Upon this arise several questions. First, What the sin against the Holy Ghost here specified was. *Answ.* It is not hard to gather this from the context, and what Mark addeth, chap. iii. 30, *Because they said, He hath an unclean spirit.* Christ was come amongst these persons to whom he speaketh; he had not only preached, but he had wrought many miraculous operations sufficient to convince them that he acted by the power and Spirit of God. They were not only convinced of it, so far as to acknowledge it, but they attributed these operations to the devil, and said he had a devil, and that he did what he did by the power of the devil. This,

out of doubt, was their sin against the Holy Ghost, maliciously speaking to the highest reproach of the Holy Spirit, contrary to the rational conviction of their own consciences. Hence ariseth a second question, Whether any such sin can be now committed. *Answ.* If there were no other texts that seem to conclude, there may be such as those, Heb. vi. 4—6; x. 26, 27; 1 John v. 16, where he speaketh of *a sin unto death,* for the forgiveness of which he would not have Christians pray. I should conclude that there is no such sin now to be committed, for we cannot have such means of conviction as the Pharisees had, Christ not being on the earth now working miracles; but it is plain from the texts before mentioned, that there is such a sin, that men and women may yet incur the guilt of. But now what that sin is hath exercised the judgment of the greatest divines to describe. I shall not repeat the various opinions about it, many of which are easily confuted; but shall determine from the guidance of the scriptures that mention it, so far as they will direct in the finding of it out. 1. It cannot be any sin that is committed ignorantly. Paul was a blasphemer, but forgiven, because he did it ignorantly. 2. It must be a sin knowingly committed against the operations of the Holy Ghost. So was this sin of the Pharisees. 3. Apostacy must be an ingredient in it: *If they fall away,* saith the apostle, Heb. vi. 6. It is a sinning wilfully after the receiving the knowledge of the truth, Heb. x. 26. 4. It should seem by this text persecution is an ingredient in it: the Pharisees did not only say this, but they spake it out of malice, designing to destroy Christ. 5. Most certain it is, that though impenitency cannot be called that sin, yet it must be an ingredient in it, for what sins we truly repent of shall be forgiven, 1 John i. 9; and therefore the apostle saith of such sinners, It is impossible they should be renewed by repentance. Upon the whole then, if any person hath been instructed in the things of God, and hath made a profession of religion and godliness, and afterwards falleth off from his profession, and becomes a bitter enemy to it; saying that those things are the effects of the devil in men, which his heart telleth him are the operations of the Holy Spirit, and be so hardy as to persecute and seek to destroy such persons for such profession: the interpretation be to those that hate us, and to the enemies of our God: if they have not committed this unpardonable sin, they have done what is very like it; and I know no way they have, but by a timely and hearty repentance to satisfy the world, or their own consciences, that they are not under this dreadful guilt. And that which confirms me in this opinion is, that we rarely hear of such persons renewed by repentance (if any instances of that nature at all can be produced). I know some have thought that this sin might be committed by words, without other overt acts, and indeed blaspheming (properly taken) can signify nothing else but evil or reproachful speaking. But these words must proceed from a malicious heart, full of rancour and revenge; for it is not every word, nor every blasphemy, that is here meant, it is (as Augustine saith) *quoddam dictum, quædam blasphemia,* a certain word, a certain blasphemy; not words spoken ignorantly or hastily, or according to our real judgment and opinion; but words spoken maliciously, in order to destroy God or Christ, if it were possible, after sufficient means of light and conviction, that the things which we speak evil of are not from the evil, but, probably at least, from the Holy Spirit of God, and yet we will impute them to the devil, in order to the defaming or destruction of those servants of God who do them, or in whom they are found. We can define nothing certain in the case, but this cometh nearest to the sin here mentioned, that shall never be forgiven in this world, or the world to come; that is, as Mark expounds it, the persons guilty shall be in danger of eternal damnation, by which he hath spoiled the papists' argument from this text for their purgatory.

33 Either make the tree good, and ^chis fruit good; or else make the tree corrupt, and his fruit corrupt: for the tree is known by *his* fruit.

c ch. 7. 17.
Luke 6. 43,
44.

We met with much the same chap. vii. 16. The words here spoken may be understood to have reference to the devil, to the scribes and Pharisees, or to Christ himself. 1. You say I do these things by the devil: you cannot but say the things I do are good; the fruit followeth the nature of the tree: the devil is evil, a corrupt tree, how can he produce good fruit? Or thus, 2. You show yourselves to be corrupt trees by the fruit you bring forth; you indeed are not lewd and profane, but put on a mask and vizard of godliness, but your fruit showeth what you are. Or, 3. If the fruit which I produce be good, why should not you judge me good? Speak things that are consistent; if the fruit be good, the tree must be good; convince me of any evil things that I do, from whence you can rationally conclude that I am a corrupt tree.

d ch. 3. 7.
& 23. 33.
e Luke 6. 45.

34 O ^dgeneration of vipers, how can ye, being evil, speak good things? ^efor out of the abundance of the heart the mouth speaketh.

35 A good man out of the good treasure of the heart bringeth forth good things: and an evil man out of the evil treasure bringeth forth evil things.

The evangelist Luke, chap. vi. 45, hath much the same with what is here. *O generation of vipers:* John had so called them, and Christ again so calleth them, Matt. xxiii. 33. A viper is of all other the most venomous and dangerous serpent. Christ, in calling them a *generation of vipers*, intimateth, that the Pharisees were generally a most mischievous faction for the souls of men. *How can ye, being evil, speak good things?* Why do I (saith he) spend my time and breath in reproving or admonishing you? you have cankered hearts, full of pride, malice, and envy, and therefore cannot ordinarily speak good things. *For out of the abundance of the heart the mouth speaketh:* what men ordinarily and deliberately do speak is from the affections and thoughts of their hearts. Hence good men out of the good treasure of their hearts speak good things, that is, most ordinarily and commonly; and evil men out of the stock of malice, revenge, envy, pride, and other lusts, which are in their hearts, speak evil things.

36 But I say unto you, That every idle word that men shall speak, they shall give account thereof in the day of judgment.

37 For by thy words thou shalt be justified, and by thy words thou shalt be condemned.

Some understand by *idle words* here, lying and deceitful words; others, contumelious and reproachful words. But the best interpreters here extend the sense further, not only from the sense of the word ἀργόν, here used, but because they judge our Saviour is here arguing from the less to the greater, convincing the Pharisees what a dreadful account they had to give for their blasphemous and reproachful words, when all must give an account even for those words which they speak to no good purpose, but vainly, without respect either to the glory of God, or the good of others, or their own necessary and lawful occasions. Hence the apostle doth not only forbid *filthiness, foolish talking,* and *jesting,* Eph. v. 4, and *corrupt communication*, Eph. iv. 29, but in the same verse commandeth that Christians' speech should be *to the use of edifying, that it may minister grace to the hearers;* and to the Colossians, chap. iv. 6, *Let your speech be alway with grace, seasoned with salt.* Nor will this seem too strict to those who consider, that any thing is abused when it is not used to the right end and use. God hath not given unto man his faculty of speech to fill the world with idle tattle and impertinent discourse, but that by it, 1. We might bless God, by prayers and praises, talking of his words and wondrous works. 2. That we might communicate our minds to men, in their or our own concerns, and so be mutually helpful one to another. *For by thy words thou shalt be justified, &c.:* what justified here signifies, appears by the word *condemned*, to which it is opposed. God will pronounce sentence for or against men in the last day, not only according to their other actions, but accordingly as they have used their tongues. If there were no other text in the Bible to prove that we have need of another righteousness, than any of our own, wherein to stand before God, this text alone would be enough, for *if a man offend not in word, the same is a perfect man*, James iii. 2.

f ch. 16. 1.
Mark 8. 11.

38 ¶ ^fThen certain of the Scribes and of the Pharisees answered, saying, Master, we would see a sign from thee.

Luke 11. 16, 29. John 2. 18. 1 Cor. 1. 22.

We read the like to this chap. xvi. 1, and Luke seemeth to relate the same history, chap. xi. 29. *Master* was the usual title which they gave to any whom they owned as a teacher. By *a sign* they mean something that might confirm unto them that he was sent of God; they expected that an extraordinary mission should be so confirmed: so John vi. 33, *What sign showest thou then, that we might see and believe thee? what dost thou work?* Moses showed them signs, (as they there go on,) he brought down for them *bread from heaven.* Had not Christ showed them signs enough? what were all the miracles he had wrought in their sight? They either speak this out of a further idle curiosity, (their eye being not satisfied with seeing,) or else they speak it in direct opposition to the whole scope and tendency of our Saviour's former discourse, which was from his miracles to prove himself truly God, and sent of God: if the latter, which seemeth from our Saviour's sharp answer most probable, the sum of what they say is this, Master, we have seen thee do wonderful works, but no other than what impostors may do by the assistance of the devil; we would see something done by thee which magicians cannot do, such as Moses did, Exod. viii. 19, when the magicians confessed they were outdone, and cried, *This is the finger of God.*

39 But he answered and said unto them, An evil and ^gadulterous generation seeketh after a sign; and there shall no sign be given to it, but the sign of the prophet Jonas:

g Is. 57. 3.
ch. 16. 4
Mark 8. 38.
John 4. 48.

40 ^hFor as Jonas was three days and three nights in the whale's belly; so shall the Son of man be three days and three nights in the heart of the earth.

h Jonah 1. 17.

An evil and adulterous generation; either called adulterous for that specifical sin, which reigned amongst them, and indeed their polygamy was hardly better; or else because of their degeneracy from Abraham, whom they so much gloried in as their father, John viii. 39, 44. *Seeketh after a sign;* not satisfied with my miracles which I do on earth, they would have a sign from heaven. God was not difficult of confirming and encouraging people's faith by signs; he gave Gideon a sign upon his asking, he gave Hezekiah and proffered Ahaz a sign without asking; but he had already given the Pharisees signs enough, and sufficient to convince them, but they would not believe, but out of curiosity would have a sign of another kind, *a sign from heaven*, as Mark expoundeth it, chap. viii. 11, such a sign as the devil could not counterfeit. *There shall no sign be given to it;* no sign of that nature, for we shall find that after this Christ wrought many miracles. But they shall have a sign when I shall be risen again from the dead, to their confusion and condemnation; when I shall answer the prophet Jonah's type of me. He was cast into the sea, and was three days and three nights in the belly of the whale, in the heart of the sea, Jonah i. 17, and then the whale *vomited* him *out upon the dry land*, chap. ii. 10. So I shall be by them violently put to death, and shall be in the grave part of three days and three nights, and then I shall rise again from the dead. But here ariseth a difficulty. Christ indeed dying the day before the Jewish sabbath, and rising the morning after, might be said to be in the grave three days, because he was there part of three days; but how can he be said to have been there three nights? for he was only in the grave the night of the Jewish sabbath, (for their sabbath began at the evening before,) and the night following, which were but two nights, either in whole or in part. *Answ.* What we call day and night made up the Jewish νυχθήμερον. It appears by Gen. i. 5, that *the evening and morning* made up *a day*. Three days and three nights is with us but the same thing with three natural days, and so it must be understood here. Christ was in the grave three natural days, that is, part of three natural days; every one of which days contained a day and a night, viz. twenty-four hours.

41 ⁱThe men of Nineveh shall rise in judgment with this generation, and ^kshall

i Luke 11. 32.
k See Jer. 3. 11. Ezek. 16. 51, 52.
Rom. 2. 27.

1 Jonah 3. 5. condemn it: ¹because they repented at the preaching of Jonas; and, behold, a greater than Jonas *is* here.

The story of the men of Nineveh we have in Jonah, chap. iii. Luke repeateth the same passage, chap. xi. 32. *The men of Nineveh shall rise in judgment*, that is, shall at the general resurrection rise, and stand up in judgment as witnesses against the scribes and Pharisees, and the other unbelieving Jews of this age, and shall be instruments as to that condemnation which God shall that day pronounce against them. Why? *Because they repented at the preaching of Jonas; and, behold, a greater than Jonas is here.* Jonas was a stranger to them, he wrought no miracles amongst them to confirm that he was sent of God, he only came and cried, *Yet forty days, and Nineveh shall be destroyed;* yet they repented, if not truly and sincerely, yet in appearance; they showed themselves to be affected with what Jonah said, his words made some impressions upon them, as that *the king arose from his throne, laid his robe from him, covered him with sackcloth, and sat in ashes,* called a fast, as Jonah iii. 5—8 But, saith our Saviour, I am greater than Jonah: I was long since prophesied of, and foretold to this people, to come; I am come; I have preached amongst them, and not only preached, but wrought many wonderful works amongst them, yet they are not so much affected as to show the least signs of repentance.

m 1 Kin. 10. 1. 2 Chron. 9. 1. Luke 11. 31.

42 ᵐThe queen of the south shall rise up in the judgment with this generation, and shall condemn it: for she came from the uttermost parts of the earth to hear the wisdom of Solomon; and, behold, a greater than Solomon *is* here.

We have the history to which this relateth 1 Kings x. 1, &c. She is here called *the queen of the south;* in the Book of Kings, and 2 Chron. ix. 1, *the queen of Sheba.* Whether this Sheba, or Saba, was in Arabia or Ethiopia, is not much material; certain it is, it was southward of Judea, and a place at a great distance. Yet, saith our Saviour, though she was a great queen, though she lived at so great a distance from Jerusalem, though she had only heard of the fame and wisdom of Solomon; yet she came in person to hear his wise discourses, either about things natural or supernatural. These wretched Jews are not put to it to take a journey, I am come amongst them, I who am greater than Solomon, who am the Eternal Wisdom, and come to discourse of heavenly wisdom to them; I am come to their doors. theirs to whom the notion of a Messiah is no new thing, they have heard of me; they are no heathens, but bred up to the knowledge of God. I have done many miracles before them, yet they will not hear nor believe me. The queen of Sheba in the day of judgment shall rise up as a witness against them, when God shall condemn them for their unbelief. The more light, and means, and obligations men have upon them to faith and holiness, the greater will their judgment and condemnation be.

n Luke 11. 24. o Job 1. 7. 1 Pet. 5. 8.

43 ⁿWhen the unclean spirit is gone out of a man, ᵒhe walketh through dry places, seeking rest, and findeth none.

44 Then he saith, I will return into my house from whence I came out; and when he is come, he findeth *it* empty, swept, and garnished.

45 Then goeth he, and taketh with himself seven other spirits more wicked than the first, and they enter in and dwell

p Heb. 6. 4. & 10. 26. 2 Pet. 2. 20, 21, 22.

there: ᵖand the last *state* of that man is worse than the first. Even so shall it be also unto this wicked generation.

The speech appeareth parabolical, the persons concerned in it are expressed in the last words, the men of that *wicked generation.* The text is thought to be well expounded by Peter, 2 Pet. ii. 20, *If after they have escaped the pollutions of the world through the knowledge of the Lord and Saviour Jesus Christ, they are again entangled therein, and overcome, the latter end is worse with them than the beginning.* Our Lord here compareth the Jews to a man out of whom the unclean spirit was gone. The devil is called *the unclean spirit*, both in regard of his own impure nature, and because his work is to tempt men to sin, which is spiritual filthiness. The Jews were a people holy to the Lord, a people distinguished from pagans by a visible profession; so as the devil in a great measure had left them. Now, saith he, the devil is an unquiet spirit, and findeth no rest if he cannot be doing mischief to men. For the phrase, *he walketh through dry places, seeking rest*, we must know, that in parabolical speeches we must not make a severe scrutiny upon every phrase. Dry places are for the most part places least inhabited, for want of the conveniencies of water. The devil cannot be at rest where he hath no mischief to do to men. *Then he saith, I will return into my house from whence I came out:* the devil so leaveth none, but he will be attempting to come into them again; and he ordinarily succeedeth where Christ hath not prepossessed the soul: all other reformation proves but a sweeping and a garnishing, while the soul is empty of Christ. It may be swept from the filth of flagitious sins, and garnished with the paint of religion, or some habits of moral virtue; but none of these will keep out the devil. *Then goeth he, and taketh with himself seven other spirits more wicked than himself, and they enter in and dwell there. Seven*, that is, many. The meaning is, he makes that man much worse than before. So (saith he) it shall be to these Jews. God gave them his laws, and so delivered them from such a dominion as the devil doth exercise over pagans. In force of this law, the scribes and Pharisees amended many things, so as they were like a house swept and garnished. God sent his Son to dwell amongst them, but him they rejected; so the house was empty, though swept and garnished. The devil will come again, and they will be ten times worse.

46 ¶ While he yet talked to the people, ᑫbehold, *his* mother and ʳhis brethren stood without, desiring to speak with him.

q Mark 3.31. Luke 8. 19, 20, 21. r ch. 13. 55. Mark 6. 3. John 2. 12. & 7. 3, 5. Acts 1. 14. 1 Cor. 9. 5. Gal. 1. 19.

47 Then one said unto him, Behold, thy mother and thy brethren stand without, desiring to speak with thee.

48 But he answered and said unto him that told him, Who is my mother? and who are my brethren?

49 And he stretched forth his hand toward his disciples, and said, Behold my mother and my brethren!

50 For ˢwhosoever shall do the will of my Father which is in heaven, the same is my brother, and sister, and mother.

s See John 15. 14. Gal. 5. 6. & 6. 15. Col. 3. 11. Heb. 2. 11.

Mark repeateth the same passage, Mark iii. 31—35. Luke repeateth it more shortly, Luke viii. 20, 21. Both Mark and Luke say more than one spake to our Saviour; first one, then others. *Thy mother and thy brethren:* most interpreters think *brethren* here signifieth no more than some of his kindred, whom the Hebrews usually called brethren. By the following words of our Saviour, ver. 48 —50, we must not understand that our Saviour slighted his mother or brethren, we are elsewhere taught what honour he gave to his parents, Luke ii. 51; yet he seemeth to speak something angrily, because he was interrupted in his work: so Luke ii. 49; John ii. 3, 4. We may show a just respect to our parents, and respect to our relations, though we do not neglect our duty to God out of respect to them. The only thing to be further learned from this paragraph, is, how dear believers and holy persons are to Christ; he counts them as dear as mother, brethren, or sisters, and thereby teacheth us the esteem we ought to have for such. Luke saith, he that heareth my word, and doth it. Matthew saith, he that doth it. It is the will of God, that we should believe on him whom he hath sent: see John i. 12; vi. 40; viii. 47. This text derogates nothing from the honour truly due to the blessed virgin, as the mother of the Messias; but it shows the madness of the papists, exalting her above Christ, whom Christ, considered only as his mother, seemeth here to set beneath every true believer, though, considered as a believer also, she hath a just preference.

CHAP. XIII

The parable of the sower, 1—9. Why Christ taught in parables, 10—17. The exposition of the parable of the sower, 18—23. The parable of the tares, 24—30; of the grain of mustard seed, 31, 32; of the leaven, 33—35. The parable of the tares expounded, 36—43. The parable of the hidden treasure, 44; of one pearl of great price, 45, 46; of a net cast into the sea, 47—52. Christ's countrymen are offended in him, 53—58.

THE same day went Jesus out of the house, ^aand sat by the sea side.

2 ^bAnd great multitudes were gathered together unto him, so that ^che went into a ship, and sat; and the whole multitude stood on the shore.

3 And he spake many things unto them in parables,

a Mark 4. 1.
b Luke 8. 4.
c Luke 5. 3.

Mark saith, chap. iv. 1, *He began again to teach by the sea-side: and there was gathered unto him a great multitude, so that he entered into a ship, and sat in the sea; and the whole multitude was by the sea on the land.* Luke, chap. viii. 4, saith no more than, *when much people were gathered together, and were come to him out of every city, he spake by a parable.* Two evangelists agree that this sermon of our Saviour's was preached out of a ship, to multitudes that stood on the shore. The occasion of his going into a ship was the throng of people, both for his own and their convenience. It is here said that he *sat*; this, we observed before, was the usual gesture of the teacher amongst the Jews. This sermon is said to have been made *the same day*, which some observe in historical narrations is to be taken strictly, and lets us know the assiduity of Christ in his work. *And he spake many things unto them in parables:* the term parable often in Scripture signifies dark sayings, or proverbial speeches, Ezek. xvii. 2; xx. 49. But in the Gospels it generally hath another sense, and signifies similitudes or comparisons of things. This being the first time we have met with the term, and the first formed and perfect parable we have met with, because we shall meet with the term often hereafter, with many formed parables, I shall here give some notes which may be not only of use to understand the following parables we shall meet with in this chapter, but in the following part of the Gospel. 1. A parable, in the gospel sense of the term, signifieth a similitude, taken from the ordinary actions of men, and made use of to inform us in one or more points of spiritual doctrines. 2. That it is not necessary to a parable that the matter contained in it should be true in matter of fact; for it is not brought to inform us in a matter of fact, but in some spiritual truth, to which it bears some proportion. This we see in Jotham's parable of the trees going to choose themselves a king, &c. 3. That it is not necessary that all the actions of men mentioned in a parable should be morally just and honest. The actions of the unjust steward, Luke xvi. 1, &c., were not so. 4. That, for the right understanding of a parable, our great care must be to consider the main scope of it, whither the story tends, and what our Saviour designed principally by the parable to instruct and teach the people by that discourse. 5. That the main scope of the parable is to be learned, either from our Saviour's general or more particular explication of it, either from the *proparabola*, or preface to it, or from the *epiparabola*, or the conclusion of it. 6. It is not to be expected that all particular actions represented in a parable should be answered by something in the explication of it. 7. Lastly, Though the scope of the parable be the main thing we are to attend unto, and in which it doth instruct us, yet it may collaterally inform us in several things besides that point which is in it chiefly attended. It is said that our Saviour *spake many things* to the multitude *in parables*, covering truths under similitudes fetched from such ordinary actions as men did or might do. This was a very ancient way of instruction, by fables or parables, as we may learn by Jotham's parable, Judg. ix. 7, 8, &c. It is now much out of use with us, but amongst the Jews was very ordinary; so as our Saviour spake to them in their own dialect. It had a double advantage upon their hearers: first, upon their memory, we being very apt to remember stories. Second, upon their minds, to put them upon studying the meaning of what they heard so delivered; and also upon their affections, similitudes contributing much to excite affection. But withal it had this disadvantage, that he who so taught was not understood of a great part of his auditory.

—Saying, ^dBehold, a sower went forth to sow;   d Luke 8. 5.

4 And when he sowed, some *seeds* fell by the way side, and the fowls came and devoured them up:

5 Some fell upon stony places, where they had not much earth: and forthwith they sprung up, because they had no deepness of earth:

6 And when the sun was up, they were scorched; and because they had no root, they withered away.

7 And some fell among thorns; and the thorns sprung up, and choked them:

8 But other fell into good ground, and brought forth fruit, some ^ean hundredfold, some sixtyfold, some thirtyfold.   e Gen. 26.12.

9 ^fWho hath ears to hear, let him hear.   f ch. 11. 15. Mark 4. 9.

There is some difference in the terms used by Mark and Luke in their relations of this parable, Mark iv. 3—8, and Luke viii. 4—8; but none that are material, nor much to be considered by us, being they are in the parable. I shall when I come to it more exactly consider what differences there are betwixt the evangelists in the terms they use in the explication which our Saviour giveth us of the parable; which he did not give before the multitude, but *when he was alone,* saith Mark, chap. iv. 10. That which our Saviour spoke to the whole multitude was this. Now whether there were indeed any such sower, yea or no, is not at all material: our Saviour's design was not to inform them in a matter of fact, but of the different success of the preaching of the word; and for this purpose he brought this similitude, leaving the generality of the hearers to study out his meaning, concluding, *He that hath ears to hear, let him hear;* which is an *epiphonema,* or conclusion of a speech, we met with before, and spake something to.

10 And the disciples came, and said unto him, Why speakest thou unto them in parables?

Luke saith, chap. viii. 9, *His disciples asked him, saying, What might this parable be?* Mark saith, chap iv. 10, *When he was alone, they that were about him with the twelve asked of him the parable.* It should seem that his twelve apostles understood his meaning, but others that with them were about him when the multitude were gone did not: they therefore desire of him, 1. That they might understand the reason why he spake to the multitude in dark sayings and similitudes, without plainly opening his meaning to them. 2. They own their own dulness of understanding, and confess that they themselves were ignorant, and therefore desired him that he would tell them the meaning of this parable, with which he had entertained the multitude. Their staying with the twelve when the generality of the multitudes were departed, argued that they came with a desire to learn and to be instructed, not out of a mere curiosity to see Christ, or in a mere formality. They show both their charity, in desiring others might be intelligibly instructed; and their piety, in desiring that they might be more fully themselves instructed.

11 He answered and said unto them, Because ^git is given unto you to know the mysteries of the kingdom of heaven, but to them it is not given.

g ch. 11. 25. & 16. 17. Mark 4. 11. 1 Cor. 2. 10. 1 John 2. 27.

12 ^hFor whosoever hath, to him shall be given, and he shall have more abundance: but whosoever hath not, from him shall be taken away even that he hath.

h ch. 25. 29 Mark 4. 25. Luke 8. 18. & 19. 26.

Mark saith, chap. iv. 11, *Unto you it is given to know the mystery of the kingdom of God: but unto them that are without, all these things are done in parables.* Luke saith

S. MATTHEW XIII

no more than, *Unto you it is given to know the mysteries of the kingdom of God: but to others in parables.* Only, chap. viii. 18, he saith, *Take heed therefore how ye hear: for whosoever hath, to him shall be given; and whosoever hath not, from him shall be taken even that which he seemeth to have. Because it is given to you, &c.;* given by my Father: God, according to the good pleasure of his will, hath given to some persons to know the mysteries of the kingdom of God, more than to others. Some here distinguish concerning the things which concern the kingdom of God. The laws of his kingdom, they say, are delivered plainly, viz. those things which are necessary to be known in order to our salvation are delivered plainly, so as we may understand them. But there are other things that belong to his kingdom not so necessary to be known in order to salvation, these God giveth to some only to know. I cannot agree to this notion. God manifested in the flesh is the great mystery of the gospel, the mystery hid from ages, yet I am sure the knowledge of Christ as such is necessary to salvation. I therefore think the emphasis lieth upon *know*. 1. There is a more general and confused knowledge of a thing; and there is a more distinct, clear, particular knowledge. 2. There is a mere notional knowledge, and there is a more effective, experimental knowledge. To you my Father hath given eternal life, and, as means in order to it, to know more clearly, particularly, and distinctly the things that concern the kingdom of God; to know and to believe in me, who am the Saviour of the world: my Father hath no such special and particular kindness for the generality of this people, and therefore he hath not given to them the same aids and assistances. *For whosoever hath, to him shall be given, and he shall have more abundance:* by him that hath, some understand, he that hath and maketh use of what he hath, and that is plainly the sense of it chap. xxv. 29, where it is the *epiparabola*, or conclusion of the parable about the talents. But though the preceding parable plainly leadeth to such a sense there, yet the preceding words seem as directly to lead to another sense here, and what is the more natural and proper signification of the word *hath*, which most naturally signifies to have a thing in our possession. He that hath, therefore, in all reason signifies, he that hath that which, ver. 11, is said to be given. He that hath the saving knowledge of the mysteries of the kingdom of God. To him that doth not so much come to hear me out of curiosity, and comprehendeth by his understanding something of my will, but hath a heart that embraceth and receiveth me, so as he believeth in me. To him that hath the seed of God in him as in good ground. *Shall be given:* that is expounded by the next words, *and he shall have more abundance;* he shall have more grace, a more full, and clear, and distinct knowledge of me, and the things which concern my kingdom. *But whosoever hath not*, hath not the seed of God, a true root of grace, in whom the seed of my word hath not fallen as in good ground, but only as in the highway, or in thorny or stony ground, *from him shall be taken away even that which he hath*. How can that be? *Answ.* It must not be understood of things in the same nature and kind; Luke expounds it, chap. viii. 18, by ὁ δοκεῖ ἔχειν, that which either to himself or to others he seemeth to have. He that hath not a truth of grace may think he hath: his hope and opinion of himself shall fail. Others may, from his gifts and parts, think he hath. God shall unmask him, taking away his common gifts, or suffering him to fall into and be overcome by foul temptations. His gifts and parts shall decay, his moral righteousness will abate by God's just dereliction of him, and withholding his restraining grace.

13 Therefore speak I to them in parables: because they seeing see not; and hearing they hear not, neither do they understand.

Neither Mark nor Luke hath this, but it directly followeth from what they have, which also followeth here; only here it is plainly asserted concerning these hearers, and given as a reason why our Lord spake to them in parables. We shall in the explication of the following words inquire in what sense it is said, This people seeing, saw not, and hearing, heard not.

i Is. 6. 9.
Ezek. 12. 2.
Mark 4. 12.
Luke 8. 10.

14 And in them is fulfilled the prophecy of Esaias, which saith, ⁱBy hear-ing ye shall hear, and shall not understand; and seeing ye shall see, and shall not perceive:

John 12. 40.
Acts 28. 26, 27. Rom.
11. 8. 2 Cor.
3. 14, 15.

15 For this people's heart is waxed gross, and *their* ears ᵏare dull of hearing, and their eyes they have closed; lest at any time they should see with *their* eyes, and hear with *their* ears, and should understand with *their* heart, and should be converted, and I should heal them.

k Heb. 5. 11.

These words of the prophet are not less than five times found in the New Testament (besides by Matthew in these verses) applied to the Jews. They are taken out of Isaiah, chap. vi. 9, 10, where they are found thus: *And he said, Go, and tell this people, Hear ye indeed, but understand not; and see ye indeed, but perceive not. Make the heart of this people fat, and make their ears heavy, and shut their eyes; lest they see with their eyes, and hear with their ears, and understand with their heart, and convert, and be healed*. It is quoted Mark iv. 12; Luke viii. 10, where the sense of the words only is quoted more shortly; John xii. 40; Acts xxviii. 26, 27; Rom. xi. 8, more largely, yet with some more difference of phrase from that of the prophet. By all of them it appeareth, either that God spake those words to the prophet, as well with reference to those Jews that were to live in the time of Christ, as to those Jews who were living when Isaiah prophesied; or at least, that the words were as true of these Jews as they were of those, so the prophecy of Isaiah was fulfilled in them. But the words are so differently related, that the prophet, and St. John, chap. xii. 39, 40, seem to make God the cause of the fatness of this people's hearts, the heaviness of their ears, and the blindness of their eyes. *Therefore they could not believe, because that Esaias said again, He hath blinded their eyes, and hardened their heart; that they should not see with their eyes, nor understand with their heart, and be converted, and I should heal them*. So also Paul speaketh, Rom. xi. 8, *God hath given them the spirit of slumber, eyes that they should not see, and ears that they should not hear*. Matthew saith, *This people's heart is waxed gross*. Matthew seemeth to speak of the more proximate cause; Isaiah, Luke, John, and Paul of the higher but remoter cause. Matthew, of their sinful act preceding; John, Luke, Paul, and Isaiah, of the judicial act of God, consequent to their sinful act. God first sent them Moses and the prophets, by whom they might have seen and known his will: they would not see, nor hear, nor understand, nor convert, nor be healed. God at last did leave them to the reprobacy of their own mind: he willed indeed the prophet to go and preach, But, saith he, this shall be all the fruit of thy ministry, it shall but make the heart of this people fat, and their ears heavy, they shall more and more shut their eyes: their time of conversion and healing is past; it is now too late, I will not convert, I will not heal them. Now (saith our Saviour) what was applicable to the Jews in the time of Isaiah, is in like manner applicable to you, and the prophet Isaiah did foretell what I should meet with. The generality of the people are a people that have so despised the grace of God, that their day of grace is over; God is resolved he will not convert nor heal them. They have had light, they have seen me and my works, they have heard my sermons and John Baptist's; in seeing they would not see, in hearing they would not hear nor understand. So they are fallen under a judicial hardness and blindness. They shall not now have the light as they have had: my Spirit shall no longer strive with them; neither shall they have a heart to make a due use of the means they have. This is doubtless the meaning of these words. And so they give a just reason why he spake to them in parables. And thus undoubtedly God doth to this day; when a people have a long time sat under a good and profitable ministry, wherein their souls have been dealt with plainly and faithfully, and they remain still ignorant, debauched, and unbelieving, God in a righteous judgment gives them over to the blindness of mind and hardness of heart under the ministry, that though it continue never so good amongst them, yet they are not affected with the word, but sleep and harden under it. Sometimes he by his providence suffers such a minister to

VOL. III—3

come amongst them as speaketh nothing but parables, things which they understand not; or smooth things, fit to smooth them up in their sinful courses, and harden them in their prejudices against Christ and holiness. A most tremendous judgment of God. When God, antecedently to this contempt, by his providence sends such a ministry as may declare his willingness they should be saved and come to the knowledge of his truth; and consequently to this contempt, and despising of his grace, so dealeth with them by his providence, either suffering their first seeming affections and edge to abate, (as the Jews are said for a while to have rejoiced in the light John brought,) or suffering such a ministry to come amongst them, as one would think God sent lest men should convert and be healed. In the mean time Christ in this text excellently sets out God's method in his dealing with souls: 1. He bringeth them to hear and see. 2. Then he makes them to understand and believe. 3. Then he converts them, reneweth and changeth their hearts. 4. Then he healeth them, pardoneth their sins, and accepts their persons, not because they are converted, but at the same time when he works faith in them, and giveth them a heart to repent.

l ch. 16. 17. Luke 10. 23, 24. John 20. 29.
m Heb. 11. 13. 1 Pet. 1. 10, 11.

16 But ¹blessed *are* your eyes, for they see: and your ears, for they hear.

17 For verily I say unto you, ᵐThat many prophets and righteous *men* have desired to see *those things* which ye see, and have not seen *them;* and to hear *those things* which ye hear, and have not heard *them.*

Luke repeateth this passage, chap. x. 23, but not as annexed to this parable. *Blessed are your eyes;* the eyes of your bodies and of your minds. With the eyes of your bodies you have seen the promised Messias, come in the flesh; and you have seen the works which I have done, confirming me to be the Messiah: and with the eyes of your minds you have understood and believed. *For many prophets and righteous men* (Luke adds, *kings*) *have desired to see those things which ye see, &c.* From the very first giving out of the promise of Christ to Adam, upon the fall, Gen. iii. 15, there was in believers an expectation of the Messiah, who being so great a good, so infinite a blessing to mankind, they could not but have a desire (if God had so pleased) to have seen him. But we are told that Abraham saw Christ's day and rejoiced. And Simeon's and Anna's expectation of him, mentioned Luke ii., lets us know that other pious souls had such desires. Our Saviour blesseth his disciples, that they had seen with the eyes of their bodies, what others had only seen afar off by the eyes of their minds, Heb. xi. 13.

n Mark 4.14. Luke 8. 11.

18 ¶ ⁿHear ye therefore the parable of the sower.

Mark addeth a little check he gave them, chap. iv. 13, *Know ye not this parable? and how then will ye know all parables?* Luke saith, *The parable is this,* that is, My meaning in and by the parable was this. You, seeing that you cannot satisfy yourselves, as the most that heard me, hearing a sound of words without understanding what they meant, and seeing *that to you it is given to know the mysteries of the kingdom of God,* and seeing that you see, God hath opened your eyes and ears to spiritual mysteries. *Hear ye therefore the parable of the sower:* my true sense and meaning in this parable, my scope in it, was to show you the different effects which the word of God preached hath upon men's hearts, and the reasons of that difference.

19 When any one heareth the word
o ch. 4. 23. °of the kingdom, and understandeth *it* not, then cometh the wicked *one,* and catcheth away that which was sown in his heart. This is he which received seed by the way side.

Mark hath this thus, chap. iv. 14, 15, *The sower soweth the word. And these are they by the way-side, where the word is sown; but when they have heard, Satan cometh immediately and taketh away the word that was sown in their hearts.* Luke hath it thus. chap. viii. 11, 12, *The seed is the word of God. Those by the way-side are they that hear; then cometh the devil, and taketh away the word out of their hearts, lest they should believe and be saved.* From Luke we learn that the seed is the word; from Mark, that the sower is the preacher, Christ in the first place, then all who derive from him as his ministers, and are exercised in preaching the gospel, which Matthew calleth *the word of the kingdom,* because it is the instrument by which God raised up Christ's kingdom on earth, both in the church, and in particular souls, and by which he prepareth men for the kingdom of glory. This is a mighty commendation of the word. The soil is the heart, the soul of man. Now there are some hearers to whom the word preached is like seed that a sower throweth upon some foot-path, or highway, the plough never turneth the earth upon it, or the harrow never goeth over it; so it lieth bare, and is trodden down by the feet of passengers, and the fowls of the air come and pick it up. So, saith our Saviour, there are some that hear the word, but never meditate upon it, never lay it to their hearts, never cover it with second thoughts; the wicked ones, the devils, who are afraid of the power of the word digested, (like the fowls of the air,) by suggesting other thoughts, or by presenting other objects to them, catch away the word that was sown in their hearts. These are they whom I compared to the highway ground receiving the seed. But some may say, How was it sown in their hearts, if the devil could thus catch it away? *Answ.* By the heart here is meant the soul, which hath several powers and faculties. Every thing we hear goeth into our heart, in some sense. As the heart may signify the imaginative power of our soul, or that power by which we take the notion of a thing, the word doth enter into sinners' hearts, so far as they spend some thoughts upon it, and gain some knowledge and notion of it, yea, they may entertain it with some sudden and temporary affection and passion: indeed it is never so in their hearts, as that they truly believe it, or that their wills are conquered into the obedience of it.

20 But he that received the seed into stony places, the same is he that heareth the word, and anon ᵖwith joy receiveth it;
p Is. 58. 2. Ezek. 33. 31, 32. John 5. 35.

21 Yet hath he not root in himself, but dureth for a while: for when tribulation or persecution ariseth because of the word, by and by ᑫhe is offended.
q ch. 11. 6. 2 Tim. 1. 15.

Both Mark and Luke have this with no difference, save only in words, Mark iv. 16, 17; Luke viii. 13. What Matthew calleth stony ground, Luke calls the rock. By the sun being up, and scorching the seed, in the parable, our Saviour meant tribulation or persecution, which Luke calleth a *time of temptation,* chap. viii. 13. *Stony places* are places where may be a little earth, but not much; he is here likened to such ground, who *heareth the word, and anon* (the Greek is εὐθὺς, which signifieth presently) *with joy receiveth it,* as Herod is said to have heard John the Baptist gladly. The word of God (as some other objects) doth often on the sudden affect some persons in whom it doth not take any deep root. A sudden passion surpriseth them, which is but like the overflowing of a brook, which is quickly down. *Yet hath he not root in himself, &c.* Our Saviour here assigneth two causes of such hearers falling away, the one internal, the other external; the former is the great cause of the latter. By *root in himself* some understand constancy, or a serious resolution and purpose of heart; but this is doubtless but the product of this root, which is the same thing which the apostle calls *the seed of God,* Job calls *the root of the matter;* a principle of grace in a heart truly touched with the love of God and of his truth. *But dureth for a while;* no longer than he thinks that he can by his profession attain the end he aimed at and propounded to himself, be it riches, or honour and reputation. *But when tribulation or persecution ariseth* for the word's sake, or *because of the word,* when he seeth that he cannot own his profession without the danger of his estate, life, liberty, places, and preferments, &c., *by and by he is offended,* made to stumble and fall, he falls off from all his former profession of the gospel.

22 ʳHe also that received seed ˢamong
r ch. 19. 23. Mark 10. 23. Luke 18. 24. 1 Tim. 6. 9. 2 Tim. 4. 10. s Jer. 4. 3.

the thorns is he that heareth the word; and the care of this world, and the deceitfulness of riches, choke the word, and he becometh unfruitful.

Mark adds, chap. iv. 19, *and the lusts of other things entering in, choke the word.* Luke saith, chap. viii. 14, *And that which fell among thorns are they, which, when they have heard, go forth, and are choked with cares, and riches, and pleasures of this life, and bring no fruit to perfection.* Under these terms, *the care of this world, the deceitfulness of riches,* and *the pleasures of this life,* or *the lusts of other things,* our Saviour comprehendeth all that which St. John calls *the lust of the eye, the lust of the flesh, and the pride of life.* The immoderate desires of our hearts after lawful things, or their desires after things prohibited and unlawful, these he compareth to thorns: as thorns in a ground choke the seed, shadowing the blade when it comes up, and keeping off the warmth of the sun, and drawing the fatness of the ground from it; so these divert men's thoughts, and draw men's affections off from the word of God, so as it bringeth forth no fruit; or if there be some little appearance of fruit, it dwindles away, and cometh to no perfection. None of these were profane, godless persons, who make no conscience of neglecting to hear the word preached; they are all hearers. Oh how strait is the way, how narrow is the gate, that leadeth to everlasting life! how few there be that find it!

23 But he that received seed into the good ground is he that heareth the word, and understandeth *it;* which also beareth fruit, and bringeth forth, some an hundredfold, some sixty, some thirty.

Mark saith much the same, chap. iv. 20. Luke saith, chap. viii. 15, *But that on the good ground are they, which in an honest and good heart, having heard the word, keep it, and bring forth fruit with patience.* To make a good Christian all these things must concur: 1. A hearing of the word. 2. An understanding or believing it. 3. A keeping of it. 4. A bringing forth of fruit. 5. A bringing forth fruit with patience. He that receiveth the seed into good ground, is he (saith Luke) *who in an honest and good heart, having heard the word, keep it. The good ground,* in this parable, is the *good and honest heart,* that is, a heart renewed and sanctified by the Spirit of God. *He heareth the word:* he (saith the apostle) who is born of God, heareth us: *faith cometh by hearing. And understandeth it.* Mark saith, *receiveth it,* that is, not in the mere notion, but by faith, and a mind willing to learn and be instructed. Luke adds, and *keepeth it,* retains the savour and impression of it upon his soul. *Which also beareth fruit,* the fruit of holiness in his life, in an obedience to the will of God; for all seed bringeth forth fruit according to his kind. Luke adds, *with patience,* by which is to be understood certainty, constancy, and perseverance, and that notwithstanding all trials and oppositions he meets with from the world, the flesh, and the devil. *Some an hundredfold, some sixty, some thirty;* not all alike. A soul may be an honest and good soul, and that (as we see here) in Christ's opinion and judgment, though it doth not bring forth fruit in the same proportion with others.

24 ¶ Another parable put he forth unto them, saying, The kingdom of heaven is likened unto a man which sowed good seed in his field:

25 But while men slept, his enemy came and sowed tares among the wheat, and went his way.

26 But when the blade was sprung up, and brought forth fruit, then appeared the tares also.

27 So the servants of the housholder came and said unto him, Sir, didst not thou sow good seed in thy field? from whence then hath it tares?

28 He said unto them, An enemy hath done this. The servants said unto him, Wilt thou then that we go and gather them up?

29 But he said, Nay; lest while ye gather up the tares, ye root up also the wheat with them.

30 Let both grow together until the harvest: and in the time of harvest I will say to the reapers, Gather ye together first the tares, and bind them in bundles to burn them: but ᵗgather the wheat into my barn.

31 ¶ Another parable put he forth unto them, saying, ᵘ The kingdom of heaven is like to a grain of mustard seed, which a man took, and sowed in his field:

32 Which indeed is the least of all seeds: but when it is grown, it is the greatest among herbs, and becometh a tree, so that the birds of the air come and lodge in the branches thereof.

33 ¶ ˣAnother parable spake he unto them; The kingdom of heaven is like † unto leaven, which a woman took, and hid in three † measures of meal, till the whole was leavened.

Here are three parables by the evangelist put together before he cometh to the explication which our Saviour giveth of the first; all of them concerning the gospel church, and the dispensation of the gospel. In the one he instructs us what we are to expect as to the mixture of persons in it while it is in this world. In the other two concerning the increase and propagation of it. The first himself expoundeth, ver. 37—43. This parable is only found in Matthew. The other two are found, shortly both of them in Luke, one in Mark; neither of them are expounded. I will therefore, without any explication of these verses at present, go on to the verses following them, all which will lead me to our Saviour's own interpretation of the first of these parables; after which I will also consider those two parables that follow here, but are neither expounded here nor in the other evangelists.

34 ʸAll these things spake Jesus unto the multitude in parables; and without a parable spake he not unto them:

35 That it might be fulfilled which was spoken by the prophet, saying, ᶻI will open my mouth in parables; ᵃI will utter things which have been kept secret from the foundation of the world.

Christ spake all the aforementioned things to the multitude, and also to his disciples, in parables, dark sayings, covering Divine and spiritual truths with fit and proper similitudes; and at this time he delivered himself wholly in this manner to them, though at other times he spake more plainly. He gave us the reason before; and by this way of speaking also he made his own disciples more diligent to attend to what they heard, and more inquisitive after the true sense and meaning of it. And thus, saith the evangelist, that which was spoken by the prophet, Psal. lxxviii. 2, was also fulfilled in Christ: not that the psalmist, whether David or Asaph, did there prophesy concerning Christ, for plainly the psalmist intended to relate the history of God's dealing with the Jews, and their behaviour toward him. Nor was it fulfilled as the type in the antitype, but as a thing of the same nature was done. The prophet delivered himself in dark sayings, so did Christ, but instead of *I will utter dark sayings of old,* the evangelist hath, *which have been kept secret from the foundation of the world;* he means the great and mysterious things of the gospel, *hid from ages and generations,* Col. i. 26; 1 Cor. ii. 7; Rom. xvi. 25, where it is called *the revelation of the mystery, which was kept secret since the world began.* As the psalmist opened his mouth in grave discourses, tending to the good of the people to whom he spake; so Christ taught the people, by revealing the mysteries of the gospel, *hid in God from the beginning of the world,* as Paul speaks to the Ephesians, Eph. iii. 9.

36 Then Jesus sent the multitude away, and went into the house: and his disciples came unto him, saying, Declare unto us the parable of the tares of the field.

The multitude went away (as most people do from sermons) never the wiser, understanding nothing of what they heard, nor caring to understand it. But there was a more conscientious part of our Saviour's auditory, who could not thus satisfy themselves; they follow Christ into the house, and entreat him to open to them *the parable of the tares of the field;* they say nothing of the other two parables, because probably they understood them, and it may be this parable did more affect them, in regard of the dreadful conclusion of it.

37 He answered and said unto them, He that soweth the good seed is the Son of man;

38 [b] The field is the world; the good seed are the children of the kingdom; but the tares are [c] the children of the wicked *one ;*

39 The enemy that sowed them is the devil; [d] the harvest is the end of the world; and the reapers are the angels.

[b] ch. 24. 14. & 28. 19. Mark 16. 15. 20. Luke 24. 47. Rom. 10. 18. Col. 1. 6. [c] Gen. 3. 13. John 8. 44. Acts 13. 10. 1 John 3. 8. [d] Joel 3. 13. Rev. 14. 15.

The design that Christ had in this parable was to show them, that though he laid a good foundation of a church in the world, calling some home to himself, and making them partakers of his effectual grace, laying the foundation of his gospel church in such as took his yoke upon them; yet in process of time, while those that should succeed him in his ministry slept, (not being so diligent and watchful as they ought to be,) the devil (who is full of envy and malice to men's souls, and is continually going about seeking whom he may devour) would sow erroneous opinions, and find a party, even in the bosom of his church, who would hearken to him, and through their lusts comply with his temptations, both to errors in doctrine and errors in practice: and it was his will, that there should be in the visible church a mixture of good and bad, such bad ones especially as men could not purge out without a danger of putting out such as were true and sincere; but there would be a time, in the end of the world, when he would come with his fan, and throughly purge his floor, and take to heaven all true and sincere souls, but turn all hypocrites into hell. This appears, by our Saviour's exposition, to have been our Saviour's plain meaning in this parable. Hence he tells us, that by the sower here he meant himself, *the Son of man.* By *the field* he meant *the world.* By *the good seed* he meant *the children of the kingdom;* such as had a true change wrought in their hearts, were truly regenerated and converted. By *the tares* he meant *the children of the wicked one,* that is, of the devil; such as did the works of the devil, John viii. 44. That *the enemy that sowed* these tares was *the devil,* who by his suggestions, presenting objects, &c., makes himself the father of all wicked men. Our Saviour here saith nothing to that part of the parable, where the tares are said to be sown *while men slept;* that was plain and intelligible enough. The devil hath a power to seduce, persuade, and allure, none to force. If particular persons kept their watch, as they might, the devil could not by his temptation force them. If magistrates and ministers kept their watches according to God's prescription, there could not be so much open wickedness in the world as there is. Neither doth our Saviour give us any particular explication of that part of the parable, which is ver. 28, 29, where the servants say to their master, *Wilt thou then that we go and gather them up.* And *he said unto them, Nay; lest while ye gather up the tares, ye root up also the wheat with them.* Our Saviour by this teacheth us, that every passage in a parable is not to be fitted by something in the explication. It was not the point that he designed in this parable to instruct them in, how far church officers might or ought to act in purging the church; but only, 1. That in the visible church they must expect a mixture, till the day of judgment. 2. That in that day he would make a perfect separation. So as those that would from this passage in the parable conclude, that all erroneous and loose persons ought to be tolerated in the church till the day of judgment, forget the common rule in divinity, that parabolical divinity is not argumentative. We can argue from nothing in a parable but from the main scope and tendency of it. However, it is bold arguing from a passage in a parable, expounded by our Saviour himself, when he hath omitted the explication of that passage; nor can any thing be concluded, but that such must not be rooted out as have such a resemblance of wheat from the outward appearance, that they cannot be rooted out without a hazard of a mistake, and a rooting up of the wheat with them. But our Saviour reserves the point of the ministerial duty in purging the church to another more proper time; he here saith nothing of that, but of his own design to purge it at *the harvest,* which he interprets, *the end of the world,* that is, the day of judgment. By *the reapers* he tells us that he meaneth *the angels.*

40 As therefore the tares are gathered and burned in the fire; so shall it be in the end of this world.

41 The Son of man shall send forth his angels, [e] and they shall gather out of his kingdom all ‖ things that offend, and them which do iniquity;

42 [f] And shall cast them into a furnace of fire: [g] there shall be wailing and gnashing of teeth.

43 [h] Then shall the righteous shine forth as the sun in the kingdom of their Father. [i] Who hath ears to hear, let him hear.

[e] ch. 18. 7. 2 Pet. 2. 1, 2. ‖ Or, *scandals.* [f] ch. 3. 12. Rev. 19. 20. & 20. 10. [g] ch. 8. 12. ver. 50. [h] Dan. 12. 3. Wisd. 3. 7. 1 Cor. 15. 42, 43, 58. [i] ver. 9.

As in the common practice of men, when they have a mind to pick their corn, and have it clean, when it is reaped, to set men to clean the wheat, and to pick out the tares, and, having tied them up in bundles, to burn them, so (saith he) I will do. I will send my angels at the day of judgment, and they shall take out of my church all impenitent sinners, all those who in this world have been scandals, and offences, and mischievous to my people, and who have made it their business to work iniquity. *And shall cast them into a furnace of fire: there shall be wailing and gnashing of teeth.* That is, into hell, which, in regard of the severe torments which the damned shall feel there, is often in Scripture compared to fire, as chap. xxv. 41, and in other texts, by which is only set out to us the dreadfulness of the punishment of the damned, that is proportioned to, if not far exceeding, that of the burning living bodies in fire. Having thus expressed the punishment of wicked men, he expoundeth what he means by gathering the wheat into his barn, viz. the taking of righteous men to heaven. *Then,* saith he, *shall the righteous,* those whom I have clothed with my righteousness, and who have lived in obedience to my will to that degree, that though they be not perfectly righteous, yet are sincere and upright, so as I have accepted them, *shine forth as the sun in the kingdom of their Father:* an expression much like that of Dan. xii. 2, 3, significative of that glorious state of the saints in heaven, which no eye having seen, nor ear having heard, no tongue is able to express. He concludeth in the same manner as he concludeth the parable of the sower, exciting his hearers to a diligent consideration and belief of what he had said.

Our Saviour adding no particular explication of the two parables delivered, ver. 31—33, the disciples not asking him to explain them, and the evangelist have put the explication of the first parable after them, it is reasonable, that though I omitted the explication of them in their proper place, yet I should add something here for the benefit of those who possibly will not be able so readily to conceive our Saviour's meaning in them without an interpreter as the disciples did, which is thought to be the reason why they asked no explication of them. The one is the parable of the *grain of mustard seed,* ver. 31, 32; the other, the parable of the *leaven hid in three measures of meal,* ver. 33. The scope of both is the same. Our Saviour intended them both to let his disciples know the success that his gospel should have over all the world, that they might not be discouraged at the little success of it at present. To this purpose he compareth it, first, to a *grain of mustard seed, which,* he saith, *is the least of all seeds,* that is, one of the least of seeds, or the least seed that produceth so great a plant; but becomes a tree so high, *that the birds of the air come and lodge in the branches thereof.* Though that small seed with us runs up to a great height, and produceth a plant which hath branches considerable enough to lodge birds which sit low, yet we must not judge of what grew in those countries by what groweth in ours; there are strange and almost incredible stories told of that plant by naturalists, as to its growth in some hot and fertile countries. Christ by this foretold his disciples, what following ages quickly verified, that the heathen should entertain the gospel, and the sound of it should go to the ends of the earth, notwithstanding its present small appearance. Upon the same score he compareth it to a little *leaven, which a woman hid in three measures of meal, till the whole* mass of meal *was leavened.* By these two expressions our Saviour also lets us know the quick and powerful nature of the word; that Christ's words are (as he said) spirit of life, and have a hidden and extraordinary virtue in them. I do not think it worth the while to inquire into the contents of these σατα, or measures of meal, and why he mentioneth but three. They are curiosities, the knowledge of which turneth to no account. Our Saviour certainly, by the expression, designed only to hint the small number of the Jews that believed in him, but foretold a far greater harvest. *The law* should *go forth out of Zion, and the word of the Lord from Jerusalem,* as Isaiah prophesied, chap. ii. 3; but *many people* (after them) should *say, Come ye, let us go up to the mountain of the house of the Lord.*

44 ¶ Again, the kingdom of heaven is like unto treasure hid in a field; the which when a man hath found, he hideth, and for joy thereof goeth and ᵏselleth all that he hath, and ˡbuyeth that field.

k Phil. 3.7,8.
l Is. 55. 1.
Rev. 3. 18.

Whatsoever belongeth to the kingdom of God, whether the word, which is called *the word of the kingdom,* or the grace and favour of God, which he by me dispenseth out under the administration of the gospel, *is like,* that is, should be adjudged, esteemed, and used like as *treasure hid in a field.* Men should do by it as they would do upon the discovery of a great sum of money, buried up in the earth, in some field not yet their own. Suppose a man had made some such discovery, what would he do? he would rejoice at it, he would hide it, he would sell all he had and buy that field. So should men do to whom there is a revelation of the gospel, and the grace thereof; they should inwardly rejoice in the revelation, and bless God for it, and, whatever it cost them, labour that they might be made partakers of that grace. Earthly possessions cannot be had without purchasing, and those who have not ready money to purchase with must raise it from the sale of something which they have; therefore our labour for the kingdom of heaven is set out under the notion of buying. But the prophet (Isa. lv. 1, 2) let us know that it is a buying *without money and without price.* However, there is some resemblance, for as in buying and selling there is a parting with something that is ours in exchange for something which is another's, so in order to the obtaining of the grace of the gospel, and the kingdom of glory, to which the remission of sins leadeth, we must part with something in order to the obtaining of it. We have no ready money, nothing by us, that is a *quid pro quo,* a valuable price for Divine grace; we must therefore part with something that we have, and it is no matter what it be, which God requireth. Where this discovery is made, the soul will part with all it hath, not only its old heart, its unlawful desires and lusts, but its riches, honours, and pleasures, if it can by no other means obtain the kingdom of heaven, that it may obtain it; they are all of no value to it. Nor is it at all necessary in order to buying, that the thing parted with be of a proportionable value. Amongst men, wedges of gold have been purchased for knives and rattles, &c.; nor doth any thing we can part with, that we may obtain the kingdom of heaven, bear any better proportion; yet it is a buying, because it is what God is pleased to accept, and upon the parting with gives us this heavenly kingdom.

45 ¶ Again, the kingdom of heaven is like unto a merchant man, seeking goodly pearls:

46 Who, when he had found ᵐ one pearl of great price, went and sold all that he had, and bought it.

m Prov. 2.4.
& 3. 14, 15.
& 8. 10, 19.

The state of the gospel dispensation is such, that men in it having a discovery of more excellent things than before they were aware of, *of life and immortality* being *brought to light through the gospel,* 2 Tim. i. 10, *grace and truth coming by Jesus Christ,* John i. 17, men and women are set upon seeking for these spiritual things, as merchants do for goodly pearls; and when God makes a discovery of Christ and his grace to the soul, it appears to them as a *pearl of great price,* of more value than all they have in the world, and they are ready to part with all to obtain Christ and his grace. Both these parables have the same scope and tendency, viz. 1. To inform us that Christ and his grace are of a great and transcendent value. 2. That under the gospel there is a clear discovery of these things to the world. 3. That where this discovery is effectually and particularly made to any soul, that soul will part with all it hath, or is worth, rather than it will miss of Christ, and his grace and glory.

47 ¶ Again, the kingdom of heaven is like unto a net, that was cast into the sea, and ⁿgathered of every kind:

n ch. 22. 10.

48 Which, when it was full, they drew to shore, and sat down, and gathered the good into vessels, but cast the bad away.

49 So shall it be at the end of the world: the angels shall come forth, and °sever the wicked from among the just,

o ch. 25. 32.

50 ᵖAnd shall cast them into the furnace of fire: there shall be wailing and gnashing of teeth.

p ver. 42.

The scope of this parable is much the same with that of the tares, to teach us, that whilst the church is in this world there will be in it a mixture of good and bad, a perfect separation of which one from another is not to be expected until the day of judgment. *Again, the kingdom of heaven.* This term signifieth the whole dispensation and administration of the gospel, both the grace dispensed in it, and the means of that grace which is administered under it. I should here interpret it of the preaching of the gospel, which is called *the word of the kingdom,* being the means by which men are gathered in both to the church visible and invisible. This our Lord here compareth to *a net,* thrown *into the sea* of the world, and gathering in of every kind, bringing in many to an outward profession, all of which shall not come to the kingdom of glory, nor are indeed true members of Christ; not members of the church invisible, though they be members of the church visible. When the end of the world shall come, and Christ shall have accomplished his design in the world, then a day of judgment shall come, and there shall be a perfect separation betwixt such as received the gospel in truth, and in the love of it, and others: the former shall be taken to heaven, and the latter thrown into hell; which he expresseth by the like phrases which he had before used in the parable of the tares, which need no further explication.

51 Jesus saith unto them, Have ye understood all these things? They say unto him, Yea, Lord.

A conscientious teacher will have a respect to the profit of his hearers. Christ here setteth us an example, asking his disciples if they had *understood all these things;* as well those parables of which he had given them no particular explication, as those he had explained. *They say unto him, Yea, Lord,* we have understood them.

52 Then said he unto them, Therefore every scribe *which is* instructed unto the kingdom of heaven is like unto a man *that is* an housholder, which bringeth forth out of his treasure ᑫ*things* new and old.

q Cant. 7. 13.

Seeing you understand these things, communicate your knowledge of them unto others, do not know for yourselves alone. *Every scribe which is instructed unto the kingdom of heaven.* The scribes amongst the Jews were not only clerks, that were employed in writing, but teachers of the law; such a one was Ezra, chap. vii. 6. Our Saviour here by *every scribe instructed unto the kingdom of God,* understandeth every good minister of the gospel, fitted to promote the kingdom of God, to be employed in the church of God: should be like a good *housholder,* that hath not his provision to seek when his guests come; but hath a full-fraught storehouse, and hath nothing to do but out of his stock and storehouse to bring out all sort of provision, according to the various palates of his guests. Ministers of the gospel should not be novices, 1 Tim. iii. 6, raw and ignorant men; but men mighty in the Scriptures, well acquainted with the writings of the Old and New Testament, and the sense of them; men that have a stock of spiritual knowledge, able readily to speak a word to the weary, and to speak to men and women's particular cases and questions.

53 ¶ And it came to pass, *that* when Jesus had finished these parables, he departed thence.

r ch. 2. 23.
Mark 6. 1.
Luke 4. 16, 23.

54 ʳAnd when he was come into his own country, he taught them in their synagogue, insomuch that they were astonished, and said, Whence hath this *man* this wisdom, and *these* mighty works?

Mark relateth this passage, chap. vi. 1—4. Our Lord went up and down preaching the gospel: he having preached unto the people in the former parables, now he departeth from the sea-side, where he preached as before, *into his own country*, most interpreters judge Nazareth; he was born in Bethlehem, but we read little or nothing of any time he spent there afterward. Nazareth was the place where he was brought up, and therefore he was called *Jesus of Nazareth*. There he preached in the synagogue, or in the synagogues of Galilee. Mark addeth, on the sabbath day. *Insomuch that they were astonished*: it is not said they repented, or believed, but they admired at him, and were astonished. *And said, Whence hath this man this wisdom, and these mighty works?* that is, a power to do these mighty works. Mark saith, *Whence hath this man these things? and what wisdom is this that is given unto him, that even such mighty works are wrought by his hands?* Astonishment and admiration flow from ignorance, and are no indications of any spiritual saving work upon men's hearts: we shall see that these Jews, notwithstanding their astonishment, are by and by scandalized, and offended at Christ.

s Is. 49. 7.
Mark 6. 3.
Luke 3. 23.
John 6. 42.
t ch. 12. 46.
u Mark 15. 40.

55 ˢIs not this the carpenter's son? is not his mother called Mary? and ᵗhis brethren, ᵘJames, and Joses, and Simon, and Judas?

56 And his sisters, are they not all with us? Whence then hath this *man* all these things?

x ch. 11. 6.
Mark 6. 3, 4.

57 And they ˣwere offended in him.

Mark saith the same, chap. vi. 3; only he saith, *Is not this the carpenter?* ὁ τέκτων; which leadeth some to think that Christ, till he was thirty years of age, wrought with Joseph upon his trade. Luke ii. 51, it is said, *that he came to Nazareth, and was subject* to his parents. Joseph was an artificer, that was certain; so τέκτων signifies; but whether a carpenter, or a smith, the word will not inform us. For the brethren of Christ and his sisters, here mentioned, the most by them understand his near relations. The Jews were offended at the meanness of our Saviour's parents and relations. *They were offended in him;* that is, these things made them stumble at him, and not receive him as the Messias, or a prophet sent from God. How unreasonable is malice and prejudice! One would have thought that their knowledge of his friends and education should have rather led them to have concluded that he must be sent from God, and more than a man, seeing that he did not come by this wisdom by any ordinary means, nor work these great works by any human power.

y Luke 4. 24.
John 4. 44.

—But Jesus said unto them, ʸA prophet is not without honour, save in his own country, and in his own house.

z Mark 6. 5, 6.

58 And ᶻhe did not many mighty works there because of their unbelief.

Mark saith, chap. vi. 4—6, *But Jesus said unto them, A prophet is not without honour, but in his own country, and among his own kin, and in his own house. And he could there do no mighty work, save that he laid his hands upon a few sick folk, and healed them. And he marvelled because of their unbelief. And he went round about the villages teaching.* Our Lord here gives another more external reason of their being scandalized at him; that is, his being so familiar with them, and conversing so long with them: familiarity ordinarily breeding contempt: to this purpose he applieth to them a proverbial speech, That *a prophet is not without honour, save in his own country.* Men are ready to undervalue, slight, and disesteem those they have been brought up and ordinarily conversed with and amongst. *He did not many mighty works there* (Mark telleth us he did some, but not many) *because of their unbelief:* he saw them a people whose hearts, through the just judgment of God, were locked and shut up under unbelief, and therefore it was to no purpose to do more miracles before them, upon whom they would have no effect; nor did this consist with what he knew of the counsels of God with reference unto them. So as he left them, and went preaching about the villages or country towns in Galilee.

CHAP. XIV.

Herod's opinion of Christ, 1, 2. *The cause and manner of John the Baptist's death,* 3—12. *Jesus departeth into a desert place, and feedeth there five thousand men with five loaves and two fishes,* 13—21. *He walketh on the sea to his disciples,* 22—33; *and landing at Gennesaret, healeth the sick who touched but the hem of his garment,* 34—36.

AT that time ᵃHerod the tetrarch heard of the fame of Jesus,

A. D. 32. beginning.
a Mark 6. 14.
Luke 9. 7.

2 And said unto his servants, This is John the Baptist; he is risen from the dead; and therefore mighty works ‖ do shew forth themselves in him.

‖ Or, are wrought by him.

This and the following history is related by Mark more largely, chap. vi. 14—30; by Luke more shortly, chap. ix. 7—9. We heard before, that the Romans, under whom the Jews now were, had altered the government of the Jews from a kingdom to a tetrarchy, or government of four. Luke telleth us who were the tetrarchs, chap. iii. 1. Herod (as we read there) was the tetrarch of Galilee. He had before this time put John Baptist to death, upon what occasion, and in what manner, we shall hear by and by. He heareth of the fame of Jesus. Luke saith he *heard of all that was done by him, and was perplexed;* that some said *John* the Baptist *was risen from the dead;* others, *that Elias had appeared;* others, *that one of the old prophets was risen again.* But Herod said, *John have I beheaded: but who is this, of whom I hear such things?* And he desired to see *him.* Mark saith, chap. vi. 14, that *king Herod heard of him; (for his name was spread abroad:) and he said, That John the Baptist was risen from the dead, and therefore mighty works do show forth themselves in him. Others said, That it is Elias. And others said, That it is a prophet, or as one of the prophets. But when Herod heard thereof, he said, It is John, whom I beheaded: he is risen from the dead.* So as it seems though others had various opinions, yet Herod was fixed in this, that this man was John the Baptist risen again from the dead. Though Luke reports him as speaking more doubtfully, (as he might do to the people,) yet Matthew and Mark speak him affirming of it more confidently (probably to his courtiers and confidants). There was an opinion amongst the heathens, that the souls of men and women, when they died, went into other bodies. Some think that Herod was infected with that, and that this is the meaning of his suspicion that John was risen from the dead; that his soul, which he had forced from his body, was gone into another body, so as it might be revenged on him. Or else he thought that John was indeed raised from the dead, (which yet by search might quickly have been known,) and therefore mighty works showed themselves in him.

3 ¶ ᵇFor Herod had laid hold on John, and bound him, and put *him* in prison for Herodias' sake, his brother Philip's wife.

A. D. 30.
b Mark 6. 17.
Luke 3. 19, 20.

Mark saith, chap. vi. 17, *for he had married her.* Whether this Philip was Herod's brother both by father and mother, is argued by some, as also whether he married her during the life of his brother: the Scripture satisfieth us not in these things, but it is most probable that Philip was his own brother, and that he at least lived in adultery with her during the life of her husband, contrary to the express law of God, Lev. xviii. 16.

c Lev. 18. 16.
& 20. 21.
4 For John said unto him, ^cIt is not lawful for thee to have her.

Mark telleth us, chap. vi. 20, that *Herod feared,* that is, reverenced and respected, *John, knowing that he was a just man and an holy, and observed him; and when he heard him, he did many things, and heard him gladly.* John was very popular, and all men counted him as a prophet; so that probably Herod sent for him to the court, and heard him there. John seeing Herod live in adultery and incest, was not able to suffer such a sin upon him, but tells him he did that which was not lawful for him to do, for God's law had forbidden such marriages. Mark addeth, that *Herodias* also *had a quarrel against him, and would have killed him; but she could not,* because of the respect which Herod had for him. But this wore off, for Matthew tells us,

d ch. 21. 26.
Luke 20. 6.
5 And when he would have put him to death, he feared the multitude, ^dbecause they counted him as a prophet.

At first he had some reverence for John because he was a good man, but either John, by the frequent checks he gave to his lust, or Herodias, by her continual importunities to Herod to revenge her of her great enemy, prevailed, and made Herod willing enough to put him to death; but now he was afraid of some popular tumult, or insurrection, because of the great esteem which the Jews generally had of John, thinking him a prophet, one sent of God to reveal his will unto men.

† Gr. in the midst.
6 But when Herod's birthday was kept, the daughter of Herodias danced † before them, and pleased Herod.

7 Whereupon he promised with an oath to give her whatsoever she would ask.

Mark relateth this more fully, but the sense is the same, chap. vi. 21—23, *And when a convenient day was come, that Herod on his birthday made a supper to his lords, high captains, and chief estates of Galilee; and when the daughter of the said Herodias came in, and danced, and pleased Herod and them that sat with him, the king said unto the damsel, Ask of me whatsoever thou wilt, and I will give it thee. And he sware unto her, Whatsoever thou shalt ask of me, I will give it thee, unto the half of my kingdom.* Those who have got over the point of lawfulness in an action, have nothing to consult but conveniency: therefore saith Mark, *when a convenient day was come,* when probably Herod should be over-merry with wine, or should be busy with his company, and not so much at leisure to consider what he did. It so happened that the daughter of this Herodias danced before Herod upon his birthday. The keeping of birthdays was usual amongst the eastern kings; Pharaoh kept his birthday, Gen. xl. 20. Some by it understand the day of the prince's coronation, or entrance upon his government, which some think is meant Hos. vii. 5, by the *day of our king,* when *the princes made him sick with bottles of wine.* The Jews reckoned them both amongst the pagan festivals, but they had derived both this and many other usages from them. Dancing was much used amongst them at their festivals. It seemeth this daughter of Herodias pleased Herod more than ordinary; he sweareth that he would give her what she would ask, to the half of his kingdom. That phrase, by Esth. v. 3, seemeth to have been ordinary with princes when they made liberal promises.

8 And she, being before instructed of her mother, said, Give me here John Baptist's head in a charger.

Mark, chap. vi. 24, 25, reports it more largely: *And she went forth, and said unto her mother, What shall I ask? And she said, The head of John the Baptist. And she came in straightway with haste to the king, and asked, saying, I will that thou give me by and by in a charger the head of John the Baptist.* The meaning is plain, so as the words need no interpreter: they let us see, 1. The power of the lust of malice and desire of revenge; surely Herodias might have prompted her to have asked something which might have done her more good than the blood of a holy and innocent man. The guilty soul is never at rest. John Baptist was a prisoner; she should not need have feared the influence of John's word to have caused a divorce, but she cannot be at rest while John is alive. 2. The great evil of wicked parents, and the contrary blessing of parents fearing God: the former, by commanding or persuading their children to sin, are great instruments towards their children's damnation; the other, by their admonitions, precepts, and instructions, great instruments of their salvation and eternal happiness. 3. We may observe the genius of flattering courtiers, not one of them interposeth to save the Baptist's life.

9 And the king was sorry: nevertheless for the oath's sake, and them which sat with him at meat, he commanded *it* to be given *her.*

10 And he sent, and beheaded John in the prison.

11 And his head was brought in a charger, and given to the damsel: and she brought *it* to her mother.

Mark relateth it more largely, chap. vi. 26—28, *And the king was exceeding sorry; yet for his oath's sake, and for their sake which sat with him, he would not reject her. And immediately the king sent an executioner, and commanded his head to be brought: and he went and beheaded him in the prison, and brought his head in a charger, and gave it to the damsel: and the damsel gave it to her mother.* The king was exceeding sorry; he could have wished she had asked something else: he was troubled; for we heard before, that although he feared not God, yet he feared the people. *Yet for his oath's sake;* not out of any religion of his oath: *Juramentum non potest esse vinculum iniquitatis.* They must be sottishly ignorant, that think their calling God to witness that they will do a thing which God hath forbidden them to do, should oblige them in any measure to the doing of the thing. But for his oath's sake, in point of honour, because his word was gone out, that he might not appear guilty of any temerity or levity; and for the sake of those that were with him, that he might not seem before them to vary from his word, or it may be, as well to gratify them as to gratify the damsel and her mother; he sends an executioner, who took off John the Baptist's head, and gave it to the damsel in a charger, who carried it to her mother. What could be more unjust, and inhuman, and bloody? John was not tried, nor condemned. It was a great festival, and should not have been profaned or defiled with blood. These things were nothing, when an unsatiable malice was to be gratified. Herodias will have her husband and his guests see that John Baptist's head in a charger was to her as pleasing a dish as any was at Herod's great feast. Thus died this great man, to satisfy the malice and lust of a lewd and imperious woman; and to teach us what we must expect, if we will be faithful to the trust which God reposeth in us.

12 And his disciples came, and took up the body, and buried it, and went and told Jesus.

The disciples of John, in testimony of their respect to their master, and of their owning of his doctrine, and grateful remembrance of him, hearing what Herod had done, came and took up John's body, and buried it in a tomb, and they soon after went and acquainted our Saviour with what had happened; which was the cause of our Saviour's withdrawing to a place where he might be less taken notice of, as we shall hear.

A. D. 32.
e ch. 16. 23.
& 12. 15.
Mark 6. 32.
Luke 9. 10.
John 6. 1, 2.
13 ¶ ^eWhen Jesus heard *of it,* he departed thence by ship into a desert place apart: and when the people had heard *thereof,* they followed him on foot out of the cities.

f ch. 9. 36.
Mark 6. 34.
14 And Jesus went forth, and saw a great multitude, and ^fwas moved with compassion toward them, and he healed their sick.

Mark hath the same, chap. vi. 32. Our Lord knew that the time for his suffering was not yet come, and possibly consulted also the safety of his disciples. The people follow him on foot; but our Saviour going by sea, how could the people follow him on foot? It is answered, that it was but a creek of the sea which our Saviour passed over, and the people by going three or four miles about might follow him on foot. He seeing a great multitude, had compassion on them, and healed the sick persons that were amongst them.

g Mark 6. 35.
Luke 9. 12.
John 6. 5.

15 ¶ g And when it was evening, his disciples came to him, saying, This is a desert place, and the time is now past; send the multitude away, that they may go into the villages, and buy themselves victuals.

The following miracle being an evident confirmation of the Godhead of Christ, is recorded by all the evangelists: by Matthew here; by Mark, chap. vi. 35, &c.; by Luke, chap. ix. 10—12, &c.; by John, chap. vi. 1—3, &c. These words lead us to it, and show us the occasion of it. Our Saviour was withdrawn to a more private place, which, because little inhabited, is called a *a desert place.* Luke saith it was near Bethsaida, Luke ix. 10. The people, as it seemeth, had been together some time. It was now afternoon, and the time of dining was past. It was evening in the Jewish sense (who called it all evening after the sun was turned, and therefore had two evenings, as those skilled in their writings tell us, betwixt which the passover was to be killed). The disciples therefore pitying the multitudes, who, they presumed, might be hungry, come to our Saviour, and move him to dismiss them, that they might get something to eat in the villages of the adjacent country.

16 But Jesus said unto them, They need not depart; give ye them to eat.

John relateth the story thus: *When Jesus lifted up his eyes, and saw a great company come unto him, he saith unto Philip, Whence shall we buy bread, that these may eat? And this he said to prove him: for he himself knew what he would do. Philip answered him, Two hundred pennyworth of bread is not sufficient for them, that every one of them may take a little. One of his disciples, Andrew, Simon Peter's brother, saith unto him, There is a lad here which hath five barley loaves and two small fishes: but what are they among so many? And Jesus said, Make the men sit down. Now there was much grass in the place. So the men sat down, in number about five thousand.*

17 And they say unto him, We have here but five loaves, and two fishes.

18 He said, Bring them hither to me.

19 And he commanded the multitude to sit down on the grass, and took the five loaves, and the two fishes, and looking up to heaven, h he blessed, and brake, and gave the loaves to *his* disciples, and the disciples to the multitude.

h ch. 15. 36.

20 And they did all eat, and were filled: and they took up of the fragments that remained twelve baskets full.

21 And they that had eaten were about five thousand men, beside women and children.

In the relation of this story by the other evangelists there is no difference in what is material; the others relate some circumstances more, as that they sat down on the grass, and *by fifties*, one saith, *by hundreds and by fifties*, &c.; but they all agree in the quantity of the provision, *five loaves and two fishes*; the number of the persons fed, *five thousand* (only one addeth, *besides women and children*); and in the number of the baskets full of fragments; and in our Saviour's lifting up his eyes to heaven, and blessing them. These are the main things observable in this history. In the history of the miracle, as there is no difference between the evangelists to be reconciled, so there is no difficulty to be explained. It is a plain relation of a matter of fact, by which our Lord evidently showed himself to be the Son of God, God blessed for ever, for he must in this necessarily exert a creating power: here must be a production of a substance or being out of a not being, or it had not been possible that five thousand men (besides women and children) should have been fed with five loaves and two fishes; and therefore some think that it is said that Christ blessed the loaves as he blessed the living creatures, Gen. i. 22; but we have not here the following words, *Be fruitful and multiply*, which inclines me rather to think, that the blessing mentioned here, upon his lifting up of his eyes to heaven, was a begging God's blessing upon their food, himself thereby paying the homage of his human nature to his Father, and teaching us, according to that, 1 Tim. iv. 4, 5, to receive the good creatures which God's providence affordeth us for our nourishment with thanksgiving, sanctifying them by prayer. By this miracle, and others of the like nature, our Saviour took from the unbelieving Jews all manner of cavil and exception to his works. Though devils might by compact give place one to another, and some exorcists of their own might seem to cast them out, yet none ever pretended to multiply bread and fish, to such a proportion as this, that such a quantity of either should feed such a number, and leave such a remainder. This history likewise further instructeth us, both concerning the low condition of Christ and his disciples, their faith in the word of Christ, and our duty, and safety in depending upon his providence while we are doing of our duty, and minding the things of the kingdom of God, and obeying the will of God. St. John observeth the fruit of this miracle, John vi. 14, *Those men, when they had seen the miracle which Jesus did, said, This is of a truth that Prophet that should come into the world.*

22 ¶ And straightway Jesus constrained his disciples to get into a ship, and to go before him unto the other side, while he sent the multitudes away.

Mark saith, chap. vi. 45, *before unto*, or over against, Bethsaida. Christ is said to have *constrained* them, to denote to us that they were not very willing to go. They were in a desert place, it was towards night, the day was far spent ere he wrought the miracle before mentioned; probably they were loth to leave Christ alone, in such a place, and at such a time. But his command was obeyed. Probably he commanded, 1. That he might better scatter the multitude, Mark vi. 45. 2. That he might prevent a tumult, for St. John tells us, that the people had a design *to take him by force* and *make him a king*, John vi. 15. 3. To make way for another miracle, to which their going by sea gave occasion, as we shall hear by and by. 4. To gain himself a private opportunity for prayer, for, Mark vi. 46, *When he had sent them away, he departed into a mountain to pray.* So also saith our evangelist.

23 i And when he had sent the multitudes away, he went up into a mountain apart to pray: k and when the evening was come, he was there alone.

i Mark 6. 46.
k John 6. 16.

John saith no more than that he departed himself into a mountain alone. Matthew and Mark say it was to pray. From whence (as from others places of holy writ) the duty of secret prayer is commended to us by the great example of our Saviour: he chooseth the mountain for it, as a place of greatest privacy and solitude. *And when the evening was come:* this confirmeth the former notion, that the Jews had two evenings. They called that part of the day after the sun had began to decline the evening, which was the evening before spoken of, interpreted by the other evangelists, when the day was well spent; and the twilight, which is here called the evening, and which is the time which we most usually call by that name.

24 But the ship was now in the midst of the sea, tossed with waves: for the wind was contrary.

25 And in the fourth watch of the night Jesus went unto them, walking on the sea.

26 And when the disciples saw him l walking on the sea, they were troubled, saying, It is a spirit; and they cried out for fear.

l Job 9. 8.

27 But straightway Jesus spake unto them, saying, Be of good cheer; it is I; be not afraid.

Whilst our Saviour was praying on the mount the ship which carried his disciples was upon the sea, that is, that creek of the sea which they were at that time passing over. A storm ariseth, not without the counsel of God, that Christ might show that both the winds and the waves were under his command. *And in the fourth watch of the night,* that is, about three hours before the rising of the sun; for though the Jews anciently divided the night into three parts, each consisting of four hours. yet being at this time under the Romans, they kept to their division of it into four parts, which they called watches, from their military guards, which they relieved every three hours. *Jesus went unto them, walking on the sea,* as if it had been firm ground. *And when the disciples saw him walking on the sea, they were troubled, saying, It is a spirit, and they cried out for fear.* By this it seemeth that the doctrine of spirits was not strange to that age, though they had a sect of Sadducees which denied it. That the devil, by God's permission, hath a power to trouble and agitate the air, and also to assume a visible shape, and in it to affright persons by sea or by land, is unquestionable. When the disciples at distance saw Christ walking on the sea, they concluded it was some such apparition. This made them cry out through fear. *But straightway Jesus spake unto them, saying, Be of good cheer; it is I; be not afraid.* Mark addeth, chap. vi. 52, *They considered not the miracle of the loaves; for their heart was hardened.* Having made so late an experience, both of the power and goodness of their Master, in their late strait for want of bread, they ought not so soon to have showed a distrust in his providence, as if he would have suffered them to have perished in the sea: that miracle did not make a due impression upon them.

28 And Peter answered him and said, Lord, if it be thou, bid me come unto thee on the water.

29 And he said, Come. And when Peter was come down out of the ship, he walked on the water, to go to Jesus.

‖ Or, *strong.* 30 But when he saw the wind ‖ boisterous, he was afraid; and beginning to sink, he cried, saying, Lord, save me.

31 And immediately Jesus stretched forth *his* hand, and caught him, and said unto him, O thou of little faith, wherefore didst thou doubt?

Peter, by saying *if it be thou,* showed that his faith was not so strong as it should have been, after he had heard his Master's voice. By his saying to him. *bid me come unto thee on the water,* he showeth a something stronger faith, and a resolution to obey his command; but his fear afterward, when the wind began to rise higher, and he began to sink, argued again the infirmity of his faith. Thus Peter is a pattern of the best believers, who though they may sometimes think that they could trust God in any state or condition, yet often mistake their own hearts, and begin to shrink in an hour of great extremity; which lets us see what need we have to pray, that God would not lead us by his providence into great temptations, much more to take heed that we do not throw ourselves into them. No man knows how he shall find his heart under a great temptation, until he hath tried it. It therefore gives us a caution, as against condemning others, so against boasting, and too much confidence as to ourselves, and lets us see how much need we have to keep our eye upon Christ and his strength in such an hour. *And immediately Jesus stretched forth his hand:* God is never far off from his people when extreme troubles are hard at hand. Christ saveth Peter, but not without a check; *O thou of little faith, wherefore didst thou doubt?* Doubting is directly contrary to faith, yet it will not conclude a soul to have no faith, only a little faith.

32 And when they were come into the ship, the wind ceased.

m Ps. 2. 7. Mark 1. 1. ch. 16. 16. & 26. 63. Luke 4. 41. John 1. 49. & 6. 69. & 11. 27. Acts 8. 37. Rom. 1. 4.

33 Then they that were in the ship came and worshipped him, saying, Of a truth ᵐthou art the Son of God.

They, that is, Christ and Peter, whom we must suppose to have walked some way with Christ upon the sea. Christ by his company making his mighty power more conspicuous; so as the Manichees had no reason to conclude, from Christ's walking on the sea, that he had no true human body, for sure Peter had; and they must ascribe little to our Saviour's Divine nature, that will not allow him to have had a power to suspend the natural motion downward, which we see in all gravity, which is an affection of all human bodies. No sooner was Christ come into the ship, but the wind ceased, in testimony of its homage to him, who bringeth the wind out of his treasuries. *They that were in the ship came and worshipped him,* paying a religious homage unto him, as he who had preserved their lives from so great a danger; and they further owned him to be *the Son of God.* This was that great point which God was bringing the world to the acknowledgment of, and we see it was done by degrees. His miracles at first only procured a veneration of him, and a faith that he had his power from God. Then he comes to be acknowledged the *Son of David* by the blind man. The miracle of the five loaves brought many to acknowledge him *that Prophet that should come into the world.* This is the first time we meet with so plain and open an acknowledgment of his being *the Son of God:* this was done not only by his disciples, but by the mariners, and the passengers in the ship, but it was far from a steady faith as to that point, which the disciples yet wanted.

34 ¶ ⁿAnd when they were gone over, they came into the land of Gennesaret. n Mark 6. 53.

35 And when the men of that place had knowledge of him, they sent out into all that country round about, and brought unto him all that were diseased;

36 And besought him that they might only touch the hem of his garment: and ᵒas many as touched were made perfectly whole.

o ch. 9. 20. Mark 3. 10. Luke 6. 19. Acts 19. 12.

Mark relateth the same, chap. vi. 53—56. with no difference considerable. Christ had been in this country before, chap. viii., and in it wrought several miracles, so as they had a former knowledge of him. As soon as they had knowledge of his being again come, they express their faith in him, and their charity towards their neighbours, in telling it abroad, and bringing sick persons to him. I know not why any should fancy any superstition in their desire to *touch the hem of his garment,* considering how Mark expresseth it, κἀν, which we translate, *if it were but the border of his garment.* It rather soundeth in my ears as a high expression of their faith; they believed there was such a fulness of virtue in Christ, that it flowed from him to every part of his garment. It was their faith in Christ, not their touch of his garment, that healed them. I am sure our Lord so far encouraged their faith, that he healed all those who touched his garment with that faith and expectation. The evangelist saith. they *were made perfectly whole.* Their faith here plainly implied not only an assent to his power, but a confidence in his goodness.

CHAP. XV

Christ reproveth the scribes and Pharisees for setting their own traditions above the commandments of God, 1—9. *He teacheth that not that which goeth into the mouth, but that which cometh out of it, defileth a man,* 10—20. *He healeth the daughter of a woman of Canaan,* 21—28; *and great multitudes near the sea of Galilee,* 29—31. *He feedeth four thousand and upwards with seven loaves and a few small fishes,* 32—39.

THEN ᵃcame to Jesus Scribes and Pharisees, which were of Jerusalem, saying, a Mark 7. 1.

2 ᵇWhy do thy disciples transgress ᶜthe tradition of the elders? for they wash not their hands when they eat bread. b Mark 7. 5. c Col. 2. 8.

Mark relateth this piece of history more largely, chap. vii. 1—5, *Then came together unto him the Pharisees, and certain of the scribes, which came from Jerusalem. And when they saw some of his disciples eat bread with defiled, that is to say, with unwashen, hands, they found fault. For the Pharisees, and all the Jews, except they wash their hands oft, eat not, holding the tradition of the elders. And when they come from the market, except they wash, they eat not. And many other things there be, which they have received to hold, as the washing of cups, and pots, brasen vessels, and of tables. Then the Pharisees and scribes asked him, Why walk not thy disciples according to the tradition of the elders, but eat bread with unwashen hands?* This portion of Scripture cannot be well understood without understanding something of the Jewish government as to matters ecclesiastical; in which the high priest was the chief. God addeth seventy men more to Moses and Aaron, Numb. xi. 25, to bear a share in the government; these were called the sanhedrim; and this was the supreme court of judicature amongst the Jews, as to all things which respected the laws of God, whether moral, judicial, or ceremonial, and every one was bound to abide by their determination. These sat in Jerusalem, but had their inferior courts in other places, from which they appealed to the sanhedrim, who finally determined, Deut. xvii. 8—13. It was the great business of this court to take care that there should be no corruption in religion. These were they therefore that sent messengers to John, when he began to preach, to inquire what he was, and by what authority he baptized, John i. 19. The Pharisees (as we before heard) had charged our Saviour's disciples with violation of the sabbath by plucking and rubbing ears of corn, and himself also with the same crime for healing the sick. It is very like these accusations were got to Jerusalem, and that these were emissaries sent from the sanhedrim to watch our Saviour, or possibly they came out of their own curiosity. They could find in our Saviour no guilt as to any violation of the law of God, but they pick a quarrel with him for some rites and ceremonies of their church, which he and his disciples were not so strict in the observation of. They say, *Why do thy disciples transgress the traditions of the elders?* The word *traditions* signifies only things delivered, and is as well applicable to the law of God as any thing else. Thus the whole law of God was but a tradition, a doctrine of life, delivered to the Jews by Moses from God: thus the apostle bids the Thessalonians, *Hold the traditions which ye have been taught, whether by word, or our epistle,* 2 Thess. ii. 15. But the term of *the elders* is that which restraineth it, for as the papists in our time hold that, besides what we have in the New Testament, the apostle delivered many things to the primitive church only by word of mouth, which have since that time been imparted to succeeding churches, to the observation of which Christians are as much obliged as to the written word, so the Jews did formerly. For though, for some tract of time, they kept to the Divine law, yet in process of time they abused that text, Deut. iv. 14, to found a new invention upon it: That while Moses was in the mount of God forty days and forty nights, God in the day time revealed to him the law written in the five books of Moses, and in the night he revealed to him several other things, as to which his will was they should not be written, for fear the heathens should transcribe them, but be delivered only by word of mouth to the sanhedrim, and be to them as much a rule of judgment as any part of the law which was written. By which means they gained themselves a liberty of making the law of God what they pleased, for their traditions were of several sorts. Some were determinations of what in the law seemed doubtful. Others were determinations of what the law left at liberty. Others they called *sepimenta legis,* rules they gave under pretence of a guard to the Divine law; for the more caution, that they might not transgress it. These things at first were not imposed as laws, but commended by way of advice and counsel, afterward they came to be looked upon as laws, and grew almost infinite. They tell us that Ezra was he who gathered those traditions together, and made the Cabbala in seventy-two books, which was kept by Gamaliel and others till the destruction of Jerusalem. A hundred and twenty years after, they tell us Rabbi Judas, the son of Simon, composed a book of them, called Misna. Three hundred years after this, they tell us R. Johanan found more, and he and others, his colleagues, collected them into a larger book, called the Jerusalem Talmud. And a hundred years after this, another rabbi made a collection of the traditions amongst the Jews that remained in Babylon, which he called the Babylonish Talmud; by which two the Jews are governed in ecclesiastical matters, all the world over, at this day. Their whole Talmud is divided into six parts. The sixth is about purifications; it containeth twelve books, and every book hath twenty or thirty chapters, all treating about the purifying of houses, clothes, vessels, human bodies, and their several parts. The Jews after the destruction of Jerusalem were in such an afflicted state, that though their Talmud was not perfected of five hundred years and more after Christ, yet it is probable they added not much to what they had in use in Christ's time. The Pharisees were very severe as to these traditions. The Sadducees kept more to the written law. But the Pharisees were in far greater credit with the Jews, therefore Paul called them the strictest sect of the Jewish religion, Acts xxvi. 5. The Jews have several ordinary sayings, that show in what esteem they had these traditions, as, *If the scribes say our right hand is our left, and our left hand our right, we are to believe them.* And, *There is more in the words of the scribes than the words of the law,* &c. These scribes and Pharisees accuse our Saviour's disciples for the violation of one of these traditions. Mark saith, that *the Pharisees, and all the Jews,* (that is, the major part of those that followed the Pharisees' faction,) *except they wash their hands oft, eat not.* They thought it sinful to eat unless they often washed their hands. The foundation of this tradition was doubtless in the Levitical law. God by that law had ordained him unclean that should touch the carcass of any unclean thing, Lev. v. 2, 3. Upon this (as some think) they had superstructed a tradition of washing their hands, pots, cups, vessels, when they had been at the market, or almost any where, for fear they, or their pots, cups, &c., should have touched any unclean person or thing. In this they were guilty of several errors: 1. Extending the law to the touching of things and persons, of whom the law had said nothing. 2. In cases where such touches happened accidentally, and were not made on purpose. 3. In thinking that the stain of sin could be washed away by a ritual action, which God never commanded. We must not think that they charge the disciples here with a neglect of a civil washing for cleanliness, but of a religious superstitious washing. Mark saith, κοιναῖς χερσί, that is, with common hands; we translate it, polluted: so Acts x. 14; xi. 8: hands not first separated to God by the religious rite of washings.

3 But he answered and said unto them, Why do ye also transgress the commandment of God by your tradition?

Mark hath the same, chap. vii. 9, though a little out of the order in which Matthew hath it: *Full well ye reject the commandment of God, that ye may keep your own tradition.* Our Saviour could have answered them, had he pleased, more strictly to their questions, but he must then either have incurred danger or odium; he therefore chooseth to answer them by another question, which struck at the root of the matter. Admit, saith he, my disciples culpable in not observing traditions, which indeed you call the traditions of the elders, but are your own, devised by you, or some like you, merely to uphold your power and authority, and to keep people in a needless subjection to you: I am sure you are far more guilty, in making traditions contrary to the law of God, or rejecting God's law to keep your traditions. And indeed this is the common guilt of those who are great zealots for traditions and rites, not commanded in the word of God. The Jewish Rabbi Jose saith, *He sinneth as much who eateth with unwashen hands, as he that lieth with an harlot.* The papists make it a greater sin for a priest to marry than to keep a concubine, and commit fornication; they make it a lesser transgression than to eat meat on a Friday.

4 For God commanded, saying, ^dHonour thy father and mother: and, ^eHe that curseth father or mother, let him die the death.

5 But ye say, Whosoever shall say to *his* father or *his* mother, ^f*It is* a gift, by whatsoever thou mightest be profited by me;

6 And honour not his father or his mother, *he shall be free.* Thus have ye made the commandment of God of none effect by your tradition.

^d Ex. 20. 12. Lev. 19. 3. Deut. 5. 16. Prov. 23. 22. Eph. 6. 2.
^e Ex. 21. 17. Lev. 20. 9. Deut. 27. 16. Prov. 20. 20. & 30. 17.
^f Mark 7. 11, 12.

Mark hath much the same, chap. vii. 10—13. Mark saith *Moses said*, which is the same with *God commanded :* God commanded by Moses. Mark saith, *It is Corban, that is to say, a gift.* Mark addeth, ver. 12, *And ye suffer him no more to do aught for his father or mother ;* which more fully showeth their crime, and expoundeth what Matthew had said more shortly. Mark adds, *and many such like things do ye.* This is an instance by which our Saviour justifieth his charge upon them, that they had made void the law of God by their traditions. The law he instanceth in is the fifth commandment, Exod. xx. 12 ; Deut. v. 16 ; which the apostle calleth *the first commandment with promise,* Eph. vi. 2 ; which God had fortified with a judicial law, wherein he had commanded, that *he who cursed his father and mother should be put to death,* Exod. xxi. 17 ; Lev. xx. 9 : he had also further threatened the violaters of this law, Prov. xx. 20. By the way, our Saviour here also lets us know, that the fifth commandment obligeth children to relieve their parents in their necessity, and this is the sense of the term *honour* in other texts of Scripture : a law of God which hath approved itself to the wisdom almost of all nations. *Liberi parentes alant aut vinciantur,* Let children relieve their parents or be put into prison, was an old Roman law. Nor did the Pharisees deny this in terms, but they had made an exception from it, which in effect made it of no use, at least such as wicked children easily might, and commonly did, elude it by : they had taught the people to say to their parents, *It is Corban, that is to say, a gift, by whatsoever thou mightest be profited by me :* and in that case, though they did not give their poor parents any thing wherewith they might relieve their necessities, yet they should be guiltless as to the fifth commandment. There is a strange variety of interpreters as to this text. Some making the sense this, That which I should relieve you with I have dedicated unto God, and therefore I cannot relieve you. Others thus, I have dedicated my estate to God, and that will be as much good and benefit to you, as if I had given it unto you. Others think that Corban was the form of an oath, from whence they form other senses. But the most free and unconstrained sense seemeth to be this : The Pharisees were a very courteous generation, and had a share in the gifts that were brought unto God for the use of the temple or otherwise ; thence they were very zealous and diligent in persuading people to make such oblations. When any pretended the need that their parents stood in of their help, they told them, that if they told their parents it was *a gift*, that they had vowed such a portion of their estate to a sacred use, that would before God excuse them for not relieving their parents ; so as the precept of honouring their parents, and relieving them in their necessities, obliged them not, if they had first given to God the things by which their parents might or ought to have been relieved. Thus he tells them, that by their traditions, under pretence of a more religious, and expounding the Divine law, they had indeed destroyed it, and made it of no effect at all.

g Mark 7. 6.

7 ᵍ *Ye* hypocrites, well did Esaias prophesy of you, saying,

h Is. 29. 13. Ezek. 33. 31.

8 ʰThis people draweth nigh unto me with their mouth, and honoureth me with *their* lips ; but their heart is far from me.

i Is. 29. 13. Col. 2. 18, —22. Tit. 1. 14.

9 But in vain they do worship me, ⁱteaching *for* doctrines the commandments of men.

The Greek is, διδάσκοντες διδασκαλίας, teaching doctrines, the commandments of men. *Ye hypocrites,* who put on an outward vizard or appearance of holiness, but have nothing in your hearts of true and severe piety, *well did Isaiah prophesy of you :* Isaiah spake to the Jews that were then in being, but what he then said of your forefathers that lived in his age, is true of you who are their children. *Saying, This people, &c.* The evangelist doth not quote the words of the prophet exactly, but his sense, and teacheth us this lesson, That whatsoever outward show and profession of religion be in and upon men, if their hearts be not right with God, and what they outwardly do proceed not from an inward principle of faith, love, and obedience in and to God, they are but hypocrites. *In vain do they worship me, &c. ;* that is, idly, and unprofitably, and to no purpose : I will not accept what they do.

Teaching doctrines, the commandments of men : he means in the worship of God, for other commandments of men are not the preacher's texts, nor doth he here mean by *commandments of men* such as backed the commandments of God, and only served to enforce them, but such as he had been speaking of, human traditions, of which God had said nothing, as washing of hands ; or such traditions as enervated the commandments of God ; such were the last mentioned.

10 ¶ ᵏAnd he called the multitude, and said unto them, Hear, and understand :

k Mark 7. 14.

11 ˡNot that which goeth into the mouth defileth a man ; but that which cometh out of the mouth, this defileth a man.

l Acts 10. 15. Rom. 14. 14, 17, 20. 1 Tim. 4. 4. Tit. 1. 15.

Mark hath the same, chap. vii. 15. Our Saviour turns off his discourse from the Pharisees and scribes, who he saw were indocible, to the multitude, in whom he discerned a more teachable temper : he useth the preface, *Hear, and understand,* as well knowing how they had been taught, and what an advantage error in possession hath. That which he tells them, and that before the scribes and Pharisees, (as will appear by the following verses,) was, that that which goeth into a man doth not defile him, but that which cometh out of him. He speaketh not of a Levitical pollution, for so he that did eat of an unclean thing might by it be defiled ; but even in such an eating it was not the flesh of the unclean bird or beast that defiled the man, but his sinful lusting after it, and eating it in disobedience to the command of God.

12 Then came his disciples, and said unto him, Knowest thou that the Pharisees were offended, after they heard this saying ?

The Pharisees' offence was, without question, at his making so light a matter at their washings ; not that they understood our Saviour as speaking against the distinction of meats, which was established by the ceremonial law, not as yet abrogated. There is nothing doth more offend hypocrites than pressing spiritual worship and homage to God, and the slighting of all external rites and actions, not attended with a suitable inward homage and devotion of heart.

13 But he answered and said, ᵐEvery plant, which my heavenly Father hath not planted, shall be rooted up.

m John 15. 2. 1 Cor. 3. 12, &c.

14 Let them alone : ⁿthey be blind leaders of the blind. And if the blind lead the blind, both shall fall into the ditch.

n Is. 9. 16. Mal. 2. 8. ch. 23. 16. Luke 6. 39.

Every plant may be understood of doctrines, practices, or persons. These scribes and Pharisees are a wretched generation, that are got into the sheepfold not at the door ; my Father never sent them, they are crept in at the windows, they are plants got into my garden, which my Father never planted there, and they must be rooted up. *Let them alone*, they are incorrigible, and blinded by their own interest against any conviction or instruction : as, Hos. iv. 17, *Ephraim is joined to idols ; let him alone :* so these men are joined to their superstitious traditions ; I will not concern myself with them. They are pretended leaders of the blind, Rom. ii. 19, but themselves are blind. I pity the poor people, for whilst the blind lead the blind they both fall into a ditch. An ignorant and unfaithful ministry is the greatest plague God can send amongst a people.

15 ᵒThen answered Peter and said unto him, Declare unto us this parable.

o Mark 7. 17.

16 And Jesus said, ᵖAre ye also yet without understanding ?

p ch. 16. 9. Mark 7. 18.

Mark saith, *his disciples asked him concerning the parable.* Peter probably began, the rest followed. Or Peter speaks in the name of the rest, for our Saviour in his answer doth not say, Art thou, but, *Are ye.* They did well in that they desired to be instructed what the meaning was of the parable, that is, the dark saying, which he used (for the Hebrews called all dark sayings parables) ; possibly they might also stumble at what our Saviour said, as tending to the destruction of the ceremonial law, about the difference of meats. But that they were no better instructed than not to understand a thing so plain and obvious, this was their fault, and argued their small improvement of our Saviour's company. God expects a proficiency in knowledge from us proportionate unto the means he giveth us.

17 Do not ye yet understand, that ^q whatsoever entereth in at the mouth goeth into the belly, and is cast out into the draught?

q 1 Cor. 6. 13.

18 But ^rthose things which proceed out of the mouth come forth from the heart; and they defile the man.

r Jam. 3. 6.

19 ^sFor out of the heart proceed evil thoughts, murders, adulteries, fornications, thefts, false witness, blasphemies:

s Gen. 6. 5. & 8. 21. Prov. 6. 14. Jer. 17. 9. Mark 7. 21.

20 These are *the things* which defile a man: but to eat with unwashen hands defileth not a man.

Mark hath this, with very small difference in words, chap. vii. 18—23; only he specifieth some more sins than Matthew enumerateth. The sum of what our Saviour saith is this: That all sin proceedeth from lust, some desires in the heart of man after things forbidden in the law of God. All the ticklings of our hearts with such thoughts, all the willings and desires of such things, though they never issue in overt acts, yet defile and pollute a man; and from these inward motions of the heart proceed those overt acts (mentioned by Matthew or Mark) of *murders, adulteries, fornications, thefts, false witness, blasphemies, deceit, lasciviousness, an evil eye, pride, foolishness*: now these things, take them in their nest, which is the heart, they defile and pollute that; take them in their passage through our lips into the world, they pollute that; take them in their overt act, they pollute the man. But to eat with unwashen hands, a thing no where forbidden by God, only by the Pharisees, who had no such authority given them from God to command any such things, this doth not pollute a man. It is possible that men may sin in not obeying the commandments of men, but it must be then in things in which God hath authorized them to command, and to determine our practice in, for the pollution lies in a disobedience to the commandment of God, not of men.

t Mark 7. 24.

21 ¶ ^tThen Jesus went thence, and departed into the coasts of Tyre and Sidon.

Mark addeth, chap. vii. 24, *and entered into an house, and would have no man know it; but he could not be hid.* Some here make a question, whether our Saviour did go into Phœnicia, (of which Tyre and Sidon were the principal cities,) or only into the coasts of Palestina, next to it: those that think he did not go into Phœnicia, are guided by his prohibition of his disciples to go into the way of the Gentiles, Matt. x. 5, and the consideration that the time was not yet come for his manifestation to the Gentiles. I rather incline to think that he went into Tyre and Sidon; and that this was a kind of a *præludium* to the calling of the Gentiles, and a prediction of what should be done more fully afterwards. It is manifest he did not go with a design to make himself public there, for Mark saith, he *would have no man know it.* But for privacy withdrew himself thither, and showed some of his miraculous operations there; and ver. 22 saith the woman that came to him was a Canaanite. Mark saith she was *a Greek, a Syrophenician by nation.* Nor is here any contradiction, for ever since the Grecian monarchy prevailed over so great a part of the world, the name of Greeks had obtained, so as they called all Greeks who were not Jews, Rom. i. 14, 16; x. 12. *A Syrophenician,* saith Mark, *by nation;* that is, one that was a native of that part of Phœnicia which is joined to Tyre and Sidon. Matthew calls her a Canaanite, or a woman of Canaan, by which though some would understand one of Cana, yet as the orthography will not agree, so Mark calling her a Greek, and a Syrophenician, inclines us rather to judge her of the stock of the old Canaanites.

22 And, behold, a woman of Canaan came out of the same coasts, and cried unto him, saying, Have mercy on me, O Lord, *thou* Son of David; my daughter is grievously vexed with a devil.

23 But he answered her not a word. And his disciples came and besought him, saying, Send her away; for she crieth after us.

Mark saith, *A certain woman, whose young daughter had an unclean spirit, heard of him, and came and fell at his feet: the woman was a Greek, a Syrophenician by nation; and she besought him that he would cast forth the devil out of her daughter. But Jesus said unto her, Let the children first be filled: for it is not meet to take the children's bread and cast it unto the dogs,* chap. vii. 25—27. Though the woman appears to have been a pagan, yet living so near Galilee, she had doubtless heard of Christ, both what he had done in casting out devils, and also that he was looked upon as the Son of David, and usually called by that name by those who went to him for any cures; she therefore gives him that title. Others think her to have been more specially enlightened, and to have called him the Son of David, not as a usual compellation given him, but as believing him to have been the true Messias promised to the Jews: nor is that impossible, for though the gospel at this time had not shined out upon any considerable number of the heathen, yet God in all times had his number amongst them; and this woman living so near to the Jews, and so near to Galilee, where our Saviour hitherto had most conversed and preached, it is not improbable that she might have received the grace as well as the sound of the gospel, so God might have kindled in her heart a true faith in the Messias. Our Saviour's commendation of her faith in the following discourse maketh this very probable. Matthew saith that *he answered her not a word.* Mark saith that he said to her, *Let the children first be filled,* &c. To the observing reader this will appear no contradiction. For by Mark it should appear, that she first came to our Saviour into the house, into which he went that he might be private, and there fell at his feet. Here Christ *answered her not a word,* took no notice of her at all. But it appeareth by Matthew that Christ soon left the house, and she followed after him upon the way. The disciples said, *Send her away; for she crieth after us.* Then it was that our Saviour said to her, *Let the children first be filled;* his disciples first interposing, saying, *Send her away; for she crieth after us.* How many of the papists think that this text patronizeth their invocation of saints departed I cannot tell, for these disciples were alive, and we do not read that she spake to any of them to intercede for her. It is certain they did move Christ on her behalf.

24 But he answered and said, ^uI am not sent but unto the lost sheep of the house of Israel.

u ch. 10. 5, 6. Acts 3. 25, 26. & 13. 46. Rom. 15. 8.

Our Lord by these words doth not deny but that he was sent as a Redeemer to more, but not as a minister, or as an *apostle,* as he is called, Heb. iii. 1. The apostle, Rom. xv. 8, saith, *that Jesus Christ was a minister of the circumcision for the truth of God to confirm the promises made unto the fathers.* Our Lord's ministry was confined to the Jews; so was the apostles', Matt. x. 5. Till some time after our Saviour's ascension the gospel was not preached generally to the Gentiles, though some particular persons might and did, both in Christ's time and in the time of the apostles, before they did go to the Gentiles, hear, receive and embrace the gospel, as we shall hear this woman did.

25 Then came she and worshipped him, saying, Lord, help me.

She here acknowledgeth his Divine power, and imploreth his help; thus showing that she believed him to be the Son of God, and a rewarder of those that sought him; and continues her request after two repulses.

26 But he answered and said, It is not meet to take the children's bread, and to cast *it* to ^xdogs.

x ch. 7. 6. Phil. 3. 2.

Mark saith, chap. vii. 27, Jesus *said unto her, Let the children first be filled; for it is not meet,* &c. By the *children* here he means the Jews, by the *dogs* he means the heathen. The Jews are called the children of the kingdom. Israel is called God's *son,* his *first-born,* Exod. iv. 22. The apostle, Rom. ix. 4, saith, to them belonged *the adoption*. By *bread* here our Saviour means the publication of the gospel, and the miracles by which the truth of the doctrine of it was confirmed; by *dogs* he means the heathen, whom the Jews did count as dogs, no members of the household of God: it was a term of contempt, 2 Sam. iii. 8; xvi. 9; 2 Kings viii. 13. When our Saviour saith, *It is not meet*, he means it is not just, nor equal. *Object.* How came it then that the gospel was ever carried to the Gentiles? Mark expounds our Saviour's meaning, or rather gives us an account of our Saviour's words, more perfectly: *Let the children first be filled; for it is not meet*, &c. The Jews are God's children, a people whom he chose out of all the nations of the earth, to whom he gave many privileges; it is his will the gospel should be first preached to them, and then to the Gentiles. Gentiles are as dogs, of whom God hath not taken such a care; but they shall have their time. Only it is not consonant to my Father's will that the gospel, and the miracles by which it is confirmed, should be exhibited unto you Gentiles, till it hath been fully preached to the Jews, and they be first filled with the sound, and with the confirmations of it.

27 And she said, Truth, Lord: yet the dogs eat of the crumbs which fall from their masters' table.

Mark reports it to the same sense, chap. vii. 28. She goeth on after three repulses, the last of which was not without a reproach, for our Lord had implicitly called her a dog. These words are as much as if she had said, Lord, I confess the Jews are children; I am a dog, a poor heathen, no proper member of the household of God; and it is truth that it seemeth unreasonable that I, being a dog, should be served before all the children are filled. Lord, I do not beg such a full manifestation of thy power and goodness for the Gentiles. I beg but a crumb of mercy for myself and poor child; and, Lord, though we do not use to give our loaves prepared for our children to the dogs that feed under our table, crumbs of our children's bread, as Mark expresseth it, yet we suffer our dogs to gather them up. Lord, I know thou hast a plenty of grace and blessing, the children may be filled, and yet I may have some crumbs. Three things are remarkable in her answer, besides her faith so eminently expressed. 1. Her humility; she owneth herself a dog. 2. Her modesty; she beggeth no more than a crumb. 3. Her fervency and importunity after three repulses. By this we learn our duty in prayer, to go to God humbly, to implore him modestly, and to be instant in prayer, going on in our duty, though we have not presently such an answer as we desire. These things, conjoined with faith, make an acceptable prayer.

28 Then Jesus answered and said unto her, O woman, great *is* thy faith: be it unto thee even as thou wilt. And her daughter was made whole from that very hour.

Mark saith, chap. vii. 29, *And he said unto her, For this saying go thy way; the devil is gone out of thy daughter. And when she was come to her house, she found the devil gone out, and her daughter laid upon the bed.* O woman! for this saying, showing the greatness of thy faith, be it unto thee as thou wilt. Go thy way; the devil is gone out of thy daughter. *And her daughter was made whole from that very hour*, as she understood when she came home to her house, she found the devil was gone out of her daughter, and her daughter was laid upon the bed. Thus the words of both the evangelists compounded make but one entire and perfect sense. The greatness of her faith appeared in two things: 1. In that she had so little means, so small a revelation; being a pagan, she ordinarily had not heard the gospel, nor seen so many of Christ's mighty works, confirming the truth of the doctrine of it. Hence it is observed, that Christ admired the faith of none but pagans, Matt. viii. 10. 2. In that she would not give over, though he gave her three repulses. So as she said, like Jacob, *I will not let thee go, until thou bless me*. And as he, like a prince, so she, like a princess, prevailed with God, and obtained the thing which she desired. But will some say, Where was her faith? what promise, what word of God, had she to assent to? God doth not speak to us outwardly, but inwardly, as undoubtedly he had to this woman, giving her some inward assurance that he was the Son of God, and both able and willing to grant her the thing she asked. Now a firm and fixed assent to any Divine revelation is faith, whether the revelation be internal or external. We from hence learn the mighty power of true faith and fervent prayer.

29 ʸAnd Jesus departed from thence, and came nigh ᶻunto the sea of Galilee; and went up into a mountain, and sat down there. _{y Mark 7. 31. z ch. 4. 18.}

30 ᵃAnd great multitudes came unto him, having with them *those that were* lame, blind, dumb, maimed, and many others, and cast them down at Jesus' feet; and he healed them: _{a Is. 35. 5, 6. ch. 11. 5. Luke 7. 22.}

31 Insomuch that the multitude wondered, when they saw the dumb to speak, the maimed to be whole, the lame to walk, and the blind to see: and they glorified the God of Israel.

Mark gives us an account of this motion of our Saviour's, chap. vii. 31—37, and mentioneth a particular miracle which our Lord wrought, either in the way, or when he came to the place where he rested; which not being mentioned by our evangelist, I shall consider when I come to that chapter in Mark. Matthew only tells us in general that he healed many, some lame, some that were blind, some that were dumb, &c. Such a general account of the miracles wrought by our Saviour we had chap. iv. 24; viii. 16; xi. 5; the evangelist not largely setting down every particular miracle wrought by our Saviour. And they glorified the Lord God of Israel. The Pharisees ascribed these operations to the devil's power, but the poor people owned them as the works of God, and gave praise unto God.

32 ¶ ᵇThen Jesus called his disciples *unto him*, and said, I have compassion on the multitude, because they continue with me now three days, and have nothing to eat: and I will not send them away fasting, lest they faint in the way. _{b Mark 8. 1.}

33 ᶜAnd his disciples say unto him, Whence should we have so much bread in the wilderness, as to fill so great a multitude? _{c 2 Kings 4. 43.}

34 And Jesus saith unto them, How many loaves have ye? And they said, Seven, and a few little fishes.

35 And he commanded the multitude to sit down on the ground.

36 And ᵈhe took the seven loaves and the fishes, and ᵉgave thanks, and brake *them*, and gave to his disciples, and the disciples to the multitude. _{d ch. 14. 19. e 1 Sam. 9. 13. Luke 22. 19.}

37 And they did all eat, and were filled: and they took up of the broken *meat* that was left seven baskets full.

38 And they that did eat were four thousand men, beside women and children.

39 ᶠAnd he sent away the multitude, and took ship, and came into the coasts of Magdala. _{f Mark 8. 10.}

Mark gives us an account of this miracle, chap. viii. 1—10. There is very little difference in their relations, only Mark saith, our Saviour went *into the parts of Dalmanutha;* Matthew saith, *into the coasts of Magdala:* most think that it was the same place, which had two names: some think one was the name of the country, the other of the city or town; others, that they were two towns near together. There are no difficulties in this history. Some question how they could fast three days; but the text doth not say so, only that at that time they had nothing to eat, having spent what they brought with them, probably in their baskets, which answers another question also, how they could get baskets in the wilderness. The miracle was of the same nature with that which we met with chap. xiv.; only there were five thousand men fed with five loaves and two fishes, here four thousand were fed with seven loaves and a few fishes; there they took up twelve, here but seven baskets full. Our Lord worketh sometimes without means, sometimes by means, and those differently proportioneth to his end, as it pleaseth him. The miraculous operations of our Saviour are amongst his *miranda et adoranda*, not his *imitanda*. These actions of his, which we are in reading to admire and adore, but are not concerned to imitate, yet something we may observe from them, both for our instruction and imitation. For our instruction, we may from this history observe the extent of Christ's compassion to his disciples, which though it is most eminently seen in what he doth for their souls, yet reacheth also to their bodies and more external wants. It also teacheth us to trust God in the doing of our duty. Those that are in a wilderness hearing Christ, shall not faint by the way before they get home. His course of giving thanks before he brake and made use of the bread, (which we observed before in the other miracle,) commendeth to us the religious custom of begging a blessing before our meat, and giving thanks to God for good things of that nature, when we have received them.

CHAP. XVI

The Pharisees require a sign, 1—4. Jesus warneth his disciples against the leaven of the Pharisees and Sadducees, and explaineth his meaning, 5—12. The people's opinion, and Peter's confession, of Christ, 13—20. Jesus foreshoweth his own death, and rebuketh Peter for dissuading him from it, 21—23. He showeth that his followers must deny themselves in prospect of a future reward, 24—28.

a ch. 12. 38.
Mark 8. 11.
Luke 11. 16.
& 12. 54,—
56.
1 Cor. 1. 22.

THE ^aPharisees also with the Sadducees came, and tempting desired him that he would shew them a sign from heaven.

What these Pharisees and Sadducees were we have had an occasion to show before in our annotations on chap. iii. 7. There was a great opposition betwixt them, as we may learn from Acts xxiii. 7, 8. The Pharisees and scribes were great zealots for their traditions; the Sadducees valued them not. The Pharisees held the resurrection, angels, and spirits; the Sadducees denied all. But they were both enemies to Christ, and combine in their designs against him. They came to him *tempting*, that is, desirous to make a trial of him; they desire *that he would show them a sign from heaven;* such a one as Moses showed them, John vi. 30, 31, bringing down bread from heaven. They had seen our Saviour showing many signs, but they had taught the people that these things might be done by the power of the devil, or by the art of man; therefore they challenge our Saviour to show them another kind of sign, a sign from heaven, that they might know he was sent of God. See Mark viii. 11.

2 He answered and said unto them, When it is evening, ye say, *It will be* fair weather: for the sky is red.

3 And in the morning, *It will be* foul weather to day: for the sky is red and lowring. O *ye* hypocrites, ye can discern the face of the sky; but can ye not *discern* the signs of the times?

You can, saith our Saviour, make observations upon the works of God in nature and common providence, and from such observations you can make conclusions; if you see the sky red in the evening, you can conclude from thence that the morrow will be fair, because you think that the redness of the sky at night speaks the clouds thin, and the air pure; and on the other side, the redness of it in the morning speaks the clouds thick, so as the sun cannot disperse them; or because you observe that generally it so proveth, though nothing be more mutable than the air. But you cannot *discern the signs of the times:* you are only dull at making observations upon the Scriptures, and the will of God revealed in them concerning me. You might observe that all the signs of the Messias are fulfilled in me: I was born of a virgin, as was prophesied by Isaiah, chap. vii. 14; in Bethlehem Judah, as was prophesied by Micah, chap. v. 2; at a time when the sceptre was departed from Judah, and the lawgiver from his feet, as was prophesied by Jacob, Gen. xlix. 10: that John the Baptist is come in the power and spirit of Elias, to prepare my way before me, as was prophesied by Malachi, chap. iv. 5; that there is one come, who openeth the eyes of the blind, and unstoppeth the ears of the deaf, and maketh the lame to leap as an hart, and the tongue of the dumb to sing, according to the prophecy, Isa. xxxv. 5, 6. All these are the signs of the time when the Messiah was to come; but these things you cannot discern, but, like a company of hypocrites, who pretend one thing and do another, you come and ask a sign, that you might believe in me, when you have so many, and yet will not believe.

4 ^bA wicked and adulterous generation b ch. 12. 39.
seeketh after a sign; and there shall no sign be given unto it, but the sign of the prophet Jonas. And he left them, and departed.

We meet with the same answer given to the Pharisees, chap. xii. 39. You pretend yourselves to be the children of Abraham, but you are bastards rather than his children; he saw my day afar off and rejoiced, you will not believe though you see me amongst you, and at your doors; he believed without any sign, you will not believe though I have showed you many signs. You shall have no such sign as you would have; the sign of the prophet Jonah is enough. But in our Lord's former reference of them to the prophet Jonah, he instanced in one particular, viz. his being three days and three nights in the belly of the whale; here he seemeth more generally to refer to Jonah as a type of him in more respects, which indeed he was. Chemnitius reckons them up thus: 1. Jonah was thrown into the sea by the mariners, to whom he had betrusted himself: Christ was delivered to death by the Jews, to whom he was specially promised. 2. Jonah was willingly thrown into the sea: Christ laid down his life, and man took it not from him. 3. Jonah by being cast into the sea saved those in the ship: Christ by his death saved the children of men. 4. Jonah after he had been in the whale's belly three days was cast up on dry land: Christ after three days rose again from the dead. 5. The Ninevites, though upon the preaching of Jonah they made a show of repentance, yet returning to their former sins were soon after destroyed; so were the Jews within forty years after Christ's ascension. So as Jonah was many ways an eminent sign and type of Christ. Our Lord having referred them to study this sign, would entertain no more discourse with them, but leaves, and departeth from them. Mark saith, chap. viii. 13, that he entering into the ship again, departed to the other side, (the ship which brought him to Dalmanutha, or Magdala,) and went into the coasts of Galilee again.

5 And ^cwhen his disciples were come c Mark 8. 14.
to the other side, they had forgotten to take bread.

6 ¶ Then Jesus said unto them, ^dTake d Luke 12.1.
heed and beware of the leaven of the Pharisees and of the Sadducees.

7 And they reasoned among themselves, saying, *It is* because we have taken no bread.

Mark saith, chap. viii. 14—16, *Now the disciples had forgotten to take bread, neither had they in the ship with them more than one loaf. And he charged them, saying, Take heed and beware of the leaven of the Pharisees, and of the leaven of Herod. And they reasoned among themselves, saying, It is because we have no bread.* The disciples went into the ship without taking a due care for provision for their bodies, which they were sensible of when they came on shore on the other side. Christ happened in the mean time to give them a caution against the doctrine of the Pharisees, and Sadducees, and Herodians, which he properly expresseth (though metaphorically) under the notion of leaven: this they understood not, but fancied that he had spoken this to them with reference to their want of bread, as if he had only given them warning, that for the making of bread to supply their necessity, they should not go to the Pharisees, or Sadducees, or Herodians, for leaven ; or that they should not go to buy any bread of the Pharisees or of the Sadducees. So dull are we to understand spiritual things, and so soon had they forgot the doctrine which our Saviour had so lately taught them, chap. xv. 17, 18, that those things which are foreign to a man, and come not out of his heart, do not defile a man, but those things only which proceed out of his heart.

8 *Which* when Jesus perceived, he said unto them, O ye of little faith, why reason ye among yourselves, because ye have brought no bread ?

e ch. 14. 17.
John 6. 9.
9 ᵉDo ye not yet understand, neither remember the five loaves of the five thousand, and how many baskets ye took up ?

f ch. 15. 34. 10 ᶠNeither the seven loaves of the four thousand, and how many baskets ye took up ?

11 How is it that ye do not understand that I spake *it* not to you concerning bread, that ye should beware of the leaven of the Pharisees and of the Sadducees ?

12 Then understood they how that he bade *them* not beware of the leaven of bread, but of the doctrine of the Pharisees and of the Sadducees.

Mark, giving us an account of this passage, chap. viii. 17—19, useth some harsher expressions : *And when Jesus knew it, he saith unto them, Why reason ye, because ye have no bread ? perceive ye not yet, neither understand ? have ye your eyes yet hardened ? Having eyes, see ye not ? and having ears, hear ye not ? And do ye not remember ? When I brake the five loaves among five thousand, how many baskets full of fragments took ye up ? They say unto him, Twelve. And when the seven among four thousand, how many baskets full of fragments took ye up ? And they said, Seven. And he said unto them, How is it that ye do not understand ?* Our Saviour here chargeth them with three things, ignorance, unbelief, forgetfulness. 1. Ignorance, in that they did not understand that his usual way was to discourse spiritual things to them under earthly similitudes, and so by leaven he must understand something else than leaven with which men use to leaven their bread. 2. Unbelief, that they having seen the power and goodness of the Lord and Master, to feed four thousand with seven loaves, and five thousand with five loaves, leaving a great remainder, and that he did this for a mixed multitude, out of a mere compassion to the wants and cravings of human nature, should not judge that he was able to provide for them, although they had brought no bread ; or doubt whether he would do it or no for them, who were much dearer to him. 3. Forgetfulness, which is often in Scripture made the mother of unbelief and disobedience, Deut. iv. 9, 23 ; xxv. 19 ; Psal. lxxviii. 11. There is nothing of difficulty in the terms, only from this history we may learn these things : 1. That God expecteth that we should not only hear and see, but understand. 2. That he looks we should not only hear for the present time, but for the time to come. Christ expected that his disciples should have learned from his doctrine about washing of hands, that he could not mean the leaven of bread, but something else, which might defile them. 3. That he is much displeased with his own people, when he discerns blindness and ignorance in them, after their more than ordinary means of knowledge. 4. That former experiences of God's power and goodness manifested for us, or to us, ought to strengthen our faith in him when we come under the like circumstances ; and a disputing or doubting after such experiences argueth but a little and very weak faith, and a hardness of heart, that the mercies of God have not made a just impression on our souls. *Then understood they how that he bade them not beware of the leaven of bread, but of the doctrine of the Pharisees and of the Sadducees.* Mark, instead of *and of the Sadducees,* hath, *and of the leaven of Herod,* which hath made some think that Herod was a Sadducee. The doctrine of the Pharisees is reducible to two heads : 1. Justification by the works of the law, and those works too according to that imperfect sense of the law they gave. 2. The obligation of the tradition of the elders ; whose traditions were also (as we have heard) some of them of that nature, that they made the law of God of no effect. The doctrine of the Sadducees we are in part told, Acts xxiii. 8. They said there was no resurrection, nor angel, nor spirit : these were principles excellently suited to men of atheistical hearts and lives, and it is more than probable that Herod and his courtiers, and some of his lords and great captains, had sucked in some of these principles, and these were the Herodians mentioned, Matt. xxii. 16 ; Mark iii. 6. These doctrines are by our Saviour compared to leaven, not only because of the sour nature of it, but also because heretics' words (as the apostle saith) eat as doth a canker, and are of a contagious nature ; as leaven doth diffuse its quality into the whole mass of meat. Our Saviour had upon this account compared the gospel to leaven, chap. xiii. 33, because by his blessing upon it it should influence the world, as we heard, chap. xiii.

13 ¶ When Jesus came into the coasts of Cæsarea Philippi, he asked his disciples, saying, ᵍWhom do men say that I the Son of man am ?   g Mark 8. 27. Luke 9. 18.

14 And they said, ʰSome *say that thou art* John the Baptist : some, Elias ; and others, Jeremias, or one of the prophets.   h ch. 14. 2. Luke 9. 7, 8, 9.

This, and the following part of this discourse, is related both by Mark and Luke. Mark hath it, chap. viii. 27, *And Jesus went out, and his disciples, into the towns of Cesarea Philippi : and by the way he asked his disciples, saying unto them, Whom do men say that I am ? And they answered, John the Baptist : but some say, Elias ; and others, One of the prophets.* Luke saith, chap. ix. 18, 19, *And it came to pass, as he was alone praying, his disciples were with him . and he asked them, saying, Whom say the people that I am ? They answering said, John the Baptist ; but some say, Elias ; and others say, that one of the old prophets is risen again.* Matthew and Mark name the place whither our Saviour was going, viz. Cesarea Philippi : it is so called partly to distinguish it from another Cesarea, and partly because it was built to the honour of Tiberius Cæsar, by Philip the tetrarch. It was a city at the bottom of Lebanon, and upon the river of Jordan. Mark saith this discourse was in the way. Luke saith, *as he was alone praying ;* but *as* must there signify *after,* for we cannot think that our Saviour would interrupt himself in prayer by this discourse, nor could he be alone praying if his disciples were with him, both which Luke saith ; so that ἐν τῷ εἶναι αὐτὸν προσευχόμενον καταμόνας were certainly translated better, after he had been praying alone, his disciples were with him : so that this discourse might be (as Mark saith) in the way, before they came to Cesarea Philippi, whither he was going. *He asked his disciples, saying, Whom do men* (or *the people,* as Luke hath it) *say that I am ?* Not that our Saviour, who knew the hearts of all, did not know, but to draw out Peter's following confession. *And they said, Some say that thou art John the Baptist :* we heard before that Herod said so. *Some, Elias :* this respected the prophecy, Mal. iv. 5. The Jews had a tradition, that before the coming of the Messias Elias should come, John i. 21. *Others, Jeremias,* (this is only in Matthew,) *or one of the prophets.* The Jews seeing Christ do such wonderful works, could not resolve themselves who he was. Herod and his court party said, that he was John the Baptist risen from the dead. They had, it seems, an opinion of some extraordinary virtues, or powers, in such as were risen from the dead. Many interpreters agree that the Jews had an opinion, that good men's souls, when they died, went into other bodies ; this made them guess that our Saviour was one of the old prophets.

15 He saith unto them, But whom say ye that I am ?   i ch. 14. 33. Mark 8. 29. Luke 9. 20. John 6. 69.

16 And Simon Peter answered and said, ⁱThou art the Christ, the Son of the living God.   & 11. 27. Acts 8, 37. & 9. 20. 1 John 4. 15. & 5. 5. Heb. 1. 2, 5.

Mark saith, chap. viii. 29, *Thou art the Christ.* Luke saith, chap. ix. 20, *Peter answering said, The Christ of God,* that is, the Messiah. You that are my disciples and apostles, what is your opinion of me ? Our Lord expects not only faith in our hearts, but the confession of our lips, Rom. x. 10. *And Simon Peter answered*, not because he had any priority amongst the apostles, but he was of a more quick and fervid temper than the rest, and so speaketh first; they silently agreed to what he said. What he saith is but little, but of that nature that it is the very foundation of the gospel. *Thou art Christ*, the Anointed, the person of old promised to the world under the name of the Messiah, Dan. ix. 25, 26. *The Son*, not by adoption, but by nature, for they believed John the Baptist, Elias, and the old prophets the sons of God by grace. It is plain Peter means more than that. *Of the living God*. Our Lord had asked, *Whom do men say that I the Son of man am?* And in the same sense he speaks to the disciples, Whom do ye say that I the Son of man am? Lord, saith Peter, we believe that thou the Son of man *art the Christ, the Son of the living God*. God is often in Scripture called *the living God*, in opposition to idols, which had eyes and saw not, ears and heard not, nor had any life in them, Gen. xvi. 13; Heb. iii. 12; ix. 14, &c. So as here we have a full and plain confession of that doctrine, which is the foundation of the gospel.

17 And Jesus answered and said unto him, Blessed art thou, Simon Bar-jona: ᵏ for flesh and blood hath not revealed *it* unto thee, but ˡmy Father which is in heaven.

k Eph. 2. 8.
1 1 Cor. 2. 10.
Gal. 1. 16.

Our Lord appeareth here to be mightily pleased with this confession of Peter and the rest of his disciples, (for we shall observe in the Gospel, that Peter was usually the first in speaking, John vi. 68,) he pronounceth him *blessed*, and giveth the reason of it afterward. *Simon Bar-jona*, that is, Simon son of Jona, or, as some would have it, son of John (they think Jona is a contraction of Johanna). Our Lord gives him the same name, John xxi. 15. *For flesh and blood hath not revealed it unto thee, but my Father which is in heaven*. By *flesh and blood* our Saviour meaneth man, and the reason and wisdom of man. Thus it is often used in Scripture, Isa. xl. 5; Gal. i. 16; Eph. vi. 12. Some note it always signifieth so when it is in Scripture opposed to God. Thou hast not learned this by tradition, or any dictates from man, nor yet by any human ratiocination, but from *my Father which is in heaven*. This confirmeth what we have Eph. ii. 8, that faith *is the gift of God*. No man cometh to the Son, but he whom the Father draweth, John vi. 44. Men may assent to things from the reports of men, or from the evidence of reason, but neither of these is faith. Faith must be an assent to a proposition upon the authority of God revealing it. Nor doth any man truly and savingly believe that Jesus Christ is the eternal Son of God, and the Saviour of the world, but he in whom God hath wrought such a persuasion; yet is not the ministry of the word needless in the case, because, as the apostle saith, *faith comes by hearing*, and ministers are God's instruments by whom men believe. No faith makes a soul blessed but that which is of the operation of God.

18 And I say also unto thee, That ᵐthou art Peter, and ⁿupon this rock I will build my Church; and ᵒthe gates of hell shall not prevail against it.

m John 1. 42.
n Eph. 2. 20.
Rev. 21. 14.
o Job 38. 17.
Ps. 9. 13.
& 107. 18.
Is. 38. 10.

And I say also unto thee, That thou art Peter: Christ gave him this name, John i. 42, when his brother Andrew first brought him to Christ. I did not give thee the name of Cephas, or Peter, for nothing, (for what Cephas signifieth in the Syriac Peter signifieth in the Greek,) I called thee Cephas, and thou art Peter, a rock. Thou shalt be a rock. This our Lord made good afterward, when he told him, that Satan had desired to winnow him like wheat, but he had prayed that his faith might not fail, Luke xxii. 32. Thou hast made a confession of faith which is a rock, even such a rock as was mentioned chap. vii. 25. And thou thyself art a rock, a steady, firm believer. *And upon this rock I will build my church*. Here is a question amongst interpreters, what, or whom, our Saviour here meaneth by *this rock*. 1. Some think that he meaneth himself, as he saith, John ii. 19, *Destroy this temple* (meaning his own body). God is often called a Rock, Deut. xxxii. 18; Psal. xviii. 2; xxxi. 3; and it is certain Christ is the foundation of the church, Isa. xxviii. 16; 1 Cor. iii. 11; 1 Pet. ii. 6.

But this sense seemeth a little hard, that our Saviour, speaking to Peter, and telling him he was a stone, or a rock, should with the same breath pass to himself, and not say, Upon myself, but *upon this rock I will build my church*. 2. The generality of protestant writers, not without the suffrage of divers of the ancients, say Peter's confession, which he had made, is the rock here spoken of. And indeed the doctrine contained in his confession is the foundation of the gospel; the whole Christian church is built upon it. 3. Others think, in regard that our Saviour directeth his speech not to all the apostles, but to Peter, and doth not say, Blessed are you, but, *Blessed art thou, Simon Bar-jona*, that here is something promised to Peter in special; but they do not think this is any priority, much less any jurisdiction, more than the rest had, but that Christ would make a more eminent and special use of him, in the building of his church, than of the rest; and they observe, that God did make a more eminent use of Peter in raising his gospel church, both amongst the Jews, Acts ii., and the Gentiles, Acts x. But yet this soundeth a little harshly, to interpret *upon this rock*, by this rock. I do therefore rather incline to interpret it in the second sense: *Upon this rock*, upon this solid and unmovable foundation of truth, which thou hast publicly made, *I will build my church*. It is true, Christ is the foundation of the church, and other foundation can no man lay. But though Christ be the foundation in one sense, the apostles are so called in another sense, Eph. ii. 20; Rev. xxi. 14: not the apostles' persons, but the doctrine which they preached. They, by their doctrine which they preached, (the sum or great point of which was what Peter here professed,) laid the foundation of the Christian church, as they were the first preachers of it to the Gentiles. In which sense soever it be taken, it makes nothing for the papists' superiority or jurisdiction of St. Peter, or his successors. It follows, *I will build my church*. By *church* is here plainly meant the whole body of believers, who all agree in this one faith. It is observable, that Christ calls it his church, not Peter's, and saith, *I will build*, not, thou shalt build. The working of faith in souls is God's work. Men are but ministers, by whom others believe. They have but a ministry towards, not a lordship over the church of God. *And the gates of hell shall not prevail against it;* that is, the power of the devil and all his instruments shall never prevail against it utterly to extinguish it, neither to extinguish true faith in the heart of any particular believer, nor to root the gospel out of the world. *The gates* is here put for the persons that sit in the gates. It was their custom to have the rulers to sit in the gates, Ruth iv. 1, 11; 2 Sam. xix. 8. Neither doth *hell* signify here the place of the damned; ᾅδης no where (except in one place, and as to that it is questionable, Luke xvi. 23) signifies so, but either death, or the graves, or the state of the dead: yet the devil is also understood here, as he *that hath the power of death*, Heb. ii. 14. The plain sense is, that our Lord would build the Christian church upon this proposition of truth, that he was the Christ, the Son of God; that Peter should be an eminent instrument in converting men to this faith; and where this faith obtained in the world, he would so far protect it, that though the devil and his instruments should by all means imaginable attempt the extinguishing of it by the total extirpation of it, the professors of it, and might as to particular places prevail; yet they should never so prevail, but to the end of the world he would have a church, a number of people called out by his apostles, and those who should succeed in their ministry, who should uphold this great truth. So as this is a plain promise for the continuance of the gospel church to the end of the world.

19 ᵖAnd I will give unto thee the keys of the kingdom of heaven: and whatsoever thou shalt bind on earth shall be bound in heaven: and whatsoever thou shalt loose on earth shall be loosed in heaven.

p ch. 18. 18.
John 20. 23.

And I will give unto thee; not unto thee exclusively, that is, to thee and no others; for as we no where read of any such power used by Peter, so our Saviour's first question, Whom think you that I am? letteth us know that his speech, though directed to Peter only, (who in the name of the rest first answered,) concerned the rest of the apostles as well as Peter. Besides, as we know that the other apostles had as well as he the key of knowledge and doctrine, and by their preaching opened the kingdom of heaven to men; so the key of discipline also was committed to the rest as well as unto him: *Whose soever sins ye remit, they are remitted unto them; and whose soever sins ye retain, they are retained,* John xx. 22, 23. *The keys of the kingdom of heaven;* the whole administration of the gospel, both with reference to the publication of the doctrine of it, and the dispensing out the ordinances of it. We read of the *key of knowledge,* which the scribes and Pharisees took away, Luke xi. 52, and the key of government: *The key of the house of David will I lay upon his shoulder,* Isa. xxii. 21, I will commit thy government into his hand; which is applied to Christ, Rev. iii. 7. The sense is, Peter, I will betrust thee, and the rest of my apostles, with the whole administration of my gospel; you shall lay the foundation of the Christian church, and administer all the affairs of it, opening the truths of my gospel to the world, and governing those who shall receive the faith of the gospel. *And whatsoever thou shalt bind on earth shall be bound in heaven; and whatsoever thou shalt loose on earth shall be loosed in heaven.* Some very learned interpreters think that our Saviour here speaketh according to the language then in use amongst the Jews; who by binding understood the determining and declaring a thing unlawful; and by loosing, declaring by doctrine, or determining by judgment, a thing unlawful, that is, such as no men's consciences were bound to do or to avoid. So as by this text an authority was given to these first planters of the gospel, to determine (by virtue of their infallible Spirit, breathed upon them, John xx. 21) concerning things to be done and to be avoided. Thus Acts xv. 28, 29, they loosed the Gentiles from the observation of the ceremonial law. Some think that by this phrase our Saviour gave to his apostles, and not to them only, but to the succeeding church, to the end of the world, a power of excommunication and absolution, to admit in and to cast out of the church, and promiseth to ratify what they do of this nature in heaven; and that this text is expounded by John xx. 23, *Whose soever sins ye remit, they are remitted; and whose soever sins ye retain, they are retained;* and that the power of the church, and of ministers in the church, as to this, is more than declarative. That the church hath a power in a due order and for just causes, to cast persons out of its communion, is plain enough from other texts; but that the church hath a power to remit sins committed against God more than declaratively, that is, declaring that upon men's repentance and faith God hath remitted, I cannot see founded in this text. Certain it is, that Christ doth not here bind himself to confirm the erroneous actions of men, either in excommunications or absolutions; nor to authorize all such actions of this nature that they do. I do therefore rather incline to think that our Saviour by this promise declared his will, that his apostles should settle the affairs of the gospel church, determining what should be lawful and unlawful, and setting rules, according to which all succeeding ministers and officers in his church should act, which our Lord would confirm in heaven. And that the ordinary power of churches in censures is rather to be derived from other texts of Scripture than this, though I will not deny but that in the general it may be here included; but I cannot think that the sense of binding and loosing here is excommunicating and absolving, but a doctrinal or judicial determination of things lawful and unlawful granted to the apostles; the not obeying or living up to whose determinations and decisions may be indeed a just cause of casting persons out of the communion of the church, as the contrary obedience and conformity to them a good ground of receiving them in again. But whether in this text be not granted to the apostles a further power than agrees to any ministers since their age I much doubt, and am very prone to believe that there is.

20 ¶ Then charged he his disciples that they should tell no man that he was Jesus the Christ.

We met with some charges of this nature before, given to those whom he had miraculously cured, that they should tell no man of it, Matt. viii. 4; ix. 30; but this seemeth to differ from them. There he only forbade the publication of his miracles; here he forbids them preaching that Jesus was the Christ, a doctrine necessary to be believed in order to people's salvation. We are not able to give an account of all our Saviour's particular actions. 1. We are sure this was a precept but of a temporary force and obligation, for we know that afterward they did sufficiently publish this abroad, only for a time he would not have it published by his disciples. We cannot certainly determine whether he forbade them, 1. Because they were not as yet fit to publish so great a truth. Or, 2. Because the time was not yet come for the publication of it. Or, 3. He would not have it published till he rose again from the dead, having triumphed over death, lest people, hearing of it before, should have had their faith shaken by his death; which seemeth very probable, because in the next words he begins to speak of his death. Or, 4. That he might hereby (as much as might be) avoid the odium and envy of the Pharisees. Or, 5. That himself might publish first this great truth of the gospel, and confirm it by his miracles.

21 ¶ From that time forth began Jesus to shew unto his disciples, how that he must go unto Jerusalem, and suffer many things of the elders and Chief Priests and Scribes, and be killed, and be raised again the third day.

Our Lord taught his hearers by degrees, as they were able to hear and to bear his instruction. He therefore first instructeth them in the truth of his Divine nature, and bringeth them to a firm and steady assent to this proposition, That he was the Christ, the Son of God. Lest they should have this faith of theirs shaken by his sufferings and death, he beginneth to instruct them as to those things, that when they saw it come to pass, they might not be offended, but wait for his resurrection from the dead.

22 Then Peter took him, and began to rebuke him, saying, † Be it far from thee, Lord: this shall not be unto thee.

Peter took our Lord aside, as we do our friend to whom we would speak something which we would not have all to hear, *and began to rebuke him;* ἐπιτιμᾶν, to reprove him, as men often do their familiar friends, when they judge they have spoken something beneath them, or that might turn to their prejudice; saying, Be it far from thee, Lord: this shall not be unto thee. The words in the Greek want the verb, so leave us in doubt whether we should translate them, Be merciful to thyself, spare thyself, or, Let God, or God shall, be merciful unto thee. The last words expound them; *this shall not be unto thee.* God shall be merciful unto thee, and help thee, this shall not betide thee. These words were undoubtedly spoken by Peter out of a good intention, and with a singular affection to his Master; but, 1. They spake him as yet ignorant of the redemption of mankind by the death of Christ, of the doctrine of the cross, and of the will of the Father concerning Christ. 2. They spake great weakness in him, to contradict him whom he had but now acknowledged to be the Christ, the Son of God. Good intentions, and good affections, will not justify evil actions. Christ takes him up smartly.

23 But he turned, and said unto Peter, Get thee behind me, *Satan: 'thou art an offence unto me: for thou savourest not the things that be of God, but those that be of men.

Peter, thou thinkest that by this discourse thou showest some kindness unto me, like a friend, but thou art in this an adversary to me; for so the word *Satan* doth signify, and is therefore ordinarily applied to the devil, who is the grand adversary of mankind. *Get thee behind me,* I abominate such advice. I told thee I *must* suffer. It was the determinate counsel of God; it is my Father's will. He is mine enemy that dissuadeth me from a free and cheerful obedience to it. I will hear no more such discourse. *For thou savourest not the things that be of God, but those that be of men.* The word is φρονεῖς, and, it may be, were better translated, Thou thinkest not of, or thou understandest not, the things that be of God, that is, the counsels of God in this matter, as to the redemption of mankind: thou considerest me only as thy Master and thy Friend, and wouldst nave no harm come to me ; thou dost not mind or think of me as the Saviour of the world, or the Redeemer of mankind, which cannot be redeemed otherwise than by my death. Though by thy intemperate affection to me thou wouldst hinder the redemption of mankind, this is not in this thing to mind, think on, or savour the things of God, but to suffer thyself to be seduced by thy carnal affection. It is a mistaken kindness to our friends, to persuade them, for our personal advantage, to do what they cannot do in consistency with their obedience to the will of God.

u ch. 10. 38.
Mark 8. 34.
Luke 9. 23.
& 14. 27.
Acts 14. 22.
1 Thess. 3. 3.
2 Tim. 3. 12.

24 ¶ "Then said Jesus unto his disciples, If any *man* will come after me, let him deny himself, and take up his cross, and follow me.

Mark hath the same, chap. viii. 34, and Luke, chap. ix. 23; only Mark saith, *when he had called the people unto him with his disciples;* Luke saith, *he said to them all.* He spake it to his disciples, but not privately, but before all the rest of the people, who at that time were present. *If any man will come after me;* that is, if any man will be my disciple : so it is expounded by Luke, chap. xiv. 26, 27, which is a text much of the same import with this, only what Matthew here calleth a denying of himself, Luke calleth hating. The disciples of others are called the followers of them. *Let him deny himself.* To deny ourselves, is to put off our natural affections towards the good things of this life, let them be pleasures, profit, honours, relations, life, or any thing which would keep us from our obedience to the will of God. Thus Christ did : the apostle saith he *pleased not himself. I seek not my own will, but the will of the Father which sent me,* John v. 30; iv. 34. *And take up his cross;* willingly and cheerfully bear those trials and afflictions which the providence of God brings him under for owning and standing to his profession, all which come under the name of *the cross,* with respect to Christ's cross, on which he suffered. *And follow me :* in his taking up the cross he shall but do as I shall do, following my example. Or else this may be looked upon as a third term of Christ's discipleship, viz. yielding a universal obedience to the commandments of Christ, or living up as near as we can to the example of Christ, 1 Pet. i. 15. This doctrine our Saviour preacheth to them upon occasion of Peter's moving him to spare himself, by which he did but indulge his own carnal affection, without respect to the will of God as to what Christ was to suffer for the redemption of mankind.

x Luke 17. 33.
John 12. 25.

25 For *whosoever will save his life shall lose it : and whosoever will lose his life for my sake shall find it.

We met with these words chap. x. 39 : see the notes there.

26 For what is a man profited, if he shall gain the whole world, and lose his own soul? or *what shall a man give in exchange for his soul ?

y Ps. 49. 7, 8.

Our interpreters, by translating the same word *soul* in this verse which they had translated *life* ver. 25, let us know that they understood it here of that essential part of man which we call the soul, in which sense it could not be understood in that verse, for it is impossible in that sense to lose our soul for Christ's sake. Some think that it hath the same sense here as in that verse, and that our Saviour argueth here from the less to the greater, thus: Men will lose any thing rather than their lives; skin for skin, and all that a man hath, for his life ; and this is but reasonable, for if a man lose his life to get the world, what will the world gotten do him good ? what can be a proportionable exchange or compensation to him for that ? Now if you value your temporary life at that rate, how much more ought you to value your eternal being and existence ! It cometh much to the same, only the sense is plainer if we take it as our translators have taken it, for otherwise part of the argument is not expressed, but left to be understood, or supplied from the next verse. So as the sense is this : Besides bodies which may be killed by persecutors, you carry about with you immortal souls of infinitely more value ; and besides a temporal life, of which you are in possession, there is an eternal state, which awaiteth you. You are creatures ordained to an eternal existence, either in misery or in happiness. Admit you could, by pleasing yourselves, denying me, shifting the cross, declining a life according to my precepts and example, prolong your temporal life, yet what will you get by it, considering that by it you must suffer loss as to your eternal happy existence, for I shall then deny you before my Father and his angels ? Can any thing you can get or save in this world be a proportionable exchange for eternal happiness ?

27 For *the Son of man shall come in the glory of his Father *with his angels; *and then he shall reward every man according to his works.

z ch. 26. 64.
Mark 8. 38.
Luke 9. 26.
a Dan. 7. 10.
Zech. 14. 5.
ch. 25. 31.
Jude 14.
b Job 34. 11.
2 Cor. 5. 10.

Ps. 62. 12.   Prov. 24. 12. Jer. 17. 10. & 32. 19. Rom. 2. 6. 1 Cor. 3. 8.
1 Pet. 1. 17. Rev. 2. 23. & 22. 12.

This verse makes it plain, that our Saviour by ψυχὴ in the former verse understood the soul of man, or eternal life, that blessed state which is prepared for the saints of God ; for he here mindeth them that there shall be a last judgment, and gives them a little description of it. 1. As to the Judge, the Son of man, him whom you now see in the shape of a man, and whom men vilify and contemn under that notion. He is to be *the Judge of quick and dead,* Acts x. 42 ; 2 Tim. iv. 1. 2. As to the splendour of it. He shall *come in the glory of his Father.* It is also his glory, John xvii. 5 ; he calls it *the glory of his Father,* because by his eternal generation he received it together with the Divine nature from his Father, and it was common to him with his Father; or because his commission for judgment was from his Father : *For the Father judgeth no man, but hath committed all judgment unto the Son,* John v. 22. *With his angels;* his holy angels, 1 Thess. i. 7. *And then he shall reward every man according to his works :* not for his works. Our Saviour is not here speaking of the cause of the reward, but the rule and measure of it : *According to his deeds,* Rom. ii. 6. *According to his labour,* 1 Cor. iii. 8. *According to that he hath done,* 2 Cor. v. 10. Not according to his faith, but works, for *faith without works is dead;* but these works must spring out of a root of faith, without which it is impossible to please God. He shall reward him, by a reward of grace, not of debt, Rom. iv. 4. Works shall be rewarded, but not as with a penny for a pennyworth, but of grace.

28 Verily I say unto you, *There be some standing here, which shall not taste of death, till they see the Son of man coming in his kingdom.

c Mark 9. 1.
Luke 9. 27.

Mark saith, chap. ix. 1, *till they have seen the kingdom of God come with power;* Luke, chap. ix. 27, saith no more than *till they see the kingdom of God. There be some standing here, which shall not taste of death,* that is, that shall not die, Heb. ii. 9. It is the same with not seeing death, John viii. 51, 52; Heb. xi. 5. The great question is, what is here meant by *the Son of man coming in his kingdom.* It cannot be meant of his second coming to judgment, spoken of immediately before, for all who stood there have long since tasted of death, yet is not that day come. Some understand it of that sight of Christ's glory which Peter, and James, and John had at Christ's transfiguration, of which we shall read in the next chapter; and I should be very inclinable to this sense, (for there was a glimpse of the glory of the Father mentioned ver. 27,) were it not for those words added by Mark, *till they have seen the kingdom of God come with power.* This inclineth others to think, that it is to be understood of Christ's showing forth his power in the destruction of Jerusalem. But the most generally received opinion, and which seemeth to be best, is, that the coming of the Son of man here meant is, his resurrection from the dead, his ascension into heaven, and sending the Holy Spirit, after which the kingdom of grace came with a mighty power, subduing all nations to the Lord Jesus Christ. He *was declared,* or determined, *to be the Son of God with power, according to the spirit of holiness, by the resurrection from the dead,* Rom. i. 4. And when, after his resurrection from the dead, they asked him, Acts i. 6, whether he would at that time *restore the kingdom to Israel,* he puts them off, and tells them for an answer, ver. 8, *But ye shall receive power, after that the Holy Ghost is come upon you: and ye shall be witnesses unto me both in Jerusalem, and in all Judea, and in Samaria, and unto the uttermost parts of the earth.* And then, ver. 9, he in their sight ascended up into heaven. Then did the kingdom of the Son of man come with power, Acts ii. 33—36, they knowing assuredly that the Son of man, whom the Jews had crucified, was *made both Lord and Christ*, as ver. 36, and, as ver. 34, 35, set at God's right hand, (according to the prophecy of David, Psal. cx. 1,) until his enemies should be made his footstool.

CHAP. XVII

The transfiguration of Christ, 1—9. He instructeth his disciples concerning the coming of Elias, 10—13; healeth the lunatic, 14—21; foretelleth his own passion, 22, 23; and payeth tribute, 24—27.

a Mark 9. 2. Luke 9. 28. AND ª after six days Jesus taketh Peter, James, and John his brother, and bringeth them up into an high mountain apart,

2 And was transfigured before them: and his face did shine as the sun, and his raiment was white as the light.

Both Mark and Luke have recorded this history. Mark saith, chap. ix. 3, *his raiment became shining, exceeding white as snow; so as no fuller on earth can white them.* Luke saith, chap. ix. 28, 29, *And it came to pass about an eight days after these sayings, he took Peter, and John, and James, and went up into a mountain to pray. And as he prayed, the fashion of his countenance was altered, and his raiment was white and glistering.* All three agree the place, upon a mountain. Matthew saith it was *six*, Luke saith *eight, days* after the preceding discourses. Luke mentioneth our Lord's praying, which neither of the others mentioneth, and saith his transfiguration began whilst that he was praying. They all agree the company that was with our Saviour, *Peter, James, and John*; which were the three our Saviour took with him when he went to pray before his passion, Matt. xxvi. 37. Peter was to be a great instrument in carrying on the works of the gospel. James was he whom Herod killed, Acts xii. 2. John was he who outlived all the apostles. He intended to have these three witnesses of his agony, Matt. xxvi. 37; he prepareth them for that, and for the future testimony they were to give him, by making them eye-witnesses of this his glorious transfiguration. This, as to his person, lay in the change of his countenance, looking gloriously as the sun, and his raiment looking extraordinarily white.

3 And, behold, there appeared unto them Moses and Elias talking with him.

4 Then answered Peter, and said unto Jesus, Lord, it is good for us to be here: if thou wilt, let us make here three tabernacles; one for thee, and one for Moses, and one for Elias.

Mark adds, chap. ix. 6, *For he wist not what to say; for they were sore afraid.* Luke addeth, chap. ix. 31—33, *who appeared in glory, and spake of his decease which he should accomplish at Jerusalem. But Peter and they that were with him were heavy with sleep: and when they were awake, they saw his glory, and the two men that stood with him. And it came to pass, as they departed from him, Peter said unto Jesus, Master, it is good for us to be here, &c.; not knowing what he said.* So as the history seemeth to be thus: After six or eight days Christ took Peter, James, and John, and went up into a mountain, and prayed. While he prayeth his disciples fall asleep. Waking, they saw him with his face shining gloriously, like the sun, and his garments white as snow, and two men talking with him about his death and passion, whom they (by revelation) knew to be Moses and Elias. They were sore afraid, and Peter, not well knowing or considering what he said, saith to Christ, *Master, it is good for us to be here: and let us make three tabernacles; one for thee, and one for Moses, and one for Elias.* It is most likely that Moses and Elias appeared in their own bodies. As to Elias, there was no difficulty, for his body was taken up to heaven in a fiery chariot. For Moses, it is said the Lord *buried him in a valley in the land of Moab, over against Beth-peor: but no man knoweth of his sepulchre unto this day,* Deut. xxxiv. 6. The devil and the archangel had a dispute about his body, Jude 9. It is very probable God raised up the body of Moses for this transfiguration testimony, that by the law and the prophets, represented in Moses, the giver of the law, and Elias, one of the most famous of the prophets, the disciples might be confirmed in their faith concerning Christ as the true Messias, and also fortified against the scandal and temptation of that ignominious death which he was soon after to undergo; and that these three apostles, being the highest number of witnesses, by the law of Moses, to confirm a thing, might be judged competent witnesses of what they saw and heard. Do not think Peter's saying, *let us make here three tabernacles*, &c., proceeded from any pleasure or satisfaction that he had from this glimpse he had of the Divine and excellent glory; for how could this consist with that fear with which Mark saith they were possessed? but that, as Mark saith, *he wist not what to say*, or, as Luke, *not knowing what he said.* Which I take to be, as a reasonable, so the best excuse can be made for the errors and weakness discovered in his speech, as if Moses and Elias, or Christ, could have dwelt there, &c.

5 ᵇ While he yet spake, behold, a bright cloud overshadowed them: and behold a voice out of the cloud, which said, ᶜThis is my beloved Son, ᵈin whom I am well pleased; ᵉhear ye him. b 2 Pet. 1.17. c ch. 3. 17. Mark 1. 11. Luke 3. 22. d Is. 42. 1. e Deut. 18. 15, 19. Acts 3. 22, 23.

Mark and Luke relate the same without any considerable variation, only Luke saith, *they feared as they entered into the cloud.* It seemeth that the cloud did encompass them, so as they seemed all as if they had been within the cloud. This still increased their fear. It is observable, that God did very often make his appearances to people in a cloud, making the clouds his chariots, Exod. xvi. 10; xl. 34; Numb. xi. 25; Psal. civ. 3; to teach us humility, not to pry too much into his secrets, who covereth himself with thick darkness, and likewise to consult our weakness, who are not able to behold him as he is. This is said to be *a bright cloud*, so differing from the cloud in which he appeared under the law, but without doubt it had something of a shadow in it, and was chosen of God for some abatement of the brightness of his glory. This cloud encompasseth Christ, Moses, and Elias, and also Peter, James, and John. *And behold a voice out of the cloud*: they saw no visible shape, no more did the Jews, Deut. iv. 15, only, as St. Peter (who saw it) expresseth it, 2 Pet. i. 17, *there came such a voice from the excellent glory.* He speaks of this very time, as may appear from ver. 18. The voice is the same which was heard upon the baptism of Christ, chap. iii. 17; only there is added to it, *hear ye him*: you need no Elias to instruct you, hear him. Thus Moses saw what he had before prophesied of, Deut. xviii. 15, 18, fulfilled: he in this ministry as a servant in the house of God had prophesied, that the Lord would raise up a prophet from amongst their brethren like unto him, and put his words into his mouth, and he should speak unto them all that God should command him, Deut. xviii. 18; and, ver. 15, *unto him ye shall hearken.* God had now fulfilled that word, and he declares that this prophet was his Son, his beloved Son, and commands them to hear him. Which words establish Christ as the only Doctor and Teacher of his church, the only one whom he had betrusted to deliver his truths and will to his people, the only one to whom Christians are to hearken: nor doth this destroy the ministers of the word, who are no more than the interpreters of what he hath said, and are no more to be regarded than as by them we hear Christ speaking more plainly and frequently unto us. This appearance of God from time to time in a cloud, and that not in any visible shape, but in an excellent glory, causing a voice to be heard, lets us see the audaciousness of those who by any pictures or images pretend to make any representation of any person in the Trinity. And this command from God to us to hear Christ, lets us also see the audacity of those who take upon them to impose upon Christians what Christ never spake.

6 ᶠAnd when the disciples heard *it*, they fell on their face, and were sore afraid. f 2 Pet. 1. 18.

7 And Jesus came and ᵍtouched them, and said, Arise, and be not afraid. g Dan. 8. 18. & 9. 21. & 10. 10, 18.

8 And when they had lifted up their eyes, they saw no man, save Jesus only.

Mark saith no more than, *And suddenly, when they had looked round about, they saw no man any more, save Jesus only with themselves.* Such is the majesty and glory of God, that a cloud will not so veil it as that a man is able to behold any appearance of it without some consternation; something more than that fear of reverence, without which none ought to draw nigh unto him. Paul *fell to the earth,* when *a light from heaven* shone upon him, Acts ix. 3, 4. The disciples here *fell on their faces, and were sore afraid.* This lets us see the goodness of God in hearkening to the people's request, Exod. xx. 19; Deut. v. 28; xviii. 16, 17, and speaking to us by men like unto ourselves: by Moses under the Old Testament; by Christ (that Prophet mentioned Deut. xviii. 15) under the New Testament, and such as he commissioned to declare his will, Heb. i. 1, 2. *And Jesus came and touched them, and said, Arise, and be not afraid.* To deliver them from the fear of a spectrum, or apparition, he toucheth them, and saith in effect, It is I; be not afraid. They look up, and see the excellent glory and the cloud was withdrawn, as also Moses and Elias, and they and their Lord were left alone; and he goeth down from the mountain with them. Whether this mountain was Tabor, or some other mountain much nearer Cesarea Philippi, is of no consequence for us to be satisfied in.

9 And as they came down from the mountain, ʰJesus charged them, saying, Tell the vision to no man, until the Son of man be risen again from the dead.

h ch. 16. 20.
Mark 8. 30.
& 9. 9.

Mark saith the same, chap. ix. 9. Luke saith, chap. ix. 36, *They kept it close, and told no man in those days any of those things which they had seen.* The other two evangelists record the precept; Luke and Mark, their obedience to it. The most probable reason of this charge given by interpreters is, lest his after-sufferings should have shaken again their faith, as to the Divine nature of Christ, before he was by his resurrection from the dead *declared to be the Son of God with power,* as the apostle speaks, Rom. i. 4.

10 And his disciples asked him, saying, ⁱWhy then say the Scribes that Elias must first come?

i Mal. 4. 5.
ch. 11. 14.
Mark 9. 11.

Before these words, Mark saith, chap. ix. 10, *And they kept that saying with themselves, questioning one with another what the rising from the dead should mean.* Then he addeth, *And they asked him, saying, Why say the scribes that Elias must first come.* The disciples (as appeareth) were as yet very imperfectly instructed in the doctrine of man's redemption by Christ, though Christ had before told them, that as Jonah was three days and three nights in the belly of the whale, so he should be three days and three nights in the belly of the earth. How dull the best of men are to apprehend spiritual mysteries, which are above the reach of our reason! The Jews had a tradition, and retain it to this day, That before the coming of the Messias Elias should come; they build it upon Mal. iv. 4, 5. That they had such an expectation appeareth by their sending to John the Baptist, John i. 21, to know if he were he, meaning Elijah the Tishbite (for him they expected); and this was their great error, and still blindeth them. The disciples had now seen Elijah, and possibly might wonder at our Saviour's forbidding them to speak of the vision, as thinking that nothing could more conduce to the receiving of him as the Messiah: or possibly they might wonder at Elijah's so soon leaving the earth, the Messiah being come, whom they expected he should come before. So as though they were fully satisfied that Christ was the true Messiah, yet they knew not how to reconcile their faith to the promise, or to their tradition built upon the promise. This causeth the question.

11 And Jesus answered and said unto them, Elias truly shall first come, and ᵏrestore all things.

k Mal. 4. 6.
Luke 1. 16, 17.

12 ˡBut I say unto you, That Elias is come already, and they knew him not, but ᵐhave done unto him whatsoever

Acts 3. 21.
l ch. 11. 14.
Mark 9. 12, 13.
m ch. 14. 3, 10.

they listed. Likewise ⁿshall also the Son of man suffer of them.

n ch.16. 21.

13 ᵒThen the disciples understood that he spake unto them of John the Baptist.

o ch. 11. 14.

Mark saith, chap. ix. 12, *He answered and told them, Elias verily comes first, and restoreth all things; and how it is written of the Son of man, that he must suffer many things, and be set at nought. But I say unto you, That Elias is indeed come, and they have done unto him whatsoever they listed, as it is written of him.* Our Saviour agreeth to the promise, but showeth their mistake as to the true sense of it. They understood the promise of Elijah the Tishbite: the promise referred only to one of his spirit, and such a one was come, that was John the Baptist, as the angel told Zacharias, Luke i. 17, *He shall go before him in the spirit and power of Elias.* Very much of the power and spirit of Elijah was evident in John. Elijah was full of zeal for God, 1 Kings xix. 10: so was John the Baptist. Did Elijah freely reprove, not only Baal's priests, but even Ahab and Jezebel? John as freely reproved Herod and Herodias, and the Pharisees and Sadducees. Was Elijah an austere man? Such was John the Baptist. Did Elijah flee unto the wilderness to save his life? John Baptist, for some time, lived and preached there. Elijah living in a corrupt time, was a great means or instrument to restore decayed religion: so was John the Baptist, in the time wherein he lived. This notwithstanding, not the Jews only, but some Christians, and that not only papists, but some protestants, think, that besides the Elias which is long since come, there is another Elias, who shall come before the end of the world. They found their opinion upon this text in a great measure, 1. Because our Saviour here saith, ἔρχεται πρῶτον, he doth come first; and Mark saith, ἐλθὼν πρῶτον, ἀποκαθιστᾷ, *coming first, restoreth all things.* Now John the Baptist was both come and gone; nor had he restored all things. Besides, they say, that John denied himself to be Elias, John i. 21; and it is plain, that not the scribes and Pharisees, but the disciples, only understood the prophecy of Elijah the Tishbite; and Malachi saith, that Elijah should come before *the terrible day of the Lord,* which day, they say, is the day of judgment, in the constant language of Scripture. But to all this is answered, 1. That the Baptist, John i. 21, only denied himself to be that Elias about which they inquired, according to their tradition. 2. That it is true, that the disciples were led away with the Jewish tradition, and looked for Elijah the Tishbite, but Christ both here and elsewhere correcteth their error. 3. That not only the day of general judgment is called the terrible day of the Lord, but the gospel time, Matt. iii. 10, when the axe was laid to the root of the tree, &c.; so Acts ii. 20; and the day of the Jews' particular judgment, which some understand hinted in those texts. 4. That our Lord first repeateth the words of Malachi, and so he saith, Elias shall come, or is coming; and then he expounds the words of Malachi of John the Baptist. 5. That the words of Mal. iv. 6 are expounded by the angel, Luke i. 16, 17, and there applied to John the Baptist. 6. That John did fulfil the words of the prophet, by endeavouring the conversion of the Jews, and prevailing in a great measure. 7. That the last words in Malachi, *lest I smite the earth with a curse,* plainly show that the text in Malachi cannot be understood of the day of judgment. And though the name of Elias be given to John, yet it is no more than the giving the name of David to the Messias, Ezek. xxxvii. 24. So as there is no other Elijah to be expected, but the Elijah prophesied of by Malachi was (as our Saviour doth expound it) John the Baptist, whom Herod had beheaded. *They knew him not,* their tradition blinded them so as they could not discern the prophecy of Malachi fulfilled in him, so did unto him *whatsoever they listed;* and, saith our Saviour, so shall they do with the Son of man, that is, with me, who am the Son of man.

14 ¶ ᵖAnd when they were come to the multitude, there came to him a *certain* man, kneeling down to him, and saying,

p Mark 9.14.
Luke 9. 37.

15 Lord, have mercy on my son: for he is lunatick, and sore vexed: for ofttimes he falleth into the fire, and oft into the water.

S. MATTHEW XVII

16 And I brought him to thy disciples, and they could not cure him.

The same history is told us both by Mark and Luke, but with considerable difference; we have it, Mark ix. 17, 18, thus, *And one of the multitude answered and said, Master, I have brought unto thee my son, which hath a dumb spirit; and wheresoever he taketh him, he teareth him: and he foameth, and gnasheth with his teeth, and pineth away: and I spake to thy disciples that they should cast him out, and they could not.* As an introduction to this, Mark saith, ver. 14—16, that when our Saviour *came to his disciples, he saw a great multitude about them, and the scribes questioning with them. And straightway all the people, when they beheld him, were greatly amazed, and running to him saluted him. And he asked the scribes, What question ye with them?* Luke gives us this account, chap. ix. 37—40, *And it came to pass, that on the next day, when they were come down from the hill, much people met him. And, behold, a man of the company cried out, saying, Master, I beseech thee, look upon my son: for he is mine only child. And, lo, a spirit taketh him, and he suddenly crieth out; and it teareth him that he foameth again, and bruising him hardly departeth from him. And I besought thy disciples to cast him out; and they could not.* When our Lord went up to the mountain where he was transfigured, he left at the foot of it the multitudes, and nine of his apostles, he took only three with him. How long he stayed there no evangelist tells us. The multitude and his disciples stayed waiting for his coming, probably not far off; some of the scribes were got to them, and they were arguing together. The day after our Lord, and Peter, James, and John, were come down from the mount, they go to the multitude, who received him with great passion, and saluted him. He beginneth to inquire what they were discoursing about; but was by and by interrupted with a certain man, who comes and falls down upon his knees before him, begging mercy for his son, who (as Matthew reports his condition) was lunatic and sore vexed, often falling into the fire, and often into the water. Mark saith, he had a dumb spirit, that it tore him, he often foamed and gnashed with his teeth. Luke saith, that it was the man's only child, that he had a spirit, that he cried out, it tare him, he foamed, and was bruised by it, &c. By the description of this young man's disease, it appeareth to have been what we call the falling sickness, wherein men fall down, foam, and beat themselves. With this disease the devil joined, so as at certain times of the moon this disease took him, and the devil acting with it, he was dumb, at least for the time, and fell sometimes into the fire, sometimes into the water, foamed, gnashed with his teeth, tore himself: this seems to have been his condition. The father (during Christ's absence) had attempted a cure by his disciples, but the text saith they could not (the reason we shall hear afterward); upon this he crieth unto Christ for his help.

17 Then Jesus answered and said, O faithless and perverse generation, how long shall I be with you? how long shall I suffer you? bring him hither to me.

18 And Jesus rebuked the devil; and he departed out of him: and the child was cured from that very hour.

Mark relates this part of the history much more largely, chap. ix. 19—27. *He answereth him, and saith, O faithless generation, how long shall I be with you? how long shall I suffer you? bring him unto me. And they brought him unto him: and when he saw him, straightway the spirit tare him; and he fell on the ground, and wallowed foaming. And he asked his father, How long is it ago since this came unto him? And he said, Of a child. And ofttimes it hath cast him into the fire, and into the waters, to destroy him: but if thou canst do any thing, have compassion on us, and help us. Jesus said unto him, If thou canst believe, all things are possible to him that believeth. And straightway the father of the child cried out, and said with tears, Lord, I believe; help thou mine unbelief. When Jesus saw that the people came running together, he rebuked the foul spirit, saying unto him, Thou dumb and deaf spirit, I charge thee, come out of him, and enter no more into him. And the spirit cried, and rent him sore, and came out of him: and he was as one dead;* insomuch that many said, He is dead. But Jesus took him by the hand, and lifted him up; and he arose. Luke relates this shorter, but addeth nothing to what is in the other evangelists, Luke ix. 41, 42. *Then Jesus answered and said, O faithless and perverse generation.* Christ here calls them so not with respect to justifying faith, but that faith which respected the Divine power as to working miracles. Every revelation of the Divine will is the object of faith; Christ had revealed to the Jews that he was sent of God, and furnished with such a power; this the Jews, and particularly the scribes, did not believe. The faith of the father of this child was but very weak in the case; no more, as we shall see afterwards, was the faith of the disciples; so as he may be understood to respect them all, though in different degrees. He calls them *perverse*, because they had so often seen and experienced his power of this nature, yet their faith was not clear and strong. He biddeth that the young man should be brought to him, and it was done. *And when he saw him,* (saith Mark,) *straightway the spirit tare him,* &c. Our Saviour could easily have prevented this, but probably he suffered it that the miracle might be more evident. However, it letteth us see how hardly the devil parteth with his possession in us in any degree, and how ready he is to run to the length of his line in doing us mischief. Christ asked his father how long he had been so vexed; his father tells him, from a child. By this also the miracle was more illustrious, which probably was the reason why Christ propounded the question. No evils are too inveterate for Christ to remove. The father reneweth his request, and in it showeth the weakness of his faith: *If* (saith he) *thou canst do any thing.* His coming to Christ, and crying to him, argued that he believed he could do something; his saying *if thou canst do any thing* speaks the weakness of his faith. Christ tells him, if he could believe, all things are possible. Nothing tieth God's hands but his creatures' unbelief. It is said, that Christ *could not* in Capernaum *do many mighty works because of their unbelief.* Upon this the father cries out, *Lord, I believe; help thou mine unbelief.* Men may truly believe, and yet have a mixture of unbelief. God rewards a weak faith, to souls labouring under the sense of their weakness, and desiring an increase of strength. Christ rebukes the spirit (called a dumb and deaf spirit, because it made the person such that was thus affected with it). Christ commands the spirit out, and so to come out as never more to enter into him. The evil spirit roars, rendeth him, comes out, and leaveth him as one dead: which still confirmeth us in his malice to mankind; he will do what harm he can when he cannot do us the harm he would.

19 Then came the disciples to Jesus apart, and said, Why could not we cast him out?

20 And Jesus said unto them, Because of your unbelief: for verily I say unto you, q If ye have faith as a grain of mustard seed, ye shall say unto this mountain, Remove hence to yonder place; and it shall remove; and nothing shall be impossible unto you.

q ch. 21. 21. Mark 11. 23. Luke 17. 6. 1 Cor. 12. 9. & 13. 2.

21 Howbeit this kind goeth not out but by prayer and fasting.

Mark repeats only what we have here ver. 19. 21. The reason assigned here by our Saviour why his disciples could not cast out this devil, was their unbelief; not their total want, but the weakness of their faith. Christ here again lets us see the power of faith, and the mischief of unbelief. I take the plain sense of the text to be this, That there is nothing which may tend to the glory of God, or to our good, but may be obtained of God by a firm exercise of faith in him. Whether our Saviour here speaketh of a faith of miracles, or no, I will not determine; I rather think that he speaketh here of any true faith: we must have the power and promise of God for its object. The promise of working miracles by a Divine power committed to them, was a particular promise made to the disciples, Matt. x., and so was only the object of their faith. But I take our Saviour's words to extend to a further latitude, though, as to miraculous operations, it was only applicable to them. There is nothing which God hath promised to give or bestow on any but faith will obtain from him, if attended by a fervent prayer, to which fasting is subservient, as preparing us to it. There are some things which are obtained by a stronger faith, and by more fervent and importunate prayers, than others are. A mercy sometimes seem to us to come out of the hand of God with more difficulty, and wrestling for it; but there is nothing within the latitude of a promise, but is to be done and obtained by the vigorous exercise of faith, and by fervent and importunate prayer. The apostles had yet but a weak and imperfect faith, and they had not used such fervent and importunate prayer in this case as they ought to have done; thence did this work appear so difficult unto them.

r ch. 16. 21.
& 20. 17.
Mark 8. 31.
& 9. 30, 31.
& 10. 33.
Luke 9. 22,
44. & 18. 31.
& 24. 6, 7.

22 ¶ ʳAnd while they abode in Galilee, Jesus said unto them, The Son of man shall be betrayed into the hands of men:

23 And they shall kill him, and the third day he shall be raised again. And they were exceeding sorry.

Mark saith, chap. ix. 30—32. *And they departed thence, and passed through Galilee; and he would not that any man should know it. For he taught his disciples, and said unto them, The Son of man is delivered into the hands of men, and they shall kill him; and after that he is killed, he shall rise the third day. But they understood not that saying, and were afraid to ask him.* Luke saith, chap. ix. 44, 45, he said unto them, *Let these sayings sink down into your ears: for the Son of man shall be delivered into the hands of men. But they understood not this saying, and it was hid from them, that they perceived it not: and they feared to ask him of that saying.* It is said that Christ taught his disciples *as they were able to hear,* Mark iv. 33. He tells them, John xvi. 12, he had many things to say unto them, but they could not bear them at that time. Christ a long time concealed the doctrine of his passion, and resurrection from the dead, from them, until he had confirmed them in the great point of his Divine power, and his being the true Messiah; now he begins to deliver this doctrine unto them, that what they should now soon see might not weaken their faith in him as the Messiah and the Son of God; partly in regard of that inveterate opinion which had possessed the generality of the Jews, that the Messiah should be a temporal prince, and should deliver the Jews from that servitude under which they were, and had for a long time been; partly in regard of the difficulty to conceive how he who was the Son of God could die. Once or twice before therefore he had begun to speak to them about his passion, chap. xvi. 21. Moses and Elias had some discourse with him about it, Luke ix. 31. The text saith, they understood it not; it was hid from them; they perceived it not; they were afraid to ask him. *They were exceeding sorry:* possibly they were sorry that they could not understand it, and reconcile it to the notion of the Messias they had drank in; for it seems hard to assert they were sorry for what Christ said about his suffering, because the Scripture saith, they understood it not, thinking our Saviour had not spoken plainly of a matter of fact which should be, but that he intended something else besides what his words seemed plainly to import.

s Mark 9. 33.
‖ Called in the original, didrachma, being in value fifteen pence: See Ex. 30. 13. & 38. 26.

24 ¶ And ˢwhen they were come to Capernaum, they that received ‖ tribute *money* came to Peter, and said, Doth not your master pay tribute?

25 He saith, Yes. And when he was come into the house, Jesus prevented him, saying, What thinkest thou, Simon? of whom do the kings of the earth take custom or tribute? of their own children, or of strangers?

26 Peter saith unto him, Of strangers. Jesus saith unto him, Then are the children free.

27 Notwithstanding, lest we should offend them, go thou to the sea, and cast an hook, and take up the fish that first cometh up; and when thou hast opened his mouth, thou shalt find ‖ a piece of money: that take, and give unto them for me and thee.

‖ Or, a *stater.* It is half an ounce of silver, value 2s. 6d. after 5s. the ounce.

The Jews were by God's law, Exod. xxx. 13, obliged to pay a half shekel, which was for the service of the sanctuary, ver. 16: this was paid every year. The half shekel amounted in our money to fifteen pence, or thereabouts. Whether this were the tribute money here demanded and paid, some doubt, and say that the Romans having the Jews now under their power, imposed this payment upon every head, as a tribute to the emperor; which being a customary payment, they thought the Jews would less stumble at, though it was changed from a sacred to a civil use, from a homage penny to God, to be a homage penny to the conquerors. The agreement of this sum with what was required by the law, together with what our Saviour saith afterward, will incline us to think that this tax was that religious tax mentioned Exod. xxx., and that the collectors were some officers deputed for that service by the priests. When Peter came into the house, our Saviour preventeth his propounding the question to him, (for Peter had before told them, Yes he did,) by asking him of whom the kings of the earth use to receive tribute, *of their own children, or of strangers?* where by *children* we must not understand their political children, that is, their subjects, but their natural children, for otherwise Peter would not have said, *Of strangers,* nor would our Saviour have answered, *Then are the children free;* for there is nothing more ordinary than for princes to receive tribute of their subjects. That which our Saviour seemeth to mean is this: This tribute is gathered for my heavenly Father. I am his Son, I am not bound to pay it. *Notwithstanding, lest we should offend them,* lest we give them occasion to say we break the law of God. *go thou to the sea,* (the sea of Galilee, which was near,) *and take up the fish that first cometh up; and when thou hast opened his mouth, thou shalt find* στατῆρα, *a piece of money,* to the value of about a half crown in English. How this money came in the mouth of the fish is a very idle dispute, considering that he that speaks was the Creator of all things. *That take, and give unto them for me and thee.* The papists, who think they have found here an argument for the primacy of Peter, because Christ paid this tribute for him, and not for the other disciples, do not only affirm what they do not know, but forget that Capernaum was the city in which Peter lived, (we heard before of Christ's curing his wife's mother there of a fever,) and that Peter was the only man of whom this tribute was demanded. This portion of Scripture affords us this instruction: That it is the duty of Christians to yield something of their own right, when they cannot insist upon and obtain it without a scandal and prejudice to the gospel, and the concern of religion. If this were required in pursuance of the law, Exod. xxx. 12, 13, and our Saviour had refused to pay it, the scribes and Pharisees would have clamoured against him as violating the law of God. If it were required as a civil tax, they would have clamoured against him as a man that went about to stir up sedition or rebellion. Having therefore first asserted his right and immunity, he departeth from it to prevent a scandal. We must never part with God's right; but to depart from our own is not only lawful, but oftentimes very advisable and expedient. Our Saviour chooseth rather to work a miracle than to give a scandal, and by this miracle he also confirmed his immunity, that he was the Son of him who is the King of kings, and so not in strictness obliged to pay it.

CHAP. XVIII

Christ proposeth a little child to his disciples for a pattern of innocence and humility, 1—6. He warneth them to avoid offences, though at the expense of a hand, a foot, or an eye, 7—9; and not to despise the little ones, whom it is the Father's will to save, 10—14. He teacheth how to treat an offending brother, 15—20, and how oft to forgive him, by the parable of a king, who punished one of his servants for refusing that mercy to his fellow which he had experienced from his lord in a larger degree, 21—35.

S. MATTHEW XVIII

^a Mark 9.33. Luke 9. 46. & 22. 24.

AT ^a the same time came the disciples unto Jesus, saying, Who is the greatest in the kingdom of heaven?

Mark, who relateth also the same history more largely, chap. ix. 33, saith, that this discourse was in the house at Capernaum, and that our Saviour began with them, asking them what they had been discoursing of by the way. That they held their peace, for they had been in the way arguing one with another who should be the greatest; they might at the same time also ask Christ the question. Luke, in whom we find the same history, speaketh of it only as a question that had arisen among themselves, chap. ix. 46. It had been the matter of their thoughts in the way, yea, and of their more private discourse also. Luke saith, Jesus knew the thoughts of their hearts. We had need set the Lord at all times before our eyes, for we are always in his sight. He encompasseth all our paths, as the psalmist saith. In the way, when we think also we cannot be overheard, he heareth us, and will call us to account for our travelling thoughts and discourses. They were at first ashamed to tell the Lord what they had been thinking and discoursing upon, for Mark saith, ver. 34, *they held their peace*. But by and by they propound the question to Christ himself; so saith Matthew. What do they mean here by *the kingdom of heaven?* or what gave them occasion to such a discourse? It is most probable that they did not in this question intend the kingdom of glory; but either the church, or gospel dispensation; or (which indeed is most likely) that earthly kingdom which the Jews thought the Messiah should exercise on the earth. The general error of their nation, about a secular kingdom, which the Messias, when he came, should exercise upon the earth, restoring the kingdom to Israel, as they phrase it, Acts i. 6, seemeth to have infected them; so as though in this they differed from the unbelieving Jews, that they owned Christ to be the promised Messiah, and the Christ the Son of God, yet they looked for a temporal kingdom which he should administer. Three times we find them in this mistake; here, and chap. xx. 21, and at our Saviour's administration of the supper, Luke xxii. 24; and by Acts i. 6 it should seem that till Christ's ascension they were not fully instructed in the nature of Christ's kingdom, but expected that after his resurrection this kingdom of his should have began; and therefore they say, *Wilt thou at this time restore the kingdom to Israel?* Some think that that which at this time raised their jealousy and stirred up their ambition, was our Saviour's promising Peter the keys of the kingdom of heaven, chap. xvi., and paying tribute for him, chap. xvii. But neither of these could be, for had not the keys been given equally the question had been determined, they needed have reasoned no more. He that had the keys was certainly to be the greatest; and for the paying of tribute, it was too minute a thing to cause such a jealousy. Besides, this discourse of theirs was by the way to Capernaum, where he now was; that was after he came to the house. But they doubtless fancied a temporal kingdom of the Messiah, in which places would be bestowed; and Christ, by his discourse about the tribute, had asserted himself a King's Son; and they conceived that after his death and resurrection (which Christ had lately been speaking of) this his kingdom would begin, which also agreeth with what we have Acts i. 6: they therefore thought it now time to speak for places. They had been arguing the point amongst themselves, and could not come to a resolution. Some of them were Christ's near kinsmen (such was James, Gal. i. 19). Some of them had more extraordinary parts; he named two of them, on this account, *the sons of thunder*. To others he had showed a more particular kindness; John is called *the beloved disciple;* Peter, James, and John were taken up to the mount to see his transfiguration. These things might cause some emulation and suspicions; they therefore come to our Saviour to be resolved. 1. How slowly do we conceive, and how hardly do we come to understand, spiritual things! we are of the earth, and we are earthly. 2. How prone are we to seek great things for ourselves, neglecting our higher spiritual and eternal concerns! This text lets us see, that even the best of men are subject to earthly-mindedness, ambition, emulation, and hardly brought truly to understand, believe, and seek the things which are above. Let us now observe how our Saviour behaveth himself towards his disciples upon this question, and what answer he makes to it.

2 And Jesus called a little child unto him, and set him in the midst of them,

3 And said, Verily I say unto you,
^bExcept ye be converted, and become as little children, ye shall not enter into the kingdom of heaven.

4 ^cWhosoever therefore shall humble himself as this little child, the same is greatest in the kingdom of heaven.

^b Ps. 131. 2. ch. 19. 14. Mark 10. 14. Luke 18. 16. 1 Cor. 14. 20 1 Pet. 2. 2.
^c ch. 20. 27. & 23. 11.

Mark saith, chap. ix. 35—37, *And he sat down, and called the twelve, and saith unto them, If any man desire to be first, the same shall be last of all, and servant of all. And he took a child, and set him in the midst of them: and when he had taken him in his arms, he said unto them*, &c. Luke saith only, that he *took the child, and set him by him*, chap. ix. 47; and adds, ver. 48, *he that is least among you all, the same shall be great*. How easy a thing had it been for our Saviour, had he intended any such primacy in the church as the papists contend for, to have said, Peter shall be the greatest! Here was a very fair opportunity for him, if he had pleased, so to have declared his will; but here is not a word of such tendency. Mark saith our Saviour, 1. *Sat down*, as the manner of their teachers was, when they taught, to denote their authority. 2. He *called the twelve*, to let them know that what he was about to speak was a grave matter, not of a particular but universal concern for them to learn, that they might teach others. He *said unto them*, (saith Mark,) *If any man desire to be first, the same shall be last of all, and servant of all;* and (which Luke adds) *he that is least among you all, the same shall be great.* You would know (saith he) who shall be greatest. He that doth not desire to be first; he who is most remote from pride and ambition; he that most contemneth the world, and the priorities and superiorities of it. The proud and ambitious man, he that seeketh great things for himself, shall be of least esteem in my kingdom; he is really least in grace, and ought to be of least esteem and repute among Christians, and he will be the last in the kingdom of glory. Then he calleth to him *a little child:* the word doth not always signify a very young child; here it doth, for, 1. He took him in his arms (saith Mark). 2. A young child was the fittest pattern to commend humility to them. This was an ancient and usual way of teaching, by types, as it were, or patterns: see Jer. xix. 10; xxvii. 2. He reads this lecture upon the child, *Verily I say unto you, Except ye be converted, and become as little children, ye shall not enter into the kingdom of heaven. Whosoever therefore shall humble himself as this little child*, &c. The prefixing *Verily* adds much to the authority of this saying. *Converted* here, στραφῆτε, doth not signify the change or conversion of a soul from a state of sin unto God, (so the apostles were already converted,) but the turning of their souls from a particular lust or error, into the opposite right way of truth and holiness: except ye repent of your pride and ambition, ye cannot be saved. The next words expound it, *and become as little children:* not as little children in all things, (which was the Anabaptists' dream in Germany, upon which they would run about the streets playing with rattles, &c.,) but, ver. 4, humbling yourselves as little children. 1. Little children know not what dominion means, and therefore affect it not, are not ambitious. 2. They are not given to boast and glory, and to prefer themselves before others. 3. They are ready to be taught and instructed. 4. They live upon their fathers' providence, and are not over-solicitous. 5. They are not malicious and vindictive. *In malice* (saith the apostle) *be ye children*. The three first are principally here intended. If ye be not thus like little children, ye will be so far from being greatest in the kingdom of God, that you will never come there at all. So as this text teacheth us all, 1. The necessity of humility in order to salvation. 2. That even converted souls have need of a daily conversion. Repentance is a work which will never be perfected till we come to die. 3. How abominable in the eyes of God ambition and pride are in any, especially in ministers of the gospel. 4. That in the church the way to be great is to be humble. 5. That true humility lieth in a mean opinion of ourselves, not minding high things, con-

84   S. MATTHEW XVIII

descending to men of low estate, not being wise in our own conceits, Rom. xii. 16; *in honour preferring one another,* ver. 10.

d ch. 10. 42. Luke 9. 48.

5 And ^dwhoso shall receive one such little child in my name receiveth me.

e Mark 9. 42. Luke 17. 1, 2.

6 ^eBut whoso shall offend one of these little ones which believe in me, it were better for him that a millstone were hanged about his neck, and *that* he were drowned in the depth of the sea.

Mark hath it thus, chap. ix. 37, *Whosoever shall receive one of such children in my name, receiveth me : and whosoever receiveth me, receiveth not me, but him that sent me.* Then he addeth, ver. 42, *And whosoever shall offend one of these little ones that believe in me, it is better for him that a millstone were hanged about his neck, and he were cast into the sea.* Our Lord having declared that the little ones before mentioned shall be greatest in the kingdom of God, here cometh to show the care which he in his providence will take for them; that their friends shall be his friends, and their enemies his enemies : Whoso receiveth such a little child, that is, a humble Christian. In the next verse it is opened by, one that believeth in me. By receiving I conceive is here to be understood the showing of any favour or kindness to them : Christ declares that he would take it as done to himself. It is much the same with chap. x. 40 —42. Mark addeth, He that receiveth me, receiveth him that sent me. The reason is, because he and his Father are one, and the Father takes any kindness done to Christ as if it were done to himself, and the Son takes any kindness or unkindness done to any humble, believing soul, as if it were done to himself: see chap. xxv. 34—46. *But whoso shall offend one of these little ones, &c.* As offending signifieth the laying of a stumbling-block before any, so it signifieth any motion or temptation to them to sin against God, whether it be by flattering or frowning arguments, though the latter seemeth rather to be understood here ; so, by offending, it signifies the doing them any harm upon Christ's account, because they own him, and make a profession of his gospel, which, besides that it is a stumbling-block upon which they fall and suffer as to their bodies and outward concerns, is also a stumbling-block to their souls, such dangers being strong temptations to Christians, to turn them aside from the right paths of truth and holiness. *It were better for him that a millstone, &c.* ; μύλος ὀνικὸς, a stone in such a mill as asses were wont to draw, because of the heaviness of it. Some think our Saviour in this phrase alludeth to some punishment of notorious malefactors, in use not amongst the Jews, but some other nations, by tying a stone about their necks, and throwing them into the sea : but whether it be such an allusion or no, is of no great moment ; the phrase signifieth a certain destruction, both in regard of the weight of the stone and the depth of the sea. He saith, It is better that a millstone, &c., because of the punishment which shall be inflicted on such persons beyond this life.

7 ¶ Woe unto the world because of

f Luke 17. 1. 1 Cor. 11. 19. g ch. 26. 24.

offences! for ^fit must needs be that offences come; but ^gwoe to that man by whom the offence cometh!

h ch. 5. 29, 30. Mark 9. 43, 45.

8 ^hWherefore if thy hand or thy foot offend thee, cut them off, and cast *them* from thee: it is better for thee to enter into life halt or maimed, rather than having two hands or two feet to be cast into everlasting fire.

9 And if thine eye offend thee, pluck it out, and cast *it* from thee: it is better for thee to enter into life with one eye, rather than having two eyes to be cast into hell fire.

By *offences* are here meant stumbling-blocks to souls, such persons or actions as are to others temptations to sin. The world, saith our Saviour, is full of temptations. Temptations to sin are on all hands, some enticing and persuading men to that which is evil, others setting them an example to it, others alluring them by promises, others by threatenings and punishments driving men to it as much as in them lieth : the world will one day find the evil and mischief of it. *It must needs be that offences come ;* God hath so ordered it in the wisdom of his providence, that he will not restrain the lusts of all men's hearts, but suffer some to walk in their own ways. Men in power will command those under them to do what is sinful, fright them by threatenings, force them (if possible) by punishments. Equals and inferiors will set examples of sin, allure, entice, and persuade. But woe be to those by whom such offences come ! Men, saith our Saviour, should be so afraid to sin, as they should rather part with the dearest things they have in the world, if they be as dear as eyes, hands, feet, rather than sin, or endure them to be occasions of sin to them. See ver. 8, 9 opened in our notes on chap. v. 29. Mark hath the same things, chap. ix. 43—48, only with the addition of this saying thrice, *Where their worm dieth not, and the fire is not quenched ;* which phrase doth but denote the eternity of sinners' misery, taken from Isa. lxvi. 24.

10 Take heed that ye despise not one of these little ones; for I say unto you, That in heaven ⁱtheir angels do always ^kbehold the face of my Father which is in heaven.

i Ps. 34. 7. Zech. 13. 7. Heb. 1. 14. k Esth. 1. 14. Luke 1. 19.

Our Saviour having before declared how dear believing souls are unto him, though their quality or parts be not like others', here he gives the world a further charge not to *despise,* that is, not to contemn or neglect them, because God the heavenly Father hath such a care of them, so as he hath given his angels a charge over them, Psal. xxxiv. 7 ; xci. 11 ; Heb. i. 14 ; which *angels* (saith he) *do always behold the face of my Father which is in heaven,* that is, are always ministering before him, and ready to execute his will and pleasure ; so as the argument is not only drawn from the indecency and undutifulness that such despising must import, but also from the danger of it. Your heavenly Father so loveth these little ones, that he hath given his angels a special charge concerning them ; and these angels being continually in the Lord's presence, are ready both to make report how they are used in the world, and likewise having commission from God to execute his vengeance upon those who neglect, despise, or affront those that he hath taken into such a special protection. Here is no ground in this text for their notion, who fancy that every particular child of God hath his proper angel to attend him. Our Saviour doth not say their several and respective angels, but *their angels ;* and if all the angels be *ministering spirits,* for the good of God's elect, Heb. i. 14, I see no great reason to contend for a particular angel for every individual amongst them. But be that as it will, the opinion hath no patronage from this text.

11 ^lFor the Son of man is come to save that which was lost.

l Luke 9. 56. & 19. 10. John 3. 17. & 12. 47.

We find the same in Luke, chap. xix. 10, but applied upon another occasion. Our Saviour here riseth higher in his argument against giving offence to his little ones. All scandal tendeth to the ruin and destruction of him to whom it is given. *Scandalum non est nisi malæ rei ædificans ad Gehennam,* saith Tertullian ; and a greater than he hath taught us the same lesson, Rom. xiv. 15 ; 1 Cor. viii. 11. Now, saith our Saviour, I am *come to save that which was lost ;* you ought therefore to take care that you be not the causes and instruments of any being lost. Or thus ; You look upon poor humble souls, that believe in me, as mean, contemptible creatures, therefore you think you may despise them : were not all those whom I came to redeem in as mean and despicable a condition ? yet I did not despise their souls. Did I come to save them, and shall it be your work to destroy them ?

12 ^mHow think ye ? if a man have an hundred sheep, and one of them be gone astray, doth he not leave the ninety and nine, and goeth into the mountains, and seeketh that which is gone astray ?

m Luke 15.4.

13 And if so be that he find it, verily I say unto you, he rejoiceth more of that *sheep,* than of the ninety and nine which went not astray.

14 Even so it is not the will of your Father

which is in heaven, that one of these little ones should perish.

We shall meet with the parable or similitude more fully, Luke xv. 4. To what purpose it is brought here our Lord hath told us, ver. 14, to show us, that it is not the will of our heavenly Father that the least and meanest believer should perish. And every scandal, or offence, (as I before showed,) hath a tendency to destroy that soul before whom it is laid, or to which it is given. Take heed, saith our Saviour, of giving scandals and offences to others, yea, though you should have observed them in something slipping and going astray. Will you be more uncharitable to men than you are to the beasts which you keep? You do not thus with a sheep; though it be gone astray you do not despise and neglect it, much less take courses to drive it further. No, you rather leave the rest, as being safe, and go, though it be into the mountains, to recover the sheep that is lost; and if you find it, have a greater passion of joy for that one sheep so recovered than for all the other. If you see some error in any of my sheep, if they do wander, should it not be your care rather to *restore such in the spirit of meekness*, as Gal. vi. 1, than to lay further stumbling-blocks before them, and give them occasion of further stumbling and falling? My Father hath done so for lost man: my coming to seek and to save that which is lost, is an evidence to you that it is not his will that one of my little ones should be lost.

ⁿ Lev. 19. 17.
Ecclus. 19. 13.
Luke 17. 3.

15 ¶ Moreover ⁿ if thy brother shall trespass against thee, go and tell him his fault between thee and him alone: if he shall hear thee, ^o thou hast gained thy brother.

^o Jam. 5. 20.
1 Pet. 3. 1.

16 But if he will not hear *thee, then* take with thee one or two more, that in ^p the mouth of two or three witnesses every word may be established.

^p Deut. 17. 6. & 19. 15.
John 8. 17.
2 Cor. 13. 1.
Heb. 10. 28.

17 And if he shall neglect to hear them, tell *it* unto the Church: but if he neglect to hear the Church, let him be unto thee as an ^q heathen man and a Publican.

^q Rom. 16. 17. 1 Cor. 5. 9. 2 Thess. 3. 6, 14. 2 John 10.

Our Saviour very appositely addeth this to his former discourse concerning avoiding offences, that none might think that by the former doctrine he had made void the law, Lev. xix. 17, which commanded all *in any wise to rebuke* their *neighbour, and not to suffer sin upon him*, pretending that it was their duty in some cases to offend any person by that law. He here telleth them that he would not be so understood, as if they might not tell offenders of their sins for fear of offending them, this had been to have withheld charity from their souls under a pretence of charity. Only in these reproofs we must keep an order, which order he here prescribes. 1. Doing it privately, betwixt them and him alone. 2. If that had not its effect, then taking two or three with them. 3. If that also proved ineffectual, then telling it to the church. 4. If that he would not *hear the church*, then, *let him be unto thee* (saith Christ) *as an heathen and a publican.*

If thy brother shall trespass against thee. By *brother* here he meaneth any Christian; for what hath the church to do to judge those that are without? 1 Cor. v. 12. *Trespass against thee.* Some interpret this of offences done so privately, that none else knoweth them but one single person; but it is objected, that then there needed no going to him, much less were there need of any witnesses, for they could prove nothing. Others therefore understand the precept of private injuries, which are in man's power to forgive, Luke xvii. 3. Others think such injuries are primarily intended, but yet the precept is not to be restrained to them, but to be understood of all offences, whether against God, ourselves, or our neighbours; and that our Saviour useth this term *against thee* only to distinguish the offences he is here speaking of from public scandals; for, 1 Tim. v. 20, it appeareth to be the will of God, that public and open sinners should be rebuked *before all, that others may fear.* The rule therefore seemeth to be given concerning private miscarriages; not such only as are done in the sight or hearing of a single person, but such as are not the matter of public fame, nor openly committed before a multitude, but being committed more secretly, are come only to the knowledge of some particular person or persons. In such cases it is the will of God, not that we should blazon and publish them, but, being certain that any Christian hath so offended, it is our duty first to go to him, and tell him of it; that is, not only tell him what thou knowest, or hast heard in matter of fact, that he hath spoken or done, but show him also the sinfulness of it. *If he shall hear thee, thou hast gained thy brother;* that is, if he confesseth the sin, and be brought to a sight of it, a sorrow for it, and a resolution against it for the time to come, thou hast gained the soul of thy brother. *But if he will not hear thee,* if he either denieth the matter of fact, that he did such a thing, or (admitting that) standeth to justify the fact, as what he might do, *then take with thee one or two more, that in the mouth of two or three witnesses every word may be established:* one or two more, either such as may be of more authority with him, whose words may probably be of more weight than thine with him, or who may witness the matter of fact if it be denied, or at least witness by charitable admonition of him, and his contumacy, if he refuseth to hearken to thee, and to repent and reform. What was the law of God in civil and judicial causes, Deut. xix. 15, God would have observed in ecclesiastical causes: *One witness shall not rise up against a man for any iniquity, or for any sin, in any sin that he sinneth: at the mouth of two witnesses, or at the mouth of three witnesses, shall the matter be established.* And so the words in Matthew should be translated, or at least understood; *every word,* that is, every matter, be confirmed. *And if he shall neglect to hear them;* either refuse to speak with them, or to suffer them to speak with him; or, hearing them with his ears, if he persists to deny the fact, or to justify the fact, as if it were no sin, or go on still in the same course; (all these things are to be understood by the term of not hearing;) if he shall not hear them, *tell it to the church.* That the term *church* is a noun of multitude is evident, and therefore cannot be understood of any particular person. Some would by the church here understand the political magistrate; but as this sense is embraced by very few, so it is very improbable that our Saviour should send Christians in that age to the civil magistrates, when they were all great haters and persecutors of the Christian religion, especially in cases that were not punishable by the judges; for no deliberate person will say, that the offences mentioned in this text were all of that nature as a civil judicature might take notice of them. Others say, that by the church is here meant the Jewish court called the Sanhedrim, which had a mixed cognizance, both of civil and ecclesiastical causes. There are three prejudices against this: 1. That the Jewish court was never in Scripture called 'Εκκλησια. 2. That it is not probable that our Saviour would direct Christians to go to the Jewish courts in such cases. 3. That the Sanhedrim was too great a court to be troubled with all scandals, though they did take cognizance of some things in religion, which were of a grand concern; such as blasphemy, idolatry, false prophets, &c. Others therefore understand it of the Christian church. Against this opinion there is this great prejudice, that there was no such thing in being at that time; but I take this to be a lighter objection than those against the two other opinions: 1. Because we need not understand our Saviour speaking with relation to the present time, but the time to come, and giving laws which should take place and abide from the gathering of the Christian church to the end of the world. Nor is it necessary that we should take the term *church* here in the strict sense, in which it is most generally used in the Scriptures of the New Testament, for the general notion of the word is only a company of people called together; and in this sense, Tell the church, is no more than, Tell the multitude, make his crime more public: now what that multitude was which our Saviour meant, would easily be understood when the churches came to be formed. But the next verse will make it more plain; ver. 18, *Verily I say unto you, Whatsoever ye shall bind on earth shall be bound in heaven, &c.* By *the church* then must be meant those who had power to bind and loose. Now though at this time there was no particular church formed, yet there were some who had a power to bind and loose. Christ had given such a power to his apostles. These were the present church, and at this time in being. They were afterwards to constitute particular churches, to whom, (when constituted,) in force of this precept, such offences were to be told. There are yet further disputes, whether this offence and contumacy be to be told only to the rulers, or to the multitude. I say, to the whole church, but first to the rulers, then by them to the multitude, not to judge of it, but for their consent in casting a person out of the communion of the church. Thus the incestuous person was first accused to Paul, then cast out by the consent of the whole church, 1 Cor. v. 3—5. For it is unreasonable to think that people should deny communion to any without knowing a justifiable cause; and to no purpose for rulers in a church to cast one out of its communion with whom the members will have communion. *If he neglect to hear the church, let him be unto thee as an heathen man and a publican;* that is, esteem him as a vile person, for so they esteemed all heathens and publicans. How far this could reach beyond having an intimacy of civil communion with them, and a communion with them in the sacrament, I cannot understand; for as Christians were licensed to a civil commerce with heathens and publicans, so neither were heathens and publicans ever, that we read of in holy writ, denied the benefit of their prayers, and hearing the apostles preach. I am very well satisfied, that the primitive church did not deny to persons excommunicated liberty to be present at the prayers of the church, but it was long after the apostles' times, and whether grounded upon any practice of theirs I much doubt. Christians had a liberty to pray for any who had not sinned the sin unto death: that they might not be present at such prayers I cannot learn from any thing in holy writ.

r ch. 16. 19.
John 20. 23.
1 Cor. 5. 4.

18 Verily I say unto you, ʳWhatsoever ye shall bind on earth shall be bound in heaven: and whatsoever ye shall loose on earth shall be loosed in heaven.

We met with this sentence, chap. xvi. 19, where we observed that by binding and loosing was signified (according to the usage of the Jews of those times) declaring of propositions true or false, or judging things lawful or unlawful. Some think that it hath no further import here; but it is the opinion of Mr. Calvin, and other very judicious interpreters, that it is here to be extended to the censures of the church, the sentence of the church pronounced justly in the case of offences; and is added, lest persons justly denied the communion of the church should contemn such censures. Christ assures these persons that such censures ought not to be slighted, for God would confirm them in heaven; as also to their absolutions, or readmissions of such persons into their communion, upon their true repentance and acknowledgment of their errors. Not that our Lord by this intended to confirm all sentences of excommunication, or to patronize any cheat or hypocrisy in any, to gain an absolution, or restoration to the church. But only, as to the first, to assure stubborn and impenitent sinners that he would ratify what his church did, according to the rule he had given them to act by. It is therefore a terrible text to those who are justly and duly cut off from the communion of the church, for notorious and scandalous sins, such as whoso committeth and doth not repent of, they shall never enter into the kingdom of God. And as comfortable to those who, being so cast out, do truly repent, and are under temptations to be swallowed up of too much sorrow. If therefore any be cast out of any church for professing or standing to any truth of the gospel, or because he will not do what is sinful, we must not understand them bound in heaven, though they be bound on earth. nor have any such excommunications any terror in them. How forcible are right words! but these arguings, what do they reprove? The church is not by this text made infallible, nor is the holy God by it engaged to defend their errors.

s ch. 5. 24
t 1 John 3. 22. & 5. 14.

19 ˢAgain I say unto you, That if two of you shall agree on earth as touching any thing that they shall ask, ᵗit shall be done for them of my Father which is in heaven.

20 For where two or three are gathered together in my name, there am I in the midst of them.

Most interpreters agree there is a connexion betwixt these verses and those immediately preceding, as if it were a further confirmation of what God had said concerning his binding and loosing in heaven whatsoever they should bind or loose on earth; and say, the asking mentioned in this verse supposeth that no church will adventure upon so grave an act as excommunication, without asking his direction or counsel; nor undertake such a thing as absolution, without the like serious asking of God pardon for the repenting sinner. Now, saith he, let the church be never so small that so joineth in prayers on this occasion, what they ask of God shall be done. Whether it hath any such reference or no, or be an independent promise of Christ's presence with his church, I shall not determine. Those who think this text hath such a particular reference, yet do also grant it a more general promise of Christ's presence with his people. Whenever they are met by his authority, or upon his account or command, whether it be for counsel, or judgment, or prayer, or the celebration of any sacred institution of his, he is in the midst of them, to protect and favour them: what they ask *shall be done for them;* that is, provided the thing asked be good, chap. vii. 11, and for a right end, James iv. 3, and in a right manner, Luke xviii.1; James i. 5—7. Christ in this text establisheth the duty of prayer in communion with others. He doth not only require of his people secret prayer, chap. vi. 6, but also praying in company with others; the gathering together of his people for prayer, whether in private families or more public congregations.

21 ¶ Then came Peter to him, and said, Lord, how oft shall my brother sin against me, and I forgive him? ᵘtill seven times?

u Luke 17.4.

22 Jesus saith unto him, I say not unto thee, Until seven times: ˣbut, Until seventy times seven.

x ch. 6. 14.
Mark 11. 25.
Col. 3. 13.

Luke hath something like this chap. xvii. 4, but it seemeth to have been spoken at another time, and upon some other occasion; yet the sense is much the same, and there are who think that Peter's mention of seven times arose from our Saviour's command there, that we should forgive our brother offending us seven times, when our Saviour by it intended not a certain and definite number, but a number uncertain and indefinite. But it is a greater question, what sinning and what forgiveness is here meant. I cannot think that our Saviour here speaketh concerning the church's absolving scandalous sinners justly excommunicated, but of the private forgiveness of injuries done to us; it is not the church, but I forgive him; for although the doors of the church ought to be as open to a repenting sinner as the doors of heaven are, yet methinks both the phrase of the text and the following parable (which seemeth to me a comment upon this text) seem to lead us to the interpretation of these verses as to private wrongs or injuries; they are properly sins against us, and such as it is in every single person's power to forgive. But it seems hard that Christians should be obliged to forgive another his private wrongs so often as he doth them, if he will go on without end multiplying affronts and injuries to us; we must therefore know, that our Saviour by this precept doth not oblige any to take his enemy into his bosom, and make him his intimate or confidant again; but only to lay aside all malice, all thoughts and desires of revenge towards him, to put on a charitable frame of spirit towards him, so as to be ready to do him any common offices of friendship. Thus far we are obliged to forgive those that do us injuries, so often as they stand in need of forgiveness. The apostle, Col. iii. 8, speaks of wrath, malice, &c., as pieces of the old man, which every true Christian hath put off, and calls upon us in malice to be children.

23 ¶ Therefore is the kingdom of heaven likened unto a certain king, which would take account of his servants.

24 And when he had begun to reckon, one was brought unto him, which owed him ten thousand ‖ talents.

‖ *A talent is 750 ounces of silver which after five shillings the ounce is 187l. 10s.*

25 But forasmuch as he had not to

S. MATTHEW XVIII

y 2 Kin. 4. 1. Neh. 5. 8. pay, his lord commanded him ʸ to be sold, and his wife, and children, and all that he had, and payment to be made.

26 The servant therefore fell down, ‖ Or, besought him. and ‖ worshipped him, saying, Lord, have patience with me, and I will pay thee all.

27 Then the lord of that servant was moved with compassion, and loosed him, and forgave him the debt.

28 But the same servant went out, and found one of his fellowservants, which ‖ The Roman penny is the eighth part of an ounce, which after five shillings the ounce is seven pence halfpenny. ch. 20. 2. owed him an hundred ‖ pence : and he laid hands on him, and took *him* by the throat, saying, Pay me that thou owest.

29 And his fellowservant fell down at his feet, and besought him, saying, Have patience with me, and I will pay thee all.

30 And he would not : but went and cast him into prison, till he should pay the debt.

31 So when his fellowservants saw what was done, they were very sorry, and came and told unto their lord all that was done.

32 Then his lord, after that he had called him, said unto him, O thou wicked servant, I forgave thee all that debt, because thou desiredst me :

33 Shouldest not thou also have had compassion on thy fellowservant, even as I had pity on thee ?

34 And his lord was wroth, and delivered him to the tormentors, till he should pay all that was due unto him.

z Prov. 21. 13. ch. 6. 12. Mark 11. 26. Jam. 2. 13. 35 ᶻSo likewise shall my heavenly Father do also unto you, if ye from your hearts forgive not every one his brother their trespasses.

All these verses (except the last) are but a parable, which (as I before showed) is a similitude brought from the usual actions of men, and made use of to open or apply some spiritual doctrine. The main scope, or the proposition of truth, which our Saviour designs to open or press, is that which is first and principally to be considered and intended; and that, as I before showed, is to be known, either by the particular explication given by our Saviour, or by what went immediately before, or followeth immediately after. The scope of this parable is plainly expressed, ver. 35, *So likewise shall my heavenly Father do also unto you, if ye from your hearts forgive not every one his brother their trespasses.* Nor is it obscurely hinted to us in what went before, where our Saviour was instructing Peter in the great duty of forgiving men their trespasses. This being agreed, as we use to say, that similitudes run not on four feet, so we are not to expect that all the actions of men, mentioned in the parable, should be answered by some correspondent actions of God : as similitudes always halt, so never more than when by them God's actions are expressed and represented to us. The main points which this parable instructeth us in are, 1. That it is our duty, especially theirs who have received forgiveness from God, to forgive their brethren. 2. That if they do not, they may justly question whether God hath forgiven them, and expect the same severity from him which they show unto their brethren. These being the main things for instruction in which this parable is brought, and which we ought chiefly to eye as the things taught us by this parable, nothing hindereth but that it may also instruct us in some other things, though we cannot raise a proposition of truth from every branch of the parable, and some things be put in according to the passions and usual dealings of men, which possibly are in them unrighteous actions, and may follow from their ungoverned passions, which will by no means agree to the pure and holy nature of God. I will pick open such terms in the parable as may be less intelligible to vulgar readers. *The kingdom of heaven ;* my administration of my kingdom : I am come to purchase remission of sins, and to dispense out remission of sins to those who are indebted to the justice of my Father; but in the application of my blood to men and women for the remission of their sins, both my Father and myself will do as a king, that took account of his servants, &c. Men must look for pardon from my Father, and benefit from me as their Redeemer, upon the following terms : see chap. vi. 15. *Ten thousand talents;* a certain for an uncertain number; a very great sum. Those who have computed it, say it amounteth to a million eight hundred and seventy-five thousand pounds. He *commanded him to be sold, and his wife, and children, and all that he had;* a thing which our law will not suffer, but in use amongst other nations, and amongst the Jews in particular, as may be learned from 2 Kings iv. 1. *And delivered him to the tormentors;* that is, to the keepers of the prison ; so the next words teach us, and the Greek word often signifieth no more, though it doth indeed sometimes. *An hundred pence,* ver. 28, signifieth a small sum, hardly exceeding in our money fifty shillings. This parable excellently instructeth us in these truths : 1. That as men, by the law of nature and God, and the laws of men, may be debtors to us, to our reputation, to our estate; so we are all debtors to the glory, honour, and justice of God. 2. That it is a vast debt we owe to God's honour and justice, to which no debt owing by any to us can bear any proportion. 3. That we have nothing to pay to God, in satisfaction for our debt. 4. That God hath a right to demand a full satisfaction of us. 5. That God, for Christ's sake, upon our application to him for mercy, will forgive us our debts. 6. That we are not so ready to forgive our brethren their little injuries, as God is to forgive us. 7. That our difficulty to forgive our brethren, after God's liberality in forgiving us, is a great charge, or will be a great charge against us in the court of heaven. 8. That we ought to set before us God's compassion towards us, and free love in forgiving us, potently to move us to forgive those who have done us injury, and to forgive them out of that consideration. 9. That we ought from our hearts to forgive men their trespasses; that is, so as not to hate them, bear them any grudge or malice, seek any private revenge upon them, or public satisfaction, beyond what they are able to give, but be ready to do them what common offices of kindness in their straits are in our power. 10. That the not doing of this will be an ill evidence to our souls, that God hath not indeed forgiven us, as well as a bar against such forgiveness; and an ill omen, that some punishment from God expecteth us in this life, to bring us to a temper more conformable to the gospel, and if not in this life, yet in the life which is to come.

CHAP. XIX

Christ healeth the sick, 1, 2 ; *answereth the question of the Pharisees concerning divorce, and the objection of his disciples to the expediency of marriage,* 3—12 ; *receiveth little children with tenderness,* 13—15 ; *instructeth a young man how to attain eternal life, and how to become perfect,* 16—22 ; *showeth how hard it is for a rich man to enter into the kingdom of God,* 23—26 ; *and promiseth great rewards to his disciples, and to all who have forsaken aught to follow him,* 27—30.

AND it came to pass, ᵃ*that* when Jesus had finished these sayings, he departed from Galilee, and came into the coasts of Judæa beyond Jordan ; A. D. 33. a Mark 10. 1. John 10. 40.

2 ᵇAnd great multitudes followed him ; and he healed them there. b ch. 12. 15.

Most interpreters agree that both Mark, chap. x. 1, and Luke, chap. ix. 51, make mention of the same motion of our Saviour out of Galilee into the province of Judea which is here expressed, though Luke and John mention, something largely, some things done in the way, of which Matthew speaketh not. *He departed from Galilee.* Our Saviour had hitherto spent his time mostly in Galilee. The country of the Jews was divided into three provinces, Galilee, Samaria, and Judea. Galilee was the more northerly part of the country, and was divided into the

Upper Galilee, which is also called *Galilee of the Gentiles,* Matt. iv. 15, and the Lower Galilee, which was contiguous to it, but lay more southerly, and adjoined to Samaria. Our Saviour dwelt at Nazareth a long time. Chorazin, Bethsaida, Capernaum, were all cities of Galilee. He is now taking his leave of this province, into which he never returned more. His next way into Judea lay through Samaria, (for Samaria lay in the middle betwixt Galilee and Judea,) and through part of it he did go, for, Luke ix. 52, 53, some inhabitants of a village belonging to the Samaritans refused to receive him. *And came into the coasts of Judea beyond Jordan.* This phrase hath caused some difficulty to interpreters, because Judea was bounded by Jordan, and had no coasts beyond it. Some say that the term *beyond Jordan* must be applied to *he came,* he came beyond Jordan to the coasts of Judea. Others say, that as men came out of Egypt, the coasts of Judea were beyond Jordan, Matt. iv. 15. But some think it should be there translated, *by Jordan:* the word πέραν signifies any border, or side of a border. *Beyond Jordan,* therefore, is on the border of Jordan, and possibly were better translated so, seeing the word will bear it, and there were no coasts of Judea beyond Jordan. It is probable that our Saviour, coming out of Galilee into Samaria, kept on the left hand near to Jordan, till he came into Judea, which also bordered on that river. Wherever he went *great multitudes followed him,* but more for healing their bodies, or for the loaves, than for the feeding or healing of their souls; so different is most people's sense of their bodily and spiritual wants. *He healed them,* the text saith; but it saith not, they believed in him.

3 ¶ The Pharisees also came unto him, tempting him, and saying unto him, Is it lawful for a man to put away his wife for every cause?

Our Saviour, though yet at some distance from Jerusalem, was come into that province where the Pharisees had the greatest power, and were in greater numbers: now they come to him, *tempting him;* where the word *tempting* rather signifies, generally, making a trial of him, than strictly, soliciting him to sin; they came (as appeareth by their question) to make a trial whether they could entrap him, and get any determination from him of a point for which they might accuse him. The question they propound to him is, *Is it lawful for a man to put away his wife for every cause?* The word here translated *cause,* signifieth not cause, or occasion, but crime also. So it may be translated crime; but they did not only put away their wives for crimes, but upon any occasion, in a sense of that text, Deut. xxiv. 1, *When a man hath taken a wife, and married her, and it come to pass that she find no favour in his eyes, because he hath found some uncleanness in her;* which the Pharisees had interpreted of any kind of deformity, or natural infirmity, not merely of moral uncleanness. Had our Saviour now answered Yes, he had contradicted what he had formerly delivered, chap. v. 32; had he denied, they had trapped him as contradicting the law of Moses, Deut. xxiv. 1, according to their interpretation of it. So they had had whereof to accuse him.

4 And he answered and said unto them, ^c Gen. 1. 27. & 5. 2. Mal. 2. 15. Have ye not read, ^c that he which made them at the beginning made them male and female,

^d Gen. 2. 24. Mark 10. 5, —9. Eph. 5. 31. e 1 Cor. 6. 6. & 7. 2. 5 And said, ^d For this cause shall a man leave father and mother, and shall cleave to his wife: and ^e they twain shall be one flesh?

6 Wherefore they are no more twain, but one flesh. What therefore God hath joined together, let not man put asunder.

Mark, chap. x. 2—9, giveth us the same history of this discourse, differing a little in the order of the words, but nothing as to the substance of his discourse. Our Saviour answereth neither Yea nor Nay to their discourse, but gives them a fair occasion to answer themselves, and tacitly chargeth them with ignorance and corruption of the law of God. He referreth them to the first institution of marriage, and for that to the book of Genesis, chap. i. 27; ii.

24. It is as much as if our Lord had said, You own the book of Genesis, as well as the book of Deuteronomy. In the book of Genesis you read the first institution of marriage: it was instituted by God himself; he made *male and female,* Gen. i. 27; he made the law of marriage, Gen. ii. 24, that *a man* should *leave his father and mother, and cleave unto his wife, and they* should *be one flesh;* from whence he concludeth that the man and wife are one flesh in God's account. From hence he leaves them to conclude, whether it was probable that Moses, whom they so reverenced, and who was so faithful in the house of God as a servant, would license them to put asunder whom God had put together; or whether they had not put an interpretation upon the law of Moses which it could not bear in consistency with the law of God. For the sense of those words, Gen. i. 27; ii. 24, see the notes on those places.

7 They say unto him, ^f Why did Moses ^f Deut. 24. 1. ch. 5. 31. then command to give a writing of divorcement, and to put her away?

8 He saith unto them, Moses because of the hardness of your hearts suffered you to put away your wives: but from the beginning it was not so.

Mark reports this a little differently, chap. x. 3, &c., as if Christ had first *said unto them, What did Moses command you? And they said, Moses suffered to write a bill of divorcement, and to put her away. And Jesus answered and said unto them, For the hardness of your heart he wrote you this precept,* &c. The substance of our Saviour's answer seemeth to be this: Moses gave you no positive command in the case, he could not make a law directly opposite to the law of my Father; but Moses saw the wantonness and wickedness of your hearts, that you would turn away your wives without any just and warrantable cause; and to restrain your extravagancies of cruelty to your wives, or disorderly turning them off upon any occasion, he made a law that none should put away his wife but upon a legal cognizance of the cause, and giving her a bill of divorce. Indeed possibly this bill of divorce was sometimes judicially granted upon irregular causes, and Moses might connive at it for the preventing of greater evils, because you were always a hard-hearted and stiff-necked people; and you by your traditions have expounded that law beyond Moses's intention, and made a bill of divorce grantable in cases which he never thought of, nor intended in that law. But the measures of lawfulness are neither to be taken from Moses's temporary toleration and connivance, nor much less from your traditions and expositions of the law of Moses, but from the original institution of marriage, and from God's original law relating to it: now God at first made but one woman for one man, and so united them that he styled them *one flesh;* so as he who puts away his wife, doth as it were divide and tear his own flesh piece from piece, which is barbarous, inhuman, and unnatural. And the law of God was not, that a man should forsake his wife whenever he had a mind to it, but that he should rather forsake his father and mother than his wife; that he should cleave to his wife, living and dwelling with her, as a man of knowledge; not hating his own flesh; loving his wife as his own body, loving and cherishing her, Eph. v. 28, 29. Now how can this possibly consist with a man's putting away his wife upon every little and trivial cause of offence or dislike unto her.

9 ^g And I say unto you, Whosoever ^g ch. 5. 32. Mark 10. 11. Luke 16. 18. 1 Cor. 7. 10, 11. shall put away his wife, except *it be* for fornication, and shall marry another, committeth adultery: and whoso marrieth her which is put away doth commit adultery.

We met with the like determination of our Lord's upon this question chap. v. 32, only there it was (instead of *committeth adultery) causeth her to commit adultery,* that is, in case she married again. Here our Lord saith the like of the husband: we have the same, Mark x. 11; Luke xvi. 18. The reason is this: Because nothing but adultery dissolveth the knot and band of marriage, though they be thus illegally separated, yet according to the law of God they are still man and wife. Some have upon these words made a question whether it be lawful for the husband or the wife separated for adultery to marry again while each other liveth. As to the party offending, it may be a question; but as to the innocent person offended, it is no question, for the adultery of the person offending hath dissolved the knot of marriage by the Divine law. It is true that the knot cannot be dissolved without the freedom of both persons each from another, but yet it seemeth against reason that both persons should have the like liberty to a second marriage. For, 1. The adulteress is by God's law a dead woman, and so in no capacity to a second marriage. 2. It is unreasonable that she should make an advantage of her own sin and error. 3. This might be the occasion of adultery, to give a wicked person a legal liberty to satisfy an extravagant lust. But for the innocent person, it is as unreasonable that he or she should be punished for the sin of another. But what our Saviour saith here, and in the other parallel texts, is undoubtedly to be understood of husbands and wives put away not for adultery, but for other light and trivial causes, for which by the law of God no divorce is allowed.

h Prov. 21. 19.

10 ¶ His disciples say unto him, [h]If the case of the man be so with *his* wife, it is not good to marry.

This is a very strange saying, and discovers to us both the imperfect state of Christ's disciples, and also the tyranny of a sinful practice grown up into a custom. The Jews had assumed a liberty of turning their wives out of doors upon every light and trivial offence or dislike; the disciples think, if this licentiousness may not be allowed it is not good to marry. So a holy institution of God, ordained for the propagation of mankind, for the restraint of extravagant lust, and for the solace and comfort of man's life, should be despised, rather than those unquiet lusts and corruptions mortified, the mortification of which would have made those irregular separations both needless and undesirable. Surely they should rather have said, If the case of a man be so with his wife, then both husbands and wives had need to learn to deny themselves, to comply each with another, to silence their brutish and boisterous passions, that, being the same flesh, they might also have one and the same spirit, and not be like a diseased piece of flesh, where humours so quarrel that one piece need be cut off to preserve the other. But the best of men have their infirmities; and, as the Hebrews said, *Spiritus Dei non semper tangit corda prophetarum*, The Spirit of God was not always upon the hearts of the prophets; so it is as true, *Spiritus Dei non semper et ubique tangit corda fidelium*, All that the saints say is not gospel. Their flesh hath its turn to speak, as well as the Spirit in them. A sinful liberty conceded, indulged, or connived at, by the laws, or by the rulers of a church or place where we live, for a long time, is not easily restrained, and even good men may for a time be carried away with the error of it, so as they cannot discern it, be convinced of it, or be brought clear of it to a conformity to the will of God.

i 1 Cor. 7. 2, 7, 9, 17.

11 But he said unto them, [i]All *men* cannot receive this saying, save *they* to whom it is given.

12 For there are some eunuchs, which were so born from *their* mother's womb: and there are some eunuchs, which were made eunuchs of men: and [k]there be eunuchs, which have made themselves eunuchs for the kingdom of heaven's sake. He that is able to receive *it*, let him receive *it*.

k 1 Cor. 7. 32, 34. & 9. 5, 15.

Our Saviour, knowing the sinful custom and practice of the Jewish nation now for many years, and giving some allowance for that, and his disciples' infirmities; so he doth not answer them severely, as what they said might deserve, but reproves them gently. What he saith amounts to thus much: You do not consider what you say. *All men*, without sinning against God, cannot abstain from marriage. An ability to live chastely without the use of marriage is a peculiar gift of God, and your saying hath no place in persons to whom God hath not given that gift, *for it is better to marry than to burn*. There are some whom God by nature hath made unfit for marriage. There are others whom men (wickedly) make unfit for it, that they may gratify their own jealousy. (Thus several courtiers were made eunuchs, and so betrusted with the care of princes' wives and concubines.) And there are some who have made themselves eunuchs, not castrating themselves, (that is wickedness,) but abstaining from marriage, and yet living chastely, (having mortified their lusts, and brought under their body,) that they might be less encumbered with the cares of the world, and be more free for the work of the ministry, or be able more to give up themselves to a holy life and spiritual conversation. But God, who by his ordinance of marriage designed to people and continue the world, hath given to persons different tempers and constitutions; so as possibly the most of men and women cannot without making use of marriage govern their lusts. As to these, marriage is not a matter of choice and deliberation, and they may and ought to use it as an appointment of God, for the ends for which he hath instituted it. If there be any who can receive this saying, who can without marriage bridle his lust, and so live in a solute and single state as not to sin against God by any extravagancy of lusts, and impure desires and affections, and desire, and shall do so, that he may be more spiritual, and serve God with less distraction, and be a more fit instrument to promote the kingdom of God in the world, let him do it.

13 ¶ [l]Then were there brought unto him little children, that he should put *his* hands on them, and pray: and the disciples rebuked them.

l Mark 10. 13. Luke 18. 15.

Mark saith, chap. x. 13, and Luke saith, chap. xviii. 15, they were brought *that he should touch them*. A doubt may from this text arise in the reader's mind, for what purpose the parents or nurses did bring these young children to Christ. It was not for baptism, for he baptized none himself, John iv. 2. It is not likely it was for healing; for though our Saviour in such cases did sometimes touch or lay his hand upon the sick persons, yet it is not likely that in that case the disciples would have rebuked them, knowing that their Master used to heal such as were brought to him. It must therefore unquestionably be, that he might bless them. Matthew here saith, *that he should put his hands on them, and pray*. The putting of hands upon persons when they blessed them, or prayed for a blessing on persons, was a very usual rite and custom amongst the Jews. *Without all contradiction* (saith the apostle, Heb. vii. 7) *the less is blessed of the better*. It was a custom amongst the Jews to bring persons to those whom they looked upon as excelling in holiness, to be blessed and commended to God by their prayers, Gen. xxvii. 4; xlviii. 14. The parents or nurses of these children by this act declared that they looked upon Christ as some great Prophet in favour with God, and whose prayers could prevail with God, and whose blessing was considerable as to these little ones. *The disciples rebuked them*, as thinking they were too troublesome to their Master, and not understanding what children in health had to do with their Master, nor perhaps having before seen such a precedent.

14 But Jesus said, Suffer little children, and forbid them not, to come unto me: for [m]of such is the kingdom of heaven.

m ch. 18. 3.

15 And he laid *his* hands on them, and departed thence.

Both Mark and Luke add something to this story. Mark saith, chap. x. 14—16, *When Jesus saw it, he was much displeased, and said unto them, Suffer the little children to come unto me, and forbid them not: for of such is the kingdom of God. Verily I say unto you, Whosoever shall not receive the kingdom of God as a little child, he shall not enter therein. And he took them up in his arms, put his hands upon them, and blessed them.* Luke saith the same, chap. xviii. 16, only he saith, he *called them unto him*, and leaves out what Mark hath, ver. 16, of Christ taking them up in his arms, putting his hands upon them, and blessing them. From this text divines will prove the baptism of children, because *theirs is the kingdom of heaven*; which whether we understand of the church, and the dispensation of the grace of Christ under the gospel, viz. that the gospel church is made up of infants as well as more adult persons, or that the grace of Christ under the gospel, viz. remission of sins through the blood of Christ, doth belong to some children, as well as to grown persons; or of the kingdom of glory, viz. children shall go to heaven as well as grown persons; the argument is well drawn from this text, Those who have a right to a membership in the church are to be baptized; or, Those who have a right to the kingdom of glory may be baptized. But one or both of these are affirmed in this text. We must take heed we do not found infant baptism upon the example of Christ in this text, for it is certain that he did not baptize these children; Mark only saith, *he took them up in his arms, put his hands upon them, and blessed them.* The argument for infant baptism from this text is founded upon his words, uttered on this occasion, not upon his practice. Mark addeth, that our Saviour told them, that unless a man received the kingdom of God as a little child, he could not enter into it. But we opened those words before, Matt. xviii. 3, where we met with the same in effect.

n Mark 10. 17.
Luke 18. 18.
o Luke 10. 25.

16 ¶ ⁿAnd, behold, one came and said unto him, °Good Master, what good thing shall I do, that I may have eternal life?

This history is reported by Mark, chap. x. 17—23, and by Luke, chap. xviii. 18—25. Mark saith, *When he was gone forth into the way, there came one running, and kneeled to him, and asked him, Good Master, what shall I do, that I may inherit eternal life?* Luke saith, *A certain ruler asked him.* Our Lord was now in his way from Galilee to Judea and to Jerusalem. There cometh a person, a ruler, whether of some of the synagogues, or in some place of civil magistracy, the Scripture saith not. He runs, he kneeleth to him, (paying him at least a civil homage, as to his superior,) he salutes him with the ordinary title they gave to their teachers, Master, Good Master; he propoundeth a grave question to him, what he should do that he might get to heaven; but yet he doth not propound the question in those terms, but, *What good thing shall I do, that I may have eternal life?* It appeareth by his respect showed to Christ at his coming, and by the question proposed, and by his going away sorrowful when our Saviour's answer did not satisfy him, that he did not come upon any captious design to entrap our Saviour, but out of a desire to learn; but yet it appeareth plainly that he was a Pharisee, or a disciple of the Pharisees; and thought his life was in his own hands, that he had a power in himself to do some good thing by which he might merit eternal life, or upon the doing of which he might at least obtain everlasting life, though not as a strict reward for his work, without any consideration of a Messias. He grants an eternal state, he declares his desire of an eternal happiness, he declares his readiness to do some *good thing* that he might obtain it.

17 And he said unto him, Why callest thou me good? *there is* none good but one, *that is,* God: but if thou wilt enter into life, keep the commandments.

Mark omitteth the latter clause, and only saith, *Thou knowest the commandments;* so saith Luke, chap. xviii. 19, 20. Our Saviour's design here was, not to show this young man by this answer the way by which it was possible that he or any other might come to heaven, but only to convince him of the errors of the Pharisaical doctrine. They would not own Christ to be God, nor to be come forth from God; they taught eternal life to be obtainable by the works of the law, and by a fulfilling of the law, according to that imperfect sense which they gave of it, of which we heard much, chap. v. Now, saith our Saviour, seeing you will not own me to be God, nor yet to have come from God, *why callest thou me good?* There is none originally, essentially, and absolutely good, but God: there is none derivatively good, but he deriveth his goodness from God. How callest thou me good, whom thou wilt neither own to be God, nor to derive from God? *But if thou wilt enter into life, keep the commandments.* This was the doctrine of the Pharisees, That men might keep the commandments. Saith our Saviour, The way to eternal life, according to your doctrine, is plain before thee. You say, men may perfectly keep the commandments of God. He that doth so shall be saved. Therefore *keep the commandments.* Not that our Saviour thought he could do it, or that there did lie a passable road to heaven that way, but that he might convince him of his error, and the need he had of a Saviour.

18 He saith unto him, Which? Jesus said, ᵖThou shalt do no murder, Thou shalt not commit adultery, Thou shalt not steal, Thou shalt not bear false witness,

19 ᑫHonour thy father and *thy* mother: and, ʳThou shalt love thy neighbour as thyself.

p Ex. 20. 13.
Deut. 5. 17.
q ch. 15. 4.
r Lev. 19. 18.
ch. 22. 39.
Rom. 13. 9.
Gal. 5. 14.
Jam. 2. 8.

Mark addeth, *defraud not,* chap. x. 19, but Luke doth not put it in, chap. xviii. 20. Three things we may observe: 1. There are no commandments mentioned but those of the second table. 2. Nor are they reckoned up in order. 3. The tenth commandment is expressed by, *Thou shalt love thy neighbour as thyself;* which elsewhere our Saviour calls the second great commandment, and makes comprehensive of all the commandments of the second table. We must not from our Saviour's order here, in the enumeration of the commandments, either conclude that the precepts of the second table are greater than those of the first, or that it is enough to keep them in order to eternal life: nor yet, that the fifth commandment is lesser than the sixth, seventh, eighth, ninth, because it is put after them. But, 1. Our Saviour had reckoned up commandments enough to convince this man that he could not by keeping the commandments hope for eternal life. 2. He had reckoned those, by some of which he intended by and by to convince him that he had not kept the commandments. 3. And those of the non-observation of which it was most easy to convince him. 4. The Pharisees looked upon these as the most vulgar and easy commandments. 5. Because love to our neighbour is an excellent evidence of our love to God. As concerning the order in which they are enumerated, it was not our Saviour's business here to show which was the greatest commandment; that he hath elsewhere determined, calling, Thou shalt love the Lord thy God with all thy heart, &c., *the first and great commandment:* here he is not solicitous about the order.

20 The young man saith unto him, All these things have I kept from my youth up: what lack I yet?

Those words, *what lack I yet?* are not in Mark or Luke. The young man understood these commandments according to the Pharisees' interpretation of them, who, as we heard, chap. v., interpreted them only as prohibiting the overt acts, not the inward lusts and motions of the heart, together with the means or occasions leading to such acts. Paul saith, he *had not known lust, except the law had said, Thou shalt not covet,* Rom. vii. 7. Men that deceive themselves with false glosses and interpretations may think they keep the commandments of God, and be very confident of a righteousness in themselves; but it is impossible others should be so. *What lack I yet?* He expected Christ should have set him some new task, and was not aware that he only wanted a better knowledge and understanding of the law to convince him of his mistake.

21 Jesus said unto him, If thou wilt be perfect, ˢgo *and* sell that thou hast, and give to the poor, and thou shalt have treasure in heaven: and come *and* follow me.

s ch. 6. 20.
Luke 12. 33.
& 16. 9.
Acts 2. 45.
& 4. 34, 35.
1 Tim. 6. 18, 19.

Mark repeats it thus, chap. x. 21, *Then Jesus beholding him loved him, and said unto him, One thing thou lackest: go thy way, sell whatsoever thou hast, and give to the poor, and thou shalt have treasure in heaven: and come, take up the cross, and follow me.* Luke, chap. xviii. 22, repeats it as Matthew, only he begins it with, *Yet lackest thou one thing.* Mark saith, that *Jesus beholding him loved him:* not with a special saving love, for he sent him away sad; upon his going he tells his disciples, that it was a very hard thing for a rich man to come to heaven; he tells him one thing was wanting to him: but he loved him with such a common love as he loveth all his creatures with, and more especially such as are better than others. All that can be concluded from hence is, that acts of moral righteousness are pleasing to God. He saith to him, *If thou wilt be perfect,* that is, in keeping the commandments of God. The papists make a great deal of stir to found upon this text their counsels of perfection; as if Christ here were advising only the young man to do something beyond what the law strictly required, in order to a more perfect state than others. But that this cannot be the sense of the words will appear to him who will diligently consider, 1. That this had been needless, for our Saviour, in directing the young man to keep the commandments in order to his obtaining everlasting life, had sufficiently declared that the keeping of the commandments was perfection enough. 2. He says, One thing is wanting to thee, that is, in order to thy obtaining everlasting life, which had not been true if our Saviour had granted him to have kept all the commandments, for he had before let him know that the keeping them was sufficient. Our Saviour therefore, by this speech, only endeavours to convince him that he had not kept all the commandments. But it may be objected, How could that be, for there was no commandment that obliged him to go sell all that he had, and give to the poor? I answer, there was a commandment that he should love the Lord his God with all his heart, and soul, and strength, which he could not do unless he had a heart ready to obey any command God should lay upon him, which our Saviour puts upon the trial by this special precept. 2. There was a commandment of God that he should love his neighbour as himself, and that he should not covet. Now not to be ready at the commandment of God liberally to relieve the poor members of Christ, argued a covetous mind, more in love with his estate than with God; so as though this was not before specially commanded, yet it was commanded generally, and that he would have understood had he rightly understood the law of God; especially having such a promise annexed as *thou shalt have treasure in heaven.* 3. Nor must all the command be taken to be included in those words, *Go sell that thou hast, and give to the poor;* but the following words must also be taken in, *and come, take up the cross, and follow me.* Perfection here is not made to lie in a voluntary poverty only, but in coming after and following of Christ, with a free taking up of the cross. In short, no man can be perfect in keeping the commandments of God, that doth not love God with all his heart, soul, and strength; nor can any man pretend to this, that hath not a heart ready to obey God in all things, whether more generally or more specially commanded. Nor can any man fulfil the duties of the second table, without first fulfilling the duties of the first; for if our love to our neighbour flow not from a love to God, it is no act of obedience, and consequently no fulfilling of the law; which is not fulfilled by mere doing the external duty of it, but by doing what is required in it out of an obedience unto God, which cannot be without a first loving God.

22 But when the young man heard that saying, he went away sorrowful: for he had great possessions.

Mark saith the same, chap. x. 22; so doth Luke, chap. xviii. 23. He was sorry that he had ever propounded the question, or that the terms were such as his covetous heart could not comply with. He would have had heaven if he could have had it cheap; or, it may be, he would have parted with something for it; but to sell all was a hard saying! Or he was sorry to see himself so confuted, and convinced that, whatsoever he dreamed, he had not kept the commandments, and had not a heart prepared to obey God in one thing. It is not said, because he loved his great possessions, but, *for he had great possessions;* yet the first is intended. It is a hard thing for us to have a great concern in the world, and not to love it more than God. *He went away;* he would hear no more of that discourse. How many would have heaven if they might have it upon their own terms! How few are willing to come up to God's terms! How false and deceitful are our hearts! they will persuade us we have done all, when indeed we have done nothing, nor are prepared to do any thing in truth and sincerity. We are not perfect, something is wanting to us, till *to will* to do whatsoever God requireth of us be present with us, though, when it comes to, we may want strength to perform.

23 ¶ Then said Jesus unto his disciples, Verily I say unto you, That [t] a rich man shall hardly enter into the kingdom of heaven.

t ch. 13. 22.
Mark 10. 24.
1 Cor. 1. 26.
1 Tim. 6. 9, 10.

24 And again I say unto you, It is easier for a camel to go through the eye of a needle, than for a rich man to enter into the kingdom of God.

Mark saith, chap. x. 23—25, *And Jesus looked round about, and saith unto his disciples, How hardly shall they that have riches enter into the kingdom of God! And the disciples were astonished at his words. But Jesus answereth again, and saith unto them, Children, how hard is it for them that trust in riches to enter into the kingdom of God! It is easier for a camel to go through the eye of a needle, than for a rich man to enter into the kingdom of God.* Luke saith, chap. xviii. 24, 25, *And when Jesus saw that he was sorrowful, he said, How hardly shall they that have riches enter into the kingdom of God! For it is easier for a camel to go through a needle's eye, than for a rich man to enter into the kingdom of God.* Our Lord, seeing the young man that came to him so briskly, with such a zeal for his soul, and appearing warmth of desire to be instructed in the right way to heaven, and asking for a task to be set him; first, what good thing he should do in order to that end, then calling for more; when our Saviour had reckoned up some commandments to be observed, *What lack I yet?* saith he; go away quite damped and sorrowful, when our Saviour said not to him, Give thy body to be burned; no, nor yet, Cut off a right hand or foot, or pluck out a right eye; only part with some of thy circumstances, *Sell that thou hast and give to the poor;* a thing he might have done, and have been a man still perfect, both as to his essential and integral parts: he hence takes occasion to discourse with his disciples the danger of riches, and the ill influence they have upon men's souls, with relation to their eternal welfare. Luke and Mark say he spake it by way of question, *How hardly?* Matthew delivereth it as spoken positively, *A rich man shall hardly enter,* &c. The sense is the same, only the interrogation seems to aggravate the difficulty, and to fortify the affirmation, as much as to say, A rich man shall very hardly enter into the kingdom of heaven. *The disciples were astonished* at this, (saith Mark,) which made our Saviour say it over again, with a little exposition, *How hard is it for them that trust in riches to enter into the kingdom of God!* Which exposition is so far from a correction or abatement of the severity of his former speech, that some judge it rather a confirmation of it, for he goes on with saying, *It is easier for a camel to go through the eye of a needle.* But why should this astonish the disciples, who had no reason upon this account to fear for themselves, who had forsaken all to follow Christ? Possibly, because it was so contrary to the common opinion of the world, who did not only, as in Malachi's time, *call the proud happy,* but thought God had scarce any favour for any but the rich; in opposition to which Christ, Luke vi. 20, 24, blesseth the poor, and pronounceth woes to the rich, as having received their consolation. As to the words themselves, the design of our Saviour in them was not to condemn riches, as in themselves damnable; nor yet to deny salvation to all rich persons: our Lord knew that Abraham, Isaac, Jacob, Job, were all rich persons, and in heaven; so was David and Solomon, &c. He also knew that riches are the gifts of God, good things, not in themselves pernicious. His design was only to show that they are dangerous temptations, soliciting and enticing our hearts into so great a love of them, and affection to them, as is not consistent with our duty with reference to God; and giving the heart of man such advantages for the lusts of pride, covetousness, ambition, luxury, (some or other of which are predominant in all souls,) that it is very hard for a rich man so far to deny himself, as to do what he must do if ever he will be saved. For those words in Mark, *them that trust in riches,* I take them rather to give the reason of the difficulty, than to be an abatement of what he had before said; for to trust in riches, is to place a happiness in them, to promise ourselves a security from them, so as to be careless of a further happiness, Psal. xlix. 6; lii. 7; 1 Tim. vi. 17. That which makes it so hard for a rich man to be saved, is the difficulty of having riches and not placing our felicity in them, being secure because of them, and having our hearts cleave unto them, so as we cannot deny ourselves in them to obey any command of God; and the suffering them to be temptations to us to pride, luxury ambition, oppression, contempt and despising of others, covetousness, &c. Upon these accounts our Saviour goeth on and saith, *It is easier for a camel to go through the eye of a needle, than for a rich man to enter into the kingdom of God.* Which doubtless was a proverbial expression, in use then amongst the Jews, to signify a thing of great difficulty, by terms importing impossibility: or else the phrase may signify an impossibility without the extraordinary influence of Divine grace, as our Saviour seemeth to expound it in the next verses.

25 When his disciples heard *it*, they were exceedingly amazed, saying, Who then can be saved?

u Gen.18.14.
Job 42. 2.
Jer. 32. 17.
Zech. 8. 6.
Luke 1. 37.
& 18. 27.

26 But Jesus beheld *them*, and said unto them, With men this is impossible; but ᵘwith God all things are possible.

Mark saith, *They were astonished out of measure, saying among themselves*, &c. All three evangelists agree in the same substance of the other words. But why are the disciples amazed? or why do they say, Who then can be saved? Are there not in all places more poor than rich persons? The disciples might reasonably conclude, that poor persons were by their poverty also exposed to many great and dangerous temptations; that even they, though they had not riches, yet might too much place felicity in them, and covet what they had not; and from hence collect a difficulty for any to get to heaven. Our Saviour saith unto them, *With men this is impossible; but with God all things are possible.* If men indeed were left all to themselves, none would be saved; the blackamoor cannot change his skin, nor the leopard his spots; but God can bring men to heaven by the mighty power of his grace: he can change a rich man's heart, and take it off from too much love of riches, and make him to despise and contemn his wealth, and to put his trust in the living God; or a poor man's heart, and make him also poor in spirit and rich in grace.

x Mark 10. 28.
Luke 18. 28.
y Deut. 33. 9. ch. 4. 20.
Luke 5. 11.

27 ¶ ˣThen answered Peter and said unto him, Behold, ʸ we have forsaken all, and followed thee; what shall we have therefore?

28 And Jesus said unto them, Verily I say unto you, That ye which have followed me, in the regeneration when the Son of man shall sit in the throne of his glory, ᶻye also shall sit upon twelve thrones, judging the twelve tribes of Israel.

z ch. 20. 21.
Luke 22. 28, 29,30. 1 Cor. 6. 2, 3.
Rev. 2. 26.

Mark and Luke repeateth the words of Peter in part, but neither of them have this part of our Lord's answer, particularly respecting his apostles. We heard before, chap. iv. 18—22, of Peter, and Andrew, and James, and John, forsaking all and following of Christ, when he called them; the others doubtless did the same. Peter observing that our Saviour laid not the stress of men's salvation either upon riches or poverty, but upon the frame of men's spirits, their humility, self-denial, their obedience to and readiness to follow him; rejoineth these words, and saith, *We have forsaken all, and followed thee; what shall we have?* Some think that he had an expectation of something in this life, according to the notion which the other Jews had, and it is apparent the disciples had some tincture of a secular kingdom, which the Messias should exercise. But considering our Lord's former discourse could not be so interpreted, and the disciples question, *Who then can be saved?* I cannot agree that. And for the same reason I cannot agree, that the coming of the Son of man in his glory, mentioned ver. 28, should be understood of his coming in his mediatory kingdom, (as some would have it,) but of his last coming, which is most properly called the coming of the Son of man in his glory, mentioned 1 Thess. iv. 15—17; Jude 14; and that the thing here promised to the apostles, is not a preference in the church, but a further degree of honour and glory in the day of judgment. *Ye which have followed me in the regeneration;* that is, at this time, while I have been by my doctrine reforming the word; in the regeneration of my church, while I have been putting it into a new state. Some make those worlds, *in the regeneration,* to refer to the next words. *In the regeneration;* that is, in the day of judgment, when Christ shall come in his glory. The apostle indeed, Acts iii. 21, calleth that day, *the times of restitution of all things.* And the prophet speaks of it as the time of the new heavens and new earth, Isa. lxvi. 22. So doth the apostle, 2 Pet. iii. 13; and John, in Rev. xxi. 1. It is not much material to which part we apply the term. *Ye which have followed me;* that is, who have followed and shall go on and follow me, for this promise cannot belong to Judas, the son of perdition. *Ye shall sit upon twelve thrones.* Judges and princes use to have assessors, that sit with them in judgment. He mentions *twelve thrones,* because he had now twelve disciples, his apostles; and though afterward Judas fell away, yet Matthias succeeded, Acts i. 26; so as the twelve thrones shall not be empty, but filled up with twelve that followed Christ, for such a one was Matthias, Acts i. 21. *Judging the twelve tribes of Israel.* Though the tribes were thirteen, yet they usually went under the notion of twelve, because Levi was not counted, as having no particular possession. That is, judging the Jews for their unbelief, and not reception of me: judging others also; but judgment shall begin at the house of God. Doubtless this promise imports, that the apostles shall have a higher place in glory at the great day than ordinary believers: yet the apostle saith *the saints shall judge the world,* 1 Cor. vi. 2.

29 ᵃAnd every one that hath forsaken houses, or brethren, or sisters, or father, or mother, or wife, or children, or lands, for my name's sake, shall receive an hundredfold, and shall inherit everlasting life.

a Mark 10. 29, 30.
Luke 18. 29, 30.

Mark saith, chap. x. 29, 30, —*for my sake, and the gospel's, but he shall receive an hundredfold now in this time, houses, and brethren, and sisters, and mothers, and children, and lands, with persecutions; and in the world to come eternal life.* Luke saith, chap. xviii. 29, 30, —*for the kingdom of God's sake, who shall not receive manifold more in this present time, and in the world to come life everlasting.* To words are a liberal promise, and we must consider, 1. To whom it is made. 2. Of what it is. The former promise respected the apostles, and was special, as appears by the number of twelve thrones. This respecteth all those that should forsake any thing, houses, brethren, lands, sisters, fathers, mothers, wife, children, for Christ; which is expressed by three phrases *(for my name's sake, for the gospel's sake, for the kingdom of God's sake)* all of the same import; rather than they will forsake me, and the profession of my gospel; rather than they will sin against God. The promise is, 1. Of *an hundredfold in this time.* 2. Of *eternal life.* We must not understand of an hundredfold in specie, but in value. Therefore Mark saith, he shall receive what he hath in this life *with persecutions.* What is therefore this hundredfold in this life? 1. Joy in the Holy Ghost, peace of conscience, the sense of God's love; so as, with the apostles, they shall rejoice that they are thought worthy to suffer any thing for the name of Christ, Acts v. 41. They shall, with Paul and Silas, Acts xvi. 25, sing in the prison; with those, Heb. x. 34, take joyfully the spoiling of their goods, knowing they have in heaven a better and an enduring substance. This inward joy and peace shall be a hundredfold more than fathers and mothers, or brethren, or sisters. 2. Contentment. They shall have a contented frame of spirit with the little that is left; though they have not so much to drink as they had, yet they shall have less thirst, Phil. iv. 11, 12. 3. God will stir up the hearts of others to supply their wants, and that supply shall be sweeter to them than their abundance was. 4. God sometimes repays them in this life, as he restored Job after his trial to greater riches. But they shall have a certain reward in another world, eternal happiness.

30 ᵇBut many *that are* first shall be last; and the last *shall* be first.

b ch. 20. 16.
& 21. 31, 32.
Mark 10. 31.
Luke 13. 30.

So saith Mark, chap. x. 31. We have much the same sentence, Luke xiii. 30, and Matt. xx. 16. The Jews that are counted now the first, nearest to the kingdom of heaven, shall have no place there; and the Gentiles, looked upon as most remote from it, shall be admitted into it. The Pharisees and great doctors, who think themselves first, that is, nearest the kingdom of heaven, shall be last; and those whom they count last, such as shall have nothing to do with heaven, shall be counted the first, shall have the preference, the chiefest place in heaven. It is a general sentence, and may be applied variously. But if we consider what discourse follows, we shall see reason to interpret it as an awakening sentence to the best of men. It is the apostles, those who had forsaken all to follow him, to whom he here saith, *But many that are first shall be last,* &c. As much as if he had said, You have forsaken all and followed me, but you had need look, and consider, from what principle, with what love, and to what end you have done it; you had need keep a watch upon yourselves, and see that you hold on, and that you have no confidence in yourselves. For many that are first in profession, first in the opinion of others, first in their own opinion and confidence, at the day of judgment will be found to be last in mine and my Father's esteem and reckoning: and many who make not so great a noise, nor have so great a name and repute in the world, and who have the lowest and meanest opinion of themselves, will be found first, and highest in my favour. The day of judgment will frustrate many expectations.

CHAP. XX

The parable of the labourers who were hired at different hours to work in the vineyard, 1—16. *Jesus foretelleth his own passion and resurrection,* 17—19: *answereth the petition of the mother of Zebedee's children, and checketh the indignation of the other disciples thereat,* 20—28. *He giveth sight to two blind men,* 29—34.

FOR the kingdom of heaven is like unto a man *that is* an housholder, which went out early in the morning to hire labourers into his vineyard.

2 And when he had agreed with the labourers for a ||penny a day, he sent them into his vineyard.

|| *The Roman penny is the eighth part of an ounce, which after five shillings the ounce is seven pence halfpenny. ch. 18. 28.*

3 And he went out about the third hour, and saw others standing idle in the marketplace,

4 And said unto them; Go ye also into the vineyard, and whatsoever is right I will give you. And they went their way.

5 Again he went out about the sixth and ninth hour, and did likewise.

6 And about the eleventh hour he went out, and found others standing idle, and saith unto them, Why stand ye here all the day idle?

7 They say unto him, Because no man hath hired us. He saith unto them, Go ye also into the vineyard; and whatsoever is right, *that* shall ye receive.

8 So when even was come, the lord of the vineyard saith unto his steward, Call the labourers, and give them *their* hire, beginning from the last unto the first.

9 And when they came that *were hired* about the eleventh hour, they received every man a penny.

10 But when the first came, they supposed that they should have received more; and they likewise received every man a penny.

11 And when they had received *it,* they murmured against the goodman of the house,

12 Saying, These last ||have wrought *but* one hour, and thou hast made them equal unto us, which have borne the burden and heat of the day.

|| *Or, have continued one hour only.*

13 But he answered one of them, and said, Friend, I do thee no wrong: didst not thou agree with me for a penny?

14 Take *that* thine *is,* and go thy way: I will give unto this last, even as unto thee.

15 ᵃIs it not lawful for me to do what I will with mine own? ᵇIs thine eye evil, because I am good?

a Rom. 9.21.
b Deu. 15. 9. Prov. 23. 6. ch. 6. 23.

16 ᶜSo the last shall be first, and the first last: ᵈfor many be called, but few chosen.

c ch. 19. 30.
d ch. 22. 14.

We find this parable only recorded by St. Matthew; nor have we any thing to guide us in understanding the scope of our Saviour in it, but the 16th verse, *So the last shall be first, and the first last: for many be called, but few chosen.* Some here by *first* understand such as are of greatest repute and estimation in the world, or who have the highest opinion of themselves. By *last* they understand persons who are of meaner note and reckoning in the world, and have lowest opinion of themselves. The former shall be last as to the love and favour of God, and any reward from him; and the other shall be first. Others by the *first* understand the Jews, who were the first people God had in the world, and more dignified than any other by privileges: by *the last,* the Gentiles, who came last into the church of God. This seems to be directly intended by our Saviour, who perfectly knew the pride and invidious temper of the Jews, who valued themselves upon their prerogative, that they were the church of God, when the world lay in wickedness; and were apt to resent as an indignity that the Gentiles should be called into the church, and be made equally partakers of spiritual privileges with them. Having now fixed the scope of the parable, the interpretation is easy.

The kingdom of heaven, that is, the sovereign dispensation of God in calling nations or persons to partake of spiritual benefits in his church, and consequently of eternal blessedness, *is like unto a man that is an householder, which went out early in the morning to hire labourers into his vineyard.* The *householder* is God the Father, compared by Christ to a husbandman, with respect to the culture of vines, John xv. 1; to one that hath a vineyard, Isa. v. 1, 2, &c. The *vineyard* is the church. The *work* is that which concerns eternal salvation, both of our own salvation, and of others that are committed to our charge, or that are within the compass of our activity to do them spiritual good. The *labourers* are, eminently, persons in office, and, generally, all that are called by the gospel. The hiring of them imports the gracious promise of the reward published in the gospel to those who will work. The *penny* is the reward, comprehensive of the spiritual privileges that persons in the church are made partakers of. Men *standing idle in the market-place,* signifies their neglect of the great and proper work for which they came into the world, to glorify God and save their souls. His going out at several times, and calling in some to the vineyard at the *third, sixth,* and *ninth hours,* implies the calling of the Jews in the early age of the world, and his sending the prophets in sundry times, when they were degenerated, to return to his service. The calling some at the *eleventh hour* particularly respects the bringing in the Gentiles by preaching the gospel, who before were without the knowledge of God and the way to life. The *even* is the time of accounts and recompence. The murmuring of some that they received no more than those that came later into the vineyard, primarily and immediately signifies the envy and vexation of the Jews, that the Gentiles should be equal partakers of the grace of God with themselves, who for so many ages had been his peculiar people. The householder's vindicating himself is from two considerations, wherein it appears that his liberality to some is perfectly consistent with his justice to all. 1. That he agreed with them for a penny, which they received: the Jews enjoyed those external privileges of God's covenant, which they so much valued themselves for, till they cut themselves off by their obstinate rejecting his grace. 2. That he might do what he pleased with his own. He was master of his own favours, and it was malignity to tax his bounty to others, which was nothing prejudicial to what was due by agreement to them. Our Saviour concludes the parable, that *the last shall be first;* the Gentiles shall be made partakers of the gospel, with the blessed privileges attending it: *and the first* shall be *last;* that is, the Jews should be deprived of those privileges. And analogically in every age, some who are first, in presumption of their own merit, in profession, and reputation, but not in real holiness, shall be last in God's account; and those who were sincere and diligent in the Christian calling, though disvalued by the world, shall be preferred before them. *For many be called, but few chosen.* This is the reason of what is said before. Many are called by the external preaching of the word into the visible communion of the church; this is the evident meaning by the reading of the parable, wherein it is said persons were called at several hours, comprehending the ministry of the prophets and the apostles, and all the succession of preachers in every age. *And few chosen;* that is, by the free and unchangeable decree of God ordained to eternal life, and to partake of saving grace in order to the obtaining it. This is the main scope of the parable.

17 ¶ ᵉ And Jesus going up to Jerusalem took the twelve disciples apart in the way, and said unto them,

ᵉ Mark 10. 32.
Luke 18. 31.
John 12. 12.

18 ᶠ Behold, we go up to Jerusalem; and the Son of man shall be betrayed unto the Chief Priests and unto the Scribes, and they shall condemn him to death,

ᶠ ch. 16. 21.

19 ᵍ And shall deliver him to the Gentiles to mock, and to scourge, and to crucify *him:* and the third day he shall rise again.

ᵍ ch. 27. 2.
Mark 15. 1, 16, &c.
Luke 23. 1.
John 18. 28, &c.
Acts 3. 13.

Both Mark and Luke give us account of this passage. Mark saith, chap. x. 32—34, *And they were in the way going up to Jerusalem; and Jesus went before them: and they were amazed; and as they followed, they were afraid. And he took again the twelve, and began to tell them what things should happen unto him, saying, Behold, we go up to Jerusalem; and the Son of man shall be delivered unto the chief priests, and unto the scribes; and they shall condemn him to death. and deliver him to the Gentiles: and they shall mock him, and shall scourge him, and shall spit upon him, and shall kill him: and the third day he shall rise again.* Luke hath it, chap. xviii. 31—34, *Then he took unto him the twelve, and said unto them, Behold, we go up to Jerusalem, and all things that are written by the prophets concerning the Son of man shall be accomplished. For he shall be delivered unto the Gentiles, and shall be mocked, and spitefully entreated, and spit on: and they shall scourge him, and put him to death: and the third day he shall rise again. And they understood none of these things: and this saying was hid from them, neither knew they the things which were spoken.* Our blessed Lord was yet upon his road from Galilee to Jerusalem; we have here an account of some of his travelling discourse, to teach us to make use of all time for edifying and profitable discourse. Mark saith, that as they went *Jesus went before them: and they were amazed; and as they followed, they were afraid.* Mark gives us no account of any formidable object in their eye. Those that think they were amazed to see him make such haste to his death, forget that Luke saith, that after our Saviour had further instructed them in this, they understood it not; but probably they knew he was going into the nest of his enemies, and this made them afraid. He calls to him the twelve, (it was not a discourse fit for a multitude,) and gives them an account very particularly of what he had twice or thrice before taught them: he had before told them of his death and resurrection, and that he should be betrayed to death; here he describes the manner, they should deliver him to the Gentiles (to Pilate and Herod); he describes his previous sufferings, he should be scourged, mocked, spit upon, and the kind of his death, he should be crucified; that when these things came to pass, they might be assured that he was God, who had so punctually foretold things to come, not existent in their causes, but mere contingencies. He comforteth them with two things: 1. That it was according to what had been foretold by the prophets. 2. That though he died, he should rise again the third day. They had need of this forewarning for a fore-arming; for considering that they now looked upon him as the Messiah, it might well pose them to think how he should die; and when they had seen all these things come to pass, it might have shaken their faith; but being so particularly foretold, the coming of them to pass rather confirmed their faith in him as the Son of God than weakened it. But Luke saith, *they understood none of these things;* that is, surely they believed none of them, the *saying was hid from them.* The words were plain enough, but they could not reconcile them to their reason, they could not conceive how he who was the Messiah could die; nor get over the prejudice of his being a temporal prince, and exercising a kingdom in this world. For his rising again the third day, they could not believe it.

20 ¶ ʰ Then came to him the mother of ⁱ Zebedee's children with her sons, worshipping *him,* and desiring a certain thing of him.

ʰ Mark 10. 35.
ⁱ ch. 4. 21.

21 And he said unto her, What wilt thou? She saith unto him, Grant that these my two sons ᵏ may sit, the one on thy right hand, and the other on the left, in thy kingdom.

ᵏ ch. 19. 28.

Mark saith, chap. x. 35, *And James and John, the sons of Zebedee, come unto him, saying, Master, we would that thou shouldest do for us whatsoever we shall desire. And he said, What would ye that I should do for you? They said unto him, Grant unto us that we may sit, one on thy right hand, the other on thy left hand, in thy glory.* Matthew's saying *in thy kingdom,* Mark, *in thy glory,* leaves us in some doubt whether these two disciples and their mother had here some carnal notion of the kingdom of heaven, because Christ had before spoken of some that should be first in it, and others last; or were in some expectation of some glorious secular kingdom, which Christ after his resurrection should exercise in the world; for that they had some such thoughts appears from Luke xxii. 24; Acts i. 6. This mother of James and John was Salome, Mark xv. 40, a constant follower of Christ, Matt. xxvii. 55, 56. Matthew saith she spake. Mark saith her two sons spake. They would first have had a general grant from Christ of whatsoever they should ask, or a certain thing. But wise men use not to grant such requests. Our Lord asks them what they would desire. Then do they betray their ambition. Was there ever a more unseasonable request, than for them to be suitors for great places to him, when he had but now told them he was going to be spit upon, scourged, condemned, crucified? Yet there was this good in it; they by it discovered a faith in him, that notwithstanding all this he should be exalted, and have a kingdom. But how carnal are our conceptions of spiritual and heavenly things, till we be taught of God a right notion of them!

22 But Jesus answered and said, Ye know not what ye ask. Are ye able to drink of ˡ the cup that I shall drink of, and to be baptized with ᵐ the baptism that I am baptized with? They say unto him, We are able.

ˡ ch. 26. 39, 42.
Mark 14. 36.
Luke 22. 42.
John 18. 11.
ᵐ Luke 12. 50.

Mark hath the same, chap. x. 38, 39. Our Saviour gently reproves them for their unadvised petition, and again mindeth them, that he was first to suffer, and then to enter into his glory, and that by much tribulation they also must enter into the kingdom of God; which was a thing fitter for their present thoughts, than sitting at his right hand and left hand, for we must *suffer with him,* if we will be *glorified together,* Rom. viii. 17. How ready are we to ask we know not what! *Are ye able to drink of the cup, &c.:* the sense is, Are you able to suffer what I am to suffer? Hereby our Saviour intimates that those who are the freest and greatest sufferers for Christ shall have the greatest rewards from him. Christ here expresseth his sufferings under the notion of drinking of a cup, and being baptized with a baptism. A *cup* is an ordinary metaphor in holy writ, by which a man's portion in this life is expressed, whether it be a portion of good things or evil, Psal. xi. 6; Isa. li. 17; Jer. xxv. 15; Lam. iv. 21; Matt. xxvi. 39, 42; John xviii. 11. Drinking of a cup is usually put for suffering, Jer. xlix. 12; Ezek. xxiii. 32; Obad. 16. The metaphor being, as some think, taken from a custom in some nations, to put malefactors to death by giving them a cup of poison to drink; or, as others think, from the lewd custom, at compotations to force men to drink off their cups. To be *baptized with the baptism that I am baptized with* hath the same import: see Luke xii. 50. Afflictions are ordinarily compared in Scripture to waters: to be baptized, is to be dipped in water; metaphorically, to be plunged in afflictions. I am, saith Christ, to be baptized with blood, overwhelmed with sufferings and afflictions; are you able to be so? *They say unto him, We are able.* This was as rashly spoken as the other. How little de we know our own strength! When Christ was apprehended, they *all forsook him and fled*, chap. xxvi. 56.

n Acts 12. 2.
Rom. 8. 17.
2 Cor. 1. 7.
Rev. 1. 9.

23 And he saith unto them, ⁿYe shall drink indeed of my cup, and be baptized with the baptism that I am baptized with: but to sit on my right hand, and

o ch. 25. 34.

on my left, is not mine to °give, but *it shall be given to them* for whom it is prepared of my Father.

Mark hath the same, chap. x. 39, 40. Our Saviour here tells them, that as he was first to suffer and then enter into his glory, so they that should be glorified with him should also first suffer with him; for none shall be crowned but those who *strive lawfully*, 2 Tim. ii. 5; and *all that will live godly in Christ Jesus shall suffer persecution*, 2 Tim. iii. 12. But who should be highest in the kingdom of glory his Father must determine, upon whose will the disposal of his kingdom, and the preferences in it, depended. This text hath been abused by those who have denied Christ's Deity, and equality to the Father, as if it served their purpose, because Christ here denieth it in his power to dispose of the kingdom of heaven; but besides that, he elsewhere asserts the contrary, John x. 28; xvii. 2. Christ doth not here speak of what was in his power, but what was his office as Mediator; so his work was to encourage them to fight the good fight, not to dispense out crowns to them. Or else he speaketh of himself as man, as he speaketh, John xiv. 28. Nor indeed doth Christ here deny that it was in his power, but only that it was in his power to give this preference to any except those for whom his Father had prepared it. Note, the Greek is, οὐκ ἔστιν ἐμὸν δοῦναι ἀλλ᾽ οἷς ἡτοίμασται, that is, is not mine to give, but to them for whom it is prepared; so that those words, *it shall be given to them*, which our translators put in, were better left out. All this was before ordered and determined by God, and he could only dispose of the kingdom of God according to the eternal counsel. Ἀλλά (which we translate *but*) hath here the force of εἰ μή, (unless,) as in Mark ix. 8; 2 Cor. ii. 5. Besides that, to show the order of the Trinity in working, acts of power and providence are usually ascribed to the Father, though by other scriptures it appears that the Son in them co-operateth with the Father.

p Mark 10. 41. Luke 22. 24, 25.

24 ᵖAnd when the ten heard *it*, they were moved with indignation against the two brethren.

Mark x. 41. Here is not yet a word of Peter's primacy, or any claim he put in for it; nor, it seemeth, had the others any apprehension of such an establishment, for then neither would James and John have put in for it, nor would all the disciples (among whom Peter was one) have been so displeased at the ambition of James and John; yet they seem to be sick of the same disease, and to have been displeased only that they had the start of the motion, and had put in their petition first.

25 But Jesus called them *unto him*, and said, Ye know that the princes of the Gentiles exercise dominion over them, and they that are great exercise authority upon them.

q 1 Pet. 5. 3.
r ch. 23. 11.
Mark 9. 35.
& 10. 43.

26 ᑫBut ⁱit shall not be so among you: but ʳwhosoever will be great among you, let him be your minister;

s ch. 18. 4.

27 ˢAnd whosoever will be chief among you, let him be your servant:

So Mark hath much the same, chap. x. 42—44. Luke hath also much the same, (but it seemeth spoken at another time,) chap. xxii. 25—27. I shall not here intermeddle with the disputes some have founded on this text: Whether there may be a civil magistracy amongst Christians; a thing undoubtedly foreign to the sense of this text. Or, Whether Christ here establisheth a party amongst ministers; which I do not think our Lord's design here. Nor yet with that other question, Whether ministers of the gospel may take upon them the exercise of any civil power. That which our Saviour here intendeth is, 1. To distinguish his kingdom from the kingdoms of the world. Those kingdoms are over men's bodies and estates; his was a spiritual kingdom, over the hearts and consciences of men. Or rather, his was a kingdom of glory, where there would be no need of rulers and magistrates, as in the government of the world, nor in any such exercise of authority as is here exercised in the government of earthly kingdoms and polities. 2. To condemn ambition and pride in his disciples, as making them most unfit for this kingdom, which is a thing he had before taught them. The way to be greatest in heaven is to be humblest, to be low and mean in our own eyes. This I think to be the properest interpretation of this text; our Lord by it correcting the erroneous opinion his disciples had of the nature of his kingdom, as also their pride and ambition, and pressing upon them other studies, than how to be the greatest in any earthly kingdom. If any do think that in this text our Lord hath some respect to the kingdom he hath upon earth, he rather checks ambition, and an affectation of superiority, than any thing else, and lets us know that such as love the pre-eminence are most unfit for it; that the work of heads of the church is but a ministry, not a domination; and that those who are fittest for it, and deserve most honour in the church, are those that least seek and affect it; and those most unworthy of that honour, who most hunt after it. But I prefer the first sense given of this text. For certainly what our Saviour here saith was not only occasioned by, but had a great relation to, the petition of James and John with their mother; and the bearing rule and exercising authority mentioned here relates to the kingdom mentioned in that petition; which I think cannot be understood of the church, which was a kingdom of Christ, which they as yet little understood: but they either meant the kingdom of glory, entertaining carnal conceptions of that, that there would be some superiority and inferiority there amongst the saints, which our Saviour here correcteth their mistake in; or else they fancied a secular kingdom, to be exercised by Christ on earth, after his resurrection from the dead. Our Saviour correcteth this mistake also, intimating that his kingdom should be of another nature, and the way to be highest in it was to be humble and low, and mean in opinions of ourselves.

t John 13. 4.
u Phil. 2. 7.
x Luke 22. 27.
y Is. 53. 10.
John 13, 14.
11. Dan. 9. 24, 26. John 11. 51, 52. 1 Tim. 2. 6. Tit. 2. 14. 1 Pet. 1. 19. z ch. 26. 28. Rom. 5. 15, 19. Heb. 9. 28.

28 ᵗEven as the ᵘSon of man came not to be ministered unto, ˣbut to minister, and ʸto give his life a ransom ᶻfor many.

So saith Mark, chap. x. 45. The apostle saith, Phil. ii. 7, *he made himself of no reputation, and took upon him the form of a servant.* Our Saviour had before taught them, that *the disciple is not above his master.* Such, saith our Saviour, as is the King in my kingdom, such must the rulers and great persons in it be. See what a kingdom I have; *I came not to be ministered unto, but to minister,* to serve the necessities of men's and women's souls and bodies; *and to give my life a ransom for many,* λύτρον, a redemption price. The apostle useth ἀντίλυτρον, which signifieth a price paid instead of another, 1 Tim. ii. 6. So as there is no further satisfaction or price to be paid for any.

a Mark 10. 46.
Luke 18. 35.

29 ᵃAnd as they departed from Jericho, a great multitude followed him.

b ch. 9. 27.

30 ¶ And, behold, ᵇtwo blind men sitting by the way side, when they heard that Jesus passed by, cried out, saying, Have mercy on us, O Lord, *thou* Son of David.

31 And the multitude rebuked them, because they should hold their peace: but they cried the

more, saying, Have mercy on us, O Lord, *thou* Son of David.

32 And Jesus stood still, and called them, and said, What will ye that I shall do unto you?

33 They say unto him, Lord, that our eyes may be opened.

34 So Jesus had compassion *on them*, and touched their eyes: and immediately their eyes received sight, and they followed him.

Mark repeateth the same story, chap. x. 46—52, with several more circumstances. 1. He mentioneth only one blind man, and nameth him *Bartimæus, the son of Timæus*. He saith, the blind man was *begging*. Mark saith, when Christ called the blind man, they said unto him, Be of good comfort, rise; he calleth thee. And he, casting away his garment, rose, and came to Jesus. He further adds, that Christ *said unto him, Go thy way; thy faith hath made thee whole.* Luke relateth the same, chap. xviii. 35—43. He saith, *As he was come nigh to Jericho.* He mentioneth but one blind man. In repeating Christ's words he saith, *Jesus said unto him, Receive thy sight: thy faith hath saved thee. And immediately he received his sight, and followed him, glorifying God: and all the people, when they saw it, gave praise unto God.* Our Lord presently gives his disciples a demonstration of what he had said, that he *came to minister*, to serve even the poorest and most despicable creatures. Jericho was a city not far from Jordan, Josh. iii. 16; it was taken, Josh. vi., and upon the division of the land fell within the lot of Benjamin, Josh. xviii. 21. Our Saviour took it in his way, from Galilee to Jerusalem. Probably these blind men, or Bartimæus at least, who alone is mentioned by Mark and Luke, hearing Christ was coming, sat first on the side of Jericho next Galilee, and then got him on the other side, as our Saviour was leaving the town. Which makes Luke say, *as he was come nigh;* and the two other evangelists say, *as he went out of Jericho*, he sat begging. Bartimæus being (as it should seem) the most known, and the most famous, is alone mentioned by Mark and Luke. Matthew (naming none) saith there were two; which Mark and Luke deny not, but knowing only the name of the one of them, they mention only one. They speak to our Saviour under the notion of the *Son of David*, by which they owned him as the true Messias; for that was a title by which the Messias was known amongst the Jews, according to the prophecies of him. They ask him for mercy; they continue in their cry, though the multitudes rebuked them, as possibly thinking they only came to ask some alms, and were too importunate, seeing our Lord seemed not to regard them. God sometimes trieth our faith by delays, how it will hold out, but he never frustrateth it. This mindeth us of our duty, to *pray without ceasing.* Christ stops, calleth them, asks them what they would have. They seem most sensible of their bodily wants, and answer, *Lord, that our eyes may be opened.* Jesus hath compassion on them, toucheth their eyes, (Christ sometimes, but not always in healing, touched the affected part,) and (as Luke saith) he said, *Receive thy sight.* The miracle is wrought; they presently are able to see. Luke addeth, that Christ said, *Thy faith hath saved thee.* We have met with the same phrase before. I have made thee whole, but thy faith in me hath prevailed with me to do it. Their faith in his power was seen, 1. In their owning him as the true Messiah; so able to do it. 2. In their imploring his mercy, and going on in their cries of that nature, though they met with a rebuke. Faith and fervent prayer do great things with God, because of his compassion. *The prayer of faith shall save the sick*, James v. 15. *The effectual fervent prayer of a righteous man availeth much*, ver. 16. Nor is any man so mean and contemptible in the world, (these two blind men were beggars,) but if they can believe on the Lord Jesus Christ, if they will lie in Christ's way, if they will cry unto him, and not give over their cries, they shall obtain at our Saviour's hands greater things than these. This miracle gaineth God glory from the multitude, and from the blind man not only praise, but a resolution to follow Christ. This should be the effect of all salvations wrought for us. Mercy is then duly improved, when it bringeth forth in our hearts glory and praise to God, and engageth us to follow the Lord Jesus Christ. Our Saviour had wrought his former miracles in Galilee, where the witnesses of them were remote; he hath now two witnesses in the province of Judea, who go along with him towards Jerusalem, where we shall find him in the next chapter.

CHAP. XXI

Christ rideth into Jerusalem upon an ass amidst the acclamations of the multitude, 1—11. *He driveth the buyers and sellers out of the temple, and healeth the diseased there,* 12—14. *His reply to the priests and scribes who took offence at the hosannas of the people,* 15, 16. *He curseth the barren fig tree, which presently withereth,* 17—22. *He silenceth the priests and elders who questioned his authority,* 23—27. *The parable of the two sons whom their father sent to work in his vineyard,* 28—32. *The parable of the vineyard let out to wicked husbandmen,* 33—46.

AND [a] when they drew nigh unto Jerusalem, and were come to Bethphage, unto [b] the mount of Olives, then sent Jesus two disciples,

a Mark 11. 1. Luke 19. 29.
b Zech. 14. 4.

2 Saying unto them, Go into the village over against you, and straightway ye shall find an ass tied, and a colt with her: loose *them*, and bring *them* unto me.

3 And if any *man* say ought unto you, ye shall say, The Lord hath need of them; and straightway he will send them.

This famous story of our Lord's entrance into Jerusalem is recorded by Mark, and Luke also: by Mark, chap. xi. 1; by Luke, chap. xix. 29. There is little difference in their relation of it thus far; afterwards we shall find more. I shall consider what they all say, that I may at once give the story perfect. Mark saith, *Bethphage and Bethany*. He saith, *ye shall find a colt tied, whereon never man sat.* Luke hardly varieth at all from Mark, at least in nothing considerable. Our Lord was come now very nigh Jerusalem; Bethany was but fifteen furlongs from Jerusalem, that was about two miles, wanting an eighth part, John xi. 18; it was the town of Lazarus, John xi. 1. Matthew names only Bethphage, which was a place at the same distance, at the foot of the Mount of Olives, so called from the plenty of olive trees growing there; this mount was betwixt Jerusalem and Bethphage. It is like our Saviour was at both these towns, for Mark and Luke nameth both. From one of them he sendeth two of his disciples to a village near hand, telling them they should there find, at their entrance in, an ass tied, with a colt, on which yet never man sat. Mark and Luke only mention the colt, because Christ rode only upon the colt. Matthew mentions the ass, for the fulfilling of the prophecy, of which we shall hear in the next verses. *Loose them, and bring them unto me. And if any man say ought unto you,* (which he knew they would, and Mark and Luke tell us they did,) *ye shall say, The Lord hath need of them.* Not, our Lord, but *the Lord* of heaven and earth, whose are the cattle upon a thousand hills, *hath need of them*: not for any weariness; he who had travelled on foot from Galilee to Bethany, could have gone the other two miles; but that he might enter into Jerusalem as was prophesied of him, Zech. ix. 9. *And straightway he will send them.* The words are so, as may be understood as a promise of Christ to send them back, but it is more likely they are intended as an assurance to the disciples that the owners would make no difficulty to send them. These instructions (considered with the success) were an evident argument of Christ's Divine nature, who could tell all particular circumstances, and also which way the heart of man would incline.

4 All this was done, that it might be fulfilled which was spoken by the prophet, saying,

5 [c] Tell ye the daughter of Sion, Behold, thy King cometh unto thee, meek, and sitting upon an ass, and a colt the foal of an ass.

c Is. 62. 11. Zech. 9. 9. John 12. 15.

The words are, Zech. ix. 9, *Rejoice greatly, O daughter of Zion; shout, O daughter of Jerusalem: behold, thy King cometh unto thee: he is just, and having salvation; lowly, and riding upon an ass, and upon a colt the foal of an ass.* The evangelist quoteth no more of them than served for his purpose. John, in the short account he giveth of this our Saviour's entrance, quoteth them shorter, John xii. 15. The former part of the words are found Isa. lxii. 11. The Jews agree this prophecy to respect the Messiah, though they were so blinded as not to see it was fulfilled in Christ. *Tell ye the daughter of Zion,* prophesy you to the Jews, to the citizens and inhabitants of Jerusalem, *Behold, thy King cometh unto thee:* thy spiritual King, having salvation, the King promised and foretold, that shall bring salvation, *cometh,* that is, shall shortly come to thee for thy profit and advantage. And you shall know him by this; he shall come עָנִי, poor, afflicted, meek, lowly, *sitting upon an ass,* an ass used to bear burdens, (so the word signifies,) *and a colt the foal of an ass:* not upon both; they are exegetical of each other; the first denoted the species of the beast, the second its age. There was not any prophecy of Christ more plainly fulfilled than this. Asses were of old beasts that great persons used to ride on, Judg. x. 4; xii. 14. But after Solomon's time the Jews got a breed of horses; so as only poor people rode upon asses, mostly reserved for burdens. Whom could the Jews possibly expect to see coming riding into Jerusalem, under the notion of a King bringing them salvation, in so little state, upon the foal of an ass, but the person prophesied of by Zechariah, chap. ix. 9, whom they themselves confess to be the Messiah? And had not there been a strange veil upon their hearts, Herod's courtiers, and Pilate's, might have understood his kingdom was not of this world, nor he such a King as threatened their grandeur.

6 ^d And the disciples went, and did as Jesus commanded them,

<small>d Mark 11. 4.</small>

Mark saith, chap. xi. 4—6, *And they went their way, and found the colt tied by the door without in a place where two ways met; and they loose him. And certain of them that stood there said unto them, What do ye, loosing the colt? And they said unto them even as Jesus had commanded: and they let them go.* Luke saith, chap. xix. 32—34, *And they that were sent went their way, and found even as he had said unto them. And as they were loosing the colt, the owners thereof said unto them, Why loose ye the colt? And they said, The Lord hath need of him.* The true obedience of Christ's disciples is to be learned from the practice of these two disciples: they dispute not the commands of their Lord, nor make objections, nor raise any disputes, nor are afraid of any danger to themselves; they went, and that speedily, and are exact to what their Lord had commanded them; accordingly they find as he had said. They loose the colt. The owner seeing them, asks why they loose the colt. They tell him the Lord had need of him.

7 And brought the ass, and the colt, and ^e put on them their clothes, and they set *him* thereon.

<small>e 2 Kings 9. 13.</small>

8 And a very great multitude spread their garments in the way; ^f others cut down branches from the trees, and strawed *them* in the way.

<small>f See Lev. 23. 40. 1 Mac. 13. 51, &c. 2 Mac. 10. 7. John 12. 13.</small>

9 And the multitudes that went before, and that followed, cried, saying, ^g Hosanna to the Son of David: ^h Blessed *is* he that cometh in the name of the Lord; Hosanna in the highest.

<small>g Ps. 118. 25. h Ps. 118. 26. ch. 23. 39.</small>

Mark saith, chap. xi. 7—10, *And they brought the colt to Jesus, and cast their garments on him; and he sat upon him. And many spread their garments in the way: and others cut down branches off the trees, and strawed them in the way. And they that went before, and they that followed, cried, saying, Hosanna; Blessed is he that cometh in the name of the Lord: blessed be the kingdom of our father David, that cometh in the name of the Lord: Hosanna in the highest.* Luke hath it yet with more circumstances, chap. xix. 35—40: *And they brought him to Jesus: and they cast their garments upon the colt, and they set Jesus thereon. And as they went, they spread their clothes in the way. And when he was come nigh, even now at the descent of the Mount of Olives, the whole multitude of the disciples began to rejoice and praise God with a loud voice for all the mighty works that they had seen; saying, Blessed be the King that cometh in the name of the Lord: peace in heaven, and glory in the highest. And some of the Pharisees from among the multitude said unto him, Master, rebuke thy disciples. And he answered and said unto them, I tell you that, if these should hold their peace, the stones would immediately cry out.* John also gives us some account of this, chap. xii. 12, 13: *On the next day much people that were come to the feast, when they had heard that Jesus was coming to Jerusalem, took branches of palm trees, and went forth to meet him, and cried, Hosanna: Blessed is the King of Israel that cometh in the name of the Lord.* They bring the ass and the colt to Jesus, who had no saddle, no costly furniture for him; they were glad to lay on the ass's back some of their garments, and to set Christ upon the colt. And in a kind of a natural country triumph, made up without any kind of art, some threw their clothes in his way, some cut down boughs of trees, *(palm trees,* saith John,) with these they bestrew the way. Christ at Bethany, in his journey, had done a famous miracle, raising up Lazarus from the dead. John saith, chap. xii. 18, the fame of this made many that were in Jerusalem, who were come thither against the passover time, (for, John xii. 1, it was but *six days before the passover,*) go out to meet him; and, joined with those who came along with him from Bethany, they cried all along as they came, *Hosanna to the Son of David: Blessed is he that cometh in the name of the Lord; Hosanna in the highest. Blessed be the kingdom of our father David. Peace in heaven, and glory in the highest.* Many of these expressions seem to be taken out of Psal. cxviii. 24 26. Their laying the garments in the way, and throwing them in the way, was a custom they used towards princes, as appears not only by many records out of profane authors, but from 2 Kings ix. 13, where the like was done to Jehu, upon his being anointed king over Israel. For the acclamations, they were also such as were usual to princes. Whether *Hosanna* signifieth, *Save now,* or, Help, we pray; or whether it was a term by which they expressed their desire of good success or prosperity to the person to whom they applied it; or whether it was the name of some song used in their festivals, or it signifies boughs, &c., is not much material: they by this acclamation acknowledged him a King, the Son of David; they blessed him, they wished him peace, honour, and glory. This was the acclamation of the multitude, who doubtless had but a small and imperfect knowledge of the Divine nature of Christ, but yet looked on him as the Son of David, as the Messiah. The Pharisees (some of which it seemeth had mixed themselves with this multitude) were troubled at the acclamation, and (as Luke tells us) speak to Christ to rebuke them; but he answereth, *If these should hold their peace, the stones would immediately cry out.* It is a proverbial expression, the sense of which is alone to be attended. The sense is this: The time is come, set by my Father for the publication of my kingdom, and declaring what I am; and when God's time is come the thing must come to pass, by one means or another. If these children of Abraham should hold their peace, God is able of these stones to raise up children to Abraham, and they should do the same thing, publish me as the Son of David, the King in Zion.

10 ⁱ And when he was come into Jerusalem, all the city was moved, saying, Who is this?

<small>i Mark 11. 15. Luke 19. 45. John 2. 13, 15.</small>

11 And the multitude said, This is Jesus ^k the prophet of Nazareth of Galilee.

<small>k ch. 2. 23. Luke 7. 16. John 6. 14. & 7. 40. & 9. 17.</small>

Such an unusual sight might well affect a great number in Jerusalem with admiration and astonishment, the people, especially, giving honour to him as a King, and calling him the Son of David; and certainly, but that the meanness of his appearance and meanness of his followers put uninterested men out of fear, and gave Herod and Pilate some security that there was no attempt on foot against the civil government, our Saviour and his followers would have been apprehended, as raisers of a sedition and rebellion. But the multitude now gave him no other title than that of Jesus the Prophet; which yet was enough to distinguish him from other prophets, for he was Jesus a Saviour, and the Prophet foretold, Deut. xviii. 15, 18, 19.

¹Mark 11.11.
Luke 19. 45.
John 2. 15.
12 ¶ ¹And Jesus went into the temple of God, and cast out all them that sold and bought in the temple, and overthrew

m Deut. 14. 25.
the tables of the ᵐmoneychangers, and the seats of them that sold doves,

13 And said unto them, It is written,

n Is. 56. 7.
o Jer. 7. 11.
Mark 11. 17.
Luke 19. 46.
ⁿMy house shall be called the house of prayer; ᵒbut ye have made it a den of thieves.

14 And the blind and the lame came to him in the temple; and he healed them.

This piece of the history is related by two of the other evangelists, but with great difference. Luke before this mentioneth a discourse upon the way, upon our Saviour's first sight of the city, and his prophecy of the destruction of it; but no other evangelist mentioning it, I shall pass it over till I come to his history. Mark hath this part of the history thus, chap. xi. 11—19, *And Jesus entered into Jerusalem, and into the temple: and when he had looked round about upon all things, and now the eventide was come, he went out unto Bethany with the twelve. And on the morrow, when they were come from Bethany, he was hungry.* (Then he relates our Saviour's cursing the barren fig tree, which I leave till I come to it in order.) *And they come to Jerusalem: and Jesus went into the temple, and began to cast out them that sold and bought in the temple, and overthrew the tables of the money-changers, and the seats of them that sold doves: and would not suffer that any man should carry any vessel through the temple. And he taught, saying unto them, Is it not written, My house shall be called of all nations the house of prayer? but ye have made it a den of thieves.—And when the even was come, he went out of the city*, ver. 19. Luke saith, chap. xix. 45—47, *And he went into the temple, and began to cast out them that sold therein, and those that bought; saying unto them, It is written, My house is the house of prayer: but ye have made it a den of thieves. And he taught daily in the temple.* It is plain by all the evangelists, that our Saviour, coming to Jerusalem five days before the passover, went every night to Bethany, about two miles off, and returned in the morning to the temple, where Luke saith that *he taught daily.* The first day it should seem, by Mark, that he only came into the temple, looked round about upon all things, and with the twelve went out to lodge at Bethany. By his going into the temple, we must understand only the outward court, for the priests and Levites only might enter into the inner court, and the holy place; and the high priest only might enter into the holiest of all. Though Mark mentions not his driving out the buyers and sellers the first day, but reciteth it as if it had been done the second day of his coming, yet the best interpreters think that it was done the first day, as Matthew and Luke seem to hint; nor is any thing more usual, than for the evangelists to set down things out of the order of time in which they were done. Some learned authors in the Hebrew learning tell us, that in the outward court was a daily market of such things as the Jews used for sacrifices, wine, salt, oil, oxen, and sheep; but it being but three or four days before the passover, the market was much greater, because of the great multitude of lambs then to be used. By the law, Exod. xxx. 12, 15, every one also was to bring a half shekel. For this purpose there were tables of money-changers, men that were furnished with half shekels to change with the people, that every one might have his half shekel; and those that so changed allowed some little profit to those that changed their money, which gain was called κόλλυβος; thence the changers were called κολλυβισταί, *money-changers*. Those *that sold doves* were there, to furnish the women that came up to their purification with their offerings, according to the law, Lev. xii. 6. This was the reason of that great market which our Lord found in the outward court of the temple; and it is not likely that our Lord should see these abuses the first day and take no notice of them, but come the next day and correct them, which makes interpreters think Mark in this relation postponed this part of the history. Here arise two questions: 1. Whether it was unlawful for them to sell these things in that part of the temple. 2. Admit it were, By what authority did our Saviour do this? To the first it must be said, That had it not been unlawful, our Saviour would not have reproved them for turning his Father's house, and the house of prayer, into a place of merchandise; nor would he have driven them out in such a zeal, overturning the tables, &c., which he had done also once before, John ii. 15. The temple was built by God's direction, not only dedicated by men, but God's acceptation of it was testified. It appeareth by John ii. 19, it was a type of Christ's body. We know there were special promises made to those that did pray toward it. God saith he had *hallowed* it, 1 Kings ix. 3; that is, separated it from common use to his service, amongst other things for a *house of prayer*, Isa. lvi. 7. Now though we read of no other things sold there but what were useful for sacrifices, yet this was a civil use, and a profanation of that holy place, because there were market-places in Jerusalem, in which these things might have been done. It had been against decency, if the temple had not been hallowed in this manner, if such things had been done in the synagogues, being places set apart and commonly used for God's worship; but to use the temple in this manner, so specially hallowed, was doubtless a great profanation of that holy place. As to the second question, By what authority our Lord, being no public magistrate, did these things, I am not so posed to determine that, he being the eternal Son of God, and now in the exercise of his regal power, as I am to give an account how it came to pass that the priests, and scribes, and Pharisees never questioned him for what he did; for if any will say, that we presently shall read of their taking counsel against him, I reply, But we read of nothing relating to this laid to his charge. Nor do we read of their questioning him when he did the same things before, an account of which we have in John ii. For though I know some say that our Saviour did this *Jure zelotarum*: that the Jews had a law, that any might punish even to death such as profaned the worship or holy things of God; which they justify from Deut. xiii. 9, and the examples of Phinehas killing Zimri and Cozbi, Numb. xxv. 6—8, and Mattaniah's killing the Jew sacrificing to idols at Modin, and the king's commissioner, of which we read in 2 Macc. ii. 24, 25: yet this doth no way give me any satisfaction: for as, on the one side, I should not have known how to have defended the act of Phinehas if God had not by and by justified him, nor do I think that the law in Deut. xiii. 9 is to be expounded of private persons; so, on the other side, if the priests, and scribes, and Pharisees had not known of some law that justified our Saviour in this act, I can hardly conceive they would have so quietly put it up, especially considering that probably their profit was concerned, if they had for gain licensed those traders to a place within the compass of the temple, as is very probable. Being therefore fully satisfied that our Saviour, who was Lord of the temple, and to whom the Spirit was given without measure, did no more than he might lawfully do, I am willingly ignorant how it came to pass that he met with no opposition in it, because God hath not pleased in his word to inform us. It is certain that he did the thing, and that it was a thing fit to be done, and that he, as the Son of God, had authority to do it; what made them take it so quietly I cannot tell, nor is it necessary for us to know, nor of any great advantage.

15 And when the Chief Priests and Scribes saw the wonderful things that he did, and the children crying in the temple, and saying, Hosanna to the Son of David; they were sore displeased,

16 And said unto him, Hearest thou what these say? And Jesus saith unto them, Yea; have ye never read, ᵖOut of the mouth of babes and sucklings thou hast perfected praise?

p Ps. 8. 2.

The other evangelists say nothing of this part of this history. The *wonderful things* here mentioned, are his healing the blind and lame, of which we read ver. 14. The cry of the children doubtless more displeased them; it was of the same nature with that of the multitude in the way, and in the streets, when our Lord came into Jerusalem; they owned Christ as the Messiah, and gave him praise, and wished all manner of felicity to him. The

S. MATTHEW XXI

Pharisees showing a displeasure at the acclamation, Christ referreth them to what was written, Psal. viii. 2: there it is, *thou hast* founded, or *ordained, strength,* that is, a solid and firm praise; a prediction that from the testimony of such weak persons, the glorious power of Christ should be proclaimed, and from such mean and despicable beginnings great and glorious things should come to pass.

17 ¶ And he left them, and went out of the city into ⁹Bethany; and he lodged there.

18 ʳNow in the morning as he returned into the city, he hungered.

19 ˢAnd when he saw †a fig tree in the way, he came to it, and found nothing thereon, but leaves only, and said unto it, Let no fruit grow on thee henceforward for ever. And presently the fig tree withered away.

20 ᵗAnd when the disciples saw *it*, they marvelled, saying, How soon is the fig tree withered away!

21 Jesus answered and said unto them, Verily I say unto you, "If ye have faith, and ˣdoubt not, ye shall not only do this *which is done* to the fig tree, ʸbut also if ye shall say unto this mountain, Be thou removed, and be thou cast into the sea; it shall be done.

22 And ᶻ all things, whatsoever ye shall ask in prayer believing, ye shall receive.

q Mark 11. 11. John 11. 18.
r Mark 11. 12.
s Mark 11. 13.
† Gr. *one fig tree.*
t Mark 11. 20.
u ch. 17. 20. Luke 17. 6.
x Jam. 1. 6.
y 1 Cor. 13.2.
z ch. 7. 7. Mark 11. 24. Luke 11. 9. Jam. 5. 16. 1 John 3. 22. & 5. 14.

Luke hath nothing of this passage, but Mark relateth it with some variation and additions: the variation is only as to time, as to which the evangelists were not curious. Matthew relates this miracle as done in the morning of the second day, as Christ and his disciples returned from Bethany; so doth Mark, chap. xi. 12: but Matthew speaks as if the disciples discerned it presently withered; Mark mentions it as not discerned to be withered till the next morning, ver. 20. Mark saith, ver. 13, *for the time of figs was not yet;* which breeds a difficulty, why our Saviour should curse the fig tree for having no fruit, when the time for its fruit was not come (of which more by and by). Mark saith, ver. 21, 22, that *Peter calling to remembrance his Master's cursing* the fig tree, *saith unto him, Master, behold, the fig tree which thou cursedst is withered away. And Jesus answering saith unto them, Have faith in God.* Then repeats the substance of what Matthew hath in ver. 21, 22; to which Mark addeth, ver. 25, 26, *And when ye stand praying, forgive, if ye have ought against any: that your Father also which is in heaven may forgive you your trespasses. But if ye do not forgive, neither will your Father which is in heaven forgive you your trespasses.* When our Lord had been in the temple, and driven out the buyers and sellers there, he went out of the city to lie at Bethany, either to avoid the noises of the city, (now very full of people, the passover being so nigh,) or to get a more private place for prayer. He returns the next morning; and being hungry, and seeing a fig tree in his way, he goes to it, finds it full of leaves, but no fruit on it. He saith unto it, Never fruit grow on thee more. Mark saith, *For the time of figs was not yet.* Why then doth our Saviour curse this tree? Some think that by *time* is here meant season (as indeed the Greek word often signifieth); these would have the meaning to be, for it was not a seasonable year for figs. But this rather augmenteth than abates the difficulty, for why should our Saviour curse it for having no figs, when the year was such as was not seasonable? Others therefore think that οὐ should be οὗ, then the English would be, Where he was was a time of figs. For this it is said, 1. That the Greek spirits and accents were ordinarily left out in ancient copies, which if they be taken away the words are the same. 2. That this was according to truth, for it was a time of green figs, at least; it being near Jerusalem, and but three or four days before

the passover, about which time they reaped their corn, as appears from Lev. xxiii. 10; Deut. xvi. 9; and it is plain from Cant. ii. 13, that in the beginning of their spring their fig trees put forth green figs. But when I consider that none of the ancient translations are according to this criticism, but as our translations, I conclude that the ancients understood it οὐ, not οὗ, and it seemeth too bold to interpret the words contrary to their unanimous sense. Others therefore tell us, that fig trees, or at least some kind of them, (like orange trees,) had leaves and fruit upon them always, some green, some half ripe, some full ripe; and that these kept on their leaves all the winter: so that our Saviour seeing leaves, might be led to it with an expectation of some fruit put forth the former year, for the time for the ripening of fruit of that kind that year was not come; and finding none, he cursed it; thereby in a type showing what should be done to barren souls, who have only leaves, no true fruit of righteousness. Or what if we should say, that he did not curse it with any respect to its want of fruit, but only to show his Divine power, working a miracle? *And presently the fig tree withered away:* as soon as our Saviour had cursed it, it began to wither. Mark tells us this was the next morning, chap. xi. 20, which made Peter say, *Master, behold, the fig tree which thou cursedst is withered away.* Matthew saith, *When the disciples saw it, they marvelled, saying, How soon is the fig tree withered away!* Upon this our Saviour telleth Peter and the rest, that if they had faith, and doubted not, they should not only do that which he had done to the fig tree, but if they said to that mountain, Be removed and cast into the sea, it should be done. This is interpreted by ver. 22, *All things, whatsoever ye shall ask in prayer believing, ye shall receive.* We met with the like expression before, Matt. xvii. 20. Mark hath the same, chap. xi. 23. Luke hath it, chap. xvii. 6. It is an expression which ought not to be strained further than to signify, that there is nothing conducive to the glory of God and our own good, but believers may receive at the hand of God, if they can believe without doubting that what they would have shall come to pass. I see no reason to discourse of a faith of miracles as different from other faith; which only thus differed, that the disciples (the apostles I mean) had a power given them, and a promise made to them, that they should be able to work miraculous operations, which is not given to other Christians serving only the particular occasions of that time, to give credit to the gospel. The general proposition is true, and shall be made good to every believer, That whatsoever good is made the matter of a promise, (such are all good things.) shall be given to believing souls, praying for them. But there were of old special promises, not made to the people of God in general, but to particular persons, for particular ends; we cannot expect to do or obtain such things now. Nothing is too big for true faith to obtain, but that faith must have a promise to lean upon, and it must be showed by prayer, as ver. 22. Mark adds, that it must be also attended with charity, a charitable heart, ready to forgive, and actually forgiving, our brethren their trespasses. But it is no more than we met with in Matthew, chap. vi. 14, 15, where we opened the sense of those words.

23 ¶ ᵃAnd when he was come into the temple, the Chief Priests and the elders of the people came unto him as he was teaching, and ᵇsaid, By what authority doest thou these things? and who gave thee this authority?

a Mark 11. 27. Luke 20. 1.
b Ex. 2. 14. Acts 4. 7. & 7. 27.

Mark hath before this, chap. xi. 18, *And the scribes and chief priests heard it,* that is, his turning the buyers and sellers out, and overturning the tables of the money-changers, *and sought how they might destroy him: for they feared him, because all the people were astonished at his doctrine.* Then he saith, ver. 27, 28, *And they come again to Jerusalem: and as he was walking in the temple, there come to him the chief priests, and the scribes, and the elders, and say unto him, By what authority doest thou these things? and who gave thee this authority to do these things?* Luke saith, chap. xix. 47, 48, *And he taught daily in the temple. But the chief priests and the scribes and the chief of the people sought to destroy him, and could not find what they might do: for all the people were very attentive to hear him.* It is plain that our Saviour went every night to Bethany, and returned to Jerusalem every morning, and daily preached in the temple. And Luke saith, *the people were very attentive to hear him;* in the Greek it is, hung upon him, hearing him. They were also much affected with the miracles which they had seen him working. So as the scribes and the elders *feared him,* saith Mark. This possibly might be one reason why they made no opposition to our Saviour, driving the buyers and sellers out of the temple, viz. for fear of the people; for we must remember they were a conquered, tributary people, and under the jurisdiction of the Romans, under whom, though they had a liberty for the exercise of their own religion, yet they had not such a power as before; it was not lawful for them to put any to death, John xviii. 31. And for the preserving of their own liberty, they were obliged to take heed of causing any tumults for matters concerning their religion. So as what they did of this nature they did by craft, rather than plainly and openly attempting it, Mark xiv. 1. It is likely they might have some previous secret counsels what method to take, mentioned both by Mark and Luke. The method, it seems, which they agreed upon, was first to send to him, to know by what authority he did those things, and who gave him such authority. This is mentioned both by Matthew and Mark. They sent such a message to John, John i. 19—21. They had often questioned him about his doctrine, and had gone by the worst, he justifying his doctrine to their faces. For the truth of his miracles, it was so evident that they could not question that. They therefore now only question his authority to preach. The question was captious enough, for if he had said, By a Divine authority, they would probably have accused him of blasphemy. For a human authority, they knew he had none, according to their rules for order, for they came from the court that should have given them such authority. Our Saviour well enough understanding their design, gives them, who would not understand his Divine mission by his miraculous operations, a wary answer.

24 And Jesus answered and said unto them, I also will ask you one thing, which if ye tell me, I in like wise will tell you by what authority I do these things.

25 The baptism of John, whence was it? from heaven, or of men? And they reasoned with themselves, saying, If we shall say, From heaven; he will say unto us, Why did ye not then believe him?

26 But if we shall say, Of men; we fear the people; ᶜfor all hold John as a prophet.

c ch. 14. 5.
Mark 6. 20.
Luke 20. 6.

27 And they answered Jesus, and said, We cannot tell. And he said unto them, Neither tell I you by what authority I do these things.

We have the same without any considerable alteration Mark xi. 27—33. Luke also records the same history, chap. xx. 1—8, with no considerable difference, only he thus prefaceth to it: *And it came to pass, that on one of those days, as he taught the people in the temple, and preached the gospel, the chief priests and the scribes came upon him with the elders:* which makes it plain, that their question principally related to our Saviour's preaching. It should seem, they had a law prohibiting any to preach in the temple without authority from the chief priests and elders. If any one think this was not an apposite answer to the question propounded to him, 1. They ought to consider, that our Saviour did truly judge they deserved no answer, for his works had testified of him that he acted by a Divine power; he should not need tell them so, in so many words. 2. In very deed there was a direct answer couched in this question of our Saviour. I pray, saith he, by what authority did John preach and baptize? They could not say, By a human authority, for they knew he was not licensed by their masters: it must follow that he acted by virtue of an extraordinary Divine mission. So do I, saith our Saviour, and have given you a greater proof of it than ever John Baptist did. But our Lord well knew that the Pharisees had a greater reverence for John the Baptist than for him, and that many of the people had a great opinion of John, indeed greater than of him; our Saviour coming *eating and drinking,* as he expresseth it, that is, being of a more free and sociable conversation, which did not so please the Pharisaical, morose, and supercilious humour: he therefore chooseth to teach them by a question, in which, as soon as they could resolve themselves, they might know by what authority he did what he did. Besides, by the baptism of John, mentioned in our Saviour's question, is not to be understood only his administration of baptism, but his doctrine, and indeed the whole of his ministry; for as his baptism is called *the baptism of repentance,* so the Pharisees here argue, that if they should say, *From heaven,* he would say, *Why then did ye not believe him?* which must be understood of his doctrine. A great part of John's doctrine was, that the Messiah was come, that Christ was he; John i. 29, he pointed to him and said, *Behold the Lamb of God which taketh away the sin of the world;* which had they believed, they would never have come to him with so silly a question. The Pharisees therefore rightly judged how they would be insnared, if they said John's baptism and doctrine was from God, for then a Divine faith was due to his words, and they must have owned Christ to be the Messiah. But why did not they say, *Of men?* The text saith, they feared the people. Those who will not fear God, shall have something to fear sordidly and slavishly. The people all owning John as a prophet, a man that had an extraordinary mission from God, and commission to reveal the mind and will of God, would have cried shame upon them had they disparaged him, as one that spake of his own head. They say, *We cannot tell.* Herein they lied. Our Saviour replies, *Neither do I tell you,* &c. Not, I cannot tell you, but I do not tell you: I will tell you no more than what John hath long since told you, and what, if you will, you and all men may know by my miracles.

28 ¶ But what think ye? A *certain* man had two sons; and he came to the first, and said, Son, go work to day in my vineyard.

29 ᵈHe answered and said, I will not: but afterward he repented, and went.

d Ecclus. 19. 21.

30 And he came to the second, and said likewise. And he answered and said, I *go,* sir: and went not.

31 Whether of them twain did the will of *his* father? They say unto him, The first. Jesus saith unto them, ᵉVerily I say unto you, That the Publicans and the harlots go into the kingdom of God before you.

e Luke 7. 29, 50.

32 For ᶠJohn came unto you in the way of righteousness, and ye believed him not: ᵍbut the Publicans and the harlots believed him: and ye, when ye had seen *it,* repented not afterward, that ye might believe him.

f ch. 3. 1, &c.

g Luke 3. 12, 13.

Matthew alone mentioneth this parable. The scope of it is taught us ver. 31, *The publicans and the harlots go* (that is, shall go) *into the kingdom of God before you,* that is, you Pharisees. Who these Pharisees and who the publicans were, we showed before, chap. iii. 7. The publicans were very odious to the Jews: see Mark ii. 16. Harlots are great sinners. By *the kingdom of God,* here, is meant that of glory. Our Lord's saying that publicans and harlots should go in before the Pharisees, doth not imply that they should follow. It only signifieth that some who had been publicans (as Matthew and Zaccheus) and harlots were in a better condition than these Pharisees. He proves it because they had done the will of God, which the Pharisees, notwithstanding all their fair profession, had not, but resisted it, and particularly in the ministry of John the Baptist, who came to them in the way of righteousness, preaching the true doctrine of righteousness, and living a holy and righteous life; upon the hearing of whose doctrine, some of the publicans and other great sinners had believed in Christ; but the Pharisees, though they heard his doctrine, saw his conversation, and saw others repent and own Christ, yet were so far from believing, that they would not repent, that they might believe; they would not be awakened to any sense of their sinful courses, nor amend any thing of their former ways, that they might receive Christ and embrace his righteousness and salvation. For although evangelical repentance is the fruit of faith, yet that repentance which lieth in a previous sense of sin, and a resolution to leave sinful courses, goeth before it. Now to illustrate and press this home upon the consciences of these Pharisees, our Saviour brings this parable, (as Nathan did to David, 2 Sam. xii. 1, 11,) that they might, being convicted, condemn themselves. Hence the parable is easily understood: The *man* mentioned is God. The *two sons* were the Pharisees, a people highly pretending obedience to the law of God, and making a great show of religion. And *the publicans and harlots*, great sinners, bad and vile people, making no pretence to religion. God saith to the one and the other, *Go, work in my vineyard*, that is, do my will, do the work I command you to do. The Pharisees, so hypocrites and formalists, by their outward pretence and profession, say, *I go, sir;* but yet go not; all their religion is a vain show, a mere outside appearance. Others by their lives declare that they will not go; but yet upon second thoughts, having their hearts touched by the finger of God, they do God's work. *Whether of them twain did the will of his father? They say unto him, The first.* This is plain; for what was the will of the father, but that they should do the work he set them to do? This the latter did not. The father's will was not only that the son should give him a cap and a knee, and compliment him, but that he should go to work in the vineyard. It is the least part of God's will that men should give him good words, be a little complimental and ceremonious toward him; but that they should repent and believe, and obey his gospel. This some publicans and harlots did; the generality of the Pharisees refused. It is a hard thing to convince a moral, righteous, civil man, that he lacks any thing to salvation; and hence it is that profane persons many times repent, believe, and are saved, when others perish in their impenitency and unbelief, because they think they have no need of repentance, or any further righteousness than they are possessed of.

33 ¶ Hear another parable: There was a certain housholder, ʰwhich planted a vineyard, and hedged it round about, and digged a winepress in it, and built a tower, and let it out to husbandmen, and ⁱwent into a far country:

h Ps. 80. 9.
Cant. 8. 11.
Is. 5. 1.
Jer. 2. 21.
Mark 12. 1.
Luke 20. 9.
i ch. 25. 14, 15.

Mark hath this parable, chap. xii. 1—9. Luke hath it, chap. xx. 9—16. Who is here intended under the notion of a *householder*, or a *man?* We are told by the prophet Isaiah, chap. v. 1, 2, it is the Lord of hosts, the God of Israel: *the house of Israel and the men of Judah* are his *vineyard*, his *pleasant plant*, ver. 7; he hedged his people by his providence. God often compareth his church to a vineyard, Deut. xxxii. 32; Psal. lxxx. 8; Jer. ii. 21. The other expressions, of making in it a wine-press, or a winefat, signify no more than that God had provided for the Jews all things necessary for use or ornament. His letting of it out to husbandmen, and going into a far country, signifies that, being himself, as to his glorious residence, in heaven, he had betrusted the church of the Jews with a high priest, and other priests and Levites.

34 And when the time of the fruit drew near, he sent his servants to the husbandmen, ᵏthat they might receive the fruits of it.

k Cant. 8. 11, 12.

35 ˡAnd the husbandmen took his servants, and beat one, and killed another, and stoned another.

l 2 Chro. 24. 21. & 36. 16.
Neh. 9. 26.
ch. 5. 12.
& 23. 34, 37.
Acts 7. 52.
1 Thess. 2. 15. Heb. 11. 36, 37.

36 Again, he sent other servants more than the first: and they did unto them likewise.

Mark agrees in the substance, but mentions three single servants sent, and then many others. The first he saith *they caught, and beat, and sent away empty*. At the second he saith *they cast stones, wounded him in the head, and sent him away shamefully handled*. The third he saith *they killed;* and for others, they did beat some, and kill some. Luke speaks to the same sense. I observed before, that we must not look to fit every particular phrase in a parable in the explication. By the *servants* here sent to the husbandmen are doubtless to be understood those extraordinary prophets, whom in the corrupt state of the Jewish church God sent to reprove the priests, and to admonish the priests, as well as the people, of the duty which they owed unto God, in obedience to his law. And the various phrases here used, to express the indignities offered to the servants, do but signify the various abuses offered to many of these prophets, of which are instances in 1 Kings xix. 10; 2 Chron. xxxvi. 16; Neh. ix. 26; Jer. xliv. 4, 5. Jeremiah was beaten and imprisoned; so was Micaiah; Zechariah slain in the temple, &c.

37 But last of all he sent unto them his son, saying, They will reverence my son.

Mark saith he had but *one son, his well beloved*, chap. xii. 6. Luke saith, chap. xx. 13, *Then said the lord of the vineyard, What shall I do? I will send my beloved son: it may be they will reverence him when they see him.* God is here brought in acting after the manner of men, using all probable means to get their rent: we must not fancy that God did not know what men would do. God, after all his prophets, sent his only Son to the Jews and to their priests, his wellbeloved Son; he said, Perhaps they will reverence my Son. These words must be understood, not as expressing what they would do, or what appeared to God probable that they would do, but as expressive of what they ought to do, and what God might reasonably expect from them.

38 But when the husbandmen saw the son, they said among themselves, ᵐThis is the heir; ⁿcome, let us kill him, and let us seize on his inheritance.

m Ps. 2. 8.
Heb. 1. 2.
n Ps. 2. 2.
ch. 26. 3.
& 27. 1.
John 11. 53.
Acts 4. 27.

39 ᵒAnd they caught him, and cast *him* out of the vineyard, and slew *him*.

o ch. 26. 50, &c. Mark 14. 46, &c. Luke 22. 54, &c. John 18. 12, &c. Acts 2. 23.

Mark and Luke have the same, with no considerable alteration. Our Lord here prophesieth his own death by the means of these wicked priests, and so both lets them know that he was not ignorant of what was in their hearts, and they had been already (as we heard before) taking counsel about, by which they might again have concluded that he was the Son of God, and one who knew their hearts; and he also lets them know, that they should not surprise him, and that he was not afraid of them. *But when the husbandmen saw the son, they said, This is the heir.* These words let the Pharisees (to whom, together with the people, he at that time spake) know that themselves knew he was the Son of God, and were convicted in their own consciences that he was the true Lord of the church. Though this was not true of all that had a hand in crucifying Christ; for Paul saith of some of them, that if they had known him, *they would not have crucified the Lord of glory;* yet it was doubtless true of many of them, and those the most knowing men amongst them. But herein did their most prodigious blindness and madness appear, that when they knew this, they should think it possible to prevent his being set as King upon the Lord's holy hill of Zion. One would think this were impossible to rational creatures. But why should we think so? How many are there in the world at this day, that are convicted in their own consciences, and do believe that the ways and people whom they prosecute to their ruin, yea, to death itself, are the truths, the ways, the people of God, yet they will be kicking against the pricks! And though God makes many of them perish in their enterprises, and suffers them not to come with hoary heads to the grave in peace, yet there ariseth another instead of this hydra, a posterity approving their doings, and thinking, though their fathers failed in this or that little policy, yet they shall prevail against God, and his inheritance shall be theirs. Wise Providence thus fitteth the saints for their crown, and suffers sinners to prepare themselves for the day of wrath.

40 When the lord therefore of the vineyard cometh, what will he do unto those husbandmen?

41 ᵖThey say unto him, ᵠHe will miserably destroy those wicked men, ʳand will let out *his* vineyard unto other husbandmen, which shall render him the fruits in their seasons.

p See Luke 20. 16.
q Luke 21. 24. Heb. 2. 3.
r Acts 13.46. & 15. 7. & 18. 6. & 28. 28.
Rom. 9, & 10, & 11.

Mark relates the latter verse as Christ's own words, chap. xii. 9; so doth Luke, chap. xx. 15, 16, adding, that *when they heard it, they said, God forbid.* It is said, to solve this difficulty, 1. That *they say unto him* must not be understood of the Pharisees, but some of the hearers; the Pharisees said only, *God forbid.* 2. Others think the Pharisees and elders did at first say as is here expressed, but our Saviour then telling them they were the men, and opening it further to them, they said, *God forbid.* It is very possible the Pharisees and elders might first say it, and that our Saviour confirming and opening their words, showing them how they had given judgment against themselves, they said, *God forbid;* so both they might say these words, and Christ also. This I take to be the most satisfactory answer. By those words also our Saviour declares, that his church should shortly be taken out of the hands of these Pharisees, and elders, and priests, and put into the hands of his apostles and a gospel ministry.

^s Ps. 118. 22. Is. 28. 16. Mark 12. 10. Luke 20. 17. Acts 4. 11. Eph. 2. 20. 1 Pet. 2. 6, 7.

42 Jesus saith unto them, ^sDid ye never read in the Scriptures, The stone which the builders rejected, the same is become the head of the corner: this is the Lord's doing, and it is marvellous in our eyes?

t ch. 8. 12.

43 Therefore say I unto you, ^tThe kingdom of God shall be taken from you, and given to a nation bringing forth the fruits thereof.

u Is. 8. 14, 15. Zech. 12. 3. Luke 20. 18. Rom. 9. 33. 1 Pet. 2. 8. x Is. 60. 12. Dan. 2. 44.

44 And whosoever ^ushall fall on this stone shall be broken: but on whomsoever it shall fall, ^xit will grind him to powder.

Mark saith, chap. xii. 10, 11, *And have ye not read this scripture, The stone which the builders rejected is become the head of the corner: this was the Lord's doing, and it is marvellous in our eyes.* Luke saith, chap. xx. 17, 18, *And he beheld them, and said, What is this then that is written, The stone which the builders rejected, the same is become the head of the corner? Whosoever shall fall upon that stone shall be broken; but on whomsoever it shall fall, it will grind him to powder.* It is more than probable that our Saviour had more words with them upon this argument than are left us upon sacred record; for John hath let us know, that we are not to expect that all he did or spake should be written, chap. xxi. 25; and as not every discourse or action, so not all words in the same discourse, nor all circumstances relating to the same action. Knowing themselves and their masters to be the husbandmen with whom the Lord had betrusted his vineyard the house of Israel, it is not reasonable to think they should be very patient to hear that God would miserably destroy them as wicked men, and commit his vineyard to the trust of others. We cannot therefore in reason imagine but that they should reply something to that, as thinking it a strange thing that he should assert, that for the rejection of him, God would reject his ancient people, and cast off the church of the Jews. To show this was nothing which ought to seem strange to them, he asks them, *Did ye never read in the Scriptures, The stone, &c.* Luke saith, *he beheld them, and said, What is this then, &c.?* as if the Pharisees had charged him with speaking without any warrant from the word of God, there was no such thing in the law or prophets. To convince them of their mistake, or at least that there was nothing in what he said which needed to appear strange to them, he saith, *Did ye never read?* or, *Have ye not read the scripture?* (so Mark relates it;) or, *What is this then?* as Luke hath it. The text he quoteth is Psal. cxviii. 22, 23. It is manifest that the Jews understood that Psalm to be a prophecy of Christ, by the people's acclamations of Hosanna; for the substance of those acclamations are in the 25th and 26th verses of that Psalm: *Save now, I beseech thee, O Lord: O Lord, I beseech thee, send now prosperity. Blessed is he that cometh in the name of the Lord.* Hoshiah na, הושיעה נא *Save, I beseech thee.* This they understood of the Messiah. This they had heard cried unto our Saviour. Saith our Saviour, In that very Psalm you may read, *The stone which the builders rejected is become the head of the corner.* Before he had compared the church to a vineyard, to show their obligation to bring forth fruit; here to a building, to denote God's dwelling in it. The builders here intended were the heads of the Jewish church, who not only by their own pretences, but by their calling, were builders, and ought to have been builders; though indeed they proved destroyers and pullers down, instead of builders. The church is elsewhere compared to a building, 1 Cor. iii. 9; Eph. ii. 21; and the teachers in it to builders, Rom. xv. 20; Gal. ii. 18. Our Lord is here compared to a *stone,* because he is the only firm foundation, *the chief corner-stone; in whom all the building fitly framed together groweth unto an holy temple in the Lord: in whom ye also are builded together for an habitation of God through the Spirit,* Eph. ii. 20—22: called by the prophet Isaiah, chap. xxviii. 16, *a stone* laid *in Zion for a foundation, a tried stone, a precious corner-stone, a sure foundation;* which is applied to Christ, Acts iv. 11; Rom. ix. 33; 1 Pet. ii. 6—8. He is become the head of the corner, that is, the chief, the principal stone in the building. Lest they should be startled at this, he addeth, *this is the Lord's doing, and it is marvellous in our eyes.* This may seem strange to you, that those who seemed to be builders and pillars should be rejected and thrown away; and no wonder, for it is *the Lord's doing.* In the reformations of churches from gross corruptions, God doth always some extraordinary things, which we are not at present able to reconcile to our reasons. Ver. 43, (which some think should have been put after the next verse,) our Lord tells them plainly, that God was removing his church from them to the Gentiles, which he calleth a people that should bring forth the fruits thereof. *And whosoever shall fall on this stone shall be broken:* there will be many that shall be offended at Christ, his person, his doctrine, his institutions, upon which account he is called a *stumbling-stone,* Rom. ix. 33. But they *shall be broken:* if they take offence at me, so as they will not believe on me, nor receive me, it will be their ruin. *But on whomsoever it shall fall, it will grind him to powder:* if they shall go on to persecute me and my members, so that I fall on them, they shall be ruined, irreparably and irrecoverably, with a more dreadful destruction.

45 And when the Chief Priests and Pharisees had heard his parables, they perceived that he spake of them.

46 But when they sought to lay hands on him, they feared the multitude, because ^ythey took him for a prophet.

y ver. 11. Luke 7. 16. John 7. 40.

Mark hath much the same, chap. xii. 12; so hath Luke, chap. xx. 19, 20: but Luke adds, *They watched him, and sent forth spies, which should feign themselves just men, that they might take hold of his words, that so they might deliver him unto the power and authority of the governor.* These wretched men were convinced in their own consciences, *they perceived that he spake of them.* They had nothing to oppose to what he said. They could not deny but that the psalmist, Psal. cxviii. 22, spake of the Messias. They could not but own that they were the builders, and that they had refused him. Yet their lusts and interests would not suffer them to obey these convictions, to receive and to embrace Christ, and prevent that ruin which was coming upon them. They durst not apprehend Christ for fear of the people. They had nothing to lay to his charge; they therefore send out spies to watch him, to see if they could catch any thing from him in discourse, whereof to accuse him before Pilate, the Roman governor in Judea at this time.

CHAP. XXII

The parable of the marriage of the king's son: the unworthiness of those that were first bidden: others called in their room: the punishment of one that came without a wedding garment, 1—14. *The captious question proposed concerning paying tribute to Cæsar, and Christ's answer,* 15—22. *He confuteth the Sadducees who questioned him touching the resurrection,* 23—33. *He showeth which are the chief commandments of the law,* 34—40. *He proposeth to the Pharisees a knotty question concerning Christ,* 41—46.

AND Jesus answered ^aand spake unto them again by parables, and said,

a Luke 14. 16. Rev. 19. 7, 9.

2 The kingdom of heaven is like unto a certain king, which made a marriage for his son,

S. MATTHEW XXII

3 And sent forth his servants to call them that were bidden to the wedding : and they would not come.

4 Again, he sent forth other servants, saying, Tell them which are bidden, Behold, I have prepared my dinner : ^bmy oxen and *my* fatlings *are* killed, and all things *are* ready: come unto the marriage.

<small>b Prov. 9. 2.</small>

5 But they made light of *it*, and went their ways, one to his farm, another to his merchandise :

6 And the remnant took his servants, and entreated *them* spitefully, and slew *them*.

7 But when the king heard *thereof*, he was wroth : and he sent forth ^chis armies, and destroyed those murderers, and burned up their city.

<small>c Dan. 9. 26.
Luke 19. 27.</small>

8 Then saith he to his servants, The wedding is ready, but they which were bidden were not ^dworthy.

<small>d ch. 10. 11,
13. Acts 13.
46.</small>

9 Go ye therefore into the highways, and as many as ye shall find, bid to the marriage.

10 So those servants went out into the highways, and ^egathered together all as many as they found, both bad and good : and the wedding was furnished with guests.

<small>e ch. 13. 38,
47.</small>

11 ¶ And when the king came in to see the guests, he saw there a man ^fwhich had not on a wedding garment :

<small>f 2 Cor. 5. 3.
Eph. 4. 24.
Col. 3. 10, 12.
Rev. 3. 4. &
16. 15. & 19. 8.</small>

12 And he saith unto him, Friend, how camest thou in hither not having a wedding garment? And he was speechless.

13 Then said the king to the servants, Bind him hand and foot, and take him away, and cast *him* ^ginto outer darkness; there shall be weeping and gnashing of teeth.

<small>g ch. 8. 12.</small>

14 ^hFor many are called, but few *are* chosen.

<small>h ch. 20. 16.</small>

Luke hath this parable, chap. xiv. 16—24, which hath made divers interpreters think that Matthew hath put it out of its due order ; for Luke reports it as spoken long before, and that not in the temple, but at a Pharisee's house where he was at dinner, and upon occasion of one of them saying, *Blessed is he that shall eat bread in the kingdom of God.* But I know no reason why we may not allow our Saviour to have used the same parable twice, in two differing companies, and upon two different occasions, especially considering there are remarkable differences in Luke's and Matthew's relation. I shall therefore leave the consideration of Luke's relation till I come to that chapter in his Gospel, where I shall meet with it in course, and consider only what Matthew saith. We must remember this is a parable, not an historical narration. The first verse tells us, *And Jesus answered and spake unto them again by parables :* he answered, that is, he began a discourse, so the word very often signifies. Our Saviour hath neither given us any particular explication of this parable, nor any *proparabola*, or *epiparabola*, any sentence before or after the parable, guiding us as to the explication, except only that short sentence, ver. 14, *For many are called, but few are chosen ;* which rather guideth us in the explication of the four latter verses than of the whole parable : yet it is not hard for us to find out our Saviour's scope in this parable. It seemeth to be double : 1. To inform those to whom he spake of the destruction suddenly coming upon the Jews, for their rejection of the gospel, and of the calling of the Gentiles. 2. To let us know, that neither amongst the Jews nor Gentiles all should be saved whom God called by the external ministration of the gospel; but those alone who, belonging to the election of grace, should be found in the day of judgment having on the wedding garment. So then, *the kingdom of heaven* here signifies, the way or equity of God in the dispensation of the gospel, or the administration of things in order to the kingdom of glory. The *king* here mentioned must be he who is the King of kings. The *marriage for his son*, is the exhibition of the covenant of grace ; which whosoever layeth hold on, Isa. lvi. 4, is by faith united to Christ; which union is often expressed in holy writ under the notion of a marriage, Psal. xlv. 10, 11 ; Eph. v. 23, &c.: or their union with him in glory, Rev. xix. 9. The persons *bidden* were the Jews. The *servants* that called them to the *wedding*, were those that were faithful amongst their ordinary teachers, or the prophets, such as Isaiah and the rest, whom they refused to hearken unto. The *other servants* might signify John the Baptist, and the twelve, and others sent out by Christ, to tell them that Christ was now come, there wanted nothing but their coming to him and receiving of him. Their making *light of it,* going *one to his farm, another to his merchandise*, and others taking the servants, entreating them spitefully, and slaying them, signifies the Jews' general refusal of the gospel, and the particular rage and malice of some of them, shown in their abusing of the Lord's prophets and messengers, and which he knew some of them would further show against Stephen and James. The king's sending forth his armies, and slaying the murderers, signified the coming of the Roman armies, and their utter destroying Jerusalem. The sending of the servants into the highways, and inviting all those whom they found to the wedding, signified the apostles going to the Gentiles, and preaching the gospel to all nations; which much enlarged the territories of the church, gathering in many who professed to accept of Christ, but not all in truth and sincerity. The king's coming to see his guests, signifieth Christ's coming at the day of the last judgment, with his fan in his hand, throughly to purge his floor. His finding one without his wedding garment, signifieth his finding many hypocrites at the day of judgment. The guests at weddings were either wont to put on their best clothes, (as we usually do,) or a particular garment which was then in use, and was worn by those who were invited to weddings. By the *wedding garment* here is meant Christ, Rom. xiii. 14, who is at this feast both the bridegroom, and the meat at the feast, and the wedding garment also, in divers respects. It is but an idle dispute, whether faith is meant, or love : neither the one nor the other separately, but faith that worketh by love ; whatsoever God requireth of us, that we may be made meet for the kingdom of God : without faith and holiness none can see God. His being *speechless* signifies, that those who have lived under the proffers of grace and salvation, and have rejected them, neither believing in the Lord Jesus Christ, nor bringing forth fruits of holiness, will be without excuse at the day of judgment. And the king's commanding his servants to *bind him hand and foot,* &c., signifieth that all such persons as live within the church, under the means of grace, yet die impenitent and unbelievers, having not by a true faith received Christ as their Saviour, and brought forth the fruits of true repentance and holiness, shall get nothing by their being within the church and externally called, but shall be thrown into hell as well as others, the pains of which are here expressed by binding hand and foot, lying in outer darkness, weeping and gnashing of teeth ; as in other places by a worm that shall never die, and a fire that shall never go out; all metaphorical expressions, signifying the vexations and intolerable punishment of the damned in hell. *For* (saith our Saviour) *many are called, but few are chosen*. We met with this expression before, chap. xx. 16, where the sense of it was not so obvious as it is here. Some by it here understand, a choice unto life eternal ; nor without reason, if that be understood by the marriage supper, as it is Rev. xix. 9 ; and it appears to be partly at least the sense of it here, in that the person without the wedding garment is doomed to eternal misery. If we by the marriage supper understand a union with Christ here, or the benefits flowing from that, we must by *chosen* here understand effectually called, being made partakers of that special distinguishing grace which bringeth salvation. The gospel is preached to many whom God doth not favour with his special grace, so as they receive it, convert, and are saved. The former part of this parable doth hint us the reason why the Jews rejected the offers of grace and salvation made to them, viz. the power that the temptations from the world, of pleasure, profit, and honour, had upon them. As the latter part also showeth us the true reason why any are saved to be from the free grace of God, viz. because they are chosen, chosen to eternal life, and particularly favoured to be made partakers of his special and distinguishing grace.

i Mark 12.13.
Luke 20. 20.

15 ¶ ¹Then went the Pharisees, and took counsel how they might entangle him in *his* talk.

Mark saith, chap. xii. 13, *They send unto him certain of the Pharisees and of the Herodians, to catch him in his words.* Luke saith, chap. xx. 20, *They watched him, and sent forth spies, which should feign themselves just men, that they might take hold of his words, that so they might deliver him unto the power and authority of the governor.* His life was what they sought for. This they had no power allowed by the Romans to take away without the sentence of Pontius Pilate, the Roman governor. That they might have something to accuse him of before him, which he might condemn him for, they first take counsel. They saw he did nothing worthy of death; they therefore issue their counsels in a resolution to send some persons to discourse with him, under the pretence of conscientious, good men, to propound some questions to him, his answer to which might give them some opportunity to accuse him of blasphemy or sedition. The men they pitch upon were some of them Pharisees, some Herodians.

16 And they sent out unto him their disciples with the Herodians, saying, Master, we know that thou art true, and teachest the way of God in truth, neither carest thou for any *man:* for thou regardest not the person of men.

17 Tell us therefore, What thinkest thou? Is it lawful to give tribute unto Cæsar, or not?

Mark hath the same, chap. xii. 14. So hath Luke, chap. xx. 21. There is a great variety of opinions, who these *Herodians* were; we read of them in an early consultation against Christ with the Pharisees, Mark iii. 6. Some think, they were foreigners of other nations, whom Herod, being tetrarch of Galilee, had brought in from contiguous pagan nations; but this is not probable, for then the Pharisees would have had nothing to do with them. Others think that they were some of Herod's guard, or soldiers; but neither is this probable, considering the issue of their counsels, to send some whom Christ should not know, nor be frighted with. Others (which is more probable) think they were some of those Jews who favoured Herod's side, and had forgotten the liberty of their country, joining with the conqueror, and taking his part. Others think they were Sadducees. Others say, that they were persons that were of a mongrel religion, made up of Judaism and Gentilism. Our Saviour bids them *beware of the leaven of the Pharisees, and of Herod,* Mark viii. 15; which maketh it probable, that the Herodians were not only courtiers, and for the Roman interest, but that they had embraced some particular doctrines, much differing from the Pharisees; it is likely they were leavened with some of the doctrine of the Sadducees, denying angels and spirits, and the resurrection. It is plain that they were some of Herod's faction; what their principles were as to religion is not so plain, nor of much concern to us to know. They begin their discourse to our Saviour with a great compliment, *Master,* a name the Jews did usually give to those whom they owned for teachers. *We know that thou art true,* one that will tell us the truth, and speak as thou thinkest to be true, *and teachest the way of God in truth, neither carest thou for any man: for thou regardest not the person of men:* thou wilt speak nothing out of fear, nor for any favour or affection; but plainly tell us what is truth, and what God would have us do in the cases we offer to thee. In these words they give us the true character of a good teacher; he must be a good man, true, one that will truly teach men the way of God, and, in the faithful discharge of their duty, not be afraid of the face of men. But herein they condemned themselves, for if our Saviour was so, why did they not believe in him, and obey what he taught them? *Tell us therefore, What thinkest thou? Is it lawful to give tribute unto Cæsar, or not?*

But how came this to be a case of conscience? What doubt could there be, whether men for their peace might not lawfully part from their own, especially such a little part of it? Some think that they spake with relation to that particular tribute which was demanded, which they think was that half shekel, Exod. xxx. 12, 15, paid by the Jews every year, which was to go for the service of the tabernacle: they say that the Romans had ordered this payment to go to the emperor, and this bred the question, Whether they might lawfully pay that which was appointed as a testimony of their homage to God, and for the service of the temple, to a profane use. I must confess I cannot so freely agree to this, wanting any good proof that the Romans exacted that payment for the emperor, and thinking it a very probable argument to the contrary, that the tables of the money-changers, who changed the people's money into half shekels fit for that payment, was now continued. And if that payment had been now altered, and turned to the use of the civil government, our Saviour's overturning those tables, and driving the money-changers out, had offered them a fair opportunity to have charged him with sedition, which they did not do upon that account. I rather therefore think the question propounded concerning the lawfulness of making any payments to the emperor, looking upon him as a usurper of authority over a free people. That the Jews were very tenacious of their liberty appears from John viii. 33; and, without doubt, the most of them paid such taxes as the Roman emperor laid upon them with no very good will. Now these hypocrites turn it into a case of conscience, God having made the Jews a free people, Whether they should not sin against God in paying these civil taxes to a pagan conqueror. There was one Theudas, and Judas, mentioned Acts v. 36, 37, who made an insurrection upon it. This was a question captious enough. For if he had said it was lawful, he had probably incurred the odium of the people, which was what they desired, for they had apprehended him before this time but for fear of them. If he had said it was not lawful, they had what they sought for, a fair opportunity for accusing him, and delivering him up to Pontius Pilate, the Roman governor at this time amongst them.

18 But Jesus perceived their wickedness, and said, Why tempt ye me, *ye* hypocrites?

19 Shew me the tribute money. And they brought unto him a ‖ penny.

20 And he saith unto them, Whose *is* this image and ‖ superscription?

‖ In value seven pence halfpenny: ch. 20. 2.
‖ Or, *inscription.*

21 They say unto him, Cæsar's. Then saith he unto them, ᵏRender therefore unto Cæsar the things which are Cæsar's; and unto God the things that are God's.

k ch. 17. 25.
Rom. 13. 7.

22 When they had heard *these words,* they marvelled, and left him, and went their way.

Mark hath the same, chap. xii. 15—17. So hath Luke, chap. xx. 23—26. Our Saviour, saith Luke, *perceived their craftiness,* how subtlely they went about to entrap him. He calls them to show him *the tribute money.* The Jews had two sorts of money, shekels and half shekels, which was money proper to them, and Roman coin, pence and sesterces. Their tribute was paid in this coin. Accordingly they bring unto him a penny, a Roman penny, as much in value as seven pence halfpenny in our coin; which it seems was the poll-money, which the Romans exacted of every head. The coining of money was always looked upon as an act of sovereign power, hence the usurpation of it is made so criminal. Most princes use to have their effigies stamped upon their coin, and some inscription about it, with their names, and some words expressive of their dominion over such places where their coin is current; so so as the admission of a prince's coin as current amongst a people was a testimony of their owning and subjection to such a prince. Such an image and superscription this piece of money had; upon which our Saviour concludes, *Render therefore unto Cæsar the things which are Cæsar's; and unto God the things that are God's.* Although Cæsar be a usurper, yet God hath given you into his hands, you have owned him by accepting his coin as current amongst you. His right and God's right are two distinct things. Religion doth not exempt you from your civil duties, and obedience to princes, in things wherein they have a power to command. Princes have power to impose tributes upon their subjects, for the maintenance and upholding of the civil government. Let Cæsar have his due, and let God have his right. You are a company of hypocrites, who by this question would make me believe you have a great zeal for God and his rights, and that you would not pay taxes that you might assert God's right over you; this is your pretence, but indeed your design is to try me, if you can persuade me, by any words of mine, to encourage you to any sedition, or acts of disloyalty to your civil governors. I see no reason for it; Cæsar hath his right, and God hath his rights; you may give them both their rights, and so you ought to do. God's kingdom is of another nature than the kingdoms of the world. His law forbiddeth no civil rights. Thus our Saviour answers their question so as he maketh them to condemn themselves, if, owning the civil magistrate's power, they did not give him his rights, and so as neither Cæsar nor yet the people had any just cause of exception against him for his words. This answer surpriseth them, they marvel and go their way, having played their game and got nothing.

l Mark 12. 18.
Luke 20. 27.
m Acts 23. 8.

23 ¶ ¹The same day came to him the Sadducees, ᵐwhich say that there is no resurrection, and asked him,

n Deut. 25. 5.

24 Saying, Master, ⁿMoses said, If a man die, having no children, his brother shall marry his wife, and raise up seed unto his brother.

o 1 6 8. 5. 8.

25 ᵒNow there were with us seven brethren: and the first, when he had married a wife, deceased, and, having no issue, left his wife unto his brother:

26 Likewise the second also, and the third, unto the †seventh.

† Gr. *seven.*

27 And last of all the woman died also.

28 Therefore in the resurrection whose wife shall she be of the seven? for they all had her.

Mark thus repeats the same history, chap. xii. 18—22. So doth Luke, chap. xx. 27—33. Concerning the Sadducees we have before spoken; they were a sect amongst the Jews much differing from the Pharisees, as may be seen, Acts xxiii. 8. Amongst other erroneous tenets, they denied the resurrection, as may be seen in that text, as well as this; and (which indeed was their fundamental error) they denied spirits, and consequently the immortality of the soul in its separate estate. Their design seemeth not so much to have been to have drawn out a discourse from our Saviour which might have touched his life, (which was the Pharisees' design,) as to have exposed him, by bringing him to an absurdity. To this purpose they put a case to our Saviour upon the law, Deut. xxv. 5, where God had ordained, for the preservation of the inheritances of the several tribes and families distinct, That if brethren dwelt together, and one of them died leaving no issue, the wife of the dead should not marry unto a stranger; her husband's brother should go in unto her, and take her to him to wife, &c. Now they either knew of, or else supposed, a case of seven brethren, successively marrying the same woman; they desire to know whose wife of the seven this woman should be in the resurrection. Instead of discovering their acuteness, and putting our Saviour upon a difficulty, they did but betray their own ignorance as to the state of the resurrection.

29 Jesus answered and said unto them,

p John 20. 9.

Ye do err, ᵖnot knowing the Scriptures, nor the power of God.

q 1 John 3. 2.

30 For in the resurrection they neither marry, nor are given in marriage, but ᑫare as the angels of God in heaven.

Mark hath the same, chap. xii. 24, 25, only he propounds it as a question, *Do ye not therefore err, because ye know not the Scriptures?* Luke saith, chap. xx. 34, 35, *And Jesus answering said unto them, The children of this world marry, and are given in marriage: but they which shall be accounted worthy to obtain that world, and the resurrection from* the dead, neither marry, nor are given in marriage: neither can they die any more: for they are equal unto the angels; and are the children of God, being the children of the resurrection. The discourse of the Sadducees was bottomed upon this mistake, that there should not only be a resurrection of bodies, but of relations too; and the state of the world to come should be like the state of this world, in, which, for the propagation and continuance of mankind, men and women marry, and are given in marriage. Now, saith our Saviour, your error is bottomed in your ignorance, *because ye know not the Scriptures,* (which indeed is the foundation of all men's errors in matter of faith,) *nor the power of God.* If you knew the power of God, you would know that God is able to raise the dead. To confirm our faith in the resurrection, the Scripture every where sendeth us to the consideration of the Divine power, Rom. viii. 11; Phil. iii. 21. If you knew the Scriptures, you would know that God will raise the dead, and the state of men in the resurrection shall not be as in this life, where men and women die daily; and in case they did not marry and give in marriage, the generation of men would quickly be extinct. *But* (saith Luke) *they who shall be accounted worthy to obtain that world, and the resurrection from the dead.* It is manifest by the first words, that the latter words are not to be understood of the general resurrection, (to which all shall come, worthy or unworthy,) but of the resurrection unto life; that resurrection which is not the mere effect of Divine providence, necessary in order to the last judgment, but that resurrection to life which is the effect of Christ's purchase. And this is observable, that the resurrection from the dead will be of so little advantage, nay, of such miserable disadvantage, to wicked men, that the Scripture sometimes speaketh of the resurrection as if it were peculiar to saints, 1 Cor vv 22; Phil. iii. 11; so in this text. Hence Luke calls them afterward, *the children of the resurrection;* not that others shall not rise, but the children of God alone shall be the favourites of the resurrection, those who shall rise as children to an eternal inheritance. Concerning the state of persons in the resurrection our Saviour thus describes it: that men and women there shall be *as the angels,* not in all things, but in the things mentioned, which are two, one of them mentioned by Matthew, both by Luke: 1. They shall not die any more. 2. They shall not marry, nor be given in marriage. The first showeth the needlessness of the latter, for one great reason of marriage was to supply the gaps which death maketh in the world; but men shall not die any more, therefore there will be no need of conjugal relations amongst men, more than among angels. *The children of this world* (saith Luke) *marry, and are given in marriage.* Marriage was only an institution for this world, and is to continue no longer than this world stands; for the state of men in another world will be such as needs it not, being a state of immortality, so not needing it for propagation; and a state for perfection, and so not needing it for mutual help in the affairs of man's life, nor a remedy against extravagant lust.

31 But as touching the resurrection of the dead, have ye not read that which was spoken unto you by God, saying,

32 ʳI am the God of Abraham, and the God of Isaac, and the God of Jacob? God is not the God of the dead, but of the living.

r Ex. 3. 6.
16. Mark 12.
26. Luke 20.
37. Acts 7.
32. Heb. 11.
16.

33 And when the multitude heard *this,* ˢthey were astonished at his doctrine.

s ch. 7. 28.

Mark hath the same, chap. xii. 26, 27; so hath Luke, chap. xx. 37, 38; only Mark and Luke mention the time when God spake these words—*in the bush,* that is, when God appeared to Moses in the burning bush, Exod. iii. 6; and Luke addeth, *for all live unto him.* Mark also saith, *Touching the dead that they rise, have ye not read in the book of Moses?* Our Saviour, in the foregoing words, had, by the by, asserted the doctrine of angels; here he asserts both the doctrine of the immortality of the soul, and also of the resurrection of the body: and though Cardinal Perron, and Maldonate the Jesuit, boldly assert that the resurrection of the body cannot be proved from hence without taking in the tradition of the church; yet, notwithstanding their confidence, those who have a greater reverence for our Saviour's words, think that not only the immortality of the soul, but the resurrection of the body also, is irrefragably proved by this argument of our Saviour's; to make out which, these things are to be observed : 1. God doth not say I have been, but *I am :* he speaketh of the time present, when he spake to Moses, and of the time to come. 2. He doth not say, I am the Lord of Abraham, Isaac, and Jacob, but *the God of :* now wherever God styles himself the God of any people or person, it always signifieth, God as a Benefactor, and one that doth and will do good to such a people or person. It is a federal expression, as where he saith to Abraham, Gen. xvii. 7, *I will be a God to thee and thy seed,* that is, of thee and of thy seed. 3. Abraham, Isaac, and Jacob, doth not signify part of Abraham, Isaac, and Jacob, but their entire persons, which consist of bodies as well as souls. 4. God is not the God of the dead, he doth not show kindness to them if they be dead, and shall rise no more. 5. In this life, Abraham, Isaac, and Jacob received no such signal kindness from God, but others might receive as great kindness as any of them did. Hence now our Lord proveth, as the immortality of their souls, so the resurrection also of their bodies, that God might show himself the God of whole Abraham, Isaac, and Jacob. Gerard saith, The argument of this text is made clear by Heb. xi. 16, *Wherefore God is not ashamed to be called their God, for he hath prepared for them a city.* This is that which made God to be truly called *their God,* because *he hath prepared for them a city,* which city they could never possess without a resurrection. It is yet further added by some, That God's promise to Abraham of the land of Canaan was in these terms, Gen. xiii. 15, *To thee will I give it, and to thy seed for ever ;* not only *to thy seed,* but *to thee :* so to Isaac, Gen. xxvi. 3 ; to Jacob, Gen. xxxv. 12 ; Exod. vi. 4, 8 ; Deut. xi. 21. The promises seemed not to be fulfilled in giving their posterity the earthly Canaan, which Abraham, Isaac, and Jacob lived not to enjoy ; but to extend to the rest prepared for the people of God, the city mentioned by the apostle, Heb. xi. 16, which God had prepared for them, to justify himself to be their God. Now this could not be prepared for their souls merely, which were but a part of them, and hardly capable of perfect happiness without a reunion with the body, there being in it such an innate desire. Nor was it reasonable that the bodies of these saints, having been sharers with their souls in their labours, should have no share in their reward from that covenant ; therefore of God with Abraham, Isaac, and Jacob, our Saviour firmly proveth their resurrection. Luke addeth, *for all live unto him.* Not live unto him only as their end, but in the same sense as Paul saith of Christ, Rom. vi. 10, *in that he liveth, he liveth unto God ;* that is, with God. So saith Luke, Abraham, Isaac, and Jacob, though dead at present, live with God ; and they, and all the children of Abraham, shall live to God, that is, with God, to all eternity. Matthew addeth, *when the multitude heard this, they were astonished at his doctrine.* Poor people, they had been used to hear discourses from the Pharisees, about the traditions of the elders, rites and ceremonies, washing hands before meat, and the necessity of washing pots and cups ; and the Sadducees, declaiming against the doctrines of angels and spirits, and the resurrection ; they were astonished to hear one instructing them in things concerning their souls, the resurrection and life eternal, and confuting their great teachers from books of Scripture owned by themselves ; for the Sadducees, though they had no great regard to the prophets, yet they owned and paid a great deference to the books of Moses.

t Mark 12. 28.

34 ¶ ᵗBut when the Pharisees had heard that he had put the Sadducees to silence, they were gathered together.

u Luke 10. 25.

35 Then one of them, *which was* ᵘa Lawyer, asked *him a question,* tempting him, and saying,

36 Master, which *is* the great commandment in the law ?

x Deut. 6. 5. & 10. 12. & 30. 6. Luke 10. 27.

37 Jesus said unto him, ˣThou shalt love the Lord thy God with all thy heart, and with all thy soul, and with all thy mind.

38 This is the first and great commandment.

39 And the second *is* like unto it, ʸThou shalt love thy neighbour as thyself.

y Lev. 19. 18. ch. 19. 19. Mark 12. 31. Luke 10. 27. Rom. 13. 9. Gal. 5. 14.

40 ᶻOn these two commandments hang all the Law and the Prophets.

z Jam. 2. 8. ch. 7. 12. 1 Tim. 1. 5.

Mark relateth this history more fully, chap. xii. 28—34. *And one of the scribes came, and having heard them reasoning together, and perceiving that he had answered them well, asked him, Which is the first commandment of all? And Jesus answered him, The first of all the commandments is, Hear, O Israel ; the Lord our God is one Lord : and thou shalt love the Lord thy God with all thy heart, and with all thy soul, and with all thy mind, and with all thy strength : this is the first commandment. And the second is like, namely this, Thou shalt love thy neighbour as thyself. There is none other commandment greater than these. And the scribe said unto him, Well, Master, thou hast said the truth : for there is one God ; and there is none other but he : and to love him with all the heart, and with all the understanding, and with all the soul, and with all the strength, and to love his neighbour as himself, is more than all whole burnt-offerings and sacrifices. And when Jesus saw that he answered discreetly, he said unto him, Thou art not far from the kingdom of God. And no man after that durst ask him any question.* Luke omitteth this history, only subjoineth to our Saviour's answer to the Sadducees, chap. xx. 39, 40, *Then certain of the scribes answering said, Master, thou hast well said. And after that they durst not ask him any question at all.* There are different opinions of interpreters concerning the design of this scribe, called by Matthew a lawyer, in coming to Christ with this question. Some think that he came upon the same errand with the others, to entangle him in his speech. Others, that he came merely out of a desire to be more fully instructed by him, and that *tempting* here signifies no more than trying him, not for a bad end, but as the queen of Sheba came to prove Solomon with hard questions, to have an experiment of his wisdom. Our Saviour's fair treating him, and the commendation he gave him, together with his fair speaking to our Saviour, and commending his answer, induce me to think that he came on no ill design. Besides that, the opinion of some, that he came hoping to hear our Saviour vilify their ritual precepts in comparison of the moral precepts, seemeth to me not probable ; for himself consents to what our Saviour saith, and addeth, that *to love the Lord our God,* &c., *is more than all burnt-offerings and sacrifices.* His question was, *Which is the first and greatest commandment?* Matthew saith, *the great ;* Mark saith, *the first :* they have both the same sense, and our Saviour puts them together, ver. 38. *Jesus said unto him, Thou shalt love the Lord thy God with all thy heart, and with all thy soul, and with all thy mind.* Mark adds, *with all thy strength.* It is to be found Deut. vi. 5, only there is not *with all thy mind.* Luke puts it in, chap. x. 27. It is but the same thing expressed in divers terms, for *with all thy soul* is comprehensive of heart, mind, and strength. Mark adds a preface : *Hear, O Israel ; the Lord our God is one Lord : thou shalt love,* &c. Those words only, 1. Stirred up the people's attention. 2. Showed the reason of the following precept, which is fully expressed in Matthew. If any ask, To which of the ten commandments is this to be referred ? it is easily answered, that it is the sum of the four first, which comprehend our duty toward God. Our Saviour's expressing them by loving God, shows us that the law of God was not fulfilled in the observation of the letter of those commandments, but doing these things which God commands out of a principle of love, the highest degrees of love to God. They idly interpret this precept, who interpret it only an obligation upon us to love God as much as we are able in our lapsed state ; the fall of man lost God no right of commanding, and telling us our duty. The law doth undoubtedly require of us love to God in the highest degree, to be showed by the acts of the whole man, in obedience to all his commandments, and that constantly. It is our only happiness that the law is in the hands of a Mediator, who hath thus perfectly fulfilled it for all those who believe in him, Rom. viii. 3, and accepteth of us the will for the deed. Thus the moral law is a schoolmaster that leadeth us unto Christ. Our Saviour justly calls this the first and great commandment, 1. Because God is to be served before our neighbour. 2. Nor can love to our neighbour flow from any other true principle than that of love to God, nor is our neighbour to be loved but for God's sake, and in subordination unto him. *And the second is like unto it,* commanding love also; so that, as the apostle saith, *love is the fulfilling of the law. Thy neighbour,* that is, every man, *as thyself;* doing as much for him as thou wouldst have him do for thee, and doing no more against him than thou wouldst willingly he should do against thee: as truly and sincerely as thyself. *On these two commandments hang all the law and the prophets:* there is nothing commanded in all the Old Testament but may be reduced to these two heads. This is the whole duty of man there commanded. The whole book of God is our rule, and we are obliged to every precept in it. Moses summed up all in the ten commandments, to which, truly interpreted, all the precepts of Scripture are reducible. Christ here brings the ten to two. The apostle brings all to one, telling us *love is the fulfilling of the law.* There is nothing forbidden in Scripture but what offends the royal law of love, either to God or man; there is nothing commanded but what will fall under it. Mark addeth, that the scribe applauds our Saviour, as having said the truth, and confessing that the fulfilling these two precepts was more than all sacrifices and burnt-offerings; in which he agreed with Samuel, who long since told Saul that *to obey was better than sacrifice;* and it needs must be so, seeing that all the true value of sacrifices lay in the obedience by them given to the will of God. Christ tells the scribe he was *not far from the kingdom of God.* He who once rightly understands the law of God, and hath cast off that silly fancy of thinking to please God with ritual things, hath made a great proficiency under that schoolmaster, who, if rightly understood, will show him the need of another righteousness than his own wherein to appear before God.

a Mark 12. 35. Luke 20. 41.

41 ¶ ªWhile the Pharisees were gathered together, Jesus asked them,

42 Saying, What think ye of Christ? whose son is he? They say unto him, *The Son* of David.

b Ecclus. 51. 10.
c Ps. 110. 1. Acts 2. 34. 1 Cor. 15. 25. Heb. 1. 13. & 10. 12, 13.

43 He saith unto them, How then doth David in spirit ᵇcall him Lord, saying,

44 ᶜ The LORD said unto my Lord, Sit thou on my right hand, till I make thine enemies thy footstool?

45 If David then call him Lord, how is he his son?

d Luke 14. 6.
e Mark 12. 34. Luke 20. 40.

46 ᵈAnd no man was able to answer him a word, ᵉneither durst any *man* from that day forth ask him any more *questions.*

Mark hath this story shortly, repeating only the substance of it, chap. xii. 35—37; adding nothing to it, but concluding, And the common people heard him gladly. Luke repeateth it as shortly, chap. xx. 41—44. For the right understanding of this discourse of our Saviour to the Pharisees, we must know, that though the Pharisees and the Jews in general did expect a Messiah or a Christ, yet they expected no more of him, or in him, than that he should be a man, the son of David, descended from his family, according to the promise, Isa. ix. 6; and dreamed only of a secular prince, who should deliver them from their enemies, and restore them to their ancient civil liberties. Christ seeing a pack of them together, took the liberty, which he had allowed them towards himself, to propound a question or two to them. His question was, *What think ye of Christ?* not of himself, but of the Messiah whom they expected; whose Son he should be. *They say unto him, The Son of David,* that is, one who should in a right line be descended from David. This was a constant and uncontrolled tradition amongst them. Hence Mark saith, the question was propounded, *How say the scribes?* Luke, *How say they that Christ is,* that is, is to be, *the Son of David?* This was a commonly received opinion amongst them, which our Saviour by the next words doth not contradict, but only argueth that he must needs be something more; for, saith he, *How then doth David in spirit call him Lord?* Psal. cx. 1. Mark saith, *David himself said by the Holy Ghost.* David was a prophet, and spake by inspiration from the Holy Ghost, Acts i. 16; ii. 30. Luke saith, *in the book of Psalms;* whence we may observe, that Psal. cx. was David's Psalm, not a Psalm composed by some other for David, as some contend. Would David have called him Lord, whom he knew to be merely his son, one that should only descend from him? He would have said, The Lord said to my son, or, will say to my son. *The Lord said,* Jehovah said, *unto my Lord, Sit thou at my right hand.* Would David, speaking prophetically by the Holy Ghost concerning the Messiah, had he believed he was to be his son, and no more, have said that Jehovah should say unto him, *Sit at my right hand,* a place of the highest honour, dignity, and favour, *until I make thine enemies thy footstool,* that is, for ever? for *until* doth not signify a determinate time. See the notes on chap. i. 25. *If David then call him Lord, how is he his son?* that is, how is he then no more than his son, no more than a mere man? Our Saviour by this argument doth neither go about to prove that the Christ was not to be the Son of David, nor that he was the Messias himself, but that their expected Messias or Christ must be more than a mere man, otherwise David would never have called him Lord, nor yet prophesied that Jehovah should call him to sit at his right hand. Matthew concludes with telling us, that as the Sadducees and the scribes were nonplussed before, so now the Pharisees' mouths were also stopped. Mark saith, *The common people heard him gladly.* Matthew saith, *No man was able to answer him a word, neither durst any man ask him any more questions.* Nor shall we hear of their troubling him with disputes any more; they now see disputing will not do their business, their next business is to consult how to take away his life; which is always the course of proud and malicious men, given over of God to ruin, to conceal their convictions, and proceed to execute their lusts and malice, rather than they will not have their ends. But before they meet with a fit opportunity we shall have some excellent discourses from our Saviour to the disciples and the multitude.

CHAP. XXIII

Christ exhorteth to observe the doctrine, but not to follow the evil examples, of the scribes and Pharisees; and particularly not to imitate their ambition, 1—12. *He pronounceth divers woes against them for their blindness and hypocrisy,* 13—33; *and prophesieth the destruction of Jerusalem,* 34—39.

THEN spake Jesus to the multitude, and to his disciples,

2 Saying, ª The Scribes and the Pharisees sit in Moses' seat:

a Neh. 8. 4, 8. Mal. 2. 7. Mark 12. 38. Luke 20. 45.

3 All therefore whatsoever they bid you observe, *that* observe and do; but do not ye after their works: for ᵇthey say, and do not.

b Rom. 2. 19, &c.

Our Lord having now done with the Pharisees, turneth his discourse to the more docible people, who (as we heard before) heard him attentively and gladly, Mark xii. 37; Luke xix. 48. Our Saviour foresaw that some unwary hearers might make two ill uses of what he had spoke against the scribes and Pharisees. 1. Some might report him an enemy to the law, the interpreters of which the Pharisees were. 2. Others might contemn the authority of the law, because he had represented these men, in whose hand the interpretation of it at present was, so truly contemptible. Whereas, on the other side, many might run into errors of practice, from the example of the scribes and Pharisees, their magistrates and teachers. Against all these mistakes he cautions them in this chapter, showing that he did not undervalue the law of Moses, nor would have his reflections on the Pharisees prejudice any thing which they taught them of it, and according to it; neither would he have his people take the copy of the law from their actions. *The scribes and the Pharisees sit in Moses's seat:* these men were the ordinary readers and interpreters of the law of God. Moses is here put for the law, as Luke xvi. 31, *If they hear not Moses and the prophets;* and so ver. 29, *They have Moses and the prophets.* Moses's seat signifieth the seat appointed for those that gave the sense of the law, or judgment upon it; thus, *Moses of old time hath in every city those that preach him, being read in the synagogues every sabbath day,* Acts xv. 21; 2 Cor. iii. 15. Their way was, while they read the Scriptures they *stood up,* (paying a particular reverence to the pure word of God,) Luke iv. 16; when they had done reading, they *sat down* and opened it. Their sitting in the seat of Moses did not signify a succession to Moses, for he had no successor, being the Mediator of the Old Testament; but the delivering and interpreting the doctrine and law of Moses. Dr. Lightfoot thinks it is rather to be understood of the chair of magistracy than the doctrinal chair. The Pharisees being exercised in that, it may be understood of both, for the reading and interpreting the law chiefly belonged to the scribes. *All therefore whatsoever they bid you observe. that observe and do;* that is, whatsoever is in Moses which they bid you observe and do. The term *all* is to be understood restrainedly, with respect to the subject matter or persons spoken of, in multitudes of scriptures. Our Saviour's cautioning his disciples so often against the leaven of these men, and their traditions, plainly showeth us that must be here the sense of it: Let not the law of God lose its authority with you because of these wicked men. He doth not command them to hear none but them, for then to what purpose did he himself preach, or send out the twelve, if none might hear them? All that can be concluded from this text is. that the law of God, or word of God, is not to be despised, whoever reads or delivereth it. He goeth on, *But do not ye after their works : for they say, and do not.* We are naturally more led by example than by precept. Men had therefore need be cautioned against ill-living teachers. *Odi philosophum qui non sapit sibi.* A man had need very well know the medicine which he taketh from a physician he seeth sick of the same disease, when he himself refuseth and abominates it. He that says and does not, may be heard, but not imitated. There may be a time when men can ordinarily hear no others, which was the present case.

c Luke 11. 46. Acts 15. 10. Gal. 6. 13.
4 ᶜFor they bind heavy burdens and grievous to be borne, and lay *them* on men's shoulders; but they *themselves* will not move them with one of their fingers.

Our Saviour saith the same of the *lawyers,* Luke xi. 46. The *burdens* here mentioned were not their traditions and ritual things, Christ would never have before commanded his disciples to observe and do them, but the things truly commanded by the law of God, especially the ceremonial law, called *a yoke,* Acts xv. 10, *which* (say the apostles) *neither our fathers nor we were able to bear.* They are, saith our Saviour, rigid exactors and pressers of the law of God upon others, but will not themselves use the least endeavours (such as the putting to of a finger) themselves to do them. 1. He blameth them that their own lives no way answered their doctrine. 2. It may be, he also blameth their too rigid pressing the law in all the minute things of it. There may be a too rigorous pressing of the law. Good teachers will be faithful in delivering the whole counsel of God, yet teaching no more than themselves will endeavour to practise; and being conscious of human infirmity, they will do it with great tenderness and compassion, joining law and gospel both together.

d ch. 6. 1, 2, 5, 16. e Num. 15. 38. Deut. 6. 8. & 22. 12. Prov. 3. 3.
5 But ᵈall their works they do for to be seen of men : ᵉthey make broad their phylacteries, and enlarge the borders of their garments,

Our Saviour had, ver. 4, blamed the Pharisees for not living up to what they taught, pressing the law of God on others, but not doing nor endeavouring to observe it themselves. Here he blames them for doing what good things they did for ostentation, *to be seen of men;* and abounding in their ritual performances of more minute concernment, in the mean time neglecting their moral duties. *All their works they do for to be seen of men;* this is their main end, to be seen of men; for this he had reflected on them, chap. vi. *They make broad their phylacteries, and enlarge the borders of their garments.* For the right understanding of this we must have recourse to Numb. xv. 37—40, *And the Lord spake unto Moses, saying, Speak unto the children of Israel, and bid them that they make them fringes in the borders of their garments throughout their generations, and that they put upon the fringe of the borders a riband of blue: and it shall be unto you for a fringe, that ye may look upon it. and remember all the commandments of the Lord, and do them; and that ye seek not after your own heart and your own eyes, after which ye use to go a whoring : that ye may remember, and do all my commandments.* Deut. xxii. 12, *Thou shalt make thee fringes upon the four quarters of thy vesture, wherewith thou coverest thyself.* In obedience to this law, the Jews did generally wear such garments that had fringes and blue ribands annexed to them. The Jews at this day do it not, because, as they pretend, they have lost the true way of dying the blue colour, required in the law. The end why God commanded them is expressed, *that ye may look upon it, and remember all the commandments of the Lord, and do them;* and be restrained from their own inventions and imaginations in God's service. They were also a note of distinction of the Jews from other people. Besides these, God commanding that they should *bind* his laws *for a sign upon their hands, and as frontlets between their eyes,* Deut. vi. 6—8, they made them parchments, in which the precepts of the law were written, which they bound to their foreheads and arms. These were called phylacteries, from φυλάττω, to keep, things wherein the law was kept. The Pharisees, for a boast how zealous keepers they were of the law of God, (than which they did nothing less,) made these phylacteries and ribands broader. and their fringes much longer, than other men's : this is that making broad their phylacteries, and enlarging the borders of their garments, which our Lord here reflects upon, done only for ostentation, and that they might be seen of men.

6 ᶠAnd love the uppermost rooms at feasts, and the chief seats in the synagogues,
f Mark 12. 38, 39. Luke 11. 43. & 20. 46. 3 John 9.

7 And greetings in the markets, and to be called of men, Rabbi, Rabbi.

We have the same applied to the scribes, Mark xii. 38, 39; Luke xi. 43. Mark addeth, *which love to go in long clothing.* Our Saviour in these words doth not blame a distinction in habits and places, for he himself hath taught us, that those who are in kings' palaces wear soft raiment; and, being often called Master and Lord, never reflected on them who called him so, as having done amiss : he only blameth the Pharisees' ambition, and silly affectation of these little things, seeking their own honour and glory, or an undue domination. There is therefore an emphasis to be put upon the word *love;* they might take salutations, and the upper rooms, if offered them as their due, for keeping civil order, but not affect them.

8 ᵍBut be not ye called Rabbi : for one is your Master, *even* Christ; and all ye are brethren.
g Jam. 3. 1. See 2 Cor. 1. 24. 1 Pet. 5. 3.

9 And call no *man* your father upon the earth : ʰfor one is your Father, which is in heaven.
h Mal. 1. 6.

10 Neither be ye called masters : for one is your Master, *even* Christ.

It is most certain that our Saviour doth not here forbid the giving of the titles of masters and fathers to his ministers, for then Paul would not have given himself the title of father, 1 Cor. iv. 15 ; nor called the Galatians his little children, Gal. iv. 19 : nor called Timothy his son, and himself his father, Phil. ii. 22 ; nor called himself a doctor of the Gentiles, 1 Tim. ii. 7 ; 2 Tim. i. 11. That which he forbids is, 1. An affectation of such titles, and hunting after them. 2. *Rem tituli,* the exercise of an absolute mastership, or a paternal, absolute power ; so as to require any to believe things because they said them, or to do things because they bid them, without seeing the things asserted, or first commanded, in the word of God. For in that sense God alone is men's Father, Christ alone their Master. Pastors and teachers in the church are all but ministers, ministers of Christ to publish his will, and to enjoin his laws; nor must any be owned as masters and fathers, to impose their laws and doctrines. This is twice repeated, because such is the corruption of human nature, that it is very prone, not only to affect these swelling titles, but also to exercise these exorbitant authorities.

i ch. 20. 26, 27.
k Job 22. 29.
Prov. 15. 33.
& 29. 23.
Luke 14. 11.
& 18. 14.
Jam. 4. 6.
1 Pet. 5. 5.

11 But ⁱhe that is greatest among you shall be your servant.

12 ᵏAnd whosoever shall exalt himself shall be abased; and he that shall humble himself shall be exalted.

We have what is in ver. 12 twice in Luke, chap. xiv. 11; xviii. 14. These verses expound what went before, and let us know, 1. That it was not a title, but the affectation of a title, which he blamed. 2. Not a doctorship, or mastership, but such a doctorship or mastership as made a man too big for the ministry of the church; such honour as lifted up the man's heart above his work. He is an infamous doctor in the church of Christ, who thinks himself too high or too great to be a minister in it. For God will abase, and men shall abase, him who exalteth himself. God resisteth, and men usually contemn and despise, the proud, especially ministers who are so. Both God shall exalt, and men shall honour, those that humble themselves, both to men, condescending to those of low degree, and to their work, thinking not the meanest ministry to souls a work beneath them.

l Luke 11. 52.

13 ¶ But ˡwoe unto you, Scribes and Pharisees, hypocrites! for ye shut up the kingdom of heaven against men: for ye neither go in *yourselves*, neither suffer ye them that are entering to go in.

Our Saviour now cometh to denounce eight woes against the teachers of those times, the scribes and Pharisees. Luke saith, chap. xi. 52, *Woe unto you, lawyers! for ye have taken away the key of knowledge: ye enter not in yourselves, and them that were entering in ye hindered.* It was written of old, that *the priest's lips should preserve knowledge:* God hath committed the key of knowledge to the ministers and guides of his church, not that they should take it away, but that the people might *seek the law at their mouths, because they are the messengers of the Lord of hosts,* Mal. ii. 7. Now saith our Saviour, you have taken it away: this Matthew calls a shutting up the kingdom of heaven against men; doing what in them lay to keep men from the knowledge of the mind and will of God, neither themselves teaching them the knowledge of God, which yet was their office and duty, nor suffering others to do it who would. You will neither go in yourselves, neither will you suffer them that are entering to go in. Yourselves are too proud, or lazy, to preach the gospel, which is the way to the kingdom of heaven, and when others would, you suffer them not; nor yet will you suffer the people, who have a heart to it, to hear it. For this he calls them *hypocrites* seven times in this chapter, they pretending to be teachers, and openers of the door to the kingdom of heaven, when indeed they did shut it; and denounceth a woe to them, comprehending that ruin which soon after came upon them and their city by the Roman armies, and that eternal damnation which slept not, and was due to them. There are no worse men in the world than hypocrites, men pretending highly to God, yet neither themselves doing their duty in embracing the gospel, nor suffering others to do it, but doing what in them lie to hinder people from the means by which they might come to the kingdom of heaven.

m Mark 12. 40. Luke 20. 47. 2 Tim. 3. 6. Tit. 1. 11.

14 Woe unto you, Scribes and Pharisees, hypocrites! ᵐfor ye devour widows' houses, and for a pretence make long prayer: therefore ye shall receive the greater damnation.

Mark hath the same, chap. xii. 40, and Luke, chap. xx. 47. If any should think that long prayers are here condemned, he will be confuted by Luke vi. 12, where he will find that *our Saviour continued all night in prayer to God.*

It is the end of their long prayers which alone our Saviour blameth, their making them a *pretence to devour widows' houses;* which whether they did as interested in the civil power, (in which it is certain the Pharisees amongst the Jews were employed,) or by virtue of their ecclesiastical power or influence, persuading silly women to give them their estates, or at least to give them a great part of them, to the service of the tabernacle, that they might pray for their souls, was an abomination to God, not only for the hypocrisy of such prayers, designed for another end than they pretended, but because God had taken upon him the special care and protection of the widows. As our Saviour had before blamed their religious acts for the ostentation in them, seeking only their own honour and applause, so he here blameth them for their covetous design in them.

15 Woe unto you, Scribes and Pharisees, hypocrites! for ye compass sea and land to make one proselyte, and when he is made, ye make him twofold more the child of hell than yourselves.

A third woe followeth, expressed in this verse, because they corrupted their proselytes, both as to doctrine and manners, so as they were twice more the children of the devil, and in danger of hell, than before. A proselyte was one who, coming from some pagan nation, relinquished idols, and worshipped one true and living God. Of these writers tell us there were two sorts; one that only professed to believe and worship one God, though he did not embrace the Jewish religion: such a one they suffered to live amongst them, and called him a *proselyte of the gate.* Others embraced the Jewish religion, and were admitted into their church, by circumcision, and baptism, and sacrifice (as their writers tell us): these they called *proselytes of righteousness.* Our Saviour saith the scribes and Pharisees compassed sea and land, that is, would take any pains, (it is a proverbial expression,) to make one a proselyte; nor was this blameworthy in them, but that which followeth, that they made him twofold more the child of hell than before; corrupting him with their false doctrine, and setting him examples of an ill life. Their business was not to turn men from sin unto God, but merely to convert them to an opinion, if they had once got them into their church, so as they could make their markets of them; never regarding their souls more, nor to press upon them the reformation of their lives, that they might be saved. Thus priests and Jesuits at this day go to China, Japan, to proselyte men to the Roman faith; and use all imaginable arts to seduce persons born and bred under the profession of the protestant religion in protestant countries, and boast much of their converts; but he who looks upon the Scriptures, and considereth the lives of the most of their converts, will easily see they are but twice more the children of hell, being licensed, by their indulgences, pardons, absolutions, nay, by their very casuists, to live most prodigious impious lives, to say nothing of their damnable errors in matters of faith.

n ch 15. 14. ver. 24.
o ch. 5. 33, 34.

16 Woe unto you, ⁿye blind guides, which say, ᵒWhosoever shall swear by the temple, it is nothing; but whosoever shall swear by the gold of the temple, he is a debtor!

p Ex. 30. 29.

17 Ye fools and blind: for whether is greater, the gold, ᵖor the temple that sanctifieth the gold?

18 And, Whosoever shall swear by the altar, it is nothing; but whosoever sweareth by the gift that is upon it, he is ||guilty.

|| Or, *debtor*, or, *bound*.

q Ex. 29. 37.

19 *Ye* fools and blind: for whether *is* greater, the gift, or ᑫthe altar that sanctifieth the gift?

20 Whoso therefore shall swear by the altar, sweareth by it, and by all things thereon.

r 1 Kin. 8. 13
2 Chron. 6. 2.
Ps. 26. 8.
& 132. 14.

21 And whoso shall swear by the temple, sweareth by it, and by ʳhim that dwelleth therein.

22 And he that shall swear by heaven,

sweareth by *the throne of God, and by him that sitteth thereon.

<small>s ch. 5. 34. Ps. 11. 4. Acts 7. 49.</small>

Our Saviour here showeth the false doctrine which the Pharisees, for their own gain, taught the people concerning oaths. God had commanded that they should fear and serve the Lord their God, and swear by his name, Deut. vi. 13; x. 20. He that sweareth by any person, or thing, doth two things: 1. He attributeth to the thing, or person, by which he sweareth, a knowledge of the heart and the secret intention. 2. He calleth upon the person, or thing, by which he sweareth, to be his judge, or to take a revenge upon him, in case he doth not believe in his heart what he affirmeth or denieth with his words to be true or false; otherwise an oath is no security at all. From whence appeareth, that it is unreasonable for any to swear by any other than God, who alone can have a knowledge of the truth, and security of the heart; and that he who sweareth by any creature committeth idolatry in his heart, and in his heart doth indeed blaspheme, paying a Divine homage to a creature, and attributing to the creature what only agreeth to the Creator. The Pharisees, as it seemeth, had taught the people, that it was lawful to swear by the creature, but all oaths by creatures did not bind to the performance of the thing promised by such oaths: if a man swear by *the temple*, or by *the altar*, it was nothing, no man was bound by such oaths to perform the thing for which such oaths were given as a security. But if any man swear by *the gold of the temple*, or by a *gift* which he brought to the altar, these oaths did bind him. By *the gold of the temple* is not to be understood the golden vessels used in the temple, nor the golden plates with which the several parts of the temple shined; but the gold which was brought as an offering into the temple, and put into the treasury there; of which, and of the gifts, the priests and officers about the temple had a considerable share, which made them equalize an oath by these to an oath made by the name of God itself. 1. Our Saviour here showed the unreasonable folly of the tradition, and calleth them for it *blind guides;* for in reason, the temple sanctifying the gold must itself be more especially holy, that is, separate for a holy use. The temple was holy, so was the altar, before the gold was brought into it, but the gold was not holy till it was brought into the holy place, and there offered. 2. He lets them know, that oaths by the creatures once made did oblige, as much as if they had been made by God himself. They were indeed sinfully made, for men ought not to have sworn by creatures; but being made, those who made them were bound to perform them, if the matter of them were not sinful. For he that swears *by the altar, swears by it, and by all the things thereon;* and he who swears *by the temple, swears by it, and by him that dwelleth therein;* and he who swears *by heaven, swears by the throne of God, and by him that sitteth thereon.* For none who sware by inanimate things could possibly be imagined to call these things, which he knew had no life, no sense, no knowledge, to be a witness to the truth of his heart, as to what he believed, or what he intended. So as though he that sweareth by the creature be a profane swearer, yet he is bound by his oath, he indeed swearing by the God of those creatures. He hath reason to repent of the profane and unlawful form of his oath, but if the matter be what he may without sin perform, he is bound by his oath to the performance of it.

23 Woe unto you, Scribes and Pharisees, hypocrites! ^tfor ye pay tithe of mint and † anise and cummin, and ^u have omitted the weightier *matters* of the law, judgment, mercy, and faith: these ought ye to have done, and not to leave the other undone.

<small>t Luke 11. 42. † Gr. ἄνηθον, dill. u 1 Sam. 15. 22. Hos. 6. 6. Mic. 6. 8. ch. 9. 13. & 12. 7.</small>

We have much the same Luke xi. 42, only there it is, *Ye tithe mint and rue and all manner of herbs, and pass over judgment and the love of God.* It is manifest by our Saviour's words in the latter part of the verse, *these ought ye to have done*, that he doth not blame the Pharisees' exactness in tithing mint, anise, rue, cummin, and all manner of herbs; but their neglecting the weightier matters of the law, faith and love to God, judgment and mercy. The Levites having no inheritance, God ordained tithes for their maintenance; of which also the poor were to have a share, Lev. xxvii. 30; Numb. xviii. 24. The Pharisee boasted, Luke xviii. 12, that he paid tithe of all he possessed. Christ here acknowledgeth that the Pharisees were exact in their paying tithes; but he blames them, 1. For their partiality, neglecting the weightier things of the law. 2. For their hypocrisy; they were only exact in these little things, that they might be taken notice of as scrupulous observers of the Divine law; while they omitted those things, which were of much more weight, which he reckoneth up: *faith*, by which some understand faith in God, but the most, faithfulness, and sincere and honest dealings with men, in opposition to fraud, and cheating, and circumventions. *Judgment*, by which he means justice, giving to every one what is their own. *Mercy*, by which he means a charitable behaviour, in helping such as are miserable and afflicted. *Love to God*, which is the true root, out of which all things should flow, and is indeed comprehensive of all our duty toward God, as well as the root of all our good works towards men.

24 *Ye* blind guides, which strain at a gnat, and swallow a camel.

It is a proverbial expression used amongst them, against such as would pretend a great niceness and scrupulosity about, and zeal for, little things, but in matters of much higher concern and moment were not nice and scrupulous at all: and this indeed is both a certain note and an ordinary practice of hypocrites. There is no man that is sincere in his obedience to God, but hath respect to all God's commandments, Psal. cxix. 6. Though some duties be greater, of more moment for the honour and glory of God, than others, which a good man will lay the greatest stress upon, yet he will neglect nothing which the law of God enjoineth him. But concerning hypocrites, these two things are always true: 1. They are partial in their pretended obedience. 2. They always lay the greatest stress upon the least things of the law, bodily labour and exercise, and those things which require least of the heart, and least self-denial.

25 Woe unto you, Scribes and Pharisees, hypocrites! ^xfor ye make clean the outside of the cup and of the platter, but within they are full of extortion and excess.

<small>x Mark 7. 4. Luke 11. 39.</small>

26 *Thou* blind Pharisee, cleanse first that *which is* within the cup and platter, that the outside of them may be clean also.

Luke hath this, chap. xi. 39, 40, as occasioned by the Pharisees wondering that he washed not before dinner; instead of *extortion and excess*, he hath *ravening and wickedness*, and addeth, *Ye fools, did not he that made that which is without make that which is within also?* But the same thing might be spoken at two several times. He speaks there to the Pharisee, with whom he dined, ver. 37. Here he speaks to the disciples and the multitude. Our Saviour's design here seemeth to me not to be a condemning of their legal or traditional washings of pots and cups, which he elsewhere reflecteth upon, but, by way of allusion only, to blame them that in their whole conversation they rather studied an external purity, than the inward purity of the heart, whereas if they would first have looked at purity of heart, the other would have followed that. A man may be outwardly pure, and inwardly filthy and impure; but no man can have a pure heart, but he will live a pure and holy life, for the external acts are but the imperate acts of the soul: *Out of the abundance of the heart the mouth speaketh*, and according to the inclinations and affections of the heart the foot moveth, the hand and all the bodily members act. For our Saviour's application of this to their traditional washings, I shall speak to it when I come to Luke xi. 39.

27 Woe unto you, Scribes and Pharisees, hypocrites! ^yfor ye are like unto whited sepulchres, which indeed appear beautiful outward, but are within full of dead *men's* bones, and of all uncleanness.

<small>y Luke 11. 44. Acts 23. 3.</small>

28 Even so ye also outwardly appear righteous

unto men, but within ye are full of hypocrisy and iniquity.

The similitude is of the same import with the other, to show that the Pharisees had only a vizard of strictness and holiness, when in the mean time their hearts were full of lusts, hypocrisy, and iniquity. The Jews had two sorts of graves; some for ordinary persons, which appeared not (to which our Saviour likened the Pharisees, Luke xi. 44); others that were covered with tombs, which were wont to be kept whited, so as they looked very fair outwardly, but had within nothing but rottenness and putrefaction. To these he compareth them in this place. They were men that made a great show, but had nothing of any inward purity or cleanness, but were full of iniquity. Thus Paul called Ananias a *whited wall*; and, Psal. v. 9, the psalmist saith of the throat of the wicked that it is *an open sepulchre*.

z Luke 11. 47.

29 ᶻWoe unto you, Scribes and Pharisees, hypocrites! because ye build the tombs of the prophets, and garnish the sepulchres of the righteous,

30 And say, If we had been in the days of our fathers, we would not have been partakers with them in the blood of the prophets.

Luke hath it, chap. xi. 47, *Woe unto you! for ye build the sepulchres of the prophets, and your fathers killed them. Truly ye bear witness that ye allow the deeds of your fathers: for they indeed killed them, and ye build their sepulchres.* It is plain by our Saviour's discourse, that the Pharisees were at great charge ofttimes to rebuild or adorn the sepulchres of the Lord's prophets, who had been slain by the Jews in former ages for testifying the truth of God, and the sepulchres of other righteous men dying for their righteousness. This they did like a company of hypocrites, to persuade the world of what they also said, that had they lived in the times of those prophets and other good men, they would have had no hand in their blood.

31 Wherefore ye be witnesses unto yourselves, that ᵃye are the children of them which killed the prophets.

a Acts 7. 51. 52. 1 Thess. 2. 15.

32 ᵇFill ye up then the measure of your fathers.

b Gen. 15. 16. 1 Thess. 2. 16.

33 *Ye* serpents, *ye* ᶜgeneration of vipers, how can ye escape the damnation of hell?

c ch. 3. 7. & 12. 34.

You (saith our Lord) confess that you are lineally descended from those who killed the prophets: you have not only their blood communicated to you, but their spirit; your behaviours and carriages towards me and my disciples have witnessed, and will yet further testify, that you are the children of those who killed the prophets in a moral as well as a natural sense; you inherit the same spirit, and are full of the same malice and rancour. They killed them, and you bury them: seeing there is no reclaiming you, go you on, fill up the measure of your fathers' sins. There is something more to be added to make the iniquity of this nation full. You are a company of serpents, vipers, that cannot escape the damnation of hell.

d ch. 21. 34, 35. Luke 11. 49.

34 ¶ᵈWherefore, behold, I send unto you prophets, and wise men, and scribes:

e Acts 5. 40. & 7. 58, 59. & 22 19. f ch. 10. 17. 2 Cor. 11. 24, 25.

and ᵉ*some* of them ye shall kill and crucify; and ᶠ*some* of them shall ye scourge in your synagogues, and persecute *them* from city to city.

g Rev. 18. 24.

35 ᵍThat upon you may come all the righteous blood shed upon the earth, ʰfrom the blood of righteous Abel unto ⁱthe blood of Zacharias son of Barachias, whom ye slew between the temple and the altar.

h Gen. 4. 8. 1 John 3. 12. i 2 Chron. 24. 20, 21.

36 Verily I say unto you, All these things shall come upon this generation.

Luke saith, chap. xi. 49—51, *Therefore also said the wisdom of God, I will send them prophets and apostles, and some of them they shall slay and persecute: that the blood of all the prophets, which was shed from the foundation of the world, may be required of this generation; from the blood of Abel unto the blood of Zacharias, which perished between the altar and the temple: verily I say unto you, It shall be required of this generation.* Luke saith, Therefore also said *the wisdom of God.* Matthew saith, *Behold, I send.* Christ is *the wisdom of God;* he here tells them he would send them *prophets, wise men, scribes.* Luke expounds it by *prophets and apostles;* men authorized by Christ to reveal unto men the will of God, and men that should be extraordinarily inspired to enable them thereunto. *Scribes,* that is, persons instructed to the kingdom of God; a new sort of scribes, but much fitter for their work than the present scribes. *And some ye shall kill and crucify, &c.:* our Lord in this only foretells what usage both himself and his apostles should meet with from them, which was fulfilled in what the Scripture telleth us of the scourging of Paul, the stoning of Stephen, the killing of James, &c., beside the crucifying of himself. *That upon you,* that is, as he expounds it, ver. 36, *upon this generation, may come all the righteous blood,* that is, the blood of righteous men, *shed upon the earth, from the blood of righteous Abel to the blood of Zacharias son of Barachias, &c.* Here arise two questions: 1. Who this *Zacharias the son of Barachias* was. 2. How it could stand with God's justice to bring the guilt of the blood of former generations upon that generation. As to the first, some have guessed the person spoken of to have been one Zacharias the son of Baruch, who was the last slain upon the taking of Jerusalem, as Josephus tells us: but our Saviour here speaks of a thing passed, not to be afterwards done. Others think it was Zacharias the father of John Baptist: but we have no proof that he died a violent death. Others think it was Zechariah, who was one of the small prophets: but there was no temple in his time. It is most probably concluded to be Zechariah, the son of Jehoiada, whom the Jews *stoned with stones at the commandment of Joash in the court of the house of the Lord,* 2 Chron. xxiv. 21. The father's name indeed doth not agree; but, first, Jehoiada (as many of the Jews had) might have two names: some think it was this same Zechariah who is called *the son of Jeberechiah,* Isa. viii. 2. Our Saviour nameth *Abel,* who lived before the law, and *Zacharias,* who lived under the law, both slain for righteousness' sake; that under them he might comprehend all the martyrs slain in those two periods. Others judge, that these two are named because we read of Abel's blood crying, Gen. iv. 10, and Zechariah's praying (when he died) that the Lord would require his blood. For the other question, it is but righteous with God to punish the sins of parents upon their children; and though such vengeance doth not ordinarily reach further than the third and fourth generation, yet where succeeding generations go on in the same sinful courses, it may reach further, and often does. Isa. lxv. 6, 7, *I will* (saith God) *recompense into their bosom your iniquities, and the iniquities of your fathers together.* That was the case here. They filled up the measure of their fathers' sins. Therefore Christ tells them, that vengeance should sleep no longer, but come upon that generation, which happened in the utter destruction of Jerusalem within less than forty years after. Our Lord concludes with a pathetical lamentation over Jerusalem, and a further confirmation of what he had said about their ruin.

37 ᵏO Jerusalem, Jerusalem, *thou* that killest the prophets, ˡand stonest them which are sent unto thee, how often would ᵐI have gathered thy children together, even as a hen gathereth her chickens ⁿunder *her* wings, and ye would not!

k Luke 13. 34. l 2 Chr. 24. 21. m Deut. 32. 11, 12. 2 Esd. 1. 30. n Ps. 17. 8. & 91. 4.

38 Behold, your house is left unto you desolate.

39 For I say unto you, Ye shall not see me henceforth, till ye shall say, ᵒBlessed *is* he that cometh in the name of the Lord.

o Ps. 118. 26. ch. 21. 9.

We have the same Luke xiii. 34, 35. *O Jerusalem, Jerusalem!* The doubling of the word showeth the vehemency of our Saviour's affection. *Thou that killest the prophets, and stonest them which are sent unto thee;* that hast killed, and abused, and art yet going on to do the like, not taking notice of the vengeance of God upon thee before for this very sin, 2 Chron. xxxvi. 16, 17; Neh. ix. 26, 27. *How often would I have gathered thee*, giving thee all external means proper to have reformed thee and reconciled thee to God, *as a hen gathereth her chickens under her wings!* which if thou hadst accepted and embraced, the chickens are not safer under the wings of the hen from the danger of a kite than thou wouldst have been from enemies. But thou wouldst not; instead of hearkening to my prophets, thou killedst them, and didst stone those sent unto thee, and so didst voluntarily reject me, and all my offers and tenders of grace, mercy, and protection, through the mere obstinacy of thy perverse will. *Behold, your house is left unto you desolate;* both the temple, in which you place such a confidence, and your own dwelling-houses, shall be destroyed, burnt, and razed down, or at least left without you as inhabitants. *For I say unto you, Ye shall not see me henceforth, till ye shall say, Blessed is he that cometh in the name of the Lord:* I will appear no more to you as a public preacher, after two or three days, for ever; and you, that the other day so envied the people's acclamations to me, *Blessed is he that cometh in the name of the Lord*, shall be glad yourselves to see *one of the days of the Son of man*, and shall say the same thing, *Blessed is he*, &c. For whereas some interpret the term *till*, &c. of the day of judgment, or the time when the Jews shall be converted, I take them to be strained interpretations. *Till* here certainly is to be interpreted, as Psal. cx. 1, and Matt. i. 25; and this comporteth with the history, for after this time our Saviour appeared in the temple publicly no more. For the disputes raised from ver. 37, about God's secret will, whether he seriously willed the salvation of the Jews, &c., I take the affirmative part to have no foundation in this text, for *would I* is plainly enough here interpreted by the foregoing word, *sending* them *prophets*, and other ministers, to persuade them to repentance and reconciliation with God; as the use of means proper to an end appear to us indications of the will of him that useth them.

CHAP. XXIV.

Christ foretelleth the destruction of the temple, 1, 2. *He showeth what signs and calamities shall go before it; and what shall happen at the time of his coming*, 3—31. *By a parable of the fig tree he marketh the certainty of the prediction*, 32—35. *No man knoweth the day and hour, which shall come suddenly*, 36—41. *We ought therefore to watch, like good servants who expect their master's coming*, 42—51.

a Mark 13. 1.
Luke 21. 5.

AND ᵃJesus went out, and departed from the temple: and his disciples came to *him* for to shew him the buildings of the temple.

2 And Jesus said unto them, See ye not all these things? verily I say unto you, ᵇThere shall not be left here one stone upon another, that shall not be thrown down.

b 1 Kin. 9. 7.
Jer. 26. 18.
Mic. 3. 12.
Luke 19. 44.

Mark saith, chap. xiii. 1, 2, *one of his disciples*. Luke saith, chap. xxi. 5, *some*. Mark saith, the disciple said, *Master, what manner of stones and what buildings are here!* Luke saith, they spake how the temple *was adorned with goodly stones and gifts*. All three evangelists agree in the substance of our Saviour's reply. Christ had now done his work in the temple, where he never came more, and was going toward the Mount of Olives, where we shall find him in the next verse. His disciples, either one of them or more, probably one in the presence of the rest, either doubting (considering the structure of the temple) whether it could be destroyed, or at least thinking it pity that so famous a structure should come to ruin, come to him, admiring the stones and buildings. Most think this was the temple builded by Zorobabel, almost six hundred years before, though it received great additions by Herod (for we have no record that that temple was ever destroyed). Incredible stories are related about the dimensions of the stones, and the ornaments of it. Our Saviour saith unto them, *Verily I say unto you, There shall not be left here one stone upon another;* that is, this brave, goodly temple shall be utterly ruined. Nor (if we may believe other histories) did this prophecy fail as to the letter of it. Titus, the Roman emperor, taking Jerusalem, about forty years after this, commanded his soldiers to spare the temple when they entered the city, but they in their rage burnt of it what was of a combustible nature; and Turnus Rufus, left general of his army when he went away, drew a plough over it, as God had said, Jer. xxvi. 18; Micah iii. 12, *Zion shall be ploughed like a field*. And when after this Alippius, by the command of Julian the apostate, attempted the rebuilding of it, with the help of the Jews, it is reported by divers, that balls or globes of fire rose up from the foundations, destroyed many of the workmen, and made the place inaccessible for any further such attempts. So justly are the Divine threatenings to be feared, whatever improbability of the contrary appeareth to us. We are very apt to be taken with the glistering prosperity of sinners, but we ought to measure the duration of it from the revelations of the Divine will, not from our own reason or fancy; to remember the temple of Jerusalem. There are no places so strong but an almighty God is able to destroy, and sin is enough to blow up. We may also observe how little God values splendid houses of prayer when they are made dens of thieves.

3 ¶ And as he sat upon the mount of Olives, ᶜthe disciples came unto him privately, saying, ᵈTell us, when shall these things be? and what *shall be* the sign of thy coming, and of the end of the world?

c Mark 13. 3.
d 1 Thess. 5. 1.

4 And Jesus answered and said unto them, ᵉTake heed that no man deceive you.

e Eph. 5. 6.
Col. 2. 8, 18.
2 Thess. 2. 3.
1 John 4. 1.

Mark saith, chap. xiii. 3—5, *And as he sat upon the mount of Olives over against the temple, Peter and James and John and Andrew asked him privately, Tell us, when shall these things be? and what shall be the sign when all these things shall be fulfilled? And Jesus answering them began to say, Take heed lest any man deceive you.* Luke saith, chap. xxi. 7, 8, *And they asked him, saying, Master, but when shall these things be? and what sign will there be when these things shall come to pass? And he said, Take heed that ye be not deceived.* Mark names the disciples which came to our Saviour privately, *Peter, James, John, and Andrew*. They seem to propound three questions to him: 1. What should be the sign of the destruction of Jerusalem? 2. Of his coming? 3. Of the end of the world? It is probable they might send these four to propound these questions to our Saviour. three of them being such to whom Christ had showed signal and special favour before. Some doubt whether the questions propounded were three or two; if but two, the coming of Christ must either be the same with the first, or with the last. Those who understand Christ's coming as a distinct period from the other two, think that the disciples refer to that secular kingdom which they fancied that the Messiah should exercise in the world. They desire to know the signs of these times, that is, prognostic signs, which might beforehand instruct them that the time was nigh, even at hand. They name two things here which time hath told us were to be at more than sixteen hundred years' distance one from the other, for historians tell us that Jerusalem was destroyed within seventy or seventy-one years after our Saviour's birth, within less than forty years after this discourse; but it is probable that they put them together, as believing that Jerusalem should not be destroyed till the day when Christ should come to judge the world, and that the end of the world and of the Jewish state should come together. And as we all are naturally curious to know things that are to come, so these disciples were in this thing particularly curious, having some particular apprehensions of the coming and kingdom of Christ, according to the mistaken notion which the Jews had of that kingdom which their expected Messiah should exercise in the world. Our blessed Lord at another time, Acts i. 7, told them it was not for them *to know the times or the seasons, which the Father hath put in his own power*. He therefore giveth them no such certain signs of these things, as they could from them certainly conclude the particular time; but yet gives them some signs from whence they might conclude, when they saw them, that the time was hastening; which signs, though some have distinguished, appropriating those in the former part of the chapter to the destruction of Jerusalem, and those in the latter part to the day of judgment, yet they rather seem in our Saviour's discourse mixed together; and time, which is the best interpreter of prophecies, must expound them to us. The destruction of Jerusalem is a thing past many hundreds of years since; so as by those histories which we have partly in holy writ, partly in other authors, it will not be hard to pick out what our Saviour intended for signs of that destruction, though there are some signs which were common signs both of that destruction and of the end of the world, and it is agreed by divines that the destruction of Jerusalem was a type of the destruction of the world, and therefore most of the signs are common to both. Paul was brought to Rome in the beginning of the reign of Nero, Acts xxvii. Other historians tell us he and Peter were put to death about the end of his reign; within a year or two after Jerusalem was destroyed. Our Saviour prefaceth his discourse of these signs with a usual caution to his disciples, *Take heed that no man deceive you.*

f Jer. 14. 14.
& 23. 21, 25.
ver. 24.
John 5. 43.
g ver. 11.

5 For ^fmany shall come in my name, saying, I am Christ; ^gand shall deceive many.

Mark hath the same, chap. xiii. 6. Luke saith, chap. xxi. 8, *Many shall come in my name, saying, I am Christ; and the time draweth near: go ye not after them.* Our Saviour seemeth to have given this as a sign common both to the destruction of Jerusalem and the end of the world, though possibly before the destruction of Jerusalem,,while the Jews were in expectation of a Messiah as a temporal prince or deliverer, there were more of them than afterward, for every one who could get a party together to colour his sedition and rebellion, gave out himself to be the Christ. Of this number are said to have been Theudas, and Judas of Galilee, mentioned by Gamaliel, Acts v. 36, 37. Amongst these some also reckon the Egyptian mentioned Acts xxi. 38, and Simon Magus, who gave out himself to be *some great one*, and the people accounted him *the great power of God.* Such there have been, and probably may be more toward the end of the world. Many were deceived by the impostors: Christ warneth his disciples concerning them.

6 And ye shall hear of wars and rumours of wars: see that ye be not troubled: for all *these things* must come to pass, but the end is not yet.

h 2 Chr. 15.
6, Is. 19. 2.
Hag. 2. 22.
Zech. 14. 13.

7 For ^hnation shall rise against nation, and kingdom against kingdom: and there shall be famines, and pestilences, and earthquakes, in divers places.

8 All these *are* the beginning of sorrows.

Mark hath the same, chap. xiii. 7, 8. Luke hath also much the same, chap. xxi. 9—11, only he addeth, *fearful sights and great signs shall there be from heaven.* Interpreters think this prophecy did chiefly respect the destruction of Jerusalem, for the time from our Saviour's death to that time was full of seditions and insurrections, both in Judea and elsewhere. The truth of our Saviour's words as to this is attested by Josephus largely, from the eleventh chapter of his second book of the Wars of the Jews to the end of the fourth book. Besides that there were great wars between Otho, and Vitellius, and Vespasian, the Roman emperor who succeeded Nero, we read of one famine, Acts xi. 28, which Agabus there prophesied should be in the time of Claudius Cæsar. Of earthquakes in several places mention is made in divers histories. Our Saviour tells them that these things should be, but the end should not be presently, which any one that will read Josephus's history of the Wars of the Jews, will see abundantly verified upon the taking of Jerusalem by the Roman armies.

i ch. 10. 17.
Mark 13. 9.
Luke 21. 12.
John 15. 20.
& 16. 2.
Acts 4. 2, 3.
& 7. 59.& 12.
1, &c. 1 Pet.
4. 16. Rev. 2. 10, 13.

9 ⁱThen shall they deliver you up to be afflicted, and shall kill you: and ye shall be hated of all nations for my name's sake.

Mark hath this thus, chap. xiii. 9, *But take heed to yourselves: for they shall deliver you up to councils; and in the synagogues ye shall be beaten: and ye shall be brought before rulers and kings for my sake, for a testimony against them.* Luke saith. chap. xxi. 12, 13, *But before all these, they shall lay their hands on you, and persecute you, delivering you up to the synagogues, and into prisons, being brought before kings and rulers for my name's sake. And it shall turn to you for a testimony.* Our Saviour, knowing that his disciples' minds still ran upon a secular kingdom, here calls off their thoughts by giving them a sign of his coming, an account of those persecutions and trials which they should undergo before his coming, either in his power to the destruction of the Jews, or in his glory at the last day: the afflictions specified are, a being hated of all nations, delivered up to councils, beating in the synagogues, casting into prisons, and being killed; all which happened to the disciples of Christ before the destruction of Jerusalem. The Christians were counted a *sect every where spoken against*, Acts xxviii. 22. Stephen was stoned, Acts vii. 59. James was killed with the sword, Acts xii. 2. Paul and Silas were imprisoned, Acts xvi. 23. Paul *five times received of the Jews forty-stripes save one;* he was *thrice beaten with rods, once stoned,* 2 Cor. xi. 24, 25. He was brought before king Agrippa and Festus. Peter and John were called before the council, Acts iv. 7; v. 21. So as all these things happened before the destruction of Jerusalem, and this may be interpreted as a sign of that great destruction; but not of that only, for the text saith, *ye shall be hated of all nations,* which came to pass afterward, when Christianity was persecuted by heathens for three hundred years together. Mark saith, this should be done *for a testimony against them,* that is, the persecutors. Luke saith, *it shall turn to you for a testimony.* The persecutions of Christians are, 1. A testimony against the persecutors, of their ingratitude, and cruelty, and hatred to the name of Christ. 2. They are a testimony to the persecuted, of their faith, and patience, and courage, &c.

10 And then shall many ^kbe offended, and shall betray one another, and shall hate one another.

k ch. 11. 6.
& 13. 57.
2 Tim. 1. 15.
& 4. 10, 16.

Mark saith, chap. xiii. 12, 13, *The brother shall betray the brother to death, and the father the son; and children shall rise up against their parents, and cause them to be put to death. And ye shall be hated of all men for my name's sake.* Luke saith, chap. xxi. 16, 17, *And ye shall be betrayed both by parents, and brethren, and kinsfolks, and friends; and some of you shall they cause to be put to death. And ye shall be hated of all men for my name's sake. Many shall be offended;* the meaning is, shall turn apostates, stumbling at these great afflictions and persecutions for the gospel. *And shall betray one another.* We read of several apostates in holy writ, such as Phigellus, Hermogenes, Demas, Hymeneus, Philetus, and others; but all things not being written that were done, we have no particular record of such treachery as is here mentioned. But it is no other than we may reasonably presume was done, though we had not been assured of it, to justify our Saviour's prediction. There is no time of great persecution but proves a time of great apostacy and some treachery. It hath been a constant observation, that no hatred flames to that degree with hatred upon the account of religion. Nor is what our Saviour here predicted more than the history of all ages of the church have justified.

11 And ^lmany false prophets shall rise, and ^mshall deceive many.

l ch. 7. 15.
Acts 20. 29.
2 Pet. 2. 1.
m 1 Tim. 4. 1. ver. 5, 24.

12 And because iniquity shall abound, the love of many shall wax cold.

Here are two signs more given: 1. The abounding of false teachers. 2. The abatements of Christians' zeal, and love to God. For the matter of the 11th verse, we shall meet with it more fully ver. 23, 24. By the aboundings of iniquity here, we may either understand the rage, and malice, and cruelty of the enemies of the gospel; or the apostacy of such as are professors. Both these are great temptations, and though they will not extinguish that holy fire which God hath kindled in good souls, yet they have oftentimes a very ill influence upon them, to abate of their former warmth in the ways of God. Or if we understand it of love to brethren, the apostacy of professors much cooleth the Christian, not knowing who they may trust and confide in as sincere. If by the abounding of iniquity we understand the abounding of profaneness in the general, (which always also aboundeth most in times of persecution,) that also hath no small influence upon Christians' warmth in their profession, to cool and abate it: see Heb. x. 25; 2 Tim. i. 15; iv. 16.

n ch. 10. 22.
Mark 13. 13.
Heb. 3. 6,14.
Rev. 2. 10.

13 ⁿBut he that shall endure unto the end, the same shall be saved.

We have the same Mark xiii. 13. We also met with it before, chap. x. 22. It is a promise to perseverance, especially to such perseverance as is joined with fortitude. He that shall not be tempted to apostacy through the afflictions of the gospel, but shall patiently and courageously endure all the sufferings which shall follow the profession of the gospel, shall be saved; if not preserved, and so saved with a temporal salvation, yet he shall be eternally saved.

o ch. 4. 23.
& 9. 35.
p Rom. 10. 18. Col. 1. 6, 23.

14 And this °Gospel of the kingdom ᵖshall be preached in all the world for a witness unto all nations; and then shall the end come.

So saith Mark, chap. xiii. 10. Some think that *the end* mentioned in the close of this verse refers to the destruction of Jerusalem; others, that it referreth to the day of judgment. If we take *world* (as it is often taken) for the Gentiles in opposition to the Jews, synecdochically, the whole being put for a great part, it is most certain, that before Jerusalem was destroyed, the gospel, which is here called the gospel of the kingdom, either because it shows the way to the kingdom of God, or because it is that sacred instrument by which Christ subdueth men's hearts to himself, was preached to the world, that is, to the Gentiles, and that to a great part of them. Paul alone had carried it from Jerusalem to Illyricum. The Romans' faith was spoken of throughout the world, Rom. i. 8. Paul saith it was *preached to every creature*, Col. i. 23: see also Rom. x. 18; xv. 16; Col. i. 6; 1 Tim. iii. 16. But others choose by *the end* here to understand the end of the world.

q Mark 13. 14.
Luke 21. 20.
r Dan. 9. 27. & 12. 11.
s Dan. 9. 23, 25.

15 ᑫWhen ye therefore shall see the abomination of desolation, spoken of by ʳDaniel the prophet, stand in the holy place, (ˢwhoso readeth, let him understand:)

Mark saith, chap. xiii. 14, *standing where it ought not*. Here are two questions: 1. What is here meant by *the abomination of desolation*. 2. What text in Daniel our Lord referreth to. As to the latter, there are three places in Daniel which mention it: chap. ix. 27, *for the overspreading of abominations,* or, as it is in the margin, with the abominable armies he shall make it desolate. Chap. xi. 31, *They shall place the abomination that maketh desolate*. Chap. xii. 11, *From the time that the daily sacrifice shall be taken away, and the abomination that maketh desolate set up*. Mr. Calvin thinks that the text in Daniel here referred to is that chap. xii. 11. Others say that it is that chap. ix. 27, contending that those two other texts speak of Antiochus, which is the very reason given by others to the contrary. It is of no great consequence to us to know which verse our Saviour referreth to. Be it which it would, it was *spoken of by Daniel the prophet;* by which quotation our Saviour doth both give his testimony to that book, as a part of holy writ, and also lets his disciples know, that what he told them was but what was prophesied of, and so must have its accomplishment, and that the Jewish worship was to cease. As to the second question, amidst the great variety of notions about it, I take theirs to be the best who understand *the abomination of desolation* to be meant of the Roman armies, which being made up of idolatrous soldiers, and having with them many abominable images, are therefore called *the abomination;* those words, *of desolation,* are added, because they were to make Jerusalem desolate; and so St. Luke, who hath not these words, possibly gives us in other words the best interpretation of them, chap. xxi. 20, *And when ye shall see Jerusalem compassed with armies, then know that the desolation thereof is nigh*. When, saith our Lord, you shall see the abominable armies *stand in the holy place*, that is, upon the holy ground, (as all Judea was,) *whoso readeth* those prophecies of the prophet Daniel, *let him understand*, that as through the righteous judgment of God he once suffered the holy place to be polluted by the abominable armies of Antiochus, which he foretold, so he will again suffer the holy place to be polluted by the abominable armies of the Romans, who shall make the holy place desolate, which was prophesied by the prophet Daniel as well as the former. Therefore, saith our Saviour, when you see the Roman armies pitch their tents before Jerusalem, be you then assured God will give Jerusalem into their hands, and then all that I have foretold shall come to pass.

16 Then let them which be in Judæa flee into the mountains:

17 Let him which is on the housetop not come down to take any thing out of his house:

18 Neither let him which is in the field return back to take his clothes.

Mark hath this, chap. xiii. 14—16. Luke saith, chap. xxi. 21, *Then let them which are in Judea flee to the mountains; and let them which are in the midst of it depart out; and let not those that are in the countriest enter thereinto*. The import of all this is no more than, Let every man with as much speed as he can shift for himself, for, as Luke saith, then the desolation of Jerusalem is nigh; *for*, as he addeth, *these are the days of vengeance, that all things which are written may be fulfilled.* Let none of you think the storm will over, for when you see this be assured the time is come when all I have spoken of this city shall be accomplished.

19 And ᵗwoe unto them that are with child, and to them that give suck in those days! t Luke 23.29.

20 But pray ye that your flight be not in the winter, neither on the sabbath day:

Mark saith nothing of the sabbath day, chap. xiii. Luke hath not what Matthew hath, ver. 20. *Woe to them* in this text is only a phrase testifying our Saviour's compassion on such, and indicative of the addition it would make to their misery, as it would retard their flight. Upon this account also, he bids them pray their flight might not be *in the winter, neither on the sabbath day*. The winter would naturally retard their motion, through the cold and moisture of it. The sabbath would be a moral hinderance, in regard of the superstitious opinion they had of the sabbath, that they might not upon that day defend themselves, nor flee from their enemies beyond the length of a sabbath day's journey, which was but two miles: our Saviour hinteth to them that their flight must be farther. When our Saviour spake this the Jewish sabbath was the day of holy rest, and he knew that although by his resurrection he should sanctify a new sabbath, yet the Jews would not for a time understand that the old sabbath was abolished. Here is therefore no establishment of the old sabbath to be observed after his resurrection; the praying that their flight might not be upon the sabbath day respected only either their remora to their flight which the sabbath would give them, (in case they should keep it as a holy rest,) or the addition of trouble it would make in their spirits, when they considered that was the day in which they were wont to go to the house of prayer, keeping it a day of holy rest unto God.

21 For ᵘthen shall be great tribulation, such as was not since the beginning of the world to this time, no, nor ever shall be. u Dan. 9. 26. & 12. 1. Joel 2. 2.

22 And except those days should be shortened, there should no flesh be saved: ˣbut for the elect's sake those days shall be shortened. x Is. 65. 8, 9. Zech. 14.2,3.

Mark hath the same in effect, chap. xiii. 19, 20. Luke speaks more particularly, chap. xxi. 23, 24. *For there shall be great distress in the land, and wrath upon this people. And they shall fall by the edge of the sword, and shall be led away captive into all nations: and Jerusalem shall be trodden down of the Gentiles, until the times of the Gentiles be fulfilled.* These verses must be understood with reference to the Jewish nation, and whoso shall read in Josephus

S. MATTHEW XXIV

the history of the wars of the Jews, will easily agree there is nothing in all the foregoing Jewish story which we have recorded in Scripture like unto it; the final destruction of them by Titus was rather an abatement of miseries they suffered by the factions within themselves, than any thing else. And thus some think that God shortened those days of their misery by sending the Roman armies to quiet the seditions and factions amongst themselves, which were more cruel one to another. God promiseth to shorten these days for the elect's sake that were amongst this sinful people. So that as the city was taken in less than six months, so was their whole country in less than eighteen months more. And if the Lord had not, in compassion to those amongst this people who belonged to his election of grace, shortened these days of calamity, both by sending the Roman armies to quiet their intestine divisions, and then giving these armies so quick a victory, none of the Jews would have been left alive, which indeed any one will judge that shall but read those histories.

y Mark 13. 21. Luke 17. 23. & 21. 8.

23 ^y Then if any man shall say unto you, Lo, here *is* Christ, or there; believe *it* not.

z Deu. 13. 1. ver. 5, 11. 2 Thess. 2. 9, 10, 11. Rev. 13. 13. a John 6. 37. & 10. 28, 29. Rom. 8. 28, 29, 30. 2 Tim. 2. 19.

24 For ^z there shall arise false Christs, and false prophets, and shall shew great signs and wonders; insomuch that, ^a if *it were* possible, they shall deceive the very elect.

25 Behold, I have told you before.

26 Wherefore if they shall say unto you, Behold, he is in the desert; go not forth: behold, *he is* in the secret chambers; believe *it* not.

Mark hath much the same, chap. xiii. 21—23. There is no doubt but that our Saviour here hath a special respect to those persons who, about the time of the destruction of Jerusalem, taking advantage of the Jewish expectation of the Messiah as a secular prince, who should restore them to liberty, (an opinion which, as we have often heard, had infected the generality of the Jews, and not a little even the disciples of Christ,) made themselves heads of parties, and pretended that they were the Messiah, the Christ, thereby to encourage people to follow them, and to stand up for their liberty; of which kind there were several mentioned both in the history of Josephus, and in the Roman history, respecting those times. Our Lord therefore cautioneth his disciples against such, and thereby taketh them off their expectation of any such secular kingdom of the Messiah as they had dreamed of. He tells them that there would such persons arise, and some of them should do great signs and wonders, insomuch that if it were possible they would deceive the elect of God; but he had prayed for them; only they must also watch and take heed, that they might not be cheated and deceived by them, though they came with never so fair pretences, for his coming would be quite of another nature, and his kingdom would be a quite other kingdom.

b Luke 17. 24.

27 ^b For as the lightning cometh out of the east, and shineth even unto the west; so shall also the coming of the Son of man be.

c Job 39. 30. Luke 17. 37.

28 ^c For wheresoever the carcase is, there will the eagles be gathered together.

Luke hath much the same, chap. xvii. 24, 37. The disagreement of interpreters about *the coming of the Son of man*, here spoken of, makes a variety in their interpretation of these verses. Some think the coming of the Son of man here spoken of was his coming to destroy Jerusalem, which, he saith, will be sudden like the lightning. which though the thunder be taken notice of aforehand, as following the lightning, yet is not taken notice of. These interpreters make *the carcass*, mentioned ver. 28, to be the body of the Jewish nation, designed to be destroyed; and *the eagles* to be the Roman armies. Job saith of the eagle, chap. xxxix. 30, *Where the slain are, there is she.* Habakkuk, chap. i. 8, saith the same of the Chaldean armies; *They shall fly as the eagle that hasteth to eat.* Some understand by the coming of Christ here, his coming in his spiritual kingdom. The preaching of the gospel shall be like the lightning; you need not listen after those that say, Lo, here is Christ, or, Lo, he is there, for my gospel shall be preached every where; and where the carcass is, where my death and resurrection shall be preached, all the elect, my sheep that hear my voice and follow me, shall be gathered together. Others understand it of Christ's coming to judgment, which is compared to lightning for the suddenness and universality of it. There, saith Christ, I shall be, and all my saints shall be gathered together. Luke seemeth to speak of this, chap. xvii. 24, 37. That phrase, *Wheresoever the carcass is, there will the eagles be gathered together*, is a proverbial speech, signifying that it will need no great labour to bring things together which are naturally joined by an innate desire either of them to the other; so that it is applicable in more cases than one. And whether that discourse in Luke were at the same time when this was I cannot say; our Saviour's discourse on this argument, Luke xxi., hath not these verses, and is a part of a discourse which is said to have been begun, at least to the Pharisees, chap. xvii. 20. But I shall further consider what Luke saith when I shall come to that chapter in him.

29 ¶ ^d Immediately after the tribulation of those days ^e shall the sun be darkened, and the moon shall not give her light, and the stars shall fall from heaven, and the powers of the heavens shall be shaken:

d Dan. 7. 11, 12. e Is. 13. 10. Ezek. 32. 7. Joel 2. 10, 31. & 3. 15. Amos 5. 20. & 8. 9. Mark 13. 24. Luke 21. 25. Acts 2. 20. Rev. 6. 12.

Mark saith, chap. xiii. 24, 25, *In those days, after that tribulation. the sun shall be darkened, and the moon shall not give her light, and the stars of heaven shall fall, and the powers that are in heaven shall be shaken.* Luke saith, chap. xxi. 25, 26, *And there shall be signs in the sun, and in the moon, and in the stars; and upon the earth distress of nations, with perplexity; the sea and the waves roaring; men's hearts failing them for fear, and for looking after those things which are coming on the earth: for the powers of heaven shall be shaken.* Interpreters are much divided in the sense of these words, whether they should be interpreted, 1. Of Christ's coming to the last judgment, and the signs of that; or, 2. Concerning the destruction of Jerusalem. Those who interpret it of the destruction of Jerusalem have the context to guide them, as also the reports of historians, of strange prodigies seen in the air and earth, before the taking of it; likewise the word *immediately after*, &c. But I am more inclinable to interpret them of the last judgment, and to think that our Saviour is now passed to satisfy the disciples about their other question, concerning the end of the world; for although Christ's coming may sometimes signify that remarkable act of his providence in the destruction of his enemies, yet the next verses speaking of his coming with great power and glory, and of his coming with his angels, and with the sound of a trumpet, and gathering his elect from the four winds, the phrases are so like the phrases by which the Scripture expresseth Christ's coming to the last judgment, 1 Cor. xv. 52; 1 Thess. iv. 16, and Christ speaking to his disciples asking of him as well about that as the destruction of Jerusalem, I should rather interpret this verse with reference to the last judgment, than the destruction of Jerusalem before spoken of, or at least that these signs should be understood common both to the one and the other, as divers of the other signs mentioned in this chapter are. Some think that the darkening of the sun and the moon here, the falling of the stars, and the shaking of the powers of heaven, are to be taken metaphorically, as signifying the great change there should be in the ecclesiastical and civil state of the Jews; and it is true that such kind of expressions do often in Scripture so signify, Isa. xiii. 10; xxiv. 23; Ezek. xxxii. 7; Joel ii. 31. But without doubt the literal sense is not to be excluded, whether we understand the text of the destruction of Jerusalem, or of his coming to his last judgment; for as historians tell of great prodigies seen before the former, so the apostle confirms us that there will be such things seen before the day of judgment, 2 Pet. iii. 10, 12.

30 ^f And then shall appear the sign of the Son of man in heaven: ^g and then shall all the tribes of the earth mourn, ^h and they shall see the Son of man com-

f Dan. 7. 13. g Zech. 12. 12. h ch. 16. 27. Mark 13. 26. Rev. 1. 7.

ing in the clouds of heaven with power and great glory.

31 ¹And he shall send his angels ‖ with a great sound of a trumpet, and they shall gather together his elect from the four winds, from one end of heaven to the other.

i ch. 13. 41. 1 Cor. 15. 52. 1 Thess. 4. 16.
‖ Or, *with a trumpet, and a great voice.*

Mark saith, chap. xiii. 26, 27, *And then shall they see the Son of man coming in the clouds with great power and glory. And then shall he send his angels, and shall gather together his elect from the four winds, from the uttermost part of the earth to the uttermost part of heaven.* Luke saith, chap. xxi. 27, 28, *And then shall they see the Son of man coming in a cloud with great power and glory. And when these things begin to come to pass, then look up, and lift up your heads; for your redemption draweth nigh.* Interpreters are also divided about these words, as about the former, some understanding them concerning the destruction of Jerusalem, and judging that by the sign of the coming of the Son of man is probably meant some prodigy or some comet seen before that destruction, which should be of that nature as it should make the Jews (here called *the tribes of the earth*) to mourn; they by the *angels* and *trumpet*, mentioned ver. 31, understanding the ministers of the gospel, who after the destruction of Jerusalem should go and preach the gospel over all the world, and so gather in the elect into the gospel church. But I cannot agree to this sense, and most interpreters expound these words of the last judgment. What is meant by the *sign of the Son of man* all are not so well agreed. Two of the evangelists say only *the Son of man*. Matthew mentions first the appearance of the sign of the Son of man, then the Son of man himself; probably it signifieth some great prodigy that shall be seen before that great and terrible day. Those things which incline me to think that the day of judgment, not the destruction of Jerusalem, is that which is spoken of in these verses, is, 1. That all the phrases are such as the Scripture useth to express Christ's coming to the last judgment: his coming in the clouds of heaven, Matt. xxvi. 64; Rev. i. 7; the tribes of the earth mourning, Rev. i. 7; his coming with the angels, and the sound of a trumpet, Matt. xxv. 31; Mark viii. 38; 1 Cor. xv. 52; 1 Thess. iv. 16; his sending his angels to gather the elect, Matt. xiii. 49. 2. The *tribes of the earth* mourning, seems to signify more than the twelve tribes of Israel. 3. That which Luke hath, *Look up, and lift up your heads; for your redemption draweth nigh*; seemeth hardly applicable to the destruction of Jerusalem, rather to *the redemption of the body*, mentioned Rom. viii. 23. For the gospel before this time was carried to the Gentiles; nor do I know that that is any where called redemption. Those things which have led some learned interpreters to expound ver. 29—31 of the destruction of Jerusalem, are, I conceive, those particles, *immediately after the tribulation of those days*, ver. 29, and the particle *then*, ver. 30; together with ver. 34, where our Saviour saith, *This generation shall not pass, till all these things be fulfilled*. But the term, *immediately after the tribulation of those days*, may signify not only the destruction of Jerusalem, but that, and all the calamities of those days that should follow that, to the end of the world: and it is very usual for prophetical scriptures to speak of things to come long after as if they were presently to come to pass, Deut. xxxii. 35; and the day of judgment is ordinarily spoken of as if it were at hand, 1 Thess. iv. 15; James v. 8; 1 John ii. 18, both to denote the certainty of it, and to keep us from security, and to let us know that a thousand years in God's sight are but as one day, 2 Pet. iii. 8. For the 34th verse, we shall give the sense of it in its order.

32 Now learn ᵏ a parable of the fig tree; When his branch is yet tender, and putteth forth leaves, ye know that summer *is* nigh:

33 So likewise ye, when ye shall see all these things, know ˡ that ‖ it is near, *even* at the doors.

34 Verily I say unto you, ᵐ This generation shall not pass, till all these things be fulfilled.

k Luke 21. 29.

1 Jam. 5. 9.
‖ Or, *he*.

m ch. 16. 28. & 23. 36. Mark 13. 30. Luke 21. 32.

35 ⁿ Heaven and earth shall pass away, but my words shall not pass away.

n Ps. 102. 26. Is. 51. 6. Jer. 31. 35, 36. ch. 5. 18. Mark 13. 31. Luke 21. 33. Heb. 1. 11.

Mark hath the very same, chap. xiii. 28—31. So hath Luke, chap. xxi. 29—33, only he saith, *the fig tree, and all the trees, when they now shoot forth, ye see and know of your own selves that summer is now nigh at hand. So likewise ye, when ye see these things come to pass, know ye that the kingdom of God is nigh at hand. Verily, &c.* By this similitude of the fig tree (called therefore by Luke *a parable*) our Saviour doth not only design to inform them that these things which he had told them should be as certain signs of the approaching of the destruction of Jerusalem, and the coming of his kingdom, as the fig trees and other trees putting forth of leaves is a sign of the approaching summer, as Cant. ii. 13; but that as the frosts, and snow, and cold of the winter, doth not hinder the trees from bringing forth fruit in the summer, so these tribulations and troubles should be so far from hindering and destroying Christ's kingdom, that they should prepare the world for it, and promote it: so that as they might know from these tribulations in Judea that the kingdom of grace was at hand, and began; so from the following tribulations upon the world they might know that his kingdom of glory was also hastening. *Verily I say unto you, This generation shall not pass, till all these things be fulfilled.* There are several notions men have of that term, *this generation*, some by it understanding mankind; others, the generation of Christians; others, the whole generation of the Jews: but doubtless our Saviour means the set of men that were at that time in the world: those who were at that time living should not all die until all these things shall be fulfilled, all that he had spoken with reference to the destruction of Jerusalem; and indeed the most of those signs which our Saviour gave, were signs common both to the destruction of Jerusalem and the last judgment, abating only Christ's personal coming in the clouds with power and glory. So that, considering that the destruction of Jerusalem was within less than forty years after our Saviour's speaking these words, so many as lived to the expiration of that number of years must see the far greater part of these things actually fulfilled, as signs of the destruction of Jerusalem; and fulfilling, as signs of the end of the world. *Heaven and earth shall pass away, but my words shall not pass away.* By this expression our Saviour confirmeth the truth of what he had said, assuring those to whom he spake, that although there should be a change of the heavens and the earth, 2 Pet. iii. 10, 12, 13, which men commonly look upon as the most stable and abiding things, yet the truth of what he had said should not fail.

36 ¶ ᵒ But of that day and hour knoweth no *man*, no, not the angels of heaven, ᵖ but my Father only.

o Mark 13. 32. Acts 1. 7. 1 Thess. 5. 2. 2 Pet. 3. 10. p Zech. 14. 7.

Mark addeth, chap. xiii. 32, *neither the Son, but the Father. Of that day and hour*, that is, the particular time when the heavens and the earth shall pass away, as he had before said, or when the end of the world shall be, which was one of the questions propounded to him by his disciples, ver. 3. *Knoweth no man*, no mere man, nor have men any reason to be troubled at it; for it is a piece of knowledge which the Father hath reserved in his own power, and his own pleasure, from the angels, who continually behold his face. Nay, I myself, as man, know it not. Nor is it more absurd, or derogating from the perfection of Christ, than for to say, that Christ, as man, was not omnipotent, or omniscient, &c. By the way, this gives a great check to the curiosity of men's inquiries after the particular time or year when the world shall have an end, or the day of judgment begin, or be.

37 But as the days of Noe *were*, so shall also the coming of the Son of man be.

38 ᑫ For as in the days that were before the flood they were eating and drinking, marrying and giving in marriage, until the day that Noe entered into the ark,

q Gen. 6. 3, 4, 5. & 7. 5. Luke 17. 26. 1 Pet. 3. 20.

39 And knew not until the flood came, and took them all away; so shall also the coming of the Son of man be.

S. MATTHEW XXIV, XXV

Luke hath much the same, chap. xvii. 26, 27, where he also saith, it shall be as *in the days of Lot;* but I shall consider what he saith, which seemeth spoken at another time, and upon another occasion, when I come to his seventeenth chapter. Two things our Saviour seemeth here to teach us: 1. That Christ's coming to the last judgment will be sudden, and not looked for; upon which account his coming is compared in Scripture to the coming of a thief, ver. 43, 44; 2 Pet. iii. 10; Rev. xvi. 15. 2. That it will be in a time of great security and debauchery: such was the time of Noah, Gen. vi. 3—5.

r Luke 17. 34, &c.

40 ʳThen shall two be in the field; the one shall be taken, and the other left.

41 Two *women shall be* grinding at the mill; the one shall be taken, and the other left.

Some refer this to the coming of Christ in his kingdom of grace; some, to his coming in the day of judgment: it is true of both those comings. God shows the freeness of his grace much in the conversion of sinners, and makes discriminations of which we can give no account, as he tells us, Luke iv. 25—27. But it seemeth here rather to be understood of that separation which Christ shall make at the day of judgment, of the sheep from the goats, the elect from the reprobates; for of that coming our Saviour seemeth to be speaking, both in the preceding and in the following words.

s ch. 25. 13. Mark 13. 33, &c. Luke 21. 36.

42 ¶ ˢWatch therefore: for ye know not what hour your Lord doth come.

t Luke12.39. 1 Thes. 5. 2. 2 Pet. 3. 10. Rev. 3. 3. & 16. 13.

43 ᵗBut know this, that if the goodman of the house had known in what watch the thief would come, he would have watched, and would not have suffered his house to be broken up.

u ch. 25. 13. 1 Thes. 5. 6.

44 ᵘTherefore be ye also ready: for in such an hour as ye think not the Son of man cometh.

Mark saith, chap. xiii. 33, *Take ye heed, watch and pray: for ye know not when the time is.* What our Lord here meaneth by watching is easily gathered, as well by what went before, where our Saviour had been speaking of the security and luxury of the old world, as by what followeth, ver. 44, where he biddeth them be always ready; and therefore Luke, chap. xxi. 34—36, expounds this thus: *And take heed to yourselves, lest at any time your hearts be overcharged with surfeiting, and drunkenness, and cares of this life, and so that day come upon you unawares. For as a snare shall it come on all them that dwell on the face of the whole earth. Watch ye therefore, and pray always, that ye may be accounted worthy to escape all these things that shall come to pass, and to stand before the Son of man.* Our Saviour in these verses, from the uncertainty of the particular time when the day of judgment shall be, presseth upon his disciples a sober, heavenly, and holy life; intimating that by such a life only they can make themselves ready for the coming of Christ, and to stand before the Son of man, when he shall appear in his power and glory. He presseth this from that which common prudence would teach any householder, viz. if he knew in what watch of the night a thief would come, to watch, and not suffer his house to be broken open; that is, in what time of the night, for the Jews divided the night into the first, second, third, and fourth watch, as the Romans divided it for relief of their military guards. Now, saith our Saviour, you, knowing that there will come such a time, and not certainly knowing at what time, stand concerned to be always watching and praying.

x Luke12.42. Acts 20. 28. 1 Cor. 4. 2. Heb. 3. 5.

45 ˣWho then is a faithful and wise servant, whom his lord hath made ruler over his houshold, to give them meat in due season?

y Rev. 16.15.

46 ʸBlessed *is* that servant, whom his lord when he cometh shall find so doing.

We have much the same, Luke xii. 42—44, whether spake at the same time, and upon the same occasion, or no, I know not. It is said there, ver. 41, that Peter gave occasion to this discourse, by saying, *Lord, speakest thou this parable unto us, or even to all?* Our Saviour replieth as here, only Luke saith, *Who is that faithful and wise steward?* the question intimates that there are but a few such. This discourse plainly referreth to the ministers of the gospel, whom Christ leaveth in trust with his church, *to give them their meat in due season.* He declareth the blessedness of those ministers that shall be found faithfully discharging their trust, and that the Lord in the day of judgment will exalt them to a much greater honour, according to that of Dan. xii. 3, *They that be wise shall shine as the brightness of the firmament; and they that turn many to righteousness as the stars for ever and ever.*

z ch. 25. 21, 23. Luke 22. 29.

47 Verily I say unto you, That ᶻhe shall make him ruler over all his goods.

48 But and if that evil servant shall say in his heart, My lord delayeth his coming;

49 And shall begin to smite *his* fellowservants, and to eat and drink with the drunken;

50 The lord of that servant shall come in a day when he looketh not for *him,* and in an hour that he is not aware of,

|| Or, cut him off.

51 And shall ||cut him asunder, and appoint *him* his portion with the hypocrites: ᵃ there shall be weeping and gnashing of teeth.

a ch. 8. 12. & 25. 30.

Luke hath much of this, chap. xii. 45, 46: *But and if that servant say in his heart, My lord delayeth his coming; and shall begin to beat the men-servants and maidens, and to eat and drink, and to be drunken; the lord of that servant will come in a day when he looketh not for him, and at an hour when he is not aware, and will appoint him his portion with the unbelievers.* If that servant prove an evil servant, presumeth upon my not making such haste to judgment as he thought I would, and shall prove a persecutor of my people, or a loose and debauched person, I will come to his particular judgment before I come to the general judgment, and at such a time as he shall not be aware of me, and destroy him, and give him his portion with such as believe not my second coming, and with such as are one thing in profession and another thing in practice, in hell, where the condition of poor creatures will be miserable as the condition of those that weep and gnash their teeth. By this parable our Saviour doth quicken his apostles, to whom he intended to leave the care of his church when he should be ascended into heaven, to a faithful care of the flock committed to their trust, and also lets us know that in succeeding ages there would arise a generation of loose and debauched ministers, and such as would persecute the sincerer professors of his gospel, who could not comply with their doctrines and lives. Of which, as all ages of the church have given a proof, so the time since popery hath prevailed in the world hath given a more plentiful and abundant proof: all which extravagancies are encouraged from their atheism, and unbelief of Christ's coming to judgment. He also showeth how severe he will be against such persons: he will come upon them before they be aware of it, and cut them in pieces. The word signifies to cut them in two pieces, as the Jews were wont to divide their sacrifices; or, (as some think,) as some pagan nations were wont to punish perfidious persons, and some more notorious malefactors. And give him his portion with unbelievers and hypocrites in hell, chap. xiii. 42; xxv. 30. The case of all persons that live secure and debauched lives because judgment is not speedily executed, will be sad; but the case of ministers that do so will be dreadful. They are a sort of sinners whom God seldom suffereth to live out half their days; and when he doth, yet they shall not escape the severest damnation of hell. They betray a greater trust, and lead multitudes to hell with them, and so are the greatest traitors against the Divine Majesty.

CHAP. XXV

The parable of the ten virgins, 1—13; *and of the talents, which a king distributed among his servants, to be improved by them,* 14—30. *A description of the last judgment,* 31—46.

THEN shall the kingdom of heaven be likened unto ten virgins, which took their lamps, and went forth to meet ᵃthe bridegroom.

2 ᵇAnd five of them were wise, and five *were* foolish.

3 They that *were* foolish took their lamps, and took no oil with them:

4 But the wise took oil in their vessels with their lamps.

5 While the bridegroom tarried, ᶜthey all slumbered and slept.

6 And at midnight ᵈthere was a cry made, Behold, the bridegroom cometh; go ye out to meet him.

7 Then all those virgins arose, and ᵉtrimmed their lamps.

8 And the foolish said unto the wise, Give us of your oil; for our lamps are ‖gone out.

9 But the wise answered, saying, *Not so;* lest there be not enough for us and you: but go ye rather to them that sell, and buy for yourselves.

10 And while they went to buy, the bridegroom came; and they that were ready went in with him to the marriage: and ᶠthe door was shut.

11 Afterward came also the other virgins, saying, ᵍLord, Lord, open to us.

12 But he answered and said, Verily I say unto you, ʰI know you not.

13 ⁱWatch therefore, for ye know neither the day nor the hour wherein the Son of man cometh.

a Eph. 5. 29, 30. Rev. 19. 7. & 21. 2, 9. *b* ch. 13. 47. & 22. 10.

c 1 Thess. 5. 6.

d ch. 24. 31. 1 Thes. 4. 16.

e Luke 12. 35.

‖ Or, *going out.*

f Luke 13. 25. g ch. 7. 21, 22, 23. h Ps. 5. 5. Hab. 1. 13. John 9. 31. i ch. 24. 42, 44. Mark 13. 33, 35. Luke 21. 36. 1 Cor. 16. 13. 1 Thess. 5. 6. 1 Pet. 5. 8. Rev. 16. 15.

For the understanding of all parables, I have formerly showed, that parables are similitudes brought from some earthly things, or actions, to illustrate some heavenly doctrine, or spiritual mysteries, and insinuate them into our practice. For the right understanding of all parables, the first and principal thing to be attended to is the scope and main end of the parable. What heavenly doctrine it is which our Saviour by that earthly similitude designeth to illustrate, or what practical thing it is which he designeth by that parable to press, I have showed. Our Saviour sometimes more particularly showeth this, expressing what he meant by the several things and actions mentioned in the parable. This he did, chap. xiii., in the parable of the *sower*, and of the *tares* of the field. But in most parables he doth not so; but from something going before or coming after gives us light enough to know what his main design was, and leaveth to us by that to interpret the several parts of the parable. Here he hath left us a sufficient light to know his meaning: 1. From his discourse in the latter end of the foregoing chapter, where he had been pressing the duty and prudence of watchfulness, from the uncertainty of the time of his coming. It is manifest that he is pursuing the same design still, by the ἐπὶ παραβολῇ, or the saying with which he closeth this parable, ver. 13, *Watch therefore, for ye know neither the day nor the hour wherein the Son of man cometh.* This watchfulness we had interpreted by an opposition to sin, both of omission and commission: taking heed of having our hearts *overcharged with surfeiting and drunkenness, and cares of this life,* Luke xxi. 34, 36; taking heed of smiting our fellow servants, eating and drinking with the drunken; discharging our trusts faithfully, ministers giving to the household of Christ their portion in due season, chap. xxiv. 45, 49; being ready for the coming of Christ, ver. 44; praying, Luke xxi. 36. This our Lord had pressed there particularly on ministers; he is here in this parable pressing the same duty on all; and in this parable further opens the duty of watchfulness, not only as opposed to slumbering and sleeping, but as comprehending a getting of ourselves ready, as he had said,

chap. xxiv. 44; and this readiness he also further openeth in this parable, under the notion of having not only lamps, but oil in our lamps. To these purposes he takes up this parable, which we shall not so well understand without understanding their usual rites and customs at weddings, which were these: 1. Their marriages were ordinarily in the night. 2. They usually had young men that attended the bridegroom, and young virgins that attended the bride at her father's house. The young men attended the bridegroom. These were called *the children of the bride-chamber*, or *the friends of the bridegroom* or bride, Mark ii. 19; John iii. 29. The wedding being in the night, there was need of lamps. When the bridegroom came, the bride-maids, who were attending the bride, went forth to meet the bridegroom, with lamps lighted, to conduct him and his companions into the house, and to her who was to be the bride. When they were entered the door was shut, and the marriage proceeded. Our Saviour now, to quicken his auditors to the watchfulness before spoken of, supposeth such a marriage, and ten virgins, the usual number at such solemnities. He supposeth these ten virgins to have been half of them wise and half foolish: the wisdom of the one he makes to lie in getting their lamps ready, and furnishing themselves in time with oil to feed them, that they might not go out, either while they waited for his coming, or in their conduct of him. The folly of the others he makes to lie in their want of this care, so as when the bridegroom came their lamps were out: they would have borrowed oil of the others, but they had none to lend them, so as they were shut out of the door of the bridal-house, and though they knocked could obtain no entrance. It is not hard now to apply the several parts of the parable to the end for which this parable is brought, provided that we do not expect that similitudes should run on four feet, or that every minute circumstance in a parable should be fitted in the explication. *The kingdom of heaven* (which in Scripture always signifies that of grace or glory) here signifieth that of grace. The state of the church is likened to *ten virgins:* these ten virgins are professors; their lamps and their going forth to meet the bridegroom, signify their joint profession of the gospel, and their expectation joyfully to meet Christ, who is the bridegroom here meant, Psal. xlv. 14; John iii. 29. *Five of them were wise, and five foolish.* This signifieth the difference of professors; some have lamps, make a profession, but have no truth of grace; others have the root of the matter in them, a true faith and love, which feeds men's profession. The bridegroom's tarrying signifies Christ's delaying to come to judgment. Their slumbering and sleeping signifies the infirmities of the best, who sleep, though their hearts wake; and the deeper security of others in their sinful state. The coming of the bridegroom at midnight signifieth Christ's coming in a dark time of troubles and afflictions, or at a time not looked for. The virgins trimming their lamps upon the cry made, signifies the care of pious souls, more especially upon any notices of Christ's coming, to prepare themselves for the meeting and reception of him. The foolish virgins late discerning that their lamps were out, and that they wanted oil, lets us know that hypocrites and formal professors will too late know that profession without a root of faith and true regeneration will serve them in no stead. Their asking the wise virgins to lend them some of their oil, with their refusal, because then they should not have enough for themselves, lets us know the woeful shifts that hypocrites will at last be put to, and how vain their hopes are, who hope to be relieved from the grace and good works of others. Their going to buy oil, and their being shut out before they returned, and knocking in vain, and in vain crying, *Lord, open to us,* lets us know, that as the tree falls so it must lie; that after our buying time in this life, mentioned Isa. lv. 1, 2, is expired, our state will be determined; that we are concerned to take the counsel of Solomon, Eccles. ix. 10, *Whatsoever thy hand findeth to do,* especially for our souls, to *do it with thy might; for there is no work, nor device, nor knowledge, nor wisdom, in the grave, whither thou goest.* Therefore we are all concerned to watch, that is, to look that we have not only lamps, but oil to feed our lamps, and to keep our lamps burning, because we know that the Bridegroom Christ will come, and we do not know at what time he will come, to the general judgment, or our particular judgment; for when we die, we can do no more to make ourselves ready for the great coming of Christ to judge the world, but must appear before him as we go out of this world. No oil after the determination of our lives will be to be bought, no further preparation of ourselves is to be made, as our life leaveth us judgment will find us.

^k Luke 19. 12.
^l ch. 21. 33.

14 ¶ ^kFor *the kingdom of heaven is* ^las a man travelling into a far country, *who* called his own servants, and delivered unto them his goods.

‖ A talent is 187*l*. 10*s*.
ch. 18. 24.
^m Rom. 12. 6. 1 Cor. 12. 7, 11, 29.
Eph. 4. 11.

15 And unto one he gave five ‖ talents, to another two, and to another one; ^mto every man according to his several ability; and straightway took his journey.

There is much the same parable Luke xix. 12, but the difference is so great in the narration, and the time, and circumstances, and scope seem so different, that the best expositors think it another, and spoken at another time, though there be much of this in that: I shall therefore leave the consideration of that in Luke, until I meet with it in him, (though some interpreters do think this the same with that,) and only consider this, as it is before us in this evangelist. By *the kingdom of heaven*, is doubtless here to be understood the economy of God's providence in his gospel dispensations. The *man travelling into a far country*, is Christ ascending up to heaven, who, *when he ascended up on high gave gifts unto men*, Eph. iv. 8. By the *goods*, which the man is said to have delivered to his servants, are to be understood the gifts which God giveth to men, being himself (as to his glorious presence, and his principal residence, which is in heaven, at a great distance from us) as a man in a far country ; for I see no reason to restrain these gifts to such as flow from Christ as Mediator, but rather choose to interpret it generally of all the gifts of God, whether of providence or grace. Whereas it is said, ver. 15, that this man divided his goods to his servants unequally, *to one five talents, to another two, to another one, to every man according to his several ability*, it signifieth only God's unequal distribution of his gifts to the sons of men, according to his own good pleasure; which is true both concerning natural parts, as wit, understanding, judgment, memory, as concerning those which the heathens call good things of fortune, as riches, honours, and dignities; Christians call them the good things of Providence; under which notion also come all acquired habits, or endowments, such as learning, knowledge, moral habits, &c., which though acquired are yet gifts, because it is the same God who gives us *power to get wealth*, as Moses speaks, Deut. viii. 18, who also gives men power to get knowledge, and upon study and meditation to comprehend the natures and causes of things, and also to govern and bridle our appetites : or the gifts of more special providence, or distinguishing grace. I take all those powers given to men, by which they are enabled to do good, or to excel others, to come under the notion of the goods here mentioned, which God distributeth unequally according to his own good pleasure, and as seemeth best to his heavenly wisdom, for the government of the world, and the ordering of the affairs of his church; of all which God will have an account one day, and reward men according to the improvement, or no improvement, which they have made of them in their several stations.

16 Then he that had received the five talents went and traded with the same, and made *them* other five talents.

17 And likewise he that *had received* two, he also gained other two.

18 But he that had received one went and digged in the earth, and hid his lord's money.

This part in the parable only showeth the different use that men and women make of those gifts, whether of common providence or of grace, especially common grace, which the Lord bestowed on them. Some make a great use of them for the profit of their Master, for the end for which God betrusted them with them, to wit, the glory of his holy name, and the salvation of their souls. Others make no use at all of them for those ends.

19 After a long time the lord of those servants cometh, and reckoneth with them.

God, in the day of judgment, will call all men to account for those gifts which he hath given them, how they have used the days of life, the measures of health, their knowledge, wit, memory, understanding, their wealth, estate, honours, dignities, relations, all their natural or acquired habits, all their enjoyments, &c., for the honour of his name, and the advantage of their own souls.

20 And so he that had received five talents came and brought other five talents, saying, Lord, thou deliveredst unto me five talents : behold, I have gained beside them five talents more.

21 His lord said unto him, Well done, *thou* good and faithful servant : thou hast been faithful over a few things, ⁿI will make thee ruler over many things : enter thou into ^othe joy of thy lord.

ⁿ ch. 24. 47. ver. 34, 46.
Luke 12. 44. & 22. 29, 30.
^o Heb. 12. 2.
2 Tim. 2. 12.
1 Pet. 1. 8.

22 He also that had received two talents came and said, Lord, thou deliveredst unto me two talents : behold, I have gained two other talents beside them.

23 His lord said unto him, ^pWell done, good and faithful servant ; thou hast been faithful over a few things, I will make thee ruler over many things : enter thou into the joy of thy lord.

p ver. 21.

This part of the parable teacheth us only these things : 1. That some persons in this world make a very good use and improvement of those gifts and good things which God hath betrusted them with, according to the measure with which God hath betrusted them. 2. That those who do so shall in the day of judgment have a liberal reward in the kingdom of glory, called here *the joy of their Lord*. That God doth not expect an equality of service from all, but a service proportionable to those gifts which God hath given men ; and those shall go to heaven who have made a due improvement of the gifts with which God hath blessed them, though it be not proportionable to the service which others, of greater parts, and who have had greater advantages and opportunities, have made : if men have but two talents, yet if they gain other two, they shall go to heaven at last, as well as those who have had five, and improved them to the gaining of other five. We must take heed of concluding from this part of the parable, that those who have most given them ordinarily do make the best improvement of them, for daily experience teacheth us the contrary, neither is the parable brought to instruct us in any such thing.

24 Then he which had received the one talent came and said, Lord, I knew thee that thou art an hard man, reaping where thou hast not sown, and gathering where thou hast not strawed.

25 And I was afraid, and went and hid thy talent in the earth : lo, *there* thou hast *that is* thine.

26 His lord answered and said unto him, *Thou* wicked and slothful servant, thou knewest that I reap where I sowed not, and gather where I have not strawed :

27 Thou oughtest therefore to have put my money to the exchangers, and *then* at my coming I should have received mine own with usury.

We must remember that we are in a parable, which (as other similitudes) cannot be expected in all things to agree with what it is brought to illustrate. This part of the parable doth chiefly instruct us in these two things : 1. That it is the genius of wicked men to lay the blame of their miscarriages upon others, ofttimes upon God himself. The unprofitable servant here pretends that the dread of his lord, as a severe man, was that which kept him from labouring, and making an improvement of the talent with which his master had intrusted him. Thus many think that if there be an election of grace, or any thing of special and distinguishing grace, and man hath not a perfect power in his own will, he shall have something to excuse himself by before God hereafter, for his not repenting, and believing God in such a case, condemning men for unbelief and impenitency, should reap where he did not sow, and gather where he did not straw. 2. Men in their excuses which they fancy, instead of excusing will but accuse and condemn themselves. The lord of the unprofitable servant tells him, that the fault lay in his own sloth and wickedness, and his dread of his lord's security was but a mere frivolous pretence and unreasonable excuse; for if he had dreaded any such thing, he would have done what he could, he would have put out his money to the exchangers, and then he should have received his own with increase. And shall not God as justly another day reply upon those who think to excuse their lewd and wicked lives, their impenitency and unbelief, from their not being elected, not having a power of themselves to repent and believe, nor receiving his efficacious grace. O you wicked and slothful wretches! did you suspect or fear you were not elected? Why then did you not give all diligence to make your calling and election sure? Do you plead the want of power in your own wills to repent and believe, and that I did not give you a special, effectual grace? But had you not a power to keep from the taverns and alehouses? to keep from lying, and cursing, and swearing, and open profanation of my sabbaths? Had not you a power to read, to hear, to pray? If you had to your utmost used the talents I gave you, and I had been wanting in my further necessary influences of grace, you might indeed have said something; but when you made no use of the talents you had, why should I trust you with more? Faith comes by reading, hearing, praying; you had a power to these things, these talents you had. Why did you not read, hear, pray, that you might believe? If you took me to be so severe a master, why did not you do what was in your power to do, that you might find me otherwise? If you had done what lay in your power to do, in the use of those talents which I gave you for that end, you might then have blamed me if I had not given you more; but you never tried my kindness in such a case. So that you are not ruined by any severity of mine, but by your own sloth, neglect, and wickedness. Thus much this parable teacheth us, that God in the recompences at the last day of judgment will be found just, and sinners will all be found liars, and their damnation will be of themselves.

28 Take therefore the talent from him, and give *it* unto him which hath ten talents.

29 ⁹ For unto every one that hath shall be given, and he shall have abundance: but from him that hath not shall be taken away even that which he hath.

q ch. 13. 12. Mark 4. 25. Luke 8. 18. & 19. 26. John 15. 2.

30 And cast ye the unprofitable servant ʳinto outer darkness: there shall be weeping and gnashing of teeth.

r ch. 8. 12. & 24. 51.

God often in this life depriveth men and women of those gifts which he hath given them, and they do not make use of for the glory of his name, and the good of their and others' souls, the great ends for which he hath betrusted them with them. But this seems not to be here intended, this text referring to the day of judgment: all therefore that we are to understand by this is, That no man's gifts, whether of nature or providence, of what advantage soever they have been to him in this life, will be of any profit to him in the day of judgment, unless he hath in this life used them to the ends for which God gave them. In that day he will lose all; and the glory of heaven shall not be the portion of them that have had great talents of learning, wit, riches, honours, spiritual gifts, or any thing of that nature, but of those only who have used these things to the honour and glory of God, and to the advantage of their own and others' souls. For all those that have been unprofitable, hell will be their portion at last, where their misery will be, as of those that live in extreme darkness, continual weeping and gnashing of teeth. The substance of what is in ver. 29 we met with chap. xiii. 12, *To him that hath shall be given,* &c.; but I think the proverbial speech here is applied differently from the application of it there. There, *him that hath* seemeth to signify, him that hath an actual possession; for it is said before, *Because it is given unto you to know the mysteries of the kingdom of heaven.* So that I take that text to contain a promise of the increase of grace to those that have the seed of God; whenas the appearances of it in others shall not last, but vanish away. Here, plainly, *him that hath* signifieth, him that maketh a good and true use of what he hath; and thus the parable expounds it. So as the sense is, He that hath any talents from God, and maketh use of them, and improveth them for the honour and glory of God, shall be rewarded with further gifts of grace or glory. But if a man *hath not*, that is, hath, but is as if he had not, making no use of what he hath for the glory of God, those gifts and talents which he hath shall be of no profit and advantage, but miserable disadvantage to him at last.

31 ¶ ˢ When the Son of man shall come in his glory, and all the holy angels with him, then shall he sit upon the throne of his glory:

s Zech. 14. 5. ch. 16. 27. & 19. 28. Mark 8. 38. Acts 1. 11. 1 Thess. 4. 16. 2 Thess. 1. 7. Jude 14. Rev. 1. 7.

32 And ᵗbefore him shall be gathered all nations: and ᵘhe shall separate them one from another, as a shepherd divideth *his* sheep from the goats:

t Rom. 14. 10. 2 Cor. 5. 10. Rev. 20. 12. u Ezek. 20. 38, & 34. 17, 20, ch.13, 49.

33 And he shall set the sheep on his right hand, but the goats on the left.

Our Saviour having spoken much before of his spiritual kingdom, which he exerciseth in his church, cometh now more plainly to tell them what kind of a kingdom he should further set up and exercise in the end of the world; far different from that which the Jews dreamed of, and his own disciples seemed to have some expectations of. *When the Son of man,* he who now appeareth to you in the form of a servant, and only as the Son of man, *shall come in his glory,* a glorious manifestation of himself; he now appeareth clothed with flesh, but he shall appear in his glory, *and all the holy angels with him;* he shall come *with ten thousand of his saints,* Jude 14, *with his mighty angels.* 2 Thess. i. 7. *Then shall he sit* (after the manner of great princes) *upon the throne of his glory;* he shall appear in great splendour: *and before him shall be gathered all nations,* that is, all persons that ever were or at that time shall be in the world; *the quick and the dead,* Acts x. 42; 2 Tim. iv. 1; 1 Pet. iv. 5. He shall send forth his angels, and say to them, who are his reapers, chap. xiii. 30, *Gather together first the tares, and bind them in bundles to burn them; but gather the wheat into my barn.* He by his angels shall separate them one from another, as a shepherd, who feedeth both sheep and goats together, at night separateth them one from another. So the saints of God, who are like sheep for whiteness, gentleness, innocency, and feed in this world together with stinking and lascivious goats, the wicked of the world, compared to goats for the filthy qualities by which they resemble them; yet at the day of judgment Christ shall separate them. *And he shall set the sheep on his right hand.* The right hand is the place of honour and dignity, and the place for favourites: then Christ shall exalt his saints to great honour and dignity, and show them his favour. *But the goats on the left;* wicked men shall rise to shame and contempt. The right-hand men of the world shall be at the left hand of Christ. It shall be then seen, that because they are people of no understanding, he that formed them will show them no favour.

34 Then shall the King say unto them on his right hand, Come, ye blessed of my Father, ˣinheritᵗ the kingdom ʸprepared for you from the foundation of the world:

x Rom. 8.17. 1 Pet. 1. 4, 9. & 3. 9. Rev. 21. 7. y ch. 20. 23. Mark 10. 40. 1 Cor. 2. 9. Heb. 11. 16.

The King, that is, he who was before called *the Son of man,* who shall then *sit on the throne of his glory;* he shall say to his saints, to those on his right hand, those whom he designs to honour and to favour, *Come, ye blessed of my Father;* you whom my Father hath blessed with all spiritual blessings in me, who were also blessed in his eternal thoughts: for there was a *kingdom prepared for you from the foundation of the world;* you have not purchased it by your works; no, it was prepared for you before ever you were. You were blessed in my Father's eternal thoughts, so he prepared a kingdom for you; and you have been blessed since with all spiritual blessings through me, so you

S. MATTHEW XXV

are now prepared for it. Therefore come and now inherit it, as that which you are foreordained and born unto, as that which is freely given you, not purchased by you.

^{z Is. 58. 7.}
^{Ezek. 18. 7.}
^{Jam. 1. 27.}

35 ^z For I was an hungred, and ye gave me meat: I was thirsty, and ye gave me

^{a Heb. 13. 2.}
^{3 John 5.}

drink: ^a I was a stranger, and ye took me in:

^{b Jam. 2. 15, 16.}
^{c 2 Tim. 1. 16.}

36 ^b Naked, and ye clothed me: I was sick, and ye visited me: ^c I was in prison, and ye came unto me.

37 Then shall the righteous answer him, saying, Lord, when saw we thee an hungred, and fed *thee?* or thirsty, and gave *thee* drink?

38 When saw we thee a stranger, and took *thee* in? or naked, and clothed *thee?*

39 Or when saw we thee sick, or in prison, and came unto thee?

^{d Prov. 14.}
^{31. & 19. 17.}
^{ch. 10 42.}
^{Mark 9. 41.}
^{Heb. 6. 10.}

40 And the King shall answer and say unto them, Verily I say unto you, ^d Inasmuch as ye have done *it* unto one of the least of these my brethren, ye have done *it* unto me.

The recompences of the last judgment are according to the tenor of our good works, and the desert of evil works. The King here gives the reason of his gracious rewarding sentence, *For I was an hungred, and ye gave me meat.* This doth not imply any desert, much less any worthiness of equality between the work and the reward; but that evangelical works, the products of unfeigned faith and love, qualify us by the covenant of grace to receive it. The causes of the reward are either, the original cause, the most free and rich mercy of God, or the meritorious, the most perfect righteousness and sacrifice of Christ; and the good works here recited are infallible signs that the performers of them are the objects of the Divine favour in predestination, and are truly united to Christ. Besides, in the gospel, which is the law of grace, God has established a necessary connexion between faith, that works by love, and the blessed reward; and accordingly evangelical works are the condition of our title, that qualifies us to obtain the kingdom of glory, freely promised for Christ's sake to obedient believers. And in this respect the dispensing the reward may be said to be an act of justice, namely, in the faithful performance of the promise; as in the forgiving sins, which is an act of pure mercy, God is said to be *faithful and just,* 1 John i. 9. Our Lord here reckons but one species of good works, instead of many, as is usual in Scripture, and he rather chooseth to instance in works of charity than of piety. 1. He knows the hardness of men's hearts; and, 2. That the poor they should have always with them, especially such as would live godly, and so be more than others out of favour with the world. 3. He knew how acceptable these were to his Father, and had a mind the world should know it, Isa. lviii. 7; Ezek. xviii. 7; Micah vi. 8; Matt. ix. 13; 1 John iii. 17. And hereby declares, that acts of charity to the souls makes us fit subjects for the Divine mercy in the day of judgment, 2 Tim. i. 18. The answer, ver. 37, *Then shall the righteous answer him, saying, &c.,* only teacheth us this, That at the great day the best of men shall blush and be ashamed to hear God speak of any good works they have done, and be swallowed up in the admiration of God's free and infinite grace, in rewarding any thing which they have done at so liberal a rate. *And the King shall answer and say unto them, &c.* This only confirmeth what we had, chap. x. 42, that Christ looketh upon acts of kindness done to the meanest godly persons, and will reward them, as if they had been done unto himself; so that though our charity must not be limited only there, yet it must be chiefly shown to those of the household of faith: other charity may be showed in obedience to the command of God, and have its reward, but none can so properly be said to be done to Christ, as that which is done to those who are his true members.

^{e Ps. 6. 8.}
^{ch. 7. 23.}
^{Luke 13. 27.}

41 Then shall he say also unto them on the left hand, ^e Depart from me, ye cursed, ^f into everlasting fire, prepared for ^g the devil and his angels:

^{f ch. 13. 40, 42.}
^{g 2 Pet. 2. 4.}
^{Jude 6.}

42 For I was an hungred, and ye gave me no meat: I was thirsty, and ye gave me no drink:

43 I was a stranger, and ye took me not in: naked, and ye clothed me not: sick, and in prison, and ye visited me not.

44 Then shall they also answer him, saying, Lord, when saw we thee an hungred, or athirst, or a stranger, or naked, or sick, or in prison, and did not minister unto thee?

45 Then shall he answer them, saying, Verily I say unto you, ^h Inasmuch as ye did *it* not to one of the least of these, ye did *it* not to me.

^{h Prov. 14.}
^{31. & 17. 5.}
^{Zech. 2. 8.}
^{Acts 9. 5.}

The great King and Judge of the whole earth had before given sentence for those on his right hand, who are now possessed of their kingdom, and sit with him to judge the world. He now comes to sentence the goats at the left hand, whose judgment is to eternal misery; lying in two things: 1. In a departure from God, so as never more to have any favour from him. 2. In a sense of pain and misery, exceeding that which fire causeth to a body consuming with it. In this life wicked men are capable of some presence of God with them, and receive several favours from God, in gifts of common providence and common grace; which might serve either as encouragements to allure them, or means to help them, in turning to God: but having abused these, the righteous God in that day will totally depart from them, and they shall receive no more tokens of kindness and favour from him; and whereas, by the advantages they had from such a presence of Divine providence, as God was pleased in this life to allow them, they lived in some degrees of pleasure and liberty, which they were not thankful for, they shall at that day be adjudged to eternal torments. Nor shall the justice of God be impeached for disproportioning eternal torments to temporary sinnings; for the infiniteness of the Majesty offended, to which satisfaction is due, is to be considered, and is so amongst men, who think it reasonable to recompense a prince or nobleman for an injury done to them with ten thousand pounds, which they would not recompense to an equal with so many shillings. Beside that, every sinner hath sinned *in suo infinito,* to the utmost line of his time, and wanted nothing but more time to have sinned more, for he had a will to have sinned infinitely. This everlasting fire is said to be *prepared for the devil and his angels;* not because it was not also prepared for men, but the evil angels were adjudged to it before man had sinned, so that man comes but into a share with the evil angels; and by this God also lets us know that they are the children of the devil by evil works, John viii. 44; 1 John iii. 8. Having determined their punishments, and pronounced their sentence, he comes to justify himself in it: *For I was an hungred, and ye gave me no meat, &c.* For here may be interpreted as a causal; for though none merits his own salvation, yet every sinner's destruction is of himself, and he meriteth his condemnation. The mentioning only of sins of omission, and those only as to acts of charity, doth not only teach us that sins of omission are enough to damn us, but that omissions of acts of charity to the distressed members of Christ are such sins, as, if not repented of, and washed off with the blood of Christ, are enough to condemn us to the pit of hell; and such things as God doth keep in mind, and will in a more special manner reckon with men for. I cannot pass by a reflection which I find almost all interpreters make upon this text: If those in the day of judgment shall be sent to hell who do not feed the poor members of Christ, and give them to drink when they are thirsty, what shall be done to those who pluck the bread out of their mouths which they have got in the sweat of their face, and spill the drink which their own labours or others' liberality hath given them to drink? If those shall have their portion with the devil and his angels who give not entertainment to them when they are banished and strangers, what shall become of them who are instruments of their banishment, and to make them strangers? If it shall go so hard with those that clothe them not when they are naked, what shall become of those who any way help to strip them naked? If those shall not escape the vengeance of God who do not visit them when they are sick, and in prison, where shall they appear who cast them into prisons, and are means of those diseases that shorten their lives, by their barbarous usages of them? Those that smite their fellow servants had need be sure that it be not for welldoing. Our Lord here tells us, that the wicked in that day will say, *When saw we thee an hungred, &c.*: they did not deny that they had refused to give bread to the hungry; but they deny that they ever saw Christ an hungred, and did not feed him. Persecutors have always ill names to give the servants of God, pretending still a great reverence for God and Christ. But mark our Lord's answer, and that with an oath: *Verily I say unto you, Inasmuch as ye did it not to one of the least of these, ye did it not to me.* It is no matter what you thought of or called those to whom you showed no mercy; you see they are here at my right hand. You might have known them to be my sheep, you saw them hear my voice, and following me: you, in casting them into prison, cast me; in starving them, you starved me; and in stripping them of their goods, you stripped me. Therefore, go, *ye cursed, into everlasting fire, prepared for the devil and his angels.*

i Dan. 12. 2.
John 5. 29.
Rom. 2. 7, &c.

46 And [i]these shall go away into everlasting punishment: but the righteous into life eternal.

So then it seems they shall rise as well as the other; though they live in the lands of the Grand Seignior, or the Great Mogul, they shall not (as some filthy dreamers have thought) have such a quiet sleep in the graves, but that the sound of the last trump shall awaken them. Nor are they out of the jurisdiction of him that shall be the Judge both of the quick and the dead. Nor shall they escape a judgment without the law, because they have sinned without the law: *For the invisible things of God from the creation of the world are clearly seen, being understood by the things that are made, even his eternal power and Godhead*, Rom. i. 20. They *shall perish* (as they have sinned) *without the law*, Rom. ii. 12. They shall go into *everlasting punishment*, not a punishment for a time, as Origen thought. But the righteous, those who shall be so adjudged, being made so in this life by the imputed righteousness of Christ, and accepted as such for their holy and sincere conversation, though in many things imperfect, shall go *into life eternal;* which doth not signify a mere eternal existence, (for so the worst of men shall live eternally, or else they could not be capable of eternal punishment,) but a happy and blessed estate, which shall never have an end: and thus *eternal life* always signifieth in Scripture, being opposed to eternal death, everlasting fire, the worm that never dieth, &c. Thus endeth Christ's kingdom of grace; or rather, thus shall begin his kingdom of glory; all his enemies being put under his feet, and none remaining but this glorious King, and those who shall be his true subjects. Of which kingdom shall be no end.

CHAP. XXVI

Christ again foretelleth his own death, 1, 2. *The rulers conspire against him,* 3—5. *A woman poureth precious ointment upon his head,* 6—13. *Judas bargaineth to betray him,* 14—16. *Christ eateth the passover, and pointeth out the traitor,* 17—25. *He instituteth his last supper,* 26—30; *foretelleth the desertion of his disciples, and Peter's denial of him,* 31—35. *His agony and prayer in the garden,* 36—46. *He is betrayed and apprehended,* 47—50. *One of the servants of the high priest hath his ear cut off; Jesus forbiddeth opposition,* 51—56. *He is carried to Caiaphas, falsely accused, examined, pronounced guilty, and treated with indignity,* 57—68. *Peter's denial and repentance,* 69—75.

AND it came to pass, when Jesus had finished all these sayings, he said unto his disciples,

a Mark 14. 1.
Luke 22. 1.
John 13. 1.

2 [a]Ye know that after two days is *the feast of* the Passover, and the Son of man is betrayed to be crucified.

Mark saith, chap. xiv. 1. *After two days was the feast of the passover, and of unleavened bread.* Luke saith, chap. xxii. 1, *Now the feast of unleavened drew nigh, which is called the passover.* For our better understanding of what the evangelists say here, and in the following part of this history, we will consider the law of the passover in its institution, which we find in Exod. xii. 3, &c.; Lev. xxiii. 4, &c.; Numb. xxviii. 16, &c. In Exod. xii., we find its first institution, and the occasion of it. Upon the tenth day of the month Nisan, they were to take up a lamb for every household; or if the household were too small, they might take in their neighbours. This lamb was to be a male without blemish, and to be kept up to the fourteenth day; then to be killed in the evening; or betwixt the two evenings, that is, as is most probably judged, some time that day after the sun began after noon to decline, before the sun did set. The flesh of this lamb was that night to be eaten, neither raw, nor sodden, but roasted with fire, with unleavened bread, and with bitter herbs: nothing was to remain till the morning; and if any did remain, it was to be burned. They were to eat it with their loins girded, their shoes on their feet, and their staff in their hands. They were to strike the blood of the lamb on the two first posts, and on the upper door-posts, of the houses where they did eat it. Seven days they were to eat unleavened bread, beginning on the fourteenth day of the month at even, and ending the one and twentieth at even. This was to be to them for a memorial of their deliverance in Egypt upon God's destroying the first-born of the Egyptians and sparing them, and their deliverance and coming out of Egypt; and was to be an ordinance unto them for ever. This may be read at large, Exod. xii. 3—20. This also was a figure of the true Passover Jesus Christ, whom the apostle calleth *our Passover,* and the evangelist calls *the Lamb of God.* The law of the passover was again repeated, Lev. xxiii. 5—8; Numb. xxviii. 16—25. The first and last of the days of unleavened bread (as may be seen there) were to be days of *an holy convocation.* There were some differences betwixt the observation of the first passover in Egypt and their after-observations of it. At the passover in Egypt the blood was to be sprinkled on the door-posts; in following times the blood and the fat were to be sprinked upon the altar: at the passover in Egypt every paschal society slew the passover in their own house; but afterwards they were all slain in the temple, and then carried to be roasted and eaten by the several societies. The passover in Egypt was to be eaten standing, with their loins girded, their shoes on their feet, and staves in their hands, in token of their being ready to take their journey out of Egypt; but in their following passovers they (in token of the liberty into which God had brought them) did eat it sitting: hence we shall find that Christ sat down with the twelve when he ate the passover. In other things the observation was much alike. They strictly kept to the time, the fourteenth day of the month Nisan or Abib, which answereth to part of our March and April. This great festival was to be kept *after two days,* saith our Saviour. Whether the two days are to be understood as including or excluding the day when he spake is uncertain, and not material for us to know; probably he spake this on the Tuesday, (as we call it,) Friday being to be the passover day. *And the Son of man is betrayed to be crucified.* Though he was not yet actually betrayed that we read of, yet he knew both what counsels his adversaries had already been taking, and were further about to take, and what was in the heart of Judas; he therefore forewarneth his disciples, that when the thing should come to pass they might not be surprised, and might know that he was the Son of God, who could foretell future contingencies, though he was also as the Son of man to be crucified.

b Ps. 2. 2.
John 11. 47.
Acts 4. 25, &c.

3 [b]Then assembled together the Chief Priests, and the Scribes, and the elders of the people, unto the palace of the High Priest, who was called Caiaphas,

4 And consulted that they might take Jesus by subtilty, and kill *him.*

5 But they said, Not on the feast *day,* lest there be an uproar among the people.

Mark, chap. xiv. 1, saith, *The chief priests and the scribes sought how they might take him by craft, and put him to death*. Luke saith much the same with Mark. They had before this been seeking how to destroy him, Luke xix. 47; nor was it the first time they had made a formal council about it, John xi. 47; but now again they met. The place is named, that was the high priest's hall; the councillors were the chief priests, scribes, and elders. The matter of their deliberation was to *kill* Christ, and how they might do it *by subtlety*, for they were afraid of the people, who had a great esteem for our Saviour, because of the many miracles he had wrought. *But they said, Not on the feast day* : that was now within two days, and in order to it the city was full of people, and they were afraid (as they were concerned, being a conquered people, and having but a precarious liberty for their religion) of causing any tumults: this awed them, not any great religion for the festival, for all things now were out of order with them. Their high priest was chosen annually, and at the will of their conquerors; some little appearance they had of their ancient religious government, but it was in no due order.

c Mark 14 3.
John 11. 1,
2. & 12. 3.
d ch. 21. 17.

6 ¶ ^cNow, when Jesus was in ^dBethany, in the house of Simon the leper,

7 There came unto him a woman having an alabaster box of very precious ointment, and poured it on his head, as he sat *at meat*.

e John 12. 4.

8 ^eBut when his disciples saw *it*, they had indignation, saying, To what purpose *is* this waste?

9 For this ointment might have been sold for much, and given to the poor.

10 When Jesus understood *it*, he said unto them, Why trouble ye the woman? for she hath wrought a good work upon me.

f Deu. 15.11.
John 12. 8.
g See ch. 18.
20. & 28. 20.
John 13. 33.
& 14. 19.
& 16. 5, 28.
& 17. 11.

11 ^fFor ye have the poor always with you; but ^gme ye have not always.

12 For in that she hath poured this ointment on my body, she did *it* for my burial.

13 Verily I say unto you, Wheresoever this Gospel shall be preached in the whole world, *there* shall also this, that this woman hath done, be told for a memorial of her.

This piece of history (or one very like it) is recorded by the three other evangelists. Mark hath it with very little difference, chap. xiv. 3—9. Instead of *for much*, ver. 9, Mark hath a precise sum, *three hundred pence*, and adds, *they murmured against her;* and some other little differences he hath in words rather than in sense. In Luke, chap. vii. 36—38, we read, *One of the Pharisees desired him that he would eat with him. And he went into the Pharisee's house, and sat down to meat.* This seemeth not to be the same history, though some think it is. *And, behold, a woman in the city, which was a sinner, when she knew that Jesus sat at meat in the Pharisee's house, brought an alabaster box of ointment, and stood at his feet behind him weeping, and began to wash his feet with tears, and did wipe them with the hairs of her head, and kissed his feet, and anointed them with ointment.* It is plain this Pharisee's name was *Simon*, by ver. 40. Luke further addeth a discourse betwixt our Saviour and this Pharisee, ver. 39—50, which I shall in its order consider. John relateth it, chap. xii. 1, 2, &c.: *Then Jesus six days before the passover came to Bethany, where Lazarus was which had been dead, whom he raised from the dead. There they made him a supper; and Martha served: but Lazarus was one of them which sat at the table with him. Then took Mary a pound of ointment of spikenard, very costly, and anointed the feet of Jesus, and wiped his feet with her hair: and the house was filled with the odour of the ointment. Then saith one of his disciples, Judas Iscariot, Simon's son, which should betray him, Why was not this ointment sold for three hundred pence, and given to the poor? This he said, not that he cared for the poor; but because he was a thief, and had the bag, and bare what was put therein. Then said Jesus, Let her alone: against the day of my burying hath she kept this. For the poor always ye have with you; but me ye have not always.* Whether all the evangelists relate one and the same or divers stories is the question. Luke's relation seemeth the most different; he saith nothing of this Simon being a leper, and relateth this history immediately after things done in Galilee. All the other three agree this passage to have fallen out at Bethany, within two miles of Jerusalem. It is very probable that Matthew, and Mark, and John recite the same story. They agree it to have happened in Bethany, at a supper in Simon's house; they agree in the kind of the ointment, and in our Saviour's discourse upon the thing. The difference in the time, John mentioning six days before the passover, and Matthew two days, will be cleared by considering, that St. John sets down the precise time when our Saviour came to Bethany, which was six days before the passover; St. Matthew sets down the time when the feast was made, which was two days before the passover; so that our Saviour had been four days in Bethany before he was entertained in the house of Simon, and anointed by Mary for his burial. When Christ came out of Galilee toward Jerusalem, he came (as we heard before) to Bethany, Mark xi. 1. There he was entertained at a supper by one Simon, who had formerly been a leper, and probably had been cured by Christ, who therefore in gratitude entertained him, and made him a supper; where (saith John) Martha served, Lazarus sat at meat, whom he had newly raised from the dead, chap. xi. There comes a woman, John saith her name was Mary, and takes a pound of the ointment of spikenard; Matthew and Mark say it was in an alabaster box. John saith she did anoint his feet, and wiped them with her hair. Matthew and Mark say nothing of her anointing his feet, but of his head only. Though therefore opinions both of ancient and modern divines be very various, some thinking that the evangelists speak but of one anointing, others, that they speak of two, others, that they speak of three, yet it seems most probable that they speak of two, one of which is mentioned by Luke a year before this, the other is mentioned by Matthew, Mark, and John. Whoso deliberately reads over the history in Luke, and compareth it with the record of it in the three others, will see reasons enough to conclude that Luke speaketh of another person, and another time, and another place; for certainly Simon the Pharisee and Simon the leper were not the same: besides, we read in Luke that Simon carped at our Saviour for letting such a sinful woman come near him; here is nothing like it in this story. I shall therefore here consider the history as reported by our evangelist, taking in what Mark and John have to make it complete. Matthew and Mark say it was *in Bethany, in the house of Simon the leper.* John mentioneth not the house, but adds that Lazarus was at the same time at supper with our Lord, and that Martha waited. It will not from hence follow that our Saviour was at the house of Lazarus, (as some think,) for as the other evangelists express another house, so John gives no suspicion of any such thing, but by mentioning the presence of Lazarus and his two sisters there, which might be, and one of them wait, though they were at the house of a friend. *There came unto him a woman*, (so say Matthew and Mark; John saith it was Mary, one of the sisters of Lazarus,) she *having an alabaster box of ointment very precious, poured it on his head as he sat at meat*. John saith the ointment was *of spikenard, very costly;* and that she *anointed his feet*, and *wiped them with her hair;* and that the quantity of it was *a pound,* so as the odour of it did fill the room. She did certainly anoint both his head and his feet. It is certain that in those Eastern countries this was a usual fashion, to entertain their guests at banquets by anointing them with oil, to which the psalmist alludeth, Psal. xxiii. 5. This woman seemeth to have exceeded the usual compliment of this nature, in the kind of oil she used, the quantity of it, and in her anointing his feet (which she possibly did instead of washing his feet, which was very usual with them); in these things she showed the greatness of her love to this guest. *When his disciples saw it, they had indignation, saying, To what purpose is this waste?* Mark adds, they murmured at the woman. They said, *This ointment might have been sold for much, and given to the poor.* Mark and John say, for *three hundred pence.* John saith it was Judas Iscariot that spake the words, and gives the reason for it, because he *bare the bag,* into which the price of the ointment (had it been sold) must have come; and *he was a thief,* he spake not this out of any regard to the poor, but to himself: it is likely other of the disciples might also think that it was too great a waste upon such a compliment. Our Lord understanding it, vindicateth the woman. 1. He tells them that she had done *a good work*. Actions not forbidden by the Divine law, nor commanded in it, take up their goodness or badness from their principles and ends; what she had done was done out of a principle of love to Christ, and for his honour and glory, so it was a good work. 2. He tells them that they had the poor with them always, but they should not have him always. A work may be good done at an extraordinary time, and upon an extraordinary occasion, which is not so if brought into ordinary practice. Christ here declares that he had no design to discourage the relief of the poor, but they would have daily occasions to do them good, but he was not long to be with them. 3. He tells them that she had poured this ointment upon him against his burial. That is, if this cost had been spent upon my dead body you would not have blamed her; for those kind of perfumes, both moist and dry, were much used in their embalming dead bodies. I am about to die, I have often told you so; you believe it not; she believeth it, and hath, out of her love to me, but bestowed such a cost upon my dying body, as you would not have blamed had it been bestowed upon my dead body: so she showed her faith in Christ's words as well as his person. Or, if this woman did not do it with any such intention, yet (saith our Saviour) she hath done the thing; I shall suddenly die, and she hath but anointed me aforehand, and is certainly as much excusable as those that spend more about bodies already dead. Finally, he tells them, that wheresoever this gospel should be preached, what she had done should be told to her honour and praise, *for a memorial of her*. Christ, seeing that her action proceeded from a hearty and burning love to him, accepteth her act as an extraordinary act of kindness to him, and proportioneth her a reward. Without love, if a man give all his goods to the poor, it signifieth nothing; but if there be love in the heart, it makes the gift acceptable. Love seldom underdoeth in an act of kindness, and it cannot overdo where Christ is the true object of it. Men, who know not our hearts, may be ready to blame us for actions which God will highly commend and reward. The evangelist having thus far digressed from his discourse, (probably to give us an account of the reason of Judas's disgust to our Saviour,) he now returneth to a discourse about what was done at the council he had told us of, ver. 3—5. The fear of an uproar amongst the people seemed to be that alone which made them shy of apprehending him on the feast day.

h Mark 14. 10. Luke 22. 3. John 13. 2, 30. i ch. 10. 4.

14 ¶ ʰThen one of the twelve, called ⁱJudas Iscariot, went unto the Chief Priests,

k Zech. 11. 12. ch. 27. 3.

15 And said *unto them*, ᵏWhat will ye give me, and I will deliver him unto you? And they covenanted with him for thirty pieces of silver.

16 And from that time he sought opportunity to betray him.

Mark saith, chap. xiv. 10, 11, *And Judas Iscariot, one of the twelve, went unto the chief priests, to betray him unto them. And when they heard it, they were glad, and promised to give him money. And he sought how he might conveniently betray him.* Luke hath this yet more fully, chap. xxii. 3—6, *Then entered Satan into Judas surnamed Iscariot, being of the number of the twelve. And he went his way, and communed with the chief priests and captains, how he might betray him unto them. And they were glad, and covenanted to give him money. And he promised, and sought opportunity to betray him unto them in the absence of the multitude.* While they were busy in council, (viz. the chief priests, and scribes, and elders,) how they might surprise Christ without making a tumult, Judas surnamed Iscariot, one of the twelve disciples of our Lord, instigated by the devil, who possibly did take advantage of Judas's discontent that the ointment was not sold, and he had not the money to put into the bag, or that Christ checked him so openly before the disciples, goes to the council, and offereth them to betray him unto them, without making any noise in the city. This being what they desired, and were consulting how to effect, they were glad of such an offer, and agreed with him for a sum of money. No evangelist but Matthew, in this place, mentioneth the particular sum, which was *thirty pieces of silver*. Interpreters do very probably think that these thirty pieces were thirty staters or shekels of the sanctuary, which being but of the value of two shillings and six-pence apiece, amounted but to three pounds fifteen shillings in our money, which was the sum appointed by the law, Exod. xxi. 32, to be paid for a servant gored to death by the beast of another, the poorest and meanest price of any person's life: Judas left it to them, and they set the meanest price imaginable. There are other opinions about the value of these pieces of silver, but this is the most probable, especially considering the mean opinion these men had of Christ, and their design and interest to depreciate him as much as might be, and that the priests were the great men in this council, who most probably agreed with him for such pieces of money as were most in use amongst the Jews. It may be a just matter of admiration that they should make so cheap a bargain with him, considering that they doubtless (had he insisted upon it) would have given him more; but there was a prophecy to be fulfilled, which we find Zech. xi. 12, 13, *So they weighed for my price thirty pieces of silver. And the Lord said unto me, Cast it unto the potter: a goodly price that I was prized at of them.* I shall have occasion, when I come to chap. xxvii. 9, to discourse that text further. The price was set by the council of Heaven, which had determined this degree of our Lord's humiliation, that as he took upon him the form of a servant, so his life should be valued at the rate of an ordinary servant's life. Though therefore Judas was covetous enough to have asked more, and it is like the malice of those councillors would have edged them to have given more, yet it was thus ordered by the Divine council. Christ must be sold cheap, that he might be the more dear to the souls of the redeemed ones. For thirty pieces of silver he covenanted with them, and they promised it to him; whether it was now paid, or when he had done his work, appeareth not. From that time, (saith Mark,) *he sought how he might conveniently betray him.* Luke expounds this ἄτερ ὄχλου, without tumult, chap. xxii. 6. He was now fixedly resolved upon his villany; his lust wanted but opportunity, which soon after offered itself.

17 ¶ ¹Now the first *day* of the *feast* of unleavened bread the disciples came to Jesus, saying unto him, Where wilt thou that we prepare for thee to eat the Passover?

l Ex. 12. 6, 18. Mark 14. 12. Luke 22. 7.

18 And he said, Go into the city to such a man, and say unto him, The Master saith, My time is at hand; I will keep the Passover at thy house with my disciples.

19 And the disciples did as Jesus had appointed them; and they made ready the Passover.

No one of the evangelists relates this history fully, but Mark relateth the former part more fully than Matthew: Mark xiv. 12—16,. *And the first day of unleavened bread, when they killed the passover, his disciples said unto him, Where wilt thou that we go and prepare that thou mayest eat the passover? And he sendeth forth two of his disciples, and saith unto them, Go ye into the city, and there shall meet you a man bearing a pitcher of water: follow him. And wheresoever he shall go in. say you to the good-man of the house, The Master saith, Where is the guest-chamber, where I shall eat the passover with my disciples? And he will show you a large upper room furnished and prepared: there make ready for us. And his disciples went forth, and came into the city, and found as he had said unto them: and they made ready the passover.* Luke chap. xxii. 7—13, differeth a little in the former part of this relation: he saith, *Then came the day of unleavened bread, when the passover must be killed. And he sent Peter and John, saying, Go and prepare us the passover, that we may eat. And they said unto him, Where wilt thou that we prepare? And he said unto them, Behold, when ye are entered into the city, there shall a man meet you,* &c.; so he goeth on, ver. 10—13, varying scarce at all from what Mark saith. The variations of the evangelists are of no moment, none contradicteth the other, only one hath some circumstances omitted by the other. Our Lord was now at Bethany, whither he went every night from Jerusalem. The day was come for the killing of the passover. What that day was, the law hath fixed, Exod. xii. 6; the fourteenth day of the first month (Nisan) in the evening; or, betwixt the two evenings, that is, as is mostly agreed, betwixt the declining of the sun after noon and the setting of the sun; for they counted one evening began when the sun was declined, which was the second evening of that day, and another evening (belonging to the ensuing day) beginning at sun-set. Betwixt these two evenings the passover was to be killed. Now this fourteenth day was called the first day of unleavened bread, though strictly it was not so, according to the Jewish account of days, from sun-set to sun-set; but it was so after the Roman account, who count the days as we do, from midnight to midnight. For the Jews began their feast of unleavened bread from their eating the passover; so as their fourteenth day must needs take in so many hours as were betwixt the setting of the sun and midnight, of the first day of unleavened bread, which held to the end of the twenty-first day; so were seven entire days with a part of another. Matthew and Mark bring in the disciples first asking our Saviour (knowing his resolution to keep the passover) where he would have it prepared. He said (Luke saith) to Peter and John, *Go into the city to such a man*, &c. Mark and Luke here supply something omitted by Matthew, for Matthew only mentioneth their going to the master of the house, and telling him from Christ, *The Master saith, My time is at hand; I will keep the passover at thy house with my disciples.* The other two evangelists mention more in their instructions; telling us, that he told them, that when they came into the city, they should see a man carrying a pitcher of water, whom they should follow into what house soever he should go in, and there they should say to the master of the house, *The Master saith, My time is at hand; I will keep the passover at thy house with my disciples.* Mark and Luke add, *Where is the guest-chamber?* No doubt but at that time most householders who had convenient houses did prepare chambers for the several passover companies. Our Lord here gave his disciples an eminent proof of his Divine nature, in so particularly telling them what they should meet with in the city, and disposing the heart of this householder to so free a reception of him. For all three evangelists agree, that the disciples did as Jesus commanded, *and found as he had said unto them. And they made ready the passover.* There was a great deal of work to be done, of which none of the evangelists say any thing. Some upon the reading of this may be thinking, Where had they the lamb? When was it offered? &c. According to the law, in Exod. xii. 3, the lamb was to be taken up the tenth day, and kept to the fourteenth; it might either be brought by those that did eat it, or bought at Jerusalem, for they had great markets for that purpose some days before the passover. Whether all the lambs thus eaten by the paschal societies were first to be brought to the temple, and then killed, and the blood sprinkled on the altar, and poured out at the foot of it, and their fat and entrails offered, I much doubt; I rather think this was only to be done with some of them, instead of all. That some were so killed by the priests, their blood so sprinkled and poured out upon and at the foot of the altar, I doubt not, though God having no temple nor altar built at that time, there be no such thing in the law, Exod. xii.; but at Hezekiah's passover, 2 Chron. xxx. 16, 17, we find the Levites killing the passover, and the priests sprinkling the blood; but, as I said before, I do not think that the priests and Levites killed the lambs for all the passover societies. The great time that it must have taken, and the vast quantity of blood there would have been, the long time it must have taken to cleanse the entrails, makes it appear impossible to be done in four or five hours, for they had no longer time to kill it in. They did not begin to kill till after the evening sacrifice, for the day was done with, and that was betwixt two and three of the clock, and they were to finish by sunset, for then the other evening began. This inclineth me to think that every lamb was not so killed and offered, only some instead of all. But what the disciples did as to these matters, the Scripture hath not told us. It is enough for us that we are told the passover was made ready, and we may be assured that nothing in the preparing of it was omitted, which by the law of God was required as to this sacred action. It was not the business of the evangelists to acquaint us with every particular circumstance, only to let us know that our Lord did keep the passover, and in the close of that feast institute his supper, to which relation our evangelist now comes.

20 ᵐNow when the even was come, he sat down with the twelve. _{m Mark 14. 17,—21. Luke 22. 14. John 13. 21.}

21 And as they did eat, he said, Verily I say unto you, that one of you shall betray me.

22 And they were exceeding sorrowful, and began every one of them to say unto him, Lord, is it I?

23 And he answered and said, ⁿHe that dippeth *his* hand with me in the dish, the same shall betray me. _{n Ps. 41. 9. Luke 22. 21. John 13. 18.}

24 The Son of man goeth °as it is written of him: but ᵖwoe unto that man by whom the Son of man is betrayed! it had been good for that man if he had not been born. _{o Ps. 22. Is. 53. Dan. 9. 26. Mark 9. 12. Luke 24. 25, 26, 46. Acts 17. 2, 3. & 26. 22, 23. 1 Cor. 15. 3. p John 17. 12.}

25 Then Judas, which betrayed him, answered and said, Master, is it I? He said unto him, Thou hast said.

Mark hath the same, chap. xiv. 17—21: *And in the evening he cometh with the twelve. And as they sat and did eat, Jesus said, Verily I say unto you, one of you which eateth with me shall betray me. And they began to be sorrowful, and to say unto him one by one, Is it I? And he answered and said unto them, It is one of the twelve, that dippeth with me in the dish. The Son of man indeed goeth as it is written of him: but woe to that man by whom the Son of man is betrayed! good were it for that man if he had never been born.* Luke saith, chap. xxii. 14—16, &c., *And when the hour was come, he sat down, and the twelve apostles with him. And he said unto them, With desire have I desired to eat this passover with you before I suffer: for I say unto you, I will not any more eat thereof, until it be fulfilled in the kingdom of God. And he took the cup, and gave thanks, and said, Take this, and divide it among yourselves: for I say unto you, I will not drink of the fruit of the vine, until the kingdom of God shall come.* Then Luke passeth to our Lord's institution of the supper. Luke mixeth the discourse about the person that should betray him with the relation about the institution of the supper, contrary to the relation both of Matthew, and Mark, and John, so as we may reasonably think that Luke misplaceth it, giving us an account of that passage, ver. 21—23, within his relation of the history of his receiving the passover, and instituting of the supper, which immediately followed each other, but not strictly in that order in which our Saviour spake them, which appeareth plainly by the other three evangelists to have been during the eating of the passover, and before the institution of the Lord's supper. For the understanding of the history, we must understand something of the Jewish order in their eating of the passover: which was this, as we have it described by the learned Doctor Lightfoot. "Their sitting at meat was commonly upon beds or couches, made for that purpose, with the table before them. Now at other meats they either sat, as we do, with their bodies erect, or when they would enlarge themselves to more freedom of feasting, or refreshing, they sat upon the beds, and leaned upon the table on their left elbow; and this or the other posture they used indifferently at other times, as they were disposed, but on the passover night they thought they were obliged to use this leaning composure, and you may take their reason for it in some of their own words. They used their leaning posture as free-men do, in memorial of their freedom. And Levi said, Because it is the manner of servants to eat standing, therefore now they eat sitting and leaning, to show that they were got out of servitude into freedom———. Upon this principle and conceit of freedom they used this manner of discumbency frequently at other times, but indispensably this night, so far different from the posture enjoined and practised at the first passover in Egypt, when they ate it with their loins girded, their shoes on their feet, their staves in their hands, and in haste, Exod. xii. 11. And as the thought of their freedom disposed them to this leaning, reposed, secure composure of their elbow upon the table, and their head leaning on their hand, so, to emblem out the matter the more highly, they laid their legs under them, sitting on them, and laying out their feet behind them." (Thus the woman, Luke vii. 38, could conveniently come at our Saviour's feet to wash, anoint, and wipe them.) "Thus removing and acquitting their legs and feet, as far as possible, from the least show of standing to attend, or readiness to go upon any one's employment, which might carry with it the least colour of servitude, or contrariety to their freedom. Now according to the manner of sitting and leaning are the texts to be understood, about the beloved disciple's leaning in the bosom of Jesus, John xiii. 23, and on the breast of Jesus, John xiii. 25; xxi. 20. Ἀνακείμενος ἐν κόλπῳ καὶ ἐπιπεσὰν, or ἐπιπεσὼν ἐπὶ τὸ στῆθος, which some translators not having observed, or at least not expressed, they have intricated the reader in such gross conceptions about this matter, as that some have thought, and some have pictured, John reposing himself or lolling on the breast of Jesus, contrary to all order and decency: whereas the manner of sitting together was only thus, Jesus leaning upon the table with his left elbow, and so turning his face and breast away from the table, on one side; John sat in the same posture next before him, with his back towards Jesus, his breast or bosom not so near as that John's back and Jesus's breast did join together, and touch one another, but at such a distance as that there was space for Jesus to use his right hand upon the table, to reach his meat at his pleasure, and so for all the rest, as they sat in like manner. For it is but a strange fancy with which some have satisfied themselves about this matter, conceiving either that they lay upon the beds before the table, one tumbling upon or before the breast of another; or if they sat leaning on the table, that they sat so close that the back of one joined to the breast of another: they sat leaning, but with such distance between each other, that the right hand of every one of them had liberty to come and go betwixt himself and his fellow, to reach his meat, as he had occasion." Thus far that learned man, in his discourse of the temple-service, in the time of our Saviour, chap. xiii. By which discourse we may learn, 1. That the Jews at the eating of the passover used the very same posture as at other times they did eat their meat in. 2. That this was not lying along, but sitting upon their legs, and sometimes leaning their head upon their left elbow, yet at such a distance one from another, as every one that sat might freely use their right hand to take their meat, and reach it to their mouths: nor did they always sit at meat so leaning, but at their pleasure leaned or not leaned; only at the paschal supper they always leaned, as an emblem of their more perfect liberty. By this we easily understand what is meant by Christ's sitting down with the twelve, after the manner of that country in eating their meat.

And as they did eat, he said. For the understanding of this we must a little inquire into the Jewish manner of eating that holy supper, which I will take out of the afore-mentioned learned author in the same book and chapter, paragraph third. "They being thus set, the first thing towards this passover supper that they went about was, that they every one drank off a cup of wine." So do their own directories and rituals about this thing inform us. Now the consideration of this is of mighty use to us to help us to understand the two cups mentioned by Luke, chap. xxii. 17, and again ver. 20. The latter was the cup which our Saviour consecrated for the institution of his supper, as is plain by the consecration of the bread mentioned immediately before it, ver. 19. The cup mentioned ver. 17 was their first cup of wine, which they drank before the passover supper, mentioned by Luke only. Our Saviour's giving thanks when he took it, was but his blessing of the whole paschal supper. Luke before this mentions some words of our Saviour, ver. 15, 16, *With desire I have desired to eat this passover with you before I suffer: for I say unto you, I will not eat any more thereof, until it be fulfilled in the kingdom of God:* that is, I am now about to suffer, I know that I am betrayed, I have therefore earnestly desired to eat this passover with you before I die, to put an end to this legal service, which hath now continued so many years, and hath all this time been but a type of me and my death, and oblation for sin, John i. 29; 1 Cor. v. 7. For this is the last passover I shall eat with you, or that you shall eat before you see those things fulfilled in gospel providences which this service doth but typify. This indeed was but the preface to the paschal supper, nor doth Luke mention more of it, only addeth, ver. 18, *For I will not drink of the fruit of the vine, until the kingdom of God shall come;* of which words I shall here say nothing, for they are doubtless by Luke put out of the true order, being both by Mark and Matthew mentioned as spoken after that our Saviour had blessed and taken the sacramental cup. So as, questionless, the 21st and 22nd verses in Luke should have been before the 18th, according to the order in which Matthew and Mark put them, and ver. 18 should be put after ver. 20, and so also both Matthew and Mark do place them. Luke mentioneth no more of the paschal supper; let us therefore return to our evangelist. *And as they did eat,* that is, the paschal supper, which (according to the law, Exod. xii. 8) was the lamb or kid roasted, which they were to eat *with unleavened bread and bitter herbs.* The Jews had a hundred traditional rites, which they observed about the paschal supper; but there seems to have none of them been of any Divine institution. The law required no more than the eating of the lamb or kid roasted, with unleavened bread and bitter herbs. As to their drink, it prescribed nothing, they were left to liberty: for their tradition of four cups of wine to be drank, &c., I cannot find any of the evangelists mentioning our Saviour's usage of any such thing, but very probably he drank wine at his pleasure, as at other meals, keeping only to the rule of the law. Now saith Matthew and Mark, *And as they did eat, he said, Verily I say unto you, that one of you shall betray me.* He had before told them the Son of man should be betrayed, chap. xvii. 22; xx. 18, where he had also told them he should be scourged, mocked, and crucified; but he now cometh to discover the traitor to them, *One of you. And they were exceeding sorrowful, and began every one to say unto him, Lord, is it I?* They were sorrowful that he should be betrayed by any, but more troubled that one of themselves should be so accursed an instrument: every one mistrusts his own heart, and saith, *Is it I?* Christ replieth, *He that dippeth his hand with me in the dish, the same shall betray me.* The dish here could be no other than the dish at the passover supper; probably the hand of Judas was at that time with our Saviour's in the dish, for we read of no more reply from any but from Judas. Our Saviour addeth, *The Son of man goeth as it is written of him: but woe unto that man by whom the Son of man is betrayed! it had been good for that man if he had not been born.* By these words our Saviour doometh the traitor, though withal he tells them, that for his suffering it was determined by God, foretold by the prophets, and so eventually necessary; he was not dragged to it, *The Son of man goeth.* But God's decree as to the thing did neither take away the liberty of Judas's will in acting, nor yet excuse the fact he did. *Woe unto that man by whom the Son of man is betrayed!* a text worthy of their study, who will not understand how God should decree to permit sin, and make a sinful act as to the event necessary, without being the author of sin. As to our Saviour's death, God had determined it, foretold it, it was necessary to be; but yet Satan put the evil motion into the heart of Judas, and Judas acted freely in the doing what he did. *Then Judas, which betrayed him, answered and said, Master, is it I? He said unto him, Thou hast said.* This (as I said) maketh it very probable that the hand of Judas was in the dish with our Saviour's, dipping in the sauce, when our Saviour spake these former words. That Judas, as well as the other disciples, was with our Lord at this action, is out of doubt. That he stayed any longer may very well be questioned, not only because John saith, chap. xiii. 30, *He then having received the sop went immediately out;* but because one cannot in reason think that his guilty conscience should suffer him to stay beyond that word, or that our Saviour would have admitted of the society of so prodigious a traitor at his last supper, the institution of which immediately followed.

26 ¶ ᑫAnd as they were eating, ʳJesus took bread, and ‖ blessed *it,* and brake *it,*

_{q Mark 11. 22. Luke 22. 19. r 1 Cor. 11. 23, 24, 25. ‖ Many Greek copies have, *gave thanks.* See Mark 6. 41.}

S. MATTHEW XXVI

and gave it to the disciples, and said, Take, eat; ^sthis is my body.

27 And he took the cup, and gave thanks, and gave it to them, saying, ^tDrink ye all of it;

28 For ^uthis is my blood ^xof the new testament, which is shed ^yfor many for the remission of sins.

29 But ^zI say unto you, I will not drink henceforth of this fruit of the vine, ^auntil that day when I drink it new with you in my Father's kingdom.

30 ^bAnd when they had sung an ‖ hymn, they went out into the mount of Olives.

s 1 Cor. 10. 16
t Mark 14. 23.
u See Ex. 24. 8. Lev. 17. 11. x Jer. 31. 31. y ch. 20. 28. Rom. 5. 15. Heb. 9. 22. z Mark 14. 25. Luke 22. 18.
a Acts 10.41.
b Mark 14. 26.
‖ Or, psalm.

Mark relates this with no considerable difference, chap. xiv. 22—26; only he saith, *they all drank of it*, and,—*shed for many for the remission of sins.* Luke saith, our Saviour upon his giving the bread, said, *This is my body which is given for you: this do in remembrance of me. Likewise also the cup after supper, saying, This cup is the new testament in my blood, which is shed for you.* From the 24th verse also to the 30th of his 22nd chapter he gives us some further discourses of our Saviour with Peter, and to his disciples; but no other evangelist mentioning them in this place, and Luke no where saying that they were spoken in the guest-chamber, I shall not consider them till I come to that chapter in Luke. *And as they were eating*, that is, while they were yet in the guest-chamber, where they had eaten the paschal lamb, (for we must not think that our Saviour interrupted them in their very act of eating the paschal lamb, with these words, and another institution,) *Jesus took bread;* without doubt unleavened bread, for this night there was no other to be found in the house of any Jew, nor yet for seven days which began from the sun-set of this night. But it will not from hence follow, that the Lord's supper must be eaten with unleavened bread. For though our Saviour be to be imitated in his actions relating to gospel worship; yet not in such of them which had a plain reference to the Jewish worship, and were there instituted for a special reason, as unleavened bread was, to put them in mind of the haste in which they came out of Egypt. Our Saviour at this time could use no other than unleavened bread, for no other was to be had. *And blessed it:* he did not only give thanks to God for it, and beg his blessing upon it, which (as we have before observed) was our Saviour's constant practice where he did eat bread, but he set it apart, and consecrated it for a part of his last supper. It seemeth very probable that this is to be understood here in the word *blessed it.* For although the Jews, and our Saviour, ordinarily used a short prayer and thanksgiving before they did eat meat, thereby showing that they owned God as the Giver of those things, and depended upon him for a blessing upon them, yet we no where read, that they did so during the same meal, as often as they put bread into their mouths. Luke (as we heard before) made a particular mention of our Saviour's blessing the paschal supper. The mentioning of our Saviour's blessing of this bread manifestly leadeth us to a new notion and institution; and the repeating of it again, ver. 27, upon his taking the cup, doth yet further confirm it: That our Saviour's blessing both the one and the other signifieth to us not only his giving thanks to God, and begging of God's blessing, as upon ordinary food, but his sanctifying the one and the other to be used as a new gospel institution, for the remembrance of his death. *And brake it, and gave it to the disciples.* Whether (as some say) the master of the Jewish feasts was wont, after begging of a blessing, thus to break bread and to give it to all the guests, I cannot tell, I know no scripture we have to assure us of it; certain it is our Saviour brake it, and did give it to his disciples. That he gave it into their mouths, they not touching it with their hands, or that he gave it into every one of their particular hands, the Scripture saith not, nor is it very probable, except we will admit that he changed the posture he was in; for let any judge how probable it is that one sitting upon his legs, leaning or not leaning, (the constant posture they used in eating, whether the paschal supper or any other meals.) keeping his posture, could reach it to eleven persons in the same posture, to put it into their several mouths, or give it particularly into every one of their hands; it is therefore more probable, that he put the dish or vessel in which the bread was from him to him that sat next to him, and so it was conveyed from hand to hand till all had taken it, after he had first spake as followeth. Those who can think otherwise, must presume that our Lord changed his posture, which I am sure is not to be proved from any place of holy writ. *And said, Take, eat; this is my body;* Luke adds, *which is given for you: this do in remembrance of me.* Paul puts all together, 1 Cor. xi. 24, only for *given* he saith *broken.* What contests have been and yet are betwixt the papists, Lutherans, and Zuinglians (since called Calvinists) about the true sense of those words, *This is my body*, every one knows. The papists make the sense this; This bread, once consecrated by the priest, is presently turned into the very body and blood of Christ, which every communicant eateth. Hence are their adorations to it, their elevations of it, their carrying it about in solemn processions, &c. The Lutherans, though they see the gross absurdities of this sense, yet say, That the true and real body and blood of Christ, in its true substance, is present with the bread and wine in the sacrament, and eaten by every communicant. Both these opinions agree in this absurdity, that Christ's body now must be no true human body; for we know that all true human bodies are subject to our senses, and so in one place that they cannot at the same time be in another, much less in a thousand or ten thousand places at the same time. But neither the papists nor the Lutherans will hear of any arguments from that head, but stick to the letter of our Saviour's words. The Zuinglians say the meaning is; This signifieth my body. In the same sense as it is said, Christ is the *way*, a *door*, a *vine*, a *shepherd;* and as it is said of the lamb, Exod. xii. 11, *It is the Lord's passover:* yet they are far from making this ordinance a bare empty sign, but do acknowledge it a sacred institution of Christ in the gospel, in the observation of which he doth vouchsafe his spiritual presence, so as every true believer worthily receiving, doth really and truly partake of the body and blood of Christ, that is, all the benefits of his blessed death and passion, which is undoubtedly all intended by our Saviour in these words: and when he saith, *Take, eat,* he means no more than that true believers should by the hand of their body take the bread, and with their bodily mouths eat it, and at the same time, by the hand and mouth of faith, receive and apply all the benefits of his blessed death and passion to their souls; and that they should do this in remembrance of him, that is, (as the apostle, 1 Cor. xi. 26, expounds it,) showing forth *the Lord's death till he come.* It followeth, *And he took the cup, and gave thanks, and gave it to them, saying, Drink ye all of it; for this is my blood of the new testament, which is shed for many for the remission of sins.* Christ's taking of the cup, and giving of thanks, were actions of the same nature with those which he used with a relation to the bread, of which I spake before. Let the papists and Lutherans say what they can, here must be two figures acknowledged in these words. The *cup* here is put for the wine in the cup; and the meaning of these words, *this is my blood of the new testament*, must be, this wine is the sign of the new covenant. Why they should not as readily acknowledge a figure in those words, *This is my body*, I cannot understand; the pronoun *this*, in the Greek, is in the neuter gender, and applicable to the term *cup*, or to the term *blood;* but it is most reasonable to interpret it, This cup, that is, the wine in this cup, is the blood of the new covenant, or testament, that is, the blood by which the new covenant is confirmed and established. Thus *the blood of the covenant* signifieth in several texts, Exod. xxiv. 8; Zech. ix. 11; Heb. ix. 20; x. 29. *Which is shed for many for the remission of sins;* to purchase remission of sins; and this lets us know, that by *many* here cannot be understood all individuals, unless we will say that Christ purchased a remission of sins for many who shall never obtain it, which how he could do, if he died in their stead, suffering the wrath of God due to them for sin, is very hard to understand. *But I say unto you, I will not drink henceforth of this fruit of the vine.* I observed before, that Luke puts these words before the institution of the supper, and some think that they properly belong to that place; but I understand no reason for it, Matthew and Mark both placing it here; nor doth it seem probable, that after these words our Saviour should presently drink of it in the institution of his supper. Some here object our Saviour's drinking after his resurrection; but besides that, it cannot be proved that he drank any wine; neither did he otherwise eat or drink at all, but to show that he was indeed risen, for he hungered and thirsted no more after his resurrection. Or else by this phrase our Saviour only meant, I will no more participate in this ordinance with you. *Until that day when I drink it new with you in my Father's kingdom,* that is, in heaven. Some will say, Shall there then be drinking of wine in heaven? *Answ.* No; neither doth the particle *until* signify any such thing. But the joys and pleasures of heaven are often metaphorically set out under the notion of sitting down to banquet, chap. viii. 11, supping, Rev. iii. 20, eating and drinking, Luke xxii. 30. Our Saviour calls this *new wine,* to signify that he did not by it mean such wine as men drink here: I will not henceforth drink of the fruit of the vine, but both you and I, in my Father's glory, shall be satisfied with rivers of pleasures, which shall be far sweeter, and more excellent, than that which is but the juice of the grape, and the fruit of the vine. *And when they had sung an hymn, they went out into the Mount of Olives.* That the Jews were wont to close their passover supper with singing a hymn I do not doubt; nor that they had some particular psalms or hymns which they used at that time to sing: but whether it were any of these that our Saviour at this time praised God with I cannot tell, much less whether he designed this praising of God with particular relation to the paschal supper, or his supper, which he had now instituted, or both. The inquiries after these things are but insignificant curiosities, fit for such as have more mind to look into the skirts of holy writ, than to find out of it what may be of profit and advantage to them. Our Saviour doubtless intended by this to instruct us, that the ordinance of his supper is a eucharistical service, wherein our souls are most highly concerned to give thanks unto God; and as singing is an external action which God hath appointed to express the inward joy and thankfulness of our hearts, so it is very proper to be used at that holy institution. *They went out into the Mount of Olives.* Our Lord knew that his time was now come when he must be actually delivered into the hands of his enemies. That he might not therefore cause any disturbance either to the master of the family wherein he was, or to the city, though it was now midnight, he goeth out of the city (the gates being either open, because of the multitude of people, very late, or else easily opened to him) to the Mount of Olives; a mountain in the way betwixt Jerusalem and Bethany, so called, as is thought, from the multitude of olive trees growing upon and about it. The evangelist as yet mentioneth nothing of Judas, who now was gone to plot his work, and will anon return to accomplish it. In the mean time let us follow our Saviour, attending to his discourses and actions.

^c Mark 14. 27. John 16. 32.
^d ch. 11. 6.
^e Zech.13.7.

31 Then saith Jesus unto them, ^c All ye shall ^dbe offended because of me this night: for it is written, ^eI will smite the shepherd, and the sheep of the flock shall be scattered abroad.

^f ch. 28. 7, 10, 16. Mark 14.28. & 16.7.

32 But after I am risen again, ^fI will go before you into Galilee.

33 Peter answered and said unto him, Though all *men* shall be offended because of thee, *yet* will I never be offended.

^g Mark 14. 30. Luke 22. 34. John 13. 38.

34 Jesus said unto him, ^gVerily I say unto thee, That this night, before the cock crow, thou shalt deny me thrice.

35 Peter said unto him, Though I should die with thee, yet will I not deny thee. Likewise also said all the disciples.

Mark hath the same, chap. xiv. 27—31, only he saith, ver. 30, *This day, even in this night, before the cock crow twice, thou shalt deny me thrice.* Luke hath it not entire, but he hath something of it, chap. xxii. 31—34, with some addition, thus, *And the Lord said, Simon, Simon, behold,*

Satan hath desired to have you, that he may sift you as wheat. But have prayed for thee, that thy faith may not fail: and when thou art converted, strengthen thy brethren. And he said unto him, Lord, I am ready to go with thee, both into prison and to death. And he said, I tell thee, Peter, the cock shall not crow this day, before that thou shalt thrice deny that thou knowest me. Those who read the evangelists, must remember that they did not write our Saviour's words from his mouth, but from their memories; and therefore must be allowed to vary in their expressions, and in circumstances, giving us only an account of the substance of words and actions, as their memories served them; from whence also it is that some of them have some circumstances not in the others. Our Saviour's design here in general, is to inform his disciples of something which would happen by and by. *All ye* (saith he) *shall be offended because of me this night.* The word *offended* is of a very large signification in holy writ; here it seems to signify disturbed or troubled, though if we take it strictly for stumbling, so as to sin, it was true enough, for that happened, (as we shall see anon,) which made them to forsake Christ and flee, which doubtless was their sin. *For it is written, I will smite the shepherd, and the sheep of the flock shall be scattered abroad.* The words are Zech. xiii. 7. The words there are imperative, *Smite the shepherd.* There are different opinions, whether that text is primarily to be understood of Christ, or it be only a proverbial speech, which the prophet made use of with another reference, which yet Christ doth apply unto himself. I do more incline to think, that Christ here interpreteth the prophecy to relate primarily to himself, for he doth not say, As it is said, but, It is written; yet, consider it as a proverbial speech, it is true of others also. But certainly our Saviour designed to uphold the spirits of his disciples, by letting them know, that though they should see the Shepherd smitten, that is, himself, who is *the good Shepherd,* John x. 11; and is called by the apostle, the *great Shepherd of the sheep,* Heb. xiii. 20, the *chief Shepherd,* 1 Pet. v. 4; yet they should not be disturbed, for, 1. It was no more than was prophesied concerning him, Zech. xiii. 7. 2. Though at present they were scattered, yet it should not be long, for he should rise again, and then he would go before them into Galilee; which was fulfilled, as we read, Mark xvi. 7. Upon these words, Peter, whom by all the gospel history we shall observe to have been of the highest courage, and forwardest to speak, saith, *Though all men shall be offended because of thee, yet will I never be offended.* These doubtless were his present thoughts, this his sudden resolution. Here now seem to come in our Saviour's words to Peter, mentioned by Luke only, chap. xxii. 31, *Simon, Simon, behold, Satan hath desired to have you, that he may sift you as wheat: but I have prayed for thee, that thy faith fail not: and when thou art converted, strengthen thy brethren. You* is in the plural number, and to be interpreted by *you all,* though our Saviour directeth his speech only to Peter, who first spake, whom he calleth by his own name, and doubleth it, to signify his earnestness in giving him warning. To *sift you.* In sifting there are two things: 1. The shaking of the corn up and down. 2. The separation of the grain from the dust, or the seeds mixed with it: Satan hath desired, or hath obtained leave of my Father, to trouble you all, shaking your faith this and that way. But I have prayed, that although the workings of your faith be suspended, and the habit of your faith be shaken, yet it may not utterly fail, but the seeds of God may abide in you: you shall not wholly fall away, but be renewed again by repentance; and *when thou art converted,* when thou hast fallen, and shalt have a sight of thy error, and be humbled for it, endeavour to strengthen thy brethren's faith. We may observe from hence, 1. That temptations are siftings. God sifts us to purge away our dross. Satan sifts us, if it were possible, to take away our wheat. 2. That the devil is the great tempter. Others may hold and move the sieve, but he is the master of the work. 3. That he hath a continual desire to be sifting in God's flour. 4. That he hath a chain upon him; he must ask God's leave to trouble his people. 5. That God often giveth him leave, but through Christ's pleadings he shall not conquer: he may sift and trouble a believer, but the believer's faith shall not fail. 6. That in the hour of temptation we stand in Christ's strength, by the virtue of his intercession. 7. That lapsed Christians, when the Lord hath restored them, ought to

S. MATTHEW XXVI.

endeavour to strengthen and establish others. Jesus saith to Peter, *Verily I say unto thee, That this night, before the cock crow, thou shalt deny me thrice.* Luke saith, *thou shalt deny that thou knowest me.* Mark saith, *before the cock crow twice;* and so interpreteth Matthew, for he denied Christ but once before the cock did crow once. How little do we know ourselves, that cannot tell what our hearts will be three or four hours! Peter was too confident of the contrary, and replieth again upon our Saviour, telling him, that if all should deny him, he would not. So also they all said, but what happened we shall hear more by and by.

h Mark 14. 32,—35.
Luke 22. 39.
John 18. 1.

36 ¶ ʰThen cometh Jesus with them unto a place called Gethsemane, and saith unto the disciples, Sit ye here, while I go and pray yonder.

Mark leaveth out *yonder,* chap. xiv. 32. Luke saith, chap. xxii. 39—41, *He came out, and went, as he was wont, to the Mount of Olives; and his disciples also followed him. And when he was at the place, he said unto them, Pray that ye enter not into temptation. And he was withdrawn from them about a stone's cast, and kneeled down, and prayed.* Whether this *Gethsemane* were the name of a garden, or of a village wherein was a garden, is not much material for us to know. In Jerusalem, they say, they had no gardens, but their gardens were without the gates. Certain it is, it was on the other side of the brook Cedron, John xviii. 1, and either in or at the foot of the Mount of Olives. Thither Christ went with his disciples, that is, eleven of them; we shall hear of the twelfth by and by. Luke saith, that he bade his disciples pray that they might not enter into temptation: these words Matthew and Mark have, after Christ's first return to them; they say he now said only, *Sit ye here, while I go and pray yonder.*

i ch. 4. 21.

37 And he took with him Peter and ⁱthe two sons of Zebedee, and began to be sorrowful and very heavy.

k John 12. 27.

38 Then saith he unto them, ᵏMy soul is exceeding sorrowful, even unto death: tarry ye here, and watch with me.

Mark names the three disciples, chap. xiv. 33, 34: *And he taketh with him Peter and James and John, and began to be sore amazed, and to be very heavy; and saith unto them, My soul is exceeding sorrowful unto death: tarry ye here, and watch.* The three witnesses of his transfiguration, chap. xvii. 1, he takes also to be witnesses of his agony. *He began to be sorrowful, and very heavy.* The words in the Greek are expressive of the greatest sorrow imaginable, which he further expresseth ver. 38, saying, *My soul is exceeding sorrowful, even unto death.* This was not wholly upon the sense of his approaching death, for he laid down his life, no man took it from him; nor yet to consider how his disciples would be left; but in the sense he had of the wrath of God due to man for sin, which he now felt, bearing our sins. So as this was a part, and a great part, of his suffering, as appears by his following earnest prayers for the passing away of that cup, his sweating as it were drops of blood, Luke xxii. 44, the angels coming and ministering unto him, Luke xxii. 43. Luke saith, he was *in an agony,* which signifieth a great inward conflict.

l Mark 14. 36. Luke 22. 42. Heb. 5. 7.
m John 12. 27.
n ch. 20. 22.
o John 5. 30. & 6. 38.
Phil. 2. 8.

39 And he went a little farther, and fell on his face, and ˡprayed, saying, ᵐO my Father, if it be possible, ⁿlet this cup pass from me: nevertheless ᵒnot as I will, but as thou *wilt.*

Mark saith, chap. xiv. 35, 36, *He went forward a little, and fell on the ground, and prayed that, if it were possible, the hour might pass from him. And he said, Abba, Father, all things are possible unto thee; take away this cup from me: nevertheless not what I will, but what thou wilt.* Luke saith, chap. xxii. 41, 42, *He was withdrawn from them about a stone's cast, and kneeled down, and prayed, saying, Father, if thou be willing, remove this cup from me: nevertheless not my will, but thine, be done.* Here are three distinct forms of words, but all agreeing in one and the same sense. Matthew saith, *He went a little farther, and fell on his face, and prayed.* He at his first motion carried but three with him, Peter, James, and John; now he leaves them, but not far,

Luke saith, *about a stone's cast.* Fervent prayer loves privacy, and Christ by this teacheth us that secret prayer is our duty. He *fell on his face;* Luke saith, he *kneeled;* he possibly at first kneeled, then fell on his face. We read in Scripture of sitting, standing, kneeling, and prostration used in prayer; the first and last rarely; standing and kneeling were the most ordinary postures. David prayed sitting in his house, 2 Sam. vii. 18. Abraham fell on his face, Gen. xvii. 17. So did Moses and Aaron, Numb. xvi. 22, 45. Prostration was ordinarily used in great passions; hardly otherwise in prayer. *Saying, O my Father, if it be possible, let this cup pass from me: nevertheless not as I will, but as thou wilt.* Mark first tells us the sum of his prayer, then saith he said, *Abba, Father, all things are possible unto thee; take away this cup from me: nevertheless not what I will, but what thou wilt.* Luke saith he said, *If thou be willing, remove this cup from me: nevertheless not my will, but thine, be done.* Luke's *if thou be willing* expounds Matthew's *if it be possible.* A thing in itself may be possible which considered in its circumstances is not so: thus, as it is in Mark, all things are to God possible; but yet it is not possible for God to alter any thing which he hath decreed, or said shall come to pass; because God is not as man, one that can lie, or repent. But it will be objected, Did not Christ know that it was not possible? Did not he himself, ver. 54, say, *thus it must be?* I answer, It is one thing what he knew as he was God, and of counsel with the Father; and another thing what he prayed for as man. Besides, our Saviour's saying, *if it be possible,* doth not suppose that he knew it was possible; it signifieth no more than this, Father, my human nature hath an aversion from this heavy stroke, so as, if it were possible, it craves of thee a discharge from this curse: *nevertheless not my will, but thine, be done.* The first clause is but the expression of the natural (but not sinful) infirmity of his flesh; the latter a perfect resignation of his will to God. In the first he tells his Father what his natural flesh would crave, if it might consist with the will of God. In the second he begs that, whatsoever his flesh craved, yet the will of God might be done. And herein he sets us a perfect pattern for our prayers for deliverance from temporal evils, viz. with a submission to the will of God. By this our Saviour doth not declare himself ignorant or uncertain of the Divine will: only as, though the person that died was God-man, yet the human nature only died; so, though the person that prayed was God-man, yet he only prayed as he was man.

40 And he cometh unto the disciples, and findeth them asleep, and saith unto Peter, What, could ye not watch with me one hour?

p Mark 13. 33. & 14. 38.
Luke 22. 40, 46. Ephes. 6. 18.

41 ᵖWatch and pray, that ye enter not into temptation: the spirit indeed *is* willing, but the flesh *is* weak.

Mark hath the same, chap. xiv. 37, 38. Luke hath nothing of our Saviour's going the second or third time, but hath some other passages, which we shall consider by and by; and telleth us but once of his finding the disciples asleep, which we shall also take notice of in their order. Whether Christ came this first time only to Peter, and James, and John, whom he had left nearer to him, or to the other eight, left at a farther distance, I cannot determine, but think the first most probable. He *saith unto Peter,* and so to James and John, *What, could ye not watch with me one hour?* You, Peter, that even now wert so resolute for me; and you, James and John, that told me, you could drink of the cup whereof I drank, and be baptized with the baptism I should be baptized with; what, do you faint the first time? *Watch and pray, that ye enter not into temptation.* Here he calls them to a greater watching, spiritual watching, in opposition to security, that they might not fall under their temptations. By watching, he directeth them to the use of such means as were within their power to use; by adding *pray,* he lets them know, that it was not in their power to stand without God's help and assistance, which must be obtained by prayer, and upon their praying should not be denied them. *The spirit indeed is willing, but the flesh is weak:* the spirit, sanctified by Divine grace, is resolved with constancy to perform its duty; but the flesh, the sensitive part, is apt to faint and fall away when terrible temptations assault us: therefore you should earnestly pray for supernatural strength, and be vigilant, lest you be surprised and overcome by them. The words also may have an immediate respect to their being overtaken with sleep in this hour of Christ's summons, though they resolved affectionately to attend him and cleave to him.

42 He went away again the second time, and prayed, saying, O my Father, if this cup may not pass away from me, except I drink it, thy will be done.

43 And he came and found them asleep again : for their eyes were heavy.

Mark saith, chap. xiv. 39, 40, *And again he went away, and prayed, and spake the same words. And when he returned, he found them asleep again, (for their eyes were heavy,) neither wist they what to answer him. Saying the same words.* How our translation came to translate this so I cannot tell, in the Greek it is τὸν αὐτὸν λόγον, which must be translated, the same word, or the same speech, not words (if that were the evangelist's sense). But that it is not, for, as it is plain our Saviour used more than one word, so it is as plain it was not the same speech, or form of words, for we have met with four different forms already : our Lord prayed but thrice, so as he could not say the same speech. But λόγον here signifies matter—speaking the same matter, or to the same sense, and thus we translate it, Mark i. 45; x. 10, and in a multitude of other texts, in correspondence with the Hebrew דבר He comes to them a second time, and findeth them asleep. So quickly did they find the truth of what he had but now taught them, that *the spirit is willing, but the flesh is weak*, for there is no doubt but they did what they could to keep themselves awake.

44 And he left them, and went away again, and prayed the third time, saying the same words.

45 Then cometh he to his disciples, and saith unto them, Sleep on now, and take *your* rest : behold, the hour is at hand, and the Son of man is betrayed into the hands of sinners.

46 Rise, let us be going : behold, he is at hand that doth betray me.

Mark saith nothing of this third praying, but saith, chap. xiv. 41, 42, *And he cometh the third time, and saith unto them, Sleep on now, and take your rest: it is enough, the hour is come ; behold, the Son of man is betrayed into the hands of sinners. Rise up, let us go ; lo, he that betrayeth me is at hand.* What the meaning of *saying the same words* is, we heard before ; praying to the same sense, or saying the same thing, or matter, though using other words, as it is plain he hid. Luke tells us, chap. xxii. 43, *there appeared an angel unto him from heaven, strengthening him.* This is not the first time we read of angels appearing and ministering to Christ. They did so, chap. iv. 11, after his conflict with the devil in the wilderness. Now an angel appeared to him in the hour of temptation. Then he had *without, troubles ;* but now he hath *within, fears*, being in a great agony. Thus it is said, John xii. 27, 28, that he being in a conflict, and praying, *Father, save me from this hour : but for this cause came I unto this hour. Father, glorify thy name. A voice was heard, saying, I have both glorified it, and will glorify it again.* There the answer was testified by a voice from heaven ; here it is by an angel. So God, Dan. ix. 21, let Daniel know his prayer was heard. Hannah knew another way, by the peace of her spirit after prayer—*her countenance was no more sad,* 1 Sam. i. 18. How the angel did strengthen him we are not told. Let no man think that he who was the Son of God needed an angel to strengthen him : he was not now exerting his Divine virtue, but by his suffering showing that he was truly man, and, as to that nature, made lower than the angels. Luke addeth, ver. 44, *And being in an agony he prayed more earnestly : and his sweat was as it were great drops of blood falling down to the ground.* These words are expressive of the great conflict of our Saviour's spirit, which was such as thrust out sweat like great drops of blood : whether they were very blood, or sweat with some mixture or tincture of blood, is very hard to determine, nor of any consequence for us to know : it is no unusual thing for bodies to breathe out sweat in ordinary conflicts of spirit ; this was much more than ordinary. Luke saith, ver. 45, 46, that *when he rose up from prayer, and was come to his disciples, he found them sleeping for sorrow, and said unto them, Why sleep ye ? rise and pray, lest ye enter into temptation.* All three evangelists agree, that Christ coming the third time found them sleeping. Luke gives one reason of it, *for sorrow.* Their sorrow, added to their watching, may be some excuse for their sleeping, though otherwise it was a time which called for more waking. The evangelists do not so well agree in what Christ said to his disciples. Luke saith, *Rise and pray, lest ye enter into temptation.* Matthew and Mark say he said, *Sleep on now, and take your rest, &c.* He might say both. Nor can we determine whether he spake those words seriously, as willing that they should take their rest, for they could be no further useful to him, whose time was now come ; he was betrayed, and the traitor was at hand : or, with some reflection upon them for their drowsiness, which the words going before, *What, could ye not watch with me one hour ?* seem to hint us.

47 ¶ And ᑫwhile he yet spake, lo, Judas, one of the twelve, came, and with him a great multitude with swords and staves, from the Chief Priests and elders of the people.

ᑫ Mark 14. 43.
Luke 22. 47.
John 18. 3.
Acts 1. 16.

Mark saith the same, chap. xiv. 43, adding also *the scribes.* Luke saith there was *a multitude*, and *Judas went before them*, adding, that he *drew near to Jesus to kiss him*, chap. xxii. 47. If any ask how Judas knew where Jesus was at that time of the night, or rather so early in the morning, John satisfieth us, chap. xviii. 2, *And Judas also, which betrayed him, knew the place : for Jesus ofttimes resorted thither with his disciples.* And then goeth on, ver. 3, *Judas then, having received a band of men and officers from the chief priests and Pharisees, cometh thither with lanterns and torches and weapons.* Those skilled in the Jewish learning tell us, that the ordinary guard of the temple belonged to the priests, and such officers as they employed ; but upon their great festivals, the Roman governor added a band of his soldiers, who yet were under the command of the priests. It is thought these officers, soldiers, and others came with a warrant to apprehend our Saviour from the Jewish sanhedrim, or highest court, which was made up of chief priests, scribes, and Pharisees, and the elders of the people : they had torches and lanterns, because it was yet dark, before the day was broke ; swords and staves, to be ready against any opposition. Judas the traitor comes before as their leader.

48 Now he that betrayed him gave them a sign, saying, Whomsoever I shall kiss, that same is he : hold him fast.

49 And forthwith he came to Jesus, and said, Hail, master ; ʳand kissed him.

ʳ 2 Sam. 20. 9.

Mark, chap. xiv. 44, 45, differs not, only instead of *hold him fast*, he hath, *lead him away safely ;* and instead of *Hail, master,* he saith, *Master, master.* There is in these words nothing difficult or doubtful : Judas had given them a sign how to know Christ, that was his kissing of him : being come where he was, he steps to our Saviour and kissed him, by which he let them know that he was the person against whom their warrant was.

50 And Jesus said unto him, ˢFriend, wherefore art thou come ? Then came they, and laid hands on Jesus, and took him.

ˢ Ps. 41. 9. & 55. 13.

Mark saith nothing of what Christ said to him. Luke, chap. xxii. 48, adds, that Christ said to him, *Judas, betrayest thou the Son of man with a kiss ?* Whether Christ used this compellation of *friend* to Judas, to mind him what he formerly had been, and still ought to have been, or as a common compellation, (as we oft use it,) is not much material. A kiss is the symbol of friendship and kindness, and therefore very improperly used by a traitor and professed enemy ; yet so used by Joab to Amasa, 2 Sam. xx. 9. That makes our Saviour ask him if he were not ashamed to betray the Son of man by a kiss. Judas, by calling him *Master, master,* acknowledged he had been once his disciple. By his kiss he pretended friendship to him, yet betrayed him. Oh the depth of desperate wickedness which is in the heart of man! especially such as apostatize from a former profession; they are commonly the worst and falsest enemies of Christ and his gospel.

t John 18.10.

51 And, behold, ᵗone of them which were with Jesus stretched out *his* hand, and drew his sword, and struck a servant of the High Priest's, and smote off his ear.

u Gen. 9. 6.
Rev. 13. 10.

52 Then said Jesus unto him, Put up again thy sword into his place: ᵘfor all they that take the sword shall perish with the sword.

53 Thinkest thou that I cannot now pray to my Father, and he shall presently give me ˣmore than twelve legions of angels?

x 2 Kin. 6.17.
Dan. 7. 10.

y Is. 53.7, &c.
ver. 24. Luke
24. 25, 44, 46.

54 But how then shall the Scriptures be fulfilled, ʸthat thus it must be?

Matthew relates this history shortly, but Mark much more, chap. xiv. 47; he saith no more than this, *And one of them that stood by drew a sword, and smote a servant of the high priest, and cut off his ear.* Luke also relates something of it, chap. xxii. 50, 51, *And one of them smote the servant of the high priest, and cut off his right ear. And Jesus answered and said, Suffer ye thus far. And he touched his ear, and healed him.* John relates the same passage with some more particulars, chap. xviii. 10. *Then Simon Peter having a sword drew it, and smote the high priest's servant, and cut off his right ear. The servant's name was Malchus. Then said Jesus unto Peter, Put up thy sword into the sheath: the cup which my Father hath given me, shall I not drink it?* If any ask, how Christ and his disciples came to have a sword, he may be satisfied that they had two, from Luke xxii. 35—38, which verses being in none of the other evangelists, I have left to be spoken to in their order. The disciples seeing the officers laying hands on Christ, as was said ver. 50, knowing *what would follow*, as Luke saith, *one of them* (St. John tells us it was Peter) drew a sword, and smote off the right ear of one of the high priest's servants. John tells us his name was Malchus. Our Saviour reproveth Peter, commanding him to put up the sword again into its sheath, and telling him, 1. That he who taketh the sword should perish with the sword. It is to be understood of private persons taking up the sword to destroy their lawful magistrates; and this lesson it teacheth all Christians. Men must have the sword given orderly into their hands, before they may use it, and that no private person can have against the supreme magistrate. 2. Secondly, (saith our Saviour,) I needed not thy help to defend me. If I were to make any defence, I could *pray to my Father*, and he should *give me more than twelve legions of angels;* there is therefore no need of thy drawing a sword in my defence. 3. The Scripture (saith he) must be fulfilled; it was prophesied of me that I should be thus used, and those prophecies must be fulfilled. Having reproved Peter, and silenced his passion, Luke tells us, he begged leave so far as to touch his ear, and he healed it; thus doing good to those that hated him, and working a miracle in the sight of them, which (had not their hearts been hardened) might have convinced them both of his innocency and his Divine power; but they take no notice of his kindness. Now he applieth himself to the multitude of his enemies.

55 In that same hour said Jesus to the multitudes, Are ye come out as against a thief with swords and staves for to take me? I sat daily with you teaching in the temple, and ye laid no hold on me.

z Lam. 4. 20.
ver. 54.
a See John
18. 15.

56 But all this was done, that the ᶻScriptures of the prophets might be fulfilled. Then ᵃall the disciples forsook him, and fled.

Mark hath the same, chap. xiv. 48—50. Luke, chap. xxii. 52, 53, hath it thus: *Then Jesus said unto the chief priests, and captains of the temple, and the elders, which were come to him, Be ye come out, as against a thief, with swords and staves? When I was daily with you in the temple, ye stretched forth no hands against me: but this is your hour, and the power of darkness.* What our evangelist reports as spoken to the rabble, Luke reports as spoken to the chief priests and captains of the temple, (that is, of the soldiers, who at that time were the guard of the temple,) some of which, it should seem, came along with the rabble, to whom our Saviour directeth his speech. *I sat daily with you teaching in the temple.* I observed before, that it was their usual manner for those that taught in the temple to sit while they taught, to testify their authority; Christ, when he came up to the passover, was wont to teach in the temple. *And ye laid no hold on me:* I did not hide myself, nor go about to raise a party to defend myself, but quietly taught in the temple. If I had been guilty of any crime, you might easily have taken me; why are you now come out against me as against a thief, upon whom you had need to raise the country? why come you against me with swords and staves, as if you thought I would make some resistance to defend myself? you never saw any such thing in me as should give you a jealousy of such a thing. *But all this was done, that the Scriptures of the prophets might be fulfilled,* the many scriptures which spake concerning the sufferings of Christ. Luke addeth, *but this is your hour, and the power of darkness,* that is, this is that which God hath determined. Wicked men and persecutors of Christ and his gospel have their hour. There is a time which God in his wise counsels hath set and determined, when for the trial of his people's faith and patience, he suffers the devil, by vile and wicked men, who are his instruments, to imprison and otherwise vex and molest his people. That such a time is their hour, and what they do is by the permission and according to the counsel of God, and but an hour, a determined and short time, are great arguments to persuade us to the exercise of faith and patience. *And the power of darkness;* a time when the prince of darkness is putting forth his power: or, *the power of darkness,* that is, a time of exceeding great darkness, of affliction to me and my disciples. Wicked men's hour is always to Christ's disciples the power of darkness. *Then all the disciples forsook him, and fled.* Probably all of them fled at first, though Peter and another came back again: or, *all* here signifieth the most of them. We never know our hearts upon the prospect of great trials, until we come to grapple with them, and to be engaged in them. These disciples had all said they would not forsake him; when it comes to the push, not one of them stands by him. But although they shrunk at first, not without the providence of God permitting them thus to fail in their duty, then governing their failures to his own glory; yet they again returned to their duty after Christ's resurrection, owned Christ, preached his gospel, and at last drank off the cup, which he drank of first, and were baptized with the baptism wherewith he was baptized. All must not be condemned for flight in a time of persecution. We must observe whether they apostatize from their profession, or whether they do not return again, before we pass a judgment against them.

b Mark 14.
53. Luke 22.
54. John 18.
12, 13, 24.

57 ¶ ᵇAnd they that had laid hold on Jesus led *him* away to Caiaphas the High Priest, where the Scribes and the elders were assembled.

Mark saith, chap. xiv. 53, *They led Jesus away to the high priest: and with him were assembled all the chief priests, and the elders, and the scribes.* Luke saith no more but, *Then took they him, and led him, and brought him into the high priest's house,* chap. xxii. 54. John saith, chap. xviii. 12, 13, *Then the band, and the captain, and the officers of the Jews, took Jesus, and bound him, and led him away to Annas first; for he was father-in-law to Caiaphas, which was the high priest that same year.* All things were now out of order in the Jewish church. Regularly, their high priests were to be such as derived from the eldest son of Aaron, and were to hold in their place for life; but they were now chosen annually, and their conquerors ruled the choice as they pleased. Yet some think, that in this the Jews kept something of their ancient form, and the high priest was chosen regularly of the house of Aaron and for life; but the Romans when they listed turned him out, and sold the place to another; and such a one was Caiaphas, who was at that time high priest, son-in-law to Annas.

Their carrying of Christ first to Annas's house, was no more than to stay there a while till Caiaphas, and the council, which was appointed to meet that morning at the house of Caiaphas, could assemble.

58 But Peter followed him afar off unto the High Priest's palace, and went in, and sat with the servants, to see the end.

Mark adds, chap. xiv. 54, *and warmed himself at the fire.* Luke saith, chap. xxii. 54, 55, *Then took they him, and led him, and brought him into the high priest's house. And Peter followed afar off. And when they had kindled a fire in the midst of the hall, and were set down together, Peter sat down among them.* John gives us a more particular account how Peter came into the hall, chap. xviii. 15, 16: *And Simon Peter followed Jesus, and so did another disciple: that disciple was known unto the high priest, and went in with Jesus into the palace of the high priest. But Peter stood at the door without. Then went out that other disciple, which was known unto the high priest, and spake unto her that kept the door, and brought in Peter.* Some think that this other disciple was John himself; but it is not probable that John and the high priest should be so well acquainted: it is more probably judged, that it was none of the twelve, but one who favoured Christ more secretly, some citizen of Jerusalem whom the high priest favoured, or at least knew by face, and had some respect for, and therefore he was admitted in, and he helped Peter in; who being come in, and a fire kindled in the hall, the rest of the company sat down and warmed themselves by the fire, Peter also sat down amongst them, being desirous to see the end.

59 Now the Chief Priests, and elders, and all the council, sought false witness against Jesus, to put him to death;

c Ps. 27. 12. & 35. 11.
Mark 14. 55.
So Acts 6. 13.
d Deu. 19. 15.

60 But found none: yea, though ᶜmany false witnesses came, *yet* found they none. At the last came ᵈtwo false witnesses.

Mark expounds this latter verse, chap. xiv. 56, *For many bare false witness against him, but their witness agreed not together.* It is plain that they had taken up a resolution to destroy Christ one way or another, but they will make a show of justice in the execution of their malice. The council being set, it is not to be thought that they had then leisure to send about for witnesses, but out of their malice they screwed and sifted such witnesses as were brought, to see if they could get of them upon thir oaths to affirm any thing against him which by their law was capital. *Many false witnesses came, yet they found none;* that is, no two agreeing in the same story, as the law required, Deut. xix. 15, for a single testimony was none. *Vox unius est vox nullius,* A single witness is no witness, or none that could testify any thing of a capital nature. Many came and witnessed trivial things, but none witnessed any thing which touched his life; till *at last came two false witnesses.*

e ch. 27. 40.
John 2. 19.

61 And said, This *fellow* said, ᵉI am able to destroy the temple of God, and to build it in three days.

Mark saith, chap. xiv. 57—59, *And there arose certain, and bare false witness against him, saying, We heard him say, I will destroy this temple that is made with hands, and within three days I will build another made without hands. But neither so did their witness agree together.* These are called by the evangelists, *false witnesses.* Our Saviour said, John ii. 19, *Destroy this temple, and in three days I will raise it up,* speaking of his body, as John tells us there, ver. 21. He did not say, *I will destroy this temple made with hands, and within three days I will build another made without hands.* But Mark saith these witnesses could not agree in their tale, or their testimony, though agreeing was not sufficient to make him guilty of a capital crime. The high priest must use some other arts.

f Mark 14. 60.

62 ᶠAnd the High Priest arose, and said unto him, Answerest thou nothing? what *is it which* these witness against thee?

g Is. 53. 7.
ch. 27. 12, 14.

63 But ᵍJesus held his peace. And the High Priest answered and said unto him, ʰI adjure thee by the living God, that thou tell us whether thou be the Christ, the Son of God.

h Lev. 5. 1.
1 Sam. 14. 24, 26.

Mark speaks to the same purpose, chap. xiv. 60, 61. The high priest expected a long defence, and so to have had matter of accusation against him out of his own mouth. Christ disappointeth him, saying nothing at all, either out of modesty, or not thinking what they said of any moment, or worthy of any reply, or perhaps seeing that they could not agree in their tale, so as what they said was of no force against him. The high priest therefore comes at last to examine him, *ex officio.* Mark saith, chap. xiv. 61, *Again the high priest asked him, and said unto him, Art thou the Christ, the Son of the Blessed.* Luke, to give us the story of Peter, from his first coming into the high priest's hall to his going out, entire, interrupteth himself a little in his relation of their dealings with Christ, and then relates some indignities offered him which the other evangelists do not mention; which seem to have been offered him where the soldiers and the rabble had been before he appeared in the council: chap. xxii. 63—67, *And the men that held Jesus mocked him, and smote him. And when they had blindfolded him, they struck him on the face, and asked him, saying, Prophesy, who is it that smote thee? And many other things blasphemously spake they against him.* And as soon as it was day, the elders of the people, and the chief priests, and the scribes came together, and led him into their council. Then he mentioneth nothing of what the witnesses said, possibly because it was nothing of moment, nothing upon which they proceeded against our Saviour for his life, but goes on, *saying, Art thou the Christ? tell us.* Matthew saith, Art thou the Christ, the Son of the living God? Mark, *the Son of the Blessed.* It is plain both from this text, and from John i. 49, that the Jews did expect a Messiah who should be the Son of the ever-living and blessed God; but whether they understood that he should be the Son of God by nature and eternal generation, or only by a more special adoption, than the whole Jewish nation was, (to whom the apostle saith belonged the adoption,) I cannot say. *I ad jure thee that thou tell us,* that is, as some say, I charge thee upon thy oath to tell me; but it doth not appear that they had given any such oath to him, the guilty person was not wont to be forced by an oath to accuse himself, neither is it very probable that our Saviour would have taken such an oath. The sense therefore seemeth to be rather, I command, or require, or charge thee, as solemnly as if thou hadst taken an oath, (as in the presence of God,) to tell us. Or, I charge thee with a terrible imprecation on thee, if thou speakest falsely, or wilt be silent, to declare if thou be the Christ, the Son of the living God.

64 Jesus saith unto him, Thou hast said: nevertheless I say unto you, ⁱHereafter shall ye see the Son of man ᵏ sitting on the right hand of power, and coming in the clouds of heaven.

i Dan. 7. 13.
ch. 16. 27.
& 24. 30.
Luke 21. 27.
& 25. 31.
John 1. 51.
Rom. 14. 10.
1 Thess. 4. 16. Rev. 1. 7.
k Ps. 110. 1.
Acts 7. 55.

Mark saith, chap. xiv. 62, *And Jesus said, I am: and ye shall see,* &c. Luke saith, chap. xxii. 67—69, *And he said unto them, If I tell you, ye will not believe: and if I also ask you, ye will not answer me, nor let me go. Hereafter shall the Son of man sit on the right hand of the power of God.* What all the evangelists say put together, makes up our Saviour's perfect answer. To what purpose (saith Christ) should I answer you? This is now but a captious question, not propounded by you to that end that you might be satisfied as to the truth, but only to insnare me, for if I should tell you I am, you would not believe it. If I should argue the matter with you, you would give me no answer. I have given you proof enough, but yet, Caiaphas, thou hast said the truth, I am the Christ, the Son of the ever-living, blessed God; and, to confirm you further, hereafter you shall see me, whom you think to be no more than the Son of man, sitting on the right hand of the power of God, and coming in the clouds of heaven. There is a time for a man to speak, and a time for him to hold his peace; in the matter of confession of truth. The seasons for silence, or speech, are to be judged from the honour and glory of God; when we cannot be silent without betraying the truth, we are bound to speak. Our Lord therefore, being so solemnly adjured in the name of God to tell them what was the truth, now confesseth, and denieth not, that he was the Son of God, and tells them, hereafter they should see it. Whether the term *hereafter* refers to the time soon following, (as ἀπ' ἄρτι, in this evangelist, and Ἀπὸ τοῦ νῦν, in Luke, seem to signify,) and be to be understood of Christ's resurrection, his ascension into heaven, the coming of the Holy Ghost, and the carrying of the gospel to all nations, or to the day of judgment (which the New Testament often speaks of as a thing at hand, and that phrase, *coming in the clouds of heaven*, seems rather to signify); or (as others think) to both, referring the sitting on the right hand of power to the former, and the coming in the clouds to the latter; is hard to determine.

1 2 Kings 18. 37. & 19. 1.

65 ¹Then the High Priest rent his clothes, saying, He hath spoken blasphemy; what further need have we of witnesses? behold, now ye have heard his blasphemy.

m Lev. 24. 16. John 19. 7.

66 What think ye? They answered and said, ᵐHe is guilty of death.

Mark hath much the same, chap. xiv. 63, 64, only he saith, *they all condemned him to be guilty of death*. Luke saith, chap. xxii. 70, 71, *Then said they all, Art thou then the Son of God? And he said unto them, Ye say that I am? And they said, What need we any further witness? for we ourselves have heard of his own mouth.* This rending of clothes was a thing very ordinary amongst the Jews, used by them in testimony of sorrow and of indignation. They used it in causes of great sorrow and mourning, even before the Israelites were formed into a nation; we find it practised by Reuben and Jacob, Gen. xxxvii. 29, 34, and by Jacob's sons, Gen. xliv. 13; by Joshua and Caleb, Numb. xiv. 6, by Jephthah, Judg. xi. 35. Indeed he that was high priest was forbidden to do it, Lev. xxi. 10, and, in order to it, to come near a dead body, ver. 11; which command yet the Jews restrain to his priestly garments, but upon other occasions he might rend his clothes, as Caiaphas here did. It was usual in case of blasphemy, both to show their sorrow for it and detestation of it, 2 Kings xix. 1; Jer. xxxvi. 24; Acts xiv. 14. So as they convicted our Saviour, not upon oaths of witnesses, but upon words which they interpreted to be blasphemy. The high priest, being but the president in this council, asks the opinion of the rest of the council. They all condemn him as guilty of a capital crime, which is here phrased *guilty of death*, that is, one who by their law ought to die.

n Is. 50. 6. & 53. 3. ch. 27. 30. o Luke 22. 63. John 19. 3. ‖ Or, *rods*. p Mark 14. 65. Luke 22. 64.

67 ⁿThen did they spit in his face, and buffeted him; and ᵒothers smote *him* with ‖ the palms of their hands,

68 Saying, ᵖProphesy unto us, thou Christ, Who is he that smote thee?

Mark hath much the same, chap. xiv. 65: *And some began to spit on him, and to cover his face, and to buffet him, and to say unto him, Prophesy: and the servants did strike him with the palms of their hands.* Though there be nothing more barbarous and inhuman than to add to the affliction of the afflicted, yet this is no more than we ordinarily see done by a rabble of brutish people; spitting in the face was but an ordinary token of contempt, Numb. xii. 14; Deut. xxv. 9. And perhaps in all these indignities Isaiah was a type of Christ, Isa. l. 6, if that text be not to be understood of Christ immediately. In the mean time, it lets us see that there is no degree or mark of contempt, or shame, or suffering which we ought to decline and grudge at for the name of Christ; who, though much more excellent than us, yet for our sake endured the cross, and despised the shame.

q Mark 14. 66. Luke 22. 55. John 18. 16, 17, 25.

69 ¶ ᑫNow Peter sat without in the palace: and a damsel came unto him, saying, Thou also wast with Jesus of Galilee.

70 But he denied before *them* all, saying, I know not what thou sayest.

Mark hath this, chap. xiv. 66, 67, only he saith, *Peter was beneath in the palace*, and *warming himself*. Luke hath this whole story before what he saith of Christ's examination and condemnation: chap. xxii. 56, 57, *But a certain maid beheld him as he sat by the fire, and earnestly looked upon him, and said, This man was also with him. And he denied him, saying, Woman, I know him not.* We before left Peter in the high priest's palace, warming himself by the fire amongst the servants. It is a dangerous thing for Christians to come into places of temptation. A maid comes to him, and chargeth him to have been with Christ, whom she calls *Jesus of Galilee:* so they called Christ sometimes *Jesus of Nazareth*, the city in Galilee where Christ lived the greatest part of his life. *He denied before them all;* so loud that all heard it. *I know not what thou sayest*, or, (as Luke saith,) *I know him not;* I neither know him, nor what thou sayest.

71 And when he was gone out into the porch, another *maid* saw him, and said unto them that were there, This *fellow* was also with Jesus of Nazareth.

72 And again he denied with an oath, I do not know the man.

Mark hath the same, chap. xiv. 70, more shortly. So Luke, chap. xxii. 58. It is like Peter, upon the first alarm, began to shift away, and was got into the porch, but there another meets him with the same charge. Here, to the former lie which he had told, and here repeateth, he adds an oath for the confirmation of what he had said. What are the best of men, when God leaves them to their own strength! But the temptation yet riseth higher.

73 And after a while came unto *him* they that stood by, and said to Peter, Surely thou also art *one* of them; for thy ʳspeech bewrayeth thee.

r Luke 22. 59.

74 Then ˢbegan he to curse and to swear, *saying*, I know not the man. And immediately the cock crew.

s Mark 14. 71.

Mark saith, chap. xiv. 70, 71, *And a little after, they that stood by said again to Peter, Surely thou art one of them: for thou art a Galilean, and thy speech agreeth thereto. But he began to curse and to swear, saying, I know not this man of whom ye speak.* Luke hath it, chap. xxii. 59, 60, *And about the space of one hour after another confidently affirmed, saying, Of a truth this fellow also was with him: for he is a Galilean. And Peter said, Man, I know not what thou sayest. And immediately, while he yet spake, the cock crew.* One spake in the name of the rest that were gathered about Peter, and he chargeth Peter confidently; and he might well, for John saith, chap. xviii. 26, that this was one of the servants of the high priest, being his kinsman whose ear Peter cut off. He said, *Did not I see thee in the garden with him?* Temptations always grow upon us in the company of wicked men. Here Peter adds to his lying, swearing and cursing; all confirming of what he had said in the denial of his Master; all in an exact fulfilling of what Christ had told Peter, ver. 34, though he was then difficult to believe it; to teach us all not to presume too far upon our own strength, but to pray that we be not led into temptation; while we stand, to take heed lest we fall; and in order to it, to avoid the society of wicked men, and places in which we probably may be tempted. To teach us also charity to lapsed brethren, and not too hastily to condemn our brethren for falling a second and a third time into the same sin; especially, while the same fit of temptation holdeth. It is added, *And immediately the cock crew*, that is, the second time; so saith Mark, chap. xiv. 72, who had mentioned the cock's first crowing, ver. 68, upon Peter's first denial of his Master.

75 And Peter remembered the word of Jesus, which said unto him, ᵗBefore the cock crow, thou shalt deny me thrice. And he went out, and wept bitterly.

t ver. 34. Mark 14. 30. Luke 22. 61, 62. John 13. 38.

Mark saith, chap. xiv. 72, *And the second time the cock crew. And Peter called to mind the word that Jesus said unto him, Before the cock crow twice, thou shalt deny me thrice. And when he thought thereon, he wept.* Luke saith, chap. xxii. 61, 62, *And the Lord turned, and looked upon*

Peter. *And Peter remembered the word of the Lord, how he had said unto him, Before the cock crow, thou shalt deny me thrice. And Peter went out, and wept bitterly.* We have in this last verse Peter's repentance, and the occasion and cause of it. A good man may fall, and that foully, but he shall not fall so as to rise no more. David lay longer than Peter under the guilt of his sin, but both of them wept bitterly. He went out of the porch ; whither he went is not said ; possibly he was afraid to what this detection of him might rise, or else sought a place (as Joseph did) to weep more privately and plentifully than he durst do, or thought convenient to do, in the porch of the high priest. That which gave occasion to this reflection was the crowing of the cock the second time, and his remembrance of the words of Jesus, ver. 34. Our memories serve us much in the business of repentance, and therefore that the soul should be without knowledge of the law of God is not good. Peter remembered what Christ had personally said to him. True penitents are still excited to repentance, by remembering the law of God, what Christ hath in his word said to them, and considering their own ways. The crowing of the cock the second time helped him to remember the words of Jesus, for he had said, *Before the cock crow twice,* &c. But the cause of his repentance is expressed by Luke, *The Lord turned, and looked upon Peter.* More must be understood by this look of Christ upon him than the mere cast of Christ's bodily eye : with that look there was a virtue which went from Christ which healed Peter, exciting his habit of grace, and assisting him in the exercise of it ; which double influence of grace is necessary to every renewed soul. Christ looked upon Judas, when Judas kissed him ; yea, and said to him, *Judas, betrayest thou the Son of man with a kiss?* yet Judas went on in his villany without remorse. He looked upon Peter, and he went out and wept bitterly. He looked only upon the face of Judas, but he looked upon the heart of Peter, as well as upon his face.

CHAP. XXVII

Christ is delivered bound to Pilate, 1, 2. *Judas hangeth himself,* 3—10. *Christ's silence before Pilate,* 11—14. *Pilate's custom at the feast, and proposal to the people,* 15—18. *His wife's message,* 19. *Being urged by the multitude, he washeth his hands in his own justification, and releasing Barabbas delivereth Jesus to be crucified,* 20— 26. *Christ is mocked of the soldiers, crowned with thorns,* 27—32, *crucified between two thieves,* 33—38, *reviled,* 39—44, *and calling upon God expireth,* 45—50. *The astonishing events which attended his death : the centurion's confession,* 51—56. *Joseph of Arimathea beggeth his body, and burieth it,* 57—61. *His sepulchre is sealed, and a watch set over it,* 62—66.

a Ps. 2. 2.
Mark 15. 1.
Luke 22. 66.
& 23. 1. John
18. 28.

WHEN the morning was come, [a] all the Chief Priests and elders of the people took counsel against Jesus to put him to death :

2 And when they had bound them, they led *him* away, and [b] delivered him to Pontius Pilate the governor.

b ch. 20. 19.
Acts 3. 13.

Mark saith, chap. xv. 1, *And straightway in the morning the chief priests held a consultation with the elders and scribes and the whole council, and bound Jesus, and carried him away, and delivered him to Pilate.* Luke saith, chap. xxiii. 1, *And the whole multitude of them arose, and led him to Pilate,* John saith, chap. xviii. 28, *Then led they Jesus from Caiaphas unto the hall of judgment : and it was early ; and they themselves went not into the judgment hall, lest they should be defiled ; but that they might eat the passover.* If any ask why, having condemned Christ, they did not put him to death. John tells us, ver. 31, it was not lawful for them to put any one to death. They had already out of their malice to Christ broken several of their own canons, or rules observed in ordinary capital causes, sitting in the night time, and upon a festival day. They must have notoriously broken another, if they had themselves on that day put him to death. It should seem by their stoning Stephen, Acts vii. 59, they had a power in some cases to put persons to death ; but Christ was to be crucified, and as to that kind of **death** they had no power : see John xviii. 31. Besides that, we must consider it was the passover day, and stoning any man to death required a concourse of people to throw stones, and they were afraid of tumults. The Roman governor had the militia in his power, and could better prevent and suppress tumults than they could do. Finally, Christ was by his death to give testimony to his kingly office ; and the Jews, as we shall hear, had this to charge him with, That he made himself a King : this was a civil cause, and to be adjudged by Pilate the Roman governor amongst them. In the morning, therefore, consulting how to put Christ to death, they delivered him to Pontius Pilate, having first bound him ; for though he was bound upon his first apprehension, yet it is probable that they had loosed him when he came into the hall of the high priest, and now bind him a second time, when they carried him before Pilate. John tells us, that they would not themselves go *into the judgment hall, lest they should be defiled ;. but that they might eat the passover ;* which words have in them a difficulty, and also give us an account of a most unaccountable superstition. For the passover, they had eaten it the night before. But we must know, that not the paschal lamb only, but all the sacrifices offered any of the seven days, were also called the passover, Deut. xvi. 1, 2, &c. It was now the first day of unleavened bread, but there were to be offerings this day of which they were to eat, which in a large sense are called the passover. But how unaccountable was the superstition of these hypocrites! They made no conscience, when they had eaten the paschal lamb in the evening, to spend the whole night in consulting how to shed innocent blood, and condemning of Christ ; but they pretend now conscience, that they will not go into a pagan's house in the morning, for that was the defilement they feared, having nothing to do to sit in judgment with him.

3 ¶ [c] Then Judas, which had betrayed him, when he saw that he was condemned, repented himself, and brought again the thirty pieces of silver to the Chief Priests and elders,

c ch. 26. 14, 15.

4 Saying, I have sinned in that I have betrayed the innocent blood. And they said, What *is that* to us ? see thou *to that.*

5 And he cast down the pieces of silver in the temple, [d] and departed, and went and hanged himself.

d 2 Sam. 17. 23. Acts 1. 18.

Matthew (who alone reports this piece of history) interrupteth his relation of our Saviour's trial before Pilate, with an account of Judas's end. We must not interpret *Then* strictly, so as to think Judas did this at the time when Christ was carried before Pilate, but some short time after ; for they went immediately from the high priest's hall to the judgment hall, and staid there until Christ was condemned by Pilate, before they returned to come into the temple. But possibly it was that day, after Pilate had condemned him, or within some short time after, that Judas (as it is said) *repented himself ;* that is, began to be terrified in his conscience for what he had done. The consciences of the worst of men will not always digest mire and dirt, but sometimes throw it up, yea, though it hath first incurably poisoned them. Sin is sweet in the mouth, but bitter in the belly. All repentance is not saving. Nor doth all confession of sin obtain remission. Judas here repents, and confesseth he had sinned, and his particular sin, in betraying an innocent person ; yet he findeth no mercy, he hath not a heart to beg forgiveness, nor to apply himself to Christ for remedy. But the answer of the chief priests and elders is very remarkable : *What is that to us? see thou to that.* Wretched Judas ! he had been the servant of these wicked men's lusts, and for a poor wages served them in the highest act of villany. He falls into a distress of conscience for what he had done. What miserable comforters do they prove ! Tempters never make good comforters. Those who are the devil's instruments, to command, entice, or allure men to sin, will afford them no relief when they come to be troubled for what they have done : nor will it now satisfy the conscience of Judas, to remember that he had a warrant for apprehending Christ, and acted ministerially. The priests will not take the money, he throws it down in the temple, and goes and hangs himself. How

S. MATTHEW XXVII

great is the power of conscience, smiting for the guilt of sin! Judas could have no hope of a better life, so as all his happiness lay in the time of this present life; yet he is not able to allow himself that. The devil that entered into his heart to tempt him, now entereth again to persuade him to put an end to his misery in this life, by hastening himself to an eternal misery. Let all apostates, turning persecutors of innocent persons, read this, and tremble. There is a difficulty of reconciling this text to that of Luke, Acts i. 18, where it is said of him, that *falling headlong, he burst asunder in the midst, and all his bowels gushed out.* That which is usually said is, that he fell from the place where he hanged himself, and with the fall burst himself. I know there are some others, who think that the word ἀπήγξατο need not be translated, he hanged himself, but he was suffocated or strangled. Some think the devil strangled him, and threw him down a precipice. Others, that he was suffocated by some disease, which caused a rupture of his body. Others think (as we translate it) that he hanged himself, and swelling, his body brake, and his bowels gushed out. Concerning the manner of his death, we can determine nothing, but that he was strangled, and his bowels gushed out; both these the Scripture asserts, but how it was we cannot certainly tell.

6 And the Chief Priests took the silver pieces, and said, It is not lawful for to put them into the treasury, because it is the price of blood.

God, Deut. xxiii. 18, had forbidden to bring the price of a whore, or a dog, into the temple; this they had interpreted of all filthy gain: upon which they thus determine, that it was not lawful for them to put the money they had given Judas, for so sordid a service as that of betraying his Master, into the chest, or place which they had, where they kept the monies given for the repairs of the temple; and in this they were right enough, perhaps, but in this they showed themselves stupidly blind hypocrites, that they saw not it was much less lawful for them, who had hired him to this sordid action, to be employed in the service of the temple, for, Isa. lii. 11, those that *bear the vessels of the Lord* ought to be holy. Thus, to justify our Saviour's words, they *strain at a gnat, and swallow a camel.*

7 And they took counsel, and bought with them the potter's field, to bury strangers in.

e Acts 1. 19.   8 Wherefore that field was called, ᵉThe field of blood, unto this day.

9 Then was fulfilled that which was spoken by Jeremy the prophet, saying, ᶠAnd they took the thirty pieces of silver, the price of him that was valued, ∥whom they of the children of Israel did value;

f Zech. 11. 12, 13.
∥ Or, whom they bought of the children of Israel.

10 And gave them for the potter's field, as the Lord appointed me.

They at last resolve what to do with the money, which was no great sum, for, as we noted before, it exceeded not three pounds fifteen shillings. They would not turn it to their own private use, for (probably) it was before taken out of the treasury; neither would they again return it into the treasury, because it had been made use of as the hire of blood. They therefore agree to buy with it a piece of ground ordinarily known by the name of *the potter's field*, probably because some potter had digged earth, and thrown the waste of his pot-kilns there, so as it was of no great value. This field the vulgar, upon this purchase of it by the priests, called many years after, *The field of blood.* Then was fulfilled that which was spoken by Jeremy the prophet. The evangelists use this term *fulfilled*, as I have before noted, in very different senses. 1. Sometimes to express the accomplishment of a prophecy. 2. Sometimes to express the fulfilling of a type, or answering it by the antitype. 3. Sometimes to express an allusion to some other scripture, mentioning some matter of fact of a like nature. For the text here quoted, we have no such text in the writings of the prophet Jeremiah, which are upon sacred record. Jeremiah indeed did buy a field by order from God, chap. xxxii. 9, to declare his faith in God's promises for the return of the Jews out of captivity, but he bought it of his uncle *Hanameel,* and for *seventeen pieces of silver;* and that

he was a potter, or that the field was called by that name, we do not read. The nearest place in the prophets to this text is Zech. xi. 12, 13, *And I said unto them, If ye think good, give me my price. So they weighed for my price thirty pieces of silver. And the Lord said unto me, Cast it unto the potter: a goodly price that I was prized at of them. And I took the thirty pieces of silver, and cast them to the potter in the house of the Lord.* It is a very hard text as it lies in the prophet to give a just account of. The prophet was one of them who prophesied after the captivity of Babylon, yet, ver. 6, he plainly prophesieth after God's destruction of the Jews and of Jerusalem. Which destruction being after that of the Chaldeans, to what it should refer, but to the last destruction of the Jews by the Romans, I cannot understand. Ver. 7, he saith, *I will feed the flock of the slaughter,* that is, the flock designed for the slaughter, or drawing near to the slaughter, *even you, O poor of the flock.* Christ came in person to feed the church of the Jews, but they also abhorred him, so that he abhorred them, and resolved to cast them quite off, ver. 8, 9. So he broke first his *staff* called *Beauty,* took away all the glory and beauty of that church. Then, as it were in indignation, he saith, *If ye think good, give me my price.* What requital will you give me for my labour amongst you? *So they weighed for my price thirty pieces of silver.* Their selling of Christ to a traitor for so much, signified their high contempt of him. *And the Lord said, Cast it unto the potter: a goodly price that I was prized at of them. And I took the thirty pieces of silver, and cast them to the potter in the house of the Lord.* The evangelist indeed doth not quote the very words of the prophet, but the substance of them. And for my part I think, that the evangelist here by fulfilling meaneth the accomplishment of the prophecy in Zechariah. For I know not what other tolerable sense to make of the prophecy, if we do not say the prophet spake in the person of Christ, foretelling his own coming amongst them, their rejection and contempt of him, and his utter rejection of them; and prophesying, as a piece of their contempt and rejection of him, their selling him to Judas for *thirty pieces of silver,* (a most contemptible price,) and God so ordering it by his providence, that this money should again be brought them, and this potter's field should be bought with it. So as I think that text was fulfilled here more than by allusion, or as it was typical to this act, and that this act was the very thing which there is prophesied, and here fulfilled. But how Matthew saith this was *spoken by Jeremy the prophet* is a harder knot. It is observable that Zechariah hath many things found in Jeremiah, and it is not improbable that the very same thing was prophesied by Jeremiah, though afterward repeated by Zechariah, and only in the writings of Zechariah left upon sacred record. Matthew having now given us an account of the fate of Judas, returneth to our Saviour, carried (as we heard) before Pilate.

11 And Jesus stood before the governor: ᵍand the governor asked him, saying, Art thou the King of the Jews? And Jesus said unto him, ʰThou sayest.

g Mark 15. 2. Luke 23. 3. John 18. 33.
h John 18. 37.
i Tim. 6. 13.

Mark hath the same, chap. xv. 2; so hath Luke, chap. xxiii. 3. John relates it more distinctly, chap. xviii. 29—32: *Pilate then went out unto them, and said, What accusation bring ye against this man? They answered and said unto him, If he were not a malefactor, we would not have delivered him up unto thee. Then said Pilate unto them, Take ye him, and judge him according to your law. The Jews therefore said unto him, It is not lawful for us to put any man to death: that the saying of Jesus might be fulfilled, which he spake, signifying what death he should die.* The other evangelists seem to have given us the story of this our Saviour's first appearance before Pilate summarily. John seems to have given us it more orderly and particularly. It is the course of all judicatures to require the accusers to speak first. Pilate therefore asketh what accusation they had brought against him. Their answer was very malapert, If he had not been a malefactor, &c. What was this to the purpose? Suppose him never so great a malefactor, must it not appear he is so before a judge condemns him? These accusers (as it seemeth) were of the same mind that the papists are, that the civil magistrate is to be executioner to the church; and when the ecclesiastical power hath condemned a man for heresy or blasphemy, the civil magistrate hath nothing to do, but without his own hearing the cause to put the person to death. But they met with a more equal judge, though he were a heathen. Say ye so, saith he, *Take him, then, and judge him according to your law.* This he either speaks as deriding them, and scorning what they would have put him upon; or else not thinking he had deserved any thing worthy of death, knowing they might without him scourge him, or inflict some lighter punishments. They reply, *It is not lawful for us to put any man to death.* It is very questionable in what sense they spake this. Those that affirm that the power of judging and determining in capital causes was before this time taken from the Jews, must affirm that Stephen was put to death in a popular tumult, for he was after this stoned to death by the Jews, Acts vii. 59; which is not probable, considering what we read of him, chap. vi. 13, 15, called before the council, and witnesses used against him, and have no record of any notice the civil magistrate took of the fact as a disorder. I therefore rather think their meaning was, This is with us a feast day, on which it is not lawful for us to put any to death without thy consent. Or, it is not lawful for us to put any to death for any civil cause, for saying he is our king; for it is manifest by the question which Pilate first put to him upon his second coming into the hall, mentioned John xviii. 33, in which all the other three evangelists agree, that they had charged him with saying, that he was the King of the Jews; to which all that he replied, which is recorded by Matthew, Mark, and Luke, is, *Thou sayest it.* I am not bound to accuse myself; who witnesses this against me? But John saith that our Saviour said, *Sayest thou this thing of thyself, or did others tell it thee of me? Pilate answered, Am I a Jew? thine own nation and the chief priests have delivered thee unto me: what hast thou done? Jesus answered, My kingdom is not of this world: if my kingdom were of this world, then would my servants fight, that I should not be delivered to the Jews: but now is my kingdom not from hence.* Our Saviour, by this answer to Pilate's question, seems to vindicate his right not to be condemned without witness, which, if others had told Pilate this, they were bound to have produced. Pilate tells him, he had it not of himself, he was no Jew, but they were those of his own nation who had delivered him to him; and therefore asketh him what he had done. Then our Saviour openeth himself, not denying that he was the King of the Jews, but telling him he was no king of this world; his kingdom was a spiritual kingdom, and he might know what King he was by his retinue, and those who took his part; for if he had laid claim to any secular kingdom, he should have had some appearing to take his part, and to fight for him to deliver him from his enemies, but he saw he had none. Pilate laying hold of his words, replies, *Art thou a king then? Jesus answered, Thou sayest that I am a king. To this end was I born, and for this cause came I into the world, that I should bear witness unto the truth. Every one that is of the truth heareth my voice. Pilate saith unto him, What is truth?* Our Saviour still useth prudence, and keeps himself upon a close guard. It had been dangerous for him directly to have owned himself a king. He therefore only tells Pilate, that he said he was a king, and that he came into the world to bear testimony to the truth; and further adds, that every one who was of the truth did hear his voice. This poseth Pilate, who had no notion of that truth which Christ spake of; he goes out as it were deriding him, saying, *What is truth?* Presently he goeth out to the Jews, ver. 38, and tells them he found in him no fault at all, and offers to release him; but this we shall meet with in our evangelist by and by: the passages hereto mentioned are only related by John; excepting only the question, *Art thou the King of the Jews?* and our Saviour's answer, *Thou sayest it*, which is reported by all.

12 And when he was accused of the Chief Priests and elders, ʲhe answered nothing.

ʲ ch. 26. 63.
John 19. 9.

13 Then said Pilate unto him, ᵏ Hearest thou not how many things they witness against thee?

ᵏ ch. 26. 63.
John 19. 10.

14 And he answered him to never a word; insomuch that the governor marvelled greatly.

Mark saith much the same, chap. xv. 3—5. These things were before Pilate went out to the people, and told them that he found no fault in him at all, and offered to release Barabbas unto them. Then seemeth to me to follow in order what we have in Luke xxiii. 5—17, in these words: *And they were the more fierce, saying, He stirreth up the people, teaching throughout all Jewry, beginning from Galilee to this place.* The constant charge which, we shall observe, was laid upon all the ministers of the gospel from Christ's time. Tertullus the Roman advocate thus charged Paul, &c. *When Pilate heard of Galilee, he asked whether the man were a Galilean. And as soon as he knew that he belonged to Herod's jurisdiction, he sent him to Herod, who himself also was at Jerusalem at that time.* After the death of Herod the Great, who died soon after our Saviour was born, (as we heard before,) the sceptre departed from Judah, there were no more kings. The government of Jewry was turned into a tetrarchy, divided into four provinces, each of which had a governor, who was called the tetrarch of that province. You have the division, and the names of the tetrarchs, Luke iii. 1, where you will find that *Herod was tetrarch of Galilee.* Our Saviour being taken within the jurisdiction of Pilate, it seemeth not to have been necessary for Pilate to have sent him to Herod, but a compliment to satisfy his curiosity. For, saith Luke, *when Herod saw Jesus, he was exceeding glad: for he was desirous to see him of a long season, because he had heard many things of him; and he hoped to have seen some miracle done by him. Then he questioned with him in many words; but he answered him nothing. And the chief priests and scribes stood and vehemently accused him. And Herod with his men of war set him at nought, and mocked him, and arrayed him in a gorgeous robe, and sent him again to Pilate. And the same day Pilate and Herod were made friends together: for before they were at enmity between themselves.* This is now all historical, and hath in it nothing difficult. Christ had spent most of his time in Galilee, (which was Herod's tetrarchy,) though Herod had not seen him, yet he had heard much of him, and had the curiosity to desire to see him, hoping that our Saviour would have wrought some miracle before him. But he failed in his expectation. He propounds several questions to him. Our Saviour being not before a proper judge, answereth him nothing. So as there was nothing done, only the chief priests and scribes followed him with incessant clamours. Herod and his guard vilify and mock him, put him on a gorgeous robe, and send him back to Pilate. All the effect of this was, Herod was pleased with Pilate's compliment, and from that day was reconciled to Pilate, though there had been a former enmity betwixt them; only, as we shall hear hereafter, Herod decreeing nothing against Christ, Pilate made some use of it, in his endeavours to have delivered our Saviour.

15 ¹ Now at *that* feast the governor was wont to release unto the people a prisoner, whom they would.

¹ Mark 15. 6.
Luke 23. 17.
John 18. 39.

16 And they had then a notable prisoner, called Barabbas.

17 Therefore when they were gathered together, Pilate said unto them, Whom will ye that I release unto you? Barabbas, or Jesus which is called Christ?

18 For he knew that for envy they had delivered him.

Mark saith, chap. xv. 6—11, *Now at that feast he released unto them one prisoner, whomsoever they desired. And there was one named Barabbas, which lay bound with them that had made insurrection with him, who had committed murder in the insurrection. And the multitude crying aloud began to desire him to do as he had ever done unto them. But Pilate answered them, saying, Will ye that I release unto you the King of the Jews? For he knew that the chief priests had delivered him for envy. But the chief priests moved the people, that he should rather release Barabbas unto them.* Luke hath this passage of the history more fully, chap. xxiii. 13—18: *And Pilate, when he had called together the chief priests and the rulers and the people, said unto them, Ye have brought this man unto me, as one that *perverteth the people: and behold, I, having examined him before you, have found no fault in this man touching those things whereof ye accuse him. No, nor yet Herod: for I sent you to him; and, lo, nothing worthy of death is done unto him. I will therefore chastise him, and release him. (For of necessity he must release one unto them at the feast.) And they cried out all at once, saying, Away with this man, and release unto us Barabbas: (who for a certain sedition made in the city, and for murder, was cast into prison.)* John saith, chap. xviii. 38—40, that when he went out he told them he found no fault in him at all. *But ye have a custom, that I should release unto you one at the passover: will ye therefore that I release unto you the King of the Jews. Then cried they all again, saying, not this man, but Barabbas. Now Barabbas was a robber.* The history is plain: Pilate discerned, upon his before-mentioned examination of Christ, that our Saviour had done nothing amiss, but was only loaded with the malice and envy of the chief priests and scribes; this made him resolve to do what in him lay to deliver him. He first tells them that they had brought him before him, accused him of many things, but had proved against him nothing criminal; that he had sent him to Herod, in whose jurisdiction he had lived, but neither did Herod find any fault in him. Now there was a custom, that ever at the passover the governor released a prisoner at the request of the people. The people desired he would keep their old custom in this particular. Pilate propoundeth to them to release the King of the Jews. The chief priests influence the people to declare their dissatisfaction at that, and to name one Barabbas, a prisoner who was a robber, and had been guilty of an insurrection, and of murder committed in the insurrection: accordingly the people cry out, *Not this man, but Barabbas.* This makes him again to return to the judgment-seat

19 ¶ When he was set down on the judgment seat, his wife sent unto him, saying, Have thou nothing to do with that just man: for I have suffered many things this day in a dream because of him.

^m Mark 15. 11. Luke 23. 18. John 18. 40. Acts 3. 14.

20 ^m But the Chief Priests and elders persuaded the multitude that they should ask Barabbas, and destroy Jesus.

Matthew only mentioneth this passage of Pilate's wife; whether it was when Pilate sat upon the judgment-seat the second time, (the story of which we have heard,) or afterward, is uncertain; nor is it material. She doubtless referreth to some late dream, which possibly she might have after her husband was gone from her, for he was called early. Whether this dream was caused by God for a further testimony of Christ's innocency, or were merely natural, cannot be determined. But still the cry holdeth, Not him, but Barabbas. So much influence had the wicked priests upon the people.

21 The governor answered and said unto them, Whether of the twain will ye that I release unto you? They said, Barabbas.

22 Pilate saith unto them, What shall I do then with Jesus which is called Christ? *They* all say unto him, Let him be crucified.

23 And the governor said, Why, what evil hath he done? But they cried out the more, saying, Let him be crucified.

Mark hath the same, chap. xv. 12—14. So also Luke saith, chap. xxiii. 20—23, *Pilate therefore, willing to release Jesus, spake again to them. But they cried, saying, Crucify him, crucify him. And he said unto them the third time, Why, what evil hath he done? I have found no cause of death in him: I will therefore chastise him, and let him go. And they were instant with loud voices, requiring that he might be crucified. And the voices of them and of the chief priests prevailed.* John, chap. xix. 1—12, hath yet more circumstances relating to the latter part of this trial, which follow: *Then Pilate therefore took Jesus, and scourged him. And the soldiers platted a crown of thorns, and put it on his head, and they put on him a purple robe, and said, Hail, King of the Jews! and they smote him with their hands. Pilate therefore went forth again, and saith unto them, Behold, I bring him forth to you, that ye may know that I find no fault in him. Then came Jesus forth, wearing the crown of thorns, and the purple robe. And Pilate saith unto them, Behold the man! When the chief priests therefore and officers saw him, they cried out, saying, Crucify him, crucify him. Pilate saith unto them, Take ye him, and crucify him: for I find no fault in him. The Jews answered him, We have a law, and by our law he ought to die, because he made himself the Son of God. When Pilate therefore heard that saying, he was the more afraid; and went again into the judgment hall, and saith unto Jesus, Whence art thou? But Jesus gave him no answer. Then saith Pilate unto them, Speakest thou not unto me? knowest thou not that I have power to crucify thee, and have power to release thee? Jesus answered, Thou couldest have no power at all against me, except it were given thee from above: therefore he that delivered me unto thee hath the greater sin. And from thenceforth Pilate sought to release him: but the Jews cried out, saying, If thou let this man go, thou art not Cæsar's friend: whosoever maketh himself a king speaketh against Cæsar.* I have not given the reader at one view what all the evangelists say, as thinking it scarce possible from them all to set down the order how things passed at this trial; but only, that I might take notice of what was remarkable in it, related from one or other of them. The reason of our reading so often of Pilate's going out, and then again coming on to the judgment-seat, seemeth to be because, as we heard before, the Jews would not come into Pilate's house, but stood at the door; and, on the other side, I conceive that he could not proceed judicially but sitting upon the tribunal, or seat of judgment. So as, though he could proceed in judgment within the house, with the attendance of his own servants, soldiers, and officers; yet, when he had any thing to propound to the Jews, he went out. We cannot think that the evangelists report all the things the Jews objected against our Saviour, nor all the questions by Pontius Pilate propounded to him. For the evangelists tellus, summarily, that they accused him of many things, and Pilate saith, *Hearest thou not how many things they witness against thee?* There was, it seems, but one thing that they most insisted upon, that was, his making himself a king, as to which we heard before how our Lord cleared himself. In the whole process of this trial these things are remarkable: 1. Our Saviour's silence. 2. Pilate's equity. 3. The rage and madness of the chief priests, scribes, and people. Our Saviour's silence confirms to us that piece of the law of nature, that no man is bound to accuse himself. Pilate's equity appears in many things: He would not condemn him without a particular hearing of his cause himself, he would not force him to accuse himself; he accepts our Saviour's vindication of himself, as to the great thing wherewith he was charged; he twice declares that he found no fault in him; he studies expedients to deliver an innocent person from their rage; he sends him to Herod, and obtains his concurrent suffrage to his innocency; he offereth to release him according to a custom they had at the passover to deliver one, whomsoever they desired; when this would not do, he caused him to be scourged, then brings him out to them again, hoping to have moved them to compassion by that lighter punishment of him. The rage and madness of the Jews, principally of the chief priests and scribes, appeared in their urging to have had our Saviour condemned without hearing; their excessive clamours against him; their preferring one before him who was a robber, a murderer, one that had made a public insurrection; their insisting so much upon the kind of death that he should die, viz. by crucifying him, though in that they did both fulfil the counsel of God, who had determined that he should be *made a curse for us,* and it was written, *Cursed is every one that hangeth on a tree,* Gal. iii. 13, and what himself had prophesied, that he should be delivered to the Gentiles, and they should mock, and scourge, and crucify him, Matt. xx. 19. But that which is most remarkable is, the providence of God, for the evidencing of our Saviour's innocency. Pilate's wife calls him a *just man.* Pilate twice tells them that he found no fault in him. They are able to say nothing when Pilate asks them, *What evil hath he done?* Herod objects nothing against him. He is merely condemned upon the brutish clamour and rage of the rabble, incensed and set on fire by the chief priests and Pharisees. The art of these his adversaries is also observable, because it is the same which the enemies of the gospel, deriving from this first pattern, have ever since observed in the execution of their malice against the preachers and faithful professors of the gospel. They durst not insist upon the doctrine which our Saviour preached, which was the true cause of their malice against him, but bring him under a charge of treason and sedition, as if he had gone about to make himself a king in opposition to the Roman emperor; though there was not the least pretence for any such thing, and if there had, none who considereth that they were a conquered people, and how zealous they upon all occasions showed themselves for their civil liberties, can imagine they had any great kindness for Cæsar. It is very observable, that malice against religion and godliness, and a desire of the extirpation of it, and the professors of it, is the predominant lust in the hearts of wicked men. To serve this, they not only deny their own reason, and principles of common justice, but deny themselves likewise in some other lusts. And herein they show themselves the true seed of the serpent, and the children of the devil, whose works they do; who, though he be the proudest spirit, yet, to destroy a soul, will abate his pride, truckle to a poor witch, and go upon her errands.

24 ¶ When Pilate saw that he could prevail nothing, but *that* rather a tumult was made, he ⁿtook water, and washed *his* hands before the multitude, saying, I am innocent of the blood of this just person: see ye *to it*.

25 Then answered all the people, and said, °His blood *be* on us, and on our children.

26 ¶ Then released he Barabbas unto them: and when ᵖhe had scourged Jesus, he delivered *him* to be crucified.

Mark saith, chap. xv. 15, *So Pilate, willing to content the people, released Barabbas unto them, and delivered Jesus, when he had scourged him, to be crucified.* Luke saith, chap. xxiii. 24, 25, *And Pilate gave sentence that it should be as they required. And he released unto them him that for sedition and murder was cast into prison, whom they had desired; but he delivered Jesus to their will.* John saith, chap. xix. 13, *When Pilate therefore heard that saying, he brought Jesus forth, and sat down in the judgment-seat in a place that is called the Pavement, but in the Hebrew, Gabbatha. And it was the preparation of the passover, and about the sixth hour: and he saith unto the Jews, Behold your King! But they cried out, Away with him, away with him, crucify him. Pilate saith unto them, Shall I crucify your King? The chief priests answered, We have no king but Cæsar. Then delivered he him therefore unto them to be crucified.* Here are three accounts given of Pilate's coming over to the Jews' desire to condemn Christ, contrary to the conviction of his own conscience, for he had twice declared that he found no fault in him. Matthew saith, he *saw he could prevail nothing, but that rather a tumult was made.* Mark saith, he did it *to content the people.* John saith, it was upon the hearing of that saying, *If thou let this man go, thou art not Cæsar's friend: whosoever maketh himself a king speaketh against Cæsar.* His fear of being accused to the emperor Tiberius, as favouring one who made himself a king, especially if his opposing the Jews in their desire of his death should have caused a tumult, was questionless the great thing that moved him to give judgment in this case contrary to his own conscience; and this is the meaning of his contenting the people, mentioned by Mark. It is plain by the whole story he had no mind to gratify or gain favour with them, but considering how jealous and suspicious a prince Tiberius was, it was Pilate's interest to quiet them, and to give them no occasion of accusing him unto the emperor. *He took water, and washed his hands before the multitude.* It was the law of God in manslaughter, where he that slew the man was not known, the priests and elders of the city that (upon measure) should be found nearest to the dead body, should take a heifer, and bring it to a rough valley, and strike off its head, and wash their hands over the head of the beheaded heifer, and say, *Our hands have not shed this blood, neither have our eyes seen it*, Deut. xxi. 1—7. Some think that Pilate, living amongst the Jews, had learned this rite from them; but others think that it was a rite used in protestations of innocency amongst other people, as well as the Jews. But it was a great fondness in Pilate, to think this excused him, and freed him from the guilt of our Saviour's death. For there was such an inseparable guilt clave to the act, as nothing could expiate but that blood which he spilt. Those who take upon them the trust of executing laws, had need to take heed what they do, for the law will not excuse them in the court of heaven, unless it be found according to the law of God. What Pilate did he did but ministerially, the law condemned, not he: but if it be understood of the law of God about blasphemy, to which the Jews undoubtedly referred, John x. 33, 36, it was misapplied. If it were a Roman law, Pilate ought to have considered the equity and justice of it, and whether the fact was proved or no. Pilate had twice owned there was no fault in him. His washing his hands could not purge him of the murder, whereof he was guilty in his condemnation; he did but protest against what he immediately was about to do. *Then answered all the people, and said, His blood be on us, and on our children:* his blood, that is, the guilt of his blood, be upon us, &c. A most sad imprecation, the effect of which hath been upon that miserable people now more than sixteen hundred years. *Then released he Barabbas unto them: and when he had scourged Jesus, &c.* The scourging was before this, and so recorded by St. John, for we cannot imagine that he was twice scourged. *He delivered him to be crucified;* not to the Jews, but to his own officers, for it was a civil crime that he was accused of before Pilate, and crucifying was a Roman punishment.

27 ᑫThen the soldiers of the governor took Jesus into the ‖ common hall, and gathered unto him the whole band *of soldiers*.

28 And they stripped him, and ʳput on him a scarlet robe.

29 ¶ ˢAnd when they had platted a crown of thorns, they put *it* upon his head, and a reed in his right hand: and they bowed the knee before him, and mocked him, saying, Hail, king of the Jews!

30 And ᵗthey spit upon him, and took the reed, and smote him on the head.

31 And after that they had mocked him, they took the robe off from him, and put his own raiment on him, ᵘand led him away to crucify *him*.

Mark hath the same, chap. xv. 17—20, only he saith they put upon him a purple robe. John seemeth to mention this a little out of order, chap. xix. 1—3, as done before his condemnation; for though some think that Matthew and Mark rather mention these things out of their due order, yet the abuses seem more likely to be done to a person who was condemned, and so dead in law, than while he was upon his trial. Writers tell us that none might be crucified before he was scourged, and that not with rods, (which was the Jewish manner,) but with whips (far more cruelly); but whether it was before or after condemnation we are not certain. He was condemned upon that article, that he should say, he was the King of the Jews. To mock him, therefore, they set a crown on his head, but of thorns; they put a sceptre into his hand, but it was of a reed; they bowed the knee before him, as was wont to princes; they put on him a robe of purple, or scarlet, both which were used by princes; in short they put upon him all the indignities and marks of scorn imaginable. When they had thus glutted themselves, they restore his own garment to him, and lead him away to the place of execution. Who can read these things with a believing heart and dry eyes, if he remembers, that our sins platted the crown of thorns set upon our Saviour's head, and made the whips with which he was scourged? Our stomachs (when we read these things) are ready to rise against the pagan soldiers; but how little did they do in comparison of what Christ suffered for our sins! Who can read these things, and not be fortified against temptations from suffering if we will own the gospel and cause of Christ? Our sufferings will come much short of what Christ hath suffered for us.

S. MATTHEW XXVII

32 ˣAnd as they came out, ʸthey found a man of Cyrene, Simon by name: him they compelled to bear his cross.

33 ᶻAnd when they were come unto a place called Golgotha, that is to say, a place of a skull,

34 ¶ ᵃThey gave him vinegar to drink mingled with gall: and when he had tasted *thereof*, he would not drink.

x Num. 15. 35. 1 Kings 21. 13. Acts 7. 58. Heb. 13. 12. y Mark 15. 21. Luke 23. 26. z Mark 15. 22. Luke 23. 33. John 19. 17. a Ps. 69. 21. See ver. 48.

Mark saith, chap. xv. 21—23, *And they compel one Simon a Cyrenian, who passed by, coming out of the country, the father of Alexander and Rufus, to bear his cross. And they bring him unto the place Golgotha, which is, being interpreted, The place of a skull. And they gave him to drink wine mingled with myrrh: but he received it not.* Luke is larger in his account of the passages betwixt his condemnation and crucifixion, chap. xxiii. 26—32. *And as they led him away, they laid hold upon one Simon, a Cyrenian, coming out of the country, and on him they laid the cross, that he might bear it after Jesus. And there followed him a great company of people, and of women, which also bewailed and lamented him. But Jesus turning unto them said, Daughters of Jerusalem, weep not for me, but weep for yourselves, and for your children. For, behold, the days are coming, in which they shall say, Blessed are the barren, and the wombs that never bare, and the paps which never gave suck. Then shall they begin to say to the mountains, Fall on us; and to the hills, Cover us. For if they do these things in a green tree, what shall be done in the dry?* And there were also two other, malefactors, led with him to be put to death. John, chap. xix. 17, saith no more than, *And he bearing his cross went forth unto a place called the place of a skull, which is called in the Hebrew Golgotha.* Matthew, and Mark, and Luke say, that a countryman, one Simon a Cyrenian, (compelled to it by the soldiers,) carried the cross after Christ. John saith, that he himself bare it. Both were doubtless true. Some say that Christ himself did carry it through the city, and when he was out of the city this Simon carried it. Others think, that Christ being wearied, Simon took it. But reason will tell us, that the cross was too heavy a piece of timber for one to bear, and therefore Simon was compelled to bear the hinder part; therefore Luke saith, he bare it after Jesus. The dispute whether this Simon was a native Jew, though an inhabitant of Cyrene, or a proselyted Cyrenian, or as yet a pagan, and whether this Cyrene was one of the ten cities comprehended in the name Decapolis, is not worth spending any words about. All the evangelists agree, that he was crucified at *Golgotha*; Luke calls it Calvary; they are both names of the same signification, *The place of a skull*; the one is the Hebrew term, the other Latin. *They gave him vinegar to drink, mingled with gall.* Mark saith, *wine mingled with myrrh.* There is so great a cognation between wine and vinegar, that it is no wonder if one evangelist calls it vinegar, another wine, which, if it be acid, is vinegar. The word translated *gall* signifies all bitterness, whether it be caused from gall or myrrh. Some think that some good people gave him wine, and the soldiers added myrrh to it. But this is a great uncertainty. Certain it is, that it was an ordinary favour they showed to dying persons, to give them some intoxicating potion, to make them less sensible of their pain. It is probable it was something of this nature; but our Saviour was not afraid to die, and so had no need of such an antidote against the pain of it; he refused it. We shall find they afterward gave him something to drink also. Luke tells us that great multitudes followed him to the place of execution, (which is still very ordinary,) lamenting him, to whom our Saviour saith, *Daughters of Jerusalem, weep not for me, but weep for yourselves, and for your children;* and then prophesieth the miseries that should follow his death, to that degree, that the barren should bless themselves; and they all should *say to the mountains, Fall on us, and to the hills, Cover us.* He bids the women weep only for themselves and for their children; for how much better is it for persons of any tenderness to have no children, than to have children, and to see them dashed against the stones, as was threatened to Babylon, Psal. cxxxvii. 9.; or to kill them for the parents'

sustenance, as it happened in Ahab's time; or to see them slain before the parents' faces, as it happened to Zedekiah, when the enemy took Jerusalem! Jer. lii. 10. The people also, he saith, should (as it was of old prophesied of those of Samaria, Hos. x. 8) cry to the mountains to cover them, and to the hills to fall on them: a proverbial expression, to signify their wishing themselves dead and under ground; or expounded by Isa. ii. 19, *And they shall go into the holes of the rocks, and into the caves of the earth, for fear of the Lord, and for the glory of his majesty, when he ariseth to shake terribly the earth.* See the like expressions, Rev. vi. 16; ix. 6, *In those days shall men seek death, and shall not find it; and shall desire to die, and death shall flee from them. For if they do these things in a green tree, what shall be done in the dry?* It is another proverbial expression, which may be understood impersonally: *If they do*, that is, if it be thus done to. If God suffers them thus to do to me, who am his Son, what shall be done to you, who are but as dry sticks, and so fitter for the fire? If judgment begin at the house of God, where shall the wicked and ungodly appear? 1 Pet. iv. 17, 18.

35 ᵇAnd they crucified him, and parted his garments, casting lots: that it might be fulfilled which was spoken by the prophet, ᶜThey parted my garments among them, and upon my vesture did they cast lots.

36 ᵈAnd sitting down they watched him there;

37 And ᵉset up over his head his accusation written, THIS IS JESUS THE KING OF THE JEWS.

b Mark 15. 24. Luke 23. 34. John 19. 24.
c Ps. 22. 18.
d ver. 54.
e Mark 15. 26. Luke 23. 38. John 19. 19.

Mark saith, chap. xv. 24—28, *When they had crucified him, they parted his garments, casting lots upon them, what every man should take. And it was the third hour, and they crucified him. And the superscription of his accusation was written over, The King of the Jews. And with him they crucified two thieves; the one on his right hand, and the other on his left. And the scripture was fulfilled, which saith, And he was numbered with the transgressors.* Luke saith, chap. xxiii. 33, 34, *And when they were come to the place which is called Calvary, there they crucified him, and the malefactors, one on the right hand, and the other on the left. Then said Jesus, Father, forgive them; for they know not what they do. And they parted his raiment, and cast lots.* John telleth us some further circumstances, chap. xix. 18—24: *Where they crucified him, and two other with him, on either side one, and Jesus in the midst. And Pilate wrote a title, and put it on the cross. And the writing was, Jesus of Nazareth the King of the Jews. This title then read many of the Jews: for the place where Jesus was crucified was nigh to the city: and it was written in Hebrew, and Greek, and Latin. Then said the chief priests of the Jews to Pilate, Write not, The King of the Jews; but that he said, I am King of the Jews. Pilate answered, What I have written I have written. Then the soldiers, when they had crucified Jesus, took his garments, and made four parts, to every soldier a part; and also his coat: now the coat was without seam, woven from the top throughout. They said therefore among themselves, Let us not rend it, but cast lots for it, whose it shall be: that the Scripture might be fulfilled, which saith, They parted my raiment among them, and for my vesture they did cast lots. These things therefore the soldiers did. And they crucified him;* that is, four soldiers, as we learn from John's narration of this matter of fact; it seemeth this business was assigned to four more especially. This crucifying was a bitter and shameful kind of death, not in use amongst the Jews, but amongst the Romans. The manner of it is not particularly known to us: but, as it is described by writers, a piece of wood was erected, which was crossed with a bar upon the top. The body of the person being fastened to the main piece of wood, his arms were extended, and nailed to the cross bar, or piece of timber, and his hands and feet were nailed. Mark saith, *it was the third hour*, which with us was about nine of the clock: so hasty they were in destroying this just person, that betwixt midnight and nine of the clock in the morning, they apprehended him, tried and condemned him in the sanhedrim, or at least in a court of high priests and elders, and then before Pilate the Roman governor, and led him to be crucified, and nailed him to his cross. The evangelists tell us, he was crucified in the middle betwixt two thieves, of whom we shall read more afterward. Several scriptures of the Old Testament were fulfilled in this crucifixion of Christ. *They pierced my hands and my feet*, Psal. xxii. 16, was fulfilled in his nailing to the cross. In his being crucified betwixt two thieves was fulfilled that, Isa. liii. 12, *He was numbered with the transgressors.* That of the psalmist, Psal. xxii. 18, *They parted my garments among them, and cast lots upon my vesture*, was fulfilled in the soldiers' parting of our Saviour's garments, as their fee. But how could they part them, and yet not rend them? Possibly they parted his other garments, and only did cast lots for his coat, or upper garment. Or, it may be, they valued it, and agreed each man's share, and then cast lots for the whole. I see no ground for their assertion, who say, that in such cases they only stripped the condemned person of his upper garment. John's relation seemeth to oppose it; he saith, *and also his coat*. Matthew, Mark, and John all agree in the inscription which Pilate drew to be put upon his cross, signifying the crime for which he died; only John puts in those words, *of Nazareth*. Thus Christ died in the attestation of his kingly office. This inscription angered the Jews; they solicit Pilate to alter it, and that it might be, Who said he was the King of the Jews. But Pilate refused, saying, *What I have written I have written.* There was nothing more pleasing to Pilate than this, (as he thought,) to deride the Jews, as having such a despicable person (as he judged him) their King. In the mean time the counsels of God have their effect; Christ in his death is declared to be the King of the Jews. Luke saith, that Christ said, *Father, forgive them; for they know what they do.* Whether these words were spoken when our Lord was first nailed to the cross, or afterward, is not much material. Luke relates them before the soldiers' parting his garments. Our Saviour by them declares himself a true Pastor and Shepherd of souls, teaching his disciples no more than he himself did practise. Chap. v. 44, he had taught his disciples to pray for them who despitefully used and persecuted them. Himself here practiseth it. The malice of men ought not to quench in Christians the grace of God. Let us now consider the passage that happened from the time he was nailed to the cross until the time of his expiration, which was more than three entire hours.

f Is. 53. 12.
Mark 15. 27.
Luke 23. 32, 33.
John 19. 18.

38 *f* Then were there two thieves crucified with him, one on the right hand, and another on the left.

g Ps. 22. 7.
& 109. 25.
Mark 15. 29.
Luke 23. 35.
h ch. 26. 61.
John 2. 19.

39 ¶ And *g* they that passed by reviled him, wagging their heads,

40 And saying, *h* Thou that destroyest the temple, and buildest *it* in three days,

i ch. 26. 63.

save thyself. *i* If thou be the Son of God, come down from the cross.

41 Likewise also the Chief Priests mocking *him*, with the Scribes and elders, said,

42 He saved others; himself he cannot save. If he be the King of Israel, let him now come down from the cross, and we will believe him.

k Ps. 22. 8.
Wisd. 2. 16, 17, 18.

43 *k* He trusted in God; let him deliver him now, if he will have him: for he said, I am the Son of God.

l Mark 15.32.
Lu e 23. 39.

44 *l* The thieves also, which were crucified with him, cast the same in his teeth.

Mark relateth this part of the history with no material circumstance differing from Matthew, chap. xv. 29—32. Luke saith, chap. xxiii. 39—43, *And one of the malefactors which were hanged railed on him, saying, If thou be Christ, save thyself and us. But the other answering rebuked him, saying, Dost not thou fear God, seeing thou art in the same condemnation? and we indeed justly; for we receive the due reward of our deeds: but this man hath done nothing amiss. And he said unto Jesus, Lord, remember me when thou comest into thy kingdom. And Jesus said unto him, Verily I say unto thee, To day shalt thou be with me in paradise.* John saith, chap. xix. 25—30. *Now there stood by the cross of Jesus his mother, and his mother's sister, Mary the wife of Cleophas, and Mary Magdalene. When Jesus therefore saw his mother, and the disciple standing by, whom he loved, he saith unto his mother, Woman, behold thy son! Then saith he to the disciple, Behold thy mother! And from that hour that disciple took her unto his own home. After this, Jesus knowing that all things were now accomplished, that the Scripture might be fulfilled saith, I thirst. Now there was set a vessel full of vinegar: and they filled a spunge with vinegar, and put it upon hyssop, and put it to his mouth. When Jesus therefore had received the vinegar, he said, It is finished.* Matthew and Mark relate more particularly what abuses our Saviour suffered while he hung dying upon the cross: 1. From passengers. 2. From the chief priests, scribes, and elders. Nothing is more inhuman than to mock such as are in the most extreme and utmost misery, and it is what we seldom hear from the worst of men; but for the chief priests and elders, the magistrates and rulers of the Jews, to be guilty of such a barbarous behaviour, is amazing. That not the ordinary priests only, but the chief priests, that is, either such as had been in the office of high priest, or else some of the most ancient and grave men of the priests; that, not the hot-headed young men amongst the Jews, but the elders of Israel, should be so rude, as not only to behave themselves indecently to a man in the extremest misery, whom they ought to have pitied, and for whom they ought at this time to have been praying, but also forgetting all reverence to God, to say, *He trusted in God, let him deliver him now, if he will have him;* jeering all faith and trusting in God, and as it were defying God's power, and saying with Nebuchadnezzar, Dan. iii. 15, *Who is that God that shall deliver you out of my hands?* this is justly surprising, and lets us see to what a height of wickedness the Jews were come, and confirms us in this, that if those who serve the Lord in public places, especially in holy things, be not the best of men, they are the worst. Having more knowledge of the will of God than others, if they have once mastered their consciences, they become the vilest of men, and the most prodigious patterns of atheism and all wickedness. It lets us also see to what a degree malice and covetousness will debauch souls, and teach us to fear sinning against our light and convictions. All this was foretold by the prophet David, Psal. xxii. 8, and so *must be.* But the necessity of the event by no means excused the sinfulness of the act, nor made God the author of these men's sins. Matthew saith, *The thieves also, which were crucified with him, cast the same in his teeth.* Luke saith, only *one of them* did so. Some think that at the first they both reviled him, but the heart of one of them was changed while he hung upon the cross; but it is no unusual thing in Scripture to use the plural number for the singular; and the number may be understood not so much to refer to the persons as their qualities, they were both thieves, though but one of them reviled our Saviour. Or what hinders, but that they both might desire Christ to put forth his power to deliver them, though one of them further reviled him, by words which the evangelists have not set down. Luke tells us, that one of these thieves rebuked his fellow, and cleared Christ's innocency. Thus God had that honour from a thief which was denied him by the chief priests and elders. He can *of stones raise up children to Abraham.* He begs of Christ to remember him when he came into his kingdom; discovering an eminent faith in Christ, he is rewarded, by Christ telling him, *To day thou shalt be with me in paradise:* a plain text to prove that souls neither sleep nor die with the body, but immediately pass into their eternal mansions. John addeth, that there stood by the cross of Jesus his mother, and her sister, Mary the wife of Cleophas, and Mary Magdalene. and mentions our Saviour's recommending his mother to the care of his beloved disciple, and tells us of John's care of her; the other three evangelists mention their being there, but standing afar off; which might both be true, they being nearer the cross at first, then removing themselves further of. John further mentioneth their giving our Saviour (upon his saying, *I thirst*) *vinegar to drink.* It is very probable this was but a kindness they did usually show to malefactors, dying that kind of death, when they were so long a time dying; but the evangelist tells us that in our Saviour's case there was a scripture to be fulfilled,

Psal. lxix. 21, *In my thirst they gave me vinegar to drink:* whether David there spake in the person of Christ, or what was at that time primarily fulfilled in David, was at that time fulfilled in Christ as his antitype, is not much material for us to know; that the text related to Christ, and was fulfilled in him, we are assured by the evangelist. This giving of Christ to drink was distinct from that we meet with before, as may appear by the many different circumstances. That he refused; this he received, and said, *It is finished:* my passion is finished, or upon the finishing.

m Amos 8. 9.
Mark 15. 33.
Luke 23. 44.

45 ᵐ Now from the sixth hour there was darkness over all the land unto the ninth hour.

n Heb. 5. 7.
o Ps. 22. 1.

46 And about the ninth hour ⁿ Jesus cried with a loud voice, saying, Eli, Eli, lama sabachthani? that is to say, ᵒ My God, my God, why hast thou forsaken me?

47 Some of them that stood there, when they heard *that*, said, This *man* calleth for Elias.

p Ps. 69. 21.
Mark 15. 36.
Luke 23. 36.
John 19. 29.

48 And straightway one of them ran, and took a spunge, ᵖ and filled *it* with vinegar, and put *it* on a reed, and gave him to drink.

49 The rest said, Let be, let us see whether Elias will come to save him.

q Mark 15. 37.
Luke 23. 46.

50 ¶ ᑫ Jesus, when he had cried again with a loud voice, yielded up the ghost.

Mark hath the same, chap. xv. 33—38. Luke saith, chap. xxiii. 44, that *it was about the sixth hour, and there was a darkness over all the earth until the ninth hour. And the sun was darkened, and the veil of the temple was rent in the midst. And when Jesus had cried with a loud voice, he said, Father, into thy hands I commend my spirit: and having said thus, he gave up the ghost.* John saith no more, chap. xix. 30, but that—*he bowed his head, and gave up the ghost.* It is said, John xix. 14, it was *about the sixth hour* when Pilate brought forth Christ to the Jews; how then could he be crucified at the third hour, and the darkness begin at the sixth? The different ways the Jews and the Romans had of counting hours, make us to be at a loss sometimes as to circumstances of time to reconcile some scriptures. But as to the present difficulty, it is said that the Jews, as they divided the night into four watches, so they also divided the day into four parts, each part having its denomination from the succeeding part, by which name all the intermediate time was called. Thus when the third hour (which with us is nine of the clock) was past, they called all the sixth hour till past twelve. Thus Pilate condemned Christ in the beginning of the sixth hour, and the darkness began at the end of it, that is, after twelve, for dividing the day into quadrants, the hours had their denomination from them. John also saith no more than *about the sixth hour*, which is true if it were some small time after. *There was darkness over all the land unto the ninth hour.* That this darkness was caused by the eclipse of the sun at that time of the day is plain enough, but that this was no eclipse in the ordinary course of nature is evident; for, 1. Whereas all eclipses use to be in the time of the new moon, this was when the moon was at the full, the fifteenth day of the month Nisan. 2. This eclipse was not seen in one part or in another, but over all the earth that was under the same hemisphere. 3. No eclipse in a natural course can last three hours. So that plainly this was a miraculous eclipse, not caused by the interposition of the moon, (as other eclipses,) but by the mighty and extraordinary power of God, which made a heathen philosopher at a great distance cry out, Either the Divine Being now suffereth, or sympathizeth with one that suffereth: he is said to have seen this eclipse in Egypt. *And about the ninth hour* (that is, about three of the clock, as we reckon the hours) *Jesus cried with a loud voice, saying, Eli, Eli, or Eloi, Eloi, lama sabachthani?* The words are Hebrew, though Mark reports them according to the Syriac corruption of the dialect. They are David's words, Psal. xxii. 1. David was a type of Christ. He that was the Son of David useth David's words, possibly spoken by David in the person of Christ. God's forsaking any person or place, must be understood with reference not to his essential presence, for so he filleth all places, and is present with all persons; but with reference to the manifestations of his providence for our good: thus when God withholds his good providence to us, either with respect to our outward or inward man, he is said to forsake us. A total forsaking either of our bodies, or of our souls, is not consistent with the being of our outward man, or the spiritual being or life of our inward man. All forsakings therefore in this life are gradual and partial. The forsaking which Christ therefore here complains of, was not the total withdrawing of Divine favour and assistance from him; that was impossible, and incompetent with the first words testifying his relation to God, and assistance in him; but it must be understood with respect to God's consolatory manifestations, and that is testified by his other words, related by Luke, *Father, into thy hands I commend my spirit.* Which words having said, *he gave up the ghost,* say Matthew, Mark, and Luke. John addeth, that he *bowed his head, and gave up the ghost:* words added, to confirm what he elsewhere said, that he laid down his life, none took it from him. His crying twice at this instant with a loud voice, argued his spirits not so spent, but he might have lived a few minutes longer, but he freely laid down his life. The people saying, *He calleth for Elias,* when he said *Eli, Eli,* spake them to be Jews, who to this day dream of an Elias to come and *restore all things.* That they no better distinguished betwixt Eli and Elias, must be attributed either to the corruption of their dialect, he saying *Eloi, Eloi,* (according to the Syriac corruption of the term,) or their too great distance from him. Their mocking him upon it was but consonant to their former behaviour toward him, while he was upon the cross. Their giving him the spunge with vinegar and hyssop we before gave an account of.

51 And, behold, ʳ the veil of the temple was rent in twain from the top to the bottom; and the earth did quake, and the rocks rent;

r Ex. 26. 31.
2 Chr. 3. 14.
Mark 15. 38.
Luke 23. 45.

52 And the graves were opened; and many bodies of the saints which slept arose,

53 And came out of the graves after his resurrection, and went into the holy city, and appeared unto many.

Mark, chap. xv. 38, mentioneth only the rending of the veil. No more doth Luke, chap. xxiii. 45. John mentioneth none of these things. It pleased God to give a testimony against this prodigious piece of wickedness by prodigious signs, both in the heavens and on the earth. In the heavens the sun, as we heard before, suffered an unusual, preternatural eclipse, which lasted three hours. In the earth, there was an earthquake, to that degree, that the rocks were rent by it. Earthquakes were sometimes no more than indications of God's power and majesty, Psal. lxviii. 8; Joel ii. 10; and some think, that by this earthquake Christ declared his Divine power. It is certain that the centurion concluded from it, *this was the Son of God*, ver. 54. But earthquakes were sometimes not only the indications of the Divine majesty and power, but also of his wrath, Psal. xviii. 7, 8; Joel iii. 16; Nah. i. 6. And such doubtless was this; to show that the earth abhorred what these men had done. Besides these, *the veil of the temple was rent:* three of the evangelists mention it. It is not much material whether this were the outward veil, or the inward veil, or hangings, which parted the most holy place from the other part of the temple, though probably it was the inner veil. By this rending of the veil God testified his wrath against the Jews, and that he was leaving his temple amongst them. The veil also was a type of Christ's flesh, Heb. x. 20: the antitype being rent, it was reasonable that the type should also be so. By this also was showed, that the temple service was now at an end, and to continue no longer, and the partition wall betwixt Jews and Gentiles was pulled down. For what Matthew speaks, ver. 52, 53, of the graves opening, and the bodies of the saints arising, &c., probably it was not till Christ's resurrection; only Matthew puts it in here, reckoning up together all the prodigious things that happened, for Matthew himself saith, ver. 53, they *came out of the graves after his resurrection*, and it is not likely that the graves opened any considerable time before they came out of their graves. These now were the prodigies which attended the death of our Saviour.

s ver. 36. Mark 15. 39. Luke 23. 47.
54 ˢ Now when the centurion, and they that were with him, watching Jesus, saw the earthquake, and those things that were done, they feared greatly, saying, Truly this was the Son of God.

55 And many women were there beholding afar off, ᵗ which followed Jesus from Galilee, ministering unto him:

t Luke 8. 2, 3.

u Mark 15. 40.
56 ᵘ Among which was Mary Magdalene, and Mary the mother of James and Joses, and the mother of Zebedee's children.

Mark saith, chap. xv. 39—41, *And when the centurion, which stood over against him, saw that he so cried out, and gave up the ghost, he said, Truly this man was the Son of God. There were also women looking on afar off: among whom was Mary Magdalene, and Mary the mother of James the less and of Joses, and Salome: (who also when he was in Galilee, followed him, and ministered unto him;) and many other women which came up with him to Jerusalem.* Luke saith, chap. xxiii. 47—49, *Now when the centurion saw what was done, he glorified God, saying, Certainly this was a righteous man. And all the people that came together to that sight, beholding the things which were done, smote their breasts, and returned. And all his acquaintance, and the women that followed him from Galilee, stood afar off, beholding these things.* We heard before, ver. 36, that the soldiers sat down and watched Christ. The centurion here mentioned was the captain of this watch; he seeing the earthquake, and all the other things that were done, saith Matthew. Mark saith, *When he saw that he so cried out, and gave up the ghost. He glorified God,* saith Luke. Matthew and Mark tell us how he said, *Truly this man was the Son of God.* Luke saith he said, *Certainly this was a righteous man:* he glorified God by a confession of the truth, to the glory of God, saying, he was a righteous man, and such a righteous man as was also the Son of God. It seems very probable that this captain, living amongst the Jews, had learned from them their expectation of a Messiah, and speaketh this with reference to that, and acknowledgeth that Christ was he. Luke addeth, that all the people that came to see that sight returned, smiting their breasts, being convinced of the great wickedness committed by their high priests, and chief priests and elders, and fearing that vengeance which followed in less than forty years. *And many women were there:* these women had followed Christ out of Galilee: two only are named here, *Mary Magdalene,* who probably had her name from Magdala a city in Galilee, *and Mary the mother of James and Joses, (James the less,* saith Mark, to distinguish him from James the son of Zebedee,) *and the mother of Zebedee's children:* these *stood afar off,* these three evangelists say. John told us, chap. xix. 25, that two of these were so near the cross, with the mother of our Lord, that he spake to them. Here we read nothing of the mother of our Lord, probably she was gone with John, to whom Christ had commended her, and the rest withdrew and stood farther off from the cross at this time. Matthew goeth on now, describing the coming of Joseph of Arimathea to beg the dead body of Christ; so doth Mark and Luke. John interposeth something tending to complete the history, chap. xix. 31—37: *The Jews therefore, because it was the preparation, that the bodies should not remain upon the cross on the sabbath day, (for that sabbath day was an high day,) besought Pilate that their legs might be broken, and that they might be taken away. Then came the soldiers, and brake the legs of the first, and of the other which was crucified with him. But when they came to Jesus, and saw that he was dead already, they brake not his legs: but one of the soldiers with a spear pierced his side, and forthwith came thereout blood and water. And he that saw it bare record, and his record is true: and he knoweth that he saith true, that ye might believe. For these things were done, that the scripture should be fulfilled, A bone of him shall not be broken. And again another scripture saith, They shall look on him whom they pierced.* The day upon which he was crucified was the fifteenth day of the month Nisan, upon the Friday, as we call it; this appeareth from this text, which saith *it was the preparation* to the Jewish sabbath; and *that sabbath,* the evangelist saith, *was a high day,* not because, as some think, the Jews put off their passover to that day, but because it was the second day of the feast of unleavened bread. It is true, John xix. 14, it is called *the preparation of the passover;* but we must remember, that all the seven days of unleavened bread were so called, as I before noted. This day was indeed the preparation to the sabbath in the paschal week, for otherwise we must say that Christ did not eat the passover the same day that the Jews did, which involves us in many inextricable difficulties, and could not be if the paschal lamb was to be killed by the priests, for they would not have killed it the day before. It is therefore most probable, that John xix. 14 must be expounded by ver. 31, and *the preparation of the passover,* ver. 14, was the preparation to the sabbath, which falling within the compass of the seven days of unleavened bread, was a great day with them, especially being the day following the eating of the paschal lamb. By the law, Deut. xxi. 23, the body of none that was hanged was to abide all night upon the tree. It was betwixt three and four of the clock in the afternoon before that Christ died; they used to set some hours apart for preparation to the sabbath, which that night began as soon as the sun was set; this therefore makes them go to Pilate, and desire that the legs of them that suffered might be broken. Pilate grants their request. The soldiers brake the legs of the two thieves, but when they came to Christ, they found him dead, and brake not his legs, but a soldier with a spear pierced his side. The evangelist takes notice of these minute things, (and assureth us he saw them, that we might believe,) that he might show us how in every point the things of old spoken of Christ were fulfilled in him. Christ was the true paschal Lamb, as to which the law was, That a bone of it should not be broken, Exod. xii. 46; Numb. ix. 12; or else the evangelist referreth to Psal. xxxiv. 20, where it is said of a righteous man, *He keepeth all his bones; not one of them is broken.* Our Saviour's side was pierced, and that also is recorded, to let us know the fulfilling of that scripture, Zech. xii. 10, *They shall look upon me whom they have pierced.*

x Mark 15. 42. Luke 23. 50. John 19. 38.
57 ˣ When the even was come, there came a rich man of Arimathæa, named Joseph, who also himself was Jesus' disciple:

58 He went to Pilate, and begged the body of Jesus. Then Pilate commanded the body to be delivered.

59 And when Joseph had taken the body, he wrapped it in a clean linen cloth,

y Is. 53. 9.
60 And ʸ laid it in his own new tomb, which he had hewn out in the rock: and he rolled a great stone to the door of the sepulchre, and departed.

61 And there was Mary Magdalene, and the other Mary, sitting over against the sepulchre.

Mark hath it, chap. xv. 42—47, *And now when the even was come, because it was the preparation, that is, the day before the sabbath, Joseph of Arimathea, an honourable counsellor, which also waited for the kingdom of God, came, and went in boldly unto Pilate, and craved the body of Jesus. And Pilate marvelled if he were already dead: and calling unto him the centurion, he asked him whether he had been any while dead. And when he knew it of the centurion, he gave the body to Joseph. And he bought fine linen and took him down, and wrapped him in the linen, and laid him in a sepulchre which was hewn out of a rock, and rolled a stone unto the door of the sepulchre. And Mary Magdalene and Mary the mother of Joses beheld where he was laid.* Luke hath it, chap. xxiii. 50—54, thus: *And behold there was a man named Joseph, a counsellor; and he was a good man, and a just: (the same had not consented to the counsel and deed of them;) he was of Arimathea, a city of the Jews: who also himself waited for the kingdom of God. This man went unto Pilate, and begged the body of Jesus. And he took it down, and wrapped it in linen, and laid it in a sepulchre that was hewn in stone, wherein never man before laid. And that day was the preparation, and the sabbath drew on.* John reports it with some additions, chap. xix. 38—42: *And after this Joseph of Arimathea, being a disciple of Jesus, but secretly for fear of the Jews, besought Pilate that he might take away the body of Jesus: and Pilate gave him leave. He came therefore, and took the body of Jesus. And there came also Nicodemus, which at the first came to Jesus by night, and brought a mixture of myrrh and aloes, about an hundred pound weight. Then took they the body of Jesus, and wound it in linen clothes with the spices, as the manner of the Jews is to bury. Now in the place where he was crucified there was a garden; and in the garden a new sepulchre, wherein was never man yet laid. There laid they Jesus therefore because of the Jews' preparation day: for the sepulchre was nigh at hand.* All four evangelists (as we see) repeat this history, one supplying what is wanting in another towards the completeness of it. Nor must we think it is for nothing so punctually related; much depended upon the world's satisfaction in the truth and certainty of his death, burial, and resurrection, they are three great articles of our faith. We have therefore here punctually described his burial, with all the circumstances of it. As it is with us, so it seems it was with them. The bodies of those who died as malefactors were taken to be in the power of the magistrates, to dispose of as they pleased, though they were ordinarily granted upon petition to their friends and relations. The person who begged the body of our Saviour is described to us by his name, Joseph; by his city, Arimathea (there it seems he was born, or had his mansion-house, though he resided in Jerusalem); by his quality, both his more exterior quality, and his more interior qualification. As for his outward quality, Matthew saith he was *a rich man*. Mark saith he was *an honourable counsellor*. Luke also calls him *a counsellor, but had not consented to the counsel and deed of them*, that is, of them who had examined and condemned Christ: whether he was a member of the Jewish sanhedrim, or of Pilate's council, (though the last be not probable,) or had been a counsellor formerly, but now was not so, is hard to determine; but his quality doubtless made his access more free to Pilate. He *went in boldly* to him, saith Mark; his quality in the city, and his love to Christ, both contributed to this boldness. For his more inward qualifications, Matthew and John both tell us he was *a disciple*, one that had learned of Christ, though John tells us, it was *secretly for fear of the Jews. Among the chief rulers many believed on him*, John xii. 42. As bad as that set of rulers was which now ruled the Jewish affairs, (and a worse could not be,) Christ had some disciples amongst them, as well as afterward in Nero's court: these, for fear of the Jews casting them out of the synagogues, durst not openly own Christ, but secretly loved him. Joseph and Nicodemus were two of them. And to let us know what the disciples of Christ are, and should be, this Joseph is described by Luke to be *a good and a just man;* by Mark, to be one who *waited for the kingdom of God;* a believer, one who, believing what Christ had said, both concerning his kingdom of grace and glory, lived in the expectation of it. This man beggeth of the governor the body of Christ. Pilate wondered that he should be so soon dead, but inquiring of the centurion, and hearing that he was dead, he commands that his body should be delivered unto Joseph. The manner of the Jews was, neither to have gardens nor burying-places within the city, but without the wall; it should appear that this Joseph had a garden place without the city, and near to the place where Christ was crucified, and in that garden he had cut out of some great stone a sepulchre for himself. Matthew calls it *his own new tomb, which he had hewn out in the rock*. The other evangelists do not call it his own new tomb, only Luke and John observe it was a sepulchre in which none ever before was laid. So as when they found him risen from the dead, they could not say it was some other body, for there was no other body in the tomb. But before they laid in the body, both Matthew and Mark observe, that Joseph wrapped it in fine linen, and John further addeth, that they embalmed the body; to which purpose it was that Nicodemus (that ruler who came to Jesus by night, of which we have the story, John iii., with whom our Saviour had a discourse about regeneration) brought the *mixture of myrrh and aloes*, of about an hundred pound weight; John adds, *as the manner of the Jews is to bury*, not ordinarily, but persons of greater note, whose estates were such as they could bear such an expense. This was the beginning of honour done unto Christ, after that he had passed through his lowest degree of humiliation. *Mary Magdalene, and the other Mary*, that is, the wife of Cleophas, of whom we heard before, stayed to see where he was laid, and took their seats over against the sepulchre. Luke saith, chap. xxiii. 55, 56, *The women also, which came with him from Galilee, followed after, and beheld the sepulchre, and how his body was laid. And they returned, and prepared spices and ointments; and rested the sabbath day, according to the commandment.* It seems they sat but a little while (as Matthew saith) right *over against the sepulchre*, but went home, and prepared spices and ointments to embalm him, but would not do it on the sabbath, which was now beginning, thinking that it would be time enough upon the first day of the week. Matthew saith, that Joseph *rolled a great stone to the door of the sepulchre, and departed.*

62 ¶ Now the next day, that followed the day of the preparation, the Chief Priests and Pharisees came together unto Pilate,

63 Saying, Sir, we remember that that deceiver said, while he was yet alive, ᶻAfter three days I will rise again.

64 Command therefore that the sepulchre be made sure until the third day, lest his disciples come by night, and steal him away, and say unto the people, He is risen from the dead: so the last error shall be worse than the first.

z ch. 16. 21. & 17. 23. & 20. 19. & 26. 61. Mark 8. 31. & 10. 34. Luke 9. 22. & 18. 33. & 24. 6, 7. John 2. 19.

65 Pilate said unto them, Ye have a watch: go your way, make *it* as sure as ye can.

66 So they went, and made the sepulchre sure, ᵃsealing the stone, and setting a watch.

a Dan. 6. 17.

This part of the history is recorded by no other evangelist: the recording it by Matthew contributeth yet further to evidence the truth of Christ's resurrection; for here was all imaginable care taken to prevent a cheat in the case. *The next day, that followed the day of the preparation*, must be the sabbath day, Mark xv. 42. These superstitious hypocrites, that quarrelled with our Saviour for his disciples (being hungry) plucking ears of corn on the sabbath day, and for his healing him that had a withered hand, chap. xii. 13, can now themselves go to Pilate, to set him on work to command that the sepulchre should be made fast to the third day. They allege that Christ, whom they impiously call *that deceiver, said, while he was alive*, that he would rise again the third day, to answer the type of the prophet Jonas, chap. xii. 39, 40. They were doubtless jealous that there was more truth in those words than they were willing to believe. They pretend also a fear lest his disciples should come privately by night, and steal his body away, and then say he was risen. But was this a probable thing, that a government should be afraid of a few poor, unarmed men? They were doubtless convicted in their own consciences that he would rise again from the dead, and to prevent his coming out of the sepulchre, they would have Pilate command that the sepulchre should be made sure. Pilate tells them, that they had a watch, a band of soldiers, which he had commanded at this time to attend them, either for the guard of the temple, or other things about which they would employ them; they might make the sepulchre as sure as they could. *So they went, and made the sepulchre sure, sealing the stone, and setting a watch.* Vain men! as if the same power that was necessary to raise and quicken the dead, could not also remove the stone, and break through the watch which they had set. But by this their excessive care and diligence, instead of preventing Christ's resurrection, as they intended, they have confirmed the truth and belief of it to all the world. So doth God take the wise in their own craftiness, and turn their wisdom into foolishness, that he may set his King upon his holy hill of Zion.

CHAP. XXVIII

Christ's resurrection is declared by an angel to the women, 1—8. Christ himself appeareth to them, 9, 10. The chief priests bribe the soldiers to report that he was stolen by the disciples, 11—15. Christ appeareth to the eleven in Galilee, 16, 17; and sendeth them to teach and baptize all nations, 18—20.

a Mark 16. 1.
Luke 24. 1.
John 20. 1.
b ch. 27. 56.

IN the ª end of the sabbath, as it began to dawn toward the first *day* of the week, came Mary Magdalene ᵇ and the other Mary to see the sepulchre.

We are now come to that part of the Gospel which treateth concerning the resurrection of Christ, and the converse which he had upon the earth for forty days, Acts i. 3, until the time of his ascension into heaven. Matthew and Mark are the shortest in this narration. I shall therefore only consider what Matthew saith, and what the other evangelists speak as to the same things which he mentioneth, leaving out what the other evangelists have (not at all mentioned by him) to be discoursed in their proper place. We heard before that Mary Magdalene and the other Mary had prepared spices and ointments to anoint the body of Christ, but the sabbath day being at hand, they would not by that unnecessary action profane the sabbath; as Luke tells us, chap. xxiii. 56, they *rested on the sabbath, according to the commandment:* The sabbath ended with them at the setting of the sun. They did not go as soon as the sabbath was ended, but after it was ended, *as it began to dawn toward the first day of the week.* The first day of the week began with them as soon as the sabbath was ended, so as the first day of the week was a third part spent; therefore Mark reports the time, chap. xvi. 1, 2, *And when the sabbath was past;* and says that *Mary Magdalene, and Mary the mother of James and Salome, had bought sweet spices, that they might come and anoint him. And very early in the morning, the first day of the week, they came unto the sepulchre at the rising of the sun.* Luke saith, chap. xxiv. 1, that *upon the first day of the week, very early in the morning, they came unto the sepulchre, bringing the spices which they had prepared, and certain others with them.* John saith, chap. xx. 1, *The first day of the week cometh Mary Magdalene early, when it was yet dark, unto the sepulchre.* As to the time, three evangelists say it was upon the first day of the week, early in the morning; about sun-rising, saith Mark; *while it was yet dark,* saith John: these now interpret Matthew's ὀψὲ σαββάτων, which doth not signify, in the evening of the sabbath, but in the evening of the sabbaths, the end of the week. The Jews, in honour to the sabbath, called all the days of the week sabbaths, the first of the sabbath, the second of the sabbath, &c.; so as ὀψὲ σαββάτων is well translated by our translators, *In the end of the sabbath,* the evening or night following the sabbath, following the seventh day, which was the sabbath. Nor is ὀψὲ to be taken here strictly for that time of the night which we call the evening, but for the whole night, which must be reckoned to continue until the sun-rising of the first day of the week; and so Matthew expounds himself, adding, *as it began to dawn toward the first day of the week,* that is, the first artificial day, as the day is accounted from sun-rising to sun-setting; otherwise it was upon the first natural day of the week, which began from the sun-setting before. Matthew mentions the coming of Mary Magdalene, and the other Mary, who, Mark saith, was the mother of James and Salome, to the sepulchre. John mentioneth only Mary Magdalene, but it is not probable she went alone, and two other evangelists say also the other Mary. Luke saith there were *certain others with them:* there might be divers with them, though one only be named by John, two by Matthew and Mark, as being the principal persons in the company. And though Matthew only mentioneth their going to see the sepulchre, yet Mark telleth us that they went also to anoint his body, and Luke saith they carried the spices prepared for that end; their faith, as it seemeth, was yet but weak as to our Saviour's resurrection.

∥ Or, *had been.*
c See Mark 16. 5.
Luke 24. 4.
John 20. 12.

2 And, behold, there ∥ was a great earthquake: for ᶜ the angel of the Lord descended from heaven, and came and rolled back the stone from the door, and sat upon it.

3 ᵈ His countenance was like lightning, and his raiment white as snow: d Dan. 10. 6.

4 And for fear of him the keepers did shake, and became as dead *men.*

Matthew alone telleth us this; all the other evangelists agree that when the women came they found the stone rolled away, which eased them of the solicitude they had as they came, saying amongst themselves, *Who shall roll us away the stone from the door of the sepulchre?* Matthew saith, an angel descended and rolled away the stone, and came and sat upon it. This angel had assumed a shape, for he appeared to those that saw him, as to *his countenance, like lightning;* as to his garment, as one clothed in exceeding white linen, white as snow. What doth the watch all this while? Matthew saith, they were afraid, shook, and became like dead men. Luke and John make mention of two angels. Indeed there needed not any angel at all to remove the stone, if this had been all he had come down for; He that was quickened by the Spirit, could by the same power have rolled away the stone; but as it was fit that the angels, who had been witnesses of his passion, should also be witnesses of his resurrection, that he who was *justified in the Spirit,* should be *seen of angels,* 1 Tim. iii. 16; so it was necessary, that the keepers might give a just account to Pilate, the chief priests, and scribes. And no wonder that they were afraid, and as dead men, whenas all apparitions of this nature naturally affright us, and they had such a conscience of guilt upon them, and might justly fear what their masters should say to them, when they found the body was missing; especially also seeing, or being sensible of, the earthquake, or great concussion of the air (for though we translate it *earthquake,* yet the Greek saith no more than σεισμος μέγας). Besides that the presence of the angels seemed reasonable to prevent a cheat, by putting some other dead body into the sepulchre, and to direct the women who were now coming towards the sepulchre, for they were not yet come: when they were come, they found the stone rolled away; and Matthew's relation, how the stone came removed, was doubtless not from them, but from the keepers, or some to whom they had related it.

5 And the angel answered and said unto the women, Fear not ye: for I know that ye seek Jesus, which was crucified.

6 He is not here: for he is risen, ᵉ as he said. Come, see the place where the Lord lay.   e ch. 12. 40. & 16. 21. & 17. 23. & 20. 19.

7 And go quickly, and tell his disciples that he is risen from the dead; and, behold, ᶠ he goeth before you into Galilee; there shall ye see him: lo, I have told you.   f ch. 26. 32. Mark 16. 7.

8 And they departed quickly from the sepulchre with fear and great joy; and did run to bring his disciples word.

Mark saith, chap. xvi. 5—8, *And entering into the sepulchre, they saw a young man sitting on the right side, clothed in a long white garment; and they were affrighted. And he saith unto them, Be not affrighted: Ye seek Jesus of Nazareth, which was crucified: he is risen; he is not here: behold the place where they laid him. But go your way, tell his disciples and Peter that he goeth before you into Galilee: there shall ye see him, as he said unto you. And they went out quickly, and fled from the sepulchre; for they trembled and were amazed: neither said they any thing to any man, for they were afraid.* Luke saith, chap. xxiv. 3—11, *And they entered in, and found not the body of the Lord Jesus. And it came to pass, as they were much perplexed thereabout, behold, two men stood by them in shining garments: and as they were afraid, and bowed down their faces to the earth, they said unto them, Why seek ye the living among the dead? he is not here, but is risen: remember how he spake unto you when he was yet in Galilee, saying, The Son of man must be delivered into the hands of sinful men, and be crucified, and the third day rise again.*

And they remembered his words, and returned from the sepulchre, and told all these things unto the eleven, and to all the rest. It was Mary Magdalene, and Joanna, and Mary the mother of James, and other women that were with them, which told these things unto the apostles. And their words seemed to them as idle tales, and they believed them not. John saith, of Mary Magdalene only, chap. xx. 2, *Then she runneth, and cometh to Simon Peter, and to the other disciple whom Jesus loved, and saith unto them, They have taken away the Lord out of the sepulchre, and we know not where they have laid him.* Matthew in this relation omitteth many things more distinctly related by the other evangelists. When the women came to the sepulchre, they first entered in; so saith Mark and Luke. It was within that they saw the angel, habited as it were in a long white, shining garment. They were affrighted, (as we naturally are upon apparitions,) they bowed down their faces to the earth. The angel bids them not to fear, he knew that they sought Jesus of Nazareth, who was crucified; *Why seek ye the living among the dead? he is not here, but is risen;* showeth to them the place where his body was laid; mindeth them of Christ's words to them in Galilee, chap. xvii. 23; bids them go tell his disciples (Mark adds, *and Peter*) that he was going before them into Galilee, and that there they should see him, as he had said unto them, chap. xxvi. 32; Mark xiv. 28. *They departed quickly from the sepulchre* (as Matthew saith) *with fear and great joy;* Mark saith, trembling and amazed. John doth not say, unbelieving, but he saith it in effect, for he saith, that they said to Simon Peter, *They have taken away the Lord out of the sepulchre, and we know not where they have laid him.* The cause of their fear and amazement was doubtless the apparition of the angel. The cause of their sudden joy was the news that he was risen, told them by the angel. It appeareth that their joy was but a sudden flash of passion, not rising from the certainty of their souls as to the truth of what they heard, because they said to the disciples, that they did not believe it, but upon second thoughts concluded that somebody had removed our Saviour's body: neither did the apostles themselves believe it, as appeareth by Luke; he saith they looked upon it as an idle tale. John saith expressly, chap. xx. 9, *As yet they knew not the scripture, that he must rise again from the dead:* they knew it notionally, but they did not give a firm and a fixed assent to it, they did not believe it. It was not, it seemeth, in the power of their wills to believe this article of Christ's resurrection; for as they had a Divine revelation of the thing from Christ himself, so we cannot but think they had mind and good will enough to believe it. But God had not given them the power of faith as to this point.

9 ¶ And as they went to tell his disciples, behold, [g]Jesus met them, saying, All hail. And they came and held him by the feet, and worshipped him.

10 Then said Jesus unto them, Be not afraid: go tell [h]my brethren that they go into Galilee, and there shall they see me.

g See Mark 16. 9. John 20. 14.

h See John 20. 17. Rom. 8. 29. Heb. 2. 11.

Matthew repeateth this very shortly. Mark saith, chap. xvi. 9–11, *Now when Jesus was risen early the first day of the week, he appeared first to Mary Magdalene, out of whom he had cast seven devils. And she went and told them that had been with him, as they mourned and wept. And they, when they had heard that he was alive, and had been seen of her, believed not.* Luke saith, chap. xxiv. 12, *Then* (that is, when Mary Magdalene and the other Mary had come and told the disciples what they had seen and heard, though at first they gave no credit to it) *arose Peter, and ran unto the sepulchre, and stooping down, he beheld the linen clothes laid by themselves, and departed, wondering in himself at that which was come to pass.* John relateth this more distinctly, in chap. xx. 3–18: *Peter therefore went forth, and that other disciple,* (whom Jesus loved, as ver. 2, and that was John himself, who wrote that Gospel, John xiii. 23,) *and came to the sepulchre. So they ran both together: and the other disciple did outrun Peter, and came first to the sepulchre. And he stooping down, and looking in, saw the linen clothes lying; yet went he not in. Then cometh Simon Peter following him, and went into the sepulchre, and seeth the linen clothes lie, and the napkin, that was* about his head, not lying with the linen clothes, but wrapped together in a place by itself. *Then went in also that other disciple, which came first to the sepulchre, and he saw, and believed. For as yet they knew not the scripture, that he must rise again from the dead. Then the disciples went away again unto their own home. But Mary stood without at the sepulchre weeping: and as she wept, she stooped down, and looked into the sepulchre, and seeth two angels in white sitting, the one at the head, and the other at the feet, where the body of Jesus had lain. And they say unto her, woman, why weepest thou? She saith unto them, Because they have taken away my Lord, and I know not where they have laid him. And when she had thus said, she turned herself back, and saw Jesus standing, and knew not that it was Jesus. Jesus saith unto her, Woman, why weepest thou? whom seekest thou? She, supposing him to be the gardener, saith unto him, Sir, if thou have borne him hence, tell me where thou hast laid him, and I will take him away. Jesus saith unto her, Mary. She turned herself, and saith unto him, Rabboni; which is to say, Master. Jesus saith unto her, Touch me not; for I am not yet ascended to my Father: but go to my brethren, and say unto them, I ascend unto my Father, and your Father; and to my God, and your God. Mary Magdalene came and told the disciples that she had seen the Lord, and that he had spoken these things unto her.* What there is particularly to be noted upon the several particulars in John's relation, I shall observe when I come to that chapter of John; I have only at present transcribed it, that from the comparing it with the other evangelists we might understand the order of this history. *And as they went to tell his disciples.* This seemeth to be their second going, and the order to be thus: When Mary and the rest came to the disciples, and told them they had been at the sepulchre, and what they had there seen and heard, they believed it not. But yet, it being close by the city, and not knowing what to think, Peter resolves to go and see, and so doth John. They both run, but John comes there first, but goes not into the sepulchre, but only looks in, and sees the linen clothes lying. Peter comes (for it was very near the gates of the city); he goeth in, seeth the linen clothes, and the napkin. Then John also adventureth to go in, and saw and believed; he is the first is said to have believed. Then they went home. But Mary stayed weeping; and now and then looking into the sepulchre, she seeth not the clothes only, but two angels sitting, the one at the head, the other at the feet, of the place where the body of Christ did lie. They ask her why she wept. She tells them, Because they had taken away her Lord, and she did not know where they had laid him. Now, saith John, when she had said thus, ἐστράφη εἰς τὰ ὀπίσω, we translate it, *She turned herself back, and saw Jesus standing,* John xx. 14; which seemeth to contradict our evangelist Matthew, who saith, *As they went to tell his disciples, behold, Jesus met them, saying, All hail.* Our translation now would make one think that Mary was still at the sepulchre, and there looking back she saw Jesus; and this seemeth either to assert that Mary saw Christ twice, once at the sepulchre, once in her return to the city, or else to contradict Matthew; but the Greek words may be translated, She was turned backward, that is, was going back to tell his disciples, and met Christ, who saluted her, saying, *All hail.* Though Mary Magdalene be only named, and possibly all the women who were with her at first did not come back with her the second time, yet it is plain she was not alone, for Matthew saith, *They came and held him by the feet, and worshipped him.* He bids her be not afraid, but go and tell his disciples they should meet him in Galilee. For the other discourse betwixt him and Mary, we shall meet with it when we come to that chapter in St. John's Gospel where it is mentioned. Mark saith, that *when they had heard he was alive, and had been seen of her, they believed not.* We do not read that the angels appeared either to Peter or John, much less that Christ as yet showed himself to them; so they had only the testimony of Mary as to these things, and their own view of the empty sepulchre, and the clothes lying by. How hard a thing it is to believe spiritual mysteries, above the reach of our reason! so hard, that no revelation of flesh and blood is sufficient to beget such a faith.

11 ¶ Now when they were going, behold, some

of the watch came into the city, and shewed unto the Chief Priests all the things that were done.

12 And when they were assembled with the elders, and had taken counsel, they gave large money unto the soldiers,

13 Saying, Say ye, His disciples came by night, and stole him *away* while we slept.

14 And if this come to the governor's ears, we will persuade him, and secure you.

15 So they took the money, and did as they were taught: and this saying is commonly reported among the Jews until this day.

No other evangelist hath this passage, which was necessary to be inserted by Matthew, 1. To satisfy readers how it could come to pass, that Matthew should know of the earthquake, or concussion of the air rather, and that an angel came and rolled away the stone; for all this was done, and Christ risen, before the women came: it came out by the watch, or by Pilate to whom the watch related it, or else by some of the priests and elders, who did not keep counsel so well as others. 2. To show the horrible wickedness of these priests and elders, that would thus cover the blood they had spilt with a lie and subornation. Thus one sin requires more to defend it. 3. To let us see how simple people will show themselves in their malice. What a story here was! If they were asleep, how could they know that Christ's disciples came by night and stole him away? Would no noise of rolling away the stone wake them? Malice will not allow men deliberation enough to show themselves wise. God infatuated these men, that succeeding ages might know they were suborned. Here we have also the ground of that fable with which the Jews presently filled all the world.

16 ¶ Then the eleven disciples went away into Galilee, into a mountain ¹where Jesus had appointed them.

j ch. 26. 32.
ver. 7.

17 And when they saw him, they worshipped him: but some doubted.

The other evangelists mention several other appearances of Christ, which we shall consider when we come to them. This was in Galilee, upon Christ's appointment either before or after his resurrection, we cannot certainly say when, or how. Some think (upon what grounds I know not, but because the evangelists mention no more) that this was the famous appearance mentioned by the apostles, when *he was seen of above five hundred brethren at once*, 1 Cor. xv. 6. The text speaks but of eleven that went into Galilee; it is possible more might meet him there, but we have no guidance of Scripture to conclude it. Some *worshipped him; but some doubted*: Thomas we know did so, so might others: but some think that it had been better translated, some had doubted; I understand no sufficient reason for it, for it is not certain that this was after his other appearances mentioned by the other evangelists.

k Dan. 7. 13, 14. ch. 11.
27. & 16. 28.
Luke 1. 32.
& 10. 22.
John 3. 35.
& 5. 22. & 13. 3. & 17. 2.
Acts 2. 36.
Rom. 14. 9.
1 Cor. 15. 27.
Eph. 1. 10, 21. Phil. 2. 9, 10. Heb. 1. 2. & 2. 8.
1 Pet. 3. 22.
Rev. 17. 14.
l Mark 16. 15.
m ls. 52. 10.
Luke 24. 47.
Acts 2. 38, 39.
Rom. 10. 18. Col. 1. 23. ‖ Or, *make disciples*, or, *Christians of all nations*. n Acts 2. 42.

18 And Jesus came and spake unto them, saying, ᵏAll power is given unto me in heaven and in earth.

19 ¶ ¹Go ye therefore, and ᵐ‖teach all nations, baptizing them in the name of the Father, and of the Son, and of the Holy Ghost:

20 ⁿTeaching them to observe all things whatsoever I have commanded you: and, lo, I am with you alway, *even unto the end of the world.* Amen.

Mark saith, chap. xvi. 15—18, *And he said unto them, Go ye into all the world, and preach the gospel to every creature. He that believeth and is baptized shall be saved; but he that believeth not shall be damned. And these signs shall follow them that believe; In my name they shall cast out devils; they shall speak with new tongues; they shall take up serpents; and if they drink any deadly thing, it shall not hurt them; they shall lay hands on the sick, and they shall recover.* Our blessed Lord in these three last verses, 1. Asserteth his power and authority. 2. He delegates a power. 3. He subjoineth a promise. The power and authority which he asserteth to himself is, *All power* both *in heaven and earth,* Acts x. 36, 42; Eph. i. 20—22; power of remission of sins, Luke xxiv. 47, of congregating, teaching, and governing his church; a power to give eternal life to whomsoever he pleased. This was inherent in him as God blessed for ever, given to him as our Mediator and Redeemer, given him when he came into the world, but more especially confirmed to him and manifested to be given him at his resurrection and ascension, Phil. ii. 9, 10. Having declared his power, he delegates it: *Go ye therefore, and teach all nations;* the Greek is μαθητεύσατε, make disciples all nations; but that must be first by preaching and instructing them in the principles of the Christian faith, and Mark expounds it, telling us our Saviour said, *Go ye into all the world, and preach the gospel to every creature,* that is, to every reasonable creature capable of hearing and receiving it. I cannot be of their mind, who think that persons may be baptized before they are taught; we want precedents of any such baptism in Scripture, though indeed we find precedents of persons baptized who had but a small degree of the knowledge of the gospel; but it should seem that they were all first taught that Jesus Christ was the Son of God, and were not baptized till they professed such belief, Acts viii. 37, and John baptized them in Jordan, *confessing their sins,* Matt. iii. 6. But it doth not therefore follow, that children of such professors are not to be baptized, for the apostles were commanded to baptize *all nations:* children are a great part of any nation, if not the greatest part, and although amongst the Jews those that were converted to the Jewish religion were first instructed in the law of God before they were circumcised, yet the fathers being once admitted, the children were circumcised at eight days old; nor were they under any covenant different from us, though we be under a more clear manifestation of the same covenant of grace, of which circumcision was a sign and seal to them, as baptism is to us. Infants are capable of the obligations of baptism, for the obligation ariseth from the equity of the thing, not from the understanding and capacity of the person; they are also capable of the same privileges, *for of such is the kingdom of God,* as our Saviour hath taught us. *All nations:* the apostles were by this precept obliged to go up and down the world preaching the gospel, but not presently. So it is plain that the apostles understood their commission, from Acts i. 8; iii. 26; xiii. 46; xviii. 6, 7; Gal. ii. 7. They were first to preach and to baptize amongst the Jews, and then thus to disciple all nations. Pastors and teachers who succeeded the apostles were not under this obligation, but were to be fixed in churches gathered, as we learn from the Acts of the Apostles, and the Epistles of the apostles. They by this commission have authority in any place to preach and to baptize, but are not under an obligation to fix no where, but to go up and down preaching in all nations. *Baptizing them in the name of the Father, and of the Son, and of the Holy Ghost.* Baptizing them is no more than washing them with water. We read of the baptism *of pots and cups,* Mark vii. 8, (we translate it *washing,*) which we know may be by dipping them in water, or by pouring or sprinkling of water upon them. It is true, the first baptisms of which we read in holy writ were by dippings of the persons baptized. It was in a hot country, where it might be at any time without the danger of persons' lives. Where it may be, we judge it reasonable, and most resembling our burial with Christ by baptism into death; but we cannot think it necessary, for God loveth mercy rather than sacrifice, and the thing signified by baptism, viz. the washing away of the soul's sins with the blood of Christ, is in Scripture expressed to us by pouring and sprinkling, Ezek. xxxvi. 25; Heb. xii. 24; 1 Pet. i. 2. *In the name of the Father, &c.;* in the Greek it is, εἰς τὸ ὄνομα, into the name. *In the name* doth not only import the naming of the names of the Father, Son, and Holy Ghost upon them, but, in the authority, or (which is indeed the chief) into the profession of the trinity of the persons in the one Divine Being: dedicating the persons baptized to God the Father, Son, and Holy Ghost, and thereby obliging them to worship and serve God the Father, Son, and Holy Ghost; for in baptism there is both a solemn dedication of the person to God, and a solemn stipulation: the person baptized either covenanting for himself that he will be the Lord's, or his parents covenanting for him that he shall be the Lord's; which covenant doth both oblige the parents to do what in them lieth in order to that end, and also the child, the parents covenanting for no more than the child was under a natural and religious obligation to perform, if such covenant had never been made by its parents on its behalf. *Teaching them to observe all things whatsoever I have commanded you.* There is a teaching must go before baptism of persons grown up; and this was the constant practice of the apostles. It is fit men should act as rational creatures, understanding what they do. And there is a teaching which must follow baptism; for baptism without obedience, and a living up to that covenant in which we are engaged, will save no soul, but lay it under a greater condemnation. The apostles might teach nothing but what Christ had commanded them, and they were bound to teach whatsoever Christ had commanded them. Here now is the rule of the baptized person's obedience. We are bound to no obedience but of the commands of Christ, and to a perfect obedience of them, under the penalty of eternal condemnation. When Mark saith, *He that believeth and is baptized shall be saved,* it doth not imply that baptism is absolutely necessary to salvation, or in the same order with faith in Christ; but that the contempt of it is damnable, as being a piece of presumptuous disobedience; and such a faith is to be understood there, under the notion of believing, as worketh by love. *And, lo, I am with you alway, even unto the end of the world:* I am and I will be with you, and those who succeed you in the work of the ministry, being called of me thereunto. I will be with you, protecting you, and upholding that ordinance, and blessing you, and all others of my faithful ministers that labour for making me and my gospel known, with success. *Unto the end of the world;* not of this age only, but of the world: my ministry begun in you shall not fail, nor shall the adding of souls to the number of them who shall be saved (as a token of my gracious presence with you) fail, till the world shall be determined, and the new heavens and the new earth shall appear. What Mark addeth concerning the signs that should follow those that believed, had a particular reference to the times immediately following Christ's ascension into heaven, and is to be understood of those miraculous operations which were to be wrought by the apostles, and others, for a further confirmation of the doctrine of the gospel by them preached. Matthew says nothing of them here. There is no promise of Christ's presence with his ministers to enable to such operations to the end of the world; but with his ministers preaching, baptizing, and teaching men to observe and to do whatsoever he hath commanded them, he hath promised to be, till time shall be no more.

THE GOSPEL ACCORDING TO

S. MARK

THE ARGUMENT

THAT the author of this compendious history of the Gospel was none of the twelve apostles, is evident to any who will read over their names, Matt. x.; Mark iii. That he was one of the seventy, whom Christ sent out afterwards, is said by some, but upon what evidence I cannot tell. That he was a disciple of Christ is out of question. There was one John surnamed Mark, Acts xii. 12; some think he was the penman of this Gospel, but others doubt it, the ancients always calling him Mark. We read of a Mark, *sister's son to Barnabas,* Col. iv. 10; and we read of Mark employed in the ministry, 2 Tim. iv. 11. Peter calls one of this name his *son,* 1 Pet. v. 13. Paul calls one of this name his *fellow labourer,* Philem. 24. He who was surnamed Mark (added to John as his prænomen) went along with Barnabas to Cyprus, upon the dissension betwixt Paul and him, Acts xv. 39. How many distinct persons are mentioned in Scripture of this name, and which of them was the evangelist, we have not light enough in Scripture to know by, (which yet we should not have wanted had it been material for us to know,) and writers give an uncertain sound concerning this evangelist. Some would have him to be one, some another. Some have thought this Gospel was dictated by Peter to Mark. We are also told, that he wrote this history at Rome, then preached the gospel in Egypt, and was the first bishop of Alexandria, where he was buried, dying in the eighth year of Nero. These are the things which men may believe, or forbear to believe, as they see reason, coming to us only upon the credit of writers who are said to have wrote what we have of their writings at least three hundred years after Mark's time. Most valuable interpreters agree him to have wrote in Greek, though a native Jew, and well understanding that language. Hierom tells us, that he wrote it at Rome upon Peter's dictating, at the desire of some Christians; but these are great uncertainties, and we want any evidence from Scripture that Peter ever came at Rome, though we know that Paul was carried thither prisoner. His history is much shorter than that of any of the other three evangelists, yet in some particular parts he added very much to Matthew's relations. He seemeth much to have compared notes with Matthew, and hath very few things which Matthew hath not, (though he omitteth many things which he hath,) which hath much shortened our annotations upon this Gospel. Matthew begins his history with the genealogy and birth of our Saviour. Luke begins his with some things that preceded the birth of John the Baptist, and of our Saviour. Mark beginneth with the preaching of John the Baptist. The Divine authority of this book never came in question, nor can come, unless Matthew and Luke be questioned also, for he hath very little that is not in one of them. That is what we are most especially to attend unto, for from thence it followeth, that what he wrote is the object of our faith, and the rule of our life, as to things practicable by us.

CHAP. I

The Gospel beginneth with the preaching of John the Baptist, 1—8. *Jesus is baptized, witnessed to from heaven,* 9—11, *and tempted of the devil,* 12, 13; *preacheth in Galilee,* 14, 15; *calleth Peter, Andrew, James, and John,* 16—22; *healeth one possessed of an unclean spirit,* 23—28, *Simon's mother-in-law,* 29—31, *and divers other diseased persons,* 32—34; *prayeth alone, and goeth on to preach,* 35—39; *cleanseth a leper,* 40—45.

THE beginning of the Gospel of Jesus Christ, ªthe Son of God;

A. D. 26.
ending.
a Matt. 14.
33. Luke 1. 35. John 1. 34.

The Gospel seems to have taken its name, εὐαγγέλιον, from the angel's words to the shepherds, Luke ii. 10, *I bring you good tidings of great joy;* for the word in the Greek signifies a good message, or good news or tidings. It sometimes signifieth the historical narration of the coming of Christ, John Baptist's and Christ's preaching, and what he did in the world, his birth, life, death, &c.; sometimes the doctrine of salvation by Christ, in opposition to that of the law; sometimes the dispensation of it, or that period of time when God began to publish *the mystery hid from ages* openly to the world. It seemeth here to signify the latter; for both Matthew and Luke seem to begin the history higher. Luke, from the history of John the Baptist and Christ, as to what things preceded their birth. Matthew, from the birth of Christ. But the dispensation of the gospel began with the preaching of John the Baptist. Before his time the doctrine of the gospel was made known to Adam, Abraham, and David; prophesied by Jacob, Isaiah, and several of the prophets; but John was the first in whom those promises and prophecies were fulfilled, the first public and plain preacher of the doctrine of the gospel; for *the law and the prophets prophesied until John: since that time the kingdom of God is preached, and every man presseth into it*, Matt. xi. 13; Luke xvi. 16. So as John's preaching was the beginning of the gospel; for though the doctrine of the gospel was before darkly made known, yet it then began to be plainly and publicly declared to the world. He was the first in whom the gospel prophecies began to have an end, as both the prophecies and the types of it had a more full completion in Christ. Two prophecies at least had their completion in John, which we find in Malachi; chap. iii. 1, which the evangelist mentioneth in the next verse, and chap. iv. 5, concerning Elias first to come, which our Saviour applies to John, Matt. xi. 14; Mark ix. 11—13, and the angel before him, Luke i. 17; besides Isaiah's prophecy, chap. xl. 3, applied unto him by Matthew, chap. iii. 3, and in the third verse of this chapter, and by John applied to himself, John i. 23. This Gospel is called *the Gospel of Jesus Christ*, because the history of Christ's birth, life, and death is the matter of it. Christ was by Matthew called *the Son of David, the son of Abraham*, to let us know that he was truly man, a native Jew, and of the royal family, and derived from those two families, to whom the promises of the Messias were made. By Mark he is called *the Son of God*, to let us know that he was more than mere man. And indeed who, but he who was the Son of God, could fully reveal his Father's will, determine the law of Moses and introduce a new way of worship, and publish a mystery of salvation, hid from all preceding ages, though not from all individual persons in them.

2 As it is written in the prophets, ^bBehold, I send my messenger before thy face, which shall prepare thy way before thee.

3 ^cThe voice of one crying in the wilderness, Prepare ye the way of the Lord, make his paths straight.

The prophets Malachi and Isaiah (saith the evangelist) prophesied of this *beginning of the gospel*. Malachi prophesied that before the great King should come unto Zion, a harbinger should come before him, to prepare his way. The angel, Luke i. 17, expounds both their prophecies, and also that Mal. iv. 5; *And he shall go before him in the spirit and power of Elias, to turn the hearts of the fathers to the children, and the disobedient to the wisdom of the just; to make ready a people prepared for the Lord*. John by his preaching turned the ears of the people to the sound of the gospel, and so prepared them for Christ. See the further explication of these words in the notes on Matt. iii. 3; xi. 10. This name given to John the Baptist, *A voice crying*, gives us the right notion of a gospel minister. Here is but a *voice crying*, speaking what God hath first suggested to him. Thus God saith to Moses, Exod. iv. 15, *Thou shalt speak unto him, and put words in his mouth; and I will be with thy mouth, and with his mouth*.

4 ^dJohn did baptize in the wilderness, and preach the baptism of repentance ‖ for the remission of sins.

5 ^eAnd there went out unto him all the land of Judæa, and they of Jerusalem, and were all baptized of him in the river of Jordan, confessing their sins.

Luke saith that John began about the fifteenth year of Tiberius Cæsar. He baptized *in the wilderness*, that is, a place little inhabited. By his baptism is not to be strictly understood baptism, but his preaching and doctrine, his whole administration; which is called *the baptism of repentance*, because repentance was the great thing he preached, a seal of which baptism was to be; the consequent of which was to be *the remission of sins*, or the argument which he used to press repentance was the remission of sins. See further the annotations on Matt. iii. 5, 6, where we before had these words.

6 And John was ^fclothed with camel's hair, and with a girdle of a skin about his loins; and he did eat ^glocusts and wild honey;

This was all explained in the notes on Matt. iii. 4.

7 And preached, saying, ^hThere cometh one mightier than I after me, the latchet of whose shoes I am not worthy to stoop down and unloose.

8 ⁱI indeed have baptized you with water: but he shall baptize you ^kwith the Holy Ghost.

We had the same, with very little difference in the phrase, Matt. iii. 11. See the notes there.

9 ^lAnd it came to pass in those days, that Jesus came from Nazareth of Galilee, and was baptized of John in Jordan.

10 ^mAnd straightway coming up out of the water, he saw the heavens ‖ opened, and the Spirit like a dove descending upon him:

11 And there came a voice from heaven, *saying*, ⁿThou art my beloved Son, in whom I am well pleased.

Christ, who, Luke ii. 51, went with his parents to *Nazareth, and was subject to them*, after he had been disputing with the doctors in the temple, now goes from Nazareth, a city in Galilee, to that part of Galilee near Jordan, or rather to Bethabara, where John was baptizing, and was baptized: see the notes on Matt. iii. 13, 16, 17; John i. 28, where this piece of history is more fully related. Luke addeth, that Christ was now about thirty years of age.

12 ^oAnd immediately the spirit driveth him into the wilderness.

13 And he was there in the wilderness forty days, tempted of Satan; and was with the wild beasts; ^pand the angels ministered unto him.

Both Matthew and Luke relate the history of our Saviour's temptations by the devil more fully. See the notes on Matt. iv. 1, 2. Mark saith *immediately*, but it is not to be taken strictly for the next moment, but after a day or two, as it should seem.

14 ^qNow after that John was put in prison, Jesus came into Galilee, ^rpreaching the Gospel of the kingdom of God,

15 And saying, ^sThe time is fulfilled, and ^tthe kingdom of God is at hand: repent ye, and believe the Gospel.

It should seem that John had but a short time wherein he exercised his public ministry: he was the son of a priest, Zacharias, Luke i. 13, and it is probable that he entered not upon his public ministry till he was thirty years of age (it was the sacerdotal age, and the age at which Luke telleth us our Saviour entered upon his public ministry). He was but about six months older than our Saviour, and was imprisoned as soon as our Saviour entered upon his ministry, indeed before we read of his entrance upon it. Upon his imprisonment, Christ beginneth to preach in Galilee the gospel by which he set up his kingdom, and which leadeth men to the kingdom of God. *And saying, The time is fulfilled*, the time determined of God for the revelation of the Messias, and the grace of the gospel through him, foretold by the prophets, Dan. ii. 44: hence Christ is said to have come in *the fulness,* and *in the dispensation of the fulness of time,* Gal. iv. 4; Eph. i. 10. *And the kingdom of God is at hand;* the gracious dispensation of God in the gospel is at hand, or hath approached. *Repent ye,* turn from the wickedness of your ways, *and believe the gospel,* or, in the gospel: to believe the gospel is one thing, to believe in the gospel (as it is here in the Greek) is another. The former phrase signifies no more than a firm and fixed assent to the proposition of the gospel; but to believe in the gospel, is to place our hope of salvation in the doctrine and promises of the gospel, which are the proximate object of our faith, though the primary object of it be the person of the Mediator. There is a repentance that must go before faith, that is the applicative of the promise of pardoning mercy to the soul; though true evangelical repentance, which is a sorrow for sin, flowing from the sense of the love of God in Christ, be the fruit and effect of faith. Our Saviour's preaching agreeth with the Baptist's, Matt. iii. 2; John iii. 23.

u Mat. 4. 18. Luke 5. 4.

16 "Now as he walked by the sea of Galilee, he saw Simon and Andrew his brother casting a net into the sea: for they were fishers.

17 And Jesus said unto them, Come ye after me, and I will make you to become fishers of men.

x Matt. 19. 27. Luke 5. 11.

18 And straightway ˣthey forsook their nets, and followed him.

y Mat. 4. 21.

19 ʸAnd when he had gone a little farther thence, he saw James the *son* of Zebedee, and John his brother, who also were in the ship mending their nets.

20 And straightway he called them: and they left their father Zebedee in the ship with the hired servants, and went after him.

We heard of the call of these four apostles before, in Matt. iv. 18—22, in the notes upon which may be found whatsoever is necessary for the explication of these verses, (having nothing new in them,) as also the reconciling of what John saith, chap. i. 40, about the calling of Andrew and Simon, to what these two evangelists say about it.

A. D. 31. z Mat. 4. 13. Luke 4. 31.

21 ᶻAnd they went into Capernaum; and straightway on the sabbath day he entered into the synagogue, and taught.

a Mat. 7. 28.

22 ᵃAnd they were astonished at his doctrine: for he taught them as one that had authority, and not as the Scribes.

We heard before that the synagogues were much of the nature of our parish churches, places where people ordinarily met together on the sabbath days, to worship God by prayer, and reading the law and the prophets, and hearing the words of exhortation, from such as the rulers of the synagogues appointed thereunto. Christ ordinarily preached in them. The evangelists often mention the people's admiring, being amazed, and astonished at his doctrine; but it is one thing for people to be astonished and amazed at a new doctrine, and to admire the preacher, another thing to believe: we read of many amongst the Jews that were affected at the hearing of Christ with astonishment and admiration, but of few that believed in him. *For he taught them as one that had authority:* a small derivative from this is yet seen in the gravity, awful presence, and authority which (as a great gift of God) we see still given to some faithful ministers of Christ, such especially as God maketh a more eminent use of in the conversion of souls; but this great preacher had the Spirit above human measure. *Not as the scribes,* the ordinary teachers of the Jews, who read their lectures of the law, but so coldly, and without life and power, as the hearts of the people were not at all affected with them, no more than with the dull telling a tale, with which neither tellers nor hearers were much affected.

b Luke 4.33.

23 ᵇAnd there was in their synagogue a man with an unclean spirit; and he cried out,

c Matt. 8.29.

24 Saying, Let *us* alone; ᶜwhat have we to do with thee, thou Jesus of Nazareth? art thou come to destroy us? I know thee who thou art, the Holy One of God.

Luke reports the same passage, chap. iv. 33, 34; he saith, *There was a man which had a spirit of an unclean devil.* The devil is called an unclean spirit in opposition to the Spirit of God, which is the Holy Spirit. The man that had this unclean spirit, or rather the unclean spirit in the man, cries out, *Let us alone; what have we to do with thee.* He doubtless feared what followed, viz. that he should be cast out. He counts himself destroyed when he cannot do mischief; like wicked men, who are the seed of this old serpent, who *sleep not, except they have done mischief; and their sleep is taken away, unless they cause some to fall,* Prov. iv. 16. The devil here owneth Christ to be *the Holy One of God.*

25 And Jesus ᵈrebuked him, saying, d ver. 34. Hold thy peace, and come out of him.

26 And when the unclean spirit ᵉhad e ch. 9. 20. torn him, and cried with a loud voice, he came out of him.

It is both here and in many other places observable, that when the devils made a confession of Christ, yet neither Christ nor his apostles would ever take any notice of it. Truth is never advantaged from the confession of known liars, as the devil was from the beginning. Christ needed not the devil's testimony, either to his holiness, or his being the Son of God, nor would he have people allow the least faith to the devil's words. Nor was he to be imposed upon by the devil's good words; he was to make no truce with him, but to destroy him and his works, he therefore chargeth him to hold his peace, and to come out. *And when the unclean spirit had torn him.* The Greek word here, σπαράξαν, is ill translated *torn,* as appears by Luke iv. 35, where it is said it did him no hurt: the word signifies no more than a violent convulsion, or shaking; and it is observed that those possessed by devils had only their members made use of by the devils, but without any wounding or laceration of them. *He cried out with a loud voice, and came out of him.* Oh how loth is the devil to part with his possession! but possibly also Christ would have him cry out with a loud voice, that his miraculous operation might be the more taken notice of.

27 And they were all amazed, insomuch that they questioned among themselves, saying, What thing is this? what new doctrine *is* this? for with authority commandeth he even the unclean spirits, and they do obey him.

The Jews had exorcists amongst them, who sometimes cast out devils by some forms of invocation they had; but Christ commanded them out; he neither did it by any kind of entreaty from any compact with the devil, nor yet by any invocation of God, but by an authoritative command. This was new to the Jews, and especially confirming a new doctrine that he had published. But still we read of no believing, no agnition of him as God, or the Son of God, or the Messias and Saviour of the world; only the generality are amazed they could not obtain of themselves to believe this new doctrine, nor yet so far command their passions, but they must be startled and amazed at it.

28 And immediately his fame spread abroad throughout all the region round about Galilee.

The *fame* of his miracles, rather than of his doctrine; by this means many were brought to him to be cured, many were brought also to hear him, some of whom believed, others were hardened.

29 ᶠAnd forthwith, when they were f Matt. 8. 14. come out of the synagogue, they entered Luke 4. 38. into the house of Simon and Andrew, with James and John.

30 But Simon's wife's mother lay sick of a fever, and anon they tell him of her.

31 And he came and took her by the hand, and lifted her up; and immediately the fever left her, and she ministered unto them.

See the notes on Matt. viii. 14, 15, where we met with this history. Our Saviour sometimes showed his power in diseases not accounted incurable. The miracle appeared, 1. In the cure of her without the use of any means. 2. In the instantaneousness of the act; she did not recover gradually, but in a moment, and to such a degree as she could minister unto them, suppose at dinner or supper, &c.

g Matt. 8.16. Luke 4. 40.
32 ᵍ And at even, when the sun did set, they brought unto him all that were diseased, and them that were possessed with devils.

33 And all the city was gathered together at the door.

h ch. 3. 12. Luke 4. 41. See Acts 16. 17, 18. ‖ Or, to say that they knew him.
34 And he healed many that were sick of divers diseases, and cast out many devils; and ʰsuffered not the devils ‖to speak, because they knew him.

It was upon the sabbath day, (as appeareth from what went before,) therefore the time is noted, *at even, when the sun did set*. Before that time, when the sabbath was determined, the Jews thought it unlawful to carry any burdens, but after sun-set they judged it lawful. The usage of the particle *all* here, ver. 32, 33, is again observable to show the vanity of those who will from general particles conclude propositions contrary to the analogy of faith, those particles being often used in a restrained sense. Luke saith, that the devils cried out, *Thou art Christ the Son of God. And he rebuking them, suffered them not to speak, because* (or that) *they knew him*. Christ desired not to be published so soon under that notion, but he much less desired the devil's testimony in the case: see ver. 25; Acts xvi. 18. The good words of the devil and his seed are indeed a defamation to Christ and his seed.

i Luke 4. 42.
35 And ⁱin the morning, rising up a great while before day, he went out, and departed into a solitary place, and there prayed.

Secret prayer stands commended to us, as by the precept of Christ, Matt. vi. 6, so by his frequent example, to teach us that our duty in prayer is not discharged without it: we are to pray with all prayer and supplication. There is in public and private prayer a more united strength and interest, but in secret prayer an advantage for more free and full communication of our souls unto God. Christ for this chooseth the morning, as the time freest from distractions and company; and a solitary place, as fittest for a secret duty.

36 And Simon and they that were with him followed after him.

37 And when they had found him, they said unto him, All *men* seek for thee.

k Luke 4. 43.
38 And he said unto them, ᵏLet us go into the next towns, that I may preach there also: for ¹therefore came I forth.

1 Is. 61. 1. John 16. 28. & 17. 4. m Mat. 4. 23. Luke 4. 44.
39 ᵐAnd he preached in their synagogues throughout all Galilee, and cast out devils.

Peter probably pitieth the multitude, because many amongst them needed Christ's presence, for their bodily infirmities. Our Saviour knew their hearts better than Peter; and that which made them so much seek for him, was either in some a curiosity to see miracles wrought, or at best but a desire of some bodily benefit from him. Whereas his working of miracles was but a secondary work, subservient to his work in preaching, and done to confirm his doctrine, and to advantage them as to their faith in him as the Messias. As therefore he refused to gratify the curiosity of the Pharisees in giving them a sign, so here our Saviour takes no notice of the multitude seeking for him, but saith to his disciples, *Let us go into the next towns, that I may preach there also; for therefore came I forth.* Paul saith that God sent him *not to baptize, but to preach*, 1 Cor. i. 17. Our Saviour saith not, *Let us go into the next towns*, that I may work miracles, but *that I may preach there also;* he doth not say he came forth to work miracles, but to preach: how it comes to pass that some are possessed of so slight an opinion of preaching as to think that it is needless, which our Saviour and St. Paul counted to be their principal work, where, in the mean time, they pretend to derive from Christ, I cannot tell. I am sure preaching was the greatest part of Christ's work; how it comes to be the least part of ministers' work since, or how any of them think it sufficient to discharge that work by journeymen, which he thought it not beneath him to do himself, may deserve their examination which make it so. We do not say that preaching is a greater work than prayer, or that it is not ministers' duty to pray; nor yet that it is greater than administering the sacrament: but this we say, we read of Christ's preaching often in the synagogues, on the mountain, in a ship; of his public praying we read not, though of his private and secret prayer often. We read expressly that he baptized none. We must have leave to think that our greatest work which our Lord and his apostles were most employed in, and do think others will be of our minds as soon as they shall understand, that if the end of preaching be not turning men from one opinion to another, but from the love and practice of sin to God, there is as much need of it as ever; and that the turning of men from one opinion to another, without a change of heart, as to the love of sin, is but a turning of men from one quarter of the devil's kingdom to another.

n Matt. 8. 2. Luke 5. 12.
40 ⁿAnd there came a leper to him, beseeching him, and kneeling down to him, and saying unto him, If thou wilt, thou canst make me clean.

41 And Jesus, moved with compassion, put forth *his* hand, and touched him, and saith unto him, I will; be thou clean.

42 And as soon as he had spoken, immediately the leprosy departed from him, and he was cleansed.

43 And he straitly charged him, and forthwith sent him away;

44 And saith unto him, See thou say nothing to any man: but go thy way, shew thyself to the Priest, and offer for thy cleansing those things ᵒwhich Moses commanded, for a testimony unto them.

o Lev. 14. 3, 4, 10. Luke 5. 14.

45 ᵖBut he went out, and began to publish *it* much, and to blaze abroad the matter, insomuch that Jesus could no more openly enter into the city, but was without in desert places: ᵍand they came to him from every quarter.

p Luke 5. 15.

q ch. 2. 13.

We before had this piece of history, Matt. viii. 2—4, to the notes upon which it is enough to refer our reader; we shall also meet with it hereafter in Luke, chap. v. Our Lord being *moved with compassion*, or affected in his bowels, (as the word signifies,) is often used as expressive of the cause of his acts of mercy: thus in curing the leper, he at once both showed himself the Son of man, one who could have compassion on our infirmities, and indeed could not but have such a commiseration toward mankind; and the Son of God, that he could in an instant, by a touch, or by the word of his power, command off a disease of so difficult cure. For his charging of him to *say nothing to any man*, we are not able to give a perfect account of it, whether it was to avoid a suspicion of ostentation, or to avoid a throng of company pressing upon him, or to avoid the odium which he knew the doing of these mighty works would bring him under with the scribes and Pharisees, until the time came for the fuller revelation of himself. Much less can we tell how to excuse the leper for doing contrary to this charge, which we find many others to have done who had the like charge, yet we read not of our Saviour's blaming them for it. Mark addeth, that his publication of it caused *that Jesus could no more openly enter into the city, but was without in desert places;* by which is to be understood only places less inhabited; some think, places near the shore, where by going into a ship (as he often did) he could more easily quit himself of the throng of people, for (as it followeth) *they came to him from every quarter.*

CHAP. II

Christ, followed by multitudes, 1, 2, healeth one sick of the palsy, 3—12; calleth Matthew from the receipt of custom, 13, 14; justifieth himself for eating with publicans and sinners, 15—17; excuseth his disciples for not fasting, 18—22; and vindicateth them for plucking the ears of corn on the sabbath day, 23—28.

a Matt. 9. 1. Luke 5. 18.
AND again ^ahe entered into Capernaum after *some* days; and it was noised that he was in the house.

2 And straightway many were gathered together, insomuch that there was no room to receive *them*, no, not so much as about the door: and he preached the word unto them.

3 And they come unto him, bringing one sick of the palsy, which was borne of four.

4 And when they could not come nigh unto him for the press, they uncovered the roof where he was: and when they had broken *it* up, they let down the bed wherein the sick of the palsy lay.

5 When Jesus saw their faith, he said unto the sick of the palsy, Son, thy sins be forgiven thee.

6 But there were certain of the Scribes sitting there, and reasoning in their hearts,

7 Why doth this *man* thus speak blasphemies? ^bwho can forgive sins but God only?

b Job 14. 4. Is. 43. 25.

8 And immediately ^cwhen Jesus perceived in his spirit that they so reasoned within themselves, he said unto them, Why reason ye these things in your hearts?

c Matt. 9. 4.

9 ^dWhether is it easier to say to the sick of the palsy, *Thy* sins be forgiven thee; or to say, Arise, and take up thy bed, and walk?

d Matt. 9. 5.

10 But that ye may know that the Son of man hath power on earth to forgive sins, (he saith to the sick of the palsy,)

11 I say unto thee, Arise, and take up thy bed, and go thy way into thine house.

12 And immediately he arose, took up the bed, and went forth before them all; insomuch that they were all amazed, and glorified God, saying, We never saw it on this fashion.

We read the history of this miracle Matt. ix. 1—8, to our notes upon which I shall refer my reader: having there taken in those passages in this evangelist's relation which Matthew had not, I shall only take notice of some few things not there touched upon. *He preached the word unto them;* the word of God, the gospel. There are other words, but that is *the word*, Matt. xiii. 20; Mark viii. 32; xvi. 20; Luke i. 2; Acts xvii. 11: the most excellent word, and the only word to be preached. *Why doth this man thus speak blasphemies? who can forgive sins but God?* so as it was on all hands then received, that none but the creditor could discharge the debt, none but God could forgive sins. But how spite cankers things! Our Saviour did not say till afterward that he forgave him his sins. What blasphemy was there in this saying, *Thy sins be forgiven thee?* But what if none but God could forgive sins? could also any but God tell unto men their thoughts? 1 Sam. xvi. 7; 1 Chron. xxviii. 9; 2 Chron. vi. 30; Psal. vii. 9; Jer. xvii. 10. That Christ could tell their thoughts was matter of demonstration to them, ver. 6, 8; why might they not also have allowed him a power to forgive sins? But they could not for this charge him with blasphemy, which was their malicious design.

e Matt. 9. 9.
13 ^eAnd he went forth again by the sea side; and all the multitude resorted unto him, and he taught them.

Still it is said he *taught them*, thereby letting his ministers know what is their great work; and therefore they should be persons *apt to teach*, as Paul directeth Timothy, 1 Tim. iii. 2.

14 ^fAnd as he passed by, he saw Levi the *son* of Alphæus sitting ‖ at the receipt of custom, and said unto him, Follow me. And he arose and followed him.

f Matt. 9. 9. Luke 5. 27. ‖ Or, at the place where the custom was received.

15 ^gAnd it came to pass, that, as Jesus sat at meat in his house, many Publicans and sinners sat also together with Jesus and his disciples: for there were many, and they followed him.

g Matt. 9.10.

16 And when the Scribes and Pharisees saw him eat with Publicans and sinners, they said unto his disciples, How is it that he eateth and drinketh with Publicans and sinners?

17 When Jesus heard *it*, he saith unto them, ^hThey that are whole have no need of the physician, but they that are sick: I came not to call the righteous, but sinners to repentance.

h Matt. 9.12, 13. & 18. 11. Luke 5. 31, 32. & 19. 10. 1 Tim. 1. 15.

We had this piece of history with some addition in Matt. ix. 9—13, where he was called *Matthew*: Mark and Luke both call him *Levi*: it was ordinary with the Jews to have two names. See the notes on Matt. ix.

18 ⁱAnd the disciples of John and of the Pharisees used to fast: and they come and say unto him, Why do the disciples of John and of the Pharisees fast, but thy disciples fast not?

i Matt. 9. 14. Luke 5. 33.

19 And Jesus said unto them, Can the children of the bridechamber fast, while the bridegroom is with them? as long as they have the bridegroom with them, they cannot fast.

20 But the days will come, when the bridegroom shall be taken away from them, and then shall they fast in those days.

21 No man also seweth a piece of ‖ new cloth on an old garment: else the new piece that filled it up taketh away from the old, and the rent is made worse.

‖ Or, raw, or, unwrought.

22 And no man putteth new wine into old bottles: else the new wine doth burst the bottles, and the wine is spilled, and the bottles will be marred: but new wine must be put into new bottles.

See all this opened in the notes on Matt. ix. 14—17. The sum of all teacheth us, 1. That fasting is an exercise suited to afflictive dispensations of Providence, and ought to be proportioned to its season. 2. That new converts are not to be discouraged by too severe exercises of religion, but to be trained up to them by degrees.

23 ^kAnd it came to pass, that he went through the corn fields on the sabbath day; and his disciples began, as they went, ^lto pluck the ears of corn.

k Matt. 12.1. Luke 6. 1.
l Deut. 23. 25.

24 And the Pharisees said unto him, Behold, why do they on the sabbath day that which is not lawful?

25 And he said unto them, Have ye never read ^mwhat David did, when he had need, and was an hungred, he, and they that were with him?

m 1 Sam.21. 6.

26 How he went into the house of God in the days of Abiathar the High Priest, and did eat the shewbread, ⁿwhich is not

n Ex. 29. 32, 33. Lev. 24. 9.

lawful to eat but for the Priests, and gave also to them which were with him?

27 And he said unto them, The sabbath was made for man, and not man for the sabbath:

°Matt. 12. 8.

28 Therefore °the Son of man is Lord also of the sabbath.

We had also this history in Matt. xii. 1—8, in our notes upon which we considered all those passages relating to it which this evangelist hath, for the explication of which I refer my reader thither. It referreth to a story, 1 Sam. xxi. 1, where Ahimelech is said to have been the high priest. Abiathar was his son, as appeareth by 1 Sam. xxii. 20, who escaped the slaughter of his father's family upon the information of Doeg the Edomite, and followed David. It was in the latter end of the priesthood of Ahimelech, and probably Abiathar assisted his father in the execution of the office, and so suddenly succeeded, that Mark calls it the time of his priesthood. Besides that those words, ἐπὶ Ἀβιαθαρ, do not necessarily signify *in the days of Abiathar*, as we translate it, no more than ἐπὶ μετοικεσίας signifies in the carrying into captivity, but about the time, or near the time; which it was, for Ahimelech was presently after it (possibly within a few days) cut off, as we read, 1 Sam. xxii. 17, 18; and Abiathar was a more noted man than his father Ahimelech, enjoying the priesthood more than forty years, and being the person who was made famous by carrying the ephod to David.

CHAP. III

Christ appealing to reason healeth the withered hand on the sabbath day, 1—5. *The Pharisees conspire his death: he retireth to the sea-side, and healeth many,* 6—12. *He chooseth his twelve apostles,* 13—19. *His friends look upon him as beside himself,* 20, 21. *He confuteth the blasphemous absurdity of the Pharisees in ascribing his casting out of devils to the power of Beelzebub,* 22—30. *Those who do the will of God he regardeth as his nearest relations,* 31—35.

a Matt. 12.9. Luke 6. 6.

AND ᵃhe entered again into the synagogue; and there was a man there which had a withered hand.

2 And they watched him, whether he would heal him on the sabbath day; that they might accuse him.

† Gr. *Arise, stand forth in the midst.*

3 And he saith unto the man which had the withered hand, †Stand forth.

4 And he saith unto them, Is it lawful to do good on the sabbath days, or to do evil? to save life, or to kill? But they held their peace.

‖ Or, *blindness.*

5 And when he had looked round about on them with anger, being grieved for the ‖hardness of their hearts, he saith unto the man, Stretch forth thine hand. And he stretched *it* out: and his hand was restored whole as the other.

See the notes upon Matt. xii. 9—13. The word πωρώσει, used ver. 5, may be understood to signify blindness, or hardness, as it may derive from πῶρος, *callus,* or πωρος, *cœcus,* but the derivation of it from the former best obtains. Hardness being a quality in a thing by which it resisteth our touch, and suffers us not to make an impression upon it, that ill condition of the soul by which it becomes rebellious, and disobedient to the will of God revealed, so as it is not affected with it, nor doth it make any impression of faith or holiness upon the soul, is usually called hardness of heart. But for the argument of this history, proving acts of mercy lawful on the sabbath day, it is fully spoken to in the notes on Matt. xii.

b Matt. 12. 14. c Matt. 22. 16.

6 ᵇAnd the Pharisees went forth, and straightway took counsel with ᶜthe Herodians against him, how they might destroy him.

7 But Jesus withdrew himself with his disciples to the sea: and a great multitude from Galilee followed him, ᵈand from Judæa, d Luke 6. 17.

8 And from Jerusalem, and from Idumæa, and *from* beyond Jordan; and they about Tyre and Sidon, a great multitude, when they had heard what great things he did, came unto him.

9 And he spake to his disciples, that a small ship should wait on him because of the multitude, lest they should throng him.

10 For he had healed many; insomuch that they ‖pressed upon him for to touch him, as many as had plagues.

‖ Or, *rushed.*

11 ᵉAnd unclean spirits, when they saw him, fell down before him, and cried, saying, ᶠThou art the Son of God.

e ch. 1. 23, 24. Luke 4. 41.

f Matt. 14. 33. ch. 1. 1.

12 And ᵍhe straitly charged them that they should not make him known.

g ch. 1. 25, 34. Matt. 12. 16.

Who these Herodians were we cannot learn plainly from holy writ; it is most probable that they were a civil faction, who took Herod's part, and were stiff for promoting his interest, and the interest of the Roman emperor, whose substitute Herod was. With these the Pharisees (in other cases their implacable enemies) mix counsels how they might destroy Christ. Christ gives place to their fury, his time being not yet come, and withdraweth himself from their sight, being followed by great multitudes, who in the fame of his miracles, or the hopes they had of receiving some good from him for themselves or for their friends, drew after him. Some of these are said to have come from Idumea, which was the country of Edom, and distinct from Judea anciently, as may be gathered from Josh. xv. 1, and Numb. xxxiv., but whether it was at this time so or no, is doubted. Our Lord commandeth the devils not to make him known, not desiring any such preachers.

13 ʰAnd he goeth up into a mountain, and calleth *unto him* whom he would: and they came unto him.

h Matt. 10.1. Luke 6. 12. & 9. 1.

14 And he ordained twelve, that they should be with him, and that he might send them forth to preach,

15 And to have power to heal sicknesses, and to cast out devils:

We have this piece of history, or rather something to which it relates, both in Matthew and in Luke, only Mark hath this peculiar to himself, that our Saviour did this upon *a mountain.* It is the opinion of Bucer, that this was the mountain at the foot of which he preached the sermon largely recorded, Matt. v.—vii., and (as some judge) more shortly by Luke, chap. vi.: he thinketh the multitude here mentioned is the same with that mentioned Matt. iv. 25, and Luke iii. 7, and that our Saviour did not go up into this mountain to preach, or ordain his disciples, but only to pray, and to discourse with some of his disciples more privately about spiritual mysteries. That it was at this time that he *continued all night in prayer to God,* Luke vi. 12; and in the morning called unto him such of his disciples as he thought fit, and discoursed with them his intentions concerning them, telling them, 1. That he had chosen them to be with him, ordinarily, to be eye and ear witnesses of what he spake and did. 2. That he designed soon after to send them out to preach; which we read he did, chap. vi. 7; Matt. x. 1; to give them a *power to heal sicknesses, and to cast out devils:* so that this chapter only mentioneth Christ's election of them, not his actual sending them, which is discoursed chap. vi., as also Matt. x. These things being privately transacted on the mountain, Bucer thinks he came down into the plain at the foot of the mountain, according to Luke vi. 17, and there preached that sermon mentioned Matt. v.—vii., as we before said. The evangelist telling us that he called to him which of his disciples he would, lets us know, that he chose them, and not they him; that the choice of them was of his free grace and mercy; and his continuing all night in prayer before this choice, lets us know the gravity of the work of choosing persons fit to be sent out to preach the gospel.

i John 1. 42.   16 And Simon ⁱ he surnamed Peter;

17 And James the *son* of Zebedee, and John the brother of James; and he surnamed them Boanerges, which is, The sons of thunder:

18 And Andrew, and Philip, and Bartholomew, and Matthew, and Thomas, and James the *son* of Alphæus, and Thaddæus, and Simon the Canaanite,

19 And Judas Iscariot, which also betrayed him: and they went ‖ into an house.

‖ Or, *home.*

Matthew nameth the apostles upon his relating the history of their mission, or sending out; Mark nameth them upon their election, or first choice. Both these evangelists agree with Luke in their names, saving that Luke calleth him Judas whom Matthew calls Lebbeus, and Mark, Thaddeus, so that he had three names. Christ changeth the name of Simon, whom he called *Cephas,* or *Peter,* John i. 42; we have the reason, Matt. xvi. 18; he also changed the names of James and John, the sons of Zebedee, calling them *Boanerges,* about the etymology of which name critics must dispute. The evangelists tell us it signifieth *Sons of thunder,* thereby minding them of their duty, to cry aloud, and to preach the gospel as on the house-tops; or perhaps declaring what he knew was in the fervour and warmth of their spirits. We must not here inquire too narrowly into the secret counsels of God, in suffering a son of perdition to come into the number of his first ministers: Christ did it not because he did not know what was in his heart, for before that he showed himself a devil, by informing against his Master, Christ told his disciples that he had chosen twelve, and one of them was a devil; nor yet because he had no others to send, he had multitudes of disciples, and he who of stones could have raised up children to Abraham, could easily have fitted out a person for this service; nor yet did he do it to let in any sots and scandalous persons into the ministry, for we read of no scandal in Judas's life. We ought to believe that God had wise ends in the permission of this, and that Christ did out of infinite wisdom do this, though we possibly are not able to give a satisfactory account in the case. What if we should say that Christ by this, 1. Instructed those that after his ascension should have the care of the church, not to pretend to judge of secret things, but only to judge as man ought to judge, according to the outward appearance, leaving the judgment of the heart to God alone. 2. God by this armeth his people against the scandal of wicked ministers, such in whom corruption may break out after their entrance into that holy function, though before no such thing appeared, that they may not think the ministerial acts performed by them to have been nullities. 3. God by this also lets us know, that the efficacy of the ordinance doth not depend upon the goodness of the spiritual state of the minister that administers. A bell may call others to hear the word, though itself receives no benefit by it. In the mean time here is no warrant either for people to choose, or the governors of a church to ordain, lewd and visibly scandalous persons. Judas was no such person; nor yet for people to own, or the governors of churches to continue, lewd and scandalous persons in the ministry, God ordinarily not blessing the labours of such. No sooner had Judas discovered himself, but he went out and hanged himself. Christ no longer allowed him his company, nor the disciples their fellowship. There is a great deal of difference with relation to our fellowship and communion, betwixt secret wickedness concealed in the heart and open and scandalous sinning, though both be alike dangerous to the soul of the sinner.

20 And the multitude cometh together again, ᵏ so that they could not so much as eat bread.

k ch. 6. 31.

21 And when his ‖ friends heard *of it,* they went out to lay hold on him: ˡfor they said, He is beside himself.

‖ Or, *kinsmen.*
l John 7. 5.
& 10. 20.

There is no small dispute who are here called our Saviour's friends, οἱ παρ' αὐτοῦ, those who were of him, whether it signifieth his neighbours, the citizens of his city, or his nearer relations, those who belonged to the family of which he was (for he had some brethren that did not *believe in him,* John vii. 5). *They went to lay hands on him,* that is, to take him from the multitude, which pressed upon him by force, (for so the word signifies,) *for they said, He is beside himself,* ἐξέστη: various senses are given of this word, but certainly the most ordinary interpretation of it doth best agree to this place. They saw our Saviour's warmth of spirit and zeal in the prosecution of that for which he came into the world, and did so well understand his person, or mission, and receiving the Spirit not by measure, that they took what he did to be the product and effect of a natural infirmity and imperfect head and disordered reason. The young prophet sent by Elisha was counted a *mad fellow* by Jehu's comrades, 2 Kings ix. 11; so was Paul by Festus, Acts xxvi. 24, or by the Corinthians, or some crept in amongst them, 2 Cor. v. 13. We are naturally inclined to inquire the causes of strange and unusual effects, and cannot always discern the true causes, and often make false guesses at them. I am not so prone as I find some to condemn these friends, or neighbours, or kinsmen of Christ, believing that they did verily believe as they spake, not yet fully understanding that the Spirit of the Lord in that measure was upon him, but through their infirmity fearing that he had been under some distraction, and charitably offering their help to him. The next words tell us of a far worse sense the scribes put upon his actions.

22 ¶ And the Scribes which came down from Jerusalem said, ᵐHe hath Beelzebub, and by the prince of the devils casteth he out devils.

m Matt. 9. 34. & 10. 25. Luke 11. 15. John 7. 20. & 8. 48, 52. & 10. 22.

23 ⁿAnd he called them *unto him,* and said unto them in parables, How can Satan cast out Satan?

n Matt. 12. 25

24 And if a kingdom be divided against itself, that kingdom cannot stand.

25 And if a house be divided against itself, that house cannot stand.

26 And if Satan rise up against himself, and be divided, he cannot stand, but hath an end.

27 ᵒNo man can enter into a strong man's house, and spoil his goods, except he will first bind the strong man; and then he will spoil his house.

o Is. 49. 24. Matt. 12. 29.

28 ᵖVerily I say unto you, All sins shall be forgiven unto the sons of men, and blasphemies wherewith soever they shall blaspheme:

p Matt. 12. 31. Luke 12. 10. 1 John 5. 16.

29 But he that shall blaspheme against the Holy Ghost hath never forgiveness, but is in danger of eternal damnation:

30 Because they said, He hath an unclean spirit.

Here is no passage in all this piece of history, but what the reader will find opened in the notes on Matt. ix. 34, and xii. 24—32, to which I refer him.

31 ¶ ᑫThere came then his brethren and his mother, and, standing without, sent unto him, calling him.

q Matt. 12. 46. Luke 8. 19.

32 And the multitude sat about him, and they said unto him, Behold, thy mother and thy brethren without seek for thee.

33 And he answered them, saying, Who is my mother, or my brethren?

34 And he looked round about on them which sat about him, and said, Behold my mother and my brethren!

35 For whosoever shall do the will of God, the same is my brother, and my sister, and mother.

See the notes on Matt. xii. 46—50.

CHAP. IV

The parable of the sower, 1—9. Why Christ taught in parables, 10—13. The exposition of the parable, 14—20. The light of knowledge is given to be communicated to others, 21—25. The kingdom of God likened to the seed which groweth imperceptibly, 26—29; and to a grain of mustard seed, 30—34. Christ stilleth a tempest by his word, 35—41.

a Matt. 13. 1. Luke 8. 4.

AND ᵃhe began again to teach by the sea side: and there was gathered unto him a great multitude, so that he entered into a ship, and sat in the sea; and the whole multitude was by the sea on the land.

2 And he taught them many things by parables, ᵇand said unto them in his doctrine,

b ch. 12. 38.

We may observe that our Saviour often preached by the sea-side, the reason of which was, doubtless, he had there the convenience by a boat or ship to quit himself of the inconvenience of the people's pressing upon him: he was now in Galilee, which bordered upon the sea. *And he taught them many things by parables, and said unto them in his doctrine.* Some of those things which our Lord taught his people by earthly similitudes are afterwards expressed, but probably he taught them many more things than the evangelists have left us upon record. *And said unto them in his doctrine:* that may be understood in a double sense; either understanding by *doctrine* his way of teaching which he affected, and made much use of, viz. by similitudes; or else thus, that he intermixed with the doctrine which he taught them several parables, some of which here follow.

3 Hearken; Behold, there went out a sower to sow:

4 And it came to pass, as he sowed, some fell by the way side, and the fowls of the air came and devoured it up.

5 And some fell on stony ground, where it had not much earth; and immediately it sprang up, because it had no depth of earth:

6 But when the sun was up, it was scorched; and because it had no root, it withered away.

7 And some fell among thorns, and the thorns grew up, and choked it, and it yielded no fruit.

c John 15. 5. Col. 1. 6.

8 And other fell on good ground, ᶜand did yield fruit that sprang up and increased; and brought forth, some thirty, and some sixty, and some an hundred.

9 And he said unto them, He that hath ears to hear, let him hear.

d Matt. 13. 10. Luke 8. 9, &c.

10 ᵈAnd when he was alone, they that were about him with the twelve asked of him the parable.

11 And he said unto them, Unto you it is given to know the mystery of the kingdom of God: but unto ᵉthem that are without, all *these* things are done in parables:

e 1 Cor. 5. 12. Col. 4. 5. 1 Thess. 4. 12. 1 Tim. 3. 7.
f Is. 6. 9. Matt. 13. 14. Luke 8. 10. John 12. 40. Acts 28. 26. Rom. 11. 8.

12 ᶠThat seeing they may see, and not perceive; and hearing they may hear, and not understand; lest at any time they should be converted, and *their* sins should be forgiven them.

13 And he said unto them, Know ye not this parable? and how then will ye know all parables?

g Mat.13. 19.

14 ¶ ᵍThe sower soweth the word.

15 And these are they by the way side, where the word is sown; but when they have heard, Satan cometh immediately, and taketh away the word that was sown in their hearts.

16 And these are they likewise which are sown on stony ground; who, when they have heard the word, immediately receive it with gladness;

17 And have no root in themselves, and so endure but for a time: afterward, when affliction or persecution ariseth for the word's sake, immediately they are offended.

18 And these are they which are sown among thorns; such as hear the word,

19 And the cares of this world, ʰand the deceitfulness of riches, and the lusts of other things entering in, choke the word, and it becometh unfruitful.

h 1 Tim. 6. 9, 17.

20 And these are they which are sown on good ground; such as hear the word, and receive *it*, and bring forth fruit, some thirtyfold, some sixty, and some an hundred.

See this parable largely opened in the notes upon Matt. xiii. 1—23. The parable is recorded both by Matthew, Mark, and Luke, and is of excellent use: 1. To show the excellency of the word of God, which is here (as in other places) called *the word*; it is the seed of God, the *good seed:* and the excellency of the ordinance of preaching, for that is the seed sown. 2. To show us the different effect of the word preached from moral discourses and philosophical disputes, from which can be expected no fruit; but where the sower soweth the word, there is yet a very different effect. Some bring forth the fruit of faith and holiness, and the abiding fruit of it, though in different degrees. But many, yea the most of those that hear it, either bring forth no fruit, or no abiding fruit, which is indeed no true fruit. The causes of this are, some men's perfunctory and careless hearing, never regarding to meditate on it, apply it to their own souls, or to hide it in their memories. Others not suffering it to sink into their hearts, and to take root in them, though it may at present a little affect them, and make them matter of discourse. Other men's thoughts being taken up with business, and the care of this world, and their hearts filled with the love of the things of this life, which they cannot part with when trouble and persecution for the owning and profession of the gospel ariseth. 3. It likewise teacheth us a sure note of unprofitable hearers of the word, as also of those whom the word is likely to profit, and have any good and saving effect upon. The former hear, but never regard whether they understand what they hear, yea or no. The others are not satisfied with hearing unless they understand; for those who went to him to know the parable, were not the twelve only, (who are often called his disciples emphatically,) but those others that were about him, to whom it was *given to know the mystery of the kingdom of God.* 4. The most of our Saviour's hearers were doubtless members of the Jewish church, yet our Saviour, ver. 11, styles the most of them *those that are without;* which teacheth us that not only such as are out of the pale of the church, but those also who are out of the degree of election, those to whom it is not given to know the mysteries of the kingdom of God, are in Christ's account *without.* For other things concerning this parable, they are fully spoken to in our notes on Matt. xiii.

21 ¶ ⁱAnd he said unto them, Is a candle brought to be put under a ‖bushel, or under a bed? and not to be set on a candlestick?

i Matt. 5. 15. Luke 8. 16. & 11. 33. ‖ The word in the original signifieth a less measure, as Matt. 5. 15.

The import of this verse may be learned from Matt. v. 15, 16, where the words are, and applied by an exhortation to holiness, being an argument drawn from the end for which men receive gifts and grace from God, which is not only for their own advantage, though (like the husbandman) those that have it reap first of their own fruit, but for the good and advantage of others also. Some think that Christ here speaketh of himself, who is the Light of the world, and therefore opened this parable unto them. But the context in Matthew guiding us to the true sense of the words, I see no reason for us to busy ourselves in searching out another, especially when the connexion is so fair with the foregoing words, where he had been describing the good ground by bringing forth fruit, *some thirty, some sixty, some a hundredfold.* What therefore the sowing the seed in the good ground, mentioned in the parable, is, that is the lighting up of a candle in this verse; and the light showed by the lighted candle, not put under a vessel, or a bed, but in a candlestick, is the same thing with the fruit before mentioned.

k Matt. 10. 26. Luke 12. 2.

22 ^k For there is nothing hid, which shall not be manifested; neither was any thing kept secret, but that it should come abroad.

l Matt. 11. 15. ver. 9.

23 ^l If any man have ears to hear, let him hear.

Our Saviour, Matt. x. 26, sending out his apostles, saith to them, *Fear them not therefore,* that is, not your enemies and persecutors: *for there is nothing covered, that shall not be revealed; and hid, that shall not be known:* the sense of which words we there said might be, though your innocency be now hid, yet it shall be made known, or though the gospel be now hid, and preached in a little corner, and kept secret, it shall be made manifest, and come abroad. Both Mark and Luke have it immediately after the parable of the sower, where it doth not seem to have the same sense as here. But more general proverbial common sayings may be variously applied to things, to which the common sense and import of them will agree. Some here apply them thus, There is nothing in the prophecies concerning me which shall not be manifested; which agrees with the sense of those who interpret the former verse concerning Christ, as if he had been giving a reason why he opened the parables to those that asked him of it. But those who interpret it to the sense which it beareth plainly, Matt. v. 15, 16, make the sense thus; For though you may play the hypocrites, and under a profession of the gospel but hide the hypocrisy, lusts, and corruptions of your hearts, yet that mask will not hold always, there will come a day of judgment, which will manifest and discover all, and bring to light the hidden things of dishonesty. What we have ver. 23 is but a usual conclusion which our Saviour hath often made of any grave and important discourses.

24 And he saith unto them, Take heed

m Matt. 7. 2. Luke 6. 38.

what ye hear: ^m with what measure ye mete, it shall be measured to you: and unto you that hear shall more be given.

n Matt. 13. 12. & 25. 29. Luke 8. 18. & 19. 26.

25 ⁿ For he that hath, to him shall be given: and he that hath not, from him shall be taken even that which he hath.

Whoso considereth the connexion of these words, *with what measure ye mete, &c.,* with the first words in the verse, *Take heed what ye hear,* and compares the former with the parallel texts, Matt. vii. 2; Luke vi. 38, will wonder what the force should be of the argument. For in both the parallel texts the latter words in this verse seem to be used as an argument to persuade them to justice and charity towards men, from the punishments of the violations of the law concerning them, by way of retaliation. Nor are there any sins so ordinarily as those of that kind so punished. But they can have no such force here, following those words, *Take heed what ye hear.* But, as I said before, there is nothing more usual than diverse applications of the same common saying, or proverbial expression. The saying is true, whether it be understood of men or of God, As we deal with God, so will God deal with us. *Take heed what ye hear.* Luke saith, *how ye hear. Take heed what ye hear;* as much as, Take heed to what you hear, that you may receive the word not as seed by the way-side, or in thorny or stony ground, but as in good ground. This seemeth rather to be the sense of our Saviour, than to give a caution by these words to men to examine what they hear, searching the Scriptures whether what they hear doth agree with them, though that also be the duty of all conscientious persons, as appeareth from Acts xvii. 11. For saith our Saviour, God will deal with you as to his providence as you deal with him. If you allow the word of God but a slightly hearing, you shall reap from it heard a very slighty profit and advantage; this appeareth to be the sense from the following words. *And unto you that hear shall more be given;* that is, unto you that hear, for so as you attend, under-

stand, believe, hearken, and obey, God will give further knowledge of Divine mysteries. *For he that hath, to him shall be given, &c.:* another general proverbial expression, which the reader may find opened in the notes on Matt. xiii. 12; xxv. 29.

26 ¶ And he said, ^o So is the kingdom of God, as if a man should cast seed into the ground;

o Matt. 13. 24.

27 And should sleep, and rise night and day, and the seed should spring and grow up, he knoweth not how.

28 For the earth bringeth forth fruit of herself; first the blade, then the ear, after that the full corn in the ear.

29 But when the fruit is ‖ brought forth, immediately ^p he putteth in the sickle, because the harvest is come.

‖ Or, *ripe.*

p Rev. 14. 15.

Our evangelist alone taketh notice of this parable, nor hath it any particular explication annexed. If we expound it with relation to what went before, the scope of it seemeth to be, to let us know that God will have an account of men for their hearing of his word, and therefore men had need to take heed what they hear, as Mark saith, and how they hear, as Luke phraseth it: thus the 29th verse expoundeth the former, with the help of our Saviour's exposition of the parable of the tares, on which he had told us, Matt. xiii. 39, *The harvest is the end of the world; and the reapers are the angels.* There is another notion of God's harvest, Matt. ix. 37; John iv. 35, where God's harvest signifies a people inclined and prepared to hear and to receive the gospel. But withal this parable of our Saviour's may be of further use to us. *So is the kingdom of God, &c.;* that is, Such is the providential dispensation of God, in gathering his church by the ministry of the word, as men's casting of seed into the ground: when the husbandman hath cast his seed into the ground, he is no more solicitous about it, nor doth he expect to discern the motion of it; but having done what is his part, he sleepeth, and riseth again, leaving the issue to God's providence. *The earth bringeth forth fruit of herself,* yet not without the influence of heaven, both in the shining of the sun and the falling of the dew and of the rain; neither doth its fruit appear presently in its full ripeness and perfection, but gradually is made perfect; first there appears the blade, the herb, then the ear, then the grain, which by degrees groweth to its full magnitude, and then hardeneth, and then the husbandman putteth in his sickle: so the ministers of the gospel ought faithfully to do their parts in sowing the seed of the gospel, then not to be too solicitous, but to leave the issue unto God. Where the seed falls upon good ground, the word will not be unfruitful: the minister of the gospel doth not presently discern the fruit of his labour, he at first, it may be, seeth nothing of it, but is ready to cry out, *I have laboured in vain;* but though the seed lie under the clods, and seems choked with the corruption of man's heart, yet if the soul be one to whom it is *given to know the mysteries of the kingdom of God,* it shall spring out, the word will be found not to be lost; but first will spring the blade, then will appear the ear: the fruit of the word preached appears by degrees, sometimes at first only by creating good inclinations in the soul, and desires to learn the way of the Lord more perfectly, then in acts further tending to perfection, at last in confirmed habits of grace. It is not thus with all, in some the word brings forth nothing but the blade, a little outward profession, which dwindleth away and dies; in some the profession holds longer, but they never come to confirmed habits of virtue and holiness. But there will come a harvest, when God will come with his sickle to reap the fruit of his seed sown; therefore men had need take heed what and how they hear. This I take to be the sense of this parable.

30 ¶ And he said, ^q Whereunto shall we liken the kingdom of God? or with what comparison shall we compare it?

q Matt. 13. 31. Luke 13. 18. Acts 2. 41. & 4. 4. 5. 14. & 19. 20.

31 *It is* like a grain of mustard seed, which, when it is sown in the earth, is less than all the seeds that be in the earth:

32 But when it is sown, it groweth up, and becometh greater than all herbs, and shooteth out great branches; so that the fowls of the air may lodge under the shadow of it.

We met with this parable Matt. xiii. 31, 32, where the reader will find we have given the sense of it. It is a prophetical parable, foretelling the great success that the gospel, which at this time was restrained to a little corner of the world, and there met with small acceptance, should have after Christ's resurrection from the dead; which prophecy we find was fulfilled in the apostles' time, and hath been further fulfilling in all ages of the world since that time.

r Matt. 13. 34. John 16. 12. 33 ʳ And with many such parables spake he the word unto them, as they were able to hear *it*.

34 But without a parable spake he not unto them: and when they were alone, he expounded all things to his disciples.

From hence we may gather that all the parables by which our Saviour instructed his hearers are not recorded by the evangelists, though many be, and some mentioned by one, some by two of them, which are not recorded by the other. *As they were able to hear it.* Christ disdained not to accommodate his style and method of preaching to his hearers' capacity, neither will any faithful minister of Christ do it: he preacheth in the best style, language, and method, that preacheth best to the capacity, understanding, and profit of his hearers. Other preachers do indeed but trifle with the greatest work under heaven, and please themselves with their own noises. That he did not speak without a parable unto them, was, 1. That he might speak with the best advantage for their understandings and their memories, and have the greater influence upon their affections; for similitudes have these three advantages. 2. That he might discern who came to hear him with a desire to learn, and be instructed by him, by their coming to him to inquire of his parables. For although some of his parables were plain, and easy to be understood, yet others of them were dark sayings, because the doctrine taught by them was more mysterious; conscientious hearers would therefore come to have the parables expounded to them; these were those *disciples* mentioned ver. 34, to whom he was wont to expound the parables in or by which he taught the multitude. For other common hearers, their contenting themselves with a mere hearing a sound of words, which they did not understand, was a sufficient indication that they made no conscience of their duty, but were such to whom it was not *given to know the mysteries of the kingdom of God*, but such upon whom the prophecy of the prophet Isaiah was to be fulfilled, chap. vi. 9, 10.

s Matt. 8. 18, 23. Luke 8. 22. 35 ˢ And the same day, when the even was come, he saith unto them, Let us pass over unto the other side.

36 And when they had sent away the multitude, they took him even as he was in the ship. And there were also with him other little ships.

37 And there arose a great storm of wind, and the waves beat into the ship, so that it was now full.

38 And he was in the hinder part of the ship, asleep on a pillow: and they awake him, and say unto him, Master, carest thou not that we perish?

39 And he arose, and rebuked the wind, and said unto the sea, Peace, be still. And the wind ceased, and there was a great calm.

40 And he said unto them, Why are ye so fearful? how is it that ye have no faith?

41 And they feared exceedingly, and said one to another, What manner of man is this, that even the wind and the sea obey him?

This piece of history is related by Matthew and Luke as well as by our evangelist, and that with no considerable variations one from another; what in it wanteth explication may be found in the notes on Matt. viii. 23—27. Christ had been preaching, and being wearied and tired with the multitude still pressing upon him, gave order to cross the sea, and to go over to the other side; then (to show us he was truly man, and took upon him the infirmities of our nature) he composeth himself to sleep *on a pillow, in the hinder part of the ship.* There happeneth a great storm of wind, not without Christ's knowledge and ordering, that he might upon this occasion both try his people's faith, and also show his Divine power in stilling the raging of the sea. As man he slept, but at the same time he was the true Watchman of Israel, who never slumbereth nor sleepeth. The storm increaseth till there was a great quantity of water come into the ship, and they were ready to perish. *In the mount of the Lord it shall be seen*, Gen. xxii. 14. God often forbears from helping his people till the last hour. Then they awake him, he ariseth, rebukes the wind and the waves, useth no means, but by the word of his power commandeth the wind and waves to be still; and he also rebuketh his disciples for want of faith, who yet did not discern that he was not man only, but the Almighty God, as appears by their words, they *said one to another, What manner of man is this?*

CHAP. V

Christ casteth out the legion of devils, and suffereth them to enter into the herd of swine, 1—20. He is entreated by Jairus to go and heal his daughter, 21—24. By the way he healeth a woman of an inveterate issue of blood, 25—34. He raiseth Jairus's daughter to life, 35—43.

AND ᵃ they came over unto the other side of the sea, into the country of the Gadarenes. a Matt. 8. 28. Luke 8. 26.

2 And when he was come out of the ship, immediately there met him out of the tombs a man with an unclean spirit,

3 Who had *his* dwelling among the tombs; and no man could bind him, no, not with chains:

4 Because that he had been often bound with fetters and chains, and the chains had been plucked asunder by him, and the fetters broken in pieces: neither could any *man* tame him.

5 And always, night and day, he was in the mountains, and in the tombs, crying, and cutting himself with stones.

6 But when he saw Jesus afar off, he ran and worshipped him,

7 And cried with a loud voice, and said, What have I to do with thee, Jesus, *thou* Son of the most high God? I adjure thee by God, that thou torment me not.

8 For he said unto him, Come out of the man, *thou* unclean spirit.

9 And he asked him, What *is* thy name? And he answered, saying, My name *is* Legion: for we are many.

10 And he besought him much that he would not send them away out of the country.

11 Now there was there nigh unto the mountains a great herd of swine feeding.

12 And all the devils besought him, saying, Send us into the swine, that we may enter into them.

13 And forthwith Jesus gave them leave. And the unclean spirits went out, and entered into the swine: and the herd ran violently down a steep place into the sea, (they were about two thousand;) and were choked in the sea.

14 And they that fed the swine fled, and told

it in the city, and in the country. And they went out to see what it was that was done.

15 And they come to Jesus, and see him that was possessed with the devil, and had the legion, sitting, and clothed, and in his right mind: and they were afraid.

16 And they that saw *it* told them how it befell to him that was possessed with the devil, and *also* concerning the swine.

b Matt. 8. 34. Acts 16. 39. 17 And ᵇthey began to pray him to depart out of their coasts.

18 And when he was come into the c Luke 8.38. ship, ᶜhe that had been possessed with the devil prayed him that he might be with him.

19 Howbeit Jesus suffered him not, but saith unto him, Go home to thy friends, and tell them how great things the Lord hath done for thee, and hath had compassion on thee.

20 And he departed, and began to publish in Decapolis how great things Jesus had done for him: and all *men* did marvel.

This famous piece of history hath the testimony of three evangelists, Matthew, Mark, and Luke. We meeting with it in Matthew, did not only largely open what passages Matthew hath about it, but what both Mark and Luke have. See the notes on Matt. viii. 28—34. We shall only annex here some short notes. Interpreters judge *the country of the Gergesenes*, and of *the Gadarenes* mentioned here, to have been the same, sometimes receiving the denomination from one city, sometimes from another in it. Why the devils are called unclean spirits, in opposition to the Holy Spirit, &c., we have formerly showed; as also why they delight to be about tombs. We have also showed his power, which (by God's permission) he exerciseth upon men: some he possesseth, and acteth the part of the soul in them (especially as to the locomotive faculty); these are properly called demoniacs, ἐνεργούμενοι. Others he afflicteth more as a foreign agent, offering violence to them. Others he more secretly influenceth, by impressions and suggestions: thus he still ordinarily *worketh in the children of disobedience*, Eph. ii. 2; nor are the people of God free from this impetus, though, being succoured by Christ, they are not so ordinarily overcome. Of the mighty power of the evil angels to break chains and fetters we need not doubt, considering that though fallen from their first righteousness, they yet have their natural power as spirits. *I adjure thee by God*, is no more than, I solemnly entreat thee; it hath not the force of, Swear unto me by God, as some would have it. Matthew mentioneth two of these demoniacs; Mark and Luke but one: there were doubtless two, but probably one of them was not so raging as the other, and therefore less taken notice of. Some think one of these men was a heathen, the other a Jew: 1. Because the term *legion*, which the demoniac gives himself, is a heathen term, signifying a squadron of soldiers, about six thousand or more, as some reckon. 2. Christ was now in a country full of heathens. 3. The woman of whose cure we next read was a Syrophenician. It is observable, that a multitude of evil spirits is called by the name of *the devil;* because, though considered as individual spirits they are many, yet in their malice and mischievous designs against mankind they are as one. Oh that the people of God were as well united in designs for his glory! Some interpreters start a question here, not very easy to be resolved, viz. What made the devils so desirous that Christ would not send them out of the country. Their answer is not improbable: That it was a paganish, ignorant, sottish place, where usually the devil hath the best markets and the greatest rule. For as it is said of Christ, that he could not do much in some places where he came because of their unbelief; so neither can the devil do much in some places, because of the faith of the gospel received by them. Hence it is observable, that as the devil is not able to play his game in any place amongst Christians, as he doth this day amongst heathens; so he hath much less power at this day in places where the word of God is more generally known, and more faithfully preached, than in other places where people are more ignorant of the Scriptures, and have less faithful and frequent preaching. In the latter he dealeth most by more inward suggestions and impressions. Our learned Dr. Lightfoot observes it probable, that this city or country was generally made up of pagans, or apostatized Jews, because they nourished so many swine, which to the Jews were unclean beasts. For other things relating to the explication of this history, see the notes on Matt. viii. 28—34.

21 ᵈAnd when Jesus was passed over d Matt. 9. 1. Luke 8. 40. again by ship unto the other side, much people gathered unto him: and he was nigh unto the sea.

22 ᵉAnd, behold, there cometh one of e Matt. 9. 18. Luke 8. 41. the rulers of the synagogue, Jairus by name; and when he saw him, he fell at his feet,

23 And besought him greatly, saying, My little daughter lieth at the point of death: *I pray thee*, come and lay thy hands on her, that she may be healed; and she shall live.

24 And *Jesus* went with him; and much people followed him, and thronged him.

This whole history also is recorded both by Matthew and Luke, and we have already, in our notes upon Matt. ix. 18, &c., fully opened the several passages of it mentioned by all the evangelists, to which we refer the reader. Christ was now come over again into Galilee, where though the temple was not, yet there were synagogues, where the people did ordinarily assemble to worship God. Nor were they without order in these synagogues; they had one whom they called the ruler of the synagogue, who directed and ordered the affairs of that particular synagogue. It is more probable that *Jairus* (here mentioned) was in that sense so called, than because he was one of the court of twenty-three which the Jews are said to have had in every city.

25 And a certain woman, ᶠwhich had f Lev. 15. 25. Matt. 9. 20. an issue of blood twelve years,

26 And had suffered many things of many physicians, and had spent all that she had, and was nothing bettered, but rather grew worse,

27 When she had heard of Jesus, came in the press behind, and touched his garment.

28 For she said, If I may touch but his clothes, I shall be whole.

29 And straightway the fountain of her blood was dried up; and she felt in *her* body that she was healed of that plague.

30 And Jesus, immediately knowing in himself that ᵍvirtue had gone out of him, g Luke 6. 19. & 8. 46. turned him about in the press, and said, Who touched my clothes?

31 And his disciples said unto him, Thou seest the multitude thronging thee, and sayest thou, Who touched me?

32 And he looked round about to see her that had done this thing.

33 But the woman fearing and trembling, knowing what was done in her, came and fell down before him, and told him all the truth.

34 And he said unto her, Daughter, ʰthy faith hath made thee whole; go in h Matt. 9.22. ch. 10. 52. Acts 14. 9. peace, and be whole of thy plague.

See the notes on Matt. ix. 18—22, upon this whole history, containing a passage which happened in the way betwixt the place where our Saviour first heard of the sickness of Jairus's daughter and his house, whither our Saviour was now going. We shall in these histories observe our Saviour propounding several questions to persons: of the matter to which they related, he could not be presumed to be ignorant, being as to his Divine nature omniscient; but he only propounded them for the bettering of the knowledge of those to whom or amongst whom he spake, that his miracles might be more fully and distinctly understood. So also he is said to have known many things (as here, *that virtue had gone out of him*) which he only knew as he was God, and knew all things. It is also observable how Christ encourageth the first rudiments of saving faith in him. All that we read of this woman is, that she said, *If I may but touch his clothes, I shall be whole:* this was much short of her owning and receiving him as her Lord and Saviour. It amounted to no more than a persuasion she had of his Divine power and goodness, and that with respect to the healing of a bodily distemper; neither doth it import her believing him to be the eternal Son of God, but one to whom God had communicated a power of healing. In this confidence she cometh unto him, and toucheth the border of his garment. She is presently healed. Christ saith, her faith had made her whole. Christ measureth her faith by the light and means she had received, and accordingly rewards it; and if the notion be true, that where he healed the body he also healed the soul, this was the beginning of a greater faith in her.

l Luke 8. 49. 35 ¹While he yet spake, there came from the ruler of the synagogue's *house certain* which said, Thy daughter is dead: why troublest thou the Master any further?

36 As soon as Jesus heard the word that was spoken, he saith unto the ruler of the synagogue, Be not afraid, only believe.

37 And he suffered no man to follow him, save Peter, and James, and John the brother of James.

38 And he cometh to the house of the ruler of the synagogue, and seeth the tumult, and them that wept and wailed greatly.

39 And when he was come in, he saith unto them, Why make ye this ado, and weep? the damsel is not dead, but
k John 11.11. ᵏsleepeth.

40 And they laughed him to scorn.
l Acts 9. 40. ¹But when he had put them all out, he taketh the father and the mother of the damsel, and them that were with him, and entereth in where the damsel was lying.

41 And he took the damsel by the hand, and said unto her, Talitha cumi; which is, being interpreted, Damsel, I say unto thee, arise.

42 And straightway the damsel arose, and walked; for she was *of the age* of twelve years. And they were astonished with a great astonishment.

m Matt. 8.4. 43 And ᵐhe charged them straitly that
& 9. 30. & 12. no man should know it; and commanded
16. & 17. 9. that something should be given her to
ch. 3. 12.
Luke 5. 14. eat.

There is nothing in this history needeth further notes for explication, than what we gave in the notes on Matt. ix., to which I here refer the reader. There is nothing more unaccountable in all the passages of our Saviour's life recorded by the evangelists, than the charges that he gave to several persons healed by him, *that no man should know it.* Especially if we consider, 1. That he did not charge all so; he bid the person possessed with the devil, ver. 19 of this chapter, go home to his friends, and tell them how great things the Lord had done for him. 2. That he could not expect to be concealed had they yielded obedience, for his miracles were done openly, and it was not likely that all would keep silence, nay, he commanded the leper to go and show himself to the priests. 3. Few of those thus charged did keep silence; nor do we ever find that Christ reflected blame on them, from which yet we cannot acquit them. But we must not think to understand the reasons of all Christ's actions and speeches; he had doubtless wise ends in doing it, though we do not understand them.

CHAP. VI

Christ is slighted by his own countrymen, 1—6. *He sendeth out the twelve with power over unclean spirits,* 7—13. *The opinions of Herod and others concerning him,* 14, 15. *John the Baptist imprisoned and beheaded by Herod at the instigation of Herodias,* 16—29. *The apostles return from their mission,* 30—33. *The miracle of five thousand fed with five loaves and two fishes,* 34—44. *Christ walketh on the sea to his disciples,* 45—52. *He landeth at Gennesaret, and healeth the sick who but touched the hem of his garment,* 53—56.

AND ᵃhe went out from thence, and came a Mat. 13.54.
into his own country; and his disciples Luke 4. 16.
follow him.

2 And when the sabbath day was come, he began to teach in the synagogue: and many hearing *him* were astonished, saying, ᵇFrom whence hath this *man* these b John 6. 42.
things? and what wisdom *is* this which is given unto him, that even such mighty works are wrought by his hands?

3 Is not this the carpenter, the son of Mary, ᶜthe brother of James, and Joses, c See Matt.
and of Juda, and Simon? and are not his Gal. 1. 19.
sisters here with us? And they ᵈwere of- d Matt. 11.6.
fended at him.

We meet with all this Matt. xiii. 53—58: see the notes there. By *his own country*, questionless, is meant Nazareth, the place of his education, though Bethlehem were the place of his birth; hence he was usually called *Jesus of Nazareth.* Luke, chap. iv. 16, nameth *Nazareth*; though I cannot be confident that this text mentioneth the same motion of our Saviour's. The constant practice of our Saviour on the sabbath days is observable: it is true, he had a liberty there to preach and expound the Scripture; but without doubt many things of a ritual nature were there done which our Lord was far from approving: their assemblies being not idolatrous, he judged it no sin to be present: the main things done there were of his Father's institution; for other things, we never read our Saviour touched at them. Still the effect of our Saviour's preaching to the Jews we find to be amazement and astonishment, but no faith. Men may be affected by the word that are not converted by it. That which troubled them was, they could not imagine whence our Saviour had his power to do those mighty works, and to speak things importing such a wisdom given unto him; they could not conceive how one that had never sat at the feet of their doctors, but had been bred up as a mechanic, should have such wisdom and knowledge, or such a power to work miraculous operations. *Is not this the carpenter?* This makes it appear probable that our Saviour did, till he was thirty years of age, work with Joseph in his trade, whether of a carpenter or a mason (for τέχνων signifies either). It is certain he did not begin to appear publicly and to preach till he was thirty years of age, and it is not probable that he lived all these years in idleness. *The son of Mary, the brother of James, and Joses, and of Juda, and Simon;* that is, the kinsman, (as most interpret it,) supposing Mary the mother of our Lord had no more children: I shall not determine it. They say these four were the children of Mary, sister to the mother of our Lord, and the wife of Cleophas. Chap. xv. 40; xvi. 1, we read of James, Joses, and Salome, as the children of that Mary; but of Judas and Simon we read not. *And they were offended at him;* that is, although they heard such things from him, and saw such mighty works done by him, as they could not but think required a Divine influence and power, yet because by their reason they could not comprehend how one who had almost thirty years lived as a mechanic amongst them, should come by any such acquaintance with or extraordinary influence from God, their passion quickly went over; and though they were more modest than, with their corrupt teachers, to say he did this by the devil, yet neither would they receive him and believe him, but slighted and despised him; as if God's influence had been tied to their schools of the prophets.

S. MARK VI

e Mat. 13.57.
John 4. 44.

4 But Jesus said unto them, ^eA prophet is not without honour, but in his own country, and among his own kin, and in his own house.

f See Gen.19. 22. & 32. 25.
Mat. 13. 58.
ch. 9. 23.

5 ^fAnd he could there do no mighty work, save that he laid his hands upon a few sick folk, and healed *them*.

g Is. 59. 16.
h Mat. 9. 35.
Luke 13. 22.

6 And ^ghe marvelled because of their unbelief. ^hAnd he went round about the villages, teaching.

Experience tells us that familiarity breedeth a contempt. Our Saviour (though there was a deeper cause) assigneth this the cause why those of Nazareth paid him no greater respect. Unbelief in us bindeth the hands of God. *He could there do no mighty works, &c.*: he could not, not from a defect of power, but the exercise of Divine power is always regulated by wisdom, and in consistency with his wisdom he could do no mighty works there: for the end of our Saviour's miracles being either to convert unbelievers to the faith of the gospel, or to confirm weak believers in it, he foresaw that the performing of miracles there would be without any saving effect, and suspended his miraculous power. Besides, he was highly provoked by their obstinate infidelity, and would not work great wonders amongst them; only he cureth a few sick persons. *And he marvelled because of their unbelief*: his Divine doctrine was so convincing, and the fame of his glorious works done in places near them was so universal and credible, that there was just cause of his rational wonder that they did not believe. Though our Saviour left them in their infidelity, he did not leave his blessed work, going *round about the villages, teaching*. Still preaching appeareth to have been our Saviour's great work, how light a thing soever some make of it. I cannot but observe how little reason men have to glory in or to trust to any external privileges: how little other aids and assistances, without the special influences of Divine grace, signify to the begetting of faith in unbelieving souls, and removing their prejudices against the doctrine of the gospel! Christ's own country is as bad as any other.

i Matt. 10.1.
ch. 3. 13, 14.
Luke 9. 1.
‖ The word signifieth *a piece of brass money, in value somewhat less than a farthing*, Matt. 10. 9. but here it is taken in general for *money*, Luke 9. 3.

7 ¶ ⁱAnd he called *unto him* the twelve, and began to send them forth by two and two; and gave them power over unclean spirits;

8 And commanded them that they should take nothing for *their* journey, save a staff only; no scrip, no bread, no ‖ money in *their* purse:

Mark had before told us of the election of the twelve, chap. iii. 14, which neither Matthew nor Luke mention: here he giveth us an account of their mission, which is mentioned by both them also. The instructions which he gave them are much the same with what we meet with in Matt. x., and there opened. He would have them, upon their first mission, commit themselves to and find the experience of the Divine providence; and therefore he chargeth them, 1. To take no money as a reward of their pains. 2. Not to go provided with any sustenance, or money to buy any; only they might take a walking-stick in their hands, for, as Matthew reports it, he forbade them taking any staves to bear burdens, as well as any scrips; or it may be he meant two staves, that if one had any way miscarried, have been broken or lost, they might have another at hand.

k Acts 12. 8.

9 But ^k*be* shod with sandals; and not put on two coats.

Go in your ordinary habits, making no provision for yourselves, as travellers, who think they may need something before their return.

l Matt.10.11.
Luke 9. 4.
& 10. 7, 8.

10 ^lAnd he said unto them, In what place soever ye enter into an house, there abide till ye depart from that place.

m Matt. 10. 14.
Luke 10.10.
n Acts 13. 51. & 18. 6.

11 ^mAnd whosoever shall not receive you, nor hear you, when ye depart thence, ⁿshake off the dust under your feet for a testimony against them. Verily I say unto you, It shall be more tolerable for Sodom †and Gomorrha in the day of judgment, than for that city.

† Gr. or

Matthew, chap. x., gives us a larger copy of the instructions given by Christ to the twelve than doth either Mark or Luke: see these things opened in the notes upon Matt. x. 12—15.

12 And they went out, and preached that men should repent.

13 And they cast out many devils, ^oand anointed with oil many that were sick, and healed *them*.

o Jam. 5. 14.

They executed both the trusts which Christ had reposed in them, preaching the gospel, and by miraculous operations confirming the doctrine which they brought to be from heaven. John Baptist, and Christ, and the twelve all preached the same doctrine, *Repent*; that is, turn from your former sinful courses, which if men do not, Christ's coming will profit them nothing. *And anointed with oil many that were sick.* James directed this *anointing with oil* also *in the name of the Lord.* It is disputed amongst learned men whether this anointing with oil was the using of oil as a medicine, having a natural virtue, (for it is certain in that country there were oils that were of great natural force for healing,) or only as sacramental and symbolical, signifying what they did was from that unction of the Spirit of Christ which they had received, not by their own power or virtue, and representing by anointing with oil, that is an excellent lenitive, the refreshing and recovery of the diseased. But it is not probable, considering that our Lord sent the disciples to confirm the doctrine of the gospel which they preached, that he should direct them in these operations to use means of a natural force and efficacy, which had at least much abated of the miracle; besides, James bids them anoint the sick with oil *in the name of the Lord*. So as they doubtless used oil as symbolical, testifying that what they did was not by their own power and virtue. Nor did the apostles always use this rite in healing. Peter and John used it not in their healing the lame man, Acts iii. 6: *In the name of Jesus Christ* (say they) *rise up and walk*. He declareth the use of it, ver. 16, only to show, that Christ's name through faith in his name was that which made the lame man whole. So that it being both a free rite, which they sometimes used and sometimes not, and a rite annexed to miraculous operations, to declare the effect was from Christ, not from their power, in a miraculous and extraordinary, not in a natural and ordinary, way of operation, the necessity of the use of it still is very impertinently urged by some, and as impertinently quoted by others, to prove the lawfulness of ritual impositions.

14 ^pAnd king Herod heard *of him;* (for his name was spread abroad:) and he said, That John the Baptist was risen from the dead, and therefore mighty works do shew forth themselves in him.

p Matt. 14. 1. Luke 9. 7.

15 ^qOthers said, That it is Elias. And others said, That it is a prophet, or as one of the prophets.

q Matt. 16. 14.
ch. 8. 28.

16 ^rBut when Herod heard *thereof*, he said, It is John, whom I beheaded: he is risen from the dead.

r Matt. 14.2.
Luke 3. 19.

17 For Herod himself had sent forth and laid hold upon John, and bound him in prison for Herodias' sake, his brother Philip's wife: for he had married her.

A. D. 30.

18 For John had said unto Herod, ^sIt is not lawful for thee to have thy brother's wife.

s Lev. 18.16.
& 20. 21.

19 Therefore Herodias had ‖ a quarrel against him, and would have killed him; but she could not:

‖ Or, *an inward grudge*.

20 For Herod ^tfeared John, knowing that he was a just man and an holy, and

t Matt. 14. 5. & 21. 6.

| Or, *kept him*, or, *saved him*.

‖ observed him; and when he heard him, he did many things, and heard him gladly.

A. D. 32.
u Matt. 14. 6.
x Gen. 40. 20.

21 ᵘAnd when a convenient day was come, that Herod ˣon his birthday made a supper to his lords, high captains, and chief *estates* of Galilee;

22 And when the daughter of the said Herodias came in, and danced, and pleased Herod and them that sat with him, the king said unto the damsel, Ask of me whatsoever thou wilt, and I will give *it* thee.

y Esth. 5. 3, 6. & 7. 2.

23 And he sware unto her, ʸWhatsoever thou shalt ask of me, I will give *it* thee, unto the half of my kingdom.

24 And she went forth, and said unto her mother, What shall I ask? And she said, The head of John the Baptist.

25 And she came in straightway with haste unto the king, and asked, saying, I will that thou give me by and by in a charger the head of John the Baptist.

z Matt. 14. 0.

26 ᶻAnd the king was exceeding sorry; *yet* for his oath's sake, and for their sakes which sat with him, he would not reject her.

‖ Or, *one of his guard*.

27 And immediately the king sent ‖an executioner, and commanded his head to be brought: and he went and beheaded him in the prison,

28 And brought his head in a charger, and gave it to the damsel: and the damsel gave it to her mother.

29 And when his disciples heard *of it*, they came and took up his corpse, and laid it in a tomb.

We meet with this history in Matt. xiv., to which I refer the reader, having there taken in the most considerable things in the relation of the same thing by Matthew or Mark. Mark calleth him *Herod the king*, whom Mark and Luke called *tetrarch.* Herod was tetrarch of Galilee, but under that title he exercised a regal power within his province. The whole history teacheth us several things. 1. The notion of a faithful minister. He is one that dareth to tell the greatest persons of what they do contrary to the plain law of God. 2. It also teacheth us the malice of souls debauched with lust. It was not enough for Herodias to have John in prison, where he could do her no great prejudice, she must also have his head cut off. 3. The ill influence of corrupt persons in princes' courts. Herod had in his government appeared no cruel, bloody man. Our Saviour in great quiet preached the gospel, and wrought miracles for the confirmation of it, within Herod's jurisdiction; in Galilee we find no inquiry made by Herod after him, no calling him in question: and for John the Baptist, he did not only tolerate him, but brought him to his court, reverenced him as a just and holy man, did many things upon his instructions, *heard him gladly;* but by the influence of Herodias (his courtiers being at least silent in the case) he is prevailed with to put him to death. 4. The arts likewise of these persons are observable; they take the advantage of his jollity on his birth-day, when in the excess of mirth it was likely he would be more easy and complying to grant their requests. 5. We may also from hence learn the mischief of rash oaths and general promises, especially when they flow from souls ignorant of the law of God; for had Herod understood any thing of that, he could not have thought that his oath could have been the bond of iniquity, or obliged him to any sinful act. 6. We may also understand the mercy of God to that people who are governed by laws, whose lives and liberties do not depend upon the will of any. 7. Lastly, We may observe how far men may go, and yet be far enough from any saving grace. They may have a reverence for godly ministers, they may hear them gladly, they may do many things. The hypocrite hath some principal lust in which he must be gratified, and cannot bear a reproof as to that.

30 ᵃAnd the apostles gathered themselves together unto Jesus, and told him all things, both what they had done, and what they had taught.

a Luke 9. 10.

When Christ chose the twelve, it is said, chap. iii. 14, 15, that *he ordained twelve, that they should be with him, and that he might send them forth to preach, and to have power to heal sicknesses, and to cast out devils.* So that till Christ's ascension, though they went out from him to preach and work miracles, yet they ordinarily were with him, receiving further instructions. When they had preached, and in his name wrought many miracles, they again returned to Christ, and gave him account both of their doctrine and of the cures they had wrought.

31 ᵇAnd he said unto them, Come ye yourselves apart into a desert place, and rest a while: for ᶜthere were many coming and going, and they had no leisure so much as to eat.

b Mat. 14. 13.
c ch. 3. 20.

32 ᵈAnd they departed into a desert place by ship privately.

d Mat. 14. 13.

33 And the people saw them departing, and many knew him, and ran afoot thither out of all cities, and outwent them, and came together unto him.

Matthew makes the cause of this motion of our Saviour's to have been his receiving the report of Herod's dealing with John the Baptist, as we often find him yielding to the fury of his adversaries. Mark assigns another reason, (as there may be several reasons or motives of and to the same action or motion,) viz. that both himself and his apostles might have a little rest. The place which he chose for his recess is called *a desert place*, not because it was wholly not inhabited, but very thinly inhabited. Luke saith it was *a desert place belonging to the city called Bethsaida*, chap. ix. 10; probably some large forest, or common pasture, which belonged to that city, and took a denomination from it. It was a place on the other side of the water, for they went to it by ship. But this water was but a lake, though called the sea of Tiberias, for the people, fetching a little further compass about, went thither on foot, and outwent the motion of the ship.

34 ᵉAnd Jesus, when he came out, saw much people, and was moved with compassion toward them, because they were as sheep not having a shepherd: and ᶠhe began to teach them many things.

e Matt. 9. 36. & 14. 14.
f Luke 9. 11.

When Christ came out of the ship, on the other side of the water, he found that the people had outwent the ship; they were come about with a desire to hear the word. He considered what miserable priests and teachers they had, so that they were indeed as sheep without a shepherd, having none but such as were as bad or worse than none. Though he was weary, and came hither for some rest and repose, yet he will deny himself as to his bodily cravings, to do good to their souls: he first preacheth to them, and teacheth them many things; then he confirmeth his doctrine by a miracle, the relation of which followeth.

35 ᵍAnd when the day was now far spent, his disciples came unto him, and said, This is a desert place, and now the time *is* far passed:

g Mat. 14. 15.
Luke 9. 12.

36 Send them away, that they may go into the country round about, and into the villages, and buy themselves bread: for they have nothing to eat.

37 He answered and said unto them, Give ye them to eat. And they say unto him, ʰShall we go and buy two hundred

h Num. 11. 13, 22.
2 Kings 4. 43.

S. MARK VI

pennyworth of bread, and give them to eat?

38 He saith unto them, How many loaves have ye? go and see. And when they knew, they say, Five, and two fishes.

39 And he commanded them to make all sit down by companies upon the green grass.

40 And they sat down in ranks, by hundreds, and by fifties.

41 And when he had taken the five loaves and the two fishes, he looked up to heaven, and blessed, and brake the loaves, and gave *them* to his disciples to set before them; and the two fishes divided he among them all.

42 And they did all eat, and were filled.

43 And they took up twelve baskets full of the fragments, and of the fishes.

44 And they that did eat of the loaves were about five thousand men.

We meet with the relation of this miracle Matt. xiv. 15—21, and shall again meet with it John vi. John relates it with some more particular circumstances, telling us it was Philip that moved our Saviour to dismiss them so seasonably, that they might provide themselves food, and making Christ to propound the questions to Philip, where they should buy bread enough for them. He also tells us that it was Andrew who told our Saviour that there was a lad there had five barley-loaves and two fishes. But all three of the evangelists agree in the main, both as to the quantity of victuals, five loaves and two fishes; and the quantity of the people fed with them, five thousand; and the number of the baskets full of fragments taken up, which was twelve. John also addeth the effect of this miracle upon the multitude, chap. vi. 14; they *said, This is of a truth that prophet that should come into the world.* For further explication of this piece of history, see the notes on Matt. xv. 15—21, and on John vi. 5—13.

45 And straightway he constrained his disciples to get into the ship, and to go to the other side before || unto Bethsaida, while he sent away the people.

46 And when he had sent them away, he departed into a mountain to pray.

If this desert where Christ was were, as Luke saith, chap. ix. 10, a desert belonging to Bethsaida, those words, εἰς τὸ πέραν πρὸς Βηθσαϊδαν, are ill translated *unto Bethsaida*, and the marginal note in our larger Bibles is better, *over against Bethsaida.* Our Saviour here first sends away his disciples by water, then he dismisseth the multitude to go to their own homes. Then he goeth up into a mountain to pray. We find Christ very often in the duty of secret prayer, very often choosing a mountain, as a place of solitude, for the performance of it, and very often making use of the night for it, which is also a time of quietness and solitude: which lets us know that secret prayer is necessary, not only for the bewailing, and confessing, and begging pardon for our secret sins, (for Christ had no such,) but for our more free and more near communion with God; for although God filleth all places, yet we shall observe that God, in his more than ordinary communion with his people, hath not admitted of company, of which Abraham, and Moses, and Jacob, and all the prophets are sufficient instances.

47 And when even was come, the ship was in the midst of the sea, and he alone on the land.

48 And he saw them toiling in rowing; for the wind was contrary unto them: and about the fourth watch of the night he cometh unto them, walking upon the sea, and would have passed by them.

49 But when they saw him walking upon the sea, they supposed it had been a spirit, and cried out:

50 For they all saw him, and were troubled. And immediately he talked with them, and saith unto them, Be of good cheer: it is I; be not afraid.

51 And he went up unto them into the ship; and the wind ceased: and they were sore amazed in themselves beyond measure, and wondered.

52 For they considered not *the miracle* of the loaves: for their heart was hardened.

See the notes on Matt. xiv. 24—33. *By the sea* here is meant the lake of Gennesaret. *The fourth watch of the night* was after four in the morning. The foregoing part of the night our Saviour had spent alone upon the mountain in prayer. *They were sore amazed in themselves, and wondered. For they considered not, &c.* Had they diligently considered by what power five loaves and two fishes were multiplied to a quantity to feed five thousand men, besides women and children, they would not have been amazed, either at the sight of Christ safely walking upon the water, or at the wind ceasing when he came into the ship; but these things had not made that due impression upon their hearts which they ought to have done. The time was not yet come when Christ would have his Divine nature fully revealed to them, and till he opened their eyes, and wrought in their hearts a full persuasion of that, it was not in their power so to apprehend it, as to give a full assent to it, and to act accordingly. This is that which is here called hardness or blindness of heart.

53 And when they had passed over, they came into the land of Gennesaret, and drew to the shore.

54 And when they were come out of the ship, straightway they knew him,

55 And ran through that whole region round about, and began to carry about in beds those that were sick, where they heard he was.

56 And whithersoever he entered, into villages, or cities, or country, they laid the sick in the streets, and besought him that they might touch if it were but the border of his garment: and as many as touched || him were made whole.

See the notes on Matt. xiv. 34—36. The charity of this people to their sick neighbours is very commendable, and instructive of us as to our duty to do good to others, as to their bodily wants and necessities, so far as we are able; but how much greater is that charity, which is showed to people's souls, inviting them to Christ that they may be spiritually healed! It was not their touching the hem of his garment, nor of his body, which healed these sick persons, those who had a hand in crucifying of him did both; it was the virtue that went out from Christ, upon the testification of their faith, by coming to him, and touching, and desiring to touch, the hem of his garment: neither is it men's coming to the congregation, and hearing the word of God, that will heal their souls, unless there goeth forth a Divine power from the Spirit of grace upon men's hungering and thirsting after Christ in his ordinances, and by faith laying hold upon the promise exhibited in the preaching of the gospel.

CHAP. VII

The Pharisees finding fault with his disciples for eating with unwashen hands, Christ reproveth them of hypocrisy, and of making void the commandments of God by the traditions of men, 1—13. *He teacheth that a man is defiled, not by that which entereth in, but by that which cometh out of him,* 14—23. *He healeth the daughter of a Syro-phenician woman,* 24—30, *and a man that was deaf and had an impediment in his speech,* 31—37.

THEN ᵃcame together unto him the Pharisees, and certain of the Scribes, which came from Jerusalem.

2 And when they saw some of his disciples eat bread with ∥defiled, that is to say, with unwashen, hands, they found fault.

3 For the Pharisees, and all the Jews, except they wash *their* hands ∥oft, eat not, holding the tradition of the elders.

4 And *when they come* from the market, except they wash, they eat not. And many other things there be, which they have received to hold, *as* the washing of cups, and ∥ pots, brasen vessels, and of ∥tables.

5 ᵇ Then the Pharisees and Scribes asked him, Why walk not thy disciples according to the tradition of the elders, but eat bread with unwashen hands?

6 He answered and said unto them, Well hath Esaias prophesied of you hypocrites, as it is written, ᶜThis people honoureth me with *their* lips, but their heart is far from me.

7 Howbeit in vain do they worship me, teaching *for* doctrines the commandments of men.

8 For laying aside the commandment of God, ye hold the tradition of men, *as* the washing of pots and cups: and many other such like things ye do.

9 And he said unto them, Full well ye ∥ reject the commandment of God, that ye may keep your own tradition.

10 For Moses said, ᵈ Honour thy father and thy mother; and, ᵉ Whoso curseth father or mother, let him die the death:

11 But ye say, If a man shall say to his father or mother, *It is* ᶠCorban, that is to say, a gift, by whatsoever thou mightest be profited by me; *he shall be free.*

12 And ye suffer him no more to do ought for his father or his mother;

13 Making the word of God of none effect through your tradition, which ye have delivered: and many such like things do ye.

See the notes upon the first nine verses of the fifteenth of Matthew. By the notion of *traditions*, our Saviour understandeth not such things as were delivered to them by God in his law, but such things as were delivered to them by the elders, that is, their rulers in the church in the former times; for, ver. 9, he opposeth traditions to God's commandments, and saith the latter were neglected by their zeal for the former: to give countenance to which traditions, as the papists would impose upon us to believe, that Christ communicated some things to his apostles, and they to the primitive churches, by word of mouth, which have been so transmitted from age to age; so the Jews pretended that God communicated his will in some things to Moses, which Moses did not publish to the people. And as the former pretend a power by Christ left to the church to determine rituals; so the Pharisees (their true predecessors) pretended a such-like power. Amongst others, besides the *divers washings* mentioned by the apostle, Heb. ix. 10, amongst the *carnal ordinances, imposed* only *until the time of reformation,* they had invented many other washings, as *sepimenta legis,* hedges to the Divine law. They washed their hands often, when they came from market, or before they did eat, not for decency and neatness, but out of religion, lest they should have been defiled by touching any heathens, or any polluted things; and not their hands only, but their pots and cups, their beds and tables, and brazen vessels; as indeed there is no stop, when once men have passed the hedge of the Divine institution, of which popery is a plentiful instance, where it is hard to discern an ordinance of God in the rubbish of their superstitious traditions. And it is very observable, that superstitious men are always more fond of, and zealous for, the traditions of men in their worship, than keeping the commandments of God. It is with the papists more heinous to violate Lent than to violate the sabbath; for a priest to marry than to commit whoredom. This zeal in them ordinarily produceth a neglect, or slight esteem, of the plain commandments of God. So it did in the Pharisees, ver. 9; upon which our Saviour calleth them *hypocrites*, ver. 6, and telleth them this worshipping of God was vain, sinful, and idle, and impertinent; there was in it a derogating from the authority of God, and arrogating of an undue authority to themselves, by their commands making those things necessary which are not so; and, as commonly it happeneth, when human inventions are over-urged and multiplied, some are urged destructive of the Divine law, so it was with those Pharisees; so they had done as to the fifth commandment, of which we have spoken plentifully in our notes on Matt. xv. 4—6. Our Saviour goeth on, showing their ignorance and blindness, in imagining that any person could be defiled by eating with unwashen hands.

14 ¶ ᵍAnd when he had called all the people *unto him*, he said unto them, Hearken unto me every one *of you*, and understand:

Our Saviour's calling *all the people unto him* before he spake what next followeth, and his prefacing that discourse with, *Hearken every one of you, and understand*, lets us know that what he was about to say was a point of great moment, well worth their learning and observation.

15 There is nothing from without a man, that entering into him can defile him: but the things which come out of him, those are they that defile the man.

16 ʰIf any man have ears to hear, let him hear.

The addition of these words, *If any man have ears to hear, let him hear*, confirm what I observed before, that our Saviour looked upon what he said as a truth of very great moment, and withal as such a notion which carnal hearts and superstitious persons had no ears to hear. This great truth was, That a man in the sight of God (for of such defilement he alone speaketh) could be defiled by nothing but what came from within him. How easily would a popish doctor have answered this, Doth not disobedience to the church's commands come from within us? Our Saviour therefore must be understood of such things as come from within in disobedience to the commands of God; such are those which he mentioneth, ver. 21, 22; for all things that come from within do not defile the man. And it is true, that a disobedience to the commands of any power, whether civil or ecclesiastical, is a thing which cometh from within and defileth a soul, if it be a disobedience in such things which God hath given them a power to command, but if not the case is otherwise.

17 ⁱAnd when he was entered into the house from the people, his disciples asked him concerning the parable.

That is, concerning this saying of his, which appeared to them dark, for a parable sometimes in Scripture signifieth no more, Psal. xlix. 4; yet one would think that our Saviour's saying was plain enough. But custom is a great tyrant. The prejudice they had received from their superstitious teachers blinded them, and locked up their souls from receiving true and spiritual instructions. We see the same thing every day. What a heinous thing do the blind papists think it is to eat flesh in Lent, or on one of their fish days! never considering by what law of God any men are restrained in such things. Our Saviour in the next words checks their blindness.

18 And he saith unto them, Are ye so without understanding also? Do ye not perceive, that whatsoever thing from without entereth into the man, *it* cannot defile him;

19 Because it entereth not into his heart, but into the belly, and goeth out into the draught, purging all meats?

20 And he said, That which cometh out of the man, that defileth the man.

^k^ Gen. 6. 5.
& 8. 21.
Matt. 15. 19.

21 ^k^ For from within, out of the heart of men, proceed evil thoughts, adulteries, fornications, murders,

† Gr. *covetousnesses, wickednesses.*

22 Thefts, † covetousness, wickedness, deceit, lasciviousness, an evil eye, blasphemy, pride, foolishness:

23 All these evil things come from within, and defile the man.

Christ checketh his disciples for understanding things no better. Ignorance is more excusable in those who are strangers to God and Christ than in those that have relation to him. In our Saviour's enumeration of those things which come out of the heart, several things are reckoned up which are the overt actions of the tongue, eye, hands; but our Saviour saith all these flow from the heart, for the actions of the outward man are but the imperate actions of the will, and things past the imaginations and understanding, before they come at the will, to be chosen or rejected. Here are but some sins reckoned instead of many, for it is true of all our evil actions, that they are first hatched in the heart, and are first entertained in our thoughts, in our understandings, then chosen by our wills, and then the bodily members are commanded by the soul to the execution of them. Mark reckoneth more than Matthew, but in both the enumerations are imperfect, and some sins are named instead of all. Nothing but sin defileth the man. Sin hath its first rise in the heart, and floweth from thence. See further the notes upon Matt. xv. 18—20.

l Mat. 15. 21.

24 ¶ ^l^ And from thence he arose, and went into the borders of Tyre and Sidon, and entered into an house, and would have no man know *it:* but he could not be hid.

25 For a *certain* woman, whose young daughter had an unclean spirit, heard of him, and came and fell at his feet:

† Or, *Gentile.*

26 The woman was a ‖ Greek, a Syrophenician by nation; and she besought him that he would cast forth the devil out of her daughter.

27 But Jesus said unto her, Let the children first be filled: for it is not meet to take the children's bread, and to cast *it* unto the dogs.

28 And she answered and said unto him, Yes, Lord: yet the dogs under the table eat of the children's crumbs.

29 And he said unto her, For this saying go thy way; the devil is gone out of thy daughter.

30 And when she was come to her house, she found the devil gone out, and her daughter laid upon the bed.

Matthew recordeth this history with several considerable additions: see Matt. xv. 21—28, where we have largely opened it.

m Matt. 15. 29.

31 ¶ ^m^ And again, departing from the coasts of Tyre and Sidon, he came unto the sea of Galilee, through the midst of the coasts of Decapolis.

n Mat. 9. 32.
Luke 11. 14.

32 And ^n^ they bring unto him one that was deaf, and had an impediment in his speech; and they beseech him to put his hand upon him.

33 And he took him aside from the multitude, and put his fingers into his ears, and ^o^ he spit, and touched his tongue;

o ch. 8. 23.
John 9. 6.

34 And ^p^ looking up to heaven, ^q^ he sighed, and saith unto him, Ephphatha, that is, Be opened.

p ch. 6. 41.
John 11. 41.
& 17. 1.
q John 11. 33, 38.

35 ^r^ And straightway his ears were opened, and the string of his tongue was loosed, and he spake plain.

r Is. 35. 5, 6.
Matt. 11. 5.

36 And ^s^ he charged them that they should tell no man: but the more he charged them, so much the more a great deal they published *it:*

s ch. 5. 43.

37 And were beyond measure astonished, saying, He hath done all things well: he maketh both the deaf to hear, and the dumb to speak.

This history is recorded by Mark only. *And again, departing from the coasts of Tyre and Sidon.* We heard, ver. 24, of his going into those coasts; some think that our Saviour did not go out of the Jewish country, though he went to *the coasts of Tyre and Sidon,* which were pagan countries. *He came unto the sea of Galilee, through the midst of the coasts of Decapolis.* That Decapolis was a union of ten cities so called, is plain by the name; but what those cities were, and whether they lay on the same side of Jordan that Galilee did, or on the other side of Jordan, is disputed; most think they lay on the Galilean side. *One that was deaf, and had an impediment in his speech:* some think that he was dumb, but the word signifies one that spake with difficulty, so as it is likely his deafness was not natural; (for all naturally deaf, are also dumb; we learning to speak by hearing;) besides that it is said after the cure, that *he spake plain.* it was probably an accidental deafness happening to him after that he could speak. Their beseeching Christ to put his hand upon him, proceeded from their observation of him very often to use that rite in his healing sick persons. *And he took him aside from the multitude,* not seeking his own glory and ostentation, *and put his fingers into his ears, and he spit, and touched his tongue.* All these things were *ex abundanti,* not necessary actions, or naturally efficacious for his cure; but our Lord sometimes used no signs or rites, sometimes these, sometimes others, as it pleased him. *And looking up to heaven, he sighed,* pitying the condition of human nature, subject to so many miseries, defects, and infirmities, and saith, *Ephphatha, that is, Be opened.* By the word of his power he made the world, and by the word of his power he upholds it, and by the same word of his power he restoreth any lapsed or decayed part of it. He speaks, and it is done. *And straightway his ears were opened:* nature obeyeth the God of nature. Concerning his charge of them not to publish it, and their disobedience to it, I have had occasion once and again to speak, and must confess I can neither satisfy myself in the reason from my own thoughts, nor from what I read in others. This miracle hath no other effect on the people than astonishment, and confession that what he did was well done; which was the common effect of Christ's preaching and miracles upon the most.

CHAP. VIII

Christ miraculously feedeth four thousand persons, 1—9. *He refuseth the Pharisees a sign,* 10—13. *He warneth his disciples against the leaven of the Pharisees and of Herod, and explaineth his meaning,* 14—21. *He giveth a blind man sight,* 22—26. *The people's opinions, and Peter's confession, of him,* 27—30. *He foreshoweth his own death, and rebuketh Peter for dissuading him from it,* 31—33. *He showeth his followers that they must deny themselves, and not be ashamed of him and his gospel,* 34—38.

a Mat. 15. 32.

IN those days ^a^ the multitude being very great, and having nothing to eat, Jesus called his disciples *unto him,* and saith unto them,

2 I have compassion on the multitude, because

they have now been with me three days, and have nothing to eat:

3 And if I send them away fasting to their own houses, they will faint by the way: for divers of them came from far.

4 And his disciples answered him, From whence can a man satisfy these *men* with bread here in the wilderness?

5 ᵇAnd he asked them, How many loaves have ye? And they said, Seven.

b Mat. 15.34. See ch. 6.38.

6 And he commanded the people to sit down on the ground: and he took the seven loaves, and gave thanks, and brake, and gave to his disciples to set before *them;* and they did set *them* before the people.

7 And they had a few small fishes: and ᶜhe blessed, and commanded to set them also before *them.*

c Mat. 14.19. ch. 6. 41.

8 So they did eat, and were filled: and they took up of the broken *meat* that was left seven baskets.

9 And they that had eaten were about four thousand: and he sent them away.

These verses give us an account of another miracle wrought by our Saviour, of the same nature with the one which we had chap. vi.; only there five thousand (besides women and children) were fed with five loaves and two fishes, here four thousand are fed with seven loaves and a few fishes; there twelve baskets full of fragments were taken up, here but seven. We meet with the same history Matt. xv. 32—38; see the notes on that place. Both miracles testified Christ to have acted by a Divine power, and were certainly wrought to prove that the doctrine which he delivered to them was from God; both of them show the compassion that he had for the sons of men, showed to them not only with relation to their spiritual, but also to their corporal wants and infirmities. In both of them is commended to us, from his great example, the religious custom of begging a blessing upon our food when we sit down to it, and receiving the good creatures of God with thanksgiving. From both of them we may learn, in the doing of our duty, not to be too solicitous what we shall eat, or what we shall drink. God will some way or other provide for those who neglect themselves to follow him. From both we may also learn our duty to take a provident care to make no waste of the good things which God lends us. These are the chief things this history affordeth us for our instruction.

10 ¶ And ᵈstraightway he entered into a ship with his disciples, and came into the parts of Dalmanutha.

d Mat. 15.39.

11 ᵉAnd the Pharisees came forth, and began to question with him, seeking of him a sign from heaven, tempting him.

e Matt. 12. 38. & 16. 1. John 6. 30.

12 And he sighed deeply in his spirit, and saith, Why doth this generation seek after a sign? verily I say unto you, There shall no sign be given unto this generation.

13 And he left them, and entering into the ship again departed to the other side.

Matthew saith, he *came into the coasts of Magdala;* it is probable they were two contiguous tracts of land. We often read of the Pharisees coming to our Saviour to ask a sign. Had they not signs? What were all the miracles he wrought but signs of his Divine power and mission? But they ask for *a sign from heaven,* such a sign as Moses, Joshua, and Elijah gave them, by this means making a trial of his Divine power. Our Saviour, who never wrought miracles to satisfy men's curiosity, but only to confirm their faith, refuseth to show them any such sign as they desired, and leaves these coasts.

14 ¶ ᶠNow *the disciples* had forgotten to take bread, neither had they in the ship with them more than one loaf.

f Mat. 16. 5.

15 ᵍAnd he charged them, saying, Take heed, beware of the leaven of the Pharisees, and *of* the leaven of Herod.

g Matt. 16.6. Luke 12. 1.

16 And they reasoned among themselves, saying, *It is* ʰbecause we have no bread.

h Mat. 16. 7.

17 And when Jesus knew *it,* he saith unto them, Why reason ye, because ye have no bread? ⁱperceive ye not yet, neither understand? have ye your heart yet hardened?

i ch. 6. 52.

18 Having eyes, see ye not? and having ears, hear ye not? and do ye not remember?

19 ᵏWhen I brake the five loaves among five thousand, how many baskets full of fragments took ye up? They say unto him, Twelve.

k Mat. 14.20. ch. 6. 43. Luke 9. 17. John 6. 13.

20 And ˡwhen the seven among four thousand, how many baskets full of fragments took ye up? And they said, Seven.

l Mat. 15.37. ver. 8.

21 And he said unto them, How is it that ᵐye do not understand?

m ch. 6. 52. ver. 17.

We met with this whole history, with some additions, in Matt. xvi. 5—12: see the notes there. It teacheth us both a lesson of human frailty, and what is our Christian duty: of our frailty, in not considering the works of the Lord for us, so as to make any use of them for the time to come. God doth his great works of providence to be had in remembrance, and that not only with respect to himself, that he might be glorified by us upon the remembrance of them, and this not only by our rejoicing in him, but also by our trusting in him, and not desponding under such-like difficulties as God by any of them hath delivered us from. And also with respect to our duty, that we might in present exigences relieve ourselves from former experiences: and if we do not thus conceive of God's dispensations, we do not perceive, nor understand, the meaning and will of God in them; though we have eyes we see not, though we have ears we hear not, and in remembering we remember not, our remembrance is of no benefit, no advantage at all unto us. Our Saviour, indeed, did not at all speak here of bodily bread; though he did bid them beware of the leaven of the Pharisees and Herod, he spake to them about the doctrine of the Pharisees, and so Matthew tells us they (after this reproof) considered, though he (after his accustomed manner) spake to them under a parabolical expression. Saith he, What though you have forgotten to bring bread, do not you know, have not I, by two miraculous operations, taught you that I am able to furnish you with bread, though you have none, or such a quantity as is very insufficient? God expecteth of us that we should so keep in mind his former dispensations of providence to us, under straits and difficulties, as to trust in him when his providence brings us again into the like difficulties, yet not declining the use of any reasonable and just means for providing for ourselves. Thus David knew, and understood, that God had delivered him from the lion and the bear, while going against Goliath, 1 Sam. xvii.; he made it a ground of his confidence : so also Psal. cxvi. 8 : and Paul, when he concluded God would deliver because he had delivered. God, when he *brake the heads of leviathan in pieces, gave him to be meat to the people inhabiting the wilderness,* Psal. lxxiv. 14 : he intends former mercies to be food for his people in following straits and exigences.

22 ¶ And he cometh to Bethsaida; and they bring a blind man unto him, and besought him to touch him.

23 And he took the blind man by the hand, and led him out of the town; and when ⁿhe had spit on his eyes, and put his hands upon him, he asked him if he saw ought.

n ch. 7. 33.

24 And he looked up, and said, I see men as trees, walking.

25 After that he put *his* hands again upon his eyes, and made him look up : and he was restored, and saw every man clearly.

26 And he sent him away to his house, saying, Neither go into the town, °nor tell *it* to any in the town.

o Mat. 8. 4. ch. 5. 43.

This miracle is only mentioned by Mark particularly, possibly because of two singularities in it: 1. With reference to the signs he used. 2. With reference to the gradual cure. Our Saviour sometimes used some signs in his miraculous operations, sometimes he used none, but by the word of his power alone healed them ; in the signs he used, to let the people understand there was nothing in them, he often varied; sometimes he laid his hands upon them, sometimes he took them by the hand, sometimes he used one sign, sometimes another. Here, 1. He takes the blind man by the hand. 2. He leads him out of the town, the inhabitants being not worthy to see a miracle : it was one of the cities upbraided by our Saviour for their impenitency and unbelief, Matt. xi. 21. 3. He spit on his eyes : so chap. vii. 33. 4. Then he twice put his hands on him. Christ was wont to heal at once; here he healeth by degrees, so as the healing of this blind man was a true pattern of his healing spiritual blindness, which usually is done gradually, but perfected at last as this bodily cure was.

p Mat. 16.13. Luke 9. 18.

27 ¶ ᵖAnd Jesus went out, and his disciples, into the towns of Cæsarea Philippi : and by the way he asked his disciples, saying unto them, Whom do men say that I am ?

q Mat. 14. 2.

28 And they answered, ᑫJohn the Baptist : but some *say*, Elias ; and others, One of the prophets.

Herod, and those that followed him, judged Christ to be John the Baptist raised from the dead, or to have the soul of John the Baptist clothed with other flesh. Others conceived him to be Elias, of whom they were in expectation that he should come before the Messias. Others thought he was Jeremias, as Matthew saith, or one of the old prophets ; they could not tell what to determine of one who appeared to them in the shape of a man, but did such things as none could do, but the Divine power either immediately, or mediately, putting forth itself in a human body.

29 And he saith unto them, But whom say ye that I am ? And Peter answereth and saith unto him, ʳThou art the Christ.

r Matt. 16.6. John 6. 69. & 11. 27. s Mat. 16.20.

30 ˢAnd he charged them that they should tell no man of him.

Luke reports no more of this than Mark, but Matthew reports it much larger, giving us a further reply of Christ to Peter : see the notes on Matt. xvi. 15—20, which we have there discoursed largely upon. I shall only say here, That if so great a point as Peter's primacy had been understood by Christ's disciples of that age to have been settled by that answer of our Saviour, it is likely two of the evangelists would not have omitted an account of it. If they had forgotten it, there is no doubt but some or other of Christ's disciples would have put them in mind of it. Our Saviour's charge that they should tell no man of him, seemeth to him, that although our Saviour was willing to be taken notice of as a prophet, yet he was not willing as yet to be taken notice of as the Messiah, or Son of God, which latter Matthew reports as added to his confession ; and perhaps both Mark and Luke, in their following words, give us the reason, for if we observe it, he immediately falls into a discourse of his suffering, and he might possibly think, that a weak faith of his Divine nature would be overthrown by the sight of his subsequent sufferings. So that he reserved the publication of himself to be the Son of God, until such time when (as the apostle saith, Rom. i. 4) he was *declared so with power, according to the spirit of holiness, by his resurrection from the dead.*

t Matt. 16. 21. & 17. 22. Luke 9. 22.

31 And ᵗhe began to teach them, that the Son of man must suffer many things, and be rejected of the elders, and *of* the Chief Priests, and Scribes, and be killed, and after three days rise again.

Our Lord is elsewhere said to have taught his disciples, according as they were able to bear, or to hear, what he spake unto them. He did not at the first teach them that he must suffer death : the doctrine of the cross of Christ was like new wine not fit to be put into old bottles ; yet necessary to be taught them, lest when they saw it soon after they should have been offended, as indeed they were to some degree, notwithstanding the premonition they had of it. With the doctrine of his suffering, he joineth also the doctrine of his resurrection the third day : so saith Matthew. Mark saith, *after three days*, μετὰ, which seemeth to be a difference between the two evangelists, and also a difficulty, when it is certain that our Saviour did not lie three entire days in the grave. But either Mark reckons the time from his first being betrayed and apprehended, so it was after three days ; and Matthew speaketh only of the time which he lay in the grave, that was but part of three days ; or else it was the fault of our translators to translate μετὰ, *after*, because indeed it often so signifies, whereas it sometimes signifies *in*, which had better fitted this text, to make it agree with Matthew. This is Grotius's and Beza's observation, (see his notes on the text,) and is abundantly justified by Matt. xxvii. 64, where his adversaries desired of Pilate that the sepulchre might be made fast ἕως τῆς τρίτης ἡμέρας, *until the third day*, because he had said while he was alive, Μετὰ τρεῖς ἡμέρας ἐγείρομαι, *After three days I will arise*, which if they had understood of after the third day fully spent, they would not have petitioned that the sepulchre should have been made fast only until the third day, but it is plain they understood it the third day he would rise. So *after three days* here is, after the third day is come, not after the third day is past, which neither agrees with Matthew nor yet with the truth. If any desire further to make out this notion, he may read the learned Beza's larger notes on this verse.

32 And he spake that saying openly. And Peter took him, and began to rebuke him.

33 But when he had turned about and looked on his disciples, he rebuked Peter, saying, Get thee behind me, Satan : for thou savourest not the things that be of God, but the things that be of men.

It is from hence manifest, that notwithstanding the confession of Peter, that he was the Christ, yet they had a very imperfect knowledge of the business of the redemption of man by the blood of Christ, and a very imperfect faith as to the hypostatical union of the Divine and human nature in the one person of the Redeemer ; for had Peter known these things he would have seen a necessity of Christ's dying and resurrection from the dead, in order to the redemption and salvation of man, and would neither have dissuaded our Saviour from it, nor doubted of the truth of what was spoken by him, who was the Truth, and could not lie. Our Saviour's telling him οὐ φρονεῖς, *thou savourest not*, might have been more favourably translated, thou understandest not, or thou mindest not, and must not be understood of a total ignorance, or regardlessness, or not relishing, but of a partial knowledge, the want of a due regard to or savour of the things of God. Thou preferrest thy carnal affection to me, and indulgest thine own desires, to the hinderance of the honour and glory of God, and the salvation of souls, which I came to purchase by these my sufferings, and so art a Satan, an adversary, to me, who came to fulfil the will of my Father, and must not therefore give the least ear to thee, who, in what thou sayest, dost but seek and take care to please thyself. This leadeth him to the following discourse.

34 ¶ And when he had called the people *unto him* with his disciples also, he said unto them, ᵘWhosoever will come after me, let him deny himself, and take up his cross, and follow me.

u Matt. 10. 38. & 16. 24. Luke 9. 23. & 14. 27.

Our Saviour hearing Peter so stumble at the news, he told him, and the rest, of the cross which himself was to endure ; and taking notice of his exceeding fondness to gratify himself, to the prejudice of a far greater good, he now tells them the law of his discipleship, that as he was not to please himself, nor to decline afflictions for the gospel, so neither must any who would be his followers; they must all deny themselves, take up the cross, and follow him. And because this was a hard saying to flesh and blood, and what was to be their certain lot, he presseth it upon them by several arguments to the end of this chapter. See more in the notes on Matt. x. 38, and xvi. 24.

x John 12. 25.
35 For ˣwhosoever will save his life shall lose it; but whosoever shall lose his life for my sake and the Gospel's, the same shall save it.

We met with this argument twice in Matthew, to the notes upon which I refer the reader. Mark adds those words, *and the gospel's*, thereby teaching us that a suffering for the sake of the gospel, with therefore owning the propositions of it, or living up to the precepts, is by Christ accounted a suffering for Christ's sake. Ψυχὴν here must signify *life*, (as it is translated,) for a man cannot lose his soul for Christ's sake and the gospel's. The meaning is, He that will deny and abandon me and my gospel, out of a desire to save his temporal life, shall lose it, or at least shall lose his soul's portion in a better life. But he that is willing to lose his life, or will run the hazard of it, for my sake, for his owning and professing me, and the faith of my gospel, or living up to the rules, shall either save it *in specie*, by the special workings of my providence for him, delivering him out of his persecutors' hands, or shall be recompensed with an eternal life, of much more value.

36 For what shall it profit a man, if he shall gain the whole world, and lose his own soul?

37 Or what shall a man give in exchange for his soul?

Luke saith, if he lose himself and be cast away. Though ψυχὴν was rightly translated *life* in the former verse, the sense justifying that translation of it there, yet here it is as truly translated *soul*; for there are many things which men value in proportion with their lives, their honour, estates, nay, many value their lusts above their lives; and Christ himself here teacheth us that his disciples ought to value his honour and glory, and their steady profession of faith and holiness, above their life, because he that will lose his life shall save it. See the notes on these words, Matt. xvi. 26.

y Mat. 10.33. Luke 9. 26. & 12. 9.
z See Rom. 1. 16. 2 Tim. 1. 8. & 2. 12.
38 ʸWhosoever therefore ᶻshall be ashamed of me and of my words in this adulterous and sinful generation; of him also shall the Son of man be ashamed, when he cometh in the glory of his Father with the holy angels.

These words occurring twice in Matthew, chap. x. 33; xvi. 27, have been before spoken to: see the notes on those texts. Luke repeats them most perfectly, as here they are recorded. Mark expounds Luke's words, where he saith that Christ *shall come in his own glory, and in his Father's, and of the holy angels*. By the *glory of the holy angels* is meant no more than attended by the holy angels, according to Matt. xiii. 41, and 1 Thess. iv., and other scriptures. Matthew saith, chap. xvi. 27, *For the Son of man shall come in the glory of his Father with his angels; and then he shall reward every man according to his works:* and chap. x. 33, *Whosoever shall deny me before men, him will I also deny before my Father which is in heaven.* There are two passions which prevail upon men to make them apostatize in a day of temptation, fear and shame. The first prevailed upon Peter, in the high priest's hall. The second we find no instance of any good man guilty of in holy writ, and it most certainly argues a rotten and a corrupt heart. When men think it beneath their honour and quality to own the despised and maligned truth and ways of God, this is not only a denial of Christ, but the most inexcusable denial of him. Nor can any such persons look for any thing less at the hands of Christ, than that he should think it much more beneath his honour and dignity in the day of judgment to own them.

CHAP. IX

The transfiguration of Christ, 2—10. He instructeth his disciples concerning the coming of Elias, 11—13. He casteth out a dumb and deaf spirit, 14—29. He foretelleth his own death and resurrection, 30—32; checketh the ambition of his disciples, 33—37; bidding them to hinder no one from working miracles in his name, and warning them to avoid offences, 38—50.

AND he said unto them, ᵃVerily I say unto you, That there be some of them that stand here, which shall not taste of death, till they have seen ᵇthe kingdom of God come with power.

a Mat.16.28. Luke 9. 27.
b Matt. 24. 30. & 25. 31. Luke 22. 18.

To *taste of death*, is the same with to die, or to begin to die, or to experience death: compare with this text Psal. xxxiv. 8; Luke xiv. 24; John viii. 52; Heb. ii. 9; vi. 4, 5; 1 Pet. ii. 3. *Till they have seen the kingdom of God come:* our evangelist addeth, *with power*. It cannot be meant of the day of judgment, unless in the type of it, which was in the destruction of Jerusalem, (of which many understand it,) for some of the apostles, more doubtless of Christ's disciples, outlived the fatal ruin of that once famous city. Others understand here by the *kingdom of God* Christ's resurrection from the dead, when Christ's kingdom began to be fully made known, Acts x. 42.

2 ¶ ᶜAnd after six days Jesus taketh *with him* Peter, and James, and John, and leadeth them up into an high mountain apart by themselves: and he was transfigured before them.

c Mat. 17. 1. Luke 9. 28.

3 And his raiment became shining, exceeding ᵈwhite as snow; so as no fuller on earth can white them.

d Dan. 7. 9. Matt. 28. 3.

4 And there appeared unto them Elias with Moses: and they were talking with Jesus.

5 And Peter answered and said to Jesus, Master, it is good for us to be here: and let us make three tabernacles; one for thee, and one for Moses, and one for Elias.

6 For he wist not what to say; for they were sore afraid.

7 And there was a cloud that overshadowed them: and a voice came out of the cloud, saying, This is my beloved Son: hear him.

8 And suddenly, when they had looked round about, they saw no man any more, save Jesus only with themselves.

9 ᵉAnd as they came down from the mountain, he charged them that they should tell no man what things they had seen, till the Son of man were risen from the dead.

e Matt. 17.9.

10 And they kept that saying with themselves, questioning one with another what the rising from the dead should mean.

Both Matthew and Luke, as well as Mark, bear record to the truth of this history: see the notes on Matt. xvii. 1—9. Our Saviour was pleased thus to fortify these three of his disciples against his passion, which they were soon to see; and also to confirm their faith as to his Divine nature. Why Moses and Elias, rather than any others, appeared, is but a curious question, of no great use to us if resolved, and not possible to be resolved. These three disciples, by this apparition, saw our Saviour owned by Moses, who gave the law, and by Elias, both of them in great repute with the Jews. The three disciples could know neither of them (dead many hundreds of years before they were in being) but by revelation: probably Christ told them who they were. What their discourse with Christ was in the general Matthew telleth us. There is no considerable thing in this evangelist's relation which we did not meet with in

Matthew, which may supersede any further labour about it here.

11 ¶ And they asked him, saying, Why say the Scribes *that Elias must first come?

f Mal. 4. 5. Matt. 17. 10.

12 And he answered and told them, Elias verily cometh first, and restoreth all things; and ᵍhow it is written of the Son of man, that he must suffer many things, and ʰbe set at nought.

g Ps. 22. 6. Is. 53. 2, &c. Dan. 9. 26.
h Luke 23.11. Phil. 2. 7.
i Matt. 11. 14. & 17. 12. Luke 1. 17.

13 But I say unto you, That ⁱElias is indeed come, and they have done unto him whatsoever they listed, as it is written of him.

Christ had been telling his disciples that he should suffer. The Jews had a prophecy, not only that the Messias should come, but that he should *be cut off, but not for himself*, Dan. ix. 26. Only this hindered the certainty of their persuasion that Christ was he, because Elias was not yet come, whom they did expect, Mal. iv. 5; for they expected the coming of Elias in person, whereas the prophecy was to be understood of one *in the spirit and power of Elias*, as the angel expounded it, Luke i. 17. They also expected that Elias, when he came, should make a great change in their world, and bring all things again into order; but still their eye was upon a secular change, and a restoring of them to that liberty of their country which they formerly enjoyed, whereas the prophecy, Mal. iv. 6, is expounded by the angel, Luke i. 16, 17, *And many of the children of Israel shall he turn to the Lord their God.——to turn the hearts of the fathers unto the children, and the disobedient to the wisdom of the just; to make ready a people prepared for the Lord.* The disciples, being Jews, were under the prejudices of these notions about Elias, so commonly received by the doctors of their church and the generality of their people. To this our Saviour answers, The thing was true, Elias (that is, one *in the spirit and power of Elias*) was, according to the prophecy of Malachi, to come before the Messias; but they had overlooked him, for indeed this Elias was come, Matt. xi. 14, and by his preaching the doctrine of repentance for the remission of sins had endeavoured to restore all things, that is, to make a great change in the hearts and lives of the Jews, but they had put him to death. He further telleth them, that John had told them of the Son of man, that he must suffer many things, and be set at nought. He did indeed tell them so, when he pointed to him passing by, and said, *Behold the Lamb of God, which taketh away* [or taketh up, or beareth] *the sins of the world*, John i. 29. So that this was no just prejudice to their believing that he was the true Messiah.

k Matt. 17. 14. Luke 9. 37.

14 ¶ ᵏAnd when he came to *his* disciples, he saw a great multitude about them, and the Scribes questioning with them.

15 And straightway all the people, when they beheld him, were greatly amazed, and running to *him* saluted him.

16 And he asked the Scribes, What question ye ‖with them?

‖ Or, *among yourselves?*

When Christ came down from the mountain of transfiguration to his disciples, whom he had left at the foot of the mountain, he saw a great multitude got together about them, and discerned some scribes (companions of the Pharisees and teachers of the law) mixing themselves with his disciples, and arguing with them. They had often attempted our Saviour to no purpose but their own shame and confusion; in his absence they fall in with his disciples, who were yet raw in the faith; over them they hope to get a great conquest. The evangelist doth not plainly tell us what the subject matter of their discourse was. Though there be no question but the scribes in this discourse pursued their design to expose and vilify Christ and his disciples, and to that purpose, taking advantage of our Saviour's absence, discoursed with them about many things, yet Mr. Calvin doth (not improbably) judge that a great part of their discourse was about our Saviour's casting out of devils, and their power in that thing derived from him, they being at the present nonplussed, and not able to exert that power in the casting out of a devil, with which one was possessed, who in our Saviour's absence was brought to them. That which maketh this probable is, not only that this act of our Saviour more troubled and galled them than any other, and put them to that miserable refuge, (out of which our Saviour had lately beaten them,) to say, That he cast out devils by Beelzebub the prince of devils; but also that when our Saviour, coming in to the timely rescue of his disciples, *asked the scribes, What question ye with them?* it is said,

17 And ˡone of the multitude answered and said, Master, I have brought unto thee my son, which hath a dumb spirit;

l Matt. 17. 14. Luke 9. 38.

18 And wheresoever he taketh him, he ‖teareth him: and he foameth, and gnasheth with his teeth, and pineth away: and I spake to thy disciples that they should cast him out; and they could not.

‖ Or, *dasheth him.*

19 He answereth him, and saith, O faithless generation, how long shall I be with you? how long shall I suffer you? bring him unto me.

20 And they brought him unto him: and ᵐwhen he saw him, straightway the spirit tare him; and he fell on the ground, and wallowed foaming.

m ch. 1. 26. Luke 9. 42.

21 And he asked his father, How long is it ago since this came unto him? And he said, Of a child.

22 And ofttimes it hath cast him into the fire, and into the waters, to destroy him: but if thou canst do any thing, have compassion on us, and help us.

23 Jesus said unto him, ⁿIf thou canst believe, all things *are* possible to him that believeth.

n Matt. 17. 20. ch.11. 23. Luke 17. 6. John 11. 40.

24 And straightway the father of the child cried out, and said with tears, Lord, I believe; help thou mine unbelief.

25 When Jesus saw that the people came running together, he rebuked the foul spirit, saying unto him, *Thou* dumb and deaf spirit, I charge thee, come out of him, and enter no more into him.

26 And *the spirit* cried, and rent him sore, and came out of him: and he was as one dead; insomuch that many said, He is dead.

27 But Jesus took him by the hand, and lifted him up; and he arose.

28 ᵒAnd when he was come into the house, his disciples asked him privately, Why could not we cast him out?

o Matt. 17. 19.

29 And he said unto them, This kind can come forth by nothing, but by prayer and fasting.

This famous history is also recorded by two other evangelists, Matthew and Luke; we have opened it in our notes on Matt. xvii. 14—21, and considered what Mark and Luke have to complete it. For our instruction we may learn several things from the consideration of it: 1. The great goodness of God in preserving us from the power of evil spirits, as also the daily working of his providence for our preservation. What but this kept this man from being destroyed by the fires and the waters into which he had been often thrown by the evil spirit? 2. That the shorter the devil's time is, the more he rageth, ver. 20. This is true, both as to the devil himself, and his instruments: Rev. xii. 12, *The devil is come down unto you, having great wrath, because he knoweth that he hath but a short time.* Thus, in the moment of conversion Christians often meet with the strongest conflicts of temptation. 3. The fault is not in Christ, but in ourselves, if we receive not that mercy from him which he hath, and which we stand in need of, and beg from him—*If* (saith Christ) *thou canst believe.* 4. God rewardeth weak faith where it is attended with a sincere desire of increase. This poor man showed a very imperfect faith in saying, *If thou canst do any thing;* but it being in some degree sincere, the Lord rewardeth it, though weak, he desiring an increase of it, and that God would from his goodness supply what was defective in his faith. 5. The great cures both of our bodies and souls in some cases, require more extraordinary and importunate addresses and applications unto God, more especially where evils are more inveterate. For other things relating to this history, see the notes on Matt. xvii. 14—21.

30 ¶ And they departed thence, and passed through Galilee; and he would not that any man should know *it*.

^p Matt. 17. 22. Luke 9. 44.

31 ^pFor he taught his disciples, and said unto them, The Son of man is delivered into the hands of men, and they shall kill him; and after that he is killed, he shall rise the third day.

32 But they understood not that saying, and were afraid to ask him.

Our Saviour, as the time of his suffering approached more nearly, did more frequently inculcate it to his disciples, that being forewarned, they might also be forearmed against the temptation of it; and we learn from Luke xxiv. 21, that all was too little, for when they saw these things come to pass they began to flag as to their faith: they said, *But we trusted that it had been he which should have redeemed Israel.* Our Saviour *said unto them, The Son of man is delivered;* which is expounded by Matt. xvii. 22, 23, *The Son of man shall be betrayed.* He was already delivered in the sure counsel of God, and what God hath revealed shall be done, because of the certainty of the effect, is often in Scripture spoken of as a thing already done. That phrase, ver. 31, *the third day,* τῇ τρίτῃ ἡμέρα, expounds that other phrase which we meet with, chap. viii. 31, μετὰ τρεῖς ἡμέρας, which we translate *after three days,* and makes the meaning of the evangelists plain to have been as we determined it.

^q Mat. 18. 1. Luke 9. 46. & 22. 24.

33 ¶ ^qAnd he came to Capernaum: and being in the house he asked them, What was it that ye disputed among yourselves by the way?

34 But they held their peace: for by the way they had disputed among themselves, who *should be* the greatest.

This ambition of the disciples we have had occasion before to discourse of, in the notes on Matt. xviii. 1. It was founded upon their mistake of the true nature of the kingdom of the Messiah, which they at this time, and a long time after, (even to the time of Christ's ascension, as appeareth by Acts i. 6,) understood of a temporal, secular kingdom, in the administration of which he should deliver the Jews from all slavery and bondage: this made their minds so often run of dignities and places which he should, in that administration, have a power to dispose of. This made the mother of Zebedee's children petition for places for her two sons.

^r Matt. 20. 26, 27. ch. 10. 43.

35 And he sat down, and called the twelve, and saith unto them, ^rIf any man desire to be first, *the same* shall be last of all, and servant of all.

^s Mat. 18. 2. ch. 10. 16.

36 And ^she took a child, and set him in the midst of them: and when he had taken him in his arms, he said unto them,

37 Whosoever shall receive one of such children in my name, receiveth me:

^t Matt. 10. 40. Luke 9. 48.

and ^twhosoever shall receive me, receiveth not me, but him that sent me.

Matthew's recital of this passage expoundeth Mark; he saith Christ said, *Except ye be converted, and become as little children, ye shall not enter into the kingdom of heaven.* *Whosoever therefore shall humble himself as this little child, the same is greatest in the kingdom of God. And whoso shall receive one such little child in my name receiveth me.* Luke also relateth this passage something more shortly, but without any contradiction to what is said by the other evangelists. The sense is plain: our Saviour's design was to check the ambition and ignorance of his disciples, never more unseasonably showed than now, when a suffering time was so hard at hand. He at first did it by word of mouth, telling them, *If any man desire to be first, he shall be last of all,* the least valuable in the eyes of God, and he would have them value such a person least. Humility is that which most exalts a soul in the eyes of Christ, and setteth it highest in his esteem. But it is observable our Lord doth not say, he that is the first, but he who desireth to be first. God is a God of order, not of confusion; there can be no order without a first as well as a last. But Christians (ministers especially, for he is here speaking to the twelve) ought to be sought out for, not to seek places of pre-eminence and dignity: he that is first in seeking them, is usually last as to any true worth deserving them, and ought last to obtain them. Then he teacheth them humility by the type of a little child, which he setteth in the midst of them, telling them they must be like that little child, (saith Matthew,) not in all things, but in the want of ambition, in a carelessness as to the great things of this life. And whosoever entertained or showed kindness to such a one, Christ would take it as done to himself; and what kindness was showed him, reached not to him only, but to his Father who sent him. There are also other things in little children commended to us in holy writ, but this is manifestly what our Saviour here intendeth. See the notes on Matt. xviii. 1—5.

^u Num. 11. 28. Luke 9. 49.

38 ¶ ^uAnd John answered him, saying, Master, we saw one casting out devils in thy name, and he followeth not us: and we forbad him, because he followeth not us.

39 But Jesus said, Forbid him not:

^x 1 Cor. 12. 3

^xfor there is no man which shall do a miracle in my name, that can lightly speak evil of me.

^y See Matt. 12. 30.

40 For ^yhe that is not against us is on our part.

Here a question ariseth worthy of our discussion a little: Seeing these miraculous operations were performed by a Divine power, and for such an end as the confirmation of Christ's Divine power, how could any one cast out devils in the name of Christ, and yet not follow him and his disciples? 1. It is apparent that this person was no enemy to Christ or his gospel, by what our Saviour saith, both ver. 39 and 40. 2. It is evident that the casting out devils was no saving effect of the Holy Spirit. Christ saith, Matt. vii. 22, that some should say, *In thy name have we cast out devils,* to whom in the day of judgment he would say, *Depart from me,* I know you not, *ye that work iniquity.* 3. It is plain that this man was no such person as Sceva's sons, of whom we read Acts xix. 14—16, for the devils resisted them, though they also used the name of Christ. It was a time exceedingly famous for some of the more extraordinary gifts of the Holy Ghost, and it is not to be wondered if some in this time, for the glory of God, received some crumbs of that plentiful benevolence, though they were but imperfect disciples, yet being no enemies. Caiaphas prophesied, John xi. 51, 52; and though I do think that the children of the Pharisees, mentioned, Matt. xii. 27, as persons that cast out devils, is best interpreted of those sent out by Christ, (the twelve and the seventy,) yet some are of another mind. Some think this man, though he did not follow Christ and his disciples as a constant companion, yet was one who favoured and had received the gospel; or else one of John's disciples, and so one who, though he was not formally joined with the followers of Christ, yet was a friend of that great Bridegroom. So as John and the rest, forbidding him, seemed to be guilty of two no small errors: 1. Envying for Christ's sake, as Joshua did for Moses's sake, Numb. xi. 28, as John's disciples did for their master's sake, John iii. 26, willing that Christ, and

S. MARK IX

those whom he sent out, should have all the honour of those miraculous operations. 2. Limiting the grace of Christ to that congregation which followed Christ, and the twelve; a thing that good men are too prone unto. How much better was the spirit of Paul, who tells us, Phil. i. 15, 18, that although some preached Christ of envy and strife, yet he rejoiced, and would rejoice, that Christ was preached, whether in pretence, or in truth. Christ would have all his people of such a spirit, as not to hinder, but commend, not to envy, but to rejoice in the doing of good by any, whether they did follow him or no. Some think that at that time it pleased God, that, for the honour of his Son Jesus Christ, he did concur with those that named his name in such miraculous operations. Sure we are that Christ reproveth John, and commandeth them not to forbid this man, giving this for a reason, That his owning the name of Christ, so far as to use it in such an operation, had at least so much kindness for him as he was no enemy, he would not curse him, nor speak evil of him; which cometh up to that of the apostle, 1 Cor. xii. 3, *No man speaking by the Spirit of God calleth Jesus accursed; and no man can say Jesus is the Lord, but by the Holy Ghost.* For he that *is not against us is on our part*: if a man be not an open enemy to Christ, he ought to be presumed to be his friend, at least so far as not to be discouraged in doing a good work.

^z Matt. 10. 42.

41 ^z For whosoever shall give you a cup of water to drink in my name, because ye belong to Christ, verily I say unto you, he shall not lose his reward.

We meet with the same in substance, Matt. x. 42: there the phrase is, *in the name of a disciple*; here it is expounded, *because ye belong to Christ. In my name*; upon my account, believing you have a relation to me.

a Mat. 18. 6. Luke 17. 1.

42 ^a And whosoever shall offend one of these little ones that believe in me, it is better for him that a millstone were hanged about his neck, and he were cast into the sea.

See the notes on Matt. xviii. 6.

b Deu. 13. 6. Matt. 5. 29. & 18. 8. || Or, *cause thee to offend:* and so ver. 45, 47.

43 ^b And if thy hand || offend thee, cut it off: it is better for thee to enter into life maimed, than having two hands to go into hell, into the fire that never shall be quenched:

c Is. 66. 24. Judith 16. 17.

44 ^c Where their worm dieth not, and the fire is not quenched.

45 And if thy foot offend thee, cut it off: it is better for thee to enter halt into life, than having two feet to be cast into hell, into the fire that never shall be quenched:

46 Where their worm dieth not, and the fire is not quenched.

|| Or, *cause thee to offend.*

47 And if thine eye || offend thee, pluck it out: it is better for thee to enter into the kingdom of God with one eye, than having two eyes to be cast into hell fire:

48 Where their worm dieth not, and the fire is not quenched.

See the notes on Matt. v. 29, 30, where the same things occur. Matthew only mentions the hand and the eye. All have the same significancy, viz. that it is better to deny ourselves in some particular satisfaction, than to hazard eternal salvation for the gratifying the appetite in it.

49 For every one shall be salted with fire, ^d and every sacrifice shall be salted with salt.

d Lev. 2. 13. Ezek. 43. 24.

The phrase of this text is so difficult, and the sense of it so necessary to be understood, that it hath deservedly exercised the parts of many interpreters, and given them a latitude to abound in interpretations. Those who would rightly understand it, 1. Must have a retrospection to the six verses immediately preceding, where our Lord had persuaded to the mortification of our most beloved and profitable or pleasant lust, under the notion of cutting off the right hand or foot offending, and plucking out the right eye, under the penalty of going into a fire that shall never be quenched: as also to the law, Lev. ii. 13, which runs thus, *And every oblation of thy meat offering shalt thou season with salt; neither shalt thou suffer the salt of the covenant of thy God to be lacking from thy meat offering: with all thine offerings thou shalt offer salt.* 2. They must next consider the nature of salt and fire. It is of the nature of salt, by drying up the over-much moisture in meats, to preserve them from putrefaction; and to cause smart to living flesh. And of fire, to separate things not of the same kind in compounded bodies, and also to cause pain and smart. 3. They must know, that *every one* in the former part of the verse is the same with *every sacrifice* in the latter part; for every man and woman living will, or shall, be a sacrifice to God. Godly men are not only priests, 1 Pet. ii. 5, 9; Rev. i. 6; v. 10, but sacrifices, Rom. xii. 1. Wicked men, though indeed they be no priests, (voluntarily giving up themselves unto God,) yet they shall be sacrifices, like the *sacrifice in Bozrah*, Isa. xxxiv. 6, or *in the north country by the river Euphrates*, Jer. xlvi. 10: see also Ezek. xxxix. 17; Zeph. i. 7. The saints are both priests and sacrifices. These things premised, the difficulty of the text is not great. Our Lord had been in the former verses persuading the mortification of men's dearest lusts, under the notions of cutting off the right hand or foot, and plucking out the right eye; and pressing this exhortation, from the eligibleness of it, rather than (keeping them) to be thrust into hell, where the worm never dies, and where the fire never goeth out. Now saith he in this verse, *For every one shall be salted with fire, and every sacrifice shall be salted with salt.* God hath a fire, and a salt, which every man must endure. He hath a purging fire, to take away men's dross and tin. Some he baptizeth *with the Holy Ghost, and with fire,* Matt. iii. 11; Luke iii. 16. And he hath a consuming, tormenting fire, a *fiery indignation, which shall devour the adversaries,* Heb. x. 27. It is true, the Lord's sacred fire of his Holy Spirit will, like fire and salt, cause smart while it purgeth out our lusts, like the cutting off of a right hand or foot; but judge you whether it be not better to endure that smart than to endure hell-fire, for every one must endure one of these. Yea, and every one must be *salted with fire.* The saints shall be seasoned with influences of grace, Eph. iv. 29; Col. iv. 6; and they shall by the Holy Spirit of God be preserved by faith through the power of God to salvation, till their purity of heart and holiness of life shall issue in an incorruptibility of being and blessed state, 1 Cor. xv. 52—54. They shall be *salted* in or *with fire,* that is, preserved in or by the holy fire of God's Holy Spirit; (nor is salting with fire so hard a metaphor as being baptized with fire seems to be, nothing being so contrary to fire as water is;) others, viz. wicked and ungodly men, who will not endure this fire, nor be salted with this salt, shall yet be salted with another fire, and with another salt, which is the fire that never goes out, mentioned ver. 44, 46, 48, which will cause them a much greater pain and smart, and in which, being separated from all their comforts and satisfactions, they shall be salted, that is (as to their beings) preserved, that they may be the objects of the eternal wrath and justice of God; for every one must go through one or the other fire, every soul must be seasoned with the one or other salt. Now judge you then whether it be not more advisable for you to be seasoned with this salt, though you indeed shall endure some smart in your acts of mortification and self-denial, than to endure hell-fire, where you will be salted too, as well as burned; that is, not tormented only, but preserved in torments, so as you shall never consume, but be ever dying; for with one or other of these fires every person, every man or woman breathing, must be salted and seasoned, as of old every sacrifice was to be with salt.

50 ^e Salt *is* good: but if the salt have lost his saltness, wherewith will ye season it? ^f Have salt in yourselves, and ^g have peace one with another.

e Mat. 5. 13. Luke 14. 34. f Eph. 4. 29. Col. 4. 6. g Rom. 12. 18. & 14. 19. 2 Cor. 13. 11. Heb. 12. 14.

We met with the former part of this verse Matt. v.: see the notes on ver. 13. In that text he compared his disciples, whether preachers or others, to salt, because by their doctrine, and holy life and example, they as it were kept the world sweet. I do not see why we should not so understand him speaking here, understanding by *salt*, persons salted, seasoned with the knowledge of the doctrine of Christ, and with the fear and love of God. These are good. But if any appearing such, apostatize, or be lazy and inactive, what are they good for? or what shall season them? *Have salt in yourselves, and have peace one with another.* Here salt is taken in a little different sense. In the former sense themselves were the salt, here they are commanded to keep salt in themselves. They could not have been salt to season others, if themselves had not first been salted with gracious habits of knowledge, faith, love, fear of God : now saith our Saviour, Keep this salt in yourselves, let not this holy fire die from the altar, take heed of losing your savour. *And have peace one with another.* It is one thing in the nature of salt to unite and knit the parts of the body salted together, so as the upholding of a union and peace one with another will declare that you have salt in yourselves. By this (saith the apostle) we know we are translated from death to life, if we love the brethren. In order to which men must avoid envy, and emulation, and contests for superiority, &c.; a contest of which nature gave the first occasion of these discourses.

CHAP. X

Christ teacheth in Judea, 1; *answereth the Pharisees' question concerning divorce,* 2—12; *blesseth the children that were brought unto him,* 13—16; *instructeth a rich man how to attain eternal life,* 17—22; *showeth how hard it is for the rich to enter into the kingdom of God,* 23—27; *promiseth rewards to all who have forsaken aught for his gospel's sake,* 28—31; *foretelleth his own death and resurrection,* 32—34; *putteth by the ambitious suit of the sons of Zebedee, and checketh the indignation of the other disciples thereat,* 35—45; *giveth sight to blind Bartimeus,* 46—52.

A. D. 33.
a Mat. 19. 1.
John 10. 40.
& 11. 7.

AND ᵃhe arose from thence, and cometh into the coasts of Judæa by the farther side of Jordan : and the people resort unto him again; and, as he was wont, he taught them again.

We have nothing in this whole chapter but what we found before in the nineteenth and twentieth chapters of Matthew. When Christ had the discourses mentioned in the former chapter, he was in Galilee; now he departeth from Galilee, passeth through Samaria, and cometh into the province of Judea, which being the chiefest, and that in which Jerusalem was, he was there more than before troubled with the scribes and Pharisees; who were now watching him in all his words and actions, that they might have somewhat whereof to accuse him.

b Mat. 19. 3.

2 ¶ ᵇAnd the Pharisees came to him, and asked him, Is it lawful for a man to put away *his* wife? tempting him.

Matthew adds, *for every cause,* that is, for any cause, unless for adultery, for so the Pharisees had interpreted the law permitting divorce, Deut. xxiv. 1, taking advantage of those words, *that she find no favour in his eyes,* and interpreting the term *uncleanness* following, of any deformity, or other cause of dislike.

3 And he answered and said unto them, What did Moses command you?

c Deu. 24. 1.
Matt. 5. 31.
& 19. 7.

4 And they said, ᶜMoses suffered to write a bill of divorcement, and to put *her* away.

5 And Jesus answered and said unto them, For the hardness of your heart he wrote you this precept.

d Gen. 1. 27.
& 5. 2.

6 But from the beginning of the creation ᵈGod made them male and female.

e Gen. 2. 24.
1 Cor. 6. 16.
Eph. 5. 31.

7 ᵉFor this cause shall a man leave his father and mother, and cleave to his wife;

8 And they twain shall be one flesh : so then they are no more twain, but one flesh.

9 What therefore God hath joined together, let not man put asunder.

The order of the discourse as recorded by Mark something differeth from that in Matthew, but the evangelists were not so accurate in that, but took care only to set down the substance of the discourse, as appears from the relation of several other parts of the history. In the notes on Matt. xix. 3—6 the reader will find whatsoever stands in need of explication opened.

10 And in the house his disciples asked him again of the same *matter.*

11 And he saith unto them, ᶠWhosoever shall put away his wife, and marry another, committeth adultery against her.

f Mat. 5. 32.
& 19. 9.
Luke 16. 18.
Rom. 7. 3.
1 Cor. 7. 10, 11.

12 And if a woman shall put away her husband, and be married to another, she committeth adultery.

Matthew, chap. v. 32; xix. 9, interpreteth this passage of Mark, by adding those words, *except it be for fornication.* None but Mark alone hath what is in ver. 12, which concerneth the woman; which hath made some doubt whether the woman, in case of the husband's adultery, may sue a divorce from him, but the most judicious interpreters say there is an equal right on both sides. I am sure the reason is equal on both sides. The adultery of the husband dissolveth the tie and covenant of marriage, as well as the adultery of the wife. It is yet a more groundless and unreasonable opinion of some from the words of this and the parallel texts, that persons divorced may not marry again; as if God's end in the law of divorce in case of adultery were merely to separate the wife from the husband's bed. Whether the person that hath given the cause for the divorce may marry again, may be more disputed, not only because such persons are dead persons in the law of God, but because such a liberty granted would open a flood-gate to iniquity of that kind, while persons weary of their correlates should by this means gratify their lusts, and also obtain their desires. But I shall not determine it. Certain it is our Saviour here speaketh only of divorces for trivial causes, which the law of God doth not warrant; and in such cases the person marrying again must necessarily commit adultery, because the band of the former union holds. As to the question, whether divorces be lawful in no cases but that of adultery, see the notes on Matt. v. and xix.

13 ¶ ᵍAnd they brought young children to him, that he should touch them : and *his* disciples rebuked those that brought *them.*

g Matt. 19. 13. Luke 18. 15.

14 But when Jesus saw *it,* he was much displeased, and said unto them, Suffer the little children to come unto me, and forbid them not : for ʰof such is the kingdom of God.

h 1 Cor. 14. 20. 1 Pet. 2. 2.

15 Verily I say unto you, ⁱWhosoever shall not receive the kingdom of God as a little child, he shall not enter therein.

i Mat. 18. 3.

16 And he took them up in his arms, put *his* hands upon them, and blessed them.

This is reported both by Matthew and Luke, only they both omit what we here have, ver. 15. By *the kingdom of God,* is doubtless to be understood the word of God, or rather the grace of Christ in the gospel : he that doth not receive it with humility and modesty, without disputing, without malice, like a little child, shall never come into heaven.

17 ¶ ᵏAnd when he was gone forth into the way, there came one running, and kneeled to him, and asked him, Good Master, what shall I do that I may inherit eternal life?

k Matt. 19. 16. Luke 18. 18.

Luke saith he was a *ruler.* His question signified, that he believed such a thing as a happy eternal existence of good souls, and that he desired it, and that he was willing to do something in order to the obtaining a share and portion in it.

18 And Jesus said unto him, Why callest thou me good? *there is* none good but one, *that is,* God.

That is, originally good, and supremely good, or perfectly good. Herein our Saviour doth not deny himself to be God, but checked him who did not believe him such, yet called him God.

19 Thou knowest the commandments, ¹Do not commit adultery, Do not kill, Do not steal, Do not bear false witness, Defraud not, Honour thy father and mother.

<small>l Exod. 20. Rom. 13. 9.</small>

20 And he answered and said unto him, Master, all these have I observed from my youth.

That is, in that latitude to which the doctors of the Jewish church at that time expounded them.

21 Then Jesus beholding him loved him, and said unto him, One thing thou lackest: go thy way, sell whatsoever thou hast, and give to the poor, and thou shalt have ᵐtreasure in heaven: and come, take up the cross, and follow me.

<small>m Mat. 6. 19, 20. & 19. 21. Luke 12. 33. & 16. 9.</small>

22 And he was sad at that saying, and went away grieved: for he had great possessions.

See the notes on Matt. xix. 21, 22. Christ had a humane compassion towards so civil a person, but showeth him, that love was the fulfilling of the law, and that love is seen in a resolution to yield a universal obedience to the will of God. Our Saviour imposeth a special precept upon him, conjoined with two general precepts concerning all the disciples of Christ, to which his not yielding obedience showed that he was mistaken in his notion, that he had from his youth kept the commandments, though it might be true according to that law interpretation of them given by the Pharisees.

23 ¶ ⁿAnd Jesus looked round about, and saith unto his disciples, How hardly shall they that have riches enter into the kingdom of God!

<small>n Mat. 19. 23. Luke 18. 24.</small>

24 And the disciples were astonished at his words. But Jesus answereth again, and saith unto them, Children, how hard is it for them °that trust in riches to enter into the kingdom of God!

<small>o Job 31. 24. Ps. 52. 7. & 62. 10. 1 Tim. 6. 17.</small>

25 It is easier for a camel to go through the eye of a needle, than for a rich man to enter into the kingdom of God.

26 And they were astonished out of measure, saying among themselves, Who then can be saved?

27 And Jesus looking upon them saith, With men *it is* impossible, but not with God: for ᵖwith God all things are possible.

<small>p Jer. 32. 17. Matt. 19. 26. Luke 1. 37.</small>

See the notes on Matt. xix. 23—26, where the same history occurred, and all the additions to it here are opened.

28 ¶ ᑫThen Peter began to say unto him, Lo, we have left all, and have followed thee.

<small>q Mat. 19. 27. Luke 18. 28.</small>

29 And Jesus answered and said, Verily I say unto you, There is no man that hath left house, or brethren, or sisters, or father, or mother, or wife, or children, or lands, for my sake, and the Gospel's,

30 ʳBut he shall receive an hundredfold now in this time, houses, and brethren, and sisters, and mothers, and children, and lands, with persecutions; and in the world to come eternal life.

<small>r 2 Chron. 25. 9. Luke 18. 30.</small>

31 ˢBut many *that are* first shall be last; and the last first.

<small>s Matt. 19. 30. & 20. 16. Luke 13. 30.</small>

See the notes on Matt. xix. 27—30. Our Saviour having blessed the poor, especially such as had stripped themselves of all for his sake and the gospel's, Peter raised up hopes to himself, who had no riches to trust in or have his heart cleave unto, and had stripped himself of all that little he had to follow Christ. Christ assures him that neither he, nor any other that had done so, should by it lose any thing; for though in this life they should have persecutions, yet they should be amply rewarded in value, if not in kind, in this world, and with infinite happiness in the next.

32 ¶ ᵗAnd they were in the way going up to Jerusalem; and Jesus went before them: and they were amazed; and as they followed, they were afraid. ᵘAnd he took again the twelve, and began to tell them what things should happen unto him,

<small>t Mat. 20. 17. Luke 18. 31.</small>
<small>u ch. 8. 31. & 9. 31. Luke 9. 22 & 18. 31.</small>

33 *Saying,* Behold, we go up to Jerusalem; and the Son of man shall be delivered unto the Chief Priests, and unto the Scribes; and they shall condemn him to death, and shall deliver him to the Gentiles:

34 And they shall mock him, and shall scourge him, and shall spit upon him, and shall kill him: and the third day he shall rise again.

See the notes on Matt. xx. 17—19. This is at least the third time that our Saviour instructeth his disciples as to his passion, toward which he was now going, and that with such a readiness, that, to the amazement of his disciples, he led the way, and outwent them. It is observable that Christ here describeth his sufferings more particularly than before. He tells them here that he should be first *delivered to the chief priests and the scribes,* and they should *condemn him.* Then they should *deliver him to the Gentiles,* (such were the Romans and Pontius Pilate,) and they should *mock him, scourge him, spit on him,* put him to death, but he should rise again the third day. Luke adds, chap. xviii. 34, *They understood none of these things: and this saying was hid from them, neither knew they the things which were spoken.* How hardly do we believe what seems contrary to our interests! But we are to hear for the time to come. This premonition was afterwards of use to them, they remembered the words of Jesus when the things were come to pass. Preachers' words are not lost, though at present they be not believed or hearkened to.

35 ¶ ˣAnd James and John, the sons of Zebedee, come unto him, saying, Master, we would that thou shouldest do for us whatsoever we shall desire.

<small>x Mat. 20. 20.</small>

36 And he said unto them, What would ye that I should do for you?

37 They said unto him, Grant unto us that we may sit, one on thy right hand, and the other on thy left hand, in thy glory.

38 But Jesus said unto them, Ye know not what ye ask: can ye drink of the cup that I drink of? and be baptized with the baptism that I am baptized with?

39 And they say unto him, We can. And Jesus said unto them, Ye shall indeed drink of the cup that I drink of; and with the baptism that I am baptized withal shall ye be baptized:

40 But to sit on my right hand and on my left hand is not mine to give; but *it shall be given to them* for whom it is prepared.

41 ʸAnd when the ten heard *it,* they

<small>y Mat. 20. 24.</small>

began to be much displeased with James and John.

See the notes on Matt. xx. 20—24, where we have the same history with little or no variation, only Matthew tells us that James and John did that by their mother which Mark reports as done by them in person; but there is nothing more ordinary even in our common discourse than to speak of that as done by ourselves, which is done by another on our behalf, at our command or solicitation. Both the evangelists agree in all the other parts of their relation, and in the following discourse also very much.

^{z Luke 22. 25.}
^{|| Or, think good.}
42 But Jesus called them *to him*, and saith unto them, ^zYe know that they which || are accounted to rule over the Gentiles exercise lordship over them; and their great ones exercise authority upon them.

^{a Matt. 20. 26, 28. ch. 9. 35. Luke 9. 48.}
43 ^aBut so shall it not be among you: but whosoever will be great among you, shall be your minister:

44 And whosoever of you will be the chiefest, shall be servant of all.

^{b John 13. 14. Phil. 2. 7. c Mat. 20.28. 1 Tim. 2. 6. Tit. 2. 14.}
45 For even ^b the Son of man came not to be ministered unto, but to minister, and ^c to give his life a ransom for many.

See the notes on Matt. xx. 25—28, where we had the same almost verbatim. Those that think it worth the while to inquire what critical men say about that phrase, οἱ δοκοῦντες ἄρχειν, which we translate *they which are accounted to rule*, may find it in Pool's Synopsis Criticorum. When all is said, doubtless the οἱ ἄρχοντες in Matthew, and οἱ δοκοῦντες ἄρχειν, and Luke's οἱ βασιλεῖς, signify the same persons. And our translators might as justifiably have translated those words, *the rulers*, as *they which are accounted to rule*, which is a translation the active participle will hardly bear.

^{d Mat.20.29. Luke 18. 35.}
46 ¶ ^dAnd they came to Jericho: and as he went out of Jericho with his disciples and a great number of people, blind Bartimæus, the son of Timæus, sat by the highway side begging.

47 And when he heard that it was Jesus of Nazareth, he began to cry out, and say, Jesus, *thou* Son of David, have mercy on me.

48 And many charged him that he should hold his peace: but he cried the more a great deal, *Thou* Son of David, have mercy on me.

49 And Jesus stood still, and commanded him to be called. And they call the blind man, saying unto him, Be of good comfort, rise; he calleth thee.

50 And he, casting away his garment, rose, and came to Jesus.

51 And Jesus answered and said unto him, What wilt thou that I should do unto thee? The blind man said unto him, Lord, that I might receive my sight.

^{e Matt. 9.22. ch. 5. 34. || Or, saved thee.}
52 And Jesus said unto him, Go thy way; ^ethy faith hath || made thee whole. And immediately he received his sight, and followed Jesus in the way.

This history is a mere narrative of a matter of fact, in the relation of which no difficulties occur which stand in need of explication. Matthew, Mark, and Luke relate it with but two considerable differences. Matthew mentioneth two blind men, the other two evangelists but one. It is probable the one was the more remarkable, and his father a person of some note, therefore he is mentioned also; the other probably some obscurer person. Luke reports it done, *as he was come nigh unto Jericho;* Matthew and Mark, *as he went out of Jericho:* but though Luke saith that he sat begging by the way as they came nigh to Jericho, yet he doth not say the miracle of his cure was wrought then. It is most probable that he followed Christ into Jericho, crying after him, and also when he went out of Jericho, and that it was as he went out of Jericho (as Matthew and Mark say) that our Saviour took notice of him, called him, and wrought the cure upon him. See further the notes on Matt. xx. 29—34.

CHAP. XI

Christ rideth into Jerusalem in triumph, 1—11; *curseth a barren fig tree,* 12—14; *driveth the buyers and sellers out of the temple,* 15—19. *The cursed fig tree is dried up: Christ exhorteth to faith in prayer, and to forgiveness of enemies,* 20—26; *and silenceth the priests and others, who called in question his authority,* 27—33.

AND ^a when they came nigh to Jerusalem, unto Bethphage and Bethany, at the mount of Olives, he sendeth forth two of his disciples. ^{a Mat. 21. 1. Luke 19. 29. John 12. 14.}

Matthew saith nothing of Bethany, mentioned by Mark and Luke. It was the town of Lazarus, John xi. 1. Some think that Bethany was rather a tract of the Mount of Olives than a town, and that Bethphage was a kind of suburbs to Jerusalem, at the remotest part of which Bethany began, but the town itself called Bethany was fifteen furlongs, near two miles, from Jerusalem. It was the place from which Christ ascended to heaven, Luke xxiv. 50, a sabbath day's journey from Jerusalem, Acts i. 12, at some distance from the town called Bethany. From this place, called still Bethany, upon the borders of Bethphage, he sent out two of his disciples.

2 And saith unto them, Go your way into the village over against you: and as soon as ye be entered into it, ye shall find a colt tied, whereon never man sat; loose him, and bring *him*.

Matthew saith *an ass and a colt*. The other evangelists speak only of the colt. The heathens, by a light of nature showing them there was a reverence and honour due to the Divine Being, were wont, in the use they made of creatures for any Divine service, to use such as they had not before used for common uses: the Philistines, 1 Sam. vi. 7, sending home the ark, set it on a new cart, and took two milch kine on which there never came yoke. But our Saviour probably made choice of such a colt for the further notice of the miracle, (colts being when first backed more unruly,) or for some other wise end which we know not.

3 And if any man say unto you, Why do ye this? say ye that the Lord hath need of him; and straightway he will send him hither.

4 And they went their way, and found the colt tied by the door without in a place where two ways met; and they loose him.

5 And certain of them that stood there said unto them, What do ye, loosing the colt?

6 And they said unto them even as Jesus had commanded: and they let them go.

See the notes on Matt. xxi. 3, &c. All along the story of our Saviour's life and actions we shall find certain indications of his Divine power and virtue: his knowing men's thoughts, and declarations of such his knowledge to them: his certain prediction of future contingencies, being able to tell persons such particulars as no man could know. How could he who was not God have told the disciples, that at their entrance into the village they should find a colt on which never man sat, that the owners would not resist strangers to take it away? Yet notwithstanding all this his disciples very imperfectly believed him to be so, until he was risen from the dead. The time was not yet come when Christ would have this published, and till he gave them a power to believe it, i. e. to have a full persuasion of it, all these moral arguments were not sufficient to work in their hearts a full persuasion. The faith of the Christians of that time seemeth to have had these three gradations: 1. They believed him a great Prophet, that had received great power from God. 2. They owned him as the Messiah, as the Son of David, and now and then they would drop some expressions arguing some persuasions that he was the Son of God. 3. Last of all, they came to a firm persuasion that he was truly God, as well as man, after that he was risen from the dead, and declared with power to be such, as the apostle saith. Yet what means imaginable could they have had more than, 1. A voice from heaven declaring it. 2. The Spirit descending in a visible shape. 3. The great miracles he had wrought by sea and land, commanding the winds and the waves, healing incurable diseases and all others in an instant without use of rational means, raising the dead, &c. 4. His telling their thoughts, foretelling future contingencies, &c. Yet all these produced in the generality of the people no more than amazement and astonishment; and in the apostles themselves, rather a disposition to such a faith, or an opinion or suspicion of such a thing, than a firm and fixed persuasion concerning it.

7 And they brought the colt to Jesus, and cast their garments on him; and he sat upon him.

b Mat. 21. 8.   8 ᵇAnd many spread their garments in the way: and others cut down branches off the trees, and strawed *them* in the way.

9 And they that went before, and they c Ps. 118. 26. that followed, cried, saying, ᶜHosanna; Blessed *is* he that cometh in the name of the Lord:

10 Blessed *be* the kingdom of our father David, that cometh in the name of d Ps. 148. 1. the Lord: ᵈHosanna in the highest.

We met with all this Matt. xxi. 8, 9: see the notes there. It appeareth by our Saviour sending for the colt, that this little rural triumph, and the acclamations attending it, were designed by him both to show the people, 1. That he was the King whom God had promised to set upon his holy hill of Zion; and, 2. That his kingdom was not of this world. For, as he elsewhere saith, if his kingdom had been of this world, his servants would have fought for him. So it may be said, You may know his kingdom that he spake of was not of this world; for if it had there would have been found a more stately beast than the colt of an ass, or at least a saddle for that; the ways would have been covered with tapestry, rather than poor men's coats and cloaks; and other heralds would have been found than a company of children and poor men, crying *Hosanna*. This was such a thing as would but have ridiculed a government to be afraid of, nor indeed (to give Pontius Pilate, the Roman governor at this time in Jerusalem, his due) do we find him the least disturbed, though the scribes and Pharisees, (which were the Jewish churchmen,) seeing their kingdom going down, were something nettled; and though they had more modesty than to bring this little triumph in judgment against him, yet their great charge was, his declaring and making himself a King, in order to which this was the greatest show he ever made.

e Mat. 21. 12.   11 ᵉAnd Jesus entered into Jerusalem, and into the temple: and when he had looked round about upon all things, and now the eventide was come, he went out unto Bethany with the twelve.

f Mat. 21. 18.   12 ¶ ᶠAnd on the morrow, when they were come from Bethany, he was hungry:

g Mat. 21. 19.   13 ᵍAnd seeing a fig tree afar off having leaves, he came, if haply he might find any thing thereon: and when he came to it, he found nothing but leaves; for the time of figs was not *yet*.

14 And Jesus answered and said unto it, No man eat fruit of thee hereafter for ever. And his disciples heard *it*.

h Mat. 21. 12.
Luke 19. 45.
John 2. 14.   15 ¶ ʰAnd they come to Jerusalem: and Jesus went into the temple, and began to cast out them that sold and bought in the temple, and overthrew the tables of the money-changers, and the seats of them that sold doves;

16 And would not suffer that any man should carry *any* vessel through the temple.

17 And he taught, saying unto them, Is it not written, ⁱMy house shall be called ‖ of all nations the house of prayer? but ᵏye have made it a den of thieves.

i Is. 56. 7.
‖ Or, *an house of prayer for all nations?*
k Jer. 7. 11.
l Matt. 21. 45. 46.
Luke 19. 47.

18 And ˡthe Scribes and Chief Priests heard *it*, and sought how they might destroy him: for they feared him, because ᵐall the people was astonished at his doctrine.

m Mat. 7. 28.
ch. 1. 22.
Luke 4. 32.

19 And when even was come, he went out of the city.

See the notes on Matt. xxi. 12—17, where having so largely spoken to this part of the history, considering also what Mark and Luke hath to complete the history, few words will be needful about it here. Though Mark seems to relate it so, as if the first day Christ came into the temple, looked about it, and did no more till he came back from Bethany (whither he went that night) the next day, yet the other evangelists' relation of it would make one think otherwise, besides that interpreters think it not probable that our Saviour the first night should only look about, and patiently see and suffer those abuses; most do therefore think that our Saviour the first day did cast out those that sold and bought in the temple. In the notes upon Matthew we have given an account of the market in the court of the Gentiles, which was the outward court of the temple, where, through the covetousness of the priests, some say there were constant shops. In the temple there were, the most holy place, into which the priests only entered, and the holy place, into which entered all the circumcised, whether native Jews or proselytes: these two places they accounted holy. But there was also a court which they called the court of the Gentiles, of which they had no such esteem, but allowed the keeping of shops and markets in it, especially before the passover. Concerning our Saviour's driving out these buyers and sellers, see the notes on Matt. xxi. 12, 13. In those notes also I have fully opened the history concerning our Saviour's cursing the barren fig tree, and given what account interpreters do give of the difficulty arising from ver. 13, as to which I have nothing to add here, save this only, offering it to learned persons to consider, whether the sense of these words, οὐ γὰρ ἦν καιρὸς συκῶν, be any more than, *for there were no figs. He found nothing but leaves, for there were no figs*, as if it had been οὐ γὰρ ἦσαν σύκα. So as καιρὸς there should neither signify the common time when figs use to be ripe, nor yet signify the seasonableness of the year for figs, but particularly relate to that tree, which at that time had no figs. But enough hath been before said as to that text.

20 ¶ ⁿAnd in the morning, as they passed by, they saw the fig tree dried up from the roots.

n Mat. 21. 19.

21 And Peter calling to remembrance saith unto him, Master, behold, the fig tree which thou cursedst is withered away.

22 And Jesus answering saith unto them, ‖ Have faith in God.

‖ Or, *Have the faith of God*.

23 For °verily I say unto you, That whosoever shall say unto this mountain, Be thou removed, and be thou cast into the sea; and shall not doubt in his heart, but shall believe that those things which he saith shall come to pass; he shall have whatsoever he saith.

o Matt. 17. 20. & 21. 21.
Luke 17. 6.

See the notes on Matt. xxi. 21. It is I confess the opinion of many excellent interpreters, whom I reverence, that the main end of our Saviour's cursing and blasting this fig tree, was to let his disciples see in a type what would be the consequent of a spiritual barrenness. That spiritual barrenness is exceedingly dangerous is out of question; our Saviour teacheth us it plainly by another parable of the fig tree, Luke xiii. 6—9, and the apostle teacheth us it, Heb. vi. 7, 8. But I see nothing to guide us to any such interpretation of this action of his, which was a miraculous operation, by which as he, 1. Plainly showed his Divine power; so, 2. These verses inform us, that it was his design to show his people the power of faith, that is, a full persuasion, that whatsoever we ask of God according to his will, and which may tend to his glory, shall be done for us. Which interpretation of this action of our Saviour's solves all the difficulties relating to this story, about which interpreters have so disquieted themselves.

24 Therefore I say unto you, *p* What things soever ye desire, when ye pray, believe that ye receive *them*, and ye shall have *them*.

p Matt. 7. 7.
Luke 11. 9.
John 14. 13.
& 15. 7.
& 16. 24.
Jam. 1. 5, 6.

25 And when ye stand praying, *q* forgive, if ye have ought against any: that your Father also which is in heaven may forgive you your trespasses.

q Mat. 6. 14.
Col. 3. 13.

26 But *r* if ye do not forgive, neither will your Father which is in heaven forgive your trespasses.

r Matt. 18. 35.

See the notes on Matt. xxi. 22; vi. 14, 15; vii. 7; in which texts we before met with what we have in these verses, teaching us the necessity of faith and charity to those who would so pray as to find acceptance with God. This also lets us know the necessity of people's full satisfaction, that what things they ask of God in prayer are according to the will of God, without which it is not possible they should pray with a full persuasion that they shall receive whatsoever they in prayer ask of God. And because it is impossible we should in this point be fully satisfied, without a Divine revelation, as to things not necessary to salvation, our faith or persuasion can rise no higher, than a full persuasion, that if things of this nature, when we ask them of God in prayer, be such as are for our good, and for God's glory, we shall receive them. The cause was otherwise as to those to whom Christ had given a power to work miracles; what they asked of that nature they must know it was the will of God to effect by them, and they could not without sin doubt of it.

27 ¶ And they come again to Jerusalem: *s* and as he was walking in the temple, there come to him the Chief Priests, and the Scribes, and the elders,

s Mat. 21. 23.
Luke 20. 1.

28 And say unto him, By what authority doest thou these things? and who gave thee this authority to do these things?

Our Lord went every night to Bethany, (two miles, or near so much,) and returned in the morning to Jerusalem. Our Saviour walked and taught in the temple. Matthew saith the priests and the scribes came to him *as he was teaching*; Mark saith, *as he was walking*: possibly he at the same time both walked and taught, for in his whole story we shall observe that he lost no time, if he were walking by the highway, or sitting in the house, wherever he was, we still find him teaching. See the notes on Matt. xxi. 23, where we had the same thing.

29 And Jesus answered and said unto them, I will also ask of you one ‖ question, and answer me, and I will tell you by what authority I do these things.

‖ Or, *thing*.

30 The baptism of John, was *it* from heaven, or of men? answer me.

31 And they reasoned with themselves, saying, If we shall say, From heaven; he will say, Why then did ye not believe him?

32 But if we shall say, Of men; they feared the people: for *t* all *men* counted John, that he was a prophet indeed.

t Matt. 3. 5.
& 14. 5.
ch. 6. 20.

33 And they answered and said unto Jesus, We cannot tell. And Jesus answering saith unto them, Neither do I tell you by what authority I do these things.

See the notes on Matt. xxi. 24—27, where are the same passages opened. *A prophet* here, ver. 32, signifieth, one extraordinarily inspired and sent of God to reveal his will, so as his baptism must needs be from heaven. This reputation John it seems universally had, so as to have denied his baptism to have been from heaven, had been to have exposed themselves to the mockings, if not the rage, of the people, which they were loth to do. If they had said, *From heaven*, they had accused themselves for not believing him, John vii. 48. This makes them choose rather to make themselves doubtful in the case, and giveth our Saviour a fitting occasion to deny them satisfaction as to what they asked of him.

CHAP. XII

In the parable of the vineyard let out to wicked husbandmen Christ foretelleth the reprobation of the Jews, and the calling of the Gentiles, 1—12. His reply to the insidious question concerning paying tribute to Cæsar, 13—17. He confuteth the Sadducees who questioned him concerning the resurrection, 18—27. He showeth which are the two great commandments of the law, 28—34. He proposeth a difficulty to the scribes concerning the character of Christ, 35—37. He cautioneth the people against their ambition and hypocrisy, 38—40; and valueth the poor widow's two mites above all the gifts of the rich, 41—44.

AND *a* he began to speak unto them by parables. A *certain* man planted a vineyard, and set an hedge about *it*, and digged *a place for* the winefat, and built a tower, and let it out to husbandmen, and went into a far country.

a Matt. 21. 33. Luke 22. 9.

2 And at the season he sent to the husbandmen a servant, that he might receive from the husbandmen of the fruit of the vineyard.

3 And they caught *him*, and beat him, and sent *him* away empty.

4 And again he sent unto them another servant; and at him they cast stones, and wounded *him* in the head, and sent *him* away shamefully handled.

5 And again he sent another; and him they killed, and many others; beating some, and killing some.

6 Having yet therefore one son, his wellbeloved, he sent him also last unto them, saying, They will reverence my son.

7 But those husbandmen said among themselves, This is the heir; come, let us kill him, and the inheritance shall be our's.

8 And they took him, and killed *him*, and cast *him* out of the vineyard.

9 What shall therefore the lord of the vineyard do? he will come and destroy the husbandmen, and will give the vineyard unto others.

10 And have ye not read this Scripture; *b* The stone which the builders rejected is become the head of the corner:

b Ps. 118. 22.

11 This was the Lord's doing, and it is marvellous in our eyes?

12 *c* And they sought to lay hold on him, but feared the people: for they knew that he had spoken the parable against them: and they left him, and went their way.

c Matt. 21. 45, 46. ch. 11. 18. John 7. 25, 30, 44.

This parable is related by Matthew, and by Luke also: see the notes on Matt. xxi. 33—46. The twelfth verse telleth us, that the rulers of the Jewish church knew that he had spoken this parable *against them*, and they needs must know it, considering what Matthew adds to this parable, (which Mark and Luke have not,) that he also told them, Matt. xxi. 43, *Therefore say I unto you, The kingdom of God shall be taken from you, and given to a nation bringing forth the fruits thereof.* By the man planting a vineyard, is to be understood God, who, Psal. lxxx. 8—11, *brought a vine out of Egypt*, and *cast out the heathen, and planted it* in the land of Canaan, and *prepared room for it, and caused it to take deep root, and it filled the land. The hills were covered with the shadow of it, and the boughs thereof were like the goodly cedars. She sent out her boughs unto the sea, and her branches unto the river.* It was a *noble vine, a right seed,* Jer. ii. 21. God planted it *in a fruitful hill; he fenced it, and gathered out the stones thereof, and built a tower in the midst of it, and also made a winepress therein: and he looked that it should bring forth grapes,* Isa. v. 1, 2. The church of the Jews then was this vineyard, which God hedged by his providence, and gave them all means necessary for the production of fruit. The servants sent to receive the fruit, so abused by the husbandmen, (as ver. 2—5,) were the prophets. 2 Chron. xxxvi. 16 is a compendious exposition of these verses. *They mocked the messengers of God, and despised his words, and misused his prophets.* The son mentioned as sent at last was Christ, and the latter part of the parable is prophetical, foretelling what they should do unto him, and also of the ruin of the Jewish nation and church, and the passing of the gospel to the Gentiles, who should more freely believe in Christ, and embrace and receive the gospel: so as they should not obtain their end; but Christ, though rejected by them, should yet be the Head of a far larger and more glorious church, according to a prophecy owned by themselves as a piece of holy writ, Psal. cxviii. 22. See more in the notes on Matt. xxi. 33, &c.

d Matt. 22. 15. Luke 20. 20.

13 ¶ [d]And they send unto him certain of the Pharisees and of the Herodians, to catch him in *his* words.

14 And when they were come, they say unto him, Master, we know that thou art true, and carest for no man: for thou regardest not the person of men, but teachest the way of God in truth: Is it lawful to give tribute to Cæsar, or not?

15 Shall we give, or shall we not give? But he, knowing their hypocrisy, said unto them, Why tempt ye me? bring me a ‖ penny, that I may see *it.*

‖ Valuing of our money seven pence halfpenny, as Matt. 18. 28.

16 And they brought *it.* And he saith unto them, Whose *is* this image and superscription? And they said unto him, Cæsar's.

17 And Jesus answering said unto them, Render to Cæsar the things that are Cæsar's, and to God the things that are God's. And they marvelled at him.

See the notes on Matt. xxii. 15—22.

e Matt. 22. 23. Luke 20. 27. f Acts 23. 8.

18 ¶ [e]Then come unto him the Sadducees, [f]which say there is no resurrection; and they asked him, saying,

The Sadducees most probably derived their name from one Sadoc, scholar to Antigonus Sochæus. It is said that the occasion of their heresy was their master's teaching them, that they must not serve God as servants for rewards. Upon which they builded their notion, that there is no resurrection, no rewards nor punishments in another life. They denied the immortality of the soul, and the resurrection of the body, and angels, and spirits, Acts xxiii. 8; attributed all to free will, denying fate and destiny; they rejected traditions, and owned no Scriptures but the five books of Moses. They seemed to be a kind of rational divines, that would own and believe nothing but what they could fathom by their reason, or was obvious to their sense; and their doctrine was excellently suited to men's lusts, who desire not to be troubled with any thoughts of a world to come. Nothing more shows the degeneracy and debauchery of human nature than this, that to gratify their sensual appetites more freely in the things of this life, they will be content to think of annihilation, (which nature not debauched abhors,) and of quitting all hopes of eternal life and happiness, that they may have a principle to warrant their living like beasts. They come to our Saviour, thinking to flout him and his hearers out of the doctrine of the resurrection, as having insuperable difficulties to clog it. But he that takes the wise in their own craftiness, shows these wise men, that all their wisdom was but folly, and their argument wholly proceeded *ex ignoratione elenchi,* from their not understanding the thing they would philosophize about.

19 Master, [g]Moses wrote unto us, If a man's brother die, and leave *his* wife behind *him,* and leave no children, that his brother should take his wife, and raise up seed unto his brother.

g Deu. 25. 5.

20 Now there were seven brethren: and the first took a wife, and dying left no seed.

21 And the second took her, and died, neither left he any seed: and the third likewise.

22 And the seven had her, and left no seed: last of all the woman died also.

23 In the resurrection therefore, when they shall rise, whose wife shall she be of them? for the seven had her to wife.

24 And Jesus answering said unto them, Do ye not therefore err, because ye know not the Scriptures, neither the power of God?

25 For when they shall rise from the dead, they neither marry, nor are given in marriage; but [h]are as the angels which are in heaven.

h 1 Cor. 15. 42, 49, 52.

26 And as touching the dead, that they rise: have ye not read in the book of Moses, how in the bush God spake unto him, saying, [i]I *am* the God of Abraham, and the God of Isaac, and the God of Jacob?

i Ex. 3. 6.

27 He is not the God of the dead, but the God of the living: ye therefore do greatly err.

The true question about the resurrection was, Whether the bodies of the dead shall rise or no? not whether they shall arise with the same qualities, affections, powers, &c. They are sown natural, but they shall rise spiritual bodies, without affections and qualities disposing them to actions only necessary for the supporting the natural life, such as hunger and thirst, &c.; or for the upholding the world, that while one generation passeth it might be supplied by another, such as an appetite to marriage, &c.: what needs this when all generations shall be determined in the everlasting world? So as in truth these learned men showed themselves dunces, wholly ignorant of what they came to argue upon. They should first have proved that there would be any need of wives, or any such thing as marriage, after the world should have an end. In the mean time our Saviour proveth the resurrection out of the writings of Moses, owned by themselves for holy writ. Without a resurrection Abraham would not be Abraham, nor Isaac Isaac, nor Jacob Jacob. See the notes on this part of the history, Matt. xxii. 24—32.

28 ¶ [k]And one of the Scribes came, and having heard them reasoning together, and perceiving that he had answered them well, asked him, Which is the first commandment of all?

k Matt. 22. 35.

29 And Jesus answered him, The first of all

the commandments is, ¹Hear, O Israel; The Lord our God is one Lord :

30 And thou shalt love the Lord thy God with all thy heart, and with all thy soul, and with all thy mind, and with all thy strength : this *is* the first commandment.

31 And the second *is* like, *namely* this, ᵐThou shalt love thy neighbour as thyself. There is none other commandment greater than these.

32 And the Scribe said unto him, Well, Master, thou hast said the truth : for there is one God ; ⁿand there is none other but he:

33 And to love him with all the heart, and with all the understanding, and with all the soul, and with all the strength, and to love *his* neighbour as himself, ᵒis more than all whole burnt offerings and sacrifices.

34 And when Jesus saw that he answered discreetly, he said unto him, Thou art not far from the kingdom of God. ᵖAnd no man after that durst ask him *any question.*

See the notes on Matt. xxii. 35—40, where whatsoever Mark here hath is opened.

35 ¶ ᑫAnd Jesus answered and said, while he taught in the temple, How say the Scribes that Christ is the Son of David ?

36 For David himself said ʳby the Holy Ghost, ˢThe LORD said to my Lord, Sit thou on my right hand, till I make thine enemies thy footstool.

37 David therefore himself calleth him Lord ; and whence is he *then* his son? And the common people heard him gladly.

See the notes on Matt. xxii. 41—46. Matthew saith that Christ spake this to the Pharisees, who were very far from acknowledging Christ God-man, or indeed expecting a Messiah that should be so. Had they owned Christ, and the hypostatical union of the two natures in him, the answer had been easy.

38 ¶ ᵗAnd ᵗhe said unto them in his doctrine, ᵘBeware of the Scribes, which love to go in long clothing, and ˣ*love* salutations in the marketplaces,

39 And the chief seats in the synagogues, and the uppermost rooms at feasts :

40 ʸWhich devour widows' houses, and for a pretence make long prayers : these shall receive greater damnation.

See the notes on Matt. xxiii. 5—7, 14. The more men and women want of real worth and value, the more they seek themselves a reputation from their habits, either the gravity, or the riches and gaudery, of them ; and the more they court titles of honour and dignity, and affect external respect. Whereas nobler souls despise these things, being like pictures well drawn, which need no superscription to tell men what or whose they are. Good men are satisfied from themselves, and as not careless of their reputation, so neither careful who men say that they are. But these verses are more fully discoursed on Matt. xxiii., to which I refer the reader for satisfaction.

41 ¶ ᶻAnd Jesus sat over against the treasury, and beheld how the people cast ‖ money ᵃinto the treasury : and many that were rich cast in much

42 And there came a certain poor widow, and she threw in two ‖ mites, which make a farthing.

43 And he called *unto him* his disciples, and saith unto them, Verily I say unto you, That ᵇthis poor widow hath cast more in, than all they which have cast into the treasury :

44 For all *they* did cast in of their abundance ; but she of her want did cast in all that she had, ᶜ*even* all her living.

This is the only piece of history in this chapter which we did not before meet with in Matthew. Luke hath this, chap. xxi. 1—4. For the understanding of this history, both as to the letter and profitable instruction arising from it, we must know, that in the temple (where our Saviour now was) there was a treasury, or rather treasuries. And famous Dr. Lightfoot saith, there were treasure chambers, called *Lesacoth*, and thirteen treasure chests, called *Shopheroth*, all called by the general name of *Corban* or *Corbonah*. Two of these chests were for the half-shekel, which every Israelite was to pay according to the law, Exod. xxx. 12, 13. There were eleven more, the inscription upon which showed what money should be put there. 1. For the price of the two turtle doves, or two young pigeons. 2. For the burnt-offering of birds. 3. For the money offered to buy wood for the altar. 4. For those who gave money to buy frankincense. 5. For those who offered gold for the mercy-seat. 6. For the residue of the money for the sin-offering. 7. For the residue of the money for a trespass-offering. 8. For the residue of an offering of birds. 9. For the surplus of a Nazarite's offering. 10. For the residue of a leper's trespass-offering. 11. For whosoever would offer an offering of the herd. The Israelites, tied to their several offerings, were not tied to provide them themselves, but they might bring sums of money, with which the priests provided them, and if there were a surpulsage, it was put into one or other of these chests. These chests were placed in that part of the temple which was called the court of the women, not because none but women might come there, but because women might go no further, as the court of the Gentiles (into which Jews came) was so called because the Gentiles might go no further. Our Lord so sat, as he observed men come and put their offerings into one of these chests. He saw many Jews that were rich casting in much money of silver, or gold, or brass, though brass money was most in use. Amongst others a poor widow came ; *she threw in two mites, which make a farthing.* As to the value of what she threw in, let us hear the learned Dr. Lightfoot in his Temple Service, chap. xix. " The weight of the piece of silver mentioned in the law, was three hundred and twenty barley-corns. The wise men added to it, and made it four hundred and eighty-four middle barley-corns. This made four Denarii ; each Denarius made six Meahs, which in Moses's time was called a Gerah. The Meah made two Pondions ; the Pondion made two Issarines or Assariusses. The Assarius, or Issarine, was the weight of four barley-corns, the weight of a mite was half a barley-corn." According to this rate, the widow's two mites made in silver the weight of a middle barley-corn. This our Saviour calls *all that she had*, and *all her living*. The Greek is *all her life*, that is, all that she had to sustain her life. Arias Montanus thinks that that which is meant is, all that she had to uphold her life for one day. For it is said, that this quantity was usually reckoned the livelihood, or a sufficiency, for a poor man for a day. Christ saith, she had cast in more than any of the rest ; not more strictly, but *pro rata*, comparing what they were able to do with what she was able to do. The two great instructions which this history affords us are, 1. That the poorer sort of people are not excused from good works, 2 Cor. viii. 2, 3. 2. That God in his acceptation of our good works looks at the heart, the will, and affections, not at the quantum of what we do : *If there be first a willing mind, it is accepted according to that a man hath, and not according to that he hath not,* 2 Cor. viii. 12. It is the obedience and love which God accepteth, not the quantum of the gift

CHAP. XIII

Christ foretelleth the destruction of the temple, 1, 2; showeth what signs and calamities should go before, 3—23, and what should happen at the time of his coming, 24—31; no man knoweth the day or hour; we must therefore watch and pray, that we may not be found unprepared, 32—37.

[a Mat. 24. 1. Luke 21. 5.] AND ᵃ as he went out of the temple, one of his disciples saith unto him, Master, see what manner of stones and what buildings *are here!*

2 And Jesus answering said unto him, [b Luke 19. 44.] Seest thou these great buildings? ᵇ there shall not be left one stone upon another, that shall not be thrown down.

The perishing nature of the splendid and gay things of this world, are fitter objects for the meditation of such as are Christ's disciples, than the splendour and magnificence of them, especially when they are the privileges of a sinful people. Sin will undermine and blow up the most famous structures. It is a good thing for Christians not to set their hearts upon them. See the notes on Matt. xxiv. 1, 2.

3 And as he sat upon the mount of Olives over against the temple, Peter and James and John and Andrew asked him privately,

[c Mat. 24. 3. Luke 21. 7.] 4 ᶜ Tell us, when shall these things be? and what *shall be* the sign when all these things shall be fulfilled?

Matthew puts two things more into the question, *What shall be the sign of thy coming, and of the end of the world?* The best of men have a great curiosity to know futurities, things that shall hereafter come to pass. All the other part of this chapter is spent by our Saviour in an answer to these three questions, according to St. Matthew, or this one question, according to Mark and Luke. Some have attempted curiously to distinguish betwixt the signs intended by our Saviour, as relating to each period. But certainly those interpreters do judge best, that think our Saviour intended to let them know, that the destruction of Jerusalem should be a type of the destruction of the world at the last day, and that the same things should go before the one, and be signs of it, that should go before the other. And whoso readeth the history of Josephus, of what happened before the destruction of Jerusalem, and after this time, will find that there were few or none of these signs, that are here mentioned, but came to pass before the dreadful destruction of that so famous place; yet we must doubtless look for many, if not all, the same things to come to pass before the general destruction of the world in the last day.

5 And Jesus answering them began to say, ᵈ Take heed lest any *man* deceive [d Jer. 29. 8. Eph. 5. 6. 1 Thes. 2. 3.] you:

6 For many shall come in my name, saying, I am *Christ;* and shall deceive many.

See the notes on Matt. xxiv. 4, 5. This is the first sign, fulfilled before the destruction of Jerusalem in part, and which hath been fulfilling ever since; and probably before the day of judgment the number of such impostors will increase.

7 And when ye shall hear of wars and rumours of wars, be ye not troubled: for *such things* must needs be; but the end *shall* not *be* yet.

8 For nation shall rise against nation, and kingdom against kingdom: and there [e Mat. 24. 8. ‖ The word in the original importeth *the pains of a woman in travail.*] shall be earthquakes in divers places, and there shall be famines and troubles: ᵉ these *are* the beginnings of ‖ sorrows.

Matthew adds *pestilences.* Luke saith, *pestilences, and fearful sights and great signs from heaven.* See the notes on Matt. xxiv. 6—8. Here are two or three more signs put together: 1. *Wars, and rumours of wars;* great commotions in nations, which though they may be at other times, yet probably may be more extraordinary before the day of judgment. 2. *Famines, pestilences,* and *earthquakes.* 3. *Fearful sights,* and apparitions in the air and the heavens. Such there were (as Josephus tells us) before the destruction of Jerusalem; and though these things be seen before the last day, yet it is most probable they will be greater before the day of judgment than at any time before; and for *fearful sights, and great signs from heaven,* they ordinarily go before some great judgment of God upon places, and therefore the observation of them by the heathen (as we learn by Livy and others) seems but to be a piece of natural religion; and Christ giving these things as signs of the approaching ruin, first of Jerusalem, then of the world, will make thinking Christians behold them with a religious fear, though not to undertake to expound them particularly or prophesy upon them. Certainly we ought to look upon them as prognosticating some great work of God, and usually of judgment upon sinners.

9 ¶ But ᶠ take heed to yourselves: for [f Mat. 10. 17, 18. & 24. 9. Rev. 2. 10.] they shall deliver you up to councils; and in the synagogues ye shall be beaten: and ye shall be brought before rulers and kings for my sake, for a testimony against them.

This, so far as concerneth those to whom Christ spake, can only be a sign of the destruction of Jerusalem; but so far as it concerneth others, it is also a sign of the end of the world. It is the fifth sign he gives them; the persecution of the ministers of Christ and the saints of God, for the preaching and profession of the gospel. See the notes on Matt. xxiv. 9.

10 And ᵍ the Gospel must first be published among all nations. [g Mat. 24. 14.]

I am prone to think that our Lord gives this not only as a sign of the destruction of Jerusalem, but of the end of the world, and the latter principally; for before the destruction of Jerusalem (which was in less than forty years after Christ's death) the gospel was not preached to *all nations,* otherwise than as *all* signifies *very many.* And I do think that all places shall have the gospel preached to them before the day of judgment, after another manner than either it was possible it should be preached to them within forty years after the death of Christ, or than many places have had it preached amongst them to this day. For though the Holy Scriptures, and ecclesiastical historians, give us a somewhat large account of the gospel being preached in Europe, Asia, and in Africa, yet we have little account from any of them of its being preached in America. I am not wholly ignorant of what those writers tell us, of Thomas the apostle's preaching to the Indians, and of Trumentius and his colleague, but there are very few preachers that any stories give an account of gone to the Indians, whither I believe the gospel must go before that Christ comes to judgment.

11 ʰ But when they shall lead *you,* and [h Mat. 10. 19. Luke 12. 11. & 21. 14.] deliver you up, take no thought beforehand what ye shall speak, neither do ye premeditate: but whatsoever shall be given you in that hour, that speak ye: for it is not ye that speak, ⁱ but the Holy [i Acts 2. 4. & 4. 8, 31.] Ghost.

See the notes on Matt. x. 19, 20. By *take no thought,* he means, take no anxious thoughts to disquiet yourselves.

12 Now ᵏ the brother shall betray the [k Mic. 7. 6. Matt. 10. 21. & 24. 10. Luke 21. 16.] brother to death, and the father the son; and children shall rise up against *their* parents, and shall cause them to be put to death.

13 ˡ And ye shall be hated of all *men* [l Matt. 24. 9. Luke 21. 17. m Dan. 12. 12. Mat. 10. 22. & 24. 13. Rev. 2. 10.] for my name's sake: but ᵐ he that shall endure unto the end, the same shall be saved.

This is but an amplification of the fifth sign, given us ver. 9, viz. a furious persecution, eminently made good in the Jewish persecution before the destruction of Jerusalem;

14 ¶ ⁿBut when ye shall see the abomination of desolation, °spoken of by Daniel the prophet, standing where it ought not, (let him that readeth understand,) then ᵖlet them that be in Judæa flee to the mountains:

15 And let him that is on the housetop not go down into the house, neither enter *therein*, to take any thing out of his house:

16 And let him that is in the field not turn back again for to take up his garment.

17 ᵠBut woe to them that are with child, and to them that give suck in those days!

18 And pray ye that your flight be not in the winter.

19 ʳFor *in* those days shall be affliction, such as was not from the beginning of the creation which God created unto this time, neither shall be.

20 And except that the Lord had shortened those days, no flesh should be saved: but for the elect's sake, whom he hath chosen, he hath shortened the days.

See the notes on Matt. xxiv. 15—22, where we have before opened all these passages. This sign doth manifestly relate to the destruction of Jerusalem, and can have no relation to the end of the world. In our notes on Matt. xxiv. we have showed what is meant by the *abomination of desolation*, and to what place in Daniel it referreth. Luke expoundeth it, chap. xxi. 20, *When ye shall see Jerusalem compassed with armies*, the Roman armies, abominable for the idols that in them were worshipped. The sign was this, When you shall see the Roman armies besieging Jerusalem, be assured God will soon deliver it into their hands, whatever vain hopes men may suggest of their holding out or driving them away. Let every one of you with all imaginable expedition shift for yourselves. God will surely deliver up the city, when that time comes. And before the taking of the city, he tells them, there shall be such affliction (by reason of their intestine factions and divisions) as never any people experienced. As to these things, see the notes on Matt. xxiv. 15—22.

21 ˢAnd then if any man shall say to you, Lo, here *is* Christ; or, lo, *he is* there; believe *him* not:

22 For false Christs and false prophets shall rise, and shall shew signs and wonders, to seduce, if *it were* possible, even the elect.

23 But ᵗtake ye heed: behold, I have foretold you all things.

See the notes on Matt. xxiv. 23—25. The history of Josephus, and those Roman historians who wrote the history of those times that went immediately before the destruction of Jerusalem, and give us account of the taking of that city, are the best commentary on these verses. It hath been often said, that the Jews were in expectation of a Messias, and are so still. But by him they understood not a person who should be God-man, and save his people from their sins, and set up a spiritual kingdom in the world, but a secular prince, who should come of the house of David, and restore them to their civil liberties. So that the name of Christ was a fair name to patronize any rebellious faction, where the leader would arrogate it to himself, especially if he could pretend to the house of David. Near the destruction of Jerusalem, several persons used these arts to draw people after them to defend themselves, and to stand up for their liberties. Our Saviour having discerned his disciples tinctured with this common error of the nation, and knowing what would come to pass, gives his disciples warning to avoid these delusions, and not to run after such pretenders, to their ruin and destruction.

24 ¶ ᵘBut in those days, after that tribulation, the sun shall be darkened, and the moon shall not give her light,

25 And the stars of heaven shall fall, and the powers that are in heaven shall be shaken.

26 ˣAnd then shall they see the Son of man coming in the clouds with great power and glory.

27 And then shall he send his angels, and shall gather together his elect from the four winds, from the uttermost part of the earth to the uttermost part of heaven.

The usage of these phrases, of the darkening the sun and the moon, and the falling of the stars, to signify the ruin of nations, and changes wrought in them; as in Isa. xiii. 10, as to the destruction of Babylon, and Ezek. xxxii. 7, to express the change the providence of God made by the destruction of Egypt, as also to signify the change made in the world by setting up the gospel, to which purpose they are used by Joel, chap. ii. 31; hath given interpreters a latitude to interpret these verses, 1. With relation to the destruction of the Jews, which made a great change as to the Jewish church and state. 2. And with reference to the change made by setting up the gospel church. But the 26th and 27th verses incline me rather to interpret them of the end of the world. For though those other expressions are used to express great changes and mutations, yet it is not said of any of them, *Then shall they see the Son of man coming in the clouds with great power and glory. And then shall he send his angels*, &c. Which phrases do so agree with those other texts, where Christ's second coming to judgment is expressed certainly, that I cannot but think our Saviour speaks here with reference to that. See Matt. xiii. 41; 1 Cor. xv. 52; 1 Thess. iv. 16; Rev. i. 7.

28 ʸNow learn a parable of the fig tree; When her branch is yet tender, and putteth forth leaves, ye know that summer is near:

29 So ye in like manner, when ye shall see these things come to pass, know that it is nigh, *even* at the doors.

30 Verily I say unto you, that this generation shall not pass, till all these things be done.

31 Heaven and earth shall pass away: but ᶻmy words shall not pass away.

See the notes on Matt. xxiv. 32—35, where we met with the same things almost word for word; so as more words need not be repeated here in the explication of these verses.

32 ¶ But of that day and *that* hour knoweth no man, no, not the angels which are in heaven, neither the Son, but the Father.

33 ᵃTake ye heed, watch and pray: for ye know not when the time is.

See the notes on Matt. xxiv. 36, 42. *Ideo latet ultimus dies ut observentur omnes dies*, God hath concealed from us the knowledge of the last day that we might watch all our days. See the notes on Matthew, in what sense Christ saith he did not know the last day and hour. Watching is opposed to sleeping. There is a natural sleep, and a spiritual sleep, of which the apostle speaks, Rom. xiii. 11; Eph. v. 14. The latter is here principally intended, to which the watching here commanded is opposed, and signifies an industrious, diligent care to keep ourselves from sin, upon a prospect of the last judgment, and the consideration of the uncertainty of the particular year or day when it shall be; together with such a bodily watching, as may be subservient unto that end, and fit us for prayer. But the watching principally intended, is a striving against sin, which is the spiritual sleep; and thus it is expounded by Luke, chap. xxi. 36, compared with ver. 34, 35.

34 ᵇ*For the Son of man is* as a man

S. MARK XIII, XIV

taking a far journey, who left his house, and gave authority to his servants, and to every man his work, and commanded the porter to watch.

^{c Matt. 24. 42, 44.} 35 ^c Watch ye therefore: for ye know not when the master of the house cometh, at even, or at midnight, or at the cock-crowing, or in the morning:

36 Lest coming suddenly he find you sleeping.

37 And what I say unto you I say unto all, Watch.

In the Greek, those words, *For the Son of man is*, are not, but those, or some such like, are necessarily to be understood to make up the sense. The watching here again twice called for is the same with that before mentioned. The sense of these verses is the same as before; the uncertainty of the time when Christ cometh to judgment should oblige all men to be diligent and industrious to keep themselves from sinning, that they may be ready at what time soever he cometh. He mentions only the four parts of the night, having spoken of sin under the notion of sleeping, and holiness under the notion of watching.

CHAP. XIV

The chief priests and scribes conspire against Christ, 1, 2. *A woman poureth precious ointment on his head*, 3—9. *Judas covenanteth to betray him*, 10, 11. *Christ eateth the passover, and showeth that one of his disciples should betray him*, 12—21. *He instituteth his last supper*, 22—26; *foretelleth the desertion of all his disciples, and Peter's denial of him*, 27—31. *His agony and prayer in the garden*, 32—42. *He is betrayed by Judas, and apprehended: his disciples flee*, 43—52. *He is carried before the council, falsely accused, examined, pronounced guilty, and treated with indignity*, 53—65. *Peter's denial, and repentance*, 66—72.

^{a Mat. 26. 2. Luke 22. 1. John 11. 55. & 13. 1.} AFTER ^a two days was *the feast of* the Passover, and of unleavened bread: and the Chief Priests and the Scribes sought how they might take him by craft, and put *him* to death.

2 But they said, Not on the feast *day*, lest there be an uproar of the people.

Matthew saith the same, only he bringeth it in as said to the disciples by Christ. This must be said upon that day in the week which we call Tuesday, for Friday was the passover day, when began the feast of unleavened bread. See other things in the notes on Matt. xxvi. 1—5.

^{b Matt. 26.6. John 12. 3. See Luke 7. 37.} 3 ¶ ^b And being in Bethany in the house of Simon the leper, as he sat at meat, there came a woman having an alabaster box of ^{|| Or, pure nard, or, liquid nard.} ointment of || spikenard very precious; and she brake the box, and poured *it* on his head.

4 And there were some that had indignation within themselves, and said, Why was this waste of the ointment made?

^{See Matt. 18. 28.} 5 For it might have been sold for more than three hundred || pence, and have been given to the poor. And they murmured against her.

6 And Jesus said, Let her alone; why trouble ye her? she hath wrought a good work on me.

^{c Deu. 15.11.} 7 For ^c ye have the poor with you always, and whensoever ye will ye may do them good: but me ye have not always.

8 She hath done what she could: she is come aforehand to anoint my body to the burying.

9 Verily I say unto you, Wheresoever this Gospel shall be preached throughout the whole world, *this* also that she hath done shall be spoken of for a memorial of her.

See the notes on Matt. xxvi. 6—13, where this piece of history is fully considered, with the differing circumstances related by our evangelist and by St. John.

10 ¶ ^d And Judas Iscariot, one of the twelve, went unto the Chief Priests, to betray him unto them. ^{d Mat. 26.14. Luke 22.3,4.}

11 And when they heard *it*, they were glad, and promised to give him money. And he sought how he might conveniently betray him.

See the notes on Matt. xxvi. 14—16.

12 ¶ ^e And the first day of unleavened bread, when they || killed the Passover, his disciples said unto him, Where wilt thou that we go and prepare that thou mayest eat the Passover? ^{e Mat. 26.17. Luke 22. 7. || Or, sacrificed.}

13 And he sendeth forth two of his disciples, and saith unto them, Go ye into the city, and there shall meet you a man bearing a pitcher of water: follow him.

14 And wheresoever he shall go in, say ye to the goodman of the house, The Master saith, Where is the guestchamber, where I shall eat the Passover with my disciples?

15 And he will shew you a large upper room furnished *and* prepared: there make ready for us.

16 And his disciples went forth, and came into the city, and found as he had said unto them: and they made ready the Passover.

See the notes on Matt. xxvi. 17—19.

17 ^f And in the evening he cometh with the twelve. ^{f Matt. 26. 20, &c.}

18 And as they sat and did eat, Jesus said, Verily I say unto you, One of you which eateth with me shall betray me.

19 And they began to be sorrowful, and to say unto him one by one, *Is* it I? and another *said*, *Is* it I?

20 And he answered and said unto them, *It is* one of the twelve, that dippeth with me in the dish.

21 ^g The Son of man indeed goeth, as it is written of him: but woe to that man by whom the Son of man is betrayed! good were it for that man if he had never been born. ^{g Mat. 26.24. Luke 22. 22.}

See the notes on Matt. xxvi. 20—25, where is opened whatever is necessary for the understanding of these words, in which nothing of moment is varied, save only that Matthew reporteth Judas as being at this time particularly discovered. John hath nothing of this, unless the supper mentioned chap. xiii. were this supper, of which more shall be said in its order.

22 ¶ ^h And as they did eat, Jesus took bread, and blessed, and brake *it*, and gave to them, and said, Take, eat: this is my body. ^{h Mat.26.26. Luke 22. 19. 1 Cor. 11.23.}

23 And he took the cup, and when he had given thanks, he gave *it* to them: and they all drank of it.

24 And he said unto them, This is my blood of the new testament, which is shed for many.

25 Verily I say unto you, I will drink no more of the fruit of the vine, until that day that I drink it new in the kingdom of God.

26 ¶ ⁱ And when they had sung an || hymn, they went out into the mount of Olives. ^{i Matt.26.30. || Or, psalm.}

See the notes on Matt. xxvi. 26—30, where the very small differences betwixt our evangelist and Matthew and Luke are also considered.

^k Mat. 26. 31.   27 ^k And Jesus saith unto them, All ye shall be offended because of me this night: for it is written, ¹I will smite the shepherd, and the sheep shall be scattered.

l Zech. 13. 7.

m ch. 16. 7.   28 But ^m after that I am risen, I will go before you into Galilee.

n Matt. 26. 33, 34. Luke 22. 33, 34. John 13. 37, 38.   29 ⁿ But Peter said unto him, Although all shall be offended, yet *will* not I.

30 And Jesus saith unto him, Verily I say unto thee, That this day, *even* in this night, before the cock crow twice, thou shalt deny me thrice.

31 But he spake the more vehemently, If I should die with thee, I will not deny thee in any wise. Likewise also said they all.

See the notes on all the discourse, Matt. xxvi. 31—35.

o Mat. 26. 36. Luke 22. 39. John 18. 1.   32 ^o And they came to a place which was named Gethsemane: and he saith to his disciples, Sit ye here, while I shall pray.

33 And he taketh with him Peter and James and John, and began to be sore amazed, and to be very heavy;

p John 12. 27.   34 And saith unto them, ^p My soul is exceeding sorrowful unto death: tarry ye here, and watch.

35 And he went forward a little, and fell on the ground, and prayed that, if it were possible, the hour might pass from him.

q Rom. 8. 15. Gal. 4. 6.
r Heb. 5. 7.
s John 5. 30. & 6. 38.   36 And he said, ^q Abba, Father, ^r all things *are* possible unto thee; take away this cup from me: ^s nevertheless not what I will, but what thou wilt.

37 And he cometh, and findeth them sleeping, and saith unto Peter, Simon, sleepest thou? couldest not thou watch one hour?

t Rom. 7. 23. Gal. 5. 17.   38 Watch ye and pray, lest ye enter into temptation. 'The spirit truly *is* ready, but the flesh *is* weak.

39 And again he went away, and prayed, and spake the same words.

40 And when he returned, he found them asleep again, (for their eyes were heavy,) neither wist they what to answer him.

u John 13. 1.   41 And he cometh the third time, and saith unto them, Sleep on now, and take *your* rest: it is enough, ^uthe hour is come; behold, the Son of man is betrayed into the hands of sinners.

x Mat. 26. 46. John 18. 1, 2.   42 ^xRise up, let us go; lo, he that betrayeth me is at hand.

See the notes on Matt. xxvi. 36—46.

y Mat. 26. 47. Luke 22. 47. John 18. 3.   43 ¶ ^yAnd immediately, while he yet spake, cometh Judas, one of the twelve, and with him a great multitude with swords and staves, from the Chief Priests and the Scribes and the elders.

44 And he that betrayed him had given them a token, saying, Whomsoever I shall kiss, that same is he; take him, and lead *him* away safely.

45 And as soon as he was come, he goeth straightway to him, and saith, Master, master; and kissed him.

See the notes on Matt. xxvi. 47—49.

46 ¶ And they laid their hands on him, and took him.

47 And one of them that stood by drew a sword, and smote a servant of the High Priest, and cut off his ear.

z Mat. 26. 55. Luke 22. 52.   48 ^zAnd Jesus answered and said unto them, Are ye come out, as against a thief, with swords and *with* staves to take me?

a Ps. 22. 6. Is. 53. 7, &c. Luke 22. 37. & 24. 44.
b Ps. 88. 8. ver. 27.   49 I was daily with you in the temple teaching, and ye took me not: but ^athe Scriptures must be fulfilled.

50 ^b And they all forsook him, and fled.

Having, to complete the history of the passion, especially as to what is said of it by Matthew, Mark, and Luke, in my notes on Matthew considered all passages relating to what Matthew saith, the things here mentioned being opened in our notes on Matt. xxvi. 50—56, need not here again be enlarged upon.

51 And there followed him a certain young man, having a linen cloth cast about *his* naked *body ;* and the young men laid hold on him:

52 And he left the linen cloth, and fled from them naked.

This part of the history is only recorded by Mark. What hath made some affirm that this was St. John I cannot tell. John was one of the eleven that were with Christ when Judas came, and though we find him asleep a little before, yet we read not that he was gone to bed, nor can conceive there was any at or near the place. The garment in which he was, in all probability, was a night garment. It is certain it was a loose garment, he could not else, when he was apprehended, have so soon quit himself of it; and being quit of that it seemeth he was quit of all, for the text saith he *fled from them naked;* nor doth the text give him the honour to call him a disciple of Christ at large. Probably it was some young man who, being in his bed, and hearing the noise of the multitude going by his lodging with swords and staves, got up, slipped on his night garment, and followed them, to see what the matter was; and they having apprehended Christ, he followed them. And possibly his unusual habit made them take the more notice of him, staying when the disciples were all fled. Nor can the reason be well given why Mark should record such a passage, unless it were to tell us what we must expect from the rage of persecutors, viz. that our own innocency should not defend us. This young man was not concerned in Christ, only came as a spectator, without any arms. But the sword of persecution useth not to distinguish perfectly. The basilisk (they say) will fly at the picture of a man.

c Mat. 26. 57. Luke 22. 54. John 18. 13.   53 ¶ ^cAnd they led Jesus away to the High Priest: and with him were assembled all the Chief Priests and the elders and the Scribes.

54 And Peter followed him afar off, even into the palace of the High Priest: and he sat with the servants, and warmed himself at the fire.

d Mat. 26. 59.   55 ^d And the Chief Priests and all the council sought for witness against Jesus to put him to death; and found none.

56 For many bare false witness against him, but their witness agreed not together.

57 And there arose certain, and bare false witness against him, saying,

e ch. 15. 29. John 2. 19.   58 We heard him say, ^eI will destroy this temple that is made with hands, and within three days I will build another made without hands.

59 But neither so did their witness agree together.

f Mat. 26. 63.   60 ^fAnd the High Priest stood up in the midst, and asked Jesus, saying, Answerest thou nothing? what *is it which* these witness against thee?

^{g Is. 53. 7.}
^{h Mat.26.63.}
61 But ^ghe held his peace, and answered nothing. ^hAgain the High Priest asked him, and said unto him, Art thou the Christ, the Son of the Blessed?

^{i Mat. 24. 30.}
^{& 26. 64.}
^{Luke 22. 69.}
62 And Jesus said, I am: ⁱand ye shall see the Son of man sitting on the right hand of power, and coming in the clouds of heaven.

63 Then the High Priest rent his clothes, and saith, What need we any further witnesses?

64 Ye have heard the blasphemy: what think ye? And they all condemned him to be guilty of death.

65 And some began to spit on him, and to cover his face, and to buffet him, and to say unto him, Prophesy: and the servants did strike him with the palms of their hands.

This history of our Saviour's examination before the high priest we had Matt. xxvi. from ver. 57—68 : see the notes there. It should seem the high priests and council were very eager upon this thing. This council seems to have sat up all night, for early in the morning they carried him (condemned by them) to Pilate, and before twelve they brought him out of the city to be crucified. These wretched hypocrites had but the evening before been taking the passover. It was now the feast of unleavened bread. This was now the first fruit of their thanksgiving to God, for bringing them out of the land of Egypt; besides that their keeping a court of judgment in a capital case on a holy day, or in the night, were things against all rules of order. But the rage of persecutors can be neither bounded by the laws of God or men. If the servants of God still be thus treated, they are in this more like Christ, who hath told them, that *the disciple is not above his master.* But see further in the notes on Matt. xxvi.

^{k Matt. 26. 58,69.}
^{Luke 22. 55.}
^{John 18. 16.}
66 ¶ ^kAnd as Peter was beneath in the palace, there cometh one of the maids of the High Priest:

67 And when she saw Peter warming himself, she looked upon him, and said, And thou also wast with Jesus of Nazareth.

68 But he denied, saying, I know not, neither understand I what thou sayest. And he went out into the porch; and the cock crew.

^{l Matt. 26. 71. Luke 22. 58. John 18. 25.}
69 ^lAnd a maid saw him again, and began to say to them that stood by, This is *one* of them.

^{m Matt. 26. 73. Luke 22. 59. John 18. 26.}
70 And he denied it again. ^mAnd a little after, they that stood by said again to Peter, Surely thou art *one* of them: ⁿfor thou art a Galilæan, and thy speech agreeth *thereto.*

^{n Acts 2. 7.}

71 But he began to curse and to swear, *saying,* I know not this man of whom ye speak.

^{o Matt. 26. 75.}
72 ^oAnd the second time the cock crew. And Peter called to mind the word that Jesus said unto him, Before the cock crow twice, thou shalt deny me thrice. And ‖when he thought thereon, he wept.

^{‖ Or, he wept abundantly, or, he began to weep.}

All four evangelists give us an account of this history of Peter's denial of his Master. We have considered what they all say, to complete the history, in our notes on Matt. xxvi. 69—75; to which I see no reason to add any thing but the observation, 1. How contemptible means God often useth to take down our pride and self-confidences. Peter, a great apostle, is here humbled by the means of two maids.

2. How naturally one sin draws on another. Peter first telleth a lie, then to lying addeth swearing and cursing. 3. How necessary it is for those that would keep from sin to keep out of sinners' company. *I am* (saith David) *a companion of them that fear thee,* Psal. cxix. 63. 4. How profitable words from God are for the time to come, though at present we find not the use and advantage of them. 5. How different the sinnings of reprobates and saints are, as to the consequences and issues. Judas sins, repents, and hangs himself; Peter goeth out and weepeth bitterly. Judas repented unto death; Peter repenteth unto life. See more with reference to this history in our notes on Matt. xxvi. 75. Thus far we have heard Christ's trial before the ecclesiastical court of the Jews. Thus far what he said chap. x. 33 is made good. He is *delivered to the chief priests, and the scribes, and they have* (as we have heard) *condemned him to death.* But he also said there,——*and they shall deliver him to the Gentiles : and they shall mock him, and shall scourge him, and shall spit upon him, and shall kill him.* We must see those words verified in the ensuing part of the history, in the next chapter.

CHAP. XV

Jesus is brought bound and accused before Pilate: his silence before the governor, 1—5. *Pilate, prevailed upon by the clamours of the people, releaseth Barabbas, and giveth up Jesus to be crucified,* 6—15. *Christ is mocked of the soldiers, crowned with thorns, and led to the place of crucifixion,* 16—23. *He is crucified between two thieves,* 24—28, *reviled,* 29—32, *and calling upon God expireth,* 33—37. *The veil of the temple rent,* 38. *The centurion's confession,* 39—41. *Joseph of Arimathea beggeth the body, and burieth it,* 42—47.

AND ^astraightway in the morning the Chief Priests held a consultation with the elders and Scribes and the whole council, and bound Jesus, and carried *him* away, and delivered *him* to Pilate.

^{a Ps. 2. 2. Matt. 27. 1. Luke 22. 66. & 23. 1. John 18. 28. Acts 3. 13. & 4. 26.}

See the notes on Matt. xxvii. 1, 2. Pontius Pilate was the Roman governor in Judea at this time, Luke iii. 1. The reasons of their carrying Christ to him, when they had condemned him to death for blasphemy, (a crime cognizable before them, as appeareth in the case of Stephen, Acts vii.,) see in our notes on Matthew. What time in the morning they carried him before Pilate is not said, only John saith it was early, and we read it was about the sixth hour, (that is, with us twelve of the clock,) when Pilate dismissed him, being by him condemned; so probably they were with Pilate by six or seven in the morning. This morning was the morning after the evening in which they had eaten the passover, and the first day of their feast of unleavened bread: so little did they regard God's ordinance.

2 ^bAnd Pilate asked him, Art thou the King of the Jews? And he answering said unto him, Thou sayest *it.*

^{b Matt. 27. 11.}

3 And the Chief Priests accused him of many things: but he answered nothing.

4 ^cAnd Pilate asked him again, saying, Answerest thou nothing? behold how many things they witness against thee.

^{c Matt. 27. 13.}

5 ^dBut Jesus yet answered nothing; so that Pilate marvelled.

^{d Is. 53. 7. John 19. 9.}

6 Now ^eat *that* feast he released unto them one prisoner, whomsoever they desired.

^{e Matt. 27. 15. Luke 23. 17. John 18. 39.}

7 And there was *one* named Barabbas, *which lay* bound with them that had made insurrection with him, who had committed murder in the insurrection.

8 And the multitude crying aloud began to desire *him to do* as he had ever done unto them.

9 But Pilate answered them, saying, Will ye that I release unto you the King of the Jews?

10 For he knew that the Chief Priests had delivered him for envy.

11 But ʳthe Chief Priests moved the people, that he should rather release Barabbas unto them.

f Matt. 27. 20. Acts 3. 14.

12 And Pilate answered and said again unto them, What will ye then that I shall do *unto him* whom ye call the King of the Jews?

13 And they cried out again, Crucify him.

14 Then Pilate said unto them, Why, what evil hath he done? And they cried out the more exceedingly, Crucify him.

15 ¶ ᵍAnd *so* Pilate, willing to content the people, released Barabbas unto them, and delivered Jesus, when he had scourged *him*, to be crucified.

g Matt. 27. 26. John 19. 1, 16.

16 ʰAnd the soldiers led him away into the hall, called Prætorium; and they call together the whole band.

h Matt. 27. 27.

17 And they clothed him with purple, and platted a crown of thorns, and put it about his *head*,

18 And began to salute him, Hail, King of the Jews!

19 And they smote him on the head with a reed, and did spit upon him, and bowing *their* knees worshipped him.

20 And when they had mocked him, they took off the purple from him, and put his own clothes on him, and led him out to crucify him.

This history of our Saviour's examination before and condemnation by Pilate, together with the indignities offered him after his condemnation, is recorded in some degree or other by all the four evangelists, by the comparing of which it will appear that Mark hath left out many material circumstances and parts of it. In our notes on Matt. xxvii. 11—31, we have compared and considered them all, and shall thither refer the reader; only observing, 1. How much more favour Christ found from a Gentile heathen than from the Jewish high priest, and not favour only, but justice also. 2. How close our Saviour kept upon his guard, not accusing himself. 3. The horrible debauchery of these priests, that they would prefer a murderer, and seditious person, before a most innocent person. 4. The weakness of a corrupt heart to resist an ordinary temptation. Pilate was convinced the prosecution was malicious, that there was no guilt in Christ; yet he must content the people, and is basely afraid of their misrepresenting him to the Roman emperor. 5. That the point upon which Christ was condemned, was his maintaining his spiritual kingdom in and over his church, for he expressly disclaimed any claim to any earthly kingdom before Pilate, as the other evangelists tell us. 6. How punctually the words of Christ are by the providence of God fulfilled; we have now heard how Christ was delivered to the Gentiles, by them mocked, scourged, spit upon, and now going to be killed. 7. How Christ hath made all our bitter waters sweet, sanctifying every cross to us, and taking the curse out of it. He was reviled, imprisoned, mocked, scourged, spit upon, and last of all killed; he hath tasted of all these bitter waters, and by that taste they are made wholesome and medicinal for us; and he hath learned us, that there is no ignominy, shame, and contempt, no indignity and species of suffering, for his sake, in which we may not boast and glory, as being thereby made conformable to the sufferings and death of Christ. And if we suffer with him, we shall be glorified together.

21 ¹And they compel one Simon a Cyrenian, who passed by, coming out of the country, the father of Alexander and Rufus, to bear his cross.

i Matt. 27. 32. Luke 23. 26.

22 ⁿAnd they bring him unto the place Golgotha, which is, being interpreted, The place of a scull.

k Mat. 27.33. Luke 23. 33. John 19. 17.

23 ¹And they gave him to drink wine mingled with myrrh: but he received *it* not.

l Mat. 27.34.

24 And when they had crucified him, ᵐthey parted his garments, casting lots upon them, what every man should take.

m Ps. 22. 18. Luke 23. 34. John 19. 23.

25 And ⁿit was the third hour, and they crucified him.

n See Matt. 27. 45. Luke 23. 44. John 19. 14.

26 And ᵒthe superscription of his accusation was written over, THE KING OF THE JEWS.

o Mat. 27.37. John 19. 19.

27 And ᵖwith him they crucify two thieves; the one on his right hand, and the other on his left.

p Mat. 27.38.

28 And the Scripture was fulfilled, which saith, ᵍAnd he was numbered with the transgressors.

q Is. 53. 12. Luke 22. 37.

29 And ʳthey that passed by railed on him, wagging their heads, and saying, Ah, ˢthou that destroyest the temple, and buildest *it* in three days,

r Ps. 22. 7.
s ch. 14. 58. John 2. 19.

30 Save thyself, and come down from the cross.

31 Likewise also the Chief Priests mocking said among themselves with the Scribes, He saved others; himself he cannot save.

32 Let Christ the King of Israel descend now from the cross, that we may see and believe. And ᵗthey that were crucified with him reviled him.

t Mat. 27.44. Luke 23. 39.

33 And ᵘwhen the sixth hour was come, there was darkness over the whole land until the ninth hour.

u Mat. 27.45. Luke 23. 44.

34 And at the ninth hour Jesus cried with a loud voice, saying, ˣEloi, Eloi, lama sabachthani? which is, being interpreted, My God, my God, why hast thou forsaken me?

x Ps. 22. 1. Matt. 27. 46.

35 And some of them that stood by, when they heard *it*, said, Behold, he calleth Elias.

36 And ʸone ran and filled a spunge full of vinegar, and put *it* on a reed, and ᶻgave him to drink, saying, Let alone; let us see whether Elias will come to take him down.

y Mat. 27.48. John 19. 29.
z Ps. 69. 21.

37 And ᵃJesus cried with a loud voice, and gave up the ghost.

a Mat. 27.50. Luke 23. 46 John 19. 30

To make this history complete, all the other evangelists must be consulted, and compared with Mark, who omitteth many considerable passages recorded by them; we have done it in our notes on Matt. xxvii. 32—50, to which I refer the reader, both for the understanding the several passages of this relation, and reconciling any small differences betwixt the relations of the several evangelists. It is the observation of some, that when in Scripture the father is made known by the son, or sons, it signifieth some more eminency in the sons than in the father. Many think that this Simon was a pagan: though it be not certain, yet it is not improbable, that this Alexander was the same who is mentioned Acts xix. 33, persecuted there by the Jews; and Rufus, he whom Paul saluteth, Rom. xvi. 13, calling him *chosen in the Lord*. They say they were both at Rome, where they judge St. Mark was when he wrote this history, and that Mark mentioneth them as those who could attest the truth of this part of the history. The father bare Christ's cross, (or one end of it,) there is all we read of him. The sons believe on him who died upon it. So free is Divine grace, fixing where it pleaseth. Concerning the wine mingled with myrrh, we spake in our notes on Matt. xxvii. Some think our Saviour's friends gave it him to refresh him; but it is most probable it was given him to intoxicate him, that he might be less sensible of the pain he should endure upon the cross: whatsoever they intended, our Saviour refused it, having wine to uphold him which they knew not of. For other things relating to this story, see the notes on Matt. xxvii. 32—50.

^b Mat. 27.51. Luke 23. 45. 38 And ^bthe veil of the temple was rent in twain from the top to the bottom.

^c Mat. 27.54. Luke 23. 47. 39 ¶ And ^cwhen the centurion, which stood over against him, saw that he so cried out, and gave up the ghost, he said, Truly this man was the Son of God.

^d Mat. 27.55. Luke 23. 49. ^e Ps. 38. 11. 40 ^dThere were also women looking on ^eafar off: among whom was Mary Magdalene, and Mary the mother of James the less and of Joses, and Salome;

^fLuke 8. 2,3. 41 (Who also, when he was in Galilee, ^ffollowed him, and ministered unto him;) and many other women which came up with him unto Jerusalem.

The prodigies happening upon the death of our Saviour, and the passages happening betwixt the time of his expiration and his burial, are more largely reported by the other evangelists than by Mark; we have put them all together, and considered the passages relating to them, in our notes on Matt. xxvii. 51—54.

^g Mat. 27.57. Luke 23. 50. John 19. 38. 42 ¶ ^gAnd now when the even was come, because it was the preparation, that is, the day before the sabbath,

43 Joseph of Arimathæa, an honour-^h Luke 2. 25, 38. able counsellor, which also ^hwaited for the kingdom of God, came, and went in boldly unto Pilate, and craved the body of Jesus.

44 And Pilate marvelled if he were already dead: and calling *unto him* the centurion, he asked him whether he had been any while dead.

45 And when he knew *it* of the centurion, he gave the body to Joseph.

ⁱ Matt. 27. 59, 60. Luke 23. 53. John 19. 40. 46 ⁱAnd he bought fine linen, and took him down, and wrapped him in the linen, and laid him in a sepulchre which was hewn out of a rock, and rolled a stone unto the door of the sepulchre.

47 And Mary Magdalene and Mary *the mother* of Joses beheld where he was laid.

The circumstances of our Saviour's honourable burial, as related by this and the other evangelists, are gathered together and opened in our notes on Matt. xxvii. 57—66.

CHAP. XVI

Christ's resurrection is declared by angels to the two Maries and Salome, 1—8. *Christ himself appeareth to Mary Magdalene,* 9—11; *to two of his disciples going into the country,* 12, 13; *and to the eleven; whom he commissioneth to preach the gospel to all the world,* 14—18. *His ascension into heaven; the gospel is preached every where, the Lord confirming the word with signs,* 19, 20.

We are now come to the history of our Saviour's resurrection, his several appearances to and converse with his disciples, from the time of his rising from the dead unto the time of his ascension up into heaven, which was forty days. Of all the evangelists, St. John is most full in his relation of this part of the history of our Saviour, which we shall consider in order; for his two last chapters are wholly spent in this part of the history: in the mean time, as we did in our notes on Matt. xxviii. take notice only of what Matthew hath upon that argument; so we shall, in the opening of this chapter of Mark, take notice only of what Mark hath not concurrent with, and completory of, what Matthew had before said (for what he hath of that nature, we shall refer the reader to our notes on Matthew). And here we will also take in what Luke hath that tends to the fuller relation of any thing which Mark hath; not meddling with what John hath, but reserving that till we come to open the fuller account of this whole history, in the twentieth and twenty-first chapters of his Gospel.

AND ^awhen the sabbath was past, Mary ^aMatt. 28.1. Luke 24. 1. Magdalene, and Mary the *mother* of ^{John 20. 1.} James, and Salome, ^bhad bought sweet ^b Luke 23. 56. spices, that they might come and anoint him.

About the time when they came, see the notes on Matt. xxviii. 1, which is also further expressed in the next verses.

2 ^cAnd very early in the morning the ^c Luke 24. 1. John 20. 1. first *day* of the week, they came unto the sepulchre at the rising of the sun.

Matthew saith, *as it began to dawn toward the first day of the week*. John saith, they came *early, when it was yet dark*. Luke also saith, *very early*. But it is manifest from the history, that they came a second time, of which Mark may speak, passing over their first coming.

3 And they said among themselves, Who shall roll us away the stone from the door of the sepulchre?

4 And when they looked, they saw that the stone was rolled away: for it was very great.

These were their thoughts as they were coming. Concerning the guard which they had set by Pilate's permission at the importunity of the Jewish priests and rulers, it is probable (the day before being the Jewish sabbath, in the observation of which the Jews were very strict) they had not heard, so were not solicitous as to them; but they knew of the stone rolled to the mouth of the sepulchre: but they were in vain solicitous; when they came they found the stone rolled away, Christ was risen before.

5 ^dAnd entering into the sepulchre, ^d Luke 24. 3. John 20. 11, they saw a young man sitting on the ^{12.} right side, clothed in a long white garment; and they were affrighted.

6 ^eAnd he saith unto them, Be not ^e Matt. 28. 5, 6, 7. affrighted: Ye seek Jesus of Nazareth, which was crucified: he is risen; he is not here: behold the place where they laid him.

7 But go your way, tell his disciples and Peter that he goeth before you into Galilee: there shall ye see him, ^fas he ^fMat. 26. 32. ch. 14. 28. said unto you.

8 And they went out quickly, and fled from the sepulchre; for they trembled and were amazed: ^gneither said they any ^g See Matt. 28. 8. thing to any *man;* for they were afraid. Luke 24. 9.

Both Luke and John mention two angels in the habit of young men. Matthew speaks of one sitting upon the stone. They might see him sitting upon the stone, and yet find him within also, the motions of angels are quick and undiscernible to our sense, or the stone might be rolled inward. That they were affrighted is no wonder, considering how apt we are to be affrighted by any apparitions. Concerning what the angel said to these women, read the notes on Matt. xxviii. 5—8. They presently flee from the sepulchre amazed, saying nothing to any till they came into the city, where they tell it to the disciples.

9 ¶ Now when *Jesus* was risen early the first *day* of the week, ^hhe appeared ^h John 20. 14. first to Mary Magdalene, ⁱout of whom he ⁱ Luke 8. 2. had cast seven devils.

10 ^k*And* she went and told them that ^k Luke 24. 10. had been with him, as they mourned and John 20. 18. wept.

11 ¹And they, when they had heard that he was alive, and had been seen of her, believed not.

l Luke 24. 11.

Concerning this appearance of Christ to Mary Magdalene, see the notes on Matt. xxviii. 9, and more fully on John xx. 14—17, who gives a more full account than any other of this appearance.

12 ¶ After that he appeared in another form ᵐunto two of them, as they walked, and went into the country.

m Luke 24. 13.

13 And they went and told *it* unto the residue: neither believed they them.

Of this appearance St. Luke gives us a very large account, chap. xxiv. 13—35. See the notes on that chapter.

14 ¶ ⁿAfterward he appeared unto the eleven as they sat ‖ at meat, and upbraided them with their unbelief and hardness of heart, because they believed not them which had seen him after he was risen.

n Luke 24. 36. John 20. 19. 1 Cor. 15. 5. ‖ Or, together.

This most probably is the appearance mentioned Luke xxiv. 36; John xx. 19. See the notes there.

15 °And he said unto them, Go ye into all the world, ᵖand preach the Gospel to every creature.

o Mat. 28. 19. John 15. 16. p Col. 1. 23.

16 ᑫHe that believeth and is baptized shall be saved; ʳbut he that believeth not shall be damned.

q John 3. 18, 36. Acts 2. 38. & 16. 30, 31, 32. Rom. 10. 9. 1 Pet. 3. 21. r John 12.48.

17 And these signs shall follow them that believe; ˢIn my name shall they cast out devils; ᵗthey shall speak with new tongues;

s Luke10.17. Acts 5. 16. & 8. 7. & 16. 18. & 19. 12. t Acts 2. 4. & 10. 46. & 19. 6. 1 Cor. 12. 10, 28.

18 ᵘThey shall take up serpents; and if they drink any deadly thing, it shall not hurt them; ˣthey shall lay hands on the sick, and they shall recover.

u Luke10.19. Acts 28. 5. x Acts 5. 15, 16. & 9. 17. & 28. 8. Jam.5.14,15.

See the notes on Matt. xxviii. 19, 20, where what we have here is largely explained.

19 ¶ So then ʸafter the Lord had spoken unto them, he was ᶻreceived up into heaven, and ᵃsat on the right hand of God.

y Acts 1. 2,3. z Luke 24. 51. a Ps. 110. 1 Acts 7. 55.

Matthew saith nothing of our Saviour's ascension. Mark speaketh of it very shortly. Luke saith, *And he led them out as far as to Bethany, and he lifted up his hands, and blessed them. And it came to pass, while he blessed them, he was parted from them, and carried up into heaven. And they worshipped him, and returned to Jerusalem with great joy.* And again gives us this part of his history most fully. Acts i. 1—12. We shall in our notes on Luke xxiv. speak more fully to this. We are told, Acts i. 3, that Christ was forty days upon the earth after his resurrection, and, ver. 9, that a cloud did receive him. He is said to sit *on the right hand of God,* to distinguish him from angels, whose places are but places of ministration.

20 And they went forth, and preached every where, the Lord working with *them,* ᵇand confirming the word with signs following. Amen.

b Acts 5. 12. & 14. 3. 1 Cor. 2. 4, 5. Heb. 2. 4.

Here is now the history of a great deal of following time, shortly epitomized in one verse. The first motion of the eleven was to Jerusalem, Luke xxiv. 52, and this was according to the express command of Christ, ver. 49. There they *were continually in the temple, praising and blessing God,* ver. 53. At Jerusalem *they went into an upper room,* Acts i. 12, 13. There they *continued with one accord in prayer and supplication,* ver. 14, and chose Matthias for the twelfth apostle. The Holy Ghost came upon them, Acts ii. Still they continued preaching to the Jews, till the Jews, by their unbelief and persecution, judging themselves unworthy of eternal life, they turned to the Gentiles, Acts xiii. 46. Of God *confirming their word,* that is, his word spoken by them, *with signs following,* the whole history of the Acts of the Apostles is an abundant proof

---

THE GOSPEL ACCORDING TO

S. LUKE

THE ARGUMENT

Concerning the penman of this history, the certain time when he wrote it, and the occasion of his writing of it, we have little in holy writ; and there is such an uncertainty in traditions, as it is hardly worth the labour to transcribe what men have but guessed at. For those who would have him to be Barnabas, or one of the seventy, they seem not to have considered what Luke himself saith, chap. i. 2, that he wrote, *as they delivered them* to him, *which from the beginning were eye-witnesses, and ministers of the word.* By which is fairly hinted to us, that he was no eye-witness, nor (from the first at least) a minister of the word. That there was one Luke contemporaneous with Paul, and his fellow labourer, appeareth from 2 Tim. iv. 11; Philem. 24; Col. iv. 14; in both which latter texts he is joined with Demas, and in Col. iv. 14, he is called *the beloved physician.* Those three texts seem all to speak of one and the same person, who, probably, at first practised physic, afterwards, being made a disciple, exercised the ministry. It is generally thought that this was he, who was the penman both of this history and of the Acts of the Apostles. Whether by nation he was a Syrian, or a Roman, or of what other nation, is but an unprofitable speculation. That he was an evangelist we know, that is, one inspired by God to transmit to the world the history of the birth, life, death, resurrection, and ascension of our Saviour; as also of the acts of the apostles, until Paul was a prisoner at Rome. For his history of the Gospel, so far as it relates to Christ himself, it containeth many remarkable things, not mentioned by the other evangelists. The generation of John Baptist; the history of Zacharias; the angel's coming to the blessed virgin; Elisabeth's exclamation, and salutation of her; the publication of Christ's birth to the shepherds, with the things spoken by them; the testimony which Simeon and Anna gave to Christ; the occasion of Joseph and Mary's going to Bethlehem; the circumstances of our Saviour's birth there; his disputing with the doctors at twelve years of age; are things reported by no other evangelist, and of great use to complete the history of John the Baptist and of Christ. Besides that he hath many parables (as those of the lost sheep, the lost groat, and of the prodigal, &c.) that are to be found in no other evangelist, together with several other parables and pieces of history; to say nothing of divers circumstances in those parables and pieces of history, which other evangelists have recorded, omitted by them. He dedicateth his book to some friend, either named Theophilus, or to whom the signification of that name (which is, *a lover of God*) in his judgment did very well agree.

The time when he wrote it is uncertain; some would have it to be written the fifteenth, some the twenty-second, some the twenty-seventh year of our Saviour. The matter written by him is of much more concern to us to know than these circumstances. We have in our annotations spoken to those things which he mentioneth, before recorded by Matthew or Mark, more shortly. To other things which we in him first meet with, more largely.

CHAP. I

Luke's preface, 1—4. An angel appeareth to Zacharias, and promiseth him a son in his old age, 5—17. Zacharias doubting is struck dumb for a sign, 18—23. His wife Elisabeth conceiveth, 24. 25. The angel's visit to Mary, 26—38. Elisabeth, saluted by Mary, prophesieth, 39—45. Mary's song of thanksgiving, 46—56. The birth and circumcision of John the Baptist, 57—63. Zacharias's mouth is opened, 64—66. His prophecy, 67—80.

FORASMUCH as many have taken in hand to set forth in order a declaration of those things which are most surely believed among us,

2 ᵃ Even as they delivered them unto us, which ᵇ from the beginning were eyewitnesses, and ministers of the word;

3 ᶜ It seemed good to me also, having had perfect understanding of all things from the very first, to write unto thee ᵈ in order, ᵉ most excellent Theophilus,

4 ᶠ That thou mightest know the certainty of those things, wherein thou hast been instructed.

a Heb. 2. 3.
1 Pet. 5. 1.
2 Pet. 1. 16.
1 John 1. 1.
b Mark 1. 1.
John 15. 27.
c Acts 15.
19, 25, 28.
1 Cor. 7. 40.
d Acts 11. 4.
e Acts 1. 1.
f John 20.31.

Luke's evangelical history hath this peculiar to itself, that whereas the histories of the other evangelists are written to the whole world, having no particular inscription, or dedication, Luke dedicates his to a particular person, named Theophilus; for though that name signifieth *one that loveth God,* yet I cannot think it is to be taken here appellatively, it being commonly used as a proper name; parents in former ages giving children names generally either expressive of their children's duty to God, (that by their names they might be put in mind of it,) or expressive of God's mercy to themselves in giving them such children. The evangelist here suggesteth, that many had taken in hand orderly to write an account of the things which were certainly believed amongst the Jews. Some think that Luke here reflecteth upon some that, even so early, had given false accounts of our Saviour's history; for there were several pretended Gospels wrote, called, The Gospel of the Nazarenes, of Thomas, Matthias, Nicodemus, and many others, which the church soon saw cause to reject. But others think that Luke doth not at all reflect, and possibly those figments were not so early; but Luke, observing that many did write this famous history, and some, possibly, for want of due information, not so exactly as they might, yet as they were delivered to them from such as *from the beginning were eye-witnesses, and ministers of the word,* but possibly might not be able so exactly to inform them, or the writers not so able duly to digest them (for most think Matthew, Mark, and John wrote after); or possibly because, there being then no printing, but all in manuscripts, because he thought his friend Theophilus (to whom he knew such a history would be grateful) might not have come to the sight of those manuscripts, he undertakes (not without the direction of the Holy Spirit, as appeared afterward) to compile a history of these things, to which he was either encouraged by the example of others, or incited by the mistakes of those who had done it ill, having the advantage perfectly to understand all things from the first. Most think that this advantage arose not from his personal knowledge, but his converse with the apostles and other ministers of Christ; for he saith no more, ver. 2, than, *even as they delivered them unto us, which from the beginning were eye-witnesses, and ministers of the word;* by which it seemeth to be hinted to us, that he was no eyewitness, nor minister of the word. To understand by *the word* in that verse Christ (whom John indeed so calleth, chap. i. 1) seemeth to me too hard, considering *the word,* in the evangelists, doth ordinarily signify the gospel, and no where Christ but in John i. 1, 2, &c. *That thou mightest know the certainty of those things, wherein thou hast been instructed;* that is, by the relation of others.

Before I pass this preface, I shall make some observations upon it. 1. That even from the beginning there were some cheats, in reporting matters of fact concerning the church. Whether Luke intended to reflect on them, or no, if we may believe any thing of ecclesiastical history, there were some false Gospels; and before the time of the Gospel there were apocryphal writings relating to the history of the Old Testament. No writings but the Scriptures deserve our faith (otherwise than they agree with them) in things of which they give us an account. 2. In Luke's time the history of the Gospel was most surely believed, as being delivered from eye-witnesses. 3. Men ought to have perfect understanding of matters of fact before they write them. Whoso writes a history upon uncertainty, imposeth upon all future ages. 4. A knowledge of certainties is what all good men ought to aim at in writing and reading. It is a mean soul that can feed upon an uncertainty, and they are as mean that spend their time in catering such food for reasonable souls. Men's understandings are given them for nobler uses than to gain the notion of a falsehood, and they are low-born souls that can spend their precious hours in such cookery, let the sauce with which they serve it up be never so artificial.

5 ¶ THERE was ᵍ in the days of Herod, the king of Judæa, a certain Priest named Zacharias, ʰ of the course of Abia: and his wife *was* of the daughters of Aaron, and her name *was* Elisabeth.

Before the Common Account called Anno Domini the sixth Year.
g Matt. 2. 1.
h 1 Chr. 24. 10, 19. Neh. 12. 4, 17.

The Holy Ghost, for infinitely wise reasons, giveth us here an account both of the time when John the Baptist was born, and also of his parentage. It was *in the days of Herod, the king of Judea,* that is, he who was the son of Antipater: not Herod the tetrarch of Galilee, of whom you read Luke iii. 1, who put John Baptist to death, that was thirty-one or thirty-two years after this. He is usually called Herod the Great; who fought his way to the government of the Jews under the Romans, and came to his throne by the slaughter of the Jewish Sanhedrim; by which means he also extinguished all the government, which till his time held in the tribe of Judah, though not in a single person, (for that was destroyed in John, soon after the time of Judas Maccabeus,) yet in a select number out of that royal tribe. So that in this Herod's time the prophecy of dying Jacob, Gen. xlix. 10, was fulfilled. The sceptre, that is, the government, departed from Judah, and the lawgiver from his feet, which was a certain sign (in order to the fulfilling of that prophecy) that Shiloh, that is, the Messias, was coming. This for the time. *A certain priest, named Zacharias;* some will have him to have been the high priest, or his deputy, but that cannot be, for the high priest was but one, and so not within the courses of the priests, but of the eldest family from Aaron; and though it be said, ver. 9, that *his lot was to burn incense,* yet it must not be understood of the incense mentioned Lev. xvi. 12. to be burned upon the yearly day of expiation, (which indeed none but the high priest might do,) but of the daily incense mentioned in the law, Exod. xxx. 7, 8, which any of the priests did in their courses. This Zacharias was *of the course of Abia.* The eldest son of Aaron was always the high priest; his other sons were priests. In a long course of time, their descendants so multiplied, that they were too many all at the same time to minister in the temple. David therefore divided them into courses, each course waited their month. 1 Chron. xxiv. 4, 5, there is an account of the distribution of the priests into twenty-four courses. In David's time the eighth course was the course of Abijah. It appeareth by Neh. xii., that after the captivity they kept the denominations of these courses, but it is probable the order of them was altered. We read of Abijah in Neh. xii. 17, but whether his was then, or at this time when Luke wrote his Gospel, the eighth course I cannot tell. It is enough for us that Zacharias was one of the ordinary priests of the course of Abia; whose office it was to serve in the temple in his course, which was the course of such as derived from the Abijah mentioned in 1 Chron. xxiv. 10. *And his wife was of the daughters of Aaron, and her name was Elisabeth.* This is added not to signify Zacharias's obedience to the Divine law, which obliged the priests to marry within their own tribes; for the reason of that law being only to prevent the confusion of the inheritances, which fell by lot to the several tribes, and by the will of God were to be so kept distinct, the tribe of Levi having no such inheritance, might intermix with any other tribe, and did so; the high priest only was obliged to marry one of his own people, Lev. xxi. 14, and Jehoiada, 2 Chron. xxii. 11, married one of the tribe of Judah; but it is added to show the honourableness of Elisabeth's stock. Moses and Aaron were the two first governors of the Israelites. Elisabeth was not only of the tribe of Levi, but descended from Aaron, whom God made the noblest family of the Levites. Her name was Elisabeth. It is a Hebrew name, Exod. vi. 23, and (as you may see there) was the very name of Aaron's wife, the *daughter of Amminadab,* and *sister of Naashon.* As it may be variously written it signifieth, *the rest,* or *the oath,* or *the rod of my God.*

^{i Gen. 7. 1. & 17. 1.
l Kings 9. 4.
2 Kings 20.3.
Job 1. 1. Acts 23. 1. & 2.
16. Phil. 3. 6.}

6 And they were both ⁱ righteous before God, walking in all the commandments and ordinances of the Lord blameless.

That they were not righteous by a perfect legal righteousness, being not guilty of any sin, is certain, for so *there is none righteous, no, not one;* but so righteous, as that God accepted them, and looked upon them as righteous; as Abraham believed, and it was imputed to him for righteousness, though he sinned in the denial of his wife, &c.; or as it is said of David, 1 Kings xv. 5, He *did that which was right in the eyes of the Lord, and turned not aside from any thing that he commanded him all the days of his life, save only in the matter of Uriah.* They also walked *in all the commandments and ordinances of the Lord blameless.* A man's blameless conversation before the world is a piece of his righteousness, but will not make up alone such a righteousness as will testify his acceptation with God, or righteousness before him; he must, in the first place, walk in the commandments and in the ordinances of God. There is a duty towards God, as well as towards men; and that duty lies in the keeping his commandments, his ordinances, for the fear of the Lord must not be taught us by the precepts of men; yea, and in all the ordinances of God, having a respect to all God's commandments; and making this his constant course and practice, not doing it by fits. He must also be blameless towards men. Here is a true pattern of what a married couple should be, especially where the husband waits at the altar, and is employed in the holy things of God. *A bishop must be blameless,* 1 Tim. iii. 2; *a deacon grave, not double-tongued, not given to much wine, not greedy of filthy lucre,* ver. 8; *blameless,* ver. 10; and, ver. 11, *Even so must their wives be grave, not slanderers, sober,* &c. Such were Zacharias and Elisabeth. Such ought all ministers of the gospel and their wives to be.

7 And they had no child, because that Elisabeth was barren, and they both were *now* well stricken in years.

Amongst all earthly blessings, there is nothing we more desire than children, in whom we have a kind of perpetuity, living in our species and in our posterity when we are dead in nature. But as God, for our trial, doth often deny us other good things which are the great objects of our desires, so he doth often deny his own people this great blessing. Sometimes he withholdeth it a long time from those to whom he at length giveth it. Barrenness in Israel was a reproach: see ver. 25, and 1 Sam. i. 6. There was a promise to Abraham of a plentiful seed; hence, amongst the Jews, she that was barren hardly thought herself, or was judged by others, a genuine daughter of Abraham. Both Zacharias and Elisabeth *were now well stricken in years.* God chooseth this woman, naturally barren, and now aged also, to be the mother of John the Baptist, therein working a double miracle; and it is observable in holy writ, that when God denied to any women children for some long time, and then opened their wombs, they were the mothers of some eminent persons, whom God made great use of. Thus it was with Sarah, Rachel, the wife of Manoah, Hannah, 1 Sam. i., and this Elisabeth.

8 And it came to pass, that while he executed the Priest's office before God ^kin the order of his course, ^{k 1 Chr. 24. 19. 2 Chr. 8. 14. & 31. 2.}

9 According to the custom of the Priest's office, his lot was ^lto burn incense when he went into the temple of the Lord. ^{l Ex. 30, 7, 8. 1 Sam. 2. 28. 1 Chr. 23. 13. 2 Chr. 29. 11.}

The priests were multiplied to an exceeding number; we find an account of more than four thousand upon the return out of the captivity of Babylon, Ezra ii. 36—39; they were doubtless afterward multiplied to a far greater number. Josephus tells us there were a thousand in a course; whether they held to twenty-four courses, as in David's time, or no, I cannot tell. There were several parts of the priestly office, which it seemeth, by this text, the priests of the course that ministered divided amongst themselves by lot. One part of their work was to burn incense morning and evening. It seems this was that part of the priestly office which Zacharias was by lot to exercise.

10 ^mAnd the whole multitude of the people were praying without at the time of incense. ^{m Lev.16.17. Rev. 8. 3, 4.}

We are told, that the order of the Jewish daily service was this: twice in the day the priests whose course it was to minister, or such of them whose lot it was, went into the holy place to burn incense, according to the law, Exod. xxx. 7. When they went in, a bell rung, to give notice that it was the hour of prayer. There were constantly there, 1. The rest of the priests of the same course. 2. The Levites. 3. Their stationary men, who represented the whole congregation, and laid their hands upon the beast slain. 4. So many more of the people as would voluntarily come; and it was very ordinary for many to go. Thus we read, Acts iii. 1, of Peter and John going into the temple at the hour of prayer. These made the *multitude,* of whom it is said, that while the priest was burning incense they were *without,* not without the temple, but in the court of Israel, without the holy place, in which the priests were burning incense, *praying;* so they used to do privately by themselves. There is a text in Ecclesiasticus, chap. l. 15, which (though it be not canonical Scripture) is as credible as any other civil history, and will much help to make the readers understand the order of the Jewish service, and what this text saith.

11 And there appeared unto him an angel of the Lord standing on the right side of ⁿthe altar of incense. ^{n Ex. 30. 1.}

Though we translate it *appeared,* yet in the Greek it is, there was seen of him. An angel indeed was there; whether the angel Gabriel or no, or in what form he appeared, it is not said. It is by some observed, that until the Urim and Thummim ceased, no angel appeared to any priest executing his office; after this, it is observed by others, that most appearances of angels to the priests were when they were employed in their service in the temple.

12 And when Zacharias saw *him,* ^ohe was troubled, and fear fell upon him. ^{o Judg. 6.22. & 13. 22. Dan. 10. 8. ver. 29. ch.2. 9. Acts 10. 4. Rev. 1. 17.}

We are naturally affrighted at sudden and unusual things, but especially at any Divine appearances, whether God himself takes a shape, or authorizeth an angel to do it. So was Daniel, chap. x. 7, 8; and Manoah and his wife, Judg. xiii. 20; and Paul, Acts ix. For though God doth not make these appearances to affright us, yet such is the imbecility of our natures, that we cannot but be shy at them, and start from them; and it is but reasonable that God should by this means both declare his own glory and majesty, and also humble his poor creatures, and make them more impressive, and receptive of his Divine revelations. It is reasonable God should keep and declare his majesty, though we keep and declare our infirmity.

13 But the angel said unto him, Fear not, Zacharias: for thy prayer is heard; and thy wife Elisabeth shall bear thee a son, and ᵖthou shalt call his name John.

p ver.60, 63.

Although the great God useth so to show himself to the best of his own people, as to imprint upon them a sacred awe of his majesty, yet he never suffereth the souls of his people to sink under those apprehensions. The first words the angel saith to Zacharias are, *Fear not, Zacharias.* I am no bad messenger to thee, but a good messenger from God, to tell thee *thy prayer is heard.* This is good news to any soul. But of what prayer the angel here speaketh is a little further question, for it follows, *and thy wife Elisabeth shall bear thee a son.* It is believed that the priest, while he burned incense, did offer up prayers, but that he had now offered up prayers to God for issue is not so probable, considering that both he and Elisabeth were well stricken in years, and probably past children. Some therefore think that those words, *and thy wife Elisabeth,* &c., are given him only as a sign that his prayers were heard; and added to signify that, as a further mercy to him than what he asked, Elisabeth should conceive. Nor do I see any reason why we should restrain the prayer mentioned to the prayer he had now made, and not expound it of those many prayers which Zacharias had before made, which though God had delayed to answer, yet the angel assures him should now be answered with relation to issue. *And thou shalt call his name John,* which is the same with Johanan in the Hebrew, and signifies *gracious.* The angel directed Joseph to call Christ's name *Jesus,* because he was to *save his people from their sins;* and he directeth Zacharias to call his son's name John, because he was to open the kingdom of grace, and to preach the grace of the gospel, through Jesus Christ.

14 And thou shalt have joy and gladness; and ᵈmany shall rejoice at his birth.

q ver. 58.

None ought to have so mean thoughts of these words of the angel, as to think that they are only expressive of that affection which commonly discovereth itself in us when God giveth us sons, especially after a long barrenness, but of a further joy and gladness his parents should have upon a spiritual account, afterwards expressed. *Many shall rejoice at his birth:* they rejoiced *in his light,* John v. 36, the glad tidings of the Messiah being come into the world, which he brought. The papists think they have a ground here for their holy-day they keep to his honour, and their apish, carnal rejoicing, which certainly was not so valuable a thing as for an angel to foretell. The angel speaks of the great acceptation with the people (many of them) which John's doctrine should have, so that, as our Saviour saith, from his days the kingdom of heaven suffered violence, and the violent did take it by force. But he further openeth his meaning in the following verses.

15 For he shall be great in the sight of the Lord, and ʳshall drink neither wine nor strong drink; and he shall be filled with the Holy Ghost, ˢeven from his mother's womb.

r Num. 6. 3. Judg. 13. 4. ch. 7. 33.
s Jer. 1. 5. Gal. 1. 15.

We have a natural ambition to be great, but it is only to be great in the sight of men; thence one man coveteth riches, another honours and reputation; but the true greatness is to be *great in the sight of the Lord,* who doth certainly judge with the truest and most infallible judgment. In God's sight he is a great man of whom God maketh a great use, especially in turning many souls to himself. Consider John separately from his work, and the concurrence of God with his work, he was a very little man, and so looked upon by the Pharisees and rulers, who would not believe in him. His father was an ordinary priest. For titles and dignities, he had none; John the Baptist was his highest title. For his clothing; he was not clothed in soft raiment, (as princes' chaplains,) he was clothed with a skin, with *camel's hair, and had a leathern girdle about his loins;* yet Christ saith of him, *Among them that are born of women, there hath not risen a greater than John the Baptist.* He had no palace, no stately habitation; he lived mostly in desert places little inhabited. Nature was his cook, that provided him locusts and wild honey. Where was his greatness, but in this—He was a great and faithful preacher of the gospel, and God blessed his labours to convert souls? They are little men that do little of the work for which God hath sent them into the world, and do little good in their generation. *He shall drink neither wine nor strong drink:* by *strong drink* is meant any drink which ordinarily intoxicateth. This was the law of the Nazarites, Numb. vi. 3. It was forbidden the priests during the time of their ministration upon pain of death, Lev. x. 9. No lovers of wine and strong drink can be great men in the sight of God. The minister of the gospel must not be one given to wine, 1 Tim. iii. 3; Tit. i. 7. *And he shall be filled with the Holy Ghost, even from his mother's womb.* This is true, both as to prophecy, (which is an extraordinary gift of the Holy Ghost,) and also of the Holy Ghost considered as a sanctifying Spirit renewing the heart. *And many of the children of Israel shall he turn to the Lord their God.* Then it seems there is another conversion besides the conversion of men from paganism. John (with the assistance of the Holy Ghost) was an instrument to turn many of the Israelites, who already verbally owned the true God, but were drenched in errors, and superstitions, and looseness of life, to the Lord their God, by repentance; and this he did by preaching both law and gospel to them. This made him a great man, for, *They that turn many to righteousness shall shine as the stars for ever and ever,* Dan. xii. 3.

16 ᵗAnd many of the children of Israel shall he turn to the Lord their God.

t Mal. 4. 5, 6.

17 ᵘAnd he shall go before him in the spirit and power of Elias, ˣto turn the hearts of the fathers to the children, and the disobedient ∥ to the wisdom of the just; to make ready a people prepared for the Lord.

u Mal. 4. 5. Matt. 11. 14.
x Mark 9. 12. x Ecclus. 48. 10.
∥ Or, *by.*

God was last spoken of, he must therefore be the *him* mentioned here, before whom John the Baptist was to go, according to the prophecy, Mal. iv. 5, 6; from whence is an evident proof that Christ was the Lord our God, before whom John the Baptist came, *in the spirit and power of Elias,* and therefore he is called *Elias,* Mal. iv. 5, as expounded by Christ, Matt. xi. 14; Mark ix. 13. The Jews' not understanding this keeps them in a vain expectation of a Messiah to this day, and of a personal coming of Elias before him. It is the observation of some learned men, that where the word *power* is added to *the Spirit,* or Holy Ghost, it signifies a more than ordinary measure and influence of the Spirit, as in this chapter, ver. 35; Acts x. 38; 1 Cor. ii. 4; 1 Thess. i. 5. But I rather think that by that phrase, *in the spirit and power,* here is meant, with the same zeal and frame of spirit that Elijah had. We have before, in our notes upon Matthew, showed in how many things John the Baptist was like Elijah, to say nothing of his habit and the severity of his life, in respect of the most corrupt time wherein they both lived, their faithfulness in their ministry, their warmth and zeal in their work, their boldness, not fearing to reprove princes for their errors, &c. *To turn the hearts of the fathers to the children.* Malachi addeth, *and the heart of the children to their fathers;* instead of which Luke hath, *and the disobedient to the wisdom of the just;* that is, to bring both young and old to repentance: the hearts of the fathers amongst the Jews to the doctrine of Christ and his apostles, their children; and the hearts of the Jews, which, with respect to Abraham, Isaac, and Jacob, and David, are children, to the doctrine which they embraced, and the ways of God wherein those just men walked, which is the doctrine of wisdom: to reconcile many amongst the Jews to that which some of them own and profess, though others of them are yet apostatized, and yet led away with the superstitions of these degenerate and corrupt times. *To make ready a people prepared for the Lord;* to acquaint this part of the world with the Messias, and to prepare them for receiving him and his doctrine, which is presently to be revealed by himself, taking off people's prejudices, and discovering and commending Christ to them. Or, by bringing men to a true repentance for their sins, and a sense of them, till which they cannot believe, to prepare them for a more internal reception of the Lord Jesus Christ. For John is said to have preached the doctrine of *repentance for the remission of sins;* and to have preached, saying, *Repent, for the kingdom of heaven is at hand.* Also defaming the Pharisees, who were the great enemies of Christ, by detecting to the people their hypocrisy. Thus he made *ready a people prepared for the Lord.*

18 And Zacharias said unto the angel, ʸWhereby shall I know this? for I am an old man, and my wife well stricken in years.

y Gen. 17. 17.

The words are much the same with those of Abraham, Gen. xv. 8, *Whereby shall I know that I shall inherit it,* viz. the land of Canaan? And Mary, ver. 34 of this chapter, when the same angel had told her she should have a child, ver. 31, saith, *How shall this be, seeing I know not a man?* Gideon also asked a sign, Judg. vi. 17. To our appearance and judgment there seemeth no great difference betwixt these and Zacharias in this place asking a sign, only Zacharias here opposeth his own sense and reason to the words of the angel, yet we shall hear a different issue of this question, or answer to it.

19 And the angel answering said unto him, I am ᶻGabriel, that stand in the presence of God; and am sent to speak unto thee, and to shew thee these glad tidings.

z Dan. 8. 16. & 9. 21, 22, 23. Matt. 18. 10. Heb. 1. 14.

20 And, behold, ᵃthou shalt be dumb, and not able to speak, until the day that these things shall be performed, because thou believest not my words, which shall be fulfilled in their season.

a Ezek. 3. 26. & 24. 27.

It is by some observed, that before the captivity of Babylon we read of no name of any angel, who have no names as we have, but assume names to declare the nature of their ministration; and that Gabriel signifieth, the power, or the strength, of God, because the declaring of the gospel, which the apostle declares *the power of God to salvation,* Rom. i. 16, seemeth to have been his peculiar ministration. We read of this Gabriel, Dan. viii. 16; ix. 21, where we find him foretelling the Messias, and the working of man's redemption; to which prophecies he doubtless refers Zacharias in saying, *I am Gabriel.* We again shall meet with him ver. 26, 27, six months after this, appearing to the virgin Mary, and telling her she should bring forth the Messiah. He addeth, *that stand in the presence of God.* As the good angels always behold the presence of our heavenly Father, (as our Saviour tells us,) and are ready to be sent about his messages, (whence is the name of *angels,*) they are called God's *ministers,* Psal. ciii. 21; civ. 4. *And am sent to speak unto thee, and to show thee these glad tidings:* God sent me on purpose to declare this thing to thee. Which when Zacharias might have known by the time and place when he appeared; at the time of prayer, at the altar in the holy place, where the evil angels used not to show themselves. *And, behold, thou shalt be dumb, and not able to speak, until the day that these things shall be performed.* Divines have perplexed themselves to give a just account of this signal punishment of so good a man; whether they have said enough to satisfaction I cannot tell. Abraham, upon the same question, was gratified with a sign, Gen. xv. 8, 9; so was Gideon, Judg. vi. 17. Where there is no difference in the words, or in a fact, there may be a great difference in the heart, and its inward habit and motions, from which those words proceed, and we must allow God to see that better than we can discern it by the words. Before Abraham's time, we read of no such experience of God's power in such cases, neither do we find that Abraham desired a sign as to this, that God would give him a child, but only as to the Lord's giving his posterity Canaan. Besides that, it is said, ver. 6, he *believed,* and it was *counted to him for righteousness;* and the apostle extolleth his faith, Rom. iv. 19—21: *Being not weak in faith, he considered not his own body now dead, when he was about an hundred years old, neither the deadness of Sarah's womb: he staggered not at the promise through unbelief; but was strong in faith, giving glory to God; being fully persuaded that, what he had promised, he was able to perform.* So as he asked not a sign for the begetting of a faith in him, he believed the Lord without a sight, only, fearing his own heart, he asked a sign for the further increase and confirmation of his faith. Besides, Zacharias's punishment was gentle, and of that nature that it also carried with it an answer to his desire: it was only the privation of speech, until the words of the angel should be fulfilled. *Because thou believest not my words.* The words of God by his messengers are to be believed, and the not believing their words, which they speak truly from him, and as so sent, is a sin God will severely punish. It is all one not to believe God, as not to believe those whom he sends, speaking what he bids them. *Which shall be fulfilled in their season.* The unbelief of men shall not make the word and promise of God of no effect; but God's promises have their seasons, before which we must not expect the accomplishment of them, Hab. ii. 3.

21 And the people waited for Zacharias, and marvelled that he tarried so long in the temple.

22 And when he came out, he could not speak unto them: and they perceived that he had seen a vision in the temple: for he beckoned unto them, and remained speechless.

23 And it came to pass, that, as soon as ᵇthe days of his ministration were accomplished, he departed to his own house.

b See 2 Kin. 11. 5. 1 Chr. 9. 25.

While the priest was in the holy place, the people were in that part of the temple called the court of Israel, or the court of the people, praying: when he had done, he came out, and blessed them according to the law, Numb. vi. 23—26, where is the form of blessing which he used; for this the people waited before they went home. Whether the angel's discourse with Zacharias was longer, or his amazement at the vision made him stay longer than the priest was wont to stay, it is uncertain; but so he did, and when he came out he was not able to pronounce the blessing, nor to speak at all, only he beckoneth to them, by which the people judged that he had seen some vision. Yet dumbness being none of those bodily defects for which by the law they were to be removed from the priest's office, nor having any great work in which he used his tongue during his ministration, which was more the work of the hands, he accomplished the days he was to minister, and then departed to his own house, for in the days of their ministration they had their lodgings in buildings appertaining to the temple.

24 And after those days his wife Elisabeth conceived, and hid herself five months, saying,

25 Thus hath the Lord dealt with me in the days wherein he looked on *me,* to ᶜtake away my reproach among men.

c Gen. 30. 23. Is. 4. 1. & 54. 1, 4.

How long *after those days* the Scripture saith not, but it is probable it was soon after, as in the case of Abraham, and in the case of Manoah's wife, Judg. xiii. 3, who conceived presently after the revelation. *And hid herself:* not that she hid herself from seeing any person, but she concealed from those whom she saw the hopes that she had of her being with child, and perhaps what her husband had let her know by writing of the revelation he had from the angel: not that she herself doubted the thing, that were unreasonable to presume, after the seeing of her husband made dumb for a sign of it, and the next words will let us know the contrary; but to avoid the discourse of people upon so unusual a thing, who might possibly think her too vain in speaking of a thing so improbable and unlikely as this was. In the mean time she did not conceal herself from God, but said, *Thus hath the Lord dealt with me,* ascribing it all to the power of God, who keepeth the key of the womb in his hand, and maketh the fruit of it his reward. *In the days wherein he looked upon me:* it is the same with ver. 48, *He hath regarded the low estate of his handmaiden.* The favour of God to his creatures is oft expressed under this notion, Psal. xxv. 18; lxxxiv. 9; cxix. 132. *To take away my reproach among men.* Barrenness is no more than a reproach amongst men; it was more especially a reproach to Jewish women, not only in regard of the expectation of being the mother of the Messias, (for none could expect that but a virgin, Isa. vii. 14, and she of the tribe of Judah, to which the Messiah was promised, and one of the house of David, to whose family he was promised as a branch,) but in regard of the special promise to Abraham, to whom a seed was promised, numerous as the dust, and as the stars, to which the barren woman could contribute nothing. It is a great mercy when God favoureth his people with any providences which take away their reproach amongst men, and a just cause for his people's thankful acknowledgment.

26 And in the sixth month the angel Gabriel was sent from God unto a city of Galilee, named Nazareth,

27 To a virgin *d* espoused to a man whose name was Joseph, of the house of David; and the virgin's name *was* Mary.

d Mat. 1. 18. ch. 2. 4, 5.

In the sixth month, that is, after Elisabeth's conception; thus it is expounded afterward, ver. 36. *The angel Gabriel*, the same angel that had appeared in the temple to Zacharias, who seemeth to have had a special ministration with reference to that part of God's will which was predictive of the Messias; he *was sent from God* (without whose command the angels do not move) *unto a city of Galilee named Nazareth*. There Joseph lived; from thence he went, chap. ii. 4. The angel came to the virgin, who is here described by her name, Mary, and her relation, she was espoused to one Joseph, who is said to be *of the house of David*. Matthew reduceth his genealogy to prove him to be so.

28 And the angel came in unto her, and said, *e* Hail, *thou that art* ‖ highly favoured, *f* the Lord *is* with thee: blessed *art* thou among women.

e Dan. 9. 23. & 10. 19. ‖ Or, *graciously accepted*, or, *much graced*: See ver. 30. *f* Judg. 6. 12.

Virgins betrothed, until the consummation of their marriage, were ordinarily kept in their friends' house: thither came this angel, and saith, *Hail, thou that art highly favoured.* The word translated *hail* signifies, Rejoice thou, or is as much as, God save thee. It is not the form of a prayer, (as the papists use it,) but an ordinary salutation, as much as, God save you, or, Good-morrow, is amongst us. *Thou that art highly favoured,* κεχαριτωμένη; the word comes originally from χάρις, which signifieth in Scripture two things: 1. The free love and favour of another bestowed on any: thus it is taken ver. 30. *thou hast found favour.* To the praise of the glory of his grace, Eph. i. 6. 2. It signifies good habits in the soul; as 2 Pet. iii. 18, *Grow in grace;* Col. iii. 16, *Singing with grace in your hearts.* Hence the verb, a participle from which the word here used is, may signify two things; either, 1. Thou hast received grace or favour from God, or, 2. Thou that art full of gracious habits. The first seems to be its sense in this place: it followeth in the verse, *blessed art thou;* so also it is expounded ver. 30, *for thou hast found favour with God.* So as the virgin was the object of Divine grace, as we are, and therefore not to be prayed to as the fountain of grace; she herself had nothing but what she received. This whole verse seemeth to be only a salutation, there is nothing of a prayer in it; the angel doth only take notice of her as a favourite of Heaven, one dear unto his Lord, with whom God was in an especial manner, and whom God blessed above the rate of those ordinary blessings with which he blesseth other women.

29 And when she saw *him*, *g* she was troubled at his saying, and cast in her mind what manner of salutation this should be.

g ver. 12.

It seemeth that she did not only hear a voice, and saw an ordinary appearance, but the appearance of the angel was attended with some manifestation of the glory of God, which affected her, and made her wonder what the meaning of this should be, that God should send an angel to her, and with such a kind of salutation.

30 And the angel said unto her, Fear not, Mary: for thou hast found favour with God.

This expounds those words, *thou that art highly favoured,* ver. 28, and lets her know that he came upon no ill design unto her, neither upon any human errand, nor yet with any message of evil tidings from God, for she was one for whom God had a favour.

31 *h* And, behold, thou shalt conceive in thy womb, and bring forth a son, and *i* shalt call his name JESUS.

h Is. 7. 14. Matt. 1. 21.
i ch. 2. 21.

32 He shall be great, *k* and shall be called the Son of the Highest: and *l* the Lord God shall give unto him the throne of his father David:

k Mark 5. 7. 2 Sam. 7. 11, 12. Is. 9. 6, 7. & 16. 5. Jer. 23. 5. Ps. 132. 11. Rev. 3. 7.

33 *m* And he shall reign over the house of Jacob for ever; and of his kingdom there shall be no end.

m Dan. 2. 44. & 7. 14, 27. Obad. 21. Mic. 4. 7. John 12. 34. Heb. 1. 8.

These three verses contain the substance of the angel's message or errand to the virgin, to tell her she should be the mother of *a Son*, by what name she should call him, and what he should be. In telling her this, who knew herself to be a virgin, one who had not known man, (as she expresseth it, ver. 34,) he plainly mindeth her that the prophecy, Isa. vii. 14, should be fulfilled in her. Thus far the angel's word signifieth a promise. *And shalt call his name Jesus:* the angel saith to Joseph, Matt. i. 21, and expounds it, adding, *for he shall save his people from their sins;* and thus the prophet expoundeth it, who saith, Isa. vii. 14, his name should be called *Immanuel.* There were two of this name before, Joshua and Jeshua, both of which were great types of Christ, as being great temporal saviours to the Israelites. The one brought them into Canaan; the other led them out of Babylon, Ezra ii. 2. But this was yet a more excellent Joshua, who was to save his people from their sins. The angel further goes on describing him, saying, *He shall be great.* Isaiah had said, chap. ix. 6, *his name shall be called Wonderful*, mighty both in words and deeds, Luke xxiv. 19. *And shall be called the Son of the Highest*, that is, the Son of God, who is often in Scripture made known by this name, Gen. xiv. 19; Psal. lxxxiii. 18; xcii. 1; Mark v. 7. *He shall be called the Son*, that is, he shall be so, for this phrase so signifieth often, Isa. i. 26; John i. 12; for he shall be known and *declared to be so*, Rom. i. 4. Peter so called him; so did the centurion who attended his cross. God himself called him so, Psal. ii. 7, and that in a sense agreeing to none but him; no, not to the angels, Heb. i. 5, much less to saints. *And the Lord God shall give unto him the throne of his father David:* not the temporal kingdom, but the spiritual kingdom over the same people over whom David ruled, from whom he is descended. It appeareth from many passages in the prophets that David's kingdom was a type of Christ's, 2 Sam. vii. 13; Psal. ii. 6; cxxxii. 11; Isa. ix. 6, 7; Amos ix. 11. Hence we find the name of David given to Christ, Jer. xxx. 9; Ezek. xxxiv. 23; xxxvii. 24; Hos. iii. 5. *And he shall reign over the house of Jacob for ever; and of his kingdom there shall be no end.* Jacob was the father of the twelve tribes of Israel; so as the house of Jacob primarily signifieth the Jews, who were the natural branches in this excellent olive. Christ's kingdom extended beyond the house of Jacob, but it began there, his law went first out of Zion, and he was in the first place sent to the lost sheep of Israel; he was the *minister of the circumcision*, Rom. xv. 8. Others were to be joined to the house of Jacob, Isa. xiv. 1. Or *Jacob*, and *the house of Jacob*, may signify the whole church, all that should believe in Christ. The rod of his strength went out of Zion, Psal. cx. 2, though his kingdom was not confined to Jacob. All believers who *worship God in the spirit, and rejoice in Christ Jesus*, are by the apostle determined *the circumcision*, Phil. iii. 3, and *he is a Jew who is one inwardly*, Rom. ii. 29. *And of his kingdom there shall be no end:* this both expounds the words *for ever*, going just before, and also distinguisheth the kingdom of Christ from all kingdoms of the world, which all shall have their periods; and also assureth us of the continuance of the gospel church, which is Christ's kingdom, till his kingdom of glory be revealed; and this agreeth with the prophecies of the Old Testament, concerning the kingdom of the Messiah, and the typical kingdom of David, Psal. cxlv. 13; Isa. ix. 7; Dan. vii. 14; Micah iv. 7.

34 Then said Mary unto the angel, How shall this be, seeing I know not a man?

There are some would excuse Mary in this reply, and tell us these words spake in her no doubt that the things spoken by the angel should not come to pass, only admiration, or a desire to be further acquainted which way God would effect such a wonder of providence. Others think her words hardly excusable from all guilt, though the more excusable because there had yet been no such precedent made in the world of the Divine power, as to cause a virgin to conceive, and bring forth a son. The next words, *seeing I know not a man*, seem to import that she understood the angel of the present or past time, that she had already conceived, or should immediately conceive, against which she objects her not having any carnal knowledge of any man. For the notion of some papists, that would from hence impose upon us to believe that Mary had vowed virginity, as if the sense of the words were, I am resolved never to know man, it is so ridiculous, that no man of ordinary sense can allow it; for, besides that there were no such vows that we ever read of amongst the Israelites, nor could any such be made but by the law of God might be rescinded, if made when the virgin was in her father's house; and besides that it is very improbable that a Jewish woman should make such a vow, in whom barrenness was such a reproach, and who looked upon it as a curse; I say, besides these things, who can have such unworthy thoughts of the blessed virgin, as to think that she should, having made such a vow, admit of an espousal to Joseph to mock him? But she certainly understood the angel as speaking of a thing in being, or which presently should be; and though she believed what the angel said, yet is desirous of further satisfaction how such a thing could be out of the ordinary course of nature.

35 And the angel answered and said unto her, ⁿThe Holy Ghost shall come upon thee, and the power of the Highest shall overshadow thee: therefore also that holy thing which shall be born of thee shall be called °the Son of God.

n Matt. 1. 20.
o Matt. 14. 33. & 26. 63, 64. Mark 1. 1. John 1. 34. & 20. 31. Acts 8. 37. Rom. 1. 4.

The Holy Ghost (who is also called here the power of the Highest) shall come upon thee; it is a phrase which signifieth a special and peculiar influence of the Holy Spirit: thus we read of the prophets, that the Spirit of the Lord came upon them, 2 Chron. xx. 14, &c., which argued a special influence of the Holy Spirit on them, efficacious, so as it put them upon a present prophesying. There is a common influence of God upon the forming of all children in the womb, Job x. 8; Psal. cxxxix. 15. But this phrase denoteth an extraordinary special influence of the Spirit, changing the order and course of nature, and giving a power to the blood of the virgin by him sanctified, to coagulate alone to the forming of the body of a child: this is more mysteriously yet expressed, by the term *overshadow thee*, which I take to be a modest phrase, signifying only a supply of man's act, by a Divine creating power, in a most miraculous manner. *Therefore also that holy thing which shall be born of thee shall be called the Son of God*, as Adam was called the son of God, chap. iii. 38, God (by his creating power) supplying as to him the place of father and mother, and to Christ supplying the place of the father, though not of the mother, for (saith the angel) he shall be *born of thee*. But yet that mass of flesh shall be a holy thing, because, though born of thee, and flesh of thy flesh, yet of thy flesh first sanctified, by the Holy Ghost coming upon and overshadowing of thee. He *shall be called* so, not that he was not so by eternal generation, (of which the angel here speaks not,) but the Word, the eternal Son of God, which was in the beginning, being thus made flesh, and personally united to thy flesh, the whole person shall be called *the Son of God*.

36 And, behold, thy cousin Elisabeth, she hath also conceived a son in her old age: and this is the sixth month with her, who was called barren.

37 For ᵖwith God nothing shall be impossible.

p Gen. 18. 14. Jer. 32. 17. Zech. 8. 6. Matt. 19. 26. Mark 10. 27. ch. 18. 27. Rom. 4. 21.

What a particular notice doth God take of the children of men! he knoweth our relations: *thy cousin Elisabeth*. Here some make a question how Elisabeth, who was one of the daughters of Aaron, ver. 5, and consequently of the tribe of Levi, could be cousin to Mary, who was of the house of David, and consequently of the tribe of Judah, (as our evangelist proveth, chap. iii.,) because of the law, Numb. xxxvi. 6, 7. But *cousin* may be taken in a large sense, as Paul calleth all the Jews his kinsmen, Rom. ix. 3; or they might be cousins in a strict sense, for the daughters of the tribe of Levi might marry into any other tribes, having no inheritance to carry away, to prevent which was the law, Numb. xxxvi. *And this is the sixth month* from her conception, by which time women use to be at some certainty about their quickening; you must not therefore think this impossible, for you know Elisabeth was counted *barren*, and was old, yet she hath conceived. *For with God nothing shall be impossible.* I bring you a message from God, to whom all things are possible. This was an ordinary saying amongst them, Nothing is impossible with God. Our Saviour useth it several times, Matt. xix. 26; Mark x. 27. Nor needed we any Scripture to prove that nothing could be impossible to him who is the first Being, the first Cause, and the Fountain of all power, and to whom all things are subject. No considerate man will from hence conclude that things are possible to God which would derogate from the perfection of the Divine Being, and are imperfections in us; nor yet that any thing is possible to God the contrary to which he hath willed, but God can do whatsoever he can will.

38 And Mary said, Behold the handmaid of the Lord; be it unto me according to thy word. And the angel departed from her.

Once have I spoken, (saith Job, chap. xl. 5.) *but I will not answer.* In like manner the virgin speaketh: I will dispute no more; I am the Lord's servant, let him do with me whatsoever he pleaseth. This phrase, *Behold the handmaid of the Lord*, doth not speak her the lady and queen of heaven, (as the papists style her,) but it speaketh her humility and readiness to give up herself to the Lord's pleasure, her assent and consent unto God. She addeth a prayer, that God would do according to what the angel had said unto her. The angel, having despatched his errand, and obtained what he came for, ascendeth into heaven.

39 And Mary arose in those days, and went into the hill country with haste, ᵠinto a city of Juda;

q Josh. 21. 9, 10, 11.

40 And entered into the house of Zacharias, and saluted Elisabeth.

Many think that this city where this Zacharias lived was Hebron, before called Kirjath-arba, Josh. xiv. 15, for that was a city in the mountainous part of Judah, one of the cities of refuge, and belonging to the priests, Josh. xx. 7; but whether it was so or no cannot be certainly determined. She probably went not only to rejoice with Elisabeth her kinswoman, but also to strengthen her own faith as to the revelation which she had received, finding that true which the angel had told her concerning her cousin Elisabeth.

41 And it came to pass, that, when Elisabeth heard the salutation of Mary, the babe leaped in her womb; and Elisabeth was filled with the Holy Ghost:

The motion of the child in the womb of the mother after her time of quickening is past, and the more than ordinary motion of it upon some extraordinary cause of joy, is no unusual thing with women in those circumstances; but doubtless as this motion was more than ordinary, so it had a more than ordinary cause, being caused from the Holy Spirit of God, and so the best interpreters judge: what is afterward said of Elisabeth, that she *was filled with the Holy Ghost*, is expounded in the next words, wherein she prophesieth, of the Spirit of prophecy.

42 And she spake out with a loud voice, and said, ʳBlessed *art* thou among women, and blessed *is* the fruit of thy womb.

r ver. 28. Judg. 5. 24.

Elisabeth useth the same words to Mary which the angel had used for her, ver. 28; that is, thou art an exceedingly happy woman, not only renowned, but one whom God hath greatly favoured and exceedingly blessed and made happy. *And blessed is the fruit of thy womb.* Though the same word be used, yet it is not to be understood of the same degree of blessing. Christ was anointed with the oil of gladness above his fellows, and blessed in another sense, and after another manner, than any creature can be said to be blessed, for the fulness of the Godhead dwelt in him bodily.

43 And whence *is* this to me, that the mother of my Lord should come to me?

Elisabeth in these words acknowledgeth both the incarnation of Christ, and the union of the Divine and human nature in the one person of the Mediator; she acknowledgeth Christ her Lord, and Mary to be his mother.

44 For, lo, as soon as the voice of thy salutation sounded in mine ears, the babe leaped in my womb for joy.

By these words Elisabeth declareth that she looked upon the motion of the child in her womb, upon Mary's salutation of her, as something more than natural.

|| Or, *which believed that there.* 45 And blessed *is* she || that believed: for there shall be a performance of those things which were told her from the Lord.

Some will have this given as a reason why Elisabeth pronounced her blessed, because she believed that what God had said should have its effect; as, chap. xi. 27, 28, when the woman blessed the womb that bare Christ, and the paps that gave him suck, Christ saith, *Yea, rather, blessed are they that hear the word of God, and keep it.* Mary was blessed not in this so much, that she brought forth Christ, as in this, that she believed in him. The words are certainly a great confirmation of what the angel had before told her, and it must needs be a great satisfaction to her to hear her kinswoman, by the Spirit of prophecy, coming extraordinarily upon her, confirming what the angel had before told her.

s 1 Sam. 2. 1. Ps. 34. 2, 3. & 35. 9. Hab. 3. 18. 46 And Mary said, *My soul doth magnify the Lord,

47 And my spirit hath rejoiced in God my Saviour.

We are now come to the famous song of the blessed virgin, upon whom also the Spirit of the Lord comes upon this occasion. She first solemnly gives praise unto God, then by various expressions declareth the power and goodness of God, showing him worthy to be praised, and lastly applieth what she had spoken more generally to the particular business of man's redemption. Our magnifying God is not by making him great, as he magnifieth us, as it is ver. 49, but by declaring and showing forth his greatness. She saith, her soul did magnify the Lord, and her spirit rejoiced. Soul and spirit are but two words signifying the same thing, and importing that she glorified God heartily, and with her whole soul, and teaching us that all praising of God with our lips is of no significancy, without the conjunction of the heart with the tongue. *In God my Saviour.* So Hannah, 1 Sam. ii. 1, *My heart rejoiceth in the Lord, mine horn is exalted in the Lord.* This is true spiritual rejoicing, when the primary object of our joy is not the sensible good, but the goodness of the Lord to us, in giving us that good thing.

t 1 Sam.1.11. Ps. 138. 6. 48 For ᵗhe hath regarded the low estate of his handmaiden: for, behold, from u Mal.3. 12. ch. 11. 27. henceforth ᵘall generations shall call me blessed.

Our translators have here rightly translated ταπείνωσιν, *low estate.* Mary doubtless doth not here commend her own humility, (as some papists would have it,) but magnifieth God for that he had respect to her who was of so mean and low a condition; for though she was of the family of David, yet that family had for many years been broken and afflicted, and she was now espoused to a carpenter, which spake her condition low and mean. though descended from the royal family of David: and thus God usually magnifieth himself; he chooseth David from the sheepfold to be king over Israel; he much delighteth to exalt such as are low; he chooseth *the foolish things of the world to confound the wise, the weak things of the world to confound the mighty, and base things of the world, and things which are despised, hath God chosen; that no flesh should glory in his presence,* 1 Cor. i. 27—29. *Henceforth* (saith Mary) *all generations shall call me blessed.* It is no mean favour of God, when God giveth us a name in the world, and that not only in the present generation, but in succeeding generations.

49 For he that is mighty ʷhath done to me great things; and ˣholy *is* his name. w Ps. 71. 19. & 126. 2, 3. x Ps. 111. 9.

That which is observable both in this verse, and in this whole song, is how the blessed virgin attributes all to God, and ascribeth nothing to herself, or any merits of her own, much like unto her father David. Psal. cxv. 1, *Not unto us, O Lord, not unto us, but unto thy name give glory, for thy mercy, and for thy truth's sake;* and herein she teacheth those generations, which she had even now said should call her blessed, how to take notice of her, viz. as one highly favoured of the Lord, one for whom God indeed had done great things, but not as one who had merited any thing at God's hand, much less as one to whom we should pay a greater devotion than to her Son, and speak to her that she should command her Son, according to the blasphemous devotion and idolatry of the papists. Mary is very careful of giving succeeding generations any occasion from her expressions for any such superstitions. *And holy is his name:* holy, that is, glorious and venerable. *His name,* that is, he himself is glorious and holy, far above the conception and comprehension of poor creatures.

50 And ʸhis mercy *is* on them that fear him from generation to generation. y Gen. 17. 7. Ex. 20. 6. Ps. 103. 17, 13.

Having celebrated God for his glory and majesty, she here celebrateth him for his mercy, which extends to all, but especially is showed to such as fear him. She certainly respecteth the promise of God to be the God of Abraham and his seed, but declareth this to be most eminently made good to those who are truly pious, all piety being expressed ordinarily in Scripture (especially in the Old Testament) under the notion of the fear of God. We have almost the same words Psal. ciii. 17. It is elsewhere expressed under the notion of thousands, Exod. xx. 6, signifying not only the extent of the Divine goodness to all his people, but the continuance of it for ever.

51 ᶻHe hath shewed strength with his arm; ᵃhe hath scattered the proud in the imagination of their hearts. z Ps. 98. 1. & 118. 15. Is. 40. 10. & 51. 9. & 52. 10. a Ps. 33. 10. 1 Pet. 5. 5.

52 ᵇHe hath put down the mighty from *their* seats, and exalted them of low degree. b 1 Sam.2. 6, &c. Job 5. 11. Ps. 113. 6.

In these verses the virgin celebrateth both the power and justice of God, as she before had done his holiness, and his mercy and goodness. The strength of a man is much seen in the effects of his arm; hence God, who hath no such parts as we have, is yet spoken of as if he had an arm, by which no more is signified than a mighty power, by which he bringeth things to pass; Exod. xv. 16; Psal. lxxxix. 13; xcviii. 1; Isa. xl. 10: so in many other texts. *He hath scattered the proud in the imagination of their hearts.* Jethro, Exod. xviii. 11, knew that *the Lord was above all gods,* because *in the thing wherein they dealt proudly he was above them.* The *proud* in Scripture often signifies wicked men, as *the humble* signifies good and holy men; but *proud,* in a strict sense, signifieth men that have a high opinion of themselves: now there is nothing that a proud man dealeth more proudly in, than in following the imaginations of his own heart. There (saith Mary) God scattereth them, turning their counsels into folly, and confounding them in their own imaginations. *He hath put down the mighty from their seats:* thus he did by Pharaoh, Nebuchadnezzar, &c.: he pulls down some, and sets up others. Promotion is not from the east, nor from the west. *And exalted them of low degree:* this is God's way; thus he exalted Moses, Joseph, Jacob, David. God thus showeth his mighty power and superintendency upon men's affairs. He doth what he pleaseth with men, yet what he doth is infinitely wise, just, and good.

53 ᶜHe hath filled the hungry with good things; and the rich he hath sent empty away. c 1 Sam.2.5. Ps. 34. 10.

In this sentence the holy virgin celebrateth the equity of

God in the government of the world, proportioning men in some degrees one to another, that the rapacious qualities of some might not gain all to them, while others have nothing. The notion of *hungry*, speaketh persons in want, and craving a supply. The notion of *rich*, signifieth persons that are full. God blesseth the poor, pitieth the needy, while he neglecteth greater persons. Some apply it to those whom Christ blesseth, Matt. v., who hunger and thirst after righteousness, and expound the rich of those who think they have no need of the righteousness of Christ. In this sense it is also true, but whether the virgin intended it here or no I know not.

54 He hath holpen his servant Israel, [d] in remembrance of *his* mercy;

55 [e] As he spake to our fathers, to Abraham, and to his seed for ever.

[d Ps. 98. 3. Jer. 31. 3, 20. e Gen. 17. 19. Ps. 132. 11. Rom. 11. 28. Gal. 3. 16.]

In these verses the blessed virgin celebrateth God's mercy together with his truth, withal she hath here a respect to God's particular goodness and mercy in the sending of the Redeemer. The word which we here translate *hath holpen*, signifieth he hath sustained, or as it were lifted up with his hand, *his servant Israel*, or his child Israel. He calleth *Ephraim* his *dear son*, his *pleasant child*, Jer. xxxi. 20; but by *Israel* he meaneth believers, those of Abraham's seed that lived in the faith, hope, and expectation of the Messiah; *the children of the promise*, Rom. ix. 8; those who are Jews *inwardly*, Rom. ii. 29; *the true circumcision*, Phil. iii. 3; *Israelites indeed*, John i. 47. This, she saith, God had done, not *in remembrance of* their merits, but *his* own mercy, Ezek. xxxvi. 32; of his own free goodness and mercy, and in the fulfilling of his promise made to Abraham, Gen. xvii. 15; the extent of which promise is declared Rom. ix. 6—9; and that *seed of Abraham*, his seed as the father of the faithful, shall be for ever, and the virtue of the promise shall hold to them for ever.

56 And Mary abode with her about three months, and returned to her own house.

It is most probable that she staid with her until she was brought to bed, not leaving her just at the time of her travail, but she staid not long after, but went home: by this time she must herself know that she was with child; and here in the true order of the history cometh in what we had Matt. i. 18—25: see the notes there.

57 Now Elisabeth's full time came that she should be delivered; and she brought forth a son.

58 And her neighbours and her cousins heard how the Lord had shewed great mercy upon her; and [f] they rejoiced with her.

[f ver. 14.]

The angel told Mary, ver. 36, that it was then *the sixth month with her;* after this Mary was with her about three months, which made up her full time; so she was delivered, and brought forth a son, to show the truth of God's promises, that we may all learn to give credit to his word. For the neighbours and kinswomen of Elisabeth to come, and to rejoice with her, was but according to the ordinary custom of friends to this day, like enough to hold to the end of the world. But the religion of persons in that age possibly is not in so ordinary a practice, I mean in the taking notice of the influence and goodness of God to those who receive such mercies. We are fallen into an age where congratulations made to friends upon any good things happening to them are ordinary, and meetings also to make merry (as they call it) upon such occasions; but ah, how little is that God, who openeth the womb, and a reward from whom children are, taken notice of! how little is his power and goodness in such providences taken notice of in such meetings, and made the subject of the discourses there had! Elisabeth's *neighbours and cousins* take notice *how the Lord had showed great mercy unto her*. The mercy of a child, of a safe delivery in the birth of a child, are great mercies, and ought to be the first and principal things taken notice of in such rejoicing meetings; otherwise the meeting is more like a meeting of pagans than of Christians.

59 And it came to pass, that [g] on the eighth day they came to circumcise the child; and they called him Zacharias, after the name of his father.

[g Gen. 17. 12. Lev. 12. 3.]

60 And his mother answered and said, [h] Not *so;* but he shall be called John.

[h ver. 13.]

61 And they said unto her, There is none of thy kindred that is called by this name.

The law for circumcision, Gen. xvii. 12; Lev. xii. 3, was strictly for it to be performed the eighth day. We find nothing commanded in Scripture, either as to the person who was to perform the office of the circumciser, or as to the place. God met Moses in the inn, and sought to kill him, because he had not circumcised his child, and Zipporah his wife did it, Exod. iv. 24, 25. It is said they afterwards did it in the synagogues, but there is no Divine law in the case. That the name was given to the child upon its circumcision appeareth not from Scripture. It is said, Gen. xxi. 3, that *Abraham called his son Isaac*, and then, ver. 4, *he circumcised his son Isaac being eight days old*. We read of no name given by Zipporah to her child when she circumcised him. But the name was at circumcision declared. It is most certain that John was circumcised in his father's house, for we find his mother was present, who at that time was not in a condition to stir abroad. They called his name *Zacharias*, whence we may observe the ancient usage of giving to children the names of their fathers and kindred. This in all probability is the reason of so many odd and unjustifiable names given to persons, such as are names of heathenish gods and goddesses, not fit to be named amongst Christians, &c. We derive from pagans, and though some heathens changed their names when they turned Christians, yet many (probably) did not, and by a long traduction (the names of parents being given to children) the names of pagan idols, such as Fortune, Diana, and the like, are by a most sordid practice made the names of Christians, a thing which certainly ought to be reformed, for it is a doing honour to those idols, if the giving a person's name to a child be (as we ordinarily account it) an honour done to the person whose name is so given. The Jews from their beginning seem to have had a religion as to this, giving names to their children either significative of God's mercy to them, or their children, or their own duty to God; and the names of the parents, or some of the kindred, were in honour to them given to their children; therefore when Elisabeth (who knew the counsel of God as to this child, either by some writing from Zacharias, or some revelation to herself) heard them call him Zacharias, and contradicted them in this thing, and named him John, they object that none of her kindred was called by that name.

62 And they made signs to his father, how he would have him called.

63 And he asked for a writing table, and wrote, saying, [i] His name is John. And they marvelled all.

[i ver. 13.]

It was the parents' place, the father's especially, to give children their names. Zacharias was dumb as yet, they therefore made signs to him; he by writing declareth that his name was *John*, that is, he was so named already by the angel, therefore there was to be no further dispute about it. The friends marvel at the consent of both the parents in the case, declining all the names of their kindred.

64 [k] And his mouth was opened immediately, and his tongue *loosed*, and he spake, and praised God.

[k ver. 20.]

The angel, ver. 20, inflicted the punishment upon him no longer than until what he had said should be performed; now it was performed, God looseth his tongue, and he praiseth God, by the song which we shall by and by meet with.

65 And fear came on all that dwelt round about them: and all these ‖ sayings were noised abroad throughout all [l] the hill country of Judæa.

[‖ Or, *things* l ver. 39]

66 And all they that heard *them* [m] laid *them* up in their hearts, saying, What manner of child shall this be! And [n] the hand of the Lord was with him.

[m ch. 2. 19, 51. n Gen. 39. 2. Ps. 80. 17. & 89. 21. Acts 11. 21.]

By *fear* here is to be understood an awe and religious reverence of God, caused by these miraculous operations. *Fear came upon every soul, and many wonders and signs were done by the apostles*, Acts ii. 43. *These sayings*, ῥήματα ταῦτα; it is a Hebraism; these doings, or matters, or things, were published throughout all the parts of Judea adjacent to the city where Zacharias dwelt, ver. 39. And those serious people that heard them pondered on them, considering the work of the Lord, and did think that this child would prove no ordinary person. *And the hand of the Lord was with him.* By *the hand of the Lord* is meant, the power of the Lord, his providence, love, favour: thus the Lord is said to have been with Samuel, 1 Sam. iii. 19. The hand of the Lord oft signifieth the power, help, and assistance of the Lord, 1 Chron. xxviii. 19; Psal. lxxx. 17. The hand of the Lord upon a person sometimes signifieth the Spirit of prophecy, Ezek. i. 3; xl. 1; but this is a different phrase, denoting only God's special favour to John, watching over and protecting him, causing him to grow up and thrive, to improve in knowledge, &c.

o Joel 2. 28. **67 And his father Zacharias ° was filled with the Holy Ghost, and prophesied, saying,**

We must not think that Zacharias was before this time destitute of the Holy Ghost, we heard the contrary before, ver. 6, but the Holy Ghost at this time came upon him by a particular and more especial impulse; as it did upon the prophets, whom the Spirit moved but at some special times to prophesy, though it at all times dwelt and wrought in them, as a holy, sanctifying Spirit. This is made good by the next words, which tell us he *prophesied;* which word signifieth any speaking for or instead of another, and is not only applicable to such speakings as are foretellings of things which shall afterward come to pass, but unto any speaking for or instead of God, in the revelation of his will made known unto us. In this prophecy there is both predictions of what should come to pass concerning John and concerning Christ, and also applications of what was before spoken of them by the prophets; and it is observed by some, that it is an epitome of all those ancient prophecies, and that there is in it a compendium of the whole doctrine of the gospel.

p 1 Kings 1.
48. Ps. 41.
13. & 72. 18.
& 106. 48.
q Ex. 3. 16.
& 4. 31.
Ps. 111. 9.
ch. 7. 16.
r Ps. 132. 17.
68 ᵖ Blessed *be* the Lord God of Israel; for ᑫ he hath visited and redeemed his people,

69 ʳ And hath raised up an horn of salvation for us in the house of his servant David;.

s Jer. 23. 5,
6. & 30. 10.
Dan. 9. 24.
Acts 3. 21.
Rom. 1. 2.
70 ˢ As he spake by the mouth of his holy prophets, which have been since the world began:

God is not the God of Israel only, but of all the nations of the earth also; but he is peculiarly called *the God of Israel*, both here and in many other places, Psal. xli. 13; lxxii. 18; cvi. 48, &c., in regard of the covenant which he had specially made with them, and the special advantages they had, mentioned by the apostle; *to them were committed the oracles of God*, Rom. iii. 2; and to them pertained *the adoption, the glory, the covenants, the giving of the law, and the service of God, and the promises*, Rom. ix. 4. Zacharias pronounceth God *blessed*, and desires that he may be blessed, that is, honoured, and celebrated, and spoken well of, for that he had *visited and redeemed his people*. The word may be extended to all God's deliverances of Israel, but it seemeth to be here more specially restrained by what followeth to the redemption by Christ. *And hath raised up an horn of salvation for us.* An horn *of salvation* signifies a mighty, powerful salvation, by a metaphor taken from beasts, which much exert their power by their horns. The beast's ten horns, Dan. vii. 7, are expounded to be ten kings, ver. 24; so Psal. lxxv. 10, where David saith he *will cut off all the horns of the wicked;* so Lam. ii. 3, where God is said to have *cut off all the horn of Israel*. *In the house of his servant David.* This agreeth to the prophecy, Jer. xxx. 9, where Christ is called *David; They shall serve the Lord their God, and David their King, whom I will raise up unto them;* who is also called *a righteous Branch raised unto David*, Jer. xxiii. 5. God is said to have raised up this horn of salvation in the house of David. The house of David was now down, lapsed and decayed. God promiseth to raise up to the Israelites a mighty salvation from the house of David. This was fulfilled in Christ. *As he spake by the mouth of his holy prophets, which have been since the world began.* All the prophets, or many of them at least, prophesied of Christ as the Son of David, and of a great salvation to be raised up to Israel from his house.

71 That we should be saved from our enemies, and from the hand of all that hate us;

72 ᵗ To perform the mercy *promised* to our fathers, and to remember his holy covenant;
t Lev. 26.42.
Ps. 98. 3. &
105. 8, 9. &
106. 45.
Ezek. 16. 60.
ver. 54.

This was that which God had told them by his prophets, that a mighty salvation should arise to them out of the house of David, by which they should be saved from their enemies. By which enemies the generality of the Jews understood their temporal enemies, made of flesh and blood. But Zacharias, speaking by the Spirit of prophecy, must needs have a truer notion of it, as it signifies our spiritual enemies. All this is attributed to God's mercy and faithfulness, his mercy freely looking upon his creatures in distress and misery, his faithfulness in remembrance of his holy covenant, made to Adam, Abraham, David, &c.; but it is more particularly explained.

73 ᵘ The oath which he sware to our father Abraham,
u Gen. 12. 3.
& 17. 4. & 22.
16, 17. Heb.
6. 13, 17.

God first gave Abraham his word, Gen. xviii. 10, then he confirmed it by his oath, Gen. xxii. 16. The apostle, to the Hebrews, saith, chap. vi. 13, *When God made promise to Abraham, because he could swear by no greater, he sware by himself.*

74 That he would grant unto us, that we being delivered out of the hand of our enemies might ˣ serve him without fear,
x Rom. 6.
18, 22.
Heb. 9. 14.
y Jer. 32. 39,
40. Ephes. 4.
24. 2 Thess.
2. 13. 2 Tim.
1. 9. Tit. 2.
12. 1 Pet. 1.
15. 2 Pet.1.4.

75 ʸ In holiness and righteousness before him, all the days of our life.

Thus Zacharias, by an infallible Spirit, expounds the covenants and oaths of God to Abraham and David, not as they appear to us at first view, as if they were promises of a mere temporal kingdom, and a victory for the Jews over their enemies, together with a splendid state for them, which was all the scribes and Pharisees, and the generality of the Jews, expected from the Messiah; but as confirming God's resolution to send the Jews a Saviour, who should save them from their sins, the guilt and dominion of them, and from the power of hell, and purchase a spiritual liberty for them to serve the Lord all their days, *without fear, in holiness and righteousness*, which indeed was the true end of the Messiah's coming. Thus far now the song of this holy man respected Christ, whom he showeth to be sent from the free grace and mercy of God, yet in performance of God's truth and faithfulness, according to his oath and promises; and to be therefore sent to deliver his people from their enemies, and to purchase for them a spiritual liberty, not to sin, but to serve the Lord without fear, in holiness and righteousness. The latter part of his prophecy respecteth John the Baptist, the new-born son of this priest and heavenly prophet.

76 And thou, child, shalt be called the prophet of the Highest: for ᶻ thou shalt go before the face of the Lord to prepare his ways;
z Is. 40. 3
Mal. 3. 1. &
4. 5. Matt. 11,
10. ver. 17.

Zacharias here foretelleth what came to pass about thirty years after, for it cannot be thought that John began his ministry before the sacerdotal age, especially considering Christ did not begin sooner, chap. iii. 23. *Thou shalt be called the prophet;* that may either signify, thou shalt be a prophet, as Matt. v. 9; John i. 12; or thou shalt be owned or taken notice of as the prophet *of the Highest*. Both were true in John. He was a prophet, (though not *that Prophet*, John i. 21,) *yea, and more than a prophet*, saith our Saviour, Matt. xi. 9. *For thou shalt go before his face to prepare his ways.* This was according to the prophecy,

Isa. xl. 3; Mal. iv. 5; and according to what John said of himself, Matt. iii. 3; Mark i. 3. See the notes on Matt. iii. 3.

77 To give knowledge of salvation unto his people ᵃ ‖by the remission of their sins,

ᵃ Mark 1. 4. ch. 3. 3.
‖ Or, for.

To preach the doctrine of repentance to men, that they may obtain remission of sins. But it seems more natural, To teach people that the only way by which they can attain salvation, is not by any righteousness of their own, but by obtaining the free pardon and remission of their sins by Christ and his righteousness, Psal. xxxii. 1; which is in short to preach the gospel, which *is the power of God to salvation to every one that believeth. For therein is the righteousness of God revealed from faith to faith,* Rom. i. 16, 17.

78 Through the ‖ tender mercy of our God; whereby the ‖ dayspring from on high hath visited us,

‖ Or, bowels of the mercy.
‖ Or, sunrising, or, branch. Num. 24. 17. Is. 11. 1. Zech. 3. 8. & 6. 12. Mal. 4. 2.

In the Greek it is, through the bowels of mercy. An ordinary expression, and very natural, to signify great and deep compassion, Gen. xliii. 30; 1 Kings iii. 26. Our remission of sin floweth from God's bowels of mercy; it dependeth not upon our satisfactions and penances, (as papists dream,) but God's free and tender love; yet God must be just, and declare his righteousness while he justifieth the ungodly. *Whereby the Day-spring from on high hath visited us, ἀνατολὴ ἐξ ὕψους.* Some think that the Greek word answereth the Hebrew word, translated the *Branch,* Jer. xxiii. 5; Zech. iii. 8: the seventy interpreters translate it by ἀνατολήν, Jer. xxxiii. 15. Those texts manifestly relate to Christ, who is called there *the Branch.* Others think it rather answereth the Hebrew word אוֹר we translate it a great *light.* Others think it should be translated *the East.* So they say Christ is called Zech. iii. 8; vi. 12; but we translate it *the Branch* in both those places. Be it *the Branch,* or *the Light,* or *Day-spring,* or *the East,* it is certain Christ is meant, who is called *the Sun of righteousness,* Mal. iv. 2. That God might be just in the remission of our sins, he sent Christ to visit us, and in our nature to die for us.

79 ᵇTo give light to them that sit in darkness and *in* the shadow of death, to guide our feet into the way of peace.

ᵇ Is. 9. 2. & 42. 7. & 49. 9. Matt. 4. 16. Acts 26. 18.

Here Zacharias showeth us the end why God visited us with his Son, *the Branch, the Light, the Day-spring, the Sun of righteousness.* Men were in the darkness of sin and ignorance, dead in trespasses and sins, at war and enmity with God; Christ came to give them the light of gospel revelations, the light of spiritual comfort and salvation, to purchase peace, and to direct them how to walk that they might have peace with God, and at last enter into peace. This he did to the Jews first, then to the Gentiles: see Isa. ix. 1, 2; lx. 1, 19.

80 And ᶜthe child grew, and waxed strong in spirit, and ᵈwas in the deserts till the day of his shewing unto Israel.

ᶜ ch. 2. 40.
ᵈ Matt. 3. 1. & 11. 7.

The evangelist having done with Zacharias's prophetical song, now cometh to tell us what became of John. He saith, *the child grew, and waxed strong in spirit.* He did not only grow in his bodily dimensions, but in the endowments of his mind. *And was in the deserts,* that is, in places very thinly inhabited, (some will have this to have been the deserts of Ziph and Maon,) *till the day of his showing unto Israel;* that is, in all probability, till he was about thirty years of age, when he came forth as a public preacher to those parts of Israel where he spent the small remaining part of his life, of which we shall hear more hereafter.

CHAP. II

Augustus taxeth all the Roman empire: Joseph goeth with Mary to be taxed at Bethlehem, 1—5. *The birth of Christ,* 6, 7. *An angel bringeth news thereof to the shepherds: the heavenly host praise God,* 8—14. *The shepherds, finding it to be as the angel had said, glorify God,* 15—20. *The circumcision of Christ,* 21. *The purifying of Mary,* 22—24. *Simeon's prophecy,* 25—35, *and Anna's, concerning Christ,* 36—38. *Jesus groweth, and increaseth in wisdom,* 39, 40. *At twelve years of age he goeth with his parents to Jerusalem, and questioneth with the doctors in the temple,* 41—50. *He is obedient to his parents,* 51, 52.

AND it came to pass in those days, that there went out a decree from Cæsar Augustus, that all the world should be ‖ taxed.

‖ Or, inrolled.

2 (ᵃ*And* this taxing was first made when Cyrenius was governor of Syria.)

ᵃ Acts 5. 37.

3 And all went to be taxed, every one into his own city.

Octavius Cæsar (called Augustus, for his prosperous achievements) was the first Roman emperor properly so called, (for Julius Cæsar had but the title of perpetual dictator,) in the forty-second year of whose reign Christ was born, (Josephus saith, in the one and thirtieth year, Antiq. cap. 10.,) Herod the Great being at that time king of Judea, being so declared by the senate of Rome near forty years before. It was the custom of the Romans to take a particular account of the numbers and qualities of all persons inhabiting countries under their jurisdiction, in order to the laying of taxes upon them. About the time of the birth of Christ there was a decree issued from the Roman emperor for such a census or account to be taken of the Jews, who, some think, are here only understood by the term, *all the world;* others think that it was a decree which reached all that part of the world which was subject to the Roman emperor. This trust it seemeth was committed to Cyrenius, governor of Syria; whether he was at that time governor, or afterwards made governor, and at this time only a commissioner for this business, is not agreed. That this Cyrenius was the same whom the Roman historians call Quirinius is pretty well agreed. Great endeavours are used to reconcile what Luke saith here to Josephus and the Roman historians, who make Varus, not Quirinius, at this time the president of Syria. Those who desire to be satisfied as to those things may read Mr. Pool's Synopsis Criticorum upon this text, &c. Where civil historians differ from what we have in holy writ, we are obliged to believe them mistaken, not the penmen of holy writ, who were guided by an infallible Spirit. Leaving therefore those disputes, and in what sense this census is called the *first,* or is said to be first begun, when Cyrenius or Quirinius was president, as being of no great concern, (for other historians grant Quirinius at this time a commissioner with Caius Cæsar, and within ten years after president, in succession to Varus,) let us rather herein observe the wonderful providence of God in the ordering of things for the fulfilling of his word, while we think of no such things, to which purpose doubtless this is premised by the evangelist. According to the counsel of God, declared by his prophets, Micah v. 2, Christ was to be born at Bethlehem, the metropolis of Judea; so the chief priests and scribes tell Herod, Matt. ii. 5. Mary his mother, and Joseph his supposed father, lived at a great distance from Bethlehem, in Nazareth, a city of Galilee. God so ordereth it, that the Roman emperor (under whose power the Jews were at this time) orders a numbering of all his subjects, either in all his dominions at the same time, or at least in Judea, and an account to be taken of their persons and qualities, in order to the laying taxes upon them, to defray the charges of the empire. The account of the Jews being to be taken according to their tribes, those who belonged to each tribe were ordered to convene in the chief city belonging to the tribe of which they were. Joseph and Mary were both of the tribe of Judah. This occasion brings them both to Bethlehem, being the chief city of their tribe, to meet the emperor's commissioners. So Christ came to be born in Bethlehem, according to the word of the Lord, from which a tittle shall not fail; and little Bethlehem becomes not the least amongst the thousands of Judah, one coming out of it to be a *Ruler in Israel, whose goings forth were of old, even from everlasting.*

4 And Joseph also went up from Galilee, out of the city of Nazareth, into Judæa, unto ᵇthe city of David, which is

ᵇ 1 Sam. 16. 1, 4. John 7. 42.

called Bethlehem; (^cbecause he was of the house and lineage of David :)

5 To be taxed with Mary ^d his espoused wife, being great with child.

6 And so it was, that, while they were there, the days were accomplished that she should be delivered.

This was the occasion of Joseph's coming to Bethlehem, who either for fear of Herod, or for the convenience of his trade, (though he belonged to the tribe of Judah, was removed into Galilee; but he yieldeth obedience to the civil magistrates, and cometh to be enrolled in the court books belonging to the Roman empire; to which by this action he acknowledgeth himself a subject; he also by this act publicly declared both himself and Mary his wife to have been of the tribe of Judah, and of the family of David. We are told it was the custom of the Romans to enrol both women and children; however, Mary's personal attendance upon this homage might have been excused by her being great with child, had not the counsel of God so ordered it, that Christ should be born there; this doubtless carried Mary along with Joseph, he having now (according to the angel's direction, Matt. i. 20, 24,) took her unto him as his wife. While they were there, Mary's time of child-bearing was *accomplished:* we have the like phrase Gen. xxv. 24.

7 And ^eshe brought forth her firstborn son, and wrapped him in swaddling clothes, and laid him in a manger; because there was no room for them in the inn.

It is Bucer's note, that in the Greek it is not *her firstborn Son,* but τὸν υἱον αὐτῆς τὸν πρωτότοκον, her Son, the first-born; he was truly her Son, and her Son first-born, but he was not called πρωτότοκον upon that account merely, for he was *the first-born of every creature,* Col. i. 15: he was the first-born also of Mary, but it cannot be from thence concluded she had more sons, for where there is but one son he is the first-born. *And wrapped him in swaddling clothes, and laid him in a manger, &c.* Whether the inn was in the city, or in the suburbs adjoining near to the city, is not material for us to know; nor, considering the occasion of meeting at Bethlehem at that day, and the numbers who upon that occasion must be there, is it at all strange, that a person of no higher visible quality than a carpenter should not find a room in the inn, but be thrust into a stable; nor was it unusual in those countries for men and women to have lodgings in the same rooms where beasts were kept. it is no more than is at this day in some places even in Europe. Here the virgin falls into her labour, brings forth her Son, and lodgeth him in a manger; God (by this) teaching all Christians to despise the high and gay things of this world. He who, though he was *in the form of God,* and *thought it not robbery to be equal with the Father,* thus making *himself of no reputation; and being found in fashion as a man,* thus humbling himself, as the apostle speaks, Phil. ii. 6—8.

8 And there were in the same country shepherds abiding in the field, keeping || watch over their flock by night.

Bethlehem was a place about which were pastures for sheep, as appears from 1 Sam. xvii. 15. There were shepherds abroad in the night (for so the word signifieth) watching over their flocks; whether the phrase signifieth (as some think) successive watches, such as are kept by soldiers, and by the priests, I cannot say. This maketh some think, that it is hardly probable that our Saviour was born in December in the midst of the winter, that being no time when shepherds use in the night to be keeping their flocks in the field.

9 And, lo, the angel of the Lord came upon them, and the glory of the Lord shone round about them: ^fand they were sore afraid.

Christ was promised to men who by their occupation were shepherds, Gen. xlvii. 3. He himself was the chief Shepherd, and the true Shepherd, John x. 11. The first publication of his birth is made to shepherds; not to shepherds that were idle, but busied in their honest vocations, keeping their flocks. This publication of his birth is made by an angel, whether the angel Gabriel before mentioned, or another, is not certain. This angel surpriseth the shepherds, cometh upon them thinking no such thing, but only minding their business. The angel comes in a glorious appearance, probably an extraordinary light, for it is said, it *shone round about them:* such an appearance of extraordinary light is Luke ix. 31, 32. That *they were sore afraid* was but natural; we are naturally affected at sudden and unusual appearances with fear and amazement.

10 And the angel said unto them, Fear not: for, behold, I bring you good tidings of great joy, ^gwhich shall be to all people.

11 ^hFor unto you is born this day in the city of David ⁱa Saviour, ^kwhich is Christ the Lord.

12 And this *shall be* a sign unto you; Ye shall find the babe wrapped in swaddling clothes, lying in a manger.

Though God, in his appearances to his people, was wont so to appear, as to show them cause to revere his majesty, yet he always supported them, that their spirits might not fail under those apprehensions and consternations. The angel bids them not to fear, for they had no reason to be afraid, he came not to bring them any affrighting tidings, but *tidings of joy,* and that not to them alone, but *to all people,* both Jews and Gentiles, for to that latitude the text may be expounded. What was that? *Unto you is born this day in the city of David a Saviour, which is Christ the Lord.* You have heard of the promises of the Messias, of a Christ that should come, and of the house of David. The promises of that nature are this day fulfilled, he is born *this very day; unto you,* but not to you alone; he had before told them that his tidings of joy should extend to all nations. *And this shall be a sign unto you,* by this you shall know the truth of what I say, and you shall know also where to find him; in *the city of David* (that is, Bethlehem, as was said before) *ye shall find the babe wrapped in swaddling clothes, lying in a manger.* Where you find such a babe, that is he, therefore be not offended at his low and mean condition, let that be no stumbling-block to you, I give it you as a sign by which you shall know him.

13 ^lAnd suddenly there was with the angel a multitude of the heavenly host praising God, and saying,

14 ^mGlory to God in the highest, and on earth ⁿpeace, ^ogood will toward men.

The nativity of our Saviour was published first by one angel, but it must be celebrated by a multitude of angels, who appear praising God upon this occasion. These are called the Lord's host, Psal. ciii. 20, 21, not only because he useth them as his arms, to destroy his enemies, but also because of the order which is amongst them. How they praised God is expressed ver. 14, they sang *Glory to God in the highest, and on earth peace, good-will toward men.* The words may be taken either judicatively, as signifying that was come to pass that day, by which God would have glory, men would have peace, and the good-will of God to the sons of men was unspeakably declared: or precatorily, the angels desiring God might have glory, and that peace might be on earth, and the good-will of God published to the sons of men. But the Vulgar Latin is most corrupt, that rendereth these words, *peace to men of good-will.* When we consider that the heavenly host was here praising God, it will appear very reasonable to interpret these words judicatively; the angels hereby declaring their apprehensions, and the truth concerning this act of providence, no act more declaring the glory of God's power, wisdom, or goodness; nor more declaring his good-will towards men, and more conducing to peace upon the earth, whether by it we understand the union of the Jews and Gentiles, or that peace of particular souls which floweth from a justification by faith in Christ; for though the text seemeth to speak of three things, *glory to God, peace on earth, and good-will toward men*, yet indeed they are but two; the two latter differing only as the cause and the effect; the goodwill of God is the cause, peace with or amongst men is the effect, Rom. v. 1; Eph. ii. 14, 15, 17.

15 And it came to pass, as the angels were gone away from them into heaven, †the shepherds said one to another, Let us now go even unto Bethlehem, and see this thing which is come to pass, which the Lord hath made known unto us.

† Gr. *the men the shepherds.*

16 And they came with haste, and found Mary, and Joseph, and the babe lying in a manger.

17 And when they had seen *it*, they made known abroad the saying which was told them concerning this child.

18 And all they that heard *it* wondered at those things which were told them by the shepherds.

It was night, yet they delayed not to go and make a search, according to the revelation of the angel; and not in vain, they *found Mary, and Joseph, and the babe.* Divine revelations never deceive the soul that gives credit to them. Heaven and earth may pass away, but nothing which God hath spoken shall pass away without its accomplishment. *When they had seen it, they made known the saying, &c:* they had no charge of secrecy upon them, so did well in publishing what was of such universal concern for men to know. Spiritual morsels ought not to be ate alone. The effect of their relation, in the generality of the people that heard it, was the same which we have often met with upon the people's seeing of Christ's miracles, viz. amazement and astonishment; we read nothing of their faith. The first was a natural effect of a strange relation. The other must have been the special operation of God.

p Gen. 37. 11. ch. 1. 66. ver. 51.

19 ᵖBut Mary kept all these things, and pondered *them* in her heart.

20 And the shepherds returned, glorifying and praising God for all the things that they had heard and seen, as it was told unto them.

The different effect of these things upon the generality of the people, upon Mary, and upon the shepherds, is worthy of our notice. The people only wondered, thinking the story of the shepherds a strange story. Mary suffereth them not to pass out of her thoughts, nor entertaineth them with a mere passion, which suddenly is extinguished; but she pondereth them in her heart, both those things she had learned from her husband, and what herself had heard from the angel, and this also, which was related to her of or by the shepherds. The shepherds return, that is, to the care of their flocks. Religion gives none a discharge from their secular duties: the disciples had a special call and command, that left their nets, and their parents, and followed Christ. The shepherds were only made occasional preachers, *pro hac vice*; they return, but *glorifying and praising God for all the things that they had heard and seen, as it was told unto them*; which argued that they gave a firm and full assent to them, and that they were the first-fruits of believers under the gospel dispensation. True faith produceth great joy and thanksgiving to God, and needs must produce joy, because of the union it maketh betwixt a soul and its desired object.

Before the Account called Anno Domini the fourth Year. q Gen. 17. 12. Lev. 12. 3. ch. 1. 59. r Mat. 1. 21, 25. ch. 1. 31.

21 ᑫAnd when eight days were accomplished for the circumcising of the child, his name was called ʳJESUS, which was so named of the angel before he was conceived in the womb.

The time prescribed by the Divine law for circumcision was the eighth day, Gen. xvii. 12; Lev. xii. 3. He was indeed the lawgiver, and as such not tied to the observance of the law. But he was also *made of a woman, made under the law*, Gal. iv. 4; and the law was, Lev. xii. 2, that *if a woman had conceived seed, and borne a man-child, in the eighth day the flesh of his foreskin should be circumcised*. He was to make himself appear the Son of Abraham; and so this was God's covenant, Gen. xvii. 10, with Abraham and his seed after him; *Every man-child among you shall be circumcised*. This law Christ was bound to fulfil, and by the fulfilling of it in this point he showed himself *a debtor to do the whole law*, Gal. v. 3, and by his observance of it he was to teach us our duty. He was to be *a minister of the circumcision*, Rom. xv. 8, and to the circumcision, which they would never have allowed him to be, had not he himself been circumcised; upon which account Paul took Timothy, *and circumcised him*, Acts xvi. 3. By his circumcision also we were to be *circumcised with the circumcision made without hands, in putting off the body of the sins of the flesh*, Col. ii. 11. It was therefore reasonable and necessary that Christ should be circumcised the eighth day. *His name was called Jesus*; it was in circumcision before witnesses publicly declared to be so, for God by his angel had given him his name, Matt. i. 21. We read of four under the Old Testament, to whom God gave names before they were born; Isaac, Gen. xvii. 19, Josiah, 1 Kings xiii. 2, Ishmael, Gen. xvi. 11, Cyrus, Isa. xliv. 28; and in the New Testament to John the Baptist, and to Jesus Christ. Which lets us know the certainty to God of future contingencies; for though the parents of Ishmael, and Isaac, John Baptist, and Christ, imposed those names in obedience to the command of God, and there was but a small time betwixt the giving of these four their names and their birth, yet the case was otherwise as to Josiah and Cyrus.

22 And when ˢthe days of her purification according to the law of Moses were accomplished, they brought him to Jerusalem, to present *him* to the Lord;

s Lev. 12. 2, 3, 4, 6.

23 (As it is written in the law of the Lord, ᵗEvery male that openeth the womb shall be called holy to the Lord;)

t Ex. 13. 2. & 22. 29. & 34. 19. Num. 3. 13. & 8. 17. & 18. 15.

24 And to offer a sacrifice according to ᵘthat which is said in the law of the Lord, A pair of turtledoves, or two young pigeons.

u Lev. 12. 2, 6, 8.

In these verses is a record of the virgin's obedience to two laws, the one concerning the purification of the woman after child-birth; the other concerning the presenting of the male child before the Lord. We have the law concerning purification, Lev. xii. throughout. The sum was, That if a woman had brought forth a male child, she should be unclean seven days, and after that continue in the blood of her purifying thirty-three days. If she brought forth a female, she was to be unclean fourteen days, and afterward to continue in the blood of her purifying sixty-six days. So that the time of the woman's purification after the birth of a female was fourscore days, for a male (which was the present case) forty. After the expiration of which time, she was to bring a lamb of a year old for a burnt-offering, and a young pigeon or a turtle-dove for a sin-offering, to the priest to the tabernacle, who was to offer it for her, and to make an atonement. If she were poor, and not able to bring a lamb, (which seems the present case,) then she was to bring only two turtle-doves, or two young pigeons, the one for a burnt-offering, the other for a sin-offering. The evangelist takes no notice of any lamb, but only *a pair of turtle-doves, or two young pigeons*; which lets us know she was poor, and so obliged by the law no further. Mary, after her forty days were expired, cometh up to the temple, to yield obedience to this law. And not so only, but also to present her child before the Lord. This depended upon two laws. We find the one Exod. xiii. 2, where, in remembrance of God's sparing the Israelites, when he smote the first-born of the Egyptians, he gave the Israelites this law: *Sanctify unto me all the first-born, whatsoever openeth the womb among the children of Israel, both of man and of beast: it is mine*. So chap. xxii. 29; xxxiv. 19. Instead of these, God took the Levites, as appears by Numb. viii. 16; yet were the first-born to be presented before the Lord, and redeemed by the payment of five shekels apiece, for all those who were above the number of the Levites, as appeareth by Numb. iii. 44—47; and five shekels was the redemption price of any male upon a singular vow, Lev. xxvii. 6. For these two ends, after six weeks, Joseph, and Mary, and Jesus come up to Jerusalem.

25 And, behold, there was a man in Jeru-

S. LUKE II

salem, whose name *was* Simeon; and the same man *was* just and devout, [x] waiting for the consolation of Israel: and the Holy Ghost was upon him.

26 And it was revealed unto him by the Holy Ghost, that he should not [y] see death, before he had seen the Lord's Christ.

27 And he came [z] by the Spirit into the temple: and when the parents brought in the child Jesus, to do for him after the custom of the law,

28 Then took he him up in his arms, and blessed God, and said,

x Is. 40. 1. Mark 15. 43. ver. 38.
y Ps. 89. 48. Heb. 11. 5.
z Matt. 4. 1.

Interpreters have spent much pains in fortifying their conjectures (for they can be no more) that this Simeon was Rabban Simeon, the son of Hillel, the father of Gamaliel, but to what purpose I cannot tell; it can hardly be thought that a man of that note should do such a thing as this so openly, and no more notice be taken of him. That which Calvin, and Brentius, and other Reformed divines do think is much more probable, that he was some ordinary, plain man, of an obscure quality as to his circumstances in the world. There was a general expectation of the Messias at this time, but very few had a right notion of him, but lived in a vain expectation of I know not what secular prince, who should bring them a temporal deliverance. These few were scarce any of them of their rabbies or rabbans, but a poor despised sort of people, whom those great doctors counted accursed, John vii. 48, 49. The revelations of Christ were to none of the Pharisees, but to Joseph, a carpenter, to Mary, a despised virgin, though of the house of David, to an ordinary priest, Zacharias, to shepherds; and why we should fancy this Simeon a principal doctor I cannot tell. The evangelist gives him his highest title, *A just man, and devout*, and one that waited *for the consolation of Israel*. One of the remnant, according to the election of grace, mentioned by the apostle; a holy and righteous man, one who waited *for the consolation of Israel*. Which is the same in sense with the character given of Joseph of Arimathea, chap. xxiii. 51, that *waited for the kingdom of God*. Simeon waited for Christ, that is meant by *the consolation of Israel*. For it is very observable, that the prophets ordinarily comforted the people of God amongst the Jews, against all their sad tidings they brought them, with the prophecies of the coming and kingdom of Christ, Isa. lxvi. 13; Jer. xxxi. 13; Zech. i. 17. Herein old Simeon showed the truth of his piety and devotion, that he believed and waited for the coming of Christ; he had a true notion of the Messiah promised, he believed that he should come, and he waited for his coming. *And it was revealed unto him, that he should not see death, before he had seen the Lord's Christ:* God by the Holy Ghost gave him this special revelation, as the reward of his faith, and the answer of his prayers, that he should live to see Christ born. The same Holy Spirit moved him to go into the temple, at that very time when Joseph and Mary brought in Christ, to present him to the Lord according to the law, and (though it be not expressed) certainly the same Spirit did intimate to him that that Child was *the Lord's Christ*. The old man takes him up in his arms, blesseth God, and saith,

a Gen. 46. 30. Phil. 1. 23.

29 Lord, [a] now lettest thou thy servant depart in peace, according to thy word:

b Is. 52. 10. ch. 3. 6.

30 For mine eyes [b] have seen thy salvation,

31 Which thou hast prepared before the face of all people;

c Is. 9. 2. & 42. 6. & 49. 6. & 60. 1, 2, 3. Matt. 4. 16. Acts 13. 47. & 28. 28.

32 [c] A light to lighten the Gentiles, and the glory of thy people Israel.

The song consists of an eulogium of Christ, whom Simeon here calls, 1. The Lord's *salvation*; 2. *A light to lighten the Gentiles*; 3. *The glory of Israel*; and a petition, that now the Lord would let him *depart in peace*. But I shall take the words in order. *Lord, now lettest thou thy servant depart in peace, according to thy word.* He desireth to die, having now lived to see what alone he desired life for. It is a speech much like Jacob's, Gen. xlvi. 30, when he had seen Joseph, whom he thought lost, but spoken here upon a much more weighty consideration. The word translated *depart*, signifies to absolve, and forgive, chap. vi. 37; to dismiss, and to deliver as from bondage and misery. It is used to express the death of good men, by the Septuagint, Gen. xv. 15; Numb. xx. 29; and the noun from it is used so by the apostle, 2 Pet. i. 15. Simeon owns God to be the Lord of his life, who had the power of it, and could alone dismiss him; and signifieth himself to be an old man, satisfied with days, willing to be at rest from the miseries of this life; but he beggeth to be dismissed, and to die in peace, that is, happily: see Gen. xv. 15; 2 Kings xxii. 20; Psal. iv. 8. *According to thy word*, that is, thy promise, mentioned ver. 26. But the putting of these words in before those words *in peace*, seems to import that he could not die in peace before he had seen God's word fulfilled to him, in which he had made him to hope. *For mine eyes have seen thy salvation*, that is, thy Christ, according to the revelation I had from thee. Simeon had a special revelation of a corporeal sight of Christ; he could not die happily till he had had that. None of us can die in peace, till we have seen the Lord's salvation with a spiritual eye, and made application of the promises of the gospel, in the more general revelation of his word. *Thy salvation, which thou hast prepared before the face of all people;* that is, the author of salvation, for there is no salvation in any other, Acts iv. 12. Simeon declares that this salvation was prepared for all people. Isa. xi. 10, he was prophesied of, as *an ensign for the people, to it shall the Gentiles seek.* So Isa. lii. 10, *The Lord hath made bare his holy arm in the eyes of all the nations; and all the ends of the earth shall see the salvation of our God.* So Psal. xcviii. 2. Simeon speaks the same thing more particularly, ver. 32, *A light to lighten the Gentiles, and the glory of thy people Israel.* All the people mentioned ver. 32 were either Gentiles or Jews. Simeon here prophesieth, that Christ should lighten the Gentiles. The state of the Gentiles (by whom were understood all the people in the world except the Jews) is often in Scripture expressed under the notion of darkness, both in respect of the ignorance of the true God which was amongst them, and of their idolatry and superstition, and their lewd and wicked lives, much proportioned to their religion. Hence Paul is said to be sent to the Gentiles, *to turn them from darkness to light*, Acts xxvi. 18. Christ is called *light;* John viii. 12, *I am the light of the world: he that followeth me shall not walk in darkness, but shall have the light of life.* So John ix. 5. Conformable to the old prophecies: Isa. lx. 1—3, *Arise, shine, for thy light is come. Behold, the darkness shall cover the earth, and gross darkness the people; but the Lord shall arise upon thee. And the Gentiles shall come to thy light.* And speaking of Christ, Isa. xlix. 6, *I will also give thee for a light to the Gentiles, that thou mayest be my salvation unto the end of the earth.* So Isa. xlii. 6, *And give thee for a covenant of the people, for a light of the Gentiles.* See Psal. xcviii. 3; Acts iii. 47. *And the glory of thy people Israel.* All the earth is the Lord's, but Israel is called his *son*, his *first-born*, Exod. iv. 22. Christ was the *minister of the circumcision*, Rom. xv. 8. To them it was that he was promised, of them it was that he was born, Rom. ix. 5. Amongst them it was that he preached and wrought miracles: *He came unto his own*, John i. 11. It was said of old, *I will place salvation in Zion for Israel my glory*, Isa. xlvi. 13. Christ is the glory of any people; the preaching of Christ, the owning and professing of Christ, a living up to his rules, this is a people's glory. And as some do this more and better than others, so in God's account they differ from others in what is true glory.

33 And Joseph and his mother marvelled at those things which were spoken of him.

Brentius notes on this text, *Non admirantur quia non credunt, sed quia credunt ideo admirantur*, They did not admire because they did not believe, but because they believed therefore they marvelled. They had revelations what Christ was; the angel had appeared to Joseph, to Mary, to Zacharias, and Elisabeth; the wise men had come from the east (if, as some think, they came so soon); yet they *marvelled;* they did not contemn and mock at these things, but certainly neither did they fully understand them, but in the general believed the Divine revelation. I do doubt whether, before Christ was *declared to be the Son of God with power, by his resurrection from the dead*, Rom. i. 4, either Mary or Christ's own disciples did steadily and firmly believe, that Christ was the eternal Son of God; though it was clear that before that time they believed him to be sent of God, and a great Prophet, nay, the promised Messias, the Christ of God, and generally believed that what was spoken of the Messias and the Christ belonged to him, but whether they did rightly understand that the Messiah was to be God-man I cannot tell. John Baptist seemeth clearest in the case. Peter also made a famous confession of it, but many things we read of Peter afterward which speak even Peter's faith in the case rather the embryo of faith than a fixed and perfect faith. But I impose nothing here on my reader, let him judge as he seeth reason; supposing a fixed firm faith in this case, yet they might marvel, for Christ is *to be admired of them that believe*.

34 And Simeon blessed them, and said unto Mary his mother, Behold, this *child* is set for the ^dfall and rising again of many in Israel; and for ^ea sign which shall be spoken against;

35 (Yea, ^fa sword shall pierce through thy own soul also,) that the thoughts of many hearts may be revealed.

d Is. 8. 14.
Hos. 14. 9.
Matt. 21. 44.
Rom. 9. 32, 33, 1 Cor. 1. 23, 24.
2 Cor. 2. 16.
1 Pet. 2. 7, 8.
e Acts 28. 22.
f Ps. 42. 10.
John 19. 25.

Simeon blessed them: some may question how it was that Simeon blessed Christ, whereas the apostle tells us, *The less is blessed of the better*, Heb. vii. 7. But we must distinguish betwixt, 1. A prophetical blessing, as Jacob blessed his sons, which was nothing but a prediction how God would bless them. 2. An authoritative blessing, as the priests blessed the people in the name of the Lord, Numb. vi.; which is nothing but a pronouncing them blessed by authority from God, whom God hath blessed. 3. A charitable or precatory blessing; praying God to bless them. Thus inferiors may bless superiors, as well as superiors may bless inferiors. The first or last, or both those, is to be understood here, not the second. *And said unto Mary his mother;* not to Joseph, who he knew was not his natural, but legal and reputed, father. *Behold, this child is set for the fall and rising again of many in Israel.* That by *the fall and rising again* is here meant the salvation and damnation of many is doubted by no valuable interpreters. The apostle so applieth Isa. viii. 14, 15, where he is said to be *for a stone of stumbling and for a rock of offence to both the houses of Israel, for a gin and for a snare to the inhabitants of Jerusalem. And many among them shall stumble, and fall, and be broken, and be snared, and be taken.* So doth Peter, 1 Pet. ii. 8. Neither is it more than Christ telleth us, John ix. 39, *For judgment I am come into this world, that they which see not might see; and that they which see might be made blind.* Accordingly the apostle saith, 2 Cor. ii. 16, that they were *to some the savour of death unto death, to others the savour of life unto life.* The reason is, because they that believe in him shall be saved, they that believe not shall be damned, Mark xvi. 16; John iii. 18, 36. This is now granted on all hands, that Christ will be the occasion of many people's damnation, even all that reject and oppose him, and believe not in him; and the cause of many people's salvation, even all that shall be saved: for there is no other name given under heaven, by which any can be saved, Acts iv. 12: see Matt. xxi. 44; 1 Pet. ii. 4, 5. And it is observable, that the salvation of souls by Christ is expressed by the term *rising;* so as all are fallen, Eph. ii. 1, and have need of the application of a greater power to them for their salvation, than an under-propping of the innate power of their wills. But the great question is about χεῖται, *is set*, whether it signifieth only an event, or some counsel and ordination of God. Let us compare it with other texts where the same word is used, Phil. i. 17; 1 Thess. iii. 3. How such great issues of providence should happen without the foreknowledge of God, or how God should have any such foreknowledge without a previous act of his will determining the thing, let any one consider; in the mean time it is freely granted, that the intervening of men's unbelief, and malice, and opposition to Christ and his gospel, is the proximate meritorious cause of the fall of any soul by occasion of him. It follows, *and for a sign which shall be spoken against;* such a mark as Job speaks of, Job xvi. 12; or such a sign as Isaiah speaks of, Isa. viii. 18. Simeon here prophesieth, that Christ, and his ministers and people, should be ridiculed, and all the arrows of ungodly men should be shot against him; which proved true in that age as to Christ and his apostles, and in succeeding ages as to all that derive from him, and will so hold to the end of the world. *Yea, a sword shall pierce through thy own soul also;* as the irons entered into the soul of Joseph, Psal. cv. 18. He tells the virgin her soul should be wounded with the reproaches and indignities which should be offered to this blessed babe, as it proved afterwards, when she heard him reviled, and saw him crucified. *That the thoughts of many hearts may be revealed.* The gospel times, especially times of persecution, will discover whom God hath chosen, and whom he hath not, by discovering the thoughts of their hearts; it will then be seen who will receive and who will reject the Messias, who is on his side and who will be against him. The term *that* doth denote the consequent, not the effect. The preaching of the gospel is the Lord's fan, by which he purgeth his floor. Persecution is the Lord's sieve, by which he winnoweth churches, and separateth the dirt, and darnel, and tares from the wheat. Gospel times and times of persecution are both of them times which make great discovery of men's spirits.

36 And there was one Anna, a prophetess, the daughter of Phanuel, of the tribe of Aser: she was of a great age, and had lived with an husband seven years from her virginity;

37 And she *was* a widow of about fourscore and four years, which departed not from the temple, but served *God* with fastings and prayers ^gnight and day.

38 And she coming in that instant gave thanks likewise unto the Lord, and spake of him to all them that ^hlooked for redemption in ‖ Jerusalem.

g Acts 26. 7.
1 Tim. 5. 5.

h Mark 15. 43. ver. 25. ch. 24. 21.
‖ Or, *Israel*.

God took care that our Saviour's nativity should be fully attested. To the testimony of the angels, the wise men, the shepherds, Simeon, here is added another. It is that of Anna, who is described here by her tribe and by her father. She was *of the tribe of Aser*, one of the meanest tribes, and of those ten tribes that were carried into the captivity of Assyria, having before made a defection (under the conduct of Jeroboam) both from the house of David and from the true worship of God. But though the generality did so, yet many particular persons removed, to enjoy the true worship of God, and joined themselves to Judah. Jer. l. 4, it was prophesied, *that the children of Israel should come, they and the children of Judah together, going and weeping, to seek the Lord their God.* What her father *Phanuel* was we read not. She is also further said to be *a prophetess.* Such there were amongst the Jews; we read of Deborah, and Miriam, and Huldah, to whom king Josiah sent. They were called prophets and prophetesses who revealed the will of God unto the people; but in the Old Testament it most generally signified, such as God enabled to foretell things which were to come. The spirit of prophecy had much failed amongst the Jews for four hundred years before Christ; about Christ's coming it began to revive. This woman seems to have been upwards of a hundred years old, if we account the eighty-four years here mentioned from her widowhood; not so, if we count them from her birth. She was but seven years married, all the rest of her life she had spent in widowhood. She *departed not from the temple night or day;* that is, she was frequently there, giving up herself wholly to religious exercises, prayer, and fasting, that she might be more fit for prayer. This woman *coming in at that instant* where Simeon took up Christ in his arms, &c., *gave thanks likewise unto the Lord, and spake of him to* such as she knew in Jerusalem, *who looked for the redemption* of Israel. There is no place where God hath had a name, but, however it be corrupted and debauched, hath a number that keep close to God. God in Ahab's time had seven thousand in Israel; and in this most corrupt time there was a Simeon and an Anna, and also others, who had a true notion and expectation of the Messiah; and these the Holy Ghost taketh more notice of than of all the Jewish doctors, all the scribes and Pharisees, whose names are enrolled, while what these persons said and did shall remain for a memorial of them wherever the gospel shall be preached to the end of the world.

39 And when they had performed all things according to the law of the Lord, they returned into Galilee, to their own city Nazareth.

If the wise men, mentioned Matt. ii. 1, had been with Herod before this time, it is more than probable that Herod would have made an end of Christ at this time, therefore certainly it was after this time. Luke saith nothing of what we have Matt. ii. 13—15, 19—23, of Joseph going into Egypt upon the admonition of the angel, nor his coming back; but both Matthew and Luke agree in their dwelling at Nazareth, which he calleth *their own city*, for there Joseph dwelt, ver. 4. How after this the wise men came to find him at Bethlehem, Matt. ii., the Scripture hath not told us. It is very idle for any to say Joseph dwelt there, for then he would not have taken up his inn there, nor been put to such a stress as to have his wife bring forth in a stable; besides, it is apparent from ver. 4 and this verse, and from Matt. ii. 23, that he dwelt at Nazareth. God, who ordered the motion of the wise men, and their instructions to be sent to Bethlehem to look for Christ, could easily find Joseph some business to be done there at that time, whether some business of his trade, or some visit to his friends, we cannot say.

i ver. 52.
ch. 1. 80.
40 ⁱAnd the child grew, and waxed strong in spirit, filled with wisdom: and the grace of God was upon him.

This verse shortly summeth up all that we have in the Gospel of the history of the first twelve years of our Saviour's life. Though there could be no accession to the perfection of the Divine nature in Christ, yet as to his human nature he was (as we are) capable of accession of habits, and wisdom and knowledge; for though the Divine nature was personally united to the human nature, yet there was no communication of properties.

k Ex. 23. 15, 17. & 34. 23. Deut. 16. 1, 16.
41 Now his parents went to Jerusalem ᵏevery year at the feast of the Passover.

The law of God enjoined all the males of the Israelites to appear at Jerusalem before him three times each year, of which the feast of unleavened bread was one; but the women seem not to have been all under the same obligation, but many of them went, of which Mary was one, but we read not of Christ's going till he was twelve years old. Some think that the women used to go once in a year, we read that Elkanah's wife went, 1 Sam. i. 5—7, but whether they generally did so or no the Scripture saith not. One thing is observable: the Pharisees, and scribes, and priests had in those days much corrupted the worship of God by their traditions, yet they retained the substance of God's institutions; we find both our Saviour and his disciples, and other people of God, not wholly forsaking the Jewish church because of its corruptions, yet we cannot think they joined with them in any thing of their willworship; from whence we may learn a tenderness as to a total separation from a church, and the lawfulness of attending divine ministrations, though attended with usages which we approve not of, provided there be no idolatry in the service.

A. D. 8.
42 And when he was twelve years old, they went up to Jerusalem after the custom of the feast.

It is said by those who are learned in the Jewish writings, that till a child was of this age he was not obliged by the law to go. We have in Scripture nothing to ascertain us in the case; it is certain that our Saviour went at this age, *after the custom of the feast*, that is, so as to be there about the fourteenth day of the month Nisan.

43 And when they had fulfilled the days, as they returned, the child Jesus tarried behind in Jerusalem; and Joseph and his mother knew not *of it*.

44 But they, supposing him to have been in the company, went a day's journey; and they sought him among *their* kinsfolk and acquaintance.

45 And when they found him not, they turned back again to Jerusalem, seeking him.

The feast of the passover, and of unleavened bread, held seven days, during which time Joseph and Mary stayed in Jerusalem, and then returned. They usually both went to and returned from these feasts in great troops, or companies. Christ tarried behind; Mary, thinking he had been in the company, missed him not; they return to Jerusalem to seek him.

46 And it came to pass, that after three days they found him in the temple, sitting in the midst of the doctors, both hearing them, and asking them questions.

After three days possibly here is to be understood from the time they first went from Jerusalem; one day they went forward in their journey, a second day they were coming back, the third day they found him; for it cannot be thought they should be in Jerusalem three days before they found him, considering that they found him in the temple, which it is likely was the first place they sought for him in. It should seem that the doctors of the law gave a general liberty to any to propound any questions to them about the law of God, to which they gave answers. But it is very probable that something more than ordinary appeared in him, that they admitted him to *sit* amongst them, for though themselves sat on benches, yet their auditors usually sat at their feet; hence we read of Paul's being brought up at the feet of Gamaliel.

l Matt. 7. 28. Mark 1. 22. ch. 4 22, 32. John 7.15,46.
47 And ˡall that heard him were astonished at his understanding and answers.

What was the subject matter of the doctors' and Christ's discourses is vainly questioned, only in the general we may be assured it was something about the Divine law; what the particular themes or subjects were is not material for us to inquire. Our Saviour so answered their questions, as they were all astonished.

48 And when they saw him, they were amazed: and his mother said unto him, Son, why hast thou thus dealt with us? behold, thy father and I have sought thee sorrowing.

Though something must be allowed to a woman's passions and a mother's indulgence, yet one would think that, especially considering where they found him, and what doing, she should not have spoken thus unto him, had she had a clear and distinct knowledge of his Divine nature, in union with her flesh: she speaks to him with the authority of a mother, *Why hast thou thus dealt with us?*

49 And he said unto them, How is it that ye sought me? wist ye not that I must be about ᵐmy Father's business? m John 2.16.

50 And ⁿthey understood not the saying which he spake unto them. n ch. 9. 45. & 18. 34.

Some read it—*that I must be in my Father's house?* then the sense must be, why did you seek me in any other place than the temple, that is, my Father's house, there lieth my business. But the phrase seemeth rather to signify as we translate it. He doth here signify that God was his Father: that Mary might have known, not only from the revelation of the angel, but because she had not known man; but she did not yet fully understand his Divine office as Mediator, and the great Prophet promised, that should reveal the will of God to people; much less did she yet fully and distinctly understand, that he was by nature the eternal Son of God: she believed so much as was revealed to her clearly concerning Christ. It is said, *they understood not the saying which he spake unto them;* they had not a clear and distinct understanding of it. In the mean time, from these words of our Saviour, and this fact of his, we may learn, that inferiors **are** not in all things under the power of their most natural superiors; particularly not in such things wherein they cannot yield obedience to them without a disobedience unto God. There are some cases wherein, instead of obeying, we are bound to hate both father and mother by our Saviour's precept.

51 And he went down with them, and came to Nazareth, and was subject unto them: but his mother °kept all these sayings in her heart.

<small>o ver. 19.
Dan. 7. 28.</small>

We left him at Nazareth, after Mary's purification, ver. 39; we find him at Nazareth now at twelve years old. We shall now read no more of him till chap. iii. 23, when he came to *be about thirty years of age.* What he did in the mean time is a business of too much curiosity for us to inquire, and of very little significancy to us if we knew. Some think he wrought with his father upon his trade. As I cannot tell how to prove it, so I know nothing against it. It is not likely he was sent to any of the schools of their prophets, as he who could argue with the doctors pertinently at twelve years of age, and to whom the Spirit was given not by measure, had no need of their instructions: so their academies were not such as we can reasonably think that Joseph and Mary should seek any education for him in them; and I know no reason why we should think, that he who abhorred not the womb of the virgin, nor a stable, nor a manger, should abhor the works of an honest vocation, and not much more abhor an idle life. But we dispute about these things in vain, being such as to which we can never be satisfied (God having hidden them from our knowledge); what is for our instruction is told us, he *was subject unto* his parents. This teacheth the greatest and highest mortals to honour their fathers and mothers; *which* (saith the apostle) *is the first commandment with promise.* Solomon honoured his mother, and behold a greater than Solomon is here, paying his homage also both to the womb that bare him, and to his (supposed) father that provided for him, and protected him. *But his mother kept all these sayings in her heart.* Mary was no forgetful hearer, some things she did not yet clearly understand, but she kept them in her heart; and those who do so as to God's word shall in time understand them.

<small>p 1 Sam. 2.
26. ver. 40.
‖ Or, *age.*</small>

52 And Jesus ᵖincreased in wisdom and ‖ stature, and in favour with God and man.

If any ask how he, who was the eternal Wisdom of the Father, (who is the only wise God,) increased in wisdom, they must know that all things in Scripture which are spoken of Christ, are not spoken with respect to his entire person, but with respect to the one or the other nature united in that person; he increased in wisdom, as he did in age, or stature, with respect to his human, not to his Divine nature. And as God daily magnified his grace and favour toward him, so he gave him favour with the neighbourhood, and people of Galilee, so as that when he came forth to be a public minister, he came forth as a bishop (the chief Bishop of souls especially) ought to do, having a good repute even of those who were without. And thus we leave our Saviour's history, for about eighteen years of which the history of the gospel tells us nothing.

CHAP. III

The preaching and baptism of John, 1—14. *His testimony of Christ,* 15—18. *Herod imprisoneth John for his free reproof,* 19, 20. *Christ is baptized, and receiveth testimony from heaven,* 21, 22. *The age and genealogy of Christ from Joseph upwards,* 23—38.

<small>A. D. 26.</small>

NOW in the fifteenth year of the reign of Tiberius Cæsar, Pontius Pilate being governor of Judæa, and Herod being tetrarch of Galilee, and his brother Philip tetrarch of Ituræa and of the region of Trachonitis, and Lysanias the tetrarch of Abilene,

<small>a John 11 49,
51. & 18. 13.
Acts 4. 6.</small>

2 ᵃAnnas and Caiaphas being the High Priests, the word of God came unto John the son of Zacharias in the wilderness.

The evangelist having given us an account both of the birth of John the Baptist and of our Saviour, and of all the prophecies preceding and attending them both, leaving the history of our Saviour a little, cometh to give us an account of the history of John the Baptist, his entrance upon his public ministry, and fulfilling of it. John the Baptist had six months' seniority of our Saviour, and probably did appear so long before him to the world as a public minister; the time of his beginning was in *the fifteenth year of the reign of Tiberius Cæsar.* Tiberius Cæsar was he who next succeeded Augustus (for all the Roman emperors after Julius Cæsar were called Cæsars, as all the kings of Egypt were called Pharaohs): he was as wicked a prince as most who ruled the Roman empire. Herod the Great (in whose time Christ was born) was some time since dead. Archelaus began to rule in his stead as a king, but the Romans changing the government from a monarchy to a tetrarchy, (that is, a government of four,) Archelaus had only the government of Judea; Herod Antipas, another son of Herod the Great, had the government of Galilee under the title of tetrarch; Philip, another son of his, had the government of Iturea and Trachonitis, under the same title of tetrarch; and one Lysanias had the government of Abilene: all four strangers. So as at this time the Jews were all under the government of foreigners, the sceptre or government was wholly departed from Judah. Archelaus was soon after sent into France, and Pontius Pilate made procurator or governor of Judea and Samaria. Annas and Caiaphas were the high priests. By the law of God, the eldest son of the family of Aaron was to be the high priest. How there came to be at this time two high priests is not agreed amongst interpreters. Those who are curious in this inquiry may see what Mr. Pool hath collected for their satisfaction in his Synopsis. We must know, that at this time the Jews were under the power of the Romans, and all things amongst them were out of order. Some say the Jews had liberty to choose their high priest, but then their conquerors would turn him out, and sell the place to another. Others say that the high priest had his deputy, who also obtained the same title. Others think, that as they had made the high priesthood an office, to which they chose one annually, (which was by God's law an office for life,) so the high priest of the former year still retained his title for another year. We are at no certainty in these things. It is certain that at this time there were two that bore the title of the high priest, upon what account we cannot tell. It appeareth from John xviii. 13, that the same men three or four years after bore this title of high priest, whether chosen again or no we know not. But this was the time when *the word of God came unto John the son of Zacharias in the wilderness;* the same John of which we heard before. The word of the Lord came to him, commanding him out to preach the gospel. It is a phrase which is often used in the Old Testament, to signify the influence of the Spirit of God upon the prophets, quickening them to their work; and signifieth to us, that no man ought to take this honour unto himself until he be called of God, nor to speak in the name of the Lord until first the word of God cometh to him.

3 ᵇAnd he came into all the country about Jordan, preaching the baptism of repentance ᶜ for the remission of sins;

<small>b Matt. 3. 1.
Mark 1. 4.

c ch. 1. 77.</small>

How long the time of John's ministry was before he was shut up by Herod in prison the Holy Scriptures do not certainly tell us; but it must be very short, for our Saviour's time was little more than three years, and we hear of his imprisonment in the beginning of our Saviour's public ministry. All that we have of John's ministry is to be found either in this chapter, or in Matt. iii., or in Mark i., or in the 1st and 3rd chapters of John. From them all it appeareth, that the sum of his doctrine was, the necessity of repentance, and faith in Christ, in order to the remission of sins. His pressing faith in Christ is most clearly declared by the evangelist John. Matthew, Mark, and Luke insist more upon his preaching the doctrine of *repentance for the remission of sins,* and baptism as an evidence of it. Which doctrine of repentance he pressed both from evangelical motives, *The kingdom of heaven is at hand,* and from legal motives, or arguments of terror, *The axe is now laid unto the root of the trees:* in this setting an example to all ministers of the gospel, showing them what should be the main subjects of their discourses, for we shall find that our Saviour preached the same doctrine, and in the same method. What is here said we before opened in our notes on Matt. iii. 2, and Mark i. 4. John did not preach that baptism was repentance, or that remission of sins was infallibly annexed to it, but that the way to obtain remission of sins was by repentance, and that baptism was an external sign and symbol of it.

4 As it is written in the book of the words of Esaias the prophet, saying, ^dThe voice of one crying in the wilderness, Prepare ye the way of the Lord, make his paths straight.

<small>d Is. 40. 3.
Matt. 3. 3.
Mark 1. 3.
John 1. 23.</small>

5 Every valley shall be filled, and every mountain and hill shall be brought low; and the crooked shall be made straight, and the rough ways *shall be* made smooth;

6 And ^eall flesh shall see the salvation of God.

<small>e Ps. 98. 2.
Is. 52. 10.
ch. 2. 10.</small>

All four of the evangelists apply that prophecy, Isa. xl. 3—5, to John the Baptist. Luke only repeats what is ver. 5, 6, and in Isa. xl. 4, 5, and he doth but shortly repeat what is in the prophet, ver. 5; the prophet saith, *And the glory of the Lord shall be revealed, and all flesh shall see it together: for the mouth of the Lord hath spoken it.* But there is nothing more usual than for the writers in the New Testament, in their quotations out of the Old Testament, to repeat the sum of the sense, not the words strictly. For the understanding of that prophecy, we must know, that there the prophet Isaiah was sent to comfort those amongst the Jews who feared God, partly with the assurance of them that they should return from Babylon, their warfare should have an end, Cyrus should deliver them; partly with the assurance of them of a far greater deliverance, in and by the coming of the Messiah (of whom Cyrus was but a type): to this purpose the prophet sets out both Cyrus, and in that type Christ's coming, as if both were present and at hand. Kings and great princes coming (especially with armies) have usually some coming before them, as pioneers, to prepare their way, by levelling rough places, and removing whatsoever is in the way of their motions, and filling up holes and ditches, &c.; nor are they far off when once their harbingers and pioneers are arrived, or are seen coming. John is here set out as a harbinger to Christ, to prepare his way, or a pioneer, to fill up ditches, throw down hills, to make rough ways smooth, and every way to prepare the way for him: that *all flesh might see the salvation of God.* And as princes that have wildernesses to pass through have more need of their pioneers to prepare and smooth their ways; so the state of the Jews being now confused, as a wilderness, and corrupt above measure, John the Baptist was sent before to cry in the wilderness, &c. This I take to be the true sense of the prophecy, and that it is mighty vain to strain these metaphorical phrases, and inquire what is meant by valleys, mountains, and crooked ways; they all most certainly signify the same thing, viz. whatsoever might be a hinderance to people's receiving of Christ; and to philosophize further about them, is but to show the luxuriancy of our wit, rather than any solidity of judgment. The whole scope of these three verses is but to show, that as kings, and princes, and governors of armies, have used to have harbingers and pioneers, or other officers, to go before them, to remove things out of the way of them and their retinue, and to prepare their way; so had Christ, and John the Baptist was the man whom the Lord pitched upon for that purpose, by his preaching to bring men to a sense of their sins, and off from their wicked courses, and to show them their need of a Saviour; that so when Christ came himself forth to preach, people might not be wholly ignorant, but in some measure prepared to receive the joyful tidings of the gospel, which he brought unto them.

7 Then said he to the multitude that came forth to be baptized of him, ^fO generation of vipers, who hath warned you to flee from the wrath to come?

<small>f Matt. 3. 7.</small>

8 Bring forth therefore fruits ‖worthy of repentance, and begin not to say within yourselves, We have Abraham to *our* father: for I say unto you, That God is

<small>‖ Or, *meet for*.</small>

able of these stones to raise up children unto Abraham.

9 And now also the axe is laid unto the root of the trees: ^gevery tree therefore which bringeth not forth good fruit is hewn down, and cast into the fire.

<small>g Mat. 7. 19.</small>

See the notes on Matt. iii. 7—10, where we met with all this with no alteration, save that Matthew saith that he spoke this to the Pharisees and Sadducees, seeing them come to his baptism: though he did especially intend them, yet he spake in the hearing of the multitude, amongst whom they were.

10 And the people asked him, saying, ^hWhat shall we do then?

<small>h Acts 2. 37.</small>

11 He answereth and saith unto them, ⁱHe that hath two coats, let him impart to him that hath none; and he that hath meat, let him do likewise.

<small>i ch. 11. 41.
2 Cor. 8. 14.
Jam. 2. 15, 16.
1 John 3. 17. & 4. 20.</small>

Although the preaching of the law doth not immediately conduce to work in us faith in Christ, yet mediately it doth, as it brings men to cry out, as those Acts ii. 37, *Men and brethren, what shall we do?* or as the jailor, Acts xvi., *Sirs, what shall we do to be saved?* John preaching God's terrors hath this effect upon the people, they ask him, *What shall we do then?* The Baptist's answer may seem a little strange to those who do not consider, that it amounts to the same with Daniel's counsel to Nebuchadnezzar, chap. iv. 27, *Wherefore, O king, let my counsel be acceptable unto thee, and break off thy sins by righteousness, and thine iniquities by showing mercy to the poor;* and what John had said, ver. 8, *Bring forth therefore fruits worthy of repentance.* Our Saviour said much the same, chap. xi. 41, *Give alms of such things as ye have;* and Peter commandeth, 1 Pet. iv. 8, *Above all things have fervent charity among yourselves; for charity shall cover the multitude of sins.* Solomon saith it *covereth all sins,* Prov. x. 12. The people's question was, *What shall we do?* what are the fruits meet for repentance, that is, truly indicative of repentance? To this now John answereth, *He that hath two coats, let him impart to him that hath none.* Which must not be interpreted, as obliging every one that had two coats to give away one; but as instructive of us, that ceremonies and ritual performances, in which that age abounded, would not serve their turn, but true and real good works, relieving the poor to their ability, out of their superfluities, from obedience and love to God; not merely pitying them, and saying to them, Go ye and be ye clothed, or be be warmed; not saying Corban, and thinking that would excuse them from relieving their parents, or other poor people, but according to their ability relieving them. John doth not here countenance Anabaptistical levelling, he only cautions them against Pharisaical hypocrisy, trusting to external privileges, such as having Abraham to their father, or some ritual and ceremonial performances, while in the mean time they neglected the weighty things of the law, of which Christ hath taught us that mercy is one.

12 Then ^kcame also Publicans to be baptized, and said unto him, Master, what shall we do?

<small>k Mat. 21. 32.
ch. 7. 29.</small>

13 And he said unto them, ^lExact no more than that which is appointed you.

<small>l ch. 19. 8.</small>

We have showed often before that the publicans were men that collected the public revenue. In all times that sort of men have been charged with exactions of what was more than their due. The Baptist, as a fruit or indication of the truth of their repentance, cautioneth them against exaction, thereby declaring, that acts of justice as well as mercy are true fruits of repentance, and that repentance is vainly pretended while men go on in the same sinful courses wherein they have formerly walked. Our Lord here doth not disapprove of the office of publicans, nor certainly was that to be condemned: if magistrates may impose taxes and payments, which without question they may, for the support of the government for our protection, there is no question but they may appoint officers under what titles they please to collect it. But both those that impose and those that collect such payments are obliged to the rule of justice; the former, to impose no more than is necessary for the end, and in a just proportion; the others, to exact no more than what is appointed them.

14 And the soldiers likewise demanded of him, saying, And what shall we do? And he said unto them, ‖ Do violence to no man, ᵐ neither accuse *any* falsely; and be content with your ‖ wages.

‖ Or, *Put no man in fear.*
ᵐ Ex. 23. 1. Lev. 19. 11.
‖ Or, *allowance.*

A good and faithful minister of Christ should be one able to bring out of his storehouse things new and old, to give every one their portion in their season, and so courageous and faithful as not to be afraid to do it, nor for any reason decline the doing of it. Such was John the Baptist. These were the Roman soldiers, kept by them to maintain their conquest of Judea. Some of these also come to hear John the Baptist preach: hearing him press repentance, and bringing forth fruits that might testify the truth of it, they ask what they should do. John saith to them, *Do violence to no man,* &c. Experience hath taught all people, that soldiers (especially employed to keep garrisons amongst a conquered people) are often very insolent, and for their own gain prone to accuse innocent persons, and the jealousy of conquerors often allows them too easy an ear; as also how apt they are by oppression to mend their short commons, or to exact upon others that they may spend luxuriously. All these are acts or species of injustice, which the Baptist lets them know must be left, if they would bring forth fruits fit for repentance. He doth not blame the employment of a soldier, but only regulates their behaviour in that employment. Wars in just causes are undoubtedly lawful under the gospel, and consequently so is the employment of a soldier; we read of several good centurions or captains of hundreds. But the soldier stands highly concerned to look, 1. That the cause be good in which he draweth his sword. 2. That he behaveth himself in it lawfully, not using any needless violence, not accusing any wrongfully, not endeavouring to mend his pay by any rapine, or unjustly taking away what is another's, either to spend in luxury, or to uphold himself in his station. From this instruction of John the Baptist, we may learn several things concerning the nature of repentance. 1. That where there is a true root of repentance, it will bring forth fruits worthy of it. 2. That acts of mercy and justice are true and proper fruits of a true repentance, without which there can be nothing of it in truth. 3. That true repentance is best discovered by our abhorrence of and declining such sinful courses as we have formerly been addicted to, and have daily temptations to from the circumstances of our lives, and those callings, and places, and courses of life wherein the providence of God had fixed us. 4. That these things, repentance and faith, are such proper effects of both, as discover the truth of those gracious habits in the soul, and without which there can be no true evidence of them.

15 And as the people were ‖ in expectation, and all men ‖ mused in their hearts of John, whether he were the Christ, or not;

‖ Or, *in suspence.*
‖ Or, *reasoned,* or, *debated.*

It being known to many what the angel had told Zacharias concerning John thirty years since, and what had miraculously happened at his circumcision, as also what Zacharias his father had prophesied concerning him; and there having been many who had observed the holiness and severity of his life all along, until he came to man's estate; and knowing that the time was fulfilled for the coming of the Messias, the sceptre being now departed from Judah, and Daniel's weeks being accomplished; and hearing him preach with that life and power which attended his ministry, as also considering his doctrine (not new in itself, being consonant to the Divine law, and the doctrine of the prophets, but) new to them, who had used to hear of rites and ceremonies, and the traditions of the elders, but little or nothing of repentance, or bringing forth fruits worthy of it; they began to reason and debate with themselves, whether John the Baptist were not the Messiah promised, and in great suspense they were about it. But John quickly satisfied them as to that, not desirous to arrogate to himself his honour, whose messenger only he was.

16 John answered, saying unto *them* all, ⁿ I indeed baptize you with water; but one mightier than I cometh, the latchet of whose shoes I am not worthy to unloose: he shall baptize you with the Holy Ghost and with fire:

ⁿ Matt. 3. 11.

17 Whose fan *is* in his hand, and he will throughly purge his floor, and ᵒ will gather the wheat into his garner; but the chaff he will burn with fire unquenchable.

ᵒ Mic. 4. 12. Matt. 13. 30.

18 And many other things in his exhortation preached he unto the people.

See the notes upon Matt. iii. 11, 12, and on Mark i. 7, 8. John the Baptist in these verses doth not only assure them that he was not the Christ, but also lets them know that Christ was coming amongst them, and that he was more excellent than he, and should *baptize* them *with the Holy Ghost and with fire;* with fire as the symbol of the Holy Ghost; so some understand it, expounding it as a prophecy of the descent of the Holy Ghost, Acts ii. 3. Others possibly better expound it of the Holy Ghost working in the souls of believers as fire, purging them, and burning up their lusts and corruptions. *And many other things in his exhortation preached he unto the people:* by which words the evangelist lets us know, that what he and the other evangelists have reported concerning John's preaching was but the sum of it.

19 ᵖ But Herod the tetrarch, being reproved by him for Herodias his brother Philip's wife, and for all the evils which Herod had done,

A. D. 30.
ᵖ Mat. 14. 3. Mark 6. 17.

20 Added yet this above all, that he shut up John in prison.

These two verses sufficiently confirm to us, that we are not to expect to find the several passages in the Gospel concerning John the Baptist set down according to the order of time in which they happened, for the evangelist sets down the imprisonment of John before the baptism of Christ, mentioned in the two next verses, which we know could not be as to the order of time, our Saviour being baptized by John. John was in so great repute, that Herod himself *heard him, did many things, and heard him gladly,* Mark vi. 20. But John was a faithful preacher, and could not but reprove him for his wicked courses, particularly for his incestuous taking of his brother Philip's wife; for he was alive when he took her, if it be true which historians tell us, that John was imprisoned in the sixteenth year of Tiberius Cæsar, and Philip died not till the twentieth; however, his brother leaving issue, (for we read Herodias had a daughter, Matt. xiv.,) it was unlawful for him to have married her, especially to turn away his own wife to take her. Matthew reporteth this history more fully, chap. xiv. 3, 4, &c.: see the notes there. It is said, that Herod *added yet this above all,* that is, above all his former or other wickedness, *that he shut up John in prison.* This spake him incorrigible in his wicked courses, resisting the remedy, or means to reduce him. A hypocrite may hear the word, and do many things; but he hath always some particular lust, as to which he must be spared, being neither willing to part with it, nor able to bear any reproof for it.

21 Now when all the people were baptized, ᵑ it came to pass, that Jesus also being baptized, and praying, the heaven was opened,

A. D. 27.
ᵑ Mat. 3. 13. John 1. 32.

22 And the Holy Ghost descended in a bodily shape like a dove upon him, and a voice came from heaven, which said, Thou art my beloved Son; in thee I am well pleased.

This history of our Saviour's baptism is reported both by Matthew and Mark, much most largely by Matthew; see the notes on Matt. iii. 13, &c. Luke only addeth those words, *and praying,* which teacheth us that prayers ought to be joined with baptism. What was the matter of his prayer we are not told, though the following words incline some not improbably to judge that he prayed for some testimony from heaven concerning him.

23 And Jesus himself began to be ʳabout thirty years of age, being (as was supposed) ˢ the son of Joseph, which was *the son* of Heli,

ʳ See Num. 4. 3, 35, 39, 43, 47.
ˢ Mat. 13. 55. John 6. 42.

Here is amongst critics a little dispute, whether our blessed Lord at his baptism (after which he soon began his public ministry) was full *thirty years of age;* ὡσεὶ and ἀρχόμενος in the Greek give occasion to the doubt. Those who judge that he was thirty complete, conceive that the age before which the priests and Levites did no service in the tabernacle of God. Numb. iv. 3 commanded the number of them to be taken *from thirty years old to fifty,* and it was done accordingly, ver. 34, 35, &c. David, in the latter end of his life, so numbered them, 1 Chron. xxiii. 3, when their number (of that age) was thirty-eight thousand; yet in that chapter, ver. 24 and 27, we find them numbered *from twenty years old and upward;* but possibly that was for some more inferior service. In conformity to this, most think that both John the Baptist and Christ entered not upon their public ministry till they were of that age; but whether they were thirty years of age complete, or current, is a question, but so little a one, as deserves no great study to resolve: the two qualifying words, ὡσεὶ and ἀρχόμενος, would incline one to think Christ was but thirty years of age current, which is advantaged by what others tell us, that the Jews ordinarily called a child two or three years old as soon as it did but enter upon its second or third year. Some think our Saviour was ten months above twenty-nine years of age when he was baptized, after which he was tempted of the devil forty days before he entered the public ministry; but these are little things. *Being (as was supposed) the son of Joseph.* Joseph was not his natural father, though so supposed by the Jews, Joseph being indeed his legal father, being married to the virgin when our Saviour was born, Matt. i. 20.

24 Which was *the son* of Matthat, which was *the son* of Levi, which was *the son* of Melchi, which was *the son* of Janna, which was *the son* of Joseph,

25 Which was *the son* of Mattathias, which was *the son* of Amos, which was *the son* of Naum, which was *the son* of Esli, which was *the son* of Nagge,

26 Which was *the son* of Maath, which was *the son* of Mattathias, which was *the son* of Semei, which was *the son* of Joseph, which was *the son* of Juda,

27 Which was *the son* of Joanna, which was *the son* of Rhesa, which was *the son* of Zorobabel, which was *the son* of Salathiel, which was *the son* of Neri,

28 Which was *the son* of Melchi, which was *the son* of Addi, which was *the son* of Cosam, which was *the son* of Elmodam, which was *the son* of Er,

29 Which was *the son* of Jose, which was *the son* of Eliezer, which was *the son* of Jorim, which was *the son* of Matthat, which was *the son* of Levi,

30 Which was *the son* of Simeon, which was *the son* of Juda, which was *the son* of Joseph, which was *the son* of Jonan, which was *the son* of Eliakim,

31 Which was *the son* of Melea, which was *the son* of Menan, which was *the son* of Mattatha, which was *the son* of ᵗ Nathan, ᵘ which was *the son* of David,

ᵗ Zech. 12. 12.
ᵘ 2 Sam. 5. 14. 1 Chron. 3. 5.

32 ˣ Which was *the son* of Jesse, which was *the son* of Obed, which was

ˣ Ruth 4. 18, &c. 1 Chron. 2. 10, &c.

the son of Booz, which was *the son* of Salmon, which was *the son* of Naasson,

33 Which was *the son* of Aminadab, which was *the son* of Aram, which was *the son* of Esrom, which was *the son* of Phares, which was *the son* of Juda,

34 Which was *the son* of Jacob, which was *the son* of Isaac, which was *the son* of Abraham, ʸ which was *the son* of Thara, which was *the son* of Nachor,

ʸ Gen. 11. 24, 26.

35 Which was *the son* of Saruch, which was *the son* of Ragau, which was *the son* of Phalec, which was *the son* of Heber, which was *the son* of Sala,

36 ᶻ Which was *the son* of Cainan, which was *the son* of Arphaxad, ᵃ which was *the son* of Sem, which was *the son* of Noe, which was *the son* of Lamech,

ᶻ See Gen. 11. 12.
ᵃ Gen. 5. 6, &c. & 11. 10, &c.

37 Which was *the son* of Mathusala, which was *the son* of Enoch, which was *the son* of Jared, which was *the son* of Maleleel, which was *the son* of Cainan,

38 Which was *the son* of Enos, which was *the son* of Seth, which was *the son* of Adam, ᵇ which was *the son* of God.

ᵇ Gen. 5. 1, 2.

There have been great disputes about the genealogy of our Saviour, as recorded both by Matthew and Luke. The adversaries of Christian religion have taken no small advantage from the seeming difference betwixt them, which even many sober writers have thought it no easy matter to reconcile. The apostle hath cautioned us against giving too much heed to *endless genealogies, which minister questions rather than godly edifying which is in faith,* 1 Tim. i. 4; yet certainly it is our duty, as well for the stopping the mouths of such as would clamour against the truth of the whole Scripture, (if not of the whole Christian religion,) as, so far as we can, to vindicate holy writ from their little cavils, and thereby also to confirm those who are weak in faith. To make these things as clear as we can: It is plain that both the evangelists agree in their design, by setting down the genealogy of our Saviour, to prove him lineally descended both from Abraham and David, the two persons to whom was made the promise of the Messiah, and the stability of his kingdom, and also in the names of the first fourteen generations, mentioned by Matthew, and here by Luke, ver. 32, 33, and to Abraham, ver. 34. Their disagreement lieth in four things. 1. In the form of the pedigree; Matthew beginning with those who were first, Luke with those who were last in order of time. But this is no valuable exception, one evangelist counts forward, another backward. 2. Matthew counts by three periods, each consisting of fourteen generations; Luke doth not: but neither is his of any moment. 3. Matthew sits down our Saviour's genealogy before he tells us any thing of his conception or birth; Luke, after his relation of his conception, birth, and baptism. 4. Matthew deriveth our Saviour's genealogy but from Abraham; Luke, from Adam. All these differences lay no foundation for any exception. Several accounts are given why Luke carrieth up the genealogy to Adam; the best seemeth to be this: that Matthew intending his history primarily for the Jews, judged it enough to prove Christ the Son of Abraham, and the Son of David; but Luke designing the information of the whole world, deriveth him from the common father of mankind. By which means he also showeth the antiquity of the gospel, and lets us know that Christ was he who was promised to Adam, before Abraham's time, and that the grace of the gospel is not limited to the seed of Abraham. Thus also Luke supplieth what was wanting in Matthew, and truly deriveth both the first and second act from God, the Father of our Lord Jesus Christ, and of us all. But besides these differences (hardly worth the taking notice of under that notion) there are some seeming contradictions in the genealogies, yet not such but I think a fair account may be given of to any who will but first consider, 1. That they all lie in what Luke hath, from ver. 23 to 31, and from the latter end of ver. 34 to the end. So that in ver. 32, 33, and part of 34, we have nothing to reconcile. 2. That these words *the son* is in the Greek only ver. 23, where Christ is said to be "the son of Joseph," but ever after it is supplied by the translators. So as the Greek runs thus: *The Son of Joseph, which was of Heli, which was of Matthat, which was of Levi, which was of Melchi,* &c. Which consideration cuts off the first cavil, how Joseph could be the son of Jacob, as Matthew saith, and the son of Heli, as Luke saith; for indeed Luke saith no more than, *And Jesus himself began to be about thirty years of age, being (as was supposed) the son of Joseph, which was the son of Heli,* ver. 23; that is, Christ was of Heli, the supposed son of Joseph, but truly of Heli, the father of Mary his mother. I know that some think Jacob was also called Heli (as it was ordinary with the Jews to have two names); others think that Joseph is called the son, because he was the son-in-law of Heli, by the marriage of the virgin Mary his daughter. (Naomi calleth those her daughters who were but her legal daughters, Ruth i. 11.) In this the most agree. But I must confess I think it is Christ, who is here said to be of Heli (though he was reputed, and generally taken, to be the son of Joseph). 3. That Luke is here deriving our Saviour, not from his supposed father Joseph, but from Mary his true mother. It is not to be conceived that Luke, after such a narration of the predictions of his conception as he had given us in the first chapter, should go to derive Christ from Joseph; and this gives us a fair account why the names are so different from David's time to the birth of Christ. Joseph (whose pedigree Matthew relates) deriving from Solomon, who was the son of David, succeeding him in the kingdom. Mary (whose pedigree Luke relates) descending from Nathan, ver. 31. 1 Chron. iii. 5 tells us he was another son of David. So as after David's time the persons named which before were the same in our Saviour's pedigree became diverse, some the progenitors of Joseph, whom Matthew reckons, others the progenitors of Mary, whom Luke nameth. This answereth the objection from the differing number of the persons from Joseph to Zorobabel (excluding them both). Matthew reckoneth but nine, Luke here reckoneth eighteen, in ver. 23—28. From Zorobabel to David Luke reckons twenty-two progenitors, Matthew but fourteen, (leaving out three kings of the half blood of Ahab, of which we gave an account in our notes on Matt. i.,) so as the Scripture nameth seventeen, though Matthew leaves out three. In two different lines, it is not impossible that one person in so many years might have so many more progenitors than another, supposing Matthew designed to reckon all, which it is plain from his leaving out three kings named in Scripture that he did not. 4. That ordinarily the Jews had two names, sometimes three. All Josiah's sons had each of them two at least. Matthew had also the name of Levi, &c. This solves the difference from ver. 27, where Rhesa is said to be the son of Zorobabel, whenas Matthew saith, chap. i. 13, Zorobabel begat Abiud. That Abraham was the son of Terah or Thara, and Terah the son of Nachor, appeareth from Gen. xi. 24, 26. That Saruch or Serug was the son of Reu or Ragau, appeareth from Gen. xi. 20; 1 Chron. i. 25. That Reu was the son of Peleg, (here called Phalec,) and Peleg the son of Eber, and Eber the son of Sala, appears from Gen. xi. 18; 1 Chron. i. 25. But in Genesis xi. we read, that Sala was the son of Arphaxad, ver. 12, whereas he is here said to be the son of Cainan, and Cainan is made the son of Arphaxad. So as Luke maketh Sala grandchild to Arphaxad; Moses makes no mention of Cainan at all, but mentions Salah as begotten by Arphaxad. Those who are curious to know what is said for the resolution of this difficulty, may read it largely both in Spanheim's Dubia Evangelica, and Mr. Pool's Synopsis Criticorum. It is a difficulty which hath exercised many very learned men, and I doubt whether ever any yet satisfied himself in the resolution of it. It is not probable that Luke should correct what Moses said; the best account I can give of it is, the Septuagint in Gen. xi. 12 have it just as Luke here hath it; and it is certain that Luke, in his quotations out of the Old Testament, doth generally follow the Septuagint, being the translation most in use among them. Beza tells us of an ancient copy of the Gospel he had, which mentioneth no Cainan. The best of it is, that it is a matter of no great moment, for the question is not, whether Sala was the son of Arphaxad, (for so he was, though Arphaxad was his grandfather, in the same sense that Christ is called the Son of Abraham, and the Son of David, and Elisabeth the daughter of Aaron, chap. i. 1,) but whether he was the immediate son of Arphaxad or Cainan; whether Moses omitted Cainan, or some transcriber of Luke added Cainan out of the Septuagint (being then the current translation among them): the last is most probable. For the other part of the genealogy, ver. 36—38, it plainly agreeth with Gen. v. 6, &c.; vi. 10. So that I must profess I see no great difficulty to reconcile the genealogies, admitting the one to give the genealogy of Joseph, and the other to give the genealogy of Mary. That indeed Mary was the daughter of Heli is not to be proved by Scripture, nor yet contradicted, but it is very probably judged so. And though we cannot prove that Cainan, mentioned ver. 36, was added out of some later copies of the Septuagint, yet it is more than probable it was so. Which two things if we admit, I see no great difficulty remaining, but a fair agreement betwixt both the evangelists. For I presume none will stumble at the alteration of some letter, or omission of some letter in a name, or addition to it in the end; there is nothing more ordinary than that, when names are mentioned in several languages.

CHAP. IV

Christ fasteth forty days, and is tempted of the devil, 1—13. *He beginneth to preach,* 14, 15. *The people of Nazareth wonder at his gracious words, but being offended go about to kill him: he escapeth by miracle,* 16—32. *He casteth out a devil,* 33—37; *healeth Simon's mother-in-law,* 38, 39; *and many other diseased persons,* 40. *The devils acknowledging him are silenced,* 41. *He preacheth through the cities of Galilee,* 42—44.

AND ᵃJesus being full of the Holy Ghost returned from Jordan, and ᵇwas led by the Spirit into the wilderness, _{a Matt. 4. 1. Mark 1. 12.} _{b ver. 14. ch. 2. 27.}

By the Holy Ghost here is to be understood the gifts of the Holy Ghost, according to the prophecy of him, Isa. xi. 1, 2. The gifts of the Holy Spirit are often in holy writ called the Spirit, Acts ii. 4; viii. 18; x. 44: and not only those that are influenced with the saving gifts and graces of the Spirit, are said to have the Spirit, and be filled; but those who received the more extraordinary powers of it, such as the gifts of prophecy, healing, &c. Others besides Christ are in Scripture said to be filled with the Spirit, Acts vi. 5; and it was so prophesied concerning John, Luke i. 15. But they had but their measure; to Christ the Spirit was given not by measure, John iii. 34. *He returned from Jordan:* there John baptized, there Christ was baptized by him. *And was led by the Spirit into the wilderness.* Ἤγετο, saith Luke. Ἀνήχθη, saith Matthew. Mark expresseth it by the word ἐκβάλλει. The words do not signify a violent motion, (for without doubt Christ went willingly,) but a potent and efficacious motion.

2 Being forty days tempted of the devil. And ᶜin those days he did eat nothing: and when they were ended, he afterward hungered. _{c Ex. 34. 28. 1 Kings 19. 8.}

See the notes on Matt. iv. 2—4.

3 And the devil said unto him, If thou be the Son of God, command this stone that it be made bread.

4 And Jesus answered him, saying, ᵈIt is written, That man shall not live by bread alone, but by every word of God. _{d Deut. 8. 3.}

See the notes on Matt. iv. 3, 4. It is very observable, that Christ here asserteth the authority of the Scriptures; and though he was full of the Holy Ghost, yet maketh the Holy Scripture his rule of action.

5 And the devil, taking him up into an high mountain, shewed unto him all the kingdoms of the world in a moment of time.

6 And the devil said unto him, All this power will I give thee, and the glory of them: for *that is delivered unto me; and to whomsoever I will I give it.

*John 12. 31. & 14. 30. Rev. 13. 2,7.

7 If thou therefore wilt ‖ worship me, all shall be thine.

‖ Or, *fall down before me.*

8 And Jesus answered and said unto him, Get thee behind me, Satan: for ᶠit is written, Thou shalt worship the Lord thy God, and him only shalt thou serve.

f Deut. 6.13. & 10. 20.

See the notes on Matt. iv. 8—10. Those words, ver. 6, *for that is delivered unto me; and to whomsoever I will I give it,* are only mentioned by Luke; where we may observe, that the devil was a liar from the beginning. The dominion over the things of the world was not given to the angels, but to man. Neither hath he any such power as he pretends to, being not able to do any thing against Job till he had obtained leave from God, nor to enter into the swine without licence first obtained from Christ.

9 ᵍAnd he brought him to Jerusalem, and set him on a pinnacle of the temple, and said unto him, If thou be the Son of God, cast thyself down from hence:

g Matt. 4. 5.

10 For ʰit is written, He shall give his angels charge over thee, to keep thee:

h Ps. 91. 11.

11 And in *their* hands they shall bear thee up, lest at any time thou dash thy foot against a stone.

12 And Jesus answering said unto him, ⁱIt is said, Thou shalt not tempt the Lord thy God.

i Deut. 6.16.

See the notes on Matt. iv. 5—7. What Matthew calls *the holy city,* Luke expoundeth *Jerusalem.*

13 And when the devil had ended all the temptation, he departed from him ᵏfor a season.

k John14.30. Heb. 4. 15.

Matthew saith, the devil left him, *and, behold, angels came and ministered unto him.* Luke saith, *he departed from him for a season, when he had ended all the temptation.* Those words, *for a season,* seem to intimate that our Saviour had further conflicts with the devil than are here mentioned; and possibly those words, *all the temptation,* may hint us, that the devil offered more temptations than the evangelist have recorded, though some affirm that all temptations fall under those which are the heads of these temptations, and think those words, *for a season,* signify until the time of his passion, when he entered into the heart of Judas, and armed all his instruments against this Captain of our salvation.

A. D. 30.

14 ¶ ˡAnd Jesus returned ᵐin the power of the Spirit into ⁿGalilee: and there went out a fame of him through all the region round about.

l Matt. 4.12. John 4. 43. m ver. 1. n Acts 10.37.

15 And he taught in their synagogues, being glorified of all.

Both Matthew and Mark make the occasion of our Saviour's going into Galilee to be his hearing that John was cast into prison. But certainly Matthew and Mark speak of a second going into Galilee, and mean by it Galilee of the Gentiles, which was in the jurisdiction of Philip, the brother of Herod Antipas. Else one might admire, why Christ should go into Galilee upon hearing that John was cast into prison; that had been for him to have thrown himself into Herod's mouth, before that his time of suffering was come; but it should seem that after his temptations, he first went to Capernaum, where he did not stay many days, John ii. 12, and then to Nazareth, which was his own country. But others think that all the evangelists speak of a second going into Galilee, which I cannot agree if Nazareth were within that Galilee which was called the Lower Galilee, and was within the jurisdiction of Herod Antipas, who was the tetrarch of Galilee, and the man that had imprisoned John, and afterwards caused him to be beheaded. *And he taught in their synagogues*: he had the reputation of a prophet, which procured him that liberty of speaking in all those places, where the Jews celebrated their public worship; *being glorified,* that is, admired and honoured, *of all.*

16 ¶ And he came to °Nazareth, where he had been brought up: and, as his custom was, ᵖhe went into the synagogue on the sabbath day, and stood up for to read.

A. D. 31. o Matt. 2. 23. & 13. 54. Mark 6. 1. p Acts 13. 14. & 17. 2.

We heard before, chap. ii. 39, 51, that Christ was brought up at Nazareth; we read of him at Nazareth, Matt. xiii. 54. But I must confess I doubt whether Matthew there, and Luke here, speak of the same time. Of the nature of the Jewish synagogues, and their order of worship there, and the reading of the Scriptures in them, we have spoken before in our notes on Matt. iv. 23.

17 And there was delivered unto him the book of the prophet Esaias. And when he had opened the book, he found the place where it was written,

18 ᑫThe Spirit of the Lord *is* upon me, because he hath anointed me to preach the Gospel to the poor; he hath sent me to heal the broken-hearted, to preach deliverance to the captives, and recovering of sight to the blind, to set at liberty them that are bruised,

q Is. 61. 1.

19 To preach the acceptable year of the Lord.

The words differ in some things from the words of the prophet out of which they are quoted, Isa. lxi. 1, where is nothing of recovering of sight to the blind; but they exactly agree with the Septuagint version, only, ver. 19, they have καλέσαι, to call, and Luke hath κηρύξαι, to preach, according to which probably the copies of the Septuagint in use with them were. It was their manner in the synagogues for the minister (an officer appointed to that purpose, see ver. 20) to bring the book of the law or of the prophets which was to be read, and to deliver it to him that officiated for that time, who, when he had read, redelivered it to the same officer to be laid up. Their writers tell us, that the books of Moses were divided into several portions, which they were tied to read in order; but for the books of the prophets, he that officiated was more at liberty to read in what place and proportion he pleased. Our Lord readeth Isa. lxi. 1, which, according to the Septuagint copy, was as Luke here translated; and by the way, this custom of the writers of the New Testament, (writing in Greek,) to quote texts out of the Old Testament, very often according to that Septuagint translation, may, first, give us some account of the difficulty we met with chap. iii., where Sala was made the son of Cainan, and the grandchild of Arphaxad, whereas Moses mentions no Cainan, Gen. xi. Luke, taking the quotation of the Septuagint, might put it in according to them, for they have it in Gen. xi. 12. Secondly, it may learn us not to be too curious as to minute things in Scripture, for had it been a thing of moment, the Holy Spirit of God had certainly never suffered Luke to write after their copy, either there or here. God never had a church in any place, but he soon stirred up some to make an interpretation of the Scriptures for their use, and so far assisted them, that though they might differ from the Hebrew text, or the Greek, in some minute things, yet they differed not in any thing of moment necessary for us to know and believe in order to salvation. And the frequent quotations we have in the New Testament out of the Septuagint, incline us to think that it is the will of God, that particular persons in churches should make use of such versions, and take them for the Holy Scriptures, not lightly and ordinarily varying from them; the translating of Scriptures, being not an ordinary ministerial gift, but the work of some stirred up by God unto it, and whom he more than ordinarily so assists, as that they have not erred in any momentous thing. If this may be admitted, we need not lay the fault upon those who transcribed Luke's copy. But let us come to the text itself. *The Spirit of the Lord is upon me, because he hath anointed me.* Anointing may signify two things: 1. The endowment of the person with gifts and abilities fit for his work. Thus, 1 John ii. 27, *the anointing* is said to *teach* us *all things;* and Christ is said, Psal. xlv. 7; Heb. i. 9, to be *anointed with the oil of gladness above his fellows,* which the Baptist seemeth to interpret, John iii. 34, *God giveth not the Spirit by measure unto him.* 2. Anointing also was a symbol of God's calling out and sending a person to the execution of an office, 2 Kings ix. 6. 3. I find also anointing used as a symbol of God's purpose and designation of a person to an employment, to the performance of which he did not presently call him; thus David was anointed, 1 Sam. xvi. 13. By *the Spirit of the Lord is upon me,* I conceive is meant, exciting and quickening Christ to the present execution of that office to which God had anointed him; that is, 1. Of old designed him; 2. Fitted him, giving him the Spirit not by measure; 3. Now called him to the exercise of it: and because the Lord had so designed him, so prepared, and now so called him, the Spirit now excited and quickened him. God stirreth up none to take upon them the office of the ministry, whom he hath not fitted with gifts for the discharge of it. But what was this employment to which Christ was anointed? Εὐαγγελίζεσθαι, *to preach the gospel to the poor.* This was the great work of our Lord and Saviour, to preach. And what? The gospel, the glad tidings of salvation. To whom? Πτωχοῖς: it is used to signify those that are mean in the world, and, by a figure, those that are miserable and afflicted; and this I should take to be the sense here, in conformity to that other phrase which our Saviour useth to John's disciples, Matt. xi. 5, and to that of the apostle, 1 Cor. i. 27. Christ was first sent to *the lost sheep of the house of Israel,* who were all at this time in a poor afflicted state and condition, and amongst them chiefly to the meaner sort. The rulers believed not on him, John vii. 48; to teach ministers what Erasmus saith, *Nulla nobis anima vilis videri debet, pro qua Dominus gloriæ mori non est dedignatus,* That they are too proud that despise the poor, and that we ought not to count any soul vile for which he who was the Lord of glory disdained not to die: we may add, to which the great Minister of the circumcision took himself to be anointed to preach. I had rather thus understand it, than of such as are poor in spirit, which seem to be understood in the next words, *he hath sent me to heal the broken-hearted,* whether wounded in the sense of sin, or melted in the sense of mercy: the whole-hearted are such as see no need of repentance, no need of a Saviour; Christ came not to heal these; *The whole need not a physician.* It followeth, *to preach deliverance to the captives;* to let them know, that are yet slaves to sin and to their lusts, that there is a way for their deliverance. *And recovering of sight to the blind;* to let all blind sinners know, that there is an eye-salve discovered, which if applied will recover their spiritual sight. *To set at liberty them that are bruised:* it is of the same significancy with binding up the broken in heart. *To preach the acceptable year of the Lord;* the true jubilee, when every soul may be set free from the bonds of its sins, 2 Cor. vi. 17; the year of God's good-will; that the time was now come, when in every nation he that feared God, and wrought righteousness, should be *accepted with him,* Acts x. 35.

20 And he closed the book, and he gave *it* again to the minister, and sat down. And the eyes of all them that were in the synagogue were fastened on him.

21 And he began to say unto them, This day is this scripture fulfilled in your ears.

Christ observeth the order used in their synagogues, when he that officiateth had read such a portion out of the law as was appointed, or out of the prophets, as he pleased, he closed the book, or the roll, and gave it again to the officer, whose work it was to bring it, and then to carry it back, and lay it up; and then sat down, while he made his exhortation upon it. This Christ did, the people being in the mean time very attentive to hear what he would say. He begins to speak, and telleth them this was a prophecy concerning him, *This day is this scripture fulfilled in your ears;* that is, it is fulfilled in me, either primarily, or as I am the antitype to Cyrus. We must not think that this was all which Christ said, but thus he began his discourse.

r Ps. 45. 2.
Matt. 13. 54.
Mark 6. 2.
ch. 2. 47.

22 And all bare him witness, and ʳ wondered at the gracious words which pro-ceeded out of his mouth. And they said, ˢ Is not this Joseph's son?   s John 6. 42.

All that heard our Saviour in the synagogue *bare him witness.* Of what? Not that he was the Messias, much less the Son of God; but they praised his discourse in opening the prophecy: they did not believe in him, but they admired the wisdom and piety of his discourses, they admired the effects of the grace of God in him, his *gracious words.* But see the wretchedness of carnal hearts, in their proneness to take up prejudices, to choke the beginnings of any convictions in themselves. They do not admire the power of Divine grace, that it could so far influence one of so mean an education as they took Christ to have had; but dreaming that the kingdom of God must come with observation, and the coming of the Messiah must be in great outward splendour and glory, they stumble at his parents, because (though of the house of David) they were of so mean a visible quality.

23 And he said unto them, Ye will surely say unto me this proverb, Physician, heal thyself: whatsoever we have heard done in ᵗ Capernaum, do also here in ᵘ thy country.   t Matt. 4. 13. & 11. 23.
u Mat. 13. 54. Mark 6. 1.

24 And he said, Verily I say unto you, No ˣ prophet is accepted in his own country.   x Mat. 13. 57. Mark 6. 4. John 4. 44.

Christ here tells those of Nazareth what was in their hearts, viz. that they in their hearts contemned him, because of the meanness of his parentage, and challenged him to confirm his doctrine by miracles, urging that Nazareth was his own country, and physicians in the first place ought to cure themselves, and their friends, and those of their own families; they therefore challenge him to work some such miracles as he had before wrought in Capernaum, as they had heard. He gives them the reason why he did no miracles amongst them, viz. because he discerned that they contemned them, as is very usual for persons, according to that common saying, *No prophet is accepted in his own country.* The reference here to some things done before this time in Capernaum, would incline us to think that after Christ's temptations he first went to Cana of Galilee, where he wrought his first miracle, John ii. 1, turning the water into wine, then to Capernaum, where he staid not many days, John ii. 12, then to Nazareth; but hearing that John was cast into prison, he removed from Nazareth to Capernaum, out of the jurisdiction of Herod, under the milder government of Philip his brother.

25 But I tell you of a truth, ʸ many widows were in Israel in the days of Elias, when the heaven was shut up three years and six months, when great famine was throughout all the land;   y 1 Kings 17. 9. & 18. 1. Jam. 5. 17.

26 But unto none of them was Elias sent, save unto Sarepta, *a city* of Sidon, unto a woman *that was* a widow.

27 ᶻ And many lepers were in Israel in the time of Eliseus the prophet; and none of them was cleansed, saving Naaman the Syrian.   z 2 Kings 5. 14.

The two stories to which our Saviour referreth are those 1 Kings xvii. 9; 2 Kings v. 14. But the question is what our Saviour intended to teach them by these stories, which made them so exceeding angry, as we shall find by and by. I answer, several things, none of which pleased them. 1. The freeness of God's distinguishing grace. That God was not bound to give to all the same aid, and means of grace, that he gave some. This is a doctrine the world was never patient to hear. That God will have mercy on whom he will have mercy. We would fain make God a debtor to us. Those of Nazareth think they had as good, if not a better, right to Christ's miracles than those of Capernaum. I tell you, saith Christ, God is a Sovereign in his acts of grace, and acteth freely, and I can do no miracles but where he will have them done. 2. That it is through the fault of men, if they receive not the benefits of Divine grace

If the Israelites would have entertained Elijah, he might have been sent to them, as well as to Sarepta. If the lepers in Israel would have sought out and come to Elisha, they might have been healed. If you would have received me, and believed in me, you might have seen what those of Capernaum did; it is because of your contempt and unbelief that I can show you no miracles. If any say, If God had put it into the hearts of the widows in Israel, or the lepers there, they would also have entertained Elijah, and have sought out and came to Elisha: why did not God put it into their hearts? To this the answer is ready: Who art thou that disputest with God? Why doth the clay reply upon the potter? Even so, O Father, for so it pleaseth thee. However, the failures of the lepers in Israel, and the widows there, and of those in Nazareth, was in a great measure in their duty, as to things within their power to do by virtue of that common grace which God denieth to none: he might justly deny his special influences, while they neglected to make use of his more common influences. 3. That in every nation he that feared God, and wrought righteousness, was ever accepted of him. God had no respect to this country, or that country; he sent Elijah to do good to a Sidonian, and Elisha to do good to a Syrian, while he neglected the ungrateful and disobedient Israelites. Thus he also not obscurely hinteth, that for their unbelief, and rejection of, and disobedience to him, God would send his gospel to the Gentiles, and reject them, which came to pass within a few years after. None of all these were grateful sounds in the ears of the men of Nazareth. You ask me (saith our Saviour) why I do not such things here at Nazareth as I did at Capernaum. I was not sent to you. No; but were not they some of the lost sheep of Israel? Ah! but Christ was no more sent to all Israel, than Elias was sent to all the widows in Israel. He was sent to preach to them all, but for any special, signal favours, he was sent but to some, and those some were such as did not proudly reject and contemn him, but receive him.

28 And all they in the synagogue, when they heard these things, were filled with wrath,

29 And rose up, and thrust him out of the city, and led him unto the ‖ brow of the hill whereon their city was built, that they might cast him down headlong.

‖ Or, *edge*.

a John 8. 59.
& 10. 39.

30 But he ªpassing through the midst of them went his way,

Unhappy Nazareth, where Christ had now lived more than thirty years! They had seen him growing up, increasing *in wisdom and stature, and in favour* both *with God and man,* chap. ii. 52; they had had the first-fruits of his ministry, and, ver. 22, they *bare him witness, and wondered at the gracious words which proceeded out of his mouth;* they knew his education, so as they could not think he had this wisdom and knowledge from any advantages of that, but must have it from Heaven; yet when they hear him preaching, and but touching them for their contempt and rejection of him, and tacitly comparing them with their forefathers in the time of Ahab, and preaching the doctrine of God's sovereign and free grace, and hinting to them that the grace of God should pass to the Gentiles, while they should be rejected, they are not able to bear him. Thus, Acts xxii. 21, the Jews heard Paul patiently, till he repeated God's commission to him to go *unto the Gentiles;* then they cried, *Away with such a fellow from the earth, for it is not fit he should live.* This was according to the old prophecy, Deut. xxxii. 21, (applied to the Jews by the apostle, Rom. x. 19,) that because they had *moved* God *to jealousy with that which is not God,* he would *move* them *to jealousy with them that are not a people, and provoke them to anger with a foolish nation.* This is further matter of observation, that wretched sinners, who cannot obtain of their lusts to be as good and holy as others, yet are ordinarily so proud, as they have no patience to hear that others are better than they, or have or shall have any more special share in God's favour. Those of Nazareth which were in the synagogue hearing these things, are filled with wrath, *thrust* Christ *out of the city,* as not fit to live among them, and go about to kill him, by throwing him down headlong from the brow of the hill upon which their city was built. *But he passing through the midst of them*

went his way. How he got out of their hands, when they had laid hold of him, the Scripture doth not tell us, nor is it our concern to be curious to inquire. We read much the like passage, John viii. 59, when the Jews had taken up stones to stone him. We know it was an easy thing for him, who was God as well as man, to quit himself of any mortal enemies; but how he did it, whether by blinding their eyes, or altering the nature of his body, and making it imperceptible by them, or by a greater strength than they, (which the Divine nature could easily supply his human nature with,) who is able to determine?

31 And ᵇcame down to Capernaum, a city of Galilee, and taught them on the sabbath days.

b Mat. 4. 13.
Mark 1. 21.

32 And they were astonished at his doctrine: ᶜfor his word was with power.

c Mat. 6. 28, 29. Tit. 2. 15.

Capernaum was a city in the other Galilee, under the jurisdiction of Philip, whither Matthew and Mark mention our Saviour's motion upon the report of the imprisonment of John. Philip is not only by historians reported of a less bloody temper than his brother Herod, but Herod having taken away his wife, it is very probable that there was no good understanding betwixt him and Philip. So that two things promised our Saviour more quiet in Philip's jurisdiction: 1. The tameness of his temper. 2. The hatred betwixt him and Herod. It appears, from ver. 23, he had been at Capernaum before, but stayed very little, hastening to his own country of Nazareth in the other Galilee: from thence he now again removeth, hearing of John's imprisonment, and seeing the baseness of his countrymen. When he came there, he keeps on his course preaching upon the Jewish sabbath, not abolished till his resurrection. It appeareth by ver. 33, that he preached in the synagogue here also. It is said that the people *were astonished at his doctrine.* Astonishment is one thing, believing is another. Men may be some ways and to some degrees affected at the word of God, that yet are far enough from believing, as the most of these Capernaites were; else Christ had never upbraided them as he did, Matt. xi. 23. *For his word was with power.* That this phrase is to be understood only of those powerful and miraculous operations, by which Christ confirmed the word which he preached to be from God, I cannot yield. It is better interpreted by Mark i. 22, *He taught them as one that had authority, not as the scribes;* and to be understood of the gravity and spirituality of his doctrine, his majesty and life in the delivering of it, and the power of God going along with it for the conviction of sinners; to all which were added his miraculous operations, of which the evangelist goeth on giving us a more particular account.

33 ¶ ᵈAnd in the synagogue there was a man, which had a spirit of an unclean devil, and cried out with a loud voice,

d Mark 1. 23.

34 Saying, ‖Let *us* alone; what have we to do with thee, *thou* Jesus of Nazareth? art thou come to destroy us? ᵉI know thee who thou art; ᶠthe Holy One of God.

‖ Or, *Away*.

e ver. 41.

f Ps. 16. 10.
Dan. 9. 24.
ch. 1. 35.

35 And Jesus rebuked him, saying, Hold thy peace, and come out of him. And when the devil had thrown him in the midst, he came out of him, and hurt him not.

36 And they were all amazed, and spake among themselves, saying, What a word *is* this! for with authority and power he commandeth the unclean spirits, and they come out.

37 And the fame of him went out into every place of the country round about.

We met with the same history related as done in Capernaum, and with the same circumstances, Mark i. 21, 22, &c., to the notes upon which we refer the reader.

38 ¶ ᵍAnd he arose out of the synagogue, and entered into Simon's house. And Simon's wife's mother was taken

g Mat. 8. 14.
Mark 1. 29.

with a great fever; and they besought him for her.

39 And he stood over her, and rebuked the fever; and it left her: and immediately she arose and ministered unto them.

We met with this history both in Matthew and Mark. See the notes on Matt. viii. 14, 15, and Mark i. 29—31.

h Mat. 8. 16. Mark 1. 32.

40 ¶ ʰNow when the sun was setting, all they that had any sick with divers diseases brought them unto him; and he laid his hands on every one of them, and healed them.

i Mark 1. 34. & 3. 11.
k Mark 1. 25, 34. ver. 34, 35.
∥ Or, to say that they knew him to be Christ.

41 ⁱAnd devils also came out of many, crying out, and saying, Thou art Christ the Son of God. And ᵏhe rebuking *them* suffered them not ∥to speak: for they knew that he was Christ.

See the notes on Mark i. 32—34, where we met with the same things.

l Mark 1. 35.

42 ˡAnd when it was day, he departed and went into a desert place: and the people sought him, and came unto him, and stayed him, that he should not depart from them.

43 And he said unto them, I must preach the kingdom of God to other cities also: for therefore am I sent.

m Mark 1. 39.

44 ᵐAnd he preached in the synagogues of Galilee.

See the notes on Mark i. 35—39, where that evangelist reports the same things that this evangelist mentioneth, only with more circumstances. Mark saith, he went out a great while before day into a solitary place to pray. He saith also that Simon and others followed him, and found him, and told him that all men sought him. Luke addeth that the others desired him not to depart from thence. They desired his stay, in order to his miracles, the healing of their sick, dispossessing demoniacs, &c. Christ replied, (as Mark saith,) *Let us go into the next towns, that I may preach there also; for therefore came I forth.* Luke saith he told them, he *must preach the gospel of the kingdom to other cities also; for therefore* he *was sent.* Accordingly, (saith Luke,) he did preach *in the synagogues of Galilee.* Mark adds also that he cast out devils. How can any think that preaching the gospel is not the great work of the minister of Christ, but prayers are to be preferred before it, or administering the sacraments greater, when it is expressly said, that Christ *baptized none, but his disciples,* John iv. 2; and Paul saith, Christ sent him *not to baptize, but to preach the gospel;* and Christ omitted opportunities of working miracles that he might preach to other cities, and only wrought miracles to confirm the doctrine he preached; and we so often read of his going about preaching and teaching, never of his praying, but alone with his disciples, or in a mountain or solitary place; (though doubtless he, or some others, did pray at their worship in the synagogues;) unless any will be so mad as to think, that the sole end of preaching was to convert men from Judaism, or paganism, to an outward owning and professing of Christ, though under that profession, by reason of their sottish ignorance and debauched lives, they remain twice more the children of the devil than many Jews and pagans are? What was Christ's great work is certainly his ministers', viz. to preach the gospel of the kingdom.

CHAP. V

Christ teacheth the people out of Simon's ship, 1—3. *The miraculous draught of fishes: Simon and the two sons of Zebedee follow him,* 4—11. *Christ cleanseth a leper,* 12—15; *prayeth in the wilderness,* 16; *answereth the reasonings of the scribes and Pharisees concerning his forgiving sins, and healeth the sick of the palsy,* 17—26; *calleth Levi from the receipt of custom,* 27, 28; *justifieth his eating with publicans and sinners,* 29—32; *excuseth his disciples from fasting for the present,* 33—35; *and illustrateth the matter by a twofold parable,* 36—39.

AND ᵃit came to pass, that, as the people pressed upon him to hear the word of God, he stood by the lake of Gennesaret,

a Mat. 4. 18. Mark 1. 16.

2 And saw two ships standing by the lake: but the fishermen were gone out of them, and were washing *their* nets.

It is by many interpreters thought that Luke in this history, to the 11th verse, doth but give us a larger account of what Matthew, chap. iv. 18, and Mark, chap. i. 16, told us shortly. The sea of Galilee (as they call it) and the lake of Gennesaret were both the same, receiving the different denomination from the opposite coasts betwixt which it was. Παρὰ τὴν λίμνην had been better translated *upon,* or *at,* than *by the lake,* for without doubt the two ships here mentioned were upon the water, though possibly fastened as usually to the shore.

3 And he entered into one of the ships, which was Simon's, and prayed him that he would thrust out a little from the land. And he sat down, and taught the people out of the ship.

4 Now when he had left speaking, he said unto Simon, ᵇLaunch out into the deep, and let down your nets for a draught.

b John 21. 6.

5 And Simon answering said unto him, Master, we have toiled all the night, and have taken nothing: nevertheless at thy word I will let down the net.

6 And when they had this done, they inclosed a great multitude of fishes: and their net brake.

7 And they beckoned unto *their* partners, which were in the other ship, that they should come and help them. And they came, and filled both the ships, so that they began to sink.

8 When Simon Peter saw *it,* he fell down at Jesus' knees, saying, ᶜDepart from me; for I am a sinful man, O Lord.

c 2 Sam. 6. 9. 1 Kin. 17. 18.

9 For he was astonished, and all that were with him, at the draught of the fishes which they had taken:

10 And so *was* also James, and John, the sons of Zebedee, which were partners with Simon. And Jesus said unto Simon, Fear not; ᵈfrom henceforth thou shalt catch men.

d Matt. 4. 19. Mark 1. 17.

11 And when they had brought their ships to land, ᵉthey forsook all, and followed him.

e Matt. 4. 20. & 19. 27. Mark 1. 18. ch. 18. 28.

Here is a plain and orderly story, related with many circumstances, tending to show us the power and influence of God upon men's successes, in their honest and ordinary callings, and also that God hath a command upon the fish in the sea; together with an account of Christ's call of Simon Peter to be a preacher of the gospel. The only difficulty is to reconcile this to what Matthew tells us, chap. iv. 18, 19, &c. Matthew's words are these: *And Jesus, walking by the sea of Galilee, saw two brethren, Simon called Peter, and Andrew his brother, casting a net into the sea: for they were fishers. And he saith unto them, Follow me, and I will make you fishers of men. And they straightway left their nets, and followed him. And going on from thence, he saw other two brethren, James the son of Zebedee, and John his brother, in a ship with Zebedee their father, mending their nets; and he called them. And they immediately left the ship, and their father, and followed him.* Mark's relation doth much agree with Matthew's. The differences are in these things: 1. Matthew and Mark speak of Christ's calling these disciples as he was walking by the sea. Luke seems to mention it as done in the ship.

Answ. Luke doth not say that Christ spake so to Simon in the ship, though he doth indeed mention those words to Simon, before he mentioneth their bringing the ship to land, because possibly he would give account of all that Christ did or spake together. 2. They might be out of the ship, walking by the sea, before he called James and John, whose call Luke doth not mention, but Matthew and Mark alone. 2. Matthew and Mark mention no ships, nor going of Christ into any, nor any draught of fishes. *Answ.* Matthew saith that he saw Simon and Andrew casting their nets into the sea. But there is nothing more ordinary than for one evangelist to relate more fully what another repeateth summarily. 3. Matthew and Mark speak of Andrew being with Simon; Luke mentioneth Simon alone. *Answ.* Luke denies not that Andrew was there, and we are sure Simon alone could not manage the nets with such a draught of fishes. 4. Matthew and Mark speak of the calling of Simon, Andrew, James, and John; Luke only of the calling of Simon. *Answ.* It doth not follow from thence that they were not called during Christ's walk by the sea after he came out of the ship: Matthew and Mark assure us they were. 5. Matthew and Mark say that James and John were mending their nets. *Answ.* Luke saith nothing to the contrary, for he doth not mention their call at that instant when Simon was. That immediately after such a draught of fishes their nets should want mending, and they be so employed, is nothing at all strange. So as it was like there was a little distance of time betwixt the call of Peter and the others; yet Luke, omitting some circumstances mentioned by Matthew and Mark, as well as adding much to this history by them omitted, saith (at least) of more than one, *they forsook all, and followed him.* Hence appeareth that there may be a coherent history, taking in what all three evangelists say, only allowing that Christ came upon the shore, and walked by the sea-side some short time, before he called James and John. The history instructeth us, 1. How good a thing it is for men to be employed in their honest callings, though never so mean. There God meets people with blessings. 2. How much it is our duty to yield obedience to God's commands, and how advantageous it will prove, how contrary soever they appear to our sense and reason. 3. Upon whom our blessing depends, let our labour be what it will. 4. That it is the work of the ministers of the gospel to catch men, to gain souls to God. 5. How powerful God's calls are: *They forsook all, and followed him.* For the difference betwixt what John saith, chap. i. 40, 41, of the call of Andrew and Simon, from what the other three evangelists say, we have spoken something in our notes on Matt. iv. 18, and shall add more when we come to that place in John. In short, John speaketh of another time, before that either of them were called to follow Christ.

f Matt. 8. 2.
Mark 1. 40.

12 ¶ ᶠAnd it came to pass, when he was in a certain city, behold a man full of leprosy: who seeing Jesus fell on *his* face, and besought him, saying, Lord, if thou wilt, thou canst make me clean.

13 And he put forth *his* hand, and touched him, saying, I will: be thou clean. And immediately the leprosy departed from him.

g Matt. 8. 4.

14 ᵍAnd he charged him to tell no man: but go, and shew thyself to the Priest, and offer for thy cleansing, ʰaccording as Moses commanded, for a testimony unto them.

h Lev. 14. 4, 10, 21, 22.

15 But so much the more went there a fame abroad of him: ⁱand great multitudes came together to hear, and to be healed by him of their infirmities.

i Matt. 4. 25.
Mark 3. 7.
John 6. 2.

See the notes on Matt. viii. 2—5, and on Mark i. 40—45. Matthew reports this miracle done when Christ *came down from the mountain,* and immediately after saith, that he *entered into Capernaum,* ver. 5. Mark also, concluding the first chapter with this piece of history, he begins the second with telling us, that *he entered into Capernaum after some days.* So that some think he was near Capernaum, within the bounds of it, when he wrought this miracle, but there is no certainty of that.

16 ¶ ᵏAnd he withdrew himself into the wilderness, and prayed.

k Mat. 14. 23.
Mark 6. 46.

We meet with Christ often commending to us the duty of secret prayer, by his own example, as he had done by his precept, Matt. vi., and always choosing for it the most private and retired places, to teach us to go and to do likewise, often to pray to our Father which seeth in secret: and his example more presseth us, because we have much more business with God in prayer than he had; he had no sins to confess, nor to beg pardon for, no need to ask for any sanctifying habits of grace, &c. It is possible also that he withdrew into desert places ofttimes to avoid all show of ostentation, or dangers of tumults, and to obtain a little rest for himself. But suppose that the reason of his motion, yet the spending of his leisurable hours in communion with his Father is very imitable for us. Christ had no idle hours, he was always either preaching or healing, thereby doing good to others; or praying, thereby paying a homage to God. If it could be said of the Roman, (with respect to his studies,) it should be much more said of Christians, They should never be less alone than when they are alone, nor less idle than when they are most at leisure from their public employments.

17 And it came to pass on a certain day, as he was teaching, that there were Pharisees and doctors of the law sitting by, which were come out of every town of Galilee, and Judæa, and Jerusalem: and the power of the Lord was *present* to heal them.

We shall observe that the scribes and Pharisees much haunted our Saviour wherever he came, either to cavil at him, or out of curiosity to see the miracles he wrought. It seems they were many of them present at this time. But here ariseth a question or two. 1. How is it said, *the power of the Lord was present* with Christ *to heal?* had not Christ this power of healing then at all times? *Answ.* Doubtless he had, for he was always *the Lord that healeth us.* The Divine nature once united to the human was never separated from Christ, but it did not always put forth itself, being as to that directed by his will. But as the end of Christ's miracles was for the confirmation of his doctrine; so we shall observe, that mostly after preaching he wrought his miraculous operations. 2. Who are here meant by *them?* by reading the words one would think *them* related to the *Pharisees and doctors of the law,* of none of which we read that they were sick, nor do we read of any cures that Christ made upon them. *Answ.* We must know that sometimes in holy writ these relative terms are put out of due order, as in Matt. xi. 1, where we have these words, *And it came to pass, when Jesus had made an end of commanding his twelve disciples, he departed thence to teach and to preach in their cities:* not in the disciples' cities; poor men, they had no cities; but in the Jewish cities, the cities of that country: yet the verse mentioneth no other persons than Jesus and the twelve disciples. So here, though the verse mentioneth no other persons present than the Pharisees and doctors of the law, yet there doubtless were many others, and some amongst them labouring under chronical distempers; of these the text is to be understood.

18 ¶ ˡAnd, behold, men brought in a bed a man which was taken with a palsy: and they sought *means* to bring him in, and to lay *him* before him.

l Matt. 9. 2.
Mark 2. 3.

19 And when they could not find by what *way* they might bring him in because of the multitude, they went upon the housetop, and let him down through the tiling with *his* couch into the midst before Jesus.

20 And when he saw their faith, he said unto him, Man, thy sins are forgiven thee.

21 ᵐAnd the Scribes and the Pharisees began to reason, saying, Who is this which

m Matt. 9 3.
Mark 2. 6, 7.

speaketh blasphemies? ⁿWho can forgive sins, but God alone?

n Ps. 32. 5.
Is. 43. 25.

22 But when Jesus perceived their thoughts, he answering said unto them, What reason ye in your hearts?

23 Whether is easier, to say, Thy sins be forgiven thee; or to say, Rise up and walk?

24 But that ye may know that the Son of man hath power upon earth to forgive sins, (he said unto the sick of the palsy,) I say unto thee, Arise, and take up thy couch, and go unto thine house.

25 And immediately he rose up before them, and took up that whereon he lay, and departed to his own house, glorifying God.

26 And they were all amazed, and they glorified God, and were filled with fear, saying, We have seen strange things to day.

See the notes on Matt. ix. 2—8, and on Mark ii. 3—12. Both those evangelists record the same story with very small alterations in the phrase, nothing in the sense. Instead of the last words, *We have seen strange things to day*, Matthew saith, *they glorified God, who had given such power unto men*. By which appeareth that all the effect this miracle had was, 1. Amazement. A thing was done; they understood not how it could be effected. 2. They apprehended a Divine power as to the effect. They therefore *glorified God, who had given such power unto men*. So as it is plain they only looked upon Christ as a great Prophet, to whom God had communicated such a Divine power, as of old he had communicated to Elijah, and then to Elisha. Lest any should stumble at what is said, that they uncovered the house, and let him down through the tiling, fancying the roofs of their houses built as ours, they must know, that the most of their houses were built (like some amongst us) with flat roofs, which were covered with some slates or stones, so as they might easily be uncovered; and this appeareth by the command of God, Deut. xxii. 8, concerning making battlements on the tops of their houses, to prevent casualties. The object of the faith here mentioned, was plainly the Divine power and goodness, but not as coming from Christ originally, as eternal God, but as an instrument by which God conveyed it to men under such miserable circumstances as this poor man was.

o Matt. 9. 9.
Mark 2. 13, 14.

27 ¶ ᵒAnd after these things he went forth, and saw a Publican, named Levi, sitting at the receipt of custom: and he said unto him, Follow me.

28 And he left all, rose up, and followed him.

p Mat. 9. 10.
Mark 2. 15.
q ch. 15. 1.

29 ᵖAnd Levi made him a great feast in his own house: and ᑫthere was a great company of Publicans and of others that sat down with them.

30 But their Scribes and Pharisees murmured against his disciples, saying, Why do ye eat and drink with Publicans and sinners?

31 And Jesus answering said unto them, They that are whole need not a physician; but they that are sick.

r Mat. 9. 13.
1 Tim. 1. 15.

32 ʳI came not to call the righteous, but sinners to repentance.

See the notes on Matt. ix. 9—13, and on Mark ii. 14—17, both which evangelists have also recorded this call of Levi; the first calls him *Matthew*; Mark and Luke call him *Levi*. There was nothing more ordinary amongst the Jews than for persons to have two names. Mark tells us his father's name also, saying he was the son of Alpheus. All agree in his employment, that he was a publican, one employed in the gathering of the public revenue, that part of it which arose from the exportation and importation of commodities; for he was *sitting at the receipt of custom*. Christ from thence calls him; he follows him, that is, gave up his name to be his disciple; in gratitude, Matthew, or Levi, invites him to a feast, and with him several other publicans and others. The other two evangelists say nothing of Matthew's preparing this feast; but it is implied in them, for they take notice of his sitting at meat in his house, and of the offence taken at it by the scribes and the Pharisees, and of our Saviour's taking notice of it, and what he said in justification of himself: see the notes before mentioned. Only Matthew adds, that our Lord also said unto them, *Go ye and learn what that meaneth, I will have mercy, and not sacrifice*. But for the explication of our Saviour's entire answer, see the notes on Matt. ix. 9—13.

33 ¶ And they said unto him, ˢWhy do the disciples of John fast often, and make prayers, and likewise *the disciples* of the Pharisees; but thine eat and drink?

s Mat. 9. 14.
Mark 2. 18.

34 And he said unto them, Can ye make the children of the bridechamber fast, while the bridegroom is with them?

35 But the days will come, when the bridegroom shall be taken away from them, and then shall they fast in those days.

36 ¶ ᵗAnd he spake also a parable unto them; No man putteth a piece of a new garment upon an old; if otherwise, then both the new maketh a rent, and the piece that was *taken* out of the new agreeth not with the old.

t Mat. 9. 16, 17. Mark 2. 21, 22.

37 And no man putteth new wine into old bottles; else the new wine will burst the bottles, and be spilled, and the bottles shall perish.

38 But new wine must be put into new bottles; and both are preserved.

39 No man also having drunk old *wine* straightway desireth new: for he saith, The old is better.

We have also both in Matthew and Mark met with this piece of history. See the notes on Matt. ix. 14—17; Mark ii. 18—22. Both Matthew and Mark say, that they were the disciples of John who came, and thus said to our Saviour. In our notes upon the two former evangelists, we have fully opened this piece of history. John the Baptist was of a more severe deportment than our Saviour thought fit to show himself; and complying more with the practices of the Pharisees (though in much more sincerity) in their exercises of discipline, the Pharisees did more easily get his disciples to join with them in this address to our Saviour; though probably John's disciples did it more out of infirmity, and the Pharisees out of malice, that they might have whereby to lessen Christ's reputation amongst the people: thus weak, though good, men are often drawn in by those who are more subtle and malicious to promote their designs. Besides, we naturally desire to be the standard to all, and that others should take their measures from us, and possibly John's disciples might have a little of that envy for their master's sake, which we find them sick of, John iii. 26. Our Lord, who might have told them that he was to be their exemplar, and not they his, dealeth more gently with them, and gives them sufficient reason why, as yet, he did not inure his disciples to those severer acts of religion: 1. Because this was all the rejoicing time they were like to have. He was now with them; when he should be gone from them, before which it would not be long, they should have time to mourn. 2. That they were but newly entered into his discipleship, and therefore not at first to be discouraged, that they might not have a temptation upon them to leave off as soon as they began. But see the notes more fully upon the same history in Matthew and Mark.

CHAP. VI

Christ allegeth Scripture in defence of his disciples plucking the ears of corn on the sabbath day, 1—5. *He appealeth to reason, and healeth the withered hand on the sabbath,*

S. LUKE VI

6—11. *He spendeth the night in prayer, and chooseth the twelve apostles*, 12—16.' *He healeth divers diseased*, 17—19; *pronounceth blessings and woes*, 20—26; *teacheth to return good for evil, and other lessons of moral duty*, 27—45; *and admonisheth to be his disciples in practice, and not in profession only*, 46—49.

^{a Mat. 12. 1.}
^{Mark 2. 23.} AND ^a it came to pass on the second sabbath after the first, that he went through the corn fields; and his disciples plucked the ears of corn, and did eat, rubbing *them* in *their* hands.

^{b Ex. 20. 10.} 2 And certain of the Pharisees said unto them, Why do ye that ^b which is not lawful to do on the sabbath days?

3 And Jesus answering them said, Have ye not read so much as this, ^{c 1 Sam. 21. 6} ^c what David did, when himself was an hungred, and they which were with him;

4 How he went into the house of God, and did take and eat the shewbread, and gave also to them that were with him; ^{d Lev. 24. 9.} ^d which it is not lawful to eat but for the Priests alone?

5 And he said unto them, That the Son of man is Lord also of the sabbath.

See the notes on Matt. xii. 1—8, and on Mark ii. 23—28. There are several guesses what day is here meant, by *the second sabbath after the first*. The Jews had several sabbaths; besides the seventh-day sabbath, which was weekly, all their festival days were called sabbaths. On the fourteenth day of the first month, at evening, began the passover; on the fifteenth day began their feast of unleavened bread, which held seven days, every one of which was called a sabbath; but the first day and the seventh day were to be days of holy convocation, in which no work was to be done that was servile, Lev. xxiii. 7. Then they had their feast of first-fruits. Fifty days after that they had their feast of pentecost. Some understand by *the second sabbath after the first*, the seventh day of the feast of unleavened bread. Others, their second great festival. It is very hard to resolve, and not material for us to know. For the history itself, see the explication in the notes on Matt. xii. 1—8.

^{e Matt. 12. 9.}
^{Mark 3. 1.}
^{See ch. 13. 14. & 14. 3.}
^{John 9. 16.} 6 ^e And it came to pass also on another sabbath, that he entered into the synagogue and taught: and there was a man whose right hand was withered.

7 And the Scribes and Pharisees watched him, whether he would heal on the sabbath day; that they might find an accusation against him.

8 But he knew their thoughts, and said to the man which had the withered hand, Rise up, and stand forth in the midst. And he arose and stood forth.

9 Then said Jesus unto them, I will ask you one thing; Is it lawful on the sabbath days to do good, or to do evil? to save life, or to destroy *it*?

10 And looking round about upon them all, he said unto the man, Stretch forth thy hand. And he did so: and his hand was restored whole as the other.

11 And they were filled with madness; and communed one with another what they might do to Jesus.

See the notes on Matt. xii. 10—13, and on Mark iii. 1—5, in both which places we met with the same history, and with some more circumstances. Mark tells us that the subject of their deliberation, what they might do to Jesus, was, *how they might destroy him;* this the evangelist maketh the effect of their madness, ἀνοίας, and he very properly so calls it. For men to answer arguments and reason with violence, is for them to act like mad-men, not like reasonable creatures; yet, to show the degeneracy of human nature, we shall observe there is nothing hath been more ordinary, when men have been conquered by reasoning, and have nothing reasonably to oppose, than to fly to violence, and with swords to cut knots which they cannot untie. Nor can there be a greater evidence of silly and brutish souls, and a baffled cause.

12 ^f And it came to pass in those days, ^{f Mat. 14. 23} that he went out into a mountain to pray, and continued all night in prayer to God.

Those who straining this text would interpret the words, ἐν τῇ προσευχῇ, for, the place of prayer, will be concerned to find us out that house of prayer which stood in this mountain, or to tell us where we shall find in holy writ any place but the temple so called, and why it should be said that *he went out into a mountain to pray*, if it were not to signify unto us, that he sought a privacy and retiredness, which he could not have had in the temple, nor in any other common place for prayer. Those interpreters certainly judge righter that say, that our Saviour, being about to send out his twelve apostles, thought so great a work should not be done without solemn prayers; he therefore seeketh a place of privacy, and goeth thither to spend some more time than ordinary in the duty of prayer, and the evangelist saith that he *continued all night;* so setting us an example what to do in great affairs, especially such as are the sending out of persons to so great an employment as that of the ministry, and by his own example commending to us what Paul afterwards commanded, Eph. vi. 18; Col. iv. 2, *Continue in prayer, and watch in the same with thanksgiving.*

13 ¶ And when it was day, he called *unto him* his disciples: ^g and of them ^{g Mat. 10. 1.} he chose twelve, whom also he named apostles;

14 Simon, (^h whom he also named ^{h John 1. 42.} Peter,) and Andrew his brother, James and John, Philip and Bartholomew,

15 Matthew and Thomas, James the *son* of Alphæus, and Simon called Zelotes,

16 And Judas ⁱ *the brother* of James, ^{i Jude 1.} and Judas Iscariot, which also was the traitor.

We have twice already met with these names of the twelve disciples, whom our Saviour called apostles, intending them not only to be with him, and to have a more special communion with him, but also to be sent out with power to preach, baptize, and to work miracles: see the notes on Matt. x. 2—4, and Mark iii. 14—19. There were amongst them two whose names were *Simon*: the one Christ named *Peter;* the other is called *Simon Zelotes* here; *Simon the Canaanite*, by Matthew and Mark. Two whose names were *James*: the one was *the son of Zebedee*, the other was *the son of Alpheus*. Two whose names were *Judas*: the one is called *Thaddeus* by Mark; *Lebbeus* and *Thaddeus*, by Matthew; *Judas the brother of James*, by Luke; (this was the penman of the Epistle of Jude;) and *Judas Iscariot, the traitor*. The other six were all of differing names. What occurs of difficulty as to their names, see opened in our notes on Matt. x. 2—4, and Mark iii. 14—19.

17 ¶ And he came down with them, and stood in the plain, and the company of his disciples, ^k and a great multitude ^{k Mat. 4. 25.} of people out of all Judæa and Jerusa- ^{Mark 3. 7.} lem, and from the sea coast of Tyre and Sidon, which came to hear him, and to be healed of their diseases;

18 And they that were vexed with unclean spirits: and they were healed.

19 And the whole multitude ^l sought ^{l Mat. 14. 36.} to touch him: for ^m there went virtue ^{m Mark 5. 30, ch. 8. 46.} out of him, and healed *them* all.

Such passages as these we meet with several times in the evangelists, who not writing a particular account of the several miracles wrought, or discourses made, by our Saviour, oftentimes they give us a general account of more than they particularly mention. Some think that Luke referreth here to Mark iii. 7, 8; but Mark seemeth rather to refer to a multitude that followed him before he went up to the mountain, which yet might be the same people coming again the next morning, and waiting for Christ's coming down from the mountain.

20 ¶ And he lifted up his eyes on his disciples, and said, "Blessed be ye poor: for your's is the kingdom of God.

21 °Blessed *are ye* that hunger now: for ye shall be filled. PBlessed *are ye* that weep now: for ye shall laugh.

22 qBlessed are ye, when men shall hate you, and when they ʳshall separate you *from their company*, and shall reproach *you*, and cast out your name as evil, for the Son of man's sake.

23 ˢRejoice ye in that day, and leap for joy: for, behold, your reward *is* great in heaven: for ᵗin the like manner did their fathers unto the prophets.

n Matt. 5. 3.
& 11. 5.
Jam. 2. 5.
o Is. 55. 1.
& 65. 13.
Matt. 5. 6.
p Is. 61. 3.
Matt. 5. 4.
q Matt.5.11.
1 Pet. 2. 19.
& 3. 14. & 4. 14.
r John 16. 2.
s Mat. 5. 12.
Acts 5. 41.
Col. 1. 24.
Jam. 1. 2.
t Acts 7. 51.

There are many that think that what Luke hath in these verses, and so to the end of this chapter, is but a shorter epitome of what Matthew hath in his 5th, 6th, and 7th chapters, and that both Matthew and Luke mean the same sermon preached at the same time. The things which favour this opinion are, 1. That sermon is said to be preached upon a mountain; this, when he came down and stood upon the plain, by which some understand only a plainer and more level part of the mountain. 2. That very many passages in the remaining part of this chapter are plainly the same with those we find in one of these three chapters in Matthew. I can hardly be of that mind: 1. Because of the phrase here used, *he came down, and stood in the plain*: it seemeth to me hard to interpret that either of the top of the mountain, (which might be a plain,) for how then could he be said to come down, or of a plainer place of the mountain. 2. The multitude described there are said to have come *from Galilee, Decapolis, Jerusalem, Judea, and beyond Jordan*. These are said to have come from *Judea, Jerusalem, and the sea-coasts of Tyre and Sidon*. But, 3. Principally from the great difference in the relations of Matthew and Luke. First, Many large discourses are not touched by Luke, viz. Christ's whole discourse in giving a true interpretation of the law, and his discourses, Matt. vi., about alms, prayer, fasting. Secondly, Luke here putteth in three verses together wherein there are woes denounced, of which Matthew saith nothing. Now though it be usual with the evangelists to relate the same discourses and miracles with some different circumstances, yet not with such considerable differences and variations. Matthew records nine blessednesses pronounced by Christ; Luke but four, and those with considerable variation from Matthew. As for those things which incline some to think it the same sermon, they do not seem to me conclusive. For what they say as to the place, it rather proves the contrary. Matthew saith it was when he had gone up into a mountain, and sat down; Luke saith, he was come down, and stood in the plain. Nor is it more considerable, that most of the passages in this chapter are to be found in the 5th, 6th, or 7th chapter of Matthew; for as they are not here exactly repeated according as Matthew recites them, so what should hinder but that our Saviour at another time, and to another auditory, might preach the same things which concern all men? Leaving therefore all to their own judgments, I see no reason to think that this discourse was but a shorter copy of the same discourse, referring to the same time and company. This being premised, let us now come to consider the words themselves, comparing them with the words recited by Matthew. *Blessed be ye poor: for yours is the kingdom of God.* Matthew saith, *Blessed are the poor in spirit: for theirs is the kingdom of heaven.* It is true, neither riches nor poverty bless or curse any man, and none that are poor are blessed if they be proud and high-minded, nor any rich man cursed but he that placeth his portion or consolation in riches; yet Christ here, by the antithesis, seems more particularly to direct his discourse to relieve his disciples discouraged by their poor and low estate in the world, by telling them that, whatever the world thought, they, being his disciples, believing in him, and following him, were in a better condition than those that were rich, and had their consolation in this life. *Blessed are ye that weep now: for ye shall laugh.* Matthew saith, *Blessed are they that mourn: for they shall be comforted.* The sense is much the same: You that are in a sad, afflicted state (being my disciples) are blessed; for there will come a time when God shall wipe tears from your eyes. *Blessed are ye that hunger now: for ye shall be filled.* Matthew saith, *Blessed are they which do hunger and thirst after righteousness.* It is true, hungering and thirsting are no blessings, but neither are they curses to a truly righteous soul, or a soul that truly seeketh after and studieth righteousness. *Blessed are ye, when men shall hate you, and when they shall separate you from their company, and shall reproach you, and cast out your name as evil, for the Son of man's sake.* Matthew saith, *Blessed are they which are persecuted for righteousness' sake: for theirs is the kingdom of heaven. Blessed are ye, when men shall revile you, and persecute you, and shall say all manner of evil against you falsely, for my sake.* It is true the general sense is the same, sufferers for the name of Christ are pronounced blessed; but the words are very different, and here are some species of persecution mentioned that Matthew mentioneth not particularly. 1. Separating the disciples. 2. Casting out their names as evil. The separating here mentioned may indeed be understood of imprisonment, or banishment, for persons under those circumstances are separated from the company of their relations and countrymen; but it may also be understood of ecclesiastical censures; and thus it agreeth both with our Saviour's prophecy, John xvi. 2, *They shall put you out of the synagogues*, and with John ix. 22, where we read of a decree they made, *that if any man did confess that Jesus was the Christ, he should be put out of the synagogue*. There are some who think that the Jews exercised no such power till the time of Ezra, when their governor was but a substitute under a pagan prince, who did not give their conquered subjects a power to put any to death, but left them to exercise any lighter punishments. I cannot subscribe to the judgment of those learned men that think so. For as it is not reasonable, that God left the church of the Jews without that power that nature clotheth every society with, to purge out of itself such as are not fit members for it; so it will not enter into my thoughts, that all were to be put to death, of whom God said so often, he, or they, shall be cut off from his, or their, people, as in case of uncircumcision, and not receiving the passover in its time. So as I do not think that the latter Jews derived this practice from a human constitution, but from a Divine law. Now we are told that the Jews had three degrees of this separation: some they merely separated from their communion; others they anathematized, that is, cursed; others they so separated, that they prayed against them, that God would make them examples of his vengeance; and some think (but I judge it but a guess) that these were those sinners unto death, for whom John would not have Christians pray, 1 John v. 16. Now it is certain that the Jews exercised not the lowest degree only, but the highest, against Christians, and also made it their business by letters, and word of mouth, to reproach them all over the world, Acts xxviii. 22. Now Christ pronounceth them, under these circumstances, blessed, if they suffered these things for his name's sake. This casting out of their names as evil, doth not only signify the blotting out their names out of the rolls of the church, but the defaming of them in the manner before mentioned, which was like to be a sore temptation to the disciples; against which he further armeth them, saying, *Rejoice ye in that day, and leap for joy: for, behold, your reward is great in heaven: for in the like manner did their fathers unto the prophets.* See the notes on Matt. v. 12.

24 ᵘBut woe unto you ˣthat are rich! for ʸye have received your consolation.

u Amos 6. 1.
Ecclus. 31.8.
Jam. 5. 1.
x ch. 12. 21.
y Matt. 6. 2, 5, 16. ch. 16. 25.

Not because you are rich, but because you are not rich towards God, because you look upon your riches as your portion, as your consolation; or, you that are rich in the opinion of your own righteousness.

z Is. 65. 13.
a Prov. 14. 13.

25 ᶻWoe unto you that are full! for ye shall hunger. ᵃWoe unto you that laugh now! for ye shall mourn and weep.

Our Saviour must be understood, either of those who are sinfully full, or at least such as are spiritually empty; those that are full are opposed to those that hunger. If we take *hunger* for a hungering and thirsting after righteousness, as Matthew speaks, those that are full are such as are filled with wind, a high opinion of their own righteousness. If we take *hunger* for a want of the necessaries of this life, then fulness signifieth either a sinfulness with drink, or meat, or ill-gotten goods, or at least for such as are spiritually empty of the knowledge or grace of God; there will come a time when they shall want, as rich Dives wanted a little water to cool his tongue. So by those *that laugh* must be understood, either those that are sinfully merry, or at least those that have no true cause of spiritual joy. By mourning and weeping, threatened to such, is either meant the vengeance of God upon them in this life, or in the world to come, where there shall be weeping, and wailing, and gnashing of teeth.

b John 15. 19.
1 John 4. 5.

26 ᵇWoe unto you, when all men shall speak well of you! for so did their fathers to the false prophets.

A good report of all, even those that are without, is a desirable thing, and what all good men ought to labour for, both by avoiding any just occasion of their speaking ill of them, and by doing all the acts of kindness and charity that may commend religion to them. But the world is so corrupt, that usually none are worse spoken of than the best men. And this is true of no sort of men more than of the ministers of the gospel; neither the prophets of old, nor John the Baptist, nor Christ, nor the apostles, could have good words from the wicked party of their several ages. The false prophets of old were in much greater credit with the generality of the Jews than the prophets of the Lord. The doctrines of the law and the gospel are so contrary to the most of men's lusts, as it is impossible that the most of the world should be reconciled to them, or to those who faithfully declare them: this the Pharisees in their age, and the papists and their friends in our age, have for some time so well understood, that as it was the business of the Pharisees in their time, so it hath been the business of the popish casuists, so to expound the law of God, as men may flatter themselves that they are no debtors to it, though they keep their several lusts; and so to interpret the gospel, that the way to heaven is made so broad that it is not easy for any to miss it.

c Ex. 23. 4.
Prov. 25. 2.
Matt. 5. 44.
ver. 35.
Rom. 12. 20.

27 ¶ ᶜBut I say unto you which hear, Love your enemies, do good to them which hate you,

d ch. 23. 34.
Acts 7. 60.

28 Bless them that curse you, and ᵈpray for them which despitefully use you.

We met with these precepts Matt. v. 44, and there discoursed the sense of them. See the notes there.

e Mat. 5. 39.

29 ᵉAnd unto him that smiteth thee on the *one* cheek offer also the other;
f 1 Cor. 6. 7. ᶠand him that taketh away thy cloke forbid not *to take thy* coat also.

We met also with a passage much like this in this verse, Matt. v. 39, 40, the general sense of which was, as I then said, a prohibition of private revenge. It is therefore there prefaced in with a more general precept, *Resist not evil.* But besides this, there seems to be in it also a prohibition of vexatious suits and molestations of others, though under a colour of law; therefore Matthew saith, *If any man will sue thee at the law, and take away thy cloak;* and it may be thought a more special precept relating to those times, when they had none but heathen magistrates, and in some measure to be expounded by 1 Cor. vi. 7, and to be a precept given with respect to the reputation of the gospel, that it might not be scandalized by Christians going to law before infidels. It is most certain it doth not forbid the use of the law, whether for the defending or recovering our just rights, only the irregular or scandalous use of it. See further the notes on Matt. v. 39.

30 ᵍGive to every man that asketh of thee; and of him that taketh away thy goods ask *them* not again.

g Deut. 15. 7, 8, 10.
Prov. 21. 26.
Matt. 5. 42.

Matthew hath much the same passage, only he saith, *Give to him that,* &c., not *to every man that asketh of thee;* and for the latter clause, he hath, *from him that would-borrow of thee turn not thou away,* which seems more agreeing to the precept, Deut. xv. 8. These precepts of our Saviour must be interpreted, not according to the strict sense of the words, as if every man were by them obliged, without regard to his own abilities, or the circumstances of the persons begging or asking of him, to give to every one that hath the confidence to ask of him; but as obliging us to liberality and charity according to our abilities, and the true needs and circumstances of our poor brethren, and in that order which God's word hath directed us; first providing for our own families, then doing good to the household of faith, then also to others, as we are able, and see any of them true objects of our charity. Nor must the second part of the verse be interpreted, as if it were a restraint of Christians from pursuing of thieves or oppressors, but as a precept prohibiting us private revenge, or too great contending for little things, &c. See the notes on Matt. v. 42.

31 ʰAnd as ye would that men should do to you, do ye also to them likewise.

h Tob. 4. 15.
Matt. 7. 12.

See the notes on Matt. vii. 12. This is the law of nature, the golden rule of all justice, and may also serve for a guide to us to expound the former verses, and some other precepts of charity in this chapter. Men in all these cases should consider what they would be glad, and think reasonable, that others should do to them, were they in their circumstances, and the others had the same ability or advantage to do good to them; and by this they should measure their acts both of justice and charity.

32 ⁱFor if ye love them which love you, what thank have ye? for sinners also love those that love them.

i Matt. 5. 46.

33 And if ye do good to them which do good to you, what thank have ye? for sinners also do even the same.

34 ᵏAnd if ye lend *to them* of whom ye hope to receive, what thank have ye? for sinners also lend to sinners, to receive as much again.

k Mat. 5. 42.

See the notes on Matt. v. 46, 47. The strength of our Saviour's argument lieth in this, That God expecteth that those who have received more grace and favour from God than others, and who make a higher profession than others, should do more in obedience to the positive commands of God, and the revelations of his will in his word, than they who live merely by the light of nature, and live up merely to the law of nature.

35 But ˡlove ye your enemies, and do good, and ᵐlend, hoping for nothing again; and your reward shall be great, and ⁿye shall be the children of the Highest: for he is kind unto the unthankful and *to* the evil.

l ver. 27.
m Ps. 37. 26.
ver. 30.
n Mat. 5. 45.

36 ᵒBe ye therefore merciful, as your Father also is merciful.

o Mat. 5. 48.

I know not how to agree, with what I find many interpreters judging, that this text is a prohibition of usury. I should rather interpret it more largely, as a command for acts of mercy, with respect to the circumstances of persons, obliging us not to withhold a charitable hand, from our fear that if we lend we shall lose what we lend, and obliging us, that if we find the circumstances of any that desireth us to lend him for his necessity such a quantity of money or goods as we can spare, and we can well enough bear the loss of, if the providence of God should render the person unable to repay us, we should not be awed by such a fear from acts of charity, but give with a resolution to lose it, if God please to disable the person to whom we lend, so as he cannot repay us. For the question about usury, as to which some conceive this text a prohibition, this is not a place to handle it in the latitude. I do not think it was ever absolutely forbidden to the Jews, they might take it of strangers, and that not only of the Canaanites, whom some say they might kill, (which I doubt after their agreement to a quiet cohabitation,) but of other strangers also who came not under the denomination of Canaanites. That argued the taking of usury to be not *malum per se*, in itself evil, but only *malum prohibitum*, an evil as forbidden; and not absolutely and universally forbidden, but respectively, only with reference to their brethren of the same church and nation; so rather to be reckoned amongst the municipal laws of the Jews, than the common laws of God for all mankind. Besides that amongst the Jews there was less need of it, partly in respect of their years of jubilee, and partly in regard their employments were chiefly in husbandry, and about cattle, which called not for such sums of money as merchandising doth. Nor is it to be referred to any of the ten commandments, unless the eighth, *Thou shalt not steal;* which forbidding sins against charity, and such sins against charity being there forbidden as are the taking away the goods of another against his will, and without a just cause, I cannot see how the lending of money for a moderate use, when it is helpful and relieving to our neighbour, should be any kind of stealing, when his good-will appeareth in the contract; nor can there be any injustice in it, where there is a *quid pro quo*, but a proportion for what I am endamaged by the loan; unless any will say it is unjust because against the law of God, which is to beg the question, this argument being brought to prove it is not contrary to the law of God. The exacting of an undue proportion for usury, or a moderate proportion, when we plainly see our brother is fallen into poverty, and cannot pay it, may be forbidden, as a sin against charity, and that love that we ought to show to our neighbours, and the mercifulness here required, ver. 36. Yet, admitting the law of God, Deut. xxiii. 19, 20, to be interpreted of all usury, (which yet seemeth hard, for then the Jews might not sell for any thing more at twelve months' time, than if they were paid presently, for the words are *usury of money, usury of victuals, usury of any thing lent upon usury*,) it concerned the Jews only betwixt themselves, not in their dealings with any strangers, which is plain, ver. 20; so also Exod. xxii. 25, where the term *poor* is also put in, as it is Lev. xxv. 35—37; by which texts the psalmist must be expounded, Psal. xv. 5. It may possibly from the equity of that law oblige us to be more kind to those that are of the same nation and church with us, than unto others, especially such as are no Christians; and amongst those that are Christians, to those that are poor, than to those who have better estates. But, as I said in the beginning, I had rather interpret the precept of the text more largely, as a general precept of mercy, from the example of our heavenly Father.

p Matt. 7. 1.   37 ^p Judge not, and ye shall not be judged: condemn not, and ye shall not be condemned: forgive, and ye shall be forgiven:

See the notes on Matt. vii. 1, and on Matt. vi. 14, where we have discoursed what private judgings are here forbidden, and what forgiving is here required.

q Prov. 19. 17.   38 ^q Give, and it shall be given unto you; good measure, pressed down, and shaken together, and running over, shall

r Ps. 79. 12.
s Matt. 7. 2.
Mark 4. 24.
Jam. 2. 13.   men give into your ^r bosom. For ^s with the same measure that ye mete withal it shall be measured to you again.

To let us know how God favoureth acts of charity and justice we shall observe, that there are no good deeds that God so rewardeth by retaliation, as such which are the products of these habits; nor any sins which God so punisheth by way of retaliation, as sins contrary to these, especially such as are more eminently contrary. This verse speaks of acts of charity. *Give, and it shall be given unto you*, and that not bare measure, but *good measure, pressed down, and shaken together, and running over*.

Nothing can more concur to make good measure, than the shaking of the bushel, the crowding and pressing down of the corn or meal with the hand, and the pouring in till the measure runneth over. So as that which is here promised, is a plentiful reward to charitable and merciful actions, either from the hand of God more mediately, God stirring up others to be as kind to us as we are to others; or more immediately, himself blessing us by his unexpected providential dispensations: to this purpose are abundance of scriptures, Deut. xxiv. 19; Psal. xli. 1—3; Prov. xi. 25; xxviii. 27; 2 Cor. ix. 6. If men will not be so just as to requite the good which their brethren have done them, having it in their power, yet God will be faithful to his promises, and by his providence take care that those who have done acts of mercy, not in a mere commiseration to human condition, but in a just obedience to his will, shall not lose by what they have done; they shall be rewarded fully and plentifully, finding again (though it may be after many days) the bread which they have cast upon the waters, according to his command.

39 And he spake a parable unto them, ^t Can the blind lead the blind? shall they not both fall into the ditch?   t Mat. 15. 14.

By *a parable* here is to be understood a proverbial saying, which hath some darkness in it, as being brought to express or signify more than the words naturally do express. Proverbial speeches are applicable to more things, and in more cases, than one. Nor is it to be expected, that in all that the evangelists give us an account of, as to the sayings of Christ, we should be able to find out an evident connexion. They, questionless, wrote much at least from their memories, and set down many sayings without respect to the time when our Saviour spake them, or the matter of his discourse immediately preceding them. We need not therefore be careful to make out the connexion of these words of his with what was before set down. In the parallel text, Matt. xv. 14, our Saviour plainly applieth these words with reference to the scribes and Pharisees, the Jewish leaders, their doctors and teachers at that time, who themselves being ignorant of the true sense of the Divine law, were not like very well to guide others, but with them to *fall into the ditch*, that is, into ruin and destruction: from whence a very probable connexion of them here with what went before may be observed; for, as appears from Matt. v., he had in the preceding verses given an interpretation of that law of God, *Thou shalt love thy neighbour as thyself*, much different from what the Pharisees had given of it, who had expounded it, Matt. v. 43, *Thou shalt love thy neighbour, and hate thine enemy;* making a great many branches of love to men more than they made. Now, (saith he,) this is the will, this is the law, of my heavenly Father. The scribes and Pharisees, your present doctors and teachers, go much below this; but listen not to them, if you mind to please God; themselves are blind, and know not the will of God, and if you follow them what can you expect more than such an event as where one blind man leads another?

40 ^u The disciple is not above his master: but every one ‖ that is perfect shall be as his master.   u Matt. 10. 24. John 13. 16. & 15. 20. ‖ Or, *shall be perfected as his master*.

This was another common saying, which our Saviour applieth, Matt. x. 24; John xv. 20, to comfort his disciples concerning their sufferings, because he was first in suffering: here he applieth it to signify their duty in doing. Some apply this with reference to the Pharisees, and so make a connexion betwixt this and the former verse, where he had said, If the blind lead the blind, they shall both fall into the ditch; for *the disciple is not above his master*, none must look to learn of another more than the teacher knoweth himself. But it is better applied to Christ, and is as much as if our Lord had said, I am your Master, you are my disciples, and by that relation engaged to learn of me, and to follow me. I have taught you no more than I am ready to practise; I am merciful, I forgive, I give, looking for nothing again. I do not look that you should do any thing above me, any thing as to which I have not set you, or shall not set you, an example; but your perfection lieth in coming as near to me as you can, in being as your Master.

41 ˣAnd why beholdest thou the mote that is in thy brother's eye, but perceivest not the beam that is in thine own eye?

42 Either how canst thou say to thy brother, Brother, let me pull out the mote that is in thine eye, when thou thyself beholdest not the beam that is in thine own eye? Thou hypocrite, ʸcast out first the beam out of thine own eye, and then shalt thou see clearly to pull out the mote that is in thy brother's eye.

marginal: x Matt. 7. 3. ; y See Prov. 18. 17.

See the notes on Matt. vii. 3—5.

43 ᶻFor a good tree bringeth not forth corrupt fruit; neither doth a corrupt tree bring forth good fruit.

44 For ᵃevery tree is known by his own fruit. For of thorns men do not gather figs, nor of a bramble bush gather they †grapes.

45 ᵇA good man out of the good treasure of his heart bringeth forth that which is good; and an evil man out of the evil treasure of his heart bringeth forth that which is evil: for ᶜof the abundance of the heart his mouth speaketh.

marginal: z Mat. 7. 16, 17. ; a Mat. 12. 33. ; † Gr. a grape. ; b Mat. 12. 35. ; c Mat. 12. 34.

See the notes on Matt. vii. 16—20. The 43rd and 44th verses are expounded in the 45th verse. Men and women here (as in other texts of Scripture) are compared to trees, with respect to their root and fruit, and the dependence the fruit hath upon the root and the nature of the tree. The heart of man is made the root, that being the principle of human actions, as the root is the principle to the fruit; for all the overt actions of a man's life are but the imperate acts of the heart and of the will. Hence it is that a will renewed and sanctified in a man, and made conformable to the will of God, doth not only will and choose the will of God, love it, desire it, and delight in it; but commandeth the tongue to direct its discourses conformable to it, and also commandeth all the members of the body, in their motions and order, to act conformably: and on the contrary, the unrenewed and unsanctified will of man doth not only reject and refuse the will of God, but directeth the tongue to words contrary to the Divine will, and all the members of the body, in their motions and order, to act without any respect to or awe of the will of God.

46 ¶ ᵈAnd why call ye me, Lord, Lord, and do not the things which I say?

47 ᵉWhosoever cometh to me, and heareth my sayings, and doeth them, I will shew you to whom he is like:

marginal: d Mal. 1. 6. Mat. 7. 21. & 25. 11. ch. 13. 25. ; e Mat. 7. 24.

48 He is like a man which built an house, and digged deep, and laid the foundation on a rock: and when the flood arose, the stream beat vehemently upon that house, and could not shake it: for it was founded upon a rock.

49 But he that heareth, and doeth not, is like a man that without a foundation built an house upon the earth; against which the stream did beat vehemently, and immediately it fell; and the ruin of that house was great.

See the notes on Matt. vii. 24—27, where we before met with the same thing. The sum is, men's hopes of salvation built upon any other but Christ alone, or built upon Christ without a sincere study and endeavour to keep the commandments of Christ, are vain hopes; and though, till a storm of affliction or temptation comes, they may please themselves a little with them, yet when they come to die, or when any notable temptation assaults them, or any great affliction cometh upon them, then they will fail them, and they will see the folly and vanity of them. *What is the hope of the hypocrite, when God taketh away his soul?* Job xxvii. 8.

CHAP. VII

Christ admireth the centurion's singular faith, and healeth his absent servant, 1—10. He raiseth to life the widow's son at Nain, 11—17; and sendeth back the messengers of John with an account of the miracles they had seen wrought by him, 18—23. His testimony of John, 24—30. He reproveth the perverseness of the people, who were not to be won either by the manners of John' or himself, 31—35. He suffereth his feet to be washed and anointed by a woman who had been a sinner; and in a parable showeth that even the worst of sinners may be forgiven upon the terms of a hearty and sincere repentance, 36—50.

NOW when he had ended all his sayings in the audience of the people, ᵃhe entered into Capernaum.

2 And a certain centurion's servant, who was dear unto him, was sick, and ready to die.

3 And when he heard of Jesus, he sent unto him the elders of the Jews, beseeching him that he would come and heal his servant.

4 And when they came to Jesus, they besought him instantly, saying, That he was worthy for whom he should do this:

5 For he loveth our nation, and he hath built us a synagogue.

6 Then Jesus went with them. And when he was now not far from the house, the centurion sent friends to him, saying unto him, Lord, trouble not thyself: for I am not worthy that thou shouldest enter under my roof:

7 Wherefore neither thought I myself worthy to come unto thee: but say in a word, and my servant shall be healed.

8 For I also am a man set under authority, having under me soldiers, and I say unto †one, Go, and he goeth; and to another, Come, and he cometh; and to my servant, Do this, and he doeth *it*.

9 When Jesus heard these things, he marvelled at him, and turned him about, and said unto the people that followed him, I say unto you, I have not found so great faith, no, not in Israel.

10 And they that were sent, returning to the house, found the servant whole that had been sick.

marginal: a Matt. 8. 5. ; † Gr. this man.

See the notes on Matt. viii. 5—13, where we have considered all the differences betwixt Matthew's and Luke's relation of this miracle. We have in it remarkable, 1. The humanity of the centurion to his servant, to teach us Christians to do the like. 2. The profitableness of good works: the centurion's love to the Jews in building them a synagogue gaineth their applications to Christ for him. 3. The humility of the centurion: he did not think himself worthy to appear in Christ's presence, nor to receive Christ into his house. 4. His faith in Christ's Divine power and goodness. It doth not appear that he believed that Christ was the eternal Son of God, but he did at least believe that he was clothed with a Divine power, or had a Divine power communicated to him from God, by which he was able, at a distance, and by no more than a word, without application of human rational means, to command off the distemper of his servant. 5. The power of faith in God, and its acceptableness to him. Christ doth not only effect the cure, but predicate his faith to be greater than he had found amongst the generality of the Jewish nation, who went for the only people of God at that day, and had much more light, and means to discern that Christ was sent of God for the good of men, than this Roman captain had.

11 ¶ And it came to pass the day after, that he went into a city called Nain; and many of his disciples went with him, and much people.

S. LUKE VII

12 Now when he came nigh to the gate of the city, behold, there was a dead man carried out, the only son of his mother, and she was a widow: and much people of the city was with her.

13 And when the Lord saw her, he had compassion on her, and said unto her, Weep not.

14 And he came and touched the ∥ bier: and they that bare *him* stood still. And he said, Young man, I say unto thee, ᵇ Arise.

∥ Or, *coffin.*

ᵇ ch. 8. 54. John 11. 43. Acts 9. 40. Rom. 4. 17.

15 And he that was dead sat up, and began to speak. And he delivered him to his mother.

Luke alone gives us an account of this miracle of our Saviour's. Matthew mentioneth only the raising from the dead of Jairus's daughter. Luke adds this. John adds that of Lazarus, John xi., by which our Lord did mightily show his Divine power, and gave us some firstfruits of the more general resurrection, as well as declared himself to be, as he elsewhere saith, the resurrection and the life. The place where this miracle was done was called *Nain.* H. Stephen, Heb., Chald., Gr. et Lat. *nomina,* &c., tells us, it was a city or town about two miles from Mount Tabor, at the foot of the lesser Mount Hermon, near to Hendor. It was the custom of the Jews to bury their dead without their cities. Christ met this dead body carrying out. He was it seems her only child, and she was a widow, so under a great affliction, God by this providence having quenched the only coal she had left in Israel. *And when the Lord saw her,* (the text saith,) *he had compassion on her, and said unto her, Weep not.* None moved him on the behalf of the widow, neither do we read that she herself spake to him; only our Saviour's bowels were moved at the sight of her sorrow, and consideration of her loss. It is observable that our Saviour wrought his healing miracles, 1. Sometimes at the motion and desire of the parties to be healed; 2. Sometimes at the desires of others on their behalf; 3. Sometimes of his own free motion, neither themselves nor others soliciting him for any such act of mercy toward them; and that in the three first miracles, (of which Matthew and Luke give us an account here and Matt. viii.,) which he wrought after his famous sermon on the mount, he gave us an instance of all these, in his healing of the leper personally beseeching him, of the centurion's servant at the entreaty of the elders of the Jews, and of the widow's son here, upon his sight of the woman's affliction, none soliciting him. Thereby showing us that we ought not to stay our hand from doing good when we have proper objects and opportunities before us, until we be importuned and solicited thereunto. Christ saying to her, *Weep not,* forbade not the natural expression of her passion, but signified a sudden and not expected resurrection, so as she should not weep without hope. This said, he cometh and toucheth the bier, or the coffin, and saith not, Young man, in the name of God, I say unto thee, Arise; but, *Young man, I say unto thee, Arise;* thereby declaring to them (would they have understood it) that he was the Son of God, and while he was on earth had a power in and from himself by the word of his mouth to command the dead to arise. His word was effective, and to evidence it, it is said, that *he that was dead sat up,* so as all might take notice of the miracle, *and began to speak. And he delivered him to his mother;* to let him know his duty to be subject to her, and the jurisdiction she had over him.

ᶜ ch. 1. 65.
ᵈ ch. 24. 19. John 4. 19. & 6. 14. & 9. 17.
ᵉ ch. 1. 68.

16 ᶜAnd there came a fear on all: and they glorified God, saying, ᵈThat a great prophet is risen up among us; and, ᵉThat God hath visited his people.

17 And this rumour of him went forth throughout all Judæa, and throughout all the region round about.

The people here saw the Divine power manifestly exerted; for the keys of the clouds, the womb, and the grave, are three keys, which their teachers had taught them were kept in God's hand alone. All sense of the Divine presence naturally fills us with fear. Some, even the worst of men, are filled with a stupid fear of astonishment and amazement. Pious persons, or those that are inclined to piety, are filled with a fear of reverence; such a fear we read of, chap. i. 65. Such was this; for it issued in a predication of the name of God, and a giving to him praise and glory; for that a great Prophet was risen amongst them. Thus far God blessed this miracle, to make them look upon Christ as a Prophet, a great Prophet; and to look upon God's act in his sending him as an act of great kindness to the Jews, for that is here plainly understood by them, saying, *God hath visited his people,* as before, Luke i. 68; and this rumour was spread abroad throughout all that country.

18 ᶠAnd the disciples of John shewed him of all these things.

ᶠ Mat. 11. 2.

19 ¶ And John calling *unto him* two of his disciples sent *them* to Jesus, saying, Art thou he that should come? or look we for another?

20 When the men were come unto him, they said, John Baptist hath sent us unto thee, saying, Art thou he that should come? or look we for another?

21 And in the same hour he cured many of *their* infirmities and plagues, and of evil spirits; and unto many *that were* blind he gave sight.

22 ᵍThen Jesus answering said unto them, Go your way, and tell John what things ye have seen and heard; ʰhow that the blind see, the lame walk, the lepers are cleansed, the deaf hear, the dead are raised, ⁱto the poor the Gospel is preached.

ᵍ Mat. 11. 5.
ʰ Is. 35. 5.
ⁱ ch. 4. 18

23 And blessed is *he,* whosoever shall not be offended in me.

See the notes on Matt. xi. 2—6.

24 ¶ ᵏAnd when the messengers of John were departed, he began to speak unto the people concerning John, What went ye out into the wilderness for to see? A reed shaken with the wind?

ᵏ Mat. 11. 7.

25 But what went ye out for to see? A man clothed in soft raiment? Behold, they which are gorgeously apparelled, and live delicately, are in kings' courts.

26 But what went ye out for to see? A prophet? Yea, I say unto you, and much more than a prophet.

27 This is *he,* of whom it is written, ˡBehold, I send my messenger before thy face, which shall prepare thy way before thee.

ˡ Mal. 3. 1.

28 For I say unto you, Among those that are born of women there is not a greater prophet than John the Baptist: but he that is least in the kingdom of God is greater than he.

See the notes on Matt. xi. 7—15, where we met with this testimony concerning John, given by our Saviour, with some considerable enlargements.

29 And all the people that heard *him,* and the Publicans, justified God, ᵐbeing baptized with the baptism of John.

ᵐ Mat. 3. 5. ch. 3. 12.

30 But the Pharisees and Lawyers ∥ rejected ⁿthe counsel of God ∥ against themselves, being not baptized of him.

∥ Or, *frustrated.*
ⁿ Acts 20 27.
∥ Or, *within themselves.*

Matthew hath not this addition to our Saviour's commendation of John, but it is of great use to introduce our Saviour's following discourse. The evangelist here divideth the hearers into two sorts. The first were the common people and the publicans; the former were despised by the Jewish doctors and rabbis, as a rude, illiterate sort of people; the latter, as a notoriously wicked sort. The second sort were the Pharisees and the lawyers; of the former, he saith, that they, *being baptized with the baptism of John, justified God*, that is, they owned, and publicly declared, and predicated the goodness and justice of God; they approved of what God had done, and blessed his name for sending amongst them such a prophet as John was, they owned and received him, and were baptized by him. Whoso believeth the message which God sendeth, and obeyeth it, he justifieth God; he that doth not, accuseth and condemneth God: see John iii. 33; 1 John v. 10. *But the Pharisees and lawyers*, that is, the scribes; not the scribes of the people, (they were but actuaries, or public notaries,) but the scribes of the law, whose office it was to interpret and give the sense of the law. These *rejected;*—the word sometimes signifies to despise, chap. x. 16; 1 Thess. iv. 8; Heb. x. 28; sometimes to disannul, as Gal. iii. 15; sometimes to reject, as Mark vi. 26; vii. 9. It is here interpreted by those words, *being not baptized of him*. We must understand the sense of ἠθετησαν by considering what is here meant by βουλὴν τοῦ Θεοῦ, *the counsel of God*, which some will understand concerning the purpose of God within himself as revealed to us. The matter seemeth to me but a strife about a word, which is sometimes taken in one sense, sometimes in another. The will of God is but one, only as every one of us keep some part of our mind to ourselves, and reveal other parts of it to our servants and children; so God, who hath determined and willed all events, concealeth some part of it from his creatures, and revealeth another part of it to them. It is the will of God that this, and that, and the other person should believe and be saved. He revealeth as to this thus much of his will, that whoso believeth shall be saved; but for that other part of his will, that this, and that, or the other man shall believe, this he concealeth, till he gives them a power to believe, and to receive the gospel, and then his will in this particular is revealed. Supposing then we here understand by βουλὴν τοῦ Θεοῦ, God's secret purpose to be understood, how is it proved that it must be understood of his secret purpose for their salvation? why should it not be understood of the secret purpose and counsel of God to give them the means of life and salvation? God from all eternity purposed to give the Jews the ministry of John the Baptist and Christ, as means for their salvation, not which should be certainly effective of it, but that should have such a tendency towards it, as without their own refusing, and opposing them, it should have been effective, and was in their own nature a proper means in order to it: they reject and refuse it; by this they rejected the counsel of God, the effect of his counsel, and so judged themselves unworthy of eternal life, by neglecting, despising, and rejecting the use of that means, which was the product of an eternal purpose to send them such means. This counsel of God is said to be *rejected* towards or *against themselves:* take it as God's act, it was towards themselves, that is, for their good; if we refer it to their act of rejection, or refusal, it was against themselves, a judging of themselves unworthy of eternal life. We cannot in this place translate it disannul, or frustrate, as Gal. iii. 15, understanding it as to the Divine act; for who can frustrate or disannul the will or purpose of man, as to an act of his own, within his power to purpose? though indeed as to the event it may be disannulled, as to any good effect as to another, if it be made to depend upon the action of another. Besides, what need any further explication of this phrase, of rejecting the counsel of God against themselves, than what followeth, *being not baptized of him*, that is, not receiving John's doctrine of repentance for the remission of sins, and bringing forth fruits worthy of amendment of life, nor submitting to baptism as a testimony of such repentance; for the baptism of John in Scripture signifieth his whole administration, the doctrine he preached, as well as the ordinance of baptism by him administered; and so must be interpreted where our Saviour asked the Pharisees whether John's baptism was from earth or from heaven, and they durst not say from heaven, lest Christ should have asked them, why then they believed him not? They were not baptized of him, is the same thing with, They would be none of his disciples.

o Mat. 11. 16. 31 ¶ And the Lord said, °Whereunto then shall I liken the men of this generation? and to what are they like?

32 They are like unto children sitting in the marketplace, and calling one to another, and saying, We have piped unto you, and ye have not danced; we have mourned to you, and ye have not wept.

33 For ᵖJohn the Baptist came neither eating bread nor drinking wine; and ye say, He hath a devil. p Matt. 3. 4. Mark 1. 6. ch. 1. 15.

34 The Son of man is come eating and drinking; and ye say, Behold a gluttonous man, and a winebibber, a friend of Publicans and sinners!

35 ᵠBut wisdom is justified of all her children. q Mat. 11.19.

See the notes on Matt. xi. 16—19, where we have this smart reflection upon the scribes and Pharisees, and the generality of the Jews. They were neither pleased full nor fasting, but censorious of the different manner of living of John and Christ. John showed a more austere and severe humour, and lived like a recluse: you had nothing else to say; you said he had a devil. I have chosen not a less innocent, but a more free converse with men of all sorts, and eat and drink as other men; of me you say that I am a wine-bibber, a glutton, a friend of publicans and sinners. Such was their perverseness, that proceeded from their enmity to the doctrine of John and Christ.

36 ¶ ʳAnd one of the Pharisees desired him that he would eat with him. And he went into the Pharisee's house, and sat down to meat. r Matt. 26. 6. Mark 14. 3. John 11. 2.

This was no small civility from a Pharisee, for the Pharisees were of all others, in the generality of them, the most desperate and implacable enemies of our Saviour. But God hath his number amongst all nations, and all sorts and orders of men. Our Saviour, as was said before, was of a free and open converse, and never refused any opportunity offered him to do good. We may soberly eat and drink with sinners pursuing such designs.

37 And, behold, a woman in the city, which was a sinner, when she knew that *Jesus* sat at meat in the Pharisee's house, brought an alabaster box of ointment,

38 And stood at his feet behind *him* weeping, and began to wash his feet with tears, and did wipe *them* with the hairs of her head, and kissed his feet, and anointed *them* with the ointment.

What hath made any interpreters imagine this was the same story which is mentioned Matt. xxvi., Mark xiv., and John xii., I cannot tell. The histories agree scarcely in any thing, unless in the bringing the alabaster box of ointment, and the anointing our Saviour's feet, whereas there was nothing in those countries more ordinary. That anointing was done in Bethany, within two miles of Jerusalem, this in Galilee. That in the house of one Simon the leper, this in the house of one Simon a Pharisee. That a little, this a great while, before our Saviour's passion. At that Judas was offended, at this Simon the Pharisee was offended. There Christ vindicates the woman from one head of argument, here from another. Questionless this is another quite different piece of history. *And, behold, a woman in the city, which was a sinner;* that is, a remarkable sinner; it is a word generally so used, and, applied to women, signifies a prostitute, or at least one of an ill report as to chastity. *Was*, referreth here to the time past, though lately past; she had lately been infamous and notorious, but it appeareth by what followeth that she was not so now, otherwise than in the opinion and vogue of the people; according to whose opinion, though uncharitable enough, *Quæ semel fuit mala, semper præsumitur esse mala in eodem genere mali*, A person who hath once been bad is always presumed so to be, through their ignorance of the power of Divine grace in changing the heart, or their malice against and envy towards those whose hearts they see so changed. But whatever this woman had been, it seems God had affected her heart with the word which Christ had preached, and filled it with the pure love of God and Christ, instead of its former fulness of impure love, and made her sins as bitter as they had been formerly pleasant to her. She hearing Christ was eating meat at the house of Simon the Pharisee, makes no noise, but cometh *behind him*, bringing *an alabaster box of ointment, and stood at his feet behind him weeping, and began to wash his feet with her tears, and did wipe them with the hairs of her head, and kissed his feet, and anointed them with the ointment.* Weeping in the sense of her sins, and so plentifully as she washed the feet of Christ with her tears, spoke a broken and a contrite heart. Wiping them with her hair; her hair, with which she had offended through wantonness, plaiting it, and adorning herself by the dress of it to allure her lovers, she now useth to testify her abhorrence of her former courses. *And kissed his feet, and anointed them with the ointment.* The kiss is a symbol of love, and not of love only, but of subjection and worship; by this she both showed her love to Christ, and also her subjection to him, she kissed Christ in the psalmist's sense, Psal. ii. 12. It was not a kiss of love only, but of reverence and subjection, like Joseph's kiss to Jacob, Gen. l. 1, Moses's kiss to Jethro, Exod. xviii. 7; nay, of the highest reverence, for such was the kiss of the Father. And to testify her adoration of him: thus the idolaters kissed the calves, Hos. xiii. 2, and Baal, 1 Kings xix. 18. Washing and anointing with oil, was a common compliment they used in those countries for cleansing and cooling the feet. She had been a great sinner, she now shows the profoundest sorrow, greatest love, humility, subjection, &c. But some may say, How could she come behind him, sitting at meat, and do this? while we sit at meat our feet are before us. This confirmeth the notion I mentioned before, in my notes on Matt. xxvi. 20, concerning the Jewish manner of sitting at meat, which was kneeling and resting their bodies upon their legs leaning backwards: admitting that, all that we here read of this woman was very easy; for his legs being thrust out backward, the soles of his feet were turned up, and she might with convenience enough come at them behind him to wash, and to wipe, and to anoint them, which it is hard to conceive how she could do, admitting him to have sat as we do, putting our feet forward under the table.

39 Now when the Pharisee which had bidden him saw *it*, he spake within himself, saying, [s] 'This man, if he were a prophet, would have known who and what manner of woman *this is* that toucheth him: for she is a sinner.

[s ch. 15. 2.]

How easily are persons (though seemingly well inclined and fair) offended, who have not the love of God rooted and grounded in their hearts! Did then all men who were prophets know persons at first sight? 1. It is certain they knew no more of people's hearts and lives than God was pleased to reveal to them, or they knew by converse with them, and observation of them. 2. Suppose she had been a sinner, might she not be a convert now? and did not her behaviour toward Christ (before mentioned) witness a change in her? 3. Admit she had been yet such a sinner, yet might not she touch Christ? This was indeed a Pharisaical error, that all not of their own religion, and all persons notorious for some sins, were in the same order as lepers, and other persons that were Levitically or legally unclean, so as none might touch them, but that contact made them also unclean. It is said also of the Samaritans, that when they met a Jew, or a Christian, they would first call out to him, Do not touch me. That there was of old such a party amongst the Jews that cried, *Stand by thyself, come not near to me, for I am holier than thou*, is plain from Isa. lxv. 5.

40 And Jesus answering said unto him, Simon, I have somewhat to say unto thee. And he saith, Master, say on.

41 There was a certain creditor which had two debtors: the one owed five hundred ‖ pence, and the other fifty.

[t See Matt. 18. 28.]

42 And when they had nothing to pay, he frankly forgave them both. Tell me therefore, which of them will love him most?

43 Simon answered and said, I suppose that *he* to whom he forgave most. And he said unto him, Thou hast rightly judged.

44 And he turned to the woman, and said unto Simon, Seest thou this woman? I entered into thine house, thou gavest me no water for my feet: but she hath washed my feet with tears, and wiped *them* with the hairs of her head.

45 Thou gavest me no kiss: but this woman since the time I came in hath not ceased to kiss my feet.

46 [t] 'My head with oil thou didst not anoint: but this woman hath anointed my feet with ointment.

[t Ps. 23. 5.]

47 [u] Wherefore I say unto thee, Her sins, which are many, are forgiven; for she loved much: but to whom little is forgiven, *the same* loveth little.

[u 1 Tim. 1. 14.]

48 And he said unto her, [x] Thy sins are forgiven.

[x Matt. 9. 2. Mark 2. 5.]

Our Saviour treateth his host civilly, but yet letteth him know, that he both knew his heart, and the heart of this poor woman, whom he had so uncharitably reflected upon. *Simon spake within himself*, ver. 39. Christ lets him know that he knew the thoughts of his heart. *I have* (saith he) *somewhat to say unto thee*. So he civilly obtaineth leave of him to speak. *Simon saith, Master, say on.* Our Saviour tells him, *There was a certain creditor*, &c. It is obvious by our Saviour's application of this parable, ver. 44—47, that he whom Christ here intendeth under the notion of a creditor is God; that one of the debtors that did owe five hundred pence (that is, a great sum) was this woman: whether Simon were intended by the other, or no, is not easily determined; but admit the other was ὁ δεῖνα, any one that was a sinner, but not so notorious a sinner, God forgives freely both the one and the other. Christ asks which would love most. Simon tells him, that debtor to whom most was forgiven. Christ tells him that he had judged rightly. Whence observe, 1. That as all sins, so all sinners, are not equal in the sight of God; all are guilty, but there are degrees in guilt. 2. That be men's sins less or greater, fewer or more, those who have least will stand in need of pardoning mercy and forgiveness. 3. That God is free in the forgiveness of all sins, be they few or more; *he frankly forgave them both*. 4. That Christ first speaketh of these two debtors as being forgiven, then of their loving much, and of their being forgiven as the cause of their loving much. 5. That much love will follow a great forgiveness; a great sinner (one, I mean, who hath been so) will hardly ever be able to satisfy himself that his much is forgiven, if he doth not find his heart very warm with love to God. 6. A true love to God and Christ will be seen in all acts, which may be demonstrative or declarative of it. Christ turns to the woman, and saith to Simon, &c. Kissing, washing of feet, anointing with oil, were usual compliments of those countries, by which men showed their respects and kindness to strangers and friends. For washing of feet, see Gen. xviii. 4; xix. 2; Judg. xix. 21; 1 Sam. xxv. 41; 1 Tim. v. 10. For anointing with oil, see Psal. xxiii. 5; xlv. 7. This woman had exceeded the usual kindness and civility of the country toward Christ: they were wont to bring their friends water to wash their feet, and possibly a piece of linen to wipe them; she washeth his feet with her tears, and drieth them with her hair. They used to anoint the head of their friends with oil, she anoints his feet. They used to kiss one another's cheeks or lips, she kisseth his feet. They kissed their friends once, she ceased not to kiss his feet. Upon this Christ, who before had forgiven her, declareth her to be forgiven, first in the hearing of Simon, then he doubleth his words unto her. He had told Simon before that the creditor had frankly forgiven them both; his adding here, *Her sins, which are many*, sufficiently evidenceth that it was she whom he intended by the debtor who owed much. Hence we may judge how little ground the papists have to urge this place to prove, that remission of sins is procured by our own merits and satisfactions. Love here is not mentioned as the cause, but as the effect of the remission of sins; and that which our Saviour here designed to instruct Simon in, was, 1. That whatsoever this woman had been, she was not now such a notorious sinner as he fancied; her sins were forgiven. 2. That God having thus favoured her with the grace of remission, had also kindled in her heart a love towards him. 3. That this love wrought in her heart in some proportion to that love which God had magnified upon her, therefore she loved much. 4. That men and women's love to God and Christ, will and ought to be according to that love which they have received from Christ. 5. That much love to God will bring a great sense of God's love to the soul, John xiv. 21. The particle ὅτι, which we translate *because*, doth not always in Scripture signify the cause, but may be translated *therefore*, or, *for what cause*: see John xiv. 17, *Ye know him; for he dwelleth in you*: the Spirit's abiding in believers is not the cause of their knowing of him, but the effect of it, so that *for*, in that place, is as much as *therefore*. So in Mark ix. 28, ὅτι is as much as *for what cause*, or, *for what reason?* We translate it, *Why could not we cast him out?* So here, *Her sins, which are many, are forgiven, for which cause*, or reason, *she loveth much*.

49 And they that sat at meat with him began to say within themselves, ʸ Who is this that forgiveth sins also?

ʸ Matt. 9. 3.
Mark 2. 7.

These were either the Pharisees, who thought that Christ blasphemed in arrogating to himself such a power as belonged to God alone; or the others, who speak this rather in admiration; but it is probable the former are here meant.

50 And he said to the woman, ᶻ Thy faith hath saved thee; go in peace.

ᶻ Mat. 9. 22.
Mark 5. 04.
& 10. 52. ch.
8. 48. &18.42.

Thy believing in me as he who have power on earth to forgive sins, and accordingly making application to me, and this thy faith working by love, Gal. v. 6, producing in thee this hearty sorrow for thy sins, a subjection unto me, and such testifications of thy love as thou art able to make, hath been an instrumental cause of that salvation, which floweth from me as the principal cause, Rom. vi. 23. We have such another expression in Matt. ix. 22; Mark v. 34; though the saving here mentioned be much more excellent than that there spoken of. Faith is profitable both for the good things of this life, and those of the life which is to come; and with reference to both, salvation is ascribed to faith, as the instrumental cause, not to obedience and love, though the faith that doth us good must work by love, and be evidenced by a holy conversation. *Go in peace*, is a phrase which was the usual valediction among the Jews, as much as our Farewell, or God be with you, they under the term of *peace* comprehending all good; but when we consider who it is that speaketh, and what immediately preceded, we have reason to think this was a more than ordinary compliment or farewell, even as much as is comprehended under the term *peace*, which, as I before said, is all good, but more especially that peace mentioned by the apostle, Rom. v. 1, as an effect of faith. Go thy way a blessed and happy woman, and in the view and sense of thy own blessedness, and be not troubled at the censures and reflections of supercilious persons, who may despise or overlook thee because thou hast been a great sinner. God hath pardoned thy sins, and this I assure thee of; only take heed to keep and maintain that peace.

CHAP. VIII

Christ preacheth through the cities, attended by his disciples, and ministered unto by devout women of their substance, 1—3. *The parable of the sower,* 4—8. *Why Christ taught in parables,* 9, 10. *The parable expounded,* 11—15. *Light is given to be improved and communicated,* 16—18. *Christ showeth whom he regardeth as his nearest relations,* 19—21; *stilleth a tempest on the sea with his word,* 22—25; *casteth out the legion of devils, and suffereth them to enter into the herd of swine; is entreated by the Gadarenes to depart, and refuseth the attendance of him whom he had healed,* 25—40; *is besought by Jairus to go and heal his daughter,* 41, 42. *By the way he healeth a woman of an inveterate issue of blood,* 43—48. *He raiseth Jairus's daughter to life,* 49—56.

AND it came to pass afterward, that he went throughout every city and village, preaching and shewing the glad tidings of the kingdom of God: and the twelve *were* with him,

2 And ᵃ certain women, which had been healed of evil spirits and infirmities, Mary called Magdalene, ᵇ out of whom went seven devils,

ᵃ Matt. 27. 55, 56.
ᵇ Mark 16. 9

3 And Joanna the wife of Chuza Herod's steward, and Susanna, and many others, which ministered unto him of their substance.

Still I cannot but observe, that preaching the gospel, and thereby showing the glad tidings of salvation, (the principal means to bring men to the kingdom of God, whether that in this life, or the kingdom of glory in the life which is to come,) was Christ's great work. His working miracles was but subservient to this, and for the confirmation of the doctrine which he preached; hence, when a people showed a contempt of his word, he refused to work any miracles before them. How any one can dream, that either praying, or government, or administering sacraments, or any thing else, should be more the work of a minister of Christ than preaching, may justly amaze any thinking soul that ever read the gospel. Christ went every where about *preaching, and the twelve were with him*, sometimes hearing, (as his disciples,) sometimes preaching; some *women* also were with him, such as *had been healed of evil spirits* and other diseases. Mary Magdalene was one, out of whom he *had cast seven devils*, that is, many devils. Most think she had her name from Magdala, a city in Galilee, where she was bred, or dwelt. It is a great error to think she was the Mary mentioned John xi., the sister of Lazarus; she lived in Bethany, near to Jerusalem. Yet it is plain from Mark xvi. that she was at Jerusalem at the time of Christ's death and resurrection; but so were many that followed him from Galilee, Mark xv. 41; Luke xxiii. 49. *And Joanna the wife of Chuza, Herod's steward*. Christ hath his elect in all places, his Joseph in Pharaoh's court, his Daniel and three children in Nebuchadnezzar's court, his saints in Nero's household, Phil. iv. 22, his Joanna in Herod's family. This was that Herod Antipas, tetrarch of Galilee, he who put John the Baptist to death, and himself with his soldiers mocked Christ; possibly his steward was as bad, but his wife was one that followed Christ, knowing that though her husband had power over her body, he had none over her soul. And they *ministered to him of their substance*. They were not ashamed to be seen following of Christ, though doubtless they met with scoffs enough. Nor were they ashamed to be reproached for their former failing; nor was Christ, because of their former lives, or the life of some of them, to have them following him. It is a glory to Christ, and to the church of Christ, to have great sinners brought to him, and brought into it; the only shame is to such as, being in the church, or pretending at least to be Christians, are debauchees still. Christ did not give himself for a people that were pure and holy, without spot or wrinkle, but *that he might sanctify* them *and cleanse* them, *with the washing of water by the word*, Eph. v. 25—27. Following Christ *they ministered to him*. This was according to Christ's doctrine, Matt. x. 10, and his apostles' after him, 1 Cor. ix. 11; 2 Cor. viii. 9; Gal. vi. 6. Some of them might be virgins, some widows, some wives, who had an allowance for themselves from their husbands; however, it could be no robbery to give of what was their husbands' to him who was the Lord of all, which either their husbands or they possessed. Nor was Christ ashamed to live upon the baskets of others, while he was providing spiritual food for the souls of all, 2 Cor. viii. 9.

4 ¶ ᶜAnd when much people were gathered together, and were come to him out of every city, he spake by a parable:

ᶜ Matt. 13. 2.
Mark 4. 1.

5 A sower went out to sow his seed: and as he sowed, some fell by the way side; and it was

trodden down, and the fowls of the air devoured it.

6 And some fell upon a rock; and as soon as it was sprung up, it withered away, because it lacked moisture.

7 And some fell among thorns; and the thorns sprang up with it, and choked it.

8 And other fell on good ground, and sprang up, and bare fruit an hundredfold. And when he had said these things, he cried, He that hath ears to hear, let him hear.

9 ᵈAnd his disciples asked him, saying, What might this parable be?   *d Mat. 13. 10. Mark 4. 10.*

10 And he said, Unto you it is given to know the mysteries of the kingdom of God: but to others in parables; ᵉthat seeing they might not see, and hearing they might not understand.   *e Is. 6. 9. Mark 4. 12.*

11 ᶠNow the parable is this: The seed is the word of God.   *f Mat. 13. 18. Mark 4. 14.*

12 Those by the way side are they that hear; then cometh the devil, and taketh away the word out of their hearts, lest they should believe and be saved.

13 They on the rock *are they*, which, when they hear, receive the word with joy; and these have no root, which for a while believe, and in time of temptation fall away.

14 And that which fell among thorns are they, which, when they have heard, go forth, and are choked with cares and riches and pleasures of *this* life, and bring no fruit to perfection.

15 But that on the good ground are they, which in an honest and good heart, having heard the word, keep *it*, and bring forth fruit with patience.

We have had this parable, Matt. xiii. and Mark iv. See the notes on both these chapters.

16 ¶ ᵍNo man, when he hath lighted a candle, covereth it with a vessel, or putteth *it* under a bed; but setteth *it* on a candlestick, that they which enter in may see the light.   *g Matt. 5.15. Mark 4. 21. ch. 11. 33.*

See the notes on Matt. v. 15, and on Mark iv. 21.

17 ʰFor nothing is secret, that shall not be made manifest; neither *any thing* hid, that shall not be known and come abroad.   *h Mat. 10.26. ch. 12. 2.*

This we have also met with twice before. See the notes on Matt. v. 15; Mark iv. 22.

18 Take heed therefore how ye hear: ⁱfor whosoever hath, to him shall be given; and whosoever hath not, from him shall be taken even that which he ‖seemeth to have.   *i Mat. 13. 12. & 25. 29. ch. 19. 26.*   *‖ Or, thinketh that he hath.*

See the notes on Mark iv. 24, and on Matt. xiii. 12; xxv. 29.

19 ¶ ᵏThen came to him *his* mother and his brethren, and could not come at him for the press.   *k Mat. 12.46. Mark 3. 31.*

20 And it was told him *by certain* which said, Thy mother and thy brethren stand without, desiring to see thee.

21 And he answered and said unto them, My mother and my brethren are these which hear the word of God, and do it.

See the notes on Matt. xii. 46—50; Mark iii. 31—35.

22 ¶ ˡNow it came to pass on a certain day, that he went into a ship with his disciples: and he said unto them, Let us go over unto the other side of the lake. And they launched forth.   *l Matt. 8. 23. Mark 4. 35.*

23 But as they sailed he fell asleep: and there came down a storm of wind on the lake; and they were filled *with water*, and were in jeopardy.

24 And they came to him, and awoke him, saying, Master, master, we perish. Then he arose, and rebuked the wind and the raging of the water: and they ceased, and there was a calm.

25 And he said unto them, Where is your faith? And they being afraid wondered, saying one to another, What manner of man is this! for he commandeth even the winds and water, and they obey him.

This whole history we have also before met with, both in Matt. viii. 23—27, and Mark iv. 35—41. See the notes upon both those chapters.

26 ¶ ᵐAnd they arrived at the country of the Gadarenes, which is over against Galilee.   *m Mat. 8. 28. Mark 5. 1.*

27 And when he went forth to land, there met him out of the city a certain man, which had devils long time, and ware no clothes, neither abode in *any* house, but in the tombs.

28 When he saw Jesus, he cried out, and fell down before him, and with a loud voice said, What have I to do with thee, Jesus, *thou* Son of God most high? I beseech thee, torment me not.

29 (For he had commanded the unclean spirit to come out of the man. For oftentimes it had caught him: and he was kept bound with chains and in fetters; and he brake the bands, and was driven of the devil into the wilderness.)

30 And Jesus asked him, saying, What is thy name? And he said, Legion: because many devils were entered into him.

31 And they besought him that he would not command them to go out ⁿinto the deep.   *n Rev. 20. 3.*

32 And there was there an herd of many swine feeding on the mountain: and they besought him that he would suffer them to enter into them. And he suffered them.

33 Then went the devils out of the man, and entered into the swine: and the herd ran violently down a steep place into the lake, and were choked.

34 When they that fed *them* saw what was done, they fled, and went and told *it* in the city and in the country.

35 Then they went out to see what was done; and came to Jesus, and found the man, out of whom the devils were departed, sitting at the feet of Jesus, clothed, and in his right mind: and they were afraid.

36 They also which saw *it* told them by what means he that was possessed of the devils was healed.

37 ¶ ᵒThen the whole multitude of the country of the Gadarenes round about ᵖbesought him to depart from them; for they were taken with great fear: and he went up into the ship, and returned back again.   *o Mat. 8. 34.*   *p Acts 16.39.*

38 Now ᑫthe man out of whom the   *q Mark 5.18.*

devils were departed besought him that he might be with him: but Jesus sent him away, saying,

39 Return to thine own house, and shew how great things God hath done unto thee. And he went his way, and published throughout the whole city how great things Jesus had done unto him.

40 And it came to pass, that, when Jesus was returned, the people *gladly* received him: for they were all waiting for him.

We have had this whole story Matt. viii. 28—34, and Mark v. 1—21. See the notes on both those chapters.

r Mat. 9. 18. Mark 5. 22.
41 ¶ ʳAnd, behold, there came a man named Jairus, and he was a ruler of the synagogue: and he fell down at Jesus' feet, and besought him that he would come into his house:

42 For he had one only daughter, about twelve years of age, and she lay a dying. But as he went the people thronged him.

s Mat. 9. 20.
43 ¶ ˢAnd a woman having an issue of blood twelve years, which had spent all her living upon physicians, neither could be healed of any,

44 Came behind *him*, and touched the border of his garment: and immediately her issue of blood stanched.

45 And Jesus said, Who touched me? When all denied, Peter and they that were with him said, Master, the multitude throng thee and press *thee*, and sayest thou, Who touched me?

46 And Jesus said, Somebody hath touched me: for I perceive that ᵗvirtue is gone out of me.

t Mark 5.30. ch. 6. 19.

47 And when the woman saw that she was not hid, she came trembling, and falling down before him, she declared unto him before all the people for what cause she had touched him, and how she was healed immediately.

48 And he said unto her, Daughter, be of good comfort: thy faith hath made thee whole; go in peace.

u Mark 5.35.
49 ¶ ᵘWhile he yet spake, there cometh one from the ruler of the synagogue's *house*, saying to him, Thy daughter is dead; trouble not the Master.

50 But when Jesus heard *it*, he answered him, saying, Fear not: believe only, and she shall be made whole.

51 And when he came into the house, he suffered no man to go in, save Peter, and James, and John, and the father and the mother of the maiden.

52 And all wept, and bewailed her: but he said, Weep not; she is not dead, ˣbut sleepeth.

x John 11. 11, 13.

53 And they laughed him to scorn, knowing that she was dead.

54 And he put them all out, and took her by the hand, and called, saying, Maid, ʸarise.

y ch. 7. 14. John 11. 43.

55 And her spirit came again, and she arose straightway: and he commanded to give her meat.

56 And her parents were astonished: but ᶻhe charged them that they should tell no man what was done.

z Matt. 8. 4. & 9. 30. Mark 5. 43.

We had both these pieces of history twice before related, by Matthew, chap. ix. 18—26, and by Mark, chap. v. 22—43, with some further circumstances. See the notes on both those chapters. Christ's saying, ver. 45, *Who touched me?* and again, ver. 46, *Somebody hath touched me; for I perceive that virtue is gone out of me;* doth not argue that Christ knew not of the woman's coming and touching him, or did not voluntarily send out that virtue that healed her; far be any such thoughts from any pious, intelligent souls: she was not healed by her touch of the border of his garment, but by his powerful will, commanding such a miraculous effect: he only spake this to bring forth the miracle into light, which was wrought secretly, so as the people took no notice of it. Healing virtue went out of Christ upon an act of his will, not necessarily. From ver. 55 is confuted the atheism of those who would make the soul to be merely the crasis, or some affection of the body; and it is proved to be a being that can subsist of itself, in a state of separation from the body. It is said, *her spirit came again;* not, Christ gave her a new spirit. Christ did not here exert a creating power; only sent forth that power with which he was clothed to raise the dead. For other things observable from this story, see the notes before mentioned upon the parallel texts.

CHAP. IX.

Christ sendeth his apostles to work miracles and preach the gospel, 1—6. *Herod desireth to see him,* 7—9. *The apostles return,* 10, 11. *Christ feedeth five thousand men with five loaves and two fishes,* 12—17. *The different opinions concerning Christ; Peter's confession of him: Christ foretelleth his own death and resurrection,* 18—22. *He showeth his followers the necessity of self-denial, and that they must not be ashamed of owning his gospel,* 23—27. *He is transfigured,* 28—36; *healeth a demoniac,* 37—42; *again foreshoweth his sufferings,* 43—45; *checketh the ambitious disputes of his disciples,* 46—48; *will not have them forbid any one to work miracles in his name,* 49, 50; *reproveth the fiery zeal of James and John against the Samaritans who would not receive him,* 51—56; *and proposeth terms to three persons who offer to follow him,* 57—62.

THEN ᵃhe called his twelve disciples together, and gave them power and authority over all devils, and to cure diseases.

a Mat. 10. 1. Mark 3. 13. & 6. 7.

2 And ᵇhe sent them to preach the kingdom of God, and to heal the sick.

b Mat.10.7,8. Mark 6. 12. ch. 10. 1, 9.

3 ᶜAnd he said unto them, Take nothing for *your* journey, neither staves, nor scrip, neither bread, neither money; neither have two coats apiece.

c Mat. 10. 9. Mark 6. 8. ch. 10. 4. & 22. 35.

4 ᵈAnd whatsoever house ye enter into, there abide, and thence depart.

d Mat. 10.11. Mark 6. 10.

5 ᵉAnd whosoever will not receive you, when ye go out of that city, ᶠshake off the very dust from your feet for a testimony against them.

e Mat. 10.14.
f Acts 13. 51.

6 ᵍAnd they departed, and went through the towns, preaching the Gospel, and healing every where.

g Mark 6.12.

We have heard of the choosing of these twelve disciples, and their names, chap. vi. 13—16; Mark iii. 14—19. Our Saviour chose them to be with him, to learn of him, and to be instructed by him, and to be witnesses of what he said and did; after some time thus spent, he sends them forth to preach the gospel, and giveth them a power to confirm the doctrine which they preached, by several miraculous operations. Matthew takes no notice of their election, only of their mission. Both Mark and Luke take notice of both. Ver. 3—6 give us an account of the instructions he gave them; we met with them all before, and a more full account of them, Matt. x., and Mark vi. 7—11. See the notes on both those places.

VOL. III—8

7 ¶ ʰNow Herod the tetrarch heard of all that was done by him: and he was perplexed, because that it was said of some, that John was risen from the dead;

8 And of some, that Elias had appeared; and of others, that one of the old prophets was risen again.

9 And Herod said, John have I beheaded: but who is this, of whom I hear such things? ⁱAnd he desired to see him.

A.D. 32.
ʰ Mat. 14.1. Mark 6, 14.

ⁱ ch. 23. 8.

This Herod was Herod Antipas, the tetrarch of Galilee, who had beheaded John the Baptist; he heareth of these great things done by Christ, and διηπόρει, saith the evangelist; it is a word that signifieth a great disturbance, and perplexity of mind, when a man is in doubt and fear, and knoweth not what counsels to take or follow: it is used Luke xxiv. 4; Acts ii. 12; v. 24; x. 17. The other evangelists say Herod himself guessed it was John the Baptist, whom he had beheaded. Oh the power of a guilty conscience! He had murdered John, now he is afraid his ghost haunted him, or that his soul was entered into another body, that it might be revenged on him. Others guessed variously. Herod knoweth not what to think, but desireth to see Christ, possibly that he might make up some judgment about him, possibly out of mere curiosity. But we read not that he did see him until Pilate sent him to him after his examination of him, Luke xxiii. 8.

10 ¶ ᵏAnd the apostles, when they were returned, told him all that they had done. ˡAnd he took them, and went aside privately into a desert place belonging to the city called Bethsaida.

ᵏ Mark 6. 30.

ˡ Mat 14.13.

11 And the people, when they knew *it*, followed him: and he received them, and spake unto them of the kingdom of God, and healed them that had need of healing.

The evangelists give us but a summary account of things. We read of the mission, or sending out, of the apostles, ver. 1. Here we read of their return, and giving their Lord an account of their discharge of the trust he had reposed in them. Being returned, our Saviour goeth with them into a place near Bethsaida, not much inhabited, and therefore called *desert*. He never wanted followers, nor a heart to receive them, and to take all opportunities to do them good. Many followed him; he receiveth them, and preacheth to them for the good of their souls, and healeth those amongst them that were sick, to teach us to join spiritual with bodily, and bodily with spiritual, alms. Spiritual alms, such as instruction, reproof, counsel, are as much better than those that relieve only bodily wants, as the soul is better than the body. Spiritual alms, without bodily relief, from such as are able to give them, are fittest for spiritual persons; carnal, ignorant people, that have no sense of spiritual things, must, like children, be allured into a good opinion of the things and ways of God by some bodily charity, and so taken by guile, and enticed to the knowledge of God.

12 ᵐAnd when the day began to wear away, then came the twelve, and said unto him, Send the multitude away, that they may go into the towns and country round about, and lodge, and get victuals: for we are here in a desert place.

ᵐ Matt. 14. 15. Mark 6. 35. John 6. 1, 5.

13 But he said unto them, Give ye them to eat. And they said, We have no more but five loaves and two fishes; except we should go and buy meat for all this people.

14 For they were about five thousand men. And he said to his disciples, Make them sit down by fifties in a company.

15 And they did so, and made them all sit down.

16 Then he took the five loaves and the two fishes, and looking up to heaven, he blessed them, and brake, and gave to the disciples to set before the multitude.

17 And they did eat, and were all filled: and there was taken up of fragments that remained to them twelve baskets.

The history of this miracle is recorded by all the four evangelists. See the notes on Matt. xiv. 15—22, and on Mark vi. 35—44. We shall again meet with it, John vi. 5—14, with some further circumstances. Luke hath nothing but what we have before met with.

18 ¶ ⁿAnd it came to pass, as he was alone praying, his disciples were with him: and he asked them, saying, Whom say the people that I am?

ⁿ Mat. 16.13. Mark 8. 27.

19 They answering said, ᵒJohn the Baptist; but some *say*, Elias; and others *say*, that one of the old prophets is risen again.

ᵒ Mat. 14. 2. ver. 7, 8.

20 He said unto them, But whom say ye that I am? ᵖPeter answering said, The Christ of God.

ᵖ Mat.16.16. John 6. 69.

21 ᵠAnd he straitly charged them, and commanded *them* to tell no man that thing;

ᵠ Mat. 16.20.

22 Saying, ʳThe Son of man must suffer many things, and be rejected of the elders and Chief Priests and Scribes, and be slain, and be raised the third day.

ʳ Mat. 16. 21. & 17. 22.

Matthew and Mark tell us this discourse passed at Cesarea Philippi (or at least one of the same import). Matthew also gives us an account of it with more circumstances. See the notes on Matt. xvi. 13—23. *As he was alone praying*; that is, free from the multitude, for the next words tell us, the *disciples were with him*. The 22nd verse is not to be found in the other evangelists; and if Luke here reported these words in the right order of time, they afford us a probable reason of what is said ver. 21, why Christ would not yet be published as the Christ, or the Son of God. Because he was to suffer, and it might much have shaken people's faith, as to that point, if they had seen the person whom they believed such suffering, and to be so despitefully used as he was; he therefore desired to be concealed as to that, until he should be declared the Son of God with power, by his resurrection from the dead.

23 ¶ ˢAnd he said to *them* all, If any *man* will come after me, let him deny himself, and take up his cross daily, and follow me.

ˢ Mat. 10.38. & 16. 24. Mark 8. 34. ch. 14. 27.

24 For whosoever will save his life shall lose it: but whosoever will lose his life for my sake, the same shall save it.

We have met with these words before, Matt. xvi. 24, 25; x. 38, 39; Mark viii. 34, 35. See the notes on those places.

25 ᵗFor what is a man advantaged, if he gain the whole world, and lose himself, or be cast away?

ᵗ Mat. 16.26. Mark 8. 36.

See the notes on Matt. xvi. 26; Mark viii. 36.

26 ᵘFor whosoever shall be ashamed of me and of my words, of him shall the Son of man be ashamed, when he shall come in his own glory, and *in his* Father's, and of the holy angels.

ᵘ Mat. 10.33. Mark 8. 38. 2 Tim. 2. 12.

27 ˣBut I tell you of a truth, there be some standing here, which shall not taste of death, till they see the kingdom of God.

ˣ Mat.16.28. Mark 9. 1.

See the notes on Matt. xvi. 28; Mark ix. 1. Luke seems here to have recorded several sayings of our Saviour, spoken not all at the same time.

28 ¶ ʸAnd it came to pass about an eight days after these ∥ sayings, he took Peter and John and James, and went up into a mountain to pray.

29 And as he prayed, the fashion of his countenance was altered, and his raiment *was* white *and* glistering.

30 And, behold, there talked with him two men, which were Moses and Elias:

31 Who appeared in glory, and spake of his decease which he should accomplish at Jerusalem.

32 But Peter and they that were with him ᶻwere heavy with sleep: and when they were awake, they saw his glory, and the two men that stood with him.

33 And it came to pass, as they departed from him, Peter said unto Jesus, Master, it is good for us to be here: and let us make three tabernacles; one for thee, and one for Moses, and one for Elias: not knowing what he said.

34 While he thus spake, there came a cloud, and overshadowed them: and they feared as they entered into the cloud.

35 And there came a voice out of the cloud, saying, ᵃThis is my beloved Son: ᵇhear him.

36 And when the voice was past, Jesus was found alone. ᶜAnd they kept *it* close, and told no man in those days any of those things which they had seen.

See the notes on Matt. xvii. 1—9, and on Mark ix. 2—10.

37 ¶ ᵈAnd it came to pass, that on the next day, when they were come down from the hill, much people met him.

38 And, behold, a man of the company cried out, saying, Master, I beseech thee, look upon my son: for he is mine only child.

39 And, lo, a spirit taketh him, and he suddenly crieth out; and it teareth him that he foameth again, and bruising him hardly departeth from him.

40 And I besought thy disciples to cast him out; and they could not.

41 And Jesus answering said, O faithless and perverse generation, how long shall I be with you, and suffer you? Bring thy son hither.

42 And as he was yet a coming, the devil threw him down, and tare *him*. And Jesus rebuked the unclean spirit, and healed the child, and delivered him again to his father.

See the notes on Matt. xvii. 14—21; Mark ix. 14—29.

43 ¶ And they were all amazed at the mighty power of God. But while they wondered every one at all things which Jesus did, he said unto his disciples,

44 ᵉLet these sayings sink down into your ears: for the Son of man shall be delivered into the hands of men.

45 ᶠBut they understood not this saying, and it was hid from them, that they perceived it not: and they feared to ask him of that saying.

Of the people's astonishment and amazement at the sight of Christ's miracles, we often hear much; of their embracing him as their Saviour, and owning him as the Christ, we read little. Thus far many of them were come, indeed the most, (the Scribes, and Pharisees, and Sadducees only excepted,) that they believed Christ was a great Prophet, a man sent of God; authorized by God to reveal his will, and empowered from God to do many things, which none but God had originally a power to do. Others were gone a step further, viz. to believe not only that he was a Prophet, but that Prophet foretold by Moses, Deut. xviii. 15; John i. 21, 45; the Christ of God, as Peter expressed it, he that should redeem Israel, Luke xxiv. 21. That they had not a true notion of the Messias, either as to his person, that the Divine and human nature were united in his person, or as to his work, that it was not to redeem Israel from their bodily servitude, but from their sins only, will appear to any from the whole history of the gospel. Nor indeed doth our Saviour hasten their faith in this revelation, I mean the perfecting and confirming of it, knowing that it would be a great shaking to their faith in him, in this notion, and indeed as the Messias, to see him so shamefully abused by the vilest abjects of the people, (as he was at his passion,) and then hanging upon the cross, and dying, until they should also see him by his own power risen from the dead, and be confirmed concerning the truth of his resurrection. Where therefore he saw this seed of precious faith springing up, as it did in Peter and divers others, who it is plain apprehended him more than man, as he did not discourage nor blame it, but highly commended it; so neither did he please to strengthen it, so as to put them out of all doubt about it, and often charged them not to publish it abroad, and bends himself to prepare them against this great obstacle, which he saw would be in their way, to wit, his sufferings. This is the second time now that in this chapter we find him inculcating it. And there was need of it, for the evangelist telleth us that *they understood it not, it was hidden from them.* They could easily understand how an ordinary prophet might be delivered into the hands of men, but how the Messias, the Christ, that Prophet, he of whom some of them believed that he was more than a mere man, how he should be thus delivered, thus suffer, they could not understand; and they saw Christ as to this point so reserved and private, and forbidding the publication of it, that they feared to be too particular with him about it.

46 ¶ ᵍThen there arose a reasoning among them, which of them should be greatest.

47 And Jesus, perceiving the thought of their heart, took a child, and set him by him,

48 And said unto them, ʰWhosoever shall receive this child in my name receiveth me: and whosoever shall receive me receiveth him that sent me: ⁱfor he that is least among you all, the same shall be great.

See the notes on Matt. xviii. 1—6; Mark ix. 33—37. This paragraph showeth what need there was of the preceding discourse, that our Saviour should prepare them with a preinforming them about his suffering, that when they saw it their faith in him as the Messiah might not fail; for they were possessed with the common notion of their country, that the Messiah should deliver them from the temporal pressures which they were under, and exercise a civil or military secular power; this made them think of places of priority and greatness, about which we often find them disputing. Our Lord, to bring them off that false notion of him and his kingdom, taketh a child, and setteth him before them, and saith, *Whosoever shall receive this child, &c.* What Luke saith must be interpreted by what we had before in Matthew and Mark. *This child*, that is, one that is as humble as this child, &c.: see the notes before mentioned.

49 ¶ ᵏAnd John answered and said, Master, we saw one casting out devils in thy name; and we forbad him, because he followeth not with us.

50 And Jesus said unto him, Forbid *him* not: for ˡhe that is not against us is for us.

S. LUKE IX

Mark saith further, that Christ added, *for there is no man, which shall do a miracle in my name, that can lightly speak evil of me:* see the notes on Mark ix. 38, 39.

51 ¶ And it came to pass, when the time was come that ᵐhe should be received up, he stedfastly set his face to go to Jerusalem,

m Mark 16. 19. Acts 1. 2.

From this to ver. 56 we have a piece of history recorded by no other evangelist but Luke; but is of great use to us, both to let us know, that our Saviour laid down his life, no man took it from him, and to let us see to what height differences about religion ordinarily arise, and what intemperateness is often found, as to them, in the spirits of the best of people, as also what is the will of our great Master as to the government of our spirits in such cases. The going up of our Saviour to Jerusalem at this time was his last journey thither. *When the time was come that he should be received up;* Ἐν τῷ συμπληροῦσθαι τας ἡμέρας τῆς ἀναλήψεως αὐτοῦ; that is, when the time was drawing nigh when Christ should ascend up into heaven; so the word is used, Mark xvi. 19; Acts i. 11; 1 Tim. iii. 16. But why doth the evangelist express it thus? why doth he not say, when he was to suffer; but skippeth over his death, and only mentioneth his ascension? 1. That is included; Christ was first to suffer, and then to enter into his glory. 2. Christ's death is called a lifting up from the earth, John xii. 32. 3. What if we should say that Christ's death is thus expressed, to let us know that the death of Christ was to him a thing that his eye was not so much upon, as the glory which he immediately was to enter into after; so as he calls his very death a taking up, as that which immediately preceded it, thereby teaching us to overlook sufferings and death, as not worthy to be named or mentioned, and to look only to that taking up into our Father's glory, which is the portion of all believers; when they die, they are but taken up from the earth: and though our bodies still stay behind a while, death having a power over us, yet of them also there shall be a taking up. Upon both which takings up our eyes should be so fixed, as to overlook all the sufferings of this life, as not worthy to be named. *He stedfastly set his face to go to Jerusalem.* Some think this was not our Saviour's last motion thither before his passion, but then it would not have been said πρόσωπον ἐστήριξε, *he set his face,* or, he confirmed his face. He was now in Galilee, Jerusalem (that killed the prophets) was the place designed for his suffering; betwixt Galilee and Jerusalem lay Samaria, through which he was to pass.

52 And sent messengers before his face: and they went, and entered into a village of the Samaritans, to make ready for them.

53 And ⁿthey did not receive him, because his face was as though he would go to Jerusalem.

n John 4. 4, 9.

The land of Canaan was by Joshua divided among all the twelve tribes of Israel, as we read in the book of Joshua, chap. xiv., xv., xvi., xvii. Saul, David, and Solomon (after the death of Joshua, the judges, and Samuel) ruled over them all; but Rehoboam the son of Solomon, following the counsel of the young men in his counsels, ten tribes revolted from the house of David, 1 Kings xii. 16—19. Jeroboam brought them to idolatry, ver. 28, 29, setting up calves at Dan and Bethel. So as that there was a perpetual difference between the Israelites and those that adhered to the house of David, both upon a civil and religious account. This held for about two hundred and sixty years. In the time of Hoshea, their last king, the king of Assyria, after a siege of three years, takes Samaria their head city. Of this we have an account, 2 Kings xvii. 6, as also of those sins which had provoked God to give them up into his hands. Ver. 24 of that chapter we read that *the king of Assyria brought men from Babylon, Cuthah, Ava, Hamath, and Sepharvaim, and placed them in the cities of Samaria instead of the children of Israel.* He removed the most of the Jews, ver. 6 of that chapter, *and placed them in Halah and in Habor by the river of Gozan, and in the cities of the Medes.* After this there were several mutations in the government of those countries. We must not imagine that all the Jews were carried away, but the chief and principal men; and we read in that 17th chapter, that a priest was sent back to instruct the new colonies how to worship the God of the country; because the lions infesting them, they conceived their non-acquaintance with the methods of worship used toward the God of that country was the cause of it, 2 Kings xvii. 26, 27. But yet the people of the several nations brought thither worshipped their several idols, as may be read there, ver. 29. After this, about a hundred and sixty years, these places came under the dominion of Cyrus, who gave the Jews a liberty to return, but it chiefly concerned those that belonged to the kingdom of Judah, for we read, Ezra i. 5, that they were *the fathers of Judah and Benjamin* that *rose up* to return. The Samaritans were their enemies as to the building of the temple, Ezra iv. 4, 5. After this, they fell under the power, first of the Grecians, then of the Romans, under which they at this time were. This old feud, both upon the account of their former civil difference, and their difference in religion, still held, so as there was a great enmity (especially occasioned by their difference in religion) betwixt those who belonged to the tribes of Judah and Benjamin, and the Samaritans, who were indeed idolaters. The Jews (for so now were they only called who adhered to the house of David) had no dealings with them, John iv. 9; though it be the opinion of some that there were common civilities betwixt them, and that the rigidness lay on the Jewish part, rather than the Samaritans'. Galilee lay beyond Samaria, and it should seem was more generally inhabited by native Jews. The king of Assyria planted his colonies (it is probable) more in that which was now more strictly called Samaria, which lay in the heart of the land; which might be the reason that the inhabitants of that part now called Samaria were more absurd and gross in their worship than the inhabitants of Galilee, amongst whom Christ so long preached. From whence (as was before said) Christ going to Jerusalem to the feast was to pass. The Samaritans refused to receive him, which ordinarily, it is said, they did not to passengers, but possibly their knowing that he was going to the feast was the cause, or his attendants might be more than they liked. When we come to John iv. we shall hear more of the religious differences betwixt the Jews and the Samaritans. This is enough to have at present noted.

54 And when his disciples James and John saw *this,* they said, Lord, wilt thou that we command fire to come down from heaven, and consume them, even as °Elias did?

o 2 Kings 1. 10, 12.

The history of Elijah to which the disciples refer, is doubtless that, 2 Kings i. 10, where Elijah, not without direction from God, called fire from heaven to destroy those captains and their fifties which the king sent to take him.

55 But he turned, and rebuked them, and said, Ye know not what manner of spirit ye are of.

56 For ᵖthe Son of man is not come to destroy men's lives, but to save *them.* And they went to another village.

p John 3. 17. & 12. 47.

The term *spirit* sometimes signifies, the inward motions, propensions, and inclinations of the soul, influenced either from the Holy Spirit of God, or from the evil spirit. So the term is used 2 Tim. i. 7. You do not (saith our Saviour) consider what kind of motions these are, which you indulge yourselves in. The case of Elijah and this case had three remarkable differences. 1. The people of Israel at that time had been in an apostasy but of few years comparatively to these Samaritans; they were fallen into it in the sight of the true worship of God, at that time upheld in Judah. They were not only stiff in it, but the king sends these captains to apprehend Elijah for declaring what God had commanded him to declare. These Samaritans were under the prejudices of antiquity, and prescription for many hundreds of years. Histories tell us, that the Samaritan temple, on Mount Gerizim, built in opposition to the temple at Jerusalem, was built by one Sanballat, Darius's governor in those parts, to be revenged on the Jews for turning his son-in-law Manasseh from the priesthood at Jerusalem, which if it be true, the Samaritans had been fixed now in their false worship more than five hundred years. Nor were these that we read of any of the heads and rulers, but probably ordinary country people, rooted so long in this corrupt way, and doing this in zeal to their own temple on Mount Gerizim, and so inclined to show no favour to those who in any devotion were going to the opposite temple. Christ pitieth them under these prejudices, and though he doth not approve of their worship, yet he did not think that the way to change their minds was to call for fire from heaven against them, nor would he be so severe against them. It is not the will of God that we should approve of any corrupt worship, and join with those that use it; but neither is it his will that we should by fire and sword go about to suppress it, and bring men off from it. Antiquity, or the practice of our forefathers, is no sufficient plea to justify any worship. (It was the Samaritans' plea, John iv. 20.) But yet where any such prejudice against the truth is, it calleth to us for mild and gentle behaviour towards such as are under those disadvantages for the receiving of the truth. 2. But, secondly, there was a difference in the call of Elijah. He was an extraordinary prophet, who did nothing of this nature but by an immediate impulse and direction; so as what he did was in zeal for God, guided by a knowledge of the will of God. The disciples had no such call. 3. The times differed; Elijah acted under the legal dispensation, which was more severe; they were under the more mild and gentle dispensation of the gospel. And in this question they did but indulge their passions, and sinful desire of revenge; therefore, saith our Saviour, *Ye know not what manner of spirit ye are of.* Our Saviour lets them know that they were under a more mild and gentle dispensation, by propounding his own example: *The Son of man* (saith he) *came not to destroy men's lives, but to save.* The term translated *lives* signifieth also souls; but if we consider the apostles' question, which was not whether they should call for fire from heaven to destroy their souls, but to destroy them as to their lives here, it will well enough justify our translators rendering it in this place *lives.* You see, saith our Saviour, by my healing the sick, raising the dead, &c., that my business is not to make my ministry ungrateful to men, by any ways prejudicing them in their outward concerns. If it were translated souls, it is yet a great truth: Christ came not to destroy men's souls, but to bring the means of salvation and eternal happiness; if they reject these, and perish, their destruction is of themselves.

q Mat. 8. 19. 57 ¶ ᑫAnd it came to pass, that, as they went in the way, a certain *man* said unto him, Lord, I will follow thee whithersoever thou goest.

58 And Jesus said unto him, Foxes have holes, and birds of the air *have* nests; but the Son of man hath not where to lay *his* head.

Matthew saith, chap. viii. 19, this man was a scribe. See the notes on Matt. viii. 19. Let those who have stately houses, and think them worth glorying in, or that they are things fit for men to value themselves upon, despising their poor brethren that want such accommodations of this life, digest this text.

r Mat. 8. 21. 59 ʳAnd he said unto another, Follow me. But he said, Lord, suffer me first to go and bury my father.

60 Jesus said unto him, Let the dead bury their dead: but go thou and preach the kingdom of God.

See the notes on Matt. viii. 21, 22. How free is Divine grace! The scribe offers to follow Christ: Christ encourageth him not. To another that made no such offer, he first speaketh, saying, *Follow me,* and will admit of no excuse.

s See 1 Kin. 19. 20. 61 And another also said, Lord, ˢI will follow thee; but let me first go bid them farewell, which are at home at my house.

62 And Jesus said unto him, No man, having put his hand to the plough, and looking back, is fit for the kingdom of God.

Matthew (who mentioned the other two) mentioneth not this third person. Some doubt whether we well translate these words, ἀποτάξασθαι τοῖς εἰς τὸν οἶκόν μου, *bid them at my house farewell;* or whether it were not better translated, to order the things or persons relating to my house. Let it be translated either way, it signifies a too much worldliness of mind in this disciple, which our Saviour checketh in the next words, saying, *No man, having put his hand to the plough, and looking back,* εἰς τὰ ὀπίσω, to the things behind, *is fit for the kingdom of God.* Some think it is an allusion to the story of Elisha's call, 1 Kings xix. 19, 20. Elijah passing by him *ploughing with twelve yoke of oxen before him, and he with the twelfth, cast his mantle upon him. And he left the oxen, and ran after Elijah, and said, Let me, I pray thee, kiss my father and my mother, and then I will follow thee.* Be that as it will, here is a plain allusion to the work of a ploughman, and a comparing of a minister of the gospel in his duty with the ploughman in his work. The ploughman is obliged to look forward to his work, or he will never draw his furrows either straight enough, or of a just depth; so must a minister of the gospel: if he be once called out of secular employments to the service of God in the ministry, he is bound to mind and attend that; that is enough to take up the whole man, and his whole strength and time, he had need of no other things to mind or look after, the things of the world are things behind him. Not that God debarreth his ministers (in case of exigence) to work for their bread with their hands, as Paul did; but they ought not, without apparent necessity, to entangle themselves with the things of this life, so as to make them their business.

CHAP. X

Christ sendeth out the seventy disciples to work miracles and to preach, 1—12. *He pronounceth a woe against Chorazin, Bethsaida, and Capernaum,* 13—16. *The seventy return with joy; Christ showeth them wherein to rejoice,* 17—20. *He thanketh his Father for having revealed his gospel to the simple only,* 21, 22. *He showeth the blessedness of those that were called into his church,* 23, 24. *He teacheth a lawyer how to attain eternal life; and by the parable of the good Samaritan showeth whom we are to consider as our neighbour,* 25—37. *He commendeth Mary's attention to his doctrine in preference to Martha's busy care to entertain him,* 38—42.

AFTER these things the Lord appointed other seventy also, and ᵃsent them two and two before his face into every city and place, whither he himself would come. a Mat. 10. 1. Mark 6. 7.

We heard before of Christ's first electing, then sending out, twelve, chap. vi. 13—16; ix. 1—6; and we heard of their return, and giving an account of their trust to their Lord, ver. 10. What their particular account was we no where read, but it was such as our Saviour judged the harvest too great for the hands of the labourers. He therefore now resolveth to send out seventy more. The names of these we have not in the evangelist, only that Christ sent them out, and that he sent them *two and two,* which might be for their better mutual assistance of each other, and also for their mutual testimony one for another. When God sent out the first conductors, and governors of his people, he sent two, Moses and Aaron. John Baptist sent two of his disciples to Christ. Christ sent two of his disciples to prepare the passover, chap. xxii. 8. There seemeth to be nothing mysterious in this. Man is a sociable creature, and it is not good for him to be alone. We cannot determine that our Saviour had any regard to the numbers of *twelve* and *seventy;* though it is certain that both those numbers amongst the Jews seem to have had a more than ordinary character, twelve being the number of the tribes of Israel, according to the promise, Gen. xvii. 20; xlix. 28; at Elim they found *twelve wells of water,* Exod. xv. 27; according to the number of the tribes were the twelve pillars, chap. xxiv. 4, and the twelve stones in the breastplate of judgment, chap. xxviii. 21; and the number of the cakes for the shew-bread was to be twelve, Lev. xxiv. 5. The princes of Israel were twelve, Numb. i. 44; and twelve men were sent to spy out the land of Canaan, Deut. i. 23. So we shall observe that in a multitude of things they kept to the number of twelve: John in his description of the new Jerusalem, which he saw in his vision, says, it had twelve gates, and at the gates twelve angels, and on the gates were the names of the twelve tribes, Rev. xxi. 12. And the wall had twelve foundations, &c., ver. 14. And for the number of seventy: Jacob's family, when they went down into Egypt, were seventy souls, Gen. xlvi. 27; they mourned for Jacob seventy days, Gen. l. 3; at Elim they met with seventy palm trees, Numb. xxxiii. 9; the posterity of Jacob was in Babylon seventy years. The Jewish sanhedrim, or great court chosen upon the advice of Jethro, is said to have consisted first of seventy, then of seventy-two persons. So as the numbers of twelve and seventy seem to have been numbers to which the Jews had some respect. Whether our Saviour, in the choice of those whom he first sent to preach the gospel, had any respect or not to the Jewish value for those numbers, or designed by it to show them, that he was about to set up a new kingdom and government, which, though differing from what they had exercised formerly, yet in some little things should have some conformity to them, we cannot determine. We shall find the same powers and authority given to these seventy as to the twelve, and the same instructions: how some come to imagine a difference of order betwixt them I cannot tell; no such thing appeareth from the instructions given the one or the other upon their first sending out.

b Matt. 9. 37, 38. John 4. 35.
c 2 Thes. 3. 1.

2 Therefore said he unto them, ^bThe harvest truly *is* great, but the labourers *are* few: ^cpray ye therefore the Lord of the harvest, that he would send forth labourers into his harvest.

See the notes on Matt. ix. 37, 38, where these words are put immediately before the sending out of the twelve. Both the twelve and the seventy, all that Christ ever sent out, were to be labourers in the Lord's harvest.

d Mat. 10. 16.
e Mat. 10. 9.
10. Mark 6.
8. ch. 9. 3.
f 2 Kings 4. 29.

3 Go your ways: ^dbehold, I send you forth as lambs among wolves.

4 ^eCarry neither purse, nor scrip, nor shoes: and ^fsalute no man by the way.

We met with these instructions before, and opened them in our notes on Matt. x. 9, 10, 16, only there we had not those words, *and salute no man by the way*. The meaning of that is no more than, make all possible speed: see 2 Kings iv. 29.

g Mat. 10. 12.

5 ^gAnd into whatsoever house ye enter, first say, Peace *be* to this house.

6 And if the son of peace be there, your peace shall rest upon it: if not, it shall turn to you again.

h Mat. 10. 11.
i 1 Cor. 10. 27.
k Mat. 10. 10.
1 Cor. 9. 4, &c.
1 Tim. 5. 18.

7 ^hAnd in the same house remain, ⁱeating and drinking such things as they give: for ^kthe labourer is worthy of his hire. Go not from house to house.

See the notes on Matt. x. 11, and on Mark vi. 10. The instructions, as to the substance of them, are the same here as there, though a little differing in the terms.

8 And into whatsoever city ye enter, and they receive you, eat such things as are set before you:

l ch. 9. 2.
m Matt. 3. 2.
& 4. 17. & 10. 7. ver. 11.

9 ^lAnd heal the sick that are therein, and say unto them, ^mThe kingdom of God is come nigh unto you.

10 But into whatsoever city ye enter, and they receive you not, go your ways out into the streets of the same, and say,

n Matt. 10. 14. ch. 9. 5. Acts 13. 51. & 18. 6.

11 ⁿEven the very dust of your city, which cleaveth on us, we do wipe off against you: notwithstanding be ye sure of this, that the kingdom of God is come nigh unto you.

o Mat. 10. 15. Mark 6. 11.

12 But I say unto you, that ^oit shall be more tolerable in that day for Sodom, than for that city.

We have met with the same instructions before in Matthew and Mark. See the notes on Matt. x. 11—15, and Mark vi. 10, 11. There is some difference in words. Matthew saith,—*inquire who in* the city *is worthy*, and, ver. 13, *if the house be worthy*; Luke saith, *if the son of peace be there*; they both mean the same thing: if there be any in it that belong to God's election of grace, any whom God intendeth by you to call, and make partakers of the peace of the gospel. For other things relating to the opening of the words, see the notes before mentioned. Only we may from hence observe for our instruction, 1. That it is the will of Christ, that his ministers should not be too solicitous for a livelihood. As the labourer is worthy of his hire, so he that sends them into his harvest will see they shall be fed. Let them look to their calling, and to the fulfilling of their ministry; God will see they shall be fed. 2. That the society of ministers of the gospel, in cities and houses, should not be with debauchees, but with those that are worthy, so far as man can judge; such as are their Master's friends and servants should be their companions. 3. Those are most worthy in places amongst whom the Son of peace is, men and women that have the most knowledge of and love for Christ. 4. The ministers of Christ ought to carry themselves with all imaginable civility, wishing good to all, and doing good to all. 5. Christ's ministers ought not to make their bellies their gods,—*eat such things as are set before you*. 6. They have a Divine licence to take and use for their necessities such things as men give them. 7. Christ expects that his people should maintain his ministers, not depriving the labourers of their hire, nor muzzling the mouths of the oxen which tread out the corn, 1 Cor. ix. 9, 10, nor preferring their servants for their worldly occasions before such as labour for their souls, and in that work are God's messengers to them, and his servants in the first place, though employed in watching for people's souls. 8. The not giving a livelihood to ministers, is a not receiving them, that is, provided the people be able. 9. People by not receiving the gospel of peace brought them by faithful ministers shall do them no hurt, their peace shall return unto them. They shall be a sweet savour unto God, even as to them that perish. Their judgment is with the Lord, and their work with their God, though they labour in vain; though Israel be not gathered, they shall be glorified. Men proportion their rewards according to successes of servants. God more justly proportioneth his rewards to men's sincerity and diligence in their labour. 10. If men refuse the gospel, yet they shall know the kingdom of God is come nigh unto them. If they will not be subject to his kingdom of grace, yet they shall be subdued by the kingdom of his power and justice. 11. There will come a day when men that have the offers of the gospel of peace, and refuse them, slighting and despising his ministers and their message, will find that they had better have lived in Sodom when it was burnt with fire and brimstone; their portion of wrath in the day of judgment will be larger and bitterer than the portion of the men of Sodom. Let all who live in our days hear and fear, and in time break off their sins by a true repentance, lest they go to hell at the highest disadvantage.

13 ^pWoe unto thee, Chorazin! woe unto thee, Bethsaida! ^qfor if the mighty works had been done in Tyre and Sidon, which have been done in you, they had a great while ago repented, sitting in sackcloth and ashes.

p Mat. 11. 21.
q Ezek. 3. 6.

14 But it shall be more tolerable for Tyre and Sidon at the judgment, than for you.

15 ^rAnd thou, Capernaum, which art ^sexalted to heaven, ^tshalt be thrust down to hell.

r Mat. 11. 23.
s See Gen. 11. 4. Deu. 1. 28. Is. 14. 13. Jer. 51. 53.
t See Eze. 26. 20. & 32. 18.

See the notes on Matt. xi. 21—24.

16 ^uHe that heareth you heareth me; and ^xhe that despiseth you despiseth me; ^yand he that despiseth me despiseth him that sent me.

u Mat. 10. 40. Mark 9. 37. John 13. 20.
x 1 Thess. 4. 8.
y John 5. 23.

See the notes on Matt. x. 40.

S. LUKE X

ver. 1. 17 ¶ And ^athe seventy returned again with joy, saying, Lord, even the devils are subject unto us through thy name.

As we before read of the twelve coming back to give Christ an account of their success, so we here have the same of the seventy. Whether this joy of the seventy was more carnal than it ought, they rather rejoicing in that new power which they had received from Christ, than in the demonstration of Christ's Divine power, and the confirmation of the doctrine of the gospel by these miraculous operations, is hard to determine; for though Christ's reply seemeth to have a check in it, yet it is so qualified by the term *rather*, ver. 20, that we cannot from thence absolutely conclude any such thing from it. Here is a difference to be observed betwixt Christ's and his disciples' casting out of devils. Christ did it in his own name, by his own word of command, power, and authority; the disciples did it in Christ's name, and by a power and authority derived from him.

a John 12. 31. & 16. 11. Rev. 9. 1. & 12. 8, 9.

18 And he said unto them, ^aI beheld Satan as lightning fall from heaven.

Lightning comes suddenly, and with thunder. The thunder of the gospel brought down the devil as lightning: and indeed this is observable, the devil is so busy in no places where the gospel prevails, as in places where that joyful sound is not come, whether we consider his power with reference to men's bodies or souls. This is one general advantage of gospel preaching, the devil will not endure the sound of it, so as to impose upon mankind, at that rate which he doth upon ignorant persons, that are heathens, or only differing from them in that they are baptized, and call themselves Christians. Christ saw this, as God, for the devil is not visible to human senses, as neither are any spirits; which showed the impudence of that popish impostor in Germany, who selling indulgences, (by which he pretended souls were delivered from purgatory,) called to the people to look up and see them fly away. But Christ could see it as God, for he certainly knew that it would be, and that it already was, the blessed effect of the gospel.

b Mark 16. 18. Acts 28. 5.

19 Behold, ^bI give unto you power to tread on serpents and scorpions, and over all the power of the enemy: and nothing shall by any means hurt you.

Christ doth here, 1. Confirm the power before given to these seventy for working miracles, that they might not think that it ceased upon the determination of their first mission. 2. He confirmeth his promise to them for his presence with them, and protection of them. Interpreters think here is a manifest allusion to Psal. xci. 13, *Thou shalt tread upon the lion and adder: the young lion and the dragon shalt thou trample under thy feet:* which must be understood figuratively, the sense being, that nothing should hurt them. This promise was more specially verified for some years in God's protection of the first ministers of the gospel, until they had done their work; and shall be fulfilled in a sense to the end of the world, according to the promise in Psal. xci. Nothing shall hurt their souls, as to the favour of God and their eternal happiness, nor their bodies, so far forth as, or so long as, God in his wisdom shall judge fit. They have a further power also given them more common to all the ministers of the gospel sent by Christ, yea, and to all Christians. They have a power over all the power of the enemy; God will not be wanting to them in a power to resist the devil, and they have a promise that, being resisted, he shall flee from them.

c Ex. 32. 32. Ps. 69. 28. Is. 4. 3. Dan. 12. 1. Phil. 4. 3. Heb. 12. 23. Rev. 13. 8. & 20. 12. & 21. 27.

20 Notwithstanding in this rejoice not, that the spirits are subject unto you; but rather rejoice, because ^cyour names are written in heaven.

It is a usual thing in holy writ, to have prohibitions delivered in general terms, which must be understood in a restrained sense. That it is so here, appeareth plainly by the word *rather*, prefixed to *rejoice*, in the latter part of the sentence. For it was doubtless a just cause of joy and rejoicing to them that Christ had honoured them with such an extraordinary gift and power, but not of so much joy as to know that their names were written in the book of life; for as the good was infinitely greater, so a proportionable joy was requisite upon the assurance of it. The expression *written in heaven*, is equivalent to the being written *in the book of life*, whereby is signified, either the certain designation of some to eternal life, or effectual calling. We read of this *book of life*, Rev. iii. 5; xx. 12, 15; xxi. 27; xxii. 19. It is called the Lamb's book, Rev. xiii. 8, and it is said it was written *from the foundation of the world;* which will justify those divines who understand it of a particular election from eternity; whereas it is objected that when amongst the twelve there was a *son of perdition*, it is unreasonable to think that all the seventy were elect vessels. It is easily answered, that our Saviour's words were true according to the usual phrase of speaking, if the generality of them only were such. Nor need our Saviour be understood as asserting all their names were so written, but only asserting the greatest cause of joy to be, if men can by their calling find that their election is sure. From our Saviour's words we may infer, 1. That there is a book of life, an election of grace. 2. That there are names written in this book; it is an election of persons. 3. That men may know that their names are written in that book, otherwise they could not rejoice; no man rejoiceth but in a good with which he hath some degree of union. 4. That this is a greater cause of joy, than for a man to know that he hath a power to cast out devils. Men may be made use of to cast out devils in Christ's name, who yet may go to the devil at last, Matt. vii. 22, 23; so cannot those whose names are written in the book of life. But I cannot understand that our Saviour in these words asserts that all the names of the seventy were written in that book. The tendency of his discourse is rather to quicken them to give all diligence to make sure of this cause of joy and rejoicing.

21 ¶ ^dIn that hour Jesus rejoiced in spirit, and said, I thank thee, O Father, Lord of heaven and earth, that thou hast hid these things from the wise and prudent, and hast revealed them unto babes: even so, Father; for so it seemed good in thy sight.

d Matt. 11. 25.

22 ^e∥All things are delivered to me of my Father: and ^fno man knoweth who the Son is, but the Father; and who the Father is, but the Son, and *he* to whom the Son will reveal *him*.

e Mat. 28. 18. John 3. 35. & 5. 27. & 17. 2. ∥ Many ancient copies add these words, *And turning to his disciples, he said,* f John 1. 18. & 6. 44, 46.

See the notes on Matt. xi. 25—27, where we met with these words of our Saviour.

23 ¶ And he turned him unto *his* disciples, and said privately, ^gBlessed *are* the eyes which see the things that ye see:

g Matt. 13. 16.

24 For I tell you, ^hthat many prophets and kings have desired to see those things which ye see, and have not seen *them;* and to hear those things which ye hear, and have not heard *them*.

h 1 Pet. 1. 10.

See the notes on Matt. xiii. 16, 17.

25 ¶ And, behold, a certain Lawyer stood up, and tempted him, saying, ⁱMaster, what shall I do to inherit eternal life?

i Matt. 19. 16. & 22. 35.

26 He said unto him, What is written in the law? how readest thou?

27 And he answering said, ^kThou shalt love the Lord thy God with all thy heart, and with all thy soul, and with all thy strength, and with all thy mind; and ^lthy neighbour as thyself.

k Deut. 6. 5.

l Lev. 19. 18.

28 And he said unto him, Thou hast answered right: this do, and ^mthou shalt live.

m Lev. 18. 5 Neh. 9. 29. Ezek. 20. 11, 13, 21. Rom. 10. 5.

These four verses would incline one to think that Luke here records the same piece of history which we met with

Matt. xxii. 35—40, and Mark xii. 28—34; (see the notes on both those texts;) but neither of those evangelists have the following part of this discourse, which makes me doubtful whether Luke speaks of the same person coming to Christ which the others mention. A lawyer he was, who came to our Saviour upon a design to tempt, that is, to make a trial of him, whether he would deliver any doctrine contrary to the law of Moses. It is plain that he fancied that the eternal life which Christ preached was to be obtained by doing what the law required. Our Saviour agreeth it, that if he did what the law required, according as he himself had given an account of it, he should live. I apprehend no absurdity, to affirm that our Saviour speaks here of living eternally. It is rather absurd to fancy that our Saviour did not answer *ad idem*, to the thing about which the question was propounded. Neither is salvation impossible because the law in itself could not give life, but because of the weakness of our flesh, so as we cannot fulfil it. So that considering our infirmity, the law serveth to us only as a schoolmaster, to bring us to Christ; and as a mark which we ought to shoot at, though we cannot shoot home; a rule to direct us in our duty, though we cannot perform or fulfil it.

n ch. 16. 15. 29 But he, willing to ⁿjustify himself, said unto Jesus, And who is my neighbour?

This lawyer's desire to justify himself spake him a hypocrite. The reason of that question, *Who is my neighbour?* was the notion of the neighbour (mentioned in the law) which the scribes and Pharisees had, who counted none their neighbours but their friends and benefactors, at least none but those that were of their own nation or particular sect; and had taught their people, that they might hate their enemies. Our Saviour (this being but a captious question, considering the received interpretation amongst them of the law of God) doth not think fit to answer his question directly, but telling him a story, maketh him answer himself.

30 And Jesus answering said, A certain *man* went down from Jerusalem to Jericho, and fell among thieves, which stripped him of his raiment, and wounded *him*, and departed, leaving *him* half dead.

31 And by chance there came down a certain Priest that way: and when he saw

o Ps. 38. 11. him, ^ohe passed by on the other side.

32 And likewise a Levite, when he was at the place, came and looked *on him*, and passed by on the other side.

p John 4. 9. 33 But a certain ^pSamaritan, as he journeyed, came where he was: and when he saw him, he had compassion *on him*,

34 And went to *him*, and bound up his wounds, pouring in oil and wine, and set him on his own beast, and brought him to an inn, and took care of him.

‖ See Matt. 20. 2. 35 And on the morrow when he departed, he took out two ‖ pence, and gave *them* to the host, and said unto him, Take care of him; and whatsoever thou spendest more, when I come again, I will repay thee.

36 Which now of these three, thinkest thou, was neighbour unto him that fell among the thieves?

37 And he said, He that shewed mercy on him. Then said Jesus unto him, Go, and do thou likewise.

It is certain that the principal scope of our Saviour in this history, or parable, was to convince the lawyer, that every one is our neighbour to whom God offereth us an opportunity of doing good, whether he be of our nation or religion or not. Every object of our mercy is our neighbour, whom God requireth us to love as ourselves. This was quite contrary to the common doctrine of the scribes' and Pharisees' interpreting the law, *Thou shalt love thy neighbour as thyself*, and excellently served our Saviour's design, to show this lawyer that he understood not, much less observed, the law of God in that manner, as that he could justify himself from the violation of it. He also by the by showeth him, that the Samaritans, whom the Jews so much abhorred, better understood the law of God, than the ecclesiastical guides of those times, who yet pretended to be teachers of it to others; for some of them by the light of nature discerned themselves obliged to do good to every one that stood in need of their help, or if not by the light of nature, yet by the light of revelation in the law of Moses; but the scribes and Pharisees, by their false interpretation of the Divine law, had taught people to omit a great part of their duty required by the Divine law, and so could not hope to be justified, or to obtain eternal life and salvation, from the observation of it.

38 ¶ Now it came to pass, as they went, that he entered into a certain village: and a certain woman named ^qMartha received him into her house. q John 11. 1. & 12. 2, 3.

39 And she had a sister called Mary, ^rwhich also ^ssat at Jesus' feet, and heard his word. r 1 Cor. 7. 32, &c. s Luke 8.35. Acts 22. 3.

Interpreters think this village was Bethany, and that this Martha and Mary were the same which are mentioned John xi. 2. Inns probably were not so frequent then, and in those places, as they are now, so as strangers were often received in private houses. Christ loseth no opportunity of preaching the gospel; while they were preparing supper, he was entertaining the family with the glad tidings of the gospel, *the feast of fat things made upon the mountain*, Isa. xxv. 6. *The lips of the righteous feed many*, Prov. x. 21. It was their fashion to have disciples sit at their doctors' feet, to hear their word; there Mary fixeth herself.

40 But Martha was cumbered about much serving, and came to him, and said, Lord, dost thou not care that my sister hath left me to serve alone? bid her therefore that she help me.

Two things are blamable in Martha: 1. That she made too much ado about the entertainment of our Saviour. That she entertained our Saviour she did well; but herein she erred, that she made her entertainment of him so troublesome, as it would not give her leave to take that advantage, which she might, or ought to have done, from the entertainment of a prophet. 2. That she is displeased with her sister because she would not lend her her hand, but chose rather to sit at Christ's feet and hear his word, and desireth Christ to send her away to her assistance.

41 And Jesus answered and said unto her, Martha, Martha, thou art careful and troubled about many things:

42 But ^tone thing is needful: and Mary hath chosen that good part, which shall not be taken away from her. t Ps. 27. 4.

Our Saviour plainly blameth Martha for her too great solicitude and trouble to provide a dinner, or supper, for him, who had meat to eat which she was not aware of, it being his meat and drink to do the will of his Father, and to preach the gospel. Interpreters much trouble themselves in determining what that *one thing* is, which our Saviour here saith *is needful*. Some think our Saviour meaneth no more than, one dish is enough; but this certainly is too low a sense. Others would have this *one thing* to be a life of meditation and contemplation, and that this was that *good part* Mary had *chosen*. If Mary had thus spent her whole life they might have said something for this. But certainly Mary's choosing to take advantage of Christ's company, rather to spend an hour or two in hearing of him, than in preparing a supper for him, will prove no such thing. I should interpret it generally, concerning the care of the soul with reference to eternity. That is certainly the one thing necessary, that was the better part, which Mary chosen, as to which Christ would not discourage her, nor any way blunt the edge of those holy desires he had kindled in her, an effect of which study and care was her sitting at the feet of Christ to hear his word.

CHAP. XI.

Christ teacheth to pray, assuring that God will give all good things to them that ask him, 1—13. *He casteth out a devil, and reproveth the blasphemy of the Pharisees, who ascribed the miracle to the power of Beelzebub,* 14—26. *He showeth who are the truly blessed,* 27, 28; *and the inexcusableness of not believing his gospel.* 29—36. *He reprehendeth the outward show of holiness in the Pharisees, and pronounceth woes against them and the scribes and lawyers,* 37—54.

A. D. 33. AND it came to pass, that, as he was praying in a certain place, when he ceased, one of his disciples said unto him, Lord, teach us to pray, as John also taught his disciples.

This seemeth to be a different time from that mentioned by Matthew, where our Saviour directed his disciples to pray; there his direction was part of his sermon on the mount. Besides, the doxology or conclusion is there left out. It is said here, *as he was praying in a certain place.* Christ looked upon all places as holy enough for prayer. It also looks as if at this time our Saviour was not at his more secret devotions, but with the twelve, (which were his family,) praying with them. *When he ceased:* this is very observable against those who pretend impulses of the Spirit, to disturb ministers in the time when they are praying and preaching; it may easily be known from what spirit such impulses are. The disciples of Christ often propounded questions to him after preaching, but never interrupting him in his work, nor before he was retired into a house. They now come to be informed about prayer, but they stay till he had first ceased. We having no account in holy writ of John's disciples asking him, or his teaching of them to pray, are more at a loss to determine whether our Saviour did intend that his disciples should use these words, as the phrase here seemeth to import, or only pray in this sense, *after this manner,* as Matthew saith; indeed nothing can be concluded from either phrase by any judicious person. For as we read in many places in Scripture, that Christ *answered and said,* when it is manifest the meaning is, he spake words to that import or sense, (the evangelists reporting the words spoken with variations of expression,) so when we pray we may say, *Our Father which art in heaven,* &c., though we do not use the same words and syllables.

2 And he said unto them, When ye
u Matt. 6. 9. pray, say, ^aOur Father which art in heaven, Hallowed be thy name. Thy kingdom come. Thy will be done, as in heaven, so in earth.

‖ Or, *for the day.* 3 Give us ‖ day by day our daily bread.

4 And forgive us our sins; for we also forgive every one that is indebted to us. And lead us not into temptation; but deliver us from evil.

See the notes on Matt. vi. 9—13. Whoso compareth this prayer as it is recorded by Matthew will find the form of words differing in more things than one; not only the doxology or conclusion is left out wholly by Luke, but for σήμερον there we have χαθ' ἡμεραν here, for ὀφειλήματα Luke hath ἁμαρτίας, for ὡς καὶ ἡμεῖς ἀφίεμεν τοις ὀφειλέταις ἡμῶν we have here καὶ γαρ αὐτοὶ ἀφίεμεν παντὶ ὀφείλοντι ἡμῖν; from whence plainly appears that our Saviour did not intend to oblige his disciples to the same syllabical words, but only to words of the same import, that is, to praying for the same things: yet that Christians have a liberty to use the same words is out of question, and as much out of question that they have a liberty to vary, still keeping their eyes upon the matter of this prayer, and not forgetting that when they go unto God in that holy duty.

5 And he said unto them, Which of you shall have a friend, and shall go unto him at midnight, and say unto him, Friend, lend me three loaves;

6 For a friend of mine ‖ in his journey ‖ Or, *out of his way.* is come to me, and I have nothing to set before him?

7 And he from within shall answer and say, Trouble me not: the door is now shut, and my children are with me in bed; I cannot rise and give thee.

8 I say unto you, ^bThough he will not b ch. 18. 1, rise and give him, because he is his friend, &c. yet because of his importunity he will rise and give him as many as he needeth.

9 ^cAnd I say unto you, Ask, and it c Matt. 7. 7. shall be given you; seek, and ye shall Mark 11. 24. find; knock, and it shall be opened unto Jam. 1. 6. you. 1 John 3. 22.

The plain meaning of our Saviour in this parable, is to teach us that we ought not only to pray, but to be importunate with God in prayer; to *continue in prayer,* as the apostle phraseth it, Col. iv. 2, and to watch *thereunto with all perseverance,* Eph. vi. 18. This in the Greek is called ἀναιδειαν, impudence, which though in our language it is generally taken in an ill sense, yet here signifieth no more than a holy boldness, or pursuing our petitions notwithstanding delays or denials. For those words, ver. 9, see the notes on Matt. vii. 7, where the same words are found.

10 For every one that asketh receiveth; and he that seeketh findeth; and to him that knocketh it shall be opened.

11 ^dIf a son shall ask bread of any of d Matt. 7. 9. you that is a father, will he give him a stone? or if *he ask* a fish, will he for a fish give him a serpent?

12 Or if he shall ask an egg, will he † offer him a scorpion? † Gr. *give.*

13 If ye then, being evil, know how to give good gifts unto your children: how much more shall *your* heavenly Father give the Holy Spirit to them that ask him?

See the notes on Matt. vii. 8—11. As our Saviour's design in the former words appeareth to be our information, that though the hand of God be full of good things proportioned to all the necessities of his creatures, yet they must not expect to have them without asking, he will for them *be inquired of by the house of Israel,* Ezek. xxxvi. 37; and all his promises for the collation of good things must be interpreted, with a supposition of people's seeking them at his hand; as also that every lazy, cold, formal praying will not obtain them at the hand of God, but the working, fervent prayer of the righteous availeth much. His design in these verses seemeth to be, to let us know, that fervent and importunate prayer will not prevail with God to give us any thing but what shall be good for us; for he knoweth that the general desire of our souls is for nothing but what is good; if we ask for things hurtful, it is but a lapse or miscarriage of our tongues, caused from the blindness and ignorance of our minds. No man knowingly will ask any thing of another that shall do him hurt; and though our children, through their want of knowledge and judgment to discern betwixt things that are good or evil for their bodies, may ask of us, and cry unto us, for things that are hurtful, yet we, who know that they would not ask for them if they had the use of their reason, and well knew their noxious quality, considering their circumstances, will not give them to them. So our heavenly Father, though he heareth us crying for such things as he knoweth (considering our circumstances) would be mischievous and hurtful to us, yet he will not give us any thing of that nature; and so in denying the words of our lips, yet answereth the general scope and designs of our souls, which is to have only what is good for us. But if we ask any thing which is good and wholesome for us, and profitable unto us, in the circumstances in which we are, we may be sure that God will give them to us, as we may that an earthly parent will deny nothing to his children crying, which is in his power to give, and which he knoweth to be good for them; for the nature of all good lieth in the conveniency and suitableness of the thing to the wants and necessities of the person that receiveth it. And every such thing must also be according to the will of God, according to his promise, Psal. lxxxiv. 11, to *withhold no good thing from them that live uprightly.* So as both God's fatherly relation, and the knowledge we have that he is a God that cannot lie nor repent, are assurances to us, that whatsoever good thing we ask we shall obtain of him, and nothing else, although we ask and cry for it. Therefore whereas Matthew saith, chap. vii. 11, *How much more shall your Father which is in heaven give good things to them that ask him!* Luke saith here, *How much more shall he give the Holy Spirit to them that ask him!*

e Matt. 9. 32. & 12. 22.

14 ¶ ᵉAnd he was casting out a devil, and it was dumb. And it came to pass, when the devil was gone out, the dumb spake; and the people wondered.

The devil is here called *dumb,* from his effect upon the demoniac, in restraining the use of his tongue.

f Mat. 9. 34. & 12. 24. † Gr. *Beelzebul,* and so ver. 18, 19.

15 But some of them said, ᶠHe casteth out devils through † Beelzebub the chief of the devils.

g Matt. 12. 38. & 16. 1.

16 And others, tempting *him,* ᵍsought of him a sign from heaven.

h Mat. 12.25. Mark 3. 24. i John 2. 25.

17 ʰBut ⁱhe, knowing their thoughts, said unto them, Every kingdom divided against itself is brought to desolation; and a house *divided* against a house falleth.

18 If Satan also be divided against himself, how shall his kingdom stand? because ye say that I cast out devils through Beelzebub.

19 And if I by Beelzebub cast out devils, by whom do your sons cast *them* out? therefore shall they be your judges.

k Ex. 8. 19.

20 But if I ᵏwith the finger of God cast out devils, no doubt the kingdom of God is come upon you.

l Mat. 12.29. Mark 3. 27.

21 ˡWhen a strong man armed keepeth his palace, his goods are in peace:

m Is. 53. 12. Col. 2. 15.

22 But ᵐwhen a stronger than he shall come upon him and overcome him, he taketh from him all his armour wherein he trusted, and divideth his spoils.

n Mat.12.30.

23 ⁿHe that is not with me is against me: and he that gathereth not with me scattereth.

See the notes on Matt. ix. 34; xii. 24—30; and on Mark iii. 22—27.

o Mat. 12.43.

24 ᵒWhen the unclean spirit is gone out of a man, he walketh through dry places, seeking rest; and finding none, he saith, I will return unto my house whence I came out.

25 And when he cometh, he findeth *it* swept and garnished.

p John 5. 14. Heb. 6. 4. & 10. 26. 2 Pet. 2. 20.

26 Then goeth he, and taketh *to him* seven other spirits more wicked than himself; and they enter in, and dwell there: and ᵖthe last *state* of that man is worse than the first.

See the notes on Matt. xii. 43—45. From these verses we may observe, 1. That the devil may in some sort and degree be cast out of persons and places, while yet in other respects they may be his house, and he may dwell in and amongst them. Their bodies, their country, may be in great measure delivered from his power, and he may yet keep possession of their souls. This ordinarily happeneth in places where the gospel is faithfully preached; though there remain abundance of men whose lives evidence that the devil hath a too great possession of their souls, yet those places, and persons inhabiting in them, are more freed from witchcraft, and the power which the devil exercises (by God's permission) upon men's and women's bodies, and cattle, &c., than other more paganish and ignorant places. He may also in a sense be said to be cast out of persons that are reclaimed from vicious and debauched lives, yet are not brought home to God, only are more enlightened, and more under the power of restraining grace; yet their souls may be his house. 2. The devil, cast out in any degree, is unquiet till (if possible) he hath recovered as full a power over and possession of men and women as he ever had. 3. If he ever recovereth it, their latter end is worse than their beginning, Heb. vi. 4; x. 26; 2 Pet. ii. 20.

27 ¶ And it came to pass, as he spake these things, a certain woman of the company lifted up her voice, and said unto him, ᑫBlessed *is* the womb that bare thee, and the paps which thou hast sucked.

q ch. 1. 28, 48.

28 But he said, Yea ʳrather, blessed *are* they that hear the word of God, and keep it.

r Matt. 7.21. ch. 8. 21. Jam. 1. 25.

We are very prone to bless persons from external priviledges, and the favours of Divine Providence, which do not at all change or affect the hearts of those to whom they are given; but God looketh with another eye upon persons. Christ doth not here deny his mother to have been blessed; her cousin Elisabeth (chap. i. 42) had pronounced her *blessed amongst women,* and the angel had before called her *highly favoured,* and told her that she had *found favour with God.* But our Saviour here declareth that her blessing did not so much lie in that her womb bare, and her paps gave suck to him, as in that she was one who heard and kept the word of God; for he pronounceth all such as did so principally blessed. Nor must we separate what God hath put together; the blessing is not pronounced to those who barely hear the word of God, the blessed and the unblessed *pariter adeunt, pariter audiunt,* they may go to church together, and hear the word together, but the blessing is to *those that hear the word of God, and keep it.* See James i. 22, 23. The word to some that hear it may be *a savour of death unto death.* The soul that through grace is made obedient to the will of God, is a more happy soul than the virgin Mary was, considered merely as the mother of Christ, without the consideration of her faith and holiness.

29 ¶ ˢAnd when the people were gathered thick together, he began to say, This is an evil generation: they seek a sign; and there shall no sign be given it, but the sign of Jonas the prophet.

s Matt. 12. 38, 39.

30 For as ᵗJonas was a sign unto the Ninevites, so shall also the Son of man be to this generation.

t Jonah 1. 17. & 2. 10.

31 ᵘThe queen of the south shall rise up in the judgment with the men of this generation, and condemn them: for she came from the utmost parts of the earth to hear the wisdom of Solomon; and, behold, a greater than Solomon *is* here.

u 1 Kings 10. 1.

32 The men of Nineve shall rise up in the judgment with this generation, and shall condemn it: for ˣthey repented at the preaching of Jonas; and, behold, a greater than Jonas *is* here.

x Jonah 3. 5.

See the notes on Matt. xii. 38—42. Matthew saith, they were the Pharisees that came to him, desiring to see a sign from heaven: they did the same again, Matt. xvi. 1. Christ was very ready to work miracles to encourage and confirm his hearers' faith, but not to satisfy unbelievers' curiosity. Instead therefore of showing them signs from heaven, he denounceth the just judgment of God against them, for their not believing in him. See further the notes upon the forementioned parallel texts.

S. LUKE XI

^{y Matt. 5. 15
Mark 4. 21.
ch. 8. 16.}

33 ^y No man, when he hath lighted a candle, putteth *it* in a secret place, neither under a ‖ bushel, but on a candlestick, that they which come in may see the light.

‖ See Matt. 5. 15.

We met with this similitude chap. viii. 16, and Matt. v. 15: see the notes on all those texts. It was a kind of proverbial speech, and so applicable to divers subjects. Some think that our Saviour bringeth in these words as a reason why he would show the Pharisees no sign, viz. because he knew it would do them no good, it had been like the lighting of a candle and putting it under a bushel, which no man doth. Others think that by it he designs to give an account why he pronounced those blessed who heard the word and did it, ver. 28, because practice, and giving light to others, is the end of all hearing.

^{z Matt. 6.22.}

34 ^z The light of the body is the eye: therefore when thine eye is single, thy whole body also is full of light; but when *thine eye* is evil, thy body also *is* full of darkness.

35 Take heed therefore that the light which is in thee be not darkness.

36 If thy whole body therefore *be* full of light, having no part dark, the whole shall be full of light, as when † the bright shining of a candle doth give thee light.

† Gr. *a candle by it's bright shining.*

See the notes upon Matt. vi. 22, 23. Our Saviour's speech in these verses is plainly both elliptical (something being in itself to be understood) and also metaphorical. The sense is this, What the eye is to the body, that the soul, the mind and affections, are to the whole man. Now look, as the eye is the organ by which light is received to guide a man's steps, so that if that be perfect, without any mixture of ill humours, &c., the body from it takes a full and right direction how to move and act; but if that be vitiated by ill humours, the man knows not how to direct his bodily steps: so if a man's soul, (which answereth the bodily eye,) more especially a man's understanding or judgment, be darkened, perverted, prejudiced, or his affections be debauched or depraved, he will not know how to move one step right in his duty; but if his understanding have a right notion of truths, and he judgeth aright concerning the things and ways of God, and his affections be not depraved, then the whole man will be in a capacity to receive the light and revelations of truth, as they shall be communicated to him, even as he who hath a perfect eye receiveth and is able to make use of the bright shining of a candle.

37 ¶ And as he spake, a certain Pharisee besought him to dine with him: and he went in, and sat down to meat.

This is the second time we meet with our Saviour at a Pharisee's house. He saith of himself, that he *came eating and drinking*, that is, allowing himself a free, though innocent, converse with all sorts of people, that he might gain some. The Pharisees were, as to the generality of them, the most bitter, stubborn, and implacable enemies Christ had, yet he refused not to go and sit at meat with a Pharisee.

^{a Mark 7. 3.}

38 And ^a when the Pharisee saw *it*, he marvelled that he had not first washed before dinner.

Matt. xv. 2, the Pharisees quarrelled with the disciples upon this account; here this Pharisee is offended at Christ himself. Mark gives us the reason of it, chap. vii. 3, *For the Pharisees, and all the Jews, except they wash their hands oft, eat not, holding the tradition of the elders*. Concerning this tradition of theirs, and the ground of it, see the notes on Matt. xv. 2, and Mark vii. 3. We would not be infallible, and therefore cannot allow others to differ from us in a rite, which hath no foundation in God's word, and wonder at those who cannot see with our eyes, nor practise according to our latitudes.

^{b Matt. 23. 25.}

39 ^b And the Lord said unto him, Now do ye Pharisees make clean the outside of the cup and the platter; but ^c your inward part is full of ravening and wickedness.

^{c Tit. 1. 15.}

40 *Ye* fools, did not he that made that which is without make that which is within also?

We have much the same, though delivered in another form, with a denunciation of a woe, Matt. xxiii. 25: see the notes on that verse. We must not imagine that our Saviour here reflecteth upon the cleansing of vessels in which we put our meat and drink, for undoubtedly, as to them, the Pharisees washed both the inside and the outside. And the conceit of them is amiss who think that by the *inward part*, ver. 39, he means the meat in their dishes, which was gotten indeed by ravening, and wickedness, extortion, &c.; for it is a hard interpretation of the inward part of the platter, to say, by it is meant the meat in the platter; but neither doth our Saviour say, the inward part of the dish, but *your inward part*, by which he plainly means the soul. Our Saviour doth therefore certainly compare the Pharisees to dishes or platters washed or scoured only on the outside, and blameth their hypocrisy in this, that they were mighty solicitous about an outside purity and cleanness, but for the inward purity of the heart and soul, they took no care at all about that; they were very scrupulous about undefiled hands, but nothing at all about having their souls and inward powers and affections undefiled. This he telleth them was most egregious folly, for God, that made the body, made the soul also, and therefore would exact a purity in the inward as well as the outward man, especially considering that he loveth truth in the inward parts.

41 ^d But rather give alms ‖ of such things as ye have; and, behold, all things are clean unto you.

^{d Is. 58. 7.
Dan. 4. 27.
ch. 12. 33.}

‖ Or, *as you are able.*

Πλὴν τὰ ἐνόντα δότε ἐλεημοσύνην. The word ἐνόντα being a word not ordinarily used in a sense which will fit this place, hath made a great abounding in their own senses amongst interpreters; some translating it, Give such things as are within for alms; others, such things as you have; others, such things as are necessary; others, such things as ye are able, as if κατὰ were to be understood before τὰ ἐνόντα, according to what you have. Others, what things remain, after the serving your own necessities, and a just restitution to those whom you have wronged. Others think it is but a connexion of our Saviour's speech, and the sense is, Moreover there is but one thing to be done, Give alms, &c., as if it were τὸ ἐνόν. I do not see but our own translation is as good as any, and κατὰ seems to be understood in the Greek. According to what you have, which is truly and justly your own, not theirs whom you have wronged, nor your creditors', nor your families', for their necessities; give alms of all that. *And, behold, all things are clean unto you.* Not, your souls are clean; though that must first be, yet our Saviour is not here directing that, or the means and methods for it; but *all things are clean to you*, you may lawfully and without guilt use them: *Unto the pure all things are pure; but unto them that are defiled and unbelieving is nothing pure*, Tit. i. 15. Our Saviour's words are a plain exhortation to repentance, that lieth in the change of our minds; and that inward change of our minds must be evidenced by the change of our actions, and particularly by a restitution in case of wrong done to any. The Pharisees were a covetous, rapacious generation, full of extortion, devouring widows' houses, &c. Their repentance was to be evidenced by contrary works; those were works of justice and mercy. God calleth to the Israelites for the first, Isa. i. 16, 17. Christ calls to the Pharisees for the latter. Such works of mercy as might evidence their hearts to be truly changed: and then, saith our Saviour, all things will be clean to you, which otherwise will not be with all your traditional superstitious washings. And needs it must be so, for no soul can repent truly without the influence and assistance of Divine grace, which God giveth not, but to those souls which are washed with the blood of Christ. So that before a soul can produce the fruits of true repentance, it must be justified by faith, and sanctified by the Spirit of holiness. Or if we understand it only of that repentance which an unjustified soul may have, yet even that may so far profit, as to have our outward things so blessed to us, that we may use them without any pollution or guilt, and have them outwardly blest to us.

S. LUKE XI

e Mat. 23. 23.

42 *But woe unto you, Pharisees! for ye tithe mint and rue and all manner of herbs, and pass over judgment and the love of God: these ought ye to have done, and not to leave the other undone.

See the notes on Matt. xxiii. 23. There are two great notes of hypocrites: 1. To be more exact in and zealous for the observation of rituals and the traditions of men, than in and for the observation of the moral law of God. 2. In matters of morality to be more exact and strict in and for little things, than for things more grave and weighty. There is no commandment of God so little as we may neglect, or despise, or disobey it; but yet there is a difference in duties, and we ought to have more regard to the greater than to the lesser.

f Matt. 23. 6.
Mark 12. 38, 39.

43 'Woe unto you, Pharisees! for ye love the uppermost seats in the synagogues, and greetings in the markets.

See the notes on Matt. xxiii. 6, 7. Their fault was not in their taking them, but in their affecting them, and in being ambitious of them. God is the God of order, and we are bound to give honour to whom honour belongs; but pride and ambition are detestable sins, especially in such as should be teachers of humility, and the vanity of all things below.

g Matt. 23. 27.
h Ps. 5. 9.

44 gWoe unto you, Scribes and Pharisees, hypocrites! hfor ye are as graves which appear not, and the men that walk over *them* are not aware *of them*.

See the notes on Matt. xxiii. 27, where our Saviour compareth the Pharisees to whited sepulchres: here he compareth them to sepulchres, but not as there to denote their hypocrisy, appearing white, but having nothing within but rottenness; but upon the account of the contagion of them, and their pollution of others that were not aware of them. To understand our Saviour, we must consider the Levitical law, Numb. xix. 16; where we shall find that not only he that touched a dead body, but he that touched a grave, was legally unclean for seven days. Christ here alludeth to that, though he be speaking not of legal, but moral uncleanness. By reason of the law afore-mentioned, the Jews took care to whiten their graves, that people might see them, and avoid that danger. To such whited sepulchres Christ compares the Pharisees, Matt. xxiii. 27. But some graves might not be whited, or the colour washed off, so as they did not appear, and men could not be aware of them, but ran into a pollution by them. To such graves he in this place compares them. They were men that externally appeared not to be what they were. The Jews took the Pharisees for great saints, (the strictest sect of their religion,) so strict they were in their duties to their traditions, &c.; which external severity and formal behaviour covered their extortion, and covetousness, and malice, and erroneous opinions, so as people did not suspect them of any such guilt.

45 ¶ Then answered one of the Lawyers, and said unto him, Master, thus saying thou reproachest us also.

This lawyer was a scribe of the law, ver. 44. The work of these men was to interpret the law; the Pharisees strictly observed their decrees and interpretations. The lawyer therefore spake rightly in thinking our Saviour's words had some reflection upon men of his order, but he woefully erred both in thinking his own order was unblamable, and also in calling our Lord's just reproof a reproaching them. But by this he gives an occasion to him, who used rightly to divide the word of God, and to give every one their portion out of it, to let them know wherein they were faulty, as well as the Pharisees.

46 And he said, Woe unto you also, *ye*

i Mat. 23. 4.

Lawyers! ifor ye lade men with burdens grievous to be borne, and ye yourselves touch not the burdens with one of your fingers.

See the notes on Matt. xxiii. 4.

47 kWoe unto you! for ye build the sepulchres of the prophets, and your fathers killed them.

k Matt. 23. 29.

48 Truly ye bear witness that ye allow the deeds of your fathers: for they indeed killed them, and ye build their sepulchres.

49 Therefore also said the wisdom of God, lI will send them prophets and apostles, and *some* of them they shall slay and persecute:

l Mat. 23. 34.

50 That the blood of all the prophets, which was shed from the foundation of the world, may be required of this generation;

51 mFrom the blood of Abel unto nthe blood of Zacharias, which perished between the altar and the temple: verily I say unto you, It shall be required of this generation.

m Gen. 4. 8.
n 2 Chron. 24. 20, 21.

See the notes on Matt. xxiii. 29—36. The Pharisees, like a company of wretched hypocrites, under a pretence of their honouring the memories of the prophets under the Old Testament, took great care to repair and to adorn their sepulchres, while in the mean time their hearts were as full of malice against the truth, and against Christ, and those who came to reveal God's will to them, as ever were their fathers against the prophets; and, saith our Saviour, I, who am the Wisdom of God, tell you, that I shall send you apostles, and prophets, and some of them you shall kill, others ye shall persecute; that all the righteous blood that hath been shed on the earth, from the blood of Abel to the blood of Zacharias, may come on you; which mind being in you, the same as in your persecuting predecessors, your building and adorning the old prophets' tombs is not (as you would have it thought) any testimony of your honour to the prophets, but rather to your fathers that killed them, a kind of trophy for the victory your fathers got over the prophets of the Lord; so as by that act you give a testimony that you own them as your fathers who killed the prophets, and glory in what they did, for if you truly honoured their memory, you would not retain the same malicious, bloody mind. It is gross hypocrisy for men to magnify the servants of God in former ages, and in the mean time to malign and persecute the servants of the same God in a present age, owning but the same truths, and living up to the same rule. See further notes on what is in these verses, in the notes on Matt. xxiii. 29—36, where the same things are said with larger circumstances. They truly honour martyrs, that live the same lives they did, and adhere to the same truths of God, in a testimony to which they died.

52 °Woe unto you, Lawyers! for ye have taken away the key of knowledge: ye enter not in yourselves, and them that were entering in ye ||hindered.

o Mat. 23. 13.

|| Or, *forbad*.

Matthew saith, chap. xxiii. 13, *for ye shut up the kingdom of heaven against men*, &c. I take the sense of these words to be, You have taken away knowledge, which is the key by which men enter into the kingdom of God. Though knowledge itself be but a common gift, and men may have great measures of it, and yet perish for ever, 1 Cor. xiii. 2, yet it is the foundation of all saving grace. *How shall they believe in him of whom they have not heard?* Rom. x. 14. So, how shall they obey a rule they do not know, or repent of those sins which they do not know to be so? So as those that are the hinderers of people's coming to the knowledge of the will of God, are the vilest instruments upon earth in hindering men's and women's salvation. The papists are highly guilty of this, in keeping their laity from the Scriptures in a language intelligible to them. But how were the scribes guilty of this? The Jews were never hindered from reading or hearing of the law; it was read in their synagogues every sabbath day. But we must know that knowledge is highly advantaged by an interpretation of the mind and will of God. But how did the scribes take away this? they preached and interpreted the law of God. *Answ.* They gave not the true sense of it, but so preached that people were scarce any whit the wiser, as to the knowledge of the law of God, only they made people understand their traditions and ceremonies: their doctrines were the traditions of men. Now they occupying the places of teachers, and no better discharging their work, instead of giving, took away knowledge from them, and proved blind leaders of the blind. Whoever they are that arrogate to themselves the office of teaching, and supplying the places of teachers, and either do not make preaching, and instruction of the people under their charge, their business, or who preach in styles and methods their people understand not, or who preach other things than what they prove to be the revealed will of God, fall deeply under the condemnation of this text. See further the notes on Matt. xxiii. 13.

53 And as he said these things unto them, the Scribes and the Pharisees began to urge *him* vehemently, and to provoke him to speak of many things:

[p Mark 12. 13.] 54 Laying wait for him, and p seeking to catch something out of his mouth, that they might accuse him.

Herein the vile genius of these wretched men was seen, Christ was become their enemy because he told them the truth; his reproofs in order to their reformation and amendment do but fill them with madness against him. Nor are wicked and malicious men at any time fair enemies. *They urge him vehemently, and provoke him to speak of many things;* they lie at the catch, in wait for him; hoping that in his many words, and answers to their many captious questions, they should hear something from him, upon which they might form an accusation against him to Pilate, the Roman governor, for his blood was that they thirsted after. If it were thus done to the green tree, let us not wonder if it be so done also to the dry. The hearts and practices of malicious and wicked men, in succeeding generations, do (as in a glass) answer the hearts of persons of their spirits and morals in preceding generations. Malice will never regard justice or equity.

CHAP. XII

Christ teacheth his disciples to avoid hypocrisy, and not to be fearful in publishing his doctrine, 1—12. *He refuseth to be judge in a civil cause, and warneth the people to beware of covetousness by the parable of a rich man, who boasted himself in his multiplied stores*, 13—21. *He exhorteth not to be over-anxious about the provisions of this life; but to seek the kingdom of God*, 22—32; *to lay up treasure in heaven by giving alms*, 33, 34; *and to be always ready against our Lord's coming*, 35—40. *By the parable of a good and a wicked steward he showeth the duty of his ministers in particular*, 41—48. *He foretelleth the divisions on account of the gospel*, 49—53; *reproveth the people for not discerning the times*, 54—56; *and showeth the danger of neglecting the means of reconciliation offered them*, 57—59.

[a Mat. 16. 6. Mark 8. 15.] IN ª the mean time, when there were gathered together an innumerable multitude of people, insomuch that they trode one upon another, he began to say unto [b Mat. 16. 12.] his disciples first of all, ᵇ Beware ye of the leaven of the Pharisees, which is hypocrisy.

We read of such a caution given to the disciples, Matt. xvi. 6. But that is not the same caution with this; there he compared their doctrine to leaven, for the aptness of it to infect others; here he compareth their lives to the same thing, and for the same reason: this appeareth to be the same sense of our Saviour here, because he saith their leaven is hypocrisy. There are none so like to do mischief to the better sort of people, as those that, under a mask and exterior disguise of severity and strictness, indulge themselves in corrupt affections and vicious inclinations.

[c Mat. 10. 26. Mark 4. 22. ch. 8. 17.] 2 ᶜ For there is nothing covered, that shall not be revealed; neither hid, that shall not be known.

It is a proverbial expression: those, and parabolical expressions, may be applied in several cases, and to several subjects: we have met with this before variously applied, Matt. x. 26; Mark iv. 22; and in this Gospel, chap. viii. 17. Here it is applied as an argument against hypocrisy, or the concealing of naughty and corrupt hearts under the vizor and disguise of demure looks, or fair conversation. In the day of judgment sinners shall walk naked, and men shall see their shame; God will in that day make known all the secrets of men's hearts, to be sure the secrets of all their hearts, whose iniquities are not forgiven, and whose sins are not covered.

3 Therefore whatsoever ye have spoken in darkness shall be heard in the light; and that which ye have spoken in the ear in closets shall be proclaimed upon the housetops.

We have something very like this Matt. x. 27, spoken by way of precept. It seemeth to be a sentence also variously applied: it may be left indifferent to the reader, whether he will understand it as a promise of the publication of the gospel, (to which purpose it seems to be spoken in the form of a precept, Matt. x. 27,) or as a further enlargement of his former discourse, ver. 2.

4 ᵈ And I say unto you ᵉ my friends, [d Mat. 10. 28. Is. 51. 7, 8, 12, 13. Jer. 1. 8. e John 15. 14, 15.] Be not afraid of them that kill the body, and after that have no more that they can do.

5 But I will forewarn you whom ye shall fear: Fear him, which after he hath killed hath power to cast into hell; yea, I say unto you, Fear him.

See the notes on Matt. x. 28, where we met with the same. From this to the 13th verse our Saviour armeth his disciples to encounter those storms of persecution which he knew they would meet with after he should be taken up into heaven. Here are two arguments in this verse: 1. The one drawn from the impotency, or limited power, of the most malicious enemies; they can *kill the body*, but can do no more. 2. From the mighty power of God, who can *cast us into hell*. Matthew saith, who can cast body and soul into hell-fire: whence is evident, 1. That there are punishments beyond this life; all men's punishments will not end with the killing of their bodies. 2. That men have souls as well as bodies, and both souls and bodies of sinners will in the resurrection be made capable of eternal punishment. 3. That the ready way to bring us under that misery, is to be more afraid of the wrath of men than of the wrath of God.

6 Are not five sparrows sold for two ‖ farthings, and not one of them is forgotten before God? [‖ See Matt. 10. 29.]

7 But even the very hairs of your head are all numbered. Fear not therefore: ye are of more value than many sparrows.

See the notes on Matt. x. 29—31. Our Saviour's third argument is brought from the providence of God, both his general providence, upholding the beings of all his creatures, so that he forgetteth not a sparrow, though a creature of so minute a value, that *two* of them *are sold for a farthing*, as Matthew saith, or *five for two farthings*, as Luke saith; yea, he so remembereth them, that one of them falls not to the ground without his knowledge and leave, saith Matthew. But besides this, God exerciseth a more special providence towards creatures, with reference to their dignity and excellency. Now, (saith our Saviour,) *you are of more value than many sparrows;* you are so as men, you are more so as my disciples, especially as my ministers and ambassadors. *The very hairs of your head are numbered;* God will regard your most minute concerns.

8 ᶠ Also I say unto you, Whosoever shall confess me before men, him shall the Son of man also confess before the angels of God: [f Mat. 10. 32. Mark 8. 38. 2 Tim. 2. 12. 1 John 2. 23.]

9 But he that denieth me before men shall be denied before the angels of God.

See the notes on Matt. x. 32, 33. Here is a fourth and

fifth argument, drawn from the rewards and punishments of such as shall confess or deny Christ before men. Confession here signifies, the owning and adhering to the truths and ways of God in a time of opposition: the reward promised is, Christ's owning those that do it at the day of judgment; *before the Father*, saith Matthew; *before the angels*, saith Luke. Christ hath no need of our owning him, his truth and ways; we may by it be profitable to ourselves, but not to him: we shall have need in the day of judgment of Christ's owning us. By the denial of Christ, is meant our apostacy from the truths or ways of God, the denial of his truths, ways, or interest in this world: it implies a persecuting of them, but signifieth something much less, a denial by words, or a forsaking and not adhering to them. The punishment will be Christ's denial of us in the day of judgment. What that signifieth Matthew tells us, chap. vii. 23, *I will profess unto them, I never knew you: depart from me,* I know you not, *ye that work iniquity.* And, *he shall say to them on his left hand, Depart from me, ye cursed, into everlasting fire, prepared for the devil and his angels,* Matt. xxv. 41. This must be understood not of such as deny him, as Peter did, in an hour of great temptation, and then go out and weep bitterly, and again return unto him, but of such as persist in such denials, and return not to confess him.

g Matt. 12. 31, 32.
Mark 3. 28.
1 John 5. 16.

10 And ᵍ whosoever shall speak a word against the Son of man, it shall be forgiven him: but unto him that blasphemeth against the Holy Ghost it shall not be forgiven.

See the notes on Matt. xii. 31, and on Mark iii. 28, 29.

h Mat. 10.19.
Mark 13. 11.
ch. 21. 14.

11 ʰ And when they bring you unto the synagogues, and *unto* magistrates, and powers, take ye no thought how or what thing ye shall answer, or what ye shall say:

12 For the Holy Ghost shall teach you in the same hour what ye ought to say.

See the notes on Matt. x. 19, 20; Mark xiii. 11.

13 ¶ And one of the company said unto him, Master, speak to my brother, that he divide the inheritance with me.

i John 18.36.

14 And he said unto him, ⁱ Man, who made me a judge or a divider over you?

This passage certainly is not recorded for nothing; if it teacheth us any thing, it is this, That matters of civil justice belong not to those whom Christ sends to preach his gospel: that work is enough for them. Christ here refuseth the office so much as of an arbitrator. A very learned author tells us, that the practice of bringing civil matters before ecclesiastical men, as judges, began in the captivity of Babylon, the Jews by that means avoiding the bringing their differences before pagan judges, which the apostle also persuadeth at large to the primitive Christians, in 1 Cor. vi. 1, 2, &c. But that the ministers of the gospel should be employed, or might be employed, in them, doth not appear by the apostle; nay, he speaks the contrary, 1 Cor. vi. 4, *Set them to judge who are least esteemed in the church:* these surely were not the elders in it. Under the Romans, the Jews had more liberty, having civil courts made up of persons of their own religion, to whom our Saviour turns over this man; being not willing to move out of his calling, as a minister of the gospel. As Christ's commissioners, it is most certain that no ministers of the gospel can intermeddle in civil judgments; whether those who are such commissioners of Christ may yet as men's commissioners act, it stands those in hand who are ambitious of such an employment, and can find leisure enough for it, and are called to it, to inquire: I shall not intermeddle in that controversy. To me, the proper work of the gospel is work enough.

k 1 Tim. 6. 7, &c.

15 And he said unto them, ᵏ Take heed, and beware of covetousness: for a man's life consisteth not in the abundance of the things which he possesseth.

The πλεονεξία, here translated *covetousness*, is an immoderate desire of having of this world's goods, which discovers itself either by unrighteous acts in procuring, or uncharitable omissions for the keeping, of the things of this life. It is that φιλαργυρία, *love of money*, which the apostle determineth to be *the root of all evil*. It is also discovered by a too much thoughtfulness what we shall eat, drink, or put on, or by the too great meltings of our hearts into our bags of gold or silver. All these come under the notion of that covetousness which is here forbidden. In short, whatsoever it is that hindereth our contentment with the portion God giveth us upon our endeavours, though it amounteth to no more than food and raiment, according to the apostle's precept, 1 Tim. vi. 8; Heb. xiii. 5. This is what Christ warneth his disciples to beware of; he gives us the reason, *for a man's life consisteth not in the abundance of what he possesseth:* which is true, whether we understand by *life* the subsisting and upholding of our life, or (as *life* is often taken) for the happiness and felicity of our lives. Abundance is not necessary to uphold our lives. *Ad manum est quod sat est,* saith Seneca, Nature is content with a little. *Sudamus ad supervacanea,* (saith he,) We sweat only to get superfluities. Nor will abundance protect our lives; it will not keep off an enemy, but rather tempt him; nor fence out a disease, but rather contribute to it, as engaging us in immoderate cares or labours to procure and keep it, or as exposing us to temptations to riot and debauchery, by which men's lives are often shortened. Nor doth the happiness of life lie in the abundance of what we possess. Some philosophers determined rightly, that something of this world's good is necessary to our happiness of life, but abundance is not. The poor are as merry, and many times more satisfied, more healthy, and at more ease, than those that have abundance. It is a golden sentence, which deserves to be engraven in every soul.

16 And he spake a parable unto them, saying, The ground of a certain rich man brought forth plentifully:

17 And he thought within himself, saying, What shall I do, because I have no room where to bestow my fruits?

18 And he said, This will I do: I will pull down my barns, and build greater; and there will I bestow all my fruits and my goods.

19 And I will say to my soul, ˡ Soul, thou hast much goods laid up for many years; take thine ease, eat, drink, *and* be merry.

l Eccl. 11. 9.
Ecclus. 11.
19. 1 Cor. 15. 32. Jam. 5.5.

20 But God said unto him, *Thou fool, this night* ‖ ᵐ thy soul shall be required of thee: ⁿ then whose shall those things be, which thou hast provided?

‖ Or, *do they require thy soul.*
m Job 20.22. & 27. 8.
Jam. 4. 14.
n Ps. 39. 6.
Jer. 17. 11.
o Mat. 6. 20. ver. 33.
1 Tim. 6. 18, 19. Jam. 2.5.

21 So *is* he that layeth up treasure for himself, ᵒ and is not rich toward God.

The evangelist lets us know, that these verses contain not a narrative of a matter of fact, but only a representation of something that is too ordinary, by a fictitious story. The scope of it is to justify what our Saviour had said in the verse immediately preceding, that a man's life lieth not in the abundance of what he possesseth; for he who hath the greatest possessions may die as soon as he who hath not where to lay down his head, and may be taken away at a time when he is enjoying the fullest satisfactions that he can promise himself, or the creature can afford him. Therefore he acteth not like a wise and rational man, that takes care to lay up for himself treasure on earth, and in the mean time neglecteth the riches of grace. The sense of the parable is to be learned from the ἐπὶ παραβολῇ, which we have ver. 21, *So is he that layeth up treasure for himself;* so foolish and unwise is he, &c. But from this parable we may make general observations: 1. That God maketh his sun to shine and his rain to fall on the just and on the unjust. Men may have laid up much earthly treasure, who are yet very poor towards God. 2. That the increase of riches increaseth care. The rich man saith, *What shall I do?* The difference betwixt the beggar and the rich man is but this: both are saying, What shall I do?

The beggar saith, What shall I do to get money? the other saith, What shall I do with it now I have it? 3. Worldly men's fruits are their goods, ver. 3; they are so in their estimation, and they are so as they are the whole portion that such should have from God. 4. Great estates and enjoyments of this life have a very enticing quality in them. (1.) They make us loth to die, and willing to think we shall live many years. (2.) They entice us to a spiritual sloth and security, and to sing a requiem to our souls. (3.) They entice us to sinful mirth and luxury; *Eat, drink, and be merry.* 5. He that hath most may have his soul taken from him in a night. 6. A man is no longer owner of the goods of this life, than he can keep an earthly possession of them. 7. When he dies, he knoweth not whose those things shall be; not whether his son or strangers shall inherit them; nor, if his son doth happen to meet with the countenance of the law, doth he know whether that son shall be a wise man or a fool. 8. Hence it appears to be the most egregious folly imaginable, for men to spend their time and strength in getting and laying up treasure upon earth, in the mean time neglecting, or not duly endeavouring, to be rich towards God; both, (1.) In that grace by which the soul is justified and accepted; and also, (2.) In that grace in the exercise of which alone he may glorify God. This latter is that which the apostle calls, a being *rich in good works, ready to distribute, willing to communicate,* &c., 1 Tim. vi. 18; where he mentioneth only one species of good works. For whereas wisdom lies in the choice of the best end, and then of the best means to obtain it, and the best circumstances in the use of those means, the worldly man failing in the first, not choosing the best end, must needs be a spiritual fool. And indeed, of all folly that is the greatest which is seen in the choice of a worse and more ignoble end, before that which is of more advantage, more noble, and excellent; as certainly the acquiring of an eternal happiness and felicity is before an acquiring a mere transitory and uncertain felicity and satisfaction.

22 ¶ And he said unto his disciples, Therefore I say unto you, ᵖTake no thought for your life, what ye shall eat; neither for the body, what ye shall put on.

p Mat. 6. 25.

23 The life is more than meat, and the body *is more* than raiment.

24 Consider the ravens: for they neither sow nor reap; which neither have storehouse nor barn; and ᑫGod feedeth them: how much more are ye better than the fowls?

q Job 38. 41. Ps. 147. 9.

25 And which of you with taking thought can add to his stature one cubit?

26 If ye then be not able to do that thing which is least, why take ye thought for the rest?

27 Consider the lilies how they grow: they toil not, they spin not; and yet I say unto you, that Solomon in all his glory was not arrayed like one of these.

28 If then God so clothe the grass, which is to day in the field, and to morrow is cast into the oven; how much more *will he clothe* you, O ye of little faith?

29 And seek not ye what ye shall eat, or what ye shall drink, ‖ neither be ye of doubtful mind.

‖ Or, *live not in careful suspence.*

30 For all these things do the nations of the world seek after: and your Father knoweth that ye have need of these things.

See the notes on Matt. vi. 25—32, where we before met with all that is here. The thoughtfulness here forbidden is not moderate, prudent thoughtfulness, or care; but, 1. A distrustful thoughtfulness; 2. Distracting or dividing cares, such as make a man live in suspense, and to be wavering as a meteor, μὴ μετεωρίζεσθε; or, 3. A thoughtfulness for high things, as some interpret that word; but possibly it better signifies such a thoughtfulness to be forbidden, as keeps the mind of man from rest, in a continual motion and fluctuation; or, 4. Any such thoughtfulness as is inconsistent with our seeking first the kingdom of God. Against this thoughtfulness our Lord arms his disciples with the consideration, 1. Of their dependence on God necessarily for their lives, which are better than meat and raiment, ver. 23. 2. Of the providence of God, which extending to all orders of creatures, particularly to such as merely have life, (such are vegetables, the grass and flowers,) and such as have only life and sense, (such are the ravens,) it cannot be reasonably presumed that it will be wanting to men, who are the most noble order of sublunary creatures, having being, life, sense, and reason (which is the image of God in man). 3. From the consideration of the vanity of this care, by which we cannot contribute a cubit to our stature. 4. From the consideration that the heathens make these things their care, whom Christians ought to excel, as knowing more, and living under more excellent hopes and promises than they have. Lastly, From the consideration of their relation to God as a Father, and their Father's knowing what they have need of, of whom therefore it were unreasonable to presume, that he should suffer them to want what is necessary for his children. See more in the notes before mentioned on Matt. vi. 25—32.

31 ¶ ʳBut rather seek ye the kingdom of God; and all these things shall be added unto you.

r Mat. 6. 33.

Matthew saith, *seek first the kingdom of God, and his righteousness; and all these things shall be added,* &c. The particle πλὴν prefixed here to ζητεῖτε, (which we translate *rather seek,*) doth expound Matthew's πρῶτον, *seek first,* and likewise expounds our Saviour's meaning, when he said, Take no thought, what ye should eat, &c.; that is, let not those be your only or principal thoughts, *quin etiam, tantum maxime,* but also, and mostly, or chiefly, *seek ye the kingdom of God,* that kingdom mentioned in the next verse, *and all these things shall be added to you;* either an affluence of them; or a sufficiency of them, with a contented, satisfied mind. See more in the notes on Matt. vi. 33.

32 Fear not, little flock; for ˢit is your Father's good pleasure to give you the kingdom.

s Mat. 11. 25, 26.

Our Saviour had mentioned a kingdom, ver. 31. How much too big a thought was this for fishermen, and others of his poor hearers, to entertain! he therefore here assureth them of the thing, that they should have a kingdom, and showeth them that their title to it was his and their Father's will; though they were a little flock, and so not likely to conquer a kingdom upon earth for themselves, yet they should have a kingdom from the free donation of him, who had kingdoms to give, and would give it to them, because he was their Father. By this kingdom can be understood nothing else but that state of honour, glory, and dignity which believers shall have in the world that is to come; which they shall have not from merit, but gift; not from the first good motions and inclinations of their own will, but from the free motions of the Divine will; and therefore they had no reason to fear that God would not provide food convenient for them. He that had provided a kingdom for them, which he would one day give unto them, would certainly provide bread for them, and give it to them.

33 ᵗSell that ye have, and give alms; ᵘprovide yourselves bags which wax not old, a treasure in the heavens that faileth not, where no thief approacheth, neither moth corrupteth.

t Mat. 19. 21. Acts 2. 45. & 4. 34.
u Mat. 6. 20. ch. 16. 9.
1 Tim. 6. 19.

34 For where your treasure is, there will your heart be also.

The immutable purpose of the Divine Being to glorify the disciples of Christ, the freedom of the Divine will in the gift of heaven and glory, are neither of them exclusive of, but include and suppose, their duty to use such due means as he hath directed them, in the use of which they shall obtain what he hath purposed for them, and promised to them; some of which are here directed and prescribed. *Sell that ye have, and give alms,* &c. It is a precept of the same import with that, Matt. xix. 21; Mark x. 21. Though possibly the precept here given to the disciples of Christ generally is not to be interpreted so strictly as seemeth to be our Saviour's meaning in those texts, as to the young man. For it seems to have been a special precept to him, laying an obligation upon him to make a present actual sale of all he had, and it is plain that he so understood it. To this Christians are not obliged generally by this precept: but to be ready at the call and command of God to part with all, for such uses as God should show them: not to set their heart on riches, Psal. lxii. 10; to be *ready to distribute*, and *willing to communicate*, 1 Tim. vi. 18; remembering that God loveth mercy rather than sacrifice, Hos. vi. 6; Matt. ix. 13. To give of our superfluities, Luke iii. 11. To *make friends* of our *mammon of unrighteousness*, Luke xvi. 9. Nay, if the necessities of the people of God be such as requires it, for the subsistence of Christians, to sell what we have, rather than others of God's people should starve, calling nothing our own in such a case; which Christians did in the primitive state of the church, Acts iv. 34—37. For the other part of ver. 33, 34, see the notes on Matt. vi. 20, 21.

x Eph. 6. 14.
1 Pet. 1. 13.
y Matt. 25.
1, &c.

35 ˣLet your loins be girded about, and ʸ*your* lights burning;

36 And ye yourselves like unto men that wait for their lord, when he will return from the wedding; that when he cometh and knocketh, they may open unto him immediately.

The first words of ver. 40, *Be ye therefore ready also*, expound ver. 35. In this sense we find the phrase used, 1 Kings xviii. 46; 2 Kings iv. 29; ix. 1; Job xxxviii. 3; xl. 7; Jer. i. 17. In those Eastern countries both masters and servants were wont to wear long garments, which they were wont to gird up, either when they went to fight, or when they were to travel, Exod. xii. 11; 1 Kings xviii. 46; or when they went about any service; see chap. xvii. 8; John xiii. 4: this was a piece of their preparation. We read of the girding about of the loins of the mind with truth, Eph. vi. 14, and with habits of grace and virtue; 1 Pet. i. 13, *Wherefore gird up the loins of your minds, be sober, and hope to the end.* The other phrase, *and your lights burning*, is of the same import, relating to the Lord's coming from the wedding, mentioned ver. 36; for in those countries their weddings were celebrated in the night. Christ's coming to judgment, whether our particular or the more general judgment, is that which is here set out to us, under the notion of a man's coming home late at night from a wedding. Nor improperly, for in this life souls are united to Christ, Eph. v. 32. When Christ shall have done his work of that nature upon the earth, that all the elect shall be gathered, then shall he come to judge the world. He would have all his people be ready for that day, and waiting for their Lord, that his coming may be welcome to them.

z Matt. 24. 46.

37 ᶻBlessed *are* those servants, whom the lord when he cometh shall find watching: verily I say unto you, that he shall gird himself, and make them to sit down to meat, and will come forth and serve them.

38 And if he shall come in the second watch, or come in the third watch, and find *them* so, blessed are those servants.

a Mat. 24. 43.
1 Thess. 5. 2.
2 Pet. 3. 10.
Rev. 3. 3.
& 16. 15.

39 ᵃAnd this know, that if the goodman of the house had known what hour the thief would come, he would have watched, and not have suffered his house to be broken through.

b Matt. 24. 44. & 25. 13.
Mark 13. 33.
ch. 21. 34, 36.
1 Thess. 5. 6.
2 Pet. 3. 12.

40 ᵇBe ye therefore ready also: for the Son of man cometh at an hour when ye think not.

The duty which Christ is here pressing upon his hearers is watchfulness, which signifieth, 1. A negation of sleep; 2. An industrious keeping ourselves awake with reference to some particular end. The end here expressed is the happy receiving of Christ, coming to judgment; from whence is evident, that the watching here intended is a spiritual watching, which is a denial of ourselves as to our lusts, and the sleep of sin, which is compared to sleep, Rom. xiii. 11; Eph. v. 14, and an industrious keeping ourselves from such sleep in order to the coming of our Lord, who will come at an hour when we think not, ver. 40; his coming is to us uncertain, and will be to many surprising. This watchfulness he presseth upon his hearers. 1. From the reward the Lord will give to such persons: *He shall gird himself, and make them to sit down to meat, and will come forth and serve them*: very high metaphorical expressions, signifying no more, than that he will put upon them a very high honour and dignity, and satisfy them with a fulness of happiness and glory, and they shall be at rest for ever. The state of glory is elsewhere set out under the notion of drinking new wine in the kingdom of God, and eating and drinking in his kingdom. 2. From the benefit which they will have by watching in this; that let the Lord come when he will, whether in the second or third watch, they will be ready, and they shall be blessed. 3. He presseth it also from the ordinary prudence of men, who if they have an intimation that a thief is coming, will watch, and prevent the mischief that might ensue by the breaking open of their houses. But concerning those words, see the notes on Matt. xxiv. 43, 44, where we met with them before used upon the same occasion.

41 ¶ Then Peter said unto him, Lord, speakest thou this parable unto us, or even to all?

42 And the Lord said, ᶜWho then is that faithful and wise steward, whom *his* lord shall make ruler over his houshold, to give *them their* portion of meat in due season?

c Matt. 24. 45. & 25. 21.
1 Cor. 4. 2.

43 Blessed *is* that servant, whom his lord when he cometh shall find so doing.

44 ᵈOf a truth I say unto you, that he will make him ruler over all that he hath.

d Matt. 24. 47.

45 ᵉBut and if that servant say in his heart, My lord delayeth his coming; and shall begin to beat the menservants and maidens, and to eat and drink, and to be drunken;

e Matt. 24. 48.

46 The lord of that servant will come in a day when he looketh not for *him*, and at an hour when he is not aware, and will ‖ cut him in sunder, and will appoint him his portion with the unbelievers.

‖ Or, *cut him off.* Matt. 24. 51.

47 And ᶠthat servant, which knew his lord's will, and prepared not *himself*, neither did according to his will, shall be beaten with many *stripes*.

f Num. 15. 30. Deu. 25. 2. John 9. 41. & 15. 22.
Acts 17. 30.
Jam. 4. 17.

48 ᵍBut he that knew not, and did commit things worthy of stripes, shall be beaten with few *stripes*. For unto whomsoever much is given, of him shall be much required: and to whom men have committed much, of him they will ask the more.

g Lev. 5. 17.
1 Tim. 1. 13.

See the notes on Matt. xxiv. 45—51, where we met with the same parable, but here expressed more largely, and with more circumstances. Matthew hath not the introduction to it which we have here, ver. 41. It was occasioned from Peter's saying to Christ, *Lord, speakest thou this parable unto us, or unto all?* Doth this duty of watchfulness concern all thy disciples, or only us, that are thine apostles, the ministers of thy gospel? The substance of what our Lord saith in answer to Peter, from ver. 42 to ver. 48, is, Peter, I spake it to all, I have not the meanest hearer but is concerned to watch against my coming; but you that are ministers of my gospel are most eminently concerned. Others are concerned, upon the pain of eternal damnation, to have the loins of their understandings girt about with truth, the loins of their minds girt with sobriety and hope, to have their lights burning, to be every way and always ready, watching against sin, abstaining from it, and industriously keeping themselves from any obedience to their lusts, in a prospect of my coming to judgment. But you that are to be ministers are more highly concerned than others. You are the rulers of my household, the stewards of my mysteries, 1 Cor. iv. 1; your work is to give the rest of my people *their portion of meat in due season;* if you faithfully do this, you shall be blessed, holding on in doing of it to your lives' end, so as your Lord find you so doing. But if any of you shall be found, who out of any atheistical principles, in not heart believing what you preach to others, but saying, either that I will not come, or not so soon but you may sleep awhile, and wake time enough to prepare for my coming; if they who should be examples to my flock, and are the rulers over them, shall give reins to their lusts, and eat with the gluttons, and drink with the drunkards; if they who should feed my flock, shall fail to the worrying of it, instead of feeding, beating my men-servants and maidens; the Lord will not spare them long, but be upon them before they are aware, καὶ διχοτομήσει, and cut them to pieces, (the word signifies to divide into two parts,) as those nations were wont to serve the vilest transgressors, traitors, and rebels, and violaters of their covenants; they shall be most severely dealt withal, ver. 47, they *shall be beaten with many stripes,* because they knew their Master's will, and did it not. Ignorance of the Divine will will not wholly excuse the sinner, he shall be beaten, but his stripes shall be few, his damnation shall be gentle compared with a minister's, that knows his Master's will, but doth it not; teacheth it to others, but doth it not himself. Our Saviour further tells them, that this just judgment of God upon lewd and scandalous ministers, is justified by the ordinary practice of men, who require much where they give much, and ask much of those to whom they have committed great trusts. God looks upon wicked, loose, and scandalous and mischievous ministers as the greatest transgressors, and he will deal with them as such. There will be degrees in the punishment as well as in the rewards of another life. Such persons as have taken upon them to be the rulers of Christ's household, the stewards of his mysteries, if they be vile and wicked, if they be not faithful in giving the servants of Christ's household their portion in its season, must expect the deepest place in the bottomless pit: they know more than others, they have more committed to their trust than others, their examples do more harm than others, their sins are greater than others, and the fiery furnace will for them be heated over seven times.

h ver. 51. 49 ¶ ʰI am come to send fire on the earth; and what will I, if it be already kindled?

Some of the ancients here by *fire* understood the Holy Ghost, or the preaching of the gospel, with those flames of love and holy affections which that causeth in the hearts of good people; but this interpretation cannot but be looked upon as strained to those who compare this verse with ver. 51—53, and the parallel text in Matt. x. 34—36. By *fire* here therefore is to be understood the dissension or *division* mentioned ver. 51, with all those persecutions, wars, &c. which are the effects of it. A prediction or threatening of persecutions or wars, or any kind of troubled state of things, is often expressed in holy writ under the notion of fire, and water, or a flood, for though fire and water are opposite in their qualities, yet they both agree in the common effect of consumption, wasting, and desolation. Christ saith he came to send it, because he foresaw this would be a certain consequent, though not a proper and natural effect, of the preaching of the gospel. Christ may be said to come to send a fire, in the same sense as he that is employed in the removal of a filthy dunghill may be said to come to send a stench; his design is to carry the muck away, and in due time he will have done it, but in the mean time it sends out a much greater stench than before it was stirred. *And what will I, if it be already kindled?* Not to take notice of what critical authors say about the signification of the particles or the phrase here used, I take the true sense to be, I desire nothing more than that it were already kindled; nor was this any more inconsistent with the goodness and holiness of Christ, than for a goldsmith to wish the fire was kindled that should separate the dross from the pure metal, or than for Christ to desire that his floor were thoroughly purged. Christ doth not desire the fire for the fire's sake, but for the sake of that effect it would have, in separating in his church the good from the bad; it was a thing he saw would be through the opposition the world would give to the preaching of the gospel, before his gospel would obtain in the world; I would, saith he, that what they do they would do quickly, that they would spit their venom, that my Father might make their wrath to praise him. Whereas some interpret it indicatively, as if the fire were already begun, εἰ ἤδη ἀνήαφη can hardly be so interpreted.

50 But ⁱI have a baptism to be baptized with; and how am I ‖ straitened till it be accomplished!   i Mat. 20. 22. Mark 10. 38. ‖ Or, *pained.*

This baptism, spoken of here by our Saviour, is the same mentioned Matt. xx. 22, 23, and can be understood of nothing but his passion, the accomplishment of which he hinteth us was to be before the fire (before mentioned) would blaze up on the earth. Concerning this he saith he was *straitened till it was accomplished:* not that he willed the influencing of the heart of Judas to betray him, the heart of Pilate to condemn him, or the hearts of the wicked Jews to accuse, condemn, and crucify him; but he willed these events, for the manifestation of the glory of his Father, in the redemption of the world by him. As the woman big with child heartily wisheth that the hour of her travail were come and over, not for the pain's sake, which she must endure, but for her own ease' sake, and the joy she should have of a child born into the world.

51 ᵏSuppose ye that I am come to give peace on earth? I tell you, Nay; ˡbut rather division: k Matt. 10. 34. ver. 49. l Mic. 7. 6. John 7. 43. & 9. 16. & 10. 19.

52 ᵐFor from henceforth there shall be five in one house divided, three against two, and two against three.   m Matt. 10. 35.

53 The father shall be divided against the son, and the son against the father; the mother against the daughter, and the daughter against the mother; the mother in law against her daughter in law, and the daughter in law against her mother in law.

See the notes on Matt. x. 34, 35. Our Saviour in these words doth but pursue the same argument which began ver. 49, to show what would be the consequences of the doctrine of the gospel. And hereby they might have understood a design in our Saviour to convince them, that the business of the Messiah whom they expect was not to exercise a temporal but a spiritual kingdom and power, not to restore to their nation a civil peace, but to purchase their peace with God, and to bring them to that joy and peace which is consequent to believing. For as to the external state of things, it would be much more troubled than it was before; our Lord foresaw how tenacious both the Jews and pagans, and in succeeding ages Christians also, would be of their idolatries and superstitious rites and usages, with whom their believing relations not complying, there would be greater feuds and animosities arise than ever were before; the father would hate the son, the son the father, &c. Before the gospel came amongst the heathens, they were entirely the devil's kingdom, which is not divided against itself. But when by Christ those who belonged to the election of grace should be separated, through the devil's rage and men's lusts, there would be continual feuds and divisions.

54 ¶ And he said also to the people, ⁿWhen ye see a cloud rise out of the west, straightway ye say, There cometh a shower; and so it is.   n Mat. 16. 2.

55 And when *ye see* the south wind blow, ye say, There will be heat; and it cometh to pass.

56 Ye hypocrites, ye can discern the face of the sky and of the earth; but how is it that ye do not discern this time?

We met with a discourse of the same nature Matt. xvi. 2, 3: see the notes there. The sense of our Saviour is, that God by his prophets had given them more certain signs and revelations of the coming of the Messiah, and of the nature of his kingdom, and the effects and consequences of it, than were written in nature of any natural effects; and upbraids their stupid ignorance and unbelief, that they could give credit to and discern the latter and not the former, whereas the former were much more certain.

57 Yea, and why even of yourselves judge ye not what is right?

o Prov. 25. 8.
Matt. 5. 25.
p See Ps. 32. 6. Is. 55. 6.

58 ¶ °When thou goest with thine adversary to the magistrate, ᴾ*as thou art* in the way, give diligence that thou mayest be delivered from him; lest he hale thee to the judge, and the judge deliver thee to the officer, and the officer cast thee into prison.

59 I tell thee, thou shalt not depart thence, till thou hast paid the very last ‖mite.

‖ See Mark 12. 42.

Our Saviour made use of this expression, Matt. v. 25, 26, to persuade peace betwixt brethren; here he useth it to persuade men to acquaint themselves with God, and be at peace. He had been treating of the last judgment; there was no fitter foundation upon which he could build an exhortation to repentance, and making our peace with God. In not doing of it, he telleth his hearers that they did not of themselves judge what was right, for if they did, they would judge themselves as much concerned to come to an agreement with God, as they did ordinarily to come to an agreement with men. Now if amongst men they had an adversary, they did not judge it prudence to stand out with him till the sentence of the judge were past, and they were imprisoned, not to come out till they had paid every farthing of the debt and charges wherein they were condemned; but to agree while they were in the way, before they came to a final judgment in the case, that so, having compounded the case, they might avoid the judgment. So in the case betwixt God and their souls, if they judged right, they would judge that it was not their wisdom to stand out till the irrevocable sentence of condemnation was passed upon them, but *in the way,* during the time of this life, they would make their peace with God, and reform their lives before that great and terrible day came. It is a sign the papists are at a woeful loss for arguments to prove purgatory, when they make use of this text, because it is said, *thou shalt not depart thence till thou hast paid the very last mite,* as if this text spake of a prison for souls from which there is an outlet. Such another argument will prove, from Psal. cx. 1, that Christ shall not sit at the right hand of his Father, because God only said to him, Sit there *until I make thine enemies thy footstool;* and that Joseph knew Mary after Christ was born, because it is said, Matt. i. 25, *he knew her not till she had brought forth her firstborn Son.* But we have before showed that that term, though it be exclusive of a time past, yet doth not determine a future time.

CHAP. XIII

Christ showeth that temporal calamities are no sure signs of sinfulness, but that others should take warning by them, and repent, 1—5. *The parable of the fig tree that was ordered to be cut down for being fruitless,* 6—9. *Christ healeth a woman that had been long bowed together, and putteth the hypocritical ruler of the synagogue to silence,* 10—17. *He likeneth the progress of the gospel to a grain of mustard seed,* 18, 19; *and to leaven,* 20—22. *Being asked of the number of the saved, he exhorteth to strive to enter in at the strait gate,* 23—30. *He will not be diverted from his course through fear of Herod; and lamenteth over the approaching desolation of Jerusalem,* 31—35.

THERE were present at that season some that told him of the Galilæans, whose blood Pilate had mingled with their sacrifices.

2 And Jesus answering said unto them, Suppose ye that these Galilæans were sinners above all the Galilæans, because they suffered such things?

3 I tell you, Nay: but, except ye repent, ye shall all likewise perish.

4 Or those eighteen, upon whom the tower in Siloam fell, and slew them, think ye that they were ‖sinners above all men that dwelt in Jerusalem?

‖ Or, debtors.
Matt. 18. 24. ch. 11. 4.

5 I tell you, Nay: but, except ye repent, ye shall all likewise perish.

The Holy Scriptures giving us no account of these two stories to which our Saviour doth here refer, and those who have wrote the history of the Jews having given us no account of them, interpreters are at a great loss to determine any thing about them. We read of one Judas of Galilee, who drew away much people after him, and perished, Acts v. 37. It is said that he seduced people from their obedience to the Roman emperor, persuading them not to acknowledge him as their governor, nor to pay tribute to the Romans. It is guessed by interpreters, that some of this faction coming up to the passover, (for they were Jews,) Pilate fell upon them, and slew them while they were sacrificing. Others think that these were some remnant of Judas's faction, but Samaritans, and slain while they were sacrificing at their temple in Mount Gerizim, and that (though Samaritans) they were called Galileans, because Judas, the head of their faction, was such. The reader is at liberty to choose which of these he thinks most probable, for I find no other account given by any. The latter is prejudiced by our Saviour's calling them Galileans, and advantaged by the desperate hatred which the Jews had to the Samaritans, which might make them more prone to censure any passages of Divine providence severe towards them. But what the certain crime or provocation was we cannot say; we are sure that *de facto* the thing was true, Pilate did mingle the blood of some Galileans with their sacrifices, of which a report was brought to Christ. We are at the same loss for those *eighteen upon whom the tower in Siloam fell.* Siloe, or Siloa, was the name of a small fountain at the foot of Mount Zion, which, as we are told, did not constantly, but at certain times, send out waters, which running through hollow places of the earth, and mines and quarries of stone, made a great noise. Isaiah mentions it, chap. viii. 6. There was also a pool in Jerusalem which had that name, and had a wall built by it, Neh. iii. 15. Christ sent the blind man to go and wash there, John ix. 7. Turrets are (as we know) very usual upon walls. It seems one of these towers fell, and slew eighteen persons, come thither either to wash themselves, or by reason of some healing virtue in those waters, upon what occasion we cannot determine; but there they perished. This story seems to have been something older than the other. Our Saviour either had heard what some people had said, or at least knew what they would say upon those accidents, for we are mightily prone to pass uncharitable judgments upon persons perishing suddenly, especially if they die by a violent death. As he therefore took all occasions to press upon them repentance, so he doth not think fit to omit one so fair; and though he doth not, by what he saith, forbid us to observe such extraordinary providences, and to whom they happen, but willeth us to hear and fear; yet he tells them, there were many Galileans as bad as they, who unless they repented, that is, being sensible of, heartily turned from, the wickedness of their ways, would perish also: thereby teaching us, 1. That punishments come upon people for their sins, and more signal punishments for more signal sinnings. 2. That although God sometimes by his providence signally punisheth some for notorious sinnings, yet he spareth more such sinners than he so signally punisheth. 3. That therefore none can conclude from such signal punishments, that such persons punished were greater sinners than they. 4. That the best use we can make of such reports, and spectacles of notorious sinners, more than ordinarily punished, is to examine ourselves, and to repent, lest we also perish.

6 ¶ He spake also this parable; ᵃA certain *man* had a fig tree planted in his vineyard; and he came and sought fruit thereon, and found none.

a Is. 5. 2.
Matt. 21. 19.

7 Then said he unto the dresser of his vine-

yard, Behold, these three years I come seeking fruit on this fig tree, and find none: cut it down; why cumbereth it the ground?

8 And he answering said unto him, Lord, let it alone this year also, till I shall dig about it, and dung *it:*

9 And if it bear fruit, *well:* and if not, *then* after that thou shalt cut it down.

This parable very fitly cohereth with the preceding discourse: there he had let his hearers know, that though God spareth some sinners, and hath a longer patience with them than others, though they be every whit as great transgressors, in expectation still that they should bring forth fruit; yet if they answer not the means which God useth with them to bring them to repentance, they shall not be spared long, but vengeance shall overtake them also. Those who think that this parable concerned not the Jews only, but all mankind, or more especially those who are in the pale of the church, judge well, provided that they allow it to have been spoken with a primary reference to that nation, amongst whom Christ had now been preaching and working miracles three years, and expected the fruits of repentance and reformation from them in vain. I do not think it any prejudice to this, that the vine-dresser begged but for one year longer, whereas after this Christ had patience with them forty years, before they were destroyed; for *one year* may not be intended strictly, (though the *three years* be,) but to signify some little time more, that the apostles might use all probable means to reclaim them, and make them more fruitful. Grotius thinks the term of *three years* is used, because every fig tree (not wholly barren) brought forth fruit one year in three; which notion (if true) of that plant is valuable, but may be of ill consequence, if any should thence conclude, that men's days of grace exceed not three years: yet thus much is observable, that when God sends a faithful minister to a place, the greatest success and blessing of his ministry is within a few of his first years in a place. The parable doubtless extendeth much further than to the people of the Jews, and learns us all these lessons: 1. That where God plants any one within the pale of his church, he looks he or she should bring forth the fruits of repentance and faith. 2. That many are so planted, yet bring forth no fruit. 3. That there is a determined time beyond which God will not bear with barren souls. 4. That barren souls are not only useless, but also spoil others; τὴν γῆν καταργεῖ, they make the soil unprofitable: a quench coal spoils the fire. 5. That faithful ministers will be very earnest with God to spare even barren souls. 6. That it is their work and duty to use all probable means to make barren souls fruitful. I will *dig about it, and dung it.* 7. That bearing fruit at last will save souls from ruin and destruction. 8. That out it every soul, though standing in God's vineyard, will at last perish eternally.

10 And he was teaching in one of the synagogues on the sabbath.

11 ¶ And, behold, there was a woman which had a spirit of infirmity eighteen years, and was bowed together, and could in no wise lift up *herself.*

12 And when Jesus saw her, he called *her to him,* and said unto her, Woman, thou art loosed from thine infirmity.

13 ᵇAnd he laid *his* hands on her: and immediately she was made straight, and glorified God.

ᵇ Mark 16. 18.
Acts 9. 17.

Though the Greek be *on the sabbaths,* which might signify any day of the week, yet it is manifest by what followeth that this miracle was wrought upon the seventh day, which was the Jewish sabbath. else the ruler of the synagogue would not have quarrelled with our Saviour about it. What is meant here, ver. 11, by *a spirit of infirmity,* would not easily be determined, whether only a very great infirmity, or an infirmity in the bringing and continuing of which upon her the devil had a great instrumentality, but for ver. 16, where she is said to be one that Satan had bound; she was a cripple, and so bowed down that she could not lift up herself, and thus she had been for eighteen years, so as the distemper was inveterate, and out of the course of ordinary cure. Christ, who, as to people's bodily infirmities, was sometimes found of those that sought him not, seeing her, calleth her to him, and saith, *Woman, thou art loosed from thy infirmity. And he laid his hands on her; and immediately she was made straight.* The inveterateness of the disease, and the instantaneousness of the cure, without the use of any means, made the miracle evident. The woman for it gave thanks to God, for that is meant by *glorified God,* she spake some things to the honour and glory of God, who had healed her.

14 And the ruler of the synagogue answered with indignation, because that Jesus had healed on the sabbath day, and said unto the people, ᶜThere are six days in which men ought to work: in them therefore come and be healed, and ᵈnot on the sabbath day.

ᶜ Ex. 20. 9.
ᵈ Mat. 12. 10. Mark 3. 2. ch. 6. 7. & 14. 3.

Answered here signifies no more than, he spake, as in a multitude of other places in the Gospels. The Jews were both very superstitious and very uneven as to the sanctification of the sabbaths: superstitious, because they would not do many things which by God's law they might do, such as applying means to heal the sick, defending themselves against enemies, &c. Uneven, because they would do divers things of equal bodily labour with those things which they pretend to scruple, one of which we shall hear our Saviour by and by instancing in. This ruler studied to defame him before the people. His pretence was, this was a work, and such a work as might be done in the six days. Let us hear how our Saviour defendeth himself.

15 The Lord then answered him, and said, *Thou* hypocrite, ᵉdoth not each one of you on the sabbath loose his ox or *his* ass from the stall, and lead *him* away to watering?

ᵉ ch. 14. 5.

16 And ought not this woman, ᶠbeing a daughter of Abraham, whom Satan hath bound, lo, these eighteen years, be loosed from this bond on the sabbath day?

ᶠ ch. 19. 9.

Our Saviour here calleth this ruler of the synagogue *hypocrite,* for his impudence in so severe a reflection on him for doing on the sabbath day a work of that nature which he himself did, and thought himself blameless in the doing of, and his friends ordinarily did, upon whom for so working he did not reflect, thereby teaching us one note of a hypocrite, viz. to reflect upon others for things which we do ourselves. This ruler of the synagogue and his party indeed did not heal on the sabbath day. But what kind of work was healing? was it not a work of mercy? what servile labour was there in it? It is only said Christ called this poor creature, and she came, not she was brought to him. What did Christ do? he only laid his hands upon her, and pronounced her loosed from her infirmity. Now the Jews would ordinarily upon the sabbath day loose a beast from the stall to go and drink at a pit, or lead it thither; was not this a greater labour? how came this to be lawful, and not that act of mercy which Christ did show to this poor creature? Their act was capable of no other excuse, than that it was an act of mercy, and a good man will show mercy to his beast: it could be no act of piety, nor of necessity; for a beast may live one day without water, or at least might have had water set by it the night before. Nay, our Lord's work of mercy was much more noble. Theirs was to a beast; his to one of mankind, to a woman, and she a Jewish woman, a daughter of Abraham, a father upon whom they much valued themselves, and their whole nation, Matt. iii. 9; John viii. 39. Their beast might not be sick; she was under an infirmity, and that no ordinary infirmity, she was in the hands of the enemy of mankind, bound by Satan; nor was her affliction of a few days' continuance, she had been so bound eighteen years.

17 And when he had said these things, all his adversaries were ashamed: and all the people

rejoiced for all the glorious things that were done by him.

It is one thing to be ashamed, another thing to be convinced, so as to confess an error; they were ashamed that they were so put to silence before the people, but we read of no confession of their error and mistake, and begging Christ's pardon. *The people rejoiced* and gave thanks to God *for all the glorious things that were done* by our Saviour.

g Mat. 13.31. Mark 4. 30.

18 ¶ ᵍThen said he, Unto what is the kingdom of God like? and whereunto shall I resemble it?

19 It is like a grain of mustard seed, which a man took, and cast into his garden; and it grew, and waxed a great tree; and the fowls of the air lodged in the branches of it.

20 And again he said, Whereunto shall I liken the kingdom of God?

f See Matt. 13. 33.

21 It is like leaven, which a woman took and hid in three ‖ measures of meal, till the whole was leavened.

See the notes on Matt. xiii. 31—33. They are two parables by which Christ foretelleth the great success of the gospel, notwithstanding the present small appearance of the efficacy of it.

h Mat. 9.35. Mark 6. 6.

22 ʰAnd he went through the cities and villages, teaching, and journeying toward Jerusalem.

Still wherever we find our blessed Lord, we find him teaching, and that not by an exemplary life only, but by word of mouth. There are different opinions whether our Saviour was now journeying towards Jerusalem with respect to the passover, or some other great festival of the Jews.

i 2 Esd. 8. 1, 3.

23 Then said one unto him, Lord, ⁱare there few that be saved? And he said unto them,

k Mat. 7. 13. l See John 7. 34. & 8. 21. & 13. 33. Rom. 9. 31.

24 ¶ ᵏStrive to enter in at the strait gate: for ¹many, I say unto you, will seek to enter in, and shall not be able.

Our Saviour hath told us, Matt. vii. 14, that *strait is the gate, and narrow is the way, that leadeth to* eternal *life, and few there be that find it.* Upon this this exhortation is founded. Ἀγωνίζεσθε, Contend, or strive, to enter in at this strait gate, a word which signifies a labouring against opposition, and the utmost endeavour of the mind and body: not that our own labouring will bring us thither, for eternal life is the gift of God, and without the influence of his grace we can do nothing effectually; but to let us know, that the Lord will give heaven to none but such as labour and strive for it, yea, and also *strive lawfully*: he tells us that *many will seek to enter, and shall not be able*; either seeking in a wrong way, or in an undue time. By this speech of our Saviour's he diverts them from that curious question, about the number of those that shall be saved. That was not so much their concern to know, as that they should be some of that number.

m Ps. 32. 6. Is. 55. 6. n Mat. 25.10.

o ch. 6. 46.

p Mat. 7. 23. & 25. 12.

25 ᵐWhen once the master of the house is risen up, and ⁿhath shut to the door, and ye begin to stand without, and to knock at the door, saying, ᵒLord, Lord, open unto us; and he shall answer and say unto you, ᵖI know you not whence ye are:

26 Then shall ye begin to say, We have eaten and drunk in thy presence, and thou hast taught in our streets.

q Mat. 7. 23. & 25. 41. ver. 25. r Ps. 6. 8. Matt. 25. 41.

27 ᑫBut he shall say, I tell you, I know you not whence ye are; ʳdepart from me, all *ye* workers of iniquity.

Our Saviour in these verses doth represent himself by a **man, who**, having invited guests to his supper, stays till all those who were invited, and accepted the invitation, were come in; then rising up, shuts the door; and after that is shut, turns a deaf ear to any that shall come knocking, let them plead for admittance what they can plead. By this parabolical expressing of himself, he both openeth in part what he meant by the foregoing words, *many will seek to enter in, and shall not be able,* and also lets us know, that there is a determinate time, wherein souls must (if ever) accept of the offers of grace and salvation, when they are made to them, which if they slip, they will not be able to obtain of God an entrance into the kingdom of heaven. *Seek the Lord while he may be found,* saith the prophet, Isa. lv. 6. *In an acceptable time have I heard thee,* saith the prophet, Isa. xlix. 8; which the apostle applieth, 2 Cor. vi. 2, to persuade men that they should not *receive the grace of God* (in the gospel) *in vain.* What this determinate time is God hath hidden from us, and it is probable that it is not the same as to all persons; we know nothing to the contrary, but while there is life there is hope, which warranteth us to preach faith and repentance to all. We are also further instructed, that no outward privileges. though Christ hath taught in our streets; no external acts of communion with Christ, though we can say we have ate and drunk with him; will justify our hopes of entrance into heaven, if in the mean time we be workers of iniquity. We had much the same Matt. vii. 21—23: see the notes there.

s Matt. 8. 12. & 13. 42. & 24. 51. t Matt. 8. 11

28 ˢThere shall be weeping and gnashing of teeth, ᵗwhen ye shall see Abraham, and Isaac, and Jacob, and all the prophets, in the kingdom of God, and you *yourselves* thrust out.

29 And they shall come from the east, and *from* the west, and from the north, and *from* the south, and shall sit down in the kingdom of God.

We have the same Matt. viii. 11, 12, only he saith only *from the east and west*: see the notes there. *Weeping and gnashing of teeth,* are usual expressions by which the pains of the damned are expressed, especially by the evangelist Matthew, chap. viii. 12; xiii. 42, 50; xxii. 13; xxiv. 51; xxv. 30. One cause of this vexation of spirit, expressed under this notion, is the Jews' sight of the rest and happiness that their relations, nay, some to whom they upon earth were enemies, should enjoy in heaven; nay, which some which were heathens should enjoy there; whereas they, who took themselves to be the only church, and to have the same right to the kingdom of heaven that children have to the inheritances of their fathers, should be cast out, as having no portion there.

u Matt. 19. 30. & 20. 16. Mark 10. 31.

30 ᵘAnd, behold, there are last which shall be first, and there are first which shall be last.

This is a sentence which our Saviour often made use of, and not always to the same purpose. See the notes on Matt. xix. 30; xx. 16; Mark x. 31. As to the sense of them here, it is plain. Our Saviour here foretelleth the conversion of the Gentiles; but yet I do not take the Gentiles to be all who are intended under the notion of the *last,* but divers others also. Men who, both in their opinion of themselves, and in reality with respect to privilege, are the *first,* whether in respect of gifts, or office, or the means of grace, or profession, will many of them be the *last,* that is, furthest off from the kingdom of God; and many who are the *last,* upon these accounts will in the day of judgment be *first,* that is, appear so, as having more of the favour of God, and be so, taken to heaven, when the others shall be cast to hell, Matt. xi. 20—24.

31 ¶ The same day there came certain of the Pharisees, saying unto him, Get thee out, and depart hence: for Herod will kill thee.

32 And he said unto them, Go ye, and tell that fox, Behold, I cast out devils, and I do cures to day and to morrow, and the third *day* ˣ I shall be perfected.

x Heb. 2. 10.

33 Nevertheless I must walk to day, and to morrow, and the *day* following: for it cannot be that a prophet perish out of Jerusalem.

It is plain from this text, that our Saviour was at this time in Galilee, for that was the tetrarchy or province of Herod Antipas, who is the Herod here mentioned. Whether these Pharisees came of their own heads, or as sent by Herod, is not so plain, nor so well agreed by interpreters. If they came of their own heads, it is certain they came not out of kindness, for the whole history of the gospel lets us know, that the Pharisees had no kindness for Christ, but were his most implacable enemies, and continually consulting how to destroy him; but they either came to scare him out of Galilee, whose repute was so great, and who did them so much mischief there, or to drive him into the trap which they had laid for him in Judea. But it is most probable that they came as secretly sent by Herod, who though of himself he be reported to be of no bloody disposition, yet upon the Pharisees' continual solicitations might be persuaded to send them on this errand, choosing rather cunningly to scare him out of his province, than by violence to fall upon him. This opinion looks more probable, because, ver. 32, our Saviour sends them back with a message to Herod, *Go ye, and tell that fox.* Herod had gained himself no reputation amongst the Jews, by his murdering John the Baptist, whom the Jews generally valued as a prophet; and probably seeing our Saviour exceeding him in popular applause, he was not willing to augment the odium which already lay upon him for that fact; yet, to gratify the Pharisees, (many of which were in his province,) he was willing, if he could effect it cleverly, and without noise, to be quit of Christ, especially considering (as we before heard) he had an opinion that he was John the Baptist risen from the dead, or the soul of John the Baptist in another body; and possibly he could not tell what might be the effect of his ghost so haunting his province. It is certain, that either he, or the Pharisees, or both, had a mind to have him gone some where else, to which purpose this message is brought to him. Our Saviour, either discerning Herod's craft in this thing, or having observed the craft he used in the whole management of his government, that he might keep favour both with the Roman emperor and with the Jews, bids them, *Go and tell that fox.* I do not much value their critical observation, who observe that it is not ἀλώπεκι ἐχείνη, but ταύτῃ, that is, this fox; from whence they would observe that our Saviour might mean the Pharisees, not Herod; nor is there any need of it to excuse our Saviour from the violation of that law of God, Exod. xxii. 28, *Thou shalt not revile the gods, nor curse the ruler of thy people;* which law Paul reflected on, Acts xxiii. 5, and pleads ignorance for his calling Ananias a *whited wall.* For we shall observe that the prophets all along (being immediately sent from God) took a further liberty than any others, in severely reproving kings and princes. Elijah tells Ahab it was he that troubled Israel; the prophets call the rulers of the Jews, *rulers of Sodom, and princes of Gomorrah,* &c. But Christ may be allowed a liberty neither lawful nor decent for other persons, not though they were prophets. But what is the message which Christ sends by these Pharisees? *Behold, I cast out devils, and I do cures to-day and to-morrow, and the third day I shall be perfected.* Tell him, saith he, what I am doing; I am freeing his subjects from molestations by evil spirits, and the encumbrances of many diseases. What do I do worthy of death? I have but a little time to trouble him, for in a little time I must die, which is that which he means by *perfected:* it is plain that those words *to-day, and to-morrow, and the third day,* must not be taken strictly, for Christ lived more than three days after this. If this will not satisfy him, tell him, saith our Saviour, that *I must walk to-day, and to-morrow, and the day following.* I know that, as to this thing, I am not under his command or power, *I must walk,* &c.; my days are not in his hands, and I know that he cannot kill me, *for it cannot be that a prophet perish out of Jerusalem.* Jerusalem is the place where I must die, not Galilee; the sanhedrin sits at Jerusalem, who alone can take cognizance of the case of false prophets, and Jerusalem is the place where the people must fill up the measure of their iniquities by spilling my blood. Upon this our Saviour breaketh out into a sad lamentation of the case of that once holy city, the praise of the whole earth.

y Mat. 23.37.   34 ʸ O Jerusalem, Jerusalem, which killest the prophets, and stonest them that are sent unto thee; how often would I have gathered thy children together, as a hen *doth gather* her brood under *her* wings, and ye would not!

35 Behold, ᶻyour house is left unto you desolate: and verily I say unto you, Ye shall not see me, until *the time* come when ye shall say, ᵃBlessed *is* he that cometh in the name of the Lord.

z Lev. 26. 31, 32. Ps. 69. 25. Is. 1. 7. Dan. 9. 27. Mic. 3. 12.
a Ps. 118. 26. Matt. 21. 9. Mark 11. 10. ch. 19. 38. John 12. 13.

See the notes on Matt. xxiii. 37—39. These five last verses afford us much for our instruction. 1. We may from them learn the craft of the enemies of the gospel, as well as their malice; they are lions, and will, like lions, tear and rend when they see an opportunity; but when they see it convenient, then they put on the fox's skin, doing the same thing by subtlety, which they durst not attempt to effect by cruelty. 2. Their malice is as much perspicuous; who but the children of the devil could have found in their hearts to have desired Christ to go out of their country, who did nothing there but innocently and diligently preach the gospel, deliver people from grievous diseases, and the power of Satan, who miserably possessed and tormented them? 3. When the most malicious enemies of God's people have done what they can, they shall finish their course, and work the time God hath set them. 4. When they have perfected their work, they shall be perfected. Death is but the perfecting of the saints, as it was the perfecting of Christ. 5. Men shall die, as at the time, so at the place, which God hath set. 6. God sending of his ministers faithfully to reveal his will to people, is a declaration of his willingness to gather them under the wings of his special favour and protection. 7. The perverse wills of men are those things which hinder men and women from being gathered. 8. Temporal judgments, and that of the severest nature, will first or last follow men's contempt of the offers of grace and salvation. 9. Those that do contemn the means of grace shall not see them long.—*Ye shall not see me.* 10. The proudest scorners and contemners of Christ and his grace shall one day wish that one would or might come unto them *in the name of the Lord,* and do but now contemn what hereafter they would be glad they might enjoy.

CHAP. XIV.

Christ healeth the dropsy on the sabbath, and justifieth his doing so, 1—6. *He recommendeth humility,* 7—11; *and hospitality toward the poor,* 12—14. *The parable of the marriage supper, and of the guests, who making excuses were excluded, and their rooms filled by others,* 15—24. *He adviseth those who are willing to be his disciples to examine beforehand their resolution in case of persecutions,* 25—33. *The unprofitableness of salt, when it hath lost its savour,* 34, 35.

AND it came to pass, as he went into the house of one of the chief Pharisees to eat bread on the sabbath day, that they watched him.

2 And, behold, there was a certain man before him which had the dropsy.

3 And Jesus answering spake unto the Lawyers and Pharisees, saying, ᵃIs it lawful to heal on the sabbath day?

a Matt. 12. 10.

4 And they held their peace. And he took *him,* and healed him, and let him go;

5 And answered them, saying, ᵇWhich of you shall have an ass or an ox fallen into a pit, and will not straightway pull him out on the sabbath day?

b Ex. 23. 5. Deut. 22. 4. ch. 13. 15.

6 And they could not answer him again to these things.

We have before observed the freedom of our Saviour's converse; sometimes he will dine with publicans, sometimes with Pharisees, becoming all things to all men that he might gain some. Christians certainly have the same liberty; the matter is not in whose houses we are, but what we do or say, how we behave ourselves there. In his going to a Pharisee's house, he gives us a great precedent of humanity and self-denial, for the Pharisees were his great enemies, and we shall observe no great kindness showed to him in the invitation of him. Whether this Pharisee be called *one of the chief of the Pharisees* because he was a member of the sanhedrim, or a ruler of a synagogue, or because he was one of the eldest and greatest repute, is not worth the inquiry. Thither Christ went *to eat bread*, that is, to take a meal with him. It is a phrase often used to signify dining, or supping, for they ordinarily under the notion of bread understood all manner of victuals. It was *on the sabbath day*. In the mean time, the evangelist tells us, *they watched him*, to wit, whether they might hear any thing from him, or see any thing in him, whereof they might accuse him. It happened *there was a man which had the dropsy*, whether casually, or brought thither on purpose by the Pharisees, the Scripture saith not; he was not there without a Divine direction, to give Christ an occasion of a miracle, and further to instruct people in the true doctrine of the sabbath. Christ upon the sabbath begins us a discourse proper for the day, asking the Pharisees if it were *lawful to heal on the sabbath day*. They make him no reply. Christ healeth him, then preacheth a doctrine to them, which he had twice before inculcated, in the case of a man who had a withered hand, Matt. xii. 10, and of the woman whom Satan had bound, of which we heard, chap. xiii. 11, viz. That works of mercy are lawful on the sabbath day. Then he justifieth his fact by the confession of their own practice, in lifting up beasts fallen into pits on the sabbath day. His argument is this: If it be lawful on the sabbath day to relieve a beast, it is much more lawful to relieve a man: but you do the former. The evangelist reports them put to silence, but saith nothing of their conviction. It is an easier thing to stop malicious persons' mouths than to remove their prejudices. Malice will ordinarily hold the conclusion, when the reason of the soul infected with it is not able to justify the premises.

7 ¶ And he put forth a parable to those which were bidden, when he marked how they chose out the chief rooms; saying unto them,

A *parable* here hath somewhat a different signification from what it more ordinarily hath in the evangelists: it usually signifies a similitude; here it signifies either a wise saying, or a dark saying, by which he intended something further than in the parable he expressed, which he expoundeth, ver. 11. We may observe from hence, that the dining of friends together on the Lord's day is not unlawful, only they ought to look to their discourses, that they be suitable to the day.

8 When thou art bidden of any *man* to a wedding, sit not down in the highest room; lest a more honourable man than thou be bidden of him;

9 And he that bade thee and him come and say to thee, Give this man place; and thou begin with shame to take the lowest room.

c Prov. 25. 6, 7.

10 ᶜ But when thou art bidden, go and sit down in the lowest room; that when he that bade thee cometh, he may say unto thee, Friend, go up higher: then shalt thou have worship in the presence of them that sit at meat with thee.

d Job 22. 29. Ps. 18. 27. Prov. 29. 23. Matt. 23. 12. ch. 18. 14. Jam. 4. 6. 1 Pet. 5. 5.

11 ᵈ For whosoever exalteth himself shall be abased; and he that humbleth himself shall be exalted.

Two or three moral instructions we have in this parable. 1. That the law of Christ justifieth none in any rudeness and incivility. 2. That the disciples of Christ ought to have a regard to their reputation, to do nothing they may be ashamed of. 3. That it is according to the will of God, that honour should be given to those to whom honour belongeth; that the more honourable persons should sit in the more honourable places. Grace gives men no exterior preference; though it makes men all glorious, yet it is within. But the more spiritual instruction (for which our Saviour put forth this parable) is in ver. 11. Our Saviour had but now, in the sight of these Pharisees, cured a man of a bodily dropsy; he is now attempting a cure of the spiritual dropsy of pride in their souls. He had before denounced a woe against the Pharisees for loving *the uppermost seats in the synagogues*, chap. xi. 43, and told us, Matt. xxiii. 6, that they *loved the uppermost rooms at feasts*, and possibly he might at this feast see something of it. He therefore applieth his discourse by pressing upon them humility, and showing them the danger of pride, which though it be a vice seated in the heart, yet by such little things discovereth itself in the outward conversation. He tells them, that God is such an enemy to pride, that he ordinarily so ordereth it in the government of the world, that usually self-exalting people are by one means or other abased, and brought to shame and contempt, and those that are low in their own eyes are exalted; and if it doth not so fall out here, yet this will be what will at the last day befall them, in the day of God's righteous judgment. See the notes on Matt. xxiii. 12. We shall meet with the same again, chap. xviii. 14.

12 ¶ Then said he also to him that bade him, When thou makest a dinner or a supper, call not thy friends, nor thy brethren, neither thy kinsmen, nor *thy* rich neighbours; lest they also bid thee again, and a recompence be made thee.

13 But when thou makest a feast, call ᵉthe poor, the maimed, the lame, the blind:

e Neh. 8. 10, 12. Tob. 2. 2. & 4. 7.

14 And thou shalt be blessed; for they cannot recompense thee: for thou shalt be recompensed at the resurrection of the just.

Many things are delivered in Scripture in the form of an absolute and universal prohibition, which must not be so understood, amongst which this is one instance. None must think that our Saviour doth here absolutely or universally forbid our invitations of our brethren, or kinsmen, or rich neighbours, or friends, to dinners or suppers with us; there was nothing more ordinarily practised amongst the Jews; Christ himself was at divers meals: but Christ by this teacheth us, 1. That this is no act of charity; it is indeed a lawful act of humanity and civility, and of a good tendency sometimes to procure amity and friendship amongst neighbours and friends, but no such act of charity as they could expect a heavenly reward for. 2. That such feastings ought not to be upheld in prejudice to our duty in relieving the poor, that is, they ought not to be maintained in such excesses and immoderate degrees, as by them we shall disable ourselves from that relief of the poor, which God requireth of us, as our duty, with respect to the estate with which he hath blessed us. 3. That we may most reasonably expect a recompence from heaven for such good works as we do, for which we are not recompensed on earth. 4. That God's recompences of us, for doing our duty in obedience to his commands, are often deferred until the resurrection of the just, but then they will not fail obedient souls.

15 ¶ And when one of them that sat at meat with him heard these things, he said unto him, ᶠBlessed *is* he that shall eat bread in the kingdom of God.

f Rev. 19. 9.

Whether this person had any gross conceptions of the kingdom of God, as a state of external happiness, and sensible satisfactions, I cannot say (though it be the opinion of some valuable interpreters): he might mean no more than, Blessed is he that shall come to heaven, and enjoy the celestial pleasures and satisfactions there; for that blessed state is called *the marriage supper of the Lamb*; and Christ spake to his disciples in this dialect, when he spake of drinking wine with them in his kingdom. But this passage both lets us know the good influence of spiritual discourse, to set the tongues of others on work, and also it lets us see what good meditations may be founded almost upon any subjects, if we have any heart thereunto. This gives our Saviour an occasion to put forth the following parable.

S. LUKE XIV

g Mat. 22. 2.

16 ᵍ Then said he unto him, A certain man made a great supper, and bade many :

h Prov. 9. 2, 5.

17 And ʰ sent his servant at supper time to say to them that were bidden, Come; for all things are now ready.

18 And they all with one *consent* began to make excuse. The first said unto him, I have bought a piece of ground, and I must needs go and see it : I pray thee have me excused.

19 And another said, I have bought five yoke of oxen, and I go to prove them : I pray thee have me excused.

20 And another said, I have married a wife, and therefore I cannot come.

21 So that servant came, and shewed his lord these things. Then the master of the house being angry said to his servant, Go out quickly into the streets and lanes of the city, and bring in hither the poor, and the maimed, and the halt, and the blind.

22 And the servant said, Lord, it is done as thou hast commanded, and yet there is room.

23 And the lord said unto the servant, Go out into the highways and hedges, and compel *them* to come in, that my house may be filled.

i Matt. 21. 43. & 22. 8. Acts 13. 46.

24 For I say unto you, ⁱThat none of those men which were bidden shall taste of my supper.

We met with the same parable Matt. xxii. 1—10, where we had the most of what is here, and many other considerable circumstances : see the notes on that chapter. Christ's primary intention by this parable was certainly to foretell the rejection of the Jews for their contempt of his gospel, and the reception of the Gentiles. They were those who were first bidden, that is, called and invited by the preaching of John the Baptist, Christ himself, and the apostles, to the receiving of Christ, that so they might be prepared for *the marriage supper of the Lamb*, mentioned Rev. xix. 9. The Gentiles, as a more rustic people, are set out under the notion of such as were in lanes, streets, and highways. It also informeth us of some great causes of men's rejection of the grace of God offered them in the ministry of the gospel : 1. Their worldly cares and businesses. 2. Their sensible enjoyments and pleasures : which did not hinder the Jews only, but one or other of which hinders the most of people still from receiving the grace of Christ tendered in the gospel. They are either not at leisure to attend to their souls, or they must enjoy things sensible and sensual in a degree in which the enjoyment of them is inconsistent with that duty which God requireth of them who would be saved. *Perimus licitis*, most men perish by their sinful use (or abuse rather) of things in themselves lawful. It may be observed also, that the two first sorts made a kind of mannerly excuse, saying, *I pray thee have me excused ;* but the last peremptorily said, *I cannot come.* Though secular employments be great diversions of us, and so hinderances of our minding things of highest concernment, yet sensual satisfactions and pleasures do most drown and swallow up the soul of man, and keep it from minding heaven and heavenly things. There have been a great many words spent about those words, *compel them to come in*, ver. 23. It appeareth to be almost the unanimous sense of the ancients, That no man ought by temporal punishments to be compelled to the profession of the true faith. Some of them have a little differed about such as, having once embraced the doctrine of the true faith, afterwards swerved from it ; though the truth of it is, they can be no more compelled than the other, for the will admits of no violence. Be the truth what it will in those points, certain it is that external compulsion hath no colour of foundation in this text. They are the ministers of the gospel that are thus spoken to, who we know by Christ's commission had no civil power committed to them. Nor do we ever read that they exercised any in order to the bringing of the Gentiles to the embracing of the faith ; nor do servants sent out to invite men to feasts (as these were) use to pull them in by head and shoulders, or to drive them in by whips and cudgels, only to use the best arguments they can to persuade them. Christ never prescribed any Spanish conversions of people. Man is presumed to be a rational creature, and taught even by nature to choose things which he sees are or may be of highest importance and concern. So that the very opening to men the riches of Divine grace, fitted to their lost and undone state, (which must also be showed them,) is a compulsion of them, or would at least be so if men by the fall were not corrupted as to their wills, so as they will not follow the dictate of their understanding. But notwithstanding the depravation and averseness of the carnal will, yet as many as the Lord will please to show mercy to, by joining the efficacious operations of his Spirit with the exterior call in the ministry of the word, shall come in. The words are ἀνάγκασον εἰσελθεῖν, make it necessary for them to come in, which no cudgels, no bodily punishments, can do, for they have their choice whether they will die or do it. It is used Matt. xiv. 22 ; Christ compelled his disciples to go into a ship, ἠνάγκασεν, yet it is certain he used no swords, or staves, or whips, or pecuniary mulcts to enforce them. A word of as high an import is used chap. xxiv. 29, of the two disciples compelling Christ to stay with them, παρεβιάσαντο. So Gal. ii. 14, ἀναγκάζεις, why dost thou force the Gentiles to Judaize ? yet it is certain Peter neither exercised nor called in the power of the magistrate to force the Gentiles. But when men began to spare their pains as to their tongues, to overpower and prevail upon men's hearts, then they began to compel them, by civil coercions, and to call in the civil magistrate, to the effecting of what they would have, while they themselves would do nothing ; and thus, contrary to all sense and reason, they expounded these words, *compel them to come in.*

25 ¶ And there went great multitudes with him : and he turned, and said unto them,

k Deut. 13. 6. & 33. 9. Matt. 10. 37. 1 Rom. 9. 13. m Rev. 12. 11.

26 ᵏIf any *man* come to me, ˡand hate not his father, and mother, and wife, and children, and brethren, and sisters, ᵐyea, and his own life also, he cannot be my disciple.

n Mat. 16. 24. Mark 8. 34. ch. 9. 23. 2 Tim. 3. 12.

27 And ⁿwhosoever doth not bear his cross, and come after me, cannot be my disciple.

We met with much the same Matt. x. 37, 38. The sum of the words is, That no man can be a true disciple of Christ, that giveth any friend, or any thing, a preference to Christ in the affections of his heart. Christ must be loved above all. It appeareth that the words must not be interpreted rigidly, for then they would oblige us to a thing, 1. Impossible in nature : *for no man ever yet hated his own flesh, but nourisheth and cherisheth it*, Eph. v. 29. Yet life is one of the things mentioned which we ought to hate. 2. It is morally impossible : for the law of God commands us to *honour* our *father and mother.* For the non-observance of, or teaching contrary to, which law, teaching the people to say, *Corban, It is a gift by whatsoever thou mightest be profited by me*, Christ so severely reflected on the Pharisees. Himself therefore doth not here teach others to hate their fathers or mothers, taking hatred in a strict and absolute sense : *If any man hate not*, signifieth here no more than, If any man doth love his father, wife, children, brethren, and sisters, yea, and his own life, more than me, *he cannot be my disciple.* Nor is this any sense put upon the term *hate*, different from what must be the sense of it in other scriptures : Gen. xxix. 31, *When the Lord saw that Leah was hated*, that is, less loved, as is expressed, ver. 30 ; so it must be interpreted in ver. 33. It also signified less loved, Deut. xxi. 15, 17 ; Matt. vi. 24 ; John xii. 25. We met with the substance of what is here, ver. 27, in Matt. x. 38, and Mark viii. 34. See the notes on those places.

o Prov. 24. 27

28 For ᵒwhich of you, intending to build a tower, sitteth not down first, and counteth the cost, whether he have *sufficient* to finish *it* ?

29 Lest haply, after he hath laid the foundation, and is not able to finish *it*, all that behold *it* begin to mock him,

30 Saying, This man began to build, and was not able to finish.

31 Or what king, going to make war against another king, sitteth not down first, and consulteth whether he be able with ten thousand to meet him that cometh against him with twenty thousand?

32 Or else, while the other is yet a great way off, he sendeth an ambassage, and desireth conditions of peace.

33 So likewise, whosoever he be of you that forsaketh not all that he hath, he cannot be my disciple.

Our Lord had in the parable of the supper showed what those things are which keep men from embracing the call of the gospel, to wit, their hearts' too much adherence to and embracing of sensible and sensual things. For the meeting of which temptation he had told them, ver. 25—27, that if they loved any thing in the world more than him, they could have no portion in him, they could not be his disciples, for (as Matthew saith) they are not worthy of him; nay, more than this, they must take up and bear their cross, and come after him. Here he directs them the best expedient in order to the performance of these duties, so hard to flesh and blood; that is, to sit down beforehand, and think what it will cost them to go through with the profession of religion. This, he tells them, ordinary prudence directeth men to, when they go about to build, or fight. As to the first, they make as good an estimate as they can of the charge. As to the latter, they consider both the charge, and the strength that they are able to produce to make opposition. So, saith he, must they do who will be his disciples: 1. Sit down and consider what it will cost them to become the Lord's building, what old foundations of nature must be digged up, what new foundation must be laid, how many stones must be laid before they can come up to a wall level to the promise wherein salvation is insured. 2. Then there must consider what oppositions they are like to meet with, from the world, the flesh, and the devil. And they must be ready to forsake all for Christ, though, it may be, they shall not be actually called out to it. Only we must remember, that in parables every branch is not to be applied. 1. We must desire no conditions of peace from our spiritual adversaries. 2. In our counting up of our strength to maintain the spiritual fight we must do as princes use to do, who use to count the forces of their allies and confederates, as well as their own: so we must not count what opposition we alone can maintain against the world, the flesh, and the devil; but what Christ (who is in covenant with us as to these fights) and we can do together. So as consideration and pre-deliberation here are not required of us upon any account to deter us from the fight, (for fight we must, or die eternally,) but to prepare us for the fight, by a firm and steady resolution, and to help us how to manage the fight, looking up to Christ for his strength and assistance in the management of it.

p Mat. 5. 13. Mark 9. 50. 34 ¶ ^pSalt *is* good: but if the salt have lost his savour, wherewith shall it be seasoned?

35 It is neither fit for the land, nor yet for the dunghill; *but* men cast it out. He that hath ears to hear, let him hear.

See the notes on Matt. v. 13; Mark ix. 50, where we met with the most of what we have in these verses. By *salt* in this place our Saviour seemeth to mean a Christian life and profession. It is a good, a noble, a great thing to be a Christian: but one that is so in an outward profession may lose his savour. Though a man cannot fall away from truth, and reality of grace, yet he may fall away from his profession; he may be given up to believe lies, and embrace damnable errors; he may shake off that dread of God which he seemed to have upon him; and then what is he good for? wherewith shall he be seasoned? He is neither fit for the land nor the dunghill: as some things will spoil dunghills, so debauched professors do but make wicked men worse, by prejudicing and hardening them against the ways and truths of God. *He that hath ears to hear, let him hear.* It is a usual epiphonema, or sentence, by which Christ often shuts up grave and weighty discourses: the sense is, You had therefore need to look about you, and to undertake the profession of my religion upon such weighty grounds and principles as will carry you through the practice of it to the end, against all the oppositions you shall meet with; for if you apostatize from your profession, you will be the worst of men, neither fit for the church nor for the world (for you will make that the worse); indeed fit for nothing but for the fire of hell.

CHAP. XV.

The Pharisees murmur at Christ for receiving sinners, 1, 2. *The parable of the lost sheep,* 3—7; *and piece of silver,* 8—10; *and of the prodigal son,* 11—32.

THEN ^adrew near unto him all the Publicans and sinners for to hear him.   a Matt. 9.10.

2 And the Pharisees and Scribes murmured, saying, This man receiveth sinners, ^band eateth with them.   b Acts 11. 3. Gal. 2. 12.

I have so often taken notice, that the term *all* in the New Testament is very often used to signify, not all the individuals of that species, or order of men, to which it is applied, but only a great and considerable number of them, that it is needless again to repeat it. None can imagine, that every individual publican and sinner in those parts, where Christ now was, came to hear Christ, but only many of them, or some of every sort. Thus publicans and harlots entered into the kingdom of God, while the children of the kingdom, and such as appeared to lie fairer for it, were cast out. The scribes, who were the interpreters of the law, and the Pharisees, who were the rigid observers of their decrees and interpretations, *murmured*, they were disturbed and troubled at it; thinking that because the law appointed no sacrifice for bold and presumptuous sinners, therefore there was no mercy in God for them, or those of whom they had such a notion, and that they were *ipso jure* excommunicated, and therefore Christ sinned in eating or drinking with them, or in any degree receiving of them; and from hence concluding he was no prophet: as if because ordinarily persons are known by their companions with whom they converse, therefore it had been a general rule; as if one might have concluded, that their doctorships were ignorant, because they conversed with them that were so, for their instruction; or could conclude, that the physician is sick, because his converse is with the sick, for their cure and healing. A man is not to be judged to be such as he converseth with necessarily, or in order to their good, which was the end of all our Saviour's converse with these sinners. Besides, were they themselves without sin? The root of their uncharitableness was their opinion of their own righteousness, from the works of the law, according to their own jejune interpretation of it. But let us hear our Saviour's reply.

3 ¶ And he spake this parable unto them, saying,

4 ^cWhat man of you, having an hundred sheep, if he lose one of them, doth not leave the ninety and nine in the wilderness, and go after that which is lost, until he find it?   c Mat. 18. 12.

5 And when he hath found *it*, he layeth *it* on his shoulders, rejoicing.

6 And when he cometh home, he calleth together *his* friends and neighbours, saying unto them, Rejoice with me; for I have found my sheep ^dwhich was lost.   d 1 Pet. 2. 10, 25.

7 I say unto you, that likewise joy shall be in heaven over one sinner that repenteth, ^emore than over ninety and nine just persons, which need no repentance.   e ch. 5. 32.

See the notes on Matt. xviii. 12, 13, where we met with the same parable, though not related with so many circumstances. The 7th verse, which is the *epiparabole*, showeth us the principal thing which our Saviour by this parable designeth to teach his hearers, and us also, viz. That Christ is so far from rejecting the greatest sinners, that repent, and flee unto his mercy, that, if it were possible, he should take a greater satisfaction in such an issue of Divine providence, than in all the glorified saints. No repenting sinner, let his sins be as many and as great as they can be, shall be unwelcome unto Christ, fleeing to him with a broken heart (resolved against his former courses) for pardon and mercy. But as it happeneth to them who by study and practice make great experiments, they can hardly find out what they mostly seek for, but in the way to it they will find out several other notions, which are of great use to them; so it will fall out to them who diligently study the parables of the gospel. Though some one truth be that the explication of which our Saviour doth chiefly intend; yet the parable will also afford some other profitable instructions, not unworthy of our notice and regard. The *man* here intended is Christ, who was the Son of man, as well as the eternal Son of God. The *hundred sheep* signifies the whole number of his elect, whether in heaven or on earth, whether yet called or hereafter to be called. The sheep going astray signifieth all the elect, who are *by nature children of wrath as well as others, dead in trespasses and sins,* Eph. ii. 1, 3. Here is mention but of *one* sheep so gone astray, though there be many, to let us know the love of Christ to every individual soul, that if but one of them had been to have been redeemed, he would have come down from heaven to have redeemed it. The *ninety-nine* left *in the wilderness* seem to me to be the glorified saints, they are the only *just persons, who need no repentance.* The countryman's going after the lost sheep till he finds it, then bringing it home upon his shoulders rejoicing, signifies the infinite love of Christ, both in leaving his Father's throne, and the society of the glorified saints and angels, to come to seek and to save that which was lost, to pay a redemption price for them; then sending his Holy Spirit and the ministers of his gospel to invite and effectually to persuade them to accept of his salvation, truly repenting of their sins; and also preserving them through his power by faith unto salvation: for it is upon his shoulders that any elect soul is brought home; it is his eye must find them, and his power that must bring them home. The countryman's rejoicing, and calling his neighbours to rejoice, &c., signifieth the satisfaction and well-pleasedness of Christ in the conversion of sinners, which is more plainly expressed ver. 7, *I say unto you, that likewise joy shall be in heaven over one sinner that repenteth, more than over ninety and nine just persons, which need no repentance.* We have much the same again ver. 10, leaving out the comparative part. There also it is, *there is joy in the presence of the angels of God.* We will consider the expressions in both the verses together; as to which there may arise these questions: *Quest.* 1. What is here meant by joy in heaven? The inhabitants of heaven are, God, the blessed angels, and the glorified saints; how can they be said to rejoice, whereas rejoicing is in us the product of a passion by which we triumph in our union to some good, which we before wanted? *Answ.* When terms expressive of our passions are applied to perfect beings, we must understand them so, as they alone can agree to such beings, separated from those excesses which they have in beings more imperfect. Joy signifieth nothing but the full satisfaction of the will in a good obtained. Thus God is said to rejoice in his people, Isa. lxii. 5. *Quest.* 2. Who are these ninety-nine just persons that need no repentance? (For the number, it is but an uncertain number put for one certain.) *Answ.* Some by such as *need no repentance* understand, such as think so of themselves, though indeed they do need it. Others understand it comparatively, such as if compared with others need no repentance. 2. Others by *repentance* understand penance; such sober persons as stand in no need of a being called to a public confession, for the satisfaction of the church offended. I had rather understand it of the glorified saints, whose society Christ left when he came to work out our redemption. For the others, it had been no great matter for Christ to have told them, that God, the holy angels and saints, rejoice more over one repenting sinner, than over ninety-nine impenitent sinners and self-righteous persons, who continually grieve him, and whom he abhorreth. But then, *Quest.* 3. How can it be said, that God, and the angels and saints, more rejoice over one repenting sinner, than over ninety-nine glorified saints? *Answ.* It is universally agreed, that Christ speaks here of God, and of the angels, after the manner of men; of whose nature it is to express more passion upon a new object that pleaseth them, than upon others that they have been long pleased with; as a parent rejoiceth more over one child recovered from the jaws of death, than over all the rest of his children. Though nothing can be new to God, that is, which he did not see and foreknow, yet some things may be new to him *in facto esse,* as done and fulfilled: and though we must not imagine any mutation or alteration of the Divine Being upon any emergency amongst men; yet to express how infinitely pleased God is, in the repentance and conversion of great sinners, he is set out as receiving an augmentation of satisfaction in the effecting of it. Such expressions as these condescended to by God for our consolation, must not be so strained by us as to occasion any unbecoming thoughts of God. *Quest.* Some query how the angels know of the conversion of a sinner; and from hence the papists would some of them infer, that they know our hearts, because that is the seat of conversion. *Answ.* Both the angels and the glorified saints also may know it by God's revealing it to them.

8 ¶ Either what woman having ten ‖ pieces of silver, if she lose one piece, doth not light a candle, and sweep the house, and seek diligently till she find *it?*

‖ *Drachma,* here translated *a piece of silver,* is the eighth part of an ounce, which cometh to seven pence halfpenny, and is equal to the Roman penny, Matt. 18. 28.

9 And when she hath found *it,* she calleth *her* friends and *her* neighbours together, saying, Rejoice with me; for I have found the piece which I had lost.

10 Likewise, I say unto you, there is joy in the presence of the angels of God over one sinner that repenteth.

This parable (as appeareth by the conclusion of it) is of the same import with the other, and needs no further explication. By both these parables our blessed Lord lets the Pharisees know the end he aimed at in conversing with publicans and sinners, viz. In order to their repentance and conversion, than which nothing could be more grateful and well-pleasing to that God who desireth not the death of a sinner, but rather that they should turn from their wickedness and live. Of the same import is also the following parable, which taketh up all the remaining part of this chapter.

11 ¶ And he said, A certain man had two sons:

12 And the younger of them said to *his* father, Father, give me the portion of goods that falleth *to me.* And he divided unto them ᶠ*his* living.

ᶠ Mark 12. 44.

13 And not many days after the younger son gathered all together, and took his journey into a far country, and there wasted his substance with riotous living.

14 And when he had spent all, there arose a mighty famine in that land; and he began to be in want.

15 And he went and joined himself to a citizen of that country; and he sent him into his fields to feed swine.

16 And he would fain have filled his belly with the husks that the swine did eat: and no man gave unto him.

The scope of this excellent parable is apparently to magnify the grace of God, who is willing to receive and to treat kindly the greatest transgressors, seriously repenting, and turning unto God; but in it we are also, 1. Instructed in the original state of man, like that of a child in his father's house, happy and wanting nothing. 2. The most miserable estate of fallen men, such especially as run to great excess of riot. 3. The true way of a sinner's returning to God. 4. The readiness of our gracious Father to receive, and his wonderful kindness in the receiving and embracing, repenting and returning sinners. 5. The envy that is sometimes found in good souls to others receiving (as they think) more favour from God than they do. 6. The gentleness and meekness of God in dealing with us, notwithstanding our infirmities and misbecoming passions. God is again here represented under the notion of a man who had two sons : some that are his children by regeneration as well as creation ; he having given them that believe a right to be called *the sons of God,* John i. 12. Others that are his sons by creation only. The latter are here represented under the notion of a younger son. This younger son is represented as dissatisfied with living in his father's house, desiring his portion, &c. All men and women by nature were equally the sons of God, being all in Adam, who was so. All men swerved from him ; in Adam all sinned, all died. But some again by grace are returned to their Father's house. Others challenge a relation to God, as his creatures, but are not of their Father's house, but desire only a portion of the good things of this life. Some desire honours, some riches, all of them life and health, &c. God, like a liberal father, gives some of these good things to one, others to another ; to some more than one kind of them : whatever they have of this nature is from him who maketh his sun to shine and his rain to fall upon the just and unjust. Wicked men, when they are thus furnished by God, quickly take their *journey into a far country,* are more alienated and estranged from God by lewd and wicked practices than they were by nature ; waste their substance, the health of their bodies, their time of life, their estates, their great and honourable capacities, by giving up themselves to lewd and riotous kinds of life, to the high dishonour of Almighty God. It pleaseth God by his providence sometimes to bring these men into straits; when they are so brought, they will take any base, sordid course to relieve themselves, rather than they will think of returning to their heavenly Father ; of themselves they will rather choose to serve swine. But if they be such as belong to God's election of grace, the providence of God will not leave them. Though there be little food for a soul in the husks of sensible satisfactions, yet they shall not have a bellyful of them. God will bring them off from satisfaction in any thing, and make every condition uneasy to them.

17 And when he came to himself, he said, How many hired servants of my father's have bread enough and to spare, and I perish with hunger !

Every sinner is beside himself ; his reason lackeys to his lust and passion, he is governed by appetite, and that rageth in him, while his understanding is blind, and cannot discern betwixt good and evil; and when he hath in any measure discerned any thing, his will is stubborn, and chooseth the evil. Conversion is but the return of a soul to itself. The first thoughts of which conversion arise from a soul's consideration, what a poor miserable creature it is, ready to perish for ever, while never a poor soul belonging to God, no, not the meanest servant in his family, wanteth any good thing that is necessary for him. These things increase in a soul thoughts of returning to his heavenly Father, through the operation of the Holy Spirit of God; for of ourselves we are not sufficient so much as to think one good thought.

18 I will arise and go to my father, and will say unto him, Father, I have sinned against heaven, and before thee,

19 And am no more worthy to be called thy son : make me as one of thy hired servants.

20 And he arose, and came to his father. But ^g when he was yet a great way off, his father saw him, and had compassion, and ran, and fell on his neck, and kissed him.

g Acts 2. 39. Eph. 2.13,17.

The way of a sinner's returning to God must be by arising, going to the Father, confessing his sins with the aggravations of them, disclaiming any goodness, any righteousness in himself, humbling himself to God's footstool. *I will arise* (saith the prodigal) *and go to my father, and will say unto him, Father, I have sinned against heaven,* *and before thee, and am no more worthy to be called thy son : make me as one of thy hired servants. And he arose, and came to his father.* He arose from the sleep and bed of sin, and came unto his father. We are not here told by whose strength, or in whose assistance, he arose and came. We must remember that our Saviour is here representing a spiritual notion by an ordinary human action ; now men have an innate power to natural motions, though not to spiritual actions. We are elsewhere told, that no man cometh to the Father, but by Christ, nor doth any man come unto the Son, but he whom the Father draweth. Every one as he is taught of the Father cometh unto the Son. And again, that though we be *saved by faith,* yet it is *not of ourselves, it is the gift of God ;* and, *it is given* to us *in the behalf of Christ to believe,* Phil. i. 29. These are but several expressions signifying, by the tender affections and gracious reception of earthly parents of a returning prodigal son, the exceeding readiness of our heavenly Father to receive penitent sinners ; he is so far from discouraging great sinners from taking up thoughts of returning unto him, that he cherisheth the embryos of such resolutions : *I said,* (saith the psalmist,) *I will confess my transgressions unto the Lord ; and thou forgavest the iniquity of my sin,* Psal. xxxii. 5. God seeth the first good motions and stirrings of our hearts towards him, and he needs must do so, for he stirreth them up in us ; there is no sacred fire upon our altar, but first cometh down from heaven. While yet the soul is far off from believing, and closing with Christ actually, and hath but some thoughts of that tendency, God looks upon it, encourageth, meeteth it as it were half way ; and indeed if he did not, our goodness would be but like a morning dew, which would quickly pass away ; our first inclinations would perish like an untimely birth, before it hath seen the light.

21 And the son said unto him, Father, I have sinned against heaven, ^h and in thy sight, and am no more worthy to be called thy son.

h Ps. 51. 4.

Now the good thoughts and resolutions of the sinner ripen into action, and the first of it is an expression of his convictions and humiliation by a humble confession of his sins, with their aggravations, as committed against God, and that in the sight of God, and this God his Father, his unworthiness so much as of the name of a son to such a Father. The petitionary part of what he resolved upon, ver. 19, is not here again repeated, but to be understood. Men may by the common grace of God, denied to no man, have some good thoughts, but they die away, and come to no maturity, unless the Holy Spirit of God breathes upon them, and maintaineth and upholdeth them in the soul ; but where the Lord designeth a thorough change in a soul, the Spirit of the Lord comes, and convinceth the soul of sin and of righteousness : and where he doth so, the resolution ripeneth into action, and produceth in the soul a true and hearty contrition, and confession of its sin, with humble petitions and a resignation of itself to the Lord's will, and a casting of itself upon God's free grace and mercy.

22 But the father said to his servants, Bring forth the best robe, and put *it* on him ; and put a ring on his hand, and shoes on *his* feet :

23 And bring hither the fatted calf, and kill *it;* and let us eat, and be merry:

24 ^i For this my son was dead, and is alive again ; he was lost, and is found. And they began to be merry.

i ver. 32. Eph. 2. 1. & 5. 14. Rev. 3. 1.

We must remember that we are in a parable where a sinner is represented to us under the notion of a prodigal son ; God, under the notion of an indulgent father ; a repenting sinner, under the notion of a prodigal returning to his father, confessing his error, petitioning his father for mercy, acknowledging he deserveth none, but casting himself upon his father's goodness and mercy. It is observed by an eminent author, that amongst all the parables this is one of the most famous, and wherein is the most full and perfect representation of the thing intended to be represented, and an applicableness of every part of the similitude to that which it is brought to represent. This part of it representeth the grace of God to truly repenting sinners. We before heard his readiness and willingness to receive them, this part lets us see the manner how he will treat them. As in case of apostacy, the seeming righteousness and profession of men shall not be remembered, Ezek. iii. 20; xxxiii. 13; so in case of a true and hearty repentance, the sins of a soul shall not be remembered, Isa. xliii. 25. The father taketh no notice of the prodigal's leaving his house, or wasting his estate riotously, but saith, *Bring forth the best robe,* τὴν στολὴν τὴν πρώτην; *and put a ring on his hand, and shoes on his feet: and bring hither the fatted calf,* τὸν μόσχον τὸν σιτευτὸν. I find some interpreters, who by the *fatted calf* are willing enough to understand Christ; yet interpreting *the best robe,* innocency, or inherent righteousness. Nor is it an ill interpretation, if we consider, that God, at the same time when he imputeth the merits of Christ to the soul for justification, doth also put his Spirit of holiness into the soul, by which being renewed in the inward man, this man brings forth the fruits of holiness unto righteousness, Ezek. xxxvi. 26, 27. But why we should not understand both the phrases of the application of Christ's merits, and the imputation of his righteousness to the soul, I cannot tell, considering, that the church of Laodicea is counselled to buy of him *white raiment,* that she might *be clothed,* Rev. iii. 18; and that those clothed with *white robes,* Rev. vii. 14, are said to *have washed their robes, and made them white in the blood of the Lamb;* and that though the habits of grace are sometimes in holy writ compared to clothing, *Be ye clothed with humility,* (saith the apostle,) yet these are not ἡ στολὴ ἡ πρώτη. I should therefore rather choose to interpret the killing of the fatted calf for the prodigal son, as representing that application of the blood of Christ, which is made to every sinner that truly repenteth, and maketh its application to God for mercy; and the best robe, as the righteousness of Christ, in that moment reckoned unto the soul (thus believing) for righteousness. Further yet, (to consider it only in the parable,) the word θύσατε, sacrifice the fatted calf, seems to signify what a great cause of thanksgiving to God, as well as joy amongst men, the conversion of a sinner is. We that are earthly parents, or ministers of the gospel, should not receive the news, or see the visible probability of a soul's being converted, and returning unto God, without offering a sacrifice of thanksgiving unto God for doing such things for men, and without a true and hearty rejoicing in ourselves. But to return again to the meaning of the parable. *Let us eat, and be merry:* consider these words as the words of a heavenly Father, they signify unto us, that the eternal God, from the day that a repenting soul hath the blood of Christ applied to it, and is clothed with his righteousness, is at peace with the soul, hath a communion with it, and that it from that time hath a true right to spiritual mirth and rejoicing; for *light is sown for the righteous, and joy for the upright in heart:* though possibly the soul at present, through temptations, cannot apprehend it, and be not actually possessed of that joy and peace which followeth believing, yet it hath a right to it, and indeed none but that soul hath any thing to do with peace. It followeth, *For this my son was dead, and is alive again; he was lost, and is found.* A sinful soul is a dead soul, as the woman *that liveth in pleasure* is said to be *dead while she liveth,* by the apostle. The conversion of a sinner is as a resurrection from the dead. Nor is any soul capable of any true mirth, till it be reconciled to God through the blood of Christ.

25 Now his elder son was in the field : and as he came and drew nigh to the house, he heard musick and dancing.

26 And he called one of the servants, and asked what these things meant.

27 And he said unto him, Thy brother is come; and thy father hath killed the fatted calf, because he hath received him safe and sound.

28 And he was angry, and would not go in : therefore came his father out, and intreated him.

29 And he answering said to *his* father, Lo, these many years do I serve thee, neither transgressed I at any time thy commandment : and yet thou never gavest me a kid, that I might make merry with my friends :

30 But as soon as this thy son was come, which hath devoured thy living with harlots, thou hast killed for him the fatted calf.

31 And he said unto him, Son, thou art ever with me, and all that I have is thine.

32 It was meet that we should make merry, and be glad : ᵏfor this thy brother was dead, and is alive again; and was lost, and is found.

ᵏ ver. 24.

This last part of the parable is not so exactly applicable to that which it is brought to represent as the former parts are, but it serveth excellently to show us that envy which is found in our hearts by nature to the spiritual good and advantage of others. Two things are observable in it: 1. Man's peevishness and envy. 2. God's meekness towards us under our frowardness. By the *elder son* some think the Jews are represented, whose peevishness to the Gentiles, and the offer of the grace of the gospel to them, is made appear to us from many places of holy writ. Others think that by the *elder son* are represented hypocrites, who swelling in an opinion of themselves, and their own righteousness, have no patience to hear that any others should be preferred in the favour of God before them. Why may we not say that all are understood by it, even the best of God's people, who, if they narrowly search their own hearts, will find something of pride and envy remaining in the best of them? and as the former prompts them to judge themselves as much deserving the favour of God, even in special particular dispensations, as any others; so the latter inclineth them to repine at such dispensations of Divine grace as others receive, and they want. two corruptions which we are as much concerned to keep a watch upon, or against, as any other; speaking both a peevishness to the honour and glory of God, a dissatisfaction in his dispensations, and an offer at the controlment of his wisdom and justice, and also a great degree of uncharitableness, our eye being evil because the Lord is good. Besides that it seemeth to put in a claim of merit; and the soul that indulgeth itself in such thoughts seems to say that it hath deserved more than it doth receive; for without such a supposition, it is the most unreasonable thing imaginable, that any person should be displeased that another should have a greater share in the favour of God than he, while he himself receives more than he can lay a claim unto, and God may do with his own what he pleaseth. The meekness of God in dealing with us under our frowardness is as much remarkable. *Son,* (saith this father in the parable,) *thou art ever with me, and all that I have is thine. It was meet that we should make merry, and be glad; for this thy brother was dead, and is alive again; was lost, and is found.* This must be understood of God ἀνθρωποπαθῶς, as spoken after the manner of men, who show greater passions upon the receiving of a good that is new to them, and possibly surprising, than they ordinarily show upon the view of a good of which they have had longer fruition; so it confirms what was before said in ver. 7, 10. We must take heed of thinking that any thing can make a change or alteration in God, but must look upon it only as an expression of God's high satisfaction and well-pleasedness in a sinner's conversion, and turning unto him; so as if it were possible any good should more than other affect the Divine Being, it would be this. So as this whole parable is of excellent use, not only to instruct sinners in their miserable state, till they be reconciled to God, but to deliver them from all temptations to fear that, heartily returning, they shall not be accepted.

CHAP. XVI

The parable of the unjust steward, 1—13. *Christ reproveth the hypocrisy of the Pharisees, who were covetous, and derided him,* 14—18. *The parable of the rich man and Lazarus the beggar,* 19—31.

AND he said also unto his disciples, There was a certain rich man, which had a steward; and the same was accused unto him that he had wasted his goods.

2 And he called him, and said unto him, How is it that I hear this of thee? give an account of thy stewardship; for thou mayest be no longer steward.

3 Then the steward said within himself, What shall I do? for my lord taketh away from me the stewardship: I cannot dig; to beg I am ashamed.

4 I am resolved what to do, that, when I am put out of the stewardship, they may receive me into their houses.

5 So he called every one of his lord's debtors *unto him*, and said unto the first, How much owest thou unto my lord?

6 And he said, An hundred ∥ measures of oil. And he said unto him, Take thy bill, and sit down quickly, and write fifty.

∥ The word *batus* in the original containeth nine gallons three quarts: See Ezek. 45. 10, 11, 14.

7 Then said he to another, And how much owest thou? And he said, An hundred ∥ measures of wheat. And he said unto him, Take thy bill, and write fourscore.

∥ The word here interpreted *a measure* in the original containeth about fourteen bushels and a pottle.

8 And the lord commended the unjust steward, because he had done wisely: for the children of this world are in their generation wiser than ᵃthe children of light.

ᵃ John 12. 36. Eph. 5. 8. 1 Thess. 5. 5.

Hierom of old thought this parable was very obscure; and Julian and other apostates, together with some of the heathen philosophers, took occasion from it to reproach the doctrine of Christ, as teaching and commanding acts of unrighteousness. But there will appear no such difficulty in it, nor cause of reproach to Christ and his doctrine from it, if we consider what I have before hinted, that it is no more necessary to a parable that all the actions in it supposed be just and honest, than that all the parts of it be true in matter of fact, whether past or possible to be; for a parable is not designed to inform us in a matter of fact, but to describe to us our duty, under a fictitious representation: nor doth every part of a parable point at some correspondent duty to be done by us; but the main scope for which it is brought is principally to be attended to by us, and other pieces of duty which may be hinted to us, are to be judged of and proved not from the parable, but from other texts of holy writ where they are inculcated. The main things in which our Saviour seemeth desirous by this parable to instruct us, are, 1. That we are but stewards of the good things God lends us, and must give an account to our Master of them. 2. That being no more than stewards intrusted with some of our Master's goods for a time, it is our highest prudence, while we have them in our trust, to make such a use of them as may be for our advantage when we give up our account. Thus we shall hear our Lord in the following verses expounding his own meaning. To this purpose he supposed a rich man to have a steward, and to have received some accusation against him, as if he had embezzled his master's goods committed to his trust. Upon which he calleth him to account, and tells him that he should be his steward no longer. He supposeth this steward to be one who had no other means of livelihood and subsistence than what his place afforded him, a man not used to labour, and too proud to beg. At length he fixed his resolution, to send for his master's debtors, and to abate their obligations, making them debtors to his master for much less than indeed they were; by this means he probably hoped, that when he was turned off from his master he should be received by them. He supposeth his master to have heard of it, and to have commended him, not for his honesty, but for his wit in providing for the time to come. What was knavery in this steward, is honest enough in those who are the stewards of our heavenly Lord's goods, suppose riches, honours, parts, health, life, or any outward accommodation, viz. to use our Lord's goods for the best profit and advantage to ourselves, during such time as we are intrusted with them. For though an earthly lord and his steward have particular divided interests, and he that maketh use of his lord's goods for his own best advantage cannot at the same time make use of them for the best advantage of his master, yet the case is different betwixt our heavenly Lord and us. It hath pleased God so to twist the interest of his glory with our highest good, that no man can better use his Master's goods for the advantage of his glory, than he who best useth them for the highest good, profit, and advantage to himself; nor doth any man better use them for his own interest, than he who best useth them for God's glory. So as here the parable halteth, by reason of the disparity betwixt the things that are compared. And though the unjust steward could not be commended for the honesty, but only for the policy, of his action, yet we who are stewards of the gifts of God, in doing the like, that is, making use of our Master's goods for our own best profit and advantage, may act not only wisely, but also honestly; and indeed Christ in this parable blameth men for not doing so: *The children of this world* (saith he) *are wiser in their generation than the children of light.* By *the children of this world*, he meaneth such as this steward was, men who regard not eternity or the concerns of their immortal souls, but only regard the things of this life, what they shall eat, or drink, or put on. By *the children of light*, he meaneth such as live under the light of the gospel, and receive the common illumination of the gospel; though if we yet understand it more strictly, of those who are *translated out of darkness into marvellous light*, it is too true, they are not so wise, and politic, and industrious for heaven, as worldly men are to obtain their ends in getting the world. He saith, *the men of this world are wiser in their generation*, that is, in their kind, as to those things about which they exercise their wit and policy, than the children of God.

9 And I say unto you, ᵇMake to yourselves friends of the ∥ mammon of unrighteousness; that, when ye fail, they may receive you into everlasting habitations.

ᵇ Dan. 4. 27. Matt. 6. 19. & 19. 21. ch. 11. 41. 1 Tim. 6. 17, 18, 19. ∥ Or, *riches*.

That by *mammon* here is meant riches is universally agreed, but whether it originally be a Chaldaic, or Syriac, or Punic word is not so well agreed. The Chaldee paraphrast useth it, Hos. v. 11; but the Hebrew there is quite otherwise, (according to our translation,) *he willingly walked after the commandment*. But if the notion of this be true, that some of those nations had an idol called Mammon, whom they made the god of riches, answering the Grecian Plutus, it fairly interprets the Chaldee paraphrast. They followed the command for idolatry, for such was Jeroboam's commandment, mentioned in that text, and from thence it might be that the Syrians and Punics called riches mammon. We have the word in the New Testament four times, thrice in this chapter, once Matt. vi. 24. It is called *the mammon of unrighteousness*, by a Hebraism; it is as much as, the unrighteous mammon: by which we must not understand ill-gotten goods, (for God hateth robbery for a burnt-offering,) we must restore such goods, not make friends of them; but riches are so called, because of the manifold temptations to sin which arise from them, upon which account they are also called *deceitful*. But others think that it is so called in opposition to *the true riches*, mentioned ver. 11. So that *the mammon of unrighteousness* is the mammon of falsehood, or hurtful riches, riches of hurtfulness (ἀδικία sometimes signifies hurt or wrong, and ἀδικεῖν, *lædere, nocere*). Of these riches, which are no true riches, and which deceive the soul, and do hurt and mischief to a soul, exposing it to temptation, Christ commands us to *make friends*; either, 1. To make God our friend, not by meriting from him any thing by our disposal of them, but by obedience to his will in our distribution of them. Or, 2. To make poor Christians our friends, so as we may have their prayers. So that, *when ye fail*, when you die, when you fail of any more comfort from them, *they may receive you into everlasting habitations;* the holy Trinity, or the blessed angels, (whose work it is, as we shall hear, to carry souls into Abraham's bosom,) may receive you into heaven.

S. LUKE XVI

<sup>c Mat. 25. 21.
ch. 19. 27.</sup> 10 ^c He that is faithful in that which is least is faithful also in much: and he that is unjust in the least is unjust also in much.

This is a usual sentence, (our Saviour made use of many such,) as to which kind of speeches it is not necessary they should be universally true, it is sufficient if they generally be so. Besides that, our Saviour plainly speaketh here according to the common opinion and judgment of men. Men ordinarily judge that he who is faithful in a little thing, of no high concern or moment, will be faithful in what is of a higher concern, or greater moment; and if they have found a person unfaithful in a small thing, they will conclude that he will be so in a greater, and not trust him: though sometimes it falls out otherwise, that one who is faithful enough in some trifling things, prove unfaithful in a greater trust, where unfaithfulness will turn more to his profit; and on the contrary, he that is unfaithful in a little thing, may prove more faithful in a greater; but none will trust to that: and that is our Saviour's design, to teach us that God will do by us as we in the like case do by our servants or neighbours.

|| Or, riches. 11 If therefore ye have not been faithful in the unrighteous || mammon, who will commit to your trust the true *riches?*

This verse now opposeth *the unrighteous mammon* to *the true riches,* which would strongly incline one to think, that by *the mammon of unrighteousness,* before mentioned, our Saviour meant only false and deceitful riches. By *the true riches* I cannot think is meant the gospel, which indeed is said to be committed to trust of the ministers, but not of all Christians. I had rather interpret it of special, effectual grace, which is of all other the true riches: and so it teacheth us this great truth, That God is justified in the denial of his special grace to those who do not make a due use of his common gifts and grace; and indeed here will lie men's damnation, because they do not make a just use of that common grace which they have, and might make a better use of it than they do. If they would be faithful in that, God would not deny them the true riches.

12 And if ye have not been faithful in that which is another man's, who shall give you that which is your own?

Let it be questioned whether ἀλλότριον might not have been translated foreign as well as *another man's,* for so interpreters expound that phrase: If you have not been faithful in things that are without you, which are little, compared with things that are within us. Yet riches are indeed properly not ours, we are but the stewards of them, and part of them are other men's, and only trusted into our hands, to dispense to them according to our Master's order. Grace is our own, especially justifying and sanctifying grace; because it is given us of God solely for our own use and advantage. We use to say, That those who have been bad servants seldom prove good masters. In the trust of our riches we are but servants; God will not give out of his special saving grace to those that abuse the trust of his common gifts and grace.

^{d Mat. 6. 24.} 13 ¶ ^d No servant can serve two masters: for either he will hate the one, and love the other; or else he will hold to the one, and despise the other. Ye cannot serve God and mammon.

See the notes on Matt. vi. 24.

^{e Mat. 23.14.} 14 And the Pharisees also, ^e who were covetous, heard all these things: and they derided him.

Concerning the Pharisees' covetousness we have often heard before; and indeed they were so from this principle, that none but the rich were happy and blessed, and that all poor people were cursed, John vii. 49; in opposition to whom some think that our Saviour, chap. vi. 20, blessed the poor. The promises relating to the Old Testament, and made to the Jews, were generally of temporal blessings, though under them spiritual mercies were also understood. As hypocrites can never endure to have their beloved lusts touched, and persons that have drank in an error have no patience to hear it contradicted; so the Pharisees had no patience to hear that doctrine, which crossed what they had taught, and struck at their darling lusts. *They derided him:* the word used signifieth a deriding with the highest degree of scorn and contempt.

15 And he said unto them, Ye are they which ^f justify yourselves before men; ^{f ch. 10. 29.} but ^g God knoweth your hearts: for ^{g Ps. 7. 9.} ^h that which is highly esteemed among ^{h 1 Sam. 16. 7.} men is abomination in the sight of God.

By justifying here is to be understood either an appearing before men as just, and strict observers of the law, or a predicating of themselves as just: You (saith our Saviour) make a fine show, and great brags amongst men; but God's eye goeth deeper, he knoweth the heart, what pride, and covetousness, and hypocrisy lodge there. Men do not know your hearts, but God knoweth them. All is not gold by God's touchstone that glittereth in man's eyes. Nay, many things which are highly esteemed amongst men, as matters of great devotion and piety and merit, and which they applaud others for, are in the sight of God no better than abominations. This highly obligeth all not to make their estimate of things from the value and estimate which men put upon them; not every thing, but many things which are highly esteemed amongst men are abomination in the sight of God.

16 ⁱ The Law and the Prophets *were* ^{i Matt. 4. 17. & 11. 12, 13.} until John: since that time the kingdom ^{ch. 7. 29.} of God is preached, and every man presseth into it.

We had the sum of these words Matt. xi. 12, 13: see the notes on those verses. The connexion of these words in this place seems to be this: Do not think it strange that I preach some doctrines to you which seem new to you, though indeed they are no other than was before contained in the precepts of the Old Testament; for the law and the prophets, the preaching of them, held but till John, since whose time the gospel hath been preached, which gives you a clearer light into the will of God than you had before; and it pleaseth God to give it a great acceptation in the world, though you reject it; *every man presseth,* that is, many press, *into it;* so as God will not want a people, though you mock and deride the gospel, instead of embracing of it, as you ought to do.

17 ^k And it is easier for heaven and ^{k Ps. 102. 26, 27. Is. 40. 8. & 51.6. Matt. 5. 18. 1 Pet. 1. 25.} earth to pass, than one tittle of the law to fail.

Neither do you scandalize me, as if I came to teach a new doctrine, contrary to the law and the prophets. I tell you the quite contrary; heaven and earth shall pass away, before one tittle of the law shall pass. Your vain interpretations of the law shall be destroyed, or amended, but the law of my Father shall remain as a certain rule of life to his people until the world shall have an end.

18 ^l Whosoever putteth away his wife, ^{l Matt. 5.32. & 19. 9. Mark 10. 11, 1 Cor. 7. 10, 11.} and marrieth another, committeth adultery: and whosoever marrieth her that is put away from *her* husband committeth adultery.

See the notes on Matt. v. 32, where this is expounded; as also in the notes on Matt. xix. 9; Mark x. 11.

19 ¶ There was a certain rich man, which was clothed in purple and fine linen, and fared sumptuously every day:

20 And there was a certain beggar named Lazarus, which was laid at his gate, full of sores,

21 And desiring to be fed with the crumbs which fell from the rich man's table: moreover the dogs came and licked his sores.

22 And it came to pass, that the beggar died, and was carried by the angels into Abraham's bosom: the rich man also died, and was buried;

It is a question of no great concern for us to be resolved

about, whether this be a history, or narrative of matter of fact, or a parable. Those that contend on either side have probable arguments for their opinion, and it may be they best judge who determine it to be neither the one nor the other, but a profitable discourse, that hath in it something of both. Our chief concern is to consider what our Lord by it designed to instruct us in. And certainly those do not judge amiss who think that this discourse hath a great reference to what went before, ver. 9, 10, where our Saviour had been exhorting his hearers to make themselves *friends of the mammon of unrighteousness*, as also to the Pharisees' deriding him for his doctrine, ver. 14; our Lord by this discourse letting them know the danger of covetousness and uncharitableness, and also letting them know that what is *highly esteemed among men* may be *abomination in the sight of God*. He telleth them there was a certain rich man, who lived in great plenty and splendour; his clothing was *purple and fine linen*, that is, exceeding costly and splendid; his fare, or diet, was delicate and *sumptuous*, and that *every day*, from whence may easily be concluded, that if he had had a heart thereunto, he might have spared something for the poor. Nor were the objects of his charity far off. *There was a certain beggar named Lazarus*, poor enough, for he was full of sores, and would have been glad of the offal of the rich man's table; but the dogs were more charitable than their master; we read of nothing which the rich man gave him, but *the dogs came and licked his sores*. What was the end of this? The beggar died, and he was by the angels carried into the bosom of Abraham, that is, into heaven; some will have the phrase signify, one of the chiefest mansions in heaven. Abraham was the father of believers, and an hospitable person while he lived upon the earth. Lazarus is expressed to have been conveyed to him. There are many things discoursed by men of wit and learning about this *Abraham's bosom*, but the best centre here, that by it is meant heaven: and from hence two great points are proved: 1. That the soul is capable of an existence separated from the body, and therefore is not, as some atheists dream, a mere affection of that, and an accident, but a distinct spiritual subsistence. 2. That the souls of the good, when they depart from their bodies, immediately pass into an eternal state of blessedness.

23 And in hell he lift up his eyes, being in torments, and seeth Abraham afar off, and Lazarus in his bosom.

24 And he cried and said, Father Abraham, have mercy on me, and send Lazarus, that he may dip the tip of his finger in water, and ᵐcool my tongue; for I ⁿam tormented in this flame.

m Zech. 14. 12.
n Is. 66. 24. Mark 9. 44, &c.

Καὶ ἐν τῷ ᾅδῃ, *And in hell*. The world hath been filled with disputes about the true signification of the word ᾅδης, which is here translated *hell*. The most probably true notion of it is, that it signifies, the state of the dead, both of the dead body, and so it often signifieth the grave, and of the departed soul. A very learned man saith, that if he mistaketh not, this is the only text in Scripture in which by it is to be understood the place of torments. The Hebrew word which is translated by this, far more often signifying the place of the blessed, whither the saints and patriarchs went when they died, than the place whither sinners went; but ver. 24 makes it appear, that here it signifies hell, properly so called, as it importeth the place of the damned. We must understand our Saviour in this whole διατύπωσις to speak to us figuratively, that by things which we understand we might comprehend spiritual things. Heaven and hell are at too great a distance for souls in each to discourse one with another: neither have souls any eyes to lift up. We are by this taught, 1. That as the souls of good men, when they leave their bodies, go into a state of eternal bliss, where are Abraham, Isaac, and Jacob, and enjoy a felicity which we are not able to express, but is set out to us under the notion of Abraham's bosom, to let us know that it is a place of rest, and communion with saints, and the same felicity which Abraham the friend of God doth enjoy: so the souls of wicked men, when they leave their bodies, shall go into a place of torments, the greatness of which being such as we are not able to conceive, they are expressed to us under the notion of being tormented by fire. 2. That it will be a great part of the misery of damned souls, to understand those to be in a state of happiness whom they in this life have scorned, despised, and abused, and, it may be, have been instruments to hasten them to those blessed mansions. 3. That there will come a time when the proudest sinners will be glad of the help of the meanest saints, if they could obtain it. *Father Abraham*, (saith the rich man,) *send Lazarus*, that Lazarus whom when alive I suffered to lie at my gate full of sores, and would not relieve. 4. That the state of the damned will be void of the least degrees of comfort and satisfaction. The rich man desireth but a cooling of his tongue with so much water as could be brought upon the tip of Lazarus's finger. 5. That the tongue is a member, the abuse of which will in another life lie very heavy upon lost souls.

25 But Abraham said, Son, °remember that thou in thy lifetime receivedst thy good things, and likewise Lazarus evil things: but now he is comforted, and thou art tormented.

o Job 21. 13. ch. 6. 24.

26 And beside all this, between us and you there is a great gulf fixed: so that they which would pass from hence to you cannot; neither can they pass to us, that *would come* from thence.

We must still remember, that all these things are spoken in a figure. The *great gulf* here mentioned, to be fixed between heaven and hell, is too wide for persons on opposite sides of it to be heard communicating their minds each to other. All that our Saviour designs to let us know is, that the circumstances of damned souls are such, that, if it were possible, they would beg the help and assistance of the meanest saints, whom they have in this life most scorned, despised, or abused; but as they will have no such opportunities as to crave any thing at their hands, so if they had, they could not receive the least relief from them; their state is determined, they are fixed for eternity, and there can be no change of their condition for the better. Abraham is here brought in calling this man *Son*, either as lineally descended from him, or being a member of that church of which he was the father. It will add to the torments of the damned, to hear and consider the former means and advantages they have been under for salvation, if they have descended from godly parents, or have been members of the church of Christ. *That in thy lifetime thou receivedst thy good things, and likewise Lazarus evil things*. The *good things* which the rich man received were no more the cause of his damnation, than the *evil things* which Lazarus met with were the cause of his salvation; but the rich man's ill use of the former, and Lazarus's good improvement of the latter, through the grace of God bestowed on him. Though it be not ordinary with God to give the same persons the upper and the nether springs, yet he sometimes doth it, of which Abraham, and Lot, and Job, and David, and Isaac, and Jacob, and Joseph of Arimathea, are some instances. But the term *thy* signifies the error of this rich man; he looked upon the good things of this life as his portion, those were the things which he set his heart upon, and let his heart run out to the neglecting the good things of another life. Lazarus received *evil things*, God gave him a mean, afflicted portion in this life; but he was found patient, and glorifying of God by a quiet and believing submission to his will under them; *now he is comforted, and thou art tormented*. So then it seemeth that departed souls do not sleep, as some have dreamed; if they did, they could neither have been capable of comfort or torment. *And besides all this, there is a great gulf fixed*, &c.; the meaning of which is no more than, 1. That the state of souls upon their separation from the bodies of men and women is determined and fixed. As the tree falls, so it lieth. 2. That there is no commerce, or intercourse, betwixt glorified and damned souls. The papists' passage from purgatory to heaven is a new-found way, or rather a new-fancied one. If purgatory be (as they pretend) a place where souls are tormented, it may be wondered how they should pass over this gulf: it seemeth Abraham did not know the way, St. Peter knew as little; this is one of his pretended vicar's new discoveries, but it is no wisdom in any souls to trust to this passage, of which Abraham knew as little as he did of our prayers passing to them, or to God for them, for there is χάσμα μέγα ἐστηριγμένον, a great gulf established.

27 Then he said, I pray thee therefore, father, that thou wouldest send him to my father's house:

28 For I have five brethren; that he may testify unto them, lest they also come into this place of torment.

Him that the rich man would not hear, when he lay at his gate full of sores, exhorting him to do good, and to distribute, to give alms of all that he had, and to make himself friends of the mammon of unrighteousness, he would now have restored to the earth again, his soul before the general resurrection reunited to his body, that he might go unto his father's house, and give them warning, that they might not come into the misery which he felt. But is there any charity in hell? Is there any there that wish well to souls upon earth? or rather, are not damned souls, like persons infected with the plague, desirous that others might be made as miserable as themselves? A grave and acute author saith, he prayeth not for them, but for himself, that he might not be the more miserable by the company of those who upon the earth were his near relations, and dear unto him. But we must remember that our Saviour here speaketh all in a figure, and that which our Saviour by these expressions designeth to instruct us in is no more than this, That although atheistical and proud and haughty souls in this life make a mock at hell, and at the wrath of God to be revealed after this life, and despise the poor servants of God, who by their doctrine, or holy life and example, would teach them better things, yet they shall find the fire of hell so hot, the wrath of God so terrible and intolerable, that if you could imagine that souls under those miseries could have the least dram of charity and good nature left in them, though they apprehend themselves past all hopes of recovery to a better state, yet they would beg that some of those faithful ministers, or godly people, whom they have rejected, despised, and abused, might be sent to every friend they have in the world, to warn them from doing as they have done, and running the hazard of those torments they feel for doing of such things. The papists, who idly go about from hence to prove a sense in departed souls of the state of their friends that are yet alive upon the earth, can derive very little comfort from that speculation out of this text; which if it could prove any thing of that nature could prove no more than that damned souls have such a sense, and might by the same argument also evince their charity. But figurative expressions must not be so closely applied. I have showed what I judge to be the true instruction from this passage.

p Is. 8. 20. & 34. 16. John 5. 39, 45. Acts 15. 21. & 17. 11.

29 Abraham saith unto him, ᵖ They have Moses and the prophets; let them hear them.

Christ here representeth to us the genius of wicked and carnal men, that would be converted by revelations and some extraordinary signs; if they could see one risen from the dead, then they would believe the resurrection; if they could see a glorified saint, or hear or see a damned soul, then they would believe a heaven and a hell: he here brings in Abraham saying, *They have Moses and the prophets; let them hear them.* God will have men believe the propositions of his word, and live up to the rule of life prescribed there, and not expect to have their curiosity satisfied by needless and extraordinary revelations. But is there then no need of the gospel to bring men to heaven? Doubtless there is, but that is included in Moses and the prophets, who all prophesied of Christ, though more darkly than he is revealed in the New Testament. *Had ye believed Moses, ye would have believed me; for he wrote of me,* John v. 46: and ver. 39, *Search the Scriptures; for in them ye think ye have eternal life: and they are they which testify of me:* now they at that time had no Scriptures to search but those of Moses and the prophets; for the New Testament was not at that time written.

30 And he said, Nay, father Abraham: but if one went unto them from the dead, they will repent.

31 And he said unto him, If they hear not Moses and the prophets, ᑫneither will they be persuaded, though one rose from the dead.

q John 12. 10, 11.

How vain is man in his imaginations! We are prone all of us to think after the rate that this rich man is here brought in speaking; that although persons be deaf to the sound of the word, yet some sensible evidence of the wrath of God would make a change in their hearts and lives. There is no such thing. There is not, possibly, in all the book of God a text that more speaks the desperate hardness of a sinner's heart than this, nor a text which looks more dreadfully upon persons sitting under the means of grace, reading and hearing the word of God, and yet find not their hearts so affected with the reading and hearing of it, as thereby to be brought to repentance, and faith, and such holiness of life as it requireth. If it were possible that such men and women should see one come out of the bottomless pit, tearing his hair, and wringing his hands, and gnashing his teeth, and bewailing his misery, and begging of them to be wise by his example, telling them for what sins he is made so miserable, and with tears and highest expressions of passion beseeching them that while they have time they would leave off those courses, acquaint themselves with God, and be at peace, that thereby good might come unto them, they would not yet believe nor repent; nor would this have any further effect upon them, than a little passion, till they could get the din out of their ears. For though sensible evidence be the highest advantage in the world to moral suasion, yet these things are under no Divine appointment to such an effect. Henceforth let us wonder no more that a drunkard sees his companion drop down dead before him, yet presently cries again, Fill the glass; that hundreds of sinners are daily hurried down to hell in their wickedness, and yet their companions take no warning. In a fight at sea or land hundreds drop, yet their companions do not fly, but are held up by their stomachs and passion, and their ears are made deaf by the noise of the drums and trumpets. So in the world hundreds of sinners drop down daily into the pit, yet the rest of their companions tumble their companions into their graves, and never consider the work of the Lord, nor consider the operation of his hands, till they also like sheep be laid in the grave, and death comes to feed upon them, and hell to devour them also. This now to those that duly consider not things, and in particular do not consider this text, seemeth strange and amazing. But it is no more to be wondered at than that hundreds read and hear the word of God, and are not by it converted and changed. It is not to be expected that any providence of God should work upon those souls any saving change, upon whom the word doth not work. That is the ordinance of God, with which the Holy Spirit joins itself, which alone can produce this change. If God works not this change thus, he will work it by nothing else; though he sometimes maketh use of such providences towards souls to whom he intendeth good, to make them observe and attend to the word better, in order to so blessed an effect.

CHAP. XVII

Christ teacheth to avoid giving occasions of offence, 1, 2; and to forgive one another, 3, 4. The power of faith, and defect of merit toward God in our best services, 5—10. Christ healeth ten lepers, 11—19; showeth the spiritual nature of the kingdom of God, 20, 21; and instructeth his disciples concerning the coming of the Son of man, 22—37.

THEN said he unto the disciples, ᵃ It is impossible but that offences will come: but woe *unto him*, through whom they come!

a Mat. 18. 6, 7. Mark 9. 42. 1 Cor. 11. 19.

2 It were better for him that a millstone were hanged about his neck, and he cast into the sea, than that he should offend one of these little ones.

See the notes on Matt. xviii. 6, 7; Mark ix. 42. This term σκάνδαλα is used in the New Testament variously; in general it signifies any thing which may be an occasion of mischief to another. Man, consisting of body and soul, may by something be made to stumble and fall, either with reference to the one, or to the other: thus, Lev. xix. 14. *Thou shalt not—put a stumblingblock before the blind:* מכשל Hebrew: so Prov. xxiv. 17. The mischief done to our souls is by sin; so as in the New Testament it often signifies any action of ours by which our brother is made to sin: which actions may be, 1. Good and necessary, and then the scandal is taken, not given. Or, 2. Wicked and abominable; hence we call some sins scandalous sins, such as give offence to others, and are examples alluring them to sin. Or, 3. Actions which in themselves are of an indifferent nature, neither commanded nor forbidden in the word. Our taking one part in these actions, rather than another, may be a scandal, that is, an offence. What our Saviour here saith is certainly true concerning all these kinds of offences: considering the complexion of the world, and the corruption which is in men's hearts, *it is impossible but that offences will come.* But I must confess that I incline to think, that the *offences* primarily intended by our Saviour here are those of the second sort; and that by them are meant persecutions of the people of God; to the authors of which our Saviour denounceth woe. So that our Saviour by this lets the world know, the special protection under which he hath taken his people;-so as though he knew there would arise those who would hurt and destroy in his holy mountain, yet he declares that they shall not go unpunished, but they had better die the most certain death imaginable, (such must be the death of him who is thrown into the sea with a millstone about his neck,) than to that degree expose himself to the vengeance of God; a guilt of that nature that there is not much more hope for him to escape God's vengeance, than there would be of a man escaping with his life whom we should see thrown into the sea with a millstone appendant to him. I do very well know that it is also highly dangerous to tempt or solicit a child of God to sin, either by our words or actions; but I do not think it the design of our Lord in this place so much to express that as the other.

b Matt. 18. 15, 21.
c Lev. 19. 17. Prov. 17. 10. Jam. 5. 19.

3 ¶ Take heed to yourselves: ᵇIf thy brother trespass against thee, ᶜrebuke him; and if he repent, forgive him.

4 And if he trespass against thee seven times in a day, and seven times in a day turn again to thee, saying, I repent; thou shalt forgive him.

Matthew hath something of the same tendency in chap. xviii. 21, 22, mentioning it as an answer to a question which Peter propounded to our Lord; but the circumstances of both relations are so different that I cannot think them the same. but do believe these words spoken at another time. This doctrine of the forgiveness of our offending brother is pressed upon us in several places in the gospel and New Testament, and that upon the gravest arguments imaginable, Matt. vi. 15; xviii. 35; Mark xi. 26; Luke vi. 37; Eph. iv. 32; from whence we may justly conclude it a duty of very high concernment for us both to understand and to live in the practice of. It signifies the laying aside of all thoughts or desire of revenge in our own cause. The precept is not exclusive of our duty in seeing the glory of God avenged upon murderers, &c.; nor yet of our seeking a just satisfaction, in a legal way, for wrongs done to us relating to our limbs or estate, so far as the person is able to do it; much less doth it require the making such a one as hath so injured us our intimate and bosom friend. That which it requireth is the laying aside all malice, or desire of revenge, upon our neighbour in a case wherein our own name or honour is concerned; and it is fitly joined to what went before, this malice, or desire of revenge, being the root of all the mischief that men voluntarily do one to another, especially of that which they do to the innocent servants of God.

5 And the apostles said unto the Lord, Increase our faith.

Though we be not to seek a connexion of all those speeches of our Lord which are recorded by the evangelists, they sometimes heaping together many of his golden sayings, without so much as regard to the order of time when he spake them, or their dependence on each other; yet he that wisely observes the preceding discourse for charity, will easily observe an excellent connexion of this verse with the former. No duty required of men and women more grates upon flesh and blood than this of forgiving injuries, nothing that the most of people find harder to put in practice; so as indeed where there is not a root of faith, this fruit will not be found. It is *faith* which *worketh by love.* Till the soul cometh steadily and fixedly to agree to those propositions of the word where this is required, as the indispensable will of God; nay, till it comes firmly to rest upon those promises, and hope for them, which are made to this duty; finally, till it comes to have received Christ, and forgiveness from him, and considers itself bound to forgive, as God for Christ's sake hath forgiven it, Eph. iv. 32; it will hardly come up to the practice of this duty. Hence it is that unregenerate men are usually implacable, malicious, always studying revenge. Nay, so imperfect are the habits and workings of faith in believers, that they often find it very difficult to forgive. The apostles therefore very properly pray, *Lord, increase our faith,* after hearing this discourse. Others make the connexion thus: Lord, we have now heard thee discoursing our duty as to love, now increase our faith, discourse to us something for the increase of that. But the former seemeth to be least strained. By the way we may observe from hence, that as the beginnings, so the increase, of our faith must be from God. In things truly and spiritually good, without him we can do nothing.

6 ᵈAnd the Lord said, If ye had faith as a grain of mustard seed, ye might say unto this sycamine tree, Be thou plucked up by the root, and be thou planted in the sea; and it should obey you.

d Matt. 17. 20. & 21. 21. Mark 9. 23. & 11. 23.

Matthew hath in effect the same, chap. xvii. 20, though he saith, *ye shall say unto this mountain:* see the notes there. I cannot be of their mind who think that our Saviour in this, and the parallel place, speaks only of a faith that works miraculous operations; the object of which must be a Divine revelation or promise made to particular persons, that they shall be able to do things (by the power of God) out of and beyond the ordinary course of nature. I do believe that in both texts our Lord designs to show the great honour he will give to the exercise of the grace of faith, so as nothing which shall be for the honour of God, and the good of those that exercise it, and which God hath promised, shall be too hard or great an achievement for it: yet will it not thence follow, that if we had faith, that is, a full persuasion, that God would do such a thing by us, and a rest and confidence in God relating to it, we might remove mountains, or cast sycamine trees into the sea; for no such faith in us now could have a promise for the object, so as such a persuasion would be no faith, but a mere presumption. But there are other things as difficult, for which all believers have promises: *Sin shall have no dominion over you. Resist the devil, and he will flee from you,* &c. And there are duties to be performed by us, as hard in the view of our natural eye as removing mountains; amongst which this of forgiving injuries is not the least, especially to some natural tempers. But, saith our Saviour, do not think it impossible to do: you have said well to me, Lord, increase our faith, for if you had faith as a grain of mustard seed, either so small as a grain of mustard seed, (if true,) or so lively and working, that had such a principle of life in it as a grain of mustard seed, you might do any duty, resist any temptation, mortify any corruption; and you that have a power given you, and a promise made you, for working miracles, might say to this sycamine tree, Be removed, &c.

7 But which of you, having a servant plowing or feeding cattle, will say unto him by and by, when he is come from the field, Go and sit down to meat?

8 And will not rather say unto him, Make ready wherewith I may sup, and gird thyself, ᵉand serve me, till I have eaten and drunken; and afterward thou shalt eat and drink?

e ch. 12. 37.

9 Doth he thank that servant because he did the things that were commanded him? I trow not.

10 So likewise ye, when ye shall have done all

those things which are commanded you, say, We are ⸁unprofitable servants: we have done that which was our duty to do.

f Job 22. 3. & 35. 7. Ps. 16. 2. Matt. 25. 30. Rom. 3. 12. & 11. 35. 1 Cor. 9. 16, 17. Philem. 11.

The 7th, 8th, and 9th verses are plainly a parable, a part of a discourse wherein our Lord, under an earthly similitude, instructeth us in a spiritual duty. This duty is easily learned from the *epiparabole*, ver. 10, and it lieth in two things: 1. That we ought to do all those things which our Lord hath commanded us. 2. That we, when we have done all, are to look for our reward, not of debt, but of grace. He illustrateth this by a similitude or parable. He supposeth a man to have a servant ploughing or feeding cattle for him. By *servants* we must understand such servants as they had in those countries, who were not day servants, or covenant servants, who are only obliged to work their hours, or according to their contracts with us; but such servants as were most usual amongst them, who were bought with their money, or taken in war, who were wholly at their master's command, and all their time was their master's, and they were obliged by their labour only to serve him: such servants our Lord supposeth to have been abroad in the field, ploughing, or sowing, or feeding cattle, and at night to be come in from their labour. He asks them which of them would think themselves obliged presently to set them to supper, (for meat, drink, and clothes were all such servants' wages,) or would not rather set them to work again, to make ready their master's supper, and then to wait upon him, tying up their long garments, which they used in those countries to wear, promising them that afterwards also they should eat and drink. And suppose they do that without murmuring, he asketh them again, whether they would take themselves obliged to thank them for doing the things which their master commanded? He tells them he supposeth they would not take themselves to be under any such obligation. Now what is the meaning of all this he tells them, ver. 10, *So likewise ye, when ye shall have done all those things which are commanded you, say, We are unprofitable servants;* for the infinitely glorious and blessed God can receive no benefit by our services; *we have done that which was our duty to do.* By which we are instructed, 1. That we are wholly the Lord's, all our time, strength, abilities; we are obliged to love the Lord with all our heart, and mind, and soul, and strength. 2. That our labour for the Lord must not cease till the Lord ceaseth commanding, till we have done all that the Lord by his revealed will lets us know we have to do. 3. That when we have done all we shall have merited nothing at God's hands; (1.) Because we are servants. (2.) Because we have but done our duty. 4. That the Lord may delay our reward till we have done all that he hath commanded us. 5. That when we have it, it is not a reward of thanks, but of grace. This parable is excellently added to the former discourses. Our Saviour had before pressed the doctrine of charity, he had also showed what must be the root of it, viz. true and lively faith; he here showeth us what we should propose to ourselves as our end in such acts, viz. not to merit at the hand of God, not merely in hope to receive a reward from him, but the glorifying of God by a faithful obedience to his will, owning him as our Lord, and ourselves as his servants, without any vain-glory or ostentation, and in all humility confessing ourselves servants, unprofitable servants, and such as have but done our duty, no, though we had done all that he commanded us; waiting for our reward with patience, and taking it at last as of his free grace with thankfulness; which is indeed requisite to the true and regular performance of every good work which we do, and our duty, if the infirmity of our flesh would allow us to do all whatsoever God hath commanded us; but much more when our performances are so lame and imperfect, that the greatest part of what we do amounteth not to the least part of what we leave undone.

11 ¶ And it came to pass, ᵍas he went to Jerusalem, that he passed through the midst of Samaria and Galilee.

12 And as he entered into a certain village, there met him ten men that were lepers, ʰwhich stood afar off:

g Luke 9. 51, 52. John 4. 4.

h Lev. 13. 46.

13 And they lifted up *their* voices, and said, Jesus, Master, have mercy on us.

Christ's nearest way from Galilee to Jerusalem was through Samaria. In a certain town ten lepers met him, for though the law forbade them any other society, yet it did not restrain them from the society of each other; probably they were got together that they might at once come to this great Physician. The leprosy was a sore disease, not so much known in our countries. We shall observe it was the disease which God made to come upon some persons, to testify his displeasure for some sin committed by them. It was threatened as the mark of God upon men for sin, Deut. xxviii. 27, —*with the scab, whereof thou canst not be healed.* God sent it upon Miriam, Numb. xii. 10, for her contempt of Moses. David curseth Joab's house with it, 2 Sam. iii. 29. Gehazi suffereth by it, for his lying and going after Naaman for a bribe, 2 Kings v. 27. King Uzziah, for usurping the priest's office, 2 Kings xv. 5. These ten lepers cry to Christ for mercy, mercy with respect to their afflictions.

14 And when he saw *them*, he said unto them, ⁱGo shew yourselves unto the Priests. And it came to pass, that, as they went, they were cleansed.

i Lev. 13. 2. & 14. 2. Matt. 8. 4. ch. 5. 14.

It was according to the Divine law, Lev. xiv. 2, that the leper in the day of his cleansing should be brought unto the priest, who was to judge whether he was healed, yea or no, and to offer the offering there prescribed. Christ sends them to the priests, partly that he might observe the law which his Father had given in the case, partly that he might have a testimony of this his miraculous operation. We shall observe that our Saviour cured some being at a distance from them, some by the word of his power only, though he were present in the same place, others by touching of them; he certainly chose thus to vary his circumstances, in actions of this nature, to let people know that the healing virtue was inherent in him, and that the proceeding of it from him was not tied to any ceremony used at the doing of the work, which he used or omitted according to his pleasure.

15 And one of them, when he saw that he was healed, turned back, and with a loud voice glorified God,

16 And fell down on *his* face at his feet, giving him thanks: and he was a Samaritan.

It is most probable that this leper first showed himself to the priest, according to the commandment and the direction of our Saviour, and then returned to give our Saviour thanks. Some think that this glorifying God here mentioned, and his giving thanks to Christ, signify the same thing. I doubt it, because nothing appeareth from this story sufficient to convince us that he looked upon Christ as God; nay, it doth not appear that his faith was risen so high as to believe him the Messiah, the Son of David; they speak to him only under the notion of *Jesus, Master*, ver. 13. It is plain they believed him at least to be a great prophet, sent from God, and clothed with a power from God. I choose rather therefore to interpret his falling down on his face at his feet, as a humble posture of reverence, which those nations did often use to compliment their superiors by, even as a posture of adoration; and that his glorifying God was a praising of him as the principal efficient cause of his healing, and his giving thanks to Christ a civil respect paid to Christ as God's instrument in the case. The evangelist addeth, *and he was a Samaritan.* Christ calls him a *stranger*, ver. 18; a stranger to the commonwealth of Israel, as all the Samaritans were.

17 And Jesus answering said, Were there not ten cleansed? but where *are* the nine?

18 There are not found that returned to give glory to God, save this stranger.

These ten lepers were a representation of all mankind; not more than one of ten that receive signal mercies from the bountiful hand of Divine Providence cometh to give God any suitable homage. Thus he maketh his sun to shine and his rain to fall upon the just and upon the unjust. Men howl to God upon their beds, but glorify him not when they are raised up. But this increpation of our Saviour lets us know, that this their way is their folly.

19 ^k And he said unto him, Arise, go thy way: thy faith hath made thee whole.

[k Mat. 9. 22. Mark 5. 34. & 10. 52. ch. 7. 50. & 8. 48. & 18. 42.]

It is a wonderful thing to observe what small rudiments and embryos of faith Christ encourageth and rewardeth. His faith appeareth to be no more than a persuasion that Christ did not do what things he did of this nature by any magical art, (as the Pharisee blasphemed,) but by the power of God, and that he was a man sent of God. This faith Christ honoureth, commendeth, rewardeth. Faith is to be measured from the revelation which he who believeth hath, and from the opposition which he encountereth: a little faith upon a little light, and maintained against a great opposition, is a great faith; though little in itself, yet great with respect to the circumstances of him or her that believeth.

20 ¶ And when he was demanded of the Pharisees, when the kingdom of God should come, he answered them and said, The kingdom of God cometh not ‖ with observation:

[‖ Or, with outward shew.]

Whether the Pharisees spake this deriding him, who in his discourses had been often mentioning a kingdom of God to come, or in simple seriousness, for they generally expected the coming of a Messiah, and a secular kingdom, which he should exercise in the earth, particularly over the Jews, (having first destroyed the Gentiles,) is very hard to determine; their mean opinion of Christ inclineth some to think the former; their generally received opinion about the kingdom of the Messiah giveth some countenance to the latter. Our Saviour's answer fitteth them, whatsoever they intended by their question: *The kingdom of God* (saith he) *cometh not μετὰ παρατηρήσεως, with observation.* The word signifies a scrupulous and superstitious observation. Thus the verb from whence it cometh signifieth, Gal. iv. 10. The verb also signifies a captious observation, Mark iii. 2; Luke vi. 7; xiv. 1; xx. 20; Acts ix. 24. But that sense cannot agree to the noun used in this place. The generality of the best interpreters agree the sense here to be, with external pomp and splendour; and therefore Beza expoundeth the noun here by a periphrasis, *ita ut observari poterit*, in such a manner as it can be observed. As if he had said, Men have taken up a false notion of my kingdom, as if it were to be a secular kingdom to be set up in the world, with a great deal of noise, and pomp, and splendour, so as men may observe it and gaze upon its coming. But that which I call my kingdom is not of this nature. Our Lord expoundeth it in the next verse: *The kingdom of God is within you;* it is of a spiritual nature, not obvious to human senses, but exercised over the hearts of my people. Whether our Saviour speaketh this in reply to the Pharisees, or (as some think) beginning a discourse with his disciples, which he further pursueth, I cannot determine.

21 ^l Neither shall they say, Lo here! or, lo there! for, behold, ^m the kingdom of God is ‖ within you.

[l ver. 23. m Rom. 14. 17. ‖ Or, among you, John 1. 26.]

The latter words of this verse seem fairly to admit of a double interpretation, as *you* here may signify the disciples of Christ, who had received Christ as their Lord, over whom he exercised a spiritual dominion and jurisdiction, or as it may respect the whole Jewish nation, amongst whom the kingdom of God was now exercised, by the preaching of the gospel, and the power of Christ put forth in the casting out devils, and other miraculous operations. I incline to the latter, as differing from those that think these words were spoken with a peculiar respect to the disciples; I rather think them a reply to the Pharisees, as corrective of their false notion and apprehension of the Messiah, as if he were yet to come, and to set up a temporal principality; for it is said, ver. 22, *And he said unto the disciples,* as if he did but then specially apply his discourse to them; *ἐν ἡμῖν* thus signifieth, chap. vii. 16; John i. 14. You (saith our Saviour) are much mistaken as to the nature of my kingdom, and indeed of the kingdom of the Messiah, in the expectation of which you live. It is not a kingdom of the same nature with the kingdoms of the world, it cometh not with pomp and splendour, for men and women to observe; they shall not say, Lo here he cometh! or, Lo there he goeth! the kingdom of God is now in the midst among you, though you observe it not.

22 And he said unto the disciples, ^n The days will come, when ye shall desire to see one of the days of the Son of man, and ye shall not see *it.*

[n See Matt. 9. 15. John 17. 12.]

Our Lord spendeth his further discourse in this chapter in a forewarning of his disciples of those great troubles which should follow his departure from them. At present the Bridegroom was with them, and they could not mourn; for many years after that he was departed from them *the days of the Son of man* continued, that is, gospel days, times wherein the gospel of Christ was freely preached to them. But (saith he) make use of that time, for it will not hold long; there will come a time *when ye shall desire to see one of the days of the Son of man, and shall not see it.* These evil days began when false Christs and false prophets rose up, which was most eminently a little before the destruction of Jerusalem, which happened about forty years after. Every factious person that had reputation enough to make himself the head and leader of a faction, taking his advantage of the common error of the Jews, that a Messiah, a Christ, was to come, who should exercise a temporal kingdom over the Jews, would pretend to be, and give out he was, the Messiah, to draw a faction after him. This is that which our Saviour saith in the next words.

23 ^o And they shall say to you, See here; or, see there: go not after *them,* nor follow *them.*

[o Mat. 24. 23. Mark 13. 21. ch. 21. 8.]

24 ^p For as the lightning, that lighteneth out of the one *part* under heaven, shineth unto the other *part* under heaven; so shall also the Son of man be in his day.

[p Matt. 24. 27.]

See the notes on Matt. xxiv. 23, 27. You will (saith our Saviour) have a great many false Christs and false prophets arise, and foolish credulous people will be deceived by them, and come and tell you, Lo, yonder is the Messiah, or, Lo, he is in another place; but believe them not. So it is in Mark xiii. 21. Follow them not, saith Luke. The Son of man shall have his day, a day when he will come in a glorious manner to judge the quick and the dead; but it will come upon the world like lightning, that suddenly shineth from one part of heaven to another, so as no man can foretell it, or observe the motion of it. Some do think that by the *day of the Son of man* here was meant the spreading of his gospel; but certainly it is a strained sense, nor was the spreading of that a thing so sudden, but more gradually and observably accomplished.

25 ^q But first must he suffer many things, and be rejected of this generation.

[q Mark 8. 31. & 9. 31. & 10. 33. ch. 9. 22.]

Before my kingdom shall appear in that glory, I *must suffer many things, and be rejected of this generation.* You may be seduced to think that I am going to put on a crown as a secular prince to deliver you from your enemies. Alas! I am going to a cross. I shall have a day, but this is mine enemies' day, and the power of darkness, both with reference to me and you. Look for nothing in or from this generation but to see me mocked, scourged, spit upon, buffeted, hanged upon a cross, rejected by men; these will be the issues of Divine providence as to this generation; look for better things hereafter, but look for no better from or in this generation.

26 ^r And as it was in the days of Noe, so shall it be also in the days of the Son of man.

[r Gen. 7. Matt. 24. 37.]

27 They did eat, they drank, they married wives, they were given in marriage, until the day that Noe entered into the ark, and the flood came, and destroyed them all.

28 ^s Likewise also as it was in the days of Lot; they did eat, they drank, they bought, they sold, they planted, they builded;

[s Gen. 19.]

S. LUKE XVII, XVIII

t Gen. 19. 16, 24.

29 But ᵗthe same day that Lot went out of Sodom it rained fire and brimstone from heaven, and destroyed *them* all.

u 2 Thess. 1. 7.

30 Even thus shall it be in the day when the Son of man ᵘ is revealed.

See the notes on Matt. xxiv. 37—39. Our blessed Lord in these verses doth both declare the surprisal of the Jews with that judgment which was coming upon them, and of the world with his coming in the day of judgment, (of which the destruction of Jerusalem was a type,) and also forewarneth them to take heed that they might not be surprised; he tells them, that *in the days of the Son of man*, (so that he speaketh of more than one day,) the day of his power in the destruction of the Jews, and in the day of judgment, the antitype to the former, it shall be as in the days of Noah and of Lot. In the days of those men, neither the men of the old world, nor the men of Sodom, would hearken either to Noah or Lot, who were preachers of righteousness to them, and gave them examples of sober and holy lives; but gave up themselves to luxury, and lived in a careless regard of any thing God was doing, until the very day that Noah went into the ark, with his family, and the flood destroyed all the rest; and till the day that Lot went out of Sodom, and fire and brimstone came down and destroyed all those who were left in Sodom. So it would be before the final ruin of the world. Till the very days came, and men felt it, the generality of men would not believe it, nor make any preparation for it. But in our Lord's propounding these two great examples to them, he also lets them know their duty and wisdom, viz. to watch, and be upon their guard, with Lot to get ready to go out of Sodom, with Noah to prepare an ark upon this admonition which he gave them. There are no such signs of approaching ruin to persons or nations, as security, and the abounding of sin and wickedness, notwithstanding the warnings which God giveth them by his messengers.

x Mat. 24.17. Mark 13. 15.

31 In that day, he ˣwhich shall be upon the housetop, and his stuff in the house, let him not come down to take it away: and he that is in the field, let him likewise not return back.

These words seem to relate singly to the destruction of Jerusalem. We had the same Matt. xxiv. 17, 18: see the notes there. They only signify the certain ruin and destruction of the place, and are our Saviour's counsel to his disciples, not to linger, or promise themselves any longer security there, notwithstanding what any false Christs or false prophets should plainly tell them, but to make as much haste away out of it as they possibly could.

y Gen. 19.26.

32 ʸRemember Lot's wife.

We have the story Gen. xix. 26. She *looked back from behind him, and she became a pillar of salt.* Lot and his family leaving Sodom, she either looked back as not believing what the angel had said, or as moved with the miserable condition of the place, or as loth to leave her estate and goods; however, in disobedience to the command of God, ver. 17, *Escape for thy life; look not behind thee, neither stay thou in all the plain; escape to the mountain, lest thou be consumed.* God turneth her into a pillar of salt. It is a dreadful caution against unbelief, disobedience, worldly-mindedness, contempt of God's threatenings, and keeping a love for the forbidden society of lewd and wicked persons.

z Matt. 10. 39. & 16. 25. Mark 8. 35. ch. 9. 24. John 12. 25.

33 ᶻWhosoever shall seek to save his life shall lose it; and whosoever shall lose his life shall preserve it.

That is, whosoever, in disobedience to my command, shall use arts to preserve his life, and whosoever, at my command, shall be ready to lose it, shall preserve it, or if he loseth his breath, he shall preserve his soul. See the notes on Matt. x. 39; xvi. 25; Mark viii. 35.

a Matt. 24. 40, 41. 1 Thess. 4. 17.

34 ᵃI tell you, in that night there shall be two *men* in one bed; the one shall be taken, and the other shall be left.

35 Two *women* shall be grinding together; the one shall be taken, and the other shall be left.

36 ‖ Two *men* shall be in the field; the one shall be taken, and the other left.

‖ This 36th verse is wanting in most of the Greek copies.

See the notes on Matt. xxiv. 40, 41. These verses seem to respect the day of judgment, and that dreadful separation which shall be in that day betwixt the sheep and the goats. It is true also of Christ's day in the preaching of the gospel; but that seemeth not to be the sense of this text. They can hardly be applied to the destruction of Jerusalem; it was so universal as hardly any were there left.

37 And they answered and said unto him, ᵇWhere, Lord? And he said unto them, Wheresoever the body *is*, thither will the eagles be gathered together.

b Job 39. 30. Matt. 24. 28.

Concerning the sense of this proverbial expression, and the various application of it by interpreters, see the notes on Matt. xxiv. 28. In our evangelist (where it is σῶμα, not πτῶμα, as in Matthew, the word there properly signifying a dead body, the word here a living body) it seems to be applied to Christ's glorious coming to judgment: Where I shall be, who am to be the Judge both of the quick and the dead, thither shall all the world be gathered before me, but my saints especially, who have eagles' eyes, senses exercised to discern betwixt good and evil, to discern me as their Redeemer, and the true Messiah; according to that, Psal. l. 5, 6, *Gather my saints together unto me; those that have made a covenant with me by sacrifice. And the heavens shall declare his righteousness: for God is judge himself.*

CHAP. XVIII

The parable of the unjust judge and the importunate widow, 1—8. *The parable of the Pharisee and publican,* 9—14. *Christ's tenderness to the little children that were brought unto him,* 15—17. *He teacheth a ruler how to attain eternal life,* 18—23. *He showeth how hard it is for the rich to enter into the kingdom of God,* 24—27; *promiseth rewards to those who have foregone aught for the gospel's sake,* 28—30; *foretelleth his own death and resurrection,* 31—34; *and giveth sight to a blind man,* 35—43.

AND he spake a parable unto them *to this end*, that men ought ᵃalways *to* pray, and not to faint;

a ch. 11. 5. & 21. 36. Rom. 12.12. Eph. 6. 18. Col. 4. 2. 1 Thes. 5. 17.

This duty of praying always is inculcated to us several times in the Epistles, as may appear from those texts quoted in the margin, which we must not interpret as an obligation upon us to be always upon our knees praying; for thus our obedience to it would be inconsistent with our obedience to other precepts of God, relating both to religious duties and civil actions, neither was Christ himself always praying: but it either, first, lets us know, that there is no time in which we may not pray; as we may pray in all places, *every where lifting up holy hands without doubting*, (as the apostle saith, 1 Tim. ii. 8,) so we must pray at any time. Or, secondly, it is as much as, pray frequently and ordinarily; as Solomon's servants are said by the queen of Sheba to stand always, that is, ordinarily and frequently, before him, 1 Kings x. 8; and the Jews are said always to have resisted the Spirit of God, Acts vii. 51; that is, very often, for they did it not in every individual act of their lives. Or else, in every part of time; knitting the morning and evening (the general parts of our time) together by prayer. Thus the morning and evening sacrifice is called the *continual burnt-offering*, Exod. xxix. 42; Neh. x. 33. Or, as it is in Eph. vi. 18, ἐν παντὶ χαιρῷ, in every season, whenever the providence of God offers us a fair season and opportunity for prayer. Or mentally praying always, intermixing good and pious ejaculations with our most earthly and sublunary occasions. Or, having our hearts at all times ready for prayer, having the fire always on the altar, (as was required under the old law,) though the sacrifice be not always offering. *And not to faint*, which is the same with that, Eph. vi. 18, *watching thereunto with all perseverance*; and Col. iv. 2, *Continue in prayer, and watch in the same.* Not fainting either by reason of God's delay to give us the things we ask of him,

256　　　　　　　　　　　　　　　　　S. LUKE XVIII

or through laziness, and remission of our duty, before our life doth determine. This is now what our Saviour designeth to teach us in this parable which followeth.

† Gr. *in a certain city.*　2 Saying, There was † in a city a judge, which feared not God, neither regarded man :

3 And there was a widow in that city ; and she came unto him, saying, Avenge me of mine adversary.

4 And he would not for a while : but afterward he said within himself, Though I fear not God, nor regard man ;

b ch. 11. 8.　5 ᵇ Yet because this widow troubleth me, I will avenge her, lest by her continual coming she weary me.

6 And the Lord said, Hear what the unjust judge saith.

c Rev. 6. 10.　7 And ᶜ shall not God avenge his own elect, which cry day and night unto him, though he bear long with them ?

d Heb. 10. 37. 2 Pet. 3. 8, 9.　8 I tell you ᵈ that he will avenge them speedily. Nevertheless when the Son of man cometh, shall he find faith on the earth ?

We have here the parable, and the interpretation thereof, both, ver. 1, in the *proparabole*, or the words immediately going before it, and also in an *epiparabole*, or some words following it, which sufficiently explain our Saviour's scope and intention in it, viz. To assure his people, that though the Lord show a great deal of patience towards wicked men, who are the enemies of his people, and doth not presently answer their cries for a deliverance of them out of their hand ; yet if they go on crying to him, he will most certainly at length deliver them. To this purpose he tells them a matter of fact, which either had happened, or might happen in the world. *There was in a city a judge, which feared not God,* &c. : from hence he concludeth, arguing from the lesser to the greater, and indeed there is an emphasis in every part of the comparison. 1. This was an unjust judge ; God is a righteous Judge. 2. He did this for a stranger ; God's people are *his own elect.* Then he assureth them, that God would *avenge them speedily.* We may from this discourse of our Saviour observe several things. 1. That all the wrongs and injuries which the people of God suffer in this life should make them fervent and frequent in prayer to God for redressing them. 2. That notwithstanding their prayers, God may bear with their enemies long, for so much time as they shall think a long time. 3. If God's people do not faint, but continue night and day crying to him, God will hear them, and avenge them of their adversaries. The power that importunity hath upon sinful men, may confirm us in this thing, and ought to engage us to pray without ceasing and fainting. *Nevertheless when the Son of man cometh, shall he find faith on the earth?* When Christ shall come to judgment, he will find very few whose hearts have not fainted ; there will be multitudes who are fallen away, through the power that temptations have upon the frailty of human nature. By *faith* here seems to be understood the true and proper effects of faith, growing out of it as the fruit out of the root. This premonition of our Saviour also served for an excellent caution to his disciples, that they would watch, and take care that they might be none of that part of the stars of heaven, which by the dragon's tail should be cast down to the earth.

9 And he spake this parable unto
e ch. 10. 29. & 16. 15. ‖ Or, *as being righteous.*　certain ᵉ which trusted in themselves ‖ that they were righteous, and despised others :

By the term *certain,* or some, he unquestionably understandeth the Pharisees and their disciples, who (as we have all along in the history of the Gospel observed) were a generation of men who were eminently guilty both of a boasting of themselves, and a scorning and despising all others.

10 Two men went up into the temple to pray ; the one a Pharisee, and the other a Publican.

Who these Pharisees, and who the Publicans, were we have had frequent occasions before to tell. The temple stood upon a hill, therefore they are said to ascend, or go up. They had in the temple set hours for prayer, as may be learned from Acts iii. 1, at which some of all sorts went up to pay that homage unto God. Our Saviour mentioneth but two, having in it no further design than by this parable to inform his disciples, how much more acceptable to God the prayers of broken, humble, contrite hearts are, though the persons possessed of them be such as have been, or at least have been reputed, great sinners, than the prayers of those who are hypocrites, and proud, and come unto God pleading their own righteousness, in order to the obtaining of his favour.

11 The Pharisee ᶠ stood and prayed　f Ps. 135. 2.
thus with himself, ᵍ God, I thank thee,　g Is. 1. 15. & 58. 2.
that I am not as other men *are,* extor-　Rev. 3. 17.
tioners, unjust, adulterers, or even as this Publican.

From hence we may observe that thanksgiving is a part of prayer. It is said he *prayed,* yet we read not of any one petition he put up. His standing while he prayed is not to be found fault with, (that was a usual posture used by persons praying,) unless the Pharisee made choice of it for ostentation, that he might be the rather taken notice of ; which was too much his fault, Matt. vi. 5. Whether the term πρὸς ἑαυτὸν, *with himself,* in this place, signifieth that he only prayed in his heart, or with a voice that could not be heard, or only that he prayed by himself, I doubt ; for though our Saviour, who knew men's thoughts, could easily repeat his prayer, supposing it only mental, or at least with a voice not audible, yet this seemeth not to suit the humour of a Pharisee, whose whole design was to be taken notice of, seen, and heard by others. He saith, *God, I thank thee, that I am not as other men, extortioners, adulterers,* &c. But was this blameworthy ? may we not bless God for his restraining grace, not suffering us to run into the same excesses of riot with other men ? Doubtless it is both lawful, and our duty, provided, 1. That we speak truth when we say it. 2. That we do not come to plead this as our righteousness before God. But this Pharisee, 1. Speaks this in the pride of his heart, in the justification of himself. 2. In the scorn and contempt of his neighbour. 3. Though he were guilty of as great sins as these, though of another kind. In the mean time we observe, that he did not attribute this negative goodness, of which he had boasted, or that positive goodness, which he will tell us of by and by, to the power of his own will. He gives thanks to God for them.

12 I fast twice in the week, I give tithes of all that I possess.

Twice in the sabbath, saith the Greek, but that is ordinary, to denominate the days of the week from the sabbath ; the meaning is, twice betwixt sabbath and sabbath. Those learned in the Jewish Rabbins tell us, that the Jews were wont to fast twice in a week, that is, the Pharisees and devouter sort of them ; once on the second, another time on the fifth day (which are those days which we call Monday and Thursday). From whence some tell us that Wednesday and Friday come to be with us fasting days or fish days. The Christians in former times, thinking it beneath them to be less in these exercises than the Jews, would have also two fasting days each week ; and those not the same with the Jews, that they might not be thought to Judaize. If that custom had any true antiquity, I doubt not but they fasted after another rate than the papists or others now do, who pretend a religion to those days. But neither was the Pharisees' practice, nor the practice of Christians, in this thing to be much admired or applauded. For fasting was always used in extraordinary cases ; and the bringing extraordinary duties into ordinary practice usually ends in a mere formality. It is a good rule, neither to make ordinary duties extraordinary or rare, nor yet extraordinary duties ordinary : the doing of the first ordinarily issueth in the loss of them, and quite leaving them off ; the latter, in a formal, lifeless performance of them. *I give tithes of all that I possess.* The emphasis lieth in the word *all.* Others paid tithe of apples, and some fruits of the earth (of which alone tithe was due); but the Pharisees would pay tithes of those things, as to which it was generally held that the law did not strictly require them, such as pot-herbs, eggs. milk, cheese. Our Saviour bare them this testimony, that they paid tithe of *mint, anise, and cummin,* Matt. xxiii. 23; *rue, and all manner of herbs,* Luke xi. 42. This Pharisee boasteth of his exactness in two things, neither of which were required particularly by the law of God. Nor did he amiss in them, if he had not omitted the weightier things of the law, as our Saviour chargeth them to have done in both the texts before mentioned. But how came these things to make him a plea for his justification before God? will he plead his righteousness, because he did things which God did not command him, while in the mean time he omitted those things which God had commanded? Or, what did these things signify, if they were not done out of a root of love? The law is, *Thou shalt love the Lord thy God with all thy heart;* and how could they be performed out of love, when love was one of the things which our Saviour chargeth them to have omitted? Of the same nature are other works, such as building of churches, and hospitals, and alms-houses: the fruit is good, if the root be good; but if they be done out of ostentation, or opinion of meriting at God's hands, men's money (notwithstanding these things) will perish with them, for heaven is not to be purchased by our money.

13 And the Publican, standing afar off, would not lift up so much as *his* eyes unto heaven, but smote upon his breast, saying, God be merciful to me a sinner.

Those who fancy the publican stood afar off from the Pharisee, because the Pharisees would suffer none but those of their sect, at least none that were under such a notoriety of disrepute as the publicans generally were, to come near them, suppose him to have been a Jew (which is not impossible): if he were a Gentile, he must stand so far off as the court of the Gentiles was from the court of Israel. This publican's humility in his address to God is described, 1. By his posture; he looked upon the earth, as one that thought himself not worthy to look toward heaven. 2. By his action; he *smote upon his breast,* as one full of sorrow and trouble. 3. By the matter and form of his prayer; he confesseth himself *a sinner;* he fleeth unto the free grace of God. Here is not a word of boasting, that he was not such or such, nor yet that he did thus or thus. He confesseth himself a sinner, a miserable sinner, and fleeth to the free grace of God; thereby instructing us how to make our applications to God, disclaiming any goodness or righteousness in ourselves, and fleeing to the alone merits of Christ, and the free grace of God in and through him.

14 I tell you, this man went down to his house justified *rather* than the other: ʰfor every one that exalteth himself shall be abased; and he that humbleth himself shall be exalted.

h Job 22. 29. Matt. 23. 12. ch. 14. 11. Jam. 4. 6. 1 Pet. 5. 5, 6.

Justified ἢ ἐχεῖνος, we translate, *rather than the other;* not that the other was at all justified by God; the other was justified by himself only, and those of his party. The publican was justified by God. It followeth, *for every one that exalteth himself shall be abased,* &c. It is another of our Saviour's sentences, often made use of by him, Matt. xxiii. 12, and in this Gospel, chap. xiv. 11. It is applied to the ordinary practice of men, but here to God in the ways of his providence; he resisteth the proud, and giveth grace to the humble. The blessed Virgin magnifieth God on this account, chap. i. 51, 52.

i Mat. 19. 13. Mark 10. 13.

15 ⁱAnd they brought unto him also infants, that he would touch them: but when *his* disciples saw *it,* they rebuked them.

16 But Jesus called them *unto him,* and said, Suffer little children to come unto me, and forbid them not: for ᵏof such is the kingdom of God.

k 1 Cor. 14. 20. 1 Pet. 2. 2.

17 ¹Verily I say unto you, Whosoever shall not receive the kingdom of God as a little child shall in no wise enter therein.

l Mark 10. 15.

See the notes on Matt. xix. 13—15; Mark x. 13—16; where we before met with this piece of history.

18 ᵐAnd a certain ruler asked him, saying, Good Master, what shall I do to inherit eternal life?

m Matt. 19. 16. Mark 10. 17.

19 And Jesus said unto him, Why callest thou me good? none *is* good, save one, *that is,* God.

20 Thou knowest the commandments, ⁿDo not commit adultery, Do not kill, Do not steal, Do not bear false witness, ᵒHonour thy father and thy mother.

n Ex. 20. 12, 16. Deut. 5. 16,—20. Rom. 13. 9. o Eph. 6. 2. Col. 3. 20.

21 And he said, All these have I kept from my youth up.

22 Now when Jesus heard these things, he said unto him, Yet lackest thou one thing: ᵖsell all that thou hast, and distribute unto the poor, and thou shalt have treasure in heaven: and come, follow me.

p Matt. 6. 19, 20. & 19. 21. 1 Tim. 6. 19.

23 And when he heard this, he was very sorrowful: for he was very rich.

24 And when Jesus saw that he was very sorrowful, he said, ᑫHow hardly shall they that have riches enter into the kingdom of God!

q Prov. 11. 28. Mat. 19. 23. Mark 10. 23.

25 For it is easier for a camel to go through a needle's eye, than for a rich man to enter into the kingdom of God.

26 And they that heard *it* said, Who then can be saved?

27 And he said, ʳThe things which are impossible with men are possible with God.

r Jer. 32. 17. Zech. 8. 6. Matt. 19. 26. ch. 1. 37.

We have met with this story at large, Matt. xix. 16—26; and with (if not the same) very like to it, Mark x. 17—27: see the notes on both those places. The history is of great use to us, 1. To show how far a man may go, that yet is a great way short of a truly good and spiritual state. He may know that nothing in this life will make him perfectly happy. He may desire eternal life, and salvation. He may go a great way in keeping the commandments of God, as to the letter of them. He may come to the ministers of the gospel to be further instructed. But herein he will fail, he will not come to Christ that he may have life, but fancy he should do something meritorious of it; he doth not aright understand the law, and that there is no going to heaven that way, but by the perfect observation of it, and therefore fancieth himself in a much better state than he is. 2. It instructeth us in this, that there is no coming to heaven by works, but by a full and perfect obedience to the whole revealed will of God. 3. That every hypocrite hath some lust or other, in which he cannot deny himself. This ruler's lust was his immoderate love of the world, and the things thereof. 4. That it is a mighty difficult thing for any persons, but especially such as have great possessions on earth, to get to heaven. 5. As difficult and almost impossible as it may appear to men, yet nothing is impossible with God. He can change the heart of the rich, and incline it to himself, as well as the heart of the poor. The rich man hath more impediments; but be men rich or poor, without the powerful influence of God upon the heart, without his free grace, no soul will be saved.

28 ˢThen Peter said, Lo, we have left all, and followed thee.

s Mat. 19. 27.

29 And he said unto them, Verily I say unto you,ᵗThere is no man that hath left house, or parents, or brethren, or wife, or children, for the kingdom of God's sake,

t Deu. 33. 9.

30 ᵘWho shall not receive manifold more in this present time, and in the world to come life everlasting.

Marginal ref: u Job 42. 10.

See the notes upon Matt. xix. 27—30, and on Mark x. 28—30. The difficulty is only to reconcile ver. 30 to God's providences. For the *everlasting life* promised *in the world to come*, that is matter of faith, and not so much as seemingly contradicted by any providence of God. But how many lose much for Christ, that in this life do not *receive manifold more*, or a hundredfold! *Answ.* It is true, if we understood it *in specie.* But the promise is not so to be interpreted. It is enough, if they do receive much more *in valore*, in value upon a true and just estimation. And this every sufferer for Christ hath, either, 1. In a joy, and peace, and assurance of God's love, which is a thousand times more. 2. Or at least in a contentment of mind with that state into which the providence of God bringeth them: this also is much more, as any will judge it a happier state never to thirst, than to have much drink to satisfy the appetite.

31 ¶ ˣThen he took *unto him* the twelve, and said unto them, Behold, we go up to Jerusalem, and all things ʸthat are written by the prophets concerning the Son of man shall be accomplished.

Marginal refs: x Matt. 16. 21. & 17. 22. & 20. 17. Mark 10. 32. y Ps. 22. Is. 53.

32 For ᶻhe shall be delivered unto the Gentiles, and shall be mocked, and spitefully entreated, and spitted on:

Marginal refs: z Matt. 27. 2. ch. 23. 1. John 18. 28. Acts 3. 13.

33 And they shall scourge *him*, and put him to death: and the third day he shall rise again.

34 ᵃAnd they understood none of these things: and this saying was hid from them, neither knew they the things which were spoken.

Marginal refs: a Mark 9.32. ch. 2. 50. & 9. 45. John 10. 6. & 12. 16.

We shall afterward, in the history of our Saviour's passion, see all these things exactly fulfilled, and our Lord here assureth his disciples, that it was but in accomplishment of all that was prophesied concerning the Messiah; nor was it any more than he had told them, chap. ix. 22, and again, ver. 44; Matt. xx. 17—19; Mark x. 32—34. Yet it is said, that *they understood none of these things.* The words were easy enough to be understood, but they could not reconcile them to the notion of the Messiah which they had drank in, they could not conceive how the Messiah, that should redeem Israel, should die, or be thus barbarously used by those whom he came to redeem, or save. We have great need to consider well what notions we entertain concerning the things of God. All this blindness and unbelief of the disciples was bottomed in the false notion of the Messiah which they had taken up. However, our Saviour thought fit to inculcate them, to prepare them against the offence they might take at them when the providence of God brought them forth. It is good for us to hear, though it be only for the time to come.

35 ¶ ᵇAnd it came to pass, that as he was come nigh unto Jericho, a certain blind man sat by the way side begging:

Marginal refs: b Mat.20.29. Mark 10. 46.

This blind man was *Bartimeus, the son of Timeus*, as Mark tells us, chap. x. 46. Matthew mentions two, the other two evangelists but one, as being more famous, either upon his own or his father's account.

36 And hearing the multitude pass by, he asked what it meant.

37 And they told him, that Jesus of Nazareth passed by.

38 And he cried, saying, Jesus, *thou* Son of David, have mercy on me.

39 And they which went before rebuked him, that he should hold his peace: but he cried so much the more, *Thou* Son of David, have mercy on me.

40 And Jesus stood, and commanded him to be brought unto him: and when he was come near, he asked him,

41 Saying, What wilt thou that I shall do unto thee? And he said, Lord, that I may receive my sight.

42 And Jesus said unto him, Receive thy sight: ᶜthy faith hath saved thee.

Marginal ref: c ch. 17. 19.

43 And immediately he received his sight, and followed him, ᵈglorifying God: and all the people, when they saw *it*, gave praise unto God.

Marginal refs: d ch. 5. 26. Acts 4. 21. & 11. 18.

See the notes on Matt. xx. 30—34, and on Mark x. 46—52, where this whole history is more fully opened. It is here again very remarkable, how much Christ attributeth to faith: *Thy faith hath saved thee*, ver. 42, which can be no otherwise understood, than of faith as the condition that was required in the person to be healed, for it is most certain that Christ by his Divine power was the efficient cause of this blind man's healing; but he exerted this Divine power upon that exercise of faith which he discerned in the blind man, whose faith seemeth to be a degree higher than that of the leper's, chap. xvii. 13, who said no more than *Jesus, Master. Jesus, thou Son of David*, was much more than this. It speaks the blind man's persuasion, that Christ was the Messiah; for it was an uncontrolled tradition amongst the Jews, that the Messiah was to be the Son of David. Christ rewards the least exercises of true faith, but much more the higher exercises of it. It doth not appear that this blind man was fully informed who the Messiah should be, viz. God-man, but so far as he knew he professeth, he calleth Jesus the *Son of David*.

CHAP. XIX

Christ visiteth Zaccheus the publican, 1—10. *The parable of a nobleman who left money with his servants to trade with in his absence,* 11—27. *Christ rideth in triumph into Jerusalem,* 28—40. *He weepeth over the city,* 41—44; *driveth the buyers and sellers out of the temple,* 45, 46; *teacheth daily therein: the rulers seek to destroy him,* 47, 48.

AND *Jesus* entered and passed through Jericho.

Jericho was a very rich city, in the tribe of Benjamin, less than twenty miles distance from Jerusalem, (whither our Saviour was going,) and less than eight miles distance from Jordan: see Numb. xxii. 1. It was the first place which Joshua sent persons to spy out, before he had conducted the Israelites over Jordan, Josh. ii. 1; he took it, chap. vi., and cursed the man that should rebuild it, for he burned it, ver. 24. He prophesied, that he who should go about to rebuild it, should *lay the foundation* of it *in his first-born, and set up the gates* thereof *in his youngest son;* which accordingly fell out in Ahab's time, to one Hiel, a Bethelite, 1 Kings xvi. 34. Through this town, or city, which now had been rebuilded many years, our Saviour passeth in his way to Jerusalem.

2 And, behold, *there was* a man named Zacchæus, which was the chief among the Publicans, and he was rich.

We have had frequent occasions to hint, that the publicans were the gatherers of the public revenue for the Romans. Amongst them there was an order of superior and inferior officers: Zaccheus was the chief of them that were in that commission. *And he was rich;* which is not to be wondered at, considering his employment; and is particularly mentioned doubtless to magnify the grace of God towards him, of which we shall by and by hear more; as well as to let us know, that though it be a hard thing for a rich man to be saved, yet with God it is possible, as we heard before, as, that though publicans were most of them rapacious and exceedingly given to extortion, and the love of money commonly increaseth with the increase of men's estate, yet Christ can change the heart of such a man, and work it into a contempt of riches, and into a freedom to part with them at the command of Christ, or where they hinder the embraces of him.

3 And he sought to see Jesus who he was; and could not for the press, because he was little of stature.

4 And he ran before, and climbed up into a sycomore tree to see him: for he was to pass that *way*.

All this was but curiosity; he saw a great crowd passing by, and asks what was the matter. The people tell him, that it was Jesus of Nazareth, that famous Prophet, whose fame had filled Judea as well as Galilee. He hath a great curiosity to see him, and runs before to find out a convenient station; but perceiving the crowd was great, and knowing that he was too low of stature to look over all their heads so well as to satisfy himself, he climbeth up upon a sycamore tree, by the way-side in which he knew that he must pass.

5 And when Jesus came to the place, he looked up, and saw him, and said unto him, Zacchæus, make haste, and come down; for to day I must abide at thy house.

I see no ground for their opinion who think that before this time Zaccheus's heart was touched with any love or affection to Christ. The evangelist seemeth to represent Zaccheus before this as a mere stranger to Christ, *he sought to see who he was*. But Christ's looks are healing looks, there went virtue along with them to convert Zaccheus, though a publican, and to recover Peter, who had denied his Master; but they must be such looks as carried with them a design to do good to souls. Christ looked upon thousands to whom his looks conveyed no spiritual saving grace. He that could heal by the hem of his garment touched, could change a heart by his look. How good a thing it is to be near the place where Christ is, whatever principle brings men thither! provided men come not as the Pharisees used to come, to execute their malice. Zaccheus was brought to the bodily view of Christ out of mere curiosity, but being there he receiveth a saving look from him. How many have had their hearts changed by gospel sermons, who never went to hear the preachers with any such desire or design! Christ's design may be executed in the conversion of sinners, though not ours. He is found of them that seek him not, and of those that inquire not after him. Preparatory dispositions in us are not necessary to the first grace. God can at the same time prepare and change the heart. Zaccheus is the first man we read of to whose house Christ (not asked) invited himself, and in it did more for Zaccheus than he expected. Oh the freeness and riches of Divine grace! which seeketh not a worthy object, but makes the object worthy, and therefore loveth it. What a word was this, *Come down; for to-day I must abide at thy house!*

6 And he made haste, and came down, and received him joyfully.

Curiosity carried Zaccheus up, but love to Christ bringeth him down; he therefore makes haste to come down, and he receiveth Christ joyfully, glad to entertain such a guest. When Christ cometh to any soul, he never brings any sorrow to it, nor any thing but glad tidings.

7 And when they saw *it*, they all murmured, saying, [a]That he was gone to be guest with a man that is a sinner.

a Mat. 9. 11.
ch. 5. 30.

All here must not be taken for every individual person, that is not to be presumed either of all the inhabitants of Jericho, or, much less, of all that were in Christ's company: amongst others Mary Magdalene was at this time in his company, who had no reason to murmur at that. But of what sort of people were these murmurers? The voice is the voice of Pharisees, who had often quarrelled at Christ for this, and of their disciples; for there were multitudes of the Jews that had drunk in the superstitions of that faction, and were more afraid of keeping company with sinners, than themselves being so; of having fellowship with their excommunicates in their houses, than of having fellowship with their, or greater, works of darkness. Our Saviour had before answered this cavil, he will now come to show them they were mistaken in the man; that he whom they counted a sinner, was a better man than themselves generally were.

8 And Zacchæus stood, and said unto the Lord; Behold, Lord, the half of my goods I give to the poor; and if I have taken any thing from any man by [b]false accusation, [c]I restore *him* fourfold.

b ch. 3. 14.
c Ex. 22. 1.
1 Sam. 12. 3.
2 Sam. 12. 6.

See here the first effects of Christ's saving looks upon any soul. The soul presently begins to cry out with the prophet, Isa. vi. 5, *Woe is me! for I am undone; because I am a man of unclean lips, and I dwell in the midst of a people of unclean lips: for mine eyes have seen the King, the Lord of hosts*. Zaccheus is now made sensible of his covetousness, and hardness of heart towards the poor, of his extortion and oppression, and resolves upon an effectual reformation. Christ never looks any soul in the face, but he looks his scandalous sinnings out of countenance. Acts of charity and justice are the first fruits of true repentance. The world, and the love of it, go out of the heart as soon as ever the true love of Christ comes into it; the soul knows that it *cannot serve God and mammon*. In case of wrong done to others, there cab be no repentance, nor (consequently) any remission, without restitution and satisfaction, so far as we know it, and are able. *I restore*, saith Zaccheus. True love to Christ never giveth him bare measure. God had no where required the giving of half a man's goods to the poor, nor the restoring of fourfold, except in case of theft, of which men were judicially convicted; in case of voluntary confession, the law was but for a fifth part, over and above the principal, as to which a person was wronged, Numb. v. 7. In case an ox were stolen, the thief was to restore fivefold, and in case of a sheep stolen four were to be restored, if the person had alienated it; if it were found alive in his hand, he was to restore double, Exod. xxii. 1, 4. In other cases he was to restore but double, if it came to the sentence of the judge, ver. 9; but in case of a voluntary confession, he was only tied to a fifth part above the principal, and to bring a trespass-offering to the Lord, Lev. vi. 1—6. This was the case of Zaccheus; being touched with the sense of his sin, he voluntarily confesseth, and promiseth the highest degree of restitution. But a true love in the soul to Christ thinks nothing too much to do in the detestation of sin, or demonstration of itself in works which may be acceptable in the sight of God.

9 And Jesus said unto him, This day is salvation come to this house, forsomuch as [d]he also is [e]a son of Abraham.

10 [f]For the Son of man is come to seek and to save that which was lost.

d Rom. 4. 11, 12, 16.
Gal 3. 7.
e ch. 13. 16.
f Mat. 18. 11.
See Mat. 10. 6. & 15. 24.

It is the opinion of some, that by *house* is here to be understood Zaccheus and his whole family. Nor can it be denied, but that God, when he poureth out the oil of grace upon the head of a family, maketh some of it to run down to the skirts of his garments. God's covenant was with Abraham and his seed. There is a blessing upon whole nations, and whole families, where the heads of them receive the gospel; but this is not to be extended beyond some gospel privileges, and the liberty of the means of grace. Σωτηρία ἐγένετο (which we translate *salvation is come*) seemeth to signify much more than this. I had rather therefore interpret *this house*, the head of this house. *Forsomuch as he also is a son of Abraham*. Here again a question ariseth, in what sense these words are to be understood, whether that he were the son of Abraham, as Abraham was the father of the Jewish nation, or as he was the father of the faithful, viz. of all those who believed, or should believe, in Christ. Those who think he was a Jew, suppose that the Romans did employ some Jews in their service, to gather the public revenue, which is not improbable, being no more than is done by all conquerors: they have also to countenance them, 1. That Zaccheus is a name of Hebrew extraction. 2. That mention of a fourfold restitution seemeth to have reference to the law of fourfold restitution, in case of a sheep stolen, and alienated, Exod. xxii. 1. 3. That the Jews did not charge our Saviour for eating with a person uncircumcised, but a person that was a scandalous sinner. These make these words to be a reason given by our Saviour why he was so kind to Zaccheus, because he also was *a son of Abraham*, one of *the lost sheep of the house of Israel*. If I could interpret σωτηρία, the means of salvation, I should incline to this sense also; but taking it to signify saving grace, which brings men to a certainty of salvation, remission of sins, and the justification of the soul of this publican, I cannot but think that by *a son of Abraham* in this text is meant a true believer, which he might be, and yet be a native Jew also. Though all Israel did not obtain, yet the election amongst them did obtain, Rom. xi. 7. All were not Israel who were of Israel. *Neither,* (saith the apostle, Rom. ix. 7.) *because they are the seed of Abraham, are they all children.* Nor were they other than Jews to whom Christ said, John viii. 39, *If ye were Abraham's children, ye would do the works of Abraham;* and, ver. 44, *Ye are of your father the devil, and the lusts of your father ye will do.* Our Saviour therefore in saying, *Forsomuch as he also is a son of Abraham,* intendeth much more than that he was a native Jew, (if indeed he were so, for that is not certain,) viz. that he was a believer, a son of Abraham considered as the father of the faithful; a genuine son of Abraham, rejoicing with him at the sight of his day, and believing with him, so as it was imputed to him for righteousness; and salvation is already come in a sure title, though not in actual possession, to every soul that is such a one. *For the Son of man* (saith he) *is come to seek and to save that which was lost.* We had the same, Matt. xviii. 11: see the notes on that place.

11 And as they heard these things, he added and spake a parable, because he was nigh to Jerusalem, and because [g] they thought that the kingdom of God should immediately appear.

g Acts 1. 6.

We noted before, that Jericho was but a hundred and fifty furlongs from Jerusalem, (which were not twenty miles,) and probably this discourse was upon the way when he was come nearer to it. But the principal occasion of the following parable was, his discerning of the opinion which possessed some of the company which went along with him, that the time was now at hand when *the kingdom of God should appear;* when Christ would put forth some eminent act of his power, in delivering them from the servitude they were in to the Romans, or in destroying the unbelieving Jews and Pharisees; or when his gospel should take a further place, and prevail in the world beyond what it yet had done. He therefore putteth forth a parable to them, wherein by a familiar similitude he lets them understand, that he was going away from them, but would come again, and then receive the kingdom: that in the mean time he would employ them, as his servants, with his goods, and when he came would take an account what use and improvement they had made of them, and then he would both reward his friends and be revenged on his enemies. The parable followeth.

h Mat.25.14. Mark 13. 34.

12 [h] He said therefore, A certain nobleman went into a far country to receive for himself a kingdom, and to return.

13 And he called his ten servants, and delivered them ten ‖ pounds, and said unto them, Occupy till I come.

‖ *Mina,* here translated a pound, is twelve ounces and an half: which according to five shillings the ounce is three pounds two shillings and sixpence. 1 John 1. 11.

14 [i] But his citizens hated him, and sent a message after him, saying, We will not have this *man* to reign over us.

† Gr. *silver,* and so ver. 23.

15 And it came to pass, that when he was returned, having received the kingdom, then he commanded these servants to be called unto him, to whom he had given the † money, that he might know how much every man had gained by trading.

16 Then came the first, saying, Lord, thy pound hath gained ten pounds.

17 And he said unto him, Well, thou good servant: because thou hast been [k] faithful in a very little, have thou authority over ten cities.

k Mat.25.21. ch. 16. 10.

18 And the second came, saying, Lord, thy pound hath gained five pounds.

19 And he said likewise to him, Be thou also over five cities.

20 And another came, saying, Lord, behold, *here is* thy pound, which I have kept laid up in a napkin:

21 [l] For I feared thee, because thou art an austere man: thou takest up that thou layedst not down, and reapest that thou didst not sow.

l Mat. 25. 24.

22 And he saith unto him, [m] Out of thine own mouth will I judge thee, *thou* wicked servant. [n] Thou knewest that I was an austere man, taking up that I laid not down, and reaping that I did not sow:

m 2 Sam. 1. 16. Job 15. 6. Matt. 12. 37.

n Matt. 25. 26.

23 Wherefore then gavest not thou my money into the bank, that at my coming I might have required mine own with usury?

24 And he said unto them that stood by, Take from him the pound, and give *it* to him that hath ten pounds.

25 (And they said unto him, Lord, he hath ten pounds.)

26 For I say unto you, [o] That unto every one which hath shall be given; and from him that hath not, even that he hath shall be taken away from him.

o Mat.13.12. & 25. 29. Mark 4. 25. ch. 8. 18.

27 But those mine enemies, which would not that I should reign over them, bring hither, and slay *them* before me.

The parable of the talents, which we had, Matt. xxv. 14—30, is of great cognation to this parable, and the doctrine of it in many things is the very same; but the circumstances of that and this relation are so differing, as I cannot think that both Matthew and Luke relate to the same time. I know nothing that hinders, but that our Saviour might twice repeat a parable which in substance is the same. Not to insist upon the examination of the words used in the Greek, (which is a work fit only for critical writers,) for the right understanding of this parable we have three things to do: 1. To inquire what special instruction our Saviour did in this parable intend to those who heard him at that time. 2. Who the persons are, represented in it under the notion of a nobleman and servants; and what the things are, represented under the notion of going into a far country, to receive a kingdom, distributing his goods, &c. 3. What general instructions from it may be collected, which inform us as well as those to whom our Lord at that time spake. The special instructions which our Lord in this parable seemeth by it to have given his disciples were these: 1. That they were mistaken in their notions or apprehensions of the sudden coming of Christ's kingdom in power and glory. He had first a great journey to go, and they had a great deal of work to do. Instead of reigning amongst them, and exalting them, he was going away from them for a long time. 2. That there would be such a manifestation of his kingdom in glory and power, when he should exalt and liberally reward his friends, and severely punish all such as should be his enemies. In order to these instructions, he taketh up this parable, or speaketh to them in the use of this similitude. 3. As to the aptness of it: The *nobleman* here mentioned was Christ, who shall hereafter be a King in the exercise of power and justice, and distribute eternal rewards and punishments; but in his state of humiliation in which he was when he thus spake to them, was but like a nobleman, a Son of man, though the chiefest of ten thousand. His going *into a far country,* signifieth his going from earth to heaven. *To receive a kingdom;* a kingdom of glory, honour, and power at the right hand of the Father. His returning signifies his coming again to judge the world at the last day. His calling his servants, and delivering to them ten pounds, signifieth his giving gifts unto men, when he should ascend up on high;

gifts of several natures, but all to be occupied, used in a spiritual trade, for the advantage of our common Lord. Not that he giveth to all alike, (which it is manifest he doth not,) for every passage in a parable is not answered in the thing which it is brought to represent or express. The citizens hating him, and sending a message after him, &c., signifies that the generality of the world are haters of Christ, and demonstrate their hatred by their refusal of his spiritual government and jurisdiction. His returning, and calling his servants to an account, signifies, that when Christ at the last day shall come to judge the world, he will have an account of every individual person, how they have used the gifts with which he hath intrusted them, whether they be longer time of life, more health than others, riches, honours, or more spiritual gifts, such as knowledge, utterance, wit, &c., or any trusty places or offices they have been in. The different account the servants brought in, signifies that men do not equally use the gifts with which the Lord blesseth them; some use them well, some ill; some bring honour and glory to God by the use of them, and that some in one degree, and some in another. Some bring him no honour or glory at all. The master's answer to them upon their accounts, lets us know that every man shall be rewarded according to his work. There will be degrees in glory, (though we cannot well open them,) as well as of punishments. The unprofitable servant's excuse for himself, signifies the great itch of proud human nature to excuse itself, and lay all the blame of its miscarriages on God, either his severity, or his not giving them enough, &c. The king's answer, ver. 22, 23, lets us know, that sinners will be found to be condemned out of their own mouths: at the last day, God will be found a righteous God, and man will be found to be the liar. What the Lord further adds, ver. 24, 26, lets us know God's liberality in rewarding his saints at last. What he saith ver. 27, concerning his enemies, assures us, that although God spareth men and women a long time, so long as while his Son is in the far country, while the heavens must contain him; yet in the day of judgment a most certain final ruin will be their portion. Hence we may easily gather what instructions are offered us in this parable. 1. That the state of Christ, when he shall come to judge the world, will be a far more glorious state than it was while he was here upon the earth. He was here in the appearance of a nobleman, but he shall then appear as a king. 2. That all the good things which we have in this life are our Lord's goods, put in trust with us to be used for his honour and glory. 3. That it must be expected that in the world there should be a great many rebels against Christ and his kingdom, a great many that shall say, *We will not have this man to rule over us.* 4. That some make greater improvements than others of what God intrusteth them with for his honour and glory, and some make no improvement at all of them. 5. That Christ, when he cometh to judge the world, will have a strict account how men have used his goods, their time of life, or health, their capacities, honours, riches, trusts, parts, &c. 6. That those shall have the highest reward in glory who have made the highest improvements; but those who have made improvements in any proportion shall have their reward. 7. That proud and wretched sinners will think in the day of judgment to wipe their own mouths, and lay all the blame of their miscarriages on God. 8. That this is their folly, God will condemn them from their own vain pleas. 9. That in the day of judgment unprofitable creatures will, besides the loss of those rewards which they might have received from God, have all their little satisfactions taken from them, in the enjoyments of which they dishonoured God. 10. That though proud sinners here oppose the law of God revealed to them, and will not suffer Christ to reign over them; yet his power they shall not be able to resist, they shall at the last day be slain before Christ's face, and become his footstool. He shall *break them with a rod of iron,* and *dash them in pieces like a potter's vessel,* Psal. ii. 9; cx. 1; and who shall then deliver them out of his hand?

28 ¶ And when he had thus spoken, p he went before, ascending up to Jerusalem. _{p Mark 10. 32.}

Jerusalem (as we before noted) stood upon a hill; those that went to it therefore ascended. This going before the company was noted by Mark, chap. x. 32; here again Luke taketh notice of it; to let us know certainly with what alacrity our Saviour managed the business of man's redemption. He knew that he was at this time to be the sufferer, and to die at Jerusalem; to show that he was freely willing, he leadeth the way.

29 q And it came to pass, when he was come nigh to Bethphage and Bethany, at the mount called *the mount* of Olives, he sent two of his disciples, _{q Mat. 21. 1. Mark 11. 1.}

30 Saying, Go ye into the village over against *you;* in the which at your entering ye shall find a colt tied, whereon yet never man sat: loose him, and bring *him hither.*

31 And if any man ask you, Why do ye loose *him?* thus shall ye say unto him, Because the Lord hath need of him.

32 And they that were sent went their way, and found even as he had said unto them.

33 And as they were loosing the colt, the owners thereof said unto them, Why loose ye the colt?

34 And they said, The Lord hath need of him.

See the notes on Matt. xxi. 1—6, and Mark xi. 1—6: we have discoursed there of Bethphage and Bethany, and whatever occurreth in this history needing any explication.

35 And they brought him to Jesus: r and they cast their garments upon the colt, and they set Jesus thereon. _{r 2 Kings 9. 13. Mat. 21. 7. Mark 11.7. John 12. 14.}

36 s And as they went, they spread their clothes in the way. _{s Matt. 21. 8.}

37 And when he was come nigh, even now at the descent of the mount of Olives, the whole multitude of the disciples began to rejoice and praise God with a loud voice for all the mighty works that they had seen;

38 Saying, t Blessed *be* the King that cometh in the name of the Lord: u peace in heaven, and glory in the highest. _{t Ps. 118. 26. ch. 13. 35. u ch. 2. 14. Eph. 2. 14.}

See the notes on Matt. xxi. 7—9; Mark xi. 7—10; both which evangelists (Mark most fully) describe this great triumph.

39 And some of the Pharisees from among the multitude said unto him, Master, rebuke thy disciples.

40 And he answered and said unto them, I tell you that, if these should hold their peace, x the stones would immediately cry out. _{x Hab. 2. 11.}

How peevish were these wretched Pharisees, to envy our Saviour this little triumph, of coming into the city upon an ass's colt, with garments under him instead of a saddle, or any stately furniture and trappings, and attended by a company of poor people throwing their garments and boughs of trees in the way! yet these they would have silenced. Our Saviour's reply, *If these should hold their peace, the stones would immediately cry out,* seemeth to have been a proverbial speech used amongst them, to signify a thing which could not be. This day was accomplished God's decree in that particular passage of providence, concerning our Saviour, which could not be defeated.

41 ¶ And when he was come near, he beheld the city, and y wept over it, _{y John 11. 35.}

Those who of old blotted out this sentence, as thinking that weeping was not becoming Christ's perfection, seem to have forgotten that he was perfect man, and a sharer in all the natural infirmities of human nature (if weeping upon the prospect of human miseries deserveth no better name than an infirmity, being an indication of love and compassion). Those who think that it was idle for him to weep for that which he might easily have helped, seem to oblige God to give out of his grace, whether men do what he hath commanded them, and is in their power to do, yea or no. Christ wept over Jerusalem as a man, compassionating these poor Jews, with respect to the miseries he saw coming upon them; as a minister of the gospel, pitying the people to whom he was primarily sent.

42 Saying, If thou hadst known, even thou, at least in this thy day, the things *which belong* unto thy peace! but now they are hid from thine eyes.

Speeches which are the products of great passion, are usually abrupt and imperfect: *If thou hadst known*, that is, Oh that thou hadst known, or, I wish that thou hadst known. We are said in Scripture not to know more than we believe, are affected with, and live up to the knowledge of. They had heard enough of the things which concerned their peace, Christ had told them to them, but they attended not to them, they believed them not, and so cared not to direct their lives according to any such notions. *At least in this thy day;* the time in which I have been preaching the gospel to thee (for so I had rather interpret it, than of this last journey of our Saviour's to Jerusalem). This was properly the Jews' day, for the first preachers of the gospel spent all their time and pains amongst them. *The things which belong unto thy peace*, that is, to thy happiness, for so the term often signifies, and it referreth as well to the happiness of the outward as of their inward man. *But now they are hid from thine eyes:* God will not suffer his Spirit always to strive with man, because he is but flesh, not fit to be always waited on by the great Majesty of heaven. First men shut their eyes against the things that do concern their peace, then God hideth them from them. No man hath more than his day, his time of grace: how long that is none can tell: if he sleepeth out that, his case is desperate, past remedy.

43 For the days shall come upon thee, that thine enemies shall ᶻcast a trench about thee, and compass thee round, and keep thee in on every side,

z Is. 29. 3, 4.
Jer. 6. 3, 6.
ch. 21. 20.

44 And ᵃshall lay thee even with the ground, and thy children within thee; and ᵇthey shall not leave in thee one stone upon another; ᶜbecause thou knewest not the time of thy visitation.

a 1 Kin. 9. 7,
8. Mic. 3. 12.
b Mat. 24. 2.
Mark 13. 2.
ch. 21. 6.
c Dan. 9. 24.
ch. 1. 68, 78.
1 Pet. 2. 12.

It is a plain prophecy of the final destruction of Jerusalem by the Roman armies, which came to pass within less than forty years after. The cause of that dreadful judgment is assigned, *because thou knewest not the time of thy visitation*. God's visitations are either of wrath or mercy; of wrath, Exod. xxxii. 34; Lev. xxvi. 16; Jer. xv. 3; of mercy, Jer. xxix. 10. It is plain that our Saviour useth the term here in the latter, not the former sense; and that by God's visitation of this people here, is meant his visiting them with his prophets, by John the Baptist, and by himself. Their not knowing of it (here intended) was their not making use of it, not receiving and embracing the gospel. The contempt of the gospel is the great cause of all those miseries which come upon people in this life, or shall come upon them in that life which is to come.

45 ᵈAnd he went into the temple, and began to cast out them that sold therein, and them that bought;

d Mat. 21. 12.
Mark 11. 11,
15. John 2.
14, 15.

46 Saying unto them, ᵉIt is written, My house is the house of prayer: but ᶠye have made it a den of thieves.

e Is. 56. 7.
f Jer. 7. 11.

We have met with this before more fully: see the notes on Matt. xxi. 12, 13; Mark xi. 15—17.

47 And he taught daily in the temple. But ᵍthe Chief Priests and the Scribes and the chief of the people sought to destroy him,

g Mark 11.
18. John 7.
19. & 8. 37.

48 And could not find what they might ∥do: for all the people ∥were very attentive to hear him.

∥ Or, *hanged on him*,
Acts 16. 14.

This our Saviour's preaching *daily* must be understood of a very few days, for it appeareth from John xii. 1, that he came to Bethany but six days before the passover; now upon the passover day he died; but for the intermediate time, it is plain from the other evangelists that he was wont to spend the day time at Jerusalem in the temple, and at night to return to Bethany. *The chief priests and the scribes and the chief of the people sought to destroy him*, only they stood in a little awe of the people, who were *very attentive to hear him*.

CHAP. XX

Christ silenceth those who questioned his authority, 1—8. *The parable of the vineyard let out to wicked husbandmen*, 9—18. *The chief priests and scribes seek matter against him: his reply to their insidious question concerning paying tribute to Cæsar*, 19—26. *He confuteth the Sadducees concerning the resurrection*, 27—40. *He propoundeth a difficulty concerning the character of Christ*, 41—44. *He warneth his disciples against the ambition and hypocrisy of the scribes*, 45—47.

AND ᵃit came to pass, *that* on one of those days, as he taught the people in the temple, and preached the Gospel, the Chief Priests and the Scribes came upon *him* with the elders,

a Mat. 21. 23.

2 And spake unto him, saying, Tell us, ᵇby what authority doest thou these things? or who is he that gave thee this authority?

b Acts 4. 7.
& 7. 27.

We have along the history of the gospel observed, that the scribes and Pharisees took all advantages imaginable against our Saviour: failing in all their acts, they now come to question his authority, which seemeth not so much to have respect to his preaching, as to his act in casting of the buyers and sellers out of the temple; for as to preaching, they seem, by the history of Scripture, to have given a great liberty, especially if any had the repute of a prophet.

3 And he answered and said unto them, I will also ask you one thing; and answer me:

4 The baptism of John, was it from heaven, or of men?

5 And they reasoned with themselves, saying, If we shall say, From heaven; he will say, Why then believed ye him not?

6 But and if we say, Of men; all the people will stone us: ᶜfor they be persuaded that John was a prophet.

c Mat. 14. 5.
& 21. 26.
ch. 7. 29.

7 And they answered, that they could not tell whence *it was*.

8 And Jesus said unto them, Neither tell I you by what authority I do these things.

See the notes on Matt. xxi. 24—27; Mark xi. 29—33. The substance of our Saviour's answer is this: From whence had John his authority? he preached and baptized; who gave him his authority? They had sent much such another message to John, John i. 19—22. Was John's authority ordinary or extraordinary? It is plain that he had no authority from them, for then they would not have sent to him to know who he was. He must therefore have it from heaven. Now if they had allowed John's call extraordinary, why should not they allow Christ's to be such, to whom John gave so large a testimony, and who confirmed his extraordinary mission by miraculous operations, which we do not read that John ever did? Besides, the Pharisees saw that if they allowed John's mission to be extraordinary, and from heaven, they had obviously exposed themselves to a check for not believing what he said; they therefore refuse to make any answer, and Christ refuseth also to satisfy them.

9 Then began he to speak to the people this parable; ᵈA certain man planted a vineyard, and let it forth to husbandmen, and went into a far country for a long time.

d Mat. 21. 33.
Mark 12. 1.

S. LUKE XX

10 And at the season he sent a servant to the husbandmen, that they should give him of the fruit of the vineyard: but the husbandmen beat him, and sent *him* away empty.

11 And again he sent another servant: and they beat him also, and entreated *him* shamefully, and sent *him* away empty.

12 And again he sent a third: and they wounded him also, and cast *him* out.

13 Then said the lord of the vineyard, What shall I do? I will send my beloved son: it may be they will reverence *him* when they see him.

14 But when the husbandmen saw him, they reasoned among themselves, saying, This is the heir: come, let us kill him, that the inheritance may be our's.

15 So they cast him out of the vineyard, and killed *him*. What therefore shall the lord of the vineyard do unto them?

16 He shall come and destroy these husbandmen, and shall give the vineyard to others. And when they heard *it*, they said, God forbid.

17 And he beheld them, and said, What is this then that is written, [e]The stone which the builders rejected, the same is become the head of the corner?

[e Ps. 118. 22. Matt. 21. 42.]

18 Whosoever shall fall upon that stone shall be broken; but [f]on whomsoever it shall fall, it will grind him to powder.

[f Dan. 2. 34, 35. Mat. 21. 44.]

We met with this parable at large both in Matt. xxi. 33—44, and in Mark xii. 1—11. Its obvious scope is to let them know, that God in righteous judgment, for the Jews' abusing the Lord's prophets, John the Baptist, and himself, who was in a few days to be killed by them, would unchurch and destroy them, and raise up to himself a church amongst the Gentiles; and that this was no more than was prophesied of, Psal. cxviii. 22.

19 ¶ And the Chief Priests and the Scribes the same hour sought to lay hands on him; and they feared the people: for they perceived that he had spoken this parable against them.

20 [g] And they watched *him*, and sent forth spies, which should feign themselves just men, that they might take hold of his words, that so they might deliver him unto the power and authority of the governor.

[g Mat. 22. 15.]

There is nothing in these verses, but what we before met with, and is opened in the notes on Matt. xxi. 45, 46, or Mark xii. 12, 13. They let us see as in a glass the spirit and genius of wicked men filled with malice against the gospel. They are continually seeking to destroy such as have any relation to Christ, and, to effect their ends, they will judge no means unfair; and their great art is to represent them as dangerous persons to the civil government: so as if good men find the same things still, they have this to comfort them, that *the disciple is not above his master, nor the servant above his lord.*

21 And they asked him, saying, [h]Master, we know that thou sayest and teachest rightly, neither acceptest thou the person *of any*, but teachest the way of God ‖ truly:

[h Mat. 22. 16. Mark 12. 14.]
[‖ Or, *of a truth.*]

22 Is it lawful for us to give tribute unto Cæsar, or no?

23 But he perceived their craftiness, and said unto them, Why tempt ye me?

24 Shew me a ‖ penny. Whose image and superscription hath it? They answered and said, Cæsar's.

[‖ See Matt. 18. 28.]

25 And he said unto them, Render therefore unto Cæsar the things which be Cæsar's, and unto God the things which be God's.

26 And they could not take hold of his words before the people: and they marvelled at his answer, and held their peace.

This piece of history we have likewise met with, both in Matt. xxii. 16—22, and Mark xii. 14—17: see the explication of it there.

27 ¶ [i]Then came to *him* certain of the Sadducees, [k]which deny that there is any resurrection; and they asked him,

[i Mat. 22. 23. Mark 12. 18.]
[k Acts 23. 6, 8.]

28 Saying, Master, [l]Moses wrote unto us, If any man's brother die, having a wife, and he die without children, that his brother should take his wife, and raise up seed unto his brother.

[l Deut. 25. 5.]

29 There were therefore seven brethren: and the first took a wife, and died without children.

30 And the second took her to wife, and he died childless.

31 And the third took her; and in like manner the seven also: and they left no children, and died.

32 Last of all the woman died also.

33 Therefore in the resurrection whose wife of them is she? for seven had her to wife.

34 And Jesus answering said unto them, The children of this world marry, and are given in marriage:

35 But they which shall be accounted worthy to obtain that world, and the resurrection from the dead, neither marry, nor are given in marriage:

36 Neither can they die any more: for [m]they are equal unto the angels; and are the children of God, [n]being the children of the resurrection.

[m 1 Cor. 15. 42, 49, 52. 1 John 3. 2. n Rom. 8.23]

37 Now that the dead are raised, [o]even Moses shewed at the bush, when he calleth the Lord the God of Abraham, and the God of Isaac, and the God of Jacob.

[o Ex. 3. 6.]

38 For he is not a God of the dead, but of the living: for [p]all live unto him.

[p Rom. 6. 10, 11.]

See the notes on Matt. xxii. 23—32, and on Mark xii. 18—27, where all the passages in this piece of history are fully opened. By *equal unto the angels*, in ver. 36, we must not understand in all things, but in the thing mentioned: 1. The number of the elect shall be perfect, so there shall be no need of marrying, or giving in marriage, to multiply the number of men. 2. There shall be no more marriages amongst men than amongst angels; *all live unto God*, ver. 38. Though Abraham, Isaac, and Jacob were dead at the speaking of those words, yet they were not so in God's eye, who was determined to raise them up in the last day, and who with the same eye beholds things past, present, and to come. But see more in the notes before mentioned.

39 ¶ Then certain of the Scribes answering said, Master, thou hast well said.

40 And after that they durst not ask him any *question at all.*

The scribes were the Jewish doctors of the Pharisees' faction, and enemies to the Sadducees; they applaud our Saviour's answer: thus as the Herodians before, (in the case of the tribute,) so the Sadducees here, are put to silence. He will now put the scribes and Pharisees to silence.

41 And he said unto them, [q]How say they that Christ is David's son?

[q Mat. 22. 42. Mark 12. 35.]

42 And David himself saith in the book

S. LUKE XX, XXI

r Ps. 110. 1.
Acts 2. 34.

of Psalms, ʳThe LORD said unto my Lord, Sit thou on my right hand,

43 Till I make thine enemies thy footstool.

44 David therefore calleth him Lord, how is he then his son?

The answer had been easy if the scribes and Pharisees, who (Matthew saith) were there also, had owned Christ to be the Son of God. But this they did not own, and so, as Matthew tells us, chap. xxii. 46, *No man was able to answer him a word, neither durst any man from that day forth ask him any more questions.* Thus Christ nonplussed all his adversaries.

s Matt. 23. 1.
Mark 12. 38.

45 ¶ ˢThen in the audience of all the people he said unto his disciples,

t Matt. 23. 5.
u ch. 11. 43.

46 ᵗBeware of the Scribes, which desire to walk in long robes, and ᵘlove greetings in the markets, and the highest seats in the synagogues, and the chief rooms at feasts;

x Matt. 23. 14.

47 ˣWhich devour widows' houses, and for a shew make long prayers: the same shall receive greater damnation.

We have met with all this before, chap. xi. 43; Matt. xxiii. 6, 7; Mark xii. 38—40. See the notes on those texts.

CHAP. XXI

Christ valueth the poor widow's two mites above all the larger offerings of the rich, 1—4; *foretelleth the destruction of the temple,* 5, 6; *the signs and calamities that should precede and accompany it,* 7—24; *and what should happen at the time of the Son of man's coming,* 25—33. *He exhorteth to watchfulness and prayer,* 34—38.

a Mark 12. 41.

AND he looked up, ᵃand saw the rich men casting their gifts into the treasury.

‖ See Mark 12. 42.

2 And he saw also a certain poor widow casting in thither two ‖ mites.

b 2 Cor. 8. 12.

3 And he said, Of a truth I say unto you, ᵇthat this poor widow hath cast in more than they all:

4 For all these have of their abundance cast in unto the offerings of God: but she of her penury hath cast in all the living that she had.

We met with this piece of history, Mark xii. 41—44. Mark telleth us, that Christ was sitting right *over against the treasury*. For other things necessary to be known to understand this piece of history, see the notes on Mark xii.

c Matt. 24. 1.
Mark 13. 1.

5 ¶ ᶜAnd as some spake of the temple, how it was adorned with goodly stones and gifts, he said,

6 *As for* these things which ye behold, the days will come, in the which

d ch. 19. 44.

ᵈthere shall not be left one stone upon another, that shall not be thrown down.

Matthew and Mark say, that some of his disciples spake these words to him, and received this answer, as he was going out of the temple. For the *goodly stones* which the disciples admired, we are told that there were some of them forty-five cubits long, five in depth, and six in breadth. The gifts here mentioned are called in the Greek, ἀναθήματα, not ἀναθέματα, nor δῶρα. The latter word, δῶρα, signified any gifts, money or plate, &c., which men voluntarily offered. Ἀναθήματα signified things accursed, or devoted to God, as all the goods of Ai were, Josh. vii. But this word signified such gifts or presents made to God, as might be hung up and exposed to open view. Our Lord, to take off his disciples' eyes from those gay and stately things, prophesieth the utter ruin of the temple, to that degree that one stone should not be left upon another; which how it was afterwards fulfilled within less than forty years, see the notes on Matt. xxiv. 1, 2, and on Mark xiii.

1, 2. God by that providence not only destroying the vain confidence of the Jews, who took their temple to be an asylum, or sanctuary, for them from the providence of God, or his justice rather; but also severely punishing them for their profanation of his holy place; and also lets them know that the time was come, when God would put an end to all types of the Messiah, and also to all that worship, *which could not make him that did the service perfect, as pertaining to the conscience; but stood only in meats and drinks, and divers washings, and carnal ordinances, imposed on them until the time of reformation*, Heb. ix. 9, 10. See further the notes on Matt. xxiv. 1, 2, and Mark xiii. 1, 2.

7 And they asked him, saying, Master, but when shall these things be? and what sign *will there be* when these things shall come to pass?

Mark saith, *Peter, James, John, and Andrew asked him privately*. Matthew brings two things more within the compass of their question, viz. *What shall be the sign of thy coming, and of the end of the world?* Our Saviour answereth this question from ver. 8 to ver. 32. The most of what he saith we have before met with in Matthew and Mark. It is the harder to distinguish betwixt the signs Christ giveth of the destruction of Jerusalem and of the day of judgment, because the signs of both are generally the same, and most divines think that God in the destruction of Jerusalem intended to give a specimen of the general conflagration, and ruin of the world at the last day; so as signs of the same kind with those seen before Jerusalem was destroyed, shall be seen before the great and terrible day of our Lord's coming to judge the world.

8 And he said, ᵉTake heed that ye be not deceived: for many shall come in my name, saying, I am *Christ;* ‖ and the time draweth near: go ye not therefore after them.

e Matt. 24. 4.
Mark 13. 5.
Eph. 5. 6.
2 Thes. 2. 3.
‖ Or, and,
The time,
Matt. 3. 2.
& 4. 17.

See the notes on Matt. xxiv. 4, 5, and on Mark xiii. 5, 6. This happened, and was abundantly fulfilled, before the destruction of Jerusalem, and probably will receive a further fulfilling in the latter end of the world. But before the destruction of Jerusalem it was, as Josephus assureth us, fulfilled in many, particularly, 1. In one Theudas, whether the same mentioned by Gamaliel, Acts v. 36, or some other of that name, is uncertain. 2. An Egyptian sorcerer, mentioned Acts xxi. 38. 3. One Dositheus, a Samaritan. 4. Another in the time of Festus's government. 5. Simon Magus is also reckoned for one, Acts viii. 9. He boasted he was *the great power of God*. Others also reckon one Menander, a disciple of Simon Magus. It is certain there were many who arrogated to themselves the name of the Messiah, to countenance their heading of a faction. There have also been many since the destruction of Jerusalem, and probably will be many more before the end of the world, 2 Tim. iv. 3; 2 Pet. ii. 1; 1 John ii. 18.

9 But when ye shall hear of wars and commotions, be not terrified: for these things must first come to pass; but the end *is* not by and by.

10 ᶠThen said he unto them, Nation shall rise against nation, and kingdom against kingdom:

f Matt. 24. 7.

11 And great earthquakes shall be in divers places, and famines, and pestilences; and fearful sights and great signs shall there be from heaven.

See the notes on Matt. xxiv. 6, 7, and Mark xiii. 8. Time is the best interpreter of prophecies: what shall be seen of these before the end of the world we are yet to observe, but the destruction of Jerusalem is past many hundreds of years since. What commotions were before that, we must learn out of civil historians, who tell us of divers. Josephus telleth us of an insurrection made by those of Judea against the Samaritans, Romans, and Syrians; and of the Romans against the Jews, to the destruction of twenty thousand Jews: as also of those of Scythopolis, who destroyed of the Jews thirteen thousand; of the Ascalonites, who destroyed of them two thousand five hundred; of those of Alexandria, who destroyed of them fifty thousand; of those of Damascus, who slew of them ten thousand. They

S. LUKE XXI

tell us also of many more seditions, during the government of Felix, Festus, Albinus, Florus, &c. The text speaks further of *earthquakes;* the Greek word signifieth no more than concussions and shakings, but historians tell us of several earthquakes that happened (though not in Judea) before the destruction of Jerusalem; one at Rome, in Nero's time; another in Asia, which destroyed three cities, &c. For *famines,* we read of one in Scripture prophesied of by Agabus, Acts xi. 28. Twelve years after Christ's death, there was another in Greece; and four years after, at Rome. For the *fearful sights, and great signs from heaven,* Josephus tells us of a comet, which for a year together in the form of a sword pointed over the city; a light that shined in the night in the temple, and made it as bright as if it had been noon-day. He tells us also of a neat beast bringing forth a lamb in the midst of the temple; of the strange opening of the gates of the temple; of visions of chariots and armed men; of a voice heard in the temple, inviting those who were there to be gone; as also of a man (whom he names) who for seven years and five months together before the siege went about crying, *Woe, woe to Jerusalem!* and could with no punishments (which they thought fit to inflict) be restrained, &c. These were great signs both from heaven and earth.

g Mark 13 9. Rev. 2. 10.
12 ᵍ But before all these, they shall lay their hands on you, and persecute *you,*
h Acts 4. 3. & 5. 18.& 12. 4. & 16. 24. i Acts 25.23. k 1 Pet.2.13.
delivering *you* up to the synagogues, and ʰ into prisons, ⁱ being brought before kings and rulers ᵏ for my name's sake.

We have all this justified from holy writ, Acts iv. 3; v. 18; xii. 4; xvi. 24. What of this shall be seen before the end of the world, time must show; though the prophecies of holy writ speak enough of that also.

l Phil. 1, 28. 2 Thes. 1. 5.
13 And ˡ it shall turn to you for a testimony.

That is, your persecution shall *turn to you for a testimony:* for a testimony against your adversaries; so as they themselves shall be brought by your confession of me to own me as the true Messiah; and their cruelty, which they mask under the vizor of religion, shall be openly detected, and it shall at last appear to all the world, that the judgments of God are just, for the cruelty they have exercised upon you. And to you it shall be for a testimony; you shall have an ampler occasion of testifying, both before kings and great men, that I am the true Messiah. Your faith, patience, and constancy shall be made more manifest; you shall also testify that my kingdom is not of this world, and that my disciples care not to expect a terrene felicity. They shall also be a testimony to you, that you expect not your portion and felicity in this, but in another life.

m Mat.10.19. Mark 13. 11. ch. 12. 11.
14 ᵐ Settle *it* therefore in your hearts, not to meditate before what ye shall answer:

15 For I will give you a mouth and wisdom, ⁿ which all your adversaries shall not be able to gainsay nor resist.
n Acts 6. 10.

See the notes on Matt. x. 19, 20; Mark xiii. 11. We must not think that our Saviour by this forbids us what is naturally impossible for us to avoid, that is, the forming of those words first in our thoughts which we speak, nor yet a prudent thinking beforehand what we should speak; but an anxious thinking what we should speak, such a thinking as should argue a distrust in God to carry us through with that testimony which he calleth us forth to give. *For,* saith he, *I will give you a mouth and wisdom.* So he promised Moses, that he would be with his mouth, and teach him what to say, Exod. iv. 12, 15. And he tells Ezekiel, that he would open his mouth, chap. iii. 27. Here he promiseth the disciples *a mouth and wisdom,* that is, such wisdom as should guide their tongues when they should be called out to testify for him. This was made good to Stephen, Acts vi. 9, 10; *the Libertines, Cyrenians, Alexandrians, those of Cilicia and Asia, were not able to resist the wisdom and spirit by which he spake.* ♦ Thus it fared with Peter and John, Acts iv. 8—13. By *resist* we must understand conquer, or victoriously resist. The enemies of the gospel have been always opposing and resisting the patrons and

witnesses of and for the truth, but never yet made a conquest: let any indifferent reader but read, and judge the accounts we have of the conflicts betwixt the papists and the protestants in the beginning of the Reformation, or betwixt the papists and the martyrs in Queen Mary's days in this nation, and judge on whose side there was most Scripture and reason. This promise hath been fulfilling from Christ's time even to this day. It is true, the enemies have been able to kill the persons of Christ's disciples; they stoned Stephen, killed James with the sword, Acts vii. 12; they crucified Peter and Andrew, stoned Philip, banished John into Patmos, flayed Bartholomew, beheaded Matthew, and various ways destroyed many in the first and most furious times, and have slain many thousands since; but the truths which they preached prevailed.

16 ᵒ And ye shall be betrayed both by parents, and brethren, and kinsfolks, and friends; and ᵖ *some* of you shall they cause to be put to death.
o Mic. 7. 6. Mark 13. 12.
p Acts 7. 59. & 12. 2.

17 And ᑫ ye shall be hated of all *men* for my name's sake.
q Mat.10.22.

See the notes on Matt. xxiv. 9, 10, and Mark xiii. 12, 13.

18 ʳ But there shall not an hair of your head perish.
r Mat. 10.30.

It is a proverbial speech, signifying that they should have no hurt or damage by any thing which their enemies should do against them. When at the last you come to cast up your accounts, you shall find you have lost nothing, and your enemies shall also find that they have gained nothing.

19 In your patience possess ye your souls.

Patience is either passive, seen in a quiet, free, and courageous suffering those evils which God will please in his providence to order us for our portion; or active, seen in a quiet believing, waiting for, and expectation of what God hath promised. *Possess your souls,* that is, yourselves; do not decline suffering for my name's sake, but live in the exercise of Christian courage and fortitude until the Lord will please to release you. In this sense James expounds this phrase, chap. i. 4, *But let patience have her perfect work, that ye may be perfect and entire, wanting nothing.* Others say, *possess your souls* is the same with, save your souls. So it seems to be expounded by Matt. xxiv. 13, and Mark xiii. 13, *But he that shall endure to the end shall be saved.*

20 ˢ And when ye shall see Jerusalem compassed with armies, then know that the desolation thereof is nigh.
s Mat. 24.15. Mark 13. 14.

21 Then let them which are in Judæa flee to the mountains; and let them which are in the midst of it depart out; and let not them that are in the countries enter thereinto.

22 For these be the days of vengeance, that ᵗ all things which are written may be fulfilled.
t Dan. 9 26, 27. Zech. 11. 1.

After our Saviour's ascension, the seditions amongst the Jews were so many, and they rebelled so often against the Romans, during the governments of Felix, Festus, Albinus, and Florus, that the Romans resolved wholly to destroy them, and to that purpose Titus Vespasian was sent with an army against them, who took the city. Our Saviour foresaw, that when that time should come there would be some vain persons full of stomach for their liberties, that would be prophesying their deliverance, and encouraging them to hold out to the last. He warneth his disciples to give no credit to them, for God would certainly deliver the city into their hands; therefore he adviseth them, as soon as they should see the city besieged, they should all shift for themselves as fast as they could, for there was no true ground to hope for any deliverance. The time of God's vengeance was come, when God would most certainly fulfil against that place whatsoever he had foretold against it.

23 ᵘ But woe unto them that are with child, and to them that give suck, in those days! for there shall be great dis-
u Mat. 24.19.

tress in the land, and wrath upon this people.

24 And they shall fall by the edge of the sword, and shall be led away captive into all nations: and Jerusalem shall be trodden down of the Gentiles, ˣuntil the times of the Gentiles be fulfilled.

x Dan. 9.27. & 12. 7. Rom. 11. 25.

Josephus tells us, that in the wars which ended in the taking of Jerusalem, by the famine and the sword there perished one million one hundred thousand Jews, and ninety-seven thousand were carried into captivity. Jerusalem ever since that time hath been *trodden down by the Gentiles*, the Romans, Saracens, Franks, and is at this day trodden of the Turks. *Until the times of the Gentiles be fulfilled.* Some from this text think, that there shall be a time when the Jews shall repossess the city of Jerusalem. Whether any such thing can be from hence gathered, I doubt. Some here by *the times of the Gentiles* understand all that time betwixt the destruction of Jerusalem and the end of the world. Others, the time when the gospel should be carried over all the world. But their opinion seemeth to me most probable, who interpret it of the time of God's patience with the Gentiles. As the Jews have filled up their measure, and now the wrath of God is come upon them to the uttermost, so the Gentiles shall have their time also. The Romans have had their time, the Turks now have their time; but their glass is also running out, there will be a fulfilling of their time too, and whether then another sort of barbarians shall possess it, or the Jews or Christians shall recover it, time must interpret.

25 ¶ ʸAnd there shall be signs in the sun, and in the moon, and in the stars; and upon the earth distress of nations, with perplexity; the sea and the waves roaring;

26 Men's hearts failing them for fear, and for looking after those things which are coming on the earth: ᶻfor the powers of heaven shall be shaken.

y Mat. 24.29. Mark 13. 24. 2 Pet. 3. 10, 12.

z Mat. 24.29.

We may easily imagine, that this was eminently fulfilled in the siege of Jerusalem, that men's hearts failed them for fear; and for prodigies, we are told of enough, both by Josephus and Tacitus, l. 5 : the latter tells us, that armies were seen fighting in the air with glistering armour, and the temple seemed all as on fire with lightning; he also tells us of the voice heard, and throwing open of the doors of the temple, before mentioned; but tells us few were affected, but built hopes upon a tradition they had, That now was the time *ut valesceret Oriens;* which was true enough, but not in their sense. But what is spoken here certainly relates to the day of judgment, before which prodigious things will be seen, 2 Pet. iii. 10, 12; and it follows,

27 And then shall they see the Son of man ᵃcoming in a cloud with power and great glory.

a Mat.24.30. Rev. 1. 7. & 14. 14.

See the notes on Matt. xxiv. 30; Mark xiii. 26.

28 And when these things begin to come to pass, then look up, and lift up your heads; for ᵇyour redemption draweth nigh.

b Rom. 8. 19, 23.

Matthew seemeth to expound this, chap. xxiv. 31 ; so doth Mark, chap. xiii. 27. Both speak to the same sense : *And he shall send his angels with a great sound of a trumpet, and they shall gather together his elect from the four winds, from one end of heaven to the other.* This is certainly to be understood of the day of judgment, when the saints shall be glorified as the sons of God by adoption, and obtain the redemption of the body, Rom. viii. 23.

29 ᶜAnd he spake to them a parable ; Behold the fig tree, and all the trees ;

c Mat. 24.32. Mark 13. 28.

30 When they now shoot forth, ye see and know of your own selves that summer is now nigh at hand.

31 So likewise ye, when ye see these things come to pass, know ye that the kingdom of God is nigh at hand.

32 Verily I say unto you, This generation shall not pass away, till all be fulfilled.

33 ᵈHeaven and earth shall pass away: but my words shall not pass away.

d Mat. 24.35.

We had this same parable both in Matthew and Mark. See the notes on Matt. xxiv. 32—35, and Mark xiii. 28—31.

34 ¶ And ᵉtake heed to yourselves, lest at any time your hearts be overcharged with surfeiting, and drunkenness, and cares of this life, and *so* that day come upon you unawares.

e Rom.13.13. 1 Thes. 5. 6. 1 Pet. 4. 7.

35 For ᶠas a snare shall it come on all them that dwell on the face of the whole earth.

f 1 Thes.5.2. 2 Pet. 3. 10. Rev. 3. 3. & 16. 15.

36 ᵍWatch ye therefore, and ʰpray always, that ye may be accounted worthy to escape all these things that shall come to pass, and ⁱto stand before the Son of man.

g Matt. 24. 42. & 25. 13. Mark 13. 33. h ch. 18. 1. i Ps. 1. 5. Eph. 6. 13.

I take the 34th verse to be a good exposition of the term *watch*, ver. 36. Avoid sin industriously, in a prospect of my coming to judgment: for sin is compared to sleep, Rom. xiii. 11 ; Eph. v. 14 ; and as he that watcheth doth not only wake, but setteth himself designedly to forbear sleep, in order to some end ; so he who keepeth the spiritual watch must set himself designedly to avoid sin, upon a prospect of Christ's coming, and the uncertainty of it. Particularly he cautioneth his disciples against luxury and worldly-mindedness. The first he expresseth under the notions of gluttony and drunkenness, which are two eminent species of it. The latter, under the notion of the *cares of this life;* not necessary and provident cares, but superfluous and distracting cares. These things he presseth them to avoid, lest they should be surprised by Christ's coming, as he tells them the most of the world would be. He further exhorteth them to *pray always;* the sense of which precept we showed largely in our notes on chap. xviii. 1. He further presseth both these duties in those words, *That ye may be accounted worthy to escape all these things that shall come to pass;* those that should come to pass at or before the destruction of Jerusalem, or afterward ; *and to stand before the Son of man,* that is, in the last judgment; for, *The ungodly shall not stand in the judgment, nor sinners in the congregation of the righteous,* Psal. i. 5.

37 ᵏAnd in the day time he was teaching in the temple ; and ˡat night he went out, and abode in the mount that is called *the mount* of Olives.

k John 8.1,2. l ch. 22. 39.

38 And all the people came early in the morning to him in the temple, for to hear him.

In these two verses our evangelist letteth us know how Christ spent those few days which he had yet to live. In the day time he was in the temple preaching ; in the evening he was on the mount of Olives praying ; to teach all those, who as under-shepherds derive from him, who is the true and chief Shepherd, how they should spend their time, preaching and praying. Though the scribes and Pharisees and Sadducees, and the chief of the Jews, maligned and despised him, yet many of the people paid him a due respect, and *came early in the morning to hear him.* In the world's reception and entertainment of Christ, that of the apostle was verified, *Not many rich, not many wise,* &c. ; *but the poor of this world hath God chosen.*

CHAP. XXII.

The chief priests and scribes conspire against Christ, 1, 2. *Judas covenanteth to betray him,* 3—6. *The apostles sent to prepare the passover: Christ eateth it with them,* 7—18; *and instituteth his last supper,* 19, 20. *He covertly point-*

S. LUKE XXII

eth out the traitor, 21—23; checketh the ambitious strife of his disciples, and promiseth them a share in his kingdom, 24—30. He telleth Peter of Satan's desire to sift him; but that his faith should be supported; and yet he should thrice deny him, 31—34. He adviseth his disciples to provide necessaries and a sword, 35—38. His agony and prayer in the garden, 39—46. He is betrayed, 47—49; healeth a servant of the high priest, whose ear was cut off, 50—53; is led to the high priest's house; Peter thrice denieth him, 54—62. Christ is scornfully used, 63—65; and brought before the council, where, confessing himself to be the Son of God, he is pronounced guilty of blasphemy, 66—71.

^{a Mat. 26. 2. Mark 14. 1.} NOW ^athe feast of unleavened bread drew nigh, which is called the Passover.

^{b Ps. 2. 2. John 11. 47. Acts 4. 27.} 2 And ^bthe Chief Priests and Scribes sought how they might kill him; for they feared the people.

See the notes on Matt. xxvi. 1—5, and on Mark xiv. 1, 2.

^{c Mat. 26. 14. Mark 14. 10. John 13. 2, 27} 3 ¶ ^cThen entered Satan into Judas surnamed Iscariot, being of the number of the twelve.

4 And he went his way, and communed with the Chief Priests and captains, how he might betray him unto them.

^{d Zech. 11. 12.} 5 And they were glad, and ^dcovenanted to give him money.

6 And he promised, and sought opportunity to betray him unto them ‖ in the absence of the multitude.

‖ Or, *without tumult.*

^{e Mat. 26. 17. Mark 14. 12} 7 ¶ ^eThen came the day of unleavened bread, when the Passover must be killed.

8 And he sent Peter and John, saying, Go and prepare us the Passover, that we may eat.

9 And they said unto him, Where wilt thou that we prepare?

10 And he said unto them, Behold, when ye are entered into the city, there shall a man meet you, bearing a pitcher of water; follow him into the house where he entereth in.

11 And ye shall say unto the goodman of the house, The Master saith unto thee, Where is the guestchamber, where I shall eat the Passover with my disciples?

12 And he shall shew you a large upper room furnished: there make ready.

13 And they went, and found as he had said unto them: and they made ready the Passover.

^{f Mat. 26. 20. Mark 14. 17.} 14 ^fAnd when the hour was come, he sat down, and the twelve apostles with him.

See the notes on Matt. xxvi. 14—19, and on Mark xiv. 10—16.

‖ Or, *I have heartily desired.*

15 And he said unto them, ‖ With desire I have desired to eat this Passover with you before I suffer:

^{g ch. 14. 15. Acts 10. 41. Rev. 19. 9.} 16 For I say unto you, I will not any more eat thereof, ^guntil it be fulfilled in the kingdom of God.

17 And he took the cup, and gave thanks, and said, Take this, and divide *it* among yourselves:

^{h Mat. 26. 29. Mark 14. 25.} 18 For ^hI say unto you, I will not drink of the fruit of the vine, until the kingdom of God shall come.

^{i Mat. 26. 26. Mark 14. 22.} 19 ¶ ⁱAnd he took bread, and gave thanks, and brake *it*, and gave unto them, saying, This is my body which is given for you: ^kthis do in remembrance of me.

^{k 1 Cor. 11. 24.}

20 Likewise also the cup after supper, saying, ^lThis cup *is* the new testament in my blood, which is shed for you.

^{l 1 Cor. 10. 16.}

21 ¶ ^mBut, behold, the hand of him that betrayeth me *is* with me on the table.

^{m Ps. 41. 9. Mat. 26. 21, 23. Mark 14. 18. John 13.}

22 ⁿAnd truly the Son of man goeth, ^oas it was determined: but woe unto that man by whom he is betrayed!

^{n Mat. 26. 24. o Acts 2. 23. & 4. 28.}

23 ^pAnd they began to enquire among themselves, which of them it was that should do this thing.

^{p Mat. 26. 22. John 13. 22, 25.}

See the notes on Matt. xxvi. 20—30, where is opened whatsoever Luke hath that is not in the other evangelists.

24 ¶ ^qAnd there was also a strife among them, which of them should be accounted the greatest.

^{q Mark 9. 34. Luke 9. 46.}

Luke only taketh notice of this strife at the time of their being in the guest-chamber. Such a strife we read of, Matt. xviii. 1; xx. 25, 26; Mark ix. 33; and in this Gospel, chap. ix. 46; by which it is apparent, that they had been more than once arguing this point. But yet most interpreters think that it is here placed by Luke out of order and some translate ἐγένετο in this text, *there had been*, not, *there was;* and indeed we can hardly think so uncharitably of the apostles, as to imagine of them, that immediately after their receiving, first the passover, then the Lord's supper, their thoughts should be taken up with things of this nature, much less that they should discourse of any such subjects as these; especially also considering what our Saviour had told them, that he was betrayed into the hands of sinners. Something of our Saviour's answer, pressing upon them brotherly love, and mutual serviceableness each to other, was very proper to this time, which our Saviour (though spoken before) might at this time repeat, and Luke prefatorily to it might take notice of this contest in this place.

25 ^rAnd he said unto them, The kings of the Gentiles exercise lordship over them; and they that exercise authority upon them are called benefactors.

^{r Mat. 20. 25. Mark 10. 42.}

26 ^sBut ye *shall* not *be* so: ^tbut he that is greatest among you, let him be as the younger; and he that is chief, as he that doth serve.

^{s Mat. 20. 26. 1 Pet. 5. 3. t ch. 9. 48.}

27 ^uFor whether *is* greater, he that sitteth at meat, or he that serveth? *is* not he that sitteth at meat? but ^xI am among you as he that serveth.

^{u ch. 12. 37. x Mat. 20. 28. John 13. 13, 14. Phil. 2. 7.}

See the notes on Matt. xx. 25—28. The sum is, our Saviour hereby teacheth all his disciples (his ministers especially) to avoid affectation of rule and dominion, as that which became heathens rather than Christians, and the kings of the Gentiles rather than the ministers of the Lord Jesus Christ. This text giveth no countenance to the levelling of all orders of men. Magistracy is an ordinance of God, and ought to be upheld. Order also in the church is to be observed, for God is the God of order; but no minister of Christ ought to affect great titles, nor to exercise a dominion or lordship. Our work is to *feed the flock of God, taking the oversight of them, not by constraint, but willingly; not for filthy lucre, but of a ready mind; neither as being lords over God's heritage, but being ensamples to the flock,* 1 Pet. v. 2, 3. *Not for that we have dominion over your faith, but are helpers of your joy,* 2 Cor. i. 24. That the ministers of Christ may not have titles given them, speaking honour and reverence due to them, I do not know. But the reason is obvious why they should not affect them to be fond of them; for pride is a vain and vicious affection, and more culpable in them than others. Their works are but a ministration to the church, in putting the laws of Christ relating to it in execution, and it is their greatest honour to be humble. Nor doth this at all degrade a minister of Christ, for even Christ himself, while he was upon the earth, was not as one that sat at meat, but as one that served.

28 Ye are they which have continued with me in ^ymy temptations.

^{y Heb. 4. 15.}

S. LUKE XXII

29 And *I appoint unto you a kingdom, as my Father hath appointed unto me;

30 That ᵃye may eat and drink at my table in my kingdom, ᵇand sit on thrones judging the twelve tribes of Israel.

These verses seem to contain (though in a few more words) the substance of what we met with Matt. xix. 28. There they are spoken as an answer to Peter, speaking on the behalf of himself and the rest of the apostles, who had forsaken all to follow Christ. Christ tells them there, that those *which had followed him, in the regeneration when the Son of man should sit on the throne of his glory, should sit upon twelve thrones, judging the twelve tribes of Israel.* That time which our Lord there calleth *the regeneration*, is the time when he had been giving a new birth to the church, reforming the world by his doctrine and holy example. That time he here calleth the time of his *temptations*, by which he meaneth trials, afflictions, and persecutions, as the word is often taken in holy writ, Gal. iv. 14; James i. 12; 2 Pet. ii. 9; Rev. iii. 10. To those of the disciples (they were eleven of the twelve) he promiseth *a kingdom*, a state of great honour and dignity, as his Father had appointed him; and therefore they might satisfy themselves with the titles and qualities of ministers and servants while they were here, and be content to meet with troubles and temptations, as he had done, to hunger and thirst, &c.; when that time came which he had appointed, they should then eat and drink at his table, they should sit also upon thrones, judging the twelve tribes of Israel. Terms expressive of that rest and satisfaction, that glory, honour, and dignity, which the saints in God shall in heaven be possessed of.

31 ¶ And the Lord said, Simon, Simon, behold, ᶜSatan hath desired *to have* you, that he may ᵈsift *you* as wheat:

32 But ᵉI have prayed for thee, that thy faith fail not: ᶠand when thou art converted, strengthen thy brethren.

Our Lord directeth his speech to Peter, as one who (as it will by and by appear) had a greater confidence of himself than the rest expressed, and as one who he foresaw would fall more foully than the rest; though it appears, that in his speech he had a respect to them all, for the word *you* is in the plural number. The devil had a mind to disturb them all by his temptations (that is here called sifting). Christ hath his fan in his hand, and will sift his church, but his sifting is to purge his floor; he sifts a particular soul, to purify it from its lusts and corruptions; but Satan sifteth the soul and the church merely to give them trouble, and to keep them from rest and quiet by continual motion and agitation. This we are all concerned to take notice of, that we may both be continually prepared for the time of our siftings, and bless God who doth not satisfy Satan's desires to sift us; for he hath the same mind to winnow us now, that he had to sift Peter and the rest of the apostles. But (saith our Saviour) *I have prayed that thy faith fail not.* There is a total and a partial failing of faith. Peter's faith did fail in part; but the seed of God did yet abide in him, his faith did not wholly fail: so will it be with the faith of every true disciple of Christ. In hours of great temptation and trial, their faith may, as to some degrees, fail, but totally it shall not: they may be perverted, but they shall again be converted. As the apostles saith of the bodies of the saints, Rom. viii. 10, 11, *And if Christ be in you, the body is dead because of sin; but the Spirit is life because of righteousness. But if the Spirit of him that raised up Jesus from the dead dwell in you, he that raised up Christ from the dead shall also quicken your mortal bodies by his Spirit that dwelleth in you:* may also be said of their souls. They have in them a body of death, and they may in an hour of great temptations fail, and their gracious habits may seem to die. But if the Spirit of God dwelleth in the soul, he will again quicken their souls by his Spirit which dwelleth in them. *And when thou art converted, strengthen thy brethren;* that is, when God hath recovered thee from thy fall, and made thee to see thy error, make an improvement of thy recovery out of the snare of the devil, by admonishing others to take heed of too much confidence in themselves, and encouraging them not to despair, though they also may fall into temptation; but that the grace of God shall be sufficient for them.

33 And he said unto him, Lord, I am ready to go with thee, both into prison, and to death.

34 ᵍAnd he said, I tell thee, Peter, the cock shall not crow this day, before that thou shalt thrice deny that thou knowest me.

This is more largely recorded by Matthew, chap. xxvi. 33—35, and by Mark, chap. xiv. 27—30. See the notes on those places.

35 ʰAnd he said unto them, When I sent you without purse, and scrip, and shoes, lacked ye any thing? And they said, Nothing.

36 Then said he unto them, But now, he that hath a purse, let him take *it*, and likewise *his* scrip: and he that hath no sword, let him sell his garment, and buy one.

37 For I say unto you, that this that is written must yet be accomplished in me, ⁱAnd he was reckoned among the transgressors: for the things concerning me have an end.

38 And they said, Lord, behold, here *are* two swords. And he said unto them, It is enough.

Those who interpret ver. 35, 36, as a precept of our Saviour's imposing a duty upon his disciples, or a counsel concerning the providing arms which they might use for the protection and defence of themselves, will not only find a difficulty to reconcile their notion of it to several other precepts, and the will of God declared by the apostles' practice, who never went about by force and arms to defend themselves in the first plantation and propagation of the gospel; but also to reconcile it to the last words of our Saviour, who said, when his disciples told him they had *two swords, It is enough;* which he would never have said, if he had intended any such thing; for two swords was much too little to have conquered that multitude of adversaries which the disciples of Christ were to meet with. Our Saviour doth doubtless speak in a figure, and all that he intendeth amounteth but to this: Hitherto I have been with you, and you have had my special protection; though you went out without a purse or a scrip, yet you have wanted nothing; though you went without a sword, yet none did you any harm. But the time is now come, when the posture of your affairs will be much altered; your friends will be few, your enemies many, therefore you stand concerned to make as good preparation as you can do in those things that are consistent with the general precepts that I have given you. The tragedy will begin with me; for what is written of me must now be accomplished, Isa. liii. 12, *He was numbered with the transgressors.* I must be brought before magistrates as a common malefactor, and hanged on a cross betwixt two thieves. And *the things concerning me* shall shortly *have an end:* you will next come upon the stage, and therefore prepare what in you lieth for the performance of your part.

39 ¶ ᵏAnd he came out, and ˡwent, as he was wont, to the mount of Olives; and his disciples also followed him.

Both Matthew and Mark say, he went to *a place called Gethsemane;* but that makes no difference, for whether Gethsemane signifieth a village, or a garden, or a valley, all agree it was at the foot of the mount of Olives. It was a place to which our Saviour had used to go ever since he came to Jerusalem, and lay in his way to Bethany. He went thither to pray, and his disciples followed him.

40 ᵐAnd when he was at the place, he said unto them, Pray that ye enter not into temptation.

When he came to the mount of Olives, he first setteth his disciples to that work, which at this day was proper for them. *Pray that ye enter not into temptation;* that, if it be the will of God, you may be delivered from such an hour of trial as I am entering into ; or, at least, that you may not be overcome by it. That my trials which you will presently be witnesses unto, and your own which you shall hereafter meet with, may have no power upon you to withdraw you from your work in the publication or profession of my gospel. The other two evangelists make mention of our Saviour's taking Peter, and James, and John with him, yet more privately. Luke mentioneth not that, but goeth on.

n Mat. 26.39.
Mark 14. 35.
41 ⁿAnd he was withdrawn from them about a stone's cast, and kneeled down, and prayed,

Whether from the eight, or from Peter, James, and John also, the evangelist doth not tell us; but some are of opinion, that he took the three disciples along to join with him in prayer, from whom some account might be given of the substance of his prayer, which followeth. I rather think he was alone.

† Gr. *willing to remove.*
o John 5. 30. & 6. 38.
42 Saying, Father, if thou be †willing, remove this cup from me : nevertheless °not my will, but thine, be done.

We have a larger account given us of our Saviour's prayer, both by Matthew and Mark, Matt. xxvi. 39—46, and Mark xiv. 35—42. See the notes there.

p Mat. 4. 11.
43 And there appeared ᵖan angel unto him from heaven, strengthening him.

q John 12.27.
Heb. 5. 7.
44 ᑫAnd being in an agony he prayed more earnestly : and his sweat was as it were great drops of blood falling down to the ground.

We have formerly opened these verses in our notes on Matt. xxvi. 44—46, where we took them in, as being a part of the history of our Saviour's praying before his passion.

45 And when he rose up from prayer, and was come to his disciples, he found them sleeping for sorrow,

46 And said unto them, Why sleep ye ?
r ver. 40. rise and ʳpray, lest ye enter into temptation.

The relations which Matthew and Mark give us are both more particular than that given us by Luke, to which we refer the reader. Luke speaketh but of his praying once ; Matthew saith he prayed thrice. Luke mentioneth nothing of his withdrawing with Peter, James, and John from the other eight; Matthew and Mark both mention it. Luke maketh mention of an angel's appearing to him, of the agony in which he was, and his sweating drops as it were of blood ; which neither Matthew nor Mark take notice of : yet we must not think, that either any one of the evangelists, or all of them together, give a perfect account of all the words our Saviour used in these prayers, only they tell us the sum of them in different words ; but see the annotations on Matt. xxvi. and Mark xiv., where we have fully considered whatsoever is said by any of the evangelists upon this argument.

s Mat. 26.47.
Mark 14. 43.
John 18. 3.
47 ¶ And while he yet spake, ˢbehold a multitude, and he that was called Judas, one of the twelve, went before them, and drew near unto Jesus to kiss him.

48 But Jesus said unto him, Judas, betrayest thou the Son of man with a kiss ?

See the notes on Matt. xxvi. 47—49, and Mark xiv. 43—45.

49 When they which were about him saw what would follow, they said unto him, Lord, shall we smite with the sword ?

t Mat. 26.51.
Mark 14. 47.
John 18. 10.
50 ¶ And ᵗone of them smote the servant of the High Priest, and cut off his right ear.

51 And Jesus answered and said, Suffer ye thus far. And he touched his ear, and healed him.

No other evangelist but John hath this passage perfect. What he hath we have opened in our notes on Matt. xxvi. 51, 52, because it tendeth to complete that part of the history there discoursed, concerning Christ's being apprehended. John relates it with more circumstances, telling us that it was Peter who drew the sword, and that his name whose ear was cut off was Malchus, and relateth some further words used by our Saviour to Peter, which we shall further consider in their places. This rash act of Peter might have cost him dear, for it made a kinsman of Malchus take such notice of him, as he was very near being accused by him, John xviii. 26. Swords are dangerous things for us to use, until God puts them into our hands. Peter ought not only to have asked his Master if he should smite with the sword, but also to have staid his hand till Christ had given him an answer.

u Mat. 26.55.
Mark 14. 48.
52 ᵘThen Jesus said unto the Chief Priests, and captains of the temple, and the elders, which were come to him, Be ye come out, as against a thief, with swords and staves ?

53 When I was daily with you in the temple, ye stretched forth no hands against me : ˣbut this is your hour, and the power of darkness.
x John 12. 27.

See the notes on Matt. xxvi. 55, and Mark xiv. 48, 49. It speaketh a great degree of rage and malice against our Saviour, that so great men, as the chief of the priests and the elders, should come out at midnight, in the company of the officers and soldiers, to apprehend Christ. From these verses it appeareth that some of them were there in the height of their zeal.

54 ¶ ʸThen took they him, and led *him,* and brought him into the High Priest's house. ᶻAnd Peter followed afar off.
y Mat. 26. 57
z Mat.26. 58.
John 18. 15.

55 ᵃAnd when they had kindled a fire in the midst of the hall, and were set down together, Peter sat down among them.
a Mat. 26 69.
Mark 14. 66.
John 18. 17, 18.

56 But a certain maid beheld him as he sat by the fire, and earnestly looked upon him, and said, This man was also with him.

57 And he denied him, saying, Woman, I know him not.

58 ᵇAnd after a little while another saw him, and said, Thou art also of them. And Peter said, Man, I am not.
b Mat. 26.71.
Mark 14. 69.
John 18. 25.

59 ᶜAnd about the space of one hour after another confidently affirmed, saying, Of a truth this *fellow* also was with him : for he is a Galilæan.
c Mat.26.73.
Mark 14. 70.
John 18. 26.

60 And Peter said, Man, I know not what thou sayest. And immediately, while he yet spake, the cock crew.

61 And the Lord turned, and looked upon Peter. ᵈAnd Peter remembered the word of the Lord, how he had said unto him, ᵉBefore the cock crow, thou shalt deny me thrice.
d Mat. 26.75.
Mark 14. 72.
e Matt. 26. 34. 75.
John 13. 38.

62 And Peter went out, and wept bitterly.

See the whole history of Peter's denial of his Master, and of his repentance, in our notes on Matt. xxvi. 69—75, where we have opened what passages relating to it are in Mark or this evangelist.

63 ¶ ᶠAnd the men that held Jesus mocked him, and smote *him.*
f Matt. 26. 67, 68.
Mark 14. 65.

64 And when they had blindfolded him, they

struck him on the face, and asked him, saying, Prophesy, who is it that smote thee?

65 And many other things blasphemously spake they against him.

Concerning these abuses offered to our Saviour, see the notes on Matt. xxvi. 67, 68, and Mark xiv. 65.

66 ¶ ᵍAnd as soon as it was day, ʰthe elders of the people and the Chief Priests and the Scribes came together, and led him into their council, saying,

67 ⁱArt thou the Christ? tell us. And he said unto them, If I tell you, ye will not believe:

68 And if I also ask *you*, ye will not answer me, nor let *me* go.

69 ᵏHereafter shall the Son of man sit on the right hand of the power of God.

70 Then said they all, Art thou then the Son of God? And he said unto them, ˡYe say that I am.

71 ᵐAnd they said, What need we any further witness? for we ourselves have heard of his own mouth.

Our blessed Lord before his death passed two trials or examinations. The one before the Jewish sanhedrim, whose proper province it was to try such as were accused as false prophets, or blasphemers. This was a kind of ecclesiastical court. The high priest was the chief judge in it, and we are told that they used to sit in his palace. The other was before Pilate, the Roman governor of Judea at that time; he principally took cognizance of criminal things, such especially as concerned the peace of the country, considered as a part of the Roman empire. These verses give an account only of the former. Blasphemy was the crime they charged upon him. We cannot from any one evangelist have a full account of either of them. In our notes on Matt. xxvi., from ver. 57 to 68, we have fully considered what all the evangelists say. See the notes on that place.

CHAP. XXIII

Jesus is accused before Pilate, who sendeth him to Herod, 1—7. Herod, disappointed in his expectations, mocketh him, and sendeth him back, 8—11. Herod and Pilate are made friends, 12. Pilate, willing to release Jesus, is prevailed on by the clamours of the people to release Barabbas, and give Jesus to be crucified, 13—25. Being led to the place of execution, Jesus biddeth the women who lamented him to weep rather for themselves and their children, 26—31. He is crucified between two malefactors, 32, 33; prayeth for his enemies, 34; is scoffed at, 35—38; reviled by one of the malefactors, but confessed by the other, to whom he promiseth a place in paradise, 39—43. The unusual darkness, and rending the veil of the temple, 44, 45. Christ crieth unto God, and expireth, 46. The centurion's confession of him, 47—49. Joseph of Arimathea beggeth his body and burieth it, 50—54. The women prepare spices, against the end of the sabbath, 55, 56.

AND ᵃthe whole multitude of them arose, and led him unto Pilate.

2 And they began to accuse him, saying, We found this *fellow* ᵇperverting the nation, and ᶜforbidding to give tribute to Cæsar, saying ᵈthat he himself is Christ a King.

3 ᵉAnd Pilate asked him, saying, Art thou the King of the Jews? And he answered him and said, Thou sayest *it*.

4 Then said Pilate to the Chief Priests and *to* the people, ᶠI find no fault in this man.

5 And they were the more fierce, saying,

He stirreth up the people, teaching throughout all Jewry, beginning from Galilee to this place.

6 When Pilate heard of Galilee, he asked whether the man were a Galilæan.

7 And as soon as he knew that he belonged unto ᵍHerod's jurisdiction, he sent him to Herod, who himself also was at Jerusalem at that time.

8 ¶ And when Herod saw Jesus, he was exceeding glad: for ʰhe was desirous to see him of a long *season*, because ⁱhe had heard many things of him; and he hoped to have seen some miracle done by him.

9 Then he questioned with him in many words; but he answered him nothing.

10 And the Chief Priests and Scribes stood and vehemently accused him.

11 ᵏAnd Herod with his men of war set him at nought, and mocked *him*, and arrayed him in a gorgeous robe, and sent him again to Pilate.

12 ¶ And the same day ˡPilate and Herod were made friends together: for before they were at enmity between themselves.

13 ¶ ᵐAnd Pilate, when he had called together the Chief Priests and the rulers and the people,

14 Said unto them, ⁿYe have brought this man unto me, as one that perverteth the people: and, behold, ᵒI, having examined *him* before you, have found no fault in this man touching those things whereof ye accuse him:

15 No, nor yet Herod: for I sent you to him; and, lo, nothing worthy of death is done unto him.

16 ᵖI will therefore chastise him, and release *him*.

17 ᵠ(For of necessity he must release one unto them at the feast.)

18 And ʳthey cried out all at once, saying, Away with this *man*, and release unto us Barabbas:

19 (Who for a certain sedition made in the city, and for murder, was cast into prison.)

20 Pilate therefore, willing to release Jesus, spake again to them.

21 But they cried, saying, Crucify *him*, crucify *him*.

22 And he said unto them the third time, Why, what evil hath he done? I have found no cause of death in him: I will therefore chastise him, and let *him* go.

23 And they were instant with loud voices, requiring that he might be crucified. And the voices of them and of the Chief Priests prevailed.

24 And ˢPilate ‖ gave sentence that it should be as they required.

25 And he released unto them him that for sedition and murder was cast into prison, whom they had desired; but he delivered Jesus to their will.

The history of our Saviour's examination and trial before Pilate, the Roman governor of Judea, is recorded by all four evangelists, nor can it be distinctly and perfectly understood without the comparing together of what they

S. LUKE XXIII

all say, which we did in our notes on Matt. xxvii., from ver. 1 to 26, where our reader will find all such passages opened as occur in any of the evangelists about it, and stand in need of explication. See the notes there. The high priests, and the chief priests, and the elders had before determined our Saviour guilty of death, for blasphemy. They stoned Stephen in that case, Acts vii. 59, without carrying him before the Roman governor at all, that we read of in that history; how came it to pass that they did not so by our Saviour, but make a double work of it? 1. Some think that that was rather done in a tumult, though he was carried before the council, Acts vi. 12, than in a regular judicial way; for conquerors in those times, though they sometimes allowed the conquered nations courts of judicature, wherein they judged in ordinary matters according to their own laws, and had judges of their own nations, yet ordinarily reserved capital causes to the cognizance of governors constituted by them; and this seemeth confirmed by John xviii. 31, where when Pilate said, *Take ye him, and judge him according to your law*, we read that the Jews replied, *It is not lawful for us to put any man to death*. 2. Others think that they had a power to put to death, but it was not lawful for them to put any to death upon the feast day: it was now the first day of unleavened bread. But the former seemeth more probable. 3. Or was it because they had sedition and treason to lay to his charge, which were crimes cognoscible only before the Roman governor? and possibly they were willing enough (knowing the reputation our Saviour had with the people) to lay the odium of his death upon Pilate, rather than take it upon themselves. 4. Whatever were the causes, it is most certain that it could be no otherwise, that all righteousness might be fulfilled. Not a word of what our Saviour said could pass away. He had foretold, Matt. xx. 18, 19; Mark x. 33, 34; Luke xviii. 32, 33, that he should not only be *betrayed to the chief priests and scribes*, and by them be *condemned to death*, but that he should be *delivered to the Gentiles, to mock, and to scourge, and to crucify him;* and indeed that way of putting to death by crucifying could only be done by the Gentiles, and that death he was to die. In the history of our Saviour's examination before Pilate is observable, 1. How much more justice and equity our Saviour found from a heathen, than from the Jewish churchmen: the latter condemn him without any proof, after all attempts of subornation, and seek to destroy him right or wrong; Pilate useth all endeavours to deliver him and set him at liberty. 2. How desperate the hatred is that groweth upon the account of religion in the hearts of wicked men; they prefer a person guilty of the highest immoralities and debaucheries, viz. sedition and murder, before the most innocent person that ever lived, who differed only from them in some points of religion, and those chiefly relating to traditions and ceremonies; but indeed he interpreted the will of God more strictly than their lusts would suffer them to interpret it, and lived another kind of life than they lived. Strictness and holiness of doctrine and life is that which enrageth the men of the world against the preachers and professors of the gospel. But see the notes on Matt. xxvii. more fully.

26 [t] And as they led him away, they laid hold upon one Simon, a Cyrenian, coming out of the country, and on him they laid the cross, that he might bear *it* after Jesus.

See the notes on Matt. xxvii. 32, and Mark xv. 21.

27 ¶ And there followed him a great company of people, and of women, which also bewailed and lamented him.

28 But Jesus turning unto them said, Daughters of Jerusalem, weep not for me, but weep for yourselves, and for your children.

29 [u] For, behold, the days are coming, in the which they shall say, Blessed *are* the barren, and the wombs that never bare, and the paps which never gave suck.

30 [x] Then shall they begin to say to the mountains, Fall on us; and to the hills, Cover us.

31 [y] For if they do these things in a green tree, what shall be done in the dry?

What is in these verses is only found in this evangelist; but being part of what happened in the way, while our Saviour was leading to his cross, we have before opened what is here in the notes on Matt. xxvii. 32—34. They are another prophecy of the dreadful calamities which happened about forty years after this, at the destruction of Jerusalem.

32 [z] And there were also two other, malefactors, led with him to be put to death.

33 And [a] when they were come to the place, which is called ‖ Calvary, there they crucified him, and the malefactors, one on the right hand, and the other on the left.

Mark saith here, *The scripture was fulfilled, which saith, And he was numbered with the transgressors.* We met with this before, both in Matthew and Mark. See the notes on Matt. xxvii. 33, 38, and also on Mark xv. 27, 28.

34 ¶ Then said Jesus, Father, [b] forgive them; for [c] they know not what they do. And [d] they parted his raiment, and cast lots.

35 And [e] the people stood beholding. And the [f] rulers also with them derided *him*, saying, He saved others; let him save himself, if he be Christ, the chosen of God.

36 And the soldiers also mocked him, coming to him, and offering him vinegar,

37 And saying, If thou be the king of the Jews, save thyself.

38 [g] And a superscription also was written over him in letters of Greek, and Latin, and Hebrew, THIS IS THE KING OF THE JEWS.

39 ¶ [h] And one of the malefactors which were hanged railed on him, saying, If thou be Christ, save thyself and us.

40 But the other answering rebuked him, saying, Dost not thou fear God, seeing thou art in the same condemnation?

41 And we indeed justly; for we receive the due reward of our deeds: but this man hath done nothing amiss.

42 And he said unto Jesus, Lord, remember me when thou comest into thy kingdom.

43 And Jesus said unto him, Verily I say unto thee, To day shalt thou be with me in paradise.

44 [i] And it was about the sixth hour, and there was a darkness over all the ‖ earth until the ninth hour.

45 And the sun was darkened, and [k] the veil of the temple was rent in the midst.

46 ¶ And when Jesus had cried with a loud voice, he said, [l] Father, into thy hands I commend my spirit: [m] and having said thus, he gave up the ghost.

See the notes on Matt. xxvii. 35—50, and on Mark xiv. 24—37. This part also of the history of our Saviour's passion is best understood by a comparing together what all the evangelists say, which we have before done in our notes on Matthew, so as we shall only observe some few things from it as here recited. *And the people stood beholding.* And the rulers also with them derided him, ver. 35. Matthew saith, chap. xxvii. 41, the chief priests, scribes, and elders were there mocking. So saith Mark, chap. xv. 31. How doth malice and hatred for religion's sake, not only outshow men's reason, but also all their moral virtue! and make nothing accounted uncharitable, unjust, or indecent to them, into whom this devil hath once entered. To say nothing of the injustice and indecencies obvious to every eye, which these men showed upon our Saviour's examination and trial: it was now the first day of the feast of unleavened bread, the day following the passover night; or, as some think, the preparation both for the weekly sabbath and for the passover, though the most judicious interpreters be of the first opinion: one of them it was, be it which it would. If atheism and irreligion had not been at the height amongst this people, had it been possible that the high priest, and the chief of the priests, and the rulers of the Jews, should have spent this day, the whole time, from break of the day till noon, in accusing or condemning Christ; and then have spent the afternoon in mocking and deriding him on the cross as he was dying, breaking all laws of humanity and decency, as well as religion? Admitting Annas and Caiaphas were not there, yet some of the chief of the priests, the scribes, and the elders were certainly there; and behaving themselves there more rudely and indecently than the common people. The people were there *beholding* him. These were there *mocking* and *deriding* a dying person. But as we say in philosophy, *corruptio optimi est pessima*; so we shall find it true, that men who are employed in sacred things, if the true fear of God be not in them, to make them the best, they are certainly the vilest and worst of men. We read of no rudenesses offered to our Saviour dying, but from the scribes, chief priests, rulers, and soldiers. These verses also afford us great proof of the immortality of the soul; otherwise the penitent thief could not that day have been with Christ in paradise, as Christ promised, ver. 43. Nor would Christ have committed his soul into his Father's hand, if it had been to have expired with the body, and have vanished into air. For other things which concern this part of the history of our Saviour's passion, see the notes before mentioned on Matt. xxvii. 35—50.

n Mat. 27. 54.
Mark 15. 39.
47 ⁿ Now when the centurion saw what was done, he glorified God, saying, Certainly this was a righteous man.

48 And all the people that came together to that sight, beholding the things which were done, smote their breasts, and returned.

o Ps. 38. 11.
Matt. 27. 55.
Mark 15. 40.
See John 19. 25.
49 º And all his acquaintance, and the women that followed him from Galilee, stood afar off, beholding these things.

For a perfect knowledge of all those things which did happen after our Saviour's nailing to the cross, till he died, and was taken down to be buried, all the evangelists must be consulted. We have made a collection of them in our notes on Matt. xxvii. 51—56, to which the reader is here referred. This passage about the centurion is taken notice of both by Matthew and Mark; only they say he said, *Truly this was the Son of God*. Luke saith that he said, *Certainly this was a righteous man*. Possibly the sense is the same, and the centurion by *the Son of God* did not mean the Son of God by eternal generation, but one highly favoured of God, a righteous man, and very dear to God, and highly beloved of him; for it must be by a very extraordinary revelation and impression if he had so early a faith in Christ as God blessed for ever. I think Mr. Calvin, on Matt. xxvi. 54, expounds it well, *Non vulgarem esse hominem, sed divinitus excitatum statuit*. The centurion determined that Christ was no ordinary person, but one stirred up by and sent of God. It is observable, that Christ had a testimony from all orders of men almost, except the scribes, and priests, and Pharisees. Pontius Pilate and Herod declared him innocent. Pilate's wife acknowledgeth him a righteous person. The thief on the cross testifieth he had *done nothing amiss*. Judas the traitor confesseth he had *betrayed innocent blood*. The centurion owneth him to be no ordinary man, but *a righteous man, the Son of God*. The multitude always owned him: they see they are now run down; they smite their breasts, say nothing, but depart. Only those that were to have been the teachers of others are blinded and hardened to their ruin.

50 ¶ ᵖAnd, behold, *there was* a man named Joseph, a counsellor; *and he was* a good man, and a just: p Mat. 27. 57. Mark 15. 42. John 19. 38.

51 (The same had not consented to the counsel and deed of them;) *he was* of Arimathæa, a city of the Jews: ᑫ who also himself waited for the kingdom of God. q Mark 15. 43. ch. 2. 25, 38.

52 This *man* went unto Pilate, and begged the body of Jesus.

53 ʳAnd he took it down, and wrapped it in linen, and laid it in a sepulchre that was hewn in stone, wherein never man before was laid. r Mat. 27. 59. Mark 15. 46.

See the notes on Matt. xxvii. 57—60.

54 And that day was ˢthe preparation, and the sabbath drew on. s Mat. 27. 62.

Greek, σάββατον ἐπέφωσκε, the sabbath shined. What preparation was here intended, whether to the weekly sabbath of the Jews, (that it was most certainly,) or to the passover also, which some will have to have been this year put off to that day, because of the concurrence of the weekly and the annual feast, I shall not determine, though the most judicious interpreters skilled in the Hebrew writings, think the passover this year was kept in its season, the night before. *And the sabbath*, that is, the seventh day, *drew on*. The Greek word signifies shined, the propriety of which term hath cost critics some pains to make out, for it rather began to be dark than lightsome, their sabbath beginning after the setting of the sun. Some think the word referred to the evening star, which began to shine. Others, that it referred to a lamp or candle, which they were wont to set up, they call it *luminare discriminationis*, the light of discrimination, which being set up in their several families, the sabbath was accounted to be begun. Others think it referred to the following day. But there need not much labour in the case, for by the same reason that it is said, the evening and the morning made the sabbath day, the sabbath might be said ἐπιφώσκειν (that is, to begin) when it began to be dark, not taking the word in a proper, but in a metaphorical sense.

55 And the women also, ᵗwhich came with him from Galilee, followed after, and ᵘbeheld the sepulchre, and how his body was laid. t ch. 8. 2. u Mark 15. 47.

56 And they returned, and ˣprepared spices and ointments; and rested the sabbath day ʸaccording to the commandment. x Mark 16. 1. y Ex. 20. 10.

See the notes on Matt. xxvii. 61. It is Beza's observation upon these verses, That Christ, being opposed by the devil and all his instruments, being now dead, leaveth two or three poor women, as it were, in the front of the battle, intending within a very short time, without much ado, to triumph over all these terrible adversaries.

CHAP. XXIV

Christ's resurrection is declared by two angels to the women that came to the sepulchre, who report it to others, but are not believed, 1—11. *Peter visiteth the sepulchre*, 12. *Christ appeareth to two disciples going to Emmaus*, 13—35; *and to the apostles, eating before them, and explaining the Scriptures concerning himself*, 36—48. *He promiseth them the Holy Ghost*, 49, *and ascendeth into heaven*, 50—53.

NOW ᵃupon the first *day* of the week, very early in the morning, they came unto the sepulchre, ᵇbringing the spices which they had prepared, and certain *others* with them. a Matt. 28. 1. Mark 16. 1. John 20. 1. b ch. 23. 56.

S. LUKE XXIV

Mary Magdalene and Mary the mother of Joses were the two women that took up their seat right over against the sepulchre, to see where Christ was laid, Matt. xxvii. 61; Mark xv. 47. They had bought spices some time of that day after they knew he must die, or else they bought them immediately after his burial, as they went home, for they rested on the sabbath day. They had now got some others into their society, and came very early upon the first day of the week, (see the notes on Matt. xxviii. 1, as to the particular time,) intending to show their last act of love to their friend by embalming his body.

c Matt. 28. 2.
Mark 16. 4.
2 ^cAnd they found the stone rolled away from the sepulchre.

The stone which Joseph had rolled to the mouth of the sepulchre, when he had laid in the body, Matt. xxvii. 60, and the Jews had sealed, ver. 66, and which, as they came walking, they were so troubled about, how they should get it removed, Mark xvi. 3. How it came to be rolled away Matthew telleth us, chap. xxviii. 2.

d ver. 23.
Mark 16. 5.
3 ^dAnd they entered in, and found not the body of the Lord Jesus.

Probably when they entered in they saw no angels, for one may reasonably suppose, that if they had they would hardly have adventured to enter in; but at their coming out, being satisfied that the body was not there, the angels made themselves visible to them; for it followeth,

4 And it came to pass, as they were much perplexed thereabout, ^ebehold, two men stood by them in shining garments:

e John 20. 12.
Acts 1. 10.

5 And as they were afraid, and bowed down *their* faces to the earth, they said unto them, Why seek ye ||the living among the dead ?

|| Or, *him that liveth.*

f Matt. 16. 21. & 17. 23. Mark 8. 31. & 9. 31. ch. 9. 22.
6 He is not here, but is risen: ^fremember how he spake unto you when he was yet in Galilee,

7 Saying, The Son of man must be delivered into the hands of sinful men, and be crucified, and the third day rise again.

g John 2. 22.
8 And ^gthey remembered his words,

These two men were two angels in human shape. See the notes on Matt. xxviii. 5—7.

h Mat. 28. 8. Mark 16. 10.
9 ^hAnd returned from the sepulchre, and told all these things unto the eleven, and to all the rest.

i ch. 8. 3.
10 It was Mary Magdalene, and ⁱJoanna, and Mary *the mother* of James, and other *women that were* with them, which told these things unto the apostles.

k Mark 16. 11. ver. 25.
11 ^kAnd their words seemed to them as idle tales, and they believed them not.

l John 20. 3, 6.
12 ^lThen arose Peter, and ran unto the sepulchre; and stooping down, he beheld the linen clothes laid by themselves, and departed, wondering in himself at that which was come to pass.

See the notes on Matt. xxviii. 8—10, but more fully on John xx. 2—9, who repeateth this piece of history more largely than the rest. It is plain that scarce any of the disciples gave credit to the first relation of the women; but yet, it being near the city, Peter and John thought it worth the while to go and see. For though Peter alone be mentioned here, yet John is mentioned, John xx. 3—5, under the notion of *that other disciple;* and he is said to have *outrun Peter,* and to have come *first to the sepulchre.* But concerning that part of the history relating to the resurrection, we shall reserve ourselves till we come to John xx. We now pass on to a piece of history relating to the evidencing of Christ's resurrection, which is neither touched by Matthew nor by Luke. Mark toucheth it shortly, chap. xvi. 12, 13, *After that he appeared in another form to two of them, as they walked, and went into the country. And they went and told it unto the residue; neither believed they them.* We shall now hear Luke giving us a more full and perfect account.

m Mark 16. 12.
13 ¶ ^mAnd, behold, two of them went that same day to a village called Emmaus, which was from Jerusalem *about* threescore furlongs.

Who those two were is variously guessed; that the name of the one was *Cleopas,* appeareth from ver. 18. Some will have the other to have been Luke, but he in the beginning of his Gospel distinguisheth himself from eyewitnesses, chap. i. 2. Some will have it to have been Nathanael; others will have it to have been Simon, from ver. 34, and 1 Cor. xv. 5. But these things are so uncertain, that all the instruction we can learn from them is the vanity and uncertainty of traditions. This Emmaus was from Jerusalem about sixty furlongs, which make seven miles and a half, according to our computation.

14 And they talked together of all these things which had happened.

There is nothing more ordinary, than for persons walking and riding upon roads to make the present news of the time the subject of their discourse. There had great things happened in Jerusalem, the death of our Saviour was such; and those things which attended his death were very extraordinary; and it is not at all to be wondered that a discourse of them should fill every mouth, especially every disciple's mouth.

15 And it came to pass, that, while they communed *together* and reasoned, ⁿJesus himself drew near, and went with them.

n Matt. 18. 20. ver. 36.

He overtook them upon the way, and joined himself to their company. It is a good thing to be discoursing of Christ, it is the way to have his presence and company with us.

16 But ^otheir eyes were holden that they should not know him.

o John 20. 14. & 21. 4.

God by his providence restrained their eyes, that though they saw a man, yet they could not discern who he was. We may learn from hence that the form or figure of Christ's body after his resurrection was not changed. His body had the same dimensions, the same quantity, colour, and figure, and was in itself a proper object for human eyes; for otherwise there had been no need for their eyes to be held. From hence also we may learn the influence which God hath upon all our members and senses, and how much we depend upon God for a daily power to exercise our natural faculties. Our Lord had no mind that these two disciples should at first discern who he was, that he might draw out their following discourses, and from them take occasion to prove from Scripture the certainty of his resurrection. From this text we may gather, how hard the Lutherans are put to it to maintain the real presence of the body of Christ, wherever the sacrament of the Lord's supper is administered; for this they must maintain, that although the body of Christ after his resurrection was the same that was crucified, and so obvious to sense, yet he had not only a power to make it insensible and invisible, which we grant, but that he hath also a power to multiply it, and make it in one and the same instant to be in so many places as his supper is administered in; and also that he willeth it at the same time to be imperceptible by any human senses in all those places: for it is apparent from hence, that it was not at all times imperceptible; it might at this time have been seen, had not the disciples' eyes been held, that they could not know him.

17 And he said unto them, What manner of communications *are* these that ye have one to another, as ye walk, and are sad ?

Not that he, from whom the secrets of no hearts are hidden, did not know what they were discoursing about, but that he had a mind to hear them repeated from them, that from their repetition of them he might take the better advantage to instruct them.

18 And the one of them, ^pwhose name was Cleopas, answering said unto him,

p John 19. 25.

Art thou only a stranger in Jerusalem, and hast not known the things which are come to pass there in these days?

19 And he said unto them, What things? And they said unto him, Concerning Jesus of Nazareth, ^q which was a prophet ^r mighty in deed and word before God and all the people:

<small>q Matt. 21. 11. ch. 7. 16. John 3. 2. & 4. 19. & 6. 14. Acts 2. 22. r Acts 7. 22.</small>

The things which had lately happened in Jerusalem were so many, and so unusual, that the disciples wonder that any one coming from Jerusalem should ask, *What things?* they therefore ask him if he were a mere stranger in Jerusalem, coming from some other country, or from some remoter parts of Judea or Galilee? or, if he were the only man who had been unconcerned in what was the common discourse both of the town and country? Still our Saviour draws out the discourse from them, by asking them, *What things?* They tell him, *Concerning Jesus of Nazareth, a Prophet mighty in deed and word;* in which phrase Stephen celebrated Moses, Acts vii. 22; that is, one who did not only in an extraordinary manner made the will of God unto men, but also did many great and mighty works, and lived a most holy and most exemplary life and conversation, so as that he was not only highly favoured of God, but in great repute and estimation also amongst the people.

<small>s ch. 23. 1. Acts 13. 27, 28.</small>

20 ^s And how the Chief Priests and our rulers delivered him to be condemned to death, and have crucified him.

<small>t ch. 1. 68. & 2. 38. Acts 1. 6.</small>

21 But we trusted ^t that it had been he which should have redeemed Israel: and beside all this, to day is the third day since these things were done.

It is from hence evident, that as yet they neither had a true notion of Christ as God-man in one person, nor yet of the Messiah, but still remained in an opinion of a temporal deliverance to be effected for the Jews by the Messiah, when he should come. The words also showed a great weakness in the disciples' faith as to Christ; they speak as if they were quite out of breath, and their faith began to fail. We were, say they, once of the mind, and maintained some hope, that this Jesus of Nazareth had been he whom God had designed for the Messiah, and now it is *the third day since these things were done*. This mention of *the third day* is a good argument to prove that these were some old disciples of Christ, who had taken notice of his promise, or prophecy, that he should rise again the third day, chap. xviii. 33. They ought to have had patience till night, and to have considered, that though the third day were begun, yet it was not yet past.

<small>u Mat. 28. 8. Mark 16. 10. ver. 9, 10. John 20. 18.</small>

22 Yea, and ^u certain women also of our company made us astonished, which were early at the sepulchre;

23 And when they found not his body, they came, saying, that they had also seen a vision of angels, which said that he was alive.

<small>x ver. 12.</small>

24 And ^x certain of them which were with us went to the sepulchre, and found *it* even so as the women had said: but him they saw not.

It is plain from the relation of these two disciples, that they had whatsoever might conduce to a moral suasion. They had the revelation of the word, from the mouth of Christ himself. They had evidences from the women, from the apparition of angels, from some among themselves, that his body was not there. The angels said he was risen. Why do they hesitate then? why do they not believe? Is the fault in the perverseness of their wills? had they no mind to believe, that the thing they had hoped, longed, waited for, was true? Certainly there was nothing they more desired. Let the patrons of the power of man's will to believe, or perform any actions spiritually good, tell us (if they can) what could hinder these disciples' actual believing the resurrection of Christ, but the impotency of their wills, God not yet pleasing to influence and assist their wills actually to believe what they had the greatest propensions and inclinations imaginable to have believed.

25 Then he said unto them, O fools, ^y and slow of heart to believe all that the prophets have spoken:

<small>y ver. 46. Acts 17. 3. 1 Pet. 1. 11. z ver. 45. a Gen. 3. 15. & 22. 18. &</small>

26 ^y Ought not Christ to have suffered these things, and to enter into his glory?

<small>26. 4 & 49. 10. Num. 21. 9. Deut. 18. 15. b Ps. 16. 9, 10, & 22. &</small>

27 ^z And beginning at ^a Moses and ^b all the prophets, he expounded unto them in all the Scriptures the things concerning himself.

<small>132. 11. Is. 7. 14, & 9. 6. & 40. 10, 11. & 50. 6. & 53. Jer. 23. 5. & 33. 14, 15. Ezek. 34. 23. & 37. 25. Dan. 9. 24. Mic. 7. 20. Mal. 3. 1. & 4. 2. See on John 1. 45.</small>

By our Saviour's form of reprehending his disciples, we may both learn, 1. That it is not every saying, *Thou fool*, but a saying of it from a root of hatred, malice, and anger, which our Saviour makes to be a breach of the sixth commandment, Matt. v. 21, 22. Our Saviour's reprehension of them was out of a principle of love, and a root of good will to them. 2. That the best of us are very *slow of heart to believe* what cometh to us upon the mere credit of a Divine revelation. It is also observable from what we have, ver. 27, that Moses and the prophets are not to be rejected by Christians; they also have much concerning Christ; out of them Christ instructeth these two disciples in the things concerning himself.

28 And they drew nigh unto the village, whither they went: and ^c he made as though he would have gone further.

<small>c See Gen. 32. 26. & 42. 7. Mark 6. 48.</small>

29 But ^d they constrained him, saying, Abide with us: for it is toward evening, and the day is far spent. And he went in to tarry with them.

<small>d Gen. 19. 3. Acts 16. 15.</small>

I do not understand how some conclude from hence the lawfulness of dissembling, or telling a lie, in some cases, because the evangelist saith our Saviour *made as though he would have gone further*, and did not; for without doubt our Saviour had gone further if the disciples had not been urgent with him to have staid: nor did he stay long there, as we shall hear by and by.

30 And it came to pass, as he sat at meat with them, ^e he took bread, and blessed *it*, and brake, and gave to them.

<small>e Mat. 14. 19.</small>

31 And their eyes were opened, and they knew him; and he ‖ vanished out of their sight.

<small>‖ Or, ceased to be seen of them. See ch. 4. 30. John 8. 59.</small>

Some would have this bread to be sacramental bread, as if our Lord at this time celebrated his supper; and some of the papists are mightily zealous for that interpretation, thinking that they have in it a mighty argument to justify their lame administration of it in one kind (for here is no mention of the cup at all); but they do not consider, that this text will prove (if it be taken with relation to the supper) more than they would have it; as, 1. That priests may consecrate without wine, which themselves will not grant, though they say that, both elements being consecrated, the people sufficiently partake if they share but in one. 2. It will also prove that a priest may consecrate without using those substantial words, *This is my body*. But it is a most improbable thing, that our Saviour coming just out of his journey should fall upon his administration of this ordinance. The text is certainly to be meant of bodily bread, which our Saviour never took without a previous blessing of it, Matt. xiv. 19. How their eyes were opened the evangelist tells us. Some think they knew him by his form of blessing. It is a wonder then they did not know him before by his style in three or four hours' discourse by the way. Others think they knew him by taking upon him the office of the master of the feast, to bless the table, and to carve to the guests. But all this is vain. He withdrew the veil from their eyes, which alone hindered their discerning him before, for the object was visible, only the medium of their sight was indisposed. *And he vanished out of their sight*. Our Saviour had now obtained his end, viz. to satisfy them that he was indeed risen; now he disappeareth, for that he had a power to make his body imperceptible to the disciples' senses is out of doubt.

S. LUKE XXIV

32 And they said one to another, Did not our heart burn within us, while he talked with us by the way, and while he opened to us the Scriptures?

There was a mighty difference, no doubt, betwixt Christ's preaching and his ministers': he preached as one who had authority, not as the scribes, not as ordinary ministers, but with more majesty and power; but as to the saving efficacy of his words, that depended upon his will; where he pleased to put forth such efficacious grace, there his words became effectual; where he did not, they were not so: Christ preached in the hearing of hundreds, who yet continued unbelievers, and perished in their unbelief. There is a great deal of difference also between one minister's preaching and another's; some kind of preaching of itself makes men's hearts to freeze, others make them to burn; but where preaching makes our heart to burn within us, Christ throws in the coal, which the best preacher doth but blow up: only the Spirit of God is pleased to work (as Erasmus saith) *secundum quod nactus est organon*, according to the instrument it worketh by, and to concur with rational and spiritual means in order to rational and spiritual ends. But wherever any soul is baptized with fire at hearing a sermon, it is also baptized with the Holy Ghost. Christ will not always cure blind eyes with clay and spittle, though he did it once. These were disciples before the fire was kindled in their hearts; Christ's preaching did but blow it up. We ought so to speak in our preaching, so to open and apply the Scriptures, as our discourses may have a rational tendency to make the hearts of our hearers to burn within them, not so as to make them dead, and sleepy, and cold, or lukewarm; and then to know that it must be Christ's work to inflame them, when we have said all that we can say.

33 And they rose up the same hour, and returned to Jerusalem, and found the eleven gathered together, and them that were with them,

34 Saying, The Lord is risen indeed, f 1 Cor. 15. 5. and ʄhath appeared to Simon.

35 And they told what things *were done* in the way, and how he was known of them in breaking of bread.

The 34th verse, compared with 1 Cor. xv. 5, makes some great authors think, that Simon was one of the two, and that Cleopas (who was the other) spake this. They make no stay at Emmaus, but come presently to Jerusalem, and acquaint the disciples, that for certain Christ was risen, and that he had appeared to them in the way, and was known of them at their breaking of bread.

g Mark 16. 14. John 20. 19. 1 Cor. 15. 5.
36 ¶ ᵍAnd as they thus spake, Jesus himself stood in the midst of them, and saith unto them, Peace *be* unto you.

Of this appearance of Christ Mark speaks, chap. xvi. 14, and John, chap. xx. 19, 20. The salutation which he useth to them was common amongst the Jews, and answereth our God save you, or God be with you. It was an apprecation of all blessing and happiness, which they comprehended under the name of peace.

37 But they were terrified and affright- h Mark 6. 49. ed, and supposed that they had seen ʰa spirit.

Spirits sometimes (by God's permission or direction) assumed human shapes. They seeing a human shape, and not able on the sudden to conceive how a human body should come into the midst among them, without any more noise or notice taken of it, were affrighted, as we usually are at the sight of apprehended apparitions. From hence we may conclude, that either the world, and the best men in it, have been in all ages deceived, and a few atheists have been wiser than them all, or there are such beings as spirits.

38 And he said unto them, Why are ye troubled? and why do thoughts arise in your hearts?

39 Behold my hands and my feet, that i John 20. 20, 27. it is I myself: ⁱhandle me, and see; for a spirit hath not flesh and bones, as ye see me have.

40 And when he had thus spoken, he shewed them *his* hands and *his* feet.

If either the papists or the Lutherans could show us Christ's hands or feet, while they impose upon us to believe that Christ's body is really present at or in the Lord's supper, they would not so fright us, nor make so many thoughts arise in us, as they do, about their apprehensions of the nature of a body. But while the papists allow us to handle and to taste the bread, and we find no such things, and the Lutherans suffer our eyes to be open, and we can see no such things, we cannot but conclude, that the body of Christ which they talk of must certainly be a spirit, which (according to our Saviour's notion) is a substance which hath neither flesh nor bones, as we see the body they would have us to believe hath not; that is to say, that the body they talk of is no body. Our Saviour here proveth that it was his true body, which appeared to them, because, 1. It had integral parts, hands and feet. 2. Because it might be seen. 3. It might be handled. 4. It had flesh and bones, which a spirit hath not. Then he shows them his hands and feet. So then our Saviour did not think that the judgment of our senses was to be rejected, concerning the nature of bodies, and his body in particular, and that in its state of exaltation, when it was raised from the dead. Do any of them say that Christ's body here came through the door, or it could not have been here? How shall that be proved? We can easily tell them how his body might be in the midst of them, though it were not discerned while he was there; even as the eyes of the two disciples were held, ver. 16, that they could not discern Christ, so the eyes of the disciples might be held now, till he was in the midst amongst them.

41 And while they yet believed not ᵏfor joy, and wondered, he said unto them, ˡHave ye here any meat? k Gen. 45. 26. l John 21. 5.

42 And they gave him a piece of a broiled fish, and of an honeycomb.

43 ᵐAnd he took *it*, and did eat before them. m Acts 10. 41.

Believed not for joy; yet if they had not now believed, they doubtless would not have rejoiced, but their faith was the cause of their joy; yet the excess of their joy was the hinderance of their faith; so dangerous are the excessive motions of our affections. Christ here gives them another evidence of the truth of his body, he *did eat before them*, though very ordinary country diet, *a piece of broiled fish, and of a honey-comb*; such a meal as we read of that he had at the lake of Tiberias, John xxi. 9. He did not eat to uphold, but only to testify, his life. Thus when he had raised the daughter of Jairus, chap. viii. 55, he bid them give her something to eat; and for this end Lazarus sat at meat with the rest, John xii. 2; and Peter proves the resurrection of Christ from their eating and drinking with him, Acts x. 41. Let not profane wits seek knots in bulrushes, inquiring what became of this meat? &c. Let them first tell us what became of the meat the angels did eat with Abraham, Gen. xviii. 8, and learn to believe, that it was easy with the power of God to annihilate again that meat, which was not necessary for the sustentation of the body of Christ, now freed from all the cravings of natural appetite, though he did eat it to satisfy them that he was truly risen from the dead.

44 And he said unto them, ⁿThese *are* the words which I spake unto you, while I was yet with you, that all things must be fulfilled, which were written in the law of Moses, and *in* the prophets, and *in* the psalms, concerning me. n Matt. 16. 21. & 17. 22. & 20. 18. Mark 8. 31. ch. 9. 22. & 18. 31. ver. 6.

The Jews ordinarily divided the Old Testament into the law, the prophets, and the holy writings, which they called the *Hagiographa*. The Book of Psalms was one of the last sort, and one of the most noted amongst them. So as by these three terms our Saviour understands all the Scriptures of the Old Testament. He tells them, that he had before his death, while he conversed with them, told them that *all things* (which were very many) which were found in any of these books concerning him must be fulfilled: he had told them so, chap. xviii. 31; Matt. xvi. 21; xvii. 22; xx. 18; Mark ix. 31; x. 34.

o Acts 16.14.   45 Then °opened he their understanding, that they might understand the Scriptures,

He did not open their understanding without the Scriptures, he sends them thither; and he knew the Scriptures would not sufficiently give them a knowledge of him, and the things of God, without the influence and illumination of his Spirit: they are truly taught of God, who are taught by his Spirit to understand the Scriptures. Christ gives a great honour to the Scriptures. The devil cheats those souls whom he persuades to cast away the Scriptures in expectation of a teaching by the Spirit. The Spirit teacheth by, not without, not contrary to, the Holy Scriptures.

p ver. 26.
Ps. 22.
Is. 50. 6. &
53. 2, &c.
Acts 17. 3.   46 And said unto them, ᵖThus it is written, and thus it behoved Christ to suffer, and to rise from the dead the third day:

All the Divine predictions are certain and infallible. The Jews did maliciously and freely prosecute our Saviour to death, and God did certainly foresee how their wills would be determined, and the event was accomplished accordingly.

q Dan. 9. 24.
Acts 13. 38,
46. 1 John 2.
12.
r Gen. 12. 3.
Ps. 22. 27.
Is. 49. 6, 22.
Jer. 31. 34.
Hos. 2. 23.
Mic. 4. 2.
Mal. 1. 11.
s John 15.27.
Acts i. 8, 22. & 2. 32. & 3. 15.   47 And that repentance and ᵍremission of sins should be preached in his name ʳamong all nations, beginning at Jerusalem.

48 And ˢye are witnesses of these things.

The few words in ver. 47 are comprehensive of the great duty of the apostles: 1. To preach *repentance and remission of sins*. 2. In Christ's *name*. 3. To *all nations*. 4. *Beginning at Jerusalem*. They were to preach *repentance*, that is, a turning from sinful courses into a course of life consonant to the will of God; and *remission of sins*, that is, upon repentance; this they were to preach *in his name*, which may refer either to their preaching; then our Saviour lets them know that they were to be his ministers, and to preach by his authority, to be *ambassadors for Christ*, 2 Cor. v. 20, stewards of his mysteries. Or else it may refer to repentance and remission of sins, which are to be preached in his name, for the sake of merits and satisfaction. They were to preach this *among all nations*. This was prophesied of plentifully, Psal. ii. 8; Isa. xlix. 6; Dan. vii. 14; Hos. ii. 23; Joel ii. 32. This was a piece of Divine revelation which Christ had till this time concealed in a great measure; when he sent out the twelve, Matt. x. 5, he commanded them not to go to the Gentiles. *Beginning at Jerusalem*, that is, amongst the Jews. He was prophesied of under the notion of a King, to be set upon the Lord's holy hill of Zion, Psal. ii. 6. So Psal. cx. 2; Isa. ii. 3; xxviii. 16; lx. 1. In pursuance of this, we shall find the apostles preaching only in Judea, till they had judged themselves *unworthy of everlasting life*, then they *turned to the Gentiles*, Acts xiii. 38, 46.

t Is. 44. 3.
Joel 2. 28.
John 14. 16,
26. & 15. 26.
& 16. 7.
Acts 1. 4.
& 2. 1, &c.   49 ¶ ᵗAnd, behold, I send the promise of my Father upon you: but tarry ye in the city of Jerusalem, until ye be endued with power from on high.

It is questioned by none, but by *the promise of the Father* our Lord meaneth the promise of the Spirit, as it came down in the days of Pentecost. This effusion of the Spirit was promised under the Old Testament, Isa. xliv. 3; Jer. xxxi. 33; Ezek. xxxvi. 27; most eminently, Joel ii. 28, the apostle himself interpreting this prophecy, Acts ii. 16—18. See also Acts i. 8, where the fulfilling of this *promise of the Father*, as it is called ver. 4, is put before—*and ye shall be witnesses unto me, both in Jerusalem, and in Judea, and in Samaria*; and is also expounded by, *But ye shall receive power, after the Holy Ghost is come upon you*. Our Lord also had said, *I will pray the Father, and he shall give you another Comforter, that he may abide with you for ever,* John xiv. 16. In this text he saith, that he will send him; so also John xv. 26; xvi. 7; thereby confirming his disciples in this, that he was equal with the Father, and that the Holy Ghost was sent by the Father and him, yet sent by the Father upon the prayer of the Son, and in his name, John xiv. 16, 26. This Holy Spirit is also called, *power from on high; the power of the Highest*, Luke i. 35. But here the gifts of the Holy Ghost may be understood, as also in Acts i. 8, where it is said this power should be received after that the Holy Ghost should come upon them: until this time should come, which was in the days of Pentecost, Acts ii. 1, the disciples were bound to stay at Jerusalem, which accordingly they did. And we may from hence conclude, that these words of our Saviour were spoken to his disciples after his appearance to them in Galilee, (of which Luke saith nothing,) which was the place where (as most think) *he was seen of above five hundred brethren at once*, 1 Cor. xv. 6.

50 ¶ And he led them out ᵘas far as to Bethany, and he lifted up his hands, and blessed them.   u Acts 1. 12.

51 ˣAnd it came to pass, while he blessed them, he was parted from them, and carried up into heaven.   x 2 Kings 2. 11. Mark 16. 19. John 20. 17. Acts 1.9. Ephes. 4. 8.

This must be understood to have happened forty days after our Saviour's resurrection, for so Luke himself tells us, Acts i. 3. *And he led them out as far as Bethany;* not the village Bethany, but that part of the mount of Olives which belonged to Bethany. Our Saviour had been often there praying; from thence he now ascendeth into heaven. *And he lifted up his hands and blessed them:* some think that by blessing here is meant praying, and the lifting up of his hands was accommodated to that religious action. Others think that blessing here signifieth a more authoritative act; and that his lifting up of his hands was a stretching out of his hands, as a sign of that effectual blessing of them. *While he blessed them, he was parted from them, and carried up into heaven;* that is, he moved upward as if he had been carried, for it is certain that our Saviour ascended by his own power. Luke saith, Acts i. 9, *He was taken up, and a cloud received him out of their sight.* As Elijah *went up to heaven in a whirlwind*, 2 Kings ii. 11, so Christ went up in a cloud; but with this difference, Christ ascended by his own power, Elijah could not without the help of an angel.

52 ʸAnd they worshipped him, and returned to Jerusalem with great joy: y Matt. 28. 9, 17.

53 And were continually ᶻin the temple, praising and blessing God. Amen.   z Acts 2. 46. & 5. 42.

We never before read of any act of adoration which the disciples performed to Christ. Their faith was now come to the highest pitch. They did no longer look upon him only as one sent of God, a great Prophet, nor only as the Son of David, the promised Messiah; in the mean time not rightly taking the notion of the Messiah, but looking upon him as one who should be a temporal saviour, and deliverer of his people; they now believe him to be the eternal Son of God, being so manifested by his resurrection from the dead, and ascension into heaven before their eyes. According to his commandment, they return to Jerusalem, full of joy: *and were continually in the temple, praising and blessing God. Amen.* It is said, Acts i. 13, 14, that being returned *they went into an upper room, and continued in prayer and supplication.* Some think that this upper room was appendant to the temple. But *continually* here may reasonably be interpreted often, or ordinarily, or at temple hours of prayer; as the morning and evening sacrifice are called the *continual burnt-offering*, Exod. xxix. 42; Numb. xxviii. 3. Their work was to praise and bless God. It is not said for what, but easily understood: as for other mercies, so more especially for his sending the Messiah for our redemption, and the confirmation and perfecting their faith in him.

THE GOSPEL ACCORDING TO

S. JOHN

THE ARGUMENT

The penman of this Gospel is generally taken to have been John the son of Zebedee, Matt. x. 2, not either John the Baptist, or John surnamed Mark, Acts xv. 37. He was a person mightily honoured by Christ's personal favours, and therefore often called *the beloved disciple;* you may read of these favours in these scriptures following, Matt. xvii. 1; Luke ix. 28; xxii. 8; John xiii. 23; xix. 26, 27; xx. 2; Acts iii. 3; iv. 13; Gal. ii. 9. Thus far the Scripture guideth us. He is thought to have gone to and continued in Asia till the third of the ten persecutions in the time of Trajan. He was by Domitian banished into Patmos, where he wrote the Revelation.

The time when he wrote this Gospel is uncertain; some think about the latter part of his life: he died the last of all the apostles, judged about a hundred years after the birth of Christ. It is said the heresies of Ebion and Cerinthus, who denied Christ's Divinity, and of the Nicolaitanes, who held many absurd things about his person, gave occasion to the writing of this Gospel; himself mentioneth the doctrine of the Nicolaitanes, Rev. ii. 6; and Ebion and Cerinthus are thought to be those antichrists which he in his Epistles reflecteth upon.

Two things are observed of him: 1. That he insists more on the proof of Christ's Divinity, than any of the evangelists; producing his miracles most evidently to prove it. 2. That he mentions very little reported by the other evangelists: to which I think may be added, that he delivereth the history of the gospel after Christ's resurrection more fully than any of them; he gives us also a more distinct account of the four passovers happening after Christ's baptism; the necessity of faith in Christ, and regeneration; the doctrine of our mystical union with Christ; the sending of the Holy Spirit, and end of his mission, and the advantage that the apostles and others should receive from it. His Gospel is most particularly remarkable for the sublimeness and mysteriousness of the matter, and sweetness of the phrase.

CHAP. I

The Divinity of Christ, 1—5. The mission of John, and end of Christ's coming, 6—13. The incarnation of the Word, 14. Christ's superior dignity witnessed by John, and evinced by his gracious dispensation, 15—18. John's record of himself to the messengers of the Jews, 19—28. His public testimony to the person of Christ, 29—34. Two of his disciples, hearing it, follow Jesus: Simon is brought to Christ, and surnamed Cephas, 35—42. Philip is called, who bringeth Nathanael to Jesus, 43—51.

a Prov. 8. 22, 23, &c.
Col. 1. 17.
1 John 1. 1.
Rev. 1. 2. & 19. 13.
IN the beginning ᵃwas the Word, and the Word was ᵇwith God, ᶜand the Word was God.

b Prov. 8. 30. ch. 17. 5. 1 John 1. 2.   c Phil. 2. 6. 1 John 5. 7.

In the beginning; in that beginning which Moses mentioneth, Gen. i. 1, the beginning of all things, when the foundations of the world were laid, Prov. viii. 27, 28; the beginning of time; for before that was no measure of time, all was eternity. *Was the Word,* that is, the eternal Son of God, the Lord Jesus Christ, of whom more is spoken afterward. Nor is Christ in this text alone called *the Word,* but 1 John i. 1, *the Word of life;* so Rev. xix. 13: and there are some who think he is so called, Luke i. 2, comparing that text with 2 Pet. i. 16, as also Psal. xxxiii. 6. Nor is it an improper term by which to express the Son of God; for it both expresseth something of his ineffable generation, as the word is begotten in our thoughts, and is the express image of them; and also his office in the revelation of his Father's will unto the sons of men, and revealing his Father to us, Matt. xi. 27: and there are some (if they be not too curious in their notion) who think by that phrase of David, 2 Sam. vii. 21, *For thy word's sake,* (expounded *for thy servant's sake,* 1 Chron. xvii. 19, which is the title of Christ, Isa. xlii. 1,) that Christ is meant. Besides, it is observed, that this term was more acceptable both to the Jews and the heathens, than the term of *Christ,* or *the Son of God,* would have been; for there was nothing more abhorred by the Jews than the latter; and the heathen writers made (as is noted by divers) a great use of this term, to express the name and the power of God. Nor is any thing more ordinary with the Chaldee paraphrast than this expression: Isa. xlv. 12, *I have made the earth;* Chald. I in my word have made the earth. So chap. xlviii. 13,

Mine hand hath laid the foundation of the earth; Chald. By my word I have laid the foundations of the earth: this is taken from Moses's describing the creation by God's word of command, *Let there be light, and there was light;* the manner of expressing it by the word command, is significative that all things were made by his eternal Word; for would any Jew deny, that God by his word created the world? The evangelist therefore calleth Christ, to whom he was about to attribute the creation, ver. 3, *the Word;* not the word of God (so the Scriptures are called); to distinguish Christ in this notion from the revelation of the Divine will to the prophets, he is only called *the Word,* though he was the Son of God. Nor is it said, that in the beginning was the Word created, (as is said of the heavens and the earth, Gen. i. 1,) but *was* the Word: this proveth the eternal existence of the Second Person in the Trinity; for what *was* in the beginning did not then begin to be: the term *the Word,* without the addition of God, speaketh him a subsistence; and it being said, that in the beginning he *was,* speaks his eternal existence; for what had a being in the beginning of time must needs be eternal, nothing being when time began but what was eternal. To this purpose are those texts, Psal. xc. 2; Prov. viii. 22—31; John xvii. 5: and Isa. xl. 4; 2 Thess. ii. 13, which two texts compared show, *In the beginning,* here used, to be the same with *before the foundation of the world:* so 2 Tim. i. 9. *The Word was with God:* lest any should say, Where was this Word before the foundations of the earth were laid? the evangelist saith, *with God;* which agreeth with Prov. viii. 27, 30. This both distinguisheth Christ from all creatures, (none of which were with God in the beginning,) and also showeth the vanity of Sabellius, and those we call quakers, who will not allow Christ to be a distinct subsistence, or person, from his Father: it also denoteth the Son's co-existence and his equality with his Father; and yet his filial relation; for God is not said to have been with the Word, but the Word was with God, which also speaks a perfect unity and consent betwixt them. *And the Word was God:* lest any should say, What but God can be eternal, or be said to have been and had an existence in the beginning of the world? the evangelist addeth, that *the Word was God:* that is, the person or subsistence spoken of and intended by him was the Divine Being, which is but one; though in it there be three distinct subsistences, all make but one and the same Divine Being. The first thing spoken here of Christ attributes to him eternity; the second speaks his relation to the Father; this speaks the oneness and sameness of his essence with that of the Father. The term *God*, which in the foregoing words is to be taken personally for God the Father, is here to be taken essentially, as it signifieth the Divine Being.

d Gen. 1. 1.   2 ᵈ The same was in the beginning with God.

These words of the evangelist are a further confirmation and explication of what the evangelist had said before; asserting the eternity of the Son, and his relation to the Father, and oneness of essence with the Father. Whether the evangelist, forewarned by the Spirit of God, did add this repetition to fore-arm Christians against those errors which did afterward trouble the church, I cannot say; but certain it is, that these words do effectually confute the Eunomians, who distinguished betwixt the Word which in the beginning was with God, and that Word by which all things were made; and the Arians, who make the Father to have existed before the Son; as also the Anomians, who would make the Father and the Son diverse both in nature and will. Some others make this verse a transition to the 4th, and the sense to be, This same was not manifest to the world from the beginning of the world, but was with God until he came to be manifested in the flesh: thus, 1 John i. 2, it is said, he *was with the Father, and was manifested unto us.* He *was manifested in the flesh,* 1 Tim. iii. 16.

e Ps. 33. 6.
Col. 1. 16.
ver. 10.
Ephes. 3. 9.
Heb. 1. 2.
Rev. 4. 11.

3 ᵉ All things were made by him; and without him was not any thing made that was made.

All things were made by him: the Divine nature and eternal existence of the Lord Christ, is evident from his efficiency in the creation of the world: what the evangelist here calleth *all things,* the apostle to the Hebrews, chap. i. 2, calleth *the worlds;* and St. Paul, Col. i. 16, calleth, *all things that are in heaven and earth, visible and invisible;* Moses calls, *the heaven and the earth,* Gen. i. 1. These were all made by the Word; not as an instrumental cause, but as a principal efficient cause; for though it be true, that the preposition διὰ is sometimes used to signify an instrumental cause; yet it is as true, that it is often used to signify the principal efficient cause; as John vi. 57; Acts iii. 16; Rom. v. 5; xi. 36; Eph. iv. 6, and in many other texts: it here only denoteth the order of the working of the holy Trinity. *Without him was not any thing made that was made;* nothing that was made, neither the heavens nor the earth, neither things visible nor invisible, were made without him. There is nothing more ordinary in holy writ, than after the laying down a universal proposition, (where no synecdoche is used,) to add also a universal negative for the confirmation of it: so Rom. iii. 12, *There is none that doeth good;* then is added, *no, not one;* Lam. ii. 2, and in many other texts. The term *without him,* doth not exclude the efficiency either of the First or Third Person in the Trinity, in the creation of all things; the Father created the world by the Son, his Word; and the creation of the world is attributed to the Spirit, Gen. i. 1; Job xxxiii. 4; Psal. xxxiii. 6.

ch. 5. 26.
1 John 5. 11.
g ch. 8. 12.
& 9. 5. & 12.
35, 46.

4 ᶠ In him was life; and ᵍ the life was the light of men.

In him was life; in this Word was life corporal, spiritual, eternal; it was in him as in the fountain. Some understand this of corporal life, both in the first being and preservation of it; it is certain that this is in Christ, for he *upholdeth all things by the word of his power,* Heb. i. 3; Acts xvii. 28; and thus it is another demonstration of the Deity of Christ. Others think that here is rather a transition from creation to redemption; *you hath he quickened,* Eph. ii. 1. Others understand it of eternal life, because our evangelist most generally taketh the term *life,* as a benefit flowing from Christ, in this sense, as chap. iii. 16, and iv. 14, and in a multitude of other texts. I know no reason why we should not understand it of all life; all life being in Christ, as God equal with the Father; and spiritual and eternal life flowing also from him in a more peculiar consideration, as Mediator. *And the life was the light of men:* but though as God he distributes life according to their degree to all his creatures, yet he is the peculiar *light of men,* enlightening their minds with light of which vegetative and sensitive creatures are not capable; so as by *light* is not here to be understood the emanations of any lucid bodies, as that of the sun or stars, for other creatures as well as men are capable of that; nor is it to be understood of the light of reason, though that be the candle of the Lord in the soul; but that light by which we discern the things of God; in which sense the apostle saith, Eph. v. 8, *Ye were darkness, but now ye are light in the Lord.* And therefore he saith *of men,* exclusively to angels, who though lightsome, noble creatures, yet had not their nature assumed by Christ, Heb. ii. 16. Besides that it is said in the next verse, that this light *shineth in darkness,* that is, amongst many men who yet had reasonable souls, but *the darkness comprehended it not.* That cannot be, that men did not comprehend reason, but even rational men comprehended not this light of supernatural revelation. So John is said to have come to testify of that light; who did not come to testify of Christ, as the author of reason. Nor is there any text of Scripture in which the term light signifieth reason.

5 And ʰ the light shineth in darkness; h ch. 3. 19. and the darkness comprehended it not.

The light shineth in darkness: he had said before, that life was in Christ, in him as in the fountain; and the life in him was the light of men, giving light to men. Now this light which was in him had its emanations (as light in the sun); *and the darkness,* that is, men of dark minds, (the abstract being put for the concrete,) *comprehended* (that is, received) *it not.* This was true concerning the Jews in former times, upon whom Christ the true Light had shined in many types and prophecies; it was also true concerning the Jews of that present age, to whom, through the favour of him who had undertaken the redemption of man, the means of grace were continued; through the blindness of their minds and hardness of their hearts, they wilfully rejected those means of illumination which God granted to them.

6 ¶ ⁱ There was a man sent from God,   A. D. 26.
whose name *was* John.   i Mal. 3. 1.
                                      Matt. 3. 1.
                                      Luke 3. 2. ver. 33.

There was a man sent from God; not the Christ, not an angel, but *a man;* yet one, than whom (as our Saviour saith) there had not risen a greater amongst those that were born of women. He did not come of his own head, but was *sent;* for it was he of whom it was written, Mal. iii. 1, *Behold, I will send my messenger before thy face,* &c., Luke vii. 27. He was not sent of men, but *from God,* foretold by the angel, as to his existence, name, work, and success, Luke i. 13—17. *Whose name was John;* his name was John, named by the angel, Luke i. 13, before he was born; by his father and mother, Luke i. 60, 63, when he was born. John signifieth *grace;* and doubtless the Baptist obtained that name, because he was to be the first and a famous preacher of the grace of the gospel which came to the world through Jesus Christ.

7 ᵏ The same came for a witness, to k Acts 19. 4. bear witness of the Light, that all *men* through him might believe.

The same came for a witness: John was called a *messenger* to denote his authority; a *witness,* to denote his work, which is the work of every true minister of the gospel. John was the first witness, and witnessed a thing wholly unknown (before him) to the generality of the world; for though the shepherds, and Simeon, and Anna, had given some testimony to Christ, when he was born, and brought into the temple to be offered to the Lord, yet that was thirty years since, and generally forgot; neither could they bear a testimony to him as an actual minister of the gospel. The apostles were to be *witnesses* to Christ, Acts i. 8; witnesses *of his resurrection,* Acts i. 22; iv. 33; v. 32; x. 41; xiii. 31. All the prophets bare witness to him, that whosoever believeth in his name should be saved, Acts x. 43. So did John also; and John further pointed to him passing by, and witnessed that it was he of whom the prophets spake. So that the apostles, and so following ministers, were and are greater witnesses than John the Baptist. The prophets witnessed that he should come, John Baptist witnessed that he was come; the apostles witnessed that he was not only come, but had died, and was again risen from the dead. *To bear witness of the Light;* for John's office was to give a testimony to Christ the true Light, mentioned before; so called, because he maketh manifest, Eph. v. 13. He revealeth his Father, Matt. xi. 27. He is *the brightness of his* Father's *glory*, Heb. i. 3, who *is light*, 1 John i. 5, and the world is by him enlightened. It was prophesied of his times, Isa. xi. 9, that *the earth should be full of the knowledge of the Lord. That all men through him might believe;* the end of John's testimony was, that multitudes of all sorts might believe by him, or by it, as an instrumental cause of their faith. If we read it *by him*, it is most proper to understand the pronoun of John the Baptist; for we are not said to believe by Christ, but *in him, in his name*, &c.

8 He was not that Light, but *was sent* to bear witness of that Light.

He was not that Light: John the Baptist was a light, as all saints are *light in the Lord*, Eph. v. 8; nay, in a peculiar sense our Saviour beareth him witness, that he *was a burning and shining light;* but he was not *that Light* before mentioned, ver. 5, that *shineth in darkness;* and again ver. 9, *which lighteth every man that cometh into the world.* John borrowed his light from that original Light; that Light was God, he was but a man sent from God. The men of the world are ordinarily in extremes, either wholly rejecting God's ministers and witnesses, or else adoring them; as the world is concerned to take heed of the former, so the ministers of Christ are also highly concerned not to admit the latter. See Luke vii. 33; Acts xiv. 13, 14; but both John here, and Paul there, were very cautious not to rob their Master of the honour due unto him alone. *But was sent to bear witness of that Light:* John, as was said before, came only *to bear witness of that Light*, that he was come, and shined forth, and was the true Light, as it followeth.

9 ¹*That* was the true Light, which lighteth every man that cometh into the world.

l ver. 4. Is. 49. 6. 1 John 2. 8.

That was the true Light: true is sometimes opposed to what is false, Eph. iv. 25; sometimes to what is typical and figurative, John i. 17; sometimes to what is not original, and of itself: in opposition to all these Christ is the *true Light;* he who alone deserved the name of light, having light in himself, and from himself, 1 John ii. 8, and shining more gloriously than the prophets or apostles. *Which lighteth every man that cometh into the world;* he lighteth not the Jews only, (as the prophets of old,) but both the Jews and Gentiles. Some understand this of the light of reason; but besides that reason is no where in holy writ called light, neither did this illumination agree to Christ as Mediator. It is rather therefore to be understood of the light of gospel revelation, which Christ caused to be made to all the world, Matt. xxviii. 19; Mark xvi. 15. Those who interpret it of the more internal illumination by the Holy Spirit of God, by which Christ is not revealed *to us* only, but *in us*, say, that Christ hath done what lay in him (as a Minister of the gospel) so to enlighten all that came into the world; and that Christ is said to enlighten every man, because none is enlightened but by him, and that some of all sorts are by him enlightened; in one of which two latter senses the terms *all* and *every man* must be interpreted in a multitude of texts in the Gospel. The words in the Greek are so, as they may either be translated as we read them, or thus, who coming into the world, enlightened every man : a more universal spiritual light, or means to come to the knowledge of God, overspreading the world after Christ's coming, than before. So John xii. 46, *I am come a light into the world.* And it is by some observed, that the phrase *cometh into the world*, doth not barely signify a being born, but being sent into the world by the Father, being sanctified, as in John x. 36; xvii. 18.

m ver. 3. Heb. 1. 2. & 11. 3.

10 He was in the world, and ᵐ the world was made by him, and the world knew him not.

He was in the world; he was in the place called *the world*, and amongst the men of the world; for so the term *world* is often taken, chap. xvi. 28; 2 Pet. iii. 6. Christ, before he came in the flesh, was in it; filling both the heavens and the earth, and sustaining it by the word of his power, and manifesting his will to it, more immediately to Moses and to the prophets, and more mediately by Moses and by the prophets. *And the world was made by him;* and the heavens and the earth, all things visible and invisible, (as was said before,) were made by him. *And the world knew him not;* and the men of the world took no notice of him, did not acknowledge him, believe in him, nor were subject to him; so the word *knew* often signifies, (according to the Hebrew idiom,) John x. 14, 15, 27; not a bare comprehension of an object in the understanding, but suitable affections: so Matt. vii. 23; 1 John iii. 1. This is not to be understood of all individual persons in the world; for Abraham, Isaac, and Jacob, and David, and many particular persons, did in this sense know him; but the generality of the world did not. The heathens did not, (who are sometimes called *the world*, distinctively from the Jews, 1 John ii. 2; 1 Cor. i. 21,) and most of the Jews did not, though some did.

11 ⁿHe came unto his own, and his own received him not.

n Luke 19. 14. Acts 3. 26. & 13. 46.

He came unto his own; Christ came into the world, which being made by him, was in the most proper sense his own; or, to the Israelites, which were as his own house, land, and possession, Psal. lxxxv. 1; John xvi. 32. The Greek word is in the plural number, and used in the places before mentioned, as also Acts xxi. 6; sometimes signifying men's proper country, sometimes their proper house. But it is a further question, what coming is here spoken of: though it be generally (or by many at least) interpreted of Christ's coming by his incarnation, yet that seemeth not to be the sense; partly, because that coming is spoken of, ver. 14; and partly, because in that sense the Jews did receive him; nor was it in their power to hinder his manifestation in the flesh. The coming therefore here mentioned seemeth to be intended of his coming by his prophets, John the Baptist, and his own personal preaching of the gospel. *And his own received him not*, whom in this way of coming they did not receive, believing neither the testimony given by his prophets, nor by the Baptist, nor by himself, John v. 43.

12 But °as many as received him, to them gave he ‖ power to become the sons of God, *even* to them that believe on his name :

o Is. 56. 5. Rom. 8. 15. Gal. 3. 26. 2 Pet. 1. 4. 1 John 3. 1. ‖ Or, *the right*, or, *privilege.*

But as many as received him; though the generality of those amongst whom Christ came received him not in the manner before expressed, yet some did own him, believed in him, and submitted to him ; and to as many as thus received him, not into their houses only, but into their hearts, *to them gave he power to become the sons of God;* he gave a power, or a right, or privilege, not that they might if they would be, but to be actually, to become, or be, the sons of God by adoption; for believers are already the sons of God, Gal. iii. 26, though it doth not yet appear what they shall be in the *adoption*, mentioned Rom. viii. 23, which the apostle calls *the redemption of our body*, viz. in the resurrection; hence the children of God are called *the children of the resurrection*, Luke xx. 36. *To them that believe on his name;* this is the privilege of all that believe in the name of Christ; by which term he opens the former term of receiving : to receive Christ, and to believe in his name, are the same thing. To believe in his name, is either to believe in him, Acts iii. 16, or in the revelation of himself in the promises of the gospel. The proposition of God's word is the object of faith of assent; but the person of the Mediator is the object of that faith which receiveth Christ; and those alone have a right to be the sons of God, and to the privileges peculiar to sons, who believe in Christ as revealed in the promises of the word of God, and there exhibited to men.

13 ᵖWhich were born, not of blood, nor of the will of the flesh, nor of the will of man, but of God.

p ch. 3. 5. Jam. 1. 18. 1 Pet. 1. 23.

Which were born, not of blood; not of the blood of men and women; or, not of the blood of Abraham (which was the boast of the Jews, *We have Abraham to our Father*). *Nor of the will of the flesh;* nor from the lusts of the flesh. *Nor of the will of man;* nor from a power in man's will, or men's free act in adopting other men's children. To be born, signifieth to receive our principle of life : those who are the children of God have not the principle of their life, as they are such, from the motions of nature, nor from the will of men. *But of God:* whatever be the sense of the former words, these words plainly affirm God to be the principal efficient, and procreant cause, of all those who are the sons of God; for faith, by which we are the children of God, Gal. iii. 26, is the work of God, John vi. 29, his gift, Phil. i. 29; and men are *born again, not of corruptible seed, but of* that which is *incorruptible,* 1 Pet. i. 23: they are sanctified and cleansed *with the washing of water by the word,* Eph. v. 26; *the washing of regeneration, and renewing of the Holy Ghost,* Tit. iii. 5.

^{q Mat. 1.16, 20. Luke 1. 31,35.& 2. 7. 1 Tim. 3. 16. r Rom. 1. 3. Gal. 4. 4. s Heb. 2.11, 14, 16, 17. t Is. 40. 5. Matt. 17. 2. ch. 2. 11. & 11. 40. 2 Pet. 1. 17. u Col. 1. 19. & 2. 3, 9.}

14 ^qAnd the Word ^rwas made ^sflesh, and dwelt among us, (and ^twe beheld his glory, the glory as of the only begotten of the Father,) ^ufull of grace and truth.

The Word was made flesh; the Son of God, called *the Word,* for the reasons before specified, was made truly man, as *flesh* often signifieth in holy writ, Gen. vi. 12; Psal. lxv. 2; Isa. xl. 5, 6; not a vile, despicable, mortal man. The evangelist rather saith he was made flesh, than he was made man, more plainly to distinguish the two natures in Christ; to assert the truth of his human nature; to let us know that Christ assumed human nature in common, not the particular nature of any; to commend the love of God, and to let us see, that his plaster was proportioned to our sore, it reached all flesh. The evangelist saith not he was changed into flesh; but, by assuming, he *was made flesh. And dwelt amongst us:* and he tabernacled amongst us; amongst us men, or amongst men that were his disciples: the word signifieth properly, he made no long stay. *And we beheld his glory;* and we beheld the signs and effects of his glory; many of which were seen, both at the time of his transfiguration, and at his passion, resurrection, and ascension; the glory of his grace, holiness, truth, miraculous operations, &c. *The glory as of the only begotten of the Father;* which glory was the glory of the only begotten of the Father; for the particle *as* here doth not signify likeness, but truth, Neh. vii. 2; Job xxiv. 14. *Full of grace and truth,* as he was God manifested in the flesh. *Grace* signifieth love and good will, out of which it was that he delivered us from the curse and rigour of the law (to which grace is opposed). He was also full of *truth,* both as truth is opposed to falsehood, and to the shadows and figures of the law; and Christ was full of truth as he was the antitype to all the ceremonies, and all the promises had and have their completion and reality in him: see chap. xiv. 17; Rom. xv. 8; 2 Cor. i. 20. Truth also may signify the sincerity and integrity of Christ's life, as he was without guile.

^{w ver. 32. ch. 3. 32. & 5. 33. x Matt. 3.11. Mark 1. 7. Luke 3. 16. ver. 27, 30. ch. 3. 31. y ch. 8. 58. Col. 1. 17.}

15 ¶ ^wJohn bare witness of him, and cried, saying, This was he of whom I spake, ^xHe that cometh after me is preferred before me: ^yfor he was before me.

John bare witness of him, and cried, saying: John was not he, but only a witness to him; and he continueth to bear witness (the verb is in the present tense); nor did he give an obscure or cold testimony, but an open, and plain, and fervent testimony, according to the prophecies, his testimony was *the voice of one crying in the wilderness. This was he of whom I spake;* he first testified that Christ was he of whom he had before spoken; possibly when he was preaching in the wilderness, and Christ came to him to be baptized of him, Matt. iii. 11, 14. *He that cometh after me is preferred before me;* he that cometh after me, in order of time, or in the ministerial office and employment, or, as if he were my disciple, John viii. 12, is become, or is made, before me. *For he was before me,* both in the eternal destination, and in respect of his Divine nature; as also in dignity and eminency, considered as a prophet, i. e. one that revealeth my Father's will. This John said before, though not in terms, yet in effect, when he said, Matt. iii. 11, *He that cometh after me is mightier than I, whose shoes I am not worthy to bear,* &c. So Mark i. 7; Luke iii. 16. This is the first thing which is here mentioned, as John's testimony concerning Christ, respecting the excellency of his person.

^{z ch. 3. 34. Eph. 1.6,7,8. Col. 1. 19. & 2. 9, 10.}

16 And of his ^zfulness have all we received, and grace for grace.

And of his fulness have all we received; of that plenty of grace which Christ hath, (who hath not the Spirit given him *by measure,* chap. iii. 34, as other saints have, Acts ii. 4, 6, 8,) we who by nature are void of grace, whether taken for the favour of God, or gracious habits, have received, as the skirts of Aaron's garment received the oil which was plentifully poured out on Aaron's head. *And grace for grace:* nor have we received drops, but grace upon grace; not only knowledge and instruction, but the love and favour of God, and spiritual habits, in proportion to the favour and grace which Christ hath (allowing for our short capacities); we have received grace freely and plentifully, all from Christ, and for his sake; which lets us see how much the grace-receiving soul is bound to acknowledge and adore Christ, and may be confirmed in the receiving of further grace, and the hopes of eternal life; and it may mind all (according to that of the apostle, 2 Cor. vi. 1) to take heed that they *receive not the grace of God in vain.*

17 For ^athe law was given by Moses, but ^bgrace and ^ctruth came by Jesus Christ.

^{a Ex. 20. 1, &c. Deut. 4. 44. & 5. 1. & 33. 4. b Rom. 3.24. & 5. 21. & 6. 14. c ch. 8. 32. & 14. 6.}

For the law was given by Moses; the law, moral and ceremonial, came not by Moses, but was given by Moses as God's minister and servant; that law by which no man can be justified, Rom. iii. 28. In this was Moses's honour, of whom you glory, chap. v. 45. God indeed made an eminent use of him, as his minister, by whom he revealed his will to you; both in matters of his worship, according to that dispensation; and in matters which concern you in your whole conversation; but yet there is an eminent difference betwixt him and Jesus Christ. The law is no where called grace, neither doth it discover any thing but duty and wrath; it showeth no remission, in case that duty be not done, nor affordeth strength for the doing of it. *But grace and truth came by Jesus Christ;* all that is from Christ; all the favour of God for the remission and pardon of sin, and for strength and assistance to the performance of duty, is (not given from God by Christ, as the law by Moses, but) from Christ as the fountain of grace; and not grace only, but *truth,* whether taken for solid and real mercy, or with respect to the law; the fulfilling of all the types and prophecies in it was by and in Christ.

18 ^dNo man hath seen God at any time; ^ethe only begotten Son, which is in the bosom of the Father, he hath declared him.

^{d Ex. 33. 20. Deut. 4. 12. Matt. 11.27. Luke 10. 22. ch. 6. 46. 1 Tim. 1. 17. & 6. 16. 1 John 4. 12, 20. e ver. 14. ch. 3. 16, 18. 1 John 4. 9.}

No man hath seen God at any time; no man hath at any time seen the essence of God with his eyes, John iv. 24; nor with the eyes of his mind understood the whole counsel and will of God, Matt. xi. 27; Rom. xi. 34. Moses indeed saw the image and representation of God, and had a more familiar converse with God than others; upon which account he is said to have talked with God face to face; Numb. xii. 7, 8, God saith he would speak unto him *mouth to mouth, even apparently;* but he tells us how in the same verse, *and the similitude of the Lord shall he behold;* and God, who had spoken to the same sense, Exod. xxxiii. 11, saith, ver. 20, *Thou canst not see my face; for there shall no man see me, and live.* Now to whom he did not discover his face, he certainly did not discover all his secret counsels. *The only begotten Son, which is in the bosom of the Father;* but he who is the only begotten and beloved Son, hath such an intimate communion with him in his nature, and such a free communication of all his counsels, as it may be said, he is continually in his bosom. *He hath declared him;* hath declared him, not only as a prophet declareth the mind and will of God, but as *the heavens declare the glory of God, and the firmament showeth his handy-work,* Psal. xix. 1; being *the brightness of his* Father's *glory, and the express image of his person,* Heb. i. 3. So as the Father can only be seen in the Son; nor is so full a revelation of the Father's will to be expected from any, as from the Son.

19 ¶ And this is ^fthe record of John, when the Jews sent Priests and Levites from Jerusalem to ask him, Who art thou?

^{A. D. 30. f ch. 5. 33.}

John's former testimony was more private to the common people; this testimony was given to a public authority. *The Jews* (most probably the rulers of the Jews, who made up their sanhedrim, or great court, answering a parliament with us, for the cognizance of false prophets belonged to them) *sent priests and Levites*, which were Pharisees, ver. 24, of the strictest sect of the Jews as to rites and ceremonies; these came from Jerusalem, where the sanhedrim constantly sat, and the chief priests were, (if the message were not from the sanhedrim itself,) to ask John Baptist who he was; that is, by what authority he preached and baptized? what kind of prophet he was? for they could not but know his name and family, he descending from a priest amongst them: and this appeareth to be their sense from what followeth.

g Luke 3. 15.
ch. 3. 28.
Acts 13. 25.

20 And ^ghe confessed, and denied not; but confessed, I am not the Christ.

And he confessed; he being asked openly and plainly, professed, *and denied not;* and did not dissemble nor halt in his speech. These negatives are in Scripture often added to affirmatives, to exclude all exceptions, Job v. 17; Psal. xl. 10—12. *But confessed:* he did not tell them once so, but again and again, because many were musing about it, Luke iii. 15. *I am not the Christ;* I am not that great Messiah which God hath promised you, and in the expectation of whom you live, Luke ii. 26, 38; xix. 11; John iv. 25. The diligence we shall constantly observe in the servants of God in holy writ, to avoid the arrogating of that honour to themselves which is due only to God and Christ; and this, together with John's steadiness and plainness, doth very well become all professors, but the ministers of the gospel especially.

h Mal. 4. 5.
Matt. 17. 10.
i Deut. 18. 15. 18.
∥ Or,
a prophet.

21 And they asked him, What then? Art thou ^hElias? And he saith, I am not. Art thou ⁱ∥that prophet? And he answered, No.

John was at Bethabara when these messengers came to him, ver. 28. They asked him if he were *Elias.* The Jews had not only an expectation of the Messias, but of Elias to come as a messenger before him, according to the prophecy, Mal. iv. 5; as appeareth, Matt. xvii. 10; Mark ix. 11; of which they had a gross conception here, that Elias should come out of heaven personally, or at least that his soul should come into another body, according to the Pythagorean opinion. Now the meaning of the prophecy was, that one should come like Elias; and this was fulfilled in John, Luke i. 17, as our Saviour tells us, Matt. xvii. 12; Mark ix. 13; but they asked the question according to that notion they had of Elias. To which John answereth, that he was not; neither that Elias that ascended in a fiery chariot to heaven; nor any body informed with Elias's soul: and thus the words of our Saviour, Matt. xvii. 12; Mark ix. 12, are easily reconciled to this text. They go on, and ask him if he were *that prophet,* or a prophet. Some think that they meant the Prophet promised, Deut. xviii. 18; but that was no other than Christ himself, which he had before denied himself to be; nor doth it appear from any text of Scripture that the Jews had any expectation of any other particular prophet; but it is plain from Luke ix. 8, that they had a notion that it was possible one of the old prophets might rise again from the dead, for so they guessed there concerning Christ. But others think that the article in the Greek here is not emphatical, and they only asked him if he were a prophet; for the Jews had a general notion, that the spirit of prophecy had left them ever since the times of Zechariah and Malachi; which they hoped was returned in John the Baptist, and about this they question him if he were a prophet. To which he answereth, *No;* neither that Prophet promised, Deut. xviii. 18, nor yet any of the old prophets risen from the dead; nor yet one like the prophets of the Old Testament, who only prophesied of a Christ to come; but, as Christ calls him, Matt. xi. 9, *more than a prophet,* one who showed and declared to them a Christ already come; for the law and the prophets prophesied but until John; the law in its types foreshowing, the prophets in their sermons foretelling, a Messiah to come; John did more. His father indeed, Luke i. 76, called him *the prophet of the Highest;* but there *prophet* is to be understood not in a strict, but in a large sense, as the term prophecy is taken, Rom. xii. 6.

And the term prophet often signifieth one that revealeth the will of God to men; in which large sense John was a prophet, and yet more than a prophet in the stricter notion of the term; and in that sense no prophet, that is, no mere prophet: so, Numb. xi. 19, Moses tells the people they should not eat flesh one, or two, or five, or ten, or twenty days, because they should eat it a whole month together.

22 Then said they unto him, Who art thou? that we may give an answer to them that sent us. What sayest thou of thyself?

Hitherto John had given them only a negative answer, and told them who he was not; he was neither Christ, nor the Elias, nor that prophet they expected; neither any of the old prophets risen from the dead; nor any prophet at all in a strict sense (as were the prophets of the Old Testament): they press him to a direct, plain, positive answer, that they might give an answer to those that sent them, who did not send them to inquire what he was not, but what he was. And there were various talks and discourses of the people about him, which they were not willing to take up and run away with; but they desired to have it from himself.

23 ^kHe said, I *am* the voice of one crying in the wilderness, Make straight the way of the Lord, as ^lsaid the prophet Esaias.

k Matt. 3. 3.
Mark 1. 3.
Luke 3 4.
ch. 3. 28.
l Is. 40. 3.

We had the same, Matt. iii. 3; Mark i. 3: see the notes there. Chemnitius thinks, that John chose rather to preach and fulfil his ministry in the wilderness, than in the temple; to make an illustrious difference betwixt himself, who was but the Lord's messenger, and whose office was but to prepare the Lord's way, and his Lord himself, of whom it was prophesied, Mal. iii. 1, *The Lord, whom ye seek, shall suddenly come to his holy temple;* upon which account Haggai prophesied, chap. ii. 9, that *the glory of* that *latter house* (built by Ezra, and Zerubbabel, and Nehemiah) should *be greater than of the former.*

24 And they which were sent were of the Pharisees.

Who these Pharisees were hath been before explained in our notes on Matt. iii. 7. They were of the strictest sect of the Jewish religion, Acts xxvi. 5. The greatest part of their councils was made up of those of this sect, as may be learned from Acts xxiii. They were the men most zealous for and tenacious of the Jewish rites; and would allow nothing to be added to the Jewish worship to what they had received concerning it, either from the law of God, or the traditions of the elders.

25 And they asked him, and said unto him, Why baptizest thou then, if thou be not that Christ, nor Elias, neither that prophet?

The Pharisees themselves would allow the Messiah, or Elias, or a prophet, to make any additions to or alterations in the worship of God, but none else: hence it is they ask, by what authority he baptized, if he were none of these? From whence we may learn, that although they might have some umbrage of that baptismal washing which was under the gospel, to commence into a sacrament, or federal sign, in the washing of their proselytes, or of Jewish children when they were circumcised; yet John's action was looked upon as new, who baptized adult Jews: now the care of the sanhedrim was to keep the worship of God uncorrupt, and the Pharisees amongst them had a particular zeal in the case, especially so far as the traditions of the elders were concerned.

26 John answered them, saying, ^mI baptize with water: ⁿbut there standeth one among you, whom ye know not;

m Mat. 3. 11.
n Mal. 3. 1.

This was no strict answer to their question, which was not, how, but why he baptized? But proper replies are often called answers in Scripture, though not apposite to the question. *I baptize with water;* I baptize you with mere water: *but there standeth one among you, whom ye know not;* but there hath stood one amongst you, ἕστηκεν, or (by a usual putting of one tense for another) there standeth one; Christ had been there with the crowd, Luke iii. 15, 21, and possibly was amongst them still when John spake these words; *whom you know not*, not so much as *ore tenus*, by face.

o ver. 15, 30.
Acts 19. 4.
27 °He it is, who coming after me is preferred before me, whose shoe's latchet I am not worthy to unloose.

John the Baptist had before told them, *He that cometh after me is preferred before me*, ver. 15 : see the notes there. He now repeateth those words; and it is observable, that the three other evangelists all put this passage before the history of Christ's coming to him to be baptized. So as it is probable that these messengers came to John as he was baptizing; and either immediately before or after Christ's baptism, Christ being yet in the crowd, he repeateth to his hearers what he had a little before said of him, that he was to be preferred before him. *Whose shoe's latchet I am not worthy to unloose ;* he here enlargeth upon it with a proverbial speech, which the other evangelists have, with a very little variation: Matthew saith, *Whose shoes I am not worthy to bear ;* that is, to perform unto him the very meanest service or office. We have such forms of speech in use at this day amongst us; when we would express the great pre-eminence of some one above another, we say of that other, He is not worthy to tie his shoes; or, to carry his shoes after him. There is a vast difference between Christ and the most excellent of his ministers; which as to baptism lieth here; the ministerial baptism is but with water; Christ baptizeth *with the Holy Ghost and with fire*, Matt. iii. 11, or, *with the Holy Ghost*, as Mark i. 8.

p Judg. 7. 24.
ch. 10. 40.
28 These things were done ᴾ in Bethabara beyond Jordan, where John was baptizing.

The evangelist had before told us what was done, these words tell us where. Some ancient writers will have the place to have been Bethany ; but they seem not to have so well considered John xi. 18, where Bethany is said to have been but fifteen furlongs from Jerusalem, and consequently on this side Jordan ; whereas the evangelist saith, that this place was περὰν, *beyond Jordan*, in the tribe of Reuben, in the country of Peræa, *where John* at this time *was baptizing*, and probably had been so for some time.

q Ex. 12. 3.
Is. 53. 7.
ver. 36.
Acts 8. 32.
1 Pet. 1. 19.
Rev. 5. 6, &c.
r Is. 53. 11.
1 Cor. 15. 3.
Gal. 1. 4. Heb. 1. 3. & 2. 17. & 9. 28. 1 Pet. 2. 24. & 3. 18. 1 John 2. 2. & 3. 5. & 4. 10.
Rev. 1. 5. ‖ Or, *beareth*.
29 ¶ The next day John seeth Jesus coming unto him, and saith, Behold ᑫ the Lamb of God, ʳ which ‖ taketh away the sin of the world.

The next day ; the most think, the day following that day when the messengers from Jerusalem had been examining the Baptist. Heinsius thinks it was the same day, and saith, the Hellenists usually so interpret ἐν ἐπαύριον, for μετὰ ταῦτα, *after these things ;* but the former sense is more generally embraced. *John seeth Jesus coming to him,* out of the wilderness, as some think, where he had been tempted by the devil ; but then it must follow, that he was not amongst the crowd, ver. 26, standing in the midst of them, when the messengers were there; and it should appear by ver. 32 and 33, that this which is here recorded happened after Christ's baptism by John (of which this evangelist saith nothing) : it seemeth rather to be understood of another coming of Christ to John after he had been baptized, when John, seeing him, pointed as it were with his finger to him, (for the term *Behold* seemeth to be here used demonstratively,) showing them the person whom he would have them cast their eye upon ; whom he calls, *the Lamb of God*, not only to denote his excellency, as we read of the *night of the Lord*, Exod. xii. 42, and *the bread of God*, Lev. xxi. 21 ; which indeed Christ was, being *without blemish*, 1 Pet. i. 19 ; but with reference to the lambs used in the Jewish sacrifices, not only at the passover, Exod. xii. 5, but in the daily sacrifice, Exod. xxix. 38 ; Lev. i. 10, or the burnt-offering ; and in the peace-offering, Lev. iii. 7, and in the sin-offering, Lev. iv. 32. He calls Christ *the Lamb of God*, probably, because divers of the priests were there to hear, and (as appears, ver. 39) it was nigh the time of their daily sacrifice ; that so he might remind them that Christ was the truth and Anti-type to all their sacrifices. *Which taketh away the sin of the world ;* ὁ αἴρων, the word signifies both to take up, and to take away : *which taketh away the sin of the world,* as God, to whom it belongs to forgive sin ; and this he did by taking it upon himself, (so it is translated, Matt. xvi. 24,) expiating it, which expiation is followed by a plenary remission, and taking it away, both the punishment of it, and the root, and body, and power of it ; redeeming them as from the grave and hell, due to man for sin ; so from a *vain conversation*, 1 Pet. i. 18 ; and not doing this for the Jews only, but for the Gentiles also, 1 John ii. 2, for many in the world, being he without whom there is no remission, Acts iv. 12. Nor doth his gracious act cease at any time, it is a work he is always doing, and which none but he can do : ministers may persuade, priests of old offered lambs and other beasts in sacrifice ; but he alone taketh away sin. So that, as what he said to the messengers of the sanhedrim gave all the honour of any valuable effect of baptism to Christ ; so, what he saith here gives him all the honour of any good effect of preaching, or any good effect of our ministry ; it is he alone, who (when we have said or done what we can) taketh away the sin of the world.

s ver. 15, 27.
30 ˢ This is he of whom I said, After me cometh a man which is preferred before me : for he was before me.

And (saith he) this is he of whom I said, (as ver. 15,) He cometh after me in order of time and ministry, but is more excellent than I am. See the notes on ver. 15.

t Mal. 3. 1.
Matt. 3. 6.
Luke 1. 17,
76, 77. & 3.
3, 4.
31 And I knew him not : but that he should be made manifest to Israel, ᵗ therefore am I come baptizing with water.

This verse is best expounded by ver. 33, where the same words are repeated, *I knew him not ;* and it is added, *but he that sent me to baptize with water, the same said unto me, Upon whom thou shalt see the Spirit descending*, &c. Lest any should think that Christ and John had compacted together to give one another credit, or that there was some near relation betwixt John and Christ, John saith, *I knew him not ;* for Christ had spent his time at home, Luke ii. 51, John had lived in desert places ; the providence of God so ordering it, that John should not know Christ so much as by face, until that time came when Christ was to be made manifest to Israel. But that God might make his Son *manifest unto Israel*, when God by an extraordinary mission sent John to baptize with water, he gave him this token, That he upon whom he should see the Spirit descending and remaining on him, as ver. 33, that was the Messiah, the Lamb of God, that should take away the sin of the world ; he who should baptize with the Holy Ghost. And *therefore* (saith John) *am I come baptizing with water.* I did not run without sending, nor introduce a new rite or sacrament without commission ; but being thus sent of God, and that I might give Christ an opportunity of coming to me, that I might see the Spirit descending and remaining upon him. From whence we learn, that none but Christ can institute a sacrament. John baptized not, till he was sent to baptize with water.

u Mat. 3. 16.
Mark 1. 10.
Luke 3. 22.
ch. 5. 32.
32 ᵘ And John bare record, saying, I saw the Spirit descending from heaven like a dove, and it abode upon him.

Saith John, According to the revelation which I had, when I received my extraordinary commission to baptize, so it fell out to me, I did see, when he was baptized, the heaven opening, and a representation of the Spirit of God (for no man can see God and live) descending. The form of the representation was like that of a dove. And it was not a mere transient sight, but it did for some time abide upon that person, in that sensible representation ; by that token I knew that he was the Son of God.

x Mat. 3. 11.
Acts 1. 5. &
2. 4. & 10. 44.
& 19. 6.
33 And I knew him not : but he that sent me to baptize with water, the same said unto me, Upon whom thou shalt see the Spirit descending, and remaining on him, ˣ the same is he which baptizeth with the Holy Ghost.

And I knew him not ; I was a stranger to him ; I knew him in a sense, when I leaped in my mother's womb, upon his mother's coming to see my mother, Luke i. 41 ; but that (as impressions made upon infants use to do) wore off. I had some impression upon me at that time when he came towards me to be baptized, which made me say to him, (as Matt. iii. 14,) *I have need to be baptized of thee, and comest thou to me?* But yet I was not certain, though I knew he was in the crowd of people, that he was the person designed, and whose work it should be to baptize with the Holy Ghost, until the same God that had given me that sign fulfilled it to me.

34 And I saw, and bare record that this is the Son of God.

But when I saw that, I could not but believe, and also bear an open testimony to the world, that this man was not mere man, but the eternal Son of that God, who sent me to baptize with water; reserving still to himself the Divine power of blessing that holy sacrament, and conferring the Holy Ghost in regenerating habits, working like fire, in purging away the dross of souls, and like water, washing away the filth of sin, Matt. iii. 11; John iii. 5.

35 ¶ Again the next day after John stood, and two of his disciples;

36 And looking upon Jesus as he walked, he saith, ʸBehold the Lamb of God!

y ver. 29.

The next day after that the messengers who came from Jerusalem had been with John, *John stood, and two of his disciples;* whether he was preaching or no it is not said; but John standing with them, saw Christ walking, whence, or whither, is not said; but as a good man is always taking opportunity to commend Christ to others, so John upon this occasion took advantage further to make Christ known to those two men, (who they were, we shall hear in the following verses,) and repeats the words he had said before, *Behold the Lamb of God!* (See the notes on ver. 27.) Thus good and faithful ministers will continually be inviting their disciples to Christ, taking them off from further consideration of themselves, and, as ministers, to show them the way to Christ.

37 And the two disciples heard him speak, and they followed Jesus.

God blessed the verbal testimony that John had given so far, that they stood in no need of any miracle to confirm it, but upon their hearing John *speak, they followed Jesus:* as yet, not as his apostles; for their call to that office was afterward (as we shall hear); nor yet, so as no more to depart from him: but there was created in them a further desire of knowledge of him and acquaintance with him.

38 Then Jesus turned, and saw them following, and saith unto them, What seek ye? They said unto him, Rabbi, (which is to say, being interpreted, Master,) where ‖ dwellest thou ?

| Or, *abidest.*

Christ, as he walked, turning back on him, and seeing two men following him, inquireth of their end, what they sought; to teach us, in all our religious motions and actions, to do the like; for the end will contribute much to specify the action, and to make it good or bad. They gave him that honourable title which was then in fashion, by and under which they were wont to speak to those upon whom they relied for instruction, whose doctrine they desired to know, and with whom they desired to converse, and to learn of him. They asked him where he abode, or where he lodged.

39 He saith unto them, Come and see. They came and saw where he dwelt, and abode with him that day: for it was ‖ about the tenth hour.

| *That was two hours before night.*

Our Lord discerning the end of their following him to be sincere and good, invites them to *come and see* where his lodging was; for he elsewhere telleth us, that he had not a house wherein to hide his head. *They came and saw* his lodgings; where, or of what nature they were, we are not told, but we never read that he during his whole pilgrimage amongst us had any stately or splendid lodgings. The text saith that these two disciples *abode with him that day;* whether only the two or three remaining hours of the same day, (for it was now about four of the clock afternoon, which answers the tenth hour according to the Jewish account,) or another whole day, being the sabbath day, (as some think,) we are not told, nor can conclude; certain it is, they abode with him the remaining part of that day, from four of the clock till night.

40 One of the two which heard John *speak,* and followed him, was ᶻAndrew, Simon Peter's brother.

z Matt. 4. 18.

Concerning the call of this Andrew to the apostleship, see Matt. iv. 18, 19, and Mark i. 16, 17. That was at another time, and in another manner: Christ here only invited them to come and see where he lodged.

41 He first findeth his own brother Simon, and saith unto him, We have found the Messias, which is, being interpreted, ‖ the Christ.

| Or, *the anointed.*

It should seem that both the disciples (after their converse with Christ at the place where he lodged) went together to look for Peter, Andrew's brother. Andrew first found him, and tells him (with great joy) that he and that other disciple had *found the Messiah,* prophesied of by Daniel, and in the expectation of whom the disciples and the Jews lived. The term *Messiah* in Hebrew is the same with *Christ* in Greek, and both signify the same with *Anointed* in English. The article in this place is emphatical, not merely prepositive, as in other places, but signifying, that Anointed; for other kings, and priests, and prophets were also anointed, and God's people are called anointed; but he was anointed with the oil of gladness above his fellows, having the Spirit not given him by measure.

42 And he brought him to Jesus. And when Jesus beheld him, he said, Thou art Simon the son of Jona: ᵃthou shalt be called Cephas, which is by interpretation, ‖ A stone.

a Mat. 16. 18.

| Or, *Peter.*

Andrew having found his brother Simon, conducts him to Jesus. Andrew, and Simon, and Philip were citizens of Bethsaida, ver. 44, which was a city of Galilee; how near to the place where John baptized, or Christ lodged, we cannot say. Probably Simon was one of John's disciples, and came to attend his ministry; so as the disciples only sought him in the crowd, and came with him to Christ. When Christ beheld him, he said, *Thou art Simon;* he knew him, and called him by name, and told him his father's name, *Jonas,* and giveth him a new name, *Cephas,* which by interpretation doth not signify a head, (as the popish disputant at Berne urged, to prove him the head of the church, as if it had been a Greek word, and came from κεφαλή; or, as he pretended, ridiculously enough, from an old Greek word, κεφάς,) but *a stone* (as this text tells us); by which name we find him called, 1 Cor. i. 12; iii. 22; ix. 5; xv. 5; Gal. ii. 9: in other places *Peter,* which signifieth a stone also, or a rock. Cephas is a Syriac word, Peter a Greek word: Christ gave him the name. Both Cephas and Peter are by interpretation, a stone. Beza thinks that our Saviour did not here give him that name, but foretell that he should be so called. Casaubon thinks that the name was here given to him, and with it a new spirit; that whereas before he was (according to his father's name Jonas, which signifies a dove) fearful and timorous, from this time forward he was as a rock, steady, firm, and full of courage and constancy: but it is a greater question how this text is to be reconciled with Matt. iv. 18—20, where Andrew and Peter are both said to be espied by Christ, *walking by the sea of Galilee;* and Luke v. 10, where Simon is reported to be called after they had taken a great draught of fish; and with Mark iii. 13, and Luke vi. 13, where all the apostles are named as called at one and the same time. Doubtless the calls were different. This in John seems rather to be a prophecy than a call. Those texts, Matt. iv. 18—20, and Luke v. 10, seem to be their calls to a discipleship. The other texts, Mark iii. 13; Luke vi. 13, respect their election to the apostleship, and the mission of them.

43 ¶ The day following Jesus would go forth into Galilee, and findeth Philip, and saith unto him, Follow me.

All this while Christ seemeth to have been in Judea,

which was the most famous province. The day after Peter had thus been with him, he had a mind to go *into Galilee*; out of that he designed to choose his disciples; and that being the country where he had been educated, he designed in a more special manner to honour it with the first fruit of his public ministry. There he *findeth Philip* (the name signifieth, a lover of horses). He calleth him to be his disciple.

b ch. 12. 21.   44 Now ᵇ Philip was of Bethsaida, the city of Andrew and Peter.

This Philip was a citizen of Bethsaida (the word signifies in the Hebrew, The house of fruits, or of huntsmen). Andrew and Peter (mentioned before) both of them lived there. It was one of those cities where Christ did *most of his mighty works*, Matt. xi. 20.

c ch. 21. 2.
d Gen. 3. 15.
& 49. 10.
Deut. 18. 18.
See on
Luke 24. 27.
e Is. 4. 2. & 7. 14. & 9. 6. & 53. 2. Mic. 5. 2. Zech. 6. 12. & 9. 9. See more on Luke 24. 27. f Matt. 2. 23. Luke 2. 4.

45 Philip findeth ᶜ Nathanael, and saith unto him, We have found him, of whom ᵈ Moses in the law, and the ᵉ prophets, did write, Jesus ᶠ of Nazareth, the son of Joseph.

Philip having himself discovered Christ, is not willing to eat his morsels alone, but desires to communicate his discovery to others; he finds (whether casually, or upon search, is not said) one Nathanael, he was of Cana in Galilee, chap. xxi. 2. (The name is a Hebrew name, signifying, The gift of God; some think it the same with Nethaneel, 1 Chron. xv. 24.) Having found him, he tells him with great joy, that they had found him of whom Moses had wrote in the law, *the Shiloh*, mentioned Gen. xlix. 10, *the Prophet*, mentioned Deut. xviii. 15, *the Branch of the Lord*, mentioned Isa. iv. 2, *the Messiah*, mentioned by Daniel, Dan. ix. 25, 26, and all the other prophets, him whom they usually called *Jesus of Nazareth*, (there he was conceived, there he was bred, Luke ii. 4, 51, though he was born in Bethlehem of Judah, ver. 4,) and who was commonly thought to be *the son of Joseph*. If Philip did only *cum vulgo loqui*, speak as was commonly said, though himself knew and believed other things, he is not to be blamed; but the most think Philip discovered here his own weakness, both in thinking Christ the son of Joseph, and to have been born at Nazareth. It is certain that the apostles themselves at first, yea, and till Christ's resurrection from the dead, had a very imperfect notion of Christ as the true Messiah. Grace may consist with great weakness as to knowledge.

g ch. 7. 41, 42, 52.   46 And Nathanael said unto him, ᵍ Can there any good thing come out of Nazareth? Philip saith unto him, Come and see.

The words of Philip begat a prejudice in Nathanael, as to what he said. It was prophesied, Micah v. 2, that the Messiah should come out of Bethlehem. So, chap. vii. 41, 42, some of the people said, *Shall Christ come out of Galilee? Hath not the Scripture said, That Christ cometh of the seed of David, and out of the town of Bethlehem, where David was?* Nazareth was not only a poor little place, (for so Bethlehem also was,) but a place which the Scripture never mentioned as the place from whence the Messiah should arise; a place that God had not honoured with the production of a prophet. By *any good thing* seems to be meant, the Messiah, or any prophet, or (more generally) any thing which is noble and excellent, and of any remark. So prone are we to think that the kingdom of God comes with observation, that we know not how to fancy how great things should be done by little means, and great persons should arise out of little, contemptible places. Whereas God chooseth *the foolish things of the world to confound the wise; and the weak things to confound the mighty; and base things of the world*, to confound the wise, 1 Cor. i. 25—28. *Philip saith unto him, Come and see*; Philip, not knowing how to answer Nathanael's objection, and to remove his prejudice, wisheth him himself to go, and make up a judgment. Wise men ought to do this, and not to take up prejudices from reports and common vogue.

h Ps. 32. 2.
& 73. 1.
ch. 8. 39.
Rom. 2. 28, 29. & 9. 6.   47 Jesus saw Nathanael coming to him, and saith of him, Behold ʰ an Israelite indeed, in whom is no guile!

They are not all Israel, which are of Israel, Rom. ix. 6. *For he is not a Jew, which is one outwardly; neither is that circumcision, which is outward in the flesh: but he is a Jew, which is one inwardly; and circumcision is that of the heart, in the spirit*, Rom. ii. 28, 29. Christ seeing Nathanael (though he was prejudiced by Philip's mistake, or the common mistake of his nation) coming to see him, and seeing not only his body and bodily motion, but his heart also, and the motions of that, saith of him, Behold one who is not only born an Israelite, but is a true Israelite, like his father Jacob, *a plain man*, Gen. xxv. 27; *in whom is no guile*; in whom there is no deceit, no doubleness of heart. Such ought Christians to be, no crafty, deceitful, doubleminded men, but men of great sincerity and plainness of heart, *laying aside all malice, and all guile*, 1 Pet. ii. 1, like *little children*, Matt. xviii. 3.

48 Nathanael saith unto him, Whence knowest thou me? Jesus answered and said unto him, Before that Philip called thee, when thou wast under the fig tree, I saw thee.

Nathanael wondereth how Christ should know him, having not been of his familiar acquaintance. Christ tells him he saw him under the fig tree, before ever Philip called him. That was a very hot country, wherein people sought shadowy places; hence we read of sitting under their own vines and fig-trees, Micah iv. 4; Zech. iii. 10; and it is likely that those being two luxuriant plants, that had large leaves, and ran out in long boughs, in hot weather they might under the covert of these plants not only sit as in an arbour to converse one with another, but also perform religious duties. Whether Christ saw him there eating and drinking, or conversing with friends, or reading, or praying, the Scripture saith not, and it is but vainly guessed; it is enough that by his telling this to him, he let him know that he saw him, though he was not in his view, and so was omnipresent and omniscient. Christ seeth us, where we are, and what we do, when we see not him; and he seeth our hearts, whether they be single or double, plain, or false and deceitful; which as in many cases it affordeth us much comfort, so it admonisheth us to be at all times in the fear of the Lord.

i Mat. 14. 33.
k Matt. 21. 5.
& 27. 11, 42.
ch. 18. 37. & 19. 3.   49 Nathanael answered and saith unto him, Rabbi, ⁱ thou art the Son of God; thou art ᵏ the King of Israel.

The term *Rabbi*, which Nathanael here giveth to Christ, is of the same significancy with Rabban, and *Rabboni*, John xx. 16, Rabban, Rabhi, Rabbi, all which signify Master, and my Master; a name which in that age they usually gave their teachers, as a title of honour, Matt. xxiii. 7, 8, titles that began about the time of our Saviour; for Buxtorf tells us, purer antiquity gave no such titles to their teachers or prophets, thinking it not possible to give those persons (extraordinarily sent of God) titles answerable to their dignity. They say, Hillel, about our Saviour's time, was the first who was so called; Rabban was counted the highest, Rabbi the next, Rabbi the least. Rabban, they say, lasted about two hundred years, given to seven after Hillel. Nathanael calls him also *the Son of God*, as Peter and the other disciples did, Matt. xiv. 33, and Peter, Matt. xvi. 16. But it appeareth, by many following passages, that they had but a faint persuasion of this, till he was *declared* so *with power, by his resurrection from the dead*, Rom. i. 4. He acknowledgeth Christ also *the King of Israel*, that is, the true Messiah. This was the title of the Messiah, Matt. xxi. 5; xxvii. 11.

50 Jesus answered and said unto him, Because I said unto thee, I saw thee under the fig tree, believest thou? thou shalt see greater things than these.

Christ encourageth the beginnings of faith in the souls of his people, and magnifies Nathanael's faith from the revelation which he had, which was but imperfect; for Christ had said no more, than that he had seen him under the fig tree before Philip called him. He tells him that he should *see greater things than these*. To him that hath, shall be given. What those greater things are, which our Lord here meaneth, he telleth him, in part at least, ver. 51.

51 And he saith unto him, Verily, verily,

S. JOHN I, II

^l Gen. 28. 12.
Matt. 4. 11.
Luke 2. 9,13.
& 22. 43. &
24. 4. Acts
1. 10.

I say unto you, ¹Hereafter ye shall see heaven open, and the angels of God ascending and descending upon the Son of man.

These things he ushers in with a *Verily, verily*, and declareth them spoken not to Nathanael alone, but *unto you;* viz. all you that are my disciples indeed, who are (like Nathanael) true Israelites, in whom there is no guile. For the terms, Amen, Amen, (by us translated, *Verily, verily*,) some of the ancients accounted them an oath; but the most learned modern writers have seen no reason to agree with them. Surely (see a large discourse about these particles in our learned Fuller, his Miscellan. l. 1. cap. 2, to which nothing need be added) if Amen is never used in the Old Testament but as a term of prayer or wishing, in the New Testament it is used to assert or affirm a thing, or as a particle of wishing and prayer. The word in the Hebrew properly signifies, *truth*, Isa. lxv. 16; whence Christ (the truth) is called *the Amen*, Rev. iii. 14. As the prophets were wont to begin their discourses with *The word of the Lord*, and *Thus saith the Lord*, to assert the truth of what they were about to say; so Christ, to show that himself was God, and spake from himself, beginneth with Amen; and Amen, Amen, sometimes: it is observed that John constantly doubles the particle, and saith Amen, Amen, that is, *Verily, verily;* either (as interpreters say) for further confirmation of the thing, or to get the greater attention, or to assert as well the truth of the speaker as of the thing spoken. Now the thing spoken followeth as a thing promised, not to Nathanael only, but to all believers, that they should *see the heavens opened, and the angels of God ascending and descending upon the Son of man.* Some think that hereby is meant the spiritual, metaphorical opening of heaven to believers by Christ. But it seems more properly to signify such an opening of the heavens as we read of, Matt. iii. 16. Some understand it of the appearances of angels to Christ at his passion, and resurrection, and ascension; but it seems rather to refer to the day of judgment, when ten thousands of angels shall wait upon Christ, as the Judge of the quick and the dead, and minister unto him; which ministration, they say, is expressed by the terms of ascending and descending, with reference (doubtless) to Jacob's vision, Gen. xxviii. 12: Jacob saw it sleeping, Nathanael and other believers shall see it with open eyes. Others interpret it more generally, viz. You shall see as many miracles as if you saw the heavens opened, and the angels ascending and descending. Others think it referreth to some further appearances of the angels to Christ in their ministration to him than the Scripture records. Christ doth not say, You shall see angels ascending and descending upon me, but *upon the Son of man;* by which our learned Lightfoot saith, he did not only declare himself to be truly man, but the Second Adam, in whom what was lost in the first was to be restored. It is observed, that only Ezekiel in the Old Testament, and Christ in the New Testament, are thus called; and that Christ was never thus called but by himself. Ezekiel was doubtless so called to distinguish him from those spiritual beings with which he often conversed: Christ, to distinguish his human nature from his Divine nature, both which (in him) made up one person. Christ's calling himself so was but a further indication of his making himself of no reputation, while he was in the form of a servant. Others think, that *the Son of man* in the gospel, used by Christ, signifies no more than I, and me; (it being usual in the Hebrew dialect for persons to speak of themselves in the third person;) so, *upon the Son of man*, is, upon me, who am truly man. Chemnitius thinks, that as the term *Messiah* (by which the people commonly called Christ) was taken out of Daniel; so this term, by Christ applied to the same person, is taken out thence too, Dan. vii. 13, where it is said, *one like the Son of man came with the clouds of heaven, and came to the Ancient of days*, &c.; and that Christ did ordinarily so call himself, to correspond with the prophecy of Daniel, to assert himself truly man, and to declare himself his Father's servant, according to the prophecy, Isa. xlii. 1.

CHAP. II

Christ turneth water into wine in Cana of Galilee, 1—11. *He goeth to Capernaum*, 12; *thence to Jerusalem, where he driveth the buyers and sellers out of the temple*, 13—17. *He giveth his own death and resurrection for a sign*, 18—22. *Many believe in him because of his miracles, but he would not trust himself unto them*, 23—25.

AND the third day there was a marriage in ᵃCana of Galilee; and the mother of Jesus was there:

ᵃ See Josh. 19. 28.

Whether it was the third day after that our Saviour had left the province of Judea, or the third day after Philip came to him, or after Peter or Nathanael came to him, is hardly worth the disputing; if it be to be interpreted with relation to ver. 43 of the former chapter, (which speaks of the day following,) it must be the third day after Simon came to Christ, there happened to be *a marriage in Cana of Galilee*. Some reckon three cities of this name; one in the lot of Manasseh, another in the lot of Ephraim, another in the lot of Asher. This Cana is concluded by most interpreters to be the same mentioned, Josh. xix. 28, which was in the tribe of Asher, which was in Galilee: some others say, it was another Cana, near to Capernaum. At this wedding feast was the virgin Mary, our Lord's mother; and it is probable that the persons for whose marriage the feast was solemnized were some of the virgin's kindred or near relations. Some think, from the virgin's taking notice of the want of wine, that it was a family where she had either a constant charge, or the charge for that day.

2 And both Jesus was called, and his disciples, to the marriage.

Whether only the five disciples mentioned in the former chapter, or some others also, the Scripture doth not say. Christ and his disciples being at this marriage feast, both lets us know that feasting at such a time is proper, and that the most severe religious persons may lawfully be present at such meetings; only they are obliged to keep to rules of frugality, modesty, and sobriety, to a breach of which possibly such meetings may give more temptations.

3 And when they wanted wine, the mother of Jesus saith unto him, They have no wine.

The word ὑστερήσαντος may as well be translated, coming short, or behind, as wanting; and so some think it is to be understood; but Mary tells Jesus, they had *no wine:* they either had none, or she discerned it came short; they had not enough. It lets us know the frugality of him who made the feast. But whether Mary told her Son of it in expectation that he should supply it by a miracle, or that he should entertain the company with some pious discourse while the want should be supplied, is not so easy to determine: that which seems to oppose the first (and most generally received) opinion, is, that this was the first miracle he wrought, which we have upon record; nor had our Saviour by any words given her hope to see any miraculous operations from him; for though some say he had, from the last verse of the former chapter, yet the words can hardly be strained to such a sense, nor doth it appear that Mary was in Judea to hear them. But yet it seems probable she had some such expectation, both from our Saviour's answer, ver. 4, and from her saying to the servants, ver. 5, *Whatsoever he say unto you, do it;* and though Christ had as yet done no public miracle, yet what the virgin might have seen of him in thirty years' time, while he lived at home with her, we cannot tell.

4 Jesus saith unto her, ᵇWoman, ᶜwhat have I to do with thee? ᵈmine hour is not yet come.

ᵇ ch. 19. 26.
ᶜ So 2 Sam. 16. 10. & 19. 22.
ᵈ ch. 7. 6.

That it was ordinary with the Jews, speaking to women, to call them by the name of their sex, is plain from Matt. xv. 28; Luke xiii. 12; xxii. 57; John iv. 21. But that, speaking to their relations, they were wont to own their relation in their compellation, sometimes is also evident, from 1 Kings ii. 20, *Ask on, my mother.* So as our Saviour's here calling the blessed virgin, *Woman*, not mother, is agreed by most to signify to her, that in this thing he

VOL. III—10

285

did not own her as his mother, and so clothed with an authority to command him. And indeed so much the next words *(what have I to do with thee?)* signify, which is a form of speech that both signifies some displeasure for her unseasonable interrupting him, and also that she had no right nor authority upon him in this thing. See the use of the same phrase, Judg. xi. 12; 2 Sam. xvi. 10; Ezra iv. 3; Matt. viii. 29; xxvii. 19. None was more obedient and respective to his parents than our Saviour, Luke ii. 51, therein fulfilling the will of God, Jer. xxxv. 13, 14; but in the business of his calling he regarded them not, Matt. xii. 48; Luke ii. 49; and hath hereby taught us our duty, to prefer our obedience to our heavenly Father before our obedience to any earthly relation, Matt. x. 37; Luke xiv. 26. He hath also hereby taught us, that the blessed virgin is not to be preferred before her Son (as the papists do). Besides this, our Lord giveth another reason for his not present hearkening to his mother, *mine hour is not yet come;* either, because the time was not yet come to work miracles publicly; or to show her, that she was not to prescribe the time to him when he should work miraculously; thereby also showing us, that for things in this life we are to submit our desires to the Divine will, and to wait God's leisure; yet by this expression he also gives her some hopes that he would in his own time supply this want.

5 His mother saith unto the servants, Whatsoever he saith unto you, do *it*.

She plainly by these words declareth her confidence that Christ (notwithstanding the repulse he gave her) would supply this want; and therefore taking no notice of Christ's reprehension of her, she orders the servants to be absolutely obedient to him, doing, without disputing, whatsoever he bid them; and indeed such is the obedience which we all owe to God and Jesus Christ.

6 And there were set there six waterpots of stone, ^eafter the manner of the purifying of the Jews, containing two or three firkins apiece.

e Mark 7. 3.

The Jews were wont in their dining-rooms to have waterpots standing; whether one for every guest (upon which account some think here were six) doth not appear. For the contents of these vessels, it is uncertain; the reason is, because the Jewish measures, both for things dry and liquid, are much unknown to us, most countries varying in their measures. According to our measures, these vessels should contain three hogsheads, or near it; but it is not probable that so great vessels of stone should stand in a room: the end of their standing there was for the people to wash in, before they did eat, Matt. xv. 2; Mark vii. 3, and to wash their vessels in, ver. 4. We are certain of the number of the vessels, but not of the contents of them. Some say, they held so much water as, being turned into wine, was enough for one hundred and fifty persons; but we can make no certain judgment of it.

7 Jesus saith unto them, Fill the waterpots with water. And they filled them up to the brim.

Either the water was defiled by some persons washing in it, or else the vessels were not full. Our Lord commands them to be filled (the water-pots, not wine vessels) *with water*, pure water; he commands them all to be filled by the servants, who could attest the miracle, that there was nothing in the vessels but pure water. Here was no new creature to be produced; he doth not therefore command the production of wine out of nothing; but only the transformation of a creature already existent into a creature of another kind. The servants dispute not his command, nor ask any reason of his command, but yield that ready and absolute obedience which we all of us owe to Divine precepts. They fill them, and so full that they could hold no more.

8 And he saith unto them, Draw out now, and bear unto the governor of the feast. And they bare *it*.

The Jews had one who was to order the affairs of their feast, and who is upon that account called the master, or *governor*, of it; to whom our Saviour directs, that some of this newly-made wine should be carried; either that they might not suspect it was by some art provided by him, or because he was of the best judgment in those affairs. The servants yield the same ready obedience to his commands which they had before yielded.

9 When the ruler of the feast had tasted ^fthe water that was made wine, and knew not whence it was: (but the servants which drew the water knew;) the govrenor of the feast called the bridegroom,

f ch. 4. 46.

Our Saviour's action, by which he turned the water into wine, being not obvious to the senses of any; but only the secret motion of his will, willing the thing to be; is not recorded, only the effect and the consequents of it are. The papists would from hence argue, that the bread in the sacrament may be called bread, though it be transubstantiated, as the water here is called water, though it were turned into wine; but it must be observed, that it is not here called water, without the addition of *that was made wine:* we have no such addition in the gospel, where the sacramental bread is called bread; it is not said, the bread which now is turned into the flesh of Christ; nor doth the Scripture any where (as here) attest any such transubstantiation. The governor of the feast had a cup of wine presented to him, but knew not whence it came; only the servants, who by Christ's command first filled the vessels, and drew out this cupful, they knew.

10 And saith unto him, Every man at the beginning doth set forth good wine; and when men have well drunk, then that which is worse: *but* thou hast kept the good wine until now.

The governor calls the bridegroom, (at whose cost the provision for the feast was to be provided,) and mindeth him, that he seemed to have done contrary to the common practice of such as made feasts; for they used to bring forth their best wine first, when men's palates were quickest, and least adulterated; and worse after that they had drank well; so the word μεθυσθῶσι signifies, as appears by the Septuagint's translation of the Hebrew word so signifying, Gen. xliii. 34; Hag. i. 6; not only men's distempering themselves with wine, which it also sometimes signifieth; and this speaketh our translation of it, 1 Cor. xi. 21, *are drunken*, something hard, the word not necessarily nor always so signifying; and they must be very uncharitable to the primitive church of Corinth, who can think that it would permit persons actually drunken to come to the Lord's table. But the custom, it seems, was, if they had any wine worse than another, to bring it out to their guests after that the edge of their palates was a little blunted with the taste of better. Now this bridegroom, as the governor of the feast (who knew nothing of the miracle) thought, had kept his briskest and most generous wine to the last; thereby giving a great approbation of the miracle, not only owning it to be true wine, but much better than they had before at the feast.

11 This beginning of miracles did Jesus in Cana of Galilee, ^gand manifested forth his glory; and his disciples believed on him.

g ch. 1. 14.

The sense is not, that this was the first miracle which Christ wrought in Cana of Galilee; but this was the first miracle which Christ wrought after he was entered upon the public ministry, and it was wrought in that Cana which is within the confines of Galilee, either in the lot of Zebulun or Asher: yet there are some who would not have it the first miracle which Christ wrought, but the first which he wrought in that place; but there is no reason for such an interpretation; for then there had been no reason for the following words, for Christ did not manifest his glory there only; though some object those wonderful or miraculous things happening at our Saviour's birth, of which we read, Matt. ii. 9; Luke ii. 9. Yet as some distinguish betwixt *mira* and *miracula*, so others give a more plain and satisfactory answer, telling us those were miraculous operations more proper to the Father and the Spirit, thereby attesting the Deity of Christ, than to Christ considered as God-man. This was the first of those miraculous operations which were wrought by Christ Jesus as Godman, by which he *manifested his glory*, the glory men-

mentioned chap. i. 14, *as of the only begotten of the Father;* his Divine majesty and power. *And his disciples,* who before believed on him, John i. 41, 45, now more firmly *believed on him,* John xiv. 1, as Mediator. In Scripture that is often said to be, which doth not commence, but increase from that time and occasion.

12 ¶ After this he went down to Capernaum, he, and his mother, and [h]his brethren, and his disciples: and they continued there not many days.

h Mat. 12.46.

Capernaum was a city lifted up to heaven, for mercies of all sorts, which Christ foretold, Matt. xi. 23, should be brought down to hell, for their contempt of his doctrine and miracles. It was in the tribe of Naphtali, whose lot was contiguous to Zebulun, and lay on the north-east of it; a place where Christ afterwards preached much, and wrought many miracles, Matt. viii. 13, 14; ix. 18; Mark ii. 1; v. 22; a place brought so low in Hierom's time, that it scarce consisted of seven poor cottages of fishermen. Thither at this time went Christ, *and his mother, and his brethren,* (by which term the Scripture often expresseth any near kinsmen,) *and his disciples;* whether only the five mentioned in the former chapter, or others also, is not said. But they did not at that time stay long there, probably because the passover time (when they were to be at Jerusalem) was so nigh, as would not admit any long stay before they began their journey; and it is likely that the company mentioned here to be with Christ at Capernaum, did also design to go along with him to the passover, of which we next read.

i Ex. 12. 14.
Deut. 16. 1,
16. ver. 23.
ch. 5. 1. & 6.
4. & 11. 55.

13 ¶ [i]And the Jews' Passover was at hand, and Jesus went up to Jerusalem,

Concerning the Jewish passover we have once and again spoken in our notes on the other evangelists. The institution of it was Exod. xii. It was to be solemnized yearly in the place which the Lord should choose, according to the law, Deut. xvi. 6. Christ, though he was not naturally subject to the law, yet to fulfil all righteousness, and to redeem his people from the curse of the law, Gal. iv. 5, kept the passover yearly, taking also advantage from the conflux of the people to Jerusalem at that time, to make himself and his doctrine more known. None of the other evangelists make mention of more than one passover betwixt the time of Christ's baptism and death: John plainly mentions three, one here, another in chap. vi. 4, the last, chap. xviii. 39; and some think that he mentioneth another, though more obscurely, chap. v. 1. Our Lord was at them all.

k Mat. 21.12.
Mark 11. 15.
Luke 19. 45.

14 [k]And found in the temple those that sold oxen and sheep and doves, and the changers of money sitting:

Matt. xxi. 12; Luke xix. 45, is a piece of history so like this, that some have questioned whether it mentioneth not the same individual matter of fact; but it is apparent that it doth not, 1. Because St. John mentioneth it as done three years before it, at the first passover; all the other evangelists mention what they report as done at the fourth passover. 2. The circumstances of the narrative make it appear. (1.) John mentions only the ejection of the sellers; all the others mention the ejection both of the buyers and sellers. (2.) Here, he only saith they had made his Father's house a place of merchandise; the others say, that whereas it was written, it should be called a house of prayer, they had made it a den of thieves. (3.) Here he only bids them that sold doves take their goods away; the others say he overturned the seats of them that sold doves: so as our Saviour plainly appeareth to have done this twice, at his first passover and at the last. For the more full explication of the parts of this history, see our notes on Matt. xxi. 12; Mark xi. 15; Luke xix. 45. The reason of their bringing oxen, and sheep, and doves into the temple, was to supply those that came afar off, and could not bring their sacrifices with them, with such sacrifices as the law required in several cases. The money-changers were there, to change the people's money into half-shekels, every one being obliged to offer his half-shekel, Exod. xxx. 13. Our Saviour did not condemn this course of accommodating of people; but blameth the covetousness of the priests, who for their private lucre had made the temple their market-place, whenas there was room enough elsewhere.

15 And when he had made a scourge of small cords, he drove them all out of the temple, and the sheep, and the oxen; and poured out the changers' money, and overthrew the tables;

It concerns not us to inquire where our Saviour had the small cords, of which he made his whip; there were doubtless cords enough at hand, taken off from beasts brought thither, though he was himself in no Franciscan habit, as the papists idly dream. But herein was the mighty power of God seen, that Christ, a single, private, obscure person, should without any more noise or opposition drive out the multitude of these hucksters, and overturn their tables. Nor I think (after the consideration of this circumstance) need we inquire by what authority he did this? It was prophesied of him, Mal. iii. 1, that he should *come to his temple;* and, ver. 3, should *sit as a refiner and purifier of silver; and purify the sons of Levi, and purge them as gold and silver.* Christ here, according to that prophecy, cometh to his temple, and begins to purge it.

16 And said unto them that sold doves, Take these things hence; make not [1]my Father's house an house of merchandise.

1 Luke 2. 49.

At this his first coming, he gives them that sold doves a liberty to take their goods away; but at the last coming, Matt. xxi. 12, it is said, he overturned their seats. Those that think this precedent sufficient to vindicate private persons' tumultuous pulling down images, seem not to consider, that Christ was no private person, (though so esteemed,) and did what he did as Lord of his house. Those who urge it as inferring magistrates' and superiors' duty in this case, urge it well; for it may well be from hence concluded, that it is the will of Christ, that places set apart for public worship, should neither wickedly be made dens of thieves, nor yet indecently made places for men to buy and sell in; though we can ascribe no such holiness to any place as to the temple, which had not only a particular dedication, but was built by God's order, his acceptation of it declared, and had peculiar promises annexed to it; besides its prefiguration of Christ (of which we shall speak more afterward); yet even nature itself teacheth, that there is a decent reverence and respect due to such places. This action of Christ's also, before he had published the doctrine of the gospel, instructs us, that those who have authority are not always to refrain from removing instruments of superstition and idolatry, or gross and indecent corruptions, until people be first by the preaching of the true doctrine persuaded willingly to part with them. But if this were to make God's house a place of merchandise for men, there to sell oxen, and sheep, and doves, and keep shops for changing money; what do papists make such houses, by their showing their relics and images to people, thereby to get money for their priests, and for selling pardons, indulgences, &c.? Never were God's houses to that degree made places of merchandise, and dens of thieves, if every one that cheateth for his profit be (as he is) a thief.

17 And his disciples remembered that it was written, [m]The zeal of thine house hath eaten me up.

m Ps. 69. 9.

The disciples, as well as the rest of the people there present, could not but be astonished at this so strange a thing, to see a single person, and he in no repute but as a private person, to make a whip, and with authority drive the buyers and sellers out of the temple, and nobody to oppose him; but they remembered the words of David, Psal. lxix. 9. Some think that John here reports what they did after Christ's resurrection; and, indeed, whoso considereth the following part of the gospel history, would think that it were so; for they did not seem so early to have had a persuasion of Christ's Divine nature, nor that he was the Messiah; or if they at this time remembered it, and apprehended that Christ was the Son of David, the impression seems to have worn off. It is a greater question whether Psal. lxix. (from whence this quotation is) is to be understood of Christ, properly and literally, or merely as the Antitype to David, of whom that Psalm is literally to be understood? Some of the Lutherans think that Psalm primarily concerned Christ. Mr. Calvin and others think it only concerned Christ as David's Antitype. The former, for their opinion, take notice of the frequent quotation of it in the New Testament, Matt. xxvii. 48; John xix. 28; Acts i. 20; Rom. xv. 3. The other urge that there are some things in that Psalm which cannot agree to Christ. The matter is not much. Zeal is nothing but a warmth of love and anger. It is good to be zealous, yea, swallowed up with zeal, in a good cause; but men must take heed of the Pharisaical zeal, not according to knowledge. Christ was zealous, but the cause was good.

18 ¶ Then answered the Jews and said unto him, ⁿWhat sign shewest thou unto us, seeing that thou doest these things?

n Mat.12.38. ch. 6. 30.

Which of the Jews, whether some of the magistrates, or the priests, (who were more specially concerned for their profit,) or the common people, or all together, is not said. They undertake not to justify their fact, nor could they deny it, but they ask him *what sign* he could show them to justify his Divine authority. For this seemeth to have been their principle, that let corruptions and abuses in a church be never so great, yet they were not to be reformed, but either by the ordinary authority of the magistrate, or by an extraordinary authority from God. Such an extraordinary authority they would acknowledge in prophets; but they expected that those who pretended to such an extraordinary Divine mission, should be able to confirm that mission by some miraculous operations, as Moses did, Exod. iv. 30. They had had no prophets now for four hundred years amongst them; the Jews required therefore a sign, 1 Cor. i. 22. The papists were at the same point with the first reformers; but they mistook, for they brought no new doctrine, but still cried, *To the law and to the testimony;* and where the true doctrine and sacraments are upheld, there is a true church, which hath power to call and send out preachers.

19 Jesus answered and said unto them, ᵒDestroy this temple, and in three days I will raise it up.

o Mat. 26.61. & 27. 40. Mark 14. 58. & 15. 29.

Our Saviour refuseth to give them any sign, but that of his resurrection the third day from the dead. This was the sign to which he afterwards referreth the Pharisees, Matt. xii. 39; Luke xi. 29. Our Saviour's words must not be understood as commanding or licensing them to destroy him, but as foretelling what they would do. It is in Scripture very ordinary to use the imperative mood for the future tense of the indicative; see Gen. xlii. 18; Deut. xxxii. 50; Isa. viii. 9, 10; liv. 1; John xiii. 27. *Destroy*, is as much as, I know you will destroy, or, If you do destroy this temple, I will build it up in three days. The resurrection of Christ from the dead is ordinarily in Scripture attributed to the Father; but here Christ saith he would do it; and the Spirit, by whom he is said to have been quickened, equally proceedeth both from the Father and the Son. Nor is this the only text where it is attributed to Christ; see chap. xx. 17, 18. It was the work of the Trinity, out of itself, and so the work of all the three Persons. These words were three years after this made a great charge against Christ, Matt. xxvi. 61; but they reported them thus, *This fellow said, I am able to destroy the temple of God, and to build it in three days.* He said only, *this temple*, meaning his body.

20 Then said the Jews, Forty and six years was this temple in building, and wilt thou rear it up in three days?

The Jews understood his words of that material temple in which they at this time were, which the best interpreters think was the temple built by Ezra and Zerubbabel; but how to make it out that it was forty-six years building, they are not well agreed. Some say, Cyrus reigned thirty, Cambyses eight, Darius six; these added together make forty-four. Others say that the Magi reigned two years more. Some reckon to Cyrus thirty-one, to his son Cambyses nine, Darius six. Others say that the years wherein the building was hindered during Artaxerxes's time, Ezra iv. 21, added to the two years of Darius, ver. 24, in whose sixth year it was finished, are reckoned together. The Jews thought it strange that our Saviour should undertake in three days to rear a bui ding which had cost their forefathers so many years.

21 But he spake ᵖof the temple of his body.

p Col. 2. 9. Heb. 8. 2. So 1 Cor. 3. 16. & 6. 19. 2 Cor. 6. 16.

But, alas, our Saviour spake not of their material temple, but of the temple of his body; which yet was proper speaking: for if the apostle calleth our bodies *the temple of God*, as he doth, 1 Cor. iii. 16; vi. 19; 2 Cor. vi. 16; it much more may be said so of the body of Christ: for as God dwelt in the temple, and there revealed his will, and would be there worshipped; how properly must the notion of *the temple* agree to Christ, in whom the fulness of the Godhead dwelt bodily, Col. ii. 9, who revealeth his Father's nature and will to men, Matt. xi. 27. and in whom all must worship him? So as the temple at Jerusalem was every way a most illustrious type of Christ, and Christ might well, speaking concerning his body, say, *Destroy this temple;* and thus Christ (would these blind Jews have seen it) drew off the Jews from glorying in their temple, Jer. vii. 4; and from the temple, which was but a type, '(as the tabernacle was before, Acts vii. 44; Heb. ix. 23, 24,) to himself, prefigured by those houses, Heb. ix. 11. Nor doth he think fit at this time to speak more plainly; for as he knew that the perverse Jews, in seeing would not see, nor bear any such doctrine; so he also knew, that his better disciples were as yet weak in faith; and none putteth new wine into old bottles.

22 When therefore he was risen from the dead, ᵠhis disciples remembered that he had said this unto them; and they believed the Scripture, and the word which Jesus had said.

q Luke 24.8.

Even Christ's own disciples at the first rather admired than perfectly understood their Lord. It is said of Christ, Luke xxiv. 45, a little before his ascension into heaven, *Then opened he their understanding, that they might understand the Scripture.* The disciples did not distinctly understand many things till after Christ's resurrection from the dead, when they saw the things accomplished, and when Christ further opened their eyes; which was also further done when the Holy Ghost came upon them in the days of Pentecost. Thus we hear for the time to come; and the seed which lieth a long time under the clods, at last springeth up through the influence of heaven upon it. *And they believed the Scripture, and the word which Jesus had said;* the disciples then more clearly and more firmly believed the Scriptures, and were able to make a clearer application and interpretation of them. By *the Scripture* here, are meant the Scriptures of the Old Testament; to which is added, *and the word which Jesus had said.* Christ's words gave them a clearer insight into the Scriptures of the Old Testament; and the harmony of the writings of the Old Testament with Christ's words under the New Testament, confirmed the disciples' faith in both.

23 ¶ Now when he was in Jerusalem at the Passover, in the feast *day*, many believed in his name, when they saw the miracles which he did.

To believe in Christ's name, and to believe in Christ himself, are one and the same thing; as it is the same to call upon God, and to call upon the name of God: so Acts iii. 16. The meaning is, that they believed the things which were published concerning his person and office : yet the periphrasis, *Believed in his name*, is not vain; but declareth a mutual relation betwixt God and the word, by the preaching of which he maketh himself known to the world. True *faith cometh by hearing, and hearing by the word of God.* I think it is to no purpose disputed here by some, whether the faith here mentioned was true faith, yea or no. It appeareth by what followeth, that it was not true justifying faith; but it was true in its kind. To make up true justifying, saving faith, which the apostle calls *the faith of God's elect*, three things are required: 1. A knowledge of the proposition of the word revealing Christ: this is acquired by reading, hearing, meditation, &c. 2. The second is assent, which is the act of the understanding, agreeing in the truth of the word revealed, when such an assent is given to a proposition, if merely upon the Divine revelation of it: this is faith, a true faith in its kind. 3. Upon this now (in those who savingly believe) the will closeth with Christ as an adequate object; for it receiveth him, accepteth him, relies on him as its Saviour, and moveth by the affections to love, desire, hope, rejoice in him; and commandeth the outward man into an obedience to his law. Now it is very possible, that, through a common influence of the Holy Spirit of God, men upon the hearing of the word, especially having the advantage of seeing miraculous operations confirming the word, may give a true assent to the proposition of the word, as a proposition of truth, and yet may never receive Christ as their Saviour, close with him, trust in him, desire, love, or obey him; this was the case of these persons, many at least of them. They believed, seeing the miracles which Christ did: they wanted a due knowledge of Christ founded in the word; neither had they any certain, steady, fixed assent, founded in the discerning the truth of the proposition; their assent was sudden, founded only upon the miracles they saw wrought; so as though they might have some confidence in him, as a famous person, and some great prince, from whom they might expect some earthly good, yet this was all, which was far enough from true saving faith.

24 But Jesus did not commit himself unto them, because he knew all *men*,

Christ did not take all these seeming believers into his bosom, nor call them after him, nor maintain any familiar fellowship and communion with them; but made haste again into Galilee, till his time was come, knowing that in so public a place of danger they were not to be trusted; for being God blessed for ever, he had knowledge of the hearts of all men.

25 And needed not that any should testify of man: for ʳhe knew what was in man.

<small>r 1 Sam.16.7. 1 Chr. 28. 9. Matt. 9. 4. Mark 2. 8. ch. 6. 64. & 16. 30. Acts 1. 24. Rev. 2. 23.</small>

And needed not any information concerning the principles and humours of all men; for he perfectly knew men, not only from their more external acts and behaviours, (as we know them,) but he knew what was in them, searching the hearts, and trying the reins, which is the property of God alone, 1 Kings viii. 39; Psal. xxxiii. 15. Here what we formerly observed is again observable, that ofttimes in holy writ, for the further confirmation of a proposition, to a universal affirmative is added a contrary negative. Here ariseth a question, agitated betwixt the Lutherans and the Calvinists, Whether Christ as man knew all things, and what is in the heart of man. They affirm it, because of the personal union of the Divine and human natures in Christ. We say, that although there be such a personal union, yet the properties of each nature remain distinct; upon which account Christ denieth that he, as the Son of man, knew the day and hour of the end of the world. Besides, by the same reason that omniscience belongeth to the human nature of Christ, omnipotence, infiniteness, and omnipresence, also must; which last indeed they affirm, seeing that without it there were not able to defend their doctrine of consubstantiation, or the presence of the body and blood of Christ, wherever the sacrament of his supper is administered; but this being a matter polemical, we shall not here discourse it. Those who would be satisfied as to what is said on either side, may find enough in Gerard, Hunnius, and Farnovius, on the Lutherans' side; and in Zanchius and others on the Calvinists' side, Zanchius de Natura and Attributis Dei, lib. 3. cap. 2. qu. 16.

CHAP. III

Christ, in a conference with Nicodemus, teacheth him the necessity of regeneration, 1—13; the efficacy of faith in his death, 14, 15; God's great love to mankind in sending his Son for their salvation, 16, 17; and the condemnation for unbelief, 18—21. Jesus baptizeth in Judea, 22, as doth John in Ænon, 23, 24. John's doctrine concerning Christ, 25—36.

THERE was a man of the Pharisees, named Nicodemus, a ruler of the Jews:

The particle *there* being put in only to fit our idiom to the Greek, where is nothing but the verb, signifies nothing to prove that what we read in this chapter was done at Jerusalem. It is a dispute amongst some interpreters, whether he was there or no. It should seem by chap. vii. 50, that Nicodemus's chief residence was there. He was one of the Pharisees, who were a sect (as we have showed before) which had their name either from a Hebrew word, which signifieth to explain, (because they were expounders of the law,) or from another word, which signifieth to divide, because they were separate from others: the opinions have both learned patrons. This man's name in Greek signifies, The victory of the people. He was either the head of a family among the Jews, or a ruler of the synagogue, or one of the sanhedrim: it seemeth most probable he is here called *a ruler* upon the last account, if we consider chap. vii. 50.

2 ᵃThe same came to Jesus by night, and said unto him, Rabbi, we know that thou art a teacher come from God: for ᵇno man can do these miracles that thou doest, except ᶜGod be with him.

<small>a ch. 7. 50. & 19. 39.
b ch. 9.16,33. Acts 2. 22.
c Acts 10. 38.</small>

He came *by night* to Christ, not, as some (too charitably) possibly may think, that he might have the freer and less interrupted communion and discourse with him; but either through fear, or possibly shame, being a master in Israel, to be looked upon as a scholar going to learn of another. He saluteth him by the name they usually gave to their teachers, (as we showed, chap. i. 49,) and saith, *we know*, by which he hinteth to us, that not only he, but others of the Pharisees also, knew that he was a teacher sent from God in a more extraordinary manner; and he giveth the reason of this their knowledge, because of those miraculous operations which he had wrought. God hath his number among all orders and sorts of men; and those that are his shall come unto Christ. There was a weakness in the faith and love of this Nicodemus; (his station amongst the Jews was a great temptation to him;) but yet there was a truth of both in him, which further discovered itself, chap. vii. 50, and more upon Christ's death, chap. xix. 39. But here ariseth a greater question, viz. How Nicodemus could conclude that Christ was a teacher sent from God, by his miracles. *Answ.* It is to be observed, that he doth not say, in the general, that no man does signs or wonders of any kind, unless the power and favour of God be with him. But he speaks particularly and eminently of those things which Jesus did; they were so great in their nature, so real and solid in their proof, so Divine in the manner of performing them by the empire of his will; so holy in their end, to confirm a doctrine most becoming the wisdom and other glorious attributes of God, and that were the verification of the prophecies concerning the Messiah, whose coming it was foretold should be with miraculous healing benefits; that there was the greatest assurance, that none without the omnipotent hand of God could do them; for it is clear by the light of reason and Scripture, that God will not assist by his almighty power the ministers of Satan, to induce those who sincerely search for truth to believe a lie. The magicians indeed performed divers wonders in Egypt, but they were outdone by Moses, to convince the spectators that he was sent from a power infinitely superior to that of evil spirits. Real miracles, that are contrary to the order and exceed the power of nature, can only be produced by creating power, and are wrought to give credit to those who are sent from God. And when God permits false miracles to be done by seducers, that would thereby obtain authority and credit amongst men, the deception is not invincible; for it is foretold expressly to give us warning, that the man of sin shall come with *lying wonders*, by *the working of Satan*, 2 Thess. ii. 9; and the heavenly doctrine of the gospel has been confirmed by real miracles, incomparably greater than all the strange things done to give credit to doctrines opposite to it.

3 Jesus answered and said unto him, Verily, verily, I say unto thee, ᵈExcept a man be born ‖ again, he cannot see the kingdom of God.

<small>d ch. 1. 13. Gal. 6. 15.
Tit. 3. 5. Jam. 1. 18. 1 Pet. 1. 23. 1 John 3. 9.
‖ Or, *from above*.</small>

We observed before, that the term *answered* doth not always in the New Testament signify a reply to a question before propounded; but sometimes no more than a reply, or the beginning of another speech: whether it doth so here or no, some question. Some think Christ here gives a strict answer to a question which Nicodemus had propounded to him, about the way to enter into the kingdom of God; which question the evangelist sets not down, but leaves to the reader to gather from the answer. Others think that our Saviour knew what he would say, and answered the thoughts of his heart. Others, that he only began a discourse to him about what was highly necessary for him, that was a master in Israel, to understand and know. He begins his discourse with *Verily, verily*, the import of which we considered, chap. i. 51. The word translated *again*, is ἄνωθεν, which often signifieth *from above*; so it signifieth, ver. 31; Jam. i. 17; iii. 15—17. It also signifieth *again*: Gal. iv. 9, *How turn ye again to the weak and beggarly elements?* That it must be so translated here, and ver. 7, appeareth from Nicodemus's answer in the next verse. But the expression of the second or new birth by this word, which also signifies *from above*, may possibly reach us, that the new birth must be wrought in the soul from above by the power of God, which is what was said before, chap. i. 12, 13, the necessity of which our Saviour presseth from the impossibility otherwise of his seeing *the kingdom of God;* by which some understand the kingdom of his glory (as the phrase is used, Luke xviii. 24, 25); others understand it of the manifestation of Christ under the gospel state, or the vigour, power, and effect of the gospel, and the grace thereof. By seeing of it, is meant enjoying, and being made partakers of it, as the term is used, Psal. xvi. 10; John xvi. 10; Rev. xviii. 7. The Jews promised their whole nation a place in the kingdom of the Messiah, as they were born of Abraham, Matt. iii. 9; and the Pharisees promised themselves much from their observation of the law, &c. Christ lets them know neither of these would do, but unless they were wholly changed in their hearts and principles (for so much being *born again* signifieth; not some partial change as to some things, and in some parts) they could never have any true share, either in the kingdom of grace in this life, or in the kingdom of glory in that life which is to come. It is usual by the civil laws of countries, that none enters into the possession of an earthly kingdom but by the right of birth; and for the obtaining the kingdom of heaven, there must be a new birth, a heavenly renovation of the whole man, soul, body, and spirit, to give him a title, by the wise and unchangeable constitution of God in the gospel, and to qualify him for the enjoyment of it.

4 Nicodemus saith unto him, How can a man be born when he is old? can he enter the second time into his mother's womb, and be born?

By the answer of Nicodemus, it should seem that he was an old man; which is also probable, because he was one of the rulers: he puts the case as to himself; I am, saith he, an old man, how should I be born? *Can a man enter the second time into his mother's womb, and be born?* How true is that of the apostle, 1 Cor. ii. 14, *The natural man receiveth not the things of the Spirit of God!* What a gross conception doth Nicodemus (though doubtless a learned as well as a great man) discover of regeneration, as if it could not be without a man's mother travailing in birth with him a second time! Nicodemus's question discovers a great deal of ignorance and weakness, but yet a great deal of simplicity and plainness in him; that he did not come, as the Pharisees generally were wont to come to Christ, to catch him by captious questions, but brought *discendi pietatem*, a pious desire to learn from him, and to be instructed by him. The Pharisees had been used to study the traditions of the elders, and spent their time about unprofitable niceties, as to the meaning of the law: so were not at all versed in the great things which concerned the kingdom of God. The like instance hath been in later ages, the popish divines spending their time generally about nice school questions, showing themselves much ignorant of spiritual things, and the great mysteries of the kingdom of God.

5 Jesus answered, Verily, verily, I say unto thee, ᵉExcept a man be born of water and *of* the Spirit, he cannot enter into the kingdom of God.

ᵉ Mark 16. 16.
Acts 2. 38.

To excite his spirit and attention, our Saviour again expresses the authority of his person, *I say;* and twice repeats the solemn asseveration, *Verily, verily*, to show the infallible certainty and importance of what he propounds, that it is a truth worthy of his most serious consideration, and to be embraced with a stedfast belief. After this preface, he declares, If any one be not born of water and the Spirit, to rectify the carnal conceit of Nicodemus about regeneration. In the 3rd verse our Saviour compared the spiritual birth with the natural, and with respect to that a renewed man is born a second time. But in this verse he expresses the cause and quality of the new birth, that distinguishes it from the natural birth, and resolves the vain, carnal objection of Nicodemus. He speaks not of the terrestrial, animal birth, but of the celestial and Divine; that is suitable to that principle from whence it proceeds, the Holy Spirit of God. There is a great difference among interpreters about the meaning of being *born of water*. The Romanists, and rigid Lutherans, understand the water in a proper sense, for the element of baptism, and from hence infer the absolute necessity of baptism for salvation; but the exposition and conclusion are both evidently contrary to the truth. Indeed the new birth is signified, represented, and sealed by baptism, it is the soul and substance of that sacred ceremony; and if our Saviour had only said, that whoever is born of water and the Spirit shall enter into the kingdom of heaven, it might have been congruously understood of baptism; because it is an undoubted truth, that all who are truly regenerated in baptism shall be saved. But our Saviour says, He that is not born of water and the Spirit cannot enter into the kingdom of heaven: the exclusion of the unsanctified is peremptory and universal. And our Saviour shows a manifest difference between an affirmative and negative proposition; when having declared, that whoever *believeth and is baptized shall be saved;* and coming to the negative, he only adds, *but he that believeth not shall be damned*, Mark xvi. 16. The reason why he does not say, Whoever is not baptized shall be condemned, is evident; for without faith it is impossible to be saved; but without baptism, even as the Romanists themselves grant, many have been saved. For if we consider the time when our Saviour spake these words, they acknowledge that believers were not then obliged to receive the baptism of Christ for salvation; for our Saviour had this conference with him some years before his death; and they hold, that before the death of Christ baptism was not necessary, neither by virtue of Divine command, nor as a means to obtain salvation; therefore the believers that lived then might enter into heaven without baptism. They also declare, that martyrdom supplies the want of baptism; and that persons instructed in the doctrine of the gospel, and. sincerely believing it, if prevented by death without being baptized, their faith and earnest desire is sufficient to qualify them for partaking of the heavenly kingdom. But if by *water* here be meant the elementary water of baptism, the words of our Saviour are directly contrary to what they assert; for neither the blood of martyrs, nor the desire and vow of receiving baptism, are the water of baptism, which they pretend is properly and literally named by our Saviour. And certainly, if. as the apostle Peter instructs us, it is not the cleansing of the flesh in the water of baptism that saveth, 1 Pet. iii. 21, it is not the mere want of it, without contempt and wilful neglect, that condemneth. By *water* then we are to understand the grace of the Holy Spirit in purifying the soul, which is fitly represented by the efficacy of water. And this purifying, refreshing virtue of the Spirit is promised in the prophecies that concern the times of the Messiah, under the mystical expression of *water*. Thus it is twofold by Isaiah, *I will pour water upon him that is thirsty, and floods upon the dry ground*, Isa. xliv. 3. And this is immediately explained, *I will pour my Spirit upon thy seed;* and the Divine birth follows, *they shall spring up as among the grass*. In the same manner the effects of the Holy Spirit are expressed by Ezekiel: *I will sprinkle clean water upon you, and ye shall be clean;* and presently after, *I will put my Spirit within you*, Ezek. xxxvi. 25, 27. Our Saviour instructing a Pharisee, to whom the prophetical writings were known, expressly uses these two words, and in the same order as they are all set down there, first *water*, and then *the Spirit*, that the latter might interpret the former; for water and the Spirit, by a usual figure when two words are employed to signify the same thing, signify spiritual water, that is, his Divine grace in renewing the soul; as when the apostle says, *in demonstration of the Spirit and of power*, to signify the powerful Spirit. Thus John the Baptist foretold of Christ, that he should *baptize with the Holy Ghost and fire*, that is, with the Spirit, that has the force and efficacy of fire to refine us from our dross and corruptions. Thus our Saviour plainly instructs Nicodemus of the absolute necessity of an inward spiritual change and renovation, thereby showing the inefficacy of all the legal washings and sprinklings, that could not purify and make white one soul, which were of high valuation among the Jews. Entering into the kingdom of God, is of the same import and sense with the seeing the kingdom of God, in the 3rd verse: that is, without regeneration no man can truly be joined with the society of the church of God, nor partake of the celestial privileges and benefits belonging to it, here and hereafter.

6 That which is born of the flesh is flesh; and that which is born of the Spirit is spirit.

That which is born of the flesh: that which is born of natural flesh; for flesh sometimes signifies the man. So the prophet saith, *All flesh is grass,* Isa. xl. 6. So Gen. vi. 12, *All flesh,* that is, all men, *had corrupted their way.* Or, that which is born of corruption, from vitiated and corrupted nature; so flesh is oft taken in Scripture, Rom. viii. 4, 5, 8, &c. *Is flesh;* that is, it bringeth forth effects proportionable to the cause; a man purely natural brings forth natural operations. Man, as man, moveth, and eateth, and drinketh, and sleepeth. Corrupted man brings forth vicious and corrupt fruit, which often are called *the works of the flesh,* Gal. v. 19. *Flesh* here signifieth the whole man, whether considered abstractly from the adventitious corruption of his nature, or as fallen in Adam, vitiated and debauched through lust. *And that which is born of the Spirit is spirit:* but that man or woman who is regenerated by the Spirit of grace is spiritual; he is *after the Spirit,* Rom. viii. 5; he is one spirit with God, 1 Cor. vi. 17; he is made *partaker of the Divine nature,* 2 Pet. i. 4; he *doth not commit sin,* 1 John iii. 9. Nothing in operation exceedeth the virtue of that cause which influenceth it; so as no man from a mere natural principle can perform a truly spiritual operation; and from hence it is absolutely necessary that man must be born of the Spirit, that he may be qualified for the kingdom of heaven.

|| Or, *from above.*

7 Marvel not that I said unto thee, Ye must be born ||again.

There is a twofold admiration, that which is joined with infidelity, and that which is the effect of faith. Our Saviour forbids Nicodemus to marvel at the doctrine of regeneration, as strange and incredible, upon an imaginary impossibility supposed by him of the thing itself. But he that believes will judge that supernatural work of the Spirit, whereby a sinful man is made a partaker of the Divine nature, worthy of the highest admiration. And what our Saviour had said in the general before, that a man must be born again, he now particularly applies to Nicodemus, with those of his order, *Ye must be born again.* For Nicodemus would easily consent that the pagans, and possibly the vulgar Jews, had need of regeneration, to partake of the kingdom of God; but that the doctors of the law, (of which number himself was,) esteemed the lights of the world, should be under the same necessity, was astonishing to him. Therefore our Saviour, to undeceive and humble him, saith, *Ye must be born again,* for that all are defiled with the corruption that is universal to mankind.

f Eccles. 11. 5.
i Cor. 2. 11.

8 f The wind bloweth where it listeth, and thou hearest the sound thereof, but canst not tell whence it cometh, and whither it goeth: so is every one that is born of the Spirit.

The word which is translated *wind,* being the same which both here and ordinarily in Scripture is translated *spirit,* hath given interpreters a great liberty to abound in their several senses. Some thinking that it should be translated, The spirit, that is, the spirit of a man, breatheth where it listeth; and that our Saviour's sense was, Nicodemus, thou needest not to wonder that thou canst not with thy senses perceive the spiritual new birth, for thou canst not understand the natural birth. Others think it should be translated, The Spirit, that is, the Spirit of God, bloweth where it listeth; but that seemeth not probable, because of these words, *so is every one that is born of the Spirit;* which will hardly be sense if we understand the first part of the verse concerning the same Spirit; and our Saviour saith, ver. 12, *If I have told you earthly things, and ye believe not:* they seem therefore best to understand it, who interpret it of a terrene spirit, particularly the wind, which is of a spiritual nature: and thus, by their translation, it is apparent that our interpreters understood it. So as, though our Saviour speaketh of the motions of the blessed Spirit, yet he speaketh of them by way of comparison, comparing them to the motion of the wind, of which he said, that it *bloweth where it listeth;* not that it is its own mover, and under no government of the First Cause; for the Psalmist tells us, Psal. cxlviii. 8, that the stormy winds fulfil God's word; nor is any such thing competible to any creature; but the original of its motion is to us imperceptible. *But canst not tell whence it cometh, and whither it goeth:* we can speak something philosophically to the cause of it, and can tell whither it bloweth, from the east, west, north, or south; but we cannot tell the particular place, where or from whence it riseth. *So is every one that is born of the Spirit:* so every one, who is regenerated from the working of the Holy Spirit of God, is changed and renewed, so as we can give ourselves or others no account of it in all points, as to the inward operation, though in the effects it be discernible.

9 Nicodemus answered and said unto him, g How can these things be?

g ch. 6. 52, 60.

Nicodemus had before spoken as if he thought it a thing impossible, understanding our Saviour of a carnal generation, which he knew could not be repeated: perceiving that he spake of a spiritual birth, he is now posed at the mystery of it; it being a thing the doctrine of which he had not been acquainted with. His carnal stupidity hindered his understanding the first lesson of Christianity, though explained by the Sun of righteousness; and his pride hindered him from confessing his ignorance; he rather judges the doctrine to be absurd and impossible. The like darkness is in every unrenewed mind; regeneration being like that new name, which none understand but those that have it.

10 Jesus answered and said unto him, Art thou a master of Israel, and knowest not these things?

Our Saviour doth not so much wonder at as upbraid the ignorance of Nicodemus, and all of his sect, who went for masters, or teachers, and that in Israel; who had the law and the prophets, and yet were ignorant of those things which were necessary to be known to every ordinary person's salvation. Will any say, But where was there any thing spoken in the books of the law and the prophets about regeneration, or a being born again? *Answ.* What other things could be meant by the circumcision of the heart, commanded by Moses, Deut. x. 16, promised in Deut. xxx. 6; by the *new heart,* and the *new spirit,* promised Ezek. xxxvi. 26; by the *clean heart* prayed for by David, Psal. li. 10? A teacher in Israel should from hence have understood the necessity of a new and of a clean heart; but the whole sect of the Pharisees were so taken up with the trifles of the rites and traditions, and the works of the law, that as to these spiritual things, of nearer and much higher concernment to people's souls, they knew and spake little of them.

11 h Verily, verily, I say unto thee, We speak that we do know, and testify that we have seen; and i ye receive not our witness.

h Mat. 11. 27
ch. 1. 18.
& 7. 16 &
8. 28. & 12.
49. & 14. 24.
i ver. 32.

Christ speaketh only of himself, though he speaketh in the plural number, for in the next verse he saith only, *If I have told you earthly things;* he lets Nicodemus know that he spake nothing but he was certain of. This he expresseth by two words, *know* and *have seen,* which are terms expressive of the greatest certainty of a thing imaginable; for the terms express a certainty of the mind, arising both from the rational deduction and sensible demonstration: and herein our Saviour lets his ministers know what is their duty to teach unto people, viz. what they know and have seen. Those that think that the doctrine of the gospel would have no certainty but for the authority of the church, stand highly concerned to reflect upon this text.

S. JOHN III

Ye receive not our witness; ye ought to believe what I tell you upon the authority of my revelation; but such is the hardness of your heart, such your stubbornness and unbelief, that you receive not my testimony.

12 If I have told you earthly things, and ye believe not, how shall ye believe, if I tell you *of* heavenly things?

If I have spoken to you plain things, and in a plain style, humbling my phrase to your apprehensions, and illustrating sublime, spiritual mysteries, which in their own nature are more remote from your apprehensions, by plain and obvious similitudes and parables, and speaking thus, you understand and believe not; what would you do if I should discourse to you sublime and spiritual things, without these advantages for your understandings?

13 And [k]no man hath ascended up to heaven, but he that came down from heaven, *even* the Son of man which is in heaven.

k Prov. 30. 4. ch. 6. 33, 38, 51, 62. & 16. 28. Acts 2. 34. 1 Cor. 15. 47. Eph. 4. 9, 10.

No man hath so ascended up to heaven, as to know the secret will and counsels of God, for of such an ascending it must be meant; otherwise, Elijah ascended up to heaven before our Saviour ascended. Thus the phrase is supposed to be used, Prov. xxx. 4. None but Christ (who as to his Divine nature came down from heaven) hath ever so ascended thither; *even the Son of man, who was in heaven;* we translate it *is,* but the participle ὤν is of the preterimperfect tense, as well as the present tense: or, *who is in heaven,* by virtue of the personal union of the two natures in' the Redeemer; as we read, Acts xx. 28, *the church, which he hath purchased with his own blood.* By reason of the personal union of the two natures in Christ, though the properties of each nature remain distinct, yet the properties of each nature are sometimes attributed to the whole person. The Lutherans have another notion, ascribing an omnipresence even to the human nature of Christ, because of its personal union with the Divine nature; and so affirm that Christ's human nature, while it was on earth, was also substantially in heaven; as, on the other side, they are as stiff in maintaining that, although Christ's human nature be now in heaven, yet it is also on earth, really and essentially present wherever the sacrament of the Lord's supper is administered; but this is to ascribe a body unto Christ which is indeed no body, according to any notion we have of a body.

14 ¶ [1]And as Moses lifted up the serpent in the wilderness, even so [m]must the Son of man be lifted up:

i Num. 21. 9.
m ch. 8. 28. & 12. 32.

The history of the lifting up of the serpent in the wilderness we have, Numb. xxi. 8, 9. The people being stung with fiery serpents, as a righteous judgment of God for their sins, as a merciful remedy God commanded Moses, ver. 8, *Make thee a fiery serpent,* (that is, the image or representation of one of those fiery serpents,) *and put it upon a pole; and it shall come to pass, that every one that is bitten, when he looketh upon it, shall live.* This brazen serpent in the wilderness was a lively type of Jesus Christ. Our Saviour having before spoken of the new birth as necessary to those who shall be saved, here comes to show it in the causes, and instanceth first in the meritorious, then in the instrumental, cause. The meritorious cause was his death; he saith, As the serpent was lifted up in the wilderness, so he, who was the Son of man, must be lifted up; that is, die upon the cross: the phrase is used twice more in this Gospel, chap. viii. 28; xii. 32, 34, in allusion, doubtless, to this type. Yet Mr. Calvin thinks the *lifted up* here more properly interpreted of the doctrine of the gospel, and by the preaching of it; and others apply it to Christ's ascension into heaven. And this he tells Nicodemus *must* be, for the fulfilling the Scripture, and the counsels of his Father.

15 That whosoever believeth in him should not perish, but [n]have eternal life.

n ver. 36. ch. 6. 47.

Here our Lord openeth the instrumental cause of justification and salvation, that is, believing εἰς αὐτὸν, *in him.* It is one thing to believe in him as a teacher, another thing to believe in him as a Saviour. The object of the first is a proposition; we believe a person when we assent and give credit to what he saith, because he saith it. The object of the latter is the person and merits of the Mediator. As the looking up to the brazen serpent healed the person, not by any physical operation, but from the goodness of God, as it was an act of obedience to the Divine institution for that end; so neither doth faith in the Mediator justify and obtain pardon for any soul from any meritorious virtue in that act, but from God's gracious ordination, that so it shall be; he hath so ordained, that whosoever shall rest upon Christ, and receive him by faith as his Mediator and Saviour, should not perish, but live for ever. There are other things besides faith necessary to salvation, such are repentance, love, and new obedience; nor is faith only mentioned because they are ingredients into it, but because faith is the root of all those, and that from which they must necessarily flow; for it is as impossible that any should truly hope, and trust in, and rest upon Christ for that life which he hath only promised to those that obey him, as it is impossible that any should indeed trust in and rest upon a man who hath promised a reward upon a condition for that reward, without any care to fulfil that condition. But by this and other places, where faith alone in Christ is mentioned as necessary to salvation, Nicodemus was taught, that no obedience to the works of the law without this faith in the Mediator would bring the soul to eternal life and salvation.

16 ¶ [o]For God so loved the world, that he gave his only begotten Son, that whosoever believeth in him should not perish, but have everlasting life.

o Rom. 5. 8. 1 John 4. 9.

For God the Father, who is the Lord of all, debtor to none, sufficient to himself, *so loved the world,* that is, Gentiles as well as Jews. There is a great contest about the signification of the term, betwixt those who contend for or against the point of universal redemption; but certain it is, that from this term no more can be solidly concluded, than from the terms *all* and *every,* which in multitudes of places are taken in a restrained sense for many, or all of such a nation or kind. As this term sometimes signifies all persons, so, in 1 John ii. 21, the Gentiles in opposition to the Jews. Nor, admitting that *the world* should signify here every living soul in the place called the world, will any thing follow from it. It is proper enough to say, A man loved such a family to such a degree that he gave his estate to it, though he never intended such a thing to every child or branch of it. So as what is truth in that so vexed a question cannot be determined from any of these universal terms; which must, when all is said that can be said, be expounded by what follows them, and by their reconcilableness to other doctrines of faith. *God so loved the world that he gave his Son* to die for a sacrifice for their sins, to die in their stead, and give a satisfaction for them to his justice. And this Son was not any of his sons by adoption, but his *only begotten Son;* not so called (as Socinians would have it) because of his singular generation of the virgin without help of man, but from his eternal generation, in whom the Gentiles should trust, Psal. ii. 12, which none ought to do, but in God alone, Deut. vi. 13; Jer. xvii. 5. *That whosoever, &c.:* the term *all* is spoken to above; these words restrain the universal term *world,* and *all,* to let us know that Christ only died for some in the world, viz. such as should believe in him. Some judge, not improbably, that Christ useth the term *world* in this verse in the same sense as in 1 John ii. 2. Our evangelist useth to take down the pride of the Jews, who dreamed that the Messiah came only for the benefit of the seed of Abraham, not for the nations of the world, he only came to destroy them; which notion also very well fitteth what we have in the next verse.

17 [p]For God sent not his Son into the world to condemn the world; but that the world through him might be saved.

p Luke 9. 56. ch. 5. 45. & 8. 15. & 12. 47.
1 John 4. 14.

The word we translate *condemn,* κρίνῃ, signifies to judge, as well as to condemn. The Jews were mistaken in their proud conceit, that Christ came to judge and destroy all those that were not of their nation; thus, chap. xii. 47, he saith, *he came not to judge, but to save the world.* Nor is this contrary to what he saith, chap. ix. 39, *For judgment I am come into this world;* for that is *ex accidenti,* from the corruption of men, shutting their eyes against the light, and hardening their hearts against the offers and tenders of Di vine grace. Christ will come in his second coming to condemn the world of unbelievers; but the tendency of his coming was not for condemnation, but to offer the grace of the gospel, and eternal life and salvation, to men in the world.

18 ¶ ^q He that believeth on him is not condemned: but he that believeth not is condemned already, because he hath not believed in the name of the only begotten Son of God.

q ch. 5. 24. & 6. 40, 47. & 20. 31.

Whoso firmly and steadily assenting to the propositions of the gospel, revealing Jesus Christ as the only and all-sufficient Saviour, commits the care of his soul unto him, trusting and hoping in him alone for eternal salvation, which no man can indeed do without doing what in him lieth to fulfil the condition upon which Christ hath promised life and salvation, that is, keeping the commandments of God, is exempted from condemnation by the law of grace. But he that believes not the doctrine of Christ, and does not upon the terms of the gospel receive him for his Saviour, is already condemned for his obstinate infidelity, which is the certain cause of damnation: as we say of one mortally wounded, that he is a dead man, though he breathes for a while; and we speak in the same manner of a malefactor, convicted and attainted of a capital crime, though the sentence be not executed; because their death is inevitable. The not believing in the only Son of God, who is able to save to the utmost all that regularly trust in him, is such a contempt of the merciful, all-sufficient, and sole means of salvation, that it is absolutely necessary, and most just, that all those who refuse to be saved by him, should perish by themselves. From this scripture arise two questions: the first concerning the heathens, who never heard of Christ. The second concerning infants, who die before they come to years of knowledge. As to the former, the apostle hath determined, Rom. ii. 12, *As many as have sinned without law shall also perish without law.* There is the same reason for those who sin without the gospel; they shall not perish for not believing *on him of whom they have not heard*, Rom. x. 14, but for not obeying such revelation of the Divine will as they had. The case of infants is excluded from this text (speaking only of adult persons). It is certain, that so many of them as belong to the election of grace shall be saved, and that by virtue of the blood of Christ; but which way God brings them to heaven is a secret to us. Some from this text have concluded, that unbelief is the only damning sin; which is no further true, than that no sin will damn that soul which shall truly believe in the Lord Jesus Christ.

19 And this is the condemnation, ^r that light is come into the world, and men loved darkness rather than light, because their deeds were evil.

r ch. 1. 4, 9. 10, 11. & 8. 12.

This is the reason, the evidence and great cause of condemnation, *that light is come into the world.* Christ is the Light, foretold by the prophet, Isa. ix. 2; xlii. 6; xlix. 6. He is styled, in the beginning of this Gospel, the true Light, chap. i. 4; that is, he hath in perfection all the excellent qualities of light; the power to enlighten the minds of men in the knowledge of saving truth, to warm the affections with the love of it, to revive the disconsolate, and to make the heavenly seed of the word to flourish and fructify in their lives. This Light is come into the world; that signifies not only his incarnation, but his revealing the merciful counsel of God for our salvation, which the clearest spirits could never have discovered; he has opened the way that leads to eternal life. But *men loved darkness rather than light;* they preferred, chose, and adhered to their ignorance and errors, before the light of life, the saving knowledge of the gospel. Their ignorance is affected and voluntary, and no colour of excuse can be alleged for it; nay, it is very culpable and guilty, by neglecting to receive instruction from the Son of God. *Because their deeds were evil;* the vices and lusts of men are the works of darkness, the fruits of their ignorance and errors; and they are so pleasant to the carnal corrupt nature, that to enjoy them securely, they obstinately reject the light of the gospel; this aggravates their sin and sentence.

20 For ^s every one that doeth evil hateth the light, neither cometh to the light, lest his deeds should be ∥ reproved.

s Job 24. 13, 17. Eph. 5. 13. ∥ Or, *discovered.*

He that makes a trade of sin, and doth evil presumptuously, loving and delighting in it, doth not love the light, nor, if he can avoid it, will come near it; for the light is that which makes things visible, and discovereth them. As it is of the nature of natural light to show things to others as they are; and therefore thieves, and adulterers, and drunkards, care not for the light, but choose the darkness for their deeds of darkness, and come as little abroad in the light as they can when they do them: so it is of the nature of Christ and his gospel to discover men's errors, both as to the obtaining of justification and eternal salvation, and the errors also of men's lives; and therefore men and women possessed of errors in their judgments, or delighting in a filthy conversation, hate Christ and his gospel; because that a discovering the right ways of God discovereth the crookedness of their ways, opposite to the truths and ways of God.

21 But he that doeth truth cometh to the light, that his deeds may be made manifest, that they are wrought in God.

Truth here is put for true things. He who purposeth, designeth, and acteth nothing but what is just, and holy, and good, and what is consonant to the will of God; he is not afraid to bring his notions and actions to the test of the Divine rule, published by him who is the true Light. For he desires that what he doth *may be made manifest*, both to himself and others, *that they are wrought in*, with, or according to, by, or through *God* (for the particle ἐν, here used, is used in all these senses, 1 Cor. vii. 39; Rev. xiv. 13). Those works are said to be wrought in, with, by, or through God, which tend to the honour and glory of God as their end, and flow from him as their cause, which are done with his strength and assistance, and for his honour and glory.

22 ¶ After these things came Jesus and his disciples into the land of Judæa; and there he tarried with them, ^t and baptized.

t ch. 4. 2.

Soon after our Saviour had had the forementioned conference with Nicodemus, which it is believed he had at Jerusalem, not (as some think) in Galilee, for then Nicodemus would hardly have come to him by night, he *came into the land of Judea.* He had before been in the province of Judea, and in the metropolis, or great city, of Judea, which was Jerusalem; but now he goeth into the country of Judea. Judah and Jerusalem are often mentioned distinctly. The chief city of a country is oft distinguished from the country, though within the same province and tribe; see Josh. viii. 1, *the king of Ai, his city, and his land;* and in particular as to Jerusalem, 2 Chron. xi. 14; xx. 17; xxxvi. 23; Ezra ii. 1; Luke v. 17; vi. 17. Christ and his disciples went into the country part of Judea, *and there he tarried with them, and baptized,* by his disciples, for himself personally baptized none; but as in our common speech, so in the language of Scripture, there is nothing more ordinary than for persons to be said themselves to do what they do by others, 1 Sam. xxvi. 11, 12; 2 Kings xxii. 16; 2 Chron. xxxiv. 24; Acts vii. 52.

23 ¶ And John also was baptizing in Ænon near to ^u Salim, because there was much water there: ^x and they came, and were baptized.

u 1 Sam. 9.4.
x Matt. 3. 5, 6.

Ænon is here said to be *near Salim*: it was the name of a city, as some think; others say, river or brook near that city: neither the river nor the city are elsewhere mentioned in Scripture; but topographers place it on the eastern part of the lot of Manasseh, not far from Bethsan or Scythopolis. There John was baptizing; because this Ænon was a brook or river that had much water, which in Judea was rare. There is no water more holy than other. John baptized in Jordan, and in Bethabara, and in Ænon. The ordinance sanctified the water, but did not require consecrated water for the due administration of it. It is from this apparent that both Christ and John baptized by dipping the body in the water, else they need not have sought places where had been a great plenty of water; yet it is probable that they did not constantly dip, from what we read of the apostles baptizing in houses, Acts ix. 17, 18; x. 47, 48. The people came to John and were baptized, that is, great numbers of them did so.

y Matt. 14. 3. 24 For ʸJohn was not yet cast into prison.

For John was yet in the exercise of his public ministry, not cast into prison, as he was soon after.

25 ¶ Then there arose a question between *some* of John's disciples and the Jews about purifying.

The Jews had so many purifyings, some legal, instituted by God, ordained by Moses as God's minister; some traditional, brought in by the Pharisees, as their washings before meat, Matt. xv.; Mark vii.; that it seemeth a hard thing to determine what the question was betwixt John's disciples and the Jews, about what purifying; and the boldest determiners in this case are no better than guessers. Some would have baptism to be meant here by *purifying*. It would much conduce to the resolution of the question if we knew what these Jews were with whom John's disciples argued. If they were of the Pharisees, it is probable the question was about John's baptism, considering the frequent washings and purifyings that they had in use amongst them. If they were other Jews, the question might be about the virtue and efficacy of the ceremonial washings, ordained by the law of God, whether they were mere types, and now to cease? whether in themselves they conduced any thing to the washing and cleansing of a soul? If these Jews were (as some think, but I know not how it can be proved) disciples of Christ, the question might be about John's and Christ's baptism. This notion seemeth to be favoured by what went before; where the evangelist had been speaking of baptism, as administered by Christ's disciples, and by John; as also from what followeth, viz. John's disciples coming to him and complaining, that Christ by his disciples baptized more than their master. But there seemeth to be this great prejudice against the notion of those learned men that have embraced that notion, viz. That the question is said to have risen betwixt *John's disciples and the Jews;* now we want an instance in Scripture, where the disciples of John are put in opposition to the disciples of Christ, and under notion of the *Jews*; the term *Jews* generally signifying that part of the people who adhered to the Judaical rites and religion; especially where (as here) it is used in opposition either to the disciples of John or of Christ. It is most probable therefore the question was, either about the washings ordained by the law of Moses, or about the traditional washings observed by the Pharisees.

26 And they came unto John, and said unto him, Rabbi, he that was with thee beyond Jordan, ᶻto whom thou barest witness, behold, the same baptizeth, and all *men* come to him.

z ch. 1. 7, 15, 27, 34.

The disciples of John coming unto him, give him the usual title, under which in that age they were wont to speak to those whom they owned as their teachers, which was *Rabbi*. Their business was to complain, that Christ, whom they do not think fit to name, nor to give him any title, but mention him as one much inferior to their master, one that came to him to Bethabara, and to whom he there gave testimony, chap. i. 7, 34, as if Christ had from him derived all his credit and reputation. Their master did not go to Christ, but he came to their master; he was not baptized of Christ, but Christ was baptized of him; he did not give testimony to their master, but their master gave testimony to him: now, say they, he baptizeth by his disciples, and multitudes, many of all sorts of people, (for the universal particle *all men* can here signify no more,) come to him. Love is jealous; they were afraid that their master's reputation would by this means flag and be diminished. Such a passage we find, Numb. xi. 28. And thus John, our Saviour's disciple, was jealous for Christ his Master, Luke ix. 49. They all sinned, as appears by the answer given by Moses to Joshua, Numb. xi. 29, and Christ's answer to John, Luke ix. 50, and by the following reply of John to these disciples, envying for his sake.

27 John answered and said, ᵃA man can ‖ receive nothing, except it be given him from heaven.

a 1 Cor. 4.
Heb. 5. 4.
Jam. 1. 17.
‖ Or, *take unto himself.*

The ministry, and the success of the ministry, must both be given a man from heaven: doth he baptize? it is a sign he is sent of God. Do all men come to him? that also is from God. An excellent corrective of ambition, envy, and jealousy: no man hath in the church of God authority, but he to whom it is given from heaven; no authority over his Son.

28 Ye yourselves bear me witness, that I said, ᵇI am not the Christ, but ᶜthat I am sent before him.

b ch. 1. 20, 27.
c Mal. 3. 1.
Mark 1. 2.
Luke 1. 17.

I appeal to you that are my disciples, Did not I always plainly tell you that I was not the Christ? It belongeth unto Christ alone, who is the Head of the church, to send out such as shall labour in it, and to restrain those that labour in it; would you have me silence or suspend him? I told you, that I was but one of his ministers, *sent before him* to prepare his way, John i. 20, 23.

29 ᵈ He that hath the bride is the bridegroom: but ᵉthe friend of the bridegroom, which standeth and heareth him, rejoiceth greatly because of the bridegroom's voice: this my joy therefore is fulfilled.

d Mat. 22. 2.
2 Cor. 11. 2.
Eph. 5. 25, 27.
Rev. 21. 9.
e Cant. 5. 1.

Christ, whose the church is by a right of redemption, and by its having given up itself to him, 2 Cor. viii. 5, he is the Bridegroom of it, Matt. xxii. 2; 2 Cor. xi. 2; Eph. v. 23, 25, 29; as his Father was the Husband of the Jewish church; it belongeth to him to give laws to it, and to order matters and affairs in it. I am but as one who is *the friend of the bridegroom*, one of *the children of the bride-chamber*, Matt. ix. 15, and have by my preaching prepared the people of the Jews for him; and instead of being troubled to hear that he is come, I rejoice greatly to hear his voice. So far am I from repining to hear that multitudes go to him, that *my joy is fulfilled;* that is, I have no greater satisfaction than to hear it.

30 He must increase, but I *must* decrease.

He must increase, in honour, and dignity, and reputation in the world; he is the rising sun, (to give you notice of which I was but as the morning star,) he must shine every day more and more. *But I must decrease;* God hath indeed used me as a prophet, yea, more than a prophet, not to foretell Christ alone, but to point him to you. I have had my time, and finished my course, and God hath given me a reputation proportioned to the work he gave me to do, and to the time in which I was to work; but I must every day decay, and grow less and less, as Christ increaseth and groweth more and more.

31 ᶠHe that cometh from above ᵍis above all: ʰhe that is of the earth is earthly, and speaketh of the earth: ⁱhe that cometh from heaven is above all.

f ver. 13.
ch. 8. 23.
g Mat. 28.18.
ch. 1. 15, 27.
Rom. 9. 5.
h 1 Cor. 15. 47.
i ch. 6. 33.
1 Cor. 15. 47. Eph. 1. 21. Phil. 2. 9.

He that cometh from heaven, (for it appeareth by the latter part of the verse, that is the sense of *from above*,) as Christ did, not only in respect of his Divine nature, but being (as to his whole person) clothed with majesty and authority from above, infinitely excelleth any one who is a mere creature: he that is of an earthly original, *speaketh of the earth*. Such as is a man's original, such is his nature, such is his discourse. Though I be sent of God, as chap. xvi. 27, and my baptism be from heaven, (so our Saviour himself testifieth, Matt. xxi. 25,) yet my original is of the earth, and my relations and expressions are suitable to a mere man: but he that is from heaven excels all, as in the dignity of his person, so in the sublimity of his knowledge.

32 And ᵏwhat he hath seen and heard, that he testifieth; and no man receiveth his testimony.

k ver. 11.
ch. 8. 26.
& 15. 15.

Another great difference which the Baptist teacheth his disciples to put betwixt his testimony and Christ's, is, that he, and so all other ministers of the gospel, testify by revelation; Christ testifieth not by revelation, but from his own personal knowledge, what himself *hath seen and heard* from his Father. See ver. 11, where our Saviour had spoken to Nicodemus much the same. So John i. 18; viii. 26; xv. 15. By these two terms is signified the most certain and infallible knowledge of those things which he testified, which made them worthy of all acceptation : but yet very few received his testimony, so as to believe in it : see John i. 11, and ver. 11 of this chapter.

33 He that hath received his testimony ¹hath set to his seal that God is true.

1 Rom. 3. 4.
1 John 5. 10.

He who hath so believed the testimony of Christ, as to accept him, and to believe in him as his Saviour, hath, by that his believing, set to his seal that God, in all his promises of the Messiah under the Old Testament, is true ; that a word hath not failed of whatsoever God hath there spoken of that nature. According to this is that 1 John v. 10, *He that believeth not God hath made him a liar ; because he believeth not the record that God gave of his Son.* This saying doth notably commend faith, and defame unbelief. Faith in Christ as the only true Mediator and Saviour, giveth testimony to the truth of God, and sealeth it. Unbelief defameth God, and doth in effect say that God is a liar.

m ch. 7. 16.

34 ᵐ For he whom God hath sent speaketh the words of God : for God giveth not the Spirit ⁿ by measure *unto him*.

n ch. 1. 16.

He whom God hath sent out of heaven, out of his bosom, not merely authorizing him as a minister, as the prophets and as John were sent, *speaketh* nothing but *the words of God.* The prophets and the apostles were sent of God in a sense, but not as Christ was sent ; they sometimes spake the words of God, when the Spirit of God came upon them ; but they sometimes spake their own words, as Nathan did to David, when he encouraged his thoughts to build a house to the Lord ; and Paul, when he said, *To the rest speak I, not the Lord ;* but whatsoever Christ spake was the words of God : for God did not give out the Spirit to him sparingly, (as out of a measure,) as he doth to his ministers or saints, who have but their proportion of revelations and graces, as was requisite for their offices to which they were called, and the several periods of time that were gradually illuminated. But in him the fulness of the Godhead dwelt bodily ; he was anointed with the oil of gladness above his fellows ; he had the spring of all in himself, not the streams only.

o Matt. 11.
27. & 28. 18.
Luke 10. 22.
ch. 5. 20, 22.
& 13. 3. & 17. 2. Heb. 2. 8.

35 ᵒ The Father loveth the Son, and hath given all things into his hand.

The eternal Father loved the world, ver. 16, but he loved the Son with a more singular and peculiar love ; so that all things were by the Father delivered to him, Matt. xi. 27, *all power in heaven and earth*, Matt. xxviii. 18 ; to give eternal life to as many as the Father had given him, John xvii. 2 ; *the keys of hell and of death*, Rev. i. 18. So as every man hath reason to receive and embrace Christ and his testimony, and to believe in him.

p Hab. 2. 4.
ch. 1. 12.
& 6. 47.
ver. 15, 16.
Rom. 1. 17.
1 John 5. 10.

36 ᵖ He that believeth on the Son hath everlasting life : and he that believeth not the Son shall not see life ; but the wrath of God abideth on him.

He that, hearing the proposition of the gospel, so agreeth to it, as with his heart he receiveth him as his Saviour, and trusteth and hopeth in him, *hath everlasting life ;* that is, a certain and just title to it, nay, in the first-fruits ; being actually delivered from condemnation, Rom. viii. 1, to which, without faith, he is exposed : he already liveth a spiritual life, Gal. ii. 20 ; and having Christ in him, hath the hope of glory, into the possession of which he shall most certainly come. But he that receiveth not the gospel published by him who is the Son of God, and doth not embrace him as his Saviour, and yield obedience to him, shall not be saved. The word here translated *believeth not*, is ἀπειθῶν, which often signifieth, one that is not obedient. But this is the command of God, That men should believe on his Son, 1 John iii. 23. The commandment doth not only respect love, but faith in the first place ; for *faith worketh by love ;* so as there is an ἀπείθεια, a disobedience in the understanding, as well as in the conversation ; and he that so believeth

not, as to obey, shall never come into heaven, which felicity is here expressed by seeing life ; as not seeing death is not dying, so not seeing life is dying. And as he was by nature a child of wrath, Eph. ii. 3, subject and exposed to the wrath of God, so that *wrath abideth on him :* being justified by faith, he hath peace with God, Rom. v. 1.

CHAP. IV

Christ talketh with a woman of Samaria, and revealeth himself unto her, 1—26. *His disciples marvel ; the woman calleth the men of her city to see him,* 27—30. *Christ showeth his own zeal to do God's work, and the blessedness of his disciples, who were to reap the fruit of his labours,* 31—38. *Many Samaritans believe on him,* 39—42. *He goeth into Galilee, and healeth a nobleman's son who lay sick at Capernaum,* 43—54.

WHEN therefore the Lord knew how the Pharisees had heard that Jesus made and ᵃ baptized more disciples than John,

a ch. 3. 22, 26.

Our Saviour knew as God, from that omniscience which is inseparable from the Divine nature, or as man, by the relation of others, that the Pharisees, (who had the greatest stroke in the sanhedrim, and the government of the church of the Jews, had received an information concerning him, that he had, by his doctrine which he preached, and confirmed by miraculous operations, made and (by his disciples) *baptized more disciples than John*, thereby initiating them into a new church.

2 (Though Jesus himself baptized not, but his disciples,)

For he himself did not personally baptize any, but left it to his disciples, himself attending to the greater work of preaching the gospel, by which men and women were made fit for the ordinance of baptism.

3 He left Judæa, and departed again into Galilee.

He left the province of Judea, which was near to Jerusalem, where the Pharisees had their chief residence and greatest power ; and went the second time into Galilee, whither he went once before, chap. i. 43, where he found Philip and Nathanael. Galilee was a province under the jurisdiction of Herod, Luke iii. 1. This motion of our Saviour's into Galilee, is reported by Matthew, chap. iv. 12, and also by Mark, chap. i. 14, and Luke, chap. iv. 14. The two former give another reason of his motion, viz. his hearing that John was cast into prison ; of which, and the cause of it, see Matt. xiv. 3—6 ; so as after that he publicly preached no more, which might possibly augment the number of Christ's disciples ; John's disciples following him. Both these causes probably concurred, to cause this motion. John, who by preaching and baptizing had laid the foundation of a gospel church in Galilee, was imprisoned ; and our Saviour knew that, the number of his disciples increasing upon John's confinement, an information had been carried against him to the Pharisees ; this made him, knowing that his time was not yet come, withdraw himself out of the province of Judea into that of Galilee, as well to supply the want there (John being in prison) as to provide for his own security.

4 And he must needs go through Samaria.

Josephus tells us that Samaria is seated between Judea and Galilee, and beginneth at a town called Ginea : see Luke ix. 51, 52 ; xvii. 11. There were two passages from Judea into Galilee ; the one was through the midst of Samaria, Luke ix. 51 ; the other through the eastern parts, by the royal valley, by Jordan, in which it is said that Sichem was. By *Samaria* must not be understood the city of Samaria, built by Omri, but the whole country so called, and possessed by the Assyrians, with a mixture of Jews amongst them. Some think that the evangelist addeth this, to excuse our Saviour for going amongst the Gentiles.

5 Then cometh he to a city of Samaria, which is called Sychar, near to the parcel of ground ᵇ that Jacob gave to his son Joseph.

b Gen. 33. 19. & 48 22.
Josh. 24. 32.

The most valuable interpreters agree, that this *Sychar* is the city called Shechem; it was originally a parcel of a field bought by Jacob of Hamor, the father of Shechem, Gen. xxxiii. 19. Jeroboam built the city there, called Shechem, 1 Kings xii. 25. It was in the lot of Mount Ephraim. Joseph's bones were there buried, Josh. xxiv. 32. Jacob gave it to his son Joseph, as a parcel above his brethren, Gen. xlviii. 22; a parcel of ground near unto which was this city called Sychar, anciently Shechem.

6 Now Jacob's well was there. Jesus therefore, being wearied with *his* journey, sat thus on the well: *and* it was about the sixth hour.

It was called Jacob's, either because he digged it, (as we read of Abraham's digging a well, Gen. xxi. 30, and Isaac, Gen. xxvi. 18,) or because he and his family used it, as ver 12. Our Lord used no horse or chariot ordinarily in his travels, but went on foot; we never read of him in a coach or chariot, but once upon the back of a beast (that was when he rode into Jerusalem upon an ass); he ordinarily travelled on foot; and the evangelist taketh notice of his weariness, to let us know that he was truly man, and subjected to weariness, and other human infirmities. And he rested himself upon the sides of the well, and it was about noon-time; for that was, according to their computation, *the sixth hour.* The 8th verse tells us his disciples were gone to the city to buy meat, so as he was alone.

7 There cometh a woman of Samaria to draw water: Jesus saith unto her, Give me to drink.

It is uncertain whether this woman was a citizen of Samaria, which city is said to be at two miles distance from this place, or one of that country, which went by that name (for Samaria was the name of that region, as well as of a city). She came not out of any design to meet with Christ there, but came to draw water; they having not pumps and wells so common as we have, were forced to travel for water for their necessary uses. Thus it often happeneth that we meet with Divine mercy when we think not of it. God is found of those who seek him not, nor inquire after him, Isa. lxv. 1; which lets us see how all our motions and actions are at the Divine disposal and government. Rachel went not to the well to meet with the tidings of a husband, but to water her father's flock; but yet there she met with Jacob, Gen. xxix. 9; as it had happened to Rebekah before, Gen. xxiv. 15. This woman (as appeareth by what followeth) was no better than a harlot; to her Christ (fleeing from the Pharisees, the great doctors of the Jews) bringeth the glad tidings of the gospel, and she receives them. So admirable are the dispensations of Divine Providence. He prevents this woman, saying unto her, *Give me to drink.*

8 (For his disciples were gone away unto the city to buy meat.)

This is added, lest any should say, How came our Saviour in this discourse with the woman of Samaria? They were travelling upon the road, and came near to Sichem. Our Lord's disciples were gone to the city to buy some food for them; in the mean time, our Saviour coming to the well, called Jacob's well, sets him down, and this Samaritan woman cometh to that well to draw water; our Saviour, being thirsty, asks of her some water to drink; this giveth occasion to the following discourse.

9 Then saith the woman of Samaria unto him, How is it that thou, being a Jew, askest drink of me, which am a woman of Samaria? for [c] the Jews have no dealings with the Samaritans.

c 2 Kings 17. 24. Luke 9. 52, 53. Acts 10. 28.

There was a great estrangement of the Jews from the Samaritans, the Samaritans having a peculiar temple built upon Mount Gerizim, in opposition to that at Jerusalem. It is said that the Jews did buy of and sell to the Samaritans, but were restrained by an order of the sanhedrim from using any familiarity with them, or borrowing or receiving any thing as a gift from them; which was the cause of this reply of the woman of Samaria, knowing our Saviour, either by his habit or by his dialect, to be a Jew: this is thought to be the sense of συγχρῶνται in this text, though it hath a larger significancy, extending to all kinds of commerce.

10 Jesus answered and said unto her, If thou knewest the gift of God, and who it is that saith to thee, Give me to drink; thou wouldest have asked of him, and he would have given thee [d] living water.

d Is. 12. 3. & 44. 3. Jer. 2. 13. Zech. 13. 1. & 14. 8.

Many by *the gift of God* here understand Christ, whom God gave to the world, chap. iii. 16; and who is the greatest gift that God ever gave to the world; so as the latter words, *who it is,* &c., expound the former. *Thou wouldst have asked of him, and he would have given thee,* either a true knowledge of the doctrine or the grace tendered in the gospel; or the Holy Spirit, called *water,* because it washeth and cleanseth the soul; and *living water,* because it is always running and flowing.

11 The woman saith unto him, Sir, thou hast nothing to draw with, and the well is deep: from whence then hast thou that living water?

What our Saviour spake metaphorically, comparing his grace, or his Spirit, or the doctrine of his gospel, to living water, this poor woman understandeth literally; and knowing that the well was very deep, (some say forty cubits,) and seeing him, as a traveller, not provided with any thing to draw with, or into, she asks him whence he had that living water? a question much like that of Nicodemus, chap. iii. 4. So ignorant are persons of spiritual things, till they are enlightened by the Holy Spirit of God.

12 Art thou greater than our father Jacob, which gave us the well, and drank thereof himself, and his children, and his cattle?

She asks him if he judged himself wiser than Jacob, whom she calleth their *father?* It is often observed, that the Samaritans would ordinarily claim kindred with the Jews when the Jews were in prosperity; but in their adversity constantly disowned any relation to them. There were some Jews, (Ephraimites especially,) mixed with a far greater number of Assyrians, which made up this body of people called the Samaritans. Now, saith the woman, Jacob, who was the father of Joseph, from whom we claim, was a wise man, and he could find no better water hereabouts for himself and family than that of this well; art thou wiser than he?

13 Jesus answered and said unto her, Whosoever drinketh of this water shall thirst again:

Our Saviour in his reply justifieth the excellency of that living water, which he had before declared to be in his power to give, and his readiness to have given to this woman, if she had asked it of him, from the perishing virtue of the water of this well, and the continuing virtue of his grace, which he compared to this living water: no man so assuaged his thirst by drinking of the water of Jacob's well, but he was subject to thirst again.

14 But [e] whosoever drinketh of the water that I shall give him shall never thirst; but the water that I shall give him [f] shall be in him a well of water springing up into everlasting life.

e ch. 6. 35, 58.

f ch. 7. 38.

But he who receiveth the Holy Spirit, and the grace thereof, though he will be daily saying, Give, give, and be continually desiring further supplies of grace, yet he shall never wholly want, never want any good thing that shall be necessary for him; the seed of God shall abide in him, and this water shall be in him a spring of water, supplying him until he come to heaven. But this text was excellently expounded by our Saviour, chap. vii. 38, 39, *He that believeth on me, as the Scripture hath said, out of his belly shall flow rivers of living water. But this spake he of the Spirit, which they that believe on him should receive.* From which it is plain, that our Saviour here by the living water he speaketh of understood the Holy Spirit.

15 [g] The woman saith unto him, Sir, give me this water, that I thirst not, neither come hither to draw.

g See ch. 6. 34. & 17. 2, 3. Rom. 6. 23. 1 John 5. 20.

I am not of their mind, who think that this woman understood our Saviour speaking about spiritual water, only she had a mind to talk; and indeed it is hard to conceive how a woman of her education, and way of life, should understand any such thing; but it is plain that she did not understand him in what he was discoursing about, but doth, as it were, deride him, believing that he had no such thing to bestow. She taketh no notice of the water which our Saviour had spoken of, springing up to eternal life; but regarding only the present life, and her ease in that, desires favour of Christ only to supply her wants in this life, and that she might live more at ease: so true is that of the apostle, Rom. viii. 5, *They that are after the flesh do mind the things of the flesh.*

16 Jesus saith unto her, Go, call thy husband, and come hither.

Not that Christ did not know, what she afterward confessed, that she lived in whoredom, and had no legitimate husband; but he said this probably to check her petulancy, and mocking at what he spake about the living water, and to bring her to a sense of her sin, that she might be more fit to receive the glad tidings of a Saviour, which he was about to publish to her; and this seems rather to be our Saviour's design in bidding her go call her husband, than (as some of the ancients thought) that he might better instruct her, or avoid any scandal to himself, by a longer private discourse with a woman alone, who was of no better reputation.

17 The woman answered and said, I have no husband. Jesus said unto her, Thou hast well said, I have no husband:

I have no husband; that is, none who is my lawful husband; she denieth not that she had one whom she used and lived with as a husband, but that she had any legal husband, to whom she clave, and to no other: still she goeth on, thinking to deceive Christ, and to put tricks upon him. Christ tells her, she in this did speak truth; he knew she had no legal husband.

18 For thou hast had five husbands, and he whom thou now hast is not thy husband: in that saidst thou truly.

He tells her, that she had *had five husbands;* whether successively, the former being dead, and she marrying another, or five from whom she had been divorced for adultery, is not agreed; the best modern interpreters judge, that she had had five men to whom she had been in marriage, but so behaved herself toward them, that either for her adultery, or some other froward behaviour towards them, they had given her a bill of divorce; and though she now used and lived with one as her husband, yet in this she said truly, because, her former husbands yet living, he was not her husband. This seemeth more properly the sense, than that after five legal husbands' death, she lived in whoredom with a sixth person. By this discovery, our Saviour both bringeth her to the sense of her sin, and also to an acknowledgment of him as the Messiah.

h Luke 7. 16. & 24. 19. ch. 6. 14. & 7. 40.

19 The woman saith unto him, Sir, [h] I perceive that thou art a prophet.

Whose office is to reveal the will of God, and to whom God revealeth secret things; one to whom the Lord maketh known himself in a vision, and speaketh in a dream, Numb. xii. 6. The woman's reply seemeth to signify both. Her acknowledgment of Christ as a prophet, upon his telling her secret things, justifieth her looking upon him as one to whom God revealed things not known ordinarily to men; and this report of her meaning appeareth by what she said, ver. 29, to her fellow-citizens, *Come, see a man, which told me all things that ever I did;* but the following verse, in which she entereth into a discourse with our Saviour about the controversy betwixt the Jews and the Samaritans about worship, lets us know that she looked upon him as a prophet in the more ordinary sense, as prophet signifies one influenced by God to reveal his mind and will unto men; and indeed there was no prophet in the former sense, but was also in the latter; though there were many prophets in the latter sense, sent of God, and enabled to reveal the will of God unto men, who were not influenced so far as to foretell things to come. The difference betwixt a hypocrite and one truly brought to a sense of sin, is very conspicuous in the example of this woman; she doth not deny her sin, as Cain, Gehazi, and Ananias and Sapphira; neither doth she discover any anger upon the discovery of it, as the scribes and Pharisees, the wicked princes of Israel and Judah, and Herod did; neither doth she go about to excuse or mitigate her sin; but she applieth herself to Christ as a prophet, to teach her what to do. The example also of this woman informs us what use we ought to make of prophets, to guide us into the right way, and faithfully to acquaint us with the will of God.

20 Our fathers worshipped in [i] this mountain; and ye say, that in [k] Jerusalem is the place where men ought to worship.

i Judg. 9. 7. k Deut. 12. 5, 11. 1 Kings 9. 3. 2 Chro. 7. 12.

Our fathers worshipped in this mountain; the mount Gerizim, which was an exceeding high mountain, and near unto Sichem. Jacob made an altar thereabouts, which he called El-elohe-Israel, Gen. xxxiii. 20. Some say that it was upon that mountain that Abraham should have offered up Isaac, Gen. xxii., but that had another name. Certain it is, that from that mountain Moses pronounced the blessings, Deut. xxvii. 12. But it is very probable that the woman had respect to none of these, but to the common usage of the Samaritans, to worship in a temple built upon this mountain, in opposition to that at Jerusalem: the story of which will be very proper here to relate, for the full understanding of this text. Sanballat was governor of Samaria, constituted by Darius; of this Sanballat we read in Nehemiah, who tells us that *one of the sons of Joiada, the son of Eliashib the high priest, was son-in-law to this Sanballat the Horonite; therefore I chased him from me,* Neh. xiii. 28. This son-in-law's name (as Josephus tells us) was Manasses. He was driven out of Jerusalem upon the account of the covenant made, Ezra x. 3, that those who had married strange wives would turn them away. The sacred story here leaving us, we must supply it out of Josephus, who (Antiq. l. 11. cap. 8.) tells us, that he being thus driven from the sacrifice, applied himself to Sanballat, and would have put his wife away, who was Sanballat's daughter; but Sanballat promised him, that if he would keep his daughter as his wife, he would not only continue him in the priesthood, but make him a high priest, and build him a temple like that at Jerusalem, upon Mount Gerizim, with the leave of Darius; upon this Manasses staid with Sanballat, and there also resorted many to him whom Nehemiah had turned out of the priesthood at Jerusalem for marrying strange wives. Sanballat was very near losing his opportunity through the favour of Darius, by the conquest of Darius by Alexander the Great. But it was regained by his brother Jaddus's stubbornness, who was high priest in Jerusalem, and refused to own the new conqueror; which advantage Sanballat took, and offered Alexander the surrender of all places in his trust to him; and being by that means ingratiated with Alexander the Great, he thereby obtained leave of him to build a temple in Mount Gerizim, where his son-in-law Manasses should be the high priest, promising Alexander that by this means the force of the Jews would be broken, so as there would be no danger of their conspiring. Accordingly he presently built this temple, and soon after died, leaving his son-in-law Manasses, brother to Jaddus the high priest in Jerusalem, high priest in this new temple, which afterwards proved an asylum or sanctuary for any who were accused amongst the Jews at Jerusalem. Thus these two temples stood for about two hundred and twenty years; then Hircanus, a high priest of the Jews at Jerusalem, destroyed it; but still they looked upon the ground as holy, and came thither to perform their devotions. With reference to this superstitious practice, the woman of Samaria saith, *Our fathers worshipped* (that is, have used time out of mind to worship) *in this mountain; and ye say, that in Jerusalem is the place where men ought to worship;* and the Jews hold, that none might worship God by sacrifice any where but at Jerusalem, according to the law, Deut. xii. 14, 26.

21 Jesus saith unto her, Woman, believe me, the hour cometh, [l] when ye shall neither in this mountain, nor yet at Jerusalem, worship the Father.

l Mal. 1. 11 1 Tim. 2. 8

Woman, thou ownest me as a prophet, whose office it is to reveal the will of God unto men; it is therefore thy duty to give credit to what I shall reveal to thee about the true and right way of worshipping God. The time is coming, yea, at hand, when you shall neither in this Mount Gerizim, (where your fathers have long worshipped God superstitiously without any direction from him,) nor yet at Jerusalem, (which is the place which the Lord made choice of for his worship,) worship my Father, or your Father. God is putting an end to both these places, and to all that worship which I shall not institute under the gospel.

m 2 Kings 17. 29.
n Is. 2. 3. Luke 24. 47. Rom. 9. 4, 5.

22 Ye worship ᵐye know not what: we know what we worship: for ⁿsalvation is of the Jews.

You have no certain rule for your worship, but only do things which your fathers did, without any revelation of the Divine will, by which you may be assured that what you do is acceptable to God. We know that God hath revealed his will, that his people should worship him at Jerusalem by such rites and performances as he himself hath instituted in his word, so as we are certain that what we do is acceptable to God : for unto the Jews (of old) were committed the oracles of God, the ordinary means of salvation ; *Out of Zion went forth the law, and the word of the Lord from Jerusalem,* Isa. ii. 3.

23 But the hour cometh, and now is, when the true worshippers shall worship the Father in °spirit ᵖand in truth: for the Father seeketh such to worship him.

o Phil. 3. 3.
p ch. 1. 17.

Under the gospel, and the kingdom of the Messiah, which is yet further coming, and is already began in the world, the true worshippers of God shall not worship him, as you Samaritans, who worship you know not what, without any rule or prescript of the word ; nor yet as the hypocritical Jews, who rest upon their sacrifices and ritual performances, as if they should purge away their sins, Psal. l. 8 ; Isa. i. 11 ; lxvi. 3 ; Micah vi. 7 ; no, nor yet as the more sincere Jews, who indeed do truly and with their hearts worship God ; but, *while the first tabernacle was yet standing, which was a figure for the time then present, by sacrifices that could not make him that did the service perfect, as pertaining to the conscience,*—*by meats and drinks, and divers ordinances, imposed on them until the time of reformation,* Heb. ix. 8—10. That time of reformation is now come, when the true worshippers of God shall offer up to him a more spiritual worship, not that carnal worship ; and a more true, and real, and solid worship : for God my Father *seeketh such to worship him,* as shall not worship him with a mere bodily labour and homage, but with their hearts and spirits ; nor with those ceremonial performances now in use by God's prescript at Jerusalem, but without them, I being come, whom all those services did but prefigure and point unto.

q 2 Cor. 3. 17.

24 ᵍGod *is* a Spirit: and they that worship him must worship *him* in spirit and in truth.

God is not a corporeal being, made up of blood, and flesh, and bones, having senses as bodies have, to be pleased with sensible things ; but he is a spiritual Being, the Father of spirits, and requireth a spiritual service proportioned to his being ; and therefore those that pay a religious homage to him, must do it with their spirits, and according to the rule that he hath prescribed, in truth and reality. This is now the will of God ; and though he required of his people under the law a more ritual, figurative service, yet that is now to cease ; and therefore the woman of Samaria need not trouble herself which was the truest worship, that at Mount Gerizim, or at Mount Zion, for both of them were very suddenly to determine, and a new and more substantial spiritual worship was to succeed, to the learning of the way and method of which she was more to attend, and not to spend her thoughts about these things which were of no significancy, and tended only to minister questions of no use.

r ver. 29, 39.

25 The woman saith unto him, I know that Messias cometh, which is called Christ: when he is come, ʳhe will tell us all things.

The woman by this reply, though a woman of Samaria, showeth herself to be a Jew, for she was one of them who lived in an expectation of one whom the Jews called the Messiah, prophesied of by Daniel under this notion, Dan. ix. 25, 26, and by the psalmist, Psal. ii. 2 ; which term *Messiah* signifieth *Christ* (that is, *anointed*) in the Greek. She had a further notion, that this Messiah should be a great Prophet, Deut. xviii. 15 ; yea, she appears to have had a further notion of the Messiah, viz. that when he came he should reveal to them the whole will of God as to the salvation of man, and the worship of God : this lets us know, that she was none of the Assyrian part of the inhabitants of Samaria. If any ask, how she, being a Samaritan, should know any thing of the Messiah, the Samaritans receiving only the five books of Moses ? it is easily answered, That even the five books of Moses make mention of the Messiah, under the notion of *the seed of the woman,* Gen. iii. 15, *the seed of Abraham,* Gen. xii. 3, *Shiloh,* Gen. xlix. 10, the *Prophet* like to Moses, Deut. xviii. 15. And for the name Messiah, she might easily learn it from other Jews, that the Person called *Shiloh,* and the *Prophet,* was called by Daniel the *Messiah.*

26 Jesus saith unto her, ˢI that speak unto thee am *he.*

s ch. 9. 37. Matt. 26. 63, 64. Mark 14. 61, 62.

The same Messiah, of whom thou declarest thyself to have some expectation, and from whom thou expectest to hear all things necessary to salvation. Some here inquire, why our Saviour maketh to this woman such a plain discovery of himself, whenas we find in the Gospel so cautious, and so often charging his disciples not to make him known. Some think our Saviour thus gratified the honesty and simplicity which he discerned in this woman, not coming to catch him, but to be instructed from him ; but possibly, if we wistfully consider those texts wherein he charged his disciples not to make him known, we shall find that the thing which he cautioned them against, was their publishing of him as the Son of God, which our Saviour desired should be concealed, till he should be so declared with power by his resurrection from the dead, Rom. i. 4 ; that his enemies, by a charge of blasphemy against him, might not cut him off before his hour was come. Now we shall observe that the Jews, though they expected a Messiah, yet had no such notion of him.

27 ¶ And upon this came his disciples, and marvelled that he talked with the woman : yet no man said, What seekest thou ? or, Why talkest thou with her ?

The disciples, as we heard before, were gone into the city Sichem to buy food, and were kept there by the providence of God till our Saviour had finished this discourse with the woman of Samaria, but came after the discourse was done. They *marvelled,* possibly at his talking with a woman in the road, (a thing forbidden by their traditions,) especially a woman of Samaria, with whom the Jews had no commerce. But yet they had so much reverence and respect for their Master, that they inquired not curiously into the matter or reason of his discourse.

28 The woman then left her waterpot, and went her way into the city, and saith to the men,

She had no sooner tasted of the living water spoken of by Christ, but she left her water-pot : thus Peter tells our Saviour, that they had left all and followed him. She goeth into the city Sichem (no doubt) or Sychar, mentioned ver. 5 ; and doth not herself enter into a long discourse with the citizens, only inviteth the citizens to come and see Christ, that they might judge from the hearing of their own ears, and the sight of their own eyes.

29 Come, see a man, ᵗwhich told me all things that ever I did : is not this the Christ ?

t ver. 25.

She invites them to him under the notion of a man, who had told her all things that she ever did. Christ doubtless had told her, and spoken to her, much more than John hath left us upon sacred record ; yet not all things she ever did, but *all things* (as often) signifies many things, and those such things as she might know that he who could tell those things could have told her all things, if they had been so proper for him to have repeated to her as those things which he did tell her. This induced her to believe that he was the Messiah ; she offereth it to their opinion and judgment.

30 Then they went out of the city, and came unto him.

Sitting still at the well, they (many of them at least) did not contemn the news as the relation of a woman, but went (possibly but out of curiosity) to see and to hear this man.

31 ¶ In the mean while his disciples prayed him, saying, Master, eat.

While the woman was fetching her citizens to come and see and hear Christ, his disciples, knowing that he must be weary and hungry with his journey, and having brought him some food out of the city, where they had been to fetch it, put him upon refreshing himself with the food they had brought.

32 But he said unto them, I have meat to eat that ye know not of.

But our blessed Lord was more intent upon gospelizing the Samaritans, than satisfying his hunger: what this meat was, he opens himself, ver. 34.

33 Therefore said the disciples one to another, Hath any man brought him *ought* to eat?

His disciples, being yet carnal, did not understand him, but thought that he had spoken of bodily nourishment. See the like instances, Matt. xvi. 7; chap. xi. 13. They were wondering how he came by meat, and who should bring it him: so hard are we to conceive of spiritual things, till God openeth our eyes.

u Job 23. 12.
ch. 6. 38.
& 17. 4.
& 19. 30.

34 Jesus saith unto them, "My meat is to do the will of him that sent me, and to finish his work.

Our Lord, without any reproof of them for their dulness in understanding, and having compassion on their infirmity and ignorance, tells them what he meant by his former words; telling them, that the doing of his Father's will, and the finishing of his work, was that which he more hungered after, and took more delight in, than in eating and drinking: this is what he sought, chap. v. 30, that which he came down from heaven for, chap. vi. 38. As the law of God was sweeter to David than the honey or the honeycomb, so the publishing of the gospel was to Jesus Christ, the calling sinners to repentance, and publishing the glad tidings of the Messiah; that was his work, which he tells his Father he had finished, chap. xvii. 4. Hereby teaching ministers, and people also, to prefer spiritual things before temporal; and the ministers of the gospel especially, to prefer the publishing of the gospel (which is their work) to any other employment whatsoever.

35 Say not ye, There are yet four months, and *then* cometh harvest? behold, I say unto you, Lift up your eyes,
x Mat. 9. 37.
Luke 10. 2.
and look on the fields; *for they are white already to harvest.

There was in those countries but four months' space betwixt seed-time and harvest; yet they fed themselves (as soon as they had sown) with the expectation of it. My harvest, saith our Saviour, is the gaining of souls for my Father: look yonder what a troop of the citizens of Sichem are coming to me, upon my revelation of myself to the woman of Samaria; I have but just sown my seed, and the fields are white to this spiritual harvest, Matt. ix. 37. In the judgment of the best interpreters, our Saviour in this verse useth a comparison, and passeth from his similitude used in the former part of the verse, fetched from a worldly harvest, to discourse of that spiritual harvest, which he by and by reaped of the citizens of Sichem coming to him; it is of that he saith, that the fields were already white, by which (as will appear from the following verses) he quickeneth his disciples to put in their sickles. Some critical authors, understanding both the former and latter part of the text of a worldly harvest, have used their wits to determine how the fields should be *white to harvest* four months before it came; but the most and best interpreters interpret the latter part of a spiritual harvest, and that will be also justified by what followeth.

y Dan. 12. 3. 36 ʸAnd he that reapeth receiveth wages, and gathereth fruit unto life eternal: that both he that soweth and he that reapeth may rejoice together.

You that are the Lord's instruments, to reap what the prophets of old, and John Baptist lately, have sown, shall not lose your labour, you shall receive wages; and your wages shall not be small, it shall be no less than eternal life: *They that turn many to righteousness, shall shine as the stars for ever and ever,* Dan. xii. 3. Thus the prophets, and John the Baptist, who sowed the seed of the gospel, and you that succeed them, and reap the fruit of what they did sow, shall have the same reward in glory, and *rejoice together. The ploughman shall overtake the reaper, and the treader of grapes him that soweth seed,* as Amos speaks, chap. ix. 13. This text is of great use to those godly ministers who faithfully sow the seed of the word, but do not in their life-time see any great effects of it; it may be it comes up when they are in their graves. The reward of a faithful preacher doth not depend upon his success in his labours, but upon his faithful discharge of his work; though one soweth and another reapeth, yet both he that soweth and he that reapeth shall rejoice together.

37 And herein is that saying true, One soweth, and another reapeth.

It was a proverbial expression, most commonly used with reference to those who unjustly invaded the rights and possessions of other men; but as applicable unto those who, by the disposing providence of God, rightly inherit the fruit of other men's labours, as the Jews inherited the land of Canaan; *A land for which ye did not labour, and cities which ye built not,* Josh. xxiv. 13. This saying (saith our Saviour) is fulfilled in you.

38 I sent you to reap that whereon ye bestowed no labour: other men laboured, and ye are entered into their labours.

I have sent you to reap that which you did not first labour for; the prophets, and John the Baptist, and myself, have sown the seed, and by their doctrine prepared for the Lord a people; you enter upon their labours, gathering them into a gospel church.

39 ¶ And many of the Samaritans of that city believed on him ᶻfor the saying z ver. 29. of the woman, which testified, He told me all that ever I did.

That city was Sichem, or Sychar, but it was within the province of Samaria, from whence it is that they had the name of Samaritans as well as Sichemites. *Many* of them, upon the testimony of the woman, That he had told her such secret passages of her life, as he could not have told her if he had not been able, if he had pleased, as well to have told her all things, *believed on him;* that is, they owned him as a prophet, and agreed to what the woman said in that particular, and were by it excited to come to see and further discourse with Christ. This justifieth what our Saviour said, that there was there a people prepared for the Lord, the fields were white unto the harvest; that they were thus far wrought upon by the discourse of a woman, and she one not of the highest reputation, and only telling them that he had told her all things she had done. Small means have great effects when God's time of working is come.

40 So when the Samaritans were come unto him, they besought him that he would tarry with them: and he abode there two days.

The Sichemites being come to Christ, had some discourse with him, as appeareth from ver. 41, 42. What the subject matter of their discourse was we are not told; we may know that it was spiritual, and something proper to excite faith in them, for believing was the effect of it. They desire that he would abide with them: thus their faith wrought by love. Our Saviour, that he might not discourage the beginning of their faith, did stay with them two days: for although, when he sent out his disciples, he commanded them not to go into the way of the Samaritans, yet himself was not obliged by that law, and did sometimes, by preaching to heathens, and converting of them, give an earnest of the calling of the Gentiles, whose fuller calling was reserved to after-times; yet, probably, the reason why he would not stay longer with them than two days, was because the time was not yet come for the fuller calling of the Gentiles, and he was not willing by a longer abode with them to give offence to the Jews, betwixt whom and the Samaritans was a rooted hatred upon the account of their differing religion.

41 And many more believed because of his own word;

Believing seemeth here to be taken in a different sense from what it was taken in ver. 39, from what followeth, ver. 42. There it seemeth only to signify a lower degree of assent, that he was a prophet, upon the woman's saying that he had told her all she had done; here it signifieth a giving credit to him as the Christ, the Saviour of the world, of which they were convinced by what they heard from himself. Thus that of the apostle, Rom. x. 17, is justified, that *faith cometh by hearing*; and the influence of Christ upon the souls of believers is also justified. We read of no miracles our Saviour wrought here; they believed not because of any signs they saw, but because of his word; wherein also they further showed themselves the first-fruit of the Gentiles, the generality of which were afterward converted to the faith of the gospel, after that miracles were ceased, by hearing the gospel preached.

42 And said unto the woman, Now we believe, not because of thy saying: for [a] we have heard *him* ourselves, and know that this is indeed the Christ, the Saviour of the world.

[a ch. 17. 8. 1 John 4. 14.]

Several things may be the occasion of faith, which are neither the principal efficient causes, nor the proper instrumental cause of it. The principal efficient cause of the faith of these Samaritans was, undoubtedly, the finger of God upon their souls, enlightening their minds with the saving knowledge of the gospel, and bowing their wills to the obedience of it. The proper instrumental cause was their hearing the words of Christ; but the occasion of this was what the woman had told them: so as, though they in a sense believed because of what she had said, because that occasioned their coming out to see and hear Christ; yet the proper instrumental cause was their hearing Christ, God upon their hearing him working in their hearts an ability and a willingness to receive and to close with Christ. Thus the church gives us the first occasion of receiving the Scriptures, and believing them to be the word of God: we, having them put into our hands by the church, read them, and find such impresses and stamps of Divinity in them, that we conclude, from our reason very probably, that they are more than human writings; but never firmly and · fixedly receive them as such, until persuaded of it by the Holy Spirit. These Samaritans do not only own Christ as a prophet, nor do they only suspect that he must be the Messias, but they profess to *know* that he was *the Christ, the Saviour of the world.*

43 ¶ Now after two days he departed thence, and went into Galilee.

Christ (as we heard before, ver. 3) was upon his journey into Galilee, only he stopped two days at Sichem to gratify the desires of the Samaritans of that city; which two days being now spent, he keepeth on in his journey. But here ariseth a question, viz. Whether he first went to Nazareth, or to Cana? For the opinion of those who think he first went to Nazareth, is quoted Matt. iv. 12. Besides, it is said that Nazareth was in his road to Cana, and, Luke iv. 24, he is said to have uttered these words there. Chemnitius thinks he went first to Cana, according to what John relateth in the following verses. And, Luke iv. 16, he is said to have gone out of Galilee to Nazareth: and besides, the next mentioned miracle is (ver. 54) said to have been Christ's second miracle, which it could not have been had he first gone to Nazareth, for, Luke iv. 23, those of Nazareth mention some miracles which he had wrought at Capernaum.

44 For [b] Jesus himself testified, that a prophet hath no honour in his own country.

[b Mat. 13. 57. Mark 6. 4. Luke 4. 24.]

Christ spake those words more than once, Matt. xiii. 57; Mark vi. 4; Luke iv. 24. But the question is, what force of reason this hath why he went into Galilee, whereas Nazareth, which was in Galilee, was his own country; for though he was born in Bethlehem, yet he was educated at Nazareth; upon which account, Luke iv. 23, it is called his own country? The best resolution of this difficulty is, that by Galilee here is to be understood, the country part of Galilee, exclusive to Nazareth; and this is not given as a reason why our Saviour went into Galilee, but why he did not go to Nazareth, but into the country part of Galilee, because Nazareth was his own country, and *a prophet is not without honour, except in his own country.*

45 Then when he was come into Galilee, the Galilæans received him, [c] having seen all the things that he did at Jerusalem at the feast: [d] for they also went unto the feast.

[c ch. 2. 23. & 3. 2.]
[d Deut. 16. 16.]

When he came not to Nazareth, but to some parts of Galilee, the Galileans entertained him hospitably; and this they did because of those miracles they had seen wrought by him at the passover feast, where Christ was, chap. ii. For these Galileans, though they lived at a great distance from Jerusalem, yet were observant of the law which commanded all the males of the Jews to be present at that solemnity. The Samaritans saw no miracle, but believed Christ upon his word. The Galileans also received Christ, but their seeing of his miracles at the feast is given as the cause of their receiving him; their faith was not so noble as that of the Samaritans. *Blessed* (saith our Saviour) *are they who have not seen, and yet have believed.*

46 So Jesus came again into Cana of Galilee, [e] where he made the water wine. And there was a certain ‖ nobleman, whose son was sick at Capernaum.

[e ch. 2. 1, 11.]
[‖ Or, *courtier*, or, *ruler*.]

Our Saviour, coming into Galilee, made choice of Cana, the place where, being at a marriage feast, he turned water into wine, chap. ii., first to fix in: the reason is not expressed, and therefore vainly guessed at by interpreters. There he worketh a second miracle, not upon the person of any one of Cana, but upon the son of one who was at Capernaum, which was a city in the tribe of Naphtali, upon the shore of the famous river Jordan. This person is described to be one that was βασιλικὸς, a *nobleman*; whether of the blood of Herod, that was tetrarch of Galilee, or some courtier or principal servant of his, it is not said.

47 When he heard that Jesus was come out of Judæa into Galilee, he went unto him, and besought him that he would come down, and heal his son: for he was at the point of death.

Christ had been in Galilee before, and in this town, and wrought a miracle, and if this courtier were a disciple of John, (as some think, but it is hard to prove,) it is probable he had been at the passover, and seen the miracles he wrought there, or at least might have heard of them from some who were there. Though it was a good way from Capernaum thither, yet his love to his son carried him, and humbled him to beseech Christ that he would come down and heal his son; by which he showed a great weakness of faith, as if he thought that Christ could not put forth his healing virtue at a distance, but his personal presence was necessary; as Naaman the Syrian thought that Elisha must come down and lay his hand upon him. His son, it seems, was in human appearance dying.

48 Then said Jesus unto him, [f] Except ye see signs and wonders, ye will not believe.

[f 1 Cor. 1. 22.]

It may seem strange to such as do not well weigh all circumstances, that our Saviour, who at other times went without asking, showed himself so hard to be entreated by this courtier, and answereth him so roughly; but we must not take ourselves to be able to give a certain account of all Christ's actions, and different dealings with persons, whose hearts he well enough knew. Thus much is certain, that our Saviour always preferred that faith which was given to his bare word, before that which waited for a miracle confirmative of that word, John xx. 29. Our Saviour saw that this courtier came to him purely upon a natural account, for the recovery of his dying son, without a desire to be instructed in his heavenly doctrine; therefore (as it may be presumed) he checks this courtier; and not him alone, but the generality of the Jews, who were only struck with admiration of his works, and drawn from curiosity, or some temporal benefit, to follow him, without a due regard of his person, or the heavenly, saving truths preached by him.

49 The nobleman saith unto him, Sir, come down ere my child die.

The courtier, though probably of spirit enough to have shown some discontent at our Saviour's no kinder answer to him before, yet was so intent upon his son's life, that he takes no notice of it, but reneweth his request, still discovering the weakness of his faith, as thinking that Christ's personal presence was necessary to the life of his son.

50 Jesus saith unto him, Go thy way; thy son liveth. And the man believed the word that Jesus had spoken unto him, and he went his way.

Our Saviour would neither discourage the weak faith of this nobleman, nor yet encourage his weakness: he healeth his son for the encouragement of his faith; he doth it by his word, without going down to him, that he might not gratify his weakness, thinking his personal presence was necessary; he bids him go, for his son was recovered (that is here meant by *liveth*). Upon this his faith groweth, and he who before only believed Christ to be a prophet, probably upon others' hearsay, now believeth his word, that is, was persuaded that his son was indeed recovered.

51 And as he was now going down, his servants met him, and told *him*, saying, Thy son liveth.

The servants that met him to bring the acceptable news of his son's recovery, knew nothing of the passages that had been betwixt Christ and their master, but merely came to tell their master what they knew would be acceptable to him.

52 Then enquired he of them the hour when he began to amend. And they said unto him, Yesterday at the seventh hour the fever left him.

He inquireth the precise time; they tell him it was about *the seventh hour*. The miracle appeared in the suddenness of the recovery, and also that it was without the application of means, at least any that could have produced so sudden an effect.

53 So the father knew that *it was* at the same hour, in the which Jesus said unto him, Thy son liveth: and himself believed, and his whole house.

The circumstance of the time when his son recovered agreeing with the very hour when Christ had said unto him, *Thy son liveth*, was a mighty confirmation to him, that he was beholden to Christ for his cure, and consequently that Christ was no ordinary man, more than a prophet, even the Son of God. This works upon his faith to a higher degree: he first-believed the report of him, then he gave credit to the word that he spake, now he believeth savingly, and not he alone, but his whole family became Christians. Such instances we have concerning Lydia, Acts xvi. 14, 15, the jailer, ver. 34, and Crispus, Acts xviii. 8.

54 This *is* again the second miracle *that* Jesus did, when he was come out of Judæa into Galilee.

His turning water into wine (chap. ii.) was the first, this was the second, and so in order of time before any of those miracles which he wrought in Galilee, of which we read, Matt. iv. 23.

CHAP. V

Christ cureth an impotent man at the pool of Bethesda on the sabbath day, 1—9. *The Jews cavil, and persecute him for it,* 10—16. *He justifieth himself by the example of God his Father,* 17, 18; *and asserteth the power and judgment committed unto him by the Father,* 19—30. *He appealeth to the testimony of John,* 31—35; *of the Father,* 36—38; *and of the Scriptures,* 39, 40. *He showeth that his humility caused their rejection of him,* 41—44; *but that in disbelieving him they disbelieved Moses also,* 45—47.

AFTER ᵃthis there was a feast of the Jews; and Jesus went up to Jerusalem.

Though there are some that think the feast mentioned here was that of Pentecost, and others that it was the feast of tabernacles, yet the most and best interpreters judge it was the feast of the passover that is here mentioned; and that this was the second passover which happened after our Saviour had entered upon his public ministry. We read of the first, chap. ii. 13; and from that verse of that chapter to this chapter the evangelist (as they think) hath been relating so much of our Saviour's actions, until the second passover, as it was the will of God we should have upon public authentic record, and had not been recorded by the other evangelists, who give a further account of his actions done this year, Matt. iv., viii., ix.; Mark i., ii.; Luke iv., v. In the time of our Saviour's public ministry (which was three years and a half) there were four passovers. The other evangelists take notice but of one of them, and that the last. John is thought to have mentioned all the four; the first, chap. ii. 13, the second in this place, the third, chap. vi. 4, the fourth, chap. xiii. 1. Another reason they give why the feast of the passover should be here intended is, because from about that time to the harvest were four months, according to what our Saviour had said, chap. iv. 35. *Jesus went up to* the passover, to *Jerusalem*, to show his obedience to his Father's law, Deut. xvi. 16.

2 Now there is at Jerusalem ᵇby the sheep ‖ *market* a pool, which is called in the Hebrew tongue Bethesda, having five porches.

We read in Scripture of *the sheep gate* in Jerusalem, Neh. iii. 1. There was also a market for sheep and other cattle, Deut. xiv. 26. Some therefore add *market*, others add *gate*, to the word in the Greek signifying *sheep*. Near to this gate or market there was *a pool*, κολυμβηθρα: some translate it, a fish-pool; others, (more properly,) a place to wash or to swim in (the word deriveth from a verb that signifies, to swim). They say there were two such pools within the compass of the mount on which the temple stood; the one eastward, called *the upper pool*, 2 Kings xviii. 17; the other westward, near to the sheep gate. The one was called *Bethesda*; the other, *the pool of Siloah, by the king's garden*, Neh. iii. 15, mentioned also by our evangelist, chap. ix. 7. They say the waters of these pools were supplied from a fountain called Siloam, which was not always full of water, but the water bubbled up in it at certain times with a great noise, coming (as was thought) through hollow places of the earth, and quarries of hard stones. These *waters of Shiloah* are mentioned, Isa. viii. 6, and said to *go softly;* from which place these waters are concluded a type of the kingdom of David and of Christ. This being admitted, it is not to be wondered that they had that healing virtue given unto them (as some judge) just about the coming of Christ; for it should appear by chap. ix. 7, that the pool of Siloam, as well as that of Bethesda, had so; for in former times it is thought to have been of use chiefly to wash garments in, and sacrifices when they were slain. Some will have them to have derived their healing virtue from thence; but that is vain, their healing virtue was doubtless derived from the Lord that healeth us. This pool *in the Hebrew* was *called Bethesda*, which some interpret, The house of pouring out, because, as some fancy, the blood of the sacrifices was there poured out; (but that is a great mistake, for that was to be poured out at the altar;) or because rain water (as some think) was poured into it; or (which is more probable) because waters were poured into it out of the conduit mentioned 2 Kings xx. 20. But others interpret it, The house of grace, mercy, &c., because of God's great goodness showed the people, in giving this healing virtue to these waters. The *five porches* belonging to this pool seem to have been five apartments for impotent men to walk in, or rest themselves in, when they came to wash themselves in the pool.

3 In these lay a great multitude of impotent folk, of blind, halt, withered, waiting for the moving of the water.

In these apartments (called here porches) there were a great number of sick persons, some labouring under one infirmity, some under another, some blind, some lame, waiting for the time the water should be troubled.

4 For an angel went down at a certain season into the pool, and troubled the water: whosoever

then first after the troubling of the water stepped in was made whole of whatsoever disease he had.

This water had not always in it this healing virtue, but only when it was *troubled*, and this was *at a certain season*, how often the Scripture hath not determined ; some will have it to be only at their great feasts, of the passover, and Pentecost, &c., but the Scripture saith no such thing. None must think that the angel appeared in any visible shape, but the rolling or troubling of the waters was a certain sign, that that was the time when alone they were medicinal ; nor were many healed at one time, but only one person, that could first get into this water, he was healed, let his disease be what it would. The waters not being constantly medicinal, but, first, at a certain time, when they were troubled ; and then, secondly, not for all, but only to him who could first get in ; and, thirdly, for any disease, of what sort or kind soever his disease was ; sufficiently confuteth the opinion of those who fancy that the waters derived this healing virtue from the entrails of the beasts offered in sacrifice being washed there ; for besides that this is denied by some, who say those entrails were washed in a room on purpose for that use within the temple ; if they had derived their healing virtue from thence in a natural, rational way, they would have exerted their virtue upon more than him who first stepped in, and not at the time only when they were troubled, nor would their virtue have extended to all kinds of diseases. Of whatever use this pool therefore was before, certain it is at this time God made use of the water in it to heal, and so as men might see that it healed not by any natural, but a miraculous operation. The Scriptures of the Old Testament make no mention of it. And it is observed by those who are versed in the Jewish Rabbins, that neither do they make the least mention of it. Which makes it very probable, that they had this virtue, not from the time of the building of the sheep gate by Shallum, Neh. iii. 15 ; nor from the time when the Asmonean family was extinct ; or the rebuilding or further building and adorning the temple by Herod ; but a little before the birth of Christ, as a figure of him being now coming, who, Zech. xiii. 1, was *a fountain opened to the house of David, and to the inhabitants of Jerusalem ;* and from whom is both our cleansing and our healing, as these waters, which before had a cleansing, and now received also a healing virtue.

5 And a certain man was there, which had an infirmity thirty and eight years.

What this man's name was, or what his circumstances in the world, or what his particular disease, we are not told ; nor is it said that he had lain there thirty-eight years, but that he had so long laboured under his weakness : which, whether it was the palsy or no, is uncertain : probably it was a disease hardly curable by human art and ordinary means ; for it cannot be thought but in that time he had used all rational means, which he finding of no value as to his case, he came and lay at this fountain, waiting for a cure in this way of miraculous operation.

6 When Jesus saw him lie, and knew that he had been now a long time *in that case*, he saith unto him, Wilt thou be made whole?

Christ, as God, knew the particular time when this infirmity seized him, which was eight years or upward before our Saviour's birth, and about the time when the temple was re-edified, or rather enlarged and further adorned, by Herod. As man, he pitieth his case ; he asketh him if he was willing to be made whole. Not that he doubted of his willingness ; for what sick man was ever unwilling to be healed? besides that, he knew that the poor man lay there for that very purpose ; but that he might make him declare his miserable, helpless state and condition, and draw out his faith and hope in himself; and from his answer take an occasion to heal him, and make the spectators more attentive to his miracle.

7 The impotent man answered him, Sir, I have no man, when the water is troubled, to put me into the pool : but while I am coming, another steppeth down before me.

What his particular impotency was the Scripture doth not tell us. Some have (not improbably) judged it the palsy, which depriveth the person of motion, by the stoppage of the animal spirits, so that without help he cannot move from one place to another, which it is manifest this poor man could not ; for he complaineth for want of help, that he could not get into the pool.

8 Jesus saith unto him, °Rise, take up thy bed, and walk. c Matt. 9. 6. Mark 2. 11. Luke 5. 24.

Our Lord will let this poor man know, that the waters and the angel derived their power from him ; and that he with a word could do as much for him, as the waters troubled by the angel could effect : he therefore bids him arise, and take up his bed and walk, that others might see and be assured that he was perfectly cured.

9 And immediately the man was made whole, and took up his bed, and walked : and ᵈ on the same day was the sabbath. d ch. 9. 14.

The man's strength returneth immediately ; he is able immediately to arise, take up his bed, and to walk. All this was done on the sabbath day ; on which day it was unlawful to carry any burdens, Jer. xvii. 21, 24 ; and by the Jewish canons it was punishable by death, or scourging. But our Saviour had a mind to let the Jews know that he was Lord of the sabbath, and what had been unlawful without his special command, became lawful by it. Neither was this against the sense of the law, though against the letter of it ; the law only prohibited civil labour, and carrying burdens for their own profit, and in the way of their trade ; it forbade the doing of nothing which was to be done as a public testimony of the goodness and mercy of God showed to persons : and by this our Saviour opens a way for his correction of their erroneous opinions about the true sanctification of the sabbath. We shall observe, that our Saviour used the like phrase to him that had the palsy, Matt. ix. 6 ; and to the centurion's daughter, Mark v. 41, *Damsel, arise* ; and to Lazarus, chap. xi. 43, *Lazarus, come forth* ; which our Saviour did for the testification of the miracle to all that should see them. It is further observed by Heinsius, that our Saviour did many miracles on the sabbath day, because that day was the usual time when the Jews were wont to consult the prophets for help, as may be learned from 2 Kings iv. 23.

10 ¶ The Jews therefore said unto him that was cured, It is the sabbath day : ᵉ it is not lawful for thee to carry *thy* bed. e Ex. 20. 10. Neh. 13. 19. Jer. 17. 21. &c. Mat. 12. 2. Mark 2. 24. & 3. 4. Luke 6. 2. & 13. 14.

That is, according to the letter of the law : they understood not that Christ was the Lord of the sabbath ; their cavil argued their want both of faith in Christ, and charity also toward their neighbour.

11 He answered them, He that made me whole, the same said unto me, Take up thy bed, and walk.

He makes them as good an answer as could well be imagined ; the sum of which was, he believed that he that had thus healed him was a prophet, and so did what he did by a Divine authority, which it was lawful for him to obey, contrary to their traditions : though who this particular person was, or what his name was, were things as yet not known to him, (as we shall by and by read,) yet he seemeth sensible that he was healed by a power more than human.

12 Then asked they him, What man is that which said unto thee, Take up thy bed, and walk?

The impotent man that was healed seemed to oppose the authority of God (by virtue of which he believed himself healed) to the authority of man, which made it unlawful for him on the sabbath day to take up his bed and walk. The Jews, taking no notice of Christ's being God, or so much as a prophet sent from God, do not ask, Who was he? but, *What man is that which said,* &c.? opposing the command of God to the command of man. It is as much as if they had said, The law of God hath commanded that no burdens should be carried on the sabbath day ; now, what is that *man* that dare teach thee or any one to do what is contrary to the law of God ?

13 And he that was healed wist not who it was : for Jesus had conveyed himself away, ∥ a multitude being in *that* place. ∥ Or, *from the multitude that was.*

Christ came as a stranger to the pool, and only wrought this miracle, so as the impotent man that was healed had no time to inquire who he was: and there being there a crowd of people, Christ had through the people conveyed himself away; so as the man could not find him, to show them the man who had so said unto him.

14 Afterward Jesus findeth him in the temple, and said unto him, Behold, thou art made whole: ᶠsin no more, lest a worse thing come unto thee.

f Mat. 12, 45. ch. 8. 11.

Jesus findeth him in the temple; walking in the outward court of the temple, or some part of it, where people ordinarily walked. He chargeth him to *sin no more, lest a worse thing* betided him; hereby letting him and us know that sin is the usual cause of diseases, and a holy walking the best preservative of health; and that God hath further revelations of his wrath against sin and sinners, than what do or can befall them in this life.

15 The man departed, and told the Jews that it was Jesus, which had made him whole.

It were very uncharitable to judge that this poor man went to the Jewish magistrates to inform against Christ, who had been so kind to him; and much more probable that he went in the simplicity of his heart, desirous both to publish what Christ had done to his honour, and also to do good to others, who might also stand in need of his help.

16 And therefore did the Jews persecute Jesus, and sought to slay him, because he had done these things on the sabbath day.

But the Jews made another use of it, seeking from hence an advantage against him, because he had violated the sabbath, which they often made a capital crime.

g ch. 9. 4. & 14. 10.

17 ¶ But Jesus answered them, ᵍMy Father worketh hitherto, and I work.

We read of no objection they made to Christ, as to what he had done, only that they persecuted him, which they might do without speaking to him: but it should seem by what we read in this verse, that some of the Jews had objected to him his violation of the sabbath (as they thought); yet, as we before noted, *answered* (in the dialect of the gospel) doth often signify no more than the beginning of a discourse upon some proper occasion offered. Our Saviour defendeth himself from the example of his Father, in the remembrance of whose resting from his work of creation on the seventh day from the beginning of the creation, the Jews kept their sabbath; who, though he rested from his work of creation, yet hitherto *worketh*, as well on the sabbath day as any other day, by his preservation of created beings: so (saith he) *I,* who am the Son of this Father, also *work; upholding all things by the word of* my power, Heb. i. 3. So that works of Divine Providence are lawful on the sabbath day; such was this. I work no other way than my Father still worketh, though he rested on the seventh day from the creation.

h ch. 7. 19.

18 Therefore the Jews ʰsought the more to kill him, because he not only had broken the sabbath, but said also that God was his Father, ⁱmaking himself equal with God.

i ch. 10. 30, 33. Phil. 2. 6.

This yet enraged the Jews more: they had before against him a charge of breaking the sabbath, or, at least, teaching another to break it (in their opinion); but now he had (as they judged) spoken blasphemy, calling God *Father;* not in the sense the Jews so called him, and all good Christians are licensed to call him; but πατέρα ἴδιον, his proper Father, or his own Father; by which (as they truly said) he made himself *equal with God.* Nor did he by that alone make himself equal with God, but he ascribed also to himself a co-operation with God, in works proper to God alone: nor did he think this any *robbery,* Phil. ii. 6. This was their charge; we shall now hear how our Saviour defendeth himself against it.

19 Then answered Jesus and said unto them, Verily, verily, I say unto you, ᵏThe Son can do nothing of himself, but what he seeth the Father do: for what things soever he doeth, these also doeth the Son likewise.

k ver. 30. ch. 8. 28. & 9. 4. & 12. 49. & 14. 10.

Consider Christ as God, so he can do nothing but what the Father doth, that is, nothing that respected created beings: for it is a known rule, That the works of the Trinity out of itself are not divided; whatsoever one person doth, the others do; though, to denote the order of the Trinity's working, some works are most ordinarily ascribed to the Father, such are the works of creation and providence; some to the Son, as redemption; some to the Holy Spirit, as sanctification; yet they are not so ascribed to any Person, but that other Scriptures justify the co-operation of all three Persons. Consider the Son as the Messias; so also it is true, that *the Son can do nothing of himself, but what he seeth the Father do.* Nor is this any diminution to the glory of Christ, nor doth it speak any impotency in him, from whence the Arians and Socinians would conclude his inferiority to his Father; but rather his perfection, that he did only what pleased the Father: so that phrase, *what he seeth the Father do,* is to be interpreted; and that term, *can do nothing,* signifies no more than, he doth or will do nothing. See such a usage of the phrase, Gen. xix. 22; Luke xvi. 2; John xii. 39. From this he leaveth them easily to conclude, that what he had done, in curing this impotent man upon the sabbath day, was the Father's work, though by him; for whatsoever the Father doth, or willeth, the same doth the Son likewise. From hence will appear an easy solution to the difficulty arising upon the first view of the words, viz. How these words can prove Christ equal with the Father, when they rather prove the contrary, because he can do nothing of himself, but what he seeth the Father do? Some seek a solution in the words *can do nothing;* he that cannot do those things which God cannot do, is equal with God. Some seek it in the word *seeth;* which they say signifieth here an identity of nature and will. Some seek the solution in the word *do,* which they say signifieth to will and consent to. The best solution is to be taken from those words, *of himself;* the Son hath done many things which he did not see the Father do, but he did them not of himself. Our Saviour's meaning is plainly this: The Son neither willeth nor can do any thing, but what the Father willeth and doth in him; therefore he is one in essence with the Father, and equal to him. *For what things soever he doeth, these also doeth the Son likewise:* the Son doth those things which the Father doth; and, as the Messias, he doth those things which the Father willeth to be done.

20 For ˡthe Father loveth the Son, and sheweth him all things that himself doeth: and he will shew him greater works than these, that ye may marvel.

l Matt. 3. 17. ch. 3. 35. 2 Pet. 1. 17.

For the Father loveth the Son; both as his Son by eternal generation, Matt. iii. 17, and also as the Messiah sent by him into the world, to finish the work the Father had given him to do: and look, as a father will make his son acquainted with all that he doth; and not only so, but communicates all his power and skill to his son, so far as he can: so the Father communicateth all his power to the Son, working all things in him, and by him; and he will in and by him work greater things than this, healing this poor man; he will by him raise the dead, &c. *That ye may marvel:* Christ knew that they would not believe, and all the effect that his miracles had upon the generality of the Jews, was but causing in them a stupefaction, amazement, and admiration, as chap. xi. 47; whereas it was their duty, not only to marvel, but to have believed also, without which their admiration did but cause that they had no cloak for their sin.

21 For as the Father raiseth up the dead, and quickeneth *them;* ᵐeven so the Son quickeneth whom he will.

m Luke 7. 14. & 8. 54. ch. 11. 25, 43.

He seemeth not to speak of what God will do in the general resurrection, but of those whom the Lord raised up from the dead in the Old Testament, by Elijah and Elisha. The giving of and restoring unto life, are things proper unto God, Deut. xxxii. 39; 1 Sam. ii. 6. *So the Son quickeneth whom he will:* God hath given unto me a power to raise from the dead whom I will; as he did raise up

Jairus's daughter, Matt. ix. 25, and the widow's son, Luke vii. 14, and Lazarus, John xi. 43. This was one of those greater works, of which our Saviour spake in the former verse.

22 For the Father judgeth no man, but ⁿhath committed all judgment unto the Son:

n Matt. 11. 27. & 28. 18. ver. 27. ch. 3. 35. & 17. 2. Acts 17. 31. 1 Pet. 4. 5.

Alone he judgeth no man, he judgeth no man but by the Son, no man without the Son; but committed all judgment in the administration of the mediatory kingdom in the church to his Son, and by his Son will judge the world at the last day.

23 That all *men* should honour the Son, even as they honour the Father. °He that honoureth not the Son honoureth not the Father which hath sent him.

o 1 John 2. 23.

That his Son might be honoured by all men, Psal. ii. 11, 12; Phil. ii. 10, with the same honour which is given to the Father; for the Son is sent by the Father, not as one inferior to him, as a servant is sent by his master, but as an equal is sent by his friend, John iv. 34; vi. 38; vii. 28. And look, as a great prince, when he sendeth his ambassador, expecteth that those to whom he is sent should give him honour, and the same honour as to himself; so doth the Father: so that *he that honoureth not the Son, honoureth not the Father which hath sent him.* It is a text which reflecteth dreadfully upon such as honour not Christ, especially the Jews and Socinians, who professedly do not honour him with the same honour with which they yet pretend to honour the Father, and are concluded by this text not in truth to honour the Father.

24 Verily, verily, I say unto you, ᵖHe that heareth my word, and believeth on him that sent me, hath everlasting life, and shall not come into condemnation; ᵠbut is passed from death unto life.

p ch. 3. 16, Is. & 6. 40, 47. & 8. 51. & 20. 31.

q 1 John 3. 14.

He that so heareth my words, that they are not a mere sound in his ears, nor affect his heart with some mere sudden and vanishing passion, but so that he gives an assent to them upon my authority; and that firmly and steadily believeth him that sent me, (the particle *on* seemeth not well put in by our translators; in the Greek it is τῷ πεμψαντί με, giveth credit to the words of my Father that sent me,) believing that I am his only begotten Son, whom he hath sent into the world, and receiving me as such, hearing me, according to the command of the voice from heaven, Matt. xvii. 5; he hath a certain title to everlasting life, and hath received the first-fruits of that harvest, Rom. viii. 23, the incorruptible seed of the word, 1 Pet. i. 23; and already sitteth *in heavenly places in Christ Jesus,* Eph. ii. 6, and hath the kingdom of God within him, Luke xvii. 21, and shall not come into that judgment which shall issue in eternal condemnation; but is passed out of a state of spiritual death into a state of spiritual life; and shall be at last eternally saved, and pass into the actual fruition and enjoyment of life eternal.

25 Verily, verily, I say unto you, The hour is coming, and now is, when ʳthe dead shall hear the voice of the Son of God: and they that hear shall live.

r ver. 28. Eph. 2. 1, 5. & 5. 14. Col. 2. 13.

The dead shall hear the voice of the Son of God: some understand this concerning the special resurrection of such bodies as Christ raised while he was upon the earth from death to life, of which number was Lazarus and the daughter of Jairus, &c. Others understand it of the general resurrection, spoken of ver. 28, 29. That which favoureth this sense is, because here is no mention of believing, but only hearing a voice. But the most and best interpreters rather understand these words of those who are dead in trespasses and sins, and the quickening and life mentioned Eph. ii. 1, which is called *the first resurrection,* Rev. xx. 5, because of what was said immediately before, that such a one *is passed from death to life;* and what was said before, *He that heareth my word,* agreeth with what is said here, of hearing the voice of Christ; and what followeth seemeth better to agree with this sense. And ver. 28, 29 speak plainly of the second and general resurrection of the body.

They that hear shall live; those who so hear the voice of Christ in the gospel, as to give a firm and steady assent to it, and, upon the credit of it, shall receive Christ as their Mediator and Saviour, shall live eternally; they do live the life of grace, and shall live the life of glory.

26 For as the Father hath life in himself; so hath he given to the Son to have life in himself;

How the eternal Father *hath life in himself,* is obvious to every capacity; for he is the First Mover, and therefore must have his life in and from himself, and not from any other; and he is the First Cause, and therefore that life which floweth from him to all created beings, must first be in him, as in its fountain. But in what sense it is said, that he hath *given to the Son to have life in himself,* whether as God, by his eternal generation, or as the Messiah and Mediator betwixt God and man, and so the fountain of spiritual life to believers, is more questioned. Those who understand it as to the Divine nature, say, that this phrase, *hath life in himself,* is expressive of the name Jehovah; and that Christ is proved to be the true Jehovah by what is here said, that he *hath life in himself.* But they distinguish betwixt having life from or by himself, and having life in himself; the text saith, it is *given* to Christ *to have life in himself.* But there are other interpreters, who seem better to understand it of Christ as Mediator, to whom it is given to have life in himself, to communicate to his creatures; and think it is well interpreted by chap. i. 4, *In him was life, and the life was the light of men.*

27 And ˢhath given him authority to execute judgment also, ᵗbecause he is the Son of man.

s ver. 22. Acts 10. 42. & 17. 31. t Dan. 7. 13, 14.

To execute judgment also; to have the power of life and death, the keys of both; to rule and govern the world, and to judge it at the last day. *Because he is the Son of man:* Acts xvii. 31, *He hath appointed a day, in the which he will judge the world in righteousness by that man whom he hath ordained,* &c. So Phil. ii. 8, *Being found in fashion as a man, he humbled himself, and became obedient unto death, even the death of the cross. Wherefore God also hath highly exalted him,* &c. Some think that the sense is, because he was that Son of man, who was the Seed of the woman, promised Gen. iii. 15; the Son of man prophesied of by Daniel, chap. vii. 13, 14. And that the term, *Son of man,* here, signifieth his office as Mediator.

28 Marvel not at this: for the hour is coming, in the which all that are in the graves shall hear his voice,

Do not marvel at this power which I tell you the Father hath given me, to execute in the world justice and judgment; to raise some particular persons from a natural death, and whom he pleaseth from the spiritual death of sin: for the hour is coming, when all those who are in the graves, shall, by an archangel, Matt. xxiv. 31; 1 Thess. iv. 16, hear my voice, commanding them to arise; and they shall obey my command.

29 ᵘAnd shall come forth; ˣthey that have done good, unto the resurrection of life; and they that have done evil, unto the resurrection of damnation.

u Is. 26. 19 1 Thess. 4. 16. 1 Cor. 15. 52. x Dan. 12. 2. Matt. 25. 32, 33, 46.

And come forth; not all to be made partakers of eternal life and glory; there shall be a resurrection unto life, which only they shall obtain *who have done good,* walking in the commandments of God; not because they have done good, as if their goodness had merited any such thing, for eternal life is *the gift of God,* Rom. vi. 23. But others, who have wrought iniquity, and died without repentance and faith in me, shall arise, that the justice of God may by me, the Judge of the quick and the dead, be executed upon them unto eternal condemnation. This Daniel, chap. xii. 2, calleth *shame, and everlasting contempt.* Our Saviour, Matt. xxv. 46, calls it *everlasting punishment.*

30 ʸI can of mine own self do nothing: as I hear, I judge: and my judgment is just; because ᶻI seek not mine own will, but the will of the Father which hath sent me.

y ver. 19.

z Mat. 26. 39. ch. 4. 34. & 6. 38.

I can of mine own self do nothing; neither considered as God, nor as Mediator. As God, the Father and Christ were one, and what one Person in the Holy Trinity doth, all do; so that he did nothing in that capacity separately from his Father. As Mediator, he did nothing of himself; he finished the work which his Father gave him to do. *As I hear, I judge; and my judgment is just;* as the Father revealed his will to him, for the administration of his mediatory kingdom in the world, so he judged; and therefore his judgment must necessarily be just and true. *Because I seek not mine own will, but the will of the Father which hath sent me;* for his will was not a will proper to himself, so as it was not also common to his Father, but diverse from the will of his Father; but as his essence, so his will, was the same with his Father; and he being by the Father sent into the world to do his will, accordingly did nothing as Mediator but what was his Father's will as well as his own, in nothing diverse from his Father's.

^{a See ch. 8. 14. Rev. 3. 14.} 31 ^aIf I bear witness of myself, my witness is not true.

This seemeth to contradict what he saith, chap. viii. 14, *Though I bear record of myself, yet my record is true:* but our Saviour here speaketh according to the common opinion of the Jews, or indeed of men, who are ready to suspect any one's testimony who testifieth of himself. He tells them, he could grant them this, though his record of himself was true, yet he could allow them their common received opinion and saying, chap. viii. 13, that the testimony of one testifying of himself is suspicious; for it is certain that a man may testify truth of himself, only such a testimony is suspicious: he tells them, he did not only testify of himself, his reputation did not stand upon his own single word.

^{b Mat. 3. 17. & 17. 5. ch. 8. 18. 1 John 5. 6, 7, 9.} 32 ¶ ^bThere is another that beareth witness of me; and I know that the witness which he witnesseth of me is true.

The Father by a voice from heaven testified of Christ, that he was his well-beloved Son, in whom he was well pleased, Matt. iii. 17. Some understand it of John the Baptist, of whom he speaketh, ver. 33. But he naming John in the next verse, it seems most proper to understand this of the Father testifying of Christ, both at his baptism, and also at his transfiguration; and to interpret the next verse, as speaking of another testimony distinct from that of John. *And* (saith our Saviour) *I know,* that is, I am fully assured, that his testimony of me is true; for God is that God who cannot lie, but is truth itself. So that I do not barely testify of myself; for my Father, whom you all own to be a God of truth, and who cannot lie, and whom know to be such, he testifieth of me, and none can contradict his testimony.

^{c ch. 1. 15, 19, 27, 32.} 33 Ye sent unto John, ^cand he bare witness unto the truth.

Ye sent priests and Levites from Jerusalem to John, chap. i. 29; he was a man of reputation among you, for all the people judged him a prophet; and he had an interest in Herod's court: *he bare witness* (he doth not say to me, but) *to the truth.*

34 But I receive not testimony from man: but these things I say, that ye might be saved.

I receive not testimony from man, that is, not for my own sake; for otherwise he did receive testimony from man, chap. xv. 27; Acts i. 8. That must be truth, to which any one can give a true testimony. John by his testimony added nothing to me. I was what I am before John testified concerning me. I only spake of John's testimony for your sake, that you might believe, and be saved.

^{d 2 Pet. 1. 19. e See Matt. 13. 20. & 21. 26. Mark 6. 20.} 35 He was a burning and ^da shining light: and ^eye were willing for a season to rejoice in his light.

I do not speak this to lessen John in any of your thoughts; he was a famous light, burning in the knowledge and love of the truth; shining both in his doctrine, in publishing the truth, and also in holiness of life and conversation. *He was not that light,* John i. 8, but he was a light, not τὸ φῶς τὸ ἀληθινόν, but λυχνος, Matt. v. 14; Luke viii. 16. And you for a small time pretended a great affection for John, and came with great zeal to hear him, Matt. iii. 5; xxi. 26; Mark i. 5, hoping that he was the Messias, or at least Elias, or that prophet in him revived again. But when they saw that John did only bear record to Christ, they grew cold in their affection, not liking either his doctrine, or the strictness of his life, or the tidings that he brought; looking for a far more splendid and glorious Messiah than Christ appeared to them to be.

36 ¶ But ^fI have greater witness than ^{f 1 John 5. 9.} *that* of John: for ^gthe works which the ^{g ch. 3. 2. & 10. 25. & 15. 24.} Father hath given me to finish, the same works that I do, bear witness of me, that the Father hath sent me.

But I have greater witness than that of John; not than that of my Father, mentioned ver. 31, 32, but *than that of John,* last mentioned; nor doth he say a truer, but a *greater witness. The works which the Father hath given me to finish;* the works which his Father sent him to do, his fulfilling of the law, his publication of the gospel, the miracles which he wrought, were all of them works which his Father had given him to finish. Christ often appealeth to the works which he had done, as sufficiently testifying of him, chap. x. 25, 37, 38; xiv. 10, 11; xv. 24. And it is plain, that the people looked upon them as a great testimony, chap. iii. 2; ix. 32, 33. The Jews avoided the force of this testimony impudently, some of them saying that he did them by the help of the devil, Matt. xii. 24; others pretending (more lately) that the Messiah was to work no miracles; but that is expressly contrary to what we have, chap. vii. 31, and is doubtless a device of later years. But it is a greater question, how the miracles of Christ *bear witness* of him; and whether they were only a probable, or a certain and infallible, testimony of his Deity. Those that think them an infallible testimony, say, 1. That he did works which none else did, John xv. 24. 2. That he did them by his own power; *There went virtue out of him, and healed them all,* Luke vi. 19. 3. That they were done in confirmation of the doctrine to that purpose which he preached, which God would not have confirmed by miracles, had not he been sent of God to work such things. Those that think they were not a certain and infallible testimony, say, 1. That the prophets and apostles also wrought miracles. 2. That our Saviour tells his apostles, they should do greater works than he had done. 3. That the doing of them from his own power, was a thing could not be known to others; so could be no testimony to them. But our Saviour did not only himself raise the dead, cast out devils, and work other miracles; but he gave others also a power to do it; which argued an original power in himself, and is more than we read of any prophets or apostles; who, though they wrought such miraculous operations, yet having not that power originally in and from themselves, could not communicate it to others.

37 And the Father himself, which hath ^{h Matt. 3. 17. & 17. 5. ch. 6. 27. & 8. 18. i Deu. 4. 12. ch. 1. 18. 1 Tim. 1. 17. 1 John 4. 12.} sent me, ^hhath borne witness of me. Ye have neither heard his voice at any time, ⁱnor seen his shape.

Hath borne witness of me; not only in my baptism, and at my transfiguration, by an audible voice from heaven, but by the voice of his prophets, by whom he spoke to your fathers. *Ye have neither heard his voice at any time, nor seen his shape;* you have no knowledge of him, nor any acquaintance with him. It is expounded, ver. 38, *Ye have not his word abiding in you:* for though indeed God appeared to the Jews in no shape or similitude; yet they (that is, their forefathers) had heard his voice, Deut. iv. 12, *speaking out of the midst of the fire,* ver. 33. God, being an incorporeal Being, hath no such organs of speech as we have, by which we declare our minds unto others; but God had formed an audible voice, by which he revealed his will unto the Jews; so as it could only be said of the Jews of that generation and their forefathers, from the time of giving the law, that they had not heard his voice; for, Exod. xx. 19, they then desired that Moses might speak to them, and that God would speak no more immediately. Accordingly, he did by the prophets speak to them; but they would not believe them, no, not when he spake to them by his Son, who knew his will, Heb. i. 1, 3.

38 And ye have not his word abiding in you: for whom he hath sent, him ye believe not.

Though they had heard the word of the Lord, their forefathers by the prophets, and in that generation by John the Baptist, (the messenger sent before Christ's face,) and now by Christ himself, whom the Father had sent; yet the word of the Lord had no place in their hearts, chap. viii. 37; it was unto them as a tale told; they received the sound of it, but it was not graven in their hearts. And this appeared, because as of themselves they had no intimacy of communion with God to know his mind; so, when the Son was sent out of the bosom of the Father to reveal God unto them, yet they would not receive him, so as to give any steady, fixed assent to what he revealed, and to yield him any just and true obedience.

k Is. 8. 20.
& 34. 16.
Luke 16. 29.
ver. 46.
Acts 17. 11.
1 Deu. 18.15,
18. Luke 24. 27. ch. 1. 45.

39 ¶ ᵏSearch the Scriptures; for in them ye think ye have eternal life: and ¹they are they which testify of me.

Search the Scriptures; the words may be read either imperatively (as our translation readeth them) or indicatively, You do search the Scriptures; that is, of the Old Testament, for the books of the New Testament were not at that time written; but as they had the books of the Old Testament, so they made use of them: Moses was read in the synagogues every sabbath day; and they (the Pharisees especially) were very well versed both in the law and the prophets. *For in them ye think ye have eternal life*; they did agree that the way of salvation and everlasting life was revealed unto them in the Holy Scriptures; nay, they did judge, that eternal life was to be obtained by their observation of the law. *They are they which testify of me:* they (saith our Saviour) are my principal testimony; he doth not only say, they testify, but *they are they which testify*. No writings but those testify of me; I principally appeal to them to give you an account of me.

m ch. 1. 11.
& 3. 19.

40 ᵐAnd ye will not come to me, that ye might have life.

You will not own, embrace, and receive me as the true Messiah and Saviour of the world, though that be the only means by which you can obtain that eternal life which you pretend to be seeking after, and rightly think that the Scripture alone can show you the way to. These two verses teach us, 1. That the Holy Scriptures are the only writings which show us the way to life eternal. 2. That not only the Scriptures of the New, but also of the Old Testament, are of use in order thereunto, though the Old Testament Scriptures show us it more darkly, and those of the New Testament show it to us more clearly. 3. That both the one and the other point us to Christ, and to the receiving and embracing of him, as our Saviour, if we would have life. 4. That it is not sufficient for us to search the Scriptures, to be versed in and acquainted with them, unless we, in obedience to them, come to Christ.

n ver. 34.
1 Thes. 2. 6.

41 ⁿI receive not honour from men.

I depend not upon the single testimony of men; or, I seek not, nor hunt after, the honour of men, nor regard what they think or say of me.

42 But I know you, that ye have not the love of God in you.

You pretend a great deal of religion, and to do many things out of love to God, and a zeal for the glory of God; but though you can cheat others, yet you cannot deceive me: I, that search the heart, and try the reins, and am a witness to your actions, know that, whatsoever you pretend, the true love of God dwelleth not in you; and that is the reason why you do not receive me.

43 I am come in my Father's name, and ye receive me not: if another shall come in his own name, him ye will receive.

I am come clothed with an authority from my Father, sent by him for this very purpose, to reveal his will to men for their salvation; I speak, I do nothing but by the authority of my Father which sent me; nor do I aim at my own glory, but the glory of him that sent me: yet you give no credit to my words, nor embrace me, as him whom God hath sent for the Saviour of man. *If another shall come in his own name, him ye will receive;* through the corruption of your hearts, and the just judgment of God, giving you up to strong delusions to believe lies, 2 Thes. ii. 11. If any seducers come, without any authority from God, never sent of him, nor speaking his words, nor seeking his glory, or your good, you will readily enough receive them.

44 °How can ye believe, which receive honour one of another, and seek not ᵖthe honour that *cometh* from God only?

o ch. 12. 43.
p Rom. 2.29.

It is evident that by receiving *honour from one another*, is here to be understood the seeking and pursuing of honour and applause from men, without regard to the praise of God: so also chap. xii. 43. For otherwise it is lawful for parents to receive honour from children, masters from servants, princes and other magistrates from people. But for men to be ambitious of honour and applause from men, in neglect of the honour and praise of God, this is highly sinful; and it cannot be expected that any such persons should so far deny themselves, and renounce their own works of righteousness, as to accept of Christ and his righteousness, and rely upon him alone for life and salvation. It is said, John xii. 42, that *among the chief rulers many believed;* yet it is added, ver. 43, *For they loved the praise of men more than the praise of God*. But these words, ver. 43, seem rather to refer to the Pharisees, mentioned in the latter part of ver. 42, where a reason is given why, though many great rulers believed, yet they did not confess Christ, because of the Pharisees. Or if those words, ver. 43, be to be applied to those of whom it is said, they believed, ver. 42, we must distinguish concerning believing, which in chap. xii. 42 signifieth no more than an assent given to him as a great prophet, upon the miracles they saw wrought by him; in this place, a true and lively faith, receiving Christ as our Mediator and Saviour.

45 Do not think that I will accuse you to the Father: ᑫthere is *one* that accuseth you, *even* Moses, in whom ye trust.

q Rom. 2.12.

There will be no need of my accusing you, you will need no other accuser than that Moses for whom you have so great a reverence, and for whose sake you contemn me. Chap. ix. 28, 29, they said, *We are Moses's disciples. We know that God spake unto Moses: as for this fellow, we know not from whence he is*. This Moses (saith our Saviour) will accuse you unto the Father.

46 For had ye believed Moses, ye would have believed me: ʳfor he wrote of me.

r Gen. 3. 15.
& 12. 3. & 18.
18. & 22. 18.
& 49. 10.
Deut. 18. 15, 18. ch. 1. 45. Acts 26. 22.

Had you given a hearty credit and understanding assent to Moses, that is, to the writings of Moses, for so the term is oft taken, Luke xvi. 31; xxiv. 27, you would have received me: as all the law of Moses pointed to and prefigured me, so he in particular wrote of me, Gen. iii. 15; Deut. xviii. 15.

47 But if ye believe not his writings, how shall ye believe my words?

But if you believe not his writings, who so plainly wrote of me, and whose writings you own, and have so great a veneration for, how can I expect that you should believe the words of one whom you so vilify and contemn? For though my words be in themselves of greater authority, yet I have not so much credit with you as Moses had. But how doth our Saviour affirm, ver. 45, that they trusted in Moses, and deny here that they did believe him? *Answ.* Some say, they believed with an implicit faith, presuming upon the merits of Abraham, Isaac, Jacob; but not with an explicit faith. Others say, they believed in the general, that whatsoever he wrote was true; but they did not believe them in the true sense of them. Tarnovius thinks, that they trusted in Moses, that they might be saved by their own works done in obedience to his law; but they did not believe him, because they rejected him of whom Moses wrote, and to whom the law of Moses was but a schoolmaster. They refused him who was *the Head of the corner*, Psal. cxviii. 22; Matt. xxi. 42.

CHAP. VI

Christ feedeth five thousand men with five loaves and two fishes, 1—14. *He withdraweth himself from the people, who would have made him a king, and walketh on the sea,*

15—21. *The multitude flocking to him, he reproveth their carnal views, and requireth their faith in him whom God hath sent,* 22—29. *They ask a sign like that of the manna in the wilderness; he declareth himself to be the bread of life from heaven, and that none can live but by eating his flesh and drinking his blood,* 30—59. *Many of his disciples taking offence thereat, he showeth his meaning to be spiritual,* 60—65. *Many leaving him, Peter in the name of the twelve professeth stedfast faith in him: Jesus pronounceth one of them to be a devil,* 66—71.

A. D. 32.
a Mat. 14.15.
Mark 6. 35.
Luke 9. 10, 12.

AFTER ᵃthese things Jesus went over the sea of Galilee, which is *the sea* of Tiberias.

Some good time (some think near a year) after the passages in the former chapter Christ went over the lake of Galilee (for the Jews called all great collections of waters seas); it is also called the lake of Tiberias, and the lake of Gennesaret, Luke v. 1. These waters received their name from the whole province whose coast they washed, so they were called *the sea of Galilee*; or the particular shore or cities they washed, so they are sometimes called *the sea of Tiberias*, sometimes *the lake of Gennesaret*. It appeareth by Mark vi. 31, that he went upon the apostles coming to give him an account of what they had done and taught.

2 And a great multitude followed him, because they saw his miracles which he did on them that were diseased.

Our Saviour (as appeareth by Mark vi. 31) only spake to his apostles to withdraw into a desert place, and to rest a while; but, ver. 33, though our Saviour went by ship, yet the people *ran afoot thither out of all cities, and outwent them, and came together unto him*. That which induced them was their knowledge of the miracles which he had wrought.

3 And Jesus went up into a mountain, and there he sat with his disciples.

b Lev. 23. 5, 7. Deut. 16. 1. ch. 2. 13. & 5. 1.

4 ᵇAnd the Passover, a feast of the Jews, was nigh.

That is, the third passover after our Saviour had entered upon his public ministry; by which we may observe, that John omitted many things spoken and done by our Saviour in the year immediately following the second passover, for he giveth us no further account than what we have in the former chapter, and in this. The other evangelists give us a more full account of them. The place whither our Saviour went seemeth to have been toward the end of the lake, so as the people could go on foot, and turn at the point of the lake, and be there before the ship could cross the water.

c Mat. 14.14.
Mark 6. 35.
Luke 9. 12.

5 ¶ ᶜWhen Jesus then lifted up *his* eyes, and saw a great company come unto him, he saith unto Philip, Whence shall we buy bread, that these may eat?

This is apparently the same history which we have met with in all the former three evangelists, Matt. xiv. 15—21; Mark vi. 35—44; Luke ix. 10—17. See the differing circumstances considered in our annotations on those chapters. The other evangelists observe, that Christ had first been preaching to them, until it was near night; and then bring in the disciples first moving him (because they had eaten nothing) to send them away to provide themselves food. This evangelist begins with some words Christ should speak to Philip.

6 And this he said to prove him: for he himself knew what he would do.

Now this he said to try what Philip would say, for he was himself resolved what to do.

d See Numb. 11. 21, 22.

7 Philip answered him, ᵈTwo hundred pennyworth of bread is not sufficient for them, that every one of them may take a little.

This discourse between our Saviour and Philip is reported by none of the other evangelists, and probably was after that which they report of the other disciples' motion to Christ to dismiss the people, because it was now towards evening. The number (as we shall find afterward) was five thousand, besides women and children; amongst whom five hundred pennyworth of bread was very little to be divided.

8 One of his disciples, Andrew, Simon Peter's brother, saith unto him,

9 There is a lad here, which hath five barley loaves, and two small fishes: ᵉbut what are they among so many?

e 2 Kings 4. 43.

10 And Jesus said, Make the men sit down. Now there was much grass in the place. So the men sat down, in number about five thousand.

11 And Jesus took the loaves; and when he had given thanks, he distributed to the disciples, and the disciples to them that were set down; and likewise of the fishes as much as they would.

12 When they were filled, he said unto his disciples, Gather up the fragments that remain, that nothing be lost.

13 Therefore they gathered *them* together, and filled twelve baskets with the fragments of the five barley loaves, which remained over and above unto them that had eaten.

The story is the same, in all substantial parts, with the relations of Matthew, Mark, and Luke, in the before-mentioned places. See the annotations on those chapters.

14 Then those men, when they had seen the miracle that Jesus did, said, This is of a truth ᶠthat prophet that should come into the world.

f Gen. 49. 10.
Deut. 18. 15, 18. Matt. 11. 3. ch. 1. 21.
& 4. 19, 25.
& 7. 40

When they had seen the miracle of Christ's multiplying five loaves and two fishes, to the feeding of five thousand persons, besides women and children; a miracle of that nature, that never any such was wrought either by Moses or any prophet, and to the working of which a creating power was necessary; this brought them to a strong persuasion that this was the Messias; for he is signified by that phrase, *that prophet that should come into the world*, as appeareth from Luke vii. 19.

15 ¶ When Jesus therefore perceived that they would come and take him by force, to make him a king, he departed again into a mountain himself alone.

This motion of Christ into a mountain alone, after he had sent away the multitude, (thus miraculously fed,) and after that his disciples had taken ship again, is mentioned by two other of the evangelists; by Matthew, chap. xiv. 23; by Mark, chap. vi. 45, 46. But this occasion of it is expressed by neither of them; who both say, that he went thither *to pray*. And indeed John (who rarely mentioneth any thing set down by the others) is judged to have recorded this history, as for the excellent discourse of our Saviour's following this miracle; so for some particular circumstances in and about the miracle, not mentioned by the other evangelists; of which, as the discourse he had with Philip was one, so this about their going about to make him a king was another. The Jews were a people exceedingly jealous of and zealous for their liberties, the Galileans especially, amongst whom our Saviour was at that time; so as they never wanted any thing but a leader for a sedition or rebellion. The Scriptures mention two, Acts v. 36, 37, under the conduct of one Theudas, and Judas of Galilee. Ecclesiastical history mentioneth more. Their error as to the Messias (whom they dreamed of as a temporal prince) gave them a colour for these insurrections, whenever they could get any to take upon him that pretence. These men seeing these great miracles wrought by Christ, particularly that of the loaves multiplied to feed five thousand, thought Christ had been such a Messias as they expected; not understanding that the kingdom of the true Messias was not to be of this world, chap. xviii. 36, but within men here, and more evident in the day of judgment, Matt. xxv. 34. But our Saviour, who never came into the world to disturb the civil order and government in it, constantly avoided the giving the least occasion for such a suspicion: when he therefore knew, either by his insight into the hearts of men, or by hearing their discourses, that they had such seditious thoughts, he withdrew himself into a mountain. How he withdrew himself, so as they did not follow him, no, not his disciples, is a matter which hath exercised the thoughts of many. The papists say, that he had a power, by virtue of the personal union of the Divine and human nature in his person, to make his body invisible, and so passed from them, not discerned by them. The Lutherans are not so confident in this, yet seem to incline it might be thus. Indeed both of them are concerned to maintain the possibility of such a thing; for without such a possibility, neither can the papists maintain their doctrine of transubstantiation, where they hold, that the bread in the sacrament of the Lord's supper is turned into the very body of Christ, and the wine into his blood (though no such thing be obvious to our senses); nor the Lutherans their doctrine of consubstantiation, who hold, that the very body and blood of Christ is really present in, with, or under the elements, though the elements be not changed into it. But the Greek words are no more than ἀνεχώρησεν πάλιν, which signify no more than that he again changed his place, which he might easily do through a multitude in a disorder, without their notice of him; and if his disciples did see him, it is not probable that they, knowing his aversion to any seditious practices, as also his custom to withdraw to places of privacy for devotion, would take any notice at all of him.

g Mat. 14. 23. Mark 6. 47.
16 ᵍAnd when even was *now* come, his disciples went down unto the sea,

This piece of history is related much more fully by the other evangelists, Matt. xiv. 23—33; Mark vi. 46—52. See the notes upon those two chapters.

17 And entered into a ship, and went over the sea toward Capernaum. And it was now dark, and Jesus was not come to them.

18 And the sea arose by reason of a great wind that blew.

19 So when they had rowed about five and twenty or thirty furlongs, they see Jesus walking on the sea, and drawing nigh unto the ship: and they were afraid.

20 But he saith unto them, It is I; be not afraid.

21 Then they willingly received him into the ship: and immediately the ship was at the land whither they went.

22 ¶ The day following, when the people which stood on the other side of the sea saw that there was none other boat there, save that one whereinto his disciples were entered, and that Jesus went not with his disciples into the boat, but *that* his disciples were gone away alone;

By *the sea* is here meant the sea of Galilee, or lake of Tiberias, or of Gennesaret. There our Saviour and his disciples had left the multitude; the disciples having taken a boat, and passing over on the other side, and Christ having followed them, the multitude, probably having gone in the night to rest themselves at their several houses, came again in the morning, expecting to have found Christ, and have seen more miracles; being disappointed, understanding that both Christ and his disciples were gone over,

23 (Howbeit there came other boats from Tiberias nigh unto the place where they did eat bread, after that the Lord had given thanks:)

24 When the people therefore saw that Jesus was not there, neither his disciples, they also took shipping, and came to Capernaum, seeking for Jesus.

They also took shipping, made use of some other boats that were come over the water, and went over to seek Jesus; not out of any love to his person or doctrine, (as we shall anon hear,) but out of a curiosity to see some further miracles wrought by him. Our Lord disappoints them, but preacheth a most admirable sermon to them.

25 And when they had found him on the other side of the sea, they said unto him, Rabbi, when camest thou hither?

26 Jesus answered them and said, Verily, verily, I say unto you, Ye seek me, not because ye saw the miracles, but because ye did eat of the loaves, and were filled.

They asked him, *When camest thou hither?* A curious and impertinent question, to which he doth not think fit to give an apposite answer, but at first letteth them know, that he knew their hearts, and what designs they had in following him; which was not to see the miraculous effects of the Divine power, the credentials of his commission from heaven, and to receive him as the true Messiah, and believe his doctrine; but they came upon so low an account as to be fed by him.

27 ‖ Labour not for the meat which perisheth, but ʰfor that meat which endureth unto everlasting life, which the Son of man shall give unto you: ⁱfor him hath God the Father sealed.

‖ Or, *Work not.*
h ver. 54. ch. 4. 14.
i Matt. 3. 17. & 17. 5. Mark 1. 11. & 9. 7. Luke 3. 22. & 9. 35. ch. 1. 33. & 5. 37. & 8. 18. Acts 2. 22. 2 Pet. 1. 17.

By the bread *which perisheth*, is not strictly to be understood bread, but whatsoever is necessary or accommodating to us in this life; all things of this nature are perishing, and perish with the using: nor is all labour as to them forbidden us; for we are to the contrary commanded, In the sweat of our face to eat our bread; and the apostle commandeth, that those that will not labour should not eat; and, Prov. xxxi. 27, the good woman is commended for not eating *the bread of idleness:* but excessive labour for these things is forbidden. So also is a first and greater labour for and seeking after them, than after *that meat which endureth to everlasting life;* under which notion also unquestionably cometh whatsoever is necessary by God's revealed will, that we may have in us the hopes of glory here, and may enter into the actual possession of that glory hereafter. Such as are, first, the knowledge of the gospel; then the believing of it, and the acceptance of that Saviour, and way of salvation, which God hath revealed in it for lost sinners; and that holiness of life which God hath made necessary to it. All which (saith he) I, who am the Son of man, (a name he ordinarily giveth to himself,) will give unto you freely. Not that you are to do nothing; no, labour for it; though it be a gift, yet it is a gift upon labour, for all your labour will not procure it; there will be a great deal of free grace seen when you have given all diligence. And Christ must give it; for the Father, in whose hand this life is, hath (as men by their seals use to confirm the commissions they give out to any persons to do any thing for them, and in their name) confirmed Christ as his commissioner, to give out this eternal life to whomsoever he pleaseth.

28 Then said they unto him, What shall we do, that we might work the works of God?

They easily understood that our Saviour did not speak of any worldly food, by his opposing the labour he mentioneth, and persuadeth for, to a labour for the world; but still they did not understand what labour he spake of, but dreamed of the works of the law; knowing of no other work which God commanded, but which was prescribed in the law; and they (probably) being some, or many of them, strict observers, especially of the law contained in ordinances, and probably many of them of the moral law also, according to the sense of it given by their teachers; in which sense the young man, Matt. xix. 20, being bid by our Saviour to keep the law, and naming most of the precepts of the second table, told him, All these things have I kept from my youth: what lack I yet? They wondered what works our Saviour meant; what labour, when he said, *Labour for that* bread, or that *meat which endureth to everlasting life;* thinking that those who kept the law (in the sense before expressed) had no more to do.

29 Jesus answered and said unto them, ᵏThis is the work of God, that ye believe on him whom he hath sent.

k 1 John 3. 23.

Our Lord calleth them to a work they never thought of,

the owning and acknowledgment of him to be the true Messiah; the embracing and receiving him as such, and trusting him with all the concerns of their souls; which was necessary, notwithstanding all their acts of obedience to the law, though most certainly productive also of that obedience, and inseparable from it. This our Saviour calleth *the work of God*, in answer to what they had said about working the works of God. Yet this will not prove that we are justified by works, because we are justified by faith; for here is no discourse concerning the causation of faith in the justification of a soul, but only concerning what is the will of God, as to all those that shall be saved.

30 They said therefore unto him, ¹What sign shewest thou then, that we may see, and believe thee? what dost thou work?

¹ Matt. 12. 38. & 16. 1. Mark 8. 11. 1 Cor. 1. 22.

They thought it reasonable, that he who brought forth a new doctrine into the world (such as faith in him was, they having never heard any such thing from their doctors the Pharisees) should confirm his mission by some miraculous operation. But this was a strange stupidity, considering the sign he had so lately showed them, of feeding five thousand with five loaves and two fishes. So it was manifest they sought for a sign, not to promote or confirm their faith, but merely to feed their curiosity; and what our Saviour said, Matt. xii. 39, *An evil and adulterous generation seeketh after a sign*, was truly applicable to them; and those words, *believe thee*, eminently confirm it; for the aforesaid miracle speaking in him a creative power, and being such as was never wrought by any creature, they were obliged to believe him, without any further sign. God ought to be believed upon his bare word.

m Ex. 16.15. Num. 11. 7. Neh. 9. 15. Wisd. 16.20. 1 Cor. 10. 3. n Ps. 78. 24, 25.

31 ᵐOur fathers did eat manna in the desert; as it is written, ⁿHe gave them bread from heaven to eat.

Here they magnify Moses; he did not bring them a law only, but confirmed it by signs from heaven to be the will of God, by obtaining for them bread to be rained from heaven to satisfy their hunger, Exod. xvi. 15; Numb. xi. 7; which is also confirmed by the psalmist, Psal. lxxviii. 25. This Moses did for the whole congregation of Israel forty years together. From hence they would seem to conclude, that they had more ground to believe Moses than Christ, who, though he had indeed lately fed five thousand with five loaves, yet had done no such thing. Not considering that Moses, in what he did, was but an instrument to obtain of God by prayer such a miracle, for supporting his people in the wilderness; and that what he had done, was done by a creating power inherent in himself, by which he multiplied that little proportion of bread which they had, to make it sufficient to feed such a quantity as five thousand, besides women and children; to which effect it bare no proportion.

32 Then Jesus said unto them, Verily, verily, I say unto you, Moses gave you not that bread from heaven; but my Father giveth you the true bread from heaven.

You are mistaken in your opinion of that manna, which indeed was bread from heaven, *spiritual meat*, (as the apostle calleth it, 1 Cor. x. 3,) but it was not given you by any power or virtue in or from Moses. Moses said otherwise; when it was first rained down, he told them, *This is the bread which the Lord hath given you to eat*, Exod. xvi. 15. It was the Lord, not Moses, that gave you that bread. Nor was that true spiritual bread; it was only spiritual (as the apostle calleth it) because it was typical, and prefigurative of me. *My Father giveth you the true bread from heaven;* it was he that gave your fathers manna, not Moses; and it is he who giveth you me, who am the true bread, of which that bread was but typical, a shadow, and a figure.

33 For the bread of God is he which cometh down from heaven, and giveth life unto the world.

Moses gave you spiritual, heavenly bread; but that was only spiritual as it was typical and prefigured me; heavenly, as it came from the lower heavens, was rained down from thence, not made upon the earth by the art of man; and was therefore called *the bread of angels;* but I am the true *bread of God*, signified by that type, who came not down from the lower, but from the highest heavens; and who do not only maintain and uphold life in men, (as that did,) but give life to men; and that not a mere natural life, but a spiritual and eternal life; and that not to the Jews only, for whose use alone manna was, but to the world.

34 °Then said they unto him, Lord, evermore give us this bread.

o See ch. 4. 15.

Most interpreters agree that they spake this seriously, that is, that they were willing enough to have such bread (if any such were to be had); but yet not conceiving aright the nature and excellency of the bread our Saviour mentioned; and this occasioned his clear explication of it in the following verse.

35 And Jesus said unto them, ᵖI am the bread of life: ᑫhe that cometh to me shall never hunger; and he that believeth on me shall never thirst.

p ver. 48, 58. q ch. 4. 14. & 7. 37.

I am the bread of life; the bread that giveth spiritual and eternal life, and the bread that upholdeth and maintaineth spiritual life; the Messiah, whom God hath sent into the world, to quicken those that are *dead in trespasses and sins*, Eph. ii. 1; and to give eternal life to as many as the Father hath given me. But those that have this life, must come unto me; which he interprets in the next phrase by believing in him. Thus he taketh them off all gross and carnal conceptions of eating and drinking in a carnal manner; and minds them to think of getting and maintaining another kind of life than they dreamed of. By believing in him, we have formerly showed is to be understood a receiving of him as the Mediator and Saviour of men, and closing with him, and committing their souls in all their spiritual concerns unto him; and he that doth so (saith he) shall never hunger nor thirst; that is, shall never want any thing necessary for him for life and eternal happiness. And for things of this life, he shall have food convenient for him; he shall *be fed*, Psal. xxxvii. 3. See such a promise, Isa. xlix. 10.

36 ʳBut I said unto you, That ye also have seen me, and believe not.

r ver. 26, 64.

You have seen me in the flesh, you have heard my doctrine, you have seen the miracles which I have wrought, confirming that doctrine, and me to be the true Messias; for I have done amongst you those works which never any man did: but you are of the generation of those of whom it was prophesied, That in seeing you should not see, nor yet perceive; for though you have seen me with your bodily eyes, and could not but conclude by what works I have done that I am the true Messiah; yet you do not own and acknowledge me as such, nor will by faith close with me, and come unto me for life and happiness.

37 ˢAll that the Father giveth me shall come to me; and ᵗhim that cometh to me I will in no wise cast out.

s ver. 45. t Mat. 24. 24. ch. 10. 28, 29. 2 Tim. 2. 19. 1 John 2. 19.

Here ariseth a great question amongst interpreters of various persuasions, what giving of the Father is here meant; whether an eternal designation of persons to eternal life, in order to the obtaining of which the persons so predestinated are given to Christ, as he who was to be the Messiah, Saviour, and Redeemer of the world; or the infusing the habits of special, saving grace, by which persons are enabled actually to believe. If the former, the words do not only infer an infallible connexion betwixt faith and eternal life and salvation; but also betwixt the decree of election and the collation of special grace, by which men are enabled to believe, and, believing, are saved. That which seemeth to favour the latter opinion is, that the verb is in the present tense; it is not, all that the Father hath given, but *all that the Father giveth;* which would incline us to think, that though in other texts the Father's giving of souls to Christ may signify his eternal election, yet in this text it rather signifieth the donation or giving the habits of special grace. But there are very learned and pious interpreters of another mind, who think by the Father's giving, is meant the Father's choosing souls in him, Eph. i. 4. Certain it is, that there are some chosen to life, and the certain means by which that life is to be obtained, Eph. i. 4, 5. And as certain it is, that persons so chosen in him, shall neither miss of that life, nor yet of that effectual means by which it shall be obtained. Whether that eternal election, or donation, be here intended or no, is not so momentous to determine. For the Jesuits' argument, that if we understand it of such an eternal gift, our Saviour rather excuseth than accuseth them for their unbelief, by telling them they could not believe, because they were not given unto him; it holdeth as strong against special grace as against particular election; so as if that were true, it could be interpreted in neither of those senses: but by their leaves it doth not at all excuse them, unless they did what in them lay to come to Christ: but this question belongs rather to polemical writers than interpreters. Certain it is, that it is such a giving here mentioned, as shall be followed by a coming to Christ; that is, believing in him, and by a true faith receiving of him. And those that do so, our Lord saith, he *will in no wise cast out*. Out of heaven, say some; others understand it of perseverance; but certainly the phrase denoteth no more than the freeness and readiness of Christ to receive every one who truly believeth in him, and to preserve him to eternal life and salvation. Who they are that are given to Christ, and that will or shall believe in him, is a secret that is known unto God alone: but this may be known to all, that Christ will not throw off any soul that is willing to receive him as its Saviour, and that no such soul shall perish for ever.

38 For I came down from heaven, ^unot to do mine own will, ^xbut the will of him that sent me.

^{u Mat. 26.39.}
^{ch. 5. 30.}
^{x ch. 4. 34.}

Our Lord confirmeth what he had before said concerning his gracious reception of believers, and preserving them by his grace in their state of grace, so that they shall not be cast out with reprobates in the day of judgment, from this, that he came not to execute any particular will of his own, but what was also the will of his Father, who sent him into the world.

39 And this is the Father's will which hath sent me, ^ythat of all which he hath given me I should lose nothing, but should raise it up again at the last day.

^{y ch. 10. 28.}
^{& 17. 12.}
^{& 18. 9.}

For this he revealeth to be his Father's will, that of all his Father had given him, he should lose none; where by the Father's giving must be meant, either his eternal act (having chosen some to eternal life) in giving them to his Son, for the work of their redemption; or, which is but the effect and product of that, the working, preserving, and upholding in them those habits and exercises of grace, by which that eternal life is to be obtained. Our Lord declareth it to be the will of his Father, that he should not suffer any of these to miscarry; but though their bodies die and turn into dust, yet Christ at the last day should come to raise the dead, and, in particular, raise them up: not that they only shall rise, (for how then shall all appear before the judgment-seat of God, to receive according to what they have done in the flesh?) but they are those alone who shall receive any benefit by the resurrection; and therefore they are called the children of the resurrection; and the resurrection is sometimes spoken of in Scripture as if it were to be peculiar to them, Phil. iii. 11. By this the certainty of the resurrection is established; it being asserted as the effect of the will of God, which none hath resisted at any time.

40 And this is the will of him that sent me, ^zthat every one which seeth the Son, and believeth on him, may have everlasting life: and I will raise him up at the last day.

^{z ver. 27, 47,}
^{54. ch. 3. 15,}
^{16. & 4. 14.}

Our Lord having asserted the will of God, as to the final issue and happiness of believers, goes on to assert the means by which, in this life using, they must obtain this life: those are, seeing the Son, and believing in him; seeing him, not with the eyes of their bodies, or seeing his miraculous operations, both which these Capernaites did, and yet did not believe, (as he told them, ver. 36,) but a seeing them with the eye of their minds, discerning him as the Messiah, and Saviour of the world; so seeing him, as to believe on him. As to these, he confirmeth it again to be the will of his Father, that they should live eternally, and that they should be raised again at the last day; and that by him, whom God had ordained to be the Judge both of the quick and the dead, Acts x. 42, which agreeth with what he had before said, chap. v. 28.

41 The Jews then murmured at him, because he said, I am the bread which came down from heaven.

The Jews were exceedingly prone to this sin of murmuring, which is a complaining either through indignation, or impatience of what men hear spoken, or see done: the thing which offended, seemeth not to be his calling himself the true bread, and the bread of life; but because he said, that he came down from heaven.

42 And they said, ^aIs not this Jesus, the son of Joseph, whose father and mother we know? how is it then that he saith, I came down from heaven?

^{a Mat. 13.55.}
^{Mark 6. 3.}
^{Luke 4. 22.}

For Capernaum, where our Saviour now was, was not far from Nazareth, where he had been educated, and lived near thirty years with Joseph his reputed father. Understanding therefore nothing of our Saviour's miraculous conception by the overshadowing of the Holy Ghost in the womb of the virgin, they were much offended at his discourse of his coming down from heaven.

43 Jesus therefore answered and said unto them, Murmur not among yourselves.

By this our Saviour gives them another proof of his Divine nature, viz. in his knowing of their hearts and thoughts; for though they were inwardly angry, and in a rage, yet we read not of any words spoken by them; but our Saviour needed not their words to tell him what was in the secret of their hearts. Our Saviour bids them not murmur at this, for he had much more than this to tell them, as followeth.

44 ^bNo man can come to me, except the Father which hath sent me draw him: and I will raise him up at the last day.

^{b Cant. 1. 4.}
^{ver. 65.}

That by drawing here is not to be understood any co-action, or force upon the will, is a thing on all hands out of question; but whether by it be only to be understood a rational drawing by arguments, (used in the ministry of the gospel,) or a further powerful influence upon the soul, inclining it to be willing and obedient, that is the question. The patrons of a power in man's will to do what is spiritually good and necessary in order to eternal life and salvation, understand it of the former only (of which the compelling, mentioned Luke xiv. 23, is to be understood, for the ministers of the gospel have no other power to compel); but in regard the drawing here mentioned is the act not of the servants, but of the Master; not of the ministers, but of the Father; it is more reasonably concluded that it here signifies a Divine power put forth upon the soul of man, by which it is made obedient to the heavenly call, and willing to close with the offer of Christ in the gospel; for though no such thing can necessarily be concluded from the word *draw*, yet it is easily concluded from the nature of the motion, in coming to Christ, which is the soul's motion to a sublime, spiritual object, to which no soul hath any power of itself; such is the darkness of the human mind, the obstinacy of the will, the depravation of the affections, unless it be illuminated and drawn by the Spirit of God. No soul is able of itself to discern spiritual things, so as to see that goodness and excellency that is in them, much less to move towards the participation of them.

45 ^cIt is written in the prophets, And they shall be all taught of God. ^dEvery man therefore that hath heard, and hath learned of the Father, cometh unto me.

^{c Is. 54. 13.}
^{Jer. 31. 34.}
^{Mic. 4. 2.}
^{Heb. 8. 10.}
^{& 10. 16.}
^{d ver. 37.}

It is written in the prophets; either in Isa. liv. 13, or in the book of the prophets; for though the words be to be found only in Isaiah, yet words of the same import are also to be found in Jeremiah, Ezekiel, Joel, and Micah. All they whom the Lord hath chosen shall be taught of God. Therefore (saith he) said I to you, *Every man that hath learned of the Father, cometh unto me.* Our Saviour proveth the doctrine which he had delivered to them, from the prophets, not because their authority was greater than his, or in any degree equal with his; but because the prophets

S. JOHN VI

and their writings were in greater authority and reputation with them.

^{e ch. 1. 18.}
^{& 5. 37.}
^{f Mat. 11. 27.}
^{Luke 10. 22.}
^{ch. 1. 18. & 7. 29. & 8. 19.}

46 ^eNot that any man hath seen the Father, ^fsave he which is of God, he hath seen the Father.

None must dream that the Father should visibly appear in the world to teach men; for the essence of God is invisible, none hath seen it at any time, saving he alone who is the only begotten Son of the Father; he hath seen the essence of the Father, he knoweth his will, and most secret counsels.

^{g ch. 3. 16, 18, 36.}
^{ver. 40.}

47 Verily, verily, I say unto you, ^gHe that believeth on me hath everlasting life.

^{h ver. 33, 35.}

48 ^hI am that bread of life.

See the notes on chap. iii. 18, and 36, and in this chapter, ver. 35.

^{i ver. 31.}

49 ⁱYour fathers did eat manna in the wilderness, and are dead.

Your fathers by nature, or in respect of unbelief, *did eat manna in the wilderness, and* they *are* naturally *dead;* (manna would not always preserve their natural life;) and those of them who were unbelievers, are also dead eternally; their eating of manna, which was a type of me, without believing in me, would not save them.

^{k ver. 51, 58.}

50 ^kThis is the bread which cometh down from heaven, that a man may eat thereof, and not die.

But I am that bread of life, who came out of the highest heavens, from the bosom of my Father; that bread, which if a man eateth thereof, he shall never die eternally. Eating Christ in this text signifieth no more than believing in him, so often before mentioned under the notion of coming to him, believing in him, &c. And believing is fitly expressed by this notion of eating; because as eating is the application of meat to our stomachs, for the sustenance of our bodily life; so believing is the application of Christ to the soul, for the beginning and increase of spiritual life, and at last obtaining life eternal.

^{l ch. 3. 13.}

51 I am the living bread ^lwhich came down from heaven: if any man eat of this bread, he shall live for ever: and

^{m Heb. 10. 5, 10.}

^mthe bread that I will give is my flesh, which I will give for the life of the world.

I am the living bread which came down from heaven: see the notes on ver. 33, and 35. Our Saviour's so often inculcating this, and what follows, lets us see both how necessary this is to be known, and also how difficult the work of believing is. Those words, *he shall live for ever*, expound those that went before in the 50th verse, *that a man may eat thereof, and not die.* His saying that the bread which he giveth is his flesh, expounds what he said before, viz. how he is the bread of life, viz. by giving his flesh, that is, his life, for the life of the world, that many might be saved; hereby showing us, that the object of our faith is a Christ crucified, 1 Cor. ii. 2.

^{n ch. 7. 43.}
^{& 9. 16.}
^{& 10. 19.}
^{o ch. 3. 9.}

52 The Jews therefore ⁿstrove among themselves, saying, ^oHow can this man give us *his* flesh to eat?

They will still understand spiritual things in a carnal sense; yet it is hard to conceive how they could imagine that Christ spake of giving them his flesh to eat, as men eat the flesh of oxen or sheep; but which way soever they did understand it indeed, their captious temper inclined them to conceal any other sense they had of it, and to represent what our Saviour said as exceedingly absurd.

^{p Matt. 26. 26, 28.}

53 Then Jesus said unto them, Verily, verily, I say unto you, Except ^pye eat the flesh of the Son of man, and drink his blood, ye have no life in you.

The short and true sense of these words is, that without a true believing in the Lord Jesus Christ, as he who died for our sins, no man hath any thing in him of true spiritual life, nor shall ever come to eternal life. Here are two questions arise from this verse and what follows. 1. Whether the flesh of Christ, that is, his human nature, giveth life, or all our life floweth from the Divine nature? That is a question betwixt the Lutherans and the Calvinists; the former affirming, that there is a quickening virtue in the human nature of Christ by virtue of its personal union with the Divine nature. It is a curious question, serving to no great edification; those who have a mind to be satisfied in it, and to read what is said on either side, may read Tarnovius on this text, and Zanchy, in his book De Incarnatione, p. 540. 2. The other is a question betwixt the papists and us, Whether this and the following verses spake any thing about the eating of the flesh and drinking the blood of Christ in the sacrament. All protestants deny it, both Lutherans and Calvinists. The papists most absurdly affirm it, to maintain their most absurd doctrine of transubstantiation. The vanity of their assertion, as to this text, appears, 1. Because it was a year and upwards after this before the sacrament of the Lord's supper was instituted; and it is very absurd to think that our Saviour should speak of an institution not in being, his doctrine about it being what it was impossible people should understand. Nor, 2. Is the proposition true, of sacramental eating; for many may have never sacramentally eaten the flesh and drank the blood of Christ, and yet be spiritually alive, and be saved eternally. Besides that mere sacramental eating the flesh and drinking the blood of Christ will not give life; but the eating here spoken of giveth life, eternal life, ver. 56, 58. 3. Besides, it is plain from ver. 29, that the eating here spoken of is believing; but it is plain, that eating the flesh and drinking the blood of Christ in the sacrament is not believing. By all which, it is apparent, that our Saviour saith nothing in this text of a sacramental eating the flesh and drinking the blood of Christ.

54 ^qWhoso eateth my flesh, and drinketh my blood, hath eternal life; and I will raise him up at the last day.

^{q ver. 27, 40, 63. ch. 4. 14.}

Hath eternal life; he hath it in a sure and just right title, and he shall have it in a certain actual possession: and in order to it, he shall have a joyful resurrection unto it at the last day. This is no more than what our Saviour had often said, particularly chap. iii. 18, 36, admitting what was before said, that by eating the flesh and drinking the blood of Christ, is to be meant believing in him; only here is a clearer discovery than was there, of the true object of that faith which justifieth, viz. a Christ crucified, for that is signified by the flesh and blood mentioned.

55 For my flesh is meat indeed, and my blood is drink indeed.

I, as a Christ crucified, not merely considered as to my Divine nature, but as to both natures united in one person, and particularly with respect to my death and suffering, am indeed the food of souls; not a tpyical food, as manna was, but a true and real food, which nourisheth them to eternal life, and the most excellent food for them. In which sense Christ is called *the true light*, chap. i. 9, and *the true vine*, chap. xv. 1.

56 He that eateth my flesh, and drinketh my blood, ^rdwelleth in me, and I in him.

^{r 1 John 3. 24. & 4. 15, 16.}

He that acknowledgeth and receiveth me, though he seeth me as a man, consisting of flesh and blood, and that particularly applieth himself to me as dying for the sins of the world, and committeth his soul in all its concerns for life and salvation to me, is united to me, and I to him: he is united to me by faith and love, Eph. iii. 17; 1 John iii. 23, 24; iv. 16; and I am united to him by a mutual love, chap. xiv. 23, and by my Holy Spirit. As our bread and meat, which we are nourished by, doth not dwell in us, and nourish, unless we eat it; so neither doth Christ do good to any soul, unless such a soul as by faith receiveth him, and believeth in him. What is said in this verse maketh it evident that these verses cannot be understood of any sacramental eating, for it is not true that Christ dwelleth in every soul, or that every soul dwelleth and abideth in Christ, who doth sacramentally eat the flesh and drink the blood of Christ. All unions are either natural or political unions. The strictest natural union is that of the head and members, the vine and the branches. The strictest political union is that of the husband and wife, Gen. ii. 24. The union betwixt Christ and a believing soul is set out by all these, chap. xv. 1; Eph. v. 30, 31; Col. i. 18. For the nature of this union, see divines who have wrote on this argument.

57 As the living Father hath sent me, and I live by the Father: so he that eateth me, even he shall live by me.

God is often in holy writ called *the living God*, not only because he hath life in himself, but because he is the fountain of life to all his creatures. Christ here declareth his Father to be *the living Father* upon the latter account, as he is the author and fountain of all life. *And I live by the Father*, saith he. Some translate it *for the Father;* as indeed the preposition διά, joined with an accusative case, (as it is here,) doth most ordinarily signify; but not always, either in profane authors, or in the dialect of Scripture, as Mark ii. 4; xii. 24; chap. iv. 41, 42. It seemeth here (as in those texts) to denote not so much the final as the efficient cause; and so better translated *by*, than *for* the Father: for Christ in this text seems to be giving his hearers an account how he came to be living bread; and to be in a capacity of giving life to the world. Saith he, I live by the Father, who by an eternal generation hath communicated to me all that life which is in him; and hath also communicated to me a quickening power, as I am Mediator, and sent by the Father into the world, to give life unto the world. Now look, as I have life in myself from him who is the fountain of life, so, according to the Father's ordination, *he that eateth me*, that is, by a true faith receiveth and closeth with me, as Mediator, *he shall live by me* both spiritually and eternally.

s ver. 49, 50, 51.

58 ⁸This is that bread which came down from heaven: not as your fathers did eat manna, and are dead: he that eateth of this bread shall live for ever.

There is no more said in this verse than ver. 49—51: see the notes on those verses. From this whole discourse it is as evident as the light, that the justification of the soul dependeth upon believing; and the spiritual life of the soul floweth not from love or obedience to the works of the law, but from faith in Jesus Christ: though it be true, that true faith cannot be without works, and no man without obedience in sincerity (though not in perfection) to the will of God, shall ever obtain eternal life and salvation; but this obedience is not faith, nor doth it enter into the justification of the soul, but is the certain and necessary product of that faith which justifieth, which cannot be justified as true and saving without obedience. In all this discourse here is no mention of love, or obedience, as that to which the promises of life everlasting and a joyful resurrection are so often made; but only of eating Christ; eating his flesh and drinking his blood; eating him as the bread which came down from heaven, &c.; which are phrases no way expressive of obedience to the works of the law, but of believing, ver. 47—49. The other texts of Scripture make it plain enough, that there can be no believing without obeying, nor any eternal life and salvation obtained without both.

59 These things said he in the synagogue, as he taught in Capernaum.

Though the state of the Jewish church at this time was corrupt enough, both as to matters of doctrine, worship, and discipline; yet it being constituted by his Father, he did not decline their assemblies either in the temple at Jerusalem, or in the places of the public worship, which were called synagogues, and were both in their cities and villages; for he had a liberty to teach in them, as appeareth both from this and many other texts; which he accordingly used, and usually spent the sabbath, or a great part of it, in those places and assemblies: yet by his presence he no way owned or declared his approbation of their corruptions, but frequently and freely reproved them; only because of those superstitious impertinencies (there being at this time no idolatry practised amongst them) he would not disown what was of God his Father among them. The same practice we shall observe amongst the apostles, till the Jews declared themselves hardened, drove them out from their synagogues, and spake evil of the way of the gospel before the multitude, Acts xix. 9. Then indeed, and not before, Paul *separated the disciples, disputing daily in the school of one Tyrannus*. This also is further to be observed in the practice of our Saviour, that although he went to the temple and the synagogues, and there joined with the Jewish worship instituted by his Father, and reproved (as he had occasion) the corruptions they had introduced and superadded; yet he did not forbear himself teaching the gospel in other places besides the temple and the synagogues. The evangelist also noteth, that the synagogue where he taught these things was in Capernaum, a city of Galilee, which in this was *exalted to heaven*, that it had not only the gospel preached in it, but by Christ himself; but for the contempt of the gospel is since *brought down to hell*, as much debased as it was before exalted, being long since reduced to a poor inconsiderable place, and at this day under the tyranny of the Mahometan prince.

60 ᵗMany therefore of his disciples, when they had heard *this*, said, This is an hard saying; who can hear it?

t ver. 66. Matt. 11. 6.

His disciples; his followers, not those that were his disciples indeed, but in name; for many followed him that did not believe in him; and many (in a sense) believed, to whom he did not commit himself, chap. ii. 23, 24. Now, many of these disciples, having heard these sayings, and being no way able to comprehend so great mysteries, nor having their eyes opened by the Spirit of illumination, said within themselves, These are sayings hard, or impossible, to be understood; who is able to hear or to understand them? or who is able to bear them?

61 When Jesus knew in himself that his disciples murmured at it, he said unto them, Doth this offend you?

Christ, though clothed with our flesh, yet being also the eternal Son of God, knew by virtue of his Divine nature, personally united to the human nature, what was in the heart of man; hence is this phrase, *knew in himself;* which is opposed to a knowledge from the hearing of his own ears, as man heareth, whether more immediately from the sound of their words, (for we read of nothing they spake audibly,) or from the relation of others, as what they had heard: he knew in himself their thoughts by his Divine prerogative and property of searching the hearts, and trying the reins, and discerning the thoughts of men afar off. Knowing their thoughts, he saith, Doth this give you occasion of stumbling?

62 ᵘ*What* and if ye shall see the Son of man ascend up where he was before?

u ch. 3. 13. Mark 16. 19. Acts 1. 9. Eph. 4. 8.

Our Saviour by these words may seem rather to increase than to abate their offence. That which stumbled them was, his calling himself the bread of life; his affirming that he came down from heaven; that he gave life to the world; that the way to obtain this life was eating his flesh and drinking his blood. How doth what he now tells them any way tend to satisfy them? He now speaks of ascending up to heaven, and asserteth that he was there before. *Answ.* The former assertions were no way to be justified but upon this foundation, that though he appeared now in the form and shape of a man, and was indeed the Son of man, yet he was also God, the eternal Son of God: he therefore here plainly asserts, that he was in heaven before he appeared as the Son of man upon the earth; and descending from thence, did assume the form of a servant; and for a further proof of this, he referreth them to what they were to see or hear (to know) within some few months after this discourse, (for this was after his third passover, which was to be the last year of his life,) viz. that he should ascend up to heaven; which it is very probable that some of them did see with their bodily eyes; for he was in Galilee when he ascended, and Capernaum was a city of that province; and when he ascended, the men of Galilee stood gazing up to heaven after him, as appears from Acts i. 11, and had a revelation, that they should see him so come again, and descend from heaven, as they had seen him go up.

63 ˣIt is the spirit that quickeneth; the flesh profiteth nothing: the words that I speak unto you, *they* are spirit, and *they* are life.

x 2 Cor. 3. 6.

As it is not the bread or flesh that a man eateth for the sustenance of his animal or natural life, that doth the main work, but the soul of a man within him, which putteth forth its virtues and powers in causing the digestion, concoction, and alteration of it, without which it nourisheth not the body; so the flesh of Christ eaten carnally can be of no profit for the nourishment of the soul: nor can the flesh of Christ considered alone, or by any virtue in it, profit; it only profiteth by virtue of the Divine nature, which being personally united to the human nature, addeth all the virtue and merit to the sufferings and actions of the human nature; so as the human nature of Christ hath all its quickening virtue from the Divine nature. It is not therefore the carnal eating of my flesh that I intended, that is a very gross conception of yours; nor can any such thing as that do you good: but the words that I speak to you, they are spiritual, and such by the belief of which you may obtain a spiritual and eternal life; for by believing those words, and obeying them, you shall come to believe in me, which is that eating my flesh and drinking my blood which I intended, not any corporeal or carnal eating.

y ver. 36.
x ch. 2. 24. 25. & 13. 11.
64 But ʸthere are some of you that believe not. For ˣJesus knew from the beginning who they were that believed not, and who should betray him.

I may say what I will to you; the Spirit quickeneth, but it doth not quicken all; it only quickeneth whomsoever it pleaseth. You understand not these things, but have most gross conceptions of sublime spiritual things; the reason is, because you believe not: though some of them, questionless, did truly believe, yet the most did not; for we read, ver. 66, that many of them *went back, and walked no more with him.* And though faith be an inward, secret act of the soul, yet Christ knew, and from the beginning, who were believers, and who were not; nay, he had a particular knowledge of that disciple who was to betray him.

a ver. 44, 45.
65 And he said, Therefore ᵃsaid I unto you, that no man can come unto me, except it were given unto him of my Father.

He said this, ver. 44: see the notes on that verse.

b ver. 60.
66 ¶ ᵇFrom that *time* many of his disciples went back, and walked no more with him.

His disciples at large, so called because they followed him, partly to hear what he would say, partly to see his miracles, followed him no more. Many professors and seeming disciples of Christ may draw back and fall from their profession, though none that truly receive Christ shall fall away, but be by the power of God preserved through faith unto salvation.

67 Then said Jesus unto the twelve, Will ye also go away?

It is probable that some stayed besides the twelve, for it is said only that many of his disciples turned back. Nor was our Saviour (who knew the hearts of all) ignorant what they would do; but he had a mind both to try them by this question, and also to convince them that there was a false brother amongst them, whose wickedness (though it lay hid from them) would in a short time discover itself.

68 Then Simon Peter answered him, Lord, to whom shall we go? thou hast
c Acts 5. 20. ᶜthe words of eternal life.

Peter, who is observed in the whole history of the gospel to have discovered the hottest and quickest spirit, and to have been first in answering questions propounded to the twelve, as Matt. xvi. 16, &c., replies, *Lord, to whom shall we go? &c.*, thereby teaching us under temptations to apostacy, first, to consider what we shall get by it, as the following words teach us, that an abiding with Christ in a steady adherence to the truths of his gospel, is the best choice that we can make.

d Mat. 16. 16. Mark 8. 29. Luke 9. 20. ch. 1. 49. & 11. 27.
69 ᵈAnd we believe and are sure that thou art that Christ, the Son of the living God.

We believe (saith Peter) *and are sure,* both from what we have heard from thee, and from the miracles which we have seen wrought by thee, *that thou art that Christ, the Son of the living God.* The very words by which St. Matthew (chap. xvi. 16) expresseth that noble confession of his, which our Saviour calleth the rock, upon which he would build his church. But notwithstanding this acknowledgment, which speaks the seeds of this faith now sown in the heart of Peter, and the hearts of the rest; yet whoso considereth the passages of the other evangelists after this, will see reason to believe, that their persuasion as to this was but faint, till Christ by his resurrection declared himself the Son of God with power.

70 Jesus answered them, ᵉHave not I e Luke 6. 13. chosen you twelve, ᶠand one of you is a f ch. 13. 27. devil?

Chosen, not to eternal life, but to the great office of an apostle. I chose but twelve amongst you, Matt. x., and of those twelve one is διάβολος, an accuser. or informer; a name by which the devil (who is the grand accuser of the brethren) is ordinarily expressed in holy writ.

71 He spake of Judas Iscariot *the son* of Simon: for he it was that should betray him, being one of the twelve.

This *he spake of Judas Iscariot,* (so called, as most think, from the name of the city where he lived,) and to distinguish him from the other Judas, the brother of James, who wrote the Epistle that goeth by his name, and is a part of holy writ: for he *being one of the twelve,* chosen and sent out with the rest to preach the gospel, and empowered by miraculous operations to confirm the truth of it; yet it was he that was to betray Christ, as we largely read in all the evangelists' relation of the passion: to teach us, that no office to which God calleth us, no gifts (except those of special grace) with which God blesseth any man, can secure him of an eternal happy state; nothing can do that but a true saving faith in Jesus Christ, with the obedience of a holy life becoming the gospel of Christ.

CHAP. VII

Jesus, exhorted by his unbelieving kinsmen to show himself at Jerusalem at the feast of tabernacles, refuseth, but afterwards goeth up in secret, 1—10. *The Jews seek him, and differ in their sentiments of him,* 11—13. *He teacheth in the temple,* 14—29. *Some are ready to lay hands on him, others believe; the rulers send officers to apprehend him,* 30—32. *Christ foretelleth his departure to the Father, and promiseth the Holy Spirit to believers,* 33—39. *Divers opinions concerning him,* 40—44. *The officers, struck with his discourse, return without him, and are rebuked by the Pharisees, who chide with Nicodemus for taking his part,* 45—53.

AFTER these things Jesus walked in Galilee: for he would not walk in Jewry, ᵃbecause the Jews sought to kill him. a ch. 5. 16, 18.

After the third passover, which happened after our Saviour had entered upon his public ministry, of which we read, chap. v. 1, and all those things which we read of, chap. v. and vi., done by our Saviour, both at the feast at Jerusalem, chap. v. and after he went into Galilee, chap. vi. 1, and had made that excellent discourse, of which we had a large account, chap. vi.; Jesus continued still to converse in Galilee, where he was; for he would not go into Judea, nor converse there, *because the Jews,* for the causes mentioned chap. v. 18, *sought to kill him.* They had two things (as appeareth from thence) against him: 1. His violation of the sabbath (as they thought) by healing him that lay at the pool of Bethesda. 2. His making himself equal with the Father.

2 ᵇNow the Jews' feast of tabernacles b Lev. 23. 34. was at hand.

The feast of tabernacles was a feast which God ordained the Jews to keep the fifteenth day of the seventh month, (which some make to answer our September, others our October,) Lev. xxiii. 34, 39, after they had gathered in the fruits of the land. It was to be kept seven days, the first and last of which days were to be kept as sabbaths; they were all the seven days to dwell in tents, or booths, in remembrance of the forty years they so dwelt in the wilderness, passing from Egypt to Canaan, as we read there, ver. 43. Now this festival was near at hand; so as we must understand the things following to have happened about the September or October before Christ's suffering, which was at the next passover; that is, the March or April following, as we count the months.

c Mat. 12.46.
Mark 3. 31.
Acts 1. 14.

3 ^c His brethren therefore said unto him, Depart hence, and go into Judæa, that thy disciples also may see the works that thou doest.

His brethren; his friends and kindred; see the notes on Matt. xii. 47, 48; either such as did believe in him, or such as did not believe; for, ver. 5, all of them did not believe in him; would have him leave Galilee, which was the far more obscure and ignoble part of the country, and go into Judea, which was the more noble and famous province; that those who in that province followed him, might also see the miracles which he wrought.

4 For *there is* no man *that* doeth any thing in secret, and he himself seeketh to be known openly. If thou do these things, shew thyself to the world.

The things which thou doest, thou doest out of a desire by them to be made known, and to spread thy own fame and glory: for this, Galilee is not a proper place, because it is an obscure part in the country. The phrase which we translate *to be known*, is in the Greek ἐν παρρησία εἶναι. The usage of it here seemeth to be something different from the use of it in other places of holy writ. It sometimes signifies confidence and security; and we translate it boldness, Acts xiii. 46; xxvi. 26; xxviii. 31; Phil. i. 20; Heb. iii. 6; x. 19. But this cannot be the sense of this text; for it were no sense to read it, seeketh to be known boldly, confidently, or securely. Sometimes we translate it *openly*, as in this text, and chap. xi. 54; Col. ii. 15. It sometimes signifieth a freedom of speech, Acts ii. 29; iv. 13; 2 Cor. vii. 4. Sometimes it signifieth clearness and plainness of speech, chap. x. 24; xi. 14. Sometimes it signifieth a speaking in public meetings, as in Mark viii. 32; chap. xviii. 20. Dr. Hammond notes, that it also sometimes signifies to speak with authority, Acts iv. 29, 31; Eph. vi. 19. Certainly the word in its primary signification signifieth a freedom and boldness of speech; which freedom and boldness is necessary to him that speaketh openly, and in public meetings; and is advantaged by the authority which any man hath to speak: hence in a secondary sense it may signify both to speak with authority, and also to speak in public assemblies; and this last I take to be here signified. It is (as our Saviour's friends tell him) both against reason, and the ordinary course of the world, for men desirous of opportunities to speak boldly and freely in public assemblies, to keep themselves in obscure places, where are no such public assemblies. They therefore advise him, that if indeed he wrought these miraculous operations, and were able to produce such effects, he would not bury up himself and his reputation in such a hole as Galilee, but show himself to the more noted and famous part of the world, which was, as to that part of the world, Jerusalem, and at the feast now, where multitudes of the people would be to celebrate the feast of tabernacles.

d Mark 3. 21.

5 For ^d neither did his brethren believe in him.

Not all his own friends and kindred; he came not only among his own countrymen, but among his own relations, and they received him not; or if they had some opinion of him, and some little hopes concerning him, yet they did not believe as they ought to have believed. Certainly there cannot be a greater proof and demonstration that faith is not of ourselves, nor a thing in our own power, no, not with all the external aids of gospel doctrine and arguments, than as is in this text. We cannot imagine but our Lord's brethren were willing enough to have believed in Christ as the true Messiah and Saviour of the world; the very honour of their family would have so far inclined them. It is impossible that they, or any others, should have had greater external means, aids, and assistances for their faith, than Christ's preaching amongst them, and confirming his doctrine by miraculous operations before them; if now they had a power in their own wills, to have looked upon Christ as the true Messiah and Saviour of the world, and accordingly to have received and embraced him, what was the matter they believed not, or as yet at least they believed not in him?

6 Then Jesus said unto them, ^e My time is not yet come: but your time is alway ready.

e ch. 2. 4.
& 8. 20.
ver. 8, 30.

My time is not yet come; the time of my death, say some; of my manifestation to the world, say others: but questionless our Saviour intends no more than his time for going up to this feast, for we shall read that he did go up afterward; but, saith he, as yet I cannot go up. *Your time is alway ready;* you may go when you please: and this he further openeth, saying,

7 ^f The world cannot hate you; but me it hateth, ^g because I testify of it, that the works thereof are evil.

f ch. 15. 19.

g ch. 3. 19.

By *the world*, our Saviour plainly understandeth the men of the world; men not regenerated, renewed, and sanctified. These men, saith he, *cannot* as yet *hate you*. There was a time afterward when this part of the world hated all the disciples of Christ, as Christ foretold, chap. xv. 18; but that was after the doctrine of the gospel was more preached, and made known to the world by the preaching of the apostles: and therefore Christ saith (in that place) that it hated him before it hated them. Christ first published the doctrine of the gospel, and so became the first object of the world's hatred on that account. These his brethren were not concerned (that we read of) at this time in the publication of it, nor had any occasion to make themselves known and odious to the world upon that account; therefore he saith, *The world* (the wicked Jews, here so called) could not be reasonably imagined to have any spite or malignity to them. *But*, saith he, *me it hateth:* that is apparent from what we met with chap. v. 18. But this was not for any fault in Christ, but only for his preaching the doctrine of the gospel, and free reproving them for the evil of their works, the corruption of their doctrine, and the errors of their life and conversation.

8 Go ye up unto this feast: I go not up yet unto this feast; ^h for my time is not yet full come.

h ch. 8. 30.
ver. 6.

Go ye up unto this feast; let not my forbearance to go up hinder your going up according to the law. *I go not up yet unto this feast;* I have some particular reasons why as yet I will not go to be there at the beginning of it. *For my time is not yet full come;* I know my time to go, when it will be most safe and proper for me. I shall be there some time during the feast, but my time is not yet come; I shall not be there at the beginning of it. It appeareth that he came not into the temple till about the middle of it, ver. 14, which was three or four days after it was began, for it held seven days, Lev. xxiii. 34. Or his time was not come, because he designed to go very privately without any notice taken of his coming; which must have been, if he had at that time gone up with his kindred and acquaintance.

9 When he had said these words unto them, he abode *still* in Galilee.

He let them take their journey to Jerusalem to the feast without him, and himself still abode in Galilee.

10 ¶ But when his brethren were gone up, then went he also up unto the feast, not openly, but as it were in secret.

He went up to show his obedience to his Father's commands, Exod. xxiii. 17. The feast of tabernacles was the same with the feast of ingathering in the end of the year, when they had gathered their labours out of the field, mentioned Exod. xxiii. 16; and that was one of those three times (as appears from that chapter) when all the males in Israel were to appear before the Lord, ver. 17. Christ being born under the law, showeth a punctual obedience to it; and therefore, in obedience to it, he would go up: but his wisdom dwelt with prudence; and therefore he did not go up openly, not in any crowd of company, so as a public notice could be taken of him; but secretly, to teach us that we are not so strictly tied up to ritual precepts, which concern only rites and circumstances of worship, that we may not abate them sometimes for the performance of moral duties. It was a moral duty incumbent upon our Saviour to preserve himself, with what wisdom and prudence he could, from the rage of his enemies, till his time should fully come to yield up himself to their rage; which was the reason why he, who went up now singly, without any company, when he went up to the last passover, where he was to suffer, went up with all imaginable boldness and alacrity, leading the way, to their amazement, Mark x. 32.

l ch. 11. 56. 11 Then ^lthe Jews sought him at the feast, and said, Where is he?

Our Saviour's constant going up to the Jewish feasts, made the rulers of the Jews, who sought to slay him at the feast of the passover, chap. v. 18, (which was but six months before this,) because he had violated the sabbath, (as they interpreted his healing the impotent man on that day, and bidding him take up his bed and walk,) and because he had made himself equal with God his Father; seek him the first days of the feast, speaking of him with great contempt and slight.

k ch. 9. 16.
& 10. 19.
l Mat. 21.46.
Luke 7. 16.
ch. 6. 14.
ver. 40.
12 And ^kthere was much murmuring among the people concerning him: for ^lsome said, He is a good man: others said, Nay; but he deceiveth the people.

Our Saviour's constant attendance at these public festivals, did not only create an expectation of his being there amongst his enemies, who therefore sought him there, that they might destroy him; but amongst the generality of the people, who had very different opinions about him. Some having heard his doctrine, and hearing nothing from him but what was good and spiritual, tending to show them the way of holiness, and the true path-way to eternal life and happiness, concluded that he was a good man; others said he was a mere impostor, one that deceived and cheated the more ignorant common people.

m ch. 9. 22.
& 12. 42.
& 19. 38.
13 Howbeit no man spake openly of him ^mfor fear of the Jews.

Though many, both of the Galileans, among whom he had conversed, and of the common people of Judea, had a very good opinion of Christ, yet the rulers of the Jews were in such a rage against him, that his friends durst not freely discourse their thoughts concerning him.

14 ¶ Now about the midst of the feast Jesus went up into the temple, and taught.

About the third or fourth day of the feast (which continued seven days) our Lord, being (as was said before) come up privately and by stealth, as it were, to Jerusalem, first appears in the temple preaching. What our Saviour at this time discoursed about the evangelist doth not tell us; but doubtless it was the things of the kingdom of God, which were the usual themes or arguments of his discourse, as we may also understand by the latter part of it. Our Lord probably deferred his preaching to the middle of the feast, partly, because the Pharisees' heat in hunting after him was now a little over; and that there might be a fuller concourse of people to hear him.

n Mat.13.54.
Mark 6. 2.
Luke 4. 22.
Acts 2. 7.
‖ Or,
learning.
15 ⁿAnd the Jews marvelled, saying, How knoweth this man ‖letters, having never learned?

Having never sat as a constant disciple at the feet of any of the Jewish doctors, nor been educated in their schools of the prophets, they wonder how he should come by such knowledge of the law of God, as he discovered in his discourses; wherein he made it appear, that he did not only know the letter of the law, but the more mysterious sense of it, the great mysteries of the kingdom of God.

o ch. 3. 11.
& 8.28. & 12.
49. & 14. 10,
24.
16 Jesus answered them, and said, ^oMy doctrine is not mine, but his that sent me.

My doctrine is not mine, considering me as the Son of man; not taught, or to be taught, me by men; not learned out of books, or by the precepts of men; not invented by me; but it is mine as it is the doctrine of the Father that sent me, and I and my Father both are one, and agree in one, 1 John v. 7, 8; and being so, there was no such need that Christ should be learned, in their sense, viz. at the feet of their doctors, and in their schools. But enthusiasts vainly argue from hence, that there is no need of human learning for him who is to be a preacher of the gospel; for Christ was not mere man, but one in whom the fulness of the Godhead dwelt bodily. No such thing will follow from the prophesying of Amos, who was a herdsman, or the apostles, who were fishermen; much less from the preaching of Christ. We must distinguish betwixt an extraordinary and an ordinary calling. And though it be truth, that the ministers of the gospel preach doctrine which is not theirs, but his that sent them; yet it doth not follow, that they must come by the knowledge of this doctrine in the same manner that Christ did, who was in the bosom of the Father, and knew his will, and came from him to communicate it to the world; nor yet in the same manner that the prophets and the apostles came to the knowledge of it, as by Christ's vocal instruction. So also by the influence of the Holy Spirit upon them in the days of Pentecost, which abode upon them.

17 ^pIf any man will do his will, he shall know of the doctrine, whether it be of God, or *whether* I speak of myself.
p Ecclus. 21.
11. ch. 8. 43.

Here our Saviour seemeth to obviate an objection which the Jews would make, viz. How they should know that the doctrine which he preached was the doctrine of God? He indeed said so, but how should they have any evidence of it? How could he make it appear to them to be of God? *If any man* (saith our Saviour) *will do his will, &c.*; that is, If any man hath a heart truly disposed to know and embrace whatsoever shall be revealed to him to be the will of God, how contrary soever it be to the interest of his own lusts, and ready to do it in all things, and live according to the prescript and revelation of it, having a serious purpose of heart to obey God in every thing; if he seeketh for truth seriously, and in the fear of the Lord, laying aside all wrath, malice, hatred, and any corrupt passions or affections; God will reveal the truth to him, so as he shall know the doctrine that is of God; and that I do not speak of or from myself, but by authority from my Father. Now, from hence indeed followeth, that corrupt affections, passions, and prejudices, and an ill life, may prejudice, yea, and will prejudice, men from receiving of the free grace of God, spiritual illuminations, and the gift of faith; so as men that give way to such prejudices, or nourish such passions, or live such lives, shall be left of God to their native blindness, and to strong delusions, and not discern the truth in the light that openly shineth in their faces. But from hence it will not follow, that a moral life, and a study of and seeking after truth, are the cause of faith, or effective of it, with the working of our own will.

18 ^qHe that speaketh of himself seeketh his own glory: but he that seeketh his glory that sent him, the same is true, and no unrighteousness is in him.
q ch. 5. 41.
& 8. 50.

Here our Saviour giveth them another note, by which they might know that his doctrine was of God, because he spake not of himself, nor sought his own glory in what he delivered. No man doth an action of and from himself, but he maketh himself the end of his action; for to what purpose should a man devise and broach new notions, but for some selfish advantage, that he may get some profit, or some honour and applause from men? But if a man acts as servant to another, and seeketh only the honour and applause of another, he is true, and cannot be presumed to have spoken of and from himself, but of and from him whose honour and glory he seeketh to advance; and in reason ought to be judged sincere and faithful in the execution of the trust committed to him, and to be without fraud and deceit, having no unrighteousness in him; there being no just cause to be presumed which should move him to speak any thing that is false. Hence also may be learned a good rule or direction, which divines ordinarily make use of to help us to judge of the truth of doctrines. Those doctrines which most tend to the advancing the honour and glory of God, and least to the advancement of the creature, those are most likely to be of God. And this also much tendeth to confirm the reputation of holy writ, and the penmen of it; for it is manifest that the penmen of it sought not their own glory in their writings, but the honour and glory of God, taking all shame to themselves.

S. JOHN VII

r Ex. 24. 3.
Deut. 33. 4.
John 1. 17.
Acts 7. 38.
s Mat. 12. 14.
Mark 3. 6.
ch. 5. 16, 18. & 10. 31, 39. & 11. 53.

19 ʳDid not Moses give you the law, and *yet* none of you keepeth the law? ˢWhy go ye about to kill me?

Moses was God's instrument in delivering his law to the people, Exod. xxiv. 3; Deut. xxxiii. 4; a law which none of them exactly kept, but daily broke. Why do you (saith our Saviour) make it such a capital crime (suppose you were not in an error, but I had in this one point of the sabbath violated the law) in me to break the law, that you for it would have my blood? how cometh it to be a more heinous offence in me to break the law in one thing, than it is in you, who violate it in so many things? Or, do not you think it a capital crime maliciously to go about to destroy an innocent person? Is not that a greater breach, think you, of the sixth commandment, than what I have done is of the fourth? supposing that had been any breach of the law at all, which indeed it was not.

20 The people answered and said,
t ch. 8. 48. 52. & 10. 20.
ᵗThou hast a devil: who goeth about to kill thee?

The Jews had an opinion, that whosoever was beside himself, and talked distractedly, was influenced with an evil spirit; so as, *Thou hast a devil*, is no more than, Thou art mad; unless we will take the phrase as a mere term of reproach, such as we ordinarily hear at this day from some men in their passions, when they hear any speak what is false, and hath no congruity with truth, according to their apprehensions, saying, The devil is in you: the former is the milder interpretation, though in that was sin enough, considering who it is that spake. *Who goeth about to kill thee?* it is very probable that the common people (to whom our Saviour was now speaking) knew nothing of the design of their rulers, mentioned chap. v. 18, so spake this innocently, (though in their passion,) having no such design in their hearts; but they ought not so peremptorily to have denied what our Saviour positively affirmed, who knew the designs and counsels of all men's hearts, though they knew them not.

21 Jesus answered and said unto them, I have done one work, and ye all marvel.

By the one miracle it is plain, by what followeth, that he meaneth healing the man who lay at the pool of Bethesda; at this, he saith, they marvelled, by which is to be understood offended, for so it is expounded by χολᾶτε, ver. 23; and to this sense is our Saviour's subsequent discourse.

u Lev 12. 3.

22 ᵘMoses therefore gave unto you circumcision; (not because it is of Moses,
x Gen. 17. 10.
ˣbut of the fathers;) and ye on the sabbath day circumcise a man.

The particle *therefore*, or, for this, διὰ τοῦτο, maketh in this verse a great difficulty, what the meaning of it should be. The most probable account of it is, that it belongeth to the former verse, which should end thus, *and ye all marvel for this*. This indeed maketh all plain; otherwise it is very hard to give an account what force it can have, if we consider it as a note of a cause. *Moses gave you circumcision*, that is, a law about circumcision; yet that law had not its rise from Moses: the law was given to your father Abraham, Gen. xvii. 10, long before Moses's time. In obedience to that law, you circumcise a male child, or a proselyte, that is, a man grown, on the sabbath day.

23 If a man on the sabbath day receive circumcision, ‖ that the law of Moses should not be broken; are ye angry at me, because ʸI have made a man every whit whole on the sabbath day?

‖ Or, *without breaking the law of Moses*.
y ch. 5. 8, 9, 16.

The strength of this whole argument seemeth to be this: If a ritual law (such was that for observation of the sabbath, given in Mount Sinai, Exod. xx.) may give place to another ritual law which is ancienter, (such was that of circumcision, given to Abraham long before,) much more ought it to give place to a law of nature written in every man's heart, viz. that it is our duty to help those that are in great degrees of misery and affliction; which is what I paid obedience to in curing the impotent man that lay at the pool of Bethesda. Do you yield this in your daily practice, that a man may be circumcised, yea, and ought to be circumcised, on the eighth day, though it happeneth to be the sabbath day; and not to do it were a violation of the law of Moses about circumcision, which was a law given you by Moses, though, before him, to Abraham also? What reason then have you to be angry with me, who on the sabbath day have only healed a man, and made him *every whit whole?* that is, (as some think,) I have not only cured him as to his body, but as to his soul; but that hardly seemeth probable; for if it were so, the Jews could have no evidence of the spiritual cure. Others therefore think that the term ὅλον ἄνθρωπον, signifieth no more than perfectly, or completely whole, as to his body.

24 ᶻJudge not according to the appearance, but judge righteous judgment.

z Deu. 1. 16.
17. Prov. 24. 23. ch. 8. 15.
Jam. 2. 1.

Do not judge persons, and condemn me for what I have done, merely out of your hatred, prejudice, and malice against me. Or, do not judge according to the first appearance of this fact. It looketh to you as a violation of the sabbath; it is not indeed so, but the performance of a duty greater than that of sanctifying the sabbath is. Judge righteously, and do not condemn in me what you yourselves do in other causes, because of your hatred to and prejudice against me; nor condemn an action which is in itself a righteous action, and not deserving condemnation.

25 Then said some of them of Jerusalem, Is not this he, whom they seek to kill?

Those who here speak are said to be of Jerusalem, (probably citizens,) who knew more of the designs and counsels of the chief priests and elders, than those who said before, ver. 20, *Thou hast a devil: who seeketh to kill thee?*

26 But, lo, he speaketh boldly, and they say nothing unto him. ᵃDo the rulers know indeed that this is the very Christ?

a ver. 48.

The first search being over, it is probable that the rulers had not heard that Christ was come up to the feast; this made the people think that they had some knowledge that he was the Messias, otherwise they would have taken some course to have restrained his so free and open discoursing: but we shall in the latter part of this chapter find that they were mistaken; for as soon as they heard where he was, and what he was doing, they used all means they could to apprehend him.

27 ᵇHowbeit we know this man whence he is: but when Christ cometh, no man knoweth whence he is.

b Mat. 13. 55.
Mark 6. 3.
Luke 4. 22.

We know this man whence he is; we know he is of Nazareth, and that Joseph is his reputed father. They also knew whence the Messias was to come, that he was to be of the family of David, of the tribe of Judah, of the town of Bethlehem: the chief priests and scribes answered Herod to that purpose, without the least hesitation, Matt. ii. 5, 6, but they had no revelation to guide them to know of what particular family he should be: thus this verse is easily reconciled to ver. 42. Others think that they spake of the second manifestation of Christ. They had a tradition, which was bottomed on holy writ, That he was to come out of Bethlehem: but then they had another tradition, that he should be taken away from thence, and hidden for some years, and then again appear as a person unknown whence he came. Which opinion, say some, was bottomed on the revelations of the Old Testament concerning a double regeneration of Christ, Isa. liii. 8, *Who shall declare his generation?* and Micah v. 2; the one of which is to be understood of his eternal generation, which none can declare; the other, as to the generation of his human nature. But the Jews not understanding that the Messiah was to be God-man, understood both of his human nature; which made them fancy, that though he was to be born at Bethlehem, according to Micah v. 2, yet he was to be carried away for some years some where; so as when he came to appear to the world, none should know whence he came, but he should appear as a man dropped down from heaven. Now Christ having been offered in the temple at his mother's purification, went back again with his parents, Luke ii. 39, came to Nazareth, and ordinarily went up to Jerusalem; there he was found disputing with the doctors, ver.

46; and at last we find him resting with his parents at Nazareth, and being subject to them; after which we read no more of him, till he came to John to be baptized: so as the Jews had known and observed the whole course of Christ's life.

28 Then cried Jesus in the temple as he taught, saying, ^cYe both know me, and ye know whence I am: and ^dI am not come of myself, but he that sent me ^eis true, ^fwhom ye know not.

Ye both know me, and ye know whence I am; you might have known me by the doctrine which I have taught, and the miracles which I have wrought among you; and you had known me, if you had not shut your eyes against the light, which shone in your face: or, you say and think that you know me. Others think that it is an irony, or as a question, Do you know me so well? If you did, you would know that I came not of myself, but was sent by my Father; and he that sent me is truth itself: but you know not the Father, and therefore cannot know me as indeed I am.

29 But ^gI know him: for I am from him, and he hath sent me.

I know him, so as no man else knoweth him, Matt. xi. 27; I know his essence, his will, his counsels, his laws; *for I am from him* by an eternal generation, his only begotten Son; and I am sent by him, as the Mediator and Saviour of the world, to declare and to execute his will and pleasure, as to man's salvation.

30 Then ^hthey sought to take him: but ⁱno man laid hands on him, because his hour was not yet come.

By this time the news was come to the sanhedrim, the great court of the Jews, to whom belonged the cognizance of church affairs, false prophets, blasphemy, violation of the sabbath, &c.: they took counsel, and used endeavours to apprehend him; or it may be, some of the ruder sort of people that were his enemies used some such endeavours, but not with any effect; for by the mighty providence of God, who had set the time when Christ should suffer, till that hour was come, mentioned also chap. viii. 20; xii. 23, there was such a restraint upon the rage of the rabble, yea, (as we shall hereafter hear,) upon the spirits of the officers, who were sent from the sanhedrim to apprehend him, that they had no power to lay hold upon him. Men shall do us no hurt, till God's time comes. A sparrow falls not to the ground without the will of our Father.

31 And ^kmany of the people believed on him, and said, When Christ cometh, will he do more miracles than these which this *man* hath done?

And many of the people believed on him; not as the true Messias; for the next words let us know, they did not believe him to be the Christ, but looked for him to come; but they gave credit to him as a great prophet sent from God; and doubted whether the miracles which he wrought were not as many and as great as ever the Messiah would do when he came. For though John reports but a few miracles wrought by Christ, yet they were such as required a Divine power to produce; such as turning the water into wine, multiplying the loaves, raising Lazarus from the dead, &c. And John tells us, chap. xx. 30; xxi. 25, that he did many more works than he hath recorded in this book; and many more are recorded by the other three evangelists. From hence may be observed the falsehood of the later Jews, who deny that the Messiah is to work any miracles; for it is apparent from hence, that they had in our Saviour's time a general expectation that great miracles should be done by the Messiah; and their expectation was truly founded upon Isa. xxxv. 5, 6, as appeareth by Matt. xi. 5.

32 ¶ The Pharisees heard that the people murmured such things concerning him; and the Pharisees and the Chief Priests sent officers to take him.

Murmured here is taken in a different sense from what it was before, and signifieth as much as whispered, or talked privately among themselves. The chief priests, who were afraid that their honour would abate amongst the people; and the Pharisees, who were afraid the credit of their traditions would be lost, if they suffered him to go on; and being more especially troubled for the miracles which he daily wrought, as chap. xi. 47; they send messengers from their great court (kept at Jerusalem) to apprehend him.

33 Then said Jesus unto them, ^lYet a little while am I with you, and *then* I go unto him that sent me.

Whether Christ spake these words to the officers sent to apprehend him, or to the people in the temple, is not much material to be known: he by them plainly declareth, that all their endeavours against him were vain and foolish; for he should yet live with them six months, (this was in September or October, he died at the next passover, which was about six months after this,) and then he should go and willingly lay down his life for the sins of the world, rise again from the dead, and ascend unto his Father who sent him into the world.

34 Ye ^mshall seek me, and shall not find *me:* and where I am, *thither* ye cannot come.

Some think the meaning is, *Ye shall seek me* to execute your malice upon me, but to no purpose, for you *shall not find me.* Or, You shall seek me to destroy me in my church, and to root out my name; but to no purpose. But the most probable sense is this: You wicked Jews, that now contemn the means of grace by me offered to you, shall one day be in distress and calamity enough; and when you are so, then you will wish I were again amongst you; but I shall be ascended to my Father, and as deaf to your prayers as above the reach of your malice. There is much the same thing said in Matt. xxiii. 39. That he here speaketh of his ascension is plain from chap. xiii. 33. He speaketh of heaven as a place where he was at that time, for so he was as to his Divine nature. It is ὑπάγω, whither I go, which makes some think it should not here be εἰμί, but εἶμι, *vado.* But others reject it, because it is a poetical word, hardly used in the New Testament.

35 Then said the Jews among themselves, Whither will he go, that we shall not find him? will he go unto ⁿthe dispersed among the ‖ Gentiles, and teach the Gentiles?

The Jews, not at all believing the Divine nature of Christ, notwithstanding all that Christ had said, and all the miracles he had wrought, are at a mighty loss to conclude what our Saviour spake of, and whither he would go; they thought he could go no where in the land of Jewry, but they should hear of him, and be able to come where he was; they conclude therefore that he would go into some pagan country. In the Greek it is, Will he go into the dispersion of the Grecians? There were two most famous dispersions, of which we read in history. The first was of the Jews, of which we read in sacred history, in the captivities of Assyria, whither the ten tribes were carried, 2 Kings xvii. 6; and Babylon, whither the two tribes were carried, 2 Kings xxiv. 14. And that of the Grecians by the Macedonians; when also many of the Jews were dispersed by Alexander the Great, and his successors. Peter directeth his Epistle *to the strangers scattered throughout Pontus, Galatia, Cappadocia, Asia, and Bithynia,* 1 Pet. i. 1. And James directs his Epistle *to the twelve tribes scattered abroad.* They fancy that our Saviour would go into some of these places, and preach; by which means the Gentiles would be taught the mysteries of the Jewish religion, which was what above all things they were impatient of hearing; and yet had reason from the prophecies of the Old Testament to fear, viz. their own rejection, and the receiving in of the Gentiles, which afterward came to pass, Rom. xi. 15.

36 What *manner of* saying is this that he said, Ye shall seek me, and shall not find *me:* and where I am, *thither* ye cannot come?

This saying stuck in their stomachs, and they knew not what sense to put upon it; owning nothing of the Divine nature of Christ.

o Lev. 23. 36.

37 °In the last day, that great *day* of the feast, Jesus stood and cried, saying, ᴾIf any man thirst, let him come unto me, and drink.

p Is. 55. 1.
ch. 6. 35.
Rev. 22. 17.

Our Saviour thinketh not fit to take any notice of their guess, whither he would go, nor replieth any thing to it. The feast of tabernacles was to hold seven days, Lev. xxiii. 34, in which they were to offer up burnt offerings, ver. 36. The eighth day was to be kept as a sabbath; there was in it to be a holy convocation, no servile labour was to be done. Christ on that day discoursed again to the people, crying aloud, and publicly, *If any man thirst, let him come unto me, and drink;* that is, If any man stand in need of any spiritual good, righteousness, strength, comfort, &c., it is to be found in me; let him come to me, by faith acknowledging, receiving, and embracing me, as the Mediator and Saviour of the world, and he shall have from me whatsoever spiritual influence of grace he stand in need of. Those who remember what our Saviour told the woman of Samaria, chap. iv. 10, 14, where he compared himself to *living water*, will easily understand this the sense of these words. The condition on our parts is expressed under the notion of thirsting; which we know is the natural appetite, craving some liquid thing to refresh the man under his drought; and it is expressive of an exceeding great passion, and so made use of both in the Old Testament and the New to signify a soul's passionate desire of spiritual things, Isa. lv. 1; Matt. v. 6.

q Deu.18.15.

38 ᑫHe that believeth on me, as the Scripture hath said, ʳout of his belly shall flow rivers of living water.

r Prov.18.4.
Is. 12.3.&44.
3. ch. 4. 14.

We have had frequent occasion to open the term of believing on Christ. It may be doubted, whether those words, *as the Scripture hath said*, be to be referred to the first or latter part of the text. If to the former, they are words expressive of that faith to which the following promise is made, which is not any assent, or slighty credit given to the word; but such a faith as the Scripture hath spoken of, as that faith which is justifying and saving. *Out of his belly shall flow rivers of living water;* the general sense of the promises, that his soul shall abound with all saving and comfortable influences of saving grace. The *belly* signifieth the heart, that part of man which is called the heart being in the belly. So Job xv. 35; Psal. xl. 8. The flowing of *rivers of water*, signifieth the plenty of spiritual influences with which believers shall be supplied; whether joy, knowledge, spiritual gifts, or graces. If any ask, where the Scripture speaketh this? I answer, in all those promises we meet with in the Old Testament, about pouring out the Spirit.

s Is. 44. 3.
Joel 2. 28.
ch. 16. 7.
Acts 2, 17, 33, 38.

39 (ˢBut this spake he of the Spirit, which they that believe on him should receive: for the Holy Ghost was not yet *given;* because that Jesus was not yet ᵗglorified.)

t ch. 12. 16.
& 16. 7.

For the evangelist tells us, that this referred to the Spirit, which believers were to receive after that Christ should be ascended into heaven. Those scriptures, Isa. xlix. 10; lviii. 11; Zech. xiv. 8, seem, among others, to be referred to in this promise of our Saviour.

u Deut. 18. 15, 18. ch. 1. 21. & 6. 14.

40 ¶ Many of the people therefore, when they heard this saying, said, Of a truth this is ᵘthe Prophet.

The Prophet mentioned Deut. xviii. 15. Some think that the Jews expected an eminent prophet, besides Elias, to come before the Messiah; and John i. 21 would incline us to think so. But others say, it cannot be proved from their writers, that they had any expectations of any but Elias and the Messiah. But the words may be read as well, this is a prophet, as this is the prophet; and I think that is the true sense of them. A prophet had now for more than four hundred years been a great rarity amongst them, they having had none but John the Baptist who had such a repute.

41 Others said, ˣThis is the Christ. But some said, Shall Christ come ʸout of Galilee?

x ch. 4. 42.
& 6. 69.
y ver. 52.
ch. 1. 46.

The people were divided in their opinions about Christ. Some of them were very well inclined to believe that he was the promised Messiah; but they stumbled at the country where alone they took notice of him. For though he came not out of Galilee, but was born in Bethlehem, Luke ii. 4, according to the prophecy of him, Micah v. 2, suitable to which was their tradition, Matt. ii. 5; yet they had seen nothing of this, though possibly they had heard some relation of it, it being two and thirty years since his birth: but he was ordinarily called Jesus of Nazareth, and of Galilee, there he had lived and been educated; so as they knew no better, probably, than that he came out of Galilee, which was contrary to the prophecy, Micah v. 2.

42 ᶻHath not the Scripture said, That Christ cometh of the seed of David, and out of the town of Bethlehem, ᵃwhere David was?

z Ps. 132.11.
Jer. 23. 5.
Mic. 5. 2.
Matt. 2. 5.
Luke 2. 4.
a 1 Sam. 16. 1, 4.

The Scriptures of the Old Testament had both described the family from whence the Messiah was to arise, viz. the family of David, Psal. cxxxii. 11, and the town, which was Bethlehem, Micah v. 2; which was David's father's town, where he lived also, till God called him out to the kingdom, 1 Sam. xvii. 15; xx. 6.

43 So ᵇthere was a division among the people because of him.

b ver. 12.
ch. 9. 16.
& 10. 19.

A division as to their opinions about him, as was before expressed.

44 And ᶜsome of them would have taken him; but no man laid hands on him.

e ver. 30.

There were some that had an ill opinion of Christ, and put on the officers that came for the purpose to apprehend him; but there was none so hardy as to do it.

45 ¶ Then came the officers to the Chief Priests and Pharisees; and they said unto them, Why have ye not brought him?

Probably the officers, Christ being amongst a multitude of the people that had a high opinion of him, durst not adventure to apprehend him. Some of them, as appeareth from what follows, were astonished at his doctrine; all of them agreed to return to their masters without him; at which they are angry, and ask them how it came to pass that they did not execute their commands, in bringing Christ before them as a malefactor, to answer what they should lay to his charge.

46 The officers answered, ᵈNever man spake like this man.

d Matt. 7.29.

With so much authority, evidence of truth, &c. Yet they did not cordially believe in Christ; being under the power of carnal and worldly affection, which only supernatural special grace could subdue. These were some of those, in whom the prophecy of Christ, Isa. xi. 4, was to be fulfilled—*He shall smite the earth with the rod of his mouth, and with the breath of his lips shall he slay the wicked.* The word of the Lord doth often restrain, astonish, and amaze those on whom it hath no powerful effect to eternal life and salvation. So it was with these poor officers.

47 Then answered them the Pharisees, Are ye also deceived?

You, who have us not only for your masters, whose commands you ought not to dispute, but to execute; but for your teachers also, from whom you might have learned better doctrine; are you seduced? For so wicked men count all who embrace not their notions, and follow not their ways.

48 ᵉHave any of the rulers or of the Pharisees believed on him?

e ch. 12. 42.
Acts 6. 7.
1 Cor. 1. 20, 26. & 2. 8.

You ought to be ruled by us, and guided by us, who are your rulers, and your teachers: so early did the doctrine of implicit faith and obedience creep into the world; which is indeed to suppose an infallibility in teachers and rulers; to whom indeed we owe all imaginable reverence, but we must live by our own faith. And though the Jews were bound to do according to the sentence that the priests and Levites in Jerusalem should show them, Deut. xvii. 10, 11; yet it must be *the sentence of the law*, and it was in civil matters, as appeareth by ver. 8, controversies *between blood and blood, plea and plea, stroke and stroke.*

49 But this people who knoweth not the law are cursed.

Out of the great pride of their hearts they vilify the people, as not learned in the law, and so were cursed, contemptible, and not to be regarded, as to their judgment and sentiments.

f ch. 3. 2.
† Gr. *to him.*

50 Nicodemus saith unto them, (ʰhe that came †to Jesus by night, being one of them,)

Of Nicodemus we read, and of his coming by night to Jesus, chap. iii. 1, 2. He now, being one of this great court, stands up to speak for Christ, yet faintly, or at least very prudently and warily. He saith no more for him than he ought to have spoken for the greatest malefactor, viz.

g Deut. 1. 17. & 17. 8, &c. & 19. 15.

51 ᵍDoth our law judge *any* man, before it hear him, and know what he doeth?

That no law of God or nature condemneth any man before they had heard him speak, or had what he did deposed by witnesses before them, that they might know what he did.

h Is. 9. 1, 2.
Matt. 4. 15.
ch. 1. 46.
ver. 41.

52 They answered and said unto him, Art thou also of Galilee? Search, and look: for ʰ out of Galilee ariseth no prophet.

Art thou also of Galilee; not that they thought Nicodemus was a Galilean; they knew him well enough; but they take up this as a term of reproach against him, for that he would offer to speak one word (though never so just) on the behalf of one against whom they had such a perfect hatred. *Search* (say they) the Scriptures, *and look* if ever there came a prophet out of Galilee. Suppose this had been truth; yet, 1. What did this concern our Saviour? who was not born in Galilee, but in Judea, in Bethlehem, the city of David, Luke ii. 4. 2. Could not God when he pleased influence one of Galilee with the Spirit of prophecy? But, 3. Neither was it true; for Nahum and Jonah were both Galileans, 2 Kings xiv. 25, compared with Josh. xix. 13, (for the tribe of Zebulun had their lot in Galilee,) Isa. ix. 1.

53 And every man went unto his own house.

As little as Nicodemus said for Christ, it put a stop to their further proceedings against Christ at present. Some think that the party of the Sadducees in the council, who valued not the Pharisees' rites and traditions, took part with Nicodemus; so as by the overruling hand of God Christ at this time escaped their wicked counsels against him. So much is certain; but what parties in the council concurred in it, is uncertain.

CHAP. VIII

Christ letteth go uncondemned the woman taken in adultery, 1—11. *He declareth himself to be the light of the world, and justifieth his doctrine against the Pharisees*, 12—30. *He promiseth freedom through knowledge of the truth to those Jews who believed on him*, 31, 32; *confuteth their vain boast of being Abraham's seed, and the children of God*, 33—47; *answereth their reviling by showing his authority and dignity*, 48—58; *and by miracle rescueth himself from their attempts to stone him*, 59.

JESUS went unto the mount of Olives.

A mountain within less than two miles of Jerusalem, whither our Saviour, when he was at Jerusalem, was wont often to withdraw, for privacy and devotion, Matt. xxiv. 3; xxvi. 30; Luke xxi. 37; xxii. 39.

2 And early in the morning he came again into the temple, and all the people came unto him; and he sat down, and taught them.

So at our Lord's last passover Luke notes, chap. xxi. 38, that *all the people came early in the morning to him in the temple, to hear him*. Our Saviour's early going into the temple to teach, and the people's diligence in coming so early to him to hear, ought to check our slothfulness in sacred business. Multitudes of people came to him; for so the universal particle *all* must be expounded in a multitude of Scriptures. *He,* after the manner of the Jewish teachers, *sat down, and taught them.* Of this custom of theirs, for their doctors, while they taught, to sit down, we have had occasion to speak before.

3 And the Scribes and Pharisees brought unto him a woman taken in adultery; and when they had set her in the midst,

There were (as they say) three sorts of scribes amongst the Jews. The first were secretaries to princes and great men; so Sheva was scribe to David, 2 Sam. xx. 25. A second sort were such as we call scriveners, or public notaries, who made instruments for people, and were employed in their more private bargains and contracts. Neither of these seem to have been of authority enough to have done this act; and besides, the Pharisees being joined with them makes it evident, that these scribes were those who expounded the law in the temple and in the synagogues, and are therefore called lawyers. They are often joined with the Pharisees in our Saviour's discourses, Matt. xxiii. 13—15, &c. And we find them often joining with them in their discourses and actions, tending to entrap our Saviour: such was their design at this time.

4 They say unto him, Master, this woman was taken in adultery, in the very act.

They bring to our Saviour a woman taken in the act of adultery, and set her before him.

5 ᵃNow Moses in the law commanded us, that such should be stoned: but what sayest thou?

a Lev. 20. 10.
Deut. 22. 22.

Moses in the law, Lev. xx. 10, commanded that such malefactors should be put to death; but we read of no law commanding this kind of death. And their rule was, that when the law had set no kind of death for an offence, there the mildest kind of death was to be their punishment, which they counted strangling to be. But they ordinarily entitled Moses to their traditional additions to the law; and death being commanded by the law, as the punishment of such offenders, they took themselves to be at liberty to determine the kind of death, as prudence and reason of state ruled them; so as, probably, they, seeing that that sin grew very frequent amongst them, appointed stoning to be the kind of death such malefactors should be put to. The manner of which we are told was this: The guilty person was to be carried up to some high place, and thrown down from thence headlong by such as witnessed against him; then they threw stones at him till they had killed him, if not killed by the fall; or covered him, if he were dead. This they tell our Saviour Moses commanded, because he had commanded in the general, that such a person should die, and their sanhedrim had determined this particular death to such malefactors. But they would know what our Saviour said to this.

6 This they said, tempting him, that they might have to accuse him. But Jesus stooped down, and with *his* finger wrote on the ground, *as though he heard them not.*

Their design was from his answer to take some colourable pretence to accuse, and either to discredit him with the people, or to expose him to the displeasure of the superior powers. If he had directed to send her to be punished by the Roman governors, who administered justice in capital causes, the people would be fired with indignation; for they looked upon them as invaders of the rights of government that belonged to the Israelites. If he had advised them to put her to death by their own power, they would have accused him of sedition, as an enemy of the Roman authority. If he had dismissed her as not worthy of death, they would have accused him to the sanhedrim, as an infringer of the law of Moses, as a favourer of dissoluteness, an enemy to civil society, and worthy of universal hatred. This malicious design, so craftily concerted, our Saviour easily discovered and defeated; whereas they thought it would require his most attentive consideration to extricate himself from the snare. He seemed not at all to attend to what they said, but, stooping down, wrote on the ground: what he wrote, or how he could write upon the floor of the temple, (which was of stone,) are very idle questions; the first not possible to be resolved, the second impertinent; for it is not said, that he made any impression upon the ground, though it be said, he wrote upon it. It appeareth plainly to have been but a divertive action, by which our Saviour signified that he gave no ear to them.

7 So when they continued asking him, he lifted up himself, and said unto them, ^b^He that is without sin among you, let him first cast a stone at her.

^b Deut. 17. 7.
Rom. 2. 1.

They will not let our Saviour alone, but importune him for an answer. He saith, *He that is without sin, let him first cast a stone at her.* The law of God was, Deut. xvii. 7, that in the execution of malefactors, *The hands of the witnesses shall be first upon him to put him to death.* In reason those who are zealous for the punishment of others, should neither be guilty of the same, nor of greater crimes, themselves. By this saying of our Saviour, we must not understand it the will of God, that those who are magistrates, and employed in executing the Lord's vengeance on malefactors, should themselves be free from all guilt, for then no justice should be done. The vengeance is God's, not theirs; it is the law of God which they execute. He only by this minds them of that compassion which ought to be found in persons prosecuting others justly, that they may execute judgment with compassion and tenderness, and such moderation as the law will allow them, considering that they are not free from guilt, but as obnoxious to the justice of God for other sins, as those poor creatures whom God hath suffered to fall into sins punishable by human judges.

8 And again he stooped down, and wrote on the ground.

When our Saviour had said this, he returneth to his former posture and action, (it being not a thing wherein he was concerned,) who was not sent into the world to be a secular judge, as not at all regarding them.

^c Rom. 2.22.

9 And they which heard *it*, ^c^being convicted by *their own* conscience, went out one by one, beginning at the eldest, *even* unto the last: and Jesus was left alone, and the woman standing in the midst.

This was an age of very great corruption as to men's lives and manners, as well as to doctrine, and corruption of worship; and as other enormities of life were very common and ordinary amongst them, so it is very probable were adulteries, and that their rulers and teachers were not without great guilt. Now, see the power of conscience, when set on work by God; these accusers' consciences were to them as a thousand witnesses; they were reproved and convicted by them, and not able to stand under the reflections of them, or to say any thing in answer to what our Saviour had said: they went away one after another; and possibly it is particularly noted that they began *at the eldest*, because the consciences of the eldest of them charged them more deeply for more and greater sins. Jesus was left not wholly alone, for the next words tell us, that the woman was still left standing in the midst; and no doubt but his apostles were there, for they constantly attended him; and no doubt divers others were also there: but the meaning is, that he was by this means quit of the scribes' and Pharisees' company, who were gone out of shame, being thus convicted by their own consciences, which told them, that whatsoever this woman was, they were no fit accusers.

10 When Jesus had lifted up himself, and saw none but the woman, he said unto her, Woman, where are those thine accusers? hath no man condemned thee?

The close of the former verse told us, that though the scribes and Pharisees were gone, yet the woman was left in the midst, expecting Christ's sentence. Christ knew well enough that the scribes and Pharisees, this poor woman's accusers, were gone; but yet he acteth warily, and calls for her accusers, and asks if no man had condemned her? thereby intimating, that the law against adultery was a just law; and if the crime were proved against her, she deserved to die; but she must first be convicted, and condemned. He asks her, If she were condemned? for then he had nothing to say.

11 She said, No man, Lord. And Jesus said unto her, ^d^Neither do I condemn thee: go, and ^e^sin no more.

^d Luke 9. 56.
& 12. 14.
ch. 3. 17.
^e ch. 5. 14.

She tells him, None had. He replieth, Neither did he. He did not acquit her, for he was not to make void the law of God; nor did he condemn her: he was neither a witness in the case, nor yet a secular judge, to whom such judgments did belong; he was only to speak to her, as the Mediator and Saviour of man. *Go,* I discharge thee, as being *coram non judice*, before one who in my present capacity am no judge to hear this cause, and to give sentence in it. *Sin no more;* whatever becometh of thee as to man's judgment, thou hast reason to fear the greater judgment of God, if thou goest on in a course of sin. Nor doth he say, Commit adultery no more; but, *sin no more.* No partial repentance or sorrow for any particular sin will suffice a penitent that hopes for any mercy from God; but a leaving off all sin, of what kind soever it be.

12 ¶ Then spake Jesus again unto them, saying, ^f^I am the light of the world: he that followeth me shall not walk in darkness, but shall have the light of life.

^f ch. 1. 4, 5,
9. & 3. 19. &
9. 5. & 12.
35, 36, 46.

I am the light of the world; this is what John the Baptist had said of Christ before, chap. i. 4, 5, and what Christ saith of himself afterward, chap. ix. 5. It was prophesied of him, that he should be *a light to the Gentiles,* and God's *salvation to the ends of the earth,* Isa. xlvi. 6. And old Simeon saith of him, Luke ii. 32, that he was to be *a light to lighten the Gentiles, and the glory of his people Israel.* Light is a thing glorious in itself, and communicative of itself unto others to guide them. So as Christ is most aptly compared to light, and spoken of under that notion; as for his own innate glory, so for the communicativeness of himself to creatures; which latter appeareth to be chiefly here intended: for he saith, that he who followed him, believing his doctrine, and obeying his precepts, living according to his direction and his example, should not be at a loss how to guide himself, nor remain in the darkness of sin, ignorance, and spiritual death; but should have that light which bringeth life along with it, and is sufficient to guide a man in all the works of a spiritual life, and at last bring him to life eternal.

13 The Pharisees therefore said unto him, ^g^Thou bearest record of thyself; thy record is not true.

^g ch. 5. 31.

It was a known rule of law, that none ought to be believed upon a testimony given to himself: this is that they object to our Saviour, that though he spake great things of himself, yet he was not to be believed in his own cause.

14 Jesus answered and said unto them, Though I bear record of myself, *yet* my record is true: for I know whence I came, and whither I go; but ^h^ye cannot tell whence I come, and whither I go.

^h See ch. 7.
28. & 9. 29.

There is a seeming difficulty to reconcile the words of our Saviour, chap. v. 31, *If I bear witness of myself, my witness is not true,* and his assertion here, *Though I bear record of myself, my record is true*: but the resolution of it is clear by considering that he speaks in the former chapter of his own single testimony with respect to them, as not of sufficient validity to authorize his Divine vocation, according to the rule of their law, that required a double testimony for confirmation of things; but here he speaks of the verity of it in itself. *For I know whence I came, and whither I go;* that is, I know from whom I have received my commission, (though secret to the world,) even from the Father: and yet, after the accomplishing of my embassy for his honour, I shall return to heaven, and be glorified with the glory I had with him before the world was, chap. xvii. 5. The reason alleged implieshis being the Son of God; and his Father's entire approbation of his office, and fidelity in the discharge of it; and the concurrent testimony

S. JOHN VIII

15 ¹Ye judge after the flesh; ᵏI judge no man.

According to my outward appearance to you, so you judge of me; or, according to your own passions, and corrupt affections. I judge no man in that manner; or, I judge no man alone, as it followeth in the next verse.

16 And yet if I judge, my judgment is true: for ¹I am not alone, but I and the Father that sent me.

My testimony is not to be looked upon as a single testimony for myself; though I do judge, yet my judgment is true; for no act of mine is a single act: I and my Father are one; and what I do, my Father also doth, that sent me into the world as his ambassador. So as if the judgment of God be true, which you all own, grant, and acknowledge; then my judgment is true, because it is not mine only, but the judgment also of that God, whom you own, acknowledge, and worship, and who sent me into the world.

17 ᵐIt is also written in your law, that the testimony of two men is true.

It is written, Deut. xvii. 6; xix. 15. God so ordered it by his Divine law, that every thing should be established by the testimony of two witnesses.

18 I am one that bear witness of myself, and ⁿthe Father that sent me beareth witness of me.

I (saith our Saviour) have two witnesses; I am one, I bear witness of myself; my Father is another, for he beareth witness of me. Our Saviour's argumentation seemeth weak, unless we look upon him as exempt from the condition of ordinary men, and no mere man, by reason of the personal union of the Divine and human nature in his person. Nor must our Saviour be understood here to distinguish himself from his Father, in respect of his Divine being, for so he and his Father are one; but in respect of his office, as he was sent, and his Father was he who sent him. And indeed in the whole he seemeth to accommodate himself to the people's apprehensions of him.

19 Then said they unto him, Where is thy Father? Jesus answered, °Ye neither know me, nor my Father: ᵖif ye had known me, ye should have known my Father also.

Thou talkest much of thy Father, where is he? We know no father which thou hast but the carpenter, Joseph; we do not look upon him as so credible a witness in the case, as to take his testimony in such a matter as this is. Christ tells them, that the reason why they did not know the Father, was because they did not know and acknowledge, receive and believe him; for if they had received and believed him, they would not then have been at such a loss to have known where his Father was, or who he was. The eternal Father is not to be known but in, and by, and through the Son.

20 These words spake Jesus in ᵠthe treasury, as he taught in the temple: and ʳno man laid hands on him; for ˢhis hour was not yet come.

The treasury was a public place in the temple; concerning which, see the notes on Matt. xxvii. 6; Mark xii. 41, 43; Luke xxi. 1. Christ taught sometimes in one part of the temple, sometimes in another: but that no man should lay hold on him, considering the search made for him in the beginning of the feast, and their sending messengers to take him, as we read chap. vii. 32, and the affront he had given to the scribes and Pharisees, of which we read in the beginning of this chapter, was very miraculous; nor can any account be given of it besides what is here given, viz. that his *hour was not yet come;* which was the reason we heard given before in the same case, chap. vii. 30. Men shall be able to do nothing against Christ, or any that belong unto him, till the time cometh that God hath set in his wise and eternal thoughts.

21 Then said Jesus again unto them, I go my way, and ᵗye shall seek me, and ᵘshall die in your sins: whither I go, ye cannot come.

The greatest part of what is said here, was said by our Saviour before, chap. vii. 34; (see the explication of it there;) only here, instead of *ye shall not find me,* is, *ye shall die in your sins;* a phrase we shall find in Ezek. iii. 18, 19, which doubtless signifieth, in the guilt of your sins, not removed from you; and is a threatening of eternal death, as well as temporal in the destruction of Jerusalem: and those who do so, cannot come into heaven, where Christ is.

22 Then said the Jews, Will he kill himself? because he saith, Whither I go, ye cannot come.

Before they guessed that he would go to the dispersed amongst the Gentiles, chap. vii. 35. Now they fancy that he would kill himself; or else speak this in mockery.

23 And he said unto them, ˣYe are from beneath; I am from above: ʸye are of this world; I am not of this world.

Ye are not only of an earthly extraction, creatures of the earth, not descended from heaven, as I am; but also of earthly spirits and principles; you savour nothing that is sublime and spiritual, and therefore you do not understand me. I tell you, *I am not of this world;* my original is not from it, nor am I to determine my being in it. I shall die, but I shall rise again from the dead, and ascend into heaven, where you cannot come. Still our Saviour asserts his Divine nature; and the stress of all, he saith, lieth there; their unbelief of which was the cause of all their disputings and errors. He had given them the greatest evidence of it imaginable in the works which he had done in their sight, which were not only above the power of nature, but such as God had never authorized, or enabled any creature to do; yet they, being destitute of supernatural grace, did not believe in him. And they were inexcusable, because that grace was denied them for their wilful corruption and wickedness, which they might have avoided by the use of that common grace which was not denied them.

24 ᶻI said therefore unto you, that ye shall die in your sins: ᵃfor if ye believe not that I am *he,* ye shall die in your sins.

In the Greek it is only, *if ye believe not that I am.* Some refer this to Christ's Divine nature; *(I am,* is the name of God, Exod. iii. 14;) but others rather think that Christ here speaketh of himself as the Messiah and Mediator, and so the object of people's faith; and he out of whom there is no salvation: the latter indeed includeth the former; for *cursed is he that trusteth in man, and maketh flesh his arm,* Jer. xvii. 5. The text plainly holds forth an impossibility of salvation for those who, under the revelations of the gospel, receive not and believe not in Christ as Mediator.

25 Then said they unto him, Who art thou? And Jesus saith unto them, Even *the same* that I said unto you from the beginning.

What good Christian will not learn to contemn the slights and reproaches of sinful men, when he readeth of a company of miscreants thus using their Lord and Master, saying to him, *Who art thou?* It is no wonder if the world, which knew him not, doth not know us. The latter part of the verse, as it lies in the Greek, is exceedingly difficult; word for word it is, The beginning, because also I speak unto you. Some think that our Saviour calleth himself *The beginning.* Others think the noun is in this place put for an adverb; of which we have many instances in Scripture, though none as to this noun. But I shall leave those who desire satisfaction as to what is said by critics about this verse, to what Mr. Pool hath collected in his Synopsis Criticorum, and only consider it as our interpreters understood it; in which form it seemeth to be a mere slighting of them, as much as if he had said, I have often enough, even from the beginning, told you who I am; I can say no more to you upon that head than I have said. I am the same, and no other, than I at first told you I was.

26 I have many things to say and to judge of you: but ᵇhe that sent me is true; and ᶜI speak to the world those things which I have heard of him.

Judging is not put here for judicial condemnation; but for reproving and accusing, which is one part of judging. You accuse and reprove me; I have many things of which I could also accuse and convince you; but let me say what I will, you will not believe me. But you will not escape the judgment of my Father, who is true, he will judge you. I speak unto men nothing but what it is his will that I should declare to them.

27 They understood not that he spake to them of the Father.

The Jews (as we are told) used to call God *The Father*, in a way of eminency: they understood that he spake to them of his Father; but they would not understand when he spake to them of his Father, or the Father, he meant God the Father of all; their minds were blinded, that they could not see, and their hearts hardened, that they could not understand.

28 Then said Jesus unto them, When ye have ᵈlifted up the Son of man, ᵉthen shall ye know that I am *he*, and ᶠ*that* I do nothing of myself; but ᵍas my Father hath taught me, I speak these things.

It is your unhappiness, that while I am alive, and preaching the gospel to you, inviting you to repentance, and faith in me, as the true Messiah, you will not believe me to be indeed what I am; but you shall lift me up upon the cross, (for that is meant by lifting up, as chap. iii. 14; xii. 32,) and when that time cometh, you shall know that I am *the light of the world*, as ver. 12; for after that, the gospel began to be preached to all nations: or, that I am the true Messiah, he whom the Father hath sent into the world. Some of you shall then know it by those signs and wonders that shall attend my death and resurrection, and to your shame and confusion: others of you shall know it to your eternal joy and salvation; believing on me then, whom you will not now acknowledge; and that what I have done, I have only done by commission from my Father, not of myself; and that what I have taught, I have had in commission from my Father to teach.

29 And ʰhe that sent me is with me: ⁱthe Father hath not left me alone; ᵏfor I do always those things that please him.

I have the presence of God with me, as I am Mediator; the Father hath not sent me into the world to do his will, and left me alone without his presence; for I do his will; I drive no separate design from my Father, but always do those things which please him. From whence all faithful ministers and Christians may learn how to conclude of God's presence with them, which they can no longer promise to themselves, than they speak and do those things that please him.

30 As he spake these words, ˡmany believed on him.

Believing on him is not here to be understood strictly of saving faith; but rather, of some preparations toward it: they began to believe that he was the true Messias, and to have more honourable thoughts than they had of him: that this was all, will appear from what we find in the following verses; and believing often signifieth no more in the New Testament than a light assent given to some propositions of the gospel relating to Christ.

31 Then said Jesus to those Jews which believed on him, If ye continue in my word, *then* are ye my disciples indeed;

Believed on him, in the sense before expressed. Our Saviour well enough saw their hearts, and in what manner they believed, and what sort of disciples they were, viz. only nominal: they have the name of disciples who come after Christ to hear him; but they are his disciples indeed, who make his doctrine the rule of their lives. He therefore tells them, That not a mere saying to him Lord, Lord, and yielding some light assent to some propositions of

truth in the gospel, would make them his disciples in truth and reality, without an abiding and continuance in the words which he taught them.

32 And ye shall know the truth, and ᵐthe truth shall make you free.

And ye shall know the truth; that is, you shall more fully and clearly know the truth; by which may be either understood Christ, who styleth himself, *The way, the truth, and the life;* or those propositions of truth which Christ hath revealed. There must be some knowledge of truth in a soul before it can believe; for *how shall they believe* (saith the apostle) *in him of whom they have not heard?* but a fuller and clearer knowledge of the truth is got by degrees, by those who studiously seek after it, and walk close with God. *And the truth shall make you free:* it appears by ver. 36, that by *the truth* he means himself; there he saith, *If the Son make you free:* and indeed, though the knowledge of the proposition of truth gives men some liberty from the bondage of ignorance and some lusts, yet it is only the saving knowledge of Christ which brings men into a perfect liberty from the law, the rigour, curse, and terror of it, and from the dominion of sin and corruption.

33 ¶ They answered him, ⁿWe be Abraham's seed, and were never in bondage to any man: how sayest thou, Ye shall be made free?

How carnally doth a carnal heart understand spiritual mysteries! Thus Nicodemus, hearing of being *born again*, grossly dreamed of entering into his mother's womb, and being born again. The woman of Samaria, hearing of *living water*, dreamed of water that should so satisfy her thirst, as that she should never come again to the well to draw. The Jews here hearing of being made free, dream of a freedom from human bondage and slavery. To what our Saviour had said, that if they knew the truth, the truth should make them free; they reply, *We are Abraham's seed, and were never in bondage to any.* Admitting that they were Abraham's seed, that is, Jews, were not the Jews in bondage, first to Pharaoh, king of Egypt; then to Nebuchadnezzar, king of Babylon? they were now in bondage to the Romans. They must either understand it of their own persons, though they were tributaries they were no slaves; or else concerning their right, they had a right to liberty though they were under an extrinsic servitude to their conquerors. This made them angry, that Christ should speak of their being *made free;* for those that are free are not in a capacity to be made free. The Jews were a people very tenacious of their liberty, and gloried much in the right they had to it.

34 Jesus answered them, Verily, verily, I say unto you, ᵒWhosoever committeth sin is the servant of sin.

Our Saviour here correcteth their mistake, letting them know, that he was not speaking about any corporal, but spiritual servitude; not of the freedom of men's bodies from the power of enemies, but of the freedom of men's souls from the slavery and dominion of lusts and corruptions. He that doth sin (saith he) is the servant of sin. The committing or doing of sin here intended, is not to be understood of single acts of sin, for in that sense who lives and sinneth not? (the righteous man sinning seven times in a day;) so as all men would be concluded the servants of sin; but of living indulgently and habitually in a course of sin, and in the practice of gross sins; in which sense workers of iniquity is to be taken, Matt. vii. 23; and this very phrase, 1 John iii. 4. And indeed, the very heathen could see, that there was no such slavery as a servitude to lusts and passions: men are *the servants of corruption*, 2 Pet. ii. 19; under the dominion of sin, Rom. vi. 20.

35 And ᵖthe servant abideth not in the house for ever: *but* the Son abideth ever.

The servant of sin abideth not in the church (which is the house of God) for ever. Look as it is with slaves, and servants; they are no fixed members of families; they may be turned out, they may be sold over to others; they abide in families according as in them they behave themselves: so you, who, as you are Abraham's seed, as you boast and glory, are now servants in the church of God; yet if you continue to be servants of sin, you shall not for ever abide in God's house; if you be not cast out of the church militant, you shall certainly be cast out of the church triumphant; that is, you shall never come there. *But the Son;* some think he speaks of himself, who was the eternal Son of God, he *abideth ever;* but I rather think he speaks of him that is a son by adoption, John i. 12; Rom. viii. 15, 16. So as this text showeth us the remarkable difference betwixt a nominal professor, and one who is a true believer: the one is but as a servant in God's house, to whom belongeth no inheritance; though while he is in the family, he enjoyeth some common privileges which a mere stranger hath no right to: the other is a son, and hath a right to the inheritance, and so shall never be cast out of the family, but abideth in it for ever.

q Rom. 8. 2.
Gal. 5. 1.
36 q If the Son therefore shall make you free, ye shall be free indeed.

If that term *the Son* in this verse be the same with *the Son* mentioned in the former verse, they must both be understood of Christ: for it is most certain, that here *the Son* can signify no more than Christ, to whom alone it belongeth to make souls free from the slavery of the law, sin, death, hell, &c. Now, saith our Saviour, this is the true freedom. Alas! what is the freedom you boast of and glory in? It is not the freedom of your inward man, if you were in the fullest actual possession of it; many a one in that sense free, hath a base, servile, slavish mind, and is a servant to corruption and lusts. It is only the freedom which I give unto souls, that is a true and perfect liberty, and is alone worthy the name of it.

37 I know that ye are Abraham's seed;
r ch. 7. 19.
ver. 40.
but r ye seek to kill me, because my word hath no place in you.

According to the flesh you are descended from Abraham, that I know; but of what advantage is or can this be to you, while in the mean time you are implacable enemies to me, and seek to murder me, who am not only an innocent person, but am the Lord of life, and came to save the world? And the root of this is your unbelief: did you receive and believe the word that I have spoken to you, you would do otherwise; but although the sound of my word pierceth your ears, and then you receive a little of it, yet it passeth not into your hearts, it hath no place within you; you do not believe it, you are not affected with it, it doth not dwell in you as it ought to do, so that you are not turned into the likeness and obedience of it. Men may be professors and members of the church of God, in whom yet the word of God hath no rooting, and findeth no true place; so as that their condition may be sad enough.

s ch. 3. 32.
& 5. 19, 30.
& 14. 10, 24.
38 s I speak that which I have seen with my Father: and ye do that which ye have seen with your father.

My Father is God; I declare unto you his mind and will; no uncertain things, but what I have seen with him, that is, what I certainly know to be his will. You declare by your actions who is your father; and as I do my Father's will, and what he teacheth me to do, so you do the works which the devil, who is your father, ver. 44, prompteth you to do.

39 They answered and said unto him,
t Matt. 3. 9.
ver. 33.
t Abraham is our father. Jesus saith unto
u Rom. 2. 28. & 9. 7.
Gal. 3. 7, 29.
them, u If ye were Abraham's children, ye would do the works of Abraham.

Abraham is our Father; this was their continual boast, as may be learned from Matt. iii. 9; glorying in their birth privilege, Abraham being the father of the whole Jewish nation; and in their church privilege, Abraham being the head of the Jewish church, and he to whom the promises were made. But Christ taketh them off this glorying, by reminding them, that the blood of Abraham running in their veins would be of little significancy to them, so long as they did not walk in Abraham's steps. Men are truly to be accounted the children of those, not from whom they are naturally descended, but whose steps they walk in, and whom they imitate in their conversations.

x ver. 37.
y ver. 26.
40 x But now ye seek to kill me, a man that hath told you the truth, y which I have heard of God: this did not Abraham.

You declare by your actions that you are very far from the spirit and temper of Abraham: I am one who, being sent of God, whom you own as your Father, have faithfully revealed the will of God to you, and have never told you any thing but the truth; and this is all my crime, for which you seek to murder me: this was none of your father Abraham's practice; so as though you have something of Abraham's blood, yet you have nothing of Abraham's spirit in you.

41 Ye do the deeds of your father. Then said they to him, We be not born of fornication; z we have one Father, even God.
z Is. 63. 16.
& 64. 8.
Mal. 1. 6.

Ye do the deeds of your father; you imitate him who is indeed your father; by whom our Saviour (as we shall hear more afterwards) meaneth the devil. This they fume at, and tell him they were not *born of fornication,* which is, in our English dialect, as much as, We are no bastards; but it hath another sense in this place, as appeareth by the next words. *We have one Father, even God;* that is, we own and worship one God, who is our Father; which makes very good interpreters think, that their meaning in those words, *We are not born of fornication,* is, We are no idolaters; idolatry in holy writ being very ordinarily compared to whoredom and fornication.

42 Jesus said unto them, a If God were your Father, ye would love me: b for I proceeded forth and came from God; c neither came I of myself, but he sent me.
a 1 John 5. 1.
b ch. 16. 27.
& 17. 8, 25.
c ch. 5. 43.
& 7. 28, 29.

This agreeth with what we have 1 John v. 1, *Every one that loveth him that begat, loveth him also that is begotten of him.* But here our Saviour rather seemeth to speak of his proceeding forth and coming from God, as sent into the world to fulfil the will of God as to the redemption of man, than of his proceeding from his Father by eternal generation. It is true, that he who loves the father will also love the child, so far forth as he resembleth his father, and acteth like unto him; and it is as true, that he who loveth him that sends a messenger will also love the messenger, executing the commission of him that sent him.

43 d Why do ye not understand my speech? *even* because ye cannot hear my word.
d ch. 7. 17.

It is manifest all along this discourse, that Christ spake riddles to the Jews, and that they understood not the import and sense of his discourse: Now (saith our Saviour) the reason is, *because ye cannot hear,* that is, believe, *my word:* they could and did hear it with their ears; they heard the sound of it, but they could not discern the spiritual sense and meaning of it: it was not given to them to know the mysteries of the kingdom of God, Matt. xiii. 11. And the reason was, because they suffered themselves to be blinded by prejudice, and by their own lusts and corrupt affections, till God gave them up to a judicial blindness, that hearing they heard, and did not understand; and seeing they saw, and did not perceive.

44 e Ye are of *your* father the devil, and the lusts of your father ye will do. He was a murderer from the beginning, and f abode not in the truth, because there is no truth in him. When he speaketh a lie, he speaketh of his own: for he is a liar, and the father of it.
e Mat. 13. 38.
1 John 3. 8.
f Jude 6.

Our Saviour now plainly tells them what he meant by their *father,* mentioned ver. 38; viz. the devil, whose children though they were not by natural traduction, yet they were by imitation, wilfully doing the things which the devil would have them do. He instanceth in two of these lusts: 1. Murder. He saith, The devil from the beginning of the world had a mind and design against the sons of men; and he ever since (as the apostle tells us, 1 Pet. v. 9) hath gone about like *a roaring lion, seeking whom he may devour.* And in this they were his true children, using all arts imaginable to destroy him whom God had sent into the world for man's salvation. In another thing also they were the true and genuine children of the devil; the devil had *no truth in him*, nor did he abide in the truth. God indeed created the angels (who afterward fell) in a state of rectitude, without unrighteousness; but they did not keep their first station. So, neither did they love the truth, nor abide in it, but were wholly false and liars, and could not abide the truth.

45 And because I tell *you* the truth, ye believe me not.

Such is your hatred to the truth, that you hate me for no other reason but because I reveal my Father's will (which is the truth) to you; than which nothing can evidence a greater hatred to truth, nor conformity and likeness to the devil. There cannot be a greater evidence of any one's hatred of the truth, than the hatred of those who tell them the truth, and for this very reason, because they do so.

46 Which of you convinceth me of sin? And if I say the truth, why do ye not believe me?

If any of you can prove that I have spoken to you any thing that is false, and not consonant to the will of my Father, do it; but which of you is able to charge me with any such thing? If there be no such thing, but I have told you what is the very truth, and the will of my Father, as to what you are to believe and do, why do you not believe me? for every reasonable soul is a debtor to truth.

g ch. 10. 26, 27. 1 John 4. 6.

47 ᵍHe that is of God heareth God's words: ye therefore hear *them* not, because ye are not of God.

He that is of God; to be of God, here, is opposed to a being not of God, and so may be understood to comprehend election, as well as regeneration. *Heareth God's words;* he heareth, acknowledgeth, believeth, and patiently submitteth to the will of God revealed in his word. The reason why you, though with your ears ye hear the word of God, yet do not in heart receive, and embrace, and believe it, nor can submit to it, *is because ye are not of God,* not chosen of him, not savingly enlightened and regenerated by him. So as this text affords us an excellent note, by which we may know whether we be regenerated, and of God, yea or no. That is, our believing and yielding obedience to the will of God revealed in his word. By this saying of our Saviour, he seemeth to acquiesce in the will of God, concerning these refractory and unbelieving Jews, notwithstanding all the pains he had taken with them to enlighten and bring them to the saving knowledge of the truth. It pleased not his Father to open their eyes that they might see, or their hearts that they might understand. This ought in like manner to satisfy all the true and faithful ministers of the gospel, when they see they have laboured in vain, and spent their strength for nothing. and in vain. When they have done all they can, they will find this of our Saviour true, That the work must be God's, and not theirs; and no more hearts will be changed, than theirs who are of God.

48 Then answered the Jews, and said unto him, Say we not well that thou art a Samaritan, and ʰhast a devil?

h ch. 7. 20. & 10. 20. ver. 52.

A Samaritan signified to the Jews as much as an impostor, or seducer; for the Jews looked upon the Samaritans as a detestable sort of men, who had corrupted the worship of God with their horrible superstitions in Mount Gerizim. *And hast a devil*; that is, art mad: see the notes on chap. vii. 20.

49 Jesus answered, I have not a devil; but I honour my Father, and ye do dishonour me.

I have not a devil; that is, I am not possessed with an evil spirit, as you blaspheme; or, (as others think,) I am not mad, I speak the words of truth and soberness, (for it is said, that the Jews held an opinion, That all who were distracted were influenced by an evil spirit, and had a devil). It is true in both senses, Christ had no devil. He did nothing that he did, but for the honour of his Father; this was but a term of scandal and reproach they cast upon Christ. In the mean time it must be observed, with how much meekness the Lamb of God received these most unworthy reproaches cast upon him; that we may learn to behave ourselves in like manner under such temptations.

i ch. 5. 41. & 7. 18.

50 And ⁱI seek not mine own glory: there is one that seeketh and judgeth.

Christ very often remindeth them of this, that in what he spake and did, he sought not his own honour and reputation; which both obviated an objection they might make against him, and also convinced them of his truth and sincerity in what he did. But, saith he, though I seek not my own honour, yet there is one who cometh himself in my honour and glory; and you must expect that he should judge and condemn you for all your hard speeches which you have spoken against me.

51 Verily, verily, I say unto you, ᵏIf a man keep my saying, he shall never see death.

k ch. 5. 24. & 11. 26.

To *see death*, in this text, signifieth to die, but in an apparently differing sense from what it is taken in Luke ii. 26, where it is to be understood of a natural death; of which it cannot be understood here, for the holiest men shall die: *The body is dead* (that is, in dying) *because of sin*; or, shall die because of sin, Rom. viii. 10. It must therefore be understood of death eternal; and in that sense the proposition is certainly true, That a holy man that keepeth the sayings of Christ shall not see death, that is, shall have eternal life; which is no more than what we have often before met with, viz. the promise of life eternal to faith and holiness.

52 Then said the Jews unto him, Now we know that thou hast a devil. ˡAbraham is dead, and the prophets; and thou sayest, If a man keep my saying, he shall never taste of death.

l Zech. 1. 5. Heb. 11. 13.

Thou hast a devil: this is the third time we have met with this blasphemous imputation from these wretched men, chap. vii. 20, in this chapter, ver. 48, and here. What we have here, may strongly incline us to believe, that by the phrase they did not intend that he was possessed with the devil; for they here declare themselves confirmed in what they said, from his speaking that which was contrary to sense and demonstration. Abraham was dead, (though the father of the faithful,) and the prophets were dead; and therefore to speak of any mortal man's not seeing death, was contrary to every day's experience, and to the experience of the holiest men who ever lived. To them therefore who understood him speaking of a natural dissolution of the soul and body, this looked like the language of one beside himself; which probably was all they meant, when they said he had a devil, unless they used it as a term of reproach and passion; of all which none can give any just account.

53 Art thou greater than our father Abraham, which is dead? and the prophets are dead: whom makest thou thyself?

If thou canst so effect it, that those who keep thy sayings shall not die, thou canst also make thyself immortal: neither Abraham nor the prophets could save themselves from death, they are all dead: what art thou? what dost thou make thyself? And by the way, this was another charge upon our Saviour, the Jews having no patience with any that should prefer himself before their father Abraham or Moses.

54 Jesus answered, ᵐIf I honour myself, my honour is nothing: ⁿit is my Father that honoureth me; of whom ye say, that he is your God:

m ch. 5. 31.
n ch. 5. 41. & 16. 14. & 17. 1. Acts 3. 13.

If I honour myself, my honour is nothing; this is much the same with what our Saviour said, chap. v. 31, which he seemed to contradict, ver. 14; (see the notes on both those places;) the meaning is, If I seek mine own honour and glory; or, If I arrogate to myself what indeed doth not belong to me; or, If I alone honour myself, which (by the next words) seemeth to be the true sense of the phrase here. My Father is he who honoureth me, by witnessing from heaven that I am his beloved Son; by sending me into the world to accomplish his work; by many signs and wonders: and you say, that this my Father is your God. If therefore you will not give credit to me and my testimony, yet you ought to give credit to him, whom you own as your God.

55 Yet ᵒye have not known him; but

o ch. 7. 28, 29.

I know him: and if I should say, I know him not, I shall be a liar like unto you: but I know him, and keep his saying.

Knowing here signifies more than a notional knowledge, or comprehending in our understanding so much of God as may by natural powers be comprehended; it signifies affections, and a conversation suitable to such a knowledge. But I (saith our Saviour) fully and perfectly know him, both as to his essence, counsels, and will, and am fully obedient to him.

p Luke 10. 24.
q Heb. 11. 13.

56 Your father Abraham ᵖrejoiced to see my day: ᵍand he saw *it*, and was glad.

You glory much in this, that you have Abraham to your father. This father of yours foresaw my coming into the world, and my dying upon the cross. He saw it by the eye of faith, in the promise which was made to him, That in his seed all the nations of the earth should be blessed. He saw it in the type of Isaac's being offered, then receiving him in a figure, Heb. xi. 19. He saw it in the light of Divine revelation. He saw my coming in the flesh; my dying upon the cross for sinners; the publication of my gospel to the whole world, by which means all the nations of the earth became blessed in his seed. And he *was glad*, with the joy of faith, which gives the soul a union with an absent object by faith made certain to it, Heb. xi. 1.

57 Then said the Jews unto him, Thou art not yet fifty years old, and hast thou seen Abraham?

Christ was at this time but three and thirty years old, and upward: they dream of Abraham's seeing him, and his seeing Abraham, with bodily eyes, of which Christ said nothing; that indeed had been a thing impossible, for Abraham was dead many hundred years before Christ appeared in the flesh to the world: neither doth our Saviour say, that he had seen Abraham, or that Abraham had seen him; but that he had seen his day, his coming in the flesh, his death, which Abraham had seen, not with bodily eyes, but with the eye of faith.

r Ex. 3. 14.
Is. 43. 13.
ch. 17. 5, 24.
Col. 1. 17.
Rev. 1. 8.

58 Jesus said unto them, Verily, verily, I say unto you, Before Abraham was, ʳI am.

Some will have the meaning to be, that Christ was before Abraham's time constituted Mediator; as he is said to be *the Lamb slain from the foundation of the world*, Rev. xiii. 8: so 1 Pet. i. 20. But thus it might have been said of any of the elect, that they were chosen before Abraham was. It is therefore undoubtedly to be understood of Christ's eternal existence, as to his Divine nature; and this will appear, as from other arguments, so from the whole scope of our Saviour's former discourse in this chapter, which was to assert his Divine nature and equality with the Father.

s ch. 10. 31, 39. & 11. 8.

59 Then ˢtook they up stones to cast at him: but Jesus hid himself, and went

t Luke 4. 30.

out of the temple, ᵗgoing through the midst of them, and so passed by.

Then took they up stones to cast at him; as they also did, chap. x. 31. It is vain to inquire where they had stones in the temple; they might be repairing some part of it, or some parts of it paved with stones might be loose, &c.; it is enough that we are assured that some they found. He did not go *through the midst of them* that were in this uproar, but first thrust himself into the more innocent crowd, then passed through the midst of them. Some make a question here, how he could pass through the midst of them? whether he made his body invisible? (so the Lutherans think;) or whether he struck his enemies with blindness, or thickened the air before their eyes? But what needs that dispute? admit some few of the rabble to be in a rage, the greatest part innocent, it is no hard thing for us to conceive how a person, discerning the disorder, may thrust himself into the more innocent crowd, and pass by, escaping the rage of his enemies.

CHAP. IX

A man that was born blind receiveth sight, 1—7. *He relateth to his neighbours the means of his cure*, 8—12. *He is brought to the Pharisees, who examine strictly into the fact, and are offended with his acknowledgment of the Divine mission of the author*, 13—33. *They excommunicate him*, 34. *He is received of Jesus, and confesseth him*, 35—38. *Christ taxeth the Pharisees with spiritual blindness*, 39—41.

AND as *Jesus* passed by, he saw a man which was blind from *his* birth.

The evangelist doth not tell us where our Saviour was passing by, but the word seemeth to import a passing by the highway-side, when he saw this poor man, who was born blind; which is particularly noted, because such blindness is judged incurable as to the art of man.

2 And his disciples asked him, saying, Master, ᵃwho did sin, this man, or his parents, that he was born blind?

a ver. 34.

The disciples' question supposed two things for truth: 1. That all bodily punishments and afflictions come upon men for sin. 2. That as some come upon them for personal sins, so others come upon them for the sins of their parents. The latter is unquestionably true: so is the former, but not universally: as there are afflictions which are punishments of sin, so there are some that are trials.

3 Jesus answered, Neither hath this man sinned, nor his parents: ᵇbut that the works of God should be made manifest in him.

b ch. 11. 4.

Our Saviour must not be understood here, as either asserting the blind man or his parents free from sin, and a degree of sin deserving such a punishment; but as speaking to his disciples' question strictly, and answering, that this affliction came not upon him, either for any personal sin of his own, (for he could not be guilty of any actual sin before he was born,) nor yet for any sin that his parents had committed: but that the works of God might be made glorious in him; both his work of power in afflicting, and his work of mercy in healing him.

4 ᶜI must work the works of him that sent me, while it is day: the night cometh, when no man can work.

c ch. 4. 34. & 5. 19, 36. & 11. 9. & 12. 35. & 17. 4.

The Father, who sent Christ into the world, gave him work to do: his general work was, to glorify God upon the earth, John xvii. 4, as by working out the redemption of man, so by revealing his will to the sons of men, and working miracles for the glorifying the name of God. Saith Christ, I have a set time to work in; that is, that which he here calleth *day*, the time wherein Christ was to live upon the earth. *The night cometh, when no man can work;* I am not to be here always, there will come a time when I must be absent from the earth, then none of this work can be done. A good argument to persuade every Christian to work while the time of his life lasteth, for the night of death will come, when no man can any longer work out his salvation; but as the tree falleth, so it must lie, Eccles. ix. 10.

5 As long as I am in the world, ᵈI am the light of the world.

d ch. 1. 5, 9. & 3. 19. & 8. 12. & 12. 35, 46.

Those words, *As long as I am in the world*, let us know what our Saviour meant by the *day*, mentioned ver. 4, viz. the time he should be in the world. Saith he, So long as I am in the world, it is a part of my work to show light to the world. Christ indeed, though he hath left the world, is yet the light of the world; but he was the light of the world, that part of the world especially where he was, in a more eminent sense, so long as the world enjoyed his bodily presence in it.

6 When he had thus spoken, ᵉhe spat on the ground, and made clay of the spittle, and he ∥anointed the eyes of the blind man with the clay,

e Mark 7. 33. & 8. 23.
∥ Or, *spread the clay upon the eyes of the blind man.*

Several mysterious allegories are found out by men of luxuriant fancies, with reference to the manner of our Saviour's curing this blind man; as if our Saviour had made choice of clay, to show, that as he at first made man of the dust of the earth, so he could again cure him with dust; and that his spittle denoted the efficacy of Christ's humanity, being now personally united to the Divine nature. Others think, he made use of spittle, because the Jews had a great opinion of the medicinal virtue of spittle; and, they say, forbade the medicinal use of it on the sabbath day, on which day this miracle was wrought. But all these things are great uncertainties, for which we want any guidance from holy writ. It is most probable, that our Saviour made use of the spittle in working this miracle because he had no water at hand, for water was a very scarce thing in those hot countries. That which we are chiefly to attend in this great miraculous operation is, Christ's demonstration of his Divine nature, for the confirmation of the truth of which he doubtless wrought this great work, as well as to show his charity to this poor creature. To this purpose, 1. He maketh choice, not of a blind man only, but one who was born so, and so incurable according to all judgment of human art. 2. He maketh use of no means that had any appearance of a natural virtue in it; nay, which was more likely to put out the eyes of one that saw, than to give sight to one that was blind.

f Neh. 3. 15.   7 And said unto him, Go, wash 'in the pool of Siloam, (which is by interpretation, Sent.) ᵍHe went his way therefore, and washed, and came seeing.

g See 2 Kin. 5. 14.

He doth not only anoint his eyes, but sendeth him also to *wash in the pool of Siloam*. We read of this pool, Neh. iii. 15; and we are told, that it was a fountain which sprang out from Mount Zion. It should seem, that there was a brook of that name, which supplied part of the city with water, Isa. viii. 6. Some think they have also found a mystery in this name, because it signifieth *sent*; and think that it hath an allusion to Shiloh, which was the Messias, mentioned Gen. xlix. 10. The name is plainly an old name, as appears from the place I noted out of Nehemiah; probably given to it anciently, in acknowledgment of the mercy of God given them, in sending them such a brook, or rivulet, from those mountains, so commodious for that great city: or, because (as some think) the water did not run always, but at certain times, as it were sent of God. We read of nothing medicinal in this water, only, as a probation of the blind man's faith and obedience, it pleased our Lord to send the blind man to wash himself there; as of old Naaman the Syrian was sent to wash in Jordan. He went, and the evangelist, to let us see that true faith joined with sincere obedience never faileth the expectation of them that exercise it, lets us know that he returned seeing.

8 ¶ The neighbours therefore, and they which before had seen him that he was blind, said, Is not this he that sat and begged?

The evangelist now reports the consequents of this miracle. He, being cured, returneth to his friends: those who lived about that place, had taken notice of his ordinary sitting there, and begging; now, seeing him perfectly recovered, they ask one another, if this were not the blind beggar that used to sit there.

9 Some said, This is he: others *said*, He is like him: *but* he said, I am *he*.

Some conclude it was he, others doubted, but did think he was like him: he puts it out of doubt, and saith that he was the man.

10 Therefore said they unto him, How were thine eyes opened?

According as is the nature of most men upon the sight of any new and strange accident, they are curious to know how it came to pass, who did it, and where he was. The blind man tells them, that he was cured.

h ver. 6, 7.   11 He answered and said, ʰA man that is called Jesus made clay, and anointed mine eyes, and said unto me, Go to the pool of Siloam, and wash: and I went and washed, and I received sight.

By one that was *called Jesus*; probably he had heard some of the people mention him by that name; and he describeth to them the manner how he did it.

12 Then said they unto him, Where is he? He said, I know not.

They would know where he was; this he knows not.

13 ¶ They brought to the Pharisees him that aforetime was blind.

Whether the neighbours, or his near relations, is not said. Nor is the place mentioned where this convention of Pharisees was, whether in the temple, or in some synagogue, or in the great court which they called the sanhedrim; nor is it material for us to inquire into.

14 And it was the sabbath day when Jesus made the clay, and opened his eyes.

It was observed before, that Christ made choice of the sabbath day, as the day wherein he did many of his mighty works. It was on the sabbath day that he cured the impotent man who lay at the pool of Bethesda, chap. v. 10; and upon the sabbath day that he cured him who had the withered hand, Matt. xii. 10; and now again upon the sabbath day that he cured him who was born blind. Possibly he chose that day, because that was a day wherein he ordinarily preached that heavenly doctrine, which he confirmed by these miraculous works; or, perhaps, that he might take occasion from thence to instruct the Jews, if they would have received instruction, in the true doctrine of the sabbath, that they might not superstitiously think that it was not lawful to do acts of mercy on the sabbath day: certain it is, that himself maketh that improvement of it, Matt. xii. Or to show them, that he was the Lord of the sabbath; and that, as his Father by his works of providence worketh on the sabbath day, so did he, being equal with his Father: by which argument he before defended himself for the cure of the impotent man on the sabbath day, John v. 17.

15 Then again the Pharisees also asked him how he had received his sight. He said unto them, He put clay upon mine eyes, and I washed, and do see.

The Pharisees asked him how he had received his sight; they had before heard it from others, but they now desire to hear it from himself; not (as appears) out of any good design, that they might be convinced of the truth of the thing, or that he who had wrought this miracle was the Son of God; but that they might have something to object against Christ, and to quarrel with him for, upon their traditions, with reference to the observation of the sabbath; of which we are told this was one, That it was unlawful for any to anoint their eyes with spittle on the sabbath day; they having a conceit that it was a medicinal application. The blind man is not ashamed to own the goodness of God to him to the Pharisees, but relateth the same story which he before had related to the people.

16 Therefore said some of the Pharisees, This man is not of God, because he keepeth not the sabbath day. Others said, ⁱHow can a man that is a sinner do such miracles? And ᵏthere was a division among them.

i ver. 33. ch. 3. 2.
k ch. 7. 12, 43. & 10. 19.

They are so far from owning Christ as God, the eternal Son of God, and equal with his Father, that they will not allow him to have any relation to God, as one sent of him. It is true, the sanctification of the sabbath is so great a piece of religion, (the whole of which is sometimes expressed by it, Isa. lvi. 4, 6,) that whoso maketh no conscience of it, may reasonably be concluded to have little or nothing of God in him: but we must rightly understand what the will of God is as to that sanctification, and not think that it lieth in a performance of some ritual services, while in the mean time we neglect moral duties. Christ had kept the sabbath, though not in that superstitious sense they thought it was to be observed, keeping to all their traditions about it. Others of the Pharisees had a something better opinion of Christ by reason of the miracles he had wrought; concluding, that if he had been so bad a man, as some of their brethren would have him taken to be, God would not have assisted him to the doing of such miraculous works as he had done. Thus the wise God made a division amongst the counsels of Christ's enemies, his work being not yet finished, nor the time come when he was to die for the redemption of man.

S. JOHN IX.

17 They say unto the blind man again, What sayest thou of him, that he hath opened thine eyes? He said, ¹He is a prophet.

^{1 ch. 4. 19. & 6. 14.}

What sayest thou of him, that he hath opened thine eyes? What opinion hast thou of this man, who hath opened thine eyes? To make the question perfect, interpreters think, there ought to be this supplement, on the sabbath day. What dost thou think of such a man as this, who would make clay, and apply it to thy cure upon the sabbath day? How can such a fact be defended? The blind man answered, *He is a prophet.* It was taken for granted by the Jews, according to their traditions, that at the command of a prophet it was lawful to violate the sabbath; which indeed is no more than, that God hath not, in giving us a law, bound up himself, but he may dispense with his own law. Their prophets had an extraordinary mission from God, and immediately revealed the will of God; so as they looked upon what they said as spoken by God himself. The blind man declareth, that he believed that Christ was a prophet; and being so, his words and actions had an extraordinary warrant, and therefore were not to be judged by ordinary rules.

18 But the Jews did not believe concerning him, that he had been blind, and received his sight, until they called the parents of him that had received his sight.

That is, the rulers of the Jews did not, or the multitude or rabble of the Jews did not; for we before heard that many of the common Jews did: they had seen him for a long time sit begging; (begging being allowed in that their corrupt and miserable state, they being tributary to the Romans; though in their settled, prosperous state, there was such a liberal provision made for their poor, that there was no beggar in Israel,) besides, they had it from his own mouth, ver. 9: but the rulers had no mind to believe it; and many others of the Jews (possibly) had been no eye-witnesses of his begging, but had only heard the relation from others: the rulers therefore send for the parents of the blind man.

19 And they asked them, saying, Is this your son, who ye say was born blind? how then doth he now see?

The parents of this man that was blind, in their answer show a great deal of discretion and prudence. Three things the Pharisees ask: 1. Whether this was their son? 2. Whether (as they said) he was indeed born blind? 3. How he came now to see? The manner of the propounding their question, *who ye say,* lets us know what answer they would have had, and that they did not send for the parents of this blind man out of a desire to know the naked truth of the thing, but hoping to fright them into a speaking doubtfully (at least) whether it was their son, yea or no; or whether he was stark blind when he was born, yea or no. But, alas! the providence of God ordering his condition to be so poor, that he was glad to beg for his livelihood, made this design vain, would his parents have gratified the Pharisees by any shuffling and indirect answer.

20 His parents answered them and said, We know that this is our son, and that he was born blind:

21 But by what means he now seeth, we know not; or who hath opened his eyes, we know not: he is of age; ask him: he shall speak for himself.

But besides this, the parents of this man proved honester and stouter than, it may be, the Pharisees did expect. They affirm, that they knew that he was their son, and that he was born blind. But for the third question, How he now saw? they avoid an answer to that, being possibly no eye-witnesses of Christ when he wrought the miracle. For this they refer them to their son, who was no babe, but a man grown, one of age, able to speak for himself; of whom they might inquire, and he was best able, as to this thing, to give them satisfaction.

^{m ch. 7. 13. & 12. 42. & 19. 38. Acts 5. 13.}

22 These *words* spake his parents, because ᵐ they feared the Jews: for the Jews had agreed already, that if any man did confess that he was Christ, he ⁿ should be put out of the synagogue.

^{n ver. 34. ch. 16. 2.}

The reason why his parents answered so very warily, and avoided saying any thing to the Pharisees' third question, which probably they could not do of their particular personal knowledge, was, that they were afraid of the rulers of the Jews. Solomon saith, *The fear of man bringeth a snare,* Prov. xxix. 25; it is often a temptation to men to deny the truth, or, at least, not to own and confess it when God calls to them for a public owning and confession of it: but nothing of that nature appeareth in this case; for it doth not appear that his parents were present when Christ wrought this great miracle; which if they were not, they were not obliged to tell the Pharisees what themselves had only received by rumour and hearsay: so that their answer seems but a prudential answer, to avoid an eminent danger. For they were not ignorant of a decree made by the Jewish sanhedrim, That if any did publicly say, or declare, that Jesus was Christ, he should be excommunicated; for that is meant by being *put out of the synagogue.*

23 Therefore said his parents, He is of age; ask him.

24 Then again called they the man that was blind, and said unto him, ᵒ Give God the praise: ᵖ we know that this man is a sinner.

^{o Josh. 7. 19. 1 Sam. 6. 5. p ver. 16.}

They were not able to obtain their design from the parents of this poor man; now they again call him, and advise him to give glory to God. Thus far they spake well, if they had been hearty and serious in what they said; for the man indeed had great reason to give God the glory, by whose power alone, exerted by his Son Christ Jesus, he had received his sight: but moral actions are made good or bad by their ends; and if we consider the end of these wretched men in this action of theirs, wherein they persuaded the poor man to his duty, the words will appear to have been spoken from hearts minding nothing less than the glory of God, and out of a design to vilify and depreciate his Son; whereas God hath set up his rest in his Son, and cannot be glorified but with, in, and through him; whom in the next words they maliciously defame, not only speaking of him contemptuously, calling him *this man,* but affirm him ἁμαρτωλὸς, not *a sinner* only, but a notorious, scandalous sinner, as that word imports.

25 He answered and said, Whether he be a sinner *or no,* I know not: one thing I know, that, whereas I was blind, now I see.

This poor man being of no higher quality than a beggar, can be presumed to have had no great education; yet his answer is as good as could be expected from one of the greatest breeding, both for security to himself, and his stout asserting what was truth. As to their charge upon our Saviour of his being a great sinner, he avoideth it, telling them, as to that he knew nothing, nor was it his concern to inquire; but this he knew, that he had wrought a great work on him, for whereas he had been blind from his mother's womb, he now had his sight by his means: so as all their frowns could not tempt him to deny the miracle wrought upon him, nor yet to speak the least in abatement of it.

26 Then said they to him again, What did he to thee? how opened he thine eyes?

They cannot frown him into a denial of the miracle wrought; he stood stoutly to affirm, that he was born blind, and that he was cured by Christ: now they put him to tell the story over again, either hoping they should entrap him, contradicting himself in his story; or, at least, find something, upon his repeating the story, for them to take advantage from, to persuade the people that it was but a cheat, and indeed there was no such miracle wrought upon him.

27 He answered them, I have told you already, and ye did not hear: wherefore would ye hear *it* again? will ye also be his disciples?

It is wonderful to see how the boldness and confidence of the poor man increased; God giving him that wisdom and courage which they were not able to resist. He refuseth to repeat the story to them, telling them he had once already told it them, but they would not give credit to him; and to what purpose was it for him to say it over again, unless they were inclined to be his disciples? Some think the form of speech implieth a hearty wishing and desiring that they would be so: but others think he speaks ironically, as if he had said, I know my repeating again the story will not induce you to be his disciples, you are resolved against that, and therefore why do you put me upon a needless trouble? And this seemeth to have been his sense by what followeth in the Pharisees' reply, full of indignation.

28 Then they reviled him, and said, Thou art his disciple; but we are Moses' disciples.

If this were all their reviling, for them to tell this poor man that he was Christ's disciple, it was a very tolerable imputation, and what the blind man had reason to glory in: their guilt in reviling is to be judged not so much from what they spake, for there was nothing of greater honour, as from what heart and spirit they spake it. A *disciple* signifies, one that followeth another, and learneth of him. To be a disciple of Christ indeed, was the greatest thing that any could glory in; yet the imputation of it to this blind man is here called a reviling: whence we may observe, that the guilt of reviling is to be judged not so much from the words which a man speaketh, as from the frame of his spirit, and design of that in the speaking of them. If a man speaketh that of another which is good and true, yet if he doth it out of a design to expose him, to do him mischief, and make him odious unto others, God doth account this reviling, because it proceedeth from the hatred of our brother in our heart, and a design to do him harm. Again, though indeed it was no reproach to be called Christ's disciple, yet they affixed this term upon this poor man out of a design to reproach him, and to expose him to the hatred of others. We are in the government of our tongues not only obliged to take heed what we say, but with what heart, and out of what design we speak it. A malicious design turns terms of the greatest honour into terms of reviling. Besides, they here oppose Christ and Moses: whereas, Moses was but the type, Christ the antitype; Moses prophesied of Christ, Christ was that Prophet which God had promised to raise up like unto him; Moses but the schoolmaster, who led them unto Christ.

29 We know that God spake unto Moses: *as for* this *fellow*, ᵠwe know not from whence he is.

q ch. 8. 14.

Concerning Moses indeed they speak honourably, and say, they knew God spake to him; yet did they know it no otherwise than by tradition, and the revelation of the will of God in the law and the prophets. For Christ, they call him τῦτον, *this fellow*; and say, they know not whence he was; that is, they know of no Divine authority that he had. They were blinded through malice and prejudice. Indeed they did know whence he was as to his human nature, for they often made that the cause of their stumbling at him; that he was of Galilee, that his father was a carpenter, and his mother called Mary: but they knew of no Divine mission or authority that he had: this they might have known also, for he did those things which no man ever did, nor could be effected by any thing less than a Divine power; but their eyes were blinded, and their hearts were judicially hardened; they studied to shut out the light by which they should have seen, and would not know whence he was.

30 The man answered and said unto them, ʳWhy herein is a marvellous thing, that ye know not from whence he is, and *yet* he hath opened mine eyes.

r ch. 3. 10.

The opening of the eyes of the blind without the application of means rationally probable for the producing such an effect, nay, by the application of means which to all human reason seemed of a quite contrary tendency; and this cure wrought upon one who was not blind by some accidental cause, but by some defect in nature, who had been so from his mother's womb, was so manifest an effect of the Divine power, that this poor man was astonished at it, that they should not understand that it was done by such a power, either immediately or mediately; especially considering the prophecy concerning the Messias, Isa. xxxv. 5, 6, to which Christ referreth John and his disciples for an evidence of it, Matt. xi. 5.

31 Now we know that ˢGod heareth not sinners: but if any man be a worshipper of God, and doeth his will, him he heareth.

s Job 27. 9. & 35. 12. Ps. 18. 41. & 34. 15. & 66. 18. Prov. 1. 28. & 15. 29. & 28. 9. Is. 1. 15. Jer. 11. 11. & 14. 12. Ezek. 8. 18. Mic. 3. 4. Zech. 7. 13.

This poor man proveth that Christ was from heaven, because he had opened his eyes; not as yet apprehending that Christ did it by putting out an immediate Divine power for his healing; but as a great prophet, obtaining such a power from God for the confirmation of the things which he delivered. *Now* (saith he) *we know that God heareth not sinners.* But the question is, what truth there is in this axiom, or proposition. Doth not God hear sinners? Then he can hear none; for who liveth, and sinneth not against God? How did he hear Ahab, and others who were notorious sinners? *Answ.* 1. By *sinners* here must be understood notorious and presumptuous sinners, that live and go on in courses of sin with hardened hearts: the word here used signifieth bold, presumptuous sinners; not such as sin merely through ignorance, weakness, or human infirmity. 2. God is under no covenant obligation to hear sinners; they can challenge no such favour upon the account of any promise: but God, out of the aboundings of his goodness, may hear them, as he heard Ahab and others; he may hear them as his creatures crying in their misery, though he hears them not as children, or upon the account of any covenant. 3. As to the sense of this maxim in this place, it seemeth to be particular and special; and the words seem to be restrained to that particular degree of favour here spoken of; God useth not to honour notorious and flagitious sinners, by giving them a power to work miracles, by which they should confirm any thing which they say. This poor man bringeth this as an argument, why Christ should not be such a notorious sinner as they spake him, because it was not God's way to honour such persons with his presence and assistance to the doing of those things which none could do but by a Divine power committed to him. Two things this man assumeth, or taketh for granted: 1. That no man can work miracles, without a power obtained of God by prayer, as we saw it was in the case of Elisha, 2 Kings iv. 33. 2. That what Christ did, he did as a man. The first is true, the second was false. He was not yet convinced of Christ's Divine nature, nor looked upon him higher than as a prophet, one sent of God, to reveal the will of God, and to work great works in the world by prayer; as to which he affirms, that if he were such a sinner as they clamoured, God would not hear him. So as the question, How far God may hear sinners, in giving them any thing they ask of him, seemeth not at all proper to this place; though it be enough clear from other scriptures, such as Psal. lxvi. 18, and Isa. i. 5, that none that live in a course of sin can expect that God should hear or give answer to their prayers, and though God may give to such sinners such things as they ask him for, which are of a mere external concern, yet it is not with respect to any promise which he hath made to them, but out of the aboundings of his own goodness. But if a man feareth God, and worketh righteousness, him the Lord heareth, accepteth, and answereth. *The secret of the Lord is with them that fear him,* Psal. xxv. 14; Prov. iii. 32.

32 Since the world began was it not heard that any man opened the eyes of one that was born blind.

He proveth Christ to be sent from God, (though it appears by ver. 33 that he looked as yet upon him in no higher notion than a man,) from the nature of the miracle that was wrought; which was not the recovery of a blind man's sight only, but giving sight to one who was born blind. Now, saith this poor man, this is such a work as was never done by Moses, or by any of the prophets who have been since the creation of the world. Some who have been blind from some accidental cause, and something which hath befallen them, films and cataracts, &c., have been cured; and possibly God by his almighty power may have given sight to one born blind; but we never heard of any such thing done by Moses, whom we magnify; nor by the prophets, for whom we have the greatest veneration.

S. JOHN IX

^{t ver. 16.} 33 ^tIf this man were not of God, he could do nothing.

If therefore this man (for still he apprehended him no more) had not some special authority from God, and there were not some special presence of God with him, he could do nothing that is of this nature. It is a work beyond the power of man, and beyond that power that we read God did ever trust any man with.

34 They answered and said unto him,
^{u ver. 2.} ^uThou wast altogether born in sins, and
‖ Or, *excommunicated him*, ver. 22. dost thou teach us? And they ‖ cast him out.

The Pharisees seeing that they could by no arts bring this poor blind man to their lure, either to deny, or speak any thing in abatement of, the miracle which Christ had wrought upon him; nor yet to agree with them, that Christ was a great sinner; fall at last to a downright railing; they tell him, he was *altogether born in sins*. So were all of them. David had taught them, that there was none righteous, no not one; and confessed concerning himself, Psal. li. 5, that he was conceived in iniquity, and that in sin his mother had brought him forth. They had learned from Job, that none can bring a clean thing out of that which is unclean; nothing can be clean that is born of a woman, Job xiv. 4. Their meaning therefore in this phrase must be something more; and possibly the adjective ὅλος, which signifieth whole, (we translate it as if it were ὅλως, *altogether*.) doth import thus much. They do not only tell this man that he was born in sin, but that he was whole or *altogether* born in sin, that is, under the guilt of sin: nor do they mean only the common corruption and contagion of human nature, derived from the loss of God's image in man upon the fall of Adam, but some notorious sin. If any say, How could they think that he was guilty of any such thing before he was born? *Answ.* It was the opinion of Pythagoras, one of the heathen philosophers, that when men and women died their souls went into other bodies that were then born, and in those bodies often suffered punishment for those enormous acts which they had been guilty of in former bodies. It is apparent that the Jews were some of them tainted with this notion, from Herod's saying, Matt. xiv. 2; Mark vi. 14, when, after the beheading of John the Baptist, he heard what great works Christ did, that John the Baptist was *risen from the dead, and therefore mighty works* did *show forth themselves in him;* by which the best interpreters think, that Herod meant no more than that John the Baptist's soul was gone into another body, according to their notion borrowed from the heathens; for it had been easy for Herod by search to have found whether John the Baptist's body was risen from the dead. So it is thought that the Pharisees here saying, *Thou wast altogether born in sins*, meant that his soul was a sordid, filthy soul, which in another body had committed vile and abominable things; and for those sins God set a mark upon him, even in his birth, and he was born blind. Or perhaps this phrase signified no more than a term of reviling; of which no great account can be given, as passionate men in the madness of their passions oft throw out words of reproach, of which neither themselves nor others can give any just and reasonable account. *And dost thou teach us?* Thou that art such a marked villain from thy mother's womb, or that art such an ignorant idiot, dost thou think thyself fit to instruct us about true and false prophets, who are of God, and who are not? Surely we are to be thy teachers, and not thou ours. *And they cast him out:* some think that casting out here signifieth no more than a turning him out of the place where they were; as the word signifieth, Acts vii. 58; xiii. 50. Others think it is here to be understood of a judicial excommunication, or casting him out of communion with the Jewish church; which latter seemeth more probable, because of the notice of it brought to our Saviour, and the notice which he took of this poor man, upon this occasion. If it had been only a turning him out of the place where they were met, it is not probable that it would have made such a noise.

35 Jesus heard that they had cast him
^{x Matt. 14. 33. & 16. 16. Mark 1. 1. ch. 10. 36. 1 John 5. 13.} out; and when he had found him, he said unto him, Dost thou believe on ^xthe Son of God?

Jesus heard that they had cast him out, as was said in the former verse, probably by excommunication. *When he had found him,* (whether casually, or upon an industrious search for him, the Scripture doth not say,) *he said unto him, Dost thou believe on the Son of God?* art thou one who art ready truly and seriously to embrace the Messiah and Saviour of the world, who must not be only the Son of man, but also the Son of God? Art thou willing to accept, receive, and close with him, and to give up thyself to his obedience?

36 He answered and said, Who is he, Lord, that I might believe on him?

It is as much as if he had said, Lord! how should I believe on him, of whom I have not heard? (So the disciples answered Paul, asking them whether they had received the Holy Ghost, *We have not so much as heard whether there be any Holy Ghost,* Acts xix. 2.) But, saith he, Lord, I am ready to believe on him, may I but know who he is. Our Lord had prepared this poor man's heart for the receiving of him; there wanted now nothing but the due revelation of the Messiah unto him. This our Saviour giveth him.

37 And Jesus said unto him, Thou hast both seen him, and ^yit is he that ^{y ch. 4. 26.} talketh with thee.

This is as much as, I am he. Thou hast not only seen him with the eyes of thy body, but thou hast had experience of his Divine virtue and power, in giving thee sight who wert born blind: thus seeing also signifieth, chap. xiv. 9. It is very observable here, that miracles do not work faith, but confirm it. The blind man had experienced here a miracle wrought upon himself, but yet he is an unbeliever, until the Lord cometh to give him the revelation of his word: *faith cometh by hearing:* but together with this word we must also conceive a mighty power to have flowed from Christ, inwardly enlightening him, and enabling him to discern the truth of what he told him, and making him yet further willing to receive him, and close with him.

38 And he said, Lord, I believe. And he worshipped him.

Now is the work of faith with power wrought in his soul: he saith, Lord, I do acknowledge and receive thee as the Son of God; I am fully persuaded that thou art more than what thou art in thy external form and appearance, more than a mere man, and I give up myself to thee, to be ruled and guided by thee. And as a testimony of this, he performed some act of external adoration to him. The word signifies prostration; he kneeled down to him, or he fell upon his face before him: we are not able to determine what particular act or posture of adoration he used; but there is nothing plainer, than that it is to be understood of such a Divine adoration and homage as is due unto God alone, for it was such as testified his faith in him as the Son of God, whom he had professed that he believed him to be, in the words immediately preceding: although therefore the word in the Greek be a word used sometimes to signify that civil respect which men show to their superiors, yet it cannot be so interpreted in this place, considering what went before.

39 ¶ And Jesus said, ^zFor judgment ^{z ch. 5.22,27. See ch. 3. 17. & 12. 47. a Mat. 13.13.} I am come into this world, ^athat they which see not might see; and that they which see might be made blind.

There is a great variety in interpreters' notions about the *judgment* here mentioned. Some think that by it is meant the Divine counsel and decree: I am come into the world, to execute the just will, and counsel, and pleasure of my Father: and the event of it is this, that some who saw not, see; and some who see, in a sense are made blind. Others understand it of condemnation; I am come to execute the judgment of condemnation: but thus it is hardly reconcilable to John iii. 17, where it is said, that *God sent not his Son to condemn the world.* The best notion of it is theirs who interpret it of the spiritual government of the world, committed to Christ, and managed by him with perfect rectitude and equity. One eminent part of this was his publishing the gospel, the law of faith. The event of which is, that many spiritually blind, and utterly unable to see the way that leads to eternal life, might (as this person that was born blind is now clear-sighted) be enlightened with the saving knowledge of the truth; and many that think they see, should by their obstinate infidelity be more blind than they were from their birth. Not that I cast any such ill influence upon them; but this happeneth through their own sore eyes. I am *the light of the world;* and as it is of the nature of light to make other things visible to men; and it hath its effect, and doth so, where men's eyes are not ill affected with humours and the like; so the light of my gospel, by which I shine in the world, makes the way of salvation by me, ordained by my Father, Acts iii. 18, evident and clear to many souls who are in darkness and the shadow of death: but it so happeneth, through the prejudices that others are prepossessed with against me, and the doctrine of my gospel by which I shine in the world, so full of ignorance, malice, and hatred against me and the doctrine which I bring; that through their own perverseness, and the righteous judgment of God, at last giving men over to their own delusions, they are made more blind. In this sense this scripture agreeth with what was prophesied by Isaiah, chap. viii. 14, *And he shall be for a sanctuary; but for a stone of stumbling and for a rock of offence to both the houses of Israel, for a gin and for a snare to the inhabitants of Jerusalem;* and the words of Simeon in Luke ii. 34, *Behold, this child is set for the fall and rising again of many in Israel;* as also with that of Paul, Rom. ix. 33.

40 And *some* of the Pharisees which were with him heard these words, [b]and said unto him, Are we blind also?

b Rom. 2.19.

The Pharisees attended our Saviour almost in all places where he went, to catch something from him whereof they might accuse him: they could not but understand, that the import of our Saviour's last words was, that this poor blind man, now not only receiving bodily sight, (though born blind,) but a spiritual illumination, by which he discerned that Christ was the Son of God, the true Messiah and Saviour of the world, was an instance of those mentioned, who, not seeing before, upon Christ's coming saw; and that themselves and their masters were an instance of those whom he intended by such as saw, and by his coming were made blind; for our Saviour had often called them blind, and so represented them to the people to whom he preached, Matt. xv. 14; Luke vi. 39. They therefore grew very angry, being very proud, and not patient to be thought or called blind, looking upon themselves as the greatest lights of the Jewish church.

41 Jesus said unto them, [c]If ye were blind, ye should have no sin: but now ye say, We see; therefore your sin remaineth.

c ch. 15. 22, 24.

If ye were blind; if your ignorance were simple, and not affected, and you were sensible that your blindness were not incurable, and your sin might be pardoned. This appeareth to be the sense from the opposition of it, *now ye say, We see,* in the latter part of the verse. They were indeed blind, as to any true and saving sight of Christ, and of the true way of salvation by believing in him; seeing (as they apprehended) a way of salvation without Christ, by the works of the law, and wilfully shutting their eyes against the glorious light of the gospel shining on them. *Ye should have no sin;* you should not have so much sin, so much guilt upon your souls, as you now have: though your ignorance had been sin, yet it had not been so great a sin as a wilful shutting your eyes against the light. *But now ye say, We see;* now that you have an opinion that you see, and boast in your knowledge of the law, as if you were the only men that saw; and upon this presumption reject the doctrine of salvation; *therefore your sin remaineth,* by it you not only conclude yourselves under the guilt of sin, but your sin remaineth upon you, not pardoned to you: which teacheth us, that without a true and saving sight of sin, and such a one as carrieth the soul out of itself to Christ for pardon and remedy, there is no hope of pardon and forgiveness from all the mercy that is in God.

CHAP. X.

Christ declareth himself to be the Door, and the good Shepherd, 1—18. *Divers opinions concerning him,* 19—21.
He proveth to the Jews by his works that he is the Christ, and asserteth his unity with the Father, 22—30. *The Jews go about to stone him: he justifieth his doctrine,* 31—38; *and escaping from them, goeth beyond Jordan, where many believe on him,* 39—42.

VERILY, verily, I say unto you, He that entereth not by the door into the sheepfold, but climbeth up some other way, the same is a thief and a robber.

In this famous parable, which reacheth to ver. 30, our Saviour seemeth to drive two great designs: 1. To prove himself the true Shepherd. 2. To prove the Pharisees and teachers of those times thieves and robbers.

It should seem, that the sheepfolds in those countries were houses, which had doors by which the entry was into them: there is no doubt but by *the sheepfold* is meant here the church of God, in which the people of God are gathered together in one. By *the door* he apparently meaneth himself, as he himself speaketh, ver. 9. Or rather, more generally, that way which God hath appointed for any that are to take charge of his church to enter. He is both the Shepherd (the true Shepherd) and the Door: the Shepherd, as the care, conduct, and government of the church belongeth to him, and is upon his shoulders: the Door, as he is he whom the Father hath ordained to be the chief Shepherd, from whom all who pretend to any right to teach or govern in the church must derive both their authority and abilities. Now saith our Saviour, Whosoever they be, that thrust themselves into the care, conduct, and government of the church, without any call or warrant from my Father or me, who am the true Door, through which whosoever entereth into the church must enter; and the chief Shepherd, from whom he must derive, or be *a thief and a robber;* his very entrance makes it appear, that his end is not to feed the flock, but to feed himself; and that he drives only private designs of advantage to himself.

2 But he that entereth in by the door is the shepherd of the sheep.

As it is amongst men, the true shepherd goes into the sheepfold by the door; so it is in the church of God. He that taketh not the honour of governing the church to himself, but being called of God, as Aaron was, he is the shepherd of the sheep. This very argument the apostle useth to prove Christ to be the true High Priest, Heb. v. 4, 5, because he *glorified not himself to be made a High Priest,* but was made one by him who said unto him, Psal. cx. 4, (quoted there also, ver. 6,) *Thou art a Priest for ever after the order of Melchisedec.* God (whose the church is, called his *heritage,* his *peculiar people,* &c.) was the Door, by which Christ, the chief Shepherd, entered into the flock; he made him *the Head of the church.* Eph. v. 23. For this he is said to be sent; and often makes himself known to us under the notion of him whom the Father hath sent. And the under-shepherds must also derive from Christ: as the Father's will in sending Christ was his door, so the will of Christ in sending others is their door; that is, their only true way of entering upon the charge of the flock of Christ. *As my Father hath sent me, even so send I you,* John xx. 21. There is a double sending; the one is extraordinary, of which mission Christ speaketh to his apostles in that place; thus the apostles and first ministers of the gospel were sent; Christ *breathed on them,* and said, *Receive ye the Holy Ghost,* chap. xx. 22: and there was yet a fuller sending of these first shepherds, in the days of Pentecost, Acts ii. 17. And there is a more ordinary sending, as to which God revealed his will, 2 Tim. ii. 2, *The things that thou hast heard of me among many witnesses, the same commit thou to faithful men, who shall be able to teach others.* Thus the apostles, Acts xiv. 23, did themselves *ordain elders in every church.* And Paul for this purpose left Titus in Crete, to *set in order the things that are wanting, and ordain elders in every city,* Tit. i. 5. Whosoever entereth into any place in the church, for the feeding and governing of it, that way which God hath directed in his word, he entereth in by the door, he is the true shepherd. Concerning Christ's title, and his way of entrance, and the first preachers of the gospel, immediately sent by Christ, and declared to be sent by the effusion of the Spirit in the days of Pentecost, there can be no question made by any who believeth the Scriptures of the Old and New Testament. This text declares, that whosoever cometh into the church with right, and as a true shepherd to it, must come in at the door, by a call from God, (as Christ was sent,) or from Christ; either by an extraordinary mission, or in such a method and order as Christ hath in his word directed, either from his own mouth, or by the mouths of his apostles, whom he, ascending up into heaven, left in the first charge of his church. This is that which every one ought in the first place to look after. We shall observe in God's whole course with his church, that in the corruption of the state of the church, when it was eminently deviated from the rule he had set, he sent some by an extraordinary mission. Such were the prophets, whose writings make up a part of Scripture. Such were the apostles, and first ministers of the gospel. Such, we say, were our first reformers in Germany, and other parts: nor is it any prejudice to it, that they were able to work no miracles; we read of no miracles wrought by the prophets of old, unless by two or three of them. Their faithful declaring the will of God, and calling men back to the plain law of God in a time when the generality were obviously departed from it; together with their spirit of courage and boldness in their work, was evidence enough that God had sent them. But this text only declareth this general truth, That every true shepherd coming into the church, must come in the right way, by the door. So the great Shepherd of the sheep did, being sent by his Father, whose the church is, to take care of it: so must all inferior shepherds do, by him whom God the Father hath made the door; according to whose directions all the affairs of the church must be ordered.

3 To him the porter openeth; and the sheep hear his voice: and he calleth his own sheep by name, and leadeth them out.

By *the porter* is understood God; or more particularly, (to show the order of the Holy Trinity in working,) the Holy Spirit, who openeth the hearts of men to receive and embrace Jesus Christ, who is the chief Shepherd; and the sheep are able to distinguish his voice from the voice of thieves and robbers. Probably they had in those countries particular words and phrases, which, their shepherds having used them to, the sheep understood, and moved according to the direction of them. Some think they had also names for their sheep, (as we have for our dogs and horses,) which they understood. Otherwise, it only signifieth that particular knowledge which Christ hath of all those that are truly his: as the former phrase signified, that judgment of discerning spirits and doctrines, which was in an eminent degree in the first ministers of the gospel, and is yet in a measure in believers; by which, though they cannot perfectly and infallibly judge concerning truth, and the will of God, in all things, yet they can in a great measure do it; and are not ordinarily led aside into pernicious and damnable errors, to the ruin of their souls. And, saith our Saviour, the true shepherd leadeth the sheep out; that is, into their pastures and true feeding-places. This is eminently true concerning Christ the chief Shepherd: when he came into the world, God opened to him the door of his church; so as though he was rejected by many, (the builders and rulers of the Jewish church in particular,) yet he was by many received; multitudes followed him; many truly believed on him, and truly heard his voice; he had a particular knowledge of them who truly were his sheep; he knew Nathanael while he was yet under the fig tree; he led them out into their true pastures, preaching the gospel of the kingdom to them, and showing them the way of life and salvation. It is in its measure true of every inferior shepherd, that truly deriveth from Christ; God giveth unto such favour in the eyes of his people. The true sheep of Christ hear them, receive and embrace the truth delivered by them. They take a particular charge of them, and they lead them to Christ, and to the embracing of his gospel; as by the holy and true doctrine which they preach to them, so by their holy lives and conversations before them.

4 And when he putteth forth his own sheep, he goeth before them, and the sheep follow him: for they know his voice.

In our country at this day, shepherds generally follow their sheep, which go before them. In other countries, as France, &c., it is otherwise at this day; the shepherds go before their flocks, and their flocks follow them, upon some sounds they make. In Palestine (which was the Jews' country) it should seem that the shepherds sometimes went before their sheep, and sometimes followed them. David followed his father's sheep, 2 Sam. vii. 8; Psal. lxxviii. 71. On the other side, God is spoken of, Psal. lxxx. 1, under the notion of the *Shepherd of Israel*, who *leadeth Joseph like a flock*. And the psalmist, Psal. xxiii. 1, speaking of God as his *Shepherd*, saith, ver. 2, *he leadeth me beside the still waters*. Christ here speaketh of himself under the notion of a shepherd that went before his sheep, and whom the sheep followed; and thereby lets us know the duty of all faithful pastors in the church, so to live, that their flocks may follow them with safety; which cannot be, unless they follow Christ, 1 Cor. xi. 1. For, saith our Saviour, those that are my true sheep, they know my voice; thereby signifying that power of discerning betwixt truth and damnable errors, which the Lord gives unto all true believers, 1 John ii. 27.

5 And a stranger will they not follow, but will flee from him: for they know not the voice of strangers.

This he further enlargeth upon, telling them, that his sheep would not follow those that did not lead them into his truth, and in his ways, for they understood not such voices. Here ariseth a question, Whether the elect of God, or such as, being truly called, and believe in Christ, are the sheep of Christ in the most strict and proper sense, may not be seduced into errors, and led away by strangers? *Answ.* First, We must distinguish betwixt single persons and the generality of believers. As in a flock the generality keep together, following the voice of the true shepherd, though some particular sheep may wander; so the generality of believers will be found keeping close to the truth and doctrine of Christ, though amongst them some particular persons may be seduced, and be led away by seducers. Secondly, We must distinguish betwixt errors and damnable errors; a pertinacious adherence to which will divide the soul from Christ, and end in the ruin of souls. Christ's sheep may follow strangers, dissembling the spiritual voice of the true Shepherd, a little way, but they will not follow them into such errors as will plunge their souls in eternal ruin and destruction. Thirdly, They may hear even this voice of strangers speaking to them perverse and damnable things; but it will be but for a short time; God will reduce and bring them back again; *they shall never perish*, ver. 28.

6 This parable spake Jesus unto them: but they understood not what things they were which he spake unto them.

Our Saviour was wont to instruct them in the mysteries of the kingdom of God by parables, that is, similitudes taken from reasonable actions of men, which might be, and were, proper to express spiritual things by. Wherefore he used this method in teaching, we are told, Matt. xiii. 10—13. They well enough understood the words in which those parables were delivered; but the inward sense, the spiritual mysteries shadowed out in those similitudes, these they understood not; neither the common sort of his disciples understood them, nor did the better sort of his disciples understand them without a further explication of them. Our Lord therefore, in the following verses, comes to give them a large explication of the parable.

7 Then said Jesus unto them again, Verily, verily, I say unto you, I am the door of the sheep.

Our Saviour had before been speaking of *the door* in another notion; there he spake of the door of the shepherd; here, of the door of the sheep: there, of the door, that is, the true and regular way of entrance into the care, conduct, and government of the church; here, of the true way of entrance, not into the church militant only, but into the church triumphant. It may be also understood of the door, or way of entrance and admission, into the church visible here upon the earth. Circumcision, baptism, external profession, are the doors into the visible church; but none, unless by Christ, that is, by a true and lively faith wrought by the Spirit of Christ in the soul, can be a true member of Christ's invisible church here upon the earth, much less a member of his glorious church in heaven.

8 All that ever came before me are thieves and robbers: but the sheep did not hear them.

This must not be understood of the prophets, but of such only as came before Christ, not being sent by him: all those that taught people another way of life and salvation, than by believing in the Messiah, who was to be revealed for the salvation of the world; all such did but seek themselves, not the good of the people's souls; and destroyed souls instead of profiting or doing them any good. But those that were mine by an eternal election, or by my special grace bestowed upon them, did not embrace them.

a ch. 14. 6.
Eph. 2. 18.

9 ᵃ I am the door: by me if any man enter in, he shall be saved, and shall go in and out, and find pasture.

Our Saviour here lets us know, that he meant by *the door*, in the former verse, the door of salvation; the way by which every man must enter into life that findeth life; not the door only by which every true pastor must enter into the church, but by which every soul that shall be saved must enter into heaven; which is the doctrine which he before taught, John iii. 16, 18, 36. And he, who so believeth in me, shall be so guided, and governed, and taught, that he shall be secure, and want nothing for the management of his whole conversation in the world. Under the notion of *pasture* here, are signified all good things that the soul can stand in need of: it is much the same promise with that chap. vi. 35, *He that cometh to me shall never hunger; and he that believeth on me shall never thirst;* and with that Psal. lxxxiv. 11; as also with the 23rd Psalm; to which Psalm our Saviour is thought in this parable to have a special reference.

10 The thief cometh not, but for to steal, and to kill, and to destroy: I am come that they might have life, and that they might have *it* more abundantly.

Look as it is with the true shepherd, that owneth the sheep, and whose the flock is; he cometh regularly into the care and conduct of it; he cometh into the sheepfold, to take care of the life and welfare of his sheep: but a thief and a robber, that climbeth into the window, and so gets into the sheepfold, he comes not there out of any good-will to the sheep, but merely, by destroying the sheep, to provide for himself. So it is with them that, without any call or derivation of authority from me, thrust themselves into the care and conduct of the church of God; they do it with no good design to the souls of people, not out of any care or respect unto their good, but merely that they may serve themselves in the ruin of my people's souls. But that is not my end in coming into the world: I am not come to destroy them, but to save them; I am come, that they might have a spiritual life, and at last eternal life; that they might live the life of grace here, and not fail of the life of glory hereafter; and not only that they may barely live, but that their life may abound, through the upholdings, strengthenings, quickenings, and comfortings of my holy and gracious Spirit; that my beloved may not only drink, but drink abundantly; not only live, but live abundantly furnished with all the affluences and accommodations of a spiritual life.

b Is. 40. 11.
Ezek. 34. 12, 23. & 37. 24.
Heb. 13. 20.
1 Pet. 2. 25. & 5. 4.

11 ᵇ I am the good shepherd: the good shepherd giveth his life for the sheep.

That good Shepherd prophesied of, Isa. xl. 11. I cannot agree with those who think that Christ here speaketh not of himself as *the good Shepherd*, with reference to his office, as he was the Messiah, but only in opposition to the hirelings after-mentioned. I can allow that he thus calleth himself, both in the one respect and the other; but I cannot allow the latter sense exclusively to the former; for what followeth is peculiar to the Messiah, of whom it was prophesied, Dan. ix. 26, that he should *be cut off, but not for himself:* and though it be true, that the true shepherd will hazard his life for his sheep, as David did, when he encountered the lion and the bear, 1 Sam. xvii. 34, 35; yet it cannot be said to be the duty of the best shepherd to lay down his life for the sheep, for the life of a man is much more valuable than the life of any beast. Our Saviour therefore, doubtless, in this place showeth wherein he was the most excellent Shepherd, far excelling the best shepherds in the world, because he was come, not only to expose, hazard, and adventure his life, but actually, willingly, and freely to lay it down.

12 But he that is an hireling, and not the shepherd, whose own the sheep are not, seeth the wolf coming, and ᶜ leaveth the sheep, and fleeth: and the wolf catcheth them, and scattereth the sheep.

c Zech. 11. 16, 17.

Those that deal in sheep, either keep them themselves, or by their near relations, as Jacob's sons, and David, and Laban's daughters did; or else they hired persons to keep them for them. There is a great deal of difference betwixt the care of an owner, and the care of a hired servant in any thing; the owner taketh a more natural, diligent care, because the whole profit of the sheep, thriving and doing well, returneth unto himself. The hired servant may be careful in his measure and degree; but no such servant will take the care that an owner will take, nor run the hazards that he will run, because he knoweth that, let the flock thrive never so well, he shall have no more than the wages he is hired for: therefore what our Saviour saith is true concerning the generality of such hired servants, they will take some care of the flocks of sheep in their trust so long as there appeareth no danger, but if any danger appeareth, they leave the sheep, and flee, and the wolf cometh, and scattereth the sheep.

13 The hireling fleeth, because he is an hireling, and careth not for the sheep.

The reason why he that is a mere hired servant, and hath no property in the sheep, fleeth, is, because he is a hireling, and doth what he doth merely for his wages; and when a danger ariseth, which his wages will not balance, he will never encounter it; he hath no property in the sheep, nor any love to them, nor care for them.

14 I am the good shepherd, and ᵈ know my *sheep*, and am known of mine.

d 2 Tim. 2. 19.

I am no hireling; the sheep are mine own; I have a true love and affection for them, which obligeth me to a just and true care of them; I know them by name, (as was said before,) by a particular distinct knowledge; or I love them, and have tender bowels for them. And as I know them, so I am mutually known, and owned, and acknowledged by them; they have heard my voice, and discerned betwixt my voice and the voice of such as are strangers, refusing to follow them, but following me, going before them. Thus our Saviour in the same parable giveth us both notes to know a true and good shepherd, and particularly to know that himself was the true, good, and most excellent Shepherd; and also notes by which we might know who they are that are the true sheep of Christ.

15 ᵉ As the Father knoweth me, even so know I the Father: ᶠ and I lay down my life for the sheep.

e Mat. 11. 27.
f ch. 15. 13.

By these words our Saviour openeth how he knew his sheep, and should be again known of them, even as the Father knoweth him, and he knows his Father: this mutual knowledge between the Father and Christ was joined with perfect love and delight. Thus our Saviour knoweth those that are his sheep, not only fully and distinctly, so as to call them all by their names; but so as to love them, delight in them; so as to be ready to lay down his life for their good, and eternal salvation. Christ, to show not only the sincerity, but the degrees, of his love to his people, doth often compare it to the love wherewith his Father loved him, chap. xv. 9; xvii. 23, 26. So that if we can believe that God the Father loved Christ his only begotten Son, we may also believe that both the Father and Christ love those that are truly the sheep of Christ. The love that Christ hath to his people is as true and as certain as the Father's love to Christ, or Christ's love to his Father; and this could be showed by no higher act than that of laying down his life, chap. xv. 13. Now, saith he, *I lay down,* that is, I am ready to lay down, or I shall shortly lay down, *my life for the sheep:* whether *sheep* can signify all and every person born into the world, is their concern more strictly to inquire, who are so tenacious of that point, That

Christ died equally for all and every man: as also, whether upon that principle that absurdity must not follow, That Christ loved those who shall yet perish eternally, with such a love as the Father loved him, and he loved the Father.

g Is. 56. 8.

16 And ^gother sheep I have, which are not of this fold: them also I must bring, and they shall hear my voice; ^hand there shall be one fold, *and* one shepherd.

h Ezek. 37. 22. Eph. 2. 14. 1 Pet. 2. 25.

And other sheep I have which are not of this fold; our Saviour meaneth the Gentiles, who belonged not to the Jewish state and church, so were not under the same laws and government; for, 1 John. ii. 2, he was not only *a propitiation* for the sins of the Jews, *but for the sins of the whole world:* he calleth those sheep, because the Lord knew who were his from eternity; and they were sheep in the counsels of God, and they were suddenly to be made his sheep by calling, the gospel being soon to be preached to all nations. *Them also* (saith he) *I must bring* in; it is so written in God's book, the promises and prophecies to that purpose must be fulfilled. They shall not only hear the voice and sound of my gospel, though going out of Zion, yet not terminated in Zion; but they shall embrace, receive, and believe that joyful sound. *And there shall be one fold, and one shepherd;* and there shall be but one church; as I am one Shepherd, so there shall be but one flock of sheep; *one body, one Spirit, one hope of our calling, one Lord, one faith, one baptism,* as there is *one God and Father of all,* as the apostle speaketh, Eph. iv. 4—6.

17 Therefore doth my Father love me, ⁱbecause I lay down my life, that I might take it again.

i Is. 53. 7, 8, 12. Heb. 2. 9.

Christ here asserteth two things. 1. That he was about to lay down his life, and should now very shortly lay it down; but yet so as he should take it again; that is, rise again from the dead; death should not have dominion over him: by which he comforteth his disciples concerning his death, declaring, (1.) That he was a freewill-offering, as he further openeth it in the next verse. (2.) That he should not perish in the grave, but rise again from the dead. 2. That therefore the Father loved him; for, (1.) By this means he declared himself with power to be the Son of God, and the Father could not but love his Son. And, (2.) By this means also *he humbled himself, and became obedient unto death, even the death of the cross,* Phil. ii. 8. So as that the Father had many reasons to love the Son; and amongst others, this obedience of his to death, even the accursed death upon the cross, to fulfil his Father's will, for the redemption and salvation of the sons of men, was not the least: and by this also he commendeth his Father's love to those that are his sheep, in that his Father loveth him with the more exceeding love, for laying down his life, to purchase their redemption and salvation.

18 No man taketh it from me, but I lay it down of myself. I have power to lay it down, and I ^khave power to take it again. ^lThis commandment have I received of my Father.

k ch. 2. 19. l ch. 6. 38. & 15. 10. Acts 2. 24, 32.

No man taketh it from me by force, without my willing it and consenting to it; the Jews and Pilate will take it from me, but not without my free and voluntary surrender of it: and this is that which we read, Acts iv. 27, 28, *For of a truth against thy holy child Jesus, whom thou hast anointed, both Herod, and Pontius Pilate, with the Gentiles, and the people of Israel, were gathered together, for to do whatsoever thy hand and thy counsel determined before to be done.* By which he asserteth his Divine power, and so comforteth his disciples against the disturbances they were like to have from the sight of his passion, at this time not many months off. And this, saith he, is the will of my Father, that which my Father hath given me commission to do, and for which he hath sent me into the world: and thus he declareth his death to be a fulfilling of his Father's purpose, and an act of obedience to his Father's will; and, indeed, in his obedience in the thing here much of the virtue of his death.

19 ¶ ^mThere was a division therefore again among the Jews for these sayings.

m ch. 7. 43. & 9. 16.

Christ by his words often caused a division amongst the Jews, so as they could not agree in their sentiments and censures about him; which was either caused through the mixture amongst them of such as truly believed with those who believed not; or else from the mixture of a more considering part amongst them with others who were more brutish, irrational, and full of passion. We met with much the same, chap. vii. 43, and again, chap. ix. 16. It is one method of God's providence for the deliverance of his servants from unreasonable men, to cause divisions among them, so as they cannot agree among themselves.

20 And many of them said, ⁿHe hath a devil, and is mad; why hear ye him?

n ch. 7. 20. & 8. 48, 52.

Some of the people said, *He hath a devil, and is mad;* for (as was said before) this was the opinion of the Jews concerning all that were mad and distracted, that it was by the influence of the devil, and they were infested with an evil spirit.

21 Others said, These are not the words of him that hath a devil. ^oCan a devil ^popen the eyes of the blind?

o Ex. 4. 11. Ps. 94. 9. & 146. 8. p ch. 9. 6, 7, 32, 33.

But others, that were less passionate and brutish in their expressions, and more thinking and considerate in passing their judgments, said, *These are not the words* (so we translate it; the word in the Greek is ῥήματα, which signifies things, and matters, as well as words; and by what follows, one would think that were the more proper translation of it here) *of him that hath a devil.* They instance in no words, but in a matter of fact; asking if a devil could open the eyes of the blind? that is, of one that was born blind; for they certainly speak with reference to that miracle which he had so lately wrought upon such a person.

22 ¶ And it was at Jerusalem the ^qfeast of the dedication, and it was winter.

q 1 Mac. 4. 59.

A. D. 33.

This verse affords two questions, which have not a little troubled interpreters. 1. What feast of dedication this was? 2. Whether dedications of places to the worship of God be warrantable or no, in that manner as they are dedicated amongst the papists at this day?

As to the first of these, that which we have about it in Scripture is this: Exod. xl. 1—15, we have God's command and direction for the hallowing, or dedication, of the sanctuary, or the tabernacle, which was the first house we read of in Scripture set apart for the public worship of God. We have a particular account of Moses's punctual obedience to that command, Lev. viii. When the temple was built by Solomon, we read of Solomon's dedication of it; but nothing of ceremony used at it, only a multitude of sacrifices offered, (which was God's ordinary worship in the Jewish church,) and a feast kept fourteen days: we read of no law that he made for the annual keeping of it, no obligation upon all the males in Israel to be present at it. As concerning the other solemn feasts which God appointed, Lev. xxiii., Solomon's feast of dedication in this differed from them, that it held double the time, for seven or eight days was the longest time that any of those feasts were kept. This temple was destroyed by the Chaldeans and Babylonians, and rebuilt by Zerubbabel, Ezra, and Nehemiah, as we read in the books known by those names. In analogy to the practice of Solomon, when they had finished the building of the temple, there was another feast of dedication kept; of which we read, Ezra vi. 16—18; but we read of nothing done in that dedication but the offering of one hundred bullocks, two hundred rams, four hundred lambs, and twelve he-goats; and setting the priests and Levites in order for the service of God. This temple was defaced by Antiochus, but not wholly ruined; and was repaired and púrified by Judas Maccabeus, of which we read, 2 Macc. ii. 23; x. 6—8; 1 Macc. iv. 52, 58; which books of Maccabees, though they be no canonical Scripture, yet are as good a piece of ecclesiastical history as any: and Josephus also giveth us an account of it, Antiq. l. 12. cap. 11. We do not read of any thing they did, saving offering sacrifices, and setting things in order, according to the law of Moses, and feasting; Josephus tells us they used all lawful pleasures. We do not read, that either God appointed an annual feast of dedication for the sanctuary; nor Solomon, nor Ezra, for either of the temples; but we read twice in the book of Maccabees, and Josephus (writing the Jewish history) tells us, that Judas Maccabeus made it a law, That the feast should be kept yearly for eight days, in memory of that mercy which God had showed them. This was without doubt the feast of dedication here mentioned: for this feast began upon the twenty-fifth day of the month Chisleu, which answereth our months of November and December, and took in part of each; so it agreeth with the text, which saith that *it was winter;* whereas Solomon's dedication was in autumn; Ezra's in the spring. Some make a question, Whether Judas Maccabeus did well in appointing this annual feast, neither Solomon nor Ezra having, that we read of, before done any such thing: and that our Saviour was not at this feast in any honour to the feast, but only to take advantage of the multitude of people that met, to preach the gospel. For my own part, as I will not defend, so I durst not condemn him: I see no more that he did in this, than was done, Esth. ix. 27, 28, as to the days of Purim. Magistrates certainly have a power to appoint public days, yea, annual days of thanksgivings, for mercies never to be forgotten. Indeed they cannot make a day holy, so as it shall be a sin against God to labour in it, or to use any pleasures (as in the case of the sabbath); but they may command the public worship of God to be performed on particular days, and men ought to attend it when with conveniency they can; only they ought to take care that such days be not spent in luxury and profaneness, and that they be for signal providences, and not so multiplied, and frequently renewing, as that the service of them degenerate into mere matter of form. Whether Christ went up in order to the feast, or because of the great concourse of people he knew would be there at that time, cannot be determined.

For the second question, it is not so much a question, whether it be lawful in a solemn and decent manner to consecrate a house to the public worship of God, by such acts of worship as God hath appointed under the gospel, such as prayer and praise, reading, preaching, and hearing the word; as whether it may be done by such rites and ceremonies as the papists do it with, for the which there is no institution. For the former, though it may be some will not agree it necessary; yet, certainly, no sober person can deny, but if a place be made for people ordinarily to meet in to worship God, there they may as well meet at the first to praise God for his mercy, and to beg his presence when they shall there meet together to worship God, and to hear his word, as they may meet there afterwards for prayer, praise, preaching, or hearing. But this satisfieth not the papists. They first do it by many superstitious ceremonies. Secondly, they plead for the holiness of the place when so consecrated. As for the ceremonies of their consecrations, or dedications, Bellarmine reckoneth up eight.

1. The painting twelve crosses in the several parts of the house to be consecrated, and lighting up twelve lamps, one at every cross; to signify the twelve apostles, who carried the banner of the cross throughout the world.

2. The bishop's knocking at the door with a pastoral staff, commanding the devil to give place, and invoking of God, the angels, and saints, to grant their presence in that place; which they make to signify the opening of people's hearts by the preaching of the gospel.

3. The scattering of ashes upon the floor of the place, upon which the bishop writes the letters of the Latin and Greek alphabet, in the figure of a cross.

4. The sprinkling the place with holy water, and lighting up wax candles.

5. The anointing of the crosses before mentioned, and painted on the walls.

6. The sprinkling of the place with a mixture of water, wine, salt, and ashes.

7. The anointing of the temple and the altar.

8. The keeping of a festival upon it. And for all these they have devised several significancies, too vain and fanciful to repeat.

For none of which we know the least warrant in holy writ; nor can we conceive how any consecration can imprint any character of holiness upon a place, or make prayers offered up in or toward it more acceptable; though we know it did so as to the temple, both because it was an eminent type of Christ, and also because of the particular promises made to it, 1 Kings ix.; which were not applicable to the synagogues, which were the Jews' ordinary meeting places for public worship; but only to the temple, upon the account before mentioned. Though we say that all places for that use ought to be used with all imaginable decency, and we ought during the public worship of God to carry ourselves in them with all reverence, because of the angels, and because of the special presence of God, promised to the assemblies of his people in his name, and for his public worship.

23 And Jesus walked in the temple 'in Solomon's porch. [r Acts 3. 11. & 5. 12.]

Of this *Solomon's porch* we read, 1 Kings vi. 3, that Solomon *built the porch before the temple of the house, twenty cubits* long, and *ten cubits* broad. This was the place where they walked in winter. Though this was destroyed when Jerusalem was destroyed by the Babylonians; yet it seemeth that there was one built that was like it, and kept that name. It should seem that it was a place better defended from the weather, than those other parts of the temple where in summer-time they used to walk.

24 Then came the Jews round about him, and said unto him, How long dost thou ‖ make us to doubt? If thou be the Christ, tell us plainly. [‖ Or, *hold us in suspense.*]

Our Saviour was at this time within three months of his crucifying: he had often before told them that he was the Light of the world, the true Shepherd; he had preached doctrine to them, from whence they might easily have concluded what he was; he had wrought works among them which none could do but by a Divine power; but he had been very wary of telling them in plain terms that he was the Messiah, the Christ; when at any time he had so declared himself to his disciples, or they had owned him as such, he still laid a charge upon them to tell no man of it, Matt. xvi. 20, &c. They therefore come to him, demanding a plain resolution in the case, as some of their minds were in some suspense about it. It was but a captious question; for had he denied it, besides that it had been the denial of a truth which he came to bear a testimony unto, they had had a great advantage to have lessened his reputation amongst those who had believed on him as such. Had he affirmed it, he had brought himself in danger of the Roman governor; for the Jews indeed expected a Messiah, a Christ, but to be a temporal prince, to deliver them from their enemies; and for him to have declared himself such a Christ as they expected, had been fatal to him. He therefore answers with his usual prudence and wariness to this question.

25 Jesus answered them, I told you, and ye believed not: ˢ the works that I do in my Father's name, they bear witness of me. [s ver. 38. ch. 3. 2. & 5. 36.]

I have in effect told it you more than once; I have told you that I am sent of the Father, &c., I have said enough for you to conclude it; but you will not understand, you will not receive it, you will not believe what I say. What need you any further witness of it, than those works which I do by Divine power; by virtue of my oneness with my Father, and of that power and authority which he hath committed to me, that by them I might confirm the doctrine which I have taught you?

26 But ᵗ ye believe not, because ye are not of my sheep, as I said unto you. [t ch. 8. 47. 1 John 4. 6.]

As many as were ordained to eternal life believed, Acts xiii. 48. Here our Saviour giveth this as one reason of the Jews' unbelief, that they were not of his sheep. Were they not Israelites? Yes, but all are not Israel that are descended of Israel. It seems a very hard interpretation that some would put upon these words, Ye believe not, because you are not teachable, and fit to be made my sheep; the words are οὐ γαρ ἐστε ἐκ των προβάτων τῶν ἐμῶν. Nor can such interpretation be paralleled from any other scripture. That by *sheep*, here, cannot be meant members of the church, is plain; for they were of the church of Israel, whom the Lord led as a flock, as the psalmist speaks, Psal lxxx. 1. That believers, and such as are truly called and sanctified, are not meant, is as plain; for then the sense would be, You believe not because you believe not; besides, our Saviour had before said, he had other sheep that were not of that fold, (by which he meant the Gentiles,) such for whom he prayed, chap. xvii. 20, being such as should believe on him. By *sheep* therefore he meaneth, certainly, such as were *ordained to life*, as Acts xiii. 48. Nor will it therefore follow, that God's not ordaining of them to life, was the near and immediate cause of their not believing; but their own stubborn and perverse wills in not repenting, that they might believe; as our Saviour tells them, Matt. xxi. 32: that is, not turning from their gross and sinful ways, which they might have done by virtue of that common grace of God which was afforded them in the gospel, by the preaching of John the Baptist, and of Christ himself.

u ver. 4, 14. 27 ^u My sheep hear my voice, and I know them, and they follow me:

This is the same which he said ver. 4: see the notes there.

28 And I give unto them eternal life;
x ch. 6. 37. & 17. 11, 12. & 18. 9. and ^x they shall never perish, neither shall any *man* pluck them out of my hand.

I do give them, and I will give them, eternal life; as soon as they shall come to hear, and believe my voice, and to follow me, they shall have a sure right and title to it; and when my Father by his providence shall remove them out of the world, and in the great day, they shall be taken up into the actual possession of it. For *they shall never perish*, but though they may fall, they shall rise again by repentance. They are in my hand, and my hand shall preserve them, none shall ever pluck them out of it; they shall be preserved through faith, by the power of God, to eternal life and salvation.

y ch. 14. 28. z ch. 17. 2, 6, &c. 29 ^y My Father, ^z which gave *them* me, is greater than all; and no *man* is able to pluck *them* out of my Father's hand.

All that are my sheep became so by my Father's donation and gift, so as my Father is equally with myself concerned in the preservation of them to that happy end, to which he hath ordained and designed them. Those that would pluck them out of my hand, and deprive them of that eternal life which I will give them, must be too strong, not for me alone, but for my Father also; which none is, for who can be too strong for omnipotence?

a ch. 17. 11, 22. 30 ^a I and *my* Father are one.

My Father and I are one, not only in counsel and will, (as John xvii. 11, 22, and believers are said to be *of one heart*, Acts iv. 32,) but in nature, power, and essence; for it is plain that our Saviour here ascribeth the preservation of his sheep, not to the will, but to the power of his Father: *None is able to pluck them out of my Father's hand*. And it is plain by what follows, that the Jews thus understood our Saviour. Some eminent protestant interpreters expound this of a oneness in consent and will, doing the same things, and driving the same design, both agreeing to preserve the sheep unto eternal life; but (with all respect unto them) I think the context implieth more, though this be not excluded.

b ch. 8. 59. 31 Then ^b the Jews took up stones again to stone him.

Tumultuously, as we read they did once before, chap. viii. 59. From whence we may learn with what design they came to Christ, ver. 24, plainly to tell them whether he were the Christ. By the law of God the false prophet was to be stoned; but he was first to be judicially tried and judged. This was but a tumultuous action of an enraged multitude.

32 Jesus answered them, Many good works have I shewed you from my Father; for which of those works do ye stone me?

The word translated *good* is of a very large signification; signifying excellent, useful, profitable, beauteous, &c., whatsoever in common speech cometh under the notion of good. I (saith our Saviour) never did harm to any of you, but I have been the instrument of a great deal of good to you. I have given sight to the blind, hearing to the deaf, healed many that were sick of grievous diseases, cast out many devils out of those which were infested with or possessed by them. Do any of these deserve any such usage at your hands? What maketh you in such a rage against me?

33 The Jews answered him, saying, For a good work we stone thee not; but for blasphemy; and because that thou, being a man, ^c makest thyself God. c ch. 5. 18.

The Jews answered him, These are not the things we are incensed against thee for; we grant that thou hast done many good works amongst us; these we gratefully acknowledge. But this is that which we are not able to bear, that whereas thou art but a mere man, by thy discourses thou makest thyself equal with God, and so art guilty of *blasphemy*; which is committed as well by arrogating to ourselves what is proper to God, as by imputing to God the natural or moral imperfections of the creature; and the blasphemer deserveth to be stoned, according to the law of God. By this it is manifest, that the Jews understood our Saviour, affirming that he and his Father were one, as asserting himself one in essence with his Father, not in will only.

34 Jesus answered them, ^d Is it not d Ps. 82. 6. written in your law, I said, Ye are gods?

This was written, Psal. lxxxii. 6. The whole Scripture of the Old Testament, being wrote by holy men, inspired of God, and directive of men's conversation before men, and towards God, is sometimes called *the law*, Psal. xix. 7. It was spoken concerning magistrates, and the governors of God's people, who, being God's deputies and vicegerents, intrusted to execute the judgments and vengeance of God, are dignified with the name of gods.

35 If he called them gods, ^e unto whom e Rom. 13. 1. the word of God came, and the Scripture cannot be broken;

If God dignified those men (and many of them were also vile and sinful men) with the title of gods, because they had a commission to govern people according to the law of God; and none must contradict what God hath said in his word; there can be no falsehood in the revelation of any part of the Divine will.

36 Say ye of him, ^f whom the Father f ch. 6. 27. g ch. 3. 17. hath sanctified, and ^g sent into the world, & 5. 36, 37. & 8. 42. Thou blasphemest; ^h because I said, I am h ch. 5. 17. 18. ver. 30. ⁱ the Son of God? i Luke 1. 35. ch. 9. 35, 37.

Suppose I were no more than a mere man, yet being *sanctified*, that is, set apart of God for the special work of man's redemption, and sent of God into the world with commission both to reveal and to do his will, yet dare you say that I blaspheme, *because I said, I am the Son of God?* In the place (viz. Psal. lxxxii. 6) where God said of magistrates, *Ye are gods*, he also added, *all of you are children of the Most High*; you have therefore no reason to rage at me, though I did say I was the Son of God; being one whom the Father hath in his eternal counsels set apart for this great and special work, and actually by his providence sent into the world for the finishing and despatching of it. But we must take heed that we do not understand our Saviour here, as if he in another sense assumed to him the title of the Son of God; it was enough for him at present to assert, that the title well enough belonged to him, if he indeed had been no more than the Son of man, as they said.

37 ^k If I do not the works of my Father, believe me not. k ch. 15. 24.

Our Saviour doth often appeal to his works to testify concerning his Divine mission and power; these works he here calleth *the works of* his *Father*; by which he doth not only mean works that are pleasing and acceptable to God, as acts of obedience to the will of God performed by men may be called, and are, chap. vi. 28, 29; nor (as I conceive) only those works which he did by commission and authority from his Father, which, chap. xvii. 4, he calleth the work which his Father had given him to do; but those works which none but God could do; such were the multiplication of the loaves, chap. vi., the curing of him who was born blind, chap. ix., &c. If (saith our Saviour) I do not do those works which no mere man ever did, give me no credit; but if I do those works which can be done by no human art or power, you have reason to believe me.

38 But if I do, though ye believe not me, ¹believe the works: that ye may know, and believe, ᵐthat the Father *is* in me, and I in him.

l ch. 5. 36. & 14. 10, 11.
m ch. 14. 10, 11. & 17. 21.

If I do such works as can be done by no less than a Divine power, being beyond the power and ability of all creatures; then, though you will not give credit to any bare affirmations of myself, because I say I am the Son of God, yet believe the things for the testimony that my works give unto it. Proper effects give testimony to the proper cause; he who doth those things which none but God can do, must needs be God, or empowered by God to do them. This is the way for you to know, be persuaded, and believe, that the Father is in me by his mighty, Divine, working power: chap. xiv. 10, *The Father that dwelleth in me, he doeth the works;* and I work in and together with him. This phrase, *The Father is in me, and I in him,* teacheth us three things concerning Christ: 1. His oneness in nature and essence with the Father. 2. His personal distinction from his Father: here are two mentioned, *the Father,* and *me:* none can properly be said to be in himself. 3. The most perfect and intimate indwelling of one of the Persons in the Holy Trinity in the other.

39 ⁿTherefore they sought again to take him: but he escaped out of their hand,

n ch. 7. 30, 44. & 8. 59.

Therefore they sought again to take him; because he said, that the Father was in him, and he in the Father; by which they well enough understood, that he asserted a union with the Father. They did not again go about to stone him, as they did before; he had sufficiently stopped their mouths as to their imputation of blasphemy; but they seek to apprehend him, with a design (no doubt) to carry him before the sanhedrim, their great court, which had cognizance of those things. But as he had once and again before, so he now again escapeth out of their hands; whether by darkening the air before their eyes, or (as some would have it) making his body invisible, by his Divine power, or what other way, the Scripture tells us not, and it is great rashness to determine.

40 And went away again beyond Jordan into the place °where John at first baptized; and there he abode.

o ch. 1. 28.

Christ's time was not yet come when he should be betrayed and crucified; it was yet three months and more to it; he saw the Jews at Jerusalem were in such a rage and fury, that there was no staying in that place: he goes beyond Jordan to Bethabara, where he found John at first baptizing, John i. 28, before he baptized in Ænon near Salim, chap. iii. 23. See the notes on John i. 28. Possibly he chose that place as being a place where John had been preparing a way for him, by turning men's hearts in some measure for receiving the gospel, and pointing out Christ to his disciples, as the Lamb of God who taketh away the sins of the world. *And there he abode:* how long he abode there we cannot tell; probably till he took his last journey from Galilee to Jerusalem; of which the other evangelists speak, Matt. xx. 17; Mark x. 32; Luke xviii. 31. What he did in Galilee during these three months John reports not, only saith,

41 And many resorted unto him, and said, John did no miracle: ᵖbut all things that John spake of this man were true.

p ch. 3. 30.

God so ordered it in the wisdom of his providence, that though Elijah and Elisha under the law wrought miracles, by which they confirmed their Divine mission; yet John, coming immediately before Christ, as his messenger and forerunner, wrought none; that so the glory of Christ in working miracles when he came might be more clear and evident. This made the people, that came to Christ while he was in Galilee, say thus amongst themselves, We paid a great veneration to John the Baptist, yet he never did those things which Christ hath done: and whatsoever John told us of this person hath proved true; he hath done, and doth, greater things than ever John did, and is in the judgment of sense to be preferred before him; should we not now believe in him? John told us he was *the Lamb of God, who takes away the sins of the world;* and told us much more concerning him, which our eyes see is true.

42 �q And many believed on him there.

q ch. 8. 30. & 11. 45.

Some believed on him as such whom John Baptist had spoken him to be; others possibly believed on him in the sense mentioned chap. ii. 23; not to the saving of their souls, but as one sent of God, a great Prophet, no ordinary man. The rage of men shall not hinder the progress of the gospel.

CHAP. XI

The sickness and death of Lazarus: Jesus raiseth him to life after he had been dead four days: many Jews believe, 1—46. *The Pharisees hold a council against Christ: Caiaphas prophesieth: Jesus retireth from places of public resort,* 47—54. *At the approach of the passover the Jews inquire about him: the rulers give orders to apprehend him,* 55—57.

NOW a certain *man* was sick, *named* Lazarus, of Bethany, the town of ᵃ Mary and her sister Martha.

a Luke 10. 38, 39.

Bethany (as appears by ver. 18) *was nigh unto Jerusalem,* not wholly at two miles distance from it: but our Saviour was not at this time in Judea, for, ver. 7, he saith to his disciples, *Let us go into Judea again.* He was at this time in Galilee, or in Peræa; and we shall find, ver. 17, that Lazarus had been in his grave four days before our Saviour got thither: so as we must allow at least six or seven days betwixt the time when Christ heard of Lazarus's sickness, and the time when he came to Bethany. This Bethany is here only described to us as the place where Martha and Mary lived, or at least where they were born. Some think that Bethany was only a part of the Mount Olivet; but others, more probably, think that it was some little town or city, standing within that part of the Mount Olivet; for it is here called a town, and, Luke x. 38, 39, the place where these two sisters lived is called a village.

2 (ᵇIt was *that* Mary which anointed the Lord with ointment, and wiped his feet with her hair, whose brother Lazarus was sick.)

b Matt. 26. 7. Mark 14. 3. ch. 12. 3.

We read of a woman, Luke vii. 37, 38, that came behind our Saviour while he was at dinner, in the house of Simon the Pharisee, brought an alabaster box of ointment, stood at his feet behind him weeping, washing his feet with her tears, and wiping them with her hair; but it appears by the story, she had been before a notorious sinner. We read of another woman, Matt. xxvi. 6, 7; Mark xiv. 3, that poured a box of ointment on our Saviour's head as he was at dinner in the house of Simon the leper: but we, in those two evangelists, read nothing of her washing his feet with her tears, or wiping them with her hair; but in the next chapter of this Gospel, ver. 3, we have a story which (whether it be the same with the other or no, I cannot tell) is that doubtless to which this verse referreth: the names and circumstances much agree. There were other Maries, (for Mary was a very ordinary name among them,) but this was that Mary which is mentioned chap. xii. 3, that anointed the Lord with ointment, &c. It was her brother was sick.

3 Therefore his sisters sent unto him, saying, Lord, behold, he whom thou lovest is sick.

Christ (as was said before) seems to have been very familiar at the house of these two sisters, and often to have made them his hostesses; and it should appear by this verse that in those visits he had showed particular kindnesses to this their brother Lazarus, who was now sick; this makes them style their brother, *he whom thou lovest.* They plead no merits either of their own or his, but only plead with him for his own goodness and love. Nor do they express in particular what they desired for their brother, though it is easily understood by their representation of his state and condition.

4 When Jesus heard *that,* he said, This sickness is not unto death, ᶜbut for the

c ch. 9. 3. ver. 40.

glory of God, that the Son of God might be glorified thereby.

God hath not sent this sickness upon Lazarus to determine his being upon the earth; or such a separation of the soul of Lazarus from his body, as there shall be no reunion of it before the general resurrection (which is our ordinary notion of death); God hath not sent this sickness for that purpose, but that he might be glorified by his Son raising him from the dead. God is glorified when his Son is glorified; and Christ is glorified when his Divine power is manifested, so as men acknowledge him to be what indeed he is.

5 Now Jesus loved Martha, and her sister, and Lazarus.

He doubtless loved them with a special, distinguishing love, as persons chosen in him to eternal life before the foundation of the world, given unto him by an eternal donation, called by him with an effectual calling, to own and receive him as their Saviour; but this text seemeth to speak of him as loving this family with a human love, which inclineth man to a complacency in an object beloved: he had a kindness for the whole family; they had showed him kindness in his state of humiliation, and he loved those that so loved him, Prov. viii. 17.

6 When he had heard therefore that d ch. 10. 40. he was sick, [d]he abode two days still in the same place where he was.

Though he loved him and his sisters with a tender love, yet he did not presently go to them, to comfort Mary and Martha in their sorrow; nor yet to cure Lazarus, and prevent his death; but stayed still two days in the place where he was. He loved Mary, and Martha, and Lazarus, but he more loved the honour and glory of his Father, which was to be manifested in his raising of Lazarus from the dead. We must not judge of Christ's love to us by his mere external dispensations of providence; nor judge that he doth not love us because he doth not presently come in to our help, at our times, and in such ways and methods as we would think reasonable.

7 Then after that saith he to *his* disciples, Let us go into Judæa again.

This lets us know, that Christ was not in Judea when he received the tidings of Lazarus's sickness, but in Peræa, or Galilee; but he presently upon it takes up thoughts of returning again into that province, and indeed he was now preparing for his last journey thither: however, the sickness of Lazarus, and his raising from the dead, was one occasion of his so soon going up; from which his disciples would have discouraged him, as followeth.

8 *His* disciples say unto him, Master, [e]the Jews of late sought to stone e ch. 10. 31. thee; and goest thou thither again?

See chap. x. 31. There were not three months elapsed since the Jews had so sought to have stoned him, and there was no reason for him to think that their fury was in any whit abated. We read in the other evangelists of other words they used (Peter especially, Matt. xvi. 22,) to dissuade our Saviour from this journey to Jerusalem. They were afraid for their Master, and they were afraid also for themselves.

9 Jesus answered, Are there not twelve ch. 9. 4. hours in the day? [f]If any man walk in the day, he stumbleth not, because he seeth the light of this world.

Look as in the day there are twelve hours, in which the sun shineth, and by giving its light directs men in their courses; so as they know how to guide their feet, and do not stumble, because they have the light of the sun, which God hath ordained, to direct men that walk up and down in the world.

g ch. 12. 35. 10 But [g]if a man walk in the night, he stumbleth, because there is no light in him.

And there is a night also, wherein if men walk they will be very prone to stumble, because they are in darkness, and have no light to guide their feet. So there is a set time for all the issues of men; a time for their peace and liberty, and a time for their troubles and sufferings. God rules and governs the world. While men are in their callings and places, faithfully discharging their trust, and finishing the work which God hath given them to do, and their time is not come for their glorifying of God by suffering, they shall not stumble, nor be given up to the rage of their eagerest enemies; they are in their callings and places, and God will be light unto them: but when their working time is over, and the time of their night is come, then they will stumble; because then God withdraweth his light from them; they are not then under such a special protection of God, who hath done his work by and with them. This is as much as he had said before, chap. viii. 20, *No man laid hands on him, for his hour was not yet come;* the twelve hours of his day were not all spent. This duty digested, is of infinite use to quiet the spirits of God's people in the worst of times; every man hath his twelve hours, his day and set time, to honour God upon the stage of the world: he shall not stumble, he shall not miscarry, while those hours are spent; he shall not die, he shall not be disabled for duty, so long as God hath aught for him to do. But every man hath his night too, when he must not expect to converse in the world without stumbling.

11 These things said he: and after h So Deut. that he saith unto them, Our friend La- 31. 16. Dan. 12. 2. zarus [h]sleepeth; but I go, that I may Matt. 9. 24. Acts 7. 60. awake him out of sleep. 1 Cor. 15. 18, 51.

There is such an analogy betwixt death and sleep, that there is nothing more ordinary than to express death by sleep in Scripture, Deut. xxxi. 16; 2 Sam. vii. 12; 1 Kings i. 21; 2 Kings xx. 21; Job vii. 21; xiv. 12; Dan. xii. 2, and in a multitude of other texts, both in the Old Testament and in the New; so as it was evident our Saviour meant he was dead, which he knew as he was God, though as yet he had received no relation of it from the friends of the deceased. *But I go* (saith our Saviour) to raise him up again from the dead, which he calls awaking him; pursuing the former metaphor, where he had compared death to a sleep.

12 Then said his disciples, Lord, if he sleep, he shall do well.

Sleeping moderately is a good sign, we know, in most diseases; this makes the disciples say, that if Lazarus slept he should do well.

13 Howbeit Jesus spake of his death: but they thought that he had spoken of taking of rest in sleep.

But that the disciples should not understand our Saviour not speaking of ordinary sleep, but of death, is wonderful, considering that there is nothing more ordinary in holy writ than to read of death expressed under this notion; but possibly by our Saviour's making such haste to him, they conceived that he was not dead, but only in an ordinary sleep, upon the abatement of his disease.

14 Then said Jesus unto them plainly, Lazarus is dead.

You will mistake me; my meaning was, not that Lazarus was fallen to rest upon the abatement of his distemper, but his soul is parted from his body.

15 And I am glad for your sakes that I was not there, to the intent ye may believe; nevertheless let us go unto him.

Had I been upon the place, my kindness to his sisters, and pity, would have prevailed far with me to have prevented his death; but it is better, for your sakes at least, and I am glad I was not there. For by this means I shall have an advantage, by putting forth my Divine power in raising him from the dead, to confirm your faith in me as the Son of God, and the true Messias; therefore, though he be dead, *let us go unto him.*

16 Then said Thomas, which is called Didymus, unto his fellowdisciples, Let us also go, that we may die with him.

Thomas and *Didymus* were names of the same signification, only Thomas was the Hebrew, and Didymus the Greek name. This is that Thomas who to the last showed a greater difficulty in believing than many others of the disciples did, chap. xx. 25. His words here signified great rashness and unbelief: *Let us also go, that we may die with him;* with Christ (say some). Seeing that our Lord will not be persuaded from going into Judea, where his life will be in apparent danger, for they will put him to death, let us also go and die with him. But it is more probable that Thomas meant with Lazarus, who, as our Saviour told them but now, was dead; and in that sense it was not only an expression of great passion, but great unbelief also. We ought not to be so affected with the death of our friends, as to wish or desire ourselves out of the world, where God hath set us in stations which we ought to keep, until God be pleased to remove us. Besides, Thomas ought to have believed our Saviour, who had told them, that though Lazarus slept the sleep of death, yet he went to awake him; which could have no other sense, than to raise him out of that sleep of death, of which he had spoken. Ah! to what errors do our passions betray us!

17 Then when Jesus came, he found that he had lain in the grave four days already.

Christ *came* to Bethany where Lazarus died; *he found he had lain in the grave four days;* so as probably Christ came not to Bethany till four days or more after the death of Lazarus, or near upon. But possibly it is better judged by others, that Christ was not yet come into Bethany, but only to the place where he met Martha; because it is said after this, ver. 30, that *Jesus was not yet come into the town, but was in that place where Martha met him;* which it is probable was at Lazarus's sepulchre, out of the town, but near it, as all the Jewish burying-places were ; where he heard from the relation of Martha how long Lazarus had been buried. Our Saviour could have come sooner had he pleased, for though Bethabara was on the other side of Jordan, (so out of the confines of Judea,) yet, if we may give any credit to those who have laboured in the study of places, it was not above four miles off. Jerusalem, so as it could not be six miles from Bethany, which our Saviour could have travelled in a less time than four or five days. Some think Lazarus died the same day news came to Christ of his sickness; after which we read, ver. 6, that he stirred not of two days; after which it was, ver. 7, that he took up thoughts of going into Judea. After this, possibly, he lingered one or two days; ver. 14, he tells them Lazarus was dead. Our Saviour was willing to protract the time, that the miracle might be more conspicuous and remarkable.

|| That is, about two miles.

18 Now Bethany was nigh unto Jerusalem, || about fifteen furlongs off:

That, as we count, wants of two miles half a quarter.

19 And many of the Jews came to Martha and Mary, to comfort them concerning their brother.

Not to pray with them for the soul of their brother departed. That departed souls are in a capacity to be advantaged by the prayers of their friends, or any such thing, are corruptions of latter times; but they had a civil usage of mourning for their friends, the time for which was anciently thirty days. They mourned for Jacob forty days, Gen. l. 3; for Aaron thirty days, Numb. xx. 29; so for Moses, Deut. xxxiv. 8. It is probable the days were fewer for persons of an inferior quality, but they had some days for all; during which days their neighbours and friends came to visit them, and relieve them in their sorrow, with such arguments as they had.

20 Then Martha, as soon as she heard that Jesus was coming, went and met him : but Mary sat *still* in the house.

It should seem by the story, Luke x. 41, that Martha had the care of the house-keeping upon her, (Mary was more retired,) so that the news of Christ's coming might come to her first. She in great joy ran out to meet him ; how far she went we are not told, but it appeareth from ver. 30 that she went out of the town.

21 Then said Martha unto Jesus, Lord, if thou hadst been here, my brother had not died.

Mary saith the same, ver. 32. They were both in an error, for Lazarus's death was appointed and determined by an eternal counsel; and he was both sick and died for a wise end, that God might be glorified, and his Son glorified in raising him from the dead ; as we were before told, ver. 4. But it lets us see the vanity of our natures, who in the loss of our friends are ready to think, if such or such means had been used, we had not lost our friends ; never considering our days are appointed, and we cannot pass the number of them. If any rational, probable means for continuing their lives be omitted, that also is not without the counsel of God, who having determined the issue, concealeth diseases, or the true and proper means for their cure, from physicians, or such as are about the sick persons. Nor did Martha and Mary fail in this only, but in that they made the Lord's presence necessary to the preserving of the life of their brother, who, had he pleased, could, though absent, have kept him from death.

22 But I know, that even now, ⁱ whatsoever thou wilt ask of God, God will give *it* thee.   i ch. 9. 31.

She showed some unbelief in her former words, but here again she showeth her faith, but not without some weakness mixed with her faith; for by these words she seemeth not to be satisfied, that the fulness of the Godhead dwelt in Christ, and that he was equal with the Father, and able by his own power to raise the dead ; her faith extendeth no further than a belief, that he was in so much favour with God, that if he would please to intercede with God, he would restore her brother to life : this she meaneth ; though the raising of persons from the dead was a thing so rare and unusual, that she dareth not to mention that particular thing, though uppermost in her thoughts.

23 Jesus saith unto her, Thy brother shall rise again.

Christ takes no notice of Martha's failings before mentioned, (he can have compassion upon his people's infirmities,) but applieth himself to the relief of her under her affliction. He doth not tell her that her brother should be raised to life presently, nor that he would do it; but only saith he *shall rise again:* to let us know, that a belief of the general resurrection is enough, and ought to be improved by us, to curb our immoderate mourning and passions for those of our friends who are dead in the Lord.

24 Martha saith unto him, ᵏ I know that he shall rise again in the resurrection at the last day.   k Luke 14. 14. ch. 5. 29.

From hence we learn, that the general resurrection of the dead is no novel doctrine. Job believed it, Job xix. 26, 27. Daniel published it, chap. xii. 2. The Pharisees owned it, though the Sadducees denied it; and possibly the Pharisees had but a confused notion of it. Martha here makes it an article of her faith.

25 Jesus said unto her, I am ˡ the resurrection, and the ᵐ life : ⁿ he that believeth in me, though he were dead, yet shall he live :

l ch. 5. 21. & 6. 39, 40, 44
m ch. 1. 4. & 6. 35. & 4. 6. Col. 3. 4. 1 John 1. 1, 2. & 5. 11.
n ch. 3. 36. 1 John 5. 10, &c.

Martha by her speech seemed not to have a true notion of Christ; she believed that there should be a general resurrection from the dead in the last day, by the mighty power of God, but she did not truly understand what influence Christ had upon this resurrection, that the raising of the dead should be the peculiar work of Christ, not without the Father, but as he was ordained by the Father to be the Judge of the quick and of the dead. Christ doth therefore here further instruct her, and tell her, he was *the resurrection;* where (as is usual in Scripture) the effect is put for the cause : *I am the resurrection,* is no more than, *I am,* and shall be, the principal cause of the resurrection : the dead shall hear the voice of the Son of God, chap. v. 28. He also adds, *and the life;* that is, the cause of life ; both that life which the dead shall in the resurrection recover, and also that eternal life which shall follow. And whosoever looketh upon me in that notion, and committeth himself unto me, though he doth die, yet he shall rise again, and live eternally; and this power being in me, I am not tied to the last day, but have a power when I please to raise the dead. Our Saviour indeed hath more in his answer than respected the present case ; but there was nothing more usual with him, than in his discourses to raise up the hearts of his people to higher things, as he doth in this place raise Martha beyond the thoughts of a resurrection of her brother's body to a natural life, to the thoughts of a spiritual and eternal life.

26 And whosoever liveth and believeth in me shall never die. Believest thou this?

He had before proved himself to be *the resurrection*, now he proveth himself to be *the life*. He saith, he that liveth, that liveth a natural life, if he be one who receiveth and embraceth me as the true Messiah and Saviour of the world, and committeth himself and all the concerns of his soul to me, shall never die. Though his body shall die because of sin, yet his spirit shall live because of righteousness; and God shall in the great day quicken again his mortal body, through the Holy Spirit which dwelleth in him, and is united to him, Rom. viii. 10, 11. He asketh Martha if she believed this. We shall observe, that our Saviour, not here only, but Matt. ix. 22, 28, before he wrought his miraculous operations, required people's faith as a prerequisite. And, Matt. xiii. 58, he could not do many mighty works in his own country, because of their unbelief. And, Matt. xvii. 20, he tells his disciples, that the reason why they could not cure the man possessed with the devil, was because of their unbelief: so great an honour hath God given to the exercise of faith.

o Mat. 16.16.
ch. 4, 42. &
6. 14, 69.
27 She saith unto him, Yea, Lord: °I believe that thou art the Christ, the Son of God, which should come into the world.

This is the nearest to the confession of Peter, Matt. xvi. 16, which our Saviour calleth, the rock upon which he would build his church, of any that we have in Scripture; yea, and more full than that, for those words, *which should come into the world*, are not in Peter's confession. The sum of this is, Martha doth here profess a full assent to our Saviour as the Messias, the Son of God; he who was prefigured, prophesied of, promised, as he who should come into the world.

28 And when she had so said, she went her way, and called Mary her sister secretly, saying, The Master is come, and calleth for thee.

Mary was left at home, while Martha went out of the town to meet Christ. It seemeth by this verse, Christ had asked for her, though that be not mentioned before. Martha goeth secretly to her, and tells her that the Master was come. (It was a name they usually called their most famous teachers by.)

29 As soon as she heard *that*, she arose quickly, and came unto him.

Mary's love and readiness to attend upon Christ, appeareth by a former story concerning her and her sister Martha, recorded Luke x. 38—40. But the present sorrow she was in for her dead brother, together with the hopes she conceived of having him restored to life by Christ's coming, added wings to her motion; therefore the evangelist saith, *she arose quickly, and came to him*.

30 Now Jesus was not yet come into the town, but was in that place where Martha met him.

p ver. 19.
31 ᵖThe Jews then which were with her in the house, and comforted her, when they saw Mary, that she rose up hastily and went out, followed her, saying, She goeth unto the grave to weep there.

32 Then when Mary was come where Jesus was, and saw him, she fell down at his feet, saying unto him, ᑫLord, if thou hadst been here, my brother had not died.

q ver. 21.

Coming, she falls down at his feet, which was a posture (as we have heard before) very usual in those countries, by which they testified both their civil respects to princes and great persons, and also which they used in the worship of God, Matt. ii. 11. Whether Mary did it upon the one account or the other, dependeth upon what we cannot know; viz. whether she at this time was fully persuaded of his Divine nature; of which the best of the disciples, till Christ's resurrection, had but a faint and uncertain persuasion. The words which she useth to him are the same which Martha used, ver. 21: see the notes there.

33 When Jesus therefore saw her weeping, and the Jews also weeping which came with her, he groaned in the spirit, and † was troubled,

† Gr. *he troubled himself.*

The apostle speaks of Christ, Heb. iv. 15, as *an High priest that can be touched with the feeling of our infirmities*, and one that *can have compassion*, Heb. v. 2. Martha's and Mary's passion for their dead brother was their infirmity; Christ is touched with the feeling of it: he, to show himself truly man, *groaned* in himself; it being natural to us to be affected with the afflictions of others, and to weep with those who weep. But here ariseth a question, whether Christ was troubled from a natural necessity, as we sometimes cannot forbear weeping to see others weep bitterly, or out of choice? Some of the ancients think it was out of choice. Mr. Calvin and others think that it was out of a natural necessity; not that he could not govern his passions (as we sometimes cannot) by reason, but that he could not, as man, forbear his passion. I shall translate what Mr. Calvin speaks, most judiciously, in the case, determining neither way, but leaving it to the reader's judgment. "But how," saith he, "do gnawing and trouble of spirit agree to that Person who was the Son of God? Because to some it looketh very absurd to say, that Christ, as one of us, is subject to human passions; they think Christ no otherwise at any time either grieved or rejoiced, than as he, so often as he thought fit, voluntarily assumed to himself those passions by a secret dispensation. Augustine thought that Christ in this sense is said to have groaned, and to have been troubled; whereas other men's passions transport them, and exercise a tyranny over them, to the disturbance of their minds: he therefore thinks the meaning is, that Christ, being otherwise sedate, and free from passions, sometimes voluntarily took these passions. But in my judgment, it is a much plainer and simpler sense of this scripture, if we say, that the Son of God, taking upon him our nature, did also freely with it put on our affections (which are our natural infirmities); so as he in nothing differed from us, but in this, that he had no sin. Nothing by this is derogated from the glory of Christ; for he voluntarily submitted to take our nature upon him, by which he became like to us in our human affections. And we must not think, that after he had voluntarily submitted to take our perfect nature upon him, that he was free from the passions and affections of it: in this he proved himself to be our Brother, that we might know that he is a Mediator for us, who can easily pardon our infirmities, and is ready to help us as to those infirmities, which he hath experienced in his own person. If any one object, That seeing our passions are sinful, it doth not agree to the nature of him who was the Son of God to share with us in them; I answer, There is a great deal of difference (as to these passions) betwixt us and Christ; for our affections are therefore faulty, because they are intemperate, and inordinate, and keep no bounds; but in Christ, though they be, yet they are composed, and moderate, and in obedience to God. The passions of men are faulty upon two accounts: 1. As they are turbulent, and not governed by the rule of moderation. 2. As they often rise without any good ground or foundation, or are not directed to a right end. They are in us a disease, because we neither grieve nor rejoice in measure, and to that degree alone which God permits and allows; many rather give the reins to their passions. And such is the vanity of our minds, that we are grieved and troubled for little or no causes, being too much addicted and cleaving to the world. There was no such thing in Christ, no passion in him ever exceeded its just bounds, or was exercised but upon a just and reasonable cause. To make this yet clearer, we must distinguish betwixt man in his creation, and the degenerate nature of man, as it is corrupted through sin. When God at first created man, he created him with natural affections, but such as were under the command of reason: that our passions are now inordinate, and rebellious, is accidental to our nature. Christ indeed took our affections upon him, but without that disorder which fell into them by the fall, which causeth us that we cannot obey them and God. He was greatly troubled, but not so as by his trouble to become disobedient to his Father. In short, if we compare our affections with his, there will appear as great a difference, as betwixt pure water and that which is dirty and filthy. And the single example of Christ is enough to make us reject the stoical apathy (or want of passion); for from whom, if not from him, should we fetch the highest rule of perfection? Let us therefore rather study to correct and tame that disorder in which our passions are entangled, and follow Christ as our guide, that we may bring them into order. Thus Paul, 1 Thess. iv. 13, doth not require of us a stony stupidity, but commands us to govern our grief, that we may not mourn as men without hope. For Christ therefore took our affections upon him, that we by his grace may be enabled to subdue whatsoever is vicious in them."

34 And said, Where have ye laid him? They said unto him, Lord, come and see.

r Luke 19. 41.

35 *r* Jesus wept.

Weeping is not of itself a sinful, but a natural passion, which (as was said before) doth very well agree with Christ, having voluntarily taken upon him our nature, and natural infirmities.

36 Then said the Jews, Behold how he loved him!

Love showeth itself, as in a complacence in the object beloved, while we enjoy it; so in a grief for it when we are deprived of it: the Jews therefore rightly concluded Christ's kindness to Lazarus, from his human affection expressed at his death.

37 And some of them said, Could not this man, *s* which opened the eyes of the blind, have caused that even this man should not have died?

s ch. 9. 6.

Some only concluded Christ's love to the deceased from his affection showed at his grave; but others made a worse conclusion, in derogation to Christ's reputation, from the miracle he had wrought, chap. ix., in restoring him that was born blind; for their speech soundeth in this sense, If he had indeed cured one that was born blind, certainly he could as well have kept this man, to whom (dead) he expresseth so great affection, clear from death. A learned interpreter therefore calleth this, a devilish sarcasm; they go about to weaken the reputation of our Saviour, from the miracle which he had wrought, apparently showing his Divine power, because he did not keep his friend from dying. It is much like the scoff with which they afterward scoffed him, while he hung upon the cross, Matt. xxvii. 42, *He saved others; himself he cannot save.* Or the words may have been spoken, if not with an irony, yet with admiration, that having cured the blind man, a stranger to him, he did not heal his sick friend; or as if they were uncertain whether his power of working miracles were not limited to some times, that he could not perform all things when he pleased. But how weak must this their argumentation be, which could stand upon no other foundation than this, That if Christ were the Son of God, he would at all times, and in all cases, have put forth his Divine power. As if God acted necessarily, not freely, governing his actions by his own wisdom, as he saw most conducing to the wise ends of his glory.

38 Jesus therefore again groaning in himself cometh to the grave. It was a cave, and a stone lay upon it.

Groaning in himself, as before, ver. 33, so showing himself yet further to be truly man, and not without human affections. He cometh to the place where Lazarus's dead body was laid, which, the evangelist telleth us, was *a cave,* or a hollow place in the earth, or some rock. And they were wont to roll some great stones to the mouth of those graves, as we see in the burial of our Saviour, Matt. xxvii. 66.

39 Jesus said, Take ye away the stone. Martha, the sister of him that was dead, saith unto him, Lord, by this time he stinketh: for he hath been *dead* four days.

Our Lord commandeth the removal of the stone, which was at the mouth of the sepulchre, that the miracle might be evident; for Lazarus to have come forth, the door of the cave being shut, and a great stone making it fast, would have looked more like an apparition than a resurrection. It is very probable that Martha thought that our Saviour commanded the removal of the stone, not in order to a commanding him to life again, but out of a curiosity to view his dead body; and therefore she objecteth the putrefaction of his body, from which the soul was now departed four days, as that which our Saviour would not be able to endure the savour of.

40 Jesus saith unto her, Said I not unto thee, that, if thou wouldest believe, thou shouldest *t* see the glory of God? t ver. 4, 23.

Christ now beginneth to open to Martha and Mary, and the rest, his resolution to raise Lazarus from the dead by and by. Christ saith that to us in his word, which he saith by a just consequence, though he doth not speak it in so many words: we do not read in this history, that Christ had spoken this in so many words and syllables, but he had spoken it in effect; he had told her, ver. 25, that he was *the resurrection and the life,* that he had power to raise dead bodies from a natural death to life; and that for those who believed in him, though they were dead, they should live. This could not be without a great manifestation of the glory of God: the power of God is his glory. *God hath spoken once,* (saith the psalmist,) *yea, twice have I heard this, that power belongeth unto God,* Psal. lxii. 11. Thou shouldest see God by me manifesting the glory of his Almighty power; God glorifying himself, and glorifying his Son. Believing brings us in experiences of God; whereas unbelief, as it were, limiteth God, and tieth up his hands.

41 Then they took away the stone *from the place* where the dead was laid. And Jesus lifted up *his* eyes, and said, Father, I thank thee that thou hast heard me.

The servants, or friends, about the grave, removeth the stone from the mouth of the cave, within which the dead corpse of Lazarus lay. Christ, before his thanksgiving to his Father, is said to have *lifted up his eyes;* a posture often used in men's addresses to God, Psal. cxxi. 1, and cxxiii. 1, as an indication of their belief that heaven is God's throne: though he filleth heaven and earth, yet heaven is his court, where he most gloriously showeth himself, the earth but his footstool. We read here of nothing that Christ had said before, yet he giveth thanks here to his Father that he had heard him. The meaning is, Thou hast willed, or pleased to grant, those things which I desired. It is very hard to determine, whether Christ had used some audible words before this, upon this occasion, in prayer to his Father, which the evangelist could not or did not set down; or whether he only groaned in his spirit, as was said before, by those groans not only expressing his sorrow for Lazarus's death, or rather sympathy with the afflictions of Mary and Martha, but also his desires to his Father, that he might be again restored to life; and his second groaning, ver. 38, was of that nature: which groanings in the saints God understandeth, knowing *the mind of the Spirit,* making *intercession for the saints according to the will of God* (as the apostle teacheth us, Rom. viii. 27); much more did the Father, who was one in nature, essence, and will with the Son, understand them in him. Nothing in these cases can be determined, much less can any conclude from hence, that there is no need of our using any words in our prayers; for although there be no simple, absolute necessity that we should use them in order to God's knowledge of what we need, and would have; for he that searcheth the heart, knows what we need, and what we desire, Matt. vi. 8; yet there is a necessity for our words, in order to our obeying God's command, Hos. xiv. 2; Luke xi. 2. There is a great deal of difference betwixt God's hearing of Christ, and hearing us: Christ and his Father have one essence, one nature, and will.

42 And I knew that thou hearest me always: but *u* because of the people which stand by I said *it,* that they may believe that thou hast sent me. u ch. 12. 30.

I know that thou always willest those things which I will; and I will nothing but what thou willest, and hast sent me to do in the world; so as in these things it is impossible but that thou shouldest always be ready to grant what I ask of thee; nay, there is no need of my asking. I only give thee thanks for the people's sake, who here stand by; who believe thee to be the true God, and to have an Almighty power; but will not as yet believe that I am thy Son, by thee sent into the world, and that I do the works which I do in thee and from thee. We read of many miracles wrought by Christ without any prayer first put up to his Father, Matt. viii. 3; ix. 6; Mark v. 41; ix. 25; Luke vii. 14, using only an authoritative word; nor need he have used any here, but only for the further conviction of the people that he was sent of God, that God whom they owned as their God: he prayeth and giveth thanks to God before them all.

43 And when he thus had spoken, he cried with a loud voice, Lazarus, come forth.

When he had groaned in his spirit, and audibly given thanks to his Father for hearing of him, and testified that he did this, not because he ever had any doubt of his Father's willing what he willed, but that the people might take notice of his favour and power with God, and that he was sent of him; *he cried with a loud voice;* not whispering, nor, like wizards, peeping and muttering, Isa. viii. 19, but speaking aloud, so as all might hear, and understand, that what was done was done by his powerful word. He calls him by his name, he bids him come forth; they were not the words that raised Lazarus, but the mighty, quickening power of Christ, which attended these words.

44 And he that was dead came forth, bound hand and foot with graveclothes: and ˣhis face was bound about with a napkin. Jesus saith unto them, Loose him, and let him go.

x ch. 20. 7.

The fashion of their dressing up the dead differeth, according to the fashion of several countries; among the Jews, we understand by this text, they tied a napkin about their head, and some clothes about their hands and feet. They wound the whole body in linen clothes with spices, chap. xix. 40; this was (as is there said) their manner to bury. So, Acts v. 6, the young men are said to have wound Ananias, and carried him out, and buried him. And this is that which certainly is meant here by these words, *bound hand and foot:* and here is a second miracle, that one so wrapped and bound up should be able to move and come forth. Christ bids, *Loose him, and let him go,* to evidence him truly recovered to life again, and that the miracle was perfectly wrought. About this miracle there are two curious questions started: 1. Whether the raising of Lazarus to life was done by the mere Divine power of Christ, or by the person of Christ; so as the human nature, being personally united to the Divine nature, had also a share in it; the Divine nature communicating its property of quickening the dead to the human nature? That it was the person of Christ that raised Lazarus, and he who did it was truly man and truly God, is out of doubt. But that there was any such communication of the properties of the Divine nature to the human nature, that it also had a share in this effect, is justly denied, and doubted by many great divines: but it is a question tending to no great profit for us to know. 2. Where Lazarus's soul was these four days wherein it was separated from the body? The Scripture hath not told us this, and it speaks too great curiosity to inquire too strictly. Though we are taught from the parable of Dives and Lazarus, that the souls of departed saints do ordinarily and immediately pass into heaven, or Abraham's bosom; yet what should hinder, but that in these cases where it appears to have been the Divine will that the souls of persons departed should again be returned into their bodies in a short time, they might by a Divine power be kept under the custody of angels, until the time of such restoration of them.

45 Then many of the Jews which came to Mary, ʸ and had seen the things which Jesus did, believed on him.

y ch. 2. 23. & 10. 42. & 12. 11, 18.

That is, which came to visit Martha and Mary in their mourning; and, coming to Mary, did go along with her to the sepulchre to meet Christ, and there meeting him, saw all the passages relating to this miracle, truly *believed on him* as the true Messiah, chap. xii. 11, 18. Or it may be, it is to be understood more largely of such a faith as is but preparatory to true and saving faith; for there was a double use of miracles. 1. To prepare men for faith, disposing them to give an ear to him, to whom God hath given so great a power; so as after the sight of them they were more fitted to hear, and inclinable to believe. 2. To confirm faith in those that believed, so as they believed the more firmly, seeing the doctrine they heard confirmed by such miraculous operations.

46 But some of them went their ways to the Pharisees, and told them what things Jesus had done.

These Jews had the same means for believing the others had; they had heard the same words from Christ, they had seen the same miracle wrought by Christ. Whence is it that any of the other Jews believed? These, instead of believing, run to the Pharisees to accuse him. Can any account be given of this, unless from the freedom of Divine grace, showing mercy where God will show mercy? Though possibly the former wickedness of these Jews was the cause of God's not giving that grace to them which he gave to others.

47 ¶ ᶻThen gathered the Chief Priests and the Pharisees a council, and said, ᵃWhat do we? for this man doeth many miracles.

z Ps. 2. 2. Matt. 26. 3. Mark 14. 1. Luke 22. 2. a ch. 12. 19. Acts 4. 16.

The chief priests and Pharisees were a great part of that great council amongst the Jews, which went under the name of the sanhedrim; and this (probably) was the council they gathered; for, ver. 49, we read, that Caiaphas, the high priest, the standing president of that court, was amongst them. The miracles wrought by Christ were the things that disturbed them, and they reflect upon themselves for conniving so long at him: what they should have improved (viz. the miracles which he wrought) to have begot or increased faith in them, they mention and misimprove to their destruction.

48 If we let him thus alone, all *men* will believe on him: and the Romans shall come and take away both our place and nation.

They are afraid, that if they should any longer suffer Christ to go on working miracles, he would have a great many followers, who upon the credit of his miracles would own him as the Messiah, and the effect and consequence of this would be, they should by the Romans (to whom they were already in subjection) be utterly deprived of that little liberty they indulged them. They say, the Romans would come (that is, with an army) and destroy their temple, which they call their *place*, their most famous place, where they met to worship God, and in which, as a token of God's presence amongst them, they so much gloried; yea, and their *nation*; that is, miserably destroy their nation, and bring it to utter ruin. Whether they really thought so or no, or only spake this as an argument to hasten the death of Christ, is not much material for us to know. There was this colour for it, the Jews were a people very prone upon all occasions to rebel, and rise up in the defence of their liberties, whenever they could get any head, to give them any countenance and conduct. They also lived in a general expectation of the Messiah, when the sceptre should be departed from Judah, (as it now was,) and when Daniel's seventy weeks, mentioned chap. ix. 24, should be determined, which were now fulfilled; so as there was about this time a general expectation of the Messiah; of whom also it is apparent they had a false notion, and generally expected under the notion of the Messiah, not the Son of God taking human nature, and to die for their redemption, and then rise again from the dead, and ascend into heaven; but a temporal prince, who, conquering all their enemies, should deliver them from all captivities and servitudes, and restore them to their ancient liberties. This their expectation was known well enough to the Roman governors, (as appeareth by Herod's question to the wise men in Matt. ii. 4,) and they were very jealous of the Jews on this account, which caused Herod's bloody act in killing the children in and about Bethlehem. So as the rulers of the Jews (according to the notion they had of the Messiah) might reasonably think, that if Jesus were taken to be the Messiah, and he went on confirming the opinion of himself by these miracles, so as people generally ran after him, the Romans would reasonably suppose they had a design to rebel, and therefore would come upon them, destroy their temple, and utterly ruin their nation. But how will they avoid this? That which they agreed upon we shall meet with ver. 53, they took counsel to put him to death. How they were led on to that fatal counsel we shall hear.

h Luke 3. 2.
ch. 18. 14.
Acts 4. 6.

49 And one of them, *named* [b] Caiaphas, being the High Priest that same year, said unto them, Ye know nothing at all,

The high priest by the Divine law was to be but one, and he the eldest son of Aaron's house; nor was he to be for a year, but for his life, as appeareth by a multitude of texts in the books of Moses: but all things were now out of order in the Jewish church; they were under the power of the Romans; all places, especially that of the high priest, were bought and sold amongst them: some say they had two high priests, others say but one, only he had an assistant, called by that name, that had a partnership in the honour. After Herod's time there was no regard to the family of Aaron, or the Asmoneans, but the Romans made what high priest they pleased; so as Josephus tells us, that the Jews, who had but thirteen high priests from Aaron's to Solomon's time, which was six hundred and twelve years; nor more than eighteen in four hundred and sixty years after, to the captivity of Babylon; nor more than fifteen from thence to the time of Antiochus, which was four hundred and fourteen years; had twenty-eight betwixt the time that Herod began to reign and Jerusalem was destroyed; of which this Caiaphas was one, and certainly the chief, (if there were two at this time,) and consequently the president of their great court, whom all attended to, and his words went a great way with the rest. He chargeth the rest of the council with folly, as not considering what was fit to be done.

c ch. 18. 14.

50 [c] Nor consider that it is expedient for us, that one man should die for the people, and that the whole nation perish not.

Never was any thing spoken more diabolically: he regards not what was their duty, nor what was lawful for them to do; whether they might upon any pretence shed innocent blood, much more the blood of one whose life was spent in nothing but a going up and down in doing good; only, like a wretched politician, who was concerned for nothing but the people's safety, he saith not, it is lawful, but, *it is expedient for us that one man*, be he never so good, never so innocent and just, *should die for the people*, that is, to save the whole nation from destruction.

51 And this spake he not of himself: but being High Priest that year, he prophesied that Jesus should die for that nation;

So far as this was a prophecy, *he spake not of himself:* take the words of Caiaphas in the sense that he spake them, they were such as might well enough come out of such a wretched mouth, speaking out of the abundance of a vile and wretched heart; *Melius pereat unus quam unitas,* That it was better that one man should die, let him be never so good, just, and innocent, than that for his sake mischief should come upon a nation. This was now suitable enough to the religion of such a high priest. But that in this (the words being capable of a double sense) Caiaphas should deliver a great truth, That this year *one should die for the people;* that is, The *Messiah* should *be cut off, but not for himself,* as we read, Dan. ix. 26; this was no more from himself, than the words which Balaam's ass spake were from itself. The Spirit of prophecy sometimes fell upon wicked men; God revealed to Pharaoh and Nebuchadnezzar (both of whom were pagans) the things which he intended to do. There was a time also when Saul (though a man rejected of God) did also prophesy; and the worst of the princes of Judah had a use of the Urim and Thummim. So also here, Caiaphas, though a vile and wicked man, was here influenced by God to prophesy, and speak an oracle. Nor are those words, *being high priest that year,* superfluously put in; for it being consistent with the holiness of God, sometimes to make use of the tongues of the worst of men to declare his will, it seems agreeable to the wisdom of God in doing it, to make use of principal men, they being persons whose words are most likely to be regarded, and so make impression upon people. The papists would from hence infer the infallibility of the pope, because he is the high priest: but they ought to prove, 1. That the office of the pope hath any foundation in the word of God. 2. That this was a gift given to particular priests, and at particular times; for the Jewish high priests were fallible enough ordinarily; witness Aaron's making the golden calf, and Urijah the altar after the pattern of Damascus, 2 Kings xvi. 10, 11. The words, *being high priest,* are not given as a reason why Caiaphas prophesied, though they are a good reason why God was pleased to choose his tongue, and overrule it beyond his own thoughts and intentions, to serve his design in this revelation. He did not prophesy intentionally, as designing such a thing, only materially: the matter of his words were indeed a Divine revelation, though his intention and scope was fit for none but a base, carnal politician. God made him a prophet in what he said, though he meant not so.

52 And [d] not for that nation only, [e] but that also he should gather together in one the children of God that were scattered abroad.

d Is. 49. 6.
1 John 2. 2.
e ch. 10. 16.
Eph. 2. 14.
15, 16, 17.

Not for that nation only; not for the Jews only. The words used in Caiaphas's speech were λαὸς and ἔθνος, words not significant of the Jews only, but of other people also: for Christ was to gather into one body all the elect of God, (who are here called *the children of God,* because they were to be so after their being begotten by the immortal seed of the word, and born again of water and the Spirit,) those that at present were *scattered abroad* over the face of the whole earth: Christ was to *gather together in one all things in heaven and earth,* Eph. i. 10. The evangelist extendeth the sense of Caiaphas's prophecy to Gentiles as well as Jews, according to the extent of the death of Christ, declared 1 John ii. 2.

53 Then from that day forth they took counsel together for to put him to death.

They had taken such counsel before; but now they were more intent than before, having found a juster pretence, viz. to prevent a sedition and rebellion; and learned of their high priest, that it was more convenient that one should die, than that a whole nation should be destroyed. The high priest had satisfied their consciences; now they make all the haste they can to put their malicious designs in execution.

54 Jesus [f] therefore walked no more openly among the Jews; but went thence unto a country near to the wilderness, into a city called [g] Ephraim, and there continued with his disciples.

f ch. 4. 1, 3.
& 7. 1.

g See 2 Chr. 13. 19.

Jesus therefore walked no more openly among the Jews; for he being the true paschal Lamb, was to be slain at that feast, and put an end to that type, and would therefore reserve himself for that time, which was now at hand. *A city called Ephraim:* what this Ephren or Ephraim was, interpreters vainly busy themselves in inquiring; it was some obscure city, and near the wilderness; some think it was in the lot of Benjamin, others think it was in the lot of Ephraim, and obtained its name from the tribe in whose lot it was. The Scripture no where mentioneth it; and it cannot be expected, but that in so many changes of government as had befallen the Jews, the names of places should be so altered, that we should be at loss for many of them: wherever it was, it is said that Christ and his disciples continued there in some privacy.

55 ¶ [h] And the Jews' Passover was nigh at hand: and many went out of the country up to Jerusalem before the Passover, to purify themselves.

h ch. 2. 13.
& 5. 1. & 6. 4.

Christ's last passover, which was the fourth after he had entered upon his public ministry, was nigh. He doth not say all, but *many went up to purify themselves.* There was no general legal purification required before men did eat the passover; but there were several legal uncleannesses, and purifications necessary to cleanse men from them; now those who had any special purification to pass, went before others, that they might have time to do what the law required of them.

i ch. 11. 7.   56 ⁱThen sought they for Jesus, and spake among themselves, as they stood in the temple, What think ye, that he will not come to the feast?

I find good interpreters expounding this verse of the friends of Christ, who having used to meet Christ at these feasts, and see some miracles wrought by him, did out of a good design seek for him, and inquire of each other whether they knew if he intended to be at the feast: yet it may also be understood of his enemies, though it seemeth something too early, being six or seven days before.

57 Now both the Chief Priests and the Pharisees had given a commandment, that, if any man knew where he were, he should shew *it*, that they might take him.

For their great court had issued out orders for the discovery and apprehending of our Saviour, if they could any way learn where he was. This was in pursuance of that wicked counsel of which we read before, ver. 53: there they decreed; now they cannot rest until they bring their bloody devices to pass, for which we shall soon find God giving them an opportunity.

CHAP. XII

Mary anointeth the feet of Jesus: Judas murmureth at the cost, 1—8. *The people flock to see Lazarus: the chief priests consult to kill him*, 9—11. *Jesus rideth into Jerusalem in triumph*, 12—19. *Certain Greeks desired to see him*, 20—22. *He showeth the benefit of his death to believers; prayeth to his Father; is answered by a voice from heaven; signifieth the manner of his death; and exhorteth to make good use of the present light*, 23—36. *The generality of the Jews believe not*, 37—41; *yet many chief rulers believe, but dare not confess him*, 42, 43. *He urgeth faith in his Divine mission*, 44—50.

THEN Jesus six days before the Passover came to Bethany, ᵃwhere Lazarus was which had been dead, whom he raised from the dead.

a ch. 11. 1, 43.

From the *country near to the wilderness*, where Jesus continued with his disciples, chap. xi. 54, he came to Bethany, within less than two miles of Jerusalem, upon the sabbath day, or possibly the night before, *six days before the passover*: it was the place where (as we read in the former chapter) Lazarus died, and was by Christ *raised from the dead.*

b Matt. 26. 6. Mark 14. 3.   2 ᵇThere they made him a supper; and Martha served: but Lazarus was one of them that sat at the table with him.

That this supper was made in Bethany is no question; but at whose house there it is questioned. Some think that it was at the house of Simon the leper. We read indeed of a supper made for our Saviour at his house, both Matt. xxvi. 6, 7. and Mark xiv. 3. and that Simon is said to have been of Bethany: only the supper here mentioned is said to have been six days before the passover, and that mentioned by Matthew and Mark seems to have been but two days before, Matt. xxvi. 2; Mark xiv. 1. That which is probably said to solve that difficulty is, the circumstances of the supper, and history about it, seem the very same, both in Matthew, Mark, and John; but it seems in Matthew and Mark to be a little put out of order; they do not say that this supper was two days before the passover, (that indeed had been a contradiction to what John doth here relate,) but both Matthew and Mark first tell us, that Christ told his disciples that the passover was to be within two days, and of the counsel taken by the chief priests and elders against Christ, and then relateth the story of this supper: John first gives us an account of this supper, which was six days before the passover; so John seems to have related it in its proper time and order.

3 Then took ᶜMary a pound of ointment of spikenard, very costly, and anointed the feet of Jesus, and wiped his feet with her hair: and the house was filled with the odour of the ointment.

c Luke 10. 38, 39. ch. 11. 2.

4 Then saith one of his disciples, Judas Iscariot, Simon's *son*, which should betray him,

5 Why was not this ointment sold for three hundred pence, and given to the poor?

6 This he said, not that he cared for the poor; but because he was a thief, and ᵈhad the bag, and bare what was put therein.

d ch. 13. 29.

7 Then said Jesus, Let her alone: against the day of my burying hath she kept this.

8 For ᵉthe poor always ye have with you; but me ye have not always.

e Matt. 26. 11. Mark 14. 7.

Both Matthew and Mark relate this story with some different circumstances: see the notes upon those two places, where all the differing circumstances are considered and explained, and the parts of this history are more largely explained.

9 Much people of the Jews therefore knew that he was there: and they came not for Jesus' sake only, but that they might see Lazarus also, ᶠwhom he had raised from the dead.

f ch. 11. 43, 44.

Bethany was so near to Jerusalem, that many of the Jews came thither, as well to see Lazarus, raised from the dead, as to see Christ: nor was this without the special providence of God, that the name of Christ might be made more famous just before his suffering.

10 ¶ ᵍBut the Chief Priests consulted that they might put Lazarus also to death;

g Luke 16. 31.

Never was there a more unreasonable madness and rage, to justify the apostle's calling of the enemies of the gospel *unreasonable men,* 2 Thess. iii. 2. Suppose that Christ had broken the sabbath, or had spoken blasphemy, yet what had Lazarus done?

11 ʰBecause that by reason of him many of the Jews went away, and believed on Jesus.

h ch. 11. 45. ver. 18.

Being raised from death to life, he possibly spake of it to the honour and glory of God; for this they consult to put him to death also; and their only reason was, *because that many of the Jews believed on Jesus* for his sake.

12 ¶ ⁱOn the next day much people that were come to the feast, when they heard that Jesus was coming to Jerusalem,

i Matt. 21. 8. Mark 11. 8. Luke 19. 35, 36, &c.

13 Took branches of palm trees, and went forth to meet him, and cried, ᵏHosanna: Blessed *is* the King of Israel that cometh in the name of the Lord.

k Ps. 118. 25, 26.

14 ˡAnd Jesus, when he had found a young ass, sat thereon; as it is written,

l Matt. 21. 7.

15 ᵐFear not, daughter of Sion: behold, thy King cometh, sitting on an ass's colt.

m Zech. 9. 9.

This whole history is much more largely reported by the other evangelists, Matt. xxi. 1—16; Mark xi. 1—10; Luke xix. 29—40: see the notes on all those places.

16 These things ⁿunderstood not his disciples at the first: ᵒbut when Jesus was glorified, ᵖthen remembered they that these things were written of him, and *that* they had done these things unto him.

n Luke 18. 34. o ch. 7. 39. p ch. 14. 26.

The evangelist, amongst others, confesseth his own ignorance also. The disciples saw the thing done, Christ riding into the city upon the foal of an ass, the people strewing of boughs, and throwing their clothes in the way; but to what purpose these things were done, or what fulfilling of prophecies was in this thing, that they understood not, so long as Christ was alive: their eyes were upon the Messiah as a temporal prince, that should come in great state and majesty, so as they were wholly blinded from seeing any thing of the truth and faithfulness of God fulfilled in this little triumph of their Lord's. But after that Christ had died, and was risen again from the dead, and ascended up to heaven, so declaring himself with power to be the Son of God; then they began to remember these things, so as to confirm their faith in him as the true Messiah, whom God had sent into the world. The word of the Lord which we hear, and the works of God which we see, though ofttimes they do not profit us, nor are improved by us at the present, yet afterward become of use and profit to us: it is therefore good to hear, and see, and observe God's words and works, and to lay them up in our hearts, as it is said Mary pondered the sayings of the angel; expecting fruit afterwards of what at present we see no fruit and effect.

17 The people therefore that was with him when he called Lazarus out of his grave, and raised him from the dead, bare record.

q ver. 11.

18 ᵠFor this cause the people also met him, for that they heard that he had done this miracle.

19 The Pharisees therefore said among themselves, ʳPerceive ye how ye prevail nothing? behold, the world is gone after him.

r ch. 11. 47, 48.

These three verses let us know the external cause of the people's coming to see Christ, which was the fame of the miracle wrought by our Saviour on Lazarus; this increased the number of those who came to see his entrance into Jerusalem; but the unseen cause was, doubtless, the influence of God upon their hearts, directing them to it, for the further glorifying of his Son before his passion. But this enraged the Pharisees, to see that their decree that those who owned Christ should be turned out of the synagogue should have no better effect: but the multitude rather more owned him, and ran after him. Here again we find the term *world* signifying many, though those many made up but a very small part of the world.

s Acts 17. 4.
t 1 Kings 8. 41, 42.
Acts 8. 27.

20 ¶ And there ˢwere certain Greeks among them ᵗthat came up to worship at the feast:

It is not easy to be determined what these *Greeks* were; whether Jews, who, being scattered in the Grecian country upon the conquests which the Grecians had made upon the Jews under Alexander the Great, and those who succeeded him, still remained in those countries, but kept so much of the religion of their country, as to come up to the passover; or Gentiles, which are ordinarily called Greeks in contradistinction to the Jews, Acts xiv. 1; xvi. 1; xviii. 17; Rom. i. 16; 1 Cor. i. 23, 24; Gal. iii. 28. But it is most probable that they were Gentiles; for though some say that the Jews would never have suffered the Gentiles to have come into the temple to worship, yet the contrary is plain from the instance of the eunuch, Acts viii. 27; who was a heathen, and came to Jerusalem to worship. And, Acts xvii. 4, we read of *a great multitude of devout Greeks;* in the Greek the word is σεβομίνων, worshipping Greeks. And it is plain that from the beginning there was a liberty for strangers, not of Israel, but such as came out of a far country, for the Lord's name's sake; and Solomon prayeth at the dedication of the temple, that the Lord would hear them, 1 Kings viii. 41—43: and there was belonging to the temple a court of the Gentiles for that purpose; it is called *the court without the temple,* Rev. xi. 2. What worship they there performed is a greater question: some think they only prayed; others think they offered sacrifices in that court, from 2 Macc. ii. 35; but certain it is, that there were divers of the Gentiles devoutly disposed, that, hearing of the Jewish temple, and the solemn worship performed there at their solemn feasts, came, some as spectators at those great conventions, others with a true design to worship the God of the Jews.

21 The same came therefore to Philip, ᵘwhich was of Bethsaida of Galilee, and desired him, saying, Sir, we would see Jesus.

u ch. 1. 44.

If these Grecians (as is probable) were Syrophenicians, their country was so near to Bethsaida of Galilee, which was Philip's town, that it is probable they might have some knowledge of him, and that might bring them to him to be spokesman; but it should seem they came only to satisfy their curiosity, for they ask for no more than that they might *see Jesus.*

22 Philip cometh and telleth Andrew: and again Andrew and Philip tell Jesus.

The news of their coming, and their errand, is brought to Christ by Philip and Andrew, who possibly might stumble at it, because they were Gentiles, and Christ had forbidden them to go into the way of the Gentiles; they therefore first acquaint him with the desire of those Greeks, before they bring them to Christ.

23 ¶ And Jesus answered them, saying, ˣThe hour is come, that the Son of man should be glorified.

x ch. 13. 32.
& 17. 1.

Christ replies, that the time was now come when he (who was the Son of God) *should be glorified;* that is, by the Gentiles receiving of the gospel, according to the many prophecies of it in the Old Testament; but he goeth on telling them that he must first die.

24 Verily, verily, I say unto you, ʸExcept a corn of wheat fall into the ground and die, it abideth alone: but if it die, it bringeth forth much fruit.

y 1 Cor. 15. 36.

Look as you see in your ordinary husbandry, the grains of wheat are first buried in the earth, and lose their form, before they spring and shoot up again, and bring forth fruit; so it must be with me; I must be first lifted up, before I shall draw men after me; I must first be crucified, before my gospel shall be preached to all nations, and the fulness of the Gentiles shall come: but if I have once died, and risen again from the dead, then you shall see this abundant fruit.

25 ᶻHe that loveth his life shall lose it; and he that hateth his life in this world shall keep it unto life eternal.

z Matt. 10. 39. & 16. 25.
Mark 8. 35.
Luke 9. 24.
& 17. 33.

We had much the same in the other evangelists, Matt. x. 39; Luke xiv. 26. Some think that our Saviour repeateth it here, to show, that as Christ first suffered, and then entered into his glory; so his disciples must also lay the foundation of their glory in their sufferings, and *through much tribulation enter into the kingdom of God,* Acts xiv. 22. Or what if we should say, that our blessed Lord doth here prophesy what sufferings would attend the first preaching of the gospel, and encourage his disciples to what he knew they must meet with and undergo, by letting them know that the ready way to lose their share in life eternal, was to be so fond of this life, and the comforts of it, as not to be ready to lay them down for him; but if any person hated, that is, less loved his life, and all that in this world is dear to him, than Christ and his service, he should, if not be preserved from enemies' rage, yet most certainly be recompensed with eternal life?

26 If any man serve me, let him follow me; and ᵃwhere I am, there shall also my servant be: if any man serve me, him will *my* Father honour.

a ch. 14. 3.
& 17. 24.
1 Thes. 4. 17.

If any man serve me, let him follow me: this is much the same with that, Matt. xvi. 24, unless following here be more restrained to suffering, *let him follow me* to my cross; for otherwise it seemeth the same with serving; we must be ready not only to do, but also to die for Christ, to follow him to the cross, if he calleth us to it. And if any man so serveth me, he shall be in heaven where I am; *If we suffer with him, we shall also be glorified together,* Rom. viii. 17. For my Father, with whom I am one in nature and essence, will honour those that are my servants; so great a thing it is to be a servant to the Son of God. The

Father will honour those that are so, and especially those who are so in suffering, with eternal life and felicity.

27 ᵇNow is my soul troubled; and what shall I say? Father, save me from this hour: ᶜbut for this cause came I unto this hour.

ᵇ Matt. 26. 38, 39. Luke 12. 50. ch. 13. 21.
ᶜ Luke 22. 53. ch. 18. 37.

Now is my soul troubled; by soul is not here to be understood only the sensitive part of the soul, but his whole human soul. So chap. xiii. 21, *He was troubled in spirit.* Our inward troubles arise from our passions; and there are passions of grief and fear, which give us most of our inward trouble; fear respecteth some evil at a distance from us; grief is caused by evil fallen upon us, or so near that we seem to be already in the power of it. The word here used is τετάρακται, which signifieth no mean, but a great and more than ordinary, degree of trouble. Christ was greatly troubled, though not so as we sometimes are, when our trouble leadeth us to despair: Christ was capable of no sinful trouble. Hence two questions arise: 1. For what the soul of Christ was troubled? 2. How such a degree of trouble could agree to the Lord Jesus Christ? He tells us, Matt. xxvi. 38, that he was *exceedingly sorrowful,* so as sorrow was one part of his trouble; and we may learn from what he afterward saith in this verse, *Father, save me from this hour,* that fear made up the other part of it. He was grieved, and he was afraid; some say it was at the apprehension of that miserable death he was to die; others say, at the sense of the Divine wrath which he was to undergo, death being not yet overcome, and his conflict with his Father's wrath for the sins of men being yet to be endured. Though Christ at this time was in the most perfect obedience to his Father's will, offering up a most acceptable and well-pleasing sacrifice unto God; yet he, sustaining our persons, had a conflict to endure even with his Father's wrath upon that account, though not upon his own personal account; for so he was at this time doing that which was most acceptable and well-pleasing in his sight. As to the second question, nothing could more agree to Christ than this, both with respect to his human nature, which had the same natural (though not sinful) infirmities which other men have; and with respect to his design and end, to help and relieve his people under their troubles of spirit; and, as the apostle saith, Heb. ii. 15, to *deliver them who through fear of death are all their lifetime subject to bondage.* So as this trouble of spirit agreed to him both as man and as Mediator. But there must be a vast difference observed betwixt this trouble of spirit in Christ, and that which is in us. Our troubles are upon reflections for our own sin, and the wrath of God due to us therefore; his trouble was for the wrath of God due to us for our sins. Our troubles are because we have personally grieved God; his was because those given to him (not he himself) had offended God. We are afraid of our eternal condemnation; he was only afraid by a natural fear of death, which naturally riseth higher according to the kind of death we die. Our troubles have mixtures of despair, distrust, sinful horrors; there was no such thing in his trouble. Our troubles in their natural tendencies are killing and destroying; only by accident, and the wise ordering of Divine providence, prove advantageous, by leading us to him, as the only remedy for troubled souls: his trouble was, in the very nature of it, not only pure and clean, but also sanative and healing. But that he was truly troubled, and that in his whole soul, and that such a trouble did very well agree to him, as to the human nature he had assumed, so to his office as our Mediator and Saviour, and the foundation of a great deal of peace, quiet, and satisfaction to us, is out of question. The chastisement of our peace in this particular lay upon him; and they were some of those stripes of his, by which we are healed. *And* (saith he) *what shall I say?* It is the natural language of a spirit troubled. *Father, save me from this hour;* this hour of my passion; it is the same with that in our Saviour's last prayer, *Let this cup pass from me;* and must be understood with the same qualifications there expressed, *if it be thy will, if it be possible,* &c. By his blessed example he hath taught us, under the distresses of our spirits, whither to flee, what to do. *For my love* (saith David to his enemies, Psal. cix. 4) *they are mine adversaries: but I give myself unto prayer;* I give up myself to prayer. God hath bidden us, Psal. l. 15, *call upon him in the day of trouble;* and St. James saith, chap. v. 13, *Is any among you afflicted? let him pray.* Herein Christ hath himself set us an example, that we should follow his steps. But how doth our Saviour pray to be saved from that hour, when for this cause he came into the world? Here was in Christ a conflict between the flesh and the Spirit; not like ours, which is betwixt corrupt flesh and the Spirit, but betwixt his natural flesh, and the natural affections of it, and his spirit; that was fully conformed to the will of God, and gets a present conquest. *But for this cause* (saith he) *came I to this hour:* he checks himself, correcteth the language of his natural flesh, acquiesceth, rejoiceth in the will of God. I was not (saith he) forced, I came of my own good-will to this hour; and I came on purpose to die for my people.

28 Father, glorify thy name. ᵈThen came there a voice from heaven, *saying,* I have both glorified *it,* and will glorify *it* again.

ᵈ Mat. 3. 17.

Father, glorify thy name; that is, make thy name glorious, make it to be known and famous over all the earth. a general petition, but such a one as all our particular requests must be reduced to, if they be according to the will of God. It is as much as, Father, do thine own will: for God is then glorified when his will is done. But it here signifies more: Not my will, but thy will be done. My flesh indeed saith, Save me from this hour; but, Father, do thy own will, let that be done concerning me which will most tend to make thy name renowned. Such a prayer never goes without an answer. *Then came there a voice from heaven, &c.;* the Lord caused a voice as from heaven to be heard. *I have glorified it;* I have by thee caused my glory to be published and proclaimed in the world, by thy preaching, by thy miracles; and I will perfect that which I have begun, *I will glorify it again;* thou shalt further glorify me by thy death, by thy resurrection from the dead, by the preaching of the gospel, and carrying it to the ends of the earth.

29 The people therefore, that stood by, and heard *it,* said that it thundered: others said, An angel spake to him.

The people said that it thundered; nor, it may be, were they mistaken, saving only in this, that they thought it was nothing else but thunder (being possibly at such a distance, as they could not distinctly hear the voice); for it was God's way, when he spake unto his people by a voice, to have that voice, for the greater declaration of the Divine majesty, attended with thunderings and lightnings: thus it was at the giving of the law upon Mount Sinai; thus we read in John's visions, Rev. iv. 5; viii. 5, of lightnings, and thunderings, and voices, which proceeded from God's throne. *Others said, An angel spake to him:* it was the general opinion of the Jews, that God always, when by voice he revealed his mind to his people, made use of an angel to do it by; hence, probably, as those who were at such a distance that they heard no voice, thought it was nothing but thunder; so those who are so nigh as, besides the thunder, to hear a voice, said, It was an angel that spake with him.

30 Jesus answered and said, ᵉThis voice came not because of me, but for your sakes.

ᵉ ch. 11. 42.

This voice came not to instruct me, I very well knew, before it came, that my Father had glorified his own name, and would do it again; it came not principally nor solely for me, but chiefly to confirm you in this great truth, that I am the Son of God, and he whom he hath sent into the world, by and in whom he designeth to glorify his own great name.

31 Now is the judgment of this world: now shall ᶠthe prince of this world be cast out.

ᶠ Mat. 12. 29. Luke 10. 18. ch. 14. 30. & 16. 11. Acts 26. 18. 2 Cor. 4. 4. Eph. 2. 2. & 6. 12.

The terms *judgment* and *world* are taken so variously in the New Testament, and particularly in this very Gospel, that they have given interpreters a great liberty to vary in their senses of this passage. It seemeth reasonable to agree, that our Saviour doth expound in this verse what the voice from heaven uttered; that the Father had already glorified his name, and would yet further glorify it. How? *Now* (saith he) *is the judgment of this world;* that is, (say some,) the condemnation of the wicked men in it: and certain it is, that the term *world* doth sometimes so signify, chap. xv. 19; xvii. 6, 9; 1 Cor. vi. 2; xi. 32. But this sense seemeth not to agree with chap. iii. 17, where Christ tells us, that this his first coming was not to condemn the world. Others do therefore here by *judgment* better understand, the dispensation of Divine providence, by which a great change or catastrophe was to be made in the world by the reformation of it; the beginning of the time of the *restitution of all things,* Acts iii. 21. But it seems best to be understood of the deliverance and vindication of mankind from the power of the devil, who had a long time held mankind in an unjust possession. The devil had got a dominion over mankind by the fall of Adam, and had exceedingly tyrannized over them, keeping the far greatest part of the world in slavery by idolatry, and keeping many others, who were no open idolaters, yet captives to his will. Now, saith our Saviour, the time is come when this shall be altered; Satan shall be bound up; I will deliver a great part of the world from the yoke of idolatry; another part of them from the power and dominion of sin. The devil, who is not by any right *the prince of this world,* but boasteth himself to be so, Matt. iv. 9, and acteth in it like a prince, powerfully working *in the children of disobedience,* Eph. ii. 2, and *as the god of this world* blinding men's eyes, 2 Cor. iv. 4, taking the world as his house, and keeping it as a strong man, Matt. xii. 29, shall be cast out of my redeemed ones; so as though he will still be going about like a roaring lion, seeking whom he may devour, and molesting the best of men by his temptations, yet he shall not prevail over them, God will bruise him under their feet; he that had the power of death shall (as to his dominion) be destroyed, and those who are in bondage through the fear of it, shall be delivered, Heb. ii. 14, 15; the tempted shall be succoured, ver. 18, and God with the temptation shall give a blessed issue. And the devil's kingdom kept up by idolatry, shall also in a great measure be destroyed in the world; many nations now under that slavery shall embrace the gospel, and throw away their idols.

g ch. 3. 14.
& 8. 28.
h Rom. 5. 18.
Heb. 2. 9.
i ch. 18. 32.

32 And I, ^gif I be lifted up from the earth, will draw ^hall *men* unto me.

33 ⁱThis he said, signifying what death he should die.

However this term of lifting up Christ is taken in some other scriptures, it is by the evangelist himself in this text expounded concerning his death, so as there is no room for any other interpretation of it in this text. The word that is used, is hardly to be found in any place (except where in Scripture it relateth to Christ) signifying to die, or put to death; but is very proper, both to express the kind of his death, which was a lifting up upon the cross, from the earth into the air; and to let us know that his death was a lifting up of his name: as it was the lowest degree of his humiliation, so it was nearest to his exaltation. It was his highest act of obedience to the will of his Father, that for which his Father *highly exalted him,* giving him *a name which is above every name,* Phil. ii. 9; and also that which made his name famous over all the world, by the preaching of the gospel; for as the apostles, so all the ministers of the gospel since their times, preach a Christ crucified. Saith our Saviour, If, or although, I be put to death by the hands of the Jews, lifted up upon the cross betwixt heaven and earth, yet this shall not hinder my Father's glorifying of himself in and by me; for instead of obscuring or hindering my Father's glory, by this I shall further promote it. For by the preaching of my cross, and publication of my gospel to all nations, and by the efficacious concurrence of my Holy Spirit, together with the preaching of the gospel, I shall draw (though not all, and every man, yet) multitudes of men and women after me, so as they shall embrace and believe in me, having died and risen up again from the dead, and being by my apostles, and other ministers of the gospel, held forth as the object of people's faith, to be by them laid hold upon in order to their eternal life and salvation. He used the term of lifting up, (saith the evangelist,) to signify the particular death he should die, by *being crucified;* in which death the bodies of the crucified abode not upon the earth, as when they were at any time stoned, or strangled, or beheaded, &c., but were lifted up from the earth to be nailed to the cross, and hung in the air until they died.

34 The people answered him, ^kWe have heard out of the law that Christ abideth for ever: and how sayest thou, The Son of man must be lifted up? who is this Son of man?

k Ps. 89. 36, 37. & 110. 4.
Is. 9. 7. & 53. 8. Ezek. 37. 25. Dan. 2. 44. & 7. 14, 27. Mic. 4. 7.

Here again *the law* is taken in a larger sense than in some places, where it is only significant of the books of Moses, in opposition to the prophets and other holy writings, as we had it before, chap. x. 34; for the places of Scripture which the people seem to refer to, seem to be Psal. cx. 4, where Christ is called *a priest for ever;* or else Dan. vii. 14, where the kingdom of the Messiah is said to be *an everlasting dominion,* which should *not pass away,* a kingdom that should *not be destroyed:* so also, Dan. ii. 44; Micah iv. 7. These old prophecies of the Messiah the people could not reconcile to what our Saviour here told them of his death; the reason was, their not understanding the true notion of the Messiah, and of his kingdom, which they fancied not to be a spiritual and eternal kingdom, but a temporal kingdom here on earth. This made them ask, how, (that is, with what consistency to those prophecies,) if he indeed were the Messias, he said, The Son of man should die; for that they understood by the term *lifted up,* which maketh it very plain, that it was a phrase they used to express that kind of death by. They ask who he meant by the Son of man.

35 Then Jesus said unto them, Yet a little while ^lis the light with you. ^mWalk while ye have the light, lest darkness come upon you: for ⁿhe that walketh in darkness knoweth not whither he goeth.

l ch. 1. 9. & 8. 12. & 9. 5.
ver. 46.
m Jer. 13. 6. Eph. 5. 8.
n ch. 11. 10. 1 John 2. 11.

Our Saviour thinketh not fit further to open himself as to that point concerning the Messiah, and his Divine nature; into a direct assertion of which he must have entered, had he given a direct answer to their questions; otherwise what they had objected might easily have been answered by our Saviour, by distinguishing betwixt the two natures in his own person: according to his Divine nature he was not to die, though he died according to his human nature; and after his suffering and resurrection, his whole person, in which both the Divine and human nature were united, were to endure for ever: but he thinks not fit to discourse this point, but returns to what John had told them, chap. i. 9, and what he himself had said, chap. ix. 5, that he was *the light of the world,* though possibly by *light* he here understandeth those beams of gospel doctrine which issued out from him as the fountain of light. Yet a little while, I, who am the great Light, and the true Light of the world, am with you: or, Yet a little while, the gospel, which is light, and directs you in the way to heaven, is with you, for within a few years (under forty) after this, their city was destroyed, and their nation ruined; and before that time the apostles were turned away from the generality of that nation to the Gentiles, Acts xiii. 46; xix. 9. He in the next verse expoundeth himself as to what he meant by walking, viz. believing: Make use of the light, both to guide your understandings and judgments, and also to direct your feet: for look on men in the world, while they have the guidance of the light of the sun, they know how to order their steps, and to direct their feet; but if once it be dark, they know not how to direct their feet in their way, but err, and stumble, and fall. So it will be with you, when I shall be gone, who am the great Light of the world while I am in the world (as he spake chap. ix. 5); and not only I gone, but the gospel, which is that light which I shall leave behind me, be gone, by my apostles turning to the Gentiles, through your perverse refusal of the salvation of it, as Acts xiii. 46; xix. 9: when you shall be utterly ruined, (as it will be at the destruction of your city,) then you will walk in darkness, having no means of salvation left you.

36 While ye have light, believe in the light, that ye may be ^othe children of light. These things spake Jesus, and departed, and ^pdid hide himself from them.

o Luke 16. 8. Eph. 5. 8.
1 Thess. 5. 5. 1 John 2. 9, 10, 11.
p ch. 8. 59. & 11. 54.

S. JOHN XII

He either expounds what he meant before, by his calling to them to walk in the light, viz. believing in him who is the true and great Light of the world; or else he declares faith in him to be their duty, as well as obedience to him, which is a point our Saviour had often before pressed. While I am amongst you, and when I shall be gone from you and the light of the gospel yet stayeth behind amongst you, embrace me, and receive me as your Saviour, and yield all obedience to the prescriptions of my gospel, *that ye may be the children of light:* this the apostle expounds and enlargeth upon, Eph. v. 8—11. After Christ had spoken these things in Jerusalem, he departed to Bethany, where he obscured himself from his enemies.

37 ¶ But though he had done so many miracles before them, yet they believed not on him:

The miracles of Christ did not work faith in any, yet they had a tendency both to prepare souls for an assent to the proposition of the gospel, and also for receiving Christ as the true Messiah and Saviour of the world, as they evidenced a Divine power in him by which he wrought those mighty works; but yet they had not this effect upon the generality of the Jews.

38 That the saying of Esaias the prophet might be fulfilled, which he spake,

q Is. 53. 1. Rom. 10. 16.

^qLord, who hath believed our report? and to whom hath the arm of the Lord been revealed?

So as that which Isaiah prophesied, Isa. liii. 1, appeared to be fulfilled in them; for the term ἵνα, which we translate *that*, doth not in Scripture always denote the final cause, with respect to the counsel and intention of God, but ofttimes the event. So chap. v. 20; Rom. v. 20; 2 Cor. i. 17. *The arm of the Lord* may either signify the gospel, which is called *the power of God to salvation,* Rom. i. 16; 1 Cor. i. 18; or else the Messiah, who is thought to be mentioned under this notion by Isaiah, chap. li. 5; lii. 10; lix. 16; lxiii. 12, because the Father worketh by him, as a man worketh by his arm, chap. i. 3, 14.

39 Therefore they could not believe, because that Esaias said again,

Some will have, *they could not believe,* to be the same with, they did not; as, Mark vi. 5, it is said Christ could not do mighty works at Nazareth; or the same with, they would not, as Gen. xix. 22; but this seemeth a hard interpretation of ἐκ ἠδύναντο. It is most certain, that in all there is a natural impotency and disability to believe; but this text seemeth to speak of a further degree of impossibility than that, occasioned through their wilful obstinacy, and God's judicial hardening of them. *Because Esaias said,* is no more than, for Esaias said; the particle doth not denote the cause influencing them, but the effect of the prophecy: God's word (saith the evangelist) must be made good, and Isaiah had prophesied of what now came to pass.

r Is. 9. 9, 10. Matt. 13. 14.

40 ^rHe hath blinded their eyes, and hardened their heart; that they should not see with *their* eyes, nor understand with *their* heart, and be converted, and I should heal them.

We have this text (than which there is not one more terrible in the whole book of God) no less than six times quoted in the New Testament, and in all places quoted and given as a reason for the Jews' unbelief in the Lord Jesus Christ, Matt. xiii. 14, 15; Mark iv. 12; Luke viii. 10; Acts xxviii. 26, 27; Rom. xi. 8. It is not quoted alike in all places, but for substance the same. The original from whence these quotations are, is Isa. vi. 9, 10. By comparing the texts we shall find several authors, instruments, or causes of these dreadful effects. In the original, the prophet Isaiah is made the instrumental cause: *Go,* (saith God,) *and make the heart of this people fat,* &c. Matthew, and Luke, in Acts xxviii. 27, mention themselves as the cause. Matthew saith, *For this people's heart is waxed gross, and their ears are dull of hearing, and their eyes have closed.* And in the Acts it is, *For the heart of this people is waxed gross, and their ears are dull of hearing, and their eyes have they closed.* All the other texts speak of it as God's act. The thing is easily thus reconciled: God sent to the Jews his prophets, and gave them the means of salvation; it is true, without the inward efficacy of his Spirit they could not savingly believe, but they did not do what was in their power to have done, nay, they did do what was in their power to have avoided, they slighted and contemned the Lord's prophets, and killed them, and stoned such as were sent unto them. Thus they first shut their own eyes, and hardened their own hearts; and as their forefathers had done in their generation, so the Jews in our Saviour Christ's time did also in their generation, shutting their eyes against the revelation of the gospel by Christ himself. They thus behaving themselves, God judicially gave them up to their own lusts, permitting their hearts to harden, and suffering them to close their own eyes, so as they could not repent, believe, or return, and be saved; not that God infused any malice into their hearts, but withdrew his grace from them after such provocations on their parts: so that as the prophets in their age laboured with them in vain, and all the event of their ministry was but the generality of that people's growing worse and more obdurate; so all the event of Christ's ministry and miracles, which he personally wrought amongst them in his age, did accidentally but increase their sin and their judgment, and ripen them for their ruin, through their wilful abuse of those sacred means of life and salvation. The judgment itself was but one, viz. a judicial hardening of them; but it is set out by a great variety of expressions, both by the prophets, and the writers of the New Testament: in Isaiah, by making their hearts fat, their ears heavy, shutting their eyes: in Matthew, making their hearts gross, their ears dull of hearing, shutting their eyes: in this text, by blinding their eyes, and hardening their hearts: in the Acts, by the same phrases as in Matthew: in Rom. xi. 8 is added, *God hath given them the spirit of slumber.* All the phrases are expressive of the same dreadful judgment of God, yet it may be expressed in this variety of phrase, to signify the distinct, particular plagues (comprehended in this one plague) which fall upon the several powers and faculties of those souls upon whom this dreadful judgment falls; blindness in the mind, stubbornness in the will, &c., vileness in the affections, reprobacy in the mind, &c.

41 ^sThese things said Esaias, when he s Is. 6. 1. saw his glory, and spake of him.

The evangelist saith, that these things *Esaias said, when he saw his glory, and spake of him.* Isaiah's sight of God's glory is described, Isa. vi. 1, *I saw the Lord sitting upon a throne, high and lifted up,* &c. The evangelist expounds this of Christ, which is an evident proof of the Deity of Christ, that he is Jehovah; for it was Jehovah whom the prophet there saw: and that the revelation of that dreadful wrath of God, did not only concern that particular age in which Isaiah lived, but the successive generation of the Jews, whom the prophet saw by the eye of prophecy would tread in the same steps, and use Christ (the Heir) as their forefathers had used him, and the prophets of that age.

42 ¶ Nevertheless among the chief rulers also many believed on him; but ^tbecause of the Pharisees they did not t ch. 7. 13. confess *him,* lest they should be put out & 9. 22. of the synagogue:

Though the Pharisees made up a great part of the sanhedrim, yet there were divers others also mixed with them, amongst which there were many of a better temper; and it may be ἀρχόντων here may not signify members of that court, but principal men in the magistracy. We must not understand by *believed,* that they believed with a saving faith; what follows will evidence the contrary; but they had some convictions upon them as to the truth of what he said, and his being the true Messias; but they durst not openly declare what themselves thought, nor publicly own and aver Christ to be what he indeed was, and they were inclinable to think he was, lest the Pharisees, who were Christ's most implacable enemies, should have put the decree they had made (of which we read, chap. ix. 22) in execution upon them.

43 ^uFor they loved the praise of men u ch. 5. 44. more than the praise of God.

For they were not willing to part with their great places in the magistracy, which brought them respect, honour, and applause from men; they valued this more than God's honouring and praising them. How hard it is for great men to enter into the kingdom of God!

x Mark 9.37. 1 Pet. 1. 21.
44 ¶ Jesus cried and said, ˣHe that believeth on me, believeth not on me, but on him that sent me.

The words, at first view, seem to contain a contradiction, and denying the same act as to the same person; as if any man could believe, and yet not believe on Christ; but there is nothing less in them. By the same figurative way of speaking God tells the prophet Samuel, 1 Sam. viii. 7. the people had not rejected Samuel, (that is, not Samuel alone,) but they had rejected him. So Mark ix. 37, *Whosoever receiveth me, receiveth not me*, (that is, not me alone,) *but him that sent me.* So 1 Thess. iv. 8. Or else thus, He that believeth on me, doth not believe on a mere man, as I appear at present to the world, but he also believeth on God that sent me. The Jews owned one God the Father, and acknowledged him the object of their faith, chap. xiv. 1, *Ye believe in God;* but they were blinded as to Christ, appearing only in the form of a man. So that our Saviour again by these words asserteth his Divine nature, his oneness and equality with his Father; so as he was also the object of their faith, as well as his Father.

y ch. 14. 9.
45 And ʸhe that seeth me seeth him that sent me.

No man hath seen God at any time; but he that by the eyes of his mind knows, and understands, and believeth in me, seeth him that sent me: or, he that seeth me in my works which I do, seeth also him that sent me, by whom I do these mighty works. Thus afterward, chap. xiv. 9, he saith to Philip, *He that hath seen me hath seen the Father;* he that hath seen me, hath not indeed seen the Divine nature and essence, but hath seen that Person who is one with the Father; *the brightness of his glory, and the express image of his person,* as the apostle speaks, Heb. i. 3.

z ver. 35, 36. ch. 3. 19. & 8. 12. & 9. 5, 39.
46 ᶻI am come a light into the world, that whosoever believeth on me should not abide in darkness.

I am come a light into the world; this is no more than what our Saviour hath often said, chap. iii. 19, and ix. 5; and it was according to the prophecy of him, Isa. xlii. 6. *That whosoever believeth on me shall not abide in darkness;* that he who receiveth and embraceth me, as his Priest and Prophet, though he may be in darkness naturally, Eph. v. 8, yet should not abide in a state of ignorance, and sin, and guilt, chap. iii. 36; viii. 31. Men and women, before they believe in Christ, are in darkness; but upon believing, they are translated out of their state of darkness into a state of marvellous light; they do not abide in darkness.

a ch. 5. 45. & 8. 15, 26. b ch. 3. 17.
47 And if any man hear my words, and believe not, ᵃI judge him not: for ᵇI came not to judge the world, but to save the world.

I judge him not; I alone judge him not, or rather, it is not my present business to pronounce sentence of condemnation against him; I am now doing the work of a Redeemer and Saviour, not of a Judge: he *is condemned already,* John iii. 18, and he hath another that accuseth and condemneth him; as the Jews had Moses, chap. v. 45, so he hath my Father as his Judge, and will be heard as his accuser (as in the next verse): I shall one day condemn him; but that is not my present business, that was not my errand in coming into the world. I came to offer the world the means, and to show them the way to salvation; if they do perish, their blood will be upon their own heads: it is not my business to condemn them.

c Luke 10. 16.
48 ᶜHe that rejecteth me, and receiveth not my words, hath one that judgeth

d Deu. 18. 19. Mark 16. 16.
him: ᵈthe word that I have spoken, the same shall judge him in the last day.

These words, *and receiveth not my words,* expound the former: not to receive in heart, to believe, and embrace the words of Christ in the gospel, is to reject Christ. So Luke x. 16, *He that heareth you heareth me; and he that despiseth you despiseth me.* And he that doth so, *hath one that judgeth him,* that is, my Father who hath sent me, and will vindicate mine honour. Nay, *the word that I have spoken* shall rise up in judgment against him at the last day, and prove that he hath judged himself unworthy of everlasting life.

e ch. 8. 38. & 14. 10.
49 For ᵉI have not spoken of myself; but the Father which sent me, he gave me a commandment, ᶠwhat I should say, and what I should speak.

f Deut. 18. 18.

I do not speak what I say to you as mere man, or any thing but what is my Father's will, and mine only as one with him, and as sent by him; I have said nothing but what my Father hath willed me to reveal to the world as his will.

50 And I know that his commandment is life everlasting: whatsoever I speak therefore, even as the Father said unto me, so I speak.

I am assured that the way to life everlasting is to obey his commandments; and that makes me speak, and deliver all that, and nothing but that, which I have in charge from my Father: *as the Father said unto me, so I speak.* Therefore look you to it, in rejecting me, you reject my Father, whom you own and acknowledge for your God; and in disobeying me, you disobey my Father, and him whom you own as your Father also.

CHAP. XIII

Jesus washeth his disciples' feet; and exhorteth them to follow his example of humility and charity, 1—17. He foretelleth the treachery of Judas, and pointeth him out to John by a token, 18—30. He speaketh of his glorification as near at hand, and commandeth his disciples to love one another, 31—35. He forewarneth Peter that he shall thrice deny him, 36—38.

a Matt. 26. 2. b ch. 12. 23. & 17. 1, 11.
NOW ᵃbefore the feast of the Passover, when Jesus knew that ᵇhis hour was come that he should depart out of this world unto the Father, having loved his own which were in the world, he loved them unto the end.

That this was the fourth passover after that he entered upon his public ministry is out of doubt, and the last he ever celebrated. We have taken notice of this evangelist's mention of the other three: but how long what follows was before the passover, which is here expressed by *before the feast,* is a great question: some will have it the day, others immediately before, as πρὸ (the very same particle) is used, Luke xi. 38, *before dinner,* and Luke xxii. 15, *before I suffer.* The resolution of it much dependeth upon another question as difficult, viz. What supper it is which is mentioned? ver. 2. Those who would be satisfied in these cases, may find a collection of what is said by most valuable interpreters in Mr. Pool's Synopsis Criticorum, upon Matt. xxvi. It is our happiness, that though some such knots occur in holy writ, yet they are about things in which our salvation is not concerned; so as without danger to our souls we may be ignorant of what is the truth about them. When Christ knew that the hour (which he had once or twice before said was not come) was now come, that he must die, rise again, and in a short time ascend to his Father; he having loved his disciples, not with a mutable, but with an unchangeable love; he resolveth upon the washing of their feet, as a demonstration of that love.

c Luke 22. 3. ver. 27.
2 And supper being ended, ᶜthe devil having now put into the heart of Judas Iscariot, Simon's *son,* to betray him;

And supper being ended; possibly it were better translated, while they were at supper, or in supper time, Greek, δείπνυ γενομένυ, but the great question is, What supper is here intended? Our most learned Lightfoot is very confident this was not the paschal supper. The most interpreters, ancient and modern, seem to be of another mind. Or it may be rather a common supper, which they ate before the passover: for whereas some think this supper was that in the house of Simon the leper, mentioned Matt. xxvi. 6, it seemeth no way probable, no circumstance inclining us to believe any such thing; and the evangelist having told us that it was after that supper that Christ rode into Jerusalem, and again went from thence, and hid himself, chap. xii. 36, and then reporting this as a thing subsequent to it in this chapter; it seemeth very clear to me, that it could not be the supper in the house of Simon the leper. Concerning the influence of the devil upon Judas, to put it into his heart to betray his Master, see Luke xxii. 3, 4.

d Matt. 11. 27. & 28. 18. ch. 3. 35. & 17. 2. Acts 2. 36. 1 Cor. 15. 27. Heb. 2. 8. e ch. 8. 42. & 16. 28.

3 Jesus knowing ^dthat the Father had given all things into his hands, and ^ethat he was come from God, and went to God;

Our translating the Greek participle εἰδώς, *knowing*, (which properly signifies having known,) createth a difficulty, viz. How Christ's knowledge of this, that the Father had given all things into his hand, should be assigned as a reason of, or motive to, his subsequent action of washing the feet of his disciples? The sense therefore must certainly be, though he knew; and so it doth not import a reason of his following action, but only signifieth Christ's great humiliation and condescension. Though he well enough knew, that *all power* was *given* him *in heaven and earth*, as in Matt. xxviii. 18; that he was his disciples' Lord, that he came from God, and was now going to God again; yet to show how much he loved his disciples, and to set them a pattern of humility, and teach them brotherly love, and that he *came not* in the estate wherein he yet was *to be ministered unto, but to minister*, Matt. xx. 28.

f Luke 22. 27. Phil. 2. 7, 8.

4 ^fHe riseth from supper, and laid aside his garments; and took a towel, and girded himself.

He riseth from supper. What supper? is the question. We are told, that the Jews had two suppers upon the paschal night, which was the 14th day of the month Nisan. The first was the passover supper, which was a religious rite in obedience to the law. The second, a common supper (as on other nights); to which our Saviour added a third, which was the Lord's supper. To me it seemeth rather that their common supper was first, then the passover supper; and that Christ arose from this common supper to do this act. Augustine understood it of the common supper; so doth Beza, Heinsius, Tarnovius, and others; which seemeth to me most probable, though others understand it of the passover supper. Whatever supper the evangelist meaneth, Christ rose up from it before it was done. Calvin, Pareus, Beza, Petargus, Tossanus, and divers others amongst the protestant interpreters; Tolet, Maldonate, and Jansenius, amongst the papists; do agree a common supper this night, besides the paschal supper, and the Lord's supper; from which it is most probable that Christ, as is here said, rose up, and laid aside his garment; that is, his outward loose garment, (for such they used,) which servants were wont to gird up when they waited at table, Luke xvii. 8: Christ laid one aside, and girding up the other, takes a towel.

5 After that he poureth water into a bason, and began to wash the disciples' feet, and to wipe *them* with the towel wherewith he was girded.

Poureth water into a bason; beginneth first to wash his disciples' feet, then to wipe them with the linen cloth he had taken. All this was done in the form of a servant; so they used to do, as to guests that came to dine or sup with their lords or masters.

6 Then cometh he to Simon Peter: and † Peter said unto him, Lord, ^gdost thou wash my feet?

† Gr. *he.* g See Matt. 3. 14.

Christ in the performance of this ceremony cometh to Simon Peter; whether first, or last, it is not said; and therefore the papists argue ill from hence, to prove the primacy of Peter over the rest of the apostles. Peter looks upon it with a modest, but sinful and superstitious, indignation. Samuel of old determined, that obedience to God is better than sacrifice; it is then certainly better than a compliment. Peter in this case ought not to have contradicted his Master out of a compliment to him, but to have suffered him to go on in this act of ministration. There may be a voluntary humility, and pretended reverence to Christ, which is indeed but superstition, and can be no other, if contrary to any revelation of the Divine will.

7 Jesus answered and said unto him, What I do thou knowest not now; ^hbut thou shalt know hereafter.

h ver. 12.

Our Lord, seeing Peter's general design good, though he mistook as to this particular act, tells him, that at present he did not understand his counsel and design in this action, but it should be more intelligible unto him afterwards; as indeed he made it by his discourse upon this his act of humiliation, ver. 13—16.

8 Peter saith unto him, Thou shalt never wash my feet. Jesus answered him, ⁱIf I wash thee not, thou hast no part with me.

i ch. 3. 5. 1 Cor. 6. 11. Eph. 5. 26. Tit. 3. 5. Heb. 10. 22.

Peter rashly replies, *Thou shalt never wash my feet.* Here was a seeming reverence for his Master, but (like the Jewish zeal mentioned by Paul, Rom. x. 2) *not according to knowledge.* Christ tells him, that except he washed him, he had no part with him; that is, he should never be saved. But will some say, Was not this too severe, for our Saviour to threaten Peter with an exclusion from a co-inheritance with him in heaven, for modestly refusing to suffer him to wash his feet? *Answ.* 1. The least disobedience not repented of, is enough to exclude a soul from the kingdom of heaven. 2. But Christ seems to take an advantage here, from this ceremony of his washing their feet, to discourse to him the necessity of his washing his soul with his blood, from the filth of sin and corruption; and of this washing it undoubtedly is that Christ here speaketh, the necessity of which is very often inculcated in holy writ.

9 Simon Peter saith unto him, Lord, not my feet only, but also *my* hands and *my* head.

Peter now understandeth what washing it is which our Saviour last spake of, and wholly submitteth to the will of his Lord and Master; acknowledging himself to be wholly defiled, and to stand in need of a washing all over: *Lord*, saith he, *not my feet only, but also my hands and my head;* that is, my whole man.

10 Jesus saith to him, He that is washed needeth not save to wash *his* feet, but is clean every whit: and ^kye are clean, but not all.

k ch. 15. 3.

Look as it is with persons that have been washing themselves in a bath, when they are washed, yet walking abroad barefoot, or with thin sandals or coverings for their feet, will be again subject to pollute and dirty their feet, so as they will have frequent need to wash them again; but they need not soon again wash their whole bodies: so it is as to souls that are washed with my blood; washed, and sanctified, justified in the name of the Lord Jesus, and by the Spirit of God, (as the apostle speaketh, 1 Cor. vi. 11,) their state is not to be renewed; they need not be justified a second time; but they will have need to have their feet washed, in regard of their remainder of sin and lust that is in them, and will be so while they are in the world, and the temptations which every where lie in the world, as snares for their feet; they will have need of a daily washing by repentance, and fresh applications of their souls to my blood, by the repeated exercises of faith, according to their renewed and repeated acts of sin. *Ye are clean;* you, who are my apostles, are clean; you are washed, you are justified, I have forgiven your sins, accepted your persons. *But not all;* the most of you are so, but not all.

11 For ^lhe knew who should betray him; therefore said he, Ye are not all clean.

l ch. 6. 64.

By these words the evangelist expounds only what our Saviour meant in the former verse, when he had told them they were not all clean; for though the disciples did not yet know that they had a traitor amongst them, Satan had before this put the design into the heart of Judas, ver. 2; and Christ, who knew all hearts, knew what was in the heart of Judas, and he soon after (as we shall hereafter in this chapter read) revealed it; yet at this time he had not revealed it to his disciples: now he begins to discover it, telling them, that though the most of them were clean, justified and sanctified, yet all of them were not so.

12 So after he had washed their feet, and had taken his garments, and was set down again, he

said unto them, Know ye what I have done to you?

After that our Saviour had finished this ceremony, and washed his disciples' feet, (some question whether all or no, but I see no reason to doubt it,) he returned again to the supper, which probably now was near finished, which certainly was the common supper which the Jews had besides the passover supper, and probably before it, though some think after it. He asketh them if they knew the meaning of this which he had done unto them; lest they should not fully understand it, he openeth it to them in the following discourse.

m Matt. 23. 8, 10. Luke 6. 46. 1 Cor. 8. 6. & 12. 3. Phil. 2. 11.

13 ^mYe call me Master and Lord: and ye say well; for *so* I am.

The disciples in their ordinary discourses called Christ *Master and Lord;* nor was it a name improper for him, for he was their Master to instruct them, their Lord to rule, guide, and govern them: now, saith our Saviour, disciples ought to obey their master, servants ought to obey their lord, and disciples also ought to imitate their master.

n Luke 22. 27.
o Rom. 12. 10. Gal. 6. 1, 2. 1 Pet. 5. 5.

14 ⁿIf I then, *your* Lord and Master, have washed your feet; °ye also ought to wash one another's feet.

I have by this my action taught you to love, and to be ready also to serve, one another, and not to think much to serve them even in the lowest and meanest offices by which you can do them good; for we must not think that these words lay a literal obligation upon Christians to wash the feet of others; washing the feet is mentioned but as *species pro genere,* a single act of service, put for all other acts by which we can be serviceable unto others: so it is also used, 1 Sam. xxv. 41; 1 Tim. v. 10. Some of the ancients seem to have judged this washing of feet to have been instituted as a sacrament, (though in an improper sense,) and from hence, though Bellarmine, Maldonate, and others deny it to be a sacrament as well as we, yet probably is the practice in use amongst the papists, to wash certain persons' feet every Thursday before Easter; a theatrical ceremony, rather than any thing of solid and profitable use. Our Saviour certainly intends no more by *ye ought to wash one another's feet,* than, ye ought to serve one another in all offices of love, and not to think yourselves too good, or too great, to do the meanest services to those who are my disciples: and this is that as to which he tells them he had set them an example that they should do as he had done, in other acts of the same kind, though not as to this specifical act.

p Mat. 11. 29. Phil. 2. 5. 1 Pet. 2. 21. 1 John 2. 6.

15 For ^pI have given you an example, that ye should do as I have done to you.

q Mat. 10. 24. Luke 6. 40. ch. 15. 20.

16 ^qVerily, verily, I say unto you, The servant is not greater than his lord; neither he that is sent greater than he that sent him.

The apostles were to take up a very high station in the gospel church, and our hearts are very prone to swell in a high opinion of ourselves, for which the nature of man taketh advantage from every thing in which we either really do excel, or can conceit that we do excel, our neighbours. Our Lord therefore, though speaking to the apostles, (some of the best of men,) yet knowing they were (like Elijah) men subject to like passions with other men, addeth this to arm them against any temptation to pride: they owned themselves as servants to Christ who was their great Lord; they had seen what he had done; he therefore applieth a proverbial expression to them, which he also made use of in other cases, as Matt. x. 24; John xv. 20; in both which places he maketh use of it to arm them against persecutions; here, to persuade them to humility, condescension, and brotherly love.

r Jam. 1. 25.

17 ^rIf ye know these things, happy are ye if ye do them.

He tells them, that it is not the bare comprehension of these things in their notion that would do them any good, unless they brought their knowledge into practice; for *to him that knoweth to do good, and doeth it not, it is sin,* James iv. 17. Faith without works is dead, and the knowledge of our Master's will, if we do it not, doth but expose us to many stripes.

18 ¶ I speak not of you all: I know whom I have chosen: but that the Scripture may be fulfilled, ^sHe that eateth bread with me hath lifted up his heel against me.

s Ps. 41. 9. Matt. 26. 23. ver. 21.

I am about to tell you what will make your ears tingle; but be of good comfort, what I shall now tell you doth not concern all of you, it concerneth but one man amongst you. *I know whom I have chosen* to the work of the apostleship; so some interpret it, as chap. vi. 70, *Have not I chosen you twelve, and one of you is a devil?* But the generality of the best interpreters understand the choosing here mentioned, of a choosing to eternal life, and perseverance in the way of God as a means in order to it, as Eph. i. 4; and so understood, here is a greater argument in this text to prove the Godhead of Christ, as the Author of eternal election: Though one of you be a devil, a traitor, yet I have chosen the rest of you to eternal life: and this is no more than was prophesied of me, and fulfilled in David as a type of me: the Scripture must have its accomplishment; that Scripture is now fulfilled in me.

19 ^t∥ Now I tell you before it come, that, when it is come to pass, ye may believe that I am *he.*

t ch. 14. 29. & 16. 4. ∥ Or, *From henceforth.*

What I now tell you should be so far from prejudicing your faith in me, that it ought rather to confirm and increase your faith in me as the true Messias; when (the thing coming to pass) you shall understand that I know the hearts, counsels, and secret thoughts of men: and when you shall see the Scriptures have their accomplishment, and those things which were long ago prophesied concerning the Messias have their just accomplishment, and fulfilling in me as the person intended in those ancient revelations.

20 ^uVerily, verily, I say unto you, He that receiveth whomsoever I send receiveth me; and he that receiveth me receiveth him that sent me.

u Matt. 10. 40. & 25. 40. Luke 10. 16.

See the notes on Matt. x. 24, the words of which place are but here repeated; either to commend to them brotherly love, and offices of love, which he had before recommended to them under the notion of washing one another's feet; or else to comfort his disciples, who might think that this treacherous villany of Judas would make them odious to the whole world: No, saith our Saviour, you are my messengers, persons sent by me; I will provide for you, there shall be those who will receive you. And I declare to all the world to encourage them, that I shall take their receiving of you as kindly as if they received me, and it shall turn to the same account, and that is all one as if they had received my Father himself, for he sent me. Some think that by these words Christ aggravateth the sin of Judas, as being committed against the Father as well as against Christ; and a most treacherous failure as to the duty of an apostle, or one dignified so much as to be sent out by Christ.

21 ^xWhen Jesus had thus said, ^yhe was troubled in spirit, and testified, and said, Verily, verily, I say unto you, that ^zone of you shall betray me.

x Mat. 26. 21. Mark 14. 18. Luke 22. 21. y ch. 12. 27.
z Acts 1. 17. 1 John 2. 19.

How, and in what sense, trouble of spirit could agree to Christ, was noted before, chap. xii. 27: see the notes on that text. This seemeth to have been rather a trouble of grief, that one of his apostles, one whom he had chosen, should commit so great a villany, than arising from fear of death; for his next words are a further discovery of the person that should betray him: he had said before, that he should be betrayed, and that it should be by one that used to eat bread with him; but now he cometh closer, and tells them that it should be by one of them, that is, one of the twelve; this was a closer discovery than he had as yet made.

22 Then the disciples looked one on another, doubting of whom he spake.

It seemeth they had no suspicion of Judas, but our Saviour telling them that it was one of them, they begin to look about one upon another, rather suspecting themselves than Judas. There may be a great deal of villany, and the greatest villany, in the hearts of professors, in whose conversation appeareth nothing that may give a just suspicion to others; and the true disciples of Christ will have so much candour and brotherly love, that they will not rashly judge and censure their brethren.

a ch. 19. 26. & 20. 2. & 21. 7, 20, 24.
23 Now ^athere was leaning on Jesus' bosom one of his disciples, whom Jesus loved.

This *leaning on Jesus' bosom*, and the *laying on Jesus' breast*, mentioned ver. 25, cannot be understood without the understanding of the usual posture the Jews used at their meals, and particularly at the paschal supper; of which we have spoken largely in our notes upon Matt. xxvi. 20: see the annotations there. Their posture seemeth to have been kneeling, and resting their bodies back upon their legs, with a leaning upon their left elbow; and this seemeth not to have been so close, but that he that so sat might use his other hand to take his meat; hence he who sat before any, sat with his back towards him, but leaning towards the bosom of the other, which is here called a leaning on (that is, towards) his bosom, and laying on his breast; for it cannot be understood of such a sitting, or leaning, as to touch the other's breast or bosom, for that would have hindered him upon whom the person so leaned from any use of his right hand to take his meat or drink. It is apparent from hence, first, that at this supper there was none but Christ and his disciples. Secondly, that they sat in this posture of leaning. These two things make it very probable, if not certain, that the supper here mentioned was either the paschal supper, or a common supper, which immediately went before, or followed after, the passover supper. For, 1. We have no record of any other supper, at which were only Christ and the twelve disciples; and, 2. If we may believe the Jewish writers, though their ordinary posture at their common meals was discumbency, that is, a kneeling on their knees, with a resting their bodies backward upon their legs; yet this posture of leaning was constantly added only upon the passover night, as a further testimony of their liberty, that they were not now servants, as in the land of Egypt. The person who sat next to our Saviour, with his back next our Saviour's bosom, was John, often in Scripture dignified with the title of the beloved disciple, and him *whom Jesus loved*, chap. xix. 26; xx. 2; xxi. 7, 20.

24 Simon Peter therefore beckoned to him, that he should ask who it should be of whom he spake.

Peter, knowing the particular affection that Christ had for John, maketh a sign to him, to ask of Christ which of them he meant, when he said, *One of you shall betray me.*

25 He then lying on Jesus' breast saith unto him, Lord, who is it?

John, accordingly, doth propound the question to Christ.

∥ Or, *morsel.*
26 Jesus answered, He it is, to whom I shall give a ∥ sop, when I have dipped *it.* And when he had dipped the sop, he gave *it* to Judas Iscariot, *the son* of Simon.

Jesus answered, He it is, to whom I shall give a sop, when I have dipped it; we have the same, though not mentioned as spoken in particular to John, Matt. xxvi. 23; Luke xxii. 21; though neither of them mention Christ's own dipping the sop; but Matthew saith, he dipped his hand with him in the dish; and Luke saith, his hand was with him on the table. Without question all the evangelists speak of the same time; for it is not reasonable to think that this discovery should be made, and Judas gone out, and that afterward he should return again to eat the passover. This maketh me very inclinable to think, that though the washing of the feet might be during the time of a common supper, preceding the passover, yet the supper they were now at was the passover supper: where, 1. Were none but he and the twelve disciples. 2. It is plain they were in that leaning posture, not used at common meals,

but on the passover nights (as Dr. Lightfoot tells us from their writings). 3. The discourse passed at the table is the very same (though not in words, yet in sense) with that mentioned by Matthew and Luke, at the passover supper. 4. It is not reasonable to think, that after such a discovery as Christ now made of the traitor, he should come again to be pointed at and exposed. Concerning the sop, what it was, hath been some question; and a learned writer of our own (but in this point I think much too critical) hath increased the difficulty, by affirming the word here used, ψωμίον, signifies a piece of bread, or the lower part or chippings of the bread; for which he quoteth Hesychius, who indeed doth say so of ψωθίον, but not ψωμίον. The learned annotator thinks ψωθίον is a false print for ψωμίον, but it cannot be: for, 1. There are in Hesychius several words in alphabetical order, between ψωθίον and this word. 2. Though ψωμίον be not in Hesychius, yet ψωμή is, and expounded by him τα μίρη, parts; now all know that this ψωμίον, which is but a diminutive derived from ψωμος or ψωμη, can signify no more than a little part, let it be of what it will; for it is manifest out of Homer, that, joined with an adjective, it signifies a mouthful of man's flesh, which came out of the Cyclops' mouth. So as the sense of these words is, He it is to whom I shall give a little part or portion of meat, when I have dipped it. And having dipped it, *he gave it to Judas the son of Simon:* not the Judas who wrote the Epistle, and who is mentioned, chap. xiv. 22, but he that was the son of Simon, called from his place which he lived in, Kiroth, *Iscariot:* by which he did as perfectly describe the traitor as if he had named him.

b Luke 22. 3. ch. 6. 70.
27 ^bAnd after the sop Satan entered into him. Then said Jesus unto him, That thou doest, do quickly.

That the devil did ever so enter into Judas as to possess him, as we read of many who were possessed, and violently acted by the devil, is more than we read any where in holy writ: the entrance into him, signifies Judas's free and willing giving up of himself to the devil's suggestions and conduct; and in this sense the devil also before this time was entered into Judas, Luke xxii. 3. But as holy men are said to be filled with the Spirit of God, who had before received the Spirit, because the Holy Spirit came after upon them with fuller and stronger impulses and motions; so though the devil had formerly been moving Judas to this vile act, and had had his consent to it, yet after he had taken this mouthful, the devil plied him with stronger motions, impulses, and suggestions: and now he had mastered his conscience, and hardened his heart, so as he was more prepared for the villany about which he had some thoughts before. He had now, with an unbelieving and unthankful heart, been eating the passover, which was a type of Christ; and had so mastered his conscience, as to come and do this, with a vile heart, reeking before with treacherous and bloody designs against his Lord and Master. See what is the effect. His heart is more vile, more treacherous, and bloody; he is twice more the servant of the devil than he was before. The sop given him by Christ was but an accidental occasion of it; as the devil took more advantage from his now hardened and further imboldened heart, and he is twice more the child of the devil than he was before. Christ, knowing this, doth not command, advise, or exhort him; but, in a detestation, bids him go and do what he was resolved to do, and which he knew would be quickly; letting him know both that he knew what was in his heart, and that he was now ready to receive the effects of his malice.

28 Now no man at the table knew for what intent he spake this unto him.

29 For some *of them* thought, because ^cJudas had the bag, that Jesus had said unto him, Buy *those things* that we have need of against the feast; or, that he should give something to the poor.

c ch. 12. 6.

How innocent are honest hearts! *Charity thinketh no evil,* saith the apostle. Although our Saviour had plainly enough deciphered him as the traitor, by telling John that he to whom he should give the sop was he, and then by giving it to Judas; yet whether they all did not hear what our Saviour said to John, or did not think of so sudden a tragedy, they do not suspect that the hour was at hand when Judas should perfect his intended villany: though they heard our Saviour bid him get him out, and do quickly what he had to do; yet Judas being he who carried that little stock of money which Christ had, chap. xii. 6, they thought that that which our Saviour bid him do, as a work he had undertaken to do, was laying out some money, either to buy some things which were necessary for them, for the seven days of the feast of unleavened bread; either for food for them to eat, or for sacrifices for them to offer; or that it was our Saviour's mind, that he should out of this little stock distribute something to the poor: they little thought that our Saviour's words argued a giving him over to perfect the treacherous designs which he had conceived in his heart.

30 He then having received the sop went immediately out: and it was night.

From hence appeareth, 1. That it is impossible to prove that Judas was with our Saviour when he instituted and celebrated the supper; though if he were, it proveth nothing of a liberty for ignorant and scandalous persons to be there, (for Judas was not such a one,) nor yet of a lawfulness for ministers of the gospel, knowing any to be such, to give the Lord's supper to them. For although Christ knew Judas's heart, yet he acted not according to his omniscience, but as the first and prime minister of the gospel, setting us an example, not to judge of secret things, but of things open only. 2. It also appeareth from hence, that it is not probable that this was any other supper than the passover supper; for if it were not, the passover supper must be after this, and this same supper preceding it. Our famous Dr. Lightfoot thinks it was a supper in Bethany, at two miles distance (or near so much) from Jerusalem. But then it must follow, 1. That John speaks nothing of the paschal supper, or the Lord's supper; and, 2. It doth by no means appear probable to me, that Judas, after such a discovery of him, should come again to eat the passover with Christ and his disciples. These things, together with what I noted before, that here is no mention made of more guests than the twelve; that the posture used (especially as to leaning) was peculiar to the paschal supper; that the discourse mentioned by this evangelist as had at this supper about the discovery of the traitor, is the same in substance (though not in terms) with what Matthew and Luke report, as passed at the passover: all these things confirm me, that it is the paschal supper that John speaketh of. Whether Judas was at the Lord's supper, which we know followed the passover immediately, depends upon the sense of the particle εὐθέως, which we translate immediately; but doth not signify necessarily such a present departure, but the action of the Lord's supper might be first over; though in reason it seemeth to me more probable, because of those words, *having received the sop, he immediately went out,* that it should be here interpreted strictly, and that shame and horror should not suffer him to stay so long, as till the action of the supper was over: though whether he were at the Lord's supper (as I said before) signifieth nothing at all to the questions about mixed communion, either as to the part of the minister administering, or the people communicating.

31 ¶ Therefore, when he was gone out, Jesus said, ᵈNow is the Son of man glorified, and ᵉGod is glorified in him.

He speaketh of that which was presently to be, as if it were already done; the meaning is, Now the time cometh when the Son of man shall immediately be glorified, by finishing the work which God hath given him to do; by rising again from the dead, and declaring himself to be the Son of God with power; by ascending up into heaven, to be glorified with the same glory which he had with the Father before the world began: and God will appear to be glorified in him, by his finishing the work which God hath given him to do, manifesting his name to the sons of men; and by the many signs and wonders which God will yet further show at the time of his death and resurrection, and by the coming down of the Holy Ghost.

32 ᶠIf God be glorified in him, God shall also glorify him in himself, and ᵍshall straightway glorify him.

God was glorified in Christ by his death upon the cross in obedience to his Father's will; (thus Peter, chap. xxi. 19, is said by his death to *glorify God;)* and as he was declared to be the Son of God; and as by him the world was brought to the knowledge of God, as by his spiritual and heavenly doctrine, so by the miracles he wrought. From hence our Lord concludeth, that God should glorify Christ *in himself;* so as the glory of the Father and the Son are the same, they are mutually glorified each in other: if the Son be glorified, the Father is also glorified; and if the Father be glorified, the Son is also glorified; the Father and the Son are mutually glorified each in other. And the Father (saith our Saviour) in a short time will further glorify him, by taking him up into heaven, and making the whole person of the Mediator glorious in heaven.

33 Little children, yet a little while I am with you. Ye shall seek me: ʰand as I said unto the Jews, Whither I go, ye cannot come; so now I say to you.

Our Saviour's time of death being very nigh, (for it was the next day,) he beginneth to speak of it to his disciples more freely and plainly, and to let them know that he, though now dying, bare a fatherly tender affection to them: he calls them *little children.* Parents have a natural affection to their children; a more tender affection to their children when little, because in their tender age they are more ignorant, and unable to provide for themselves. We find this compellation used by Christ's apostles, Gal. iv. 19; 1 John ii. 1, 28. And he tells them, that he had but now a little time to be with them before his death, and not long after his resurrection; in which, too, his converse was not such with them as it hitherto had been. *Whither I go, ye cannot come;* he told this to the Jews in chap. vii. 34, and now he tells them the same, that they would miss him when he was gone, and should seek him; but even the disciples at present could not follow him to heaven, whither he was going. The unbelieving Jews should never follow him thither, but even those who were his disciples, who were born again, and whom he loved as little children are beloved by their parents, should not yet follow him; his work in the world was done, but they had yet a great deal of work in it to do.

34 ⁱA new commandment I give unto you, That ye love one another; as I have loved you, that ye also love one another.

The commandment of loving one another is strictly no new commandment, we find it in the law of Moses, Lev. xix. 18; often pressed in the New Testament, chap. xv. 17; Eph. v. 2; 1 John iv. 21. St. John in his First Epistle saith, it is *no new commandment,* chap. ii. 7; see also 2 Epist. 6. It is therefore called *a new commandment,* either because of the excellency of it, as *new* seemeth to be taken, Psal. xxxiii. 3; Isa. lxv. 17; Matt. xxvi. 29; or because it is expounded in the gospel in a new manner, pressed more plainly and in new arguments, and urged by a new example of their Lord and Master.

35 ᵏBy this shall all *men* know that ye are my disciples, if ye have love one to another.

A disciple hath his name, either from learning from his master, or from following his master and treading in his steps: take it in either sense, loving one another is a certain note of being Christ's disciples; for as Christ continually pressed this by his precepts, so he set them his own example, by showing the greatest love to them he could show.

36 ¶ Simon Peter said unto him, Lord, whither goest thou? Jesus answered him, Whither I go, thou canst not follow me now; but ˡthou shalt follow me afterwards.

Peter yet understood not his Lord and Master, and therefore asked him whither he went? Our Saviour spake of his ascension into heaven, after his suffering death upon the cross; whither he tells Peter he could not at present follow him, but afterwards should. Believers shall be ever with the Lord, but they must wait the Lord's time, and first finish the work which he hath given them to do upon the earth.

[m Matt. 26. 33, 34, 35. Mark 14. 29, 30, 31. Luke 22. 33, 34.] 37 Peter said unto him, Lord, why cannot I follow thee now? I will [m] lay down my life for thy sake.

Still Peter doth not understand our Saviour, but fancieth some earthly motion from the place where he was; but it should seem by what followeth, that he thought our Saviour spake of some motion which might be very dangerous to him; and therefore he adds, according to his usual courage and mettle, expressed on all occasions, *I will lay down my life for thy sake:* we had such a resolution of his, Matt. xxvi. 33, 35.

38 Jesus answered him, Wilt thou lay down thy life for my sake? Verily, verily, I say unto thee, The cock shall not crow, till thou hast denied me thrice.

Mark saith, *before the cock crow twice.* So the other three evangelists must be expounded, who say no more than *before the cock crow,* not mentioning how often; but the history makes it good, that our Saviour meant twice, for it was not before the second crowing of the cock that Peter *went out, and wept bitterly.*

CHAP. XIV

Christ comforteth his disciples with the promise of a heavenly mansion, 1—4. *He professeth himself the way, the truth, and the life,* 5—7; *and that he is one with the Father,* 8—11. *He promiseth them power to do greater works than his own, and the grant of all that they should ask in his name,* 12—14. *He requireth their obedience as a proof of their love, and giveth them a promise of the Comforter, the Holy Ghost,* 15—26. *He leaveth his peace with them,* 27—31.

The three ensuing chapters contain either one or more consolatory discourses of our Saviour to his disciples, (as appeareth from the first verse of this chapter,) made, as is probable, to them in the guest chamber (at least that part of them which we have in this chapter); for we read of no motion of our Saviour's till we come to the last verse of this chapter. That which troubled them was, what he had told them in the close of the former chapter, that he was going from them. By our Saviour's discourse in this and the two following chapters, it should seem that there were three things that troubled them. 1. The sense of their loss as to his bodily presence. 2. The fear, that with the loss of that they should also lose those spiritual influences which they had received from him, and upon which their souls had lived. 3. The prospect of those storms of troubles and persecutions, which were likely to follow his departure from them; for if we wisely consider what our Saviour saith in these three following chapters, it all tends to comfort them as to troubles that might arise in their spirits, upon one or other of these accounts: the general proposition is laid down in the first verse of this chapter.

[a ver. 27. ch. 16. 3, 22.] LET [a] not your heart be troubled: ye believe in God, believe also in me.

Let not your heart be troubled, through grief, or fear, which are the two passions which ordinarily most disturb our minds. Our Saviour himself was troubled, but not sinfully; his trouble neither arose from unbelief, nor yet was in an undue measure; it was (as one well expresseth it) like the mere agitation of clear water, where was no mud at the bottom: but our trouble is like the stirring of water that hath a great deal of mud at the bottom, which upon the roiling, riseth up, and maketh the whole body of the water in the vessel impure, roiled and muddy. It is this sinful trouble, caused from these two passions, and rising up to an immoderate degree, and mixed with a great deal of unbelief and distrust in God, against which our Saviour here cautioneth his disciples; and the remedy he prescribes against those afflicting passions, is a believing in God, and a believing on him. The two latter passages in the verse are so penned in the Greek, that they may be read four ways; for the verb *believe,* twice repeated, may be read either indicatively or imperatively, or the one may be read indicatively and the other imperatively; so as they may be translated, You believe in God, you believe also in me. And so they teach us, that there is no such remedy for inward troubles, as a believing in God, and a believing in Jesus Christ; and those that do so, have no just reason for any excessive heart-troubles. Or else they may be read, Believe in God, believe in me: or else as we read them, *Ye believe in God, believe also in me:* or, Believe in God, ye believe in me. But the disciples' faith in Christ as Mediator, and God-man, being yet weak, and their weakness being what our Saviour hath ordinarily blamed, not magnified, or commended, the best interpreters judge the sense which our translators give to be the best sense; and judge that our Saviour doth inculcate to them his Divine nature, and again offer himself to them as the proper object of their faith. You (saith he) own it for your duty to trust in God, as your Creator, and he that provideth for you: *believe also in me,* as God equal with my Father; and in me, as the Messiah, your Mediator and Redeemer: so as you have one to take care of all your concerns, both those of your bodies, and those of your souls also, so as you have nothing to be immoderately and excessively, or distrustfully, troubled for; therefore *let not your hearts be troubled;* only, without care or distrust, commit yourselves to me.

2 In my Father's house are many mansions: if *it were* not *so,* I would have told you. [b] I go to prepare a place for you. [b ch. 13. 33, 36.]

Our Lord's first argument brought to comfort them, from the place whither he was going, and the end of his going thither. The place whither he was going was his *Father's house,* so as they needed not to be troubled for him, he was but going home; nor was God his Father only, but theirs also, as he afterwards saith, *I go to my Father, and your Father.* And here he tells them, that in his Father's house there was not only a mansion, that is, an abiding place for him, but for many others also. *Our days on the earth* (saith David, 1 Chron. xxix. 15) *are as a shadow, and there is no abiding;* but in heaven there are μοναί, abiding places. *We shall* (saith the apostle, 1 Thess. iv. 17) *be ever with the Lord.* And the mansions there are *many;* there is room enough for all believers. I would not have deceived you; if there had been no place in heaven but for me, I would have told you of it; but there are many mansions there. *I go to prepare a place for you:* the place was prepared of old; those who shall be saved, were of old ordained unto life. That *kingdom* was *prepared for* them *before the foundation of the world;* that is, in the counsels and immutable purpose of God. These mansions for believers in heaven were to be *sprinkled with blood:* the sprinkling of *the tabernacle, and all the vessels of the ministry,* were typical of it; *but the heavenly things themselves with better sacrifices than these,* saith the apostle, Heb. ix. 21, 23. By his resurrection from the dead, and becoming the first-fruits of those that sleep; by his ascension into heaven, as our *forerunner,* Heb. vi. 20; by his sitting at the right hand of God, and making intercession for us; he prepareth for us a place in heaven. And thus he comforteth his disciples, (as to the want of his bodily presence,) as from the consideration of the place whither he went, so from the end of his going thither, which was, to do those acts which were necessary in order to his disciples' inheriting those blessed mansions which were prepared for them from before the foundation of the world.

3 And if I go and prepare a place for you, [c] I will come again, and receive you unto myself; that [d] where I am, *there* ye may be also. [c ver. 18, 28 Acts 1. 11. d ch. 12. 26. & 17. 24. 1 Thess. 4. 17.]

The particle *if* in this place denoteth no uncertainty of the thing whereof he had before assured them; but in this place hath either the force of although, or after that: When, or after that, I have died, ascended, and by all these acts, as also by my intercession, shall have made places in heaven fully ready for you, I will in the last day return again, as Judge of the quick and the dead, and take you up into heaven, 1 Thess. iv. 16, 17; that you may be made partakers of my glory, John xvii. 22. This is called, Rom. viii. 17, a being *glorified together* with him; and elsewhere, a reigning with him. So as this is a third argument by which our Lord comforteth his disciples as to their trouble conceived for the want of his bodily presence with them, from the certainty of his return to them, and the end and consequent of his return: the end was to receive them to himself; the consequent, their eternal abiding with Christ where he was.

4 And whither I go ye know, and the way ye know.

Christ, ver. 33 of the former chapter, had dignified his disciples with the familiar, loving title of *little children*. It is pleasant to consider how he continueth his discourse to them in such a dialect as a mother would speak to a little child crying after her, seeing her preparing herself to go abroad. The child cries: the mother bids it be still, she is but going to such a friend's house. It still cries: she tells it, she is but going to prepare a place for it there where it shall be much happier than it is at home. It is not yet satisfied: she tells it again, that though she goes, she will come again, and then it shall go along with her, and she will part no more from it. The child is yet impatient: she again endeavoureth to still it, telling it that it knoweth whither she goeth, and it knows the way, by which, if need be, it may come to her.

5 Thomas saith unto him, Lord, we know not whither thou goest; and how can we know the way?

Reason tells every one, that he who knoweth not the term whither a person is going, must needs be ignorant of the way. It is plain, that Thomas, and so (probably) divers others of the apostles, notwithstanding what our Saviour had so plainly told them, ver. 2, yet dreamed of some earthly motion our Saviour was making, which makes Thomas to speak thus: so dull are we, and hard to conceive of spiritual things. But will some say, Doth not Thomas here contradict his Master, who had told them, ver. 4, that they both knew whither he went, and the way also? *Answ.* Some think that our Saviour meant no more than they ought to have known, both whither he went, and the way also; active verbs in Scripture phrase, often signifying no more than duty, or ability. But possibly others answer better, They had some knowledge, but it was more confused and general; not distinct, particular, or certain.

e Heb. 9. 8.
f ch. 1. 17.
& 8. 32.
g ch. 1. 4.
& 11. 25.
h ch. 10. 9.

6 Jesus saith unto him, I am ᵉthe way, ᶠthe truth, and ᵍthe life: ʰno man cometh unto the Father, but by me.

Christ was his own *way* to his Father; *By his own blood he entered in once into the holy place*, Heb. ix. 12. See Luke xxiv. 26; Phil. ii. 8. But both the former words, where the apostle spake of the way they should go, and the following words, hint to us, that Christ is here speaking of their way, not his own. As to them, he saith, *I am the way*; that is, the way by which those must get to heaven who will ever come there. Christ is our way to heaven by the doctrine which he taught; by his death, by which he purchased this heavenly inheritance for us; by his holy life and conversation, setting us an example that we should follow his steps; by the influence of his Spirit, guiding us to, and assisting us in, those holy actions by which we must come unto glory. He is *the truth*; that is, say some, the true way to life eternal: but he is *the truth* as to his doctrine, the gospel being *the word of truth*, Eph. i. 13: and as truth signifies reality and accomplishment, in opposition to the prophecies and promises, all being but words till they were in him fulfilled; in which sense we read of the *true tabernacle*, and the *true holy places*, Heb. viii. 2; ix. 24: or as truth is opposed to falsehood, as *truth* is taken John viii. 44; Rom. iii. 7. And he is *the life*, the Author and Giver of eternal life, John xi. 25; 1 John v. 11; and the purchaser of it by his death; he who by his doctrine showeth the way to it, and by his Holy Spirit begins it, and carrieth it on to perfection. The Jews thought the way to it was by the law of Moses; but our Saviour beateth his disciples out of that opinion: for if the law could have given life, Christ had died in vain, as the apostle argueth. Therefore (saith he) there is no coming to the Father *but by me*; no way for you or any other, to come to heaven, but by receiving, and embracing, and believing in me.

7 ⁱIf ye had known me, ye should have known my Father also: and from henceforth ye know him, and have seen him. i ch. 8. 19.

If ye had known me as you ought to have known me, as I am indeed the eternal Son of God, sent by my Father into the world, you should have known my Father, with whom I am equal, and one and the same God, so as in knowing one of us, you must have known both: but you stick in my outward form and appearance, while I appear to you in the form of a man; and you stick in your prejudices sucked in from the notion you have of the Messiah, expecting I know not what temporal prince: these things blind you as to my Divine nature, (personally united to my human nature,) that you see nothing of my Godhead, which if you had clearly known and believed, you would not have been at a loss to know the Father, the brightness of whose glory, and the express image of whose person, I am, though my glory be veiled by my human nature. And if you will yet believe what I say, from henceforth you do know the Father, and you have seen the Father so oft as you have seen me.

8 Philip saith unto him, Lord, shew us the Father, and it sufficeth us.

Still Philip understandeth not our Saviour, and further discovereth a very gross conception of the Divine Being, as if it could be seen with mortal eyes; whereas God had told Moses, Exod. xxxiii. 20, *Thou canst not see my face; for there shall no man see me, and live*. It is a hard thing to determine what degrees of ignorance are consistent or inconsistent with saving grace in souls; the resolution of which doth much depend upon those degrees of revelation and means of knowledge which men have.

9 Jesus saith unto him, Have I been so long time with you, and yet hast thou not known me, Philip? ᵏhe that hath seen me hath seen the Father; and how sayest thou *then*, Shew us the Father? k ch. 12. 45. Col. 1. 15. Heb. i. 3.

Our Saviour still insisteth upon the oneness of himself with his Father, and the personal union of the Divine and human nature in him; for otherwise the apostles might have been with Christ a long time, and known him, and yet not have seen nor known the Father. But that supposed, none that had seen Christ, but must have seen the Father also, there being but one God.

10 Believest thou not that ˡI am in the Father, and the Father in me? the words that I speak unto you ᵐI speak not of myself: but the Father that dwelleth in me, he doeth the works. l ver. 20. ch. 10. 38. & 17. 21, 23. m ch. 5. 19. & 7. 16. & 8. 28. & 12. 49.

I am in the Father, and the Father in me. It is the opinion of Mr. Calvin, that these words are not here spoken so much to express his Divine nature and being, (for so Christ is no more known to us than his Father,) as to express his manner of revealing it. Yet is the Divine nature of Christ fully proved from hence. Others judge, that these words do clearly signify both the distinction of persons, for nothing is in itself, and also the union of the persons in the Divine Being. He proveth his union with the Father, because he spake not those words which he spake of himself; that is, not of himself solely; he revealed but his Father's will, and declared his Father's mind; and because the works which he did, he did not by his own sole power, without the concurrence of his Father's power in those operations.

11 Believe me that I *am* in the Father, and the Father in me: ⁿor else believe me for the very works' sake. n ch. 5. 36. & 10. 38.

Believe my words (for that is your duty); but yet if you will not believe my words, declaring to you my union with my Father, yet when you see me doing such works as none but God can do, believe me for their sake. It is true, that both the prophets and the apostles spake God's words, not their own, to the people, and also did many great and mighty works; but still their doctrine led unto another, that was Christ; and their miracles were not wrought in their own names, but in the name of Christ. Elijah raised the Shunammite's dead child to life by prayer to God that he would do it; and the apostles bid the lame man arise and walk, in the name of the Lord Jesus Christ. Christ's doctrine terminated in himself; he called men to believe in him, and he wrought miracles by his own power, and by a virtue proceeding out of and from himself, though by the power of his Father also, because he and his Father were one in essence.

o Mat. 21. 21.
Mark 16. 17.
Luke 10. 17.
12 °Verily, verily, I say unto you, He that believeth on me, the works that I do shall he do also; and greater *works* than these shall he do; because I go unto my Father.

He that believeth on me; not every individual soul that believeth on me; but some of those, particularly you that are my apostles, and shall be filled with the Holy Ghost in the days of Pentecost; you shall preach the gospel, and work miracles for the confirmation of the truth of the doctrine of it. Yea, and you shall do *greater works* than I have done: not more or greater miracles: the truth of that may be justly questioned; for what miracle was ever done by the apostles greater than that of raising Lazarus? Much less do I think that it is to be understood of speaking with divers tongues. It is rather to be understood of their successful carrying the gospel to the Gentiles, by which the whole world, almost, was brought to the obedience of the faith of Christ. We never read that Christ which we read of Peter, viz. his converting three thousand at one sermon. *Because I go unto my Father*, he afterwards expoundeth, telling us, that if he did not go away, the Comforter would not come. The pouring out of the Spirit in the days of Pentecost, was the proximate cause of those great works. Now Christ's going to the Father had an influence upon that mission of the Holy Spirit.

p Matt. 7. 7.
& 21. 22.
Mark 11. 24.
Luke 11. 9.
ch. 15. 7, 16.
& 16. 23, 24.
Jam. 1. 5. 1 John 3. 22. & 5. 14.
13 ᵖAnd whatsoever ye shall ask in my name, that will I do, that the Father may be glorified in the Son.

The *whatsoever*, in this text, must be limited by what the will of God hath revealed in other texts, as to the matter of our prayers; viz. they must be things that are for our good; such things as we stand in need of, and as God hath given us a liberty to ask: and indeed no other things can be asked in the name of the Lord Jesus Christ; for to ask in Christ's name, signifieth not only the making use of his sacred name in our prayers, (though the constant practice of the church in prayer, hath evidenced it the general opinion of divines, that this is a part of the sense,) but also in asking for his merits, and such things as shall be conformable to his will, and for his glory. Whatsoever (saith he) you shall ask of this nature, I will do. He doth not say, my Father will do, but I will do it; to testify his Divine power, and oneness in power with his Father. *That the Father may be glorified in the Son:* God hath set up his rest in Christ, and will be glorified in and through him; and hath therefore given him all power in heaven and earth.

14 If ye shall ask any thing in my name, I will do *it*.

The words are doubled for the further confirmation of them, that we might not doubt when we put up our petitions to God in the name of the Lord Jesus Christ, according to the will of God.

q ver. 21, 23.
ch. 15. 10, 14.
1 John 5. 3.
15 ¶ ᵠIf ye love me, keep my commandments.

Do not show your love to me in mourning, and being troubled for my going from you; but show it by your obedience to what I have commanded you. True love must not evaporate in compliment, but discover itself in a strict observance of the commandments of God.

r ch. 15. 26.
& 16. 7.
Rom. 8. 15, 26.
16 And I will pray the Father, and ʳhe shall give you another Comforter, that he may abide with you for ever;

This verse containeth a new argument by which our Saviour relieveth his disciples under their affliction for the want of his bodily presence; that is, the mission of the Holy Spirit, *another Comforter*, as our translation reads it. For this he saith that he *will pray the Father;* not that himself had no concern in the mission of the blessed Spirit; for himself telleth us, chap. xvi. 7, that he would send him; only for the attestation, 1. Of his human nature; 2. Of himself, as our Mediator; and, 3. Of his Father's concern, as well as his own, in sending the Holy Spirit; he here saith, *I will pray the Father, and he shall send you another Comforter*. That term *another*, signifieth the personal distinction of the Third from the First and Second Person in the blessed Trinity. And the name here given to the blessed Spirit, Παράκλητον, (which we too narrowly translate *comforter*,) is a term exceedingly proper to signify all the operations of the blessed Spirit in and upon the souls of his people. The same word, 1 John ii. 1, where it is applied to Christ, (as here it is to the Spirit,) is there much better translated *Advocate;* and it is most probable that our translators here translate it *Comforter*, because he is here promised to the disciples troubled, as fitted to their present distress. The verb from whence the word deriveth, signifies not to comfort only, but to exhort, and to be an advocate for another. Now it belongs to the office of an advocate to suggest to his client what may be for his advantage; which is also the office of the blessed Spirit: if he seeth his client in an error, to reprove and to convince him; which is also the work of the Spirit, John xvi. 8: if he seeth him weak and discouraged, to uphold, strengthen, and encourage him; this is also the Spirit's work, Eph. iii. 16: if he seeth him running into an error, to restrain him; if he findeth him dull and heavy, to quicken him; if he seeth him ready to be run down, to defend him; if he hath any thing to do in the court, to prepare and draw it up for him, and, as occasion serveth, to speak for him. All these things (as might be largely showed) fall within the office of an advocate, and under the comprehensive term here used. And (saith our Saviour) he shall *abide with you for ever:* I shall be with you but for a while, but he shall abide with you to eternity (as some observe this word is constantly used by this evangelist). So that the promise of the Spirit is not to be restrained only to the apostles and their successors in the ministry, or to be understood only of those extraordinary gifts bestowed on the apostles and first ministers of the gospel; but to be extended further, both with reference to persons and influences: and without doubt the influences of the Spirit, both as to gifts and graces, both upon ministers and more private Christians, are much more plentiful since the sending of the Holy Ghost, after Christ's ascension, in the days of Pentecost, than ever they were before: not as to particular persons; a David, a Solomon, or some particular persons, might have greater measures than any or the most have since had; but as to the generality of ministers and Christians. Doubtless, since the pouring out of the Spirit in the days of Pentecost, there have been greater measures of the gifts and graces of the Holy Spirit given out, and will be to the end of the world, than ever was in any age before Christ's ascension; which is no more than what was prophesied, Isa. xliv. 3; Joel ii. 28, applied to the days of Pentecost, Acts ii. 17, but not to be limited to that time or age, either for gifts or gracious habits: for as the extraordinary gifts and powers held in some degree after the apostles' age, (if we may give any credit to ecclesiastical history,) so both in those ages, and ever since, as to the generality both of ministers and Christians, (that is, such as are mentioned ver. 15, that love Christ, and keep his commandments,) there have been fuller measures of gifts, of more constant, standing use for the church, such as those of knowledge and utterance, &c., and also of inward graces, than ever before was.

17 *Even* ˢthe Spirit of truth; ᵗwhom the world cannot receive, because it seeth him not, neither knoweth him: but ye know him; for he dwelleth with you, ᵘand shall be in you.

s ch. 15. 26.
& 16. 13.
1 John 4. 6.
t 1 Cor. 2. 14.
u 1 John 2. 27.

He here explaineth himself, and tells them, that by that other Comforter, mentioned ver. 16. he meant the Spirit; whom he here calls *the Spirit of truth*, either because he is a Spirit that declareth and revealeth the truth, as in 1 John v. 6, or because he teacheth us truth, 1 John ii. 27, he guideth us into all truth, John xvi. 13; or in opposition to the lying spirit of the devil, 1 Kings xxii. 22. Most probably the Holy Spirit is here called *the Spirit of truth*, because of the efficiency he hath as to it. It is he who hath revealed all the truth contained in the Scriptures to the world. Holy men wrote as they were inspired by him, Acts i. 16; 2 Pet. i. 21. It is he that more particularly and specially revealeth truth to the particular soul, 1 Cor. ii. 12; hence persons enlightened, are said to be *made partakers of the Holy Ghost*, Heb. vi. 4. He leadeth his people into truth, chap. xvi. 13; he sealeth and confirmeth truth to the soul: hence we read of the *demonstration of the Spirit*, 1 Cor. ii. 4. This Spirit of truth, *the world*, that is, men of carnal hearts, that are of the world, and in whom worldly lusts predominate, 1 John ii. 16; chap. xvii. 9; this world, through natural impotency, 1 Cor. ii. 14, through wisdom, 1 Cor. i. 21, through lusts and passions, *cannot receive*, that is, be made partakers of; because it neither seeth him, who is not to be seen with mortal eyes, nor knoweth him affectionately and experimentally; he being not to be known by men whose hearts are carnal and full of lusts: *but ye know him* believingly, experimentally, affectionately, savingly; for he dwelleth in you by a mystical union, Rom. viii. 11; 1 Cor. vi. 17; and he shall abide with you, by his dwelling in you, and influences upon you.

18 ˣI will not leave you ‖ comfortless: ʸI will come to you. [x Mat. 28.20. ‖ Or, *orphans*. y ver. 3, 28.]

Comfortless; the word in the Greek is, orphans, persons without father and mother, who for the most part are the most comfortless persons; therefore it is translated *comfortless*: Christ hath a care, not only of the people's salvation and life, but also of their comforts while they are here; he will not leave his people without proportionable comfort for their distresses. *I will come to you*; in the Greek it is, I do come to you, to denote the certainty and the suddenness of his coming; which is either to be understood of his resurrection, which was (as we know) after the absence of three days; or, which is more probable, (for after his resurrection he stayed with them but a few days,) in and by his blessed Spirit, (for the Spirit is called the Spirit of Christ,) who was to come, and to abide with them for ever. Though it may also have a reference to his coming again to judge both the quick and the dead, to receive them to himself, that (as he said before) they might always be where he was; but the two former senses are understood as more specially relating to their present distresses, upon account of his bodily absence from them.

19 Yet a little while, and the world seeth me no more; but, ʸye see me: ᵃbecause I live, ye shall live also. [z ch. 16. 16. a 1 Cor. 15. 20.]

The world seeth me now only with fleshly eyes; it will be but a little while, and the men of the world shall be able to see me no more; I shall be crucified, and laid in the grave; and though I shall rise again, yet I shall not be seen of them: (we read of no appearances of him after his resurrection, but to his disciples:) *but ye see me*, or shall see me; so they did often after his resurrection with their bodily eyes; or it may be understood of a spiritual sight by the eye of faith, or of a sight of experience; as seeing often in Scripture signifieth enjoying. *Because I live*, that is, I shall live by my resurrection from the dead, and by my glorious ascension into heaven, *you also shall live* the life of grace here; and though your bodies must die, because of sin, yet your souls shall upon the death of your bodies live; and in the resurrection, both your souls and bodies shall live, and together be glorified with me: all this grace and mercy shall flow out to you from me as Mediator, and because I live.

20 At that day ye shall know that ᵇI am in my Father, and ye in me, and I in you. [b ver. 10. ch. 10. 38. & 17. 21, 23, 26.]

Some understand our Saviour here speaking of the day of his resurrection; others interpret it of the days of Pentecost, when there should be such an effusion of the blessed Spirit: but the following words discover, that it is best interpreted of the day of judgment, and the general resurrection: for they speak of two great mysteries, which the disciples should understand in that day which is here spoken of; to wit, the personal union of Christ with his Father, and the mystical union of believers with Christ: as to both which, though the apostles and believers knew much more after Christ's resurrection, and the pouring forth of the Spirit in the days of Pentecost, than they knew before those times; yet it is a very imperfect knowledge they ever had, or yet have, of those mysterious unions; but in the resurrection we shall understand these things clearly.

21 ᶜHe that hath my commandments, and keepeth them, he it is that loveth me: and he that loveth me shall be loved of my Father, and I will love him, and will manifest myself to him. [c ver. 15, 23. 1 John 2. 5. & 5. 3.]

He that hath my commandments and keepeth them, he it is that loveth me: our Lord here doth repeat what he had before said, ver. 15, declaring that there is no infallible indication of our love to Christ, but obedience, which is here expressed under two notions. 1. Having Christ's commandments and keeping them: they must both concur to make a true indication of our love to Christ. It is possible that men may have Christ's commandments in their ears, in their notion, in their mouths, and yet not keep them; they may hear them, they may know and remember them, they may talk of them, yet they may not keep them; for keeping them denotes universal, diligent and industrious, steady and constant obedience to them; and this alone will speak our love to Christ. And if any man thus declareth his love to Christ, Christ declareth, that both he and his Father will take a pleasure and delight in him to do him good; and he shall not live only under the real benefits of his love to him, but under the sensible manifestations of it. Here is no mention of the Spirit's coming with the Father and the Son, because the Son dwelleth in us by the Spirit.

22 ᵈJudas saith unto him, not Iscariot, Lord, how is it that thou wilt manifest thyself unto us, and not unto the world? [d Luke 6. 16.]

Jude the brother of James, Jude 1, the son of Alpheus; not Judas the son of Simon, who, from the city whence he was, was called Iscariot, and was the traitor; asks our Saviour, how it was, or wherefore it was, that he would manifest himself to them, and not to the world? This question either proceeded out of ignorance, not aright understanding of what manifestation of himself Christ here spake; or out of a pious desire that all might be made partakers of the same grace with them; or out of the apostle's modest opinion of himself and his brethren; as if he had said, Lord, what are we that thou shouldest speak of any more special manifestation of thy love to us, than to the rest of the world? or out of a deep admiration of God's unsearchable judgments in leaving some of the world, while he made choice of others to dignify with such special distinguishing favours, hiding those things from the wise and prudent which he revealed to babes.

23 Jesus answered and said unto him, ᵉIf a man love me, he will keep my words: and my Father will love him, ᶠand we will come unto him, and make our abode with him. [e ver. 15. f 1 John 2. 24. Rev. 3. 20.]

If any man love Christ, he will keep Christ's words; that is, he will study and endeavour to keep the commandments of Christ; for if nothing evidenced a true love to Christ but a perfect obedience to his will, none could comfort himself from his obedience, or conclude his love to Christ from it; but he that loveth Christ, will make it his business to be obedient to him in those things that he hath commanded, and are within his power. *And my Father will love him*; and my Father will manifest his love to him in further dispensations of his grace; for it cannot be understood of God's eternal love, nor yet of his love in justification and regeneration; for till the man or woman be justified and regenerated, he will never study and endeavour obedience to the will of God. This love of God is the cause, not the effect of our obedience; but *love* in this verse must be expounded by *manifesting* in the former verse; and this is certain, that the manifestations of Divine love to our souls depend upon our walking with God. This is also meant by God the Father and Christ's coming to those that love him, and keep his commandments; viz. a coming in the sweet influences of Divine grace, suited to the soul's various necessities: nay, our Lord promiseth, not only his and his Father's coming to, but their making an abode with such as love him, and keep his commandments. Here the abiding of the First and Second Person in the Trinity with believers; the abiding of the Third Person with them is also promised, ver. 16; which all make that presence of God with them, so often promised to them in holy writ. Thus our Saviour answereth one part of what Judas said, *How is it that thou wilt manifest thyself to us?* Because, saith our Saviour, you love me, and keep my words: for though no love, no works of ours, foreseen or seen, be the cause of eternal love, or the first grace; yet it is so much a cause of further grace, especially in the sensible manifestations of it, that no soul must expect it that doth not love Christ, and keep his words. He also further gives them a reason, as to the second thing he asked, why he did not manifest himself to the world?

24 He that loveth me not keepeth not my sayings: and ᵍthe word which ye hear is not mine, but the Father's which sent me.

g ver. 10. ch. 5. 19, 38. & 7. 16. & 8. 28. & 12. 49.

Because they did not love him, nor keep his sayings, their sin was aggravated; because the words which he spake were not his will only, but the will of his Father who had sent him into the world, to reveal his will to the sons of men.

25 These things have I spoken unto you, being *yet* present with you.

That is, as to his bodily presence: For more than three years I have been fulfilling a ministry amongst you, and have spoken many things to you.

26 But ʰthe Comforter, *which is* the Holy Ghost, whom the Father will send in my name, ⁱhe shall teach you all things, and bring all things to your remembrance, whatsoever I have said unto you.

h ver. 16. Luke 24. 49. ch. 15. 26. & 16. 7.
i ch. 2. 22. & 12. 16. & 16. 13. 1 John 2. 20, 27.

The word is the same which was so translated before; (see the import of it, ver. 16, 17;) he is there called *the Comforter*, and *the Spirit of truth;* here, *the Holy Spirit.* The Father here is said to send in the name, that is, with the authority and upon the mediation, of the Lord Jesus Christ: and two pieces of the Spirit's work, besides comforting, are here expressed. *He shall teach you all things;* he shall more fully explain to you all things. Three of the apostles themselves had already in this chapter discovered great degrees of ignorance as to the doctrine of the Trinity, Christ's union or oneness with his Father, &c. You shall not be left (saith our Saviour) in this ignorance; for when the Holy Spirit shall come, he shall more fully and perfectly instruct you in all things, in which I have already instructed you, and which are necessary for you to know in order to your eternal happiness. *And bring all things to your remembrance, whatsoever I have said unto you;* and shall bring to your remembrance the things I have taught you, so as you shall more fully and clearly understand them; and though you may have forgotten them, yet they shall by the Holy Spirit be revived in your memories; so as they shall not be like water spilt on the ground, which cannot again be gathered up, but like seed sown in the earth; which, though it may at present rot, and die under the clods, or at least not spring up, yet it shall spring up, and bring forth desired fruit. It is one great work of the Holy Spirit, to bring the revelations of holy writ to our remembrance, and withal to clear to us the sense of them, and confirm our faith in them, and chiefly quicken us to practise what is our duty: but it is to be observed, that the Spirit doth not make revelations of new notions; it only brings to our remembrance what Christ hath said, and further revealeth what was before in the word revealed, though possibly particular persons were ignorant of such revelations of the word: so things may be new, and newly revealed to us, which in themselves are not so. There are no new truths, but particular persons may have new discoveries of old truth, which they had before misapprehensions of.

k Phil. 4. 7. Col. 3. 15.
l ver. 1.

27 ᵏPeace I leave with you, my peace I give unto you: not as the world giveth, give I unto you. ˡLet not your heart be troubled, neither let it be afraid.

Peace be with you, or to you, was the Jewish common salutation, 1 Sam. xxv. 6; under that general name they comprehended all manner of good: with this good wish they both saluted their friends when they met them, and took their farewell of them when they left them. Christ, being now about to take his leave for a time of his disciples, wisheth them *peace;* nay, he doth not only wish it to them, but he *leaves* it to them; he giveth it them as a legacy; and that in another kind of peace, and in another manner, than was common. He therefore calls it his peace revealed in the gospel, Eph. vi. 15; purchased with his blood, Rom. v. 1; brought to the soul by his Spirit, by which we are sealed to the day of redemption. Christ's peace is either union or reconciliation with God, or the copy of it, which is a quiet of conscience, and assurance of his love; or a union with men by brotherly love, so often commended and pressed by Christ. Nor doth Christ give this peace as the men of the world give peace; who often wish peace earnestly, never considering what it is they say; often falsely, formally wishing peace, when they are about to strike those to whom they wish it under the fifth rib; and when they are most serious, wish it, but cannot give it. Christ leaves it to his disciples for a legacy, giveth it to them as a gift; if they want it, it is their own fault: therefore, as in the first verse, so here again he saith, *Let not your heart be troubled;* and adds, *neither let it be afraid.* Fear is one of those passions which most usually and potently doth disturb the hearts and minds of men; but there was no reason it should have this ill influence on Christ's disciples, because he had left them peace for his legacy, and the gifts of God are without repentance; and, *if God be for us,* (saith the apostle, Rom. viii. 31,) *who,* or what, *can be against us?*

28 Ye have heard how ᵐI said unto you, I go away, and come *again* unto you. If ye loved me, ye would rejoice, because I said, ⁿI go unto the Father: for ᵒmy Father is greater than I.

m ver. 3, 18.
n ver. 12. ch. 16. 16. & 20. 17.
o See ch. 5. 18. & 10. 30. Phil. 2. 6.

Ye have heard how I said unto you, I go away, and come again unto you; they had heard our Saviour saying so, ver. 3. It is of the nature of true love, to rejoice in the good of the object beloved, as much as in its own, nay, before its own. Saith our Saviour, *if ye loved me,* that is, as ye ought to love me, (for our Lord had before owned that they did love him, giving it as a reason why he rather revealed himself and manifested himself to them, than to the world, ver. 23,) you would not have been so unreasonably disturbed at my telling you that I shall leave you; because I not only told you that I would come again to you, but because I told you that I was going to my Father, ver. 2; from whom though I was never separated, as I am God over all blessed for ever, yet my human nature was yet never glorified with him; so that I shall be there much happier than here; being highly exalted, and having a name given me *above every name,* Phil. ii. 9. *For my Father is greater than I;* not greater in essence, (as the Arians and Socinians would have it,) he had many times before asserted the contrary; but greater, 1. Either as to the order amongst the Divine Persons; because the Father begat, the Son is begotten; the Father is he from whom the Son proceeded by eternal generation: in which sense, divers of the ancients, amongst whom Athanasius, Cyril, and Augustine, and some modern interpreters, understand it. Or, 2. As a Mediator sent from the Father, so he is greater than I. Or, 3. In respect of my present state, while I am here in the form of a servant; and in my state of humiliation: which seemeth to be the best interpretation, if we consider the words before, *ye would rejoice, because I said, I go unto the Father;* for the true reason of that joy must have been, because Christ in his glorious state of exaltation would be much more happy than he had been in his state of humiliation, while he was exposed to the scoffs, reproaches, and injuries of men, the temptations of Satan, &c.

29 And ᵖnow I have told you before it come to pass, that, when it is come to pass, ye might believe.

p ch. 13. 19. & 16. 4.

Evils that surprise us are always the most heavy, and load our spirits. Saith our Saviour, Before these things come to pass, I have given you notice of them, that, when you see them come to pass, you might not be overwhelmed with sorrow and trouble, to the hinderance of your faith in me; but understanding that I have told you the truth, before the thing come to pass, you may be assured that I am not mere man, but truly God; and receive and embrace me, and rest upon me as your Saviour.

30 Hereafter I will not talk much with you: ^qfor the prince of this world cometh, and hath nothing in me.

^q ch. 12. 31. & 16. 11.

I shall not have much time hereafter to reveal my mind to you, my suffering is very near; the devil, who is *the prince of this world*, chap. xii. 31; (see the notes there;) xvi. 11; Eph. vi. 12; he *cometh* by the evil angels, or rather by vile and wicked men, as his instruments, Judas and the soldiers. He doth not say wherefore he came, but it is easily understood. And he *hath nothing in me* that he can justly fault, and take advantage against me, for he findeth no guilt in me to give him any advantage against me; I shall die as an innocent person, and be cut off, but not for myself, (as it was prophesied of the Messiah, Dan. ix. 26,) but (as it is there, ver. 24,) *to finish transgression, and to make reconciliation for iniquity, and to bring in everlasting righteousness.*

31 But that the world may know that I love the Father; and ^ras the Father gave me commandment, even so I do. Arise, let us go hence.

^r ch. 10. 18. Phil. 2. 8. Heb. 5. 8.

I die not for my own sin; but *being found in fashion as a man, I humbled myself, and became obedient unto death, even the death of the cross,* (as Phil. ii. 8,) to let the world know, that I love the Father, and am obedient to him, doing even so as he hath commanded me. *Arise, let us go hence;* arise from supper, (after which they were wont sometimes to lengthen out discourse,) the supper in Bethany, as some think; but to me it seems more probable (as I said before) to be the passover supper, and the Lord's supper which immediately followed that; and *let us go hence,* out of the guest chamber, where the passover was to be administered. So as it is most probable, that the discourses in the two next chapters were as they went along in the way to Mount Olivet. In this discourse our Saviour hath most applied himself to relieve his disciples upon their disturbance for their want of our Saviour's bodily presence.

CHAP. XV

Under the parable of a vine Christ setteth forth God's government of his church, and exhorteth his disciples to abide in his faith and doctrine, 1—11. *He commandeth them to love one another, according to the great love he had showed for them,* 12—17; *forewarneth them of the hatred and persecution of the world,* 18—25; *and telleth them of the testimony which the Holy Ghost, and they also, should bear to him,* 26, 27.

As our Saviour in the former chapter had chiefly spent his discourse for the relief of his disciples under their trouble for the want of his bodily presence, so he seemeth in this chiefly to bend his discourse for the comfort of them under their disturbance, for fear they should, together with the want of the comfort they had in his bodily presence, want also his spiritual influences; to prevent which, he compareth himself to a vine, then to the branches; and showeth by that similitude the near union they had with him, and the influence he would and must have upon them, so long as they did abide with him. From the 18th verse to the end he comforts them by a variety of arguments against that black storm of persecution, which he had so often told them would arise after his departure from them, from the hatred of the world, of wicked men, both Jews and Gentiles, that were enemies to the cross of Christ; as to which he comforts them by a variety of arguments to the end of the chapter, and continueth his discourse of that nature also in the following chapter.

I AM the true vine, and my Father is the husbandman.

Christ had but newly come from his last supper, wherein he had sanctified the fruit of the vine, by setting it apart as one of the elements in that holy sacrament, and told them, that he would no more drink of the fruit of the vine, until the kingdom of God should come, Luke xxii. 18. This (as some suppose) gave occasion to this parable, or discourse about the vine. Others think, that in his passage from the guest chamber to the Mount Olivet he saw a vine, which gave occasion to this discourse, it being with him very ordinary to graft spiritual discourses upon sensible objects occasionally occurring; as, chap. iv., he raised a discourse of living water upon the sight of the water at Jacob's well, and the woman's discourse about it; and, chap. vi., he founded another discourse concerning the bread of life, upon the loaves that were multiplied. Whatever the occasion was, (of which we can affirm nothing certainly), certain it is, that the notion of a vine, with respect to the root and body of it, (for he calls his disciples the branches,) excellently agreeth to Christ, whether in respect of his present low condition, and mean appearance to the world, (as a vine hath less beauty than most plants,) or in respect of its exceeding fruitfulness; or as it is the basis and foundation of the branches, in which they are, and thrive, and are fruitful; which seemeth here to be chiefly intended; as all the branches are united to the vine, in it they live, bud, bear fruit. There are three principal things which our Saviour teacheth us by this similitude: 1. That we have no ability to do good but from Christ. 2. That believers have a true and real union with the Lord Jesus, which while they uphold by faith and holiness, they shall not want his influence upon them, nor his Father's care over them, in purging them, that they may bring forth much fruit. 3. That if any professing him prove unfruitful, God will take them away; they shall wither, be cast into the fire, and burned. He calls himself *the true vine,* to show them that their fruit was not in themselves, but must be found in him; or that their fruit could not proceed from Moses, the observance of the ritual or moral law given them by him; but it must flow from their spiritual union with him, and that influence of grace which should flow from that union. Or else *true* (as sometimes it doth in Scripture) may signify excellent. As he compareth himself to *the true vine,* by which he signifieth to us that he is the true root and support of our spiritual life and fruit; so he compareth his Father to *the husbandman,* to let us know, that his people are not only under his, but under his Father's care; which he afterwards more particularly openeth. He also, ver. 2, compareth believers, or members of the church, to branches in a vine.

2 ^aEvery branch in me that beareth not fruit he taketh away: and every *branch* that beareth fruit, he purgeth it, that it may bring forth more fruit.

^a Mat. 15. 13.

And concerning his Father's care, he tells us, that as the good vine-dresser cutteth off those branches in the vine which bring forth no fruit, so his Father will take away such branches in him as bring forth no fruit. But here ariseth a question, viz. Whether, or how, any can be branches in Christ, and yet bring forth no fruit? *Answ.* 1. Some say, there is no need of translating the words so, which may as well be translated, Every branch not bringing forth fruit in me. Indeed no true fruit can be brought forth but in Christ; but yet much that looks like fruit, much that men may call fruit, may be brought forth without any true spiritual union with Christ. All acts of moral discipline, or any acts of formal profession in religion, may be brought forth without any true root and foundation in Christ; and God will in the end discover and cut off, those who bring forth no other fruit. But, 2. Men may be said to be branches in him, by a sacramental implantation, being baptized into him, Rom. vi. 3; and are hereby members of the visible church, and make a visible profession of adhering to him, with respect to their own good opinion and persuasions of themselves, though they be not so in respect of any true, spiritual, and real implantation. But those who in the last sense are not in him, bring forth no fruit unto perfection, and God will cut them off, either by withdrawing his restraining grace, and giving them up to strong delusions to believe lies; or to a reprobate mind, and vile lusts and affections; or by taking away their gifts; or some way or other, so as they shall never have an eternal communion with God in glory. But if any man bringeth forth true spiritual fruit in Christ, him God the Father will purge, by the sprinkling of Christ's blood yet further upon his conscience, Heb. x. 22; and by his Holy Spirit working on him like fire, to purge away his dross, and like water, to purge away his filth; and by his word, 1 Pet. i. 22, by faith, Acts xv. 9, by crosses and trials, Isa. i. 25; xxvii. 9; that he may be more fruitful in works of holiness and righteousness.

3 [b] Now ye are clean through the word which I have spoken unto you.

b ch. 13. 10. & 17. 17. Eph. 5. 26. 1 Pet. i. 22.

Now that the traitor is gone out from you, ye are all clean; not by any works which you do, much less upon the account of any legal and ceremonial rites and purifyings; but through my word, your believing and obeying, Eph. v. 26; 1 Pet. i. 22. Our cleansing is in holy writ attributed sometimes to the blood of Christ, sometimes to the Spirit, sometimes to the word. By the blood of Christ we are made clean as to justification, washed; but yet we had need wash our feet, contracting soil every day in a sinful world, from which we are cleansed by the purifying virtue of the Holy Spirit, working by and together with the word, which purgeth us of our dross, and maketh us obedient to the will of God.

c Col. 1. 23. 1 John 2. 6.

4 [c] Abide in me, and I in you. As the branch cannot bear fruit of itself, except it abide in the vine; no more can ye, except ye abide in me.

This our abiding in Christ is expounded, by an abiding in his words, ver. 7, by abiding in his love, ver. 10, an abiding in his Spirit, 1 John ii. 27, a walking as Christ walked, 1 John ii. 6, an abiding in the light, ver. 10, not sinning, 1 John iii. 6. The exhortation is, without doubt, to a holiness of life and conversation, by which our union and communion with Christ is upheld and maintained, and which is in itself an abiding in the love of Christ: nor is there a want of sufficient reason for this exhortation, though our union with Christ cannot be dissolved, nor our communion with him wholly interrupted; because, 1. It must be upheld and maintained on our part by the exercises of faith and holiness. 2. The sense of it in our souls may be eclipsed, and wholly fail, Psal. xxii. i. 3. We may fall away foully, though neither totally, (as Lutherans say,) because the seed of God abideth in the believer; nor yet finally (as papists say). We had need therefore of all exhortations and arguments imaginable, to persuade us to do what in us lieth that we may abide in him. We have a great encouragement to the use of all possible endeavours to abide in the love of God, from the promise annexed, *and I in you;* that is, I will abide in you; do you strive, and I will help you to perfect; do you fight, and I will help you to overcome; I will continue to you such gradual influences of grace, as shall be sufficient for you; grace wherein and whereby you shall stand, Rom. v. 2. You shall be *kept by the power of God through faith to salvation,* 1 Pet. i. 5. But look as it is with the branch, it cannot bear fruit of itself; but if it be once separated from the influences of the stock, it dies and withers; so it will be with you, you can bring forth no fruit unless you abide in me.

5 I am the vine, ye *are* the branches: He that abideth in me, and I in him, the same bringeth forth much [d] fruit: for without me ye can do nothing.

d Hos. 14. 8. Phil. 1. 11. & 4. 13. ‖ Or, *severed from me,* Acts 4. 12.

I am the vine, ye are the branches; that is, I am as the vine, you are as the branches: without the continual influence of the vine upon the branches, they bring forth no fruit; but that influence continuing, no plant is more fruitful than a vine is: so without the continual influence of my Spirit of grace upon you, you will be altogether barren and unfruitful; but if you have that influence, you will not be fruitful only, but very fruitful: for without my continuing such influence, you will not only be able to do little, but you will be able to do nothing that is truly and spiritually good and acceptable in the sight of God.

e Matt. 3. 10. & 7. 19.

6 If a man abide not in me, [e] he is cast forth as a branch, and is withered; and men gather them, and cast *them* into the fire, and they are burned.

Our Lord yet pursueth the metaphor of the vine, the branches, and the husbandman: Look (saith he) as it is with a vine, when the time of pruning the vine cometh, the vine-dresser cutteth off the fruitless, luxuriant branches, and throweth them by; which being done, their greenness presently abateth, and they wither, and after a time some come and gather them up, and cast them into some fire, where they are burned: so it will be with you; if you do not bring forth fruit, God will take from you his common influences, which have for a while made you to look speciously; and your profession, or your parts and gifts, will wither and decay; and in the day of judgment the angels shall gather you up, and God shall cast you into hell, Matt. xiii. 40, 41, where you shall perish as miserably, nay, infinitely more miserably, than if you were burned with fire.

7 If ye abide in me, and my words abide in you, [f] ye shall ask what ye will, and it shall be done unto you.

f ver. 16. ch. 14. 13, 14. & 16. 23.

Here our Lord expounds what he meaneth by that abiding in him which he before mentioned by another phrase, *and my words abide in you,* my precepts and promises; so as you by faith embrace the promises, and by obedience live up to the precepts which I have given you: for without these, though the words of Christ may come unto men in the preaching of the gospel, their ears may receive the sound of them, yet the word doth not dwell and abide in the soul: but if the word abides in the souls of men and women, then they may in prayer ask of God what they will, keeping to the conditions and limitations elsewhere required in holy writ, according to God's will, 1 John v. 14, believing, Matt. xxi. 22, in the name of Christ, chap. xiv. 13, 14, for the honour and glory of God, (to which end all our actions must be directed,) and they shall be granted to them.

8 [g] Herein is my Father glorified, that ye bear much fruit; [h] so shall ye be my disciples.

g Mat. 5. 16. Phil. 1. 11. *h* ch. 8. 31. & 13. 35.

Here are two arguments to press his disciples' abiding in him, that so they might bring forth much fruit. 1. *Herein* (saith our Saviour) *is my Father glorified.* The glorifying of God is the great end of our lives, 1 Cor. x. 31. God is glorified by men and women's bringing forth much fruit, Matt. v. 16, the *fruit unto holiness,* Rom. vi. 22: fruit is the product of the plant, from the natural moisture that is in it, nourished and augmented by the fatness of the earth in which it stands, and by the warmth of the sun drawn out to the producing of such effects, according to the nature of the plant. According to the different nature of plants they bring forth various fruits, Matt. vii. 16—18. Hence we read of the fruit of sin unto death, and the fruit of righteousness unto life. The first is every man's natural fruit, until he be ingrafted into Christ: being ingrafted into him, the soul having a new nature given to it, being regenerated and renewed by the Holy Ghost, it no longer bringeth forth fruit from its old principle, and according to its old nature, but from its new principle, and according to its new nature. As the cultivated earth, that is ploughed and harrowed, doth not bring forth weeds and ordinary grass, according to its nature, but bringeth forth fruit according to the seed that is cast into it, yet not without the influence of heaven, both with respect to the dew of it, and the warmth which it hath from the sun; so the soul, being regenerated, the fallow ground of it being ploughed up, and the seed of righteousness being sown in it, no more brings forth the weeds of lusts and corruptions, or only ordinary acts of human nature, but it brings forth fruits according to its new nature, and the new seed of the word now sown in it, and dwelling in it. And look, as it tendeth to the honour of the husbandman, when the ground by him ploughed and manured brings forth much fruit; so it tendeth to the honour and glory of God, when the souls renewed, manured, and influenced by him, bring forth much of the fruit of righteousness and holiness. And though men must be Christ's disciples before they bring forth any fruit, yet their bringing forth much fruit is that which alone can evidence and make them appear to be the disciples of Christ. And often in Scripture being signifieth appearing, as John viii. 31; Rom. iii. 4.

9 As the Father hath loved me, so have I loved you: continue ye in my love.

What our Saviour before called an abiding in him, and his words abiding in us, and a bearing and bringing forth much fruit, he here calleth a continuing in his love; though indeed this phrase also may be interpreted by a continuance in the favour of God and Christ, in that state of love into which God hath put the souls of those who are his true disciples: but I had rather interpret it of that love wherewith they loved Christ, than that wherewith Christ loved them. So the former words are an argument to persuade perseverance, or a continuance in those acts of holiness by which men alone can show their true love to Jesus Christ, from Christ's love to them, which he there expresseth, *As the Father hath loved me, so have I loved you;* where the particle *as* is only a note of comparison, but doth not denote an equality; only signifieth truth and greatness; as truly and sincerely as the Father loveth me: or, I have loved you with a great love, bearing some proportion to the love wherewith my Father loveth me. The Father's love to Christ is eternal, immutable, constant, full and perfect, wise and just, free; in all these respects Christ loveth his people as the Father loveth him: this ought to engage them again to love him, and so to walk as they may continue in that state of favour into which his goodness hath advanced them.

^{i ch. 14. 15, 21, 23.} **10 ⁱIf ye keep my commandments, ye shall abide in my love; even as I have kept my Father's commandments, and abide in his love.**

Abiding in Christ's love, in this verse, may be interpreted as before; either actively, you shall continue your love to me, according to what we had, chap. xiv. 15; obedience to the commandments of Christ being the only way to show and declare the truth of our love to Christ. Or else passively, you shall keep yourselves in my favour, I will love you. Thus I abide in my Father's love; I do not show love to my Father by my words and expressions only, nor by performance of some ceremonial, ritual services, which he hath required; but by fulfilling his whole will and counsel, by yielding an obedience to him in all things. I love you as my Father loveth me; and you must abide in my love by the same ways and means that I abide in my Father's love. The disciple is not above his master, nor the servant above his lord.

11 These things have I spoken unto ^{k ch. 16. 24. & 17. 13. 1 John 1. 4.} **you, that my joy might remain in you, and ^kthat your joy might be full.**

The end of my pressing so much the duty of holiness upon you, under the notions of abiding in me, abiding in my love, in my words, bringing forth much fruit, &c. is, that I might have a continual cause to rejoice in you. Joy is nothing else but the satisfaction of the reasonable soul in its union with an object which it loved and desired. Christ, willing and desiring the perfection of his disciples, according to the rational workings of human nature, is properly said to rejoice in the satisfaction of his will; in which sense joy and rejoicing are often in Scripture attributed to God. Nor doth Christ press them to this, that he might rejoice in them, but also that their joy might be full; that joy and peace which attends and follows believing, Rom. xv. 13; called the *peace of God*, Col. iii. 15; a peace *which passeth all understanding*, Phil. iv. 7. No man maketh Christ to rejoice over him, but he thereby also procureth unspeakable joy and peace to himself; as no man grieveth his Spirit, but also purchaseth grief and sadness to himself in the latter end.

^{l ch. 13. 34. 1 Thes. 4. 9. 1 Pet. 4. 8. 1 John 3. 11. & 4. 21.} **12 ^lThis is my commandment, That ye love one another, as I have loved you.**

This is that which our Lord called the *new commandment*, chap. xiii. 34: see the notes there. He had before pressed the keeping of his words, continuing and abiding in his words, keeping his commandments, &c. Here he tells them what was his commandment: not his only commandment, but that which he laid a very great stress upon; a commandment most necessary to be pressed, because so necessary to keep up and uphold his church in the world, (love being the very ligament of that society,) and because there was a greater failure in obedience to this than in some others, as may be learned from our Saviour's correction of the Pharisees' interpretation of that law, Matt. v. This he presseth to a higher degree, as he had loved them; not that it is possible that our love to our brethren can rise up in any proportion to that love wherewith Christ hath loved us; but to mind us to eye him, to press forward toward this mark. *As* here again doth not signify equality, but a comparison; as truly and sincerely as I have loved you, and pressing after the highest degree of love.

13 ^mGreater love hath no man than ^{m ch. 10. 11, 15. Rom. 5. 7, 8. Eph. 5. 2. 1 John 3. 16.} **this, that a man lay down his life for his friends.**

The reason of this is, because life is the greatest earthly good to men under ordinary circumstances: *Skin for skin, yea, all that a man hath will he give for his life*, Job ii. 4. Now it is impossible that a man should show a greater love to another, than by parting with the greatest good he is in possession of for his sake. Hence our Saviour proves, that he loved them with the greatest love, because he for their sake was about to part with what in the common judgment of men is the greatest good. The greatness of the love of Christ to us is from hence often commended to us in Scripture; and our mutual love to our brethren is pressed upon this argument, Eph. v. 2; 1 John iii. 16. But how did Christ lay down his life for his friends, when the Scripture tells us, that *the just* died *for the unjust*, 1 Pet. iii. 18, and that *while we were enemies, we were reconciled unto God by the death of his Son*, Rom. v. 10? *Answ. Friends* must not here be taken as a name of relation, but only as it signifieth the objects of love; persons we have set our love upon, whether they mutually love us or no; as the world was the object of that love in God, which moved him to send his only begotten Son, John iii. 16. Though they for whom Christ died were enemies by their wicked works, yet by his death they were reconciled. But possibly the first answer is best; for by Christ's death they were only meritoriously reconciled, and after this enemies to God, till they received the word of reconciliation, and believed in Christ.

14 ⁿYe are my friends, if ye do whatsoever I command you. ^{n ch. 14. 15, 23. See Mat. 12. 50.}

Our Lord presseth obedience to his commandments as a means, and indeed the only means, by which we can declare our love to Christ; and also useth a new argument to press their obedience, from his assuming them into the state and dignity of his friends.

15 Henceforth I call you not servants; for the servant knoweth not what his lord doeth: but I have called you friends; ^ofor all things that I have heard of my Father I have made known unto you. ^{o See Gen. 18. 17. ch. 17. 26. Acts 20. 27.}

By his saying, *I call you not servants*, he doth not discharge them of that duty and service which they owed to him; for in pressing them to obey his commandments, he declareth that duty they owed to him; he only showeth that they were no ordinary servants, but taken into a state of dignity, favour, and familiarity, beyond that of servants, and that he had not treated them like servants, but like intimate, familiar friends. For look as ordinary masters in the world communicate their counsels and whole heart to their friends, especially in things which are of any concern, or may be of any advantage for them to know and understand; whereas they keep themselves at a distance from servants, and they only know so much of their minds as is by them to be done in their masters' service: so he had not only revealed to them their duty, what was to be by them done in his service, but had been more free, giving to them *to know the mysteries of the kingdom of heaven*, as he told them, Matt. xiii. 11; as well telling them his Father's counsels on the behalf of them, and whatsoever he might communicate to them, as his Father's will, what he would have them to do in obedience to his commandments.

16 ^pYe have not chosen me, but I have chosen you, and ^qordained you, that ye should go and bring forth fruit, and *that* your fruit should remain: that ^rwhatso- ^{p ch. 6. 70. & 13. 18. 1 John 4. 10, 19. q Mat. 28. 19. Mark 16. 15. Col. 1. 6. r ver. 7. ch. 14. 13.}

ever ye shall ask of the Father in my name, he may give it you.

Ye have not chosen me to be your Lord, Master, Saviour, *but I have chosen and ordained you;* so we have it in our translation; but the Greek is, ἔθηκα, I have set you, or placed you in a station. What choosing Christ here speaks of is doubted amongst various divines. Some think that our Saviour here speaks of his choice of them to the apostleship, as Luke vi. 13; chap. vi. 70: those who thus understand it, understand by going and bringing forth fruit, the apostles' going out, preaching, and baptizing all nations, bringing forth fruit amongst the Gentiles. But others understand it of election to eternal life, and the means necessary to it; for our Saviour brings this as an argument of his greatest love: Judas was in the first sense chosen, yet not beloved with any such love: and this seemeth to be favoured by chap. xiii. 18, *I speak not of you all; I know whom I have chosen:* and certain it is, Augustine and others of the ancients from hence proved the freedom of election and special grace. Both senses may be united, for the eleven (to whom Christ was now speaking) were chosen in both senses; they were chosen for this end, to *bring forth fruit* amongst the Gentiles, turning many to righteousness, and that they might bring forth the fruit of holiness, in obedience to the gospel of Christ. Yea, not only to bring forth fruit, but that they might persevere in bringing forth fruit; and that thus doing, they might have a freedom of access to the throne of grace, and obtain whatsoever they should ask of the Father, in the name, for the merits, and through the mediation of the Lord Jesus Christ. See the notes on chap. xiv. 13, 14.

s ver. 12.   17 ˢThese things I command you, that ye love one another.

This is but the repetition of the same precept we before had; unless we will understand it as a more special charge upon them, considered as ministers of the gospel; the mutual love of ministers being highly necessary for the good and peace of the church of God, over which God hath set them.

t 1 John 3. 1, 13.   18 ᵗIf the world hate you, ye know that it hated me before *it hated* you.

In the latter part of this chapter our Lord cometh to comfort those who were his true disciples, against that third trouble, from the prospect they had of that hatred which the world would pour out and execute upon them, as soon as he should be withdrawn from them. Hatred is rooted and originated in the heart, and is properly a displeasure that the mind taketh at a person, which, fermenting and boiling in the mind, breeds an abhorrence of that person, anger, and malice, and a desire to do him mischief, and root him out; and then breaks out at the lips, by lying, slanders, calumnies, cursings, wishing of evil, &c.; and is executed by the hands, doing to such persons all the harm and mischief within the power of him that hateth: all this is to be understood under the general term *hate*. By *the world* here must be meant wicked men, in opposition to good men, who are often in Scripture called *the world*, because they are of the earth, earthly; they relish and savour nothing but worldly things, and pursue nothing but worldly designs. Against this our Saviour comforts them; first by telling them, that this part of the world hated him before it hated them, which must needs be so, because they hated them as his disciples, and for that very reason.

u 1 John 4. 5. 19 ᵘIf ye were of the world, the world
x ch. 17. 14.   would love his own: but ˣbecause ye are not of the world, but I have chosen you out of the world, therefore the world hateth you.

Men and women may be in the world, yet not of the world. *Of the world* here signifies carnal men, such as are like to the men of the world in their studies, designs, counsels, affections; as *of the devil*, and *of God*, signifies, chap. viii. 44, 47. If you had affections, lusts, and dispositions like them, and drove no other designs than they drive, you might expect, that as it is of the nature of all men to love such as are like to them in manners and studies; so they would love you, take a delight in you, be kind to you, and do you all offices of love: but because you are not of such tempers, dispositions, and inclinations; but that I, having chosen you out of the world, have given you new hearts, new frames and dispositions, quite contrary to theirs; therefore the world, disliking you, and seeing that your principles are quite opposite to theirs, abhor and hate you, and will be ready to do you all that evil and mischief, which is the product of a rooted hatred and malice in the heart. This is a second argument by which our Lord comforts them. It is drawn from the cause and root of that hatred which they would meet with: it was not for their faults or sins, but because they were the objects of Christ's love, which being also shed abroad in their hearts by the Holy Ghost, produced again in them holy affections and dispositions, making them wholly unlike to men in the world.

20 Remember the word that I said unto you, ʸThe servant is not greater than his lord. If they have persecuted me, they will also persecute you; ᶻif they have kept my saying, they will keep your's also.   y Mat. 10. 24. Luke 6. 40. ch. 13. 16.
                                               z Ezek. 3. 7.

The word that I said unto you, chap. xiii. 16, to press you to humility, and a mutual serving of one another in love; and which I spake to you, Matt. x. 24, when I first sent you out; and I spake it then to you upon the very same account that I now speak it. You that are my servants cannot look to fare better with the world than I that am your Master; you know they have hated me, you must expect they should persecute you: if there be any of them whose hearts God shall incline to keep my sayings, they will also keep your words, which are but my sayings explained to them, and further pressed upon them.

21 But ᵃall these things will they do unto you for my name's sake, because they know not him that sent me.   a Matt. 10. 22. & 24. 9. ch. 16. 3.

For my name's sake here signifies no more than for my sake, as Matt. x. 22; for your preaching, owning, and professing me and my gospel. And this they would not do, if they had any true knowledge of faith in or love for him that sent me: for knowing, (as hath been often said,) in holy writ, and particularly in this Gospel, signifieth not the bare comprehension of the object by our understanding, but such a comprehension of it as is operative and efficacious to the bringing forth of all such effects as are proper to such a knowledge and comprehension. So as this text containeth two arguments more to arm them against the hatred of the world: the first, from the honourableness of the cause, for Christ's name's sake; the second, from the ignorance and blindness of the persons.

22 ᵇIf I had not come and spoken unto them, they had not had sin: ᶜbut now they have no ‖ cloke for their sin.   b ch. 9. 41.
                                               c Rom. 1. 20. Jam. 4. 17.
                                               ‖ Or, *excuse*.

They had not had this particular sin, of not knowing him that sent me; or they had not had such degrees of sin as they now have; or they had had more to say in excuse, or for a cover for their sin. Ignorance of the will of God will not excuse sinners wholly, but it will excuse them in part. And this last seemeth to be the sense of the words by the latter part of the verse, because it is opposed to a having no cloak nor excuse for their sin. If Christ had not come in his incarnation, in his preaching the gospel, &c., they could not have been guilty of that hatred and malice which they showed against him, which was their greatest guilt; and they would have had this to say, Lord, we knew not what Christ was, as Matt. xxv. 44: but now, saith our Saviour, they have no cloak, no colour, no pretence; I am come, I have revealed my Father's mind and will to them, yet they will not receive me; no, though I have done those works before them which no man ever did, nor could do but by a Divine power.

23 ᵈHe that hateth me hateth my Father also.   d 1 John 2. 23.

This agreeth with what we had, chap. v. 23. It is a common error of the world, that many in it would pretend to love God, while yet they are manifest haters of Christ and his gospel. Now, saith our Saviour, this is impossible; whosoever hateth him who is sent, hateth also him that sent him. God the Father and Christ are one, and no man can hate Christ, or be an enemy to Christ, but he must be an enemy to his Father: and as this is an aggravation of their sin, so it is a great argument of consolation to the disciples of Christ, that those who should be their enemies were such as were in reality God's enemies.

e ch. 3, 2. & 7. 31. & 9. 32.
24 If I had not done among them *the works which none other man did, they had not had sin: but now have they both seen and hated both me and my Father.

Our Saviour often appealeth to his works, both to own his mission from God, and also to prove the Jews inexcusable in their not receiving and embracing him; for which latter purpose he mentions them here, and saith, that he had done such works as no man did, and by his own power and virtue. Christ did some works such as we do not read that ever man did; as the multiplying of the loaves, the giving sight to those that were born blind, the healing of so many desperate diseases: and for such as he did which God had also given men a power to do, he did them in a quite different manner from that in which men did them. Elisha raised the Shunammite's child to life; but it was by prayer. Peter cured the lame man, Acts iii. 6; but it was *in the name of Jesus Christ of Nazareth*. We read indeed of Christ's praying at the raising of Lazarus; but his ordinary way was by his word of command, which was a quite different way than that used by those men by whom miracles had been wrought. Besides, it is manifest that the generality of the Jews did not look upon Christ as one sent from God, though many of them did: and admit that there had been nothing in the miracles wrought by Christ, more than Elijah, or Elisha, or the prophets had done; yet it had been sufficient for to have convinced them, that he acted by a Divine power, and must be sent and authorized by and from God to do what he did. Now saith our Saviour, If I had not done before their faces such works as no man could do but by a power derived from God, and some such as God never authorized men to do, their sin had been nothing to what now it is: but now they have understood that I am sent from my Father; and knowing this, yet going on in their most malicious designs against me, they both declare a hatred and malice against my Father who sent me, and me as sent by him.

25 But *this cometh to pass*, that the word might be fulfilled that is written
f Ps. 35. 19. & 69. 4.
in their law, 'They hated me without a cause.

The particle *that* here again denoteth not the final cause, but only the consequent; and the *law* here signifieth not strictly the law of Moses, but the whole Scripture, in which sense we have once and again met with the term. Saith our Saviour, This is no more than was prophesied of me by the prophet David; or no more than was fulfilled in me, being first done to David as my type: which also hath the force of another argument to uphold and encourage his disciples under their sufferings, that they were but the fulfilling of prophecies, no more than was foretold in holy writ.

g Luke 24. 49. ch. 14. 17, 26. & 16. 7, 13. Acts 2. 33.
26 ᵍBut when the Comforter is come, whom I will send unto you from the Father, *even* the Spirit of truth, which
h 1 John 5.6.
proceedeth from the Father, ʰhe shall testify of me:

Concerning the Holy Ghost as a Comforter we have spoken largely, chap. xiv. 16, 26; as also his mission from the Father and the Son, and in what sense he is called *the Spirit of truth*: see the notes on those verses. What proceeding from the Father is here meant, is questioned amongst divines: some understand it only of his coming out from the Father, and being poured out upon the disciples in the days of Pentecost: others understand it of the Holy Spirit's eternal proceeding. Those that interpret it of the first, urge the use of the Greek word, here used to signify God's manifestation of himself by some external sign, as they say the Septuagint useth the same word. They also urge the same use of a parallel word, chap. viii. 42; xvi. 28. But the generality of the best interpreters think it is best understood of the eternal procession of the Holy Spirit:
1. Because Christ here distinguisheth the Spirit's proceeding from the Father from his sending. 2. Having himself promised to send the Spirit, he seemeth further to describe him as proceeding from the Father. 3. The word here used is not any where used in the New Testament to signify a temporal mission. Some will say, But doth not the Spirit proceed from the Son? *Answ.* The Greek Church in latter ages hath denied this, and this is the principal text they rest on; but those churches that are more orthodox have constantly affirmed it: 1. Because he here saith he would send it. 2. Because he is often called *the Spirit of Christ*, Rom. viii. 9; Gal. iv. 6. 3. Because otherwise there were no personal relation between Christ and the Spirit. Our Saviour here having first said he would send him, here only nameth his proceeding from the Father; that they might not suspect his testimony, or think that he spake arrogantly. *He shall testify of me;* the Spirit, he saith, should testify of him, both by those gifts with which he was to fill the apostles, and to the hearts of God's people.

27 And ⁱye also shall bear witness,
i Luke 24.48. Acts 1. 8, 21, 22. & 2. 32. & 3. 15. & 4. 20, 33. & 5. 32. & 10. 39. & 13. 31. 1 Pet. 5. 1. 2 Pet. 1. 16. k Luke 1. 2. 1 John 1. 1, 2.
because ᵏye have been with me from the beginning.

He adds also, they should testify, &c.: the apostles, and their successors, by the preaching of the gospel; but particularly the apostles, Acts x. 39; 1 John i. 2, 3, being chosen witnesses, Acts x. 41. And they were competent witnesses, because they had been with Christ from the beginning of his public ministry. We shall find the testimony of his apostles and of the Holy Ghost both joined together, Acts v. 32.

CHAP. XVI

Christ warneth his disciples of their sufferings for his sake, 1—4. He comforteth them by a promise of the Holy Ghost, 5—15. He intimateth his death, resurrection, and ascension, telling them that their sorrow should soon be succeeded by joy, and that their prayers in his name would be accepted of the Father, 16—28. His disciples confess their faith in him; he foretelleth their desertion of him, and promiseth them peace in him amidst their tribulation in the world, 29—33.

THESE things have I spoken unto you,
a Matt. 11. 6. & 24. 10. & 26. 31.
that ye ªshould not be offended.

That is, that when you see these storms of persecution arise, and fall heavily upon you, they may not give you any occasion, or be any temptation to you, to desist from your duty, and be afraid or ashamed to own me, and the profession of my gospel. Evils unthought of we are not ordinarily prepared for, so as, being surprised by them, they the more sink us. *Offended* here therefore may signify, either immoderate trouble and affliction, or being tempted to any apostasy, or remission of duty.

2 ᵇThey shall put you out of the synagogues: yea, the time cometh, ᶜthat whosoever killeth you will think that he doeth God service.
b ch. 9. 22, 34. & 12. 42. c Acts 8. 1. & 9. 1. & 26. 9, 10, 11.

The term *synagogue*, as it is used often in Scripture to signify those places of public worship which they had in country towns and cities, is proper to the Jews; but as it signifieth an assembly of people met together in any place, it as well agreeth to other people as to them. Our Lord here, in pursuit of the argument which he hath been upon from the 18th verse of the former chapter, forewarneth his disciples, that when he should be taken from them, the Jews first should excommunicate them as heretics, or schismatics: and I know not why what our Saviour here saith may not also be extended as a prophecy of what hath since been done, and is yet doing, under the tyranny of the pope. As also the latter clause, which, though at first applicable to the Jews, who stoned Stephen upon a charge of blasphemy, in which it is apparent that they thought they did God good service, and doubtless slew many others; yet certainly it also referred to others, even as many as shall do the same thing to the end of the world.

3 And ᵈthese things will they do unto you, because they have not known the Father, nor me.
d ch. 15. 21. Rom. 10. 2. 1 Cor. 2. 8. 1 Tim. 1. 13.

This is but what our Lord said as to his Father, ver. 21 of the former chapter, (see the notes on that verse,) and teacheth us, that all persecutions of good men speak in persecutors an ignorance both of God the Father and of Christ; and whoever they are that continue in such ignorance under the light of the gospel, though they be baptized, and make never so great a profession of religion, yet will be under daily temptations to turn persecutors; for ignorance is here made the cause of persecution. And it is some alleviation of trouble to God's suffering people, to consider that the persons that are the cause of their sufferings neither know God the Father, nor Jesus Christ; and it is no wonder, if they know not God, that they will not know, love, nor approve of them.

e ch. 13. 19. & 14. 29.

4 But ᵉthese things have I told you, that when the time shall come, ye may remember that I told you of them. And

f See Matt. 9. 15.

ᶠthese things I said not unto you at the beginning, because I was with you.

Whatsoever I have discovered to you formerly, of my going to my Father, the coming of the Holy Ghost, your sufferings from the world, I have told you of before; you will see that they will most certainly come to pass: then you will remember what I have said unto you; and I have told you them on purpose that you may remember them, and thereby know, that although I am in the form of a man, yet I also am God blessed for ever, and did know things that should afterward come to pass, and could tell you the truth about them. And having been with you, I have not from the first of your converse with me told you these things; that is, those which relate to the world's dealing with you (which he had told them, Matt. x. 16, &c., but that was after some good while's converse with them); nor yet had he spoken to them at first about his death, resurrection, and ascension, because he was with them, and to stay with them some time, during which time he bare the brunt of all; the whole hatred of the Jews was poured out upon him: and for those other things relating to his death, and ascension, and the sending of the Spirit, he, who taught his disciples as they were able to bear them, Mark iv. 33, had concealed these things till by his other doctrine he had prepared them to receive this revelation, and there was a necessity of his relieving them against his bodily absence, by the promise of that other Comforter the Holy Ghost.

g ver. 10, 16. ch. 7. 33. & 13. 3. &14. 28.

5 But now ᵍI go my way to him that sent me; and none of you asketh me, Whither goest thou?

Though I did not tell you this from the beginning, for many wise reasons; yet I now tell you, that I must die, but shall rise again from the dead, and go to my Father who sent me into the world to finish that work which I now have done, and so am returning from whence I came. And though indeed some of you have cursorily asked me whither I go, (as Peter, chap. xiii. 36,) yet none of you seem to understand, or so seriously as you ought to inquire, whither I go, or so much to be busied in the thoughts of that.

h ver. 22. ch. 14. 1.

6 But because I have said these things unto you, ʰsorrow hath filled your heart.

But all your thoughts are taken up about yourselves, what you shall do for want of my bodily presence; and sorrow for that hath so overwhelmed your hearts, that you cannot enough deliberate with yourselves, as to consider either mine or your own advantages, from my death, resurrection, and ascension.

7 Nevertheless I tell you the truth; It is expedient for you that I go away:

i ch. 7. 39. & 14. 16, 26. & 15. 26. k Acts 2.33. Eph. 4. 8.

for if I go not away, ⁱthe Comforter will not come unto you; but ᵏif I depart, I will send him unto you.

He doth not say it was expedient for him, though this was truth; for his human nature was not till his ascension glorified, as afterward, chap. xvii. 5; but he saith it was expedient for them. The saints may desire a dissolution, but it is for their own advantage, Phil. i. 23. Christ desires it for their advantage; because the Holy Spirit could not come upon them (as in the days of Pentecost) until he by his death had made reconciliation for iniquity; and God had so ordered the counsels of eternity, that Christ should first die, rise again, and ascend into heaven, and then he would pour out his Spirit upon all flesh, as one eminent fruit of Christ's meritorious death and passion, Acts ii. 32, 33; Eph. iv. 11. We are not able to give certain reasons of the counsels of God; but the reasonableness of them in this very particular may easily be concluded: that the sending of the Spirit might appear to be the fruit of Christ's death: that the Messiah's influence upon the sending of him jointly with the Father, might appear; for he was to be sent from Christ glorified, chap. vii. 39: that the Spirit might glorify Christ, as we have it, ver. 14; for (saith that verse) *He shall receive of mine, and shall show it unto you:* and that the world might better understand the mystery of the Trinity. The Father was by all owned to be in heaven. The Son ascended up to heaven in the presence of many witnesses. The Spirit descended from heaven with great majesty and glory, as may be read. Acts ii. 2, 3.

8 And when he is come, he will ‖reprove the world of sin, and of righteousness, and of judgment:

‖ Or, convince.

When the Holy Spirit is come in the days of Pentecost, he, by his inward operation in men's hearts, and by his gifts bestowed upon you that are his apostles, *will reprove the world*. By *the world* here, may be meant all men and women, as it is used in some texts; neither is the operation of the Spirit here mentioned to be restrained to carnal and wicked men. The word translated *reprove*, 1. Lets us know, that the Holy Ghost is here mentioned, not in the notion mentioned chap. xiv. 16, as a *Comforter*, but in the larger notion, (there mentioned,) as an Advocate; which possibly had been a better translation of it, ver. 7, than *Comforter*, as we translate it; for it is not the proper work of the Spirit considered as a Comforter to reprove, but it is proper enough to the notion of an Advocate to do it. The word here translated *reprove* doth often so signify, and is so translated, Luke iii. 19; chap. iii. 20; Eph. v. 11, 13. It signifieth real rebukes, Heb. xii. 5; Rev. iii. 19. But it also signifieth to convince, John viii. 9, 46; 1 Cor. xiv. 24; 2 Tim. iv. 2; Tit. i. 9; and in several other texts. Yet it is one thing to convince the understanding and judgment; another thing to prevail upon the will, by reason of the total corruption of our souls; so that we will not embrace what we confess is truth, nor do what we know is best; but, through the stubbornness of our will, we resist the light and conviction of our understandings. The Holy Spirit is here promised, not only (as before) to lead men into truth, by a work of illumination, but to bow the hearts and wills of some in the world, to the embracing of it, and living up to it, while others yet remain without excuse. The things of which the Spirit is promised to convince the world, are *sin, righteousness, and judgment*, which are further opened in the following verses.

9 ¹Of sin, because they believe not on me;

1 Acts 2. 22, —37.

Here may arise some doubt, whether these words import that the Holy Ghost should convince the world of sin in general, or of that particular sin of not believing on the Lord Jesus Christ: the first seemeth best to agree with the 8th verse, where convincing of sin is mentioned, without the addition which we have here; and it also best agreeth with the effect of the Spirit, for the Holy Spirit doth not convince the world of one sin only. The second seemeth to be favoured by the addition of those words, *because they believe not on me;* which yet may be understood only as a particular great instance of sin, of which the Spirit convinceth the world. It was the great sin of that age, that, though Christ was come into the world, and had given such manifest evidence that he was sent of his Father, yet the generality of the men and women in that part of the world into which he was come, would not receive and embrace him as the true Messiah. Now, saith our Saviour, when I am gone to my Father, I will send the Spirit, and he, by his gifts given to my apostles, shall so convince a great part of the world, that they shall have nothing to say, but be wholly inexcusable in their not receiving me as the true

Messiah and Saviour of the world. Others he shall, by his inward influence upon their hearts, so convince of sin in not believing on me, that they shall believe on me, and be saved.

m Acts 2. 32.
n ch. 3. 14.
& 5. 32.

10 ᵐ Of righteousness, ⁿbecause I go to my Father, and ye see me no more ;

A second thing of which the Spirit is promised to convince the world, is *righteousness*, by which all interpreters agree is meant the righteousness of Christ. Only some would have it to be understood of Christ's personal righteousness, which is inherent in him ; upon which account he is called the *just One*, the *righteous One*, &c. Then the sense is this : The Jews now say I have a devil, and cast out devils by Beelzebub ; they accuse me as an impostor and seducer, call me a friend of publicans and sinners ; but when the Holy Spirit which I will send shall come, he shall convince the world that I was a just and righteous person, and not such a one as they have vilely represented me : which was fulfilled in a great measure, Acts ii., iii., when so many were converted and joined to the church. 2. But the best interpreters understand it of that righteousness of Christ which is communicated to men in justification, of which so much is spoken in holy writ, Isa. liii. 11 ; lvi. 1 ; Jer. xxiii. 6 ; Dan. ix. 24 ; and in many other texts : so as the Spirit is here promised as instructing the world in that true righteousness by which a soul can be justified ; and therein both correcting the errors of the pagan world, who thought the light of nature enough to show them the way to heaven ; and also of the Jewish world, who thought the righteousness of the law sufficient ; by showing them, that no righteousness would do it but the righteousness of Christ, reckoned unto them for righteousness, and apprehended by faith. Christ's going to his Father, did both evidence him to be a just and righteous person, however wicked men in the world had represented and traduced him, for his Father would not have received him if he had not been such a person ; and also evidence that, as was prophesied of the Messias, Dan. ix. 24, he had finished *the transgression*, made *an end of sin*, made *reconciliation for iniquity*, and brought in *everlasting righteousness* : for it could not be imagined, that he should have an access to his Father before he had finished the work which his Father had given him to do, chap. xvii. 4. *And* (saith our Saviour) *ye see me no more ;* that is, after my ascension you shall see me no more ; or after my death you shall see me no more, to have any such ordinary converse with me as hitherto you have had : for I shall not ascend to return again to you ; but to sit at the right hand of my Father, till I return again to the last judgment.

o Acts 26. 18.
p Luke 10. 18. ch. 12. 31.
Eph. 2. 2.
Col. 2. 15. Heb. 2. 14.

11 ᵒOf judgment, because ᵖthe prince of this world is judged.

The third thing to convince the world of which the Spirit is promised, is *judgment*. There is a great variety amongst interpreters in their senses, what is to be understood by judgment in this text. Mr. Calvin thinks that by it is to be understood a right order of things : the devil, who is the prince of the world, had made a great disorder and confusion in the world ; Christ, having judged him, brought in a reformation, and restored things into order again. Others understand the term, of that judicial power which Christ obtained after his ascension into heaven, when the Lord said unto him, *Sit thou at my right hand, until I make thine enemies thy footstool*, Psal. cx. 1 ; Acts ii. 34, 35. Others understand it of that government which Christ exerciseth over and upon the souls of his people, once delivered out of the power of Satan by the obedience of Christ's death. Others understand it of that *all power* given to Christ *in heaven and earth*, mentioned Matt. xxviii. 18 ; Phil. ii. 9, 10. Others understand it of that perverse and corrupt judgment which the world exercised upon Christ and his apostles. Others understand it of the judgment of condemnation : the world should by the Spirit be convinced, that they lay in wickedness, and exposed to eternal condemnation, when they should see their father the devil, who arrogates to himself the title of the prince of the world, and exerciseth a tyranny over them, cast out, and overcome.

q Mark 4. 33.
1 Cor. 3. 2.
Heb. 5. 12.

12 I have yet many things to say unto you, ᑫbut ye cannot bear them now.

Not any new articles of doctrine or faith, for, chap. xv. 15, he had told them that he had made known unto them all things which he had heard of the Father of that nature ; but some things (probably) which concerned them with reference to their office as apostles, the constitution, state, and government of the church : *but*, saith he, *ye cannot bear them now ;* in regard of their passion, or rather of their more imperfect state.

13 Howbeit when he, ʳthe Spirit of truth, is come, ˢhe will guide you into all truth : for he shall not speak of himself ; but whatsoever he shall hear, *that* shall he speak : and he will shew you things to come.

r ch. 14. 17. & 15. 26.
s ch. 14. 26.
1 John 2. 20, 27.

The word which we here translate *guide*, ὁδηγήσει, is a word of great emphasis ; it strictly signifieth to be a guide of the way, not only to discover truth as the object of the understanding, but the bowing of the will to the obedience of it. It is said, that the Spirit should *guide* the apostles *into all truth ;* that is, all necessary truth, whatsoever Christ had revealed to them, because in their present state they were not able to bear it ; whatsoever should be fit for them to know, in order to their planting, ordering, and governing the church of God, which Christ had not, while he was with them, acquainted them with ; and people were to expect from the apostles, upon whom the Spirit should come in the days of Pentecost, and so influence them, that in those things they should not be at a loss to understand the will of God, which they should communicate unto others. And they ought to look upon what the apostles so revealed, as the mind of Christ ; for the Holy Spirit should *not speak* merely *of himself*, but as from Christ, with whom he was essentially one ; as also from the Father : whatsoever the Father and the Son willed he should communicate, that he should reveal to the apostles : and he shall reveal to you *things* that are *to come*, being in you the Spirit of prophecy. The apostles in their Epistles, and in the book of Revelation, showed not indeed all things, but many things which were and are to come to pass.

14 He shall glorify me : for he shall receive of mine, and shall shew *it* unto you.

That is, he shall make me famous in the world ; as by the extraordinary gifts which he shall dispense and give out, so particularly by showing you things to come : for he shall guide and lead you into no other truth, but that which I have revealed, or which it is my will he should make known and reveal.

15 ᵗAll things that the Father hath are mine : therefore said I, that he shall take of mine, and shew *it* unto you.

t Mat. 11. 27. ch. 3. 35. & 13. 3. & 17. 10.

All the Divine essence, wisdom, power, which is in the Father, are mine ; I am, in all things that concern the Deity, one and equal with the Father ; and that was the reason that I said that he should *take of mine, and show it to you ;* which is the same as if I had said, he shall take of my Father's, and shall show it to you ; for all that the Father hath is mine ; I and my Father are one in essence, wisdom, power, &c.

16 ᵘA little while, and ye shall not see me : and again, a little while, and ye shall see me, ʷbecause I go to the Father.

u ver. 10. ch. 7. 33. & 13. 33. & 14. 19.
w ver. 28. ch. 13. 3.

I must die, and so for two or three days you shall not see me ; but after that you shall see me again, when I shall be risen from the dead : but because of the last words, *because I go to the Father*, which seem to give a reason of the first clause ; possibly by the *little while* first mentioned, our Saviour means the whole time from the speaking of those words to his ascension into heaven, for all that time was not more than six weeks ; and by the *little while* mentioned in the latter part of the verse, our Saviour intends the whole time from his ascension until his coming to judgment : and so the reason is proper which is added, *because I go unto the Father ;* for being so ascended, and sat down at the right hand of God, we are told that there he must sit, till God hath made all his enemies his footstool ; and by the apostle, that the last enemy to be destroyed is death ; and, Acts iii. 21, *Whom the heaven must receive until the times of restitution of all things, which God hath spoken by the mouth of all his holy prophets since the world began*

17 Then said *some* of his disciples among themselves, What is this that he saith unto us, A little while, and ye shall not see me: and again, a little while, and ye shall see me: and, Because I go to the Father?

Christ had used much the same expression to the Jews, chap. vii. 33, *Yet a little while I am with you;* he had spoken the same to his disciples, chap. xiii. 33; yet it is plain from this verse, that his disciples did not understand him. What need the best of us have of the illuminations of the blessed Spirit, rightly to conceive of and understand spiritual things! These doctrines of his death, resurrection, and ascension, and coming to judgment, our Lord had inculcated to his disciples, not only in the two texts aforementioned, but also chap. viii. 21; xii. 33, 36; xiv. 2, 4, 12, 28; and in this chapter, ver. 5, 7.

18 They said therefore, What is this that he saith, A little while? we cannot tell what he saith.

Still they do not understand what he meant. Who shall hereafter arrogate to man's reason or understanding a power to comprehend spiritual mysteries? Had not the disciples reasonable souls? will any say they had no mind to understand them? certainly none can say so. Some lay the fault of the disciples not understanding these things upon the obscurity of our Saviour's phrase, and his parabolical expression of them, others, in their ignorance of our Saviour's resurrection from the dead; others, in their not understanding the circumstance of time: but certainly it is best imputed to the disciples' inability to conceive of these things, and the prejudices of their national error concerning the temporal kingdom of the Messias. Let it lie where it will, the weakness of the disciples may be reasonably conceived not to be greater than is incident to the best of men; and if they were so dull of hearing and understanding, we may reasonably conceive that we are not free from the like impotency and infirmity.

19 Now Jesus knew that they were desirous to ask him, and said unto them, Do ye inquire among yourselves of that I said, A little while, and ye shall not see me: and again, a little while, and ye shall see me?

In the terms of this verse there is nothing difficult, but in the matter of it there is much instructive. We learn from hence, 1. That though good men may as to some points be ignorant as to the mind and will of God, yet they will be desirous of further instruction in it. To be willingly and contentedly ignorant, is not consistent with a root of saving grace. 2. Christ knows the desires of our hearts, before they are made known to him by the words of our lips; but yet it will not follow, that we may satisfy ourselves with inward, secret desires, without making them known by our lips; for God requireth the calves of our lips, as well as the desires and groans of our inward man. 3. Christ is very ready to teach those whose hearts he seeth desirous to learn; therefore he saith, *Do ye inquire among yourselves?* &c. Are you inquisitive? I am ready to teach and to instruct you.

20 Verily, verily, I say unto you, That ye shall weep and lament, but the world shall rejoice: and ye shall be sorrowful, but your sorrow shall be turned into joy.

Our Saviour's reply is no literal answer to their question, or exposition of the term which appeared so difficult to them to understand; but yet it is a substantial answer, by which he lets them know, that he should be absent from them for some time, which time would be to them a time of mourning and sadness, as he had before told them; that when the Bridegroom should be taken from them, then they should mourn; that that time would be to the wicked part of the world a time of mirth and jollity: but their sorrow should be turned into joy when they should see him again, both upon his resurrection, and in the general resurrection. The time of this life is the worldling's hour, and for the most part *the power of darkness* to such as love and fear God; but as the worldling's joy shall at last be turned into sorrow, (they *compass themselves about with sparks,* but they shall at last *lie down in sorrow,* Isa. l. 11,) so the godly man's sorrow shall be turned into joy: Christ will say to the good servant, *Enter thou into the joy of thy Lord,* Matt. xxv. 23.

21 ˣA woman when she is in travail hath sorrow, because her hour is come: but as soon as she is delivered of the child, she remembereth no more the anguish, for joy that a man is born into the world. ˣ Is. 26. 17.

Our Lord compareth the state of the church in this life, and more especially in those first and most furious times, to the state of a woman that is big with child, and in her travail; when, he saith, she hath sorrow, that is, great pain, because God, when he cursed the woman for her transgression, made this her portion, Gen. iii. 16, *I will greatly multiply thy sorrow and thy conception; in sorrow thou shalt bring forth children;* and when her weeks are fulfilled, her hour is come to feel the effect of this curse, the fruit of the first woman's transgression: but no sooner is she delivered of a child, but she forgetteth all her throes and pains, for joy of a child born into the world. Such (saith our Saviour to his disciples) is your state; you are as a woman in travail; so will all those that believe in me be, to the end of the world.

22 ʸAnd ye now therefore have sorrow: but I will see you again, and ᶻyour heart shall rejoice, and your joy no man taketh from you.
ʸ ver. 6. ᶻ Luke 24. 41, 52. ch. 14. 1, 27. & 20. 20. Acts 2. 46. & 13. 52. 1 Pet. 1. 8.

The whole church, Rev. xii. 1, 2, is compared to a woman with child, crying, travailing in birth, and pained to be delivered. During this time of your travail you must have sorrow. *All those that will live godly in Christ Jesus must suffer persecution,* 2 Tim. iii. 12. *It is appointed* for all *men once to die,* Heb. ix. 27. It is appointed for God's people (especially under some periods of time) to be dying daily, *killed all the day long,* as the apostle expresseth the state of Christians in his time, Rom. viii. 36, quoting Psal. xliv. 22, which showeth the state of the church in the Old Testament to have been the same. But (saith our Saviour) it is but as the hour of the woman's travail; it will be sharp, very sharp, but it shall be short; for *I will see you again, and* then *your heart shall rejoice;* which cannot be understood of Christ's seeing them again after his resurrection; for before that time we read of few or no sufferings of the apostles or other disciples. It must therefore be understood, either of the visitation of his Spirit, filling their hearts with joy and peace, or the visitation of his providence: or rather, of Christ's coming to the last judgment, when all that have believed in Christ shall see him with joy unspeakable; and then all tears shall be wiped away from their eyes, and they shall enter into the joy of their Lord, and sigh and sorrow no more, nor shall it be in the power of all their enemies to deprive them of their joy.

23 And in that day ye shall ask me nothing. ᵃVerily, verily, I say unto you, Whatsoever ye shall ask the Father in my name, he will give *it* you. ᵃ Matt. 7. 7. ch. 14. 13. & 15. 16.

That the day here spoken of is that before mentioned, ver. 22, when Christ promised to see them again, and that their hearts should rejoice, is without question; but what that day is (as we before showed) is not so well agreed: some understand it of the general resurrection, when Christ shall come to judgment, when all asking for satisfaction as to any thing of which we doubt shall cease; and this seemeth at first the plainest sense: You shall then be made perfect; as you shall want nothing, so you shall ask nothing. But because of the following words, which plainly refer to the time of this life, others distinguish concerning asking, and by asking here understand, asking by way of question, for further information, not by way of prayer for supply: and indeed the Greek word enforceth that sense; for it is not αἰτήσετε, which signifieth to ask or beg, as in prayer; but ἐρωτήσετε, which signifieth to ask for a resolution in case of doubting. Now though it be true, that in the day of judgment, when we shall see Christ as he is, and know God as we are known, we shall have no occasion to ask any questions; yet because the following words speak of an asking in prayer, which is proper to this life, it should seem that the day here mentioned is some time before the last judgment: what that should be, is the question. It is certainly best understood of the time after the effusion or pouring out of the Spirit in the days of Pentecost; of which time it was prophesied by Joel, chap. ii. 28, that God would *pour out his Spirit on all flesh;* their *sons and* their *daughters* should *prophesy,* their *old men* should *dream dreams,* and their *young men* should *see visions,* Acts ii. 17; and to which time Isaiah had a respect in his prophecy, chap. xi. 9, that *the earth* should *be full of the knowledge of the Lord, as the waters cover the sea.* So as these words, *ye shall ask me nothing in that day,* signify the great light that should, upon the coming down of the Holy Spirit, shine in upon their souls, so that they should no longer have any such doubts as they now had; and sound much the same thing that we have, 1 John ii. 27, *But the anointing* (by which is meant the Holy Spirit) *which ye have received of him abideth in you, and ye need not that any man teach you; but as the same anointing teacheth you of all things.* We must not too rigidly interpret our Saviour's words here, as if they were a promise of such a state in this life, when either the present or succeeding disciples of Christ should be so filled with knowledge, as they should have no further doubts, or need not to ask any thing of Christ, that is, to be resolved in any thing. Our Saviour here speaketh only comparatively, to signify the great difference there would be as to knowledge, betwixt them in their present state, and what should be after the pouring out of the Holy Spirit: they should then fully understand what Christ meant by his saying, *A little while, and ye shall not see me: and again, a little while, and ye shall see me, because I go to the Father:* and should not need ask him questions about that, or many other things which they were now at a loss about: as Jer. xxxi. 34, where the prophet saith, *They shall teach no more every man his neighbour, and every man his brother, saying, Know the Lord: for they shall all know me, from the least to the greatest.* It must not be interpreted (as some have done) to signify a needlessness of ministerial teaching; so neither must this text be interpreted to signify a needlessness of an inquiry of Christ for further satisfaction; but only as signifying the vast difference in the degrees of knowledge, after the Holy Spirit should be poured forth, from what was even in the best men before that time. In the latter part of the text another word is used, it is not ἐρωτήσετε, but αἰτήσετε. Our Saviour there plainly speaketh of their asking in prayer; and the promise is, that to supply the defects of their knowledge, and the want of his personal instruction, they should obtain by prayer from the Father all that was necessary for their discharge of the prophetical office, Matt. vii. 7; chap. xv. 7; xvi. 24. See the notes on those texts.

24 Hitherto have ye asked nothing in my name: ask, and ye shall receive, ᵇthat your joy may be full. ᵇch. 15. 11.

All the prayers of believers under the Old Testament were accepted upon the account of the Mediator, who was typified by the temple, and the ark, where their solemn worship was performed by Divine appointment; but the explicit naming of him was not usual in their requests. Indeed the prophet Daniel enforced his requests for the Lord's sake, which may peculiarly respect the Messias, the promised Mediator. Our Saviour, in the form of prayer dictated to his disciples, gave no direction of addressing themselves to God in his name. But now he was ready to accomplish the will of his Father, by offering himself as an expiatory sacrifice for sin, and thereby reconciling God to them; and the prevalency of his intercession depending upon his meritorious, all-sufficient sufferings, he directs and encourages them to pray with a humble confidence in his name for all the blessings they stand in need of. And it is matter of exceeding joy, that notwithstanding their unworthiness of the least favours, yet they are assured of obtaining their petitions offered up in his name; for the Father was so pleased with his voluntary obedience to the death of the cross, that no blessing is so good or great, but he most willingly bestows for his sake to all humble supplicants.

25 These things have I spoken unto you in ‖ proverbs: but the time cometh, when I shall no more speak unto you in ‖ proverbs, but I shall shew you plainly of the Father. ‖ Or, *parables.* ‖ Or, *parables.*

That by *proverbs* is meant any dark sayings, is plain from the opposition in the text of that term *plainly.* Christ had spoken, though not all things, yet many things to them in dark phrases, and under many figurative expressions; *but* (saith he) *the time cometh, when I shall show you plainly of the Father:* that time is either Christ's second coming, or after the pouring out of the Spirit, which latter is most probably what our Saviour doth here intend, because of those great measures of knowledge which at and after that time were given out. He had before given to his disciples *to know the mysteries of the kingdom of heaven,* far beyond others, Matt. xiii. 11; but yet it appears by chap. xiv., and many other texts, that they had a very confused and imperfect knowledge of the Trinity, and Christ's oneness with the Father, and their mutual personal relation one to another.

26 ᶜAt that day ye shall ask in my name: and I say not unto you, that I will pray the Father for you: ᶜver. 23.

When the Spirit shall come, then you shall fully and clearly understand how to put up your prayers to the Father in my name: hitherto have you done it imperfectly, not fully understanding what you did; but when I shall have poured out my Spirit, then you shall fully understand what it is to pray in my name, and you shall accordingly do it. He doth not deny that he would ask the Father; for the Scripture elsewhere plainly expresseth it, Rom. viii. 34; Heb. vii. 25; but he only tells them, that he said not so to them; the reason of which he tells us in the next words.

27 ᵈFor the Father himself loveth you, because ye have loved me, and ᵉhave believed that I came out from God. ᵈch. 14. 21, 23. ᵉver. 30, ch. 3. 13. & 17. 8.

I need not tell you (to beget in you a confidence that your prayers should be heard) that I will pray to the Father for you; for my Father himself hath such a love for you, that you may from thence alone conclude that he will hear you. And though my Father's love to you be an everlasting love, which hath no cause in the creature; yet as to the manifestations of my Father's love, they are further drawn forth by the love which he seeth you bear to me, and by your receiving me, who am the Messiah, and came forth from God, to perform the work of man's redemption.

28 ᶠI came forth from the Father, and am come into the world: again, I leave the world, and go to the Father. ᶠch. 13. 3.

Though I be in the world, yet my original is not from the world; I am one with my Father, equal with him, God blessed for ever. I came forth from him, as one sent in the fulness of time, to discharge the office of the Messias; the world, the place so called, was neither my original, nor yet is my home. I am presently leaving the world again, and going to my Father.

29 His disciples said unto him, Lo, now speakest thou plainly, and speakest no ‖ proverb. ‖ Or, *parable.*

Our Saviour having now plainly told them that he was leaving the world, put an end to their inquiries whither he was going, and satisfied them that in his former expressions of going away, not for a while to be seen, he meant no earthly motion: this they confess had no obscurity at all in it; These words are so intelligible, that there is no reason for any of us to ask thee any thing about the sense of them.

30 Now are we sure that ᵍthou knowest all things, and needest not that any man should ask thee: by this ʰwe believe that thou camest forth from God. ᵍch. 21. 17. ʰver. 27. ch. 17. 8.

This confirmeth us in that faith, or persuasion, which we before had, though it was in us but weak, that indeed thou art come forth from God.

31 Jesus answered them, Do ye now believe?

Some read the words, (not as a question,) You do now believe. It is well you believe at last, you had reason enough to have believed before this time.

32 ⁱBehold, the hour cometh, yea, is now come, that ye shall be scattered, ᵏevery man to ‖his own, and shall leave me alone: and ˡyet I am not alone, because the Father is with me.

Though you profess that now you do believe, you had need look to your faith; there is yet a trying time coming upon you, when your faith will waver, and you, who have been so long my followers, will leave me to shift for myself, and every one of you shift for yourselves: this came to pass presently after, Matt. xxvi. 56. Those who think they stand, had need take heed lest they fall; those who think their faith strongest, ought to be thinking with themselves, what they shall do, how they shall be able to stand, in a day of sharp trial. Many in a calm time appear to be professors and believers, who, when affliction and persecution ariseth for the gospel's sake, will fall away, and leave Christ alone. Yet (saith our Saviour) *I am not alone, because the Father is with me.* No man is alone who hath the presence of God with him. Christ knew that in all his sufferings he should have the presence and assistance of his heavenly Father.

33 These things I have spoken unto you, that ᵐin me ye might have peace. ⁿIn the world ye shall have tribulation: °but be of good cheer; ᵖI have overcome the world.

By *peace* here is not so much to be understood peace with God; which yet we have from Christ, and through Christ, according to Rom. v. 1, *Being justified by faith, we have peace with God through our Lord Jesus Christ;* nor yet peace of conscience, which is the copy of our peace with God; as a peace of mind, a quiet, serene, calm temper, which indeed is the effect of the other, as the cause: that you might not be troubled and disturbed, neither for my sake, nor yet for your own. Though in the world ye meet with troubles, which you will certainly do, because the world hateth you, *be of good cheer*, (saith he,) *I have overcome the world;* where by *world* is to be understood, all temptations from it, whether from the flatteries or from the frowns and troubles of it. We are said to overcome the world, but we overcome it as soldiers, fighting under Christ, who is the Captain of our salvation, and his victory is our victory, 1 John iv. 4; v. 4, 5. Christ overcame the prince of the world, and cast him out, as we heard before; and he hath overcome sin, and we in him, in the midst of all tribulations, *are more than conquerors through him that loved us*, Rom. viii. 37.

This was our Saviour's last sermon which we have upon sacred record in holy writ.

CHAP. XVII

Christ prayeth to his Father to glorify him, 1—5; *and to preserve his apostles in unity of faith,* 6—14, *and from all evil,* 15, 16; *and to sanctify them with the word of truth,* 17—19; *and for the perfect union of all believers, and their admission to a share of his glory in heaven,* 20—26.

THESE words spake Jesus, and lifted up his eyes to heaven, and said, Father, ᵃthe hour is come; glorify thy Son, that thy Son also may glorify thee:

When our Lord had finished his discourses, of which we have had a large account in chap. xiv.—xvi., he goes to prayer. As he taught us when we pray to direct our petitions to the Father, so in this he setteth us an example; and before he speaketh it is said he *lifted up his eyes to heaven*, as his Father's mansion-house, who, though he filleth heaven and earth, yet doth in heaven most manifest his glory: and therefore, teaching us to pray, he commandeth us to say, *Our Father which art in heaven;* not exclusively, as if God were not on earth also; but eminently, as heaven is the place where he most gloriously manifests himself. Lifting up the eyes was a usual gesture in prayer, and but an indication of the soul's being lifted up, Psal. cxxi. 1; cxxiii. 1; yet no necessary gesture, for we shall at another time find our Saviour falling upon his face when he prayed, Matt. xxvi. 39; Mark xiv. 35. The lifting up of the soul to God, wherein the main and spiritual part of prayer lies, doth not necessarily require the lifting up of the eyes. The publican cast down his eyes upon the earth, in the sense of his unworthiness. Our Lord lifted up his eyes, and said, *Father, the hour is come;* that is, the hour of my passion, the time wherein thou hast determined that I should die; now make thy Son glorious, by raising me from the dead, by taking me up to heaven, or by giving me assistance from thee to do the work which I have to do, to drink this bitter cup: that so I, being risen again from the dead, and ascending up to heaven, may make thy name famous by publishing thy justice, goodness, and truth, upon the preaching of the gospel to all nations.

2 ᵇAs thou hast given him power over all flesh, that he should give eternal life to as many ᶜas thou hast given him.

I see no reason for any to contend here, that by *all flesh* the elect only, who shall be eternally saved, are to be understood; Christ's power undoubtedly extendeth further than to the elect, though to them only for salvation; he hath a power over reprobates and unbelievers to condemn them, as well as over his elect, to bring them to eternal life and salvation. The former part of the text speaketh of the more general power and authority, by which the Father had already made Christ glorious; putting all things under his feet, and causing all knees to bow down unto him; which are other phrases by which the same things are expressed, 1 Cor. xv. 27; Phil. ii. 10. This general power our Saviour executeth according to the counsels of God, with respect to their faith or unbelief. As to those given to Christ, that he should die in their stead, and with the price of his blood purchase eternal life for them; Christ executeth his power in giving them eternal life: under which notion (as appeareth from many other scriptures) is comprehended, not the end only, which is eternal life and happiness, but all the necessary means in order to that end; from whence we are to observe, that eternal life is a free gift, that the Son gives only to such as the Father hath given him by his eternal counsels; so that all shall not be saved; for the term *as many as*, &c., is plainly restrictive, and limits the gift to a certain number. And to examine our right to it, we need not ascend up into heaven, to search the rolls of the eternal counsels; for all whom the Father hath given him shall come unto him, and not only receive him as their High Priest, but give up themselves to be ruled and guided by him, by the efficacious working of the Spirit of his grace. By such a receiving of Christ, and giving up of ourselves to his conduct and government, we shall know whether we be of the number of those that are given to Christ; and till we find this, we have no reason to conclude it, but to fear and suspect the contrary.

3 And ᵈthis is life eternal, that they might know thee ᵉthe only true God, and Jesus Christ, ᶠwhom thou hast sent.

Those who deny the Divine nature of Christ, think they have a mighty argument from this text, where Christ, (as they say,) speaking to his Father, calleth him *the only true God.* But divines answer, that the term *only,* or alone, is not to be applied to *thee*, but to the term *God*; and the sense this, To know thee to be that God which is the only true God: and this appeareth from 1 John v. 20, where Christ is said to be the true God, which he could not be if the Father were the only true God, considered as another from the Son. The term *only,* or alone, is not exclusive of the other two Persons in the Trinity, but only of idols, the gods of the heathen, which are no gods; so 1 Tim. vi. 15, 16, and many other Scriptures: so Matt. xi. 27, where it is said, that *none knoweth the Son, but the Father; neither knoweth any the Father, save the Son;* where the negative doth not exclude the Holy Spirit. Besides, the term *alone* is in Scripture observed not always to exclude all others, as Mark vi. 47. Our Saviour saith, it is life eternal to know him who is the only true God, that is, it is the way to eternal life, which is an ordinary figure used in holy writ. He adds, *and Jesus Christ, whom thou hast sent;* by which he lets us know, that the Father cannot be savingly known, but in and by the Son. Knowing, in this verse, signifieth not the mere comprehending of God and of Christ in men's notions; but the receiving Christ, believing in him, loving and obeying him, &c.

g ch. 13. 31. & 14. 13.
h ch. 4. 34. & 5. 36. & 9. 3. & 19. 30.
i ch. 14. 31. & 15. 10.

4 ᵍI have glorified thee on the earth: ʰI have finished the work ⁱwhich thou gavest me to do.

I have glorified thee on the earth; by preaching the gospel, by living up to the rule of thy law, by the miracles which I have wrought. God could not be glorified by Christ, by the addition of any thing to his essential glory; only by manifesting to the world his Father's goodness, justice, mercy, truth, wisdom, and other of his attributes. One way by which he had glorified his Father, is expressed, viz. by finishing the work which he had given him in commission. But how could Christ say this, who had not yet died for the sins of men, which was the principal piece of his work? *Answ.* It was so nigh, that he speaks of it as already done: so, ver. 11, he saith. *I am no more in the world,* because he was to be so little a time in the world. Again, he speaks of what he was fully resolved to do, as if it were already done.

k ch. 1. 1, 2. & 10. 30. & 14. 9. Phil. 2. 6. Col. 1. 15, 17. Heb. 1. 3, 10.

5 And now, O Father, glorify thou me with thine own self with the glory ᵏwhich I had with thee before the world was.

Let the glory which, as to my Divine nature, I had with thee before the foundation of the world, be communicated also to my human nature, that my whole person may be made glorious. From hence is easily concluded, against those who deny the Godhead of Christ, that Christ was glorified with his Father before the world was, which he could not have been if he had not been eternal God. He here begs of his Father, that that glory might shine upon his person as Mediator.

l ver. 26.
22. 22.
m ver. 2,9,11. ch. 6. 37, 39. & 10. 29. & 15. 19.

6 ˡI have manifested thy name unto the men ᵐwhich thou gavest me out of the world: thine they were, and thou gavest them me; and they have kept thy word.

Here he openeth this former phrase, *I have glorified thee on the earth:* it was done by manifesting the Lord's name, proclaiming his goodness and mercy, publishing his will, making famous all whereby God can be made known: this Christ did both by his words and by his works. This he had done (as he saith) to all those whom the Father had given him; whom the Father had given him by an act of his eternal counsel, and by inclining their hearts to own and receive him when he came into the world. He tells his Father, that his they were, his chosen ones; and he had given them unto Christ, that he should redeem them with his blood, and take the care of their salvation: and he saith, When I came and revealed thy will unto them, they have not stubbornly and obstinately, as the generality of the Jews, shut their eyes against the light, and rebelled against thy will revealed; but they have heard, received, embraced, and obeyed thy word.

7 Now they have known that all things whatsoever thou hast given me are of thee.

They have thus far made proficiency in the doctrine which I have taught them; that though the Pharisees say, that I *cast out devils by Beelzebub the prince of devils,* yet they believe, and are persuaded, that the doctrine which I have taught them is from thee, and that it is by a Divine power that I have wrought those miracles which I have wrought; and so I have manifested thy name unto them, and they have received the manifestation and revelation of thy name unto them.

n ch. 8. 28. & 12. 49. & 14. 10.
o ver. 25, ch. 16. 27, 30.

8 For I have given unto them the words ⁿwhich thou gavest me; and they have received *them,* ᵒand have known surely that I came out from thee, and they have believed that thou didst send me.

Our Lord here doth both justify himself, and commend those whom in this former part of his prayer he is commending to his Father. He justifieth himself, that he had not delivered any thing to them but what he had from his Father; thereby teaching all those who claim the name of his ministers what is their duty, viz. to give to their hearers no word but what God hath given them. If Christ confined his discourses to words which his Father had given him, certainly we ought to do so also. We are not to speak what we list, nor what men would have us; we are tied up to God's word. He commendeth these his disciples, that they had *received them;* not only the sound of them in their ears, not only the notion of them in their understandings, but they had embraced and believed them; and had, from the force and authority of them, given credit to him as the true Messias, who *came out* and was sent from God. Though they were not yet come up to a perfect faith in him as the eternal Son of God, yet they believed him one that came from God, and was sent of God as the promised Messiah; which seemeth to have been that degree of faith which Christ most insisted upon as to his disciples, until by his resurrection from the dead he declared himself to be the Son of God with power; though all along this Gospel, his discourses,and the miracles which he wrought, had a particular tendency to prove himself one with the Father, and the eternal Son of God; and the disciples had some weak persuasion of this truth.

9 I pray for them: ᵖI pray not for the world, but for them which thou hast given me; for they are thine.

p 1 John 5. 19.

The world seemeth here to signify all mankind, for whom Christ in this place doth not pray; though some interpret it of reprobates, others of unbelievers. Christ afterward prayeth for the world, ver. 20; that is, for such who, though they at present were unbelievers, yet should be brought to believe by the apostles' ministry. But to teach us to distinguish in our prayer, our Saviour here distinguisheth, and prayeth for some things for his chosen ones, which he doth not pray for on the behalf of others: these he describeth to be such as his Father (whose they were) had given him, either by an eternal donation, or by working faith in them.

10 And all mine are thine, and ᑫthine are mine; and I am glorified in them.

q ch. 16. 15.

In the Greek the adjectives are of the neuter gender, so as the sense is not, All my friends, or all my disciples, are thine also; but, All my things are thine, and all thy things are mine; which is no more than he hath before often said. Christ and his Father have all things common, neither of them have any thing that is not the other's: they are one, and they agree in one; they have the same essence, the same will, the same attributes, the same friends. *And I am* (saith our Saviour) *glorified,* or made glorious, *in them,* by their owning, receiving, and embracing me, and accepting me as their Saviour. So as this verse containeth two arguments more, enforcing his petition on the behalf of his elect: 1. His Father's propriety in them, as well as his. 2. Their love to him, and the glory which redounded to him from their faith and holiness.

11 ʳAnd now I am no more in the world, but these are in the world, and I come to thee. Holy Father, ˢkeep through thine own name those whom thou hast given me, ᵗthat they may be one, ᵘas we *are.*

r ch. 13. 1. & 16. 28.
s 1 Pet. 1. 5. Jude 1.
t ver. 21, &c.
u ch. 10. 30.

The term *world* in this verse signifies not the men of the world, nor any particular party of them, (as it often signifies,) but the habitable part of the earth. Our Saviour saith he is *no more in the world,* because he was to continue on the earth but a very small time; *but* (saith he) *these* my disciples *are* like to abide *in the world* when I have left it; they will stand in need of this help, to be armed against all the temptations they will meet with from the world. I am coming to thee, therefore I commend them to thee, beseeching thee, that thou through thy power wouldst keep those, who, in giving themselves up to me, have also given themselves up to thee; let their owning thy name (which is as a strong tower, Prov. xviii. 10) keep them from all the temptations and dangers to which they will be exposed in the world, wherein they are to live and converse; *that they may be one*, one body, and in one Spirit; that they may own one Lord, one faith, one baptism, &c.; that they may be one in love and affection, *as we are*; in some proportion to that union which is betwixt thee and me, though not in an equality. This prayer of our Saviour's doth both oblige all those who in any sincerity own Christ, to study union both in opinion and affection; and also give us ground of hopes, that there is a time coming, when there shall be greater measure of it than we have seen in those miserably divided times wherein we have lived, and do yet live.

12 While I was with them in the world, *I kept them in thy name: those that thou gavest me I have kept, and ʸnone of them is lost, ᶻbut the son of perdition; ᵃthat the Scripture might be fulfilled.

Christ speaks here of himself as one who had already died, was risen, and ascended, though none of all these things were past, because they were so suddenly to come to pass. I have, (saith our Saviour,) for all the time that I have abode in the world, and conversed with them, *kept them in thy name*, i. e. in the steady owning and profession of thy truth; or (if we read it, through thy name) it signifieth through thy power, and the influence of thy grace. I have not so kept all that came to hear me, but all *those whom thou gavest me by the act of thy eternal counsel*; or *whom thou gavest me* to be my apostles: and none of them is proved an apostate, but *the son of perdition*: none of them is lost whom thou gavest me by thy eternal gift, none of them whom thou gavest me to be my apostles, but one who, though he was my apostle, and in that sense given to me, yet was never given me by thy eternal gift, as one to be by me redeemed, and brought to eternal life and salvation; for he was a *son of perdition*: we have this term applied to antichrist, 2 Thess. ii. 3. As *the son of death*, 2 Sam. xii. 5, signifies one appointed to die, or that deserveth to die; and *the child of hell*, Matt. xxiii. 15, signifieth one who deserveth hell; so *the son of perdition* may either signify one destined to perdition, or one that walketh in the high and right road to perdition, or rather both; one who being passed over in God's eternal counsels, as to such as shall be saved, hath by his own wilful apostacy brought himself to eternal perdition, or into such a guilt as I know thou wilt destroy him. And by this the Holy Scripture is fulfilled, Psal. cix. 8, for that is the portion of Scripture here intended, as is apparent from Acts i. 20, where the apostle applieth that text to Judas, who is here spoken of. Other scriptures also were thus fulfilled, as Psal. xli. 9, compared with John xiii. 18.

13 And now come I to thee; and these things I speak in the world, that they might have my joy fulfilled in themselves.

He speaketh still in the present tense. These words were not fulfilled six weeks after this, for he conversed with his disciples forty days after his resurrection, Acts i. 3; but Christ was now shortly coming, therefore he saith, *I come*. And, saith he, while I am in the world, *I speak these things*; I put up this prayer, that the joy of my people may not be diminished by my going from them, but that when they can no longer (as hitherto) rejoice in my bodily presence with them, they may yet rejoice that I am ascended to my Father, that they stand commended to the care of thee, my Father, by this my last prayer.

14 ᵇI have given them thy word; ᶜand the world hath hated them, because they are not of the world, ᵈeven as I am not of the world.

I take more to be understood here, by Christ's giving his word unto his disciples, than his preaching the gospel in their ears: otherwise Christ had no more given these his disciples his word, than he had given it to many thousands of others who were yet in the world, and whom the world hated not. The sense therefore is, I have not only preached thy word in their ears, but I have opened their hearts to receive and believe it, and bowed their wills to a compliance with it; so that the word dwelleth in their hearts, is ingrafted in them, and they are turned into the likeness of it. And here it is observable, that when any soul is given to Christ by his Father, Christ will most certainly, first or last, give unto that soul his word in that sense; that is, so as it shall receive, believe it, and be turned into the likeness of it. And for this *the world hath hated them*, for thy word hath made them to be of another spirit from carnal, loose, and worldly men; they have other affections, other inclinations, other designs and studies; *they are not of the world* in that respect *as I am not of the world*: though in other respects not so; for Christ, as to his original, was not of the world, which they were, *of the earth, earthy*.

15 I pray not that thou shouldest take them out of the world, but ᵉthat thou shouldest keep them from the evil.

Christ doth not pray that his Father would take up his saints out of this sinful and troublesome world into heaven, because he knew that they were to be of use to him for a time in the world; but he prays that the Lord would keep them from the evil one, (so some would have it translated,) or from the evil thing; by which we must not understand what is penally and afflictively evil, but only what is sinfully evil: and by his example he hath directed us how we ought to pray; not for death, nor absolutely for a deliverance from the evils and miseries of this life; but that we may be delivered from those temptations to sin, to which a multitude of sharp trials and afflictions will expose even the best of men.

16 ᶠThey are not of the world, even as I am not of the world.

This is the same thing which he had said before, ver. 14, which he again repeateth, either to fix it in their memories, that they, calling it to their minds, might direct their lives accordingly, or be thereby fortified against the hatred and malice of the world; for which purpose he told them so before, chap. xv. 19, and again in this chapter, ver. 14: see the notes on ver. 14.

17 ᵍSanctify them through thy truth: ʰthy word is truth.

It is doubted amongst interpreters, whether sanctifying in this place signifieth the consecrating, deputing, or setting the apostles apart, and preparing them for the work of the ministry in which they were to be employed, as the word signifies, Jer. i. 5; or the strengthening and confirming their habits of grace, so as they might be able to encounter the temptations they should meet with from the hatred or opposition of the world; or the perfecting of them in holiness. Mr. Calvin saith our Saviour here prayeth that God would appropriate them unto himself. And he showeth how this is done, *through*, or in, *thy truth;* that is, some say, through thy truth engraven and imprinted upon their hearts by thy Holy Spirit, which was promised to lead and to guide them into all truth, chap. xvi. 13: say others, through thy Spirit, which indeed is the Sanctifier; and we have met with twice, called, *the Spirit of truth*, chap. xiv. 17. Some say, *Sanctify them through thy truth*, is no more than, Sanctify them truly, in opposition to that legal sanctification of priests, &c., of which we read in the books of Exodus and Leviticus. Others would have it, to thy truth, that is, to the preaching of thy gospel. But our translation seems to come nearest the meaning; *through thy truth*, that is, through the knowledge of thy truth; as the Gentiles are said to have had their hearts purified by faith, Acts xv. 9. He opens what he meant by *truth*, adding, *thy word is truth;* that is, thy word and gospel, which I have preached to them, is truth (the abstract, as some think, for the concrete); that is, it is most true: it is not like the doctrine of false prophets, nor like the doctrine of the Pharisees, which is partly true, partly false; but it is truth itself: and though indeed it is the blood of Christ which cleanseth and purifieth the heart, yet this is applied to the conscience by the Spirit, which is the Sanctifier, in and through the word of God preached and applied to the soul.

18 ⁱAs thou hast sent me into the world, even so have I also sent them into the world.

That is, My Father, they have not thrust themselves into their employment, they have not run without sending; for as I am thine apostle, as I was sent by thee, so I have sent them. The apostles indeed were not sent for the same end in all things that Christ was sent; who was sent to purchase salvation for men, as well as to preach the gospel: but they were sent in part for the same work for which Christ was sent, and they were sent by him who had authority to send them; and as it is but reasonable for princes to protect those whom themselves send upon their embassies, so it was but reasonable that God should defend and protect those whom his Son had sent out as his ambassadors.

k 1 Cor. 1. 2,
30. 1 Thess.
4. 7. Heb.
10. 10.
║ Or, *truly sanctified*.

19 And *k* for their sakes I sanctify myself, that they also might be ║ sanctified through the truth.

I sanctify myself, here, is no more than, I set myself apart, as a sacrifice acceptable and well-pleasing in the sight of God: and indeed sanctifying, in the ancient notion of it under the law, did ordinarily signify the setting of persons and things apart to the special service of God; which was done legally by certain ritual performances and ceremonies, and is still done inwardly and spiritually by regeneration, and renewing of the hearts of men and women by the efficacious working of the Holy Ghost. Christ saith, that for his disciples' sake he sanctified himself, being both the Priest and the sacrifice. Christ set apart himself as a sacrifice for his people, *that they might be sanctified*: not only our eternal life and happiness, but all the means to it, fell within the counsel of God; hence we are said to be chosen of Christ, *that we should be holy and without blame before him in love*, Eph. i. 4; and within the purchase of Christ: hence the apostle saith, Eph. v. 25, 26, that he *gave himself for* his church, *that he might sanctify and cleanse it with the washing of water*: and our Saviour here saith, that he set apart himself for a sacrifice for our sins, that his people *might be sanctified through the truth*; that is, by receiving the truth, not in their ears only, but in their hearts, in the love of it, and bringing forth the fruits of it in all holiness of life and conversation.

20 Neither pray I for these alone, but for them also which shall believe on me through their word;

Two things are evident from this verse. 1. That Christ did not pray for any reprobates, not for any that were and should die unbelievers: he prayed before for those who actually did believe; he prayeth here for them that should believe; but we never read that he prayed for any others. Now whether he laid down his life for those for whom he would not pray, lieth upon them to consider, who are so confident that he died for all and every man. 2. That by persons given to Christ, cannot be understood believers as such; for Christ here prayeth for those that were no actual believers, but should believe. 3. That faith cometh by hearing; Christ here prayeth for those that should believe *through their word*, that is, the apostles' preaching the gospel.

l ver. 11, 22,
23. ch. 10.16.
Rom. 12. 5.
Gal. 3. 28.
m ch. 10. 38.
& 14. 11.

21 *l* That they all may be one; as *m* thou, Father, *art* in me, and I in thee, that they also may be one in us: that the world may believe that thou hast sent me.

Our Saviour here prayeth on the behalf of such as should believe on him, that they might *be one* in faith, and one in brotherly love. Whoso considereth this as a piece of Christ's prayer for believers, and that St. Paul hardly wrote one epistle to the primitive apostolical churches in which he did not press this by most potent arguments, cannot but nourish some hopes, (how improbable soever it appears at present,) that all the sincere disciples of Christ shall one day arrive at the keeping of the unity of the Spirit in the bond of peace, and likewise look upon themselves in point of duty obliged to endeavour it. To which pitch of perfection possibly Christians might soon arrive, if superiors would, after the example of the apostle, Acts xv. 28, lay upon their inferiors no more than *necessary things*; and equals would learn to contend for truth in love, and to walk with their brethren so far as they have attained; and as to other things, to forbear one another in love; and wherein any of their brethren are otherwise minded, then they are to wait till God shall reveal it to them, Phil. iii. 15. But this is not all the union which Christ prayeth for;

he also prayeth that they might be one in the Father and the Son; that is, that they might believe; for faith is that grace by which we are united to, and made one with, God and Christ; though others interpret it of obedience, or such things wherein God the Father and Christ are one, &c. For although so many as are ordained to life shall believe, yet that they might believe is matter of prayer: this our Saviour prayeth for, for the further glory of God, which is that which he meaneth by the world's believing that God had sent him; there being no greater evidence that Christ is the true Messiah, than the general acceptance of the doctrine of the gospel, which he brought throughout the world; for who can imagine, that a new doctrine brought into the world by one of no greater reputation than Christ had in the world, and propagated by persons of no greater quality than the apostles were, should obtain in the greatest part of the world, if he that first introduced it had not been first sent by God into the world, and the apostles had not been extraordinarily influenced and assisted by God as to the propagation of it, after Christ was ascended into heaven?

22 And the glory which thou gavest me I have given them; *n* that they may be one, even as we are one: *n* ch. 14. 20. 1 John 1. 3. & 3. 24.

By *glory* here some understand the heavenly glory; but then they must understand the oneness mentioned in the latter part of the verse, of the union which the saints shall have with Christ and his Father in glory, in another world. Others understand the Divine nature, of which the apostle, 2 Pet. i. 4, saith, believers are made partakers: this seemeth to come nearer, for the more men and women are made partakers of that, the more they will study the unity of the Spirit. Others understand the power of working miracles, by which Christ is said to have *manifested his glory*, chap. ii. 11; and the effect of this power is called *the glory of God*, chap. xi. 40. Others understand the preaching of the gospel, in which *the ministration of the Spirit is glorious*, 2 Cor. iii. 8; and the faithful ministers of the gospel are called *the glory of Christ*, 2 Cor. viii. 23. *That they may be one, even as we are one;* our Saviour either again repeats his prayer, that they might be one; or else declareth that he had communicated his power, his glory to them, that they might be one, as he and his Father are one.

23 I in them, and thou in me, *o* that they may be made perfect in one; and that the world may know that thou hast sent me, and hast loved them, as thou hast loved me. *o* Col. 3. 14.

I in them; not only as my Divine nature is united to their flesh, but as I have made them partakers of my Spirit, and of the Divine nature; as I have loved them with a special and peculiar love, and am the head, they the members; I the vine, they the branches. *And thou in me,* the fulness of the Godhead dwelling in me bodily; I being the brightness of thy glory, the express image of thy person; thou also doing whatsoever I do, and accepting and approving of it, as chap. xiv. 10. *That they may be made perfect in one;* the Greek is, εἰς ἕν, into one; in one body, whereof Christ is the Head; which body is the church, keeping a unity of faith; all believing the same things in matter of faith, and those things no other than what thou hast revealed, and I have revealed as from thee. This, O Father, will be a great evidence, both that thou hast sent me, when the world shall see thee bowing men's hearts to the obedience of the truth of thy gospel; and that thou hast loved them with a tender and everlasting love, as thou hast loved me.

24 *p* Father, I will that they also, whom thou hast given me, be with me where I am; that they may behold my glory, which thou hast given me: *q* for thou lovedst me before the foundation of the world. *p* ch. 12. 26. & 14. 3. 1 Thes. 4. 17. *q* ver. 5.

Here our Saviour willeth his disciples eternal life; or rather prayeth to his Father, that he would preserve his disciples unto, and at last bestow upon them, eternal life and salvation; so as the phrase, *whom thou hast given me,* is not to be restrained to the apostles, but to be extended to all those who, belonging to the election of grace, shall hereafter be made heirs of glory, and have everlasting life and happiness. This he expresseth under the notion of being with him where he is, as chap. xiv. 3; which is called a being *ever with the Lord*, 1 Thess. iv. 17; and certainly this is the highest happiness, to be where the Son of God is. *That they may behold my glory*, is the same thing with, that they may be made partakers of my glory: as to see death, is, in Scripture phrase, to die; and to see life, is to live; so, to behold the glory of God, is to be glorified. *For*, saith our Saviour, *thou lovedst me before the foundation of the world*, both as thy only begotten Son, and as the person in whom thou hast chosen all them, and whom thou hast set apart to be the Mediator between God and man; and therefore I know that thou wilt glorify me, and that thou wilt in this thing hear my prayers, and glorify them also, whom thou hast given to me to be redeemed by my blood.

25 O righteous Father, ʳthe world hath not known thee: but ˢI have known thee, and ᵗthese have known that thou hast sent me.

r ch. 15. 21. & 16. 3.
s ch. 7. 29. & 8. 55. & 10. 15.
t ver. 8.
ch. 16. 27.

It is observed, that the servants of God, in holy writ, have used in their prayers to give unto God such compellations as have been suitable to the things which they have begged of God in their prayers, and proper to express their faith in God, for the hearing of such their prayers: Christ here calls his Father by the name of *righteous*, with relation to the argument which he here useth, which is from his disciples' knowledge of him; under which term (as very often before) is comprehended their acceptance of him, believing in him, love to him, &c. Father, saith he, thou art righteous; it is a piece of thy righteousness to *render to every man according to his work*, Job xxxiv. 11; Psal. lxii. 12; Prov. xxiv. 12. *The world hath not known thee;* the men of the world hate thee, are ignorant of thee, rebellious against thee; *but I have known thee;* I have known thee, and have made thee known, and I have been obedient to thy will; and these my disciples have known me, and known, that is, received, embraced me, as one sent by thee, as the Messiah.

26 ᵘAnd I have declared unto them thy name, and will declare *it*: that the love ˣwherewith thou hast loved me may be in them, and I in them.

u ver. 6. ch. 15. 15.
x ch. 15. 9.

By the *name* of God, is to be understood God himself, and whatsoever God hath made himself known by his word and gospel, his attributes and perfections. And after my resurrection, I will yet further declare it to them, who are yet in a great measure ignorant and imperfect in their notions of thee; that thy love wherewith thou hast loved me may be further communicated to them, and be derived to them, and abide in and upon them for ever; because I am in them (so some would have it read, though the word be καγώ, which properly is, *and I*, as we translate it). The words are but a repetition of what our Lord hath often said, and illustrated, chap. xv. 9, by the parable of the vine and the branches; and teach us this lesson, that Christ must be in those souls who can pretend to any share in that love of God wherewith he hath loved Christ: *Know ye not your own selves, how that Jesus Christ is in you, except ye be reprobates?* 2 Cor. xiii. 5.

CHAP. XVIII.

Judas betrayeth Jesus: the officers and soldiers at Christ's word fall to the ground, 1—9. *Peter cutteth off Malchus's ear,* 10, 11. *Jesus is led bound to Annas and Caiaphas,* 12—14. *Peter denieth him,* 15—18. *Jesus is examined by the high priest, and struck by one of the officers,* 19—24. *Peter denieth him the second and third time,* 25—27. *Jesus, brought before Pilate, and examined, confesseth his kingdom not to be of this world; Pilate, testifying his innocence, and offering to release him, the Jews prefer Barabbas,* 28—40.

Having so largely discoursed the history of our Saviour's passion, in our notes upon the 26th and 27th chapters of Matthew, where (to make the history entire) we compared what the other evangelists also have about it; I shall refer the reader to the notes upon those two chapters, and be the shorter in the notes upon this and the following chapters.

WHEN Jesus had spoken these words, ᵃhe went forth with his disciples over ᵇthe brook Cedron, where was a garden, into the which he entered, and his disciples.

a Mat. 26. 36. Mark 14. 32. Luke 22. 39. b 2 Sam. 15. 23.

Matthew hath nothing of those discourses, and prayer, which we have had in the four last chapters; no more have any of the other evangelists, who yet all mention his going into the mount of Olives, after his celebration of his last supper, Matt. xxvi. 30; Mark xiv. 26; Luke xxii. 39. Our evangelist saith, he went over the brook Cedron into a garden. The others say nothing of a garden, but mention his coming to a place called Gethsemane. It is probable that this village was at the foot of Mount Olivet; and the garden mentioned was a garden near that village, and belonging to it (for they had not their gardens within their towns, but without): now the way to this was over the brook Cedron; of which brook we read, 2 Sam. xv. 23; David passed over it when he fled from Absalom; and 1 Kings ii. 37, where it is mentioned as Shimei's limit, which he might not pass. This brook was in the way towards the mount of Olives; which being passed, he with his disciples went into a garden belonging to the town Gethsemane.

2 And Judas also, which betrayed him, knew the place: ᶜfor Jesus oft-times resorted thither with his disciples.

c Luke 21. 37. & 22. 39.

We read that Christ, when he was at Jerusalem, was wont at night for privacy to retire to the mount of Olives, Luke xxi. 37; xxii. 39; and it should seem that he was wont ordinarily to go to this garden, which made Judas know the particular place where he might find him.

3 ᵈJudas then, having received a band *of men* and officers from the Chief Priests and Pharisees, cometh thither with lanterns and torches and weapons.

d Mat. 26. 47. Mark 14. 43. Luke 22. 47. Acts 1. 16.

The evangelist here passeth over all mentioned by the other evangelists about Judas's going to the high priests, and contracting with them, and cometh to relate his coming to apprehend him with a band of men that he had obtained from the chief priests and Pharisees for that purpose. By *band* we must not understand a Roman cohort, as the word signifies, but such a convenient number out of that band (probably) which at the time of the passover guarded the temple, as was sufficient to take him: they came with *lanterns and torches*, (though it were the time of full moon,) to make the strictest search; and with *weapons*, fearing where no fear was; for Judas (their leader) could have told them that he was not wont to go with any great company to the mount of Olives.

4 Jesus therefore, knowing all things that should come upon him, went forth, and said unto them, Whom seek ye?

This evangelist saith nothing of what the other evangelists mention, of the sign that Judas had given them, by which they should know him; nor of Judas's kissing of him, or our Saviour's reply to him. (John, all along his Gospel, mentioneth very little of what is recorded by the other evangelists.) It must be supposed, that after Judas had kissed our Saviour, our Saviour himself came forth, and asked him whom they looked for; hereby showing that he laid down his life, and no man took it from him: he could easily have delivered himself out of their hands, (though I think they are too charitable to Judas, who think that it was that which made Judas discover him; not that he designed his death,) he had once and again before so escaped them; but now his hour was come, he freely offers himself unto his enemies, and asketh whom they looked for.

5 They answered him, Jesus of Nazareth. Jesus saith unto them, I am *he*. And Judas also, which betrayed him, stood with them.

They tell him, *Jesus of Nazareth*. Christ was born in *Bethlehem of Judea*, Matt. ii. 1; but his father and mother lived at Nazareth, a city of Galilee, Luke ii. 4, 39, where he lived with them, ver. 51; hence he was called *Jesus of*

Nazareth, from the place where he lived, and most ordinarily conversed. Matt. xxi. 11; xxvi. 71; Mark i. 24; x. 47; xiv. 67; xvi. 6. Christ replieth that he was the man; and it is particularly noted, that Judas was with this armed company.

6 As soon then as he had said unto them, I am *he,* they went backward, and fell to the ground.

For a further evidence to the world that Christ was the Son of the Everlasting Father, it pleased God in all the periods of his life to show forth by him some acts of the Divine power. What had Christ said or done here to prostrate his armed adversaries? He had only asked them whom they looked for; and hearing that it was for him, told them he was the man : they are struck with a terror, and instead of apprehending him, start from him, and fall down to the ground. If there were so much majesty in and such an effect of the voice of Christ in one of the lowest acts of his humiliation, what will the voice of a glorified Christ be to sinners, when he shall return as a Judge to condemn the world! And what will the effect of that be upon his enemies! How easily might our Saviour have escaped, now that his enemies were fallen to the ground! But he suffered them to rise up again, to take him, and to carry him away, to show that he had laid down his life freely.

7 Then asked he them again, Whom seek ye? And they said, Jesus of Nazareth.

8 Jesus answered, I have told you that I am *he:* if therefore ye seek me, let these go their way :

Our Saviour's question, and their answer, are the same as before. They fell down, but they rose up again, and go on in their wicked purpose. This is the genius of all sinners; they may be under some convictions and terrors, but they get out of them, if God doth not concur by his Spirit, and sanctify them as means to make a thorough change in their hearts. Though those words, *let these go their way,* might be interpreted of the armed men that came with the officers, of whom there seemed no such need to carry away an unarmed man; yet the next words make it evident that they are to be understood of his disciples, being persons against whom they had no warrant. Our Lord hath a care of his disciples, that they might not suffer with him.

9 That the saying might be fulfilled, which he spake, ^e Of them which thou gavest me have I lost none.

e ch. 17. 12.

But were those words of our Saviour, *Of them which thou gavest me have I lost none,* to be understood as to a temporary losing, or of an eternal destruction? Some of the ancients were of opinion, that they were to be understood of a losing with reference to a spiritual and eternal state; but that they were applicable also to a losing as to this life. I think that they are applicable to both, and that in this text they are primarily to be understood of a losing as to a temporal death and destruction. It was Christ's purpose, that eleven of his twelve apostles should outlive him, receive the promise of the Father in the pouring out of the Spirit, and be his instruments to carry the gospel over a great part of the world : this they could not have done had they been put to death at this time; he therefore resolved not to lose them in this sense, but to uphold and preserve their lives, for these ends to which he had designed them; and therefore he said to these officers, You have the person whom ye seek for; for these my disciples, you have nothing against them, let them go away : and by his power upon their hearts he effected it, so that they had a liberty to forsake him, and to flee and to shift for themselves.

f Mat. 26. 51. Mark 14. 47. Luke 22. 49, 50.

10 ^f Then Simon Peter having a sword drew it, and smote the High Priest's servant, and cut off his right ear. The servant's name was Malchus.

It is thought that this action of Peter's was before the apprehension of our Saviour, though after the discovery of it, as our evangelist reports it; because upon the apprehension of our Saviour, both Matthew, chap. xxvi. 56, and Mark chap. xiv. 50, agree, that the disciples fled; and it can hardly be thought that if Peter had seen his Master apprehended he would have adventured upon so daring and provocative an action; nor could Christ, had he been first bound, have stretched out his hand, to have touched his ear, and healed it. Lest any should wonder how Peter came by a sword, we may read, Luke xxii. 38, that the disciples had *two swords* amongst them, probably brought out of Galilee for the defence of themselves and their Master against assaults from robbers in that long journey.

11 Then said Jesus unto Peter, Put up thy sword into the sheath : ^g the cup which my Father hath given me, shall I not drink it?

g Mat. 20. 22. & 26. 39, 42.

The other evangelists report this part of the history with many more circumstances; particularly our Saviour's miraculous healing Malchus again; see the notes on Matt. xxvi. 51—54; Mark xiv. 47—49; Luke xxii. 50, 51. With what pretence some, both of the ancient and modern writers, think that Peter did not sin in this action, I do not understand, when our Saviour did not only (as John saith) command him to put up his sword again into its sheath, but also (as Matthew tells us, chap. xxvi. 52) told him, that *all they that take the sword,* that is, without commission from God, *shall perish with the sword.* He used that argument, according to the other evangelists. This evangelist tells us of another, *The cup which my Father hath given me, shall I not drink it?* that is, shall I not freely and cheerfully submit to the will of God in suffering what he willeth me to suffer? The term *cup* is often in Scripture used to signify people's measure and proportion of affliction and suffering, which God allotteth them ; (possibly the metaphor is taken from the custom of some nations, to put some kinds of malefactors to death by giving them a cup of poison;) see the notes on Matt. xx. 22; xxvi. 39. It is a good argument to quiet our spirits roiled by any afflictive providences : they are but a cup, and the cup our Father hath given us.

12 Then the band and the captain and officers of the Jews took Jesus, and bound him,

As is usual for officers to do with ordinary malefactors which are great criminals; they put no difference between Christ and the most villanous thieves and murderers. There are many conjectures why Christ was first led to Annas, whereas Caiaphas was the high priest that year, not Annas (as the next words tell us); but it is uncertain whether it was because his house was very near, and in the way to Caiaphas's house, or that he lived in the same house with his son-in-law; or out of an honour and respect to him, being the high priest's father, or to please the old man's peevish eyes with such a sight, or by this means to draw Annas to the trial of Christ, or because he had had a more than ordinary hand about the apprehending him, or to take direction from him what to do : we cannot give a certain account why they used this method; we are only certain they did it, and that they did not carry him before him as high priest; for the next words tell us,

13 And ^hled him away to ⁱAnnas first; for he was father in law to Caiaphas, which was the High Priest that same year. ||

h See Matt. 26. 57. i Luke 3. 2 || *And Annas sent Christ bound unto Caiaphas the High Priest,* ver. 24.

That his son-in-law Caiaphas was the high priest that year; which we had also before, chap. xi. 51, where we discoursed more largely about the disorder of the Jews, in that most corrupt time, when that place was bestowed without regard to the family of Aaron, and bought and sold, or conferred at the will of their conquerors. See the notes on chap. xi. 51.

14 ^kNow Caiaphas was he, which gave counsel to the Jews, that it was expedient that one man should die for the people.

k ch. 11. 50.

Of his giving that counsel, and the wickedness of it, (though it proved an oracle beyond his intention,) we discoursed before : see the notes on chap. xi. 51. The meaning of the high priest was, that right or wrong, whether they had any just accusation against Christ or no, yet they might for expediency put him to death, because his death might prevent mutinies and seditions amongst the people.

15 ¶ ^l And Simon Peter followed Jesus, and *so did* another disciple : that disciple was known unto the High Priest, and

l Mat. 26. 58. Mark 14. 54. Luke 22. 54.

went in with Jesus into the palace of the High Priest.

When Christ was apprehended, the other evangelists tell us, *all the disciples forsook him and fled;* but it should seem that Peter, who all along the gospel history hath appeared more forward, and bold, and daring than any of the rest, came back ; but who that other disciple was that went in with him, and in favour of whom Peter was admitted, we are not told. It is but a conjecture of those who think that it was John, for John was a Galilean as well as Peter, and would have been as much to be questioned upon that account as Peter was. They judge more probably who think it was the master of the house where Christ had ate the passover, and celebrated his supper ; or some person of note in Jerusalem, who by reason of his reputation might have more free access to the chief magistrate than one of the apostles, who were but mean persons in the account of the Jews. This disciple, whoever he was, was one that had some familiarity and acquaintance with Caiaphas, which it is no way probable that either John or any of the apostles had.

m Mat 26.69.
Mark 14. 66.
Luke 22 54.

16 ᵐ But Peter stood at the door without. Then went out that other disciple, which was known unto the High Priest, and spake unto her that kept the door, and brought in Peter.

This further confirmeth the conjecture of those, who think that other disciple was none of the apostles, but a favourer of Christ, that lived in Jerusalem, and was of some repute either for estate or place ; so as he had not only an acquaintance with the high priest, but also with his family; and could gain admittance into his palace, not only for himself, but also for his friend.

17 Then saith the damsel that kept the door unto Peter, Art not thou also *one* of this man's disciples? He saith, I am not.

This is Peter's first denial of his Master ; betwixt which and his second denial (of which John saith nothing till he comes to ver. 26) the evangelist interposeth many things not mentioned by the other evangelists.

18 And the servants and officers stood there, who had made a fire of coals; for it was cold : and they warmed themselves : and Peter stood with them, and warmed himself.

Here is nothing in this verse which needeth any explication, unless any should ask how it could be cold weather at that time of the year, (about April 14,) especially in a country where it now was the time of harvest ? which may easily be resolved. It was now about three of the clock in the morning, and we know that in summer (the spring especially) nights are cold ; besides that in those countries that are more equinoctial, the nights are longer, and consequently colder towards the morning, as the air hath had more time to cool.

19 ¶ The High Priest then asked Jesus of his disciples, and of his doctrine.

Questions about sedition or rebellion belonged not to the judge of this court, but fell under the cognizance of the Roman governor, they being now a conquered people, and tributary to the Romans ; who, though themselves heathens, granted the Jews their liberty as to religion, and courts in order thereunto ; as also a liberty of courts for civil causes : the high priest therefore saith nothing to Christ about his being a King, but only inquireth of him about his doctrine. What particular questions he propounded to him we do not read ; only in general he inquired about the doctrine he had preached, and the disciples he had sent out, which was one and the same cause, to see if he could bring him under the guilt of a false prophet ; for that, and blasphemy, and idolatry, were three principal causes that fell under the cognizance of this court, as appeareth from Deut. xiii.

n Mat.26.55.
Luke 4. 15.
ch. 7. 14. 26,
28. & 8. 2.

20 Jesus answered him, ⁿ I spake openly to the world ; I ever taught in the synagogue, and in the temple, whither the Jews always resort ; and in secret have I said nothing.

I spake openly to the world ; to all sorts of men, my enemies as well as my friends. *I ever taught in the synagogue, and in the temple, whither the Jews always resort ;* the Jews for instruction do use to resort to the temple, which was in Jerusalem, and whither three times in the year all the males were wont to come from all parts of the country : and in the public assemblies of the Jews, and in the places where they use to meet. *And in secret have I said nothing ;* I have said nothing in secret contrary to the doctrine which I have publicly taught ; though I have preached in other places, yet it hath been the same thing which I have said in public.

21 Why askest thou me ? ask them which heard me, what I have said unto them : behold, they know what I said.

We are told by those that have written about the Jewish order in their courts of judgment, that their capital causes always began with the defensative part ; and that it was lawful for any to speak for the defendants for a whole day together ; (though they did not observe this in the cause of Christ ;) and their method was not to put the defendants to accuse themselves, but to examine witnesses against them. Our Saviour therefore appeals to their own order, and says, *Why askest thou me ?* It was, saith he, no secret action ; I spake publicly, ask them that heard me speak ; they know what doctrine I preached, and can accuse me if I delivered any false doctrine.

22 And when he had thus spoken, one of the officers which stood by ᵒ struck Jesus ‖ with the palm of his hand, saying, Answerest thou the High Priest so ?

o Jer. 20. 2.
Acts 23. 2.
‖ Or, *with a rod.*

This lets us see in what indecent disorder the Jewish government was at this time, that an inferior officer dared to strike a supposed criminal, standing before the judgment-seat, and defending himself by their own known rules and methods ; for what had our Saviour said or done, more than making use of the liberty their own law allowed ; not confessing any thing against himself, but putting them upon the proof of what they laid to his charge ? Yet we read of no notice taken of this disorder.

23 Jesus answered him, If I have spoken evil, bear witness of the evil : but if well, why smitest thou me ?

Our Saviour could easily have revenged himself upon this officer ; but, to teach us our duty, he only gently reproves him, and lets him know that he did not behave himself as one ought to do in the face of a court of justice, where he had both a liberty and a present opportunity to have accused him, if he had spoken ill ; and if he had spoken well, there was no reason for his striking him.

24 ᵖ Now Annas had sent him bound unto Caiaphas the High Priest.

p Mat. 26.57.

These words are only to let us know, that these things were not done before Annas, but before Caiaphas the high priest, to whom (as to his proper judge) Annas had sent him bound, as he was at first brought to him.

25 And Simon Peter stood and warmed himself. ᑫ They said therefore unto him, Art not thou also *one* of his disciples ? He denied *it*, and said, I am not.

q Matt. 26. 69, 71.
Mark 14. 69.
Luke 22. 58.

26 One of the servants of the High Priest, being *his* kinsman whose ear Peter cut off, saith, Did not I see thee in the garden with him ?

27 Peter then denied again : and ʳ immediately the cock crew.

r Mat.26. 74.
Mark 14. 72.
Luke 22. 60.
ch. 13. 38.

This history of Peter's denial of his Master the second time we have before met with, Matt. xxvi. 71, 72 ; Mark xiv. 69, 70 ; Luke xxii. 58, 59, with several circumstances not mentioned by John. See the notes upon Matt. xxvi. 69, &c.

28 ¶ ˢ Then led they Jesus from Caia-

s Matt. 27.2
Mark 15. 1.
Luke 23. 1 Acts 3. 13.

S. JOHN XIX

|Or, *Pilate's house*, Matt. 27. 27.
t Acts 10. 28. & 11. 3.

phas unto ‖ the hall of judgment: and it was early; 'and they themselves went not into the judgment hall, lest they should be defiled; but that they might eat the Passover.

The chief priests having in their sanhedrim done with our Saviour's case, and judged him worthy of death, as we read, Matt. xxvi. 66; Mark xiv. 64; which two evangelists, with Luke, relate this history of Christ's trial before the sanhedrim, with many more circumstances than John doth; (see the notes on those texts;) they now lead him from the ecclesiastical court to the court of the civil magistrate; either kept in Pilate's house, who was the present civil governor under the Romans, or some where at least where he sat as judge, which was therefore called *the hall of judgment. And it was early;* how early it was we cannot tell, but probably about five or six of the clock. The Jews would not go into the judgment-hall, that they might not be defiled, for they accounted it a legal pollution and uncleanness to come into a heathen's house, or to touch any thing which a heathen had touched: now the reason is assigned why they were afraid of contracting any legal pollution, viz. that they might the passover. *Object.* But had they not eaten the passover the night before? that was the time prescribed by the law, to the letter of which there is no doubt but that our Saviour strictly kept himself. *Answ.* Some say that they had not, because the day wherein they should have eaten it this year falling the day before their sabbath, the passover was put off to be kept on the sabbath, that two great festivals might not be kept two days successively; so as, though our Saviour kept it at the time appointed by the law, yet the Jews did not. But this is denied by other very learned men, who tell us the Jews never altered their day for keeping their passover, neither for the succeeding sabbath, nor any other reason. They say therefore, that by *the passover* which is mentioned in this verse is to be understood the feast, mentioned Numb. xxviii. 17, which was to be kept *the fifteenth day*, which day was a day of great solemnity with them from the morning to the evening; all the seven days they also offered various sacrifices, which all went under the name of the passover, because they followed in the days of the paschal feast. Thus the term *passover* is taken, Deut. xvi. 2, *Thou shalt therefore sacrifice the passover unto the Lord thy God, of the flock and the herd.* According to this notion, the meaning of those words, *that they might eat the passover*, is, that they might proceed in their paschal solemnity, keeping the feast according to the law. Be it as it will, these hypocrites in it notoriously discovered their hypocrisy, scrupling what caused a legal uncleanness, and not at all scrupling either immediately before their eating the passover, or presently after it, in their great festival to defile themselves with the guilt of innocent blood; nay, had Christ been such a malefactor as they pretended, yet the bringing him into judgment, their prosecuting, and accusing, and condemning him, and assisting in his crucifying, were not works fit for the day before such a solemnity, or the day after it, which was so great a festival: but there is nothing more ordinary, than for persons over zealous as to rituals, to be as remiss with reference to moral duties.

29 Pilate then went out unto them, and said, What accusation bring ye against this man?

The Roman governor humoureth them in their superstition (the Romans having granted them the liberty of their religion): they scruple to go into the ordinary place of judgment; he goes out to them, and calls for their *accusation* of Christ, according to the ordinary and regular course of judgments.

30 They answered and said unto him, If he were not a malefactor, we would not have delivered him up unto thee.

They had in their sanhedrim before judged him guilty of blasphemy, Matt. xxvi. 65, but this they durst not mention, lest Pilate should have rejected them, as being not concerned in questions of their law; they therefore only exclaimed against him in the general as a great malefactor, but of what kind they do not say. It should seem they would have had Pilate have added his civil authority to confirm and execute their ecclesiastical censure, without so much as hearing any thing of the cause (as at this day frequent in popish countries); but they met with a more equal judge.

31 Then said Pilate unto them, Take ye him, and judge him according to your law. The Jews therefore said unto him, It is not lawful for us to put any man to death:

Take ye him, and judge him according to your law; I will judge no man before myself first hear and judge of his crime; you have a law amongst yourselves, and a liberty to question and judge men upon it, proceed against him according to your law. They reply, *It is not lawful for us to put any man to death.* We are assured by such as are exercised in the Jewish writings, that the power of putting any to death was taken away from the Jews forty years before the destruction of Jerusalem. Some say it was not taken away by the Romans, but by their own court. They thought it so horrid a thing to put an Israelite to death, that wickedness of all sorts grew to such a height amongst them, through the impunity, or too light punishment, of criminals, that their courts durst not execute their just authority. And at last their great court determined against the putting any to death; nor (as they say) was any put to death by the Jews, but in some popular tumult, after their court had prejudiced the person by pronouncing him guilty of blasphemy, or some capital crime; which seemeth the case of Stephen, Acts vii.

32 ᵘThat the saying of Jesus might be fulfilled, which he spake, signifying what death he should die. ᵘ Mat. 20.19. ch. 12. 32, 33.

Christ had before this time told his disciples that he should die, and that by the death of the cross, as we read, Matt. xx. 19. God by his providence ordereth things accordingly, to let us know that the Scripture might be fulfilled to every tittle. Crucifying was no Jewish but a Roman death; had the Jews put him to death, they would have stoned him; but he must remove the curse from us, by being made *a curse for us*, being *hanged on a tree*, which was looked upon as an accursed death, Gal. iii. 13. The Jews therefore knowing nothing of this counsel of God, yet execute it by refusing themselves to put him to death, and putting it off to Pilate, though possibly their design was but to avoid the odium of it. Thus God maketh the wrath of men to praise him.

33 ˣ Then Pilate entered into the judgment hall again, and called Jesus, and said unto him, Art thou the King of the Jews? ˣ Mat. 27.11.

Then Pilate entered into the judgment-hall again, the ordinary place of judicature, from whence we read before he went out, in civility to the Jews, whose superstition (as we before heard) kept them from going there during the festival. He called Jesus to him privately, and asks him, if he owned himself to be *the King of the Jews?* the confessing of which (for without doubt they had suggested some such thing to Pilate, and could not prove it) had brought Christ under Pilate's power, he being governor for the Romans, and so concerned to inquire upon any that pretended to any regal power over that conquered people.

34 Jesus answered him, Sayest thou this thing of thyself, or did others tell it thee of me?

Our Saviour neither affirmeth nor denieth: though we are bound, whenever we speak, to speak the truth, yet we are not bound at all times to speak the whole truth. Our Saviour desireth to be satisfied from Pilate, whether he asked him as a private person for his own satisfaction, or as a judge, having received any such accusation against him? for if he asked him as a judge, he was bound to call them to the proof of what they had charged him with.

35 Pilate answered, Am I a Jew? Thine own nation and the Chief Priests have delivered thee unto me: what hast thou done?

The sum of this is no more than that he did not devise this captious question, for he was no Jew, not concerned in nor regarding what they had in their books of the law and the prophets; but he was accused to him by those of his own nation, and he was desirous to find out the truth, and to know what he had done.

36 ʸJesus answered, ᶻMy kingdom is not of this world: if my kingdom were of this world, then would my servants fight, that I should not be delivered to the Jews: but now is my kingdom not from hence.

My kingdom is not of this world; that is, I cannot deny but that I am the King of the Jews, but not in the sense they take it, not such a king as they look for in their Messiah; my kingdom is spiritual, over the hearts and minds of men, not earthly and worldly. And of this thou thyself mayst be convinced; for was there ever an earthly prince apprehended and bound for whom none of his subjects would take up arms? Here is none of my disciples takes up arms, or offereth to fight for me; which is a plain evidence, that I pretend to no kingly power in disturbance of the Roman government.

37 Pilate therefore said unto him, Art thou a king then? Jesus answered, Thou sayest that I am a king. To this end was I born, and for this cause came I into the world, that I should bear witness unto the truth. Every one that ᵃis of the truth heareth my voice.

Art thou a king then? Pilate seems to have spoken this rather in derision and mockery, than out of any desire to catch him in his words. Christ neither owneth himself to be a king, nor yet denieth it, but tells Pilate that he said so; and to this end he was born, and for this cause he came into the world, to bear testimony to the truth: i. e. I cannot deny but that I have a spiritual kingdom, that is truth, and I must attest the truth; it was a part of my errand into the world; and every one who is by Divine grace disposed to believe and love the truth, will hear and obey my doctrine.

38 Pilate saith unto him, What is truth? And when he had said this, he went out again unto the Jews, and saith unto them, ᵇI find in him no fault *at all.*

Pilate (as profane persons use to do) thought that our Saviour, speaking of truth, and a spiritual kingdom, did but cant, and therefore asking him what he meant by truth, he never stays for an answer, but goes out again to the Jews, whom he had left without the door of the judgment-hall, and tells them he found no fault in him. Whatever the quality of the kingdom was of which our Saviour spake, he judged that his pretensions to it were not prejudicial to the authority of the emperor, nor the tranquillity of the state, and would have dismissed him from their unjust prosecution.

39 ᶜBut ye have a custom, that I should release unto you one at the passover: will ye therefore that I release unto you the King of the Jews?

Whence this custom came is uncertain; most probably from the Romans, who in some honour of this great festival of the Jews, and in humour of them, granted them the life of any criminal whom they desired. Pilate propounds Christ as the prisoner whom he had most mind to release, perceiving that his prosecution was of malice, rather than for any just cause.

40 ᵈThen cried they all again, saying, Not this man, but Barabbas. ᵉNow Barabbas was a robber.

But such was the malice of his adversaries, that though Barabbas was one that had committed murder in an insurrection, yet they choose him rather than Christ. See the notes on Matt. xxvii. 15—18.

CHAP. XIX

Jesus is scourged, crowned with thorns, mocked, and buffeted by the soldiers, 1—4. *Pilate declareth his innocence:* *the Jews charge him with assuming the title of the Son of God,* 5—7. *Pilate upon further examination is more desirous to release him, but, overcome with the clamours of the Jews, delivereth him to be crucified,* 8—16. *He is led to Golgotha, and crucified between two malefactors,* 17, 18. *Pilate's inscription on his cross,* 19—22. *The soldiers part his garments,* 23, 24. *He commendeth his mother to John,* 25—27; *receiveth vinegar to drink, and dieth,* 28—30. *The legs of the others are broken, and the side of Jesus pierced,* 31—37. *Joseph of Arimathea beggeth his body, and, assisted by Nicodemus, burieth it,* 28—42.

THEN ᵃPilate therefore took Jesus, and scourged *him.*

It was the custom of the Romans, when any one was to be crucified, first to scourge him; but (as it appears) Pilate ordered it, hoping that, though he could not prevail by any other art with them, yet by this he might; and they might possibly be satisfied with this lighter punishment; for it appeareth by ver. 4 and 12, that Pilate had a mind to release him, if he could have satisfied the Jews; though he had not courage enough to oppose the stream, and to do what himself thought was just, in despite of their opposition.

2 And the soldiers platted a crown of thorns, and put *it* on his head, and they put on him a purple robe,

The other evangelists also mention a reed put into his right hand. The crown, and the purple robe, and a sceptre, are all regal ensigns; they give them to Christ in derision of his pretence to a kingdom, and in the mean time themselves proclaim what he had said, that his kingdom was not of this world; for though earthly kings wear crowns, yet they use to be of gold, not of thorns; and their sceptres use to be gold, not reeds.

3 And said, Hail, King of the Jews! and they smote him with their hands.

They mocked him when they said, *Hail, King of the Jews!* but yet spake a great truth, though not in their sense. The other evangelists speak of more indignities offered him: see the notes on Mark xv. 19.

4 Pilate therefore went forth again, and saith unto them, Behold, I bring him forth to you, ᵇthat ye may know that I find no fault in him.

Pilate appeareth convinced in his own conscience that Christ had done nothing worthy either of death or bonds, and a great while resisted that strong temptation which he was under to please the people, and to secure his own station, lest any complaint made to the Roman emperor against him should have prejudiced him.

5 Then came Jesus forth, wearing the crown of thorns, and the purple robe. And *Pilate* saith unto them, Behold the man!

He therefore, after Jesus had been scourged, and dressed up in this mock dress, brings him out again to the people to move their pity.

6 ᶜWhen the Chief Priests therefore and officers saw him, they cried out, saying, Crucify *him,* crucify *him.* Pilate saith unto them, Take ye him, and crucify *him:* for I find no fault in him.

Our Lord findeth more compassion from Pilate, though a heathen, than he found from those of his own nation; yea, those that pretended highest to religion amongst them: Pilate would have saved him; they cry out for his blood. Pilate leaves another testimony behind him, that what he did, at last overborne with a great temptation, he did contrary to the conviction of his own conscience, and as yet declineth the guilt of innocent blood.

7 The Jews answered him, ᵈWe have a law, and by our law he ought to die, because ᵉhe made himself the Son of God.

The *law* they mean, is the law for putting false prophets to death, Deut. xviii. 20. By *the Son of God* here, they mean the eternal Son of God, in all things equal with his Father; otherwise it was a term applicable to themselves, whom God calls his son, his first-born, &c. Now for any in this sense to arrogate to himself this title who indeed was not so, was blasphemy, and that in the highest degree, and brought him under the notion of a false prophet of the deepest dye: but this was injuriously applied to Christ, who thought it no robbery to be equal with the Father, and who was so declared by God himself at his baptism and transfiguration; and who had made his Divine power appear by such works as no mere man ever did.

8 ¶ When Pilate therefore heard that saying, he was the more afraid;

It should seem that the Romans permitted judgments to the Jews according to their own laws, which the Roman governor was to see executed; or else, seeing the rabble in such a heat and disorder, he feared some breaking out.

9 And went again into the judgment hall, and saith unto Jesus, Whence art thou? [f]But Jesus gave him no answer.

[f Is. 53. 7. Matt. 27. 12, 14.]

Our Lord, who knew the secrets of all men's hearts, very well knew, that though Pilate had for some time withstood his temptations, yet he would at last yield; he also was ready to lay down his life, as he knew was determined for him; having therefore made a reasonable defence, he thinks fit to add no more of that nature.

10 Then saith Pilate unto him, Speakest thou not unto me? knowest thou not that I have power to crucify thee, and have power to release thee?

Pilate seemeth something displeased that Christ would be no more free: men in worldly power are too prone to forget from whom they derive it.

11 Jesus answered, [g]Thou couldest have no power *at all* against me, except it were given thee from above: therefore he that delivered me unto thee hath the greater sin.

[g Luke 22. 53. ch. 7. 30.]

Our Lord checketh Pilate modestly for boasting of his authority as a judge to absolve or condemn him; declaring, that all the power he had was derived from God, who in his eternal counsels had determined this thing, which must therefore come to pass: but withal lets him know, that this neither excused him, nor much less the Jews, who were to execute the Divine purposes. Pilate was to look to God's revealed will, not his secret counsels, of which he could have no knowledge; but he saith, they who had delivered him to him had the greater sin: he did act but as a judge upon their accusations; they procured the false witness, they would not be satisfied without his blood, and they sinned against much more light.

12 And from thenceforth Pilate sought to release him: but the Jews cried out, saying, [h]If thou let this man go, thou art not Cæsar's friend: [i]whosoever maketh himself a king speaketh against Cæsar.

[h Luke 23. 2.]
[i Acts 17. 7.]

He *sought* all fair and plausible means *to release him*, being convinced in his own conscience that he was an innocent man: but the Jews double their clamours, and (according to the usual acts of sycophants) quit their charge as to religion, though that was the true and real cause of all their malice, and pursue only the charge which was proper for the cognizance of the Roman governor, of sedition or rebellion; and tacitly accuse Pilate as a traitor, and being false to his trust, if he should let our Saviour go; for no man could set up himself as a king, but he must proclaim himself a traitor to the Roman emperor.

13 ¶ When Pilate therefore heard that saying, he brought Jesus forth, and sat down in the judgment seat in a place that is called the Pavement, but in the Hebrew, Gabbatha.

That saying, that if he let Jesus go he was not Cæsar's friend. Pilate was a man that loved the honour that was from men more than the honour and praise which is from God; he was more afraid of losing his place than his soul, and could no longer resist the temptation he was under. *He brought Jesus forth, and sat down in a place called the Pavement,* because it was paved with stone, *but in the Hebrew,* (mixed with the Syriac,) *Gabbatha,* that is, a high place; for it was their manner to have their judgment-seats higher than other parts of the room where they were.

14 And [k]it was the preparation of the Passover, and about the sixth hour: and he saith unto the Jews, Behold your King!

[k Mat. 27. 62.]

The preparation to any feast signifies the day before it, because on that day they prepared whatsoever according to the law was necessary for the solemnization. Some much doubt whether in this place *the passover* signifies strictly the paschal supper, which it could not do if the Jews strictly this year kept to the law; for the fourteenth day of the month Nisan at evening was the time when most certainly Christ kept it, who ate it the night before. It is therefore more probably thought, that by *the passover* here is meant their great festival, which was upon the fifteenth day. (See the notes on chap. xviii. 28.) John tells us it was *about the sixth hour;* that is, in the latter part of the interval between nine o'clock in the morning and twelve at noon: for the division of the day according to the Jews was in four parts; the first was from the rising of the sun till our nine in the morning, and was called the third hour; the other was from the third hour to the sixth, that is, twelve o'clock at noon; the third division was from their sixth hour to the ninth, that is, three o'clock with us in the afternoon; the fourth division was from the ninth hour to sun-set, that is, with us six o'clock in the evening, when the sun is in the equinox. Now, not only the time when any of these hours came was called either the third or sixth hour, but the space of three hours allotted to each division was so called, when the next division began: so the time of our Saviour's crucifixion is recorded by Mark to be *the third hour;* that is, the whole space from nine o'clock to twelve was not quite gone, though it was near at an end; and by the evangelist here it is said, that it was *about the sixth hour,* that is, near our twelve o'clock. And thus the different relations are clearly reconciled.

15 But they cried out, Away with *him*, away with *him*, crucify him. Pilate saith unto them, Shall I crucify your King? The Chief Priests answered, [l]We have no king but Cæsar.

[l Gen. 49. 10.]

The more Pilate sought to quiet them, the more they rage, contrary to all dictates of reason; when God hath determined a thing, all things shall concur to bring it about. Pilate mocks them when he saith, *Shall I crucify your King?* Yet so fierce was their malice against Christ, that to compel the governor to condemn him, (though there were not a people under heaven more zealous for their liberties, nor more impatient of a foreign yoke,) they cry out, *We have no king but Cæsar;* that is, the Roman emperor, who had conquered them.

16 [m]Then delivered he him therefore unto them to be crucified. And they took Jesus, and led *him* away.

[m Matt. 27. 26, 31. Mark 15. 15. Luke 23. 24.]

This must be at or about twelve of the clock, for that must be signified by *the sixth hour,* ver. 14. Pilate condemned him, and delivered him to the executioner, who (as the manner is in such cases) *led him away.*

17 [n]And he bearing his cross [o]went forth into a place called *the place* of a skull, which is called in the Hebrew Golgotha:

[n Matt. 27. 31, 33. Mark 15. 21, 22. Luke 23. 26, 33.]
[o Num. 15. 36. Heb. 13. 12.]

See the notes on Matt. xxvii. 31—33, where whatsoever needs expounding in this verse may be found, and this text is reconciled to that, which telleth us, that one Simon, a man of Cyrene, bore his cross. Their places of execution (as usually with us) were without their cities.

18 Where they crucified him, and two other with him, on either side one, and Jesus in the midst.

See the notes on Matt. xxvii. 38.

19 ¶ [p]And Pilate wrote a title, and put *it* on the cross. And the writing

[p Mat. 27. 37. Mark 15. 26. Luke 23. 38.]

S. JOHN XIX

was, JESUS OF NAZARETH THE KING OF THE JEWS.

See the notes on Matt. xxvii. 37.

20 This title then read many of the Jews: for the place where Jesus was crucified was nigh to the city: and it was written in Hebrew, *and* Greek, *and* Latin.

The place where Jesus was crucified was nigh to the city; as all their places of execution were, within two furlongs, or thereabouts. *It was written in Hebrew, and Greek, and Latin;* it was written in all three languages, that not the Jews only, but all such strangers as were come up to the feast, might understand it.

21 Then said the Chief Priests of the Jews to Pilate, Write not, The King of the Jews; but that he said, I am King of the Jews.

The Jews thought it would be a disgrace to them, that Christ should be reported abroad as their king, therefore they desire an alteration of the writing.

22 Pilate answered, What I have written I have written.

But Pilate refuseth to gratify them, and lets them know he would not be directed by them what to write, nor alter any thing of it.

23 ¶ ᵃThen the soldiers, when they had crucified Jesus, took his garments, and made four parts, to every soldier a part; and also *his* coat: now the coat was without seam, ∥ woven from the top throughout.

[q Mat. 27.35. Mark 15. 24. Luke 23. 34.]
[∥ Or, *wrought*.]

Both Matthew, chap. xxvii. 35, and Mark, chap. xv. 24, mention this parting of Christ's garments amongst them, which must be understood of his inward garments; which some tell us might easily be done, because their garments were made up of four parts. But his outward garment, which is called his coat, was all of a piece.

24 They said therefore among themselves, Let us not rend it, but cast lots for it, whose it shall be: that the Scripture might be fulfilled, which saith, ʳThey parted my raiment among them, and for my vesture they did cast lots. These things therefore the soldiers did.

[r Ps. 22. 18.]

This made them choose rather to cast lots for that, than to divide it, as they had done his inward garments. But there was something more in it than the soldiers knew; Christ hereby proved a true Antitype to David, who said of himself figuratively, Psal. xxii. 18, *They part my garments among them, and cast lots upon my vesture;* by which he meant no more, than that his enemies loaded themselves with his spoils: those words which figuratively were true of David, proved literally true as to Christ. Thus vile and wicked men are fulfilling the Scriptures when they little think of it.

25 ¶ ˢNow there stood by the cross of Jesus his mother, and his mother's sister, Mary the *wife* of ∥ᵗCleophas, and Mary Magdalene.

[s Mat. 27.55. Mark 15. 40. Luke 23. 49.]
[∥ Or, *Clopas*. t Luke 24.18.]

These words *the wife* are not in the Greek, but supplied by our translators; which leaves it doubtful whether that Mary was the wife, or the mother, or the daughter of Cleophas.

26 When Jesus therefore saw his mother, and ᵘthe disciple standing by, whom he loved, he saith unto his mother, ˣWoman, behold thy son!

[u ch. 13. 23. & 20. 2. & 21. 7, 20, 24. x ch. 2. 4.]

We have often heard that John was the beloved disciple, and usually expressed under the notion of him whom Jesus loved. Our Lord commendeth his mother to the care of John, whom he had ordered to take care of her, as if he had been her own son: this letteth us know that Joseph was at this time dead, otherwise it is not probable that Christ would have committed his mother to any other guardian.

27 Then saith he to the disciple, Behold thy mother! And from that hour that disciple took her ʸunto his own home.

[y ch. 1. 11. & 16. 32.]

He also reciprocally commendeth his mother to John, to be cared for as his own mother. From that time Mary went home, and lived with John.

28 ¶ After this, Jesus knowing that all things were now accomplished, ᶻthat the Scripture might be fulfilled, saith, I thirst.

[z Ps. 69. 21.]

29 Now there was set a vessel full of vinegar: and ᵃthey filled a spunge with vinegar, and put *it* upon hyssop, and put *it* to his mouth.

[a Mat. 27. 48.]

David said, Psal. lxix. 21, to signify his enemies multiplying afflictions upon him, *They gave me also gall for my meat; and in my thirst they gave me vinegar to drink;* which he spake metaphorically. Part of these words were without a figure literally fulfilled in Christ, who was the Son of David; for he crying out upon the cross that he thirsted, there being no other liquor at hand, or this being set on purpose for this end, they dip a spunge in it, and give it to him to drink; whether to stupify his sense, or to prolong his life in those torments, or barely to quench his thirst, is hard to determine. It is probable that it was such a kind of refreshment as they allowed to ordinary malefactors in his circumstances, the particulars of which usage we are not able to determine.

30 When Jesus therefore had received the vinegar, he said, ᵇIt is finished: and he bowed his head, and gave up the ghost.

[b ch. 17. 4.]

When Christ had tasted the vinegar, *he said, It is finished;* that is, I have now done and suffered all things which lay upon me in this life to do and suffer. Having said this, *he bowed his head, and gave up the ghost.* They are terms expressive of death, and our Saviour's free surrender of his soul unto his Father.

31 The Jews therefore, ᶜbecause it was the preparation, ᵈthat the bodies should not remain upon the cross on the sabbath day, (for that sabbath day was an high day,) besought Pilate that their legs might be broken, and *that* they might be taken away.

[c ver. 42. Mark 15. 42. d Deu.21.23.]

It was the preparation; not to the passover, (for that was celebrated the night before,) but to the weekly sabbath; and they judged according to the law, Deut. xxi. 23, that the land should be defiled if the persons executed were not buried that day, but their bodies should remain on the tree all night, especially on the sabbath, which began immediately after sun-set. And this sabbath was a more than ordinary sabbath, for it was not only the weekly sabbath, but also their second day of unleavened bread; which, and the last day, were both very solemn days, as may be seen, Lev. xxiii. This makes them come and beseech Pilate that the bodies might be taken down, and in order to it, *that their legs might be broken,* lest any life remaining in them they should revive and escape.

32 Then came the soldiers, and brake the legs of the first, and of the other which was crucified with him.

33 But when they came to Jesus, and saw that he was dead already, they brake not his legs:

They brake the two other malefactors' legs, but not Christ's, because they found him dead. It is very possible in a natural course, that of three men dying in the same manner, one may die sooner than another; but it is but rationally presumed, that the cause of our Saviour's quicker death, was not the failure of his spirits sooner, but his own voluntary surrender of his soul.

34 But one of the soldiers with a spear pierced his side, and forthwith ᵉcame thereout blood and water.

e 1 John 5. 6, 8.

But one of the soldiers, to make sure of him, *pierced his side,* out of which it is said that there presently came forth *blood and water.* That there should come out blood is no wonder, nor yet that there should come forth water. Blood being congealed, it is ordinary to see water on the top of the vessel where it is. And besides, anatomists tell us, that in the hollow part of the breast there are watery as well as bloody humours in the membrane that encompasseth the heart, which being pierced, and the water let out, the living creature dieth necessarily. But yet in regard of the next words, *He that saw it bare record, and he knoweth that he saith true,* &c., most divines think, that there was some mystery in this water and blood which came out of Christ's side pierced. Some would have the two sacraments of the gospel signified by this water and blood. Christ is said to have come *by water and blood,* 1 John v. 6 ; that is, say interpreters, he brought in a true expiation of sins by his blood, and the laver of regeneration, washing the soul from its filthiness : and thus be proved the true Antitype, answering the Jewish types in sacrifices and divers washings.

35 And he that saw *it* bare record, and his record is true : and he knoweth that he saith true, that ye might believe.

Nor was this a fable, for John *saw it,* and *bare record,* and knew it to be true ; and published it, that men might believe that it was him in whom all the legal types and figures had their completion.

f Ex. 12. 46. Num. 9. 12. Ps. 34. 20.

36 For these things were done, ᶠthat the Scripture should be fulfilled, A bone of him shall not be broken.

Nor was there any thing of this but in fulfilling of the Scripture ; for it was God's law about the passover, Exod. xii. 46 ; Numb. ix. 12, concerning the paschal lamb, (which was a type of Christ, chap. i. 29 ; 1 Cor. v. 7,) that a bone of it should not be broken. So as by this breaking no bone of Christ's body, they might have understood that he was figured out by the paschal lamb.

37 And again another Scripture saith, ᵍThey shall look on him whom they pierced.

g Ps. 22. 16, 17. Zech. 12. 10. Rev. 1.7.

So also by seeing Christ's side pierced, (a thing not very usual,) they might have understood, that he was the person mentioned, Zech. xii. 10.

h Mat.27.57. Mark 15. 42. Luke 23. 50.

38 ¶ ʰAnd after this Joseph of Arimathæa, being a disciple of Jesus, but secretly ⁱfor fear of the Jews, besought Pilate that he might take away the body of Jesus : and Pilate gave *him* leave. He came therefore, and took the body of Jesus.

i ch. 9. 22. & 12. 42.

See the notes on Matt. xxvii. 57—59.

k ch. 3. 1, 2. & 7. 50.

39 And there came also ᵏNicodemus, which at the first came to Jesus by night, and brought a mixture of myrrh and aloes, about an hundred pound *weight.*

The history of Nicodemus coming by night to our Saviour, and of their discourse together, we had chap. iii. 1—21. We again heard of him standing up for Christ in the sanhedrim, chap. vii. 50. We read no more of him till now, where he shows his love to his dead body ; bringing a hundred pounds weight of myrrh and aloes, which were both of them drugs used in embalming dead bodies, as also in perfuming other things, Psal. xlv. 8.

40 Then took they the body of Jesus, and ˡwound it in linen clothes with the spices, as the manner of the Jews is to bury.

l Acts 5. 6.

That is, persons of fashion.

41 Now in the place where he was crucified there was a garden ; and in the garden a new sepulchre, wherein was never man yet laid.

As all their gardens were out of the city, so also their burial places, which usually were vaults, or caves within the earth.

42 ᵐThere laid they Jesus therefore ⁿbecause of the Jews' preparation *day ;* for the sepulchre was nigh at hand.

m Is. 53. 9. n ver. 31.

There they immediately buried Christ, because the time strictly called the *preparation* (for the whole day was so called) was nigh at hand. See a fuller account of the history of our Saviour's passion, death, and burial, in the notes on Matt. xxvii., where what is said by all the evangelists is compared together, and made one complete history.

CHAP. XX

Mary Magdalene, seeing the stone taken away from the sepulchre, runneth to tell Peter and John, who go thither, and find not the body, 1—10. *Mary seeth two angels sitting in the sepulchre ; Jesus himself appeareth to her,* 11—18. *He appeareth to his disciples,* 19—23. *The incredulity of Thomas,* 24, 25. *Jesus appeareth again to the disciples, and satisfieth the doubts of Thomas ; who confesseth him,* 26—29. *The sufficiency of what is written for a ground of salvation,* 30, 31.

The evangelist St. John giving a fuller account than the other evangelists of Christ's resurrection, and his converse upon the earth forty days, until he ascended up into heaven, we have in our notes on the other evangelists been shorter, reserving ourselves for a fuller account of it till we should come to these two last chapters of this evangelist.

THE ᵃfirst *day* of the week cometh Mary Magdalene early, when it was yet dark, unto the sepulchre, and seeth the stone taken away from the sepulchre.

a Mat. 28. 1. Mark 16. 1. Luke 24. 1.

Matthew saith, *In the end of the sabbath, as it began to dawn toward the first day of the week ;* he also mentioneth another Mary in company with Mary Magdalene. Mark tells us that other *Mary was the mother of James and Salome.* Luke saith, *they came,* referring to the *women which came with him from Galilee,* chap. xxiii. 55. For the time, Luke saith it was *upon the first day of the week ;* Mark saith it was *when the sabbath was past ;* our evangelist saith it was *when it was yet dark ;* so that Matthew's ὀψὲ δὲ σαββάτων, which we translate, *in the end of the sabbath,* must be interpreted by Mark, *when the sabbath was past ;* and indeed Matthew plainly expounds himself, adding, *as it began to dawn toward the first day of the week ;* which must be seven or eight hours after the Jewish sabbath was ended, for that ended with the setting of the sun the night before. The other evangelists tell us, that the design of their coming was to show their last act of love, in anointing or embalming the body of Jesus ; for which purpose they had bought materials the night wherein he was crucified, but rested on the sabbath day, which ending about sun-set, probably they slept some hours, and early in the morning, in the twilight, they come with their spices. Hence appears, that there is no contradiction at all betwixt the four evangelists about the time of these women's coming to the sepulchre. Matthew saith it was about the dawning of the first day of the week ; Mark saith it was when the sabbath was past ; Luke saith it was upon the first day of the week ; so saith John : which would make one admire that so many words should have been spent by divines in untying a knot here, where there is indeed none. Though John, in his history of our Saviour's burial, saith nothing of any stone rolled to the mouth of the sepulchre ; yet Matthew doth ; and of the Jews' sealing of it, and setting a watch, Matt. xxvii. 64—66. Mark (chap. xvi. 3) tells us also, that these women were thoughtful as they came, who should roll the stone away ; and Matthew also tells us how it came rolled away, viz. by an angel. John saith nothing but that the stone was rolled away. So then the history runs thus : Early on the first day of the week an angel, in a glorious appearance, (described by Mark,) cometh down, rolleth away the stone from the mouth of the sepulchre, and Christ ariseth : soon after, these women came with spices, and were thoughtful as they came who

S. JOHN XX 379

should roll away the stone; but when they came to the sepulchre they found that, as to that, their cares were needless, for the stone was rolled away to their hands.

2 Then she runneth, and cometh to Simon Peter, and to the ᵇother disciple, whom Jesus loved, and saith unto them, They have taken away the Lord out of the sepulchre, and we know not where they have laid him.

ᵇ ch. 13. 23. & 19. 26. & 21. 7, 20, 24.

Then she runneth; that is, Mary Magdalene ran into the city to tell Peter; and that seemeth to be the reason why John mentions only her going to the sepulchre: but yet Luke (chap. xxiv. 10) makes not Mary Magdalene only, but Joanna, and Mary the mother of James, the reporters of the news to the apostles; but possibly she was the forwardest and first reporter of it. She came to the eleven, and told all these things to them, Luke xxiv. 9, but possibly her chief discourse was with Simon Peter, and John, the beloved disciple: she complains to them that her Lord was removed out of the sepulchre, whither and by whom she knew not. But how did they know that? Mark saith, they entered into the sepulchre, chap. xvi. 5. Or if that were after, as it should seem by ver. 11 of this chapter; they guessed that the body was gone when they saw the stone rolled away, and the door open.

3 ᶜPeter therefore went forth, and that other disciple, and came to the sepulchre.

ᶜ Luke 24. 12.

4 So they ran both together: and the other disciple did outrun Peter, and came first to the sepulchre.

Luke, chap. xxiv. 12, mentions Peter's going only, upon Mary Magdalene's report; but he must be expounded by this evangelist, who expressly saith, that Peter and John went together, and that John outran Peter, and got first to the sepulchre.

5 And he stooping down, *and looking in*, saw ᵈthe linen clothes lying; yet went he not in.

ᵈ ch. 19. 40.

John stooped down and looked into the sepulchre, and saw the linen clothes lying, but he would not adventure to go in.

6 Then cometh Simon Peter following him, and went into the sepulchre, and seeth the linen clothes lie,

7 And ᵉthe napkin, that was about his head, not lying with the linen clothes, but wrapped together in a place by itself.

ᵉ ch. 11. 44.

But Peter, who all along the Gospel appears to have been the boldest spirit, goeth into the cave, and seeth all the linen clothes lying there, and the napkin that was about his head lying by itself.

8 Then went in also that other disciple, which came first to the sepulchre, and he saw, and believed.

John seeing Peter adventure in, adventureth also, and seeth the same things, and believeth that Christ was risen from the dead; or (as some think) that, as the women had said, somebody had taken him away.

9 For as yet they knew not the ᶠScripture, that he must rise again from the dead.

ᶠ Ps. 16. 10. Acts 2. 25, —31. & 13. 34, 35.

That is, they did not fully understand those scriptures of the Old Testament, Psal. ii. 2, and xvi. 10, and cx., and the types of the Old Testament, by which Christ's resurrection was foretold and prefigured.

10 Then the disciples went away again unto their own home.

Peter and John, when they had been within the sepulchre, and seen that the body was not there, went home; believing verily that what the women at first told them was true, that somebody had removed the body out of the sepulchre; whither, they knew not.

11 ¶ ᵍBut Mary stood without at the sepulchre weeping: and as she wept,

ᵍ Mark 16. 5.

she stooped down, *and looked* into the sepulchre,

That the Mary here mentioned was Mary Magdalene appeareth from ver. 14, compared with Mark xvi. 9, which saith, he appeared first to Mary Magdalene.

12 And seeth two angels in white sitting, the one at the head, and the other at the feet, where the body of Jesus had lain.

13 And they say unto her, Woman, why weepest thou? She saith unto them, Because they have taken away my Lord, and I know not where they have laid him.

The other evangelists differing in their accounts of this part of the history, have raised some questions here not easily to be resolved. Matthew reports thus, chap. xxviii. 2—9, *And, behold, there was a great earthquake; for the angel of the Lord descended from heaven, and came and rolled back the stone from the door, and sat upon it. His countenance was like lightning, and his raiment white as snow: and for fear of him the keepers did shake, and became as dead men. And the angel answered and said unto the women, Fear not ye: for I know that ye seek Jesus, which was crucified. He is not here: for he is risen, as he said. Come, see the place where the Lord lay. And go quickly and tell his disciples that he is risen from the dead; and, behold, he goeth before you into Galilee; there shall ye see him; lo, I have told you. And they departed quickly from the sepulchre with fear and great joy; and did run to bring his disciples word. And as they went to tell his disciples, behold, Jesus met them,* &c. Mark saith, chap. xvi. 2—8, *And very early in the morning the first day of the week, they came unto the sepulchre at the rising of the sun.* Where by *the rising of the sun* must not be understood its rising above the horizon; but after midnight, (as the learned Casaubon hath noted,) when the sun and stars begin to ascend. *And they said among themselves, Who shall roll us away the stone from the door of the sepulchre? And when they looked, they saw that the stone was rolled away: for it was very great. And entering into the sepulchre, they saw a young man sitting on the right side, clothed in a long white garment; and they were affrighted. And he saith unto them, Be not affrighted: ye seek Jesus of Nazareth, which was crucified: he is risen; he is not here: behold the place where they laid him. But go your way, tell his disciples and Peter that he goeth before you into Galilee: there shall ye see him, as he said unto you. And they went out quickly, and fled from the sepulchre; for they trembled and were amazed: neither said they any thing to any man; for they were afraid.* Luke reports this part of the history thus, chap. xxiv. 1—12, *Now upon the first day of the week, very early in the morning, they came unto the sepulchre, bringing the spices which they had prepared, and certain others with them. And they found the stone rolled away from the sepulchre. And they entered in, and found not the body of the Lord Jesus. And it came to pass as they were much perplexed thereabout, behold, two men stood by them in shining garments: and as they were afraid, and bowed down their faces to the earth, they said unto them, Why seek ye the living among the dead? he is not here, but is risen: remember how he spake unto you when he was yet in Galilee, saying, The Son of man must be delivered into the hands of sinful men, and be crucified, and the third day rise again. And they remembered his words, and returned from the sepulchre, and told all these things unto the eleven, and to all the rest. It was Mary Magdalene, and Joanna, and Mary the mother of James, and other women that were with them, which told these things unto the apostles. And their words seemed to them as idle tales, and they believed them not. Then arose Peter, and ran unto the sepulchre, and stooping down, he beheld the linen clothes laid by themselves, and departed, wondering in himself at that which was come to pass.* Concerning the persons that went to the sepulchre, and the time of their going, there is (as we have showed) little difficulty in reconciling the evangelists. The greatest difference seemeth to be about the angels that Mary saw; whether she saw two apparitions of angels, or but one, and one angel, or two; and concerning the time when she saw them, whether before or after that Peter and John had been in the sepulchre. Matthew saith, the stone was rolled away, and the angel sat upon the stone; this must be without the sepulchre. Mark saith, *they, entering into the sepulchre, saw* (an angel in the shape of) *a young man sitting,* &c. Luke and John speak of two angels; but seen in the sepulchre, not without it. There is no doubt but the apparition was of two angels; one of which might be seen without first, sitting upon the stone, to let the women know that he had rolled it away: both of them within, sitting one at the head, the other at the feet, of the place where the body of Jesus lay. But the greatest question is, Whether the woman saw the angels before that Peter and John had been at the sepulchre, or after? Some think that it was before, but it is no way probable; for it can hardly be thought but that if they had seen the angel at the first, they would have told the eleven of it, or Peter and John at least; nor would Mary have told Peter and John (as ver. 2) they had taken away her Lord, &c., for the angels told them he was risen. So that although by some of the others' relation, who say nothing of Peter and John's coming to the sepulchre, it seems as if the women saw the angel before their coming to satisfy themselves, yet indeed it was after. The women first came, saw the door open, the stone rolled away, &c. In a fright they ran back, and told it the disciples. Peter and John came to see, and being satisfied, return, leaving Mary still standing at the sepulchre weeping; then she stooping down and looking into the sepulchre, both saw the angel sitting on the stone, and also the two angels within the sepulchre, who fully revealed the resurrection to her.

h Matt. 28.9.
Mark 16. 9.
i Luke 24.16, 31. ch. 21. 4.

14 ʰAnd when she had thus said, she turned herself back, and saw Jesus standing, and ⁱknew not that it was Jesus.

And presently Christ himself appeareth to her, though at first she did not know him.

15 Jesus saith unto her, Woman, why weepest thou? whom seekest thou? She, supposing him to be the gardener, saith unto him, Sir, if thou have borne him hence, tell me where thou hast laid him, and I will take him away.

Either these words passed before the angels had told her that he was risen, Mark xvi. 6; Luke xxiv. 5, 6; or (which is most probable) Mary was hard to believe what the angels had told her so lately; but coming out of the sepulchre, Christ appeareth to her, whom she knew not, but thought him to have been the person that had the charge of that garden where Christ was buried, and that he for his own conveniency had removed the dead body; she therefore desires to know where he had disposed of it, having a mind to remove it to some honourable place of burial.

16 Jesus saith unto her, Mary. She turned herself, and saith unto him, Rabboni; which is to say, Master.

Christ calleth her by name, making such a sound as he certainly knew she understood. She calleth him *Rabboni*, which is as much as to say, My Master.

17 Jesus saith unto her, Touch me not; for I am not yet ascended to my Father: but go to ᵏmy brethren, and say unto them, ˡI ascend unto my Father, and your Father; and *to* ᵐmy God, and your God.

k Ps. 22. 22.
Matt. 28. 10.
Rom. 8. 29.
Heb. 2. 11.
l ch. 16. 28.
m Eph. 1.17.

There are in this verse two no mean difficulties: the one about the sense of the prohibition, when our Saviour forbade this woman to touch him; when after his resurrection (Matt. xxviii. 9) he suffered the women to hold him by the feet, and himself (ver. 27 of this chapter) called Thomas to thrust his hand into the hole of his side. There are many opinions about it: the best seems to be the opinion of those who think that our Saviour saw Mary too fond, and too much in the embraces of her Lord, as if she thought he had been raised up to such a converse with them as he had before his death; and this error is all which he tasks her of, not forbidding her any kind of touching him, so far as to satisfy herself that he was truly risen from the dead, but restraining any such gross conception. The other difficulty, What force of a reason there could be for her not touching him because he had not yet ascended?

is much solved by that answer to the former; reminding Mary that he was to ascend to his Father, though he had not yet ascended, and therefore not to be enjoyed by them with so much freedom and familiarity as before. But (saith he) go and tell *my brethren*, that is, my disciples; whom the apostle tells us he is not ashamed to call brethren, Heb. ii. 11, 12; that *I ascend*, that is, I shall shortly ascend, *to my Father and your Father, to my God and your God:* though I shall very suddenly leave them, yet I shall go but to my Father and my God, and to their Father and their God.

18 ⁿMary Magdalene came and told the disciples that she had seen the Lord, and *that* he had spoken these things unto her.

n Mat. 28.10.
Luke 24. 10.

This was that first appearance of our Lord after his resurrection to Mary Magdalene, after that he was risen from the dead, mentioned Mark xvi. 9, 10, which she reported to the disciples; but Mark saith, they believed her not, ver. 11. Matthew tells us of another appearance of his, chap. xxviii. 9, to the women as they went from the sepulchre, when they *held him by the feet, and worshipped him.* Luke tells us of a third appearance to the two disciples as they were going to Emmaus; which is also shortly touched by Mark, chap. xvi. 12, 13; but it is there said that they believed them not. John mentioneth neither of these. These were all the same day that he rose, so was also the next, which is mentioned by our evangelist in the following verses.

19 ¶ ᵒThen the same day at evening, being the first *day* of the week, when the doors were shut where the disciples were assembled for fear of the Jews, came Jesus and stood in the midst, and saith unto them, Peace *be* unto you.

o Mark 16. 14. Luke 24. 36. 1 Cor.15. 5.

Luke expounds this verse, chap. xxiv. 29, where the two disciples told Christ it was *towards evening, and the day* was *far spent;* for the Jews called the afternoon evening, as well as the time after sun-set; and John tells us expressly, it was yet *the first day of the week*. This appearance is unquestionably the same mentioned Luke xxiv. 36. For it is said, the two disciples went immediately to Jerusalem, where they *found the eleven gathered together*, and discoursed of the Lord's appearance to them; and while they spake, Jesus came and *stood in the midst of them, and said unto them,* (as here), Peace be unto you. The disciples had shut the doors of the place where they met, *for fear of the Jews.* Here is a great question betwixt the Lutherans and Calvinists, how Christ came in amongst them when the doors were shut? whether he went through the doors remaining shut? which the Lutherans stiffly maintain, as a strong proof of the possibility of the real presence of the body of Christ in, with, or under the elements of the Lord's supper; though we object, that this is to destroy the nature of Christ's body, and to assign him a body which indeed is no body, being not obvious to the sense, nor confined to a place; and which must pierce another body, which is contrary to the nature of a body according to our notion of bodies. The Lutherans object, 1. That here is a plain mention of the doors being shut. 2. No mention of the opening of them. 3. Nor of Christ's entrance upon opening any doors, windows, roof, or by any ordinary way, as men use to enter into houses. 4. Nor, had he so entered, would there have been any occasion for the disciples taking him for a *spirit*, as it is plain they did, Luke xxiv. 37. The Calvinists on the other side object, 1. That it is not said that he went through the doors. 2. That if he had gone through the doors, he would not presently have called to them to have seen him, and handled him; by which he evidenced that his body had such dimensions as our bodies have, and so could not go through a door shut. In the Lutherans' reason, the fourth is only considerable, the three first have no force, because all circumstances of actions are not recorded in holy writ. Nor is there much force in the fourth, for the doors by his miraculous power opened and shut, and he showed himself in the midst of them, and used to them the usual salutation amongst the Jews, *Peace be unto you.*

20 And when he had so said, he shewed unto

S. JOHN XX

p ch. 16. 22. them *his* hands and his side. ᵖThen were the disciples glad, when they saw the Lord.

He showed unto them his hands and his side; Luke adds his *feet* too; those parts of his body where were the most undeniable marks of the death he had suffered upon the cross. Then to disciples, who gave little credit to what Mary Magdalene, and the other woman, and the two disciples going to Emmaus, had reported, believed; seeing the Lord, and being exceeding glad at this confirmation of their faith.

q Mat. 28. 18. ch. 17. 18, 19. Heb. 3. 1. 2 Tim. 2. 2.
21 Then said Jesus to them again, Peace *be* unto you: ᑫas *my* Father hath sent me, even so send I you.

Peace be unto you; the repeating of this salutation speaketh it more than an ordinary compliment, or form of salutation. It signifieth his reconciliation to them, notwithstanding their error in forsaking him, and fleeing; it prepared their attention for the great things that he was now about to speak to them; it also signified, that he was about to preach the gospel of peace to all nations. *As my Father hath sent me, even so send I you;* I have now fulfilled my ministry, and am now going to my Father who sent me: now by the same authority that I am sent, I send you, to gather, instruct, and govern my church; I send, or I will send, you clothed with the same authority with which I am clothed, and for the same ends in part for which I was sent.

22 And when he had said this, he breathed on *them*, and saith unto them, Receive ye the Holy Ghost:

The apostles could not but be apprehensive how great a work their Lord had laid upon them, in sending them as his Father had sent him, to carry the gospel over the world; *Who* (said Paul afterward) *is sufficient for these things?* Our Lord therefore fortifies them with an earnest of that more plentiful effusion of the Spirit, which they afterward received in the days of Pentecost. They before this had received the Spirit as a Spirit of sanctification, and had received a power to work miracles. They did not till after this receive the gift of tongues, &c. But he here assures them of the presence of the Holy Spirit with them, in their more ordinary ministry, in instructing and governing the church. This conferring of the Spirit upon them he confirms to them by breathing, as an exterior sign or symbol. The name, *Spirit,* signifieth a breath; and it is said, that in the creation God *breathed into* Adam *the breath of life.* Christ breatheth into his apostles the Holy Spirit; thereby showing, that the Holy Spirit proceedeth, as from the Father, so also from him; as the breath of a man proceedeth from him. He also useth words, expounding his action in breathing, and carrying with them an authority, which being once spoken, the thing was done.

r Matt. 10. 19. & 18. 18.
23 ʳWhose soever sins ye remit, they are remitted unto them; *and* whose soever *sins* ye retain, they are retained.

Whether Matt. xviii. 18 be a parallel text to this, I doubt: see the notes on that verse. Our Lord here speaks of the sins of persons, *Whose soever sins ye remit,* &c.; he saith there, *Whatsoever ye shall bind or loose.* This text hath caused a great deal of contest. All remission of sins is either authoritative; so it is most true, that none can forgive sin but God; and if we had no Scripture to prove it, yet reason will tell us none can discharge the debtor but the creditor, to whom the debt is owing: or else ministerial; thus he who is not the creditor (amongst men) may remit a debt by virtue of a letter of attorney made to him, authorizing him so to do. The question therefore amongst divines is, Whether Christ in this text hath given authority to his ministers actually to discharge men of the guilt of their sins; or only to declare unto them, that if their repentance and faith be true, their sins are really forgiven them? The former is by many contended for; but it doth not seem reasonable, 1. That God should betrust men with such a piece of his prerogative. 2. That God, who knoweth the falsehood of men's hearts, and the inability in the best ministers to judge of the truth of any man's faith or repentance, as also the passions to which they are subject, should give unto any of the sons of men an absolute power under him, and in his name, to discharge any from the guilt of sin; for certain it is, that without true repentance and faith in Christ no man hath his sins forgiven; so as no minister, that knoweth not the hearts of men, can possibly speak with any certainty to any man, saying, his sins are forgiven. What knowledge the apostles might have by the Spirit of discerning, we cannot say. But certain it is, none hath any such certainty of knowledge now of the truth of any man, declaring his faith and true repentance; from whence it is to me apparent, that no man hath any further power from Christ, than to declare to them, that if indeed they truly believe and repent, their sins are really forgiven. Only the minister, being Christ's interpreter and ambassador, and better able to judge of true faith and repentance than others, (though not certainly and infallibly,) such declarations from a faithful, able minister, are of more weight and authority than from others. And this is the most I can conceive should be in this matter; and that if by those words any further power be granted to the apostles, it was by reason of that power of *discerning of spirits,* 1 Cor. xii. 10, which ordinary ministers since the apostles' times, or in latter ages, cannot with any modesty pretend unto.

24 ¶ But Thomas, one of the twelve, ˢcalled Didymus, was not with them when Jesus came. s ch. 11. 16.

Whether Thomas had ever, since they all forsook our Saviour in the garden and fled, returned again to a communion with the rest, or was absent through some occasion, is not said; but upon this some have started a question, Whether Thomas, being absent, received the Holy Ghost at this time as the rest did? Some think he did not, because of his unbelief. Some of the ancients think he did; for, Numb. xi. 26, 27, when God gave out the Spirit to the seventy elders, Eldad and Medad, though absent, had their share of it, ver. 27. The matter is not much.

25 The other disciples therefore said unto him, We have seen the Lord. But he said unto them, Except I shall see in his hands the print of the nails, and put my finger into the print of the nails, and thrust my hand into his side, I will not believe.

It is not said what disciples, whether any of the apostles, or some others, told Thomas of this appearing of the Lord unto them. But Thomas eminently declareth his unbelief, which argues him as yet much ignorant of the Deity of Christ, and having given too little heed to what Christ had told them of his rising again the third day.

26 ¶ And after eight days again his disciples were within, and Thomas with them: *then* came Jesus, the doors being shut, and stood in the midst, and said, Peace *be* unto you.

After eight days signifieth here the eighth day from the resurrection, counting the day wherein Christ rose for one; as we call those third day agues which have but one day's intermission, and those quartan agues which have but two days' intermission; so it is said, Mark viii. 31, *after three days he shall rise again,* that is, the third day. This appears the most probable sense of the phrase: the disciples beginning from Christ's resurrection to keep the first day of the week for the weekly sabbath, and having met on the resurrection day, met again that day sevennight, hoping (probably) for such a presence of Christ with them in their meeting as they had before experienced; nor was their expectation vain. It appears also further, from Acts xx. 7, and 1 Cor. xvi. 2, that the Christians were wont ordinarily to meet together the first day of the week for religious exercises; which from Christ's resurrection, or institution, or both, is thought to be called *the Lord's day,* Rev. i. 10. Nor indeed do we read in all the Scripture of any congregation of Christians on the Jewish sabbath, but upon this day; though, indeed, we find that the apostles (and possibly some other Christians) did meet together with the Jews in their synagogues on their sabbath; but we have not so much as one instance after the resurrection of any congregation, where Christians only were assembled upon the Jewish sabbath. Thomas at this time

27 Then saith he to Thomas, Reach hither thy finger, and behold my hands; ^t and ^treach hither thy hand, and thrust *it* into my side: and be not faithless, but believing.

<small>t 1 John 1. 1.</small>

We had need take heed what we speak wherever we are. Christ had not after his resurrection so ordinary and frequent a converse with his disciples as before. This is the fifth time that we read of Christ's appearing to them since his resurrection. He knew what words of unbelief Thomas had uttered, and accordingly applieth himself to him, in a wonderful condescension to his weakness; he bids him reach his finger, and his hands, and behold his hands, and thrust his hands into his side. So pitiful is our Lord, and compassionate towards the infirmities of his people.

28 And Thomas answered and said unto him, My Lord and my God.

My Lord, to whom I wholly yield and give up my self; *and my God*, in whom I believe. It is observed, that this is the first time that in the Gospel the name of *God* is given to Christ; he was now by his resurrection *declared to be the Son of God with power*, Rom. i. 4. So as Thomas did not show more weakness and unbelief at the first, than he showed faith at last, being the first that acknowledged Christ as *God over all blessed for ever*, the object of people's faith and confidence, and his Lord, to whom he freely yielded up himself as a servant, to be guided and conducted by him.

29 Jesus saith unto him, Thomas, because thou hast seen me, thou hast believed: ^ublessed *are* they that have not seen, and *yet* have believed.

<small>u 2 Cor. 5. 7. 1 Pet. 1. 8.</small>

Thou believest that I am risen from the dead upon the testimony of thy senses; thou doest well in that: thou hast seen, thou hast felt me; but it is a more noble faith to believe without any such sensible evidence. Faith is properly an assent given to a proposition upon the testimony of revelation, which if it be but human it is no more than a human faith; as we give credit to what our neighbours tell us, though we have not seen it with our own eyes, nor heard it with our ears immediately, nor had it made evident to any of our senses. If the revelation to which the assent is given be from God, we call the assent that is given to it a Divine faith; so that to give credit to a thing upon the evidence of sense, is properly no believing, otherwise than as sense confirms what we have before received by a Divine revelation. This is a sure rule, that by how much our faith stands in less need of an external evidence of sense, the stronger it is.

<small>x ch. 21. 25.</small>

30 ¶ ^xAnd many other signs truly did Jesus in the presence of his disciples, which are not written in this book:

This passage plainly refers to whatsoever signs we read of in any part of St. John's Gospel; and lets us know, that the evangelist could have added abundance more to the history of the miracles which Christ wrought upon the earth.

<small>y Luke 1. 4.</small>

31 ^yBut these are written, that ye might believe that Jesus is the Christ, the Son of God; ^zand that believing ye might have life through his name.

<small>z ch. 3. 15, 16. & 5. 24. 1 Pet. 1. 9.</small>

But he had wrote these to induce his readers to believe that Jesus Christ was the Son of God; a thing of so great concernment to them, that their eternal life depended upon it; for through his name alone eternal life is to be obtained, Acts iv. 12.

CHAP. XXI

Christ appeareth to his disciples at the sea of Tiberias, and maketh himself known by a great draught of fishes, 1—11. *He eateth before them,* 12—14. *He thrice repeateth his charge to Peter to feed his flock; foretelleth the manner of his death; and rebuketh his curiosity concerning John,* 15—23. *John asserteth the truth of his testimony, and that Jesus did many acts besides, too numerous to be recorded,* 24, 25.

AFTER these things Jesus shewed himself again to the disciples at the sea of Tiberias; and on this wise shewed he *himself*.

After three several appearances of Christ to his disciples, which hitherto were all of them in Jerusalem, Christ showed himself again to them in Galilee, whither he had ordered his disciples to go, promising there to meet them, Matt. xxvi. 32; Mark xvi. 7. Here the occasion and circumstances of this his third appearance are related by St. John.

2 There were together Simon Peter, and Thomas called Didymus, and ^aNathanael of Cana in Galilee, and ^bthe *sons* of Zebedee, and two other of his disciples.

<small>a ch. 1. 45. b Mat. 4. 21.</small>

All the disciples were either there in several places, or going thither, according to Christ's direction before mentioned: but either these seven were there before the rest, or else they lodged together, or near one another; so as these only are here mentioned as being together at this time, and so witnesses of this miracle which followeth.

3 Simon Peter saith unto them, I go a fishing. They say unto him, We also go with thee. They went forth, and entered into a ship immediately; and that night they caught nothing.

Peter and divers others were fishermen, as we have formerly heard, and had boats which they so employed. Though they were called to the work of the ministry, yet, churches not yet being gathered and constituted able to maintain them, they did not judge it unlawful to employ themselves in honest vocations, which might bring in something of a livelihood; no more did Paul afterward. The others resolve to go with Peter. They went, but *that night caught nothing;* the providence of God so ordering it, that Christ's Divine power might be seen in commanding fish into their nets.

4 But when the morning was now come, Jesus stood on the shore: but the disciples ^cknew not that it was Jesus.

<small>c ch. 20. 14.</small>

Probably their distance from him was the cause that they did not know him, though they had seen him once and again since his resurrection from the dead: others think, that by the providence of God *their eyes were holden that they should not know him*, as Luke xxiv. 16.

5 Then ^dJesus saith unto them, ‖ Children, have ye any meat? They answered him, No.

<small>d Luke 24. 41. ‖ Or, Sirs.</small>

He asketh them if they had any thing to eat, not because he knew not, but in order to what he intended to do, to make them more attentive to the miracle which he by and by intended to work.

6 And he said unto them, ^eCast the net on the right side of the ship, and ye shall find. They cast therefore, and now they were not able to draw it for the multitude of fishes.

<small>e Luke 5. 4, 6, 7.</small>

Though they had before laboured in vain, yet their Master's command encourageth them to go to work again; then they take a multitude of fishes; a presage, say some, of that great success which the apostles should have in their fishing for men.

7 Therefore ^fthat disciple whom Jesus loved saith unto Peter, It is the Lord. Now when Simon Peter heard that it was the Lord, he girt *his* fisher's coat *unto him,* (for he was naked,) and did cast himself into the sea.

<small>f ch. 13. 23. & 20. 2.</small>

There is a great dispute amongst critical writers what this *fisher's coat* was; whether a loose coat, or the garment next his skin, or a fisherman's slop. It is a point not worth the disputing: it was some garment that might modestly

S. JOHN XXI

cover him when he came to Jesus, and yet not hinder him in his swimming.

8 And the other disciples came in a little ship; (for they were not far from land, but as it were two hundred cubits,) dragging the net with fishes.

The other disciples came in a little fishing-boat, dragging the net with fishes; probably, because it was too heavy to be lifted up into the boat.

9 As soon then as they were come to land, they saw a fire of coals there, and fish laid thereon, and bread.

As to the question whence this fish came, there are three opinions: some think that our Saviour caught it out of the sea without a net, or by his power commanded it to come to his service; others think that the history is transposed, and this verse should in its true order come after the eleventh; but it is most probable that Christ by his Divine power created the fish, as well as the coals and the bread.

10 Jesus saith unto them, Bring of the fish which ye have now caught.

11 Simon Peter went up, and drew the net to land full of great fishes, an hundred and fifty and three: and for all there were so many, yet was not the net broken.

In this one miracle there is a complication of miracles. 1. That having fished all night and caught nothing, they should at Christ's command throw out the net on the side of the ship next the shore, and so most unlikely to have plenty of fish, and catch so many. 2. That before their fish could be brought on shore, they should see a fish broiling on coals, and bread lying by. 3. That notwithstanding the multitude of fish, the net should not be broken.

g Acts 10.41. 12 Jesus saith unto them, g Come *and* dine. And none of the disciples durst ask him, Who art thou? knowing that it was the Lord.

It was in the morning, and may as well be translated, Come and break your fasts, as *Come and dine.* They now knew it was the Lord, if not by his face and voice, yet by this miracle; therefore they durst not ask him, for fear of a sharp reproof, after he had by such a miraculous operation made himself known to them.

13 Jesus then cometh, and taketh bread, and giveth them, and fish likewise.

Those who question whether our Saviour himself did eat, seem not to consider what is written Acts x. 41, where it is expressly said, *he did eat and drink with them after he rose from the dead;* which he doubtless did, to show that he was truly risen from the dead, and his seeming body was not a phantasm, and mere apparition of a body, but the same true body which was crucified, though now more glorious, and not clothed with those infirmities which it had before his death; from whence it only followeth, that he did not eat to satisfy his hunger, but only to confirm the truth of his resurrection. He did before this eat with some of them, Luke xxiv. 30.

h See ch. 20. 19, 26. 14 This is now h the third time that Jesus shewed himself to his disciples, after that he was risen from the dead.

The third time; that is, the third day, for upon his resurrection day he showed himself, 1. To Mary Magdalene, chap. xx. 14. 2. To the two disciples going to Emmaus, Luke xxiv. 15, 31. 3. To the women going to tell his disciples, Matt. xxviii. 9. 4. In the evening to his disciples, met, chap. xx. 19. All these are by John counted for one time, because they were upon one and the same day. That day seven-night he appeared to them again, chap. xx. 26. After this *at the sea of Tiberias,* mentioned in this chapter.

15 ¶ So when they had dined, Jesus saith to Simon Peter, Simon, *son* of Jonas, lovest thou me more than these? He saith unto him, Yea, Lord; thou knowest that I love thee. He saith unto him, Feed my lambs.

Lovest thou me more than these? more than the rest of my disciples love me? for so Peter had professed, when he told our Saviour, Matt. xxvi. 33, *Though all men should be offended because of thee, yet will I never be offended.* Peter now having by his temptation learned more humility and modesty, doth not reply, Lord, thou knowest that I love thee more than these; he only averreth the truth and sincerity, not the degree of his love. Christ replies, *Feed my lambs:* by which he understands his people, his church; not the pastors of it, (as if Christ by this had made Peter the chief pastor over the rest of the apostles,) but the community. The papists from this text argue for Peter's primacy and authority over his fellow apostles, as well as over the members of the church. But Christ said not to Peter only, but to all the rest of the eleven, Matt. xxviii. 19; Mark xvi. 15, Go ye, preach the gospel to all nations; and it was to the rest as well as to Peter that he said, chap. xx. 23, *Whose soever sins ye remit, they are remitted.* So as it is apparent, whether feeding only signifies instructing, or feeding by doctrine, or (as most judge) comprehends government, and signifies that universal charge which ministers have over the church, the same power which Peter had was also committed to the other disciples.

16 He saith to him again the second time, Simon, *son* of Jonas, lovest thou me? He saith unto him, Yea, Lord; thou knowest that I love thee. i He saith unto him, Feed my sheep.

i Acts 20. 28. Heb. 13. 20. 1 Pet. 2. 25. & 5. 2, 4.

17 He saith unto him the third time, Simon, *son* of Jonas, lovest thou me? Peter was grieved because he said unto him the third time, Lovest thou me? And he said unto him, Lord, k thou knowest all things; thou knowest that I love thee. Jesus saith unto him, Feed my sheep.

k ch. 2. 24, 25. & 16. 30.

Divines here raise a question, why our Saviour propounds this question thrice to Peter. The most of the ancients agree, that it was because Peter had thrice denied him. Some say, it was to show his great love to his church, which he could not commit to Peter but after three inquiries if he truly loved him, who was the Lord of it. Others refer it to the three ways by which good pastors ought to feed the church; prayer, preaching, and a holy life. Others think, that it hath reference to the three flocks that Peter was to feed; the Jews in Judea, the Gentiles, the dispersed amongst the Gentiles.

18 l Verily, verily, I say unto thee, When thou wast young, thou girdedst thyself, and walkedst whither thou wouldest: but when thou shalt be old, thou shalt stretch forth thy hands, and another shall gird thee, and carry *thee* whither thou wouldest not.

l ch. 13. 36. Acts 12. 3, 4.

19 This spake he, signifying m by what death he should glorify God. And when he had spoken this, he saith unto him, Follow me.

m 2 Pet. 1. 14.

The 19th verse gives us the general scope of ver. 18, viz. that it was a prediction of that particular death by which Peter should die, which was (if we may believe what the ancients have generally reported, and we can have no other proof) by crucifying; in which kind of death the hands of the person crucified are stretched out and nailed to the cross. But which way he died we cannot certainly affirm. The evangelist assureth us, that our Saviour spake these words with reference to that kind of death by which Peter as a martyr was to glorify God; nor is it any objection against his martyrdom, that our Saviour here saith, that he should be carried whither he would not; for he was not better than his Lord, whose spirit was willing, and flesh weak. Whether our Saviour by this command, *Follow me,* intended the imitation of him, his death, or the particular kind of his death, is uncertain; unless we will allow this text to be interpreted by chap. xiii. 36, and 2 Pet. i. 14.

20 Then Peter, turning about, seeth the disciple n whom Jesus loved follow-

n ch. 13. 23, 25. & 20. 2.

ing; which also leaned on his breast at supper, and said, Lord, which is he that betrayeth thee?

That is, he saw John, whom we have often before heard so described.

21 Peter seeing him saith to Jesus, Lord, and what *shall* this man *do?*

Do is not in the Greek, nor possibly is so properly added: the sense is, What shall become of this man? what shall be his fate? what shall he suffer?

○ Matt. 16. 27, 28. & 25. 31. 1 Cor. 4. 5. & 11. 26. Rev. 2. 25. & 3. 11. & 22. 7, 20.

22 Jesus saith unto him, If I will that he tarry °till I come, what *is that* to thee? follow thou me.

Our Lord only checketh the curiosity of Peter, and minds him to attend things which himself was concerned in; telling him, he was not concerned what became of John, whether he should die, or abide upon the earth until Christ's second coming: it was Peter's concern, without regarding what others did, or what became of them, himself to execute his Master's command, and follow his example.

23 Then went this saying abroad among the brethren, that that disciple should not die: yet Jesus said not unto him, He shall not die; but, If I will that he tarry till I come, what *is that* to thee?

But the disciples, knowing the particular kindness our Saviour had for John, upon these words, not duly attended to, concluded John should abide upon the earth to the second coming of Christ.

24 This is the disciple which testifieth of these things, and wrote these things: and ᵖwe know that his testimony is true.

p ch. 19. 35. 3 John 12.

John, who wrote this Gospel, was that disciple whom Jesus loved, who leaned on our Saviour's breast at supper, and inquired who should betray Christ; of whom Peter spake, ver. 21, and who testifieth these things, both concerning Peter, and concerning himself, and the church: the ancient church knew his testimony was true.

25 ᑫAnd there are also many other things which Jesus did, the which, if they should be written every one, ʳI suppose that even the world itself could not contain the books that should be written. Amen.

q ch. 20. 30.

r Amos 7. 10.

But none must imagine that all Christ's sermons, or miracles, are recorded in this book, or in any of the other Gospels; the world would have been too much filled with books, if all spoke or done by our Saviour had been written. There is so much written as it pleased God we should know, or was necessary for us to know for the true ends of such revelation; to beget and increase faith in us, and to promote and direct holiness.

THE

ACTS OF THE APOSTLES

THE ARGUMENT

This book hath been held by all Christians to be canonical, and esteemed, though amongst the hardest, yet amongst the brightest jewels that shine in the word of God. It is a history concerning the church of Christ in its infancy, and shows God's wonderful care for it, and powerful providence over it. It begins where the Gospel ends, which the same author (St. Luke) had wrote; and is of great use to prevent and confute all feigned stories concerning the lives and doctrine of the holy apostles. St. Luke having accompanied St. Paul, and having been an eye-witness, and an ear-witness, was certainly the fittest to record what that great apostle did and said; and if most of this book be taken up concerning him, it is because (speaking of the rest of the apostles, 1 Cor. xv. 10) he *laboured more than they all*. In this book there is an account of many sermons, preached by the apostles and apostolical men, upon the most necessary parts of our holy religion, as the death, resurrection, and ascension of our blessed Saviour; of God's mercy through him, and of the life to come, &c.; and withal, how holy men lived answerably to their profession and hope. Who, when we read these things, seem to speak unto us, and tell us, (what they say was inscribed upon the statue of some deified hero,) *Si feceritis sicut nos, eritis sicut nos;* If ye shall do as we have done, and suffer as we have suffered, then ye shall be (glorious and happy) as we are.

CHAP. I

Christ, after his resurrection, having given instructions to his apostles, and commanded them to wait in Jerusalem the coming of the Holy Ghost, ascendeth into heaven in their sight, 1—9. *Two angels warn them to depart, and to look for his second coming,* 10, 11. *They return, and give themselves unto prayer,* 12—14. *Peter exhorting to fill up the place of the traitor Judas, Matthias is chosen by lot to be an apostle,* 15—26.

a Luke 1. 3.

THE former treatise have I made, O ᵃTheophilus, of all that Jesus began both to do and teach,

The former treatise have I made; this refers unto the Gospel wrote by this evangelist, St. Luke, who was undoubtedly the penman of this book, which bears testimony unto and confirms (if need were) that other. *Theophilus;* esteemed the same name with Jedidiah, signifying beloved of God, or one that loved God. Who he was is not certain; some have taken the name appellatively. It is evident by the epithet given unto him, Luke i. 3, that he was one of great authority, having the same title which Tertullus gives unto Festus, Acts xxiv. 3, and the chief captain unto Felix, Acts xxiii. 26. Although *not many noble are called,* 1 Cor. i. 26, yet God extends his grace unto some of all conditions. *Of all that Jesus began both to do and teach;* this is the sum of the Gospel, viz. a history of the life, doctrine, and death of our blessed Saviour; although every particular word or deed of our Saviour's could not be expressed, John xxi. 25, yet the evangelist was faithful in withholding nothing which was necessary for the church to know, and leaving no room for unwritten traditions.

2 ᵇUntil the day in which he was taken up, after that he through the Holy Ghost ᶜhad given commandments unto the apostles whom he had chosen:

b Mark 16. 19. Luke 9. 51. & 24. 51. ver. 9. 1 Tim. 3. 16. c Mat. 28. 19. Mark 16. 15. John 20. 21. ch. 10. 41, 42.

The day in which he was taken up; that is, the day of

his ascension. This is a translation from the former book (his Gospel) unto this, showing how far he had proceeded in setting down the doctrine of our salvation. *After that he through the Holy Ghost had given commandments unto the apostles whom he had chosen;* which words may be referred, either to the commandments he gave, or the choice he made of the apostles; both being by the Holy Ghost. The apostles had their doctrine from God, and were appointed to publish it by God; especially to publish the gospel to the whole world, Matt. xxviii. 19; and to continue at Jerusalem till the coming of the Holy Ghost, Luke xxiv. 49.

3 ᵈTo whom also he shewed himself alive after his passion by many infallible proofs, being seen of them forty days, and speaking of the things pertaining to the kingdom of God:

To whom, i. e. the apostles, *he showed himself alive after his passion by many infallible proofs;* eating, drinking, speaking, walking with them; nay, showing them his very wounds, and permitting them to be touched; God suffering Thomas's infidelity to contribute to the strengthening of our faith. *Being seen of them forty days;* not continually, but upon occasion as he pleased; it was so long from his resurrection to his ascension; and the same space in which God showed himself unto Moses in Mount Sinai. So long also he was pleased to stay with them, that he might more abundantly testify the truth of his humanity, and of his resurrection. *And speaking of the things pertaining to the kingdom of God;* either his kingdom in heaven, the church triumphant, or his kingdom on earth, the church militant; what future bliss and happiness he was going to prepare, and what means they ought to use towards the obtaining of it.

4 ᵉAnd, ‖ being assembled together with *them,* commanded them that they should not depart from Jerusalem, but wait for the promise of the Father, ᶠwhich, saith he, ye have heard of me.

And being assembled together with them; by his order, or conversing frequently with them, as those that table together. *Commanded them that they should not depart from Jerusalem:* otherwise the apostles would have abhorred Jerusalem, as reeking afresh in the blood of our Lord. And there Christ chose to pour out his Spirit, that he might show forth his glory in the same place where he suffered ignominy: there Christ would have his apostles to abide, that they might be nigher to Mount Olivet, from whence he was to ascend; as also that both his ascension, and the coming of the Holy Ghost, might more publicly be manifest; and that that prophecy, Isa. ii. 3, might be fulfilled. *The promise of the Father; of my Father,* Luke xxiv. 49; that is, the Holy Spirit, promised by our Saviour in his Father's name, John xiv. 26; and may well be called *the promise,* without which all other promises would be of no value unto us.

5 ᵍFor John truly baptized with water; ʰbut ye shall be baptized with the Holy Ghost not many days hence.

For John truly baptized with water, Matt. iii. 11; water being of a purifying nature, plentiful, and easy to come by. *But ye shall be baptized with the Holy Ghost;* his gifts and graces, which were (as water on baptized persons) largely bestowed upon them on the day of Pentecost: 1. That the apostles and all others might be assured of the doctrine of the Gospel. 2. That they might be enabled to fulfil their ministry, and obey our Saviour's commands left with them. *Not many days hence;* it was but ten days after his ascension; but our Saviour would not prefix a certain day, that they might watch every day.

6 When they therefore were come together, they asked of him, saying, ⁱLord, wilt thou at this time ᵏrestore again the kingdom to Israel?

When they therefore were come together; either the one hundred and twenty, mentioned ver. 15, or the five hundred, mentioned 1 Cor. xv. 6. That they might more readily obtain an answer, they join in the question, *Lord, wilt thou at this time restore again the kingdom to Israel?* which was taken away by the Romans, and by Herod, and they expected should be restored to them by the Messiah; understanding the prophecy, Dan. vii. 27, to this purpose.

7 And he said unto them, ¹It is not for you to know the times or the seasons, which the Father hath put in his own power.

Our Saviour blames their curiosity about such things as are not necessary to be known; and yet though our Saviour does not in his answer tell them what they desired to know, he tells them what is more expedient for them to know. The petition of wicked men, nay, of devils, (as when they crave to go into the swine,) is sometimes granted according to their will. But the prayer of the disciples of Christ is answered to their best advantage, though it does not seem to agree to the matter of their desire. *It is not for you to know the times or the seasons;* how long any mercy shall be deferred; when it shall be given. *The Father;* who is *fons et origo Deitatis;* to whom Christ, especially as Mediator, and in our stead, refers all things.

8 ᵐBut ye shall receive ‖ power, ⁿafter that the Holy Ghost is come upon you: and ᵒye shall be witnesses unto me both in Jerusalem, and in all Judæa, and in Samaria, and unto the uttermost part of the earth.

But ye shall receive power, after that the Holy Ghost is come upon you; not till then, not of their own strength, but of God's grace, as appeared by Peter's denying and the others' leaving of our Saviour. *And ye shall be witnesses unto me,* that I am indeed the promised Messiah; and of my doctrine, life, death, resurrection, and ascension, which ye shall testify to all the world by your preaching and holy living, working miracles. *Both in Jerusalem, and in all Judea, and in Samaria;* places where your testimony shall be most opposed. These words are both a command, to tell the apostles what they ought to do, and a prediction of what they should be enabled to do.

9 ᵖAnd when he had spoken these things, while they beheld, ᵠhe was taken up; and a cloud received him out of their sight.

Mark xvi. 19; Luke xxiv. 51. As he did not actually give up his life till all was fulfilled, so he did not leave the world till all was revealed by him that was necessary for us. *While they beheld;* that they might be eye-witnesses, and most unexceptionable. *He was taken up;* not by an external help of angels, but by his own power, and the agility of his now glorious body. *And a cloud received him out of their sight:* this, though a true cloud, yet was a more than ordinarily glorious one, suitable to the majesty of him that used it.

10 And while they looked stedfastly toward heaven as he went up, behold, two men stood by them ʳin white apparel;

Christ's ascent was the more leisurely, that he might delight their eyes and mind; but especially confirm their faith the more. *Behold, two men stood by them,* angels in the shape of men, *in white apparel;* which angels ordinarily appeared in, to show they retained their native purity, as also to represent the joyfulness of the errand they were usually sent upon.

11 Which also said, ˢYe men of Galilee, why stand ye gazing up into heaven? this same Jesus, which is taken up from you into heaven, ᵗshall so come in like manner as ye have seen him go into heaven.

Which also said; the two angels (in the form of men) before mentioned. *Ye men of Galilee;* that is, the apostles, who were of that country. *Why stand ye gazing up into heaven?* they are roused out of the ecstasy they were in at that glorious sight, to learn what was so much to their and our advantage. *Shall so come:* 1. Visibly. 2. In a cloud. 3. By his own power. 4. With the like majesty. 5. With the same soul and body.

u Luke 24. 52.

12 ᵘThen returned they unto Jerusalem from the mount called Olivet, which is from Jerusalem a sabbath day's journey.

From the mount called Olivet, which Bethany was a part of, as situate towards the bottom of it, remoter from Jerusalem. Hence Luke xxiv. 50, differs not from this place. From hence the rather our Lord ascended, that he might receive his glory nigh the place where he began his suffering, (in the garden where he endured his agony, and was betrayed,) and in the view of Jerusalem, where he had been condemned and scorned. *A sabbath day's journey;* about a mile or two, or such a space as, by God's appointment, was betwixt the ark and the people, Josh. iii. 4.

x ch. 9. 37, 39. & 20. 8.
y Matt. 10. 2, 3, 4.

13 And when they were come in, they went up ˣinto an upper room, where abode both ʸPeter, and James, and John, and Andrew, Philip, and Thomas, Bartholomew, and Matthew, James *the son* of Alphæus, and ᶻSimon Zelotes, and ᵃJudas *the brother* of James.

z Luke 6. 15.
a Jude 1.

And when they were come in, to the city, and to the house, *they went up into an upper room;* the same probably where they had kept the passover, and partook of the Lord's supper; howsoever, for its largeness capable to receive so many. *Peter,* as elder, and first called to the apostleship, is generally first named; and here especially his name is put first, and their names are repeated, to show, that though they fell in forsaking of Christ, they did rise again in professing of him; and that, notwithstanding their apostacy, they were continued after their recovery in their former office and dignity.

b ch. 2. 1, 46.
c Luke 23. 49, 55. & 24. 10.
d Mat.13.55.

14 ᵇThese all continued with one accord in prayer and supplication, with ᶜthe women, and Mary the mother of Jesus, and with ᵈhis brethren.

These all continued with one accord, with great resolution, notwithstanding all opposition and contradiction they met with, *in prayer and supplication,* for mercies they wanted, or preventing of the evils they feared. *The women;* their wives, or such women especially as we read of Matt. xxvii. 55, 56. *His brethren;* that is, his relations and kinsmen, which frequently in Scripture are called brethren.

15 ¶ And in those days Peter stood up in the midst of the disciples, and said,

e Rev. 3. 4.

(the number ᵉof the names together were about an hundred and twenty,)

In those days, betwixt our Saviour's ascension and Pentecost. *Peter,* as generally, spake for and amongst the apostles; but now especially, to express his zeal and faithfulness to our Saviour, whom he had so lately denied, he being also designed the minister of the circumcision, which place he began now to execute. *The number of the names,* or persons, *together were about an hundred and twenty;* probably Christ had converted many men, but these might be either men of name or quality, or meant of such as, ver. 21, had accompanied with Christ and his apostles, and were designed for the ministry.

16 Men *and* brethren, this Scripture must needs have been fulfilled, ᶠwhich the Holy Ghost by the mouth of David spake before concerning Judas, ᵍwhich was guide to them that took Jesus.

f Ps. 41. 9.
John 13. 18.
g Luke 22. 47.
John 18. 3.

Men and brethren, an ordinary compellation; speaker and auditors were Hebrews of the Hebrews. *This Scripture,* viz. Psal. xli. 9, *must needs have been fulfilled;* yet God's foreknowledge and prediction excused not Judas's sin. *Which was guide to them that took Jesus;* not only leading them in the way when they took our Saviour, but being director of their counsels against him. This the apostle premises to abate the offence that the horrible fall of Judas might have occasioned.

17 For ʰhe was numbered with us, and had obtained part of ⁱthis ministry.

h Mat. 10. 4.
Luke 6. 16.
i ver. 25.
ch. 12. 25.
& 20. 24. & 21. 19.

Numbered with us; being one of the twelve apostles. *Had obtained,* ἔλαχε; not as if Judas was made an apostle by lot, as Matthias afterwards; but by the providence of God, by which every lot and casual matter is governed: and to show that the dignity did not befall him, or any of the other apostles, because of their descent, (from Aaron,) or from nature, or from any desert whatsoever, but merely from God's good will and pleasure. *Part of this ministry;* then the apostles' office is ministerial, and they were not lords over God's heritage.

18 ᵏNow this man purchased a field with ˡthe reward of iniquity; and falling headlong, he burst asunder in the midst, and all his bowels gushed out.

k Matt. 27. 5, 7, 8.
l Mat. 26. 15.
2 Pet. 2. 15.

Purchased a field; which Judas might have agreed for at that price, and yet the chief priests bought, (as Matt. xxvii. 7,) by a strange providence, leading of them to that purchase; howsoever, eventually he bought it, as throwing back to them their money which paid for it, Matt. xxvii. 5. *Falling headlong, he burst asunder;* it is said he hanged himself, which implying only his death by suffocation, whether he died out of horror of his fact, or laying violent hands on himself in such circumstances as may agree with this relation, it is not material to determine.

19 And it was known unto all the dwellers at Jerusalem; insomuch as that field is called in their proper tongue, Aceldama, that is to say, The field of blood.

Their proper tongue; the Syriac language then in use after the Babylonish captivity. *The field of blood;* as bought with the price of Christ's blood, and sprinkled with his own blood.

20 For it is written in the book of Psalms, ᵐLet his habitation be desolate, and let no man dwell therein: and ⁿhis ‖ bishoprick let another take.

m Ps. 69. 25.
n Ps. 109. 8.
‖ Or, *office,* or, *charge.*

For it is written in the book of Psalms; viz. Psal. lxix. 25. What there is in general spoken by David concerning his enemies, is here applied particularly to Judas, who betrayed our Saviour; whose type David was, as Doeg was of Judas. *His bishopric;* his charge or office, or prefecture, as of a shepherd over his flock.

21 Wherefore of these men which have companied with us all the time that the Lord Jesus went in and out among us,

There were to be twelve apostles in the Christian church, to answer unto the twelve patriarchs and twelve tribes in the Jewish church. *Companied with us,* in ordinary conversation, *Went in and out among us;* in discharge of his ministry, and gathering of disciples among us.

22 ᵒBeginning from the baptism of John, unto that same day that ᵖhe was taken up from us, must one be ordained ᵍto be a witness with us of his resurrection.

o Mark 1. 1.
p ver. 9.
q John 15. 27. ver. 8.
ch. 4. 33.

Beginning from the baptism of John; when Christ was baptized by him, and by that consecration began the ministry, and publishing of the gospel (which the history of his immaculate conception did preface to). *A witness with us of his resurrection;* all other things being consummated in that, it being the most difficult to be believed; and therefore God was pleased to attest it by so many eye-witnesses.

23 And they appointed two, Joseph called ʳBarsabas, who was surnamed Justus, and Matthias.

r ch. 15. 22.

Joseph, or Joses, the same name called *Barsabas* in their common tongue, and *Justus* (probably for his integrity) amongst the Romans, who then ruled over them. *Matthias;* some think the same with Nathanael.

24 And they prayed, and said, Thou, Lord, ˢwhich knowest the hearts of all

s 1 Sam. 16. 7. 1 Chr. 28. 9. & 29. 17.
Jer. 11. 20.
& 17. 10. ch. 15. 8. Rev. 2. 23.

men, shew whether of these two thou hast chosen,

The other apostles being chosen by God immediately, it was necessary that he who was to act in the same office, should be chosen after the same manner. *Knowest the hearts*, which is God's prerogative only; all others may be, and often are, mistaken by outward appearances.

t ver. 17. 25 ᵗ That he may take part of this ministry and apostleship, from which Judas by transgression fell, that he might go to his own place.

Ministry and apostleship, κλῆρον, or every one's station in the world, is ordered by the providence of God, and their part or portion is assigned to them; and so the apostleship was unto the apostles. *His own place*; hell, or destruction, not intended by Judas, but righteously by God appointed for him: whilst he was in the world (especially after his betraying of our Saviour) he was a usurper in it; and as bad as the world was, it was too good for him. That these words should be understood of Matthias's succeeding to the apostleship of Judas as into his own place, is the less probable, because as yet he was not chosen into it.

26 And they gave forth their lots; and the lot fell upon Matthias; and he was numbered with the eleven apostles.

They gave forth their lots; the manner is not so certain, nor necessary to be known; but the whole disposing of the lot being from the Lord, as Prov. xvi. 33, they were thus as it were immediately chosen by God, and were consecrated by Christ himself; no apostle ordaining another, but all of them being called and ordained by Christ. *He was numbered with the eleven apostles;* tho rest of the apostles, and the whole church, agreeing with that Divine choice which was made.

CHAP. II

The descent of the Holy Ghost upon the apostles on the day of Pentecost: they speak divers languages, to the general amazement, but some deride them, 1—13. *Peter showeth that the inspiration spoken of by Joel was now fulfilled; that Jesus, whom they had crucified, was now risen from the dead, and ascended into heaven, according to David's predictions, and had shed forth the promise of the Holy Spirit in full proof of his being the Messias,* 14—36. *A great number are converted by Peter's preaching,* 37—40; *who, being baptized, converse devoutly and charitably together, the apostles working many miracles, and God daily increasing the church,* 41—47.

a Lev. 23. 15.
Deut. 16. 9.
ch. 20. 16.
b ch. 1. 14.

AND when ᵃ the day of Pentecost was fully come, ᵇ they were all with one accord in one place.

Pentecost; this feast was fifty days after the feast of unleavened bread, or passover, as Lev. xxiii. 16, whence it had its name, and was called *the feast of weeks*, Exod. xxxiv. 22, because it was to be observed seven weeks after the feast of unleavened bread, Deut. xvi. 9. It was the feast of *the first-fruits of wheat harvest*, Exod. xxxiv. 22; and on this day (to answer the type) the Spirit was poured out in such a plentiful manner, as the first-fruits of Christ's ascending into heaven: besides, the law was given on this day, Exod. xix. 1, 11, and it was expedient that the gospel (Christ's law) should be published on the same day: and it being on the first day of the week, it did recommend and honour the Lord's day, as our Saviour had before by his resurrection on that day. *With one accord;* as if they had but one mind, as sent in so many bodies. *In one place;* probably that mentioned chap. i. 13.

2 And suddenly there came a sound from heaven as of a rushing mighty wind,
c ch. 4. 31. and ᶜ it filled all the house where they were sitting.

Suddenly, the apostles themselves not expecting it, *there came a sound from heaven as of a rushing mighty wind;* to prepare them to attend the more unto what they should hear and see afterwards; also to signify the unexpected and powerful progress which the gospel should have: it may be, to cause the greater concourse to that place, it being a usual manner; and God would make this miracle more public. *It filled all the house;* to show that the Spirit should be bestowed on them that were met there, and on all the church throughout the world.

3 And there appeared unto them cloven tongues like as of fire, and it sat upon each of them.

Cloven tongues; to signify the variety of languages which the apostles should be enabled to speak, to qualify them to preach the gospel unto all nations, and to remove the obstacle which the confusion of tongues caused. *Like as of fire;* which represented, 1. The light that the apostles should impart; 2. The fervent heat and zeal which they should be endowed with; 3. The gospel's spreading in the world, and carrying all before it, prevailing over all errors; 4. The purity and holiness which they and all that preach the gospel ought to appear withal. *And it sat upon each of them;* remained, as far as was necessary for the founding of the Christian religion; and was not, as the gift of prophecy, bestowed only occasionally, as on Nathan, Samuel.

d ch. 1. 5.
e Mark 16.
17. ch. 10.
46. & 19. 6.
1 Cor. 12.10,
28, 30. & 13.
1. & 14. 2,
&c.

4 And ᵈ they were all filled with the Holy Ghost, and began ᵉ to speak with other tongues, as the Spirit gave them utterance.

Filled with the Holy Ghost; those gifts and graces which proceeded from him; the apostles having them all in a more excellent manner than formerly, and the gift of tongues superadded. *With other tongues*, than what were vernacular or natural to them. *As the Spirit gave them utterance;* ἀποφθέγγεσθαι, signifies more than barely to speak, implying they speak each language in its perfection, after an excellent, eloquent, and powerful manner, as from the Holy Ghost, whose works are perfect; *non vox hominem sonat.*

5 And there were dwelling at Jerusalem Jews, devout men, out of every nation under heaven.

Not only constant inhabitants, but such as had on occasion their lodgings there; partly out of a constant respect, which both Jews and proselytes had for that place, (for the temple and their worship' sake; it being also a place for learning and education, as appears by the colleges and synagogues mentioned, chap. vi. 9,) but especially now the concourse from all parts must needs have been very great, it being one of those times in which all the males were to appear before God: to which might be added, the great expectation they had of the Messiah made them to omit no occasion of inquiring concerning him, the prophecies concerning the time of his coming being fulfilled, and they could not be ignorant of the many and great things concerning the true Messiah. *Out of every nation under heaven;* whither the Jews had been dispersed in the two or three greater or other lesser dispersions. Thus in part was fulfilled what was prophesied, Isa. xliii. 5.

6 Now † when this was noised abroad, the multitude came together, and were ‖ confounded, because that every man heard them speak in his own language.

† Gr. *when this voice was made.*
‖ Or, *troubled in mind.*

Noised abroad; either the miraculous winds were heard, or the report of what had happened was spread abroad. *Were confounded;* either out of shame that they had slain Christ, whom God thus extraordinarily glorified; or out of admiration at so extraordinary a matter. *Every man heard them speak in his own language;* probably, not that the same words spoken by the apostles were diversified according to every one's understanding, for then the miracle had been wrought in their auditors, and not in the apostles; but that the apostles did speak to every one in their proper and most intelligible language: and this was the gift of tongues, which for some time after also was continued in the church.

7 And they were all amazed and marvelled, saying one to another, Behold, are not all these which speak ᶠ Galilæans? f ch. 1. 11.

Without literature, or good education, they being worse thought of on that account than the ordinary sort of that nation were; besides, they thought no prophet was to be expected from Galilee, John i. 46.

8 And how hear we every man in our own tongue, wherein we were born?

Διάλεκτος signifies commonly a different way of speaking, or pronouncing in the same language; as our southern and northern men differ in some words and pronunciation, though speaking both the English tongue. God's works being most perfect, the apostles might speak, not only the same language which all understood, but in the same idiom and propriety of speech which agreed to every one best.

9 Parthians, and Medes, and Elamites, and the dwellers in Mesopotamia, and in Judæa, and Cappadocia, in Pontus, and Asia,

Elamites; descended from Elam, Gen. x. 22, thought to be the Persians. *Mesopotamia;* between the two rivers, Tigris and Euphrates. *Judea;* the apostles being Galileans, spake a distinct dialect from the rest of the Jews, till now enabled to speak as they did. *Asia;* some particular district, at that time especially so called, as 1 Pet. i. 1; otherwise the places before-named are in Asia in a larger sense.

10 Phrygia, and Pamphylia, in Egypt, and in the parts of Libya about Cyrene, and strangers of Rome, Jews and proselytes,

Strangers of Rome, who came either to Jerusalem to worship, or for any other business. It is evident that many in or about the city of Rome had embraced the Jewish religion; and of them it may be understood. *Jews:* the others, mentioned ver. 9, were such as then dwelt in Judea; these were such as lived elsewhere, only now came to worship or sojourn there. *Proselytes;* these were of two sorts: the one, such as came over from paganism unto the Jewish religion, and were bound only to observe the precepts of Noah, and enjoyed a liberty to buy and sell, live and converse, amongst the Jews: hence they were called *proselytes of the gate.* The other were called *proselytes of righteousness;* for these were circumcised, and took upon them the observation of the whole law of Moses, and had all the privileges belonging to the people of God.

11 Cretes and Arabians, we do hear them speak in our tongues the wonderful works of God.

Cretes; such as belonged to the island of Crete, now called Candia. *The wonderful works of God;* those things which God had wonderfully wrought, especially the resurrection of our blessed Saviour from the dead, which was a most wonderful work, and the main argument whereby the world was converted, and unto which the apostles bare witness.

12 And they were all amazed, and were in doubt, saying one to another, What meaneth this?

They were all amazed; so ver. 7; ἐξίσταντο, they were as in an ecstasy, (the object was too strong for the faculty,) they could not fathom the cause or reason of these wonderful things; and therefore they desire one of another to be resolved concerning them.

13 Others mocking said, These men are full of new wine.

Others; viz. the scribes and Pharisees, and also the inhabitants of Jewry and Jerusalem; who not understanding the languages of other nations, might think the apostles did but babble, and talk idly or rudely, when they spake with other tongues. *New wine,* or sweet wine; which done, may inebriate; and might be had at that time, though the full vintage was not yet.

14 ¶ But Peter, standing up with the eleven, lifted up his voice, and said unto them, Ye men of Judæa, and all *ye* that dwell at Jerusalem, be this known unto you, and hearken to my words:

Peter standing up; it speaks his extraordinary courage; after his stumbling and fall, he runs the faster, being recovered; and begins to verify his name which our Lord had given him, showing himself as firm and stedfast as a rock. *With the eleven;* the other apostles, probably, spake too in divers languages; but by reason of the shortness of St. Luke's intended narrative, and it being to the same purpose, their sermons are omitted. *Men of Judea;* such as came from other parts of the country. *Ye that dwell at Jerusalem;* such as were constant inhabitants in that city.

15 For these are not drunken, as ye suppose, ᵍseeing it is *but* the third hour of the day. ^{g 1 Thess. 5. 7.}

For these; this proves that the other apostles spake as well as Peter, and were vindicated by him. *Are not drunken;* he mildly and solidly confutes their calumny. *The third hour of the day,* which answers to our nine o'clock in the morning, and was the ordinary time for their morning sacrifice and prayer, before which time they did not eat or drink any thing; nay, it is thought on festival days it was usual with them not to eat or drink until the sixth hour, that is, noon-time, that they might be more intent upon and fit for the service of the day. How little soever (to our shame) such an argument would be of proof now, it was in their more sober times very conclusive.

16 But this is that which was spoken by the prophet Joel;

God does ordinarily, before that he sends his judgments, and does his *strange work,* endeavour to reclaim them by mercies: not only Joel, but Isaiah, Jeremiah, and Ezekiel, and others, prophesied before the destruction of that people and country by Nebuchadnezzar; but now, before the final and total ruin, God sent greater and more than these, and endued them with a greater measure of the Spirit, clearer and fuller light to forewarn them of and deliver them from wrath to come.

17 ʰAnd it shall come to pass in the last days, saith God, ⁱI will pour out of my Spirit upon all flesh: and your sons and ᵏyour daughters shall prophesy, and your young men shall see visions, and your old men shall dream dreams: ^{h Is. 44. 3. Ezek. 11. 19. & 36. 27. Joel 2. 28, 29. Zech. 12. 10. John 7. 38. i ch. 10. 45. k ch. 21. 9.}

In the last days; in the time of the Messiah, called *the last days* frequently, 2 Tim. iii. 1; Heb. i. 2; 2 Pet. iii. 3; as also called *the last time,* 1 Pet. i. 5; 1 John ii. 18; Jude 18; because we are now under the last and most perfect dispensation of the things of God, and no other is to be looked for until the consummation of all things. *I will pour out of my Spirit;* before the Spirit was given in lesser measures, and comparatively but by drops, *here a little, and there a little;* now more largely, even to overflow. *Upon all flesh;* all sorts of men, as well Gentiles as Jews, contrary unto their proud conceit, that God dwelt in none out of the land of Israel. *Daughters shall prophesy;* fulfilled in Anna the prophetess, Luke ii. 36, and in the four daughters of Philip, chap. xxi. 9. *Visions;* these were formerly either representations more inward to their mind, as Isaiah's and Jeremiah's were; or more outward, to their bodily eye, as Belshazzar's was, Dan. v. 5, and such as Peter had, chap. x. 11. *Dreams;* by dreams God sometimes manifested his will, as to Joseph; but this is by St. Peter accommodated to the gospel times. The prophets spake suitably to them unto whom they preached; and the apostle rightly understands by these expressions, the manifold and more clear revelation of the will of God in Christ.

18 And on my servants and on my handmaidens I will pour out in those days of my Spirit; ˡand they shall prophesy: ^{l ch. 21. 4, 9, 10. 1 Cor. 12. 10, 28, & 14. 1, &c.}

On my servants and on my handmaidens; to show what all ought to be, that hope to receive any benefit or comfort from the promises of God, either in the law or gospel, the Old or New Testament: viz. such as seek and serve God; but to the disobedient and unbelieving there is not a comfortable word in all the book of God. Some read without the pronoun, on servants and handmaids; to show that God doth not despise men of the lowest rank and condition in the world, but that the promise of the Spirit is made unto them also.

19 ᵐAnd I will shew wonders in hea- ^{m Joel 2. 30, 31.}

THE ACTS II

ven above, and signs in the earth beneath; blood, and fire, and vapour of smoke:

As St. Peter had declared the promises unto such as would be drawn by the cords of love; so here, on the other side, he useth threatenings, and declares the terrors of the Lord, if so that they will be persuaded. These *wonders* were such as did precede the destruction of Jerusalem, or shall forerun the destruction of the whole world.

20 ⁿ The sun shall be turned into darkness, and the moon into blood, before that great and notable day of the Lord come:

n Mat. 24. 29. Mark 13. 24. Luke 21. 25.

The sun shall be turned into darkness, and the moon into blood; this agrees with the other words in the fore-cited prophecy, Joel ii. 31. How these amazing signs shall be fulfilled, whether literally, and by what means; or whether only that the consternation and dread upon men shall be so great, as expecting the change of the whole frame of nature, is not so material for us to know, as it is to be always prepared for it. *Great and notable day;* ἐπιφανῆ, manifest and illustrious day; and it may be taken in a comfortable sense, and will be a comfortable day indeed, to all that preparedly wait for it; for it is the *day of the Lord*, it is Christ's day, in which he will be magnified over his enemies, and in his friends, children, and servants.

21 And it shall come to pass, *that* ^owhosoever shall call on the name of the Lord shall be saved.

o Rom. 10. 13.

That he may prepare thus a people for the Lord, the apostle shows by what means they and we may escape. Pray in faith unto him. The name is that whereby any one is known; and the Lord's name is his attributes, goodness, power, wisdom, faithfulness, &c. *The name of the Lord is a strong tower: the righteous runneth into it, and is safe*, Prov. xviii. 10.

22 Ye men of Israel, hear these words; Jesus of Nazareth, a man approved of God among you ^pby miracles and wonders and signs, which God did by him in the midst of you, as ye yourselves also know:

p John 3. 2. & 14. 10, 11. ch. 10. 38. Heb. 2. 4.

Jesus of Nazareth; for so Pilate had called our Saviour through contempt, in his superscription on the cross: and that they might certainly know of whom he spake, and that he was not now (as formerly) ashamed to own him, he mentions our Saviour under that name here. *Approved;* demonstrated, and beyond any contradiction proved, to be the Messiah: for this was that great truth St. Peter preached upon, that Christ, whom Pilate had condemned, and called Jesus of Nazareth, was indeed the Son of God, and the true Messiah. *Miracles and wonders and signs;* the critical difference is not so material; it was ordinary to add many words to show the greatness of the matter spoken of; indeed all sorts of wonderful works Christ did, and so many, and so great, as no variety of words can express. *As ye yourselves also know;* those that are not convinced are self-condemned.

23 Him, ^qbeing delivered by the determinate counsel and foreknowledge of God, ^rye have taken, and by wicked hands have crucified and slain:

q Mat. 26. 24. Luke 22. 22. & 24. 44. ch. 3. 18. & 4. 28. r ch. 5. 30.

Him, being delivered by the determinate counsel and foreknowledge of God: that the apostle might take away the offence of the cross of Christ, he declares unto them that he did not suffer by chance, but by the wise and holy providence of God, who had ordered, and by his prophets foretold, what he should suffer before he did enter into glory, Luke xxiv. 26. Yet this did no way excuse those who were instrumental in his death; for notwithstanding God's determinate counsel concerning it, he tells the Jews, *ye have taken, &c.* The determination of God, as it does not necessitate it, so it does not excuse any from sin. *Have crucified,* by the Romans, who were truly ἄνομοι, without any law of God. What the Jews urged or occasioned the Romans to do, is charged justly upon them as their act.

24 ^sWhom God hath raised up, having loosed the pains of death: because it was not possible that he should be holden of it.

s ver. 32. ch. 3. 15. & 4. 10. & 10. 40. & 13. 30, 34. & 17. 31. Rom. 4. 24. & 8. 11. 1 Cor. 6. 14. & 15. 2 Cor. 4. 14. Gal. 1. 1. Eph. 1. 20. Col. 2. 12. 1 Thes. 1. 10. Heb. 13. 20. 1 Pet. 1. 21.

Whom God hath raised up: Christ rose by his own power as God: it being, perhaps, too strong meat to be given at first to such who were under so great prejudices against our Saviour; but by consequence in the following discourse he sufficiently shows it. *Loosed;* the same word חבל variously pointed, signifying either a cord or pain, the metaphor of loosing agrees with it. *The pains of death:* though our Lord endured no more pain after he had said, *It is finished*, and had yielded up the ghost; yet whilst he was in the grave, being under the power of death, the pains of death are said to be loosed at his resurrection. *It was not possible that he should be holden of it* long, much less for ever; being such a one as David spake of.

25 For David speaketh concerning him, ^tI foresaw the Lord always before my face, for he is on my right hand, that I should not be moved:

t Ps. 16. 8.

David speaketh concerning him, Psal. xvi. 8. *I foresaw the Lord always before my face:* in the psalm it is, *I have set the Lord:* the apostle following the reading of the Seventy, then in use and known; and to the same sense; for by faith we both see God, and place our confidence in in him; David, and especially our Saviour, doing and enduring all things as in the sight of God, whom he knew to be both careful of him, and ready to help him. Thus, in all troubles, there is no such approved comfort, as the seeing or acknowledging the will of God concerning them, his power to preserve us under them, and his promises to deliver us from them. Christ, and all that are Christ's, do conflict under the eye and in the sight of God, as soldiers whilst their general looks on. *On my right hand;* the place of the advocate for one that is accused or endangered.

26 Therefore did my heart rejoice, and my tongue was glad; moreover also my flesh shall rest in hope:

Therefore, because of God's nearness to or presence with him, *did my heart rejoice;* Christ's and his people's joy is solid and true, real and inward, and may bear the test, *res severa est verum gaudium. My tongue;* in Psal. xvi. 9, it is *my glory,* as the tongue is frequently called; communicating our thoughts or apprehensions by speech, being the excellency of a reasonable creature. *My flesh;* or my body. *Shall rest;* or be in the grave, as in a tabernacle, ordinarily a movable, always no durable abiding place. *In hope;* that is, of the resurrection, and going out of that tabernacle of the grave.

27 Because thou wilt not leave my soul in hell, neither wilt thou suffer thine Holy One to see corruption.

My soul; that is, me: the soul is put for the person, as Rom. xiii. 1, *Let every soul be subject;* and sometimes for a dead body, as Lev. xix. 28; Numb. v. 2, and in divers other places, נפש that signifies a soul, is so used. *In hell;* the word ἄδης is put either for the grave, or for the place of the damned. Being these words are alleged as a proof of Christ's resurrection, and that our Saviour's soul was certainly in paradise, where he promised to the penitent thief that he should be with him, it seems rather to be meant of the grave, which, according to this prophecy, could not hold our blessed Saviour's body so long as that it should corrupt in it. If David by his *soul* here did mean our Saviour, because he was as it were the soul of his soul, and life of his life, it shows how he did, and how we ought to value him. *Thine Holy One;* as being anointed, sanctified, and sent by God.

28 Thou hast made known to me the ways of life; thou shalt make me full of joy with thy countenance.

Thou hast made known to me; God is frequently said to make those mercies known to us which he bestows upon us. *The ways of life;* of a true life, which is life indeed. David in these words celebrates God's delivering of him from his grievous afflictions and exile; in which

THE ACTS II

he was looked upon by others, and by himself, as a dead man, yet was brought again to see the temple, and enjoy the ordinances of God, without which his life was as no life unto him. So our Saviour, after his death and passion, arose, and ascended into heaven, and lives for ever to make intercession for us. *With thy countenance;* that is, with thy presence, or manifestation of thy love and favour.

|| Or, *I may.*
u 1 Kings 2. 10. ch. 13. 36.

29 Men *and* brethren, || let me freely speak unto you ᵘof the patriarch David, that he is both dead and buried, and his sepulchre is with us unto this day.

Men and brethren; St. Peter bespeaks this attention and favour, intimating he was one of the same nation with themselves, than which nothing could more recommend him. *David* was had in great veneration, and his memory very precious amongst this people, as was Abraham's, Isaac's, and Jacob's; who were the chief of their fathers. *He is both dead and buried;* as in 1 Kings ii. 10, and elsewhere, is recorded of him, which they firmly believed. *His sepulchre,* or monument, *is with us;* either not wholly spoiled by the barbarous enemies, who had destroyed Jerusalem; or rather repaired after the captivity, to keep up the memory of so great and good a man. But by this it appeared, that David did not speak these things concerning himself, who must needs have seen corruption, (themselves being witnesses,) for on that account they respected his tomb, as being the repository of his ashes.

x 2 Sam. 7. 12, 13. Ps. 132. 11. Luke 1. 32, 69. Rom. 1. 3. 2 Tim. 2. 8.

30 Therefore being a prophet, ˣand knowing that God had sworn with an oath to him, that of the fruit of his loins, according to the flesh, he would raise up Christ to sit on his throne;

Had sworn with an oath; not barely had sworn, which had been sufficient; but to show the excellency of the matter, and the necessity of our believing of it, as also the solemnity of the words, Psal. cxxxii. 11. *Of the fruit of his loins;* such as should descend from him, as the virgin Mary did. *According to the flesh;* as to his human nature, which our Saviour did truly partake of, being in the form of a servant. *He would raise up Christ,* by the power of the Holy Ghost in the womb of his virgin mother, as to his incarnation; and by the same power out of the grave, in his resurrection. *To sit on his throne;* as Luke i. 32, 33: not as a temporal king, for his kingdom is not of this world; but as David ruled over all the people of God, so does Christ, and shall do for ever.

y Ps. 16. 10. ch. 13. 35.

31 He seeing this before spake of the resurrection of Christ, ʸthat his soul was not left in hell, neither his flesh did see corruption.

He seeing this before; by a prophetical eye, unto which any thing that was revealed was as certain and manifest, as aught could be to the eye of the body. By the same prophetical Spirit, and with the same certainty, which he spake of the incarnation, he *spake* also *of the resurrection of Christ.* Of the rest, see ver. 27.

z ver. 24.
a ch. 1. 8.

32 This Jesus hath God raised up, ᵃwhereof we all are witnesses.

This Jesus, whom ye crucified, and we preach. *Whereof we all are witnesses:* they had now received the power spoken of and promised chap. i. 6, and testify what they had heard, and seen, and felt, and all agree in; though they could get nothing by it, but hatred and persecution, nay, death.

b ch. 5. 31. Phil. 2. 9. Heb. 10. 12. c John 14. 26. & 15. 26. & 16. 7. 13. & 1. 4. d ch. 10. 45. Eph. 4. 8.

33 Therefore ᵇbeing by the right hand of God exalted, and ᶜhaving received of the Father the promise of the Holy Ghost, he ᵈhath shed forth this, which ye now see and hear.

By the right hand of God, that is, by the power of God, spoken after the manner of men, the right hand being that we commonly do any thing with. Some read *at* the right hand of God; and then the apostle preaches Christ's ascension too, and his being justified by God, though he had been condemned by men. *Having received of the Father the promise of the Holy Ghost:* Psal. lxviii. 18. *Which ye now see,* in the fiery cloven tongues; *and hear,* in the divers languages which are spoken.

34 For David is not ascended into the heavens: but he saith himself, ᵉThe LORD said unto my Lord, Sit thou on my right hand,

e Ps. 110. 1. Matt. 22. 44. 1 Cor. 15. 25. Eph. 1. 20. Heb. 1. 13.

For David is not ascended into the heavens; hence St. Peter here proves, that these words, spoken by David, were not principally to be understood concerning himself, but concerning Christ the Messiah; for David, as to his body, was in the sepulchre, which on that account was kept amongst them. *The Lord said unto my Lord;* the eternal Father unto his eternal Son, who was now made flesh—hence our Saviour proves his Divinity, Matt. xxii. 45. The words here referred to are Psal. cx. 1.

35 Until I make thy foes thy footstool.

Christ is commissioned and empowered to reign over and govern all creatures, and all their actions, till the consummation of all things, so long as the world lasts, in which he, his people, and truths, will have enemies, Eph. i. 20—22; 1 Cor. xv. 27, 28.

36 Therefore let all the house of Israel know assuredly, that God ᶠhath made that same Jesus, whom ye have crucified, both Lord and Christ.

f ch. 5. 31

This is the conclusion which the apostle infers from the premises, applying what he had said very close and home, or it would not in all likelihood have had so good an effect. *Ye have crucified;* ye are the men. *Lord* over all the creatures, beyond what the first Adam was; *and Christ,* King over all the people of God, to rule in them, and reign for them; for to this purpose he was the Christ, or the Anointed of God, declared by God to be so, and owned for such by all that believed in him.

37 ¶ Now when they heard *this,* ᵍthey were pricked in their heart, and said unto Peter and to the rest of the apostles, Men *and* brethren, what shall we do?

g Zech. 12. 10. Luke 3. 10. ch. 9. 6. & 16. 30.

They were pricked in their heart; so great and true their grief, they were concerned as if they had been run through: (the pains the mind suffer are most acute:) this was foretold, Zech. xii. 10. *Men and brethren;* an ordinary compellation which the apostle had given them, ver. 29. *What shall we do?* not, What shall we say, or believe? conversion, if real, goes further than profession, and is in heart and deed, not in speech and word only: they desire to know if there be any hope, that such sinners as they might obtain forgiveness of their sins.

38 Then Peter said unto them, ʰRepent, and be baptized every one of you in the name of Jesus Christ for the remission of sins, and ye shall receive the gift of the Holy Ghost.

h Luke 24. 47. ch. 3. 19

Repent, which includes amendment of life, Matt. iii. 8; Luke iii. 8. *In the name of Jesus Christ;* not excluding the name of the Father and the Holy Ghost, in whose name, as well as in the name of the Son, they were to baptize, Matt. xxviii. 19: but the name of Jesus is here mentioned, because they had not yet known (but persecuted and slain) him, whom henceforward they must profess; and that they look for pardon and salvation only through him. *For the remission of sins;* thus Saul, or Paul, is said to wash away his sins by baptism, chap. xxii. 16; and this apostle elsewhere says, that baptism saves us, 1 Pet. iii. 21; which he explains to be, *not the putting away of the filth of the flesh, but the answer of a good conscience,* &c. *The gift of the Holy Ghost:* 1. His internal gifts, confirmation and strengthening in the faith. 2. External gifts, as that of speaking with tongues, which they heard. Both, or either of these, according to their conditions or stations, God would bestow upon them.

39 For the promise is unto you, and ⁱto your children, and ᵏto all that are afar off, *even* as many as the Lord our God shall call.

i Joel 2. 28. k ch. 10. 45. & 11. 15, 18. & 14. 27. & 15. 3, 8, 14. Eph. 2. 13, 17

For the promise is unto you; lest they should doubt of pardon and grace, their sin having been so great. St. Peter here gives them a ground of hope, they being the descendants from Abraham, unto whom especially this was promised, Jer. xxxi. 34. *And to all that are afar off;* that is, to the Gentiles as well as to the Jews, who were said to be a people near unto God, as the Gentiles were said to be afar off, Isa. lvii. 19; Eph. ii. 13. *Even as many as the Lord our God shall call;* vocation, whether external by the word only, or internal by the Spirit also, depends on the pleasure of God; but the same promises of pardon and acceptance upon repentance made unto the Jews, are as effectually to be trusted unto by any of the Gentiles, as by any formerly amongst the Jews.

40 And with many other words did he testify and exhort, saying, Save yourselves from this untoward generation.

Many other words: the sermons of the apostles, or of our Saviour, are not all set down by the holy writers; but only so much as God saw necessary for his church to know and believe. *Testify and exhort;* using God's name and authority, and calling him as it were to witness. *Save yourselves:* no less than the salvation of our souls depends upon our forsaking wicked and profane persons in their ungodly courses. *From this untoward generation;* the whole world lies in wickedness; but especially the scribes and Pharisees, and other such declared enemies of Christ Jesus.

41 ¶ Then they that gladly received his word were baptized: and the same day there were added *unto them* about three thousand souls.

They that gladly received his word; some still remained in their unbelief and hardness of heart; though never men spake as the apostles now spake, with divers tongues, &c. *Unto them;* to the church, or the hundred and twenty formerly mentioned, chap. i. 15. This was the effect of Christ's prayer for his persecutors, Luke xxiii. 34; and of the promise of the Spirit now fulfilled, whereby in the day of his power they were made willing.

42 ¹And they continued stedfastly in the apostles' doctrine and fellowship, and in breaking of bread, and in prayers.

They continued stedfastly, speaks the reality of their conversion, and that they were not only for the present affected with what they had heard and seen. These three parts of worship were frequently, if not always, in those purer times used together: though some understand by *breaking of bread,* their civil fellowship and community, yet breaking being a holy rite used by our Saviour, at the institution of his supper, Matt. xxvi. 26, and breaking of bread being here put in conjunction with preaching and praying, the celebration of the eucharist, if not only meant, is chiefly to be understood in this place. *Prayers;* all those kinds of prayers mentioned by St. Paul, 1 Tim. ii. 1, as also their frequent praying, is implied. Thus, by a united force, they laboured to pull down mercies upon themselves and others, and to do violence unto the kingdom of heaven.

43 And fear came upon every soul: and ᵐmany wonders and signs were done by the apostles.

Upon every soul; that is, upon every man; not only on them that were present, and persuaded to believe on Christ, whom the apostles preached; but on such also as were informed of those miraculous things which now happened; so that by this means the apostles were had in great esteem and respect by the people.

44 And all that believed were together, and ⁿhad all things common;

All that believed were together; not that they lived together in one house or street, but that they met (and that frequently) together in the holy exercises of their religion; and that manner of some, which St. Paul speaks of, Heb. x. 25, to forsake the assembling of themselves together, was a sin not yet known in the church. *And had all things common;* this was only at that place, Jerusalem, and at that time, when the wants of some, and the charity of others, may well be presumed to be extraordinary; and there is no such thing as community of goods here required or practised. Christ's gospel does not destroy the law; and the eighth commandment is still in force, which it could not be, if there were no propriety, or *meum* and *tuum,* now; nay, after this, the possession which Ananias sold is adjudged by this apostle to have been Ananias's own, and so was the money too which he had received for it, chap. v. 4. And these *all things* which they had in common, must either be restrained to such things as every one freely laid aside for the poor; or that it speaks the extraordinary charitable disposition of those new converts, that they would rather have parted with any thing, nay, with their all, than that any of their poor brethren should have wanted.

45 And sold their possessions and goods, and ᵒparted them to all *men,* as every man had need.

Those proportions of their estate they set apart to this charitable work; whether they did arise out of the sale of house or land, called *possessions,* or of any chattels or movable estate, called here *goods*: but that they did not divest themselves of all property, appears in that we find soon after this, chap. xii. 12, Mary the mother of St. Mark to have a house; and Lydia, after she was baptized, did not renounce any propriety in her house, chap. xvi. 15, but entreated St. Paul, and those who were with him, to come into her house, &c.

46 ᵖAnd they continuing daily with one accord ᑫin the temple, and ʳbreaking bread ‖ from house to house, did eat their meat with gladness and singleness of heart,

In the temple; in the court and porches of the temple, whither the people did use to resort at the time of the morning and evening sacrifice and prayers, that by means of the great concourse at such times they might have the better opportunity to preach the gospel amongst them; casting that net where they found most fish. *Breaking bread;* not only celebrating the eucharist, but their love-feasts which they usually had at that time, as 1 Cor. xi. 21, 22. *From house to house;* now here, now there, as they could conveniently; the richer also entertaining their poorer brethren at their tables. *Did eat their meat with gladness and singleness of heart:* if the former words be understood of the Lord's supper, then these words speak the great spiritual strength, cheer, and comfort they got by it: if we understand them of the ordinary meats which they willingly bestowed one upon another, the rich were more than recompensed with inward peace and satisfaction, for what they gave unto their poor brethren.

47 Praising God, and ˢhaving favour with all the people. And ᵗthe Lord added to the Church daily such as should be saved.

Praising God; acknowledging him who teacheth one to want, and another to abound. *Having favour with all the people;* that is, generally to be understood, amongst them that continued yet without the pale of the church; the goodness, meekness, and patience of the apostles, and the rest of the believers, did wonderfully prevail to beget a good opinion of them. *The Lord added to the church;* salvation is (to be sure) only from the Lord; not Peter's sermons, no, nor the miracles of fiery cloven tongues, and the rushing mighty wind, could have converted any, but Δεῖ τι ἔνδον, that which was signified there, viz. the powerful operation of the Spirit of God in their hearts.

CHAP. III

The lame man healed by Peter and John, 1--11. *Peter declareth to the people that this cure was not wrought by any power or holiness in himself or John, but by the power of God through faith in the name of Jesus, whom they had ignorantly crucified, but whom God had raised from the dead according to the Scriptures; and exhorteth them by faith to seek remission of sins and salvation in Jesus, whose coming had been spoken of by Moses and all the prophets,* 12--26.

THE ACTS III

a ch. 2. 46.
b Ps. 55. 17.

NOW Peter and John went up together ^ainto the temple at the hour of prayer, ^bbeing the ninth *hour*.

Went up together into the temple; not to communicate with the Jews in their worship, which was now antiquated, but that they might have a larger field to sow the seed of the gospel into; and therefore it was most probably upon some sabbath or festival day, and not unlikely in the evening of that great day of Pentecost (of which in the former chapter). *At the hour of prayer:* that God must be worshipped, and daily prayed unto, the law of nature and positive law of God requires; but, says Maimonides, there is no obligation by virtue of any command of God, unto any number of prayers, nor to any certain prayers, nor to any definite time of prayer. Howsoever, they did usually pray thrice a day, and thought each of those three times recommended unto them by one of the patriarchs, Abraham, Isaac, and Jacob. Howsoever, the time of offering up the morning and evening sacrifice was recommended or commanded by God, as a time of prayer; a sacrifice being an actual prayer, as the other is real or verbal. *The ninth hour;* about three o'clock in the afternoon, the time of the evening sacrifice.

c ch. 14. 8.

2 And ^ca certain man lame from his mother's womb was carried, whom they laid daily at the gate of the temple which is called Beautiful, ^dto ask alms of them that entered into the temple;

d John 9. 8.

Lame from his mother's womb, and not by any casualty, that so the miracle might be the greater, and the power of the God of nature appear. *They laid daily;* by which it was manifest, that it could not be by any correspondence betwixt the apostles and the lame man upon this occasion. *At the gate of the temple;* where there must needs be the greater notice taken of him; none going in or out but such as might see him. *Called Beautiful,* for the excellency of the workmanship: it was at the entering into the second court, or the court of the Jews from that of the Gentiles. This man, out of pride, being unwilling to beg of the Gentiles, though proselyted, (whom they did contemn,) or out of policy, hoping to receive more of the Jews, whom he is nearer related to, *asked alms of them that entered into the temple.* Poverty is no sign of God's disfavour (our blessed Redeemer is in an especial manner called *Caput pauperum*); but lameness in this man, divers miseries and calamities in others, bring them to the knowledge of Christ, and salvation through him.

3 Who seeing Peter and John about to go into the temple asked an alms.

Seeing, though lame: every one hath something that is truly valuable, and matter of praise and thanks unto God.

4 And Peter, fastening his eyes upon him with John, said, Look on us.

The eye affects the heart, and speaks the compassion he had of this poor man, whom he did not disdain thoroughly and seriously to behold: he excites the lame man's expectation, and requires his attention, that he might the more mind the manner and means of his cure, and be the better prepared to give God the glory of it.

5 And he gave heed unto them, expecting to receive something of them.

Gave heed, with his eyes and mind too, being intent upon the apostles; this he was commanded to do, and it succeeds beyond all hopes. Thus we receive of God daily more than we can ask or think.

6 Then Peter said, Silver and gold have I none; but such as I have give I thee: ^eIn the name of Jesus Christ of Nazareth rise up and walk.

e ch. 4. 10.

Silver and gold have I none; that is, at hand, or about me; neither had he much elsewhere; the apostles abounded indeed, but in grace, not in riches. *Such as I have;* a power from Christ to heal. *Give I thee;* I apply it to thee, and will make it effectual for thee. *In the name,* in the power, or at the command, *of Jesus Christ,* and trusting unto his promised assistance, who can speak to things that are not as if they were. *Jesus Christ of Nazareth;* our Saviour was usually so called, and being known by that name, the apostle does not decline it, though it had been by many (without cause) given him by way of reproach.

7 And he took him by the right hand, and lifted *him* up: and immediately his feet and ancle bones received strength.

He took him by the right hand; not disdaining to take hold of a poor cripple or beggar; as also being fully persuaded of Christ's presence with him for his cure. *And immediately,* that it might the more evidently appear that this was the work of God, who can without means, and on a sudden, bring aught to perfection, *his feet and ancle bones,* whence his lameness did proceed, *received strength:* thus God can say unto the weak, Be strong.

8 And he ^fleaping up stood, and walked, and entered with them into the temple, walking, and leaping, and praising God.

f Is. 35. 6.

Thus was fulfilled the prophecy of Isaiah, chap. xxxv. 6, *Then shall the lame man leap as an hart;* and thus the lame man manifested that he was perfectly cured, though in an instant, *walking, and leaping, and praising God,* to whom alone he attributed that sudden and perfect (and therefore miraculous) cure; nay, he attributes nothing unto the means; the apostle's words he knew did little or nothing, but God is all in all unto him: and he leaped, to evidence the truth of the miracle that was wrought upon him, and that his soul rejoiced in God his Saviour.

9 ^gAnd all the people saw him walking and praising God:

g ch. 4. 16, 21.

This miracle was so publicly done, that none could deny the matter of fact; which the enemies of the gospel are forced to confess, chap. iv. 16.

10 And they knew that it was he which ^hsat for alms at the Beautiful gate of the temple: and they were filled with wonder and amazement at that which had happened unto him.

h Like John 9. 8.

They knew that it was he; the very same lame beggar, probably notoriously known to many. *They were filled with wonder and amazement at that which had happened unto him;* being so much contrary to what they had seen him but a little while before, when he had begged their alms; and, as he reasoned well, John ix. 32, *Since the world began was it not heard that any man opened the eyes of one that was born blind;* so it was never heard, that any strengthened thus the feet of him that was born lame.

11 And as the lame man which was healed held Peter and John, all the people ran together unto them in the porch ⁱthat is called Solomon's, greatly wondering.

i John 10. 23. ch. 5. 12.

Held Peter and John, in an ecstasy of thankfulness unto them, they having been the instruments of so great a mercy from God towards him; as also out of fear, lest when they were gone he might relapse: he that found so great a change in himself, could not but be as much surprised as they that saw the change upon him. *The porch that is called Solomon's;* not that which was built by Solomon, for that was destroyed by the Babylonians, as the rest of the temple was, 2 Kings xxv. 9; unless some part of this porch might not be consumed by the fire, when the other parts of the temple were burned, some morsel often escaping the jaws of that devouring element, fire; or it may be it was built in the re-edification of the temple, in the same place where Solomon's porch had stood, and thence called by the former name that was so much renowned. If any wonder that a porch should hold so many thousands of people, inasmuch as five thousand of them are said to be converted, chap. iv. 4; this porch is thought not only to have been the court of the Gentiles, and that of the Jews, that is, the outward and inward court; but to have contained a great part of the court of the Gentiles, if the whole court of the Gentiles might not be so called, as being indeed but a porch, or an entrance into the court of the Jews.

THE ACTS III

12 ¶ And when Peter saw *it*, he answered unto the people, Ye men of Israel, why marvel ye at this? or why look ye so earnestly on us, as though by our own power or holiness we had made this man to walk?

He answered, for he said, an ordinary Hebraism, though no question was put unto him; thus the evangelist tells us that our Saviour *answered and said*, when there was no previous question spoken of, Matt. xi. 25. Nay, *Jesus answered and said unto* the fig tree, Mark xi. 14; that is, he spake powerfully unto it. *Ye men of Israel;* an ingratiating compellation, they ever valuing themselves and others on that account. *By our own power or holiness:* holiness, were it never so real and great in men, cannot cause the least miracle, although it is itself, all things considered, a very great one.

13 ᵏ The God of Abraham, and of Isaac, and of Jacob, the God of our fathers, ¹hath glorified his Son Jesus; whom ye ᵐ delivered up, and ⁿ denied him in the presence of Pilate, when he was determined to let *him* go.

k ch. 5. 30.
1 John 7. 39.
& 12. 16. &
17. 1.
m Mat. 27. 2.
n Mat. 27. 20.
Mark 15. 11.
Luke 23. 18,
20, 21. John
18. 40. & 19.
15. ch. 13. 28.

The God of Abraham, and of Isaac, and of Jacob; he mentions them, because the promise of the Messiah was made to them. *Hath glorified his Son Jesus;* or his servant, for so also he is called, Isa. liii. 11; and that he might redeem us, he took upon him the form of a servant, and was obedient to the death of the cross, and did that great work of redemption which God sent him into the world to do. *Whom ye delivered up;* the rulers, at whose command our blessed Saviour was apprehended, bound, and delivered unto Pilate, Matt. xxvii. 1, 2. *And denied him;* this is charged upon the common sort of people also, who were earnest in crying, Matt. xxvii. 25, *His blood be on us, and on our children.* Their sin is here ripped up, and their sore searched to the quick, that they might entertain the word of salvation with the greater attention and desire.

14 But ye denied ᵒthe Holy One ᵖand the Just, and desired a murderer to be granted unto you;

o Ps. 16. 10.
Mark 1. 24.
Luke 1. 35.
ch. 2. 27. &
4. 27.
p ch. 7. 52.
& 22. 14.

But ye denied the Holy One; Christ the anointed, when they cried out as with one voice, *We have no king but Cæsar*, John xix. 15; disclaiming our Redeemer, and his being anointed over them. *And desired a murderer;* to wit, Barabbas, crying out, *Not this man, but Barabbas*, John xviii. 40; which much aggravated their impiety; when the choice was given unto them of two, so vastly different, the just Jesus, and the murderous Barabbas, they chose the latter, to their destruction and confusion unto this present day. Where will blindness of mind and hardness of heart end!

15 And killed the ‖ Prince of life, ᑫwhom God hath raised from the dead; ʳwhereof we are witnesses.

‖ Or, *Author*,
Heb. 2. 10.
& 5. 9.
1 John 5. 11.
q ch. 2. 24.
r ch. 2. 32.

The Prince of life; as God, he is the Author of our temporal life too, in whom we live, and move, &c., and in whose hand is our breath; but Christ, as Mediator, is the guide and way to eternal life, John xiv. 6. These are said to have killed our Saviour, though neither Herod, nor Pilate, nor probably many (if any) of them that nailed him to the cross, were present; but it was done for their sakes, and at their desires, and therefore by their means; and it is here charged upon them, as done by them.

16 ˢAnd his name through faith in his name hath made this man strong, whom ye see and know: yea, the faith which is by him hath given him this perfect soundness in the presence of you all.

s Matt. 9. 22.
ch. 4. 10.
& 14. 9.

His name; his power; for by it he is known, as men or things are by their several names; or the *name* of Christ is put for Christ himself, as the name of God is put for God commonly. *Through faith in his name;* calling by faith on the name of Christ, being thoroughly persuaded that he could and would heal this cripple. *The faith which is by him;* not only faith, as on Christ as its object, but by and from Christ as its author; faith being twice made mention of in this cure, there being required faith in Peter to heal, and in the lame man to be healed.

17 And now, brethren, I wot that ᵗthrough ignorance ye did *it*, as *did* also your rulers.

t Luke 23. 34. John 16. 3. ch. 13. 27.
1 Cor. 2. 8.
1 Tim. 1. 13.

Lest the corrosive in ver. 13—15 should pierce too far, to prevent despair in his auditors the apostle useth in this verse a lenitive, calling them yet *brethren*, though guilty of so great a mistake in their judgment, and fault in their practice. *Through ignorance ye did it;* whatsoever they did against Christ, whom St. Peter preached, was out of a double error: 1. About the place of Christ's birth, supposing him to have been born at Nazareth. 2. They were ignorant of the nature of his kingdom. *As did also your rulers;* whose fault was the greater, as having seduced others, &c.; yet St. Peter opens a door of hope by repentance, even for them also.

18 But ᵘthose things, which God before had shewed ˣby the mouth of all his prophets, that Christ should suffer, he hath so fulfilled.

u Luke 24. 44. ch. 26.
22.
x Ps. 22. Is. 50. 6. & 53. 5, &c. Dan. 9. 26. 1 Pet. 1. 10, 11.

The prophets did all speak the same things, as if they had spoken out of one *mouth*, as they did speak by one Spirit. God used the ignorance of some, and the malice of others, for his own holy ends: and that it was prophesied *that Christ should suffer*, is very plain, Isa. l. 5—7.

19 ¶ ʸRepent ye therefore, and be converted, that your sins may be blotted out, when the times of refreshing shall come from the presence of the Lord;

y ch. 2. 38.

Repent ye therefore, and be converted; this is the true end, use, and application, both of the preceding miracle and sermon, to persuade unto repentance and conversion. *That your sins may be blotted out;* alluding to the manner of writing upon tables in those times, and not much disagreeing from what is in use amongst us, who write upon paper or parchment. There is a book of remembrance, and a record of all our sins kept: *The sin of Judah is written with a pen of iron, and with the point of a diamond*, Jer. xvii. 1. When sin is pardoned, it is said to be *blotted out*, Isa. xliv. 22; and not to be found any more, though it should be *sought for*, Jer. l. 20. *Times of refreshing;* or, times of cooling; as afflictions are called a fiery trial, so deliverance from them is a season of refreshing or cooling. Such a time of refreshing shall come in this life, commonly from many troubles; but when this life ends, a deliverance comes from all afflictions to them that truly fear and serve God. *Shall come from the presence of the Lord;* God's presence is the cause and ground from whence all the refreshment his people take do arise; heaven would not be heaven (a place of bliss and glory) without it: and as God is the object of our beatitude, so he is the giver of all comfort, and his Spirit is the only Comforter.

20 And he shall send Jesus Christ, which before was preached unto you:

To remove all evils and miseries from his people; when that Sun shines all clouds and mists are scattered. This refers especially to Christ's second coming, which is here promised, to encourage us to do good, and to deter us from doing evil; as also to move us to repentance, and to comfort us when penitent.

21 ᶻWhom the heaven must receive until the times of ᵃrestitution of all things, ᵇwhich God hath spoken by the mouth of all his holy prophets since the world began.

z ch. 1. 11.
a Mat. 17. 11.
b Luke 1. 70.

Whom the heaven must receive; that is, contain after it hath received him, as a real place doth a true body; for such Christ's body was, which was received into heaven: and heaven is the palace and throne of this King of kings and Lord of lords, where he shall reign until he hath put all his enemies under his feet, 1 Cor. xv. 25. *Until the times of restitution of all things;* or restoration of all things, when all things shall be restored to that condition from which sin put them: for the fall hath maimed and disordered the whole universe; and probably there is not that excellency in any of the creatures which there was at first, before man (for whom they were made) by his sin brought death to himself, and as it were a dead colour over all them; this makes the whole creation groan and travail in pain until now, Rom. viii. 22. But the end of the world will be a time of *restitution of all things* unto man especially, who shall be then restored unto God, and to a blessed immortality: for unless this be granted, all their preaching and prophesying was in vain, 1 Cor. xv. 14.

22 For Moses truly said unto the fathers, c Deut. 18. 15, 18, 19. ch. 7. 37. ᶜA prophet shall the Lord your God raise up unto you of your brethren, like unto me; him shall ye hear in all things whatsoever he shall say unto you.

For Moses truly said unto the fathers; their ancestors in the wilderness, Deut. xviii. 15, as also in the 18th verse. St. Peter names here but one of their prophets, but a most remarkable one. *Like unto me;* 1. In wisdom. 2. In miracles. 3. In being a Mediator betwixt God and his people. 4. In their being both out of their brethren, i. e. of the seed of Abraham. 5. In that they were both sent from God after an extraordinary manner. *Him shall ye hear in all things;* if any prophet did come amongst them, and did foretell future things which came to pass, or did work a real miracle, they were bound to believe him, if he did not endeavour to draw them to worship a false god; and by consequence they were bound to have believed our Saviour, who taught them only to fear that true God, whom the law and all the prophets had spoken of.

23 And it shall come to pass, *that* every soul, which will not hear that prophet, shall be destroyed from among the people.

Every soul; that is, every one. *Hear that prophet;* that is, believe and obey him. *Shall be destroyed from among the people;* as those that disobeyed Moses were destroyed, many perishing by strange and sudden deaths; we read of Korah, Dathan, and Abiram, and all that belonged to them, swallowed up for this sin, Numb. xvi. The apostle demands, *How shall we escape, if we neglect so great salvation?* Heb. ii. 3. For a greater than Moses is here, and God hath undertaken to require it of every one that will not hearken unto him, Deut. xviii. 19.

24 Yea, and all the prophets from Samuel and those that follow after, as many as have spoken, have likewise foretold of these days.

Though there were some prophets betwixt Moses and Samuel, yet they were but such as prophesied in some particular exigences and cases; and in Samuel's days *the word of the Lord was precious,* or rare, 1 Sam. iii. 1; but then David, that lively type of Christ, appearing at the throne, the Messiah began to be more discovered in and by him: besides, Samuel was the first who wrote his prophecies, and erected the schools of the prophets, and therefore he is first mentioned; and the date of the prophets is here begun from him.

d ch. 2. 39. Rom. 9. 4. 8. & 15. 8. Gal. 3. 26. e Gen. 12. 3. & 18. 18. & 22. 18. & 26. 4. & 28. 14. Gal. 3. 8. 25 ᵈYe are the children of the prophets, and of the covenant which God made with our fathers, saying unto Abraham, ᵉAnd in thy seed shall all the kindreds of the earth be blessed.

Children of the prophets; the patriarchs, Abraham, Isaac, and Jacob, are called *prophets,* Psal. cv. 15, and did prophesy, foretelling things to come, &c. The disciples of the prophets are also called their children, or *sons,* 2 Kings ii. 3; and so these pretended and desired to be accounted. Children *of the covenant* are such unto whom the covenant belongs, which God made with Abraham and his seed; hence they are called *the children of the promise,* Rom. ix. 8; Gal. iv. 28; and *the children of the kingdom,* Matt. viii. 12. And this covenant of God with Abraham was the cause, that notwithstanding all the sore and heavy calamities of that people, God did always preserve some, and there was a remnant saved. *Kindreds;* families, or nations. *Be blessed:* through Christ, who is this seed of Abraham, all mercies in this world, and eternal life in the world to come, are bestowed; grace and glory, and every good thing.

26 ᶠUnto you first God, having raised up his Son Jesus, ᵍsent him to bless you, ʰin turning away every one of you from his iniquities. f Matt. 10. 5. & 15. 24. Luke 24. 47. ch. 13. 32, 33, 46. g ver. 22. h Mat. 1. 21.

Unto you first; the Jews and inhabitants of Jerusalem, who are the lost sheep of the house of Israel. St. Peter did not yet know that the Gentiles should be called, until he was taught it by the vision, Acts x.; and though our Saviour had told the apostles that they should be his *witnesses unto the uttermost part of the earth,* Acts i. 8, they understood it only of those of their own nation, scattered or dispersed abroad, 1 Pet. i. 1. *Raised up his Son Jesus;* which word does not only refer to the resurrection of Christ, but to his being constituted and appointed to be a Prince and a Saviour; thus it is said, *a great prophet is risen up amongst us,* Luke vii. 16; and, God *hath raised up a horn of salvation,* Luke i. 69. Howsoever, it is by virtue of Christ's being raised from the dead, and carried into his kingdom, that we are blessed. *In turning away every one of you from his iniquities;* this is the greatest blessing indeed; hence our Saviour hath his name imposed by God on him, Matt. i. 21, and was called Jesus, because he saves his people from their sins; and without this being saved from our sins, nothing can be a blessing to us, Isa. iii. 11; and, *There is no peace, saith my God, to the wicked,* Isa. lvii. 21. Add to this, that if any be turned from their iniquities, it is through the blessing of God in Christ.

CHAP. IV

The rulers of the Jews, offended with the teaching of Peter and John, imprison them, 1—4. *Being brought before the council, Peter boldly avoucheth the late cure to have been wrought in the name of Jesus, and that men can be saved by no other name,* 5—12. *The council, struck with the boldness of the two apostles, after conferring together, dismiss them with a threatening charge to speak no more in the name of Jesus,* 13—22. *The church betaketh itself to prayer,* 23—30. *The presence of the Holy Ghost is signified by the house shaking, and the apostles thereby imboldened to speak the word,* 31. *The unity and charity of the church, who have their possessions in common,* 32—37.

AND as they spake unto the people, the priests, and the ‖captain of the temple, and the Sadducees, came upon them, ‖ Or, *ruler.* Luke 22. 4. ch. 5. 24.

The captain of the temple; the commander over those soldiers who were appointed to guard the temple, and provide that no disorder might happen, by reason of the multitudes that came to worship there; and most probably was a Roman, and not of the Jewish nation, much less the chief of any of the courses of the priests, to whom this term cannot agree. *The Sadducees;* these were most inveterate against the gospel, whose main article is the resurrection, which they denied: and thus each man, Jews and Gentiles, agree against Christ, as was foretold, Psal. ii. 1, 2.

2 ᵃBeing grieved that they taught the people, and preached through Jesus the resurrection from the dead. a Mat. 22 23. Acts 23. 8.

Being grieved; or angry to such a degree that it was a great trouble to them. The doctrine of *the resurrection* alone could not but vex the Sadducees, who denied it; but it did more afflict them, that the apostles *preached* it *through Jesus;* asserting, not only the resurrection of our Saviour, which the Jews gave so much money unto the soldiers to hinder the report of, Matt. xxviii. 12, 13, but also that Christ was the author of the resurrection, and the first-fruits of them that sleep; and because they inferred from Christ's resurrection that his disciples should rise from the dead also.

3 And they laid hands on them, and put *them* in hold unto the next day: for it was now eventide.

Put them in hold; some think this not to have been so strait a custody as that of a prison, but that rather the apostles were delivered to some who promised that they should be forthcoming. The prediction of our Saviour began now to be fulfilled, Luke xxi. 12. *They shall lay their hands on you, and persecute you.* Howsoever, God was pleased to suffer persecution to come by degrees on his church; after the sun was down, (Christ was gone from them,) it was not presently pitch-darkness with them. God always remembers his people's condition, and his own promise, and lays no more upon them than they are able to bear.

4 Howbeit many of them which heard the word believed; and the number of the men was about five thousand.

Faith cometh by hearing, and hearing by the word of God, Rom. x. 17. It being the ordinary means which God hath appointed; the apostles themselves make use of it towards the conviction of this people. The number of the hearers is not intended to be set here, or in any other place; but either these *five thousand* were such as were converted at this sermon, or rather the number converted by St. Peter's former sermon, chap. ii. 14—40, were at this sermon made thus many; howsoever, the increase which God gave was very great.

5 ¶ And it came to pass on the morrow, that their rulers, and elders, and Scribes,

Their rulers; the sanhedrim, or great council. *Elders and scribes;* the magistrates of the city, scribes, doctors, or teachers of the law, &c.; howsoever these might be distinguished, they are all as one against the doctrine of the gospel, and endeavour to put out the light as soon as it began to shine, as Herod would have killed Christ in the manger.

6 And [b]Annas the High Priest, and Caiaphas, and John, and Alexander, and as many as were of the kindred of the High Priest, were gathered together at Jerusalem.

b Luke 3. 2. John 11. 49. & 18. 13.

Annas the high priest, and Caiaphas; both these are said to be high priests, Luke iii. 2; whether they bare this office by turn each other year, as some think, or that the Roman power put in and out whom they pleased, and in courtesy he that was laid aside still retained the title during his life, is not very material. *John,* thought to be the son of Annas. *Alexander,* a man of great repute amongst them, as Josephus says. *As many as were of the kindred of the high priest;* their relation many times preferring them to a place in their great council, or sanhedrim. *Were gathered together at Jerusalem;* or in Jerusalem; either such as were in the city, being called together on such an extraordinary occasion; or else they sent also unto men of greatest note, that lived nigh thereunto.

7 And when they had set them in the midst, they asked, [c]By what power, or by what name, have ye done this?

c Ex. 2. 14. Matt. 21. 23. ch. 7. 27.

When they had set them in the midst; the sanhedrim, or great council, did sit in a circular form; and the apostles being to answer for themselves, were placed so as they might better hear and be heard. *By what power;* natural, or supernatural and Divine? *By what name?* at whose command, or in whose authority? they inquire whether they did pretend to be prophets, or persons extraordinarily sent, &c. Though the miracle which they had wrought showed sufficiently by whose power it was done, yet of this they were willingly ignorant, and inquire only that they might find matter out of the apostles' own mouths, for which they might blame or punish them.

8 [d]Then Peter, filled with the Holy Ghost, said unto them, Ye rulers of the people, and elders of Israel,

d Luke 12. 11, 12.

Filled with the Holy Ghost; guiding and strengthening of him in what he did speak, by which so mightily Peter differed from himself, that though formerly he was afraid of a servant, and denied our Saviour, now he is not afraid before the rulers to confess him. *Rulers of the people, and elders of Israel:* see ver. 5. These were especially the great council, in imitation of the seventy, which Moses appointed by God's command to help him in the burden of his government, Numb. xi. 16, 24.

9 If we this day be examined of the good deed done to the impotent man, by what means he is made whole;

Examined; juridically called in question; it is a forensical word. *Of the good deed;* though they disputed not the authority of the court, yet they assert their integrity; that it was no other than a good deed they had done, which rulers ought not to be a terror unto, Rom. xiii. 3. *By what means,* that is, in the words of the question which was propounded unto them, ver. 7, by what power, or by what name, *he is made whole?*

10 Be it known unto you all, and to all the people of Israel, [e]that by the name of Jesus Christ of Nazareth, whom ye crucified, [f]whom God raised from the dead, *even* by him doth this man stand here before you whole.

e ch. 3. 6, 16.
f ch. 2. 24.

• *Be it known unto you all, and to all the people of Israel;* the apostles are not dismayed, but make their boldness, spoken of ver. 13, to appear; they preach Christ to all of them, and wish they could make him known to all others. *Jesus Christ of Nazareth:* see chap. ii. 22. *Whom God raised;* i. e. God the Father: our Surety was discharged by God himself, who had laid him in the prison of the grave for our debts. *This man stand here before you whole;* the lame man that was made whole being present, and an ocular demonstration of the miracle wrought upon him.

11 [g]This is the stone which was set at nought of you builders, which is become the head of the corner.

g Ps. 118. 22. Is. 28. 16. Matt. 21. 42.

Alluding to Psal. cxviii. 22, in which there is a prophecy of what was now fulfilled: see chap. ii. 23. *You builders;* so by their office they were, and ought to have been so indeed, and are here so called, that they might be minded of their duty, viz. to increase, strengthen, and beautify the building, and not to demolish, weaken, or deface it. *The head of the corner;* or the corner-stone: Christ is frequently so called, Matt. xxi. 42; Mark xii. 10; and that, 1. Because he sustains and upholds the whole building. 2. He is a *rock* or stone *of offence,* Rom. ix. 33; as many run upon and are hurt by a corner-stone. 3. He is most precious, 1 Pet. ii. 6, as the corner-stones are usually the largest, firmest, and best. 4. Christ is a light to lighten the Gentiles, as well as the glory of the people of Israel; and both Gentile and Jew are united in him, and saved by him, as the corner-stone is equally necessary for both sides, which are united in it, and borne up by it.

12 [h]Neither is there salvation in any other: for there is none other name under heaven given among men, whereby we must be saved.

h Matt. 1. 21. ch. 10. 43. 1 Tim. 2. 5, 6.

Neither is there salvation, for soul or body, *in any other* person or thing. *For there is none other name;* because in distress men did usually call upon their false gods by name, as, *O Baal, hear us,* 1 Kings xviii. 26. *Under heaven;* whether patriarch or prophet, priest or king; especially referring unto Moses, in whom they did trust; and therefore under the gospel especially we must lift up our hearts.

13 ¶ Now when they saw the boldness of Peter and John, [i]and perceived that they were unlearned and ignorant men, they marvelled; and they took knowledge of them, that they had been with Jesus.

i Mat. 11. 25. 1 Cor. 1. 27.

They were unlearned; not wholly unlearned, but such as were without any polite learning, or more than ordinary education, such as every one amongst them had. *Ignorant men;* idiots, so the Greek word, from whence ours come, signifying such as were brought up at home, and never acted in a larger sphere than the walls of their own house; having never been magistrates, or teachers of the law, or any way public persons; and spake only their mother tongue. *They took knowledge of them, that they had been with Jesus;* which these rulers might easily take notice of, many of them frequenting his company too, Matt. xxi. 23; Luke xviii. 18; John xii. 42.

14 And beholding the man which was healed ᵏstanding with them, they could say nothing against it.

k ch. 3. 11.

Standing; whereas, before he was either carried, or was forced to lay down. *They could say nothing against it;* they could not deny but that it was a good deed, and that it was miraculously done.

15 But when they had commanded them to go aside out of the council, they conferred among themselves,

To go aside out of the council; the place where the council met; for the apostles were not dismissed to go away at their liberty. *They conferred among themselves;* it was their joint endeavour to stifle the gospel, and would now consult about the best expedient, but they would not let the apostles hear, lest they might discover the weakness of their proofs against them, and against the truth.

1 John 11. 47.

16 Saying, ¹What shall we do to these men? for that indeed a notable miracle hath been done by them *is* ᵐmanifest to all them that dwell in Jerusalem; and we cannot deny it.

m ch. 3. 9, 10.

What shall we do? at what a loss are these great men, about the manner of their proceeding with the apostles! they might seem to have the victory in their hands, and yet they are evidently overcome by three witnesses; viz. by both the apostles and the lame man, and especially by the evidence of this fact itself: though they did not boggle at being unjust, yet they were loth to seem to be so, and therefore they take counsel to hide it, or palliate it before men; more valuing their credit, than the salvation of their own or other men's souls.

17 But that it spread no further among the people, let us straitly threaten them, that they speak henceforth to no man in this name.

Straitly threaten them; the pleonasm here used implies a very sore and heavy threatening, as of the most grievous punishment upon the most heinous fact. *That they speak henceforth to no man in this name;* either, 1. By preaching; or, 2. By praying in it; or, 3. By doing miracles again by it.

n Again, ch. 5. 40.

18 ⁿAnd they called them, and commanded them not to speak at all nor teach in the name of Jesus.

Not to speak at all; neither privately nor publicly. *Nor teach in the name of Jesus;* as his apostles and ministers sent from him.

19 But Peter and John answered and said unto them, °Whether it be right in the sight of God to hearken unto you more than unto God, judge ye.

o ch. 5. 29.

Peter and John answered; both spake by one and the same Spirit, and agreed in one and the same answer; they are not solicitous what will best bring them off at present, but *said unto them, Whether it be right in the sight of God,* from whom nothing is hid, and who is the avenger of all wrong, *to hearken unto you more than unto God, judge ye.* The apostles seem to refer to a commonly received rule amongst their rabbins, which also they make use of, chap. v. 29, *We ought to obey God rather than men.* In the greatest matters of our most holy religion, God hath not left himself without a witness, or a thousand witnesses, in our own breasts and consciences, Amos ii. 11.

p ch. 1. 8. & 2. 32. q ch. 22. 15. 1 John 1. 1, 3.

20 ᵖFor we cannot but speak the things which ᑫwe have seen and heard.

We cannot but speak; in a moral, not in a physical sense; they could not restrain speaking, because of the necessity which was laid upon them, and the woe which would have befallen them, if they had not preached the gospel, 1 Cor. ix. 16. If any man denies to bear testimony for man to a truth, he sins; how much more does he sin, who forbears to witness for God, and at the command or the sending of God!

21 So when they had further threatened them, they let them go, finding nothing how they might punish them, ʳbecause of the people: for all *men* glorified God for ˢthat which was done.

r Mat. 21. 26. Luke 20. 6, 19. & 22. 2. ch. 5. 26. s ch. 3. 7, 8.

They let them go for the present; for amongst them no acquittal was so peremptory or absolute, but that they might be tried again for the same fact upon further evidence. *Because of the people;* it was not the sense of the evil or sin, nor the apprehensions of God's displeasure and wrath, which deterred them; but the fear or favour of the people. The corruptions that are in the world are overruled for the good of God's children in it. *All men glorified God;* not only such as believed, but others also, could not but confess that this was the hand of God which had made the lame to walk, and rejoice in it, and by consequence have a very great veneration for the apostles, who were the instruments of it.

22 For the man was above forty years old, on whom this miracle of healing was shewed.

Therefore, 1. The harder to be cured. 2. The man was the more credible, who had so long known what it was to be without the use of his limbs, which now he enjoyed. 3. Whom they could not themselves but have often seen and heard begging. But if he had laid so many years in the porch of the temple through which our Saviour frequently entered, how came it to pass that he was not cured before? we do not read that our Saviour denied any who came for cure. There need no other answer, but that all times and seasons are in God's hands, who justly forbore to send deliverance till this very time, and now mercifully sent it; especially reserving this miracle for the confirmation of the truth of the gospel, and of the apostles themselves in the preaching of it.

23 ¶ And being let go, ᵗthey went to their own company, and reported all that the Chief Priests and elders had said unto them.

t ch. 12. 12.

They went to their own company, the rest of the apostles and believers, who have a special propriety and delight in one another; sheep with sheep, and goats with goats: though the separation will be made at the last day, the foundation of it is laid here. *And reported all;* to forewarn them of what they might expect, and encourage them to hope for the like deliverance. *Chief priests;* to what hath been said concerning them might be added, that these, it may be, were the first or chief in the courses, which David divided the priests into, which division was observed till our Saviour's time, Luke i. 5.

24 And when they had heard that, they lifted up their voice to God with one accord, and said, Lord, ᵘthou *art* God, which hast made heaven, and earth, and the sea, and all that in them is:

u 2 Kings 19. 15.

And when they, their own company, believers, unto whom they went, *heard that, they lifted up their voice to God with one accord;* either jointly, with one heart and spirit, agreeing in the same words, or saying Amen to the same thing. *And said, Lord;* they begin prayer with such a reverend compellation, as suited best to the matter of their prayer and praises: whether by *Lord* they meant their Saviour, who was usually so called by them, or God the Father, (because the word here is not Κύριε, but Δέσποτα), is not material; for when any person in the Trinity is invoked, the others are included; for we worship the Trinity in Unity, and the Unity in Trinity. *Which made heaven and earth, &c.;* the creation and government of the world, is a good consideration to confirm us under all things that befall us here.

25 Who by the mouth of thy servant David hast said, ˣWhy did the heathen rage, and the people imagine vain things?

x Ps. 2. 1.

Who by the mouth of thy servant David; through the Holy Ghost by the mouth of David; so it is read in many ancient copies; and shows, that what David and other holy men spake, was from the Holy Ghost, and is to be attended unto and believed as spoken by him. *Servant,* or son; David's relation to God is mentioned as a greater dignity than his being ruler over so great a people. *Why did the heathen rage, and the people imagine vain things?* it shows the unreasonable fury wherewith the enemies of God persecute his people, without cause, but what themselves imagine or make, and the event failing of their end; for *all things work for good to them that love God*, Rom. viii. 28; and the blood of martyrs have been found to be the seed of the church. These words are quoted out of Psal. ii. 1.

26 The kings of the earth stood up, and the rulers were gathered together against the Lord, and against his Christ.

These words do not vary in sense from what we read, Psal. ii. 2, but are the same for substance. *The kings;* not only such who in a strict sense we call kings, but any chief governors, as Herod and Pilate were. *The rulers;* the sanhedrim, or great council of the Jews. *Against the Lord;* God looks upon it as done against him, whatsoever is done against them that fear him; thus the Israelites are said to be *gathered together against the Lord*, Numb. xvi. 11, who were gathered against Moses and Aaron. *And against his Christ;* our Saviour was at the right hand of his Father, but they who afflict his members afflict him; he cries from heaven to Saul. *Why persecutest thou me?* chap. ix. 4; and had before told his disciples, *He that despiseth you despiseth me*, Luke x. 16.

y Matt. 26. 3.
Luke 22. 2.
& 23. 1, 8.
z Luke 1. 35.
a Luke 4. 18.
John 10. 36.

27 For ^y of a truth against ^z thy holy child Jesus, ^a whom thou hast anointed, both Herod, and Pontius Pilate, with the Gentiles, and the people of Israel, were gathered together,

Thy holy child; it speaks Christ's dearness to God as a child, and obeying of God as a servant. *Whom thou hast anointed,* to be a King, Priest, and Prophet to his church. *Both Herod and Pontius Pilate, &c.* a strange agreement against Christ, his truths, and people; Gentiles and Jews never combined so together before. Henceforth it is no dishonour to any, if they follow that which is good, to have great and many enemies, for so had our Saviour: nor is it any honour to any to persecute and despise such; so did Herod, Pilate, Judas, &c.

b ch. 2. 23.
& 3. 18.

28 ^b For to do whatsoever thy hand and thy counsel determined before to be done.

The apostles mind not so much second causes in what our Saviour or themselves suffered, but see and acknowledge God in all; who makes a straight line with a crooked stick; and is holy, wise, and good in overruling and permitting the greatest evils; and does deserve to have praise for all things, Eph. v. 20: see chap. ii. 23. *Thy hand and thy counsel;* thy power and right to dispose of all persons and things; alluding to Lev. xvi. 8: as the lot cast for the two goats (the disposing of which being from the Lord, Prov. xvi. 33) did determine which of the goats should be sacrificed, and which should escape; so it was not without a Divine disposition, that Christ was made a sin-offering for us; though this no way excuses the wicked instruments of his death and suffering.

c ver. 13, 31.
ch. 9. 27.
& 13. 46. &
14. 3. & 19.
8. & 26. 26.
& 28. 31.
Eph. 6. 19.

29 And now, Lord, behold their threatenings: and grant unto thy servants, ^c that with all boldness they may speak thy word,

Behold their threatenings; they had acknowledged God the Maker of heaven, ver. 24, and accordingly here they desire that from heaven his dwelling-place he would behold them and their sufferings; as all things are visible to such as sit above us. *With all boldness;* freeness, or presence of mind, here translated *boldness*, which in a good cause (for Christ and his truth) is (as all good gifts) *from the Father of lights*, James i. 17; and our Saviour hath promised that it shall be given unto us in that hour what to say, Luke xii. 11, 12.

d ch. 2. 43.
& 5. 12.
e ch. 3. 6, 16.
f ver. 27.

30 By stretching forth thine hand to heal; ^d and that signs and wonders may be done ^e by the name of ^f thy holy child Jesus.

By stretching forth thine hand; they desire nothing else to imbolden them, but God's owning them and their work.

That signs and wonders may be done: miracles were then necessary, as being the seal of their commission from God; they desire to have this patent with them, to show as often as occasion served. *By the name of thy holy child Jesus;* by the power and authority of Christ; for Christ alone they sought to advance and magnify, and not themselves, by all the wonders they wrought.

31 ¶ And when they had prayed, ^g the place was shaken where they were assembled together; and they were all filled with the Holy Ghost, ^h and they spake the word of God with boldness.

g ch. 2. 2, 4.
& 16. 26.

h ver. 29.

The place was shaken; miraculously moved up and down, as on the waves of the sea, to evidence God's presence with them, and acceptance of them and their prayers in an extraordinary manner. *They were all filled with the Holy Ghost;* according to their conditions, whether apostles (for whom these prayers were especially made) or private believers. *They spake the word of God with boldness:* this was the grace they asked, ver. 29. God gave it them, and with it all other graces necessary for them. In their difficulties and wants, the greatest and holiest in the church of God must go to God to be supplied, and prayer is the most successful means.

32 And the multitude of them that believed ⁱ were of one heart and of one soul: ^k neither said any *of them* that ought of the things which he possessed was his own; but they had all things common.

i ch. 5. 12.
Rom. 15. 5.
6. 2 Cor. 13.
11. Phil. 1.
27. & 2. 2.
1 Pet. 3. 8.
k ch. 2. 44.

Were of one heart and of one soul; as if one heart and one soul had moved that multitude; to be sure there was one Spirit in them all, that is, the Spirit of God, by whose grace they agreed in all truths, and in hearty affections towards one another; insomuch, that they were as willing that what they had might be enjoyed by their necessitous brethren as by themselves. The community of goods was not commanded, but left at liberty, and was chosen as most expedient at such a time in that place; that it was not even then commanded, we may see, chap. v. 4; neither was it practised any where but at Jerusalem; and it was the rather practised there, that believers might show what credit they gave to our Saviour's prediction concerning the destruction of that place, in which they did not care to have or retain any thing. There might be something too to command this practice of the church in that season: the whole church, upon the matter, being in Jerusalem, and consisting of such as lived afar off, and were by persecution to be driven suddenly farther, had not such a means been yielded to it must have perished, without a miracle.

33 And with ^l great power gave the apostles ^m witness of the resurrection of the Lord Jesus: and ⁿ great grace was upon them all.

l ch. 1. 8.

m ch. 1. 22.

n ch. 2. 47.

With great power; by sundry miracles which they wrought, as also by their boldness with which they spake; it being no small wonder to see and hear such illiterate men testifying the truths of the gospel amidst so many learned rabbins. *The resurrection* was the greatest point in controversy, which being granted, all things concerning Christ and the gospel could not be denied; and therefore here it is especially mentioned. *Great grace;* favour and acceptation; men could not but think well of their doctrine and ways, whom they saw so innocent and holy, meek and good; especially God's grace was manifest in their words and actions.

34 Neither was there any among them that lacked: ^o for as many as were possessors of lands or houses sold them, and brought the prices of the things that were sold,

o ch. 2. 45.

So far forth as might relieve the present necessities of believers; not that every one parted with all that he had, for that had taken away (at least) the use and force of the eighth commandment; for where there is no propriety there can be no theft. Now Christ came not to dissolve any law, but to fulfil it: the meaning then is, that these early Christians would not only part with their revenue, but, rather than their brethren should want, they would and did sell their fee-simple. See chap. ii. 44.

p ver. 37. ch. 5. 2.
q ch. 2. 45. & 6. 1.
35 ᵖ And laid *them* down at the apostles' feet: ᑫ and distribution was made unto every man according as he had need.

Laid them down at the apostles' feet; submitted them to the apostles' disposal : this metaphor is used, 1 Cor. xv. 27, *He hath put all things under his feet. According as he had need;* the poor man's want is the fittest measure for our relief.

36 And Joses, who by the apostles was surnamed Barnabas, (which is, being interpreted, The son of consolation,) a Levite, *and* of the country of Cyprus,

Joses; some read Joseph ; the Hebrew names, when turned into Greek, meet with divers terminations or endings. *Surnamed Barnabas ;* full of consolation ; not only in that he gave so liberally towards the relief of the poor, parting with his possessions for them ; but that he excelled in propounding inward and spiritual comfort unto poor and rich, being of a mild disposition, and fitted to handle gently such wounds as the terrors of the law had made. Though *a Levite* he might have land, either in right of his wife, or given to him and his ancestors ; as we read was to Phinehas, Josh. xxiv. 33 ; otherwise the Lord was the Levites' portion in an especial manner. The Jews being dispersed all over the known world, some dwelt in *Cyprus,* as Joses's parents; Saul's parents dwelt at Tarsus ; though at this time both Saul and Joses dwell in Jerusalem.

r ver. 34, 35.
ch. 5. 1, 2.
37 ʳ Having land, sold *it*, and brought the money, and laid *it* at the apostles' feet.

This is an instance of what was said ver. 34, 35 ; and Joses probably is instanced in it, either because he sold a greater quantity of land, as having large possessions, or as being one of the first that was remarkable in this kind of charity. *Laid it at the apostles' feet :* see ver. 35.

CHAP. V

Ananias and Sapphira, profanely tempting the Holy Ghost with a lie, at Peter's rebuke fall down dead, 1—11. *The apostles work many miracles, to the great increase of the faith,* 12—16. *They are all imprisoned, but released by an angel, and sent to preach openly in the temple : being brought before the council,* 17—28, *they support their witness with great freedom,* 29—32. *The council are restrained from killing them by the advice of Gamaliel, but beat and dismiss them with a charge not to speak in the name of Jesus,* 33—40. *They rejoice in their sufferings, and cease not to preach Christ both in public and private,* 41, 42.

BUT a certain man named Ananias, with Sapphira his wife, sold a possession,

A dreadful instance of God's indignation against hypocrisy and sacrilege, which we have an infallible testimony of ; which is the more remarkable, because such sins escape punishment from men, either as not known, or not disliked ; yet the *damnation* of such as are guilty of them *slumbereth not,* 2 Pet. ii. 3, it being the glory of God to search out matters further than men can, or list to do. *A possession ;* an estate, house, or farm.

2 And kept back *part* of the price,
a ch. 4. 37.
his wife also being privy *to it,* ᵃand brought a certain part, and laid *it* at the apostles' feet.

Kept back part of the price, when they had vowed the whole to God and his service, which made it a robbing of God, whatsoever pretence they might possibly have of detaining some part for their own necessities in old age, or time of sickness ; arguing a great distrust in that God, whom, when they had made their vow, they pretended to give themselves and their substance unto. *His wife also being privy to it ;* her subjection to her husband not excusing her partaking in his sin and punishment. *Brought* *a certain part ;* their ambition carried them thus far, they would seem devout, charitable, &c., and their covetousness hindered them from going farther. *Laid it at the apostles' feet :* see chap. iv. 35.

3 ᵇ But Peter said, Ananias, why hath
b Num. 30.2. Deut. 23. 21. Eccles. 5. 4.
ᶜSatan filled thine heart ∥to lie to the
c Luke 22. 3.
Holy Ghost, and to keep back *part* of the
∥ Or, to deceive. ver. 9.
price of the land ?

But Peter said ; Peter knew this deceit by the inspiration of the Holy Ghost ; it being most probably not otherwise likely ever to be discovered. *Satan filled thine heart :* as when the heart is filled with hot spirits it is daring and bold, so when Satan filled their heart these wretches venture upon desperate courses and provoking sins. *To lie to the Holy Ghost ;* this sin is said to be lying to the Holy Ghost, 1. Because against their own consciences, and the Spirit of God too witnessing with their spirits, Rom. ix. 1. As also, 2. Because they pretended to holiness, and the service of God, when they intended only to serve their own turns ; now the Spirit is in a peculiar manner the Spirit of holiness, and the author of it in us, whom they pretended to have been moved by, but falsely. And, lastly, Defrauding the poor members of Christ of their right, (for so by their vow it became,) they lied to the Holy Ghost, who constitutes and establishes the church, and accepteth these gifts as given to God, and not to men.

4 Whiles it remained, was it not thine own ? and after it was sold, was it not in thine own power ? why hast thou conceived this thing in thine heart ? thou hast not lied unto men, but unto God.

Whiles it remained, was it not thine own ? a sufficient argument, that there was no command (even then) to necessitate them to part with their estates, but only what the present and eminent necessity of the church did persuade them voluntarily unto. The doubling of this expostulation makes the conviction the more forcible. *In thine own power ;* as a steward under God, to do what thou wouldest with it according to his will ; and none are, or can be, otherwise disposers of what they possess. *Why hast thou conceived this thing in thine heart ?* it seems hence, that it was a deliberate and propensed iniquity. *Thou hast not lied unto men, but unto God :* in that lying unto God is so often charged, and no express mention is made of Ananias's vow, some excuse him of sacrilege, and charge him the more deeply with ambition, covetousness, lying, and hypocrisy, to the apostles, whom he intended to deceive.

5 And Ananias hearing these words
ᵈfell down, and gave up the ghost : and
d ver. 10, 11.
great fear came on all them that heard these things.

Fell down and gave up the ghost ; expired and died. Some instances of God's extraordinary judgments upon sinners were in the beginning of the Jewish church ; as upon the man that gathered sticks on the sabbath day, Numb. xv. 35, and upon Nadab and Abihu, Lev. x. 1, 2 ; and so here in the beginning of the Christian church ; to be as marks to teach us to shun such sins, and to teach us that the God with whom we have to do is greatly to be feared. And this miraculous way of punishing notorious sinners in the church, was accommodated to such a time, in which magistrates were so far from defending the church, that they themselves were the greatest enemies unto it. *And great fear came on all them that heard these things :* let others also hear, and fear, and do so no more.

6 And the young men arose, ᵉwound
e John 19.40.
him up, and carried *him* out, and buried *him.*

The young men ; such as were present at that time, and fittest for that employ. *Wound him up ;* according as they were wont to do to such as they intended to prepare for sepulture. Read what was done to the body of our Saviour, Mark xv. 46.

7 And it was about the space of three hours after, when his wife, not knowing what was done, came in.

THE ACTS V   399

About the space of three hours after; this circumstance is expressed to confirm the truth of this history. *Not knowing what was done;* not suspecting any such thing, she was the less inquisitive; and such a consternation and dread was upon all that were there, that they durst not tell her, lest they should offend Peter; also, probably, lest they should with so sudden and sad news grieve her. *Came in;* into the church, or place, where they were met together.

8 And Peter answered unto her, Tell me whether ye sold the land for so much? And she said, Yea, for so much.

Peter answered; an ordinary Hebraism, by which one that speaketh first is said to answer, if it be tending towards any discourse especially. *For so much;* the certain price is not mentioned, as not being necessary to the intent of the Holy Ghost in this narrative; but be it more or less, it was the same which her husband had said the land was sold for. *She said, Yea;* she had agreed with her husband what to say; and one sin draws on another, till it ends in perdition.

9 Then Peter said unto her, How is it that ye have agreed together [f] to tempt the Spirit of the Lord? behold, the feet of them which have buried thy husband *are* at the door, and shall carry thee out.

f ver. 3. Matt. 4. 7.

To tempt the Spirit of the Lord; this expression, of tempting God, or the Spirit of God, is not used amongst profane writers; and this sin is not (at least to such a degree) committed amongst pagans and heathens, and is to be dreaded by all that profess the gospel. As often as men sin against their conscience, and their consciences condemn them in what they do, so often they dare, tempt, or try, whether God be omniscient, and knows of, or holy and powerful, and will punish, their sins; which they find at last to their cost. *The feet of them which have buried thy husband, are at the door;* this the apostle foretells ere it came to pass, the more to confirm his authority and the truth of the gospel. *Shall carry thee out,* after thou art dead, to thy burial.

g ver. 5.

10 [g] Then fell she down straightway at his feet, and yielded up the ghost: and the young men came in, and found her dead, and, carrying *her* forth, buried *her* by her husband.

The same sins meet with the same punishment; God is no respecter of persons, Jew or Gentile, male or female.

h ver. 5. ch. 2. 43. & 19. 17.

11 [h] And great fear came upon all the Church, and upon as many as heard these things.

Thus upon the smiting of so many men in and about Beth-shemesh, 1 Sam. vi. 20, they wisely demand, *Who is able to stand before this holy Lord God?* and upon the slaying of Uzzah, 2 Sam. vi. 9, *David was afraid of the Lord. Discite justitiam moniti.* As many as heard these things, out of the pale of the church: God's judgments do restrain in a great measure wicked men.

i ch. 2. 43. & 14. 3. & 19. 11. Rom. 15. 19. 2 Cor. 12. 12. Heb. 2. 4.
k ch. 3. 11. & 4. 32.

12 ¶ And [i] by the hands of the apostles were many signs and wonders wrought among the people; ([k] and they were all with one accord in Solomon's porch.

By the hands of the apostles; by the apostles' ministry: though they were holy and excellent men, they were but instruments; the power they acted by was God's; which also they had prayed for, and acknowledged, chap. iv. 30. *Among the people;* generally among the meaner sort, according to that question, *Have any of the rulers believed on him?* John vii. 48. *Not many mighty, not many noble, are called,* 1 Cor. i. 26. *In Solomon's porch;* a large and capacious place, where they might with greatest convenience hear and see what was done and said.

l John 9. 22. & 12. 42. & 19. 38.
m ch. 2. 47. & 4. 21.

13 And [l] of the rest durst no man join himself to them: [m] but the people magnified them.

Of the rest; such who were not of the common sort of people, and here seem to be distinguished from them: or, *of the rest* (more largely) who had not joined themselves to the church, being amazed at this judgment on these two hypocrites, durst not make a formal show of religion, unless they had a thorough persuasion in their mind concerning the truth of it, and a firm resolution in their conversation to live answerably unto it.

14 And believers were the more added to the Lord, multitudes both of men and women.)

This explains the former verse, and helps us against mistaking it, for this wonderful judgment was so far from being a hinderance to the truth of the gospel, that it is turned to the furtherance of it; for though great men, and such as were insincere, were terrified from owning Christ and his doctrine, others did more readily embrace them by reason of it.

15 Insomuch that they brought forth the sick ‖ into the streets, and laid *them* on beds and couches, [n] that at the least the shadow of Peter passing by might overshadow some of them.

‖ Or, *in every street.*
n Matt. 9. 21. & 14. 36. ch. 19. 12.

Into the streets; into every street generally taken, it being a common practice where they came, and not in one street only. These weak and unlikely means did more show the power to be of God, and was the greater confirmation to the truth of the gospel; and thus was fulfilled what our Saviour had promised to the apostles, and such as should believe in him, John xiv. 12, that they should do greater works than he did.

16 There came also a multitude *out* of the cities round about unto Jerusalem, bringing [o] sick folks, and them which were vexed with unclean spirits: and they were healed every one.

o Mark 16. 17, 18. John 14. 12.

The variety and grievousness of these evils did but the more commend the power which was present with the apostles. *They were healed every one;* an evidence that these cures were not wrought by second causes, for the best medicines do not always succeed; as also, in that they were perfectly and suddenly cured who were thus miraculously cured, the God of nature restoring nature beyond what means and art could do.

17 ¶ [p] Then the High Priest rose up, and all they that were with him, (which is the sect of the Sadducees,) and were filled with ‖ indignation,

p ch. 4. 1, 2, 6.
‖ Or, *envy.*

Then the high priest rose up; moved at the report of these things, went out of the council to observe what was done. *And all they that were with him;* there were both Pharisees and Sadducees in their sanhedrim or great council, as appears Acts xxiii. 6; but the high priest and a great part were at this time Sadducees. *Indignation,* or zeal, which is the best when kindled (as the fire on the altar) from heaven, regularly acting for God's truth and word; and the worst when inflamed by carnal affections, and set upon wrong objects for self-ends. The pique these Sadducees had against the apostles and their doctrine, was, because they taught the resurrection, which the Sadducees denied.

18 [q] And laid their hands on the apostles, and put them in the common prison.

q Luke 21. 12.

See chap. iv. 3.

19 But [r] the angel of the Lord by night opened the prison doors, and brought them forth, and said,

r ch. 12. 7. & 16. 26.

God useth the ministry of angels, though he might otherwise do what pleaseth him. An angel rolled away the stone from the door of the sepulchre. Angels ministered to Christ, Matt. iv. 11; and are *all ministering spirits, sent forth to minister for them who shall be heirs of salvation,* Heb. i. 14; and encamp round about them that fear God, Psal. xxxiv. 7. *Opened the prison doors;* and shut them again, after that the apostles were gone out, as appears ver. 23.

20 Go, stand and speak in the temple to the people [s] all the words of this life.

s John 6. 68. & 17. 3. 1 John 5. 11.

Stand; the word implies courage and stedfastness of mind, as well as such a posture of the body. *All the words;*

without preferring some acceptable truths before others more ungrateful, if necessary towards their salvation. Christ for a time did limit them; they might not tell any *that he was Jesus the Christ*, Matt. xvi. 20, nor the vision which they had seen in his transfiguration, Matt. xvii. 9. Now this prohibition is taken off. Thus the sun does not shine in his full glory all at once. *This life;* some admit of an hypallage, and join the pronoun to the other substantive, reading in this place, *these words of life;* and the rather because by *this life* is ordinarily understood the present, temporary life, as in 1 Cor. xv. 19: but there needs not this translatitious sense; by *this life*, the angel might very well understand eternal life and salvation, for that was it which the Sadducees denied, and for the preaching of which life the apostles were imprisoned.

21 And when they heard *that*, they entered into the temple early in the morning, and taught. ᵗBut the High Priest came, and they that were with him, and called the council together, and all the senate of the children of Israel, and sent to the prison to have them brought.

t ch. 4. 5, 6.

When they heard that; having received a command from God, they resolved to obey him rather than man. *Early in the morning;* taking the first opportunity, though they could not but be sensible of the danger they ran into. *The council;* the sanhedrim, or great council. *The senate;* the judges of their inferior courts, or the chief amongst the priests or senators; either living in the city, or coming thither upon that festival occasion.

22 But when the officers came, and found them not in the prison, they returned, and told,

These men, thus sent to hinder the spreading of the gospel, could not but be a means of confirming it, when they saw, and declared what they found; so easily can God make use of what is intended against his truth and people unto the advantage of either.

23 Saying, The prison truly found we shut with all safety, and the keepers standing without before the doors: but when we had opened, we found no man within.

All means imaginable were used to secure their prisoners; but when God will deliver, what can keep them? when God will work, who can hinder? Job xi. 10. It is strange, that so great evidence of the innocency of the apostles, and truth of their doctrine, should be ineffectual; but prejudice is insuperable, unless to the mighty power of the grace of God; and this blindness cannot be cured, but by God's *Ephphatha.*

24 Now when the High Priest and ᵘthe captain of the temple and the Chief Priests heard these things, they doubted of them whereunto this would grow.

u Luke 22. 4. ch. 4. 1.

The captain of the temple; the commander over the soldiers who were set to guard the temple, either to secure the treasure there, or to be in a readiness to suppress any tumult thereabouts; Pilate speaks of this, Matt. xxvii. 65. *The chief priests;* the heads of the families, or chief of the courses of the priests. *They doubted of them;* by what means these wonderful things were done; for they were loth to see and acknowledge God in them.

25 Then came one and told them, saying, Behold, the men whom ye put in prison are standing in the temple, and teaching the people.

So true is that in Isa. viii. 10, *Take counsel together, and it shall come to nought.* But, *The counsel of the Lord standeth for ever*, Psal. xxxiii. 11.

26 Then went the captain with the officers, and brought them without violence: ˣfor they feared the people, lest they should have been stoned.

x Mat. 21. 26.

Brought them without violence; they might, peradventure, think it needless or impossible to bind *them* against their wills, who had opened the prison, and so miraculously came out: however, another more certain reason is given of it; *they feared the people;* they feared men more than God, who had done so great things amongst them.

27 And when they had brought them, they set *them* before the council: and the High Priest asked them,

When they are about to do the greatest injuries, they pretend to right; and will not judge them, without giving them leave to answer for themselves.

28 Saying, ʸDid not we straitly command you that ye should not teach in this name? and, behold, ye have filled Jerusalem with your doctrine, ᶻand intend to bring this man's ᵃblood upon us.

y ch. 4. 18.
z ch. 2. 23, 36. & 3. 15. & 7. 52.
a Matt. 23. 35. & 27. 25.

Did not we straitly command you? as indeed they had, chap. iv. 18; hence they aggravated the apostles' crime, as done out of malice, and not out of ignorance. *This name,* and *this man's blood*, are odious reflections, full of contumely against our blessed Saviour, as if he had not been worthy the naming by them. *To bring this man's blood upon us;* they shunned not the sin of murder, but are afraid or ashamed of the imputation of it: as many scruple not to commit that wickedness which they would be loth to be thought guilty of. *Blood;* the punishment of his blood-shedding.

29 ¶ Then Peter and the *other* apostles answered and said, ᵇWe ought to obey God rather than man.

b ch. 4. 19.

This they all agree in, and it is the common sense of all considering men; as Socrates in his apology told the Athenians, I embrace and love you, O Athenians, and yet I will obey God rather than you. This the apostles had formerly asserted, chap. iv. 19.

30 ᶜThe God of our fathers raised up Jesus, whom ye slew and ᵈhanged on a tree.

c ch. 3. 13, 15. & 22. 14.
d ch. 10. 39. & 13. 29.
Gal. 3. 13.
1 Pet. 2. 24.

The God of our fathers; this is the rather mentioned by the apostle, that they might not think our Saviour, or they his ministers, preached any other God unto them, but him whom they had worshipped from their forefathers. *Hanged on a tree;* a tree, or wood, which is rather mentioned than a cross, that the allusion to Deut. xxi. 23 might be more full, where he that is hanged on a tree is accursed; and in that Christ was *made a curse for us*, Gal. iii. 13.

31 ᵉHim hath God exalted with his right hand *to be* ᶠa Prince and ᵍa Saviour, ʰfor to give repentance to Israel, and forgiveness of sins.

e ch. 2. 33, 36.
Phil. 2. 9.
Heb. 2. 10.
& 12. 2.
f ch. 3. 15.
g Matt. 1. 21.
h Luke 24. 47. ch. 3. 26.
& 13. 38. Eph. 1. 7. Col. 1. 14.

Him hath God exalted with his right hand: see chap. ii. 33. *A Prince;* to conquer and subdue all his enemies, to defend and protect his subjects. *A Saviour;* to save from sin, according to his name, *Jesus*, Matt. i. 21; viz. from the condemnation that is due unto it, and the pollution that is acquired by it. *To give repentance;* repentance is the gift of God; and nothing does more avail with us to repent, than the loss of Christ, (his bitter suffering and death,) by whom the world is crucified unto us, Gal. vi. 14: and if repentance includes newness of life, (as it does,) who would not walk in that way which our blessed Lord hath recommended, and in which only we can enjoy him; that doing as he did, we may come at last to be where he is? *And forgiveness of sins,* which never fails to accompany true repentance, and is therefore also called *repentance unto life,* chap. xi. 18.

32 And ⁱwe are his witnesses of these things; and *so is* also the Holy Ghost, ᵏwhom God hath given to them that obey him.

i John 15. 26, 27.
k ch. 2. 4. & 10. 44.

We are his witnesses; they refuse not to bear their testimony for Christ, who witnessed a good profession for us. *So is also the Holy Ghost;* the Holy Ghost does witness, 1. By the apostles; through his grace and strength they bear their record. 2. By all the miracles that were wrought, for they were only done by his power. 3. By enabling any to believe these things; which belief is his work. 4. Not to say that the Holy Ghost was a witness of the things concerning Christ at his baptism, and the several attestations he gave, *saying, This is my beloved Son,* Matt. iii. 17. *Obey him;* some read, believe in him, which is to the same purpose; for there is no true repentance where there is no faith; nor no saving faith where there is no repentance and amendment.

33 ¶ ¹When they heard *that*, they were cut *to the heart*, and took counsel to slay them.

^{l ch. 2. 37. & 7. 54.}

They were cut to the heart; they grinned with their teeth, visibly showing the rage and fury that was within them, by which they were as sawn and divided asunder; malice and rage being a grievous torment to the cruel and malicious, ὁ γαρ μεγας πόνος τὸ μὴ ζῆν καλῶς.

34 Then stood there up one in the council, a Pharisee, named ᵐGamaliel, a doctor of the law, had in reputation among all the people, and commanded to put the apostles forth a little space;

^{m ch. 22. 3.}

A Pharisee; this sect was accounted more mild than the Sadducees. *Named Gamaliel;* it is thought that this man was the same at whose feet Paul sat, chap. xxii. 3: that he was the instructor to Barnabas and St. Stephen, with many other stories concerning him, are doubtful; howsoever, God made use of him, though as yet an enemy to his church and people, to plead for and protect them to his power. God can effect any thing without or against means, and suddenly to make such as were against him to be for him and his truth. *Commanded to put the apostles forth;* that they might consult amongst themselves what to do with them: thus chap. iv. 15.

35 And said unto them, Ye men of Israel, take heed to yourselves what ye intend to do as touching these men.

A wise and good caution; for he that injures another brings the worse mischief upon himself, both in the sense of having done evil, and in being exposed to the revenging hand of God, whose property vengeance is, Heb. x. 30.

36 For before these days rose up Theudas, boasting himself to be somebody; to whom a number of men, about four hundred, joined themselves: who was slain; and all, as many as ‖ obeyed him, were scattered, and brought to nought.

The third Year before the Account called Anno Domini.

‖ Or, *believed.*

Before these days; probably under the reign of Augustus, as he whom Josephus mentions was another under the reign of Claudius. *Theudas;* some suppose it a contracted name of Theodorus, as Demas is thought to be of Demetrius; though others think it to be of a Hebrew original.

37 After this man rose up Judas of Galilee in the days of the taxing, and drew away much people after him: he also perished; and all, *even* as many as obeyed him, were dispersed.

Judas of Galilee; whether this was the same Judas who was called Gaulonite, from the place of his birth, a town in or near Galilee, and Galileus, from the province itself in which he was born, it is not so material to discuss, Josephus makes mention of two of this name. *The taxing;* setting down all their names at the command of the Roman emperor, whereby, 1. They professed themselves to be his subjects. 2. They paid him a certain rate, in token of subjection, for every head, as poll-money. 3. By this means he knew the number of his subjects, and the strength or weakness of every province. This was another tax than that mentioned Luke ii. 2, which is there called the first.

38 And now I say unto you, Refrain from these men, and let them alone: ⁿfor if this counsel or this work be of men, it will come to nought:

^{n Prov. 21. 30. Is. 8. 10. Matt. 15. 13.}

And now I say unto you; he undertakes to advise them what they should do in the present case. *Refrain from these men;* have nothing to do with them, as Pilate's wife advised him concerning our Saviour, Matt. xxvii. 19. Gamaliel interposes, partly out of his moderate and mild disposition; partly out of fear, lest if they slew the apostles they might incense the Romans, who were very jealous of their authority, and had taken away the power of capital punishments from the Jews. *For if this counsel or this work be of men, it will come to nought;* this argument, or dilemma, which Gamaliel uses for the sparing of the apostles, is of force either way; as that question our Saviour propounds concerning the baptism of John, Matt. xxi. 25. This first part is evident, for that building must needs fall which is built upon the sand, Matt. vii. 27.

39 °But if it be of God, ye cannot overthrow it; lest haply ye be found even ᵖto fight against God.

^{o Luke 21. 15. 1 Cor. 1. 25.}
^{p ch. 7. 51. & 9. 5. & 23. 9.}

The other part of the dilemma. *The counsel of the Lord, that shall stand,* Prov. xix. 21; Isa. xlvi. 10; and it must needs be so, for all power is his, in whom we live and move, chap. xvii. 28. *Fight against God;* they who afflict and contend with his people unjustly, though they little think so, set themselves against God, who will overcome at the last, and triumph over his and his people's enemies.

40 And to him they agreed: and when they had ᑫcalled the apostles, ʳand beaten *them*, they commanded that they should not speak in the name of Jesus, and let them go.

^{q ch. 4. 18.}
^{r Matt. 10. 17. & 23. 34. Mark 13 Q}

To him they agreed; they yielded to his reason and argument, being persuaded and convinced by it. *Beaten them;* this was what our Saviour had foretold them, Matt. x. 17; and thus the husbandmen took the householder's servants and beat them, Matt. xxi. 35. They had power yet left them by the Romans to punish offenders in their synagogues, but not capitally nor publicly. In this they left the good advice of Gamaliel, who had warned them not to fight against God.

41 ¶ And they departed from the presence of the council, ˢrejoicing that they were counted worthy to suffer shame for his name.

^{s Mat. 5. 12. Rom. 5. 3. 2 Cor 12. 10. Phil. 1. 29. Heb. 10. 34. Jam. 1. 2. 1 Pet. 4. 13, 16.}

Rejoicing; it argued full persuasion of the truth, and great resolution to abide by it, that they could account so foul a disgrace for Christ's sake to be an honour. *That they were counted worthy to suffer;* it is a condescension and favour, when God uses any to give testimony unto his truth, although it be by their suffering: Phil. i. 29, *Unto you it is given, not only to believe, but to suffer;* as if to suffer for Christ were as great, if not a greater gift than to believe in him. *Shame;* scourging being a servile and disgraceful punishment. *For his name;* Christ's name, or for Christ's sake, to assert his truth, &c.: some do not read the pronoun, but *the name,* put absolutely for God, as was usual amongst the Jews, out of reverence to God's name, lest they should profane it.

42 And daily ᵗin the temple, and in every house, ᵘthey ceased not to teach and preach Jesus Christ.

^{t ch. 2. 46.}
^{u ch. 4. 20, 29.}

This is the same with what we read Acts xx. 20, *publicly, and from house to house;* that is, in the temple, and public places, they preached unto the Jews; and in more private places, (or houses,) where they saw it needful; unto such they conversed with. They visited their flock, and instructed, exhorted, comforted them as their condition required. See the power of the grace of God; these were the men who forsook Christ when the soldiers came to apprehend him, they durst not be seen in his company; yet now they profess his name, and abide by their profession, though they are derided and beaten for it.

CHAP. VI

The apostles, that the poor might not be neglected, recommend, 1—4, *and with the church's consent ordain, seven chosen men, deacons,* 5, 6. *The word of God prevaileth,* 7. *Stephen, full of faith and the Holy Ghost, confuting those with whom he disputed, is brought before the council, and by suborned evidence falsely accused of blasphemy against the law and the temple,* 8—15.

THE ACTS VI

^{a ch. 2. 41.}
^{& 4. 4. & 5.}
^{14. & ver. 7.}
^{b ch. 9. 29.}
^{& 11. 20.}
^{c ch. 4. 35.}

AND in those days, ^a when the number of the disciples was multiplied, there arose a murmuring of the ^b Grecians against the Hebrews, because their widows were neglected ^c in the daily ministration.

Grecians; these were not such as are elsewhere called Greeks, either as being of that nation, or more generally taken for all Gentiles at large; but they were (as to their authority) Jews, and descended from such of them who, in several national calamities, were forced (or chose) to leave their country, and fly to Alexandria, and divers other places; yet kept themselves unmixed with other nations, retaining the knowledge of God, and coming to worship upon the solemn feasts; only, disusing the Hebrew language, they were more acquainted with the Greek tongue, (then commonly spoken every where,) and used the Holy Scripture translated into that language, which made them the rather called Hellenists or Grecians. *Their widows were neglected in the daily ministration;* they were not taken, as others, into the college, or number of widows, who in that time had some care of the poor; or rather, because they were not so largely allowed, or carefully looked after; for those that sold their goods, being Hebrews, they might not be so tender over the Hellenists, whose estates laying farther off, could not so readily be sold for the relief of themselves or others.

2 Then the twelve called the multitude of the disciples *unto them,* and said, ^d It is not reason that we should leave the word of God, and serve tables.

^{J Ex. 18. 17.}

The twelve; for such was their number now again, Matthias having supplied the place of Judas; this is that blessed number, or the root of it, which God hath so much magnified. *The word of God;* preaching of the word, and other duties belonging to it. *Serve tables;* either providing for the agapæ and love-feasts, or distributing to the necessities whereby they might be fed, and their tables provided.

^{e Deut. 1.13.}
^{ch. 1. 21. &}
^{16. 2.}
^{1 Tim. 3. 7.}

3 Wherefore, brethren, ^e look ye out among you seven men of honest report, full of the Holy Ghost and wisdom, whom we may appoint over this business.

Look ye out among you seven men; as carefully and circumspectly as ye would in any cases of your own concerns. *Of honest report;* a good direction, that obliges to this day, in all elections of any for the service of God and his church. *Full of the Holy Ghost;* of the gifts and graces of the Holy Ghost, which were not bestowed on the apostles only. *And wisdom;* or prudence, and skill in the word of God, which only is able to make a man wise unto salvation, 2 Tim. iii. 15.

^{f ch. 2. 42.}

4 But we ^f will give ourselves continually to prayer, and to the ministry of the word.

We will give ourselves continually; we will stick close, and with perseverance, to this work. *To prayer, and to the ministry of the word;* the two great employs of a minister of Jesus Christ; to pray unto God for the people, and to speak unto the people from the Lord: these, though great businesses, they durst not delegate from themselves unto others to perform for them.

5 ¶ And the saying pleased the whole multitude: and they chose Stephen, ^g a man full of faith and of the Holy Ghost, and ^h Philip, and Prochorus, and Nicanor, and Timon, and Parmenas, and ⁱ Nicolas a proselyte of Antioch:

^{g ch. 11. 24.}
^{h ch. 8. 5,}
^{26, & 21. 8.}
^{i Rev. 2. 6, 15.}

All these being Greek names, it is likely they were all Hellenists, and descended from Hebrew parents, but born in foreign countries; or amongst the Jews they might have other names, which St. Luke, writing this history, translated into Greek. *A proselyte of Antioch:* see chap. ii. 10.

6 Whom they set before the apostles: and

^k when they had prayed, ^l they laid *their* hands on them.

^{k ch. 1. 24.}
^{l ch. 8. 17. &}
^{9. 17. & 13. 3.}
^{1 Tim. 4. 14. & 5. 22. 2 Tim. 1. 6.}

When they had prayed; prayer is the salt which seasoneth and sanctifieth all things. *They laid their hands on them;* a rite used in the church of old, 1. In their sacrifices, Exod. xxix. 15; 2. In their blessings, Gen. xlviii. 14; 3. In their designations unto a charge or office; thus Moses on Joshua, Numb. xxvii. 18: and from thence it was more easily derived unto the gospel church; our Saviour blessing thus the children which were brought unto him, Matt. xix. 13; and thus also were ministers ordained in the primitive times, 1 Tim. v. 22.

7 And ^m the word of God increased; and the number of the disciples multiplied in Jerusalem greatly; and a great company ⁿ of the Priests were obedient to the faith.

^{m ch. 12. 24.}
^{& 19. 20.}
^{Col. 1. 6.}
^{n John 12. 42.}

A great company of the priests; none so violent opposers of the gospel as these were (their interest in all likelihood, heightening their opposition); yet great is truth, especially the Spirit of truth, and did prevail; and though in itself the number might not be so great as to be called a great multitude, yet, considering who they were that were converted, it was very wonderful, and the few might pass for many. *Were obedient to the faith;* Christianity is not a bare speculation, but a practical religion; and we believe no more than we practise: *Fac quod dicis et fides est,* Aug.

8 And Stephen, full of faith and power, did great wonders and miracles among the people.

Full of faith and power; enabled to preach, dispute, do, and suffer all things through Christ. *Did great wonders and miracles among the people;* of whom he cured many; or, *among the people,* in that he did these wonders publicly.

9 ¶ Then there arose certain of the synagogue, which is called *the synagogue* of the Libertines, and Cyrenians, and Alexandrians, and of them of Cilicia and of Asia, disputing with Stephen.

Certain of the synagogue; synagogues were as colleges in our universities, being used for instruction and learning; and were distinguished according to the persons that frequented them. *Libertines;* some think these were natives of a certain country in Africa, from whence they were so called; but more probably they were such as were manumitted or made free, (as the word is commonly used for such,) and in a middle condition between such as were free-born and such as were bond-slaves, and might desire to frequent with those of their own rank. *Cyrenians, &c.;* the Jews spake of no less than four hundred and eighty synagogues at Jerusalem; a vast number, and probably increased by them: though several places are called Cyrene, this (from whence they took their name) was in Africa in all likelihood, it being joined with that of the Alexandrians. So God pleased to sever the Hellenists, (or Jews by traduction,) for the Gentiles were not yet called, that they might all hear the gospel in the language they understood best.

10 And ^o they were not able to resist the wisdom and the spirit by which he spake.

^{o Luke 21. 15. ch. 5. 32.}
^{See Exod. 4. 12. Is. 54. 17.}

Not able to resist; they did oppose it, but ineffectually. *The wisdom: The foolishness of God is wiser than men,* 1 Cor. i. 25. What then is his wisdom, through which this holy man spake? *The spirit;* the Holy Ghost directing him, and putting a Divine power upon what he spake, according to the promise, Matt. x. 20.

11 ^p Then they suborned men, which said, We have heard him speak blasphemous words against Moses, and *against* God.

^{p 1 Kings 21. 10, 13. Matt. 26. 59, 60.}

What these *blasphemous words* were, we have, ver. 14; which show, that the veil was yet over their hearts, and that they could not endure to hear, that the shadows must flee away when the sun is risen, and the types be abolished when the substance of the things typified is exhibited; for this truth was all the blasphemy this holy martyr was guilty of.

12 And they stirred up the people, and the elders, and the Scribes, and came upon *him*, and caught him, and brought *him* to the council,

Being overcome by reason and arguments, they betake themselves to all the evil arts imaginable; they suborn witnesses against St. Stephen, as was done against Naboth, and (that we read of) never before; they make the people, and the number, (which is usually the worst,) on their side; then they complain of him to the priests, &c.; and lest any, or all these, should fail, they lay violent hands on him themselves. Sin goes on as a current, and never stops, unless an Almighty word be spoken unto it to go no further.

13 And set up false witnesses, which said, This man ceaseth not to speak blasphemous words against this holy place, and the law:

They mingled in their testimony false things with truths, as they who witnessed against our Saviour had done. St. Stephen might possibly have inculcated what our Saviour had foretold, Luke xix. 43, 44, and both have been very innocent; for neither of them spake with any abhorrence of, much less blasphemy against, the law or the temple; but in that the witnesses perverted and added to their words, they are deservedly branded as *false witnesses. Falsus in uno, falsus in omnibus,* is a granted maxim in the case of witness-bearing.

q ch. 25. 8.
r Dan. 9. 26.
‖ Or, *rites.*

14 qFor we have heard him say, that this Jesus of Nazareth shall r destroy this place, and shall change the ‖ customs which Moses delivered us.

This place; that is, the temple. Jeremiah had foretold this long ago, and did escape, though very narrowly, Jer. xxvi. 12—16; Daniel had prophesied of the destruction both of *the city and the sanctuary,* Dan. ix. 26; and yet these were in great respect amongst them: and none could speak more plainly of the calling of the Gentiles than Malachi, chap. i. 11: and yet when the apostles came to apply these very things more home and close, they could not endure them.

15 And all that sat in the council, looking stedfastly on him, saw his face as it had been the face of an angel.

With an extraordinary lustre and radiancy, above what appears in men, whereby they might be distinguished, as Matt. xxviii. 2, 3, affecting the beholders with admiration; thus Moses's face did shine.

CHAP. VII

Stephen, called upon to answer the charge against him, relateth how God called Abraham, and gave him and his seed the land of Canaan by promise, 1—8: *how Joseph was sold by his brethren, and Jacob with his family went down into Egypt,* 9—16: *how, when they were oppressed by the Egyptians, Moses was born, and sent to deliver Israel out of Egypt,* 17—36: *that this same Moses witnessed of Christ, received the law, and experienced the disobedience and idolatry of their forefathers,* 37—43; *who had the tabernacle of witness, till Solomon built the temple,* 44—50. *He reproacheth his hearers with imitating their fathers' rebellion against God, and persecution of his prophets, by having themselves murdered Christ, and transgressed the law they had received,* 51—53. *Stung with reproach, they stone him, looking up with faith unto God, and calling upon Jesus to receive his soul, and forgive his persecutors,* 54—60.

THEN said the High Priest, Are these things so?

Then said the high priest; who was resolved to condemn any, right or wrong, that should profess Christ, as appears John xix. 22. *Are these things so?* that he might seem just, he gives him a kind of liberty to answer for himself; not to defend his doctrine, but to know out of his own mouth whether he preached it, or no.

a ch. 22. 1.

2 And he said, aMen, brethren, and fathers, hearken; The God of glory appeared unto our father Abraham, when he was in Mesopotamia, before he dwelt in Charran,

Brethren; to take away any prejudice they might have conceived against him, and to recommend, not his person so much as his doctrine to them, he calls them *brethren*; 1. As hoping in the same promises with them; 2. Observing the same law; 3. Worshipping the same God. *Fathers;* a word of respect; especially the elder amongst them, or his judges: thus the Roman senators were called fathers; and magistrates ought to be reverenced as the fathers of their country. *The God of glory;* who is also called, Psal. xxiv. 7, *the King of glory;* from whom all glory descends to angels or men. By this, and what follows, St. Stephen would show that he honoured the true God, and thought respectfully of the law, the temple, and the patriarchs, whom he was accused to contemn and disgrace. He names *Abraham,* because he was accounted the first father and patriarch of the Jews, and had the first clear promise that the Messiah should come of his seed. *Mesopotamia* is sometimes taken strictly for that country which lies betwixt the two rivers, Tigris and Euphrates, from whence it had its name; sometimes more largely, including Chaldea; and so it is taken here. *Charran;* a city of the Parthians, in the borders of Mesopotamia, towards the land of Canaan.

3 And said unto him, bGet thee out of thy country, and from thy kindred, and come into the land which I shall shew thee.

b Gen. 12. 1.

This command given unto Abraham we read of, Gen. xii. 1, 5, 6; and it is here the rather spoken of by St. Stephen, to prove that Abraham was in the favour of God, and did truly serve him, before he ever saw the land of Canaan, and before the ceremonial law was given by Moses, and, much more, before the temple was built; and therefore it could not be blasphemy in him to hold that God might be served without those ceremonies, and worshipped elsewhere than in Jerusalem. *The land which I shall show thee;* this was the glory of Abraham's faith, that it submitted absolutely to God, and enabled Abraham to go he knew not whither, Heb. xi. 8, for God did not so much as name the place he would have him go unto.

4 Then ccame he out of the land of the Chaldæans, and dwelt in Charran: and from thence, when his father was dead, he removed him into this land, wherein ye now dwell.

c Gen. 11. 31. & 12. 4, 5.

Abraham had as great a love to his kindred and native country as others have; but he had a greater faith, which made him yield to God's call and command, and follow from place to place the will of God, who is said here to have removed Abraham, and does choose the inheritance and habitation for his people, Psal. xlvii. 4.

5 And he gave him none inheritance in it, no, not *so much as* to set his foot on: dyet he promised that he would give it to him for a possession, and to his seed after him, when *as yet* he had no child.

d Gen. 12. 7. & 13. 15. & 15. 3, 18. & 17. 8, & 26. 3.

He gave him none inheritance in it; it is true that Abraham had a field, and the cave of Mach-pelah, Gen. xxiii. 9; but that was of no use to Abraham whilst alive, but to bury him in when dead; besides, it was not as an inheritance by God's gift, but it was purchased with his money. *Not so much as to set his foot on;* whereby the least parcel of ground is meant: hence St. Stephen would prove, that Abraham's happiness, and theirs too, if they rightly understood it, did not depend upon the enjoyment of that place and country. *And to his seed after him;* faith met with a double difficulty, not only Abraham must believe he should have all that country given him for an inheritance, in which he had not a foot of land, but he must also believe that it should be his seed's after him, whenas he had no children; but thus faith is *the evidence of things not seen,* Heb. xi. 1.

6 And God spake on this wise, eThat his seed should sojourn in a strange land; and that they should bring them into

e Gen. 15. 13, 16.

THE ACTS VII

f Ex. 12. 40.
Gal. 3. 17.
bondage, and entreat *them* evil [f]four hundred years.

Should sojourn in a strange land, as men which dwell in houses that are not their own; which seem to contradict the promise mentioned in the foregoing verse; but it is only to make Abraham the more believe against hope in hope, as it is said, Rom. iv. 18: though there were never so many difficulties more, for what God hath promised faith would overcome them all. This very space of *four hundred years* is also mentioned, Gen. xv. 13; which is thus computed: from the birth of Isaac (the promised seed) to the birth of Jacob, sixty years; from Jacob's birth to his going into Egypt, one hundred and thirty years; from thence to their deliverance out of Egypt, two hundred and ten years; this period is accounted, Exod. xii. 40, 41, to be four hundred and thirty years; which also St. Paul reckons by, Gal. iii. 17; but then thirty years is added unto the account, being the space of time betwixt the first promise made unto Abraham of this seed, and the birth of Isaac, in whom the promise was to be fulfilled; St. Stephen here reckoning only from the birth of Isaac.

7 And the nation to whom they shall be in bondage will I judge, said God: and after that shall they come forth, and g Ex. 3. 12. [g]serve me in this place.

Will I judge, or punish; and so the Egyptians were punished, not by human means, but by Divine power, and with God's own immediate hand, and that in the fulness of time, the very night in which God's promise was to take effect: and therefore it is *a night to be much observed*, Exod. xii. 42, as showing, that the sabbath of his people, and the destruction of his enemies, slumber not, 2 Pet. ii. 3. *Serve me in this place;* in Mount Horeb. The reason why God delivers his people is, that they may serve him, as Luke i. 74, 75; and so long as God hath any work for them to do in this world, he will preserve and deliver them.

h Gen. 17.
9, 10, 11.
i Gen. 21. 2, 3, 4.
k Gen. 25. 26.
l Gen. 29. 31, &c. & 30. 5, &c. & 35. 18, 23.
8 [h]And he gave him the covenant of circumcision: [i]and so *Abraham* begat Isaac, and circumcised him the eighth day; [k]and Isaac *begat* Jacob; and [l]Jacob *begat* the twelve patriarchs.

He gave him, Abraham, of whom he was speaking, *the covenant of circumcision ;* of which covenant, circumcision was the sign and seal, by which, on the part of Abraham and his seed, it was stipulated, that they should put off all carnal affections. *Begat Isaac*, after the promise: so that the promises were not given for Isaac's sake, but Isaac was given for the promise' sake; which made these things more fit to represent gospel grace, of which St. Stephen was preaching. *The twelve patriarchs ;* the heads of the tribes, from whom they were denominated. Of this genealogy, see Matt. i. 1, 2, &c., and the history of it in Genesis.

m Gen. 37.
4, 11, 28.
Ps. 105. 17.
n Gen. 39. 2,
21, 23.
9 [m]And the patriarchs, moved with envy, sold Joseph into Egypt: [n]but God was with him,

Moved with envy ; enraged: the holy martyr accommodates his apology so, as that they may yet have occasion to reflect on themselves; for as they had sold our Saviour unto strangers, so had their fathers *sold Joseph. But God was with him*, to favour and bless him; for God's presence brings all good along with it: with this he comforts himself and others, that it was not without example or precedent that God should be with such whom their persecutors could not endure.

o Gen. 41.
37. & 42. 6.
10 And delivered him out of all his afflictions, [o]and gave him favour and wisdom in the sight of Pharaoh king of Egypt; and he made him governor over Egypt and all his house.

And delivered him out of all his afflictions; the effect of God's presence with him, which to his people is always in an especial manner, not only as he is with all other creatures, but as the soul is with the body, most effectually, so is God with them. *And gave him favour and wisdom in the sight of Pharaoh :* thus God brought Daniel into favour, Dan. i. 9, and hath all hearts in his hands.

11 [p]Now there came a dearth over all the land of Egypt and Chanaan, and great affliction: and our fathers found no sustenance. p Gen. 41. 54.

A dearth ; this is mentioned, Gen. xli. 54, &c. *And great affliction ;* as seldom any mischief comes alone, rapine and many diseases follow famine. *Found no sustenance ;* any coarse diet, grass or herbs.

12 [q]But when Jacob heard that there was corn in Egypt, he sent out our fathers first. q Gen. 42. 1.

The history is known, Gen. xlii. *Our fathers ;* our progenitors, Jacob's sons, from whom we are descended.

13 [r]And at the second *time* Joseph was made known to his brethren; and Joseph's kindred was made known unto Pharaoh. r Gen. 45. 4, 16.

Upon their second coming into Egypt, Gen. xlv. 3, 4, 16, Joseph made himself known unto them. *Joseph's kindred was made known unto Pharaoh ;* for the continuance of their sustenance, and fulfilling of what was foretold.

14 [s]Then sent Joseph, and called his father Jacob to *him*, and [t]all his kindred, threescore and fifteen souls. s Gen. 45. 9, 27.
t Gen. 46. 27.
Deut. 10. 22.

All his kindred ; his affinity, and not consanguinity only, which may be the reason why, though in Gen. xlvi. 26 it is said, that all *the souls that came with Jacob into Egypt were threescore and six*, (it being then added, they were all such as *came out of his loins,)* yet it is said they were seventy persons, Gen. xlvi. 27, Jacob, Joseph, and Joseph's two sons (who were also of the promised seed) being added unto the number. In this account of St. Stephen, his sons' wives might be added, which make up seventy-five. There are other accounts of this difference; but it is not of any consequence as to faith and holy living, which are only necessary unto salvation: the wonderful increase to so many hundred thousands of men, besides children, spoken of, Exod. xii. 37, notwithstanding the barbarous cruelty of the Egyptians, is to be admired. *Souls ;* the nobler and better part, by which they are numbered, and according unto which they are esteemed by God.

15 [u]So Jacob went down into Egypt, [w]and died, he, and our fathers, u Gen. 46. 5.
w Gen. 49. 33. Ex. 1. 6.

Which St. Stephen puts them in mind of the rather, that he might insinuate, no country, nor place, nor temple, were so necessary, but that (notwithstanding they had none of them) their forefathers did live and die in the fear and favour of God, although in Egypt, out of the Promised Land, &c.

16 And [x]were carried over into Sychem, and laid in [y]the sepulchre that Abraham bought for a sum of money of the sons of Emmor *the father* of Sychem. x Ex. 13. 19.
Josh. 24. 32.
y Gen. 23.
16. & 35. 19.

That they carried Joseph to bury him in Canaan, according to the oath he made them take, Gen. l. 25, is certain; and that this was desired to be done for him out of faith, Heb. xi. 22; but is not so certain (unless this place be so understood) that the rest of the patriarchs were so translated after their death: yet it is very likely; for, first, They had as much reason to desire it as Joseph had; they believed the same promises, and had an interest in that land as well as he. Secondly, Their posterity bore the same respect unto them that Joseph's family did to him. Thirdly, It seems alike reasonable, that none of those twelve heirs to the land of Canaan should be left in the land of bondage. This place is acknowledged to be most difficult, and the difficulties are better not to be mentioned than ill solved, which the nature of these notes (not to mention other reasons) might occasion: whosoever will consider the intended shortness of the story, with the usual idioms of the Hebrew language, from which it was deduced, may take this as a paraphrase upon the whole verse: And Jacob and our fathers died, and were removed to Sychem, and were laid in sepulchres, in that which Abraham bought for money, and in that which was bought of the sons of Emmor, the father of Sychem. *Dr. Lightfoot*, in *locum.*

17 But when *the time of the promise drew nigh, which God had sworn to Abraham, ªthe people grew and multiplied in Egypt,

z Gen. 15. 13. ver. 6.
a Ex. 1. 7, 8, 9. Ps. 105. 24, 25.

Of the promise; of the fulfilling of the promise, either of the increase of his seed, or of their deliverance out of bondage, for both were promised, Gen. xxii. 17; though at that very time there were the greatest endeavours to hinder either when God accomplished both.

18 Till another king arose, which knew not Joseph.

These words are taken from the Septuagint, Exod. i. 8.

19 The same dealt subtilly with our kindred, and evil entreated our fathers, ᵇso that they cast out their young children, to the end they might not live.

b Ex. 1. 22.

Pharaoh resolves to *deal* (as he thought) *wisely*, Exod. i. 10, and it is acknowledged that the Egyptians dealt subtilly with them, Psal. cv. 25. For they do not at once destroy them, which might have been hazardous, the Israelites being so numerous; neither could Egypt well spare at once so many inhabitants; (too great and sudden evacuations cause swoonings;) but they endeavour their ruin by degrees: 1. Wasting them by hard labours. 2. Commanding the midwives privately to kill their males. 3. Casting out, or exposing, any whom they found spared. Yet this people, attempted upon by so many secret and open means to bring them to destruction, God did preserve; and so he will his church, (which they did typify,) maugre all the endeavours the most potent malice can use against it.

20 ᶜIn which time Moses was born, and ᵈwas ‖ exceeding fair, and nourished up in his father's house three months:

c Ex. 2. 2.
d Heb. 11.23.
‖ Or, *fair to God.*

Exceeding fair, or, fair to God; which though some understand of the inward beauty of the mind, (which is indeed the most admirable,) yet in this place there is no more to be understood by it, than the wonderful beauty of his body, which God bestowed in an extraordinary measure upon him, that it might be a means to attract the care and pity of Pharaoh's daughter, as it afterwards came to pass: besides, that which is eminent in any kind, is, by a Hebraism, said to be of God: upon this account Nineveh is called a city of God, Jonah iii. 3; and we read of Rachel's great wrestlings, or wrestlings of God, Gen. xxx. 8. Josephus says, that Moses was so beautiful, that all who passed by left the business they were about to gaze at him, Antiq. ii. 5.

21 And ᵉwhen he was cast out, Pharaoh's daughter took him up, and nourished him for her own son.

e Ex. 2. 3, —10.

Was cast out; exposed and left, Exod. ii. 2, &c.; now was the time for God to take him up, as in Psal. xxvii. 10. *Pharaoh's daughter*, an enemy to God's Israel; yet God did make use of her to bring up and educate Moses, who was their deliverer, adopting him for her son, Exod. ii. 10, and giving him education accordingly.

22 And Moses was learned in all the wisdom of the Egyptians, and was ᶠmighty in words and in deeds.

f Luke 24.19.

Learned in all the wisdom of the Egyptians; the Egyptians were anciently famous for learning, especially in astronomy, and some other parts of philosophy. *Mighty in words;* he was eloquent. *And in deeds;* his deeds were equal to his words; he could do, as well as say, what became him.

23 ᵍAnd when he was full forty years old, it came into his heart to visit his brethren the children of Israel.

g Ex. 2. 11, 12.

Forty years old; this age of Moses is not set down in his history, but they might have it by tradition, which is here confirmed unto us by the holy penman: these forty years Moses spent in Pharaoh's court. *It came into his heart;* it speaks these thoughts and resolutions to have been from God, that such a great courtier should so far debase himself; therefore this is deservedly attributed unto his faith, Heb. xi. 24, which is *the gift of God*, Eph. ii. 8.

24 And seeing one *of them* suffer wrong, he defended *him*, and avenged him that was oppressed, and smote the Egyptian:

This fact of Moses some defend by the law of nature, which allows us to protect the innocent; but many things we know were done by an extraordinary warrant, which we are not to imitate; nor by our own authority to avenge ourselves or others.

25 ‖ For he supposed his brethren would have understood how that God by his hand would deliver them: but they understood not.

‖ Or, *Now.*

This they might have inferred, 1. From his extraordinary deliverance out of the Egyptians' hands, and out of the river, when young. 2. From his readiness to defend them: it was wonderful, that such a one as he was, and might have been, should mind them. 3. From the drawing near of the time of their deliverance, which they could not, without negligence, be wholly ignorant of. *By his hand;* by his means and ministry. *But they understood not:* stupidity is frequently charged upon this people: they then did not receive Moses, as these now would not receive Christ.

26 ʰAnd the next day he shewed himself unto them as they strove, and would have set them at one again, saying, Sirs, ye are brethren; why do ye wrong one to another?

h Ex. 2. 13.

He shewed himself; as one appointed by God to deliver them, which he had evidenced before. *Would have set them at one again;* with great earnestness, and as far as words could do, he compelled them. *Saying, Sirs, ye are brethren;* these words are not mentioned, Exod. ii. 13, but something otherwise than here; but the sense is here and there the same. *Brethren*, not so much being all descended from Abraham and the patriarchs; but in that they all worshipped one and the same God, which is the greatest obligation to concord and agreement that can be; and if any offence be given, or trespass committed, it obliges us as much to pass it by and pardon it: *Forgive the trespass of the servants of the God of thy father*, Gen. l. 17.

27 But he that did his neighbour wrong thrust him away, saying, ⁱWho made thee a ruler and a judge over us?

i See Luke 12. 14. ch. 4. 7.

The injurious are most averse from peace, and one sin makes way for another. This was a causeless cavil, especially from such a one as had known what Moses had done, as an essay of his being the deliverer of God's Israel.

28 Wilt thou kill me, as thou diddest the Egyptian yesterday?

He charges this great crime upon Moses, to hinder him from further reproving of him: though recrimination do not make him, or any other, more innocent; yet men ordinarily use it, as if it were some satisfaction to them that they are not wicked alone, but that others are as bad or worse: this better befits an Egyptian than an Israelite.

29 ᵏThen fled Moses at this saying, and was a stranger in the land of Madian, where he begat two sons.

k Ex. 2. 15, 22. & 4. 20. & 18. 3, 4.

Then fled Moses; knowing that what he had done to the Egyptian would be discovered to Pharaoh, and his life in danger. *The land of Madian;* inhabited by the posterity of Midian, Abraham's son by Keturah, Gen. xxv. 1, 2. Moses was forty years in Egypt, forty years in Midian, with Jethro or Jether, who was called also Reuel, Exod. ii. 18, and Hobab, Numb. x. 29, and the other forty years in the wilderness, which make up the hundred and twenty years of his life, Deut. xxxiv. 7. This makes to St. Stephen's purpose, to prove that God is always with them that fear him, in what country or place soever; as he was with Abraham in Mesopotamia, and with his people in Egypt, so with Moses in Midian.

30 ˡAnd when forty years were expired, there appeared to him in the wilderness of mount Sina an angel of the Lord in a flame of fire in a bush.

l Ex. 3. 2.

Forty years; so long it pleased God to try Moses's faith, and his people's patience. *Mount Sinai,* in the desert of Arabia, where the law was afterwards delivered, Exod. xviii. 5; xix. 3. *An angel;* not a created, but the uncreated Angel; the Angel of the new covenant, as may be seen ver. 32, and by Moses putting off his shoes because the place was holy, Exod. iii. 2, 5; he is also in the 4th verse of that chapter called the Lord. God still appeared in such a manner as was most instructive to them he appeared to, and to us; as here in *a flame of fire in a bush,* to show that he was with his people in all their sufferings, and would so provide, that they should not be consumed by them; they might be purified, but should not be destroyed.

31 When Moses saw *it,* he wondered at the sight: and as he drew near to behold *it,* the voice of the Lord came unto him,

He wondered at the sight; seeing the bush on a flame, and not consumed, contrary to the nature of devouring flames; that he might be convinced of God's presence, and made the more attentive to what God should say, and prepared to yield obedience unto it.

32 *Saying,* ᵐI *am* the God of thy fathers, the God of Abraham, and the God of Isaac, and the God of Jacob. Then Moses trembled, and durst not behold.

I am the God of thy fathers; that he might know from whom he had his commission, and by whom he was to be sent. *The God of Abraham, &c.;* mention is made of these, because God had made unto them the promise of delivering their posterity, which he was now about to do, the time being fully come. *Moses trembled:* all great admiration hath some fear joined with it: God's appearing, though in mercy, was ever full of terror and amazement; what will his appearing be, when he shall come in judgment to render vengeance! who then shall be able to abide?

33 ⁿ Then said the Lord to him, Put off thy shoes from thy feet: for the place where thou standest is holy ground.

Put off thy shoes; either out of reverence to the Divine presence, as Josh. v. 15, or that thereby he might show that he resigned himself wholly to God's will and disposal; as in Ruth iv. 7, the kinsman, by pulling off his shoe and giving it to Boaz, did resign all his right he might have had to Ruth and the inheritance. *Holy ground,* whilst God manifested his presence there.

34 ° I have seen, I have seen the affliction of my people which is in Egypt, and I have heard their groaning, and am come down to deliver them. And now come, I will send thee into Egypt.

I have seen, I have seen; seeing I have seen, I have attentively seen and considered; it is doubled to show the certainty of it: if earthly parents, especially, look after their children when weak, much more our heavenly Father. *I have heard their groaning;* though but sighs, and scarce framed into words. *Am come down;* spoken after the manner of men, according unto which God is said to come down unto any when he delivers them from their troubles, and to go from them when he leaves them in them: see Exod. iii. 7, 8, from which place, according to the reading of the Septuagint, these words are taken.

35 This Moses whom they refused, saying, Who made thee a ruler and a judge? the same did God send *to be* a ruler and a deliverer ᵖ by the hand of the angel which appeared to him in the bush.

A deliverer; or, a redeemer; but only as a type of Christ, *in whom* alone *we have redemption through his blood,* Eph. i. 7; as Moses by the blood of the paschal lamb brought forth and saved the people of Israel. *The hands of the angel;* the power of the angel; it was not Moses, but God, that wrought so great salvation.

36 ᵠ He brought them out, after that he had ʳ shewed wonders and signs in the land of Egypt, ˢ and in the Red sea, ᵗ and in the wilderness forty years.

After that he had showed wonders and signs: God could with the least word or motion of his will save his people; but he chooseth so to do his wonderful works, that they may be had in remembrance. *In the Red sea;* it is not agreed why it is so called; but this name of that sea is mentioned in profane authors. This whole verse, as divers others, refer to the history of it in Exodus, from the beginning to the 15th chapter.

37 ¶ This is that Moses, which said unto the children of Israel, ᵘ A prophet shall the Lord your God raise up unto you of your brethren, ∥ like unto me; ˣ him shall ye hear.

St. Stephen would show, that he was so far from speaking against Moses, as they falsely imagined, that he recommended none but him, whom Moses had so long before spoken of. *A prophet;* Christ the Messiah, and Head of the prophets: see chap. iii. 22. *Him shall ye hear;* or obey.

38 ʸ This is he, that was in the Church in the wilderness with ᶻ the angel which spake to him in the mount Sina, and *with* our fathers: ᵃ who received the lively ᵇ oracles to give unto us:

In the church in the wilderness; or congregation; with the rest of the people in all their difficult journey. *The angel;* see ver. 30 of this chapter. *The lively oracles;* God's law and word is so called, as the only rule to walk by unto life, Deut. xxxii. 47: it is there said to be our life; and it is the only ordinary means of a spiritual and holy life, which it begets and preserves.

39 To whom our fathers would not obey, but thrust *him* from them, and in their hearts turned back again into Egypt,

Their glory being in their fathers, St. Stephen reminds them that many of them rebelled against God and his servant Moses; as they (their posterity) now were rebellious against Christ, who came to save them, as Moses before had done; but from a greater bondage, and by more valuable means. *In their hearts turned back again into Egypt;* not so much towards that country, or food they had there, (garlick and onions,) as towards their idolatry and superstition; as in the following verse appears.

40 ᶜ Saying unto Aaron, Make us gods to go before us: for *as for* this Moses, which brought us out of the land of Egypt, we wot not what is become of him.

Make us gods; according to the Egyptians, who held that there were many gods, and divers degrees of gods; they therefore speak in the plural number. *This Moses:* though they confess the great deliverance wrought by Moses's means, yet how contemptibly do they speak of him! *We wot not what is become of him:* they could not but know that Moses was gone up into the mount unto God, at his command, and had not forgotten them, but had left Aaron and Hur to govern them; yet they soon forgot both God and Moses, notwithstanding the large and late experience they had of his wonders: this is left upon record against them, Psal. cvi. 13, 21.

41 ᵈ And they made a calf in those days, and offered sacrifice unto the idol, and rejoiced in the works of their own hands.

They made a calf; in imitation of the Egyptians, who worshipped their god Apis in that, or the like form of an ox. *The idol;* the calf which they had made, which they could not be so sottish as to terminate their worship in, knowing that they themselves had made it, and it had not made them; yet they are for this charged to have committed idolatry, 1 Cor. x. 6, 7. *Rejoiced;* which joy they express by feasting, singing, and dancing, Exod. xxxii. 6. *The works of their own hands;* so this idol, and idols generally, are called, Psal. cxv. 4; cxxxv. 15; which is enough to speak their emptiness and vanity; vain man can make but vain gods.

42 Then [e]God turned, and gave them up to worship [f]the host of heaven; as it is written in the book of the prophets, [g]O ye house of Israel, have ye offered to me slain beasts and sacrifices *by the space of* forty years in the wilderness?

[e Ps. 81. 12. Ezek. 20. 25, 39. Rom. 1. 24. 2 Thess. 2. 11.
f Deut. 4. 19. & 17. 3. 2 Kings 17. 16. & 21. 3. Jer. 19. 13.
g Amos 5. 25, 26.]

Then God turned, from being as a Father to them, to be a Judge over them, to punish them; whereas formerly he had blessed them. *And gave them up;* this was indeed to deliver them to Satan; God withholding his grace which they had abused, Rom. i. 24, 25, and giving them up, (to fall from one sin unto another,) though not positively, yet permissively. *The host of heaven;* the angels are so called, Luke ii. 13; but it is rather here to be understood of the sun, moon, and stars, which are called so, Deut. xvii. 3; Isa. xl. 26. *In the book of the prophets:* the words here referred to are in Amos v. 25. It is said to be *in the book*, in the singular number, because the twelve small prophets are by the Jews mentioned but as one book. *Have ye offered to me slain beasts,* &c.: this positive question does vehemently deny that they had offered any sacrifices unto God whilst they were in the wilderness; but at the same time they offered sacrifices unto idols; for when they had corrupted God's worship, their sacrifices were as no sacrifices unto him, Isa. i. 11; xliii. 23.

43 Yea, ye took up the tabernacle of Moloch, and the star of your god Remphan, figures which ye made to worship them: and I will carry you away beyond Babylon.

Took up the tabernacle, on their shoulders, as they did the ark. *Of Moloch;* the idol of the children of Ammon, which the Israelites were especially forbidden to worship, Lev. xviii. 21; xx. 2; yet they did ordinarily worship him, 2 Chron. xxviii. 3; Jer. vii. 31; and there was a high place built by Solomon for him, 1 Kings xi. 7. *The tabernacle of Moloch* was either a chest or press in which that idol was put, or the chapels into which the worshippers of Moloch were admitted, according to the quality of the offering which they brought. Which of the planets they intended to honour hereby, whether the sun, or Mars, or Saturn, it matters not so much; any of these, or any other of their gods, might be called Moloch, taking the word appellatively. *Remphan*, in the place here cited, is called by the prophet, *Chiun;* which is one and the same idol in both places, the prophet calling it by its name then in use; and St. Stephen, like unto the name the Septuagint had called it by: whether Saturn was intended by this, as some think, or Hercules, as others, it is not our present business to inquire. *Figures;* images and representatives of the hosts of heaven, or of the planets. *Beyond Babylon;* the prophet Amos saith, *beyond Damascus*, Amos v. 27: here St. Stephen does not contradict the prophet, for they who were carried away beyond Babylon must needs be carried away beyond Damascus, as the ten captive tribes were, unto whom this was threatened.

44 Our fathers had the tabernacle of witness in the wilderness, as he had appointed, ‖ speaking unto Moses, [h]that he should make it according to the fashion that he had seen.

[‖ Or, *who spake*.
h Ex. 25. 40. & 26. 30. Heb. 8. 5.]

The tabernacle of witness; called also *the tabernacle of the congregation*, Exod. xxxiii. 7, because about it on all solemn occasions the people assembled. Here it is called *the tabernacle of witness*, because God here testified or witnessed his glorious presence; and especially because in it the ark of the covenant, the law, and the testimony were kept. *According to the fashion that he had seen*, Exod. xxv. 40; Heb. viii. 5. Moses was charged not to vary from the prescript; God being jealous of his own appointments. Now this is the rather spoken of by St. Stephen, that he might prove that the place where God was worshipped in had varied, and therefore might also now be changed.

45 [i]Which also our fathers ‖that came after brought in with Jesus into the possession of the Gentiles, [k]whom God drave out before the face of our fathers, unto the days of David;

[i Josh. 3. 14.
‖ Or, *having received*.
k Neh. 9. 24. Ps. 44. 2. & 78. 55. ch. 13. 19.]

Jesus, or Joshua, it being the same name, as appears also, Heb. iv. 8, only Jesus is more according to the Greek use: Joshua was a type of Jesus, and agreed with him in his name, and in the reason of his name; he having also saved the people, and brought them into the promised rest; yet the difference is as great between them as betwixt the heavenly Canaan and the earthly. *Before the face of our fathers;* they were not able to look upon an Israelite, whilst God was for them.

46 [l]Who found favour before God, and [m]desired to find a tabernacle for the God of Jacob.

[l 1 Sam. 16. 1. 2 Sam.7.1.
m Ps. 89. 19. ch. 13. 22.
n 1 Kings 8. 17. 1 Chron. 22. 7. Ps. 132. 4, 5.]

Found favour before God; as Luke i. 30. *Desired to find a tabernacle for the God of Jacob;* it was David's earnest request, that he might any ways glorify God, especially in his worship, and that he might know where the ark should rest, and where the temple was to be built, as Psalm cxxxii. declares throughout.

47 [n]But Solomon built him an house.

[n 1 Kings 6. 1. & 8. 20. 1 Chron. 17. 12. 2 Chron. 3. 1.]

1 Kings vi. 9; 2 Chron. iii. 1, 2. *An house;* a fixed and stable structure, not movable, as the tabernacle was.

48 Howbeit [o]the most High dwelleth not in temples made with hands; as saith the prophet,

[o 1 Kings 8. 27. 2 Chron. 2. 6. & 6. 18. ch. 17. 24.]

This is also St. Paul's doctrine, chap. xvii. 24, which divers amongst the wiser heathens were persuaded of; for God cannot be comprehended in any place, no, not where he is worshipped; and therefore they did foolishly conceive that the worship of God was so tied to the temple, as if he himself had been included in it. *In temples;* the primitive Christians abstained from calling the places of their assembling by the name of temples; and were charged by their pagan enemies for having no altars, or temples, or images.

49 [p]Heaven *is* my throne, and earth *is* my footstool: what house will ye build me? saith the Lord: or what *is* the place of my rest?

[p Is. 66. 1, 2. Matt. 5. 34, 35. & 23. 22.]

The place referred unto, is Isa. lxvi. 1. *What house will ye build me*, that shall be big enough for one so great as God is? 1 Kings viii. 27.

50 Hath not my hand made all these things?

As appears in the history of the creation, Gen. i. 1. It is spoken unto our capacity after the manner of men, and implies that God is too great to stand in need of temples or offerings; and that what worship he requires, is not for his own sake, for our righteousness cannot profit him; but for man's sake, that he might be exercised in the duties of religion and devotion.

51 ¶ Ye [q]stiffnecked and [r]uncircumcised in heart and ears, ye do always resist the Holy Ghost: as your fathers *did*, so *do* ye.

[q Ex. 32. 9. & 33. 3.
Is. 48. 4.
r Lev. 26. 41. Deut. 10. 16. Jer. 4. 4. & 6. 10. & 9. 26. Ezek. 44. 9.]

Stiff-necked; a metaphor taken from heifers that are unaccustomed to the yoke. *Uncircumcised in heart;* such as had still depraved affections, which they ought to have put away rather than the foreskin of their flesh; for they were commanded to circumcise their hearts, Deut. x. 16, which also God promised to do for his people, Deut. xxx. 6. And St. Paul was not the first who spake of a twofold circumcision, Rom. ii. 28, 29; but God looked always to the inward and spiritual part of his own ordinances, and men's observance of them. *And ears;* such as were not so much as willing to hear and know their duty. *Ye do always resist the Holy Ghost*, speaking by his prophets and ministers, and exhorting to true and serious piety: by this St. Stephen would abate their glorying in circumcision, which they so much boasted of. *As your fathers did, so do ye:* thus the prophet Ezekiel, chap. xvi. 44, unto which may be here alluded, *As is the mother, so is her daughter.*

52 [s]Which of the prophets have not your fathers persecuted? and they have slain them which shewed before of the

[s 2 Chron. 36. 16. Matt. 21. 35. & 23. 34, 37. 1 Thess. 2. 15.]

coming of ᵗthe Just One; of whom ye have been now the betrayers and murderers:

Which of the prophets have not your fathers persecuted? this is the rather said to stain all their glory from succession, and their ancestors, Matt. v. 12; xxiii. 31, 37. *The Just One;* our Saviour deservedly, and by way of eminence, is so called; as not only being himself just, and fulfilling all righteousness, but being *The Lord our Righteousness,* Jer. xxiii. 6, and is *of God made unto us, wisdom, righteousness, sanctification, and redemption,* 1 Cor. i. 30. This word is used in a forensic sense, and is the same with innocent, and opposite to guilty; whereby St. Stephen vindicates our Saviour, notwithstanding the unjust sentence passed here upon him. *The betrayers,* in hiring Judas, *and murderers,* in that they excited Pilate to condemn him, and abetted the soldiers and others in executing of him.

53 ᵘWho have received the law by the disposition of angels, and have not kept *it*.

The disposition of angels; or ministry of angels; the commandments were published from them ministerially; or the Son of God, (called an Angel, ver. 35,) accompanied with the militia of heaven, (for it is a military metaphor,) did in the midst of that glorious retinue give the law, Deut. xxxiii. 2; Psal. lxviii. 8; Gal. iii. 13, 19. *And have not kept it;* they transgressed the law, though so gloriously delivered by angels; and therefore it was no wonder if they despised the gospel, that was published by so mean and contemptible ministers.

54 ¶ ˣWhen they heard these things, they were cut to the heart, and they gnashed on him with *their* teeth.

See chap. v. 33. *They were cut to the heart;* they were angry to madness. *They gnashed on him with their teeth:* gnashing of teeth is the curse of the damned, Matt. viii. 12, which men by their sins do prepare for. This corrosive was applied by a skilful hand, would they have endured the cure.

55 But he, ʸbeing full of the Holy Ghost, looked up stedfastly into heaven, and saw the glory of God, and Jesus standing on the right hand of God,

Full of the Holy Ghost; filled with grace suitable to his present trial and suffering. *The glory of God;* the glorious God, or so much of the throne and glory of God as mortal eyes are capable for to see. *Jesus standing on the right hand of God;* being justified by God, though condemned by Pilate; and *standing* ready to assist and comfort all that should suffer for his sake.

56 And said, Behold, ᶻI see the heavens opened, and the ᵃSon of man standing on the right hand of God.

I see the heavens opened; God not suffering any distance to hinder this refreshing sight. *The Son of man;* so Christ is frequently called; and St. Stephen would by this inform them, how vain they were in striving against Christ or his truth. *Standing on the right hand of God,* as an Advocate, Soldier, or Captain for Stephen; or as one showing the prize unto him, which he was now running for, and had need to be encouraged with the sight of. But it seems strange that St. Stephen should tell the Jews of this heavenly vision, being they did not see it, although in the same place with him; but this he might do, 1. Out of his ardent love to Christ, desiring to magnify him. 2. To invite his enemies to repentance, now heaven was opened, and Christ's arms were stretched out to receive them. 3. To hinder any from being afraid to own Christ and his truths. 4. To terrify the most obdurate amongst them, by showing them their Judge, and minding them of his avenger. 5. That he might assert himself to be an eye-witness of Christ's being risen again from the dead, which they made such difficulty to believe.

57 Then they cried out with a loud voice, and stopped their ears, and ran upon him with one accord,

They cried out; the rabble, or multitude. *Stopped their ears;* that they might show their great detestation of what was said, and might not contract any guilt from it. *And ran upon him with one accord:* this violence and fury was both against the law of God and the law of the land; and the number of zealots (there were some amongst that people eminently so called) provoked the Romans to destroy both city and temple.

58 And ᵇcast *him* out of the city, ᶜand stoned *him:* and ᵈthe witnesses laid down their clothes at a young man's feet, whose name was Saul.

Cast him out of the city; that the city might not be polluted with his blasphemy. *Stoned him;* this punishment was appointed for such as seduced them to the worship of false gods, Deut. xiii. 6, 10; and though all power of capital punishment was taken from them, as they themselves confess, John xviii. 31, yet what will not popular rage attempt? *The witnesses;* who were by the law to cast the first stones, Deut. xvii. 7, whereby the witnesses, if they had not testified true, did take upon themselves the guilt of the blood that was spilt, and freed the people, who only followed them in the execution. *Laid down their clothes;* their upper garments, that they might carry and cast down the heavier stones.

59 And they stoned Stephen, ᵉcalling upon *God,* and saying, Lord Jesus, ᶠreceive my spirit.

Stephen called upon him whom he saw standing, and that was our Saviour. *My spirit;* or, my soul: thus our Saviour commended his spirit into his Father's hands, Luke xxiii. 46; and this disciple imitates his Master, and comforts himself with this, that to be sure his soul should be safe, whatever became of his body.

60 And he ᵍkneeled down, and cried with a loud voice, ʰLord, lay not this sin to their charge. And when he had said this, he fell asleep.

He kneeled down; a posture used in most earnest prayers; and if so, he prayed at least as earnestly for his enemies as for himself, he praying for them kneeling, and for himself standing. *Lay not this sin to their charge;* do not weigh it, reckon or impute it, that it may not remain against them, to hinder their conversion. This our Saviour commanded, Matt. v. 44, this he practised, Luke xxiii. 34; and whosoever can thus pray for his enemies, and do good for evil, hath a great evidence that the Spirit of Christ is in him. *He fell asleep;* he died; his death being thus expressed, in that, 1. He died quietly, as one fallen into a sleep. 2. Because of his certain hope of the resurrection. 3. As easily to be raised again by Christ, as one that sleeps is to be awaked by us. 4. It is an ordinary Hebraism to express death by sleep; which made St. Luke use it amongst them, with whom it was frequently thus expressed.

CHAP. VIII

The disciples being dispersed by reason of a great persecution at Jerusalem, a church is planted by Philip in Samaria, 1—8. *Simon the sorcerer is baptized, with many others,* 9—13. *Peter and John are sent thither, who by prayer and imposition of hands give the Holy Ghost,* 14—17. *Simon offereth money for the like power, is sharply reproved by Peter for his wickedness and hypocrisy, and admonished to repent: the apostles return to Jerusalem, having preached the word,* 18—25. *Philip is sent by an angel to convert and baptize an Ethiopian eunuch,* 26—40.

AND ᵃSaul was consenting unto his death. And at that time there was a great persecution against the church which was at Jerusalem; and ᵇthey were all scattered abroad throughout the regions of Judæa and Samaria, except the apostles.

Consenting unto his death; well-pleased with it, (as the

THE ACTS VIII

word implies,) and did approve it in thought, word, and deed, Acts xxii. 4, 20; which is here noted in the beginning of the narrative concerning this great apostle, that we might consider οἶος ἐξ οἴου, what a great change the grace of God did make; which was by him, and is by us the more to be acknowledged and magnified. *A great persecution against the church;* not, as heretofore, against the apostles only; but now it was against the whole church. *All scattered abroad;* the multitude of believers, at least as many as could flee; which was allowed, or rather commanded, Matt. x. 23, when they were persecuted in one city, to flee unto another; especially such as were teachers amongst them (besides the apostles) were forced to remove from Jerusalem, and by this means did publish the gospel in all places whither they came; so that what was intended for the hinderance, God did overrule towards the furtherance, of the gospel; as he did afterwards, Phil. i. 12, and still does, and ever will do. *Except the apostles;* who were commanded to stay at Jerusalem, chap. i. 4; there they were to make their beginning, Luke xxiv. 47, and from thence to proceed unto other parts, Isa. ii. 3; and whilst God had any work for them to do at Jerusalem, they knew that God could and would defend and maintain them in the midst of their enemies, as he had done the bush in the fire, Exod. iii. 3.

2 And devout men carried Stephen *to his burial,* and ^c made great lamentation over him.

<sup>c Gen. 23. 2.
& 50. 10.
2 Sam. 3. 31.</sup>

It was an argument that they were *devout* (religious) indeed, that they durst, amongst such a multitude of persecutors and furious zealots, own their esteem for St. Stephen. It was piacular amongst the Jews, to touch the dead corpse of such a one as was put to death for blasphemy; and these perform such funeral rites for him, as were used for such only as were of note and eminency. *Made great lamentation over him*, as the Jews were wont to do at the funeral, especially of eminent persons: thus it was done at Jacob's interment, Gen. l. 10; and thus had been done more lately at Lazarus's funeral, John xi., even by our Saviour himself, ver. 35: which lamentation was the greater, because of the church's loss at such a time.

3 As for Saul, ^d he made havock of the Church, entering into every house, and haling men and women committed *them* to prison.

<sup>d ch. 7. 58.
& 9. 1, 13,
21. & 22. 4.
& 26. 10, 11.
1 Cor. 15. 9.
Gal. 1. 13.
Phil. 3. 6.
1 Tim. 1. 13.</sup>

He made havoc of the church; Saul was a degree beyond the ordinary sort of persecutors, and was, as he does acknowledge himself, eminently *injurious*, 1 Tim. i. 13. *Entering into every house;* house after house, sparing none. *Haling men and women;* as by the hair of their heads. *Committed them to prison;* this to be sure the Jews had yet retained power from the Romans to do. All this is but as a foil, to illustrate more the riches of God's mercy towards Saul.

4 Therefore ^e they that were scattered abroad went every where preaching the word.

<sup>e Mat. 10.23.
ch. 11. 19.</sup>

Now the partition-wall was about to be broken down, and the Gentiles to be taken into the pale of the church, God provides this strange means towards it. The disciples are forced to flee for their lives out of Jerusalem, and have an opportunity to preach Christ and the gospel wheresoever they came: thus God can make light to come out of darkness, and makes Japheth to dwell in the tents of Shem, Gen. ix. 27.

5 Then ^f Philip went down to the city of Samaria, and preached Christ unto them.

^{f ch. 6. 5.}

Philip; not the apostle, but the deacon of that name; for the apostles remained at Jerusalem, as ver. 1. *Samaria* is a name both of a city and a country, so called from the chief city, 1 Kings xvi. 24: here it is taken for that city, or at least a city in that country. *Preached Christ;* the doctrine of Christ, his miraculous birth, holy life and death, and glorious resurrection and ascension, together with remission of sins only by faith in his name, &c.

6 And the people with one accord gave heed unto those things which Philip spake, hearing and seeing the miracles which he did.

Gave heed; a good preparation towards their conversion, seeing *faith cometh by hearing*, Rom. x. 17. *Hearing and seeing the miracles which he did;* these miracles were as so many evidences of the truth he spake, by which he showed God's authority for what he said.

7 For ^g unclean spirits, crying with loud voice, came out of many that were possessed *with them:* and many taken with palsies, and that were lame, were healed.

^{g Mark 16. 17.}

Unclean spirits, crying with loud voice; this is frequently mentioned, as Matt. viii. 29; Mark i. 26; iii. 11; v. 8; Luke iv. 41, to show how loth these evil spirits are to be forbid and kept from tormenting and destroying of us; and they are called *unclean spirits*, because they delight in sin, and instigate men unto it, which is spiritual uncleanness, and defile the soul. *Taken with palsies*, and other diseases and infirmities: this was promised, Mark xvi. 17, 18, that they which believe should cure in Christ's name, or by his power.

8 And there was great joy in that city.

Great joy; not only for the cures wrought upon their bodies, but much more for the word of reconciliation and salvation preached unto their souls: *joy in the Holy Ghost*, is one of the effects of the kingdom of God, Rom. xiv. 17. *In that city;* the despised Samaria rejoices, and the formerly beloved city of Jerusalem repines, at the gospel; such strange alterations does the free grace of God make.

9 But there was a certain man, called Simon, which beforetime in the same city ^h used sorcery, and bewitched the people of Samaria, ⁱ giving out that himself was some great one:

<sup>h ch. 13. 6.
i ch. 5. 36.</sup>

Used sorcery; magical enchantments, as a wizard. *Bewitched the people;* caused them, as men in an ecstasy, to be amazed at and afraid of him. *Some great one;* as if he had been God, or at least had some great favour with him, and had received some extraordinary power from him. Ecclesiastical histories speak much of him, and tell us that he had a statue set up in Rome for him, inscribed, To Simon the holy God.

10 To whom they all gave heed, from the least to the greatest, saying, This man is the great power of God.

From the least to the greatest; showing how general their mis-persuasion was; and no condition is exempt from the grossest mistakes, if not prevented by the grace of God. *This man is the great power of God;* it is said of this Simon, that he gave out himself to be that god, which any nation held to be the chiefest; and that he was the Messias of the Jews, and the God of the Gentiles.

11 And to him they had regard, because that of long time he had bewitched them with sorceries.

They had regard; they acquiesced in what he said, and yielded obedience unto it; not only attending to his words with their ears, but with their hearts: so true is that which our Saviour says, John v. 43, *If any man come in his own name, him will ye receive.* These Samaritans shall rise up in judgment against most men, who do not thus regard what was said by Christ, and such as he hath sent. *Bewitched them;* made them as out of their wits; they were not themselves, and could not act their reason. *With sorceries;* such wonders as by the permission of God, and Satan's power, he did.

12 But when they believed Philip preaching the things ^k concerning the kingdom of God, and the name of Jesus Christ, they were baptized, both men and women.

^{k ch. 1. 3.}

When they believed; before they were baptized, being adult and strangers from the covenant, they must first evidence their right unto it, and profess their faith in Christ,

THE ACTS VIII

and testify their conversation. *Concerning the kingdom of God;* the kingdom of grace, and the kingdom of his glory, which is one and the same, being begun here, but consummated in heaven hereafter. *Both men and women;* women under the gospel are as capable of this seal of the covenant as men.

13 Then Simon himself believed also: and when he was baptized, he continued with Philip, and wondered, beholding the † miracles and signs which were done.

† Gr. *signs and great miracles.*

Simon himself believed; Simon believed with an historical faith, that it was indeed true, that our Saviour had done miracles, and did rise from the dead; but his faith, to be sure, was dead all the while; neither did he believe with his heart, or purpose to live according to the law of Christ, which is the life of faith. *He continued with Philip;* kept him constantly company, and was amongst the forwardest of the professors of Christ's faith. *And wondered, beholding the miracles and signs which were done;* thus the magicians of Egypt were brought to acknowledge the finger of God, Exod. viii. 19, although their hearts were hardened.

14 Now when the apostles which were at Jerusalem heard that Samaria had received the word of God, they sent unto them Peter and John:

These were sent that they might further confirm the doctrine which Philip had preached amongst the Samaritans, and by apostolical authority constitute a church in Samaria.

15 Who, when they were come down, prayed for them, ¹that they might receive the Holy Ghost:

l ch. 2. 38.

They; Peter and John. *Prayed for them;* in this particular they did not pray for all that believed, amongst whom there were several women, ver. 12. *That they might receive the Holy Ghost;* those extraordinary gifts of tongues, of prophesying, of working miracles, &c. See chap. x. 45.

16 (For ᵐas yet he was fallen upon none of them: only ⁿthey were baptized in ᵒthe name of the Lord Jesus.)

m ch. 19. 2.
n Mat. 28.19.
ch. 2. 38.
o ch. 10. 48.
& 19. 5.

For as yet he was fallen upon none of them; by which it is plain that the Holy Ghost as the author of saving grace, is not here meant, for so he was fallen upon all them that did believe, for faith is the gift of God; but he was not yet bestowed upon them as the author of those extraordinary gifts mentioned chap. ii. 4. *They were baptized in the name of the Lord Jesus:* 1. They were baptized by his authority and commission, Matt. xxviii. 19. 2. By baptism they now belong unto and are united with him; they are *baptized into Jesus Christ,* Rom. vi. 3.

17 Then ᵖlaid they *their* hands on them, and they received the Holy Ghost.

p ch. 6. 6.
& 19. 6.
Heb. 6. 2.

That this laying on of the hands of the apostles was not intended here as any rite whereby the apostles did confirm some, or ordain others, seems evident from the context. *They received the Holy Ghost;* the power of speaking with tongues, and working of miracles; which throughout this book is so often spoken of in this acceptation.

18 And when Simon saw that through laying on of the apostles' hands the Holy Ghost was given, he offered them money,

The Holy Ghost; those extraordinary gifts before mentioned; for this appeared visibly and audibly, and by this indeed was signified the great change God's Spirit makes where he comes. *He offered them money;* this notorious hypocrite values these outward gifts; how much more valuable are the inward and spiritual gifts of God!

19 Saying, Give me also this power, that on whomsoever I lay hands, he may receive the Holy Ghost.

Such an extraordinary power of working miracles he did not desire that he might glorify God, or confirm the truths of the gospel (now professed by him); but out of an insatiable desire of gain, and ambition to keep up his reputation, seeing how the apostles had done beyond what he was able to do.

20 But Peter said unto him, Thy money perish with thee, because ᑫthou hast thought that ʳthe gift of God may be purchased with money.

q Matt. 10. 8.
See 2 Kings 5. 16.
r ch. 2. 38.
& 10. 45.
& 11. 17.

Thy money perish with thee; a formal execration or curse, not only on his money, but also upon Simon himself; but always to be conditional, viz. unless he repented. *Thou hast thought:* our hearts are to be watched over; our thoughts may be exceeding sinful, as here, which made his words or desires to be so ill taken.

21 Thou hast neither part nor lot in this matter: for thy heart is not right in the sight of God.

Neither part nor lot in this matter; no inheritance or share in such a thing as this, to wit, either in the receiving or conferring the Holy Ghost; or in that eternal life which we preach; thou hast no part in it, neither art thou fit to be a minister of it. *Thy heart is not right in the sight of God:* the apostle had the gift of *discerning of spirits,* which is mentioned 1 Cor. xii. 10; which might cause the execration in the foregoing verse, and in divers other places of Scripture, 2 Tim. iv. 14.

22 Repent therefore of this thy wickedness, and pray God, ˢif perhaps the thought of thine heart may be forgiven thee.

s Dan. 4. 27.
2 Tim. 2. 25.

The only remedy and help in his (otherwise) desperate case. This is not spoken as if it were doubtful whether true repentance should obtain pardon, but whether Simon Magus's repentance were true. Repentance is a condition under which God proposeth our pardon and forgiveness, but it is far from being the cause of it.

23 For I perceive that thou art in ᵗthe gall of bitterness, and *in* the bond of iniquity.

t Heb. 12. 15.

The gall of bitterness; the same with *gall and wormwood,* Deut. xxix. 18: or gall and bitterness; signifying a very bad constitution and disposition of soul or mind, such as may be compared unto that meat which the gall of any creature hath corrupted. And for Simon Magus to be *in the gall of bitterness,* is yet worse than to have the gall of bitterness in him; as to be *born in sin,* which the Pharisees upbraided the blind man with, John xi. 34, denotes more intended thereby than that he had sin from his birth in him: thus David bewails that he was *shapen in iniquity,* Psal. li. 5; and thus may those expressions of St. Paul be understood, of being *in the flesh,* and being in the *Spirit,* Rom. viii. 9. This also shows (if any sensible or outward thing could show it) what a bitter and poisonous thing sin is, no gall so bitter, no poison so deadly. *The bond of iniquity;* either the judgment St. Peter had threatened to deter him from sin was this bond, or his sin itself might be rather so called: thus we read of *the bands of wickedness,* Isa. lviii. 6. One sin is twisted with another, hard to be severed or broken, and draws on judgment powerfully.

24 Then answered Simon, and said, ᵘ"Pray ye to the Lord for me, that none of these things which ye have spoken come upon me.

u Gen. 20. 7, 17.
Ex. 8. 8.
Num. 21. 7.
1 Kin. 13. 6.
Job 42. 8.
Jam. 5. 16.

Simon Magus was convinced that he was indeed such as the apostles had spoken him to be; and knowing them to be powerful with God, he desires this of them. He feigns himself to be a true penitent, being terrified with the threatening of St. Peter, ver. 20, and probably fearing the punishment of Ananias and Sapphira might befall him, which it is likely he had heard of.

25 And they, when they had testified and preached the word of the Lord, returned to Jerusalem, and preached the Gospel in many villages of the Samaritans.

Not only in the chief city, but in the smallest villages, these great apostles spend their pains; for so it was promised unto them that they should receive power to do, chap. i. 8.

26 And the angel of the Lord spake unto Philip, saying, Arise, and go toward the south

unto the way that goeth down from Jerusalem unto Gaza, which is desert.

Some speak of two Gazas, one distinguished from the other by this epithet of *desert*; but rather there were two ways unto one and the same Gaza, and that it was not the city but the way unto it, which is called desert; by which difference, here mentioned, the angel admonishes Philip not to go the ordinary road, but the more unusual road over the mountains, which was rarely travelled over, but was now necessary to be gone in to meet with the eunuch. God telleth our wanderings, and ordereth our steps.

27 And he arose and went: and, behold, ˣa man of Ethiopia, an eunuch of great authority under Candace queen of the Ethiopians, who had the charge of all her treasure, and ʸhad come to Jerusalem for to worship,

ˣ Zeph. 3. 10.

ʸ John 12. 20.

A man of Ethiopia: the Ethiopians were the most despicable unto the Jews; and Homer calls them, ἔσχατοι ἀνδρῶν; but God would now show that there is no difference of nations with him; but in every nation, he that worketh righteousness shall be accepted, chap. x. 35. *An eunuch;* in great esteem in courts, especially to attend on queens, to avoid all suspicion: here that prophecy was fulfilled, Isa. lvi. 4, 5: though both in the Hebrew and (anciently) in the Greek tongue, a eunuch signified more largely, viz. any attendant in the chamber. *Candace;* a name common to the queens of that country; as all the kings of Egypt were called Pharaohs, and the emperors of Germany are called Cæsars. *Come to Jerusalem for to worship;* being a proselyte, he had been to worship God in that solemn festival of the passover.

28 Was returning, and sitting in his chariot read Esaias the prophet.

He had some knowledge of the true God, whom he came to worship, and he endeavours after more: and to him that thus hath, shall be given; and they that thus seek, shall find. God will rather work a miracle, than that any that sincerely desire and faithfully endeavour to know him, or his will, should be disappointed.

29 Then the Spirit said unto Philip, Go near, and join thyself to this chariot.

The Spirit said, either by the ministry of an angel, as ver. 26, or by inspiration immediately by himself. *Go near;* so near that you may speak with him that sits in it. *Join thyself to this chariot;* stick close unto it, and leave it not.

30 And Philip ran thither to *him,* and heard him read the prophet Esaias, and said, Understandest thou what thou readest?

Philip ran thither to him; hastening to obey the Divine command, and coveting to gain a soul. *Heard him read the prophet Esaias,* with a loud voice, it is like, to instruct some of his attendants. *Understandest thou what thou readest?* without understanding our reading is but as the tinkling of a cymbal.

31 And he said, How can I, except some man should guide me? And he desired Philip that he would come up and sit with him.

A wonderful modesty and humility in so great a man: he takes well Philip's interposing, and questioning with him; he acknowledges his ignorance, and desires further instruction, and condescends to be taught by one so much his inferior.

32 The place of the Scripture which he read was this, ᶻHe was led as a sheep to the slaughter; and like a lamb dumb before his shearer, so opened he not his mouth:

ᶻ Is. 53. 7, 8.

God's providence is remarkable, that the eunuch should be reading this very scripture, which contains such fundamental truths, and which he had most need for to be informed of. The words referred unto are in Isa. liii. 7. Whether read in the Hebrew tongue, which the eunuch might have learned of many Jews living in Ethiopia; or whether they were read out of the translation of the Seventy, which was then in common use, is not so necessary an inquiry; both being to the same intent and purpose. Christ was indeed *as a sheep* for his patience, not opening his mouth to defend his own case; but especially he was as a sheep in being a sacrifice for us, the true paschal Lamb that causeth the destroyer to pass from us; and yet he is our Shepherd too, to supply and preserve us, Psal. xxiii. 1.

33 In his humiliation his judgment was taken away: and who shall declare his generation? for his life is taken from the earth.

In his humiliation; when our blessed Saviour was in his lowest condition, and the utmost degree of his exinanition; his soul being made a sacrifice for us, and suffering that desertion for a time we had merited for ever, and his body laid in the grave as in a prison; then *his judgment,* the punishment which was inflicted upon him in our stead, *was taken away;* for he brake the bonds of death, and opened the prison-door: this was foretold, although in somewhat differing expressions, by the prophet Isaiah, chap. liii. 7, 8. *Who shall declare his generation?* those that shall be brought forth by this travail of his soul are innumerable, or his own eternal generation (who could do such great things as overcame death itself for us) is inexpressible: but by *generation* others (more to the scope of this place) understand Christ's duration, or abiding, notwithstanding that he died; γενεά, does often signify duration; and thus it is an ordinary expression with the prophet, Isa. xxxiv. 10, 17, *from generation to generation:* now none can comprehend that eternal duration of Christ, who dies no more, Rom. vi. 9, and of whose kingdom there is no end, Luke i. 33. *For his life is taken from the earth;* Christ acquired his glory by his suffering; his very exceeding great weight of glory was indeed wrought for him by his afflictions, (as for us, 2 Cor. iv. 17,) his becoming obedient unto the death was the cause why he was so highly exalted, Phil. ii. 8, 9.

34 And the eunuch answered Philip, and said, I pray thee, of whom speaketh the prophet this? of himself, or of some other man?

Of whom speaketh the prophet this? the modestly inquisitive man does get understanding; this question (God so ordering it) brings in the discourse concerning our Saviour. *Of himself, or of some other man?* this the eunuch might well make a question, because Isaiah himself suffered much under Manasseh.

35 Then Philip opened his mouth, ᵃand began at the same Scripture, and preached unto him Jesus.

ᵃ Luke 24. 27. ch. 18. 28.

Opened his mouth; so they were said to do when they began to speak of some weighty matter. *Began at the same Scripture;* showing that the prophet, in that most signal prophecy, Isa. liii., could not mean such things of himself, nor of Jeremiah, or of any other. *Preached unto him Jesus;* things in that prophecy are applicable unto our blessed Saviour, but to none else.

36 And as they went on *their* way, they came unto a certain water: and the eunuch said, See, *here is* water; ᵇwhat doth hinder me to be baptized?

ᵇ ch. 10. 47.

A certain water; this water is supposed to be a fountain in a town called Bethsora, or a river called Eleutherus, which in that road must needs be passed over; it being otherwise very dry, and water very scarce there. *What doth hinder me to be baptized?* although it was not expressly mentioned, Philip had informed this eunuch concerning baptism, its nature and use, which made him express such desire after it; which else he had not done.

37 And Philip said, ᶜIf thou believest with all thine heart, thou mayest. And he answered and said, ᵈI believe that Jesus Christ is the Son of God.

ᶜ Matt. 28. 19. Mark 16. 16. ᵈ Mat. 16.16. John 6. 69. & 9. 35, 38. & 11. 27. ch. 9. 20. 1 John 4. 15. & 5. 5, 13.

With all thine heart: a verbal profession is not a sufficient believing, Rom. x. 10; though we can discern no other, yet God can, and will not be mocked: Philip, in God's name, requires a faith with all the heart, and not such as Simon Magus had, who is said to believe, and be baptized, ver. 13. *I believe that Jesus Christ is the Son of God;* this was the only thing necessary, either then or now, if rightly understood. The eunuch was instructed concerning God out of the law, and was one of them that waited for his salvation; which here he acknowledgeth to be only found in Christ, whom he owns to be the Messiah, who made *his soul an offering for sin,* Isa. liii. 10, and did bear *our griefs, and carried our sorrows,* ver. 4, and *was wounded for our transgressions,* ver. 5 ; for all these things Philip had told him were meant of our Saviour, which he did believe were so to be understood.

38 And he commanded the chariot to stand still: and they went down both into the water, both Philip and the eunuch; and he baptized him.

In hot countries this was usual, to baptize by dipping the body in the water; and to this the apostle alludes, when he tells the Corinthians, 1 Cor. vi. 11, that they are washed: but God will have mercy, and not sacrifice; sprinkling being as effectual as washing, and as significative also, representing the sprinkling of the blood of the paschal lamb, of which we read, Exod. xii. 3, which presignified the sprinkling the blood of Jesus, that Lamb of God which taketh away the sins of the world ; and our hearts must by it be *sprinkled from an evil conscience,* Heb. x. 22. It is not the more or the less of the outward element which makes the sacraments effectual ; but they are effectual only as they are God's appointments, and attended upon according to his will.

39 And when they were come up out of the water, ᵉthe Spirit of the Lord caught away Philip, that the eunuch saw him no more: and he went on his way rejoicing.

e 1 Kings 18. 12. 2 Kings 2. 16. Ezek. 3. 12, 14.

Philip was suddenly and extraordinarily taken away from the eunuch's sight and company, that thereby the eunuch might be the more assured of the truth of those things which had been taught by him. The *rejoicing* was the effect of his faith ; being now justified, he had *peace with God through our Lord Jesus Christ,* Rom. v. 1.

40 But Philip was found at Azotus : and passing through he preached in all the cities, till he came to Cæsarea.

Philip was set down by the Spirit at Ashdod of the Philistines, which is called by the Septuagint *Azotus:* names of persons and places do in tract of time vary. This place had been famous for the idol Dagon, 1 Sam. v. 3, and for being a chief place of the Philistines, those enemies to God's church ; but Christ, when he comes, can cast Satan out of his strongest holds. This Azotus is accounted thirty-four miles from Gaza.

CHAP. IX

Saul, going towards Damascus, is encompassed with a light from heaven, falleth to the earth, is called by Christ, and led blind to Damascus, 1—9. *Ananias is sent to him, by whom he is restored to sight, and baptized: he straightway preacheth Christ boldly,* 10—22. *The Jews of Damascus seek to kill him,* 23—25. *He goeth to Jerusalem, and is brought to the apostles by Barnabas: preaching boldly against the Grecians, he is again in danger of his life, and is sent to Tarsus,* 26—30. *The church hath rest, and is multiplied,* 31. *Peter cureth Eneas of the palsy at Lydda,* 32—35 ; *and raiseth Tabitha to life at Joppa,* 36—43.

A. D. 35. a ch. 8. 3. Gal. 1. 13. 1 Tim. 1. 13.

AND ᵃSaul, yet breathing out threatenings and slaughter against the disciples of the Lord, went unto the High Priest,

St. Luke intending a narrative of the wonderful conversion of St. Paul, lets us know what manner of person he was before his conversion, that none might despond of the grace of God, who earnestly and heartily seek it. *Breathing out threatenings and slaughter;* so full of rage within, that the stream was outwardly apparent, which that inward fire had sent forth : nothing less than destruction of the church is aimed at by its enemies ; whilst Saul was one of them he hunted after their precious life too. *The high priest;* who did usually preside in their great council, in which they took cognizance of such matters ; the blood of Stephen did not quench their thirst, but increased it ; they would spill more still.

2 And desired of him letters to Damascus to the synagogues, that if he found any †of this way, whether they were men or women, he might bring them bound unto Jerusalem.

† Gr. *of the way:* So ch. 19. 9, 23.

To the synagogues ; this council, though it sat at Jerusalem, had a power (whether commanding or recommending) over all the synagogues within or without Judea. *Of this way;* this was eminently so called, being the way of God, and the way of life, and the only right and true way : any profession, persuasion, or manner of life, is called a way frequently in Scripture, 1 Kings xv. 26 ; Psal. xci. 11. *Men or women ;* it speaks their extraordinary rage, that would not spare the weaker sex, who are generally spared on that account. *Bring them bound ;* which shows that he carried many with him, to the further aggravation of his sin. *Unto Jerusalem ;* where they had power to judge of such things, and out of which it was impossible that a prophet should perish, Luke xiii. 33.

3 And ᵇas he journeyed, he came near Damascus : and suddenly there shined round about him a light from heaven :

b ch. 22. 6. & 26. 12. 1 Cor. 15. 8.

He was near to Damascus before this wonderful vision, that, being struck blind, he might be the sooner led thither; as also, that the miracle might be more easily and publicly known, Damascus being the chief city of Syria ; and, though about six days' journey from Jerusalem, inhabited by many Jews. This was done at noon-day, the rather, that the light which Paul saw might appear to be beyond that which the sun gives ; and this light was a symbol of that inward light, wherewith his mind was now to be enlightened ; as also of the purity of the doctrine he was to preach, and holiness of his life which he was to lead ; and most probably it was caused by the glorified body of Christ, which appeared unto him.

4 And he fell to the earth, and heard a voice saying unto him, Saul, Saul, ᶜwhy persecutest thou me ?

c Matt. 25. 40, &c.

Saul *fell to the earth,* struck with the amazing light and terrible voice of Christ; as also with the sense of the presence of God, which he knew was thus reverenced by Daniel, chap. viii. 17 ; x. 9. *Saul, Saul;* the name Saul is the rather mentioned, to mind him and us of his persecuting of Christ in his members, as his name-sake had persecuted David, who was a type of Christ ; and it is ingeminated, or doubled, not only to rouse and awaken Saul, but to testify his love to him, and commiseration of him. *Why persecutest thou me?* Christ was in heaven, beyond Saul's rage ; but Christ and his church make but one body. Thus Christ says, I was hungry and thirsty, Matt. xxv. 35. And in all their afflictions he is afflicted, Isa. lxiii. 9. But *me* is here emphatically spoken, as if our Saviour had minded him of his great love and mercy to him, in dying and suffering for him ; and why then should he persecute him ?

5 And he said, Who art thou, Lord ? And the Lord said, I am Jesus whom thou persecutest : ᵈ*it is* hard for thee to kick against the pricks.

d ch. 5. 39.

Who art thou, Lord? Saul was in a great consternation and doubting, whether it was God, or an angel. *Jesus whom thou persecutest:* though he did not intend this persecution against Christ, yet our Saviour looks upon the good or evil done unto his members as done unto himself. *It is hard for thee to kick against the pricks:* this kicking against the pricks is a proverbial speech, taken either from oxen or slaves, whom they used with goads to prick on to their work, which when they kicked against, or opposed themselves to, they did not hurt the goads or pricks, but themselves ; so shall all persecutors find that their mischiefs recoil upon themselves ; Christ and his members shall be

THE ACTS IX

made more glorious by it: this metaphor is common in Scripture, Deut. xxxii. 15; 1 Sam. ii. 29. *The pricks* Saul had kicked against, were the sermons and miracles of St. Stephen and others.

e Luke 3. 10.
ch. 2. 37.
& 16. 30.

6 And he trembling and astonished said, Lord, ^e what wilt thou have me to do? And the Lord *said* unto him, Arise, and go into the city, and it shall be told thee what thou must do.

Lord, what wilt thou have me to do? Saul, being thoroughly humbled, and brought to resign himself wholly to God, makes this question, giving up himself as a white paper, for Christ to write what he would upon: he had thought he had done God good service, (as it is said many persecutors should think so too, John xvi. 2,) but he is now powerfully brought off from his obstinacy in that persuasion. *Go into the city;* Damascus, which was near at hand. Whether Christ revealed his gospel now unto him, or in the three days in which he remained blind in Damascus, ver. 9, is not so certain; but it is certain that he was Χριστο διδακτος, taught immediately by Christ himself, as he testifies, Gal. i. 12, and in that, without any further instruction, he was baptized, ver. 17, 18: yet many things might be left for Ananias to confirm him in; and God, by this sending of him to Ananias, would honour his own ordinance, and recommend the ministry and use of means, which are *the power of God unto salvation*, Rom. i. 16: and thus, though God could have instructed Cornelius by the angel which appeared unto him, chap. x. 3, yet he is commanded to send for Peter, and to hear from him what he ought to do, ver. 5, 6.

f Dan. 10. 7.
See ch. 22.
9. & 26. 13.

7 And ^f the men which journeyed with him stood speechless, hearing a voice, but seeing no man.

Stood speechless: in chap. xxvi. 14, these men are said to be fallen to the earth as well as Saul, which they might at first be, and now rose up; or rather, by standing still here is only meant, they, being sorely amazed, remained in the place in which they were, without going forward: thus the angel forbade Lot and his family to stay or stand in the plain, Gen. xix. 17, meaning that they should hasten forward. *Hearing a voice;* the greater difficulty is, to reconcile these words with chap. xxii. 9, where it is expressly said, that these men did not hear the voice; but it is there added, *of him that spake* unto Saul; so that they might hear the voice of Saul, as it is said in this place, and wonder whom he spake unto, or what he spake about, they not hearing the voice of him that spake unto him, as in chap. xxii. 9 it is said: and it seems very likely that they should not hear the voice of Christ, for we read not that any of them were converted; and being left in their infidelity, they were in some respects the more undeniable witnesses of a great part of that miracle. But if it be understood of the voice of Christ in both places, then they might hear it, as it is said here, inarticulately, or the noise which that voice made; but not hear it articulately, or so as to understand it, as in a parallel case, John xii. 29, the people are said to hear the voice that spake unto Christ from heaven, yet they heard so confusedly, as that they thought it had only been thunder. To be sure, they who are converted, and they who are not converted, by the word of God, may hear the word; but after a very different manner; they that are converted by it only hearing it inwardly, spiritually, effectually. *But seeing no man;* these fellow travellers with St. Paul are said to see no man, but the expression here imports their doing their utmost for to see him that spake: thus God made a difference, Dan. x. 7, in the vision we read of there.

8 And Saul arose from the earth; and when his eyes were opened, he saw no man: but they led him by the hand, and brought *him* into Damascus.

When his eyes were opened; when he opened his eyes as at other times, when he did rise to see, the glorious light had so dazzled him, that he could see nothing: thus Saul was, and all men are, before their conversion; he had the shape of a man, and of one learned in the law, when notwithstanding he is blind, and sees or knows nothing as he ought to know.

9 And he was three days without sight, and neither did eat nor drink.

Some have thought that in these three days Paul had that rapture into the third heavens, which he speaks of, 2 Cor. xii. 2; but that seems rather to have been afterwards; God would, however, by this humble and try him, and excite his dependence wholly upon him, and that he might value his restored sight the more. *Neither did eat nor drink;* that by fasting he might be more intent in prayer; for fasting does prepare for prayer, and therefore fasting and prayer are so often put together, Matt. xvii. 21; Acts xiii. 3. In those places they could fast longer without prejudice to their health, than amongst us, and, as I might add, were more willing to fast for any spiritual advantage than we are.

10 ¶ And there was a certain disciple at Damascus, ^g named Ananias; and to him said the Lord in a vision, Ananias. And he said, Behold, I *am here*, Lord.

g ch. 22. 12.

Ananias; he was of good repute for zeal and holiness, as appears, chap. xxii. 12, but whether he was one of the seventy disciples which our Saviour sent out, Luke x. 1, as some will have, is not certain. *He said, Behold, I am here, Lord;* thereby showing his willingness to be sent on God's message, and to do as God should bid him, as Samuel to Eli, 1 Sam. iii. 5.

11 And the Lord *said* unto him, Arise, and go into the street which is called Straight, and enquire in the house of Judas for *one* called Saul, ^h of Tarsus: for, behold, he prayeth,

h ch. 21. 39.
& 22. 3.

Inquire in the house of Judas for one called Saul. God telleth our wanderings, and knoweth our abode, and mindeth his, especially in their sorrows, which was Saul's case. *For, behold, he prayeth;* he spent those three days, spoken of ver. 9, in acts of great humiliation, in which he would also not taste any food; this is revealed to Ananias, that he might not fear to go unto him. A great change! Is Saul also amongst them that pray? A greater wonder than that the other Saul was formerly amongst the prophets.

12 And hath seen in a vision a man named Ananias coming in, and putting *his* hand on him, that he might receive his sight.

If this verse be the words of St. Luke, continuing the history, then they must be included in a parenthesis, the sense being entire without them; but they seem to be the words of the Lord continued to Ananias, telling him how he had provided for his welcome to Saul, contrary to his expectation.

13 Then Ananias answered, Lord, I have heard by many of this man, ⁱ how much evil he hath done to thy saints at Jerusalem:

i ver. 1.

I have heard by many of this man; his design and commission could not but be noised abroad. *Thy saints:* the disciples of Christ are called saints, because, 1. They are dedicated unto the Lord in their baptism. 2. They are called unto holiness. 3. They did then live holily and exemplarily. 4. And so must all that hope for any benefit by their being disciples of Christ, &c.

14 And here he hath authority from the Chief Priests to bind all ^k that call on thy name.

k ver. 21.
ch. 7. 59.
& 22. 16.
1 Cor. 1. 2.
2 Tim. 2. 22.

Here Ananias shows the strengh of his excuse; for flesh and blood cried in him, as in Moses, Exod. iv. 13, *Send by him whom thou wilt send.*

15 But the Lord said unto him, Go thy way: for ^l he is a chosen vessel unto me, to bear my name before ^m the Gentiles, and ⁿ kings, and the children of Israel:

l ch. 13. 2.
& 22. 21.
& 26. 17.
Rom. 1. 1.
1 Cor. 15. 10.
Gal. i. 15.
Eph. 3. 7, 8.
1 Tim. 2. 7.
2 Tim. 1. 11.

m Rom. 1. 5. & 11. 13. Gal. 2. 7, 8. n ch. 25. 22, 23. & 26. 1, &c.

He is a chosen vessel: the whole world is God's fabric, and the church especially is his house: not only in the whole world, but in the visible church, there are all sorts of utensils, some for higher, others for meaner uses; Saul was to be a vessel unto honour, Rom. ix. 21, into which the treasures of God's word were to be put, 2 Cor. iv. 7, though he was but an earthen vessel: Saul was indeed chosen by God to preach the gospel, Gal. i. 15, 16, to suffer for Christ's name's sake, 1 Thess. iii. 3. *To bear my name before the Gentiles:* this mystery of the calling of the Gentiles began now to spread abroad, and to be made more known, which was hid in those promises, Isa. xlix. 6; Jer. i. 10.

o ch. 20. 23.
& 21. 11.
2 Cor. 11. 23.

16 For °I will shew him how great things he must suffer for my name's sake.

He shall suffer as great things as he ever did cause or inflict; the hatred of his own countrymen the Jews, and the fury of the Gentiles: see the catalogue of them, 2 Cor. xi. 23—27. And were there ever so many sufferings heaped upon one man? And yet, though all these were foretold unto him, and certainly foreknown by him, he would preach the gospel for all that: much was forgiven him, and he loved much.

p ch. 22. 12, 13.
q ch. 8. 17.

17 ᵖAnd Ananias went his way, and entered into the house; and ᑫputting his hands on him said, Brother Saul, the Lord, *even* Jesus, that appeared unto thee in the way as thou camest, hath sent

r ch. 2. 4. &
4. 31. & 8. 17.
& 13. 52.

me, that thou mightest receive thy sight, and ʳbe filled with the Holy Ghost.

Entered into the house; the house of Judas, with whom Saul lodged, as ver. 11. *Putting his hands on him;* concerning this, see chap. vi. 6, besides on what may be said of this imposition of hands elsewhere: the curing of St. Paul's blindness was one reason of putting his hands on him here, for so it was ordinarily done towards the sick or infirm; they laid their hands upon them to heal them, as it was promised that they should do, Mark xvi. 18. *Brother Saul;* Saul was become Ananias's brother, as professing the same faith, and heir of the same promise with him. *Jesus, that appeared unto thee in the way;* Ananias mentions what had happened to Paul in the way, that Saul might be assured that he was sent from God, for none else could have told him what had happened.

18 And immediately there fell from his eyes as it had been scales: and he received sight forthwith, and arose, and was baptized.

Scales, as scales of fish: it was no ordinary blindness, nor from any ordinary cause, and could not have been cured by common means.

19 And when he had received meat, he was strengthened. ˢThen was Saul certain days with the disciples which were at Damascus.

s ch. 26. 20.

St. Paul could not but be much weakened with his journey, fear, grief, fasting, and constant praying; and now he takes a prudent care of his health, that he might be further enabled for the service of God, to what place soever he should be appointed. *With the disciples:* Saul is no sooner changed, but he changeth his company and acquaintance; he resorts to none of the rabbies of the Jews, but to the disciples of Christ; he would love any, learn of any, that had Christ for their Master.

20 And straightway he preached Christ in the synagogues, ᵗthat he is the Son of God.

t ch. 8. 37.

He preached Christ in the synagogues; the apostles spake unto the Jews first, either that they might convert them, or at least take away all excuse from them. *That he is the Son of God;* which doubtless he spake largely unto, though it be not here expressed; but he had an abundance in his heart, having tasted the power of the grace of God in Christ, and out of his heart his mouth spake.

21 But all that heard *him* were amazed, and said; ᵘIs not this he that destroyed them which called on this name in Jerusalem, and came hither for that intent,

u ch. 8. 3.
ver. 1. Gal. 1.
13, 23.

that he might bring them bound unto the Chief Priests?

This great change is a most unaccountable thing, and might truly cause amazement; but *ex quovis ligno fit Mercurius, cum digitus Dei sit statuarius.* Nothing is too hard for that God in whose hand Saul's heart was.

22 But Saul increased the more in strength, ˣand confounded the Jews which dwelt at Damascus, proving that this is very Christ.

x ch. 18. 28.

Increased the more in strength; true grace thrives by exercise and opposition: the word here used many take to be a metaphor from builders, who, in erecting their fabrics, fit one piece or part to another, and then bring them and join them together; thus St. Paul did, in bringing forth or quoting the promises in the Old Testament, and showing their exactly being fulfilled in the New Testament, or in the gospel of our Saviour Jesus Christ; and he spake with such an evidence and demonstration of the Spirit, that he did, as it were, constrain men to be of his opinion. *Proving that this is very Christ;* which was the sum of the gospel.

23 ¶ And after that many days were fulfilled, ʸthe Jews took counsel to kill him:

A. D. 37.
y ch. 23. 12.
& 25. 3.
2 Cor. 11. 26.

Many days; God would not presently expose him to conflicts, but inure him to suffer by degrees; as also it pleased God to spare him so long nigh unto that place where he had wrought so great a miracle for him, the sense of which might the more be upon himself and others also; for he continued here three years, excepting only a journey into Arabia, as may be seen, Gal. i. 17, 18.

24 ᶻBut their laying await was known of Saul. And they watched the gates day and night to kill him.

z 2 Cor. 11. 32.

Their laying await; the Jews, who stirred up Aretas the king of Damascus against Paul, 2 Cor. xi. 32, 33: now began those things to be fulfilled, foretold ver. 16.

25 Then the disciples took him by night, and ᵃlet *him* down by the wall in a basket.

a So Josh. 2. 15. 1 Sam. 19. 12.

As Rahab did the spies, Josh. ii. 15, and Michal did David, 1 Sam. xix. 12.

26 And ᵇwhen Saul was come to Jerusalem, he assayed to join himself to the disciples: but they were all afraid of him, and believed not that he was a disciple.

b ch. 22. 17.
Gal. 1. 17, 18.

To join himself to, to be admitted to intimate fellowship and communion with, *the disciples. They were all afraid of him;* Paul was sufficiently known by name and face at Jerusalem, and many had felt his rage. *And believed not that he was a disciple;* but how could the disciples be ignorant of his conversion so long, if it was three years after, as it seems by Gal. i. 18? To answer which may be considered, 1. The great distance betwixt Jerusalem and Damascus, six days' journey. 2. The little correspondence betwixt the kings of those places, Herod and Aretas. 3. The persecution which was at Jerusalem might hinder the converts of Damascus from going thither. 4. Paul might have spent a great part of the three years in his journey amongst the Arabians, of which before.

27 ᶜBut Barnabas took him, and brought *him* to the apostles, and declared unto them how he had seen the Lord in the way, and that he had spoken to him, ᵈand how he had preached boldly at Damascus in the name of Jesus.

c ch. 4. 36.
& 13. 2.

d ver. 20, 22.

Of *Barnabas* mention is made, chap. iv. 36, who is thought to have been Paul's fellow disciple under Gamaliel. *Brought him to the apostles;* these apostles, to whom Barnabas brought Paul, were Peter and James, as Gal. i. 18, 19, who being the apostles of the circumcision, or having Judea under their charge, were abiding at Jerusalem, whilst the other apostles probably were absent, being founding of churches elsewhere. *He had seen the Lord, &c.:* some take these things to have been related by Paul,

THE ACTS IX

others by Barnabas, who testified these things concerning Paul.

e Gal. 1. 18.

28 And °he was with them coming in and going out at Jerusalem.

Living amongst them, and freely conversing with them; that is, with Peter, and James, and the rest of the believers, who had now no suspicion of him.

29 And he spake boldly in the name of the Lord Jesus, and disputed against the ᶠGrecians: ᵍbut they went about to slay him.

f ch. 6. 1. & 11. 20.
g ver. 23.
2 Cor. 11. 26.

Disputed against the Grecians; Hellenists, of which chap. vi. 1, such as were born in foreign parts, but of Jewish parents; these Paul chose rather to dispute with, because these had raised the persecution against Stephen, and Paul had furthered them in it; and he was very desirous to unweave that web, and give them an antidote unto whom he had formerly given poison; being especially concerned for their souls, whom he had helped to destroy.

30 *Which* when the brethren knew, they brought him down to Cæsarea, and sent him forth to Tarsus.

Cæsarea; there were two towns of this name, one a coast town, spoken of, chap. viii. 40; the other was called Cæsarea Philippi, nigh Mount Lebanon. *Tarsus,* St. Paul's birth-place, where amongst his relations and acquaintance they might hope he would be safe.

h See ch. 8. 1.

31 ʰThen had the churches rest throughout all Judæa and Galilee and Samaria, and were edified; and walking in the fear of the Lord, and in the comfort of the Holy Ghost, were multiplied.

Then had the churches rest; when Paul was sent away, against whom they had the greater spite, as having been as zealous a persecutor as any amongst them. *And were edified:* the church is frequently compared to a building, and every believer to the temple of God, 1 Cor. iii. 16, and vi. 19, which God dwells in; from whence this metaphor is taken. *Walking in the fear of the Lord:* walking is a progressive motion, and so is building and adding to a structure till it come to perfection; which signifies that these believers increased daily in the knowledge of God, in true piety and charity, &c. *In the comfort of the Holy Ghost;* the word also signifies the exhortation of the Holy Ghost; such exhortations as were given from God by the apostles: to be sure, the comforts of the Spirit are not without our obedience to the commandments of God; and it seems to be given here as the reason why the churches were edified, and did thus increase, because believers walked in the fear of the Lord; and nothing persuades more effectually to the embracing of religion, than the holy living of such as make profession of it.

A. D. 38.
i ch. 8. 14.

32 ¶ And it came to pass, as Peter passed ⁱthroughout all *quarters,* he came down also to the saints which dwelt at Lydda.

Throughout all quarters, where the disciples that were dispersed had planted churches. *Saints:* see ver. 13. *Lydda;* a little town about the west bank of the Jordan, not far from the Mediterranean Sea.

33 And there he found a certain man named Æneas, which had kept his bed eight years, and was sick of the palsy.

It is supposed this *Æneas* was a Jew, though now living at Lydda; and that St. Luke here names him by the name the Grecians called him by, he being amongst his own countrymen called Hillel. *Kept his bed eight years;* to show the difficulty of the cure, and greatness of the miracle.

k ch. 3. 6, 16.
& 4. 10.

34 And Peter said unto him, Æneas, ᵏJesus Christ maketh thee whole: arise, and make thy bed. And he arose immediately.

Jesus Christ maketh thee whole: these words are not a prayer, (though they were not spoken without Peter's lifting up his heart to Christ in prayer,) but a promise to this sick man of health and recovery, declaring from whom he should receive it, that he might know whom to acknowledge and thank for it. *Arise, and make thy bed:* our Saviour bids the sick of the palsy to arise, and take up his bed, Mark ii. 11; and so he commands the impotent man, John v. 8. Here St. Peter bids this paralytic to make his bed; which seems more strange, being he was commanded to arise, so that now he should have no need of having his bed made; but it is easily answered, that being it was only intended to show how fully he was cured, the making of his bed did as much prove, both to himself and others, that he was recovered, as any thing else could do.

35 And all that dwelt in Lydda and ˡSaron saw him, and ᵐturned to the Lord.

l 1 Chron. 5. 16.
m ch. 11. 21.

Lydda: see ver. 32. *Saron* is the name of a city, 1 Chron. v. 16, but here it is rather the name of a country, (which the masculine article usually shows,) lying between Mount Tabor and the lake of Tiberias, a very fruitful plain, 1 Chron. xxvii. 29; Cant. ii. 1. *Turned to the Lord;* to the owning of his truth. Error (if in fundamentals) keeps us from God.

36 ¶ Now there was at Joppa a certain disciple named Tabitha, which by interpretation is called ‖ Dorcas: this woman was full ⁿ of good works and almsdeeds which she did.

‖ Or, *Doe, or, Roe.*
n 1 Tim. 2. 10. Tit. 3. 8.

Joppa, a post town: see chap. x. 5. These circumstances of places and persons are set down to evidence the certainty of the history. *Tabitha,* according to the Syriac dialect, then in use amongst the Jews, and *Dorcas,* as she was called amongst the Greeks; it being common for the same person to have two names, one Hebrew and the other Greek, as Thomas, who was called Didymus, and Cephas, who was called Peter. *Full of good works;* she was rich in good works, which are the best riches, last longest, and go farthest.

37 And it came to pass in those days, that she was sick, and died: whom when they had washed, they laid *her* in °an upper chamber.

o ch. 1. 13.

They washed the dead, and anointed them, to fit them for their burying, and especially to show their hope of the resurrection; which some think St. Paul alludes unto, 1 Cor. xv. 29.

38 And forasmuch as Lydda was nigh to Joppa, and the disciples had heard that Peter was there, they sent unto him two men, desiring *him* that he would not ‖ delay to come to them.

‖ Or, *be grieved.*

They sent for Peter, that he might come to comfort those that were concerned in the great loss of so good a woman, and, it may be, not without some hopes of her recovery by a miracle from St. Peter; which is the likelier, because they so much hasten his coming to them, she being already dead, and they preparing for her burial.

39 Then Peter arose and went with them. When he was come, they brought him into the upper chamber: and all the widows stood by him weeping, and shewing the coats and garments which Dorcas made, while she was with them.

It was strange that Peter should be sent for, or that he should go on such an account, viz. to raise one that was dead; but God, who had ordered this miracle for the manifestation of his truth and glory, so wrought in their hearts, that they did this out of faith; though if others should think to imitate it, it would be but presumption. *Weeping;* here needed no mourning women to be hired; the death of this good woman was a common loss: these coats were made by Dorcas in her lifetime, to clothe the poor and naked with.

40 But Peter ᵖput them all forth, and ᑫkneeled down, and prayed; and turning *him* to the body ʳsaid, Tabitha, arise. And she opened her eyes: and when she saw Peter, she sat up.

p Mat. 9. 25.
q ch. 7. 60.
r Mark 5. 41, 42.
John 11. 43.

Peter put them all forth; Peter put them out, that he might pray the more earnestly, without distraction or interruption; thus Elisha shut the door to him when he prayed for the Shunammite's son, 2 Kings iv. 33. *Kneeled down;* this his kneeling is mentioned, to recommend reverence in our praying unto God. *And prayed:* Peter, by his betaking himself unto prayer, would show, that he could do nothing by his own power, but it must come from above; and he had every mercy as much precariously, and by prayer, as any others.

41 And he gave her *his* hand, and lifted her up, and when he had called the saints and widows, he presented her alive.

The saints and widows; such who had sent for him, and now were gathered together to see what effects his prayers might have. *Presented her alive,* and in perfect health, as all were that were miraculously cured; for the Lord's works are perfect, Deut. xxxii. 4.

s John 11. 45. & 12. 11.

42 And it was known throughout all Joppa; [s]and many believed in the Lord.

This cure was wrought, and all the other miracles were done, to be a means to make the gospel to be believed, which he published, and was an undeniable proof that this doctrine was from heaven; for none could do such things unless God were with him, or rather, unless God did them by him; so that this miracle wrought by St. Peter did more good to the souls of many, than to the body of this relieved woman.

t ch. 10. 6.

43 And it came to pass, that he tarried many days in Joppa with one [t]Simon a tanner.

The miracle had only prepared them to receive his doctrine, which Peter tarried some time with them to instruct them in: the miracle had prepared the ground, and now he takes this season to sow the seed of the word into it.

CHAP. X.

Cornelius, a devout centurion, being commanded by an angel, sendeth for Peter, 1—8; *who in the mean time is prepared by a heavenly vision,* 9—16; *and, receiving a command from the Spirit, goeth with the messengers to Cæsarea,* 17—24. *Cornelius receiveth him with great respect, and showeth the occasion of his sending for him,* 25—33. *Peter preacheth Christ to him and his company,* 34—43. *The Holy Ghost falleth on them, whereupon they are baptized,* 44—48.

A. D. 41.

THERE was a certain man in Cæsarea called Cornelius, a centurion of the band called the Italian *band*,

In Cæsarea; in Cæsarea Palestine, as it was called in contra-distinction to Cæsarea Philippi. *Cornelius;* a Roman by his name; which name was ordinarily to be found amongst the families of the Scipios and Syllas. A *band* answers either to a regiment amongst us, or to a legion amongst the Romans (this latter was far greater than the former). It was *called the Italian band,* as being composed of Italian soldiers, and might be used as a guard of the proconsul, who dwelt at Cæsarea, who was that Felix we read of, chap. xxiii. 24.

a ver. 22. ch. 8. 2. & 22. 12. b ver. 35.

2 [a]*A* devout *man,* and one that [b]feared God with all his house, which gave much alms to the people, and prayed to God alway.

A devout man; this Cornelius was a proselyte of the gate, or such as observed the seven precepts of Noah, and lived without giving any offence to the Jews. *With all his house;* it was a very good sign that he feared God, in that he engaged all his house to do the like, at least outwardly, which was as much as he could do: this was spoken by God in Abraham's commendation, Gen. xviii. 19. *Prayed to God alway;* he did not neglect the seasons of prayer, especially the time of offering the morning and evening sacrifice, which by prayer they desired to partake the benefit of, by which Christ our sacrifice, and his merits, were figured unto them. Cornelius indeed prayed always, or at all times, taking time in a moral sense, for the seasons and opportunities for such a duty; (as we are commanded to give thanks always, Eph. v. 20;) but he could not pray always, or at all times, taking time in a natural sense, for then he must have neglected all other duties; however, his endeavour was to keep his heart always in a praying disposition.

c ver. 30. ch. 11. 13.

3 [c]He saw in a vision evidently about the ninth hour of the day an angel of God coming in to him, and saying unto him, Cornelius.

In a vision; not in a dream or rapture, but sensibly and plainly. *About the ninth hour;* their ninth hour was with us about three o'clock in the afternoon, being the ordinary time for the evening sacrifice; and, by consequence, their time of prayer, chap. iii. 1. And this devout man doth not seek God's face in vain; Cornelius had been faithful in a little, and God would give him much; rather than he should want further instruction, who had improved what he had already, God here sends an angel, and soon after an apostle unto him.

4 And when he looked on him, he was afraid, and said, What is it, Lord? And he said unto him, Thy prayers and thine alms are come up for a memorial before God.

He was afraid; the angel appeared in so great splendour: all admiration hath some fear with it. *And said, What is it, Lord?* this is equivalent to What wilt thou have me to do? and shows that Cornelius was prepared to hear the message. *Thy prayers and thine alms;* prayer and alms are joined together in our Saviour's discourse concerning them, Matt. vi., and in the apostle's order about them, 1 Cor. xvi. 1: alms are our sacrifices now under the gospel, Phil. iv. 18; Heb. xiii. 16. *Are come up for a memorial before God;* an allusion to the offering up of incense under the law; the smoke of the incense did ascend, and so David desires that his prayers might ascend to God-ward, Psal. cxli. 2: thus, under the gospel, prayers are resembled to incense, Rev. viii. 3. That prayers are said to come up for a memorial, is but the pursuance of the same metaphor; for, Lev. ii. 2, the frankincense, &c. was the memorial there commanded to be burned; and all this only to represent unto us how well-pleasing the prayers of his people are unto God through Christ, and that God keeps in remembrance all those things they thus desire of him, and in his time and measure (which are the best circumstances) bestows all upon them: but let not prayers and alms, which God here hath put together, be put asunder, and in due time we shall reap.

5 And now send men to Joppa, and call for *one* Simon, whose surname is Peter:

Joppa, a town that was memorable for Jonah's taking ship there, when he would flee from God, and decline his message, Jonah i. 3. The angel could have declared the gospel, and instructed Cornelius; but he sends him to Peter, God being willing to honour the means of his own institution.

d ch. 9. 43. e ch. 11. 14.

6 He lodgeth with one [d]Simon a tanner, whose house is by the sea side: [e]he shall tell thee what thou oughtest to do.

These particulars, when found true by Cornelius, did very much advantage him towards his believing what Peter in the name of the Lord did tell him.

7 And when the angel which spake unto Cornelius was departed, he called two of his houshold servants, and a devout soldier of them that waited on him continually;

Two of his household servants; these servants doubtless Cornelius had instructed, as appears ver. 2, and God blesses him with faithful and successful service from them. *A devout soldier;* no condition, or temptation, too hard for the grace of God to overcome; both centurion and soldier are willing to hazard all they had, rather than not to obey God, and come to the knowledge of Jesus Christ. *Waited on him continually;* this soldier, for his religion's sake, and his holy life, was taken into nearer attendance on Cornelius; it is no small matter to have one near us that hath power with God.

8 And when he had declared all *these* things unto them, he sent them to Joppa.

Thus on Cornelius's side all things are disposed towards his receiving of the gospel; and the same providence, at the same time, disposes all things on Peter's part towards his coming to publish it: for

9 ¶ On the morrow, as they went on their journey, and drew nigh unto the city, [f ch. 11. 5, &c.] [f]Peter went up upon the housetop to pray about the sixth hour:

These houses were flat on the tops, and therefore they were commanded to make battlements for them, Deut. xxii. 8. *Peter went up upon the housetop to pray*, that he might from thence view the temple, which was a type of Christ, through whom only we and our prayers can be acceptable unto God; hence, 1 Kings viii. 30, &c., there is so often mention made of praying towards the city, and towards the place which God should choose; this Daniel practised, though upon the hazard of his life, when both city and temple were ruined, Dan. vi. 10. *The sixth hour* with them is high noon, or mid-day, and is accounted one of the three times of prayer, (see chap. iii. 1,) and was, as the Jews say, recommended to them by Isaac; howsoever, it was the time when they might begin to prepare the evening sacrifice: none of these causes need to be assigned, for doubtless this blessed apostle did *watch unto prayer*, 1 Pet. iv. 7, and desirously laid hold upon all opportunities to pour out his soul unto God.

10 And he became very hungry, and would have eaten: but while they made ready, he fell into a trance,

He became very hungry; he might be more than ordinarily hungry, to fit or suit the vision, which is hereafter mentioned. *He fell into a trance:* the most excellent way of God's manifesting himself unto man, is by a trance; (and they reckon seven ways, in which God makes himself known unto man;) but what this trance was is diversly expressed: it is certain, that in it the soul was, as it were, absent from the body, drawn off from the perception of earthly and sensible things, and enabled unto the perception of heavenly mysteries: in such an ecstasy was St. Paul, 2 Cor. xii. 2, and St. John, Rev. i. 10, who is therefore said to be *in the Spirit*.

[g ch. 7. 56. Rev. 19. 11.] 11 And [g]saw heaven opened, and a certain vessel descending unto him, as it had been a great sheet knit at the four corners, and let down to the earth:

And saw heaven; either visibly to his corporal eyes, as to St. Stephen's; or rather mentally, more suitably to the rapture mentioned in the former verse. *Opened;* which might signify, that heaven, that was shut to the children of men by the first Adam, was now by Christ, the Second Adam, opened to all believers. *Vessel;* this word is taken for any utensil commonly used about the house; and, with the *sheet* here spoken of, bears an analogy to a table and table-cloth amongst us. *Knit at the four corners;* so gathered up or knit, that the viands, ver. 12, might not fall down. And this Peter saw to come from heaven, to show that the liberty of taking Cornelius and other Gentiles into the church, did come from thence only.

12 Wherein were all manner of four-footed beasts of the earth, and wild beasts, and creeping things, and fowls of the air.

As well unclean beasts, such as were forbidden by the law, as clean, such as by the law might be eaten.

13 And there came a voice to him, Rise, Peter; kill, and eat.

Of that thou seest, without any exception, whether they be clean, or (formerly) unclean creatures. The moral of which command is, that he might now converse with Jews and Gentiles indifferently, and preach unto these also the word of life.

[h Lev. 11. 4. & 20. 25. Deut. 14. 3, 7. Ezek. 4. 14.] 14 But Peter said, Not so, Lord; [h]for I have never eaten any thing that is common or unclean.

These words may signify one and the same thing, and the latter explain the former; showing that those things are said to be common, which the law, by forbidding them, had made unclean. Others make some difference; and by things common, understand all sorts of creatures, which were forbidden to the Jews, but were commonly fed upon by all nations round about them; and by things unclean, they understand such as by accident became so, as when any of the creatures permitted for use was strangled.

15 And the voice *spake* unto him again [i Matt. 15. 11. ver. 28. Rom. 14. 14, 17, 20. 1 Cor. 10. 25. 1 Tim. 4. 4. Tit. 1. 15.] the second time, [i]What God hath cleansed, *that* call not thou common.

Do not make in thy esteem, or practice, as *common*, that is, polluted. The Jews did imagine, that by unclean creatures were meant the Gentiles, as by clean creatures things would have themselves to be understood; howsoever, they opposed common unto holy; indeed a holy man is (as they called him) a singular man: it was God that cleansed Cornelius, turning him from idolatry to the worship of the true God, from darkness unto light.

16 This was done thrice: and the vessel was received up again into heaven.

Whereby this great mystery of the conversion of the Gentiles, and taking them into the church, might be the more confirmed, and fixed in St. Peter's mind.

17 Now while Peter doubted in himself what this vision which he had seen should mean, behold, the men which were sent from Cornelius had made enquiry for Simon's house, and stood before the gate,

Doubted in himself; recollecting himself; for the vision had so affected him, that it had put him into a kind of ecstasy, out of which when he came to himself, *behold, the men;* the two servants and the soldier which Cornelius had sent.

18 And called, and asked whether Simon, which was surnamed Peter, were lodged there.

Being strangers, they address themselves to such of the house as came to the door.

19 ¶ While Peter thought on the vision, [k]the Spirit said unto him, Behold, three men seek thee. [k ch. 11. 12.]

Thought on the vision; set himself to meditate upon that he had seen and heard. *The Spirit said unto him;* the Holy Spirit informs him further. Thus whosoever meditates carefully upon what he hears from God's word, God will never leave him without sufficient instruction.

20 [l]Arise therefore, and get thee down, [l ch. 15. 7.] and go with them, doubting nothing: for I have sent them.

Arise therefore; immediately put thyself upon the journey. *Doubting nothing;* spend no time in disputing within thyself, because that they, unto whom thou art sent, are not Jews.

21 Then Peter went down to the men which were sent unto him from Cornelius; and said, Behold, I am he whom ye seek: what *is* the cause wherefore ye are come?

Peter being in no small consternation, and not perfectly knowing whither all this tended, makes the more exact inquiry.

22 And they said, [m]Cornelius the centurion, a just man, and one that feareth [m ver. 1, 2, &c.] God, and [n]of good report among all the [n ch. 22. 12.] nation of the Jews, was warned from God by an holy angel to send for thee into his house, and to hear words of thee.

That they might speed in their message, they labour to prevent all prejudice Peter might have against Cornelius, who was a Gentile by title; telling him, 1. That he was *a just man,* as is said of Joseph, Matt. i. 19. 2. That he worshipped the true God the same with the Jews, and not the false gods of the Gentiles. 3. That he was reputed a pious and good man, and so it would be no disparagement to the apostles to go unto him. *Was warned from God:* this argument St. Peter could not deny. When God's command is evident, his people are determined and resolved.

23 Then called he them in, and lodged *them.* And on the morrow Peter went away with them, °and certain brethren from Joppa accompanied him.

o ver. 45. ch. 11. 12.

And on the morrow Peter went away with them; he delays not to obey the heavenly vision ; but as Abraham took his journey the very next morning after that he had received the command, Gen. xxii. 3, so did Peter here, and *bis dat qui cito dat,* he doubles his obedience that obeys speedily and cheerfully. *And certain brethren from Joppa accompanied him;* these brethren were six in number, as chap. xi. 12 ; who might undertake this journey, 1. Out of respect to Peter, to accompany him. 2. Being moved at the extraordinary visions that were spoken of. But especially, 3. Disposed by the providence of God to accompany St. Peter, that they might testify the grace of God that was come unto the Gentiles, when it might be afterwards questioned.

24 And the morrow after they entered into Cæsarea. And Cornelius waited for them, and had called together his kinsmen and near friends.

Joppa was about fifteen leagues from Cæsarea, so that the next day after they set out they might easily come from Joppa thither. *His kinsmen;* his relations. *And near friends;* and such as he had the greatest love and kindness for ; he thought that he could not express it better, than by giving them an opportunity to hear the word of life, and to gain instruction for their souls : and probably those here spoken of were reckoned as friends, and near friends, by Cornelius, because they were such as with him had forsaken all pagan idolatry, and were worshippers of the true and living God.

25 And as Peter was coming in, Cornelius met him, and fell down at his feet, and worshipped *him.*

As Peter was coming in, Cornelius met him; into Cornelius's house, for he hastened to meet with him. *Worshipped him;* Cornelius worshipped with the most humble civil worship; but he could not think him to be God, and therefore he did give him no Divine worship, he having forsaken the idolatry of the Gentiles ; but might perhaps think him to have been an angel, and intended to worship him accordingly, for which he is blamed in the following verse.

p ch. 14. 14, 15. Rev. 19. 10. & 22. 9.

26 But Peter took him up, saying, ᵖStand up; I myself also am a man.

It is certain that Peter did think this worship Cornelius gave him to have exceeded ; and here he blames him for it, telling him, he was but a man like unto him ; and he needed not give any further reason of his reproof, for man must adore, but by no means may be adored ; no, nor take too much honour unto himself.

27 And as he talked with him, he went in, and found many that were come together.

As he talked with him; they went talking together into the house, probably of the goodness of God, that they should be directed so happily unto one another ; for they could not but see and acknowledge God in it.

28 And he said unto them, Ye know how ᵍthat it is an unlawful thing for a man that is a Jew to keep company, or come unto one of another nation ; but ʳGod hath shewed me that I should not call any man common or unclean.

q John 4. 9. & 18. 28. ch. 11. 3. Gal. 2. 12, 14.

r ch. 15. 8, 9. Eph. 3. 6.

God himself did erect a partition-wall betwixt his people and other nations, Jews and Gentiles ; hence by God's own command the Jews might not have any familiar converse with the Gentiles, especially they might not marry with them. The Jews themselves had made this partition-wall much larger, and they held it unlawful to eat with any of the Gentiles, or to go so much as into their houses ; hence that objection made upon this occasion against St. Peter, chap. xi. 3. *Unclean;* no man is now unclean by any ceremonial uncleanness, because he is not circumcised, or because he is not sprinkled with the blood of bulls, Heb. ix. 13 ; yet sin hath defiled the whole mass of mankind, and they are equally by nature morally unclean.

29 Therefore came I *unto you* without gainsaying, as soon as I was sent for : I ask therefore for what intent ye have sent for me ?

Gainsaying, or delay. *I ask therefore for what intent ye have sent for me?* Peter did in a great measure know the business he came about, partly by the vision and its interpretation, partly by what he might have heard from them that Cornelius sent for him, unto whom Cornelius had declared the whole matter, as we find, ver. 8 ; yet Peter's question is but necessary, for to give Cornelius an opportunity to acquaint his friends, who were met there, with all that had passed.

30 And Cornelius said, Four days ago I was fasting until this hour ; and at the ninth hour I prayed in my house, and, behold, ˢa man stood before me ᵗin bright clothing,

s ch. 1. 10. t Matt. 28. 3. Mark 16. 5. Luke 24. 4.

Four days ago I was fasting until this hour; Cornelius does not intend to declare by this how long he had fasted ; but he tells him when he, being fasting, saw the vision, which was four days before, at the same time of the day. *The ninth hour,* which was a time of prayer, it being the time of offering the evening sacrifice : see chap. iii. 1. *A man,* in appearance, but an angel indeed, as in the 3rd verse. *In bright clothing;* why angels appeared in bright or white raiment, see chap. i. 10.

31 And said, Cornelius, ᵘthy prayer is heard, ˣand thine alms are had in remembrance in the sight of God.

u ver. 4, &c. Dan. 10. 12. x Heb. 6. 10.

Alms; of which see the 4th verse. *In the sight of God;* unto which, not only the outward gift, but the inward affection, is visible ; and this is peculiarly in the sight of God, the other may be seen also by men.

32 Send therefore to Joppa, and call hither Simon, whose surname is Peter ; he is lodged in the house of *one* Simon a tanner by the sea side : who, when he cometh, shall speak unto thee.

The substance of this verse is in the 5th and 6th verses before-going. Cornelius might say this to excuse his sending for Peter, being a stranger to him ; as also to encourage Peter to speak in such a matter as God had appeared in.

33 Immediately therefore I sent to thee ; and thou hast well done that thou art come. Now therefore are we all here present before God, to hear all things that are commanded thee of God.

Immediately therefore I sent to thee; as a hungry soul delays not to send for food, as soon as he knows where to have it. *Thou hast well done that thou art come;* which does not only approve of St. Peter's coming, but thank him for it. *Present before God;* we will set ourselves to attend to thy words, as if we saw God looking upon us, whom we call to witness that we are ready to do whatsoever he shall require of us. Thus it becomes every one that would profit by the word of God, to attend upon it. Men do not behave themselves as before God, and therefore they enjoy nothing less than God in an ordinance, and are as if God had taken no notice of them.

34 ¶ Then Peter opened *his* mouth, and said, ʸOf a truth I perceive that God is no respecter of persons :

y Deut. 10. 17. 2 Chro. 19. 7. Job 34. 19. Rom. 2. 11. Gal. 2. 6. Eph. 6. 9. Col. 3. 25. 1 Pet. 1. 17.

Opened his mouth; an expression used (as formerly) in matters of great moment, as Matt. v. 2. *God is no respecter of persons;* God does not accept of one because he is a Jew, and respect another because he is a Gentile ; though St. Paul, being prejudiced by his education, had been carried along with that error of the Jews ; against which, notwithstanding, God had declared himself even unto them, Deut. x. 17, which is also confirmed unto us in

THE ACTS X

the New Testament, Rom. ii. 11; 1 Pet. i. 17: so that our being of any nation or any condition, rich or poor, honoured or despised, on the one side recommends us not unto God, and on the other side it will not hinder us from being accepted with the Lord.

z ch. 15. 9. Rom. 2. 13, 27. & 3. 22, 29, & 10. 12, 13. 1 Cor. 12. 13. Gal. 3. 28. Eph. 2. 13, 18. & 3. 6.

35 But [z] in every nation he that feareth him, and worketh righteousness, is accepted with him.

In every nation; even though Romans or Italians, of which nation Cornelius was, and might probably be worse thought of by the Jews, because they supposed themselves to have been hardly used by them. *Feareth him, and worketh righteousness;* these two particulars include the observation of both tables of the law: the fearing of God comprehends piety, that is, the true worship of the true God; and working righteousness, includes all the duties to our neighbour; and both describe a truly good and holy man, such as Cornelius was; unto whose case this is to be applied.

a Is. 57. 19. Eph. 2. 14, 16, 17. Col. 1. 20. b Mat. 28. 18. Rom. 10. 12. 1 Cor. 15. 27. Eph. 1. 20, 22. 1 Pet. 3. 22. Rev. 17. 14. & 19. 16.

36 The word which *God* sent unto the children of Israel, [a] preaching peace by Jesus Christ: ([b] he is Lord of all:)

The word; the word of reconciliation betwixt God and man, not only betwixt God and the Jews, but betwixt him and the Gentiles also, he had *sent unto Israel* by his prophets formerly. God is said to create *peace to him that is afar off,* the Gentile, as well as *to him that is near,* the Jew, Isa. lvii. 19; and that salvation was not limited to the Jews only, Psal. lxxii. 7, 8; Isa. xlix. 6, might be known unto them by the examples of Melchizedek, Job, and Naaman, who did no ways belong unto them; but this was now more manifest; God preaching this peace betwixt himself and all nations indifferently, 1. By Christ in his own person preaching this, Matt. viii. 11, and telling them that by his death he would draw all men unto him, John xii. 32. 2. This peace is preached to be had by Christ, or only through Christ, by the angels themselves, Luke ii. 14. And, 3. By all the apostles and ministers of the gospel. Speaking to the Gentiles, St. Paul says, *Ye who were afar off are made nigh by the blood of Christ,* Eph. ii. 13; and it was their constant doctrine, that there was no name under heaven by which men could be saved, but the name of Christ, chap. iv. 12; and that it was all one whether they were Greeks or Jews, &c., *but Christ is all, and in all,* Col. iii. 11: so that in this doctrine there is an exact harmony betwixt the Old and New Testaments, the prophets and the apostles. *He is Lord of all;* Christ is Lord, not of the Jews, or one people, only; but of the Gentiles, all nations, also, as Matt. xxviii. 19, 20; Rom. iii. 29.

37 That word, *I say,* ye know, which was published throughout all Judæa, and

c Luke 4. 14.

[c] began from Galilee, after the baptism which John preached;

They had heard of the doctrine of the gospel by common fame and report, which could not but spread abroad; all might know that Christ and his apostles did preach, though these might be ignorant of the particular doctrines which they taught, and which Peter was now sent to instruct them in: or by *the word* (in a usual Hebraism) the matter of the gospel may be meant, as the life, death, and resurrection of our blessed Saviour, which they could not but have heard several reports of. *After the baptism which John preached;* who, as the Elijah who was promised, Mal. iv. 5, was the forerunner of the Lord.

d Luke 4. 18. ch. 2. 22. & 4. 27. Heb. 1. 9.

38 How [d] God anointed Jesus of Nazareth with the Holy Ghost and with power: who went about doing good, and healing all that were oppressed of the

e John 3. 2.

devil; [e] for God was with him.

God anointed Jesus: it was usual to anoint their kings, priests, and prophets, unto all which offices Christ was anointed by his Father; hence called Christ, as in the Old Testament the Messiah. *Of Nazareth:* the apostle is not ashamed of this name, though given to our Saviour by way of contempt; he gloried in the cross of Christ. *With the Holy Ghost and with power;* Christ was endued with the Almighty Spirit of God, and with the power of it. *Who went about doing good:* all the miracles our blessed Saviour wrought, were works of mercy, for the benefit and relief of those upon whom he wrought them: he could have wrought miracles to destroy and ruin such as would not believe in him, which he was often provoked unto; nay, his apostles would have had him but to permit them by fire from heaven to destroy the Samaritans, Luke ix. 54, and he would not. *Healing all that were oppressed of the devil:* the deliverances our Saviour so often wrought upon such as were possessed of devils, was to show unto them that he was come to destroy the works of the devil, and to cast him out of the souls of men who were spiritually possessed by him; which also our Saviour did, so that it was a happy calamity for them, which brought them to Christ. *For God was with him;* God was with our Saviour, 1. By his might and power doing such miracles. 2. In his extraordinary love to him, Matt. iii. 17, and always hearing of him, John xi. 42. And also, 3. God was with Christ οὐσιωδῶς, in the fulness of the Godhead, Col. ii. 9.

39 And [f] we are witnesses of all things which he did both in the land of the Jews, and in Jerusalem; [g] whom they slew and hanged on a tree:

f ch. 2. 32.
g ch. 5. 30.

We are witnesses; the apostles, whom Christ had chosen to go in and out with him, and to be eye and ear witnesses of all that was done by him, or against him. *Whom they slew:* their killing of our Saviour is the rather here spoken of, to show how rightfully the Jews were now to be forsaken, and that they had no cause to complain of the calling in of the Gentiles, being themselves had in such a manner rejected Christ; but especially, that they who were here met, and we, all might consider, how much it cost our blessed Saviour to deliver us from sin and hell. He was *made a curse for us,* Gal. iii. 13, as Deut. xxi. 23, that the blessing of Abraham might come upon us, Gal. iii. 14.

40 Him [h] God raised up the third day, and shewed him openly;

h ch. 2. 24.

Lest these Gentiles be deterred from believing in Christ, and take offence at his cross, St. Peter preached unto them the resurrection, which suddenly and powerfully followed. And this he tells them was unquestionable, as appeared by all the ways that any thing can be proved by; Christ was seen, and heard, and felt after his resurrection, as the beloved disciple tells us, 1 John i. 1, and manifested his victory over death for us.

41 [i] Not to all the people, but unto witnesses chosen before of God, *even* to us, [k] who did eat and drink with him after he rose from the dead.

i John 14. 17, 22. ch. 13. 31.
k Luke 24. 30, 43. John 21. 13.

Not to all the people: Christ after his resurrection appeared not to the wicked Jews, for being to suffer no more, his enemies were not vouchsafed a sight of him; and thus he did not manifest himself unto the world, John xiv. 22. *But unto witnesses;* these witnesses were the apostles, who were chosen by God himself immediately; and the vacancy supplied by lot, which was at God's direction, chap. i. 24, 26. The metaphor here used is taken from the ordinary way then in use of choosing men into offices, which is here alluded to. *Eat and drink with him:* though in the gospel history we do not read that our Saviour drank after he rose again; yet it is sufficiently implied, being he did eat, and make a meal with his disciples, Luke xxiv. 30, 42, 43; John xxi. 12; and eating is put in Scripture for the whole refection, Matt. xv. 2, compared with Luke vii. 36.

42 And [l] he commanded us to preach unto the people, and to testify [m] that it is he which was ordained of God *to be* the Judge [n] of quick and dead.

l Mat. 28. 19, 20. ch. 1. 8.
m John 5. 22, 27. ch. 17. 31. n Rom. 14. 9, 19. 2 Cor. 5. 10. 2 Tim. 4. 1. 1 Pet. 4. 5.

Our Saviour gave this charge to his apostles before his ascension, Matt. xxviii. 19; Mark xvi. 15; Luke xxiv. 47; and foretold that they should execute this his charge, chap. i. 8. *Ordained of God to be the Judge:* that God hath ordained to judge the world by Jesus Christ, Scripture abundantly testifies, John v. 26, 27; 2 Tim. iv. 1; 1 Pet. iv. 5. And this is here spoken of the apostle, and was given in charge by our Saviour to be principally preached of by them all, because the resurrection of Christ, and the glory of his kingdom in this world, is clouded by the blindness and hardness of men; as also, because it is of the greatest concernment unto all, that at any time hear the word of God, to be persuaded of this, that Christ, whose gospel and word they hear, will judge them according unto it. *Quick;* such as shall be alive at the coming of our Lord to judgment, 1 Thess. iv. 15.

o Is. 53. 11.
Jer. 31. 34.
Dan. 9. 24.
Mic. 7. 18.
Zech. 13. 1.
Mal. 4. 2.
ch. 26. 22.
p ch. 15. 9.
& 26. 18. Rom. 10. 11. Gal. 3. 22.

43 °To him give all the prophets witness, that through his name ᵖwhosoever believeth in him shall receive remission of sins.

This our Saviour had told his apostles, which St. Peter here preaches to his auditors. It was included in the very first promise recorded by Moses, Gen. iii. 15, The seed of the woman shall break the serpent's head; and so continued through all ages of the church, to be manifest in such degrees as it pleased the wisdom of God to make it known: it is certain that all the ceremonial law concerning sacrifices did testify this very thing; for by it, it did appear, that without shedding of blood there was no remission of sin, as Heb. ix. 22; and it is manifest by the light of nature, that the blood of bulls and goats could not take away sins, as Heb. x. 4. But *through* Christ's *name*, for his sake, and by virtue of his merit, who died for our sins, and rose again for our justification, Rom. iv. 25, we *shall receive remission of sins*, Heb. ix. 13, 14.

q ch. 4. 31.
& 8. 15, 16,
17. & 11. 15.

44 ¶ While Peter yet spake these words, ᵠthe Holy Ghost fell on all them which heard the word.

While Peter yet spake these words, that God might miraculously show his approbation of what Peter had said, and to assure Peter of the real conversion of these Gentiles, which all the Jews did make such a difficulty to believe, *the Holy Ghost fell on all them which heard the word;* such fiery tongues in a visible shape as had appeared unto the apostles, chap. ii. 3, whereby the inward powerful effects of the Spirit upon their hearts was signified. What wonderful effects had this short sermon! And doubtless, were practisers but as sincere, and hearers as intent, now-a-days, as then, we should find that the hand of the Lord is not shortened.

r ver. 23.
s ch. 11. 18.
Gal. 3. 14.

45 ʳAnd they of the circumcision which believed were astonished, as many as came with Peter, ˢbecause that on the Gentiles also was poured out the gift of the Holy Ghost.

They of the circumcision; such as were not only themselves circumcised, but born of circumcised parents, who are thus called, Gal. ii. 12. These, not minding, or understanding, the many predictions of the calling of the Gentiles, thought that Christ was only promised unto the Jews; and were amazed to see now such an argument as might convince them to the contrary. *Poured out,* speaks the abundant measure in which the Holy Ghost was given unto them.

46 For they heard them speak with tongues, and magnify God. Then answered Peter,

With tongues; with variety of languages, or strange tongues, as in the day of Pentecost, chap. ii. 6. *Answered;* an ordinary Hebraism for speaking, though the first part of any discourse. And Peter, knowing that these miraculous fiery tongues did show that these men did partake of the same Spirit from whom the apostles had received them, he makes an inference from thence.

t ch. 11. 17.
& 15. 8, 9.
Rom. 10. 12.

47 Can any man forbid water, that these should not be baptized, which have received the Holy Ghost ᵗas well as we?

This question, as chap. viii. 36, is without question, and denies that any can forbid water, that is, in order to baptize such as these. As if the apostle had argued thus: They that have the grace signified or promised,

have a right unto the seal of the promise: but these Gentiles have the grace signified or promised in baptism; they had the inward part, and therefore the outward part could not be denied unto them. He that hath the inheritance, may claim the writings, wax, and parchment that belong unto it.

u 1 Cor. 1. 17.
x ch. 2. 38.
& 8. 16.

48 "And he commanded them to be baptized ˣin the name of the Lord. Then prayed they him to tarry certain days.

In the name of the Lord; that is, in the name of our Saviour. But this does not imply, but that they were baptized according to our Saviour's prescription, Matt. xxviii. 19: but the Jews by their baptism were become the Lord's, and had given up their names to Jesus Christ; under which title, *the Lord,* not only our Saviour, but the Father who anointed him, and the Spirit by whom he was anointed, is to be understood. *Then prayed they;* Cornelius and the rest of his friends, which he caused to be present. At their entreaty, Peter, and others that came with him, (as chap. xi. 12,) tarried there, that they might further instruct, confirm, and comfort them; (as the best have ever need to learn, and to grow in grace and knowledge;) and by this Peter showed that he looked upon himself and others as not bound to observe those precepts, (of the wise men, as they called them,) forbidding them all familiarity with the uncircumcised.

CHAP. XI

Peter, being accused for conversing with the Gentiles, maketh his defence; the church is satisfied, and glorifieth God, 1—18. The gospel having spread as far as Phenice, Cyprus, and Antioch, 19—21, Barnabas is sent thither, who fetcheth Saul from Tarsus: many people are taught at Antioch, where the disciples are first called Christians, 22—26. Agabus prophesieth a dearth: the disciples send relief from Antioch to the brethren in Judea by Barnabas and Saul, 27—30.

AND the apostles and brethren that were in Judæa heard that the Gentiles had also received the word of God.

And brethren; the rest of the believers, who had not only one God to their Father, but one church to their mother, and were born of the same Spirit, and were fed by the same milk of the word of God. *The Gentiles had also received the word of God;* this was a most incredible thing unto them who were of the seed of Abraham according to the flesh, and were not acquainted with that mystery that Abraham should have a seed of his faith, upon whom all the promises were entailed. These looked upon the Gentiles as most execrable persons, such as the apostle describes, Eph. ii. 12, that had no hope, and were without God; and therefore no less than a miracle, and that well attested, as this was, could make them change their opinion.

a ch. 10. 45.
Gal. 2. 12.

2 And when Peter was come up to Jerusalem, ᵃthey that were of the circumcision contended with him,

They that were of the circumcision; they were such Jews as conversed with them of the church, and argued against them for taking in the Gentiles into any fellowship with them. But it may be that the believing Jews might for a time be very weak, and offended at it, until they were further satisfied by the following relation of St. Peter: till then they disputed, and brought what arguments they could against it.

b ch. 10. 28.
c Gal. 2. 12.

3 Saying, ᵇThou wentest in to men uncircumcised, ᶜand didst eat with them.

This is the objection they make against Peter, That, contrary to the tradition of their elders, and precept of their wise men, he had familiarly conversed with the Gentiles: see chap. x. 28. This they look upon as piacular, although no conversation in order to the gaining of the Gentiles unto God was ever forbidden, but only such as might withdraw the Jews from God.

d Luke 1. 3.

4 But Peter rehearsed *the matter* from the beginning, and expounded *it* ᵈby order unto them, saying,

This great apostle condescends to the least and weakest amongst them, and gives an account of what he had done, and the reasons that moved him unto it, if by any means he might gain some, and confirm others.

e ch. 10. 9, &c.

5 ᵉI was in the city of Joppa praying: and in a trance I saw a vision, A certain vessel descend, as it had been a great sheet, let down from heaven by four corners; and it came even to me:

See this whole narration spoken to in the foregoing chapter. *It came even to me;* to show that he was especially concerned in this vision, it being for his instruction and regulation.

6 Upon the which when I had fastened mine eyes, I considered, and saw fourfooted beasts of the earth, and wild beasts, and creeping things, and fowls of the air.

Fastened mine eyes; it speaketh his great intention of mind upon it; God so ordering of it, that it might leave the greater impression upon him.

7 And I heard a voice saying unto me, Arise, Peter; slay and eat.

He might now use them without any distinction indifferently.

8 But I said, Not so, Lord: for nothing common or unclean hath at any time entered into my mouth.

St. Peter here avoucheth that he had lived in this ceremonial righteousness, though he thought himself far from being justified thereby. *Hath at any time entered into my mouth;* he abstained from all the appearances of that evil.

9 But the voice answered me again from heaven, What God hath cleansed, *that* call not thou common.

This is twice spoken to St. Peter, that it might be the more unquestionable with him and others, it seeming otherwise very strange; and, it may be, therefore twice by St. Luke recorded.

10 And this was done three times: and all were drawn up again into heaven.

This was done three times; for the same reason but now mentioned, that God might more abundantly manifest this mystery of the calling in of the Gentiles, which had been so long hid. *All were drawn up again into heaven;* all this was from heaven; unto which also it tended, namely, to bring the Gentiles thither.

11 And, behold, immediately there were three men already come unto the house where I was, sent from Cæsarea unto me.

So many sent, and such a journey willingly undertaken, for to gain instruction in the way of life.

f John 16. 13. ch. 10. 19. & 15. 7. g ch. 10. 23.

12 And ᶠthe spirit bade me go with them, nothing doubting. Moreover ᵍ these six brethren accompanied me, and we entered into the man's house:

These six brethren accompanied me; whom they might hear testify the same thing, that in the mouths of so many it might be established. *We entered into the man's house:* the man meant is Cornelius, concerning the entry into whose house, and converse with him, the doubt or controversy was that he was now speaking to.

h ch. 10. 30.

13 ʰAnd he shewed us how he had seen an angel in his house, which stood and said unto him, Send men to Joppa, and call for Simon, whose surname is Peter;

An angel, who, by reason of his appearing a man, is, in chap. x. 30, called *a man.*

14 Who shall tell thee words, whereby thou and all thy house shall be saved.

God promises that upon his obedience to this oracle, in sending for Peter, he should tell him those things that were necessary to be known by him and his whole family unto their salvation. Whatsoever was formerly the case of such as obeyed the precepts of Noah, (as they were called,) after Christ is come, and preached unto the world, there is no other way unto salvation but through him.

15 And as I began to speak, the Holy Ghost fell on them, ⁱas on us at the beginning.

i ch. 2. 4.

As I began to speak; whilst Peter was speaking, as chap. i. 1. *The Holy Ghost fell on them,* as in the day of Pentecost, chap. ii. 4, he had fallen on the apostles; either visibly, by fiery cloven tongues; or rather by extraordinarily enduing them with the gift of tongues; enabling the most illiterate amongst them to speak in any language needful for any to understand towards their salvation.

16 Then remembered I the word of the Lord, how that he said, ᵏJohn indeed baptized with water; but ˡye shall be baptized with the Holy Ghost.

k Matt. 3. 11. John 1. 26, 33. ch. 1. 5. & 19. 4. l Is. 44. 3. Joel 2. 28. & 3. 18.

Of the Lord; of Christ, who is every where so called. *He said;* but these words seem rather spoken by St. John himself, Matt. iii. 11; Mark i. 8; which makes no difference; for, first, Whatsoever a disciple of Christ says in his name, it is as if it were spoken by himself: *He that heareth you, heareth me.* But, secondly, Though this was spoken by the Baptist, it was spoken by our Saviour also, chap. i. 5. *John indeed baptized with water; but ye shall be baptized with the Holy Ghost;* by which the great difference is implied betwixt outward baptism (administered by whomsoever, though the Baptist himself) and the inward baptism of the Holy Ghost, which, as fire, separates powerfully the scum and dross of sin from us. *With the Holy Ghost;* the extraordinary gifts of the Spirit.

17 ᵐForasmuch then as God gave them the like gift as *he did* unto us, who believed on the Lord Jesus Christ; ⁿwhat was I, that I could withstand God?

m ch. 15. 8, 9 n ch. 10. 47.

The apostle's argument is cogent: They who have the grace signified by baptism, ought to have the seal of that grace; but the Gentiles had the grace signified by baptism. Or, they who have the inward baptism, may not be denied the outward. As he that hath a right to an inheritance, cannot without injustice be denied the writings and seals thereunto belonging. To deny baptism unto any unto whom it doth belong, is to *withstand God,* and to keep back the token of God's love from such unto whom it is sent.

18 When they heard these things, they held their peace, and glorified God, saying, ᵒThen hath God also to the Gentiles granted repentance unto life.

o Rom. 10. 12, 13. & 15. 9, 16.

They held their peace; they were fully satisfied with the reason St. Peter had given them of his admitting the Gentiles unto baptism, and fellowship with him; wisely inferring from what Peter had said, that what he had done was of God, who was to be acknowledged in it. *Then hath God also to the Gentiles granted repentance:* repentance is the gift of God, as well as faith, or any other grace, 2 Tim. ii. 25; nor can the greatest guilt affect the heart with true godly sorrow, until God hath quickened it. It is called *repentance unto life,* because God hath appointed that it should precede our entrance into life.

19 ¶ ᵖNow they which were scattered abroad upon the persecution that arose about Stephen travelled as far as Phenice, and Cyprus, and Antioch, preaching the word to none but unto the Jews only.

p ch. 8. 1.

So true hath it been from the beginning of the gospel, that *sanguis martyrum est semen ecclesiæ.* St. Stephen's death, and the persecution upon it, was a great means of disseminating the gospel. Thus all things work for good. *Phenice;* the country about Tyre. *Cyprus;* an island in the Mediterranean Sea. *Antioch;* the metropolis of Syria. This explains what was briefly said, chap. viii. 4, and showed what places the disciples were scattered into, and preached in. They preached to *the Jews only,* because they were not yet persuaded of the calling of the Gentiles; God suffering them to be enlightened by degrees.

20 And some of them were men of Cyprus and Cyrene, which, when they were come to Antioch, spake unto ᵍthe Grecians, preaching the Lord Jesus.

^q ch. 6. 1. & 9. 29.

Men of Cyprus and Cyrene; they were such as were born in Cyprus and Cyrene, but had their habitation in Jerusalem, and now upon the persecution there fled unto Antioch; which by this means in time became the Jerusalem of the Gentile Christians, whither their greatest resort was. *Spake unto the Grecians:* here they of the dispersion taught not only such Hellenists as are spoken of, chap. vi. 1, who were born of Hebrew parents, though living out of the country of Judea; but such also amongst the Gentiles, (who are generally called Greeks since Alexander's time, who conquered all those nations round about, and brought in his own language amongst them,) who, forsaking idolatry, and worshipping the true God, were called σεβόμενοι, devout or religious persons, such as Cornelius is said to be, chap. x. 2. And thus God by degrees brought in the knowledge of himself, and his Son Jesus Christ. *Preaching the Lord Jesus;* which knowledge only is that which is necessary unto salvation, and that only which Saul determined to know, 1 Cor. ii. 2.

21 And ʳthe hand of the Lord was with them: and a great number believed, and ˢturned unto the Lord.

^r Luke 1. 66. ch. 2. 47.
^s ch. 9. 35.

The hand of the Lord; the power, assistance, and working of God, expressed by the hand. which is the organ or instrument men use in working. This hand or work of God was manifest, first, In the miracles which they wrought. Secondly, In the conversion of any by these miracles. For these alone cannot soften a heart; as appeared in Pharaoh, whose heart was hardened by them. *A great number believed, and turned unto the Lord;* faith and conversion are wrought by the hand of the Lord, and are his work. But in vain is faith pretended unto, when there is no change in heart and life. What God hath put together, none may put asunder.

A. D. 42.

22 ¶ Then tidings of these things came unto the ears of the church which was in Jerusalem: and they sent forth ᵗBarnabas, that he should go as far as Antioch.

^t ch. 9. 27.

Came unto the ears of the church; this pleonasm seems emphatical, to show with what readiness and delight the church heard the news of the conversion of so many to Christ. Of *Barnabas* we read, chap. iv. 36, who had given such an earnest of love to God, and true faith in Christ, for whose sake he sold what he had.

23 Who, when he came, and had seen the grace of God, was glad, and ᵘexhorted them all, that with purpose of heart they would cleave unto the Lord.

^u ch. 13. 43. & 14. 22.

The grace of God; which appeared in their conversion, being made manifest by their professions, and answered by their pious lives and conversations; for all which they might cry, Grace, grace. By *the grace of God,* is also to be understood the increasing of the church, and adding to it such as should be saved. *Was glad;* this is matter of joy in heaven, Luke xv. 7, and of all such as are learning their lesson, and preparing for that blissful place. *With purpose of heart;* firm and fixed resolution, that come what can come, tribulation or distress, life or death, they would keep close to the profession of the truth of Christ. This *purpose of heart* is the same with the whole heart elsewhere; which must *cleave unto the Lord;* be joined, or stick close, to God's truth and ways.

24 For he was a good man, and ˣfull of the Holy Ghost and of faith: ʸand much people was added unto the Lord.

^x ch. 6. 5.
^y ver. 21. ch. 5. 14.

Barnabas is here described to be beyond what the Jews called a righteous man, who would say to his neighbour, That which is yours is yours, and that which is mine is mine; meaning such as would do no wrong. But Barnabas, as the good man in their esteem, (such a one as the apostle speaks of, Rom. v. 7, for whom one would dare to die,) had actually made, and not called only, that which was his his poor neighbours', selling what he had to bestow upon them, as chap. iv. 37. *Much people was added unto the Lord;* his good works, accompanying his good preaching, might be a great means of the conversion of so many.

25 Then departed Barnabas to ᶻTarsus, for to seek Saul:

A. D. 43.
^z ch. 9. 30.

Saul, or Paul, being Barnabas's friend and acquaintance, whom Barnabas had brought to the knowledge of the apostles, chap. ix. 27; he goes now to seek him, that they might advise and strengthen one another in the work of the Lord.

26 And when he had found him, he brought him unto Antioch. And it came to pass, that a whole year they assembled themselves ‖ with the church, and taught much people. And the disciples were called Christians first in Antioch.

‖ Or, *in the church.*

A whole year they assembled themselves: frequency of meeting to partake of the ordinances of God, is the great reason why the gospel was so prevalent in this place. *The disciples were called Christians first in Antioch;* which will be renowned so long as the world lasts, because here the banner of Christ was first publicly set up, and men listed under him: and this by Divine authority, for the word imports no less. And that it was not a name they gave themselves, much less was it a name the enemies of Christianity gave unto the professors of it, for they called them Nazarenes, or Galileans, out of contempt. But God would have Christ's disciples to be called Christians: not only as scholars were amongst the Greeks called from their masters, (viz. Platonists, Pythagoreans, &c.,) to teach us whom we profess to learn of, and to be instructed by; but to mind us of our unction; for Christians are anointed ones, 1 John ii. 27, and are made by Christ (in a spiritual sense) *kings and priests unto God and his Father,* Rev. i. 6.

27 ¶ And in these days came ᵃprophets from Jerusalem unto Antioch.

^a ch. 2. 17. & 13. 1. & 15. 32. & 21. 9. 1 Cor. 12. 28. Eph. 4. 11.

These here meant were enabled to foretell things to come; a gift which God did furnish some of his church with on such an extraordinary occasion, Eph. iv. 11, whereby they did beforehand signify future things for the good of the church, as here.

28 And there stood up one of them named ᵇAgabus, and signified by the spirit that there should be great dearth throughout all the world: which came to pass in the days of Claudius Cæsar.

^b ch. 21. 10.

By the Spirit; by a resolution from the Spirit, as one of his gifts, and not by judicial astrology, or any other means real or pretended; for it is a prerogative of God only to foretell things to come, as Isa. xli. 22, 23. *Which came to pass in the days of Claudius Cesar:* this famine Suetonius and other heathen writers make mention of, though some place it in one year, and some in another year, of Claudius's reign. It may be there were divers famines, or one might continue divers years; but thus God, who provided for the patriarchs by means of Joseph's foreseeing of the scarcity in Egypt and elsewhere, provides for his church now also by a like prediction. God's omniscience is exerted for his church's preservation.

29 Then the disciples, every man according to his ability, determined to send ᶜrelief unto the brethren which dwelt in Judæa:

^c Rom. 15. 26. 1 Cor. 16. 1. 2 Cor. 9. 1.

Every man according to his ability; which is the measure whereby we must mete out unto others: we are to give alms of such things as we have, or according as we are able, Luke xi. 41. These *brethren,* or believers, *in Judea,* were very poor, by reason of the extraordinary malice and persecution of the Jews against them, and therefore recommended by St. Paul unto them of Achaia, (especially to the Corinthians,) and to the believers in Macedonia.

30 ᵈWhich also they did, and sent it to

^d ch. 12. 25.

the elders by the hands of Barnabas and Saul.

A. D. 44.

To the elders; to the apostles; or if they (as it is probable) were gone out of Jerusalem, to the governors or chief of the churches; for the famine being to come over all Judea, it is most probable that the other churches, besides that in Jerusalem, did partake of this bounty.

CHAP. XII

King Herod persecuteth the Christians, killeth James, and imprisoneth Peter, who, upon the prayers of the church, is delivered by an angel, 1—19. *Herod, in his pride assuming the glory due to God, is smitten by an angel, and dieth miserably,* 20—23. *After his death the word of God prospereth,* 24. *Barnabas and Saul return to Antioch,* 25.

NOW about that time Herod the king || stretched forth *his* hands to vex certain of the Church.

| Or, *began.*

There were several Herods mentioned in Scripture, being all of the family of Herod the Great, (by whose name they were called,) as Herod that killed the children in Bethlehem, called Hecolonita; another that beheaded St. John, and derided our Saviour, this Herod was surnamed Antipas: the Herod here spoken of was called Agrippa; the son, or, as others think, the nephew, of Aristobulus, and was the father of that Agrippa we read of, chap. xxv. 26, being viceroy, or king, under the Roman emperor. This Herod did not only kill some, but punished others with banishment and blows; and especially the governors of the church, knowing how much all suffer in them.

2 And he killed James [a] the brother of John with the sword.

a Matt. 4.21. & 20. 23.

Who had especially the care of the church at Jerusalem: one eminent amongst the apostles, and one of the sons of thunder, (or Boanerges,) for his zealous and earnest preaching, and therefore the more hated by Herod: so that which our Saviour had foretold him came now to pass, Matt. xx. 23, that he drank of the cup our Saviour did drink of. There was another James, who wrote the Epistle known by his name, and was called James the Less; because, as some think, he was brought to the knowledge of Christ after the other, of whom we read, Mark xv. 40.

3 And because he saw it pleased the Jews, he proceeded further to take Peter also. (Then were [b] the days of unleavened bread.)

b Ex. 12. 14, 15. & 23. 15.

All the posterity of Herod the Great, by his example, studied chiefly to please the Roman emperors, and to gratify the Jews, whether by right or wrong. *The days of unleavened bread;* or the passover, which festival solemnity lasted eight days; and God overruled the hypocrisy of Herod (for he did not out of piety observe this time) for the preservation of Peter; and Herod might fear some tumult of the people, in so great a concourse, upon Peter's death, for which he did defer it: however, the perverseness of the Jews is very remarkable, who were mad with rage against Christ and his apostles, at such times in which they pretended to serve the God of love and peace.

4 And [c] when he had apprehended him, he put *him* in prison, and delivered *him* to four quaternions of soldiers to keep him; intending after Easter to bring him forth to the people.

c John 21.18.

Four quaternions of soldiers: there were sixteen soldiers appointed to keep Peter; the Romans using four soldiers at a time to keep sentry, and the Jews dividing their nights into four watches, there were enough to relieve the other, and to set a new watch as often as was required for every night; of which four at a time, two were with the prisoner, and perhaps, for the greater security, bound with the same chain, and two did always stand at the door or gate; and this they might the rather do, out of great caution, having heard what miracles Peter did, and that he had been delivered by an angel out of prison, chap. v. 19. *After Easter;* that day in which the paschal lamb was eat, on which the Jews would put none to death, that they might not eclipse the joy of that day. *Bring him forth to the people;* to do with him what they would, leaving him to their mercy, or rather cruelty.

5 Peter therefore was kept in prison: but || prayer was made without ceasing of the Church unto God for him.

|| Or, *instant and earnest prayer was made.* 2 Cor. 1. 11. Eph. 6. 18. 1 Thess. 5. 17.

Peter therefore was kept in prison, till a fit time to offer him up as a sacrifice unto the people: so basely do wicked men stoop for their ends. *But prayer was made:* the only help or hope poor Christians had, was from prayer *(preces et lachrymæ);* there are no quaternions of soldiers can keep the passage shut that is towards heaven. *Without ceasing;* continued, long prayers, without intermission; but also fervent and earnest prayers, ὁλοψυχῶς, with all the might of their souls; remembering the apostle now in bonds, as bound with him, Heb. xiii. 3.

6 And when Herod would have brought him forth, the same night Peter was sleeping between two soldiers, bound with two chains: and the keepers before the door kept the prison.

Brought him forth, to be put to death. *The same night:* this is a night to be remembered, as that in which God delivered his Israel out of Egypt: when both were come to the utmost extremity, and at the pit's brink, then so God does his marvellous work of deliverance, that it ought to be had in remembrance, Psal. cv. 5. *Peter was sleeping:* innocency hath this advantage, and a good conscience acquiesces in the providence of God; it hath God to its friend; and if he be for us, who can be against us? *Bound with two chains:* see ver. 4: to which may be added, that with one chain St. Peter's right hand was bound to the soldier's left; with the other chain his left hand to the other soldier's right; for so was their manner for their greater security, that they might not let the prisoner escape: thus persecutors are skilful to destroy; but no device can avail against any whom God will save.

7 And, behold, [d] the angel of the Lord came upon *him*, and a light shined in the prison: and he smote Peter on the side, and raised him up, saying, Arise up quickly. And his chains fell off from *his* hands.

d ch. 5. 19.

The angel of the Lord, whose office it is to minister for the heirs of salvation, Heb. i. 14, and who willingly fulfil this will of the Lord. *Came upon him,* as Luke ii. 9, suddenly and unexpectedly. *A light shined in the prison;* whether this light was from the bright body the angel assumed, or from some other cause, we are not told, and therefore it is not necessary for us to know; but it was a light only to Peter, but darkness to his keepers; as the pillar of fire enlightened only the Israelites; which made them both the more strange and miraculous. The angel *smote Peter* (as one jogs, or gently strikes another) to awaken him; thus God was waking, though Peter slept; and by his providence watches over all his people for their preservation. *His chains fell off from his hands;* chains could not hold any whom God will have free; every thing loses its force when God suspends or withdraws his concurrence.

8 And the angel said unto him, Gird thyself, and bind on thy sandals. And so he did. And he saith unto him, Cast thy garment about thee, and follow me.

Gird thyself; the custom being to wear long garments, they were not so fit to go about any business until they had girt their garments to them; hence Jeremiah is commanded to get a girdle about him, Jer. xiii. 1, when he was to be sent on God's errand. The *sandals* were little other than sole-leathers, bound or fastened with thongs. *Thy garment;* the uppermost vest, answerable to a cloak amongst us. God furnishes his people thus with necessaries, and he will have them use them, so far as they are able to serve them, even then when he is working of miracles for their deliverances.

9 And he went out, and followed him; and ᵉwist not that it was true which was done by the angel; but thought ᶠhe saw a vision.

e Ps. 126. 1.
f ch. 10. 3. 17. & 11. 5.

The greatness and suddenness of the deliverance was such, as it amazed him, it seemed incredible unto him: not that he questioned God's power or goodness; but knowing that he was to suffer for Christ's name's sake, he might the rather not look for such a deliverance, and when it came, be as one that dreams, as Psal. cxxvi. 1: God therefore bringing his people to such extremities, that his salvation might be the more astonishing.

10 When they were past the first and the second ward, they came unto the iron gate that leadeth unto the city; ᵍwhich opened to them of his own accord: and they went out, and passed on through one street; and forthwith the angel departed from him.

g ch. 16. 26.

The first and the second ward; guard or sentinels. *The iron gate that leadeth unto the city;* the outermost gate that led out of the prison into the city, not that the prison itself was out of the city. *Which opened to them of his own accord:* God worketh a series of miracles in their fit place and time; he could have done them all together, and have opened his iron gate beforehand, when he conducted Peter through the first, then through the second watch; but it is good for Peter, and us, to be convinced that we stand every moment in need of God's conduct and deliverance.

11 And when Peter was come to himself, he said, Now I know of a surety, that ʰthe Lord hath sent his angel, and ⁱhath delivered me out of the hand of Herod, and *from* all the expectation of the people of the Jews.

h Ps. 34. 7. Dan. 3. 28. & 6. 22. Heb. 1. 14.
i Job 5. 19. Ps. 33. 18, 19. & 34. 22. & 41. 2. & 97. 10. 2 Cor. 1. 10. 2 Pet. 2. 9.

When Peter was come to himself, out of that amazement which so many wonderful things had wrought in him, that he could compose himself to reflect upon what he had heard and seen, he knew his deliverance was real and effectual. *Delivered me;* from Herod, who had resolved to have killed him, as he had done James, ver. 2; and from the people's expectation, who had heard the report of Herod's resolution, and longed for the fulfilling of it.

12 And when he had considered *the thing,* ᵏhe came to the house of Mary the mother of ˡJohn, whose surname was Mark; where many were gathered together ᵐpraying.

k ch. 4. 23.
l ch. 15. 37.
m ver. 5.

Peter, being delivered, meditates upon the greatness of the danger that he had been in, and the goodness of God that had delivered him, and this whilst walking in the street, and going along: no place can exclude good thoughts and holy meditations. *The mother of John;* the mother is here described by the son, as the more known person; here the parent gains reputation, and to be remembered in this Scripture, for her son's sake. Thus a wise son made a glad mother, as Prov. x. 1. *Mark;* some think this was he that wrote the Gospel called by his name. *Many were gathered together:* in this time of persecution the Christians met secretly, and in small numbers, as they could; these here mentioned are thought to be private Christians, because it appears by the 17th verse, that James, &c. were not there.

13 And as Peter knocked at the door of the gate, a damsel came ‖ to hearken, named Rhoda.

‖ Or, *to ask who was there.*

The door of the gate; this was the outermost door to the porch, or court before the house. *A damsel came to hearken;* being in great fear of a surprisal, they ordered one to observe, and give an answer unto any that should come to the house; which was the more heedfully done, because it was at an unseasonable time of the night; yet these holy men broke their rest, and exposed themselves to many fears and dangers, rather than not to assemble to serve God, when they could not serve him otherwise.

14 And when she knew Peter's voice, she opened not the gate for gladness, but ran in, and told how Peter stood before the gate.

She opened not the gate for gladness; as one from herself, not knowing what to do for gladness. Great and sudden passions have caused strange ecstasies, and death itself sometimes; the spirits in grief flowing too fast unto the heart to fortify it, and in joy leaving the heart as fast, to meet the object that causeth it.

15 And they said unto her, Thou art mad. But she constantly affirmed that it was even so. Then said they, ⁿIt is his angel.

n Gen. 48. 16. Matt. 18. 10.

Thou art mad; thou speakest thou knowest not what; thinking her, out of fear, to have been discomposed in her mind. *It is his angel:* some have thought, that by Peter's angel no other was meant than some messenger from Peter, which they might expect from him in such a case as he was in; now though ἄγγελος (the word here) signifies a messenger or an angel, indifferently, yet how could Rhoda then know it to have been Peter's voice? a messenger's voice being no more like his that sent him than another man's. They did probably mean some angel that had assumed Peter's shape, and imitated his voice: and the Jews having had a constant opinion, that at least every good man hath a guardian angel which God appoints to him for a means of his preservation, might be apt to imagine that this was that angel whose charge St. Peter was, Matt. xviii. 10. Though that angel spoken of, Gen. xlviii. 16, most probably was the angel of the new covenant, and not a created angel, being Jacob blesseth in his name; yet the opinion of tutelar angels, though not certain or needful, is to this day thought probable.

16 But Peter continued knocking: and when they had opened *the door,* and saw him, they were astonished.

Peter continued knocking; Peter might be unwilling to have his entrance into the house deferred, 1. Out of fear of being taken again, and his life concerned upon it. 2. Out of an earnest desire to see the brethren, whom he might hope to meet with there. 3. Out of zeal to declare the mercy of God towards him; this fire was kindled in him, and he sought vent for it.

17 But he, ᵒbeckoning unto them with the hand to hold their peace, declared unto them how the Lord had brought him out of the prison. And he said, Go shew these things unto James, and to the brethren. And he departed, and went into another place.

o ch. 13. 16. & 19. 33. & 21. 40.

Beckoning; it was usual by the motion of the hand both to desire silence and to crave audience. *How the Lord had brought him out;* Peter gives God the glory, though an angel had been the means of his delivery. *James;* this James was the son of Alpheus, Matt. x. 3; Mark iii. 18, and succeeded the other James, (the brother of John, of whom, ver. 2,) in governing the church at Jerusalem. *Went into another place;* Peter could not but know he should be sought after, and therefore durst not abide in one place, lest he should ruin himself, and endanger his friends that should harbour him. Thus the great apostle, as David formerly, was hunted, *as one hunteth a partridge in the mountains,* 1 Sam. xxvi. 20.

18 Now as soon as it was day, there was no small stir among the soldiers, what was become of Peter.

The soldiers, who were bound with Peter in the same chains, could not but miss him as soon as they did awake, and with admiration find the chains still holding them, though loosened from Peter. What strange imaginations they might have, is not to be expressed, though some guess at it.

19 And when Herod had sought for him, and found him not, he examined the keepers, and commanded that *they* should be put to death. And

THE ACTS XII, XIII

he went down from Judæa to Cæsarea, and *there* abode.

He examined the keepers; that is, judicially; proceeding against them for the escape of St. Peter. *Commanded that they should be put to death;* they were sentenced to be led away, and it is most probably thought, unto the place of execution. The instruments in persecution God many times meets with in this world, and sometimes by the persecutors themselves.

20 ¶ And Herod ‖ was highly displeased with them of Tyre and Sidon: but they came with one accord to him, and, having made Blastus † the king's chamberlain their friend, desired peace; because ᵖtheir country was nourished by the king's *country*.

‖ Or, *bare an hostile mind, intending war.*
† Gr. *that was over the king's bed-chamber.*
p 1 Kings 5. 9, 11.
Ezek. 27. 17.

Tyre and Sidon; these were two coast towns in Phœnicia, famous, especially the former, for their great trading; and being rich, might be insolent, or possibly might tempt Herod to a war against them, whose conquest would pay the charge of it. *The king's chamberlain,* or chief of his bed-chamber. *Desired peace,* or begged pardon; there being no war yet begun. *Their country was nourished by the king's country;* these cities lying upon the sea, had little land belonging to them, and of old were forced to have their provision from other places, especially from Judæa; thus Solomon gave Hiram, king of Tyre, twenty thousand measures of wheat for his household, and twenty measures of pure oil yearly, 1 Kings v. 9, 11; and long after that, they of Judah and Israel are said to have traded with their wheat in Tyre, Ezek. xxvii. 17.

21 And upon a set day Herod, arrayed in royal apparel, sat upon his throne, and made an oration unto them.

Upon a set day; this was (says Josephus, cap. 19. lib. 7) the second day of the sports or games, which Herod had instituted in honour of the emperor Claudius; or, it may be, such a day as Herod had appointed to determine the difference betwixt him and the Tyrians. *Royal apparel;* such, saith Josephus, as were made of silver, woven with extraordinary art, and did reflect strangely the beams of the sun shining upon it. *Sat upon his throne;* an elevated place, from whence he might the better be seen and heard.

22 And the people gave a shout, *saying, It is* the voice of a god, and not of a man.

These impious flatterers destroy whom they exalt; for God will pull down his rivals.

23 And immediately the angel of the Lord ᵠsmote him, because ʳhe gave not God the glory: and he was eaten of worms, and gave up the ghost.

q 1 Sam. 25. 38. 2 Sam. 24. 17.
r Ps. 115. 1.

An angel had delivered Peter, and here an angel destroys Herod: all that heavenly host fulfil God's will for the deliverance of his church, and the destruction of his enemies. *He gave not God the glory;* priding himself in the acclamation the people had made, and not attributing his eloquence and glory to God, as the giver of them; or rather, not repressing or punishing their blasphemy; whereas Peter durst not accept of undue honour from Cornelius, chap. x. 26, nor the angel from St. John, Rev. xix. 10; xxii. 9. *He was eaten of worms;* either breeding in his bowels, or in his flesh, after a more unusual manner; as it is recorded of Herod the Great, that he was eaten up of lice. No creature so little or contemptible, but it can execute God's judgments on whom he please.

24 ¶ But ˢthe word of God grew and multiplied.

s Is. 55. 11. ch. 6. 7. & 19. 20. Col. 1. 6.

Grew; the word of God is compared here to seed, as in our Saviour's parable, Matt. xiii. 19. *Multiplied;* the number of believers multiplied through the word, which was sown, as seed is scattered abroad. So true it is, that persecutors, by their pulling down of the church, do but build it up.

25 And Barnabas and Saul returned from Jerusalem, when they had fulfilled *their* ‖ ministry, and ᵗ took with them ᵘ John, whose surname was Mark.

‖ Or, *charge.* ch. 11. 29, 30.
t ch. 13. 5, 13. & 15. 37.
u ver. 12.

From Jerusalem; they returned unto Antioch, from whence they were sent, chap. xi. 26, 30, to carry the benevolence of the church of Antioch to that of Judea. *Their ministry;* this was the ministry or service they were appointed to do. *John;* of whom before, ver. 12.

CHAP. XIII

Barnabas and Saul, being set apart with fasting and prayer, are sent forth by the Holy Ghost to the work of their calling, 1—5. *At Paphos, Elymas the sorcerer, opposing the Gospel, is smitten with blindness, and the deputy Sergius Paulus converted to the faith,* 6—12. *Paul and his company come to Antioch in Pisidia: Paul preacheth Christ, and the necessity of faith in him unto justification,* 13—41. *The Gentiles desire to hear the word again: many are converted,* 42, 43. *The envious Jews gainsay and blaspheme: the apostles profess to turn to the Gentiles, of whom many believe,* 44—49. *The Jews raise a persecution, and expel Paul and Barnabas, who go to Iconium,* 50—52.

NOW there were ᵃin the church that was at Antioch certain prophets and teachers; as ᵇBarnabas, and Simeon that was called Niger, and ᶜLucius of Cyrene, and Manaen, ‖ which had been brought up with Herod the tetrarch, and Saul.

A. D. 45.
a ch. 11. 27. & 14. 26. & 15. 35.
b ch. 11. 22, —26.
c Rom. 16. 21.
‖ Or, *Herod's foster-brother.*

The church that was at Antioch; the true church, which hath a being, and whose Builder and Maker is God. Other churches (as that of the circumcision) are no churches or congregations of the faithful. *Prophets and teachers;* these two offices might be in the same person, as he that had the gift of prophecy, and could foretell things to come, might be a teacher to instruct the people; but yet they were frequently appertaining to several persons, one excelling in one gift, another in another. *Simeon that was called Niger;* this Simeon is thus distinguished from Simon Peter, and from Simon the Canaanite, this name of *Niger* being given him by the Romans. *Lucius;* this hath been thought the name of Luke, it being more after the Latin termination; and that it might be he that wrote the Gospel called by his name, and this book of the Acts. However, we meet with this name, Rom. xvi. 21; and St. Paul sends salutation unto him that was so called. *Of Cyrene;* born at a place so called, or brought up in the synagogue of the Cyrenians; of which, chap. vi. 9. Either this *Manaen* was Herod's foster-brother. or had the same tutors and instructors with him, their education being together. This *Herod* was Herod Antipas, who set at nought our Saviour, and killed the Baptist. And yet Manaen, as another Moses, kept his integrity in that Pharaoh's court; and, as Moses, he choose rather *to suffer affliction with the people of God, than to enjoy the pleasures of sin for a season,* Heb. xi. 25. Thus there was an Obadiah in Ahab's house, 1 Kings xviii. 3, and divers believe in Nero's family, Phil. iv. 22.

2 As they ministered to the Lord, and fasted, the Holy Ghost said, ᵈSeparate me Barnabas and Saul for the work ᵉwhereunto I have called them.

d Num. 8. 14. ch. 9. 15. & 22. 21. Rom. 1. 1. Gal. 1. 15. & 2. 9.
e Matt. 9. 38 ch. 14. 26.
Rom. 10. 15. Eph. 3. 7, 8. 1 Tim. 2. 7. 2 Tim. 1. 11. Heb. 5. 4.

Ministered; the word importeth the exercise of any public office, sacred or civil. But in the former verse mention being made of prophets and teachers, these words are in sense too conjoined with them; and inform us, that they were preaching to and instructing of the people, (for there is no ministry or service which God likes better than to convert and save souls,) and, that all might be more effectual, as being done with greater earnestness and intention of mind, whilst they fasted. *The Holy Ghost said;* by some inward instinct in those prophets before spoken of, who had warrant to declare it as from him. *Separate me Barnabas and Saul;* these two were to be separated: as the first-born under the law, Exod. xiii. 12, and after them, or in their stead, the Levites, Numb. iii. 12; so were Paul and Barnabas in especial manner separated for the calling in of the Gentiles, that great ministry or service which God had for them to do.

3 And ᶠwhen they had fasted and pray- f ch. 6. 6.

ed, and laid *their* hands on them, they sent *them* away.

When they had fasted and prayed; a good preparation to enter into any business with, whereby they acknowledged that all success must come from God. Our blessed Saviour himself would not enter upon his ministry till he had fasted forty days, Matt. iv. ver. 2, compared with ver. 17. *Laid their hands on them;* Barnabas and Saul being called to be apostles already, this laying on of their hands upon them signifies, first, Their being set apart to this particular employment they were now to be sent about. Secondly, The approbation of the church to that heavenly call they had. Thirdly, Their praying for God's blessing upon them, and success upon the work they went for.

4 ¶ So they, being sent forth by the Holy Ghost, departed unto Seleucia; and g ch. 4. 36. from thence they sailed to g Cyprus.

Seleucia; a sea town of Cilicia, nigh unto Antioch, and over against Cyprus, built by Seleucus, and was a town of some note, but mentioned here only as in their passage to Cyprus.

5 And when they were at Salamis, h ver. 46. h they preached the word of God in the synagogues of the Jews: and they had i ch. 12. 25. & 15. 37. also i John to *their* minister.

Salamis; the chief city of Cyprus, now called Famagusta, situate on the east side of the island, over against Syria. *They preached,* here and elsewhere, *in the synagogues,* either because they found no other such convenient places to preach in; (these being large structures, and many resorting to them;) or rather, because though they were sent unto the Gentiles, yet it was not till after the Jews should have refused the gospel, as may be seen throughout all this book, and in the conclusion of it, chap. xxviii. 28. *They had also John to their minister:* as chap. xii. 25.

6 And when they had gone through k ch. 8. 9. the isle unto Paphos, they found k a certain sorcerer, a false prophet, a Jew, whose name *was* Bar-jesus:

Unto Paphos; this city was on the west end of Cyprus, so that going from Salamis they went through the island: this place was famous for the worshipping of Venus. *A certain sorcerer;* there were many magicians about this time amongst the Jews, who by their false miracles endeavoured to bring the real miracles of our Saviour into contempt. As the magicians and sorcerers of Egypt, by their enchantments, for a while did seem to do such wonders as Moses had wrought by the finger of God, Exod. vii. 11.

7 Which was with the deputy of the country, Sergius Paulus, a prudent man; who called for Barnabas and Saul, and desired to hear the word of God.

The deputy of the country; whether he was pro-consul or proprietor, it is in effect the same; for he it was that governed the land. *Desired to hear the word of God;* this desire was extraordinary, and wrought by God, in order to the fitting him for the further mercy of his conversion and salvation. Where such a desire is, it shall be granted: *Ask, and it shall be given you,* Luke xi. 9.

i Ex. 7. 11. 8 But l Elymas the sorcerer (for so is 2 Tim. 3. 8. his name by interpretation) withstood them, seeking to turn away the deputy from the faith.

Elymas; this is another name of him that was called Bar-jesus, which was not unusual, as *Simon Bar-jona,* Matt. xvi. 17. This *Elymas* may be taken appellatively, and signifies the magician or *sorcerer;* but being it was a proper name unto others we read of, it may be so here.

9 Then Saul, (who also *is called* Paul,) m ch. 4. 8. m filled with the Holy Ghost, set his eyes on him,

It is observable, that St. Luke never before called this great apostle by the name of Paul, and henceforth never calls him by the name of Saul. Though there be no great difference in these names, *Saul* might be more acceptable to the Jews, amongst whom hitherto he had conversed; and *Paul* a more pleasing name unto the Gentiles, unto whom he was now sent, and with whom for the future he should most converse. He was called *Saul* as he was a Jew born, a Hebrew of the Hebrews; and *Paul,* as he was a denizen of Rome; the Romans having that name in good account in several of their chief families. *Filled with the Holy Ghost;* zeal for God's glory, and faith and power to work the ensuing miracle.

10 And said, O full of all subtilty and all mischief, n *thou* child of the devil, n Mat. 13. 38. John 8. 44. *thou* enemy of all righteousness, wilt 1 John 3. 8. thou not cease to pervert the right ways of the Lord?

Mischief; ῥᾳδιουργία signifies a facility or readiness in doing mischief, and that such who are given to sorcery are easily drawn to commit any kind of sin whatsoever. *Thou child of the devil;* because he did his work who is the destroyer, in hindering what he could the salvation of Sergius Paulus and his family. *To pervert the right ways of the Lord;* to make the way of God crooked, which is straight; and rugged, when indeed it is smooth: that is, to lay what rubs he could to keep any from coming unto, or continuing in, the ways of God.

11 And now, behold, o the hand of the o Ex. 9. 3. 1 Sam. 5. 6. Lord *is* upon thee, and thou shalt be blind, not seeing the sun for a season. And immediately there fell on him a mist and a darkness; and he went about seeking some to lead him by the hand.

The hand of the Lord is put for any powerful action of God, whether in mercy or judgment: here it is put for the Divine power wherewith God strikes his enemies. God did in judgment remember mercy, inflicting this blindness only *for a season,* that it might be rather a medicine than a punishment.

12 Then the deputy, when he saw what was done, believed, being astonished at the doctrine of the Lord.

The gospel which Paul preached; finding in it (though a wise man) depths beyond his fathoming; and all accompanied with such a power in doing of miracles, and changing of hearts and lives, as might well amaze so prudent and considering a man.

13 Now when Paul and his company loosed from Paphos, they came to Perga in Pamphylia: and p John departing from p ch. 15. 38. them returned to Jerusalem.

Perga, a city *in Pamphylia:* not that there were any other cities of that name; but because this region was more commonly known, it being a country in the Lesser Asia, bordering on Cilicia. The departure of John (of whom before, ver. 5, and chap. xii. 25) was blameworthy, as chap. xv. 38. Some think he shunned that labour and suffering which he saw attended the gospel; others suppose that he returned to Jerusalem out of too fond an affection for his mother, who lived there; and it may be that he, retaining a great aversion from the Gentiles, might abhor to go amongst them: however, *let him that standeth take heed lest he fall.*

14 ¶ But when they departed from Perga, they came to Antioch in Pisidia, and q went into the synagogue on the q ch. 16. 13 & 17. 2. sabbath day, and sat down. & 18. 4.

Antioch in Pisidia; so called to distinguish it from the other Antioch, mentioned in the 1st verse, which was a city in Syria, as this in Pisidia, next to, or part of, Pamphylia. *Went into the synagogue on the sabbath day;* either to join with the Jews in their worship, which was not then unlawful; or to get an opportunity more publicly to preach the gospel unto them: they were no sooner come thither, but they mind that great business they went about.

15 And r after the reading of the Law r Luke 4. 16. ver. 27. and the Prophets the rulers of the syna-

THE ACTS XIII

gogue sent unto them, saying, *Ye* men *and* brethren, if ye have ªany word of exhortation for the people, say on.

s Heb. 13.22.

The reading of the law was commanded by Moses; and they say that Ezra commanded the reading of *the prophets* also in their synagogues, which was used, as we may see in the 27th verse; and so divided into several sections, that once a year they might be all read over. *The rulers of the synagogue;* they were such as had the oversight of this service of God in their synagogues, that it might be performed according to the prescription. *Men and brethren;* a usual compellation which the Jews gave one another, owning them to serve the same God, and professing a suitable respect for them. *If ye have any word of exhortation for the people, say on;* after the reading before spoken of, there followed a sermon, or exhortation; which the apostles are desired to make, the rulers of the synagogue, as it is supposed, having had some previous knowledge of them.

t ch. 12. 17.
u ver. 26, 42, 43.
ch. 10. 35.

16 Then Paul stood up, and ᵗbeckoning with *his* hand said, Men of Israel, and ᵘye that fear God, give audience.

Beckoning with his hand, to procure silence and attention, as chap. xii. 17. *And ye that fear God;* besides the native Jews, the proselytes, and such out of all nations who left the idolatry of the Gentiles, and served the only true God, met together in the worship of God; these were the σεβόμενοι, spoken of chap. xvii. 4. It shows also what they are to do that would hear the word of the Lord with profit; viz. to attend unto it in the fear of his name.

17 The God of this people of Israel

x Deut. 7. 6, 7.
y Ex. 1. 1.
Ps. 1[0]5, 23, 24, ch. 7. 17.
z Ex. 6. 6.
& 13. 14, 16.

ˣchose our fathers, and exalted the people ʸwhen they dwelt as strangers in the land of Egypt, ᶻand with an high arm brought he them out of it.

The God of this people of Israel; God was the God of Israel after a peculiar manner. *Chose our fathers;* having chosen them before all nations, to make him known unto them, to be served and worshipped by them. *And exalted the people;* and God exalted them in the time of Joseph, and whilst the memory of that great preservation wrought by his means did continue, till another king arose that knew not Joseph. *An high arm;* the many miracles done by the power of God towards the Israelites' deliverance out of Egypt. By which the apostle would have them remember, that they owed all which they challenged from their progenitors to the grace and blessing of God only, and that God may do with his own as he please.

a Ex. 16. 35.
Num. 14. 33, 34.
Ps. 95. 9, 10.
ch. 7. 36.
† Gr.

18 And ªabout the time of forty years †suffered he their manners in the wilderness.

ἐτροποφόρησεν, perhaps for ἐτροφοφόρησεν, *bore,* or, *fed them, as a nurse beareth*, or, *feedeth her child*, Deut. 1. 31. 2 Mac. 7. 27. according to the LXX. and so Chrysostom.

This is recorded, Psal. xcv. 10, and remembered by the apostle, Heb. iii. 8, 9, and to be admired through all ages, that God should be so patient, or a people could be so perverse. Some instead of ἐτροποφόρησεν, read ἐτροφοφόρησεν, there being but one letter difference, (and such as are usually changed into one another,) and then it speaks God's providing for this people all that while, and carrying them as in his bosom, as a nurse bears the sucking child, Numb. xi. 12; Deut. i. 31; or as an eagle beareth her young ones on her wings, Deut. xxxii. 11, 12. But it seems God did not bear with their fathers, but destroyed them in the wilderness, 1 Cor. x. 5. First, God bare long with those that perished. Secondly, The succeeding generation took not that warning which did become them, but followed their fathers' steps; and whilst one generation was wearing away, and another coming, this space of forty years was spent, through the abundant compassion of God towards them, who did not consume them, as they tempted him to do, in a moment.

b Deut. 7. 1.
c Josh. 14.
1, 2. Ps. 78.
55.

19 And when ᵇhe had destroyed seven nations in the land of Chanaan, ᶜhe divided their land to them by lot.

These *seven nations* are mentioned, Josh. iii. 10. He *divided their land to them by lot;* the lot being disposed only as God would, Prov. xvi. 33. And it was but reasonable that God, having miraculously got this land, (for the Israelites did rather go to take possession of it than to fight for it,) and assumed a special right unto it, that he should divide it to whom he pleased, and in what proportions he thought good.

20 And after that ᵈhe gave *unto them* judges about the space of four hundred and fifty years, ᵉuntil Samuel the prophet.

d Judg. 2. 16.
e 1 Sam. 3. 20.

These *judges* were persons deputed by God to govern and deliver that people; their commission was attested usually by some extraordinary thing done by them, and their power (as being mediately from God) was absolute. The computation of years here mentioned hath been very much controverted. That which hath the greatest probability with it, is, either, first, to have recourse to the 17th verse, and begin this era there, with God's choosing of their fathers; and ending it at the time of the decision of the land by lot, as ver. 19; for from the birth of Isaac, to this distribution of the land, are reckoned four hundred and forty-seven years; which may well be said here, *about four hundred and fifty years:* but then the sense is, *after that* such things mentioned in the 17th, 18th, and 19th verses were done; which were in the compass of four hundred and fifty years, God then gave them judges. Or, as others do refer these words to what follows, and begin the era or computation from the going of the children of Israel out of Egypt, and ending it at the expulsion of the Jebusites out of Jerusalem, which may make up this account. But then this passage of St. Paul is not intended to show how long the judges ruled, but when it was, or about what time that they ruled; as also to show what a long time it took up to gain that people a quiet possession of that promised inheritance, their sins still keeping good things from them.

21 ᶠAnd afterward they desired a king: and God gave unto them Saul the son of Cis, a man of the tribe of Benjamin, by the space of forty years.

f 1 Sam. 8. 5. & 10. 1.

Their great sin in desiring a king was, because by that desire they rejected God, who had at that very time a prophet (Samuel) by whom he governed them, 1 Sam. viii. 7; x. 19. They had been under a theocracy ever since they came out of Egypt, their laws and their governors being appointed by God; had their condition been as that of other nations, their desire had not been a provocation. These words, *by the space of forty years*, are to be joined with the foregoing verse, and the other foregoing words in the verse read with a parenthesis: and thus they show how long Samuel the prophet (as he is here called) exercised his prophetical office, which was the space here mentioned, partly before Saul was anointed king, and in part afterward; in which, as another Moses, he cared for, and went in and out before, the people of God, the like space of forty years. This computation of St. Paul might also agree more with the Septuagint, and be according to the then current account, which (not being of more consequence) St. Paul would not controvert at this time, having greater matters to speak of unto them.

22 And ᵍwhen he had removed him, ʰhe raised up unto them David to be their king; to whom also he gave testimony, and said, ⁱI have found David the *son of* Jesse, ᵏa man after mine own heart, which shall fulfil all my will.

g 1 Sam. 15. 23, 26, 28.
h 1 Sam. 16. 1.
Hos. 13. 11.
h 1 Sam. 16. 13. 2 Sam. 2. 4. & 5. 3.
i Ps. 89. 20.
k 1 Sam. 13. 14. ch. 7. 46.

He had removed him; God had taken Saul away by death; for he would not suffer David to hasten it. *After mine own heart;* favoured or beloved by me, and obedient to me; *my servant,* as God speaks of him, Psal. lxxxix. 20. *Which shall fulfil all my will;* and here, that he should fulfil all God's will, to wit, in governing his people; for he hath a testimonial upon record in God's word, Psal. lxxviii. 72. He that is according to God's heart, fulfils all the will of God, and does nothing by partiality; but if it be God's will either for him to do or to suffer any thing, he is ready to set his fiat to it; as he daily prays (understandingly) that the will of the Lord may be done.

23 ¹Of this man's seed hath God according ᵐ to *his* promise raised unto Israel ⁿ a Saviour, Jesus :

Christ was the Son of David, and so frequently called, Matt. i. 1 ; Luke xviii. 38, 39, with reference unto the promise made, Isa. xi. 1, spoken of, chap. ii. 30 ; Rom. i. 3. *Raised unto Israel a Saviour ;* because he lived amongst the Jews, and salvation was first offered unto them by him, as ver. 46. *Jesus ;* our Saviour's name is added to show that he truly was according to his name, and what he was said to be, as Matt. i. 21.

24 ° When John had first preached before his coming the baptism of repentance to all the people of Israel.

John the Baptist did not speak of Christ's coming, as the other apostles had done, as of a thing a great way off, or at a distance of time ; but he spake of it as of a present matter, before his and their faces, and in their view ; *Behold the Lamb of God!* John i. 29, 36. *The baptism of repentance ;* so it is called, Matt. iii. 2, 8 ; Mark i. 4 ; Luke iii. 3 ; repentance being a due qualification for such as hope to receive the mercies of God in Christ unto life eternal.

25 And as John fulfilled his course, he said, ᵖ Whom think ye that I am? I am not *he*. But, behold, there cometh one after me, whose shoes of *his* feet I am not worthy to loose.

Fulfilled his course ; the course of his ministry, or of his life : in respect of either, he ran as one in a race. *I am not he ;* that is, the Messias, which they were in such expectation of, and so inquisitive about. *There cometh one after me ;* Christ began his life (as to the flesh) after John ; and he began his ministry after him, and in that respect may be said to come after him. *Whose shoes of his feet I am not worthy to loose ;* a proverbial expression, whereby the meanest office is implied, which the disciples or servants could do for their masters, Matt. iii. 11. The sense of these words we have, John i. 20, 27.

26 Men *and* brethren, children of the stock of Abraham, and whosoever among you feareth God, ᑫ to you is the word of this salvation sent.

Men and brethren ; he speaks to the Jews according as the manner was amongst them ; to the Jews he became as a Jew. *Whosoever among you feareth God ;* some think the devout Pisidians, or men of that country, are here meant ; but rather it may insinuate the apostle's hope concerning these Jews, that they were such as feared God, which hope they ought the rather to have carefully answered. *The word of this salvation* : 1. Christ, who is the incarnate Word, or the Word made flesh, John i. 14 ; or the Gospel, which is glad tidings of salvation ; as if the apostle had minded them, that it was not any business which belonged unto others alone, which he was speaking about : but of such things as pertained unto their salvation ; and such a salvation *(this salvation)*; as never greater was or ever will be published, this is certain, that we are concerned in it for ourselves, if we accept or neglect this salvation, it is for ourselves. Oh that in this respect self-interest were more prevalent with us !

27 For they that dwell at Jerusalem, and their rulers, ʳ because they knew him not, nor yet the voices of the prophets ˢ which are read every sabbath day, ᵗ they have fulfilled *them* in condemning *him*.

They ; the common people, and *their rulers ;* great council, both had a hand in our Saviour's death. But if so great a fault was capable of any alleviation, the apostle gladly mentions it, that it was done out of ignorance ; they knew neither Christ the Word, nor the word (of the Gospel) concerning Christ, though, that they may be made sensible that this their ignorance was not invincible, he minds them that it was their sin, having had means whereby they might have come unto the knowledge of Christ. *Fulfilled them :* see chap. iv. 28 ; Luke xxiv. 25, 26.

28 ᵘ And though they found no cause of death *in him*, ˣ yet desired they Pilate that he should be slain.

Though they found no cause of death in him ; he was a Lamb without blemish ; neither had he offended the rabble that was so slanderous against him, unless by such vast goodness and kindness towards them he branded them for ingratitude. *Yet desired they Pilate that he should be slain*, Matt. xxvii. 22. The Jews did condemn him, but they could not put him to death, the Romans, under whom they were subject, having reserved the power of life and death wholly unto themselves ; and therefore they desired Pilate to confirm their sentence, and to cause it to be executed.

29 ʸ And when they had fulfilled all that was written of him, ᶻ they took *him* down from the tree, and laid *him* in a sepulchre.

All that was written of him ; as the giving him vinegar to drink, piercing his side, &c., Psal. lxix. 21 ; John xix. 28—30. *From the tree :* see chap. v. 30. *They laid him in a sepulchre ;* Joseph of Arimathea, and Nicodemus, Matt. xxvii. 60 ; John xix. 39.

30 ᵃ But God raised him from the dead :

Lest they should be offended at our Saviour's dying so shameful and cursed a death, and to take away the scandal of the cross, he shows, that his resurrection was as glorious as his death could be ignominious, being by it *declared to be the Son of God with power*, Rom. i. 4.

31 And ᵇ he was seen many days of them which came up with him ᶜ from Galilee to Jerusalem, ᵈ who are his witnesses unto the people.

Seen many days ; forty days betwixt his resurrection and ascension, chap. i. 3. Christ was seen, not only by the apostles, but of the Galilean women which came up with him unto Jerusalem, Matt. xxviii. 1, and by above five hundred at once, 1 Cor. xv. 6 ; so plentifully would God have this great article of our faith and object of our hope to be confirmed unto us.

32 And we declare unto you glad tidings, how that ᵉ the promise which was made unto the fathers,

Glad tidings ; or the gospel, which is nothing else but the glad tidings of our salvation from sin and hell. *The promise which was made unto the fathers ;* this promise was frequently made and renewed to their ancestors, and typified by many deliverances, especially from Egypt and Babylon.

33 God hath fulfilled the same unto us their children, in that he hath raised up Jesus again ; as it is also written in the second psalm, ᶠ Thou art my Son, this day have I begotten thee.

Raised up Jesus again ; some refer these words to the incarnation, others to the resurrection, of our Saviour : our translators lay the stress upon the preposition, with which the verb is compounded, and by adding *again*, intend it to be understood of the resurrection ; and there is ground for it in the context ; for the resurrection of Christ is that which in the 30th verse is propounded by St. Paul as his theme or argument to preach upon. *Thou art my Son ;* these words quoted, though they do not seem to be a proof of Christ's resurrection at the first view, yet if we weigh them well, they answer St. Paul's purpose : *Thou art my Son*, Psal. ii. 7, is ushered in with, *I have made thee king*, ver. 6, and followed with, *I will give thee the heathen for thine inheritance ;* which was in an especial manner to be fulfilled after the resurrection, as our Saviour manifests, Matt. xxviii. 18, 19. *This day have I begotten thee ;* not as if Christ at his resurrection began to be the Son of God ; but then he was manifested to be so, Rom. i. 4 ; which before, whilst he was in a suffering condition, was not so apparent. Some of the ancients have understood these words, of the eternal generation of the Son of God; eternity being an everlasting point, and one and the same day for ever.

34 And as concerning that he raised him up from the dead, *now* no more to return to corruption, he said on this wise, ᵍ I will give you the sure † mercies of David.

g Is. 55. 3.
† Gr. *τὰ ὅσια, holy,* or, *just things;* which word the LXX. both in the place of Is. 55. 3. and in many others, use for that which is in the Hebrew, *mercies.*

The former verse was not intended so much by St. Paul for a proof of the resurrection, as it was to show how faithful God was in fulfilling that promise there spoken of; here the apostle's design is, to evince Christ's resurrection, and that it was agreeable to the prophesies which were concerning him. *I will give you the sure mercies of David;* these words are found, Isa. lv. 3, and *the sure mercies of David* there and here spoken of, are such mercies as were promised to David (David being to be taken positively). Now the mercies which were promised to David are all included or surmounted in this, that by this Son of David (our Lord and Saviour, frequently and truly so called) God would erect and establish an everlasting kingdom; which could not be done, unless Christ rose again, and obtained the victory over death and the grave. All the promises God hath made unto his church in any age concerning Christ, are sure and faithful, holy and just; the words have been variously rendered and changed; but no words can sufficiently express their stability and excellency.

35 Wherefore he saith also in another *psalm,* ʰ Thou shalt not suffer thine Holy One to see corruption.

h Ps. 16. 10. ch. 2. 31.

These words are quoted out of Psal. xvi. 10, 11: see chap. ii. 27.

36 For David, ‖after he had served his own generation by the will of God, ⁱ fell on sleep, and was laid unto his fathers, and saw corruption.

‖ Or, *after he had in his own age served the will of God.* ver. 22. Ps. 78. 72. i 1 Kings 2. 10. ch. 2. 29.

Some point these words otherwise, reading them thus; *David, after he had served his generation, by the will of God fell asleep:* which contains indeed a truth, viz. that God hath appointed every one's time in the world, and that the issue of life and death are his; but thus they would prove little to David's praise, for who dies otherwise but according to the determinate counsel of God? But this is remembered to David's glory, that, according to the will of God, he was a public good, and he lived and governed by the rule and square of God's word; notwithstanding which he fell asleep, and saw death, but such as did not deserve so terrible a name. *Laid unto his fathers;* buried amongst his ancestors; *and saw corruption;* and his body corrupted as theirs. Now this verse explains the former, and draws the argument home, in that it proves, that the words before mentioned could not be meant of David, but of one that he typified and represented.

37 But he, whom God raised again, saw no corruption.

God raised again; that is, on the third day, according to the gospel. *Saw no corruption;* was not under the power of death so long as to be preyed upon so far by it.

38 ¶ Be it known unto you therefore, men *and* brethren, that ᵏ through this man is preached unto you the forgiveness of sins:

k Jer. 31. 34. Dan. 9. 24. Luke 24. 47. 1 John 2. 12.

Men and brethren; the usual compellation given in these cases. *This man;* having spoken concerning Christ's resurrection, which only can be meant of him in his human nature, here, according unto that nature, the apostle calls him *man. The forgiveness of sins;* as in chap. x. 43. This *forgiveness of sins* is that which the apostle so much would recommend to all to seek after, and magnify Christ for, it being only through him; and he could not be overcome by death, who could deliver us from sin.

39 And ˡ by him all that believe are justified from all things, from which ye could not be justified by the law of Moses.

l Is. 53. 11. Rom. 3. 28. & 8. 3. Heb. 7. 19.

Are justified; it is a forensic word, opposed to condemned; all that believe in Christ with the heart, by his merit and mediation shall be absolved, and shall not come into condemnation: and thus this agrees with the former words, and shows us whence remission of sins is to be had. If any will take this word as signifying also to be purged from sin; yet it is evident, that the law can bring neither of these benefits unto us. The law declares what is sin, and what the curse is that is due unto sin, but not how to be delivered from them; it shows the spot, but not how to wash it off; and the sore, but not how to heal it; but, on the other side, we are bidden to *glory in the Lord,* (Jesus,) *who of God is made unto us wisdom, righteousness, sanctification, and redemption,* 1 Cor. i. 30, 31. *From all things, from which ye could not be justified by the law of Moses;* to which may be added, that there were some sins which by the ceremonial law there was no sacrifice appointed for; and for such sins which a sacrifice was appointed for, it was not possible that the blood of bulls and goats should take them away, Heb. x. 4; which may make us more to admire the grace of the gospel, by which *we are sanctified through the offering of the body of Jesus Christ once for all,* Heb. x. 10.

40 Beware therefore, lest that come upon you, which is spoken of in ᵐ the prophets;

m Is. 29. 14. Hab. 1. 5.

Hab. i. 5. He cautions these Jews, lest the same thing threatened by the prophet to their fathers come also upon them; for sin is as odious unto God as ever, and God is as jealous of his honour, which sin robs him of, as ever he was.

41 Behold, ye despisers, and wonder, and perish: for I work a work in your days, a work which ye shall in no wise believe, though a man declare it unto you.

These words are cited from that place in Habakkuk, according to the reading of the Septuagint, St. Paul not being willing to alter the words, the Jews that were dispersed being so used to that translation, especially the sense being the same with the original Hebrew. This quotation of the apostle might also be taken from Isa. xxviii. 14, 16. *Ye despisers;* for which cause, in that place of Habakkuk they are commanded to consider the heathen, and are sent to school unto them they contemned so much, who had had God for their teacher, had they not despised his word. *And wonder;* grow pale for shame and fear. *And perish;* ye shall be destroyed by the Romans your enemies, as your ancestors were by their enemies. *A work in your days;* this work was a work of God's just revenge on them then, by the Chaldeans; but threatened to come on these (without repentance) by the Romans. *Which ye shall in no wise believe, though a man declare it unto you;* which destruction should be so great, that it was incredible to them now, though it should have been told them.

42 And when the Jews were gone out of the synagogue, the Gentiles besought that these words might be preached to them † the next sabbath.

† Gr. *in the week between,* or, *in the sabbath between.*

When the Jews were gone out of the synagogue; or, as some read, the apostles, Paul and Barnabas, were gone out of the synagogue of the Jews. *The Gentiles;* proselytes, or such devout persons formerly spoken of, who had relinquished paganism, and came to be instructed in the knowledge of the true God by the Jews. *The next sabbath;* or in some day betwixt the sabbaths: the apostles took all advantages, if there were a festival, which was also called a sabbath, Lev. xvi. 31, and in the 23rd chapter of Leviticus, frequently; they would preach in season and out of season: howsoever, because we find the apostles did meet again with them on that day seven-night after, it is most probable that their desire was so to be understood. See ver. 44.

43 Now when the congregation was broken up, many of the Jews and religious proselytes followed Paul and Barnabas: who, speaking to them, ⁿ per-

n ch. 11. 23. & 14. 22.

THE ACTS XIII, XIV

^o Tit. 2. 11.
Heb. 12. 15.
1 Pet. 5. 12. suaded them to continue in °the grace of God.

The congregation was broken up; the congregation was dissolved, by the offence the Jews generally had taken at the doctrine of the apostles. *Religious proselytes;* these proselytes were so called, from their coming over from paganism to own the true God: see chap. ii. 10. *In the grace of God;* this grace of God the apostles so earnestly exhorted them to continue in, was, 1. Their present state of being firmly resolved to serve God, whatsoever opposition or temptation they should meet with to the contrary, which was wrought in them by the grace of God, 2. The doctrine of justification by the grace of God, which St. Paul had preached unto them, ver. 39. Or, 3. The whole gospel, and doctrine therein contained, which is called *the grace of God,* Heb. xii. 15, and *the true grace wherein we stand,* 1 Pet. v. 12.

44 ¶ And the next sabbath day came almost the whole city together to hear the word of God.

The citizens generally resorted thither. *To hear the word of God;* some out of curiosity, some to cavil at it, though some also out of love to it; here was doubtless a mixed congregation.

45 But when the Jews saw the multitudes, they were filled with envy, and ^pspake against those things which were spoken by Paul, contradicting and blaspheming.

p ch. 18. 6.
1 Pet. 4. 4.
Jude 10.

The Jews could not endure that the Gentiles should be equalled to them, being as much concerned against the Gentiles being exalted, as against their own being depressed. *Envy,* as a vicious humour, made them disrelish the wholesomest and most saving truths. *Contradicting and blaspheming;* contradicting the doctrine of the gospel, and blaspheming the preaching of it; or going from one degree of opposition unto another, until they came to the highest enmity against both.

46 Then Paul and Barnabas waxed bold, and said, ^q It was necessary that the word of God should first have been spoken to you: but ^rseeing ye put it from you, and judge yourselves unworthy of everlasting life, lo, ^swe turn to the Gentiles.

q Mat. 10. 6.
ch. 3. 26.
ver. 26.
Rom. 1. 16.
r Ex. 32. 10.
Deut. 32. 21.
Is. 55. 5.
Mat. 21. 43.
Rom. 10. 19.
s ch. 18. 6.
& 28. 28.

Waxed bold; being nothing affrighted with the reproaches and blasphemies they met with, which but increased their zeal, as a little water does the fire in the smith's forge. *It was necessary;* there was a necessity that the word of God should be first preached to the Jews, 1. Because Christ was promised to the children and heirs of their ancestors. 2. Because Christ did command it to be thus preached, Matt. x. 5, 6; Luke xxiv. 47; Acts i. 8. 3. Christ himself thus preached it, declaring that he was *not sent* (comparatively) *but to the lost sheep of the house of Israel,* Matt. xv. 24. *And judge yourselves unworthy of everlasting life;* by this their contradicting and blaspheming, they show as evidently that they are thus unworthy of everlasting life, as if a judge had determined so, or passed such a sentence upon his tribunal, or judgment-seat.

47 For so hath the Lord commanded us, *saying,* ^tI have set thee to be a light of the Gentiles, that thou shouldest be for salvation unto the ends of the earth.

t Is. 42. 6.
& 49. 6.
Luke 2. 32.

Because that prophecy must be fulfilled which we find, Isa. xlix. 6, the apostle infers aright, that they were *commanded* to publish Christ unto the Gentiles; for *how shall they believe in him of whom they have not heard? and how shall they hear without a preacher?* Rom. x. 14. *I have set thee to be a light;* all knowledge is ignorance, and all light is darkness, without Christ.

48 And when the Gentiles heard this, they were glad, and glorified the word of the Lord: ^uand as many as were ordained to eternal life believed.

u ch. 2. 47.

When the Gentiles heard this they were glad; there can be no true rest or peace in any to whom Christ is not manifested; the apostle telling us, that *we have peace with God through our Lord Jesus Christ,* Rom. v. 1; and the kingdom of God is peace and joy in the Holy Ghost. *Glorified the word of the Lord;* they magnified the goodness of God, which appeared in the gospel unto them. *As many as were ordained to eternal life, believed;* God, who ordered the end, ordereth the means, and gives them opportunities to hear the word, and by it graciously worketh faith in them whom he hath appointed to eternal life; without which faith, purging the heart, there is no hope of life eternal.

49 And the word of the Lord was published throughout all the region.

The word of the Lord, concerning salvation to be found only by Christ, and the Gentiles to be admitted to partake of that salvation. *Was published throughout all the region;* like *leaven, which a woman took, and hid in three measures of meal, till the whole was leavened,* Matt. xiii. 33.

50 But the Jews stirred up the devout and honourable women, and the chief men of the city, and ^xraised persecution against Paul and Barnabas, and expelled them out of their coasts.

x 2 Tim. 3. 11.

The devout; σεβόμενοι, as was said of the men, such as had relinquished the idolatry of their country and ancestors, and acknowledged the true God, the Maker of heaven and earth. *Honourable women;* of great repute and esteem; women being accounted more earnest in what way soever they take; and to be sure Eve was first seduced, and in the transgression. *The chief men of the city;* in some cities there were but five, in some ten, in others twenty, in whose hands the government of the city was ordinarily put; and these the persecutors (knowing what an influence their authority must needs have) by all means labour to seduce.

51 ^yBut they shook off the dust of their feet against them, and came unto Iconium.

y Mat. 10. 14.
Mark 6. 11.
Luke 9. 5.
ch. 18. 6.

This was according to our Saviour's command, Matt. x. 14; Mark vi. 11; Luke ix. 5, so often is it mentioned, and so considerable a matter it is for us to know, and dread the punishment appointed for such as refuse the gospel, and contemn the salvation offered by it. What this was symbolical of is not expressed. The Hebrew proverb says, The dust of an ethnic city or country doth pollute a man; and they might by this represent, that the inhabitants of such a city or place, who did not entertain the gospel, and the ministers thereof, they would repute as the vilest sinners, and they should by God be dealt with accordingly. *Iconium:* see chap. xiv. 1.

52 And the disciples ^zwere filled with joy, and with the Holy Ghost.

z Matt. 5. 12.
John 16. 22.
ch. 2. 46.

The disciples; either Paul and Barnabas in a more especial manner, or, also such as at Perga had believed the gospel, and came with them to Antioch, *were filled with joy,* so as no place was left for meaner contentments: First, By reason of the pardon of their sins. Secondly, The promise made to them of everlasting life. Thirdly, The gifts of the Holy Ghost which they had, at that time, as an earnest and pledge to assure the other unto them.

CHAP. XIV

Paul and Barnabas are persecuted from Iconium by the malice of the unbelieving Jews, 1—7. *At Lystra they heal an impotent man, and refuse divine honours with abhorrence,* 8—18. *Paul is stoned at the instigation of the Jews, but escapeth alive with Barnabas to Derbe,* 19, 20. *Having passed through divers places, and confirmed the churches in faith and patience, they return to Antioch, and give an account of their ministry,* 21—28.

AND it came to pass in Iconium, that they went both together into the synagogue of the Jews, and so spake, that a great multitude both of the Jews and also of the Greeks believed.

Iconium, a city in Lycaonia. *They went both together;*

THE ACTS XIV

Paul and Barnabas, as they were wont to do, showing as great constancy in performing of their duty, as their enemies did obstinacy in persecuting them for it. *So spake;* with such evidence and *demonstration of the Spirit and of power. The Greeks :* see chap. xiii. 43.

2 But the unbelieving Jews stirred up the Gentiles, and made their minds evil affected against the brethren.

The unbelieving, or disobedient, *Jews,* who did not believe the truths or obey the precepts of the gospel, *stirred up the Gentiles;* urging, persuading, and pressing of them, who of themselves (though as yet ignorant of Christ, and his word) would not have been so cruel. *The brethren;* the apostles themselves, and others that were converted by them, whose common father God through Christ was, and were accordingly endeared one to another.

3 Long time therefore abode they speaking boldly in the Lord, [a] which gave testimony unto the word of his grace, and granted signs and wonders to be done by their hands.

a Mark 16. 20. Heb. 2. 4.

Long time therefore abode they, to strengthen the new converts against the opposition they met with in the way of Christ, willingly partaking with them in their afflictions for Christ's sake. *Speaking boldly;* with great courage, and humble confidence, as knowing in whom they had believed. *In the Lord;* first, In the Lord's cause, a business which he had sent them about. Secondly, And in the Lord's strength, who enabled them in it. *The word of his grace;* the gospel: first, Wherein the grace of God is manifested. Secondly, Whereby it is offered. Thirdly, Wherewith, to such as receive, it is conveyed. Fourthly, And out of grace disputed and allowed to some, hidden and withdrawn from others. *Granted signs and wonders to be done by their hands;* God, by his miraculous confirming the doctrine of the apostles, showed that it was from him.

A. D. 46.

4 But the multitude of the city was divided: and part held with the Jews, and part with the [b] apostles.

b ch. 13. 3.

Was divided; as it was about our Saviour and his doctrine, John vii. 43. *The apostles;* Paul and Barnabas, who were called to be apostles, 1 Cor. ix. 5, 6.

5 And when there was an assault made both of the Gentiles, and also of the Jews with their rulers, [c] to use *them* despitefully, and to stone them,

c 2 Tim. 3. 11.

Rulers, such as were called *the chief men of the city,* chap. xiii. 50. *To use them despitefully;* thus they that were called to the marriage of the king's son, Matt. xxii. 6, entreated the servants despitefully. *And to stone them;* they would have used them as such who were not worthy to live, and then have taken away their lives from them, as they did by our Saviour; first they spat upon him, and then crucified him.

d Mat. 10.23.

6 They were ware of *it*, and [d] fled unto Lystra and Derbe, cities of Lycaonia, and unto the region that lieth round about:

And fled; the apostles did not flee so much to save their lives, as to husband their time best for the glory of God in other places; and this they were commanded to do, Matt. x. 23, *When they persecute you in this city, flee ye into another. Lystra and Derbe;* these were cities further in the country of Lycaonia than Iconium was. *Lycaonia;* a part of the Lesser Asia, nigh unto the mountain Taurus.

7 And there they preached the Gospel.

Thus was verified what St. Paul observed, Phil. i. 12, that all those things fell out *unto the furtherance of the gospel,* which spread the further for the scattering of the apostles and preachers of it; and thousands had not heard of Christ, if persecution had not driven the ministers of the gospel unto them: God working good out of evil, and causing the sun, when it leaves one part, to shine upon another.

e ch. 3. 2.

8 ¶ [e] And there sat a certain man at Lystra, impotent in his feet, being a cripple from his mother's womb, who never had walked:

Such defects as are from nature, are incurable by art, and only to be helped immediately by the God of nature. *Who never had walked;* this is observed and enlarged upon, to make the miracle the more appear to be the only work of God: see chap. iii. 2.

9 The same heard Paul speak: who stedfastly beholding him, and [f] perceiving that he had faith to be healed,

f Matt. 8. 10. & 9. 28, 29.

This Paul might know by a prophetical Spirit; and that extraordinary gift of discerning of spirits might be in this case bestowed upon him. But withal, it is not unlikely but this lame man's attention to the word, eyes, gesture, and countenance, might speak as much.

10 Said with a loud voice, [g] Stand upright on thy feet. And he leaped and walked.

g Is. 35. 6.

As chap. iii. 6, 8, to shew that he was perfectly recovered of this lameness; as all miraculous cures (being the work of God) were perfect.

11 And when the people saw what Paul had done, they lifted up their voices, saying in the speech of Lycaonia, [h] The gods are come down to us in the likeness of men.

h ch. 8. 10. & 28. 6.

In the speech of Lycaonia; which was a dialect of the Greek tongue, that language being in the Lesser Asia ordinarily spoken. *The gods are come down to us in the likeness of men;* the heathens (especially their poets) did frequently believe such kind of apparitions; probably at first from the appearing of angels unto the patriarchs and others, which by tradition they might have heard of.

12 And they called Barnabas, Jupiter; and Paul, Mercurius, because he was the chief speaker.

Jupiter; whom the heathens took for their chief God. *Mercury* was feigned to be the messenger of their gods, and therefore represented with wings; as also the interpreter of the gods, which caused their applying of his name to Paul.

13 Then the priest of Jupiter, which was before their city, brought oxen and garlands unto the gates, [i] and would have done sacrifice with the people.

i Dan. 2. 46.

Before their city; the temple of Jupiter, whom they took for the patron of their city, was in the suburbs. *Garlands;* these were usually in the form of crowns put upon the oxen which they intended to sacrifice; and, by this sign, showed that they were dedicated to Jupiter, whom the heathen blasphemously called, The king of kings, and placed him sitting in his chair, or throne, with a crown on his head. *Unto the gates;* the gates or doors of the house where the apostles lodged.

14 *Which* when the apostles, Barnabas and Paul, heard *of*, [k] they rent their clothes, and ran in among the people, crying out,

k Mat.26.65.

They rent their clothes; which was a sign of their greatest detestation of, and sorrow for, such abominations. *And ran in among the people, crying out;* expressing their greatest zeal for the glory of God, and earnestness to hinder the idolatry of this people.

15 And saying, Sirs, [l] why do ye these things? [m] We also are men of like passions with you, and preach unto you that ye should turn from [n] these vanities [o] unto the living God, [p] which made heaven, and earth, and the sea, and all things that are therein:

l ch. 10. 26. m Jam. 5. 17. Rev. 19. 10. n 1 Sam. 12. 21. 1 Kings 16. 13. Jer. 14. 22. Amos 2.4.1 Cor.8.4. o 1 Thess. 1. 9. p Gen. 1. 1. Ps. 33. 6. & 146. 6. Rev. 14. 7.

We also are men of like passions with you; we stand in need of food and raiment, are liable to diseases and death, as well as you. *Vanities;* so idols are frequently called, 1 Kings xvi. 13, 26; Jer. xiv. 22, because they disappoint the hopes that are placed in them, and are empty of any good which is expected from them, and have nothing but what vain men (their makers) bestow upon them. *The living God;* the true God is called *the living God,* Deut. v. 26; Josh. iii. 10, in opposition to those false gods, who usually were only dead men, which out of love or fear were deified; as also in that he lives from himself, and gives life to every living creature. *Which made heaven, &c.:* by this also the true God is distinguished from false gods, as Jer. x. 11, 12; and is a good argument against all idol worship; for Divine worship is a tribute we owe and pay to him that made us, Psal. c. 3, 4. It should be considered with what a respective compellation the apostles speak unto this heathen rabble, calling them, *Sirs,* or masters; a term surely then not unlawful to be given to our equals or betters.

16 q Who in times past suffered all nations to walk in their own ways.

There were two main objections which these heathen idolaters might make against the gospel, and the worship of the true God: and they are, first, from the antiquity, secondly, from the universality, of that false worship; both which the apostle here gives a critical answer unto, telling them, that the reason why so many, and for so long a time had followed idols, was from the just judgment of God upon them, as Psal. lxxxi. 12; Rom. i. 24, 28. *Their own ways;* ways of our choosing, and not of God's commanding, are false ways.

17 r Nevertheless he left not himself without witness, in that he did good, and s gave us rain from heaven, and fruitful seasons, filling our hearts with food and gladness.

These words are to prevent that cavil, Why does God yet complain? and inform them, that though God had not given them, nor their ancestors, his laws written in tables of stone, as he had given to the Jews; yet they had the law written in their hearts, which they had not obeyed, though God's manifold mercies, his works of creation and providence, had testified unto them, that he only was to be feared and worshipped. How many witnesses hath God against sinful man, when every creature and providence speaks his power, wisdom, goodness, &c., and call upon us to love and obey him? Every creature tells us that God made it, &c.

18 And with these sayings scarce restrained they the people, that they had not done sacrifice unto them.

So hard a matter it is to persuade any to leave off these sins they are accustomed unto, or to rectify such errors in religion which men are brought up in.

19 ¶ t And there came thither *certain Jews from Antioch and Iconium, who* persuaded the people, u and, having stoned Paul, drew *him* out of the city, supposing he had been dead.

Certain Jews; such as mention was made of, chap. xiii. 50. *Persuaded the people;* a strange and incredible fickleness; but that we know how the same multitude who cried *Hosanna,* did more suddenly alter their note, and cry against our Saviour, *Crucify him, crucify him;* so uncertain a thing is worldly honour. *Stoned Paul;* the malice of Satan is every way great; if he cannot destroy the souls of these blessed apostles, by making of them to accept of Divine worship, he will do his utmost to kill their bodies.

20 Howbeit, as the disciples stood round about him, he rose up, and came into the city: and the next day he departed with Barnabas to Derbe.

Stood round about him; either in order to bury him, thinking him to be dead, as well as his persecutors did; or else to defend him, as much as possibly they could, from the rage of his enemies in that popular fury. Their spite was most against Paul, because he spake most, and preached unto them the way of life. *He rose up;* being by the power of God suddenly restored to his strength again. *Derbe;* a city near to Lycaonia, some say in it.

21 And when they had preached the Gospel to that city, x and † had taught many, they returned again to Lystra, and to Iconium, and Antioch,

Had taught many; had made many disciples by teaching, and also by baptizing of them, Matt. xxviii. 19. For as by circumcision they were made Moses's disciples, so by baptism they are made Christ's disciples.

22 Confirming the souls of the disciples, *and* y exhorting them to continue in the faith, and that z we must through much tribulation enter into the kingdom of God.

It is not enough to sow the seed of the word, but it must be watered also, frequent endeavours must be used that it may be fruitful. Thus the apostles return to visit such as they had preached unto; the persecution they had endured, increasing their resolution for God, and their strength from him. Lest they should be offended at what they saw St. Paul had endured, or themselves might be called to endure, they preach unto them the doctrine of the cross, not hiding from them the miseries which in this world the profession of Christ and his truths might bring upon them. God hath indeed dealt all along thus with his people. The troubles which the Israelites met with in the wilderness, in their journey towards an earthly Canaan, did typify the calamities which God's people will meet with in this world, as they journey towards the heavenly Canaan, or Jerusalem which is above.

23 And when they had a ordained them elders in every church, and had prayed with fasting, they commended them to the Lord, on whom they believed.

Ordained; the word properly signifies a stretching out of the hand, such as was used when they gave their suffrages in the election of their magistrates, whereby was showed for whom they gave their voice; and afterwards it was commonly used for to constitute or appoint, or, as here, to ordain to any office or place; which might the rather be done by stretching out or laying on of the hands of the apostles, because by that means the Holy Ghost (or a power of working miracles) was frequently bestowed, chap. viii. 17, 18, which in those times was necessary to authorize their doctrine to the infidel world. *Elders;* such as might instruct and govern the church. *They commended them;* they commended the disciples as their jewels and chiefest treasure; as all sufferers are to commit their very souls to God, 1 Pet. iv. 19. *To the Lord;* to Christ, the best and faithful Keeper, that he should keep and further them in grace and goodness; to whose providence they wholly had committed themselves.

24 And after they had passed throughout Pisidia, they came to Pamphylia.

Going the same way back which they had come, as appear by chap. xiii. 13, 14.

25 And when they had preached the word in Perga, they went down into Attalia:

The word; the gospel, the word of the Lord; or Christ, who is the word, and who is the sum of what the ministers of the gospel preach about. *Perga:* mentioned chap. xiii. 13; a city, or as some, a country, in Pamphylia, by the sea-side. But the bounds of provinces were often altered by the Romans, and some made larger, and others lesser.

26 And thence sailed to Antioch, b from whence they had been c recommended to the grace of God for the work which they fulfilled.

Antioch; that Antioch which was in Syria, as appears chap. xiii. 1—3, to which this relates; and is a sufficient proof that they had not sought God in vain, and that there is no better preparation or provision towards any business, than faithful prayer unto God concerning it; doing our duty, and leaving the event unto his disposing.

27 And when they were come, and had gathered the church together, d they rehearsed all that God had done with them, and how he had e opened the door of faith unto the Gentiles.

All that God had done with them; God being with them, and they being labourers with God, 1 Cor. iii. 9; 2 Cor.

vi. 1. They showed how much God had honoured them in making them his instruments in the conversion of so many souls. *He had opened the door of faith unto the Gentiles;* he had given the Gentiles an opportunity of knowing and believing the gospel. The fleece alone had been wet before, and all the ground round about it dry; and now all the ground is wet, and that fleece was dry; to allude to Judg. vi. 37—40, by which this mystery was presignified, and can only be resolved by that of our Saviour, Matt. xi. 25, 26, *Even so, Father; for so it seemed good in thy sight.*

28 And there they abode long time with the disciples.

To confirm them, as ver. 22; and also, as our Saviour withdrew himself from the multitudes, they chose there to refresh themselves a while, out of the heat of contention and persecution.

CHAP. XV

Great dissensions arise about circumcising the Gentiles: Paul and Barnabas are sent to consult the apostles and elders at Jerusalem, 1—4. *The matter is debated in a council there*, 5, 6. *Peter declareth his opinion*, 7—11. *Paul and Barnabas report the miracles they had wrought among the Gentiles*, 12. *James pronounceth sentence in favour of the Gentiles, requiring of them abstinence only in a few particulars*, 13—21. *Letters are sent with the determination by messengers to the churches, which are received with joy*, 22—35. *Paul and Barnabas propose to visit together the churches they had planted, but disagree, and travel different ways*, 36—41.

A. D. 51.
a Gal. 2. 12.
b John 7. 22. ver. 5.
Gal. 5. 2.
Phil. 3. 2.
Col. 2. 8, 11, 16.
c Gen. 17. 10.
Lev. 12. 3.

AND [a]certain men which came down from Judæa taught the brethren, *and said*, [b] Except ye be circumcised [c] after the manner of Moses, ye cannot be saved.

Certain men; these were such as did pretend to believe, but were false brethren; some think Cerinthus to have been of them. *The brethren;* the Gentiles who were converted unto the faith of Christ, or Proselytes of the gate (as they were called) who were not circumcised, and now professing the true faith. These the pharisaical professors would have excluded from any hopes of salvation, although circumcision was not commanded but unto the posterity of Abraham, Gen. xvii. 10—13, and Abraham himself was justified before he was circumcised, Rom. iv. 10. *After the manner of Moses;* according unto the law of Moses: for God by him did renew and establish that ordinance unto that people, although it was long before his time both commanded and practised, John vii. 22.

A. D. 52.
d Gal. 2. 1.

2 When therefore Paul and Barnabas had no small dissension and disputation with them, they determined that [d] Paul and Barnabas, and certain other of them, should go up to Jerusalem unto the apostles and elders about this question.

Paul, that meek apostle, who was willing to become all things unto all men, yet he enters into a holy war with them that would introduce circumcision into the Christian church; because, 1. He would have no works of the law to be an ingredient into our salvation; but the free grace of God in Christ to be all in all. 2. That our freedom from all the ceremonial law, acquired by the death of Christ, might not be diminished. 3. That the spreading of the gospel might not be hindered, but that Christ might be accepted and honoured amongst all. Now if circumcision had been retained, it would have kept possession for all the other ceremonies to have continued, or re-entered, there being the same reason for the one as for the other, and the circumcised person was obliged by his circumcision to observe them all, Gal. v. 3, 4. *They determined;* the church at Antioch, where this controversy was moved. *Unto the apostles;* James, Peter, and John, who are thought to have been then at Jerusalem, the rest being probably gone to preach Christ in other parts.

3 And [e]being brought on their way by the church, they passed through Phenice and Samaria, [f]declaring the conversion of the Gentiles: and they caused great joy unto all the brethren.

e Rom. 15. 24. 1 Cor. 16. 6, 11.
f ch. 14. 27.

Brought on their way by the church; the brethren or believers of Antioch, out of respect, went part of the way with them; as also thereby showing, that Paul and Barnabas did not go upon their own business or mind only, and that there was no dissension betwixt them and the church there. *The conversion of the Gentiles;* it is a conversion or turning indeed from error to truth, from impurity to holiness; that is, *from darkness to light, and from the power of Satan unto* the ever-living *God*, chap. xxvi. 18. *They caused great joy unto all the brethren;* nothing more rejoices a good man, than the bringing of souls unto God, and the enlarging of the kingdom of Jesus Christ.

4 And when they were come to Jerusalem, they were received of the church, and *of* the apostles and elders, and [g]they declared all things that God had done with them.

g ver. 12.
ch. 14. 27.
& 21. 19.

They were received of the church; they were owned with respect and thankfulness, for their great work and labour in the Lord's vineyard. *All things that God had done with them:* see chap. xiv. 27.

5 But there ‖ rose up certain of the sect of the Pharisees which believed, saying, [h]That it was needful to circumcise them, and to command *them* to keep the law of Moses.

A. D. 52.
‖ Or, rose up, said they, certain.
h ver. 1.

If these words be taken for St. Luke's, the penman of this book, then they declare, that in the church of Jerusalem there were some that did abet the opinion of the necessity of circumcision; but if, (as most probably we may,) we take them for the words of St. Paul, they then are part of his narrative to the church there, of what had happened at Antioch. *The sect of the Pharisees;* these Pharisees were a sect amongst the Jews, (so called from פרש *separavit*, and may be Englished, separatists,) separating from converse with others, by reason of an opinion they had of their own holiness, Luke xviii. 11.

6 ¶ And the apostles and elders came together for to consider of this matter.

The apostles and elders, unto whom Paul and Barnabas were sent about the decision of this question, ver. 2, *came together for to consider of this matter;* they had been informed of it, and now they met to deliberate about it.

7 And when there had been much disputing, Peter rose up, and said unto them, [i]Men *and* brethren, ye know how that a good while ago God made choice among us, that the Gentiles by my mouth should hear the word of the Gospel, and believe.

i ch. 10. 20.
& 11. 12.

Much disputing; they argued on both sides, and considered what might be said for either opinion: some of them that met here seem at first to have been for the retaining of circumcision; for we *know but in part*, and from the collision of adverse parties such sparks fly out, that many a man hath lighted his candle at them. *A good while ago;* from the beginning of our having received our commission to preach, as Matt. xxviii. 19; or more particularly, from the time of Cornelius's conversion, chap. x. 22; xi. 12, which is thought to have been about fourteen or fifteen years before, that Peter preached Christ, by the command of God, unto the Gentiles.

8 And God, [k]which knoweth the hearts, bare them witness, [l]giving them the Holy Ghost, even as *he did* unto us;

k 1 Chron. 28. 9. ch. 1. 24.
l ch. 10. 44.

Which knoweth the hearts; God knew the desires of the Gentiles, that they did sincerely desire to please God, and to see his salvation. This great attribute David improved, 1 Chron. xxix. 17, and highly recommended his son Solomon to consider of, 1 Chron. xxviii. 9; which, if believed, would make us also to serve God *with a perfect heart and a willing mind.* *Giving them the Holy Ghost;* God himself was a witness for these Gentiles beyond all exception, when he gave them the ordinary and extraordinary gifts of the Holy Ghost; by which he testified, that they belonged to Christ, whose Spirit this was. Thus *the testimony of Jesus is the spirit of prophecy,* Rev. xix. 10; and the Spirit, according to our Saviour's promise, John xv. 26, doth testify of him.

9 ᵐAnd put no difference between us and them, ⁿpurifying their hearts by faith.

[m Rom. 10. 11.]
[n ch. 10. 15. 28, 43.]
[1 Cor. 1. 2. 1 Pet. 1. 22.]

God had now broken down the middle wall of partition betwixt Jew and Gentile, Eph. ii. 14, and distributed his graces to these also, which was signified by the rending of the veil from the top to the bottom, Matt. xxvii. 51, whereby such as were formerly without, might see and enjoy the benefit of those great things which had been hidden under those shadows and types. *Purifying their hearts,* from idolatry, and other impieties in which they had lived; which is the inward circumcision of the heart; and, whosoever is thus cleansed, ought not to be reputed amongst the unclean. *By faith;* faith is the instrument, God is the efficient cause, of our justification and renovation.

10 Now therefore why tempt ye God, ᵒto put a yoke upon the neck of the disciples, which neither our fathers nor we were able to bear?

[o Matt. 23. 4. Gal. 5. 1.]

Why tempt ye God? why would you make a doubt of, and put it to a trial, whether God did in good earnest admit the Gentiles to his favour, and whether he remains firm and constant in such his kindness towards them? They did tempt God also, by disliking the calling of the Gentiles, and would have brought God's will, were it possible, unto theirs; not submitting their wills, as they ought, unto God's: for he that sins in any kind, does tempt God; that is, he tries God's patience, power, and righteousness. *A yoke;* so the law of ceremonies is called, Gal. v. 1, and was a yoke indeed, if we consider, 1. Their variety; 2. Their difficulty; 3. Their chargeableness; 4. Their inefficacy, being only shadows of good things to come, Col. ii. 17.

11 But ᵖwe believe that through the grace of the Lord Jesus Christ we shall be saved, even as they.

[p Rom. 3. 24. Eph. 2. 8. Tit. 2. 11. & 3. 4, 5.]

The grace of the Lord Jesus Christ; all saving grace may be well so called, it being purchased only by Christ, and bestowed upon us from the Father through Christ. *Even as they;* the Jews their fathers; these were saved through the grace of the Messiah which was to come; and the apostle urges this (against the imposing of the law) to the Jews, because neither their ancestors nor themselves could be justified by the law, but only by grace.

12 ¶ Then all the multitude kept silence, and gave audience to Barnabas and Paul, declaring what miracles and wonders God had ᑫwrought among the Gentiles by them.

[q ch. 14. 27.]

All the multitude; the apostles and elders themselves gave attention to what Barnabas and Paul declared, and by their silence did tacitly approve of what they had said. *Miracles and wonders;* the conversion of the Gentiles in itself, and not only the signs which did attend it, is truly wonderful: the saving of any one soul is a miraculous work.

13 ¶ And after they had held their peace, ʳJames answered, saying, Men *and* brethren, hearken unto me:

[r ch. 12. 17.]

After they had held their peace; Barnabas and Paul had finished their narrative. *James,* who was surnamed the Just, and was the son of Alpheus, and a kinsman to our Saviour, now being president of this council. *Answered;* that is, began to speak.

14 ˢSimeon hath declared how God at the first did visit the Gentiles, to take out of them a people for his name.

[s ver. 7.]

Simeon, or Simon, the name of Peter; but St. Luke,

being himself a Hebrew, writes it according as they pronounced it, and not so contracted as the Greeks wrote it. *A people;* there were some at all times probably amongst the Gentiles who did fear God, as Job and his three friends; but they did not make a people, or such a number as is here spoken of. *For his name:* God takes out of the world *a people for his name,* that is, 1. For himself; as, Prov. xviii. 10, *the name of the Lord* is put for the Lord himself. 2. For to call upon his name, as also for to be called by his name. 3. For his glory and honour, and to magnify his name.

15 And to this agree the words of the prophets; as it is written,

The prophets; in the plural number, though only one cited: it is an ordinary enallage; but it also shows the harmony amongst the prophets, they all speaking by one Spirit; what one said is as if all had said it.

16 ᵗAfter this I will return, and will build again the tabernacle of David, which is fallen down; and I will build again the ruins thereof, and I will set it up:

[t Amos 9. 11, 12.]

After this; in the days of the Messiah. *I will return:* the word may be taken in both voices. If actively, it signifies God's returning unto the Gentiles, from whom he had departed. If passively, it foreshows their returning unto God, whom they had forsaken. *The tabernacle;* the house, expressed by a tabernacle, (as frequently in Scripture,) because that anciently they dwelt only in tabernacles; and here for the throne of David, who was a type of Christ, whose kingdom is over all. God does promise less than he does perform, for he did not only restore the tabernacle of David, in Christ, but raised it to a far greater splendour and glory in its spiritual state. And though St. James here does not exactly keep unto the words of the prophet, he speaks their sense and meaning.

17 That the residue of men might seek after the Lord, and all the Gentiles, upon whom my name is called, saith the Lord, who doeth all these things.

In the prophet it is *the remnant of Edom,* Amos ix. 12, which is here called *the residue of men;* for as Jacob, or Israel, shadowed out the church, so Edom, or Esau, (the other son of Isaac,) represented those who were rejected, Rom. ix. 13. The prophet also adds, by way of explication, *all the heathen;* as the apostle does here, *all the Gentiles. Upon whom my name is called;* who shall be mine, or appropriated unto me; also called by his name, they being called Christians from Christ, whom they believed in. *Saith the Lord, who doeth all these things;* the calling of the Gentiles was God's work, and therefore so far from being excepted against, that it ought to be marvellous in our eyes.

18 Known unto God are all his works from the beginning of the world.

This the apostle adds, that they might not be offended with the seeming novelty and surprise of the calling of the Gentiles, and abrogation of the ceremonies; for it was no other than what God had before determined to do, and therefore they ought to rest satisfied in the wise and holy appointments of God.

19 Wherefore ᵘmy sentence is, that we trouble not them, which from among the Gentiles ˣare turned to God:

[u See ver. 28.]
[x 1 Thes. 1. 9.]

St. James here gives his opinion, confirming and approving what Peter had done in conversing with and baptizing of the Gentiles; whom he would not have afflicted or disturbed with such things as were not necessary, lest that it should hinder the conversion of the Gentiles, and the church should lose the substance for a shadow.

20 But that we write unto them, that they abstain ʸfrom pollutions of idols, and ᶻfrom fornication, and *from* things strangled, ᵃand *from* blood.

[y Gen. 35. 2. Ex. 20. 3, 23. Ezek. 20. 30. 1 Cor. 8. 1. Rev. 2. 14, 20. & 10. 20, 28.]
[z 1 Cor. 6. 9.]
[a Gen. 9. 4. Lev. 3. 17.]

18. Gal. 5. 19. Eph. 5. 3. Col. 3. 5. 1 Thess. 4. 3. 1 Pet. 4. 3. Deut. 12. 16, 23.

That they abstain from pollutions of idols; eating of meat that was offered to idols, (as ver. 29,) in a case of scandal, and for the present state of the church, was forbid, though afterwards in other cases indulged, 1 Cor. x. 27. *Fornication* is here mentioned amongst indifferent things; not that it ever was so, but because it was amongst the Gentiles reputed to be so, even by them who punished adultery severely. By these two, some think all sins against both the tables of the law to be forbidden, because by one sin against each table all the sins against any command may synecdochically be understood. *From things strangled;* such creatures as had not their blood let out, and therefore were not to be fed upon, by the law of God, Gen. ix. 4, given as soon as the use of flesh was allowed for food. *And from blood;* they were also much more to abstain from blood, when shed out of the body of any slain creature, Lev. iii. 17; Deut. xii. 23. That blood was forbidden might be to teach them meekness, and to abstain from revenge. It is certain, that such nations as feed on blood are most barbarous and cruel. It is also probable, that these being included in the precepts which they called, The precepts of Adam, or Noah, and to which all the proselytes of the gate were obliged to yield obedience, the apostle would have the observance of them to be continued upon them that came from amongst them over unto Christianity. For though all these ceremonies were dead, (with Christ,) yet they were not then deadly, and did wait a time for their more decent burial. If any wonder that the council did not treat of and write about greater matters; as of worshipping God the Father, through the Son; of denying of ourselves, and taking up the cross; he ought to consider, that the question they met upon was about other matters, and that those great things were never in question amongst such as feared God.

21 b ch. 13. 15, 27. For Moses of old time hath in every city them that preach him, b being read in the synagogues every sabbath day.

The reason why St. James would not have the ceremonies buried as soon as they were dead, was because the Jews had been so long confirmed in them, and bare such a love unto them; and he would purchase concord betwixt them and the Gentile converts; though the Gentiles should bear with some inconvenience into the bargain, as not presently using all the liberty which through Christ they had a right unto.

22 Then pleased it the apostles and elders, with the whole church, to send chosen men of their own company to Antioch with Paul and Barnabas; namely,
c ch. 1. 23. Judas surnamed c Barsabas, and Silas, chief men among the brethren:

The apostles and elders, with the whole church; a happy concord, all agreeing as one man, by one Spirit. *To send chosen men of their own company;* that Paul and Barnabas might be the better credited, and that by such as had been of a contrary judgment: so hard it is to remove suspicions, and to root out pre-conceived opinions. *Judas surnamed Barsabas;* the brother of that Joseph mentioned chap. i. 23. *Silas,* called Silvanus also. *Chief men among the brethren;* noted for their holy living, or great knowledge, or office in the church.

23 And they wrote *letters* by them after this manner; The apostles and elders and brethren *send* greeting unto the brethren which are of the Gentiles in Antioch and Syria and Cilicia:

The apostles and elders and brethren; the letter was wrote in the name of them all, that it might have the greater force, and better acceptance; that so strong a cord might not be broken by the false apostles. *Of the Gentiles;* such as out of Gentilism, or paganism, were converted unto Christ; to whom the determination of this case was of the greatest concern; their right of belonging unto Christ, and having any hopes of salvation, being questioned, unless they would be circumcised.

d ver. 1. Gal. 2. 4. & 5. 12. Tit. 1. 10, 11. 24 Forasmuch as we have heard, that d certain which went out from us have troubled you with words, subverting your souls, saying, *Ye must* be circumcised, and keep the law: to whom we gave no *such* commandment:

Certain which went out from us; for these false apostles were such as came from Judea, ver. 1, that is, from the church there. It is Satan's great policy to divide, that he may rule; he will have at least one share where there is more than one. No such sad divisions as church divisions, when that some of ourselves preach *perverse things,* as chap. xx. 30. *Have troubled you with words;* as if in the professing of Christianity there would be no salvation unless Judaism be embraced, and circumcision admitted. No greater trouble to a considerate mind, than about the concern of salvation, when they say, Where is thy God? *Saying, Ye must be circumcised, and keep the law;* these they did well put together; for by circumcision they engaged to the observance of the whole law of Moses; and by the decreeing the omission, that whole law of ceremonies is declared void, and of no effect. What truth and unity build up, discord and error pull down.

25 It seemed good unto us, being assembled with one accord, to send chosen men unto you with our beloved Barnabas and Paul,

With one accord; with one mind, as if they had all but one soul, (they had but one Spirit, the Spirit of truth,) as chap. ii. 1; v. 12; their unanimity adding great strength to the decree they sent.

26 e Men that have hazarded their lives for the name of our Lord Jesus Christ. e ch. 13. 50. & 14. 19. 1 Cor. 15. 30. 2 Cor. 11. 23, 26.

Because that the false apostles at Antioch had vilified Paul and Barnabas, and opposed their doctrine and practice in admitting of the Gentiles by baptism into the church, the council here at Jerusalem take occasion to vindicate and to commend them, especially for their suffering so much for Christ, of which we read, chap. xiii. 50; xiv. 19: it being most reasonable to believe, that they had not done or said any thing for their own sakes, who had done and suffered so much for Christ and his truth's sake. *For the name of our Lord Jesus Christ;* for Christ's honour, and the truth of his gospel.

27 We have sent therefore Judas and Silas, who shall also tell *you* the same things by † mouth. † Gr. *word.*

They shall inform you of the truth of what is contained in this epistle, that you may be more assured it is not forged or counterfeited. Of these men, see ver. 22.

28 For it seemed good to the Holy Ghost, and to us, to lay upon you no greater burden than these necessary things;

To the Holy Ghost, and to us; that is, unto us, assisted by the Holy Ghost. The Holy Ghost is deservedly first mentioned, that the apostles might testify that they desired to say, write, or do nothing in which they had not the Spirit of God directing of them: and they mention the Spirit, that the Antiochians, unto whom they wrote, might be assured they were not human inventions which they recommended, but that they had the authority of God for them. *Unto us;* as ministers, or God's stewards, who acquainted them with these things, in discharge of their duty, and that they might appear themselves to be faithful. *Burden;* the yoke spoken of, ver. 10. *Necessary things:* to be sure, several of the things here spoken of are not absolutely necessary unto salvation, or simply, and in their own nature, necessary, as to abstain from blood, &c.; but though they are not necessary always and at all times, yet in this place, and at this time, they were necessary for the peace of the church, and to avoid giving of offence to the converted Jews, and to nourish brotherly love betwixt them and the Gentiles.

29 f That ye abstain from meats offered to idols, and g from blood, and from things strangled, and from fornication: from which if ye keep yourselves, ye shall do well. Fare ye well. f ver. 20. ch. 21. 25. Rev. 2. 14, 20. g Lev. 17.14.

Of these see more largely, ver. 20. *From meats offered*

to idols; they were wont to carry home and feast upon part of the sacrifices they had offered unto their false gods; nay, they did not, without reproach, eat of any greater beasts, (as oxen and sheep,) but they always first offered some of them unto their idols. And it was accounted no small impiety to eat ἄθυτα ἱερὰ, part of any beasts which they had not first offered up to some or other of their gods. *From blood;* for this reason they might not eat of any thing that died of itself, as Deut. xiv. 21, because the blood was not gone out of it. *From fornication;* mentioned here, because so commonly practised amongst the Gentiles, and yet not esteemed a sin. Hence also, 1 Thess. iv. 3, the apostle lays a very great charge against it. *Fare ye well;* the ordinary apprecation wherewith their letters were concluded, in which they wished health and strength to the party they wrote unto: instead of which word, some ancient copies read, φερόμενοι ἐν Πνεύματι Ἁγίῳ; which is rendered, Walk in the Holy Ghost; or, the Holy Ghost carrying, or enabling of you: a wish or prayer becoming these holy men that made it. They who have found the necessity of the Spirit's assistance, desire it above all things for such as they wish well unto.

30 So when they were dismissed, they came to Antioch: and when they had gathered the multitude together, they delivered the epistle:
When they were dismissed; Paul, Barnabas, Judas, and Silas; which two last were sent with the former. *Gathered the multitude together;* from whom they were sent, ver. 1, 2, and that this determination of the council might be more publicly known, as all things concerning our common salvation ought to be.

31 *Which* when they had read, they rejoiced for the ‖ consolation.

‖ Or, *exhortation.*

It could not but much rejoice the Gentile believers, that they were exempted from circumcision, and the ceremonial law. And it gladdened the believing Jews also, that the controversy was determined, and concord established amongst them. But much more might they all rejoice to understand the grace of the gospel; and that we are not justified by the deeds of the law, but by faith in Christ, Rom. v. 1. *Consolation;* this word also signifies exhortation, and it was matter of joy to be put upon such excellent duties as our most holy religion recommends, and to be deterred from such erroneous evils as it forbids. All that God requires of us being only to *eschew evil, and do good,* Isa. i. 16, 17; 1 Pet. iii. 11.

32 And Judas and Silas, being prophets also themselves, [h] exhorted the brethren with many words, and confirmed *them.*

h ch. 14. 22. & 18. 23.

Prophets; not properly so called, from any gift of foretelling things to come, but as doctors and teachers in the church, Eph. iv. 11, expounding Moses and the prophets, and showing how and what they speak concerning Christ: proving out of them, that he was the Messiah, as Philip had done, chap. viii. 35. *Confirmed them:* see chap. xiv. 22; xviii. 23.

33 And after they had tarried *there* a space, they were let [i] go in peace from the brethren unto the apostles.

i 1 Cor.16.11. Heb. 11. 31.

A space; a competent time; some make this space to be a year. *They were let go in peace;* they were dismissed with earnest prayers for them; for by *peace* is meant all kind of good, which they desired for them, as Matt. x. 13. *Unto the apostles;* such of them as were at Jerusalem, who also had sent them.

34 Notwithstanding it pleased Silas to abide there still.
Though, having performed his message, he was discharged, and might have returned; yet, for the further benefit of that church, he continued at Antioch.

35 [k] Paul also and Barnabas continued in Antioch, teaching and preaching the word of the Lord, with many others also.

k ch. 13. 1.

Judas only returned to Jerusalem, to acquaint the apostles with the reception their letter had met with, and what obedience was readily given to their decrees; so that when these went away the church at Antioch was not left destitute of faithful pastors. When God gives the word, great is the multitude of preachers, Psal. lxviii. 11.

36 ¶ And some days after Paul said unto Barnabas, Let us go again and visit our brethren [l] in every city where we have preached the word of the Lord, *and* see how they do.

A. D. 53.

l ch. 13. 4, 13, 14, 51. & 14. 1, 6, 24, 25.

It is not enough that they had sown good seed, but they must take care lest it be plucked up, and tares sown in the stead of it, by the wicked one, Matt. xiii. 19. A husbandman's work is never at an end, neither is the labourer's in God's vineyard. *See how they do;* not so much looking after their bodily welfare, as how their souls fared, whether they continued in the faith, and integrity of life.

37 And Barnabas determined to take with them [m] John, whose surname was Mark.

m ch. 12. 12, 25 & 13. 5. Col. 4. 10. 2 Tim. 4. 11. Philem. 24.

This John, or *Mark,* was *sister's son to Barnabas,* as Col. iv. 10.

38 But Paul thought not good to take him with them, [n] who departed from them from Pamphylia, and went not with them to the work.

n ch. 13. 13.

This deserting of Paul and Barnabas by John, is mentioned chap. xiii. 13. *To the work;* the work unto which the Spirit had called them, chap. xiii. 2, which was to offer life and salvation unto the Gentiles, and to gather them into the fold of Jesus Christ. This objection was very considerable, and ought to have weighed more than this John's propinquity, or nearness in blood, unto Barnabas.

39 And the contention was so sharp between them, that they departed asunder one from the other: and so Barnabas took Mark, and sailed unto Cyprus;

They departed asunder; as Abraham and Lot parted, Gen. xiii. 9, yet keeping the unity of the Spirit in the bond of peace; loving of and praying for one another, as we may judge, being both good men. But they verified here what they had said at Lystra, chap. xiv. 15, *We are men of like passions with you;* yet God overruled these very divisions betwixt Paul and Barnabas for his own glory, and the enlargement of the kingdom of Jesus Christ, several places being by this means blessed with the gospel. And this reflection upon this John Mark, is thought to have made him for the future more diligent and valiant in the cause of the gospel, which occasioned that kind salutation from St. Paul unto him, Col. iv. 10. *Cyprus;* an island in the Mediterranean Sea.

40 And Paul chose Silas, and departed, [o] being recommended by the brethren unto the grace of God.

o ch. 14. 26.

The favour of God, as chap. xiv. 26, which the wisest and holiest men stand in need of in all their undertakings; as also his gracious conduct and assistance.

41 And he went through Syria and Cilicia, [p] confirming the churches.

p ch. 16. 5.

Syria and Cilicia; where there were several brethren by reason of the dispersion that was upon Stephen's death, chap. xi. 19; and unto whom also the fore-recited letter was written, chap. xv. 23. *Confirming the churches;* putting them in mind of the gospel of Christ, which they had heard and believed; and encouraging of them to persevere in the profession of it, and being ready to answer any objection that could be brought against it.

CHAP. XVI

Paul having circumcised Timothy, and taken him for his companion, passeth through divers countries, 1—8; *and is directed by a vision to go into Macedonia,* 9—13. *He converteth Lydia,* 14, 15; *and casteth out a spirit of divination,* 16—18. *He and Silas are whipped and imprisoned,* 19—24. *The prison doors are thrown open by an earth-*

THE ACTS XVI

quake at midnight: the jailer, prevented by Paul from killing himself, is converted, 25—34. They are released by the magistrates, 35—40.

a ch. 14. 6.
b ch. 19. 22.
Rom. 16. 21.
1 Cor. 4. 17.
Phil. 2. 19.
1 Thes. 3. 2.
1 Tim. 1. 2.
2 Tim. 1. 2.
c 2 Tim. 1. 5.

THEN came he to [a] Derbe and Lystra: and, behold, a certain disciple was there, [b] named Timotheus, [c] the son of a certain woman, which was a Jewess, and believed; but his father was a Greek:

Derbe and Lystra; of these cities see chap. xiv. 6. *Timotheus;* who was known unto Paul from his childhood, 2 Tim. i. 5, and accompanied him in many journeys, 2 Tim. iii. 10, 11, and is called by him, his *work-fellow,* Rom. xvi. 21. *A certain woman,* called Eunice; being one of them that had *believed* in Christ in Judea, and had a holy woman to her mother, named Lois. *His father was a Greek:* although it was not lawful for a Jew to marry a woman of another nation, yet some think that a Jewess might marry to a stranger, as Esther married to Ahasuerus. *A Greek;* of Gentile extraction, and therefore not circumcised; yet he is accounted to have been a proselyte.

d ch. 6. 3.

2 Which [d] was well reported of by the brethren that were at Lystra and Iconium.

Though Timothy was well known unto Paul, yet he would not ordain him without the testimony of others concerning him, of his holy life, and knowledge in the Scripture, 2 Tim. iii. 15, which he did excel in.

3 Him would Paul have to go forth with him; and [e] took and circumcised him because of the Jews which were in those quarters: for they knew all that his father was a Greek.

e 1 Cor.9.20.
Gal. 2. 3.
See Gal. 5. 2.

Circumcised him because of the Jews, who could not yet be persuaded that the law of circumcision was abrogated. Paul, who became all things to all men, that he might save some, circumcised Timothy that he might not offend the Jewish converts, 1 Cor. ix. 22, but would not circumcise Titus, Gal. ii. 3, lest that he should harden them, and offend the Gentiles. These indifferent things require a single eye, to the edifying of the church, and the salvation of souls. Timothy was uncircumcised, although his mother was a Jewess; for according to their Talmudists, the mother could not cause her child to be circumcised against the mind of the father.

4 And as they went through the cities, they delivered them the decrees for to keep, [f] that were ordained of the apostles and elders which were at Jerusalem.

f ch. 15. 28, 29.

The decrees; the determination of the council, mentioned chap. xv. 20, 29. *Ordained of the apostles and elders;* by common consent, and not of one only. whosoever he were.

g ch. 15. 41.

5 And [g] so were the churches established in the faith, and increased in number daily.

Established in the faith; being rightly persuaded in the nature and use of things indifferent; and, in general, of things necessary to be believed. *And increased in number daily;* so that this visitation of the churches had a double benefit. First, it strengthened them that were already converted. Secondly, it added more unto their number.

6 Now when they had gone throughout Phrygia and the region of Galatia, and were forbidden of the Holy Ghost to preach the word in Asia,

Phrygia and *Galatia* were parts of Asia Minor. They *were forbidden of the Holy Ghost* by some revelation, though the manner is not known, *to preach the word in Asia,* for that time; though afterwards Paul preached there about two years together, chap. xix. 10. Thus God (the great Householder) orders the candle to be removed from one room unto another; sends, or takes away, the light of the gospel, to whom, and as often, as he pleaseth. Our calling, as well as our election, is free; and we may say with our Saviour, Matt. xi. 26, *Even so, Father; for so it seemed good in thy sight.*

7 After they were come to Mysia, they assayed to go into Bithynia: but the Spirit suffered them not.

Mysia; a little country near Troas. *Bithynia;* another province nigh unto the same place, over against Thracia, bordering upon the Black Sea. *The Spirit;* the Spirit of Jesus, or of God, as some copies read. *Suffered them not;* the journeyings of them that preached the gospel, as well as their words, were directed by God; they might not say, Do, or Go, but according to the will of God.

8 And they passing by Mysia [h] came down to Troas.

h 2 Cor. 2.12.
2 Tim. 4. 13.

Either the relics of the famous city of Troy, or the country thereabouts, in which the city of Antigonia was built.

9 And a vision appeared to Paul in the night; There stood a [i] man of Macedonia, and prayed him, saying, Come over into Macedonia, and help us.

i ch. 10. 30.

A man; an angel in the appearance and likeness (in habit and demeanour) of one of that country. *Macedonia;* a Grecian province in Europe, extending to the Archipelago. *Help us;* as to our souls, with the saving light of the gospel: God sends the ministers of the gospel to help such as would otherwise perish: with the gospel, salvation comes.

10 And after he had seen the vision, immediately we endeavoured to go [k] into Macedonia, assuredly gathering that the Lord had called us for to preach the Gospel unto them.

k 2 Cor. 2. 13.

Immediately; as soon as God's will was manifested, they make no delay, not objecting against the journey. *We endeavoured to go;* St. Luke, the penman of this book was one of them that went, (the others were Paul, Silas, and Timotheus,) and therefore speaks in the plural number.

11 Therefore loosing from Troas, we came with a straight course to Samothracia, and the next *day* to Neapolis;

Samothracia; an island so called, because the inhabitants came partly out of Thrace, and partly from Samos. This *Neapolis* was a city in the confines of Thrace and Macedonia.

12 And from thence to [l] Philippi, which is ‖ the chief city of that part of Macedonia, *and* a colony: and we were in that city abiding certain days.

l Phil. 1. 1.

‖ Or, *the first.*

Philippi; a city so called from Philip, the father of Alexander the Great, who repaired a ruined town, and caused it to be called by his name. *The chief city of that part of Macedonia;* or the first city in the passage from Samothracia unto Macedonia. *A colony;* where many Roman citizens went to inhabit, and whose inhabitants had the freedom of the city of Rome. To the church in this city Paul wrote an Epistle.

13 And on the † sabbath we went out of the city by a river side, where prayer was wont to be made; and we sat down, and spake unto the women which resorted *thither.*

† Gr. *sabbath day.*

In those places where there were not enough to build a synagogue, or could not obtain leave to do it, the Jews in those countries chose more private places to meet in, which usually were near rivers, or by the sea-side, removed from the noise and observance of the multitude; and these places were called προσευχαί, from the prayers which were usually made there; and to one of these Paul and the rest went, taking that occasion to meet with them whom they might preach the word of life unto. The *women* are here named, as being more numerous in those oratories, or such as most willingly heard and attended unto what was spoken.

14 ¶ And a certain woman named Lydia, a seller of purple, of the city of Thyatira, which worshipped God, heard *us:* whose [m] heart the Lord opened, that

m Luke 24. 45.

THE ACTS XVI

she attended unto the things which were spoken of Paul.

Lydia; so called from the country of that name, she being born at *Thyatira,* a city therein, and now lived with her family at Philippi. *Worshipped God;* being a proselyte, and one of them who had left the heathenish idolatry, and owned the one only and true God; but as yet unacquainted with the gospel of his Son our Saviour. *Heart,* in Scripture sense, signifies both the understanding and the will: thus, *With the heart man believeth unto righteousness,* Rom. x. 10. Her understanding was enlightened, her heart changed; she now loved what she before hated, and hated what before she loved. *The Lord opened;* this was the Lord's work; according unto what our Saviour himself had said, John vi. 44, *No man can come to me, except the Father which hath sent me draw him.* And yet we may in a sense open our hearts, by using such means as God hath promised to succeed for that purpose, Rev. iii. 20; and especially when, in a sense of our inability and necessity, we implore the free grace of God, and engage him to work in us according unto all his good pleasure. Otherwise creating a clean heart within us, as it is called, Psal. li. 10, is beyond the power of nature. *She attended:* hearing is an instructive sense, and faith cometh by it, Rom. x. 17, but it must then be accompanied with attention.

15 And when she was baptized, and her houshold, she besought *us,* saying, If ye have judged me to be faithful to the Lord, come into my house, and abide there. And ⁿshe constrained us.

n Gen. 19. 3. & 33. 11. Judg. 19. 21. Luke 24. 29. Heb. 13. 2.

And her household; when Lydia had right to baptism, by reason of her faith in Jesus Christ, all her family, whom she could undertake to bring up in the knowledge of Christ, were admitted to that ordinance also; as all the servants, and such others as were born in his house, or bought with his money, were circumcised with Abraham, Gen. xvii. 12, 13. Now the gospel does not contract in any respect, but enlarges, the privileges of believers in all things. And if they might under the law have their children and servants admitted into a covenant with God, (which could not but rejoice religious parents and masters, who value the relation they and theirs have to God, above all earthly things,) surely under the gospel none of our families are excluded, unless they wilfully exclude themselves. *She constrained us;* as the two disciples that were going to Emmaus constrained our Saviour, Luke xxiv. 29, with all earnest entreaties and loving violence.

16 ¶ And it came to pass, as we went to prayer, a certain damsel ᵒpossessed with a spirit ‖ of divination met us, which brought her masters ᵖmuch gain by soothsaying:

o 1 Sam. 28. 7. ‖ Or, of *Python.* p ch. 19. 24.

Went to prayer; went towards the place where their public prayers were usually made. *Of divination;* or, of Python, the name of Apollo, from the place where he was worshipped, (which was afterwards called Delphi,) and from whom all evil spirits, that pretended to divination, were called Pythons; as that the woman made use of to delude Saul by, 1 Sam. xxviii. 7.

17 The same followed Paul and us, and cried, saying, These men are the servants of the most high God, which shew unto us the way of salvation.

The devil might be forced by God to confess this; or, he might do it voluntarily by God's permission: First, To draw men on to believe him in other things, being he commended the servants of God, and spake the truth in this. Secondly, That, by flattering St. Paul, he might puff him up, and occasion him to sin. But an evil spirit, (or an evil man,) when he dissembles as if he were good, is then worst of all.

18 And this did she many days. But Paul, ᑫbeing grieved, turned and said to the spirit, I command thee in the name of Jesus Christ to come out of her. ʳAnd he came out the same hour.

q See Mark 1. 25, 34.
r Mark 16. 17.

St. Paul was *grieved,* either for the maid's sake, who suffered so much by her being possessed with this spirit, or, for their sakes who were seduced by him. St. Paul (as our Saviour had done, Mark i. 25) refuseth the testimony of the devil; for he being the father of lies, John viii. 44, makes every thing he says to be suspected; as it is a usual punishment of liars, that they are not believed when they speak the truth; and the devil never speaks any truth but with an intention to deceive. *In the name of Jesus Christ;* by the authority and power of Christ.

19 ¶ And ˢwhen her masters saw that the hope of their gains was gone, ᵗthey caught Paul and Silas, and ᵘdrew *them* into the ‖ marketplace unto the rulers,

s ch. 19. 25, 26.
t 2 Cor. 6. 5.
u Mat. 10. 18.
‖ Or, *court.*

Her masters; for she was a servant, or slave; and being very advantageous, might have many that had a share in her. *Their gains;* the profit could not but be considerable, for they were to come with *the rewards of divination in their hands,* as they did to Balaam, Numb. xxii. 7. *Rulers:* see the next verse.

20 And brought them to the magistrates, saying, These men, being Jews, ˣdo exceedingly trouble our city,

x 1 Kings 18. 17.
ch. 17. 6.

Magistrates, the same who are called *rulers;* and the word here shows, that they were under the power of the sword, and ruled by the Romans; though the rulers spoken of in the former verse might be the civil magistrates of the city, and the magistrates here mentioned might be the commanders of the forces therein. They carried them, as they did our Saviour, from one to the other, the more to disgrace them, and to obtain the greater punishment for them. They mention their *being Jews,* because it was a most odious name unto all men, by reason of their different opinions in religion, and diversity of manners in conversation from all.

21 And teach customs, which are not lawful for us to receive, neither to observe, being Romans.

There was at Philippi, as appears ver. 12, a colony of the Romans, and they were governed by their laws, by which they might make no innovation in religion without the consent of the senate, and afterwards of their emperors; which here these persecutors allege.

22 And the multitude rose up together against them: and the magistrates rent off their clothes, ʸand commanded to beat *them.*

y 2 Cor. 6. 5. & 11. 23, 25. 1 Thes. 2. 2.

The multitude; generality and unanimity alone cannot authorize opinions or practices. *Rent off their clothes;* Paul's and Silas's clothes, to disgrace them the more, or in order unto their being scourged; though some think that the magistrates rent their own clothes, in detestation of the pretended blasphemy which was laid to Paul's charge, as the high priest did, Mark xiv. 63.

23 And when they had laid many stripes upon them, they cast *them* into prison, charging the jailor to keep them safely:

Laid many stripes upon them; partly by the lictors or executioners, and partly by the furious rabble. *The jailer;* this jailer's name (of whose conversion we read hereafter) was Stephanas, as may appear if you compare 1 Cor. i. 16 with what follows by St. Luke in this story. Of him also we read, 1 Cor. xvi. 15, 17.

24 Who, having received such a charge, thrust them into the inner prison, and made their feet fast in the stocks.

Thus they dealt with Joseph, Gen. xxxix. 20, compared with Psal. cv. 18, and with Jeremiah, and with John Baptist. *Sanctorum sors est, et non moleste ferenda.*

25 ¶ And at midnight Paul and Silas prayed, and sang praises unto God: and the prisoners heard them.

No time or place where prayer is not acceptable unto God, and prevalent with him; nay, it sounds the sweeter when on the waters of affliction a good man pours it forth

THE ACTS XVI

unto God. *Sang praises unto God*, that they were counted worthy to suffer for Christ: and being all things are over-ruled for the good, and conduce to the advantage, of them that love God, Rom. viii. 28, they owe unto God thanks for all things through Jesus Christ, which is also required of them, Eph. v. 20.

a ch. 4. 31.

26 ªAnd suddenly there was a great earthquake, so that the foundations of the prison were shaken: and immediately

a ch. 5. 19. & 12. 7, 10.

ªall the doors were opened, and every one's bands were loosed.

Suddenly; how soon is prayer answered, when the fulness of time is come! So nigh is God unto all that call upon him, Psal. xxxiv. 17; cxlv. 18. *There was a great earthquake*; an earthquake did usually precede some wonderful matter, as Matt. xxviii. 2. And although God could have delivered these his servants without an earthquake, yet, to show the more that their deliverance was his work, and it was no artifice or force of their own, he manifested his power after this manner. *Every one's bands were loosed*; either by the earthquake, or some secret power of an angel, or by God himself immediately, that the apostles and others might know that the souls of men should be loosed and set free by them, whose bodies for that purpose were now freed by God.

27 And the keeper of the prison awaking out of his sleep, and seeing the prison doors open, he drew out his sword, and would have killed himself, supposing that the prisoners had been fled.

Awaking out of his sleep, by the earthquake, which being upon an extraordinary occasion, could not fail to do all that God intended by it. *Would have killed himself*, for fear of suffering a more cruel death; for all jailers, who let any prisoner escape, were to suffer the same punishment that the prisoners were thought to have deserved; and self-murder was very ordinary amongst both the Romans and Grecians. But whatsoever their philosophers have said of it, it must needs have been a very great provocation against God, to show so great an aversion from God's will, disposing of them and their concerns in this world, and challenging or daring of him to do worse by them in the world to come. Men must have sad comforts, and take desperate resolutions, that come to this at once.

28 But Paul cried with a loud voice, saying, Do thyself no harm: for we are all here.

The other prisoners were smitten with amazement; neither did they mind (or it might have been kept from them) that the doors were opened, and their chains loosed: but as for the apostles, the same God who wrought this deliverance for them, might inform them of the intent of it; that by this means the conversion of the jailer and his family was intended; and that their doctrine might be magnified, which had been so much vilified.

29 Then he called for a light, and sprang in, and came trembling, and fell down before Paul and Silas,

He called for a light, or lights, which prisons are not usually without. *Came trembling*: what a sudden and great change can God make! he comes trembling to those feet which he had put into the stocks so lately. *Fell down before Paul and Silas*; by which he would give a civil respect unto them, it being an ordinary rite amongst the Eastern nations (as endless examples in Scripture witness) to pay their respects; and from them it spread itself into Greece: which respect Paul and Silas do not refuse, because it was barely civil, and did show the humility and brokenness of the jailer's heart. Yet Peter would not accept of the like from Cornelius, chap. x. 25, 26, because it was more than a bare civil respect which Cornelius would have given him.

b Luke 3. 10. ch. 2. 37. & 9. 6.

30 And brought them out, and said, ᵇSirs, what must I do to be saved?

Brought them out, into his own apartment in the prison, or to some more open and free place. *Sirs*; a term of respect given by the Romans and Grecians to such whom they honoured, as now the jailer did these seemingly most contemptible men. *What must I do to be saved?* he might have some knowledge of a future state, which he here inquires after, 1. By the very light of nature. 2. By tradition. 3. By the doctrine of the philosophers. 4. By his frequenting with Jews and proselytes. Men under fears, and in dangers, as to the things of this world, are brought to look after another world (as every one prays in a storm): but this is only when God is pleased to sanctify such fears and disasters; otherwise all the plagues of Egypt do but harden them the more, Exod. vii. 3.

31 And they said, ᶜBelieve on the Lord Jesus Christ, and thou shalt be saved, and thy house.

c John 3. 16, 36. & 6. 47 1 John 5. 10.

Believe on the Lord Jesus Christ; this is the sum of the gospel. Christ, apprehended by faith, serves for *wisdom, righteousness, sanctification, and redemption*, as 1 Cor. i. 30. But then this precious faith must be such as works by love, as purifies the heart, chap. xv. 9, as *overcometh the world*, 1 John v. 4, as quenches *the fiery darts of the devil*, Eph. vi. 16, and is deservedly called, a *most holy faith*, Jude 20. *Thou shalt be saved, and thy house*; thou shalt by this means come to obtain that life thou dost so much desire after; and not only thyself, but (God gives more than we ask) thy children and family shall be saved; inasmuch as the covenant, where it is entered into, is not only with them, but with their children.

32 And they spake unto him the word of the Lord, and to all that were in his house.

Expounding more at large that which they had briefly propounded in the foregoing verse, as concerning the natures and offices of Christ; especially his suffering for our sins, and rising again for our justification. *To all that were in his house;* their fellow prisoners not exempted, unto whom it was a joyful confinement, being by this means made God's freemen.

33 And he took them the same hour of the night, and washed *their* stripes; and was baptized, he and all his, straightway.

The same hour of the night; he did not delay to show forth the fruits of his faith, and real conversion. *And washed their stripes;* which his stripes had made, using such means as might assuage their pain, and heal their wounds. *He and all his:* see on ver. 15, and 32. Of baptism administered without any delay, upon their profession of faith in Christ, we have had examples, chap. viii. 38, and x. 47, and in the 15th verse of this chapter.

34 And when he had brought them into his house, ᵈhe set meat before them, and rejoiced, believing in God with all his house.

d Luke 5. 29. & 19. 6.

Into his house; which was close unto, or a separate part of, the prison, into which they did ascend, being before in a low dungeon. *He set meat before them;* Paul and Silas had been long fasting, and in any season of the night it was a mercy to them to have a table spread for them. *Rejoiced;* finding the effects of his faith, peace with God, and joy in the Holy Ghost; which was not a little augmented, in that he had his family admitted into the covenant of God's grace, they also believing, and being baptized.

35 And when it was day, the magistrates sent the serjeants, saying, Let those men go.

The serjeants; their messengers, or officers, which did carry a mace, or a rod, from whence they had their name. *Saying, Let those men go;* probably being terrified with the earthquake, which if it had not been general, they could not yet have heard of. Their consciences might also accuse them for having unjustly punished them for a good deed which they had done, only to gratify the rage of the multitude; as also because they had acted against the custom of the Romans, (though they did not yet know that they had the privilege of Roman citizens,) and had beaten strangers without any legal trial, or form of law.

36 And the keeper of the prison told this saying to Paul, The magistrates have sent to let you go: now therefore depart, and go in peace.

Told this saying to Paul; being glad that he might release them. Neither does he bid them go, as desirous to be rid of them; but, not requiring any fees, he lets them go to preach the gospel, and fulfil their ministry, with his prayers and good wishes.

37 But Paul said unto them, They have beaten us openly uncondemned, ^ebeing Romans, and have cast *us* into prison; and now do they thrust us out privily? nay verily; but let them come themselves and fetch us out.

e ch. 22. 25.

Paul said unto them, the officers who were sent to the prison with the message about their liberty. *They have beaten us;* the magistrates, who commanded them to be beaten, are justly charged with the beating of them, as if they had themselves done it. *Openly;* it was no small aggravation of their injustice, and these holy men's sufferings, that they had, for the greater spite unto them, openly scourged them. *Uncondemned;* for they were not tried, or permitted to speak for themselves. *Being Romans;* having the privilege of Roman citizens, which was sometimes given to whole communities. Now such by their laws might not be bound, much less beaten, (and least of all uncondemned,) without the consent of the Romans. *Let them come themselves and fetch us out;* this the apostle stands upon, not so much for his own, as for the gospel's sake, that it might not be noised abroad, that the preachers of it were wicked and vile men, and did deserve such ignominious punishment. Though they were as innocent as doves, it became them also to be as wise as serpents.

38 And the serjeants told these words unto the magistrates: and they feared, when they heard that they were Romans.

For the Romans (under whom these magistrates were) made it by their laws to be treason thus to abuse any of their citizens. God overruled their fear of man for the deliverance of his servants.

39 And they came and besought them, and brought *them* out, and ^fdesired *them* to depart out of the city.

f Matt. 8. 34.

Two things the magistrates had to desire of them: 1. That they would excuse the wrong done unto them, which they feared lest the Romans might revenge. 2. That, to avoid further mischiefs, (as they thought,) they would leave the city. But the words here used do signify, also, that they comforted them, as well as besought, or exhorted them: both by word and deed they sought to make amends for the injury they had offered unto them; and desired them to depart for their own safety, lest the people should express their rage and madness against them.

40 And they went out of the prison, ^gand entered into *the house of* Lydia: and when they had seen the brethren, they comforted them, and departed.

g ver. 14.

Entered into the house of Lydia; of whom, ver. 14. They do not shun dangers, so as to neglect their duty. *They comforted them,* in respect of the tribulation they had endured, and were still to endure; or exhorted them to prepare for suffering, and to submit unto God in it, and to make a holy use of it.

CHAP. XVII.

Paul preaching in the synagogue at Thessalonica, some believe, both Jews and Greeks, 1—4. *The unbelieving Jews raise an uproar,* 5—9. *Paul and Silas are sent to Berea: the Berean Jews are commended for searching the Scriptures,* 10—12. *The Jews of Thessalonica follow and drive Paul from Berea,* 13—15. *At Athens Paul disputing is carried before the court of Areopagus,* 16—21. *He preacheth the living God, to the Athenians unknown: his general call to repentance; the resurrection of Christ; and his coming to judgment,* 22—31. *Some mock, others believe,* 32—34.

NOW when they had passed through Amphipolis and Apollonia, they came to Thessalonica, where was a synagogue of the Jews:

Amphipolis, a city near to Philippi; so called, because the sea came up to it on both sides. *Apollonia,* a city near to Thessalonica. This *Thessalonica* was one of the chiefest cities of Macedonia: unto the church in this place St. Paul wrote two of his Epistles. This city was built by Philip, in memory of a victory he obtained over the Thessali. *Where was a synagogue of the Jews:* it seems that there was no synagogue in either of the other places, but that the Jews of the other cities resorted unto the synagogue in this, all these three cities being in Macedonia. The sending away of Paul and Silas, chap. xvi. 39, to gratify the mad multitude, was a means to bring the word of salvation to those places.

2 And Paul, as his manner was, ^awent in unto them, and three sabbath days reasoned with them out of the Scriptures,

a Luke 4. 16. ch. 9. 20. & 13. 5, 14. & 14. 1. & 16. 13. & 19. 8.

As his manner was; who was faithful unto him that had called him, and took all occasions to do his Master's work. *Out of the Scriptures;* the law and the prophets, which they owned to be of Divine authority; and from the Holy Scriptures alone, all knowledge in the things of God and of our salvation must be fetched. If any speak of these matters not according to them, *it is because they have no light in them,* Isa. viii. 20. What scriptures St. Paul alleged are not set down; but they were such as our Saviour had made use of, Luke xxiv. 27, for the same purpose. This was customary with Paul, to preach these things unto the Jews first, as chap xiii. 46, till they had put the word of God from them by their incredulity.

3 Opening and alledging, ^bthat Christ must needs have suffered, and risen again from the dead; and that this Jesus, ‖whom I preach unto you, is Christ.

b Luke 24. 26, 46. ch. 18. 28. Gal. 3. 1. ‖ Or, *whom,* said he, *I preach.*

Opening the scriptures which he had quoted. The very entrance into God's word giveth light, Psal. cxix. 130. *And alleging, that Christ must needs have suffered;* making the truth concerning our Saviour, which he preached, so plain to the eye of their understanding, as any thing which is exposed to the view of our bodily eyes. Comparing the words of the prophets concerning Christ, with those things which were done and suffered by him, Psal. xxii. 6; Isa. liii. throughout; Matt. xvi. 21; Luke xxiv. 26, 46. *That this Jesus, whom I preach unto you, is Christ;* that Jesus whom Paul preached was the true and only Messiah, and that what was written of the Messiah was fulfilled in him.

4 ^cAnd some of them believed, and consorted with Paul and ^dSilas; and of the devout Greeks a great multitude, and of the chief women not a few.

c ch. 28. 24. *d* ch. 15. 22, 27, 32, 40.

Consorted with Paul and Silas; were so affected towards them, as that they were willing to take the same part or lot with them. The word imports the nearest and most intimate friendship and union; even such as is conjugal. *Devout Greeks;* such of that nation as were become proselytes, who had renounced the idolatry and wicked conversation of the heathen, amongst whom they lived; and had joined themselves to the Jews; at least so far as to hear the law and the prophets read and expounded in their synagogues; and did worship but one God, and did injury unto none. Of these we frequently read in this book; as ver. 17; chap. xiii. 42, 43. *Of the chief women not a few;* a considerable number of these believed; yet, chap. xiii. 50, such had stirred up persecution against Paul and Barnabas.

5 ¶ But the Jews which believed not, moved with envy, took unto them certain lewd fellows of the baser sort, and gathered a company, and set all the city on an uproar, and assaulted the house of ^eJason, and sought to bring them out to the people.

e Rom. 16. 21.

Believed not; or were not convinced, or persuaded by St. Paul's sermons and arguments. *Moved with envy,* or zeal; which, as fire in the chimney, its due place, is useful and necessary; but when scattered abroad, and out of its place, is most dangerous and destructive. *Lewd fellows;*

such as stand in markets and public places, gazing, and having nothing to do. *Of the baser sort:* to what mean and base acts do not blind zeal and the rage of persecutors descend! *Jason;* some think this to be the Greek name which the Hellenists did use for Joshua, or Jesus. This man was one of the dispersion, who came from Judea into Syria, and from thence into Macedonia; and is famous, so far as the word of God is preached, for being the host to Paul and Silas; and is mentioned, Rom. xvi. 21. *To bring them out to the people,* for to slay them. Nothing but their blood could quench the thirst of their persecutors; but having no just cause for the spilling of it, they are willing to have others to bear the odium of it.

6 And when they found them not, they drew Jason and certain brethren unto the rulers of the city, crying, ᶠThese that have turned the world upside down are come hither also;

f ch. 16. 20.

Being withdrawn, to avoid the popular rage against them, they charge innovation upon them, as knowing how jealous rulers are of any alteration. Thus whatsoever mischief befell the state, or whatsoever was odious and abominable, was in the primitive times still charged upon the Christians. The enemies of God's church clothe his servants in beasts' skins, (painting and representing them in what forms they please,) that every one may hunt and worry them.

7 Whom Jason hath received: and these all do contrary to the decrees of Cæsar, ᵍsaying that there is another king, *one* Jesus.

g Luke 23. 2.
John 19. 12.
1 Pet. 2. 15.

Hath received; privily, and with design. *Contrary to the decrees of Cæsar:* the Romans, before they were brought under their emperors, (and after that,) did not suffer any to be called king without their allowance and approbation; which was also much valued by such unto whom that honour was bestowed by them. *Another king,* besides Cæsar, who was called the lord of the world. This is like to the charge laid against our Saviour; but most maliciously both then and now, and wholly against their own consciences; for they themselves expected the Messiah to be a king, and refused and rejected him because his kingdom was a spiritual kingdom, and not of this world, John xviii. 36, 37.

8 And they troubled the people and the rulers of the city, when they heard these things.

They troubled the people; hearing something to have been done against the Roman state, under whom they were, and not knowing what it might come to, or how it might be construed. *And the rulers;* for fear of an insurrection and tumult.

9 And when they had taken security of Jason, and of the other, they let them go.

Had taken security; either being satisfied with their answer, or having bail for their appearance, if need were; the word only hinting their being satisfied, or contented, as Mark xv. 15.

10 ¶ And ʰthe brethren immediately sent away Paul and Silas by night unto Berea: who coming *thither* went into the synagogue of the Jews.

h ch. 9. 25.
ver. 14.

Berea; a city of Macedonia, not far from Pella and Thessalonica. *Went into the synagogue of the Jews;* they went still first unto the lost sheep of the house of Israel; in which Paul's invincible love, which he speaks of, Rom. ix. 2, 3, does manifestly appear. The Jews had every where endeavoured his destruction; he still requites them (what he may) in promoting their salvation.

11 These were more noble than those in Thessalonica, in that they received the word with all readiness of mind, and ⁱsearched the Scriptures daily, whether those things were so.

i Is. 34. 16.
Luke 16. 29.
John 5. 39.

The Jews of Berea did excel those of Thessalonica, not so much in birth as in disposition: they were not so prejudiced and obstinate; they patiently heard Paul; they seriously thought upon what he had said, and compared it with the Scriptures. And thus God gave them the preparation of the heart; and they brought their empty vessels. No wonder then that the oil of grace ran into them, and filled them. The Jews call their learned men, the sons of nobles; and according to that expression, these Bereans, that had acted so ingenuously and wisely, were said to be *more noble. Searched the Scriptures daily, whether those things were so:* truth dares abide the test; only false wares need a dark shop to put them off in. The Scriptures only are our infallible rule; for they come from God, 2 Tim. iii. 16, *who cannot lie,* Titus i. 2.

12 Therefore many of them believed; also of honourable women which were Greeks, and of men, not a few.

God blessing his own gifts, and giving still unto them that had, and made use of them. And would we also *lay aside all filthiness, and superfluity of naughtiness, and receive with meekness the ingrafted word, which is able to save our souls,* James i. 21, we should find the hand of the Lord not to be shortened, but his word as powerful, as piercing, as converting as ever.

13 But when the Jews of Thessalonica had knowledge that the word of God was preached of Paul at Berea, they came thither also, and stirred up the people.

As the waves are stirred with the wind; a fit metaphor to represent the fickle multitude by, that, as the sea, now rolls one way, then another; or as tottering buildings, that shake with every wind.

14 ᵏAnd then immediately the brethren sent away Paul to go as it were to the sea: but Silas and Timotheus abode there still.

k Matt. 10. 23.

To go as it were to the sea; that they might give over the pursuit of him; or, at least, be disappointed if they did pursue him, being he went on foot to Athens. *But Silas and Timotheus abode there still;* the fury of the persecutors not being so hot against them as against Paul, who was more known or maligned than Silas or Timotheus: or these might abide there longer, having their relations in Macedonia.

15 And they that conducted Paul brought him unto Athens: and ˡreceiving a commandment unto Silas and Timotheus for to come to him with all speed, they departed.

l ch. 18. 5

They that conducted Paul; who accompanied, and had undertaken to secure him. *Athens;* the Greece of Greece, or the eye of Greece; as Greece was accounted the eye of the world; and yet, with all its learning, did not attain to saving knowledge, until Paul came and preached it. Satan's malice still causes the gospel to spread.

16 ¶ Now while Paul waited for them at Athens, ᵐhis spirit was stirred in him, when he saw the city ∥wholly given to idolatry.

A. D. 54.
m 2 Pet. 2. 8.
∥ Or, *full of idols.*

His spirit was stirred in him; moved, and sharpened, being highly affected with divers passions: 1. With grief, for so learned, and yet blind and miserable a place. 2. With zeal, and a holy desire to instruct and inform it. 3. With anger and indignation against the idolatry and sin that abounded in it. *Wholly given to idolatry;* or, as the marginal reading hath, full of idols. For we read, that there were more idols in Athens than in all Greece besides; and that it was easier to find a god there (that is, an idol) than a man; their images being as numerous as their inhabitants.

17 Therefore disputed he in the synagogue with the Jews, and with the devout persons, and in the market daily with them that met with him.

Therefore disputed he in the synagogue with the Jews; as ver. 2, still giving the Jews, if there were any, the priority; or, by having that means an opportunity to speak unto the proselytes of the Gentiles, who are the *devout persons* here meant: see chap. xiii. 43. *In the market,* because of the concourse thither; throwing the net of the

Gospel where there were most fish; and he himself preaching, as he exhorted others to do, in season and out of season, 2 Tim. iv. 2.

18 Then certain philosophers of the Epicureans, and of the Stoicks, encountered him. And some said, What will this ||babbler say? other some, He seemeth to be a setter forth of strange gods: because he preached unto them Jesus, and the resurrection.

|| Or, *base fellow*.

Both these sects of philosophers were the most opposite to Christianity of all others: 1. The *Epicureans* (so called from one Epicurus) did generally deny, that the world was made, or that it is governed, by God; as also, that there were any rewards or punishments for men after death, holding nothing to be good but what was so to their senses: and if so, were indeed swine rather than men. 2. The *Stoics* were so called from the place where they met at first; and held as bad opinions as the other did; and denied that their wise men were inferior to their gods, and in some respect preferred them before their gods; which their Seneca was not free from, Epist. 73. And no wonder if such men oppose the gospel what they may. *What will this babbler say?* they make Paul so contemptible, comparing him to such as live by the off-falls of corn, which was used to be gathered up as they fell down in measuring, and left to be fed upon by the meanest and poorest of the people. *A setter forth of strange gods;* they might amongst the Athenians bring in by public authority as many gods as they would, but none out of their private opinions; which was the fault charged upon Socrates. *And the resurrection;* so ignorantly, or maliciously, did they pervert St. Paul's words, that they accuse him for making the resurrection a god too. Probably they heard him often naming the word, and magnifying of the resurrection, as without which we were without hope.

19 And they took him, and brought him unto ||Areopagus, saying, May we know what this new doctrine, whereof thou speakest, *is?*

|| Or, *Mars' hill. It was the highest court in Athens.*

The city of Athens was divided into five wards, or parts; one of which was called *Areopagus,* from the temple of Mars, which stood upon a hill in it: nigh unto which temple, or in some part of it, was their chiefest court kept; and here they judged of all religious affairs: here they condemned Diagoras, Protagoras, and Socrates; and hither they bring Paul, though rather to inquire of him (there being the resort of learned men) concerning his doctrine, than to condemn him for it.

20 For thou bringest certain strange things to our ears: we would know therefore what these things mean.

The greatest objection which these men had against the gospel was, that it was strange and new. That it is not new was apparent, it having been in the Old Testament (as the ripe fruit is in the blossom) so long ago; and their own superstitions were but so many apish imitations of God's worship. And if these things were strange unto them, they might thank themselves, who had not made due inquiring after them; and had, by their not improving the light of nature, provoked God to withhold further manifestations unto them, Rom. i. 24, 28.

21 (For all the Athenians and strangers which were there spent their time in nothing else, but either to tell, or to hear some new thing.)

Strangers which were there; which must needs have been a considerable number, Athens being then a famous haven town and university; and these strangers might easily take this itch after news from the natives, who are noted for it by Theophrastus, Demosthenes, &c.

22 ¶ Then Paul stood in the midst of ||Mars' hill, and said, *Ye* men of Athens, I perceive that in all things ye are too superstitious.

|| Or, *the court of the Areopagites.*

Mars' hill: see ver. 19. *Too superstitious;* sometimes this word is taken in a good sense; many then, as now, taking superstition to be religion. But it is often taken in a bad sense: thus Theophrastus says, that a truly pious man is a friend of God; ὅδε δεισιδαίμων κόλαξ Θεῶ, but the superstitious man is a flatterer of God. Now this word being then of a kind of middle signification, the apostle would seem not to bear too hard upon the Athenians, who were devout and religious, according to the measure of their knowledge, and whom he desired to win by love and gentleness.

23 For as I passed by, and beheld your ||devotions, I found an altar with this inscription, TO THE UNKNOWN GOD. Whom therefore ye ignorantly worship, him declare I unto you.

|| Or, *gods that ye worship,* 2 Thess. 2. 4.

Devotions; any thing unto which Divine worship and honour is given. *To the unknown God:* it is storied, that in a plague time, when the Athenians had wearied themselves with their supplications unto all the gods of their country, they were advised by Epaminondas (a devout man amongst them) to erect an altar unto that god who had the power over that disease, whosoever he was; which because they did not know, and would be sure not to omit in their devotions, they erected an altar unto him under the name of *The unknown God.* Some say, there was a more general inscription, To the gods of Asia, Europe, and Africa, to the unknown and strange gods; though the inscription the apostle mentions in the singular number, might be usual too: for the Athenians, who entertained all manner of gods, fearing lest there should be any which they had not heard of, for their greater security, as they imagined, would have an altar for such also. Now this *unknown God,* St. Paul says, which was worshipped by them, was the true God: for, 1. They had an apprehension that Christ was the true God, whilst that wonderful eclipse at his death was effectually considered amongst them. Hence it is said, that Dionysius cried out, *Deus ignotus in carne patitur.* Now the unknown God suffers in the flesh. 2. The God of the Jews, whose name the Jews took to be so ineffable that they would not undertake to speak it, and who was not wholly unknown to Plato and Pythagoras, and who is truly invisible and incomprehensible, might upon that account be thus styled amongst them.

24 ⁿGod that made the world and all things therein, seeing that he is ᵒLord of heaven and earth, ᵖdwelleth not in temples made with hands;

n ch. 14. 15.
o Matt.11.25.
p ch. 7. 48.

God that made the world; this seems to be directed against the Epicureans, who held, that the world was without beginning. *Dwelleth not in temples made with hands;* as if he could be tied to them, or circumcised by them: yet God did in some respect dwell in his temple, where he did manifest himself more clearly than in other places; but that was a type of heaven, the throne of God.

25 Neither is worshipped with men's hands, ᵠas though he needed any thing, seeing ʳhe giveth to all life, and breath, and all things;

q Ps. 50. 8.
r Gen. 2. 7.
Num. 16.22.
Job 12. 10. &
27. 3. & 33.
4. Is. 42. 5.
& 57. 16.
Zech. 12. 1.

As though he needed any thing; God is not worshipped or served by holy men, because he wants their service, or any thing that can be offered unto him by them; but because it is their duty and advantage to be employed in his service and worship, Psal. l. 10, 11. *Life, and breath; the breath of life,* Gen. ii. 7. And in this respect God is called *the God of the spirits of all flesh,* Numb. xvi. 22; as the cause of life and breath in all creatures, but especially in man; which made that charge so great against Belshazzar, Dan. v. 23, that his breath was in God's hand, and yet he had not glorified him.

26 And hath made of one blood all nations of men for to dwell on all the face of the earth, and hath determined the times before appointed, and ˢthe bounds of their habitation;

s Deut. 32. 8.

Hath made of one blood: 1. To teach all charity and compassion towards one another, being so nearly allied to one another. 2. As also to admire God more in that va-

THE ACTS XVII

riety that appears in men's shapes and voices, but especially in the dispositions of their minds; whenas they all come from one stock and stem. *Hath determined the times, &c.:* the apostle asserts the providence of God against these Athenian philosophers, that nothing comes by chance, or a fatuitous concourse of atoms; but that God is in every thing, though men know it not, or rather will not consider it, Job vii. 1; xiv. 5, 14. This doctrine was preached by Moses, who tells the people, that God is their life, and the length of their days, that they might love him, and obey his voice, and cleave unto him, Deut. xxx. 20.

t Rom. 1. 20.
27 ^tThat they should seek the Lord, if haply they might feel after him, and
u ch. 14. 17.
find him, ^uthough he be not far from every one of us:

That they should seek the Lord: the apostle tells these philosophers, to whom he spake, the true use of their philosophy, to improve their knowledge of natural things, to beget in them by it an admiration of the God of nature; for as from him, so for him are all things, Rom. xi. 36. *If haply they might feel after him, and find him;* and although God himself is incorporeal, yet the things which he made are palpable; and did they seek as they ought, they might find out a great deal of God by the creatures, in which his wisdom, power, and goodness are manifested, Rom. i. 20. *Though he be not far from every one of us;* God filleth all things, especially he is near in the effects of his wisdom, goodness, and faithfulness, by which he orders and disposes of all things, to the falling off of a hair from our heads.

x Col. 1. 17. Heb. 1. 3.
y Tit. 1. 12.
28 For ^xin him we live, and move, and have our being; ^yas certain also of your own poets have said, For we are also his offspring.

In him we live, &c.; he is the God that made us, that preserves us, and not we ourselves; he keeps us as in the hollow of his hand, and compasseth our paths. Our breath is in our nostrils, and when we send it forth we have none to take in again, unless God furnish us with it, as out of his own hand. *As certain also of your own poets;* Aratus, a Greek poet: not that St. Paul thought to derive any authority from these poets unto what he had said, but that he might shame them the more by the testimony of their allowed authors. Such quotations as these are (as the bringing in of a Greek into the temple) very rare; yet, besides this, we meet with the like, 1 Cor. xv. 33; Tit. i. 12.

29 Forasmuch then as we are the off-
z Is. 40. 18.
spring of God, ^zwe ought not to think that the Godhead is like unto gold, or silver, or stone, graven by art and man's device.

We are the offspring of God; this is spoken by the apostle in a poetical expression, according unto what he had cited. We are indeed the children, and in our souls bear the image of God. But as many as have the Spirit of adoption, they partake of God's holiness, and imitate his goodness, and are more like unto him, by whom they are *begotten again unto a lively hope,* 1 Pet. i. 3; and at the resurrection they will appear unto all to be his children, when they shall be acknowledged his heirs, and coheirs with Jesus Christ, Rom. viii. 17. *We ought not to think that the Godhead is like unto gold, or silver:* taking man in his natural principles, consisting of soul and body, he is not made of gold and silver; much less can God be made of them. Our soul, in which we bear the image of God, cannot be expressed by any graving or painting; much less God, whose image it is. There are two things to be considered in every image: its matter, and its form or shape. The matter of an image, let it be never so precious, is much inferior to man; for it lies in the earth, (be it gold or silver,) for man to trample upon, until he dig it up, and take it out. As for the form of the image, it is that which men please to give it, and man is a kind of creator of it; howsoever, it is his workmanship, and the work is more ignoble than the workman, at least not to be adored by him. *By art and man's device;* according to man's will and pleasure, for the image cannot determine itself to be made as it would.

30 And ^athe times of this ignorance God winked at; but ^bnow commandeth all men every where to repent:
a ch. 14. 16. Rom. 3. 25.
b Luke 24. 47. Tit. 2. 11, 12.
1 Pet. i. 14. & 4. 3.

The times of this ignorance God winked at; to prevent an objection, lest any should think that they might continue in their unbelief, and fare as well as their progenitors, God is said to have overlooked them; as if he had counted them unworthy of his care and providence, and therefore he did not correct or instruct them. When any are left to go on in their sin, without God's instruction or correction, it is a sad sign that God scorns to look upon them, or to use any means to recover them. *But now commandeth all men every where to repent:* under the gospel we are so far from having liberty to do what we list, that we are more nearly concerned to repent and become holy, Rom. xiii. 11; Tit. ii. 11, 12; 1 Pet. i. 14, 15; and all men, every where, without exception of time or place, are under this command of repentance; and cursed indeed will he be that does not observe it.

31 Because he hath appointed a day, in the which ^che will judge the world in righteousness by *that* man whom he hath ordained; *whereof* he hath ∥ given assurance unto all *men,* in that ^d he hath raised him from the dead.
c ch. 10. 42. Rom. 2. 16. & 14. 10.
∥ Or, *offered faith.*
d ch. 2. 24.

He hath appointed a day, in the which he will judge the world: that God will judge the world his enemies have with trembling acknowledged, but when God will judge the world he hath concealed from his friends; yet the time is already set, Psal. xcvi. 13; 2 Cor. v. 10, and we ought to be daily prepared for it. *In righteousness:* shall not the Judge of all the world do right? *By that man whom he hath ordained;* our blessed Saviour, called here *man,* suitably to his death and resurrection, which St. Paul preached of; as also as man he is thus highly exalted for his debasing of himself for our sakes, Phil. ii. 9—11. *Whereof he hath given assurance unto all men, in that he hath raised him from the dead;* an undeniable proof or argument, it being so difficult a matter to believe a world to come, when we see all things remain as they did in this world; and especially to believe, that in the general judgment Christ, whom they had judged, condemned, and executed, should be Judge: God therefore did glorify him, by raising him from the dead, that they and we might not be faithless, but believe, Rom. i. 4.

32 ¶ And when they heard of the resurrection of the dead, some mocked: and others said, We will hear thee again of this *matter.*

Some mocked; the Epicureans, whom Paul had spoken against in his doctrine of the resurrection from the dead, and judgment to come. *Others said, We will hear thee again of this matter;* it is thought the Stoics, who did not think the resurrection to be impossible, but did acknowledge rewards and punishments in the world to come; yet, though this seem most likely, the grace of God is free and powerful, and can subdue any unto itself. We are sure that there are different soils into which the seed of the word is cast, Matt. xiii.

33 So Paul departed from among them.

Leaving what he had said to God's blessing and their consideration.

34 Howbeit certain men clave unto him, and believed: among the which *was* Dionysius the Areopagite, and a woman named Damaris, and others with them.

Clave unto him, in more than ordinary friendship; they were as glued to him; great was their love to the apostle, by whom their eyes were opened, nay, by whose ministry they were raised from the dead. *Dionysius the Areopagite;* one of that great council mentioned ver. 19, whose conversion might have a great influence on many. *Damaris;* who is thought to have been an honourable woman; such are mentioned ver. 12: or she might have been specially eminent for some grace or goodness she excelled in, and therefore hath a name upon record in the word of God.

CHAP. XVIII

Paul worketh for his subsistence, and preacheth Christ at Corinth, first to the Jews, and, upon their opposing and blaspheming, to the Gentiles with more success, 1—8. He is encouraged by the Lord in a vision, and abideth there a long time, 9—11. The Jews accuse him before Gallio the deputy, who will have nothing to do with them, 12—17. Paul passeth from city to city, confirming the disciples, 18—23. Apollos, instructed more perfectly in the Christian doctrine by Aquila and Priscilla, preacheth it at Ephesus, and afterward in Achaia, with great efficacy, 24—28.

AFTER these things Paul departed from Athens, and came to Corinth;
The metropolis of Achaia, being a rich sea town, and situate in the very isthmus which joins Peloponnesus unto Achaia; made a Roman colony, and now flourishing with learned men. Here St. Paul gathered a famous church, unto which he wrote two of his Epistles.

2 And found a certain Jew named [a] Aquila, born in Pontus, lately come from Italy, with his wife Priscilla; (because that Claudius had commanded all Jews to depart from Rome:) and came unto them.

[a] Rom. 16.
3 1 Cor. 16.
19. 2 Tim. 4. 19.

Pontus; a country between Cappadocia and the Black Sea, Acts ii. 9, whither the progenitors of Aquila, in one of the dispersions, might flee from Judea to inhabit there. *Claudius;* the Roman emperor, who, at the beginning of his reign, gave liberty to the Jews freely to exercise their religion, but about eight years after took away that privilege from them; which Suetonius makes mention of, though very much mistaking the reason. With the Jews, it is thought that the Christians were banished too; for the pagan Romans did not care to distinguish betwixt them, they both worshipping but one God, and agreeing in opposing their idolatry.

3 And because he was of the same craft, he abode with them, [b] and wrought: for by their occupation they were tentmakers.

b ch. 20. 34.
1 Cor. 4. 12.
1 Thes. 2. 9.
2 Thes. 3. 8.

Of the same craft; the most learned amongst the Jews did always learn some handicraft, and it was one of those things which they held a father was bound to do for his child, viz. to teach him some trade. And one of their rabbi's sayings is, That whosoever does not teach his child a trade, does as bad as if he did teach him to play the thief. *And wrought;* St. Paul wrought with his hands, not so much because as yet there was no church there that could maintain him, but, 1. Because he would not be burdensome unto them, they being probably most mean persons that believed there, as appears, 1 Cor. i. 26. Or, 2. That he might show how that he did not covet theirs. but them, and to gain nothing but souls amongst them. Yet he asserted his right, and the right of ministers, by Divine appointment, to live of the gospel, 1 Cor. ix. 6, 11, 12. *Tent-makers;* tents were used by soldiers, and in those hot countries by others also, being usually made of skins sewn together to keep off the violence of the weather.

c ch. 17. 2.

4 [c] And he reasoned in the synagogue every sabbath, and persuaded the Jews and the Greeks.

He reasoned in the synagogue; or argued and disputed, giving his reasons out of Scripture, and answering their objections. *And persuaded the Jews;* not only using cogent arguments, but, as some understand the verb, such as did prevail upon them. *And the Greeks;* not such as were of the Jewish race, and after the dispersion used the Scripture in the Greek tongue; but such as were Gentile Greeks, Greeks by descent.

d ch. 17. 14, 15.
e Job 32. 18.
ch. 17. 3.
ver. 28.
|| Or, is the Christ.

5 And [d] when Silas and Timotheus were come from Macedonia, Paul was [e] pressed in the spirit, and testified to the Jews that Jesus || *was* Christ.

Were come from Macedonia; according as was ordered by him, chap. xvii. 14, 15. *Pressed in the spirit;* more than ordinarily affected, the Spirit of God influencing his spirit, so that he felt an anguish or pain at the heart, as 2 Cor. ii. 4; such was his grief for the contumacy of the Jews, so great was his desire that they might be saved. *Jesus was Christ:* 1. The Christ, or anointed, that excelled all other Christs or anointed ones, being anointed with oil above measure. 2. The Christ that was promised by the prophets.

6 And [f] when they opposed themselves, and blasphemed, [g] he shook *his* raiment, and said unto them, [h] Your blood *be* upon your own heads; [i] I *am* clean: [k] from henceforth I will go unto the Gentiles.

f ch. 13. 45.
1 Pet. 4. 4.
g Neh. 5. 13.
Mat. 10. 14.
ch. 13. 51.
h Lev. 20. 9, 11, 12.
2 Sam. 1. 16.
Ezek. 18. 13. & 33. 4.
i Ezek. 3. 18, 19. & 33. 9. ch. 20. 26.   k ch. 13. 46. & 28. 28.

Blasphemed; they blasphemed Paul, miscalling of him, but especially Christ, whose dishonour grieved Paul most. *He shook his raiment;* his upper garment, as the manner was, Matt. xxvi. 65, that none of the dust of that place where such blasphemy was spoken might stick unto him. See chap. xiii. 51. *Your blood be upon your own heads;* or, You are guilty of your own deaths and damnation, 2 Sam. i. 16; Matt. xxvii. 25; *Felo de se.* This expression is borrowed from the witnesses laying their hands on the head of the guilty person; or the sacrificer's laying his hand on the head of the beast which was to be slain, Exod. xxix. 10; Lev. i. 4. *I am clean;* free from their blood, or the loss of their souls, having warned them, and shown the way of life unto them. Ezek. xxxiii. 4; he had blown the trumpet, and warned the people.

7 ¶ And he departed thence, and entered into a certain *man's* house, named Justus, *one* that worshipped God, whose house joined hard to the synagogue.

Justus; some read Titus, some both Titus and Justus, making Justus a surname, as Acts i. 23; Col. iv. 11; after the manner of the Romans. *One that worshipped God;* had forsaken the polytheism of the heathen.

8 [l] And Crispus, the chief ruler of the synagogue, believed on the Lord with all his house; and many of the Corinthians hearing believed, and were baptized.

l 1 Cor. 1. 14.

The chief ruler: there were several rulers in a synagogue, which we find frequent mention of, as Matt. ix. 18; Mark v. 22. Their office and place was, to advise and give order about the affairs of the synagogue, that all things might be performed according to their prescribed rules. *Many of the Corinthians believed;* amongst whom are reckoned Gaius, Sosthenes, 1 Cor. i. 1, and Epenetus, Rom. xvi. 5.

9 Then [m] spake the Lord to Paul in the night by a vision, Be not afraid, but speak, and hold not thy peace;

m ch. 23. 11.

In the night by a vision; as chap. xvi. 9; it may be, by an angel. *Speak, and hold not thy peace;* it is doubled again and again, as of greatest consequence, 1. To the Corinthians, whose salvation by this means might be procured. 2. To Paul himself, whose soul, howsoever, should be delivered, he having discharged his duty, chap. xx. 26, 27. The fierceness of the enemies of God and his truth, should kindle a greater fervour in his servants for his glory. Should Satan have better servants than God? Should they dare for their master beyond what the servants of God are willing to do or suffer for him? Isa. lxii. 1; Jer. i. 17, 18.

10 [n] For I am with thee, and no man shall set on thee to hurt thee: for I have much people in this city.

n Jer. 1. 18, 19.
Matt. 28. 20.

Christ, in this vision, useth two arguments to persuade Paul to continue preaching the gospel at Corinth: 1. Because he would be with him, to supply, support, and deliver him; as it is promised to Jeremiah, Jer. i. 19, and to all the faithful ministers of Christ, Matt. xxviii. 20. This promise was fulfilled to Paul, and to other of God's servants; whatsoever troubles they met with, even when they were killed, they were not hurt, Rom. viii. 36—39. The other reason why Paul was commanded to tarry was, because there were many that God would have called by his ministry; and thus

THE ACTS XVIII

those who were not his people God calleth his people, as Hos. i. 10; ii. 23.

† Gr. *sat there.* 11 And he †continued *there* a year and six months, teaching the word of God among them.

He sat there as his fixed place; which implies his continuance and constancy in the work of the ministry.

A. D. 55. ending. 12 ¶ And when Gallio was the deputy of Achaia, the Jews made insurrection with one accord against Paul, and brought him to the judgment seat,

This *Gallio* was brother to that deservedly famous Seneca, (who was tutor to Nero,) and hath great commendations given him, as being a man of excellent disposition, beloved by all men, an enemy to all vice, and especially a hater of flattery. *Deputy of Achaia;* this man was proconsul, governing Achaia and all Greece absolutely, or with the power of a consul. *With one accord;* wicked men in their evil deeds are unanimous, for Satan knows that his kingdom would not stand if it were once divided.

13 Saying, This *fellow* persuadeth men to worship God contrary to the law.

Contrary to the law, of the Romans, who, to avoid tumults and confusions, did forbid any to set up any new worship without leave; and the Jews in these parts having here no power to punish St. Paul as they had at Jerusalem, maliciously incite the governor against him. Or by *the law* here may be meant the law of Moses, which they accuse Paul to have broken, and so not to be comprehended in that licence which they had to exercise their religion.

14 And when Paul was now about to open *his* mouth, Gallio said unto the Jews, °If it were a matter of wrong or wicked lewdness, O *ye* Jews, reason would that I should bear with you:

To open his mouth; to make his apology, and to speak in his own defence. *A matter of wrong;* as murder, theft, or any such injury, which judges do usually determine of. *Reason would that I should bear with you;* I would endure any trouble to hear and understand it, I should think it my duty to suffer you to say as much as you would in your case.

15 But if it be a question of words and names, and *of* your law, look ye *to it;* for I will be no judge of such *matters.*

A question of words; which have been spoken about the controversies of religion. *And names;* as, whether Jesus was to be called Christ or the Messiah; and whether his disciples might be called Christians. *And of your law;* concerning circumcision, as whether none may be saved without it. *I will be no judge of such matters;* he acknowledges his unfitness and unwillingness to determine such things as did not belong unto him, or he did not understand.

16 And he drave them from the judgment seat.

He commanded them to be gone, having dismissed their case; and, if need were, added threatening and force.

p 1 Cor. 1. 1. 17 Then all the Greeks took ᵖ Sosthenes, the chief ruler of the synagogue, and beat *him* before the judgment seat. And Gallio cared for none of those things.

All the Greeks; not the converted Greeks, though St. Austin thought they beat Sosthenes, as an enemy to Paul, (yet surely they had not so learned Christ,) but the unbelieving or Gentile Greeks, who cared for neither Paul nor Jews, but favoured Gallio, who would have them driven away. *Sosthenes;* some think him to have been the same with Crispus, ver. 8; others, to have succeeded him in that office; and some think that he was chief ruler of another synagogue (for in great cities there might be more than one); and others, that there might be several called chief rulers over one and the same synagogue. *Gallio cared for none of those things;* either slighting the Jews and all their controversies, or prudently declined intermeddling with them.

18 ¶ And Paul *after this* tarried *there* yet a good while, and then took his leave of the brethren, and sailed thence into Syria, and with him Priscilla and Aquila; having ᑫshorn *his* head in ʳCenchrea: for he had a vow.

q Num. 6. 18. ch. 21. 24. r Rom. 16. 1.

A good while; a year and a half in all, as some think, which is mentioned ver. 11, by a prolepsis; or, besides that year and a half there spoken of. *Took his leave of the brethren;* ordering every thing as if he were to have taken his last farewell of them, as it fell out accordingly: howsoever, holy men live in a constant expectation of their dissolution. *Priscilla and Aquila:* that the wife's name is here put before the husband's, have caused various conjectures; and it is observed, that in St. Paul's Epistles, whereas there are three times only mention of them both together, viz. Rom. xvi. 3; 1 Cor. xvi. 19; 2 Tim. iv. 19, the wife's name is twice placed first, to show, that in Christ Jesus *there is neither male nor female,* Gal. iii. 28. *Cenchrea;* which was a town at the entering into the haven belonging to Corinth, Rom. xvi. 1. *For he had a vow;* to wit, St. Paul had; and therefore had shaven his head, according unto the law, Numb. vi. 18. To the Jews he became as a Jew.

19 And he came to Ephesus, and left them there: but he himself entered into the synagogue, and reasoned with the Jews.

Ephesus; the metropolis of the Lesser Asia, where afterwards that famous church was, unto which St. Paul wrote an Epistle, as also St. John wrote another, Rev. ii. 1. *Left them there;* that is, Aquila and Priscilla at Ephesus, to confirm the believing Ephesians; whilst Paul *entered into the synagogue, and reasoned with the Jews;* out of an extraordinary love for his nation, although he had suffered all those indignities from them, yet he would give them precept upon precept, and line upon line.

20 When they desired *him* to tarry longer time with them, he consented not;

They desired; that is, Aquila and Priscilla, whom Paul would not yield unto. *He consented not;* by God's wonderful providence, which overrules all our inclinations; Paul having greater things to do and suffer for the glory of God elsewhere.

21 But bade them farewell, saying, ˢI must by all means keep this feast that cometh in Jerusalem: but I will return again unto you, ᵗif God will. And he sailed from Ephesus.

s ch. 19. 21. & 20. 16.

t 1 Cor. 4. 19. Heb. 6. 3. Jam. 4. 15.

This feast; the feast of the passover; which is meant where feast is put absolutely, unless some after-expression qualifies it: not that this holy man did out of conscience to the feast intend to observe it, for *Christ is the end of the law* to them that believe, Rom. x. 4; but because of the vast concourse from all places to Jerusalem at that time, which would give him an opportunity of making Christ known to such multitudes, and to gain their souls unto him. *If God will;* though he was an apostle, and had the Spirit of prophecy, and might know whether he should return or no, yet he does not absolutely promise them to return to them, but conditionally, if the Lord will; to teach us what caution we should use in all our promises and resolutions, as Jam. iv. 15, being we know not what a day may bring forth. Besides, in our owning of God's will and pleasure, we acknowledge a providence of God in all things, especially in our concerns, which we desire to refer all unto.

22 And when he had landed at Cæsarea, and gone up, and saluted the church, he went down to Antioch.

A. D. 56.

Cæsarea; not that Cæsarea that was in Syria, but that which was in Palestine, called Cæsarea Stratonis; and which was the safest way to Jerusalem; for the way by Joppa, though shorter, was accounted more dangerous. *The church;* either the church of Cæsarea in his journey, or that at Jerusalem at his journey's end, which for its populousness might be called eminently, *the church.* *Antioch;* that Antioch that was in Syria.

VOL. III—15

THE ACTS XVIII, XIX

23 And after he had spent some time *there*, he departed, and went over *all* the country of "Galatia and Phrygia in order, ˣstrengthening all the disciples.

Had spent some time there; this work might take up the constant care and indefatigable pains of the apostle. *Galatia;* where he had converted many. *Phrygia:* see chap. xvi. 6. *Strengthening all the disciples;* though the seed be duly sown, yet it must be seasonably watered; and *redit labor actus in orbem.*

24 ¶ ʸAnd a certain Jew named Apollos, born at Alexandria, an eloquent man, *and* mighty in the Scriptures, came to Ephesus.

Apollos; who is thought also to be called Apelles, Rom. xvi. 10. *Born at Alexandria;* his parents having lived there. *An eloquent man;* a rational, prudent, and learned man. Though the kingdom of God is not in any *excellency of speech*, 1 Cor. ii. 1, 4, yet this Egyptian jewel may be used to adorn the tabernacle. *Mighty in the Scriptures;* in quoting, explaining, and urging of them.

25 This man was instructed in the way of the Lord; and being ᶻfervent in the spirit, he spake and taught diligently the things of the Lord, ᵃknowing only the baptism of John.

Instructed; catechised, or taught, *viva voce*. *In the way of the Lord;* Christ, who hath by his precepts and example taught us the way to happiness. *Fervent in the spirit;* very zealous to promote God's glory, and men's salvation, as Rom. xii. 11. *Knowing only the baptism of John;* who baptized with water, but could not baptize with the Holy Ghost, Matt. iii. 11; that is, they had not those extraordinary gifts of the Holy Ghost which followed upon baptism after that Christ was ascended, and the Spirit poured out, chap. ii. 4. But John was a preacher of repentance, and of faith in Christ, pointing at the Lamb of God; and he baptized his disciples into this doctrine; which is the same with the baptism and belief of the apostles afterwards; only now they knew many things more fully than were revealed in the Baptist's time.

26 And he began to speak boldly in the synagogue: whom when Aquila and Priscilla had heard, they took him unto *them*, and expounded unto him the way of God more perfectly.

If we allow Priscilla to have contributed towards the instruction of Apollos, as doubtless we may, it is certain it was only in private discourse; which being joined with a meek and humble behaviour, might be very effectual for the conversion of souls, 1 Pet. iii. 1, 2. Thus Timothy was indebted for his knowledge in the things of God to his mother and grandmother, 2 Tim. i. 5. But otherwise it is not lawful for a woman to teach, 1 Tim. ii. 11, 12.

27 And when he was disposed to pass into Achaia, the brethren wrote, exhorting the disciples to receive him: who, when he was come, ᵇhelped them much which had believed through grace:

To pass into Achaia; to Corinth, which was in Achaia. *The brethren wrote;* who were at Ephesus. *Helped them much which had believed through grace;* Apollos helped them much by his eloquence, zeal, and constancy, which all are the gifts of God; but, especially, that they believed was through grace; for *faith is the gift of God*, Eph. ii. 8, and it was given unto them to believe, Phil. i. 29.

28 For he mightily convinced the Jews, *and that* publickly, ᶜ shewing by the Scriptures that Jesus ‖ was Christ.

Mightily; with great constancy, perseverance, and enduring of opposition. *Showing by the Scriptures that Jesus was Christ;* as chap. xvii. 3. Some think that Christ ought to be the subject, and Jesus the predicate; and then the sense is, that Jesus is our Lord, Jesus, or Saviour. The Messiah, that was sent from God, is the Saviour of the world.

CHAP. XIX.

The Holy Ghost is conferred by Paul on twelve of John's disciples, 1—7. *He preacheth at Ephesus, first in the synagogue, and afterwards in a private school for two years; God confirming the word by special miracles,* 8—12. *Certain Jewish exorcists, attempting to cast out a devil in the name of Jesus, are sent off naked and wounded: the gospel gaineth credit, and magical books are burned,* 13—20. *Paul proposing to depart soon, Demetrius and the silversmiths raise an uproar against him, which is with some difficulty appeased,* 21—41.

AND it came to pass, that, while ᵃApollos was at Corinth, Paul having passed through ᵇthe upper coasts came to Ephesus: and finding certain disciples,

The upper coasts; the north parts, in which were Pontus, Bithynia, Phrygia, and Galatia, chap. xviii. 23.

2 He said unto them, Have ye received the Holy Ghost since ye believed? And they said unto him, ᶜWe have not so much as heard whether there be any Holy Ghost.

Have ye received the Holy Ghost? the extraordinary gifts of the Holy Ghost, as prophesying, speaking with tongues, healing of the sick, &c., as appears by ver. 6, and John vii. 39; for it could not be, that they, who were instructed and baptized by John, should be ignorant of the essence or person of the Holy Ghost; for the Baptist had seen him descending upon our Saviour; as is remembered by all the evangelists which speak of his baptism, Matt. iii. 16; Mark i. 10; Luke iii. 22; besides other scriptures which testified of him; and St. John had spoken of him unto all he baptized, that our Saviour would baptize them *with the Holy Ghost and with fire*, John i. 32, 33. *We have not so much as heard whether there be any Holy Ghost:* this answer must be understood, according to the question, of those gifts now mentioned; and which by the imposition of the hands of the apostles were given, especially at the ordination of such as were sent to preach the gospel, it being necessary for the planting of the church, those miraculous gifts assuring those unto whom they preached, that their doctrine was from heaven; as also to assure the apostles themselves of the success of their ministry, and the conversion of such they preached unto, as chap. x. 44, 47. And this acceptation of these words is paralleled, 1 Sam. iii. 7, where it is said, that *Samuel did not yet know the Lord;* the meaning is, that he knew not that God was wont so to speak unto any; otherwise, that holy man, as young as he was, both knew God, and served him.

3 And he said unto them, Unto what then were ye baptized? And they said, ᵈUnto John's baptism.

Unto what then were ye baptized? what doctrine did you make profession of? and what religion did you seal unto at your baptism? *Unto John's baptism;* the doctrine that John taught, and the religion that he professed and preached. Thus the Jews are said to be *baptized unto Moses*, 1 Cor. x. 2, being engaged to believe the doctrine and observe the law delivered by Moses. Now the Baptist, as chap. xviii. 25, preached indeed Christ; but many things concerning him he could not preach, unless as of things to come; as his death, and resurrection: the Baptist being beheaded before our Saviour's death, and the Holy Ghost was not poured out in that extraordinary manner until after our Saviour's resurrection and ascension; which pouring out of the Spirit, these disciples at Ephesus, having been baptized by John in Judea, and afterwards returning home, might not have heard of.

4 Then said Paul, ᵉJohn verily baptized with the baptism of repentance, saying unto the people, that they should believe on him which should come after him, that is, on Christ Jesus.

The baptism of repentance; at which the Baptist did exhort them to repentance, and they by it were obliged to repent; by which is manifest, that the baptism of John and of Christ (which he commanded) are one and the same. John's baptism did respect Christ, and oblige the baptized to believe in him, as also to repent; and more, it was a seal unto them of the remission of their sins, as is expressly observed, Mark i. 4: so that the baptism of John, and the baptism of the apostles afterward, had the same sign and the same thing signified in them both (the inward and outward part, the heavenly and earthly part, were the same in both); as also they had both the same end; and therefore they were both the same. Add to this, that unless the Baptist's and the apostles' baptism were the same, Christ and his members (the church) are not baptized with the same baptism. It must be acknowledged that there are some circumstances in which they differ; John's baptism respected Christ to come; that is, in the exercise of his ministry (which was not so fully exercised till after John's death); but especially, those great things (his death, resurrection, and ascension, &c.) were to come after John's time, which now are accomplished. *On Christ Jesus;* including the Father and the Holy Ghost, and mentioning Christ, to difference his baptisms from the several baptizings and washings then in use.

5 When they heard *this*, they were baptized ᶠin the name of the Lord Jesus.

ᶠ ch. 8. 16.

The disciples, or those that John preached to, (for these Ephesians were not amongst those few that Paul baptized, 1 Cor. i. 14,) who when they heard what the Baptist said in the foregoing verse, they were baptized; as in the same terms it is said, chap. ii. 37, *when they heard* what St. Peter had said, *they were pricked in their heart,* &c., and were baptized. As for Paul's imposing his hands upon them that are said here to be baptized, it might very well be, that the twelve disciples, ver. 7, might have been baptized by John, and now receive the Holy Ghost in those extraordinary gifts by the laying on of the hands of St. Paul: for to what end should these disciples, who were baptized with St. John's baptism, be again baptized by Paul? It is true, they had further manifestations of the mystery of the gospel brought unto them; but if men should be baptized for every degree of knowledge or grace which they do acquire, how many baptisms had they need to have, who ought daily to grow in grace and in knowledge! It is evident, that the apostles themselves were only baptized with the baptism of John, for there were none else to baptize them. And baptism being an ordinance for our regeneration and new birth, as we can be born but once in the flesh, we can be but once also born in the Spirit; and no more may Christians be baptized twice, than the Jews could be twice circumcised.

6 And when Paul had ᵍlaid *his* hands upon them, the Holy Ghost came on them; and ʰthey spake with tongues, and prophesied.

ᵍ ch. 6. 6. & 8. 17.
ʰ ch. 2. 4. & 10. 46.

Laid his hands upon them; thereby ordaining and authorizing of them to preach the gospel. *The Holy Ghost came on them;* in those extraordinary gifts of tongues, &c., whereby they were fitted to preach the gospel unto any nation or people unto whom they should be sent. *Prophesied;* they prophesied, either in its proper sense, being enabled to foretell things that were to come; or in a larger and more improper sense, praising and magnifying of God, and declaring the hidden mysteries of the gospel; expounding the Scriptures, especially the prophecies concerning Christ, as 1 Cor. xiv. 1.

7 And all the men were about twelve.

Or exactly twelve; answering to the apostles, and that blessed number so often mentioned in Scripture.

8 ⁱAnd he went into the synagogue, and spake boldly for the space of three months, disputing and persuading the things ᵏconcerning the kingdom of God.

ⁱ ch. 17. 2. & 18. 4.
ᵏ ch. 1. 3. & 28. 23.

The synagogue of the Jews at Ephesus. For in the greater cities the Jews had their synagogues, in which they had their prayers, read, and expounded the law; as also a school for teaching of their theology, in which they treated of hard questions, and more difficult matters; which might occasion the apostle's frequenting that place. *The kingdom of God;* the gospel; which is so called, Rom. xiv. 17, because the kingdom of grace is by it set up in us here, and we are fitted by it for the kingdom of glory hereafter. But it might be also so called, because the Jews had dreamed of a political kingdom of the Messiah, and the Christians would own that Christ was indeed a King, but that his kingdom was a spiritual kingdom.

9 But ¹when divers were hardened, and believed not, but spake evil ᵐof that way before the multitude, he departed from them, and separated the disciples, disputing daily in the school of one Tyrannus.

A. D. 57.
1 2 Tim. 1. 15. 2 Pet. 2. 2. Jude 10.
ᵐ See ch. 9. 2. & 22. 4. & 24. 14. ver. 23.

Divers were hardened; the sun hardeneth what it doth not soften, and causeth a stench from dunghills, as well as a sweet smell from the mountains of spices; and Christ is for the falling, as well as for the rising of many. *That way;* so the doctrine of the gospel is called, by reason of its excellency above other ways. By *way* the Hebrews understand any course or means to an end. Hence we read of *the way of peace, the way of salvation, the way of the Lord. He departed from them;* not frequenting any more the synagogue of the Jews, where they met only with contradiction of their doctrine, and blasphemy against their Saviour. *Tyrannus;* some have taken this word appellatively, as denoting some great man, or ruler, who maintained a school, or place for instruction; but it is rather a proper name of some private teacher amongst them: for the Jews had not only public schools, where their consistories did meet, but private schools, where their law was taught.

10 And ⁿthis continued by the space of two years; so that all they which dwelt in Asia heard the word of the Lord Jesus, both Jews and Greeks.

ⁿ See ch. 20. 31.

All they; many of all sorts. *Asia;* Asia the Lesser, or Asia strictly so called, lying about Ephesus: the heathens came thither to worship their Diana; the Jews came thither about their affairs, either in their trades, or law-suits. *The word of the Lord Jesus;* the gospel, which is the word concerning the Lord Jesus; or, the word which he appointed to be preached and published.

11 And ᵒGod wrought special miracles by the hands of Paul:

ᵒ Mark 16. 20. ch. 14. 3.

Special miracles; not common or ordinary things, or such as might happen by chance. *By the hands of Paul;* as chap. v. 12; by his means and ministry.

12 ᵖSo that from his body were brought unto the sick handkerchiefs or aprons, and the diseases departed from them, and the evil spirits went out of them.

ᵖ ch. 5. 15. See 2 Kings 4. 29.

Handkerchiefs or aprons; our habit and attire being so different from what was used so long since, it cannot but occasion some variety in rendering these words; which some think to signify two things; and some, but one and the same part of their clothes or dress: the words are both originally Latin; the former so called from its use to wipe away sweat; the other, from its being usually tied about such as wore it. *The diseases departed from them;* God by such small and unlikely means wrought these miracles: 1. That the power of Christ (whom Paul preached) might the more clearly appear. And, 2. That such as were absent might have a high value for Christ and the gospel, though they had never seen Paul, or heard him preach. Such extraordinary works were also wrought by God to magnify the words preached by Peter, chap. v. 15, as our Saviour had foretold and promised, John xiv. 12.

13 ¶ ᑫThen certain of the vagabond Jews, exorcists, ʳtook upon them to call over them which had evil spirits the name of the Lord Jesus, saying, We adjure you by Jesus whom Paul preacheth.

A. D. 58.
ᑫ Mat. 12.27.
ʳ See Mark 9. 38. Luke 9. 49.

Vagabond Jews; who wandered up and down, making it their trade and livelihood; as jugglers amongst us. *Exorcists;* so called from their obtesting the evil spirits in the name of God. Of these Josephus tells strange stories,

Antiq. lib. 8, and thinks that the way of their exorcising was derived unto them from Solomon, and that they used the name of the God of Abraham, Isaac, and Jacob; as also of Zebaoth, and Adonai, as Origen tells us. Some think, that though there is certainly no power in the words and syllables which they pronounced, yet that the true God, being rather willing to be known and owned by those names, than that any should call on the names of the false gods, did sometimes put forth his power in casting out of devils at such times, as Matt. xii. 27. Howsoever, there being no warrant in the word of God for any such practice, and no promise to act faith in prayer upon, were the words never so serious, and the name of God and his attributes never so much (seemingly) manifested, it is a most abominable impiety. *The name of the Lord Jesus;* instead of, or together with, those other names formerly mentioned.

14 And there were seven sons of *one* Sceva, a Jew, *and* chief of the Priests, which did so.

One of the chief of the twenty-four courses into which the priests were divided, 1 Chron. xxiv. 4, or such as (according to the corruption of those times) had been high priests, and were laid aside, or were of the high priest's family, and hoped to succeed him.

15 And the evil spirit answered and said, Jesus I know, and Paul I know; but who are ye?

I acknowledge that Jesus hath power to command me to go hence; and I know that Paul, as his minister, hath authority over me; but what pretensions have ye to command me now? Though the devil is a liar, and the father of lies, yet none lie to their own disadvantage, but rather to their advantage, as they take it; and Satan may therefore be believed in what he here says, because it is to his disgrace, that, will he, nill he, he is under the command of God, though but signified to him by the least of his ministers or servants.

16 And the man in whom the evil spirit was leaped on them, and overcame them, and prevailed against them, so that they fled out of that house naked and wounded.

Leaped on them, &c.; by the power of the evil spirit, which by the permission of God did act in him, Matt. viii. 28; Mark v. 4; Luke viii. 29. Satan retains still his natural power, though he hath wholly lost his moral or spiritual power unto any good: and that his violence proceeded no further, is to be ascribed only to the bounds which God had set him, which he, being in chains, could not exceed or go beyond; not for his want of malice, but power.

17 And this was known to all the Jews and Greeks also dwelling at Ephesus; and *fear fell on them all, and the name of the Lord Jesus was magnified.

Fear fell on them all; they feared (after this example of God's not holding them guiltless that had taken his name in vain) to profane the name of Christ, and much more to blaspheme or speak against it. *The name of the Lord Jesus was magnified;* his authority, which the unclean spirit could not resist; and his doctrine and ministers, whose defence God had undertaken.

18 And many that believed came, and *confessed, and shewed their deeds.

Many that believed came; that believed the power which God alone had over Satan, and were convinced of their sin and danger in being led captive by him. *And confessed, and showed their deeds;* openly declared their evil deeds. They durst keep the devil's counsel no longer, but expose and manifest it, that their sores being laid open, the balm of the gospel might more effectually be put into them. Thus *with the mouth confession is made unto salvation,* Rom. x. 10.

19 Many of them also which used curious arts brought their books together, and burned them before all *men:* and they counted the price of them, and found *it* fifty thousand *pieces* of silver.

Thus their good works justified their faith, without which it had been dead, James ii. 24, 26. *Curious arts;* or rather idle and vain arts, as judicial astrology, calculating nativities, and all magical arts, which the Ephesians, of all others, were most addicted to and famous for; and may be here called *curious arts,* because they were so called by the Ephesians, who practised them; as also because these arts are about curiosities, not necessary for us to know. Otherwise they are diabolical arts, or rather devilish cheats. *Brought their books together, and burned them:* these books were not sold, and the price of them brought unto the apostles, because it was looked upon as the price of a whore, which was an abomination, and might not be offered unto God, Deut. xxiii. 18. *Fifty thousand pieces of silver:* what this sum amounts to is not so certain, because it is not agreed what these pieces were. Some make them Roman or Grecian coin; and others understand by them shekels, which are the Jewish money, and would make this sum so much the greater. Take them for so many pence, a piece of money commonly so called, which weighed the eighth part of an ounce of silver, as Matt. xviii. 28, they make six thousand two hundred and fifty ounces of silver, or so many crowns, and so much more as silver is worth more per ounce. Such indignation have true converts against the sins they have been guilty of, that they will not retain any thing that might occasion their return unto them; were it a right eye, they would pull it out.

20 "So mightily grew the word of God and prevailed.

The increase which the seed of the word had made was very remarkable; or it is a great instance of the power of God's word, when it makes men willing to part with their beloved and accustomed sins, and not to stand upon saving or gaining; as Isa. lv. 11.

21 ¶ *After these things were ended, Paul *purposed in the spirit, when he had passed through Macedonia and Achaia, to go to Jerusalem, saying, After I have been there, *I must also see Rome.

Paul purposed in the spirit; resolved with himself, or purposed in his heart, as Dan. i. 8. Yet in this his determination he had the influence and guidance of the Holy Ghost, and that in a more than ordinary manner; as we may see by the continued series of this history, how he came to all these places here mentioned. Paul travelled through these countries, and went to these cities, because he hoped for a greater harvest, where he might scatter the seed so far abroad.

22 So he sent into Macedonia two of *them that ministered unto him, Timotheus and *Erastus; but he himself stayed in Asia for a season.

Ministered unto him; this great apostle had not any to minister unto him out of state, but out of necessity, being he could not himself attend to all the offices of the church. These were employed by Paul, not so much to procure any accommodation for himself by the way, as to further a collection for the poor brethren at Jerusalem, 2 Cor. ix. 3, 4. *Erastus:* there seems to have been two of this name mentioned in Scripture: the one, Rom. xvi. 23, and the other, 2 Tim. iv. 20: the latter is here spoken of. *In Asia;* in Ephesus, which was in Asia, where Paul now was.

23 And *the same time there arose no small stir about *that way.

And the same time; when all things seemed to have been quiet: so uncertain are the servants of Christ to have any quiet here. *That way;* the doctrine of the gospel, as chap. xviii. 25.

24 For a certain *man* named Demetrius, a silversmith, which made silver shrines for Diana, brought *no small gain unto the craftsmen;

These shrines were only, either, 1. Portraits of the temple of Diana, in which was graven, or by any other art represented, that famous structure, which was afterwards burnt by Erostratus: or, 2. they were medals in which their idol Diana was expressed according to her image, spoken of, ver. 35. And they are called here, temples, or *shrines,* because they did resemble and represent that shrine or temple. And these the superstitious people carried home to their houses and friends; not only to evidence what a pilgrimage they had performed, but to incite the more their devotions towards this idol.

25 Whom he called together with the workmen of like occupation, and said, Sirs, ye know that by this craft we have our wealth.

Gain, getting or keeping a livelihood, are great temptations, and, a little pretext of piety with them, keep up the superstition and false worship that abound in the world.

26 Moreover ye see and hear, that not alone at Ephesus, but almost throughout all Asia, this Paul hath persuaded and turned away much people, saying that *they be no gods, which are made with hands.

f Ps. 115. 4. Is. 44. 10, —20. Jer. 10. 3.

He tells them indeed what was St. Paul's doctrine; but he conceals the reasons of his doctrine; for there can be nothing more evident to any considering man, than that there is but one God who made all things; as Psal. cxv. 3, 4; Jer. x. 10.

27 So that not only this our craft is in danger to be set at nought; but also that the temple of the great goddess Diana should be despised, and her magnificence should be destroyed, whom all Asia and the world worshippeth.

Not only this our craft is in danger to be set at nought; not only that we shall have no more to do, and be without work; but that it will be a reproach unto us to have had such an employment. *But also that the temple of the great goddess Diana should be despised;* this is made an aggravation to the loss of their all, that religion should suffer too. How much more ought it to concern those who have a sure foundation for what they do profess! *All Asia*, this temple is said to have been burnt down the same day that Alexander was born, and that it was two hundred and twenty years in re-building, at the charge of all Asia. *The world worshippeth;* though the Romans might worship any god (of those multitudes) which they allowed, yet they might leave their estates only to a very few amongst them; but Diana of the Ephesians was one of those few; as also one of those twelve whom they accounted *dii* or *deæ majorum gentium,* gods and goddesses of the highest quality, or first rank.

28 And when they heard *these sayings*, they were full of wrath, and cried out, saying, Great is Diana of the Ephesians.

The argument from their profit wrought very much upon them, especially meeting with their prejudicate opinions, having pretended antiquity and universality to confirm them. *Saying, Great is Diana of the Ephesians;* to show their abhorrence of what Paul had taught; and desiring her glory might be perpetual, whom Paul thought not worthy to be honoured at all.

29 And the whole city was filled with confusion: and having caught ᵍGaius and ʰAristarchus, men of Macedonia, Paul's companions in travel, they rushed with one accord into the theatre.

g Rom. 16. 23. 1 Cor. 1. 14. h ch. 20. 4. & 27. 2. Col. 4. 10. Philem. 24.

Filled with confusion; tumults and noise; all conditions of men, high and low, promiscuously being met in such uproars. *Gaius;* one born at Derbe, but living at Thessalonica, as chap. xx. 4. *Aristarchus;* of whom we read, chap. xxvii. 2; Col. iv. 10. *The theatre;* a place or structure built for public uses; whence, 1. Their sports or plays in any public solemnity were beheld. 2. Their speeches or orations in their common assemblies were heard. 3. Where they punished also their malefactors; it being accommodated with several steps or seats higher than one another, and of vast extent for these purposes. Hither, according to their custom, they resort, to hear if any one would speak upon this occasion to them; or rather, to get these Christians condemned and executed for their supposed sacrilege and blasphemy.

30 And when Paul would have entered in unto the people, the disciples suffered him not.

Paul would have entered in unto the people; being desirous either to appease the tumult; or, if the worst came of it, to die for Christ's sake. *The disciples suffered him not*, by their entreaties; to whom this good apostle's life, from whom they had received the faith, was more dear than their own.

31 And certain of the chief of Asia, which were his friends, sent unto him, desiring *him* that he would not adventure himself into the theatre.

Certain of the chief of Asia; such as had the oversight of the plays and shows in honour of their idol gods, and were usually their priests; and were of four countries, from whence they had their names of Asiarchs, Bithynarchs, Syriarchs, and Cappadociarchs. Whosoever these were, the providence of God is to be adored, who could out of his greatest enemies raise up deliverers for his servants.

32 Some therefore cried one thing, and some another: for the assembly was confused; and the more part knew not wherefore they were come together.

An excellent description of a popular tumult. Whether this *assembly* was afterwards made legal by the magistrates resorting thither, (though it was not called by their authority,) and is therefore called here, ἐκκλησία, is not so useful to inquire.

33 And they drew Alexander out of the multitude, the Jews putting him forward. And ⁱAlexander ᵏbeckoned with the hand, and would have made his defence unto the people.

i 1 Tim. 1. 20. 2 Tim. 4. 14. k ch. 12. 17.

They drew Alexander out of the multitude, where he could not be seen and heard, unto some more convenient place, from whence he might make a vindication or defence for them; and that most likely in behalf of the Jews, who were equally obnoxious to the rage of the people for being against their idolatry, as the Christians were. This *Alexander* is thought to have been that Alexander of whom we read, 1 Tim. i. 20; 2 Tim. iv. 14: though some think that this was another of that name. *Beckoned with the hand,* to procure silence; as chap. xii. 17.

34 But when they knew that he was a Jew, all with one voice about the space of two hours cried out, Great *is* Diana of the Ephesians.

A Jew, and by consequence an enemy to their idolatry; and, as they might imagine at least, a friend to St. Paul. *All with one voice;* unanimity makes not the cause to be good, if it were bad at first.

35 And when the townclerk had appeased the people, he said, Ye men of Ephesus, what man is there that knoweth not how that the city of the Ephesians is † a worshipper of the great goddess Diana, and of the *image* which fell down from Jupiter?

† Gr. *the temple keeper.*

Town-clerk, or secretary, who registered their acts, and intervened in all their meetings. *Is a worshipper;* each country and city had their peculiar gods, which they worshipped, and took for their patrons, as Ephesus did this goddess Diana. But the word here signifies a sacrist, or one that looks to the temple to keep it clean; especially that hath the charge of more solemn shows or sports in honour of any supposed deity: and these Ephesians took it to be their no small glory, that they were employed in such as belonged to Diana. *The image which fell down from Jupiter;* though the maker's name (Canetias) is upon record, yet it having lasted whilst the temple was six or seven times repaired, at least, if not renewed, and none ever remembering when it first was brought in amongst them, the crafty priests persuaded the credulous people that it was fallen from heaven, thereby getting more honour unto it, and profit to themselves.

36 Seeing then that these things cannot be spoken against, ye ought to be quiet, and to do nothing rashly.

He did more cunningly than honestly endeavour to evade their clamour, and still their rage, by telling them (how fallaciously soever,) that neither Paul, nor any other Christian or Jew, had any quarrel with their goddess or worship. For they indeed were against all images that were made with hands; but theirs was not such a one, it being fallen down from heaven. We must consider he was but a pagan; and his design was only to still the people; and *populus vult decipi.*

37 For ye have brought hither these men, which are neither robbers of churches, nor yet blasphemers of your goddess.

Neither robbers of churches; for they had not entered into their temple. *Nor yet blasphemers of your goddess;* Paul had barely preached this truth amongst them, not upbraiding them for their idolatry; as Michael, the archangel, brought no railing accusation against the devil, when he contended with him, Jude 9.

38 Wherefore if Demetrius, and the craftsmen which are with him, have a matter against any man, ∥ the law is open, and there are deputies: let them implead one another.

∥ Or, *the court days are kept.*

The law is open; which is fittest to determine all questions and controversies; for men would be partial to their own cause, and every one challenge to be in the right. *Deputies;* who, under the Roman emperors or consuls, had power to hear and determine of all matters. *Let them implead one another;* that so both parties may be heard.

39 But if ye enquire any thing concerning other matters, it shall be determined in a ∥lawful assembly.

∥ Or, *ordinary.*

Other matters; relating to the good government of the city, or maintaining the established religion, which ought not in such a confused manner to be treated of, but in an assembly called by lawful authority, which the Romans did usually call, at least, three times every month.

40 For we are in danger to be called in question for this day's uproar, there being no cause whereby we may give an account of this concourse.

He wisely minds them of their danger; for being under the power of the Romans, it was no less than the loss of their liberties to abet any faction or sedition; and to make a concourse or meeting tumultuously together, was capital, unless it were upon the sudden invasion of an enemy, or to put out some raging fire.

41 And when he had thus spoken, he dismissed the assembly.

The people were persuaded quietly to depart to their homes. Thus God one way or other, sometimes by friends, and sometimes by foes, kept his church and people from being ruined; and his hand is not shortened.

CHAP. XX

Paul goeth to Macedonia, and having passed over divers countries cometh to Troas, 1—6; *where, as he preached long, Eutychus falleth out of a window, and is taken up dead: Paul restoreth him to life,* 7—12. *He continueth his travels,* 13—16. *At Miletus he calleth to him the elders of the church of Ephesus, and taketh a solemn and affectionate leave of them, exhorting them to look well to their charge, and commending them to God's grace,* 17—35. *He prayeth with them, and departeth,* 36—38.

AND after the uproar was ceased, Paul called unto *him* the disciples, and embraced *them*, and [a] departed for to go into Macedonia.

a 1 Cor. 16. 5. 1 Tim. 1. 3.

Embraced them; took his farewell of them, and, as the manner of those countries was in meeting and parting with friends, he kissed them: as Luke vii. 45, and far more anciently, Gen. xxxi. 55. And this was the true ground of that kiss of peace, or the holy kiss, recommended Rom xvi. 16; 1 Cor. xiii. 12, and elsewhere, which was only a civility then in use. *Departed for to go into Macedonia;* yielding to the present fury of Demetrius; not so much for his own safety, as for the good of the church, that it might not be further persecuted for his sake; and that elsewhere it might by his ministry be enlarged and built up.

2 And when he had gone over those parts, and had given them much exhortation, he came into Greece. A. D. 60.

Much exhortation; which after so great a stir and opposition against them, the disciples could not but stand in great need of, that they might not be offended at the cross of Christ: and also mingling consolations with his exhortations, as the word indifferently signifies, as the case would well bear, there being a special blessing promised unto such as are *persecuted for righteousness' sake,* Matt. v. 10; 1 Pet. iii. 14. *Came into Greece;* Attica, in which province Athens was: otherwise Macedonia was in Greece largely taken.

3 And *there* abode three months. And [b] when the Jews laid wait for him, as he was about to sail into Syria, he purposed to return through Macedonia.

b ch. 9. 23. & 23. 12. & 25. 3. 2 Cor. 11. 26.

The Jews laid wait for him; some have thought that their laying in wait might be to rob him of the collections which he carried with him for the saints at Jerusalem; but most likely it was rather to take away his life, whom they hated for his zeal and diligence in the gospel. *He purposed to return;* shunning their treachery and plotting against him. He would not tempt God by running into dangers, though his cause were never so good. *Through Macedonia;* being the same way that he had come to Corinth.

4 And there accompanied him into Asia Sopater of Berea; and of the Thessalonians, [c]Aristarchus and Secundus; and [d]Gaius of Derbe, and [e]Timotheus; and of Asia, [f]Tychicus and [g]Trophimus.

c ch. 19. 29. & 27. 2. Col. 4. 10. d ch. 19. 29. e ch. 16. 1. f Eph. 6. 21. Col. 4. 7. 2 Tim. 4. 12. Tit. 3. 12. g ch. 21. 29. 2 Tim. 4. 20.

There accompanied him into Asia; their names are set down, as being men called and known at that time in the churches, and that what they did for this holy apostle might be remembered in all ages. *Sopater;* who is called also *Sosipater,* Rom. xvi. 21. It is added in some copies, that he was the son of Pyrrhus; which in Greek is the same with Rufus in Latin. *Berea;* a city of Macedonia, chap. xvii. 10. *Aristarchus;* of whom, chap. xix. 29, as also of the others, mention hath been formerly made. *Of Asia;* of Ephesus, a city in Asia. *Tychicus;* of whom, Eph. vi. 21; Col. iv. 7; 2 Tim. iv. 12; and of *Trophimus* we read, chap. xxi. 29; 2 Tim. iv. 20. These seem to have been the apostles or messengers of the churches, spoken of 2 Cor. viii. 23; in the number of whom St. Luke is to be reckoned, but being the penman of this book, he declines mentioning of himself by name; but his praise will be for ever in the gospel, 2 Cor. viii. 18, 19.

5 These going before tarried for us at Troas.

Us; whereby it appears, that St. Luke was one of them that accompanied St. Paul, though neither here nor elsewhere doth he express his own name. *Troas;* either the city of Troy, or the country thereabout so called.

6 And we sailed away from Philippi after [h]the days of unleavened bread, and came unto them [i]to Troas in five days; where we abode seven days.

h Ex. 12. 14, 15. & 23. 15. i ch. 16. 2 Cor. 2. 12. 2 Tim. 4. 13.

From Philippi; where they embarked, and sailed on the river first, then on the sea. *After the days of unleavened bread;* though St. Paul would not have the Gentile converts to be burdened with the ceremonial law, yet, that he might not offend the Jews, for a while he complied with their rites, chap. xviii. 21, they being indeed dead, but not yet deadly; and therefore he stays his journey all the time of the passover solemnity, instructing them in the mean while of the nature and use of such things.

7 And upon [k]the first *day* of the week, when the disciples came together [l]to break bread, Paul preached unto them, ready to depart on the morrow; and continued his speech until midnight.

k 1 Cor. 16. 2. Rev. 1. 10. l ch. 2. 42, 46. 1 Cor 10, 16. & 11. 20, &c.

The first day of the week; this was the day which the Lord had made, it being called from his resurrection, which was on this day, *the Lord's day,* Rev. i. 10. On this day the disciples met, and Christ honoured them with his presence, John xx. 19, 26. And when he was ascended, this day was appointed for the Christians to meet in, 1 Cor. xvi. 2; which must necessarily infer the abrogation of the Saturday, or Jewish sabbath: for it being part of the command, *Six days shalt thou labour,* they could not in ordinary have rested the last day of the week and the first day too, without sinning against the law of God. *To break bread;* to take a meal in common together, which they called *agapæ,* or the love-feast, so great a harmony and natural love was manifested in it; which was concluded with celebrating the Lord's suppei; and this is chiefly, if not only, intended in this place. The love-feasts being abused, were soon laid aside; but the other must continue until the Lord come, 1 Cor. xi. 26. *Continued his speech until midnight;* a long sermon indeed, at least it would be now thought so; and yet we must have the same spirit, or we are not members of that catholic church.

m ch. 1. 13.   8 And there were many lights ᵐ in the upper chamber, where they were gathered together.

There were many lights; there being many present; and it being in the night, because of the persecution that the Christians met with. Lest they should be reproached for doing any thing indecently, they by this means exposed themselves, and all that was done amongst them, to the common view and notice of all. *In the upper chamber;* where it is supposed they did ordinarily meet; as chap. i. 13.

9 And there sat in a window a certain young man named Eutychus, being fallen into a deep sleep: and as Paul was long preaching, he sunk down with sleep, and fell down from the third loft, and was taken up dead.

Preaching; discoursing and arguing; for it does not seem to have been a continued speech, by the word here used. *Fell down from the third loft;* this fall is thought by some to have been caused by Satan, (through God's permission,) that he might the more disturb Paul, and hinder, or put an end to, his sermon; which by the ensuing miracle God turned to a quite contrary effect.

n 1 Kings 17. 21.
2 Kings 4. 34.
o Matt. 9.24.

10 And Paul went down, and ⁿ fell on him, and embracing *him* said, ᵒ Trouble not yourselves; for his life is in him.

Fell on him; as Elijah on the widow of Zarephath's dead son, 1 Kings xvii. 21, and Elisha on the Shunammite's son, 2 Kings iv. 34. *His life is in him;* not but that he had been really dead, as ver. 9, but that upon the apostle's prayer (which is to be understood, though it is not here expressed) God had restored the young man to life; or howsoever, because St. Paul knew infallibly he should presently be restored to life, even whilst he spake.

11 When he therefore was come up again, and had broken bread, and eaten, and talked a long while, even till break of day, so he departed.

Had broken bread; either in the eucharist, as ver. 7, or in taking his ordinary refection and breakfast. *Talked a long while, even till break of day;* this was of long continuance, and speaks the patience and zeal of Christians in those times, and will rise up in judgment against a careless and negligent generation. *He departed;* going that part of his journey on foot, as the rest of his company did go by sea, as ver. 13.

12 And they brought the young man alive, and were not a little comforted.

They rejoiced not only that the young man was restored to life, but that by this means the gospel was attested to, and many confirmed in the belief of it.

13 ¶ And we went before to ship, and sailed unto Assos, there intending to take in Paul: for so had he appointed, minding himself to go afoot.

Assos; a city in Mysia, called also Apollonia, not far from Troas either by water or land. *Minding himself to go afoot;* Paul's going on foot might be the rather, that so he might have the better opportunity to scatter the seed of the gospel as he went, going through towns and villages, and conversing still with some or other, more than in sea journeys can be expected. So greedy of winning souls to Christ was this holy man, that he ordered every step, as near as he could, towards it. But St. Paul might desire to go alone thus on foot, that he might enjoy more free and full communion with God, having only God and his own soul to converse with.

14 And when he met with us at Assos, we took him in, and came to Mitylene.

An island, as also a city in it so called, in the Ægean Sea. Some think the island is called Lesbos, in which this Mitylene is.

15 And we sailed thence, and came the next *day* over against Chios; and the next *day* we arrived at Samos, and tarried at Trogyllium; and the next *day* we came to Miletus.

Chios; a noted island betwixt Lesbos and Samos in the Ægean Sea. *Samos;* in Ionia; for there are several other islands of this name. *Trogyllium;* a promontory not far from Samos. *Miletus;* a sea town upon the continent or firm land of Ionia.

16 For Paul had determined to sail by Ephesus, because he would not spend the time in Asia: for ᵖ he hasted, if it were possible for him, ᵠ to be at Jerusalem ʳ the day of Pentecost.

p ch. 18. 21. & 19. 21.
q ch. 21. 4, 12. q ch. 24. 17.
r ch. 2. 1.
1 Cor. 16. 8.

Ephesus was not so far from Miletus; but lest he should hinder his journey, he would not go thither. *If it were possible for him;* or, as chap. xviii. 21, if the Lord would; for his endeavour should not be wanting. *To be at Jerusalem the day of Pentecost;* not that he placed any religion in the observing this feast, which was abrogated and done away by being fulfilled, chap. ii.; but because of the vast concourse of people at all those solemn feasts, when his opportunities to magnify Christ and his truths might be the greater.

17 ¶ And from Miletus he sent to Ephesus, and called the elders of the church.

The governors and pastors of it; *elders* being here a title not respecting their age, but their place; and they might be the twelve spoken of, chap. xix. 7.

18 And when they were come to him, he said unto them, Ye know, ˢ from the first day that I came into Asia, after what manner I have been with you at all seasons,

s ch. 18. 19. & 19. 1, 10.

Asia; strictly and properly so called; or that part of the Lesser Asia whose metropolis was Ephesus. *After what manner I have been with you at all seasons;* a singular form for a good man to use, if he must of necessity leave his charge or flock, when his conscience does not accuse him. St. Paul spake not this as boasting of what he had done, or how he had been amongst them; but setting his example before them and others, to be imitated, and calling them for to witness the truth of it.

19 Serving the Lord with all humility of mind, and with many tears, and temptations, which befell me ᵗ by the lying in wait of the Jews:

t ver. 3.

Serving the Lord; in his apostleship or public ministry; of which, if any ever could, he might have gloried; yet in this office he clothes himself *with humility,* as the most becoming garment for a minister of Jesus Christ: though so high, yet so low. We need not cry, (as one did, though ironically,) Fie, St. Paul! but fie upon all such as pretend to succeed in his dignity, and do not at all imitate him in his humility. *With many tears;* he shed tears of compassion over the ignorant and blind, hard and perverse. It grieved him to see how large a dominion the god of this world had, and what a little part was left for his dear Lord and Master, Christ Jesus. *Temptations;* afflictions and troubles, which befell him for Christ and the gospel's sake; which are so called, James i. 2; 1 Pet. i. 6.

20 *And* how "I kept back nothing that was profitable *unto you*, but have shewed you, and have taught you publickly, and from house to house,

I kept back nothing that was profitable unto you; useful in order to eternal life to be known or hoped for, or to be done; shunning no labour or danger; concealing nothing out of fear or hope of advantage. *Taught you publicly;* in the public synagogues and schools. *And from house to house;* privately, as chap. ii. 46; not only speaking publicly and in general, but secretly and particularly, as every one's condition did require, exhorting some, reproving others. And indeed a good shepherd will labour to understand the state of his flock, and to supply them with what is necessary and suitable for them. Jacob says, Gen. xxxi. 39, that he bare the loss, and was fain to answer for all the sheep unto Laban. And of how much more value are the souls of men, to be sure, in God's sight, who will require an account of them!

21 ˣTestifying both to the Jews, and also to the Greeks, ʸrepentance toward God, and faith toward our Lord Jesus Christ.

Testifying to all sorts and conditions of men, for there is no difference with God, that repentance would be accepted from them by God, and that he was ready to give repentance unto them, as chap. xi. 18; and that faith in the Lord Jesus Christ was the true saving faith, there being no other name given whereby we may be saved. Upon these two depends the whole gospel, and our salvation by it.

22 And now, behold, ᶻI go bound in the spirit unto Jerusalem, not knowing the things that shall befall me there:

Bound in the spirit; as powerfully persuaded by a Divine instinct, to undertake this journey, as if I were led or drawn to it by forcible means; being bound to obey God in all things, whom I take to be my God and Guide, my Sun and Shield: and I do not desire so much to act, as to be acted by him. This St. Paul says, not as if he was drawn unto this journey against his will, but lest any should attempt to dissuade him from it, or that he should seem to have slighted the predictions of the prophets, mentioned chap. xxi. 11, 12. Nay, he might say this, as being as certain of his bonds as if he felt them already. Such things are foretold to such as know the veracity of God, they are as present. Howsoever, he was content to be bound, to suffer, nay, to die for Christ. And as he is poor in spirit who crucifies the world, and is willing to want, if God sees good; so he is bound in spirit, who is thus willing to be bound for the name of Christ. Howsoever, these words speak his firm resolution to take this journey upon him. *Not knowing the things that shall befall me there;* what the event shall be, in what measure he should be bound, and how long; he left it unto God's good will and pleasure.

23 Save that ᵃthe Holy Ghost witnesseth in every city, saying that bonds and afflictions ǁabide me.

1. Those that were endued with the Spirit of prophecy, in every city, foretold his sufferings; as chap. xxi. 4, 11. 2. He did suffer more or less in every city or place he came to; so great was the malice of the Jews against him.

24 But ᵇnone of these things move me, neither count I my life dear unto myself, ᶜso that I might finish my course with joy, ᵈand the ministry, ᵉwhich I have received of the Lord Jesus, to testify the Gospel of the grace of God.

None of these things move me; they cannot deter me from my duty. *Neither count I my life dear unto myself;* I am so far from fearing bonds, that I would not fear death itself. He is said to account his life precious, or dear, that spares it; as 2 Kings i. 13, 14. *My course;* his general course of Christianity, or the special course of his ministry; in either of which there is a race to be run, and a prize to be got, 2 Tim. iv. 7. It implies the great and constant labour that all Christians must take in their general calling, and especially ministers in their particular calling, 1 Cor. ix. 24. *With joy;* which ariseth from the testimony of a good conscience, which only is true joy; the other is madness, Eccles. ii. 2. *The ministry;* his apostleship, so called, chap. i. 25; vi. 4. *The gospel of the grace of God;* so the gospel is called, because bestowed upon any nation or people by God's mere grace only. And also it declares the grace of God in Christ Jesus to repenting and believing sinners.

25 And now, behold, ᶠI know that ye all, among whom I have gone preaching the kingdom of God, shall see my face no more.

This is thought to have been spoken by St. Paul, as his present purpose and resolution only, as Rom. xv. 24. *The kingdom of God;* the gospel, by which his kingdom is set up in the minds and hearts of men.

26 Wherefore I take you to record this day, that I *am* ᵍpure from the blood of all *men.*

I take you to record; I testify and affirm unto you; and I dare appeal unto yourselves concerning it. *I am pure from the blood of all men;* from the guilt of destroying their souls; none of them have perished through my fault, having faithfully showed unto them the way of life, and earnestly persuaded them to walk in it. Thus, according as the Lord told Ezekiel, chap. iii. 19, the prophet that hath warned the wicked man, hath delivered his own soul.

27 For ʰI have not shunned to declare unto you all ⁱthe counsel of God.

God's decree, to save all that believe in Christ; or the whole doctrine of Christianity, as it directs to a holy life; whatsoever God requires of any one in order to a blessed eternity. This is that which the Pharisees rejected, Luke vii. 30; and so do all wicked and ungodly men, who refuse to take God's counsel, or to obey his command.

28 ¶ ᵏTake heed therefore unto yourselves, and to all the flock, over the which the Holy Ghost ˡhath made you overseers, to feed the Church of God, ᵐwhich he hath purchased ⁿwith his own blood.

Take heed therefore unto yourselves; be mindful of your own salvation: for he that neglects his own, will not be careful of the salvation of another. *The Holy Ghost hath made you overseers;* 1. By his choosing and nominating of them, which was then by a special instinct, or immediate warrant from the Spirit, chap. i. 24; xiii. 2. Or, 2. Because they were constituted by the apostles, who were filled with the Spirit, enabling them to the choice of such persons, chap. xiv. 23. But also, 3. Whosoever is set apart to this office, according to the will of God, is made an overseer by the Holy Ghost; God owning his institutions, and concurring with them. *Overseers;* the same who (ver. 17) are called *elders;* they were certainly such as had the government and care of the church committed unto them. *To feed;* as a shepherd does, (for the apostle continues here the metaphor,) Jer. xxiii. 4; John xxi. 16, 17. *The church of God;* our Saviour is so called; for *the Word was God,* John i. 1. *Which he hath purchased;* Christ by his bloody death hath redeemed his church, and obtained power to gather it, to rule over it, to protect and preserve it, Isa. liii. 10; Phil. ii. 8—10. *With his own blood;* the blood of Christ, called truly the blood of God, there being in Christ two natures in one person, and a communion of the properties of each nature. If Christ had not been man, he could have had no blood to shed: had he not been God, the blood which he shed could not have been a sufficient price of redemption. Oh the depth of the riches of the wisdom and knowledge of God, who found out such a ransom; and the breadth, and length, and depth, and height of the love of Christ, who paid this ransom for us! Rom. xi. 33; Eph. iii. 18, 19.

29 For I know this, that after my departing ᵒshall grievous wolves enter in among you, not sparing the flock.

THE ACTS XX, XXI

My departing; either out of this country, or out of this life. *Grievous wolves;* so false teachers and persecutors are called, the one destroying the body, the other the soul. In this the metaphor is persisted in; the disciples of Christ being as sheep or lambs, their enemies are by our Saviour himself called wolves, Matt. vii. 15.

p 1 Tim.1.20.
1 John 2. 19.

30 Also ᵖ of your own selves shall men arise, speaking perverse things, to draw away disciples after them.

Of your own selves shall men arise; whilst Paul yet lived, and was only departed from that place. Several seducers may be reckoned up, as Nicolas the deacon, (from whom it is thought the sect of the Nicolaitanes came, Rev. ii. 6,) Hymenæus, Alexander, Phygellus, and Hermogenes, 1 Tim. i. 20; 2 Tim. i. 15. *Speaking perverse things;* perverting Scripture; establishing their false doctrines by Scripture, which they wrest to their purpose. *To draw away disciples;* as members are forcibly plucked from their body; which speak the cruelty and violence of these heretics, and the tenderness of the church towards her members, being loth to part from them. *After them;* thus false teachers gain indeed disciples to themselves, but not unto the Lord.

31 Therefore watch, and remember,
q ch. 19. 10. that ᑫ by the space of three years I ceased not to warn every one night and day with tears.

Watch; take heed yourselves, and warn others to take heed. *By the space of three years;* from St. Paul's first coming to Ephesus it was three years current, and now almost complete, chap. xix. 8, 10; xx. 3. *With tears;* a great, and no feigned πάθος; as Christ wept over Jerusalem, Luke xix. 41, so St. Paul over the unbelieving Jews; it went to his heart to think that they could not be saved. See how St. Paul loved souls, and pitied souls.

r Heb. 9.
s ch. 9. 31.
t ch. 26. 18.
Eph. 1. 18.
Col. 1. 12.
& 3. 24.
Heb. 9. 15.
1 Pet. 1. 4.

32 And now, brethren, I commend you to God, and ʳ to the word of his grace, which is able ˢ to build you up, and to give you ᵗ an inheritance among all them which are sanctified.

I commend you to God; it being so hard a matter to escape so many snares and dangers, the apostle prays to God for them, who is able to keep them by his power, *through faith, unto salvation,* 1 Pet. i. 5; and it is in vain to look after any meaner defence. *The word of his grace;* the gospel, which leads us to the rock upon which we must build, if we would not be moved when the storm comes. *Build you up;* increasing the number of believers, and augmenting their graces. God is said to build, and so is his word, both concurring: the gospel builds, as a means appointed by God; and God builds, who blesses that means. Hence he is called *the God of all grace,* 1 Pet. v. 10. *An inheritance;* heaven is called an inheritance, because we have it only by adoption, and it is given only unto children, Rom. viii. 17; as also, because it is a firm and lasting possession, not for a term of years, or a certain time, but for ever and ever. *Which are sanctified;* for without holiness none shall see God, Heb. xii. 14.

u 1 Sam.12.3.
1 Cor. 9. 12.
2 Cor. 7. 2.
& 11. 9.
& 12. 17.

33 ᵘ I have coveted no man's silver, or gold, or apparel.

Having spoken of the heavenly inheritance, he tells them how willing he was to have his reward hereafter, and to waive receiving his wages here. In this, St. Paul imitates Moses, Numb. xvi. 15, and Samuel, 1 Sam. xii. 3, 5.

x ch. 18. 3.
1 Cor. 4. 12.
1 Thess. 2. 9.
2 Thess. 3. 8.

34 Yea, ye yourselves know, ˣ that these hands have ministered unto my necessities, and to them that were with me.

St. Paul working hard (as they all knew) for a livelihood, chap. xviii. 3; 1 Cor. iv. 12; 1 Thess. ii. 9; which he gives an account of, 2 Thess. iii. 8, to have been done only that in such a juncture, they being poor, and the false teachers watching all advantages against him, he might not then be chargeable to them.

y Rom. 15. 1.
1 Cor. 9. 12.
2 Cor. 11. 9.
12. & 12. 13.
Eph. 4. 28.
1 Thess. 4.
11. & 5. 14. 2 Thess. 3. 8.

35 I have shewed you all things, ʸ how that so labouring ye ought to support the weak, and to remember the words of the Lord Jesus, how he said, It is more blessed to give than to receive.

I have showed you all things; as ver. 27. *So labouring;* with more than ordinary pains and constancy. *To support;* that they do not fall; or, being fallen, that they may rise again. The word imports the stretching out of the hand to retain any that are going away, or to hold up any that are falling. *The weak;* in knowledge, faith, or any other grace. *The words of the Lord Jesus;* Paul might have these words by the relation of others who heard them spoken by our Saviour; for all things that he said or did could not be written, John xx. 30. *It is more blessed to give than to receive;* not so much in that giving speaks abundance and affluence, but as it shows our charity and goodness, in which we resemble and imitate God. The substance of these words which are attributed to our Saviour, though not the terms, may be found in divers places, as Luke vi. 38; xvi. 9.

36 ¶ And when he had thus spoken, he ᶻ kneeled down, and prayed with them all.

z ch. 7. 60.
& 21. 5.

He kneeled down; a posture of great humility, becoming prayer, and frequently used on such occasions, especially in a time of great trouble and distress. Although bodily exercise alone do not profit, 1 Tim. iv. 8, yet we may, and must on occasion, in prayer bow the knee, lift up the hand and eye; 1. Because it is a reasonable thing to give our bodies in his service to God that made them. 2. By this we may show that we are not ashamed to serve and own God before men. And, 3. These outward signs do sometimes stir up our own and others' devotion.

37 And they all wept sore, and ᵃ fell on Paul's neck, and kissed him,

a Gen. 45.
14. & 46. 29.

As they used to do their friends when they took their leave of them: see Gen. xlv. 14, 15.

38 Sorrowing most of all for the words ᵇ which he spake, that they should see his face no more. And they accompanied him unto the ship.

b ver. 25.

The loss of a faithful and painful minister is a public loss, and many are concerned in it; besides, they had found great benefit by his ministry, and could not but be sensible of their missing of it. Add to this, Paul's gracious and humble conversation, and the sense of many good offices done by him, could not but have endeared him unto them. *They accompanied him unto the ship;* enjoying him as long and as far as they could, and expressing their last and utmost kindness unto him.

CHAP. XXI

Paul, journeying to Jerusalem, calleth at the house of Philip the evangelist, whose four daughters prophesied, 1—9. *Agabus foretelling what should befall him at Jerusalem, he will not be dissuaded from going thither,* 10—16. *Arriving at Jerusalem, he is persuaded to purify himself in the temple* 17—26; *where he is set upon by the Jews of Asia, and in danger of losing his life in an uproar, but is rescued by the chief captain, and carried to the castle in chains,* 27—36. *He requesteth, and is permitted, to speak to the people,* 37—40.

AND it came to pass, that after we were gotten from them, and had launched, we came with a straight course unto Coos, and the *day* following unto Rhodes, and from thence unto Patara:

Were gotten from them; had parted with them, as dearest friends and relations do one from the other, with much difficulty and reluctance. *Coos;* an island in the Mediterranean Sea, nigh unto Crete, where Hippocrates and Apelles are said to have been born. *Rhodes;* another island in the same sea, of great fame for the Colossus, or vast image of brass, which was there, accounted one of the wonders of the world. *Patara;* a haven town of Lycia, and its metropolis.

2 And finding a ship sailing over unto Phenicia, we went aboard, and set forth.

Sailing over unto Phenicia; whose master and mariners intended such a voyage. *Phenicia;* a country in Syria, situate nigh the sea, and bordering upon Palestine, whose chief city was Tyre.

3 Now when we had discovered Cyprus, we left it on the left hand, and sailed into Syria, and landed at Tyre: for there the ship was to unlade her burden.

Cyprus; another island in the Mediterranean. *Unlade her burden;* of goods and merchandise which she had taken in at Ephesus.

4 And finding disciples, we tarried there seven days: a who said to Paul through the Spirit, that he should not go up to Jerusalem.

a ver. 12. ch. 20. 23.

Seven days; they tarried the rather so long, that they might worship and serve the Lord on his day together. *Through the Spirit;* by the Spirit of prophecy they foretold his sufferings at Jerusalem, which afterward accordingly befell unto him; and they, being ignorant of his undertaking that journey at God's command, out of commiseration and pity dissuade St. Paul from going to such a place, where they foresaw that he should suffer so much: and this, it is said, they did *through the Spirit,* because they had that foreknowledge of all his sufferings from the Spirit; and knowing but in part, being ignorant of that special command Paul had had to go to Jerusalem, they did, according to what they knew, dissuade Paul from that journey. But, they knowing that their prophecy about St. Paul's sufferings must be fulfilled, and the Spirit by which they spake could not err or be mistaken, how came they to dissuade St. Paul from going to Jerusalem? It may be answered, that they might think this prediction of his sufferings to be only conditional, in case he went to Jerusalem; as David was told, that the men of Keilah would deliver him to Saul, 1 Sam. xxiii. 11, 12; that is, in case he had trusted himself amongst them.

5 And when we had accomplished those days, we departed and went our way; and they all brought us on our way, with wives and children, till *we were* b out of the city: and b we kneeled down on the shore, and prayed.

b ch. 20. 36.

They all brought us on our way; to show their greater respect unto him, being loth to part with him so long as it was possible for them to enjoy him; so that they did not despise his temptation that was in the flesh, Gal. iv. 14; but it is truly strange what follows, that he was received by them *as an angel of God, even as Christ Jesus.* *Kneeled down on the shore;* this the Jews on extraordinary occasions were wont to do, whilst the temple itself were standing, viz. make every place a place of prayer in such a case, chap. xx. 36.

6 And when we had taken our leave one of another, we took ship; and they c returned c home again.

c John 1. 11.

Had taken our leave one of another; as chap. xx. 1, embracing one another at their parting.

7 And when we had finished *our* course from Tyre, we came to Ptolemais, and saluted the brethren, and abode with them one day.

We came to Ptolemais; so far forth as to Ptolemais, a city in Phenicia, so called from one of the Ptolemies, king of Egypt; and is thought to be the same with Accho, mentioned Judg. i. 31, which ancient name is yet retained in the Syriac translation.

8 And the next *day* we that were of Paul's company departed, and came unto Cæsarea: and we entered into the house of Philip d the evangelist, e which was *one* of the seven; and abode with him.

d Eph. 4.11. 2 Tim. 4. 5.
e ch. 6. 5. &
8. 26, 40.

Cæsarea; that which was called Cæsarea Stratonis, to distinguish it from Cæsarea Philippi, at the foot of Mount Libanus, as also from another city of that name in Cappadocia; they having been all so called in honour of Cæsar, to flatter and perpetuate that family. The Cæsarea here spoken of was in Palestine, and is mentioned chap. x. 1; xviii. 22. *The evangelist;* whose office and charge it was to publish the gospel, which Timothy is exhorted to do, 2 Tim. iv. 5. This office is placed between that of an apostle and of a pastor and teacher, Eph. iv. 11, and was not so confined to a certain place or people as the latter of these were. *One of the seven;* of the seven deacons; of which see chap. vi. 5. Which office of a deacon Philip having well discharged, did purchase to himself this good degree, as 1 Tim. iii. 13.

9 And the same man had four daughters, virgins, f which did prophesy.

f Joel 2. 28. ch. 2. 17.

Virgins; by their father's and their own voluntary determination, as 1 Cor. vii. 37; neither is it said whether they continued in that state. but they were so. *Which did prophesy;* not by expounding the prophecies or word of God, for no woman is suffered to teach publicly, 1 Cor. xiv. 34; 1 Tim. ii. 12; but rather foretelling things to come, which gift God did not debar that sex from; especially it having been promised, Joel ii. 28, and in part fulfilled before, chap. ii. 17; by which God would show the enlargement of his mercies, and plenty of his Spirit, reserved for the times of the gospel.

10 And as we tarried *there* many days, there came down from Judæa a certain prophet, named g Agabus.

g ch. 11. 28.

Of whom mention is made, chap. xi. 28; of whose prophecy they could not be ignorant, by reason of the great collection which, on that account, was made for the poor at Jerusalem.

11 And when he was come unto us, he took Paul's girdle, and bound his own hands and feet, and said, Thus saith the Holy Ghost, h So shall the Jews at Jerusalem bind the man that owneth this girdle, and shall deliver *him* into the hands of the Gentiles.

h ver. 33. ch. 20, 23.

Took Paul's girdle; it was ordinary amongst the prophets to confirm, or at least to exemplify, their prophecies by outward signs and symbols, as Isa. xx. 2; Jer. xiii. 1; Ezek. xii. 5. But that of Jer. xxvii. 2, is a parallel unto this; where the prophet is commanded to make bonds and yokes, and to put them upon his neck, to foreshow the subjection of all those nations unto Nebuchadnezzar. *Thus saith the Holy Ghost;* none of all the sufferings foreshown concerning St. Paul, or others of God's children and servants, but are ordered by God, who knows them altogether; and they came not out of the dust, or by casualty, or chance, so as not to have been the matter of God's foreknowledge and counsel, Eph. i. 11. *The Gentiles;* the Roman powers at Jerusalem, and afterwards at Rome.

12 And when we heard these things, both we, and they of that place, besought him not to go up to Jerusalem.

They of that place; the converts or believers that were in Cæsarea, pitying him, and having a tender affection for him: see ver. 4. *Besought him* with tears, so earnest were they, as in the following verse.

13 Then Paul answered, i What mean ye to weep and to break mine heart? for I am ready not to be bound only, but also to die at Jerusalem for the name of the Lord Jesus.

i ch. 20. 24.

What mean ye to weep, and to break mine heart? a strange strife, who should overcome by loving most, as in that betwixt David and Jonathan, 1 Sam. xx. 41, 42. This undaunted champion, who did not seem to feel any of his own afflictions and miseries, yet grieves for the grief and sympathy of others, and bears a double weight in his burdens; one directly and immediately from them, as lying upon himself; the other mediately, as recoiling from others (who suffered with him) unto him again. *But also to die;* as Christ's love for us was stronger than death, Cant. viii. 6, so must our love be to him again, or it is not of the same nature with his, nor begotten by it. *For the name of the Lord Jesus;* his truth, and glory.

14 And when he would not be persuaded, we ceased, saying, ᵏThe will of the Lord be done.

ᵏ Matt. 6. 10. & 26. 42.
Luke 11. 2. & 22. 42.

We ceased; as having done their utmost, and what became them. *Saying, The will of the Lord be done;* they commit the event unto God: thus we pray daily, that God's will may be done, Matt. vi. 10; Luke xi. 2; and thus our Saviour, not only by his precept, but by his example, hath taught us, Matt. xxvi. 42; Luke xxii. 42; and when God's will is done, our will is done also, if the mind and spirit be in us that was in Christ, Phil. ii. 5, and otherwise we are none of his, Rom. viii. 9.

15 And after those days we took up our carriages, and went up to Jerusalem.

As they do pack up that are to remove to another house or place, not intending to come thither any more again; this also did show their readiness of mind to endure and suffer all things, as loss of relations and friends, and all accommodations, for Christ.

16 There went with us also *certain* of the disciples of Cæsarea, and brought with them one Mnason of Cyprus, an old disciple, with whom we should lodge.

Either this Mnason was in their company, or rather they were brought by the disciples of Cæsarea to the house of this Mnason, who was one of them that was converted when Paul and Barnabas were at Cyprus, chap. xiii. 4; and lodgings being scarce at Jerusalem, (when all the males were to appear there in those three annual solemnities,) it was no small kindness to be provided for by him.

ˡ ch. 15. 4

17 ˡAnd when we were come to Jerusalem, the brethren received us gladly.

It is thought, that by *brethren* in this place, and ver. 7, they are meant, who, being believers, were formed into a church with its several officers, and that they are called *disciples* only, ver. 4, who, living dispersed, and in smaller numbers, could not constitute such a church; but surely whatsoever there is of privilege and happiness in this spiritual fraternity, that truly catholic charity that was in the apostles and other holy men, would not so confine it, as to exclude any from enjoying of it, who did not exclude themselves by greater crimes than their paucity in number, or the consequences of that, could amount unto.

18 And the *day* following Paul went in with us unto ᵐJames; and all the elders were present.

ᵐ ch. 15. 13.
Gal. 1. 19. & 2. 9.

James, one of the apostles, though some think that he was a kinsman of our Saviour's, and at this time bishop of Jerusalem. *Elders;* as chap. xv. 6, 23, not so called for their age, but dignity or place in the church.

19 And when he had saluted them, ⁿ he declared particularly what things God had wrought among the Gentiles ᵒby his ministry.

ⁿ ch. 15. 4, 12. Rom. 15. 18, 19.
ᵒ ch. 1. 17. & 20. 24.

God had so done those marvellous works, that they ought to be had in remembrance; and this was said by the apostle, that God might not lose the glory, nor the church the benefit, of any of those great things which God had wrought: otherwise, St. Paul acknowledges that he was *the least of the apostles,* and *not meet to be called an apostle,* 1 Cor. xv. 9; and all his power was ministerial, he was only an instrument in God's hand, to be acted by him, as chap. xx. 24.

20 And when they heard *it,* they glorified the Lord, and said unto him, Thou seest, brother, how many thousands of Jews there are which believe; and they are all ᵖzealous of the law:

ᵖ ch. 22. 3.
Rom. 10. 2.
Gal. 1. 14.

Glorified the Lord; acknowledging all in that great work of the conversion of the Gentiles to have been from God; and that Paul that had planted, and Apollos that had watered, were nothing, 1 Cor. iii. 6, 7. *Thousands of Jews;* tens of thousands, as the word does usually signify; a definite for an indefinite number, signifying very many: and considering out of what small beginnings, and by what despicable means, and all within the space of about five and twenty years, this grain of mustard seed had spread itself; and add to this, that they were Jews, that obstinate and prejudiced generation, who are here spoken of, and they were then so many, so wonderfully many, who believed. *All zealous of the law,* of ceremonies, and concerning forbidden meats, &c. For the decree of the apostles, chap. xv. 29, concerning these things, did only respect such as were converted from paganism to the faith of Christ; and the Jews that were converted before the dispersion by Adrian, the Roman emperor, many years after this time, did not thoroughly understand their freedom from that law, but were under the burden of it, as appears by several ecclesiastical writers.

21 And they are informed of thee, that thou teachest all the Jews which are among the Gentiles to forsake Moses, saying that they ought not to circumcise *their* children, neither to walk after the customs.

Informed of thee; instructed or catechised concerning thee; the zealots had made it their business to instil such aspersions and odious reflections against Paul, as if their accusations had been the fundamental truths of their religion. *Moses;* the ceremonial law, given by his ministry. *To walk,* to live, to act in their course of life, *after the customs* of their fathers, or the rituals of Moses.

22 What is it therefore? the multitude must needs come together: for they will hear that thou art come.

What is it therefore? it cannot be otherwise; or, what else remains to be done? *The multitude must needs come together;* all the faithful must meet; for the magistrates then being pagan, and enemies both to the church and the gospel; in matters of great moment, especially when there was any fear of a schism, the whole multitude of believers were gathered together to consult about it.

23 Do therefore this that we say to thee: We have four men which have a vow on them;

Vows were either, first, such as men did make in gratitude for any deliverance they had received, as from sickness, storms, or any imminent dangers: or, secondly, to enable them the better to serve God on any occasion; and then they were bound to keep themselves from all those things which were forbidden to the Nazarite, as wine and strong drink, and to nourish their hair, as the Nazarites were bound to do. This vow they made for a certain time, and not perpetual: the law concerning it you may see, Numb. vi. 2—5.

24 Them take, and purify thyself with them, and be at charges with them, that they may ᑫshave *their* heads: and all may know that those things, whereof they were informed concerning thee, are nothing; but *that* thou thyself also walkest orderly, and keepest the law.

ᑫ Num. 6. 2, 13, 18.
ch. 18. 18.

Purify thyself; they advise Paul to perform all those rites required of a Nazarite, the observation of which did legally purify him. *Be at charges with them;* these charges were about the threefold sacrifice which were to be offered, two turtles or young pigeons, a lamb, unleavened bread, and cakes of fine flour, as Numb. vi. 10—12, 15: and the other four, spoken of ver. 23, being poor, they require Paul here to bear their charges also, that so he might appear to be the chief amongst them, and the more zealous in their law, to take away the scandal that was taken up by the Jews against him; these ceremonies being as yet not deadly, or evil, though they were dead and indifferent. *Shave their heads;* which was done at the end of their separation, and was the accomplishment of all; and they burned the hair which they shaved off under their sacrifices, to show, that all their legal performances were only acceptable unto God through Jesus Christ, who was sacrificed for us, 1 Cor. v. 7; Heb. x. 12. *Walkest orderly, and keepest the law;* livest according to the law of Moses, contrary unto what they reported of thee.

25 As touching the Gentiles which believe, *we have written *and* concluded that they observe no such thing, save only that they keep themselves from *things* offered to idols, and from blood, and from strangled, and from fornication.

r ch. 15. 20, 29.

These ceremonies (after their accomplishment in Christ) not being at all necessary, they were not imposed upon any that received the faith of Christ from amongst the Gentiles, or other nations; only suffered for a while unto the Jews that turned to Christ, for the hardness of their hearts, and inveterate zeal for them. *Things offered to idols, &c.:* of these things, see chap. xv. 29.

26 Then Paul took the men, and the next day purifying himself with them *entered into the temple, ᵗto signify the accomplishment of the days of purification, until that an offering should be offered for every one of them.

s ch. 24. 18.
t Num. 6. 13.

Paul agrees to their advice, and follows it; and having set such a time for his vow as might end with the other four men's, he, with the four mentioned, signify to the priest (who was concerned to know it, because of the sacrifices that were to be offered for them,) that the time of their separation was fulfilled, which is here called *the days of purification*, for the reason intimated, ver. 23. *Until that an offering should be offered for every one of them* : intending to abide in the temple until all those rites were performed which were required of them.

27 And when the seven days were almost ended, ᵘthe Jews which were of Asia, when they saw him in the temple, stirred up all the people, and ˣlaid hands on him,

u ch. 24. 18.
x ch. 26. 21.

The seven days; either, 1. After his coming to Jerusalem; or rather, 2. Of his vow; for it is thought that his vow of separation was but for seven days; or, 3. The seven days of that feast of Pentecost which he came unto. *The Jews which were of Asia;* who were implacably set against him wheresoever he went, as chap. xiv. 19; xvii. 5. These Jews dwelt at Ephesus and elsewhere, but were come to observe the feast at Jerusalem. *Laid hands on him;* by violence, and against law.

28 Crying out, Men of Israel, help: This is the man, ʸthat teacheth all *men* every where against the people, and the law, and this place: and further brought Greeks also into the temple, and hath polluted this holy place.

y ch. 24. 5, 6.

Men of Israel; minding them by this compellation, of their being a peculiar people unto God, and that none might be admitted with them in his worship. A charge is laid against St Paul consisting of divers articles, but all false; for he was a most zealous lover of that people, and taught them nothing but the true use and meaning of the law: but thus they had done to our Saviour, Matt. xxvi. 61, and to St. Stephen, chap. vi. 13. *Into the temple;* that is, into the court of the Jews, which is so far unlawful, that they might have killed a Roman if he had come in there; and every one was warned by an inscription upon the pillars, Μὴ δεῖν ἀλλόφυλον ἐντὸς τῦ ἁγίυ παριέναι, That no stranger or foreigner might come into that holy place.

29 (For they had seen before with him in the city ᶻTrophimus an Ephesian, whom they supposed that Paul had brought into the temple.)

z ch. 20. 4.

For they had seen; the Jews of Asia, who could not but know Trophimus; and he following of Paul in this journey, either ignorantly or maliciously they accuse the apostle for taking him into the temple with him; which was only their surmise, and the issue of their enraged jealousy.

a ch. 26. 21.

30 And ᵃall the city was moved, and the people ran together: and they took Paul, and drew him out of the temple: and forthwith the doors were shut.

And all the city was moved; there was a general concourse from all parts. *Tantum religio poterat*, no such heats as such are which are moved about religion; whilst *the wisdom that is from above, is first pure, then peaceable*, James iii. 17. *Drew him out of the temple;* lest by their uproar they should occasion any of the Gentiles to come in there to quell them; or, intending to kill Paul, they drew him thence, that he might not pollute that holy place with his blood: thus they strain at a gnat, being unwilling to pollute the temple; but they would swallow a camel, not sticking to shed the blood of the innocent. *The doors were shut;* either by the keeper of the doors, or by the soldiers of the temple.

31 And as they went about to kill him, tidings came unto the chief captain of the band, that all Jerusalem was in an uproar.

The chief captain; the commander-in-chief over all the soldiers there; or one that had the command over a thousand. At the three great feasts there was usually a considerable number of soldiers at Jerusalem; the confluence from all parts being then so great, and the Jews so impatient of any yoke or government, the Romans durst not trust such multitudes without some check upon them. Thus at the passover, when they took and crucified our Saviour, these soldiers were made use of, John xviii. 12.

32 ᵇ Who immediately took soldiers and centurions, and ran down unto them: and when they saw the chief captain and the soldiers, they left beating of Paul.

b ch. 23. 27.
& 24. 7.

A wonderful providence of God for Paul's preservation, that the chief captain should be so near, as to be able to hinder the massacring of Paul; and especially that he should be defended and preserved by one that was a stranger to him, and an enemy to his religion! *They left beating of Paul*, lest they should have been set upon by the soldiers, for breaking the peace, &c. The fear of man caused them to forbear what the fear of God could not.

33 Then the chief captain came near, and took him, and ᶜcommanded *him* to be bound with two chains; and demanded who he was, and what he had done.

c ver. 11.
ch. 20. 23.

Bound with two chains; whether as Peter was, see chap. xii. 6. or that he was bound with one upon his feet, and with the other upon his hands, it was exactly fulfilled what Agabus had prophesied concerning him, ver. 11. So does God provide, that not one word of his servants, which they speak from him, shall fail; and that St. Paul should be heard before he was condemned.

34 And some cried one thing, some another, among the multitude: and when he could not know the certainty for the tumult, he commanded him to be carried into the castle.

Some cried one thing, some another; as is usual in popular commotions, they agreed in doing mischief, but not in the reason of it. *Into the castle* called Antonia, because it was built in honour of Mark Antony, on the north side of the temple.

35 And when he came upon the stairs, so it was, that he was borne of the soldiers for the violence of the people.

When he came upon the stairs, in the ascent to the castle, *he was borne of the soldiers;* either because the press was so great, he being in the midst of them; or being taken up by them, to secure him from the fury of the enraged multitude.

36 For the multitude of the people followed after, crying, ᵈAway with him.

d Luke 23. 18. John 19. 15. ch. 22. 22.

That is, Kill him; for that was indeed to take him out of their way. The same speech they used against our Saviour, Luke xxiii. 18; John xix. 15, when they desired his death.

37 And as Paul was to be led into the castle,

THE ACTS XXI. XXII

he said unto the chief captain, May I speak unto thee? Who said, Canst thou speak Greek?

May I speak unto thee? a common expression in that language, whereby he craves leave, and bespeaks attention. *Canst thou speak Greek?* after the Grecian empire, their language became and continued to be very common in Asia and Egypt, and very well known amongst all the Romans of any education or quality.

This Egyptian rose A. D. 55.
e See ch. 5. 36.

38 ᵉ Art not thou that Egyptian, which before these days madest an uproar, and leddest out into the wilderness four thousand men that were murderers?

That Egyptian; a famous ringleader of a rebellious crew, as some think, in the reign of Tiberius; but as others, in the thirteenth year of the emperor Claudius, and continued till under Nero's reign, and came, from these four thousand mentioned here at his first setting up, to have thirty thousand followers; pretending himself to be a prophet; of whom Josephus, Antiq. lib. 20. cap. 11. *Murderers,* or assassins, that did wear daggers or stilettos.

f ch. 9. 11. & 22. 3.

39 But Paul said, ᶠI am a man *which am* a Jew of Tarsus, *a city* in Cilicia, a citizen of no mean city: and, I beseech thee, suffer me to speak unto the people.

No mean city; it being the metropolis, or chief city, in Cilicia, built by Perseus, as some think; howsoever, having the privilege of the Roman freedom; as chap. xxii. 28. *I beseech thee;* St. Paul begs leave to speak unto the people, that he might not seem to affect popularity, or to be guilty of any insurrection or tumult. Thus he had leave also of Agrippa, before that he made that famous apology, chap. xxvi. 1.

40 And when he had given him licence, Paul stood on the stairs, and
g ch. 12. 17. ᵍ beckoned with the hand unto the people. And when there was made a great silence, he spake unto *them* in the Hebrew tongue, saying,

Paul stood on the stairs; as he was now about to be carried into the castle Antonia, before mentioned. *And beckoned with the hand;* signifying that he craved their audience; as chap. xii. 17; xiii. 16. *He spake unto them in the Hebrew tongue;* the Hebrew tongue being understood by all of them, and most grateful unto them. Yet this was not the pure and ancient Hebrew, which had been corrupted ever since their captivity; but the Syriac tongue, which they there learned, was called Hebrew, it having at first been derived from the Hebrew, and being then in use by those who were Hebrews.

CHAP. XXII

Paul declareth at large the manner of his conversion and call to the apostleship, 1—21. *At the very mentioning of the Gentiles the people exclaim furiously against him: whereupon the chief captain ordereth to examine him by scourging,* 22—24; *which he avoideth by pleading the privilege of a Roman citizen,* 25—29. *He is brought before the Jewish council,* 30.

a ch. 7. 2. MEN, ᵃbrethren, and fathers, hear ye my defence *which I make* now unto you.

Although they were wicked men, and cruel persecutors, St. Paul giveth them their titles of respect, which by the places God had put them in, are due unto them: see on chap. vii. 2.

2 (And when they heard that he spake in the Hebrew tongue to them, they kept the more silence: and he saith,)

The Hebrew tongue; the ordinary Hebrew; that which was taken for Hebrew, and spoken by the Hebrews after their return from the captivity, though mixed with the Syriac; as chap. xxi. 40. *They kept the more silence;* it being more grateful unto them to hear Paul speak in their mother tongue, especially they having so great a prejudice against all other nations and languages.

3 ᵇI am verily a man *which am* a Jew, born in Tarsus, *a city* in Cilicia, yet brought up in this city ᶜat the feet of ᵈGamaliel, *and* taught ᵉaccording to the perfect manner of the law of the fathers, and ᶠwas zealous toward God, ᵍas ye all are this day.

b ch. 21. 39. 2 Cor. 11. 22. Phil. 3. 5.
c Deu. 33. 3. 2 Kings 4. 38. Luke 10. 39.
d ch. 5. 34. e ch. 26. 5. f ch. 21. 20. Gal. 1. 14. g Rom. 10. 2.

At the feet; the apostle alludes unto the posture that the disciples of any rabbi, or teacher, in those times did use; the master sitting in some high or elevated place, did teach his scholars, who sat at his feet on the ground; and as they grew in knowledge, were advanced to sit nearer to their master: see Deut. xxxiii. 3. Abraham is thus said to be called to God's foot, Isa. xli. 2; and Mary sat at our Saviour's feet, Luke x. 39. *Of Gamaliel;* the same Gamaliel who made that moderating speech in the apostle's behalf, chap. v. 34. *The perfect manner of the law;* this perfect manner of the law is Pharisaism, in which the apostle was brought up, and before his conversion made a profession of, Phil. iii. 5. Not that the apostle reckoned upon any perfection in this profession; but because, as chap. xxvi. 5, it was the most strait sect of their religion, observing a great deal of punctuality and accurateness, making what they called a hedge about the law. *Of the fathers;* not observing only the law, which was given by God to their fathers by the hand of Moses; but the traditions of their fathers he was exceeding zealous in; as Gal. i. 14. *Zealous toward God;* or, as some copies read, zealous toward the law; both in the same sense. His zeal for the law was sincere, not out of by-ends, but out of his love to God, though it was *not according to knowledge,* Rom. x. 2. It was truly according unto what he knew or believed, but it was not according to true knowledge.

4 ʰAnd I persecuted this way unto the death, binding and delivering into prisons both men and women.

h ch. 8. 3. & 26. 9, 10, 11. Phil. 3. 6. 1 Tim. 1. 13.

This way; the doctrine and practice of Christianity. *Unto the death;* as much as in him lies, being one of the most furious persecutors, that hunted for the precious life, *breathing out threatenings and slaughters* with every breath, chap. ix. 1.

5 As also the High Priest doth bear me witness, and ⁱall the estate of the elders: ᵏfrom whom also I received letters unto the brethren, and went to Damascus, to bring them which were there bound unto Jerusalem, for to be punished.

i Luke 22. 66. ch. 4. 5. k ch. 9. 2. & 26. 10, 12.

The estate of the elders; their sanhedrim or great council. *Letters;* commission or orders. *The brethren;* the Jews of Damascus are called brethren, because descended from the patriarchs as well as he. And still, as ver. 1, he would overcome that stubborn people with civility, heaping up coals of fire on their heads, Rom. xii. 20, that they might be melted, and then formed after a more excellent manner.

6 And ˡit came to pass, that, as I made my journey, and was come nigh unto Damascus about noon, suddenly there shone from heaven a great light round about me.

l ch. 9. 3. & 26. 12, 13.

As lightning it suddenly encompassed him. But see chap. ix., from the 3rd verse; where this history is set down by St. Luke. And here little more can be taken notice of, than some small variety in the expressions.

7 And I fell unto the ground, and heard a voice saying unto me, Saul, Saul, why persecutest thou me?

Saul, Saul; as men that call another earnestly repeat his name; as when the angel of the Lord called *Abraham, Abraham,* Gen. xxii. 11.

8 And I answered, Who art thou, Lord? And he said unto me, I am Jesus of Nazareth, whom thou persecutest.

I am Jesus of Nazareth; that contemned (though not contemptible) name is owned by Christ from heaven, that they might not be ashamed when they were reproached by it on earth. Of the rest, see chap. ix. 5.

9 And ^mthey that were with me saw indeed the light, and were afraid; but they heard not the voice of him that spake to me.

^{m ch. 9. 7.}
^{Dan. 10. 7.}

Of this, see chap. ix. 7. This may be added to what was formerly said, that the men who travelled with Paul may be said not to have heard the voice of him that spake, because they did not understand it, or obey it; they were not converted, as Paul was, by it; the Hebrew language putting hearing for obeying, as in many scriptures; and both St. Paul, who here spake, and Luke, who penned this history, understood exactly the proprieties of that tongue.

10 And I said, What shall I do, Lord? And the Lord said unto me, Arise, and go into Damascus; and there it shall be told thee of all things which are appointed for thee to do.

See chap. ix. 6. Such things as Ananias told him from Christ, were as if Christ himself had told him them; and by Ananias our Saviour satisfied St. Paul's question, *What shall I do, Lord?*

11 And when I could not see for the glory of that light, being led by the hand of them that were with me, I came into Damascus.

I could not see for the glory of that light; the excellency of the object overpowering his sight. It was a strange work of God that enabled St. Stephen to see Christ, who is now so glorious, chap. vii. 55. And it will be according to God's wonderful power, when at the resurrection we shall be enabled to look upon Christ in his greatest glory. Behold the goodness and severity of God upon Paul: severity upon him in striking of him with blindness in his body; but goodness indeed to him, in enlightening, converting, and saving of his soul.

12 And ⁿone Ananias, a devout man ^oaccording to the law, ^ohaving a good report of all the ^pJews which dwelt *there,*

^{n ch. 9. 17.}
^{o ch. 9. 22.}
^{p 1 Tim. 3. 7.}

According to the law; this is added to distinguish him from a proselyte, and to let them know that he had received the gospel, not from a convert out of Gentilism, (who though they admitted, yet they had a greater jealousy over, and less kindness for,) but from one like unto themselves in all things.

13 Came unto me, and stood, and said unto me, Brother Saul, receive thy sight. And the same hour I looked up upon him.

Stood; that in this posture he might more conveniently put his hands upon Paul; which we read that he now did, chap. ix. 17, and was ordinarily done upon the miraculous curing of any. *The same hour;* or, as chap. ix. 18, *immediately.* The suddenness of the cures spake the power from whence they came: none but God saves and delivers after this manner.

14 And he said, ^qThe God of our fathers ^rhath chosen thee, that thou shouldest know his will, and ^ssee ^tthat Just One, and ^ushouldest hear the voice of his mouth.

^{q ch. 3. 13. & 5. 30.}
^{r ch. 9. 15. & 26. 16.}
^{s 1 Cor. 9. 1. & 15. 8.}
^{t ch. 3. 14. & 7. 52.}
^{u 1 Cor. 11. 23. Gal. 1. 12.}

The God of our fathers; nothing could please the people better than to hear God so styled; for this they gloried in, above all things, that they and theirs had God to their Father, John viii. 41. And nothing could better suit St. Paul's purpose, who would not lie under that scandal of endeavouring an apostacy from the Jewish religion, (for the gospel which he preached was but the substance and perfection of the law,) or that he served or worshipped any other God than the God of Abraham. *Hath chosen thee;* he hath taken thee, as by the hand, and by his wonderful providence brought thee into that condition in which thou art. *See that Just One;* Christ is the Holy One, spotless and without blemish; God's *righteous servant,* Isa. liii. 11. But this is here the rather spoken, that he might convince them of their sin in putting our Lord to death: for though he sweetened his speech to them in what he might, he would not flatter them to their destruction; like a skilful surgeon, he would not heal too fast. Now Paul saw Christ with the eye of his mind, it being enlightened to believe in him; and he saw him in his journey also with the eyes of his body. Some read, τὸ, not τὸν δίκαιον. And then Ananias tells St. Paul, that he was sent to show him that which was just and right in God's sight; which he, being blinded by his zeal for the law, could not perceive.

15 ^xFor thou shalt be his witness unto all men of ^ywhat thou hast seen and heard.

^{x ch. 23. 11.}
^{y ch. 4. 20. & 26. 16.}

His witness; the apostles were in a more special manner Christ's witnesses; as Luke xxiv. 48; John i. 7; Acts i. 8; God giving them extraordinary gifts, not for their own sakes chiefly, but to profit others withal; as the tree bears not fruit, nor the field yields its increase, for itself. *Of what thou hast seen and heard;* not that St. Paul's commission extended only to the publishing this wonder at his conversion: for he was intrusted with the gospel, and had that treasure in his earthen vessel: but this miracle is expressly mentioned, because it was unto him and others a great confirmation of the truths which he believed himself, and recommended to the faith of others. And therefore in the course of his ministry he mentions this frequently; as here in this place, and before king Agrippa, chap. xxvi. 16; and 1 Cor. ix. 1; as also 1 Cor. xv. 8.

16 And now why tarriest thou? arise, and be baptized, ^zand wash away thy sins, ^acalling on the name of the Lord.

^{z ch. 2. 38. Heb. 10. 22.}
^{a ch. 9. 14. Rom. 10. 13.}

Wash away thy sins; as washing causeth the spots to disappear, and to be as if they had not been, Isa. i. 18; so does pardoning mercy, or remission of sins, which accompanieth baptism, as in the due receiver, Matt. iii. 11; 1 Pet. iii. 21, 22. Where true faith is, together with the profession of it by baptism, there is salvation promised, Mark xvi. 16. In the mean while it is not the water, (for that only signifies,) but it is the blood of Christ, which is thereby signified, that cleanseth us from our sins, as 1 John i. 7. Yet sacraments are not empty and deceitful signs; but God accompanieth his own ordinances with his power from on high, and makes them effectual for those great things for which he instituted and appointed them. *Calling on the name of the Lord;* Christ, to whom by baptism he was to be dedicated.

17 And ^bit came to pass, that, when I was come again to Jerusalem, even while I prayed in the temple, I was in a trance;

^{b ch. 9. 26. 2 Cor. 12. 2.}

This was probably about three years after his conversion, as Gal. i. 18, and was one of the *visions and revelations* he makes mention of, 2 Cor. xii. 1. *A trance;* a rapture and ecstasy, as chap. x. 10.

18 And ^csaw him saying unto me, ^dMake haste, and get thee quickly out of Jerusalem: for they will not receive thy testimony concerning me.

^{c ver. 14.}
^{d Mat.10.14.}

Get thee quickly out of Jerusalem; this St. Paul takes notice of, that it might appear unto the Jews that he did not out of choice, or because he bare a grudge against them, decline them, and preach to the Gentiles. *For they will not receive thy testimony concerning me;* as if Christ had said, They who were appointed unto life, and were curable, are already cured; but the rest who are hardened, nothing remains for them but utter destruction.

19 And I said, Lord, ^ethey know that I imprisoned and ^fbeat in every synagogue them that believed on thee:

^{e ver. 4. ch. 8. 3.}
^{f Mat. 10.17.}

This was Paul's objection which he made against the will of God concerning his leaving Jerusalem, and the Jews in it; and shows how apt carnal reason is in the very best men to set up itself against the wisdom of God, and to argue for what we fancy best to be done, or left undone. The sum of his reasoning is this, That he was most likely to do more good amongst the Jews than amongst the Gentiles, whither God was sending of him, because the Jews

THE ACTS XXII

knew how zealous he had been not only to observe the law himself, but to procure its observation by all others; and that it was no less than a miracle which changed his mind about it. He shows also by this his great love unto the Jews, whom he would have staid with, had it been at his choice, and did only remove from by God's command.

g ch. 7. 58.   20 ᵍAnd when the blood of thy martyr Stephen was shed, I also was standing by, and ʰconsenting unto his death, and kept the raiment of them that slew him.

h Luke 11. 48. ch. 8. 1. Rom. 1. 32.

Martyr is a Greek word, that signifies a witness; and is here, and since by the ecclesiastical writers, appropriated unto such as suffer death for the testimony they give to the truths of God, or doctrine of the gospel. *Consenting unto his death;* as chap. viii. 1. *Of them that slew him;* that is, of the witnesses against Stephen, as chap. vii. 58. For the witnesses did slay him not only by the testimony which they gave against him, but they were to be the first who stoned him. *Slew him;* or murdered him.

i ch. 9. 15. & 13. 2, 46, 47. & 18. 6. & 26. 17. Rom. 1. 5. & 11. 13. &   21 And he said unto me, Depart: ⁱfor I will send thee far hence unto the Gentiles.

15. 16. Gal. 1. 15, 16. & 2. 7, 8. Eph. 3. 7, 8. 1 Tim. 2. 7. 2 Tim. 1. 11.

God repeats his command, and by that answers all Paul's reasonings; whatsoever the event be, whether the Gentiles will hear, or whether they will forbear, he must go unto them. When the will of God is manifest we must do it, whatsoever success we are like to have. *I will send thee far hence;* this was verified; God sent Paul, and he went very far, as appears, chap. ix. 15; Rom. xv. 19; Gal. i. 17; ii. 8.

22 And they gave him audience unto this word, and *then* lifted up their voices, and said, ᵏAway with such a *fellow* from the earth: for it is not fit that ˡhe should live.

k ch. 21. 36.
l ch. 25. 24.

They gave him audience unto this word; they had heard all the rest of St. Paul's discourse without any gainsaying, either thinking it did not much concern them whether it were true or false, or else, being convinced of the truth of it, they were silent; but when the mercy of God unto any but themselves is mentioned, they are not able to bear with it. Though they themselves refused the offers of God's mercy, yet they could not endure that it should be tendered unto others; especially that others should be preferred before them in the tendering of it. *Away with such a fellow from the earth;* that is, Kill him; encouraging one another to so barbarous a murder, or exciting their rulers unto it.

23 And as they cried out, and cast off *their* clothes, and threw dust into the air,

Cast off their clothes; they that stoned the blasphemer cast off their upper garments, that they might be the readier to do that execution, and carry the heavier stones; as chap. vii. 58. They might also cast or rend them off, in sign of grief and detestation of Paul's (supposed) blasphemy. *Threw dust into the air;* out of raging madness, having no stones at present in that place to throw at him; or stamping on the ground first with their feet, and taking thence the loosened earth, threw it up, to show that Paul had sinned against heaven, and provoked the God who dwells there; and that he was not worthy to tread on the earth, which, as well as they could, they took from him.

24 The chief captain commanded him to be brought into the castle, and bade that he should be examined by scourging; that he might know wherefore they cried so against him.

The chief captain; of whom, chap. xxi. 31. *The castle,* or fort, called Antonia, as chap. xxi. 34. *By scourging;* or torturing, (being put to the question, as the French expression is, agreeable to the Greek word here used,) which went no further than by scourging; which was for this purpose used upon the blessed body of our Saviour, Matt. xxvii. 26. The chief captain took it for granted that he was some notorious malefactor whom all cried out against injuriously, accounting *vox populi* to be *vox Dei;* and because in that confusion he could not know the certainty from his accusers, he would wrest a confession out of St. Paul, whom they accused.

25 And as they bound him with thongs, Paul said unto the centurion that stood by, ᵐIs it lawful for you to scourge a man that is a Roman, and uncondemned?

m ch. 16. 37.

They bound him with thongs; they who were to be scourged were bound to a post or column (amongst the Jews) of a cubit and a half high, inclining downwards upon it; and these thongs were such wherewith they bound Paul to this column or pillar; and with such also they intended to scourge him. *Is it lawful for you to scourge a man that is a Roman, and uncondemned?* that is, it is not lawful to scourge a Roman; much less, uncondemned: see on chap. xvi. 37. This latter, the laws of no nation that was civilized did ever allow.

26 When the centurion heard *that*, he went and told the chief captain, saying, Take heed what thou doest: for this man is a Roman.

There were several centurions under one chief captain, or chiliarch, as there are several captains under one colonel; and this centurion might be deputed to examine Paul. The reason why they presently desisted from binding Paul, and informed the commander-in-chief of what he had alleged, might be, because as it was very penal to challenge this privilege falsely, so it was treason for any to deny it to such to whom it was due.

27 Then the chief captain came, and said unto him, Tell me, art thou a Roman? He said, Yea.

It is very reasonable that a good man should make use of such lawful privileges as the place in which he lives doth afford, and in his condition may be allowed. And it is part of that wisdom our Saviour does recommend, if it does not destroy the innocence of the dove, Matt. x. 16.

28 And the chief captain answered, With a great sum obtained I this freedom. And Paul said, But I was *free* born.

The historian relates, that the emperor Claudius sold this privilege to such foreigners as had not by any notable service merited to have it conferred upon them. At first it cost them very much to obtain it, as it did this chief captain; but afterwards it was more cheap and contemptible. *I was free born;* though Paul was born of Hebrew parents, yet he was born at Tarsus, to the natives of which town Augustus had given this privilege, for the assistance that the citizens afforded him in his wars with Brutus and Cassius; or, as some will have it, for favouring of Julius Cæsar, this privilege was granted unto that place by him: and they, on the other side, to continue the sense of his favour, caused their town to be called Juliopolis, or the city of Julius.

29 Then straightway they departed from him which should have ‖ examined him: and the chief captain also was afraid, after he knew that he was a Roman, and because he had bound him.

‖ Or, tortured him.

They departed from him, who had bound him, and would have scourged him. *The chief captain also was afraid;* the crime of breaking the privileges of the Roman citizens being accounted no less than treason, and a sin, as they called it, against the majesty of that people; as afterwards it was as great an offence against their emperors.

30 On the morrow, because he would have known the certainty wherefore he was accused of the Jews, he loosed him from *his* bands, and commanded the Chief Priests and all their council to appear, and brought Paul down, and set him before them.

He loosed him from his bands; that he might not continue, after knowledge, in that (accounted) crime of binding a Roman citizen; as also that Paul might speak with the greater liberty and freedom in his own defence. *The chief priests;* the chief of the four and twenty courses amongst the priests, according to their families, or such as in place and dignity did excel in the sanhedrim.

CHAP. XXIII.

Paul, pleading his integrity, is smitten at the command of the high priest, whom he reproveth of injustice, 1—5. *By declaring himself a Pharisee, and questioned for the hope of the resurrection, he causeth a division in the council,* 6—9. *He is carried back to the castle, and encouraged by the Lord in a vision,* 10, 11. *A conspiracy against him is discovered to the chief captain,* 12—22; *who sendeth him under a guard with a letter to Felix the governor at Cæsarea,* 23—35.

a ch. 24. 16. 1 Cor. 4. 4. 2 Cor. 1. 12. & 4. 2. 2 Tim. 1. 3. Heb. 13. 18.

AND Paul, earnestly beholding the council, said, Men *and* brethren, [a] I have lived in all good conscience before God until this day.

Said, Men and brethren; acknowledging himself to have descended from the patriarchs as well as they; and bespeaks, as much as he could, their favour and attention. *I have lived in all good conscience;* not that he thought himself to have been without sin or fault, for he acknowledges and bewails his captivity to the law of sin, Rom. vii. 23, 24; but that he was not conscious to himself of any notorious impiety (as sacrilege, which they accused him of); nay, he had not suffered willingly any sin to be, much less to reign, in him. And as for his persecuting of the Christians, he did it not to flatter any with it, or upon any sinister design whatsoever, but thinking to serve God by it, 1 Tim. i. 13. *Before God;* in the sense of God's seeing of him, and whom St. Paul acknowledges to be the searcher and knower of the heart and conscience.

b 1 Kings 22. 24. Jer. 20. 2. John 18. 22.

2 And the High Priest Ananias commanded them that stood by him [b] to smite him on the mouth.

Them that stood by him; the officers, probably. *To smite him on the mouth;* thus Micaiah was smote by Zedekiah the false prophet, 1 Kings xxii. 24, and Jeremiah by Pashur, Jer. xx. 2; and our blessed Lord escaped not this suffering and indignity, John xviii. 22. Now this was the rather inflicted on Paul, because of his protesting of his innocency, which did reflect upon the council, as being injurious; but it was indeed no more than what was necessary in his own just defence, and for the glory of the gospel.

3 Then said Paul unto him, God shall smite thee, *thou* whited wall: for sittest thou to judge me after the law, and [c] commandest me to be smitten contrary to the law?

c Lev. 19. 35. Deut. 25. 1, 2. John 7. 51.

Thou whited wall; an excellent similitude to represent wicked men, especially hypocrites, by, who counterfeit God's glory and worship, whilst they intend only their own profit or grandeur. Thus our Saviour compared the scribes and Pharisees unto *whited sepulchres*, Matt. xxiii. 27. Whited sepulchres and walls, though they seem fair and comely, have within nothing but rottenness and useless rubbish. Now these words are not to be looked upon as a curse or imprecation upon the high priest, which does not consist with the temper of the gospel; but they are rather to be taken as a prophecy or prediction, St. Paul having on occasion had the gift of prophecy amongst the other gifts of the Holy Ghost. And accordingly it is observed, that this high priest either died, or was put out of his place, soon after. And thus Paul's imprecation upon Alexander the coppersmith, mentioned 2 Tim. iv. 14, is to be understood; as also several other curses (seemingly wished) by holy men, especially in the Psalms, as Psal. cix. 6, 7, &c., and many other places, which are by no means for our imitation; neither were they spoken so much as the wishes or prayers of such as uttered them, as their prophecies or predictions; which we know came to pass; as that now mentioned was fulfilled in the person of Judas. *Contrary to the law;* it was contrary to all law, Divine and human, that any should be punished before that he was heard; and especially to their own judicial law, which in matters of this nature they were yet governed by under the Romans. Now the Jews were first to hear and inquire diligently, whether the matter any were accused of were true, before they might give sentence, or inflict any punishment upon them, Deut. xvii. 4.

4 And they that stood by said, Revilest thou God's High Priest?

These partial parasites take no notice of the real injury done unto Paul by the high priest, and readily catch at the seeming calumny spoke by Paul against him.

5 Then said Paul, [d] I wist not, brethren, that he was the High Priest: for it is written, [e] Thou shalt not speak evil of the ruler of thy people.

d ch. 24. 17.
e Ex. 22. 28. Eccles. 10. 20. 2 Pet. 2. 10. Jude 8.

I wist not, brethren, that he was the high priest; Paul does not here ironically say this, because the high priest had, contrary to his place and office, caused him to be smitten; but either, 1. Because he knew now no high priest on earth, but only Christ in heaven to be our High Priest, Heb. viii. 1. Or rather, 2. Because the high priests being so often changed, (insomuch as in one year sometimes they had had three,) and they being in a confusion at this time, and not meeting or sitting in their due place and order, Paul might very well be ignorant who that was, who in such a multitude had commanded that they should smite him. *Thou shalt not speak evil of the ruler of thy people;* the scripture here cited by St. Paul, is Exod. xxii. 28.

6 But when Paul perceived that the one part were Sadducees, and the other Pharisees, he cried out in the council, Men *and* brethren, [f] I am a Pharisee, the son of a Pharisee: [g] of the hope and resurrection of the dead I am called in question.

f ch. 26. 5. Phil. 3. 5.
g ch. 24. 15, 21. & 26. 6. & 28. 20.

I am a Pharisee; in his former profession, opinion, and conversation; and now also in the points that were controverted betwixt them: and St. Paul, with his dove-like innocency, does in this but make use of the serpentine subtlety, to preserve himself, and to gain credit unto the truths of the gospel. *The son of a Pharisee;* the son of Pharisees, in the plural; either for several descents his ancestors had been of that sect; or that both his father and his mother were of it. *Of the hope and resurrection;* or, for the hope of the resurrection; an hendyadis: although he did not agree with the Pharisees in all their opinions, yet in this he did; and the resurrection was the common subject he preached upon: and the gospel does give us the best proof and evidence of it; insomuch that Paul was taxed for preaching *Jesus and the resurrection,* chap. xvii. 18; and unless there be a resurrection, his preaching was vain, and his faith vain, 1 Cor. xv. 13, 14.

7 And when he had so said, there arose a dissension between the Pharisees and the Sadducees: and the multitude was divided.

Not only of the common people, or standers-by, but of the senators and judges; God by this means dividing and infatuating of them, that they could not bring about Paul's intended destruction.

8 [h] For the Sadducees say that there is no resurrection, neither angel, nor spirit: but the Pharisees confess both.

h Mat. 22. 23. Mark 12. 18. Luke 20. 27.

The Sadducees say that there is no resurrection; against this our Saviour argued, Matt. xxii. 23, &c. *Neither angel;* it seems strange that they should deny that there were angels, whereas they owned the Pentateuch, or five books of Moses, in which mention is made frequently of angels: but it seems that they understood those places allegorically, either for good instincts, or apparitions caused by God to manifest his mind by them unto men, wresting those places to their own destruction. *Nor spirit;* they denied the existence of the soul of man, as different from the crasis and temperament of his body; and therefore believed that the soul perished with the body. Nay, they were so far from believing there was any spirit, that they held, blasphemously, that God himself was corporeal. *But the Pharisees confess both;* the three things here mentioned, which the Sadducees denied, may be well spoken of as but two, viz. the resurrection and the existence of spirits. When men sin with much obstinacy against supernatural light, God justly withdraws from them even natural light, and they are

THE ACTS XXIII

9 And there arose a great cry: and the Scribes *that were* of the Pharisees' part arose, and strove, saying, ⁱ We find no evil in this man: but ᵏ if a spirit or an angel hath spoken to him, ˡ let us not fight against God.

i ch. 25. 25. & 26. 31.
k ch. 22. 7, 17, 18.
l ch. 5. 39.

Scribe is a name denoting an office or place; and *the scribes* were men skilled in the law. *A spirit or an angel;* some take the latter to be exegetical of the former, and that by a spirit is only meant an angel; by such messengers God many times sending his messages to the children of men. Yet others by *spirit* understand prophetical revelation, and the Spirit of prophecy, which was expected to be shed abroad in large measures about that time; as appears, John vii. 39. *Let us not fight against God:* see chap. v. 39.

10 And when there arose a great dissension, the chief captain, fearing lest Paul should have been pulled in pieces of them, commanded the soldiers to go down, and to take him by force from among them, and to bring *him* into the castle.

A great dissension: feuds about pretended religion are usually among all men very sharp, because their opinions, being the issues of their own brains, are more beloved than their children, the fruit of their bodies. *Commanded the soldiers to go down;* from the fort or castle, unto which there was an ascent or stair, to go up and down by.

m ch. 18. 9. & 27. 23, 24.

11 And ᵐ the night following the Lord stood by him, and said, Be of good cheer, Paul: for as thou hast testified of me in Jerusalem, so must thou bear witness also at Rome.

The Lord stood by him; in a revelation appearing inwardly to his mind; which is the rather thought to have been so, because it is here said to have been in the night; but whether by vision or revelation, it is all one as to this purpose, and neither were unfrequent unto Paul, 2 Cor. xii. 1. *Be of good cheer:* so true is it what our Saviour had promised and foretold, John xvi. 33, *In the world ye shall have tribulation*, but *in me ye shall have peace.*

n ver. 21, 30. ch. 25. 3.

12 And when it was day, ⁿ certain of the Jews banded together, and bound themselves ∥ under a curse, saying that they would neither eat nor drink till they had killed Paul.

∥ Or, *with an oath of execration.*

If they did not kill Paul before they did eat or drink any more, they wished that they might become a *cherem*, or anathema; as Jericho and the inhabitants thereof were, being devoted to utter ruin and destruction. Or, if they did not execute this their wicked design, they would yield themselves to be anathematized, or excommunicated, as those that had broken their pact or agreement.

13 And they were more than forty which had made this conspiracy.

They made themselves sure (they thought) of killing Paul; there were above forty to one. The church's enemies are unanimous and resolute. As David formerly, so might now Paul say, *They that are mad against me are sworn against me,* Psal. cii. 8.

14 And they came to the Chief Priests and elders, and said, We have bound ourselves under a great curse, that we will eat nothing until we have slain Paul.

They came to the chief priests and elders, whose place and office it was to have dissuaded such an abominable murder: *For the priest's lips should keep knowledge,* Mal. ii. 7. And they could not but have been guilty of the blood of St. Paul, had it been shed, who by encouraging the design became accessory unto it. But they had drank blood very largely before now; viz. the blood of St. Stephen, and the blood of our Saviour; and it is no wonder that they thirst for more: such wild beasts, (rather than men,) when they have once tasted of blood, are never satisfied with it. But at what a low ebb was religion, when the chief priests themselves combine with assassins!

15 Now therefore ye with the council signify to the chief captain that he bring him down unto you to morrow, as though ye would enquire something more perfectly concerning him: and we, or ever he come near, are ready to kill him.

Ye with the council; the chief priests are to join with the council in this desire to the chief captain; for they had no authority to command him. *As though ye would inquire something more perfectly concerning him:* the plot against Paul's life was laid very deep, and not easily to be discovered; it being usual to send for prisoners to re-examine them, especially when religion and the public peace are concerned, as they pretended that here they were. *Or ever he come near:* the space between the castle and the place where the council met, being considerable, it gave the greater advantage to the conspirators.

16 And when Paul's sister's son heard of their lying in wait, he went and entered into the castle, and told Paul.

Paul's sister's son, who is thought to have been one of Paul's company: but the hatred against Paul by the Jews being so general, because of his (supposed) profaning of the temple, they were not so curious who they spake to of this confederacy and design. Or rather, there is no counsel against God: the very *birds of the air*, if need were, *shall carry the voice, and that which hath wings shall tell the matter*, Eccles. x. 20. For *he that sitteth in the heavens shall laugh: the Lord shall have them in derision*, Psal. ii. 4.

17 Then Paul called one of the centurions unto *him*, and said, Bring this young man unto the chief captain: for he hath a certain thing to tell him.

The chief captain having the command of a thousand soldiers, there were ten captains under him: one of these Paul intrusts with his message to the chief captain, not making any particular request unto the chief captain, supposing him to have so much of the Roman justice in him, that when he understood his case, he would provide for his safety; which he was not mistaken in.

18 So he took him, and brought *him* to the chief captain, and said, Paul the prisoner called me unto *him*, and prayed me to bring this young man unto thee, who hath something to say unto thee.

The centurion took Paul's kinsman, and went with him, as he was desired, unto the chief captain, that there might be no mistake, but that he might hear all out of the young man's own mouth, and be the more affected with it. *The prisoner*, or, the chained; for it was customary to chain their prisoners for their greater security. And God is now remembering of Paul in his bonds.

19 Then the chief captain took him by the hand, and went *with him* aside privately, and asked *him*, What is that thou hast to tell me?

He *took him by the hand*, as a token of courtesy; these commanders showing an excellent example of humanity and pity towards their inferiors and supposed criminals. There are several reasons given of this great civility here used, as the chief captain's naturally meek temper; or his policy to satisfy for the injury he had done to Paul, in binding him, being a Roman; nay, some think that he, as well as Felix the governor, hoped for money to be given unto him, chap. xxiv. 26: but all these are but guesses. It is sure, whatever any of these causes were or were not, God is to be seen and acknowledged in it, who hath the hearts of all men in his hands, and turneth them as it pleaseth him, Prov. xxi. 1.

20 And he said, ᵒ The Jews have agreed to desire thee that thou wouldest bring down Paul to morrow into the council,

ᵒ ver. 12.

as though they would enquire somewhat of him more perfectly.

The Jews; both the council, and those forty and upwards spoken of, ver. 12, 13.

21 But do not thou yield unto them: for there lie in wait for him of them more than forty men, which have bound themselves with an oath, that they will neither eat nor drink till they have killed him: and now are they ready, looking for a promise from thee.

Do not thou yield unto them; this the young man desires out of his care for his uncle's (Paul's) preservation, as also touched with the horror of the fact if it should have been executed; and howsoever, by this means he delivers his own soul, having done his utmost to hinder it. *Now are they ready, looking for a promise from thee;* the match is laid, the hand is as it were lifted up, nothing is wanting to Paul's destruction but the chief captain's consent, which the Jews assuredly expected, it being but a small courtesy to grant them, to examine a prisoner, especially such a one as upon their complaint was committed in a case cognizable by them: but, *Deus e machina, Take counsel together, and it shall come to nought; speak the word, and it shall not stand; for God is with us,* Isa. viii. 10.

22 So the chief captain *then* let the young man depart, and charged *him, See thou* tell no man that thou hast shewed these things to me.

The chief captain shows by this his care, both for St. Paul, and for the young man too; for had it been known that he had discovered their conspiracy, they would have sought his life, and might divers ways have taken it away; and as for Paul, being disappointed in this, they would have made other attempts against him.

23 And he called unto *him* two centurions, saying, Make ready two hundred soldiers to go to Cæsarea, and horsemen threescore and ten, and spearmen two hundred, at the third hour of the night;

Make ready two hundred soldiers; two hundred were the usual proportion or number of men which were under the two centurions; so that they were commanded to have their companies in readiness. *And horsemen threescore and ten;* horsemen being usually added for defence of their foot-soldiers. *Spearmen,* as they are called here, were such as handled, or threw, their javelins or darts with their right hand. Some think them to have been such as our serjeants, who take men into custody; others, that they were soldiers raised out of foreign nations, and lightly armed. *At the third hour of the night;* partly because in those hot countries it is very troublesome to travel by day, and partly for the greater security of Paul and such as went with him.

24 And provide *them* beasts, that they may set Paul on, and bring *him* safe unto Felix the governor.

What a strong guard and retinue does God by his providence get together for the safe-guarding of Paul! None of all these intended the least good unto him; but God can make use of them as effectually as if they had had the greatest good will for him.

25 And he wrote a letter after this manner:

It is not certain whether the following words were the letter itself, or only the sum or contents of the letter.

26 Claudius Lysias unto the most excellent governor Felix *sendeth* greeting.

Most excellent; a title given to persons of great eminency, as, Luke i. 3, it is given to Theophilus, unto whom also this book of the Acts is inscribed, chap. i. 1. This *Felix* was brother to one Pallas, who together with Narcissus (the other of the emperor Claudius's favourites) managed all public affairs, and are by the historians branded for all the mischiefs of that calamitous time. This Felix and his brother Pallas were born slaves, and manumitted by Claudius, and were such as are exalted; as often Providence will show the power it hath in pulling down and setting up whom it pleaseth.

27 ᵖThis man was taken of the Jews, p ch. 21. 33. & 24. 7.
and should have been killed of them: then came I with an army, and rescued him, having understood that he was a Roman.

He represents Paul's case fairly and indifferently, God overruling his heart and pen; but withal, he conceals his binding of him, and instead thereof magnifies his care of him, being a Roman; and probably being touched with a sense of his fault, he represents Paul's case the better.

28 ᑫAnd when I would have known q ch. 22. 30.
the cause wherefore they accused him, I brought him forth into their council:

The council understanding those questions (as he thought) best, and having yet retained some power from the Romans concerning them.

29 Whom I perceived to be accused ʳof questions of their law, ˢbut to have r ch. 18. 15. & 25. 19.
nothing laid to his charge worthy of death s ch. 26. 31.
or of bonds.

According to the Roman laws, or imperial constitutions. That he undervalued the great things in question concerning our blessed Saviour's death and resurrection, and the whole gospel, it is not to be wondered at; he spake and wrote as a pagan; and God overruled his very slighting of these controversies for Paul's advantage, he being by that means preserved from the rage of his enemies.

30 And ᵗwhen it was told me how that t ver. 20.
the Jews laid wait for the man, I sent straightway to thee, and ᵘgave command- u ch. 24. 8. & 25. 6.
ment to his accusers also to say before thee what *they had* against him. Farewell.

The Jews laid wait for the man; this reflects upon the Jews, as being seditious, and ready to attempt against the government; as also gives the governor an account why he troubled him with this prisoner, and why he sent so great a guard with him. *Farewell;* the usual prayer wherewith they ended their letters, as chap. xv. 29.

31 Then the soldiers, as it was commanded them, took Paul, and brought *him* by night to Antipatris.

Not that they came to Antipatris by night; but they began that journey by night, as ver. 23, and went as much of it as they could by night, for fear of being discovered, and attempted upon by the Jews. This *Antipatris* was built by Herod the Great, and so called in memory of his father Antipater; it was about seventeen leagues from Jerusalem, pleasantly situated upon the Mediterranean Sea, between Joppa and Cæsarea.

32 On the morrow they left the horsemen to go with him, and returned to the castle:

The footmen returned to the castle or fort of Antonia in Jerusalem, from whence they did set out, there being no fear of any such design upon Paul at that distance from Jerusalem, which the horsemen might not easily avoid.

33 Who, when they came to Cæsarea, and delivered the epistle to the governor, presented Paul also before him.

Cæsarea; Cæsarea Stratonis, as it was called, to difference it from the other. They *presented Paul,* as being their charge, whom they had safely kept, and now delivered according to appointment.

34 And when the governor had read *the letter,* he asked of what province he was. And when he understood that *he was* of ˣCilicia; x ch. 21. 39.

He asked of what province he was; Palestine and the countries thereabouts being divided into several heptarchies or jurisdictions, the governors were very loth to infringe the limits of one another. *Of Cilicia;* a country in Asia Minor, in which was Tarsus where Paul was born, and from his birth-place he is reckoned to belong to that province.

35 ʸI will hear thee, said he, when thine accusers are also come. And he commanded him to be kept in ᶻHerod's judgment hall.

I will hear thee thoroughly, the whole matter, as the preposition διὰ, here used, does import; and as it is commanded unto all judges, Deut. i. 16. *When thine accusers are also come;* for this the dictate of nature did teach the very heathen, that both parties ought to be heard before any thing were determined: *Qui aliquid statuerit parte inaudita altera:* That whosoever pronounced any sentence before both sides were fully heard, were the sentence never so just, yet the judge was unjust. *Herod's judgment-hall;* a palace where the governors were lodged, built by Herod the Great, when, in honour, or flattery, of Augustus, after he had fortified the city, he caused it to be called Cesarea.

CHAP. XXIV

Paul is accused before Felix by Tertullus in the name of the Jews, 1—9. He answereth in defence of his life and doctrine, 10—21. The hearing is deferred, 22, 23. Paul preaching freely before the governor and his wife; Felix trembleth, 24, 25. Felix hopeth for a bribe to release Paul, but in vain; and going out of his office leaveth him bound, 26, 27.

AND after ᵃfive days ᵇAnanias the High Priest descended with the elders, and *with* a certain orator *named* Tertullus, who informed the governor against Paul.

After five days, from the time that Paul was come to Cæsarea: the malice and fury of the persecutors was very great, they stick not at any travail and pains to do mischief; and surely we ought to be as earnest in doing good, or their zeal will condemn us. *A certain orator;* a lawyer to form the indictment against Paul, or to aggravate his fault, and to desire judgment upon him. Such advocates usually were the chiefest orators, as Demosthenes in Greece, and Cicero at Rome; and Tertullus seems to have been a crafts-master, whom the Jews hired to draw up an accusation against Paul.

2 And when he was called forth, Tertullus began to accuse *him,* saying, Seeing that by thee we enjoy great quietness, and that very worthy deeds are done unto this nation by thy providence,

When he was called forth; when Paul was sent for to appear, being under the custody of the soldiers who brought him to Cæsarea. *Seeing that by thee, &c.:* it being one of the rules of art, which an orator seldom forgets, to endeavour to obtain the judge's favour, Tertullus commends Felix, who indeed had delivered that country from some robbers (like banditti, or moss-troopers) that did infest it; but is commended for little else amongst the historians, who brand him for extraordinary covetousness and cruelty.

3 We accept *it* always, and in all places, most noble Felix, with all thankfulness.

We accept it; we commend and admire it. It is most certain, that inferiors enjoy many benefits by the means of their governors, who bear the burden for the people, watching and caring for them; and that a bad government is better than none; and therefore not only Tertullus, (who may well be thought to speak out of flattery,) but St. Paul himself, ver. 10, speaks with great respect unto Felix.

4 Notwithstanding, that I be not further tedious unto thee, I pray thee that thou wouldest hear us of thy clemency a few words.

Be not further tedious unto thee; hinder thee, or take thee away from other occasions: this is another artifice of an orator, to promise brevity, especially when he speaks to men of employment or business.

5 ᶜFor we have found this man *a* pestilent *fellow,* and a mover of sedition among all the Jews throughout the world, and a ringleader of the sect of the Nazarenes:

A pestilent fellow; a pest, or plague, the abstract being put for the concrete, as implying, that no word he could use could properly signify the mischievousness of that man, whom he falsely charges with *sedition* (not that the Jews would have disliked him for that, had it been true, but) to make St. Paul the more odious, and in danger of his life. *The sect,* or heresy, which in common use was then taken more favourably, for any doctrine. *Of the Nazarenes;* of the Christians; for they who out of Judea were called Christians, in Judea were called Nazarenes. The Jews did call our Saviour and his followers thus, it being accounted an ignominious term; and they who were born at Nazareth disgraced by it, as appears by Nathanael's question, *Can there any good thing come out of Nazareth?* John i. 46. Yet this name is most glorious, as imposed upon our Saviour by God himself, Matt. ii. 23.

6 ᵈWho also hath gone about to profane the temple: whom we took, and would ᵉhave judged according to our law.

Hath gone about to profane the temple; by bringing into the temple (as they falsely suggested) uncircumcised persons: but Tertullus does not mention this, or show in what Paul had profaned the temple; for Felix himself being uncircumcised, it would have reflected upon him too much, to be accounted, by the Jews, amongst such profane ones, as were enough to defile their temple and worship. *Would have judged according to our law;* they had a law, it seems, whereby it was death to bring strangers into the temple; and some think, that by the Romans they had yet power allowed them to put it in execution: see chap. xxi. 28. And this was their aim all along, viz. to take away his life.

7 ᶠBut the chief captain Lysias came upon *us,* and with great violence took *him* away out of our hands,

So they call the bringing of soldiers, to hinder them from acting violently; and as far as they dare, they accuse Lysias, whom they thought not to favour them.

8 ᵍCommanding his accusers to come unto thee: by examining of whom thyself mayest take knowledge of all these things, whereof we accuse him.

By examining of whom; not that the Jews would have any witnesses produced, and fairly examined; but the pronoun being singular, it refers to Paul, whom Tertullus would have examined, and put to the question, or racked, that he might confess what they would have had him guilty of: or it is as if he had said, (so impudent is impiety,) that Paul himself could not deny (if he were asked) the accusation which was brought against him.

9 And the Jews also assented, saying that these things were so.

The high priest, and the rest of the senate that came with him, acknowledged (as the manner was) that Tertullus had spoken their sense, and what they had to say; and some think that this their assent went further, and that they offered themselves as witnesses to the truth of what he had said.

10 Then Paul, after that the governor had beckoned unto him to speak, answered, Forasmuch as I know that thou hast been of many years a judge unto this nation, I do the more cheerfully answer for myself:

Beckoned unto him, by some sign with his hand. Though St. Paul would not flatter Felix with notorious untruths, as Tertullus had done, yet he speaks very respectfully, and mentions his continuance in the government; the rather, because, if he had been so seditious a person as Tertullus would have represented him to have been, Felix could not but have heard of him, and of any mischief that had been done by him.

11 Because that thou mayest understand, that there are yet but twelve days since I went up to Jerusalem ʰfor to worship.

That thou mayest understand, either by what thou hast

heard already, or by what the witnesses, when examined, will declare. *There are yet but twelve days since I went up to Jerusalem*; there were but twelve days since Paul's coming to Jerusalem; seven of them he had spent there, until the time of his purification was accomplished; and the other five days he had been in custody, and at Cæsarea: by which St. Paul proves how unlikely it was, that in so short a time he, being a stranger in those parts, should raise any tumults. *For to worship*; he being so far from designing any mischief, that he only intended to worship God.

i ch. 25. 6. & 28. 17.
12 ¹And they neither found me in the temple disputing with any man, neither raising up the people, neither in the synagogues, nor in the city:

Disputing, or discoursing. Although it seems not to have been unlawful, after the sacrifices were offered, to discourse about the meaning of any place in the law or the prophets; for thus our Saviour is said to have heard and asked questions of the doctors in the temple, Luke ii. 46; yet St. Paul would hereby show how far he was from doing aught that was unlawful, in that he had forborne to go to the utmost of what might have been lawful.

13 Neither can they prove the things whereof they now accuse me.

They could not prove either of those crimes they charged him with, viz. 1. Raising of sedition; or, 2. Profaning of the temple, which they had accused him of.

k See Amos 8. 14. ch. 9. 2.
l 2 Tim. 1. 3.
m ch. 26. 22. & 28. 23.
14 But this I confess unto thee, that after ᵏthe way which they call heresy, so worship I the ˡGod of my fathers, believing all things which are written in ᵐthe Law and in the Prophets:

But this I confess; he makes here a good confession, and is indeed a follower of Christ, who *before Pontius Pilate* is said to have *witnessed a good confession*, 1 Tim. vi. 13. *Heresy*; this word is of a middle signification, being sometimes taken in a good sense, as chap. xxvi. 5, and thus the Greeks did use it sometimes when they spake of their philosophers; though the Jews called the doctrine of Christ so in the worst acceptation of the word; which doctrine this blessed apostle is not ashamed to own. Yet he does withal truly assert, that he worshipped no other God than the God of his fathers, but worshipped him whom Abraham, Isaac, and Jacob (whom they so much gloried in) had worshipped; and that he had no other religion than what was taught in the law and the prophets, from whom they themselves had received theirs.

n ch. 23. 6. & 26. 6, 7. & 28. 20.
o Dan. 12. 2. John 5. 28, 29.
15 And ⁿhave hope toward God, which they themselves also allow, ᵒthat there shall be a resurrection of the dead, both of the just and unjust.

Which they themselves also allow; the wiser sort amongst them, the Pharisees, (though bad was the best,) and yet they were not for this opinion persecuted by the Sadducees. *A resurrection of the dead*; the resurrection of the dead is again owned as the chief matter Paul preached upon, and in which all his other doctrines and opinions did centre, it being indeed the foundation of that faith and manners, 1 Cor. xv. 13, of that belief and holy life, which St. Paul preached up. *Both of the just and unjust*; that both sorts, even that all such, rise again at the last day, we have assurance given, Matt. xxv. 32, 33; John v. 28, 29; which was also foretold expressly unto the Jews, Dan. xii. 2, though it hath found so many since amongst them that have denied it.

p ch. 23. 1.
16 And ᵖherein do I exercise myself, to have always a conscience void of offence toward God, and *toward* men.

And herein; or at this time, and in this business; or for this reason, to wit, because I believe the resurrection. *I exercise myself*; I am altogether taken up with it; this is my one thing necessary, Luke x. 42. *To have always a conscience void of offence toward God, and toward men*; that I may not offend God or man in any thing; but that I may be without blame at the judgment-seat of God, or man. They only are blessed and happy, whose belief concerning another world makes them endeavour after holiness in this world.

17 Now after many years ᵍI came to bring alms to my nation, and offerings.
q ch. 11. 29, 30. & 20, 16. Rom. 15. 25. 2 Cor. 8. 4. Gal. 2. 10.

After many years; it is thought fourteen years, which we find mentioned, Gal. ii. 1; and therefore the more unlike to have any seditious practices there, where he had so little acquaintance. *I came to bring alms to my nation*; and he was so far from designing mischief to his nation, that his charity to them put him upon this journey. *And offerings*; which in his condescension to the Jews, and hoping to gain their good will, he brought according to the law; as chap. xxi. 26. For whilst Jerusalem and the temple stood, those offerings were in a sort permitted; but God, in that general destruction of both city and temple, put an end to them all.

18 ʳWhereupon certain Jews from Asia found me purified in the temple, neither with multitude, nor with tumult.
r ch. 21. 26, 27. & 26. 21.

Whereupon; upon my bringing up those alms now mentioned; whilst I was employed for the good of my countrymen who now accuse me. *Purified in the temple*; performing all things which the law did require of Nazarites, or those who had made a vow, and in which their legal purification did consist. *Neither with multitude, nor with tumult*; the multitude was of their own gathering together; and the tumult, if any, was made by themselves. It is no new thing that Christians should be charged with those mischiefs which their enemies themselves did to make them odious.

19 ˢWho ought to have been here before thee, and object, if they had ought against me.
s ch. 23. 30. & 25. 16.

Who ought to have been here; the Jews of Asia, who had caused all this stir, having seen Trophimus with Paul in the streets of Jerusalem, and maliciously presuming that he had brought him into the temple with him. Now these were the only proper witnesses, who might therefore be now absent, because they could testify nothing to the purpose, and when they thought seriously upon it, their consciences might accuse them for the clamour they had made against the apostle, chap. xxi. 28. As for the other Jews, they could only testify by hearsay, which is not sufficient.

20 Or else let these same *here* say, if they have found any evil doing in me, while I stood before the council,

St. Paul is willing to allow the present Jews' testimony about such things as they could know, having themselves heard and seen them; which was what passed in the council when Paul was brought before it, chap. xxiii. 1, 9. The sense of a Deity was more quick upon men; and they might then be trusted under the security of an oath.

21 Except it be for this one voice, that I cried standing among them, ᵗTouching the resurrection of the dead I am called in question by you this day.
t ch. 23. 6. & 28. 20.

As if he had said, Let them object, if they can, any other fault: but if this be a fault, to hold the resurrection of the dead, I do acknowledge it, and there need no other proof concerning it: not that he held any evil to be in this opinion; but he speaks ironically, knowing that they durst not renew their quarrel about it.

22 And when Felix heard these things, having more perfect knowledge of *that* way, he deferred them, and said, When ᵘLysias the chief captain shall come down, I will know the uttermost of your matter.
u ver. 7.

Some understand by *that way*, 1. The custom or manner of the priests to calumniate Paul; or, 2. The religion of Moses, and how and in what it differed from the religion of Christ: either of which Felix might know, and by either of them conclude Paul to be innocent. But, 3. By *that way*, as frequently in this book, chap. ix. 2, and xxii. 4, is meant the Christian religion itself, which Felix, not only from Paul's apology, and Lysias's account of the whole matter, but by divers other means, (it having made so great a noise in the world,) could not be ignorant of. Some

THE ACTS XXIV, XXV

read, he deferred them till he could have a more perfect knowledge of that way, and till Lysias, the chief captain, should come down. For there being two things laid to Paul's charge; 1. His evil opinions in matters of religion; and, 2. His causing a sedition: as to the first, Felix would not determine it till he had had better information about those things which St. Paul was accused for to hold. As to the latter, it being matter of fact, which Lysias was present at, he would hear his testimony or evidence, looking upon him as one indifferent and unconcerned betwixt them.

23 And he commanded a centurion to keep Paul, and to let *him* have liberty, and *that he should forbid none of his acquaintance to minister or come unto him.

x ch. 27. 3. & 28. 16.

To let him have liberty; not so confined as to be kept in a dungeon, or more inward prison; but to have the liberty of the prison, yet so as with a chain about him; as appears, chap. xxvi. 29; xxviii. 20. *Acquaintance;* relations or disciples; for there was a church at Cæsarea, chap. x. 48; xxi. 8. When it is expedient for us, God can add the comforts of these outward enjoyments, relations and friends, unto us; and that his and our enemies shall contribute towards it.

24 And after certain days, when Felix came with his wife Drusilla, which was a Jewess, he sent for Paul, and heard him concerning the faith in Christ.

Felix came with his wife; having been out of town to meet and conduct his wife. *Drusilla;* who was daughter of Herod the Great, and sister of that Agrippa of whom mention is made in the two following chapters; a most libidinous woman, who had left her husband Aziz, and, whilst he yet lived, was married to this Felix, who was taken with her beauty. Yet Paul preached *the faith in Christ,* the gospel, unto such, not knowing what persons, or in what hour, God might call.

25 And as he reasoned of righteousness, temperance, and judgment to come, Felix trembled, and answered, Go thy way for this time; when I have a convenient season, I will call for thee.

These two, *righteousness* and *temperance,* the Christian religion do indispensably require; and all true worship without these, will not make up our most holy religion, or give to any the title of a religious or a holy man. But Paul chose rather to discourse of those than any other virtues, because Felix was most defective in them. He would lay his plaster where there was a sore, though it pained the patient, and he should get little thanks for his labour. Had great men but such faithful preachers, it might contribute very much to hinder them in their career of sin, and by that means help to mend the world. *Temperance;* or continence; the want of which is charged upon both these great persons, being taxed by historians for adultery; so that Paul preaches here as John Baptist did once to Herod, very suitably, though not gratefully. Yet in the discharge of his duty he meets with no trouble, not so much as a reproach, which probably the sense of the judgment to come might contribute to. *Judgment to come;* whatsoever is present, this is certainly to come: and the secret reflections that wicked men have upon it in the midst of their fullest enjoyments, mingle fears and terrors with them. Hence their *surda vulnera,* misgivings and inward guilt; as its contrary, *the peace of God, passeth all understanding.* *Go thy way for this time;* Felix, not liking such discourse, the subject being too quick and searching for him, put it off longer. And so men put off the consideration of their duties, and of the judgment that will pass upon every one according unto what he hath done in the flesh, till the Judge be, as it were, set, and their case called.

y Ex. 23. 8.

26 He hoped also that money should have been given him of Paul, that he might loose him: wherefore he sent for him the oftener, and communed with him.

This speaks the charge to be true that the historians give of Felix concerning his covetousness; for taking hold of that part of Paul's accusation, ver. 5, that he was the ring-leader of the sect of the Nazarenes, he supposed that, there being so many thousands of them, they would give large sums for the life and liberty of this their supposed captain. This did speak Felix (according to his birth) to be of a servile and base spirit, that for money could transgress the laws of God, and the Roman laws too.

27 But after two years Porcius Festus came into Felix' room: and Felix, *will- ing to shew the Jews a pleasure, left Paul bound.

A. D. 62.
z Ex. 23. 2.
ch. 12. 3.
& 25. 9, 14.

After two years, either from Paul's being in bonds, which history St. Luke is here setting down; or, as others, after Felix had been governor two years over Judea; for that St. Paul speaks, ver. 10, is not thought to have been true as to this place, though he had governed the neighbouring parts some years before. *The Jews* had accused Felix unto the emperor for his barbarous cruelty and exactions, insomuch that had it not been for his brother Pallas (a great favourite) he had lost his life: yet he did not wholly escape punishment, but was sent bound by Festus, his successor, unto Nero. *Sic transit gloria mundi;* and, *Man being in honour continueth not*

CHAP. XXV

The Jews accuse Paul to Festus, first at Jerusalem, and afterwards at Cæsarea, 1—7. *He answereth for himself, and appealeth to Cæsar; his appeal is admitted,* 8—12. *Festus being visited by king Agrippa openeth the matter to him, who desireth to hear Paul,* 13—22. *Paul is brought forth; Festus declareth he found nothing in him worthy of death,* 23—27.

NOW when Festus was come into the province, after three days he ascended from Cæsarea to Jerusalem.

Province; so the Romans called any country which they had conquered with their arms, and unto which they sent a governor, which at this time was Festus, being now set over Judea in Felix's room. *Cæsarea* had been the place of residence for the Roman governors, by reason of its strength and situation, chap. xxiii. 23.

2 ᵃThen the High Priest and the chief of the Jews informed him against Paul, and besought him,

a ch. 24. 1.
ver. 15.

The chief of the Jews; the same who are called the elders, chap. xxiv. 1. *Informed him against Paul;* continued their accusation and prosecution of Paul. So restless is the rage and enmity the adversaries of truth have against the professors of it.

3 And desired favour against him, that he would send for him to Jerusalem, ᵇlaying wait in the way to kill him.

b ch. 23. 12, 15.

Desired favour; though it seems to have been but justice, that they might be allowed to try Paul for such crimes as were within their cognizance; yet that they might the more easily obtain their desire, they beg it as a favour. *Laying wait in the way to kill him;* which did worse become magistrates and priests than any men, to act thus against the law of nature, and to be sure also against the law of the land, to hire ruffians to assassinate Paul.

4 But Festus answered, that Paul should be kept at Cæsarea, and that he himself would depart shortly *thither.*

It is most probable that Festus had been informed by Felix of the Jews' malice against Paul; for Felix having been accused by the Jews unto the emperor, might be supposed to have recriminated wheresoever he had any opportunity; and in all the time of his government they were not guilty of a worse fact than their design against Paul, it being sedition, and intended murder of one who had the privilege of a Roman citizen. *He himself would depart shortly thither;* the governors kept their courts wheresoever they came.

5 Let them therefore, said he, which among you are able, go down with *me,* and accuse this

man, ᵉif there be any wickedness in him.

c ch. 18. 14.
ver. 18.

Which among you are able; fit to prosecute Paul in your behalf; as Tertullus was, whom the Jews had carried with them formerly, chap. xxiv. 1. *Go down with me;* because Jerusalem was in a mountainous part of the country, and much of it built upon a hill. *Wickedness;* the word properly signifies a foolish thing; but it is also taken for a wicked thing; all sin being folly, and grace wisdom; as they are frequently called in Scripture, though the world hath another opinion of them, many abhorring to be accounted fools, and yet care not though they appear most wicked.

6 And when he had tarried among them ∥more than ten days, he went down unto Cæsarea; and the next day sitting on the judgment seat commanded Paul to be brought.

∥ Or, as some copies read, no more than eight or ten days.

More than ten days; the margin gives an account of a diverse reading, unto which might be added another, viz. eight or ten days; which reading many follow, and is according unto the usual expression of such a short space of time, which need not to be exactly set down. Thus though God hath provided so, as there is little or no variety in setting down those truths or doctrines in Scripture which concern faith and manners, or our believing and holy living; yet in circumstances which (though they pertain to complete the history or genealogies in Scripture) are not necessary to be so exactly known, God left them not so, designed to exercise us in this state, wherein *we know* but *in part,* 1 Cor. xiii. 9. Fundamental truths are not of such a depth but a lamb may wade or walk in them; but there are less material things of such a profundity, that an elephant may swim in them, and men of the highest understanding and deepest reach must cry out, ὦ Βάθος.

7 And when he was come, the Jews which came down from Jerusalem stood round about, ᵈand laid many and grievous complaints against Paul, which they could not prove.

d Mark 15. 3. Luke 23. 2, 10. ch. 24. 5, 13.

When he was come; the judge sat, and the prisoner brought. *The Jews which came down from Jerusalem;* his accusers, which were many, and came with a full cry against him, *stood round about* him, or about the judgment-seat. *Many and grievous complaints;* what these accusations were, appears in the next verse by Paul's answer; but they could not demonstrate them, or make them evident; and if it were sufficient to accuse, no man could be innocent.

8 While he answered for himself, ᵉNeither against the law of the Jews, neither against the temple, nor yet against Cæsar, have I offended any thing at all.

e ch. 6. 13. & 24. 12. & 28. 17.

Paul answers unto the three crimes which he was charged with: 1. He had not offended against the law, having been always a religious observer of it: nor, 2. Against the te.nple, which he went into devoutly, and upon a religious account: nor, 3. Against Cæsar; having never taught any rebellion, nor said or done any thing against his government.

9 But Festus, ᶠwilling to do the Jews a pleasure, answered Paul, and said, ᵍWilt thou go up to Jerusalem, and there be judged of these things before me?

f ch. 24. 27.
g ver. 20.

Willing to do the Jews a pleasure; as his predecessor, Felix, before him, chap. xxiv. 27, to gain popular applause, and the good will of that nation; especially Felix having been displaced upon the complaint of the Jews against him. *Answered,* or spake to *Paul;* as chap. iii. 12. *Wilt thou go up to Jerusalem, &c.:* Festus apparently inclines to favour the Jews, though he does not command, but ask this of Paul; he being privileged as a Roman, could not against his will be forced to acknowledge the Jews for competent judges.

10 Then said Paul, I stand at Cæsar's judgment seat, where I ought to be judged: to the Jews have I done no wrong, as thou very well knowest.

Paul might justly suspect his judges, and the place where they would have him judged, and also his journey thither, knowing with what difficulty, and not without a great guard, he came from thence. *I stand at Cæsar's judgment-seat;* he was now before Cæsar's tribunal, whose vicegerent Festus was; and he only ought to judge a Roman citizen. *As thou very well knowest;* Festus might know that Paul had done the Jews no wrong, from the relation Felix had made unto him, as also from such as were with Felix when Paul's case was heard.

11 ʰFor if I be an offender, or have committed any thing worthy of death, I refuse not to die: but if there be none of these things whereof these accuse me, no man may deliver me unto them. ⁱI appeal unto Cæsar.

h ver. 25. ch. 18. 14. & 23. 29. & 26. 31.
i ch. 26. 32. & 28. 19.

If I be an offender; if I have injured the Jews, and my fault be *worthy of death,* such as by law deserves death, I beg no favour. *No man may deliver me unto them;* according to law, (which the Romans did punctually observe,) before sentence was passed. *I appeal unto Cæsar:* it was lawful for any that had that privilege of the Roman citizens, to appeal; neither might they be tried against their wills in any province out of Rome. Now Paul might appeal unto Cæsar, 1. To make Cæsar more favourable unto himself, and to other Christians. 2. Because he thought it more safe for himself and for the church. 3. He was in part admonished to do it by Christ himself, who had told him that he must bear witness of him at Rome, chap. xxiii. 11.

12 Then Festus, when he had conferred with the council, answered, Hast thou appealed unto Cæsar? unto Cæsar shalt thou go.

Conferred with the council; either of the Jews, and those of the sanhedrim, that he might inform them of the law or custom of the Romans, and how that he could not but admit of St. Paul's appeal; or with his own council; it being usual with the Roman presidents to do nothing of moment without the advice of their council, or assistants. *Hast thou appealed unto Cæsar?* or without an interrogation, Thou hast appealed unto Cæsar; which Festus was glad of, that without danger on the one hand, or ill-will on the other, he might get rid of that difficult business.

13 And after certain days king Agrippa and Bernice came unto Cæsarea to salute Festus.

This *Agrippa* is called by Josephus, the younger, and was the son of Herod Agrippa, or Agrippa the Great, who in this book of the Acts is called Herod, whose death is mentioned, chap. xii. 23. But this Agrippa was brother to Drusilla and Bernice, here spoken of, and lived in incest with her, whom Juvenal in his satire speaks of:

Barbarus incestæ dedit hunc Agrippa sorori.

14 And when they had been there many days, Festus declared Paul's cause unto the king, saying, ᵏThere is a certain man left in bonds by Felix:

k ch. 24. 27.

Festus declared Paul's cause unto the king; either amongst common discourse, or matter of novelty, and for the strangeness of it, or for his advice about it. Howsoever, by this means the wickedness of the Jews was published, and the safety of St. Paul provided for, and God's design of publishing the gospel at Rome itself furthered.

15 ˡAbout whom, when I was at Jerusalem, the Chief Priests and the elders of the Jews informed *me,* desiring *to have* judgment against him.

l ver. 2, 3.

To wit, judgment of death upon Paul, that he might be sentenced according to the crimes they had laid against him; δίκη being put for καταδίκη. Neither do they at all mind that St. Paul's case was not yet heard; they would rather have had him condemned unheard, as they had gotten our Saviour to be condemned, though the judge declared that he found no fault in him, Luke xxiii. 4 ; which their unjust desire appears by Festus's answer.

m ver. 4, 5. 16 ᵐTo whom I answered, It is not the manner of the Romans to deliver any man to die, before that he which is accused have the accusers face to face, and have licence to answer for himself concerning the crime laid against him.

To condemn any man *indicta causa*, without sufficient cause alleged and proved, is not only against the laws of the Romans, but of the Jews, Deut. xvii. 4; nay, against the law of nature and of all nations. Yet malice had so far blinded the enemies of St. Paul, that they go about such things as a heathen reproves, and the very light of nature condemns.

17 Therefore, when they were come n ver. 6. hither, ⁿwithout any delay on the morrow I sat on the judgment seat, and commanded the man to be brought forth.

Festus had gratified the Jews in what lawfully he might, not detaining them at charges from their habitations : and that not only commends Festus's own justice, but Paul's innocence ; for if Paul had not appeared guiltless, he would have left him to the rage of the Jews, whom he desired to gratify what he could.

18 Against whom when the accusers stood up, they brought none accusation of such things as I supposed :

For Festus, knowing how Paul had been prosecuted by the Jews before Felix, and what charge they had been at, and what journeys they had made about him, could not think less than that he was a capital offender.

o ch. 18. 15. & 23. 29. 19 ᵒBut had certain questions against him of their own superstition, and of one Jesus, which was dead, whom Paul affirmed to be alive.

Superstition ; so this heathen governor profanely calls the religion and worship of God's own institution, and that in the presence of Agrippa and Bernice, who were both Jews, or, at least, brought up amongst them. *To be alive ;* to have been raised again from the dead ; acknowledging, with them, that he had been indeed dead.

∥ Or, *I was doubtful how to enquire hereof.* 20 And because ∥ I doubted of such manner of questions, I asked *him* whether he would go to Jerusalem, and there be judged of these matters.

Festus pretends, that he knew not by what rule those cases were to be decided, nor before what judges ; whether before himself or the Jewish sanhedrim. But this is only his pretension : the true cause why he would not acquit Paul, though he knew him to be innocent, we read, ver. 9, viz. that he might *do the Jews a pleasure*. He asked Paul this question, *Whether he would go to Jerusalem?* but with a resolution to have sent him whether he would or no, had he not appealed ; but then he durst not : for in certain cases none could hinder appeals, from any judge, to the people in the former times, or to their emperor in the latter times.

21 But when Paul had appealed to be ∥ Or, *judgment.* reserved unto the ∥ hearing of Augustus, I commanded him to be kept till I might send him to Cæsar.

Augustus : the emperor who now reigned, and to whom Paul appealed, was Nero, who was called Augustus ; this title being at first appropriated to Octavius, who succeeded Julius Cæsar ; but out of honour unto him, or because of its signification, it became an appellative, and was given unto all the emperors successively : nay, the emperor of Germany to this day is called *Semper Augustus*. *Cæsar ;* as from Octavius the emperors of Rome had the name of Augustus, so from the first emperor, Julius, they have the name of Cæsars. This word Cæsar, which was the proper name of the first emperor, is, in acknowledgment of him, made an appellative to all his successors.

p See ch. 9. 15 22 Then ᵖAgrippa said unto Festus, I would also hear the man myself. To morrow, said he, thou shalt hear him.

Agrippa being well acquainted with the Jewish religion, if not a Jew, could not but have heard of our Saviour, his doctrine, death, and resurrection ; and yet makes this desire but out of curiosity ; as Herod desired to hear John Baptist, Mark vi. 20, and to see our Saviour, Luke xxiii. 8.

23 And on the morrow, when Agrippa was come, and Bernice, with great pomp, and was entered into the place of hearing, with the chief captains, and principal men of the city, at Festus' commandment Paul was brought forth.

With great pomp ; the state, attire, and retinue used in this solemnity is much undervalued by the term the Holy Ghost here gives it (φαντασία) ; intimating, that all worldly glory is but in opinion and appearance merely, and that as a show it passeth away. *Paul was brought forth ;* here is a great difference indeed between these great persons thus adorned and accompanied on the one side, and Paul, the prisoner, (δέσμιος, the chained, as he is called, chap. xxiii. 18,) on the other side ; yet holy Paul, with great reason, prefers his condition before theirs. He does not desire to partake with them in their ease and splendour, but with Christ in his disgrace and sufferings, Phil. iii. 10.

24 And Festus said, King Agrippa, and all men which are here present with us, ye see this man, about whom ᑫall the q ver. 2, 3, 7. multitude of the Jews have dealt with me, both at Jerusalem, and *also* here, crying that he ought ʳnot to live any r ch. 22. 22. longer.

Well might Paul be aghast, to be friendless in so great a multitude, and to be shown and pointed at as a monster, being *made a spectacle unto the world, and to angels, and to men*, as 1 Cor. iv. 9. But he found surely the benefit and efficacy of that promise, Matt. xxviii. 20, *I am with you alway, even unto the end of the world.*

25 But when I found that ˢhe had s ch. 23. 9, committed nothing worthy of death, ᵗand 29. & 26. 31. t ver. 11, 12. that he himself hath appealed to Augustus, I have determined to send him.

The calumny of the Jews adds to the reputation of St. Paul : so many enemies, and so long in finding or making a fault that might reach his life, and yet to be disappointed ! Paul and his religion are vindicated by the testimony of Lysias, the chief captain, chap. xxiii. 29, and of Felix, the governor, chap. xxiv. 25, and here by Festus, as afterwards by Agrippa too, chap. xxvi. 32. So mighty is truth and innocence, that they do prevail sooner or later.

26 Of whom I have no certain thing to write unto my lord. Wherefore I have brought him forth before you, and specially before thee, O king Agrippa, that, after examination had, I might have somewhat to write.

My lord ; Nero, the present emperor, whose deputy Festus was in this province ; though some of the former emperors refused this name, as savouring of too much arbitrariness, the latter did accept of it. *Specially before thee ;* Agrippa, being brought up in the knowledge of the Jewish law, though it was not his business to judge Paul's case, yet he might instruct and inform the judge about it.

27 For it seemeth to be unreasonable to send a prisoner, and not withal to signify the crimes *laid* against him.

So great a clamour, so hot a pursuit, and yet after all this the judge (who would willingly have condemned Paul, and gratified the Jews) knows not wherefore all this stir had been : but the more must he have been self-condemned, that durst not absolve or free a prisoner who was detained only by the power and multitude of his adversaries.

CHAP. XXVI

Paul, in the presence of Agrippa, declareth his life from his childhood, his wonderful conversion, and call to the apostleship, and his preaching of Christ according to the scripture doctrine, 1—23. Festus chargeth him with madness: his modest reply, and address to Agrippa, who confesseth himself almost a Christian, 24—29. The whole company pronounce him innocent, 30—32.

THEN Agrippa said unto Paul, Thou art permitted to speak for thyself. Then Paul stretched forth the hand, and answered for himself:

This stretching forth of his hand was, 1. To obtain silence of others whilst he spake; or, 2. To show his innocence, whilst he uses this modest confidence; or, 3. As other orators, when they begin to speak, move their hands. The providence of God wonderfully procures Paul a liberty to publish the gospel, and to make his case and religion known.

2 I think myself happy, king Agrippa, because I shall answer for myself this day before thee touching all the things whereof I am accused of the Jews:

I think myself happy; Paul thought it to be his advantage to speak before Agrippa, who could not be unacquainted with the law or the prophets, by which St. Paul would have his case determined. *Before thee;* though Agrippa was not as judge in this place, yet his opinion and judgment could not but prevail much with Festus.

3 Especially *because I know* thee to be expert in all customs and questions which are among the Jews: wherefore I beseech thee to hear me patiently.

This is not flattery, but a plain confession of what was true; for Agrippa, by reason of his birth and breeding, could not be wholly ignorant of those things in question; 1. About the Messiah; 2. About the resurrection; 3. About the giving of the Holy Ghost. *I beseech thee to hear me patiently;* it being a matter that concerned religion, and the life and liberty of a man, nothing but ignorance or impiety could take him off from attending unto it.

4 My manner of life from my youth, which was at the first among mine own nation at Jerusalem, know all the Jews;

Paul appeals to his enemies, the Jews themselves, whether they could tax him with any enormity whilst he was of their persuasion; whereby he vindicates his holy religion from being the sink and offscouring of other religions, as some would make it; as also to intimate, that it was his religion which made him so hateful unto them, and not any ill practices done by him.

5 Which knew me from the beginning, if they would testify, that after ª the most straitest sect of our religion I lived a Pharisee.

a ch. 22. 3. & 23. 6. & 24. 15, 22. Phil. 3. 5.

This heresy, sect, opinion, or way of the Pharisees, St. Paul rightly commends, if we consider it comparatively with the other sects of the Sadducees and Essenes: he had called this before, chap. xxii. 3, the most exact *manner of the law of the fathers;* for it is certain it was more learned and strict, and came nigher to the truth in many things, than the other did.

6 ᵇ And now I stand and am judged for the hope of ᶜ the promise made of God unto our fathers:

b ch. 23. 6. c Gen. 3. 15. & 22. 18. & 26. 4. & 49. 10. Deut. 18. 15. 2 Sam. 7. 12. Ps. 132. 11. Is. 4. 2. & 7. 14. & 9. 6. & 40. 10. Jer. 23. 5. & 33. 14, 15. 16. Ezek. 34. 23. & 37. 24. Dan. 9. 24. Mic. 7. 20. ch. 13. 32. Rom. 15. 8. Tit. 2. 13.

I stand; the posture of such as are held for guilty. *The hope of the promise;* St. Paul brings in the discourse of the resurrection, which, as hath been observed, is the foundation of all religion, 1 Cor. xv. 14; chap. xxiii. 6; xxiv. 15; and now it is called *the hope of the promise,* because God's promise did raise them up to this hope: for God having promised to be the God of Abraham, Isaac, and Jacob, gave them rather less than others in this world; neither had they any propriety in all the Promised Land, but only to a burying-place; whence they might certainly infer, that there was another life to be expected, in which God would make this his word good. Paul was also *judged for the hope of the promise,* taking this hope for the salvation which Christ did purchase, and Paul preach, which was also promised unto the fathers, though mostly under types and obscure representations. The sum is, Paul was judged for one of those two articles of our faith, viz. the resurrection of the body, or a life everlasting.

7 Unto which *promise* ᵈ our twelve tribes, instantly serving *God* †ᵉ day and night, ᶠ hope to come. For which hope's sake, king Agrippa, I am accused of the Jews.

d Jam. 1. 1. † Gr. *night and day.* e Luke 2. 37. 1 Tim. 5. 5. 1 Thess. 3. 10. f Phil. 3. 11.

Twelve tribes; so St. Paul still reckons them, notwithstanding that ten tribes had been led captive, without returning again to this day. Yet, 1. There were many left by the king of Assyria in their own land; and though for a while they joined themselves unto the Samaritans rather than to the Jews, yet a century or two before our Saviour's time they returned to the Jewish religion and worship, at least very many of them. 2. Though the ten tribes never returned (as tribes) entirely back again, yet many of them doubtless had that love for their religion and country, as they took all opportunities of coming back. 3. At their first defection in Jeroboam's time, God touched the hearts of a great many, who rather changed their habitation than their religion. So that St. James might well dedicate his Epistle to the twelve tribes, for there were some who at the dispersion were scattered out of every tribe. *Instantly serving God day and night;* now these, with great intention and earnestness of desire, (as when any stretcheth himself to his utmost length to take hold of aught,) endeavoured to obtain that very salvation which God had promised, and the gospel revealed.

8 Why should it be thought a thing incredible with you, that God should raise the dead?

This St. Paul seems to have spoken in regard of Festus, and many others there present, who were heathens; or to any of the Sadducees, if any such were amongst them: as for Agrippa, He believed the prophets, ver. 27, and had out of them learned and observed this promise, ver. 7. However, God did not leave himself without a witness to testify so much unto all, as should make the doctrine of the resurrection credible, whensoever it should be revealed unto them. The works of creation evidence it; for he that can give life unto that which had it not, can restore it unto that which had it: and the works of providence attest it; in every spring there is a resurrection of such plants or trees as seemed dead; nay, the bread which we daily feed on, was made of that grain, which was not quickened except it died, 1 Cor. xv. 36.

9 ᵍ I verily thought with myself, that I ought to do many things contrary to the name of Jesus of Nazareth.

g John 16. 2. 1 Tim. 1. 13.

The name of Jesus; the religion which teacheth Christ is to be worshipped, and his name to be magnified. *Jesus of Nazareth;* so they called our Saviour, of which see chap. xxii. 8.

10 ʰ Which thing I also did in Jerusalem: and many of the saints did I shut up in prison, having received authority ⁱ from the Chief Priests; and when they were put to death, I gave my voice against them.

h ch. 8. 3. Gal. 1. 13. i ch. 9. 14, 21. & 22. 5.

The saints; the professors of the religion of the holy Jesus, who are *called to be saints,* Rom. i. 7, and have him for the great example of holiness, who fulfilled all righteousness; and from him they have the Spirit of holiness; being sanctified in him, 1 Cor. i. 2; and whosoever hath not his Spirit, *he is none of his,* Rom. viii. 9. *I gave my voice against them:* Paul was not one of the council, nor, that we read of, in any office or place to judge any person; besides, the Jews are thought to have had no power of life and death; and that St. Stephen was slain rather in a popular tumult, than legally: but Paul may be said to do this, by carrying the suffrages or sentence to the Ro-

THE ACTS XXVI

man president, or any others, to get it executed (for so the words will bear); and howsoever, by his approving, rejoicing at, and delighting in their condemnation, (which was indeed giving his voice, as much as he could, against them,) this was verified.

k ch. 22. 19.

11 ᵏ And I punished them oft in every synagogue, and compelled *them* to blaspheme ; and being exceedingly mad against them, I persecuted *them* even unto strange cities.

Paul confesses that he *compelled them to blaspheme*, either, 1. By the torments he made them to be put unto ; or, 2. By his own example ; for he confessed that he had been a blasphemer himself, 1 Tim. i. 13. This blasphemy was either, 1. Denying of Christ to be the Messiah ; or, 2. Cursing or execrating of Christ, and acknowledging that he was justly condemned. *I persecuted them even unto strange cities;* drove them out of Jerusalem and Judea; and, according to what Paul then believed, he drave them from the worship of the true God, and said in effect, as David's adversaries when they expelled him from Jerusalem, *Go, and serve other gods,* 1 Sam. xxvi. 19.

l ch. 9. 3. & 22. 6.

12 ¹ Whereupon as I went to Damascus with authority and commission from the Chief Priests,

With procuratory letters recommending him to the Jews abroad, and deputing him as their agent.

13 At midday, O king, I saw in the way a light from heaven, above the brightness of the sun, shining round about me and them which journeyed with me.

At mid-day; this appeared at noon-day, that it might not be suspected to be a dream or fancy. *Above the brightness of the sun;* our Saviour's face in the transfiguration *did shine as the sun,* Matt. xvii. 2, and he was yet on earth in his mortal body ; how much more resplendent must it have been now, when he appeared from heaven with his glorious body ! And if the righteous shall shine as the sun, Dan. xii. 3 ; Matt. xiii. 43 ; how much more does their Prince and Saviour ! See concerning this history, chap. ix. 3, &c., and chap. xxii. 6, &c.

14 And when we were all fallen to the earth, I heard a voice speaking unto me, and saying in the Hebrew tongue, Saul, Saul, why persecutest thou me ? *it is* hard for thee to kick against the pricks.

In the Hebrew tongue; whereby it appears, that Paul spake not now before Agrippa in the Hebrew tongue, as he did before the Jews at Jerusalem, chap. xxi. 40. *It is hard for thee to kick against the pricks :* this is a proverb borrowed from the Greeks, as some think, but used in many languages, denoting any who endeavour such things as will ruin or detriment themselves : and so do all persecutors ; for they cannot harden themselves against God, his truth, or servants, and prosper, Job ix. 4. Not to speak of other pricks, there is never an attribute in God, nor ever a faculty in their own souls, but they kick against, and will be themselves at last pricked by.

15 And I said, Who art thou, Lord ? And he said, I am Jesus whom thou persecutest.

The foot is trod upon on earth, and the Head cries out out from heaven, as chap. ix. 5.

16 But rise, and stand upon thy feet : for I have appeared unto thee for this m ch. 22. 15. purpose, ᵐ to make thee a minister and a witness both of these things which thou hast seen, and of those things in the which I will appear unto thee ;

Stand upon thy feet; as Daniel was bidden by the angel, Dan. x. 11, to mitigate his consternation and fear. *Of those things in the which I will appear unto thee :* St. Paul accordingly had many visions and revelations, chap. xviii. 9 ; xxiii. 11 ; 2 Cor. xii. 2 ; as he was more abundant in his sufferings for Christ, so in consolations from Christ, 2 Cor. i. 5.

17 Delivering thee from the people, and *from* the Gentiles, ⁿ unto whom now I send thee,

n ch. 22. 21.

From the people ; from this people of the Jews, so in some copies it is expressed ; howsoever, by the antithesis, *and from the Gentiles,* it is plainly to be understood : and God undertakes no less hereby, than to deliver Paul, and all his faithful servants, from all evils and enemies. But how is this performed ? and where is the promise ? St. Paul was sorely persecuted by the Jews, and at last put to death by the Gentiles. But so long as it would be a mercy, and a true deliverance to Paul, God wrought many such for him ; and that, rather than fail, miraculously too ; no chains, no iron gates could detain him. When he had finished his course, and done the work he was sent for, it would not have been a deliverance, to have been kept longer from his reward, and the prize he had ran for.

18 ᵒ To open their eyes, *and* ᵖ to turn them from darkness to light, and *from* the power of Satan unto God, ᵠ that they may receive forgiveness of sins, and ʳ inheritance among them which are ˢ sanctified by faith that is in me.

o Is. 35. 5. & 42. 7. Luke 1. 79. John 8. 12. 2 Cor. 4. 4. Eph. 1. 18. 1 Thes. 5. 5. p 2 Cor. 6. 14. Eph. 4. 18. & 5. 8. Col. 1. 13. 1 Pet. 2. 9. s ch. 20. 32.

25. q Luke 1. 77. r Eph. 1. 11. Col. 1. 12.

To open their eyes ; the eyes of their minds, that they might know God, and their duty towards him. Our Saviour assures Paul, that he should do that for the souls of men which he should find effected in his own body, being made to see. Now though this be only the work of God, yet, to honour the ministry, he is pleased to attribute it unto his ministers, as being the instruments he ordinarily worketh it by ; and who are hence called co-workers with God, 2 Cor. vi. 1. *To turn them from darkness to light ;* this was signified by the glorious light which came from the body of our glorified Redeemer, which appeared unto him. *The power of Satan ;* so are all sins, for by them Satan rules in the children of disobedience, Eph. ii. 2. *That they may receive forgiveness of sins ;* thereby intimating, that their former sins (how grievous soever) should not hinder their salvation, who received the gospel in the love and power of it. *By faith that is in me ;* by faith which purifieth the heart ; but this may be referred, either to our being sanctified, or to our receiving of the inheritance, for both are by faith ; and as without faith we are no better, and do no better, so we shall receive no better, than other men.

19 Whereupon, O king Agrippa, I was not disobedient unto the heavenly vision :

I was not incredulous, I believed God, and yielded to his call, as Isa. l. 5, which cannot be counted a fault in me ; and yet this is all that can be charged upon me.

20 But ᵗ shewed first unto them of Damascus, and at Jerusalem, and throughout all the coasts of Judæa, and *then* to the Gentiles, that they should repent and turn to God, and do ᵘ works meet for repentance.

t ch. 9. 20, 22, 29. & 11. 26. & 13, & 14, & 16, & 17, & 18, & 19, & 20, & 21.

u Matt. 3. 8.

Showed first unto them of Damascus ; nigh unto which place he was first converted, taking the first opportunity to preach Christ : out of the abundance of his heart his mouth speaking. *And turn to God :* as sin is a turning from God, so repentance is a turning (or rather returning) unto God. *Do works meet for repentance ;* such as became a true penitent ; for as we must show our faith by our works, James ii. 18, so we must show our repentance by our works also : for to say we are grieved for sin, and we hate sin, and yet to live in it, is but to deceive ourselves, and (what in us lay) to mock God.

21 For these causes ˣ the Jews caught me in the temple, and went about to kill *me*.

x ch. 21. 30, 31.

By violent hands and indirect means, as we see, chap. xxi. 31, and as they had done unto our Saviour, chap. v. 30, where the same word is used.

22 Having therefore obtained help of God, I continue unto this day, witnessing both to small

and great, saying none other things than those ʸwhich the prophets and ᶻMoses did say should come:

^y Luke 24. 27, 44. ch. 24. 14. & 28. 23. Rom. 3. 21. z John 5. 46.

I continue unto this day : that Paul continued till then alive, notwithstanding all the fraud and force of his enemies, is acknowledged by him to be from God; from whence he infers towards his justification, that what he had done was but in a becoming gratitude towards that God who had maintained him in life unto that very day. *Witnessing both to small and great;* witnessing to all sorts, princes or people; implying, that the truths of the gospel, and the things of God, concerned Agrippa as well as the meanest of his auditors; and indeed with God there is no respect of persons, and that we *are all one in Christ Jesus,* Gal. iii. 28. *The prophets and Moses;* Moses was himself also a prophet, but he is here made especial mention of, because of his excellency above the other prophets, (unto whom God spake face to face,) as also because he was the lawgiver to the Jews, and to whom, upon all occasions, they pretended to yield obedience.

23 ᵃThat Christ should suffer, *and* ᵇthat he should be the first that should rise from the dead, and ᶜshould shew light unto the people, and to the Gentiles.

^a Luke 24. 26, 46. b 1 Cor. 15. 20. Col. 1. 18. Rev. 1. 5. c Luke 2. 32.

The sufferings of Christ were taught by Moses in all the commands about sacrifices, and more plainly by Isaiah in all the 53rd chapter; insomuch, that this was acknowledged by Tryphon, disputing with Justin Martyr, although the generality of Jews, both then and now, do stiffly deny it. The carnal Jews do not like to hear of a spiritual kingdom. *The first that should rise from the dead ;* Christ was the first that did rise to an immortal life ; others that were restored to life, died again : besides, Christ is deservedly called the first, by reason of his dignity and eminency, and in that he rose as a head and fountain of life to others, even to all that live and believe in him. *Show light;* all the word of God is light; but especially the gospel, which discovers a plain and open way unto salvation. *Unto the people, and to the Gentiles ;* to both Jews and Gentiles, as ver. 17.

24 And as he thus spake for himself, Festus said with a loud voice, Paul, ᵈthou art beside thyself; much learning doth make thee mad.

^d 2 Kings 9. 11. John 10. 20. 1 Cor. 1. 23. & 2. 13. 14. & 4. 10.

Thou art beside thyself; this was the opinion of Festus concerning Paul, and such is the opinion of carnal and worldly men concerning such as are truly godly; as the prophet who came to Jehu was counted a *mad fellow,* 2 Kings ix. 11, and the friends of our Saviour thought him to be *beside himself,* Mark iii. 21. And it cannot be otherwise; for good men and bad men have quite different apprehensions concerning most things; and what one calls good, the other accounts evil ; and what is wisdom to the one, is madness to the other. *Much learning doth make thee mad;* much study many times increasing melancholy, which a sedentary and thoughtful life is most exposed unto. Paul is reckoned to have been skilful in the Hebrew, Syriac, Greek, and Latin tongues; to have been well read in the poets; and certainly he was an excellent orator, as appears all along in his defence he made for his doctrine, and his life : but there was yet somewhat more than all this; Festus might feel a more than ordinary effect from Paul's words, and not knowing of the Spirit by which he spake did attribute it to his learning, or madness, or to any thing but the true cause of it.

25 But he said, I am not mad, most noble Festus; but speak forth the words of truth and soberness.

St. Paul with all meekness makes his reply to the governor, and not taking notice of his sharp censuring of him, returns an answer in most respectful terms unto him ; as his blessed Master, *who, when he was reviled, reviled not again,* 1 Pet. ii. 23. *Soberness,* in contradiction to madness; modestly waiving the reflection, and denying the charge Festus had laid upon him.

26 ' For the king knoweth of these things, before whom also I speak freely : for I am persuaded that none of these things are hidden from him ; for this thing was not done in a corner.

Agrippa, being educated in Judea, could not but hear of the life and doctrine, death and resurrection, of our Saviour; as also of the miracles done by him, and by his disciples; for, as our Saviour says, he ever taught openly, John xviii. 20.

27 King Agrippa, believest thou the prophets ? I know that thou believest.

A rhetorical insinuation, that could not but much affect the king, and leave a sensible impression on his heart. St. Paul answers the question which he had propounded, and that in favour of Agrippa ; or rather blames himself for making that a question ; but his cryptical inference would then be, If you believe the prophets, why do you not believe Christ of whom they prophesied ?

28 Then Agrippa said unto Paul, Almost thou persuadest me to be a Christian.

Some think that these words were spoken ironically, or scoffingly ; as if Agrippa had said, Thou wouldst have me in so short a space (for so ἐν ὀλίγῳ may be translated) to be brought to profess Christ: some think it unlikely that such a one as Agrippa would speak so plainly as we translate it, in such a place, before such an auditory: but the danger seems not to have been so great from these words; and if it had been greater, who knows the power of that conviction under which Agrippa at that time was? and Paul's rejoinder do suppose the words to be spoken in the sense we read them.

29 And Paul said, ᵉI would to God, that not only thou, but also all that hear me this day, were both almost, and altogether such as I am, except these bonds.

^e 1 Cor. 7. 7.

Paul, knowing how little it would avail any to be almost a Christian, wisheth their perfection in that profession, that they might not, with the Laodiceans, be neither hot nor cold, Rev. iii. 16 ; nor, with the Israelites, halt between God and Baal, 1 Kings xviii. 21. *Except these bonds:* some think that by *bonds* St. Paul means only his guard wherewith he was surrounded ; but it is certain that St. Paul was bound, in the most literal sense, with chains, as chap. xxiv. 27 ; and he wishes his auditors all the good that was in him, and to be freed from all the evils that were upon him.

30 And when he had thus spoken, the king rose up, and the governor, and Bernice, and they that sat with them :

Agrippa, Festus, and the queen, together with the governor's council, although they had heard this excellent discourse from the most learned apostle, like the blackamoor or leopard, they cannot change their spots, or skin, Jer. xiii. 23 : having sinned against former manifestations of God's will, this, for aught we read, became ineffectual unto them.

31 And when they were gone aside, they talked between themselves, saying, ᶠThis man doeth nothing worthy of death or of bonds.

^f ch. 23. 9. 29. & 25. 25.

Gone aside ; either to their houses, or to some apartment nigh to the tribunal. They acquit Paul ; for as yet Nero had not made those bloody laws. whereby the profession of Christianity was made capital.

32 Then said Agrippa unto Festus, This man might have been set at liberty, ᵍif he had not appealed unto Cæsar.

^g ch. 25. 11.

These judges and great men do, by their opinion concerning Paul, condemn the Jews, whom they declare to have no cause for the prosecuting of him ; and so those caitiffs returned to Jerusalem, not only with their labour for their pains, but being branded by the sentence of so many eminent personages, not to say tormented with the guilt of so foul a fact in their own conscience. Such honour have all persecutors ! But, withal, these great men seem to be self-condemned, in that they own Paul's innocence, and yet dare not set him free for fear of the Jews; for as for this excuse from his appealing to Cæsar, it bound up them indeed from condemning Paul till Cæsar had heard

THE ACTS XXVII

him; but they could not be bound by it from acquitting or freeing of him; for Paul might have withdrawn his appeal, and enjoyed his liberty, if they had pleased, at any time: but what popularity, or self-ends, put them upon, they are willing to varnish over with pretence of lawfulness and necessity.

CHAP. XXVII

Paul is conducted in a ship toward Rome, 1—8. He foretells the danger of the voyage, but is not credited, 9—11. The ship setting sail against his advice is tossed with a tempest, 12—20. Paul comforteth his fellow travellers with assurance of having their lives saved, but foretelleth a shipwreck; all which is verified by the event, 21—44.

a ch. 25. 12, 25. AND when [a]it was determined that we should sail into Italy, they delivered Paul and certain other prisoners unto *one* named Julius, a centurion of Augustus' band.

It was determined; upon the solemn hearing of Paul's case, it was resolved by Festus and Agrippa, with the rest that were taken by Festus to advise concerning it. *Julius;* thought to have been a freed-man of the family of Julius, who thence took his name. *A centurion of Augustus' band;* as Cornelius was *a centurion of the Italian band:* see chap. x. 1. This band, or regiment, was called Augustus's (or the emperor's) because (as some will) it was part of his guard.

2 And entering into a ship of Adramyttium, we launched, meaning to sail b ch. 19. 29. by the coasts of Asia; *one* [b]Aristarchus, a Macedonian of Thessalonica, being with us.

Adramyttium; a city in Mysia, a province in the Lesser Asia, almost over against Mitylene, of a pestilent air. *Meaning to sail by the coasts of Asia;* the ship did belong to Adramyttium, and designed a trading voyage along the coasts of Asia. *Aristarchus;* this Aristarchus seems to have been a man of some note, who accompanied St. Paul (together with Luke, the holy penman of this book, and of the Gospel so called) throughout his journey, and none else that we read of. This Aristarchus was one of them that was laid hold on in the uproar at Ephesus, chap. xix. 29; and having partook of Paul's afflictions in all his travels, was at last his fellow prisoner at Rome, Col. iv. 10. *Thessalonica;* of this city mention is made, chap. xvii. 1.

3 And the next *day* we touched at c ch. 24. 23. & 28. 16. Sidon. And Julius [c]courteously entreated Paul, and gave *him* liberty to go unto his friends to refresh himself.

Sidon; a city in Phenicia, bordering upon Palestine, mentioned Matt. xi. 21, and Acts xii. 20. *Julius courteously entreated Paul;* as Felix had commanded that centurion to whom he committed him, chap. xxiv. 23. *And gave him liberty to go unto his friends to refresh himself;* though Paul went with a soldier to guard him, as their manner was, yet it was a great favour that he might converse with his friends, and receive from them such refreshments towards his journey as he stood in need of. Now Paul indeed experienced the truth of God's word, chap. xviii. 10, that he was with him: and it is wonderful to consider the presence of God with Paul all along: which things are our examples, that we also may put our trust in God, who hath said he will not leave us nor forsake us, Heb. xiii. 5, 6.

4 And when we had launched from thence, we sailed under Cyprus, because the winds were contrary.

Launched; or put to sea. *Cyprus;* a noted island in the Mediterranean Sea, of which we read, chap. xi. 19; xiii. 4. Their nearest way from Sidon to Myra had been to have left Cyprus on the right hand, but by reason of the winds they were forced to go almost round about the island, leaving it on the left hand.

5 And when we had sailed over the sea of Cilicia and Pamphylia, we came to Myra, *a city* of Lycia.

The sea of Cilicia and Pamphylia; that part of the Mediterranean that borders on those provinces. *Cilicia;* of which see chap. vi. 9; xv. 23, 41. *Pamphylia;* mention is made of this province, chap. ii. 10; xiii. 13. *Lycia;* another province in the lesser Asia, bordering on Pamphylia.

6 And there the centurion found a ship of Alexandria sailing into Italy; and he put us therein.

Alexandria; a famous port town in Egypt, formerly called No, of which we read, Jer. xlvi. 25: unto this place the ship did belong, which was now in the road or haven of Myra, intending for Italy, whither they carried corn, and Persian and Indian commodities, from thence.

7 And when we had sailed slowly many days, and scarce were come over against Cnidus, the wind not suffering us, we sailed under ‖ Crete, over against Sal- ‖ Or, *Candy.* mone;

Had sailed slowly many days; the wind being contrary, or at least very bare, and, it may be, their ship much laden. *Cnidus;* a city or promontory over against *Crete,* which is now called Candia, a known island in the Mediterranean. *Salmone;* a sea town in Candia, or the easterly promontory there, so called.

8 And, hardly passing it, came unto a place which is called The fair havens; nigh whereunto was the city *of* Lasea.

The fair havens; or, the fair or good shore, that being accounted the best which is safest for ships to ride in or enter into. A place of this name remains to this day (as some tell us) in the island of Candia. *Lasea;* called Lasos, and more inland; yet some think that this town is not certainly known, not having been mentioned by any ancient geographer.

9 Now when much time was spent, d The fast was on the and when sailing was now dangerous, tenth day of the seventh [d]because the fast was now already past, month, Lev. 23. 27, Paul admonished *them,* 29.

This *fast* was not any necessitated abstinence, but a religious fast, as the word here used does most commonly signify; and the article being put to it, it may well denote some eminent and known fast. We read, that amongst the Jews several fasts were observed; as the fast of the fourth month, of the fifth month, of the seventh, and of the tenth month, Zech. viii. 19. But that of the seventh month did far exceed them all, it being the day in which the priest was to make an atonement for the people; and they were strictly commanded to afflict their souls in it, Lev. xvi. 29; xxiii. 27. (Thus when we look up to him whom by our sins we have pierced, we must mourn, Zech. xii. 10.) Now this fast was to be observed on the tenth day of Tisri, or their seventh month (which is made up of part of September and part of October); and then this day, which might well be called *the fast,* fell about the beginning of October; after which time, until March, they did not usually venture on the seas, especially their ships not being so able to bear a storm as ours are, and the art of navigation being not yet in any reasonable degree found out amongst them.

10 And said unto them, Sirs, I perceive that this voyage will be with ‖ hurt ‖ Or, *injury.* and much damage, not only of the lading and ship, but also of our lives.

Paul did not say this so much by reason of the time of the year, and the tempests which do usually attend it, as by a prophetical spirit: God intending to provide for Paul in this tedious and difficult journey, endues him with the gift of prophecy; which (especially when they saw it verified) could not but beget a great respect toward him, and might be a means of salvation to many that were with him. *But also of our lives;* so it had been, their lives had been lost as well as the ship and goods, had not God given the lives of all in the ship unto Paul, and saved them for his sake; as ver. 24.

11 Nevertheless the centurion believed the master and the owner of the ship, more than those things which were spoken by Paul.

The centurion believed those whom he thought best skilled in those things (as every one in his own art); and if he had not heard of Paul's condition and extraordinary qualification, he was doubtless the more to be excused.

12 And because the haven was not commodious to winter in, the more part advised to depart thence also, if by any means they might attain to Phenice, *and there* to winter; *which is* an haven of Crete, and lieth toward the south west and north west.

This *Phenice* was a port town in Candia, and not the country in Syria. *Lieth toward the south-west and north-west;* being on the south part of that island, having a bay or road like unto a half-moon or crescent, one horn or part of it (admitting entrance into it) toward the south-west, and the other toward the north-west.

13 And when the south wind blew softly, supposing that they had obtained *their* purpose, loosing *thence*, they sailed close by Crete.

The south wind being ordinarily most mild, and at that time not high, they sailed along the shore of Candia, not being afraid to be driven upon it.

|| Or, *beat.*   14 But not long after there || arose against it a tempestuous wind, called Euroclydon.

There arose against it; Crete or Candia; so that they were in the greater danger, having a sea-shore. *Called Euroclydon;* this some will have to have been a whirlwind; but the word signifies only, the tempestuous east, or the north-east, which is a contrary wind unto any that would go from Crete to Italy.

15 And when the ship was caught, and could not bear up into the wind, we let *her* drive.

The ship was caught; being forced from Crete, and no longer at the command of the mariners, but in the sole power of the winds. *And could not bear up into the wind;* the ship could not keep her course, the winds being contrary, so that her prow or head (part whereof was called the eye of the ship, and on which its name was formerly, as now at the stern, inscribed) could not bear up according as their course did require; whence that expression, ἀντοφθαλμειν τῶ ἀνέμω, which is here used.

Sic quo non voluit, sed quo rapit impetus undæ.

16 And running under a certain island which is called Clauda, we had much work to come by the boat:

Clauda; called also Claudos, and by some Gaudos, and now Gozo, an island near unto Crete. *We had much work to come by the boat;* in this stress of weather they would take up the boat, lest it should have been staved or beat in pieces against the ship.

17 Which when they had taken up, they used helps, undergirding the ship; and, fearing lest they should fall into the quicksands, strake sail, and so were driven.

They used helps; not only using all instruments fit for their purpose, but all hands were employed too. *Undergirding the ship,* with cables, to keep the sides of the ship the closer and faster together. *The quicksands:* there were two quicksands especially famous in Africa, the one the greater, the other the lesser, called Syrtes, because these mountains of sand under water did seem, as it were, to draw and suck up ships, they were so soon swallowed up by them. *Strake sail;* by the word here used, sails and their tackle, or the top-mast, may be understood decks.

18 And we being exceedingly tossed with a tempest, the next *day* they lightened the ship;

Casting out the merchandise or lading which was in it, that the ship, being so much lighter, might not so readily strike upon a rock, or be swallowed up of the quicksands, it drawing so much the less water.

19 And the third *day* ᵉwe cast out ᵉ Jonah 1. 5. with our own hands the tackling of the ship.

All the ship's furniture which it had either for ornament or defence, and not their ballast or lumber only: so willingly do men part with all things for their lives; which yet are but short, and, at best, mixed with care and sorrow, Job xiv. 1, 2.

20 And when neither sun nor stars in many days appeared, and no small tempest lay on *us*, all hope that we should be saved was then taken away.

Neither sun nor stars in many days appeared; which shows the greatness of their misery, which had not the ordinary refreshments from the sight of the sun to relieve it. For that the sun does cheer, is one reason why our Saviour is called *the Sun of righteousness*, Mal. iv. 2. *All hope that we should be saved was then taken away;* there remained no hope in the eye of reason, or reckoning upon second causes, or natural events.

21 But after long abstinence Paul stood forth in the midst of them, and said, Sirs, ye should have hearkened unto me, and not have loosed from Crete, and to have gained this harm and loss.

After long abstinence: these did not abstain from their meals for any want; for they had sufficient provision, as appears, ver. 38; nor because the storm or tempest tossing the ship, and them in it, took away their stomach, for the sea-men, at least, were not so long troubled with that sea-sickness: but, 1. Their continually being employed, working for their lives. Or, 2. Their fear of perishing, and sense of a future state, might take up their thoughts so effectually, that they minded nothing else. Hence it hath been said, that whosoever cannot pray should go to sea, and there he would learn it; for *in their affliction they will seek me early,* saith the Lord, Hos. v. 15. *Ye should have hearkened unto me;* being Paul had foretold this that now befell them, as ver. 10, they were bound to have believed him; which they not doing, are now deservedly punished. *Have gained this harm and loss;* harm and loss, misery and calamity, is all that disobedience and God gets at last, whatsoever it may promise us to tempt us with.

22 And now I exhort you to be of good cheer: for there shall be no loss of *any man's* life among you, but of the ship.

Provided they would do as he required of them: see ver. 31. In God's promises there is a tacit condition, which from the nature of the thing is to be understood; as in that which was made to Eli, mentioned 1 Sam. ii. 30. Paul did foretell this so particularly, that when it was come to pass, he might gain the more reputation to the truth of the gospel which he preached, and more glory to that God whom he worshipped.

23 ᶠFor there stood by me this night ᶠ ch. 23. 11. the angel of God, whose I am, and ᵍ Dan. 6. 16. ᵍwhom I serve,   Rom. 1. 9. 2 Tim. 1. 3.

A good introduction to recommend the true God, and the gospel of his Son. Paul, who knew the certainty of what he had predicted, owns himself to be now in the service of God, that not unto him, but unto God, may be given the glory.

24 Saying, Fear not, Paul; thou must be brought before Cæsar: and, lo, God hath given thee all them that sail with thee.

The message which God's angels bring from God unto his people, is, *Fear not.* Thus unto Daniel, Dan. x. 12, 19; and thus unto the holy women that attended at our Lord's sepulchre, Matt. xxviii. 5. There are *all ministering spirits,* Heb. i. 14. *Thou must be brought before;* it is a forensic word, showing that Paul must be heard and tried by Cæsar. *God hath given thee all them that sail with thee;* graciously bestowed all thy fellow travellers upon thee at thy request: for it is implied, that Paul had prayed for them, and begged their lives of God; as Esther had the lives of her people at the hands of King Ahasuerus, Esth. vii. 3. There is a remarkable difference between Paul and Jonah in a storm, though Jonah professes as much as Paul does in the preceding verse, Jonah i. 9; but it was little more than a profession in Jonah, but Paul was actually in the fear and service of God; and doubtless there was as great a difference in their breasts during the storm. The true fear and service of God brings with it great peace and inward satisfaction, which, when any leave, they must, at least so long, be strangers unto, for *there is no peace unto the wicked*, Isa. xlviii. 22.

25 Wherefore, sirs, be of good cheer: [h] for I believe God, that it shall be even as it was told me.

[h Luke 1. 45. Rom. 4. 20, 21. 2 Tim. i. 12.]

Paul, having had experience of the power and faithfulness of God, and known his name, professeth to trust in him; and recommends God's veracity unto them, as worthy to be relied upon. What a great deal of good does one holy man do in a place. These hundreds of men fare the better both in soul and body for holy Paul.

[i ch. 28. 1.] 26 Howbeit [i] we must be cast upon a certain island.

This was given by Paul as a sign unto them of the truth of what he had said, which, when it came to pass, might induce them to believe the rest; which probably it did, and saved Paul from being killed by the soldiers, ver. 42. Thus God preserves his people, and delivers Paul, and brings all his safely off at the last, but it is by tempests and storms. It may be they must suffer shipwreck of all they have in this world first. *Augusta per angusta*. Through many tribulations we must enter into the kingdom of God, as St. Paul had taught others, Acts xiv. 22, he experienced to be true himself. There was no truth more experimented than this.

27 But when the fourteenth night was come, as we were driven up and down in Adria, about midnight the shipmen deemed that they drew near to some country;

In Adria; not in the Adriatic Bay, or Gulf of Venice, which divides Italy and Dalmatia, though that be also so called; but this name is sometimes extended to those parts of the Mediterranean Sea which border on Sicily, and Ionia in Greece, and must be passed over by such as go from Crete, or Candia, to Melita, or Malta.

28 And sounded, and found *it* twenty fathoms: and when they had gone a little further, they sounded again, and found *it* fifteen fathoms.

Found it twenty fathoms: a fathom is the distance betwixt the end of the middle finger on the one hand, from the end of the middle finger on the other hand, when the arms are stretched out; which is ordinarily accounted about six feet in measure. *Found it fifteen fathoms*; coming into more shallow places they might reasonably conclude that they were near unto the land.

29 Then fearing lest they should have fallen upon rocks, they cast four anchors out of the stern, and wished for the day.

Fallen upon rocks; of which there are very many in these seas, especially about the islands. *Cast four anchors*; which show how great the tempest was, that they needed so many anchors. *Wished for the day*; that they might the better discover whereabouts they were.

30 And as the shipmen were about to flee out of the ship, when they had let down the boat into the sea, under colour as though they would have cast anchors out of the foreship,

Had let down the boat; that they might betake themselves into it, after they had left the ship: for, ver. 17, they had taken up the boat, and secured that against this or the like occasion. *As though they would have cast anchors out of the foreship*; dissembling the true reason of their going into the boat to make their escape.

31 Paul said to the centurion and to the soldiers, Except these abide in the ship, ye cannot be saved.

Notwithstanding the promise mentioned, ver. 24, that they should all be saved, they must use means, so far as means can be used, although the efficaciousness and truth of the promise do no ways depend upon the virtue of the means; but the means are made effectual by virtue of the promise. Yet whosoever neglects means upon any pretext of a promise, he does tempt God, but does not rightly believe in him. *These*; as it were pointing unto the mariners, and such as were useful in such a case.

32 Then the soldiers cut off the ropes of the boat, and let her fall off.

The centurion and soldiers, agreeing to what Paul had said, did this to take away all thoughts of escaping from the mariners, and leaving all upon what Paul had promised to them in the name of his God.

33 And while the day was coming on, Paul besought *them* all to take meat, saying, This day is the fourteenth day that ye have tarried and continued fasting, having taken nothing.

While the day was coming on; all the night after the mariners were disappointed in their project to escape. So hard a matter it was to abate their fear of being presently destroyed; and so great influence hath the apprehension of present death, and judgment which follows it, upon the minds of men. *The fourteenth day;* not as if they had wholly eaten nothing all that while, (for it is commonly held, that none can fast above half so long without danger of death,) but because in all that space they had held no set meal, as they were wont to do; and what they did eat was very little, and only in extreme necessity, without any desire or taste; so great was their anguish.

34 Wherefore I pray you to take *some* meat: for this is for your health: for [k] there shall not an hair fall from the head of any of you.

[k 1 Kings i. 52. Matt. 10. 30. Luke 12. 7. & 21. 18.]

This is for your health; that they might be stronger to endure that pain and perform that labour which was necessary towards their escape; for God would have them to use all means for their deliverance. *For there shall not an hair fall from the head of any of you;* a proverbial speech used by the Jews, as 1 Kings i. 52, signifying that they should not suffer the least detriment in their bodies, much less the loss of their lives. Thus God numbereth our hairs, and his providence extendeth over every one of them, as Matt. x. 30; Luke xxi. 18.

35 And when he had thus spoken, he took bread, and [l] gave thanks to God in presence of them all: and when he had broken *it*, he began to eat.

[l 1 Sam. 9. 13. Matt. 15. 36. Mark 8. 6. John 6. 11. 1 Tim. 4. 3, 4.]

Paul thanks God for their preservation hitherto: and there is no such encouragement to hope for future deliverances, as when God doth give us hearts to thank him for deliverances already enjoyed. But he thanked God also for giving them in their necessity such food to nourish and strengthen them, Matt. xiv. 19; xv. 36; Mark viii. 6, 19, and one season more to enjoy it. The acknowledging of God in all things we enjoy, doth sanctify them to us: otherwise they do defile us; for we usurp them; we holding them by no other tenor but in *franc-almoine*, from God: neither can they be serviceable unto us, if God withholds his blessing. Hence the Jews would not eat until Samuel had thus blessed their food, 1 Sam. ix. 13. And our Saviour himself, to give us an example, gives thanks before he would have the miraculous loaves and fishes distributed, John vi. 11.

36 Then were they all of good cheer, and they also took *some* meat.

Believing Paul's words, promising in the name of that God whom he served, that they should all be preserved; believing, they did rejoice. Now Paul, a prisoner, a neglected and contemned person, comes to be valued and credited. Whilst they sailed with a prosperous gale, neither God, nor his poor prisoner and chained apostle, is thought upon; but in a storm or tempest they are glad to believe and follow his direction. God's stars shine in the night, and are seen in affliction.

THE ACTS XXVII, XXVIII

^m ch. 2. 41. & 7. 14.
Rom. 13. 1.
1 Pet. 3. 20.

37 And we were in all in the ship two hundred threescore and sixteen ^m souls.

That is, so many persons; as chap. ii. 41; vii. 14; Rom. xiii. 1; the soul being the noblest part, and the body following its condition, whatsoever it be: if the soul be holy, the body shall be glorious. But it is not so on the other side: the soul is not hereafter as the body is here; for Dives's body fared well, was fed and arrayed sumptuously, and yet his soul was miserably tormented, Luke xvi. 19, 24.

38 And when they had eaten enough, they lightened the ship, and cast out the wheat into the sea.

Cast out the wheat, the provision they had for their sustenance. This is the third time that they lightened the ship, being willing that all their goods should perish for them, rather than with them. Or these heathens were so far persuaded by St. Paul, that they ventured their lives upon the credit of what he had foretold them; and parted with their food, and all they had to live upon, only upon his word, that they should want them in the ship no more.

39 And when it was day, they knew not the land: but they discovered a certain creek with a shore, into the which they were minded, if it were possible, to thrust in the ship.

They knew not the land; in so long and violent a tempest, thinking every moment to be swallowed up, they could keep no reckoning of the ship's running or way; neither were charts or maps so usual (if they had any at all) in those times. A certain creek; a bay, or bosom of the sea, having land on each side, where they judged it most likely for them to get on shore; using still all means for their safety.

‖ Or, *cut the anchors, they left them in the sea, &c.*

40 And when they had ‖ taken up the anchors, they committed *themselves* unto the sea, and loosed the rudder bands, and hoised up the mainsail to the wind, and made toward shore.

Loosed the rudder bands; rudders is in the plural number put for the singular: or rather, in those times they having two rudders, (as by several passages amongst the ancients do appear,) they were both loosed, that now they might use them to direct the ship to the best advantage in making the shore, they having been tied whilst they were adrift, or at anchor. Hoised up the mainsail, which they had let down, or struck, ver. 17, and now, that they might make some use of the winds, to get nigher to the shore, they hoisted up. As God doth instruct the ploughman, Isa. xxviii. 26, so he teacheth the mariner, and every one in their calling.

41 And falling into a place where two seas met, ⁿ they ran the ship aground; and the forepart stuck fast, and remained unmoveable, but the hinder part was broken with the violence of the waves.

ⁿ 2 Cor. 11. 25.

A place where two seas met; a shoal, sand, or isthmus, where the sea was on both sides of it. They were now in the greatest extremity; and God suffers them to fall into it before he sends them deliverance, that he might have the more glory by it.

42 And the soldiers' counsel was to kill the prisoners, lest any of them should swim out, and escape.

This speaks their great ingratitude, that they would take away Paul's life, who had preserved theirs. But Christ's apostles and ministers must not look for their reward in this life; though men cannot, or do not, recompense them, they shall be recompensed at the resurrection of the just, Luke xiv. 14.

43 But the centurion, willing to save Paul, kept them from *their* purpose; and commanded that they which could swim should cast *themselves* first *into the sea*, and get to land:

The centurion, willing to save Paul; because Paul was a Roman citizen, whose death he durst not be accessory unto. It may be also, that this centurion, (if there were no more,) as the Samaritan that was cleansed, did this in thankfulness unto Paul. Should cast themselves first into the sea, and get to land; that they might be helpful to others in getting on shore.

44 And the rest, some on boards, and some on *broken pieces* of the ship. And so it came to pass, ^o that they escaped all safe to land.

^o ver. 22.

Some on boards, and some on broken pieces of the ship; still using means, though it was of God only that they had them, and that they were effectual to them. In this history is lively verified that of the psalmist, Psal. cvii. 18—20, Their soul abhorreth all manner of meat; and they draw near unto the gates of death. Then they cry unto the Lord in their trouble, and he saveth them out of their distresses. He sent his word, and healed them, and delivered them from their destructions. And what follows but, ver. 21, Oh that men would praise the Lord for his goodness, and for his wonderful works to the children of men! God hath a tribute of praise which is due unto him from the readers of this story, that they would acknowledge that there is none else who can deliver after this manner, Dan. iii. 29; and then to be sure they will desire that this God might be their God for ever and ever, Psal. xlviii. 14.

CHAP. XXVIII

Paul and his company, after their shipwreck, are kindly entertained by the barbarians of Melita, 1, 2. *A viper fastening on his hand without hurting him, the people, who at first thought ill of him, believed him a god,* 3—6. *He healeth the father of Publius, and other sick persons in the island,* 7—10. *Paul and his company depart, and arrive at Rome; where Paul is left with a guard in a house of his own,* 11—16. *He calleth the Jews together, and showeth the occasion of his coming,* 17—22. *He preacheth Christ to them, of whom some believe, others believe not,* 23—29. *He continueth for two whole years to preach the gospel without interruption,* 30, 31.

AND when they were escaped, then they knew that ^a the island was called Melita.

^a ch. 27. 26.

The island; this was foretold by Paul, chap. xxvii. 26; and therefore though the mariners knew not the land, ver. 39, and were not able to direct the ship, as ver. 15, yet God so ordered it, that not a word spoken by Paul did fall to the ground, but the wind and sea obey him. Melita; now called Malta, a little island between Sicily and Africa. There is another obscure island in Illyricum that was called by this name, which some have mistook for this place of Paul's shipwreck, by reason that this tempest was in the Adriatic Sea: but not only the Gulf of Venice, but the sea about Sicily, and this coast, was so called, as Strabo witnesseth. See chap. xxvii. 27.

2 And the ^b barbarous people shewed us no little kindness: for they kindled a fire, and received us every one, because of the present rain, and because of the cold.

^b Rom. 1. 14. 1 Cor. 14. 11. Col. 3. 11.

The barbarous people; so the Grecians and Romans called all other nations that did not receive their customs, nor speak their language, 1 Cor. xiv. 11; and to this day the African coast over against this island is called Barbary. For they kindled a fire, &c.: how far is this humanity of heathens beyond that inhumanity which some that are called Christians use towards those that are shipwrecked, and their goods that come on shore!

3 And when Paul had gathered a bundle of sticks, and laid *them* on the fire, there came a viper out of the heat, and fastened on his hand.

A viper; a creature so venomous, that not only its biting, but (some say) its breath, is deadly: this, upon the warmth of the fire, being benumbed with the cold, and now refreshed, began to stir itself. Fastened on his hand; as it used to do when it biteth. God by this miracle prepares this people not only to be civil and courteous unto Paul, but to believe the gospel which he preached, wheresoever

THE ACTS XXVIII

he went. And this wonderful work of God was (as God's seal to his ministry) to show his authority to be from him.

4 And when the barbarians saw the *venomous* beast hang on his hand, they said among themselves, No doubt this man is a murderer, whom, though he hath escaped the sea, yet vengeance suffereth not to live.

Venomous; so the viper is called by that appellative word, from whence also comes *theriaca*, or treacle, which is made out of flesh, or trochusses, of vipers. And if men can make an antidote out of poison, much more can God bring good out of evil. *This man is a murderer;* it is a strange sense that men by the light of nature had of Divine vengeance, especially of God's revenging of murder. Hence they called one of their furies Tisiphone, as one that punished and revenged murder. Yet they were to blame in this case, 1. Because they confine the punishment of wicked men wholly unto this life. 2. In that they did not expect the event; they judged before they knew what would be the end of Paul afterwards. 3. They erred, in that they measured the goodness or badness of a man's state or cause by his prosperity or adversity.

e Mark 16.18.
Luke 10. 19.

5 And he shook off the beast into the fire, and ᶜfelt no harm.

As Daniel in the lion's den. God is the God of nature, and the most natural properties are restrained when he pleases, and cannot be exerted without his concurrence. Thus the promises our blessed Saviour made, Mark xvi. 18; Luke x. 19, were fulfilled according to the letter.

6 Howbeit they looked when he should have swollen, or fallen down dead suddenly: but after they had looked a great while, and saw no harm come to him, they changed their minds, and ᵈsaid that he was a god.

d ch. 14. 11.

Should have swollen; the word signifies primarily to be burnt, and then by burning or scalding to swell, which is accounted the ordinary symptom of the biting of a viper; to swell or blister, as if the part was burnt with fire. *Or fallen down dead suddenly;* in those places where there is much more heat, there is more venom in these vipers. And though some are said to live several days after they are bit by them, yet others die very suddenly upon their biting; as the known story of Cleopatra testifies; and condemned persons were sometimes put to death by vipers set unto their breasts. *And said that he was a god;* a strange extreme; so uncertain and unequal are men's minds.

7 In the same quarters were possessions of the chief man of the island, whose name was Publius; who received us, and lodged us three days courteously.

This Publius is thought to have been governor for the Romans in this island. Howsoever, he was a man of great account and estate, that could provide for so many as were in the ship, and receive them into his own house.

e Jam. 5.
14. 15.
f Mark 6. 5.
& 7. 32.
& 16. 18.
Luke 4. 40.
ch. 19. 11, 12.
1 Cor. 12. 9,
28.

8 And it came to pass, that the father of Publius lay sick of a fever and of a bloody flux: to whom Paul entered in, and ᵉprayed, and ᶠlaid his hands on him, and healed him.

A bloody flux; a painful and dangerous disease; the torment in the bowels frequently causing a fever. *And prayed;* Paul could do nothing of himself, and therefore begs of God the recovery of Publius's father. It is God only that kills and makes alive, 1 Sam. ii. 6. *Laid his hands on him;* this imposition of hands was commonly used in miraculous cures. as Matt. ix. 18; Mark vi. 5; and is joined with prayer, Matt. xix. 13, which it might be a symbol of. Thus Publius was well paid for what he did for Paul and his company. Relieving of the poor and distressed is frequently rewarded in this world, and not only in the world to come. And God now recommends the gospel and the ministry of Paul by this miracle also: for none could do such things as these, unless God were with him.

9 So when this was done, others also, which had diseases in the island, came, and were healed:

The fame of this cure, wrought so suddenly, perfectly, and only with the laying on of Paul's hands, could not but spread far and near; especially being done upon the governor: and men are usually very careful about their bodily health and welfare. So that their diseases were blessed occasions to bring them to the knowledge of God in Christ, whom Paul preached; and they might have perished eternally if they had not perished (or been thus near unto perishing) temporally.

10 Who also honoured us with many ᵍhonours; and when we departed, they laded *us* with such things as were necessary.

g Mat. 15. 6.
1 Tim. 5. 17.

They who were cured, rewarded or presented the apostle and his company very liberally. And this was the effect of that inward respect and real esteem they had for them; and was a fruit of their faith.

11 And after three months we departed in a ship of Alexandria, which had wintered in the isle, whose sign was Castor and Pollux.

A. D. 63.

These *three months* that St. Paul staid at Malta, he spent like a true labourer in the Lord's vineyard, planting a church that was famous for its stedfastness in the truth. *Had wintered in the isle;* it was their wont to lay up their ships all the winter season; as we may see, chap. xxvii. 12. And to this day the galleys seldom go out on those seas in winter. *Castor and Pollux;* feigned to be the sons of Jupiter, and to have the ordering of tempests, and the care of mariners, and were chosen for the patrons of that ship, by the pagan owners of it.

12 And landing at Syracuse, we tarried *there* three days.

Syracuse; the chief city of Sicily, famous for Archimedes. *We tarried there three days;* probably to sell some of their wares, the ship making a trading voyage.

13 And from thence we fetched a compass, and came to Rhegium: and after one day the south wind blew, and we came the next day to Puteoli:

Rhegium; a city in the kingdom of Naples, over against Messina in Sicily; so called because that Sicily was believed to be thereabouts rent and plucked from the main land, unto which they held it to have been formerly joined, until by a tempest it became an island. *Puteoli* is a sea town not far from Naples.

14 Where we found brethren, and were desired to tarry with them seven days: and so we went toward Rome.

Where we found brethren; Christians, as some think, for so they mutually called one another. But it is not so probable that any should profess Christianity so near unto Rome, and that it should be no more known or believed in Rome. Others therefore think that the apostle means Jews, whom he calls *brethren* (being, as himself, descended from Abraham); for so he calls the Jews he found at Rome, ver. 17; who yet called the Christians a sect, adding, that it was every where spoken against, ver. 22. *Rome* is known to be the chief city in Italy, and to have been the empress of the world, and famous for the church to whom St. Paul wrote his Epistle, known by its inscription unto them.

15 And from thence, when the brethren heard of us, they came to meet us as far as Appii forum, and The three taverns: whom when Paul saw, he thanked God, and took courage.

Appii forum; a place about one and fifty miles, or seventeen leagues, from Rome; so called from Appius Claudius, who made a way from Rome thither, called from his name, The Appian Way; and had his statue there set up; which is the reason why it is called thus: for the Romans did call those places *fora*, were such statues were placed. (The concourse to see those statues might bring them to become markets.) *The three taverns;* as that was a place of resort for the buying and selling of other commodities, so this for the affording of necessary provision; a little town, hence so called, about three and thirty miles, or eleven leagues, from Rome. So that some came a greater, some a lesser way to meet with Paul, and show their respect unto him. These brethren are thought to have been converted by such as at the day of Pentecost were present when those miracles were wrought, chap. ii. 10, it being expressly said, that there were strangers from Rome. *Took courage;* God moving so many not to be ashamed of his bonds.

16 And when we came to Rome, the centurion delivered the prisoners to the captain of the guard: but ʰ Paul was suffered to dwell by himself with a soldier that kept him.

h ch. 24. 25. & 27. 3.

The captain of the guard; the *præfectus prætorio,* being commander-in-chief over the soldiers, and unto whom the prisoners of state were usually committed. *Paul was suffered to dwell by himself;* God by this means giving Paul an opportunity to go abroad at his pleasure; though chained, as ver. 20, yet he might preach the gospel, and that was not bound, 2 Tim. ii. 9. And now God is with Paul, as he was with Joseph, in prison, Gen. xxxix. 21, and procures him favour.

17 And it came to pass, that after three days Paul called the chief of the Jews together: and when they were come together, he said unto them, Men *and* brethren, ⁱ though I have committed nothing against the people, or customs of our fathers, yet ᵏ was I delivered prisoner from Jerusalem into the hands of the Romans.

i ch. 24. 12, 13. & 25. 8.

k ch. 21. 33.

Paul called the chief of the Jews together; Paul does this not only out of an extraordinary love which he had for that people, but also because the apostles were commanded to *go rather to the lost sheep of the house of Israel,* Matt. x. 5, 6. The whole economy of the gospel is a doing good for evil. So did our Saviour, who is the author and subject of it; and so must his messengers or ministers do, or they are not like to do any good at all; for the world will hate them, 1 John iii. 13.

18 Who, ˡ when they had examined me, would have let *me* go, because there was no cause of death in me.

l ch. 22. 24. & 24. 10. & 25. 8. & 26. 31.

Examined me; as Festus did in the presence of king Agrippa, chap. xxv. 26, who, they were both unbelievers, yet justified Paul, acknowledging that he had not committed any thing worthy of bonds, much less of death. Thus our Saviour was declared innocent by Pilate, Luke xxiii. 4, 14.

19 But when the Jews spake against *it,* ᵐ I was constrained to appeal unto Cæsar; not that I had ought to accuse my nation of.

m ch. 25. 11.

The Jews spake against it; the Jews used all their oratory and interest against Paul, both before Felix and Festus. And had it been in Festus's power, (which after Paul's appeal it was not,) he would have sacrificed Paul to the malice of the Jews; and by that means got their favour, whom he had so incensed against them. *Not that I had aught to accuse my nation of;* Paul did not so much want matter, as mind, to accuse the Jews; and he declares, that whatsoever he had suffered, his intentions were not to calumniate them, but to vindicate himself.

20 For this cause therefore have I called for you, to see *you,* and to speak with *you:* because that ⁿ for the hope of Israel I am bound with ᵒ this chain.

n ch. 26. 6, 7. o ch. 26. 29. Eph. 3. 1. & 4. 1. & 6. 20. 2 Tim. 1. 16. & 2. 9. Philem. 10, 13.

For the hope of Israel: see chap. xxiii. 6; xxiv. 21. This *hope* is either, 1. Of the resurrection, as in the forementioned places; and chap. xxvi. 6, 7; or, 2. The Messiah; Christ is the hope of Israel, so they pretended for many ages, and him now Paul preached. *I am bound with this chain;* for though he had his liberty to go abroad, yet he was chained with his right hand to the soldier's left hand who went with him, and could not possibly be loosened unwittingly from him.

21 And they said unto him, We neither received letters out of Judæa concerning thee, neither any of the brethren that came shewed or spake any harm of thee.

The high priest, and the rest of them that had persecuted Paul, did either despond of their cause, when it should come to be impartially heard; or were supine and negligent in a matter which they pretended so highly to concern their religion; but self-ends, their present ease and reputation, were the main matters they contended for.

22 But we desire to hear of thee what thou thinkest: for as concerning this sect, we know that every where ᵖ it is spoken against.

p Luke 2. 34. ch. 24. 5, 14. 1 Pet. 2. 12. & 4. 14.

Sect, or heresy, for so they called the Christian religion, chap. xxiv. 5, 14. *Every where it is spoken against;* of all conditions of men, governors and people, and in all places; as, Luke ii. 34, Christ is said to be *a sign that shall be spoken against.*

23 And when they had appointed him a day, there came many to him into *his* lodging; ᵠ to whom he expounded and testified the kingdom of God, persuading them concerning Jesus, ʳ both out of the Law of Moses, and *out of* the Prophets, from morning till evening.

q Luke 24. 27. ch. 17. 3. & 19. 8.

r See on ch. 26. 6, 22.

His lodging; the house which he had hired, as ver. 16, and 30. *He expounded and testified the kingdom of God;* Paul expounded the Scriptures, and by them proved our Saviour to be the Messiah; and that the kingdom of the Messiah, which God had promised, and Moses and the prophets had foretold, was now come. *Persuading them concerning Jesus;* using such proofs and arguments as were cogent enough to prove what he asserted; and which also did thoroughly persuade or prevail with several of them. *From morning till evening;* thus Paul *laboured more abundantly,* 1 Cor. xv. 10.

24 And ˢ some believed the things which were spoken, and some believed not.

s ch. 14. 4. & 17. 4. & 19. 9.

Thus there are different soils into which the word is cast, as appears in the parable of the sower, Matt. xiii. 19, 20, &c. Thus Paul found by experience what he says, 2 Thess. iii. 2, that *all men have not faith;* and *the word* preached doth *not profit,* unless it be *mixed with faith in them that hear it,* Heb. iv. 2.

25 And when they agreed not among themselves, they departed, after that Paul had spoken one word, Well spake the Holy Ghost by Esaias the prophet unto our fathers,

They agreed not among themselves; thus Christ came to *send fire on the earth,* Luke xii. 49: not that the gospel does this in itself; for it is *the gospel of peace,* Eph. vi. 15, not only betwixt God and man, but betwixt man and man; and if its precepts were observed, love, meekness, and goodness would banish all hatred, pride, and contention out of the hearts and lives of men; but this arises out of the corruption that is in man, and from the evil one that sows his tares amongst us. *After that Paul had spoken one word;* Paul spake this eminent and remarkable word, or sentence, that they might (if possible) be pricked in their hearts at the hearing of God's judgments denounced against them.

26 Saying, ᵗ Go unto this people, and say, Hearing ye shall hear, and shall not understand; and seeing ye shall see, and not perceive:

t Is. 6. 9. Jer. 5. 21. Ezek. 12. 2. Matt. 13. 14, 15. Mark 4. 12. Luke 8. 10. John 12. 40. Rom. 11. 8.

As their fathers did hear the many prophecies concerning the miseries and calamities which for their sins were to come upon them, as also concerning the Messiah which was to come, but did not believe them or entertain them as they ought; so these their children (through the righteous judgment of God) inherited their fathers' sins, and should be heirs also of their punishments. Thus we see, that *Scriptura prophetica sæpius impletur;* and what was spoken and fulfilled in that generation so long before, was also in this so many hundred years after.

27 For the heart of this people is waxed gross, and their ears are dull of hearing, and their eyes have they closed; lest they should see with *their* eyes, and hear with *their* ears, and understand with *their* heart, and should be converted, and I should heal them.

Though God did forsake this people, (being first forsaken of them,) and withdraw his gratuitous assistance from them, yet it is all justly charged upon them, they having by their sins said unto God, *Depart from us, for we desire not the knowledge of thy ways,* Job xxi. 14. *Their eyes have they closed;* they winked, as those that were loth to see, though they could not but see, the truths Paul preached concerning the Messiah; prejudicate opinions and self-conceit hindering them from coming unto the acknowledgment of them. *I should heal them,* or pardon them; for by guilt the soul is wounded.

28 Be it known therefore unto you, that the salvation of God is sent "unto the Gentiles, and *that* they will hear it.

u Matt. 21. 41, 43. ch. 13. 46, 47. & 18. 6. & 22. 21. & 26. 17, 18. Rom. 11. 11.

The salvation of God; so the gospel is called; because, 1. The finding of it out, 2. The preparing of it by sending his Son, 3. The revealing of it, and, 4. Its efficacy, is only of God. *Is sent unto the Gentiles;* as by our Saviour's commission, Matt. xxviii. 19, and Luke xxiv. 47, does appear. And Paul had by experience found the effects of it, as may be seen in all this book of his travels, where we may find many of the Gentiles were obedient unto the word, which the Jews gainsaid and blasphemed.

29 And when he had said these words, the Jews departed, and had great reasoning among themselves.

Some accusing of Paul, others vindicating of him; some believing, as ver. 24, others not believing; our Saviour, and his gospel too, being for the rising and falling of many.

A. D. 65. 30 And Paul dwelt two whole years in his own hired house, and received all that came in unto him,

Of what nation or quality soever they were, Paul preached salvation to them upon the gospel condition of faith and holiness; and in that imitated God and our Saviour, who refuse none that thus come unto him. And though Paul might have had greater security from trouble by the Jews if he would have desisted, yet a necessity was laid upon him, and a woe unto him if he did not preach the gospel, as 1 Cor. ix. 16, which may abundantly excuse and justify him.

31 ˣPreaching the kingdom of God, and teaching those things which concern the Lord Jesus Christ, with all confidence, no man forbidding him.

x ch. 4. 31. Eph. 6. 19.

The kingdom of God; the gospel is so called; as also Paul preached that kingdom of God which is to come at the end of the world, which falls in with the subject he was so often upon, concerning the resurrection; which if men did but believe effectually, all the other ends of preaching would be easily obtained. *Those things which concern the Lord Jesus Christ;* Christ's precepts and miracles, his death and resurrection. *No man forbidding him:* God, who puts bounds to the raging sea, had stopped the Jews' malice, and bidden it go no further; and he who delivered Daniel from the lions, had delivered Paul from Nero, and would have delivered him, had not his death been more for the glory of God, and the good of Paul himself, than his life; which at last he offered in confirmation of the truths which he had preached; which he foresaw, 2 Tim. iv. 6, and, as Eusebius says, it came to pass accordingly.

This book may be called, not only πράξεις, but τέρατα; not only the Acts, but the wonders, of the Apostles: though the holy penman and the apostles meekly contented themselves with that name by which at present it is called, yet what wonders are contained in it! not only such as were wrought *by* the apostles, but *for* them, to deliver, preserve, and encourage them; insomuch as the attempt to silence them, and to hinder the progress of the gospel preached by them, proved as vain as if men had endeavoured to hinder the sun from shining, or the wind from blowing.

Now unto him, who is able to work so as none can hinder, be all honour and glory, dominion and power, for ever and ever. Amen.

THE EPISTLE OF PAUL THE APOSTLE

TO THE

ROMANS

THE ARGUMENT

THE penman of this Epistle, viz. Paul, was so called (as some think) because he was little or low of stature. Others suppose he had this name first given him upon the converting of Sergius Paulus the deputy; of which see Acts xii., and Hierom. Com. in Ep. ad Philem. But others are of opinion, that his name was not changed at all, and that he had two names, as all those Jews had who were freemen of Rome. The text in Acts xiii. 9 doth favour this opinion; there you read of Saul, who was also called Paul. (So John was surnamed, or also called, Mark, Acts xii. 12, 25.) And because he was the apostle of the Gentiles, and his work lay mostly amongst them, he was called at last altogether by his surname, or Roman title.

As to the order of it: all are agreed, that it was not written as it is placed in our Bibles: that the Epistles to the Thessalonians, to the Corinthians, and other of his Epistles, were written before this; and the reason why it is placed before the other Epistles is, because of the dignity of the Romans, to whom it was directed; Rome being, at that time, the imperial city: or, because of the prolixity and largeness of it, this being the longest of all the Epistles: or, because of the excellency and fulness of it; so full and excellent is this Epistle, that some have called it "the marrow of divinity." Chrysostom had such an esteem of it, that he caused it to be read to him twice every week. Melancthon called it "the confession of the churches;" he is reported to have gone over it ten several times in his ordinary lectures. Mr. Perkins adviseth, in the reading of the Scriptures, to begin with the Gospel of John, and this Epistle to the Romans, as being the keys of the New Testament.

The subject-matter of it seems to be much the same with the Epistle to the Galatians. The body of this Epistle (not to speak any thing of the preface, or conclusion) is partly doctrinal, and partly practical. In the doctrinal part, the apostle handles (and that purposely, and at large) that fundamental article of a sinner's justification in the sight of God: so that this Epistle (as one saith) is the proper seat of that doctrine; and from hence it is principally to be learned. Here we are taught the way and manner of our justification before God, that we are *justified by faith, without the deeds of the law*, by a righteousness which is imputed to us, and not by any righteousness inherent in us. This is proved in the first four chapters, by many irrefragable arguments, and vindicated from all objections. And then it is amplified in the seven following chapters. The amplification is first from the glorious effects and sweetest privileges of justification by faith, viz. *peace with God*, which no tribulation can hinder or interrupt, chap. v. 1—10. Then there is rejoicing with God, as reconciled through Jesus Christ, the Second Adam, who doth abundantly transcend the first Adam in many particulars, chap. v. 11—21. Then there is sanctification, in both the parts of it, as mortification and death to sin; and vivification, or newness of life, chap. vi. throughout. The next is freedom from the law, as the first husband, now dead, chap. vii. throughout. And in the 8th chapter you have divers other privileges closely couched, as non-condemnation, adoption, the indwelling of the Spirit, the co-operations of all things for good, the certainty of the love of God, together with the triumph we have over all our enemies upon that account. Further, this doctrine of justification is amplified from the remote cause of it; and that is, God's predestination or eternal counsel. This is brought in to obviate an objection against this doctrine, as not true, because the Jewish nation (God's ancient people) received it not. Thereupon the apostle shows, that justification belonged not to the whole nation of the Jews, but only to the elect amongst them; the rest being rejected of God till the fulness of the Gentiles were come in; and then the Jews should more generally believe and be converted. This you have at large in the 9th, 10th, and 11th chapters. The practical part of this Epistle follows, in which you have many useful exhortations, from the beginning of the 12th chapter to the 14th verse of the 15th chapter. These are either more general, or more particular, showing Christians how they should behave themselves with respect to the church of Christ, and the fellowship thereof, every one attending upon the calling and ministry wherein God hath placed him, chap. xii.; with respect to the civil society, and the government which God had set over them in the world, yielding all subjection thereunto, chap. xiii.; and with respect to their brethren and neighbours, exercising Christian charity towards all, avoiding censoriousness on the one hand and offences on the other, chap. xiv., xv. These duties he largely presseth, interweaving now and then many ethical and theological aphorisms, of which in their proper place.

CHAP. I

Paul, commending to the Romans his calling, greeteth them, 1—7; and professeth his concern for, and desire of coming to see them, 8—15. He showeth that the gospel is for the justification of all mankind through faith, 16, 17. And having premised that sinners in general are obnoxious to God's wrath, he describeth at large the corruption of the Gentile world, 18—32.

A. D. 60.
a Acts 22. 21.
1 Cor. 1. 1.
Gal. 1. 1.
1 Tim. 1. 11.
& 2. 7.
2 Tim. 1. 11. b Acts 9. 15. & 13. 2. Gal. 1. 15.

PAUL, a servant of Jesus Christ, ª called *to be* an apostle, ᵇ separated unto the Gospel of God,

A servant of Jesus Christ, is a higher title than monarch of the world: several great emperors styled themselves Christ's vassals. He so calls himself, either in respect of his condition, which was common with him to all true Christians; or else in respect of his office. Of old, they who were in great offices were called *the servants of God*: see Josh. i. 1; Neh. i. 6; Psal. cxxxii. 10. Or else in respect of his singular and miraculous conversion: by reason of which, he thought himself so obliged to Christ, that he wholly addicted or devoted himself to his service. *Called to be an apostle;* appointed to that high office by the immediate call of Christ himself: see Gal. i. 1; Tit. i. 3. The history of this call you have in Acts ix. 15. Two things are couched in this phrase: 1. That he did not take this honour to himself, but was thereunto appointed and called of God. 2. That this apostolical dignity was not by any desert of his, but by grace only, and the free gift of him that calleth. It was formerly matter of admiration, and so it became a proverb in Israel, *Is Saul also among the prophets?* And we may say, with great astonishment, Is Saul also among the apostles? He that a little before had seen him doing what he is recorded to have done, Acts xxvi. 10, 11, would never have dreamed of any such thing. *Separated;* either from his mother's womb, in the purpose of God, Gal. i. 15; so Jeremiah of old, Jer. i. 5. Or else it may have respect to Acts xiii. 2, where the Holy Ghost did actually order he should be separated for the work to which he had called him. The Greek word, in both places, is the same. Or else it may respect the more immediate commission he had from Christ himself, Acts ix. 15; xxvi. 16—18. Some think he alludes to the name of Pharisee, which is from separating: when he was a Pharisee, he was separated to the law of God; and now, being a Christian, he was separated to the gospel of God. *Unto the gospel of God;* that is, to the preaching and publishing of it. The gospel is sometimes called *the gospel of God*, as in this place; and sometimes *the gospel of Christ*, as in the 16th verse of this chapter: it is said to be the gospel of God, because he is the author of it, it is not a human invention; and it is said to be the gospel of Christ, because he is the matter and subject of it.

2 (ᶜ Which he had promised afore ᵈ by his prophets in the holy Scriptures,)

c See on Acts 26. 6.
Tit. 1. 2.
d ch. 3. 21.
& 16. 26. Gal. 3. 8.

Which he had promised; the meaning is not, that the history of the gospel was promised by the prophets, but that Jesus Christ, with all his benefits, (which is the direct subject of the gospel history and revelation,) was promised or foreshown by them. *Afore;* this word is added to prevent the imputation of novelty: q. d. Let none object and say, the gospel is a new and modern doctrine; for it was promised or foretold of old, by all the *prophets which have been since the world began*, Luke i. 70. *By his prophets:* by *prophets* we may understand, not only those that were commonly dignified with that title, but all those also whom God condescended to converse with in a familiar manner, revealing his secrets to them: that such are called prophets, see Gen. xx. 7; Psal. cv. 15. *In the holy Scriptures;* to wit, of the Old Testament; he hath respect to the oracles and promises therein contained, concerning Christ and his kingdom; chiefly to Gen. iii. 15; xlix. 8, 10; Deut. xviii. 18; Psal. xvi. 10; xxii.; xl.; cx. 1; Isa. vii. 14; ix. 6; liii.; lxiii. 1—3; Dan. ix. 24—26; Micah v. 2; Zech. ix. 9; Mal. iii. 1, &c. He hereby intimates, that there is a great harmony and consent betwixt the prophets and apostles, the doctrine of the Old Testament and the New; see Luke xxiv. 44; John xii. 16; Acts x. 43. Our modern translators include this verse in a parenthesis; the ancients did not.

3 Concerning his Son Jesus Christ our Lord, ᵉ which was ᶠ made of the seed of David according to the flesh;

e Mat. 1. 6, 16.
Luke 1. 32. Acts 2. 30.
2 Tim. 2. 8.
f John 1. 14. Gal. 4. 4.

Concerning his Son Jesus Christ our Lord: this phrase either respects the Holy Scriptures, mentioned immediately before in the 2nd verse; the sum and substance of them is, concerning the Messiah, the Son of God: or else it respects the gospel, that was spoken of in the 1st verse; the 2nd verse being only a parenthesis, as was before hinted; then the meaning is, that the apostle Paul was separated to the gospel of God, which only or mainly concerns his Son Jesus Christ. And this seems to show the excellency of the gospel, that it doth not treat of vulgar and ordinary matters, as of the gods of the Gentiles, or the actions of Alexander, Cæsar, the Scipios, or such-like heroes; but of the Son of God himself. *Which was made;* i. e. as he afterwards expresseth it, according to the flesh, or his human nature: in regard of his Divine subsistence, he was begotten and not made; in regard of his manhood, he was made and not begotten. When he says the Son of God *was made*, &c., it is undeniably implied, that he did exist before his incarnation, and was the Son of God before he was the Son of man. This place proves clearly these two truths: 1. That in the person of Jesus Christ there are two natures. 2. That there is betwixt these a communication of properties; here the Son of God is said to be made of the seed of David; and elsewhere the Son of man is said to have come down from heaven: see John iii. 13: compare John vi. 62; Acts xx. 28; 1 Cor. ii. 8. *Of the seed of David*; i. e. of the virgin Mary, who was of David's lineage and posterity; the promise was expressly, that the Messiah should be *of the fruit of his loins*, Acts ii. 30, compared with Isa. xi. 1; Jer. xxiii. 5; Ezek. xxxiv. 24. Yea, this promise was so fully known to the Jews, that when they spake of the Messiah, they called him *the Son of David*: see Matt. xxi. 9; xxii. 42; Mark x. 47, 48; John vii. 42. Hence it is that the evangelists, Matthew and Luke, are so careful and industrious to prove, that the virgin Mary, and Joseph to whom she was espoused, did come of David's line and race.

+ Gr. *determined.*
g Acts 13.33.
h Heb. 9. 14.

4 And †ᵍ declared *to be* the Son of God with power, according ʰ to the spirit of holiness, by the resurrection from the dead:

Not made the Son of God, as he was said before to be *made of the seed of David*; but *declared*, or demonstrated, *to be the Son of God*. *With power*: this refers either to the word *declared*, and then the meaning is, he was powerfully or miraculously declared to be the Son of God; the Greek word ordinarily signifies a miracle in the New Testament: or else it refers to the last words, *the Son of God*; and then the sense is, he was declared to be the powerful and omnipotent Son of God, of the same power and majesty with the Father. By *the spirit of holiness*, some would understand the Third Person in the blessed Trinity, which is often called the Holy Spirit, and here the Spirit of holiness; but others, and they more rightly, do understand the Deity and Divine nature of Christ; this is called the *Spirit*, 1 Tim. iii. 16; 1 Pet. iii. 18; and *the eternal Spirit*, Heb. ix. 14; and here it is called *the Spirit of holiness*, or the most Holy Spirit, and that, probably, because of its effects; for thereby he sanctified his natural body, and still sanctifies his mystical body, the church. That this is the meaning is evident, by the opposition between the flesh and the Spirit: as *according to the flesh*, in the former verse, did signify his human nature; so *according to the Spirit*, in this verse, doth signify his Divine nature. See the like antithesis in 1 Tim. iii. 16; 1 Pet. iii. 18. *By the resurrection from the dead*: because it is said, the resurrection *of* the dead, not *from* the dead, some would understand the words of Lazarus, and others, who by the power of Christ were raised from the dead; and others would understand the words of those who were raised with Christ, when he himself arose: see Matt. xxvii. 52, 53. But in Scripture *the resurrection of the dead*, is put for the resurrection from the dead; see 1 Cor. xv. 42; Heb. vi. 2; and hereby is meant the resurrection of Christ himself: he rose again from the dead, and thereby declared or manifested himself to be the Son of God with power: see John ii. 19, 21; v. 26; x. 18; 1 Cor. xv. 4. And though it be said in Scripture, that the Father raised him from the dead, Acts ii. 24; xiii. 30, 33; yet that doth not hinder but by his own power he raised himself; seeing the Father and he were one, and the works of the Three Persons in one and the same Essence are undivided.

i ch. 12. 3.
& 15. 15.
1 Cor. 15. 10.
Gal. 1. 15.
& 2. 9.
Eph. 3. 8.
‖ Or, *to the obedience of faith.*   k Acts 6. 7. ch. 16. 26. l Acts 9. 15.

5 By whom ⁱ we have received grace and apostleship, ‖ for ᵏ obedience to the faith among all nations, ˡ for his name:

By whom; or of whom; by whom, as Mediator, or of whom, as Author and Giver. *Grace and apostleship*: some make these two distinct gifts; the one common, which is grace; the other special, which is apostleship: others think, that, by an hendiadis, he means the grace of apostleship; which he so calls, because it was conferred upon him, not for any desert of his, but by the mere favour and free grace of God. It is his manner to call his apostleship by the name or style of *grace*: see chap. xv. 15; Gal. ii. 9; Eph. iii. 2, 8. *For obedience to the faith*; you have the same phrase, chap. xvi. 26, and there it is rendered *for the obedience of faith*. By *faith* here some understand the gospel or doctrine of faith; it hath this sense, Acts vi. 7; Jude 3, &c.; and then the meaning is, God, of his mere grace, hath given me this office, that I might bring the nations to believe, and work in them obedience to the doctrine of the gospel. Others understand the grace of faith; and then the meaning is, I have received this office, that I might bring the nations to believe, and so to obey the gospel. Therefore obedience is joined with faith, because by faith we obey the commands of God; and faith itself consists in obedience, and is the great command of the gospel. *Among all nations*; according to the general commission, Matt. xxviii. 19, and a more special commission to this apostle; see Acts ix. 15; Gal. ii. 7, 8; 1 Tim. ii. 7; 2 Tim. i. 11. *For his name*; that the nations might believe in his name; so some: others suppose these words are added to declare the end of Paul's preaching and apostleship, which was to set forth the glory and praise of Christ: see 2 Thess. i. 12.

6 Among whom are ye also the called of Jesus Christ:

Among whom are ye also; the Romans are in this number, and a part of the nations to whom I have a commission, and for whom I have received the grace of apostleship. He adds this, to show his warrant for writing to them, he did it by virtue of his office; as also to humble them; for though they were Romans, and such as bore the greatest sway in the world, yet they were formerly pagans and idolaters. *The called of Jesus Christ*: though such were some of you, to wit, heathen idolaters; yet now you are Christians, and *the called of Jesus Christ*: called outwardly by his word, and inwardly by his Spirit. By effectual calling you are become his disciples and followers.

m ch. 9. 24.
1 Cor 1. 2.
1 Thess. 4. 7.
n 1 Cor. 1. 3.
2 Cor. 1. 2.
Gal. 1. 3.

7 To all that be in Rome, beloved of God, ᵐ called *to be* saints: ⁿ Grace to you and peace from God our Father, and the Lord Jesus Christ.

To all that be in Rome; he doth not direct this Epistle to all that there inhabited, as to the emperor and senate, &c.; but to the church, and all the Christians there, as appears by the two following phrases. He wrote not to those only which were Romans by nation, but to all the faithful, whether Jews or Gentiles, bond or free, for they were all one and alike in Christ. They are deceived that think this Epistle, because directed to the Romans, was written in Latin. The Greek tongue was well understood in that city. Juvenal calls Rome a Greek city, because the inhabitants, as well natives as strangers, did some of them use, and most of them understand, that language. *Called to be saints*, or, called saints; though there might be hypocrites amongst them, yet they were denominated from the better part. The Jews of old were only accounted a holy nation or people; and the Gentiles, common or unclean; but now that difference is taken away, faith in Jesus Christ, and effectual calling, makes the Gentiles holy as well as the Jews. The name *saint* doth not denote a perfection in holiness, but one that is devoted and consecrated to God, who is holy in heart and life, though he hath many imperfections. *Grace to you, and peace*: under these two words, *grace* and *peace*, are comprehended all spiritual and temporal blessings. It is a usual salutation or benediction in the Epistles of this apostle: see 1 Cor. i. 3; 2 Cor. i. 2; Gal. i. 3; Eph. i. 2; Phil. i. 2; Col. i. 2; 2 Thess. i. 2; 1 Tim. i. 2; Tit. i. 4; Philem. 3. See the like in the Epistles of Peter, 1 Pet. i. 2; 2 Pet. i. 2. See also 2 John 3; Rev. i. 4. *From God our Father, and the Lord Jesus Christ*: why is there no mention made here of the Holy Ghost? *Answ*. Because he is implied in his gifts: grace and peace are the fruits and gifts of the Holy Spirit. In other salutations the Holy Ghost is expressed; see 2 Cor. xiii. 14; and here, when the Father and Son are named, he is plainly implied.

o 1 Cor. 1. 4.
Phil. 1. 3.
Col. 1. 3, 4.
p 1 Thes. 1. 2.
Philem. 4.
p ch. 16. 19.
1 Thess. 1. 8.

8 First, ᵒ I thank my God through Jesus Christ for you all, that ᵖ your faith is spoken of throughout the whole world.

First, here, is not a word of order, for there follows no

secondly, &c.; but it serves to show, that here the Epistle begins, for all before was but a preface or inscription: q. d. In the first place. See the like, 1 Tim. ii. 1. *Throughout the whole world*, that is, through many parts of it; it is a figurative speech: see the like, John xii. 19. Or else, by *the whole world* may be understood the Roman empire, which ruled at that time over a great part of the known world. See the like, Luke ii. 1. Besides, there was a resort to Rome from all parts of the world, and so this report might be diffused far and near. The faith of the gospel at Rome made it more famous than all its victories and triumphs. Oh, how is Rome degenerated! We may take up the complaint concerning her which we find, Isa. i. 11, 12. The Romanists urge this place to prove Rome the mother church; but without reason: the church of Thessalonica had as high a eulogy: see 1 Thess. i. 8.

q ch. 9. 1.
2 Cor. 1. 23.
Phil. 1. 8.
1 Thess. 2 5.
r Acts 27. 23.
2 Tim. 1. 3.
|| Or, *in my spirit*,
John 4. 23, 24. Phil. 3. 3. s 1 Thess. 3. 10.

9 For qGod is my witness, rwhom I serve || with my spirit in the Gospel of his Son, that sithout ceasing I make mention of you always in my prayers;

God is my witness; in these words there is the force, if not the form, of an oath. See the like, 2 Cor. i. 18; xi. 31; Gal. i. 20. His great love and care of them was a hidden thing, and known only to God; to him therefore he appeals for the truth thereof. Oaths, in certain cases, are allowable under the New Testament, as well as the Old. *With my spirit*, i. e. sincerely, or with my whole heart: see Eph. vi. 6; 2 Tim. i. 3. *Without ceasing*, i. e. as often as he prayed. This was a great indication of his hearty affection to them.

t ch. 15. 23, 32. 1 Thess. 3. 10.
u Jam. 4. 15.

10 tMaking request, if by any means now at length I might have a prosperous journey uby the will of God to come unto you.

Making request; this was one thing he requested of God, that what he had long desired and designed might happily (if it seemed good in God's sight) be at last accomplished, that he might come in person to them. This desire of Paul to see the Romans might be one cause of that appeal which he made to Rome, Acts xxv. 10, 11. *By the will of God*; he adds this, because, in publishing the gospel, he followed the order which God, by his Spirit, prescribed him: see Acts xvi. 7, 9, 10.

x ch. 15. 29.

11 For I long to see you, that xI may impart unto you some spiritual gift, to the end ye may be established;

He declares his end in desiring to see them; it was not his own profit, but their edification. By *some spiritual gift*, he means some one or other of those gifts of the Spirit, of which particular mention is made, 1 Cor. xii. 7—11. *To the end ye may be established*: q. d. I do not intend to bring any new doctrine to you, but to confirm and establish you in that which you have already heard and received. Establishing grace is that which all Christians stand in need of. See Rom. xvi. 25; 1 Thess. iii. 8, 13; 2 Thess. ii. 15—17.

|| Or, *in you*.
y Tit. 1. 4.
2 Pet. 1. 1.

12 That is, that I may be comforted together || with you by ythe mutual faith both of you and me.

This is added to qualify what he had said before, lest he should seem to arrogate too much to himself; he tells them, he hoped not only to comfort them, but to be comforted by them. The meanest of Christ's members may contribute somewhat to the edifying even of an apostle. The apostle John did hope to be quickened and comforted by the graces of a woman and her children, 2 John 12. Great is the benefit of the communion of saints. *By the mutual faith both of you and me*; i. e. by the faith which you and I have in Jesus Christ; which he elsewhere calls *the common faith*, and *the faith of God's elect*. All true comfort springs from faith.

z ch. 15. 23.
a See Acts 16. 7.
1 Thess. 2. 18.
b Phil. 4. 17.
|| Or, *in y u*.

13 Now I would not have you ignorant, brethren, that zoftentimes I purposed to come unto you, (but awas let hitherto,) that I might have some bfruit || among you also, even as among other Gentiles.

He prevents a cavil; they might say, If Paul hath such a longing desire to see us, why doth he not come to us? To this he answers, it was not for want of will or affection; for he often intended and attempted it. *But was let hitherto*; either by Satan, as 1 Thess. ii. 18; or by the Holy Spirit otherwise disposing of him, as Acts xvi. 6, 7; Rom. xv. 22. It is possible that he might be hindered also by his own infirmities, or by others' necessities and entreaties, Acts x. 48; xvi. 15; xxviii. 14. *That I might have some fruit*, i. e. of my ministry and calling, as the apostle of the uncircumcision. He hoped the gospel he should preach among them would have good success, and bring forth fruit in them, as it had done in other churches of the Gentiles. See Col. i. 6.

14 cI am debtor both to the Greeks, and to the Barbarians; both to the wise, and to the unwise. c 1 Cor. 9. 16.

I am debtor; as being obliged by virtue of my calling, and as being intrusted by God with talents to that purpose. You are not beholden to me for this desire, as if it were an arbitrary favour, for it is my bounden duty. *Both to the Greeks, and to the Barbarians*; i. e. to all nations, which he divides into these two sorts, *Greeks* and *Barbarians*. The Jews he mentions not, because he was the doctor of the Gentiles. *Both to the wise, and to the unwise*; by these he understands particular persons among the Greeks and Barbarians, for there were among either of them some wise, and some unwise. The gospel is adapted to all sorts of persons, whether wise or simple.

15 So, as much as in me is, I am ready to preach the Gospel to you that are at Rome also.

q. d. I have preached it at Antioch, at Athens, at Ephesus, at Corinth, &c.; and I am ready (if God permit) to preach it in the most splendid city of Rome likewise. So the reason is not in myself, or in my own will, why I have not come to you all this while.

d Ps. 40. 9, 10. Mark 8. 38. 2 Tim. 1. 8.
e 1 Cor. 1. 18, & 15. 2.
f Luke 2. 30, 31, 32. & 24. 47. Acts 3. 26. & 13. 26, 46. ch. 2. 9.

16 For dI am not ashamed of the Gospel of Christ: for eit is the power of God unto salvation to every one that believeth; fto the Jew first, and also to the Greek.

Though Rome be the head of the empire, and the Romans bear the name of wise and learned persons; and though the gospel hath the show of simplicity, and is foolishness to the wise men of this world; yet *I am not ashamed* to own and publish this *gospel of Christ*. I do not shrink back, and withdraw myself, as men do from those things whereof they are ashamed. Neither indeed need I, because, how mean soever it seems to be to carnal eyes, yet *it is the power of God unto salvation*, &c.; not the essential power of God, but the organical power. See the like, 1 Cor. i. 18. The meaning is, it is a powerful means ordained of God for this purpose. Touching the efficacy and excellent power of the gospel for the conversion and salvation of the souls of men, see Isa. liii. 1; 1 Cor. iv. 15; 2 Cor. iv. 7; x. 4, 5; Heb. iv. 12; James i. 21. *To every one that believeth*; the gospel is offered unto all, but it profiteth unto salvation only those that believe; as a medicine is only effectual to those who receive or apply it. *To the Jew first, and also to the Greek*; the gospel was first to be published to the Jews, and then to the Gentiles, whom he here calls Greeks: see Luke xxiv. 47; Acts i. 8. This order the apostles accordingly kept and observed, Acts xiii. 46.

g ch. 3. 21.
h Hab. 2. 4.
John 3. 36.
Gal. 3. 11.
Phil. 3. 9.
Heb. 10. 38.

17 For gtherein is the righteousness of God revealed from faith to faith: as it is written, hThe just shall live by faith.

It will give light to this whole Epistle, to explain what is here meant by *the righteousness of God*. Some do thereby understand the whole doctrine of salvation and eternal life, which is revealed in the gospel; and they make it the same with *the faith of God*, chap. iii. 3, and with *the truth of God*, chap. iii. 7. Others, by *the righteousness of God*, do understand that righteousness whereby a man is justified, or stands just and righteous in the sight of God: and it is called *the righteousness of God*, to distinguish it from our own righteousness, chap. x. 3, and because it is appointed, approved, and accepted by him, it being such as he himself can fi..d no fault with. Further, it is called *the righteousness of God*, because it was performed by him, who is God as well as man, and imputed unto us: hence he is said to be *made righteousness* unto us, and we are said to *be made the righteousness of God in him;* we having his righteousness, as he had our sins, viz. by imputation. This is often called *the righteousness of faith*, because by faith it is apprehended and applied. And again, it is called *the law of righteousness*, chap. ix. 31, in opposition to that law of righteousness whereby the unbelieving Jews sought to be justified. *Revealed;* the law of God discovers no such way of justifying a sinner, nor is it taught by reason or philosophy: the gospel only makes a revelation of it; which occasioned the apostle's glorying in it. *From faith to faith:* this apostle seems to delight in such repetitions, and there is an elegancy in them: see chap. vi. 19; 2 Cor. ii. 16; iii. 18. The words are variously interpreted: from the faith of the Old Testament to the New; so that no person ever was or shall be justified in any other way. Or, from a lesser faith to a greater; not noting two faiths, but one and the same faith increasing to perfection. He saith not, from faith to works, or from works to faith; but *from faith to faith*, i. e. only by faith. The words *to be* must be understood: q. d. The gospel reveals the righteousness of God *to be* from faith to faith. The beginning, the continuance, the accomplishment of our justification is wholly absolved by faith. *The just shall live by faith:* some refer these words, *by faith*, to the subject of this proposition, *the just;* and thus they render it, *The just by faith shall live;* and so read, the foregoing proposition is the better proved thereby. There is some difficulty to understand the fitness of this testimony to prove the conclusion in hand; for it is evident, that the prophet Habakkuk, in whom these words are found, doth speak of a temporal preservation; and what is that to eternal life? *Answ.* The Babylonian captivity figured out our spiritual bondage under sin and Satan; and deliverance from that calamity did shadow forth our deliverance from hell, to be procured by Christ: compare Isa. xl. 2—4, with Matt. iii. 3. Again, general sentences applied to particular cases, are not thereby restrained to those particulars, but still retain the generality of their nature: see Matt. xix. 6. Again, one and the same faith apprehends and gives us interest in all the promises of God; and as by it we live in temporal dangers, so by it we are freed from eternal destruction.

i Acts 17. 30. Eph. 5. 6. Col. 3. 6.

18 ¹For the wrath of God is revealed from heaven against all ungodliness and unrighteousness of men, who hold the truth in unrighteousness;

He proceeds to prove the principal proposition laid down in the foregoing verse; the causal particle *for* implies as much. Men must be justified by the righteousness of God, because they have no righteousness of their own to justify them, they themselves are all unrighteous. This he proves both of the Gentiles and Jews. He begins with the Gentiles, and proves it upon them, from this verse to the 17th verse of the 2nd chapter; and then he proves it upon the Jews also, from thence to the end of the 3rd chapter. *The wrath of God is revealed;* it is revealed in the word of God, or rather, by the judgments which he inflicteth. *From heaven;* i. e. from God in heaven. Plagues and judgments spring not out of the dust, proceed not originally from second causes, much less do they come by chance. *Against all ungodliness and unrighteousness of men:* the abstract is put for the concrete; he means unrighteous and ungodly men; but he chooseth this way of speaking, because God, when he punisheth, aims at the sins of men; and would not punish their persons, but for their sins. By *ungodliness*, understand sins against the first table, which are mentioned ver. 21, 23: by *unrighteousness*, sins against the second, of which there is mention at large, from ver. 26 to the end of the chapter. *Who hold the truth in unrighteousness:* by *truth*, understand all that light which is left in man since the fall. There are in all men some common notions of God, his nature and will; some common principles also of equity and charity towards men, which nature itself teacheth, and upon which the consciences of the Gentiles did accuse or excuse them. These natural notions concerning God and their neighbour they did not obey and follow, but wickedly suppressed them. They imprisoned the truth which they acknowledged, that they might sin the more securely. The metaphor is taken from tyrants, who oppress the innocent, and imprison them: so the Gentiles did by the truth which they had by nature, they kept it in and under.

19 Because ᵏ that which may be known of God is manifest ‖ in them; for ¹God hath shewed *it* unto them.

k Acts 14. 17. ‖ Or, *to them.* 1 John 1. 9.

That which may be known of God; or, that which is knowable of God, viz. by the light of nature. The apostle, by a prolepsis, prevents an objection which some might make in excuse of the Gentiles: how could they suffocate or suppress the truth, seeing they wanted the Scripture, and were without the knowledge of it? To this he answers, that they were not wholly without knowledge, for that which might be known of God was manifest in them, and revealed to them. *Is manifest in them,* i. e. in their heart and minds; see chap. ii. 15: or, to and among them; as appears by many of their learned writers, who have left behind them many clear discourses, and wise essays and sayings, about this matter, though they themselves did act contrary thereunto. *For God hath shewed it unto them;* i. e. as before, by the light of nature in their consciences, or by the consideration of the creatures, as it follows in the next verse.

20 For ᵐ the invisible things of him from the creation of the world are clearly seen, being understood by the things that are made, *even* his eternal power and Godhead; ‖ so that they are without excuse:

m Ps. 19. 1, &c. Acts 14. 17. & 17. 27.
‖ Or, *that they may be.*

Because it might be further objected in behalf of the Gentiles, that the notions of God imprinted in their nature are so weak, that they may be well excused; therefore the apostle adds, that the certainty of them is further confirmed by the book of the creatures, which was written before them in capital letters, so that he that runs may read. *The invisible things of him:* the apostle tells us afterwards himself what he means by the invisible things of God, viz. his being and his attributes, particularly his eternity and almighty power; to which we might add, his wisdom, goodness, &c. These, though invisible in themselves, yet are discernible by his works, and that ever since the creation of the world. By what they see created, they may easily collect or understand, that there is an eternal and almighty Creator; they may argue from the effects to the cause. *So that they are without excuse:* some render it, that they may be without excuse; but it is better rendered in our translation: the meaning is not, that God gave them that knowledge for this end and purpose, that they might be inexcusable, for they might catch even at that for an excuse; but the plain sense is this, that God hath given all men such means of knowledge as sufficeth to leave them without excuse, there can be no pretence of ignorance.

21 Because that, when they knew God, they glorified *him* not as God, neither were thankful; but ⁿ became vain in their imaginations, and their foolish heart was darkened.

n 2 Kings 17. 15. Jer 2. 5. Eph. 4. 17, 18.

Because; either this must be referred to the words immediately foregoing, and then it is a reason why the Gentiles are inexcusable, *because that, when they knew God, they glorified him not as God,* &c.; or else it refers to ver. 18; and then it is a proof of their withholding the truth in unrighteousness, *because*, &c. *They knew God;* they had a natural knowledge of God, it was taught them, as before, by the light of nature, and by the book of the creatures. Though this was not sufficient to save them, yet it was sufficient to leave them without excuse. *They glorified him not as God;* they did not conceive of him and worship him as became his Divine excellencies and perfections; see Psal. xxix. 2. *Neither were thankful;* they did not own God to be the Author and Giver of all the good things they enjoyed, and return him thanks accordingly; but referred all to chance and fortune, their own prudence and providence, the influence of the stars, &c. *But became vain in their imaginations,* or reasonings. This hath chief respect to the conception and opinions that the heathen framed to themselves of the Divine Being. For though some denied there was a God, and others doubted thereof, yet generally it was acknowledged by them; yea, some owned a multiplicity of gods, and those either corporeal or incorporeal. Others acknowledged but one God, as Plato, Aristotle, &c.; but then they either denied his providence, as the Peripatetics, or tied him to second or inferior causes, as the Stoics. This is the vanity which the apostle here speaketh of. Note also, that idols, the frame of idle brains, are called *vanities*: see Deut. xxxii. 21; Jer. x. 15; Acts xiv. 15. *And their foolish heart was darkened*: by the *heart* is meant the mind, their very understandings were darkened, the natural reason in them was obscured. This was a just judgment upon them for their abuse of knowledge, and pride, of which in the next verse.

o Jer. 10. 14.   **22** °Professing themselves to be wise, they became fools,

Some think, that all along this context the apostle hath reference to the Gnostics, a sort of heretics in the first age, (of which see Dr. Hammond *in locum*,) and that the meaning of the words is this, That they, assuming the title of Gnostics, of knowing men, and of men wiser than others, have proved more sottish than any. Others think the words refer to the heathen philosophers, who though they were learned and wise in secular and natural things, yet they became fools in spiritual and heavenly matters; though they well understood the creature, yet they erred concerning the Creator. And as fools delight in toys, neglecting things of great value; so they set up puppets and idols of their own devising, in the room of the true God; which the apostle gives us in the next verse, as a demonstration of their folly. Socrates, who was accounted one of the wisest amongst them, desired his friends, when he was about to die, to offer for him a cock to Æsculapius, which he had vowed.

p Deut. 4. 16, &c.
Ps. 106. 20.
Is. 40. 18, 26.
Jer. 2. 11.
Ezek. 8. 10.
Acts 17. 29.   **23** And changed the glory of the uncorruptible ᵖGod into an image made like to corruptible man, and to birds, and fourfooted beasts, and creeping things.

Changed the glory of the uncorruptible God; you have the same phrase, Psal. cvi. 20; Jer. ii. 11; and from thence it is borrowed. *Into an image made like to corruptible man, &c.*: the apostle proceedeth from the more worthy to the less worthy creatures, that the grossness of their idolatry might the better appear; and these four are put for all other kinds. This gross idolatry of the heathen in worshipping such images as are here spoken of, was practised by the Israelites; see Ezek. viii. 10, 11: and so it is by the Romanists to this day; nor doth it avail them to say, they do not worship images, but the true God in or before those images; for the same plea was made by the idolaters of old. Symmachus, in a learned oration, wherein he craved of the emperors Valentinian and Theodosius the restitution of the Roman gods, affirms, that they had respect only to one God; but they had divers ways to bring them to that God: they did not hold such things as they worshipped to be God, but in them they said they worshipped the true God. That worship which is intended to God by an image, is not the worship of God, but of the image. Compare Psal. cvi. 19, 20, with Exod. xxxii. 4, 5.

q Ps. 81. 12.
Wisd. 12. 23.
Acts 7. 42.
Eph. 4. 18,
19. 2 Thess.
2. 11, 12.
r 1 Cor. 6. 18.
1 Thess. 4. 4.
1 Pet. 4. 3.   s Lev. 18. 22.   **24** ᑫWherefore God also gave them up to uncleanness through the lusts of their own hearts, ʳto dishonour their own bodies ˢbetween themselves:

. Wherefore; their impiety was the cause of what followed: this is repeated again, that it may be the better observed. The contempt of God and of religion is the cause of all wickedness. *God also gave them up;* this phrase is thrice used in this context, viz. ver. 24, 26, 28: it seems to be taken out of Psal. lxxxi. 12. Some think his giving them up, is only his withdrawing his grace from them, and permitting them to sin; but there seems to be more in it than a bare subtraction or permission. He did not only leave them to themselves, but, in a judicial way, he put them into the hands of Satan, and of their own lusts; as it is said, Psal. lxix. 27, he added iniquity to their iniquity, making the latter iniquity a punishment of the former. *Between themselves;* some read it, in themselves, and some read it, one among another; so the same word is rendered, Eph. iv. 32; Col. iii. 13. The apostle here speaks more generally of all kinds of pollution and uncleanness that was committed by them, whether natural or unnatural.

25 Who changed ᵗthe truth of God ᵘinto a lie, and worshipped and served the creature ‖ more than the Creator, who is blessed for ever. Amen.   t 1 Thes. 1. 9.
1 John 5. 20.
u Is. 44. 20.
Jer. 10. 14.
& 13. 25.
Amos 2. 4.
‖ *Or, rather.*

Who changed the truth of God into a lie; i. e. the God of truth, or the true God, into an idol, which is a lie, which seems to be that which it is not: or else, by *the truth of God,* understand those true sentiments and notions that they had of God, and were taught them, as before, by the light of nature, and the book of the creatures; these they changed into lying imaginations and conceits. *And worshipped and served the creature more than the Creator;* or, besides the Creator: some understand it comparatively, they worshipped one more than the other; others exclusively, they worshipped one and not the other. They were guilty of two great errors; one was in their minds, they changed the truth of God into a lie; the other in their wills, they served the creature more than the Creator. *Who is blessed for ever. Amen:* when the Hebrews of old made mention of the true God, they were wont to add these words, Let him be blessed for ever.

26 For this cause God gave them up unto ˣvile affections: for even their women did change the natural use into that which is against nature: x Lev. 18. 22, 23.
Eph. 5. 12.
Jude 10.

For this cause; i. e. for their idolatry and uncleanness both, for now their idolatry is aggravated by the uncleanness accompanying it. *Vile affections;* Gr. affections of dishonour, i. e. the most dishonourable and shameful affections; for as we are exhorted, 1 Thess. iv. 4, 5, to possess our vessels in honour, that is, to withhold our body from uncleanness; so they that give up themselves to uncleanness, dishonour themselves and their own bodies; see 1 Cor. vi. 18: if they, as this scripture tells us, that commit fornication dishonour their own bodies; then much more do they that practise the unnatural uncleanness hereafter mentioned. *For even their women, &c.;* i. e. γυναῖκες ἀνδρίζονται, so Clem. Alexandr. *Ad præposteros et sodomiticos concubitus sese maribus prostituerunt.* See Paræus: a filthy practice not to be named, Eph. v. 3.

27 And likewise also the men, leaving the natural use of the woman, burned in their lust one toward another; men with men working that which is unseemly, and receiving in themselves that recompence of their error which was meet.

This was the sin of the Sodomites of old, for which they were destroyed, Gen. xix. 5: see Lev. xviii. 22. How meet was it that they who had forsaken the Author of nature, should be given up not to keep the order of nature; that they who had changed the glory of God into the similitude of beasts, should be left to do those things which beasts themselves abhorred! God only concurred as a just judge in punishing foregoing with following sins: see ver. 25.

28 ʸAnd even as they did not like ‖ to retain God in *their* knowledge, God gave them over to ‖ a reprobate mind, to do those things ᶻwhich are not convenient;   y Wisd. 14.
22, 23, &c.
‖ *Or, to acknowledge.*
‖ *Or, a mind void of judgment.*
z Eph. 5. 4.

To retain God in their knowledge; or, to have God in acknowledgment. The apostle proceeds to show the analogy betwixt their sin and their punishment. The evil he here taxed them with is much the same with that in ver. 21; though they had some knowledge of God, yet they did not acknowledge him as God, by glorifying him, and giving thanks to him; it did not seem good to them so to do. *God gave them over to a reprobate mind;* or, an injudicious mind, a mind void of judgment. It is just and equal, that he, who in his judgment disapproves of God, should be left either to be of a corrupt judgment, or of none at all. The word may be taken passively, for a mind disapproved of

God; or actively, for a mind which disapproves of all good. They were not given up to this reprobate mind all at once, but by degrees. First, they were given up to *their own hearts' lusts*, ver. 24; then, to *vile affections*, ver. 26; and then, lastly, to a mind void of judgment; to such an evil habit, that they could do nothing but evil.

29 Being filled with all unrighteousness, fornication, wickedness, covetousness, maliciousness; full of envy, murder, debate, deceit, malignity; whisperers,

Now follow the sins against the second table, which reigned amongst the Gentiles; amongst which *unrighteousness* is as the fountain, from whence the rest as streams do flow. This is the genus that comprehends all the evils hereafter enumerated. It is not to be supposed that all the following vices were found in every individual person; but the meaning is, that all were guilty of some, and some were guilty of all of them. *Fornication, wickedness;* in the Greek there is an elegant paronomasia, πορνεία, πονηρία. So there are two more in the following verses, φθόνε, φόνε, ἀσύνετοι, ἀσύνθετοι. The design of the apostle is, to set down a particular vice; therefore, instead of *wickedness*, some read troublesomeness, or a desire to procure trouble and molestation to another. The devil is called ὁ πονηρος, the troublesome one. *Maliciousness;* or, mischievousness, the better to distinguish it from envy. *Malignity;* or, morosity and churlishness, taking all things in the worser part. *Whisperers:* whisperers speak evil privily of others; backbiters, openly.

30 Backbiters, haters of God, despiteful, proud, boasters, inventors of evil things, disobedient to parents,

Haters of God; the original word hath a passive termination, and therefore some read it, hated of God. But words passive are sometimes actively taken: see 2 Pet. i. 3. And the apostle here intendeth a catalogue of the Gentiles' sins, whereof this was one: see Psal. lxxxi. 15. *Despiteful;* or, injurious. *Inventors of evil things;* they were not contented with old usual evils, but they invented new; whether we refer this to evils of pain, or evils of sin, we may find examples thereof amongst the heathen. Phalaris propounded a reward to him that could devise a new torment; and Sardanapalus offered rewards to such as could find out new venereal pleasures. *Disobedient to parents*, either natural or political.

31 Without understanding, covenant-breakers, ||without natural affection, implacable, unmerciful :

|| Or, *unsociable*.

Without understanding; or, without conscience; σύνεσις, or συνείδησις, being much the same. *Without natural affection;* this evil also reigned amongst the Gentiles, who sacrificed their very children to their idols, and otherwise exposed them to ruin: see 2 Tim. iii. 3. *Implacable;* or, irreconcilable and vindictive.

a ch. 2. 2.

32 Who ªknowing the judgment of God, that they which commit such things ᵇare worthy of death, not only do the same, but ||ᶜhave pleasure in them that do them.

b ch. 6. 21.
|| Or, *consent with them*.
c Hos. 7. 3.
Ps. 50. 18.

Knowing the judgment of God; i. e. his just law and statute, or his justice in punishing sin and sinners. This the Gentiles knew by the light of nature, and by the examples of God's justice in the world. *That they which commit such things are worthy of death;* the barbarians of Melita judged murder worthy of death, Acts xxviii. 4: see Acts xxiii. 29; xxvi. 31. The heathen also had some knowledge of future and everlasting punishment, as appears by their writings: and were persuaded that the sins beforementioned, and such-like, did really deserve it. *Have pleasure in them that do them;* or, patronize and applaud such; see Psal. x. 3. This is set last, as worst of all; it is the highest degree of wickedness: such come nearest the devil, who take pleasure in evil because it is evil.

CHAP. II

They that condemn sin in others, and are guilty of the like themselves, cannot escape God's judgment, 1—5; *which will be according to every man's deserts, without distinction of Jew or Gentile*, 6—13. *The Gentiles are not left without a rule of conduct*, 14—16. *The Jew, who boasteth of greater light, is doubly criminal in sinning against it*, 17—24; *nor will circumcision profit him, except he keep the law*, 25—29.

THEREFORE thou art ªinexcusable, O man, whosoever thou art that judgest : ᵇfor wherein thou judgest another, thou condemnest thyself; for thou that judgest doest the same things.

a ch. 1. 20.
b 2 Sam. 12. 5, 6, 7.
Matt. 7. 1, 2.
John 8. 9.

It is much disputed to whom the apostle directs his discourse in the beginning of this chapter. Some think that having discovered the sins of the Gentiles in the former chapter, he here useth a transition, and turneth himself to the Jews, and lays open their more secret wickedness and hypocrisy. But the particle *therefore* in the front of the chapter, doth seem to intimate, that this is inferred from what went before, and is a continuance of the same argument. It is of the Gentiles then that he is still discoursing, and he begins by name to deal with the Jews, ver. 17. Some think he speaks more particularly of such as were judges and magistrates amongst the Gentiles, who, though they made laws for to judge and punish others for such and such crimes, did yet commit the same themselves. Some think he intends more especially such as were philosophers, and men renowned for virtue, as Socrates, Aristides, Fabricius, Cato, Seneca, &c., which last, as is said, was well known to the apostle. These, in their speeches and writings, did censure the evil manners of others, and yet were as bad themselves. As Cato is said to have used extortion, prostituted his wife, and to have laid violent hands upon himself; and yet he was affirmed by Velleius to be *homo virtuti simillimus*, a most virtuous man. But the received opinion is, that the apostle in general doth tax all such as censure and find fault with others, and yet are guilty of the same things themselves. *Thou art inexcusable, O man, whosoever thou art that judgest:* q. d. Thou art without all excuse, that dost assent and subscribe to the righteous judgment of God, that they who do such things as are mentioned in the foregoing chapter, are worthy of death, and yet doest the same thyself; if not openly, yet secretly and inwardly thou art guilty of the same or as great sins. Thou canst make no apology or pretence, why the sentence of death and condemnation, which is due to others, should not likewise pass upon thee. *For wherein thou judgest another, thou condemnest thyself;* i. e. in that very thing, or by that very law, whereby thou censurest and condemnest others, thou pronouncest sentence against thyself; thy own mouth condemns thee in the person of another: see Matt. vii. 3; xxi. 40, 41, 45; John viii. 4, 9.

2 But we are sure that the judgment of God is according to truth against them which commit such things.

We know assuredly, and it is evident, both from Scripture and reason, that God's judgment, both here and hereafter, is true and upright; see 1 Sam. xvi. 7. He judgeth righteous judgment; he judgeth of persons and things, not as they are in appearance, but as they are in reality. *Against them which commit such things;* this indefinite manner of speaking includeth both those that judge others, and those who, for the aforementioned sins, are subject to the censures of others.

3 And thinkest thou this, O man, that judgest them which do such things, and doest the same, that thou shalt escape the judgment of God ?

When other men's facts escape not thy censure, who art but a man; what folly and madness is it to imagine, that thine own evil deeds should escape the judgment of God ! See 1 John iii. 20.

4 Or despisest thou ᶜthe riches of his goodness and ᵈforbearance and ᵉlong-

c ch. 9. 23.
Eph. 1. 7.
& 2. 4, 7.
d ch. 3. 25.
e Ex. 34. 6.

suffering; *not knowing that the goodness of God leadeth thee to repentance?*

f Is. 30. 18.
2 Pet. 3. 9, 15.

Here he taxeth such as thought God approved of their persons and courses, at least that he would not regard or punish their evil actions, because he had hitherto forborne them, and heaped up abundance of worldly blessings upon them, as he did upon the Romans especially, above other people. It is common for men to grow secure, and promise themselves impunity, when God forbears them, and gives them outward prosperity : see Psal. l. 21 ; lv. 19 ; Eccles. viii. 11 ; Hos. xii. 8. *Despisest thou?* the word signifies, to think amiss ; he despiseth the goodness of God, who thinks otherwise of it than he should, that it is extended to him for other ends than it is : or, to despise the goodness of God, is, to turn it into wantonness. *The riches of his goodness ;* i. e. The abundance of his goodness : see chap. ix. 23 ; Eph. i. 7, 18 ; ii. 4. 7 ; iii. 8. *Forbearance and long-suffering ;* God's long-suffering is a further degree of his forbearance : the Scripture speaks much of this attribute of God, and of his abounding therein, Exod. xxxiv. 6 ; Numb. xiv. 11, 18 ; Psal. lxxxvi. 15 ; Matt. xxiii. 37 ; Rom. ix. 22 ; 1 Tim. i. 16 ; 1 Pet. iii. 20. *The goodness of God leadeth thee to repentance ;* that is one great end of God's goodness and forbearance ; see Hos. xi. 4 ; 2 Pet. iii. 9. God's goodness is abused when it is not used and improved to this end.

5 But after thy hardness and impenitent heart [g] **treasurest up unto thyself wrath against the day of wrath and revelation of the righteous judgment of God ;**

g Deut. 32. 34. Jam. 5.3.

Treasurest up unto thyself wrath against the day of wrath ; this passage seems to respect Deut. xxxii. 34, 35, or Job xxxvi. 13. You have a parallel place, James v. 3. The meaning is, Thou provokest more and more the wrath of God against thee ; by heaping up sins, thou heapest up judgments of God upon thyself : just as men add to their treasure of wealth, so dost thou add to thy treasure of punishment. *Revelation of the righteous judgment of God ;* this is a periphrasis of the day of judgment, or of the last day : then will God visit for those sins that here escape punishment ; then the justice and equity of his proceedings shall appear, and all shall have reason to approve thereof.

6 [h] **Who will render to every man according to his deeds :**

h Job 34. 11.
Ps. 62.12.
Prov. 24. 12.
Jer. 17. 10.
& 32. 19, Matt. 16. 27. ch. 14. 12. 1 Cor. 3. 8. 2 Cor. 5. 10. Rev. 2, 23. & 20. 12. & 22. 12.

This proves what he had said, that the judgment of God, in that day, will be according to righteousness, or most *righteous judgment.* Parallel places you will find, Psal. lxii. 12 ; Matt. xvi. 27 ; 2 Cor. v. 10 ; Rev. xxii. 12. The papists from hence infer the merit of works ; but the reward to the godly is a reward of grace, and not of debt. The word ἀποδοῦναι imports not only a just retribution, but a free gift, as in Matt. xx. 8, and elsewhere. Good works are the rule of his proceeding, not the cause of his retribution : see Luke xvii. 10.

7 To them who by patient continuance in well doing seek for glory and honour and immortality, eternal life :

What he had laid down in general, he amplifies more particularly. *Patient continuance ;* or perseverance *in well-doing,* which implies patience : see Matt. x. 22 ; xxiv. 13 ; Heb. x. 36. *Immortality ;* or incorruption : he adds this to show, that the *glory and honour* he speaks of was not such as the Gentiles usually sought, who made worldly glory the scope of their actions ; but it was eternal in the heavens, and such as never fades away. *Eternal life ;* i. e. God will render eternal life to such : the word *render* must be supplied out of the former verse.

8 But unto them that are contentious, i **and** l **do not obey the truth, but obey unrighteousness, indignation and wrath,**

i Job 24. 13.
ch. 1. 18.
2 Thes. 1. 8.

That are contentious ; or, that are of contention : so, *they of the circumcision,* for such as are circumcised, Acts x. 45 ; Gal. ii. 12. By *contentious,* understand such as are refractory and self-willed ; that, from a spirit of contradiction, will not be persuaded ; that strive and kick against the righteousness of God, from an opinion of their own righteousness, Hos. iv. 4. *Do not obey the truth :* see chap. i. 18, and the note there. *But obey unrighteousness ;* that are the servants of sin, and of corruption, chap. vi. 12 ; 2 Pet. ii. 19. *Indignation and wrath ;* these two differ only in degree : thereby understand the judgments of God upon the wicked, which are the effects of his anger : the cause is commonly put for the effect.

9 Tribulation and anguish, upon every soul of man that doeth evil, of the Jew [k] **first, and also of the † Gentile ;**

k Amos 3. 2.
Luke 12. 47,
48. 1 Pet. 4. 17.
† Gr. Greek.

Tribulation and anguish ; the word *render* is here again understood, he shall render tribulation and anguish. Some refer the former to the punishment of sin, the latter to the punishment of loss ; or the one to the unquenchable fire, the other to the never-dying worm : it seems to be a rhetorical exaggeration : see Psal. xi. 6 ; Mark ix. 43—48. *Every soul of man ;* a double Hebraism : first, the soul is put for the person, as Gen. xii. 5 ; xiv. 21 ; xvii. 14 ; xxxvi. 6 ; xlvi. 26. Secondly, *every soul of man,* is put for the soul of every man ; as before, chap. i. 18, *all unrighteousness of men,* is put for the unrighteousness of all men. The soul of man shall not be punished only, but chiefly. *Of the Jew first, and also of the Gentile ;* the Jew is first placed in order of punishment, because he better knew God's will, and had more helps : see Matt. xi. 22, 24 ; Luke xii. 47.

10 [l] **But glory, honour, and peace, to every man that worketh good, to the Jew first, and also to the † Gentile :**

l 1 Pet. 1. 7.
† Gr. Greek.

Peace ; what he called immortality, ver. 7, he now calls *peace ;* which word, according to the usual acceptation of it amongst the Hebrews, is comprehensive of all good and happiness, both here and hereafter. *To the Jew first, and also to the Gentile ;* as the ungodly and unbelieving Jews shall have the first place in punishment, so those that believe and are godly amongst them shall have the first place in reward, though yet, for the reason mentioned in the next verse, the godly and believing Gentiles shall share with them therein.

11 For [m] **there is no respect of persons with God.**

m Deut. 10. 17. 2 Chron. 19. 7. Job 34. 19. Acts 10. 34. Gal. 2. 6. Eph. 6. 9. Col. 3. 25. 1 Pet. i. 17.

This seems to be borrowed from 2 Chron. xix. 7, and Deut. x. 17. You have the same again, Acts x. 34 ; see Job xxxiv. 19 ; Gal. ii. 6 ; iii. 28 ; Eph. vi. 9 ; 1 Pet. i. 17. *Obj.* God loved Jacob, and hated Esau, when they were yet unborn, and had done neither good nor evil. *Answ.* This was not properly a respecting of persons, because God did not this as a judge, but as an elector : so the apostle states it, Rom. ix. 11—13. God is gracious to whom he will be gracious, and may do what he will with his own.

12 For as many as have sinned without law shall also perish without law : and as many as have sinned in the law shall be judged by the law ;

By the former he means the Gentiles, by the latter, the Jews ; the like distribution he makes, 1 Cor. ix. 20, 21. *In the law ;* i. e. under the law, or against it.

13 (For [n] **not the hearers of the law *are* just before God, but the doers of the law shall be justified.**

n Mat. 7. 21.
Jam. 1. 22, 23, 25.
1 John 3. 7.

This and the two following verses are included in a parenthesis, and they serve to obviate an objection against what was said, ver. 12. The Jews might plead, that they were superior to the Gentiles, and should be exempted or privileged in judgment, forasmuch as they knew and professed the law of God, which the Gentiles did not. To this he says, that to know and learn the law was not sufficient, unless in all things they yielded obedience to it, which they neither did nor could. The scope of the apostle is not simply to show how sinners are now justified in the sight of God ; but to show what is requisite to justification according to the tenor of the law, and that is, to do all that is written therein, and to continue so to do. And if there be any man that can bring such perfect and constant obedience of his own performing, he shall be justified by God ; but inasmuch as no man, neither natural nor regenerate, can so fulfil the law, he must seek for justification in some other way. The text, thus expounded, doth no way militate with chap. iii. 30, and Gal. iii. 11, which at first reading it seems to do. And it further shows, that the Jews are comprehended under the general curse, as well as the Gentiles, and are bound to have recourse to the righteousness of God by faith.

14 For when the Gentiles, which have not the law, do by nature the things contained in the law, these, having not the law, are a law unto themselves:

Here he preoccupates the Gentiles' plea. They might object, that having not the law, they could not transgress, nor be culpable in judgment: see chap. iv. 15. To this he says, that though they had not the law written in tables of stone, as the Jews had, yet they had a law written in their hearts, which was a copy or counterpart of the other, and had in a manner the effects of it; for thereby they were instructed to do well, and debarred from doing evil, which are the two properties of all laws. *Do by nature;* nature is opposed to Scripture and special revelation: by the direction of the law, and light of nature, they did many things which the law of Moses commanded, and forbore many things which it forbade. *Are a law unto themselves;* i. e. they have in themselves such principles of reason and rules of equity, as are to them instead of a law, prescribing what they ought to do and avoid.

15 Which shew the work of the law written in their hearts, ‖ their conscience also bearing witness, and *their* thoughts ‖ the mean while accusing or else excusing one another;)

‖ Or, *the conscience witnessing with them.*
‖ Or, *between themselves.*

By *the work of the law,* either understand the sum of the law, which is, To love God above all, and our neighbour as ourselves; or the office of the law, which consists in directing what to do, and what to leave undone; or the external actions which the law prescribes. *Written in their hearts;* this seems to be a covenant promise and privilege, Jer. xxxi. 33; how then is it predicated of the Gentiles? Answ. Jeremiah speaks there of a special and supernatural inscription or writing in the heart by grace; and the apostle here, of that which is common and natural. *Their thoughts the mean while accusing or else excusing one another;* interchangeably, now one way, anon another. Not as though the thoughts did, at the same time, strive together about the same fact; nor is it meant of divers men, as if good men were excused, and bad men accused, by their own thoughts; but in the same persons there were accusing or excusing thoughts and consciences, as their actions were evil or good.

16 [o] In the day when God shall judge the secrets of men [p] by Jesus Christ [q] according to my Gospel.

o Eccles. 12. 14. Mat. 25. 31. John 12. 48. ch. 3. 6. 1 Cor. 4. 5. Rev. 20. 12.
p John 5. 22. Acts 10. 42. & 17. 31. 2 Tim. 4. 1, 8. 1 Pet. 4. 5. q ch. 16. 25. 1 Tim. 1. 11. 2 Tim. 2. 8.

These words may be referred to the 12th verse, and so they express the time when Jews and Gentiles shall be judged. Though some annex them to the words immediately preceding: q. d. Now the consciences of men do testify for or against them, and their thoughts accuse or excuse them; but in the day of judgment they will do it more especially. *Shall judge the secrets of men;* so that the most secret sins shall not escape the notice and censure of the Judge: see Eccles. xii. 14; 1 Cor. iv. 5. *My gospel;* i. e. the gospel which I preach. So, John xii. 48, our Saviour calls his word, his disciples' word. He calls it his gospel, not as the author, but as the publisher of it; it was not his in respect of revelation, but in regard of dispensation, chap. xvi. 25; 1 Cor. ix. 17; 2 Cor. v. 18, 19; 2 Tim. ii. 8. As for the fiction of a Gospel written by Paul, as was by Matthew, Mark, &c., the papists themselves begin to be ashamed of it.

17 Behold, [r] thou art called a Jew, and [s] restest in the law, [t] and makest thy boast of God,

r Matt. 3. 9. John 8. 33.
ch. 9. 6, 7. 2 Cor. 11. 22.
s Mic. 3. 11. ch. 9. 4.
t Is. 45. 25. & 48. 2. John 8. 41.

He now comes to deal more particularly and expressly with the Jews, reciting their privileges, in which they trusted, and of which they boasted; and shows, that notwithstanding them, they stood in as much need of the righteousness of God as the Gentiles did. *Thou;* he speaks in the singular number, that every one might make the readier application of what he said. *Art called a Jew;* so called from Judah; as of old, Hebrews from Heber, and Israelites from Israel: the title was honourable in those days, and imported a confessor or worshipper of one God. Thou art so called, but art not so indeed: see ver. 28, and Rev. ii. 9. *Restest in the law;* puttest thy trust in it. *Makest thy boast of God;* that he is thy God, and in covenant with thee; and that thou hast a peculiar interest in him: see John viii. 41. The phrase seems to be borrowed from Isa. xlv. 25.

18 And [u] knowest *his* will, and ‖ [x] approvest the things that are more excellent, being instructed out of the law;

u Deut. 4. 8. Ps. 147. 19, 20.
‖ Or, *triest the things that differ.*
x Phil. 1. 10.

19 And [y] art confident that thou thyself art a guide of the blind, a light of them which are in darkness,

y Matt. 15. 14. & 23. 16, 17, 19, 24. John 9. 34, 40, 41.

Art confident; thou dost proudly arrogate all that follows to thyself, and conceitest that thou hast all the points of the law in thy breast, and full knowledge of all the secrets thereof.

20 An instructor of the foolish, a teacher of babes, [z] which hast the form of knowledge and of the truth in the law.

z ch. 6. 17. 2 Tim. 1. 13. & 3. 5.

Babes; such as have little or no knowledge. *The form of knowledge;* a scheme or system of notions, a compendious model or method, which is artificially composed; such as tutors and professors of arts and sciences, do read over again and again to their pupils and auditors.

21 [a] Thou therefore which teachest another, teachest thou not thyself? thou that preachest a man should not steal, dost thou steal?

a Ps. 50. 16, &c. Matt. 23. 3, &c.

Teachest thou not thyself? q. d. Dost not thou thyself do what thou pressest upon others? see Matt. xxiii. 3. *Dost thou steal?* the Jews were infamous of old for this sin, Psal. l. 18; Matt. xxiii. 14.

22 Thou that sayest a man should not commit adultery, dost thou commit adultery? thou that abhorrest idols, [b] dost thou commit sacrilege?

b Mal. 3. 8.

Dost thou commit adultery? to this sin also the Jews were greatly addicted: see Psal. l. 18; Jer. v. 8. *Dost thou commit sacrilege?* here he varies the crime; he does not say, Dost thou commit idolatry, but sacrilege. The Jews, after their return out of captivity, kept themselves free from idolatry; but it seems they were guilty of a sin that was near akin to it. Here it may be questioned, what the sacrilege was that the Jews were guilty of. Some think, their covetousness is here taxed, which is a kind of idolatry. The Jews took those things which were consecrated to idols, and which, by the law of God, should have been destroyed, and turned them to their private advantage. Others think, that their sacrilege consisted in withholding from God that which they should have consecrated and offered up to him; see 1 Sam. ii. 13; Mal. iii. 8, 9: they converted to their own use such things as were dedicated to God. Much to the same purpose is their opinion, that think it consisted in robbing God of his due. By the imperial law in the code, it is declared sacrilege to take from the emperor any thing that is his; it ought to be much more accounted sacrilege to deal so with God. Some think their sacrilege lay in polluting the worship of God, and making his commands of no effect, through their corrupt additions and traditions.

23 Thou that [c] makest thy boast of the law, through breaking the law dishonourest thou God?

c ver. 17.

Dost thou bring a reproach upon religion, and give occasion to the Gentiles to blaspheme his name? so it follows, in the next words.

24 For the name of God is blasphemed among the Gentiles through you, as it is written.

Through you; because of your and your forefathers' sins. *As it is written:* the apostle doth not tell them where it was written; he supposeth they were not ignorant of it: see Isa. lii. 5; Ezek. xxxvi. 20, 23.

25 For circumcision verily profiteth, if thou keep the law: but if thou be a breaker of the law, thy circumcision is made uncircumcision.

The Jews might object, If the former privileges availed not to righteousness and salvation, yet circumcision at least might stand them in some stead. In answer whereunto you have, 1. A concession; circumcision indeed is profitable. 2. A limitation; *if thou keep the law;* which is illustrated by a large antithesis, ver. 26, 27. 3. A distinction; circumcision is of two sorts, outward and literal, inward and spiritual; the latter stands in force, and hath acceptation with God, ver. 28, 29. *If thou keep the law;* if thou keep it perfectly, to which circumcision obligeth, Gal. v. 3; or if thou use thy utmost care and endeavour so to do. *But if thou be a breaker of the law, thy circumcision is made uncircumcision;* i. e. if otherwise thou transgress the law, thy circumcision avails thee nothing, it gives thee no privilege above the uncircumcised. A wicked Jew is to God as an Ethiopian, Amos ix. 7. The apostle corrects the carnal confidence and hypocrisy of the Jews, who valued themselves upon the account of this outward ceremony, and thought it sufficient to be circumcised in the flesh. Some think the apostle hath respect in these words to the time of the law, whilst circumcision was an ordinary sacrament of the covenant; then indeed it was profitable and available; but now, in the times of the gospel, it is abrogated: see Gal. v. 2, 6.

26 Therefore if the uncircumcision keep the righteousness of the law, shall not his uncircumcision be counted for circumcision?

The uncircumcision; i. e. the uncircumcised; a figurative and frequent way of speaking: see chap. iii. 30; iv. 9. *Keep the righteousness of the law;* which none of them ever did; but admit they could, or else, which some of them have done, in sincerity, though with manifold imperfections; such as the two centurions, one of which is mentioned in the Gospel of Luke, the other in the Acts: if in this sense the uncircumcised keep the righteousness of the law, shall they not be all one in the account of God as if they were circumcised? See Rom. iv. 10.

27 And shall not uncircumcision which is by nature, if it fulfil the law, judge thee, who by the letter and circumcision dost transgress the law?

Uncircumcision which is by nature; a periphrasis of the Gentiles, who want circumcision, or are by nature without it. *Fulfil the law;* here is another word; before it was *keep,* but now it is *fulfil the law:* though the word be varied, yet the sense is the same: see James ii. 8. *Judge thee;* i. e. rise up in judgment against thee; or else, shall he not do it by his example? as in Matt. xii. 41, 42, the men of Nineveh, and the queen of Sheba, shall judge the Israelites. The meaning is, the obedient Gentile shall condemn the disobedient Jew. *By the letter and circumcision dost transgress the law;* i. e. the outward literal circumcision; or, by the *letter* understand the law; see 2 Cor. iii. 6. The sense is, by means of the law and circumcision, and resting in them, as pledges of the love of God, (so ver. 17,) they are the more secure and bold in sinning against God; it is to them an occasion of transgression.

28 For he is not a Jew, which is one outwardly; neither *is that* circumcision, which is outward in the flesh:

He is not a Jew; a right or true Jew, who is heir of the promises made to the fathers. *That is one outwardly;* the word *only* is to be understood: see 1 Cor. i. 17. *Neither is that circumcision;* the right and true circumcision, which God principally requires, and is available unto salvation: that circumcision is not much to be accounted of which is only the cutting off an outward skin.

29 But he *is* a Jew, which is one inwardly; and circumcision *is that* of the heart, in the spirit, *and* not in the letter; whose praise *is* not of men, but of God.

He is a right and true Jew, an Israelite indeed, that hath taken away the foreskin of his heart, Jer. iv. 4; that is cleansed from all corrupt affections, and hath laid aside all superfluity of naughtiness; that worshippeth God in the Spirit, rejoiceth in Christ Jesus, and hath no confidence in the flesh. Such are the circumcision and Jews indeed: see Phil. iii. 3.

CHAP. III

The Jew's prerogative, 1, 2; *which is not vacated by the unbelief of some,* 3, 4; *nor is God's justice impeached in punishing their sinfulness,* 5—8. *The law itself convinceth the Jews also universally of sin,* 9—19; *so that no flesh is justified by the deeds of the law,* 20; *but all indiscriminately by God's grace through faith in Christ,* 21—30: *yet without annulling the obligations of the law,* 31.

WHAT advantage then hath the Jew? or what profit *is there* of circumcision?

What advantage then hath the Jew? an elegant prolepsis or anticipation of what might be objected against the apostle's assertion in the foregoing words. If the Jews (might some object) lie equally exposed to condemnation with the Gentiles, then they have no excellency above them. Or thus, If external things do not commend us to God, (as it is affirmed, chap. ii. 28, 29,) but the Gentiles are brought into the church without them, then the Jews have no prerogative above the Gentiles, though God hath owned them so long for his peculiar people. *What profit is there of circumcision?* i. e. what is the use of it, or for what end was it instituted, seeing the uncircumcised are brought in and accepted, as being circumcised notwithstanding, and lean in heart?

2 Much every way: chiefly, because that unto them were committed the oracles of God.

He answers the before-mentioned objection by a liberal and free concession. The answer doth particularly relate to the first member of the objection, though comprehending the other. *Chiefly;* this word is not to be referred to the order of speech, as chap. i. 8, for he doth not begin any discourse here; nor to the number of privileges and advantages, for he names but one in all; but to the quality, and so the excellency, of this privilege here spoken of; q. d. It is the chief of all. *Unto them were committed the oracles of God:* profane writers make this word to signify the answer that was given by the demons, or heathen gods; and yet the Holy Ghost doth not disdain to make use of this word, (as well as divers others,) though abused to heathenish superstition. The sense is, To the Jews were credited, or given in custody, the Holy Scriptures, containing all the books of the Old Testament, in particular the legal covenant, or law of God, given on Mount Sinai, which Stephen calls the *lively oracles,* Acts vii. 38; more especially yet the fundamental articles of religion, and doctrines of grace, and salvation by the Messias, called *the oracles of God,* Heb. v. 12, though more hid, it is true, in types, promises, and predictions.

3 For what if some did not believe? shall their unbelief make the faith of God without effect?

If some did not believe; if some did remain in infidelity, Acts xxviii. 24, if they would give no credit to the oracle, and to the promise of a Messiah. *The faith of God;* i. e. the truth and faithfulness of God, Psal. xxxiii. 4. The whole verse is another prolepsis. The implied objection is this, That the Jews are nothing the better for these oracles, or have no advantage by them, if by unbelief they have rendered themselves unworthy or incapable of benefit by them. The answer to this is anticipated by propounding another question; Can the infidelity of some be any hinderance of God's performing his promise to others, to his chosen ones? The interrogation is a negation, q. d. It cannot be, as the following words show: see 2 Tim. ii. 13.

^{d Job 40. 8.}
^{e John 3. 33.}
^{f Ps. 62. 9.}
^{& 116. 11.}
^{g Ps. 51. 4.}

4 ^dGod forbid: yea, let ^eGod be true, but ^fevery man a liar; as it is written, ^gThat thou mightest be justified in thy sayings, and mightest overcome when thou art judged.

God forbid; the negation that was closely couched in the former verse, is in this expressed by a note of indignation, and of the greatest detestation. *Let God be true;* let him remain or appear faithful to his promises and covenant; or, let him be acknowledged to be so, according to the frequent testimonies of Scripture: see Numb. xxiii. 19; Tit. i. 2; Heb. vi. 17, 18. *But every man a liar;* or, although every man should be a liar; or, whatsoever we say of men, who are all mutable creatures, who are liable to mistakes in their own natures, and so may easily deceive others: see Psal. cxvi. 11. *That thou mightest be justified in thy sayings;* that thou mightest be acknowledged just in thy promises and threatenings; in which sense the word is used in divers places, Matt. xi. 19; Luke vii. 29, 35; x. 29. *Mightest overcome;* that thou mightest be clear or pure, so it is in the Psalm. The apostle honours the Seventy, which was the common translation, and minds the sense rather than the words. He that is clear, is like to overcome in a just judgment. *When thou art judged;* or, when thou judgest: the word may be taken actively or passively; i. e. when thou dost execute judgment upon any, or, when any do presume to censure you.

5 But if our unrighteousness commend the righteousness of God, what shall we say? *Is* God unrighteous who taketh vengeance? (^hI speak as a man)

^{h ch. 6. 19.}
^{Gal. 3. 15.}

But if our unrighteousness commend the righteousness of God; an anticipation of another objection, which might be made upon the preceding words: that if the faithfulness of God, in keeping his promises, doth appear in and notwithstanding the unfaithfulness of men, then we gather thus much, that the fidelity of God is rendered a great deal more commendable by the perfidiousness of man. *What shall we say?* thus we object, or this will be the inconvenience. *Is God unrighteous who taketh vengeance?* i. e. then God is unjust in punishing the Jews, or any other wicked men, for that which tends to his own glory, and the commendations of his veracity. *I speak as a man;* this is the language of carnal men, and such blasphemy they speak; I recite the objection of some men, and speak after their carnal manner.

^{i Gen. 18. 25.}
^{Job 8. 3. &}
^{34. 17.}

6 God forbid: for then ⁱhow shall God judge the world?

God forbid; he rejects the cavil with his usual note of detestation, as not thinking it worthy of answer. *For then how shall God judge the world?* q. d. If God were in the least unrighteous, how could he govern the world at present, and judge it at last in righteousness? which is affirmed, Psal. xcvi. 13; xcviii. 9. Or, how could he be God and supreme, if he were not just by his nature and essence, and his will the very rule of righteousness: see Gen. xviii. 25; Job xxxiv. 12.

7 For if the truth of God hath more abounded through my lie unto his glory; why yet am I also judged as a sinner?

By *truth* he means the faithfulness and veracity of God; as by *lie*, the perfidiousness and inconstancy of man; *ut supra et alibi. Why yet am I also judged as a sinner?* q. d. If more glory accrues to the name of God by my wickedness, what reason is there that I should be punished, and proceeded against as an offender, who have occasioned this further glory to God? The apostle doth plainly personate in this place a wicked objector, or he speaks in the name and person of such a one. This way of speaking and writing is very frequent among all authors; and it is found sometimes with the penmen of the Holy Scriptures: see Eccles. iii. 19—22; 1 Cor. xv. 32. The apostle tells the Corinthians, 1 Cor. iv. 6, that in a figure he transferred some things to himself and to Apollos for their sakes, that they might not be puffed up; he counted such schemes and figures as these to be most profitable and efficacious to the reader.

8 And not *rather*, (as we be slanderously reported, and as some affirm that we say,) ^kLet us do evil, that good may come? whose damnation is just.

^{k ch. 5. 20.}
^{& 6. 1, 15.}

The placing of these words makes them sound harshly, and consequently causeth obscurity. Critics make a great stir about them, some including them in a parenthesis, others affirming there is a transposition in them. They seem to be a refutation to the former cavil, and must be accommodated to that sense. It is as if the apostle should have said, If sinners deserve no punishment, because God reaps glory to himself by their sins; then that is a good proverb, or saying, which is in some men's mouths, and we ourselves are slandered with it, as if it were our opinion and doctrine, That we may do evil, that good may come of it. But this saying is generally exploded; none dare to vouch it, and therefore the former cavil is of no force. *Whose damnation is just;* i. e. their damnation is just, who teach such doctrine, and practise accordingly; who *do evil, that good may come of it.* The apostle doth not vouchsafe to refute this absurd saying, but simply condemns it, and those that put it in practice. Or else his meaning in these words is this, that they justly deserve damnation, who calumniate the apostles and publishers of the gospel, and raise false reports and slanders of them: their damnation is just, who affirm we say or hold, That evil may be done, that good may come thereof.

9 What then? are we better *than they?* No, in no wise: for we have before †proved both Jews and Gentiles, that ^lthey are all under sin;

^{† Gr. charged.}
^{ch. 1, 28, &c.}
^{& 2. 1, &c.}
^{l ver. 23.}
^{Gal. 3. 22.}

What then? are we better than they? the apostle here returns to the argument that he had been handling in the beginning of the chapter. He brings in the Jews propounding a question. Seeing it was confessed that the oracles of God were committed to them, then it followed, that they excelled the Gentiles, and stood upon better ground than they. *No, in no wise;* he doth not contradict himself as to what he had said of the Jews' prerogative, ver. 2. They did indeed excel the Gentiles as to some external benefits, of which you have a larger account, chap. ix. 4, 5, but not upon the account of any evangelical righteousness, or their own supposed merit. *We have before proved;* viz. separately and apart, in the foregoing chapters; and the same is now to be asserted of *both Jews and Gentiles*, conjunctly and together; that notwithstanding the Jews boasted of their law, and the Gentiles of their philosophy, yet as to the evangelical faith and righteousness, they were both in the same case. *Under sin;* under the power of sin, but chiefly under the guilt of sin: see ver. 19.

10 As it is written, ^mThere is none righteous, no, not one:

^{m Ps. 14. 1,}
^{2, 3. & 53. 1.}

As it is written; viz. in several places of Scripture, which he quotes in the following verses, giving us the sense, though not so strictly tying himself to the words; and this is a proper proof, to the Jews at least, whom he had called a little before the keepers of these oracles. *There is none righteous, no, not one:* the more general proof with which he begins, is taken out of Psal. xiv. 11, and liii. 1, upon which places see the annotations.

11 There is none that understandeth, there is none that seeketh after God.

There is none that understandeth; a more particular proof of the corruption of the soul, and the faculties thereof; and first of the mind, taken out of the forecited Psalms, which may be compared with the scriptures which speak of the ignorance and blindness of the mind, Deut. xxxii. 29; Job xxxii. 9; Isa. i. 3; Jer. iv. 22; x. 14. *There is none that seeketh after God;* a proof of the corruption of the will, which follows also in the forecited Psalms.

12 They are all gone out of the way, they are

together become unprofitable; there is none that doeth good, no, not one.

They are all gone out of the way; viz. of truth, or life: see Psal. xiv. 3; xxxvi. 4; lviii. 3. This doth illustrate the former charge. *They are together become unprofitable;* unuseful, and, which is more noisome, fit only for the dunghill, as the word signifies: this follows also in Psal. xiv.: see Job xv. 16. *There is none that doeth good, no, not one;* the same as ver. 10, though more exactly according to the words of the Psalm, where also it is twice repeated: see Psal. xiv. 1, 3.

n Ps. 5. 9.
Jer. 5. 16.
13 ⁿTheir throat *is* an open sepulchre; with their tongues they have used deceit;

o Ps. 140. 3.
°the poison of asps *is* under their lips:

Their throat is an open sepulchre; he proceeds to instance in the corruption of man with respect to the members of his body; and he mentions the organs of speech in four several expressions, much to the same purpose: the first is allegorical, taken out of Psal. v. 9, upon which see the annotations. *With their tongues they have used deceit;* this text doth plainly express the corruption of the tongue, because of lies, calumnies, perjuries, flatteries; and it is taken out of Jer. ix. 3—5. *The poison of asps is under their lips:* the third expression is allegorical, as the first, taken out of Psal. cxl. 3, upon which see the annotations.

p Ps. 10. 7.
14 ᵖWhose mouth *is* full of cursing and bitterness:

This last and very plain expression of the corruption of the tongue, is taken out of Psal. x. 7: see notes there.

q Prov. 1.16.
Is. 59. 7, 8.
15 ᑫTheir feet *are* swift to shed blood:

If we consider this member also, we may see the corruption of man; witness that testimony, Prov. i. 16, and Isa. lix. 7; on both which see annotations.

16 Destruction and misery *are* in their ways:

17 And the way of peace have they not known:

Both which assertions lie together, and follow in that Isa. lix. 7, 8.

r Ps. 36. 1.
18 ʳThere is no fear of God before their eyes.

This last assertion gives us one true cause of all the aforesaid evils, taken out of Psal. xxxvi. 1: see notes there.

s John 10.34.
& 15. 25.
t Job 5. 16.
Ps. 107. 42.
Ezek. 16. 63.
ch. 1. 20.
& 2. 1.
u ver. 9, 23.
ch. 2. 2.
‖ Or, *subject to the judgment of God.*

19 Now we know that what things soever ˢthe law saith, it saith to them who are under the law: that ᵗevery mouth may be stopped, and ᵘall the world may become ‖ guilty before God.

Another anticipation of an objection, to this purpose: All these testimonies (might the Jews say) do not concern us, they concern the impure and Gentile world only, unless possibly some profane wretches amongst ourselves also. But to this the apostle says, We know (which some think hath the force of an asseveration) that whatsoever the law of God, more especially the Mosaical law, or more generally all that is contained in the Scripture, saith of the wickedness and defection of mankind, it saith to the Jews more particularly, to whom the law was given, and who are under the conduct of it; much the same with that phrase, chap. ii. 12: see chap. vi. 15; 1 Cor. ix. 20. *That every mouth may be stopped;* i. e. hindered from boasting, to which the Jews were so prone; or rather, that conscience might so press them, that they should silently, or as it were speechless, expect their own damnation, without being able to frame any excuse: see Psal. lxiii. 11; Ezek. xvi. 63; Matt. xxii. 12. *And all the world may become guilty before God;* that Jews and Gentiles, and all mankind, as depraved, might be obnoxious to the judgment and condemnation of God: see ver. 9, and John iii. 18.

x Ps. 143. 2.
Acts 13. 39.
Gal. 2. 16.
& 3. 11.
Eph. 2. 8, 9.
Tit. 3. 5.
y ch. 7. 7.
20 Therefore ˣby the deeds of the law there shall no flesh be justified in his sight: for ʸby the law *is* the knowledge of sin.

Therefore; i. e. Seeing the Gentiles, by the law of nature, and the Jews, by the written law, are thus subject to the judgment of God; and seeing no one is able to fulfil the law, and satisfy for the breach of it; *therefore, &c.* *By the deeds of the law;* he means the moral law, and not the ceremonial law only or chiefly; even that law that forbids theft and adultery, as chap. ii. and concupiscence, as chap. vii.; and by which, as this text says, *is the knowledge of sin;* to which Gentiles as well as Jews are obliged, and by which therefore they are condemned. *No flesh;* a common synecdoche: see Gen. vi. 3, 12, and elsewhere. The same with *no man living,* in the psalmist; especially being depraved with original corruption, which is called *flesh* in Scripture. *Be justified in his sight;* or be discharged in the court of heaven: the phrase is taken from Psal. cxliii. 2, see annotations there. *For by the law is the knowledge of sin:* lest any should think that the law hereupon is useless, he goes on to show its use, but a quite contrary one to what they intended. It convinceth us of our guilt, and therefore is far from being our righteousness, chap. vii. 7; 1 Cor. xv. 56.

z Acts 15.11.
ch. 1. 17.
Phil. 3. 9.
Heb. 11. 4.
&c.
a John 5. 46.
21 But now ᶻthe righteousness of God without the law is manifested, ᵃbeing witnessed by the Law ᵇand the Prophets;
Acts 26. 22. b ch. 1. 2. 1 Pet. 1. 10.

But now: q. d. Though justification be not by the law, yet it is to be obtained in another way, as follows. *The righteousness of God:* see chap. i. 17. *Without the law;* inasmuch as the law, pressing obedience to be performed by us in our own persons, seems plainly ignorant of the righteousness of another imputed to us. *Is manifested;* this righteousness nevertheless is revealed plainly, now since the coming of Christ, and in the gospel, as in chap. i. 17. *Being witnessed by the law and the prophets;* that there may be no suspicion of novelty: see John v. 46, 47. The testimonies he refers to are very numerous: see Gen. iii. 15; xv. 6; xxii. 17, 18; Isa. liii.; Jer. xxxi. 31, 33; Dan. ix. 24, 25. See the same argument used, Acts xxiv. 14; xxvi. 22; xxviii. 23.

22 Even the righteousness of God *which is* ᶜby faith of Jesus Christ unto all and upon all them that believe: for ᵈthere is no difference:

c ch. 4. throughout.
d ch. 10. 12.
Gal. 3. 28.
Col. 3. 11.

He mentions *the righteousness of God* again, that he may further explain it, by the means or instrument by which it is received, viz. *faith;* see chap. iv. 11, 12; ix. 30; Phil. iii. 9; where there are several expressions to the same purpose, that this righteousness is without the law indeed, but it is by the hand of that faith by which we believe in Jesus, called therefore here, the *faith of Jesus Christ.* *Unto all and upon all them that believe;* whether they be Jews or Gentiles, if they believe, excluding the self-justiciaries amongst the one, and the philosophers amongst the other. *For there is no difference;* they are not justified two several ways: see ver. 9.

23 For ᵉall have sinned, and come short of the glory of God;

e ver. 9.
ch. 11. 32.
Gal. 3. 22.

For all have sinned: q. d. No wonder there is no difference, when both the one and the other have the guilt of Adam's transgression imputed to them, and have original corruption inherent in them, from whence proceed very many actual transgressions. *And come short of the glory of God;* i. e. of the glorious image of God, in which man was at first created; or, of communion with God, in which the glory of a rational creature doth consist; or rather, of the eternal glory, which they come short of, as men that run a race are weary, and fall short of the mark.

24 Being justified freely ᶠby his grace ᵍthrough the redemption that is in Christ Jesus:

f ch. 4. 16.
Eph. 2. 8.
Tit. 3. 5, 7.
g Matt. 20. 28. Eph. 1. 7.
Col. 1. 14. 1 Tim. 2. 6. Heb. 9. 12. 1 Pet. 1. 18, 19.

Being justified freely by his grace; i. e. Being in this case, they can by no means be acquitted and freed from the accusation and condemnation of the law, but in the way and manner that follows. He mentions the great moving cause of justification first, (which doth comprehend also the principal efficient,) that it is without any cause or merit in us; and by the free favour of God to undeserving, ill-deserving creatures, Eph. i. 6, 7; ii. 8; Tit. iii. 7. *Through the redemption that is in Christ Jesus:* the meritorious cause is expressed by a metaphor taken from military proceedings, where captives taken in war, and under the power of another, are redeemed upon a valuable price laid down : see Matt. xx. 28 ; Mark x. 45 ; 1 Tim. ii. 6 ; Heb. ix. 12.

|| Or, *fore-ordained.*
h Lev. 16. 15.
1 John 2. 2. & 4. 10.
i Col. 1. 20.
k Acts 13. 38, 39.
1 Tim. 1. 15.
|| Or, *passing over.* 1 Acts 17. 30. Heb. 9. 15.

25 Whom God hath || set forth [h] *to be* a propitiation through faith [i] in his blood, to declare his righteousness [k] for the || remission of [l] sins that are past, through the forbearance of God ;

Whom God hath set forth ; i. e. God the Father hath proposed this *Jesus,* in the eternal counsel, and covenant of redemption, Eph. i. 9 ; 1 Pet. i. 20, 21 ; or in the types and shadows of the old tabernacle ; and hath now at last shown him openly to the world. *To be a propitiation,* or atonement, 1 John ii. 2. He alludes to the mercy-seat sprinkled with blood, which was typical of this great atonement; and from whence God showed himself so propitious and favourable to sinners, Lev. xvi. 2 ; Numb. vii. 89. *Through faith in his blood:* he goes on to show the instrumental cause of justification, to wit, *faith ;* i. e. the close adherence and most submissive dependence of the sinner; together with the peculiarity of the object of faith, viz. the *blood,* i. e. the death and sacrifice, of Christ ; in contra-distinction to his dominion, (with which yet on other accounts faith is so much concerned,) and in opposition to the blood of beasts slain and sacrificed. *To declare his righteousness;* i. e. for the showing forth either of his goodness and mercy; see 1 Sam. xii. 7, 8, 10 ; Psal. xxxvi. 10 ; or of his faithfulness in his promises, and fulfilling all types and prophecies; or else of his vindictive justice, in the just proceedings of God against sin, which he hath condemned in his Son, though he justify the sinner. Or further, it may be understood of the righteousness of faith, of which ver. 22, which is hereby shown to be his ; and to manifest itself in the forgiveness of sins, which is so declared as to be exhibited. *For the remission of sins that are past, through the forbearance of God ;* he means, either the sins committed before justification, while God bore so patiently with the sinner, and did not presently take the forfeiture ; or else the sins committed under the Old Testament, before the proposed propitiation was exposed to the world, when God so indulged our fathers, as to pardon them upon the account of what was to come : see Heb. ix. 15—18.

26 To declare, *I say,* at this time his righteousness : that he might be just, and the justifier of him which believeth in Jesus.

To declare, I say, at this time his righteousness ; he repeats the final cause of justification, viz. the making the aforesaid declaration of the righteousness of God, in the time of the gospel, and dispensation and ministry thereof, 2 Cor. vi. 2, which is taken out of Isa. xlix. 8. *That he might be just, and the justifier of him which believeth in Jesus ;* i. e. that no wrong might be done to the essential purity of his nature, or rectitude of his will ; nor yet to his immediate justice, by which he cannot but hate sin, and abhor the sinner as such ; though in the mean time he gives a discharge to him that is of the faith of Jesus, (as it is in the original,) or of the number of those that believe, and cast themselves upon a Saviour.

m ch. 2. 17, 23. & 4. 2.
1 Cor. 1. 29,
31. Ephes. 2. 9.

27 [m] Where *is* boasting then ? It is excluded. By what law ? of works ? Nay : but by the law of faith.

Where is boasting then? the apostle doth, as it were, insult over them : q. d. Where is now the former boasting of the Jews, as if they were so much better than the Gentiles ? or what is become of the ground of boasting, that they, or either of them, might think they had in the law, or philosophy, or any moral performances ? see Jer. ix. 23, 24. *It is excluded. By what law? of works?* if it be inquired upon what account this boasting is excluded, we answer plainly, It cannot be by that law that commands works, as the condition of acceptance and justification, and tells us nothing by whom that condition should be fulfilled ; the law being become weak to us, for such a purpose, by reason of sin, chap. viii. 3. *Nay : but by the law of faith ;* i. e. the gospel law which requires faith, by which the righteousness of Christ is imputed to us, and attained by us. And this is called a *law of faith,* as some think, in condescension to the Jews' custom of speaking, who are so much delighted with the name of the law ; and so that he might not be suspected of novelty : but, as most, it is a Hebraism, denoting no more than the doctrine or prescript of faith.

28 Therefore we conclude [n] that a man is justified by faith without the deeds of the law.

n Acts 13. 38, 39.
ver. 20, 21, 22. ch. 8. 3.
Gal. 2. 16.

Here is the conclusion of the whole matter that he had been discoursing of, from chap. i. 17 to this very place. When he says, *we conclude,* he means, we have reasoned or argued well, as logicians do ; or this is the full account that we have taken, and summed up, after the manner of arithmeticians. *A man is justified by faith without the deeds of the law;* a phrase equivalent to that which is so much spoken against, that we are justified by faith only ; as if we should say, That God is to be worshipped, excluding angels, idols, images, &c., it would be as much as to say, God is to be worshipped only.

29 *Is he* the God of the Jews only ? *is he* not also of the Gentiles ? Yes, of the Gentiles also :

By answering his own proposed questions, he plainly shows us, that the covenant of grace, by which God is God of his people, does not belong to the Jews only, that they only should have justification and bliss, but to the Gentiles also, according to the promise, Gen. xvii. 5 ; xxii. 18 ; Psal. ii. 8 ; Isa. xi. 10, 12, and many others ; which promises are more especially to be accomplished, now the wall of partition is broken down, as Eph. ii. 13, 14.

30 Seeing [o] *it is* one God, which shall justify the circumcision by faith, and uncircumcision through faith.

o ch. 10. 12, 13. Gal. 3. 8, 20, 28.

That it may not be thought that God is variable in the action of justifying sinners, but that it might be known that he is one, i. e. unchangeable, he shows, that both the circumcised Jews and uncircumcised Gentiles are justified by the same God in Christ, and by the same way and manner, viz. by and through faith, with no more difference than there is betwixt these two phrases, (*by faith* and *through faith,*) which cannot be distinguished the one from the other.

31 Do we then make void the law through faith ? God forbid : yea, we establish the law.

Do we then make void the law through faith? a very material objection is here to be anticipated and answered, viz. that by establishing justification by faith alone the law is rendered useless, and the obligation thereto destroyed. *God forbid : yea, we establish the law :* having rejected this objection, by his usual note of abhorrency, he proceeds to show, that nothing more establisheth the law, inasmuch as by faith we attain a perfect righteousness, we are interested in the most complete obedience of Christ to the moral law ; and that hereby every type, promise, and prophecy is fulfilled ; see Matt. v. 17 ; Luke xvi. 17 : and we ourselves also being enabled thereunto by a gospel spirit, have a more exact conformity to the law, though we cannot reach to a fulfilling of it.

CHAP. IV

Abraham himself was justified by faith, 1—8 : *which was imputed to him for righteousness before circumcision, that he might be the common father of believers, whether circumcised or not,* 9—12. *The promise was not given him through the law, else had it been void from the very nature of the law ; but being of faith by grace is sure to all the destined seed, and not to those of the law only,* 13—17. *The acceptableness of Abraham's faith,* 18—22; *which stands recorded not for his sake only, but for the sake of all who shall profess a like faith in God through Christ,* 23—25.

WHAT shall we then say that [a] Abraham, our father as pertaining to the flesh, hath found ?

a Is. 51. 2.
Matt. 3. 9.
John 8. 33, 39. 2 Cor. 11. 22.

The apostle proceeds to prove his main conclusion, chap. iii. 28, which is, that a sinner is justified by faith without works, from the example of Abraham. He was a man that had faith and works both, yet he was justified by faith, and not by works ; and who doubts but the children are justified after the same manner that their father was: there is but one way of justification; this is the connexion. *As pertaining to the flesh:* these words may either be referred to *father;* and then they import no more but that Abraham was their father according to the flesh, chap. ix. 5. Or else they may be referred to the following word *found;* and then the question is, What hath Abraham found, i. e. got or attained, according to the flesh? The sense is, What hath he got by his righteousness, which stands in works, and are done in the flesh? Abraham obtained not righteousness by any works, ceremonial or moral. So the word *flesh* is taken, (see Phil. iii. 3, 4,) when under the word flesh came circumcision, our own righteousness, which is by the law, or whatsoever is or may be opposed to that righteousness which is by the faith of Christ.

b ch. 3. 20, 27, 28.

2 For if Abraham were ᵇjustified by works, he hath *whereof* to glory; but not before God.

He hath whereof to glory; he hath cause or matter of glorying and boasting; he hath something from whence he may take occasion of so doing. *But not before God;* something must be supplied to fill up the sense, i. e. he hath nothing whereof to glory before God. The argument of the apostle might be thus formed: If Abraham had obtained justification by works, he should have had somewhat whereof he might glory before God: but he had nothing whereof to glory before God; therefore he was not justified by works. God's way of justifying sinners is such, as shuts out all glorying and boasting, as he had before laid down, chap. iii. 27.

c Gen. 15. 6.
Gal. 3. 6.
Jam. 2. 23.

3 For what saith the Scripture? ᶜAbraham believed God, and it was counted unto him for righteousness.

The scripture referred to is in Gen. xv. 6. The apostle a little varies the words; in Genesis it is *he believed in God,* but here *he believed God:* again, in Genesis it is expressed actively, *he counted it to him for righteousness;* but here passively, *it was counted to him for righteousness.* The answer is, That the apostle in both followed the Septuagint, which was then more in use than the Hebrew text; and both are capable of an easy reconciliation, the difference being more in sound than in sense. *Abraham believed God;* i. e. the promises of God: that he would be his *shield and exceeding great reward,* Gen. xv. 1; that he would give him an heir of his body, ver. 4; that he would multiply his seed, ver. 5, whereby he understood not only his fleshly seed, but also the Messiah, the Saviour of the world, which was to come of his loins; *He took on him the seed of Abraham,* Heb. ii. 16. And besides these promises in Gen. xv., he believed that promise which was made him, Gen. xii. 3, That in him and his seed all families of the earth should be blessed. That in these promises the Messiah is understood, is evident from Gal. iii. 8, 16; and that Abraham had an eye to him is evident, without exception, from John viii. 56. *It was counted unto him for righteousness;* i. e. he was justified thereby: to have faith imputed for righteousness, and to be justified by faith, is the same thing. Faith is not our righteousness materially, but objectively and organically, as it apprehends and implies the righteousness of Christ, which is the matter of our justification. Our adversaries the papists oppose the imputation of Christ's righteousness to us; they cavil at the very word, and call it putative righteousness: and yet the apostle useth the word ten times in this chapter, and in the same sense that we take it. But how shall we reconcile our apostle with St. James, about the manner of Abraham's justification: he says expressly, James ii. 21, that *Abraham our father was justified by works, when he offered his son Isaac;* and thence he infers, ver. 24, that *by works a man is justified, and not by faith only.* They are easily reconciled, forasmuch as the one discourseth of the cause of our justification before God; the other, of the signs of justification before men. The one speaks of the imputation of righteousness; the other, of the declaration of righteousness. The one speaks of the office of faith; the other, of the quality of faith. The one speaks of the justification of the person; the other, of the faith of that person. The one speaks of Abraham to be justified; the other, of Abraham already justified.

4 Now ᵈto him that worketh is the reward not reckoned of grace, but of debt. d ch. 11. 6.

He proceeds to prove, that Abraham was not justified by works, but by faith, and free grace, and so had no cause of boasting. This he illustrates by a comparison betwixt one that *worketh,* and one that *worketh not, but believeth.* *To him that worketh;* i. e. to him that worketh with a design or intent to obtain or merit justification by his works, for else he that believeth also worketh; only he is said not to work, *secundum quid,* after a sort, to the end or intent that he might merit by it. *Is the reward not reckoned of grace, but of debt;* he speaks this by way of supposition, in case he should have fulfilled the condition of perfect obedience: and yet, to speak properly, there is no reward, as a due debt from God to him that worketh, Rom. xi. 35; only he speaks after the manner of men, and useth a civil maxim, taken from human affairs.

5 But to him that worketh not, but believeth on him that justifieth ᵉthe ungodly, his faith is counted for righteousness. e Josh. 24. 2.

To him that worketh not; i. e. to him that worketh not to the end or intent before mentioned, or with respect to justification, but takes the other way to be justified and saved, and that is, the way of believing. *That justifieth the ungodly;* that makes him, who is wicked in himself, just and righteous in Christ; or justifies him that was ungodly, but after justification is made godly. By *ungodly,* some would understand such as want that perfection of godliness, as they may build the hopes of justification upon; because the proposition is drawn from the instance of Abraham, a man not void of godliness. *His faith is counted for righteousness;* not considered in itself as a work, but in relation to Christ, the object of it, and as an act of receiving and applying him; as eating nourisheth, though it be the meat that doth it.

6 Even as David also describeth the blessedness of the man, unto whom God imputeth righteousness without works,

To the example of Abraham taken from Moses, he adjoins the testimony of David, that so he might more fully prove what he had asserted, chap. iii. 21: both the one and the other were of great authority amongst the Jews. Here it may be objected, that David no where says, that he is blessed *unto whom God imputeth righteousness without works. Answ.* Though the words be no where extant in David, yet the sense is, as appears in what follows.

7 *Saying,* ᶠBlessed *are* they whose iniquities are forgiven, and whose sins are covered. f Ps. 32. 1, 2.

This testimony is taken out of Psal. xxxii. 1, and it is well enough accommodated to the occasion, for those two, to remit sin, and to impute righteousness, are inseparable. The one is put here figuratively for the other. They mistake, who take occasion from hence to make justification to consist only in remission of sin: the text will not bear it. The apostle's design is, not hereby to declare the full nature of justification, which he had done before; but only to prove the freedom of it from any respect to works, in the instance of this principal and essential part of it. Remission of sin and the imputation of righteousness differ, as the cause and the effect. Remission of sin presupposeth imputation of righteousness; and he that hath his sins remitted, hath Christ's righteousness first imputed, that so they may be remitted and forgiven to sinners.

8 Blessed *is* the man to whom the Lord will not impute sin.

The same thing is expressed three several ways; there are three things in sin to be considered: 1. There is an offence against God, which is said to be *forgiven.* 2. There is a filthiness in sin, which is said to be *covered.* 3. There is guilt in it, which is said not to be *imputed.*

9 *Cometh* this blessedness then upon the circumcision *only,* or upon the uncircumcision also? for we say that faith was reckoned to Abraham for righteousness.

This word *cometh* is not in the original, but it is aptly inserted by our translators. *Circumcision* again is put for the circumcised, and *uncircumcision* for the uncircumcised: see chap. ii. 28. *For we say*; q. d. This we have proved, and it is on all hands confessed, *that faith was reckoned to Abraham for righteousness*: now, therefore, the question is, whether this blessedness of justification belongs to the circumcised only, or to the uncircumcised also.

10 How was it then reckoned? when he was in circumcision, or in uncircumcision? Not in circumcision, but in uncircumcision.

And if this be the question, the way to resolve it, is, to consider in what circumstances Abraham was when his faith was thus reckoned to him for righteousness; it was a long time before he was circumcised. The promise to which Abraham's faith had respect, was made to him fourteen years, at least, before his circumcision: compare Gen. xv. 2, and xvii. 24, 25: also see Gen. xvi. 16. If the blessedness, therefore, of justification was not annexed to circumcision, the Gentiles are no less capable of it than the Jews.

g Gen. 17.10.

11 And [g] he received the sign of circumcision, a seal of the righteousness of the faith which *he had yet* being uncircumcised: that [h] he might be the father of all them that believe, though they be not circumcised; that righteousness might be imputed unto them also:

h Luke 19.9. ver. 12, 16. Gal. 3. 7.

The sign of circumcision; or, circumcision, which is a sign. Two things are here affirmed of circumcision: 1. That it was a *sign*. Of what? Of the circumcision of the heart, of original sin and its cure. 2. That it was a *seal*. Of what? *Of the righteousness of faith:* of the meaning of which, see the notes on chap. i. 17. This is a periphrasis of the covenant of grace, wherein righteousness is promised, and made over to us in a way of believing: and this is not the only place where *the righteousness of faith* is put for the new covenant; see chap. x. 6, and the notes there. Circumcision is called a *seal*, because it was a confirmation of the covenant of grace, and the righteousness therein promised. The common use of a seal amongst men is to confirm and ratify a matter, and make it more firm and sure: it is joined often with an earnest, which is for the same end and purpose. The Corinthians' conversion is said to be the seal of Paul's apostleship; i. e. it was a confirmation of it, and made it more evident that he was sent of God. What the apostle says of an oath, that we may say of a seal; it is for confirmation, and for putting things out of controversy. When God made a promise to Abraham, he confirmed it with an oath; and when he made a covenant with him, and with his seed, he confirmed it by a seal, and that was circumcision, which he calls in Genesis the *covenant* of God, and here, the *seal* thereof. And what is said of circumcision is not spoken of it barely as circumcision, but as a sacrament; and it shows the nature and use of all sacraments, both of the Old Testament and New, that they are seals of the new covenant. That which the apostle mentions here of circumcision, hath nothing proper and peculiar in it to circumcision as such; but it may, with equal reason, be applied to any other sacrament: it belongs as well to the passover, yea, to baptism, and the Lord's supper: e. g. The apostle first calls circumcision a *sign;* so was the passover, so is baptism, and the Lord's supper. Again, he calls it *a seal of the righteousness of faith*, or of the new covenant, as before; and so is each of the other sacraments: take, for instance, the Lord's supper; our Saviour calls the *cup* therein *the new testament*, or covenant, that is, it is a seal and confirmation thereof. And what is here affirmed of Abraham, may be affirmed as well of the eunuch, or the jailer, or any baptized person; he received the sign of baptism, a seal of the righteousness of faith, and of remission of sins, &c. *That he might be the father of all them that believe;* i. e. that he might be known or declared to be the father of such: see the like phrase, Matt. v. 45. Though many of the fathers did believe before Abraham, yet none of them are said to be the fathers of the faithful, as Abraham was, because God made to none of them the like promise, concerning their posterity, as he did to Abraham. See the next verse.

12 And the father of circumcision to them who are not of the circumcision only, but who also walk in the steps of that faith of our father Abraham, which *he had* being *yet* uncircumcised.

The former verse tells you he was the father of the believing Gentiles, for the covenant was made with him, for all his believing seed, when he was uncircumcised, which shows, that righteousness is and may be imputed to them also without any outward circumcision: and then he is the father of the believing Jews; especially of as many of them as unto circumcision do add the imitation of his faith; who, besides circumcision, which they derived from him, do also transcribe his divine copy, and follow his example of faith and obedience; who leave their sins, as he did his country; who believe all God's promises, and adhere to him against all temptations to the contrary.

13 For the promise, that he should be the [i] heir of the world, *was* not to Abraham, or to his seed, through the law, but through the righteousness of faith.

i Gen. 17. 4, &c. Gal. 3. 29.

Some by *the world* do understand, the world of the faithful, or believers dispersed over all the world: and so in effect it is the same which he said before, that Abraham should be the father of all that believe, whether of the circumcision or uncircumcision. Others by *the world* do understand the land of Canaan, under which also heaven was typically promised and comprehended: see Heb. iv. 3; xi. 9, 10, 16. This, by a synecdoche, is put for all the world; and so also Tabor and Hermon are put for the east and west of the whole world, Psal. lxxxix. 12. This was promised to Abraham and to his seed, Gen. xii. 7; xv. 18. *Was not to Abraham, or to his seed, through the law, but through the righteousness of faith;* i. e. it was not made to Abraham because he had merited it by keeping the law; but because he had believed God, and obtained the righteousness of faith. In the whole verse is couched an argument for justification by faith without works, which is the apostle's drift; and it may be thus formed: If the promise of inheritance to Abraham and his seed was to be accomplished not by legal obedience, but by the righteousness of faith; then it follows, that we are justified by faith, and not by works; but the promise of inheritance to Abraham and his seed was to be accomplished, not by the law, but by the righteousness of faith.

14 For [k] if they which are of the law be heirs, faith is made void, and the promise made of none effect:

k Gal. 3. 18.

i. e. If they that trust to the fulfilling of the law, be heirs of the promise of God, and so the inheritance come by works; then faith is to no purpose, neither is there any use of it; and so also the promises which are made to believers are vain and useless. This is the sum of this verse; a more particular explication follows. *If they which are of the law:* compare this with Gal. iii. 9, 10. There the apostle sorts them that seek righteousness and salvation into two kinds. First, some are *of faith*, and they are such as seek salvation in that way. Again, others are *of the works of the law*, and they are such as seek salvation by means thereof. These phrases, of *the law*, and of *the works of the law*, are all one. *Be heirs;* that is, of the promises of God; of the heavenly rest, of which, as before, Canaan was a type. *Faith is made void;* i. e. if they which seek the inheritance of the law can by the law obtain it, then there is no use of faith: to what end should we by faith go out of ourselves to seek righteousness and salvation in Christ, if we could obtain it by the legal obedience? See the like, Gal. v. 4. *And the promise made of none effect;* i. e. the promise itself, which was made to Abraham and his seed, that also is ineffectual, and brought to nought; no man shall be saved by it; forasmuch as the law can bring no man to the obtaining of what is promised.

15 Because [l] the law worketh wrath: for where no law is, *there is* no transgression.

l ch. 3. 20. & 5. 13, 20. & 7. 8, 10, 11. 1 Cor. 15 56. 2 Cor. 3. 7, 9. Gal. 3. 10, 19. 1 John 3. 4.

The law worketh wrath; i. e. the wrath of God: and this

it doth not of itself, but occasionally, in respect of our disobedience. This is a confirmation of what was said in the foregoing verse, that the inheritance is not by the law, and the works thereof; he proves it from the effect and work of the law, such as it hath in all men since the fall; it worketh wrath; it is so far from entitling men to the promised blessing, that it exposeth men to the curse and wrath of God, Gal. iii. 10. *For where no law is, there is no transgression*: q. d. And that it worketh wrath is evident, because it discovers and occasions transgressions, betwixt which and God's wrath there is an inseparable connexion. This assertion is simply true of things indifferent, as were all ceremonial observations before the law required them, for then before the law it was no sin to omit them: but of things which are evil in their own nature, it must be understood respectively, and after a sort; that is, there was no such great transgression before the law was given, as afterwards. The reasons are; Because we are naturally bent to do that which is forbidden us; and so by the reproofs of the law, the stubbornness of man's heart is increased. As also, because by the law comes the clear knowledge of man's duty; and so the servant that knows his master's will, and doth it not, is worthy of the more stripes.

16 Therefore *it is* of faith, that *it might be* ᵐby grace; ⁿto the end the promise might be sure to all the seed; not to that only which is of the law, but to that also which is of the faith of Abraham; ᵒwho is the father of us all,

ᵐ ch. 3. 24.
ⁿ Gal. 3. 22.

ᵒ Is. 51. 2.
ch. 9. 8.

Here are two new arguments to prove that the inheritance is not of the law, but of faith. *It is of faith, that it might be by grace*; for to be justified by faith and by grace are all one with the apostle. Again, that *the promise might be sure to all the seed*; whereas if it were of the law, it would be unsure and uncertain, because of man's weakness, who is not able to perform it. Abraham's seed is of two sorts. One sort is of the law, to wit, the Jews. Another sort is of such as walk in the steps of Abraham's faith, whether Jews or Gentiles. To all these the promise must be sure; which cannot be, if the law be made the condition or the means of the inheritance.

17 (As it is written, ᵖI have made thee a father of many nations,) ‖ before him whom he believed, *even* God, ᵍwho quickeneth the dead, and calleth those ʳthings which be not as though they were.

ᵖ Gen. 17. 5.
‖ Or, *like unto him.*
ᵍ ch. 8. 11.
Eph. 2, 1, 5.
ʳ ch. 9. 26.
1 Cor. 1. 28.
1 Pet. 2. 10.

Before him whom he believed; i. e. in the sight or esteem of God. He was not the *father of many nations* by carnal generation in the sight of men, but by spiritual cognation in the sight of God. Or, as it may be read, like unto God, after his example: and then the meaning is, that God so honoured Abraham's faith, that he made him a father, in some respects like himself. As God is a universal Father, not of one, but of all nations, so was Abraham. Again, As God is their spiritual Father, not by carnal generation, so was Abraham also. *Even God, who quickeneth the dead, and calleth those things which be not as though they were;* i. e. Abraham believed in him as omnipotent. His omnipotency is described by two great effects of it. The one in making that to have a being again, which had ceased to be, as in the resurrection. The other, in causing that to be which never was; or to make all things of nothing, as in the creation: he expresseth this by calling things, to intimate the great facility of this work to God: he only spoke, and it was done; he commanded, and all was created. And as Abraham thus generally believed the power of God, so it is likely he made a particular application of it to his own state at present; as he believed that God could raise the dead, so, that he could raise him seed out of his own dead body, and Sarah's dead womb. And as he believed that God could create things out of nothing, so, that he could give him seed that had none; yea, and make the Gentiles a people that were not a people.

18 Who against hope believed in hope, that he might become the father of many nations, according to that which was spoken, ˢSo shall thy seed be.

ˢ Gen. 15. 5.

Here the apostle digresseth a little from his principal argument, and falls into a commendation of Abraham's faith. *Who against hope believed in hope:* Abraham, when he had no natural or rational grounds of hope, either in respect of himself or Sarah his wife, did yet believe and hope he should have a son; and so be a root or stock, from whence many nations should spring: and this faith and hope of his was grounded upon the power and faithfulness of God. *So shall thy seed be;* so as the stars of heaven for multitude, which must be supplied out of the promise, in Gen. xv. 5.

19 And being not weak in faith, ᵗhe considered not his own body now dead, when he was about an hundred years old, neither yet the deadness of Sarah's womb:

ᵗ Gen. 17. 17. & 18. 11.
Heb. 11. 11, 12.

He regarded not the impotency of his own body, which was as it were dead, because of his age, in respect of any desires or powers of generation. Abraham several years after married Keturah, by whom he had divers children; how then doth the apostle say his body was now dead, or unable for generation? Some say that the deadness of Abraham's body was only in his own opinion. Augustine hath two answers: 1. That his body was not dead simply, but in respect of Sarah; he might be able to beget children of a younger woman. 2. His body was revived, and he received a new generative faculty of God. Another question may be moved, and that is, how the apostle could say that Abraham *considered not his own body*, being *dead;* seeing we read, Gen. xvii. 17, that Abraham, upon the promise of a son, *fell upon his face, and laughed, and said in his heart, Shall a child be born unto him that is an hundred years old?* &c. Some answer, that Abraham at first doubted, but afterwards he recollected himself, and got over that unbelief; his faith overcame all difficulties. Others say, that he doubted not at all of the truth of God's promise, but was uncertain only how it should be understood, whether properly or figuratively: see Gen. xvii. 19. Others say, that these words of Abraham are not words of doubting, but inquiring; they proceed from a desire to be further instructed how that thing should be. It was a question like that of the virgin Mary's, How shall these things be? Augustine says, that Abraham's laughter was not like Sarah's. Hers proceeded from distrust; his, from joy and admiration.

20 He staggered not at the promise of God through unbelief; but was strong in faith, giving glory to God;

The promise of God; viz. in Gen. xv. 5, and xvii. 16. *Giving glory to God;* as all do that rely upon the power and promise of God, setting to their seals that he is true.

21 And being fully persuaded that, what he had promised, ᵘhe was able also to perform.

ᵘ Ps. 115. 3.
Luke 1. 37, 45. Heb. 11. 19.

He looked upon God as one that was perfectly able to do whatever he had promised, and as one that was most faithful, and sure never to fail in the performance; collecting nothing else from the difficulty and improbability of the matter, but that it was the fitter for an Almighty power to effect.

22 And therefore it was imputed to him for righteousness.

See ver. 3. By reason of his faith he was as sufficiently disposed and qualified for the obtaining of the promise, as if he had had all the righteousness required by the law.

23 Now ˣit was not written for his sake alone, that it was imputed to him;

ˣ ch. 15. 4.
1 Cor. 10. 6, 11.

24 But for us also, to whom it shall be imputed, if we believe ʸon him that raised up Jesus our Lord from the dead;

ʸ Acts 2. 24.
& 13. 30.

Here it may be inquired, If Abraham's faith did justify him, and it was imputed to him for righteousness, what doth this concern us? The apostle answers, it was recorded of him for our sakes; see chap. xv. 4; and to us there shall be the like imputation, if we believe in God, *that raised up Jesus our Lord from the dead*. This a greater act of faith than Abraham's was. And the nature of justifying faith lies rather in affiance, or in putting trust in God through our Lord Jesus Christ, than in assent, or in giving credit, to the truth of his promise. *Quest.* Why doth the apostle single out this act of raising Christ from the dead to describe the Father by? *Answ.* To maintain the proportion betwixt the faith of Abraham and the faith of his seed; that as his respected the power of God, in raising, as it were, the dead, so in like sort should ours. So some. But the apostle speaks as if there were some special reason and ground for confidence in God for justification in this act of raising Christ from the dead; and indeed nothing is more fit to establish our faith in persuasion of our justification than this; for when God raised up our Lord Jesus Christ, having loosed the pains of death, he gave full assurance that his justice is fully satisfied for our sins. Had not Christ Jesus, our surety, paid the utmost farthing that was due for our sins, he had still continued in prison, and under the power of death. Hence it is that the apostle Peter tells us, 1 Pet. i. 3, that God *hath begotten us to a lively hope* of the heavenly inheritance *by the resurrection of Christ from the dead;* there being no more effectual means to persuade us of the pardon of sin, of reconciliation with God, and of acceptance to eternal life, than that Jesus Christ, our surety and sponsor, is risen from the dead.

z Is. 53. 5, 6. ch. 3. 25. &
5. 6. & 8. 32.
2 Cor. 5. 21.
Gal. 1. 4.
1 Pet. 2. 24.
& 3. 18. Heb. 9. 28.

25 [z] Who was delivered for our offences, and [a] was raised again for our justification.

a 1 Cor. 15. 17. 1 Pet. 1. 21.

Who was delivered; he saith *delivered* rather than crucified, to lead us by the hand to the first cause thereof, the determinate counsel of the blessed Trinity: see Acts ii. 23; iv. 27, 28; Rom. viii. 32. *For our offences;* i. e. for the expiating of them, Isa. liii. 10. *And was raised again for our justification;* not that his death had no hand in our justification; see Rom. iii. 24; but because our justification, which was begun in his death, was perfected in his resurrection. Christ did meritoriously work our justification and salvation by his death and passion, but the efficacy and perfection thereof with respect to us depend on his resurrection. By his death he paid our debt, in his resurrection he received our acquittance, Isa. liii. 8; when he was discharged, we in him, and together with him, received our discharge from the guilt and punishment of all our sins. This one verse is an abridgement of the whole gospel.

CHAP. V

Being justified by faith, we have peace with God, 1; *we glory in our hopes,* 2, *and in present afflictions,* 3—5; *from the best experience of God's love, looking with more assurance for final salvation.* 6—10: *we glory in God also, to whom we are reconciled by Christ,* 11. *As sin and death came upon all men by Adam, so the grace of God, which justifieth unto life, cometh more abundantly unto all mankind through Christ,* 12—19. *Under the law sin abounded unto death; but grace hath much more abounded unto life,* 20, 21.

a Is. 32. 17.
John 16. 33.
ch. 3. 28, 30.
b Eph. 2. 14.
Col. 1. 20.

THEREFORE [a] being justified by faith, we have [b] peace with God through our Lord Jesus Christ:

Hitherto of the cause and manner of our justification; now follow the benefits and effects. *Being justified by faith;* as he had before asserted and proved particularly, in chap. iii. 28; iv. 24. *We have peace with God;* i. e. we have reconciliation with God, who before were utter enemies to him, Col. i. 21; he is now become our Friend, as he was Abraham's. *Through our Lord Jesus Christ,* who is the only Mediator of reconciliation: see 2 Cor. v. 19; Eph. ii. 14—16; Col. i. 20; 1 Tim. ii. 5.

c John 10. 9.
& 14. 6.
Ephes. 2. 18.
& 3. 12.
Heb. 10. 19.
d 1 Cor. 15.1.
e Heb. 3. 6.

2 [c] By whom also we have access by faith into this grace [d] wherein we stand, and [e] rejoice in hope of the glory of God.

We have not only reconciliation with God by Jesus Christ, but also by faith in him we are admitted to his presence, his grace and favour. One may be reconciled to his prince, and yet not to be brought into his presence: witness Absalom, &c. See Eph. ii. 18; iii. 12; 1 Pet. iii. 18. *This grace* is either that whereof he spake, chap. iii. 24; or else rather it may be understood of that excellent state of reconciliation, friendship, and favour with God, which God hath graciously bestowed upon us. *Wherein we stand;* or, in which we stand or abide, not stirring a foot for any temptation or persecution: a metaphor from soldiers keeping their station in fight. A man may obtain his prince's favour, and lose it again; but, &c. *And rejoice in hope of the glory of God;* in the glory hoped for, a Hebraism; see Luke x. 20; 1 Pet. i. 8, 9; even in that glory which God hath promised, and which consists in the enjoyment of him.

3 And not only *so,* but [f] we glory in tribulations also: [g] knowing that tribulation worketh patience;

f Matt. 5. 11, 12. Acts 5. 41. 2 Cor. 12. 10.
Phil. 2. 17.
Jam. 1. 2, 12. 1 Pet. 3. 14. g Jam. 1. 3.

We glory in tribulations also; as old soldiers do in their scars of honour: see Gal. vi. 17; 2 Cor. xii. 9—11. Believers do not only glory in their future happiness, but in their present sufferings and afflictions: yet not so much in affliction itself, as in the issue and fruitful effects thereof, of which he speaks in what follows. *Knowing,* finding by experience, *that tribulation worketh patience;* not as if affliction of itself and in its own nature did this, for in many it hath a contrary operation; but God, who is the author and giver of patience, chap. v. 15, doth make use of it for this purpose; it is a means sanctified of God for the exercising, obtaining, and increasing thereof.

4 [h] And patience, experience; and experience, hope:

h Jam. 1. 12.

And patience, experience; viz. of God's sustentation and care of us, and of his faithfulness in fulfilling his promises, Psal. xci. 15; Isa. xliii. 2; 2 Cor. i. 4, 5; as also of our own sincerity, and strength to endure and persevere, Matt. xiii. 21. *And experience, hope;* i. e. of the glory of God, as before in ver. 2, or hope of further mercy and seasonable deliverance. Believers find and feel that God hath delivered them, and doth deliver them, and in him they trust and hope that he will still deliver them.

5 [i] And hope maketh not ashamed; [k] because the love of God is shed abroad in our hearts by the Holy Ghost which is given unto us.

i Phil. 1. 20.
k 2 Cor. 1.
22. Gal. 4. 6.
Ephes. 1. 13, 14.

And hope maketh not ashamed; it doth not disappoint or deceive us. Frustrated hopes fill men with shame and confusion, Job vi. 19, 20. This passage seems to be taken out of Psal. xxii. 5. *Because, &c.;* this is either rendered as the reason of all that went before; Therefore the justified by faith have peace with God, access to him by faith, hope of glory, joy in tribulation, &c., because the love of God is shed abroad in their hearts: or else it is a reason of what immediately preceded; Therefore hope maketh not ashamed, because the love of God is shed abroad, &c. *The love of God;* understand it either actively, of our love to God, or rather passively, of his love to us, (of which he speaks, ver. 8,) and of the sense thereof. *Is shed abroad in our hearts;* is greatly manifested, or abundantly poured forth: a frequent metaphor, both in the Old and New Testament: see Isa. xliv. 3; Joel ii. 28; Zech. xii. 10; John vii. 38; Acts ii. 17. *By the Holy Ghost which is given unto us;* not excluding the Father and Son; it is the more proper work of the Spirit, both to make us feel the love of God, and to fill our hearts with love to God.

6 For when we were yet without strength, ‖ in due time [l] Christ died for the ungodly.

‖ Or, *according to the time,* Gal. 4. 4.
l ver. 8.
ch. 4. 25.

Without strength; utterly unable to help or redeem ourselves. *In due time;* some read it, according to the time, and refer this clause to the foregoing words, making this to be the sense, When we were weak in time past, or in the time of the law, before grace appeared, then Christ died, &c. Others rather refer it to the following words, and so our translation carries it, that in due time, i. e. *in the fulness of time,* as Gal. iv. 4, or in the time that was before decreed and prefixed by the Father. The Scripture every where speaks of a certain season or hour assigned for the death of Christ: see Matt. xxvi. 45; John viii. 20; xii. 27; xvii. 1. *Christ died for the ungodly;* i. e. for the sake, or instead of, such as were enemies to God, (as ver. 10,) and so could deserve no such favour from him.

7 For scarcely for a righteous man will one die: yet peradventure for a good man some would even dare to die.

He amplifies the love of Christ in dying for the ungodly, and shows that it is unparalleled and without example. By *a good man* you must understand one that is very kind and bountiful, or one that is very useful and profitable; that is, a public and common good. Instances may be given of those that have sacrificed their lives for such. Lilloe stepped between the murderer and king Edward his master. Nicholas Ribische lost his life to preserve Prince Maurice at the siege of Pista.

^{m John 15. 13. 1 Pet. 3. 18. 1 John 3. 16. & 4. 9, 10.} **8 But ^m God commendeth his love toward us, in that, while we were yet sinners, Christ died for us.**

God commendeth his love toward us; i. e. he declareth or confirmeth it by this, as a most certain sign, he makes it most conspicuous or illustrious: see John iii. 16; 1 John iv. 9, 10. *In that, while we were yet sinners, Christ died for us;* i. e. in a state of sin, and under the guilt and power of sin. Believers in some sense are still sinners, 1 John i. 8, but their sins being pardoned and subdued, they go no longer under that denomination. Sinners in Scripture are said to be those in whom sin dwells and reigns; see John ix. 31. Such we were by nature. Yea, we were not only sinners, but enemies to God, which further commendeth the love of Christ in dying for us: there is no greater love amongst men, than when one layeth down his life for his friends; but herein Christ's love excelled, that he gave his life for his enemies.

^{n ch. 3. 25. Eph. 2. 13. Heb. 9. 14. 1 John 1. 7. o ch. 1. 18. 1 Thes. 1. 10.} **9 Much more then, being now justified ⁿ by his blood, we shall be saved ^o from wrath through him.**

The apostle's arguing is cogent, for it is more to justify and reconcile sinners, than to save them being justified; Christ therefore having done the former, he will much more do the latter. *By his blood;* i. e. by faith in his blood or sufferings. *From wrath;* the Greek reads it with an article, from that wrath, whereby is meant the wrath to come, or eternal punishment.

^{p ch. 6. 32. q 2 Cor. 5. 18, 19. Eph. 2. 16. Col. 1. 20, 21. r John 5. 26. & 14. 19. 2 Cor. 4. 10, 11.} **10 For ^p if, when we were enemies, ^q we were reconciled to God by the death of his Son, much more, being reconciled, we shall be saved ^r by his life.**

We were reconciled to God; put into a capacity of reconciliation, God being by Christ's death made reconcilable, and also actually reconciled, when we believe, through the merits of the death of Christ. *We shall be saved by his life;* i. e. by the resurrection to life. Salvation is ascribed to the resurrection and life of Christ, because he thereby doth perfect our salvation, he ever living to make intercession for us, Heb. vii. 25; and because by his resurrection and life we shall be raised to eternal life at that day.

^{s ch. 2. 17. & 3. 29, 30. Gal. 4. 9. || Or, reconciliation, ver. 10. 2 Cor. 5. 18, 19.} **11 And not only so, but we also ^s joy in God through our Lord Jesus Christ, by whom we have now received the || atonement.**

And not only so, &c.: q. d. We do not only rejoice in the hope of glory, and in tribulation, of which he had spoken, ver. 2, 3, (all that fell in between being a long parenthesis,) but we rejoice and glory in God himself, who is become our God and merciful Father in Jesus Christ. *By whom we have now received the atonement;* this is rendered as the reason why we should rejoice in God through Jesus Christ; for by him God is atoned or reconciled, satisfaction being made for our sins in his blood. The particle *now* hath its emphasis, to show the privilege of those who live in these times of the gospel.

^{t Gen. 3. 6. 1 Cor. 15. 21. u Gen. 2. 17. ch. 6. 23. 1 Cor. 15. 21. || Or, in whom.} **12 Wherefore, as ^t by one man sin entered into the world, and ^u death by sin; and so death passed upon all men, || for that all have sinned:**

From this verse to the end of the chapter, the apostle makes a large comparison between the first and Second Adam, which he joins to what he had said by the causal particle *wherefore:* q. d. Seeing things are as I have already said, it is evident, that what was lost by Adam is restored by Christ. This verse seems to be lame and imperfect; the reddition is wanting in the comparison; for unto this, *as by one man sin entered into the world,* there should be added, so by Christ, &c. But the reddition, or second part of the comparison, is suspended, by reason of a long parenthesis intervening to the 18th and 19th verses, where the apostle sets down both parts of the comparison. *By one man:* viz. Adam. *Obj.* Eve first sinned, 1 Tim. ii. 14. *Answ.* He is not showing the order how sin first entered into the world, but how it was propagated to mankind. Therefore he mentions the man, because he is the head of the woman, and the covenant was made with him: or, *man* may be used collectively, both for man and woman; as when God said, *Let us make man,* &c. *Sin;* it is to be understood of our first parents' actual sin, in eating the forbidden fruit; this alone was it that affected their posterity, and made them sinners, ver. 19. *Entered into the world;* understand the inhabitants of the world; the thing containing, by a usual metonymy, is put for the thing contained. *And death by sin;* as the due reward thereof. *Death* here may be taken in its full latitude, for temporal, spiritual, and eternal death. *And so death passed upon all men;* seized upon all, of all sorts, infants as well as others. *For that all have sinned;* others read it thus, in which all have sinned, i. e. in which one man; and so it is a full proof that Adam was a public person, and that in him all his posterity sinned and fell. He was our representative, and we were all in him, as a town or county in a parliament man; and although we chose him not, yet God chose for us. The words ἐφ' ᾧ are rendered *in which,* in other places, and the preposition ἐπὶ is put for ἐν; see Mark ii. 4; Heb. ix. 10: and if our translation be retained, it is much to the same sense; for if such die as never committed any actual sin themselves, (as infants do,) then it will follow that they sinned in this one man, in whose loins they were: as Levi is said to have paid tithes in Abraham's loins, Heb. vii. 9.

13 (For until the law sin was in the world: but ^x sin is not imputed when there is no law. ^{x ch. 4. 15. 1 John 3. 4.}

For until the law sin was in the world: q. d. It appears that all have sinned, because sin was always in the world, not only after the law was given by Moses, but also before, even from the beginning of the world till that time. *But sin is not imputed when there is no law:* q. d. It appears there was a law before the law of Moses, for if there had been no law all that while, then sin would not have been imputed to men, so as to make them liable to punishment or death; but sin was imputed or charged upon men before the law of Moses, and death passed upon all. Therefore there must have been a law, by the transgression of which men were sinners, before that time. And that was either the law of nature, or the positive law which God gave to Adam, the transgression whereof is imputed to all, as we shall see, ver. 19. Some think the apostle doth here obviate a cavil: q. d. Let no man think that sin began to have its being together with the law, for there was sin before there was any written law to forbid it. The same acts that were forbidden afterwards by the law, were before committed, and were really sinful in the sight of God. But sin was not so well known, nor so strictly charged upon the sinner, as it is since the law was given. It was not imputed comparatively, though absolutely it was, as may appear by many instances, as the drowning of the world, the destruction of Sodom, &c.

14 Nevertheless death reigned from Adam to Moses, even over them that had not sinned after the similitude of Adam's transgression, ^y who is the figure of him that was to come. ^{y 1 Cor. 15. 21, 22, 45.}

He proceeds to prove his assertion in the foregoing verse, that sin was in the world before the law, because *death,* which is the wages of sin, *did reign,* and had power over all mankind, *from Adam to Moses,* which was about two thousand five hundred years. *Even over them that had not sinned after the similitude of Adam's transgression;* i. e.

over very infants, that had not actually sinned as Adam did. But though infants did not sin like Adam, yet they sinned in Adam; the guilt of his sin was imputed to them, else death could have had no power over them. Infants (as one saith) are not altogether innocents; the very first sheet or blanket wherewith they are covered is woven of sin and shame, of blood and filth, Ezek. xvi. 4, 6. *Who is the figure of him that was to come;* of his offspring, (so some,) which came of him in after-times; his posterity (as before) was represented in his person: but others better expound it of Christ, who is the Second Adam; and of whom Adam was a figure or type, not in respect of such things as were personal to either of them, but of that which by them redounded to others. The first Adam was the original of man's natural and earthly being; the Second Adam, of his spiritual and heavenly. By the first, sin and death came into the world; by the Second, righteousness and life.

15 But not as the offence, so also *is* the free gift. For if through the offence of one many be dead, much more the grace of God, and the gift by grace, *which* [z Is. 53. 11. Mat. 20. 28. & 26. 28.] *is* by one man, Jesus Christ, hath abounded [z] unto many.

But not as the offence, so also is the free gift: q. d. But yet the resemblance betwixt the first and Second Adam is not so exact as to admit of no difference; differences there are, but they are to great advantage on Christ's part: e. g. Compare Adam's sin and Christ's obedience, in respect of their efficacy and virtue, and you will find a great difference. *For if through the offence of one many be dead, much more the grace of God, and the gift by grace, which is by one man, Jesus Christ, hath abounded unto many:* the obedience of Christ (which is the product of his grace and favour) is much more powerful to justification and salvation, than the sin of Adam was to condemnation. If the transgression of mere man was able to pull down death and wrath upon all his natural seed, then the obedience of one, which is God as well as man, will much more abundantly avail to procure pardon and life for all his spiritual seed. He doth not give the pre-eminence unto the grace of Christ in respect of the number, but of the more powerful efficacy and virtue.

16 And not as *it was* by one that sinned, *so is* the gift: for the judgment *was* by one to condemnation, but the free gift *is* of many offences unto justification.

q. d. As there is a difference between Adam and Christ in respect of their persons, so also in respect of their acts, and the extent thereof; for one sin of Adam did condemn us; the mischief arose from one offence; but the free gift and grace of Christ doth absolve us not only from that one fault, but from all other faults and offences; it reacheth to the pardon, not only of original sin, but of all other personal and actual sins.

‖ Or, *by one offence.*

17 For if ‖ by one man's offence death reigned by one; much more they which receive abundance of grace and of the gift of righteousness shall reign in life by one, Jesus Christ.)

Here he shows the difference in respect of the effects and consequents of their acts. If by means of one man and his one offence death had power over all mankind, then much more shall the grace and gift of righteousness, which is by Jesus Christ alone, obtain eternal life for all that have received abundant grace and mercy from him.

‖ Or, *by one offence.*

18 Therefore as ‖ by the offence of one *judgment came* upon all men to condemnation; even so ‖ by the righteousness of one *the free gift came* [a] upon all men unto justification of life.

‖ Or, *by one righteousness.* a John 12. 32. Heb. 2. 9.

Here, after a long parenthesis, the apostle returns to what he had begun to say in ver. 12; and now he makes the comparison full in both members, which there, by reason of intervening matter, was left imperfect, as I before hinted. *Judgment;* guilt, which exposeth to judgment. *Came upon all men;* all the posterity, or natural seed, of the first Adam. *The free gift;* that which all along he calls *the free gift,* seems to be the benefit believers have by Christ's obedience. *Came upon all men;* not all universally, but all sorts of men indifferently, Gentiles as well as Jews; or all that are his spiritual seed. Or *all men* here is put for many men; see elsewhere, Luke vi. 26; Acts xxii. 15. *Many* is sometimes put for *all,* as Dan. xii. 2, and again *all* for *many;* and indeed these two words, *all* and *many,* seem to be used reciprocally by this context in particular, ver. 15, and 19.

19 For as by one man's disobedience many were made sinners, so by the obedience of one shall many be made righteous.

One man's; i. e. Adam's: see the notes on ver. 12. *Many;* i. e. all, as before; many is here opposed to one, or a few; the meaning is, Though Adam was but one, yet he infected many others, his sin rested not in his own person. *Were made sinners;* brought into a state of sin. This is more than when all the world were said to sin in him. The word is used to signify great and heinous sinners. The apostle here informs us of that which all philosophy was ignorant of, viz. the imputation of Adam's sin, and our natural pollution flowing from it. Yea, this was more than the naked history of man's fall by Moses did discover; there indeed we see the cause of death, how that came upon all mankind; but that Adam's sin was accounted to us, that by his disobedience we are involved in sin and misery, that is not clearly revealed in the books of Moses. We are beholden to the gospel, and particularly to this text and context, for the more full discovery hereof. *By the obedience of one;* i. e. of Christ. He leaves out the word man, either for brevity sake, or because Christ was not a mere man, as Adam was. Here the apostle concludes the collation he had made between Adam and Christ, whom he had all along represented as two public persons, or as two common roots or fountains, the one of sin and death, the other of righteousness and life. And indeed there are throughout the context (as one observes) several textual and grammatical obscurities, as also redundant and defective expressions, which are not unusual with this apostle, whose matter runneth from him like a torrent, and cannot be so well bounded by words. Another saith, upon the consideration of the difficulties in this context, We do not need Theseus's twine of thread, but the Holy Ghost, and that light by which this Epistle was wrote, to guide us into the understanding of it.

20 Moreover [b] the law entered, that the offence might abound. But where sin abounded, grace did much [c] more abound:

b John 15. 22. ch. 3. 20. & 4. 15. & 7. 8. Gal. 3. 19, 23. c Luke 7. 47. 1 Tim. 1. 14.

Here he shows the reason why the law was given; although (as it is in ver. 13) before that time sin was in the world, it was *that the offence might abound;* either strictly, the offence of that one man, or rather largely, the offence of every man. The particle ἵνα (rendered *that,*) is to be taken either causally, and so it is interpreted by Gal. iii. 19, where it is said, *the law was added because of transgressions,* that thereby the guilt and punishment of sin being more fully discovered, the riches of God's free grace and mercy might be the more admired; or else eventually, it so falls out by accident, or by reason of man's corruption, that sin is thereby increased or augmented. *The law is holy, just, and good,* (as chap. vii. 12,) how then doth that increase sin? Either as it irritates the sinner, chap. iii. 20; and vii. 8, 11, or makes manifest the sin, chap. vii. 7, 13; thereby sin is known to be, as indeed it is, out of measure sinful. *But where sin abounded, grace did much more abound:* this is added by way of correction, to mitigate the former assertion, and it lays down a second end of giving the law; the former was the increase and manifestation of sin, the latter is the abounding or superabounding of God's grace. There is this difference to be observed; that the first end is universal, for in all men, both good and bad, the law worketh the increase and knowledge of sin; but the other is particular, and peculiar to the elect; to them only the grace of God is superabundant after that they have abounded in sin, and by how much the greater is their guilt, by so much the greater is the grace of God in the free forgiveness thereof.

21 That as sin hath reigned unto death, even so might grace reign through righteousness unto eternal life by Jesus Christ our Lord.

Before he ascribed dominion and reign to death, now to sin; the reason is evident, because death indeed reigneth by sin. Before also he had made the comparison betwixt Adam and Christ, here it is betwixt sin and grace, the power of one and of the other. The sum is, that as sin hath prevailed over all mankind to bring death upon man, not only a temporal but eternal death, so the grace of Christ prevails, and becomes effectual, to confer upon us eternal life. *Righteousness*; i. e. imputed or imparted. *By Jesus Christ our Lord:* see how sweetly the end answers the beginning of this chapter, and how Jesus Christ is both the Author and Finisher of all.

CHAP. VI

Though justified by grace, we may not live in sin; since the very figure of baptism requireth us to die with Christ unto sin, that we may lead a new life of holiness unto God, 1—13. *The dispensation of grace freeth us from the dominion of sin; but we are still the servants of sin, if we obey it; therefore being freed from sin, we are bound unto holiness,* 14—20. *The end and wages of sin is death; but the fruit of holiness through God's grace is eternal life,* 21—23.

a ch. 3. 8. ver. 15.

WHAT shall we say then? ^aShall we continue in sin, that grace may abound?

Another anticipation; this Epistle abounds therewith. The apostle here prevents an objection, which might be occasioned, either by the foregoing doctrine in general, concerning justification by the free grace of God, and by a righteousness imputed to us; or by what he said more particularly in the close of the foregoing chapter, that *where sin abounded, grace did much more abound.* Some might hence infer, that there was no need then of inherent righteousness, that persons might abide and abound in sin, that so grace might be the more exalted in the forgiveness thereof. The apostle Jude speaks, Jude 4, of some that made this ill improvement of the grace of God. Those that draw such inferences from the premises, they put a false construction upon the apostle's doctrine, and a paralogism or fallacy upon themselves. They make the apostle's words more general than he meant or intended them: for the abounding of sin is not the occasion of the abounding of grace in all, but only in some, even in those who confess and forsake their sins. And they apply that to the time to come which the apostle only uttered of the time past. The abounding of sin in men before their conversion and calling, doth commend and exalt the abundant grace of God, in the forgiveness thereof; but not so if sin abound in them after they are converted and called. He propounds this objection by way of interrogation, partly to show his dislike that his doctrine should be so perverted, and partly to show the peace of his own conscience, that he was far from such a thought.

b ver. 11. ch. 7. 4. Gal. 2. 19. & 6. 14.

2 God forbid. How shall we, that are ^bdead to sin, live any longer therein?

God forbid; be it not, or far be it; he rejects any such inference or consequence, as unworthy of an answer: q. d. Away with all such doctrines, as, under pretence of advancing grace, do promote sin, or obstruct a godly life. This phrase is frequent with the apostle, when he is speaking of any absurdity: see chap. iii. 4, 6, 31. *How:* by this particle he shows the impossibility, or the incongruity, of the thing: see Matt. vi. 28; Gal. iv. 9. The following argument is very convincing, and may be thus formed: They whose property it is to be dead to sin, cannot any longer live therein; but the justified by faith are dead to sin. They are said to be *dead to sin,* who do not live under the power and dominion of it; who mortify sin, and suffer it (so far as they can) to have no life or power in it. Fall into it they may, but live and lie in it they cannot. It is not falling into the water that drowns a man, but it is his lying in it; so it is not falling into sin that damns a man, but it is his living in it.

3 Know ye not, that ^cso many of us as ‖ were baptized into Jesus Christ ^dwere baptized into his death?

c Col. 3. 3. 1 Pet. 2. 24. ‖ Or, *are.* d 1 Cor. 15. 29.

Know ye not? q. d. This is a truth which you ought not to be ignorant of, and which confirms what I say. *Baptized into Jesus Christ:* to be baptized into Christ, is either to be baptized in the name of Christ; see Acts x. 48, and xix. 5; or else it is, incorporated, ingrafted, or planted into Christ, and so to be made members of his mystical body by baptism. *Baptized into his death:* to be baptized into the death of Christ, is to have fellowship with him in his death, or to have the efficacy of his death sealed up to us; and that is the blessed privilege of as many as are baptized or planted into Christ; they are not only partakers of the merit of his death for justification, but of the efficacy of his death for mortification. See a parallel place, Gal. iii. 27.

4 Therefore we are ^eburied with him by baptism into death: that ^flike as Christ was raised up from the dead by ^gthe glory of the Father, ^heven so we also should walk in newness of life.

e Col. 2. 12. f eh. 8. 11. 1 Cor. 6. 14. 2 Cor. 13. 4. g John 2. 11. & 11. 40. h Gal. 6. 15 Eph. 4. 22, 23, 24. Col. 3. 10.

Therefore: q. d. Because we are thus dead with Christ, therefore, &c. *We are buried with him;* i. e. we have communion with him in his burial also, which represents a farther degree of the destruction of sin, by putting it, as it were, out of our sight, Gen. xxiii. 4, and having no more to do with it. *By baptism into death:* he seems here to allude to the manner of baptizing in those warm Eastern countries, which was to dip or plunge the party baptized, and so were to bury him for a while under water. See the like phrase, Col. ii. 12. Baptism doth not only represent our mortification and death to sin, but our progress and perseverance therein. Burial implies a continuing under death; so is mortification a continual dying unto sin. *That like as Christ was raised up from the dead;* look as, after the death and burial of Christ, there followed his resurrection, so it must be with us; we must have communion with, and conformity to, the Lord Jesus Christ in his resurrection as well as in his death; both these are represented and sealed to us by the sacrament of baptism. *By the glory of the Father;* i. e. by the power of the Father, which is called, Col. i. 11, *his glorious power.* God is said elsewhere to have raised him *by his power,* 1 Cor. vi. 14; and in 2 Cor. xiii. 4, he is said to live *by the power of God.* Some read it thus, he was raised from the dead, to the glory of the Father. The preposition διὰ is sometimes rendered *to:* see 1 Pet. i. 3. *Walk in newness of life;* i. e. live a new life, being actuated by new principles, aiming at new ends, and bringing forth new fruits of holiness: see chap. vii. 6.

5 ⁱFor if we have been planted together in the likeness of his death, we shall be also *in the likeness of his* resurrection:

i Phil. 3. 10, 11.

He prosecutes what he had before propounded, and illustrates it by an apt similitude, which is taken from grafting or planting. He takes it for granted, that believers are *planted together in the likeness of* Christ's *death,* i. e. are made conformable to him in his death: see Phil. iii. 10. Christ died, and believers die; the one a natural, the other a spiritual death: the one by way of expiation, suffering, and satisfying for the sins of others; the other by way of mortification, killing and crucifying their own sins. *We shall be also in the likeness of his resurrection:* in the original the sentence is elliptical and imperfect, the words running thus, *we shall be of his resurrection;* our translation therefore fills up the sense with a word borrowed from the preceding clause. See the like, John v. 36, *I have a greater witness than of John,* i. e. than that witness of John. The sense of the whole is this, That believers are not only dead, but risen with Christ, Col. iii. 1. They partake of such a resurrection as resembles his; as Christ arose from the dead to a new life, so we rise from dead works to *walk in newness of life,* ver. 4. Moreover, they are raised and quickened by a power and virtue that flows from Christ and his resurrection: this is that virtue which the apostle Paul so earnestly desired to be made a partaker of, Phil. iii. 10. The graft revives with the stock in the spring, and that by a virtue which it receives from the stock; so as a believer is raised to newness of life, by virtue flowing from Christ, into whom he is ingrafted. *Quest.* Why doth he say believers *shall be* planted, &c.? Are they not so already, upon their believing in Christ? *Answ.* The apostle rather chooseth to speak in the future, than in the present tense; rather *we shall be*, than we are, or have been; because the work is only begun; it daily increaseth more and more, until it comes to a full perfection in heaven.

k Gal. 2. 20.
& 5. 24. & 6.
14. Eph. 4. 22.
Col. 3. 5, 9.
l Col. 2. 11.

6 Knowing this, that ^k our old man is crucified with *him*, that ^l the body of sin might be destroyed, that henceforth we should not serve sin.

By the *old man* is meant, that corrupt and polluted nature which we derive from Adam, the first man: see Eph. iv. 22; Col. iii. 9, 10. The old and new man are opposites; as then the new man is the image of God repaired in us; so the old man is a depravation of that image of God, and a universal pollution of the whole man. *Is crucified with him;* by virtue of our union with him, and by means of his death and crucifixion: see Gal. ii. 20. *The body of sin* is the very same that he called before the old man. The corrupt nature is sometimes called *the body*, chap. viii. 13, sometimes a *body of death*, chap. vii. 24, and here *the body of sin*. It is indeed a mere mass and lump of sin; it is not one sin, but all sin seminally. It is with respect to this body of sin, that particular lusts and corruptions are called *members*, Col. iii. 5. *Might be destroyed;* weakened more and more, till at last it be destroyed. *That henceforth we should not serve sin;* as we did before regeneration, and as they still do who voluntarily commit it, John viii. 34. They do not only act sin, but are acted by it, having as many lords as lusts, Tit. iii. 3. See more of this, ver. 16.

m 1 Pet. 4. 1.
† Gr. *justified.*

7 For ^m he that is dead is † freed from sin.

He that is dead, i. e. to *sin, is freed from* it; not only in respect of the guilt thereof, which sense the marginal reading of the word seems to respect, but also in regard of the service of it. This agrees best with the context; look, as he that is dead is freed and discharged from the authority of those who had dominion over him in his lifetime, so it is with those that are dead to sin. There is a parallel place, 1 Pet. iv. 1.

n 2 Tim. 2. 11.

8 Now ⁿ if we be dead with Christ, we believe that we shall also live with him:

i. e. If we have fellowship with Christ in his death, we have reason to believe we shall have fellowship with him also in his resurrection and life: see ver. 5. Though everlasting be not excluded, yet a spiritual life is principally intended; we shall so live with Christ, as no more to return to dead works. The next words show this to be the sense.

o Rev. 1. 18.

9 Knowing that ^o Christ being raised from the dead dieth no more; death hath no more dominion over him.

q. d. Of this you know you have an example or copy in Christ himself; he so rose again, as never more to come under the power of death.

p Heb. 9. 27, 28.
q Luke 20. 38.

10 For in that he died, ^p he died unto sin once: but in that he liveth, ^q he liveth unto God.

For when *he died unto sin*, i. e. to take away sin, he died but once; see Heb. ix. 28, and x. 10, 14; but when he rose again from the dead, he lived with God for ever an immortal, endless life. By this phrase is expressed that eternal and indissoluble union which the Son hath with the Father.

11 Likewise reckon ye also yourselves to be ^r dead indeed unto sin, but ^s alive unto God through Jesus Christ our Lord.

r ver. 2.
s Gal. 2. 19.

So we in like manner must make account, that by virtue of his death we are dead to sin, and by virtue of his resurrection are alive to God, and so alive as never to resume our former courses, or return again to our former sins. *Through Jesus Christ our Lord;* or, in Jesus Christ our Lord; i. e. after the similitude of Jesus Christ, who so lives as to die no more. Or else this phrase imports that Jesus Christ is the root of our spiritual life; even as the scion lives in the stock, so believers are alive unto God in Jesus Christ, receiving from him that virtue whereby their spiritual life is begun, maintained, and perfected.

12 ^t Let not sin therefore reign in your mortal body, that ye should obey it in the lusts thereof.

t Ps. 19. 13.
& 119. 133.

Let not sin therefore: q. d. Seeing this is the case, that you are dead to sin, baptized into Christ, are planted together into the likeness of his death, &c., therefore the rather hearken to and obey the following exhortation. By *sin* he means the sin or corruption of our nature, the same that before he called the *old man*, and the *body of sin*. There are remainders thereof in the regenerate; in them it is mortified, but not eradicated; therefore to them this exhortation is not unnecessary. *Reign;* he doth not say, let it not be or reside, but let it not reign or preside; let it not bear sway or have dominion in you; let it not have the upper hand of the motions of the Spirit of God. *In your mortal body;* the body (called here a *mortal* or frail *body*) is put by a synecdoche for the whole man; and he the rather makes mention of the body, because the parts and members thereof are the usual instruments of sin. Therefore it follows in the next verse, *Neither yield your members as instruments of unrighteousness. That ye should obey it in the lusts thereof;* i. e. that you should obey sin in the lust of the body. The gender of the relative article of the Greek, requires it should be so read and understood. The meaning is not as if lusts were in the body alone, for Christ teacheth the contrary, Matt. xv. 19, 20; but because all sinful lusts do mostly show and manifest themselves in and through the body, Gal. v. 19.

13 Neither yield ye your ^u members *as* † instruments of unrighteousness unto sin: but ^x yield yourselves unto God, as those that are alive from the dead, and your members *as* instruments of righteousness unto God.

u ch. 7. 5.
Col. 3. 5.
Jam. 4. 1.
† Gr. *arms*, or, *weapons*.
x ch. 12. 1.
1 Pet. 2. 24.
& 4. 2.

He fitly compares our bodily members to tools that artificers work, or weapons that soldiers fight withal; for as those, so these, may be used well or ill: e. g. With the hand one man giveth an alms, another stealeth; with the tongue one man blesseth, another curseth. By members here we are not only to understand the parts of the body, as the hands, eyes, ears, &c.; but also the faculties of the soul, as the understanding, will, affections, &c. These bear some proportion to the bodily members, as the understanding to the eye, &c. All of them must be employed by us as weapons to fight, not under the command of Satan for sin, but under the command of God for righteousness. *As those that are alive from the dead:* these words contain a reason why we should not serve sin and Satan, but bequeath and dedicate ourselves to the service of God, because we are endued with a spiritual life, after a spiritual death; or because we have received so great a benefit as to be raised in Christ from the death and power of sin.

14 For ^y sin shall not have dominion over you: for ye are not under the law, but under grace.

y ch. 7. 4, 6.
& 8. 2.
Gal. 5. 18.

In the 12th verse it was an exhortation, but in this it is a promise, that sin shall not reign in and over us. Rebel it may, but reign it shall not in the regenerate. It hath lost its absolute and uncontrolled power. It fares with sin in such as with those beasts in Dan. vii. 12, who, though their lives were prolonged for a season, had their dominion taken away. It is an encouragement to fight, when we are sure of victory. *For ye are not under the law, but under grace:* he adds this as a reason of what he had asserted and promised: you are not under a legal, but gospel dispensation; so some expound the words; *grace* is often put for the gospel: or, you are not under the old but the new covenant. *The law* and *grace* thus differ; the one condemns the sinner, the other absolves him; the one requires perfect, the other accepts sincere, obedience; the one prescribes what we must do, the other assists us in the doing of our duty. This last seems to be the genuine sense: q. d. You may be sure sin shall have no dominion over you; for you are not under the law, which forbids sin, but gives no power against it, or which requires obedience, and gives no strength to perform it (like the Egyptian taskmasters, who required bricks but gave no straw); but under the gospel or covenant of grace, where sin is not only forbidden, but the sinner is enabled to resist and overcome it. *Quest.* But what shall be said of the godly in the times of the law; were not they under grace? *Answ.* They were, Acts xv. 11; Heb. iv. 2; but not in the same degree. The godly had help and assistance under the law, but they had it not by the law. How believers are said not to be under the law: see chap. vii. 4.

z 1 Cor. 9.21. 15 What then? shall we sin, ᶻbecause we are not under the law, but under grace? God forbid.

What then? doth it follow from hence that we are lawless, and may live as we list? *God forbid:* q. d. No, by no means, the premises afford no such conclusion; though we are not under the curse and rigour of the law, yet we are under its directions and discipline: the gospel allows of sin no more than the law. The apostle is careful, both here and elsewhere, to prevent licentiousness, or the abuse of Christian liberty: see Gal. v. 13; 1 Pet. ii. 16: see also ver. 1, and the notes there.

a Matt. 6.24.
John 8. 34.
2 Pet. 2. 19. 16 Know ye not, that ᵃto whom ye yield yourselves servants to obey, his servants ye are to whom ye obey; whether of sin unto death, or of obedience unto righteousness?

He refutes the aforementioned cavil by a common axiom, that every one knows and apprehends. *Of obedience unto righteousness;* which will be rewarded with eternal life. But why doth he not say of obedience unto life? then the antithesis had been more plain and full. Because though sin be the cause of death, yet obedience is not the cause of life, (as ver. 23,) but only the way to it.

17 But God be thanked, that ye were the servants of sin, but ye have obeyed
b 2 Tim.1.13.
+ Gr. where-
to ye were
delivered. from the heart ᵇthat form of doctrine † which was delivered you.

But God be thanked, that ye were the servants of sin: q. d. But as for you, God be thanked, that though once you were the servants of sin, viz. when you were ignorant and unregenerate, yet now you are freed from that bondage, and set at liberty from the power and dominion of sin. *But ye have obeyed from the heart that form of doctrine which was delivered you:* this phrase expresseth the efficacy of Divine doctrine in the hearts of believers; it changeth and fashioneth their hearts according to its likeness, 2 Cor. iii. 18. Hence in James i. 21, it is called an *ingrafted word;* it turns the heart and life of the hearer into its own nature, as the stock doth the scion that is ingrafted into it. The doctrine of the gospel is the mould, and the hearer is the metal, which, when it is melted and cast into the mould, receives its form and figure.

c John 8.32.
1 Cor. 7. 22.
Gal. 5. 1.
1 Pet. 2. 16. 18 Being then ᶜmade free from sin, ye became the servants of righteousness.

Made free from sin; i. e. the servitude of sin; having received a manumission from that hard and evil master, you have given up yourselves to a better and more ingenuous service.

19 I speak after the manner of men because of the infirmity of your flesh: for as ye have yielded your members servants to uncleanness and to iniquity unto iniquity; even so now yield your members servants to righteousness unto holiness.

I speak after the manner of men because of the infirmity of your flesh: q. d. I accommodate myself to your capacity, because of the weakness of your understanding in spiritual things; therefore I use this familiar similitude of service and freedom, that by these secular and civil things you might the better understand such as are spiritual: see John iii. 12. *For as ye have yielded, &c.:* q. d. The great thing that I desire of you (and it is most reasonable) is this, that you would be as sedulous and careful now to obey God, as you have formerly been to obey and serve sin; to do good, as you have been to do evil. *To unclean-*

ness; to fleshly lusts, which defile you. *To iniquity unto iniquity;* i. e. adding one sin to another; or else by the former you may understand original, by the latter actual sin. He useth three words about the service of sin, and but two about the service of God; wicked men take great pains for hell; oh that we would take the same for heaven.

20 For when ye were ᵈthe servants of sin, ye were free † from righteousness. d John 8.34.
+ Gr. to
righteous-
ness.

q. d. When you served sin, you knew that God and righteousness had no whit of your service; why then should sin have any of your service now, when you have delivered up yourselves to righteousness, or godliness, to be the observant followers thereof? Why should not ye now abstain as strictly from all sin, as then ye did from all good?

21 ᵉWhat fruit had ye then in those things whereof ye are now ashamed? for ᶠthe end of those things *is* death. e ch. 7. 5.

f ch. 1. 32.

q. d. And this will be much more equal and reasonable, if you consider these three things: 1. How little fruit and satisfaction your former sins have afforded you in the very time of committing them. 2. How nothing but shame and sorrow doth follow upon the remembrance of them. 3. How death, yea, eternal death and damnation, (unless pardoning grace and mercy prevent it,) will be the certain conclusion of them. And whether these things are true or no, I appeal to yourselves.

22 But now ᵍbeing made free from sin, and become servants to God, ye have your fruit unto holiness, and the end everlasting life. g John 8. 32.

q. d. But now, on the contrary, being set at liberty from the service of sin, and admitted to be the servants of God, you plainly perceive a difference: for, 1. In your lifetime you increase in grace and holiness, and that is no small fruit or advantage; and then, 2. At your death you shall have everlasting life.

23 For ʰthe wages of sin *is* death; but ⁱthe gift of God *is* eternal life through Jesus Christ our Lord. h Gen. 2. 17.
ch. 5. 12.
Jam. 1. 15.
i ch. 2. 7.
& 5. 17, 21.
1 Pet. 1. 4.

q. d. Now therefore compare the office of both these services together, and you shall easily see which master is best to serve and obey; the wages that sin will pay you, in the end is death; but the reward that God will freely bestow upon you (if you be his servants) *is eternal life through Jesus Christ our Lord. Wages;* the word properly signifies victuals. The Romans of old paid their soldiers with provision and victuals in recompence of their service; afterward they gave them money, but still the old term was retained, and now it is used to signify any reward or stipend whatsoever. *Is death:* by *death* here we must understand not only temporal, but also and more especially eternal death, as appears by the opposition it hath to *eternal life:* this is the just and true hire of sin. *The gift of God is eternal life;* he doth not say that eternal life is the wages of righteousness, but that it is the gracious or free gift of God. He varies the phrase on purpose, to show that we attain not eternal life by our own merits, our own works or worthiness, but by the gift or grace of God; for which cause he also addeth, *through Jesus Christ our Lord.* See Aug. lib. de Gratia et Libero Arbitrio, c. 9. Let the papists (if they can) reconcile this text to their distinction of mortal and venial sins, and to their doctrine of the meritoriousness of good works.

CHAP. VII

No law having power over a person longer than he liveth, 1—3, we therefore, being become dead to the law by the body of Christ, are left free to place ourselves under a happier dispensation, 4. For the law, through the prevalency of corrupt passions, could only serve as an instrument of sin unto death; although it be in itself holy, and just, and good, 5—13; as is manifest by our reason approving the precepts of it, whilst our depraved nature is unable to put them in practice, 14—23. The wretchedness of man in such a situation, and God's mercy in his deliverance from it through Christ, 24, 25.

KNOW ye not, brethren, (for I speak to them that know the law,) how that the law hath dominion over a man as long as he liveth?

The apostle, having showed in a former chapter how believers are freed from the dominion of sin, proceeds in this chapter to declare, that they are free also from the yoke of the Mosaical law, because that was dead to them, and they to it. This he illustrates, and proceeds by the familiar allegory of a husband and his wife: Look, as a wife is free from her husband when he is dead, and may then marry another, and be no adulteress; so believers are dead to the law, and are free to be married to another, even to Christ, that is raised from the dead, that upon their marriage they may bring forth fruit unto God. By *the law* here he means the law of wedlock, or the law of Moses about that matter, as appears by the instance given in the next verse. The word *man* here is common to both sexes, and may be applied to either, for both are subject to the aforementioned law.

a 1 Cor. 7. 39.

2 For ^a the woman which hath an husband is bound by the law to *her* husband so long as he liveth; but if the husband be dead, she is loosed from the law of *her* husband.

He here exemplifies and illustrates the foregoing assertion. *The woman is bound by the law to her husband so long as he liveth*: see a parallel place, 1 Cor. vii. 39. This is the general rule, yet there is an exception in the case of fornication or desertion: see Matt. v. 32; 1 Cor. vii. 15. *From the law of her husband;* from the obligation of the law of marriage.

b Mat. 5. 32.

3 So then ^b if, while *her* husband liveth, she be married to another man, she shall be called an adulteress: but if her husband be dead, she is free from that law; so that she is no adulteress, though she be married to another man.

c ch. 8. 2.
Gal. 2. 19.
& 5. 18.
Ephes. 2. 15.
Col. 2. 14.
d Gal. 5. 22.

4 Wherefore, my brethren, ye also are become ^c dead to the law by the body of Christ; that ye should be married to another, *even* to him who is raised from the dead, that we should ^d bring forth fruit unto God.

Ye also are become dead to the law; i. e. ye are taken off from all hopes of justification by it, and from your confidence in obedience to it, Gal. ii. 19. The opposition seems to require that he should have said, the law is dead to us; but these two phrases are much the same. *Quest.* What law doth he mean? *Answ.* Not only the ceremonial, but the moral law, for in that he instanceth, ver. 7. The moral law is in force still; Christ came to confirm, and not to destroy it; but believers are freed from the malediction, from the rigid exaction, and from the irritation thereof. Of this last he speaks, ver. 8, 9, and from it we are freed but in part. *By the body of Christ;* i. e. by the sacrifice of Christ's body upon the cross; thereby he delivered us from the law, in the sense before mentioned. *Fruit unto God;* i. e. fruits of holiness and good works, to the glory and praise of God.

+ Gr. *passions.*
e ch. 6. 13.
f ch. 6. 21.
Gal. 5. 19.
Jam. 1. 15.

5 For when we were in the flesh, the † motions of sins, which were by the law, ^e did work in our members ^f to bring forth fruit unto death.

For: q. d. For bringing forth of which fruit unto God, we have now better helps than formerly we had; or we are in much better circumstances than formerly we were: and so he proceeds to show how our present state doth differ from the former. *When we were in the flesh;* i. e. in our carnal, fleshly state, before we were regenerated, or under the carnal pedagogy of the law; for in the next verse he speaks of our being *now delivered from the law. The motions of sins which were by the law;* i. e. the corrupt inclinations to sin, which are drawn forth by the law, as ill vapours are raised out of a dunghill by the sun; or which are irritated by the law; of which by and by. *Did work*

in our members: see chap. vi. 13, 16. *To bring forth fruit unto death;* i. e. such ill fruit as ends in death, chap. vi. 21.

6 But now we are delivered from the law, ‖ that being dead wherein we were held; that we should serve ^g in newness of spirit, and not *in* the oldness of the letter.

‖ Or, *being dead to that,* ch. 6. 2.
ver. 4.
g ch. 2. 29.
2 Cor. 3. 6.

But now; i. e. being brought out of our fleshly state. *We are delivered from the law:* see the notes on ver. 4. *That being dead wherein we were held;* the relative is not in the Greek text, but it is well supplied to fill up the sense. The antecedent must be either sin or the law; by both of these we were held or detained whilst unregenerate; but now neither of these have any power to hold us with. Some read it, he being dead; the old man, of which he spake in the foregoing chapter. *That we should serve in newness of spirit;* i. e. that we should serve God, or Jesus Christ, our new husband, in true holiness, which is wrought in us by the renewing of the Spirit; or serve him in a new spiritual manner. *And not in the oldness of the letter;* i. e. not in an outward and ceremonial manner, according to the letter of the law; which service, or way of worship, is now antiquated, and grown out of date. The word *oldness* insinuates the abolishing thereof, because of insufficiency, Heb. viii. 13.

7 What shall we say then? *Is* the law sin? God forbid. Nay, ^h I had not known sin, but by the law: for I had not known ‖ lust, except the law had said, ⁱ Thou shalt not covet.

h ch. 3. 20.
‖ Or, *concupiscence.*
i Ex. 20. 17.
Deut. 5. 21.
Acts 20. 33.
ch. 13. 9.

Is the law sin? God forbid: here is another anticipation of an objection, which might arise from what the apostle had said, ver. 5, that sin was powerful in us by the law. Some might object and say, that the law then was sin, i. e. that it was the cause of it, and a factor for it. To this he answers, by his usual note of detestation, *God forbid. Nay, I had not known sin, but by the law;* i. e. I had not known it so clearly and effectually, so as to humble and drive me to Christ; for otherwise, nature itself teacheth a difference of good and evil in many things. He adds this as a reason why the law cannot be the cause of sin, because it discovers and reproves sin, it detects and damns it; and that it so doth, he proves from his own experience. *For I had not known lust;* i. e. I had not known it to be sin. By *lust* here some understand that concupiscence which the schoolmen call unformed concupiscence, which hath not the consent of the will: for the concupiscence to which we consent, the heathens themselves know to be sinful; but that which hath not the consent of the will, or the first motions to sin, they held to be no sin; as neither did the Pharisees, amongst whom Paul lived; nor do the papists to this very day. Some by *lust* understand original sin, which is the fountain from whence all particular lusts flow; the hot furnace from which all sinful motions, as so many sparks, continually arise: this is called *lust,* likewise, in James i. 14; and this is forbidden in every commandment; for where any of sin is prohibited, there the root also is prohibited; but more particularly it is forbidden in the tenth commandment. *Except the law had said, Thou shalt not covet:* some understand the law in general; but the article used in the Greek seems to restrain it to a particular precept. Besides, they are the very words of the tenth commandment. But why doth he not mention the objects that are specified in that commandment, as, *thy neighbour's house, wife,* &c.? The answer is, That that was not material; for the apostle speaking of inward concupiscence, which without the law is latent and undiscovered, it was enough to name the sin itself, seeing the objects about which it is conversant are of all sorts, and can hardly be numbered.

8 But ^k sin, taking occasion by the commandment, wrought in me all manner of concupiscence. For ^l without the law sin *was* dead.

k ch. 4. 15.
& 5. 20.
l 1 Cor. 15. 56.

But sin; i. e. the corruption of our nature, the depraved bent and bias of the soul, called before *lust. Taking occa-*

ROMANS VII

sion by the commandment; i. e. being stirred up or drawn forth by the prohibition of the law. The law did not properly give occasion, but sin took it. The law (as before) is not the cause of sin, though by accident it is the occasion of it. In a dropsy, it is not the drink that is to be blamed for increasing the disease, but the ill habit of body. Such is the depravedness of man's nature, that the things which are forbidden are the more desired: the more the law would dam up the torrent of sinful lusts, the higher do they swell. The law was given to restrain sin, but through our corruption it falls out contrarily. The law inhibiting sin, and not giving power to avoid it, our impetuous lusts take occasion or advantage from thence, the more eagerly to pursue it. *Wrought in me all manner of concupiscence;* i. e. inordinate affections and inclinations of all sorts. *For without the law;* i. e. without the knowledge of the law. *Sin was dead;* i. e. comparatively dead. Sin hath not so much power, either to terrify the conscience, or to stir up inordinate affections; it is like a sleepy lion, that stirs not.

9 For I was alive without the law once: but when the commandment came sin revived, and I died.

For I was alive without the law once: q. d. Take me, if you please, for an instance. Before I knew the law aright, and understood the Divine and spiritual meaning of it, or whilst the law stood afar off, and was not brought home to my conscience, *I was alive,* that is, in my own conceit; I thought myself in as good condition as any man living; my conscience never gave me any trouble. So it was with me once, or heretofore, when I was a Pharisee, or in an unregenerate state. *But when the commandment came;* i. e. when it came nearer to my conscience; when I came to know and understand the spiritual meaning and extent of it, that it condemned sinful lusts, affections, and inclinations. *Sin revived;* i. e. its sinfulness and guilt appeared, and I had a lively sense thereof imprinted upon my soul; or my corruptions began to gather head, and seemed, as it were, to receive new vigour and life. *And I died;* i. e. in my own opinion and feeling. I felt my conscience deadly wounded. I was convinced I was in a state of death and damnation. I lost the confidence I formerly had of my good estate.

10 And the commandment, ᵐ which *was ordained* to life, I found *to be* unto death. [m Lev. 18. 5. Ezek. 20. 11, 13, 21. 2 Cor. 3. 7.]

q. d. So it came to pass, that the commandment, which was ordained to be a rule of life, and, if I could have kept it, a means of life also, chap. x. 5; Gal. iii. 12, I found it to be to me (through my corruption and transgression) an occasion of death; it bound me over to punishment; and so, by accident, it tendeth to death. Some by *life* and *death,* here, understand peace and perturbation of spirit.

11 For sin, taking occasion by the commandment, deceived me, and by it slew *me.*

For sin, taking occasion by the commandment: see the notes on ver. 8. *Deceived me;* i. e. seduced and drew me aside, Heb. iii. 13; James i. 14. *And by it slew me;* i. e. it drove me into despair, or delivered me over to death and damnation, and made me obnoxious thereunto.

12 Wherefore ⁿ the law *is* holy, and the commandment holy, and just, and good. [n Ps. 19. 8. & 119. 38, 137. 1 Tim. 1. 8.]

Wherefore the law is holy; and so the objection, ver. 7, was a groundless objection: for though the law were the occasion of sin, or were made advantage of by sin, as ver. 8, yet it was not the cause of it; that, on all hands, is acknowledged to be holy, &c. *The law;* the law in all the branches of it. *The commandment;* particularly the preceptive part of the law, and every particular precept. *Holy, and just, and good:* the three epithets here given the law of God may be thus distinguished; it is *holy* in respect of the ceremonial part, it is *just* in respect of the judicial part, and *good* in respect of the moral part of it. Or else the law is *holy,* as it teacheth us our duty unto God; *just,* as it showeth us our duty to our neighbour; *good,* in regard of the effect and end, as it works goodness in the observer thereof, and is conducive to his temporal and eternal good.

13 Was then that which is good made death unto me? God forbid. But sin, that it might appear sin, working death in me by that which is good; that sin by the commandment might become exceeding sinful.

Was then that which is good made death unto me? God forbid: another anticipation. The apostle denies that the holy law was in its own nature deadly, or the cause of death to him; the fault was not in the law, but in his own depraved nature: but the plain case is this that follows. *But sin, that it might appear sin, working death in me by that which is good;* that sin, that so it might appear every way like itself, wrought death in him, by occasion of that law, which yet itself is holy, just, and good. *That sin by the commandment might become exceeding sinful;* so as hereupon sin, which in the time of his ignorance and unregeneracy seemed not worthy of any notice, appeared to be exceeding foul and sinful. Sin is so evil, that he cannot call it by a worse name than its own. Jerome thinketh, that the apostle here commits a solecism, by joining an adjective of the masculine gender with a substantive of the feminine; but Beza and Erasmus have observed, that this is usual in the Attic dialect. See the like, chap. i. 20. Some read sinner for *sinful,* and make the apostle to speak of sin as of a certain person; and therefore all along the context sin is said to work, to be dead, to revive, to deceive, to kill, &c., which is properly attributed to persons, and not to things.

14 For we know that the law is spiritual: but I am carnal, ° sold under sin. [o 1 Kings 21. 20, 25. 2 Kin. 17. 17. 1 Mac. 1. 15.]

He goes on to clear the law, and excuse it, giving it another commendation, that it is *spiritual;* i. e. it requires such obedience as is not only outward, but inward and spiritual; it forbids spiritual as well as fleshly sins. Read Christ's exposition of it, in the 5th of St. Matthew. *I am carnal;* i. e. in part, because of the remainders of sin and of the flesh that are still in me; in respect of which, those who are regenerated are said to be carnal. Compare 1 Cor. i. 2, with 1 Cor. iii. 1. *Sold under sin:* he did not actively sell himself to sin, or to commit sin, which is said of Ahab, 1 Kings xxi. 20, 25, and of the idolatrous Israelites, 2 Kings xvii. 17. He was not sin's servant or slave; but many times he was sin's captive against his will; see ver. 23. Against his will and consent, he was still subject to the violent lusts and assaults of sin, and not able wholly to free himself: though he always made stout resistance, yet many times he was overcome. Hitherto the apostle hath spoken of the power of the law and sin in unregenerate persons, even as he himself had experienced whilst he was yet in such a state; but now he cometh to speak of himself as he then was, and to declare what power the remainders of sinful flesh had still in him, though regenerated, and in part renewed. That the following part of this chapter is to be applied to a regenerate person, is evident, because the apostle (speaking of himself in the former verses) useth the preter-perfect tense, or speaketh of that which was past; but here he changeth the tense, and speaketh of the present time. From the 7th verse to the 14th, he tells us how it had been with him formerly; and then from the 14th verse to the end, he relates how it was with him now; *I was* so and so, *I am* thus and thus. The changing of the tense and time doth plainly argue a change in the person. They that list to be further satisfied in this point, may find it fully discussed in our own language, by Mr. Anthony Burgess, in his excellent discourse of Original Sin, part iv. c. 3, and by Dr. Willet, in his Hexalta in locum; and they that understand the Latin tongue, may find it argued *pro* and *con,* in Synops. Critic. &c., and by Aug. Retractat. lib. i. c. 23; Contra Julian. lib. v. c. 11.

15 For that which I do I †allow not: for ᵖ what I would, that do I not; but what I hate, that do I. [† Gr. *know,* Ps. 1. 6. p Gal. 5. 17.]

For that which I do; i. e. what I do contrary to the command of God. *I allow not:* in the Greek it is, I know not: q. d. Many times I am surprised and overtaken, not knowing or considering what I do. Or when he says, I know not, his meaning is, (as our translation renders it,) *I allow* or approve *not.* So the word is used, Matt. vii. 23, and elsewhere: q. d. Even now, in my converted and regenerate state, I am many times greatly divided, and feel a strife or combat in myself; so that the good I would do upon the motions of God's Spirit in me, I do not; and the evil that

I hate, and am utterly averse to, so far as I am regenerated, that I do. See a parallel place, Gal. v. 17. *But what I hate, that do I:* he doth not speak here so much of outward actions, as of inward motions and affections: he doth not speak of gross sins, as drunkenness, uncleanness, &c., but of such infirmities as flow from the polluted nature, and from which we can never be thoroughly cleansed in this life.

16 If then I do that which I would not, I consent unto the law that *it is* good.

This very thing is an argument, that the law is such as I have before asserted, ver. 12, 14. This shows my consent to the holiness and goodness of the law; I vote with it, and for it, as the only rule of right or righteousness.

17 Now then it is no more I that do it, but sin that dwelleth in me.

It is no more I that do it; i. e. it is not I as spiritual or renewed, it is not my whole self, *but it is sin that dwelleth in me,* that inhabits in me as a troublesome inmate, that I cannot get rid of, that will not out so long as the house stands; as the fretting leprosy in the walls of a house would not out till the house itself were demolished. It is such an inhabitant as is never from home; it is not in us as a stranger for a season, but it makes its constant abode with us.

q Gen. 6. 5. & 8. 21.

18 For I know that ^q in me (that is, in my flesh,) dwelleth no good thing: for to will is present with me; but *how* to perform that which is good I find not.

In my flesh; i. e. in my fleshly part, or my nature in and of itself. *No good thing;* no goodness at all, or no spiritual good. *For to will is present with me;* i. e. I can, so long and so far as I follow the motions of God's Spirit, will that which is good; *but how to perform the good* that I would, *I find no* power or might, at least to perform it in that manner that I desire: the meaning is not that he never did the good he desired; but it often so fell out, he began many good things, but he could not go thorough-stitch with them.

19 For the good that I would I do not: but the evil which I would not, that I do.

20 Now if I do that I would not, it is no more I that do it, but sin that dwelleth in me.

These two verses are a repetition of what he had said, ver. 15, 17. Every new man is two men; there is in him an I and an I. The apostle in his unregenerate state, could make no such distinction as now he doth.

21 I find then a law, that, when I would do good, evil is present with me.

This verse hath greatly vexed interpreters. The apostle speaking simply and abstractly of *a law,* the question is, What law he means? Some take the word improperly, for a decree or condition, which was imposed upon him, and to which he was necessarily subject, that when he would do good, evil should be present with him. Others by *law* here do understand the law of sin; of which he speaks afterwards, ver. 23, 25. Sin is like a law, and so powerful and imperious in its commands and dictates, that we have much ado, the best of us, to resist it, and shake off its yoke. q. d. I find by sad experience such a forcible power in sin, that when I would do good, I am hindered, and cannot do it so freely and fully as I desire. Others by *law* here do understand the law of God; and those that so understand it, have given no less than eight interpretations, to make the grammatical connexion: the best is of those that say the preposition κατὰ is understood, a frequent ellipsis in the Greek tongue, (see James i. 26,) and then the sense is this; I find that when, according to the law or command of God, I would do good, evil is present with me. *Evil is present with me;* another periphrasis of original sin, of which there are many in this chapter. Just now it was the sin that dwelleth in us, and here it is the evil that is present with us: it inheres and adheres, or hangs upon us continually. It is adjacent, so the Greek word signifies, and always at hand; we carry it about with us at all times, and in all places; whithersoever we go, it follows us; or, as it is here, in our doing of good it is a very great impediment to us.

22 For I ^r delight in the law of God after ^s the inward man: r Ps. 1. 2. s 2 Cor. 4. 16. Eph. 3. 16. Col. 3. 9, 10.

This shows yet more expressly that the apostle speaketh in the person of a regenerate man, or of himself as regenerate. Certainly, to *delight in the law of God* is an inseparable property of such a one: see Psal. i. 2, and cxix. 77, 111. *The inward man;* i. e. the new man, or regenerate part within me: this is called *the hidden man of the heart,* 1 Pet. iii. 4: see chap. ii. 29; 2 Cor. iv. 16.

23 But ^t I see another law in ^u my members, warring against the law of my mind, and bringing me into captivity to the law of sin which is in my members. t Gal. 5. 17. u ch. 6. 13, 19.

Another law in my members; i. e. a law quite different from *the law of God,* mentioned in the foregoing verse. By the *law in* the *members* understand natural corruption, which, like a law, commandeth and inclineth by sensual rewards and punishments; and by the *law in* the *mind* understand a principle of grace, which, as a law, as well as the other, commandeth and inclineth to that which is good. The *law in* the *members* and the *law in* the *mind,* are the same that are called *flesh* and *Spirit,* Gal. v. 17. These two laws and principles are in all regenerate persons, and are directly contrary to one another; hence there is continual warring and combating betwixt them, as is expressed in both these places, as also in James iv. 1; 1 Pet. ii. 11. *Bringing me into captivity to the law of sin;* i. e. drawing and hurrying me to the commission of sin, against my will and consent. He pursues the metaphor; the flesh doth not only war in the regenerate, but many times it overcomes and hath success: see ver. 15. *To the law of sin which is in my members;* i. e. to itself. The antecedent is put in the room of the relative: see Gen. ix. 16, and elsewhere. The *law in the members* and the *law of sin in* the *members* are the same.

24 O wretched man that I am! who shall deliver me from ∥ the body of this death? ∥ Or, *this body of death.*

O wretched man that I am! the word signifies one wearied out with continual combats. *Who shall deliver me?* it is not the voice of one desponding or doubting, but of one breathing and panting after deliverance: the like pathetical exclamations are frequent: see Psal. lv. 6. One calls this verse, *gemitus sanctorum,* the groan of the godly. *From the body of this death;* or, from this body of death; or, by a Hebraism, from this dead body, this carcass of sin, to which I am inseparably fastened, as noisome every whit to my soul as a dead carcass to my senses. This is another circumlocution, or denomination of original sin. It is called *the body of sin,* chap. vi. 6, and here *the body of death;* it tends and binds over to death.

25 ^x I thank God through Jesus Christ our Lord. So then with the mind I myself serve the law of God; but with the flesh the law of sin. x 1 Cor. 15. 57.

I thank God; who hath already delivered me from the slavery and dominion of sin; so that though it wars against me, I still resist it, and, by the strength of Christ, do frequently overcome it, 1 Cor. xv. 57. *So then with the mind I myself serve the law of God; but with the flesh the law of sin:* this is the conclusion the apostle maketh of this experimental discourse. q. d. So far as I am renewed, I yield obedience to the law of God; and so far as I am unregenerate, I obey the dictates and suggestions of the law of sin. *Object.* No man can serve two contrary masters. *Answ.* The apostle did not serve these two in the same part, or the same renewed faculty; nor did he do it at the same time, ordinarily; and for the most part he served the law of God, though sometimes, through the power of temptation and in-dwelling corruption, he was enforced, against his will, to serve the law of sin.

CHAP. VIII

Under the gospel we are free from condemnation, walking after the Spirit, 1—4. *The evil of being carnally minded, and the good of being spiritually minded,* 5—8. *Chris-*

tians have God's Spirit to guide and assist them, 9—11; by which if they mortify the flesh, they shall live, 12, 13. For they that are led by the Spirit are sons of God, and heirs of glory, 14—18; whose manifestation the world hath long earnestly looked for, hoping to be rescued thereby from the bondage of corruption, 19—22. And even they who have the first-fruits of the Spirit do still long after it, 23; being hitherto saved by hope only, 24, 25: the Spirit in the mean time aiding their infirmities in prayer, 26, 27. Nevertheless the final good of them that fear God is all along pursued, being fore-ordained of God, and brought about according to the course of his providence, 28—30. The ground and assurance of the Christian's hope, 31—39.

THERE is therefore now no condemnation to them which are in Christ Jesus, who [a]walk not after the flesh, but after the Spirit.

a ver. 4.
Gal. 5. 16, 25.

There is therefore now; seeing things are so as I have said, since believers do not allow themselves in sin, chap. vii. 15, and are in part delivered from it, as ver. 25, therefore it follows as it is here. No condemnation; or no one condemnation. He doth not say, there is no matter of condemnation, or nothing damnable in them that are in Christ, there is enough and enough of that; but he says, there is no actual condemnation to such: see John iii. 18; v. 24. There is a meiosis in the words, more is understood than is expressed; he means, that justification and eternal salvation is the portion of such. The positive is included in the negative; it is God's condemnation only, from which such as are in Christ are exempted; they are nevertheless condemned and censured by men, and sometimes by their own consciences too. To them which are in Christ Jesus; so we fill it up, but in the original it is only, to them in Christ Jesus. The phrase imports, that there is a mystical and spiritual union betwixt Christ and believers. This is sometimes expressed by Christ's being in them, ver. 10; 2 Cor. xiii. 5; Col. i. 17; and here by their being in Christ: see 1 Cor. i. 30; 1 John v. 20. Christ is in believers by his Spirit, and believers are in Christ by faith. Who walk not after the flesh, but after the Spirit: this clause describes the persons who are united to Christ, or who are exempted from condemnation; they are such as walk not, &c. By flesh understand the corrupt nature that is in man: see chap. vii. 18, 25; John iii. 6; Gal. v. 17: to walk after it, is to be led and guided by the motions of it. That is, it is not their principle and guide, there is another nature or principle in them, by which they are guided and acted; and what that is the next words tell you. By the Spirit some understand the person of the Spirit; others, the grace of the Spirit, the new or divine nature (as it is called) which is implanted in the soul in the work of regeneration: this is called the Spirit, Matt. xxvi. 41; John iii. 6; Gal. v. 17. To walk after the Spirit, is to be led and guided by the counsels and motions thereof. It is to regulate and order the whole conversation according to the rule of the new creature, or according to the line and square of God's word and Spirit. You have the same phrase, Gal. v. 16, 25. To walk after the Spirit, is not only now and then to have some good motions, or to do some good actions, but it is to persevere and go forward therein; walking is a continued and progressive motion. The connexion of these two shows that negative holiness is not enough; we must not only abstain from evil, but do good.

2 For [b]the law of [c]the Spirit of life in Christ Jesus hath made me free from [d]the law of sin and death.

b John 8. 36.
ch. 6. 18, 22.
Gal. 2. 19.
& 5. 1.
c 1 Cor. 15. 45. 2 Cor. 3. 6.
d ch. 7. 24, 25.

The law of the Spirit of life; some understand hereby the doctrine of the gospel, which is called the law of the Spirit of life, because it is the ministry of the Spirit and of life. Others understand the efficacy and power of that grace and holiness, wherewith the living and quickening Spirit of God hath filled the human nature of Christ. Others rather understand a regenerating and working the new and heavenly life in the soul, with great power and efficacy. In Christ Jesus; i. e. which was poured out upon him, and doth still reside in him after a very eminent manner: see Isa. xi. 2; Luke iv. 1. Or, in Christ Jesus, is as much as by Christ Jesus; it is he that gives and conveys this Spirit, how, when and to whom he pleaseth. Hath made me free from the law of sin: by sin here he aims chiefly at original sin; he doth not say, that those who are in Christ are simply and absolutely delivered from sin, but from the law of sin; i. e. the power, dominion, and tyranny thereof. And death; i. e. from sin that is deadly, or of a deadly nature; as the Spirit of life is the living Spirit, so sin and death is no more, say some, than deadly sin. Others take death to be distinct from sin, and think he speaks of a double deliverance; and then by death they understand eternal or the second death: see Rev. xx. 6. The sense of the whole is this: That the mighty power of the renewing and quickening Spirit did free the apostle, and doth free all believers, from the command and rule of sin, so that it doth not reign over them, as formerly it did; and being thus freed from the power of sin, they are also freed from the power of death and eternal condemnation. So it seems as a proof of the foregoing proposition, That there is no condemnation to them, &c.

3 For [e]what the law could not do, in that it was weak through the flesh, [f]God sending his own Son in the likeness of sinful flesh, and ‖ for sin, condemned sin in the flesh:

e Acts 13. 39.
ch. 3. 20.
Heb. 7. 18, 19. & 10. 1, 2, 10, 14.
f Gal. 3. 13.
2 Cor. 5. 21.
‖ Or, by a sacrifice for sin.

In this verse is a further proof of the main proposition in ver. 1. There are two things in sin that may endanger us as to condemnation, the power and the guilt of it. As to the freeing us from the former, viz. the power of sin, of that he had spoken in the foregoing verse; as to taking away the guilt of sin, of that he speaks in this verse. For what the law could not do: by the law here he means the moral law, the righteousness whereof is to be fulfilled in us, ver. 4. What is it the law cannot do? There are several answers; but this is principally meant, it cannot justify us before God. It can condemn us, but it cannot exempt us from condemnation: see Acts xiii. 38, 39; Gal. iii. 21; Heb. vii. 18, 19. In that it was weak through the flesh: by flesh, as before, we must understand the corrupt nature; that is, every man since the fall. This is that which puts a weakness and inability upon the law. The impotency of the law is not from itself, but from the condition of the subject with whom it hath to do. The law is weak to us, because we are weak to it: the sun cannot give light to a blind eye, not from any impotency in itself, but merely from the incapacity of the subject it shines upon. God sending his own Son: to justify and save fallen man, was impossible for the law to do; therefore God will find out another way, that shall do it effectually. What his own law cannot do, his own Son can; and therefore him he will send. In the likeness of sinful flesh; i. e. such flesh as sin hath made now to be subject to many infirmities and weaknesses. Flesh in this clause carries quite another sense than it did in the first verse; and in the former part of this verse, than it doth in the following verse; there it is taken morally for the corrupt nature of man, here physically for the human nature of Christ. The word likeness is to be linked, not with flesh, but with sinful flesh; he had true and real flesh, but he had only the appearance and likeness of sinful flesh: see 2 Cor. v. 21; Heb. iv. 15; vii. 26; 1 Pet. i. 19. And for sin; either this clause is to be joined to what goes before, and then the sense is, that God sent his Son in the likeness of sinful flesh, that he might take away sin. Or else it is joined to what follows, and then there is an ellipsis in it; something is cut off, or left out, which must be understood. The margin of our common Bibles insert the word sacrifice: q. d. By a sacrifice for sin, or by a sin-offering, he condemned sin. &c. This ellipsis is usual in Scripture. Isa. liii. 10, When thou shalt make his soul sin; that is, (as our translation renders it,) an offering for sin. Ezek. xlv. 19, The priest shall take of the blood of the sin; we read it, of the sin-offering. See the like in Hos. iv. 8; 2 Cor. v. 21; Heb. x. 6. Condemned sin in the flesh; the Syriac reads it, in his flesh. The meaning is, that God severely punished sin, and inflicted the curse and penalty of it, that was due to us, in and upon the person of his own Son; God laid on him the iniquities of us all, and he bore them in his body upon a tree: see Gal. iii. 13; 1 Pet. ii. 24.

4 That the righteousness of the law might

^{g ver. 1.} be fulfilled in us, ^g who walk not after the flesh, but after the Spirit.

That the righteousness of the law might be fulfilled in us: here is another end of God's sending his Son, as before; it was that he might perfectly fulfil the righteousness of the law in or for us, which for us ourselves to do in our own persons was utterly impossible; and yet upon which (as being imputed unto them, and accepted of God on our behalf) we shall be accounted just and righteous, as if we had done it ourselves. Christ's being a sacrifice for sin was not sufficient to answer all the ends and demands of the law; there must be doing of what it commanded, as well as suffering of what it threatened: therefore Christ was sent for both, and both were accomplished by him; and what he did and suffered is accounted unto us as if we had done and suffered it. This is the imputed righteousness which was so often spoken of, chap. iv.; and in reference to this he is said to be *made righteousness* for us, 1 Cor. i. 30, and we are said to be *made the righteousness of God in him*, chap. v. 19; 2 Cor. v. 21. *Who walk not after the flesh, but after the Spirit:* this was the description before of those that had union with Christ, and exemption from condemnation; and it is again set down, as the description of those who partake of the righteousness of Christ in this way of imputation; and it is added here again, to stave off all others from laying claim to this grace. None but holy walkers can warrantably apply Christ's fulfilling or satisfying the law to themselves: because Christ hath fulfilled the righteousness of the law for us, none may infer there is nothing for us to do, we may live as we list; for though Christ hath fulfilled the law in all respects, yet all those for whom he hath so done, or have benefit thereby, are, and must be, such as *walk not after the flesh, but after the Spirit:* for the opening of which terms, see ver. 1.

^{h John 3. 6.}
^{1 Cor. 2. 14.} 5 For ^h they that are after the flesh do mind the things of the flesh; but they ^{i Gal. 5. 22, 25.} that are after the Spirit ⁱ the things of the Spirit.

For they that are after the flesh; i. e. that are carnal and unregenerate persons, in a mere natural state. *Do mind the things of the flesh;* either such things as are absolutely evil, and are called, *the works of the flesh,* Gal. v. 19—21; or else such things as are occasionally evil, as riches, honours, pleasures, &c. These are also called *the things of the flesh,* and are such as carnal persons mind; i. e. they savour, affect, and take delight in them. *But they that are after the Spirit;* i. e. that are spiritual and regenerate, in whom the Spirit dwells. *The things of the Spirit;* i. e. they mind spiritual and heavenly things, they relish them most of all; see Psal. iv. 7; lxxiii. 25.

^{k ch. 6. 21.}
^{ver. 13.}
^{Gal. 6. 8.}
^{† Gr. the minding of the flesh:}
^{So ver. 7. + Gr. the minding of the Spirit.} 6 For ^k †to be carnally minded *is* death; but †to be spiritually minded *is* life and peace.

In this verse we have an account of the different end of those that are carnal and spiritual, as in the former we had a description of their different carriage and disposition. *For to be carnally minded is death;* i. e. to be of that temper before described, ver. 5; to *mind* and affect *the things of the flesh,* doth cause death, or will end in it: the second or eternal death is chiefly intended. *But to be spiritually minded;* i. e. to mind and savour the things of the Spirit, to find a sweetness and excellency therein, so as that the bent and inclination of the mind shall be thereto. *Is life and peace;* it is the way to eternal life hereafter, and to a sound peace here, Psal. cxix. 165; Prov. iii. 17; Gal. vi. 16.

^{Gr. the minding of the flesh.}
^{l Jam. 4. 4.}
^{m 1 Cor. 2. 14.} 7 Because †^l the carnal mind *is* enmity against God: for it is not subject to the law of God, ^m neither indeed can be.

q. d. Neither can the carnal man look for any better issue, *because the carnal mind is enmity against God.* He doth not say it is an enemy, but in the abstract, it is *enmity,* which heightens and intends the sense: an enemy may be reconciled, as Esau was to Jacob; but enmity cannot be reconciled; as black may be made white, but blackness cannot. *For it is not subject to the law of God, neither indeed can be:* this is rendered as a reason of the foregoing assertion, and it is, taken from the property of enmity. Those that are at enmity, cross each other's wills, and will not submit to one another: and the carnal mind is rebellious in the highest degree against the will of God, unless it be changed and renewed; it is impossible it should be otherwise; there is in it a moral impotency to obedience: see John viii. 43; 1 Cor. ii. 14.

8 So then they that are in the flesh cannot please God.

So then; this verse is a consectary, or it follows from that which went before. *They that are in the flesh;* not they which are married, as a pope once expounded it; the next verse refels such an absurd conception; but they that are carnal and unregenerate; the same with those who, in ver. 5, are said to be *after the flesh. Cannot please God;* neither they, nor any thing they do, is pleasing unto him; their best works are dead works, and silken sins (as one expresseth it): it must be understood with this limitation, so long as they continue in such a state: see Psal. v. 4, 5; Heb. xi. 6.

9 But ye are not in the flesh, but in the Spirit, if so be that ⁿ the Spirit of God dwell in you. Now if any man have not ^o the Spirit of Christ, he is none of his. ^{n 1 Cor. 3. 16. & 6. 19.} ^{o John 3. 34. Gal. 4. 6. Phil. 1. 19. 1 Pet. 1. 11.}

Here he applies what he had laid down more generally to the believing Romans in particular. *Not in the flesh, but in the Spirit;* i. e. not *after the flesh,* but *after the Spirit,* (as in ver. 5,) or not carnally, but spiritually minded. *If so be that;* the conjunction here is causal, not conditional; it may be rendered, seeing that, or forasmuch as: see ver. 17, 31; 2 Thess. i. 6. *The Spirit of God dwell in you;* the Spirit of God dwells in the regenerate, not only by the immensity of his presence, so he is every where and in all things; but by the presence and efficacy of his grace. The indwelling of the Spirit in believers denotes two things: 1. His ruling in them: where a man dwells as Lord, there he doth command and bear rule. 2. His abiding in them, and that for ever, John xiv. 16. *If any man have not the Spirit of Christ, he is none of his;* if he has not the same Spirit which in the former part of the verse is called *the Spirit of God:* it is called the Spirit of Christ, because it proceeds from him, and is procured by him, John xiv. 26; xvi. 7; Gal. iv. 6. When he saith such a one is none of Christ's, he means, that he doth not peculiarly belong to Christ, he hath no special interest in him, is no true member of him. As a merchant sets his seal upon his goods, so doth Christ his Spirit upon his followers, Eph. i. 13.

10 And if Christ *be* in you, the body *is* dead because of sin; but the Spirit *is* life because of righteousness.

If Christ be in you; before he said, the Spirit of God and Christ dwelt in them; here, Christ himself. Christ dwells in believers by his Spirit. *The body is dead because of sin:* by *body* some understand the corrupt and unregenerate part in the godly, as if that were as good as dead in them. But others take the word in its proper signification, and think no more is meant thereby than that the bodies, even of believers, are mortal bodies; so they are called in the next verse: they are subject to death as the bodies of other men. *But the Spirit is life:* some by *Spirit* here do understand the Spirit of God; and he *is life,* that is, he will quicken and raise up your bodies again to an immortal life. Others by *Spirit* do understand the soul, yet not simply and absolutely considered, but as renewed by grace; that *is life,* or that doth live; it lives a life of grace here, and it shall live a life of glory hereafter. *Because of righteousness;* by *righteousness* here understand, either imputed righteousness, which gives us a right and title to salvation; or inherent righteousness, which is a necessary condition required in every person that shall indeed be saved. The sum is, If you be Christians indeed, though your bodies die, yet your souls shall live, and that for ever; and your dead bodies shall not finally perish, but shall certainly be raised again; so it follows in the next verse.

11 But if the Spirit of ^p him that raised up Jesus from the dead dwell in you, ^q he that raised up Christ from the dead shall ^{p Acts 2. 24.} ^{q ch. 6. 4, 5. 1 Cor. 6. 14. 2 Cor. 4. 14. Ephes. 2. 5.}

‖ Or, because of his Spirit.
also quicken your mortal bodies ‖ by his Spirit that dwelleth in you.

Him that raised up Jesus from the dead; a periphrasis of God the Father. The Son raised himself, John ii. 19; x. 18; and yet the Father is said here to raise him from the dead: see notes on chap. i. 4. *Quicken your mortal bodies;* raise them from a state of mortality, and all the attendants, to a glorious immortal life. *By his Spirit that dwelleth in you:* q. d. If you are sanctified by the Spirit, you shall be raised up by the Spirit also, as Christ was. The wicked also shall be raised at the last day. But the righteous shall be raised after a peculiar manner; they shall be raised, as by the almighty power of God, so by virtue of their union with Christ as his members, and by virtue of their relation to the Spirit as his temples. They only shall partake of a resurrection that is desirable and beneficial to them. Therefore it is called emphatically *the resurrection of the just,* Luke xiv. 14; and these two are joined together, as belonging one to the other; *the children of God,* and *the children of the resurrection,* Luke xx. 36.

r ch. 6.7,14.

12 ʳTherefore, brethren, we are debtors, not to the flesh, to live after the flesh.

Therefore; this illative particle sends us to the things before delivered: q. d. Seeing we are not in the flesh, but have the Spirit of God dwelling in us; not only sanctifying and enlivening our souls for the present, but raising and quickening our bodies for the time to come; *therefore we are debtors, not to the flesh, to live after the flesh;* i. e. we are not debtors to sin, or the corrupt and sinful nature that is in us; we owe it no service, there is nothing due to it from believers, but blows, and the blue eye that the apostle gave it. The antithesis is omitted, but it is necessarily implied and understood; and that is, that we are debtors to the Spirit, to live and walk after it.

s ver. 6.
Gal. 6. 8.

13 ˢFor if ye live after the flesh, ye shall die: but if ye through the Spirit do

t Eph. 4. 22.
Col. 3. 5.

ᵗmortify the deeds of the body, ye shall live.

If ye live after the flesh, ye shall die; viz. eternally, and never partake of the glorious resurrection before spoken of. The godly themselves need this caution; they must not think, that because they are elected and justified, &c., that therefore they may do and live as they list. *Through the Spirit;* i. e. by the grace and assistance of the Spirit. *Mortify;* i. e. kill and put to death. It is not enough to forbear the actings of sin, but we must kill and crucify it. Sin may be left upon many considerations, and yet not mortified. Evil deeds are called *the deeds of the body,* because the body is so instrumental in the doing thereof. There are some, that by *body* here do understand the corrupt nature, the same that before in many places he calls the flesh: this was called, chap. vi. 6, *the body of sin,* and here it is called *the body. Ye shall live;* viz. eternally. See a parallel place, chap. vi. 22; Gal. vi. 8: see ver. 6.

u Gal. 5. 18.

14 For ᵘas many as are led by the Spirit of God, they are the sons of God.

This proves the latter part of the foregoing verse: Such as by the Spirit do mortify sin, shall live, for *they are the sons of God;* and that appears, because they *are led by the Spirit of God.* He doth not say, as many as live by the Spirit, but, *as are led by the Spirit;* to show (says one) that the Spirit must be the guide and ruler of our life, as the pilot is of the ship, and as a rider is of his horse. The phrase is borrowed (says another) either from those who are guided and directed as a blind man in his way; or from those who, wanting strength of their own, are borne and carried of others: so we are both ways led by the Spirit, for we can neither see our way, unless the Spirit direct us; nor have we strength to walk in it, unless the Spirit assist and draw us along. The Spirit leads and draws us irresistibly and necessarily, and yet not violently or against our wills; though we were unwilling before, yet we are made willing afterwards; so willing, that we desire and pray to be led by the Spirit. See Psal. xxv. 5; cxliii. 10; Cant. i. 4.

x 1 Cor. 2.12.
Heb. 2. 15.
y 2 Tim. 1. 7.
1 John 4. 18.

15 For ˣye have not received the spirit of bondage again ʸto fear; but ye have received the ᶻSpirit of adoption, whereby we cry, ᵃAbba, Father.

z Is. 56. 5.
Gal. 4. 5, 6.
a Mark 14. 36.

This verse proves the former, that we *are led by the Spirit of God,* and are his children, and that by an effect of the Spirit in them, which is to enable them to call God Father. He doth not here speak of two distinct Spirits, but one and the same Spirit of God, in different persons and at different times, is both *the spirit of bondage* and *the Spirit of adoption. The spirit of bondage* seems to respect either that state of servitude, which the people of God were under in the time of the ceremonial law; see Gal. iv. 3, 9; or it respects the publishing of the moral law upon Mount Sinai, which was with horror and fear. Compare Exod. xix. 16, with Heb. xii. 18—21: see Gal. iv. 24. Or else it respects that horror and slavish fear, which the Spirit of God doth work in men's hearts and consciences, by the ministry of the law, when he opens the eyes of men to see they are in bondage and slavery to sin and Satan, and that they are subject and obnoxious to the wrath and vengeance of God; this is many times preparatory and introductory to their conversion; but when they are regenerated they are delivered from it: see Luke i. 74; Heb. ii. 15; 1 John iv. 18. *Object.* Many of God's children are full of doubts and fears. *Answ.* These are not always from the suggestions of God's Spirit, but the misgivings of their own spirits. Some distinguish between the spirit of bondage and desertion; the children of God are delivered from the former, but exercised with the latter. The Spirit of God is called *the Spirit of adoption,* both because he works and effects it in us, and because he testifies and assures it to us. He might have said, the Spirit of liberty; the antithesis required it; but he said as much, when he called him *the Spirit of adoption,* for children are free. *Whereby we cry, Abba, Father;* or, by whom we cry. Acceptable prayer is wrought in us by the Spirit, ver. 26. *Abba* is a Hebrew or Syriac word, signifying Father; why then is the word *Father* added in the Greek? To signify, that God is the Father both of Jews and Gentiles, chap. iii. 29; x. 12; or to show the double paternity that is in God, he is the Father of all men by creation, of believers only by grace and regeneration: or, rather, to denote the importunity and earnestness which ought to be in prayer; and so it agrees with the former word, crying. Ingeminations carry an earnestness with them. There are two places more where these two words are repeated or used together, Mark xiv. 36; Gal. iv. 6.

16 ᵇThe Spirit itself beareth witness with our spirit, that we are the children of God:

b 2 Cor. 1. 22. & 5. 5.
Eph. 1. 13.
& 4. 30.

The Spirit of adoption doth not only excite us to call upon God as our Father, but it doth ascertain and assure us (as before) that we are his children. And this it doth not by an outward voice, as God the Father to Jesus Christ; nor by an angel, as to Daniel, and the virgin Mary; but by an inward and secret suggestion, whereby he raiseth our hearts to this persuasion, that God is our Father, and we are his children. This is not the testimony of the graces and operations of the Spirit, but of the Spirit itself. Conceive it thus; A man's own spirit doth witness to him his adoption, he finds in himself, upon diligent search and examination, the manifest signs and tokens thereof. But this testimony of itself is weak, and Satan hath many ways and wiles to invalidate it; therefore, for more assurance, it is confirmed by another and greater testimony, and that is of the Spirit himself; he witnesseth with our spirits, and seals it up unto us; he first works grace in our hearts, and then witnesseth to it. This testimony is not alike in all believers, nor in any one of them at all times; it is better felt than expressed. He witnesseth to our spirit (so some read) by a distinct and immediate testimony, and witnesseth with our spirit (so the word properly signifies) by a conjunctive and concurrent testimony.

17 And if children, then heirs; ᶜheirs of God, and joint-heirs with Christ; ᵈif so be that we suffer with *him,* that we may be also glorified together.

c Acts 26.18.
Gal. 4. 7.
d Acts 14. 22.
Phil. 1. 29.
2 Tim. 2. 11, 12.

And if children, then heirs; there is a parallel text in Gal. iv. 7. It is not so with the children of earthly princes: see 2 Chron. xxi. 3. *Joint-heirs with Christ;* or co-heirs with Christ; he is our elder Brother, and is not ashamed to call us brethren: the inheritance is his by nature, ours by grace. *If so be that we suffer with him;* the cross of Christ is the condition of our heavenly inheritance. The pronoun *him* is not in the original, but fitly supplied in our translation. Suffering *with him,* is much the same with suffering for him: suffering believers do but pledge Christ in the cup that he began to them. *That we may be also glorified together;* or, glorified with him, not with equal glory, but according to our proportion; he was glorified in this way, Luke xxiv. 26, and so must we. Three things are implied in our being *glorified together:* 1. Conformity; we shall in some measure be like him in glory: see John xvii. 22; Phil. iii. 21. 2. Concomitancy; we shall be present with him in glory, John xvii. 24; 1 Thess. iv. 17. 3. Conveyance; our glory will be from him; his glory will reflect on us, and we shall shine in his beams.

e 2 Cor. 4.17.
1 Pet. 1. 6, 7.
& 4. 13.

18 For I reckon that ^e the sufferings of this present time *are* not worthy *to be compared* with the glory which shall be revealed in us.

For I reckon; i. e. I make account, I certainly conclude: see chap. iii. 28. The word is borrowed either from arithmeticians, who by casting their accounts do find the true and total sum; or from logicians, who by considering the premises do draw the conclusion. *Not worthy to be compared;* the word properly signifieth that part of the balance which goeth down: q. d. If the sufferings of this life be weighed with the glory to come, they will be light in comparison. These words, *to be compared,* are supplied in our translation to make up the sense. *Revealed in us;* it is revealed to us, and it shall be revealed in us. This text is a confutation of the popish doctrine of merit and human satisfaction.

f 2 Pet. 3.13.
g 1 John 3. 2.

19 For ^f the earnest expectation of the creature waiteth for the ^g manifestation of the sons of God.

The apostle Peter, speaking of the Epistles of our apostle, in 2 Pet. iii. 16, saith, that there are *some things* in them *hard to be understood;* and some think, by reflecting upon some particular passages in that chapter, he doth more especially respect this context; there is indeed a great deal of obscurity in it. *The creature:* this word is four times used in this and the three following verses, only in the 22nd verse it is rendered *creation;* that is the subject of which all that followeth is predicated. One main question therefore is this, Of what creature the apostle here speaks? Divers answers are or may be given; I will fix upon two only. 1. By *the creature,* or *the creation,* (and, ver. 22, *the whole creation,* or every creature,) is meant all mankind, both Jews and Gentiles, and especially the latter: see Mark xvi. 15; there Christ gives it in commission to *preach the gospel to every creature;* it is the same word. And in 1 Pet. ii. 13, they are commanded to *submit* themselves *to every ordinance of man:* in the original it is, to every human creature, the same word which is in the text before us: he means the Gentile or heathen magistrates in authority over them. In the Scripture the Gentiles are sometimes called *the world,* chap. xi. 12, 15, and sometimes *the creature,* or *the creation.* 2. By *the creature* is meant the whole world with all the creatures therein, or the whole frame and body of the creation. *The creature* in this sense, by a prosopopœia, is here spoken of as a rational person; it is usual with the Spirit of God, in Scripture, to fasten upon unreasonable creatures such expressions as are proper only to those that are reasonable: see Psal. xcvi. 11, 12; Hab. ii. 11; James v. 4. So here *the creature* (in this sense) is said to expect, wait, &c. *Waiteth;* the expectation of the creature expecteth: a Hebrew pleonasm: it expecteth with the head lift up or stretched out, Phil. i. 20. *The manifestation of the sons of God;* i. e. the time when the sons of God shall be manifested. The Arabic interpreter puts the word *glory* into the text, and reads the word thus, *The earnest expectation of the creature waiteth for the manifestation of the glory of the sons of God;* their glory for the present is hidden, but it shall be discovered and manifested, 2 Cor. iii. 18. *The creature,* in the sense of the word as above, *waiteth* for this, because then it shall be restored to its primitive liberty and lustre, at that time there will be a *restitution of all things,* Acts iii. 21. But those who understand *the creature* in the first sense, do put a quite different interpretation upon this last clause; and that is, that the Gentile world are now earnestly expecting and waiting to see what the Jews will do, whether they will discover themselves to be *the sons of God,* or not, by their receiving or rejecting Christ.

20 For ^h the creature was made subject to vanity, not willingly, but by reason of him who hath subjected *the same* in hope,

h ver. 22.
Gen. 3. 19.

If these words be understood of the world, and all the creatures therein contained, then they show the creature's present condition; it is *subject to vanity,* and that, either in regard of its insufficiency, it falling short of that for which it was first created and ordained; then a thing is said to be vain, when it doth not answer or reach its proper end: or in respect of its transitoriness and uncertainty, of which see 1 Cor. vii. 31; Heb. i. 11, 12; 1 John ii. 17. The next verse tells us it is subject to *the bondage of corruption* as well as vanity. Now this must needs be an unwilling subjection, therefore it is here said it is *not* subject *willingly,* i. e. of its own accord, or of its proper instinct and inclination. What the will is in those that are rational, the inclination is in those things that are natural; how comes it then into this condition? The next clause tells us, it is *by reason of him who hath subjected the same in hope:* i. e. God, for the sin of man, hath cursed the creature, and subjected it to vanity and corruption: see Gen. iii. 17; iv. 12; Lev. xxvi. 19, 20. And though he hath done this, yet there is ground to expect and hope that the creature shall return again to its former estate wherein it was created; that it shall be delivered and restored into a better condition, as in the next verse. Those that by *the creature* understand the Gentile world, give a different interpretation of these words; they say that the Gentiles are *made subject to vanity,* i. e. to idolatry, or a vain, superstitious worship, (idols are called *vanities,* Acts xiv. 15,) or to a miserable, wretched estate; that (as Hesychius notes) is the import of the word *vanity.* And this not so much of their own accord, or by their own free choice, but by the power and malice of Satan, to whom they are justly given up of God; he rules in their hearts, carries them captive at his will, subjects them to all villany and misery. And it is reasonable to suppose of these poor heathens, that they are willing to be rescued (at least some, and a considerable number of them) from under this vanity and slavery, as it is said, ver. 22. *Quest.* But if he that thus subjects them be the devil, how is he said to do this *in hope? Answ.* These words, *in hope,* belong to the end of the former verse; all the rest of this verse being read or included in a parenthesis: q. d. The creature attends the manifestations of the sons of God in hope: meanwhile it is subject to vanity, &c.

21 Because the creature itself also shall be delivered from the bondage of corruption into the glorious liberty of the children of God.

If this verse be understood of the heavens and the earth, and the things therein, the meaning is, that the creatures, in their kind, and according to their capacity, shall be partakers of that liberty and freedom, which in the children of God is accompanied with unspeakable glory; they shall not partake with the saints in glory, but of that liberty, which in the saints hath great glory attending it, and superadded to it. The creature, at the day of judgment, shall be restored (as before) to that condition of liberty which it had in its first creation; as, when it was made at first, it was free from all vanity, bondage, and corruption, so it shall be again at the time of the general resurrection: see Acts iii. 19, 21; 2 Pet. iii. 13. Those that by *the creature* would understand the Gentile world, give the sense of this verse, That the very heathens also shall, by the gospel and grace of Christ, be rescued from those courses of sin and corruption, to which they have been long enslaved, into that glorious condition not only of free-men, redeemed by Christ out of their bondage to sin and Satan, but even of the sons of God, to have right to his favour, and that neverfading inheritance.

22 For we know that ‖ the whole creation ⁱ groaneth and travaileth in pain together until now.

‖ Or, *every creature,*
Mark 16. 15.
Col. 1. 23.
i Jer. 12. 11.

If here again the heavens and the earth, with what is therein, be understood, then the apostle further enlargeth upon their present state and condition; before they waited and expected deliverance, now they groan and travail in pain. They also are metaphorical expressions; one is taken for a man who hath upon him a heavy burden, another from a woman that is near her delivery. And this they do *until now*; i. e. from the fall of Adam to this present day. They that understand the words of the Gentile world, thus interpret them: We, the apostles and ministers of Jesus Christ, do find by experience, that the Gentiles are very forward to receive the gospel when they hear it, whilst the Jews generally reject it. The Gentile world is, as it were, in pangs of travail ever since Christ's time till now, ready to bring forth sons and daughters to God.

^{k 2 Cor. 5. 5.}
^{Eph. 1. 14.}
^{l 2 Cor. 5. 2,}
^{4.}
^{m Luke 20.}
^{36.}
^{n Luke 21.}
^{28.}
^{Eph. 4. 30.}

23 And not only *they*, but ourselves also, which have ^k the firstfruits of the Spirit, ^l even we ourselves groan within ourselves, ^m waiting for the adoption, *to wit*, the ⁿ redemption of our body.

The apostle had asserted and concluded, ver. 18, that there is a future glory to be revealed hereafter in the saints, such as infinitely transcendeth their sufferings now; and this he had confirmed from the earnest expectation of the creature, (the pronoun *they* is not in the original,) and now he further confirms it from the expectation which is in believers themselves. *The first-fruits of the Spirit*; hereby he means that righteousness, joy, and peace, which believers have in this life; these are the fruits of the Spirit, and called *first-fruits* in regard of their order; and in regard of their quantity, they are but a handful in comparison of the whole, little in regard of the fulness which they shall have in heaven; and in regard also of their signification, the grace and comforts of the Spirit of God in this life are pledges to us of that abundance and fulness of joy, which we shall partake of in the life to come, as the firstfruits of the Jews were an evidence to them of the ensuing crop. *Groan within ourselves*; among ourselves, say some, but it is better read in our translation, *within ourselves*. It expresseth the manner of the saints groaning under sin and affliction; it is inward, and from the heart. *Waiting for the adoption:* now we are the sons of God; why then should we wait for what we have already? *Answ.* We have the right, but not the full possession, of our inheritance: the apostle himself explains his meaning in the next words. *The redemption of our body*; i. e. our perfect deliverance from sin and misery; this phrase is used in other places; see Luke xxi. 28; Eph. iv. 30. But why *of our body*, and not of our souls? Because their souls would be in actual possession of the inheritance before that day, or because the miseries and troubles of this life are conveyed to the whole man by the body, so that the redemption of the body is in effect the redemption of the whole man.

24 For we are saved by hope: but
^{o 2 Cor. 5. 7.}
^{Heb. 11. 1.}
^o hope that is seen is not hope: for what a man seeth, why doth he yet hope for?

Though we certainly believe there is such a redemption or salvation belonging to us, according to the promise of God, yet for the present we have no possession of it; all the salvation we have at present is in *hope*, which, according to the nature of it, is of things not yet enjoyed, for vision or possession puts an end to hope; no man hopeth for what he seeth and enjoyeth.

25 But if we hope for that we see not, *then* do we with patience wait for *it*.

q. d. If we indeed hope for redemption and salvation, which is out of sight, then it is meet that we do with patience digest and bear all our present evils and sufferings; true hope is accompanied always with a patient waiting for the things hoped for; therefore you read of the *patience of hope*, 1 Thess. i. 3: see Heb. vi. 12; x. 36.

26 Likewise the Spirit also helpeth our
^{p Mat. 20. 22.}
^{Jam. 4. 3.}
^{q Zech. 12.}
^{10.}
^{Eph. 6. 18.}
infirmities: for ^p we know not what we should pray for as we ought: but ^q the Spirit itself maketh intercession for us with groanings which cannot be uttered.

Likewise: this referreth us, either to the work of the Spirit, before noted, ver. 11; he quickeneth, and he likewise helpeth: or rather, to *hope*, in the foregoing verse; hope helpeth to patience, so also the Spirit. *Helpeth our infirmities;* the word imports such help, as when another of greater strength steps in, and sustains the burden that lies too heavy upon our shoulders; or it is borrowed from nurses, that help their little children that are unable to go, upholding them by their hands or sleeves. *For we know not what we should pray for as we ought:* one way whereby the Spirit helps us, is by teaching us to pray. Prayer doth greatly relieve us under the cross, and is a great refuge in trouble: but we knowing not how to pray *as we ought*, either in regard of matter or manner, herein therefore the Spirit aids or helps us, as it followeth. But how is it said *we know not what to pray for*, when we have the Lord's prayer. which contains a perfect rule and summary of all things meet to be prayed for? Though the Lord's prayer be a rule in general, yet we may be to seek in particulars? God's own children many times ask they know not what; see Job vi. 8; Jonah iv. 3; Mark x. 38; 2 Cor. xii. 8. *But the Spirit itself maketh intercession for us :* there is a twofold intercession, one of Christ, of which we read, ver. 34; the other of the Spirit, of which this place speaks. How doth the Spirit make intercession for us? *Answ.* By making intercession in us, or by helping us to pray. The Spirit is called, Zech. xii. 10, *the Spirit of supplications*. It is by him, ver. 15. that *we cry, Abba, Father:* he cries so in our hearts; Gal. iv. 6, *God hath sent forth the Spirit of his Son into your hearts, crying, Abba, Father*. The Spirit of our Father speaketh in us, Matt. x. 20: he suggesteth to us what we should pray for; he helpeth us to suitable dispositions, and many times to suitable expressions in prayer: see Eph. vi. 18; Jude 20. *With groanings which cannot be uttered;* with inward sighs and groans, which cannot be expressed by words. There may be prayer, where there is no speech or vocal expression. A man may cry, and that mightily to God, when he uttereth never a word: see Exod. xiv. 15; 1 Sam. i. 13.

27 And ^r he that searcheth the hearts
^{r 1 Chron. 28. 9.}
^{Ps. 7. 9.}
^{Prov. 17. 3.}
^{Jer. 11. 20.}
^{& 17. 10.}
^{& 20. 12.}
^{Acts 1. 24.}
knoweth what *is* the mind of the Spirit, || because he maketh intercession for the saints ^s according to *the will of* God.
^{1 Thess. 2. 4. Rev. 2. 23.} ^{|| Or, that.} ^{s 1 John 5. 14.}

He that searcheth the hearts; this phrase is a periphrasis of God, and is spoken of him after the manner of men. God doth not properly search or inquire into any thing; but because amongst men knowledge comes by searching, therefore, by way of resemblance, this is attributed to God, though that which is intended by it is only this, that God knoweth the heart, Jer. xvii. 10; Acts i. 24. *Knoweth what is the mind of the Spirit*, both with the knowledge of apprehension and approbation. *Maketh intercession for the saints according to the will of God :* our prayers shall be sure to speed, if they are of this sort, 1 John v. 14, 15. Praying according to the will of God, respects, 1. The matter of our prayers. 2. The manner of our praying. 3. The end thereof, James iv. 3.

28 And we know that all things work together for good to them that love God, to them ^t who are the called according to
^{t ch. 9. 11, 23, 24.}
^{2 Tim. 1. 9.}
his purpose.

Another argument to comfort us under the cross, from the benefits of it; *We know that all things, &c.* It is not matter of guess only and conjecture, but of certainty and assurance. How is this known? 1. By the testimony of God; the Scripture tells us as much, Psal. cxxviii. 1, 2; Isa. iii. 10. 2. By our own experience; we are assured of it by the event and effects of all things, both upon ourselves and others. *All things*, even sin itself; because from their falls, God's children arise more humble and careful. Afflictions are chiefly intended; the worst and crossest providences, those things that are evil in themselves, they *work for good* to the children of God. *Work together;* here is their operation, and their co-operation: First, they *work together* with God. What the apostle says of himself and others in the ministry, 2 Cor. vi. 1, that may be said of other things, especially of afflictions; they are *workers together* with God. Some read the words thus, God co-operates all to good. Again, they *work together* with us; we ourselves must concur, and be active herein; we must labour and endeavour to get good out of every providence. Once more, they *work together* amongst themselves, or one with another. Take this or that providence singly, or by itself, and you shall not see the good it doth; but take it in its conjunction and connexion with others, and then you may perceive it. One exemplifies it thus, As in matter of physic, if you take such and such simples alone, they may poison rather than cure; but then take them in their composition, as they are made up by the direction of a skilful physician, and so they prove an excellent medicine. *For good;* sometimes for temporal good, Gen. l. 20; always for spiritual and eternal good, which is best of all. All occurrences of providence shall serve to bring them nearer to God here, and to heaven hereafter. *According to his purpose:* these words are added to show the ground and reason of God's calling us; which is nothing else but his own *purpose* and good pleasure; it is not according to our worthiness, but *his purpose:* see 2 Tim. i. 9.

29 For whom ^uhe did foreknow, ^xhe also did predestinate ^y*to be* conformed to the image of his Son, ^zthat he might be the firstborn among many brethren.

u See Ex. 33. 12, 17. Ps. 1. 6. Jer. 1. 5. Matt. 7. 23. ch. 11. 2. 2 Tim. 2. 19. 1 Pet. 1. 2. x Eph. 1. 5, 11. y John 17. 22. 2 Cor. 3. 18. Phil. 3. 21. 1 John 3. 2. z Col. 1. 15, 18. Heb. 1. 6. Rev. 1. 5.

Having let fall a word in the former verse concerning the *purpose* of God, he thinks good, in what follows, to pursue that subject, and a little to enlarge upon it. *Whom he did foreknow;* i. e. with a knowledge of approbation; for otherwise, he foreknew all persons and things: or, whom he did foreknow for his own, John x. 14, 27; chap. xi. 2; 2 Tim. ii. 19. This *foreknowledge of God* is the ground of our election: see 1 Pet. i. 2. *He also did predestinate to be conformed to the image of his Son;* whom he was pleased to approve of, and to pitch his free love and favour upon, he severed from the common lump and mass of mankind, and did appoint them *to be conformed to the image of his Son;* i. e. to be conformed to him in holiness and sufferings here, and in glory hereafter: see 1 Cor. xv. 49; 2 Cor. iii. 18; Eph. i. 4—6; Phil. iii. 20, 21; 1 John iii. 2. *That he might be the first-born among many brethren;* this is the limitation of the forementioned conformity; though there be a likeness in us unto Christ, yet there is not an equality; he still retaineth the dignity of the first-born, and hath a double, yea, a far greater portion; he is Head and Ruler of all the family in heaven and in earth, Psal. xlv. 7, 8.

30 Moreover whom he did predestinate, them he also ^acalled: and whom he called, them he also ^bjustified: and whom he justified, them he also ^cglorified.

a ch. 1. 6. & 9. 24. Eph. 4. 4. Heb. 9. 15. 1 Pet. 2. 9. b 1 Cor. 6. 11. c John 17. 22. Eph. 2. 6.

He hath already given them the beginning and pledge thereof in grace; and will in due time bring them to the possession of eternal life and glory. Some, under this term of glorification would have sanctification included; because, otherwise, they think there is a great defect in this chain of salvation, here set down by the apostle, of which sanctification is one special link; but this is rather to be couched and included in effectual calling, which is the third link, and already spoken of.

31 What shall we then say to these things? ^dIf God be for us, who *can be* against us?

d Num. 14. 9. Ps. 118. 6.

What shall we then say to these things? some refer this question to what is said in the verses immediately preceding: others, to what he had said, ver. 28; and others go higher, and refer it to all that he said before. Some by *these things* understand afflictions and sufferings more especially; What shall we say to these, or what need we be disheartened by these? For if God, &c. *If God be for us;* i. e. seeing God is for us; it is a note of certainty, not of ambiguity; see ver. 9. He takes it for granted, as that which cannot be denied; see Psal. xlvi. 7, 11; cxviii. 6, 7. *Who can be against us?* i. e. none can; none can be against us successfully, none can be against us safely; such will harm themselves more than us: see Psal. lvi. 4. Maximilian, the emperor, so admired this sentence, that he caused it to be written over the table where he used to dine and sup; that having it often in his eye, he might have it also in his mind.

32 ^eHe that spared not his own Son, but ^fdelivered him up for us all, how shall he not with him also freely give us all things?

e ch. 5. 6, 10. f ch. 4. 25.

He that spared not his own Son: this phrase either shows the bounty of God, that he did not withhold Christ; or the severity of God, that he did not favour, but afflict and punish him, Isa. liii. 4, 5, 11. *But delivered him up:* see Acts ii. 23. This doth not excuse Judas, no, nor Pilate and the Jews; though they executed God's purpose, yet they acted their own malice and wickedness. *For us all;* this plainly refers to such persons as he had before mentioned, such as God foreknew, predestinated, called, &c., which is not all men in general, but a set number of persons in particular: it is an expression both of latitude and restriction; of latitude, in the word *all;* of restriction, in the word *us*. *How shall he not with him also freely give us all things?* q. d. Without question he will; it may be confidently inferred and concluded, He that hath given the greater, will not stick to give the less. Christ is more than all the world, or than all other gifts and blessings whatsoever.

33 Who shall lay any thing to the charge of God's elect? ^g*It is* God that justifieth.

g Is. 50. 8, 9. Rev. 12. 10, 11.

Who shall lay any thing to the charge of God's elect? who can implead such, or put in any accusation against them? There is nothing to accuse them of, they are justified; and there is none to accuse them, *It is* God that *justifieth;* the Supreme Judge hath absolved them. This seems to be taken out of Isa. l. 8, 9. They were Christ's words there, and spoken of God's justifying him; they are every believer's words here, and intended of God's justifying them. Here seems to be two reasons of their indemnity; one is implied, i. e. God's electing them: the other expressed, i. e. God's justifying and acquitting of them.

34 ^hWho *is* he that condemneth? *It is* Christ that died, yea rather, that is risen again, ⁱwho is even at the right hand of God, ^kwho also maketh intercession for us.

h Job 34. 29. i Mark 16. 19. Col. 3. 1. Heb. 1. 3. & 8. 1. & 12. 1. 1 Pet. 3. 22. k Heb. 7. 25. & 9. 24. 1 John 2. 1.

Who is he that condemneth? as none can accuse the elect of God, so much less can any condemn them, see ver. 1. *It is Christ that died;* and it is he that is the Judge, and must condemn them, if they be condemned. His death frees them from condemnation; thereby he hath made a sufficient atonement and satisfaction for all their sins; and that which hath long ago satisfied in heaven for the sins of all the elect, may very well serve to satisfy the heart and conscience of a believing sinner here on earth. Such a one may thrown down the gauntlet, as the apostle doth, and challenge all the world. Let conscience, carnal reason, law, sin, hell, and devils, bring forth all they can, it will not be sufficient to condemnation; and that because of Christ's death and satisfaction. *Yea rather, that is risen again:* the resurrection of Christ hath a special influence upon our justification, and therefore the apostle puts a *rather* upon it, and that comparatively to the death of Christ: see chap. iv. 25, and the notes there. *Who is even at the right hand of God, who also maketh intercession for us:* faith finds matter of triumph, not only from Christ's death and resurrection, but from his session at the right hand of God, and intercession for us.

35 Who shall separate us from the love of Christ? shall tribulation, or distress, or persecution, or famine, or nakedness, or peril, or sword?

Who shall separate us? he continues his triumph: he doth not say what, but *who;* though he instanceth in things, and not in persons, yet it is expressed personally, because that these things do commonly do us hurt in the improvement of persons, whether of Satan or wicked men, who are instrumental thereunto. *From the love of Christ;* understand it either actively, from our love of him; or passively, from his love of us: the latter seems to be chiefly intended; *Who shall separate us from the love of Christ,* or from the sense and manifestation thereof? *Shall tribulation, &c.?* he makes an enumeration of particular evils, of seven in number; and he begins with the lesser, and riseth to the greater; placing them in order, not casually, but by choice. The word *tribulation* signifies any thing that presseth or pincheth us. *Or distress?* the word properly signifies straitness of place, and is transferred from the body to the mind, to point out the anguish or perplexity thereof. *Or persecution;* the word properly signifies a driving from place to place; banishment is implied therein, if not chiefly intended: see Matt. x. 23. *Or peril;* any danger or hazard of life, in any kind whatsoever: see 2 Cor. xi. 26. *Or sword;* this is put figuratively for death itself, especially violent death.

l Ps. 44. 22.
1 Cor. 15. 30, 31.
2 Cor. 4. 11.

36 As it is written, ¹For thy sake we are killed all the day long; we are accounted as sheep for the slaughter.

He cites this testimony to prove that none of the forementioned evils, no, not death itself, can separate believers from the love of Christ: it is taken out of Psal. xliv. 22. The argument seems to be this: The saints of old have endured all manner of sufferings, and yet were not separated from the love of God; therefore such sufferings cannot separate them now. *For thy sake;* not for our sins' sake, but for Christ's, or *for righteousness' sake,* Matt. v. 10; x. 18, 39; 1 Pet. iii. 14. *We are killed:* how could they say this? Killing takes away all complaining, and makes the parties so dealt with incapable of saying how it is with them. This expression notes the danger and desperateness of their condition. It is usual in Scripture to set forth an eminent danger under the notion of death: see 1 Cor. xv. 31; 2 Cor. i. 10; iv. 11. *All the day long;* i. e. continually, without ceasing: see Psal. xxxviii. 6, 12; lxxi. 24; lxxiii. 14; Prov. xxiii. 17; chap. x. 21. *We are accounted as sheep for the slaughter;* i. e. we are designed for destruction. Our enemies make account they can destroy us, as men do sheep, that they have by them in the slaughter-house. They reckon they have us at command, and can cut us off when they list. Or rather thus, they make no reckoning of our destruction; they make no more of killing us, than butchers do of killing sheep: our death is very cheap in their account, Psal. xliv. 11, 12. Here let me insert a tragical story of the Christians of Calabria, that suffered persecution, A. D. 1560. They were all shut up in one house together, as in a sheepfold: an executioner comes in, and among them takes one, and blindfolds him with a muffler about his eyes, and so leadeth him forth to a larger place, where he commandeth him to kneel down; which being done, he cutteth his throat, and so leaveth him half dead; and taking his butcher's knife and muffler, all of gore blood, he cometh again to the rest, and so leading them one after another, he despatcheth them, to the number of eighty-eight, no otherwise than a butcher doth his sheep. *Fox's Acts and Monuments.*

m 1 Cor. 15. 57.
2 Cor. 2. 14.
1 John 4. 4.
& 5. 4, 5.
Rev. 12. 11.

37 ᵐNay, in all these things we are more than conquerors through him that loved us.

Nay, in all these things; i. e. in *tribulation, distress,* &c. as before, ver. 35. *We are more than conquerors;* or, we overcome. We conquer when we ourselves are conquered; we conquer by those which are wont to conquer others; we beat our enemies with their own weapons. The meaning seems to be this: The devil aims, in all the sufferings of God's children, to draw them off from Christ, to make them murmur, despair, &c.; but in this he is defeated and disappointed, for God inspires his children with such a generous and noble spirit, that sufferings abate not their zeal and patience, but rather increase them. "We Christians laugh at your cruelty, and grow the more resolute," said one of Julian's nobles to him. *Through him that loved us:* a short description of Christ, together with a reason of a Christian's success. The conquest he hath over sin, and over sufferings also, is not from himself, or his own strength, but from Christ, &c.: see chap. vii. 24, 25; 1 Cor. xv. 57; 2 Cor. ii. 14; 2 Tim. iv. 17.

n Eph. 1. 21.
& 6. 12.
Col. 1. 16.
& 2. 15.
1 Pet. 3. 22.

38 For I am persuaded, that neither death, nor life, nor angels, nor ⁿprincipalities, nor powers, nor things present, nor things to come,

For I am persuaded; or, I am fully assured, not by any special revelation, but by *the same spirit of faith,* which is common to all believers, 2 Cor. iv. 13. *Neither death, nor life;* i. e. neither fear of death, nor hope of life. *Nor angels.* 1. The evil angels; for the good angels would not attempt the separating us from the love of Christ. 2. There are some, that think the good angels to be also here intended; and they understand it by way of supposition: q. d. If they should endeavour such a thing, they would never effect it: and thus they make the apostle here to argue, as he doth in another place, Gal. i. 8. *Nor principalities, nor powers;* some would have the evil angels to be here intended, and the good angels in what went before; in Col. ii. 15, they are thus termed: but others, by *principalities and powers,* do rather understand persecuting princes and potentates. *Nor things present, nor things to come;* i. e. the evils and pressures that are upon us now, or that shall be upon us hereafter. He makes no mention of the things past, for they are overcome already.

39 Nor height, nor depth, nor any other creature, shall be able to separate us from the love of God, which is in Christ Jesus our Lord.

Nor height, nor depth; i. e. neither the height of honour and worldly advancement, nor the depth of disgrace and worldly abasement. Some take *height* and *depth* for a comprehensive expression, which the Scripture useth, when he takes in all, and leaves nothing out. *Nor any other creature;* this is added to the rest, as an &c. at the end of a sentence; and to supply whatever our fancies might, in this case, frame to themselves. Or the apostle here makes an end of his induction; and because it had been endless to reckon up all the creatures, he closeth in this manner, If there be any other creature. *Shall be able to separate us from the love of God, which is in Christ Jesus our Lord;* which he bears to us, as members of Christ, and by faith united to him: see ver. 35, and the notes there.

CHAP. IX.

Paul professeth an unfeigned sorrow for the Jewish nation, 1—5; but proveth by instances from Scripture that the promise to Abraham did not necessarily include all his descendants, 6—13; asserting that there is no unrighteousness in God's bestowing his unmerited bounty on whom he pleaseth, 14—18; and that he was unquestionably free to suspend his judgments, where deserved, either for the more signal display of his power in taking vengeance on some, or of his mercy in calling others to glory, 19—24. The calling of the Gentiles, and rejection of the Jews, foretold, 26—29. Accordingly, the Gentiles have attained the righteousness of faith, which the Jews refused, 30, 31. The cause of such refusal, 32, 33.

a ch. 1. 9.
2 Cor. 1. 23.
& 11. 31. &
12. 19.
Gal. 1. 20.
Phil. 1. 8. 1 Tim. 2. 7.

I ᵃSAY the truth in Christ, I lie not, my conscience also bearing me witness in the Holy Ghost,

The apostle being about to treat of the rejection of the Jews and the calling of the Gentiles, before he enters upon it, he premiseth a preface, to prepare the minds of the Jews to a patient reading or hearing the same; and in this preface, he solemnly protesteth his love to his nation, and his hearty grief for their rejection, that so it might the better appear, that these things were not written out of any spleen or malice, but out of conscience towards God and the truth.

I say the truth in Christ; or, by Christ: so the word *in* is taken, Matt. v. 34—36. This is the form of an oath, which the Scripture elsewhere useth in matters of importance: see Gen. xxii. 16; Dan. xii. 7; Eph. iv. 17. *I lie not;* this is added for confirmation, or to gain the greater credit to what he said or swore. It was the manner of the Hebrews, to an affirmative to add a negative: see 1 Sam. iii. 18; John i. 20. *My conscience also bearing me witness;* as being for this purpose placed in man by God, and is instead of a thousand witnesses. *In the Holy Ghost;* i. e. in the presence of the Holy Ghost, who is privy to what I say, and who is a witness also to the truth thereof: or, as some, by the guidance of the Holy Ghost, who cannot lie.

2 ᵇThat I have great heaviness and continual sorrow in my heart.

ᵇ ch. 10. 1.

His grief for his nation and people he expresseth, 1. By the greatness of it; it was such as a woman hath in travail; so the word imports. 2. By the continuance of it; it was *continual*, or without intermission. 3. By the seat of it; it was in his *heart*, and not outward in his face. The cause he doth not here set down, but it is easily gathered from what follows, viz. the obstinacy and infidelity, together with the rejection, of the Jews.

3 For ᶜI could wish that myself were ‖accursed from Christ for my brethren, my kinsmen according to the flesh:

ᶜ Ex. 32. 32.
‖ Or, *separated*.

I could wish that myself were accursed from Christ; or, separated from Christ. This verse hath greatly vexed interpreters. Some read it, I did wish myself accursed from Christ: q. d. Before my conversion, I was willing to be accursed from Christ, to be a violent persecutor of the Christians, and so to be held of them as accursed for my brethren's sake. The vulgar Latin, and many Romanists, thus render the word ηὐχόμην in the text; but the generality of interpreters read it as we do, not indicatively, but potentially; and they make an ellipsis in the words, ηὐχόμην *pro* ηὐχοίμην ἄν; the like is frequent; see Acts xxv. 22; 1 Cor. ii. 8; 2 Cor. xi. 1. But then still the difficulty is, how, and in what sense, the apostle wished himself *accursed*, or separated *from Christ*. The received opinion is, that out of zeal to the glory of God, and love to his brethren, he was willing to be damned, that they all might be saved. Many of the ancients did thus expound this place: "Christ became a curse for us; and what marvel is it" (says one) "if the Lord would be made a curse for the servants, that a servant should be willing to become an anathema for the brethren." "He doth not wish" (says another) "for his brethren's sake to be separated from the love and grace of Christ, but from the comforts of Christ, and the future happiness that we have by him: he is content to lose his part in the heavenly glory, if that might promote the glory of Christ, which would be more illustrated by the saving a whole nation, than a particular person: q. d. If this might be the fruit of it, if it would gain this end, I could, methinks, be content to part with all my hopes in Christ, even my eternal happiness, upon condition my brethren might be partakers thereof; so passionate and abundant love have I to and for them." This exposition is not satisfactory; therefore some think the apostle here speaks of being accursed only for a season, or of being an anathema in this world. An anathema sometimes signifieth corporal death and destruction: of old, in times of common calamity, they were wont to sacrifice men to their idols and infernal gods, for the pacifying of their anger; such a sacrifice they called *anathema*, which is the word here used: q. d. For my brethren's sake, that so they might be saved, I could be content to be cut off, to be made a sacrifice, to die the worst of deaths. But if this be admitted, how then is that clause to be understood, *from Christ?* it is not, I could wish myself an anathema, but an anathema from Christ. To this they answer that favour this interpretation, That instead of *from Christ*, you may read, by Christ: q. d. I could be content to be cut off or destroyed by Christ, that my brethren might be saved. This sense of the words suits well with the zeal and kindness of Moses to his brethren, Exod. xxxii. 32; rather than they should not be pardoned and spared, he prays. that God would blot him out of the book that he had written: see annotations there. There is yet another, and a more probable, interpretation of this wish of the apostle. It is as if he had said, I could be willing to be separated or excommunicated from the church of Christ, for the sake and salvation of my country and nation. Anathema (says Hesychius) signifies ἀκοινώνητος, excommunicate; 1 Cor. xvi. 22, *If any man love not the Lord Jesus Christ, let him be anathema;* let him be removed from the Christian assemblies, deprived of those Christian privileges that are afforded there. Gal. i. 8, 9, Let him be an anathema that teacheth another gospel; i. e. turned out of the church of Christ, and avoided by all true Christians. If this sense be admitted, then *from Christ* must signify, from the body of Christ; and so the word *Christ* is used, 1 Cor. xii. 12; Gal. iii. 27. Christ being the Head of the body, he that is cut off from the body may be truly enough said to be cut off from Christ. Thus the apostle Paul, who was accused and persecuted by the Jews, for having made a defection from the law of Moses, and setting up Christian assemblies in opposition to their Judaical service, doth fitly express his kindness and love to them, in wishing himself deprived of those most valuable privileges, on condition they might be partakers thereof. To this it may be added, that in the primitive times, this anathematizing, or excommunicating, was attended with delivering up to Satan, and that with destruction of the flesh, with very sharp and severe punishments upon the bodies of men. And so *anathema*, in this notion, may be taken with this improvement, and may contain all those temporal calamities that he was willing to endure and undergo for their good: see D. H. in loc. *My kinsmen according to the flesh;* so the Jews were by natural descent: see Gen. xxix. 14.

VOL. III—17

4 ᵈWho are Israelites; ᵉto whom *pertaineth* the adoption, and ᶠthe glory, and ᵍthe ‖covenants, and ʰthe giving of the law, and ⁱthe service *of God*, and ᵏthe promises;

ᵈ Deut. 7. 6. ᵉ Ex. 4. 22.
Deut. 14. 1. Jer. 31. 9.
ᶠ 1 Sam. 4. 21. 1 Kings 8. 11. Ps. 63. 2. & 78. 61.
ᵍ Acts 3. 25. Heb. 8. 8, 9,
10. ‖ Or, *testaments*. ʰ Ps. 147. 19. ⁱ Heb. 9. 1. ᵏ Acts 13. 32. ch. 3. 2. Eph. 2. 12.

In this and the following verse, he rehearseth the privileges and advantages the Jews had from God, above all other nations of the earth; and this he doth to show, that he had good reason to make such a wish, as in the foregoing verse; as also, that what he should declare concerning the Jews, and their ejection, did not proceed from any disrespect or disesteem of them.

Israelites; i. e. the offspring of that holy patriarch Israel: this was the Jews' first title of honour, that they descended from him, who by God himself was surnamed Israel, or *a prince* that had *power with God, and prevailed*, Gen. xxxii. 28. *The adoption;* adoption is not here to be understood as before, in chap. viii. 15, or as in Eph. i. 5, and elsewhere. But thereby we must understand the peculiar privilege of the seed of Jacob; that they, of all the nations of the earth, were pitched upon to be nearly related to God, to be his *children* (as they are called) and his *firstborn:* see Exod. iv. 22; Deut. xiv. 1; Jer. xxxi. 9, 20; Matt. xv. 26. *The glory;* the ark and the temple; so called, because in them God did manifest his glorious presence, 1 Sam. iv. 21, 22; Psal. xxvi. 8; lxxviii. 61. *The covenants;* some understand by covenants, the tables of the law: see Heb. ix. 4. Others rather understand the covenant made with Abraham, Gen. xv. 8; xvii. 2, 7; and with the Jewish nation, Exod. xxiv. 7, 8; xxxiv. 27, &c. Circumcision also may be intended, for that is called God's covenant, Gen. xvii. 10. *The giving of the law;* the judicial, ceremonial, but especially the moral law. This is spoken of as a great privilege, Deut. iv. 8, 32. It may refer both to the law itself, and to the circumstances, also, with which the law was given. *The service of God;* the true manner of worshipping God, which was a great privilege. Other nations knew there was a God, and that he must be worshipped, but they knew not how; and so they ran into superstition and idolatry. *The promises;* of this life, and that to come; particularly of the Messiah, and of the benefits and blessings by him. These are found in Moses and the prophets, and were entailed upon the Jews and their children, Acts ii. 39; Eph. ii. 12, till God at last cut off the entail.

5 ˡWhose *are* the fathers, and ᵐof whom as concerning the flesh Christ came, ⁿwho is over all, God blessed for ever. Amen.

ˡ Deut. 10. 15. ch. 11. 28.
ᵐ Luke 3. 23. ch. 1. 3. ⁿ Jer. 23. 6. John 1. 1.
Acts 20. 28. Heb. 1. 8. 1 John 5. 20.

Whose are the fathers; who are lineally descended of the holy patriarchs, Abraham, Isaac, and Jacob, with other holy fathers and prophets, and of the same blood. This was also a great privilege, of which the Jews boasted. *Of whom as concerning the flesh Christ came;* or out of whom; understand the people of the Jews, not the fathers. The meaning is, Christ took his human nature of their stock. It is the great honour of mankind, that Christ took not the nature of angels, but of man; and it is a great honour to the nation of the Jews, that he took the seed of Abraham their father. *Who is over all, God blessed for ever;* this is the fullest place to express the two natures that are in the person of our Redeemer, the Lord Jesus Christ; he was God as well as man: yea, this is the title by which the one and supreme God was known amongst the Jews.

o Num. 23. 19. ch. 3. 3.
p John 8. 39. ch. 2, 28, 29. & 4. 12, 16. Gal. 6. 16.

6 °Not as though the word of God hath taken none effect. For ᴾthey *are* not all Israel, which are of Israel :

An objection is here obviated: the Jews might object and say, If they were cast off and rejected, then God is unfaithful, and all his promises made to Abraham, Isaac, and Jacob, and their seed, are ineffectual. To this he answers by a distinction of Israelites. Some are Israelites only in respect of their carnal generation; and others, again, are true Israelites, children of the promise, and of the faith of Abraham: see chap. ii. 28, 29. Now the promises of God were made to the true Israelites, and in all such it is effectual: and under the name of *Israel*, or true Israelites, all those are comprehended, who imitate the faith of Abraham, and walk in his steps, whether they descended from him by fleshly generation or not. This he further asserts in the following verse.

q Gal. 4. 23.
r Gen. 21. 12. Heb. 11. 18.

7 ᑫNeither, because they are the seed of Abraham, *are they* all children: but, In ʳIsaac shall thy seed be called.

He had before made a difference of Israelites, and now he makes a difference of the seed of Abraham. This was ever and anon in the mouths of the Jews, *We are Abraham's seed*, John viii. 33. But here he tells them, that all Abraham's seed were not the children of the promise; for it was said to Sarah, Gen. xxi. 12, that the promised seed should be confined to Isaac's line, of his issue should the Messiah come, and all the true seed of Abraham, who are born after the manner of Isaac, by the word and promise of God. And as Ishmael, though Abraham's natural seed, was cast out, and therein was a type of those who are born only according to the flesh; so Isaac is a type of Abraham's spiritual seed, who are born not of the power of nature, but by virtue of the promise of God.

8 That is, They which are the children of the flesh, these *are* not the children

s Gal. 4. 28.

of God: but ˢthe children of the promise are counted for the seed.

q. d. That I may speak more plainly, all those that are the children of Abraham according to the flesh, are not therefore the adopted children of God; it is not their blood, but their faith, must make them such. There are some of Abraham's seed, that are selected from the rest, to whom the promise was made, who are therefore called *children of the promise;* and of this sort are all they who are *born after the Spirit*, (as Isaac is said to be, Gal. iv. 29,) whether Jews or Gentiles. The sense of this verse is fully expressed, Gal. iii. 8, 14, 29: see Gal. iv. 28.

t Gen. 18. 10, 14.

9 For this *is* the word of promise, ᵗAt this time will I come, and Sarah shall have a son.

The birth of Isaac was a thing extraordinary; for which, neither Abraham nor Sarah had any ground to hope, but only that promise made, Gen. xviii. 10, in these words, *At this time*, or according to this time, i. e. the time of bearing children after conception, *will I come, and Sarah shall have a son;* i. e. I will manifest my power in fulfilling my promise of giving thee a son. By which it is clear, that the birth of Isaac was an effect of God's promise, and nothing else. So that they to whom the promise belong, (whosoever they be,) they are the seed of Abraham, and, upon the obedience of faith, shall be accepted for the children of God. The apostle Peter tells women, (whether Jews or Gentiles, it matters not,) that by well-doing they become the daughters of Sarah.

u Gen. 25. 21.

10 And not only *this;* but when ᵘRebecca also had conceived by one, *even* by our father Isaac;

And not only this; some read it, And not only she; the particle *this* is not in the Greek. *When Rebecca also had conceived by one, even by our father Isaac:* this instance is added, because there might be some objection against the former; as if there were some reason why God chose Isaac, and refused Ishmael. Isaac was born of a free-woman, and when Abraham was uncircumcised: besides, Ishmael no sooner came to years, but he showed some tokens of perverseness, and of a wicked spirit. Therefore, in this and the three following verses, he gives another, which was beyond all exception; and that is in Esau and Jacob, betwixt whom there was no disparity, either in birth or in works: they had both one and the same mother; Rebecca conceived with them at one and the same time, and that by no other person than our father Isaac; and yet the one of these is chosen, and the other refused. This now was an undeniable proof, that the promise belongs not to all the children of Abraham, or of Isaac, according to the flesh; all the seed of neither are the children of the promise.

11 (For *the children* being not yet born, neither having done any good or evil, that the purpose of God according to election might stand, not of works, but of ˣhim that calleth;)

x ch. 4. 17. & 8. 28.

For the children being not yet born: q. d. As there was nothing in the birth of those twins, so neither in their works, that occasioned the difference that God made betwixt them; for when God spake of what should happen to them, they were unborn, and had done neither good nor evil. *Neither having done any good or evil;* he means, actual good or evil, such as might difference them one from another. As for original sin, they were both alike tainted therewith. *That the purpose of God;* this purpose of God is to be understood about reprobation, or (if you will) rejection, or preterition, as well as about election. *Might stand;* be firm or stable. *Not of works*, either done or foreseen. *But of him that calleth;* i. e. of the good pleasure and undeserved favour of God, who also effectually calleth those that he hath elected, as chap. viii. 30. See a parallel place, 2 Tim. i. 9.

12 It was said unto her, ʸThe ‖ elder shall serve the ‖ younger.

y Gen. 25. 23.
‖ Or, *greater.*
‖ Or, *lesser.*

This verse is to be read with the 10th, the whole 11th verse being a parenthesis. Then when she resorted to the Lord for counsel, about the struggling of the children in her womb, it was told her, or revealed to her of God, that *the elder should serve the younger:* of the sense of which words, see annotations on Gen. xxv. 23, where they are recorded.

13 As it is written, ᶻJacob have I loved, but Esau have I hated.

z Mal. 1. 2, 3. See Deut. 21. 15. Prov. 13. 24. Matt. 10. 37. Luke 14. 26. John 12. 25.

The foregoing oracle is expounded by another, taken out of Mal. i. 2, 3; see the annotations there. Because the foregoing passage of Esau's serving Jacob doth not seem so full and clear, to betoken the election of Jacob, and the rejection of Esau, in the purpose of God, therefore the apostle brings this place to explain the former; and proves that the service or subjection of Esau to Jacob, was accompanied with God's eternal and undeserved love of the one, and his just and righteous hatred of the other. There are some, that by Esau and Jacob do understand their posterity, and not their persons; that say, the love and hatred of God, in the forecited text, doth only or chiefly respect temporal things; God loved Jacob, i. e. he gave him the Land of Promise; but hated Esau, i. e. he gave him a dry and barren country, and made his mountain waste: that by God's hating Esau, is only meant he loved him less than Jacob, &c. Such should consider, that the scope of the apostle is to show, that some are the children of God, and of the promise, and not others; and they must not make him cite testimonies out of the Old Testament impertinently. Much is written *pro* and *con* upon this argument. But I remember, he that writes a commentary must not too far involve himself in controversy.

14 What shall we say then ? ᵃ *Is there* unrighteousness with God ? God forbid.

a Deut. 32. 4. 2 Chr. 19. 7. Job 8. 3. & 34. 10. Ps. 92. 15.

Another anticipation of an objection. Some might object and say, If God elect some, and reject others, their case being the same, or their persons being in themselves equal and alike, then he is unjust and partial. To this he answers, 1. More generally, with his repeated note of detestation, *God forbid;* the Syriac translator reads it, God forgive; noting thereby the heinousness of such a thought: and then he answers this cavil more particularly; showing, 1. That God is not unjust in electing some, ver. 15, 16. And, 2. That he is not unjust in rejecting others, ver. 17.

b Ex. 33. 19.   15 For he saith to Moses, ^b I will have mercy on whom I will have mercy, and I will have compassion on whom I will have compassion.

q. d. God is not chargeable with any injustice in electing some, and not others; for this is an act of mere mercy and compassion, and that can be no violation of justice. To prove this, he cites a testimony out of Exod. xxxiii. 19, which see. There he tells Moses, that the good pleasure of his will was the only rule of all his favourable and merciful dealings with the children of men. The same thing is intended and expressed in two several phrases: and the ingemination imports the freeness of God's mercy; nothing moves him thereunto, but his own gracious inclination; and also the arbitrariness thereof: it depends only upon his good will and pleasure. The sum is, if God show mercy to some, and not to others, he cannot be accused of injustice, because he injures none; nor is he obliged or indebted to any.

16 So then *it is* not of him that willeth, nor of him that runneth, but of God that sheweth mercy.

q. d. God's election is not of Jacob's, or of any other man's, willing or running; i. e. it is not from his good desires or deeds, his good inclinations or actions, or from the foresight thereof; but it is of God's mere mercy and good pleasure. This text wounds Pelagianism under the fifth rib. *Nec volenti, nec volanti,* was the motto of a noble personage.

c See Gal. 3. 8, 22.
d Ex. 9. 16.   17 For ^c the Scripture saith unto Pharaoh, ^d Even for this same purpose have I raised thee up, that I might shew my power in thee, and that my name might be declared throughout all the earth.

This verse shows, that God is not unjust in rejecting others of equal condition with the elect; for the proof of which, he cites a testimony out of Exod. ix. 16. This verse must be joined with the 14th. *God forbid; for the Scripture saith,* i. e. God saith in the Scripture, *Even for this same purpose have I raised thee up;* i. e. I have created or promoted thee to be king in Egypt. Or, (as some,) I have raised or stirred thee up to oppress my people. Or, I have hardened thee, as it follows in the next verse, and given thee up to thy own rebellious and obstinate mind. *That I might show my power in thee, &c.:* I have done what I have done for this very end, that the whole world may ring of my power and glory. And this shows, that it is not unjust in God to reject sinners of the children of men, because thereby he furthers his own glory. For this end all things are made, and all things are accordingly ordered and disposed, Prov. xvi. 4.

18 Therefore hath he mercy on whom he will *have mercy,* and whom he will he hardeneth.

This verse is a short repetition of the foregoing argument. *Therefore hath he mercy on whom he will have mercy:* see ver. 15, and the notes there. *And whom he will he hardeneth;* i. e. in a judicial way. Besides natural hardness, which is in all men, and is hereditary to them; and habitual hardness, which is contracted by a custom in sin, as a path is hardened by the continual trampling of passengers; there is judicial or judiciary hardness, which is inflicted by God as a punishment. Men harden their own hearts sinfully, (so it is thrice said of Pharaoh in Exodus, that he hardened his own heart, Exod. iii. 15, 32; ix. 34,) and then God hardens their hearts judicially: so it is often said of God in Exodus, that he hardened Pharaoh's heart, Exod. vii. 13; ix. 12; x. 1, 20, 27; xiv. 8. God is not said properly to harden the hearts of men; i. e. he doth not make their soft hearts hard, nor doth he put hardness into the hearts of men, (as our adversaries slanderously report us to affirm,) nor doth he barely permit or suffer them to be hardened (which is the opinion of the papists about this matter); but two ways may he be said to harden sinners: 1. By forsaking them, and not softening their hearts: as darkness follows upon the sun's withdrawing of his light, so doth hardness upon God's withholding his softening influence. 2. By punishing them; he inflicts further hardness, as a punishment of former hardness; and this he infuseth not, but it is effected either, 1. By Satan, to whom hardened sinners are delivered up; or, 2. By themselves, they being given over to their own hearts' lusts; or, 3. By God's word and works, which accidentally harden the hearts of men, as might be shown.

19 Thou wilt say then unto me, Why doth he yet find fault? For ^e who hath resisted his will?
e 2 Chr. 20.6. Job 9. 12. & 23. 13. Dan. 4. 35.

Here he obviates a third objection or cavil. The first was, that God is unfaithful, ver. 6; the second, that God is unjust, ver. 14; now the third is, that God is severe and cruel. Some might object and say, If God, in those courses which he takes with men and sinners, doth follow only his own will and pleasure, and all things are done thereafter; why then doth he complain of sinners, and find fault with them? It seems it is his will to reject them; and who hath resisted, or can make resistance thereunto? It seems to be a common saying amongst the Hebrews, that None can withstand God: see 2 Chron. xx. 6, and elsewhere.

20 Nay but, O man, who art thou that ∥ repliest against God? ^f Shall the thing formed say to him that formed *it,* Why hast thou made me thus?
∥ Or, *answerest again,* or, *disputest with God?* Job 33. 13.
f Is. 29. 16. & 45. 9. & 64. 8.

Here follows the answer to this cavil; which is either personal to the caviller, in this and the next verse, or real to the cavil, in the two following verses. *Nay but, O man, who art thou that repliest against God?* the apostle seems to speak these words with some warmth, as if his spirit and zeal was stirred at the sauciness of the caviller: q. d. Dost thou consider what thou art? Thou art but a man, a piece of living clay, a little breathing dust, a contemptible worm in comparison; and darest thou to word it with God, to dispute with thy Maker, to question or call him to an account? You may argue matters with your fellow creatures, but not with your Creator: see Isa. xlv. 9, 10, from whence this seems to be borrowed, and Job xl. 2. *Shall the thing formed say to him that formed it, Why hast thou made me thus?* q. d. Shall the wood quarrel with the carpenter, the iron with the smith; or, as it is in the next verse, the clay with the potter?

21 Hath not the ^g potter power over the clay, of the same lump to make ^h one vessel unto honour, and another unto dishonour?
g Prov. 16.4. Jer. 18. 6. Wisd. 15. 7.
h 2 Tim. 2. 20.

He argueth from the less to the greater, that if a potter hath power over his clay, to form it as he pleaseth, then God hath much more power over his creatures, to form them or order them as he listeth. God's authority over his creature, is greater than that of a potter over his clay. The potter made not his clay; but both clay and potter are made by God. Here is something implied, that as there is no difference in the matter or lump out of which the potter frameth diversity of vessels, so there is no difference in mankind; all men are alike by nature, and in the same corrupt state; both those who are elected, and those who are rejected, that are made vessels of mercy, or vessels of wrath. And here is this expressed, that as the potter maketh vessels of honour or dishonour, of nobler or viler use, out of the same lump, as he listeth, and is not bound to give a reason of his so doing to his pots; so God may choose some, and reject others, and give no account thereof unto his creatures. The potter takes nothing from the clay, of what form soever he makes it; and the Creator doth no wrong to the creature, however he doth dispose of it.

22 *What* if God, willing to shew *his* wrath, and to make his power known, endured with much longsuffering ⁱ the vessels of wrath ∥ ^k fitted to destruction:
i 1 Thes.5.9.
∥ Or, *made up.*
k 1 Pet. 2. 8. Jude 4.

In this and in the next verse, is a real answer to the cavil in ver. 19. The apostle having spoken before of God's absolute right and power over his creatures, to dispose of them at his pleasure, as the potter doth his clay; lest any should tax God with tyranny and partiality towards his creatures, he subjoineth the reasons of his different proceedings with the one and with the other. q. d. What hast thou to answer or object against God, if he take a severe course with some? seeing, 1. He thereby manifesteth his great displeasure against sin, and his power to take vengeance of sinners. Seeing, 2. He bears long with them in their sins; exerciseth great patience towards them in the midst of their provocations, giving them space to repent, if they can or will. And seeing, 3. They are *vessels of wrath, fitted to destruction*; partly by themselves, and their own sensual courses; partly by God's righteous judgment, who gives them up thereunto.

23 And that he might make known ¹the riches of his glory on the vessels of mercy, which he had ᵐafore prepared unto glory,

l ch. 2. 4. Eph. 1. 7. Col. 1. 27.
m ch. 8. 28, 29, 30.

q. d. Again, on the other side, what hast thou to say, if he proceed more mercifully with others? seeing, 1. He thereby manifesteth *the riches of his glory*, or his glorious grace; and seeing, 2. They are *vessels of mercy, which he had afore prepared unto glory*; i. e. he had done it by election from eternity, and by regeneration and sanctification of the Spirit in time. He speaks here of two sorts of *vessels*, some of *wrath*, and some of *mercy*, as he had before spoken of *vessels of honour*, and of *dishonour*. Concerning the latter, he speaks passively, that they are *fitted to destruction*: see ver. 22. Concerning the former, he speaks actively, that God hath *prepared* them *unto glory*.

24 Even us, whom he hath called, ⁿnot of the Jews only, but also of the Gentiles?

n ch. 3. 29.

Hitherto he hath been showing, that the promise was never made or meant to the carnal seed of Abraham. This argument he began, ver. 6, 7, and he continues it (using several apostrophes and amplifications, which were to his purpose) till he comes to these words; and here he tells you plainly who are the true seed of Abraham, and the children of the promise, even the called of God of all nations, whether Jews or Gentiles. And he takes occasion to fall into it, by speaking of some in the foregoing verse, that were *vessels of mercy, afore prepared unto glory*: now here, in this verse, he tells you, who these are; (and to be sure they are the persons he is inquiring after, viz. the spiritual seed of Abraham, and the children of the promise;) he says, they are such as God *called*; i. e. effectually called, *not of the Jews only, but also of the Gentiles*; and that this is so, he further proves in the following verse.

25 As he saith also in Osee, ᵒI will call them my people, which were not my people; and her beloved, which was not beloved.

o Hos. 2. 23. 1 Pet. 2. 10.

Here the apostle proves, that the Gentiles were children of the promise, or that the promise belonged to them, as well as to the Jews: and because the Jews could not endure to hear of this, he cites two testimonies out of Hosea, to convince them: one is in this verse, and it is taken out of Hosea ii. 23; the other is in the following verse.

26 ᵖAnd it shall come to pass, *that* in the place where it was said unto them, Ye *are* not my people; there shall they be called the children of the living God.

p Hos. 1. 10.

This testimony is taken out of Hosea i. 10; and it is as if he had said, This that I affirm concerning the conversion and calling of the Gentiles, is nothing else but what the prophet Hosea long ago did preach to our fathers. Some think, these places in Hosea do speak primarily of the Jews, and but secondarily, or by consequence, of the Gentiles. Others think, that they speak chiefly of the Gentiles; those terms *(not beloved*, and *not a people)* being in Scripture mostly used of them.

27 Esaias also crieth concerning Israel, ᑫThough the number of the children of Israel be as the sand of the sea, ʳa remnant shall be saved:

q Is. 10. 22, 23.
r ch. 11. 5.

In this and the two next verses he proves, that it was foretold of old, by Esaias the prophet, that God should pass by the greatest part of the Jews, and save only a remnant, or a few of them. *Crieth*; hereby is noted the prophet's zeal, or his openness and plainness. The testimony recorded, is found in Isa. x. 22, 23. *As the sand of the sea*; for number or multitude, for so the promise was to Abraham, Gen. xxii. 17; xxxii. 12. *Shall be saved:* Isaiah saith, *shall return*; i. e. from the captivity, or from sin, as it is, Isa. x. 21. This shows, none can be saved but they who return and repent.

28 For he will finish ‖ the work, and cut *it* short in righteousness: ˢbecause a short work will the Lord make upon the earth.

‖ Or, *the account*.
s Is. 28. 22.

This verse is also found in that forecited place, Isa. x. 22, 23. The apostle in this, and in the other citations, follows the Seventy, which was a received translation, and had been in request about three hundred years, though in this, and in other places, it is very different from the Hebrew text. That which God is said to *finish*, and *cut short*, is his *work*; the Greek is λογος, which signifies his word, or the account, as some read it. This is brought in as a reason why a remnant only should be saved; because God would shorten the account, or (as we read it) make *a short work*, in the Jewish world. He would bring a sudden destruction upon that people. Sennacherib and the Assyrians, or Titus Vespasian and the Romans, shall make a complete and speedy conquest of them; few of them shall remain, the greater part being involved, first in infidelity, then in destruction. The apostle makes those few to be a type of God's elect among that people, that should be saved by faith in Jesus Christ.

29 And as Esaias said before, ᵗExcept the Lord of Sabaoth had left us a seed, ᵘwe had been as Sodoma, and been made like unto Gomorrha.

t Is. 1. 9. Lam. 3. 22.
u Is. 13. 19. Jer. 50. 40.

As Esaias said before; in Isa. i. 9. *The Lord of sabaoth*; or, of hosts: the mighty God, whose hosts all creatures are, which execute his will, as soldiers the will of their commander. *Had left us a seed:* he means by *a seed*, the same that he meant before by *a remnant*, a small number. These were left as a little seed, out of a great heap of corn: that which is chosen, and left for seed, is little in comparison of the whole crop. *We had been as Sodoma, and been made like unto Gomorrha;* i. e. utterly wasted and destroyed as they were, Jer. l. 40.

30 What shall we say then? ˣThat the Gentiles, which followed not after righteousness, have attained to righteousness, ʸeven the righteousness which is of faith.

x ch. 4. 11. & 10. 20.
y ch. 1. 17.

This is the conclusion of the apostle's discourse about the election of some and the rejection of others; as also about the calling of the Gentiles and the casting off the Jews. *Which followed not after righteousness;* that never minded or regarded it; instead of following after it, they fled from it. They were full of all unrighteousness, chap. i. 18, to the end; Eph. ii. 2, 3. *The righteousness which is of faith;* viz. gospel righteousness, or the righteousness of Christ, which is received by true faith.

31 But Israel, ᶻwhich followed after the law of righteousness, ᵃhath not attained to the law of righteousness.

z ch. 10. 2. & 11. 7.
a Gal. 5. 4.

Israel, which followed after the law of righteousness; i. e. the unbelieving Jews, who paid great reverence to the law of God, regarding and observing the outward precepts and ceremonies thereof. *Hath not attained to the law of righteousness;* they came short of that righteousness which the law requires, which God will accept, and which is to be attained, not by works, but by faith, as it follows in the next verse.

32 Wherefore? Because *they sought it* not by faith, but as it were by the works of the law. For ᵇthey stumbled at that stumblingstone;

b Luke 2. 34. 1 Cor. 1. 23.

Here is the reason of the foregoing seeming paradox; why they, who *followed after the law of righteousness*, should not attain it, rather than other. *Because they sought it not* aright; they sought it not in a way of believing, but of working. These two are opposed in the business of justification, as before at large, in chap. iii. and iv. *As it were by the works of the law;* i. e. as if they could have attained righteousness or justification in that way, which it was impossible to do. *They stumbled at that stumblingstone;* i. e. the true Messiah : q. d. So far were they from seeking righteousness by Christ, that, on the contrary, they took offence at him, to their own destruction, Mark vi. 3; 1 Cor. i. 23. They thought it impossible that he should give them a righteousness better than their own. This happened to them according to the prophecy that went before them : so it followeth;

<small>c Ps. 118. 22.
Is. 8. 14.
& 28. 16.
Matt. 21. 42.
1 Pet. 2. 6, 7, 8.
d ch. 10. 11.
‖ Or, confounded.</small>

33 As it is written, ^cBehold, I lay in Sion a stumblingstone and rock of offence: and ^dwhosoever believeth on him shall not be ‖ ashamed.

As it is written; viz. in Isa. viii. 14, and xxviii. 16; to which prophecy also the apostle Peter refers, in 1 Pet. ii. 6—8. *A stumbling-stone;* Jesus Christ is properly a corner-stone, elect and precious; but accidentally and eventually a stumbling-stone, Luke ii. 34. *Ashamed;* or confounded. Isaiah saith, *he that believeth;* the apostle, *whosoever believeth;* which is much the same: an indefinite proposition is equivalent to a universal. The prophet saith, *He that believeth shall not make haste;* the apostle, *he shall not be ashamed.* He that is rash and hasty will at last be ashamed and confounded.

CHAP. X

Paul's prayer for Israel, who were misled by blind zeal, 1—3. *The difference between justification by the law and by faith explained from Scripture,* 4—10. *Salvation open to all that believe, both Jews and Gentiles,* 11—13. *The necessity of preaching to the Gentiles inferred,* 14—18. *God's acceptance of the Gentiles known before to the Jews,* 19, 20; *as also their own refusal of his offered mercy,* 21.

BRETHREN, my heart's desire and prayer to God for Israel is, that they might be saved.

The apostle begins this chapter with another prolepsis, or rhetorical insinuation, professing his unfeigned love of his nation, and his hearty desire of their salvation : q. d. As before, (c. g.) so now again I declare openly, (O ye Christian Jews, my brethren,) that whatever the generality of the Jews do think of me, as if I hated them, or were their enemy; yet there is none more passionately and tenderly affected to them than I am : and from hence it is, that I do so heartily desire and pray to God, for all that people, that they might be saved. *That they might be saved;* that they may obtain eternal salvation, and escape that deluge of wrath and destruction that hangs over their heads.

<small>a Acts 21. 20. & 22. 3. Gal. 1. 14. & 4. 17. See ch. 9. 31.</small>

2 For I bear them record ^athat they have a zeal of God, but not according to knowledge.

For I bear them record, i. e. I must testify this of them, or many of them, *that they have a zeal of God;* that they have a fervent desire to maintain the law of God, with all the Mosaical rites and ceremonies, as thinking thereby to promote the glory of God. *But not according to knowledge;* i. e. true and right knowledge. Though it be a warm, yet it is a blind zeal. They know not the will of God, or what that righteousness is which he will accept. They know not for what end the law and worship of God, under the Old Testament, was instituted. They knew not that Christ, in, and by whom, that law is fulfilled.

<small>b ch. 1. 17. & 9. 30.
c Phil. 3. 9.</small>

3 For they being ignorant of ^bGod's righteousness, and going about to establish their own ^crighteousness, have not submitted themselves unto the righteousness of God.

They being ignorant of God's righteousness: here he shows more particularly what knowledge the Jews wanted. They knew not *the righteousness of God;* of which see chap. i. 17, with the notes there. This was abundantly manifested, being witnessed by the law and the prophets, chap. iii. 21; and a thing very needful to be known, as being that wherein man's happiness consisted; but they were ignorant of it. *Going about to establish their own righteousness;* their personal and inherent righteousness, a homemade righteousness, which is of their own spinning; this they designed to set up in the room of God's righteousness. *Have not submitted themselves to the righteousness of God;* this notes the pride that accompanied their ignorance, and that is in the hearts of men by nature. They will not go abroad for that which they think they have, or may have, at home. They will not be beholden to another for that which they suppose they have in themselves. They have righteousness enough of their own working; and therefore they reject and withdraw themselves from that which is of God's appointing.

4 For ^dChrist *is* the end of the law for righteousness to every one that believeth. <small>d Matt. 5.17. Gal. 3. 24.</small>

He proves that the Jews were ignorant of the righteousness of God, because they were ignorant of Christ, the true *end of the law. Christ is the end of the law :* q. d. The law was given for this end, that sinners being thereby brought to the knowledge of their sins, and their lost and damned estate, by reason thereof, should fly to Christ and his righteousness for refuge; see Gal. iii. 19, 24. Or else, *Christ is the end of the law;* i. e. the perfection and consummation thereof. The word is taken in this sense, 1 Tim. i. 5. He perfected the ceremonial law, as being the substance whereof all the ceremonies of the law were shadows; they all referred to him as their scope and end. He perfected also the moral law, partly by his active obedience, fulfilling all the righteousness thereof, partly by his passive obedience, bearing the curse and punishment of the law, which was due to us. Whatever the law required that we should do or suffer, he hath perfected it on our behalf : see chap. viii. 4.

5 For Moses describeth the righteousness which is of the law, ^eThat the man which doeth those things shall live by them. <small>e Lev. 18. 5. Neh. 9. 29. Ezek. 20. 11, 13. 21. Gal. 3. 12.</small>

In this and the following verses, he shows the great difference that is between the righteousness of the law and the righteousness of faith; and this difference is taught us in the books of Moses himself. As for the righteousness of the law, that is plainly described by Moses, Lev. xviii. 5; and it tells us expressly, That the man who doth personally, perfectly, and constantly observe and do whatsoever the law requires, shall be rewarded with eternal life : see chap. ii. 13, and the notes there. And on the contrary, it implies thus much, That whoso fails, or falls short, shall incur death and damnation. This also it declares in other places, Deut. xxvii. 26; Gal. iii. 10. This is a hard saying; who can hear it? It shuts us all out of heaven, it turns us into hell, it lays upon us impossible conditions. Let us hearken therefore to the righteousness of faith; of which in the next.

6 But the righteousness which is of faith speaketh on this wise, ^fSay not in thine heart, Who shall ascend into heaven? (that is, to bring Christ down *from above :*) <small>f Deut. 30. 12, 13.</small>

The righteousness which is of faith speaketh on this wise: by a prosopopœia (a frequent figure in Scripture) he puts the person of a reasonable creature upon the righteousness of faith, and bringeth it in speaking and declaring itself as followeth; or else the meaning is, that the Scripture, or Moses, speaketh thus of the righteousness of faith. These words are taken out of Deut. xxx. 12, 13. The question is, Whether Paul doth properly allege this place in Deuteronomy, or only allude to it? Some think the latter, that Moses directly speaks of the law, and that the apostle, by an allusion, or by way of accommodation, applies it unto faith; hence it is, that he doth not cite the very words of Moses, but alters and adds to them, as best served his purpose. But others think, that this would extenuate the force of St. Paul's argument, if he should only allude unto this testimony of Moses, and not confirm that which he intended by the same. Therefore their opinion is, that these words are properly cited; and that Moses himself, in that place, doth speak (though very obscurely) of the righteousness of faith; yea, the foregoing words in that 30th chapter of Deuteronomy do belong to the times of the gospel. Some of the Jewish rabbis have confessed, that Moses in that chapter, especially the beginning of it, hath reference to the days of the Messiah. He speaks there of the Israelites being driven among all nations, and unto the utmost parts of heaven, which chiefly happened to them a little after the ascension of Christ, and will abide upon them till their conversion, of which see the 11th chapter of this Epistle; and then God will restore them again to the Land of Promise, to that Jerusalem which is from above, the true church of Jesus Christ; then he will circumcise their hearts, and the hearts of their seed, to love the Lord with all their heart, and with all their soul; then will the Lord rejoice over them to do them good, as he rejoiced over their fathers; then, according to God's covenant promise, the law of God shall be written in their hearts; it shall not be hidden, or afar off, but nigh them, in their mouths, and in their hearts. Thus the apostle convinceth the Jews by a testimony out of Moses, in whom they trusted. *Say not in thine heart*; i. e. think not anxiously and despondingly within thyself. *Who shall ascend into heaven?* i. e. to learn the will of God there concerning our righteousness and salvation, and then teach it to us; or, to see if there be any admission or room for such as I am there, and to carry me thither. *That is, to bring Christ down from above;* this is in effect to deny that Christ has already come down from heaven to reveal it to us; and that he must now come to do it: or else, this is as much as to deny that Christ hath already descended from heaven, to procure and purchase salvation for us; and that he must come down again for that purpose. It were to deny the ascension of Christ into heaven; for he is gone thither, not as a private, but as a public person: he is gone thither as our Head, and thither he will bring all his members; he is there as our forerunner, as one that is gone before to prepare a place for us. For Christians to distrust their going to heaven, is to doubt whether Christ be in heaven; he had never gone thither if he had not perfected our redemption and salvation here.

7 Or, Who shall descend into the deep? (that is, to bring up Christ again from the dead.)

Who shall descend into the deep? by *the deep*, here, understand hell: see Luke viii. 31; Rev. ix. 1; xx. 1, 3. q. d. Do not inquire distrustfully, and despairingly, whether thou shalt go to hell, or who shall go thither, to see, and bring the word, if such as thou are there. *That is, to bring up Christ again from the dead;* this were in effect to frustrate and make void the death of Christ; it is as much as to say, he never died for us, or he must come again, and suffer, and shed his blood for the remission of our sins. He died to deliver us from death and damnation; he endured the wrath of God, that we may escape it. The sense of the whole is this, That the doctrine of justification by faith, doth not propose such difficult and impossible terms, as the doctrine of justification by works. The righteousness of the law, that speaks terror, and puts us into a continual fear of hell, and despair of heaven; but the righteousness of faith, that speaks comfort, and forbids all amazing fear and troubles about our salvation or damnation.

g Deut. 30. 14.
8 But what saith it? ᵍThe word is nigh thee, *even* in thy mouth, and in thy heart: that is, the word of faith, which we preach;

But what saith it? i. e. what saith the text in Deut. xxx. 14? or what saith the righteousness of faith? what is its style and language? In the 6th and 7th verses he did but tell us what it said not, but here he tells us what it saith. *The word is nigh thee;* i. e. the matter required of thee, in order to life and salvation. He seems in these words to declare the readiness and easiness of the way of salvation. as taught us in the gospel, and by the righteousness of faith. God requires no hard thing of us, to cross the seas, to climb the mountains, to take long and painful journeys, to find it out. The way of salvation under the gospel hath but a short cut; it requires not so much the labour of the hand, as the confession of the mouth, and the belief of the heart: or, *The word* that teacheth it is at hand, it is as if it were *in thy mouth and heart:* a proverbial speech, (as some think,) to show the readiness of it. *That is, the word of faith, which we preach:* by *the word of faith*, he means the gospel, and the doctrine of it: and the gospel is so called, either effectively, because it works faith; or objectively, because it is a received faith, and is the proper object of it.

9 That ʰif thou shalt confess with thy mouth the Lord Jesus, and shalt believe in thine heart that God hath raised him from the dead, thou shalt be saved.
h Mat. 10. 32. Luke 12. 8. Acts 8. 37.

q. d. There are but these two things, which the gospel principally requires in order to our salvation: the one is, the confession of Christ with our mouths, and that in spite of all persecution and danger, to own him for our Lord, and for our Jesus; and to declare, that we are and will be ruled and saved by him, and by him only. The other is, to believe in our hearts, *that God hath raised him from the dead*. This article of the resurrection of Christ presupposeth all the rest, and fasteneth together, as by a link, all the antecedents and consequents of it; his ascension, session at the right hand of God, and intercession, which followed after. This article therefore, by a figure, is put for all the rest; and this is mentioned, because the death and passion of Christ had availed us nothing, unless he had risen again; for thereby he obtained a perfect victory over sin, death, and damnation, for all the elect. This is the principal ground of our justification, as hath been said, chap. iv. 25.

10 For with the heart man believeth unto righteousness; and with the mouth confession is made unto salvation.

With the heart man believeth; in the former verse confession was set first; in this, believing. Faith indeed goes before confession; *I believed*, says the psalmist, and the apostle after him, *therefore have I spoken;* yet our faith is discerned and known by our confession. *Unto righteousness;* i. e. unto justification. This phrase may be expounded by chap. iv. 5, or ix. 30. *With the mouth confession is made unto salvation:* our adversaries the papists make great use of this text, to prove that good works, as confession, &c., are the cause of salvation; whereas confession is required here, not as the cause, but as the means thereof. The apostle makes faith here to be the cause, as well of salvation, as justification; because confession of the mouth, to which salvation is here ascribed, is itself an effect or fruit of faith; and so, according to that known rule in logic, the cause of the cause, is the cause of that which is caused thereby.

11 For the Scripture saith, ⁱWhosoever believeth on him shall not be ashamed.
i Is. 28. 16. & 49. 23. Jer. 17. 7. ch. 9. 33.

The saving effect of faith and confession, spoken of immediately before, is here proved by Scripture. Either he refers to Isa. xxviii. 16, or Psal. xxv. 3; or else he means, that this is the general doctrine of the Scripture. See notes on chap. ix. 33.

12 For ᵏthere is no difference between the Jew and the Greek: for ˡthe same Lord over all ᵐis rich unto all that call upon him.
k ch. 3. 22. Acts 15. 9. Gal. 3. 28. l Acts 10. 36. ch. 3. 29. 1 Tim. 2. 5. m Eph. 1. 7. & 2. 4, 7.

For there is no difference between the Jew and the Greek: he gives a reason for that universal term, *whosoever*, which he had added in the precedent verse, and is not found in Isaiah, as was noted before, in chap. ix. 33. *The same Lord over all;* these words are a reason why there is no difference now betwixt Jew and Greek. This title is to be referred more especially to Jesus Christ, who was called Lord, ver. 9, and is called, *Lord of all*, Acts x. 36. He is Head of all the elect, in all nations of the world. *Is rich unto all;* i. e. is bountiful unto all. So that the Jews need not envy the calling or coming of the Gentiles; they have never the less themselves; the Lord hath an inexhaustible store of grace and mercy. The fountain is above our thirst. *That call upon him;* not to all, hand over head, but to such as call upon him in faith.

13 ⁿFor whosoever shall call ᵒupon the name of the Lord shall be saved.
n Joel 2. 32. Acts 2. 21. o Acts 9. 14.

That *the Lord is rich unto all that call upon him*, is confirmed here by a testimony out of Joel ii. 32, which is also cited by St. Peter, Acts ii. 21. The apostle's argument may be thus formed: If whosoever calls on the name of the Lord shall be saved, then the Lord is rich to all that call upon him; for no riches are comparable to salvation; but the former is true, therefore the latter. *Whosoever*, whether Jew or Gentile, *shall call upon the name of the Lord shall be saved;* i. e. on him whose name is the Lord. Jesus Christ is principally meant, as appears by many passages in the prophet. Compare this with 1 Cor. i. 2.

14 How then shall they call on him in whom they have not believed? and how shall they believe in him of whom they have not heard? and how shall they hear ᵖwithout a preacher?

p Tit. 1. 3.

The connexion of this verse and the following verses of this chapter is very obscure. Some connect these words with the 12th verse. There he said, *There is no difference between Jew and Greek*, &c. And this he proves, because the means to attain salvation by the true invocation of God hath been made common to all; and consequently faith, and so, from time to time, the hearing and preaching the word of God, according as the one is occasioned by the other. Others make this the coherence: Seeing the righteousness of faith is the only true righteousness, and doth, in common, by the promise of God, belong to Jew and Gentile (as hath been said); it was therefore necessary, that some must be sent of God to both people, which is the ordinary way and means to beget faith, and to bring men to Christ. His way of arguing is such, as logicians call *sorites;* rhetoricians, a gradation; and it is very forcible and demonstrative: q. d. God hath, by his prophets, promised salvation indifferently to Jew and Gentile; but without calling on him, there is no salvation; and without faith, there is no prayer; and without hearing, there is no faith; and without a preacher, there is no hearing; and without solemn mission, there can be no preacher. His manner of speaking all along is by way of interrogation, which is the more convincing, because it carries in it a kind of an appeal to the persons spoken to; every interrogation is equivalent to a negation.

How then shall they call on him in whom they have not believed? there is no foundation then for the popish doctrine of invocating saints and angels. *How shall they believe in him of whom they have not heard?* amongst the elect of God, there may be some that are born deaf; and in these, God doth supply the want of outward means in an extraordinary way: but ordinarily, hearing is as necessary to faith, as faith is to prayer, or prayer to salvation.

15 And how shall they preach, except they be sent? as it is written, ᑫHow beautiful are the feet of them that preach the Gospel of peace, and bring glad tidings of good things!

q Is. 52. 7. Nah. 1. 15.

How shall they preach, except they be sent? viz. immediately, by God or Christ, as the prophets and the apostles: see Gal. i. 1. Or mediately, by men; i. e. by such as have authority from Christ to separate and ordain others to this work. Without this orderly mission, or ordination, how can they preach? saith the apostle; i. e. how can they do it duly or profitably, or in the name and by the authority of Christ? For otherwise, there were, and still are, those that run before they are sent, Jer. xxiii. 21. *How beautiful are the feet of them!* their arrival or approach. The persons of such are meant, though their feet be named, because they carried them up and down to do this work. The scripture referred to is found in Isa. lii. 7. The apostle here leaveth the Septuagint, and followeth the Hebrew text; yet he doth not cite the place in all points as the prophet hath it. He leaveth out some words, as *upon the mountains*, which had respect to the situation of Jerusalem; and he changeth the number, turning the singular into the plural. *Object.* But the text in Isaiah speaks of such a messenger as was sent to publish the deliverance of the Jews from the bondage of the Assyrians. *Answ.* Though that be granted, it is applied and accommodated aptly enough to the preaching of peace and salvation by Christ; because that deliverance (as all other temporal deliverances) had its foundation in the redemption purchased by Christ.

16 But ʳthey have not all obeyed the Gospel. For Esaias saith, ˢLord, who hath believed † our ‖ report?

r ch. 3. 3. Heb. 4. 2.
s Is. 63. 1. John 12. 38.
† Gr. *the hearing of us.* ‖ Or, *preaching?*

But they have not all obeyed the gospel: he here preventeth a cavil of the Jews. Thus they might reason: If the apostles and preachers of the gospel are sent with so great authority from God, and bring such a welcome message, how comes it to pass that so few receive it, and yield obedience thereunto? To this he answers, that it need not seem strange, because it was foretold long ago by the prophet, Isa. liii. 1. It is not to be understood as if this was the cause of their unbelief, because Isaiah said thus. The particle *for* doth not show the cause, but the consequence: it was not because the prophet so said, that they did not believe; but because they believed not, the prophet so foretold. *Lord;* this is added by the Seventy for explanation. *Who hath believed our report?* i. e. very few, none in comparison. Compare this with John iii. 32.

17 So then faith *cometh* by hearing, and hearing by the word of God.

This is the conclusion of the former gradation, ver. 14. He speaketh here of the ordinary means whereby faith is wrought; not confining or limiting the Spirit of God, who worketh, or may work, by extraordinary means, yea, without any means at all. See the notes on ver. 14. *By the word of God;* by the command of God: q. d. The gospel could not be lawfully preached to them, for them to hear it, but by God's command; and therefore the apostles and others, in preaching the gospel to the Gentiles, had good authority for what they did.

18 But I say, Have they not heard? Yes verily, ᵗtheir sound went into all the earth, ᵘand their words unto the ends of the world.

t Ps. 19. 4. Matt. 24. 14. & 28. 19. Mark 16. 15. Col. 1. 6, 23.
u See 1 Kin. 18. 10. Matt. 4. 8.

He answers an objection, that some one might make in behalf of the Jews, to excuse them; that they could not believe, because they had not heard; and faith, as in the foregoing verse, comes by hearing. To this he answers, that the gospel was published to the whole world; therefore the Jews must needs have heard it. That the gospel had been preached all the world over, he proves by a testimony taken out of Psal. xix. 4: q. d. David tells you, that all have heard, or might hear; for the sound of the gospel is gone out into all the earth. *Object.* But David speaks of the works of God, as the heavens, the firmament, &c. *Answ.* Some think the apostle only alludes to this place in the 19th Psalm, and doth not allege it. Others think, that the psalmist doth literally and historically speak of the heavens, &c.; and prophetically of the apostles, and preachers of the gospel. By *all the earth*, in this verse, you may understand the greatest part of it; and by *the ends of the world*, the remote parts thereof.

19 But I say, Did not Israel know? First Moses saith, ˣI will provoke you to jealousy by *them that are* no people, *and* by a ʸfoolish nation I will anger you.

x Deut. 32. 21. ch. 11. 11.
y Tit. 3. 3.

Here he proves by three testimonies out of the Old Testament, that the Jews must needs have heard the sound of the gospel, together with the Gentiles; only they rejected it, when the other embraced it. And so he layeth the ground of what he was purposed to handle in the following chapter, concerning the receiving of the Gentiles, and the casting off, and after calling, of the Jews.

Did not Israel know; here something must be supplied to make up the sense: either God, or the gospel, or the righteousness of faith, or the conversion of the Gentiles. The Israelites could not well pretend ignorance, considering what Moses and Isaiah had said, in whom, or in whose writings, they were conversant. *Moses saith;* viz. in Deut. xxxii. 21. Still he follows the translation of the Seventy. *I will provoke you to jealousy by them that are no people, and by a foolish nation I will anger you;* here God threateneth the Jews, that he would punish them with *jealousy* and *anger*, by preferring the Gentiles before them; at the sight whereof, their hearts should be sore vexed; to behold all their privileges taken from them, and given to a people whom they accounted most vile and despicable, to be *no people* in regard of them, to be dogs and beasts rather than men: see Acts xiii. 45. Read the cited place in Deuteronomy and you will find that God speaks of this as a fit punishment upon the Jews for their idolatry. They had chosen to themselves such as were no gods; and therefore, to requite them, God would take to him such as were no people: they had chosen to themselves (as it were) another husband; and God, to be even with them, had chosen another wife.

20 But Esaias is very bold, and saith, ˣI was found of them that sought me not; I was made manifest unto them that asked not after me.   ˣ Is. 65. 1. ch. 9. 30.

Esaias is very bold; i. e. he speaks more boldly concerning the calling of the Gentiles, and the casting off the Jews. He used a holy freedom, though it cost him dear; Jerome saith, he was sawn asunder with a wooden saw. This is a commendable property in a preacher: see Acts iv. 13; xxviii. 31. *And saith:* viz. in Isa. lxv. 1. The apostle in this citation differs in some words, both from the Hebrew text and the Seventy, as may appear to him that will compare them together. *I was found of them that sought me not;* compare this with chap. ix. 30, and see the notes there. *I was made manifest unto them that asked not after me;* compare this with Eph. ii. 2. The advantage and advancement of the Gentiles was altogether of free grace, and an effect of God's free election.

21 But to Israel he saith, ᵃAll day long I have stretched forth my hands unto a disobedient and gainsaying people.   ᵃ Is. 65. 2.

But to Israel he saith; viz. in Isa. lxv. 2. In the former verse there is a consolatory prophecy, foretelling the vocation of ignorant and profane Gentiles; and in this, there is a menacing prophecy, threatening the rejecting of the rebellious and stubborn Jews. *All day long;* from the time of their first calling to their dissipation. *I have stretched forth my hands;* as a father holds forth his arms to receive a rebellious son. Compare this with Matt. xxiii. 37. *Unto a disobedient and gainsaying people;* the prophet Isaiah hath but one word, *rebellious,* and the apostle renders it by these two words, *disobedient and gainsaying:* they were disobedient in heart, and gainsaying with their tongues, contrary to those two gracious qualifications, mentioned ver. 9, 10, belief in the heart, and the confession of the mouth. Compare this with Acts vii. 51, 52; xiii. 45; xix. 9.

CHAP. XI

God hath not so far cast off all Israel, but that a remnant is saved by grace, not by works, 1—6. *The judicial blindness of the rest is prophesied of in Scripture,* 7—10. *The consequence both of their fall and conversion with regard to the Gentile world,* 11—16. *The Gentiles are cautioned not to insult the Jews, but to make a proper use of the example both of God's goodness and severity,* 17—22. *The Jews may, and shall in time, believe and be saved,* 23—32. *God's judgments and ways are unsearchable,* 33—36.

I SAY then, ᵃHath God cast away his people? God forbid. For ᵇI also am an Israelite, of the seed of Abraham, *of* the tribe of Benjamin.   ᵃ 1 Sam. 12. 22. Jer. 31. 37.   ᵇ 2 Cor. 11. 22. Phil. 3. 5.

The apostle having shown, in the end of the foregoing chapter, that the Jews were for their obstinacy rejected, and the Gentiles called, he here prevents or answers an objection. Some might be ready to say, If this be so, then God hath cast away his covenant people, which he hath promised not to do; see Psal. xciv. 14. To this he answers, first, by his accustomed form of denial, *God forbid;* and then he proceeds to show, that the rejection of the Jews was neither total nor final. That it was not total, he proves, first, by a particular instance in the following words. *I also am an Israelite;* i. e. I am a Jew by descent, of the seed of Abraham according to the flesh, and yet am not cast off by God. *Of the tribe of Benjamin:* some think this is added to intimate, that he was born of an honourable tribe, out of which king Saul sprang, 1 Sam. ix. 1, and Esther the queen, Esth. ii. 5. Others think this is added for a contrary reason; lest his calling should be ascribed to the dignity of his tribe, he says, he was of Benjamin, the last and least of all the tribes. And others rather think, that this particular recital of his genealogy is only to show, that he was a Jew by nature and nation, and not a proselyte converted to the faith: see Phil. iii. 5.

2 God hath not cast away his people which ᶜhe foreknew. Wot ye not what the Scripture saith † of Elias? how he maketh intercession to God against Israel, saying,   ᶜ ch. 8. 29.   † Gr. *in Elias?*

God hath not cast away his people which he foreknew: here he makes a further answer to the forementioned objection: by way of distinction, he distinguisheth the people of God into such as are foreknown, and such as are not foreknown: and as for the former of these, he says, they are not rejected of God. By such as are foreknown of God, he means those that are elected and predestinated to eternal life, chap. viii. 29: a foreknowledge with approbation is implied and intended, John x. 14; 2 Tim. ii. 19. *Wot ye not what the Scripture saith of Elias?* here is a third answer to the objection in the 1st verse, and it is taken from an instance in Elias, which the Jews were well acquainted with. He cites or brings a book case for it. And he the rather brings this instance, lest the Jews should accuse him of insolency, for that he had spoken before only of himself; and therefore he gives them to understand, that there were many other believing Israelites, as well as himself, though possibly they were unknown to them. You know (saith he) *what the Scripture saith of Elias,* 1 Kings xix. *How he maketh intercession to God against Israel:* i. e. against the ten tribes, who were generally revolted from God, and fallen to idolatry: against those he complained, or those he impeached, ripping up their impieties, as in the following words.

3 ᵈLord, they have killed thy prophets, and digged down thine altars; and I am left alone, and they seek my life.   ᵈ 1 Kings 19. 10, 14.

See 1 Kings xix. 10, 14. *Digged down thine altars:* these were not the altars of the high places, for they are commended that cast them down; nor the altars in the temple at Jerusalem, for they were out of the reach of the ten tribes, against whom Elias complains: but such altars (say some) as the godly of the ten tribes did build to serve God with, when they were not permitted to go up to Jerusalem; in which case the building of private altars (as some learned Jews have affirmed) was allowed. Or else by *altars* you may understand such altars as Elias himself, by the special commandment of God, had erected. Others, by digging down God's altars, do understand their corrupting and destroying the true worship of God; and the words are to be taken synecdochically, or metonomically, the sign being put for the thing signified. *I am left alone;* so it was, for aught he knew; for few, if any, did publicly own the true worship of God: so general was the defection of the ten tribes in those days.

4 But what saith the answer of God unto him? ᵉI have reserved to myself seven thousand men, who have not bowed the knee to *the image of* Baal.   ᵉ 1 Kings 19. 18.

The answer of God; the word properly signifieth the oracle, or answer of God given in the tabernacle from the mercy-seat; but it is generally taken for any Divine answer, or direction received from God: see Matt. ii. 12; Heb. xi. 7, where the same word is used. The apostle doth not repeat the whole *answer of God,* as it is recorded in 1 Kings xix. 15—18, but so much only as was pertinent to his purpose. *I have reserved to myself;* he saith not, They have reserved themselves, but, *I have reserved* them: q. d. Of my own free grace I have kept them from idolatry and apostacy. *Seven thousand men;* a certain number for an uncertain. There were doubtless women amongst them; but they are noted by the more worthy sex. *Who have not bowed the knee to the image of Baal;* the word *image* is not in the Greek; but the article being of the feminine gender, it was necessarily understood.

f ch. 9. 27.

5 ᶠEven so then at this present time also there is a remnant according to the election of grace.

q. d. As it was in the times of Elias, so it is now; *there is a remnant* of the Jews, which God hath graciously elected; therefore their rejection is not total, which was the thing to be proved. Though those that believe are few in respect of those that believe not, as a remnant is but little in respect of the whole piece, yet there are many thousands of them, as James said to Paul, Acts xxi. 20, *Thou seest, brother, how many thousands of Jews there are which believe.*

g ch. 4. 4, 5.
Gal. 5. 4.
See Deut. 9. 4, 5.

6 And ᵍif by grace, then *is it* no more of works: otherwise grace is no more grace. But if *it be* of works, then is it no more grace: otherwise work is no more work.

This verse depends upon the former; and though it doth not seem to appertain to the argument the apostle had in hand, yet, by the direction of the Spirit, he takes the little occasion that is offered, to show, that election and vocation are only by grace, and not by works. This he had spoken to before, chap. iv. 4, 5; ix. 11; but he toucheth upon it again: and here he delivers a truth, which the Jews of old either could not, or would not, understand; i. e. that there is no mixing of the merit of good works and the free grace of God, but one of these doth exclude and destroy the nature of the other; for if election and calling were both of grace and works, (as some that call themselves Christians, as well as the Jews, affirm,) then grace is no grace, and works are no works. For whatsoever proceedeth of grace, that cometh freely, and not of debt; but what cometh by merit of works, that cometh by debt; but now debt and no debt, or that which is free, and by desert, are quite contrary things. Therefore to say, that men are elected and called, partly of grace and partly of the merit of foreseen works, that were to put things together that cannot agree, to make debt no debt, merit no merit, works no works, grace no grace; and so, to affirm and deny one and the same thing.

h ch. 9. 31.
& 10. 3.

7 What then? ʰIsrael hath not obtained that which he seeketh for; but the election hath obtained it, and the rest were ǁ blinded.

ǁ Or, *hardened*, 2 Cor. 3. 14.

What then? q. d. My discourse comes to this, or this is the sum of it. *Israel hath not obtained that which he seeketh for;* i. e. the body of the Jewish nation, seeking righteousness and life by the works of the law, have not obtained it, or they have not hit the mark; they aimed at it, but they shot wide; they took a great deal of pains to little or no purpose: see chap. ix. 31. *The election;* i. e. the elect; the abstract for the concrete: so before, *circumcision* for the circumcised. *The rest were blinded;* i. e. those who are not elected; they are left, by God's just judgment, to their own ignorance and obdurateness; as also to Satan, who doth increase it in them, 2 Cor. iv. 4. The antithesis requires that he should have said, The rest have not obtained; but he speaks this of purpose to show the cause of their not obtaining, i. e. their own blindness of mind and hardness of heart.

i Is. 29. 10.
ǁ Or, *remorse*.
k Deut. 29. 4. Is. 6. 9.
Jer. 5. 21.
Ezek. 12. 2.
Matt. 13. 14.
John 12. 40. Acts 28. 26, 27.

8 (According as it is written, ⁱGod hath given them the spirit of ǁ slumber, ᵏ eyes that they should not see, and ears that they should not hear;) unto this day.

It is written; viz. in Isa. vi. 9; xxix. 10. *The spirit of slumber;* the word signifieth, such a dead sleep, as those have, who are pricked or stung with venomous beasts, out of which they hardly or never awake. *Unto this day:* q. d. So it was of old, and so it is still. Or else these words (the former being included in a parenthesis) may be joined with the last words of the foregoing verse, thus, *the rest were blinded unto this day.*

l Ps. 69. 22.

9 And David saith, ˡLet their table be made a snare, and a trap, and a stumblingblock, and a recompence unto them:

10 ᵐLet their eyes be darkened, that they may not see, and bow down their back alway.

m Ps. 69. 23.

David saith; viz. in Psal. lxix. 22, 23. The apostle tieth not himself to the very words of the psalmist, but being guided by the same Spirit by which David wrote, he adds and alters some words, without diminishing the sense. *Let their table be made a snare, &c.:* some take these words for a prayer; others, a prophecy. David, in the person of Christ, (of whom he was a type,) doth complain and prophesy of the extreme injuries and oppressions wherewith the Jews (his own people) should vex him; as that they should give him *gall for meat,* and in his thirst, give him *vinegar to drink,* ver. 21. Therefore, by way of imprecation, he prayeth down the wrath of God upon them: particularly, he prophesies or prays, that all their most pleasant things might be turned to their destruction; that their understandings might be darkened, so as they shall discern nothing of heavenly things; that they might savour nothing but earthly things, and be unable to lift up their heads and hearts to God, and to his gospel. Now David having, by the Spirit of prophecy, prayed down such miseries upon the Jews, they must be fulfilled; therefore the general unbelief and hardness of heart that is amongst that people is not to be wondered at.

11 I say then, Have they stumbled that they should fall? God forbid: but rather ⁿthrough their fall salvation *is* come unto the Gentiles, for to provoke them to jealousy.

n Acts 13. 46. & 18. 6. & 22. 18, 21. & 28. 24, 28. ch. 10. 19.

Hitherto he hath showed that the rejection of the Jews is not total. Now he comes to prove that it is not final; that before the end of the world they shall be generally called and converted; that they, together with the Gentiles that believe, shall make one sheepfold, and one flock under one Shepherd, the Lord Jesus Christ. And for the proving of this, divers arguments are brought by the apostle, (who alone plainly handles this secret,) on which he insisteth the longer, for the comfort of the poor Jews, as also for the administration and information of the Gentiles. *Have they stumbled that they should fall? God forbid:* here is another prolepsis or anticipation. The Jews might say, If the case be thus, that these holy prophets, Isaiah and David, have foretold our blindness and stumbling, then we are in a hopeless condition, and that for ever. To this he answers, that they have not so stumbled as that they should finally fall, so as never to rise again; far be it from me to affirm any such things: God hath revealed the contrary to me; that he will one day call the Jews again, and restore them to his favour. *Through their fall salvation is come unto the Gentiles:* q. d. Out of the forementioned evil there ariseth this good, that the gospel (being rejected by the Jews) is preached to the Gentiles, and they are thereby called and brought to salvation: see Acts xiii. 42, 46. Because now at first a few Jews only, and a multitude of Gentiles, are converted, it hath so fallen out, that the ceremonial law is the more easily abrogated, and the doctrine of the gospel and the grace of God is the better established. *To provoke them to jealousy;* i. e. the Jews who embrace not the gospel: q. d. This grace that God hath bestowed upon the Gentiles, he will make use of in his appointed time, as a prick of holy jealousy to the Jews; he will by means thereof stir them up to a holy indignation and emulation, to see themselves so far outstripped by those whom they contemned, and thereupon to embrace the gospel, and become the people of God again. Thus, as God hath ordered that the casting away of the Jews should be an occasion of the calling of the Gentiles; so again, on the other hand, the calling of the Gentiles shall be an occasion of the restoring of the Jews.

12 Now if the fall of them *be* the riches of the world, and the ǁ diminishing of them the riches of the Gentiles; how much more their fulness?

ǁ Or, *decay*, *or, loss.*

Another anticipation. The apostle having showed, that

the falling away of the Jews was an occasion of the coming in of the Gentiles, it might be objected, that the conversion of the Jews might likewise be an occasion of the falling away of the Gentiles. To this he answers negatively, and confirms his answer by an argument from the less to the greater; that if their fall and diminution were the riches of the Gentiles, their calling again would be so much more: q. d. If God hath made use of the fall and rejection of the Jews, for an occasion of pouring out the riches or abundance of his grace upon the nations; and if the number of believing Jews, being so very small, (which is meant by their *diminishing*,) hath occasioned the conversion of such a multitude of Gentiles; then how much more will their fulness have the effect! *How much more their fulness!* i. e. their general conversion, the coming in of the Jews, shall so fill the world with wonder, and the gospel with lustre, that a much further accession will be made even to the number of the believing Gentiles.

o Acts 9. 15.
& 13. 2. & 22.
21. ch. 15.
16. Gal. 1.
16. & 2. 2.
7, 8, 9.
Eph. 3. 8. 1 Tim. 2. 7. 2 Tim. 1. 11.

13 For I speak to you Gentiles, inasmuch as ° I am the apostle of the Gentiles, I magnify mine office:

i. e. *I speak to you* of being rich in the faith above the Jews, because I challenge a special interest in you, *inasmuch as I am* appointed to be *the apostle of the Gentiles*, and am sent chiefly unto them: see chap. xv. 16; Acts ix. 15; xiii. 2; xxii. 21; xxvi. 17; Gal. i. 16; ii. 7; Eph. iii. 8; 2 Tim. i. 11. And therefore, in thus setting forth your privileges and blessings, *I magnify mine office.*

p 1 Cor. 7.
16. & 9. 22.
1 Tim. 4. 16.
Jam. 5. 20.

14 If by any means I may provoke to emulation *them which are* my flesh, and ᵖ might save some of them.

q. d. And I thus extol God's favour and mercy to you, that it may be a means (if God please) to provoke the Jews, that are my own flesh and blood, to a holy emulation or jealousy, (see ver. 11,) when they shall see the Gentiles possess what was promised to them. *Quest.* How doth he say, that he may save some of them? is not God the author of salvation? *Answ.* Yes; but he hath given his ministers to be instruments therein, and called them fellow workers with himself, 2 Cor. vi. 1 : see 1 Tim. iv. 16.

15 For if the casting away of them *be* the reconciling of the world, what *shall* the receiving *of them be*, but life from the dead?

This verse contains an argument to prove the calling of the Jews; not a new one, but that repeated which you had before, ver. 12; the substance is the same, only the terms differ : there he spake of the fall and diminishing of the Jews, here, of their casting away; there it was the riches, here it is the reconciling of the world : q. d. If the rejection of the Jews brought great profit to the Gentiles, their reception and restoration will bring abundantly more. *Be the reconciling of the world;* i. e. an occasion of preaching the gospel to the Gentiles, by means of which they were reconciled to God. The gospel is *the ministry of reconciliation*, 2 Cor. v. 18—20. *The receiving of them*, into the favour of God and the bosom of the church. *Life from the dead;* a proverbial speech, to signify a great change for the better. The conversion of that people and nation, will strengthen the things that are languishing and like to die in the Christian church. It will confirm the faith of the Gentiles, and reconcile all their differences in religion, and occasion a more thorough reformation amongst them : there will be a much more happy and flourishing estate of the church, even such as shall be in the end of the world, at the resurrection of the dead.

q Lev. 23. 10.
Num. 15. 18,
19, 20, 21.

16 For if ᵠthe firstfruit *be* holy, the lump *is* also *holy*: and if the root *be* holy, so *are* the branches.

Here is another argument to prove the Jews are not finally rejected, because of the covenant made with their fathers. *If the first-fruit be holy :* some make a difference between *the first-fruit*, and *the root*, in the latter part of the verse. By *the first-fruit* they understand the apostles and other godly Jews, that were at first converted to the Christian faith ; and by *the root* they understand Abraham and the patriarchs. Others take them for the same, and understand Abraham, Isaac, and Jacob, with the rest of the patriarchs, to be both *the first-fruit* and *the root*. *The lump is also holy ;* by *lump*, and *branches*, he means the people of the Jews that descended of these holy patriarchs, and sprung from them, as branches from a root. The great question is, In what sense they are said to be *holy?* or of what holiness doth he speak? It is not meant of inherent, but of federal, or covenant holiness; all in an outward and visible covenant with God, were called *holy :* see Exod. xix. 6 ; Dan. viii. 24. Many common things are called *holy* in Scripture, because dedicated to God and to his service ; yea, Jerusalem, though a place of great wickedness, is called a *holy city*, Matt. xxvii. 53. In such a sense as this, the Jews are still a holy people ; they have an hereditary kind of dedication to God ; they have a federal holiness, and relation to God, as being for ever separated to him, in the loins of their progenitors ; this can never be wholly forfeited, as being granted to all the posterity of the holy patriarchs : therefore they are called *the children of the covenant, which God made with their fathers*, Acts iii. 25 : see Acts ii. 39. So then God will remember in his own time, his covenant with the Jews, the posterity of Abraham, &c., who are *beloved for the fathers' sakes*, ver. 28. Therefore, in the mean time, they should not look on themselves with desperation ; nor should the Gentiles look on them with disdain, as it follows in the next words.

17 And if ʳsome of the branches be broken off, ˢand thou, being a wild olive tree, wert graffed in ∥ among them, and with them partakest of the root and fatness of the olive tree;

r Jer. 11. 16.
s Acts 2. 39.
Eph. 2. 12, 13.
∥ Or, *for them.*

In this, and some following verses, the apostle digresseth a little, and takes occasion to prevent the insulting of the Gentiles over the Jews ; as also to persuade them to take warning by their example. *If some of the branches be broken off;* the unbelieving Jews. *And thou;* a believing Gentile : though he speaks as to a particular person, yet he means the whole body of the believing Gentiles. *Being a wild olive tree;* a scion taken from a wild olive tree ; i. e. from the heathenish and unbelieving world. *Wert graffed in among them;* the believing Jews. Some read, for them, or in the place of the branches that are broken off. *And with them partakest of the root and fatness of the olive tree :* by *the root* he means Abraham, &c. as before : by *the olive tree* he means the church of Christ ; by *the root*, or sap of the root, and by the *fatness of the olive tree*, he means, all the promises and privileges, the graces and ordinances, the spiritual blessings and benefits, which belonged to Abraham and his seed, or to the true church of God.

18 ᵗBoast not against the branches. But if thou boast, thou bearest not the root, but the root thee.

t 1 Cor. 10. 12.

Boast not against the branches ; i. e. against the Jews, who, because of their unbelief, are broken off ; as if by nature thou wert better than they, or more worthy of that grace which is bestowed on thee. The word signifies, Throw not up thy neck, do not carry thyself scornfully and insultingly. *But if thou boast, thou bearest not the root, but the root thee :* q. d. If any will needs be so insolent, let them know and consider, that as the root is not beholden to the branches, but the branches to the root ; so the good things that the Gentiles have, they received from the Jews, and not the Jews from them : the Gentile church is incorporated into the Jewish, and not the Jewish into the Gentile. Or else the meaning is, Despise not the Jews, for they are the natural branches of the root that bears them. If thou insultest over the branches, thou dost in a manner lift up thyself against the root, that once bore them, and now bears thee ; even Abraham, who is the father of all them that believe. Abraham is not the root, simply and absolutely, but relatively, or by way of relation to his posterity and offspring.

19 Thou wilt say then, The branches were broken off, that I might be graffed in.

20 Well ; because of unbelief they were broken off, and thou standest by faith. ᵘ Be not highminded, but ˣ fear :

u ch. 12. 16.
x Prov. 28. 14. Is. 66. 2. Phil. 2. 12.

Here he brings in the Gentiles, alleging a reason for their

insulting over the Jews; because the Jews were broken off, that they might give place, or make way, for them; and the less worthy do always give place to the more worthy. To this he answers, first, by way of concession: Well, (saith he,) it is true, and I do not deny it, that the Jews *were broken off*, that the Gentiles *might be graffed in.* But then he further adds, by way of correction or negation, that the worthiness of the Gentiles was not the cause why the Jews were broken off; but it was *because of* their own *unbelief;* they would not accept of Christ, John i. 11; they went *about to establish their own righteousness,* and would *not submit themselves to the righteousness of God,* as it is in chap. x. 3. Therefore, if you Gentiles shall reason after this manner, you plainly put a fallacy upon yourselves, and take that for a cause which is none : you do not distinguish between the cause and the event; it fell out, indeed, that the Jews, being cast off, the Gentiles were received in, but this was not the cause of that. *And thou standest by faith :* q. d. Neither is thy worthiness the cause of thy present standing in the room of the Jews, or of having thy station in the church of Christ; but it is thy believing in that Christ whom the Jews rejected. By *faith* thou wast first ingrafted, and still continuest in the good olive tree. *Be not high-minded, but fear :* q. d. Be advised, and take heed of being self-conceited and secure; if thou fall into their fault, thou mayst expect the same fate. Therefore stand in awe, and sin not; thou art subject to unbelief and apostacy, as well as they.

21 For if God spared not the natural branches, *take heed* lest he also spare not thee.

This verse is a reason of the forementioned admonition : q. d. If God proceeded with so much severity against his ancient people the Jews, you Gentiles may in reason expect as great severity, if you take not heed to yourselves, and to your standing.

22 Behold therefore the goodness and severity of God: on them which fell, severity; but toward thee, goodness, ʸ if thou continue in *his* goodness: otherwise ᶻ thou also shalt be cut off.

ʸ 1 Cor. 15. 2. Heb. 3. 6, 14.
ᶻ John 15. 2.

In this verse, he further persuades the Gentiles to humility and godly fear, and suggesteth several reasons for it. The first is taken from the example of God's *severity* to the Jews; they falling into apostacy and unbelief, are generally cut off and cast away. A second reason is taken from the free grace and undeserved goodness of God to the poor Gentiles, who were mercifully planted or grafted in the room of the Jews. A third reason is taken from the condition of their present standing, which is, if they *continue in his goodness;* i. e. if they continue in that state wherein his goodness hath set them. Some think the cause is here put for the effect, the *goodness* of God for faith, which was wrought in them by the goodness or grace of God. The antithesis, in the next verse, shows this to be the sense; for there he speaks of the Jews not continuing or abiding still in unbelief. A fourth reason is from the danger that would follow; if, through pride and security, they should fall and miscarry, they would be cut off, as the Jews, the natural branches, are. Some observe the change of the word; the Jews are said to be *broken off,* but the Gentiles would be *cut off;* they would, as it were, be stocked up by the roots: but that seems too critical and curious.

23 And they also, ᵃ if they abide not in unbelief, shall be graffed in : for God is able to graff them in again.

ᵃ 2 Cor. 3. 16.

Here he adds another argument, to repress the arrogance and insulting of the Gentiles; and it is taken from the hope of the Jews' restoration. Though for the present they seem to be in a desperate and forlorn condition, yet the restoring and re-ingrafting of them into the church is not impossible. The great obstacle is their unbelief, which God is able to remove. The same God that rejected them is able to restore them; to him all things are possible, he can cause dead and dry bones to live. An argument from the power of God (and that in the very words of this text) is frequently made use of in Scripture, to excite hope and assurance, chap. iv. 21; xiv. 4; 2 Cor. ix. 8; 2 Tim. i. 12; Heb. ii. 18; xi. 19.

24 For if thou wert cut out of the olive tree which is wild by nature, and wert graffed contrary to nature into a good olive tree : how much more shall these, which be the natural *branches,* be graffed into their own olive tree ?

He here shows the probability, as well as possibility, of the Jews' conversion, because God hath done that which is more unlikely : q. d. If the Gentiles, which were a kind of wild olive branches, were grafted into a good olive tree, the church of God, which is contrary to nature, seeing men use to graft a good scion into a wild stock, (as an apple into a crab,) and not a wild scion into a good stock ; how much more shall the Jews, which are the natural branches, yea, branches of that olive tree into which the Gentiles are now ingrafted, be grafted into their own olive tree, to which formerly they did belong ! according to the custom of grafting which was common amongst them, to graft one tree upon another of the same kind; and grounded on Lev. xix. 19.

25 For I would not, brethren, that ye should be ignorant of this mystery, lest ye should be ᵇ wise in your own conceits; that ᶜ ‖ blindness in part is happened to Israel, ᵈ until the fulness of the Gentiles be come in.

ᵇ ch. 12. 16.
ᶜ ver. 7. 2 Cor. 3. 14.
‖ Or, *hardness.*
ᵈ Luke 21. 24. Rev. 7. 9.

Here he shows there is not only a possibility and probability, but a certainty of the Jews' conversion and calling. This he calleth a *mystery,* or a secret; though it was revealed in the Scripture, (as you will hear,) yet it was not understood; nay, the manner, the number, and the time of their conversion, is still concealed and hid from us. The calling of the Gentiles was a mystery, and a great secret ; see Eph. iii. 3; and so is the calling and restoration of the Jews. There are three particulars of this *mystery,* which he makes known to the Gentiles (and he doth it the rather, lest they should swell with a high conceit of themselves, and proudly despise the Jews) : two of them are in this verse; and the first is, *that blindness is happened to Israel in part* only; i. e. they were not all blinded or hardened; or this blindness should not last always, but for a time. The latter sense agrees best with the word *mystery ;* for it was no secret that some of the Jews believed; this was told them before, ver. 2, 5, 7. Secondly, another part of this *mystery* was, that this blindness of the Jews should continue till *the fulness of the Gentiles came in.* By *fulness* here, (as in ver. 12,) understand a great number or multitude of the Gentiles ; greater, by far, than was in the apostles' days. There is another exposition of this clause, which I submit to consideration : by *the Gentiles,* here, you may understand the Romans, or the Roman monarchy and power ; (see Acts iv. 27 ; xxi. 11 ;) and by the coming in of their fulness may be understood, the full time of their reign and continuance ; after which their ruin follows. And so here is foretold the time of the calling of the Jews, which will be soon after the destruction of antichrist and the Roman monarchy. *Query,* Whether this doth not agree with the prediction of our Saviour ? Luke xxi. 24.

26 And so all Israel shall be saved : as it is written, ᵉ There shall come out of Sion the Deliverer, and shall turn away ungodliness from Jacob :

ᵉ Is. 59. 20. See Ps. 14. 7.

Here is a third and chief part of the aforementioned *mystery,* that in the end, *all Israel shall be saved.* By *Israel* is not meant the whole church of God, consisting of Jews and Gentiles ; so that word is used, Gal. vi. 16, and elsewhere ; for then, what he spake would have been no mystery at all : but by *Israel* here (as in the precedent verse) you must understand, the nation and people of the Jews. And by *all Israel* is not meant every individual Israelite, but many, or (it may be) the greatest part of them. So *all* is to be taken in Scripture : see John vi. 45 ; 1 Tim. ii. 6, and elsewhere. Look, as when he speaks of the conversion of the Gentiles, and the coming in of their fulness, there are many (too many of them) still unconverted ; so, notwithstanding the general calling of the Jews, a great many of them may remain uncalled. *As it is written ;* the apostle had this by revelation, but he proves it also by Scripture.

All are not agreed from whence these testimonies are taken; the former is found (with some little variation) in Isa. lix. 20: as for the latter, some think it is taken from Jer. xxxi. 33. Others think, that he joineth two places in Isaiah together, (as he did before, ver. 8,) and the last words are taken out of Isa. xxvii. 9. The Seventy have the very words used by the apostle. These prophecies and promises, though they were in part fulfilled when Christ came in the flesh, (see Acts iii. 26,) yet there will be a more full and complete accomplishment thereof upon the Jewish nation and people towards the end of the world.

f Is. 27. 9.
Jer. 31. 31,
&c. Heb. 8.
8. & 10. 10.

27 f For this *is* my covenant unto them, when I shall take away their sins.

28 As concerning the Gospel, *they are* enemies for your sakes : but as touching the election, *they are* g beloved for the fathers' sakes.

g Deut. 7.
8. & 9. 5.
& 10. 15.

Here an objection is obviated : the Gentiles might object and say, The Jews can never return and be saved, forasmuch as they have rejected the gospel, and are therefore hated of God. To this he answers by way of concession, that it was true indeed, they had rejected the gospel, and for this they were rejected and hated of God; but this happened well to the Gentiles, and was to their advantage, for the Jews' refusal of the gospel brought it sooner to them: see ver. 11. Or else the meaning is, They are enemies of God, and of his gospel ; and the rather reject it, because you Gentiles embrace it ; they think the worse of the gospel because you believe and profess it. Then he adds by way of correction, that they were not yet in such desperate circumstances ; but in regard of *election, they are beloved for the fathers' sakes.* By *election* he means, either God's choosing them to eternal life ; or rather, his choosing that nation and people, above all other nations and people of the world, to be his peculiar people : see Deut. vii. 6 ; Psal. cxxxv. 4 ; Acts xiii. 46. And by God's love to them, he means his love of good will which he had to that people still, for their fathers' sakes: not because of the merit of their fathers, but because of the covenant made with their fathers ; because they are descended of those fathers, to whom God had promised, that he would be their God, and the God of their seed after them ; aye, and of their seed's seed for ever; which promises of God, the infidelity of many of them cannot wholly frustrate.

29 For the gifts and calling of God *are* h without repentance.

h Num. 23. 19.

These words, considered simply and abstractedly, afford this truth ; That the special gifts of God, his election, justification, adoption, and in particular effectual calling, are irrevocable. God never repents of giving, nor we of receiving them. It is otherwise with common gifts and graces, 1 Sam. xv. 11. But if you consider these words relatively, as you respect what went before, the sense seems to be this ; That *the gifts and calling of God,* whereby he was pleased to adopt the posterity of Abraham, and to engage himself by covenant to them, are inviolable, and are such as shall never be reversed or repented of.

i Eph. 2. 2.
Col. 3. 7.
|| Or, *obeyed.*

30 For as ye i in times past have not || believed God, yet have now obtained mercy through their unbelief:

31 Even so have these also now not || believed, that through your mercy they also may obtain mercy.

|| Or, *obeyed.*

This is the last argument, to prove the conversion and calling of the Jews, which is further confirmed, ver. 32. The argument is taken from the like dealing of God with the Gentiles ; after a long time of infidelity, he received them to mercy ; therefore he will also at last receive the Jews. He argues from the less to the greater ; If the infidelity of the Jews was the occasion of mercy to the Gentiles, much more shall the mercy showed to the Gentiles be an occasion of showing mercy to the Jews : q. d. There is more force in that which is good, to produce a good effect, than in that which is evil, to have a good event: therefore, if the unbelief of the Jews had so good an event, as to occasion the conversion of the Gentiles, why may we not think, that the calling of the Gentiles will contribute to the conversion of the Jews ? see ver. 11, 14. When the Jews shall see the Gentiles' mercy, i. e. God's mercy to them ; how the whole world flourisheth under the profession of Christianity ; how the Messias is in vain expected by them ; how their nation is dispersed, &c.; then they shall at last come in and cleave to Christ, and be mercifully received by him.

32 For k God hath || concluded them all in unbelief, that he might have mercy upon all.

k ch. 3. 9.
Gal. 3. 22.
|| Or, *shut them all up together.*

q. d. God hath, in just judgment, shut up both Jews and Gentiles, equally and successively, in unbelief, as in a prison, that so, in his own time, he might fulfil the counsel of his will, in showing undeserved mercy unto all; i. e. unto both Jews and Gentiles ; first the Jews, and then the Gentiles ; and then at last, both to Jews and Gentiles. By *all* here he means, those that shall believe, whether of one sort or of the other, as appears from that parallel place, Gal. iii. 22. Luther, in a very great conflict, had much support from this text.

33 O the depth of the riches both of the wisdom and knowledge of God ! l how unsearchable *are* his judgments, and m his ways past finding out !

l Ps. 36. 6.
m Job 11. 7.
Ps. 92. 5.

In this and the following verses is the conclusion of all that he had delivered, especially in this and the two preceding chapters. He had spoken of many profound mysteries, and answered many critical questions ; and here he makes a pause, and falls into an admiration of God, his abundant wisdom and knowledge. He seems here to be like a man that wades into the waters, till he begins to feel no bottom, and then he cries out, *Oh the depth !* and goes no farther. *Oh the depth of the riches both of the wisdom and knowledge of God !* i. e. the unmeasurable, inconceivable abundance of his *wisdom and knowledge.* Some distinguish these two ; others take them for the same : see Col. ii. 3. *How unsearchable are his judgments, and his ways past finding out !* Some distinguish betwixt the *judgments* and *ways* of God ; by the former, understanding his decrees and purposes concerning nations or persons ; by the latter, the methods of his providence in his dealings with them : others think the same thing is meant, by an ingemination, which is familiar amongst the Hebrews. He says of God's *judgments,* that they are *unsearchable;* therefore not to be complained of, censured, or to be narrowly pried into ; and of his *ways,* that they are *past finding out ;* the same in sense with *unsearchable :* it is a metaphor from hounds, that have no footstep or scent of the game which they pursue : nor can men trace the Lord, or find out the reason of his doings ; as none can line out the way of a ship in the sea, or an eagle in the air, &c. Some restrain the sense to the ways of God in disposing and ordering the election and rejection of men.

34 n For who hath known the mind of the Lord ? or o who hath been his counsellor ?

n Job 15. 8.
Is. 40. 13.
Jer. 23. 18.
Wisd. 9. 13.
1 Cor. 2. 16.
o Job 36. 22.

i. e. Who knoweth what God is about to do ? or who hath given his advice about the doing of it ? This is taken out of Isa. xl. 13, 14.

35 Or p who hath first given to him, and it shall be recompensed unto him again ?

p Job 35. 7.
& 41. 11.

q. d. If any man hath obliged God, by any thing he hath done for him, he shall have an ample reward : alluding (as some think) to Job xli. 11. But seeing this cannot be, and that God is indebted unto none, therefore the salvation of all is of mere grace and mercy ; and there is no cause of complaining, if he deal more bountifully with some than with others.

36 For q of him, and through him, and to him, *are* all things : r to † whom *be* glory for ever. Amen.

q 1 Cor. 8. 6.
Col. 1. 16.
r Gal. 1. 5.
1 Tim. 1. 17.
2 Tim. 4. 18.
Heb. 13. 21.
1 Pet. 5. 11. 2 Pet. 3. 18. Jude 25. Rev. 1. 6. † Gr. *him.*

For of him, and through him, and to him, are all things ; i. e. *all things* are *of him,* as the efficient cause ; *through him,* as the disposing cause ; *to him,* as the final cause. They are *of him,* without any other motive ; *through him,* without any assistance ; and *to him,* without any other end,

i. e. for his sake alone. *To whom be glory for ever. Amen:* a usual doxology in Scripture: see Gal. i. 5; 2 Tim. iv. 18; Heb. xiii. 21; 1 Pet. v. 11.

CHAP. XII

Paul exhorteth to holiness and conformity to God's will; and to think soberly of the gifts allotted every man respectively, 1—3. *We are all members of one body in Christ,* 4, 5; *and should diligently exercise our several gifts for the common benefit,* 6—8. *Sundry practical duties recommended,* 9—18. *Revenge is specially forbidden, and to do good for evil enjoined,* 19—21.

a 2 Cor. 10 1.
b 1 Pet. 2. 5.
c Ps. 50. 13, 14. ch. 6. 13, 16, 19. 1 Cor. 6. 13. 20.
d Heb. 10.20.

1 ª BESEECH you therefore, brethren, by the mercies of God, ᵇ that ye ᶜ present your bodies ᵈ a living sacrifice, holy, acceptable unto God, *which is* your reasonable service.

Hitherto the apostle hath discoursed of matters of faith; in this and the following chapters he sets down precepts of holy life. *By the mercies of God:* he useth the word in the plural number, to amplify and set forth the manifold mercies of God, in election, justification, adoption, &c.: q. d. Seeing you Gentiles have received so many and so great mercies from God; seeing he hath preferred you to his ancient people the Jews, and hath chosen and called you, when he hath rejected them; as you value these mercies, let the consideration of them engage you to all manner of holiness and new obedience. *That ye present;* that you give, dedicate, and offer up, as spiritual priests. *Your bodies;* yourselves, or, your whole man; a part is put for the whole; the body is named, because it is the soul's instrument in the service of God. *A living sacrifice;* the sacrifices of old were presented alive to God, and their blood was shed at the feet of the altar: a beast that died of itself, or was torn by wild beasts, was not so much as to be eaten, Exod. xxii 31; Lev. xxii. 8. Conformable hereunto, God will have us offer up ourselves *a living sacrifice;* i. e. we must be quickened and alive to God, and not dead in sins and trespasses. *Holy;* as the sacrifices under the law were to be without blemish or defect, Exod. xii. 5; Lev. i. 10; Deut. xv. 21. *Acceptable unto God;* or, well-pleasing unto God. So were the appointed sacrifices under the law, Lev. i. 9; so was the sacrifice of Christ the Lamb of God, Eph. v. 2; and so are all spiritual sacrifices under the gospel, Phil. iv. 18; Heb. xiii. 16. *Which is your reasonable service;* or, which is agreeable to reason; nothing is more reasonable, than that you should devote yourselves to God in this manner. Some think this is added, to show a difference between the sacrifice here required, and that of the Jews, which was of unreasonable beasts. Others, by *reasonable service,* understand spiritual service, and expound this place by 1 Pet. ii. 5, where you read of *spiritual sacrifices acceptable to God by Jesus Christ.* Others think, that by *reasonable* you must understand such service as is according to the word of God; and this suits best with the Greek phrase in the text, λογικὴν λατρείαν. The same word is used, 1 Pet. ii. 2, and there it is rendered the *milk of the word,* and not reasonable milk. And so the service or worship here spoken of is opposed to that *will worship,* of which you read in Col. ii. 23.

e 1 Pet. 1. 14.
f Eph. 1. 18. & 4. 23.
Col. i. 21, 22. & 3. 10.
g Eph. 5. 10, 17. 1 Thess. 4. 3.

2 And ᵉ be not conformed to this world: but ᶠ be ye transformed by the renewing of your mind, that ye may ᵍ prove what *is* that good, and acceptable, and perfect, will of God.

Be not conformed to this world; do not fashion or accommodate yourselves to the corrupt principles, customs, or courses of worldly and wicked men; and what they are, you will find in chap. xiii. 13; Eph. iv. 18, 19; 1 Pet. iv. 3. You have somewhat the like counsel, Exod. xxiii. 2; 1 Pet. i. 14. *Be ye transformed by the renewing of your mind:* q. d. Be you regenerated, and changed in your whole man; beginning at the mind, by which the Spirit of God worketh upon the inferior faculties of the soul: see Eph. iv. 23. *That ye may prove what is that good, and acceptable, and perfect, will of God:* by prove, understand discerning: by the *will of God,* his revealed will in his word; and so it best accords with the *reasonable service,* spoken of ver. 1, and with the scope of the text itself; which is, to exhort unto holiness and obedience, which is according to the rule of the word. He annexeth three adjuncts to the will or word of God: it is *good;* revealed only for our benefit. It is *acceptable;* i. e. by obedience thereunto we shall be accepted. It is *perfect,* and the observance thereof will make us so too, 2 Tim. iii. 17. There are different readings of these words, but all to the same sense. Some thus, that you may prove the will of God, which to do, is good, acceptable, and perfect. Others thus, that you may prove what the will of God is, and what is good, acceptable, and perfect.

h ch. 1. 5. & 15. 15. 1 Cor. 3. 10. & 15. 10. Gal. 2. 9. Eph. 3, 2.7, 8. i Prov.25.27. Eccles. 7.16. ch. 11. 20. † Gr. *to sobriety.*
k 1 Cor. 12.7, 11. Eph. 4. 7.

3 For I say, ʰ through the grace given unto me, to every man that is among you, ⁱ not to think *of himself* more highly than he ought to think; but to think †soberly, according as God hath dealt ᵏ to every man the measure of faith.

Before he exhorted to a holy life in general, now he comes to more particular exhortations. *I say;* i. e. I enjoin and command; see Gal. v. 16. I do not only beseech you, as ver. 1, but I also require you, as one that hath authority. *Through the grace given unto me:* see on chap. i. 5. *To every man that is among you;* more particularly, to him that hath any particular gift or office in the church. *Not to think of himself more highly than he ought to think;* i. e. not to be drunk with a proud and overweening conceit of himself, his own wisdom, ability, &c. *But to think soberly,* or modestly; let him contain himself within bounds, and not take upon him what doth not belong to him; let him not contemn others, and pretend to more than he hath. There is an elegant paronomasia in the Greek, which our language cannot reach. *According as God hath dealt to every man the measure of faith: faith* here is put for the knowledge of God and Christ, and all other spiritual gifts and graces bestowed upon the faithful; these are called *faith,* because they are given with faith, and exercised by faith: of these, God deals to every man his *measure* or portion; not all gifts to one, nor the same gift to every one in the same measure or proportion: see ver. 6; Eph. iv. 7.

l 1 Cor. 12. 12. Eph. 4. 16.

4 For ˡ as we have many members in one body, and all members have not the same office:

m 1 Cor. 10. 17. & 12 20, 27. Eph. 1. 23. & 4. 25.

5 So ᵐ we, *being* many, are one body in Christ, and every one members one of another.

These verses are a reason against arrogancy. All Christians are *members of one* and the same *body;* therefore, they should not pride themselves in their gifts, but employ them for the common good. It is with the church, the mystical body of Christ, as with a natural body that hath many members, and all these *have not the same office,* or the same action or operation (as the word signifieth); the eye hath one office, the ear another, the hand a third, &c. So the church of Christ, though one body in him who is the Head, hath many members; many in regard of their persons, and many in regard of their offices, which are various and diverse; and which is more, the members are every one *members one of another;* i. e. they are joint and fellow members; as they have a common relation to the same Head, so a mutual relation to one another. Therefore Christians, especially church officers, should not contemn one another, or intrude upon the office of each other; but all should use their gifts to the good and edification of others.

n 1 Cor. 12. 4. 1 Pet. 4. 10, 11. o ver. 3.
p Acts 11.27. 1 Cor. 12. 10, 28. & 13. 2. & 14. 1, 6, 29, 31.

6 ⁿ Having then gifts differing ᵒ according to the grace that is given to us, whether ᵖ prophecy, *let us* prophesy according to the proportion of faith;

Having then gifts differing according to the grace that is given to us; or, seeing we have different gifts and offices, according as the grace of God hath bestowed them upon us, let us use them aright. This is added to prevent pride and envy: none should be proud of that he hath himself, or envy what another hath, seeing all is of grace. *Whether prophecy, let us prophesy;* the words, *let us prophesy,* are not in the text; but they are put in by our translators, to fill up the sense. There is an ellipsis in the words, and something must be inserted. Some make the supply from the last words in the foregoing verse, Let us be one another's members in prophesying, teaching, exhorting, &c. Others think it ought to be supplied out of ver. 3: q. d. Whether we have prophecy, let us be wise unto sobriety in prophesying; and so in all the rest that follow: in all the several gifts and offices, he showeth how they should behave themselves. The Greek scholiast will have supplied in them all, *let us persevere*. By prophesying, in this place, you may understand an extraordinary gift that some had in understanding Divine mysteries and Old Testament prophecies, with a wonderful dexterity in applying the same; to which was joined sometimes the revelation of secret and future things: see Acts xi. 27; xxi. 9. *According to the proportion of faith;* i. e. they that have this gift of prophesying, must exercise it according to the measure of knowledge, in heavenly mysteries, that God hath given them; or else, in their prophesying they must have regard to the articles of Christian faith, and see that they regulate themselves according thereunto. Some think he calls the Holy Scripture in general, an analogy or proportion of faith; by these, the false prophets of old were discerned, if they delivered any thing contrary thereunto, Deut. xiii. 1, &c. Others think he speaks of certain principles, or heads of Christian religion, (see Heb. vi. 1,) from which the prophets and others were not to swerve; yea, some think he aims at the symbol and creed, called the Apostles', which, from the beginning, was called the analogy of faith.

q Acts 13. 1.
Eph. 4. 11.
Gal. 6. 6.
1 Tim. 5. 17.

7 Or ministry, *let us wait* on our ministering: or ^qhe that teacheth, on teaching;

Ministry; under this word are comprehended all ordinary ecclesiastical functions, which afterwards divideth into two sorts; the first relating to the word; the second, to other pious works. *Let us wait on our ministering:* the words, *let us wait*, are not in the text, but fitly supplied: q. d. Let all that be called to the office of the ministry be diligent in it, and attend to it: see Acts xx. 28; 1 Pet. v. 2. *Teaching*, in the latter end of this verse, and *exhortation*, in the beginning of the next, are mentioned as the two great works of those that minister and labour in the word and doctrine. Some think they are distinct offices; see Eph. iv. 11; and that in the primitive church, where they had variety of ministers, some had the office of teachers, and chiefly exercised themselves in instructing their hearers in the principles of religion, in laying down sound doctrine and confuting of errors: others had the office of pastors, and attended chiefly to exhortation and admonition; pressing points of practice, and making application thereof. Others think that they are distinct gifts, but not diverse offices; some have a gift to teach, that have none to exhort, and *e contra*. The apostle, ver. 6, calls them *differing gifts:* sometimes these two are found in the same persons, and they are excellently gifted both for teaching and exhorting.

r Acts 15. 32.
1 Cor. 14. 3.
s Matt. 6. 1, 2, 3.
‖ Or, *imparteth*.
t Or, *liberally*.
2 Cor. 8. 2.
t Acts 20. 28.

8 Or ^rhe that exhorteth, on exhortation: ^she that ‖ giveth, *let him do it* ‖ with simplicity; ^the that ruleth, with diligence; he that sheweth mercy, ^uwith cheerfulness.

1 Tim. 5. 17. Heb. 13. 7, 24. 1 Pet. 5. 2. u 2 Cor. 9. 7.

Exhortation: see the notes on the foregoing verse. *He that giveth, let him do it with simplicity;* i. e. he that hath the office of collecting and distributing the church alms, (which was the deacons' work or charge, Acts vi. 1, &c.,) let him discharge it *with simplicity*, or with *singleness of heart;* (so the word is rendered, Eph. vi. 5;) let him do it faithfully and impartially, and without favour or affection. *He that ruleth;* or he that is a president, and set over others. There is great difference amongst expositors, who is meant by this ruler. It is not meant of state rulers, (of them he treats in the next chapter,) but of church rulers. Some understand, all church officers in general. Others think, such are meant as were not properly pastors and teachers, but together with them had the oversight of the church, to rule the same; to regulate misdemeanors, to pacify differences, to administer discipline in admonition and censures; these they call seniors or elders, or the censors of manners; and are the same the apostle calls *governments*, or governors, 1 Cor. xii. 28; see 1 Tim. v. 17. *He that showeth mercy, with cheerfulness:* some understand this generally of all Christians, that they should be charitable, and that with cheerfulness. But the apostle is yet speaking of the special offices of the church. It cannot be meant of deacons, forasmuch as he had spoken of them before in this very verse. Such therefore may be intended, as had the care assigned them of the sick and impotent, of prisoners and strangers, &c.; see 1 Tim. v. 10; the same, it may be, that he calleth *helps* in 1 Cor. xii. 28. This charge he directeth them to discharge with cheerfulness; without being weary of that troublesome work, or being sour and froward to those they had to do with.

9 ^x*Let* love be without dissimulation. ^yAbhor that which is evil; cleave to that which is good.

x 1 Tim. 1. 5.
1 Pet. 1. 22.
y Ps. 34. 14.
& 36. 4. &
97. 10.
Amos 5. 15.

The former exhortations respect church officers in particular; those that follow concern all Christians in general. He begins with *love*, because that is a radical grace; other graces, and gracious actions, do spring from it, and must be accompanied with it. By *love* here, you may understand the love of God, or of our neighbour: the latter seems chiefly to be intended. The great requisite in love is this, that it be *without dissimulation*, or (as the word is) without hypocrisy; i. e. that it be sincere and unfeigned, 2 Cor. vi. 6; 1 Pet. i. 22. It must not be *in word* and *in tongue* only, *but in deed and in truth*, 1 John iii. 18. *Abhor that which is evil;* do not only avoid it, but hate it, and that as hell itself. The simple verb imports extreme detestation, and it is aggravated by the composition: see Psal. cxix. 104; Amos v. 15. *Cleave to that which is good;* be glued to it; so the word signifieth. Things that are glued together are hardly disjoined. The same word is used of the union and conjunction between man and wife: see Matt. xix. 5; Eph. v. 31.

10 ^z*Be* kindly affected one to another ‖ with brotherly love; ^ain honour preferring one another; *brethren.*

z Heb. 13. 1.
1 Pet. 1. 22.
& 2. 17. & 3. 8.
2 Pet. 1. 7.
‖ Or, *in the love of the brethren.*
a Phil. 2. 3. 1 Pet. 5. 5.

Be kindly affected one to another; Christians ought to have such affection one to another, as parents have to their children, and as all creatures have to their young: so much the word here used imports. *In honour preferring one another:* this clause is expounded by Phil. ii. 3. It is exemplified in Abraham, Gen. xiii. 9. Most desire preference and honour before others, which is contrary to the good counsel in this text. Some read it, prevent one another; do not tarry till others honour you, but do you go before them in this expression of *brotherly love*, and be examples to them.

11 Not slothful in business; fervent in spirit; serving the Lord;

Not slothful in business; this clause may be expounded by Eccles. ix. 10: q. d. In all the duties of thy particular and general calling, in every thing that respects the glory of God, thine own or neighbours' good, take heed of slothfulness: see Matt. xxv. 26, 27; Heb. vi. 12. *Fervent in spirit;* this is added to the former, as the cure of it. Zeal and fervency will drive away sloth. This spiritual warmth is often recommended to us in Scripture; see Gal. iv. 18; Rev. iii. 19. See examples of it in Psal. lxix. 9; John ii. 17; iv. 34; Acts xviii. 25. *Serving the Lord;* i. e. diligently performing all things that are required to his service and honour: see Psal. ii. 11; Eph. vi. 7. Some copies read it, serving the times, in such a sense as it is in Eph. v. 16, and Col. iv. 5.

12 ^bRejoicing in hope; ^cpatient in tribulation; ^dcontinuing instant in prayer;

b Luke 10. 20.
ch. 5. 2. & 15. 13. Phil. 3. 1. & 4. 4.
1 Thess. 5. 16. Heb. 3. 6. 1 Pet. 4. 13. c Luke 21. 19. 1 Tim. 6. 11. Heb. 10. 36. & 12. 1. Jam. 1. 4. & 5. 7. 1 Pet. 2. 19, 20. d Luke 18. 1. Acts 2. 42. & 12. 5. Col. 4. 2. Eph. 6. 18. 1 Thess. 1. 17.

Rejoicing in hope; i. e. in hope of deliverance here in due time, and of eternal salvation hereafter: see on chap. v. 2. *Continuing instant in prayer;* be instant and constant in the duty. A metaphor from hounds, that give not over the game till they have got it: see Luke xviii. 1; Eph. vi. 18; Col. iv. 2; 1 Thess. v. 17.

13 ᵉDistributing to the necessity of saints; ᶠgiven to hospitality.

Necessity; the word signifieth uses. The saints must be succoured in things useful, as well as necessary. This apostle, in his Second Epistle to the Corinthians, spends two whole chapters about this sort of charity, in relieving the poor saints; viz. the 8th and 9th chapters: see also Gal. vi. 10; Heb. xiii. 16. *Given to hospitality;* or, as the word may be rendered, pursue hospitality; hunt after it, as Abraham and Lot did, Gen. xviii. 1, 2; xix. 1, 2. Concerning this duty of accommodating strangers, (which is here meant by hospitality,) see Deut. x. 18, 19; Isa. lviii. 7; 1 Tim. iii. 2; Tit. i. 8; Heb. xiii. 2; 1 Pet. iv. 9.

14 ᵍBless them which persecute you: bless, and curse not.

Bless them which persecute you; i. e. pray for them, and wish well to them. This is borrowed from Matt. v. 44; Luke vi. 28: see the like in 1 Pet. iii. 9. This is commended to us by the example of Christ himself, Isa. liii. 12; Luke xxiii. 34; 1 Pet. ii. 23; of Stephen, Acts vii. 60; of Paul, and the primitive Christians, 1 Cor. iv. 12. *Bless, and curse not:* his doubting the exhortation shows the difficulty of the duty; it is contrary to corrupt nature: and it denotes the constancy of it; we must persevere therein. When he saith, *curse not,* he means, wish no evil to your enemies. *Object.* The prophets and apostles went contrary to this: see 2 Kings ii. 24; Psal. lxix. 22, 23; Acts viii. 20; xiii. 10, 11; xxiii. 3. *Answ.* These did it by a special vocation and instinct of the Spirit.

15 ʰRejoice with them that do rejoice, and weep with them that weep.

i. e. Be touched with your neighbour's good or evil, as if it were your own. The reason of this sympathy, or fellow feeling, is rendered by the apostle, 1 Cor. xii. 26, 27; Because we are members one of another, therefore, if *one member suffer, all the members suffer with it;* and if *one member be honoured, all the members rejoice with it.* Examples hereof we have in Luke i. 58; 2 Cor. xi. 29: see Heb. xiii. 3.

16 ⁱ*Be* of the same mind one toward another. ᵏMind not high things, but ‖ condescend to men of low estate. ˡBe not wise in your own conceits.

‖ Or, *be contented with mean things.* 1 Prov. 3. 7. & 26, 12. Is. 5. 21. ch. 11. 25.

Be of the same mind one toward another: this exhortation respects not so much unity in judgment, as in affection: q. d. Bear the same good respect to others, as others bear to thee; let there be a mutual agreement in your desires and good wishes one for another: see chap. xv. 5; Phil. ii. 2; 1 Pet. iii. 8. *Mind not high things;* i. e. things above your capacities and callings. Take heed of ambitious aspirings: remember what David said (one every way above you) in Psal. cxxxi. 1. *Condescend to men of low estate:* the word *low* only is in the Greek; the other words are put in by our translators: and it may be referred, either to things, and so it answers to *high things,* in the foregoing clause; or it may be referred to persons, according to our translation; and then the sense is, that we should not despise our poor brethren, but stoop to the lowest offices of Christian kindness. *Be not wise in your own conceits;* this seems to be taken from Prov. iii. 7: see ver. 3.

17 ᵐRecompense to no man evil for evil. ⁿProvide things honest in the sight of all men.

Recompense to no man evil for evil; our Saviour teacheth the same doctrine in other words, Matt. v. 39, 40: see parallel places in Prov. xx. 22; 1 Thess. v. 15; 1 Pet. iii. 9. See more against retaliating injuries and private revenge in the three last verses of this chapter. Revenge is so sweet to flesh and blood, that men are very hardly dissuaded from it. *Provide things honest in the sight of all men:* q. d. Look carefully, as to your conscience before God, so to your honour and reputation with men. Let all your words and actions be justifiable, and unexceptionable, that evil men may have no occasion to reproach you as evil-doers. See a parallel place, 2 Cor. viii. 21. See also Phil. iv. 8; 1 Pet. iii. 16.

18 If it be possible, as much as lieth in you, ᵒlive peaceably with all men.

The duty to which he exhorts in this verse, is a peaceable and quiet behaviour towards all men, as well infidels as Christians; those who are bad, as well as those who are good. The like exhortations we have, Heb. xii. 14. And to the discharge of this duty he annexeth a double limitation; first, *If it be possible;* secondly, *As much as lieth in you:* q. d. It may so fall out, that some men are of such froward and unpeaceable tempers, that it is impossible to live peaceably with them, or by them: or such conditions of peace may be offered as are not lawful for you to accept; it will not stand with the truth and glory of God, with a good conscience, to agree with them. But, however, do your part, let there be no default in you why you should not live in peace with all men whatsoever.

19 Dearly beloved, ᵖavenge not yourselves, but *rather* give place unto wrath: for it is written, ᑫVengeance *is* mine; I will repay, saith the Lord.

Dearly beloved; he useth this friendly compellation, the better to persuade to the following duty, which is so hard to flesh and blood. *Avenge not yourselves:* you had an exhortation to this purpose, ver. 17; but considering the proneness of corrupt nature to private and personal revenge, he renews his exhortation, and enlargeth upon it. This seems to be borrowed from Lev. xix. 18. *But rather give place unto wrath;* i. e. say some, your own wrath: q. d. Be not angry, or suffer not your anger to hurry you to revenge; give way a little, and walk aside, as Ahasuerus did, when his wrath kindled against Haman. Others refer it to the wrath of those who wrong us; decline their wrath, as David did Saul's; put up wrongs and injuries. But it is better referred to the wrath of God, which they seem to prevent who seek revenge: q. d. Suffer God to vindicate and right you, to avenge you of your adversaries; commit your cause to him, and do not take his work out of his hand. This sense agrees well with what follows. *For it is written;* viz. in Deut. xxxii. 35. This is cited also, Psal. xciv. 1; Nahum i. 2; Heb. x. 30.

20 ʳTherefore if thine enemy hunger, feed him; if he thirst, give him drink: for in so doing thou shalt heap coals of fire on his head.

If thine enemy hunger, feed him; if he thirst, give him drink: q. d. Instead of rendering evil for evil to thine adversary, do him good for evil: see following verse. *Thou shalt heap coals of fire on his head;* i. e. either make him relent, or bring down the greater vengeance from God upon him. This is taken out of Prov. xxv. 21, 22; see the notes there.

21 Be not overcome of evil, but overcome evil with good.

This verse is a Divine aphorism: therein the apostle anticipates an objection. Some might be ready to say, If we should follow this advice we should be counted cowards and dastards, &c. To this he answers, that it is the ready way to be triumphers and conquerors. By *evil,* here, he means, the wrongs and injuries of men; and to be *overcome of evil,* is to be moved and provoked thereby to impatience or malice. When it is thus with a man, he is overcome, or conquered: in revenge of injuries, he is a loser that gets the better. Therefore he exhorts us, rather to *overcome evil with good;* that is a noble victory indeed: this is the way, not to be even with him that wrongs us, but to be above him. Thus David overcame Saul, and Elisha the bands of Syria. This is the way to overcome ourselves, and our adversaries too: ourselves, in denying our lusts that egg us on to revenge; our adversaries, in winning them to relent and acknowledge their miscarriages.

CHAP. XIII

Subjection to magistrates enforced, 1—6. *We must render to all their dues,* 7; *only love is a debt we must always*

ROMANS XIII

owe, and virtually containeth the whole law, 8—10. Rioting, drunkenness, and other works of darkness must be put away, as much out of season under the gospel, 11—14.

^a Tit. 3. 1.
1 Pet. 2. 13.
^b Prov. 8. 15, 16. Dan. 2. 21. & 4. 32.
Wisd. 6. 3.
John 19. 11.
∥ Or, *ordered*.

LET every soul ^a be subject unto the higher powers. For ^b there is no power but of God: the powers that be are ∥ ordained of God.

The former chapter is called by some St. Paul's ethics, and this his politics. He having said, in the latter end of the foregoing chapter, that Christians must not avenge themselves, but refer all to God, who says, that vengeance is his, and he will repay it; some might infer from hence, that it was not lawful for magistrates to right the wronged, and avenge them of their adversaries; or for Christians to make use of them to such a purpose; therefore, to set us right in this matter, he falls into the following discourse. Others think, that the apostle having spoken in several places concerning Christians' liberty, lest what he had said should be misconstrued, as if he meant that Christians were freed from subjection to the powers that were over them, he seasonably insists upon the doctrine and duty of obedience to authority; which point is more fully handled in this context than in any other place besides.

Let every soul; i. e. every person. In the first verse of the foregoing chapter the body was put for the whole man; here, the soul; and when he says every person, it is plain that ecclesiastical persons are not exempted. *Be subject:* he doth not say, be obedient, but be subject; which is a general word, (as some have noted,) comprehending all other duties and services. This subjection must be limited only to lawful things; otherwise, we must answer as they did, Acts iv. 19: or as Polycarpus did; when he was required to blaspheme Christ, and swear by the fortune of Cæsar, he peremptorily refused, and said, We are taught to give honour to princes and potentates, but such honour as is not contrary to true religion. *Unto the higher powers:* though he speaks of things, he means persons; and he calls them *rulers* in the 3rd verse, whom he calls *powers* in this verse. So in Luke xii. 11, Christ tells his disciples, they should be brought before *magistrates and powers;* it is the same word, and it is plain he means persons in power. Chrysostom notes, that he rather speaks of our subjection to powers, than persons in power; because, that howsoever their power be abused, their authority must be acknowledged and obeyed. He speaks of *powers,* in the plural number, because there are divers sorts and kinds thereof, as monarchy, aristocracy, democracy: under which soever of these we live, we must be subject thereunto. By *higher powers,* he means the supreme powers; so the word is rendered, 1 Pet. ii. 13. To them, and to those that are authorized by them, we must submit, for that is all one as if we did it to themselves, 1 Tim. ii. 2; 1 Pet. ii. 14. There are other inferior powers, which are also of God, as parents, masters, &c.; but of these he doth not speak in this place. *For there is no power but of God:* this is a reason of the foregoing injunction: q. d. That which hath God for its author, is to be acknowledged and submitted to; but magistracy hath God for its author: ergo. He speaketh not here of the person, nor of the abuse, nor of the manner of getting into power, but of the thing itself, viz. magistracy and authority: and he says, it is of God; he instituted the office, and he appointeth or permitteth the person that executes it. This clause is attested and illustrated by Prov. viii. 15; Dan. iv. 32; John xix. 11. *The powers that be are ordained of God:* this passage is an exemplification of the former. Erasmus thinks it was inserted by some interpreter, by way of explanation; but it is found in all ancient copies, therefore that conceit of his is without foundation. The emphasis of this sentence seems to lie in the word *ordained;* power and civil authority is not simply from God, as all other things are, but it is ordained by him. This word (as one observes) implieth two things; invention, and ratification. God invented and devised this order, that some should rule, and others obey; and he maintaineth and upholdeth it.

^c Tit. 3. 1.

2 Whosoever therefore resisteth ^c the power, resisteth the ordinance of God: and they that resist shall receive to themselves damnation.

Whosoever therefore resisteth the power, resisteth the ordinance of God: these words are, either an argument to enforce the subjection enjoined in the former part of the foregoing verse; q. d. You may not resist; therefore, you must be subject: or else, they are an inference from the latter part of it; q. d. Seeing the civil power is of God, and of his ordination; therefore, it must not be resisted or opposed. To resist authority, is to wage war against God himself. *Damnation;* the word properly signifieth judgment, and it is applied in Scripture, either to human and temporal punishment, as Luke xxiii. 40; 1 Cor. vi. 7; 1 Pet. iv. 17; or else to Divine and eternal punishment, as Luke xx. 47; Heb. vi. 2; 2 Pet ii. 3. Accordingly, it may be understood of eternal punishment, that the resister of authority shall receive from God; or of temporal punishment, that he shall receive from the magistrate.

3 For rulers are not a terror to good works, but to the evil. Wilt thou then not be afraid of the power? ^d do that which is good, and thou shalt have praise of the same:

^d 1 Pet. 2. 14. & 3. 13.

This verse contains a further argument for subjection to the higher powers, and it is taken from the benefit thereof, or from the end of magistracy, which is for the punishment of evil, and the encouragement of good works: see 1 Pet. ii. 14. When he says, that *rulers are not a terror to good works,* he means, they are not so ordinarily; or they were not ordained for that end, but the contrary. Or else, by *are not* understand they ought not so to be. *Wilt thou then not be afraid of the power? do that which is good, and thou shalt have praise of the same:* q. d. Wouldst thou be free from fear of being punished by the magistrate? do that which is good, and thou shalt not only be free from fear, but sure of praise and reward: see Prov. xiv. 35; xvi. 13. By *good* he means, not that which is so theologically, but morally: q. d. Live honestly, hurt no man in word or deed, give to every man his due, &c. This is good in the sight of all men, of heathens themselves.

4 For he is the minister of God to thee for good. But if thou do that which is evil, be afraid; for he beareth not the sword in vain: for he is the minister of God, a revenger to *execute* wrath upon him that doeth evil.

For he is the minister of God to thee for good: q. d. That is the end of his office, and for this reason God hath invested him with his authority. The Scripture applieth the same title to him that preacheth the word, and to him that beareth the sword; both are God's ministers, and there is one common end of their ministry, which is the good and welfare of mankind. *But if thou do that which is evil, be afraid; for he beareth not the sword in vain:* this is the reason why he that trangresseth the moral law of God, or the wholesome laws of the country where he lives, should be afraid of the magistrate, because *he beareth not the sword in vain.* The *sword* is figuratively put for power and authority: he alludes to the custom of princes, who had certain officers going before them, bearing the ensigns of their authority: q. d. The magistrate hath not his authority for nothing, or for no purpose; but that he may punish the evil, as well as defend the good. *For he is the minister of God, a revenger to execute wrath upon him that doeth evil:* here is another reason why evil-doers (as before) should be afraid of the magistrate; or rather, the same reason in other and plainer words; because he is God's officer to execute wrath upon him that doeth evil; he is in God's room upon earth, and doth the work which primarily belongeth unto him: see chap. xii. 19. By *wrath,* here, understand punishment: so in Luke xxi. 23; chap. ii. 8. The word *execute* is not in the text, but aptly enough supplied by our translators.

5 Wherefore ^e ye must needs be subject, not only for wrath, ^f but also for conscience sake.

^e Eccles. 8.2.
^f 1 Pet. 2. 19.

q. d. Seeing things are so as I have said; that magistracy is of God, that it is his ordinance, that it is for the benefit of mankind, and that it is armed with the sword; therefore there is a necessity of subjection, and that for a double reason: first, from fear of wrath, or punishment from the magistrate. Secondly, and more especially, from the obligation of conscience, because God hath so commanded; and to err in this particular, is to offend God, and to wound our own consciences: see 1 Sam. xxiv. 5; Eccles. viii. 2; 1 Pet. ii. 13.

6 For for this cause pay ye tribute also: for they are God's ministers, attending continually upon this very thing.

For this cause, i. e. in token, or in testimony, of that subjection you owe to magistracy, *pay ye tribute:* the word is plural in the original, and thereby is intended all taxes and burdens, which are legally and customarily imposed. *For they are God's ministers, attending continually upon this very thing:* this is a reason why tribute should be paid to rulers; but it is for the support of their authority, and a due recompence for their great care and industry. When he says, they attend *continually upon this very thing*, the meaning is not, they attend always upon the receiving of tribute; but it is to be understood of the duty of magistrates, which is, to be continually promoting the good and welfare of their subjects; to encourage the good, and punish the evil-doer, which is the very thing he had been before speaking of.

g Mat. 22. 21.
Mark 12. 17.
Luke 20. 25.

7 [g] Render therefore to all their dues: tribute to whom tribute *is due;* custom to whom custom; fear to whom fear; honour to whom honour.

This verse concludes his discourse about the civil powers. When he saith, *Render to all their dues*, he doth not mean all men, but all magistrates, whatever they be for quality, either good or bad; or whatever they be for degree, either supreme or subordinate. Render to them their dues; i. e, whatever of right belongs to them: see Matt. xxii. 21. There are two things that more especially belong to rulers, and are due from those that are under them: the one is maintenance; the other is reverence. The first is expressed here by *tribute* and *custom;* if these two differ, then the former is a tax laid upon the substance, the latter upon the person. The second, by *fear* and *honour; fear* notes inward, and *honour* outward, reverence and respect. *Fear* is the magistrate's due by reason of his authority; *honour*, by reason of his dignity.

h ver. 10.
Cal. 5. 14.
Col. 3. 14.
1 Tim. 1. 5.
Jam. 2. 8.

8 Owe no man any thing, but to love one another: for [h] he that loveth another hath fulfilled the law.

Having treated of special duties belonging to superiors, he now comes to that which is more general, and belongs to all. *Owe no man any thing;* neither your superiors, nor your equals and inferiors; render and pay to every person what is due to him, let his rank and quality be what it will. *But to love one another:* q. d. Only there is one debt that you can never fully discharge; that you must be ever paying, yet ever owing; and that is *love. For he that loveth another hath fulfilled the law:* this is a reason why we should love one another, and be still paying that debt; and it is taken from the excellency of love: *he that loveth another* (i. e. he that doth it in deed and in truth) *hath fulfilled the law;* he means, the second table of the law, as the next verse showeth; he hath done what is required therein.

i Ex. 20. 13,
&c. Deut. 5.
17. &c.
Mat. 19. 18.

9 For this, [i] Thou shalt not commit adultery, Thou shalt not kill, Thou shalt not steal, Thou shalt not bear false witness, Thou shalt not covet; and *if there*

k Lev. 19. 18.
Matt. 22. 39.
Mark 12. 31.
Gal. 5. 14.
Jam. 2. 8.

be any other commandment, it is briefly comprehended in this saying, namely, [k] Thou shalt love thy neighbour as thyself.

This verse proves, that love is the fulfilling of the law. It is done by an induction or enumeration of the particular precepts of the second table. The fifth is not mentioned, because the Jews made that commandment a part of the first table; so some: or because he had treated before of duty to the higher powers and superiors, under which parents are comprehended; so others. It may be, he would only mention the negative precepts, as being most contrary to love. But, why doth he mention the seventh commandment before the sixth? Because of the commonness of adultery amongst the Romans; so some: because of the odiousness of it; so others. Hence *adultery* is first named amongst *the works of the flesh*, Gal. v. 19. Possibly it is, because the Seventy, in Exodus, rehearse the commandments in this very order. The tenth commandment is summed up in one word, *Thou shalt not covet;* it seems, then, it is but one commandment. and their opinion is ridiculous who divide it into two. When he says, *if there be any other commandment?* he means a commandment of the same nature, requiring us to pay what we owe one to another; *ergo*, to honour our parents; or he means, any other in the Scripture, though not expressed in the decalogue. All commandments respecting our neighbour are summed up in this one, *Thou shalt love thy neighbour as thyself:* see Matt. xxii. 39; Gal. v. 14; 1 Tim. i. 5.

10 Love worketh no ill to his neighbour: therefore [l] love *is* the fulfilling of the law.

l Mat. 22. 40.
ver. 8.

This verse is an argument to prove what was proposed, ver. 8. It may thus be formed: That which *worketh no ill,* or doth no hurt to our *neighbour*, fulfilleth the law: but *love worketh no ill to his neighbour; ergo*. That this is the property of love, see 1 Cor. xiii. 4, 5. When he saith, Love doth no hurt, this is implied, that it doth good to his neighbour. Where only negatives are mentioned, the affirmative also is included; and the negative only is set down in this place, that it may the better correspond with the foregoing verse.

11 And that, knowing the time, that now *it is* high time [m] to awake out of sleep: for now *is* our salvation nearer than when we believed.

m 1 Cor. 15.
34. Eph. 5.
14. 1 Thess.
5. 5, 6.

And that; or, moreover; the speech is elliptical, something must be understood, as, I say, or add: q. d. Unto this exhortation to Christian love, I further add what followeth. *Knowing the time;* i. e. considering it is a time of great trial, or time of gospel light. *Now it is high time to awake out of sleep;* i. e. to shake off slothfulness, security, and all former sinful courses. See the like, 1 Cor. xv. 34; Eph. v. 14; 1 Thess. v. 6—8. q. d. Consider, now it is the hour or season to awake or rise up, to lay aside your night-clothes, as it is in the following verse. *Now is our salvation nearer than when we believed;* or, salvation is nearer to us than when we first began to believe. Some would understand it of temporal salvation, and deliverance from those persecutions which befell the Christians in the infancy of the church; from these they were saved and delivered by the destruction of the Jews their persecutors. This was foretold by Christ, and expected by the Christians; and it was nigher at hand than when they first embraced the Christian faith. But most understand it of eternal salvation, which he says was nearer than when they first believed. In which words is couched another argument to awaken or stir up the believing Romans; the first was taken from the consideration of the time or season; the second, from the nearness of the word. Therefore it should be with them as with those that run in a race; the nearer they come to the goal, the faster they run, lest others should get before them.

12 The night is far spent, the day is at hand; [n] let us therefore cast off the works of darkness, and [o] let us put on the armour of light.

n Eph. 5. 11.
Col. 3. 8.
o Eph. 6. 13.
1 Thess. 5. 8.

The night is far spent, the day is at hand: some, by *night* and *day*, do understand the night of Jewish persecution and the day of deliverance and salvation; see Heb. x. 25. Others, by *night*, understand the time of ignorance and infidelity; this, he says, *is far spent*, or for the greatest part it is past and gone: darkness is not perfectly done away in this life amongst believers themselves, 1 Cor. xiii. 9, 10. By *day*, they understand the time of gospel light and saving knowledge: so in the next verse, and in 1 Thess v. 5. This, he says, *is at hand*, or is come nigh; it was dawning upon the world, and would shine brighter and brighter, till its more perfect day. *Let us therefore cast off the works of darkness;* i. e. all our former sins, which are called *works of darkness*, here, and in Eph. v. 11

They are so called, because they are usually committed by those that are in ignorance and darkness; and because some sins, such as he speaks of in the next verse, were wont to be committed in the darkness of the night, men being ashamed of them in the day time: see Job xxiv. 15; 1 Thess. v. 7. These he exhorts the believing Romans to *cast off*: the word implieth, haste and hatred, Isa. xxx. 22; xxxi. 7. *And let us put on the armour of light*; i. e. all Christian graces, which are bright and shining in the eyes of the world, Matt. v. 16; and which will be as so much Christian armour, to defend us against sin, and all the assaults of Satan.

13 ᵖLet us walk ‖ honestly, as in the day; ᵍnot in rioting and drunkenness, ʳnot in chambering and wantonness, ˢnot in strife and envying.

Let us walk honestly, as in the day: q. d. Let us behave ourselves decently, and with a holy shamefacedness, as becomes those to whom the grace of God, and the glorious light of the gospel, hath appeared. This honest walking is expressed by three adverbs in Tit. ii. 12; i. e. *soberly, righteously, godly*. He enumerates divers vices, which are contrary to this honest walking, and he sets them down by pairs. He makes three pairs of them: the first is *rioting and drunkenness*; by which he means intemperance, or excess in eating and drinking: see Luke xxi. 34. The second is *chambering and wantonness*; by which he means actual uncleanness, and all lustful and lascivious dalliances: see Gal. v. 19; Eph. v. 3; Col. iii. 5; 1 Thess. iv. 3—5, 7; 1 Pet. iv. 3. The third pair is *strife and envying*. All these vices are twisted and connected: intemperance causeth uncleanness, and both cause contention and emulation, Prov. xxiii. 29, 30. The famous St. Augustine confesseth, that he was converted by reading and pondering this text.

14 But ᵗput ye on the Lord Jesus Christ, and ᵘmake not provision for the flesh, to *fulfil* the lusts *thereof*.

Put ye on the Lord Jesus Christ; he exhorted, ver. 12, to *put on the armour of light*; now, to *put on Jesus Christ*. This is necessary, for though grace may help to defend, yet it is Christ and his righteousness only that can cover us (as a garment doth our nakedness) in the sight of God. To *put on Christ*, is to receive him and rest upon him by faith; as also to profess and imitate him. You have the same phrase, Gal. iii. 27. *Make not provision for the flesh, to fulfil the lusts thereof*: by *flesh*, here, some understand the corrupt nature; others, the body. When he says, *make not provision for the flesh*, he doth not mean, that they should not provide things necessary for the body; this is allowed, Eph. v. 29; 1 Tim. v. 23; we are no where commanded to neglect or macerate our bodies; but he means, that we should not gratify it in its sinful lusts or lustings: see 1 Cor. xi. 27. Sustain it we may, but pamper it we may not: we must not care, cater, or make projects for the flesh, to fulfil its inordinacies and cravings.

CHAP. XIV

Directions to treat a weak brother kindly, and not to despise or censure one another in matters of indifference, 1—6. *Christ's right to our best services, whether we live or die*, 6—9. *We must all be answerable for our respective conduct at his judgment-seat*, 10—12. *We must be careful not to use our Christian liberty to the hurt or offence of tender consciences*, 13—23.

HIM that ᵃis weak in the faith receive ye, *but* ‖not to doubtful disputations.

In this chapter and part of the next, the apostle treats of some lesser matters of religion, about which there were great contentions in the church of Rome. Some of the Jews, though they embraced the gospel, did stiffly adhere still to the Mosaical ceremonies; and though a difference in meats and days should be conscientiously observed, yet they were ready to censure those that were contrary-minded, as profane persons, and contemners of the law of God.

On the other side, the believing Gentiles, being better instructed about their Christian liberty, when they saw the Jews insisting upon such things as these, that had never any real goodness in them, and were now abrogated by Christ, they were ready to despise them as ignorant and superstitious, and to deny communion with them. The apostle therefore doth seasonably endeavour to arbitrate this matter, and make peace amongst them.

Him that is weak in the faith; that is, wavering and unsettled in some lesser points of faith, particularly in the doctrine of Christian liberty, and freedom from the ceremonial law: he means, the scrupulous and erroneous Judaizer, though yet, in proportion, it may be applied to other scrupulous and doubting Christians. *Receive ye*; or, receive him to you, take him into your bosoms, admit him to communion with you, bear with his weakness, better instruct him with the spirit of meekness: see chap. xv. 1; Phil. iii. 15, 16. Bucer received all, though differing from him in some opinions, in whom he found, *aliquid Christi*, any thing of Christ. *But not to doubtful disputations*: q. d. Do not entertain him with disputes and vain janglings, which will not edify, but perplex and prejudice him. Do not make him question sick, as it is in 1 Tim. vi. 4. This passage may be expounded by Tit. iii. 9. The marginal reading would make this to be the sense, that a scrupulous Christian should be received unto communion; yet not so as to encourage him to judge and condemn the thoughts of those that differ from him.

2 For one believeth that he ᵇmay eat all things: another, who is weak, eateth herbs.

One believeth that he may eat all things; i. e. one that is informed aright of his Christian liberty, is fully persuaded, and that upon good grounds, that he may eat any thing that is wholesome, though forbidden by the ceremonial law; that there is now no difference of clean and unclean meats: see Matt. xv. 11; Acts x. 12—15. *Another, who is weak, eateth herbs*; i. e. he that (as before) *is weak in faith*, and not so well informed, such a one, for fear of offending God by eating any thing that is forbidden, will rather content himself with the meanest diet. The meaning is not, as if any, in those times, thought it lawful only to eat herbs, and so abstained altogether from other meats; but they would rather satisfy themselves with herbs, and other fruits of the earth, in which the law of Moses made no difference, than eat meats that were forbidden, or not cleansed from blood, or offered to idols, &c.: see Dan. i. 8.

3 Let not him that eateth despise him that eateth not; and ᶜlet not him which eateth not judge him that eateth: for God hath received him.

Let not him that eateth despise him that eateth not; i. e. Let not him that makes use of his liberty in eating any thing indifferently, vilify or contemn him that is of a contrary mind, as one that is ignorant and over-scrupulous; and let not him that forbears such meats as were of old forbidden, judge and condemn him that is contrary-minded, as profane and over-venturous; notwithstanding such little difference in opinion, let one Christian love and communicate with another. *For God hath received him*: it is disputed, whether this be meant of the weak or strong Christian; the word *judge*, which immediately goes before and follows after, carries it rather for the latter. But some think it is meant of both. He that eateth, and he that eateth not, is received by God into his church and family, and indifferently accepted with him, upon another and a higher account.

4 ᵈWho art thou that judgest another man's servant? to his own master he standeth or falleth. Yea, he shall be holden up: for God is able to make him stand.

Who art thou that judgest another man's servant? to his own master he standeth or falleth: a sharp reprehension of the forementioned evil. You have the like, James iv. 12. q. d. This phrase is repugnant not only to the law of God, but to the very law of nature, which tells us, that one man must not condemn the servant of another, over whom he hath no right or power; much less may any man condemn him that is the Lord's servant. Every Christian hath Christ alone for his own or his proper Master; and it is his judgment by which he must abide; it is to him that he standeth or falleth, that he doth well or ill. *Yea, he shall be holden up: for God is able to make him stand:* q. d. If (as thou thinkest) he be fallen or falling, he shall be upheld and supported; *for God is able,* &c. But how doth this follow, because God can make him stand, therefore he shall be holden up? *Answ.* It is a rule in divinity, that in all God's promises, his power is joined with his will; so that where the latter is once revealed, there is no question of the former: now of the word of God in this matter, there was no doubt; for he had said, ver. 3, that God had *received him.* You had the like way of arguing, chap. xi. 23, where the apostle proves the calling of the Jews by an argument taken from the power of God, because he is able to graft them in again: see chap. iv. 21; Heb. x. 23.

e Gal. 4. 10. Col. 2. 16.

5 ^e One man esteemeth one day above another: another esteemeth every day

‖ Or, *fully assured.*

alike. Let every man be ‖ fully persuaded in his own mind.

One man esteemeth one day above another: another esteemeth every day alike: there were differences in the church of Rome about the observation of days, as well as the choice of meats; and in this he endeavours an accommodation as well as in the other. The converted Jew was of opinion, that the festival days appointed in Moses's law, were holier than other days, and that they should still be observed: see Gal. iv. 10; Col. ii. 16. On the other side, the believing Gentile was of opinion, that the difference in days under the Old Testament was now ceased, and he (the text says) esteemed or approved of all days. The word *alike* is not in the original, but it is aptly supplied by our translators. *Let every man be fully persuaded in his own mind;* i. e. Let every man be satisfied as to the grounds of his practice; let him act by his own, and not another man's, judgment and conscience; let him be so fully assured in his own mind of the lawfulness of what he doth, as to find no doubting or scrupulous hesitations in the doing of it; let him be able to say as the apostle himself doth, ver. 14. The reason of this counsel you have, ver. 23. He that doth what he thinks is a sin, is an offender against God, whether it be a sin or no. And yet a man may sin in that wherein he is fully persuaded he sinneth not. A full persuasion must be had, but it is not sufficient to make an action good or lawful.

f Gal. 4. 10. ‖ Or, *observeth.*

6 He that ^f ‖ regardeth the day, regardeth *it* unto the Lord; and he that regardeth not the day, to the Lord he doth not regard *it.* He that eateth, eat-

g 1 Cor. 10. 31. 1 Tim. 4. 3.

eth to the Lord, for ^g he giveth God thanks; and he that eateth not, to the Lord he eateth not, and giveth God thanks.

In this verse you have a reason why Christians should not censure one another, upon an account of different opinions and practices, because they have all the same end and scope, which is the pleasing and glorifying of God. It is with regard to him that they eat, or eat not; that they observe those festival days, or observe them not; and so far both are on both sides to be commended; for that indeed should be our end, in all our actions, to glorify and please the Lord: see 1 Cor. x. 31; Col. iii. 17. *He giveth God thanks;* i. e. he is thankful unto God for the bountiful and free use of his creatures. Some would ground that laudable practice of giving thanks at meals upon this text, but it hath a clearer warrant from Matt. xiv. 19; xv. 36; xxvi. 26; Acts xxvii. 35. *He eateth not, and giveth God thanks;* because he hath meat enough besides, which he is not forbidden, 1 Cor. x. 28.

h 1 Cor. 6. 19, 20. Gal. 2. 20. 1 Thes. 5. 10. 1 Pet. 4. 2.

7 For ^h none of us liveth to himself, and no man dieth to himself.

8 For whether we live, we live unto the Lord; and whether we die, we die unto the Lord: whether we live therefore, or die, we are the Lord's.

Here he proves what he had before asserted, that Christians have regard to God and his glory in their particular actions; and that from their general end and design, which is to devote themselves, and their whole life, and death, to God. He tells them first, in the negative, that *none of us,* i. e. that none of us Christians and believers, do live or die to ourselves; we are not our own lords, nor at our own disposal: and then, in the affirmative, he shows, that we live or die to the Lord; we spend our lives in his service, and part with them at his appointment. His glory is the white, at which we aim, living or dying: he is the centre, in which all the lines in the whole circumference of our lives do meet, 2 Cor. v. 9; Phil. i. 21. *Whether we live therefore, or die, we are the Lord's:* this is an inference from what he had said before: q. d. At all times, and in all estates, whether of health or sickness, abundance or poverty, life or death, we are the Lord's property, and at his disposal; he hath an absolute dominion over us, living or dying; in this world, or in the next.

9 For ⁱ to this end Christ both died, i 2 Cor. 5. 15. and rose, and revived, that he might be ^k Lord both of the dead and living. k Acts 10. 36.

To this end Christ both died, and rose: q. d. This is the fruit that accrues to Christ, by his death and resurrection, *that he might,* &c. *And revived:* the Vulgar Latin leaves out this word. Chrysostom left out the former word, he *arose.* Ambrose inverts the order of the words, and reads them thus, To this end he lived, and died, and rose again. Some think the preter tense is here put for the present tense: he *revived,* i. e. he still lives, to intercede for us, and to exercise dominion over us. Others think that Christ's reviving here doth denote that new state of life which he had after his resurrection. *That he might be Lord both of the dead and living;* or, that he may govern and lord it (ἵνα κυριεύσῃ) over all his, whether dead or alive; that he might obtain dominion, or rather the exercise of his dominion, over them. As God, he hath a universal dominion over all; but as Mediator, he hath a more special dominion over all the Father gave to him: this dominion he purchased at his death, and he had the full exercise of it when he rose again, Matt. xxviii. 18; Phil. ii. 9, 10.

10 But why dost thou judge thy brother? or why dost thou set at nought thy brother? for ^l we shall all stand before the judgment seat of Christ.

l Mat. 25. 31, 32. Acts 10. 42. & 17. 31. 2 Cor. 5. 10. Jude 14, 15.

He goes on to persuade them to a mutual forbearance, to dehort them from condemning or contemning one another about indifferent things. He suggests two arguments against it in this verse; one (which is more implied) is taken from the relation they bore one to another; they were brethren, not by natural generation, but by regeneration and adoption; they had the same Father, even God. The second argument is more plainly expressed; and it is taken from the consideration of the day of judgment, when all shall stand before Christ's judgment-seat; see 2 Cor. v. 10; *all,* both the strong and the weak; and then he will determine who hath done well or ill. In the mean while, who art thou that darest to usurp his place or office? The interrogation hath the force of a strong denial; q. d. Have you no more grace, charity, or wisdom, than so to do.

11 For it is written, ^m *As* I live, saith m Is. 45. 23. the Lord, every knee shall bow to me, Phil. 2. 10. and every tongue shall confess to God.

This verse proves what was before asserted, that all must *stand before the judgment-seat of Christ.* The proof is from Isa. xlv. 23. The prophet speaks only of God's swearing; the apostle sets down the form of his oath; which form is frequently mentioned in Scripture: see Numb. xiv. 21, 28; Jer. xxii. 24; Ezek. v. 11; xiv. 16, 18; xx. 3. And instead of *every tongue shall swear;* the apostle, following the Seventy, saith, *every tongue shall confess;* and we are told, Phil. ii. 11, what it shall confess, viz. *that Jesus Christ is Lord.* That which is generally spoken of Jehovah being here in a peculiar manner applied to Christ, it evidently showeth, that he is supreme Judge, and sovereign Lord, unto whom all knees must bow in token of subjection; and before whose tribunal all persons, will they, or will they not, must appear.

12 So then ⁿevery one of us shall give account of himself to God.

n Mat. 12. 36. Gal. 6. 5. 1 Pet. 4. 5.

Here you have the end of our standing before the judgment-seat of Christ, which is to give account: see Matt. xii. 36; 1 Pet. iv. 5. He saith, *Every one of us shall give account*, whether he be great or small, strong or weak; and that he *shall give account of himself*; i. e. of his own actions, and not another's. He shall give account of himself in his natural capacity, as a man; and in his capacity, as a rich or great man; and in his religious capacity, as one that hath enjoyed such education, such means of grace, &c. *Object.* Pastors must give account for their flock, Heb. xiii. 17. *Answ.* Pastors shall give account of their negligence, and want of care, whereby they suffered their sheep or flock to miscarry; but every particular sheep also shall give account of his own personal wanderings.

13 Let us not therefore judge one another any more: but judge this rather, that ᵒno man put a stumblingblock or an occasion to fall in *his* brother's way.

o 1 Cor. 8. 9, 13. & 10. 32.

Let us not therefore judge one another any more: q. d. Seeing all must be judged by Christ, let us no more judge one another, but mend this fault for time to come. *But judge this rather:* hitherto his counsel was more general, respecting both the strong and the weak. Here he begins, in a more particular manner, to apply himself to the more strong and knowing Christians; counselling them to take heed, lest, by the abuse of their Christian liberty, they should be an offence to them that were weak and more ignorant. He entereth upon this with an elegant transition, making use of the same word in a different sense; for he doth not speak contraries, when he says, *judge not, but judge;* for the word in the former part of the verse signifies, to condemn and censure; but here, in the following part, to deliberate or consider: q. d. Instead of judging others, let us look upon this as a rule for ourselves, and our own deportment, that we put no stumblingblock, &c. *That no man put a stumblingblock or an occasion to fall in his brother's way:* q. d. Take heed of offending your brethren in any kind; do not, by an unseasonable use of your liberty, either drive them from their Christian profession, or provoke them to imitate you, and so to sin against their consciences. You have a parallel text, 1 Cor. viii. 9. There he speaks only of a stumblingblock; here he adds an occasion of falling, or, as it is in the original, a scandal. Though these two words do differ in their etymologies, yet they have one and the same signification. The latter word, as Stephanus observes, is peculiar to Holy Scripture, and seldom, if ever, used in any common author: it signifieth, properly, the bridge in a trap, which, by its falling down, catcheth a creature in a snare, and so occasions its ruin; and from thence it is used to denote any thing which is an occasion to others of stumbling or falling; any thing whereby we so offend another, as that he is hindered from good, drawn into or confirmed in evil. Scandal, or offence, is either passive or active. Passive scandal is, when that which is good is, by reason of man's corruption, an occasion of falling to him. So Christ himself, and his doctrine, was a scandal to the Jews: see 1 Cor. i. 23; 1 Pet. ii. 8. Active scandal is, when any thing is done or said which gives occasion of offence to others, when it is an occasion of grief, or of sin to them, ver. 15, 21. This occasion may be administered, either by evil counsel, Matt. xvi. 23; Rev. ii. 14; or by evil example, Isa. ix. 16; Matt. xv. 14; or by the abuse of Christian liberty in things indifferent, 1 Cor. viii. 9.

14 I know, and am persuaded by the Lord Jesus, ᵖthat *there is* nothing †unclean of itself: but ᑫto him that esteemeth any thing to be †unclean, to him *it is* unclean.

p Acts 10. 15. ver. 2, 20. 1 Cor. 10. 25. 1 Tim. 4. 4. Tit. 1. 15. † Gr. common. q 1 Cor. 8. 7, 10. † Gr. common.

Here he obviates an objection. Some might say, they were thoroughly persuaded, that no meat was unclean in itself, and therefore they might, and would, use their liberty in eating any thing that was before them. To this the apostle answers, first, by way of concession; he grants what they say is true, and tells them, that for his own part he knew it full well, and was himself assured of it; and that he had this assurance from *the Lord Jesus;* i. e. that he was instructed therein by his word and Spirit. *That there is nothing unclean of itself;* i. e. that no meat was unclean in itself; it was not so in its own nature: see Gen. i. 31; ix. 3. Some creatures might be unwholesome, but none were in themselves unclean: to the Jews they were not unclean by nature, but by a positive law, which law was now antiquated and out of doors: see Col. ii. 16, 17; 1 Tim. iv. 3, 4. *But to him that esteemeth any thing to be unclean, to him it is unclean:* this he adds by way of restriction, that though no meat was unclean in itself, yet it was so to him that thought it to be unclean. If a man shall believe that there is yet a difference in meats, that some are still unclean, and that by virtue of God's prohibition, it would be evil in him to eat such meats, because he therein acts against his conscience, and doth that which he himself thinks to be a sin: see ver. 23.

15 But if thy brother be grieved with *thy* meat, now walkest thou not †charitably. ʳDestroy not him with thy meat, for whom Christ died.

† Gr. according to charity. r 1 Cor. 8. 11.

In this verse you have two reasons to induce the strong not to offend the weak: First, it is contrary to charity; to grieve a brother upon the score of meats, is to walk uncharitably; it is a violation of the royal law of love, which is against the grieving or offending others, 1 Cor. xiii. 4. Two ways are weak Christians grieved, when others do unseasonably use their liberty. 1. They think such do offend God in eating that which he hath forbidden; and this is matter of grief to those that fear God, to see others transgress his laws. 2. They may be drawn by their example to do the like, against their own light and conscience; and this afterwards causeth grief and trouble; their consciences hereby are galled and wounded, 1 Cor. viii. 12. *Destroy not him with thy meat, for whom Christ died:* this is the second reason why Christians should not use their liberty to the offence of others; it may occasion their ruin and destruction: q. d. Hereby, as much as in you lies, you take a course to destroy them for whom Christ died. You will alienate and estrange them from the Christian religion, or you will draw them into sin, and induce them (as before) to act against their consciences, and so hazard their salvation. See a parallel place, 1 Cor. viii. 11. Here a question may arise, whether any can perish for whom Christ died? The answer is, They cannot; and for this the Scripture is express, in John x. 28. See also Matt. xxiv. 24; John vi. 39; 1 Pet. i. 5. How then is this text to be understood? The apostle doth not speak of those for whom Christ indeed did die, but of such as, in the judgment of charity, are held to be of that number. We must account all those who confess the faith of Christ, for such as he hath redeemed by his death.

16 ˢLet not then your good be evil spoken of:

s ch. 12. 17.

Here is another argument against offences; it will cause our *good* to be blasphemed, or *evil spoken of.* Some, by *good* here, would understand the Christian faith, or the gospel in general; but others do rather understand it of our Christian liberty in particular: q. d. Give none occasion for this great privilege of your Christian liberty to be traduced; use it so, as that neither the weak Christian nor the infidel may reproach or accuse you as licentious or contentious: see 1 Cor. x. 29, 30.

17 ᵗFor the kingdom of God is not meat and drink; but righteousness, and peace, and joy in the Holy Ghost.

t 1 Cor. 8. 8.

This verse contains a new argument to persuade Christians not to strive about meats, or such-like things; and that is, that the *kingdom of God* doth not consist in these, but in weightier matters. By the *kingdom of God,* you may understand the gospel, or true religion and godliness; that kingdom which God erects in the hearts of men, Luke xvii. 21; 1 Cor. iv. 20. When he saith, *the kingdom of God is not meat and drink,* he means, that it doth not stand or consist therein. *Meat and drink* are put by a synecdoche for all things of an indifferent or middle nature; such things as, the apostle elsewhere says, *commend us not to God,* 1 Cor. viii. 8:

they are no part of his worship and service ; the kingdom of God, or godliness, is not promoted, either by the use or the forbearance thereof: see Gal. v. 6 ; 1 Tim. iv. 8. *But righteousness, and peace, and joy:* here he tells you positively wherein the kingdom of God consisteth ; not in outward observations, but in inward graces and gracious dispositions. He doth not reckon up all, but contents himself with these three, *righteousness, peace, and joy.* By *righteousness,* some understand that which is imputed, of which you read, chap. iv. : others, rather, that which is implanted and inherent; it is the same with holiness, both the habit of it in the heart, and the exercise of it in the life. By *peace,* some think, he means peace with God, or peace of conscience ; others, that he rather means peace with men ; or, if you will, peaceableness, or Christian concord and unity. This suits best with what follows, ver. 19, and it is often commended to us in Scripture. By *joy* may be understood that spiritual comfort, which ariseth from a present feeling of the favour of God, or from a well-grounded hope of future salvation; as also, the comfort and delight which Christians take in the good and welfare of each other. He that loveth his brother, rejoiceth in his welfare, 1 Cor. xiii. 6 ; and therefore will not offend, or occasion him to sin. *In the Holy Ghost;* this is added, to show the efficient cause of these graces, which is the Spirit of God ; and to distinguish this righteousness, peace, and joy, from that which is merely civil and carnal.

18 For he that in these things serveth Christ *is* acceptable to God, and approved of men. u 2 Cor. 8.21.

This proves the foregoing assertion, that *the kingdom of God* consisteth in *righteousness, peace, and joy,* because *he that serveth Christ in* and by *these things, is accepted of God, and approved of men ;* this cannot be affirmed of meat and drink, &c. When he says, that the serving of Christ in these things is approved of men, he means of such as are godly, and of sound judgment; for of others they are often hated and reviled for the exercise of these very graces : and yet righteousness and peaceableness have oftentimes their praise from the wicked themselves : see 1 Sam. ii. 26 ; Prov. iii. 4 ; Luke ii. 52 ; Acts ii. 47.

19 ˣLet us therefore follow after the things which make for peace, and things wherewith ʸone may edify another. x Ps. 34. 14. ch. 12 18. y ch. 15. 2. 1 Cor. 14. 12. 1 Thes. 5. 11.

This verse is the application of the foregoing discourse, in which you have an exhortation to the practice of two great duties. The one is peace, or peaceableness ; the other is mutual edification. He had persuaded before to peace with all men, chap. xii. 18 ; and here he speaks more especially of peace and concord amongst brethren : see 2 Cor. xiii. 11 ; Eph. iv. 3 ; Col. iii. 15 ; 1 Thess. v. 13 ; Heb. xii. 14. This peace is very necessary, and Christians should endeavour all things that will promote it, and avoid all things that will obstruct it. And they must not only live peaceably, but profitably one with another. They should build one another up in grace and knowledge.

20 ᶻ For meat destroy not the work of God. ᵃ All things indeed *are* pure ; ᵇ but *it is* evil for that man who eateth with offence. z ver. 15. a Mat. 15.11. Acts 10. 15. ver. 14. Tit. 1. 15. b 1 Cor. 8. 9, 10, 11, 12.

For meat destroy not the work of God: here you have a further argument against scandals : q. d. For so inconsiderable a matter as eating a little meat, or for the use of an indifferent thing, do not destroy the work of God. By *the work of God,* some understand the soul of a brother ; that is styled God's work by way of eminency: it was one of the chiefest works of the creation, and made, as it were, with the consultation of the whole Trinity ; the image of God, after a sort, was engraven therein : and if this be the sense, it is a repetition of the argument in ver. 15. But by *the work of God,* in this place, other things may be understood ; e. g. the unity and peace which God worketh amongst believers of different persuasions in indifferent things ; or else the work of grace, or faith, which God hath wrought by his mighty power in the hearts of men : see John vi. 29 ; 1 Thess. i. 3. *The work of God,* in either of these senses, may be disturbed or hindered by the abuse of Christian liberty; and he that scandalizeth his brother, goes about, as much as in him lieth, to dissolve and demolish that which hath God alone for its author and worker. *All things indeed are pure ; but it is evil for that man who eateth with offence :* here you have a concession and an exception : he granteth, that *all things are pure* and clean ; i. e. in themselves, or in their own nature; see ver. 14 ; 1 Cor. vi. 12 ; Tit. i. 15 : but then he addeth, that *it is evil for,* or to, *that man who eateth with offence,* or that offends another with his eating : it is not evil simply in itself, but accidentally, by reason of scandal.

21 *It is* good neither to eat ᶜflesh, nor to drink wine, nor *any thing* whereby thy brother stumbleth, or is offended, or is made weak. c 1 Cor. 8. 13.

The apostle proceedeth to enlarge his doctrine touching this particular, beyond the controversy that occasioned this his discourse ; for he showeth, that to avoid the scandal or offence of our brethren, we are to abstain, not only from things prohibited by the law, but also from things that are not prohibited thereby ; as from *flesh* or *wine,* or any indifferent thing whatsoever. These words, *any thing,* are not in the original, but they are understood, and well supplied in our translation. Thus to do, he says, *is good,* as the contrary, in the foregoing verse, was said to be *evil:* it is good in regard of God, to whom it is acceptable and pleasing ; and in regard of our brethren, to whom it is profitable and advantageous; the positive (it may be) is put for the comparative ; it is good, for it is better : see Matt. xviii. 8, 9. *Whereby thy brother stumbleth, or is offended, or is made weak:* some distinguish these three words, *stumbleth, is offended, made weak,* making the first to be the greater, and the last the lesser injury : others will have the first to be the lesser, and the last the greater injury. But there are those that think they all three do signify the same thing ; and the Syriac interpreter renders them all by one word, viz. is offended : and the same thing may be expressed by divers words, to insinuate the great care we should take, that we do not *put a stumblingblock* (as it is ver. 13) or an occasion of falling into our brother's way. The apostle seems to practise what he here prescribeth, in 1 Cor. viii. 13.

22 Hast thou faith ? have *it* to thyself before God. ᵈ Happy *is* he that condemneth not himself in that thing which he alloweth. d 1 John 3. 21.

Hast thou faith ? have it to thyself before God: some read the first clause without an interrogation, thou hast faith ; either way the sense is the same. The apostle here anticipates an objection. The stronger Christian might be ready to say, as it is in ver. 14, *I know and am persuaded by the Lord Jesus, that nothing is unclean of itself ;* I firmly believe, that now, under the gospel, all meats are lawful, and that I have liberty to use or eat what I please ; and is it not fit that my practice should be agreeable to my belief, that I should act according to my judgment ? To this he answereth, that if a man hath such a faith or persuasion, he should not unseasonably discover it to the offence of his brother, but rather conceal it. He doth not speak of faith in the fundamentals of religion, this must be professed and acknowledged, let who will be offended ; but of faith in indifferent things (which are the subject matter he is treating of) : our belief or persuasion therein is not to be unseasonably uttered or declared, so as to occasion scandal or contention. *Happy is he that condemneth not himself in that thing which he alloweth;* an excellent aphorism respecting all, especially the stronger and more knowing Christian : the sense is, He is a happy man, that, when he knoweth a thing to be lawful, he doth so manage the practice of it, that he hath therein no reason to accuse or condemn himself : or else, that doth not inwardly condemn himself, for doing that against his conscience, which he openly alloweth or practiseth : such a one is happy in this respect, because he is free from those terrors that torment those who act against their consciences.

23 And he that ‖ doubteth is damned if he eat, because *he eateth* not of faith : for ᵉwhatsoever *is* not of faith is sin. ‖ Or, *discerneth and putteth a difference between meats.* e Tit. 1. 15.

In this verse is another aphorism, respecting especially

the weaker Christian. *He that doubteth* of the lawfulness of any meat, whether he may or may not eat it, *is damned if he eat,* i. e. his own conscience condemns him, or he makes himself liable to damnation, *because he eateth not of faith.* The word *eateth* is not in the original, but it is aptly inserted by our translators. What a man doth doubtingly, he doth sinfully: he showeth a wicked heart, that is not afraid of sin, but in great readiness to commit it. *For whatsoever is not of faith is sin;* this is a confirmation of the foregoing assertion. By *faith* here is meant knowledge, or full persuasion, as ver. 22: q. d. Whatever a man doth with a wavering mind, without being persuaded that it is pleasing to God, and warranted by his word, he sinneth in the doing of it. Though we may not nourish doubts and scruples, yet we must not act against them. An erring conscience binds us to act nothing contrary to it: he sins that doth any thing against it, though the fact or thing done should not be sinful. Nature itself teacheth as much: that is a known saying of Cicero, *Quod dubitas, æquum sit an iniquum, ne feceris,* If thou doubtest whether a thing be lawful or not lawful, thou shalt not do it. See Heb. xi. 6.

CHAP. XV

We ought, in condescension to the weak, to give up our own will for our neighbour's good, after the example of Christ, 1—3. *The intent of the Scriptures,* 4. *Paul prayeth for unanimity among Christians,* 5, 6. *Exhorteth to receive one the other, as Christ did all, both Jews and Gentiles,* 6—12; *and wisheth them all joy, peace, and hope,* 13. *He apologizeth for his freedom in admonishing them, as he was the apostle of the Gentiles,* 14—16; *and showeth the success and extensiveness of his labours,* 17—21. *He excuseth his not coming to them before, and promiseth them a visit on his return from Jerusalem,* 23—29. *He requesteth their prayers,* 30—33.

a Gal. 6. 1.
b ch. 14. 1.
WE [a] then that are strong ought to bear the [b] infirmities of the weak, and not to please ourselves.

We then that are strong: the particle *then* showeth, that what followeth is inferred from what went before. By the *strong,* he means those who have attained to a good measure of knowledge and understanding, that are instructed in the Christian faith, and particularly in the doctrine of Christian liberty. He putteth himself in the number, not out of ambition, but that he may propose himself an example of the following duty. *Ought;* i. e. we are obliged and bound both by the law of God and nature. *To bear the infirmities of the weak:* by the *weak,* he means those who are weak in faith and knowledge, chap. xiv. 1. By their *infirmities,* he means their ignorance, frowardness, censoriousness, &c. He doth not speak of heresies and manifest enormities; but of such errors in doctrine and life, which proceed from ignorance or common infirmity. When he says, we must *bear* their infirmities, his meaning is, that we must bear with them, as we do with children or sick persons in their waywardness: though it be a great burden to us, yet we must bear it; we must not impatiently contradict them, but prudently instruct them: see Exod. xxiii. 5; 1 Cor. ix. 22; Gal. vi. 2. *And not to please ourselves:* q. d. We ought not to do what we please in indifferent things, and to act according to our own sentiments without any regard to others; we should not please ourselves in a proud reflecting upon our own knowledge, and in contemning of others because of their ignorance; we should not stand upon the terms of our liberty and contentment, but rather, for the sake of others, depart a little from our own right.

c 1 Cor. 9. 19, 22. & 10. 24, 33. & 13. 5.
Phil. 2. 4, 5.
d ch. 14. 19.
2 [c] Let every one of us please his neighbour for *his* good [d] to edification.

Having said we must not please ourselves, he immediately subjoins, we must please others, viz. *every one his neighbour:* he means, that we should condescend and accommodate ourselves to others, and give them satisfaction in all things; at least so far as may tend to their good and edification. You had a like passage, chap. xiv. 19. The apostle exhorts the Corinthians to a practice somewhat like this, 1 Cor. x. 24; and he leads them the way by his own example, 1 Cor. ix. 19; x. 33. There is a pleasing of men which is sinful, and there is a pleasing of men which is lawful; and that is, when it is limited, as in this text.

3 [e] For even Christ pleased not himself; but, as it is written, [f] The reproaches of them that reproached thee fell on me.
e Mat. 26. 39. John 5. 30. & 6. 38.
f Ps. 69. 9.

For even Christ pleased not himself: he backs his exhortation in the 1st verse, with an argument taken from the practice of our Lord himself, who is our perfect pattern, and hath left us an example, that we should follow his steps: see John xiii. 15, 34; 1 Pet. ii. 21; 1 John ii. 6; iv. 17. By Christ's not pleasing himself, is meant his not indulging or sparing himself; he did not seek his own ease, nor to satisfy the inclination of the human nature, which abhorreth pain, and the destruction of itself. He took such a course all along as sufficiently demonstrated that he respected our benefit, and not his own. *But;* here is an ellipsis, something must be supplied to fill up the sense: either the meaning is, he pleased not himself, but others; or, he pleased not himself, but bore our infirmities and reproaches: or else, he pleased not himself, but it happened to him; or he so carried himself that it might be truly applied to him, which is written, &c. *As it is written;* viz. in Psal. lxix. 9. That David uttered these words in the person of Christ, or as a type of him, may appear from John ii. 17. Interpreters are divided about accommodating this testimony to the occasion for which it is brought. Either the meaning is, that Christ did willingly expose himself to all the reproaches and contumelies of men, in obedience to his Father's will; or else, that he had the same concernments with God the Father, so that what befell God did also befall him; he was as tender of the Father's honour as of his own: or else, that the sins of men, which are the things that cast reproach upon God, were taken by Christ upon himself, and he bore them in his body upon a tree. Seeing then that Christ hath done so much for our sakes, and hath not sought his own ease and benefit, we ought also to seek the good of others, and to deny ourselves: see Phil. ii. 6—8.

4 For [g] whatsoever things were written aforetime were written for our learning, that we through patience and comfort of the Scriptures might have hope.
g ch. 4. 23, 24. 1 Cor. 9. 9, 10. & 10. 11. 2 Tim. 3. 16, 17.

Lest any should think, that the testimony before alleged concerneth only David or Christ, he showeth that it belongeth also unto us; that we may learn by their example to bear the infirmities of the weak, and not to please ourselves. Yea, he takes occasion from hence to inform us of the general use of the Scriptures, that whatsoever is written, in this or any other place, is written for our learning and instruction; we are concerned not only in all the precepts, but in all the promises, Heb. xiii. 5, menaces, Acts xiii. 40, 41, rewards, chap. iv. 24, and punishments, 1 Cor. x. 11, therein mentioned and declared: and though this passage is more especially to be understood of the Scriptures of the Old Testament, yet it is true also of the Scriptures of the New Testament; they, being written by the same Spirit, are profitable for the same ends: see 2 Tim. iii. 16. *That we through patience and comfort of the Scriptures might have hope;* he proceeds to show more particularly the use and benefit of the Holy Scripture, which is, to confirm our hope and assurance of eternal life; see 1 John v. 13. He saith, *the patience and comfort of the Scriptures,* because they are both wrought in us by means thereof: see Rev. iii. 10. We are armed with patience, and furnished with consolations, from the examples and promises contained therein. It may be, the *hope* he here speaks of is to be understood not only of eternal life, but of salvation and deliverance in this life: q. d. One principal use of the Scriptures is this, that by the examples we find there of the patience of holy men, and of God's relieving and comforting them in their distresses, we might be confident that God will relieve and comfort us also in due time.

5 [h] Now the God of patience and consolation grant you to be likeminded one toward another ‖ according to Christ Jesus:
h ch. 12. 16. 1 Cor. 1. 10. Phil. 3. 16.
‖ Or, *after the example of.*

Now the God of patience and consolation: he is called,

the God of all grace, 1 Pet. v. 10, *the God of hope,* ver. 13, *the God of peace,* ver. 33, *the God of love and peace,* 2 Cor. xiii. 11, and here, *the God of patience and consolation:* the meaning is, he is the author and worker thereof. You read in the former verse of the *patience and comfort of the Scriptures;* and here he showeth that the Scriptures do not work these of themselves, but God doth it in and by them. *Grant you to be like-minded one towards another;* this is that to which he had exhorted them, chap. xii. 16. See the like, 1 Cor. i. 10; 2 Cor. xiii. 11; Eph. iv. 3; Phil. ii. 2. God is the author, as of patience and consolation, so of peace and concord: the grace of unity and charity is his gift; he maketh men of one mind and of one heart, and for this he should be inquired of by his saints and people to do it for them. *According to Christ Jesus;* i. e. according to his doctrine, command, or example.

i Acts 4. 24, 32.　6 That ye may ⁱ with one mind *and* one mouth glorify God, even the Father of our Lord Jesus Christ.

That ye may with one mind and one mouth glorify God: q. d. I further pray, that you may not only be like-minded one towards another, but *that ye may with one mouth glorify God;* that whether you be Gentiles or Jews, strong or weak in the faith, you may agree and be unanimous in his worship and service; that not only *with one mind,* but *with one mouth,* or as if you had all but one mouth, you may pray unto God and praise him: that is one way of glorifying God, Psal. l. 23, and it seems to be chiefly intended in this place. See Acts iv. 32, what accord and unanimity there was among the primitive Christians. *Even the Father of our Lord Jesus Christ;* a usual periphrasis of God in the New Testament: see 2 Cor. i. 3; xi. 31; Eph. i. 3; Col. i. 3; 1 Pet. i. 3. God is the Father of Christ, first, as he is the Son of God; so he begat him by an eternal and ineffable generation, John iii. 16; 1 John iv. 9. Secondly, as he is man; so he created him, Luke i. 35. Thirdly, as he is Mediator; so he appointed him to and qualified him for that office, Psal. xl. 8; John xx. 17. This compellation of God includes all our comfort and happiness, for he is our Father because he is the Father of Jesus Christ. It is added here by way of limitation, to distinguish the true God from the false gods of the earth; and by way of explanation, to show how God will be glorified and worshipped under the gospel, viz. as the God and Father of our Lord Jesus Christ.

k ch. 14. 1, 3.
l ch. 5. 2.　7 Wherefore ^k receive ye one another, ^l as Christ also received us to the glory of God.

Wherefore receive ye one another: see chap. xiv. 1, 3. He ends this discourse with the same terms in which he began it. Before, the strong only were charged to receive the weak, but here both are charged alike; the strong must receive the weak, and the weak the strong; they must all have communion one with another, continuing in brotherly love, accounting one another for brethren, exercising mutual forbearance and long-suffering. *As Christ also received us;* i. e. after the example of Christ, who beareth with the infirmities of his followers, putting no difference betwixt Jews and Gentiles. The particle *as* noteth quality, not equality; there is no proportion betwixt the infinite love of Christ and the scanty charity of man. See the like, Matt. v. 48; Eph. v. 2. *To the glory of God;* some join this with the former clause, that we should *receive one another to the glory of God:* God is glorified by that brotherly love and concord that is amongst his people. Others join it with the latter clause, that *Christ hath received us to the glory of God;* i. e. to make us partakers of the glory of God, or to declare and manifest the glory of God's truth to the Jews, and mercy to the Gentiles, as he showeth in the following verses.

m Mat. 15.24. John 1. 11. Acts 3. 25, 26, & 13 46. n ch. 3. 3. 2 Cor. 1. 20.　8 Now I say that ^m Jesus Christ was a minister of the circumcision for the truth of God, ⁿ to confirm the promises *made* unto the fathers:

He explains himself, and declares more at large, how Christ received both Jews and Gentiles, thereby to admonish them to receive one another. As for the Jews, whom he calls here *the circumcision,* see chap. iii. 30; iv 9, 12, he saith, Christ became *a minister* unto them; see Matt. xx. 28. He exercised his ministry in the days of his flesh amongst them only, Matt. xv. 24. He went indeed now and then into the coasts of Samaria to make way for the calling of the Gentiles, but his chief abode was in Jewry. *For the truth of God;* or, because of the truth of God, that his truth or faithfulness might not fail. *To confirm the promises made to the fathers;* i. e. the promises of the Messiah, made first to Adam, then to Abraham and to David, that the Messiah should come of their loins, that in their seed all the nations of the earth should be blessed.

9 And ^o that the Gentiles might glorify　o John 10.16.
God for *his* mercy; as it is written, ^p For　ch. 9. 23.
this cause I will confess to thee among　p Ps. 18. 49.
the Gentiles, and sing unto thy name.

Here he proves the second part, that Christ hath also received the Gentiles. There is a plain ellipsis in the words; this is understood, that there were promises made of or to the Gentiles, and Christ came to confirm them also. The sum of these promises was this, *that the Gentiles* should *glorify God for his mercy.* Some have observed how the truth of God is spoken of in the foregoing verse with respect to the Jews, and the mercy of God with respect to the Gentiles; not that the one was without the other; for the salvation of the Jews, as it was of truth, so of mercy also, Micah vii. 20; and the vocation of the Gentiles, as it was of mercy, so also of truth; for there were many promises of God concerning that matter, but mercy is predicated of the Gentiles, because that attribute of God appeared more eminently in their conversion and calling. You had the like distribution and difference in chap. iv. 25; x. 10. *As it is written:* because the Jews were hardly persuaded of the mercy of God to the Gentiles, therefore he proves it by divers Scripture testimonies. This first is taken out of Psal. xviii. 49: see the notes there. David speaks this in the person of Christ. In the Psalm it is, *I will give thanks to thee;* but here, according to the LXX., *I will confess to thee,* or celebrate thee *among the Gentiles.* They then are received to mercy, forasmuch as it was foretold they should celebrate or praise God for his mercy.

10 And again he saith, ^q Rejoice, ye　q Deu. 32.43.
Gentiles, with his people.

This is taken out of Deut. xxxii. 43. Here it is evidently implied, that the Gentiles should become the people of God, and join with the Jews in his worship and service, and rejoice in the sense of his goodness and mercy to them. The partition-wall is now taken away, and they both became one sheepfold under one Shepherd.

11 And again, ^r Praise the Lord, all ye　r Ps. 117. 1.
Gentiles; and laud him, all ye people.

This is found in Psal. cxvii. 1. There the Gentiles are willed to praise God, which they could not do unless they knew him aright, and had obtained mercy from him.

12 And again, Esaias saith, ^s There　s Is. 11. 1,
shall be a root of Jesse, and he that shall　10. Rev. 5. 5. & 22. 16.
rise to reign over the Gentiles; in him
shall the Gentiles trust.

And again Esaias saith; viz. in Isa. xi. 10: see the notes there. This is a plain prophecy of the conversion of the Gentiles; their being received to mercy is implied in the former testimonies, but here it is expressed. The Son of David (the Saviour) shall rise and spring out of Jesse's root, and reign over the Gentiles by his word and Spirit. He shall gather them by the preaching of his cross, as by an ensign, and they, as it is in the prophet, shall *seek* to him; or, as it is here, shall *trust* or hope in him. The apostle, as he is wont, doth follow the LXX., which makes some little variation from the Hebrew text; but it is rather in sound than in sense. You have other prophecies and promises of the Gentiles' mercy, as Isa. xlii. 1, 6; xlix. 22; lx. 3, 5; but the apostle thought, that these he had mentioned were sufficient for his purpose.

13 Now the God of hope fill you with
all ^t joy and peace in believing, that ye　t ch. 12. 12.
may abound in hope, through the power　& 14. 17.
of the Holy Ghost.

He finisheth here his long discourse about brotherly love and concord with a short and pithy prayer. Having said before, that the Gentiles should hope in God, he takes occasion from hence to style him, *The God of hope.* He is so, both objective, as being the only object of our hope, see Psal. cxlvi. 5; Jer. xvii. 7; 1 Tim. vi. 17; and effective, as being the only author of it, 1 Pet. i. 3. *With all joy and peace in believing;* i. e. with much inward joy and peace, which riseth in the heart through a lively faith in Christ; or else, with all comfort and concord in the Christian faith. In this he prays they may *abound;* instead of those contentions that had been amongst them, he desires they may be filled with those things, wherein he told them, chap. xiv. 17, *the kingdom of God* consisted. *That ye may abound in hope through the power of the Holy Ghost;* he doth not say, that you may have hope, but that you may abound therein, that you may arrive to a plerophory or *full assurance of hope,* as it is in Heb. vi. 11. Such hope as may be like an anchor to the soul, to keep it safe and steady in the midst of storms and tempests. This hope is wrought in us by no less power and virtue than that of the Holy Ghost. See before.

u 2 Pet. 1. 12. 1 John 2. 21.
w 1 Cor. 8. 1, 7, 10.

14 And "I myself also am persuaded of you, my brethren, that ye also are full of goodness, "filled with all knowledge, able also to admonish one another.

Here begins the epilogue or conclusion of this excellent Epistle, wherein the apostle makes an apology, first for his manner of writing to them, and then for his not coming to them himself. His first apology is ushered in with a singular commendation of the Christians at Rome; he began with their commendation, chap. i. 8, and he ends with the same. There are three things which he commends them for. The first is their *goodness;* thus it is numbered among *the fruits of the Spirit,* Gal. v. 22. It may be taken more largely, and so it comprehends all grace and virtue; or else more strictly, and so it is put for kindness, gentleness, and charity, in forbearing and forgiving others. The second is *all-knowledge;* i. e. in things necessary, or in matters relating to Christian liberty; or, by *all knowledge,* he means a large measure and proportion of it. The third is ability *to admonish one another,* to inform others in things about which they were ignorant, or to reprehend others for things about which they were negligent. Though there were many weak and ignorant persons among them, yet there were others of whom he was persuaded and fully assured they were thus qualified: see 1 Cor. i. 5.

x ch. 1. 5. & 12. 3. Gal. 1. 15. Eph. 3. 7, 8.

15 Nevertheless, brethren, I have written the more boldly unto you in some sort, as putting you in mind, * because of the grace that is given to me of God,

q. d. Though I am thus persuaded of you, or of many of you, yet I thought good to write to you *in some sort,* or in part, or a little the more boldly and freely, that I may stir you up to the practise of that which you know already: see 2 Pet. i. 12, 13; iii. 1. This he speaks to allay the sharpness of his former reprehensions, and that what he had written might be the better digested; for all men more easily endure to be noted of negligence, than of malice or ignorance. And further he tells them, he could do no less, *because of the grace that* was *given him of God;* i. e. because of his apostolical office and authority: see chap. i. 5; xii. 3.

y ch. 11. 13. Gal. 2. 7, 8, 9. 1 Tim. 2. 7. 2 Tim. 1. 11. Phil. 2. 17. ‖ Or, *sacrificing.* z Is. 66. 20. Phil. 2. 17.

16 That ʸI should be the minister of Jesus Christ to the Gentiles, ministering the Gospel of God, that the ‖ ᶻ offering up of the Gentiles might be acceptable, being sanctified by the Holy Ghost.

He proceeds to speak more particularly of his office and calling, which he had mentioned more generally in the foregoing words. *The minister of Jesus Christ to the Gentiles:* see the notes on chap. xi. 13. See also Gal. ii. 7, 8; 2 Tim. i. 11. *Ministering the gospel of God;* i. e. preaching of it. Some read it consecrating, or working, in the holy service of the gospel of God. It is an allusion to the work or office of the priests under the law. The Jews and Gentiles, they both boasted of their priesthood and sacrifices: the apostle therefore showeth, that his ministry was far more excellent, being not occupied in sacrificing of beasts, but in offering up living men to be a holy sacrifice to God. *That the offering up of the Gentiles might be acceptable:* some understand it actively, that the Gentiles might offer up themselves, as it is in chap. xii. 1; or that they might offer up acceptable sacrifices to God, according to Mal. i. 11. But it is better understood passively, that the apostle, converting them by his ministry, might present or offer them to God, as an acceptable oblation: see Isa. lxvi. 20. *Being sanctified by the Holy Ghost;* not by any priest on earth, but even by the Holy Ghost himself; as the oblations of old had their external and legal purifyings, so this oblation is purified or *sanctified by the Holy Ghost.*

17 I have therefore whereof I may glory through Jesus Christ ᵃ in those things which pertain to God.   a Heb. 5. 1.

q. d. Having received this grace of apostleship, and having had great success in my labours, multitudes being converted by my ministry, *I have whereof to glory,* or, I have matter of glorying and rejoicing. But then he adds, that this glorying of his was not in himself, but in and *through Jesus Christ,* by whose grace he did what he did: see 1 Cor. xv. 10. And also, that it was not in any thing that concerned himself, but in things pertaining to God, which concerned his worship and service, and wherein his ministry consisted. In the foregoing verse he described his apostleship in terms that were borrowed from the Levitical priesthood; and here, contriving the same metaphor, he calleth the execution of his function, a performing of things pertaining to God, which is that for which the priests of old were ordained, Heb. v. 1.

18 For I will not dare to speak of any of those things ᵇ which Christ hath not wrought by me, ᶜ to make the Gentiles obedient, by word and deed,   b Acts 21. 19. Gal. 2. 8. c ch. 1. 5. & 16. 26.

q. d. I dare not speak of more than is true, or of any thing that was not really done by me: or else the meaning is, I dare not speak of any thing that I have done of myself, I acknowledge that, whatever good hath come to the Gentiles by my means, it was wrought by Christ, whose instrument I have only been: see 1 Cor. iii. 5. *By word and deed:* some join these words to the obedience of the Gentiles; by the preaching of the gospel they were made obedient in word and deed. But they are better joined with the former words; Christ wrought in and by the apostle Paul, both by word and deed. By *word* is understood his public preaching, and private instruction; and by *deed,* the example of his good works, or godly life: or else, by *deed* ye may understand the miracles that he wrought, and the labour and travail that he underwent; of which in the following verse.

19 ᵈ Through mighty signs and wonders, by the power of the Spirit of God; so that from Jerusalem, and round about unto Illyricum, I have fully preached the Gospel of Christ.   d Acts 19. 11. 2 Cor. 12. 12.

Through mighty signs and wonders; or, by the power of signs and wonders, which served to confirm my commission from God, and the truth of what I preached, and so helped forward the obedience and conversion of the Gentiles: see 2 Cor. xii. 12. If there be any difference betwixt *signs and wonders,* it is only gradual. I find them often conjoined in Scripture, Matt. xxiv. 24; John iv. 48; Acts ii. 43; v. 12; vii. 36; xiv. 3. *By the power of the Spirit of God;* which blessed the words, deeds, and miracles of the apostle, and wrought effectually by them in the Gentiles. The word δύναμις, *power,* or virtue, is twice used in this verse: it is first applied to signs and wonders, to show their efficacy; and then to the Spirit of God, to show that he was the efficient cause of that efficacy. *So that from Jerusalem, and round about unto Illyricum:* this showeth the pains and travail of the apostle, to bring the Gentiles to the obedience of faith. Illyricum is said to be in the utmost parts of Greece, bordering upon the sea, which is thereupon called Illyricum Mare. It is thought to be the country now called Sclavonia, and that is distant from Jerusalem about three hundred and fifty German miles, which make above a thousand English miles; yet it seems he did not travel in a direct and straight line, but round about, or in a circle, as the word imports, fetching a circuit. Some writers have given us out of the Acts a particular history of his peregrination from Damascus, where he began his ministry: he went into Arabia, and after three years returned to Damascus, and from thence to Jerusalem; from Jerusalem he went to Cæsarea, and so to Tarsus; from Tarsus Barnabas brought him to Antioch, and from thence to Jerusalem, to carry relief to the Jews. From Jerusalem they returned to Antioch; from Antioch he and Barnabas went to Seleucia, then to Cyprus, and to some cities of Pamphylia, and so to another Antioch in Pisidia; from thence to Lycaonia, and then returned to Antioch, from whence they had been recommended by the church. From Antioch they were sent to Jerusalem about the question of the circumcision, and returned to Antioch with the apostles' decree. From thence he went through Syria and Cilicia, visiting the churches. Then he went through Phrygia, Galatia, and Mysia; then to Troas, where by a vision he was called unto Macedonia, and so came into the parts of Europe; first to Philippi in Macedonia, then to Thessalonica; from thence to Athens, and then to Corinth; from thence to Ephesus; and going to visit the churches of Galatia and Phrygia, returned to Ephesus. From Ephesus he went again to Macedonia; from thence to Troas and Miletus; and thence, by Tyrus and Cæsarea, and other cities, he came to Jerusalem, where he was taken and put in bonds. Thus you have an account of the apostle's travels, which he abridgeth here, when he says, that it was *from Jerusalem round about unto Illyricum*. *I have fully preached the gospel of Christ;* i. e. I have filled all these countries with the gospel of Christ. The word signifieth to fulfil; see Col. iv. 17. This he calleth the finishing his ministry, Acts xx. 24.

20 Yea, so have I strived to preach the Gospel, not where Christ was named, ^elest I should build upon another man's foundation:

e 2 Cor. 10. 13, 15, 16.

f Is. 52. 15.

21 But as it is written, ^fTo whom he was not spoken of, they shall see: and they that have not heard shall understand.

He gives a reason why he chose to preach the gospel in these places, because Christ had not been named or preached there before; this, he saith, was his ambition, and a thing that he greatly coveted; he was unwilling to *build upon another man's foundation*, to put his sickle into another's harvest, to derive the glory to himself which would be due to others, 2 Cor. x. 15, 16. Again, another reason why he preached the gospel where Christ had not been named, was this, that so by him, as an apostle of Christ, and in his ministry, that scripture might be fulfilled, which you have in Isa. lii. 15, *To whom he was not spoken of, they shall see,* &c. See the notes there.

g ch. 1. 13.
1 Thess. 2. 17, 18.
‖ Or, *many ways*, or, *oftentimes*.

22 For which cause also ^gI have been ‖ much hindered from coming to you.

Hitherto he hath excused his manner of writing, now he makes an apology for his not coming unto them. They at Rome might be ready to say, If he had travelled into so many countries, why could he not all this while give us a visit? To this he answers, it was not from any want of respect or good will to them, but for another cause, which he had already assigned, and that was, the preaching of Christ where he had not been named; for this cause, he says, he had been much hindered: he looked upon that as the more necessary work; the planting of churches is more than the watering of them. He told them, chap. i. 13, of his being hindered from coming to them, and now he acquaints them more particularly with the reason, which he concealed before. The word (τὰ πολλὰ) rendered *much*, signifieth many; and it implies that he was many times hindered, and many ways; but this was the chief.

23 But now having no more place in these parts, and ^hhaving a great desire these many years to come unto you;

h Acts 19.21. ver. 32.
ch. 1. 11.

Having given the reason why he came not to them hitherto, in the following words he assures them he would do it hereafter. And here he saith he was the more inclined so to do, first, Because he had no more place in those parts, i. e. as before, in those places where Christ had not been named, or his gospel preached, he had no new churches there to found, and he had ordained elders in every city to build upon his foundation. The word rendered *parts*, signifies climates; i. e. places which lie on divers elevations of the pole. And then, secondly, Because he had long longed so to do, he had desired it for many years, chap. i. 10, 11.

24 Whensoever I take my journey into Spain, I will come to you: for I trust to see you in my journey, ⁱand to be brought on my way thitherward by you, if first I be somewhat filled † with your *company*.

i Acts 15. 3.

† Gr. *with you*, ver. 32.

Here he sets down the time when he would visit them, i. e. when he took his journey into Spain. He saith, he trusted he should see them then; he was not assured of it, he had no revelation from God concerning it, he could make no absolute promise. See ver. 28. *And to be brought on my way thitherward by you;* i. e. by some of you; this he did promise himself from them, and indeed it was usually done by the churches he visited; see Acts xvii. 15: not that he affected any train or pomp, but it was done for his guidance and safety, as he travelled through unknown and dangerous ways. *If first I be somewhat filled with your company:* this he adds, lest they should think he meant to make no stay with them; he gives them to understand, that he did not intend to leave them, till they were mutually filled and satisfied with one another's company and society.

25 But now ^kI go unto Jerusalem to minister unto the saints.

k Acts 19.21. & 20. 22. & 24. 17.

Some might be ready to say, If Paul hath no more place in those parts where he is, and hath such a longing desire to see us, why then doth he not presently come to us? To this he answers, that for the present he could not come, because he had a weighty affair upon his hands, which was to go up to Jerusalem to minister to the saints; i. e. to carry thither certain collections and contributions from the Gentile churches for their relief. He useth a participle of the present tense in the original, to show that this work is now in hand, and it would not stay or hold him long. Though indeed his work was to preach the gospel, and not to serve tables; yet it seems likely that the churches of the Gentiles, who were moved by him to this contribution, had committed the same to his care, 2 Cor. viii. 4.

26 For ^lit hath pleased them of Macedonia and Achaia to make a certain contribution for the poor saints which are at Jerusalem.

l 1 Cor. 16.1, 2. 2 Cor. 8. 1. & 9. 2, 12.

For the understanding of these words, you need only to read 2 Cor. viii. 1, and ix. 2. When he saith, *it hath pleased them*, it is implied, that it was not extorted or squeezed out of them; but that it proceeded from a ready and willing mind, and that they took delight therein. The word here rendered *contribution*, properly signifieth communication, which implieth a mutual exchange or intercourse between the givers and the receivers; the one contributing alms, the other prayers and intercessions to God. He speaks elsewhere of communicating *concerning giving and receiving*, Phil. iv. 15.

27 It hath pleased them verily; and their debtors they are. For ^mif the Gentiles have been made partakers of their spiritual things, ⁿtheir duty is also to minister unto them in carnal things.

m ch. 11. 17.

n 1 Cor. 9.11. Gal. 6. 6.

It hath pleased them verily; he makes this repetition, as to commend the Grecians, so also to admonish the Romans to the like benevolence. *And their debtors they are;* i. e. the Gentiles are debtors to the Jews; though what they sent them was a gift, yet it was also a debt, it was due by the law of charity, chap. xiii. 8, and by the law of gratitude and equity; they had received from them, and they were obliged in some sort to make returns to them. *For if the Gentiles have been made partakers of their spiritual things, their duty is also to minister unto them in carnal things:* by the *spiritual things* of the Jews, of which the Gentiles were *made partakers*, you may understand all those things of which mention is made, chap. ix. 4, 5; more particularly, the gospel, with the ministry and ordinances thereof: the gospel was first preached to the Jews, and from Jerusalem it was spread abroad among the Gentiles: see Luke xxiv. 47; Acts i. 4, 8. By the *carnal things* of the Gentiles, you may understand their gold and silver, with all things needful for the sustentation of the body: you have a parallel place in 1 Cor. ix. 7.

28 When therefore I have performed this, and have sealed to them ° this fruit, I will come by you into Spain.

o Phil. 4. 17.

When therefore I have performed this, and have sealed to them this fruit; i. e. After that I have despatched this business, and safely delivered the alms of the Greek churches to the Jews, wherewith I am intrusted; it is put into my hands as a treasure sealed in a bag or chest, that it may not be diminished or embezzled: he calls it *fruit*, because it proceeded from their faith and love, and because it would abound to their account, Phil. iv. 17; it would benefit them that received it, but much more them that gave it. *I will come by you into Spain;* i. e. I will take you, or your city, in my way thither. He told them as much before, ver. 24. This he really intended, but it is generally concluded that he was prevented, that he never went this journey into Spain. The purposes of men are ruled and over-ruled by the providence of God, Prov. xvi. 9.

p ch. 1. 11.

29 ᵖ And I am sure that, when I come unto you, I shall come in the fulness of the blessing of the Gospel of Christ.

i. e. As some expound it, I shall find you furnished with all spiritual and gospel blessings: this sense agrees with ver. 14. But others rather think, that he speaks of what he should bring with him, and not of what he should find there: therefore it may better be expounded by chap. i. 11, 12. He assures himself he should impart unto them much knowledge, grace, and comfort; that he should enrich and fill them with all *the blessings of the gospel of Christ.*

30 Now I beseech you, brethren, for the Lord Jesus Christ's sake, and ᵍ for the love of the Spirit, ʳ that ye strive together with me in *your* prayers to God for me;

q Phil. 2. 1.
r 2 Cor. 1.11. Col. 4. 12.

In the conclusion, he commends himself to their prayers. This is usual with him in his other Epistles: see Eph. vi. 18—20; Col. iv. 3; 2 Thess. iii. 1; Heb. xiii. 18. *I beseech you, brethren, for the Lord Jesus Christ's sake:* q. d. If not for my sake, yet for his sake, who is most dear to you. *And for the love of the Spirit:* q. d. If you love the Spirit of God; or rather, if the grace of love be wrought in you by the Spirit, show it in this thing. This pathetical way of speaking is frequent with this apostle: see chap. xii. 1; Phil. ii. 1. *That ye strive together with me in your prayers to God for me;* that you strive as those that be in an agony; it is a military word: he bespeaks their earnest and importunate prayers in his behalf. Jacob prayed after this manner; so did Elijah, and Epaphras, Col. iv. 12. He prayed himself, and he desired them to join with him, and help him, as Aaron and Hur helped Moses.

s 2 Thess. 3. 2.

31 ˢ That I may be delivered from them that ‖ do not believe in Judæa; and that ᵗ my service which *I have* for Jerusalem may be accepted of the saints;

‖ Or, *are disobedient.*
t 2 Cor. 8. 4.

Here are two things more particularly, which he desires them to beg of God in his behalf. First, That he may be delivered from them that did not believe, or were disobedient and refractory, in Judea. He knew the Jews were incensed against him; that troubles did abide him or wait for him in Judea, whither he was going; see Acts xx. 23. And it happened accordingly, for the Jews went about to kill him, Acts xxi. 31. Therefore it is that he desires their prayers, that he might be *delivered from them;* see 2 Thess. iii. 2. Secondly, That the alms he brought the poor saints at Jerusalem might be taken by them in good part; that they might be reconciled, both to the Gentile churches that sent it, and to him that brought it. It detracts greatly from a gift, when it comes, either from one, or by one, against whom we are prejudiced.

32 ᵘ That I may come unto you with joy ˣ by the will of God, and may with you be ʸ refreshed.

u ch. 1. 10.
x Acts 18. 21.
1 Cor. 4. 19.
Jam. 4. 15.
y 1 Cor. 16. 18. 2 Cor. 7. 13. 2 Tim. 1. 16. Philem. 7. 20.

That I may come unto you with joy by the will of God: q. d. This would be a means to make me come unto you with the more comfort, if God will, or if God grant it to our prayers. This condition, if God will, he had before inserted upon this very occasion, chap. i. 10. See the like, 1 Cor. iv. 19; James iv. 13, 15. This he did to free himself from the suspicion of inconstancy, in case it should fall out otherwise; as also to show, that always, and in all things, he referred himself to the good pleasure and providence of God. *And may with you be refreshed;* i. e. with your company and converse. This hath the same sense with chap. i. 12: see the notes there.

33 Now ᶻ the God of peace *be* with you all. Amen. Phil. 4. 9. 1 Thess. 5. 23. 2 Thess. 3. 16. Heb. 13. 20.

z ch. 16. 20.
1 Cor. 14. 33.
2 Cor. 13. 11.

The God of peace; this is a frequent title of God in Scripture; he is called *the God of peace,* chap. xvi. 20; 2 Cor. xiii. 11; Phil. iv. 9; 1 Thess. v. 23; 2 Thess. iii. 16; Heb. xiii. 20. Here it fits his great argument, which was to persuade the believing Romans to be at peace amongst themselves, and not to contend about indifferent things. *Be with you all:* three times in this chapter doth the apostle lift up a prayer for the believing Romans; see ver. 5, 13; and this is more comprehensive than the other two. If God be with us, no good thing can be wanting to us. God's presence is inclusive of all good, and exclusive of all evil. *Amen:* see chap. xvi. 27.

CHAP. XVI

Paul commendeth Phebe to the Christians at Rome, 1, 2; *and sendeth salutations to many by name,* 3—16. *He warneth them to take heed of those who cause divisions and offences,* 17—20. *After sundry salutations,* 21—24, *he concludeth with praise to God,* 25—27.

I COMMEND unto you Phebe our sister, which is a servant of the church which is at ᵃ Cenchrea:

a Acts 18. 18.

This chapter is in the nature of a postscript. The apostle begins it with the recommendation of a certain woman to them. She went upon some occasion to Rome, and by her (as some have supposed) this Epistle was sent to the church there. *Phebe:* the poets called the moon Phœbe, as they did the sun Phœbus. This name is likely to have been imposed by her parents, being Gentiles. *Our sister;* i. e. in Christ, and by the profession of the same faith: see James ii. 16. *Cenchrea;* a port or haven belonging to Corinth, on the east side towards Asia: there was another on the west side towards Italy, called Lechea. By reason of this double haven, Corinth was called by the poets, *Bi maris.* Here Paul paid a vow, which he had made, Acts xviii. 18. Here also he preached and converted many, amongst whom this Phebe (as is probable) was one. When he saith, she was *servant of the church,* it is not meant she was a deaconness, or one of the college of widows, of whom he speaketh, 1 Tim. v. 9. But she served the church, in harbouring and succouring the saints that were driven out of their country; yea, as appears by the next verse, she was a succourer of the ministers of the gospel, and of the apostle himself. We read, Luke viii. 3, of some that *ministered unto* the Lord *of their substance;* there the same word is used. And this Phebe seems to have been employed in the same works; she ministered unto Paul as Onesiphorus did, 2 Tim. i. 18; there the same word is used again.

2 ᵇ That ye receive her in the Lord, as becometh saints, and that ye assist her in whatsoever business she hath need of you: for she hath been a succourer of many, and of myself also.

b Phil. 2. 29.
3 John 5, 6.

Receive her in the Lord; i. e. in the Lord's name, or for the Lord's sake: see Matt. xviii. 5. Or else it is as if he had said, Receive her Christianly. *As becometh saints;* as it is fit that saints should be received, or as it is fit for them, who profess themselves to be saints, to receive one another. *That ye assist her in whatsoever business she hath need of you;* that you stand by her, and afford her your counsel, or any other assistance. She might have some business in the emperor's court, by reason of fraud, oppression, or some unjust vexations; and there might be those amongst them that could stand her in some stead. There were Christians of Cæsar's household, Phil. iv. 22. *For she hath been a succourer of many, and of myself also :* the word signifieth a patroness. She had been hospitable to many, and in particular, to the apostle himself. This showeth she was a woman of some account : it was but equal that the saints at Rome should assist her, who had been assistant unto so many others.

c Acts 18. 2, 18, 26.
2 Tim. 4. 19.
3 Greet c Priscilla and Aquila my helpers in Christ Jesus :

In the next place, he saluteth several persons by name; the first are *Priscilla and Aquila.* Sometimes she is called *Prisca,* 2 Tim. iv. 19; and by a diminutive, *Priscilla.* This was usual amongst the Romans. So Livia was called Livilla ; Tullia, Tulliola ; Petrona, Petronella, &c. The wife is named before her husband ; so she is, Acts xviii. 18; 2 Tim. iv. 19. Some think she was first called ; others, that she was most renowned for her zeal and charity. We need not to be curious in our inquiry after the reason ; we find in other places Aquila is set before Priscilla, Acts xviii. 2, 26 ; 1 Cor. xvi. 12. Hence it may appear how weakly the papists argue for Peter's primacy, because he was placed first on the catalogue of the apostles ; for by the same argument, the wife should be preferred before her husband. This Aquila was a Jew of Pontus, and by occupation a tent-maker : with him the apostle Paul abode and wrought at Corinth, Acts xviii. 2, 3. Though Claudius the emperor had commanded the Jews to depart from Rome, yet now, it seems, they were returned thither again ; possibly, because Claudius was dead, or because that severe edict was relaxed. *My helpers in Christ Jesus;* in propagating the gospel in their place and calling, and as they had opportunity. Though they preached not publicly, yet they furthered the gospel many ways privately : see Acts xviii. 26.

4 Who have for my life laid down their own necks : unto whom not only I give thanks, but also all the churches of the Gentiles.

Who have for my life laid down their own necks ; i. e. they hazarded their own lives to save mine. The Scripture speaks of this as the duty of Christians, 1 John iii. 16. He refers (it may be) to that uproar that was at Corinth, of which see Acts xviii. 12 ; or that in Asia, of which see Acts xix. 23. *Unto whom not only I give thanks, but also all the churches of the Gentiles;* because he was the apostle of the Gentiles, and his preservation redounded to the benefit of them all.

d 1 Cor. 16.19.
Col. 4. 15.
Philem. 2.
5 Likewise *greet* d the church that is in their house. Salute my wellbeloved
e 1 Cor. 16. 15.
Epenetus, who is e the firstfruits of Achaia unto Christ.

Likewise greet the church that is in their house ; the word *greet* is supplied to fill up the sense : q. d. Declare my good-will to them, and desires of their welfare. You have the same salutations, 1 Cor. xvi. 19 ; and the like in Col. iv. 15; Philem. 2. By *the church in their house,* is generally understood, their family or household ; which he calls a church, because of the godly order and religious worship that was exercised amongst them. May Aquila and Priscilla be a pattern unto other housekeepers ; may the families of Christians be every where as little churches. The house of George, prince of Anhalt, for the good and godly order therein observed, was said to be, as well a church as a court. There are some that think, that by *the church in their house,* is meant the Christians that were wont to assemble there for solemn worship ; but this is not likely, because of the particular salutations of so many in the following verses. *Salute my well-beloved Epenetus: Epenetus,* in the Greek tongue, is laudable and praiseworthy ; so was this person, both in name and in deed. *Who is the first-fruits of Achaia unto Christ :* the same is affirmed of *the house of Stephanas,* 1 Cor. xvi. 15. The meaning may be this, Epenetus was the first person, and Stephanas's family was the first family, that embraced the faith of Christ in the region of Achaia. This is a singular commendation ; God's soul desires such first-ripe fruits, Micah vii. 1.

6 Greet Mary, who bestowed much labour on us.

Greet Mary : this was a common name, but the person here meant was of special note. Ignatius highly commends one of this name, giving her an ample character for wisdom and godliness. *Who bestowed much labour on us ;* this is the commendation the apostle gives of this woman : it is to be understood of her labour and service in providing food and other necessaries for the entertainment of the faithful, especially the preachers of the gospel ; which he acknowledgeth as done to himself, though he had not been at Rome, because of the communion of saints. Some think this woman dwelt before at Corinth, or Antioch, or in some other places, where she had ministered unto the apostle Paul himself.

7 Salute Andronicus and Junia, my kinsmen, and my fellowprisoners, who are of note among the apostles, who also f were in Christ before me. f Gal. 1. 22.

Salute Andronicus and Junia; it may be rendered Junius. Some think this Junia was a woman, and the wife of Andronicus ; others take them both for men. *My kinsmen ;* so he calls them, either because they were Jews, chap. ix. 3 ; or because they were of the same tribe ; or because they were more nearly related to him by consanguinity and affinity. *My fellow prisoners ;* i. e. they had been imprisoned for the gospel, as well as he : the apostle had been often in prison himself, 2 Cor. xi. 23. We read, Acts xvi. 23, of his being imprisoned at Philippi, and it may be these two were his fellow prisoners, for we read of other prisoners there besides Paul and Silas, ver. 25, 26. *Who are of note among the apostles ;* i. e. they were well known to the apostles, and were in good esteem with them : not only the twelve, together with Paul and Barnabas, but other teachers are sometimes called *apostles,* or *messengers ;* see 2 Cor. viii. 33 ; Phil. ii. 25. Some have thought these two, Andronicus and Junia, were of the number of the seventy disciples, who are mentioned Luke x. 1. Others, that they were of the one hundred and twenty, who are mentioned Acts i. 15 ; or of those that were converted by the first preaching of Peter, and the rest, Acts ii. 41 ; iv. 4. By what follows, it appeareth they were of considerable standing in Christianity. *Who also were in Christ before me :* there are three things for which he commends these two persons : the first is, their sufferings for Christ ; the second is, their fame among the apostles ; and the third is, their forwardness in conversion. This was Mnason's commendation, Acts xxi. 16. When he saith, they *were in Christ,* he intimates the virtue and power of faith, to incorporate us into Christ, as branches into a vine.

8 Great Amplias my beloved in the Lord.

Some translations call him Ampliatus ; it is a Roman name. *My beloved in the Lord;* this is added, to show that he did not love him for his riches, or any outward respect, but for the Lord's sake ; for the grace of Christ, which appeared in him.

9 Salute Urbane, our helper in Christ, and Stachys my beloved.

Urbane ; this also is a Roman name ; it was coveted afterwards by many bishops of Rome. *Our helper in Christ ;* the same that was said of Aquila and Priscilla, ver. 3. Possibly he might be one of their teachers. *Stachys my beloved ;* this is a Greek name, which signifieth an ear of corn. Some have reported, he was the first bishop of Constantinople : he was doubtless a person eminent in grace and gifts, or else the apostle would never have dignified him with this additional commendation, that he was *beloved* of him, or dear to him.

10 Salute Apelles approved in Christ. Salute them which are of Aristobulus' || houshold. ∥ Or, friends.

Origen supposeth this *Apelles* to be Apollos, of whom you read, Acts xviii. 24, and in other places. Epiphanius saith, he was teacher in the churches of Smyrna before

Polycarpus. *Approved in Christ;* one who hath showed himself a faithful and sincere Christian, who hath given many proofs of his sincerity, zeal, and constancy. This is a high encomium; to be *in Christ* is much, to be *approved in Christ* is more: tried gold is most precious. In a time of trial, to stand fast, and hold his own, is a Christian's greatest praise. *Salute them which are of Aristobulus' household;* the word *household* is not in the Greek, but is added to fill up the sense; you have the like in the next verse, and in 1 Cor. i. 11. Aristobulus himself is not saluted; either he was dead, or as yet unconverted to the faith of Christ; but it seems there were several Christians in or belonging to his family, whom the apostle here salutes. See the next verse.

11 Salute Herodion my kinsman. Greet them that be of the ‖ *houshold* of Narcissus, which are in the Lord.

‖ Or, friends.

Salute Herodion my kinsman: see ver. 7. *Greet them that be of the household of Narcissus:* this *Narcissus* is reported by Suetonius to have been in great favour with Claudius the emperor, and to have abounded in wealth, so that he was worth ten millions. He was a wicked man himself, yet it seems he had divers good Christians in his family. So we read that there were saints in Nero's house or court, Phil. iv. 22. To what a degree of wickedness are they arrived, who will not suffer a religious person to dwell in their houses! This shows, that good Christians may serve wicked masters with a good conscience. *Which are in the Lord;* this may be added, because that all in Narcissus's family were not Christians, or members of the church of Christ.

12 Salute Tryphena and Tryphosa, who labour in the Lord. Salute the beloved Persis, which laboured much in the Lord.

He salutes several women as well as men: you read before of Priscilla, ver. 3; of Mary, ver. 6; and now he adds three more in this verse. He saith of the two first, that they *laboured in the Lord;* i. e. in the service of Christ and his church, according to their place and power. See the notes on ver. 6. *Salute the beloved Persis, which laboured much in the Lord;* he gives this woman a higher commendation, calling her *the beloved Persis;* see ver. 8. He saith of the other two, that they *laboured;* but of this, that she hath *laboured much in the Lord,* noting some special favour or service for which she is here commended.

g 2 John 1.

13 Salute Rufus [g] chosen in the Lord, and his mother and mine.

Salute Rufus; the same (it may be) of whom you may read, Mark xv. 21. *Chosen in the Lord;* a choice Christian, one eminent for gifts and graces. So, 2 John 1, you read of an *elect lady:* he is supposed not to speak here of eternal election. *And his mother and mine; his mother* by nature, *mine* by affection: she hath tendered me as a mother her son: see 1 Tim. v. 2.

14 Salute Asyncritus, Phlegon, Hermas, Patrobas, Hermes, and the brethren which are with them.

i. e. The Christians that are their domestics, or that dwell with them.

15 Salute Philologus, and Julia, Nereus, and his sister, and Olympas, and all the saints which are with them.

Julia; probably the wife of *Philologus. Olympas;* this is thought to be the name of a man, rather than of a woman. *All the saints which are with them;* that are in their several families: see ver. 14. There were, doubtless, many more Christians in the church of Rome, but either they were of no great note, or else not known to the apostle: and indeed it is matter of admiration, that he, who was never at Rome, should know the name and proper characters of so many there. And because he sendeth salutations to so many brethren at Rome, and makes no mention of Peter, it may be rationally inferred, that Peter was not there at the writing of this Epistle. It is questionable whether ever he were there at all; but it is without question, that he came not thither in the beginning of Claudius's reign, and in the forty-fifth year of our Lord, as the Romanists report; nor was he bishop there for the space of five and twenty years, as they affirm.

16 [h] Salute one another with an holy kiss. The churches of Christ salute you.

h 1 Cor. 16. 20. 2 Cor. 13. 12. 1 Thes. 5. 26. 1 Pet. 5. 14.

From greeting them himself, he proceeds to exhort them to greet or *salute one another:* this he adviseth them to do *with an holy kiss.* You have the same exhortation, 1 Cor. xvi. 20; 2 Cor. xiii. 12; 1 Thess. v. 26. This the apostle Peter calls *a kiss of charity,* 1 Pet. v. 14. Kissing is accounted a great symbol of love and concord: q. d. You have been much troubled with dissensions, about meats and days, &c.; therefore I beseech you that, forgetting all former offences, you would manifest for the future all signs of love to and peace with one another. Kissing was an old custom amongst the Hebrews; we find it used by the patriarchs, Gen. xxvii. 26; xxix. 11. It is still retained more or less in all countries. The primitive Christians did use it in their assemblies; so Tertullian testifieth, Lib. Dec.; and they did it especially in receiving the eucharist. So Chrysostom witnesseth, Hom. 77. in John xvi. "We do well," saith he, "to kiss in the mysteries, that we may become one." This custom, for good reasons, is laid down, and the Romanists, in room of it, keep up a foolish and superstitious ceremony, which is to kiss the pax in the mass. *The churches of Christ salute you:* he sends, besides his own, the salutations of others also to the Christians at Rome; and that, first, of whole churches, and by and by of particular persons, ver. 21—23. By *churches,* here, he principally means, the churches in Greece, where he then was, of whose good affection to the Christian Romans he was well assured.

17 Now I beseech you, brethren, mark them [i] which cause divisions and offences contrary to the doctrine which ye have learned; and [k] avoid them.

i Acts 15. 1, 5, 24. 1 Tim. 6. 3.
k 1 Cor. 5. 9. 11. 2 Thes. 3. 6, 14. 2 Tim. 3. 5. Tit. 3. 10. 2 John 10.

He shuts up the Epistle with a seasonable admonition, which he reserved to the last, that it might be the better remembered: it is, to beware of those that *cause divisions and offences.* By the former, some understand those that corrupt the doctrine of the church; by the latter, those that violate the discipline thereof: others refer *divisions* to faith, and *offences* to manners. There are that like neither of these distinctions, but think he only cautions them against church dividers; and mentions scandal or offences as the effect or fruit of church divisions. He seems to aim more especially at those who, together with the Christian faith, did obtrude upon believers the ceremonies of the law, as necessary to salvation; of these he often complains as enemies to the gospel and cross of Christ: see Gal. i. 7; Phil. iii. 2, 18, 19; Tit. i. 10. *Contrary to the doctrine which ye have learned;* i. e. that you have learned from those that first taught you and converted you to Christ: q. d. You have been instructed in the true doctrine of Christ; and there are some that would innovate and teach another doctrine, that broach opinions that are contrary, or, at least, beside the doctrine which is pure and apostolical, and so make divisions and factions amongst you: of such as those he speaks what follows. *And avoid them;* here are two precepts with respect to innovators and church dividers. The first is, that they should be marked. The word signifies such a marking, as a watchman useth that standeth on a tower to descry enemies; he marketh diligently all comers, and giveth notice accordingly, for the safety of the place. The second is, that they should be avoided, or declined: the like counsel is given, 2 Thess. iii. 6, 14; 1 Tim. vi. 3—5; 2 Tim. iii. 5; Tit. iii. 10; 2 John 10. The sum is, the church should excommunicate them, and all sound Christians should turn away from them, and shun their society, that they may be ashamed.

18 For they that are such serve not our Lord Jesus Christ, but [l] their own belly; and [m] by good words and fair speeches deceive the hearts of the simple.

l Phil. 3. 19. 1 Tim. 6. 5.
m Col. 2. 4.
2 Tim. 3. 6. Tit. 1. 10. 2 Pet. 2. 3.

In this verse you have a reason of the foregoing admonition, together with a description of the seducers, whom they should mark and avoid. He says, they are such as *serve not our Lord Jesus Christ, but their own belly;* i. e. they serve themselves rather than Christ. Though they pretend to be the servants of Jesus Christ, and give themselves out for his ministers, yet they aim at nothing but their own commodity and advantage. A further account you have of such persons in Phil. iii. 19; 1 Tim. vi. 5; Tit. i. 11; 2 Pet. ii. 3. *By good words and fair speeches deceive the hearts of the simple*: q. d. As Satan insinuated into Eve, by pretending he wished her good; so these seducers pretend they aim at nothing but the good and benefit of those with whom they have to do: with smooth and flattering words, they praise both the persons and doings of those whom they would insnare, (so much the word εὐλογία, here used, imports,) and by this means they impose upon *the simple*, i. e. the over-credulous and unwary, who do not mistrust any deceit or hurt. The word here rendered *simple*, properly signifies such as are not evil, or that are incautious, and not suspicious.

n ch. 1. 8.

19 For ⁿ your obedience is come abroad unto all *men*. I am glad therefore on your behalf: but yet I would have you ᵒ wise unto that which is good, and ∥ simple concerning evil.

o Mat. 10.16.
1 Cor. 14. 20.
∥ Or, *harmless*.

For your obedience is come abroad unto all men: q. d. As for you, your ready embracing of the gospel, and conformity thereunto, is generally taken notice of by all that mind such things: see the like, chap. i. 8; 1 Thess. i. 8. *I am glad therefore on your behalf;* I rejoice to hear of your soundness and teachableness; I do not therefore speak this to accuse, but to caution you. *But yet I would have you wise unto that which is good, and simple concerning evil*: q. d. Take heed that you be not cheated by seducers, that they do not abuse your tractableness to draw you into errors. He exhorts them to join prudence with simplicity; to be so harmless and simple as not to invent false doctrine, and yet to be so wise and skilful as to be able to discern truth from falsehood; to be so innocent as not to deceive, and so prudent as not to be deceived: see Matt. x. 16. He prays for the Philippians, that they may have this discretion, Phil. i. 9, 10, and exhorts the Thessalonians thereunto, 1 Thess. v. 21.

p ch. 15. 33.
q Gen. 3. 15.
∥ Or, *tread*.
r ver. 24.
1 Cor. 16. 23.
2 Cor. 13. 14.
Phil. 4. 23.
1 Thes. 5. 28.
2 Thess. 3. 18. Rev. 22. 21.

20 And ᵖ the God of peace ᵠ shall ∥ bruise Satan under your feet shortly. ʳ The grace of our Lord Jesus Christ *be* with you. Amen.

And, &c.: q. d. And to encourage you to be watchful, I dare promise you shall be successful. *The God of peace;* so he is called, chap. xv. 33. *Shall bruise Satan under your feet*: the word signifies to bruise by treading: it imports the conquest that the Lord gives his people over Satan and all his wicked instruments, that divide, seduce, or oppress his people; the promise is that they shall overcome him and them; they shall deal by Satan and his agents, as Joshua and his captains did by those five kings, Josh. x. 24: see Rev. xxii. 11. This promise plainly bears upon the first grand promise, in Gen. iii. 15, that Jesus Christ, the Seed of the woman, should bruise the head of the serpent; for it is by virtue of his bruising the head of Satan, that he is subdued and brought under our feet. The seed of the woman, in their own persons, as well as in their representative, shall bruise the serpent's head. *Shortly*, or suddenly; though now he rage, yet ere long he shall be thrown down. Some refer this to the day of judgment: others, to the time of Constantine, who overthrew idolatry; and that it is not only a promise, but a prophecy also of the conversion of the Roman empire. There are that think that the apostle doth comfort here the believing Romans, by telling them, that the dissensions raised amongst them by means of Satan's malice and subtlety, should be shortly quenched and reconciled; and that it was effected partly by this Epistle, and partly by the apostle's labours afterwards amongst them. *The grace of our Lord Jesus Christ be with you*: as he began this Epistle with wishing them *grace and peace*, so he ends it. He had said, chap. xv. 33, *The God of peace be with you;* and here he saith, *The grace of our Lord Jesus Christ be with you*. He was once and again shutting up his Epistle, but having more room and time, he makes some short additions and supplements, as it is usual with those that write epistles. This salutation he was wont in the end of every Epistle to write with his own hand, 2 Thess. iii. 17. It is repeated, ver. 24. Hereby he intimates the necessity of the grace of Christ, therefore he prayeth for it again and again. See the notes on chap. i. 7.

21 ˢ Timotheus my workfellow, and ᵗ Lucius, and ᵘ Jason, and ˣ Sosipater, my kinsmen, salute you.

s Acts 16. 1. Col. 1. 1.
Phil. 2. 19.
1 Thess. 3. 2.
1 Tim. 1. 2.
Heb. 13. 23.
t Acts 13. 1. u Acts 17. 5. x Acts 20. 4.

As before he saluted divers persons himself, so now he sendeth the salutation of others to the church of Rome. This he doth to show the mutual amity and love that is and ought to be betwixt Christians; though they are divided in respect of place, yet not in respect of affection and goodwill. He begins with *Timotheus*, or Timothy, whom he calls his *work-fellow*, or fellow helper, viz. in preaching and propagating the gospel of Christ. This shows the humility of the apostle, that he dignifies so young a man with this title. This is he to whom he wrote afterwards two Epistles; you may read more of him, Acts xvi., and elsewhere. *Lucius:* Origen and some others are of opinion that this was Luke the evangelist, who was the inseparable companion of the apostle Paul, and was with him about this very time. as appears by Acts xx. 5; and here he is called Lucius, according to the Roman inflexion. Others think that this was Lucius of Cyrene, of whom you read, Acts xiii. 1. *Jason;* this was Paul's host at Thessalonica, Acts xvii. 5, 7; the same, as some think, that is called Secundus, Acts xx. 4, the one being his Hebrew, the other his Roman name. *Sosipater;* the same that is called Sopater of Berea, Acts xx. 4. *My kinsmen:* see ver. 7.

22 I Tertius, who wrote *this* epistle, salute you in the Lord.

Tertius; this was the apostle's scribe or amanuensis, *who wrote this Epistle*, either from his mouth, or from his papers: he put in this salutation by the apostle's licence. *Salute you in the Lord;* i. e. I wish you safety from the Lord.

23 ʸ Gaius mine host, and of the whole church, saluteth you. ᶻ Erastus the chamberlain of the city saluteth you, and Quartus a brother.

y 1 Cor. 1. 14.
z Acts 19. 22.
2 Tim. 4. 20.

Gaius: we read of more than one that bore this name; there was Gaius of Macedonia, of whom you read, Acts xix. 29; there was Gaius of Derbe, of whom you read, Acts xx. 4; he is most likely the person here meant. There was one of this name whom Paul baptized at Corinth, 1 Cor. i. 14; and there was another Gaius, to whom St. John wrote his Third Epistle: whether any of those were the same, or whether they were all different persons, is uncertain. *Mine host, and of the whole church;* i. e. he entertained the apostle, and all Christian strangers that passed that way. That Gaius to whom the apostle John wrote, is commended for the like hospitality, 3 John 5, 6. *Erastus the chamberlain of the city;* or the receiver or steward of the city; one that had the management of the city's stock or public treasure. The city was Corinth, from whence the apostle wrote this Epistle. There *Erastus* is said to abide, 2 Tim. iv. 20, possibly to attend upon his office. Yet we find, Acts xix. 22, that he was one of them that ministered to the apostle, and was sent by him hither and thither, as he had occasion, which would not well consist with his being chamberlain or steward of so great a city; therefore some are of opinion, that he is so called, because that had been his office in time past. So *Abigail* is called *the wife of Nabal*, 2 Sam. iii. 3, because she formerly stood in that relation to him. *Quartus;* this is no word of number, but it was his name: we had Tertius in the foregoing verse; and we read of Secundus, Acts xx. 4. Histories also speak of the name of Quintus, and Sextus, &c.

24 ᵃ The grace of our Lord Jesus Christ *be* with you all. Amen.

a ver. 20.
1 Thes. 5. 28.

These words are the very same which you had, ver. 20, only the word *all* is added. Some have thought, that the former was written with the hand of Tertius, the scribe or notary, and this with the apostle's own hand. He seems to be like a loving and tender father, who bids his children farewell once and again; and being loth to leave them, returns a second and a third time to discourse with them.

538

ROMANS XVI

^b Eph. 3. 20.
1 Thess. 3. 13.
2 Thess. 2.
17. & 3. 3.
Jude 24.
c ch. 2. 16.
d Eph. 1. 9.
& 3. 3, 4, 5.
Col. 1. 27.
e 1 Cor. 2. 7.
Eph. 3. 5, 9.
Col. 1. 26.

25 Now ^bto him that is of power to stablish you ^caccording to my Gospel, and the preaching of Jesus Christ, ^daccording to the revelation of the mystery, ^ewhich was kept secret since the world began,

He concludes all with an excellent doxology; wherein, first, he describes God, and then he ascribes eternal glory to him. He describes him by two of his attributes or perfections: the first is his *power;* He is able to establish you; i. e. in grace and in truth; to keep you from falling into sin and into error. The Scripture often attributes our establishment unto God: see 1 Thess. iii. 13; 2 Thess. ii. 17; iii. 3; 1 Pet. v. 10. Our own weakness and Satan's power are such, that unless God did establish us, we should soon totter and fall: see chap. xiv. 4, and the notes there. Our establishment is further amplified by the instrumental cause thereof, which is the *gospel;* touching which, several things are here to be noted. First, He calls it *my gospel,* because he was the preacher and publisher thereof: see chap. ii. 16, and the notes there. Secondly, he calls it *the preaching of Jesus Christ:* which may be taken actively, for the preaching of our Lord himself; so the doctrine of salvation is called, the word that was *spoken by the Lord,* Heb. ii. 3: see Matt. iv. 23; ix. 35. Or rather passively, for the gospel which was preached concerning Jesus Christ: see chap. i. 1, 3, and the notes there. Thirdly, He calls it a *mystery, which was kept secret since the world began, but now is made manifest:* see parallel places, 1 Cor. ii. 7; Eph. iii. 9; Col. i. 26. Some restrain this to the calling of the Gentiles; but it is better understood of the whole doctrine of the gospel, concerning the Trinity, the incarnation of the Son of God, &c., which, although it was in some sort made known under the Old Testament, yet, in respect of the present light and revelation, it was a hidden *mystery.*

f Eph. 1. 9.
2 Tim. 1. 10.
Tit. 1. 2, 3.
1 Pet. 1. 20.

26 But ^fnow is made manifest, and by the Scriptures of the prophets, according to the commandment of the everlasting God, made known to all nations for ^gthe obedience of faith:

g Acts 6. 7.
ch. 1. 5.
& 15. 18.

Concerning the *revelation* of this *mystery,* four things are further recorded: 1. The means whereby it was made known; viz. *the Scriptures of the prophets;* see Acts x. 43; xvi. 32; xxviii. 23. 2. The authority by which it was made known; *the commandment of the everlasting God.* 3. The persons to whom it was made known; the Gentiles, or the inhabitants of *all nations.* 4. The end for which it was made known; viz. *for the obedience of faith;* i. e. that it may be believed and obeyed: see chap. i. 5; xv. 18.

27 To ^hGod only wise, *be* glory through Jesus Christ for ever. Amen.

h 1 Tim. 1.
17. & 6. 16.
Jude 25.

The second attribute in the description of God, is his wisdom; he is said to be *wise,* and *only wise.* See the like, 1 Tim. i. 17; Jude 25. So he is said to be *only true,* John xvii. 3, and to be *the only Potentate,* 1 Tim. vi. 15, and *only* to have *immortality,* 1 Tim. vi. 16. And this doth not exclude the wisdom of the Son, and of the Holy Spirit, but the wisdom of the creatures. He is said to be *only wise,* because none is as wise as he, and all the wisdom of others is from him; the wisdom of men and angels is but a ray from his light. Again, he is said to be *only wise,* because he is originally wise; his wisdom is of himself; yea, his wisdom is himself. *Be glory through Jesus Christ for ever:* here he ascribes eternal glory to God. You had the same before, chap. xi. 36. Only here is added, *through Jesus Christ,* to show that our praise and thanksgiving is accepted of God through him: see chap. i. 7; Eph. iii. 20, 21. *Amen:* this word is six times before used in this Epistle; chap. i. 25; ix. 5; xi. 36; xv. 33; xvi. 20, 24. It is a Hebrew word, but retained in all languages. It cannot be translated without losing much of its weight. It may be taken three ways: 1. As a name, and so it is a name of Christ, Rev. iii. 14. 2. As an adverb; so it is used in the beginning of speech, and signifies verily; or in the end of speech, and so it notes assent. Therefore it was used of old by the Jews, not only at prayer, but at all the sermons and expositions of their rabbins, to testify that they assented and agreed to all that they taught: see 1 Cor. xiv. 16. 3. As a verb; and so it is as much as, So be it, having the nature of a prayer: hence Jeremiah said *Amen* to the prophecy of Hananiah, though false, concerning the sudden return from the Babylonish captivity, to show how earnestly he desired it might be so, Jer. xxviii. 6.

¶ Written to the Romans from Corinthus, *and sent* by Phebe servant of the church at Cenchrea.

This was not added by the apostle Paul, nor by Tertius his amanuensis, but by a later and unknown hand; yet there is nothing in the Epistle itself, nor in any ancient or modern writer, that may induce us to question the verity thereof.

THE FIRST EPISTLE OF PAUL THE APOSTLE

TO THE

CORINTHIANS

THE ARGUMENT

CORINTH (the inhabitants of which are called Corinthians) was an eminent city of Achaia, (that Achaia which is now called the Morea,) and was situated on an isthmus, or neck of land, betwixt the Ægean and Ionian Seas; so was very convenient for merchandise, and by merchandise came to great riches, which gave them great temptations to luxury, drunkenness, whoredom, &c. They were very infamous for the latter, as we read in writers, and grown to that impudence, that they made the increase of harlots a part of their prayers to their idols, and made the bringing of harlots into the city a part of their vows. Lais was a harlot amongst them, very famous in civil history. And as pride usually attendeth wealth, so they also were a people very proud and puffed up. They were also anciently famous for pagan learning, and had amongst them Stoics and Epicureans, who laughed at the resurrection of the body, and looked upon incest, adultery, and fornication, as very venial things, if at all unlawful. We read of Paul's first coming thither from Athens, Acts xviii. 1, where, ver. 11, he continued eighteen months; there he converted Crispus, ver. 8, and Sosthenes, and many believed and were baptized. Paul went from thence to Ephesus, ver. 18, 19. To the church thus planted at Corinth Paul writeth this Epistle, at what time is not certain; but he is thought to have written it from Ephesus, whither he came, Acts xix. 1, the second time, and, as appears from ver. 10, was going and coming to and from that city between two and three years. The occasion of his writing this Epistle will appear to any who consideringly reads it. He had heard from some who were *of the house of Chloe,* chap. i. 11, of factions and contentions that were amongst them, and had heard it reported that they suffered an incestuous person to abide in their communion, chap. v. 1. They had also written to him for his resolution in several cases and questions about marriage, divorce, &c. He had also heard of several disorders amongst them relating to their communion in the Lord's supper, and of some amongst them who denied the resurrection. For the allaying of these heats, and quieting their divisions, and for the direction of them in those cases about which they wrote to him, and the setting them right in the doctrine of the resurrection, and directing them in the true and profitable use of their gifts, and in the right celebration of the Lord's supper, and the quickening the exercise of their charity, he writes this Epistle; which is supposed to be placed in our Bibles next to the Epistle to the Romans, (though plainly written in order of time before,) because that as that Epistle most fully discourseth the doctrine of justification, so this most fully resolves questions concerning church order and government. It is a book of holy writ concerning the Divine authority of which there was never any doubt, nor hath any portion of holy writ (for the quantity of it) a greater variety of matter, nor more of those δυσνόητα, *things hard to be understood,* which St. Peter (2 Epist. iii. 16) tells us are in this apostle's Epistles; the difficulty of which much ariseth from our ignorance of some rites used in the primitive church, but long since disused, and the usages of that country different from ours.

CHAP. I

After saluting the church at Corinth, 1—3, *and thanking God for his grace toward them,* 4—9, *Paul exhorteth them to unity,* 10, *and reproveth their dissensions,* 11—16. *The plain doctrine of the gospel, how foolish soever in the eyes of the world, is the power and wisdom of God to the salvation of believers,* 17—25. *God, to take away human boasting, hath not called the wise, the mighty, the noble; but the foolish, the weak, the despised among men,* 26—29. *Christ is our wisdom, righteousness, sanctification, and redemption,* 30, 31.

A. D. 59.
a Rom. 1. 1.
b 2 Cor. 1. 1.
Eph. 1. 1.
Col. 1. 1.
c Acts 18. 17.

PAUL, ᵃcalled *to be* an apostle of Jesus Christ ᵇthrough the will of God, and ᶜSosthenes our brother,

Paul, called to be an apostle of Jesus Christ: our common custom is to subscribe our name to the bottom of our letters; it seems by the apostolical Epistles, that their fashion was otherwise: he elsewhere telleth us, that it was his *token in every epistle,* which makes some doubt, whether that to the Hebrews was wrote by him; but others think it is there concealed, for the particular spite the Jews had to him. He had the name of Saul as well as Paul, as we read, Acts vii. 58; ix. 1: whether he had two names, (as many of the Jews had,) or Saul was the name by which he was called before his conversion, and Paul his name after he was converted, (for Paul is a Roman name, nor do we read that after his conversion he was ever called by the name of Saul,) is not worth our disputing. He was a man of Tarsus in Cilicia, by his nation a Jew, both by father and mother; an Hebrew of the Hebrews, of the tribe of Benjamin, a Pharisee, bred up at the feet of Gamaliel, one of their great doctors; he was also citizen of Rome, as himself tells us, Acts xxi. 39; xxii. 3, 27; Phil. iii. 5; by his trade a tent-maker, Acts xviii. 3; a great zealot for the Jewish ceremonies and law, and upon that score a great persecutor, consenting to the death of Stephen, and breathing out threatenings against Christians. Of his miraculous conversion we read, Acts ix., as also of his being called to be an apostle, not one of those first sent out by Christ, but yet called: he gives king Agrippa a full account of his calling, Acts xxvi. 12—19. *Through the will of God;* so as he was an apostle by *the will of God,* God's special revelation from heaven: he did not thrust himself into the employment, but was sent of God in an extraordinary manner; not only mediately, (as all ministers are,) but by an immediate call and mission. *And Sosthenes our brother:* in the salutation prefixed to this Epistle, he joineth *Sosthenes,* whom he calls his *brother.* Of this Sosthenes we read, Acts xviii. 17; he was a *chief ruler of the synagogue,* but converted to Christianity; Paul disdaineth not to call him his *brother.*

d Jude 1.
e John 17. 19.
Acts 15. 9.
f Rom. 1. 7.
2 Tim. 1. 9
g Acts 9. 14, 21. & 22. 16.
2 Tim. 2. 22.
h ch. 8. 6.
i Rom. 3. 22.
& 10. 12.

2 Unto the church of God which is at Corinth, ᵈto them that ᵉare sanctified in Christ Jesus, ᶠcalled *to be* saints, with all that in every place ᵍcall upon the name of Jesus Christ ʰour Lord, ⁱboth their's and our's:

Unto the church of God which is at Corinth; unto those in Corinth who having received the doctrine of the gospel, and owned Jesus Christ as their Saviour, were united in one ecclesiastical body for the worship of God, and communion one with another. Corinth was a famous city in Achaia, (which Achaia was joined to Greece by a neck of land betwixt the Ægean and Ionian Seas,) it grew the most famous mart of all Greece. Paul came thither from Athens, Acts xviii. 1. *Crispus, the chief ruler of the synagogue there, believed,* upon Paul's preaching; so did *many Corinthians, and were baptized,* ver. 9. He stayed there eighteen months, ver. 11; there Sosthenes (mentioned ver. 1) was converted; from thence Paul went to Ephesus, ver. 19. These believers were those here called *the church of God at Corinth,* to whom he writes this Epistle (as it should seem from chap. xvi. 8) from Ephesus, where Paul stayed three years, Acts xx. 31. The members of this church the apostle calleth such *as are sanctified in Christ Jesus, called to be saints:* whether by the term the apostle meaneth only such as by the preaching of the gospel were separated from the heathens at Corinth, and professed faith in Christ, (as, Acts xv. 9, the apostle saith the Gentiles' hearts were purified by faith,) or such in Corinth as were really regenerated, and had their hearts renewed and changed, is not easy to determine: both of them are saints by calling; the former are called externally by the preaching of the gospel, the other internally and effectually by the operation of the Spirit of grace. It is most probable, that St. Paul intended this Epistle for the whole body of those that professed the Christian religion in Corinth, though in writing of it he had a more special respect to those who were truly sanctified in Christ by the renewing of the Holy Ghost. Nor doth Paul only respect those that lived in Corinth, but he directs his Epistle to all those who in any place of Achaia called *upon the name of Jesus Christ,* whom he calleth their Lord, and *our Lord:* which is an eminent place to prove the Divine nature of Christ; he is not only called *our Lord,* our common Lord, but he is made the object of invocation and Divine worship: and it teacheth us, that none but such as call upon the name of Jesus Christ our Lord, are fit matter for a gospel church; which both excludes such as deny the Godhead of Christ, and such as live without God in the world, without performance of religious homage to God the Father and the Lord Jesus Christ, and owning him as their Lord.

k Rom. 1. 7.
2 Cor. 1. 2.
Eph. 1. 2.
1 Pet. 1. 2.

3 ᵏGrace *be* unto you, and peace, from God our Father, and *from* the Lord Jesus Christ.

This is the common salutation in all Paul's Epistles, only in one or two *mercy* is also added. *Grace* signifies free love. *Peace* signifies either a reconciliation with God, or brotherly love and unity each with other: see the notes on Rom. i. 7. The apostle wisheth them spiritual blessings, and the greatest spiritual blessings, *grace and peace,* and that not from and with men, but *from God our Father, and the Lord Jesus Christ.*

l Rom. 1. 8.

4 ˡI thank my God always on your behalf, for the grace of God which is given you by Jesus Christ;

Lest his former salutation should be misapprehended by them, as signifying that he thought they were without grace, he here cleareth his meaning by blessing God for that grace which they had received: but no man hath so much grace, but he is still capable of more, and stands in need of further influences; therefore, as he here blesseth God for the grace of God, which they by Jesus Christ received; so he before prayed for *grace and peace* for them, *from God our Father, and from the Lord Jesus Christ*. Christ is both the Author and Finisher of our faith, he giveth both to will and to do. The beginnings, increases, and finishings of grace are all from him. Grace is indeed from God the Father, but by Jesus Christ; it floweth from him who is Love, but it is through his Well-beloved. No man hath the love of God, but by and through Jesus Christ.

5 That in every thing ye are enriched by him, ᵐin all utterance, and *in* all knowledge;

^{m ch. 12. 8.}
^{2 Cor. 8. 7.}

In every thing; in every grace and in every good gift, (for he is manifestly speaking of spiritual things,) so as this general particle must not be extended to the things of this life, but restrained either to spiritual gifts, or spiritual, sanctifying habits. Thus we read of *the riches of grace*, Eph. i. 7, and of *the riches of Christ*, Eph. iii. 8: nor is the metaphor improper, whether we consider *riches* as signifying plenty or abundance, or that which accommodateth a man in this life, and is fitted to men's wants, to give them a supply. *In all utterance*; the word may be translated, in every thing, or, in all speech; but the first having been said before, it seems more proper here to translate it, in all word or speech, or *in all utterance*, as we translate it. If it be taken in the first sense, the gospel is by it understood, the doctrine of the gospel preached amongst them by Paul and Apollos, who *preached among the Gentiles the riches of Christ*, Eph. iii. 8. If we interpret it *utterance*, which our translators prefer, it signifies an ability to utter that knowledge which God hath given us, to the glory of God and the good of others, either in prayer or spiritual discourses. *And in all knowledge*: some by *knowledge* here understand the gift of prophecy; but it more properly signifies the ability God had given them to comprehend in their understanding the mysteries of the gospel, the great and deep things of God. The apostle blesseth God both for the illumination of their minds by the ministry of the gospel, so as they knew the things of God, and also for the ability which God had given them to communicate this their knowledge to others.

6 Even as ⁿthe testimony of Christ was confirmed in you:

^{n ch. 2. 1.}
^{2 Tim. 1. 8.}
^{Rev. 1. 2.}

By which *knowledge* and *utterance the testimony of Christ*, that is, the gospel, which containeth both the testimony which Christ had given of himself, and which the apostles had given concerning Christ; (the gospel is called *the testimony of God*, chap. ii. 1; 2 Tim. i. 8;) others understand the gifts of the Spirit (for the Spirit is one of the witnesses upon earth, 1 John v. 8); *was confirmed in you*; by the miraculous operations wrought by the apostles, as some think; but the way of confirmation here spoken of by the apostle seemeth rather to be understood of their *knowledge* and *utterance*. The gospel, and the doctrine of it, and the mission of the Holy Spirit, were confirmed to them and to the world by the knowledge which God had given the apostles, and these Corinthians, of the great things of God; and their ability to communicate this knowledge unto others, for the honour of God, and the good of others.

7 So that ye come behind in no gift; ᵒwaiting for the †coming of our Lord Jesus Christ:

^{o Phil. 3. 20.}
^{Tit. 2. 13.}
^{2 Pet. 3. 12.}
^{†Gr. revelation.}
^{Col. 3. 4.}

Not that every one of them was filled with all the gifts of the blessed Spirit; but one excelled in one gift, another excelled in another, as the apostle expounds himself, chap. xii. 7, 8; neither doth the apostle assert them perfect in their gifts, but saith that they came behind-hand, or were defective, in no gift; but were all *waiting for the* second *coming of the Lord Jesus Christ* to judgment, of which he mindeth them, to encourage them to go on as they had began.

8 ᵖWho shall also confirm you unto the end, ᑫ*that ye may be* blameless in the day of our Lord Jesus Christ.

^{p 1 Thess. 3. 13.}
^{q Col. 1. 22.}
^{1 Thes. 5.23.}

Which *Lord Jesus Christ*, (mentioned immediately before,) or which *God* who *is faithful*, (mentioned immediately after, ver. 9,) *shall confirm* your habits of grace *unto the end*, approving himself the finisher of your faith (you being not wanting in your duty and endeavour): so as either you shall not fall, or at least not totally and finally, but so as you shall rise again, and appear in the day of our Lord Jesus without blame, so as he will accept you as if you had never sinned against him.

9 ʳGod *is* faithful, by whom ye were called unto ˢthe fellowship of his Son Jesus Christ our Lord.

^{r Is. 49. 7.}
^{ch. 10. 13.}
^{1 Thes. 5.24.}
^{2 Thes. 3. 3.}
^{Heb. 10. 23.}
^{s John 15. 4. & 17. 21. 1 John 1. 3. & 4. 13.}

God is faithful: faithfulness is the same with veracity or truth to a man's word, which renders a person fit to be credited. It is a great attribute of God, chap. x. 13; 1 Thess. v. 24. This implieth promises of God for the perseverance of believers, of which there are many to be found in holy writ. But these promises concern not all, but such only whom God hath chosen out of the world, calling them to a communion with Christ, which necessarily supposeth union with him. So as here is another argument to confirm them that God would keep them to the end, so as they should be blameless in the day of Christ; because God had called them into that state of grace wherein they were, and would not leave his work in them imperfect; he had called them *unto the fellowship of Jesus Christ*; see 1 John i. 3; into a state of friendship with Christ, and into a state of union with him, into such a state as he would daily by his Spirit be communicating the blessed influences of his grace unto them.

10 Now I beseech you, brethren, by the name of our Lord Jesus Christ, ᵗthat ye all speak the same thing, and *that* there be no † divisions among you; but *that* ye be perfectly joined together in the same mind and in the same judgment.

^{t Rom. 12. 16. & 15. 5.}
^{2 Cor. 13. 11.}
^{Phil. 2. 2.}
^{& 3. 16.}
^{1 Pet. 3. 8,}
^{†Gr. schisms,}
^{ch. 11. 18.}

By the name of our Lord Jesus Christ, is as much as, by Christ, by the authority of Christ, for this is his will; or, by the love which you bear to the Lord Jesus Christ, who hath so often recommended to you peace with, and brotherly love towards, one another. *That ye all speak the same thing*; that in matters of doctrine you all *speak the same thing* (for it is capable of no other sense); and that you neither be divided in sentiments or opinions, nor yet in affection, *that there may be no divisions among you;* which is also further evidenced by the last phrase, being *joined together in the same mind and in the same judgment*. A union in affection is the necessary and indispensable duty of all those that are the disciples of Christ, and such a duty as not only concerns Christians of the same nation, with relation one to another, but also Christians of all nations, and may be attained, if by our lusts we do not hinder it. A union in opinion, as to the fundamental truths of religion, is (though not so easy, yet) what the church of God hath in a great measure arrived at. But for a union in every particular proposition of truth, is not a thing to be expected, though we all are to labour for it: God hath neither given unto all the same means, nor the same natural capacities.

11 For it hath been declared unto me of you, my brethren, by them *which are of the house* of Chloe, that there are contentions among you.

The apostle cometh to show one reason, as why he wrote to them, so also why in the preceding verse he so zealously pressed unity upon them, because of an information he had received from some of the family of Chloe; for it is far more probable that Chloe was the name of a person, head of a family in Corinth, than of a city or town. *There are contentions among you:* what their divisions were about, the next verses will tell us.

12 Now this I say, ᵘthat every one of you saith, I am of Paul; and I of ˣApollos; and I of ʸCephas; and I of Christ.

^{u ch. 3. 4.}
^{x Acts 18. 24.}
^{& 19. 1.}
^{ch. 16. 12.}
^{y John 1. 42.}

Every one here signifieth no more than many of you, or several of you; so chap. xiv. 26: from whence, those that think they have such a mighty argument from Heb. ii. 9, where is the same particle, to prove Christ's dying for all individuals, may undeceive themselves, and find that they have need of better arguments to prove their assertion. *I*

I. CORINTHIANS I

am of Paul, and I of Apollos, and I of Cephas, and I of Christ: we may from hence observe, that the divisions amongst the Corinthians were not in matters of faith, but occasioned from their having men's persons in admiration. This was probably caused either from God's making of *Paul* the instrument of some of their conversion, *Apollos* the instrument of others' conversion, and *Peter* the instrument of others', or else from the difference of their gifts. Of this Apollos we read, Acts xviii. 24; he was a *Jew* of *Alexandria*, who (as may be seen there, ver. 28) *mightily convinced the Jews, and that publicly*, and probably was as useful to the Corinthians. One minister of Christ may be justly preferred to another. We ought to honour those most whom God most honoureth, either by a more plentiful giving out of his Spirit, or by a more plentiful success upon their labours; but we ought not so far to appropriate any ministers to ourselves, as for them to despise others. We are not bound to make every minister our pastor, but we are bound to have a just respect for every minister, who by his doctrine and holy life answereth his profession and holy calling.

z 2 Cor. 11. 4. Eph. 4. 5.

13 Is Christ divided? was Paul crucified for you? or were ye baptized in the name of Paul?

How came these parties? there is but one Christ, but one that was crucified for you, but one into whose name, into a faith in whom, and a profession of whom, you were baptized. Peter baptized you into the name of Christ, so did I; I did not list those whom I baptized under any banner of my own, but under Christ's banner. The Head is but one, and the body ought not to be divided.

a Acts 18. 8. b Rom. 16. 23.

14 I thank God that I baptized none of you, but [a]Crispus and [b]Gaius;

Concerning the apostle's baptizing Crispus we read, Acts xviii. 8; he was *the chief ruler of the synagogue* of the Jews: why Paul thanks God that he baptized not many, he tells us, ver. 15.

15 Lest any should say that I had baptized in mine own name.

Because by that providence of God it so fell out, that very few of them could pretend any such thing, as that he had baptized any in his own name.

c ch. 16. 15, 17.

16 And I baptized also the houshold of [c]Stephanas: besides, I know not whether I baptized any other.

He correcteth himself, remembering that he also *baptized the household of Stephanas*, which (chap. xvi. 15) he calleth *the first-fruits of Achaia*, a family that had *addicted themselves to the ministry of the saints. Besides, I know not whether I baptized any other;* he did not remember that he had baptized any more at Corinth, though it is very probable he had baptized many more in other parts of the world, where he had been travelling.

d ch. 2. 1, 4, 13. 2 Pet. 1. 16. || Or, *speech*.

17 For Christ sent me not to baptize, but to preach the Gospel: [d]not with wisdom of || words, lest the cross of Christ should be made of none effect.

For Christ sent me not to baptize, but to preach the Gospel; baptism was not his principal work, not the main business for which Paul was sent; it was his work, otherwise he would not have baptized Crispus, and Gaius, or the household of Stephanas, but preaching was his principal work. It is very probable others (besides the apostles) baptized. It is hard to conceive how three thousand should in a day be added to the church, if Peter had baptized them all, Acts ii. 41. The apostle goes on, telling us how he preached the gospel, and thereby instructing all faithful ministers how they ought to preach. *Not with wisdom of words*, or speech. *Wisdom of words* must signify either what we call rhetoric, or logic, delivering the mysteries of the gospel in lofty, tunable expressions, or going about to evidence them from rational demonstrations and arguments. This was the way (he saith) to have taken away all authority from the doctrine of the cross of Christ: Divine faith being nothing else but the soul's assent to the Divine revelation because it is such, is not furthered, but hindered, by the arguing the object of it from the principles of reason, and the colouring of it with high-flown words and trim phrases. There is a decent expression to be used in the communicating the will of God unto men; but we must take heed that we do not diminish the authority of God's revealed will, either by puerile flourishings of words, or philosophical argumentation.

18 For the preaching of the cross is to [e]them that perish [f]foolishness; but unto us [g]which are saved it is the [h]power of God.

e 2 Cor. 2. 15. f Acts 17. 18. ch. 2. 14. g eh. 15. 2. h Rom. 1. 16. ver. 24.

For the preaching of the cross is to them that perish foolishness: I know (saith the apostle) that plain discourses about a Christ crucified are to some persons foolish things, and accounted canting; but to whom are they so? to those who, if they be not some that shall perish eternally, yet are some of those who at present are in a perishing estate; these indeed count sermons of Christ silly, foolish things. *But unto us which are saved it is the power of God;* but to those who shall be eternally saved, and are at present in the true road to eternal life and salvation, it is, that is, the preaching of the gospel is, that institution of God by which he showeth his power in the salvation of those who shall be saved. The apostle saith the same, Rom. i. 16.

19 For it is written, [i]I will destroy the wisdom of the wise, and will bring to nothing the understanding of the prudent.

i Job 5. 12, 13. Is. 29. 14. Jer. 8. 9.

What Isaiah said of the wise men among the Jews in his time, is applicable to the wise men among the heathen, God will destroy their wisdom, and make their understanding appear to be no better than foolishness. So as it is not at all to be admired, if the philosophers of this world count the gospel, and the preaching of it, foolishness; the taking away the wisdom and understanding of men worldly wise, is but an ordinary dispensation of God's providence, no more than God threatened to do in Isaiah's time to the men of that generation.

20 [k]Where *is* the wise? where *is* the scribe? where *is* the disputer of this world? [l]hath not God made foolish the wisdom of this world?

k Is. 33. 18. l Job 12. 17, 20, 24. Is. 44. 25. Rom. 1. 22.

Where is the wise? where is the scribe? he alludeth again to that, Isa. xxxiii. 18, *Where is the scribe? where is the receiver?* Where are the wise men amongst the heathens? where are the scribes, the learned men in the law, amongst the Jews? *Where is the disputer of this world?* where are those amongst Jews or Gentiles that are the great inquirers into the reasons and natures of things, and manage debates and disputes about them? They understand nothing of the mysteries of the gospel, or the way of salvation, which God holds out to the world in and through Jesus Christ. Or, where are they? what have they done by all their philosophy and moral doctrine, as to the turning of men from sin unto God, from ways of iniquity unto ways of righteousness, in comparison of what we, the ministers of Christ, have done by preaching the doctrine of the gospel, and the cross of Christ? *Hath not God made foolish the wisdom of this world?* do not you see how God hath fooled the wisdom of the world? making it to appear vain and contemptible, and of no use, as to the saving of men's souls; making choice of none of their doctors and great rabbis, to carry that doctrine abroad in the world; and convincing men that, without faith in Christ, all that can be learned from them will be of no avail to the soul.

21 [m]For after that in the wisdom of God the world by wisdom knew not God, it pleased God by the foolishness of preaching to save them that believe.

m Rom. 1. 20, 21, 28. See Matt. 11. 25. Luke 10. 21.

For after that in the wisdom of God: some here, by *the wisdom of God*, understand Jesus Christ, and make the sense thus: When he who is the Wisdom of God came and preached to the world. Others understand the gospel, which is so called, ver. 24, and chap. ii. 7. But I take *the wisdom of God* in this text to signify the wise administrations of Divine Providence in the government of the world to his wise ends. *The world by wisdom knew not God;* the unregenerate part of the world would not come to a knowledge of and an acquaintance with God, in that way whereby he chose to reveal himself in and through Jesus Christ,

VOL. III—18

as to which they were hindered by their own reasonings and knowledge, and apprehended skill in things, and capacity to comprehend them. *It pleased God by the foolishness of preaching to save them that believe;* it pleased God to institute the great ordinance of preaching the gospel, which they count *foolishness,* as the sacred means by which he would bring all those that give credit to the revelation of it, and receive Christ held forth in it, to eternal life and salvation.

22 For the ⁿJews require a sign, and the Greeks seek after wisdom:

The Jews were not without some true Divine revelation, and owned the true God, and only desired some miraculous operation from Christ, Matt. xii. 38; John iv. 48, to confirm them that Christ was sent from God: without signs and wonders they would not believe; giving no credit at all to the words of Christ. And *the Greeks,* (by whom the apostle understands the Gentiles,) especially the more learned part of them, (for Greece was at this time very famous for human literature,) they sought after the demonstration of all things from natural causes and rational arguments, and despised every thing which could not so be made out unto them.

23 But we preach Christ crucified, °unto the Jews a stumblingblock, and unto the Greeks ᵖfoolishness;

But we preach Christ crucified; we that are the ministers of Christ, come and preach to them, that there was one hanged upon a cross at Jerusalem, who is the Saviour of the world, and was not cut off for his own sins, but for the sins of his people. *Unto the Jews a stumblingblock;* the Jews are stumbled at this, looking for a Messiah that should be a great temporal Prince; and besides, accounting it an ignominious thing to believe in one as their Saviour whom they had caused to be crucified. *And unto the Greeks foolishness;* and the Greeks, the most learned among the Gentiles, look upon it as a foolish, idle story, that one who was and is God blessed for ever, should be crucified.

24 But unto them which are called, both Jews and Greeks, Christ ᑫthe power of God, and ʳthe wisdom of God.

Blessed be God, Christ is not to all the Jews a stumblingblock, nor to all the Greeks is he foolishness; for to so many of them as *are called,* (not by the external call of the gospel, but only by the internal call and effectual operation of the Spirit,) let them be of one nation or another, by their country, Jews or pagans, Christ is so far from being foolishness, that Christ, and the doctrine of the gospel, appear to them *the power of God, and the wisdom of God.*

25 Because the foolishness of God is wiser than men; and the weakness of God is stronger than men.

The foolishness of God is wiser than men; the least things that are the products of the wisdom of God, or the contrivance of God for man's salvation, which the sinful and silly world calls *foolishness,* are infinitely more wise, and have more wisdom in them, than the wisest imaginations, counsels, and contrivances of men. *And the weakness of God is stronger than men;* and those things and means which God hath instituted in order to an end, have in them more virtue, power, and efficacy in order to the production of God's intended effects, than any such means as appear to men's eyes of reason to have the greatest strength, virtue, and efficacy. Whence we may observe, that the efficacy of preaching for the changing and converting souls, dependeth upon the efficacy of God working in and by that holy institution, which usually attendeth the ministry of those who are not only called and sent out by men, but by God, being fitted for their work, and faithfully discharging of it.

26 For ye see your calling, brethren, how that ˢnot many wise men after the flesh, not many mighty, not many noble, *are called:*

To prove that this is the method of Divine Providence, to make use of seemingly infirm and weak means to produce his great effects, you need not look further than yourselves; look upon the whole body of your church at Corinth, it is not made up of many that have a reputation for the wise men or the noble men of your city. Some indeed were such; Crispus, the ruler of the synagogue, was converted, and Sosthenes; but the generality were men of very ordinary repute.

27 But ᵗGod hath chosen the foolish things of the world to confound the wise; and God hath chosen the weak things of the world to confound the things which are mighty;

God hath even amongst you chosen persons that are in the account of the world as foolish things, to put the wise to shame; and persons of weak esteem, to confound those that are mighty in the repute of the world.

28 And base things of the world, and things which are despised, hath God chosen, *yea,* and ᵘthings which are not, ˣto bring to nought things that are:

Things which are not in the world's account, *to bring to nought things which are* in high esteem.

29 ʸThat no flesh should glory in his presence.

And God doth this in infinite wisdom, consulting his own honour and glory, that none might say, that God hath chosen them because they were nobler born, or in higher repute and esteem in the world, than others, but that the freeness of Divine grace might be seen in all God's acts of grace.

30 But of him are ye in Christ Jesus, who of God is made unto us ᶻwisdom, and ᵃrighteousness, and ᵇsanctification, and ᶜredemption:

But of him are ye in Christ Jesus; of his grace ye are implanted into Christ, and believe in him. You are *of him,* not by creation only, as all creatures are, but by redemption and regeneration, which is *in Christ Jesus, who of God is made unto us wisdom;* the principal means by which we come to the knowledge of God, and an acquaintance with his will; for he *is the image of the invisible God,* Col. i. 15. *The brightness of his* Father's *glory, and the express image of his person,* Heb. i. 3. *God hath shined in our hearts, to give the light of the knowledge of the glory of God in the face of Jesus Christ,* 2 Cor. iv. 6. So that *he who hath seen him, hath seen the Father,* John xiv. 9. *All the treasures of wisdom and knowledge are hid in him,* Col. ii. 3. And *no man knoweth the Father, save the Son, and he to whomsoever the Son will reveal him,* Matt. xi. 27. Thus, though God destroyed the wisdom of the wise, yet the Corinthians were not without wisdom; for God had made Christ to them *wisdom,* both causally, being the author of wisdom to them; and objectively, their wisdom lay in their knowledge of him, and in a fellowship and communion with him. And whereas they wanted a righteousness in which they might stand before God justified and accepted, God had also made Christ to them *righteousness: Sending his own Son in the likeness of sinful flesh, and for sin, condemned sin in the flesh; that the righteousness of the law might be fulfilled in us,* Rom. viii. 3, 4. *And sanctification* also, believers being renewed and sanctified by his Spirit. *And* he is also made *redemption:* where by re*demption* is meant *the redemption of the body,* mentioned Rom. viii. 23; so as *redemption* here signifies the same with resurrection of the body. Christ is *the resurrection, and the life,* John xi. 25.

31 That, according as it is written, ᵈHe that glorieth, let him glory in the Lord.

God doth this, or hath done this, for this end, that man should have nothing to glory in, neither wisdom, nor righteousness, nor sanctification, nor redemption, but should *glory in the Lord;* acknowledging that whatsoever wisdom, righteousness, or holiness he hath, it is all from God, in and through the Lord Jesus Christ.

CHAP. II

Paul declareth that he used not human learning and eloquence in preaching the gospel to his converts, that their faith, being built on the testimony of the Spirit, and on miracles, might be solely ascribed to God, 1—5. The gospel doth contain God's wise, but secret, counsel for bringing men to glory; which no natural abilities could discover, but the Spirit of God only, by which it was revealed to the apostles, 6—13. Upon this account, both the doctrine and its teachers are held in disesteem by the mere natural man, who is not duly qualified to judge of and discern them, 14—16.

AND I, brethren, when I came to you, ^acame not with excellency of speech or of wisdom, declaring unto you ^bthe testimony of God.

a ch. 1. 17. ver. 4, 13. 2 Cor. 10. 10. & 11. 6. b ch. 1. 6.

It should seem by the apostle's so often declaring against that vanity, that even that age much admired a style, and ministers in sacred things delivering their minds, not in a mere decent, but in a lofty, high-flown phrase; and that they vilified St. Paul, because his phrase did not so tickle their ears. The apostle had declared against this, chap. i. 17; there he called it the *wisdom of words*; here he calls it an *excellency of speech*: ver. 4, the *enticing words of man's wisdom*: chap. iv. 19, *the speech of them which are puffed up*; puffed up with conceits of their own parts and abilities. St. Paul declares, that this was not his way of preaching, he came to declare to them the gospel, which he calleth *the testimony of God*: this needed no fine words, and excellent phrase and language, to set it forth.

2 For I determined not to know any thing among you, ^csave Jesus Christ, and him crucified.

c Gal. 6. 14. Phil. 3. 8.

I did not value myself upon any piece of knowledge I had attained, saving only that of *Christ, and him crucified*; or, I determined with myself to carry myself amongst you, as if I knew nothing of arts, or sciences, or languages, but only *Christ, and him crucified*; not to make any thing else the subject of my public discourses. I was acquainted with the Jewish law, rites, and traditions, with the heathen poets and philosophers; I troubled you with none of these in my pulpit discourses; my whole business was to open to you the mysteries of the gospel, and to bring you to a knowledge of and an acquaintance with Jesus Christ; this was my end, and the means I used were proportionable to it.

3 And ^dI was with you ^ein weakness, and in fear, and in much trembling.

d Acts 18. 1, 6, 12. e 2 Cor. 4. 7. & 10. 1, 10. & 11. 30. & 12. 5, 9. Gal. 4. 13.

Either in a weakness of style, I used a plain, low, intelligible style, studying rather to be understood by all than admired by any. Or in weakness of state, in a mean and low condition; for we read, Acts xviii. 3, that he wrought with his hands at Corinth; so Acts xx. 34. Or it may be, in a weak state of body; or it may be he means humbleness of mind and modesty, which to worldly eyes looks like a weakness of mind. And in much fear and trembling, either with respect to the Jews, and the danger he was exposed to from them, or with respect to the greatness of his work, lest they should refuse the grace of the gospel, by him brought and offered to them. So as (saith he) you might see that all the work was God's, I but a poor instrument, contemptible with respect to my outward quality, appearing poor and mean, in my phrase and style, and whole behaviour amongst you.

4 And my speech and my preaching ^fwas not with ||enticing words of man's wisdom, ^gbut in demonstration of the Spirit and of power:

f ver. 1. ch. 1. 17. 2 Pet. 1. 16. || Or, *persuasible*. g Rom. 15. 19. 1 Thess. 1. 5.

Either here Paul's *speech and preaching* signify the same thing, (expressed by two words,) or else *speech* referreth to his more private conferences and discourses with them, and *preaching* signifieth the more public acts of his ministry; neither of them was *with* the persuasive or *enticing words of man's wisdom*. What these persuasive words of man's wisdom are, will quickly appear to any that considers there are but two human arts that pretend to any thing of persuading; rhetoric, and logic, or the art of reasoning. Rhetoric persuadeth more weakly, working more upon the affections than upon the understanding and judgment. Logic, or the art of reasoning, more strongly, working upon the understanding and judgment, and teaching men to conclude from connate natural principles. Now, saith Paul, my preaching was neither of these ways. I neither studied neat and fine words and phrases, nor did I make it my work to demonstrate gospel propositions to you from principles of natural reason. *Object.* Ought not then ministers now to use such words? *Answ.* A learned popish writer saith, that "at that time it was the will of God that his ministers should use plain speech; but it is otherwise now; the using of words studiously composed and ordered, being now the ordinary way to persuade others." But, 1. After this rate any thing of the will of God may be evaded; it is but saying, that it was the will of God indeed then, but not now. 2. The thing is false. It was then, as much as now, the ordinary way of persuading to use rhetorical phrases and rational demonstrations. 3. Although now this be the ordinary method of persuading men of learning and capacities, yet for the generality of people it is not so. 4. The apostle's reason holds now as much as ever. It is the way to make Christians' faith stand *in the wisdom of men*, not *in the power of God*. *Object.* Ought then ministers to use no study, but talk whatever comes at their tongue's end, and to use no reason to prove what they say? *Answ.* By no means. 1. It is one thing to study matter, another thing to study words. 2. Nay, it is one thing to study a decency in words, another to study a gaudery of phrase. It is an old and true saying, *Verba sequuntur res*, Words will follow matter, if the preacher be but of ordinary parts. In the study of words we have but two things to attend: (1.) That we speak intelligibly, so as all the people may understand. (2.) That we speak gravely and decently. All other study of words and phrases in a divine is but folly and vanity. 3. We ought to use our reason in our preaching; but reason works two ways: (1.) Either making conclusions from natural and philosophical principles; (2.) Or, from Scriptural principles. We ought to study to conclude as strongly as we can what we say from principles of revelation, comparing spiritual things with spiritual, but not from all natural and philosophical principles; for so we shall conclude, there is no Trinity in the Unity of the Divine Being, because, according to natural principles, three cannot be one, nor one three; and against the resurrection, because there can be no regress from a privation to a habit, &c. 4. Again, it is one thing to use our natural reason, *ex abundanti*, as an auxiliary help to illustrate and confirm what is first confirmed by Divine revelation; another thing to use it as a foundation upon which we build a spiritual conclusion, or as the main proof of it. Paul's preaching was in words intelligible to his hearers, and decent enough, and with reason enough, but not concluding upon natural principles, nor making any proofs of that nature the foundation upon which he built his gospel conclusions. *But in demonstration of the Spirit;* by which Grotius and some others understand miracles, by which the doctrine of the gospel was at first confirmed; but Vorstius and many others better understand by it the Holy Ghost's powerful and inward persuasion of men's minds, of the truth of what was preached by Paul. All ministers' preaching makes propositions of gospel truth appear no more than probable; the Spirit only demonstrates them, working in souls such a persuasion and confirmation of the truth of them, as the soul can no longer deny or dispute, or withstand the conviction of them. *And of power:* by this term also some understand the power of working miracles; but it is much better by others interpreted of that authority, which the word of God preached by Paul had, and preached by faithful ministers still hath, upon the souls and consciences of those that hear it. As it is said, Matt. vii. 29, Christ *taught them as one having authority*. And it is said of Stephen, Acts vi. 10, *They were not able to resist the wisdom and the spirit by which he spake*. So the gospel preached by Paul came to people, *not in word only, but also in power, and in the Holy Ghost, and in much assurance*, 1 Thess. i. 5: and was *quick, and powerful, and sharper than any two-edged sword, piercing even to the dividing asunder of soul and spirit, and of the joints and marrow, and is a discerner of the thoughts and intents of the heart*, Heb. iv. 12.

And thus every faithful minister, with whose labours God goeth along in the conversion of souls, yet preacheth *in the demonstration of the Spirit and of power.* Nor indeed can those miracles, by which Christ and his apostles confirmed the truth of the doctrine of the gospel, though they were a mighty proof, be, in any propriety of speech, called a *demonstration;* which, properly, is a proof in which the mind fully acquiesceth, so that it no longer denieth or disputeth the thing so proved, but gives a firm and full assent to it: the miracles wrought by Christ himself never had that effect; the Pharisees and the generality of the Jews believed not that Christ was the true Messiah and the Son of God, notwithstanding his miracles. Nothing but the inward powerful impression of the Spirit of God, persuading the heart of the truth of gospel principles, can possibly amount to a *demonstration,* bringing the minds of men, though never so judicious and prepared, to a certainty of the thing revealed, and a rest, so as they can no longer deny, resist, dispute, or contradict it. With this Paul's preaching was attended, not to every individual person to whom he preached, but to many, even as many as should be saved: he delivered the doctrine of the gospel freely, plainly, and boldly, not resting upon the force of his rhetoric and persuasive words, nor yet upon the natural force of his reasoning and argumentation; but leaving the demonstration and evidencing of the truth of what he said to the powerful internal impression and persuasion of the holy and blessed Spirit of God, who worketh powerfully.

† Gr. *be.*
h 2 Cor. 4. 7. & 6. 7.

5 That your faith should not †stand in the wisdom of men, but ʰin the power of God.

Faith properly signifieth our assent to a thing that is told us, and because it is told us. If the revelation be from man, it is no more than a human faith. If it be from God, and we believe the thing because God hath revealed it to us, this is a Divine faith. So as indeed it is impossible that a Divine faith should rest in the wisdom of men. If we could make gospel propositions evident to the outward senses, or evident to such principles of reason as are connatural to us, or upon such conclusions as we make upon such principles, yet no assent of this nature could be faith, which is an assent given to a Divine revelation purely because of such revelation. An assent other ways given may be sensible demonstration, or rational demonstration, or knowledge, or opinion; but Divine faith it cannot be, that must be bottomed in the power of God. Nor ought any thing more to be the care of the ministers of the gospel than this, as to call men to believe, so to endeavour that their faith may *not stand in the wisdom of men:* nothing but a human faith can do so. This will show every conscientious minister the vanity of not proving what he saith from holy writ: all other preaching is but either dictating, as if men were to believe what the preacher saith upon his authority; or philosophizing, acting the part of a philosopher or orator at Athens, not the part of a minister of the gospel.

i ch. 14. 20. Eph. 4. 13. Phil. 3. 15. Heb. 5. 14. k ch. 1. 20. & 3. 19. ver. 1, 13. 2 Cor. 1. 12. Jam. 3. 15. l ch. 1. 28.

6 Howbeit we speak wisdom among them ⁱthat are perfect: yet not ᵏthe wisdom of this world, nor of the princes of this world, ˡthat come to nought:

Lest what the apostle had seemed to speak before in defamation of wisdom, should reflect upon the gospel, and give some people occasion to justify against it their impious charge of folly, the apostle here something corrects himself, affirming that he and the rest of the apostles spake *wisdom,* and what would be so judged by such as were *perfect;* not absolutely, for so there is no man perfect, but comparatively, that is, persons who *have their senses exercised to discern* betwixt *good and evil,* Heb. v. 14, or such as are of a true, sound judgment, and are able to discern what is true wisdom. To such, saith the apostle, *we speak wisdom;* and it needs must be so; for wisdom being a habit directing men to use the best means in order to the best end, the salvation of men's souls being the best end, that doctrine which directs the best means in order to it, must necessarily be wisdom, and the purest and highest wisdom. *Yet not the wisdom of this world, nor of the princes of this world, that come to nought;* but, saith he, not what the philosophers, or cunning men, or politicians of the world count wisdom; for all their wisdom is of no significancy at all, in order to the best end, the salvation of men's souls, and it will all vanish, and come to nothing at last.

7 But we speak the wisdom of God in a mystery, *even* the hidden *wisdom,* ᵐ which God ordained before the world unto our glory:

m Rom. 16. 25, 26. Eph. 3. 5, 9. Col. 1. 26. 2 Tim. 1. 9.

But we speak the wisdom of God in a mystery; we preach the gospel, where the righteousness in which alone men can another day appear, and be accepted before God, is revealed from faith to faith. It is indeed a sacred secret, a mystery to many men, but it is *the wisdom of God,* a doctrine directing the best means to the best end of man. *Even the hidden wisdom, which God ordained before the world unto our glory:* it is *hidden wisdom:* it was ordained of God before the world for our glory, the way of salvation for man, which he had from all eternity ordained and decreed; but it lay hidden in the secret counsels of God till the latter ages of the world, when it pleased God to send forth his Son into the world to publish it, and after him to appoint us to be the preachers and publishers of it.

8 ⁿWhich none of the princes of this world knew: for ᵒhad they known *it,* they would not have crucified the Lord of glory.

n Mat. 11. 25. John 7. 48. o Acts 13. 27. 2 Cor. 3. 14. o Luke 23. 34. Acts 3. 17. See John 16. 3.

Which none of the princes of this world knew; which Divine wisdom neither Caiaphas, nor Pontius Pilate, nor any considerable number of the rulers of this age, whether amongst the Jews or amongst the heathens, understood, though they heard of it. *For had they known it, they would not have crucified the Lord of glory;* for if they had so known it, as to have believed and been persuaded of it, they would never have nailed to the cross that person, who was the Head and Fountain of it, and *the Lord of glory;* both with respect to his Divine nature, as to which he was God blessed for ever, and also as Mediator, being the Author of glory to those who believe. Nor would this ignorance at all excuse their crucifying of Christ, because it was not invincible, they had means sufficient by which they might have come to the knowledge of him, and have understood what he was; so as their ignorance was affected and voluntary.

9 But as it is written, ᵖEye hath not seen, nor ear heard, neither have entered into the heart of man, the things which God hath prepared for them that love him.

p Is. 64. 4.

The place where this is written is by all agreed to be Isa. lxiv. 4, where the words are, *For since the beginning of the world men have not heard, nor perceived by the ear, neither hath the eye seen, O God, beside thee, what he hath prepared for him that waiteth for him.* It is so usual with the penmen of holy writ to quote the sense of texts in the Old Testament, not tying themselves to letters and syllables, that it is mightily vain for any to object against this quotation, as no where written in the Old Testament, but taken out of some apocryphal writings. The sense of what is written, Isa. lxiv. 4, is plainly the same with what he speaketh in this place; the greatest difference is, the apostle saith, *them that love him;* the prophet, *him that waiteth for him* (which is the certain product and effect of love). The whole 64th chapter of Isaiah, and some chapters following, treat concerning Christ; so doth this text. Christ and his benefits are to be understood here, by *the things which God hath prepared for them that love him;* which are set out as things not obvious to sense, nor to be comprehended by reason. It could never have entered into the heart of men to conceive, that God should give his only begotten Son out of his own bosom, to take upon him our nature, and to die upon the cross; or, that Christ should so far humble himself, and become obedient unto death.

10 But ᑫGod hath revealed *them* unto us by his Spirit: for the Spirit searcheth all things, yea, the deep things of God.

q Mat. 13. 11. & 16. 17. John 14. 26. & 16. 13. 1 John 2. 27.

God hath revealed them unto us by his Spirit; God by his Spirit hath opened our understandings to understand the

Holy Scriptures, the types and prophecies of Christ, and what the holy prophets have spoken of him both as to his person and offices. *For the Spirit searcheth all things, yea, the deep things of God;* for the Holy Spirit being the third person in the blessed Trinity, and so equal with the Father and the Son, *searcheth the deep things of God*, and so is able to reveal to us all the counsels of God, whatsoever God would have men to understand concerning the Lord Jesus Christ. So as this text is an evident proof of the Deity of the Holy Spirit, he searching the deep things of God, and being alone able to reveal them unto men, so as they shall acknowledge, comprehend, and believe them.

11 For what man knoweth the things of a man, ʳsave the spirit of man which is in him? ˢeven so the things of God knoweth no man, but the Spirit of God.

r Prov. 20. 27. & 27. 19. Jer. 17. 9. s Rom. 11. 33, 34.

Look, as it is with a man, no man knoweth his secret thoughts, and counsels, and meanings, save only his own soul that is within him; so it is as to the things of God, until God by his Spirit hath revealed them to men, none knoweth them but the Holy Spirit of God. It is true as it is with man; when he hath by his tongue discovered his mind to others, they know it so far as he hath so delivered it; but there is no man that discovereth all his thoughts and counsels: so God having in his word revealed his will, so far as he hath plainly revealed it men may know it; but there are *deep things of God*, mysteries in Scripture, which, till the Spirit of God hath revealed to men, they know not nor understand; for none knoweth them originally, *but the Spirit of God*, who is himself God, and *searcheth the deep things of God*.

12 Now we have received, not the spirit of the world, but ᵗthe spirit which is of God; that we might know the things that are freely given to us of God.

t Rom. 8. 15.

By *the spirit of the world* some understand the devil, that evil spirit which is in the world, and ruleth those that are worldly, carnal men: others understand a mere human spirit, by which men understand and comprehend mere worldly things. The sense certainly is, we have not a mere worldly instruction and tutoring, we are not taught and instructed from the world; (so *the spirit* is put for the effects of the spirit of the world;) but we are taught and instructed by the Holy Spirit, by which we are taught and *know the things that are freely given to us of God*, whether they be Divine mysteries, or Divine benefits, both what God hath done for us, and what God hath wrought in us.

13 ᵘWhich things also we speak, not in the words which man's wisdom teacheth, but which the Holy Ghost teacheth; comparing spiritual things with spiritual.

u 2 Pet. 1. 16. See ch. 1. 17. ver. ᵃ

Reason and all practice directeth men to speak and write of subjects in a style and phrase fitted to the matter about which they write or discourse. Our subjects, saith the apostle, were sublime, spiritual subjects; therefore I did not discourse them like an orator, with an *excellency of speech or of wisdom*, (as ver. 1,) or with the *enticing* or persuasive *words of man's wisdom*, (as he had said, ver. 4,) nor with *words which man's wisdom teacheth*, (which is his phrase here,) but with words which the Holy Ghost hath taught us, either in holy writ, or by its impressions upon our minds, where they are first formed. *Comparing spiritual things with spiritual;* fitting spiritual things to spiritual persons who are able to understand them, or fitting spiritual language to spiritual matter, speaking the oracles of God *as the oracles of God*, 1 Pet. iv. 11; not declaiming like an orator, nor arguing philosophically like an Athenian philosopher, but using a familiar, plain, spiritual style, giving you the naked truths of God without any paint or gaudery of phrase.

14 ˣBut the natural man receiveth not the things of the Spirit of God: ʸfor they are foolishness unto him: ᶻneither can he know *them*, because they are spiritually discerned.

x Mat. 16. 23. y ch. 1. 18, 23. z Rom. 8. 5, 6, 7. Jude 19.

There are great disputes here, who is meant by *the natural man*, ψυχικὸς ἄνθρωπος. Some think that by *the natural man* here is meant the carnal man: thus, chap. xv. 44, the *natural body* is opposed to the *spiritual body;* besides, they say, that in the constant phrase of holy writ, man, who is made up of flesh and spirit, as his essential parts, hath constantly his denomination from one of them, and all men in the world are either carnal or spiritual, and that the Greek word ψυχὴ signifies that soul and life which is common to all men, from whence all common motions and affections are, and is opposed to the Holy Spirit, which dwells in the souls of them that are sanctified, by which they are led and guided, &c. Thus, say they, the natural man is one who is a servant to his lusts and corruption, under the perfect government of his soul considered merely as natural, all whose motions in that estate of sin and corruption are inordinate. Others think that the apostle here speaks of such as are weak in the faith, little ones, babes in Christ, who had need of milk, not of strong meat, and are natural men in comparison of those more spiritual and perfect. In this sense indeed the apostle, chap. iii. 4, calleth them *carnal*. But there is nothing more plain, than that the apostle, under the notion of ψυχικὸς ἄνθρωπος (which we translate *natural man*) here, understands all such as were not perfect and spiritual, such to whom God hath not by his Spirit revealed the deep things of God, ver. 10; such as had only received *the spirit of the world*, not *the spirit of God*, by which alone men come to *know the things that are freely given* them *of God*, as ver. 12. *Receiveth not the things of the Spirit of God:* all these, though some of them are much better than others, having their minds more cultivated and adorned with worldly knowledge and wisdom, yet do not in their hearts (though they may with their ears) receive, that is, believe, embrace, and close with or approve of, spiritual and Divine mysteries, such doctrines as are purely matters of faith, standing upon a Divine revelation. *For they are foolishness unto him;* for men of wit and reason count them all *foolishness*, being neither demonstrable by sense or natural reason. *Neither can he know them, because they are spiritually discerned;* neither can any man, no otherwise taught and instructed, so comprehend them, as to give a firm and fixed assent to them, or in heart approve them, because they are only to be seen and discerned in a spiritual light, the Holy Spirit of God, which is *the Spirit of wisdom and revelation in the knowledge of Christ*, enlightening their understandings, that they may *know the hope of his calling, and what is the riches of the glory of his inheritance in the saints, and what is the exceeding greatness of his power to* them *that believe, according to the working of his mighty power*, &c., Eph. i. 17—19. Thus therefore the apostle gives a reason of what he had said, ver. 8, that *none of the princes of the world knew the wisdom of God*.

15 ᵃBut he that is spiritual ‖judgeth all things, yet he himself is ‖judged of no man.

a Prov. 28. 5. 1 Thes. 5. 21. 1 John 4. 1. ‖ Or, *discerneth*. ‖ Or, *discerned*.

He that is spiritual, in this verse, is opposed to *the natural man*, in the former verse, πνευματικὸς to ψυχικὸς. So that by *spiritual* here is understood, he that is taught by the Spirit of God, and is by him specially and savingly enlightened. *Judgeth* or discerneth *all things*, that is, of this nature, the mysteries of God, which concern man's eternal life and salvation; not that every good Christian hath any such perfect judgment or power of discerning, but according to the measure of illumination which he hath received. *Yet he himself is judged of no man;* it may as well be translated, of nothing; and the term *judged* might as well have been translated *examined*, or *searched*, as it is in Acts iv. 9; xii. 19; xvii. 11; xxiv. 8; or condemned. The wisdom that is of God is not to be subjected to the wisdom of men, nor to be judged of any man, but only the spiritual man. The truth, which the spiritual man owneth and professeth, dependeth only upon God and his word, and is not subjected to the authority and judgment of men, nor the dictates of human reason: so as the spiritual man, so far forth as he is spiritual, is neither judged by any man nor by any thing. There are some that by *he himself* understand the Spirit of God; he indeed *is judged of no man*, nor of any thing; but that seemeth a much more strained sense.

16 ᵇFor who hath known the mind of the Lord, that he †may instruct him? ᶜBut we have the mind of Christ.

b Job 15. 8. Is. 40. 13. Jer. 23. 18. Wisd. 9. 13. Rom. 11. 34. † Gr. *shall*. c John 15. 15.

For who hath known the mind of the Lord, that he may instruct him? this phrase is taken out of Isa. xl. 13, and was quoted by our apostle before, Rom. xi. 34 : the sense of it, as here used, is, For what natural man, that never was taught and enlightened by the Spirit of God, could ever know the secret counsels of God, and the Divine mysteries of man's salvation ? Nor can any instruct him what to do. It is by some observed, that συμβιβάσει signifies, by arguments to bring one over to be of his mind, which indeed is a kind of instruction. *But* (saith the apostle) *we*, who have the Spirit of God given to us, dwelling and working in us, and instructing us, we *have the mind of Christ;* for the Spirit of Christ, which is our teacher, knoweth his mind, and hath revealed it unto us.

CHAP. III.

Paul showeth that he could not instruct the Corinthians in the higher doctrines of Christianity because of their carnal mind, 1, 2 ; *which temper discovered itself in their factions,* 3, 4. *The most eminent preachers of the gospel are but instruments employed by God in building his church,* 5—9. *Paul hath laid the only true foundation, Christ Jesus ; and others must take heed what they build thereon,* 10—15. *Christians are God's temple, not to be defiled,* 16, 17. *Worldly wisdom is foolishness with God,* 18—20. *They that are Christ's must not glory in men,* 21—23.

a ch. 2. 15.
b ch. 2. 14.
c Heb. 5. 13.

AND I, brethren, could not speak unto you as unto ªspiritual, but as unto ᵇcarnal, *even* as unto ᶜbabes in Christ.

The apostle plainly returneth in this chapter to reprove them for their divisions and factions, for which he had begun to reprove them, chap. i. 11 ; and (as some think) here he anticipateth an objection, which they might have made against him, against his reproving and judging of them, whereas *he that is spiritual* (as he had now said) *is judged of no man. I,* (saith he,) *brethren, could not speak unto you as unto spiritual,* that is, as to Christians who had made any great proficiency in the ways of God, and had arrived to any just degrees of spiritual perfection ; *but as unto carnal,* that is, persons who, though you are not under the full conduct and government of your flesh and sensitive appetite, yet are far from being perfect, either in faith or holiness. *In Christ,* but not as grown men, but *as babes,* as the apostle fully explaineth this term, Heb. v. 12, 13, such as had need be taught again *which are the first principles of the oracles of God ; and have need of milk, and not of strong meat: for every one that useth milk is unskilful in the word of righteousness ; for he is a babe.*

d Heb. 5. 12, 13.
1 Pet. 2. 2.
e John 16. 12.

2 I have fed you with ᵈmilk, and not with meat : ᵉfor hitherto ye were not able *to bear it,* neither yet now are ye able.

Milk signifies what the apostle to the Hebrews calls *the first principles of the oracles of God,* and so is opposed to sublime spiritual doctrines, here set out under the notion of *meat;* called *strong meat,* Heb. v. 14, fit for those of *full age:* as young children's stomachs will not endure strong meat, so neither are sublime spiritual mysteries fit for new converts, until they have *senses exercised to discern good and evil;* and therefore the apostle gives this as a reason, why he had not communicated the deep things of God to them, because as yet they had not been able to bear the notion of them, nor indeed were they yet able : it should seem that there were many in the church of Corinth, who though they were true Christians, yet were not grown and judicious Christians, but had great imperfections, as indeed it will further appear in this Epistle.

f ch. 1. 11. & 11. 18.
Gal. 5. 20, 21.
Jam. 3. 16.
‖ Or, *factions*.
† Gr. *according to man.*

3 For ye are yet carnal : for ᶠwhereas *there is* among you envying, and strife, and ‖ divisions, are ye not carnal, and walk † as men ?

For ye are yet carnal; not wholly carnal, but in a great measure so, not having your lusts and corrupt affections entirely subdued to the will of God, nor yet so much subdued as some other Christians have, and you ought to have.

As an evidence of this he mindeth them of the *envying, strifes, and divisions* that were amongst them. *Strife* and *envyings* are reckoned amongst *the works of the flesh,* Gal. v. 19—21 ; they are all opposite to love, in which the perfection of a Christian lieth. He told us before what strifes and contentions he meant, and tells us it again in the next verse.

4 For while one saith, ᵍI am of Paul ; and another, I *am* of Apollos ; are ye not carnal ?

g ch. 1. 12.

Not that Christians in so large a city as Corinth might not put themselves under several pastors, or, as to themselves, prefer one before another, either in respect of the more eminent gifts of God bestowed upon one, (as doubtless Paul was preferable to Apollos,) or in respect of the more suitableness of one man's gifts to their capacities than another : but their adherence so to one minister of the gospel, that for his sake they vilified and despised all others, that were also true and faithful servants of God in the work of his gospel, this was their sin, and spake them to have vicious and corrupt affections, and to walk more like men than like saints, not having a true notion of the ministers of Christ, nor behaving themselves towards them as they ought to do.

5 Who then is Paul, and who *is* Apollos, but ʰministers by whom ye believed, ⁱeven as the Lord gave to every man ?

h ch. 4. 1.
2 Cor. 3. 3.
i Rom. 12. 3,
6. 1 Pet. 4. 11.

Neither Paul, nor yet Apollos, are authors of faith to you, but only instruments ; it is the Lord that giveth to every man a power to believe ; or else that latter phrase, *as the Lord gave to every man,* may be understood of ministers, whose abilities to the work of the ministry, and success in it, both depend upon God. The sense of the words is this, then : God giveth unto his ministers variety of gifts, and different success ; but yet neither one nor the other of them are more than the servants of Christ in their ministry, persons whom God maketh use of to call upon and to prevail with men, to give credit to the doctrine of the gospel, and to receive and accept of Christ. The work is the Lord's, not theirs.

6 ᵏI have planted, ˡApollos watered ; ᵐbut God gave the increase.

k Acts 18. 4, 8, 11. ch. 4.
15. & 9. 1. &
15. 1. 2 Cor. 10. 14, 15. l Acts 18. 24, 27. & 19. 1. m ch. 1. 30. & 15. 10. 2 Cor. 3. 5.

God honoured me first to preach the gospel amongst you, Acts xviii. &c., and blessed my preaching to convert you unto Christ ; then I left you : Apollos stayed behind, and he *watered* what I had *planted,* daily preaching amongst you ; see Acts xviii. 24—26 ; he was a further means to build you up in faith and holiness ; but God increased, or *gave the increase,* God gave the power by which you brought forth any fruit. The similitude is drawn from planters, whether husbandmen or gardeners ; they plant, they water, but the growing, the budding, the bringing forth flowers or fruit by the plant, doth much more depend upon the soil in which it stands, the influence of heaven upon it, by the beams of the sun, and the drops of the dew and rain, and the internal virtue which the God of nature hath created in the plant, than upon the hand of him that planteth, or him who useth his watering-pot to water it. So it is with souls ; one minister is used for conversion, or the first changing of souls ; another is used for edification, or further building up of souls ; but both conversion and edification are infinitely more from the new heart and new nature, which God giveth to souls, and from the influence of the Sun of righteousness by the Spirit of grace, working in and upon the soul, than from any minister, who is but God's instrument in those works.

7 So then ⁿneither is he that planteth any thing, neither he that watereth ; but God that giveth the increase.

n 2 Cor. 12. 11. Gal. 6. 3.

So that, look as it is in earthly plantations, God hath the greatest influence upon the growth and fruitfulness of the plant, and the husbandman or gardener is nothing in comparison with God, who hath given to the plant planted its life and nature, by which it shooteth up, buddeth, and bringeth forth fruit, and maketh his sun to shine and his rain to fall upon it : so it is in the spiritual plantation, God is the principal efficient Cause, we are little instrumental

I. CORINTHIANS III

causes in God's hand, nothing in comparison with God. *I have planted, Apollos* hath *watered;* but if we see a soul changed, or grow, and make any spiritual proficiency, we must say, *Not unto us, O Lord, not unto us, but unto thy name* be given the *glory :* God hath done the main work ; we have not done any thing in comparison with him. These words do no more tend to vilify the ministry of the gospel, or make it useless, than, taking them in their native sense, as they respect earthly plantations, they would prove, that there is no need of the husbandman's or gardener's hand to plant or to water plants, because all that he doth of that nature is to no purpose, unless God first gives to the plant its proper nature and virtue, and then followeth the planting with the influence of the sun, dew, and rain. But yet it is observable, that the apostle doth not say, the man himself gives the increase, from the good use of the power that is naturally in his own will, but *God giveth the increase;* which argues the necessity of special grace both to conversion and edification, superadded to the best preaching of his ministers. Though Paul himself by preaching plants, and Apollos watereth, yet God must make the soul to increase with the increase of God. Hence the apostle argueth their unreasonableness, in adoring one minister, and magnifying him above another, when indeed neither the one nor the other had any principal efficiency in the production of the blessed effect, but a mere instrumental causation, the effect of which depended upon the sole blessing of God, in comparison with whom, in this working, neither the one nor the other minister was any thing.

8 Now he that planteth and he that watereth are one : °and every man shall receive his own reward according to his own labour.

o Ps. 62. 12.
Rom. 2. 6.
ch. 4. 5.
Gal. 6. 4, 5.
Rev. 2. 23.
& 22. 12.

The ministers of Christ, though one be used in planting and another in watering, one in laying the foundation and another in building thereupon, yet *are one;* one in their office and work, one in their ministry, being all servants to Christ, who is one ; all serving one and the same Lord, all doing the same business, proposing the same end, and with all their might labouring towards it ; and therefore, as they ought not to divide into parties and factions, so you ought not for their sakes to be so divided. Yet they are not so one, but that one may labour more than another, and be honoured by God with more success than another, and every one shall receive a reward proportioned to his labour : the apostle saith not, according to the success of his labour, (that is not in his power,) but, *according to his labour.*

p Acts 15. 4.
2 Cor. 6. 1.
|| Or, *tillage.*
q Eph. 2. 20.
Col. 2. 7.
Heb. 3. 3, 4.
1 Pet. 2. 5.

9 For ᵖwe are labourers together with God: ye are God's ‖ husbandry, *ye are* ᑫGod's building.

Though compared with God we are nothing, yet our station is no mean station; God works as the principal efficient Cause, we work with God as his instruments ; God worketh one way, by his secret influence upon the heart, we another way, by publication of the gospel in people's ears, but the scope and end of the work is the same. The Lord is said to work with his ministers, Mark xvi. 20, and they are here said to work with him. Hence he proveth what he had before said, that they should be rewarded ; God will not suffer those who work with him to be without their reward : as also that they were *one,* for they are all *labourers together with God.* Yet do not think yourselves our husbandry, for you are *God's husbandry:* thus God's people, Isa. lxi. 3, are called *the planting of the Lord. God's building :* thus the church is called *the house of God,* 1 Tim. iii. 15. Still the apostle minds them, that they were God's, not their minister's ; it was God to whom they were beholden for their conversion, for their edification, &c.

r Rom. 1. 5.
& 12. 3.

10 ʳAccording to the grace of God which is given unto me, as a wise masterbuilder, I have laid ˢthe foundation, and another buildeth thereon. But ᵗlet every man take heed how he buildeth thereupon.

s Rom. 15.
20. ver. 6.
ch. 4. 15.
Rev. 21. 14.
t 1 Pet. 4. 11.

According to the grace of God which is given unto me : Χάριν here signifies either the ability which God hath given Paul to preach the gospel, or the apostolical office, to which God had called him ; he maketh both to proceed from God, and to be the effects of his free love and favour to him. According to this he saith, Look, *as a wise master-builder* first layeth the foundation, then buildeth upon the foundation which he hath laid ; so *I,* being the first whom God pleased to employ in this his work at Corinth, *have laid the foundation,* that is, have first preached the gospel in this famous city : thus the first preaching of the gospel is called, a *laying the foundation,* Rom. xv. 20 ; Heb. vi. 1. *Another buildeth thereon;* afterwards Apollos and other ministers further carried on that work of preaching the gospel amongst them. *But let every man take heed how he buildeth thereupon ;* but (saith he) whoever cometh to preach after me had need take heed what he buildeth ; for, Gal. i. 8, *though we, or an angel from heaven, preach any other gospel unto you than that which we have preached unto you, let him be accursed.*

11 For other foundation can no man lay than ᵘthat is laid, ˣwhich is Jesus Christ.

u Is. 28. 16.
Matt. 16. 18.
2 Cor. 11. 4.
Gal. 1. 7.
x Eph. 2. 20.

Can in this text doth not signify a mere natural power, but a rightful power: No man by any just right or authority can lay any other foundation, can preach any other doctrine of salvation, than that which I have already preached, which is the doctrine of salvation by Jesus Christ. *Neither is there salvation in any other; for there is none other name under heaven given among men, whereby we must be saved,* Acts iv. 12.

12 Now if any man build upon this foundation gold, silver, precious stones, wood, hay, stubble ;

The apostle is discoursing metaphorically, he had compared the church of Corinth to a building, ver. 9, and called them there *God's building;* they were built upon the doctrine of the gospel, the doctrine of the apostles and prophets, who had preached Christ to them, this was the foundation ; and had told us, that none, by any pretence of right, could lay any other foundation. But there was to be a superstructure upon this foundation, which might be of various materials : he names six ; three very good and excellent, *gold, silver,* and *precious stones ;* three others vile and invaluable, *wood, hay, stubble.* By these he either means good or bad works, or rather, good or bad doctrines. Good doctrine is signified by the *gold, silver,* and *precious stones* mentioned ; bad doctrine by the *wood, hay,* and *stubble* mentioned ; by which may be understood various degrees of bad doctrine, as some doctrines are more pernicious and damnable than others, though the others also be false, unprofitable, trivial, and of no significancy to the good of souls, but bad, as they are unprofitable.

13 ʸEvery man's work shall be made manifest: for the day ᶻshall declare it, because ᵃit †shall be revealed by fire ; and the fire shall try every man's work of what sort it is.

y ch. 4. 5.
z 1 Pet. 1.
7. & 4. 12.
a Luke 2. 35.
† Gr.
is revealed.

Now, saith he, there will come a time when *every man's,* that is, every teacher's, *work,* or doctrine, *shall be made manifest.* As the metal is brought to the touchstone to be tried, whether it be gold or silver, or some baser metal ; so there will come a time, when all doctrines shall be tried and made manifest, whether they be of God or no. *For the day shall declare it :* what day shall declare it is not so steadily agreed by interpreters. Some by a *day* here understand a long time, in process of time it shall be declared ; as indeed erroneous doctrines have not used to obtain or prevail long : Dagon falls before the ark. Others understand it of a day of adversity and great affliction, the day of God's vengeance ; and indeed thus it is often seen, a false faith, or a lie believed, will not carry a man through the difficulties which he meeteth with in an evil day : the truths of the gospel are of that nature, that they will give a soul relief and support in a day of affliction, and under God's severest dispensations, but errors and falsehoods will not do it. Others understand by *the day* here mentioned, the day of judgment, which is indeed often called *the day of the Lord,* chap. i. 8, and described by fire, Joel ii. 3 ; 2 Thess. i. 8 ; 2 Pet. iii. 10 ; but this text saith not *the day of the Lord,* but only *the day.* It seemeth, therefore, rather

547

to signify the bright shining out of the gospel; for the text seemeth to speak of such a manifestation as shall be in this life, not in the day of judgment. *Because it shall be revealed by fire;* the same thing is also to be understood. *The fire shall try every man's work of what sort it is:* by *the fire* here mentioned, not the fire of God's wrath, or the fire of affliction and adversity, nor the fire of the last judgment, but the truth of the gospel shining forth in the world, and burning up the dross and stubble of corrupt, false doctrine, that shall bring all the doctrines which men teach, to the trial.

14 If any man's work abide which he hath built thereupon, ^bhe shall receive a reward.

b ch. 4. 5.

If any preacher keeps the foundation, and the doctrine which he hath built upon the true foundation prove consonant to the will of Christ, God will reward him for his labour: he shall hear the voice saying, *Well done, good and faithful servant, enter thou into the joy of thy Lord.*

15 If any man's work shall be burned, he shall suffer loss: but he himself shall be saved; ^cyet so as by fire.

c Jude 23.

But if his work do not abide, if it shall appear upon the more clear and bright shining out of the truth of the gospel, that though he hath held the foundation right, yet he hath built upon it wood, hay, and stubble, mixed fables, and idle stories, and corrupt doctrine with the doctrine of the gospel, *he shall suffer loss* by it, either by the afflicting hand of God, or by a loss of his reputation, or some other way. But yet God will not cast off a soul for every such error, if he keeps to the main foundation, Jesus Christ; *he shall be saved,* though it be *as by fire,* that is, with difficulty; which certainly is a more natural sense of this text, than those give, who interpret *as by fire,* of the fire of the gospel, or the fire of purgatory, of which the papists understand it. For, 1. It is, and always hath been, a proverbial form of speech to express a thing obtained by difficulty; we say, It is got out of the fire, &c. 2. For the fire of purgatory, it is a fiction, and mere imaginary thing, and of no further significancy than to make the pope's chimney smoke. 3. That pretended fire only purgeth venial sins; this fire trieth every man's work, the gold as well as the stubble.

d ch. 6. 19.
2 Cor. 6. 16.
Eph. 2. 21,
22. Heb. 3. 6.
1 Pet. 2. 5.

16 ^d Know ye not that ye are the temple of God, and *that* the Spirit of God dwelleth in you?

The apostle, ver. 9, had called the church of Corinth, and the particular members of it, *God's building;* after this he had enlarged in a discourse concerning the builders, and the foundation and superstructure upon that foundation; now he returns again to speak of the whole church, whom he here calleth *the temple of God,* with a manifest allusion to that noble and splendid house which Solomon first built, and was afterwards rebuilt by Zerubbabel, Ezra, and Nehemiah at Jerusalem, as the public place for the Jewish church to meet in to worship God according to the prescript of the Levitical law: in which house God was said to dwell, because there he met his people, and blessed them, and there he gave answers to them from the mercy-seat. He calls them *the temple of God,* because they were built, that is, effectually called, for this very end, that they might be *to the praise of the glory of his grace, wherein he hath made us accepted in the beloved,* Eph. i. 6 : and, as the apostle Peter further expoundeth this text, 1 Pet. ii. 5, the people of God are *a spiritual house, an holy priesthood, to offer up spiritual sacrifices, acceptable to God by Jesus Christ.* And God by his Spirit dwelt in them, both by his person, and by his gifts and graces, which is a far more noble dwelling in them than the dwelling of God was in the Jewish temple. From this text may be fetched an evident proof of the Divine nature, of the Third Person in the blessed Trinity; for he is not only called here *the Spirit of God,* but he is said to dwell in the saints: which dwelling of God in his people, is that very thing which maketh them *the temple of God;* and those who are here called *the temple of God,* are, chap. vi. 19, called *the temple of the Holy Ghost.*

‖ Or, *destroy.*

17 If any man ‖ defile the temple of God, him shall God destroy; for the temple of God is holy, which *temple* ye are.

If any man defile the temple of God, him shall God destroy; the word which we translate *defile* and *destroy* (for the Greek word is the same for both) signifieth to violate, corrupt, or destroy. Our translators generally render it *corrupt,* chap. xv. 33; 2 Cor. vii. 2; xi. 3; Eph. iv. 22; Jude 10; Rev. xix. 2. The people of God, who are here called *the temple of God,* are defiled, either by imbibing false doctrine, or being tempted to any looseness of life and conversation. Now, (saith the apostle,) if any one goeth about to do this, which all preachers do who teach any false doctrine, or any principles that lead to a liberty for the flesh, or lead to an ill and scandalous life, God shall destroy those men. *For the temple of God is holy;* for as the temple of God of old was a place built and set apart for holy uses, and therefore not without great peril to be abused and profaned; so those that are the people of God, are by God called and set apart in a more immediate, eminent manner for the honour and glory of God, and therefore cannot be debauched or defiled by any as instruments in that action, without exceeding great peril and hazard to them that endeavour and attempt any such thing.

18 ^e Let no man deceive himself. If any man among you seemeth to be wise in this world, let him become a fool, that he may be wise.

e Prov. 5. 7.
Is. 5. 21.

Let no man deceive himself: there are some that, with their eloquence and flourishes of words, or with their philosophical notions and reasonings, (which, Col. ii. 8, the apostle calls *vain deceit,*) or with their traditions *after the rudiments of the world,* (as the apostle addeth in that place,) would cheat and deceive your souls, under a pretence of making you wonderfully wise: *the wisdom of the world is foolishness with God. If any man among you seemeth to be wise in this world;* if any of you seemeth unto others, or seemeth unto himself, that is, thinketh that he is endued with what the world calleth wisdom. *Let him become a fool, that he may be wise;* if ever he would be truly wise, wise unto God, and to eternal life and salvation, let him be contented, by the wise men and philosophers of this world, to be looked upon as a fool; and let him be willing to deny himself in any notions or opinions of his own, which he hath taken up upon the credit of his natural reason and philosophical principles, which agree not with the Divine revelation, that so he may be truly and spiritually wise, truly understanding, savouring, and believing what God hath in his word revealed, and is alone able to make the man of God wise to salvation, thoroughly furnished unto every good work.

19 For ^fthe wisdom of this world is foolishness with God. For it is written, ^g He taketh the wise in their own craftiness.

f ch. 1. 20. & 2. 6.

g Job 5. 13.

For the wisdom of this world is foolishness with God; God accounteth that folly which the world calleth wisdom, and indeed it is so (for God cannot err, nor be mistaken in his judgment): the philosophers and wise men of the world propose the happiness of man as their end, which indeed is the true end which all men aim at, and do propound to themselves; true wisdom directeth the best means in order to the best end. Whatsoever directeth not to the best end, or to what is not the best means in order to that end, is not wisdom, but real folly; worldly wisdom neither directeth to the best end, for it looks at no further happiness than that of this life, nor yet to the best means, and therefore is truly, what God accounts it, *foolishness. For it is written,* He taketh the wise in their own craftiness; and to see the wise and learned men of the world thus err both in their judgment and practice, is no wonder at all; for God is set out of old by Eliphaz, as one that *taketh the wise in their own craftiness,* Job v. 13.

20 And again, ^h The Lord knoweth the thoughts of the wise, that they are vain.

h Ps. 94. 11.

And again, it was said by the psalmist, Psal. xciv. 11, that *The Lord knoweth the thoughts of man, that they are vanity:* man's counsels, imaginations, reasonings, they are

I. CORINTHIANS III, IV

all vanity; they propose to themselves ends which they cannot attain, and pursue them by means that are inefficacious with reference to their ends.

^{i ch. 1. 12. & 4. 6. ver. 4, 5, 6. k 2 Cor. 4. 5, 15.}

21 Therefore ⁱ let no man glory in men. For ^k all things are your's;

Seeing, therefore, that Christ is but one, his ministers but one, and no more than *ministers by whom ye believed*, ver. 5; and the principal efficiency of any saving work begun, or carried on in your souls to any degree of perfection, is from God, and the minister's work in that effect nothing compared with his; seeing you are *God's husbandry, God's building*, not merely man's, and *the temple of God*, not men's temple; leave your glorying *in men*, and saying *I am of Paul*, or *I am of Apollos*; glory only in this, that *ye are Christ's*: besides, *all things are yours;* why do you glory in a particular minister, when all is yours? as if two joint-heirs in an estate should glory in this or that particular house or enclosure, when the whole estate is jointly theirs, all theirs.

22 Whether Paul, or Apollos, or Cephas, or the world, or life, or death, or things present, or things to come; all are your's;

^{l Rom. 14. 8. ch. 11. 3. 2 Cor. 10. 7 Gal. 3. 29.}

23 And ^l ye are Christ's; and Christ *is* God's.

Here are in these two verses three things asserted: 1. The believer's title to *all things*. 2. The specialty of their title. 3. The force of the apostle's argument from hence, why they should not *glory in men*. He had said before, *All things are yours*, which he repeats again, ver. 22: they have a right and title to all things, and all things are for their good, use, and advantage. Amongst these he first reckons ministers: every one of them might lay a claim to Paul, to Apollos, to Peter; for they were all servants of Christ for the use of the church, a part of which they were. Then he goes on, and saith, *the world*, that is, the things of the world, are theirs; that is, whatsoever portion of them the providence of God orderly disposed to them, they had a true title to it, and it was for their use and advantage; so were the lives and deaths of God's ministers, their own lives and deaths, all *things present*, and all *things* that were *to come*, they were all theirs by a just title; if the providence of God gave them to them in an orderly way, they might comfortably use them. They themselves were *Christ's*; they were not of Paul, nor of Apollos, nor of Peter. He that had the bride was the bridegroom; these ministers were but the friends of their bridegroom. *And Christ is God's*, the Son of God by an eternal generation; the servant of God as man, and born under the law, so yielding obedience to his Father; the Messiah or Anointed, and sent of God as Mediator. All things are God's, by God given to Christ, by Christ given to and sanctified for you; that makes the believers' special title to all things. The men of the world derive their title to what they have from God alone, as Creator; they derive not from Christ, as being ingrafted and implanted into him. Hence the apostle rightly concludes their vanity, in glorying in their relation to this or that special apostle or minister, whereas they had a true and just right to the labours of all ministers, and ought to look upon all faithful ministers as God's gifts to his whole church, and for the advantage and benefit of all: yet this hindereth not, but that people ought to have their particular pastors and teachers, to whom they ought ordinarily to attend in their ministry; but they ought not to have their persons in such admiration, as for them to despise or slight any other faithful ministers, nor to make parties and factions in the church of God.

CHAP. IV

Paul showeth in what account such as he should be held, of whose fidelity it should be left to God to judge, 1—5. *He dissuadeth the Corinthians from valuing themselves in one teacher above another, since all had their respective distinctions from God*, 6, 7. *To their self-sufficient vanity he opposeth his own despised and afflicted state*, 8—13; *warning them, as their only father in Christ, and urging them to follow him*, 14—16. *For the same cause he sent Timotheus, and meant soon to follow in person, when he would inquire into the authority of such as opposed him*, 17—21.

LET a man so account of us, as of ^a the ministers of Christ, ^b and stewards of the mysteries of God.

^{a Mat. 24. 45. ch. 3. 5. & 9. 17. 2 Cor. 6. 4. Col. 1. 25. b Luke 12. 42. Tit. 1. 7. 1 Pet. 4. 10.}

The apostle here gives us the right notion of the preachers of the gospel; they are but *ministers*, that is, servants, so as the honour that is proper to their Master, for a principal efficiency in the conversion and building up of souls, belongeth not to them; they are *ministers of Christ*, so have their primary relation to him, and only a secondary relation to the church to which they are ministers; they are *ministers of Christ*, and so in that ministration can only execute what are originally his commands, though those commands of Christ may also be enforced by men: ministers of the gospel, not of the law, upon whom lies a primary obligation to preach Christ and his gospel unto people. They are also *stewards of the mysteries of God*, such to whom God hath committed his word and sacraments to dispense out unto his church. The word *mystery* signifieth any thing that is secret, but more especially it signifieth a Divine secret, represented by signs and figures; or a religious secret, not obvious to every capacity or understanding. Thus we read of the *mysteries of the kingdom of heaven*, Matt. xiii. 11; *the mystery of godliness*, 1 Tim. iii. 16; *the mystery of Christ*, Eph. iii. 4. *The wisdom of God*, Col. ii. 2; the incarnation of Christ, 1 Tim. iii. 16; the calling of the Gentiles, Eph. iii. 4; the *resurrection from the dead*, 1 Cor. xv. 21; Christ's mystical union and communion with his church, Eph. v. 32; the sublime counsels of God, 1 Cor. xiii. 2, are all called *mysteries*. Ministers are the stewards of the mysterious doctrines and institutions of Christ, which we usually comprehend under the terms of the word and sacraments.

2 Moreover it is required in stewards, that a man be found faithful.

It is required of all servants, but especially of chief servants, such as stewards are, who are intrusted with their masters' goods, to be dispensed out to others. The faithfulness of a steward in dispensing out his master's goods lies in his giving them out according to his master's order, giving to every one their portion, not detaining any thing from others which it is his master's will they should have; as Paul gloried, Acts xx. 20, 27, that he had *kept back* from the Ephesians *nothing that was profitable* for them, nor *shunned to declare* to them *all the counsel of God;* not giving holy things to dogs, or casting pearls before swine, contrary to Christ's direction, Matt. vii. 6.

3 But with me it is a very small thing that I should be judged of you, or of man's †judgment: yea, I judge not mine own self.

^{† Gr. day. ch. 3. 13.}

Those who said, *I am of Apollos, and I* am *of Cephas*, did at least tacitly judge Paul, and prefer Apollos and Cephas before him; and it is probable, and will appear also from other parts of these Epistles, that they passed very indecent censures concerning Paul: he therefore tells them, that he valued very little what they or any other men said of him. In the Greek it is, *of man's day*; but it is generally thought that our translators have given us the true sense, in translating it *man's judgment, day* being put for *judgment*; as Jer. xvii. 16, where *woeful day* signifies woeful judgment. So *the day of the Lord* in Scripture often signifieth the Lord's judgment: the reason of that form of speech seems to be, because persons cited to a court of judgment use to be cited to appear on a certain day. *Yea, I judge not mine own self;* yea, saith the apostle, I pronounce no sentence for myself, I leave myself to the judgment of God. I may be deceived in my judgment concerning myself, and therefore I will affirm nothing as to myself.

4 For I know nothing by myself; ^c yet am I not hereby justified: but he that judgeth me is the Lord.

^{c Job 9. 2. Ps. 130. 3. & 143. 2. Prov. 21. 2. Rom. 3. 28. & 4. 2.}

I know nothing by myself; nothing amiss, nothing that is evil; yet this must not be interpreted universally, as if St. Paul knew nothing that was evil and sinful by himself;

himself, Rom. vii., tells us the contrary; but it must be understood with respect to his discharge of his ministerial office: I do not know any thing wherein I have wilfully failed in the discharge of my ministry; yet even as to that I durst not stand upon my own righteousness and justification before God, I may have sinned ignorantly, or have forgotten some things wherein I did offend. *But he that judgeth me is the Lord;* God knoweth more of me than I know of myself, and it is he that judgeth, and must judge me. Though in this text Paul doth not speak of his whole life and conversation, but only of his conversation with respect to his ministry; yet the conclusion from hence, that no man can be justified from his own works, is good; for if a man cannot be justified from his conscience not rebuking him for his errors in one part of his conversation, he cannot be justified from his conscience not rebuking' him for his whole conversation. For he that keepeth the whole law, if he offendeth but in one point, must be guilty of all, because the law curseth him who continueth not in every point of the law to do it.

d Matt. 7. 1. Rom. 2. 1, 16. & 14. 4, 10, 13. Rev. 20. 12. e ch. 3. 13.

5 ^dTherefore judge nothing before the time, until the Lord come, ^ewho both will bring to light the hidden things of darkness, and will make manifest the counsels of the hearts: and ^fthen shall every man have praise of God.

f Rom. 2. 29. 2 Cor. 5. 10.

Therefore judge nothing before the time, until the Lord come; seeing that the judgment of secret things belongs to God, *judge nothing before the time,* which God hath set to judge all things. The works of the flesh are manifest, and men may judge of them; but for secret things, of which it is impossible that those who do not know the hearts of men should make up a judgment, do not judge of them before the time, when God will certainly come to judge all men. *Who both will bring to light the hidden things of darkness, and will make manifest the counsels of the hearts:* if men cloak *the hidden things of darkness* with the cover of hypocrisy and fair pretences, they will at that day be most certainly uncovered, and the secret thoughts, counsels, and imaginations of men's hearts shall in that day be made manifest. *And then shall every man have praise of God;* and then those that have done well, every of them *shall have praise of God;* as, on the contrary, (which is understood, though not here expressed,) those that are hypocrites, and whose hearts have been full of evil thoughts and counsels, shall by God be put to shame and exposed to contempt.

g ch. 1. 12. & 3. 4.

6 And these things, brethren, ^gI have in a figure transferred to myself and *to* Apollos for your sakes; ^hthat ye might learn in us not to think *of men* above that which is written, that no one of you ⁱbe puffed up for one against another.

h Rom. 12. 3.

i ch. 3. 21. & 5. 2, 6.

And these things, brethren, I have in a figure transferred to myself and to Apollos for your sakes: by these words the apostle lets us know, that though he had said, chap. i. 12, that some of them said, We are of Paul, and others, We are of Apollos; yet the names of Paul and of Apollos were but used to represent other of their teachers, which were the heads of those factions which were amongst them. In very deed there were none of them that said, We are of Paul or of Apollos, (for those that were the disciples of Paul and Apollos were better taught,) but they had other teachers amongst them as to whom they made factions, whom Paul had a mind to reprove, with their followers; and to avoid all odium, that both they and their hearers might take no offence at his free reproving of them, he makes use of his own name, and that of Apollos, and speaketh to the hearers of these teachers, as if they were his own and Apollos's disciples; that those whom the reproof and admonition concerned properly, might be reproved under the reproof of others. *That you might learn in us not to think of men above that which is written;* and that (as the apostle saith) all the church of Corinth, as well ministers as people, might learn to have humble opinions and thoughts of themselves, not to think of themselves above what, by the rules of God's word, was written in the Old Testament they ought to think; or above what he had before writen in this Epistle, or to the Romans, chap. xii. 3. *That no one of you be puffed up for one against another;* and that none of them, whether ministers or private Christians, might be *puffed up.* The word signifieth to be swelled or blown up as a bladder or a pair of bellows, which is extended with wind: it is used in this chapter, ver. 18, 19; chap. viii. 1; Col. ii. 18.

7 For who †maketh thee to differ *from another?* and ^k what hast thou that thou didst not receive? now if thou didst receive *it,* why dost thou glory, as if thou hadst not received *it?*

† Gr. distinguisheth thee.
k John 3. 27. Jam. 1. 17. 1 Pet. 4. 10.

It is apparent that pride was the reigning sin of many in this church of Corinth; pride, by reason of those parts and gifts wherein they excelled, whether they were natural or acquired habits, or common gifts of the Spirit which were infused: to abate this tumour, the apostle minds them to consider, whence they had these gifts from which they took occasion so to exalt and prefer themselves; whether they were the authors of them to themselves, or did receive them from God. *Now if thou didst receive it, why dost thou glory, as if thou hadst not received it?* it became none of them to glory in what they had received from another, and were beholden to another for. What the apostle here speaketh concerning natural or spiritual abilities, is applicable to all good things; and the consideration here prompted, is a potent consideration to abate the pride and swelling of a man's heart upon any account whatsoever; for there is nothing wherein a man differeth or is distinguished from another, or wherein he excelleth another, but it is given him from God; be it riches, honour, natural or spiritual gifts and abilities, they are all received from the gift of God, who gives a man *power to get wealth,* Deut. viii. 18; who *putteth down one and setteth up another,* Psal. lxxv. 7: and, as the apostle saith in this Epistle, chap. xii. 7—9, gives *the manifestation of the Spirit to every man to profit withal: to one by the Spirit the word of wisdom; to another the word of knowledge; to another faith; to another the gifts of healing,* &c., all *by the same Spirit.*

8 Now ye are full, ^lnow ye are rich, ye have reigned as kings without us: and I would to God ye did reign, that we also might reign with you.

l Rev. 3. 17.

Now ye are full, now *ye are rich;* you that are the teachers at Corinth, or you that are the members of the church there, think yourselves full of knowledge and wisdom, so as you stand in need of no further learning or instruction. *Ye have reigned as kings without us;* ye think now you have got a kingdom, and are arrived at the top of felicity. *And I would to God ye did reign, that we also might reign with you;* I am so far from envying you, that I wish it were so, and we might have a share with you. The apostle speaketh this ironically, not that he indeed thought they were so, but reflecting on their vain and too good an opinion of themselves.

9 For I think that God hath set forth ‖ us the apostles last, ^m as it were appointed to death: for ⁿ we are made a †spectacle unto the world, and to angels, and to men.

‖ Or, us the last apostles, as. m Ps. 44. 22. Rom. 8. 36. ch. 15. 30, 31. 2 Cor. 4. 11. & 6. 9.
n Heb. 10. 33.
† Gr. theatre.

For I think that God hath set forth us the apostles last, as it were appointed to death; the lot of us who are the apostles of Christ is not so externally happy, but a lot of poverty and misery, as if we were the worst of men, men *appointed to death.* *For we are made a spectacle unto the world, and to angels, and to men;* to be a mere sight or gazing-stock to the world, angels, or men. Some think that the apostle here hath a reference to the barbarous practice of the Romans, who first exposed and carried about for a sight those persons that were condemned to fight with wild beasts, that by them they might be torn in pieces. You are happy men, saith the apostle, if you can own Christ, and profess Christianity, and yet be in such credit and favour with the world, so full, and so rich, and so like princes: we are those whom God hath honoured to be his apostles and the first ministers of the gospel; our lot and portion is far otherwise.

I. CORINTHIANS IV

10 °We *are* ᵖfools for Christ's sake, but ye *are* wise in Christ; ᵠwe *are* weak, but ye *are* strong; ye *are* honourable, but we *are* despised.

We are accounted fools for Christ's sake by the wise men of the world, and we are willing to be·so accounted; but you think yourselves *wise*, and yet *in Christ. We are weak* in the opinion of men, we suffer evil, and do not resist; *but ye* account yourselves, and are by the world accounted, *strong:* ye are accounted noble and *honourable, but we are despised* and contemptible.

11 ʳEven unto this present hour we both hunger, and thirst, and ˢare naked, and ᵗare buffeted, and have no certain dwellingplace;

Our state in the world is low and mean; though you be full, we are hungry and thirsty; though you be richly clothed, yet we *are* next to *naked*, clothed with rags; though you be hugged and embraced by the men of the world, yet we *are buffeted;* though you have rich and famous houses, yet we *have no certain dwelling-place*. Thus it hath been with us from the beginning of our profession of Christ, and thus it is with us at this day, saith the apostle: from whence he gives these Corinthians and their false teachers a just reason to suspect themselves, whether they were true and sincere professors, yea or no, and to consider how it came to pass, that their lot in the world was so different from the lot of those whom the Lord had dignified with the title and office of his apostles. The condition of the most faithful and able ministers and the most sincere Christians that have been in the world, hath always been a mean and afflicted state and condition.

12 ᵘAnd labour, working with our own hands: ˣbeing reviled, we bless; being persecuted, we suffer it:

And labour, working with our hands; we do not only labour in the word and doctrine, but we labour with our hands, that we might not be burdensome to the church, our hands ministering to our necessities, Acts xx. 34; though, as he saith, chap. ix. 4, they had a *power to eat and drink*, that is, a right to have demanded meat and drink of them, and might have forbore *working;* for *who goeth a warfare at his own charges?* ver. 6, 7. Whence we may observe, that though the ministers of Christ ought to be maintained by the churches to which they relate, and they sin if they neglect it; yet where this either is not done through men's sinful neglect of them, or cannot be done through the poverty of the members of such churches, it is lawful for them to labour with their hands. *Being reviled, we bless;* we are reviled and spoken ill of, but we do not revile others, but speak well of them, and wish well to them. *Being persecuted, we suffer it;* though we be hunted and pursued to the endangering of our lives and liberties, yet we do make no resistance, but patiently *suffer it.* By this the apostle showeth them the duty of Christians, as well as their lot and portion in this life; and also tacitly reflecteth on them and their teachers, who were some of those that thus reviled the apostles; and though they did not, it may be, smite them with their hands, yet they persecuted them with their tongues; and leaves it to their consideration, whether the apostles or they lived more up to the rule of Christianity given by Christ, Matt. v. 39—41.

13 Being defamed, we intreat: ʸwe are made as the filth of the earth, *and are* the offscouring of all things unto this day.

Being defamed, we entreat: we are blasphemed, Gr. that is, spoken evil of, which is the same with *defamed* in our language, men speak all manner of evil of us to take away our reputation; but *we entreat* God for them: the word signifieth to exhort, entreat, comfort, we exercise ourselves in all pious and charitable offices toward them, who are most uncharitable toward us. *We are made as the filth of the earth, and are the offscouring of all things unto this day:* here are two words used, which signify the most vile, abject, contemptible things in the world, excrements, sweepings of houses. The apostle by these two words signifies, that no persons could be more base, vile, and contemptible than they were, nothing more despised, or in less esteem: he speaketh not this as complaining, or in any discontent at what he saw was the will of God concerning them; but to show them the difference betwixt the apostles, and them and their teachers, and possibly reflecting upon them, as being in some degree guilty of this scorn and contempt of them, or at least, more than they ought, neglecting them under these mean and afflictive circumstances.

14 I write not these things to shame you, but ᶻas my beloved sons I warn *you.*

I tell you not of this to make you blush, as having had any hand in these indignities which are put upon us, nor yet *to shame you* (though possibly you have reason to be ashamed, either for your neglect of us, or for your adding to our affliction); I look upon you as my *sons*, and sons whom I love: I only write to *warn you*, both of your duty, to have some respect for us, and of your sin, if you have neglected us beyond what was your duty to have done.

15 For though ye have ten thousand instructers in Christ, yet *have ye* not many fathers: for ᵃin Christ Jesus I have begotten you through the Gospel.

The great lesson of this text is, That people ought to have a tender respect for those ministers whom God hath honoured with their first conversion, and bringing them home to Christ. God may make use of a multitude of ministers to instruct Christians, and carry on his work in their souls to perfection; but he maketh use of some particular minister at first to convince them, and be an instrument in the changing of their hearts; such they ought to have a great value for, they are their spiritual *fathers* in a proper sense. *For*, saith the apostle, *in Christ Jesus I have begotten you through the gospel:* where we have regeneration (as it signifieth a new state) set out in its causes. The principal efficient cause is *Christ Jesus;* the instrumental cause is the minister of the gospel; the means is the doctrine of the gospel, or the preaching of the gospel. *In Christ Jesus* signifieth here by the grace of Christ Jesus; those who are born again, are not born of flesh or of blood, but of the will of God, John i. 13, and by the influence of Christ upon their hearts; though God makes use of the minister of the gospel as his instrument, and the minister makes use of the word and the preaching of the gospel, as the sacred means which God hath appointed to that end, 1 Pet. i. 23. All these causes unite and concur in the work of regeneration.

16 Wherefore I beseech you, ᵇbe ye followers of me.

I might as a father command you, but *I beseech you, be ye followers of me,* in preserving the unity and promoting the holiness of the church. He expounds this, chap. xi. 1, *Be ye followers of me, as I am of Christ.* Holiness of life and conversation is necessary to a true minister of Christ; for their people ought not only to be their hearers, but their followers; they are *ensamples to the flock,* 1 Pet. v. 3, and ought to be examples of believers, *in word, in conversation, in charity, in spirit, in faith, in purity,* 1 Tim. iv. 12; in all things showing themselves patterns of good works; *in doctrine showing uncorruptness, gravity, sincerity,* &c., Tit. ii. 7. Those who teach well and live ill, are no good ministers of Christ; they cannot say unto people, *Be ye followers of me.*

17 For this cause have I sent unto you ᶜTimotheus, ᵈwho is my beloved son, and faithful in the Lord, who shall bring you ᵉinto remembrance of my ways which be in Christ, as I ᶠteach every where ᵍin every church.

This Timothy Paul found at Lystra, Acts xvi. 1. *His father was a Greek*, his mother *a Jewess*, therefore Paul circumcised him; her name was Eunice, the daughter of Lois, 2 Tim. i. 5. Paul took him along with him in his travels. He was ordained by the imposition *of the hands of the presbytery,* 1 Tim. iv. 14; 2 Tim. i. 6. Paul calls him his *beloved son,* either because he was his spiritual son, or because he was by him instructed in the gospel: he calls him his *own son in the faith*, 1 Tim. i. 2. *Faithful in the Lord*, because he was faithful in the work of the Lord, in the business of the ministry. *Who shall bring you into remembrance of my ways which be in Christ, as I teach every where in every church;* he (saith the apostle) shall bring to your remembrance my ways in the Lord, he shall acquaint you with both what doctrine I have preached and what course of life I have lived; how I have preached to every church, what rules I have given for the ordering of every church, and how I have walked before and toward them.

h ch. 5. 2.   18 ʰ Now some are puffed up, as though I would not come to you.

I hear that some of your teachers, and some of your members, are so conceited of themselves, that they would persuade you that I durst not see their faces, or come to discourse with them face to face, and therefore *would not come unto you.*

i Acts 19. 21.
ch. 16. 5.
2 Cor. 1. 15,
23.
k Acts 18.21.
Rom. 15. 32.
Heb. 6. 3.
Jam. 4. 15.

19 ⁱ But I will come to you shortly, ᵏ if the Lord will, and will know, not the speech of them which are puffed up, but the power.

But I will come to you shortly: Paul intended in his journey to Rome to pass through Macedonia and Achaia, but he knew that God could hinder him, and therefore he adds, *if the Lord will:* neither did Paul go to them so soon as he intended, but had time before he went to write another Epistle, as we shall afterwards find. All Christians are bound, when they promise or resolve upon any journeys, to understand, *if God will,* and to have in their thoughts the power of God to hinder them, and to speak with submission to his pleasure, who counteth their steps and telleth their wanderings, and orderth their steps; though they be not strictly bound at all times to use this form of speech. *And will know, not the speech of them which are puffed up, but the power:* and when I come, then I shall understand these teachers of yours, who so vilify me; I shall not regard so much their fine words and philosophical reasonings, as what there is of spiritual life and power in them; either in their doctrine or life, how conducive it is to the ends of the gospel, and how consonant to the truth of the gospel, what good they do amongst you, what manner of lives they live: these are the things that my eyes shall be upon, and which I shall regard.

l ch. 2. 4.
1 Thess.1.5.

20 For ˡ the kingdom of God *is* not in word, but in power.

The kingdom of God in the church, or *the kingdom of God* in the particular soul. God hath not sent his ministers to subdue souls to himself by fine, florid words and phrases, but by a lively preaching the gospel, while his power attends their plain preaching; and the power and efficacy of the preachers' doctrine appeareth in their holy life and conversation, so as their people cannot say to them, *Physician, heal thyself,* as to those spiritual diseases which thou wouldst cure us of. So the kingdom of God in particular souls doth not appear in words, but in the power which the word of God hath upon men's hearts, in subduing their lusts and corruptions, and bringing their hearts into a subjection to his will.

m 2Cor. 10.
2. & 13. 10.

21 What will ye? ᵐ shall I come unto you with a rod, or in love, and *in* the spirit of meekness?

Which will ye rather choose? that I should come unto you as a father cometh to his child under some guilt for which he must punish and correct him, or as a father cometh to his child that hath done nothing provoking his displeasure, in love, and meekly? I am not willing to come to you to correct and punish any of you by ecclesiastical censures, which are a rod which Christ hath intrusted to me; I had rather come in love and meekness, that we might mutually rejoice in each other's society.

CHAP. V.

Paul reproveth a scandalous incest committed and protected from censure in the church at Corinth, 1, 2; *and by his authority in Christ excommunicateth the offender* 3—5.

The necessity of purging out the old leaven, 6—8. *Christians guilty of notorious crimes are not to be consorted with,* 9—13.

IT is reported commonly *that there is* fornication among you, and such fornication as is not so much as ᵃ named among the Gentiles, ᵇ that one should have his ᶜ father's wife.

a Eph. 5. 3.
b Lev. 18. 8.
Deut. 22. 30.
& 27. 20.
c 2 Cor. 7. 12.

The apostle here giveth a reason of the question which he propounded in the former chapter, whether they would be willing that, when he came to them, he should come unto them with a rod? because such horrid wickedness was committed amongst them, as he, being an apostle to whom Christ had intrusted the government of his church, could not pass over without correction: he instanceth here in one, which he calleth *fornication;* by which word is often in Scripture to be understood all species of uncleanness, though, in strict speaking, we by *fornication* understand the uncleanness of a single person, as by *adultery* we understand the uncleanness of a person married, and by *incest* the uncleanness of a person with some near relation, as a mother, a sister: in strict speaking, the sin here reflected on was incest; but the Scripture by this word comprehends all species of unlawful mixtures. *Such fornication as is not so much as named among the Gentiles:* this sin he aggravates by saying, that the Gentiles by the light of nature discerned and declined such an abomination; by whom is not to be understood the more brutish part, but the more civilized part of the heathen, such as the Romans, &c. were. *That one should have his father's wife:* by having *his father's wife,* in this place, is not to be understood, the marrying of his father's wife, his father being dead; but the using of his father's wife as his wife while his father was yet alive, (as some judicious interpreters think,) because hardly any nation would have endured a son openly to have married the widow of his father. And in 2 Cor. vii. 12, there is mention made not only of one *that had done,* but of another *that had suffered* the *wrong;* which latter must be the father himself: so as there was both incest and whoredom in this fact.

2 ᵈ And ye are puffed up, and have not rather ᵉ mourned, that he that hath done this deed might be taken away from among you.

d ch. 4. 18.
e 2 Cor. 7. 7, 10.

And ye are puffed up; you are so conceited of your own parts and gifts, and are so full of your contentions about the preference of ministers, and things of little concernment to your souls and the interest of the church, that you have not been able to find leisure to deal with this scandalous person, as a church of Christ ought to have done. This seemeth rather the reason of their not mourning, than any rejoicing in iniquity, as if they had thought the gospel had opened that door against this licentiousness which the law had shut, or triumphed in this incestuous person, being one of their teachers (which can hardly be thought). *And have not rather mourned, that he that hath done this deed might be taken away from among you:* they ought rather to have mourned, keeping times of fasting and prayer, on the behalf of this scandalous member amongst them, that his sin might (upon his due sense of it, and repentance for it) have been forgiven him, and the blot upon their church, by their having such a one in their fellowship, might be washed out, by his being cast out of their fellowship and communion. It was no time for them to glory in their gifts, and be puffed up with the parts of their teachers or members, when they had such a blot upon them by a putrid member that was amongst them. They had a great deal more cause for humiliation, than for pride and glorying.

3 ᶠ For I verily, as absent in body, but present in spirit, have ‖ judged already, as though I were present, *concerning* him that hath so done this deed,

f Col. 2. 5.
‖ Or, determined.

Though I be absent as to my bodily presence, yet God having intrusted me with a superintendency and care over his church amongst you, out of the care and solicitude which I have for you, as well as the other churches of Christ, and in discharge of that trust which God hath re-

I. CORINTHIANS V

posed in me, I do determine, and have determined as much as if I were present amongst you, what ought to be done by you concerning this person so notoriously scandalous.

4 In the name of our Lord Jesus Christ, when ye are gathered together, and my spirit, ^g with the power of our Lord Jesus Christ,

^g Matt. 16. 19. & 18. 18. John 20. 23. 2 Cor. 2. 10. & 13. 3, 10.

In the name of our Lord Jesus Christ; either having solemnly called upon the name of the Lord Jesus Christ for his counsel and direction, or blessing your action, that it may be of spiritual advantage to the party concerned; or according to the command of Christ, or by his authority, or for his glory. It may be referred either to what went before, I have judged or determined by the authority of Christ; or to what follows after. *When ye are gathered together, and my spirit;* when you are gathered together by the authority, or according to the institution, of Jesus Christ, and my spirit with you, you having my judgment in the case. *With the power of our Lord Jesus Christ;* and the power and authority of Christ committed to me, and to you, as a church of Christ.

5 ^h To deliver such an one unto ⁱ Satan for the destruction of the flesh, that the spirit may be saved in the day of the Lord Jesus.

h Job 2. 6. Ps. 109. 6. 1 Tim. 1. 20. i Acts 26. 18.

What this delivering to Satan is, (of which also we read, 1 Tim. i. 20,) is something doubted by interpreters. That by it is to be understood excommunication, or casting out of the communion of the church, can hardly be doubted by any that considereth, 1. That the apostle speaketh of an action which might be, and ought to have been, done by the church of Corinth when they met together, and for the not doing of which the apostle blameth them. 2. That the end of the action was, taking away the scandalous person from the midst amongst them, ver. 2; purging out the old leaven, that they might become a new lump, ver. 7. 3. It was a punishment inflicted by many. Those, therefore, who interpret the phrase of an extraordinary power given the apostles or primitive churches, miraculously to give up the scandalous person to the power of the devil, to be afflicted, tormented, or vexed by him, (though not unto death,) seem not to have considered, that the apostle would not have blamed the church of Corinth for not working a miracle, and that we no where read of any such power committed to any church of Christ; and one would in reason think, that persons under such circumstances should rather be pitied and helped, than shunned and avoided. The only question therefore is, Why the apostle expresseth excommunication under the notion of being delivered to Satan? Some have thought that the reason is, because God was so pleased to ratify the just censures of his church, delivering such persons as were cast out of it into the hands of Satan, to be vexed and tormented by him; and that this might be in some particular cases, none can deny, but that this was an ordinary dispensation of Providence as to all excommunicated persons, wants better proof than any have yet showed us. It appears to me a more probable account of this phrase which others have given us, telling us, that Satan is called the god of the world, and the prince of the world, as world is taken in opposition to the church of God; so as delivering to Satan, is no more than our Saviour's— *If he neglect to hear the church, let him be unto thee as an heathen man and a publican,* Matt. xviii. 17. Only for the further terror of it, the apostle expresseth it by this phrase of delivering up to Satan; thereby letting us know, how dreadful a thing it is to be out of God's special protection, and shut out from the ordinary means of grace and salvation, and exposed to the temptations of our grand adversary the devil, which is the state of all those who are out of the church, either having never been members of it, or, according to the rules of Christ, cast out of the communion of it. *For the destruction of the flesh, that the spirit may be saved in the day of the Lord Jesus:* the end of excommunication is not for the destruction of the person of him who is cast out, but for the destruction of his flesh, that is, his lusts, which are often in Scripture called flesh, or the maceration and affliction of his body through grief and sorrow; for a determination of his fleshly being cannot be here understood by *the destruction of the flesh,* for that is no effect of excommunication; and those who interpret the delivery to Satan, of an extraordinary punishment, which the apostles or church in the primitive times had a power to inflict, make it to terminate not in the death, but in the torments only, of the person so punished. Again, the apostle mentioneth this punishment as a means to the eternal salvation of this person's soul in the day of Christ. There is no text in Scripture which more clearly asserts and opens the ordinance and nature of excommunication, than this text doth. As to those who are to inflict it, it lets us know, that it is to be done by the church, *when gathered together;* though the elders of the church may put the church upon it, and decree it, yet the consent and approbation of the whole church must be to it; and indeed it is vain for the officers of a church to cast any out of a communion, when the members of that communion will yet have communion with him or them so cast out. It also lets us know, that it is a censure by which men are not shut out of the fellowship of men as men, but of men as Christians, as a church of Christ, in such religious actions and duties as concern them, considered as such a body: excommunication doth not make it unlawful for persons to buy and sell with the persons excommunicated, but to eat and drink at the Lord's table with them, or have communion with them in acts proper to a church as the church of Christ. The excommunicated person is in something a better condition than a heathen, for he is not to be counted *as an enemy, but admonished as a brother,* 2 Thess. iii. 15. Heathens also may hear the word; he is only to be avoided in acts of church fellowship; and as to intimate communion, though it be not religious, as appeareth from this chapter, ver. 11, and from 2 Thess. iii. 14. Further, we are taught from hence, that none ought to be excommunicated but for notorious, scandalous sins, nor without a solemn invocation on the name of Christ, inquiring his will in the case. We are further taught, that the person that is duly excommunicated is in a miserable state, he is delivered up to Satan, cast out of God's special protection, which is peculiar to his church, and oftentimes exposed to formidable temptations. Finally, we are from this text instructed, that excommunication ought to be so administered, as may best tend to the saving of the soul of him that falls under that censure: men's end in excommunications should not be the ruin of persons in their health or estates, only the humbling of them, and bringing them to a sense of their sins, and a true repentance; and all means in order to that end should be used, even to such as are cast out of any church, such are repeated admonitions, the prayers of the church for them, &c.

6 ^k Your glorying *is* not good. Know ye not that ^l a little leaven leaveneth the whole lump?

k ver. 2. ch. 3. 21. & 4. 19. Jam. 4. 16. l ch. 15. 33. Gal. 5. 9. 2 Tim. 2. 17.

You boast and glory because you have men of parts amongst you, persons whom the world count wise; *your glorying is not good;* what do you glory for, when you have such a scandalous person amongst you, and take no care to cast him out? Can you be ignorant, that as *a little leaven* taken into the midst of the meal, and there kept, presently soureth the whole mass, and *leaveneth the whole lump;* so one notorious, scandalous sinner detained in the bosom of a church, casts a blot upon the whole church?

7 Purge out therefore the old leaven, that ye may be a new lump, as ye are unleavened. For even ^m Christ our ⁿ Passover ‖ is sacrificed for us:

m Is. 53. 7. John 1. 29. ch. 15. 3. 1 Pet. 1. 19. Rev. 5. 6, 12. n John 19. 14. ‖ Or, *is slain.*

Purge out therefore the old leaven: if the article τὴν in this place be emphatical (as some think) it ought to have been translated this old leaven, that is, the incestuous person, whose communion with you influenceth your whole communion, which is defiled by it, through your church's neglect of their duty with reference to him. If the article be not to be taken emphatically, these words may be understood as spoken to every individual member of this church, and is no more than *put off the old man;* the lusts and corruptions of our hearts, as well as false doctrine, being compared to leaven, which influence our whole man, as leaven doth the whole mass of meal. The first seemeth to be most proper to this place, if we consider what went before, and that the apostle is speaking to the whole church, and had been before speaking of an act to be done by them

I. CORINTHIANS V

not singly, but when they should be gathered together in a church assembly; these he commands to purge out the old leaven, that is, this incestuous person. *That ye may be a new lump;* that they might be truly a Christian church, reformed from such things as no way agreed with the doctrine and profession of the gospel. *As ye are unleavened;* as you are or should be unleavened, like the Jews, who at the passover kept the feast of unleavened bread, when for seven days together they might have no leavened bread in any of their houses, Lev. xxiii. 6. *For even Christ our Passover is sacrificed for us;* for though the feast of the Jewish passover be ceased, and you be tied to none of those Levitical observations, yet you are under as high an obligation; for Christ, who is the true paschal Lamb, is slain or sacrificed for us, and your old man should be crucified with him, and you no longer serve sin.

o Ex. 12. 15. & 13. 6.
‖ Or, *holyday.*
p Deut.16.3.
q Matt. 16. 6, 12.
Mark 8. 15.
Luke 12. 1.

8 Therefore °let us keep ‖the feast, ᵖnot with old leaven, neither ᵠwith the leaven of malice and wickedness; but with the unleavened *bread* of sincerity and truth.

Therefore let us keep the feast: here is a manifest allusion to the feast of the Jewish passover, which was immediately followed with the feast of unleavened bread for seven days. As the passover prefigured Christ, who is our paschal Lamb, whose flesh we eat and whose blood we drink by believing, and sacramentally in the Lord's supper; so the Jewish subsequent feast of unleavened bread prefigured all the days of a Christian's life, which are to be spent, *not with the old leaven, neither with the leaven of malice and wickedness; but with the unleavened bread of sincerity and truth:* which may be either understood of those evil and good habits which they signify, and so let us know the duty of every particular Christian to take heed of any malice or wickedness; or else (which seemeth most proper to this place) the abstract is put for the concrete, *malice and wickedness* for wicked and malicious men, and *sincerity and truth* for persons that are true and sincere. So that we are from hence taught, both the duty of every particular Christian, considering that Christ hath died as a sacrifice for his sin, to live up to the rule which he hath given us, abhorring malice and all wickedness, and acting truth and sincerity; and also the duty of every true church of Christ, to keep their communion pure from the society of wicked and malicious men, and made up of men of truth and sincerity. The latter seemeth to be principally intended.

r See ver. 2.
7. 2 Cor. 6.
14. Eph. 5.
11. 2 Thess. 3. 14.

9 I wrote unto you in an epistle ʳnot to company with fornicators:

It should seem that Paul had wrote so in some former epistle which he had directed to this church, which is lost; for we must think that Paul wrote more epistles to the several churches than those left us upon record in holy writ (yet so as not to undermine the perfection of the Holy Scriptures). By *fornicators* are meant any sorts of unclean persons known to them; and the keeping company with them, which the apostle had prohibited to the Corinthians, was not a mere fellowship with them in their works of darkness, but any intimacy of communion with any such persons.

s ch. 10. 27.
t ch. 1. 20.
u John 17. 15. 1 John 5. 19.

10 ˢYet not altogether with the fornicators ᵗ of this world, or with the covetous, or extortioners, or with idolaters; for then must ye needs go ᵘout of the world.

Yet not altogether with the fornicators of this world; I did not intend that admonition as to such persons as were no Christians, no members of the church (so this term *world* is used, John xv. 19; xvii. 14; and so it is to be interpreted here). He extendeth this admonition to other scandalous sinners, such as *covetous* persons, by which he understandeth such as by any open and scandalous acts discover their too great love of money, whether by oppression, or by cheating and defrauding, &c.; *or extortioners,* as such exact more than their due; *or with idolaters,* by which he understandeth such as worship images: and under these few species of scandalous sinners here mentioned, the apostle understands all others alike scandalous. *For then must ye* needs go *out of the world;* for (saith he) you could have no commerce nor trading with men in the world, if you might keep no company with such as these. Which is true at this day, when the world is much more Christianized than it was at that time.

11 But now I have written unto you not to keep company, ˣif any man that is called a brother be a fornicator, or covetous, or an idolater, or a railer, or a drunkard, or an extortioner; with such an one ʸno not to eat.

x Mat. 18.17.
Rom. 16. 17.
2 Thess. 3
6, 14.
2 John 10.

y Gal. 2. 12.

Of late there have been some disputes what eating is here intended, whether at the Lord's table, or at our common tables. Intimacy of communion is that which undoubtedly is here signified by eating; and the apostle's meaning is, that the members of this church should forbear any unnecessary fellowship and communion with any persons that went under the name of Christians, and yet indulged themselves in any notorious and scandalous courses of life; of which he reckoneth up several sorts. 1. Unclean persons, noted for any kind of uncleanness. 2. Covetous persons; by which he understands all such as, out of their too great love of money, either scandalously sought to add to their heap, or to detain what was others' just due. 3. Idolaters; by which he understands such as out of fear, or to gain favour with the heathen amongst whom they lived, would frequent and perform Divine worship in the idol's temple. 4. Railers, such as used their tongues intemperately and scandalously, to the prejudice of others' reputation. 5. Drunkards; under which notion he comprehends all such as drank hot liquors intemperately, whether they had such an effect upon them as to deprive them of the use of their reason or no. 6. Extortioners, viz. such as, being in any place, exacted more than was their due of those that were under their power. But yet by this interpretation the argument is not lost against eating with such at the table of the Lord, which is no more necessary communion with them, than civil eating is; for neither hath God spread that table for any such, neither ought any church to endure any such persons in its communion: nor are any Christians bound for ever to abide in the communion of that church, which shall wilfully neglect the purging out of such old leaven. Admitting this precept prohibitive of a civil intimacy with scandalous persons, though they be called brethren, it holds *a fortiori,* as a stronger argument against religious communion with such, in ordinances to which, apparently, they have no proximate right.

12 For what have I to do to judge ᶻthem also that are without? do not ye judge ᵃthem that are within?

z Mark 4.11.
Col. 4. 5.
1 Thes.4.12.
1 Tim. 3. 7.
a ch. 6. 1, 2, 3, 4.

For what have I to do to judge them also that are without? my jurisdiction extendeth not to heathens; God hath intrusted to me not the government of the world, but the government of his church. *Do not ye judge them that are within?* nor would I have you concern yourselves further, than in judging your own members, those that are within the pale of your church, and who, by a voluntary joining with you, have given you a power over them.

13 But them that are without God judgeth. Therefore ᵇput away from among yourselves that wicked person.

b Deut. 13. 5. & 17. 7.
& 21. 21. &
22. 21,22, 24.

But them that are without God judgeth; for heathens that live brutish and scandalous lives, God will judge them; the church hath nothing to do with them, they never gave up themselves to them, and are only under the justice of God in the administrations of his providence. *Therefore put away from among yourselves that wicked person:* do you, therefore, what belongs to you to do. This incestuous person, besides his subjection to God's judgment, who is the Judge of all, whether within or without the church, is subjected also to your judicature; therefore use that power which God hath given you, and put away from amongst you that evil person. The conclusion of this discourse helps us clearly to understand those former precepts, *Purge out the old leaven,* ver. 7, and, *Let us keep the feast, not with the old leaven,* ver. 8; that they are not so properly to be interpreted of particular Christians' purging

I. CORINTHIANS VI

out their lusts and corruptions, (though that be every good Christian's duty,) as of every Christian church's duty to purge themselves of flagitious and scandalous persons.

CHAP. VI

The Corinthians are reproved for bringing their controversies before heathen judges, which they ought to decide among themselves, 1—6. There would be no occasion for lawsuits, if men acted up to the principles of the gospel, 9; which exclude from the kingdom of God all notorious transgressors of the moral law, 7—11. All lawful things are not expedient, 12—14; but fornication is a gross offence against our bodies, which are members of Christ, temples of the Holy Ghost, and not our own to dispose of otherwise than to God's glory, 15—20.

DARE any of you, having a matter against another, go to law before the unjust, and not before the saints?

The apostle having already sharply reflected upon this church for their pride, and contentions, and divisions, (which were branches from that root,) and for their vilifying him who was their spiritual father, and magnifying their instructors above him, as also for their looseness in their church discipline; he cometh in this chapter to another thing, viz. their going to law before pagan judges; for such was the misery of those times, that they had no other, though some think that they might have had, the pagan persecutions being as yet not begun. The apostle speaks of this as a thing which he wondered that they durst be guilty of, that they should be no more tender of the glory of God in the reputation of the Christian religion, and should not rather choose arbitrators amongst the members of their church, to hear and determine such differences as arose amongst them, than give pagans an occasion to reproach the Christian religion for the contentions and feuds of Christians. The reputation of the gospel and the professors of it being the thing for which Paul was here concerned, and upon the account of which he thus speaketh; it becometh Christians yet to consider, whether what he saith concerneth not them, where either the judges, or the generality of the auditors in such judgments, may probably reproach religion, or that way of God which they own, for their trivial and uncharitable contentions.

2 Do ye not know that [a] the saints shall judge the world? and if the world shall be judged by you, are ye unworthy to judge the smallest matters?

[a Ps. 49. 14. Dan. 7. 22. Mat. 19. 28. Luke 22. 30. Rev. 2. 26. & 3. 21. & 20. 4.]

If indeed the Corinthians had had no other competent judges, they might have been excused in making use of infidel judges; but, saith the apostle, you have other persons competent enough, whom you may (by your submission to them) make judges; for you *know that the saints shall judge the world;* in the same sense (as some think) as Christ saith the Ninevites and the queen of the south should rise up in judgment against the Jews, and condemn them; but certainly there is something more than that in it; when the apostle said, the saints should judge the world, he intended to say something of them which was not common to some heathens with them. Others therefore think, that the saints in the day of judgment shall judge the world, approving the sentence of Christ pronounced against the world, and as being assessors with Christ, which indeed is what Christ said of the apostles, Matt. xix. 28; Luke xxii. 39. Others think, that the phrase only signifieth a great honour and dignity, to which the saints shall be advanced. A late learned and very critical author hath another notion of the saints' judging the world here spoken of, interpreting it of a time when the secular judgment of the world should be given to the saints, which was prophesied by Daniel, chap. vii. 18, 27, and therefore might be known by them. If this be the sense, it is either a prophecy of God's giving the government of the world into the hands of Christians, (which fell out after this in Constantine's time,) or else it signifies such a time towards the end of the world, as those that expect a fifth monarchy speak of, when those that are true saints, in the strictest sense, shall have the government of the world; which seemeth not probable, considering what the Scripture speaks of persecutions, and wars, and disorders, rather increasing than abating towards the end of the world. The apostle therefore here seemeth rather to speak of the saints judging the world in the last day, approving the sentence of Christ the Judge of the quick and the dead; or else to prophesy of that time, when Christianity should so far obtain in the world, that the government either of the whole world, or of a great part of it, should be in the hands of Chrstians. From whence the apostle strongly concludeth the competency of Christians to arbitrate and determine little matters of difference amongst Christians, in their commerce and civil dealings one with another.

3 Know ye not that we shall [b] judge angels? how much more things that pertain to this life?

[b 2 Pet. 2. 4. Jude 6.]

That the saints shall judge angels, is here so plainly asserted, as a thing within their knowledge, that none can doubt it; but how, or when, or what angels, is not so easily determined. The best interpreters understand it of the evil angels, that is, the devils, whom the saints shall judge at the last day, agreeing with the Judge of the whole earth in the sentence which he shall then give against the evil angels, confining them to the bottomless pit, who, while this world lasteth, have a greater liberty as princes of the air, to rove abroad in the air, and to work mightily in the children of disobedience. Others understand the judging of angels here mentioned, of the spoiling of the devils of the kingdom that they exercise in the world, in the places where the gospel hath not prevailed, by lying oracles, and seducing men to idolatry, and the worshipping of devils: in which sense Christ said, *Now shall the prince of this world be cast out,* John xii. 31. From hence the apostle argues the competency of their brethren to judge of and to determine those little matters which were in difference betwixt them, being but *things* concerning *this life,* and so of far less consequence than the judging of the world and the evil angels at the last day.

4 [c] If then ye have judgments of things pertaining to this life, set them to judge who are least esteemed in the church.

[c ch. 5. 12.]

If then ye have judgment of things pertaining to this life, that is, if you have any cause of suing or impleading one another for things that pertain to this life, be they of what nature they will, *set them to judge who are least esteemed in the church;* rather commit the umpirage and determination of such little differences to the meanest members of your church, than go to contend before pagans and infidels: or do not employ your teachers about them, who have higher work to be employed in; but employ those who are of a lower order in the church, and whose business and concerns lie in secular affairs.

5 I speak to your shame. Is it so, that there is not a wise man among you? no, not one that shall be able to judge between his brethren?

6 But brother goeth to law with brother, and that before the unbelievers.

I do not speak this, as if I would have you make choice of the meanest persons among you to arbitrate and determine all matters that may be in difference betwixt you; but it would be a shame to you if, amongst you all, there could not be found one man whom you can judge wise enough to determine differences betwixt you about things of this life, without bringing one another into pagan courts, to the reproach and scandal of the religion which you profess: make use of any, yea, the meanest Christians, in such judgments, rather than infidels and unbelievers, who will make use of your differences to the reproaching of the holy name of God.

7 Now therefore there is utterly a fault among you, because ye go to law one with another. [d] Why do ye not rather take wrong? why do ye not rather *suffer yourselves to* be defrauded?

[d Prov. 20. 22. Matt. 5. 39, 40. Luke 6. 29. Rom. 12. 17, 19. 1 Thes. 5. 15.]

Now therefore there is utterly a fault among you, because ye go to law one with another; not that it is simply unlawful for men to make use of human laws, and courts, and methods of judicature; for even the laws of men are good, if they be lawfully used: and the word here used by the apostle is ἥττημα, which signifieth rather an impotency or weakness of mind and affections, a defect or diminution from perfection, than any scandalous sin. Going to law with brethren (though lawful in itself) may be made unlawful by circumstances: 1. When it is before judges that are unbelievers, so as men's going to law before them tends to the reproach of religion, the credit and reputation of the gospel ought to be dearer to us than any little secular concern. This was the case in this place. 2. When it is for little matters, such as a coat or a cloak. It is against the law of charity to do another a great wrong to recover to ourselves a little that is our right. 3. When we cannot do it without wrath, anger, impatience, covetousness, or desire of revenge. It is a thing possible to go to law without sin, but what very few do, through that corruption which cleaveth to corrupt nature. *Why do ye not rather take wrong? why do ye not rather suffer yourselves to be defrauded?* it is therefore far more becoming conscientious Christians to take a little wrong, and to suffer themselves to be cheated of their right, especially under such circumstances, where the credit of the gospel and religion must lose more than they can get. And to do otherwise speaks ἥττημα, a defect or imperfection in Christians, and is not without its guilt. If, by their contentiousness, they do not show themselves so bad as some would make them, who hold all contendings at law amongst Christians unlawful, yet they do not show themselves so good as the rule of Christianity requireth them to be, Matt. v. 39, 40; Luke vi. 29; Rom. xii. 19.

8 Nay, ye do wrong, and defraud, ᵉand that *your* brethren.

ᵉ 1 Thess. 4. 6.

The apostle riseth higher in his charge against them; he had before only charged them for want of self-denial, that they could not bear or suffer wrong; he now chargeth them for doing wrong and defrauding, and that not heathens, (which yet had been bad enough,) but Christians that were their brethren, whom they had the highest obligations upon them imaginable to love, and to do good to. And indeed this charge followeth directly upon the other: for as in war, one army always are murderers, or guilty of the blood which they spill; so in suing at law, (which is a civil war betwixt the two parties,) either the one or the other party suing must do wrong, either putting his brother to trouble and expense, to recover of him what is not his right, or that he might withhold from him what is truly and indeed his right, either of which is indeed a doing of wrong or defrauding.

9 Know ye not that the unrighteous shall not inherit the kingdom of God? Be not deceived: ᶠneither fornicators, nor idolaters, nor adulterers, nor effeminate, nor abusers of themselves with mankind,

ᶠ ch. 15. 50. Gal. 5. 21. Eph. 5. 5. 1 Tim. 1. 9. Heb. 12. 14. & 13. 4. Rev. 22. 15.

That by *the kingdom of God* is here meant the kingdom of glory, the happiness of another life, is plain, because he speaketh in the future tense; this kingdom, he saith, *the unrighteous*, that is, those who so live and die, *shall not inherit*. If we take the term *unrighteous* here to be a generical term, the species, or some of the principal species, of which are afterwards enumerated, it signifieth here the same with notoriously wicked men. But if we take it to signify persons guilty of acts of injustice towards themselves or others, it cannot be here understood as a general term, relating to all those species of sinners after enumerated; for so *idolaters* cannot properly be called unrighteous, but ungodly men. *Be not deceived*, (saith the apostle,) either by any false teachers, or by the many ill examples of such sinners that you daily have, nor by magistrates' connivance at these sins. *Neither fornicators;* neither such as, being single persons, commit uncleanness with others (for here the apostle distinguisheth these sinners from adulterers, whom he mentioneth afterward). *Nor idolaters;* nor such as either worship the creature instead of God, or worship the true God before images. *Nor adulterers;* nor such as, being married persons, break their marriage covenant, and commit uncleanness with such as are not their yokefellows. *Nor effeminate persons;* nor persons that give up themselves to lasciviousness, burning continually in lusts. *Nor abusers of themselves with mankind;* nor such as are guilty of the sin of Sodom, a sin not to be named amongst Christians or men.

10 Nor thieves, nor covetous, nor drunkards, nor revilers, nor extortioners, shall inherit the kingdom of God.

Nor thieves; nor such as take away the goods of their neighbours clandestinely, or by violence, without their consent or any just authority. *Nor covetous;* nor persons who discover themselves excessively to love money, by their endeavours to get it into their hands any way, by oppression, cheating, or defrauding others. *Nor drunkards;* nor persons that make drinking their business, and use it excessively, without regard to the law and rules of temperance and sobriety. *Nor revilers;* nor persons that use their tongues intemperately, railing at others, and reviling them with reproachful and opprobrious names. *Nor extortioners;* nor any such as by violence wring out of people's hands what is not their due. None of these, not repenting of these sinful courses, and turning from them into a contrary course of life, shall ever come into heaven.

11 And such were ᵍsome of you: ʰbut ye are washed, but ye are sanctified, but ye are justified in the name of the Lord Jesus, and by the Spirit of our God.

ᵍ ch. 12. 2. Eph. 2. 2. & 4. 22. & 5. 8. Col. 3. 7. Tit. 3. 3. ʰ ch. 1. 30. Heb. 10. 22.

In the two last verses the apostle had pronounced a terrible sentence, especially to the Corinthians, who, having been heathens lately, had wallowed in a great deal of this guilt; he therefore here, that they might be humbled, and have low thoughts of themselves, and not be puffed up, (as he had before charged them,) mindeth them, that some of them had been guilty of some of these enormous sins, some of them of one or some of them, and others of other of them. But, that they might not despair in their reflections upon that guilt, he tells them, they were *washed*, not only with the baptism of water, but with the baptism of the blood of Christ, and with the baptism of the Holy Ghost, *born again of water and of the Spirit*, John iii. 5; yea, and not only washed, but *sanctified*, filled with new, spiritual habits, through the renewing of the Holy Ghost: having obtained a true righteousness, in which they might stand and appear before God, even the righteousness of Christ, reckoned unto them for righteousness; *justified* through the merits of the Lord Jesus Christ, and *sanctified* through the Spirit of holiness. So that the washing, first mentioned in this verse, seemeth to be a generical term, comprehending both justification, remission of sin, and deliverance from the guilt of it; and also regeneration and sanctification, which is the proper effect of the Spirit of grace, creating in the soul new habits and dispositions, by which it is enabled and inclined, as to die unto sin, so to live unto God. This the apostle doth not say of them all, (for it is very probable there were in this church some hypocrites,) but of some of them.

12 ⁱAll things are lawful unto me, but all things are not ǁexpedient: all things are lawful for me, but I will not be brought under the power of any.

ⁱ ch. 10. 23. ǁ Or, *profitable.*

The words of this text are not so difficult in themselves, as it is to make out the connexion they have with, and the dependence they have upon, what went before and what followeth after. Some, thinking that they refer unto what the apostle had said before about their going to law before infidels in the first seven verses, lest any should say, Is it not then lawful for men to sue at law for their just dues and rights? the apostle answers, Admit it be, yet Christians ought not only to consider what is strictly lawful and just, but they ought to consider circumstances; for, *Quicquid non expedit, in quantum non expedit non licet,* is an old and good rule; An action that is in itself lawful, may be by circumstances made sinful and unlawful; and that was the case as to the Christians going to law before infidels. But others, and those the most, think that the apostle here begins a new head of discourse to dissuade them from the sin of fornication, and from an intemperate use of meat and drink, as being provocative of lust, and disposing them to that sin. Now, lest they should say, Is it not lawful then to eat and drink liberally, must we eat and drink for bare necessity? he

I. CORINTHIANS VI

answereth, *All things are lawful for me;* that is, all things which are not forbidden by the law of God may be used, may be done, under fair circumstances; but circumstances may alter the case, *all things* may not be *expedient* to be used or done by all persons, or at all times. The Corinthians might possibly conclude too much from what he had told them, that they were *washed, justified,* and *sanctified,* viz. that now all things were *lawful* to them, at least all things not simply and absolutely condemned in the word of God: the apostle correcteth their mistake, by telling them they were to have a regard to expedience, and the profit of others, the neglect of which might make things that were in themselves lawful to become unlawful. Besides that, they must take heed that they did not make such a use, even of lawful things, as to *be brought under the power of* them; which men are, when they become potent temptations to them to sin against God any way.

k Mat. 15. 17.
Rom. 14. 17.
Col. 2. 22, 23.

13 [k] Meats for the belly, and the belly for meats: but God shall destroy both it and them. Now the body *is* not for fornication, but [l] for the Lord; [m] and the Lord for the body.

l ver. 15, 19,
20. 1 Thess.
4. 3, 7.
m Eph. 5. 23.

The beginning of this verse seemeth to give a great light to our true understanding of the former verse, and maketh it very probable that the apostle spake with reference to the free use of meats and drinks, when he said, *All things are lawful for me.* Though God hath ordained *meats for* the filling of *the belly,* and hath made *the belly for* the receptacle of *meats,* for the nourishment of the body, so as the use of meats and drinks is lawful; yet when we see that the free use of them proveth inexpedient, as too much pampering the body, and disposing it to wantonness, so far as they do so they are to be avoided. Others make the connexion thus: All your contests are but for things which concern the belly, for meats and drinks, for perishing things, now, in things of this nature, all things that are lawful are not expedient. Others say, that the apostle here answereth or obviateth what the Nicolaitanes or the Epicureans held, that all sorts of meats and drinks were lawful, yea, fornication itself. The apostle grants the first, but denieth the second, there being not a parity of reason for the lawfulness of meats and drinks, and of fornication. He tells them, God had ordained meats for the belly of man, and had created the stomach and belly for the reception of meats for the nourishment of man's body, and the preservation of his life; yet they ought to use them lawfully, and to consider expedience in the use of them, and not too eagerly to contend for them, for *God shall destroy both* the belly, and the use of meats as to the belly. In the resurrection, as men shall not marry, nor give in marriage, so they shall hunger and thirst no more. But God had not created *the body* of a man *for fornication,* but for himself, that men by and with it might glorify his name, by doing his will. And *the Lord* is *for the body,* as the Head of it, to guide and direct the use of the several members of it; and as the Saviour of it, to raise it up at the last day, as he further declareth in the next words.

n Rom. 6. 5,
8. & 6. 11.
2 Cor. 4. 14.
o Eph. 1. 19,
20.

14 And [n] God hath both raised up the Lord, and will also raise up us [o] by his own power.

And God hath both raised up the Lord; the Lord Jesus Christ, as the first-fruits of those that sleep, from whose resurrection the apostle largely proveth our resurrection, chap. xv. *And will also raise up us by his own power:* God will raise up his saints by his own Almighty power.

p Rom. 12. 5.
ch. 12. 27.
Eph. 4. 12,
15, 16. & 5.
30.

15 Know ye not that [p] your bodies are the members of Christ? shall I then take the members of Christ, and make *them* the members of an harlot? God forbid.

Christ is united to the person of the believer, and he is the Head of the church, which is his mystical body; so that the *bodies* of believers *are* in a sense *the members of Christ,* and should be used by us as the members of Christ, which we should not rend from him: but he that doth commit fornication, rends his body from Christ, and maketh it *the member of an harlot;* for as the man and wife are *one flesh* by Divine ordination, Gen. ii. 24, so the fornicator and the harlot are one flesh by an impure conjunction.

16 What? know ye not that he which is joined to an harlot is one body? for [q] two, saith he, shall be one flesh.

q Gen. 2. 24.
Matt. 19. 5.
Eph. 5. 31.

The conjunction of the husband and wife, mentioned Gen. ii. 24, and the conjunction of the fornicator and the harlot, differ not as to the species of the act, only as to the morality of it; the former is an honest and lawful act, the other a dishonest and filthy act. So that he that is wickedly joined to a harlot, maketh himself one flesh with her with whom he committeth that folly and lewdness, and he must needs by it separate his body from its membership with Christ, whose holiness will admit no such union.

17 [r] But he that is joined unto the Lord is one spirit.

r John 17.
21, 22, 23.
Eph. 4. 4.
& 5. 30.

This phrase *joined unto the Lord,* is thought to be taken out of Deut. x. 20, *To him shalt thou cleave.* He that hath attained to that mystical union which is betwixt Christ and every one that is a true believer, is not essentially, but spiritually and mystically, *one spirit* with Christ; his spirit is united to the Spirit of Christ, and he is one by him in faith and love, and by obedience, Christ and he have one will, and he is ruled and governed by Christ: therefore you must take heed what you do in making your bodies the members of harlots, which they cannot be, and the members of Christ also.

18 [s] Flee fornication. Every sin that a man doeth is without the body; but he that committeth fornication sinneth [t] against his own body.

s Rom. 6.
12, 13.
Heb. 13. 4.

t Rom. 1. 24.
1 Thes. 4. 4.

The apostle cometh to a new argument, by which he presseth them to flee the sin of uncleanness. It is observed by some, that this sin is peculiarly to be resisted, not so much by resisting it, and pondering arguments against it, as by flying from it, avoiding all occasions of it, and not suffering our thoughts to feed upon it; but the apostle's argument is, because other sins are *without the body,* that is, the body hath not such a blemish and note or mark of infamy laid upon it by any other sin as by this: in drunkenness the liquor, in gluttony the meat, in other sins something without a man's self is that which is abused, but the body itself is the thing which is abused in this filthy sin. So he that is guilty of it, *sinneth* not only against his wife, with whom he is one flesh, but *against his body,* which he abuseth in this vile and sinful act, and upon which he imprints a mark of infamy and disgrace, a blot not to be washed out but with the blood of Christ. So as though by other sins men may sin against their own bodies, yet by no sin so eminently as by this sin. Other sins have their seat in the mind and soul; the body, and commonly some particular member of the body, is but the servant of the soul in the execution and committing of them; but lust, though indeed it ariseth from the heart, yet it is committed more in the body than any other sin is.

19 What? [u] know ye not that your body is the temple of the Holy Ghost *which is* in you, which ye have of God, [x] and ye are not your own?

u ch. 3. 16.
2 Cor. 6. 16.

x Rom. 14.
7, 8.

The apostle, chap. iii. 16, had called the church of Corinth, *the temple of God,* and there made use of it to dissuade them from dissensions and divisions, because by them they defiled and destroyed the temple of God; here he calls the members of that church, *the temple of the Holy Ghost,* which strongly proveth the Holy Ghost to be God: he makes use of it here as an argument to dissuade them from the sin of fornication. God's temple was built for his habitation upon earth, the place which he chose most to manifest himself in to his people, and for a place wherein his people were to pay him that external homage and worship, which he required of them under the law. So as the apostle's calling them *the temple of the Holy Ghost,* both minded them of the favour God had bestowed on them, and also of that homage and duty which they with their bodies were to pay unto God; the latter they could not perform, nor hope for the former, while they lived in the practice of a sin so contrary to the will of God. Besides, he mindeth them, that their bodies were not their own, they had them of God: they had them from God by creation; and they were upheld by the daily workings of his providence in

I. CORINTHIANS VI, VII

their upholding and preservation; God had not given them their bodies for this use, *the body* was *not for fornication*, as he had told them, ver. 13. So as in abusing their bodies, they abused what was not their own, nor in their own power to use, as they listed to use them; but to be used only for those ends, and in that manner, that he who had given them had prescribed and directed: and in these abuses there was a kind of sacrilege; as God of old charged the Jews, Ezek. xvi. 17—19, that they had taken the *jewels of* his *gold and* his *silver*, to make *images, and commit* spiritual *whoredom with them;* and they had taken his *meat*, his *fine flour*, his *oil*, and *incense to set before them,* &c.

y Acts 20.28. ch. 7. 23. Gal. 3. 13. Heb. 9. 12. 1 Pet. 1. 18. 19. 2 Pet. 2. 1. Rev. 5. 9.

20 For ʸye are bought with a price: therefore glorify God in your body, and in your spirit, which are God's.

For ye are bought with a price; what price this is that is here mentioned Peter tells us, both negatively and positively, 1 Pet. i. 18, 19: *Forasmuch as ye know that ye were not redeemed with corruptible things, as silver and gold, from your vain conversation received by tradition from your fathers; but with the precious blood of Christ, as of a lamb without blemish and without spot.* So he argueth with them against this sin from their redemption, it being suitable to reason, that those who are redeemed out of any slavery or captivity, should be the servants of him who redeemed them, not of those tyrants from whom they are redeemed; such are our lusts and corruptions, from which we are redeemed, as well as from that curse and wrath, which is the consequent of them. *Therefore glorify God in your body, and in your spirit, which are God's;* therefore, (saith the apostle,) you who are redeemed with a price, and with such a price, are bound to *glorify God*, as by speaking well of his name, so by obeying his will, Matt. v. 16. And this you are bound to do, not with your bodies or your spirits only, but in or with your bodies and spirits also, that is, with your whole man; for both of them are God's, by a manifold right, not that of creation and providence only, but of redemption also: with which exhortation the apostle finisheth this discourse, and cometh to give them an answer to some questions about which they had wrote unto him.

CHAP. VII

Marriage is to be used as a remedy against fornication, 1—9. *Christ hath forbidden to dissolve the bond thereof,* 10, 11. *Directions how to act where one of the parties is an unbeliever,* 12—16. *Every man must abide in and fulfil the duties of the state wherein he was called,* 17—24. *Directions concerning the marriage of virgins, respecting the distress of the times,* 25—38; *and concerning the second marriage of widows,* 39, 40.

a ver. 8, 26.

NOW concerning the things whereof ye wrote unto me: ᵃ*It is* good for a man not to touch a woman.

It seemeth, that though this church was very much corrupted, yet some of them retained a reverence for this great apostle, and had wrote one or more letters to him about some points, to which he returneth answer. It seemeth that one thing they had wrote to him about, was about marriage; not about the lawfulness of marrying, (that *doctrine of devils* was not broached so early in the world,) but concerning the advisableness of marriage, and men's use of their wives, in that afflicted state of the church. The apostle answereth, that *it is good for a man not to touch a woman*. When he saith, *It is good*, he means only more convenient, or better, with respect to the troubled state of the church, or that persons might be more at liberty for the service of God and the duties of religion. Upon these accounts it were more convenient for a man not to marry, for that he meaneth by touching a woman.

2 Nevertheless, *to avoid* fornication, let every man have his own wife, and let every woman have her own husband.

Nevertheless, to avoid fornication; in the Greek it is, Because of fornications; the sense of which can be no other than this which our translators give. The word is in the plural number, to signify that that which he meaneth by this term, is all sorts of impurities and uncleannesses, which are the products of the lusts of the flesh. These are sins of that nature and species, that if we cannot choose what in respect of some circumstances would be more convenient, we must balk it, rather than run into such a guilt. The apostle doth therefore determine, that in this case it was every man's duty to marry, and every woman's likewise; the reason of which must be, because God had ordained marriage as a means to bridle men, and restrain them from extravagant lusts. *His own wife, her own husband;* a clear place against polygamy.

3 ᵇLet the husband render unto the wife due benevolence: and likewise also the wife unto the husband.

b Ex. 21. 10. 1 Pet. 3. 7.

The word translated *due benevolence*, signifieth due goodwill or kindness, but from ver. 5, it appeareth what the apostle meaneth: Moses, Exod. xxi. 10, calleth it, the *duty of marriage;* both of them using a modest term in expressing the conjugal act, as we shall observe the Scripture always doing, when there is occasion to mention what men of profane hearts are ready to make a scoff at. The apostle maketh this the mutual duty both of husband and wife, under due circumstances, therefore useth the word *render*, which implieth the thing required to be an act of justice.

4 The wife hath not power of her own body, but the husband: and likewise also the husband hath not power of his own body, but the wife.

He gives the reason of it; because marriage takes away from each married person the power over his or her own body, and giveth it to their correlate. The apostle seemeth here to answer a question propounded to him by some members of this church, Whether, though they were married, the husband and wife might not forbear each other's bed, and make us of their society each with other merely for helps in other things, such as getting an estate, looking after the affairs of a family, &c.? which the apostle doth by no means judge advisable.

5 ᶜDefraud ye not one the other, except *it be* with consent for a time, that ye may give yourselves to fasting and prayer; and come together again, that ᵈSatan tempt you not for your incontinency.

c Joel 2. 16. Zech. 7. 3. See Ex. 19. 15. 1 Sam. 21. 4, 5.

d 1 Thes. 3. 5.

Defraud not one the other; that is, Withhold not yourselves one from another; which he rightly calls defrauding one another, because he had before declared it a debt; and further declared, that neither the husband nor the wife had a power over their own bodies, but the power of either of their bodies was in their correlate. He adds, *except it be with consent*, mutual consent, and then it is indeed no defrauding; and *for a time*, for a religious end, *that* they might *give themselves to fasting and prayer:* not that this abstinence is necessary to us by any Divine precept, to prepare us for solemn prayer, (for such only is here spoken of,) for then the apostle would not have made consent necessary in this case; but the Jews were commanded it, Exod. xix. 15, as a preparation to their hearing of the law; and it was a piece of the legal purification, as appeareth from 1 Sam. xxi. 4, as to which Christians were at liberty, and might observe or not observe it, as they agreed. *And come together again, that Satan tempt you not for your incontinency:* then he requires, that they should return to their former course, not defrauding one another, lest the devil, observing their abstinence, should tempt them to unlawful mixtures, seeing their inability to contain themselves within the bounds of temperance and chastity.

6 But I speak this by permission, ᵉ*and* not of commandment.

e ver. 12, 25. 2 Cor. 8. 8. & 11. 17.

Some refer these words to all that had gone before in this chapter; but the best interpreters rather refer them to what went immediately before in the preceding verse, declaring, that he had no express command from God, as to those things of abstaining for a time for fasting and prayer, and then coming together again, but he spake what he judged equitable and reasonable; but as to particular per-

I. CORINTHIANS VII

sons, they ought to judge and govern themselves according to their particular circumstances.

f Acts 26. 29.
g ch. 9. 5.
h Mat. 19. 12.
ch. 12. 11.

7 For ^fI would that all men were ^geven as I myself. But ^hevery man hath his proper gift of God, one after this manner, and another after that.

I would that all men were even as I myself: I would, in this place, can signify no more than, I could wish or desire, (if it were the will of God,) that all Christians had the gift of continency, which God (blessed be his name) hath given me: that this is meant, is plain by the next words, and ver. 9: it is apparent that Paul did not will this absolutely, for that had been to have willed the dissolution of the world, as well as the church, within the compass of that age. *But every man hath his proper gift of God, one after this manner, and another after that:* But, saith the apostle, every one hath not the gift of continency, one hath it, another hath it not; which is the same thing which our Saviour said in reply to his disciples, saying, *If the case of the man be so with his wife, it is not good to marry. All men cannot receive this saying, save they to whom it is given,* Matt. xix. 10.

i ver. 1, 26.

8 I say therefore to the unmarried and widows, ⁱIt is good for them if they abide even as I.

By *the unmarried and widows,* it is apparent that Paul means virgins that were never married, and such as, having been once married, had lost their husbands: though the first word, in the Greek, had been significative enough of persons in both these states; yet the apostle's using of two words, makes it past dispute; when he saith, it is good for such to be as he was, his meaning is, that it was better with respect to the present circumstances of Christians, or it was convenient, in which notion *good* is often taken, not for what is absolutely good; and indeed the nature of all good lieth in the conveniency or suitableness of the thing so called to us; and though in the Divine precepts there is always such a suitableness, so as they must be always good, yet in other things, which God hath left to our liberty, (such as is this of marriage,) a thing may be good or evil, as the circumstances of several persons, yea, of the same person, may vary. St. Paul considereth only the circumstances of the world common to all Christians, and upon them, determines this goodness, supposing the circumstances of the particular person not to rule otherwise. His not saying, it is good for them not to marry, but to be as he was, hath bred a question of no great import to be determined, Whether Paul was ever married or no? in the determination of which the ancients could not agree; but it is not worth spending our time about, considering that all agree he was at this time unmarried, which is all he doth here mean: if St. Paul was never married, we are sure Peter was, for we read of his *wife's mother sick of a fever,* Mark i. 30.

k 1 Tim. 5. 14.

9 But ^kif they cannot contain, let them marry: for it is better to marry than to burn.

That St. Paul's saying, *It is good,* &c. did not signify, it is the will of God, or, (as the papists would have it,) it is my counsel in order to your further perfection, is plain by his precept for them to marry if they could not contain; and this likewise lets us see that second marriages are not only lawful, but may be an incumbent duty, that is, if they who are concerned as to them cannot contain themselves within the bounds and rule of chastity, which must not only be interpreted with reference to acts of uncleanness. This is contradicted by the reason given by the apostle, determining that marriage was much more eligible than burning, which term signifies the inward fervour and eager inclinations of the mind, not the acts only of the outward man.

l See ver. 12, 26, 40.
m Mal. 2. 14, 16. Mat. 5. 32, & 19. 6, 9. Mark 10. 11, 12. Luke 16. 18.

10 And unto the married I command, ^l*yet* not I, but the Lord, ^mLet not the wife depart from *her* husband:

The apostle had spoke to the married before, but in another case, he now returneth in his discourse to them again, speaking to another case, which it should seem they had put to him; what it was is not plainly expressed, but it may easily be gathered from ver. 12, 13, as also from the apostle's determination in this verse: or it was this, Whether it was lawful for the husband to depart from his wife, or the wife from her husband, unless it were in the case of adultery; for though here be nothing spoken as to that case, yet it plainly must be excepted, as determined before by our Saviour; but as the Jews, so the heathens amongst whom these Corinthians lived, had entertained much too mean thoughts about the marriage bond, indulging themselves in a liberty to break it for every slight cause; and it should seem by ver. 12, 13, it was judged by them a sufficient cause, if one of them were not converted to the faith of Christ. Now in this case, saith the apostle, *I command,* and what I tell you is the will of God; it is not I alone who command it, but you are to look upon it as the will of God concerning you, though revealed to you by me that am the minister of God to you. *Let not the wife depart from her husband;* she may be divorced from her husband in case of fornication, but let her not for any other cause make a voluntary secession.

11 But and if she depart, let her remain unmarried, or be reconciled to *her* husband: and let not the husband put away *his* wife.

How our translators came to translate χωρισθῇ, which is manifestly a verb passive, *if she depart,* I cannot tell. It signifieth, if she be departed, and so is as well significative of a being parted from her husband by a judicial act of divorce, as of a voluntary departing. The Jews were wont to give bills of divorce to their wives for any trivial cause. The word is to be interpreted as well of any legal divorce, not according to the true meaning of the Divine law, as concerning a voluntary secession; in which case the apostle commandeth that she should marry to no other: the reason is plain, because no such cause of divorce broke the bond of marriage; she was yet the wife of her former husband in God's eye and account, and committed adultery if she married to another, as our Saviour had determined, Matt. v. 32; xix. 9. But he gives her a liberty to *be reconciled to her husband.* In case that a woman put away by her husband became another man's wife, by the law, Deut. xxiv. 4, she might not (though that latter husband died) return to her former husband; but in case she remained unmarried, she might be reconciled to him. *And let not the husband put away his wife;* the apostle giveth the same precept concerning husbands.

n ver. 6.

12 But to the rest speak I, ⁿnot the Lord: If any brother hath a wife that believeth not, and she be pleased to dwell with him, let him not put her away.

But to the rest speak I, not the Lord; either as to the other part of your Epistle, or as to the cases of the rest mentioned in your Epistle, I shall give you my advice so far as I am instructed by the Holy Spirit of God, though our Lord Jesus Christ hath set no certain rule concerning them. *If any brother hath a wife that believeth not: that believeth not,* both here and ver. 13, signifieth, that hath not embraced the Christian faith, but still remaineth a pagan. *And she be pleased to dwell with him;* if there be no other matter of difference betwixt such persons, save only in matter of religion, *let him not* for that *put her away.* If a Christian man or woman had their choice to make, it were unlawful for either of them to make choice of a pagan for their yoke-fellow; but if, after marriage, either the husband or the wife embraceth the Christian faith, the other correlate still abiding a pagan, their difference in religion is not a sufficient ground for a separation: this seemeth to be the apostle's meaning. The case seemeth a little different in the opinion of some divines, when the idolater or idolatress blasphemeth God and the true religion, and is continually tempting the correlate to apostacy: but it is hard to determine against the plain precept of so great an apostle, especially considering the reason by which he backeth his precept.

13 And the woman which hath an husband that believeth not, and if he be pleased to dwell with her, let her not leave him.

14 For the unbelieving husband is sanctified by the wife, and the unbelieving wife is

a Mal. 2. 15. sanctified by the husband: else °were your children unclean; but now are they holy.

Sanctifying, in holy writ, generally signifieth the separation or setting apart of a person or thing from a common, to and for a holy use, whether it be by some external rites and ceremonies, or by the infusing of some inward spiritual habits. In this place it seemeth to have a different sense from what it usually hath in holy writ; for it can neither signify the sanctification of the person by infused habits of grace; for neither is the unbelieving husband thus sanctified by the believing wife, neither is the unbelieving wife thus sanctified by the believing husband; nor are either of them thus set apart for the service of God by any legal rites: which hath made a great difference in the notions of interpreters, how *the unbelieving husband is sanctified by the believing wife*, or *the unbelieving wife, by the believing husband.* Some think it signifies no more than prepared for God, as *sanctified* signifies, Isa. xiii. 3. Others think they are sanctified by a moral denomination. I rather think it signifies, brought into such a state, that the believer, without offence to the law of God, may continue in a married estate with such a yoke-fellow; and the state of marriage is a holy state, notwithstanding the disparity with reference to religion. *Else were your children unclean;* otherwise, he saith, the children begotten and born of such parents would be unclean, in the same state that the children of pagan parents are without the church, not within the covenant, not under the promise. In one sense all children are unclean, i. e. children of wrath, born in sin, and brought forth in iniquity; but all are not in this sense unclean, some are within the covenant of grace, within the church, capable of baptism. *But now are they holy;* these are those that are called *holy;* not as inwardly renewed and sanctified, but relatively, in the same sense that all the Jewish nation are called *a holy people:* and possibly this may give us a further light to understand the term *sanctified,* in the former part of the verse. The unbelieving husband is so far sanctified by the believing wife, and the unbelieving wife so far sanctified by the believing husband, that as they may lawfully continue in their married relation, and live together as man and wife, so the issue coming from them both shall be by God counted in covenant with him, and have a right to baptism, which is one of the seals of that covenant, as well as those children both whose parents are believers.

p Rom. 12. 18. & 14. 19. ch. 14. 33. Heb. 12. 14. + Gr. *in peace.*
15 But if the unbelieving depart, let him depart. A brother or a sister is not under bondage in such *cases:* but God hath called us ᵖ† to peace.

If the unbelieving husband or the unbelieving wife will leave his or her correlate, that is, so leave them as to return no more to live as a husband or as a wife with her or him that is Christian, *let him depart.* Such a person hath broken the bond of marriage, and in such cases Christians are *not under bondage,* they are not tied by law to fetch them again, nor by the laws of God to keep themselves unmarried for their perverseness. But it may be objected, that nothing but adultery, by the Divine law, breaketh that bond. *Answ.* That is denied. Nothing but adultery is a justifiable cause of divorce: no man may put away his wife, nor any wife put away her husband, but for adultery. But the husband's voluntary leaving his wife, or the wife's voluntary leaving her husband, with a resolution to return no more to them, breaks also the bond of marriage, frustrating it as to the ends for which God hath appointed it; and, after all due means used to bring again the party departing to their duty, doth certainly free the correlate. So that although nothing can justify repudiation, or putting away a wife or a husband, and marrying another, but the adultery of the person so divorced and repudiated; yet the departure either of husband or wife without the other's consent for a long time, and refusal to return after all due means used, especially if the party so going away doth it out of a hatred and abomination of the other's religion, will justify the persons so deserted, after due waiting and use of means to reduce him or her to their duty, wholly to cast off the person deserting; for no Christian in such a case, by God's law, is under bondage. *But God hath called us to peace;* for God hath called Christians unto peace, and in his ordinance of marriage aimed at the quiet and peace of his people in their service of him in their families and relations; and therefore as Christians ought not to disturb the peace of their own consciences, turning away their relations, though they be unbelievers; yet neither are they bound, if such will leave them, to court their own continual trouble and disturbance.

16 For what knowest thou, O wife, whether thou shalt ᑫsave *thy* husband? q 1 Pet. 3. 1. or †how knowest thou, O man, whether † Gr. *what.* thou shalt save *thy* wife?

The apostle having before determined the lawfulness of a Christian husband's or wife's abiding in a state of marriage with a wife or husband that was an infidel, if she or he were willing to abide with the believer, now argues the great advantage which might be from it, for the glory of God, and the good of the soul of such husband or wife. *What knowest thou, O wife?* saith he; it is not certain that God will so far bless thy converse with thy husband or wife, as that thou shalt, by thy instruction, admonition, or example, be an occasion or instrument to bring them to Christ; but it is neither impossible nor improbable, and their willingness (notwithstanding their difference from thee in religion) yet to abide with thee, may give thee some hopes that they will hearken to thee. They are often (in the language of holy writ) said to save others, who are instrumental to bring them to Christ, chap. ix. 22; 1 Tim. iv. 16; James v. 20. We ought to bear with many inconveniences to ourselves, where our bearing with them may any way promote the glory of God or the good of souls.

17 But as God hath distributed to every man, as the Lord hath called every one, so let him walk. And ʳso ordain I r ch. 4. 17. 2 Cor. 11. 28. in all churches.

Calling in this place signifieth that station and course of life, wherein by the providence of God any man is set. Some think, that this precept hath a special reference to what went before, as if the sense were this, If God by his providence hath so ordered it that thy heart be changed, thy wife's or thy husband's heart being not yet changed, but he or she remaining pagans, yet let not this cause any separation betwixt you, but, unless the unbeliever will depart, live yet as man and wife together, mutually performing conjugal offices each to other. But the following verses, (ver. 21, 22,) where the apostle speaks of *called being a servant,* show this interpretation to be too narrow. The sense of the text is, that the profession of Christianity is consistent with any honest calling or course of life, and it is the will of God that Christians should not pretend their profession of religion, to excuse them from the duties of any relation wherein they are set. *And so ordain I in all churches;* this is a universal rule, and concerned not the church of Corinth only, but all other churches of Christ, being an apostolical constitution.

18 Is any man called being circumcised? let him ˢnot become uncircumcised. s 1 Mac. 1. 15. Is any called in uncircumcision? t Acts 15. 1, 5, 19, 24, 28. ᵗlet him not be circumcised. Gal. 5. 2.

Is any one who was a native Jew, and so circumcised according to the Jewish law, converted (while he is in that state) to the faith of Christ? let him not affect the state of him that, having been formerly a Gentile, was never circumcised. On the other side, is any, being a native Gentile, and so not circumcised, converted to Christianity? let not him affect the state of one converted from Judaism, who was circumcised. This is, doubtless, the sense of the verse, not, (as some would have it,) let him not endeavour by art to make himself uncircumcised, which was the wicked practice of some, (for a better compliance with the Gentiles,) of whom we read, 1 Macc. i. 15.

19 ᵘCircumcision is nothing, and un- u Gal. 5. 6. & 6. 15. circumcision is nothing, but ˣthe keeping x John 15.14. 1 John 2. 3. of the commandments of God. & 3. 24.

Circumcision was an ordinance of God, a sign of God's covenant, as necessary to salvation in its time, as the fufilling of any precept of the law contained in ordinances: and uncircumcision also was something; for by the law relating to that ordinance, the uncircumcised male is determined to have broken God's covenant, and determined to a cutting off, Gen. xvii. 10—14. But in the present state of the church, circumcision was of no value or moment in the business of salvation: *In Christ Jesus neither circumcision availeth any thing, nor uncircumcision, but faith which worketh by love,* Gal. v. 6.

20 Let every man abide in the same calling wherein he was called.

Let every man abide in the same state and condition of life in which he was when he was first converted to the faith of Christ, that is, supposing that he was in an honest course of life; for we read in the Acts that the conjurers burnt their books, and unlawful courses of life must not be adhered to after men have once given up their names to Christ. The apostle's design is only to show, that the profession of Christianity maketh no state of life unlawful, which was before that profession lawful, nor dischargeth any from such as were before the duties of persons in their circumstances and relations. They too far strain this text, who interpret it into an obligation upon all men, not to alter that particular way and course of life and trading to which they were educated, and in which they formerly have been engaged; though such a thing be of too great moment and consequence for any to do without just advice and deliberation. The world is a mutable thing, and trades and particular courses of life wear out, and what will now bring in a due livelihood, possibly seven years hence will not furnish any with bread; and it is unreasonable in such a case to think, that the rule of Christian profession ties up a man under these changes of providence to such a particular course of life, as he cannot, in it, in the sweat of his face eat his bread.

21 Art thou called *being* a servant? care not for it: but if thou mayest be made free, use *it* rather.

Art thou called being a servant? care not for it: if while thou art a servant to another in any honest employment, thou art converted to the Christian religion, let it not trouble thee, mind it not. A man may be the servant of Christ, and yet a servant to men in any honest employment. *But if thou mayest be made free,* by the favour of thy friends, with the consent of thy master, *use it rather;* that is, (say some,) rather choose to be a servant still, (which indeed in some cases may be the duty of a good Christian,) that is, if thou seest, that in that station thou canst better serve God and the interest of thy master's or other souls. But it is more probable the sense is, make use of thy liberty rather; for certain it is, that the free-man is ordinarily at more advantage for the service of God than he that is a servant.

22 For he that is called in the Lord, *being* a servant, is ʸ the Lord's † freeman: likewise also he that is called, *being* free, is ᶻ Christ's servant.

y John 8. 36.
Rom. 6. 18.
22. Philem. 16.
† Gr. *made free.*
z ch. 9. 21.
Gal. 5. 13.
Eph. 6. 6. 1 Pet. 2. 16.

For the state of a servant to men no way prejudiceth a man as to his spiritual liberty; a servant and a free-man, considered with reference to Christ, are both one; a servant may be as near the kingdom of heaven as a free-man; and let a man be in never so good a state of civil liberty, yet, if he be a Christian, he is still a servant of Christ, and bound in all things to obey him. As to the new man, *there is neither bond nor free, but Christ is all and in all.*

a ch. 6. 20.
1 Pet. 1. 18, 19. See Lev. 25. 42.

23 ᵃ Ye are bought with a price; be not ye the servants of men.

What *price* we *are bought with,* we heard, chap. vi. 20: the apostle there pressed it upon us as our duty to glorify God with our bodies and our spirits; here he presseth upon us another duty, viz. upon that consideration not to be *the servants of men;* by which some think he forbiddeth the selling themselves as slaves to infidels; others think that he only forbiddeth *eye-service,* as the apostle calls it, Eph. vi. 6; while in the mean time they might be the servants of men, if they served them *as the servants of Christ, doing the will of God from the heart; with good will doing service, as to the Lord, and not to men.* But the most probable interpretation is, Be not servants to the lusts of men: wherein you can serve men, and in the same actions also serve God, and be obedient to his will, you may be the servants of men; but be not servants of men in such actions wherein, to serve them, you must disobey God.

24 Brethren, ᵇ let every man, wherein he is called, therein abide with God.

b ver. 20.

In whatsoever state or condition, whether he be married or unmarried, whether he be a master or a servant, whether he were before circumcised or uncircumcised, let him not think Christianity obligeth him to alter it; he may abide in it, only he must *abide* in it *with God,* as one who remembereth God's eye is upon him, and seeth him, and that he is bound to approve himself in it unto God, and to keep a good conscience towards him, as one that is a member of the church of God, and under the laws of it.

25 Now concerning virgins ᶜ I have no commandment of the Lord: yet I give my judgment, as one ᵈ that hath obtained mercy of the Lord ᵉ to be faithful.

c ver. 6, 10, 40. 2 Cor. 8. 8, 10.
d 1 Tim. 1. 16.
e ch. 4. 2. 1 Tim. 1. 12.

He had before spoken to married persons and widows, now he comes to speak *concerning virgins;* and though he mentions only the female sex, yet the following words show that his advice extended to both. As to them he saith, he had no special direction from Christ, none that would suit the case of every virgin; but yet he would give his advice, what seemed to him best. And he would have them look upon him *as one that* himself had received *mercy from the Lord,* and as he desired to be faithful in the discharge of his trust, so might and ought to have credit given him in what he said. In which sense we read in Scripture of *a faithful saying, a faithful Creator, a faithful man,* &c.

26 I suppose therefore that this is good for the present ǁ distress, *I say,* ᶠ that it *is* good for a man so to be.

ǁ Or, *necessity.*
f ver. 1, 8.

Good here signifieth convenient, (as before,) if other circumstances of particular persons make it not sinful; or better with respect to *the present distress* or necessity: by which, without doubt, the apostle meaneth, not the common necessities of all men that are born once to die, (which is the more easy the fewer relations we have to part from,) nor yet of family troubles and concerns, for there is none who hath a family in this world to look after, but will have trouble in the flesh; but the continual troubles with which the church of God was disquieted, as the ark upon the waters, and the more special troubles of the primitive church; for though their great persecutions from the heathen were not, possibly, at that time begun, yet Christ had foretold them, and the apostles had them in a very near prospect (Paul is thought to have died the tenth or eleventh year of Nero). For this present necessity or distress, the apostle gives his opinion, that it was convenient and better, for those that could honestly abstain from marriage, to keep themselves in their single and unmarried condition.

27 Art thou bound unto a wife? seek not to be loosed. Art thou loosed from a wife? seek not a wife.

Art thou bound by marriage, or bound by contract, do not use any sinful ways to be loosed from that bond, either by divorce or by a voluntary departure: if the unbeliever will depart, he or she may, you are not obliged to court their stay, but do not you put him or her away. Are you free from a wife, either as yet unmarried, or by the hand of God separated, in case you can without sin, abstain. If your circumstances be such as they do not oblige you to marriage, do not seek a wife; the times are like to be full of trouble and difficulty. Our Master said, *Woe unto them that are with child, and to them that give suck in those days!* Matt. xxiv. 19.

28 But and if thou marry, thou hast not sinned; and if a virgin marry, she hath not sinned. Nevertheless such shall have trouble in the flesh: but I spare you.

I would not have you mistake me, as if I judged marriage sinful for persons in any state or condition, or of any sex; but those that are married in any time, will find troubles about the things of this life, and those that marry in such times as these are, and you are like further to see, will

I. CORINTHIANS VII

meet with more than ordinary troubles of this nature: I only would spare you, and have you keep yourselves as free as you can: or, *I spare you* any further discourse of that nature, not willing to torment you before the time cometh.

29 But ᵍ this I say, brethren, the time *is* short: it remaineth, that both they that have wives be as though they had none ;

<small>ᵍ Rom. 13. 11.
1 Pet. 4. 7.
2 Pet. 3. 8,9.</small>

He had before spoken to what concerned some, now he comes to what concerneth all. *The time* (saith he) *is short;* furled up, like sails when the mariner comes near his port. He either meaneth the time of this life, or the time of the world's duration; we often find the apostles speaking of their times as the last times (and in these senses all are concerned): or the time of the church's rest and tranquillity, which they had hitherto enjoyed in a far more perfect degree than they enjoyed them soon after this, when ten persecutions followed immediately one upon the neck of another. *It remaineth, that both they that have wives be as though they had none;* therefore (saith the apostle) it is the concernment of all Christians, not to indulge themselves too much in the pleasures and contentments of this life; but if ye be married, or shall marry, you will be concerned to keep your hearts as loose from the contentment and satisfaction men use to take in their wives, as if you had no wives at all.

30 And they that weep, as though they wept not ; and they that rejoice, as though they rejoiced not ; and they that buy, as though they possessed not ;

And they that weep, as though they wept not; this consideration also should weigh with those who have a more afflicted portion in this life, and are mourners for the loss of their near relations ; they have but lost what they could not long have kept, and for the time they kept them must have enjoyed them, probably, with a great deal of sorrow and bitterness. *And they that rejoice, as though they rejoiced not;* and so for any of those who rejoiced in any worldly enjoyments, the shortness of the time they are like to have them to rejoice in, should admonish them to govern and moderate their joy, for it is like to be but like the crackling of thorns under a pot. *And that they buy as though they possessed not ;* and those that have liberal possessions of good things in this life, they should look upon them as none of theirs, and use them as not like to be their possessions long.

31 And they that use this world, as not ʰ abusing *it :* for ⁱ the fashion of this world passeth away.

<small>ʰ ch. 9. 18.
ⁱ Ps. 39. 6.
Jam. 1. 10. & 4. 14.
1 Pet. 1. 24. & 4. 7.
1 John 2. 17.</small>

And they that use this world, as not abusing it: while you have any thing of this world's goods you may use them, yea, you must use them, without them you cannot live in the world ; but the consideration how little the time is you are like to have them to use, should govern you in the use of them, so as you ought to take heed you do not use them to any other purpose, or for any other end, than that for which God hath appointed and given them to you. *For the fashion of this world passeth away;* for this world is like a stage or theatre where are diversities of scenes, and the present scene abideth but for a little time, then passeth, and another scene or figure of things appeareth : those who appear this day in the form of princes and nobles, to-morrow appear as beggars, and persons of a low estate and degree.

32 But I would have you without carefulness. ᵏ He that is unmarried careth for the things † that belong to the Lord, how he may please the Lord :

<small>ᵏ 1 Tim. 5.5.
† Gr. of the Lord, as ver. 34.</small>

But I would have you without carefulness; the reason why I have advised (during the present distressed estate of the church) a single rather than a married life, for those to whom God hath given the gift of continency, is, that those who are Christians might live as free from such cares as divide and distract men's and women's minds, as they possibly can. *He that is unmarried careth for the things that belong to the Lord, how he may please the Lord:* the single person that hath a spiritual heart, disposed to pious performances, being free from other distractions and cares, caused by worldly occasions, will spend all his thoughts about his duty toward God, and how to please him.

33 But he that is married careth for the things that are of the world, how he may please *his* wife.

But he that is married hath other things which he must take care about ; for besides that he is obliged to provide for his family, husbands and wives are under some obligations to please each other by divertisements, which, though not in themselves sinful, yet take up time, which those free from such relations may spend more religiously.

34 There is difference *also* between a wife and a virgin. The unmarried woman ˡ careth for the things of the Lord, that she may be holy both in body and in spirit : but she that is married careth for the things of the world, how she may please *her* husband.

<small>ˡ Luke 10. 40, &c.</small>

There is the same difference betwixt a married woman and a single woman, as there is betwixt a married man and a single man. If a woman be unmarried, and be piously disposed, she hath leisure and opportunity enough to mind the things of God ; but if she be married, she will then be obliged to attend secular affairs, to take care for her family, and to please her husband. It is the same thing that was before said of the man. The sense is, that a conjugal relation draws along with it many diversions, from which a single life is free.

35 And this I speak for your own profit ; not that I may cast a snare upon you, but for that which is comely, and that ye may attend upon the Lord without distraction.

And this I speak for your own profit; for your advantage both as to your converse in the world, and also for your religious conversation, and the performance of those duties which you owe unto God ; for those that are married must meet with more troubles and cares in this life, and cannot have so much time and leisure for religious duties, as others have that are not entangled in the domestic cares of a family. *Not that I may cast a snare upon you;* yet I would not bring you under a snare, imposing what God hath not imposed, and obliging you where God hath not obliged you. *But for that which is comely;* the word here is εὐσχημον, it strictly signifies a thing of a good figure, and is translated in Scripture *honourable,* Mark xv. 43 ; Acts xiii. 50 ; xvii. 11 ; where it signifies what is of a fair and good repute in the eye of the world ; which is also the sense of it, chap. xii. 24, where we read of the *comely parts* of man's body ; but in this place the word signifies most largely, the same with profitable and convenient. For marriage is a state which neither is in itself indecent, nor ever was so reputed in the world by any nation, and the Scripture tells us, that *marriage is honourable* amongst *all,* Heb. xiii. 4. The word therefore here is of the same significancy with συμφέρον, which in the beginning of the verse is translated *profit,* and chap. vi. 12, is translated *expedient. And that you may attend upon the Lord without distraction ;* the phrase in the Greek is very difficult to be translated properly into our English language, word for word it is, to sit well to the Lord without distraction ; our translators render it, *attend upon the Lord.* We have something like it in our language, when we express our diligent attendance to a thing, under the notion of sitting close to a business ; which is opposed to such an attendance to business as we give when we have many avocations and callings away, so as we cannot sit close to it. The apostle saith, that this was the end of his advising those who could contain not to marry under that state of things in the world referring to the church, that they might with more ease and conveniency attend to the great concerns of their souls, without those distracting and dividing thoughts which they must have who were entangled with domestic businesses and relations.

36 But if any man think that he behaveth himself uncomely toward his virgin, if she pass the flower of *her* age, and need so require, let him do what he will, he sinneth not : let them marry.

But if any man think that he behaveth himself uncomely: there is a general and a particular uncomeliness ; some things are uncomely with respect to all persons; of such things the apostle doth not here speak; but of a particular uncomeliness with respect to the circumstances of particular persons. Neither doth *uncomely* here signify a mere indecency and unhandsomeness, but such a behaviour as suiteth not the general rules of the gospel, which judgment is to be ruled by the circumstances of persons, as they more or less desire marriage. *If she pass the flower of her age;* if she be of marriageable years, or rather, if she beginneth to grow old, *and need so require*, and be desirous of marriage, so as the parent seeth reason to fear that, if he gives her not in marriage, she will so dispose of herself without asking her father's advice or leave, or be exposed, possibly, to worse temptations: which two things seem to interpret that term, *if need so require*. *Let him do what he will, he sinneth not: let them marry;* in such a case as this a Christian parent shall not sin, if he disposeth her in marriage: let her marry to such a person as she loveth, and her parent seeth proper for her. He speaks in the plural number, because marriage is betwixt two persons. The reason of this determination is, because the apostle, in his former discourse, had no where condemned a married estate during the present distress of things, as sinful or unlawful, but only as inexpedient, or not so expedient as a single life during the present distress; he had before determined, ver. 9, that it was *better to marry than to burn*. Now no inexpediency of a thing can balance what is plainly sinful. If therefore the case be such, that a man or woman must marry, or sin, through marriage brings with it more care and trouble, yet it is to be preferred before plain sinning.

37 Nethertheless he that standeth stedfast in his heart, having no necessity, but hath power over his own will, and hath so decreed in his heart that he will keep his virgin, doeth well.

Nevertheless he that standeth stedfast in his heart; if a man be resolved to keep his daughter a virgin, not uncertain in his own mind, and wavering what he should do, upon a just consideration of circumstances; *having no necessity;* and doth not see a necessity to dispose of her, either for the avoiding some sin against God, or for the better providing for himself and the rest of his family; *but hath power over his own will;* but hath a perfect freedom in his own will, so that his will be not contradicted by his daughter's fondness of a married life; for in such a case the father, though he would willingly not dispose of his daughter in marriage, yet ought to be overruled by the will of his daughter, and so hath not a power over his own will, being forced by the rules of religion to take care of the soul and spiritual welfare of his child; for though the parent hath a great power over his child, and ought to consent to the marriage of his child, yet he hath no such power as wholly to hinder them from marriage. *And hath so decreed in his heart that he will keep his virgin;* if he be fully resolved, upon a due consideration of all circumstances, and the virgin be satisfied, and yields up herself in the case to her father's pleasure, in such a case, if the father doth not put her upon marriage, but resolves to keep her unmarried, he *doeth well;* that is, not only he shall not sin against God, but he doth that which is more eligible, considering the present circumstances of things, and better than if he did find out a husband for her, and give her to him (as it is expounded in the next verse).

m Heb. 13.4. 38 ᵐ So then he that giveth *her* in marriage doeth well; but he that giveth *her* not in marriage doeth better.

So then he that giveth her in marriage doeth well: there is no general rule for all parents in this case, where the duty or sin of parents may arise from their or their children's different circumstances. But supposing that a parent, having duly weighed all circumstances, be fully resolved, and he finds the child's will concurring, that she can forbear, and is willing to do in the case what her parent desires; in such a case as this, if the parent disposeth her in marriage, I cannot say he sinneth, but he doth what he may do. *But he that giveth her not in marriage doeth better;* but with reference to the present state of things in the church and in the world, and with reference to the young woman's liberty for the service of God, he doth better, if he doth not so dispose her. The thing is in itself **indifferent, and Christians must be in it ruled and inclined one way or another** from circumstances.

39 ⁿ The wife is bound by the law as n Rom. 7.2. long as her husband liveth; but if her husband be dead, she is at liberty to be married to whom she will; ° only in the o 2 Cor.6.14. Lord.

The apostle all along this chapter hath been speaking to several cases, which the church of Corinth had put to him concerning marriage; some that concerned persons already married, others that concerned such as were single, having been never married; he shutteth up his discourse with advice which relateth to such as had lost their husbands, with reference to second marriages. As to this he determineth, that no woman might marry again while her first husband lived; that is, unless her husband be legally divorced from her for adultery, or unless her husband, being a heathen, had voluntarily deserted her: but if her husband were dead, she might marry to whom she would; yet she was not at such liberty, as that she might marry an unbeliever. Unbelievers are either heathens, or Christians in name, but such as are idolaters, or profane persons, or heretics, who hold such tenets as are inconsistent with any true faith in Jesus Christ. This phrase, *only in the Lord*, seemeth to oblige godly women, not only to avoid marrying with heathens, but with nominal Christians; that is, such who, although they have been baptized, and own Christ with their tongues, yet hold such damnable opinions, or live such profane lives, or worship God in such an idolatrous manner, as is inconsistent with any true faith in Christ. The reason of the precept holds as well to the latter as to the former.

40 But she is happier if she so abide, ᵖ after my judgment: and ᑫ I think also p ver. 25. that I have the Spirit of God. q 1 Thes.4.8.

But if other circumstances concur, that a widow can abide without marriage without waxing wanton, and running into temptation, and so as to manage her outward concerns without the help of a husband, my opinion is, that she is more happy if she keeps herself a widow, and doth not marry again; not more happy because more holy, or in a fairer road to the kingdom of heaven, but upon the two accounts before mentioned; more happy because free from troubles and distractions, and because she will be more free and at liberty to mind heavenly things. *And I think also that I have the Spirit of God;* and, saith he, I think I know as much of the mind of the Holy Spirit of God, as either those who teach you otherwise, or who may have opinions contrary to mine in this case.

CHAP. VIII.

The preference of charity to knowledge, 1—3. *An idol is nothing in the esteem of those who have right notions of one God, and of one Lord Jesus Christ,* 4—6. *But it is sin in those, who by an indiscreet use of their knowledge, in eating meats offered to idols, tempt weaker consciences to offend,* 7—13.

NOW ᵃ as touching things offered unto a Acts 15.20, idols, we know that we all have ᵇ know- 29, ch. 10.19. ledge. ᶜ Knowledge puffeth up, but 14, 22. charity edifieth. 3, 10.

The apostle proceedeth to a new argument, about which the Corinthians had wrote to him, viz. about the eating of meat *offered to idols*. Of this meat offered to idols we have this account given us: Feasts upon sacrifices were very usual amongst the heathens; they first offered oxen, sheep, or other cattle to the idol; then the priest offered a part, burning it upon the idol's altar; other part they restored to the offerers, or took it to themselves. The priests made a feast in the idol's temple of their parts, and invited friends to it. The offerers either so feasted with the part restored to them in the idol's temple, or carried it home, and there feasted their neighbours with it; or else carried it into the market, and sold it (as other meat) in the shambles. The question was, Whether it was lawful for Christians, being

I. CORINTHIANS VIII

invited to these feasts by those amongst whom they lived, to go to them, and to eat of such meat, whether it were in the idol's temple, or at the pagans' houses; or if any such meat were bought in the shambles, whether they might eat of that? Some amongst the Christians at Corinth thought any of these were lawful, because they knew an idol was nothing but a block, or piece of wood or stone, so could not defile any thing. The apostle tells them, that he knew very many of them had good degrees of *knowledge*, and every one understood that an idol was nothing; but yet he warneth them to take heed they were not puffed up with their knowledge, that is, swelled in such a confident opinion of it, that they thought they could not be mistaken, and be betrayed, by their conceit of it, to do that which is sinful; for *charity edifieth*. Charity signifieth either love to God, or love to our neighbour; here the latter seemeth to be intended, and the sense is, That they were not only concerned in the good of their own souls, but of their neighbours' also, and to do that which might tend to their profit and edification, not to their ruin and destruction.

d ch. 13. 8, 9.
12. Gal. 6. 3.
1 Tim. 6. 4.

2 And ^d if any man think that he knoweth any thing, he knoweth nothing yet as he ought to know.

Let it be in this or any other matter, if any man be proud of his knowledge, and be conceited that he knoweth enough, and needeth none to instruct him, he may commit have a notion of things, but it will do him no good; a man ought to use his knowledge for the glory of God, and the edification of others. Let a man have never so large a notion of things, if he be not humble, if he useth not his knowledge to the honour of God and the advantage of others, *he knoweth nothing as he ought to know* it. Knowledge is a talent not to be laid up in a napkin.

e Ex. 33. 12,
17. Nah. 1. 7.
Matt. 7. 23.
Gal. 4. 9.
2 Tim. 2. 19.

3 But if any man love God, ^e the same is known of him.

It is of much more advantage to a soul to be known of God, that is, owned, acknowledged, and approved, than to comprehend much of the things of God in its notion. A man may know much of God, and yet be one to whom God will one day say, Depart from me, I know you not, you workers of iniquity: but if any man love God, that man is beloved of God, and shall be owned and acknowledged by him. In this sense *know* is taken in a multitude of scriptures: see John xvii. 3. Our translators render this word *allow*, Rom. vii. 15.

f Is. 41. 24.
ch. 10. 19.
g Deu. 4. 39.
& 6. 4. Is. 44.
8. Mark 12.
29. ver. 6.
Eph. 4. 6.
1 Tim. 2. 5.

4 As concerning therefore the eating of those things that are offered in sacrifice unto idols, we know that ^f an idol *is* nothing in the world, ^g and that *there is* none other God but one.

Those things that are offered in sacrifice unto idols; meat which is part of that sacrifice which hath been offered to an idol, whether it be to be eaten in the idol's temple, or in a private house. *We know that an idol is nothing in the world;* we know that an image, or an idol, the representation of some other thing, though in respect of the matter it be something, either wood, stone, or earth, and in respect of form it be something, yet it is nothing formally, or representatively; though it is set up to represent to us a Deity, there is nothing of a Divine nature, or the representation of a Divine nature, in it. It *is nothing* of what the poor blind heathen take it to be, and therefore in the Hebrew it hath its name from a word אל that signifieth nothing, Job xiii. 14; Zech. xi. 17: or it *is nothing* that can either sanctify or pollute any meat that is set before it. And we know *that there is none other God but one:* the apostle may be conceived to have spoken these words as from himself, granting what those said who took themselves to be men of knowledge; or else in the language of those who thus spake, repeating their words.

h John 10. 34.

5 For though there be that are ^h called gods, whether in heaven or in earth, (as there be gods many, and lords many,)

There are many whom heathens call gods, and whom God himself calleth gods: the angels that are in heaven are called *God's host*, Gen. xxxii. 2; *the heavenly host*, Luke ii. 13; *the sons of God*, Job i. 6; ii. 1. Magistrates are also called *gods*, Psal. lxxxii. 6, because God hath committed a great part of his power unto them. Thus there are many gods and many lords.

6 But ⁱ to us *there is but* one God, the Father, ^k of whom *are* all things, and we ∥ in him; and ^l one Lord Jesus Christ, ^m by whom *are* all things, and we by him.

i Mal. 2. 10.
Eph. 4. 6.
k Acts 17. 28.
Rom. 11. 36.
∥ Or, *for him*.
l John 13. 13.
Acts 2. 36.
ch. 12. 3.
m John 1. 3. Col. 1. 6. Heb. 1. 2.

Whatever the idolatrous heathens think or believe, to us (who are Christians) *there is but one* who is truly and essentially *God*, (though indeed there be more than one person in the Deity,) *the Father*, who is the Fountain of the Deity, communicating his Divine nature to the other two persons, and *of whom are all things*. It is a term which signifieth the primary Cause and Author of all things: we subsist in him, according to that of the apostle, Acts xvii. 28, *In him we live, and move, and have our being ;* and we are for him, created for his honour and glory, as the phrase may also be translated. *And one Lord Jesus Christ, by whom are all things*. He is the second person in the holy Trinity. It is the observation of a learned author, That though the name of God be often given to Christ, yet no where by Paul where he maketh mention of God the Father; from whence he concludes, that the term of *Lord* given to Christ, signifieth his pre-eminence above all things, (the Father excepted,) according to what the apostle speaks, chap. xv. 27. By this Christ, saith the apostle, *are all things: All things were made by him, and without him was not any thing made that was made*, John i. 3; yet the difference of the phrase is observable, to denote to us the order of working in the holy Trinity. All things are of the Father by the Son. *And we by him ;* and we (saith the apostle) are by the Son created, redeemed, &c.

7 Howbeit *there is* not in every man that knowledge: for some ⁿ with conscience of the idol unto this hour eat *it* as a thing offered unto an idol; and their conscience being weak is ^o defiled.

n ch. 10. 28, 29.

o Rom. 14. 14, 23.

Though some of you know that there is but one living and true God, and that an idol is nothing in the world, and meat is neither sanctified nor polluted by being set before it; yet every one doth not know so much : and though the gospel have been a long time preached amongst them, yet to this day they may have some superstitious opinion of the idol, and then their conscience will be defiled or polluted. It is much the same case at this day as to the business of image-worship, or veneration of images, and invocation of saints, amongst the papists. The wisest and most knowing of them will declaim against giving Divine adoration to the image, or to the saint, and tell us that they worship the true and living God upon the sight of the image only, and make use of the name of the saint only to desire him, or her, to pray to God for them. Now not to meddle with that question, Whether in our worshipping the true God, it be lawful to set a creature before us as our motive or incitement to worship, or use any Mediator but Christ? yet the things are unlawful, upon the same account that the apostle here determines it unlawful for stronger Christians to eat meat offered to idols, though they knew and professed that an idol was nothing; for all people that come so to worship have not that knowledge; there are, without doubt, multitudes of simple people amongst the papists, that, plainly, in this kind of veneration and adoration venerate and adore the creature; and so their consciences are defiled by idolatry, because they have not such knowledge as others have, supposing that what those others did were lawful as to their practice, which indeed it is not.

8 But ^p meat commendeth us not to God: for neither, if we eat, ∥ are we the better; neither, if we eat not, ∥ are we the worse.

p Rom. 14. 17.
∥ Or, *have we the more*.
∥ Or, *have we the less*.

The apostle here speaketh in the person either of those teachers amongst them, or those more private persons amongst them, who made no difficulty of eating meat offered to idols; they objected, that meat, or the eating of meat, was not the thing which commended any man to God; they were not the better if they did eat, or the worse if they did not eat. The apostle himself had asserted this, Rom. xiv. 17, that *the kingdom of God was not meat or drink; but righteousness, and peace, and joy in the Holy Ghost.*

q Gal. 5. 13.
∥ Or, *power*.
r Rom. 14. 13, 20.

9 But ^q take heed lest by any means this ∥ liberty of your's become ^r a stumblingblock to them that are weak.

The word ἐξουσία is here well translated *liberty*, though it also signifieth right, and seems in either sense rather to signify a supposed than a real liberty or right; for we shall see in the next verse, that the apostle is here speaking of their eating in the idol's temple, which, chap. x. 21, he determineth to be a having a communion with devils, and therefore could not be lawful; the apostle therefore seemeth here only to suppose (as they pretended) that in their eating simply in the idol's temple they did not sin, because by eating men are not made the worse; yet, as we shall see afterwards, he declareth their action was not free from guilt, as it was a violation of that brotherly love which they were obliged to show to their neighbour.

s 1 Mac. 1.47.
t ch. 10. 28, 32.
† Gr. *edified*.

10 For if any man see thee which hast knowledge sit at meat in ^s the idol's temple, shall not ^t the conscience of him which is weak be † emboldened to eat those things which are offered to idols;

Here the apostle showeth how they sinned in eating meat in the idol's temple, which had been before offered to the idol, admitting the thing in itself lawful, (which indeed it was not,) viz. accidentally, by laying a stumblingblock before their brethren, who either were really weak in their knowledge, or, at least, they were looked upon as such. For (saith he) if any see thee, who, they think, hast knowledge, or who boastest of thy knowledge, sit at meat in the idol's temple, will not he by it be encouraged to do the same, though possibly he judgeth it is not lawful? The word translated *emboldened*, is the same which is elsewhere often in the New Testament translated *edified*: it metaphorically signifies to make a progress or proficiency either in good or evil (though this be the only text in the New Testament where it is taken in an ill sense). This the apostle determines sinful; which lets us know the obligation that lieth upon every good Christian, not to use his liberty to the prejudice of others' souls, by doing any actions which we may do or let alone, which done by us may probably become a snare to them.

u Rom. 14. 15, 20.

11 And ^u through thy knowledge shall the weak brother perish, for whom Christ died?

Through thy knowledge, in this place, is, by occasion of thy knowledge. God hath not given people knowledge that they thereby should be a means to harm and to destroy, but to do good, and to save others; it is a most absurd thing for any to use their knowledge, therefore, to the destruction of others. *Shall the weak brother perish?* by *perish* is here meant, be led into sin, by acting contrary to the judgment of his own conscience; for, (as the apostle saith, Rom. xiv. 23,) *He that doubteth is damned if he eat, for whatsoever is not of faith*, that is, done out of a firm persuasion in the party doing that it is lawful, *is sin*. *For whom Christ died;* though he be weak, yet if he be a true believer, Christ died for him, and there can be nothing more contrary to the duty of a charitable Christian, than to be a means to damn him whom Christ came down from heaven and died for, that he might save him.

x Mat. 25.40, 45.

12 But ^x when ye sin so against the brethren, and wound their weak conscience, ye sin against Christ.

But when ye sin so against the brethren: sin is properly against God, for it is a breach of the Divine law; but the violations of that part of the Divine law which concerneth our duty to our neighbour, are called sins against our brethren, that is, sins against God in matters which concern our duty towards our brethren. *And wound their weak conscience;* the giving the weak judgments of others, by your examples, an occasion of sin, by venturing upon actions which they think sinful, is that which is here called a beating, or a wounding, their weak consciences, because it is indeed a hurting and defiling of them. *Ye sin against Christ;* this the apostle determineth to be a sinning against Christ; both against the law of Christ, concerning loving one another, and against the love of Christ, who, in dying for the weakest believers, hath showed the highest degree of love imaginable to them; whom they are far from following, who will not abate themselves a small matter of liberty, where the use of it this or that way may very probably be an occasion of sin and ruin to their brethren's souls.

13 Wherefore, ^y if meat make my brother to offend, I will eat no flesh while the world standeth, lest I make my brother to offend.

y Rom. 14. 21.
2 Cor. 11. 29.

If meat make my brother to offend; suppose therefore it were lawful for me to eat flesh offered to idols, yet if I cannot do it but I shall make my brother sin, I will forbear. Others understand it more generally, not of the meat before mentioned, but of all flesh: I will rather live upon bread and herbs; by which expression the apostle doth not suppose, that there can ever be such a case when there shall be any such need, but only declares how much a good Christian should do, to prevent his brother's sinning against God. *I will eat no flesh while the world standeth, lest I make my brother to offend:* those expressions, Matt. v. 29, of plucking out the right eye, and cutting off the right hand, are much of the same nature; both those phrases and this phrase signify only, that we ought to do any thing, and to deny ourselves in any thing, rather than ourselves to sin, or be wilful occasions to others of sin.

From this discourse of the apostle it is very plain, that it is the duty of Christians, in any matters where they are by the law of God at liberty whether they will do a thing or no, to take that part which they see will give least occasion of sin unto their brethren, and to avoid that part which, if they will take, they see they shall by taking it give occasion to others to sin, though they be themselves never so well satisfied as to the lawfulness of their action (provided the action be only lawful, not necessary, and what by the law of God they are bound to do, or to avoid). But here two grave questions arise: 1. Whether the command of superiors doth not here alter the case? Admit a thing be in itself by us judged lawful, what by God's law we may do, or let alone; and our superiors command us to do, or to avoid that thing: we on the other side see, that if we do it, or avoid it, we shall very probably be occasion to make our brethren sin, who doubt of the lawfulness of the thing. The question is, What is to be done in this case? That the law of God commanding love to our brethren equally concerneth high and low, is out of doubt; so that no superior ought more to command any to do what it is evident he cannot do without making his brother to offend, than the inferior ought to do it: but the question is, What is the inferior's duty, if commanded? 2. A second question is, Suppose that, in such a case, I am commanded to do what I judge I may lawfully do, were it not for making my brother, by my example, to offend, and by the command of men I am obliged to do it, or to ruin myself and family; what is my duty in this case? In both these cases there seems to be a collision of precepts. In the first case the precept of loving our neighbours seems to dash against the many precepts for obeying superiors; in the other case, it seems to dash against the precept for providing for ourselves and families; so as the question is, Which precepts lay here the greatest obligation, where both cannot be obeyed? But we leave these questions to casuists. The determination of what is the will of God in either of them, will require a great many more words than what is fit to encumber annotations with, especially considering that neither of them properly falls into the explication of this text, where it is certain that the Corinthians were at a perfect liberty, and had no superiors that commanded them so to eat, (had the thing been in itself lawful,) neither were they under any necessity, either to eat that meat, or to starve themselves or families; they had other flesh besides that to eat. In this case the duty of Christians is plainly determined by the apostle.

CHAP. IX.

Paul vindicateth his apostolical character, 1, 2, *and right to a maintenance from the churches,* 3—14 ; *though he relinquished that right for the furtherance of the gospel, not content with doing only his indispensable duty,* 15—18 ; *but voluntarily subjecting himself in many points, where he was otherwise free, in order thereby to win over more converts to Christ,* 19—23. *Those who contend for a corruptible crown use much labour and abstinence,* 24, 25. *So doth the apostle strive for one that is incorruptible,* 26, 27.

In the greater part of this chapter, the apostle proceedeth in his former discourse, not speaking particularly to the case of eating meat offered to idols, but to the general point, viz. That it is our duty to abate of our liberty, when we see we cannot use it without harm to other Christians. And here he proposeth to them his own example, who had restrained himself in three things, to two of which he had a liberty, and yet avoided it, and that not to prevent their sinning, but only their suffering, and that, too, only by being by him over-burdened : 1. As to eating and drinking. 2. Abstaining from marriage, by which he might have been more chargeable to them. 3. Requiring maintenance of them for his labour amongst them. As to both which he declares he had from God's law a liberty, but had forborne to use that part from which the church in that state might be prejudiced.

a Acts 9. 15. & 13. 2. & 26. 17. 2 Cor. 12. 12. Gal. 2. 7, 8. 1 Tim. 2. 7. 2 Tim. 1. 11. b Acts 9. 3, 17. & 18. 9. & 22. 14, 18. & 23. 11. ch. 15. 8. c ch. 3. 6. & 4. 15.

^a AM I not an apostle ? am I not free ? ^bhave I not seen Jesus Christ our Lord ? ^care not ye my work in the Lord ?

Am I not an apostle ? some that are puffed up or seduced, will, it may be, deny that I am an apostle, a preacher of the gospel of the greatest eminency, immediately sent out by Christ to preach his gospel ; but will any of you deny it ? *Am I not free?* have I not the same liberty that any of you have in things wherein the law of God hath no more determined me than you ? What charter of liberty hath God given to any of you more than he hath to me ? *Have I not seen Jesus Christ?* did not I see Christ in my going to Damascus ? Acts ix. 5 ; xxii. 13, 14 ; and when I was in my ecstasy, when I was rapt into the third heavens ? 2 Cor. xii. 2—4 ; in prison ? Acts xxiii. 11. He was the only apostle we read of, who saw Christ after his ascension. *Are not ye my work in the Lord?* if others will not look upon me as an apostle, God having wrought nothing upon their souls by my ministry, yet you, whose faith is my work, though in the Lord, as the principal efficient Cause, yet by me as God's instrument, cannot deny me to be so : if my having seen Jesus Christ, and being immediately sent out by him, be not enough to prove me so to you, yet the effects of my ministry upon you puts it past your denial.

2 If I be not an apostle unto others, yet doubtless I am to you : for ^dthe seal of mine apostleship are ye in the Lord.

d 2 Cor. 3. 2. & 12. 12.

He had, ver. 1, told them they were his *work in the Lord,* from whence he concludes here, that he was *an apostle,* that is, one sent of Christ to them for the good of their souls, whatever he was to others. You, saith he, as to yourselves at least, are *the seal* of my apostolical office ; it hath a confirmation in you by the effect, as the writing is confirmed by the seal. For how can you think, that the blessing of the Lord should go along with my preaching, to turn you from pagan idolatry, and your lewd courses of life, to the true Christian religion, and to a holy life and conversation, if God had not sent me. There is no such argument to prove a minister sent of Christ, as the success of his ministry in the conversion of souls unto God. It is true, we cannot conclude, that a minister is no true minister if he be able to produce no such seals of his calling ; for the spiritual seed may for a time lie under the clods, and changes may be wrought in hearts, which are not published to the world ; and even Isaiah may be sent to make the hearts of people fat. But where those seals can be produced, it is a most certain sign that the minister is a true minister, that is, one sent of God ; for he could be no instrument to do such works if God were not with him ; and if God had not sent him, he would not be with him so blessing his ministry. Yet it is possible the man may have his personal errors ; for though some men doubt, whether an instance can be given of one openly and scandalously wicked, whom God ever honoured to be his instrument to convert souls, yet it would be rashly affirmed by any to say, that Judas (though a son of perdition, but not scandalous till the last) was an instrument to convert none.

3 Mine answer to them that do examine me is this,

These words may be understood in a double reference : either to what went before ; then the sense is this : To those that examine me about my apostleship, this is my answer ; That I have seen the Lord, that you are my work in the Lord, and the seal of my ministry. Or with reference to the words that follow ; then the sense is this : If any man examine me, how I myself practise the doctrine which I preach to others, and determine myself as to my liberty for the good and profit of others, I give them the following answer.

4 ^eHave we not power to eat and to drink ?

e ver. 14. 1 Thess. 2. 6. 2 Thess. 3. 9.

Could I not eat and drink of such things offered to idols as well as you ? Have not I as great a knowledge, and as much liberty ? Yet, you see, I forbear. But the generality of interpreters rather incline to interpret it by what followeth : then, though it be here shortly expressed, and more fully opened afterward, yet the sense is, Have not I power to ask a maintenance of you, by which I should be enabled to eat and drink ?

5 Have we not power to lead about a sister, a || wife, as well as other apostles, and *as* ^fthe brethren of the Lord, and ^gCephas ?

|| Or, *woman.* f Mat. 13. 55. Mark 6. 3. Luke 6. 15. Gal. 1. 19. g Matt. 8. 14.

Have we not power to lead about a sister, a wife? those that by those terms, ἀδελφὴν, γυναῖκα, understand, not (as we translate it) *a sister, a wife,* but a woman, that should out of her estate have contributed to the apostle's maintenance, (as *Joanna the wife of Chuza Herod's steward, and Susanna, and many others,* followed Christ, and *ministered to him of their substance,* Luke viii. 3,) seem not to consider, 1. That such women would have been no burden, but a help to the church (which is quite contrary to the apostle's sense). 2. That the term *lead about,* imports a conjugal relation to the woman. 3. That if this had been the sense, it had been enough to have said, to lead about a woman ; he should not need have said, *a sister, a woman.* 4. That such leading about a woman, not their wife, had been scandalous. 5. That the very phrase, *a sister, a wife,* answers the phrase, Acts xxiii. 1, *Men, brethren,* which signifies no more than, O ye Christian men ; as *a sister, a wife,* signifies here a Christian wife. 6. That we no where read, that Peter, James, John, Judas, (here called *the brethren of the Lord,*) or any of the other apostles, ever in their travels carried about with them any such rich matrons, not their wives, who (as those, Luke viii. 3) ministered to them of their substance. Our interpreters have therefore justly translated it, *a sister, a wife ;* and the sense is, Have I not power to marry ? Yet the phrase teaches us two things : 1. That Christians have no power, that is, no lawful power, to marry such as are no Christians ; their wives must be their sisters also in Christ. 2. That husbands and wives ought to be undivided companions one to another. *As well as other apostles, and as the brethren of the Lord, and Cephas :* he instanceth in several apostles that were married, Peter, (called *Cephas,*) James, John, and Judas the son of Alpheus, Christ's kinsmen. Whence we may observe, that ministers may lawfully marry, no law of God hath restrained them more than others. The popish doctrine *forbidding to marry,* is by the apostle determined to be a *doctrine of devils,* 1 Tim. iv. 1, 3.

6 Or I only and Barnabas, ^hhave not we power to forbear working ?

h 2 Thess. 3. 8, 9.

Are I and Barnabas the only apostles who are obliged for our livelihood to work with our hands ? as Paul did, Acts xviii. 3, making tents. We certainly, as well as the rest of the apostles, if we would run out to the utmost end of the line of our liberty in things, without having any regard to the circumstances of our brethren, might forbear working with our hands, and expect that those amongst whom we labour should maintain us.

7 Who [i] goeth a warfare any time at his own charges? who [k] planteth a vineyard, and eateth not of the fruit thereof? or who [l] feedeth a flock, and eateth not of the milk of the flock?

Who goeth a warfare any time at his own charges? the work of the ministry is *a warfare*, the minister's work in that age was so in a more eminent manner, as the opposition to those first ministers of the gospel, both from the Jews and from the heathens, was greater than what ministers have in later ages met with. Now, saith the apostle, none that lists an army, expects that his soldiers should maintain themselves without any pay. *Who planteth a vineyard, and eateth not of the fruit thereof?* it is like the planting of a vineyard. The church, in Scripture, is called a vineyard, Isa. v. 1, 2. The plants are the Lord's, but he useth ministers' hands in the planting of them: none planteth a vineyard, but in expectation of some fruit; none employeth servants to plant a vineyard, but he resolveth to uphold them with food and raiment, while they are in his work. *Or who feedeth a flock, and eateth not of the milk of the flock?* the church is compared to a flock: saith the apostle, No man feeds a flock, either personally, or by his servants, but he eateth, or alloweth his servants to eat, *of the milk of the flock.* By these three instances, commonly known amongst men, the apostle showeth the reasonableness, that the ministers of the gospel should be maintained by the people, to whom they are ministers.

8 Say I these things as a man? or saith not the law the same also?

That is, I do not speak this only rationally, or by a fallible spirit, nor do I build this assertion alone upon instances known and familiar amongst men. As this is highly reasonable, and conformable to what the very light of nature showeth, and the law of nature obligeth men to in other cases, where men take others off their own work to attend theirs; so it is according to the will of God, which is the highest reason.

9 For it is written in the law of Moses, [m] Thou shalt not muzzle the mouth of the ox that treadeth out the corn. Doth God take care for oxen?

Art being not so improved formerly as now, nor in all places as in some places; they were wont anciently, both in the land of Judea, and since in Greece, and (as is said) at this day in some places of France, to tread out their corn by the feet of oxen: and by the law of Moses, Deut. xxv. 4, it should seem that some too covetous persons would muzzle the mouths of their oxen, that while they trod out the corn, they might eat none of it; which God, looking upon as an act of cruelty or unmercifulness, forbade his ancient people the Jews. Now, saith the apostle, *Doth God take care for oxen?* that is, more for oxen than for ministers or men? For God doth take care for oxen, he preserveth both man and beast; he takes care, as our Saviour elsewhere teacheth us, for the sparrows, for the fowls of the air, for the grass of the field, and therefore for oxen, which are a degree of creatures more noble: but by the same reason we must conclude, that he taketh a greater care for men, especially such as he employeth in his more immediate service.

10 Or saith he *it* altogether for our sakes? For our sakes, no doubt, *this* is written: that [n] he that ploweth should plow in hope; and that he that thresheth in hope should be partaker of his hope.

Not that the law, Deut. xxv. 4, did primarily reveal God's will for the maintenance of ministers; for undoubtedly it did primarily oblige them, according to the letter of it, not to deal cruelly and unmercifully with the beasts they made use of; but as they took them off from getting their food, by taking them up to tread out corn for them; so, while they did it, they should not starve them, but give them leave moderately to eat of it. But (saith the apostle) the reason of it doth much more oblige with respect to men, especially such men as are employed in a ministry for your souls. *That he that plougheth should plough in hope;* that as he who plougheth for another, plougheth in hope to get bread for himself, from the wages for which he covenanteth; *and that he that thresheth in hope should be partaker of his hope;* and so also doth the thresher thresh in hope: so we that are the Lord's ploughmen, working together with him (though in a far inferior degree of causation) in the ploughing up the fallow grounds of men's hearts, and sowing the seed of righteousness in men's souls; and the Lord's threshers, by our labours, exhortations, arguments, &c., beating the fruits of good works, to the glory of God, out of those amongst whom we labour; might also labour in some hope of a livelihood for ourselves, while we are doing the Lord's work and his people's.

11 [o] If we have sown unto you spiritual things, *is it* a great thing if we shall reap your carnal things?

By *spiritual things* the apostle meaneth the doctrine and sacraments of the gospel; which are called *spiritual things,* because they come from heaven, they affect the soul and spirit of a man, they tend to make men spiritual, they prepare the soul for heaven. By *carnal things* he means things which only serve our bodies, which are our carnal, fleshly part. From the inequality of these things, and the excellency of the former above the latter, the apostle argueth the reasonableness of ministers' maintenance from their people, they giving them *quid pro quo,* a just compensation for such allowance, yea, what was of much more value; for there is a great disproportion between things spiritual and things carnal, the former much excelling the latter: so as the minister of the gospel had the odds of them, giving people things of a much greater and more excellent value, for things of a much less and inferior value.

12 If others be partakers of *this* power over you, *are* not we rather? [p] Nevertheless we have not used this power; but suffer all things, [q] lest we should hinder the Gospel of Christ.

If others be partakers of this power over you, are not we rather? those false apostles or teachers, which were amongst the Corinthians, did (as it seemeth) exercise this power, that is, required maintenance of the people; saith the apostle, Are not we by the same right possessed of such a power? might not we as reasonably expect such a maintenance? *Object.* But might not they have said, No, you are not; they are constantly residing amongst us, and instructing us, &c.? *Answ.* This arguing of the apostle lets us know, that the primitive churches were not only obliged to maintain their own pastors, but those also who were general officers to the church, and by the appointment of God were not to fix and abide in any one place, but had the care of all the churches upon them. And it may also teach us, that though Christians be in the first place obliged to take care of their own pastors, yet they are not to limit their charity to them, but also to take what care their ability will allow them of others, whose labours have at any time been useful to them, or may be useful to any other part of the church of God. *Nevertheless we have not used this power; but suffer all things, lest we should hinder the gospel of Christ:* Yet, saith the apostle, though we have this power or liberty, neither I nor Barnabas have made use of it, but suffer all those evils that come upon our not using it, hunger, thirst, labour, lest we should hinder the progress of the gospel, while some might for the charge decline hearing us, or others might charge us with covetousness, &c.

13 [r] Do ye not know that they which minister about holy things || live *of the things* of the temple? and they which wait at the altar are partakers with the altar?

You may understand what is the mind and will of God under the New Testament, by reflecting upon what appeareth to you to have been his mind and will under the Old Testament: God had a ministry under the Old Testament, the tribe of Levi was it; and God there ordained and appointed a livelihood for them, Numb. xviii. 20; Deut. x. 9; xviii. 1, so as they needed not (as other men) to labour with their hands to get bread to eat.

14 Even so *hath the Lord ordained that they which preach the Gospel should live of the Gospel.

<small>a Mat. 10.10.
Luke 10. 7.
t Gal. 6. 6.
1 Tim. 5. 17.</small>

God's will is the same under the New Testament that it was under the Old; it is not as to the people a matter of liberty, so as men may choose whether they will maintain their ministers or no, there is an ordinance of God in the case: it is the will of God, that those who are taken off from worldly employments, and spend their time in the study and preaching of the gospel, should have a livelihood from their labour.

15 But "I have used none of these things: neither have I written these things, that it should be so done unto me: for *it were better for me to die, than that any man should make my glorying void.

<small>u ver. 12.
Acts 18. 3.
& 20. 34.
ch. 4. 12.
1 Thess. 2. 9.
2 Thess. 3. 8.
x 2 Cor. 11. 10.</small>

Though I have such a liberty to marry as well as others, and a liberty to demand a maintenance of those to whom I preach the gospel, yet I have done neither. Nor do I now write to that purpose, that I would now impose a burden upon you to raise me a maintenance. I know I am calumniated by some, as if by preaching the gospel I only sought my own profit and advantage: I have gloried in the contrary, Acts xx. 33, 34; so ver. 18 of this chapter; and I look upon it as my great honour, that I can preach the gospel freely, and I had rather die by starving than lose this advantage of glorying. And if I for your profit, and for the advantage of the gospel, abate of my liberty, should not you abate of yours, to keep your weak brethren from destroying their souls by sinning against God?

16 For though I preach the Gospel, I have nothing to glory of: for ʸnecessity is laid upon me; yea, woe is unto me, if I preach not the Gospel!

<small>y Rom. 1. 14.</small>

For though I preach the gospel, I have nothing to glory of; though I do preach the gospel, yet I have no reason at all to glory; all that I have to glory in is, that I have preached it freely (which your false apostles and teachers do not); for the preaching of the gospel, considered without that circumstance, I have no reason to glory in that, for I am in it but a servant. *For necessity is laid upon me; yea, woe is unto me, if I preach not the gospel!* I am under the necessity of a Divine precept to do that, and exposed to dreadful penalties and woes if I do not do that; there is therefore no thanks I can claim upon that account; all that I can glory in is, that I do it without charge to those to whom I preach it. Some make a doubt, whether there lieth the same necessity upon ministers now to preach the gospel, and they be liable to the same dangers and penalties, if they do it not. I see no reason at all to doubt it; for what necessity lay upon Paul, or any of the apostles, but a necessity of precept, that is, they were obliged to obey the command of God in the case, and liable to such penalties in case of neglect, as men are subject to that obey not the command of God, in fulfilling the duties of their relations? The same necessity, the same danger, is yet incumbent upon every minister; or else we must say, that the precepts commanding ministers to preach concerned the apostles only, or that there is now no such order of men as ministers (both which are indeed said by Socinians). If there be such an ordinance of God as the ministry, ministers are under the precepts given to ministers, one of which is to preach: if they be under the same precepts, there is the same necessity upon them of obeying them, that was upon Paul, and they are, in case of disobedience, subjected to the same woes and penalties. Indeed, every minister is not bound to go up and down the world to preach, his relation is to a particular flock; that travelling to carry the gospel about the world was peculiar to the apostles, for the first plantation of the gospel; but so was not preaching; if it had, Timothy and Titus would have had no such charge as to that work. It is true, ministers are not bound to preach in others' houses without their leave; therefore we read very little of the apostles preaching in the temple and synagogues, nor without the leave of the Jews. But Paul judged himself bound to preach *in the school of Tyrannus,* Acts xix. 9, and *in his own hired house* at Rome, Acts xxviii. 30, 31. For the circumstance of numbers, to which they are bound to preach, the Holy Scripture hath no where determined, and ministers are left to be guided by their own prudence according to circumstances; but preach they must, if they be called of God; he hath sent them to it, fitted them for the work, and they have taken it upon them, and woe will be to every minister, so called and sent of God, if he doth not fulfil his ministry, as he hath opportunity and wisdom, considering circumstances, in order to the end which he is to aim at and to act for.

17 For if I do this thing willingly, ᶻI have a reward: but if against my will, ᵃa dispensation *of the Gospel* is committed unto me.

<small>z ch. 3. 8, 14.
a ch. 4. 1.
Gal. 2. 7.
Phil. 1. 17.
Col. 1. 25.</small>

For if I do this thing willingly, I have a reward; if I who have a liberty to take a maintenance for my labour in the gospel, yet notwithstanding preach it freely, out of a free and cheerful mind, desirous to promote the honour and glory of Christ, I then may expect a reward: *but if against my will, a dispensation of the gospel is committed unto me;* but if I only preach the gospel because there is a necessity laid upon me, all that can be said of me is, that there is such a dispensation committed to me. The strength of the apostle's argument seems to lie here, That no man can reasonably expect thanks, or any extraordinary reward, for doing what he is obliged by his superior's command under a great penalty to do. The apostle was obliged by such a precept, and under such penalties, to preach the gospel; therefore he desired not only to do it, but to do it willingly and readily, a greater testimony of which could not be, than for him to do it without desiring or expecting any reward for his pains, but what God of his free grace should give him; this made this matter of glorying to him, which he desired might not be in vain. So that though the word ἑκών here be truly translated *willingly,* and opposed to ἄκων, which is as truly translated unwillingly, yet it seems to comprehend without charge, and taking nothing for his pains, as a demonstration of his willingness to and cheerful performance of his work; which being a thing as to which God had laid him under no necessity by any precept, was matter of glorying to him against the false apostles, who did otherwise; and also a ground for him to expect a greater reward from God, than those who, though they did the same work, yet did it not from the like free and cheerful spirit.

18 What is my reward then? *Verily that,* ᵇwhen I preach the Gospel, I may make the Gospel of Christ without charge, that I ᶜabuse not my power in the Gospel.

<small>b ch. 10. 33.
2 Cor. 4. 5.
& 11. 7.
c ch. 7. 31.</small>

What is my reward then? what then is the ground of my expectation of a greater reward? or wherein is the glorying I before mentioned? Not in the performance of the work, for as to that, I am under a necessity to do it, and under a penalty if I neglect it: but it lieth here, *that when I preach the gospel, I do it freely,* and *make it without charge;* a thing which, as to the substance of the work, he was not by any law of God bound to do, yet was not this in Paul a work of supererogation; for circumstances might so rule, and, doubtless, Paul apprehended they did so, that it might be his duty so to do. For though the minister may lawfully take maintenance from the people, where he cannot support himself without their assistance; yet if the case be such, that he can subsist without it, and the people be so poor that they are not able to give it; or if he seeth it will hinder the gospel, keeping many from coming within the sound of what must be chargeable to them, and open the mouths of enemies; it is matter of duty to him, under such circumstances, to preach freely. Though, considering the thing in itself, separately from such circumstances, the minister may lawfully enough require and expect such maintenance. *That* (saith the apostle) *I abuse not my power in the gospel.* Some think that the word here translated *abuse,* might better have been translated *use,* as it signified, chap. vii. 31. But it generally signifies abuse, so as there is no reason to vary from the common usage of it; according to which it teaches us this remarkable lesson, that so to use a liberty which God hath left us as to actions, as that by our use of it the glory of God or the good of others is hindered, is to abuse it, that is, not to use it to that true end for which God hath intrusted us with it. For this is

I. CORINTHIANS IX

certain, that God hath intrusted us with no power or liberty to be used to the prejudice of his glory, which is the great end of our lives, or to the prejudice of the spiritual good and advantage of others. All such use of our liberty in any thing is indeed an abuse of it.

d ver. 1.
e Gal. 5. 13.
f Mat. 18. 15.
1 Pet. 3. 1.

19 For though I be ^dfree from all *men*, yet have ^eI made myself servant unto all, ^fthat I might gain the more.

For though I be free from all men; the word *men* is not in the Greek, but is supplied by our interpreters. Some make *things* the substantive, and restrain it to the things of the ceremonial law. It may be understood both of men and things; he was born no man's servant, nor by God's law made a servant to any men's humours, and as free as to many other things, as he was to have taken maintenance of the churches, for the pains he bestowed amongst them. *Yet have I made myself servant unto all, that I might gain the more;* yet (saith he) observe my practice, that I might gain men to Christ, (so the apostle several times calleth converting souls, bringing them in love with the gospel, and into a road that may bring them to heaven, which we ought to account the greatest gain in the world, as it appeareth from Dan. xii. 3,) I have become, or made myself, the servant of all; not the servants of their lusts and corruptions, (that is the way to lose men's souls, and destroy them, not to gain them,) but a servant to their weaknesses and infirmities, so far as they were not sinful: I have denied myself in my liberty, and determined myself to that part in my actions, which I saw would most oblige, profit, and endear them to me, and to bring them more in love with the gospel.

g Acts 16. 3.
& 18. 18. &
21. 23, &c.

20 And ^gunto the Jews I became as a Jew, that I might gain the Jews; to them that are under the law, as under the law, that I might gain them that are under the law;

The ceremonial law died with Christ, Eph. ii. 15, 16, wherefore Christians were not obliged to the performance and observation of it after the death of Christ; but it pleased God for a time to indulge the Jews in the observance of those rites, until they could clearly see, and be fully persuaded of, their liberty from it, with which Christ had made them free; and it was some good time before all those, who from Judaism had turned to Christianity, could be thus persuaded, as we may learn from Gal. iv. 21, they desired to be under the law. To such, saith the apostle, *I became as a Jew,* that is, I observed some rites which the ceremonial law (peculiar to the Jews) required; an instance of which we have, Acts xxi. 23—26, where we find Paul purifying himself (according to the rites of the ceremonial law) with four men which had a vow upon them. The Jews before Christ's death were *under the law;* many of them, though converted to the Christian religion after the death of Christ, apprehended themselves under the law, not as yet seeing the liberty with which Christ had made them free: saith the apostle, I, knowing the will of God, for a time, that the Jews should be indulged as to their weakness, *became as* one of them *under the law, that I might gain them,* that is, reconcile them to the Christian religion, and in some measure prepare them for the receiving the gospel. We have an instance of this in Paul's practice, Acts xvi. 3, where he circumcised Timothy, because his mother was a Jewess, that he might not irritate the Jews in those quarters, nor estrange them from the doctrine of the gospel. In all this Paul did nothing that was sinful, but only determined himself as to the liberty which God had given him, when he might do or forbear, either doing or forbearing to do, as he saw the one or the other made most for the honour and glory of God in the winning of souls.

h Gal. 3. 2.
i Rom. 2. 12, 14.
k ch. 7. 22.

21 ^hTo ⁱthem that are without law, as without law, (^kbeing not without law to God, but under the law to Christ,) that I might gain them that are without law.

It is manifest by the opposition of *them that are without law,* mentioned in this verse, to *them under the law,* mentioned in the former verse, that as by the latter the Jews are understood, so by the former the Gentiles are to be understood, who were under no obligation to the observance either of the ceremonial law or judicial law, given to the Jews; the one to guide that nation in the matters of worship till Christ should come; the other to guide them in matters of civil justice, as well as criminal causes, as matters of plea and trespass: so that the term ἀνόμοις here signifieth differently from what it signifieth in many other scriptures; where it signifieth men that live as they list, without any regard to any laws of God or men, as Mark xv. 28; Luke xxii. 37; Acts ii. 23; 2 Thess. ii. 8; 1 Tim. i. 9, &c. This the apostle makes appear by the next words, where he tells us, he was *not without law to God, but under the law to Christ:* though to the Gentiles he behaved himself as if he himself had been a Gentile, that is, forbearing the observances of the Levitical law, to which the Gentiles had never any obligation at all, yet he did not behave himself as one that had no regard to the law of God, that was yet in force and obligatory, but acknowledged himself to be under that, though a servant of Christ's; so that he abated nothing of his necessary duty, only denied himself in some things as to which the law of God had left him a liberty, both to the Jews and Gentiles, propounding to himself the same end as to both, that is, the gaining of their souls to Christ.

22 ^lTo the weak became I as weak, that I might gain the weak: ^mI am made all things to all *men*, ⁿthat I might by all means save some.

l Rom. 15. 1.
2 Cor. 11. 29.
m ch. 10. 33.
n Rom. 11. 14. ch. 7. 16.

To the weak became I as weak, that I might gain the weak; to those that I observed weak in knowledge and faith, who had not such a firm persuasion of the lawfulness of some things, (suppose circumcision, purifyings required by the law of Moses, &c.,) *I became as weak,* that is, I yielded to them; and the things being to me matters of liberty, which I knew I might do, or not do, and be no transgressor of God's law, they being not able to comply with me, I complied with them, abating my liberty to gratify their consciences; though I knew that it was weakness in them, yet I indulged it, and made my more knowledge serve them in their weakness, so that I might not lose them. *I am made all things to all men, that I might by all means save some;* thus, that I might be an instrument in any degree to save them, according to the various persuasions of several Christians I behaved myself towards them; doing nothing to gratify them, by doing of which I knew, or had the least jealousy, I should offend God; but not refusing any thing, either as to doing or forbearing, (which by the law of God I saw I might do or forbear,) where I saw the least hopes, by such doing or forbearing, to do the souls of those good, in order to their eternal salvation, with whom I was, and for whose sake I so did, or forbore any thing. Oh the humility and charity of this great apostle! what an example hath he set to all! for none can pretend to a greater superiority over men, as to spiritual things, than he unquestionably had.

23 And this I do for the Gospel's sake, that I might be partaker thereof with *you*.

Paul had two great ends which he aimed at in this denial of himself in these points of liberty; the one was the doing good to the souls both of Jews and Gentiles, this he had before instanced in; the other was the glory of God, which is that which he here meaneth by this phrase, *for the gospel's sake,* which he before expounded, ver. 12, *lest we should hinder the gospel of Christ.* By Paul's tenacious adhering to one part in a thing wherein he had liberty, the gospel, that is, the progress or success of the gospel, might have been hindered, both by the reproaches of enemies, and also by the alienation and estrangement of the hearts of weaker Christians, or laying stumblingblocks before them, at which they might fall, being emboldened by the examples of their guides, to do what, though lawful in itself, yet they judged unlawful. *That I might be partaker thereof with you;* I did it, saith he, that I might bring you into the fellowship of the gospel: I had rather so interpret it, than of the reward of the gospel, as it pleaseth some. The humility of the great apostle is very remarkable; he disdaineth not to be συγκοίνωνος, a *partaker* in the gospel with the meanest members of the church; he is not ashamed to call those brethren whom his Lord and Master is not ashamed so to call.

I. CORINTHIANS IX

^o Gal. 2. 2. &
5. 7. Phil. 2.
16. & 3. 14.
2 Tim. 4. 7.
Heb. 12. 1.

24 Know ye not that they which run in a race run all, but one receiveth the prize? °So run, that ye may obtain.

The apostle presseth all his former discourse by minding them of the difficulty of getting to heaven, and of the obligation that lay upon them to be the first in the spiritual race. To this purpose he fetcheth a similitude from what they saw daily, in the practice of those who frequented those games by which the Romans and Corinthians were wont to divert themselves. They had several, known by the names of the Olympian, Pythian, Nemean, and Isthmian games, the latter of which were most proper' to Greece. At these games there were several that ran races, either on foot or on horseback; and several that wrestled. The reward was a crown, or garland: and for those that ran, we read that the crown or garland was hung up at the end of the race, and those who, running on foot or on horseback, could first lay hold upon it, and take it down, had it, so as though many ran, yet but one had the crown. So, he saith, it is as to getting to heaven; men might think it was a light matter, but they who would have the crown of glory must run for it. and it was a work which required so much striving and labour, that not many would have that crown: which is the same with that which our Saviour saith, Luke xiii. 24. *For many will seek to enter in, and shall not be able.* 2 Tim. ii. 5. *If a man strive for masteries, yet is he not crowned, except he strive lawfully.* Therefore, saith the apostle, make it your business, *so to run, that you may obtain;* not only to do things in themselves lawful or good, but which are so clothed with all their circumstances, and in the best manner, for the glory of God, and the good of others.

^p Eph. 6.12.
1 Tim. 6. 12.
2 Tim. 2. 5.
& 4. 7.
^q 2 Tim. 4.8.
James 1. 12.
1 Pet. 1. 4.
& 5. 4. Rev.
2. 10. & 3.11.

25 And every man that ^p striveth for the mastery is temperate in all things. Now they *do it* to obtain a corruptible crown; but we ^q an incorruptible.

This is not all that is required of men that would go to heaven, that they do not make an ill use of their liberty, using it to the dishonour of God, or to the prejudice of others; but look as it is with wrestlers in those games in practice amongst you, they are *temperate in all things;* in the use of meats and drinks, or any pleasures, though in themselves lawful, they will so use them, as may best serve their end, upholding the strength of their body for the motion they are to use, and yet not clogging them, or so using them, that they shall indispose them to, or hinder them in, that motion which they are to use. We, that are Christians, and striving for heaven, should also do the like, so behaving ourselves in the use of meats, drinks, apparel, pleasures, as the things, so used by us, may serve us in our business for heaven, and be no clog or hinderance to us. And we have reason so to do, or we shall be shamed by those gamesters; for they in that manner deny, restrain, and govern themselves to get a crown, which, when they have, is a pitiful, corruptible, perishing thing; we do it for a crown that is *incorruptible: An inheritance incorruptible, and undefiled, and that fadeth not away, reserved in heaven for you,* as the apostle speaketh, 1 Pet. i. 4.

^r 2 Tim. 2.5.

26 I therefore so run, ^r not as uncertainly; so fight I, not as one that beateth the air:

The apostle proposeth his own example. As it is observed in country work, he that only bids his servants do work, and puts not his own hand to it, or at least doth not attend and overlook them in their work, hath little done: so it is as observable in spiritual work, that a minister of the gospel, who only, in the pulpit, dictates duty to others, but, out of it, doth nothing of himself, seldom doth any good by his preaching. People not naturally inclined to any spiritual duty, have the old proverb, *Physician, cure thyself,* at their tongue's end, and are hard to believe that teacher, who doth not in some measure live up to his own doctrine. Therefore, saith the apostle, *I run;* I am in the same race with you, and running to the same mark and for the same prize. I give you no other counsel than I myself take; I endeavour so to live, so in all things to behave myself, as I may not be at uncertainties whether I please God by my actions, or shall get to heaven, yea or no. I am a fellow soldier with you, fighting against sin; I make it my great business, not so to fight, so to resist sin, as if I did *beat the air;* that is, get no more fruit, profit, or advantage by it, than if I threw stones against the wind, or with a staff did beat the air. It is not every running, or every fighting, that will bring a man to heaven; it must be a running with all our might, and continuing our motion till we come to the end of our race; a fighting with all our might, and that against all sin.

27 ^s But I keep under my body, and ^t bring *it* into subjection: lest that by any means, when I have preached to others, I myself should be ^u a castaway.

^s Rom. 8.13.
Col. 3. 5.
^t Rom. 6.18, 19.
^u Jer. 6. 30.
2 Cor.13.5,6.

Here the apostle informs us how he ran, that he might not run uncertainly; how he fought, so as he might not be like one beating the air: *I* (saith he) *keep under my body, and bring it into subjection.* By *body,* here, we must not understand only the apostle's fleshly part (which we usually call our body); no, nor only our more gross and filthy affections and lusts (as some of the schoolmen have thought); but what the apostle elsewhere calleth the *old man,* under which notion cometh the sinful inclinations of our will, and corrupt dictates of reason, as it is in man since the fall. All this, as it cometh under the notion of *the flesh* in many other places of Scripture, and of *our members which are upon the earth,* Col. iii. 5; so it cometh here under the notion of the *body;* and, indeed, is that which our apostle calleth *the body of death,* Rom. vii. 24. This was the object of the apostle's action; the object about which he was exercised. For his action, or exercise about this object, is expressed by two words, ὑπωπιάζω and δυλαγωγῶ· the former word (as some think) is borrowed from the practice of those that fought in the afore-mentioned games, who knocked and beat one another till they were black and blue, and forced to yield themselves conquered. The second word signifieth to make one a servant, to bring one under command, so as he will do what another would have him do. By these two words the apostle expresseth that mortification, which he declareth himself to have lived in the practice of, that he might not in his race for heaven run uncertainly, nor in his spiritual fight lose his labour, and reap no more profit than one should reap that spends his time in beating the air. Their sense, who think that this duty of Paul was discharged by acts of mere external discipline, such as fasting, wearing sackcloth, beating themselves, &c., is much too short; these things reach not to the mind of man, his corrupt affections and lusts, which give life to the extravagancy of the bodily members, though indeed they may some of them be good means in order to the greater work. Paul's meaning was, that he made it his work to deny his sensitive appetite such gratifyings as it would have; to resist the extravagant motions of his will, yea, of his own corrupt reason, so far as they were in any thing contrary to the holy will of God; though, in order to this, he also used fasting and prayer, and such acts of external discipline as his wisdom taught him were any way proper to this end. And this he tells us that he did, *lest,* while he *preached to others,* he himself *should be a castaway:* from whence we may observe, that Paul thought such a thing possible, that one who all his life had been preaching to others, to bring them to heaven, might himself be thrown into hell at last; and if it had not, our Saviour would never have told us, that he would at the last day say to some, Depart from me, I know you not, you workers of iniquity; who for their admittance had pleaded, We have prophesied in thy name, Matt. vii. 22, 23. Nor must we question but Judas, whom our Saviour calls a *son of perdition,* was a lost man as to eternity, though it be certain that he, as well as the other apostles, was a preacher of the gospel: yea, so far is this from being impossible, that it was the opinion of Chrysostom, that few ministers would be saved. We may also further observe, that such ministers as indulge their body, giving themselves liberties, either more externally in meats, drinks, apparel, pleasures; or more internally, indulging themselves in sinful speculations, notions, affections, inclinations; take a quite contrary road to heaven than Paul took, and think they have a great deal more liberty to the flesh than St. Paul thought he had, or than he durst use.

CHAP. X.

The Jews who came out of Egypt had all sacraments typical of ours, yet many of them perished through sin, 1—5. *Their examples should serve, as they were intended, for our admonition,* 6—12. *God will not suffer his servants to be tempted beyond their strength,* 13. *Christians must flee idolatry, and not by partaking of idol sacrifices own fellowship with devils,* 14—22. *Even in the use of things lawful we should consult the good of others,* 23—30; *and refer all we do to God's glory,* 31; *careful to give none offence, after the apostle's own example,* 32, 33.

^a Ex. 13. 21. & 40. 34. Num. 9. 18. & 14. 14. Deut. 1. 33. Neh. 9. 12, 19. Ps. 78. 14. & 105. 39.
^b Ex. 14 22. Num. 33. 8. Josh. 4. 23. Ps. 78. 13.

MOREOVER, brethren, I would not that ye should be ignorant, how that all our fathers were under ^athe cloud, and all passed through ^bthe sea;

The apostle saw that many in this church of Corinth were puffed up with their knowledge, and other gifts and great privileges with which God had blessed them; as also with the opinion of their being a gospel church, and some of the first-fruits of the Gentiles unto Christ, and might therefore think, that they needed not to be pressed to such degrees of strictness and watchfulness; therefore, to beat them off from this confidence and vain presumption, the apostle here sets before them the example of the church of the Jews: when he tells them, he would not have them ignorant, his meaning is, he would have them know and remember, he would have them well acquainted with and to reflect upon this, that all the Jews in Moses's time, whom he calls their *fathers*, not according to the flesh, for the Corinthians were not descended from Jews, but with respect to the covenant, and their relation they stood unto God, as they were the only people God had on earth; these, he saith, were all of them (the whole camp of Israel) under very great privileges, of which he reckoneth divers: they were under the conduct of the cloud, Exod. xiii. 21; and they all obtained the favour of God so far for them, as to divide the Red Sea, so as they passed through it upon dry ground.

2 And were all baptized unto Moses in the cloud and in the sea;

There are two great difficulties in this verse: 1. What is meant by *Moses*. 2. How and why the Israelites are said to be *baptized unto Moses.* Some understand by *Moses* the person of Moses; others, the law or doctrine of Moses. Those who by *Moses* understand the person of Moses, are divided in their opinions, whether the preposition εἰς, which signifieth divers things, were better translated *by*, or *into*, or *unto*, or *together with.* Some think it were better translated *by*, and thus all the Jews were baptized by Moses in the cloud and in the sea, that is, by his ministry; and thus this very particle is translated, Acts vii. 53; xix. 3. Some think it were better translated *in Moses;* that is, Moses going before them, when they were under the conduct of the cloud, and when they passed through the Red Sea. Others judge it better translated *into Moses;* that is, either Moses going before them; or, as Moses was a type of Christ, Gal. iii. 19. Some would have the particle here to signify *together with.* Others, *even unto Moses*, Moses himself not being excepted from that baptism in the cloud and in the sea. Others by *Moses* here understand the doctrine and law of Moses: thus the term *Moses* is used, Luke xvi. 29; Acts xv. 21. So they say, that to be *baptized unto Moses*, is to believe Moses so far, as to follow his conduct through the sea, and under the cloud. The second difficulty is, to resolve what is meant by being *baptized.* The word signifieth, in the common acceptation of it, a being washed: in the ecclesiastical acceptation, it signifies a holy institution of the New Testament, according to which Christians are initiated into the church of God, by washing them in the name of the Father, Son, and Holy Ghost. Now how could the Jews be said either to be washed (that is, baptized) either in Moses, or by Moses, or with Moses, or into Moses; whenas the history of the Old Testament tells us, that both Moses and all the Israelites went through the sea on dry ground, and we do not read that the cloud, under the conduct of which the Israelites journeyed, ever poured down any water with which the Jews, or Moses their leader, could be washed. *Answ.* Some think, that the cloud which, passing over the Israelites, was all darkness to their enemies, yet poured down water for the refreshing of the Israelites, as it passed over their heads, and that this is hinted to us by the psalmist, Psal. lxviii. 7—9. Others think, that the apostle applieth the term of baptism to a privilege of which the old Israelites had as much reason to glory, as the Corinthians had of their baptism, properly so called. Others say, that the Israelites' walking under the cloud and through the sea, which was darkness and destruction to their adversaries, was a figure of baptism, the seal of the New Testament, by which Christ's victory over our spiritual enemies is confirmed to us, and in that respect the apostle maketh use of this term *baptized*. Others, most probably, think, that the apostle useth this term, in regard of the great analogy betwixt baptism, as it was then used, the persons going down into the waters, and being dipped in them; and the Israelites going down into the sea, the great receptacle of water; though the waters at that time were gathered on heaps on either side of them, yet they seemed buried in the waters, as persons in that age were when they were baptized; and for being baptized in the cloud, there is a great probability that the cloud did shower down rain, according to what is quoted out of the psalmist.

3 And did all eat the same ^cspiritual meat;

^c Ex. 16. 15, 35. Neh. 9. 15, 20. Ps. 78. 24.

Those of the Jews that perished in the wilderness, did all eat the same manna which Caleb and Joshua ate of, who went into Canaan; or, those Jews that so perished in the wilderness did eat the same spiritual meat that we do, they in the type, we in the antitype. Manna is called *spiritual meat:* 1. Because it was bread which came down from heaven, the habitation of spiritual beings, John vi. 31. 2. It was miraculously produced. 3. Because it was angels' food, given out by their ministry. 4. But principally, because it signified Christ, who was *the true bread from heaven*, John vi. 32.

4 And did all drink the same ^dspiritual drink: for they drank of that spiritual Rock that ‖ followed them: and that Rock was Christ.

^d Ex. 17. 6. Num. 20. 11. Ps. 78. 15. ‖ Or, *went with them,* Deut. 9. 21. Ps. 105. 41.

And all the Jews, as well those that perished in the wilderness, as those that were preserved to go into Canaan, they drank of the water which came out of the rock, of which we read, Exod. xvii. 6; Numb. xx. 11; which water was *spiritual drink* in the same respects that the manna was *spiritual meat*, being miraculously produced, and being a figure of Christ. For, saith the apostle, *that rock was Christ;* that is, that rock did signify or prefigure Christ; the rock was Christ in the same sense that the bread in the Lord's supper is the body of Christ, that is, a sign which by Divine institution did signify Christ. Here ariseth a question in what sense it is said, that the *rock followed them?* That by the rock is to be understood the water that God made to flow out of the rock, is evident; but though we read of water twice fetched out of the rock upon Moses smiting of it; once at Rephidim, before they came so far as Mount Sinai, Exod. xvii. 6; another time at Kadesh, Numb. xx. 7, 8; yet we no where read in the history of the Jewish journeyings to Canaan, that the rock followed them. But this is not the only thing that we read in the New Testament relating to the history of the Old Testament, with some circumstances which we do not find recorded there; it is enough that it is plainly asserted here, and it must be presumed, or how can we imagine that the Israelites were supplied with water for forty years together? Whereas some object, that if the water, which came out of the rock at Rephidim, had followed them, there would have been no need of Moses striking the rock at Kadesh; it is answered, that God, to try them, probably caused the water to stop. For the analogy betwixt the rock and Christ, divines make it to lie in these particulars: 1. That Christ is the firm and unmovable foundation of his church, called therefore *a stone, a tried stone*, Isa. xxviii. 16; Rom. ix. 33; 1 Pet. ii. 6. 2. As this rock sent out no water for the refreshment of the Israelites, till Moses had struck it; so all the benefit we have from Christ as Mediator, floweth from him as *smitten of God*, and *afflicted.* 3. As the water of the rock served both for cleansing, and upholding life in satisfying thirst; so the blood of Christ is useful to the soul, both for washing from the guilt of sin, and the upholding spiritual life in a soul. 4. As the rock that followed the Israelites afforded water not only to that generation that were alive and present when the rock was smitten, but to all the succeeding generations, until the Israelites came into Canaan; so the blood of Christ is useful not only to his people in this or that place or age, but to all that shall believe in him, and that till they shall come into the heavenly Canaan.

e Num. 14. 29, 32, 35. & 26. 64, 65. Ps. 106. 26. Heb. 3. 17. Jude 5.

5 But with many of them God was not well pleased: for they [e] were overthrown in the wilderness.

But with many of them God was not well pleased; these many were no less than that whole generation, which were at that time twenty years old and upward, according to the threatening, Numb. xiv. 28. 29; of the acccomplishment of which we read, Numb. xxvi. 64, 65. *For they were overthrown in the wilderness;* as an instance of God's being displeased with them, he giveth their falling in the wilderness. It is very possible, that many of these were the objects of God's eternal and special love, and eternally saved, notwithstanding their joining with worse men in their rebellion and murmuring; but that signal judgment of God upon them was enough to prove, that their being *baptized unto Moses in the cloud and in the sea,* and being made partakers of those great privileges of eating *spiritual meat,* and drinking *spiritual drink,* typifying Christ, did not set them out of the danger of God's judgments, which is the use the apostle maketh of it.

+ Gr. our *figures.* f Num. 11.4, 33, 34 Ps. 106. 14.

6 Now these things were †our examples, to the intent we should not lust after evil things, as [f] they also lusted.

Our examples; our types or patterns (as the Greek word signifies): we may, by God's dispensations to them, learn what God will be to us: as they were patterns to us, of persons enjoying great spiritual privileges; so they are also examples or patterns to show us what we may expect from God, and to deter us from such practices, as brought the vengeance of God upon them; which were their sinful lustings or desirings of things which God had forbidden, as they did the flesh-pots, and onions, and garlic of Egypt, and to return thither again, Numb. xi. 4, 5, 33; xiv. 2—4.

g ver. 14. h Ex. 32. 6.

7 [g] Neither be ye idolaters, as were some of them; as it is written, [h] The people sat down to eat and drink, and rose up to play.

Neither be ye idolaters, as were some of them; the people of Israel, being first enticed to whoredom with the daughters of Moab, were after that invited *to the sacrifices of their gods, and did eat, and bowed down to their gods,* Numb. xxv. 2; so, either worshipped the creature instead of the Creator, or worshipped the Creator in and by the creature. *As it is written, The people sat down to eat and drink, and rose up to play;* thus it is written in Exod. xxxii. 6; which history mentioneth another idolatry they were guilty of, in worshipping the golden calf. They were wont to have feasts after their sacrifices, and pastimes and diversions after such feasts; and particularly we are told in the history concerning the golden calf, that they danced before it. Stephen saith, Acts vii. 41, they *rejoiced in the works of their own hands.*

i ch. 6. 18. Rev. 2. 14. k Num. 25. 1, 9. Ps. 106. 22.

8 [i] Neither let us commit fornication, as some of them committed, and [k] fell in one day three and twenty thousand.

The story to which this verse relates is that, Numb. xxv. 1—9. When Balaam could not curse the Israelites, he advised the debauching of them by the Moabitish women, first enticing them to fornication and adultery, then to idolatry: and they were enticed, which caused a plague amongst them, which destroyed amongst them *in one day three and twenty thousand,* saith our apostle: Moses saith, that there died *twenty and four thousand.* There are many guesses for the clearing of that seeming contradiction. Some say, that Moses mentioneth not *one day,* there might in all die twenty-four thousand, but not all the same day, nor possibly by the same death. But nothing is in Scripture more ordinary, than to speak of things or persons in round numbers, though something over or under; and also to speak according to the common reckoning of people, who also may talk variously. Some might report twenty-three, some twenty-four thousand: or possibly Paul chose to mention the lesser rather than the greater round number. The sense of Moses might be, about twenty-four thousand, or near up to that number, all of which probably had not been guilty of adultery or fornication. Paul saith, there died twenty-three thousand. If there did die twenty-four thousand, there must needs die twenty-three thousand.

9 Neither let us tempt Christ, as [l] some of them also tempted, and [m] were destroyed of serpents.

l Ex. 17. 2, 7. Num. 21. 5. Deut. 6. 16. Ps. 78. 18, 56. & 95. 9. & 106. 14. m Num. 21. 6.

To *tempt,* in the general notion of the term, signifies to make a trial; applied unto God, it signifieth to make a trial of God, either with reference to his power, Psal. lxxviii. 18—20, or to his truth and goodness: not to be satisfied with God's word, but to challenge him to a sensible demonstration, is to tempt God. Or else to *tempt* may signify more generally, to provoke God; for indeed all notorious sinning against God is a tempting of God, not believing the wrath of God, which he hath revealed in his word against sin, till men feel it. The term *Christ* here is very remarkable to prove Christ's Divine nature and existence before he was incarnate; for the same person who is here called *Christ,* is called *God,* Psal. cvi. 14, and Jehovah also in the same Psalm; neither could they have tempted Christ at that time, if at that time he had not been existent. *Were destroyed of serpents;* by *serpents* he meaneth the fiery serpents; we have the history, Numb. xxi. 6—9.

10 Neither murmur ye, as [n] some of them also murmured, and [o] were destroyed of [p] the destroyer.

n Ex. 16. 2. & 17. 2. Num. 14. 2, 29. & 16. 41. o Num. 14. 37. & 16. 49. p Ex. 12. 23. 2 Sam. 24. 16. 1 Chron. 21. 15.

Murmuring signifies the speaking against a person or thing, out of dislike, impatience, or discontent. It was a sin the Jews were very much guilty of, as may be read, Exod. xv. 24; xvi. 7, 8; xvii. 3; Numb. xiv. 27; xvi. 11, 41. The apostle may either refer to all their murmurings, when he saith they *were* (as the punishment of their sin) *destroyed of the destroyer,* or to that more universal murmuring upon the ill report the spies brought up of the land of Canaan, of which we read, Numb. xiv.

11 Now all these things happened unto them for ‖ ensamples: and [q] they are written for our admonition, [r] upon whom the ends of the world are come.

‖ Or, *types.* q Rom. 15. 4. ch. 9. 10. r ch. 7. 29. Phil. 4. 5. Heb. 10. 25, 37. 1 John 2. 18.

Now all these things happened to them for ensamples; all these dispensations of Divine providence in the revelations of Divine wrath against several sorts of sinners, happened to the Jews, who were God's first and ancient people, and enjoyed those great privileges which were before mentioned, not only as just punishments upon them for their sins, but as examples or types, to let the succeeding world know what they should find God towards such kind of sinners. *And they are written for our admonition;* and God in his wise providence hath ordered the record of them in holy writ, that others who should live afterward might read, and hear, and fear, and take warning, and beware of such wicked actions, as pulled down such vengeance upon a people, than which none can plead a nearer relation to God, or the receiving of greater favours and privileges from him. *Upon whom the ends of the world are come:* the apostles ordinarily in their epistles speak of the world as nigh to an end in their age, though it hath since continued more than sixteen hundred years; which would incline one to think, that they thought it would have been at an end before this time, but had no such revelation from God. So true is that of our Saviour, that *of that day and hour knoweth no man;* and it should teach us to beware of too particular determinations in the case, which the apostles did not make, though they spake of theirs as the last times, and themselves as such upon whom the ends of the world were come.

12 Wherefore [s] let him that thinketh he standeth take heed lest he fall.

s Rom. 11. 20.

Let him that thinketh he standeth, either in a right and sound judgment and opinion of things, or in a state of favour with God, or confirmed in a holy course of life and conversation; standeth in grace, Rom. v. 2. A man may stand in these things, and he may but think that he standeth: be it as it will, he is concerned to *take heed lest he fall.* He may but think he standeth, and if so, he will fall : he may really stand in a right judgment and opinion of things, and be a member of the church of Christ, and yet may fall into errors and some loose practices, so as to bring down Divine vengeance upon himself; he may have God's favour so far as concerns external privileges, and yet perish, as many of the Jews did in the instances before mentioned : nay, he may really stand in a state of justification and regeneration, and yet may fall, though not totally and finally, yet foully, so as to lose his peace, and bring God's severe judgments upon him. Therefore he that thinketh that he standeth, whether his apprehensions be false or true, had need use all means and caution that he may not fall, and that because, if he keepeth his standing, it must be by the use of due means, which God hath appointed in order to that end, though he be also *kept by the power of God unto salvation,* 1 Pet. i. 5.

13 There hath no temptation taken you but ‖ such as is common to man : but ᵗGod *is* faithful, ᵘwho will not suffer you to be tempted above that ye are able ; but will with the temptation also ˣmake a way to escape, that ye may be able to bear *it.*

‖ Or, *moderate.*
t ch. 1. 9.
u Ps. 125. 3.
2 Pet. 2. 9.

x Jer. 29. 11.

There hath no temptation taken you : temptation (as hath been said before) signifieth in the general notion of it no more than trials, and is often so used in holy writ. Now, in regard we are tried either by afflictive providences, or by motions made to us, either from God, or our own lusts, or the devil, or men of the world; temptations, in Scripture, sometimes signify afflictions, as James i. 2 ; 1 Pet. i. 6 ; sometimes, motions made to us by God, Gen. xxii. 1, 2 ; both which sorts of temptations are good in themselves. Sometimes the term signifies motions made by the lusts and unrenewed part of our own souls, or by the devil, or by sinful men in the world; these are sinful temptations, and what we most ordinarily call by that name. Whether the apostle here means all or some of these, cannot certainly be determined ; what he saith is true of all, and therefore that is the safest interpretation of the term in this place. Though he had not been before speaking indeed of afflictive temptations, he had before affrighted them with minding them of the possibility of their falling, though they did stand, or thought they stood, and cautioned them to take heed : here he comforteth them, by minding them, that no temptation had befallen them, *but what was* incident and *common to man,* ἀνθρώπινος, and they could not expect to be freed from the common fate of mankind : then he minds them, that that God who had promised strength and assistance to his people, Matt. vii. 11 ; Luke xi. 13 ; 2 Cor. i. 18 ; 1 Thess. v. 4 ; 2 Thess. iii. 3, was one that would be as good as his word, being *faithful,* and would not suffer them to be tempted above their strength, and ability to oppose and resist ; yea, and would *make a way to escape,* both the evil of the temptation, that it should not overbear them to a total ruin of their souls, and likewise the burdensome and afflictive evil, that it should not continually lie upon them, provided they used their just endeavours, and (as he had said before) took heed lest they fell.

y ver. 7.
2 Cor. 6. 17.
1 John 5. 21.

14 Wherefore, my dearly beloved, ʸflee from idolatry.

The apostle would have them avoid all sin, but *idolatry* more especially, keeping at the utmost distance imaginable from that, being of all sins in its kind the greatest transgression ; upon which account it is often in Scripture compared to whoredom. Though we ought to be afraid of and to decline all sin ; yet as God hath revealed his wrath against any particular sin more than other, so every good Christian is obliged more to detest and abhor that sin. How the Corinthians were concerned in this caution, we shall read afterwards, ver. 20. For though idolatry be properly where the failure is in the ultimate or mediate object of our worship, and the creature is made either the ultimate term of our worship, or the medium in and by which we worship the Creator ; yet there are many other ways by which we may be partakers of the sins of others, and this sin of idolatry in particular : and idolatry being a sin of the greatest magnitude, from which they were bound to keep the furthest distance, they were bound to take heed of being partakers of other men's sins of this kind.

15 I speak as to ᶻwise men ; judge ye what I say.

z ch. 8. 1.

As to the present case, you are persons that understand the principles of Christian religion, I will make you judges in this case.

16 ᵃThe cup of blessing which we bless, is it not the communion of the blood of Christ ? ᵇThe bread which we break, is it not the communion of the body of Christ ?

a Matt. 26. 26, 27, 28.
b Acts 2. 42, 46. ch. 11. 23, 24.

It is on all hands agreed, that the apostle is here speaking of believers communicating in the sacrament of the Lord's supper. By *the cup of blessing,* he meaneth the cup there, which he so calleth, because we in the taking of it bless the Lord, who gave his Son to die for us, and Christ, for that great love which he showed in dying for us : we are said to *bless* it, because we, by solemn prayer in the consecration of it, set it apart for that sacred use, and beg of God to bless it to us. This *cup* (saith the apostle) *is the communion of the blood of Christ.* The *cup* is put for the wine in the cup (which is very ordinary). *The cup,* or wine, *of blessing,* signifieth that cup of wine to which the blessing is added, or with which in that holy institution we thankfully remember the death of Christ, and bless his name for that great mercy ; and the wine or *cup of blessing,* also, here signifieth our religious action in drinking of that cup of wine so blessed. This, saith he, is *the communion of the blood of Christ ;* that is, it is an action whereby and wherein Christ communicates himself and his grace to us, and we communicate our souls to him ; so that Christ and believers in that action have a mutual communion one with another. And as it is with the one element in that holy sacrament, so it is also with the other. *The bread* which the minister breaketh (according to the institution and example of Christ) for the church to make use of in the celebration of the Lord's supper, that is, their action in eating of that bread so broken and divided amongst them, *is the communion of the body of Christ ;* an action wherein Christians have a fellowship and communion with Christ.

17 For ᶜwe *being* many are one bread, *and* one body : for we are all partakers of that one bread.

c Rom. 12. 5. ch. 12. 27.

Believers, though *many,* yet *are one body,* and declare themselves to be one body mystical, by their fellowship together in the ordinance of the Lord's supper ; as the bread they there eat is *one bread,* though it be made up of many grains of corn, which come into the composition of that loaf or piece of bread which is so broken, distributed, and eaten ; and the wine they drink is one cup, one body of wine, though it be made up of many particular grapes. And they declare themselves to be one body, by their joint partaking *of that one bread.* Some have from hence fetched an argument to prove the unlawfulness of communicating with scandalous sinners at the Lord's table, because we declare ourselves one body with those that communicate : but whether it will (if examined) be cogent enough, I doubt ; for *one body* signifieth no more than one church, and that not invisible, but visible. So as we only declare ourselves to be fellow members of the visible church with those with whom we partake in that ordinance, and the visible church may consist of persons that are bad mixed with the good. So as though, undoubtedly, scandalously wicked persons ought to be excluded from the holy table, yea, and no unbeliever hath a right to it ; yet it may reasonably be doubted, whether those that partake with unbelievers, do by it own themselves to be unbelievers ; they only own themselves members of that church wherein there are some unbelievers. But the scope of the apostle is from hence to argue, that by a parity of reason, those that communicated with an idolatrous assembly in their sacrifices, declared themselves by that action to be one body with those idolaters.

18 Behold ᵈIsrael ᵉafter the flesh :

d Rom. 4. 12. Gal. 6. 16.
e Rom. 4. 1. & 9. 3, 5. 2 Cor. 11. 18.

VOL. III—19

I. CORINTHIANS X

^f Lev. 3. 3. & 7. 15. ^f are not they which eat of the sacrifices partakers of the altar?

Israel after the flesh was the whole seed of Jacob, the whole body of the Jewish church; for believers only were Israelites after the Spirit, Rom. ix. 6, called *the Israel of God,* Gal. vi. 16. *Are not they which eat of the sacrifices partakers of the altar?* if in the Jewish church any persons ate of the flesh of sacrifices offered upon God's altar, did they not by that act manifest that they were members of the Jewish church, and owned that God to whom those sacrifices were offered, and that way of worship by which God was so worshipped? By the same reason these Corinthians eating of the flesh of those beasts in the idol's temple, which had been offered unto idols, did by that act declare their owning of the idol, and that idolatrous worship which had been there performed, and were really partakers of the idolatrous altar.

^g ch. 8. 4. 19 What say I then? ^g that the idol is any thing, or that which is offered in sacrifice to idols is any thing?

I do not by this contradict what I before said, nor now affirm that an idol is any thing, or the sacrifices offered to it any thing. An idol hath nothing in it of a Deity, nor can it either sanctify or pollute any thing that is set before it; the error is in your action, as you communicate with such as are idolaters; it is your own action that polluteth you, not the idol, nor yet the meat set before it.

20 But *I say,* that the things which ^h Lev. 17. 7. Deut. 32. 17. Ps. 106. 57. Rev. 9. 20. the Gentiles ^h sacrifice, they sacrifice to devils, and not to God: and I would not that ye should have fellowship with devils.

The heathens might not intentionally offer sacrifices to devils, (such a thing can hardly be supposed of men,) but actually they offered sacrifices to devils: for they were devils, that is, evil angels, which deluded the poor heathen, and gave answers from the images and statues which they worshipped, believing the true God to be in them: which answers they accounted for oracles. Besides, the apostle saith, they sacrificed to devils, because in God's esteem it was so, though not in their intention; God judgeth of men's acts of worship and homage pretendedly done unto him, not according to their intention, but according to the truth and reality of the thing: now, really the heathen in their sacrifices paid a homage to devils, though such a thing was far from their intention; and this deserves the consideration, both of the papists, who worship images, and also of those protestants (if any such be) who would excuse the papists in their idolatries from their intentions. The nature of idolatry doth not lie in men's intending to worship the creature instead of the Creator, (there were hardly every any such idolaters in the world,) but in their actual doing of the thing; and except they can find a direct rule in holy writ ordering the adoration of the Creator in the creature, or before the creature, it is much to be feared, that in the last day God will judge their homage performed to the creature, not to him. Now, saith the apostle, you had need take heed that, by this action, you prove not yourselves to have *fellowship with devils,* instead of Christ and the true and living God.

ⁱ 2 Cor. 6. 15, 16. ^k Deu. 32.38. 21 ⁱ Ye cannot drink the cup of the Lord, and ^k the cup of devils: ye cannot be partakers of the Lord's table, and of the table of devils.

The cup of the Lord: we may either take the phrase as signifying all religious communion under one great act of religion, or as particularly signifying having a communion with Christ in the ordinance of the Lord's supper, which is called *the cup of the Lord,* either because God hath instituted and appointed the drinking of it, or because it is done for the honour, glory, and remembrance of our Lord Christ, to remember his death until he come, as the apostle speaketh, chap. xi. 26. This apostle tells them they could not drink of, that is, not rightly, and with a good conscience; or not really; no man that is an idolater, or hath communion with idolaters in their idolatrous acts, can have communion with Christ. The same is meant by *the Lord's table,* and *the table of devils.* So as I cannot see how either an idolatrous church can be a true church, or an idolater a true Christian, unless we will assert, that a body of people may be a true church, that can have no communion with Christ; or a man may be a true Christian, and yet have no communion with Christ. Idolatry, doubtless, both divides the soul from Christ, as he is the Head of a believer, and as he is the Head of the church. To call any body of idolaters a true church, either morally, or metaphysically, is to say to those, Ammi, You are the Lord's people, to whom God hath said, Lo-ammi. Let them be what they will, the name of a church belongeth not to them, if (as the apostle affirmeth) they can have no communion with Christ.

22 Do we ^l provoke the Lord to jealousy? ^m are we stronger than he? ^l Deu. 32.21. ^m Ezek. 22. 14.

Jealousy is a violent passion in a man, not bearing a companion or a rival as to a thing or person which he loveth. It is in holy writ applied unto God, not to signify any such extravagancy, excess, or vehemence, as attendeth that passion in men, but only his just displeasure at the giving that homage to any creature which is due to him alone. It is most applied to God to express his anger against those who give Divine homage to idols; the worship of God being a great piece of his *glory* which he hath said he *will not give to another, nor his praise to graven images,* Isa. xlii. 8. Hence divines observe, that jealousy is attributed to God in the second commandment, which concerns the more external worship of God, to deter men from the violation of it, Exod. xx. 5. So Exod. xxxiv. 14; Deut. iv. 24; v. 9; vi. 16, and in many other texts, it signifieth, that the worship of God is a thing that he is very tender of, and that his will is to endure no creature to share with him in it, and that his wrath shall flame against that man that offers to make any creature such a sharer. So that it is not safe for any to do any thing of that nature, unless he could fancy himself to be *stronger* than God; for he that doth it, must expect the power and strength of God to be engaged against him. Thus the apostle had dissuaded them from eating meat sacrificed to idols in the idol's temple, from the impiety of it, it being a species of idolatry, against which God hath signally revealed his wrath. He returns in the following verses to an argument, by which he had before dissuaded it, chap. viii., as it was against charity, and the duty of love, in which they were indebted to their brethren.

23 ⁿ All things are lawful for me, but all things are not expedient: all things are lawful for me, but all things edify not. ⁿ ch. 6. 12.

All things here must necessarily signify many things, or, at least, (as some think,) all those things I have spoken of, to eat meat offered to idols, &c. But if we interpret it in the latter sense, it is not true without limitations; for the apostle had but now determined, that to eat meat offered to idols in the idol's temple, was to have communion with devils. I had rather therefore interpret *all* by many, as that universal particle must be interpreted in a great multitude of scriptures. So as the sense is, There are many things that are lawful which are not expedient; that is, considered in themselves, under due circumstances, they are lawful, but considered in such and such circumstances, are not so, because they are not for the profit or good, but the hurt and disadvantage, of others. Thus the apostle himself expounds it in the latter clause of the verse, where he saith, they *edify not,* that is, they tend not to promote the gospel, or the faith and holiness of particular Christians.

24 ^o Let no man seek his own, but every man another's *wealth.* ^o Rom. 15. 1, 2. ver. 33. ch. 13. 5. Phil. 2. 4,21.

It is the duty of every one who is a disciple of Christ, not merely to look at his own pleasure or profit, but the profit and advantage of others. *Charity seeketh not her own,* (saith the apostle, chap. xiii. 5,) that is, it seeketh not its own with the prejudice of another. So as admit that in this practice there were nothing looked like idolatry and impiety towards God, yet charity or love to your brethren ought to deter you.

25 ^p Whatsoever is sold in the shambles, *that* eat, asking no question for conscience sake: ^p Bar. 6. 26. 1 Tim. 4. 4.

I. CORINTHIANS X

It is possible that butchers, before they brought their meat into the market, might offer some part of it to the idol; or it is possible that the priests, who had a share in the beasts offered to idols, or the people that had offered such beasts, who also had a share returned them, might out of covetousness come and bring it to be sold in the market. The apostle directeth the Corinthians in such cases to make no scruple, but eat of it, if it were commonly sold in the shambles; which argued, that the thing in itself, considered nakedly, was not sinful. But yet he would have them in that case ask no questions, whence it came? or whether it had not been offered to an idol? for the sake of other men's consciences, lest some others standing by should take notice that they bought and ate such meat. Or their own consciences, lest, though the thing in itself, so separated from a sacred use, and returned to its common use, might be lawfully eaten, yet their consciences should afterwards reflect upon them for the doing of it.

26 For ^qthe earth *is* the Lord's, and the fulness thereof.

q Ex. 19. 5.
Deut. 10. 14.
Ps. 24. 1. & 50. 12. ver. 28.

This sentence is taken out of Psal. xxiv. 1. The earth is God's, or the Lord Christ's, who hath sanctified all things for the use of man, and all the variety of creatures that are in it are sanctified by him. An idol cannot pollute any kind of meat, it hath no such malign influence upon any thing; you may pollute yourselves by your action, eating it in the idol's temple, at an idolater's feast immediately upon his sacrifice, but the idol itself is no operative thing, nor can cause an ill quality in the meat; let the meat be once returned to its common use, (the idolater's sacred mysteries being over,) it is the Lord's, what he hath appointed for the use of man. In the idol's temple they took the meat out of the devil's hand, that was indeed unlawful; but if it were once returned to its common use, and sold in the market, they took it out of the hand of God's common providence, and *every creature of God is good, and nothing to be refused, if it be received with thanksgiving*, 1 Tim. iv. 4.

27 If any of them that believe not bid you *to a feast*, and ye be disposed to go; ^rwhatsoever is set before you, eat, asking no question for conscience sake.

r Luke 10. 7.

The apostle puts another case, in which they might lawfully enough eat of meat offered to an idol; that was in case any of their neighbours, that were heathens, invited them to dinner or supper in a private house (some add, or in the idol's temple, if it were a feast of friendship, not a feast upon a sacrifice; but I doubt that, and also whether in the idol-temples there were any feasts but upon sacrifices): he determineth it lawful for them to go and eat whatsoever was set before them; but in this case he would also have them *ask no questions for conscience sake*.

28 But if any man say unto you, This is offered in sacrifice unto idols, eat not ^sfor his sake that shewed it, and for conscience sake: for ^tthe earth *is* the Lord's, and the fulness thereof:

s ch. 8. 10, 12.
t Deu. 10. 14.
Ps. 24. 1.
ver. 26.

The meat being out of the idol's temple, and returned to a common use, there could be no impiety in eating it, no communion with devils, and partaking of the table of devils, in and by such an action; but yet there might be a breach of charity in the action, that is, in case one were there present, who knew that it had been so offered to the idol, and declared his offence, by telling the Christian that was about to eat, that that meat had been so offered: in that case the apostle commandeth Christians not to eat, and that partly *for his sake that shewed it*, lest they should lay a stumbling-block before him, and by their example imbolden him that showed it to do the like, though he doubted the lawfulness of it; and likewise *for conscience sake*, that is, for their own conscience sake, which through weakness might afterward trouble them for it, though without just cause. He gives that as a reason for it, because *the earth is the Lord's, and the fulness thereof*, that is, because there was other meat enough to eat. This passage, taken out of the psalmist, had a something different application, ver. 26; there the apostle used it to justify the lawfulness of their eating such meat, returned again to a common use, and exposed to sale in the shambles; here he useth it to dissuade them from eating, if any let them know it had been offered to the idol.

29 Conscience, I say, not thine own, but of the other: for ^uwhy is my liberty judged of another *man's* conscience?

u Rom. 14. 16.

By reason of what we had, ver. 28, (where the apostle forbade eating these meats, in case any at the feast told them they had been offered to idols, both for his sake that told him so, and also for conscience sake,) it is most reasonable to interpret those words *not thine own* in this verse, not thine own only, there being frequent instances in Scripture where the negative particle must be so restrained, as John iv. 42; chap. vi. 27, 38. *For why is my liberty judged of another man's conscience?* for why should my practice in a thing wherein I have a liberty, be censured or condemned by the conscience of another, he being persuaded that what I do, and judge that I have a liberty to do, and may do lawfully, is done by me sinfully, and I by him accounted a transgressor for it; so as though I do a thing that is honest, yet it is not honest in the sight of all men, or of good report; whereas Christians are obliged, Rom. xii. 17, to *provide things honest in the sight of all men*, not in their own sight merely, and to do those things that are *lovely* and of *good report*, Phil. iii. 8.

30 For if I by ‖ grace be a partaker, why am I evil spoken of for that ^xfor which I give thanks?

‖ Or, *thanksgiving.*
x Rom. 14. 6.
1 Tim. 4. 3, 4.

If I by grace be a partaker; if I by the goodness of God, whose the earth is, and the fulness thereof; or by the grace of knowledge, by which God hath given me to understand that I may do that, as to which others less knowing stumble; can eat such meat (out of the idol's temple) as part of it hath been offered to the idol, or with thanksgiving partake of such meat, (for so χάρις signifies, Luke vi. 32; chap. xvii. 9,) *why am I* blasphemed, or *evil spoken of, for that for which I* can *give God thanks?* That is, I ought not to cause another to speak evil of me for using of meat, but rather than run that danger, to abstain from such meat which I could otherwise eat of, and give God thanks: for in so doing I should but abuse my liberty, and instead of giving God thanks, I should grievously offend God, not at all consulting his glory.

31 ^yWhether therefore ye eat, or drink, or whatsoever ye do, do all to the glory of God.

y Col. 3. 17.
1 Pet. 4. 11.

The apostle, in these three last verses, layeth down three rules, to direct Christians how to use their liberty as to things that are of an indifferent nature, neither in themselves commanded nor forbidden in the word of God. His first rule is in this verse, to do whatsoever we do *to the glory of God*. This is a general rule, not to be restrained to the eating of meat offered to idols, of which the former discourse had been. It is a general rule, not applicable alone to eating and drinking, but to all other human actions. The reasonableness of this rule appeareth from our consideration, that the glory of God was the end of our creation; *The Lord hath made all things for himself*, Prov. xvi. 4: and indeed it is impossible it should be otherwise; for whereas every reasonable agent both propounds to himself some end of his actions, and the best end he can imagine, it is impossible but that God also, in creating man, should propound to himself some end, and there being no better end than his own glory, he could propound no other unto himself. The glory of God being the end which he propounded to himself in creating man, it must needs follow, that that must be the chief and greatest end which any man can propound to himself in his actions. God is then glorified by us, when by our means, or by occasion of us, he is well spoken of in the world, or by our obedience to his will: this our Saviour hath taught us, John xvii. 4, 6. No man in any of his actions hath a liberty from this rule; so as though a man, as to many things, hath a liberty to marry or not to marry, to eat meats or not to eat them, to wear this apparel or not to wear it; yet he is not even in such things as these so at liberty, but he ought to look about, and to consider circumstances, which will be most for the honour of God, the credit of the gospel, and reputation of religion. And the judgment of this is to be made from circumstances, the difference of which may make that unlawful which otherwise would be lawful, and that lawful which under other circumstances would be unlawful.

z Rom. 14.
13. ch. 8. 13.
2 Cor. 6. 3.
† Gr. *Greeks.*
a Acts 20. 28.
ch. 11. 22. 1 Tim. 3. 5.

32 ᶻGive none offence, neither to the Jews, nor to the † Gentiles, nor to ᵃthe Church of God:

We use to say, that men are offended when they are grieved or angered; but these offences are not here meant, (as appears by the Greek phrase, Ἀπρόσκοποι γίνεσθε,) but give no occasion of sin or stumbling. This care he commands us, with reference to all men; for at that time all the world fell under one of these denominations, they were either *Jews*, or *Gentiles*, (that is, heathens,) or *the church of God* (that is, Christians). It was always a hard matter, if not a thing impossible, for Christians to carry themselves so as not to anger those that were no Christians; but it was not impossible for them so to behave themselves, as not to be to them any just occasion of sin. Much less ought conscientious Christians to give offence to Christians, that made up the church of God, and were with them members of the same mystical body, of which Christ is the Head.

b Rom. 15. 2.
ch. 9. 19, 22.
c ver. 24.

33 Even as ᵇI please all *men* in all things, ᶜnot seeking mine own profit, but the *profit* of many, that they may be saved.

Even as I please all men in all things; that is, in all things wherein the law of God hath left me a liberty; for Paul pleased no man, either in the omission of any thing which God had commanded him to do, or in the doing of any thing which God had forbidden him to do. *Not seeking mine own profit, but the profit of many, that they may be saved;* not seeking my own advantage, either the satisfaction of my own mind or humour, or my own gain, but the advantage of others, especially in matters that may any way affect them as to their eternal salvation. Thus Paul, like a good shepherd, goeth out before the sheep, and leadeth them, and, as every true minister should be, is himself an example to the flock of Christ. And this is a third rule to be observed by Christians, as to the use of the liberty which God's law hath left them as to any particular actions; notwithstanding that liberty, yet they ought to have respect to the spiritual good and salvation of others, and to do that part which their judgments inform them will be, as least to the spiritual damage and detriment, so most to the spiritual good and profit, of the souls of others with whom they converse.

CHAP. XI

Paul exhorteth the Corinthians to follow him, as he did Christ, 1. *He praiseth them for observing the rules he had given them,* 2; *and forbiddeth men to pray or prophesy with heads covered, and women with heads uncovered; the covering of the head being a token of subjection,* 3—16. *He blameth them for abuses in their religious assemblies, particularly for their divisions,* 17—19, *and profanation of the Lord's supper,* 20—22. *He remindeth them of the first institution thereof, and showeth the danger of partaking of it unworthily,* 23—34.

a ch. 4. 16.
Ephes. 5. 1.
Phil. 3. 17.
1 Thess. 1. 6.
2 Thess. 3. 9.

BE ᵃye followers of me, even as I also am of Christ.

Interpreters judge, that these words do properly belong to the foregoing chapter, in the last verse of which he had propounded his own example to them; but whether they be applied to that chapter or this, is not much material. They teach us, that the examples of the apostles are part of our rule; yet the modesty of the apostle is remarkable, who requires of his people no further to follow him than as he followed Christ: nor indeed ought any man to require more of those that are under his charge, than to follow him so far forth as he imitates the Lord Jesus Christ.

b ch. 4. 17.
c ch. 7. 17.
∥ Or, *traditions.*
2 Thess. 2. 15. & 3. 6.

2 Now I praise you, brethren, ᵇthat ye remember me in all things, and ᶜkeep the ∥ ordinances, as I delivered *them* to you.

That ye remember me in all things; that you remember my doctrine, the precepts and instructions that I gave you; *and keep the ordinances:* so we translate it; the Greek word is παραδόσεις. The word signifieth any thing that is doctrinally delivered, or taught men, whether it concerns faith or manners. It is thought, that in this text it doth not signify what the apostle had delivered to them with respect to faith, or their moral conversation, but with respect to matters of order, because such is the next instance which the apostle mentioneth, about *praying or prophesying* with the *head covered*, or *uncovered;* and undoubtedly any precepts of that nature from one guided by an infallible Spirit ought to be observed. The apostle doth not command them to keep any traditions, which others should to the end of the world deliver to them, he only praiseth them for keeping those which he had delivered. There is a great question betwixt us and the papists, about the obligation that lieth upon Christians to observe unwritten traditions; that is, such rites and observances as they tell us were apostolical, and the traditions of the primitive church, though they can show us no Scripture for them; but no Christian disputes his obligation to keep apostolical traditions; only we are at a loss to know how to prove those traditions apostolical, of which we find nothing in the writings of the apostles: it is praiseworthy to keep apostolical traditions; but for others, or such as do not appear to us to be so, it is but a work of supererogation: where hath God required any such thing at people's hands?

d Ephes. 5. 23.
e Gen. 3. 16.
1 Tim. 2. 11, 12. 1 Pet. 3. 1, 5, 6.
f John 14. 28.
ch. 3. 23. &
15. 27, 28. Phil. 2. 7, 8, 9.

3 But I would have you know, that ᵈthe head of every man is Christ; and ᵉthe head of the woman *is* the man; and ᶠthe head of Christ *is* God.

The abuse which the apostle is reflecting upon in this and the following verses, is women's praying or prophesying with their heads uncovered, against which the apostle strongly argueth. His argument seemeth to be this, That the woman in religious services ought to behave herself as a person in subjection to her husband, and accordingly to use such a gesture, as, according to the guise and custom of that country, testified such a subjection; to this purpose he tells us in this verse, *that the head of every man is Christ.* Christ, considered as God according to his Divine nature, is the Head of all men and women too in the world; but the text seemeth rather to speak of Christ as Mediator: so the apostle tells us, Eph. v. 23, he is *the Head of the church;* and the New Testament often speaks of Christ in that notion, and of believers as his members: in this sense, by *every man*, we must understand no more than every Christian, every member of the church. *The head of the woman is the man;* the man is called the head of the woman, because by God's ordinance he is to rule over her, Gen. iii. 16; he hath an excellency above the woman, and a power over her. *The head of Christ is God;* and God is the Head of Christ, not in respect of his essence and Divine nature, but in respect of his office as Mediator; as the man is the head of the woman, not in respect of a different and more excellent essence and nature, (for they are both of the same nature,) but in respect of office and place, as God hath set him over the woman. Nor indeed could those who deny the Divine nature of Christ, easily have brought a text more against their own assertion, than this, which rather proveth, that God the Father and the Lord Jesus Christ are equal in nature and essence, than different; for surely the head is not of a different, but the same nature with the members. Nor doth Christ's subjection to his Father at all argue an inequality, or difference from him in nature and essence, more than the subjection of subjects to a prince argue any such thing. The apostle then determines this to be the order which God hath set: God is the Head of Christ; Christ is the Head of his church, and every one that is a member of it; and man is the head of the woman, he to whom the woman ought to be subject, as the church is subject to Christ, and Christ is subject to his Father; and from hence he argueth as followeth.

g ch. 12. 10, 28. & 14. 1, &c.

4 Every man praying or ᵍprophesying, having *his* head covered, dishonoureth his head.

By *every man praying or prophesying*, some (amongst whom the learned Beza) understand not only he that ministereth in prayer, or in opening and applying the Scriptures, whether from a previous meditation and study of them, or from the extraordinary revelation of the Holy Spirit, which they had in those primitive times; but also all those that were present at those actions. The reason they give is, Because the reason given by the apostle for his assertion, is such as is common to the people, as well as to him that ministereth; and the woman was forbidden to speak in the church, 1 Tim. ii. 12. But our learned Bishop Hall assures us, he cannot agree with those of this mind. And indeed it is an unreasonable interpretation; for though those who join with others in prayer may be said to pray, yet those that hear one preaching or expounding Scripture, can in no propriety of speech be said to prophesy. Nor is any such usage of the term to be paralleled, neither are the reasons they bring cogent; for though the reason of the precept may concern the people as well as the minister, yet it doth not follow that the rule or precept must necessarily do so too. And although the woman be forbidden to teach in ordinary cases, yet it did not concern those who were immediately and extraordinarily inspired, according to the prophecy, Joel ii. 28, applied, Acts ii. 17. *Having his head covered;* i. e. with a hat or cap, or such covering of the head as is in use in the country wherein he liveth. It is not to be understood of the natural covering of the head, which is our hair; nor yet of any other covering which is necessary for the preservation of life and health; but such a covering as he might spare, and is ornamental to him according to the fashion of the country. *Dishonoureth his head;* either dishonoureth Christ who is his Head, and whom he ought to represent, and doth as it were make the church the head to Christ, which is subject to him, while by covering his head he declares a subjection in his ministration. Or he dishonoureth his own head, (so many interpret it,) to wit, he betrayeth his superiority, lesseneth himself as to that power and dignity which God hath clothed him with, by using a posture which is a token of inferiority and subjection. Interpreters rightly agree, that this and the following verses are to be interpreted from the customs of countries; and all that can be concluded from this verse is, that it is the duty of men employed in Divine ministrations, to look to behave themselves as those who are to represent the Lord Jesus Christ, behaving themselves with a just authority and gravity that becometh his ambassadors, which decent gravity is to be judged from the common opinion and account of the country wherein they live. So as all which this text requires of Christian ministers, is authority and gravity, and what are external indications of it. Our learned Dr. Lightfoot observeth, that the Jewish priests were wont in the worship of God to veil their heads; so that Christian ministers praying or prophesying with their heads covered, Judaized, which he judgeth the reason of the apostle's assertion. The heathens also, both Romans and Grecians, were wont to minister in their sacred things with their heads covered. Some think this was the reason why the Christians used the contrary gesture; but the apostle's arguing from the man's headship, seemeth to import that the reason of this assertion of the apostle was, because in Corinth the uncovered head was a sign of authority. At this day the Mahometans (or Turks) speak to their superiors covered, and so are covered also in their religious performances. The custom with us in these western parts is quite otherwise; the uncovering of the head is a sign or token of subjection: hence ministers pray and preach with their heads uncovered, to denote their subjection to God and Christ: but yet this custom is not uniform, for in France the Reformed ministers preach with their heads covered; as they pray uncovered, to express their reverence and subjection to God, so they preach covered, as representing Christ, the great Teacher, from whom they derive, and whom they represent. Nothing in this is a further rule to Christians, than that it is the duty of ministers, in praying and preaching, to use postures and habits that are not naturally, nor according to the custom of the place where they live, uncomely and irreverent, and so looked upon. It is only the general observation of decency (which cannot by any be created, but ariseth either from nature, or custom, and prescription) which this text of the apostle maketh to be the duty of all Christians; though as to the Corinthians, he particularly required the man's ministering in sacred things with his head uncovered, either to avoid the habit or posture used by Jews and pagans; or for the showing of his dignity and superiority over the woman, (whom we shall by and by find commanded to pray or prophesy covered,) or that he represented Christ who was the Head of the church. The uncovering of the head being with them as much a sign of subjection, as it is with us of superiority and pre-eminence.

5 But [h] every woman that prayeth or prophesieth with *her* head uncovered dishonoureth her head: for that is even all one as if she were [i] shaven.

[h] Acts 21. 9.
[i] Deut.21.12.

But every woman that prayeth or prophesieth: though the woman be forbidden *to teach*, and commanded *to be in silence*, 1 Tim. ii. 12; yet that text must be understood of ordinary women, and in ordinary cases, not concerning such as prophesied from an extraordinary impulse or motion of the Spirit. We read of women prophetesses both in the Old and New Testament; such was Huldah in Josiah's time, and Anna, of whom we read Luke ii. 36; and we read that Philip *had four daughters that did prophesy*, Acts xxi. 9. *With her head uncovered:* the uncovered head here (as before) must signify not covered with some artificial covering, such as our quoifs, hats, hoods, or veils, &c., or with her own hair, not hanging loose, but artificially used so as to be a covering. *Dishonoureth her head;* dishonoureth either her husband, who is her political or economical head, for by that habit she behaveth herself as if she were not one in subjection, and seemeth to usurp an undue authority over the man; or her natural head, it being in those places accounted an immodest thing for a woman to appear in public uncovered. It is observed of Rebekah, when she met Isaac, Gen. xxiv. 65, *She took a veil, and covered herself*. *For that is even all one as if she were shaven;* for, saith the apostle, yourselves would judge it an uncomely thing for a woman to be shaven, now to pray or to prophesy with the head uncovered, is all one. This last clause will incline us to think, that by the uncovered head in this verse, is not only to be understood uncovered with some other covering besides her hair, but with her hair dishevelled, hanging loose at its length, for else it is not all one to have the head uncovered with a hat, or hood, or quoif, and to be shaven; for the apostle afterward saith, ver. 15, her hair is given to her for a covering or a veil: so that possibly that which the apostle here reflecteth upon, is women's coming into the public assemblies with their hair hanging loosely down, and not decently wound up so as to make a covering for the head; which, we are told, was the practice of those beastly she-priests of Bacchus, who, like frantic persons, performed those pretendedly religious rites with their hair so hanging loose, and were called *manades*, because they behaved themselves more like mad persons than such as were in the actual use of their reason: something like which, it is most probable, some women in the Christian church at Corinth affected, against which the apostle here argueth.

6 For if the woman be not covered, let her also be shorn: but if it be [k] a shame for a woman to be shorn or shaven, let her be covered.

[k] Num. 5.18. Deut. 22. 5.

For if the woman be not covered, let her also be shorn: nature itself teacheth, that it is a shameful sight to see a woman revealing the mind and will of God, by an extraordinary pretended revelation, in so indecent a manner, as with her hair all hanging down; let her hair be either shaven off, or at least cut after the manner of men's hair, if she will neither tie it up artificially, so as to make it a covering for her head, nor put on a veil to cover her: for though a woman prophesying from an extraordinary impulse, be not under the common law of women not speaking in the public assembly, but keeping silence; yet she is under the law of nature to do no such grave and solemn actions in such a rude manner, that from the light of nature, or the common account of all that live in that place, she should be judged to be irreverent and brutish in her religious action. From this text a question hath been started, Whether Christian women may lawfully go without any other covering upon their heads than their hair? I must confess, I see not how such a question can have any bottom in this text, where the apostle is not speaking of women's ordinary habiting themselves, but only when they prayed and prophesied, and (if I mistake not) when they ministered in prayer and prophecy (as was said before). We now have no such prophetesses; so as I think that question about the lawfulness of women's going without any other covering upon their heads than their hair, must be determined from other texts, not this, and is best determined from circumstances; for God having given to the woman her hair for a covering and an ornament, I cannot see how it should be simply unlawful; accidentally it may, from the circumstances of pride in her heart that so dresseth herself, or lust and wantonness in others' hearts; or other circumstances of ill designs and intentions in the woman so dressing herself. *But if it be a shame for a woman to be shorn or shaven, let her be covered;* if nature teacheth us that it is a shame for a woman to be shorn or shaven, it also teacheth us that it is a shame for her to be uncovered, either with her hair, or some artificial covering; which latter seemeth rather to be meant in this place, because divines think, that the face is that part of the head which the apostle here intendeth should be covered in their religious actions, which is not covered with the hair, but with a veil, &c.

7 For a man indeed ought not to cover his head, forasmuch as [1]he is the image and glory of God: but the woman is the glory of the man.

l Gen. 1. 26, 27. & 5. 1. & 9. 6.

For a man indeed ought not to cover his head; covering the head being in those countries a token of subjection, a man ought to uphold the power, pre-eminence, and authority with which God hath invested him, and not to cover his head, further than it is naturally covered with hair. *Forasmuch as he is the image and glory of God;* because he hath a peculiar cause of glorying in God, as he to whom alone he is subject, and therefore ought by no habits or postures to show himself in subjection to others: or because God glorieth in him, as a most excellent piece of his workmanship: God is represented in man. Paul useth to call that one's glory wherein he glorieth, 2 Cor. i. 12, 14; 1 Thess. ii. 20. So David calleth God his *glory;* and Solomon tells us, Prov. xvii. 6, that *the glory of children are their fathers.* So as the apostle here useth a double argument for the man's not covering of his head: 1. Because the man is immediately subject to God, and therefore ought not by any habits, or civil rites, to show his natural subjection to men, that are not by nature his superiors (for we must not think, that the apostle by this argument forbiddeth subjection to natural, economical, or political superiors). 2. Because God glorieth in man. *But the woman is the glory of the man,* created for the honour of the man, and for his help and assistance, and originally made out of man, so as man may glory of her, as Adam did of Eve, Gen. ii. 23, *This is now bone of my bone, and flesh of my flesh.* The glory of God ought to be revealed and uncovered, manifested to all: the glory of the man ought to be hidden and concealed.

8 For [m]the man is not of the woman; but the woman of the man.

m Gen. 2. 21, 22.

Here the apostle openeth or proveth what he had before said of the woman's being *the glory of the man;* the woman was made of the man; the man was not made of a rib taken out of the woman, but the woman was made of a rib taken out of the man; we have the history, Gen. ii. 21, 22; and from hence the apostle argueth her subjection to the man.

9 [n]Neither was the man created for the woman; but the woman for the man.

n Gen. 2. 18, 21, 23.

We have this expounded, Gen. ii. 18, where God said, *It is not good that man should be alone; I will make him an help meet for him.* God did not first create the woman, and then make man a meet help for her; but he first made the man, and then the woman, that she might be a meet help for him. Now it is a rule in reason, That whosoever or whatsoever is made for another person or thing, is less excellent than that person or thing for which the other is made. *For the man,* signifies to serve and help the man.

10 For this cause ought the woman °to have ‖power on *her* head [p]because of the angels.

o Gen. 24. 64. ‖ That is, a covering, in sign that she is under the power of her husband. p Eccles. 5. 6.

By *power on her head* is here to be understood (as some think) a covering on her head, in sign that she is under the power of her husband: the thing signified is here put for the sign, as the sign is often put for the thing signified. Thus the ark, which is called, *the ark of* God's *strength,* Psal. cxxxii. 8, is itself called *his strength,* 1 Chron. xvi. 11. But others here by *head* do not understand the woman's natural head, but her husband, or the man, who is the political head of the woman; and by having *power* on him, understand her exercising of her power in him, testifying it by covering her head; and think this text well expounded by 1 Tim. ii. 12, where the apostle forbiddeth the woman to *usurp authority over the man.* He addeth another reason, *because of the angels.* By *angels* here some understand God himself, who by the ministry of angels created man and woman in this order, and put this law upon the woman. Others understand those messengers which the man sent sometimes, by whom the woman was betrothed (but this was a custom only in use amongst the Jews). Others here by *angels* understand the ministers and officers of the church, who are sometimes in holy writ called *angels.* Others understand the evil angels, who watch to take advantage to tempt men from objects appearing beautiful to unchaste thoughts, &c. But the most and best interpreters understand here by *angels,* the good angels; for the apostle would hardly have spoken of devils under the notion of angels, especially speaking to deter persons from actions; and so it teaches us, that the good angels, who are ministering spirits for the good of God's elect, at all times have a special ministration, or at least are more particularly present, in the assemblies of people for religious worship, observing the persons, carriage, and demeanour; the sense of which ought to awe all persons attending those services, from any indecent and unworthy behaviour.

11 Nevertheless [q]neither is the man without the woman, neither the woman without the man, in the Lord.

q Gal. 3. 28.

Lest the man, upon the apostle's discourse of his pre-eminence and dignity over the woman, should wax proud and insolent, and carry himself too imperiously, the apostle addeth this, that they both stand in need of each other's help, so as neither of them could well be without the other, either as to matters that concern God, or that concern the world; the Lord so ordering and disposing it, that they should be mutual helps one to another. Or else the sense is, they are equal in the Lord as to a state of grace, in Christ there is *neither male nor female:* though there be a difference betwixt a man and woman in other things, and the man hath the priority and superiority; yet when we come to consider them as to their spiritual state, and in their spiritual reference, there is no difference.

12 For as the woman *is* of the man, even so *is* the man also by the woman; [r]but all things of God.

r Rom. 11. 36.

The man hath a priority to the woman, being first created, and a superiority over her upon that account, she being made for him, not he for her, this is indeed the man's advantage; but on the other side, since the creation of the first man, all men are by the woman, who conceives them in her womb, suckles them at her breasts, is concerned in their education while children, and dandled upon her knees; the man therefore hath no reason to despise and too much to trample upon the woman: and *all* these *things* are *of God,* by the wise ordering and disposing of God; so as neither hath the man, by reason of his prerogative, in being first created, and the end for which the woman was created, any cause to insult and triumph over the woman; neither hath the woman any cause, by reason of her prerogative, that the man is by her, any cause to triumph over the man; but both of them ought to look upon themselves as having their prerogatives from God, and in the use of them to behave themselves according to the will of God, behaving themselves in their respective stations as it is the will of God they should behave themselves, the woman being subject to the man, and testifying by all the signs of it, and the man carrying himself towards the woman as he who is the image and glory of God.

13 Judge in yourselves: is it comely that a woman pray unto God uncovered?

I. CORINTHIANS XI

No man is truly and thoroughly convinced of an error, till he be convicted by his own conscience. It is therefore very usual in holy writ for God, by his sacred penmen, to make appeals unto men's own consciences, and put them to judge within themselves, to examine a thing by their own reason, and according to the dictates of that to give sentence for or against themselves. The thing as to which he would have them judge within themselves, and accordingly pronounce sentence, was, whether it were a decent thing for women to pray to God with their hair all hanging loose about their shoulders, or without any veil, or covering for their head and face.

14 Doth not even nature itself teach you, that, if a man have long hair, it is a shame unto him?

He tells them, that they could not judge this as a thing comely, for nature itself taught them, that it is a shame for a man to wear long hair. By *nature* here some understand the law of nature, according to which it would have an intrinsic evil in it, which it is plain it hath not; for then neither must the Nazarites have used it, (as they did,) neither would it be lawful for the sake of men's health or life. Others understand by *nature* the law of nations; but neither is this true, for in many nations men wear hair at the utmost length. Others understand common sense, or the light and judgment of that natural reason which since the fall is left in man; but this must be the same in all men, and we know that all men do not judge this shameful. Others therefore by *nature* here understand a common custom, which (as they say) maketh as it were a second nature; so the term is taken, Rom. xi. 24: but it cannot so signify here; for there neither is, nor ever was, such a universal custom in any place, that none in it wore long hair. Others by *nature* here understand natural inclination; but neither can this be the sense, for there is in some men, as well as in women, a natural propension and inclination to wear their hair at excessive lengths. Others here by *nature* understand the difference of the sex, as they take this word to be used, Rom. i. 26; the distinction of the sexes teacheth us this: and this seemeth to be the most probable sense of this text. The apostle arguing, that as the male and female sex are artificially distinguished by garments, and it was the will of God they should be so, so they should also be distinguished by the wearing of their hair; and it was no less shame for a man to wear his hair like a woman, than to wear garments like a woman.

15 But if a woman have long hair, it is a glory to her: for *her* hair is given her for a ǁ covering.

‖ Or, *veil.*

But, he saith, *if a woman have long hair, it is a glory to her.* Long hair is comely for the woman, and accounted to her for a beauty or ornament, for God hath *given her her hair for a covering.* There have been books written about the lawfulness or unlawfulness of men's wearing long hair, and the due or undue lengths of men's hair, the substance of which were too much to transcribe here. That which in these verses seemeth to be commended to us, as the will of God in this matter, is, 1. That men and women should so order their hair, as by it to preserve the distinction of sexes. 2. That men should not wear their hair after the manner of women, either dishevelled, or curled, and tricked up about their heads, which speaks too much of an unmanly and effeminate temper, much more was what became not Christians. And if this be forbidden men, as to the use of their own hair, they stand concerned to consider whether it be lawful for them thus to wear and adorn themselves with the hair of other men and women.

s 1 Tim. 6. 4.
t ch. 7. 17. & 14. 33.

16 But ˢ if any man seem to be contentious, we have no such custom, ᵗ neither the churches of God.

If any man seem to be contentious; if any man hath a mind to quarrel out of a love to show his wit in discoursing what may be said on the other side, or out of a desire to hold up a party, and contradict us. *We have no such custom,* of women's praying or prophesying with their heads uncovered, or men's praying or prophesying with their heads covered; or we have no such custom of contending for these little frivolous things; *neither* any of *the churches of God;* and good Christians, in their practices, ought, in things of this nature, to have an eye and regard to the custom of their own church, and also of other Christian churches. Thus the apostle closeth this discourse, and proceedeth in the next verses to tax other abuses which were crept into this famous church.

17 Now in this that I declare *unto you* I praise *you* not, that ye come together not for the better, but for the worse.

Now in this that I declare unto you I praise you not; I come now to another thing of greater consequence, as to which I must much blame you; I am so far from being able to commend or approve of what you do, that I must for it smartly reflect upon you. *That ye come together not for the better, but for the worse;* that when you meet in your church assemblies, for the performance of your religious duties, to pray, preach, hear, or receive the holy sacrament, you so meet and behave yourselves, as your meeting tends to the increase of your sin, rather than to the increase of your grace, and the promoting the work of God in yourselves and the souls of others.

18 For first of all, when ye come together in the church, ᵘ I hear that there be ǁ divisions among you; and I partly believe it.

u ch. 1. 10, 11, 12. & 3. 3.
ǁ Or, *schisms.*

In the church, here, must signify the religious assembly; for at this time there were no temples built for Christians, but they met in private houses, as the iniquity of those times would bear: yet others think the place is here meant where the church was wont to meet, and say, that the Christians had a certain stated place, though in a private house, where they used to meet. But it is not very probable that they should, in the midst of heathens, be so quiet and secure as to meet either constantly, or ordinarily, in any one certain and stated place, so denominated. What schisms, or *divisions,* the apostle meaneth, he expoundeth in the following verses; either they quarrelled about meats, or drinks, or their order in sitting down, or the time when they should begin, or did not stay till they were all met.

19 For ˣ there must be also ǁ heresies among you, ʸ that they which are approved may be made manifest among you.

x Mat. 18. 7. Luke 17. 1. Acts 20. 30. 1 Tim. 4. 1. 2 Pet. 2. 1, 2.
ǁ Or, *sects.*
y Luke 2. 35. 1 John 2. 19. See Deut. 13. 3.

There must be; it is not simply and absolutely necessary that there should be such divisions amongst you, (they are caused from the free acts of men's corrupt wills,) but yet these things do not fall out by chance, but through the providence of God, who hath so immutably ordered and decreed, to suffer Satan to show his malice, and men to discover the lusts and corruptions of their own hearts. *Heresies:* though heresy be a term that, by ecclesiastical usage, is restrained to signify perverse opinions in matter of doctrine, as to which men are stubborn and tenacious; yet it is manifest, that the word is not natively so to be restrained, neither can it reasonably be here so interpreted, but signifies the same thing with *schisms* and *divisions* before mentioned: for though (as will appear from chap, xv.) there were corrupt opinions amongst them in matters of doctrine, yet it is unreasonable to understand the apostle here, as speaking with reference to them, these words being brought as a reason why he was inclined to believe that there were such schisms or divisions amongst them, because there must be heresies. *That they which are approved may be made manifest among you:* God hath his wise end in suffering breaches and divisions, that such as are true and sincere Christians, opposing themselves to such violations of charity, might appear to you to be true and sincere, and to have the love of God dwelling, working, and prevailing in them.

20 When ye come together therefore into one place, ǁ *this* is not to eat the Lord's supper.

ǁ Or, *ye cannot eat.*

The Greek words do not necessarily signify *into one place,* they may as well be translated, for the same thing, and possibly that were the better translation of them in this place; divisions appearing the worse amongst persons that met as one and the same body, and for one and the same grave action, and that such an action as declared them one body, and laid upon them the highest obligation to brotherly love imaginable. *This is not to eat the Lord's supper:* some words must be here supplied to complete the sense. *This is not to eat;* that is, as you do it is indeed not to do it; to eat the Lord's supper in an unlawful manner, is not to eat it. It is called *the Lord's supper,* either because he ordained and instituted it, or because it was instituted for the remembrance of his death, ver. 26; Luke xxii. 19. Some think that the sacrament of the Lord's supper is here meant, and so one would think, by comparing what is here with ver. 23, 24. Others say, that the love feast is here intended, which ordinarily preceded the Lord's supper; the reason they give is, because the abuses here mentioned, viz. not staying one for another till the whole church were met, one eating plentifully, another sparingly, some being hungry while others had ate and drank enough, could not be at the Lord's supper, where the minister beginneth not till the whole church be assembled, and where there is no such liberal eating and drinking. To this purpose we are told, that by an ancient custom in Greece (within which Corinth was) the rich men offered some things to their idols, (which after that action the poor had for their relief,) and made feasts in the idol's temples, of which all had a liberty to eat. That the Christians imitated this practice of theirs, and the rich amongst them upon the Lord's days made feasts, at which both poor and rich Christians might be, and the poor carried away what was left. But this church growing corrupt every way, and having got teachers to their humours, they at these feasts neglected the poor, inviting only the rich to them, and also exceeding in their provision for their rich guests. These feasts were called feasts of love, or love feasts, either because, 1. Love to God was that which (pretendedly at least) caused them. 2. Or because they were representations of our Lord's last supper, in which he first ate the paschal lamb, then instituted what we call the Lord's supper; or because they immediately preceded or followed the administration of the Lord's supper, from whence the love feast, being immediately before or after it, had also the same name. But if we allow this, we must make the love feasts also Christ's institution, and instituted in remembrance of him, neither of which can be proved. The meaning must be, You cannot rightly communicate at the Lord's table, when immediately before or after that table, at your love feast, you are guilty of such disorderly actions. In the mean time, only what Christ instituted for remembrance of his death is what the apostle calls *the Lord's supper.*

21 For in eating every one taketh before *other* his own supper: and one is hungry, and ᵃ another is drunken.

a 2 Pet.2. 13.
Jude 12.

There was at this time in most of the Christian church a Jewish party, viz. such as were converted from Judaism to Christianity, and had a tang of the old cask, being too tenacious of some Jewish rites. These looked upon the Lord's supper as an appurtenance to the passover, immediately after which we know that Christ at first instituted his supper. As therefore Christ did eat the paschal supper before the Lord's supper; so they, in imitation of him, though they forbore the paschal lamb, yet would have a supper of their own to precede the Lord's supper, and having provided it at home, would bring it to the place where the church was to meet; and their poor brethren contributing nothing to the charge of that supper, they would not stay for them, but took this their *own supper:* so it came to pass, that the poorer Christians were *hungry,* had none or very little share in their feast, while others, the richer part of the church, had too much; for I take our translation of this word, μεθύει, to be very hard and uncharitable. Hard, because the word doth not necessarily so signify, only drinking beyond what is strictly necessary, and our translators themselves, John ii. 10, render it *well drunk.* Uncharitable, because it certainly must be very uncharitably presumed of this church of Corinth, that they should suffer persons, at that time actually drunk, to come to the Lord's table.

22 What? have ye not houses to eat and to drink in? or despise ye ᵃ the Church of God, and ᵇ shame ‖ them that have not? What shall I say to you? shall I praise you in this? I praise *you* not.

a ch. 10. 32.
b James 2. 6.
‖ Or,
them that are poor.

What? have ye not houses to eat and to drink in? hence evidently appears, that these love feasts were kept in the place where the assembly met for the public worship of God; for the apostle would have them (if they would continue them) kept in their private houses: and he doth not only blame the abuses of these feasts, but the feasts themselves as kept in the place where the church met, or as having in them any pretence to any thing of religion: meet they might, friendly to eat and to drink, but their private houses were the fittest places for that. *Or despise ye the church of God?* or do you despise the place (as some think) where the church of God meeteth, or the people met in that place, by carrying yourselves so disorderly in such a grave assembly; or the poorer part of the church, who, though poorer, are a part of the church, redeemed by the blood of Christ? the next words would incline us to think that the sense; for it followeth, *and shame them that have not,* that is, that have not estates to contribute to such feasts, and so are forced to go away without any due refreshment.

23 For ᶜI have received of the Lord that which also I delivered unto you, ᵈ That the Lord Jesus the *same* night in which he was betrayed took bread:

c ch. 15. 3.
Gal. 1. 1, 11, 12.
d Mat.26.26.
Mark 14. 22.
Luke 22. 19.

About these love feasts preceding the Lord's supper, I have received nothing from the Lord, you have taken the practice up from the Jews or heathens: I do not know that it is unlawful for you civilly to feast, and eat and drink in your private houses; but to come to make such feasts immediately before you religiously eat and drink at the Lord's table, I have received no order from the Lord for any such practice. I have told you what I received from the Lord, which is no more than, *That the Lord Jesus the same night in which he was betrayed took bread:* see this in the evangelists, Matt. xxvi. 26; Mark xiv. 22; Luke xxii. 19; where all these words are opened. Some think that Paul received this from the Lord by immediate revelation (as it is thought Moses received the history we have in Genesis and part of Exodus, which relates to a time before he was born, or arrived at man's estate). Others think that he received it from St. Luke's writings (for the words are quoted according to his Gospel). Others think he received it from some other of the apostles. Certain it is, that he did receive it from the Lord; how, is uncertain.

24 And when he had given thanks, he brake *it,* and said, Take, eat: this is my body, which is broken for you: this do ‖ in remembrance of me.

‖ Or, *for a remembrance.*

25 After the same manner also *he took* the cup, when he had supped, saying, This cup is the new testament in my blood: this do ye, as oft as ye drink *it,* in remembrance of me.

These words we also met with, Luke xxii. 19, 20, and in the other evangelists' narration of the institution of the supper. See the explication of them in the notes on those texts.

26 For as often as ye eat this bread, and drink this cup, ‖ ye do shew the Lord's death ᵉ till he come.

‖ Or, *shew ye.*
e John 14. 3.
& 21. 22.
Acts 1. 11.
ch. 4. 5.
& 15. 23. 1 Thess. 4. 16. 2 Thess. 1. 10. Jude 14. Rev. 1. 7.

From hence it appears, that the bread and wine is not (as papists say) transubstantiated, or turned into the very substance of the flesh and blood of Christ, when the communicants eat it and drink it. It is still the same bread and cup it was. The end of the institution is but to commemorate Christ's death; and upon that account the waiting upon God in this ordinance, will be a standing duty incumbent upon Christians, until Christ shall come to judgment. Some think, show ye, is a better translation of the verb, than (as we translate it) *ye do show;* wherefore so behave yourselves at this ordinance, as those who know what they have to do in it, that is, to show forth the death of the Lord Jesus Christ.

I. CORINTHIANS XI, XII

f Num. 9. 10, 13. John 6. 51. c 3, 64. & 13. 27, ch. 10. 21.

27 ᶠWherefore whosoever shall eat this bread, and drink *this* cup of the Lord, unworthily, shall be guilty of the body and blood of the Lord.

Divines agree, that the unworthiness here spoken of, respecteth not the person of the receiver so much as the manner of the receiving; in which sense, a person that is worthy may receive this ordinance *unworthily :* it is variously expounded, without due religion and reverence, without faith and love, without proposing a right end in the action, under the guilt of any known sin not repented of, &c. *Shall he guilty of the body and blood of the Lord;* shall incur the guilt of the profanation of this sacred institution ; for an abuse offered to a sign, reacheth to that of which it is a sign ; as the abuse of a king's seal, or picture, is justly accounted an abuse of the king himself, whose seal and picture it is. Some carry it higher; he shall be punished, as if he had crucified Christ, the profanation of Christ's ordinance reflecting upon Christ himself.

g 2 Cor. 13. 5. Gal. 6. 4.

28 But ᵍlet a man examine himself, and so let him eat of *that* bread, and drink of *that* cup.

He is to examine himself about his knowledge, whether he rightly understands what Christ is, what the nature of the sacrament is, what he doth in that sacred action ; about his faith, love, repentance, new obedience, whether he be such a one as God hath prepared that holy table for ; it is the children's bread, and not for dogs ; a table Christ hath spread for his friends, not for his enemies. *And so let him eat, &c.;* having so examined himself, not otherwise. Whence it appears, that neither children in age or understanding, nor persons not in the use of their reason, nor unbelievers, nor persons under the guilt of sins not repented of, have any right to the Lord's supper: accordingly was the practice of all the primitive churches, and all rightly reformed churches. Whether they ought, if they will presume to come, to be kept away by the officers of the church, and how, and by whom? whether good Christians may communicate with such at the holy table? and after what previous duty performed? are questions that belong not to this text.

‖ Or, *judgment,* Rom. 13. 2.

29 For he that eateth and drinketh unworthily, eateth and drinketh ‖ damnation to himself, not discerning the Lord's body.

He that eateth and drinketh unworthily ; in the sense before mentioned, either having no remote right or no present right to partake in that ordinance, being an unbeliever, or a resolved unholy or ignorant person; or irreverently and irreligiously. He *eateth and drinketh* κρῖμα, *damnation,* or judgment, it is no matter which we translate it ; for if he bringeth God's judgments upon him in this life, they will end in eternal damnation, without a timely repentance ; but it is *to himself,* not to him that is at the same table with him, unless he hath been guilty of some neglect of his duty to him. *Not discerning the Lord's body ;* and his guilt lieth here, that he doth not discern and distinguish betwixt ordinary and common bread, and that bread which is the representation of the Lord's body, but useth the one as carelessly, and with as little preparation and regard to what he doth, as he useth the other.

30 For this cause many *are* weak and sickly among you, and many sleep.

You, it may be, are not aware of it, but look upon other causes why so many amongst you are sick, and weak, and die immaturely ; but I, as the apostle of Jesus Christ, (and so know the mind and will of God,) assure you, that this your irreverent and irreligious profanation of this holy ordinance, is one great cause of so many among you being sick, and weak, and dying in unripe age. Some think that the word *sleep* argues that they were godly, penitent Christians that so died, (for the death of wicked men is hardly called sleeping any where in holy writ,) to let us know, that even good people, who yet may be saved, may bring judgments in this life upon themselves, as by the profanation of God's name in other ordinances, so more especially by their profanation of it in this ordinance of the supper.

31 For ʰif we would judge ourselves, we should not be judged.

h Ps. 32. 5. 1 John 1. 9.

This word *judge* in Scripture signifies all parts of judgment, examining, accusing, condemning, &c. : here it signifies accusing ourselves, condemning ourselves ; discriminating ourselves, by the renewings of faith and repentance, from unbelievers, impenitent and profane persons : if we would thus judge ourselves, God would not accuse or condemn us.

32 But when we are judged, ⁱwe are chastened of the Lord, that we should not be condemned with the world.

i Ps. 94. 12. 13. Heb. 12. 5,—11.

Lest they be terrified at what he had said, and look upon their afflictions as indications of God's displeasure against them to that degree, that he would not look any more upon them as his children ; he tells them, that when God's people are afflicted with the evils of this life, sickness, &c., God doth not deal with them so much as a Judge, as a Father, who chasteneth the child whom he loveth, and scourgeth whom he receiveth, Heb. xii. 6—8 ; and doth it for a good end, to prevent the eternal condemnation of the soul with the impenitent sinners of the world, giving us our hell in this life, that we may escape it in the life to come.

33 Wherefore, my brethren, when ye come together to eat, tarry one for another.

The apostle concludes this discourse with an exhortation to them, for the time to come to take heed of these irreligious and irreverent behaviours, with relation to the Lord's supper ; that they should not take the sacrament before the whole church were met together, the rich should stay for the poor, and not receive it in parties, but as one body eat that one bread.

34 And if any man ᵏ hunger, let him eat at ˡhome ; that ye come not together unto ‖ condemnation. And the rest ᵐ will I set in order when ⁿ I come.

k ver. 21. l ver. 22. ‖ Or, *judgment.* m ch. 7. 17. Tit. 1. 5. n ch. 4. 19.

And if any one hungered, they should not make the place where they met together for the solemn worship of God, a place for eating and drinking at feasts, but eat at home ; lest, by these disorderly and irreverent actions, they incurred the displeasure of God, and brought down the judgment of God upon themselves. Lastly, he minds them, that if there were any other things of this nature, which he had not spoken to, he did design suddenly to come to them, and then he would set them in order, by giving them rules about them.

CHAP. XII

Paul teacheth that none can own Christ but by the Holy Ghost, 1—3 ; *whose gifts are diverse,* 4—6, *and dealt out to different persons to profit withal,* 7—11. *As many members make up one natural body, so Christians in general form one mystical body,* 12, 13 : *and as every member is equally a part of the natural body, and hath a necessary function allotted it,* 14—26 ; *so is it with Christ's body, the church ; to the several members of which God hath assigned different gifts and offices for the general good,* 27—31.

NOW ᵃ concerning spiritual *gifts,* brethren, I would not have you ignorant.

a ch. 14. 1, 37.

The word *gifts* is not in the Greek, but supplied by our interpreters. In the Greek is no more than *concerning spirituals,* which is equally applicable to spiritual offices, or administrations, operations, and gifts ; of all which he afterward treateth something, but mostly concerning gifts, which are chiefly spoken of in this chapter : and our translators agree with the best interpreters, in supplying the text with the word *gifts.* This church eminently abounded in these abilities to spiritual actions given them of God (for *spiritual gifts* signifies nothing else) ; and as they abounded in them, so they erred much in the abuse or ill use of them, as we shall afterward read in this chapter. Therefore the apostle tells them, that as to them, he would not have them *ignorant,* either of the favour of God in enriching them with them, as he had said, chap. i. 5, or yet

I. CORINTHIANS XII

in the due and right use of them, so as God might have glory from their good use of them: or of the errors that they had ran into, or might further run into, in the ill use of them.

^b ch. 6. 11.
Eph. 2.11,12.
1 Thess. 1. 9.
Tit. 3. 3.
1 Pet. 4. 3.
c Ps. 115. 5.

2 Ye know ^b that ye were Gentiles, carried away unto these ^c dumb idols, even as ye were led.

Ye know that ye were Gentiles; so they were still in respect of their birth and country; but he speaketh with reference to their religion and way of worship. *Carried away unto these dumb idols;* carried away by your idol-priests, and by the examples of your friends and neighbours, to idols, which, though they seem to you to speak, and to tell you of things to come, yet indeed have mouths and speak not, only the devil spake from them. *Even as ye were led;* wherein you acted not under the conduct of reason, nor as became reasonable creatures, but you were blindly led by the dictates of priests, or by the examples of others. This the apostle puts them in mind of, to let them know, that all those excellent gifts with which they were now endued, as he had told them, chap. i. 5, 6, they had received from God since their conversion to Christianity, and from the Spirit of Christ; for before their conversion they were like brute beasts, knowing nothing, but led by others.

3 Wherefore I give you to understand,
^d Mark 9. 39.
1 John 4. 2, 3.
∥ Or, *ana-thema.*
e Mat. 16.17.
John 15. 26.
2 Cor. 3. 5.

^d that no man speaking by the Spirit of God calleth Jesus ∥ accursed: and ^e *that* no man can say that Jesus is the Lord, but by the Holy Ghost.

The apostle proveth that they had received their spiritual gifts from the Spirit of God, because when they had not received this Spirit, they blasphemed the Christian religion, and called Christ *accursed,* which could not be done by any that spake *by the Spirit of God;* for there being but one God, and the Holy Spirit being one of the three persons in the Divine Being, and Jesus Christ another, and the eternal Son of God, it could not be but he that called Christ accursed, as the Jews and the heathens did, must blaspheme God, which none could do by the influence of that Holy Spirit, who was one of the persons in the blessed Trinity: and as by this the apostle lets them know, that they were now acted by another spirit than they were in their Gentile state; so he also lets them know, that those heathens, amongst whom they lived, were not acted by the Spirit of God, but by the evil spirit. On the other side, he saith, that *no man can say that Jesus is the Lord, but by the Holy Ghost.* There is a double saying that Jesus is the Lord: 1. When men only say it with their lips, but do not believe it in their hearts, are not affected with what they say, nor do pay that homage of faith and obedience to him, which should correspond with such a profession: thus men say Christ is the Lord, who preach him or discourse of him as men, though they do not in heart believe in him, receive or embrace him, or live up to the holy rules of life which he hath given; thus Judas, Caiaphas, and others, said Christ was the Lord; this they could not do *but by the Holy Ghost,* that is, the gifts of the Holy Ghost, which are common, which those might have who were never renewed by the Holy Ghost. So these Corinthians generally going thus far verbally to acknowledge Christ the Lord, it was an argument they had thus far been influenced by the Holy Ghost. 2. There is a serious and saving saying *that Jesus is the Lord,* when men do not only with their lips speak these words, and other words to the same sense, but heartily acknowledge him, believe in him, love him, obey him, and call upon him, professing him as they ought to do, and so as may be of advantage to them to life and salvation. No man now doth this but by the Holy Ghost renewing and sanctifying him, and blessing him with and helping him in the exercise of such habits. We shall observe in holy writ, that some verbs signify not the action only, but the action with its due quality: thus, hearing sometimes signifieth to hear so, as withal to believe. Calling *upon the name of the Lord,* Rom. x. 13, signifieth a calling aright. Confessing, 1 John iv. 15, signifies a confessing with faith and love. So the verb *say* in this text may signify such a saying or speaking, as is attended with faith, love, and due obedience.

4 Now ^f there are diversities of gifts, but ^g the same Spirit.
f Rom. 12. 4, &c.
Heb. 2. 4.
1 Pet. 4. 10. g Ephes. 4. 4.

Gifts signifieth the same thing with habits, or powers, or abilities to actions; our actions being either natural, as eating, drinking, sleeping, &c., or moral, or spiritual. These powers are either natural, which are in an ordinary course of providence bred with us, as the infant hath a power to eat, drink, sleep, cry, &c.: or acquired, and that by imitation, or human learning, as the child gets a habit of speaking, or a power to write, understand languages, arts, and sciences: or infused; and those are either merely infused, as faith, love, and all habits truly spiritual are, and therefore called graces, or spiritual gifts of the highest natures; or else such as are obtained by the use of means on our parts, but yet not without the influence of the Holy Spirit of God; such are abilities to pray, preach, &c. There are some common powers, that is, such as those might have, who should never be saved, which might be merely infused, and were extraordinary in those first times of the gospel; such as the gift of tongues, prophecy, healing, &c. These powers, especially such as are not natural and common to all in an ordinary course of providence, nor acquired merely by imitation, or study, or the teaching of others, but infused either in whole or in part, are those which the apostle here calleth *gifts:* and he saith there is a diversity of them; there was the gift of prophecy, of healing, of tongues, &c.; but he tells them, this diversity of gifts flowed all from one and the same Spirit, the Spirit was not diverse, though his influences were divers.

5 ^h And there are differences of ∥ administrations, but the same Lord.
h Rom. 12. 6, 7, 8.
Ephes. 4. 11.
∥ Or, *ministeries.*

There are divers offices or ministries in the church of God; one ministereth in the office of an elder, another in the office of a deacon; one in one service of the church, another in another service; but there is but one Lord to whom they minister; they all serve the great Lord of the church, Jesus Christ, though in divers orders and places of ministration.

6 And there are diversities of operations, but it is the same God ⁱ which worketh all in all. i Eph. 1. 23.

Operations and *administrations* both differ from *gifts,* as acts from habits. Habits and powers, by which men performed holy offices in the church, or wrought miracles, are called *gifts.* The acts or exercise of these powers are called *administrations* and *operations.* These latter differ one from another, as the former signify standing and continuing acts in the church; *operations,* ἐνεργήματα, rather signify miraculous effects, such as healing the sick without the application of ordinary means, speaking with divers tongues, &c. The apostle tells them, that as there was a diversity of gifts, or powers, and a diversity of acts in the constant service of the church, by which men exercised those gifts or powers they had in the performance of them; so there were diversities of operations, by which men used those extraordinary gifts or powers, which God gave some in the first plantation of the church, for the sake of such as believed not. But it was *the same God* that wrought them all, and in all, though all did not do, or could not do, the same things.

7 ^k But the manifestation of the Spirit is given to every man to profit withal.
k Rom. 12. 6, 7, 8.
ch. 14. 26.
Eph. 4. 7.
1 Pet. 4. 10, 11.

He here calleth gifts, *the manifestation of the Spirit,* partly to let them know, that these powers flowed from the Holy Spirit apparently, they having no such powers while they were heathens, and carried after dumb idols, as they were led; and partly to let all know, that these gifts and powers were evident proofs both of Christ's ascension, and of the promise of the Father and of Christ in sending the Holy Spirit, Acts i. 4; xvi. 7, 8; Eph. iv. 8. These gifts he tells them were *given to every man;* where *every* signifieth each one; for the same gifts or powers were not given to all, but to those to whom they were given, they were given not to puff them up, or to give them matter to boast of, but to do good withal to the church of Christ. No man hath any power or gift given him of God, either for his own hurt, or the hurt of others, but only for his own good, and the good of others.

I. CORINTHIANS XII

^{1 ch. 2. 6, 7.}
^{m ch. 1. 5. & 13. 2.}
^{2 Cor. 8. 7.}

8 For to one is given by the Spirit ¹the word of wisdom; to another ᵐthe word of knowledge by the same Spirit;

There are different apprehensions as to the particular gifts here enumerated, and it is no wonder, these extraordinary gifts being ceased, if we be now at a loss to determine what is to be understood by the terms whereby they are expressed. Some by *the word of wisdom*, here, understand a faculty to deliver grave sentences; others, an ability to open the deep mysteries of religion; others, a singular knowledge of spiritual things, joined with a great authority, &c.; others, an ability to explain the deep wisdom of God. But it is most probable, that he meaneth by it what we ordinarily understand by wisdom, viz. a faculty, from a good judgment of the circumstances of actions, to do them at the best time, and in the best manner, wherein they may be serviceable to their ends. It is as uncertain, whether by *the word of knowledge* he meaneth a capacity to comprehend things in our knowledge, or to communicate it to others, or the actual communication of it by preaching, which was the work of the pastors and teachers; or the prophetical knowledge of future contingencies; or an ability to speak of spiritual things doctrinally, without any great faculty of applying them.

^{n Mat.17.19, 20. ch. 13. 2.}
^{2 Cor. 4. 13.}
^{o Mark 16.}
^{18. Jam.5.14.}

9 ⁿTo another faith by the same Spirit; to another ᵒthe gifts of healing by the same Spirit;

To another, he saith, is given *faith*: by which cannot be understood that faith which is common to all Christians, for he is speaking of such gifts as were given to some Christians, not to all; he must therefore mean, either a faith of miracles, that is, a persuasion that God would work a miracle in this or that case, or a great knowledge in the matters of faith, or a great confidence and boldness in the discharge of their office. *To another the gifts of healing*, of healing diseases miraculously, without the application of ordinary rational medicines.

^{p ver. 28,29.}
^{Mark 16. 17.}
^{Gal. 3. 5.}
^{q Rom.12.6. ch. 13. 2.}
^{& 14. 1, &c.}
^{r ch. 14. 29.}
^{1 John 4. 1.}
^{s Acts 2. 4. & 10. 46. ch. 13. 1.}

10 ᵖTo another the working of miracles; to another ᵠprophecy; ʳto another discerning of spirits; to another ˢ*divers kinds* of tongues; to another the interpretation of tongues:

To another the working of miracles, of other sorts, such as the inflicting punishments on sinners, casting out devils, &c. *To another prophecy*, which in the general signifieth the revelation of the will of God, whether by the foretelling future contingencies, or opening the Scriptures by preaching or teaching. *To another discerning of spirits;* a power wherein God, for the further authority and credit of his gospel in the primitive times, communicated to some men something of his own prerogative to discern men's inward thoughts and hearts, and to make up a judgment of their truth and sincerity, or contrariwise of their falsehood and hypocrisy. *To another divers kinds of tongues*, that is, a power to discourse with men in their several languages, as we read in Acts ii. 8. *To another the interpretation of tongues:* this is made a diverse gift from an ability to speak with divers tongues; possibly some of those that spake with divers tongues could not interpret what they said.

^{t Rom.12.6. ch. 7. 7.}
^{2 Cor. 10. 13.}
^{Eph. 4. 7.}
^{u John 3. 8.}
^{Heb. 2. 4.}

11 But all these worketh that one and the selfsame Spirit, ᵗdividing to every man severally ᵘas he will.

Though the Spirit of God be but one, from whom these several powers and abilities flow; yet he doth not give all this variety of gifts to all Christians, but one to this man, another to another, as the same Holy Spirit pleaseth, for the glory of God, or the good of the church.

^{x Rom. 12. 4, 5. Eph. 4. 4; 16.}
^{y ver. 27. Gal. 3. 16.}

12 For ˣas the body is one, and hath many members, and all the members of that one body, being many, are one body; ʸso also is Christ.

For as it is in the body natural, the integral parts, or members of it, are *many*, yet *the body is* but *one;* so it is in the spiritual body, the church, which is that mystical body of which Christ is the Head. The members of the church may be many, and there may be in several members of the church a diversity of gifts, of administrations, and operations, yet the church is but one, yea, Christ and the church make up but one mystical body, of which he is the Head, and they are the members; and therefore the several members, having several gifts, or several offices, or several powers and operations, had no reason, for their difference in such gifts, or powers, or offices, to envy one another, or to despise each other, or glory over one another; for they were but one body, and had all the same Head, though they had from the same Spirit divers abilities, offices, and powers for several operations.

^{z Rom. 6. 5.}
^{a Gal. 3. 28.}
^{Eph. 2. 13, 14, 16.}
^{Col. 3. 11.}
^{† Gr. Greeks.}
^{b John 6. 63. & 7. 37, 38, 39.}

13 For ᶻby one Spirit are we all baptized into one body, ᵃwhether *we be* Jews or †Gentiles, whether *we be* bond or free; and ᵇhave been all made to drink into one Spirit.

The apostle proveth the oneness of the church, as the body of Christ, from the same sacraments of the New Testament instituted for all Christians, and wherein they jointly partake. He saith, we are *baptized into one body*, by which he must mean the universal church, for Christ is the Head of that; particular churches are but parts of that church, of which Christ is the Head. Let men be of what nation they will, whether Jews or Gentiles, turning to the Christian religion, and of what condition they will, when they are baptized they are by it made members of that one body, of which Christ is the Head; though for the more convenient administration of, and participation in, the ordinances, they are divided into smaller societies, which also have the denomination of churches; as the smallest drop of water may be called water, though there be but one element of water. *And*, saith the apostle, we *have been all made to drink into one Spirit;* which some interpret as if it were, we have all drank of one Spirit, that is, been made partakers of one Spirit, whose benefits are sometimes set out under the notion of water, *living water*, John iv. 10, 14; vii. 38, 39; and so in the Old Testament, Isa. xii. 3; Ezek. xlvii. But many others choose rather to interpret drinking in this place, of drinking at the table of the Lord, partaking of that whole action being set out here by one particular act there performed. This is probable, considering that the apostle, in the former part of the verse, had been speaking of the other sacrament of the gospel, and that he, speaking of the Lord's supper. chap. x. 17, had used this expression, *For we being many, are one bread, and one body.*

14 For the body is not one member, but many.

As the natural body is *totum integrale*, a whole consisting of many members; so the body spiritual, the mystical body of Christ, is not made up of one single member, but of many members.

15 If the foot shall say, Because I am not the hand, I am not of the body; is it therefore not of the body?

16 And if the ear shall say, Because I am not the eye, I am not of the body; is it therefore not of the body?

It should seem by these expressions, that one great cause of those divisions, which the apostle had charged the church of Corinth with, was their difference in *gifts, administrations*, and *operations;* which was to that degree, that either those who were higher in gifts and administrations, and more famous for their miraculous operations, despised and vilified those that were inferior to them; or those who were lower in gifts, or in their stations in the church, or their power to work miracles, would not own themselves members of the church at Corinth, because they were in those low and inferior orders and degrees. The apostle argueth the unreasonableness of this, by a further comparing of the natural with the spiritual mystical body, the church, and showeth, that it was altogether as unreasonable for men to disclaim the church, and their relation to it, because they had not the most eminent gifts, or were not in the most eminent places and offices, as for the foot to say, it was not of the body, because it was not the hand; or for the ear to say, it was not of the body, because it was not the eye.

17 If the whole body *were* an eye, where *were*

the hearing.? If the whole *were* hearing, where *were* the smelling?

There are several actions to be performed by the body of a man, either for the support and the upholding of it in life, or for the accommodation of it while it lives; seeing, hearing, and smelling (which are the three actions here mentioned) are not indeed necessary for the upholding of life, but they are highly useful for a man's better being, and the accommodation of bodily life; therefore there is need of a variety of bodily members, organs or instruments of sight as well as of hearing, and organs of smelling as well as hearing; the wise God hath created no member of man's body in vain, each one hath its use in order to the being or well-being of the body: so it is in the church of God, as the apostle, ver. 27, argueth; but he goeth yet further on, first, in his comparison of the natural and mystical body.

c ver. 28.
d Rom. 12. 3. ch. 3. 5. ver. 11.

18 But now hath ^cGod set the members every one of them in the body, ^das it hath pleased him.

The infinitely wise God, who hath made the body of man, and ordered all the members of the body for several uses and offices, either for the upholding or accommodating the life of man, hath likewise appointed the order in the body in which every member shall stand; that the head should be uppermost for the better guidance of the whole body; the feet lowermost to tread upon the earth, and to bear the weight of the whole body: and none must repine at the wisdom of God, which hath not only created man's body, (consisting of a variety of members,) but also appointed every member its place, and there setteth it, that it cannot shift its station or office.

19 And if they were all one member, where *were* the body?

The body is a whole consisting of many members, it could not therefore be a body if there were but only one member. Or how could the body perform the several actions necessary either for the being or the well-being of it, if it consisted but of one member?

20 But now *are they* many members, yet but one body.

The multiplicity of members, having several uses and offices for the service of the whole body, do not make a multiplicity of bodies, the body still is but one.

21 And the eye cannot say unto the hand, I have no need of thee: nor again the head to the feet, I have no need of you.

He names two of the most noble and useful members of the body, *the head* and *the eye*, which yet cannot tell the hands or the feet they have no need of them: the wise God having created nothing in vain, but made every member in the body of a man for use, as to the whole, so to the several parts of the body; the hand is useful to the eye, and the feet are of use to the head. The application of this similitude, which the apostle so much enlargeth upon, we shall have, ver. 27, &c.

22 Nay, much more those members of the body, which seem to be more feeble, are necessary:

By *feeble* the apostle here doth not only mean most weak, but which seem to us most abject and contemptible; in which sense the word is used, 2 Cor. xii. 10; such are the belly and the entrails; the eye also is a feeble member, &c.; yet these parts are most necessary for the use of the body, being such without the use of which the body cannot live.

23 And those *members* of the body, which we think to be less honourable,

| Or, *put on*.

upon these we || bestow more abundant honour; and our uncomely *parts* have more abundant comeliness.

All know what those parts of the body are, which are commonly judged *less honourable* and less comely; upon these we bestow more abundant honour and comeliness, by hiding them and covering them, that they are not, as the hands, and face, and head, (which we esteem more honour-able parts of the body,) exposed to the public view of those with whom we converse.

24 For our comely *parts* have no need: but God hath tempered the body together, having given more abundant honour to that *part* which lacked:

God hath, in the wisdom of his providence, so ordered it, that as we have some parts of our body which are judged uncomely, and not for those noble uses that others are; so we have other parts that are, for use, more noble, yet in common repute more ignoble and uncomely: and the same wise God so built the body of man, as of both these to make a temperament so as they all concur in the composition of the same body, and more abundant honour in covering and clothing them is given to those parts, that, in the judgment of men, seemed most to lack honour, that their uncomeliness might by some artificial means be taken away.

25 That there should be no || schism in the body; but *that* the members should have the same care one for another.

|| Or, *division*.

By *schism* is here meant division, and that also must be expounded figuratively, and it is expounded in the next words, *that the members should have the same care one for another;* that though the members differ in honour and office, yet they might mutually take care for each other, as if they were all in an equal degree of honour.

26 And whether one member suffer, all the members suffer with it; or one member be honoured, all the members rejoice with it.

From this union of the members in the body natural, of all the members proceedeth a natural sympathy, that if one member suffereth, all are afflicted, and ready to contribute to the relief and help each of other; and likewise the honour that is reflected on the body, is reflected on all the parts, and all rejoice in the good that affecteth any one single member.

27 Now ^eye are the body of Christ, and ^fmembers in particular.

e Rom. 12.5. Eph. l. 23, & 4. 12. & 5. 23, 30. Col. 1. 24. f Eph. 5. 30.

Considering you in the whole as a church, so *ye are the body of Christ:* considering you particularly as individual believers, so ye are *members* of Christ. Some think ἐκ μέρους signifies in part, intending that true believers amongst them were members of Christ, but not others. The apostle, in these words, beginneth to apply to them what he had before discoursed concerning the body natural, and the parts thereof; you are the mystical body of Christ, which hath a great analogy with that natural body which you carry about with you.

28 And ^gGod hath set some in the Church, first ^hapostles, secondarily ⁱprophets, thirdly teachers, after that ^kmiracles, then ^lgifts of healings, ^mhelps, ⁿgovernments, || diversities of tongues.

g Eph. 4. 11. h Eph. 2. 20. & 3. 5. i Acts 13. 1. Rom. 12. 6. k ver. 10. l ver. 9. m Num. 11. 17. n Rom. 12.8. 1 Tim. 5. 17. Heb. 13. 17, 24. || Or, *kinds*, ver. 10.

The apostle, Eph. iv. 11, seemeth to make a different enumeration; there he saith, *And he gave some, apostles; and some, prophets; and some, evangelists; and some, pastors and teachers.* He mentioneth here only three of those there mentioned, viz. *apostles, prophets, teachers.* He reckoneth up there *evangelists,* whom he doth not here mention. He here first mentioneth *apostles,* by whom he meaneth those servants of God who were sent out by Christ to lay the first foundations of the gospel church, and upon whom a universal care lay over all the churches of Christ, having not only a power in all places to preach and administer the sacraments, but to give rules of order, and direct in matters of government; though particular churches had a power of government within themselves, otherwise the apostle would not have blamed this church for not casting out the incestuous person. *Prophets* signify persons (as I have before noted) that revealed the mind and will of God to people, whether it were by an extraordinary impulse and revelation, or in an ordinary course of teaching; whether they revealed things to come, or opened the mind and will of God already revealed. But in this text, and in Eph. iv. 11, *prophets* seem to signify, either such as from the Spirit of God foretold future contingencies, (such was Agabus, of whom we read in the Acts of the Apostles, and others in the primitive church,) or else such as interpreted Scripture by extraordinary and immediate revelation. Some think that *prophets* signify the ordinary pastors of churches; but they seem rather to be comprehended under the next term of *teachers*, unless we had better grounds than we have to distinguish betwixt pastors and teachers, making the work of the teacher to speak by way of doctrine and explication, and the work of the pastor to speak practically. *Thirdly teachers*: some by these understand governors of schools; others, such ministers whose work was only to expound the Scriptures, or the mysteries of salvation: but the apostle, in this enumeration, (which is the largest we have in Scripture,) not mentioning pastors, it seemeth to me that he means the fixed and ordinary ministers of churches, or the elders, whom the apostles left in every city, which by their ministry had received the gospel. *After that miracles;* after that such as he empowered to work miraculous operations, and those of more remarkable nature, for otherwise the *healings* next mentioned come under that notion also. *Then gifts of healings;* then such persons as he gave a power to in an extraordinary way to heal the sick. Who the apostle means by *helps*, and by *governments*, is very hard to determine. Certain it is, that he doth not mean the civil magistrates; for the time was not yet come for kings to be nursing fathers, and queens nursing mothers to the gospel church. But whether he meaneth deacons, or widows, elsewhere mentioned, as helpful in the case of the poor, or some that assisted the pastors in the government of the church, or some that were extraordinary helps to the apostles in the first plantation of the church, is very hard to determine. *Diversities of tongues;* such as spake with divers tongues, that faculty being a gift, as we heard before, not given to all, but to some in the primitive church. The apostle, by this enumeration, showeth what he meant by those *diversities of gifts, differences of administrations,* and *diversities of operations,* of which he spake in ver. 4—6.

29 *Are* all apostles? *are* all prophets? [Or, *powers*.] *are* all teachers? *are* all ‖ workers of miracles?

30 Have all the gifts of healing? do all speak with tongues? do all interpret?

That is, all are not, nor can be, any more than all the body can be an ear, or an eye, or a hand, or a foot: you cannot expect, that in a governed body all should be governors; and you see by experience, that all cannot work miracles, prophesy, speak with tongues, or heal those that are sick.

o ch. 14. 1, 39. 31 But °covet earnestly the best gifts: and yet shew I unto you a more excellent way.

But covet earnestly the best gifts: the word may be translated indicatively, Ye do covet the best gifts; or as we translate it, imperatively, Covet ye; I would have you be covetous to excel in the best gifts, that is, those which will make you most useful and profitable to the church of God. *And yet show I unto you a more excellent way;* but yet (saith he) gifts are not the best things, the habits of saving grace are much more valuable than gifts; love to God and your neighbour ought to be by you preferred before gifts. To a discourse of which the apostle thus shortly passeth.

CHAP. XIII

All gifts, how excellent soever, without charity are nothing worth, 1—3. *The praises of charity,* 4—12; *and its preference to faith and hope,* 13.

THOUGH I speak with the tongues of men and of angels, and have not charity, I am become *as* sounding brass, or a tinkling cymbal.

The apostle had promised, in the close of the former chapter, to show them a more excellent thing than gifts, or a more excellent course than that they were so hotly pursuing, in their emulation of the best gifts; he now cometh to show them that way, that course: the way was that of love; the course was the study and pursuing methods how to show their love to God and to one another. For (saith the apostle) *though I speak,* that is, if I could speak, or admit I did speak, *with the tongues* used in all the nations of the world, and with the tongues *of angels;* by which some understand the best and most excellent ways of expressing ourselves. Angels have no tongues, nor make any articulate audible sounds, by which they understand one another; but yet there is certainly a society or intercourse among angels, which could not be upheld without some way amongst them to communicate their minds and wills each to other. How this is we cannot tell: some of the schoolmen say, it is by way of impression: that way God, indeed, communicates his mind sometimes to his people, making secret impressions of his will upon their minds and understandings; but whether angels can do the like, or what their way is of communicating their minds each to other, is a great secret, and we ought to be willingly ignorant of what God hath not pleased, in any part of his revealed will, to tell us. Neither do I judge it a question proper to this place, where the *tongues of angels* unquestionably signify the best and most excellent ways of expressing and communicating ourselves to others; as manna is called *angels' food,* Psal. lxxviii. 25, that is, the most excellent food, for angels, being spiritual substances, need no food, have no mouths to eat, nor bellies to fill; and this the apostle meaneth. Though I could express myself, or communicate my mind to others, in the most excellent way, or in the greatest variety of expression, yet if I have not ἀγάπην, which we translate, *charity,* but possibly might be better translated love, because we usually by charity (in common speech) understand that indication of brotherly love, which is in act sof bounty, feeding the hungry, clothing the naked, giving to those that are in want; which it is possible that men do out of mere humanity, or a superstitious opinion of meriting thereby, without any true root of love to our neighbour, which is never true if it doth not grow out of a love to God. If I want love, (saith the apostle,) a true root of love to men, flowing from a true love to God, and out of obedience to his precept, I am but *as sounding brass or a tinkling cymbal,* that is, I only make a noise, but it will conduce nothing to my salvation, it will be of no use to me; but if I have this true root of love, then it will be of avail to me. And thus the apostle proveth, that the habit of love to God and man in the heart, is far more excellent than the gift of tongues, which many of the Corinthians had, or coveted, or boasted in, despising those who had it not.

2 And though I have *the gift of* [a] prophecy, and understand all mysteries, and all knowledge; and though I have all faith, [b] so that I could remove mountains, and have not charity, I am nothing.

[a] ch. 12. 8, 9, 10, 28. & 14. 1, &c. See Matt. 7. 22.
[b] Mat. 17. 20. Mark 11. 23. Luke 17. 6.

And though I have the gift of prophecy: it hath been before showed, that *the gift of prophecy,* signifieth an extraordinary power or faculty, by which men in those primitive times were enabled to reveal the mind and will of God, either as to future contingencies, or things which should afterwards come to pass in the world, or by further explication or application of the mind and will of God already revealed in holy writ. *And understand all mysteries, and all knowledge:* though, saith the apostle, I have a vast knowledge, and could in any notion comprehend the most sublime and hidden things, whether Divine or human. *And though I have all faith* (except that which is saving and justifying). *So that I could remove mountains:* he further opens what faith he meant, viz. faith of miracles, a firm persuasion that God would upon my prayer work things beyond the power, and contrary to the course, of nature: the apostle alludeth to the words of our Saviour, Matt. xvii. 20. *And have not charity, I am nothing;* yet, saith he, if I have not love, that true love to God and men, by which that faith which is profitable to salvation worketh and showeth itself, it will all signify nothing, be of no profit nor avail unto me in order to my eternal salvation; I may perish for ever, notwithstanding such gifts.

3 And [c] though I bestow all my goods to feed *the poor,* and though I give my body to be burned, and have not charity, it profiteth me nothing.

[c] Mat. 6. 1, 2.

The apostle proceedeth from common gifts, powers, and habits, to actions, and instanceth in two; the first of which might be a great service to men; the latter, an appearance of a great service to God. *Though I bestow all my goods to feed the poor;* though, saith he, I feed the poor with my goods, and that not sparingly, but liberally, so as I spend all my estate in that way, and make myself as poor as they: *and though I give my body to be burned;* though I die in the cause of Christ, for the testimony of his gospel, or for owning of his ways; and that by the sharpest and most cruel sort of death, burning; and be not dragged to the stake, but freely give up myself to that cruel kind of death: *and have not charity, it profiteth me nothing;* yet if I have not a root and principle of love to God in my heart, that carrieth me out to these actions and these sufferings, they all will signify nothing to me, as to my eternal salvation and happiness. From whence we may observe, that, 1. The highest acts of beneficence or bounty towards men, (which we usually call good works,) are not meritorious at the hand of God, and may be separated from a true root of saving grace in the soul. 2. That the greatest sufferings for and in the cause of religion, may be separated from a true root and principle of saving grace. 3. That no actions, no sufferings, are sufficient to entitle any soul to heaven, further than they proceed from a principle of true love to God, and a desire to obey and to please him in what we do. Faith and love must be the roots and principles of all those works which are truly good, and acceptable to God, and which will be of any profit or avail to us with reference to our eternal happiness.

d Prov. 10. 12. 1 Pet. 4. 8.
|| Or, *is not rash.*

4 ᵈ Charity suffereth long, *and* is kind; charity envieth not; charity || vaunteth not itself, is not puffed up,

Lest the Corinthians should say to the apostle, What is this love you discourse of? or how shall we know if we have it? the apostle here gives thirteen notes of a charitable person. *Charity suffereth long:* by love or *charity* he either meaneth a charitable person, a soul possessed of that love, which he had been commending; or if we take the term plainly, to signify the habit itself, the meaning is, it is a habit or power in the soul, enabling and inclining it to do these things: to suffer long, not to be too quick and tetchy with brethren that may offend or displease us; the charitable man will withhold and restrain his wrath, not be rash in the expressions of it, and hasty to revenge. *And is kind;* it disposeth a man to desire to deserve well of all, and to do good to all, as he hath occasion and opportunity; so as it is impossible there should be in a man any thing more opposite to this grace, than a currish, churlish temper, with a study and desire to do others mischief. *Charity envieth not;* though a charitable person seeth others in a higher and more prosperous condition than himself, yet it doth not trouble him, but he is glad at the preferment, good, and prosperity of other men, however it fareth with himself. Every envious man, that is displeased and angry at another's faring well, is an uncharitable man, there is no true root of love to God or to his neighbour in his heart. *Vaunteth not itself;* he doth not prefer himself before others, ambitiously glorying or boasting, and acting rashly to promote his own glory, and satisfy his own intemperate desires or lusts. He *is not puffed up,* proudly lifting up himself above others, and swelling with high conceits of himself.

5 Doth not behave itself unseemly,

e ch. 10. 24. Phil. 2. 4.

ᵉseeketh not her own, is not easily provoked, thinketh no evil;

Doth not behave itself unseemly; he doth not behave himself towards any in an uncomely or unbeseeming manner, and will do nothing towards his brother, which in the opinion of men shall be a filthy or indecent action. *Seeketh not her own;* he doth not seek what is his own, that is, what is for his own profit or advantage only; he hath an eye to the good and advantage of his brother, as well as his own profit and advantage. Such a man *is not easily provoked;* he is not without his passions, but he is not governed by his passions, and overruled by them to fly out extravagantly against his brother upon every light and trivial occasion; he knows how to bear injuries, and is willing rather to bear lesser wrongs, losses, and injuries, than to do any thing in revenge of himself, or to the more remarkable prejudice of his neighbour. He *thinketh no evil,* that is, no mischief, nothing that may be hurtful and prejudicial to his neighbour. Or else, he doth not rashly suspect his neighbour for doing evil (which possibly may be the better interpretation); and so it teacheth us, that lightly to take up evil reports of our neighbours, is a violation of charity; for the man that hath a true love to his brother, though he may believe evil of his brother, and charge him with evil, when it evidently appears to him that he is guilty; yet before that be evident to him, he will not suspect, nor think any such things of him.

6 ᶠRejoiceth not in iniquity, but ᵍrejoiceth || in the truth;

f Ps. 10. 3. Rom. 1. 32.
g 2 John 4.
|| Or, *with the truth.*

He doth not rejoice in the sinful falls of others, but he rejoiceth in all truth, and the success and prospering of truth in the world; or in the manifestation of any person's truth, or innocency, and righteousness.

7 ʰBeareth all things, believeth all things, hopeth all things, endureth all things.

h Rom. 15. 1. Gal. 6. 2.
2 Tim. 2. 24.

The charitable man *beareth all* injuries with patience; he *believeth all things* that are good of his brother, so far is he from being credulous to his prejudice; *endureth all things* that a good man ought to endure, that is, any evils done to himself. In the same sense Solomon saith, Prov. x. 12, *Love covereth all sins.*

8 Charity never faileth: but whether *there be* prophecies, they shall fail; whether *there be* tongues, they shall cease; whether *there be* knowledge, it shall vanish away.

The apostle, from another argument, commendeth the grace of love, viz. its never failing; it shall go with us into another world, and have its use and exercise there, where there will be no prophesying, no speaking with divers tongues, but there the saints shall love God. And this maketh it evident, that by charity, or love, (before mentioned,) the apostle doth not singly mean bounty or beneficence to those that stand in need of those good things of this life, in which we can help them. *Whether there be knowledge, it shall vanish away:* by *knowledge,* here, some understand the communicating of knowledge to the church by preaching: others, the means we now have by meditating in and study of the Scriptures: others, better, of the imperfect degrees of our knowledge, or the way of our procuring it: the following verses would incline us to interpret it of the former, though it be true also of the latter.

9 ⁱFor we know in part, and we prophesy in part.

i ch. 8. 2.

For we know in part; it was truly said, as to things human, that the greatest part of those things that we know, is the least part of those things which we are ignorant of. A great measure of Divine things is also unknown to us, and the knowledge of them reserved for the resurrection and day of judgment, John xiv. 20. *And we prophesy in part;* nor can the communication of our knowledge to that, be larger than what we by prophecy communicate; we having ourselves but a short and imperfect communication of Divine things, we can communicate but an imperfect degree of knowledge to others.

10 But when that which is perfect is come, then that which is in part shall be done away.

But when we come to heaven, we shall be in such a state, as nothing shall or can be added to us; then our partial and imperfect knowledge shall be swallowed up in a knowledge perfect and complete.

11 When I was a child, I spake as a child, I understood as a child, I ||thought as a child: but when I became a man, I put away childish things.

|| Or, *reasoned.*

The apostle compareth the state of believers in this life, compared with their state in another life, to the state of a child, compared to that of a man. Look, as one, when he is a child, knoweth things imperfectly, and discourseth of them in the style and according to the knowledge of a child; but when he is grown up, he discourseth of them at another rate, according to the degree of knowledge which

I. CORINTHIANS XIII, XIV

he hath acquired by instruction of others, or his own experience and observation : so it is with all of us ; in this life we, like children, have a poor, low, imperfect knowledge of spiritual things, and accordingly discourse of them ; but when we come to heaven, we shall know them and discourse of them in a more perfect manner.

12 For [k] now we see through a glass, † darkly ; but then [l] face to face : now I know in part ; but then shall I know even as also I am known.

k 2 Cor. 3. 18. & 5. 7. Phil. 3. 12.
† Gr. in a riddle.
l Mat. 18. 10. 1 John 3. 2.

The apostle pursues his former theme, comparing the imperfect state of believers, as to knowledge in this life, with what shall be in the life that is to come. In this life it is as in a looking-glass, (where we only see the images and imperfect representations of things,) and darkly, in a riddle ; it is but a little knowledge that we have, and what we have we get with a great deal of difficulty ; but in heaven we shall have such knowledge as two men have who see one another face to face, and shall know God fully, in some measure, though not in the same degree, of the fulness and perfections wherein God knoweth us.

13 And now abideth faith, hope, charity, these three ; but the greatest of these *is* charity.

Take us according to our state in this life, we have, and shall have, the exercise of three graces : *faith,* to evidence unto us those things which we do not see, either by the eye of sense or reason ; *hope,* by which we wait for the receiving of them ; and *love,* by which we delight ourselves in God, and show obedience to the will of God. But of all these, love is *the greatest,* either in respect of its use and profitableness unto men, or in respect of its duration and abiding (which last the apostle seemeth chiefly to intend). *Faith* shall cease when we come to the vision of God ; and *hope,* when we come to the fruition of God in glory ; *love* also will cease, as to some acts, but never as to a pleasure and a delighting in God ; that will be to eternity.

CHAP. XIV.

Prophecy, for its greater tendency to edification, is preferred before speaking with tongues, 1—5. *Tongues not understood, like indistinct musical sounds, are of no service to the hearers,* 6—11. *All gifts should be referred to edification,* 12—20. *Tongues are of use for the conviction of unbelievers,* 21, 22 ; *but in the assemblies of the church prophecy is more useful,* 23—25. *Rules for the orderly exercise of spiritual gifts in the church,* 26—33. *Women are forbidden to speak there,* 34—38. *An exhortation to use each gift freely, but with decency and order,* 39, 40.

FOLLOW after charity, and [a] desire spiritual *gifts,* [b] but rather that ye may prophesy.

a ch. 12. 31.
b Num. 11. 25, 29.

Follow after charity; that love to God and your brethren, concerning which I have been speaking so much, as preferable to all common gifts, follow that with your utmost diligence, (as to which they could use no means but prayer and a holy life,) as the persecutors follow you ; for it is the same word that is ordinarily used to signify the violent prosecution of persecutors, though it be applied also to things which we ought eagerly to follow, Rom. ix. 31 ; xiv. 19. *But rather that ye may prophesy;* but rather, or principally that you may be able to reveal the mind and will of God unto others. Some think, by foretelling things to come ; but that is not very probable, such an ability of prophesying being given but to few until the New Testament : it is therefore more probable, that he speaketh of an ability to open the Scriptures, either by immediate revelation, (as to which they could use no means but prayer and a holy life,) or by ordinary meditation, and study of the Scriptures. For though the former species of prophesying, by prediction of future things, when the truth of it was justified by such prophecies' accomplishment, was of great use to confirm the doctrine of the gospel ; yet the latter was of greater and more general use for the good of others, which makes the apostle put them upon the coveting and earnest desire of that faculty or ability, because, of all others, it made them most eminently and generally useful to others, as well those within the church, as those without ; and thus the apostle expoundeth himself, ver. 3.

2 For he that [c] speaketh in an *unknown* tongue speaketh not unto men, but unto God : for no man † understandeth *him;* howbeit in the spirit he speaketh mysteries.

c Acts 2. 4. & 10. 46.
† Gr. *heareth.* Acts 22. 9.

For he that speaketh in an unknown tongue; by a *tongue* (for *unknown* is not in the Greek, but necessarily added by our translators, for he speaketh of such a language) he meaneth a language not known to all, or at least not to the most of them that hear him. It may be asked, what unknown language the apostle here meaneth ? Shall we think that any pastors or teachers in the church of Corinth were so vain, as to preach in the Arabic, Scythian, or Parthian language to a people who understood only the Greek ? Our learned Lightfoot thinks this not probable, and that if any had been so vain for ostentation, the apostle would rather have chid them for suffering such an abuse, and have forbidden such further practice, than have given direction, than if any so spake he should interpret, as he doth, ver. 5. He rather thinks, therefore, that the apostle meaneth the Hebrew tongue ; the use of which, though it was by this time much lost through the Jews' mixture with other nations, yet was restored in a great measure to the guides of churches, for their better understanding the Scriptures of the Old Testament ; and continued amongst the Jews in their reading of the law in the synagogues. Now there being many Jews in this church, and the service of God being ordinarily in the Jewish synagogues performed in that language, it is very probable, that some of these Jews that were Christianized (to show their skill) might, when they spake to the whole church of Corinth, use to speak in Hebrew, though few or none understood that language. The apostle saith, he that did so, spake *not unto men,* that is, not to those men who did not understand that language, not to the generality of his hearers, though possibly here and there some might understand him, *but unto God,* who being the Author of all languages, must necessarily know the significancy of all words in them : for (he saith) scarce any man understood him. *Howbeit in the spirit he speaketh mysteries;* howbeit he may speak mysterious things to himself, and to the understanding of his own soul and spirit. Others think that it was possible, that some who thus spake, being but the instruments of the Holy Spirit, might not themselves understand all which they said ; but that is hardly probable.

3 But he that prophesieth speaketh unto men *to* edification, and exhortation, and comfort.

Speaketh unto men; that is, to the understanding of men, and for the good and profit of men. *To edification;* for their increase in knowledge and all habits of grace. *And exhortation;* to quicken them in the exercise and practice of such duties as God hath, in his word, required of them. *And comfort;* and for the relief of them under their burdens, to support and uphold their troubled or wounded spirits. These expressions make it probable, that the apostle, by prophecy in this text, understands ministerial preaching ; which more properly tends *to edification, exhortation, and comfort,* than the foretelling of things to come.

4 He that speaketh in an *unknown* tongue edifieth himself ; but he that prophesieth edifieth the church.

He that speaketh in an unknown tongue edifieth himself; knowledge or understanding of the things that any man speaketh, is necessary to the improvement of them, by their being a means to promote faith and love ; for how shall what men say in the least promote, either my faith in God or Christ, or my love to him, if I understand not what they say ? *How shall they believe in him of whom they have not heard?* Rom. x. 14. So that, though he that speaketh in an unknown tongue may (if he understand what he says) have his own heart affected with what he saith, yet it is not possible he should affect another. *But he that prophesieth edifieth the church;* but he that preacheth in an intelligible language and style to all that hear him, he doth what in him lieth to edify all those that hear him.

5 I would that ye all spake with tongues, but rather that ye prophesied: for greater *is* he that prophesieth than he that speaketh with tongues, except he interpret, that the church may receive edifying.

I would, in this place, signifies no more than either. I could wish, or I could be content that you could all speak with tongues, if God pleased. It should seem by this speech of the apostle's, that this speaking in unknown tongues was that extraordinary gift, which, above all others, this church, or the several members of it, were proud and ambitious of. St. Paul tells them, that if God pleased he wished they could all do it. But of the two, he rather wished them all a power to open and apply the Holy Scriptures to men's understandings and conscience. He addeth the reason, because it was a more honourable gift and work, and made men truly greater. But he adds, *except he interpret,* for then he prophesied also. *That,* saith he, *the church,* that is, those that heard him prophesying, *may receive edifying.* Whence we learn, 1. That spiritual growth, and proficiency in Divine knowledge and habits of grace, ought to be the great end of all preachers; and whoso doth not propound this as his end, abuseth his office, and trifles in a pulpit. 2. That whoso maketh this his end, will make it his business, to the best of his skill, to use such a language. style, and method, as the generality of his hearers may best understand; for without their understanding, there can be no edifying. And this lets us see the vanity of using much Latin, or Greek, or a lofty style, or a cryptic method, not obvious to poor people in popular sermons, where the people understand not those languages; or philosophical ratiocinations before a plain people that understand none of these things. Such preaching is neither justifiable by reason, nor by the practice either of Christ or his apostles.

6 Now, brethren, if I come unto you speaking with tongues, what shall I profit you, except I shall speak to you either by ᵈrevelation, or by knowledge, or by prophesying, or by doctrine?

ᵈ ver. 26.

God hath given me an ability to speak with tongues; suppose I should come to you speaking in the Arabian, Scythian, or Parthian language, what good would it do you? how should it any way *profit you, except I shall speak to you either by revelation, or by knowledge, or by prophesying, or by doctrine?* Some make these four things distinct each from other; others think that they all signify no more, than the interpreting mentioned in the former verse. Those who distinguish them say, by *revelation* is meant the explication of the types and figures of the Old Testament; or some such revelation as John had in Patmos; or the expounding the mysteries of the gospel. By *knowledge* they understand the knowledge of history, or any other ordinary knowledge. By *prophesying,* the explication of the difficult texts of Scripture. By *doctrine,* catechetical or practical doctrine. But these are all but uncertain guesses; the sense is plainly no more, than, if I should come speaking with unknown tongues, and no way by interpretation make what I say intelligible unto you.

7 And even things without life giving sound, whether pipe or harp, except they give a distinction in the ‖ sounds, how shall it be known what is piped or harped?

‖ Or, *tunes.*

In the sounds which are artificially made by the use of wind music, or other music, nothing could be understood, if art had not also devised a distinction in the sounds; that one sound should signify one thing, another sound should signify another thing: so unless the voice of the teacher be significant to, and understood by, the person instructed or taught, the sound is of no use at all.

8 For if the trumpet give an uncertain sound, who shall prepare himself to the battle?

The trumpet is made use of in battles, and that variously; it is used to give soldiers notice to march on against the enemy, and also to sound a retreat: if there were not a distinction in the one sound, and in the other, how should the soldier know when to go forward, and when to come back, by the sound of it? To instruct them what to do, the trumpet must not only sound, but sound intelligibly to those that hear it, which it could not, if there were no distinction in the sound.

9 So likewise ye, except ye utter by the tongue words † easy to be understood, how shall it be known what is spoken? for ye shall speak into the air.

† Gr. *significant.*

By λόγον εὔσημον is meant words which signify well to those that hear them; for words may be significant enough in themselves, yet nothing at all significant to them that hear them, being unlearned; such sounds of words can contribute nothing to people's knowledge, but are so much lost labour. This is a text that deserveth the thoughts of those who affect in preaching, if not the use of languages, yet the use of a style, or method, which not one of many of those who hear them understand. It is all one to speak in an unknown tongue, as in a style or method that people do not understand; and truly, such are the generality of ministers' hearers, that words most significant in themselves, and to learned ears, are least significant to them, being hardest to be understood; so as they know nothing of what they say, and the minister doth but, as to the far greater number of people, beat the air (which is a dreadful meditation).

10 There are, it may be, so many kinds of voices in the world, and none of them *is* without signification.

The whole earth was originally *of one language. and of one speech,* Gen. xi. 1; but upon the building of Babel, ver. 7, God confounded their languages, so as they did not understand one another. They being scattered abroad, had different languages; so as now there are in the world many languages, and the words in every language are significant to those that understand that language.

11 Therefore if I know not the meaning of the voice, I shall be unto him that speaketh a barbarian, and he that speaketh *shall be* a barbarian unto me.

But if a man doth not understand the language, the words are not significant unto him, I shall neither understand him, nor will he understand me; for a barbarian cannot understand one of another nation, till he hath learned the language of that nation; nor can a man of another nation understand a barbarian till he hath learned his language.

12 Even so ye, forasmuch as ye are zealous † of spiritual *gifts,* seek that ye may excel to the edifying of the church.

† Gr. *of spirits.*

This proves that the members of the church of Corinth were very ambitious of *spiritual gifts.* The particle ὅτω, which our translation here renders *so,* plainly signifies therefore in this place. In the Greek it is, because, or *forasmuch as ye are zealous of* spirits; the efficient is put for the effect, the Spirit, which is the author of those gifts, for the gifts themselves. *Seek that ye may excel to the edifying of the church;* seek that ye may excel in them, and that will be, if you most desire those which tend to the edifying the church, and use those with which God hath blessed you in the best order and manner for that end. From whence it is observable, that the improvement of the people to whom we preach in the knowledge of God, and in faith and obedience, is the great end which we ought to propose to ourselves in the discharge of our office, and in the use of our gifts.

13 Wherefore let him that speaketh in an *unknown* tongue pray that he may interpret.

To *interpret* here signifieth no more, than to render that intelligible to people, which he first uttereth in an unknown tongue. But what need he *pray* for that? Hath not every man that can speak a power to speak his native language, as well as a foreign language? Some say, therefore, that ἵνα in this place signifies also, let him pray and also interpret; but this seemeth hard: nor can I think those that had a faculty to speak in an unknown tongue, might some of them not themselves understand what they said, and so had need to pray that they might interpret: but they might be puffed up with their gift, and think it beneath them to

I. CORINTHIANS XIV

interpret, and then they had need to pray that they might have humility enough to interpret. Others think, that by interpreting in this place, is meant something more than bare translating, or turning the words into the common language of the place, viz. the opening and applying of the Scriptures, an ability to which was a distinct gift; which they who would have, had need pray that God would open their eyes to understand the mysteries of his law.

14 For if I pray in an *unknown* tongue, my spirit prayeth, but my understanding is unfruitful.

From this and the former verse, the papists would justify the lawfulness of their Latin service, which none or few of the common people understand ; and they seem to have a little advantage from the opinion of some of the ancients, That some of those who spake with tongues, did not themselves understand what they uttered, but the Spirit of God only made use of their tongues as machines. But these are apprehensions much beneath the Spirit of light and truth, that it should make use of the tongue of a man for an end neither profitable to the man himself, nor others. Besides, how is it then true which we had, ver. 4, that he who spake in an unknown tongue edifieth himself? Nay, how can it be true, which is here said, that such a man's *spirit prayeth?* nor is it here said, *my understanding is* dark or blind, but *unfruitful;* that is, though myself understand, yet my knowledge bringeth forth no fruit to the advantage or good of others. *My spirit prayeth,* but others cannot pray with me.

15 What is it then? I will pray with the spirit, and I will pray with the understanding also: [e] **I will sing with the spirit, and I will sing** [f] **with the understanding also.**

e Eph. 5. 19.
Col. 3. 16.
f Ps. 47. 7.

What is to be done then? *I will* (saith the apostle) *pray with the spirit;* that is, either use the extraordinary influences of the Spirit of God upon me; or with my own spirit, with the inward attention of my thoughts, and the utmost intension of my mind, and the greatest devotion and fervour of affections. *And I will pray with the understanding also;* but I will so pray, that myself and others may understand what I say; I will neither so pray, that myself shall not understand what I say, nor yet so, that others shall not understand me. *Understanding* is here taken in a passive sense, though the active sense of the term be not to be excluded. The same thing he also saith of singing, to let us know, that all our religious acts in public assemblies ought to be so performed, that others may be benefited by them, which they cannot be, if they do not understand what we say, whether it be in preaching, praying, or singing.

16 Else when thou shalt bless with the spirit, how shall he that occupieth the room of the unlearned say Amen [g] **at thy giving of thanks, seeing he understandeth not what thou sayest?**

g ch. 11. 24.

Else when thou shalt bless with the spirit: blessing is expounded in the latter part of the verse, *giving of thanks* to God, which is either in prayer, (for thanksgiving is a part of prayer,) or in singing of psalms. Blessing *with the spirit* either signifieth giving of thanks with the inward man, or giving of thanks in an unknown tongue, by the extraordinary influence of the Spirit of God. *How shall he that occupieth the room of the unlearned say Amen at thy giving of thanks?* it is plain from hence, 1. That the teachers had in the apostolical churches distinct places and seats from the common hearers, for their better convenience in speaking, that they might so speak as all might hear, understand, and be profited. 2. That in those churches there was one only who used to speak audibly, and the work of the others was only from a devout heart to *say Amen,* wishing or praying that God would do what, in the name of all, he that ministered had asked of God for them. So 1 Chron. xvi. 36; Neh. v. 13: viii. 6; Psal. cvi. 48. *Seeing he understandeth not what thou sayest:* people ought not to say *Amen* to any thing, unless they understand that petition, or those petitions, to which, in the worship of God, they add their *Amen,* which word makes the petitions theirs, being a particle of wishing, as well as affirming.

17 For thou verily givest thanks well, but the other is not edified.

Otherwise, saith the apostle, it is possible that thou mayst give thanks well; but others get no good by it, nor can make any good and spiritual improvement of it.

18 I thank my God, I speak with tongues more than ye all:

Our Saviour, in the parable of the good shepherd, gives us this as his character, that the sheep hear his voice, and follow him, John x. 4; and we shall observe this great apostle every where propounding himself for imitation to them. They are bad shepherds over God's flock, that must only be heard, but not followed. The apostle lets them know, that God had not left him without the gift of speaking with divers tongues, nay, he had it in a more eminent manner than they all; put them all together, they could not speak with so many tongues as he did.

19 Yet in the church I had rather speak five words with my understanding, that *by my voice* I might teach others also, than ten thousand words in an *unknown* tongue.

Yet he had so great a regard to the end of his ministry, teaching others, and communicating Divine knowledge to them, that he had rather speak a little tending to that end, than never so much in a language which those to whom he spake did not understand.

20 Brethren, [h] **be not children in understanding: howbeit in malice** [i] **be ye children, but in understanding be** [†] **men.**

h Ps. 131. 2. Matt. 11. 25. & 18. 3. & 19. 14. Rom. 16. 19. ch. 3. 1. Eph. 4.
i4. Heb. 5. 19, 12   i Matt. 18. 3. 1 Pet. 2. 2.   † Gr. *perfect,* or, *of a ripe age.* ch. 2. 6.

Be not children in understanding; in understanding the differences of gifts, and which are more excellent, or of the right use of gifts. *Howbeit in malice be ye children, but in understanding be men;* you are commanded indeed in something to be like little children, Matt. xviii. 3, but it is not to be understood with relation to knowledge and understanding, but with reference to innocence and malice, which is opposite to it; ye ought to study to be men in understanding, though with respect to innocence ye ought to be as little children.

21 [k] **In the law it is** [l] **written, With *men* of other tongues and other lips will I speak unto this people; and yet for all that will they not hear me, saith the Lord.**

k John 10. 34.
l Is. 28. 11, 12.

In the law it is written: by *the law* here is meant the Old Testament, (as in many other texts, John x. 34; xv. 25,) so called (as some think) in opposition to the words of the scribes. The words following are quoted out of Isa. xxviii. 11, 12, *For with stammering lips and another tongue will he speak to this people. To whom he said, This is the rest wherewith ye may cause the weary to rest; and this is the refreshing: yet they would not hear.* But there is nothing more ordinary, than for the penmen of the Scriptures of the New Testament to quote passages out of the Old, keeping not so much to the words as to the sense; nor quoting them all, but so many of them as serve for their purposes. The words in the prophet are a threatening, that because God had brought the Jews into Canaan, and promised them rest there, upon their obedience to his commandments, and they would not hear, he would now take another course with them, speaking to them with men of stammering lips, and of another language; meaning the Chaldeans and Babylonians, with whom in captivity they conversed afterwards for seventy years. The sense is much the same (as some think); for they that speak to others in and with strange tongues, are like those that stammer at others, which looks more like a mocking them than an instructing them. Others make the gift of tongues, under the New Testament, to be within the prophecy of Isaiah; as if the prophet's words contained both a threatening, to speak to the Israelites with the strange tongues of the Chaldeans; and a promise under the gospel, to speak to them with the tongues of the apostles and others, tuned to various tunes, as men of several nations could understand. Others make this the sense, as if the prophet complained, that the people were so mad, that they regarded no more God speaking to them, than they would have regarded one chattering with a strange tongue. And they think, the apostle checks them for being so ambitious of speaking with strange tongues, whenas their being so spoken to was by the prophet threatened as a judgment upon them. *And yet they will not hear me,* nor hearken to and obey me.

22 Wherefore tongues are for a sign, not to them that believe, but to them that believe not: but prophesying *serveth* not for them that believe not, but for them which believe.

Wherefore tongues are for a sign, &c.; that is, an eminent product of Divine providence for the confirmation of the truth of the doctrine of the gospel; signifying that the doctrine which was so delivered in every nation's language, must be from heaven, from whence the first ministers must have their power so to speak; yet, doubtless, they were not only for a sign, being also a means, by which the knowledge of the gospel was conveyed unto those who could not have understood what the apostles and first ministers of the gospel said, had they not spoken to them in the language of the hearers. When he saith, *prophesying serveth not for them that believe not,* the meaning is, not only for them that believe not; for prophesying is certainly of use to them that believe not, for their conversion, as well as *for them that believe,* for their edification.

23 If therefore the whole church be come together into one place, and all speak with tongues, and there come in *those that are* unlearned, or unbelievers, m Acts 2. 13. ᵐ will they not say that ye are mad?

Be come together into one place; the phrase signifieth to one place, or for one and the same work; the first seemeth to be meant here by what followeth. *And all speak with tongues:* some think that the apostle here, by all speaking with tongues, understands all, or many of them, confusedly talking together; and indeed that is an error we shall find the apostle afterward reflecting upon them for; but here I do not think it is intended, but only, many of you, one after another, because of what the apostle speaketh of prophesying, ver. 24. For if *all* prophesied in that sense, talking at the same time together confusedly, and unbelievers came in and heard, they would also, instead of being convinced, say they were mad. *And there come in those that are unlearned, or unbelievers;* those that are heathens, or that did not understand the language you discoursed in. *Will they not say that ye are mad?* would they not say you were men that had lost the use of your reason, to talk to men in a language you yourselves knew they understood nothing of?

24 But if all prophesy, and there come in one that believeth not, or *one* unlearned, he is convinced of all, he is judged of all:

But if all prophesy: all here certainly is not to be understood of every one in the assembly, for all were not prophets, chap. xii. 29, nor could the speaking of a great number be judged orderly by the light of nature: it here must signify any, one or more, successively, interpret or apply the Holy Scriptures. *He is convinced of all;* the heathens will see an order in this, and will stand still to hear and be convinced. *He is judged of all;* seeing their wicked life and false religion judged and condemned by all those that so prophesy.

25 And thus are the secrets of his heart made manifest; and so falling down on *his* face he will worship God, and report n Is. 45. 14. Zech. 8. 23. ⁿ that God is in you of a truth.

God either, by an extraordinary providence, discovering to him that prophesieth the secrets of such a sinner's heart, and causing him that prophesieth to make them manifest; or, by a more ordinary providence, (often experienced at this day,) directing the preacher to such subjects and discourses, as he that cometh to hear shall think directed to himself, and confess that he is the man, and be convinced of his errors, and converted, and turn to the Christian religion, and report that God indeed is amongst you. So as prophesying will have these two great advantages of speaking with tongues, God will be more glorified, and the souls of others will be more profited; which makes the gift of prophesying much preferable to the gift of tongues.

26 How is it then, brethren? when ye come together, every one of you hath a psalm, ᵒ hath a doctrine, hath a tongue, hath a revelation, hath an interpretation. ᵖ Let all things be done unto edifying. c ver. 6. ch. 12. 8, 9, 10. p ch. 12. 7. 2 Cor. 12. 19. Eph. 4. 12.

By what followeth in the two next verses, one would think that some of them, in their church meetings, were so absurd, as, being endued with several gifts, they would be using them all together, one singing, another preaching, a third speaking with tongues, &c.; but this is so apparent a confusion, that one must be very uncharitable to this famous church, to presume that they should be so absurd. Others therefore rather think, that those endued with several gifts, (of which he reckoneth five, under which he comprehendeth all others,) were every one contending for his course to exercise his gift; one, for spending the time in singing the psalm he had made; another, for spending the time in hearing his doctrinal discourse; a third, for the spending it in hearing his discourse in an unknown tongue; a fourth, for the spending it in hearing his revelation; a fifth, for the spending it in hearing his interpretation; or at least desiring the time might be protracted, until they had been all successively heard. *Let all things be done unto edifying:* to prevent this and other disorders, the apostle giveth several rules. The first is, That all things should be so done, as might tend best to promote in men faith and holiness; that is and ought to be the main and chief end of those who any way minister in sacred things.

27 If any man speak in an *unknown* tongue, *let it be* by two, or at the most *by* three, and *that* by course; and let one interpret.

Concerning the use of their gift of tongues, he directeth three things: 1. That every one that had it should not be ambitious to show it at all times, but *two or three at most* at a time. 2. That they should do it *by course,* not together, confusedly. 3. Not without *one to interpret,* that people might understand. For though these were extraordinary gifts, flowing from a more than ordinary influence of the Spirit of God, yet they were abiding habits, not coming upon them at some certain times, by an impulse; for then they would not have been under human government, as it is apparent this gift of tongues was, else Paul could not have so governed himself in the use of it, as he lets us know he did, ver. 19.

28 But if there be no interpreter, let him keep silence in the church; and let him speak to himself, and to God.

If he hath a mind to use this gift, he may use it *to God,* who understands all languages, by *himself;* but *let him keep silence* in the assembly of Christians, where he is not understood.

29 Let the prophets speak two or three, and.�q let the other judge. q ch. 12. 10.

That is, two or three successively, the one beginning to speak when the others have done, and two or three at the same church assembly; and if there be more present, let them sit still and judge of the truth of what he saith.

30 If *any thing* be revealed to another that sitteth by, ʳ let the first hold his peace. r 1 Thess. 5. 19, 20.

There were two modes or sorts of prophecies; the one ordinary, when the teacher came to those assemblies furnished with a revelation from some previous impression of God upon him, enabling him to give the sense of some scripture, or to open some Divine truth; not as we are, but by some influence of the Holy Spirit upon him, without the use of such means as we use. The other was, by some present afflatus or impression. The apostle seems not to speak of the latter; or if of both, he plainly lets them know, that even such a one was under the government of natural order, and obliged to do nothing confusedly and tumultuously, but might, without any offence to God, stay until the other had finished his discourse.

I. CORINTHIANS XIV

31 For ye may all prophesy one by one, that all may learn, and all may be comforted.

Ye may not all prophesy in the same day, or hour, or moment of time, but orderly and successively *ye may all prophesy*, the end of it being for the instruction and consolation of all; which may mind you so to govern yourselves in the exercise of that gift, as not to lose your end, *but that all may learn, and all may be comforted*. Which lets us know, that though their receiving the gift of prophecy obliged them to an exercise of it, yet it did not oblige them to an exercise of it in or at this or that particular time.

a 1 John 4. 1.

32 And *the spirits of the prophets are subject to the prophets.

By *the spirits of the prophets* the apostle either meaneth their spiritual gifts, as to the use and exercise of them, and the actions to be done by them; or, the actions themselves, or interpretations pretendedly done and given by the exercise of those gifts, their doctrines; or, that instinct, or impetus, by which they pretend themselves to be moved to prophesy: these (he saith) *are subject to the prophets* themselves, so as they may themselves govern their gifts, or (which most think is the rather here intended) they are subject to the judgment and censure of others that are endued with the same gift. But here ariseth a difficulty, how the gifts of the Holy Spirit, flowing immediately from the Spirit, should be subject to any human judgment or censure? This indeed they could not, if the Divine revelation to this or that man were full and perfect, and ran as clearly in the stream always, as it was in the fountain. But God giveth his Spirit to us but by measure, and in the exercise of our gifts there is always *aliquid humani*, something of our own; and this maketh them *subject to the prophets*, viz. whether what they pretended to have from the Spirit of God were indeed from it, yea or no? Prophets were obliged to prophesy, Rom. xii. 6, but *according to the* analogy *of faith*: now, whether they did so or no, might be judged by other prophets, according to that rule. Others think this text is to be interpreted restrainedly, viz. as to this thing in this matter of plain, natural order, commanding, while one speaks, all the rest to hold their peace.

† Gr. *tumult*, or, *unquietness*.
t ch. 11. 16.

33 For God is not *the author* of †confusion, but of peace, ᵗas in all churches of the saints.

Here he showeth the principle upon which he said, that *the spirits of the prophets are subject to the prophets*: what any prophets speak is not so certain, or at least not more certain, than this, that nothing which is *confusion* can be from God. Now, for two or three to speak together in a public assembly, is a confusion, and a breach of order, of which God cannot be the author; therefore, in such a thing as that, the spirits of the prophets must be subject to other prophets; and there is a general rule which concerneth not only the church of Corinth, but all churches.

u 1 Tim. 2. 11, 12.

34 ᵘLet your women keep silence in the churches: for it is not permitted unto them to speak; but ˣ*they are commanded* to be under obedience, as also saith the ʸlaw.

x ch. 11. 3. Eph. 5. 22. Col. 3. 18. Tit. 2. 5. 1 Pet. 3. 1.
y Gen. 3. 16.

This rule must be restrained to ordinary prophesyings; for certainly, if the Spirit of prophecy came upon a woman in the church, she might speak. Anna, who was a prophetess, in the temple *gave thanks to the Lord, and spake of him to all them that looked for redemption in Jerusalem*, Luke ii. 38: and I cannot tell how Philip's daughters prophesied, if they did not speak in the presence of many, Acts xxi. 9. The reason that is given why women should *keep silence*, is, because *they are commanded to be under obedience*. This apostle speaketh much the same thing, 1 Tim. ii. 11, 12, because it looked like a usurping authority over the man; which indeed is true, if it had been the ordinary practice of women to speak in the assemblies of the church; but not so, if some particular women sometimes spake upon an extraordinary impulse or impression. The law to which the apostle here refers, is thought to be that, Gen. iii. 16, where the woman is commanded to be subject to her husband, and it is said, that he should rule over her; yet that law did neither restrain Miriam from prophesying, Exod. xv. 20, nor yet Huldah, to whom Josiah himself sent, 2 Chron. xxxiv. 22, of whom it is also said, that *she dwelt in the college*. But setting aside that extraordinary case of a special afflatus, it was, doubtless, unlawful for a woman to speak in the church.

35 And if they will learn any thing, let them ask their husbands at home: for it is a shame for women to speak in the church.

This must be understood of speaking to the congregation, for the instructing them, or speaking in the congregation to the minister, or any of the people, for her own instruction, for the woman might, doubtless, say Amen to the public prayers, and also sing with the congregation to the honour and glory of God. But for her to speak in an ordinary course of prophecy to instruct people, or to call aloud to the minister, or any members in the assembly of the church, to be satisfied in any thing wherein she was in doubt, this she is forbidden.

36 What? came the word of God out from you? or came it unto you only?

These words look like a smart reflection upon divers members of this church of Corinth, who thought themselves wiser than all the world besides; and the apostle might foresee, that out of the high opinion they had of themselves they would much contemn and slight his directions. He therefore asks them, what they thought of themselves? whether they thought themselves the only churches in the world, or were the first that believed in Christ, so that the gospel went out from them, and they might give law to all churches? There were churches at Jerusalem, and in several other places, before there was any church at Corinth, so as the gospel came unto them from other churches, and did not go out from them to other churches.

37 ᶻIf any man think himself to be a prophet, or spiritual, let him acknowledge that the things that I write unto you are the commandments of the Lord.

z 2 Cor. 10. 7
1 John 4. 6.

If there be any amongst you who hath a conceit that he is inspired by God, and from that inspiration understandeth the mind and will of God, he must acknowledge, that I also am an apostle, and know the mind and will of God as well as he; and being so, that what I tell you *are the commandments of the Lord*.

38 But if any man be ignorant, let him be ignorant.

If any one will pretend ignorance in this, he is wilfully ignorant; for my own part, I will concern myself no further about him, but leave him and him also to the judgment of God; *let him be ignorant*. In some copies it is, he shall not be known: in the day of judgment Christ shall say unto him, Depart from me, I know you not.

39 Wherefore, brethren, ᵃcovet to prophesy, and forbid not to speak with tongues.

a ch. 12. 31.
¹ Thes. 5. 20.

The apostle concludeth his discourse, summarily repeating all that he before had said. He had, ver. 2, encouraged their desire of spiritual gifts; all along the chapter he hath been magnifying the gift of prophecy above the gift of tongues, as being of much more general use, and more for the profit of others; but he minds them here, that he did not forbid those to whom God had given the gift of tongues, to make use of it at due times, and in a due manner and order.

40 ᵇLet all things be done decently and in order.

b ver. 33.

He forbade them not to speak with tongues, provided they did it decently and orderly, as all other things ought to be done in so grave an assembly as that of the church, and so grave an action as the worship of God. For women to prophesy in the public assemblies, was an indecent thing; he had said, ver. 35, that it was *a shame*. For many of them to speak together, confusedly, making a noise, that was disorderly. Nor did this decency or indecency, order or disorder, arise from obeying or disobeying the apostolical constitution, but from the law of God, the light of nature, the common usage of all the churches of Christians, as ver. 33. All things ought so to be done, (especially in religious assemblies and actions,) as they may not be judged by the law of God, or the light of nature, or the common custom of other churches, to be done indecently or confusedly, without order. It is very observable, that though the apostle, in these things, hath given rules, yet he hath determined nothing shameful or uncomely, but what he hath made to appear so, either from the Divine law, (as in the case of the women's prophesying, ver. 34,) or from nature and reason, (as in the case of many speaking at the same time,) it being useless to the end, which was teaching and instructing those to whom they spake, and what unbelievers would count the effect of madness, ver. 23.

CHAP. XV

From the truth of Christ's resurrection Paul inferreth the necessity of our own, 1—19. Christ the first-fruits, being raised, shall be followed in due order by those that are his, 20—23; till having subdued all enemies, he shall give up the kingdom to God the Father, 24—28. If there be no resurrection of the dead, in vain is it for any one to risk his life, as the apostle did continually, 29—34. The manner of the resurrection, 35—50. The change which shall be wrought at the last day in the bodies both of the dead and the living, 51—57. An exhortation to stedfast faith and perseverance in our duty, 58.

MOREOVER, brethren, I declare unto you the Gospel [a] which I preached unto you, which also ye have received, and [b] wherein ye stand;

[a] Gal. 1. 11.
[b] Rom. 5. 2.

The apostle, towards the conclusion of his Epistle, comes to reprove the Corinthians for an error in the doctrine of the resurrection from the dead; an error, though last mentioned, yet of all the most momentous. The resurrection of the body in the last day is an article of faith, to the firm belief of which reason speaketh not sufficiently, and therefore it was denied by many philosophers and worldly wise men, Acts xvii. 18. It should seem, that some in the church of Corinth had sucked in some of their notions; the apostle, therefore, in this chapter setteth himself to confirm that article of the Christian faith. To this purpose he begins, telling them, that that which he declared unto them was *the gospel*, that is, that doctrine of the gospel which he had before preached to them, and which they had heard, and believed, and embraced as the truth of God, and wherein the greatest part yet stood firm to their former profession, though some of them had been seduced and warped.

2 [c] By which also ye are saved, if ye ‖ keep in memory † what I preached unto you, unless [d] ye have believed in vain.

[c] Rom. 1. 16. ch. 1. 21.
‖ Or, *hold fast.*
† Gr. *by what speech.*
[d] Gal. 3. 4.

By which also ye are saved; by the believing, receiving, of which doctrine, you are already in the way to salvation (as it is said, John iii. 18, *He that believeth on him is not condemned;* and ver. 36, *He hath everlasting life,* and shall be eternally saved): but not unless ye persevere (for that is meant by keeping *in memory* the doctrine which I have *preached unto you);* and this you must do, or your believing will signify nothing, but be *in vain* to your souls.

3 For [e] I delivered unto you first of all that [f] which I also received, how that Christ died for our sins [g] according to the Scriptures;

[e] ch. 11. 2, 23.
[f] Gal. 1. 12.
[g] Ps. 22. 15, &c. Is. 53. 5, 6, &c. Dan. 9. 26. Zech. 13. 7. Luke 24. 26, 46. Acts 3. 18. & 26. 23. 1 Pet. 1. 11. & 2. 24.

For I, in my preaching, delivered it to you as one of the principal articles of the Christian faith, which I received, either from Christ *by revelation,* (as he saith, Gal. i. 12,) or from Ananias, Acts ix. 17, *how that Christ died for our sins,* Rom. iv. 25, that is, that he might satisfy the Divine justice for our sins, and make an atonement for us. And this is *according to the Scriptures* of the Old Testament, where it was foretold, Isa. liii. 5, *He was wounded for our transgressions, and bruised for our iniquities;* and Dan. ix. 26, that the *Messiah* should *be cut off, but not for himself.*

4 And that he was buried, and that he rose again the third day [h] according to the Scriptures:

[h] Ps. 2. 7. & 16. 10. Is. 53. 10. Hos. 6. 2. Luke 24. 26, 46. Acts 2. 25,—31. & 13. 33, 34, 35. & 26. 22, 23. 1 Pet. 1. 11.

Not the death only, but the burial of Christ, and his resurrection again from the dead, were (though more darkly) revealed in the Scriptures of the Old Testament. Jonah and Isaac were both of them types of this; David prophesied, that God would not leave his *soul in hell,* nor suffer his *Holy One to see corruption,* Psal. xvi. 10; which Peter applieth to Christ, Acts ii. 31: so chap. xiii. 35. So that the doctrine of the New Testament in these things agreeth with the doctrine of the Old; with this only difference, that the Old Testament contained the New Testament in a mystery, and the New Testament was the Old Testament more fully and clearly revealed.

5 [i] And that he was seen of Cephas, then [k] of the twelve:

[i] Luke 24. 34.
[k] Mat. 28. 17. Mark 16. 14. Luke 24. 36. John 20. 19, 26. Acts 10. 41.

We read not in the history of the gospel of Christ's appearing unto Peter, unless he were one of those to whom Christ appeared, as they were going to Emmaus; for which there is this probability, because when they came to Jerusalem, they told the rest, that the Lord was risen, and had appeared unto Simon, Luke xxiv. 34 (if Simon Peter be there meant). His appearance to the whole number of the disciples we have recorded, John xx. 19: they are called *twelve,* (though Judas was now dead, and Thomas at that time was not there,) because twelve was the number that God had appointed the college of apostles to consist of; so, Gen. xlii. 13, the children of Jacob said they were *twelve brethren,* though they thought at that time that Joseph (who made the twelfth) was dead. This is much more probably the sense, than the fancy of some, that Barnabas, who was afterward chosen to supply the room of Judas, being at that time a disciple, might at that time be with them; for admit he were, yet Thomas, we are sure, was at that time absent.

6 After that, he was seen of above five hundred brethren at once; of whom the greater part remain unto this present, but some are fallen asleep.

Of this appearance to *above five hundred brethren at once* the Gospels say nothing; but it is probably thought to be understood of that great meeting of the disciples in Galilee, where our Saviour promised to meet them, Matt. xxvi. 32; xxviii. 7, after his resurrection. Wherever it was, the apostle saith, that the greater part of them were yet in a capacity to give a living testimony to the resurrection of Christ, though some of them were dead.

7 After that, he was seen of James; then [l] of all the apostles.

[l] Luke 24. 50. Acts 1. 3, 4.

The Scripture tells us nothing, in the history of the gospel, of Christ's appearing to *James;* but we read of two appearances to the apostles besides these, which the apostle had before mentioned.

8 [m] And last of all he was seen of me also, as of ‖ one born out of due time.

[m] Acts 9. 4, 17. & 22. 14, 18. ch. 9. 1.
‖ Or, *an abortive.*

Last of all the apostles, or, it may be, last of all persons; for after Stephen we read of none but St. Paul who saw Christ. Stephen, as they were stoning him, cried out, *Behold, I see the heavens opened, and the Son of man standing on the right hand of God,* Acts vii. 56. We read of Paul's hearing a voice from him, Acts ix. 4, and no doubt but he had a bodily sight of him, for he here reckoneth himself amongst those that were eye-witnesses. Nor is it any objection against it, that he was struck blind, for that was after his sight of Christ, not before. He calls himself an abortive, or *one born out of due time,* either because he was added to the number of the twelve; or in respect to his new birth, he being converted (as he tells us afterward) after that he had been a persecutor of the church of Christ, after the descending of the Holy Ghost; or, it may be, because his conversion was sudden, like the abortive birth of a woman.

9 For I am [n] the least of the apostles, that am not meet to be called an apostle, because [o] I persecuted the Church of God.

[n] Eph. 3. 8.
[o] Acts 8. 3. & 9. 1. Gal. 1. 13. Phil. 3. 6. 1 Tim. 1. 13.

I. CORINTHIANS XV

The least, not in dignity, or gifts, or labours; (he tells us, that he had *laboured more than all,* he had made the gospel to abound *from Jerusalem to Illyricum;* he hath in this Epistle let us know, that he spake with tongues more than they all;) but deserving the least esteem, as he afterward expoundeth himself, telling us, that he was not worthy of the name of an apostle. He gives the reason, because he had before been a persecutor of the church of God, the history of which we have, Acts ix. 1—3.

p Eph. 2. 7, 8.   10 But ᵖby the grace of God I am
q 2 Cor. 11. 23. & 12. 11.   what I am: and his grace which *was be-*
r Mat. 10. 20.   *stowed* upon me was not in vain; but ᑫI
Rom. 15. 18, 19. 2 Cor. 3. 5. Gal. 2. 8.   laboured more abundantly than they all:
Eph. 3. 7. Phil. 2. 13.   ʳyet not I, but the grace of God which was with me.

By the grace of God I am what I am; by the free love and goodness of God, I, that was before a blasphemer, and a persecutor, and injurious, have obtained mercy; and though it was impossible for me any more to requite and answer, than at first to merit, that love, yet his grace in me hath produced some fruit, and hath not been wholly in vain; for in the discharge of my ministry, as an apostle, I have abundantly laboured, though not more than all the rest of the apostles taken together, yet more than any one of them all, who were my fellow apostles: what these labours were, he told us, Rom. xv. 19; and more fully, 2 Cor. vi. 4—10. But lest he should be thought to arrogate any thing to himself, and the power or good use of his own will, he addeth, *yet not I, but the grace of God which was with me.* Grace seemeth, in the latter part of the verse, to be taken in something a different sense from what it was in the former part: here it signifies the free love and favour of God; though it may also there be understood of those gracious habits, which were the effects of that free love and mercy; here it plainly signifies those gracious habits which were infused into Paul, together with the gracious influences of the Holy Spirit, by which he was enabled to reduce those habits into acts. Paul had something in the acts he had done considered as a man, but yet so little, as in these spiritual acts he denieth his own efficiency, and attributeth all to Divine grace, either exciting him to his actions, or preventing, or working in and with him, and assisting him, and giving him all that success he had had.

11 Therefore whether *it were* I or they, so we preach, and so ye believed.

Whether it were I or they; whether I or any other of the apostles preached amongst you. *So we preach, and so ye believed:* this was one great point that we preached amongst you, that Christ was risen again from the dead. This we held forth to you as the object of your faith, this you received and closed with as the object of your faith; we did not only preach to you, that Christ died for our sins, but that he rose again for our justification. Neither was your faith objected only in Christ, as one that was crucified and had died, but as one that was risen from the dead. Thus Peter preached, Acts ii. 31; iii. 15; iv. 10; v. 30; and Stephen, Acts vii. 56; and Peter, Acts x. 40; and Paul, Acts xiii. 37; xvii. 3, 31; and so all the apostles.

12 Now if Christ be preached that he rose from the dead, how say some among you that there is no resurrection of the dead?

The apostle having laid a good foundation, proving the resurrection of Christ by a plentiful testimony of those who saw him after that he was risen from the dead; and minded them, that this was the doctrine of the gospel, which both they and all the rest of the apostles had with one consent preached to them; he comes to build upon it, and from this, as a main argument, to prove, that there must needs be a resurrection from the dead; and beginneth with a reflection upon some in that church who denied it. Who those were we are not told: some think they were *Hymeneus and Philetus,* mentioned 2 Tim. ii. 17, 18, who held *that the resurrection was past;* others think he reflects on Cerinthus, who was one of the leaders of those heretics we read of, who after Simon Magus denied the resurrection; others think they were some of the Sadducees, of whom we read in the Acts, that they denied the resurrection, or some of the Pharisees, who denied the resurrection of Christians, looking on them as apostates; others think they were some who had been tinctured, at least, with the doctrine of the pagan philosophers. We cannot certainly determine who, but certain it is some there were; and the apostle argues them in this thing to assert absurdly, upon this supposition, that Christ was risen.

13 But if there be no resurrection of the dead, ˢthen is Christ not risen: s 1 Thess. 4. 14.

If (saith the apostle) *there be no resurrection of the dead, then is Christ not risen.* But some will possibly say, How doth this follow? Suppose it true, that Christ be risen, how doth it follow, that the dead shall rise? The force of it lieth in several things: 1. Christ, as he saith, ver. 20, is *the first-fruits of them that slept,* the exemplary cause of our resurrection. 2. If we consider Christ as the Head, it is unreasonable, that the Head should be risen from the dead, and the members yet held of death, when it is the office of the Head to communicate sense, life, and motion to the members. Again, the argument is strong from the consideration of the end of Christ's resurrection, which was to show his victory over death, that the dead might hear his voice and live, and that he might be the Judge of the quick and the dead (which he could not have been, if the dead did not rise). Now though it be true, that Christ's headship to his church, and the apostle's argument from thence, will not prove the resurrection of the wicked, yet, (besides that the resurrection of believers is the main thing the apostle here proveth, having elsewhere abundantly proved the general resurrection,) the consideration here of Christ's being raised, that he might be the Judge both of the quick and of the dead, will prove the resurrection of the wicked, as well as of believers.

14 And if Christ be not risen, then *is* our preaching vain, and your faith *is* also vain.

Now, (saith the apostle,) if Christ be not raised, in what a case are you! and we also, who have preached his resurrection to you! Our preaching is vain and false, and your faith is so also, for the object of it faileth, which is a Christ risen from the dead.

15 Yea, and we are found false witnesses of God; because ᵗwe have testified of God that he raised up Christ: t Acts 2. 24, 32. & 4. 10, 33. & 13. 30. whom he raised not up, if so be that the dead rise not.

16 For if the dead rise not, then is not Christ raised:

There is nothing in these two verses but what the apostle had before said, viz. That if Christ were not risen, the apostles' preaching and the Corinthians' believing were both of them vain and false. Only what the apostle, in the former verse, called preaching, he here calleth witnessing, *We are* (saith he) *false witnesses of God.* To be false witnesses for men, or in the name of men, is against the ninth commandment, and a sin of no ordinary magnitude; but to be a false witness of God, is a much higher sin. This title of *witnesses* was at first given to the apostles by Christ, Acts i. 8; afterwards often (especially in the Acts) applied to them, Acts i. 22; ii. 32; iv. 33; v. 32; x. 39, 41: particularly Paul applieth it to himself, Acts xxii. 15; xxvi. 16. It is true, the apostles, who either saw Christ while he was on earth after his resurrection, or in heaven, as Paul did, Acts ix., were in the strictest sense eye-witnesses; but yet in a larger sense this notion agreeth to all ministers, who testify, upon the hearing of the ears, and upon reading the Scriptures, the same thing which the apostles testified, though not upon the same evidence. Now to affirm a thing, as from God, for truth, which is in itself false, is a very high transgression; which (saith the apostle) we must be guilty of, if Christ be not raised; and *if the dead rise not, then is not Christ raised.*

17 And if Christ be not raised, your faith *is* vain; ᵘye are yet in your sins.   u Rom. 4. 25.

That is, ye are yet in your estate of nature, under the guilt and condemning power of your sins, which are not yet pardoned to you; for no sins are remitted, but upon believing in the Lord Jesus Christ, which none can do, if Christ be not risen from the dead; for by that he was *declared to be the Son of God with power.* Rom. i. 4: his death declared him to be truly man, it was his resurrection that manifested him to be truly God, God over all blessed for ever, and so the proper object of people's faith.

18 Then they also which are fallen asleep in Christ are perished.

Some think that the term *in Christ* in this text, is of the same significancy with for the sake of Christ, which would restrain it to martyrs; but I know no reason for that, because what is said is true of all; for it is plain, from what was said before, that if Christ be not risen from the dead, all that die must die in their sins, there being no object for their faith to work or lay hold upon; the door of salvation remaineth as fast shut as ever, so as those whom they looked upon as being asleep in Christ, must necessarily perish, if Christ be not risen; there is no forerunner entered into the heavens for us.

t 2 Tim. 3. 12.   **19 ᵗIf in this life only we have hope in Christ, we are of all men most miserable.**

The apostle here argueth the resurrection of believers from a new head. It is not reasonable for any to imagine, that those who believe in Jesus Christ should of all others be the most miserable; but this they must be, if there be no resurrection from the dead. He enlargeth upon this head or argument further, ver. 30, 31. The reason of it is, because it must then follow, that they could have no hope in Christ beyond this life; and the condition of the apostles, and the generality of Christians, at least in those first and furious times, was a most afflicted state and condition. The apostle was *in jeopardy every hour,* ver. 30, he died daily, ver. 31. If any say, How doth this follow? for their souls might be in glory, though their bodies, once dead, were not raised? It is answered, 1. That it still must hold as to their bodily, fleshy part. 2. That those who denied the resurrection of the body, denied also the immortality of the soul. 3. That Paul speaketh upon the supposition of the Divine ordination; God having so ordered it, that the death of Christ, without his resurrection, should be of no avail to us to save either soul or body; and that our souls and bodies should not be separately, but jointly, glorified upon their re-union in the end of the world: 1 Pet. i. 3, we are said to be *begotten to a lively hope by the resurrection of Jesus Christ from the dead.*

y 1 Pet. 1. 3.   **20 But now ʸis Christ risen from the**
z Acts 26. 23.   **dead, *and* become ᶻthe firstfruits of them**
ver. 23. Col. 1.
18. Rev. 1. 5.   **that slept.**

The apostle returneth to his former argument, to discourse concerning the resurrection of Christ, who is by him called the *first-fruits of them that slept;* not of all that shall rise, (as some think,) for it will be hard to prove, that any benefit of Christ's death or resurrection, after this life, belongs to wicked men: nor is it usual for the penmen of holy writ to express the death of unbelievers under the gentle notion of a sleep; and, Col. i. 18, Christ is called *the first-born from the dead,* as he is *the Head of the church.* It is rather spoken with reference to believers; the resurrection of wicked men, flowing rather from God's providence, in order to the manifestation of his justice in the last judgment, than from the mediation of Christ. But here a question ariseth, How Christ is said to be the first-fruits of those that sleep, whenas we read of divers in Scripture that were raised from the dead before Christ was so raised? *Answ.* 1. Christ was the first that rose again by his own power and virtue. 2. He was the first who rose again, and died no more. 3. He was the first in respect of dignity. 4. He was the first-fruits of them that sleep, by his resurrection making a way for the resurrection of others, even of all such as were members of him; as the offering of the first-fruits, under the law, sanctified the whole crop.

a Rom. 5. 12,   **21 For ᵃsince by man *came* death, ᵇby**
17.
b John 11. 25.   **man *came* also the resurrection of the**
Rom. 6. 23.   **dead.**

Since by one man, viz. Adam, (who is also styled *the son of God,* Luke iii. 38, because he had neither father nor mother,) came man's subjection to mortality, sicknesses, and death here, and eternal death and misery in another world; it pleased God that by one, who though he was the eternal, only begotten Son of God, yet was also made man, and was flesh of our flesh, the resurrection of those that are believers, and asleep in Christ, should come, Heb. ii. 14.

22 For as in Adam all die, even so in Christ shall all be made alive.

As in the first Adam all men, that were in him, became subject both to temporal death, and all the afflictions and miseries of this life, which are so many little deaths, Rom. viii. 36, and forerunners of natural death, or attendants upon it; and also to that eternal death, which is the consequent of the guilt of sin, Rom. vi. 23: so in Christ, that is, through the merits of his death, and through his resurrection, all that are in him, being chosen in him, given to him, and by faith implanted into him, are not only spiritually made alive, (being *passed from death unto life,* 1 John iii. 14,) but shall be raised from the dead unto eternal life. But though this text doth not prove the general resurrection, (being only intended of believers, that are members of Christ,) yet it doth not oppose it. But that the *all* here mentioned is no more than all believers, appeareth not only from the term *in Christ* in this verse, but from the whole following discourse; which is only concerning the resurrection of believers to life, not that of the wicked to eternal condemnation.

23 But ᶜevery man in his own order: c ver. 20.
                                                  1 Thess. 4.
Christ the firstfruits; afterward they that 15, 16, 17.
are Christ's at his coming.

In his own order, either with respect to time, or dignity, lest any should say, If Christ's resurrection be the cause of the resurrection of believers, then why did not all the saints, that were in the graves, rise with Christ? The apostle saith, God had appointed an order, and this order was, that they that were dead, or should be dead, before Christ's second coming, should not prevent one another, 1 Thess. iv. 15, &c. Besides, the order which God had set was, That Christ should be *the first-fruits* of this harvest, rising first from the dead, so as to die no more. *Afterward they that are Christ's at his coming;* then believers, that are members of Christ, by faith implanted into him, should also rise, but not before his second coming.

24 Then *cometh* the end, when he shall have delivered up ᵈthe kingdom to d Dan. 7. 14,
God, even the Father; when he shall 27.
have put down all rule and all authority and power.

Then cometh the end; the end of all the miseries and afflictions which believers meet with in this life, or the end of all our preaching and ministry, the end of the world, or the end of man; or rather, (as the next words seem to interpret it,) the end of that mediatory kingdom of Christ, which he now administereth instead of his Father, and shall manage to the end of the world. *When he shall have delivered up the kingdom to God, even the Father:* Christ shall then deliver up those keys of life, and hell, and death to his Father, yet shall not Christ's kingdom cease (for the prophet saith, Isa. ix. 7, that of it *there shall be no end):* Christ's essential kingdom, which is his dominion, which he hath and exerciseth over all created beings, together with his Father, and the Holy Spirit, (all being but one Divine essence,) that shall hold and abide for ever; but his mediatory kingdom, by which he ruleth over his church in the midst of his enemies, that shall cease, and be delivered up unto the Father. So that Christ's delivering up the kingdom to his Father, proveth no inferiority of Christ to his Father, more than his Father's committing that mediatory kingdom to him can prove his Father's not reigning, or inferiority to him, which it certainly doth not. It signifieth only the ceasing of that dispensation, or Christ's exercise of his mediatory kingdom on earth, in the rule and government of the church, and subduing his and his people's enemies. *When he shall have put down all rule and all authority and power;* then shall all rule and authority of kings and princes of the earth cease, and all the ministration of good angels, and power of evil angels; so shall all ministrations and governments in the church militant here on earth, and all those that are the enemies of the church shall be subdued and brought under.

I. CORINTHIANS XV

^{e Ps. 110. 1.
Acts 2. 34.
35. Eph. 1.
22. Heb. 1.
13. & 10. 13.}

25 For he must reign, ^e till he hath put all enemies under his feet.

God hath so decreed, (and what he hath said must come to pass,) that Christ should, as Mediator, exercise a kingdom and government in the world, until he hath subdued all the enemies of his gospel and people; all those who have said, he shall not rule over them; the whole world that lieth in wickedness, the devil, and all his instruments: this he proveth from the words of the psalmist, Psal. cx. 1. The term *until* doth not signify the determination of Christ's kingdom then, though his mediatory kingdom on earth will then be determined. He shall still reign, but not as now, in the midst of his enemies, and in the exercise of his kingdom in the conquest and subduing of them.

^{f 2 Tim.1.10.
Rev. 20. 14.}

26 ^f The last enemy *that* shall be destroyed *is* death.

If death be an enemy, (as we usually judge,) that also must be destroyed; and there is no other way to destroy death, but by the causing of a resurrection from the dead. So that the apostle proveth the resurrection from the necessity of Christ's reigning until all his enemies be destroyed, of which death is one; for it keeps the bodies of the members of Christ from their union with their souls, and with Christ, who is the Head of the whole believer, the body as well as the soul.

^{g Ps. 8. 6.
Matt. 28. 18.
Heb. 2. 8.
1 Pet. 3. 22.}

27 For he ^g hath put all things under his feet. But when he saith, All things are put under *him, it is* manifest that he is excepted, which did put all things under him.

The apostle referreth to Psal. viii. 6, where the psalmist adoreth God for the privileges given man in his creation; amongst which this is one, that God had *put all things under his feet*: the psalmist afterward expounds that universal particle, ver. 7, 8, by *all sheep and oxen, yea, and the beasts of the field, the fowls of the air, and the fish of the sea.* But that that psalm, or some passages at least in it, are to be understood of Christ, appeareth from Heb. ii. 6—8, where the penman applieth it to him, as doth the apostle here; under whose feet all things are put in a much larger sense, and therefore the apostle expounds the affirmative, Heb. ii. 8, by a negative, *he left nothing that is not put under him.* But lest men of perverse minds should conclude, that then the Father also is put under Christ, the apostle addeth, that when he saith, he hath put all things under his feet, the Father himself, who is the person that put all things under him, is not to be included.

^{h Phil. 3. 21.
i ch. 3. 23.
& 11. 3.}

28 ^h And when all things shall be subdued unto him, then ⁱ shall the Son also himself be subject unto him that put all things under him, that God may be all in all.

The Son's subjection to his Father, which is mentioned in this place, doth no where prove his inequality of essence or power with his Father; it only signifieth what was spoken before, that Christ should deliver up his mediatory kingdom to his Father; so manifesting, that whatsoever he had done in the office of Mediator, was done in the name of his Father, and by his power and authority; and that as he was man, he was subject to his Father. Suppose (saith Pareus) a king should have one only son, whom he should take into a partnership with him in his majesty and kingdom; but yet so, that the king should still have the pre-eminence of a father, the son only the dignity of a son in such power and authority: after which this king, having some subjects risen up in rebellion against him, should send his son with armies and his authority against them; he should despatch the work, and at his return yield up his commission to his father, yet still retaining the same nature he had, and authority with which his Father had before clothed him, as a partner in the kingdom and government with him. *That God* (saith the apostle) *may be all in all;* instead of all things which the heart of man can wish; or that God may exercise a full and perfect empire and government over all things; that the incomprehensible glory of God may fill all the elect. But is not God in this world all in all? *Answ.* He is; but he doth not so appear ruling in the midst of his enemies here. 2. The government will be altered; God here is sole King of the world, but he partly ruleth it by Christ, as Mediator, whose mediatory kingdom shall then cease, and nothing shall appear but the essential kingdom of God; the power by which the Father, the Son, and the Holy Ghost (three persons, though but one God) shall govern and rule all things, when all this sublunary world shall cease.

29 Else what shall they do which are baptized for the dead, if the dead rise not at all? why are they then baptized for the dead?

A very difficult text, and variously expounded. The terms baptize, and baptism, signify no more in their original and native signification, than to wash, and a washing: the *washing of pots and cups,* in use amongst the Jews, is, in the Greek, the baptisms of pots and cups. But the most usual acceptation of baptism in Scripture, is to signify one of the sacraments of the New Testament; that sacred action, by which one is washed according to the institution of Christ, *in the name of the Father, the Son, and the Holy Ghost.* It is also metaphorically used by our Saviour in the Gospels, Matt. xx. 22, 23; Mark x. 38, 39; Luke xii. 50, to signify a suffering for the name of Christ. And it is also used thus metaphorically, to signify the action of the Holy Ghost in cleansing and renewing our hearts, Matt. iii. 11, 12; John iii. 5. The last usage of the term is by no means applicable here. The question is, Whether the apostle meaneth here only, Why are men washed for the dead? or why are men baptized religiously for the dead? or why are men baptized with blood for the dead? For the popish notion, that baptism here signifies any religious actions, as fastings, and prayers, and penances for those that are in purgatory, there is no such usage of the term in Scripture; for though in Scripture it signifies sometimes sufferings from the hands of others, as in Matt. xx. 22, 23; Mark x. 38, 39, yet it no where signifies penances, or such sufferings as men impose upon themselves for the dead. Nor doth Paul here say, To what purpose do men baptize themselves? but *why are they baptized for the dead?* 1. Those that think the term here signifies washing, *what shall they do who are* washed *for the dead?* tell us, that it being a custom in many countries, for neatness and cleanliness, to wash dead bodies, the primitive Christians used that ceremony as a religious rite, and a testification of their belief of the resurrection. That such a custom was in use amongst Christians, is plain from Acts ix. 37: but that they used it as religious rite, or a testimony of their faith in the resurrection, appeareth not. And though it be ὑπὲρ τῶν νεκρῶν, yet they say ὑπὲρ is so used, Rom. xv. 8, *for the truth of God,* expounded by the next word, *to confirm the promises.* 2. Those that think, that by baptizing, in this text, the sacrament of baptism is to be understood, give us more than one account. Some say, that whereas they were wont in the primitive church, before they admitted persons into a full communion with the church, to keep them for some time under catechism, in which time they were called *catechumeni;* if such fell sick, and in danger of death, they baptized them; or if they died suddenly, they baptized some other for them, in testimony of their hope of the joyful resurrection of such a person to eternal life. Now admit this were an error of practice in them, as to this ordinance; yet if any such thing were in practice in this church, the argument of the apostle was good against them. But how shall any such thing be made appear to us, that there was such an early corruption in this church? Others say, that some, believing the resurrection, would upon their death-beds be baptized, in testimony of it, from whence they had the name of *clinici*. Others say, To be *baptized for the dead,* signifieth to be baptized when they were dying, and so as good as dead. Mr. Calvin chooseth this sense: but the question is, Whether the Greek phrase ὑπὲρ τῶν νεκρῶν will bear it? Others tell us of a custom in use in the primitive church, to baptize persons over the graves of the martyrs, as a testimony of their belief of the resurrection. That there was anciently such a custom, I doubt not; and I believe that the custom with us in reading of prayers over dead bodies at the grave, doth much more probably derive from this ancient usage, than the papists' praying for the dead; but that there was any such custom so ancient as the apostles' times, I very much doubt. There are yet two other senses given of this difficult phrase, either of which seemeth to me much more probable than any of these. To the first we are led by the next verse, *And why stand we in jeopardy every hour?* which inclineth many good interpreters to think, that the baptism here mentioned, is that baptism with blood mentioned by our Saviour, Matt. xx. 22, 23; and so the sense is no more than, if there be no resurrection of the dead, why do we die daily? why are we killed all the day long? for we do that in hope of a blessed resurrection. The only objections against this are, 1. That none but Christ himself useth the word in this sense (which seemeth a light exception). 2. That ὑπὲρ τῶν νεκρῶν is hardly capable of that sense; but yet our learned Dr. Lightfoot brings parallels of such a usage of the preposition out of the LXX. Others observe, that the apostle, in this whole chapter, is discoursing of the resurrection of believers unto life, and they are such dead alone, that he here speaketh of, for whom he saith any were baptized. Now, it is plain from Scripture, that baptism is a seal of the resurrection, signifying to believers, that they shall be made partakers of the death and resurrection of Christ (the resurrection being strongly proved from God's covenant, of which baptism is a seal, Luke xx. 37, 38); and being so, it confirmed the covenant, not only to the persons baptized, but to the whole church, as well the triumphant as the militant part of it; as well with reference to those of it that were dead, as those that were living. So that so often as baptism was administered in the church, so often God repeated the covenant made to his whole church, that he was the God of believers and of their seed: so that all who to this day are baptized, are baptized for the dead, that is, for the confirmation of God's covenant to his whole church, as well that part of it which is dead, as that part which is yet alive; and it testifieth, that those that sleep in Christ (although dead) yet live in the promise of the resurrection, because God is their God, and he is not the *God of the dead, but of the living*, as our Saviour speaketh in Luke xx. 38. In this variety amongst learned men about the true sense of this place, I shall leave the reader to his own judgment, although to me the two last seem to be most probable.

k 2 Cor. 11. 26. Gal. 5.11.

30 And ^kwhy stand we in jeopardy every hour?

We are the veriest fools in nature, if there be no resurrection of believers unto life; for it is in the firm belief and hopes of that, that we are in danger of our lives, and all that we have, every hour of our lives.

‖ Some read, our.
l 1 Thess. 2. 19.
m Rom. 8. 36. ch. 4. 9. 2 Cor. 4. 10, 11. & 11. 23.

31 I protest by ‖ ^lyour rejoicing which I have in Christ Jesus our Lord, ^mI die daily.

What is meant here by *your rejoicing which I have*, is something doubted; some understanding it of the apostle's rejoicing in them as believers, whom he had been an instrument to convert, and bring home to Christ; others, of their rejoicing in him (which seems not probable, many of them so much despising and vilifying him) : others understand it of their glorying against him, and triumphing over him, and that this was one of his sufferings which he instanceth in, which he underwent in hope of a resurrection. The words are not an oath, (for here God is not called to witness,) they are only an attestation. As the prophets sometimes call heaven and earth to witness, so here he calls their *rejoicing* to witness; and this rejoicing seems to be the joy of those who amongst them truly rejoiced in Jesus Christ, for which also he rejoiced daily, they being the seal of his apostleship. That which he solemnly affirms, is, that he died daily; not only was ready to die daily, but in the same sense that he elsewhere saith, he was in *deaths often*, and that they were *killed all the day long*; suffering such afflictions as were near akin to death, and led on to death, as their end.

‖ Or, to speak *after the manner of men*.
n 2 Cor. 1. 8. o Is. 22. 13. & 56. 12. Eccles. 2. 24. Wisd. 2. 6. Luke 12. 19.

32 If ‖after the manner of men ⁿI have fought with beasts at Ephesus, what advantageth it me, if the dead rise not? ^olet us eat and drink; for to morrow we die.

Concerning this fight of the apostle with *beasts at Ephesus*, there are two opinions; some thinking that he indeed fought with beasts, and we know that in those countries such a punishment was in use, to bring out malefactors to fight with wild beasts; but as we read in the Acts of no such dealings with Paul, so that being a punishment rather for their slaves and vilest men, it can hardly be thought that Paul, who was a free-man of Rome, should be exposed to it. They seem therefore better to understand it, who interpret it of his conflict with men, who in their conditions and manners were like beasts; and that he doth not speak here of his scuffle with Demetrius, mentioned Acts xix., but some other conflict he had there, of which the Scripture giveth us no large account, but it seems to be generally and obscurely mentioned in the next Epistle, chap. i. 8, for this Epistle was wrote after his contest with Demetrius. By that phrase, *after the manner of men*, some think he means, as men use to fight; some have other notions of it: the sense seems to be plainly this, If I have fought with beastly men at Ephesus after the manner that men fight with beasts, exposing my body to their rage and fury, what profit is it to me, if the dead rise not? I have opposed myself to their fury out of a hope for a joyful resurrection; but if there shall be no such resurrection, the epicures, that resolve to stick at nothing, nor to deny themselves in any sensual satisfaction from meat and drink, have the best of it; all men had then best sing their song, *Let us eat and drink*, for we have but a little time to eat and to drink in; we know that we shall die, and there will be an end of us.

33 Be not deceived: ^pevil communi- p ch. 5. 6.
cations corrupt good manners.

Do not suffer yourselves to be abused with evil and corrupt discourses of those philosophers amongst whom you converse, who argue from innate principles of reason against articles of faith; though you may judge that they talk but for discourse sake, yet their communication or discourse is naught, and will influence men as to things of practice, and debauch men in their morals. It is a verse or saying taken out of, or at least found in, one of the pagan poets; but containing in it much truth.

34 ^qAwake to righteousness, and sin q Rom.13.11.
not; ^rfor some have not the knowledge Eph. 5. 14.
of God: ^sI speak *this* to your shame.   r 1 Thes.4.5.
                                              s ch. 6. 5.

Awake to righteousness, and sin not: sin is in Scripture compared to sleep, Rom. xiii. 11; Eph. v. 14, and that very properly; for as the natural senses are bound up in natural sleep, so the sinner's spiritual senses are locked up, so that he doth not exercise them to discern betwixt good and evil; and as he that is asleep is void of all care and fear, is secure, so the sinner is secure and void of fear. And repentance is set out under the notion of awaking; we are not only concerned to eschew evil, but to do good; not only to awake from sin, but to *righteousness*, that is, to a holy life and conversation, that is it which is here called *righteousness*, all spiritual rectitude being to be judged from the soul's conformity to the Divine rule; hence sin is called a crooked way, because it will not agree with the rule of God's word. *For some have not the knowledge of God*; for some amongst you have not a due and saving knowledge of God, or a right apprehension of the things of God; *I speak this to your shame*; though it be a shame for them that have it not, considering the light and means of knowledge which you have had by my ministry, and the ministry of others who have been amongst you.

35 But some *man* will say, ^tHow are t Ezek. 37. 3.
the dead raised up? and with what body
do they come?

Some of your vain philosophers, who are resolved to give credit to nothing upon the account of a bare Divine revelation, unless they can give a further rational account of it in the circumstances, will be ready to object and say, How is it possible, that those very bodies which are putrefied, and turned into dust, and that dust, it may be, scattered to the four winds, should be raised up? And if the same bodies shall not again rise, what kind of bodies shall the believers have in the resurrection? Shall they be bodies that will need meat, and drink, and clothes, as our present bodies do? or what other bodies shall they be?

I. CORINTHIANS XV

u John 12. 21.

36 *Thou* fool, ^u that which thou sowest is not quickened, except it die:
He saith not, *Thou fool*, in anger, (which is that using of this term which our Saviour saith, Matt. v. 22, brings a man under the danger of hell fire,) but in the way of a grave and authoritative reproof, calling them fools for their want of a due understanding of the things and ways of God. He lets them know, that they might as well ask, how the grain of wheat, which they ordinarily sowed in their field, did rise again; for that grain also rotteth under the clods of the earth, under which it is buried, before it again riseth.

37 And that which thou sowest, thou sowest not that body that shall be, but bare grain, it may chance of wheat, or of some other *grain*:
And when it again riseth, or shooteth up, it is not bare grain, without either stalk or ear, which was the body by them sown.

38 But God giveth it a body as it hath pleased him, and to every seed his own body.
But God giveth to every grain, or kind of seed, such a kind of body as it pleaseth him, and a several body, according to the nature of the grain; yet none will deny, but it is the seed sown which cometh up, though with a different body, in respect of some qualities.

39 All flesh *is* not the same flesh: but *there is* one *kind of* flesh of men, another flesh of beasts, another of fishes, *and* another of birds.
Flesh is a kind of body, but it is of various degrees of dignity and excellency, in respect of the qualities of it: the flesh of men is of a differing excellency from the flesh of beasts; and there is a difference in natural qualities betwixt the corporeal substances of beasts, and of fishes, and birds; yet they are all bodies, they are all flesh; our distinction betwixt flesh and fish, is but according to our idiom or propriety of speaking; we read of the flesh of fish, Lev. xi. 10, 11.

40 *There are* also celestial bodies, and bodies terrestrial: but the glory of the celestial *is* one, and the *glory* of the terrestrial *is* another.
There are also celestial bodies; such are the sun, the moon, and the stars. *And bodies terrestrial;* men, beasts, birds, fishes, the elements, stones, &c. *But the glory of the celestial is one, and the glory of the terrestrial is another;* now betwixt these two species of bodies, in respect of qualities, there is a very great difference; the glory of the heavenly bodies is much greater than the glory of the earthy bodies that are compounded of the elements.

41 *There is* one glory of the sun, and another glory of the moon, and another glory of the stars: for *one* star differeth from *another* star in glory.
Amongst the celestial bodies there is a great deal of difference with respect to the qualities; one of them is in glory much differing from another, the glory of the moon is not like the glory of the sun, and the glory of a star is much beneath the glory both of the sun and of the moon; yea, one star is more glorious than another: yet they are all bodies, though of different species and qualities.

x Dan. 12. 3. Matt. 13. 43.

42 ^x So also *is* the resurrection of the dead. It is sown in corruption; it is raised in incorruption:
So also is the resurrection of the dead; that is, so shall it be, as to the bodies of the saints, in the resurrection. The same bodies of the saints shall rise, though with qualities, and in a condition, much different from what they were when they fell; as the same grain of wheat shooteth up, though with another body: and as there is a difference betwixt celestial and terrestrial bodies, and betwixt celestial bodies themselves; so there will be a difference betwixt the bodies of the saints, now that they are only of the earth, earthy, from what they shall be in the resurrection; which difference he openeth in several particulars. *It is sown in corruption, it is raised in incorruption: it is sown,* that is, it dieth and is buried in such a state, that it is subject to putrefaction; but when it shall be again raised from the dead, it shall be subject to no putrefaction or corruption; so ver. 52, *The dead shall be raised incorruptible.*

y Phil. 3. 21.

43 ^y It is sown in dishonour; it is raised in glory: it is sown in weakness; it is raised in power:
It is sown in dishonour; it is raised in glory: there is nothing more uncomely, unlovely, and loathsome than a dead body; but it will not be so when it shall be raised again, then it shall be a beautiful, comely body. We shall rise in a full and perfect age, (as is generally thought,) and without those defects and deformities which may here make our bodies appear unlovely. Daniel says, chap. xii. 3, the righteous *shall shine as the stars*: Christ saith, Matt. xiii. 43, they shall *shine like the sun*: the apostle saith, Phil. iii. 21, we shall be made *like unto his glorious body.* Three things make the body beautiful, a perfection of parts, the well putting them together and proportioning them one to another, and a well-tempered, cheerly spirit; all these will concur in the bodies of saints in the resurrection. The schoolmen determine, that much of the beauty of the saints' bodies in the resurrection, will flow from their perfect sight of God, and the reflection of God upon them. *It is sown in weakness; it is raised in power:* when it dieth it is a frail, weak body, unable to resist injuries; but it shall rise a strong body, with quick senses, and subject to no more weaknesses.

44 It is sown a natural body; it is raised a spiritual body. There is a natural body, and there is a spiritual body.
It is sown a natural body; such a body as all living creatures have by nature, which is upheld by the actions of the soul that quickeneth it; both the vegetative powers, by which it is nourished by the use of meat and drink, the eating, concocting, and digesting it, &c.; and the sensitive powers, &c. But it shall be *raised a spiritual body;* spiritual, not as to the substance of it, (for in that sense a spiritual body is a contradiction,) but in respect of the qualities and conditions of it, Matt. xxii. 30; Luke xx. 35, 36. Bodies which, in respect of many new qualities they shall have, shall be more like angels and other spirits, than human bodies; beautiful, incorruptible, free from infirmities, not subject to hunger, or thirst, or injuries from cold or heat, &c.; not using meat, drink, clothes, physic, or marriage; free, active, and nimble as spirits, 1 Thess. iv. 17. *Spiritual*, because they shall perfectly obey the soul made perfect, and be by it commanded to spiritual actions only; of subtile, spiritual, refined constitutions.

z Gen. 2. 7. a Rom. 5. 14. b John 5. 21. & 6. 33, 39, 40, 54, 57. Phil. 3. 21. Col. 3. 4.

45 And so it is written, The first man Adam ^z was made a living soul; ^a the last Adam *was made* ^b a quickening spirit.
The first part is written in Gen. ii. 7, God *breathed into* man's *nostrils the breath of life, and* so he *became a living soul;* that is, a living substance, living an animal, natural life, by virtue of that breath of life which God breathed into him. *The last Adam,* by which he meaneth Christ, who in time was after the first Adam, and was born in the last days, and was the last common Head; as Adam was the first, with respect of natural and carnal propagation, so Christ was the last Head, in respect of grace and spiritual regeneration, he *was made a quickening spirit:* he was *made* so, not when he was conceived and born, for he had a body subject to the same natural infirmities that ours are; but upon his resurrection from the dead, when, though he had the same body, in respect of the substance of it, yet it differed in qualities, and was much more spiritual; with which body he ascended up into heaven, clothed with a power, as to quicken souls with a spiritual life, so also to quicken our mortal bodies at his second coming, when he shall raise the dead out of their graves.

46 Howbeit that *was* not first which is spiritual, but that which is natural; and afterward that which is spiritual.
Christ, the spiritual Adam, was not first in order of time, but the natural Adam, God in his providence rising from more imperfect to more perfect dispensations: and so it is as to God's providences relating unto us; we have first natural bodies, we are born with such, we grow up and

die with such, but then we shall rise again with others, in respect of more excellent qualities and endowments.

^c John 3. 31.
^d Gen. 2. 7. & 3. 19.
^e John 3. 13, 31.

47 ^c The first man *is* of the earth, ^d earthy: the second man *is* the Lord ^e from heaven.

Adam, who was the first man, was of the earth, Gen. ii. 7, and was of an earthy constitution, like unto the earth out of which he was formed; but Christ had another original: for though his body was formed in the womb of the virgin, and he was flesh of her flesh, yet she conceived by the Holy Ghost overshadowing her, and Christ had an eternal generation (as to his Divine nature) from his Father.

48 As *is* the earthy, such *are* they also ^f Phil. 3. 20, 21. that are earthy: ^f and as *is* the heavenly, such *are* they also that are heavenly.

Such a body as Adam had, (which was earthy,) such all the sons of Adam have; and such a body as Christ now hath since his resurrection, (which is a heavenly body,) such a body also shall believers, who are heavenly, have in the resurrection.

^g Gen. 5. 3.
^h Rom. 8.29.
2 Cor. 3. 18, & 4. 11.
Phil. 3. 21.
1 John 3. 2.

49 And ^g as we have borne the image of the earthy, ^h we shall also bear the image of the heavenly.

And as believers, being the natural sons of the first Adam, have borne his image, had such bodies as he had while they lived here; so they shall also in the resurrection bear the image of the heavenly, the image of Christ; that is, have such bodies as was Christ's body after that he was again risen from the dead.

ⁱ Mat. 16.17.
John 3. 3, 5.

50 Now this I say, brethren, that ⁱ flesh and blood cannot inherit the kingdom of God; neither doth corruption inherit incorruption.

Flesh and blood do not here signify sin, the unrenewed nature, (as some would have it,) but our bodies, in their present natural, corruptible, frail, mortal state; so the terms signify, Eph. vi. 12; Heb. ii. 14. Flesh and blood shall inherit the kingdom of God, (else our bodies could not be glorified,) but our body, as in its present state, till changed and altered as to qualities, till it be made a spiritual body, shall not inherit the kingdom of God. The latter words give a reason why *flesh and blood cannot inherit the kingdom of God*; because it is *corruption*, that is, subject to natural corruption and putrefaction, and the heavenly state of *incorruption*; the bodies of believers therefore must be raised up in that state of incorruption mentioned ver. 42, before they can be capable of inheriting the kingdom of God.

51 Behold, I shew you a mystery;
^k 1 Thess. 4. 15, 16, 17.
1 Phil. 3. 21.

^k We shall not all sleep, ^l but we shall all be changed,

They might object, How can this be? there will be many saints alive in the world at the day when Christ shall come to judge the world, they will have natural bodies, such as they were born with, and grew up with in the world until that time. Saith the apostle, I now tell you a secret thing; for so the term *mystery* signifieth, Rom. xi. 25; xvi. 25, and in many other texts. *We shall not all sleep* any long sleep: some think all shall die, but some for a very short time, and then they shall revive. *But we shall all be changed*, either dying for time, or by some other work of God, their natural, corruptible bodies shall be turned into spiritual bodies, not capable of corruption.

52 In a moment, in the twinkling of
^m Zech.9.14.
Mat. 24. 31.
John 5. 25.
1 Thes. 4. 16.

an eye, at the last trump: ^m for the trumpet shall sound, and the dead shall be raised incorruptible, and we shall be changed.

This change will be on the sudden, *in a moment;* either upon the will and command of Christ, which shall be as effectual to call persons out of their graves, as a trumpet is to call persons together; or rather, upon a sound made like to the sound of a trumpet, as it was at the giving of the law upon Sinai, Exod. xix. 16. We read of this last trump, Matt. xxiv. 31; 1 Thess. iv. 16. There shall (saith the apostle) be such a sound made; and upon the making of it, the saints, that are dead, shall be raised out of their graves; not with such bodies as they carried thither, (which were corruptible,) but with such bodies as shall be no more subject to corruption; and those who at that time shall be alive, shall one way or another be *changed*, and be also put into an incorruptible state.

53 For this corruptible must put on incorruption, and ⁿ this mortal *must* put on immortality.
ⁿ 2 Cor. 5. 4.

God hath so decreed, that our flesh and blood, in the state wherein now it is, shall not be glorified; it shall be the same body as to the substance, but not as to the qualities; it is now *corruptible* and *mortal*, it must be put into a state of *incorruption* and *immortality*, before it can enter into the kingdom of heaven.

54 So when this corruptible shall have put on incorruption, and this mortal shall have put on immortality, then shall be brought to pass the saying that is written, ^o Death is swallowed up in victory.
^o Is. 25. 8.
Heb. 2. 14.
15. Rev. 20. 14.

That is, in an eternal and continuing victory; the saints shall die no more. The quotation which the apostle bringeth, is out of those two texts, Isa. xxv. 8; Hos. xiii. 14; which two texts, the apostle saith, at that day will have a more full, perfect, and eminent accomplishment, than ever they before had.

55 ^p O death, where *is* thy sting? O ‖ grave, where *is* thy victory?
^p Hos. 13.14.
‖ Or, *hell*.

The apostle, in the contemplation of this blessed day, triumpheth over death, in a metaphorical phrase, *Where is thy sting?* what hurt canst thou now do unto believers, more than a wasp, or hornet, or bee, that hath lost its sting? *O grave*, or O hell, (the same word signifieth both,) *where now is thy victory?* The conqueror of all flesh is now conquered, the spoiler of all men is spoiled; it had got a victory, but now, O death, where is thy victory?

56 The sting of death *is* sin; and ^q the strength of sin *is* the law.
^q Rom.4.15. & 5. 13. & 7. 5, 13.

The sting of death is sin; if it were not for sin, death could have no power over man; sin is that which giveth death a power to hurt the children of men: *The wages of sin is death*, Rom. vi. 23. *And the strength of sin is the law;* and without the law there could be no transgression. The law is so far from taking away the guilt of sin, that, through the corruption of our natures, strongly inclining us to what is forbidden, it addeth strength to sin; *sin* (as the apostle saith, Rom. vii. 8) *taking occasion by the commandment*, and working in us *all manner of concupiscence*.

57 ^r But thanks *be* to God, which giveth us ^s the victory through our Lord Jesus Christ.
^r Rom. 7.25.
^s 1 John 5.4, 5.

The victory over sin and over death, we have both through the death and the resurrection of our Lord Jesus Christ; who by his death both delivered us from the guilt of sin, and also from the power of sin; and who through death destroyed him who had the power of death, even the devil.

58 ^t Therefore, my beloved brethren, be ye stedfast, unmoveable, always abounding in the work of the Lord, forasmuch as ye know ^u that your labour is not in vain in the Lord.
^t 2 Pet. 3. 14.
^u ch. 3. 8.

The apostle concludeth his discourse, proving the resurrection of the body from the dead, founding upon it an exhortation to holiness, which is here called *the work of the Lord*, because it is made up of works done by us at the command of Christ, and with direct respect to his glory in obedience to his will. He mindeth them not only to do these things, but to do them *stedfastly*, not by fits, but never turning aside from them either one way or another; and *unmovably*, so as no temptations, either from dangers, or rewards, or false teachers, should shake their faith, as to the principles that lead unto such a holy life, this especially of the resurrection from the dead. *For as much as ye know that your labour is not in vain in the Lord;* because they knew, that through the grace of God, and the merits of Christ, such works as these should not want their reward; for though the work of God be wages to itself, and Christians should not serve God merely for wages, yet it is lawful for them (as for Moses) to have an eye to *the recompence of reward;* and a greater reward than this of the resurrection of the body to eternal life, and that in a state of immortality and incorruption, in a spiritual and honourable estate, could not be.

CHAP. XVI

Paul directeth the Corinthians how to proceed in their collections for the relief of the brethren at Jerusalem, 1—4. *He mentioneth his design of visiting them,* 5—9; *and commendeth Timothy, who was coming to them,* 10—12. *After some seasonable admonitions,* 13—18, *he closeth the Epistle with divers salutations,* 19—24.

a Acts 11.29. & 24. 17.
Rom. 15. 26.
2 Cor. 8. 4.
& 9. 1, 12.
Gal. 2. 10.

NOW concerning ^athe collection for the saints, as I have given order to the churches of Galatia, even so do ye.

The business of relieving the poor members of the church, is a moral duty, a sacrifice with which God is well pleased, Phil. iv. 18; our faith must work by this love. The apostle, in several Epistles, was very solicitous about this; he mentioneth it, Rom. xv. 26; Gal. ii. 10, as well as in this Epistle. Besides that our Saviour had foretold, that the state of the church would be such, that they should have the poor always with them; Agabus, Acts xi. 28, had prophesied of a famine, which (some think) raged at this time; and besides, the persecution at Jerusalem had scattered the brethren abroad, and being out of their country and employments, they could not but be at a loss for a livelihood, and so need the charitable contribution of other churches under better circumstances, as they were at this time in Greece. The churches of Galatia and Macedonia had been very liberal this way; and the apostle, by their example, quickens the churches both at Rome and Corinth, Rom. xv. 26; 2 Cor. viii. 4. As to this he had (as he saith) *given order to the churches of Galatia,* which, it is thought, he did in his journey through Galatia, Acts xvi. 6; and he ordereth the church at Corinth to follow that order, which followeth.

b Acts 20. 7.
Rev. 1. 10.

2 ^bUpon the first *day* of the week let every one of you lay by him in store, as *God* hath prospered him, that there be no gatherings when I come.

From hence both divers of the ancients, and very many late divines, argue for the change of the sabbath from the seventh day of the week to the first. It is plain from hence, that the gospel churches were wont to assemble upon that day; nor do we read in Scripture of any assembly of Christians for religious worship on any other day. On this day the apostle orders collections for the poor saints to be made, accordingly as God had prospered any in their employments; he directeth that they should every one lay by him something, not doing what he did with any ostentation, but having it ready when it should be called for: this he calls a treasuring (so it is in the Greek); monies laid by for charitable uses are treasures, both with respect to those for whom they are laid up, and also for ourselves; for he that giveth to the poor, layeth up for himself treasures in heaven. He would have *no gatherings when* he came, either to avoid the scandal of his being chargeable to them, or that he would have no delay, but when he came it might be in a readiness to be presently sent away.

c 2 Cor. 8. 19.

3 And when I come, ^cwhomsoever ye shall approve by *your* letters, them will I send to bring your †liberality unto Jerusalem.

† Gr. *gift,* 2 Cor. 8. 4, 6, 19.

The word here translated *liberality,* is the same which signifieth grace; their charity is called by that name, either because it flowed from their free love towards their poor brethren, (though living at a great distance from them,) or because their sense of the free love and grace of God to

them, was that which moved them to that charitable act, 2 Cor. viii. 9.

4 ^dAnd if it be meet that I go also, they shall go with me.

d 2 Cor. 8. 4, 19.

To encourage them to the more free and liberal contribution, he promiseth them himself to go along with those that carried it, if it were thought meet.

5 Now I will come unto you, ^ewhen I shall pass through Macedonia: for I do pass through Macedonia.

e Acts 19. 21. 2 Cor. 1. 16.

Whether Paul, according to this promise, did go to Corinth, some question, because of what we read, 2 Cor. i. 15, 16. But others think, that he speaketh there of another journey, which he intended thither; and that he did go in a fulfilling of this promise, because we read, Acts xx., that he went into Greece, and spent there a considerable time; during which it is very probable that he did not omit to visit the church of Corinth.

6 And it may be that I will abide, yea, and winter with you, that ye may ^fbring me on my journey whithersoever I go.

f Acts 15. 3. & 17. 15. & 21. 5. Rom. 15. 24. & 4. 19. 2 Cor. 1. 16.

He did stay in Greece three months, Acts xx. 3, but it is believed some things hindered him, that he did not winter at Corinth. It was the custom for some members of the gospel churches, to accompany the apostles some part of their way when they went from them to any other places, in token of their kindness and respect to them, Acts xv. 3; xvii. 15; xx. 38.

7 For I will not see you now by the way; but I trust to tarry a while with you, ^gif the Lord permit.

g Acts 18. 21. ch. 4. 19. Jam. 4. 15.

I will not see you in my passage into Macedonia, for then I shall have no time to stay long with you; and I hope to gain a time when I shall stay longer with you; but all this must be understood with submission to God's will, who can hinder, and order my journeys, and determine my purposes, as he pleaseth. James teaches us, when we declare our resolutions to go to this or that place, to add, *If the Lord will;* and our apostle observeth that rule, Rom. i. 10.

8 But I will tarry at Ephesus until Pentecost.

He altered this resolution afterward, for, Acts xx. 16, *he hasted, if it were possible, to be at Jerusalem the day of Pentecost.* Pentecost was a Jewish feast, and not named here as a feast then celebrated by Christians, but as a known period of time; for the Jews computing time from their festivals, Christians who lived amongst them, and had some of them been converted from their religion, computed also their time from the Jewish festivals.

9 For ^ha great door and effectual is opened unto me, and ⁱthere are many adversaries.

h Acts 14. 27. 2 Cor. 2. 12. Col. 4. 3. Rev. 3. 8. i Acts 19. 9.

For God hath opened to me at Ephesus a great opportunity to preach the gospel, which I have reason to hope will also be effectual for the conversion of many souls. What this door of hope was, whether God had let him know there were many souls in that place prepared for receiving the gospel; or that some eminent persons for authority or learning, whom many were like to follow, were there already converted; or that he looked upon that famous city as like to be a place where many might be converted; is not told us. *And* (saith the apostle) *there are many adversaries,* (as it will appear to those that read Acts xix. and xx.,) therefore there was need of the presence of the apostle himself, whose authority might better stop their mouths, than the more inferior pastors could. What would have affrighted others from going or staying there, this great apostle mentions as an argument to cause him to make haste to go thither, and to tarry there for some time.

10 Now ^kif Timotheus come, see that he may be with you without fear: for ^lhe worketh the work of the Lord, as I also *do.*

k Acts 19. 22. ch. 4. 17. l Rom. 16. 21. Phil. 2. 20, 22. 1 Thess. 3. 2.

He had told them, chap. iv. 17, that he had sent Timothy unto them, whom he there calleth his *beloved son, and faithful in the Lord.* Here he bespeaketh his welcome and security. It is probable he had it in commission from Paul to visit divers other churches in his journey to them, and therefore he speaketh of his coming as uncertain, but chargeth them, that if he did come, they would take care of him, that he might not be exposed to danger or trouble from any party amongst them. *For he worketh the work of the Lord, as I also do;* for (saith he) he is a minister of the gospel, and engaged in the same work of the Lord that I am.

m 1 Tim. 4. 12.
n Acts 15.33.

11 ᵐLet no man therefore despise him: but conduct him forth ⁿin peace, that he may come unto me: for I look for him with the brethren.

Let no man therefore despise him; either because he is a very young man, 1 Tim. iv. 12, or upon any other account. *But conduct him forth in peace, that he may come unto me;* but when he cometh away, show him the respect you use to show me, conduct him in his way. *For I look for him with the brethren;* for I have need of his help here, in carrying on the business of the gospel; and therefore I, with the brethren here, expect him; or, I expect him with the rest of the brethren, who are in like manner employed abroad in carrying about the gospel.

o ch. 1. 12. & 3. 5.

12 As touching *our* brother ᵒApollos, I greatly desired him to come unto you with the brethren: but his will was not at all to come at this time; but he will come when he shall have convenient time.

Apollos (as may be seen, Acts xviii. 27) was known to them, and had been a preacher amongst them, and was grateful to many of them; he was *an eloquent man, mighty in the Scriptures, instructed in the way of the Lord, and fervent in the spirit,* Acts xviii. 24—28; he was one of those from whom some of this church denominated themselves, chap. iii. 4. For these reasons Paul would have persuaded him to go and visit this church, (which some think that he had left, because of those contentions and divisions which were amongst them,) but he had no mind to go at that time; though it is said, that he afterwards did return again to them, when Paul, by his Epistle, had quieted those divisions, and allayed their heats.

p Mat. 24.42. & 25. 13.
1 Thess. 5. 6.
1 Pet. 5. 8.

13 ᵖWatch ye, ᵠstand fast in the faith, quit you like men, ʳbe strong.

q ch. 15. 1. Phil. l. 27. & 4. 1. 1 Thess. 3. 8. 2 Thess. 2. 15.   r Eph. 6. 10. Col. 1. 11.

Watch ye: watching, in its usual acceptation, signifieth a forbearing of sleep; and that in order to some end. Sin is set out under the notion of sleep, Eph. v. 14; so that spiritual watching signifies a diligent abstaining from sin, and from whatsoever may be to us a temptation to sin against God, in order to the perfecting of holiness, and the obtaining life and immortality. *Stand fast in the faith;* be steady in the profession of the truth, and holding close to the doctrine of faith. *Quit you like men, be strong;* you are as soldiers fighting against the world, the flesh, and the devil; do not behave yourselves like children, whom the least opposition will terrify and throw down; but like men, with a spiritual courage and fortitude, becoming such who have so good a Captain, and so good a cause.

s ch. 14. 1.
1 Pet. 4. 8.

14 ˢLet all your things be done with charity.

Charity (as hath been before discoursed) is a term comprehensive both of love to God, and to our neighbour; the failure of this in their divisions and contentions, and satisfying their own judgments and humours, without regard to the consciences of others, and having no regard to the profit of others, is that which the apostle, in this Epistle, had once and again blamed in the members of this church; in the conclusion of his Epistle, he therefore again recommends to them the getting and exercising of this habit.

15 I beseech you, brethren, (ye know

t ch. 1. 16.
u Rom. 16.5.

ᵗthe house of Stephanas, that it is ᵘthe firstfruits of Achaia, and *that* they have

x 2 Cor. 8. 4. & 9. 1.
Heb. 6. 10.

addicted themselves to ˣthe ministry of the saints,)

Of this *Stephanas* we read before, chap. i. 16; his family was one of those few families which Paul baptized: he is here called *the first-fruits of Achaia,* because (as it should seem) he was one of the first of all those who in that country received the gospel. He further saith of him, that he had given up himself *to the ministry of the saints,* either in preaching the gospel, or (which is more probable) in the proper employment of a deacon, in relieving such amongst the saints (whether of that or other churches) as were in want.

16 ʸThat ye submit yourselves unto y Heb. 13.17.
such, and to every one that helpeth with *us,* and ᶻlaboureth. z Heb. 6. 10.

He adviseth them to reverence him, and all such as were helpers and labourers of that nature, and wrought with the apostles in the work of the gospel.

17 I am glad of the coming of Stephanas and Fortunatus and Achaicus: ᵃfor that which was lacking on your part a 2 Cor. 11. 9. Phil. 2. 30.
they have supplied. Philem. 13.

18 ᵇFor they have refreshed my spirit b Col. 4. 8.
and your's: therefore ᶜacknowledge ye c 1 Thess. 5. 12.
them that are such. Phil. 2. 29.

It should seem that this church had sent these three persons to Paul at this time (as most think) at Ephesus, to acquaint him with the state of their churches; these men supplied the want of that whole church's coming, or they made a report to the apostle of the Corinthians more fully than they had done in their letters. He adds, that they had *refreshed* his *spirit,* not with bringing him any money, (for the apostle hath told us, chap. ix. 15, that he gloried in this, that he had preached the gospel to them freely, without being any charge to them,) but by their visit, and the conference that he had had with them about the state of that church. The apostle addeth, that they had refreshed their spirits also; intimating, that their joy was his, and that what was a refreshing to him, ought also to be so to them; he therefore recommendeth these men, and such as they were, to be reverenced and respected by this church.

19 The churches of Asia salute you. Aquila and Priscilla salute you much in the Lord, ᵈwith the church that is in their d Rom. 16. 5, 15.
house. Philem. 2.

He meaneth the Lesser Asia, in which was Ephesus; from whence it is more probable (according to the Arabic and Syriac opinion) that this Epistle was written, than from Philippi (according to the copy followed by our translators). And that which further adds to that probability is, that the apostle mentioneth the salutations of *Aquila and Priscilla,* as persons that were at that time with him; now, that they lived at Ephesus, or at least went thither with Paul, and tarried there, appeareth from Acts xviii. 19: their saluting the church of Corinth *in the Lord,* signifies their wishing them all spiritual blessings in and from Christ. But what is meant by *the church in their house,* which joined with Paul in this salutation, is not so plain : we read the like, Col. iv. 15, of the church in Nymphas's house; and in Philemon's house, Philem. 2; and the same again of this Aquila and Priscilla, Rom. xvi. 5. Some think that it signifieth no more, than that their whole families had received the Christian faith; others think, that divers other Christians sojourned with them; others, that the church was wont to meet in some room in their house: but the last is not probable, either that in those times the church kept their meetings in any one stated place, or that Christians then had such spacious houses as could afford a room large enough for the whole church to meet in.

20 All the brethren greet you. ᵉGreet e Rom. 16. 16.
ye one another with an holy kiss.

This proveth no more, than that as it is in use with us to salute one another with a kiss when we meet; so it was in use in those times and countries to do the like, in token of love and friendship. It is called *the kiss of charity,* 1 Pet. v. 14. The apostle requireth, that in these salutations they should have chaste and holy thoughts. This seemeth to be all meant by the *holy kiss,* mentioned Rom. xvi. 16 ; 2 Cor. xiii. 12; 1 Thess. v. 26, and here.

21 ᶠThe salutation of *me* Paul with f Col. 4. 18. 2 Thes. 3.17.
mine own hand.

These words are judged to signify to us, that though the

former part of the Epistle was written out of Paul's copy by some others, yet the three last verses were written by him with his own hand.

g Eph. 6. 24. 22 If any man ᵍ love not the Lord
h Gal. 1. 8, 9. Jesus Christ, ʰ let him be Anathema
i Jude 14, 15. ⁱ Maran-atha.

If any man love not the Lord Jesus Christ: love is an affection of the heart, but discernible by overt acts: the meaning is, If any man, by any notorious acts, declareth that he loveth not the Lord Jesus, whether he be a hypocrite, owning the name of Christ, but living in a contempt of and disobedience to his commandments; or an apostate, who showeth his want of love to Christ by denying him in an hour of danger and persecution, or an open enemy and persecutor of Christ and his gospel. *Let him be Anathema Maran-atha;* let him be accursed, let him be looked upon as a detestable and abominable person. Some tell us, that the Jews having three excommunications, this word signifieth their highest degree, by which the person was given up to the judgment and vengeance of God; but others say, there is no such term to be found among them, and that the term *Maran-atha* signifies no more than, The Lord is come. Let the Jews and other vain persons say what they will, the Lord is come; and if any love him not, let him be looked on as a detestable person.

23 ᵏ The grace of our Lord Jesus Christ *be* with you.   k Rom. 16. 20.

That is, The Lord Jesus favour you, and bless you with all spiritual blessings: this is the apostle's ordinary salutation, Rom. xvi. 24.

24 My love *be* with you all in Christ Jesus. Amen.

As I love you, so I desire to be again beloved of you in Christ sincerely. Or, I love you all in Christ, and for Christ's sake; or, I wish that my love may abide in and with you.

¶ The first *epistle* to the Corinthians was written from Philippi by Stephanas, and Fortunatus, and Achaicus, and Timotheus.

These words are no part of Scripture; and (as was said before) it is much more probable, that this Epistle was written from Ephesus than from Philippi, though it might be sent by these, or some of these, men named.

THE SECOND EPISTLE OF PAUL THE APOSTLE

TO THE

CORINTHIANS

THE ARGUMENT

CONCERNING the sacred penman as well of this as the former Epistle, and the church to whom this as well as that Epistle was sent, enough hath been said before. It is plain, that the apostle, when he wrote it, was in Macedonia; probably at Philippi, which was the first city of Macedonia, Acts xvi. 12, whither Paul went after the uproar that Demetrius had made at Ephesus, of which we read, Acts xx. 1. The occasion of his writing this Second Epistle seemeth to be, partly the false teachers' aspersing him, 1. As an inconstant man, because he had promised to come in person to Corinth, and was not yet come; the reason of which he showeth, chap. i., was not levity, but the troubles he met with in Asia, and his desire to hear they had first reformed the abuses he had taxed them for. 2. As an imperious man, because of the incestuous person against whom he had wrote; which charge he avoids, by showing the necessity of his writing in that manner, and giving new orders for the restoring him, upon the repentance he had showed. 3. As a proud and vain-glorious man. 4. As a contemptible person; base in his person, as he expresseth it. The further occasions of his writing were, To commend them for their kind reception of and compliance with the precepts and admonitions of his former Epistle, and their kind reception of Titus: as also to exhort them to a liberal contribution to the necessities of the saints in Judea, to which they had showed their forwardness a year before: and his hearing that there was yet a party amongst them bad enough, that went on in vilifying him and his authority, as well as in other sinful courses; against whom he vindicateth himself, magnifying his office, assuring them he was about to come to Corinth; when they should find him present such as, being absent, he had by his letters declared himself, if they were not reformed. The substance therefore of this Epistle is partly apologetical, or excusatory, where he excuseth himself for his not coming to Corinth so soon as he thought, and for his so severe writing as to the incestuous person: partly hortatory, where he persuadeth them, more generally, to walk worthy of the gospel; more specially, chap. viii. and ix., to a liberal contribution to the saints: partly minatory, or threatening, where he threateneth severity against those whom, when he came amongst them, he should find contumacious and impenitent offenders. He concludes the Epistle (as usually) with a salutation of them, pious exhortations to them, and a prayer for them.

CHAP. I

Paul saluteth the Corinthians, 1, 2; *and blesseth God for the comforts and deliverances given him, not solely for his own sake, but for the comfort and encouragement of others also,* 3—7. *He telleth them of a deliverance he had lately had from a great danger in Asia, and expresseth his trust in God's protection for the future through their prayers,* 8—11. *He calleth both his own conscience and theirs to witness his sincerity in preaching the gospel,* 12—14; *and excuseth his not coming to them, as not proceeding from lightness,* 15—22, *but from lenity towards them,* 23, 24.

PAUL, ᵃ an apostle of Jesus Christ by the will of God, and Timothy *our* brother, unto the church of God which is at Corinth, ᵇ with all the saints which are in all Achaia: A. D. 60.
a 1 Cor. 1. 1.
Eph. 1. 1.
Col. 1. 1.
1 Tim. 1. 1.
2 Tim. 1. 1.
b Phil. 1. 1.
Col. 1. 2.

The will of God here doth not signify the bare permission, but the calling and precept of God; he was *called to be an apostle*, Rom. i. 1; 1 Cor. i. 1, making him *a minister and a witness*, Acts xxvi. 16. His joining of *Timothy* with him, showeth both the great humility of the apostle, and his desire to give him a reputation in the churches, though he was a very young man. The Epistle is not directed only

II. CORINTHIANS I

to the church of God which was at Corinth, (the metropolis of Peloponnesus,) but also to all those Christians which lived in Achaia: by which name probably he doth not understand all Greece, (though that anciently had that name, from one Achæus, that was king there, from whom the Grecians had the name of Achivi,) but that region of Peloponnesus which lay in a neck of land between the Ægean and Ionian Seas; which obtained that name in a more special and restrained sense.

c Rom. 1. 7.
1 Cor. 1. 3.
Gal. 1. 3.
Phil. 1. 2.
Col. 1. 2.
1 Thess. 1. 1.
2 Thess. 1. 2. Philem. 3.

2 ^c Grace *be* to you and peace from God our Father, and *from* the Lord Jesus Christ.

This was the apostle's common salutation, Rom. i. 7. See the notes on the former Epistle, chap. i. 3; where it is observable, that not the Father only, but the Lord Jesus Christ is invoked, and made the Author of *grace*, which is the free love of God, and of *peace*, which signifieth either reconciliation with God upon the free pardon of our sin, or union with men, and brotherly love amongst themselves. The heathens used to begin their epistles with wishing one another health and prosperity; but the apostle hath shown us a more Christian way, and more suited to the faith of Christians, who believe the love and favour of God the greatest and most desirable blessings.

d Eph. 1. 3.
1 Pet. 1. 3.

3 ^d Blessed *be* God, even the Father of our Lord Jesus Christ, the Father of mercies, and the God of all comfort;

It is a usual form of thanksgiving, Rom. i. 25; ix. 5. It is in use with us, signifying our sincere and hearty desire that both we ourselves might be enabled, and others by our examples might be quickened, to speak well of God, and to praise his name. This God is called *the Father of our Lord Jesus Christ*, that is, by eternal generation: he is also called *the Father of mercies*, because he is the Fountain of all that good which floweth to poor creatures. And upon the same account he is also called *the God of all comfort*.

4 Who comforteth us in all our tribulation, that we may be able to comfort them which are in any trouble by the comfort, wherewith we ourselves are comforted of God.

Who comforteth us in all our tribulation; us, who are the ministers of the gospel, (as it may appear by what followeth,) for the apostle saith, that God doth it, that ministers might, from the comforts wherewith God had comforted them, be able to comfort his people when they are under any trouble, either of body or mind, by the same methods and arguments which the Holy Spirit had used and brought to their minds under trouble to relieve any of them. Two things are observable from this verse: 1. That the apostle attributeth all the support, relief, and comfort, which he had under any tribulation, to God, as the Fountain and Author of all mercy; for though possibly our comforts may be caused from the application of some promises in holy writ, either called to our minds by the act of our own minds, or brought to our remembrance by some others; yet it is God who must make those plasters to stick, and to become healing and sanative to our souls: so that he is the principal efficient cause, though the Scriptures, or men, may be instrumental causes. 2. That the gifts, graces, and mercies that God bestowed upon his ministers, are bestowed upon them, not merely for their own use, but for the use and good of others; to enable them to be serviceable in doing good to others' souls.

e Acts 9. 4.
ch. 4. 10.
Col. 1. 24.

5 For as ^e the sufferings of Christ abound in us, so our consolation also aboundeth by Christ.

He calleth his and the other apostles' sufferings, *the sufferings of Christ*, either because they were sufferings for Christ, that is, for doing the work which Christ had given them to do; or his and their personal sufferings, as members of that body of which Christ is the Head. Christ calleth Saul's persecuting the saints, a persecuting of himself, Acts ix. 4. Thus we read of Paul's filling up *that which is behind of the afflictions of Christ*, Col. i. 24. *So our consolation also aboundeth by Christ*; but, saith the apostle, blessed be God, as we have many sufferings for Christ, so also we have many consolations by Christ. Christ, as God, is the efficient cause of the saints' consolation; as Mediator, dying for us, he is the meritorious cause; and it is by his Spirit (who is called the Comforter) that they are applied to us.

6 And whether we be afflicted, ^f *it is* for your consolation and salvation, which ‖ is effectual in the enduring of the same sufferings which we also suffer: or whether we be comforted, *it is* for your consolation and salvation.

f ch. 4. 15.
‖ Or, is wrought.

And whether we be afflicted, it is for your consolation and salvation; our sufferings tend to *your consolation and salvation,* your souls being upheld and supported by the sight of our boldness, and courage, and confidence in our sufferings: thus, Phil. i. 13, 14, *My bonds in Christ are manifest in all the palace, and in all other places; and many of the brethren in the Lord, waxing confident by my bonds, are much more bold to speak the word without fear.* And his sufferings also were for their salvation, as they encouraged them to suffer also; and, if we suffer with him, we shall reign with him; and our light and momentary afflictions shall work *for us a far more exceeding and eternal weight of glory*, chap. iv. 17. *Which is effectual in the enduring of the same sufferings which we also suffer;* and (saith the apostle) our suffering hath had a good effect amongst you, while you, with faith and patience, endure sufferings of the same sort which we endure and suffer. *Or whether we be comforted, it is for your consolation and salvation;* and if we be supported, upheld, and comforted under our sufferings, the advantage of this also redoundeth to you, as you are encouraged to suffer for the gospel and profession of Christ, from seeing how God supporteth us under our sufferings.

7 And our hope of you *is* stedfast, knowing, that ^g as ye are partakers of the sufferings, so *shall ye be* also of the consolation.

g Rom. 8.17.
2 Tim. 2. 12.

We have a *stedfast hope* of you, that as you have endured sufferings for Christ and his gospel, so you will still endure them, as we have done. And we know, *that as you are partakers of the sufferings* of Christ and his gospel, so you shall also share in those Divine consolations that those feel who endure such sufferings.

8 For we would not, brethren, have you ignorant of ^h our trouble which came to us in Asia, that we were pressed out of measure, above strength, insomuch that we despaired even of life:

h Acts 19.23.
1 Cor. 15. 32.
& 16. 9.

We are at a great loss to determine what these troubles were in Asia, of which the apostle doth here speak. We read of several troubles Paul met with in Asia: it was there he was in danger through the tumult raised by Demetrius, Acts xix. 23. It was there (at Ephesus) where he fought with beasts after the manner of men, as he told us in the former Epistle, chap. xv. 32. Whoso readeth chap. xix. and xx. of the Acts, will find the largest account we have in Scripture of the troubles Paul met with in Asia. But this Epistle is thought to have been written at a time that will not agree to the time of those troubles; therefore they are thought to have been some troubles of which we have a mention no where else in holy writ. *We were pressed out of measure, above strength, insomuch that we despaired even of life:* whatsoever they were, this text tells us they were very great, and above his natural strength to have borne; some think, above the strength of ordinary Christians, insomuch that if the apostle had not found the more than ordinary assistances of the Spirit of God, he could not have stood under them.

9 But we had the ‖ sentence of death in ourselves, that we should ⁱ not trust in ourselves, but in God which raiseth the dead:

‖ Or, answer.
i Jer. 17. 5, 7.

But we had the sentence of death in ourselves; we verily thought we should have been killed; and so it is expounded by the last words of the former verse, *we despaired even of life*. And this God did to teach us, that we should, when we are in dangers, look above the creature, and have no confidence in created means, but only look up to him, who *raiseth the dead;* as Abraham offered up Isaac, Heb. xi. 17—19, *accounting that God was able to raise him up, even from the dead.* Abraham had a promise to bottom such a faith upon; God had told him, *That in Isaac his seed should be called:* so had Paul, God having revealed to him, that he had a further work for him to do. So have not all Christians; we do not know our courses, nor what work God hath in his eternal counsels laid out for us, and therefore cannot be confident of deliverances in this life by the Almighty power of God; but yet we, under our greatest trials, may trust in God, who will certainly raise us from the dead; of which faith we have an instance in Job, chap. xix. 25—27. However, for our comfort in our distresses we may observe, That God, in his great deliverances of his people, useth to suffer them first to be brought to the greatest extremities; that in the mount of the Lord it may be seen, and that they may learn to know that their salvations are from him; more from his Almighty power, than from the virtue of any means they can use, though yet it be our duty to use what lawful means his providence affordeth us.

k 2 Pet. 2. 9. 10 ᵏWho delivered us from so great a death, and doth deliver: in whom we trust that he will yet deliver *us;*

So great a death, in this text, signifies no more than so great a trial of affliction; as he elsewhere saith, he was *in deaths often*, that is, in dangers of death. Nor (saith the apostle) were we only at that time in danger of our lives, nor had we only at that time an experience of God's power, goodness, and faithfulness in our deliverance; but we are *in jeopardy every hour*, and experience the power of God in our deliverance yet every day. And it being for the advantage of the church of Christ, that our lives should be prolonged, (though we desire rather to be dissolved, and to be with Christ,) we are confident *that he will yet deliver.* Former experiences of God's goodness in delivering us out of troubles, ought to increase our faith, and beget a confidence in us, that God will yet deliver us, if it may be for his own glory, and our good.

l Rom.15 30. Phil. 1. 19. Philem. 22. m ch. 4. 15. 11 Ye also ˡhelping together by prayer for us, that ᵐ for the gift *bestowed* upon us by the means of many persons thanks may be given by many on our behalf.

Ye also helping together by prayer for us: faith ought not to hinder prayer; nor doth God's principal efficiency, as to any mercy or deliverance bestowed upon us, give a *supersedeas* to us, as to the use of any means, whether natural or spiritual, by which the mercy may be obtained. Nor are the prayers of the meanest saints useless for the greatest, or beneath their desires; men and women's favour with God depends not upon their order, station, and repute in the world. *That for the gift bestowed upon us by the means of many persons thanks may be given by many on our behalf:* by the gift here he means the deliverance before mentioned; which he calls a *gift*, to denote, not only God's principal efficiency in it, but his free bestowing of it: this gift (saith he) is *bestowed by the means of many*, because obtained upon the intercession or prayers of many. God doth therefore bestow mercies upon particular persons at the intercession of many others on their behalf, that he may not only have the praises of those persons upon whom he so bestoweth the mercy, but of those who have been so praying. The apostle hereby hinteth to us, that we ought no more to forget to give thanks for others, for whom God hath heard us, than to pray for them when in distress.

12 For our rejoicing is this, the testimony of our conscience, that in simplicity n ch. 2. 17. & 4. 2. o 1 Cor. 2. 4, 13. and ⁿgodly sincerity, ᵒnot with fleshly wisdom, but by the grace of God, we have had our conversation in the world, and more abundantly to you-ward.

He declareth the confidence that he had, that he should not want their prayers, because his own heart told him, to his joy and satisfaction, that however others might reproach him, as if he had carried himself deceitfully, or craftily, yet he had not done so, but had lived in the world in all *simplicity and sincerity of God* (so the Greek is). Simplicity is opposed to double-mindedness; where there is a composition in a man, a mixture of truth and falsehood, fairness in speech and falsehood in heart or action. Sincerity is opposed to hypocrisy. It is said to be of God, because he is the God of truth, hath commanded it, approveth it, worketh it, and disposeth the heart of man to it. This is opposed to *fleshly wisdom*, which prompteth a man to seek his own ends any way, good or bad. *But* (saith the apostle) *we have had our conversation in the world*, not by the guidance of any such corrupt habit or principle, but *by the grace of God*, the love and fear of God dwelling in us; or, we have done this, not of ourselves, but by the guidance and assistance of Divine grace, helping us so to live, and to have our conversation in the world. *And more abundantly to you-ward;* and more especially you are our witnesses of this, amongst whom we have preached the gospel freely, so as we have not made it chargeable to you.

13 For we write none other things unto you, than what ye read or acknowledge; and I trust ye shall acknowledge even to the end;

I do not tell you stories; the things which I write, and which you read, either in my Epistles to you, or to the r churches of Christ, are what you know, must own and acknowledge, to be truth; and I hope you shall acknowledge them to be so to the end both of my life and yours.

14 As also ye have acknowledged us in part, ᵖthat we are your rejoicing, even as ᑫye also *are* our's in the day of the Lord Jesus. p ch. 5. 12. q Phil. 2.16. & 4. 1. 1 Thess. 2. 19, 20.

In part, may either refer to persons or things; part of you have so owned and acknowledged us, though o heis of you have abused us. Or you have *in part*, or at some times, owned us, that you had cause to bless God for us, and to rejoice that God ever sent us to preach the gospel amongst you. And as some have owned us as their joy, or all of you have at some times acknowledged us as such, so you are also *our rejoicing;* we rejoice that God hath made our labour successful to your souls, and I trust, in the day when the Lord Jesus shall come to judge the world, you shall be more our rejoicing.

15 And in this confidence ʳI was minded to come unto you before, that ye might have ˢa second ‖ benefit; r 1 Cor. 4.19. s Rom. 1.11. ‖ Or, *grace*.

Being confident that my presence with you would be matter of rejoicing both to you and also to me, I purposed to come unto you before I went into Macedonia, visiting you shortly in my journey thither, that so you might have a second longer visit in kindness to you. We find, Acts xvi. 9, that Paul received his first call into Macedonia in a vision; we read again of his passing through Macedonia to go to Jerusalem: the apostle seemeth to speak here of the latter.

16 And to pass by you into Macedonia, and ᵗto come again out of Macedonia unto you, and of you to be brought on my way toward Judæa. t 1 Cor 16. 5, 6.

He had purposed to take Corinth in his way unto Macedonia, and after he had finished his business in Macedonia, his resolutions were to have come back to Corinth, and to stay with them some time, hoping to have some of their company some part of the way toward Judea: but it seems, though he thus purposed, yet God had otherwise ordered his motions.

17 When I therefore was thus minded, did I use lightness? or the things that I purpose, do I purpose ᵘaccording to the flesh, that with me there should be yea yea, and nay nay? u ch. 10. 2.

When I therefore was thus minded, did I use lightness? though the apostle doth not in so many words tell us so, yet it is apparent from this verse, that some of the Corinthians had taken occasion from his not coming at this time to Corinth, to charge him with levity and inconstancy, as if his words were not to be regarded. It is very observable, how little things the men of the world will take advantage from, to vilify and lessen the reputation of God's faithful ministers and people. How many others might have promised to be in such a place at such a time, and have failed, without the reproach of the men of the world! who would have been so charitable to them, as to have excused them, by saying, They spake according to their present intentions and resolutions, but they were hindered by the providence of God; but if Paul fails, they will interpret it to be from the lightness and inconstancy of his mind: so charitable is the world to its own; so uncharitable to those who are not of the world, but by God called out of the world. From this imputation the apostle cleareth himself, denying that he used *lightness*, and that his not coming proceeded from any levity or inconstancy of mind; for he did fully purpose to have come. *Or the things that I purpose, do I purpose according to the flesh?* or (saith he) did I purpose after the manner of carnal men, who make no conscience of their word, who promise and deny both in a breath? *That with me there should be yea yea, and nay nay;* should there be in me such a spirit, as to speak a thing with my lips which my heart doth not agree to? This lets us know, that truth and steadiness are things which do highly commend either a minister or a Christian, but especially him who is a minister of the gospel.

¹ Or, preaching.
18 But *as* God *is* true, our ∥ word toward you was not yea and nay.

As God is true to his promises, so he hath taught me to be true to mine. Some make these words not to be merely declarative of the truth of God, but a kind of an oath, or calling the God of truth to witness, that his *word toward* them; by which some understand the gospel, or the word which he had preached amongst them (and of that indeed he speaketh in the next verse); but to me it seemeth much less strained, to interpret Paul's *word*, in this verse, of that word of promise of which he had before spoken, the promise which he owned before that he had made them of his coming to them. That *word*, he saith, *was not yea and nay*, that is, he did not make it with a quite contrary intention; but when he promised, he faithfully intended to have justified his word, and indeed to have come; but the providence of God, to which all men are subjected, had otherwise ordered him and disposed of him; which was the cause why he had not yet been as good as his word. It is very observable, how careful this great apostle was to clear himself from any imputations of levity and falsehood; and it should teach us to be careful to maintain our reputation in the world for truth and steadiness.

x Mark 1. 1. Luke 1. 35. Acts 9. 20.
19 For ˣthe Son of God, Jesus Christ, who was preached among you by us, even by me and Silvanus and Timo-
y Heb. 13. 8.
theus, was not yea and nay, ʸbut in him was yea.

The apostle here giveth a reason why he had made truth and sincerity so much his business (which reason obligeth us also, who are as much bound as he to study a conformity to Christ); saith he, The Son of God, who was preached among you, that is, Jesus Christ; who, though (as some observe) he is in these Epistles no where called God, but Lord, is here called *the Son of God;* which can be understood in no other sense, than by eternal generation; for those who are only the sons of God by adoption, are not the subjects of ministers' preaching. We read of this *Silvanus*, 1 Thess. i. 1; 1 Pet. v. 12: some think that he was the same person who is called Silas, Acts xvi. 19. Of *Timothy* we have heard before. They were both ministers, who (as well as Apollos before mentioned) had laboured in the gospel amongst the Corinthians. *Was not yea and nay, but in him was yea:* now (saith the apostle) that Christ, whom both I, and other ministers of the gospel, have preached to you, is not uncertain and unconstant, one thing at one time, and in one place, another thing at another time, and in another place. He was only one and the same; his doctrine was always certain and uniform, and consistent with itself; and our conversation ought to be suitable to him and his doctrine.

z Rom. 15. 8, 9.
20 ᶻFor all the promises of God in him *are* yea, and in him Amen, unto the glory of God by us.

As Christ was *yea*, and all his doctrine certain and uniform, so *all the promises of God are yea;* the promises of the Messiah have their yea and Amen in him; all the promises of grace, whatsoever is promised to believers, shall be verified by him, that so God may be glorified, and have from men the honour of being always esteemed a true and faithful God, one that cannot fail and falsify his word. But how are the promises of God yea and Amen in Christ by us? *Answ.* As the ministers of the gospel are the ministers of Christ for the explication and application of them. The promises are from the Father, through Christ as the meritorious cause, and internally applied by the Holy Spirit, while they are more externally applied by the ministers of the gospel.

21 Now he which stablisheth us with you in Christ, and ᵃhath anointed us, *is* God;
a 1 John 2. 20, 27.

The anointing here mentioned is, doubtless, the same mentioned by St. John, 1 John ii. 20, 27, by which is understood the Holy Spirit: so as God's anointing his people signifies his giving them his Holy Spirit, to dwell and to work in them; which Holy Spirit diffuseth itself throughout the whole soul of the believer, as the oil of old poured out upon the heads of the kings, high priests, and prophets. Believers are said to be *anointed*, because God hath, by his Spirit given to them, declared, that he hath set them apart to be kings and priests, a royal priesthood. The same God also *establisheth* their souls both in faith and love, and all *in Christ;* in him as our Head, and through him as the meritorious cause of all that grace wherein we stand. It is observable, that how much soever vain man may ascribe to the power of man's will, yet the blessed apostle attributeth all to God; both our anointing, the first infusion of gracious habits, and also our establishing. It is grace by which we stand.

22 Who ᵇhath also sealed us, and ᶜgiven the earnest of the Spirit in our hearts.
b Eph. 1. 13. & 4. 30.
2 Tim. 2. 19. Rev. 2. 17.
c ch. 5. 5. Eph. 1. 14.

The use of a seal is for confirmation of the thing to which it is affixed; the effect of it is the making the impression of itself upon the wax: so as sealing us, both in this and other texts, signifies both the confirmation of the love of God to our souls, and also the renewing and sanctification of our natures, imprinting the image of God upon our souls, making us (as the apostle Peter saith, 2 Pet. i. 4) *partakers of the Divine nature;* but the first seemeth probably to be most intended here. *And given the earnest of the Spirit in our hearts:* we have the same expression, chap. v. 5; Eph. i. 14. We read of *the first-fruits of the Spirit,* Rom. viii. 23. The giving unto believers the Holy Spirit, and those saving spiritual habits which are his effects in the soul, are both the first-fruits and an earnest; for as the first-fruits assured the harvest, and the earnest is a sure pledge of the bargain, when those who give it are honest and faithful; so the sanctifying habits, wrought in the soul by the Spirit of holiness, are a certain pledge of that glory which shall be the portion of believers.

23 Moreover ᵈI call God for a record upon my soul, ᵉthat to spare you I came not as yet unto Corinth.
d Rom. 1. 9. ch. 11. 31.
Gal. 1. 20. Phil. 1. 8.
e 1 Cor. 4. 21.
ch. 2. 3. & 12. 20. & 13. 2, 10.

Here is a perfect form of an oath, which is nothing else but a solemn calling of God to witness the truth of what we speak, whether promising or asserting. Those words, *upon my soul,* also have the force of an imprecation; but it is in a very serious thing: the apostle was deeply charged with levity, for not making good his promise in coming; and because he reasonably presumed, that some amongst them would be difficult to believe the true cause, to gain credit with them, he takes a voluntary oath, which in weighty matters is lawful (though sometimes it be done not before a magistrate). The thing he thus attests is, That he hitherto had forborne to come out of kindness to them; to *spare* them, (as he phraseth it,) which may either be understood of their purses, for he could not have gone without some charge to them, though he took no standing salary from them for preaching: or (as others possibly judge better) to spare their persons; for if he had come before they had reformed those abuses that were amongst them, he must (as he before spake) have come unto them *with a rod.*

f 1 Cor. 3. 5.
1 Pet. 5. 3.
g Rom. 11. 20.
1 Cor. 15. 1.

24 Not for ᶠthat we have dominion over your faith, but are helpers of your joy: for ᵍby faith ye stand.

Not for that we have dominion over your faith; not (say some) that we pretend or boast of any dominion over you because of your faith, as if upon that account we would be chargeable, and exact monies of you. But their interpretation is better, who think that by these words the apostle removes from himself, and much more from all inferior ministers, any power of imposing upon people to believe any thing, but what God had in his word revealed as the object of faith. He had in the verse before used the phrase *spare you*, which he thought might sound harsh in their ears, and give some occasion to carp at him, as if he designed some lordly power over them : No, (saith the apostle,) though I speak of sparing you, I intend no exercise of lordly power, *but* only to promote *your joy*, by removing those things which hinder your true rejoicing. Your present glorying is not good, while these disorders, contrary to the will of God, are amongst you ; and you are full of contentions and divisions, which hinder your comfortable society and communion together, as one body. *For by faith ye stand ;* the most of you stand in the faith (so some interpret this). I should rather make this the sense, by faith you must stand ; if you err in matters of faith, (as some of this church had done in the business of the resurrection, as the apostle told us in the 15th chapter of the First Epistle,) you fall ; you no longer stand than you keep the faith pure and uncorrupt. For, because of their errors as to the resurrection, I cannot tell how to make the apostle's sense to be what some learned men make it to bear, that he had nothing to blame in them in matters of faith, but only in some things referring to order ; and therefore they need not to suspect his exercise of any dominion over their faith.

CHAP. II.

Paul, having shown a motive of tenderness for not coming to Corinth, as also for writing his former Epistle, 1—5, *declareth himself satisfied with the censure inflicted on the incestuous person, and desireth them to forgive and comfort him,* 6—9 ; *as he himself had forgiven him in Christ's name,* 10, 11. *His uneasiness for not finding Titus at Troas had caused him to go forthwith into Macedonia,* 12, 13. *He blesseth God for the successfulness of his labours every where,* 14—16 ; *professing his sincerity and disinterestedness before God,* 17.

a ch. 1. 23.
& 12. 20, 21.
& 13. 10.

BUT I determined this with myself, ᵃ that I would not come again to you in heaviness.

One reason why I put off my formerly intended journey to you, was, that I might give you time to repent, and reform those disorders that were amongst you, that my coming to you might neither cause heaviness in you, seeing me come with a rod, to chide and reprove you ; nor yet in myself, who do not delight in censures and chidings, but must myself have been sad to have seen such errors and disorders amongst you, as I must by my paternal and apostolical authority have corrected.

2 For if I make you sorry, who is he then that maketh me glad, but the same which is made sorry by me ?

When I am there, I have no refreshment or joy in that part of the citizens who are pagans, all my joy is in that part which are Christians, and constitute the church of God in that city : so as I could have had no pleasure or joy in my being there, if I had have had nothing but occasion of sadness and heaviness from you, in whom was all my expectation of any joy or refreshing.

b ch. 12. 21.

3 And I wrote this same unto you, lest, when I came, ᵇ I should have sorrow from them of whom I ought to rejoice ;

ᶜhaving confidence in you all, that my joy is *the joy* of you all.

c ch. 7. 16.
& 8. 22.
Gal. 5. 10.

This hath been the cause of my writing this Second Epistle to you, before I myself came in person, that you might have a time more fully and perfectly to reform such things as are amiss amongst you, and I have formerly given you notice of ; lest when I come, instead of rejoicing in you, as I ought to do, or having any just occasion so to do, I might meet with what would give me nothing but trouble and sadness ; which would not only be grievous to me, but would be contrary to your duty, for *I ought to rejoice* in you, and you ought so to behave yourselves, that I may have cause to rejoice in you. And I have confidence in the most of you, or in all you who are sincere, that you would all be glad to see me glad and cheerful, rejoicing in my society with you.

4 For out of much affliction and anguish of heart I wrote unto you with many tears ; ᵈ not that ye should be grieved, but that ye might know the love which I have more abundantly unto you.

d ch. 7. 8, 9, 12.

Every man that deriveth from God, is in this made partaker of the Divine nature, that like as God doth not grieve willingly, nor willingly afflict the children of men, so neither will he ; but if, by reason of his office or trust reposed in him, he be under an obligation sometimes to speak smartly, or to chastise and punish others for their errors, yet he will so do it as one that hath no pleasure and delight in it. Thus the good judge weepeth, or at least showeth sorrow and compassion, when he giveth sentence against malefactors. So, this great apostle, to whom God had committed a care over all the Christian churches, saw a necessity of reproving this church that was at Corinth, for enduring the incestuous person in their communion, and not casting him out; for their errors about the resurrection, for their divisions, schisms, and contentions, &c. : but he professeth that he did this *with many tears ;* and those not shed in hypocrisy, but forced from the anguish and affliction of his heart ; that he had nothing less in his design, than to put them to any excessive grief or trouble, but what he wrote was out of a principle of love and good will, both to the welfare of their whole church, and to the good of the particular souls of those that were the members of that church. Ministers or others do no good by their censures or reproofs, if they do not so dispense them, as people may see that what they do, or say, is out of their abundant love to their souls.

5 But ᵉ if any have caused grief, he hath not ᶠgrieved me, but in part: that I may not overcharge you all.

e 1 Cor. 5. 1.

f Gal. 4. 12.

The particle *if* doth not here signify any doubting or uncertainty (for the incestuous person, of whom the apostle here, and in the following verses, speaks, had certainly caused grief both to the apostle, and also the church whereof he was a member). It is as much as although ; or the apostle speaketh in this form, because by his repentance his grief was much allayed. But how doth the apostle say, that he had grieved him *but in part?* Some think he saith so, because the apostle's grief for his sin was now turned into joy by his repentance : others think, that those words, *in part*, signify that it was not the whole church that had grieved him, but only a part of it, viz. this incestuous person, and those who took part with him. Others say, the apostle saith, *in part*, to let us know, that it was not a grief to him only, but to them also. The last would bid very fair for the sense of the place, if the apostle had not in his First Epistle, chap. v. 2, said that they were puffed up, and had not mourned. So as I judge the second more like to be the sense of the apostle ; viz. that it was not the whole church that had grieved him, but a part of it only : and therefore the next words are added, *that I may not overcharge you all*, that is, that I might not lead you all with that imputation, as if you were all involved in it.

6 Sufficient to such a man *is* this ‖ punishment, which *was inflicted* ᵍ of many.

‖ Or, *censure*.

g 1 Cor. 5. 4, 5. 1 Tim. 5. 20.

This verse maketh it clear, that by *any*, ver. 5, he meaneth the incestuous person, mentioned in the First Epistle, chap. v., whom he had ordered to be cast out, and delivered to Satan; which (as appeareth from this verse) they had done, which is the *punishment* mentioned in this verse. They who think, that the punishment here mentioned was not excommunication, but another being delivered to Satan, and vexed by him, 1. Beg a grave question, viz. Whether delivering to Satan in this place signifieth any more than a casting of the person out of Christ's kingdom on earth, (which is his church,) and making him one of the world again, of which Satan is the god? 2. They seem not to consider, that if this church had delivered him to Satan, they could have done no more: so as the apostle would not have said, *Sufficient is this punishment,* when it was the greatest that they could inflict. Some object, that it is not probable that the apostle (had he been cast out of the communion of the church, for so notorious a crime) would have given order for his being restored in so short a time, as was that betwixt his writing the First and this his Second Epistle. 1. Some think, that he was as yet only under a suspension, and the church had not proceeded to excommunication: this opinion is favoured by the Greek word here used, which is ἐπιτιμία, the gentlest of all the words in use in that language to express punishment by. 2. Though in the times following the apostles', a longer time was set after excommunication, for testifying the repentance of sinners notoriously scandalous, before the church did again admit them into her fellowship; yet that it was so in the apostles' time, is more than appears. Possibly it might be so ordered afterwards, when, as the church multiplied, so sin more abounded; and they might, from many experiences of relapses, be quickened to make such orders. 3. The gift of discerning spirits was more usual in the apostles' times than afterward; so that though in following times, when the apostles were dead, and the extraordinary gift of discerning spirits was failed or abated, the church being not able any other way to judge of the truth of sinners' repentance, than from their changed life and conversation, which asked time, might set a longer time for such penitents; yet there might not be the same reason for the apostles doing it. 4. Notwithstanding any thing that appears, there might be the distance of a year or two betwixt Paul's writing these two Epistles. *Which was inflicted of many:* who these many were, by whom the apostle saith this punishment was inflicted, is a little disputed; whether the presbytery, or the community. Their opinion seemeth (to me) best, who think that the officers of the church of Corinth heard and judged of matters of faith, and reported it to the community; but he was not cast out without the consent and approbation of the community.

h Gal. 6. 1.   7 ʰ So that contrariwise ye *ought* rather to forgive *him,* and comfort *him,* lest perhaps such a one should be swallowed up with overmuch sorrow.

So that contrariwise ye ought rather to forgive him, and comfort him: forgiveness in this place doth not signify the taking away or remitting of the guilt of sin, (that is God's work, not man's,) but remitting of the punishment. And this maketh that probable, that they had not as yet proceeded with this person to excommunication, only kept him (like a suspected leper, without the camp) out of a a communion with the church: or if they had actually cast him out, forgiving here can signify nothing but restoring him again to a full communion with them; which is also the comforting which is here mentioned. *Lest perhaps such a one should be swallowed up with overmuch sorrow:* it is plain from hence, that the apostle had intelligence that this person expressed abundant sorrow; otherwise he would not have expressed his fear of his being drowned in his own tears. Though the condition of such, at this day, is sad enough, who are regularly cast out of the communion of any true church of Christ, for crimes which deserve such a punishment, yet we must imagine it much sadder then. Now churches are multiplied, whole cities and nations are Christianized, and though a person be cast out of a church, yet it is not so taken notice of, but he may yet have converse with other Christians, &c.: but there, the greater part of the city being heathens, and the whole countries of Achaia and Greece (contiguous to it) being heathens; one cast out of the communion of the church (if he had the least sense of religion) could not but be deeply afflicted to be in such a case, as none but heathens and professed idolaters would keep him company, or have any intimacy with him.

8 Wherefore I beseech you that ye would confirm *your* love toward him.

That you would restore him to a communion with you in your church assemblies, and take him into the bosom of your church again, and be (as before) friendly towards him. The word which we translate *confirm,* is κυρῶσαι, which signifieth authoritatively to establish or confirm. Some observe, that the apostle speaks to them as judges, to gain their good opinion, and make them more pliable, whereas he might authoritatively have absolved him. It is hard to say what authority the apostles had, or had not, to excommunicate; but we want a precedent in holy writ of the apostles, or any of them, exercising such a power, as being absent, and so in no capacity to hear the proof of any fact against scandalous persons. Paul (1 Cor. v.) writes to the church of Corinth to do it, and doth only himself command them to do their duty; and here again he writeth to them to forgive him, and restore him. There being no mention, either in the former Epistle, or here, of any command that the incestuous person should put away his wife taken unlawfully, or that he did any such thing in testification of his repentance, makes it very probable, that his crime was not using his father's wife as his wife, but as his harlot; had it been otherwise, we should, very probably, have read of something in the one or the other place, signifying such a command of the apostle, or the thing done by him.

9 For to this end also did I write, that I might know the proof of you, whether ye be ⁱ obedient in all things.   i ch. 7. 15. & 10. 6.

As for other ends, so for this also I wrote my former Epistle to you, and I now write this Second Epistle to you also, that I might have an experiment of you, what regard you would show to that apostolical authority wherewith God hath invested me.

10 To whom ye forgive any thing, I *forgive* also: for if I forgave any thing, to whom I forgave *it,* for your sakes *forgave I it* ‖ in the person of Christ;   ‖ Or, *in the sight.*

The word so often repeated in this verse, and translated *forgive,* is χαρίζομαι, which signifies to give, or gratify, or do a kindness, as well as to forgive; so as it needeth not always to be interpreted of any judicial act of absolution. If you see reason to remit any thing of the punishment inflicted upon the incestuous person, I am satisfied with what you do, I shall take no offence at you for it. If I have showed any favour to any person amongst you that hath fallen under my reproof and chastisement, it hath been for your sake, for the good and advantage of your church, or upon their motion and intercession; and I have done it sincerely in the sight of Christ (the Greek is, in the face of Christ).

11 Lest Satan should get an advantage of us: for we are not ignorant of his devices.

As I have done it in kindness to you, so I have also done it for the advantage both of that person, who is so forgiven, and of your whole church, which is concerned in the welfare or miscarriage of every individual member. *Lest Satan should get an advantage of us:* the Greek is, That we be not overcome by Satan: πλεονεκτεῖν properly signifies to get again, or to gain a superiority, to get the upper hand. The advantage Satan was like to get by their continuing severity to this offender, was either by his over-much grief, or by the hardening of his heart; so as he, seeing no probability to be restored again to his communion with the church, should be exposed, either to temptations to some desperate courses, (which are often the effects of minds full of sorrow and discontent,) or else to courses of idolatry or looseness, in giving up himself to the devil's kingdom in the world, because he could not be admitted into the church, which is the kingdom of Christ. *For* (saith the apostle) *we are not ignorant of his devices,* νοήματα, his thoughts and counsels, how he continually walketh about both like *a roaring lion, seeking whom he may devour;* and like an *old serpent,* seeking whom and how he may deceive. This lets us know, with how much prudence those who are trusted with the souls of others, ought to manage their reproofs, or severe dealings with others : the end of all these is the amendment and reformation of such persons, not their spiritual ruin and destruction; and all reproofs and censures must be given, and made, and managed with reference to that end. We have not only the concern of God's glory (which is the main) to be looked at, but the good also of their souls, whom we so reprove, censure, or alienate ourselves from : and indeed, without consulting this, we cannot consult God's glory; who hath told us, that he desireth not the death of a sinner, but rather that he should turn from his wickedness and live : and therefore we must have an eye about us, and beneath us, to the devil, as well as above us, to God ; and prudently judge how such afflictive and harsh actions may be so done by us, that in the mean time Satan get no advantage, and we lose the souls of those with whom we so deal, instead of gaining them to God ; which is the main and principal end we ought in all those actions to aim at, 1 Cor. v. 5 ; so 1 Tim. i. 20.

k Acts 16. 8. & 20. 6. 1 1 Cor. 16. 9.
12 Furthermore, ^k when I came to Troas to *preach* Christ's Gospel, and ^l a door was opened unto me of the Lord,

This *Troas* was either the city, or the whole country, called Troy or Ilium, or the lesser Phrygia. We read of Paul's going thither by sea from Philippi, Acts xx. 6, and of his having been there, 2 Tim. iv. 13. He tells us, that the business why he went thither, was to preach the gospel; for it was not the apostles' business to stay, as fixed ministers, in any one place, but to carry the gospel up and down the world to several places; which they did by virtue of their general commission to go, preach, and baptize all nations; though sometimes they had a more special call and commission, as Paul had to go into Macedonia. The *door opened*, either signifieth the free liberty he had there to preach, or the great success which God gave him in his work; which he elsewhere calleth an *effectual door.*

m ch. 7. 5, 6.
13 ^m I had no rest in my spirit, because I found not Titus my brother : but taking my leave of them, I went from thence into Macedonia.

He tells us, that when he came there, he was much troubled because he did not find his brother Titus; where the humility of this great apostle is considerable, in that he disdained not to call *Titus* (a person, though a minister, yet much inferior to him as an apostle) *brother*. Several reasons are given of Paul's trouble. That which is most probable is, that he did expect at Troas to have met with Titus come from Corinth, from whom he might more perfectly have understood the affairs of that church : not finding him there, he tells us he went forward into Macedonia; whither, after the uproar at Ephesus, he designed to go, (as we read, Acts xx. 1,) but went first into Greece, and stayed there three months, intending to come to Macedonia in his return, ver. 3.

14 Now thanks *be* unto God, which always causeth us to triumph in Christ,
n Cant. 1. 3.
and maketh manifest ⁿ the savour of his knowledge by us in every place.

Now thanks be unto God, which always causeth us to triumph in Christ : the translation of the Greek here is not certain; for to translate it word for word, it is, But thanks be to God always, triumphing us in Christ; which makes it uncertain, whether there be not a defect of a preposition, upon the supply of which it would be, who triumpheth over us in Christ, having subdued our hearts to the kingdom and obedience of Christ. But the most interpreters rather agree with our translators, and think the sense of the apostle is, *who maketh us to triumph*. In the Hebrew there is a conjugation, where the active verb signifieth to make another to do a thing ; and there are several instances brought by learned men out of the Septuagint, where the active verb in the Greek also hath that sense ; that which cometh nearest it in the original in holy writ, is that, Rom. viii. 26, where the Spirit is said to make *intercession for us*, because it causeth us to make intercession. According to this, the sense is, Blessed be God, who though we meet with many enemies, yet through Christ he maketh us *more than con-querors*, Rom. viii. 37, so that we are not overcome by any of them, but, on the contrary, we triumph over them as conquered by us. *And maketh manifest the savour of his knowledge by us in every place ;* and this by manifesting by us in every place *the savour of* the *knowledge* of Christ; that is, of the gospel. He calleth it a *savour*, either with allusion to that sweet perfumed ointment, with which the high priest, under the law, was anointed, Exod. xxx. 23; Psal. cxxxiii. 2 ; or with reference to the incense used also under the law ; or with relation to Solomon's expression, Cant. i. 3, where we read of *the savour of* Christ's *good ointments*, and that his name is as an ointment poured forth. By the savour of the knowledge of Christ here mentioned, the apostle plainly meaneth the reputation or good report that the gospel had in every place : see Hos. xiv. 7.

15 For we are unto God a sweet savour of Christ, ^o in them that are saved,
o 1 Cor. 1. 18.
and ^p in them that perish :
p ch. 4. 3.

For the God whom we serve doth not judge of us, nor will reward us, according to our success, but according to our faithfulness and diligence in his work. We give unto all a good savour by our doctrine ; and our labours are a sweet savour in the nostrils of God, whatever effects they have upon souls. God accepteth of our labours as to good men, to whom we are instruments of eternal life and salvation ; and though others despise the gospel, and refuse the sweet sound of it, yet as to them also we are a sweet savour in the nostrils of God : Though Israel be not saved, (saith the prophet, Isa. xlix. 5,) yet I shall be glorified. It is not for any neglect in us, as to our duty, if any perish, but from their own wilfulness and perverseness.

16 ^q To the one *we are* the savour of
q Luke 2.34. John 9. 39. 1 Pet. 2. 7, 8.
death unto death ; and to the other the savour of life unto life. And ^r who *is* sufficient for these things ?
r 1 Cor. 15. 10. ch. 3. 5, 6.

As sweet smells, which are to some pleasant and comfortable, are to others pernicious and deadly; so it is with the sweet savour of the gospel. The report which we in all places make of Christ, to some, through their unbelief and hardness of heart, and fondness of their lusts, proveth but *the savour of death unto death*, hardening their hearts to their eternal ruin and destruction; but to such who, being ordained to eternal life, believe our reports, and embrace the gospel, and live up to the precepts and rule of it, our preaching proves a cause of spiritual and of eternal life, to which that leadeth. *And who is sufficient for these things?* and oh how great a work is this ! What man, what angel, is sufficient for it? It is a mighty work to preach the gospel as we ought to preach it.

17 For we are not as many, which
∥ Or, *deal deceitfully with.* s ch. 4. 2. & 11. 13. 2 Pet. 2. 3. t ch. 1. 12. & 4. 2. ∥ Or, *of.*
∥ ^s corrupt the word of God : but as ^t of sincerity, but as of God, in the sight of God speak we ∥ in Christ.

Lest the false apostles and teachers in this church should slight this exclamation of the apostle's, and the pretended difficulty he made of the ministerial work, the apostle adds these words : I confess (saith he) it is no very difficult thing to speak of Christ, and pretend to preach and do as much as I do ; but there are many καπηλεύοντες, we translate it, *corrupt the word ;* the Greek word signifies, to sell wine or victuals for money ; and because such kind of people make no conscience to deceive, cheat, and deal fraudulently with their customers, it is sometimes used to signify corrupting or deceiving. We are not (saith the apostle) of the number of those who in preaching merely serve their own bellies, and turn the church into a tavern or victualling-house, making a gain of the gospel, and discoursing a little while in a pulpit for gain; and so making no conscience, either what they speak, or how they speak. But we speak by authority from Christ, and in Christ's name; clothed with his authority, and as his ambassadors; and so dare not say any thing unto people, and deliver to his people what he never gave us any commission to speak, nor yet to speak whatever cometh at our tongue's end ; but we must remember that we are *in the sight of God*, and speak as from God of God ; and that not fraudulently, but sincerely ; sincerely aiming at the glory of God in what we do, and the salvation of the souls of them to whom we speak. This is a great work, first to consult the mind and will of God, and find it out by study and meditation; then faithfully to communicate it unto people, without any vain or corrupt mixtures (which do but adulterate the word preached); then to apply it to the consciences of those that hear us. *Who is sufficient for these things?* that is, to discharge the office of the ministry in the preaching of the gospel, as men ought to preach it.

CHAP. III

To obviate the imputation of vain-glory, Paul showeth that the gifts and graces of the Corinthians were a sufficient commendation of his ministry, 1—3, *the efficacy of which he ascribeth entirely to God,* 4, 5. *He proveth the superior excellency of the gospel ministry to that of the law,* 6—11; *and thereupon justifieth his plain speaking, as under a dispensation of greater light and liberty than that of Moses,* 12—18.

a ch. 5. 12.
& 10. 8, 12.
& 12. 11.

b Acts 18.27.

1 DO [a] we begin again to commend ourselves? or need we, as some *others*, [b] epistles of commendation to you, or *letters* of commendation from you?

The apostle, in the former Epistle, had spoken much in the vindication of himself and of his office; he seeth reason to return again to something of the like discourse, being provoked by the many imputations which the false apostles and teachers, in this church, had laid upon him: therefore he saith, *Do we begin again?* Or else these words may have a special reference to the last verse of the former chapter; where he had commended himself, as being none of those who corrupted the word of God, but had preached as of God, and in the sight of God. No, (saith the apostle,) though some others stand in need of commendatory letters, and are very careful to procure them, (by which *others* he very probably means the false apostles and teachers, which were Paul's great enemies,) yet I trust I need not any letters commendatory to recommend me to you, any more than letters of recommendation from you to commend me unto any other churches of Christ.

c 1 Cor. 9. 2.

2 [c] Ye are our epistle written in our hearts, known and read of all men :

Your Christianity, and embracing of the gospel of Christ, your faith and holiness, are instead of an epistle to me, to let the world know, both with what faithfulness, and with what blessing of God, and success upon my labours, I have preached the gospel; and you are such an epistle as I do not carry about in my pockets, or lay up in my closet, but it is written in my heart, where I carry continually both a thankful and honourable remembrance of you. Nor are you only taken notice of by me as a famous church, to the planting and watering of which God hath blessed my labours, and the labours of other ministers; but, as he saith to the Romans, chap. i. 8, *Your faith is spoken of throughout the whole world*, so he saith here. *Ye are our epistle, known and read of all men;* that is, all Christians take notice of you as a church to which God hath particularly blessed my ministry; so as I need no other recommendation than what I have from your receiving, and the proficiency you have made in, the gospel. Nothing so commends a minister as the proficiency of his people.

d 1 Cor. 3. 5.
e Ex. 24. 12.
& 34. 1.
f Ps. 40. 8.
Jer. 31. 33.
Ezek. 11. 19.
& 36. 26.
Heb. 8. 10.

3 *Forasmuch as ye are* manifestly declared to be the epistle of Christ [d] ministered by us, written not with ink, but with the Spirit of the living God; not [e] in tables of stone, but [f] in fleshy tables of the heart.

He had told them before that they were his epistle, his epistle recommendatory, the change which God had wrought in their hearts did more recommend him than all the epistles in the world could; but here he tells them that they were *the epistle of Christ*, it was Christ that wrote his law in their hearts, (which writing was that which commended the apostle, who himself had but a ministration in the work,) nor was it a writing *with ink*, but the impression of *the Spirit of the living God.* An epistle *not written in tables of stone, but in* the *fleshy tables of the heart:* he alludeth to the writing of the law, which was written in *tables of stone*, Exod. xxxi. 18, and also to the promises, Ezek. xi. 19; xxxvi. 26. That work of grace in the hearts of these Corinthians, which recommended the apostle, was wrought by Christ, and the apostles were but ministers in the working of it; it was a work more admirable than the writing of the law in tables of stone, and this work (he saith) was *manifestly declared.*

4 And such trust have we through Christ to God-ward :

We are not infallible in the case; but I tell you what confidence we have, hoping in God concerning you, through the merits of Jesus Christ.

g John 15. 5.
ch. 2. 16.
h 1 Cor. 15. 10. Phil. 2. 13.

5 [g] Not that we are sufficient of ourselves to think any thing as of ourselves; but [h] our sufficiency *is* of God;

I would not have you think that we judge ourselves sufficient to work a change in the hearts of men; we are so far from that, that we have no sufficiency so much as to think one good thought, which is the lowest human act. Though the subject, upon which the apostle is here discoursing, be a sufficiency to work a work of grace in the hearts of men; yet here is a strong proof to prove the impotency of man's will unto any thing that is truly and spiritually good: for though the apostle declares here his own and all other ministers' insufficiency to the change of any man's heart, yet he proveth it by an argument, concluding from the lesser to the greater; for if they be not sufficient of themselves, and as of themselves, to think any thing which is truly and spiritually good, they are then much less sufficient for so great a work as the conversion of souls. Nor doth that term, *as of ourselves*, any thing alter the matter; for if we can think good thoughts, in any sense, *as of ourselves*, it is not *of God*, in the sense which the apostle is speaking of; who is not here speaking of God as the God of nature, (from whom indeed we derive our power of thinking,) but as the God of grace, from whom we derive our power of thinking holy thoughts, and such as are truly and spiritually good. The apostle determineth all our sufficiency to spiritually good actions to be from God, our sufficiency to the lowest (which is thinking good thoughts) as well as to those of the highest sort; amongst which must those actions be accounted, by which men are made workers together with God, in the bringing of souls out of darkness into marvellous light; opening their eyes, turning them *from darkness to light, and from the power of Satan unto God*, Acts xxvi. 18. Our sufficiency to think any thoughts, or to do any natural or moral actions, is from God, as he is the God of nature. But it appeareth from all the preceding discourse, that our apostle is here speaking of that sufficiency which floweth from God through the mediation of Christ: our power of thinking floweth from the providence of God towards all men; and if that had been all which the apostle had meant in saying, *our sufficiency is from God*, it had been no more than what they might have learned from the heathen philosophers, who would have acknowledged, that all men's sufficiency to natural actions is from the Divine Being, or the first Mover.

i 1 Cor. 3. 5.
& 15. 10. ch.
5. 18. Eph.
3. 7. Col. 1.
25, 29.
1 Tim. 1. 11,
12. 2 Tim.
1. 11.

6 Who also hath made us able [i] ministers of [k] the new testament; not [l] of the letter, but of the spirit : for [m] the letter killeth, [n] but the spirit ∥ giveth life.

k Jer. 31. 31. Matt. 26. 28. Heb. 8. 6, 8. l Rom. 2. 27, 29. & 7. 6. m Rom. 3. 20. & 4. 15. & 7. 9, 10, 11. Gal. 3. 10. n John 6. 63. Rom. 8. 2. ∥ Or, *quickeneth.*

This verse plainly openeth what he had said before, and lets us know what sufficiency of God that was of which he there spake. He hath (saith the apostle) not found, but *made us* sufficient. We were men before, and, through the creating power and providence of God, we had an ability to think and to speak; but God *hath made us* sufficient, by a supervening act and influence of his grace, to be *ministers of the new testament*, that is, of the gospel; which being the new revelation of the Divine will, and confirmed by the death of Christ, is called the new testament. *Not of the letter, but of the Spirit :* by *the letter*, here, the apostle understandeth the law; for the law is called *the letter*, Rom. ii. 27; vii. 6: *Who by the letter and circumcision dost transgress the law;* that is, While thou, by some external acts, professest a subjection to the law (particularly by circumcision) in a multitude of other actions, (which are more valuable in the sight of God than those external acts,) thou transgressest the law. The law, in opposition to the gospel, is called *the letter*, sometimes a dead letter; because it was only a revelation of the will of God concerning man's duty, no revelation of God's grace, either in pardoning men their omissions of duty, and doing acts contrary to duty, or assisting men to the performance of their duty. As the gospel is also called *the Spirit*, both in opposition to the carnal ordinances of the law, and because Christ is the matter, subject, and argument of it; and chiefly because, that the preaching of it is so far attended by the Spirit of grace, that where men do not turn their ears from the hearing of it, nor shut their eyes against the light of it, nor harden their hearts against the precepts and rule of it, it becomes (through the free grace of God) effectual to change their hearts, and to turn them *from the power of Satan unto God*, and to make them truly spiritual and holy. *For the letter* (that is, the law) *killeth*; the law showeth men their duty, accuseth, condemneth, and denounceth the wrath of God against men for not doing their duty, but gives no strength for the doing of it. But the *spirit* (that is, the gospel) *giveth life*: the gospel, in the letter of it, showeth the way to life; and the gospel, in the hand of the Spirit, or with the Spirit, working together with it, (the Holy Spirit using it as its instrument,) giveth life; both that life which is spiritual, and that which is eternal, as it prepareth the soul for life and immortality.

o Rom. 7. 10.
p Ex. 34. 1, 28. Deut. 10. 1, &c.
q Ex. 34. 29, 30, 35.

7 But if ° the ministration of death, ᵖ written *and* engraven in stones, was glorious, ᵠ so that the children of Israel could not stedfastly behold the face of Moses for the glory of his countenance; which *glory* was to be done away:

The apostle is manifestly comparing the ministry of the gospel with the ministry of the law, and showing the excellency of the former above the latter. In the former verse he had called the law, *the letter*; and the gospel, in opposition to it, he had called, *the spirit*: here he calleth the ministration of the law, *the ministration of death*; because it only showed man his duty, or things to be done, but gave no strength or help by which he should do them; only cursing man, but showing him no way by which he might escape that curse: so it did kill men, and led them to eternal death and condemnation, without showing them any means of life and salvation. He also undervalueth the law, in comparison with the gospel, as being only *written and engraven in stones*; whereas (as he had said before) the gospel is written *in the fleshy tables of* men's hearts. Yet (saith he) the ministration of the law (which was indeed but the *ministration of death*) *was glorious*: there was a great deal of the glory and majesty of God attended the giving of the law, of which we read, Exod. xix. *So that the children of Israel could not stedfastly behold the face of Moses for the glory of his countenance*: of this we read, Exod. xxxiv. 29, 30, *When Aaron and all the children of Israel saw Moses, behold, the skin of his face shone; and they were afraid to come nigh him*. So as it was glorious to be but a minister of the law, that is, of the revelation of the will of God, as to man's duty, *which glory* (saith the apostle) *was to be done away*: Moses's face did not always so shine, neither was the glory of his ministration to abide always, but to cease by the coming in of the new covenant.

r Gal. 3. 5.

8 How shall not ʳ the ministration of the spirit be rather glorious?

How shall not that ministration, which is more spiritual, and the effects of which are much more spiritual, be accounted much more glorious? Thus the apostle doth not only magnify the gospel above the law, but he also magnifieth his offices in the ministration of the gospel; which ministration he reasonably concludeth to be a more glorious ministration than that which Moses had, in whom the Jews so much gloried.

s Rom. 1. 17. & 3. 21.

9 For if the ministration of condemnation *be* glory, much more doth the ministration ˢ of righteousness exceed in glory.

What the apostle before called *the ministration of death*, he here calleth *the ministration of condemnation*; and therein gives us a reason why he called it the ministration of death, because it led unto eternal death, as showing men sin, so accusing and condemning men for sinful acts. If it pleased God (saith the apostle) to make that ministration glorious, that the minister of the law (Moses) appeared so glorious in the eyes of Aaron and of the people; *the ministration of righteousness* (by which he means the gospel) must needs be more exceedingly glorious. He tells us, Rom. i. 16, 17, that he was *not ashamed of the gospel—for therein is the righteousness of God revealed from faith to faith*; that is, the righteousness wherein a soul must stand and appear righteous before God. *The ministration of righteousness* signifieth the ministration of that gospel, that doctrine, which revealeth righteousness. *Righteousness* is here opposed to *condemnation*; and therefore signifieth that which is opposed to it, viz. justification. For God doth not so freely remit sins, but that he declares his righteousness in the remission of them; and will show himself just, while he showeth himself *the justifier of him that believeth in Jesus*, Rom. iii. 26. And from hence it appeareth, that the gospel is called the ministration of righteousness, because he that ministereth in it exhibiteth the righteousness to Christ to be reckoned to the soul, as that whereby it must be justified; for God could not otherwise declare his righteousness in the remission of sins, nor show himself just in justifying the ungodly. This ministration (he saith) must needs be more glorious in the eyes of men than the ministration of the law; for that ministration afforded nothing but terror and death, this affordeth relief, and comfort, and life.

10 For even that which was made glorious had no glory in this respect, by reason of the glory that excelleth.

The law had in it something of intrinsic glory and excellency, as it was the revelation of the will of God to and concerning his creatures; there was an inseparable glory attending it upon that account: and it was made glorious in the ministration of it; as it pleased God that the giving of it should be attended with thunder and lightning, fire and smoke, and an earthquake, and a voice like to the sound of a trumpet, as we read, Exod. xix. 16—18: this was an accidental and adventitious glory, and made that which was glorious in itself, glorious also in the eyes of the people, that saw and heard these things. But yet, saith the apostle, if we compare it with the glory of the gospel, it had comparatively no glory; so much doth that excel. For though the law was the revelation of the Divine will, as well as the gospel, yet the law was the revelation of the Divine will but as to duty, and wrath, in case of the non-performance of that duty: but the gospel is the revelation of the Divine will, as to grace and mercy, as to remission of sin, and eternal life. And although the gospel came not into the world as the law, with thunder, and lightning, and earthquakes; yet that was ushered in by angels, foretelling the birth and office of John the Baptist, and of Christ; by the great sign of the virgin's conceiving and bringing forth a Son; by a voice from heaven, proclaiming Christ the Father's only begotten Son, in whom he was well pleased. But that which the apostle doth here principally intend, is the exceeding excellency of it, in regard of its further usefulness and comfortable nature.

11 For if that which was done away *was* glorious, much more that which remaineth *is* glorious.

The apostle, by another argument, proveth the ministration of the gospel to be much more glorious than the ministration of the law, because it is more durable and abiding. The strength of the argument dependeth upon this principle, that any durable good is more excellent and glorious than that which is but transitory, and for a time. The ministration of the law is done away; the law, contained in ordinances, is itself done away, and therefore the ministration of it must needs cease. There are now no priests and Levites, no worldly sanctuary, nor any ministrations in it, or relating to it. But our Saviour hath told us, that the gospel shall be preached to the end of the world; so as that ministration must (according to all principles of reason) be more glorious, as that which is eternal is more glorious than that which is fluid and vanishing.

II. CORINTHIANS III

^{t ch. 7. 4.}
^{Eph. 6. 19.}
^{‖ Or, *boldness*.}

12 Seeing then that we have such hope, ^twe use great ‖ plainness of speech:

Hope here signifieth nothing but a confident, certain expectation of something that is hereafter to come to pass. The term *such* referreth to something which went before: the sense is, We being in a certain confident expectation, that our ministration of the gospel shall not cease, as the ministration of the law hath done; and that the doctrine of the gospel brings in not a temporary, but an everlasting righteousness; that there shall never be any righteousness revealed, wherein any soul can stand righteous before God, but that which is revealed in the gospel to be *from faith to faith*; we are neither ashamed nor afraid to preach the gospel with all freedom and boldness. We do not, as Moses, cover ourselves with a veil when we preach the gospel to people, but we speak what God hath given to us in commission to speak, unconcernedly as to any terrors or affrightments from men: we know, that great is the truth which we preach, and that it shall prevail and outlive all the rage and madness of the enemies of it.

^{u Ex. 34. 33, 35.}

13 And not as Moses, ^u*which* put a vail over his face, that the children of Israel could not stedfastly look to ^xthe end of that which is abolished:

^{x Rom. 10. 4.}
^{Gal. 3. 23.}

We have the history to which this passage of the apostle relateth, in Exod. xxxiv. 33, 35, where we read, that *when Moses had done speaking, he put a veil on his face*. The apostle here elegantly turns that passage into an allegory, and opens to us a mystery hidden under that piece of history. That shining of Moses's face, in a type, prefigured the shining of Him who was to be the light of the world; as he was from eternity *the brightness of his Father's glory*. Moses's covering himself with a veil, signifies God's hiding the mystery of Christ from ages. Moses did not put a veil on his face for that end, that the children of Israel might not look upon him; but this was the event of it, which also prefigured the blinding of the Jews; they first shut their eyes and would not see, then God judicially sealed their eyes that they should not see, that Christ was *the end of the law for righteousness*, the true Messiah, and the Mediator betwixt God and man; they could not (as the apostle expresseth it) see *to the end of that which is abolished;* to the end of the legal dispensation, to the end of all the types of Christ which were in the Levitical law. Now, (saith the apostle,) we do not do so, but make it our business to preach the gospel with as much openness, and plainness, and freedom, as is imaginable. The whole history of the gospel justifieth what this text affirmeth concerning the Jews; that they could not see that Christ, by his coming, had put an end to the law, and the righteousness thereof. We find upon all occasions how much the Pharisees, and those who adhered to that sect, stuck in the law, to the hinderance of their receiving of, or believing in, the Lord Jesus Christ.

^{y Is. 6. 10.}
^{Matt. 13. 11, 14. John 12. 40. Acts 28. 26. Rom. 11. 7, 8, 25.}
^{ch. 4. 4.}

14 But ^ytheir minds were blinded: for until this day remaineth the same vail untaken away in the reading of the old testament; which *vail* is done away in Christ.

Here the apostle expoundeth what he meant before by the mystical veil, viz. the blinding of the eyes of the Jews; of which we read often in the New Testament, Matt. xiii. 14; Mark iv. 12; Luke viii. 10; John xii. 40; Acts xxviii. 26; Rom. xi. 8: see the notes upon all those texts. And (saith the apostle) to this day the veil remaineth not taken away; that veil, which was signified by the veil with which Moses covered his face. *In the reading of the Old Testament*, is, when the Old Testament is read: some part of which was wont to be read in the synagogues every sabbath day. But we shall meet with this in the next verse more fully. But (saith he) this *veil is done away in Christ*. It is really taken away upon the coming of Christ; that is, the veil, that covered the face of Christ, is now truly taken away upon his coming; the types are fulfilled in him, as their complement and antitype; the prophecies are fulfilled in him, as he whom they concerned, and of whom the prophets spake. But the veil, that is drawn over men's hearts, is not taken away, till they come to receive Jesus Christ, as the end of the law for righteousness, to close with him,

and to believe in him. God hath taken the veil off from Christ, by sending him personally to fulfil all righteousness; but Christ profiteth nothing particular souls, until they come to believe in him, then it is taken away from their souls, and not before. Which was the reason that it remained still upon the Jews, among whom he came, as among his own, but they received him not.

15 But even unto this day, when Moses is read, the vail is upon their heart.

The veil, mystically signified by the veil upon Moses's face, which hindereth them from seeing or discerning the Messiah to be come. But why doth he say, *when Moses*, that is, the books of Moses, or rather of the Old Testament, are *read?* Possibly he thereby hinteth, that it was their duty, when in the synagogues they heard the chapters of the Old Testament read, which contain the types and prophecies of Christ, they ought to have looked through those veils, and have considered Christ as the end of those things; so the law, as a schoolmaster, should have led them to Christ: but it was quite otherwise. When they heard those portions of the Old Testament read, through the veil upon their hearts, they could not see through the veil of those types, prophecies, and ritual performances, but rested in them as things in the performance of which they laid their righteousness. Or, if they before had some little convictions upon their spirits, yet when they again came into the synagogues, and heard the law read, the veil again appeared over their hearts, so as they could not see Christ.

^{z Ex. 34. 34.}
^{Rom. 11. 23, 26.}
^{a Is. 25. 7.}

16 Nevertheless ^zwhen it shall turn to the Lord, ^athe vail shall be taken away.

When it shall turn, may be understood of the whole, or of the generality (at least) of the Jews; when they shall be converted to the faith of Christ, or when any particular person shall be converted to Christ, then *the veil shall be taken away;* not the veil with which God covered and veiled the mysteries of the gospel, (that was already taken away upon Christ's coming in the flesh,) but the veil of blindness, which they had drawn over their own souls. Though the light of the gospel shineth clearly, and Christ be unveiled, yet until men, by a true faith, receive Christ, and turn from sinful courses to the obedience of the gospel, they see little or nothing of Christ. The taking away of this veil, and the turning to the Lord, are things done in souls at the same time; therefore nothing is to be concluded here, from the apostle's naming the removal of the impediment, after the effect of which that is a cause.

^{b ver. 6.}
^{1 Cor. 15. 45.}

17 Now ^bthe Lord is that Spirit: and where the Spirit of the Lord *is*, there *is* liberty.

The Lord Christ was a man, but not a mere man; but one who had the Divine nature personally united to his human nature, which is called the *Spirit*, Mark ii. 8. But some think, that the article here is not merely prepositive, but emphatical; and so referreth to ver. 6, where the gospel (the substance of which is Christ) was called *the Spirit*. So it is judged by some, that the apostle preventeth a question which some might have propounded, viz. how the veil should be taken away by men's turning unto the Lord? Saith the apostle, *The Lord is that Spirit*, or he is that Spirit mentioned ver. 18; he is a Spirit, and he gives out of the Spirit unto his people, the Spirit of holiness and sanctification. *And where the Spirit of the Lord is*, (that holy, sanctifying Spirit, which is often called the Spirit of Christ,) *there is liberty;* for our Saviour told the Jews, John viii. 36, *If the Son make you free*, then *shall ye be free indeed:* a liberty from the yoke of the law, from sin, death, hell; but the liberty which seemeth here to be chiefly intended, is a liberty from that blindness and hardness which is upon men's hearts, until they have received the Holy Spirit.

^{c 1 Cor. 13. 12.}
^{d ch. 4. 4, 6. 1 Tim. 1. 11.}
^{e Rom. 8. 29. 1 Cor. 15. 49. Col. 3. 10.}
^{‖ Or, *of the Lord the Spirit.*}

18 But we all, with open face beholding ^cas in a glass ^dthe glory of the Lord, ^eare changed into the same image from glory to glory, *even* as ‖ by the Spirit of the Lord.

Some by *we* here understand all believers; others think it is better understood of ministers: but the universal particle *all* rather guideth us to interpret it of the whole body of believers, of whom the apostle saith, that they *all behold the glory of God with open face;* that is, not under those dark types, shadows, and prophecies, that he was of old revealed under, but as in a looking-glass, which represents the face as at hand; not as in a perspective, which showeth things afar off. We behold him in the glass of the gospel, fully opened and preached; and this sight of Christ in the gospel is not a mere useless sight, but such a sight as changeth the soul into the image and likeness of Christ, *from glory to glory;* carrying on the souls of believers from one degree of grace to another; or making such a glorious change in the heart, as shall not be blotted out until a soul cometh into those possessions of glory which God hath prepared for his people. And all this is done *by the Spirit of the Lord,* working with the word of God in the mouths of his ministers, but so as the Spirit hath the principal agency and efficiency in the work.

CHAP. IV

Paul declareth his unwearied zeal and integrity in preaching the gospel, 1, 2; *so that if any see not the truth of it, it must be owing to their corrupt hearts, not to want of clear light,* 3—6. *The weakness and sufferings he was exposed to redounded to the praise of God's power,* 7—11. *That which animated him in undergoing them for the church's sake, was the assurance of a more exceeding and eternal reward,* 12—18.

THEREFORE seeing we have ᵃ this ministry, ᵇ as we have received mercy, we faint not;

It is the opinion of Beza, that the traducers of this great apostle took advantage from his great trials and afflictions, by reason of them, to conclude him no such man as he was by some represented; and that the apostle upon that takes advantage to magnify his office. God (saith he) having intrusted us with so glorious a ministration, as I have proved that of the gospel to be, according to the measure and proportion of gifts and graces which God hath bestowed upon us, or by reason of that infinite grace and mercy which God hath showed us, in calling us to so honourable a station and office, though we meet with many adversaries, many afflictions, many difficulties, yet we bear up and sink not under them, nor faint in our spirits because of them.

2 But have renounced the hidden things of † dishonesty, not walking in craftiness, ᶜ nor handling the word of God deceitfully; but ᵈ by manifestation of the truth ᵉ commending ourselves to every man's conscience in the sight of God.

But have renounced the hidden things of dishonesty; though we be exposed to many sorrows and sufferings, it is not for any dishonest or unwarrantable behaviour amongst men; nay, we have not only declined openly dishonest actions, but any secret or hidden dishonest behaviour. Possibly he reflecteth upon those, whether teachers or others in this church, who, though they behaved themselves very speciously in their more external conversation, yet it was a shame to speak what things were done of them in secret. We (saith the apostle) have renounced all secret, dishonest, shameful actions. *Not walking in craftiness;* it hath not been our design to carry ourselves craftily, to cheat people with a fair outside and external demeanour. *Nor handling the word of God deceitfully;* nor in our ministry have we cheated and deceived people, instead of instructing them in the truth; crying, Peace, peace, when God hath said, There is no peace to the wicked, and tempering our discourses to all men's humours; not speaking right things, but smooth things. *But by manifestation of the truth commending ourselves to every man's conscience in the sight of God;* our business, in the course of our ministry, hath been to commend ourselves to every man's conscience, as in the sight of God, by manifesting to them the truth of God.

3 But if our Gospel be hid, ᶠ it is hid to them that are lost:

The apostle call the gospel *his gospel,* because of his instrumentality in the promoting and publishing of it. His meaning is, If the doctrine of the gospel, which I am an instrument to preach, be hidden, so as there yet be any souls that do not understand, receive, and believe it, the fault is not in the word we preach, nor yet in our preaching of it, (which hath been in all simplicity and plainness, without craftiness or deceit,) but in themselves, who favour and indulge their lusts to that degree, as that they deserve to be lost, or are at present in their sinful state; in which sense all men are in the parables compared to the lost sheep, or lost groats; and Christ is said to have come to seek and to save those that are lost. Men, mad upon their lusts, may not understand the doctrine of the gospel which we preach; but others understand and believe it. I had rather understand the term *lost* in this sense, than as expressing reprobates; for it seemeth something harsh to make this phrase to signify that God had no more in Corinth at this time that belonged to the election of grace, than those that were already converted; or that all those that were at this time hypocrites in this famous church, were such as perished eternally. Yet the words of the next verse seem rather to favour their notion, who by *lost* here understand reprobates.

4 In whom ᵍ the god of this world ʰ hath blinded the minds of them which believe not, lest ⁱ the light of the glorious Gospel of Christ, ᵏ who is the image of God, should shine unto them.

Though some, by *the god of this world,* understand the true and living God, the Lord of heaven and earth; yet the notion of the most interpreters, that it is the devil who is here called *the god of this world,* because he ruleth over the greatest part of the world, and they are his servants and slaves, is most consonant to Scripture: for though we no where else find him called the god of this world, yet our Saviour twice calls him *the prince of this world,* John xii. 31; xiv. 30; and our apostle, Eph. ii. 2, calls him *the prince of the power of the air.* The effect also doth more properly belong to the devil, than unto God, who no otherwise blindeth the eyes of them than either permissively, by suffering them to shut their own eyes, or judicially. And the apostle declares, that those who are so blinded are such persons as *believe not.* He further declareth the end of the devil's agency in blinding men's eyes with errors, malice, and prejudice, *lest the light of the glorious gospel of Christ, who is the image of God,* the express image of his person, (considered as to his Divine nature,) *should shine unto them,* that is, into their hearts.

5 ¹ For we preach not ourselves, but Christ Jesus the Lord; and ᵐ ourselves your servants for Jesus' sake.

For we preach not ourselves: for a man to preach himself, is to preach the devices and imaginations of his own heart, instead of the revealed will of God; to make his discourses the evomitions of his own lusts and passions; or to make himself the end of his preaching; preaching merely for filthy lucre sake, or to supply himself with bread, or for the ostentation of his own wit, and learning, and parts. *But we preach Christ Jesus the Lord;* we preach what he hath commanded us to preach, and he is the subject of our discourses; we either preach what Christ is, or declare in our preaching what he hath done and suffered for sinners, or what he hath commanded us to do in order to our and your obtaining of life and salvation through him. And in our preaching, though in the first place we are Christ's servants, who hath commanded us to go and preach, and who is the subject matter of our preaching, and whose honour and glory is the end of all our preaching; yet we are also *your servants:* really so, not in that we serve your lusts and humours, and speak smooth things, such as may be pleasing to your humours; but *for Jesus' sake,* because in revealing the will of God to you, and in publishing the grace of the gospel to you, we do you the highest service we can in your eternal concerns.

6 For God, ⁿ who commanded the light to shine out of darkness, † hath ᵒ shined in our hearts, to *give* ᵖ the light of the

knowledge of the glory of God in the face of Jesus Christ.

The Holy Ghost in the New Testament often compareth the work of the new creation by Jesus Christ, to the work of God in the old creation; intimating to us, that the latter is as great a work of providence and Divine power, as the former: Eph. iv. 24, *the new man, after God,* is said to be *created in righteousness and true holiness.* For as that is a creation which is a making of something out of nothing, (as God created the heavens and the earth,) so the production of one thing out of another, which hath no fitness or aptitude to receive such a form, is also a true creation, and requireth an Almighty power. God made *light to shine out of darkness,* Gen. i. 2, 3: so (saith the apostle) he hath made Christ (who is the Light of the world) to shine into our hearts, to give us the true knowledge of God, and of his glory, the glory of his grace. *In the face of Jesus Christ;* that is, by which we attain the clear and certain knowledge of God: as a man is distinctly known by or from his face, God is clearly and distinctly known only in and by Christ.

q ch. 5. 1.
r 1 Cor. 2. 5.
ch. 12. 9.

7 But we have this treasure in ⁹ earthen vessels, ʳ that the excellency of the power may be of God, and not of us.

By the *treasure* here mentioned, the apostle meaneth either his ministration, or apostolical office, which he before had proved glorious, more glorious than that of the law; or else, that *light of the knowledge of the glory of God,* which (as he had before said) God had made to shine into their hearts *in the face of Jesus Christ.* This treasure (saith he) we, even we that are the apostles of the Lord, have in our souls, which are clothed with bodies; and these not made of iron, or stone, or any other matter not capable of impressions of violence, but made of earth, like earthen pots or shells, that easily receive impressions of violence, and are presently broken in pieces. *That the excellency of the power may be of God, and not of us;* that the world may see, that whatsoever powerful effects are wrought by us, they are the work of the excellent power of God; not done by us, but by him; that he, not we, might have all the glory.

s ch. 7, 5.
‖ Or, not altogether without help, or, means.

8 *We are* ˢ troubled on every side, yet not distressed; *we are* perplexed, but ‖ not in despair;

We are troubled on every side; we are many ways, indeed every way, afflicted, afflicted with all sorts of afflictions; *yet not distressed;* but yet we are not like persons cooped up into a strait place, so as they are not able to turn them, nor know which way to move (so the word signifies). *We are perplexed;* the word signifies doubting, uncertain what shall become of us, or how God will dispose of us; full of anxious, troublesome thoughts about what shall be our lot in the world; *but not in despair;* but yet not despairing of the help, presence, support, and assistance of God.

t Ps. 37. 24.

9 Persecuted, but not forsaken; ᵗ cast down, but not destroyed;

Persecuted; violently pursued and prosecuted by such as are the adversaries of the gospel, and enemies to our Lord Jesus, because of our profession of him, and preaching his gospel; *but yet not forsaken* of God, nor wholly of men; God, by the inward influences of his Holy Spirit, supporting, upholding, and comforting us; and also, by his providence, raising us up some friends that stick by us. *Cast down,* either in our own thoughts, (as it is the nature of worldly troubles and afflictions to sink men's thoughts,) or cast down by the violence of men, thrown to the earth; *but not destroyed;* but yet we live, and are by the mighty power of God preserved, that we are not utterly destroyed.

u 1 Cor. 15. 31. ch. 1. 5.
9. Gal. 6. 17.
Phil. 3. 10.
x Rom. 8.17.
2 Tim. 2. 11,
12. 1 Pet. 4. 13.

10 ᵘ Always bearing about in the body the dying of the Lord Jesus, ˣ that the life also of Jesus might be made manifest in our body.

A Christian beareth about with him *the dying of the Lord Jesus* in his mind and soul, while he fetches strength from it to deaden his heart unto sin; being *buried with Christ into death,* and *planted in the likeness of his death;* having his *old man crucified with him, that the body of sin might be destroyed, that henceforth* he *may not serve sin,* Rom. vi.

4—6.. He also beareth about with him *the dying of the Lord Jesus in his body;* either in a representation, while in his sufferings he is made conformable to the death of Christ, Phil. iii. 10; or in his own real sufferings, which he calleth *the dying of the Lord Jesus,* because they were for Christ's sake, and because Christ sympathizeth with them therein, he being afflicted in all their afflictions; yea, and Christ (as the apostle expresseth it, Phil. i. 20,) is magnified in their body, by death, as well as by life. This the apostle tells us he did, *that the life also of Jesus might be made manifest in his body:* by the life of Christ must be here understood, either the resurrection of Christ, and that life which he now liveth in heaven with his Father; or that quickening power of the Spirit of Christ, which then mightily showeth itself in believers, when they are not overwhelmed by the waters of affliction, nor conquered by their sufferings; but in, and over all, are more than conquerors, through that mighty power of Christ which showeth forth itself in them: or (as some think) that lively virtue and power of Christ, which showeth itself in the efficacy of the apostles' ministry; by which so many thousands of souls were brought in to Christ, which was not the effect of their own virtue, but of the life of Christ manifested in their body. But the apostle having before spoken of his sufferings, it seems best interpreted of that living power put forth by Christ, in upholding the earthly vessels of his apostles, notwithstanding all the knocks they met with, to carry about that heavenly treasure with which God had intrusted them.

11 For we which live ʸ are alway delivered unto death for Jesus' sake, that the life also of Jesus might be made manifest in our mortal flesh.

y Ps. 44. 22.
Rom. 8. 36.
1 Cor. 15. 31, 49.

We who are yet alive, as having breath still in our bodies; in another sense we do not live, viz. as life signifies prosperity and happiness; for we *are always delivered unto death,* that is, under continual threats and dangers of death, so that we have always the sentence of death in ourselves; *for Jesus' sake,* for our owning, preaching, and professing Christ, and the doctrine of the gospel. We are not delivered to death for evil-doing, nor merely as innocent persons, but for well-doing; and that in the noblest sense, for obeying the commands and for publishing the gospel of Christ. *That the life also of Jesus might be made manifest in our mortal flesh;* and the infinitely wise providence of God permitteth this, that he might make manifest in our mortal flesh, that Christ is risen from the dead, and liveth for ever, making intercession for us; and, as a living Head, giving necessary influences of strength, support, and comfort, as to all those who are his members, so more particularly to us, who are some of the principal members of that mystical body, of which he is the Head. So that our sufferings are so far from being an evidence against the truth of our doctrine and of our ministration, that they are rather an evidence of the truth of both; as testifying, that he whom we preach, having died for our sins, is also risen for our justification, and exalted at the right hand of God; from whence he dispenseth his spiritual influences, to the souls of all his people, so to our souls in particular, by which we are enabled, without fainting, to suffer such things with boldness, courage, and patience.

12 So then ᶻ death worketh in us, but life in you.

z ch. 13. 9.

You see the difference betwixt us and you; either the real difference, or the fancied difference. We are killed all the day long, in deaths often, delivered to death always; you are rich, and full, and want nothing; *life,* that is, security, happiness, and prosperity, attends you. Or the fancied difference: You bless yourselves, that you are not in so much jeopardy as we are, and some of you are ready to curse us, because vipers stick to our hands, and we are in continually renewed and repeated troubles. Very good interpreters think these words a smart ironical expression, by which the apostle reflecteth upon a party in this church, who from his sufferings concluded against the truth of his doctrine, or his favour with God; and for themselves, because of their immunity and freedom from such sufferings. Others think the sense this, our death is your life; our sufferings are your spiritual advantage.

II. CORINTHIANS IV, V

^a Rom. 1. 12.
2 Pet. 1. 1.
^b Ps. 116. 10.

13 We having ^a the same spirit of faith, according as it is written, ^b I believed, and therefore have I spoken; we also believe, and therefore speak;

The same spirit of faith signifieth the same faith, or faith proceeding from the same spirit; thus, Isa. xi. 2, *the spirit of wisdom and understanding, the spirit of counsel and might, the spirit of knowledge and of the fear of the Lord*, signifieth wisdom, understanding, counsel, might, knowledge, &c. It is a question whom the apostle meaneth when he saith, *We having the same faith*. Some think he meaneth the saints under the Old Testament, whose faith was the same with the faith of believers under the New Testament; and that which guideth them to that interpretation, is the apostle's following quotation out of Psal. cxvi. 10. But the scope of the quotation seemeth to be, to prove that all good men will speak as they believe; they therefore seem better to interpret the text, that make this the sense of it: Though God, in the wisdom of his providence, hath assigned us in this world a different lot from you, that you are full, we empty; you in prosperity, we in adversity; yet we are partakers of the same faith with you, and are acted from the same spirit that you are: and as David's spirit guided him to a profession of his faith, and a speaking what he believed; so we also speak, and must speak, according to what we believe. And this is manifestly the sense of the words, if we consider what followeth in the next verse.

^c Rom. 8. 11.
1 Cor. 6. 14.

14 Knowing that ^c he which raised up the Lord Jesus shall raise up us also by Jesus, and shall present *us* with you.

Knowing that God the Father, who raised up the Lord Jesus from the dead, as the first-fruits of them that sleep, shall likewise, by the virtue of his resurrection, and by a power flowing from him, as now alive, and sitting at the right hand of God, quicken our mortal bodies; that both our souls and bodies may be presented with you, to be both eternally glorified: this maketh us that we do not fear death, but are unconcerned, although by wicked men we every day be delivered to it, and brought within the danger and sight of it; still the resurrection of Christ is made the foundation of our resurrection, and a firm ground for our faith of it. And we are from this text confirmed in the truth of this, that although the lot of God's people in this life be very different, (some are poor, some rich, some in prosperity, some in adversity, and encompassed with sorrows and afflictions,) yet if they have all the same faith, they shall all meet in the resurrection, and shall, by Christ, be all presented unto God as persons redeemed by him, and washed with his blood, and who shall be glorified together.

^d 1 Cor. 3. 21. ch. 1. 6.
Col. 1. 24.
2 Tim. 2. 10.
^e ch. 1. 11.
& 8. 19. &
9. 11, 12.

15 For ^d all things *are* for your sakes, that ^e the abundant grace might through the thanksgiving of many redound to the glory of God.

All things that Christ hath done and suffered, his death, and his resurrection from the dead, and all things that I have done or suffered, all *are for your sakes*; that the greater benefit it be which you receive from God, the greater praise, honour, and glory might redound to him by *the thanksgiving of many*; for God can be no otherwise glorified by us, than by the predicating of his mercy and goodness, and the praising of him for the mercies which we receive from him. The more God doth good unto, the more honour, praise, and glory redoundeth to his name.

^f Rom. 7. 22.
Eph. 3. 16.
Col. 3. 10.
1 Pet. 3. 4.

16 For which cause we faint not; but though our outward man perish, yet ^f the inward *man* is renewed day by day.

Because of this double advantage which accrueth from our sufferings, viz. the furthering of the good of your souls, and the promoting the glory of God from the thanksgivings of many, though we suffer many harsh and bitter things, yet we do not faint nor sink under the burden of our trials; but though, as to our outward man, we are every day dying persons, daily decaying as to the strength, and vigour, and prosperity of our outward man, yet the strength and comfort of our souls and spirits reneweth day by day; we are every day stronger and stronger as to the managing of our spiritual fight, and every day more cheered and comforted in our holy course.

17 For ^g our light affliction, which is but for a moment, worketh for us a far more exceeding *and* eternal weight of glory;

^g Matt. 5. 12.
Rom. 8. 18.
1 Pet. 1. 6.
& 5. 10.

The apostle in these words wonderfully lesseneth his own, and the rest of the apostles', and all other Christians' sufferings for the gospel: he calleth them *light*, not that they were so in themselves, but with respect to that *weight of glory* which he mentioneth in the latter part of the verse: he calleth them momentary, *but for a moment*, with reference to that eternity which is mentioned. The *afflictions* are *light*, the *glory* will be a *weight;* the *afflictions* are *but for a moment*, the *glory* shall be *eternal*. And (saith the apostle) *our affliction worketh for us* this *glory:* the glory will not only be a consequent of these afflictions, but these afflictions will be a cause of it; not a meritorious cause, (for what proportion is there betwixt momentary afflictions and eternal glory? betwixt light afflictions and a weight of glory, an exceeding weight of glory?) but a cause in respect of the infinite goodness and mercy of God, and in respect of the truth and faithfulness of God.

18 ^h While we look not at the things which are seen, but at the things which are not seen: for the things which are seen *are* temporal; but the things which are not seen *are* eternal.

^h Rom. 8. 24.
ch. 5. 7.
Heb. 11. 1.

Two things support the spirits of Christians under trials; 1. The eyeing of him who is invisible; this supported Moses, Heb. xi. 27, *He endured, as seeing him who is invisible*. 2. The seeing by the eye of faith the things which are invisible; the things which God hath prepared in another world for those that love him; the things which eye hath not seen, nor hath it entered into the heart of man to conceive. *For* (saith the apostle) *the things which are seen*, which fall under the senses of men, they *are* but *temporal*, and of a temporary duration; but the invisible things, the *exceeding and eternal weight of glory*, which are before mentioned, they are of an eternal duration, and therefore much to be preferred before those things which endure but for a moment.

CHAP. V

Paul declareth that, in assured hope of a blessed immortality hereafter, he was indifferent to life, and laboured only to approve himself to Christ, 1—9: *that knowing the general judgment that would follow, and the terrors of it, he was solicitous to persuade men,* 10, 11: *that this was said not by way of boasting, but purely to furnish the Corinthians with a reply in his justification against false pretenders,* 12, 13: *that, moved by the love of Christ, he was become dead to all former regards,* 14—16; *and all things being now made new by God in Christ reconciling the world to himself,* 17—19, *he, as ambassador for Christ, besought men to embrace the offered reconciliation,* 20, 21.

FOR we know that if ^a our earthly house of *this* tabernacle were dissolved, we have a building of God, an house not made with hands, eternal in the heavens.

^a Job 4. 19.
ch. 4. 7.
2 Pet. 1. 13, 14.

The apostle had before said, that he looked at the things not seen; in this verse he openeth himself, and showeth what those unseen things are: *We* (saith he) *know*, we have a certain persuasion, we doubt not of it, but that if our body were dissolved. This body he calleth an *earthly house*, either because it is made of the dust of the earth, into which it must again be resolved; or because it is only the habitation of the soul, so long as the soul is on this side of heaven; and therefore he calleth it also, the *earthly house of this tabernacle*. A tabernacle is a moving house or booth built up for a time. This tabernacle (saith the apostle) must be pulled down, and taken in pieces; and we are certain, that if it be dissolved, *we have a building of God*, either a blessed, eternal mansion, (according to that of our Saviour, John xiv. 2, *In my Father's house are many mansions,)* or else, God will give us a spiritual, glorious, incorruptible body; not *a house made with hands,* nor a house that shall be dissolved and any more pulled down, but which shall be *eternal in the heavens;* in such a state, as that it shall be incorruptible, and no more subject to any corruption or decay.

b Rom. 8.23. 2 For in this [b] we groan, earnestly desiring to be clothed upon with our house which is from heaven:

We are so confident of such a blessed state, that we passionately desire to be invested into it; and this groaning is also an evidence of it, for the desire of grace shall not be made frustrate; desirous that our mortality may put on immortality, and our corruption may put on incorruption. It is against the nature of man to desire death, which is the stripping or unclothing the soul of flesh; but not to desire that the garment of immortality may be put upon mortality, which is that our house from heaven, which is mentioned in ver. 1.

c Rev. 3. 18. & 16. 15. 3 If so be that [c] being clothed we shall not be found naked.

Some make the clothing here spoken of different from the clothing before mentioned; and make this verse restrictive of what the apostle had before said, of the certainty which some have of being clothed upon with a glorious body. *If so be* (saith the apostle) *we shall not be found naked,* but *clothed,* i. e. with the wedding-garment of Christ's righteousness; for concerning those that do not die in the Lord, that do not watch, and keep their garments, it is said, Rev. xvi. 15, they shall walk naked, and men shall see their shame. But considering the clothing before mentioned was not this clothing, but the superinducing of an immortal, incorruptible, glorious state of body, upon our mortal, corruptible state, some judicious interpreters think, that the clothing here mentioned is the clothing of the soul with the body. It is manifest that the apostles apprehended Christ's second coming much nearer than it hath proved. Therefore he saith, 1 Thess. iv. 15, *We that are alive* (supposing that generation might live) to Christ's second coming; and 1 Cor. xv. 51, *We shall not all sleep, but we shall all be changed.* This some think (and that not improbably) is the cause of this passage; the sense of which they judge to be this: If so be that we be, at the resurrection, found in the flesh, clothed still with our bodies, and shall not be found naked, that is, stripped of our flesh, and dead before that time.

4 For we that are in *this* tabernacle do groan, being burdened: not for that d 1 Cor. 15. 53, 54. we would be unclothed, but [d] clothed upon, that mortality might be swallowed up of life.

By *tabernacle,* he meaneth (as he had before expounded it) the earthly house of our body. *Do groan;* both a groaning of grief, and also of desire. *Being burdened;* either with the body of flesh; or with sin, *the body of death,* Rom. vii. 24; or with the load of trials and afflictions. *Not that we would be unclothed,* that is, die, be unclothed of our flesh, (nature abhorreth death, and flieth from it,) *but clothed upon;* which is expounded, 1 Cor. xv. 54, our *corruptible* having *put on incorruption,* and our *mortal* having *put on immortality.* And this confirmeth what was observed before, that the apostles had some persuasion, (though not from any Divine revelation of that hour,) that the resurrection, and day of judgment, would be before the determination of that age and generation; that so we might come into the possession of eternal life (for that the apostle meaneth by *mortality* being *swallowed up of life).* Death is not desirable for its own sake, but upon the account of that immortal life into which it leadeth the souls of believers; nor (as was said before) doth the apostle here directly desire death, (which is that which in this verse he calleth unclothing,) but rather the change mentioned 1 Cor. xv. 52, which he here calleth a clothing upon.

e Is. 29. 23. Eph. 2. 10. f Rom. 8. 23. ch. 1. 22. Eph. 1. 14. & 4. 30. 5 Now [e] he that hath wrought us for the selfsame thing *is* God, who also [f] hath given unto us the earnest of the Spirit.

The selfsame thing is the life, the eternal life, mentioned in the former verse; the *house in the heavens, not made with hands,* ver. 1. God *hath wrought us for* it (as some interpret the text) in creation, and by his providence, forming our bodies in the womb: but it is much better interpreted by others concerning regeneration; for in the first birth (without respect to the decree of election) God hath no more wrought us for it, than the worst of men. The apostle therefore is, doubtless, to be understood, as speaking concerning the work of grace, which is here attributed to God; we have not wrought ourselves into or up to any fitness or any grounded expectation of the future blessed and glorious estate; but it is God who hath prepared us for it, and wrought such a lively hope of it in us. *Who also hath given unto us the earnest of the Spirit;* and hath also given us his Holy Spirit as the pledge and earnest of it; (concerning this, see chap. i. 22;) he hath given us his Spirit to dwell and to work in us, and to assure us of what we speak of, viz. the house in the heavens, the building of God, that is not made with hands. The Spirit of grace given to the people of God, working and dwelling in them, is a certain pledge of that glory and life eternal, which he hath prepared for them.

6 Therefore *we are* always confident, knowing that, whilst we are at home in the body, we are absent from the Lord:

We are always full of courage and comfort, being confident of this glory, and the swallowing up of mortality in life: for we know, that while we are in our earthly home (which is our body) we are farthest off from that which is our true home, (which is heaven,) from the vision and fruition of God; for believers are but *strangers and pilgrims on the earth,* desiring *a better country, that is,* an *heavenly,* Heb. xi. 13, 16.

7 (For [g] we walk by faith, not by sight:) g Rom. 8. 24, 25. ch. 4. 18. 1 Cor. 13. 12. Heb. 11. 1.

That is, we live, and order our conversations, *not by sight,* or any evidence of sense, but *by faith,* which is described by the apostle, Heb. xi. 1, to be *the substance of things hoped for, the evidence of things not seen.* We see nothing here by the eye of sense but mortality, corruption, and misery; but by faith we see another more excellent and glorious state, and we order our life according to our faith, and sight of things that are invisible: or *sight* here may be taken more strictly for the beatific vision prepared in heaven for the saints.

8 We are confident, *I say,* and [h] willing rather to be absent from the body, and to be present with the Lord. h Phil. 1. 23.

We are confident of such a blessed state, and this makes us willing to be out of this body, that we might have the glorious presence and enjoyment of God to all eternity.

9 Wherefore we || labour, that, whether present or absent, we may be accepted of him. || Or, *endeavour.*

Having such a hope, yea, not such a hope only, but such an assurance and confidence, *we labour,* both actively, doing the will of God, and passively, submitting to the will of God in all afflictive providences; that while we are in the body, and absent from the Lord, *we may be accepted of him;* as we know we shall be, when we shall be present with him, in another sense than we now are.

10 [i] For we must all appear before the judgment seat of Christ; [k] that every one may receive the things *done* in *his* body, according to that he hath done, whether *it be* good or bad. i Matt. 25. 31, 32. Rom. 14. 10. k Rom. 2. 6. Gal. 6. 7. Eph. 6. 8. Col. 3. 24, 25. Rev. 22. 12.

The apostle declareth, either the ground of his confidence, or, rather, the reason of his and other believers' labour, so to behave themselves, as that, both in life and death, they might be accepted of God; that was, his knowledge and firm belief of the last judgment. It is called *the judgment-seat of Christ,* because he it is whom God hath appointed to be the *judge* both *of* the *quick and* the *dead,* Acts x. 42. The word translated *appear,* is πεφανερῶσθαι, which signifieth to be made manifest, and so signifieth not only to appear, but to be inquired into, searched, and examined, and narrowly sifted: and this lets us know, that those texts which speak of believers not being judged, or not coming into judgment, must not be understood of the judgment of inquiry, (for all shall come into that judgment,) but of the judgment of condemnation. And it lets us also know the vanity of their opinion, who think that pagans shall not rise again in the last day. *That every one may receive the things done in his body, according to that he hath done, whether it be good or bad:* the end of this judgment is declared, that every man may receive according to what he hath done in his body; that is, according to the thoughts he hath thought, the words that he hath spoken, the actions which he hath done, during the time that his soul dwelt upon the earth in his body; whether the things which he did in that state were good, and such things as God required; or sinful, and contrary to the revealed will of God. What this receiving means, we are told, Matt. xxv. 46, *These shall go away into everlasting punishment, but the righteous into life eternal.* Hence we read. John v. 29, of a *resurrection of life,* and a *resurrection of damnation.*

l Job 31. 23.
Heb. 10. 31.
Jude 23.
m ch. 4. 2.

11 Knowing therefore ¹the terror of the Lord, we persuade men; but ᵐwe are made manifest unto God; and I trust also are made manifest in your consciences.

We believing and being fully persuaded, that there shall be such a great and terrible day of the Lord, when there shall be such a narrow inquiry and search into whatsoever men have thought, spoke, or done in the flesh; *we persuade men* to believe in the Lord Jesus Christ, to walk according to the rule of the gospel, to be charitable towards us, and not to censure or judge us, or use against us hard speeches. If any will not be persuaded to think well of us, yet the sincerity of our hearts and ways is *made manifest unto God;* he knoweth what we are, and how we have behaved ourselves: and *I trust* we have so behaved ourselves, that we are not only made manifest unto God, but we *are made manifest in your consciences;* so as your consciences will bear us a testimony, how we have behaved ourselves amongst you.

n ch. 3. 1.

12 For ⁿwe commend not ourselves again unto you, but give you occasion

o ch. 1. 14.

°to glory on our behalf, that ye may have somewhat to *answer* them which glory

‖ Gr. in the face.

† in appearance, and not in heart.

I do not speak this to commend myself unto you; he had before declared, that he trusted that he was made manifest to their consciences, and so needed not further to commend himself. But (saith he) I speak it only to *give you occasion to glory,* to glory in me as the apostle of Christ unto you, or to defend me against the scandals and reproaches of those that reproach me, when themselves have no true inward cause of glorying, though they have in outward appearance, in respect of their riches, wit, wisdom, or the like.

p ch. 11. 1, 16, 17. & 12. 6, 11.

13 For ᵖwhether we be beside ourselves, *it is* to God: or whether we be sober, *it is* for your cause.

It should seem, that some amongst the Corinthians, amongst other reproaches, had reproached Paul for a madman; either taking advantage of the warmth and fervour of his spirit, or of those ecstasies in which he sometimes was; or of his speaking things which they could not apprehend and understand: as the Roman governor, in the Acts, told him, *Much learning hath made thee mad.* The apostle tells them, that if indeed he was beside himself in any of their opinion, it was *to God,* that is, for the honour and glory of God: or if he was sober, it was for their sake; in what temper soever he was, it was either for service to God, or them.

14 For the love of Christ constraineth

q Rom. 5. 15.

us; because we thus judge, that ᑫif one died for all, then were all dead:

The *love of Christ* signifieth either that love towards the sons of men which was in Christ before the foundation of the world; for even then (as Solomon telleth us, Prov. viii. 31) he was *rejoicing in the habitable part of the earth, and his delight was with the sons of men:* which love showed itself in time, in his coming and assuming our natures, and dying upon the cross for us; John xv. 13, *Greater love hath no man than this, that a man lay down his life for his friends.* Or else it signifieth that habit of love to Christ, which is in every believer; for it is true of either of these, that they constrain a believer's soul. *Because* (saith the apostle) *we thus account,* or reason, *that if one died for all. All* here is interpreted according to the various notions of men, about the extent of the death of Christ. Some by the term understanding all individuals; some, all the elect, or all those that should believe in Christ; others, some of all nations, Jews or Gentiles. Be it as it will, that point is not to be determined by this universal particle, which is as often in Scripture used in a more general sense. The apostle here concludeth, *that if one died for all, then were all dead;* which is to be understood of a spiritual death, as Eph. ii. 1. And the apostle's argument dependeth upon this, that if all, for whom Christ died, had not been dead in sin, there then had been no need of his dying for to expiate their sin, and to redeem them from the guilt and power of it; but be they what they would, for whom Christ died, whether all individuals, or all the elect only, his dying for them was a manifest evidence that they were dead.

15 And *that* he died for all, ʳthat they which live should not henceforth live unto themselves, but unto him which died for them, and rose again.

r Rom. 6. 11, 12. & 14. 7, 8.
1 Cor. 6. 19.
Gal. 2. 20.
1 Thes. 5. 10.
1 Pet. 4. 2.

And he died for all those for whom he died, not only to redeem them from the guilt of sin, but also from their vain conversation; that they which live by his grace, might not make themselves the end of their life, and live to serve themselves, and gratify their own corrupt inclinations; but might make the service of Christ, the honour and glory of him who died for them, and also rose again from the dead, the end of their lives; arguing the reasonableness of a holy and Christian life, from the love and end of Christ in dying for them; according to that, Rom. xiv. 7, 8, *For none of us liveth to himself, and no man dieth to himself. For whether we live, we live unto the Lord; and whether we die, we die unto the Lord: whether we live, therefore, or die, we are the Lord's.* This is one way by which a believer fetcheth strength from the death of Christ to die unto sin, and from his resurrection to live unto newness of life; he concluding, If Christ died, and rose again for him, that then he was once dead in trespasses and sins; and therefore he judgeth himself obliged, now that he is made spiritually alive, not to live to himself, or serve his own profit, honour, reputation, lusts, or passions, but to live in obedience to him, and to the honour and glory of him, who died to redeem him from the guilt and power of sin, and rose again to quicken him to newness of life and conversation, to the honour and glory of his Redeemer.

16 ˢWherefore henceforth know we no man after the flesh: yea, though we have known Christ after the flesh, ᵗyet now henceforth know we *him* no more.

s Mat. 12. 50.
John 15. 14.
Gal. 5. 6.
Phil. 3. 7, 8.
Col. 3. 11.
t John 6. 63.

Wherefore henceforth know we no man after the flesh: words of sense in Scripture ordinarily signify more than the act of that sense which they express; particularly this term *know* ordinarily signifieth to approve' and acknowledge; and so it signifies here. We *know,* that is, we regard, we acknowledge no man in the discharge of our office; we regard no man with respect to any external fleshly consideration. Under which notion he comprehends all things not spiritual, whether carnal relations, riches, &c. *Yea, though we have known Christ after the flesh;* not from any sight of him, for we read not that Paul at any time saw Christ, but, Acts ix., when he saw him, not according to the flesh, but as exalted at the right hand of God: but by the hearing of the ear Paul had known Christ, as one that had lived in the flesh, and who had conversed with men for above thirty years; *yet* (saith he) *we know him no more,* we shall neither see nor hear him any more in the flesh; we now only know him as he hath a glorious body, with which he sitteth at the right hand of God.

17 Therefore if any man ᵘ*be* in Christ,

u Rom. 8. 9,
& 16. 7.
Gal. 6. 15.

II. CORINTHIANS V, VI

‖ Or, let him be.
x Gal. 5. 6. & 6. 15.
y Is. 43. 18, 19. & 65. 17. Eph. 2. 15. Rev. 21. 5.

‖ *he is* ˣa new creature: ʸold things are passed away; behold, all things are become new.

If any man be in Christ, is as much as, if any man be implanted or ingrafted into Christ, by faith united to him, *he is a new creature;* (the Greek is, a new creation;) a phrase which argueth the greatest change imaginable, and such a one as can be wrought in the soul by no other power than the power of God. We have the same expression, Gal. vi. 15. The ellipsis of the verb makes some translate it, *Let him be a new creature,* supplying ἔϛω for ἐϛί. But the next words show us, that the apostle is speaking of what is past, *Old things are passed away,* old affections, passions, notions, &c. He hath the same soul, but new qualities, new apprehensions in his understanding, new inclinations in his will and affections, new thoughts, counsels, and designs. The predicate showeth, that the term, *be in Christ,* cannot be understood of those that are only in the church, and turned from paganism to the Christian faith; for there are many such in the world, in whom there is no new creation, and who have in them nothing of this new creature.

z Rom. 5. 10. Eph. 2. 16. Col. 1. 20. 1 John 2. 2. & 4. 10.

18 And all things *are* of God, ᶻwho hath reconciled us to himself by Jesus Christ, and hath given to us the ministry of reconciliation;

And all things are of God; this change, which is wrought in our hearts, is not of ourselves, but wrought in us by the great and mighty power of God: so John i. 13, *Which were born, not of blood, nor of the will of the flesh, nor of the will of man, but of God;* of God, as the principal efficient Cause. *Who hath reconciled us to himself by Jesus Christ;* who, by the blood of his Son Jesus Christ, meritoriously, and by the Spirit of Christ, actually, hath reconciled us unto himself; of enemies hath made us friends. *And hath given to us the ministry of reconciliation;* hath intrusted us with the preaching of the gospel. It is God that hath reconciled us; it is Christ by whom we are reconciled, his blood is the price of our reconciliation; but he committed to his apostles, and so to the successive ministers of the gospel, *the ministry of reconciliation*, that is, the ministry of the gospel, by which this reconciliation is published to such as are yet enemies to God. They have but a ministration in it; God hath appointed them to publish and to declare it, and to entreat men to be reconciled unto him.

a Rom. 3. 24, 25.

19 To wit, that ᵃGod was in Christ, reconciling the world unto himself, not imputing their trespasses unto them; and hath †committed unto us the word of reconciliation.

+ Gr. put in us.

God was in Christ, reconciling the world unto himself; by *world,* here, some would understand all mankind, and by *reconciling,* no more than making God reconcilable; but this proceedeth from an over-fondness of their principle of Christ's dying for all, and every man. For as it is manifest from a multitude of scriptures, that *world* is many times taken in a much more limited and restrained sense; so there is nothing here that guides us to interpret it in such a latitude; nay, that which followeth, doth manifestly so restrain it; for God was not in Christ, reconciling the world to himself, that is, every man and woman in the world, so as not to impute their sins to them. This the apostle here affirmeth; which makes it manifest, that by *world* here is meant many, some of all sorts, as well Gentiles as Jews; even so many as he pleaseth not to impute their sins unto. *And hath committed unto us the word of reconciliation:* now, (saith the apostle,) the dispensing and publishing that word, by which this reconciliation is made known to the children of men, God hath committed to us; to us, that are apostles, and so to the ministers of the gospel that shall succeed us in the work of the ministry. This mightily commendeth the gospel, and the preaching of it, that it is the word by which, as a means, souls are reconciled unto God.

b Job 33. 23. Mal. 2. 7. ch. 3. 6. Eph. 6. 20. c ch. 6. 1.

20 Now then we are ᵇambassadors for Christ, as ᶜthough God did beseech *you* by us: we pray *you* in Christ's stead, be ye reconciled to God.

The apostle here giveth us a true notion, not only of apostles, which were the first and principal ministers of the gospel, but of all other ministers; teaching us what all ministers should be, and what all true ministers of the gospel are. They *are ambassadors for Christ.* There is by nature an enmity betwixt the creature and God; he naturally hateth God, and God is angry with him. Those *that were sometime alienated, and enemies* in their *minds by wicked works, Christ hath reconciled in the body of his flesh through death,* Col. i. 21, 22; he hath purchased a reconciliation for them. But yet, till they have received Christ as their Lord and Saviour, they are not actually recovered to God by him. God does by men, as great princes do by such as they are at enmity with; he sends his ministers to them, who are his ambassadors; and as all ambassadors represent the person of him whose ambassadors they are, and speak in his name, and as in his stead, persuading to peace; so these speak as in Christ's name, and in God's stead; their business is to beseech men to be reconciled unto God, to lay down their arms, and to accept of the terms of the gospel for peace and reconciliation.

d Is. 53. 6, 9, 12. Gal 3. 13. 1 Pet. 2. 22, 24. 1 John 3. 5. e Rom. 1. 17. & 5. 19. & 10. 3.

21 For ᵈhe hath made him *to be* sin for us, who knew no sin; that we might be made ᵉthe righteousness of God in him.

For he hath made him to be sin for us, who knew no sin: Christ *knew* no sin, as he was guilty of no sin; *Which of you* (saith he, John viii. 46) *convinceth me of sin?* 1 Pet. ii. 22, He *did no sin, neither was guile found in his mouth:* but God *made him to be sin for us. He was numbered with the transgressors,* Isa. liii. 12. Our sins were reckoned to him; so as though personally he was no sinner, yet by imputation he was, and God dealt with him as such; for he was made a sacrifice for our sins, a sin-offering; so answering the type in the law, Lev. iv. 3, 25, 29; v. 6; vii. 2. *That we might be made the righteousness of God in him;* that so his righteousness might be imputed to us, and we might be made righteous with such a righteousness as those souls must have whom God will accept. As Christ was not made sin by any sin inherent in him, so neither are we made righteous by any righteousness inherent in us, but by the righteousness of Christ imputed to us; as he was a sinner by the sins of his people reckoned and imputed unto him.

CHAP. VI

Paul entreateth the Corinthians not to frustrate God's grace, 1, 2; setting forth his own inoffensive, faithful, and patient demeanour in the discharge of his ministry, 3—10: of which he telleth them he spake more freely out of the great love he bare them, 11, 12; challenging the like affection from them in return, 13. He dissuadeth from any intimate connexions with unbelievers, 14, 15. Christians are the temples of the living God, 16—18.

a 1 Cor. 3. 9. b ch. 5. 20. c Heb. 12. 15.

WE then, *as* ᵃworkers together *with him,* ᵇbeseech *you* also ᶜthat ye receive not the grace of God in vain.

We then, as workers together with him: ministers of the gospel are fellow workers together with Christ; though but as instruments, serving him as the principal Agent, and efficient Cause: he trod the wine-press of his Father's wrath alone, and had no partner in the purchase of man's salvation; but in the application of the purchased salvation, he admits of fellow workers. Though the internal work be his alone, and the effects of his Spirit upon the souls of those whose hearts are changed; yet there is a ministerial part, which lieth in exhortation and argument, by the ear conveyed to the soul; thus ministers work together with Christ. And without him they can do nothing: they are workers, but they must have Christ work with them, or they will find that they labour in vain. *Beseech you also that ye receive not the grace of God in vain:* grace signifieth any free gift; and it is in the New Testament variously applied; but here it signifies, the doctrine of the gospel, held forth in the preaching of it, which these Corinthians had received with the ears of their bodies. And this was Paul's, and should be every godly minister's, work, not with

II. CORINTHIANS VI.

roughness, but with all mildness and gentleness, to beseech those to whom they preach the gospel, that they would believe and embrace it, and live up to the holy rules of it; without which, (as to their souls' benefit,) all the kindness of God, in affording them the gospel and means of grace, is in vain, and lost: though God yet hath his end, and his ministers shall be *a sweet savour to God,* as well with reference to them that perish, as those who shall be saved. For the effectual grace of God in the heart, that cannot be received in vain; nor is that here spoken of.

d Is. 49. 8.

2 (For he saith, ^d I have heard thee in a time accepted, and in the day of salvation have I succoured thee: behold, now *is* the accepted time; behold, now *is* the day of salvation.)

For he saith, I have heard thee in a time accepted, and in the day of salvation have I succoured thee: the words here quoted, are taken out of the prophet Isaiah, chap. xlix. 8, according to the Septuagint's translation. Though some think, that the apostle here doth but accommodate to the spiritual salvation brought in by Christ, a temporal salvation mentioned, and primarily intended; yet the most and best interpreters rather judge that whole chapter in Isaiah to refer to Christ, and that the salvation there mentioned, is to be understood of the spiritual salvation of the gospel; of which also the apostle speaketh here, and maketh these words (as in the prophet) the words of God the Father to Christ his Son; testifying both his assistance of him in the accomplishment of the work of man's redemption, and his acceptance of him; according to which sense, the *accepted time* is the same with what the apostle calls, *the fulness of time,* Gal. iv. 4; (though it may also be so called in the same sense that the apostle calleth the gospel *a faithful saying, worthy of all acceptation,* 1 Tim. i. 15;) in which sense the gospel time was prophesied of as an acceptable time, Gen. xlix. 10; Hag. i. 8. *Behold, now is the accepted time; behold, now is the day of salvation;* now is that accepted or acceptable time, now is that day of salvation, spoken of by the prophet; therefore you are concerned to receive this grace of the gospel, and to live up to the rule of it.

e Rom. 14. 13. 1 Cor. 9. 12. & 10. 32.

3 ^e Giving no offence in any thing, that the ministry be not blamed:

Giving no offence in any thing: to give no offence signifies, to avoid all actions which may be occasion of spiritual stumbling unto others, i. e. to make them to sin against God, or estrange their hearts from Christ, and the owning and profession of his gospel. These words may be understood as a general precept given to all Christians; so it agreeth with 1 Cor. x. 30, 32; or (which the following verses seem most to favour) as referring to himself and Timothy, and other ministers of the gospel; like true pastors of the church of Christ, going out before the flock, and showing in their example what they ought to be. *That the ministry be not blamed; the ministry* here may either signify the office of the ministry, or the subject of it, the gospel, which, chap. v. 18, is called *the ministry of reconciliation:* not only the office of the ministry, but the gospel itself, suffereth by the scandalous conversation of ministers and private Christians; ignorant persons being not able, or not willing, to distinguish betwixt the faults of persons and the faults of a doctrine or office.

† Gr. commending. ch. 4. 2. f 1 Cor. 4. 1.

4 But in all *things* † approving ourselves ^f as the ministers of God, in much patience, in afflictions, in necessities, in distresses,

But in all things approving ourselves as the ministers of God: ministers of the gospel are in the first place to be considered as *the ministers of God;* secondarily. as ministers and servants of the church; which they ought to serve so far, as in serving it they do obey Christ. None can approve or commend themselves for ministers of God that live a scandalous life; God hath not sent them to lay stumblingblocks in, but to remove them out of, the way of men. *In much patience; patience* signifies an enduring of evils quietly and cheerfully, at the command of God; or when we see it is the will of God, we should patiently submit to put our necks into the heaviest yokes. The apostle goes on reckoning up several species of those evils: *afflictions* is a general term, signifying any evils that wear out our bodies. *Necessities* signify any bodily wants of food, or raiment, or whatever is for the use of man's life. *Distresses* signify, properly, a man's being straitened, or thrust up in a place, so as that he knoweth not how to steer himself; and, metaphorically, a want of counsel, not knowing what to do, or which way to turn ourselves.

5 ^g In stripes, in imprisonments, ‖ in tumults, in labours, in watchings, in fastings;

g ch. 11. 23, &c. ‖ Or, in tossings to and fro.

In stripes: the apostle, chap. xi. 23, tells us he was *in stripes above measure;* and ver. 24, that *of the Jews* he *five times received forty stripes save one:* we read of his *many stripes,* Acts xvi. 23. *In imprisonments;* of the imprisonment of him and Silas, Acts xvi. 23, which was not the only time before the writing of this Epistle, as appeareth by this verse. *In tumults,* or seditions raised by the Jews and the heathens; we have a record of one at Ephesus, Acts xix., caused by Demetrius: others, by *tumults,* here, understand unfixed and uncertain habitations, tossing to and fro, so as they could be quiet in no place; but the former seemeth rather the sense of the word, as Luke xxi. 9; 1 Cor. xiv. 33. *In labours;* he either means labours with his hands, (which Paul was sometimes put to, as Acts xviii. 3; xx. 34,) or travels and journeys. The word is a general word, significative of any pains that men take. *In watchings;* religious watching, chap. xi. 27. *In fastings,* as acts of discipline, by which he kept under his body. and brought it into subjection, as he told us, 1 Cor. ix. 27.

6 By pureness, by knowledge, by longsuffering, by kindness, by the Holy Ghost, by love unfeigned,

By pureness: as the apostle in the former words had declared the patience of his conversation, in the enduring of the afflictions of the gospel; so in this verse he declares the more internal holiness of it, under the general notion of *pureness;* showed in his knowledge, faith, gentleness, kindness, or goodness towards all men. The word translated *pureness,* signifieth rather the universal rectitude of his heart and ways, than (as some think) the habit or exercise of any particular virtue. In or *by knowledge;* a right understanding and notion of spiritual things; if it doth not here signify faith, which is a superstructure on this foundation, and that habit which hath a special influence upon purifying the heart, Acts xv. 9. Without knowledge there can be no purity, Prov. xix. 2. *By long-suffering;* the apostle means, not being easily provoked by such as had offended him, or done him wrong. *By kindness;* the word translated *kindness,* signifies generally any goodness by which a man may show himself either sweet and pleasant, or useful and profitable, unto his neighbour. *By the Holy Ghost:* thus the apostle showeth how he behaved himself; but not through his own strength, but through the influence and assistance of the Holy Ghost. *By love unfeigned;* the *love unfeigned* here mentioned, is a general term, signifying that habit of grace wrought in his soul by the Holy Spirit of God, which was the principle of the *long-suffering* and *kindness* before mentioned.

7 ^h By the word of truth, by ⁱ the power of God, by ^k the armour of righteousness on the right hand and on the left,

h ch. 4. 2. & 7. 14. i 1 Cor. 2. 4. k ch. 10. 4. Eph. 6. 11,13. 2 Tim. 4. 7.

By the word of truth; living up to and keeping our eye upon the word of God, which is the word of truth: this seemeth to be the sense, rather than speaking truth to every one, as some have thought. *By the power of God;* by the efficacious working of the Spirit of God upon our hearts, enabling us to live up to the doctrine we preach. Some understand here, by *the power of God,* that extraordinary power of working miracles, which God gave the apostles; others, thereby, what the apostle calls *the power of God unto salvation,* Rom. i. 16. It may be understood of the first and the last joined together; for the gospel is no otherwise the power of God to salvation, than as it is attended to the souls of those to whom it is so made powerful, with the inward, powerful, efficacious working of the Holy Spirit. *By the armour of righteousness;* he means a good conscience, (which cannot be without a universal rectitude, or uprightness of life,) which is a defence against all temptations, either from prosperity or from adversity. In which sense that of Solomon is true, *He that walketh uprightly, walketh surely*, Prov. x. 9: and David prayeth, Psal. xxv. 21, *Let integrity and uprightness preserve me.*

8 By honour and dishonour, by evil report and good report: as deceivers, and *yet* true;

By honour and dishonour; we depart not from our integrity, whether we be honoured or dishonoured. *By evil report and good report;* well or evilly reported of. This hath from the beginning been the lot of all the faithful ministers of Christ; some have given them honour, others have cast reproach upon them; some have given a good report of them, some an evil report. *As deceivers, and yet true;* some have represented them as impostors, and such as deceived the people; others have spoken of them as true men: their business is to go through good report and bad report, honour and dishonour, still holding fast their integrity.

l ch. 4. 2. & 5. 11. & 11. 6.
m 1 Cor. 4. 9. ch. 1. 9. & 4. 10, 11.
n Ps. 118. 18.

9 As unknown, and ¹*yet* well known; ᵐ as dying, and, behold, we live; ⁿ as chastened, and not killed;

As unknown, and yet well known; dealt with by Jews and heathens as persons wholly unknown to them, though we be sufficiently known; or being such whom the world knoweth not, as to our state towards God, and interest in him, though it knows us well enough as to our other circumstances. *As dying, and, behold, we live;* so hunted and persecuted, as that we appear every day dying; yet such hath been the power of God's providence, that we yet live. *As chastened, and not killed;* and though our heavenly Father chasteneth us, yet we are not utterly consumed: the apostle alludeth to that, Psal. cxviii. 18, *The Lord hath chastened me sore; but he hath not given me over to death.*

10 As sorrowful, yet alway rejoicing; as poor, yet making many rich; as having nothing, and *yet* possessing all things.

As sorrowful, yet alway rejoicing; appearing to others as persons drowned in griefs and sorrows, yet we are always rejoicing in God, (Hab. iii. 17, 18,) and in the testimony of a good conscience, chap. i. 12. *As poor, yet making many rich;* in outward appearance poor, having no abundance of the good things of this life; yet making many rich in knowledge and grace, God by us dispensing to them the riches of his grace. *As having nothing, and yet possessing all things: as having nothing,* no houses, no lands, no silver or gold, Acts iii. 6; yet being as well satisfied and contented, as if all things were ours; as well satisfied with that little which we have, as the men of the world are with their abundance; *possessing all things* in Christ, though having little in the creature.

o ch. 7. 3.

11 O *ye* Corinthians, our mouth is open unto you, ° our heart is enlarged.

Our mouth is open to speak freely to you, and to communicate to you the whole will and counsel of God; *our heart is enlarged* both by the love that I have towards you, and by the rejoicing that I have in you. This enlargement of my heart is that which openeth my lips, and makes me speak freely to you, both in admonishing you of your errors, and in exhorting you to your duty.

p ch. 12. 15.

12 Ye are not straitened in us, but ᵖ ye are straitened in your own bowels.

Ye are not straitened in us; if you cannot mutually rejoice in me, and what I write, or if you do not repay me the like affection, the fault is not in me; I have done my duty, and that too from a true principle of love to you. *But ye are straitened in your own bowels;* but it is through mistakes and misapprehensions in yourselves, your not aright conceiving of me in the discharge of my apostolical office. Or the cause of your trouble and sorrow is from yourselves, upon your suffering the incestuous person, and other scandalous persons, to abide in your communion; which was an error I could not but take notice of, according to that apostolical authority which God hath committed to me.

13 Now for a recompence in the same, (ᑫ I speak as unto *my* children,) be ye also enlarged.

q 1 Cor. 4. 14.

Be ye also enlarged, both in love to me, and also in obedience; it is but a just recompence for that great affection which I have borne, and upon all occasions showed to you; and also for that faithfulness which I have showed in discharging the duty of my relation to you. For I speak as a father unto children, it being but reasonable, that children should recompense to their fathers their love to them, and be as exact and faithful in their duty to their parents, as their parents are in their duty towards them.

14 ʳ Be ye not unequally yoked together with unbelievers: for ˢ what fellowship hath righteousness with unrighteousness? and what communion hath light with darkness?

r Deut. 7. 2, 3
1 Cor. 5. 9.
& 7. 39.
s 1 Sam. 5. 2, 3. 1 Kings 18. 21.
Ecclus. 13. 17. 1 Cor. 10. 21. Eph. 5. 7, 11.

Be ye not unequally yoked together with unbelievers: they too much restrain the sense of this general precept, who either limit it to religious communion with idolaters, or to civil communion in marriages. The precept is delivered in a term of more general significancy, than to be limited by either of these, though both of them, questionless, be comprehended in it: μὴ γίνεσθε ἑτεροζυγοῦντες, do not become such as in the same yoke draw another way. It is a metaphor drawn from horses or oxen; which should draw together, being in the same yoke, neither standing still, nor yet holding back. It is a general precept, prohibitive of all unnecessary communion and intimate fellowship with such, as either in matters of faith or worship, or in their lives and conversations, declare themselves to be unbelievers; for why we should expound ἀπίστοις of infidels merely, I cannot tell, especially considering that the apostle, 1 Cor. v. 9—11, seems to allow a further communion with a heathen, than with a notoriously scandalous Christian. So as this precept may reasonably be interpreted by those in the former Epistle, of marrying with such, eating with them at idol-feasts, or at the Lord's table, (as chap. v.,) maintaining intimate communion with them, &c. *For what fellowship hath righteousness with unrighteousness? and what communion hath light with darkness?* the reason he giveth, is, because they could have no comfortable communion with such; they were *righteousness,* those persons were *unrighteousness;* they were *light,* such persons were *darkness,* that is, full of the darkness of sin and ignorance. In the mean time, this precept ought not to be extended to a total avoiding of commerce with, or being in the company of, either heathens, or scandalous persons; for as to that, the same apostle had before determined it lawful, 1 Cor. v. 11. Whatever communion with such persons is either necessary from the law of God or nature, or for the support and upholding of human life and society, is lawful even with such persons; but all other is unlawful.

15 And what concord hath Christ with Belial? or what part hath he that believeth with an infidel?

And what concord hath Christ with Belial? by *Belial,* in this text, very good interpreters understand the devil, judging that the apostle here opposeth Christ, who is the Head of believers and of the church, to him who is the head of all unbelievers, and the god of the world. The term is used only in this place in the New Testament, but very often in the Old Testament, to express men notoriously wicked and scandalous, Deut. xiii. 13; Judg. xix. 22; 1 Sam. i. 16; ii. 12; xxv. 17; 2 Sam. xvi. 7; 2 Chron. xiii. 7. The Hebrews themselves are not agreed in the etymology of it; Psal. ci. 3, a *wicked thing* is called a *thing of Belial* (as may be seen in the margin of our bibles); so as the argument is drawn from our duty of conformity to our Head; Christ hath no fellowship with the devil, therefore we ought to have no unnecessary communion with such who manifest themselves to be of their father the devil, by their doing his works; nor hath Christ any communion with the sons of Belial. *Or what part hath he that believeth with an infidel?* what part or portion, that is, what society or communion, hath a believer with one that believeth not? what hath he to do with him? It was a usual phrase amongst the Jews, Josh. xxii. 25, 27. Some by this *part* understand, what portion in the life to come? in which sense it teacheth us, that we should maintain intimate and elective communion in this life only with such as we would gladly have our portion with in another life. But the most judicious interpreters think this is not intended in this place.

t 1 Cor. 3. 16.
& 6. 19. Eph. 2. 21, 22.
Heb. 3. 6.
u Ex. 29. 45.
Lev. 26. 12.
Jer. 31. 33.
& 32. 38.
Ezek. 11. 20.
& 36. 28. &
37. 26, &c.
Zech. 8. 8.
& 13. 9.

16 And what agreement hath the temple of God with idols? for ^t ye are the temple of the living God; as God hath said, "I will dwell in them, and walk in them; and I will be their God, and they shall be my people.

And what agreement hath the temple of God with idols? this particular instance giveth some expositors occasion to interpret ver. 14, of communion with idolaters in such acts of religion as are proper to them; but nothing hinders but that that precept may be interpreted more generally, though the apostle gives this as one particular instance, wherein he would have them avoid communion with unbelievers. *For ye are the temple of the living God;* the argument is drawn from what the apostle had before asserted, 1 Cor. iii. 16; vi. 19, their being the temples of the Holy Ghost; which he proveth from Lev. xxvi. 12; Ezek. xxxvii. 26, 27. *As God hath said, I will dwell in them, and walk in them; and I will be their God, and they shall be my people:* not that what the apostle meaneth here, is the literal meaning of Lev. xxvi. 11, 12; for it is manifest, that God by Moses there is speaking not of God's dwelling in the persons of believers, or in his church, but of that gracious presence and manifestation of himself to his people in the tabernacle erected by his order. Some therefore think, that the place here alluded to, though not quoted verbatim, is that, Ezek. xxxvii. 26, 27, which is a promise respecting the kingdom of Christ; where God promiseth to *make a covenant of peace* with his people, and saith, *I will place them, and multiply them, and will set my sanctuary in the midst of them for evermore. My tabernacle also shall be with them: yea, I will be their God, and they shall be my people.* The words, as they are here quoted, are entirely to be found in no one text of holy writ; it is sufficient that they are to be found there in parts. Nor doth this text so properly speak of God's dwelling in particular believers, as of his dwelling in the churches of his people; therefore, though he speaks of many, *ye are,* yet *temple* is in the singular number. These many are but one body; the church in which God dwelleth, and with which he hath communion, which is expressed by *walk in them;* as in Rev. ii. 1, he is said to *walk in the midst of the golden candlesticks.* Nor is the term *living* vainly added to *God;* for besides that he is usually so called, as being ever-living, and the Fountain of all life; it also showeth the opposition betwixt him and idols, which are dead things: and therefore God could have no more communion with idols, than the living can have with the dead; nor could they have communion with the living God and dead idols. Nor could they be the people of the living God, and the people or worshippers of dead idols; so as those that were idolaters must lose the advantage of that covenant wherein God had said, *I will be their God, and they shall be my people.*

x Is. 52. 11.
ch. 7. 1.
Rev. 18. 4.

17 ^xWherefore come out from among them, and be ye separate, saith the Lord, and touch not the unclean *thing;* and I will receive you,

The apostle here quoteth words out of the Old Testament, no where to be found there syllabically, without variation, but keeping to the sense of them, which is a thing very usual with the penmen of the New Testament. The first quotation seemeth to be taken from Isa. lii. 11, *Depart ye, depart ye, go ye out from thence, touch no unclean thing; go ye out of the midst of her; be ye clean, that bear the vessels of the Lord.* Interpreters are not agreed as to the term from whence the prophet there admonisheth the Jews to depart: some make it to be their former sinful courses; others make it to be the kingdom of the devil and antichrist; others make it to be literal Babylon; the prophet foreseeing, that when the Jews should have a liberty given them to leave Babylon, (which happened in the time of Cyrus the Persian monarch,) some of them (now as it were incorporated with the Chaldeans) would linger, and find a difficulty to pluck up their stakes in Babylon, though it were in order to their return to Jerusalem, heretofore the joy and praise of the whole earth. Whatever was the prophet's meaning, certain it is, the apostolical precept cannot be interpreted of a leaving literal Babylon, for neither the Christian Jews, nor Gentiles, were at this time there; he must therefore be understood of a mystical Babylon. And the sense must be this, *Come out and be ye separate* from those with whom your souls will be in as much danger as the Jews were in the literal Babylon. But whether by these are to be understood idolaters only, or all notorious scandalous livers, is the question. The true determination of which, I conceive, dependeth upon the sense of those words, *Come out, be ye separated;* which words, I think, are not fully interpreted by those that follow, *touch not the unclean thing;* for, doubtless, the former words are a precept concerning the means to be used in order to that as an end, it being a hard thing to touch pitch, and not to be defiled therewith. On the other side, they interpret it too rigidly, who make it to be a prohibition of all commerce or company with such persons; for this is contrary to the apostolical doctrine in his former Epistle to this church, where he had allowed, chap. v., a civil commerce and traffic with the worst of men; and, chap. vii., had forbidden the separation of Christians and heathens, once joined in marriage, unless the unbeliever first departed. The text therefore must be understood only of elective and unnecessary, intimate communion; and is much the same with that, ver. 14, *Be ye not unequally yoked with unbelievers.* So as that it doth by no means justify the withdrawing of all civil or religious communion from those whose judgments or practice in all things we cannot approve; it only justifieth our withdrawing our communion from idolaters, and from notorious scandalous sinners in such duties and actions, or in such degrees, as we are under no obligation to have fellowship and communion with them in; and our forbearing to touch their unclean things in that fellowship and communion which we are allowed with them, having no fellowship with them in their unfruitful works of darkness, but reproving them, even while in civil things, and some religious actions, we have some fellowship with them.

18 ^yAnd will be a Father unto you, and ye shall be my sons and daughters, saith the Lord Almighty.

y Jer. 31. 1, 9.
Rev. 21. 7.

The latter words, which are a promise of God's reception of them who for his sake withdraw from a sinful communion with idolaters and scandalous persons, are taken out of Jer. xxxi. 1, 9, and teach us this, That none can reasonably expect that God should fulfil his covenant with them, who make no conscience of fulfilling their part in it with him; nor claim the benefits of a Father, who perform not the duties of his children: but on the contrary, those who are conscientious in the discharge of their duties of filial obedience, may expect from him both the kindness and the protection of a Father; which is the more valuable because he is the *Lord God Almighty,* who wants no power to protect them, or so to influence them, as to make them in all things happy, as the children of so great a Father.

CHAP. VII

Paul exhorteth the Corinthians to purity of life, 1; *and to receive him, who had done nothing to forfeit their esteem,* 2. *He repeateth the assurance of his love for them, and showeth what comfort he had received in all his troubles from the report which Titus had brought of their good dispositions toward him,* 3—7: *so that, upon the whole, he did not repent of having grieved them a little by letter, considering the good effects which that godly sorrow had produced,* 8—12. *Above all, he rejoiced to observe the good impressions which their behaviour, so answerable to his former boastings of them, had left in the mind of Titus,* 13—16.

HAVING ^atherefore these promises, dearly beloved, let us cleanse ourselves from all filthiness of the flesh and spirit, perfecting holiness in the fear of God.

a ch. 6. 17, 18.
1 John 3. 3.

Having therefore these promises; i. e. of God's dwelling in us, and walking with us; of God's being our Father, and making and owning us as his sons; which promises are made to true penitents that will touch no unclean thing. *Let us cleanse ourselves from all filthiness of the flesh and the spirit;* let us, through the assistance of Divine grace, endeavour to cleanse ourselves, or keep ourselves clean, not only from fleshly filthiness, such as are sins of intemperance, drunkenness, uncleanness; but also from spiritual filthiness, extravagant passions, corrupt affections, pride, envy, rash anger, idolatry, contention, division. *Perfecting holiness in the fear of God;* and that, because we are not only obliged to holiness, but to perfect holiness, in, or through, the fear of the Lord; awing our hearts, lest we should profane the temple of the Lord, or behave ourselves as undutiful sons to so good a Father. So far are God's promises, and our belief of them, or affiance in God for the fulfilling of them, from hindering us in the practice and exercise of holiness, that there can be no more potent motive to persuade the perfection of holiness; and that not only from the argument of Divine love, contained in the promises, but from the consideration of the persons to whom, and the conditions upon which, the promises are made.

2 Receive us; we have wronged no man, we have corrupted no man, [b] we have defrauded no man.

b Acts 20. 33. ch. 12. 17.

Receive us; let us have a room in your hearts and esteem, or (more generally) accept us, as you ought to receive and accept the ministers of Christ. As our heart is enlarged towards you, so let your hearts be enlarged towards us; we have done nothing to alienate your hearts from us. *We have wronged no man;* we have done no harm to any of you, we have not been like the shepherds that merely take the fleece, and eat the flesh of the flock: Acts xx. 33, *I have coveted no man's silver, or gold, or apparel. We have corrupted no man;* we have corrupted none by any false doctrine, or by flattering speeches, or by bribes or gifts. *We have defrauded no man;* we have cheated or defrauded no man. By which vindication of or apology for himself and his fellow labourers, it is not improbably judged, that the apostle reflecteth upon those false apostles and teachers that were crept into this church, who had wronged him, corrupted them, and been too busy in other ways to pick their pockets. Nothing becometh more a minister of the gospel, than innocency and righteousness; nothing more commends him unto his people: for though they are easily persuaded that an innocent and just man must be a pious man, yet they are difficultly persuaded, (and there is no reason for it,) that an unjust or mischievous man can be so. Men are so mad of their lusts, that ofttimes teachers who will favour them in them, though never so unjust and unrighteous in their actings, shall find more favour with them, than the most righteous person that will not spare them as to their Herodias. But he who will entertain the least hopes to bring men off from their lusts and sinful practices, is concerned above all men to be innocent and righteous.

3 I speak not *this* to condemn *you:* for [c] I have said before, that ye are in our hearts to die and live with *you.*

c ch. 6. 11, 12.

The apostle deals very tenderly with this church, which was (as he knew very well) full of many touchy members; who upon all occasions were ready to reflect upon him, and to take occasion from any expressions of his in letters, as well as other things, to that purpose; to obviate whose whisperings, the apostle tells them, that he did not speak this to reflect upon or expose them, as if they had wronged or defrauded him; for the love which he bare to them was such, as would admit of no such thing; he so loved them, as that he could live and die with them.

4 [d] Great *is* my boldness of speech toward you, [e] great *is* my glorying of you; [f] I am filled with comfort, I am exceeding joyful in all our tribulation.

d ch. 3. 12.
e 1 Cor. 1. 4. ch. 1. 14.
f ch. 1. 4.
Phil. 2. 17.
Col. 1. 24.

Great is my boldness of speech toward you; because I so dearly love you, therefore I speak so boldly and freely to you (as men use to speak most freely to those whom they most love). *Great is my glorying of you;* I boast of your obedience to others, and therefore would be far from exposing you. And this I do not feignedly, for *I am filled with comfort* on your behalf (a further account of this he giveth us afterward). *I am exceeding joyful in all our tribulation;* yea, (saith he,) the report I have received of your carriage and behaviour, upon your receipt of my former Epistle, hath filled me with a joy that balanceth all the affliction and tribulation that I meet with for the gospel. So good news to a faithful minister is the repentance and reformation of any member or members that belong to his flock; whereas the hireling, or false teacher, is not much concerned whether the souls of his people do well or ill.

5 For, [g] when we were come into Macedonia, our flesh had no rest, but [h] we were troubled on every side; [i] without *were* fightings, within *were* fears.

g ch. 2. 13.
h ch. 4. 8.
i Deu. 32. 25.

Of this motion of the apostle's *into Macedonia,* what he did and suffered there, we have a short account, Acts xx. He saith his *flesh had no rest,* he met with incessant storms of persecution; and was *troubled* both by Jews and Gentiles in all places where he came. *Without were fightings;* by persons that were without the Christian church; such were the generality of the Jews and Gentiles; *within were fears;* and by false brethren within, or with his own fears, lest those violent dealings should be temptations to Christians, being yet tender and young in the faith, to relapse and apostatize.

6 Nevertheless [k] God, that comforteth those that are cast down, comforted us by [l] the coming of Titus;

k ch. 1. 4.
l See ch. 2. 13.

God, that comforteth those that are cast down: it is observable, how careful the apostle is to ascribe all the supports and reliefs of his spirit unto God. Nor is this notion, or name, of God unuseful to any that fear him, who through any casualties or contingences of this life shall happen to be cast down. It advantageth our faith in prayer, in any such straits, to consider God as having taken to himself the name of him that comforteth those that are cast down. *Comforted us by the coming of Titus:* it is only the coming of Titus, his fellow labourer, and one dear to him, that he mentioneth in this verse, as the means of his support and relief; yet he entitleth God to his comfort under his dejection. God comforteth his people variously, sometimes by his good word, sometimes by his providence; be what will the instrumental cause, God is the principal efficient.

7 And not by his coming only, but by the consolation wherewith he was comforted in you, when he told us your earnest desire, your mourning, your fervent mind toward me; so that I rejoiced the more.

And not by his coming only, but by the consolation wherewith he was comforted in you: I was glad to see Titus, but that was the least of that consolation which he brought me. You had before much comforted and rejoiced him, and he being come to me, made me a partaker of his consolation, upon his beholding or being a witness to *your earnest desire,* to give me satisfaction in the things about which I wrote to you; *your mourning,* either for those scandals amongst you, of which I have given you notice; or for my afflicted state and condition; or for the offence you had given me, which caused me to write that sharp letter to you. *Your fervent mind toward me; so that I rejoiced the more:* your earnest desire to give me satisfaction, and yield obedience to my admonitions, or to maintain and defend my honour and reputation against such as had impeached and wounded it; these things much augmented my rejoicing in and over you. Nothing so much rejoiceth the heart of a conscientious, faithful minister of Christ, as to see his people's obedience to the doctrine of the gospel, which he is an instrument to communicate to them.

8 For though I made you sorry with a letter, I do not repent, [m] though I did repent: for I perceive that the same epistle hath made you sorry, though *it were* but for a season.

m ch. 2. 4.

For though I made you sorry with a letter; the apostle doubtless meaneth the former Epistle to this church. *I do*

II. CORINTHIANS VII

not repent, though *I did repent:* as to which, he saith, that although he was sometimes troubled, because (probably) he understood that some truly pious persons in this church were troubled at it, as thinking themselves intended in the reprehensions of it; for which effect, or mistake, (he saith,) he was once sorry, being troubled that he should do any thing to grieve them, whom he so affectionately loved; yet now he tells them he was not sorry. *The same epistle hath made you sorry, though it were but for a season;* and their sorrow was but a temporary sorrow, until they could reform those abuses, which they were made sensible of by that Epistle, and give the apostle that wrote it just satisfaction.

9 Now I rejoice, not that ye were made sorry, but that ye sorrowed to repentance: for ye were made sorry ‖ after a godly manner, that ye might receive damage by us in nothing.

‖ Or, *according to God.*

Now I rejoice, not that ye were made sorry, but that ye sorrowed to repentance: the apostle takes all advantages to insinuate himself into the good opinion and affections of the members of this famous church, and to obviate any misrepresentations of him to them from those false teachers that were crept in amongst them. Lest they should take some advantage from his saying, that he repented not that he had made them sorry, he here openeth himself, and tells them, he did not rejoice in their sorrow, but in the blessed product and effect of it; which was their reformation of those abuses and errors which he had reproved them for, the effect of which reproof was this their sorrow for a little season. And that they *were made sorry after a godly manner;* they did but sow in tears, they reaped in joy; they had a wet seed-time, but a fair harvest. They sorrowed with a sorrow according to God; the cause of their sorrow was their sin, the root of it a love to God, the manner of it such as was agreeable to the will of God. *That ye might receive damage by us in nothing;* the wise God so governing things by his providence, that nothing which the apostle spake or wrote should prove detrimental, but rather advantageous, to this church which he so loved.

10 For ⁿgodly sorrow worketh repentance to salvation not to be repented of: ᵒbut the sorrow of the world worketh death.

n 2 Sam. 12. 13. Matt. 26. 75.
o Prov. 17. 22.

Godly sorrow; that sorrow which is according to God, either commanded by him, (as sorrow for our own or others' sins, or for the judgments of God, as they are the indications of God's wrath and displeasure for sin,) or which he, as the God of grace, worketh in the soul, touching the heart by the finger of his Spirit, Zech. xii. 10. Or that sorrow whose end is the glory of God, in the reformation of the person sorrowing, by a hatred and detestation of sin, and a hearty turning from it. *Worketh repentance to salvation not to be repented of;* it is not repentance, but it produceth that change of heart and life which is repentance; and shall not be imperfect, but perfect, which shall issue in the salvation of the soul, and will never be repented of. Never did any when he came to die repent of true repentance; nor is it possible that reasonable souls should repent of what issueth in their eternal salvation. *But the sorrow of the world worketh death;* but all sorrow except this is but *the sorrow of the world,* the effect of which is ofttimes natural death; while men bow down under their burdens, and through impatience destroy themselves, or at least so fix their thoughts upon sad objects, and so afflict themselves with them, that they bring themselves into diseases tending to death. It also worketh spiritual death; as it indisposeth men for their duty, (as it was in the case of Elijah,) and is a temptation to them to be angry against God, (as in the case of Jonah,) to fret, murmur, and repine against God's providence: and by this means it also worketh towards eternal death, which is the wages belonging to sin.

11 For behold this selfsame thing, that ye sorrowed after a godly sort, what carefulness it wrought in you, yea, *what* clearing of yourselves, yea, *what* indignation, yea, *what* fear, yea, *what* vehement desire, yea, *what* zeal, yea, *what* revenge! In all *things* ye have approved yourselves to be clear in this matter.

The apostle having showed the mischievous effects of worldly sorrow, all which he comprehended under the word *death,* here showeth the blessed effects of that sorrow which is according to God. *What carefulness it wrought in you!* the first he mentioneth is great *carefulness,* both to make our peace with God for our former violations of his law, (using all means he hath prescribed and directed thereunto,) and also to preserve our peace, by avoiding the like breaches for the time to come. *What clearing of yourselves!* the Corinthians' sorrow might work in some of them a *clearing* or purging themselves of that guilt which other members of that church had incurred. But there is another clearing of ourselves, which true repentance worketh, not by denying the fact, but by confessing it, with taking shame to ourselves; which, though it be not a clearing of a person from the fact, yet, through Divine grace, joined with a reformation, it is a clearing him from the guilt thereof. *What indignation!* what a displeasure against yourselves for your follies! *What fear!* not so much of the wrath of God, as lest you should again fall into the like temptations, and be overcome by them. *What vehement desire!* what hearty prayers to God, that for the time to come you might be kept from the like temptations! *What zeal!* what warmth and great degrees of all sanctified affections; love to God, hatred of sin, fear of offending God, desire to please him! *What revenge!* what acts of discipline, fasting, denying of yourselves in some lawful things wherein you may have offended, or the too free use of which may have been to you occasions of offending. *In all things ye have approved yourselves to be clear in this matter;* by these acts, though some of you have been to be blamed, yet the body of you have showed yourselves clear of this matter; or though all of you have been formerly too guilty of some things I have charged you with, yet you have cleared yourselves both to God, who imputeth no sin to him that confesseth his sin and forsaketh it, and to me, who am abundantly satisfied with your declared sorrow, repentance, and reformation.

12 Wherefore, though I wrote unto you, *I did it* not for his cause that had done the wrong, nor for his cause that suffered wrong, ᵖbut that our care for you in the sight of God might appear unto you.

p ch. 2. 4.

I did it not for his cause that had done the wrong; for the cause of him that had abused his father's wife, not out of any particular hatred or ill-will I had to him; *nor for his cause that suffered wrong;* nor for the sake of him whose wife was so abused; nor for my own sake, who had been so abused, and suffered wrong by you. *But that our care for you in the sight of God might appear to you;* but only out of a love to your souls, and a care I had for you, that in all things you might approve yourselves unto God. Or possibly this text is more generally be interpreted, without respect either to the incestuous person in particular, or to his father; and the sense of the verse no more than this: Though in my former Epistle I wrote something sharply to you, yet I did it not in any passion, nor was I drawn aside by any prejudice or hatred of any person, nor out of any partial affection to any, as to any thing for which I blamed you; but out of that general love and affection which I have to you all, which produceth in me a care of and a solicitude for you, that you might do no evil; which care I was willing should appear to you.

13 Therefore we were comforted in your comfort: yea, and exceedingly the more joyed we for the joy of Titus, because his spirit ᑫwas refreshed by you all.

q Rom. 15. 32.

We were comforted in your comfort; the comfort which your letters brought us, and so came from you; or the comfort which you received upon your reformation of those things which were amiss amongst you. And we also *joyed for the joy* that *Titus* conceived, upon his understanding of your affairs, and your ready obedience to the Epistle which I wrote to you: such is the union betwixt the true members of Christ, that they are comforted with one another's comforts, and afflicted with one another's sorrows and griefs.

14 For if I have boasted any thing to him of you, I am not ashamed; but as we spake all things to you in truth, even so our boasting, which *I made* before Titus, is found a truth.

The apostle here multiplieth expressions to sweeten the Corinthians, by all manner of ways declaring his value for and affection towards them. It appeareth by this, that the apostle had at some time before spoken something to Titus in commendation of this church of Corinth, which he here calleth a *boasting* of them; he now again boasted, that he had said nothing but the truth, which Titus had experienced, and reported to him.

† Gr. *bowels*, ch. 6. 12.
r ch. 2. 9. Phil. 2. 12.

15 And his † inward affection is more abundant toward you, whilst he remembereth ʳ the obedience of you all, how with fear and trembling ye received him.

By your obedience to my admonitions and exhortations, you have not only obliged me in a debt of love to you, but Titus also; who joyfully remembers, with what *fear and trembling you received him*, lest he should find any thing amongst you that should grieve and offend him.

s 2 Thes. 3. 4. Philem. 8, 21.

16 I rejoice therefore that ˢ I have confidence in you in all *things*.

That I can write and speak to you with confidence that you will hearken to my admonitions and exhortations, and that I can confidently boast and glory concerning you.

CHAP. VIII

Paul extolleth the liberal contributions of the Macedonian churches for the relief of the brethren in Judea, 1—5; and recommendeth the like charity to the Corinthians, as well beseeming their other graces, 6—8; enforced by Christ's example, 9; consistent with the alacrity they had already expressed therein, 10—12; and a precedent which might in time be of use to themselves, 13—15. He letteth them know the willingness of Titus to come and further this good work among them; and commendeth him to their love, together with the brethren, men of special worth, who were sent with him on the same errand, 16—24.

MOREOVER, brethren, we do you to wit of the grace of God bestowed on the churches of Macedonia;

The apostle in this chapter proceedeth to a new argument, viz. the pressing of this church to acts of charity. This is that which he here calleth *the grace of God bestowed on the churches of Macedonia*, putting the cause for the effect. Bounty or liberality to the poor saints and members of Christ, as such, floweth from that habit of love by which men are taught of God to love one another; for though men, from a natural goodness, or habits of moral virtue, may relieve men as men, compassionating persons in misery; yet none, from any such principle, do good to any members of the household of faith, as such; such rather feel from them the effects of their hatred, in taking what is their own from them.

a Mark 12. 44.
† Gr. *simplicity*. ch. 9. 11.

2 How that in a great trial of affliction the abundance of their joy and ᵃ their deep poverty abounded unto the riches of their † liberality.

In a great trial of affliction; how great the afflictions of the churches in Macedonia were, both from the Jews and pagans, may be read in chap. xvi. and xvii. of the Acts. Afflictions are called trials, because under them God maketh a trial of our faith, patience, and constancy; and the devil also, ordinarily, by them trieth to draw out our lusts and corruptions. *The abundance of their joy and their deep poverty abounded unto the riches of their liberality;* God made their inward peace and joy in the Holy Ghost so to abound in them under their trials, that though they were poor, (deeply poor,) yet they abounded in the riches of liberality; not ministering to the necessities of their poor brethren in proportion to their abilities, or as might have been expected from men under their circumstances, but showing themselves rich in their liberality, though poor in their estates, and as to what they had of this world's goods.

3 For to *their* power, I bear record, yea, and beyond *their* power *they were* willing of themselves;

Two things the apostle commendeth in the charity of the churches of Macedonia: first, the quantity of their gift, which, he saith, was *to their power, yea,* (on his knowledge,) *beyond* what they were able. Secondly, their freedom in the action; so as they did not need the apostle's exhortations and arguments, but did it of themselves freely and cheerfully.

4 Praying us with much intreaty that we would receive the gift, and *take upon us* ᵇ the fellowship of the ministering to the saints.

b Acts 11. 29. & 24. 17. Rom. 15. 25, 26. 1 Cor. 16. 1, 3, 4. ch. 9. 1.

Bringing what they had freely collected amongst themselves to the apostles, and importuning them to receive it at their hands, and to take upon them the work of distributing it.

5 And *this they did*, not as we hoped, but first gave their own selves to the Lord, and unto us by the will of God.

We might have hoped for something from them, though they were in that poor afflicted condition; but what they brought was much beyond what we could hope for, or expect from them. Or else this phrase may refer to what followeth: they did not only bring us their *gift*, but they also *gave* up *themselves* to us, to be disposed of for the good of the church, according to the will of God; for they first gave themselves up to the Lord, devoting themselves to his service and glory, and then to us, the will of God so ruling and directing them.

6 Insomuch that ᶜ we desired Titus, that as he had begun, so he would also finish in you the same ‖ grace also.

c ver. 17. ch. 12. 18.
‖ Or, *gift*. ver. 4, 19.

The same grace, in this place, signifieth no more than the same gift, or the same good work, in collecting in the church of Corinth. If by *grace* here be understood the grace of God, the cause is put for the effect (as we had it in the first verse); but τῠ Θεῠ being not here added, possibly it had been better translated gift, or free contribution; for how a minister should finish the grace of God, is hard to conceive; and the phrase is at best very hard, but he may be an instrument for completing a good work, which is done from a habit of Divine grace, by exhortations and arguments, which he may use to press the performance of it. Titus (it seemeth) had been diligent in some other places to make this collection; going to Corinth, the apostle presseth him to go on with it there also.

7 Therefore, as ᵈ ye abound in every *thing, in* faith, and utterance, and knowledge, and *in* all diligence, and *in* your love to us, *see* ᵉ that ye abound in this grace also.

d 1 Cor. 1. 5. & 12. 13.
e ch. 9. 8.

Though the apostle made little use of oratory in his ordinary discourses and epistles, yet he knew how to use it when it might be of probable advantage for the ends which he aimed at, viz. the glory of God, and the good of the souls that were under his care. He did not turn divinity into mere words and rhetorical flourishes; yet he made use of these sometimes, as a waiting-maid to divinity. Being therefore to press upon these Corinthians this great duty of charity, he insinuateth himself into them, by telling them, that they abounded in all other spiritual habits: *Faith*, by which they had both steadily assented to the truth of gospel propositions, and also received Christ. *Utterance*, by which they were enabled either to speak with tongues, or to God in prayer, or to men by prophecy and exhortation. *Knowledge*, both of things Divine and human. And in *love* to the ministers of the gospel, which, if it did not appear in all, yet it did in many of them. And from hence he fetcheth an argument to press them to be complete in this habit of grace. The force of the apostle's argument lies, in the duty of all Christians to strive after perfection, and that natural desire, which is in all ingenuous people, to be

II. CORINTHIANS VIII

perfect in that good of which they have a taste in less perfect degrees.

f 1 Cor. 7. 6.

8 ^fI speak not by commandment, but by occasion of the forwardness of others, and to prove the sincerity of your love.

I do not speak in an imperious way, as one that commandeth you; or rather, God hath no where given an express command as to the quantum of what you should give; but *the forwardness of others* makes me thus speak to you, as not being willing you should in good works come behind any churches; and that I might *prove the sincerity of your love*, to God, to me, and to the poor afflicted saints that are in Judea. Though God hath not directed the particular sums we should give to those that are in need, yet he hath given us general rules; That we should give *as God hath prospered us*, 1 Cor. xvi. 2; and so as there may be some *equality*, as the apostle speaketh, ver. 14. So, as the sincerity of our love to God dependeth in some measure upon the proportion of what we give at his command, so doth also the sincerity of our love to those poor members of Christ that are in want; that there may be a moderate supply for their want, from our abundance.

9 For ye know the grace of our Lord Jesus Christ, ^g that, though he was rich, yet for your sakes he became poor, that ye through his poverty might be rich.

g Mat. 8. 20.
Luke 9. 58.
Phil. 2. 6, 7.

For ye know the grace of our Lord Jesus Christ; call to mind the free love of your Lord and Master Jesus Christ, which you know, believing the gospel, which gives you a true account of it, and having in your own souls experienced the blessed effects of it. *He was rich,* being the *Heir of all things,* the Lord of the whole creation, Heb. i. 2, all things were put under his feet. *Yet for your sakes he became poor;* yet that he might accomplish the work of your redemption, and purchase his Father's love for you, he took upon him the form of a servant, stripped himself of his robes of glory, and clothed himself with the rags of flesh, denied himself in the use of his creatures, had not where to lay down his head, was maintained from alms, people ministering to him of their substance. *That ye through his poverty might be rich;* and all this that you might be made rich, with the riches of grace and glory; rich in the love of God, and in the habits of Divine grace; which was all effected by his poverty, by his making himself of no reputation, and humbling himself. If after your knowledge of this, by receiving and believing the gospel, and experiencing this, in those riches of spiritual gifts and graces and hopes of glory which you have, you shall yet be found strait-hearted in compassionating the poverty and afflicted state of his poor members, or strait-handed in ministering unto them, how will you in any measure answer this great love, or conform to this great example?

h 1 Cor. 7. 25.
i Prov. 19.17.
Matt. 10. 42.
1 Tim. 6. 18, 19.
Heb. 13. 16.
†Gr. *willing.*
k ch. 9. 2.

10 And herein ^h I give *my* advice: for ⁱ this is expedient for you, who have begun before, not only to do, but also to be †^k forward a year ago.

Giving to those that were in want, was matter of precept (it being what the law of God and nature did require); but giving as the Macedonians had given, not only to, but beyond, their ability, was not so. Or, possibly, the apostle's saying, *I give my advice,* doth not suppose what he advised to be no commanded duty; friends may advise us to what is our duty to do. *For,* saith the apostle, *this is expedient for you;* for your profit, or for your honour and reputation. A precept alone ought to oblige us to this doing of the thing commanded, but the profit, credit, and honour of the action adds an edge to the duty, and layeth us under a double obligation; the first, of obedience to God; the second, of being wise for ourselves. *Who have begun before, not only to do, but also to be forward a year ago:* the apostle proveth the expediency of it from the concern of their reputation in it; that they might not be thought to have gone backward, or to become weary of well-doing, in regard they had begun this charitable work some time before. *Object.* But how cometh he here to put doing before willing (for so it is in the Greek, *not only to do, but also* θέλειν, to will)? Some tell us these hysterologies, or putting things after which should in order be before, are usual in holy writ;

but possibly it is better answered by others, that θέλειν here doth not signify the mere inclination of the will, but a forwardness, (thus our translators understood it, and therefore translate it *to be forward,)* or a spontaneous willingness, without arguments used by others to persuade them to it. So as the sense is this, You not only began to do the thing a year ago, but you did it of your own accord, without our exhortations and arguments, of your own free mind and will; so as if you should now be behind-hand, it would be a reproach to you. This sense is favoured by the next verse, what he here calls a willing, he there calls *a readiness to will.*

11 Now therefore perform the doing *of it;* that as *there was* a readiness to will, so *there may be* a performance also out of that which ye have.

Ye showed yourselves some time since free to will the thing which I am now pressing you unto, you have now opportunity to do it, and the example of other churches going before you in the doing of it; show yourselves now constant by *the doing of it;* that seeing God hath given you something of this world's goods, and that in proportions beyond your poor brethren, as you pretended a great readiness a great while since to relieve them, so you may by your performance justify that it was not all a mere pretence.

12 For ^l if there be first a willing mind, *it is* accepted according to that a man hath, *and* not according to that he hath not.

l Mark 12. 43, 44.
Luke 21. 3.

He had before directed them to give out of that which they had, that is, in a proportion to what God had blessed them with; for he tells them that it is the willing mind which God accepteth, not the quantity of the gift. God doth not require of people things not in their power, yet bare velleities, or pretended willings, are not accepted; there must be an acting according to our power to justify the sincerity of our willing mind, and men vainly pretend to will that towards the performance of which they never move. Though God requireth not of us things that are not within our power, yet he requireth of us the putting forth of our power in doing what he hath commanded us, so far as we are able; which indeed can alone justify the willingness of our mind to be more than a mere pretence. A present impotency, if contracted by our own fault, will not excuse us from the performance of those acts as to which it doth extend, to which some are bound by the just laws of God or men; but it is very unreasonable to think it should excuse us as to those acts to which it doth not extend, and as to which it cannot be pleaded.

13 For *I mean* not that other men be eased, and ye burdened:

I do not press you to such proportions in giving as should make your afflicted brethren rich, and you poor.

14 But by an equality, *that* now at this time your abundance *may be a supply* for their want, that their abundance also may be *a supply* for your want: that there may be equality:

But by an equality; but only to bring you and them to some equality, that they might not starve while you have plenty, and what you may well enough spare. *That now at this time your abundance may be a supply for their want;* I do not urge you to make your necessaries a supply for others' wants; I would only have a supply for their wants out of your abundance. *That their abundance also may be a supply for your want:* some by *their abundance* understand their aboundings in the good things of this life: they are now in distress by reason of the great famine that is in Judea, or by reason of the great storm of persecution that is there raised against Christians; yet God may turn the scales, he may send a famine in those parts where you live, and there may be plenty in Judea; then their abundance may supply your wants. Others interpret *their abundance* of the aboundings of their grace, which may quicken them up to pray for you, for the supply of such grace to you as you stand in need of. *That* so *there may be an equality,* they being instruments of spiritual blessings to you, as you are instruments of temporal blessings and good things to them.

m Ex. 16.18. 15 As it is written, ᵐHe that *had gathered* much had nothing over; and he that *had gathered* little had no lack.

This quotation would incline us to think, that the *abundance* mentioned in the latter part of the former verse, as also the *equality* mentioned in the end of it, is rather to be understood with reference to the good things of this life, than with reference to spiritual blessings, or to temporal and spiritual put together, balancing one another to make an equality. For certain it is, that this quotation referreth to manna, which was the bread God afforded for the bodies of his people in the wilderness, though, considered typically, it is rightly by the apostle called *spiritual meat,* 1 Cor. x. 3; signifying that bread which came down from heaven, which Moses could not give, as Christ tells us, John vi. 32, 58. These words are quoted from Exod. xvi. 18, though more agreeably to the Septuagint than to our translation. The history is this: The manna being fallen, the text saith, ver. 17, that *some gathered more, some less;* but it so fell out, by the providence of God ordering it, that when they came and measured what they had gathered, *he that gathered much had nothing over, and he that gathered little had no lack.* Now of this the apostle makes an argument to press the Corinthians to this charitable act. The force of which lies in this: As it was in the case of manna; there were some that gathered more, others that gathered less, yet all had enough; so it will be as to the riches of the world that men gather, though some gather more, and others gather less, yet men will find, that those that have gathered little, (have less estates than others,) using what they have to the glory of God, and according to the Divine rule, will have no lack; and those that have gathered much, if they do not distribute it according to the will of God, will find that they have nothing over; God will shrink their heap into some equality to those whom at God's command they would not relieve: Eccles. v. 10, *He that loveth silver shall not be satisfied with silver.* The wisdom of the Divine providence hath not ordained levelling, nor made all men equal in their portions of the good things of this life; but he hath willed such an equality as every one may eat, (unless he or she that will not work,) either from the sweat of their own faces, or from the charity of others. Besides, nature craveth no great things, but is satisfied with a little; so that he that hath gathered little shall have no lack, if he can but moderate the excesses of his appetite; and he that hath gathered much hath nothing over, what is either necessary for himself and his family, or what he ought to part with for the relief of others at the command of God.

16 But thanks *be* to God, which put the same earnest care into the heart of Titus for you.

n ver. 6. 17 For indeed he accepted ⁿthe exhortation; but being more forward, of his own accord he went unto you.

The apostle, by his exhortation, put Titus upon this employment of making at Corinth an extraordinary collection for the poor Christians that were in Judea; but it should seem, that when he did it, Titus let him know, that he was before resolved upon it: so as, though he went at the entreaty of the apostle, yet he went also of his own accord, having resolved upon the work before the apostle spoke to him of it. To let us know, that we are not sufficient of ourselves so much as to think one good thought, he gives *thanks to God* for putting this *earnest care into the heart of Titus.*

o ch. 12. 18. 18 And we have sent with him ᵒthe brother, whose praise *is* in the Gospel throughout all the churches;

Who this other *brother* was, whether Luke, or Barnabas, or Silas, or Apollos, or Mark, is not much material; it is plain, whoever he was, that he was a brother and a minister, one who had a good repute for preaching the gospel.

p 1 Cor. 16. 3, 4.
∥ Or, *gift.*
ver. 4, 6, 7.
ch. 9. 8.
q ch. 4. 15.

19 And not *that* only, but who was also ᵖchosen of the churches to travel with us with this ∥grace, which is administered by us ᑫto the glory of the same Lord, and *declaration of* your ready mind:

And that he was *chosen by the churches* to go along with Paul and Titus, to carry the charity of other churches to the distressed Christians in Judea; which charity is here again called *grace,* for the reason before mentioned, ver. 1. He declares that their end in this administration, was *the glory of God,* and the proof and *declaration* of these Corinthians' sincerity of brotherly love, and *ready mind* to yield obedience to the will of God declared to them.

20 Avoiding this, that no man should blame us in this abundance which is administered by us:

I have sent more than one as witnesses of what is done in this service, that none might reflect upon those trusted with the charity of divers churches, as if they converted any part of it to their own private use, and did not distribute it to those for whom it was given. The apostle here commendeth to all ministers and Christians, a prudent foresight of such scandalous imputations, as they may be exposed to (be their sincerity what it will) from the men of the world, who have no good-will towards them; and a provision against them. Paul could have trusted Titus in the distribution of these alms, but he did not know what the world might say, had he discharged the trust alone; he therefore takes in one with him, to be a witness of his actions.

21 ʳProviding for honest things, not only in the sight of the Lord, but also in the sight of men.

r Rom. 12. 17. Phil. 4. 8. 1 Pet. 2, 12.

He had said the same, Rom. xii. 17. In both places he instructeth us, what is the great duty of all Christians, but of ministers especially, (who are as cities built upon a hill, and cannot be hid, and against whom ill men are much more ready to open their mouths, than against private Christians of a more obscure condition,) viz. to *provide things honest, not only in the sight of God,* (having an eye, that in our actions we do nothing which God hath forbidden us, nor omit any thing which God hath commanded us,) but also looking that in our conversation we (as much as in us lies) do those things which have a good report amongst men, Phil. iv. 8. For besides that we are obliged to give no offence to Jews or Gentiles, nor any way to alienate them from the ways of God, we are also obliged to do what in us lieth to win and gain them to Christ; to which, the doing of actions which they account dishonest (though, it may be, some are not so upon a strict inquiry) is no fitting mean.

22 And we have sent with them our brother, whom we have oftentimes proved diligent in many things, but now much more diligent, upon the great confidence which ∥ *I have* in you.

∥ Or, *he hath.*

This *brother* is uncertainly guessed at, nor is it at all material for us to know whether it were Epenetus, or Apollos, or Sosthenes, or any other; it is sufficient for us to know, that he was a brother, and one of whose diligence and faithfulness the apostle, and the churches where Paul now was, had had experience; and that he was now very ready and forward to be employed in this service, upon the apostle's recommendation of this church unto him.

23 Whether *any do enquire* of Titus, *he is* my partner and fellowhelper concerning you: or our brethren *be enquired of, they are* ˢthe messengers of the churches, *and* the glory of Christ.

s Phil. 2. 25.

This verse contains the apostle's credential letters, given to Titus, and the other two persons, sent about the business of making this collection in the church of Corinth. Many, in matters where the drawing of their purses is solicited and concerned, are very scrupulous and inquisitive, seeking all advantages to excuse themselves; one while pleading their own poverty, another while objecting against the state, or want, or quality of those for whom they are solicited; again, questioning whether their charity shall ever come to those persons for whom it is desired, objecting against the persons intrusted with the conveyance or distribution of it. The apostle having, therefore, before obviated some objections, he here obviateth the last mentioned, letting them know, that the persons intrusted with this service were unexceptionable persons. He calleth Titus his *partner and fellow-helper concerning* them, that is, in the business of the gospel, and promoting the salvation of their souls. For the others, he tells them they were such as *the churches* had thought fit to make their *messengers;* so had the credit of the churches, whose messengers they were, who would not have intrusted them if they had not judged them faithful. He calleth either the churches, or them, *the glory of Christ.* If the words be to be understood of the *messengers.* (which seemeth the fairest application of them,) the meaning is, that they were instruments of the glory of Christ: or persons who, by their grace, did bring much glory to Christ. Every one that excelleth in the habits or exercise of grace, is the glory of Christ, because without Christ he can do nothing of that nature: *I live; yet not I, but Christ liveth in me,* Gal. ii. 20. The acts and exercises of grace are indeed our acts, but the power by which we do them is from Christ: we glory in Christ, and by our holy conversations glorify Christ; and Christ glorieth in every pious and holy person, as God did concerning Job, chap. i. 8; ii. 3.

24 Wherefore shew ye to them, and before the churches, the proof of your love, and of our ᵗboasting on your behalf.

t ch. 7. 14. & 9. 2.

The chapter concludeth with an exhortation to their liberality, backed with a heap of arguments. 1. It would be an evidence of their love to God, to their afflicted brethren, and to the apostle. 2. It would be a proof of it to those messengers of the churches, and to the churches whose messengers they were. 3. It would evidence that the apostle had not, to Titus and others, boasted on their behalf in vain.

CHAP. IX

Paul showeth the reason why, though he knew the forwardness of the Corinthians, he had sent the brethren beforehand to make up their collections against his coming, 1—5. *He stirreth them up to give bountifully and cheerfully, as a likely means to increase their store,* 6—11; *and as productive of many thanksgivings unto God,* 12—15.

a Acts 11. 29. Rom. 15. 26. 1 Cor. 16. 1. ch. 8. 4. Gal. 2. 10.

FOR as touching ᵃthe ministering to the saints, it is superfluous for me to write to you:

I should think the particle γὰρ, here translated *for,* had been better translated *but,* as in 1 Pet. iv. 15, and 2 Pet. i. 9, our translators do render it. So these words contain an elegant revocation of himself from the argument he had dwelt upon in the whole former chapter, and the sense amounts to this: But to what purpose do I multiply words to you, to persuade you to minister to the saints in distress? as to you, *it is superfluous.* By this art letting them know, that he had no doubt, but a confident expectation, concerning them; the suggesting of which hath also the force of another argument, that they might not deceive the apostle's good opinion and confidence of them.

b ch. 8. 19. c ch. 8. 24. d ch. 8. 10.

2 For I know ᵇthe forwardness of your mind, ᶜfor which I boast of you to them of Macedonia, that ᵈAchaia was ready a year ago; and your zeal hath provoked very many.

He gives them the reason why he judgeth it superfluous to write to them, because they had a forward mind of themselves, and needed not to be spurred on. This the apostle tells them that he knew, (he had told them of it, chap. viii. 10,) he knew it either from themselves, or from some that came from them unto him; and he had boasted of them for this their forwardness in this good work to the churches of Macedonia. *And your zeal hath provoked very many;* he tells them, that their warmth unto, and in, this work, had kindled a heat in many in those parts where he was. Having therefore been so forward in this good work, and so good instruments to kindle a heat in others, he would not have them now come behind others, or grow cold in it.

3 ᵉYet have I sent the brethren, lest our boasting of you should be in vain in this behalf; that, as I said, ye may be ready:

e ch. 8. 6. 17, 18, 22.

I did not send the brethren so much to move you to this work, or quicken you to it, for you yourselves purposed it a year ago, and showed a forwardness in it; the motion proceeded from yourselves, and you showed a readiness to it, which gave me occasion to boast of you to the churches of Macedonia; but I thought you might forget it. and I would not have *our boasting in vain on this behalf.* And besides, I would have the work done, that your alms might not be to gather when I come, (as he had said, 1 Cor. xvi. 2,) but might be in a readiness to be taken and carried away; for that is signified here by being *ready,* not that readiness of mind of which he had before spoken, and which he had before mentioned as what he had found in them.

4 Lest haply if they of Macedonia come with me, and find you unprepared, we (that we say not, ye) should be ashamed in this same confident boasting.

For if I should come, and any of the members of the churches of Macedonia, who have heard me boasting of you as a people very forward in this charitable work, and when they are come they should find you had done nothing, only talked much of your readiness, both I should be ashamed, and you also might see some cause to blush, which I, who consult your honour and reputation equally with my own, would prevent.

5 Therefore I thought it necessary to exhort the brethren, that they would go before unto you, and make up beforehand your † bounty, ‖ whereof ye had notice before, that the same might be ready, as *a matter of* bounty, and not as *of* covetousness.

† Gr. *blessing.* Gen. 33. 11. 1 Sam. 25. 27. 2 Kings 5. 15. ‖ Or, *which hath been so much spoken of before.*

This was the cause why I judged it reasonable to send the three brethren, before mentioned, unto you, that they might make up your bounty; προκαταρτίσωσι, not so much to move, quicken, or exhort you to it, as to hasten the despatch and perfecting of it, that your money might be ready gathered. The word which we translate *bounty,* in the Greek signifieth blessing, which agreeth with the Hebrew dialect. Abigail's present to David in his distress is called ברכה, a *blessing,* 1 Sam. xxv. 27: so Jacob called his present to his brother Esau, Gen. xxxiii. 11. Such kind of reliefs are called a *blessing* in both the Hebrew and the Greek tongue: 1. Because they are a part of God's blessing upon him that gives, Psal. xxiv. 5. 2. Because the giving of them is a recognition or acknowledgment how far God hath blessed persons, they giving as the Lord hath prospered them, 1 Cor. xvi. 2. 3. Because they are an indication of the blessing, or well-wishing, of him that giveth to him that receiveth the gift. 4. Because they are a real doing good to the person that receiveth them, an actual blessing of him. 5. Possibly they are (in him that gives) an effectual, real blessing of God; for we then bless God with what we have, when we use and improve it for the ends for which he hath given it to us. It is very observable, that a liberal, free giving to the relief of the servants of God in distress, is called χάρις and εὐλογία, *grace* and *blessing;* a heart to it being created in us from the free grace of God, and the work itself being a real, actual blessing of God with our substance, and the fruit of our increase: which two things well digested, will be potent arguments to charity with every soul that knoweth any thing of God, or hath any love for God. *That the same might be ready;* that the same may be ready gathered, not to gather when I come. As a blessing, we translate it, *as a matter of bounty:* the sense is the same. *Not as of covetousness:* the meaning is, I have also sent the brethren, that they may persuade you to a free and liberal contribution, a giving that may look like a blessing, not as proceeding from a narrow heart, in which the love of money prevaileth above the love of God. Giving to the distressed saints of God sparingly, and disproportionately to what estate we have, no ways looks like a blessing; he that so gives, doth not, according to the apostle's phrase, give ὡς εὐλογίαν· for he neither gives as the Lord hath blessed and prospered him, nor yet according to what God requires of him; for he withholds a part of what he ought to part with: neither doth he bless his brother; he doth him some little good, but blessing another signifies a more liberal doing good to him.

^f Prov. 11. 24. & 19. 17. & 22. 9. Gal. 6. 7, 9.

6 ^fBut this *I say*, He which soweth sparingly shall reap also sparingly; and he which soweth bountifully shall reap also bountifully.

Whereas covetous persons think all lost which they give to charitable uses, the apostle correcteth their mistake, by letting them know, that it is no more lost than the seed is which the husbandman casteth into his ground, which bringeth forth thirty, sixty, or sometimes a hundred-fold; though with this difference, that whereas the husbandman's crop dependeth upon the goodness and preparedness of his ground, it is not so with this spiritual crop; a man shall not reap according to the nature of the soil in which he casts his seed; for he that giveth to a prophet or to a righteous man, in the name of a prophet or a righteous man, (though he may be mistaken in the person to whom he so giveth,) yet shall he receive the reward of a prophet and of a righteous man. But this spiritual sower shall receive according to the quantity of seed which he soweth: he that soweth niggardly and sparingly shall reap accordingly; he that soweth liberally shall reap liberally: from whence we may be confirmed, that the rewards of another life will not be equal, but bear some proportion to the good works which men have done here.

^g Deu. 15. 7. ^h Ex. 25. 2. & 35. 5. Prov. 11. 25. Ecclus. 35. 9. 10. Rom. 12. 8. ch. 8. 12.

7 Every man according as he purposeth in his heart, *so let him give;* ^gnot grudgingly, or of necessity: for ^hGod loveth a cheerful giver.

Let not any give out of any awe of us, nor as it were forced by our authority, but as God shall put it into his heart, and as he hath purposed in himself, and is inclined from himself, without any grudging or unwillingness; not because he thinks he must give, but out of choice: for God loveth one that giveth with freedom and cheerfulness, not him that giveth as it were by constraint, or upon force; it is the will and affection of the giver, not the quantity of the gift, that God looks at. The apostle, by naming God and his acceptance in the case, lets the Corinthians know, that God was concerned in what they thus gave, it was not given to men only; according to that, *He that hath pity upon the poor lendeth unto the Lord; and that which he hath given will he pay him again*, Prov. xix. 17.

ⁱ Prov. 11. 24, 25. & 28. 27. Phil. 4. 19.

8 ⁱAnd God *is* able to make all grace abound toward you; that ye, always having all sufficiency in all *things*, may abound to every good work:

Having made God, in the verse before, a debtor to those who, by giving to poor distressed saints, would make him their creditor, he here proveth him to be no insolvent debtor, but able to do much more for them, than they in this thing should do at his command out of love to him. He *is* (saith he) *able to make all grace to abound toward you:* the word translated *grace*, signifieth all sorts of gifts, whether of a temporal or spiritual nature; and being here applied to God, (who is the Author of all gifts,) it may very properly be interpreted concerning both. God is able to repay you in temporal things what you thus lend him, and so to pay you in specie; and he is able to pay you in value, by spiritual habits and influences. *That ye, always having all sufficiency in all things, may abound to every good work;* that you may have a sufficiency in all things, so as that you may abound to and in every good work.

^k Ps. 112. 9.

9 (As it is written, ^kHe hath dispersed abroad; he hath given to the poor: his righteousness remaineth for ever.

As in the former verse the apostle had asserted God's sufficiency to repay them what they should lend him, so he here asserteth God's readiness and willingness. This he confirmeth from a promise taken out of Psal. cxii. 9, where also is further added, *his horn shall be exalted with honour.* Concerning the merciful man, it is true that Solomon saith,

Prov. xi. 24, *There is that scattereth, and yet increaseth.* The psalmist saith, *His righteousness endureth for ever:* by which term some understand his bounty or liberality: I had rather understand by it here his obedience to the command of God in his free distribution to the poor; this remaineth in God's book of remembrance for ever, God will not forget this *labour of love*, Heb. vi. 10. The friends which he maketh with his *mammon of righteousness*, shall receive him *into everlasting habitations*, Luke xvi. 9. A man's riches cannot remain for ever, but his righteousness, in the distribution of them according to the command of God, that shall remain for ever.

10 Now he that ^lministereth seed to the sower both minister bread for *your* food, and multiply your seed sown, and increase the fruits of your ^mrighteousness;)

^l Is. 55. 10. ^m Hos. 10. 12. Matt. 6. 1.

The God, whose providence and blessing maketh rich, and who giveth this seed to the sower, supply you with whatsoever you stand in need of for this life, and give you a heart to multiply that spiritual seed, by which the fruits of your righteousness shall be increased. Some Greek copies read these words in the future tense, according to which reading they are a formal promise, both of good things, whereby they might show their charity, and also of a free and large heart, disposing them to that exercise of grace. Our translators render it in the form of a prayer; which yet being the prayer of the apostle, put up in faith, doth virtually contain a promise both of a temporal and a spiritual increase.

11 Being enriched in every thing to all ‖ †bountifulness, ⁿ which causeth through us thanksgiving to God.

‖ Or, *liberality*. † Gr. *simplicity*. ch. 1. 2. ⁿ ch. 1. 11. & 4. 15.

The word here translated *bountifulness*, signifies simplicity, in opposition to deceit and fraud. We had it before, chap. viii. 2; so Rom. xii. 8: so, James i. 5, God is said to give ἁπλῶς, simply (we translate it *liberally*). We have in these two chapters met with three words, by which the bounty of Christians to persons in distress is expressed; *grace, blessing, simplicity*, χάρις, εὐλογία, ἁπλότης. The first lets us know the true root of all acceptable giving to those who are in distress, that must be free love: the second expresseth the true end, blessing God and our neighbour; serving the glory and commands of God, and the necessities of our brethren: this third expresseth the manner how we must give, that is, with simplicity. It is no true liberality where simplicity is wanting, that a man doth not what he doth with a plain heart and design to obey God and do good to his brother. *Which causeth through us thanksgiving to God;* as a further argument to press them to this liberality, he tells them, that it would cause them that were the apostles and ministers of Christ, to offer thanksgiving unto God.

12 For the administration of this service not only ^osupplieth the want of the saints, but is abundant also by many thanksgivings unto God;

^o ch. 8. 14.

No man ought to live to himself; the two great ends of every Christian's life ought to be, the glory of God, and the good of others, especially such as belong to the household of faith. This service (saith the apostle) serveth both those ends: 1. It supplieth the necessities of the saints; and, 2. It causeth thanksgivings to God by many persons, and upon many accounts; which he further openeth in the following verses.

13 Whiles by the experiment of this ministration they ^pglorify God for your professed subjection unto the Gospel of Christ, and for *your* liberal ^qdistribution unto them, and unto all *men:*

^p Matt. 5. 16. ^q Heb. 13. 16.

Whiles by the experiment of this ministration, upon their receiving of what you sent them, *they glorify God for your professed subjection unto the gospel of Christ;* they will see how ready you are to obey the gospel of Christ, (which hath in so many places called you to this duty,) and this will give them occasion of blessing God, who in the day of his power hath made such a willing people, willing at God's command, and in consideration of the love of Christ, to strip themselves to clothe his naked members, to restrain their own appetites to feed them. The grace of God bestowed on others, is matter of great thanksgiving to every gracious heart. *And for your liberal distribution unto them, and unto all men:* another cause of thanksgiving will be God's moving your hearts towards them; they will see reason to bless God, who hath raised them up such friends in their great straits; so as they will both bless God on your behalf, for his grace bestowed on you, that out of the Gentiles he hath picked out a people so subject to the law of his gospel; and also on their own behalf, that God hath stirred up a people to compassionate them in their deep distresses.

r ch. 8. 1.   14 And by their prayer for you, which long after you for the exceeding *grace of God in you.*

Another way by which the glory of God will be promoted, by your simple, free, and liberal contribution, is, that by this he will have more prayers, which also will redound to your advantage, for it will procure prayers for you; and not prayers only, but a great deal of fervent love; so as they will long after your good, and after your acquaintance, when they shall receive such an experiment of *the exceeding grace of God in you.*

s Jam. 1. 17.   15 Thanks *be* unto God *for his unspeakable gift.

Interpreters are not agreed what the apostle here meaneth by God's *unspeakable gift.* Some by it understand Christ, who is *the gift of God,* and the Fountain of all grace; and to this the epithet *unspeakable* doth best agree. Others understand the gospel, by which the hearts of men are subdued, effectually disposed, and inclined to obey the will of God. Others think it is to be understood of that habit of brotherly love, which from the Spirit of Christ, by the gospel, was wrought in the hearts of these Corinthians. If the last be meant, (to which the most incline,) the apostle declareth his firm persuasion of them, that they would obey him in this thing, and giveth God thanks for giving them such a heart. Seeing the contribution was not yet made, though a year before they had declared their readiness to it, I should rather incline to interpret it concerning Christ; and that the apostle concludeth this whole discourse about contributing to the relief of these poor members of Christ, with a general doxology, or blessing of God for Jesus Christ, who is the Author and Finisher of all grace, without such a particular reference to the preceding discourse; yet hereby hinting to them, that without the influence of his grace they would, they could do nothing.

CHAP. X

Paul entreateth the Corinthians not to leave him cause to exert against them that spiritual power, with which he was armed, and meant to chastise those who undervalued his person and apostolical character, 1—11. *He pointeth out the difference between those who, for want of looking beyond themselves, were arrogant and vain, intruding into, and taking merit from, the labours of others, and himself, who kept strictly within the province allotted him by God, and, avoiding self-commendation, sought honour from the commendation of Christ,* 12—18.

Hitherto the apostle, who in his former Epistle had blamed this church for so many things, and dealt sharply with them, in this Epistle hath treated them as if they had been a people that had had no faults, or none but what, in obedience to his former Epistle, they had reformed, and become a new lump: which argueth, that the major part of the members of it were a good and an obedient people, by whose prevalent vote they had reformed much that was amiss. But in these four last chapters, to let us know that there was yet some of the old leaven amongst them, he useth another style; taking notice, that he understood there was amongst them another (though possibly the lesser) party who had much vilified him; and justifying himself against their whisperings and calumnies, not without some sharp reflections upon them.

a Rom. 12.1.   NOW ᵃI Paul myself beseech you by the meekness and gentleness of Christ, ᵇwho ‖ in presence *am* base among you, but being absent am bold toward you:

b ver. 10. ch. 12. 5, 7, 9. ‖ Or. in outward appearance.

Now I Paul myself beseech you by the meekness and gentleness of Christ: meekness respecteth the spirit or inward man, being a virtue that moderateth inward anger and rash passions. *Gentleness* more respecteth the outward conversation. The apostle mentioneth both these virtues, as eminent in Christ, who is our great example, and to whom all Christians are bound to be conformable. *Who in presence am base among you, but being absent am bold toward you:* he here repeateth the words of those who, in this church, reproached him; they reported him a man, who, when he was there in presence with them, was lowly and humble enough; but when he was absent from them, then he wrote imperiously and confidently enough. The sense of the words is plainly this: I Paul, (of whom some amongst you say, that when I am there with you I am low and humble enough, even to some degrees of baseness; but when I am absent, then I write like a lord, boldly and confidently,) I beseech you to consider the temper of our common Lord and Saviour, to remember how free he was from rash anger and passion, how gentle he was in his conversation; and by the obligation that is upon you, to love and practise those virtues which you saw, or have heard of, in him.

2 But I beseech *you,* ᶜthat I may not be bold when I am present with that confidence, wherewith I think to be bold against some, which ‖ think of us as if we walked according to the flesh.

c 1 Cor. 4. 21. ch. 13. 2, 10. ‖ Or, reckon.

It is true, (saith the apostle,) when I have been with you I have made it my business to behave myself with all obliging sweetness, not using that authority which I might have used; and I beseech you, as not to blame me for that, (remembering the meekness and gentleness of Christ,) so by your conversation not to force me to another kind of conversation amongst you; that you would not constrain me to a severer behaviour towards you when I am present with you, to be so free with some of you, as at present I am resolved to be; such, I mean, as have traduced me, as if I *walked according to the flesh,* that is, not guided by the Holy Spirit of God, and the directions of his word, but by some external, carnal considerations, respecting my own profit, pleasure, or reputation, indulging my own passions or corrupt affections. Walking *after the flesh* is opposed to a walking *after the Spirit,* Rom. viii. 1. He walketh *after the flesh,* to whom the fleshly appetite is the principle, rule, and end of his actions; as he, on the contrary, to whom those habits of grace which are wrought in the soul by the Holy Spirit, or the Spirit himself more immediately by his motions or impulses, are the principle of his actions, and the word dictated by the Spirit is the rule of his actions, and the glory of God is the end of his actions, is truly said to walk *after the Spirit.*

3 For though we walk in the flesh, we do not war after the flesh:

There is a great difference betwixt walking in the flesh, and warring after the flesh. The best of men in this life walk in the flesh, as their souls are not in a state of separation from, but union with, the body; but they do not walk after the flesh, as their fleshly appetite is not the principle of their actions, nor the satisfaction of it the end of their actions. The apostle, in the latter part of the verse, changeth the verb; in the former part he called our conversation, a walking; in the latter part he calleth it a warring; which he describeth negatively in this verse, positively in the following verses. In calling it a warring, he lets us know that it is, and will be, a life of opposition, in which a Christian will have many enemies; though his hand be against none, yet many hands will be against him. But though they be men of strife and contention, in a passive sense, yet they are not so in an active sense, according to the usual notion of warring; for they war not after the flesh, neither as fleshly men, nor in a carnal, fleshly manner, nor yet for fleshly ends. The men of the world war for their honour and glory, or for revenge and satisfaction of their lusts, or for the enlarging of their territories and dominions; but *we do not* thus *war after the flesh.*

4 (^d For the weapons ^e of our warfare *are* not carnal, but ^f mighty ‖ through God ^g to the pulling down of strong holds ;)

<small>d Eph. 6. 13.
1 Thes. 5. 8.
e 1 Tim. 1. 18.
2 Tim. 2. 3.
f Acts 7. 22.
1 Cor. 2. 5. ch. 6. 7. & 13. 3, 4.   ‖ Or, *to God.*   g Jer. 1. 10.</small>

As our end is spiritual, so are our means ; the means by which we manage our spiritual fight are spiritual. Whether by these *weapons* he meaneth the word of God, and his preaching the gospel, or the censures of the church duly administered, it is true, they are not of a carnal nature, or fitted to the subduing of men's bodies, and bringing them into subjection ; they are of a spiritual nature, and have their effects upon the mind and inward part of a man ; yet, through the concurrence of Divine grace, there is in them a mighty force and power, to pull down *strong holds :* by which metaphorical expression he understands whatsoever opposeth the gospel, and seemeth to defend and uphold men in their sinful courses; subduing the will of man, which is so strong a hold that all the power of hell cannot storm it.

5 ^h Casting down ‖ imaginations, and every high thing that exalteth itself against the knowledge of God, and bringing into captivity every thought to the obedience of Christ ;

<small>h 1 Cor. 1. 19. & 3. 19.
‖ Or, *reasonings.*</small>

Casting down imaginations ; λογισμὸς, reasonings ; *and every high thing,* every height of reasoning, *that exalteth itself against the knowledge of God.* The great troublers of this church of Corinth were the heathen philosophers, and such as had sucked in their principles ; with whose notions, which were conclusions drawn from reason not sanctified and subdued to the will of God, divers doctrines of faith would not agree. St. Paul tells them, that the gospel, (which was the great weapon of his warfare,) through the power of God, was mighty to pull down the strong holds which unbelief had in the carnal understanding of men, to overthrow their reasonings, the heights of them, which exalted themselves against the doctrine of faith ; and to bring πᾶν νόημα, *every thought,* or counsel, *into a captivity to the obedience of Christ :* so as whatsoever was revealed by the apostles from the Spirit of God, men readily agreed and yielded obedience to ; whatever their thoughts or reasonings about it were, they gave credit to it ; not because it appeared rational to them, but upon the Divine authority of the revelation ; submitting their reason to that, and believing it the most rational thing in the world, that they should believe what God affirmed, and do what God commanded ; and this blessed effect the gospel had in all those who heartily embraced it : for indeed to give an assent to a proposition, merely upon a sensible or rational demonstration, is no faith, that is, no Divine faith. Truly to believe, in a Divine sense, is to assent to a proposition upon the credit of the revelation, though we cannot make it out by our reason : and this it is to have our thoughts brought into a captivity to the obedience of Christ. That whereas reason, as it is since the fall subjected in man, riseth up in arms against several Divine propositions, and saith, How can these things be ? how can one be three, and three one ? how could the Divine and human nature unite in one person ? how can the dead rise ? &c. : the believer *audit verbum Dei et tacet,* readeth these things, and others of the like nature, plainly asserted in holy writ, and chides down his reason ; resolving to give credit to these things merely because God hath said them, who cannot lie. Thus our νοήματα, thoughts, counsels, reasonings, deliberations, conclusions, all the product of our understanding, is brought into a captivity to the obedience of Christ; and reason itself, which is the governess and mistress of the soul of man, is made a captive to revelation. And in this appeared the mighty power of the weapons of the apostle's warfare.

6 ⁱ And having in a readiness to revenge all disobedience, when ^k your obedience is fulfilled.

<small>i ch. 13. 2, 10.
k ch. 2. 9. & 7. 15.</small>

The apostle certainly means by this, excommunication ; which was the rod which he had before mentioned, asking them if they would he should come unto them with a rod. This rod he here threateneth them with ; telling them, that he had another weapon of his warfare, of a spiritual nature too, to be used against such as preferred themselves to be believers, but walked disorderly ; only he at present spared them, because though a great part of them were obedient, yet there were some amongst them of whose obedience he could not yet glory ; but yet he hoped well, and therefore should wait until, by the use of all fair means, (such as exhortations and arguments,) he had reduced as many of them as he could unto obedience. But that being done, God had intrusted him with another weapon, with which he would, in the name and by the authority of God, revenge his glory upon the disobedience of others. Herein the apostle hath set a rule and a pattern to all churches, where are multitudes that walk disorderly ; not to be too hasty in excommunicating them, but to proceed gradually ; first using all fair means, and waiting with all patience, for the reducing them to their duty, who will by any gentle and fair means be reduced ; and then revenging the honour and glory of God only upon such as will not be reclaimed.

7 ^l Do ye look on things after the outward appearance ? ^m If any man trust to himself that he is Christ's, let him of himself think this again, that, as he *is* Christ's, even so *are* ⁿ we Christ's.

<small>l John 7. 24. ch. 5. 12. & 11. 18.
m 1 Cor. 14. 37.
1 John 4. 6.
n 1 Cor. 3. 23. & 9. 1. ch. 11. 23.</small>

Are ye so weak as to judge of persons and things merely from their faces, pretences, or outward appearances ? and to magnify these false apostles and teachers, merely because they set forth and magnify themselves, or because they take up a great breadth in the world, and live in a little state and splendour ? If any of them do judge that he is the servant or the minister of Christ, why should he not think the same of me ? what hath he to say to prove his relation to Christ more than I have ? what hath he to glory in upon that account more than I have ?

8 For though I should boast somewhat more ^o of our authority, which the Lord hath given us for edification, and not for your destruction, ^p I should not be ashamed :

<small>o ch. 13. 10.
p ch. 7. 14. & 12. 6.</small>

Here is a remarkable maxim, a rule from which all ecclesiastical superiors ought to measure their actions : God hath given to no superiors a power for *destruction* of the flock, but only for *edification ;* so as that no such can pretend to a power received from God, to do or exact any thing which may any ways hinder the salvation of the souls put under their trust ; they ought to command or exact nothing, nor to do any thing, but what may probably tend to the promoting of people's faith, and holiness, and eternal salvation. This maxim the apostle puts in in a parenthesis in this verse, to sweeten what he had before spoken, concerning his readiness to revenge the disobedience of such who should appear to be stubborn and contumacious. But he tells them, he *should not be ashamed* if he did *boast somewhat more of* a just and due *authority* than the false apostles and teachers had, who vilified him ; for he was an apostle, and had a more immediate authority than they who were ordinary teachers.

9 That I may not seem as if I would terrify you by letters.

This was one imputation upon the apostle, as we may learn by the next verse. I tell you, saith the apostle, that I have an authority, and a further authority than those who vilify me can pretend unto : but I also tell you, I have no authority to do any harm to any of you ; all the authority I have is for your edification, as much as lieth in me to promote the business of your salvation ; so that I need not be reported as one that went about to terrify you by my letters ; yet I know there are some who so represent me unto you.

10 For *his* letters, † say they, *are* weighty and powerful ; but ^q *his* bodily presence *is* weak, and *his* ^r speech contemptible.

<small>† Gr. *saith he.*
q 1 Cor. 2. 3, 4. ver. 1. ch. 12. 5, 7, 9. Gal. 4. 13.
r 1 Cor. 1. 17. & 2. 1, 4. ch. 11. 6.</small>

There are some amongst you that tell you, that indeed (when absent) I write severely, and with authority ; but when I am there with you, neither my behaviour, nor my speech, speaks any such authority.

11 Let such an one think this, that, such as we are in word by letters when we are absent, such *will we be* also in deed when we are present.

I would have no such person think so of me, for he shall find me the same in deed when I come, that I have spoken myself to be by my letters. I do not write vainly, merely to terrify you, but what I truly intend to do, and when I come he shall find that I will do.

s ch. 3. 1. & 5. 12.

12 ˢFor we dare not make ourselves of the number, or compare ourselves with some that commend themselves: but they measuring themselves by themselves, and comparing themselves among themselves, ‖ are not wise.

‖ Or, *understand it not.*

This whole verse is a reflection upon the false teachers of the church of Corinth, from whose manners Paul purgeth himself. I (saith he) durst not, as some others, magnify myself, nor compare myself with those that do so. Neither is it any wisdom in them to contemn and despise others, in comparison of themselves; for observe what measures they take, they only measure themselves by themselves, and compare themselves amongst themselves, that is, with birds of their own feather, such as are like unto themselves, and of their own faction and party; which no wise men would do.

t ver. 15.

13 ᵗBut we will not boast of things without *our* measure, but according to the measure of the ‖ rule which God hath distributed to us, a measure to reach even unto you.

‖ Or, *line.*

The apostle may be understood as speaking both of spiritual gifts, and also of his travels to the several places whither he had gone preaching the gospel. He reflecteth still upon the false teachers who were crept into this church; who (as it should seem) had much boasted of their gifts and abilities, and of their labours and successes. In opposition to whom, he saith, that he boasted not *without* his *measure,* or, (as it is in the Greek, τὰ ἄμετρα,) unmeasurable things; but he kept himself within *the measure of the rule;* that is, according to that regular measure which God hath set us. Which *measure* extendeth *even to you.* You have those amongst you who boast unmeasurably of the gifts which they have, and of the great things which they do; I durst not do so (saith the apostle); God hath given me a measure and a rule, according to that I have acted, and of those actings only I will glory. And in my so doing I can boast of you, for to you my measure and line hath reached; God hath made me an instrument to raise him up a church amongst you.

14 For we stretch not ourselves beyond *our measure,* as though we reached not unto you: ᵘfor we are come as far as to you also in *preaching* the Gospel of Christ:

u 1 Cor. 3. 5, 10. & 4. 15. & 9. 1.

For in our boasting of you as our converts, amongst whom I have preached the gospel, and God hath made my preaching successful; *we stretch not ourselves beyond our measure,* and arrogate that to ourselves which belongeth not to us: for the thing is true, and ye know that in our *preaching the gospel we have come as far as unto you,* and that God hath given our labours success amongst you.

15 Not boasting of things without *our* measure, *that is,* ˣ of other men's labours; but having hope, when your faith is increased, that we shall be ‖ enlarged by you according to our rule abundantly,

x Rom. 15. 20.

‖ Or, *magnified in you.*

So that although we have boasted of you, we have not boasted *of things without our measure;* that is, of things that are not, or (as the apostle expounds himself) of things that were not done by him but by other men; for his line did reach unto them, and his labours had been employed and made successful amongst them. And he declares his hope, that when the gospel should have had its full success amongst them, and their *faith* should be *increased,* (either by the addition of more persons to the church amongst them, or by the perfecting of their faith, and other graces,) they, who were apostles and the ministers of the gospel to them, should by it be magnified, or made great; to wit, by their means, who using much navigation, would have opportunities to commend the gospel, and the ministry of it, to other people, amongst whom they should come: wherein yet they should not exceed their rule; for though ordinary ministers be fixed in particular churches and places, yet the apostles' rule was to go and preach the gospel over the whole world, being tied to no certain people or places.

16 To preach the Gospel in the *regions* beyond you, *and* not to boast in another man's ‖line of things made ready to our hand.

‖ Or, *rule.*

To preach the gospel in the regions beyond you; the apostle here expoundeth what he meaneth by the term magnified, or *enlarged,* in the preceding verse, viz. to have a door opened to preach the gospel in places whither it was not yet come. God honoureth persons when he maketh them instruments to bring any to an acquaintance with, and to the embracing of, his gospel, who formerly had been ignorant of it, and not acquainted with it. *And not to boast in another man's line of things made ready to our hand:* he here seemeth to reflect on the false teachers crept into this church, who had nothing to boast in but a pretended building, upon other men's foundations, and carrying on a work by others made ready to their hands; and seemeth to prefer the work of conversion, and an instrumentality in that, before an instrumentality merely in edification, and carrying on the work of God already begun in people's souls.

17 ʸBut he that glorieth, let him glory in the Lord.

y Is. 65. 16. Jer. 9. 24. 1 Cor. 1. 31.

But we have none of us any thing to glory in, neither I Paul who plant, nor Apollos who watereth; whether God maketh use of us as the first planters of the gospel, or as instruments to carry on the work of the gospel already planted, we have nothing of our own to glory in. *God giveth the increase;* we have therefore no reason to glory in ourselves, or in our own performances, but only to give thanks to God, who maketh use of us, poor earthly vessels, to carry about and distribute that heavenly treasure, by which he maketh souls rich in faith and good works : all that we do is only instrumentally; God is all, and in all, as to primary efficiency.

18 For ᶻnot he that commendeth himself is approved, but ᵃwhom the Lord commendeth.

z Prov. 27. 2.
a Rom. 2.29. 1 Cor. 4. 5.

Solomon saith, Prov. xxvii. 2, *Let another man praise thee, and not thine own mouth; a stranger, and not thine own lips.* Self-commendation is an ungrateful sound to ingenuous ears; no man thinks another a jot the better for his commending himself, but always hath the worse opinion of him for such boasting; but this text speaketh of a higher approbation, viz. from God. No man is approved of God for his speaking well of himself; the business is, who they are who approve themselves in the work which God hath committed to them; to whom the Lord will say, Well done, good and faithful servants: to whom the apostle refers both himself, and those who magnified themselves, but vilified him.

CHAP. XI

Paul unwillingly entereth upon a commendation of himself, out of jealousy lest the Corinthians should be perverted by false apostles from the pure doctrine of Christ, 1—4. *He showeth that he was in all respects equal to the chiefest apostles,* 5, 6: *that he declined being chargeable to them, not for want of love toward them, but to cut off occasion from those deceitful workers of taking shelter under his example,* 7—15: *that he was not inferior to those, whom they so patiently submitted to, in any of their boasted prerogatives,* 16—22; *but as a minister of Christ, in labours and sufferings for the gospel's sake, was abundantly their superior,* 23—33.

II. CORINTHIANS XI

1 WOULD to God ye could bear with me a little in *my* folly: and indeed ‖ bear with me.

That which the apostle here calls his *folly*, was his speaking so much in his own commendation; which indeed is no better than folly, unless there be a great reason; which was here, for it was the false teachers, vilifying his person and office, that put him upon it. The verb in the latter part of the verse, may be read either imperatively, (and so we translate it,) as if it were an entreaty of them to excuse him in speaking so much good of himself; or indicatively, you do bear with me.

2 For I am jealous over you with godly jealousy: for I have espoused you to one husband, that I may present *you as* a chaste virgin to Christ.

Jealousy is a passion in a person which makes him impatient of any rival or partner in the thing or person beloved. The apostle tells them, that he was *jealous over them*, and thereby lets them know, that he so passionately loved them, as that he was not patient that any should pretend more kindness to them than he had for them; and withal, that he had some fear of them, lest they should be perverted and drawn away from the simplicity of the gospel; upon this account he calls it a *godly jealousy*. For (saith he) I have been instrumental to bring you to Christ; this he calls an espousing of them, the union of persons with Christ being expressed in Scripture under the notion of a marriage, Eph. v. 23, &c. And he expresseth his earnest desire to *present* them *to Christ* uncorrupted, like *a chaste virgin*.

3 But I fear, lest by any means, as the serpent beguiled Eve through his subtilty, so your minds should be corrupted from the simplicity that is in Christ.

In all jealousy there is a mixture of love and fear: the apostle's love to this church, together with his earnest desire to present them in the day of judgment unto Christ pure and uncorrupted, caused him to write; because he was afraid, lest that as the serpent by his subtlety deceived Eve, so some subtle seducers should corrupt them, and so withdraw them from the simplicity of their faith in Christ, and obedience to him. This danger was partly from the pagan philosophers, mixing their philosophical notions with the plain doctrine of the gospel; and partly from some that were tenacious of the Judaical rites, and would not understand the abolition of the ceremonial law.

4 For if he that cometh preacheth another Jesus, whom we have not preached, or *if* ye receive another spirit, which ye have not received, or another Gospel, which ye have not accepted, ye might well bear ‖ with *him*.

How our translators have interpreted καλῶς ἠνείχεσθε, *ye might well bear*, I cannot tell: the words manifestly are to be interpreted, you have well borne, and so are plainly a reflection upon some in this church, who had patiently endured false teachers, who had preached other doctrine than what Paul had preached. And this the apostle giveth as a reason of his fear, lest they should be corrupted and drawn away from the simplicity of the gospel. This certainly is more obviously the sense of the words, than what others incline to, who make the sense this: If any other could come to you, who could preach to you a better Jesus, a more excellent Saviour, than we have done; or a more excellent spirit than him whom you have received; or a more excellent doctrine than the doctrine of the gospel, which we have preached; you might bear with him. For I see no pretence to interpret the verb as in the potential mood, it is manifestly the indicative mood; and declareth, not what they might do, but what they had done; which made the apostle jealous of them, lest they should be perverted. And our Saviour, John v. 43, hath taught us, that those who with the most difficulty receive those who come to them in God's name, are always most easy to receive those who come in their own name, without any due authority or commission from God.

5 For I suppose I was not a whit behind the very chiefest apostles.

The apostle, doubtless, meaneth those that were the true apostles of our Lord, those who were immediately sent out by him to preach the gospel, behind whom the apostle was not, either in respect of ministerial gifts and graces, or in respect of labours, or in respect of success which God had given him in his work. One method that false teachers used to vilify Paul, was by magnifying some others of the apostles above him, and preferring them before him; which makes him, both here, and in Gal. ii., and Rom. xi. 13, to magnify his office, by showing them, there was no reason why they should make a difference betwixt him and other apostles; for he had the same immediate call, was intrusted with the same power, furnished and adorned with the same gifts, in labours (as he elsewhere saith) he had been more than they all; nor had God been wanting in giving him success in his labours, proportionable to the chiefest of them: so as he *was not a whit behind* them.

6 But though *I be* rude in speech, yet not in knowledge; but we have been throughly made manifest among you in all things.

But though I be rude in speech; admit (saith the apostle) that I be no orator, speaking to you in high language, or in a neat style and phrase; either having no faculty that way, or, if I have, yet choosing rather to speak plainly, and home to your consciences, than floridly, to tickle your ears with a fine sound and chiming of words. *Yet not in knowledge;* yet, I bless God, I am not defective in knowledge; and, as God hath enlightened me with a large knowledge of his will, so I have communicated to you the whole counsel of God. *But we have been throughly made manifest among you in all things;* and in all things, which may declare me an apostle, one sent of Christ about the business of the gospel, I have been made manifest amongst you; preaching amongst you the whole doctrine of the gospel, and having been an instrument to convert many of you from paganism to Christianity.

7 Have I committed an offence in abasing myself that ye might be exalted, because I have preached to you the Gospel of God freely?

What is it that hath made you take such offence at me; seeing you cannot say, that either in my call, or in my gifts and graces, or in my labours, or in the success of my labours, I have been inferior to the chiefest of the apostles? Doth this offend you, that for your sake I have veiled my authority, and departed from my right? which makes some of you say, I am base in presence. Is it for my putting you to no charge in my preaching the gospel? This was a thing wherein he gloried, and told them, 1 Cor. ix. 6, 12, 15, that he would rather die, than have his glorying void in this particular.

8 I robbed other churches, taking wages *of them*, to do you service.

He interpreteth the term of *robbed other churches*, by a *taking wages of them;* which indeed is no robbery, as he had proved, 1 Cor. ix. All the robbery that was in it lay in this, that his maintenance, in strictness of right, should have been proportionably from this, as well as from other churches; but for some reasons (which he thinks fit to conceal) he refused to receive any thing from this church; but spared them, and lived upon the maintenance he had from other churches, while he was doing them service. Either he saw the members of this church were poor, or that there were some in this church who would sooner have taken advantage to reproach him for it, and so have hindered the success of the gospel. Whatever it was that caused the apostle to do it, certain it is, that he did it, and make it a great piece of his glorying.

9 And when I was present with you, and wanted, I was chargeable to no man: for that which was lacking to me the brethren which came from Macedonia supplied: and in all *things* I have kept myself from being burdensome unto you, and *so* will I keep *myself*.

The word which we translate *chargeable*, signifies to benumb; I benumbed no man: or, (as others,) I was not myself more benumbed in any thing. If we take it in the first-mentioned sense, it lets us see a reason why Paul refused to take wages of the church of Corinth, lest he should cool and benumb them as to the receiving of the gospel, when they saw it would prove chargeable to them. If in the latter sense, the apostle seems to reflect upon such whom wages only edged to their work, who preached merely for gain and filthy lucre. To distinguish himself from such hirelings, he tells them, that when he was with them, and laboured amongst them in preaching the gospel, he put them to no charge; yet he was not slothful in his work, but as laborious as those who did take wages. As to himself, he had want enough whilst he was amongst them; but the providence of God ordered him a supply from the churches of Macedonia, and by that means he kept himself from being burdensome to them; and, he tells them, so he was resolved that he would still be.

10 *As the truth of Christ is in me, †ᵃno man shall stop me of this boasting in the regions of Achaia.

r Rom. 9. 1.
† Gr. *this boasting shall not be stopped in me.*
a 1 Cor. 9. 15.

The apostle often repeateth this, glorying much in it, that in this region of Achaia he had preached the gospel without charge to the hearers: he did so also at Thessalonica, 1 Thess. ii. 5, 6, 9; but concerning them, he saith, what he no where saith of the Corinthians, that they received the word in much affliction; which might, probably, be the cause. It is most likely that he either discerned this people to be more covetous, and too much lovers of their money: or that there was a generation among them, who, if he had taken wages for his labours, would have reproached him as one that was a hireling, and who did all that he did for money. And, indeed, himself seemeth in the next verses to give this as a reason.

11 Wherefore? ᵗbecause I love you not? God knoweth.

t ch. 6. 11. & 7. 3. & 12. 15.

Can you possibly interpret my not being chargeable to you, as proceeding from a want of love in me to you? God knoweth the contrary.

12 But what I do, that I will do, ᵘthat I may cut off occasion from them which desire occasion; that wherein they glory, they may be found even as we.

u 1 Cor. 9. 12.

I know (saith the apostle) that there are some amongst you who, out of their hatred to me, would seek any occasion to asperse me to justify themselves. If I had (as I might) have taken wages amongst you for my labours, they would either have taken occasion from it to have aspersed me, (as doing what I did from a mercenary spirit,) or at least to have justified themselves in their exactings upon you. I had a mind to prevent any such occasions of boasting. *That wherein they glory, they may be found even as we:* it should seem by these words, that some teachers in this church, being (possibly) men of estates, required no maintenance of the people; and would have taken advantage against the apostle, if he had taken any: or, possibly, some others exacted upon them unreasonably, who, had Paul taken wages, would have justified themselves by his example. The apostle therefore was resolved to cut off from them any pretence or occasion of boasting, and to do whatever any of them did, in sparing the Corinthians as to the business of their purses.

13 For such ˣ*are* false apostles, ʸdeceitful workers, transforming themselves into the apostles of Christ.

x Acts 15. 24. Rom. 16. 18. Gal. 1. 7. & 6. 12. Phil. 1. 15. 2 Pet. 2. 1. 1 John 4. 1. Rev. 2. 2.   y ch. 2. 17. Phil. 3. 2. Tit. 1. 10, 11.

For such are false apostles; that is, persons pretending to be sent of Christ, but were indeed never sent of him. *Deceitful workers;* persons whose work is but to cheat and deceive you; and that both with reference to their call and authority which they pretend to, and also to the doctrine which they bring. *Transforming themselves into the apostles of Christ;* they were never apostles of Christ, only they put themselves into such a shape and form, that they might have more advantage to deceive.

14 And no marvel; for Satan himself is transformed into ᶻan angel of light.

z Gal. 1. 8.

It is not at all to be wondered, that the emissaries of Satan dissemble, and pretend themselves to be what they are not, for even Satan himself, who is the prince of darkness, in order to the deceiving and seducing of souls, transformeth himself *into an angel of light;* that is, puts on the appearance and form of a good angel. He calls them *angels of light,* because they were wont to appear in a lightsome brightness; or because of that glory in which they behold the face of God; or because of those great measures of heavenly knowledge which those blessed spirits have. All tempted souls have an experiment of this; for none is tempted to evil under the appearance of evil, (evil as evil being what a reasonable soul cannot be courted to). The devil therefore, in all his temptations to sin, though his end be to ruin and destroy, yet appeareth as *an angel of light;* moving the soul to evil under the notion and appearance of good.

15 Therefore *it is* no great thing if his ministers also be transformed as the ᵃministers of righteousness; ᵇwhose end shall be according to their works.

a ch. 3. 9.
b Phil. 3. 19.

It is no wonder if there be like servants, like masters: and as the devil, in order to the deceiving of souls, pretends to what he is not, viz. a friend to them; so those who seek their own profit, not your good, show themselves to be *his ministers,* driving the same design with him, also do the like, and change their shapes, pretending themselves to be ministers of the gospel, and to aim at the good of your souls, by teaching you the way *of righteousness;* but God will one day judge of their works, and their reward at last will be *according to their works.*

16 ᶜI say again, Let no man think me a fool; if otherwise, yet as a fool ‖receive me, that I may boast myself a little.

c ver. 1. ch. 12. 6, 11.
‖ Or, *suffer.*

I say again, Let no man think me a fool: I know that he, who is much in magnifying and praising himself, ordinarily is judged to be a fool; but though I do so, let me not lie under that imputation. There is a time for all things; a time for a man to cease from his own praises, and a time for him to praise himself. The time for the latter is, when the glory of God, or our own just vindication, is concerned; both which concurred here: the apostle was out of measure vilified by these false apostles; and the glory of God was eminently concerned, that so great an apostle and instrument in promoting the gospel, should not be exposed to contempt, as a mean and despicable person, or as an impostor and deceiver. *If otherwise, yet as a fool receive me, that I may boast myself a little;* but if you will judge me a fool, be it so; yet receive me as such, while I boast a little.

17 That which I speak, ᵈI speak *it* not after the Lord, but as it were foolishly, ᵉin this confidence of boasting.

d 1 Cor. 7. 6, 12.
e ch. 9. 4.

That which I speak, I speak it not after the Lord; I do not pretend to have any special command of God, to speak what I shall now say in my own commendation; God hath left that to our liberty, which we may use, or not use, as circumstances of time, place, and occasion direct. Or, I do not speak according to the ordinary practice of Christians and ministers of the gospel; whose ordinary practice is to abase and vilify, not to exalt and set forth themselves, according to the more general rules of the word. Yet what the apostle saith was not contrary to the Lord, or to the directions of his word, which hath no where commanded us to vilify ourselves, or to conceal what God hath wrought in us and by us. *But as it were foolishly, in this confidence of boasting:* this my confident boasting hath an appearance of foolishness in it, though really it be not so; for nothing can be truly called foolishness, which hath a direct and immediate tendency to the glory of God, and is designed for that end.

18 ᶠSeeing that many glory after the flesh, I will glory also.

f Phil. 3. 3, 4.

By *the flesh* is meant, carnal and external things; which though they be the gifts and favours of God, yet do not at all commend a man to God. The apostle saith, there are *many that glory after the flesh;* and there needs must be such in all places, because there are many that *walk after*

II. CORINTHIANS XI

the flesh: now, it is but natural for men to boast and glory in those attainments, which it hath been the business of their lives to pursue after. Such there were, doubtless, in this famous church, who gloried that they were native Jews, or in their riches, or in their knowledge and learning. Now, though (saith the apostle) I know there is nothing in these things truly to be gloried in, yet, others glorying in them, *I will glory also;* and let them know, that if I thought these things worth the glorying in, I have as much to glory in of that nature as any of them have.

g 1 Cor. 4. 10.

19 For ye suffer fools gladly, ^g seeing ye *yourselves* are wise.

Ye freely suffer others foolishly glorying and boasting of themselves, therefore do ye suffer me therein to judge yourselves wise, and it belongs to the wise to bear with such as are not so wise as themselves.

h Gal. 2. 4. & 4. 9.

20 For ye suffer, ^h if a man bring you into bondage, if a man devour *you,* if a man take *of you,* if a man exalt himself, if a man smite you on the face.

If any domineer over you, as if you were their slaves, or if any bring you into subjection to the rites of the ceremonial law; if they *devour* and make a prey of you, take wages of you, and do nothing without hire; if they carry themselves proudly, exalting themselves above you; nay, if they *smite you,* you will suffer and bear with such: this is more than to bear with a little folly and indiscretion in me. This is observable, that men of corrupt hearts and loose lives will better bear with teachers that will humour and spare them in their lusts, than with such as are faithful to their souls in instructing and reproving them, though they carry themselves with the greatest innocency and justice towards them.

i ch. 10. 10.

21 I speak as concerning reproach, ⁱ as though we had been weak. Howbeit

k Phil. 3. 4.

^k whereinsoever any is bold, (I speak foolishly,) I am bold also.

I speak as to those reproaches they cast on me, who am by them represented to you as though I were weak and contemptible; as indeed I am, as to my person, but not as to my doctrine, and the miracles I have wrought amongst you. And being some of them are so confident in boasting what they are, and what they have done and suffered; let me be a little bold as well as they, in telling you what I am, and what I have done and suffered.

l Acts 22. 3. Rom. 11. 1. Phil. 3. 5.

22 Are they Hebrews? ^l so *am* I. Are they Israelites? so *am* I. Are they the seed of Abraham? so *am* I.

Are they Hebrews? so am I: this would incline us to think, that some, at least, of those corrupt teachers, upon whom the apostle hath so much reflected, were Jews; who had endeavoured to corrupt the Gentile churches with their traditions, and imposing on them the ceremonial rites of the Jewish church. Others think otherwise, and that the words import no more than this; Do they glory in the antiquity of their stock and parentage, as descending from Abraham? I have as much upon that account to glory in as they; for although I was born, not in Judea, but *in Tarsus, a city of Cilicia,* Acts xxii. 3, yet I was a *Jew, an Hebrew of the Hebrews,* Phil. iii. 5. *Are they Israelites?* will they derive from Jacob, to whom God gave the name of Israel, from whence all his posterity were called Israelites? *so am I,* (saith he,) I can derive from Jacob as well as they. *Are they the seed of Abraham? so am I:* will they glory in this, that they are *the seed of Abraham?* (this was a great boast of the Jews, as we learn from Matt. iii. 9, and John viii;) saith the apostle, I have on that account as much to glory in as they. Some here inquire, What difference there is in these three things? for to be a Hebrew, and an Israelite, and of the seed of Abraham, seem all to signify the same thing. Nor indeed have we any need to assign any difference, it seemeth to be but the same thing amplified in three phrases. But others distinguish more subtlely, and think the first may signify a glorying in the ancientness of their pedigree, or in their ability to speak in the Hebrew tongue; the second, may refer to the nation of which they were; the third, to the promise made to Abraham and his seed.

23 Are they ministers of Christ? (I speak as a fool) I *am* more; ^m in labours more abundant, ⁿ in stripes above measure, in prisons more frequent, ^o in deaths oft.

m 1C or. 15. 10.
n Acts 9. 16. & 20. 23. & 21. 11. ch. 6. 4, 5.
o 1 Cor. 15. 30, 31, 32. ch. 1. 9, 10. & 4. 11. & 6. 9.

Will they glory in this, that they are *ministers of Christ,* employed as the servants of Christ in preaching the gospel? I should not boast about this, (in that I may seem to *speak as a fool,)* but I am much more a minister than they, both with respect to my call to the work, and also my performing of it. I had a more immediate call and mission to the work than what they can boast of, and I have done more in that work than any of them have done. *In labours more abundant;* I have travelled more to preach it, I have laboured more in the propagation of it. *In stripes above measure, in prisons more frequent;* I have suffered more for the preaching of it, I have been oftener whipped, oftener imprisoned, than any of them ever were: see chap. vi. 4, 5. *In deaths oft;* I have been oftener in hazard of my life: he calls dangers threatening death, *deaths,* as chap. i. 10.

24 Of the Jews five times received I ^p forty *stripes* save one.

p Deu. 25. 3.

God, to restrain the passions of his people, which might carry them out to cruelty in the punishments of malefactors, forbade the Jewish magistrates to give any malefactor above forty stripes; (so many they might give them by the Divine law, Deut. xxv. 3;) but they had made an order, that none should receive above thirty-nine. This was amongst their constitutions which they called *sepimenta legis,* hedges to the Divine law; which indeed was a violation of the law: for that did not oblige them to give every malefactor, that had not deserved death, so many stripes; it gave them only a liberty to go so far, but they were not to exceed. Some think, that they punished every such malefactor with thirty-nine stripes: others, more rationally, think, that they did not so, but thirty-nine was the highest number they laid upon any. And it is most probable, that, out of their hatred to the apostle, they laid as many stripes upon him as their constitution would suffer them to do.

25 Thrice was I ^q beaten with rods, ^r once was I stoned, thrice I ^s suffered shipwreck, a night and a day I have been in the deep;

q Acts 16.22.
r Acts 14. 19.
s Acts 27. 41.

Thrice was I beaten with rods; this was by the pagans, for the Jews whipped malefactors with a whip which had three cords. We read of one of these times, Acts xvi. 23; and of a second, Acts xxi. 24. when the captain commanded he should be so punished, but he avoided it, by pleading he was a citizen of Rome. *Once was I stoned:* of his stoning, read Acts xiv. 19, it was by a popular tumult at Lystra. *Thrice I suffered shipwreck:* we read but of one time that Paul suffered shipwreck, Acts xxvii. 18; which was none of the three times here mentioned, for it was after the writing of this Epistle. But though many of the acts and sufferings of this apostle were written, yet all were not. *A night and a day I have been in the deep:* some by the *deep* here understand the inner prison, mentioned Acts xvi. 24, or some deep dungeon; but more probably he means, some time when, after a shipwreck, he might be put twenty-four hours to swim up and down the sea upon some broken part of the ship. It refers to some eminent danger Paul was in, of which the Scripture in no other place maketh mention particularly.

26 *In* journeyings often, *in* perils of waters, *in* perils of robbers, ^t *in* perils by mine own countrymen, ^u *in* perils by the heathen, *in* perils in the city, *in* perils in the wilderness, *in* perils in the sea, *in* perils among false brethren;

t Acts 9. 23. & 13. 50. & 14. 5. & 17. 5. & 20. 3. & 21. 31. & 28. 10, 11. & 25. 3.
u Acts 14. 5. & 19. 23.

In journeyings often; in travellings from place to place for the propagation of the gospel. *In perils of waters;* in the Greek, rivers, which were many in those countries through which he travelled. *Of robbers;* such as waited to rob passengers by the high-way. *By mine own countrymen,* the Jews, who were mortal enemies to Paul, whom they looked upon as an apostate from their religion. *In the city;* in many cities where he preached the gospel, as we find in the Acts of the Apostles. *In the wilderness;* in wildernesses through which he was forced to pass. *In the sea;* storms and shipwrecks. *Among false brethren;* false teachers and private persons, who corrupted the Christian religion, and were as great enemies to the apostle as any he had.

x Acts 20. 31. ch. 6. 5.
y 1 Cor. 4. 11.

27 In weariness and painfulness, [x]in watchings often, [y]in hunger and thirst, in fastings often, in cold and nakedness.

The apostle reckons up several afflictive evils, ordinarily incident to such as travel in foreign countries. Of this nature were the *weariness and painfulness,* the *hunger and thirst,* the *cold and nakedness,* here mentioned. He also mentioneth *watchings* and *fastings,* as voluntary acts of discipline, which he used for the end mentioned, 1 Cor. ix. 27, for the keeping under his body, and bringing it into subjection, and that he might the better attend and discharge the work of the ministry.

z See Acts 20. 18, &c. Rom. 1. 14.

28 Beside those things that are without, that which cometh upon me daily, [z]the care of all the churches.

By the *things that are without,* the apostle meaneth either those evils which happened to him from persons that had no relation to the Christian church, but were persons *without,* (as the phrase is used, 1 Cor. v. 13,) or else such kinds of troubles and afflictions as very little influenced his mind, but only affected his outward man: such were his labours, travels, journeyings, imprisonment, stripes, before mentioned. *Beside* these (he saith) there lay upon him an inward *care* and solicitude for *all the* Christian *churches;* and this was a *daily* care. For an apostle differed from an ordinary pastor, not only in his immediate call from Christ, but also in his work; there lay an obligation upon such to go up and down preaching the gospel, and they further had, both a power, and also an obligation, to superintend all other churches, and to direct the affairs of them relating to order and government: and thereupon they were mightily concerned about their doing well or ill.

a 1 Cor. 8. 13. & 9. 22.

29 [a]Who is weak, and I am not weak? who is offended, and I burn not?

Who, may be either, what church? or, what particular Christian in any church? *Is weak,* ἀσθενεῖ, through outward afflictions, or in respect of inward spiritual troubles, *and I am not weak,* and I do not sympathize with that church, or with that person? *Who is offended,* or scandalized, under temptations to be seduced and fall into sin, *and I burn not,* and I am not on fire with a holy zeal for the glory of God, and the good of his soul, if possible to keep him upright? By which the apostle doth not only show us what was his own holy temper, but what should be the temper of every faithful minister, as to his province, or that part of the church over which he is concerned to watch; viz. to have a true compassion to every member of it, to watch over his flock, inquiring diligently into the state of it; to have a quick sense of any evils under which they, or any of them, labour. This is indeed the duty of ever private member, but more especially of him whose office is to feed any part of the flock of Christ, Rom. xii. 15. In this the members of the spiritual, mystical body of Christ should answer to the members of the body natural, to which our apostle before resembled it.

b ch. 12. 5, 9, 10.

30 If I must needs glory, [b]I will glory of the things which concern mine infirmities.

The apostle here calleth the things which he had suffered for the gospel, and the propagation of it, his *infirmities;* and saith, that he chose those things to glory in. He would not glory of the divers tongues with which he spake, nor of the miracles which he had wrought; but being by the ill tongues of his adversaries put upon glorying, he chose to glory of what he had suffered for God. For as the mighty power of Christ was seen in supporting him, and carrying him through so many hazards and difficulties; so these things, probably, were such as his adversaries could not much glory in. Besides, that these things had not that natural tendency to lift up his mind above its due measures, as gifts had, which sometimes puff up (as the apostle saith concerning knowledge); and also these were things which flesh and blood commonly startleth at, and flieth from: that his gifts and miraculous operations spake the power of God in him, and the kindness of God to him, in enabling him to such effects, rather than any goodness in himself; but his patient bearing the cross spake in him great measures of faith, patience, and self-denial, and love to God; and so really were greater and truer causes of boasting, than those things could be.

31 [c]The God and Father of our Lord Jesus Christ, [d]which is blessed for evermore, knoweth that I lie not.

c Rom. 1. 9. & 9. 1. ch 1.
23. Gal. 1. 2.
1 Thess. 2. 5.
d Rom. 9. 5.

Whether this phrase be the form of an oath, or a mere assertion of God's knowledge of the heart, is a point not worth the arguing. If we look upon it in the former notion, it is no profane oath, because made in the name of God; nor no vain oath, because it is used in a grave and serious matter, and for the satisfaction of those who were not very easy to believe the apostle in this matter. But I had rather take it as a solemn assertion of God's particular knowledge of the truth of his heart in what he had said. The term *blessed for evermore,* may either be applied to the Father, or to Jesus Christ. It is applied to the Creator, Rom. i. 25, and to Jesus Christ, Rom. ix. 5. It is here so used, as that it is applicable either to the First or Second Person. The usage of it in these three texts, is an undeniable argument to prove the Godhead of Christ. The apostle, in these words, seemeth rather to refer to what he had said before, of his various labours and sufferings, than to that which followeth; which was but a single thing, and a danger rather than a suffering.

32 [e]In Damascus the governor under Aretas the king kept the city of the Damascenes with a garrison, desirous to apprehend me:

e Acts 9. 24, 25.

33 And through a window in a basket was I let down by the wall, and escaped his hands.

Luke hath shortly given us the history of this danger, Acts ix. 23—25. Soon after Paul was converted from the Jewish to the Christian religion, he, disputing with the Jews which dwelt at Damascus, confounded them by his arguments, proving Jesus was the Christ, as we read there, ver. 21. This so enraged them, as that they sought to kill him, ver. 23. And (as we learn from this text) to effect their design, they had by some acts or other brought over the governor to favour their design; which governor was a substitute under Aretas the king, who was father-in-law to Herod; for (as Josephus tells us) Herod put away his wife, the daughter of this Aretas, when he took Herodias. The Jews had got this deputy heathen governor so much on their side, that he shut up the gates, keeping his soldiers in arms. But (as St. Luke tells us, Acts ix. 24) Paul coming to the knowledge of this design, though they watched the gates day and night, yet he found a way of escape by the help of those Christians, who at that time were in Damascus; ver. 25, *The disciples took him by night, and let him down by the wall in a basket.* Two questions are started upon this passage of Paul's life: 1. Whether it was lawful for him to flee? But besides the particular licence our Lord, in this case, had given his first ministers, Matt. x. 23, Paul did in this case no more than what divines make lawful for a more ordinary minister, viz. to flee, when the persecution was directed against him in particular, leaving sufficient supply behind him. The second question raised is, Whether, it being against human laws to go over the walls of a city or garrison, Paul did not sin in this escape? But that is easily answered; for, 1. This was lawful in some cases. 2. God's glory, and the good of souls, were more concerned in Paul's life, than to have it sacrificed to a punctilio of obedience to a human law made upon a mere politic consideration.

CHAP. XII

Paul showeth that, though he had been favoured with visions and revelations, 1—4, *yet for commendation of his apostleship he chose rather to glory in his infirmities,* 5—10; *blaming the Corinthians, who had seen in him all the signs of an apostle, for forcing him to such vain boasting,* 11—13. *He telleth them of his design of visiting them again with the same disinterestedness and fatherly affection as before,* 14, 15. *He justifieth himself from any crafty extortion by his messengers,* 16—19; *and expresseth his fears, lest, both to his sorrow and theirs, he should find many notorious disorders still unredressed among them,* 20, 21.

† Gr. For I will come.

IT is not expedient for me doubtless to glory. † I will come to visions and revelations of the Lord.

It is not expedient for me doubtless to glory; it is neither comely, nor of any advantage to myself, to glory; nor would I do it but in this case of necessity, where glorying is necessary for the glory of God, and for your good, to vindicate myself to you from the imputations that some others lay upon me. *I will come to visions and revelations of the Lord:* do any of them boast of visions and revelations from God? I have something of that nature to glory in as well as they. Some make this difference betwixt *visions,* and *revelations;* that *visions* signify apparitions, the meaning of which, those that see them do not understand; *revelations* signify the discoveries of the mind and will of God to persons immediately, either by dreams, or by some audible voice, which may be without any object represented to the eye. Pharaoh and Nebuchadnezzar seem to have had such visions as they did not understand, till interpreted by Joseph and Daniel; but undoubtedly Paul's visions were not such. The difference therefore seems rather to be, that in all visions which good and holy men had, there was a revelation; but every revelation did not suppose a vision.

a Rom. 16. 7.
ch. 5. 17.
Gal. 1. 22.

b Acts 22. 17.
A. D. 46.
at Lystra,
Acts 14. 6.

2 I knew a man ᵃin Christ about fourteen years ago, (whether in the body, I cannot tell; or whether out of the body, I cannot tell: God knoweth;) such an one ᵇcaught up to the third heaven.

Some doubt whether ἐν Χριστῷ, in this place, be so well translated *in Christ,* (so signifying, that the person spoken of was a Christian, one that had embraced the gospel,) as *by Christ,* (as the particle is sometimes used,) so signifying, that this vision was given to him by the grace and favour of Christ. The *man* he speaketh of was, doubtless, himself, otherwise it had been to him no cause or ground of glorying at all. Thus several times in Scripture, the penmen thereof speaking in commendation of themselves, they speak in the third person instead of the first. In his saying, it was *about fourteen years ago,* and in that we do not read that he did ever before publish it, he avoids the imputation of any boasting and glorying; and showeth, that had he not been now constrained, for the glory of God, and the vindication of his own reputation, to have spoken of it, he would not now have mentioned it. *Whether in the body, I cannot tell; or whether out of the body, I cannot tell:* what the circumstances of the apostle were in this ecstasy, he professeth not to know; and therefore it seems too bold for us curiously to inquire, or positively to determine about it. It is not very probable that his soul was separated from his body; but whether his body was, by some angel, carried up to the sight of this vision, or things absent were made present to him, the apostle himself, being deprived of the use of his senses, could not tell. But *such an one* (he saith) he knew, *caught up to the third heaven;* by which he means the highest heavens, where God most manifesteth his glory, where the blessed angels see his face, and where are the just souls made perfect. The Scripture, dividing the world into the earth and the heavens, calleth all heaven that is not earth or water; hence it mentioneth an aerial heaven (which is all that space betwixt the earth and the place where the planets and fixed stars are); hence we read of *the fowls of the heaven,* Dan. iv. 12, of *the windows of heaven,* Gen. vii. 11, of a *starry heaven,* where the stars are, which are therefore called *the stars of the heaven,* Gen. xxii. 17; and then the *highest heaven;* which was meant in the Lord's prayer, when we pray, *Our Father which art in heaven;* and is called *the heaven of heavens.* This is the heaven here spoken of.

3 And I knew such a man, (whether in the body, or out of the body, I cannot tell: God knoweth;)

4 How that he was caught up into ᶜparadise, and heard unspeakable words, which it is not ‖ lawful for a man to utter.

c Luke 23. 43.

‖ Or, *possible.*

How that he was caught up into paradise: some by *paradise* understand a place distinct from *the third heaven* before mentioned, and think the apostle here speaks of more visions than one; but they speak much more probably, who interpret it of *the third heaven* before mentioned, called *paradise,* in regard of the delight and pleasures of it. Thus the term is used by our Saviour to the thief upon the cross, Luke xxiii. 43, and thus it is used, Rev. ii. 7. *And heard unspeakable words;* what these *unspeakable words,* or things, were, which the apostle heard in this ecstasy, is vainly inquired; whenas the apostle hath told us twice, that he could not tell *whether he was in or out of the body;* and that the words or things were such as were *unspeakable. Which it is not lawful for a man to utter;* such as were either impossible to be uttered, or at least which he was prohibited to utter; so they could be made known to none but only to him that heard them. If any inquireth, for what purpose God showed them to Paul, if he might not communicate them for the good of others? the answer is easy; that this vision might be for his own confirmation, as sent of God, and for his consolation under all those hazards and dangers which he was to undergo in the ministry of the gospel, to which God had called him.

5 Of such an one will I glory: ᵈyet of myself I will not glory, but in mine infirmities.

d ch. 11. 30.

Of such an one will I glory: the apostle, as appeareth by what followeth, speaketh of himself; but he does it in a third person. The meaning is, that that man who had been thus dignified of God, in such revelations and visions, might well glory of such a favour; but *yet* (saith he) *of myself will I not glory.* But how doth the apostle say, that of himself he will not glory, if he were the person intended? *Answ.* Some say, he distinguisheth concerning himself; as to his inward man, his soul, (which was rapt into the third heavens,) he did glory; but as to his body, or outward man, he would not glory in any thing which he had done, but only in what he had suffered. I should rather interpret it thus: In this the Lord greatly dignified me; but here was nothing of myself; of myself therefore I will not glory in any thing, except those things which I have suffered for the name of God.

6 For ᵉthough I would desire to glory, I shall not be a fool; for I will say the truth: but *now* I forbear, lest any man should think of me above that which he seeth me *to be,* or *that* he heareth of me.

e ch. 10. 8.
& 11. 16.

If I should have a mind to glory, I should not be a fool; for I would not glory in things that were not true. And though a man, in speaking things of himself which are true, may sometimes betray folly (viz. where he doth it merely to set forth himself, and make himself to appear a greater person than indeed he is); yet for a man to glory of himself, where the honour of God is concerned in the vindication of himself from reproaches and calumnies, speaks not any folly. *But* (saith the apostle) *I forbear,* having no desire that any *should think of me above what he seeth in me, or heareth of me* from others' mouths, and not mine own.

7 And lest I should be exalted above measure through the abundance of the revelations, there was given to me a ᶠthorn in the flesh, ᵍthe messenger of Satan to buffet me, lest I should be exalted above measure.

f See Ezek. 28. 24. Gal. 4. 13, 14.
g Job 2. 7.
Luke 13. 16.

The best of God's people have in them a root of pride, or a disposition to be *exalted above measure,* upon their receipt of favours from God not common to others; of which nature extraordinary revelations are none of the meanest, especially when they are multiplied, as it seems they were here to Paul. To prevent the breaking out of which, the apostle here tells us, that he had *a thorn in the flesh* given him. It is variously guessed what this was; he calleth it *a thorn in the flesh;* but whether (supposing *flesh* to be here strictly taken) he meaneth some disease affecting his body with pain and smart, and if so, what that specifical disease was, is no where revealed, and very uncertainly conjectured: or whether (taking *flesh* in a large sense, for his state in the flesh) he meaneth some motions to sin made to him from the devil; the importunity of which made them very grievous and afflictive to him, being *in the flesh:* or (as others think) motions to sin from his own lusts; which God suffered to stir in him, withholding such influence of his grace, by which he ordinarily kept them under, and in subjection; is very uncertain. The last mentioned seem to be least probable. For although the devil hath an influence upon our lusts, to excite and educe them into acts, yet it seems not according to the language of holy writ, to call these *messengers of Satan;* neither is it probable, that St. Paul would have reckoned these amongst the gifts of God unto him: nor was this an infirmity which he would have gloried in, or which would have commended him; nor doth the term *buffet* so well agree to this sense. It seems therefore more properly to be interpreted, either of some great bodily affliction, or some diabolical importunate temptation, with which God, after these abundant revelations, suffered this great apostle to be infested; that he might be kept humble, and not lifted up upon this great favour which God had showed him; which, considering the danger of pride, might well be reckoned amongst the gifts of God to this great apostle. And so he here gives another reason why he would not glory in the abundance of his revelations, because God by this providence had let him know, that his will was, that he should walk humbly notwithstanding them; and it had been very improper for him, being immediately upon this favour humbled by such a providence, to have lifted up himself by reason of it.

h See Deut. 3. 23,—27. Matt. 26. 44. 8 ^h **For this thing I besought the Lord thrice that it might depart from me.**

For the removal of this affliction, (of what nature soever it was,) for the taking of this thorn out of my flesh, I prayed often. It is lawful for us to pray for the removal of bodily evils, though such prayer must be always attended with a due submission to the wisdom and will of God; they being not evils in themselves, but such trials as God intendeth for our good, (as it was here in Paul's case,) and which issue in our spiritual advantage.

9 **And he said unto me, My grace is sufficient for thee: for my strength is made perfect in weakness. Most gladly therefore ⁱ will I rather glory in my infirmities, ^k that the power of Christ may rest upon me.**

i ch. 11. 30.
k 1 Pet. 4. 14.

And he said unto me, My grace is sufficient for thee: Paul prayed, and God answered, not *in specie,* (doing the very thing for him which he asked,) but *in valore,* giving him what was every whit as valuable. His answer was, *My grace* (my love and favour, not that which the apostle had already received, but which God was resolved further to show him, strengthening and supporting him under his trials, as also comforting and refreshing him) shall be enough for thee, to uphold thee under the present trial which is so burdensome to thee. *For my strength is made perfect in weakness;* for my Divine power, in upholding and supporting my people, is never so glorious as when they are under weaknesses in themselves. When they are sensible of the greatest impotency in themselves, then I delight most to exert and put forth my power in them and for them, my power then is most evident and conspicuous, and will be best acknowledged by my people. *Therefore* (saith the apostle) *I will* choose *to glory in my infirmities, that the power of Christ may rest upon me.* Those dispensations of providence, in which the souls of men have the greatest experiences of the power and strength of Christ, are most to be gloried in; but such are states of infirmities. This text confirmeth Christ to be God blessed for ever; for by his power it is that we are supported under trials, his strength it is which is made perfect in the weakness of poor creatures.

l Rom. 5. 3.
ch. 7. 4.

10 **Therefore ^l I take pleasure in infirmities, in reproaches, in necessities, in persecutions, in distresses for Christ's sake: ^m for when I am weak, then am I strong.**

m ch. 13. 4.

Amongst other reasons why I rather choose to glory in what I suffer for Christ, (which is what he here calleth *infirmities,* and further openeth by *reproaches, necessities, persecutions,* and *distresses for Christ's sake,)* this is one; that I never find myself more *strong* in the habits and acts of the grace that is in me, than *when I am* thus made *weak.* What the apostle here saith of himself, the people of God have ever since his time ordinarily experienced: then it is that they are made strong in the exercises of faith, and patience, and love to God. A child of God seldom walks so much in the view of God as his God, and in the view of his own sincerity, as when, as to his outward condition and circumstances in the world, he walks in the dark and seeth no light.

11 **I am become ⁿ a fool in glorying; ye have compelled me: for I ought to have been commended of you: for ^o in nothing am I behind the very chiefest apostles, though ^p I be nothing.**

n ch. 11. 1, 16, 17.
o ch. 11. 5. Gal. 2. 6, 7, 8.
p 1 Cor. 3. 7. & 15. 8, 9. Eph. 3. 8.

I am become a fool in glorying; I may amongst some of you (who interpret all things I say into the worst sense) gain nothing but the reputation of a weak man, wanting understanding, for speaking so much in my own commendation (contrary to the rules of modesty in ordinary cases). *Ye have compelled me;* but it is not matter of choice, but of necessity to me; the ill-will which some amongst you have to my honour and reputation, and continual defaming me as a vile and contemptible person, hath constrained me, for the honour of Christ, (whose apostle I am,) and the vindication of my own reputation, to boast in this manner; at least to relate what God hath done for, and in, and by me. *For I ought to have been commended of you;* it was your duty to have vindicated me from the aspersions cast upon me; so others' mouths should have praised me, and not my own: I must speak, because you hold your peace, or do worse in calumniating me. *For in nothing am I behind the very chiefest apostles, though I be nothing;* for you cannot but say that I, neither in my apostolical call and commission, nor yet in my gifts and graces, nor in my labours, nor in my sufferings, come behind those that are commonly thought to be *the chiefest* of the *apostles; though* (in some of your opinions) *I be nothing;* or indeed, of or from myself, am nothing; doing all that I do through Christ that strengtheneth me, and by the grace of God being what I am.

12 ^q **Truly the signs of an apostle were wrought among you in all patience, in signs, and wonders, and mighty deeds.**

q Rom. 15. 18, 19.
1 Cor. 9. 2. ch. 4. 2. & 6. 4. & 11. 6.

I had not only a call to my apostleship, (of which indeed you were no witnesses,) but I amongst you evidenced my call by such *signs,* as were sufficient to declare me to you to be a true apostle. Amongst these, he reckons, 1. *Patience;* 2. Miracles. The first refers to those many labours which he had, in travelling to propagate the gospel, in preaching, writing, &c.; this manifested him called of God to the work. 2. Miraculous operations were another sign; for though the working of miracles was not restrained to the apostolical office, yet when they were wrought in confirmation of the doctrine which the apostle had first preached, and so were a seal of his ministry, they were truly signs of his apostleship; it being no way probable, that the God of truth would have communicated his power to men for the confirmation of lies, or of an employment to which he had never called them.

13 ^r **For what is it wherein you were inferior to other churches, except it be that ^s I myself was not burdensome to you? forgive me ^t this wrong.**

r 1 Cor. 1. 7.
s 1 Cor. 9.12. ch. 11. 9.
t ch. 11. 7.

Wherein have not you been used as any other gospel churches were, where Peter, or James, or any other of the apostles have laboured? Hath not the same doctrine been preached to you? Have not as great miracles been wrought amongst you? Hath not the Holy Ghost been as plentifully shed abroad amongst you, to enrich you with all spiritual gifts, so as you have come behind in no gospel benefit? I know of nothing in which it hath not fared with you as with other churches, except in this; that whereas in other churches the apostles, or their pastors, have been burdensome to them, taking stipends and salaries for their pains, I have forborne it, and have not at all charged you. If this be a *wrong* to you, I hope it is not of that nature, but I may obtain a pardon for it. The reasons of the apostle's thus sparing the church of Corinth more than some other churches, we have before guessed at.

u ch. 13. 1.
x Acts 20.33.
1 Cor. 10. 33.
y 1 Cor. 4. 14, 15.

14 ᵘ Behold, the third time I am ready to come to you; and I will not be burdensome to you: for ˣ I seek not your's, but you: ʸ for the children ought not to lay up for the parents, but the parents for the children.

Behold, the third time I am ready to come to you: we read in holy writ but of two journeys which the apostle made to Corinth, Acts xviii. 1; xx. 2, and the latter is believed to have been after the writing of this Epistle. We must not think that all these motions are set down in Scripture. It is manifest that Paul had thoughts of going oftener, Acts xix. 21; 1 Cor. xvi. 5; chap. i. 15. Man purposeth, but God disposeth. For which reason, James adviseth us to add, *If the Lord will,* to our expressions testifying our resolutions. *And I will not be burdensome to you*; he lets them know, that he was coming to them with the same resolutions he had before taken up, not to put them to any charge. *For I seek not yours, but you*; for that, which should be the design of every faithful minister, was his design; viz. the gaining of their souls to Christ, and protecting of them, that in the day of judgment he might present them as a pure and chaste virgin unto Christ. His business was not to enrich himself by them; he sought the good of their souls, not their estates. *For the children ought not to lay up for the parents*: he looked upon them as his children, upon himself as their parent. And though indeed children ought to relieve their parents, if in want, yet it is not the course of the world for children to lay up for their parents. *But the parents for the children;* but, on the contrary, it is the course of parents to maintain their children, and to lay up for them.

z 1 Thess. 2.
8. Phil. 2. 17.
a John 10. 11. ch. 1. 6.
Col. 1. 24.
2 Tim. 2. 10.
† Gr. *your souls*. b ch. 6, 12, 13.

15 And ᶻ I will very gladly spend and be spent ᵃ for † you; though ᵇ the more abundantly I love you, the less I be loved.

And I will very gladly spend and be spent for you; I am so far from desiring your money, that, if I had it, I would willingly spend it for you; and I do spend my strength for you, willing to die in your service, labouring for the good of your immortal souls. *Though the more abundantly I love you, the less I be loved;* but I am very unhappy as to some of you, who will not rightly understand me, but love me the less, the more they see my love to them.

c ch. 11. 9.

16 But be it so, ᶜ I did not burden you: nevertheless, being crafty, I caught you with guile.

I hear what some say, It is true, that when I was myself with you, I laid no burden upon you, did not put upon you any collection for me; but, like a crafty man, I set others to take money of you for my use; so as, what I did not by myself, I did by those whom I employed. This appeareth to be the sense by what followeth in the next verse, where he appealeth to them for his vindication of this particular.

d ch. 7. 2.

17 ᵈ Did I make a gain of you by any of them whom I sent unto you?

e ch. 8. 6, 16, 22.
f ch. 8. 18.

18 ᵉ I desired Titus, and with *him* I sent a ᶠ brother. Did Titus make a gain of you? walked we not in the same spirit? *walked we* not in the same steps?

The apostle, to avoid or wipe off this imputation, appealeth to themselves to name any person (whom he had sent unto them) that had taken any thing of them for his use. He saith, that he *desired Titus* to come to them: of this desire we read before, chap. viii. 6, 16, 18, 22. *With him* (he saith) he *sent* another *brother:* this is that brother, of whom he had said, ver. 18, that his *praise* was *in the gospel throughout all the churches.* Some guess it was Luke, but there is no certainty of that. He appeals to them, whether either of these made *a gain* of them? that is, took any thing of them: and whether they did not walk *in the same spirit,* and *in the same steps?* whether they did not show the same generosity and freedom? and by their behaviour amongst them did not show, that they did not seek what was theirs, (to be enriched by their estates,) but them; to communicate the riches of grace to their souls? The circumstances of God's providence may be such towards faithful ministers, as that they may be constrained to make use of others to do their work; but such, so near as they can judge, will never make use of any therein, but such as are of *the same spirit* with themselves, and walk in *the same steps.*

g ch. 5. 12.
h Rom. 9. 1. ch. 11. 31.
i 1 Cor. 10. 33.

19 ᵍ Again, think ye that we excuse ourselves unto you? ʰ we speak before God in Christ: ⁱ but *we do* all things, dearly beloved, for your edifying.

Think ye that we excuse ourselves unto you? some of you may think, that I speak all this in my own defence, and seek only my own credit and reputation amongst you. I do not so. *We speak before God in Christ;* I speak as a Christian, as one who knows that God knoweth, seeth, and observeth what I say; searching my heart, and trying my reins. *But we do all things, dearly beloved, for your edifying;* all that I say I speak for your good, that you may be built up in faith, and love, and all other graces: a great hinderance to which, is prejudice against me, and such as are the ministers of the gospel to you; which I therefore desire (what in me lieth) to prevent and obviate. The apostle, not only here, but in several other parts of these and other his Epistles, declares what ought to be the great end of him, and all other ministers, viz. the edification of people; the conversion of the unconverted, and the perfecting of those in whom the foundation is laid, building them up in all good spiritual habits; both of these come under the notion of edification. If we consider Christ as the Foundation, conversion is edification; the building up of souls upon Christ, who is the gospel foundation; and *other foundation can no man lay.* If we consider the infusion of the first habits of grace into the soul as the foundation, edification signifies a going on from faith to faith; a growing in grace and in the knowledge of the Lord Jesus Christ, a going on to perfection. The true minister of Christ ought to make edification in both of these senses his end, and his great end; for by this means is God glorified, the souls of his people benefited, and eternally saved.

k 1 Cor. 4. 21. ch. 10. 2. & 13. 2, 10.

20 For I fear, lest, when I come, I shall not find you such as I would, and *that* ᵏ I shall be found unto you such as ye would not: lest *there be* debates, envyings, wraths, strifes, backbitings, whisperings, swellings, tumults:

For I fear, lest, when I come, I shall not find you such as I would; a good man, especially a faithful minister of the gospel, will be concerned at the sins of others, and as to their spiritual welfare. A profane person either rejoiceth in the sins of others, or at least is unconcerned for them; but a good man cannot be so, as knowing the sins of others reflect dishonour upon God. *And that I shall be found unto you such as ye would not;* he also cannot delight in the punishments of others, or doing any thing which may be ungrateful to them. Paul feareth lest the miscarriages of this church should enforce from him some acts of severity. He instanceth in some particular disorders in the members of this church, which he feared that he should find amongst them not amended; all the effects of pride and passion. *Debates,* or contentions, such as he had taxed them for, 1 Cor. i. 11; iii. 3. *Envyings,* or heats of passion; envying of one another for their gifts, &c. The other things which he mentioneth, are all sins against that brotherly love which ought to be found amongst Christians, and tending to ruptures amongst them; and teach us how contrary these are to the duty of Christians, who are one body.

l ch. 2. 1, 4.

21 *And* lest, when I come again, my God ˡ will humble me among you, and

II. CORINTHIANS XII, XIII

ᵐ ch. 13. 2. *that* I shall bewail many ᵐwhich have sinned already, and have not repented of ⁿ 1 Cor. 5. 1. the uncleanness and ⁿfornication and lasciviousness which they have committed.

From hence it appeareth, that this church of Corinth, though it had many in it, without doubt, who were true and sincere Christians, yet had also many it which were otherwise; yea. many that were scandalous; for such are those mentioned in this verse. Again, the apostle's mentioning of *many* that had committed *uncleanness, fornication, and lasciviousness,* and *not repented;* whenas he had only given order for the excommunication of one incestuous person, 1 Cor. v., and in this Epistle, chap. ii., had given order for the restoring him upon his repentance; lets us know, that the governors of churches ought to use a great deal of prudence in the administering of church censures. We are also further taught, that nothing more afflicteth a godly person, who hath the charge of the souls of others, than to see them go on in courses of sin without repentance. Whether bewailing, in this verse, implieth proceeding to ecclesiastical censures,· (as several interpreters think,) I doubt; for as the word doth not necessarily imply it, so his sparing use of that rod, which he could (though absent) have as well used against other unclean persons as one incestuous person; and choosing rather that the sentence should be declared against him by the church in his absence, than by himself when present; inclineth me to think, that by bewailing, here, he only means a Christian, afflictive sense of their miscarriages; whereas his desire was, that he might have a cheerful, comfortable journey to and abode with them. But yet, in the next chapter, he seemeth to threaten something more against some particular offenders.

CHAP. XIII

Paul threateneth to vindicate his authority at his coming by punishing severely unreclaimed offenders, 1—4. *He adviseth the Corinthians to try if they had as good proofs of their faith, as he trusted to have of his mission,* 5, 6. *He wisheth that by a blameless conversation they might prevent him from using sharpness toward them, whatever became of his proofs,* 7—10. *He concludeth with an exhortation, salutation, and prayer,* 11—14.

a ch. 12. 14.
b Num. 35. 30. Deut. 17. 6. & 19. 15. Matt. 18. 16. John 8. 17. Heb. 10. 28.

THIS is ᵃthe third *time* I am coming to you. ᵇIn the mouth of two or three witnesses shall every word be established.

Not *the third time* when he was upon his journey, (for he was not now travelling.) but the third time that he had taken up thoughts of, and was preparing for, such a journey : which, it may be, he hinteth to them, that they might be the more afraid to continue in those sinful courses which he had blamed them for. *In the mouth of two or three witnesses shall every word be established :* he alludeth to the law of God, Deut. xix. 15, concerning witnesses in any case. God ordered, that the testimony of two or three persons should determine all questions in their law; and that should be taken for certain and established, which such a number of persons asserted. The apostle would from hence have them conclude, that he would certainly come, because this was *the third time* that he had resolved upon it, and was preparing for it.

c ch. 10. 2.

2 ᶜI told you before, and foretell you, as if I were present, the second time ; and being absent now I write to them d ch. 12. 21. ᵈwhich heretofore have sinned, and to all e ch. 1. 23. other, that, if I come again, ᵉI will not spare :

I told you in my former Epistle, and now (though I be yet absent) I tell you beforehand, as though *I were present* amongst you. *I write to them which heretofore have sinned, and to all other;* I write this for the sake of those who have already sinned scandalously; and not for theirs only, but for the sake of others, who may have temptations so to offend. *That, if I come again, I will not spare;* that, if I do come, and find any such who walk in courses of sin,

and are hardened in them, so as all that I have said will not bring them to remorse and reformation, *I will not spare* them, either as to sharp reprehensions. or as to ecclesiastical censures; according to the trust which Christ hath reposed in me. Some extend this further, to a power of inflicting bodily pains; but it is not clear that the apostles were intrusted with any such power ordinarily, though sometimes they did exert such a power; as appeareth, both from the instances of Ananias and Sapphira, Acts v., and that of Elymas, Acts xiii. 8—11.

3 Since ye seek a proof of Christ ᶠspeaking in me, which to you-ward is not weak, but is mighty ᵍin you.

f Mat. 10. 20. 1 Cor. 5. 4. ch. 2. 10. g 1 Cor. 9. 2.

Christ (saith the apostle) hath openly showed his power in my ministry, speaking to you; how else came your hearts to be turned from dumb idols to serve the living God? how came you to be furnished with those excellent gifts wherewith you abound? But, seeing all this is not judged a sufficient proof of Christ's *speaking in me* to you, but you are yet doubting whether I am an apostle or no, and calling for *a proof of Christ in me ;* I will, if I come, and find any that have lived scandalously, and are impenitent, show you another proof of that power and authority with which Christ hath trusted me. Which must be understood, either of his miraculous power to inflict some bodily afflictions upon them, or (which is more probable) of his power as an apostle to cut them off from the communion of gospel churches.

4 ʰFor though he was crucified through weakness, yet ⁱhe liveth by the power of God. For ᵏwe also are weak ∥in him, but we shall live with him by the power of God toward you.

h Phil. 2. 7, 8. 1 Pet. 3. 18. i Rom. 6. 4. k See ch. 10. 3, 4. ∥ Or, with him.

He had before said, that Christ in him was *not weak, but mighty;* here he showeth, that there was a time when Christ himself was weak, in a low and contemptible state, in which state *he was crucified;* his state of weakness subjected him to a death upon the cross: but, *by the power of God,* he rose again from the dead, ascended up into heaven, where he *liveth* for ever to make intercession for us. *For we also are weak in him;* in conformity to Christ (he saith) he and the rest of the apostles were *weak;* in a low, abject, contemptible condition, exposed to reproaches, deaths, &c. *But we shall live;* which some understand of life eternal, consequent to the resurrection of believers; but others better, of the life and vigour of the apostle's ministry. Through *the mighty power of God,* flowing from a living Christ, who hath ascended up on high, and given gifts unto men, our ministry shall be a living, powerful, efficacious ministry *toward you.*

5 ˡExamine yourselves, whether ye be in the faith; prove your own selves. Know ye not your own selves, ᵐhow that Jesus Christ is in you, except ye be ⁿreprobates?

l 1 Cor. 1l. 28. m Rom. 8. 10. Gal. 4. 19. n 1 Cor. 9. 27.

Examine yourselves : it is most commonly seen, that those who are most busy to desire or inquire after a proof of Christ in others, are tardiest in making an inquiry after Christ's being in themselves. The apostle therefore calleth the censorious part of this church, who desired *a proof of Christ* in him, to examine themselves. *Whether ye be in the faith;* whether they had any true faith; such as works by love, and purifies the heart. For he knew that they were baptized, and Christians in outward profession; nor is he blaming them for any apostacy from the doctrine of faith, only for an ill life, which evidenceth their faith not to be the *faith of God's elect,* a faith of the *operation of God,* &c. *Prove your own selves :* he doubleth the exhortation upon them, possibly for this end, to let them know, that if they found themselves in the faith, they could not reasonably doubt whether he himself was in the faith, or no, whom God had made the instrument to convert them. *Know ye not your own selves :* he commends to them the knowledge of themselves, as being a far more desirable piece of knowledge than the knowledge of other men; as to what they are, or what their state is towards God. *How that Jesus Christ is in you, except ye be reprobates?* in the inquiry after this, he bids them to inquire, whether Christ was in them, yea or

VOL. III—21

no? The name of Christ was named upon them in their baptism, Christ had been preached to them; this the apostle knew; but all this might be, and yet Christ not dwell in their hearts by faith. This is the great point the apostle directs them to examine and prove themselves about, whether Christ was in them by a lively faith? apprehended and applied as their Saviour, ruling and governing them as their Lord and King? He lets them know the importance of this inquiry, telling them that Jesus Christ must be in them, if they were not *reprobates*. But (some might say) how could the apostle conclude this? though at present Christ was not in them, and they as yet were no more than formal professors, yet might not God open their eyes, and work in them afterwards a more full and effectual change? *Answ.* 1. The apostle might be allowed to know more than ordinary ministers can know. He had before said, *If our gospel be hid, it is hid to them that are lost.* 2. When the gospel and the means of grace have been for some considerable time in a place, it is much to be feared, that those who have not in that time felt the saving power and effect of it upon their hearts, never shall. It is ordinarily observed, that where God blesseth the ministry of any to convert souls, their greatest harvest is in the first years of their ministry. 3. Some think, that the word ἀδόκιμοι should not be translated *reprobates*, but rather, not approved by God. If Christ be not in the soul by faith, it cannot be approved of God, because *without faith it is impossible to please God*. But we generally translate the word by *reprobate, rejected, cast-away*, 1 Cor. ix. 27; 2 Tim. iii. 8; Tit. i. 16; Heb. vi. 8. It seemeth to signify persons given over by God to a stupidity of mind, &c. So as the apostle here useth a very close argument, to put them upon a search into their own hearts and states, to see if they could find Christ dwelling in them; for otherwise, (considering their long profession, and the revelation of Christ to them,) it would be a ground of fear, that they were such as God had cast off for ever. However, as to their present state, they had no ground to conclude better, whatever mercy God might afterwards show them. Men's sitting and continuing long under the means of grace, and an outward profession, without a saving knowledge of Christ, and true savour of the truth, and a reformation of their lives according to the rules and directions of the gospel, is not indeed an infallible sign that he who formed them will never show them any favour; but it is a very great presumption that it will be so with such. Which should therefore strongly engage them to be very often and very seriously proving themselves, as to this thing, whether they be in Christ, and whether they have a true, saving faith?

6 But I trust that ye shall know that we are not reprobates.

You make a doubt whether Christ be in us, and you would fain know how it may be evidenced that he is so. If Christ be not in us we must be reprobates. *But I trust that ye shall know*, either in this life, by the evident signs of my apostleship, (which when I come I shall give you,) and by the life and power of my ministry amongst you; or in another life, when the sheep shall stand at God's right hand, and the goats at his left; that (whatsoever you think or say of us) we are none of those who are rejected and disapproved of God.

7 Now I pray to God that ye do no evil; not that we should appear approved, but that ye should do that which is honest, though °we be as reprobates.

o ch. 6. 9.

Now I pray to God that ye do no evil; I do not desire that when I come I may find objects for my severity, upon whom I may show a proof of Christ in me, by exercising that authority upon them with which Christ hath intrusted me: no, on the contrary, I heartily pray that ye may be holy and blameless, *without spot or wrinkle. Not that we should appear approved;* neither do I desire this for my own sake, that I may be *approved*, but I singly desire it for your good. *But that ye should do that which is honest, though we be as reprobates;* that you may do that which is good; and then do you, and let the world, think of me as a reprobate, or what they will.

8 For we can do nothing against the truth, but for the truth.

Truth in this place notes integrity of life and conversation; truth in action, opposed to hypocrisy, or scandalous living. He had before prayed, that they might *do no evil;* which if they did not, they need not fear his coming with a rod; for though he had a power from Christ to punish, yet he had no power to punish such as did well; his power was to be used for them, not against them. As the law was not made for the righteous, and the civil magistrate is not ordained of God for the terror of those that do well, but only of those that do evil; so neither did Christ ever ordain ecclesiastical censures for the punishment of good and holy men. And indeed here is the just boundary of all civil and ecclesiastical power; no magistrate or minister, acting as Christ's servants, *can* (lawfully, or as by any commission from him) do any thing *against the truth*, or those that own, defend, and practise it; the power with which they are trusted is for edification, not destruction.

9 For we are glad, ᵖwhen we are weak, and ye are strong: and this also we wish, ᵍ*even* your perfection.

p 1 Cor. 4. 10. ch. 11. 30. & 12. 5, 9, 10. q 1 Thess. 3. 10.

Some by *weak* here understand a moral impotency; as the apostle had said, he could not do any thing against the truth, that is, rightly and justly he could not: and by *strong* here, a spiritual strength, a reformation, growth, and proficiency in grace. These make the sense to be this; I am so far from coming with a desire to show amongst you my apostolical power in punishing offenders, as that I should be glad to find you so strong in the exercise of grace, that I should find none to punish; that men be made weak (as to the putting forth that power) by your spiritual strength. I incline to a more general interpretation. The apostle by this purgeth himself from any thing of vain-glory, or seeking himself; Though (saith he) I be weak, (as some amongst you report me,) yet if you be truly strong, I shall heartily rejoice therein. For I wish nothing more than *your perfection;* my reputation is nothing to me compared with that.

10 ʳTherefore I write these things being absent, lest being present ˢI should use sharpness, ᵗaccording to the power which the Lord hath given me to edification, and not to destruction.

r 1 Cor. 4. 21. ch. 2. 3. & 10. 2. & 12. 20, 21. s Tit. 1. 13. t ch. 10. 8.

The apostle here lets them know with how much tenderness he dealt with them; and whereas they might have charged him with sharpness in his letters, he assures them, that he therefore had so wrote, that he might prevent sharper dealings with them when he should come to them, by their hearkening to the admonitions of his letter; for otherwise, he tells them, that after he came he must deal more sharply with them in the execution of that power with which Christ had intrusted him. Yet he further tells them, that that power was for their good, not for their harm; for their edification, not for their destruction: which is the same with what he had said, chap. x. 8, and in the verse immediately preceding.

11 Finally, brethren, farewell. Be perfect, be of good comfort, ᵘbe of one mind, live in peace; and the God of love ˣand peace shall be with you.

u Rom. 12. 16, 18 & 15. 5. 1 Cor. 1. 10. Phil. 2. 2. & 3. 16. 1 Pet. 3. 8. x Rom. 15. 33.

Finally, brethren, farewell: the apostle shutteth up his Epistle according to the ordinary form of conclusions of letters, wishing all happiness to them: but he addeth something as a Christian, and a minister of the gospel. *Be perfect:* the word καταρτίζεσθε signifies to be compact, or united, as members of the same body, or parts of the same house; the perfection of a society lying much in the union of it. The perfection the apostle presseth here, seemeth to be the perfection of the body of the church, by the restoring of such as were separated from its communion, or had, through a spirit of contention, withdrawn themselves, rather than the perfection of the particular members of it, in the habits and exercises of grace. The Greek word seemeth that way to carry the sense; it properly signifies, the putting of members loosed from their joints into their proper place again, and such a perfection as followeth upon such an action, or any action proportionable to it. *Be of good comfort;* the word imports exhorted, comforted, confirmed: be exhorted to yield obedience to my precepts, or counsels; be comforted in all the trials or afflictions you do meet with, or may further meet with, for your profession of the gospel; be confirmed in the truths and holy ways of God. *Be of one mind;* if possible, of one and the same judgment in the truths of God; however, as pursuing the same scope and end; be one in affection. *Live in peace,* free from those contentions and divisions, those debates, and strifes, and wraths, and envyings, which I have before told you of as faults among you. This is the way for to have the presence of God with you, for he is not the God of hatred and strife, but *the God of love and peace;* who hath commanded love and peace amongst those that are brethren, and will be present among them only who live in obedience to his royal law of love.

12 [y] Greet one another with an holy kiss.

[y] Rom. 16. 16. 1 Cor. 16. 20. 1 Thess. 5. 26. 1 Pet. 5. 14.

See the notes on Rom. xvi. 16; 1 Cor. xvi. 20. It was an ancient custom and of common use, when friends met, for them (as a token of mutual love and friendship) to kiss each other: the Christians used it also at their ecclesiastical assemblings. It must not be looked upon as a precept, obliging all Christians to do the like; but only as directing those that then did use it, to use it innocently, chastely, sincerely, and holily.

13 All the saints salute you.

That is, all about me in these parts of Macedonia wish you all happiness, and by me send the remembrance of their love and respects to you.

[z] Rom. 16. 24. [a] Phil. 2. 1.

14 [z] The grace of the Lord Jesus Christ, and the love of God, and [a] the communion of the Holy Ghost, *be* with you all. Amen.

The free love of our *Lord Jesus Christ,* shown in the application of his redemption; that *grace* which floweth from him as the Fountain of grace, or cometh by him as the Mediator between God and man; *the* actual *love of God;* that good-will by which God the Father embraceth creatures in Christ, and for his sake; and all the gracious communications of the Holy Spirit of God, (by which he strengtheneth, quickeneth, or comforteth the souls of God's people,) *be with you all.* Whether you value me or no, I heartily wish you well, and all the best things. In this text is an eminent proof of the Trinity, all the Persons being distinctly named in it (as in the commission about baptism). The apostle calleth the Father, *God;* the Son, *Lord:* he attributeth *love* to the Father; (moved by which he sent his only begotten Son into the world, John iii. 16;) *grace* to the Son, who loved us freely, and died for the fellowship or *communion of the Holy Ghost,* by whom the Father and Son communicate their love and grace to the saints. *Amen* is here used as a particle of wishing or desiring the thing before mentioned; it is the same with, Let it so be. Whether added by the apostle, or subjoined by the church of Corinth, upon the reading this Epistle among them, (as some think,) is not material.

¶ The second *epistle* to the Corinthians was written from Philippi, *a city* of Macedonia, by Titus and Lucas.

If the subscriptions to the apostolical Epistles were parts of the text and holy writ, we have it here determined, who that other brother was, mentioned chap. viii. 22, sent along with Titus to carry this letter, and the benevolence of the churches of Macedonia. But it is observed, that even in this subscription there is a certain evidence, that the subscriptions of the Epistles are no part of canonical writ; for in some Greek copies it is said to be sent by Paul and Timothy; whereas Paul was the writer of it, not the messenger, and in Macedonia when it was sent; and Timothy is joined with him in the writing, chap. i. 1.

THE EPISTLE OF PAUL THE APOSTLE

TO THE

GALATIANS

THE ARGUMENT.

GALATIA (to the churches in which country this Epistle is directed) is by all agreed to be a part of Asia the Lesser, now under the power of the Turks, and by them called Chiangare. Geographers tell us, it is bounded on the west by Phrygia the Greater, (now called Germian,) Bithynia, (now called Becksangel,) and Asia Propria, a country of Anatolia; on the south, with Pisidia, (now called Versacgeli,) and Licaonia (now called Cogni); on the east, with Cappadocia (now called Amasia); and on the north, with Paphlagonia (now called Bolli). The whole country was anciently called Gallo-Grecia, from some French, who, leaving their country and coming to inhabit there, gave it that name. It had in it several cities, amongst which geographers reckon Ancyra, Synopa, Pompeiopolis, Claudiopolis, Nicopolis, Laodicea, to which also some count Antioch. When or by whose ministry this people first received the gospel, we do not read. Paul travelled thither, Acts xvi. 6, but was at that time *forbidden of the Holy Ghost to preach* there; but, Acts xviii. 23, it is said, that when *he had spent some time at Antioch, he departed, and went over all the country of Galatia and Phrygia in order, strengthening all the disciples.* This was about two years after that he was forbidden to preach there, in which time the gospel was planted and disciples made in this country.

At what time Paul wrote this Epistle to them is very uncertain; some think that it was written much at the same time when the Epistle to the Romans was written (the argument being much the same with that of that Epistle). Others think it was written at Rome during his last imprisonment, because he saith, chap. vi. 17, that he bare in his *body the marks of the Lord Jesus.* It is manifest that it was written at some distance of time after the first plantation of the gospel there, for the enemy had had time to sow tares.

The occasion of writing it, was partly to reprove the members of this church, for their apostacy from the doctrine of the gospel, as to justification; partly to set them right again in it, and to vindicate himself from the aspersions and imputations which their false teachers had cast upon him, in order to their better success with their new doctrine.

The new doctrine brought in by these false teachers, was the necessity of circumcision, and other works of the law, as well as faith in Christ, in order to the justification of the sinner before God; which they pressed rather upon a politic, than any religious consideration, as being the way to avoid that persecution which at that time attended all Christians; from which imputation, those who were circumcised, though they also professed faith in Christ, saved themselves. To buoy up themselves they vilified the apostle Paul to these churches, as being no apostle, one that had learned all which he knew from James, and Peter, and John; yet varied from them as to his doctrine and practice, yea, from himself also.

The two first chapters of this Epistle are mostly spent in the apostle's vindication of himself; proving himself to be a true apostle, and not to have learned what he taught from Peter, or James, or John, but that he had it by revelation from Jesus Christ. In the two following chapters he proves the doctrine of justification *by faith in Christ*, (in opposition to the justification taught by these false teachers, *by the works of the law*,) by various arguments. In the two last chapters, he presseth their standing fast in the liberty wherewith Christ had made them free, together with several other things, which are the common duties of all Christians. Then closeth his Epistle, with praying grace, mercy, and peace, to be their, and all true Christians', portion.

CHAP. I

After saluting the churches of Galatia, 1—5, *Paul testifieth his surprise that they should so soon have forsaken the truth of the gospel which he had taught them,* 6, 7; *and pronounceth those accursed who preach any other gospel,* 8, 9. *He showeth that his doctrine was not concerted to please men, but came to him by immediate revelation from God,* 10—12: *to confirm which he relateth his conversation before his calling,* 13, 14, *and what steps he had taken immediately thereupon,* 15—24.

A. D. 58. PAUL, an apostle, (ªnot of men, neither by man, but ᵇby Jesus Christ, and God the Father, ᶜwho raised him from the dead;)

a ver. 11, 12.
b Acts 9. 6.
& 22. 10, 15,
21. & 26. 16.
Tit. 1. 3. c Acts 2. 24.

The term *apostle*, in its native signification, signifieth no more then one sent; in its ecclesiastical use, it signifies one extraordinarily sent to preach the gospel; of these some were sent either more immediately by Christ, (as the twelve were sent, Matt. x. 1; Mark iii. 14; Luke ix. 1,) or more mediately, as Matthias, who was sent by the suffrage of the other apostles to supply the place of Judas, Acts i. 25, 26, and Barnabas, and Silas, and others were. Paul saith he was sent *not of men, neither by man*, that is, not merely; for he was also sent by men to his particular province, Acts xiii. 3; *but* he was immediately sent *by Jesus Christ,* (as we read, Acts ix., and xxvi. 14—17, of which also he gives us an account in this chapter, ver. 15—17,) *and* by *God the Father* also, *who*, he saith, *raised* Christ *from the dead.* By this phrase the apostle doth not only assert Christ's resurrection, and the influence of the Father upon his resurrection, (though he rose by his own power, and took up his own life again, and was also quickened by the Spirit,) but he also showeth a specialty in his call to the apostleship. As it differed from the call of ordinary ministers, who are called by men (though their ministry be not merely of men); so it differed from the call of the rest of the apostles, being made by Christ not in his state of humiliation, (as the twelve were called, Matt. x.,) but in his state of exaltation, after he was raised from the dead, and sat down on the right hand of God.

d Phil. 2. 22.
& 4. 21.
e 1 Cor. 16. 1.

2 And all the brethren ᵈwhich are with me, ᵉunto the churches of Galatia:

He writeth not only in his own name, but in the name of all those other Christians that were with him in the place where he now was (whether Rome or Corinth, or some other place, is uncertain); with whose consent and privity probably he wrote, possibly at their instigation, and whose common consent in that doctrine of faith which he handleth, (as well as in other things about which he writeth,) he here declareth. Some think that the apostle forbears the term *saints*, or *sanctified in Christ Jesus*, &c., commonly used in his other Epistles, because of that apostasy for which he designed to reprove them; but it is implied in the term *churches.* Galatia was a large country, and had in it many famous cities; it was neither wholly Christian, nor yet such as to the major part; but there were in it several particular congregations of Christians, which he calleth *churches;* every congregation of Christians using to meet together to worship God, being a church, a particular church, though all such congregations make up but one universal visible church. Nor, being guilty of no idolatry, though corrupted in some particular points of doctrine, and those of moment, doth the apostle deny them the name of churches, though he sharply rebuketh them for their errors.

f Rom. 1. 7.
1 Cor. 1. 3.
2 Cor. 1. 2.
Eph. 1. 2.
Phil. 1. 2.
Col. 1. 2.
1 Thess. 1. 1. 2 Thess. 1. 2. 2 John 3.

3 ᶠGrace *be* to you and peace from God the Father, and *from* our Lord Jesus Christ,

A common, as well as religious and Christian, form of salutation; Paul's mark in every Epistle, and used by him without any variation, (except in his Epistles to Timothy and Titus, where he only adds *mercy* &c.,) the want of which, as also of his name, offers some grounds to doubt whether he wrote the Epistle to the Hebrews. Paul had used it in the beginning of his Epistle to the Romans, and both the Epistles to the Corinthians: see the notes on Rom. i. 7; 1 Cor. i. 3; 2 Cor. i. 2. It teaches us, in our common discourses, whether epistolary or otherwise, to speak to our friends like Christians, who understand and believe that the *grace, mercy, and peace from God*, are the most desirable good things.

4 ᵍWho gave himself for our sins, that he might deliver us ʰ from this present evil world, according to the will of God and our Father:

g Mat. 20. 28.
Rom. 4. 25.
ch. 2. 20.
Tit. 2. 14.
h See Is. 65.
17 John 15.
19. & 17. 14.
Heb. 2. 5. & 6. 5. 1 John 5. 19.

Which Christ, though he was put to death by Pilate and the Jews, yet he was not compelled to die; for he laid down his life, no man took it from him, John x. 17, 18. Sometimes it is said, he died for our sins, as Rom. v. 8; sometimes, that he *gave himself*, (meaning, to death,) as in Eph. v. 2, 25; 1 Tim. ii. 6; Tit. ii. 14: he was given by his Father, and he gave himself by his own free and spontaneous act. *For our sins*, must be interpreted by other scriptures: here is the defect of a word here, which the Socinians would have to be remission; others, expiation (of which remission is a consequent). Both, doubtless, are to be understood, and something more also, which is expressed in the following words of the verse. Remission of sins is granted to be the effect of the death of Christ, but not the primary and sole effect thereof; but consequential to the *propitiation*, mentioned Rom. iii. 25; the *redemption*, Eph. i. 7; the *sacrifice,* Heb. x. 12: both which texts show the absurdity of the Socinians, in quoting those texts to favour their notion of Christ's dying for the remission of our sins, without giving the justice of God satisfaction. And though some other texts mention Christ's dying for our sins, without mention of such expiation, propitiation, redemption, or satisfaction; yet they must be interpreted by the latitude of the end of Christ's death (expressed in other scriptures) relating to sin. Which is not only expiation, and remission, but the delivery of us from the lusts and corruptions of *this present evil world.* The apostle here deciphers this world, by calling it *present* and *evil*: by the first, he hinteth to us, that there is a world to come; by the latter, he showeth the sinful practices of the greatest part of men, (for by *world* he means the corruption of persons living in the world,) they are evil; and this was one end of Christ's death, to deliver his saints from their evil practices and examples; thus, 1 Pet. i. 18, we are said to be by the blood of Christ *redeemed from a vain conversation received by tradition from* our *fathers.* This (he saith) was done *according to the will of God;* the Greek word is θέλημα, not διαθήκην: the will of God is his decree, purpose, or good pleasure, so as it signifieth both his eternal purpose, (according to Eph. i. 4,) and his present pleasure or consent. I see no ground for the Socinian criticism, who would have us understand by it, God's testament, or present will for things to be done after death; the word importeth no more than God's eternal purpose, as to the redemption of man by the blood of Christ, and his well-pleasedness with his undertaking and performance of that work; this God he calleth *our Father*, not with respect to creation so much as adoption.

5 To whom *be* glory for ever and ever. Amen.

To which Father, (yet not excluding the Son,) for so great benefits bestowed upon us, be honour, and praise, from age to age, and to all eternity. The term *Amen*, being always used in Scripture either as a term of assertion, to aver the truth of a thing, or as a term of wishing, may here be understood in either or both senses; the apostle using it either to assert the glorifying of God to be our duty, and a homage we owe to God; or to signify his hearty desire that this homage may from all hands be paid unto him.

6 I marvel that ye are so soon removed ⁱfrom him that called you into the grace of Christ unto another Gospel:

i ch. 5. 8.

The apostle here beginneth the matter and substance of his Epistle, with a reprehension of this church; which in some things is much qualified, in other things much aggravated. His expressing his reproof by the word *marvel*, hath in it something of mitigation, and signifieth his better hopes concerning them. The term *removed*, also, mollifies the reproof, the apostle thereby rather charging their apostacy upon their seducers, than upon them who were seduced; though they were not to be excused for their so yielding to the temptation, and that in so short a time, either after their first conversion, or after the first attempts upon them to seduce them; and herein was the aggravation of their guilt, that they very little resisted the temptation, but were presently overthrown by it. But it was a greater aggravation of their guilt, that they suffered themselves to be removed *from him that called* them. Interpreters doubt whether this be to be understood of God, or of Paul; and if of God, whether of the First or of the Second Person. That which inclineth some to think that Paul meant himself, was his instrumentality in the conversion of these Galatians; and his complaints of them in this Epistle, for their deserting his doctrine, and alienation from him; but then the substantive to the participle must be understood, and the call must be understood of the external call only, by the ministry of the word. It therefore seemeth rather to be understood of God; the apostles generally ascribing calling to God, chap. v. 8; 1 Thess. v. 24; 2 Thess. ii. 14; 1 Pet. i. 2, 15; 2 Pet. i. 3. Nor doth it seem proper to refer the action to Christ, because the apostles ordinarily ascribe calling to the First Person in the Trinity, calling us *by Christ*, as Rom. viii. 30; 2 Thess. ii. 13, 14, 16; 2 Tim. i. 9; 1 Pet. v. 10; besides, *the grace of Christ* is here made the term to which they are called. And though this would supply the participle with a substantive in the text, without understanding one, yet it seems both too remote, and also to alter the sense of the text; making it to run thus, from Christ that called you into grace, instead of *him that called you into the grace of Christ.* By which grace the apostle doubtless means not the doctrine of the gospel only, (though that be sometimes called grace,) but all the benefits of the gospel, justification, reconciliation, adoption; which are all properly called the grace of Christ, as being the purchase of his blood. *Unto another gospel;* that is, to the embracing of other doctrine, differing from the doctrine of the gospel, though it be brought to you by seducers under that notion; showing you another pretended way of salvation than by the merits of Jesus Christ, whereas God hath *given no other name under heaven, neither is there salvation in any other*, Acts iv. 12.

k 2 Cor. 11. 4. 1 Acts 15. 1, 24. 2 Cor. 2. 17. & 11. 13. ch. 5. 10, 12.

7 ^kWhich is not another; but there be some ^lthat trouble you, and would pervert the Gospel of Christ.

Which is not another; another doctrine it is, but another doctrine or glad tidings of salvation, or another gospel of Christ, it is not; for there is no other. In and by the new notions they bring they do but *trouble you*, and *pervert the* true doctrine of *the gospel;* though they use the name of Christ, and of his gospel, they do it falsely; for by making the works of the law, and the observance of them, necessary to be by you observed in order to your salvation, they quite destroy and pervert the glad tidings of salvation; viz. that we are saved by Christ alone and faith in him, and by a righteousness without these works.

m 1 Cor. 16. 22.

8 But though ^mwe, or an angel from heaven, preach any other Gospel unto you than that which we have preached unto you, let him be accursed.

9 As we said before, so say I now again, If any *man* preach any other Gospel unto you ⁿthan that ye have received, let him be accursed.

n Deut. 4. 2. & 12. 32. Prov. 30. 6. Rev. 22. 18.

The apostle, by this vehement expression, doth no more suppose it possible that a heavenly angel should publish to them any other way of salvation than what he had published, than that he himself might so contradict his own doctrine. He only by it declares his certainty of the truth, which he had delivered to them; it was not to be contradicted either by man or angel; and further teacheth us, that additions to the doctrines of the gospel make another gospel; God neither allowing us to add to, nor to diminish from, Divine revelations; for of this nature were the corruptions crept into this church. These seducers owned Christ and the doctrine of the gospel; only teaching the Jewish circumcision, and other ceremonial rites, as necessary to be observed in order to people's salvation, they made the pretended gospel (which they taught) to be another gospel than that which Paul had preached, and which believers in this church had received. In saying *let him be accursed*, he also saith that he who doth this shall be accursed; for the apostle would neither himself curse, nor direct others to curse, whom he did not know the Lord would curse, and look upon as cursed. These two verses look dreadfully upon the papacy, where many doctrines are published, and necessary to be received, which Paul never preached, nor are to be found in any part of Divine writ.

10 For ^odo I now ^ppersuade men, or God? or ^qdo I seek to please men? for if I yet pleased men, I should not be the servant of Christ.

o 1 Thes. 2. 4. p 1 Sam. 24. 7. Matt. 28. 14. 1 John 3. 9. q 1Thes.2.4. Jam. 4. 4.

For do I now persuade men, or God? there is an emphasis in the particle *now*, since I became a Christian, and was made an apostle; while I was a Pharisee I did otherwise, but since I became an apostle of Jesus Christ, do I persuade you to hear what men say, or what God saith? Or (as others) do I persuade the things of men, their notions and doctrines, or the things of God? Or do I in my preaching aim at the gratifying or the pleasing of men, or the pleasing of God? The last is plainly said in the next words, *do I seek to please men?* which must not be understood in the full latitude of the term, but restrainedly, do I seek to please and humour men in things wherein they teach and act contrary to God? It is the duty of inferiors to please their superiors, and of all good ministers and Christians, to please their brethren, so far as may tend to the advantage of their souls; or in civil things, so as to maintain a friendly and peaceable society; but they ought not to do any thing in humour to them, by which God may be displeased. In which sense it is that the apostle adds, *For if I pleased men*, that is, in saying as they say, and doing as they do, without regard to pleasing or displeasing of Christ, *I should not* show myself *the servant of Christ;* for his servants we are whom we obey, and our Lord hath taught us, that no man can serve two masters, that is, commanding contrary things.

11 ^rBut I certify you, brethren, that the Gospel which was preached of me is not after man.

r 1 Cor. 15. 1.

He calls them *brethren*, though some of them were revolted, because they owned Christ, and makes known or declares to them, (so the word is translated, Luke ii. 15; John xv. 15; xvii. 26,) that the doctrine of the gospel, which he had preached unto them, was no human invention or fiction, nor rested upon human authority, but was from God, immediately revealed to him: and herein he reflecteth upon the false teachers that had seduced them, and, in order to that, vilified him, as being but a disciple to some other of the apostles, yet teaching otherwise than they taught. I would have you know (saith he) that it is otherwise; the gospel which I preached *is not after man.* He fully openeth his own meaning in this phrase, in the next words.

12 For ^sI neither received it of man, neither was I taught *it*, but ^tby the revelation of Jesus Christ.

s 1Cor. 15.1, 3. ver. 1. t Eph. 3. 3.

Not *of man*, as my first and sole instructor, not only at

second-hand, from Peter, James, or John, as the false teachers had suggested, *nor was I taught it* otherwise than *by the* immediate *revelation of Jesus Christ. Revelation* signifieth the discovery of something which is secret (as the gospel, and doctrine of it, is called a *mystery hid from ages*). It may be objected, that Paul was instructed by Ananias, Acts ix. 17. But this prejudiceth nothing the truth of what the apostle saith in this place, neither do we read of much that Ananias said to him in a way of instruction; it is only said, that he laid *his hands on him*, and he was *filled with the Holy Ghost*. When, or where, he had these revelations, the apostle saith not; probably while he lay in a trance, blind, and neither eating nor drinking for three days, Acts ix. 9. Others think it was when he was caught up into the third heaven, 2 Cor. xii. 2. Certain it is, that St. Paul had revelations from Christ, Acts xxii. 17, 18 ; xxvi. 15—18. Revelation signifies an immediate conveying of the knowledge of Divine things to a person, without human means ; and in that Paul ascribes the revelation of the gospel to Jesus Christ, he plainly asserts the Divine nature of the Lord Jesus Christ.

13 For ye have heard of my conversation in time past in the Jews' religion, how that ᵘbeyond measure I persecuted the Church of God, and ˣwasted it :

It will be no difficult thing for you to believe, that I had never preached the gospel without a Divine revelation of the truth of it, if you do but reflect upon my former conversation ; for you cannot but have heard, that I was born a Jew, educated in the Jewish religion, and was a zealous defender of it, so as I persecuted the Christians beyond measure. This unmeasurable persecution is expressed by Luke more particularly, Acts viii. 3, *He made havoc of the church, entering into every house, and haling men and women, committed them to prison ;* and Acts ix. 1, *He breathed out threatenings and slaughter against the disciples of the Lord,* &c. He wasted the church like an enemy that useth fire and sword, and all means to destroy. The word here used is ἐπόρθουν, which signifies to make a devastation; the word used in Acts viii. is ἐλυμαίνετο· both words signify the most ruinating hostile actions. And this he saith was his conversation, or constant practice, so as they might reasonably think, that something more than human had made a change in him, that he should now be a preacher of that doctrine, which he had before so abominated as that his whole business was to root out those that professed it.

14 And profited in the Jews' religion above many my †equals in mine own nation, ʸbeing more exceedingly zealous ᶻof the traditions of my fathers.

The word here used, and translated *profited*, may be interpreted either of his own personal proficiency, and going on in the Jewish religion, or of his propagating of it, and making that to go on, which seemeth to be the sense of the same word, 2 Tim. ii. 16. And it is observed, that active verbs in the Greek in imitation of the Heb. con. Pihil., sometimes signify to do an action oneself, sometimes to make others do it ; and Paul's wasting the Christian church had a rational tendency to uphold and propagate Judaism, the propagation of which was the end designed by it ; this he saith he did above others of his countrymen, that were his equals in years. By this also he lets them know, that his persecuting the Christian church was not a passionate act, or for a gain to himself, but from an erroneous judgment, he verily thought that he ought to do what he did against Jesus of Nazareth, and his disciples. He addeth, that he was *more exceedingly zealous of the traditions of* the *fathers ;* by which he understands not only the rites of the ceremonial law, but the whole body of their constitutions, which the rulers of their church had made, under the notion of *sepimenta legis*, hedges or fences to the laws of God, to keep men at a distance from the violation of them ; and other constitutions also, of which they had an innumerable. Paul was a Pharisee, *(the son of a Pharisee,* Acts xxiii. 6,) bred up at the feet of Gamaliel (one of the doctors of their law) ; this was the strictest sect (for ceremonies) of their religion : and this his zeal for traditions, is that which he calleth a progress, or profiting in the Jewish religion, and was a cause of the propagation of that religion.

15 But when it pleased God, ᵃwho separated me from my mother's womb, and called *me* by his grace,

Here are two acts predicated of God, with relation to Paul : the first is a separating of him from the womb ; the same was said of two of the great prophets, Isaiah and Jeremiah, Isa. xlix. 1 ; Jer. i. 5. The apostle here is not speaking of God's decree, predestinating him to eternal life, but of his determining him to the work of an apostle. God predetermineth men to the stations they shall take up in the world ; especially such who are to take up stations wherein they are to be eminently useful and serviceable to him. The second act predicated of God is his calling of Paul : this is an act in time, and lieth much in the preparing of persons for the work allotted to them, and in inclining the heart to it. Thus God called Paul, fitting him for the work of the ministry, and inclining him to it ; to which he added his immediate command from heaven, that he should go and preach the gospel. Both these acts of God are ascribed to his good pleasure and grace, nothing but his mere free love and favour moving him, either to separate, or to call Paul to this high and great employment.

16 ᵇTo reveal his Son in me, that ᶜI might preach him among the heathen ; immediately I conferred not with ᵈflesh and blood :

When it pleased God to discover Christ his Son (by an eternal generation) to me, whom neither naturally, nor from any instruction in my education, was acquainted with any thing of Christ, but, according to the common prejudices of those of my own country, looked upon him as a mere man, and an impostor ; and also revealed to me the end of that discovery, not only that I myself should receive and embrace him, but that I should publish him amongst the heathens (where he intimates the specialty of his separation and call) ; I, saith he, immediately advised with no mortal man living, (for that is signified by *flesh and blood*, Matt. xvi. 17 ; 1 Cor. xv. 50,) but resolved with myself to address myself to that work and employment to which I had such a special call from God.

17 Neither went I up to Jerusalem to them which were apostles before me ; but I went into Arabia, and returned again unto Damascus.

As Jerusalem was the place for the oracle of the law, under the Old Testament ; so it also was for the gospel upon the first publication of it. There the disciples were ; they returned thither after they had seen Christ ascend to heaven, Luke xxiv. 52 ; from thence they were not to depart, but to *wait* there *for the promise of the Father*, Acts i. 4. There the Holy Ghost came down upon them, Acts ii. ; there they continued till the persecution scattered them ; there was the college of the apostles. Paul saith, that, upon his conversion, he did not go up thither, nor till *three years after* (as he tells us in the next verse); but he *went into Arabia*, amongst the heathens, and the most wild and barbarous heathens, for such were the Arabians. Luke, in the Acts, tells us nothing of this. From hence it was easy to conclude, that Paul had not his commission from the other apostles that were before him, for he saw none of them till he had been a preacher of the gospel to the wild Arabians three years. And then he *returned to Damascus :* the word is ὑπέστρεψα, which is by some observed to signify his being compelled to return, (as they judge,) by some persecution raised amongst the heathens ; but of this the Scripture saith nothing.

18 Then after three years ᵉI ∥ went up to Jerusalem to see Peter, and abode with him fifteen days.

These *three years* were spent partly in Arabia, partly at Damascus, whither he returned ; and he, being there, was not idle, but, as Luke informs us, *preached Christ in the synagogues, confounded the Jews, proving that this was the very Christ*, which made *the Jews* take *counsel to kill him :* here it was that he escaped them, by being *let down* over *the wall in a basket*, Acts ix. 20, 22—25. Then he *went* to *Jerusalem*, where his conversion, and call to preach the gospel, was not heard of, (possibly in regard of the remoteness of Arabia, where he had spent most of those three years; or in regard of the troubled state of the church at Jerusalem at this time,) insomuch that the disciples were afraid to admit him to join with them, until Barnabas had given testimony concerning him, Acts ix. 27. He tells us here that he stayed there but *fifteen days;* during which time Luke tells us, Acts ix. 29, *he spake boldly in the name of the Lord Jesus, and disputed against the Grecians.*

f 1 Cor. 9. 5.
g Mat. 13.55.
Mark 6. 3.

19 But ^fother of the apostles saw I none, save ^gJames the Lord's brother.

The apostles were at this time scattered, either through the persecution, or for the fulfilling of the work of their apostleship; so as probably there were at this time no more of the apostles at Jerusalem, except Peter, and James the less, the son of Alpheus, who is here called the brother of our Lord, as is generally thought, according to the Hebrew idiom, who were wont to call near kinsmen, brethren. Upon another journey which Paul made to Jerusalem, he saw others (as we shall hear in the next chapter); but that was several years after this his first journey thither.

20 Now the things which I write unto

h Rom. 9. 1. you, ^hbehold, before God, I lie not.

Whether those words, *before God*, make this sentence an oath, is not material to determine; they are either an oath, or a very serious asseveration. If the apostle designed to call God for a witness, to the correspondence of his words with the truth of the things he had spoken, they make up an assertory oath, which was lawful enough (though privately taken) in so serious a matter as this, where the apostle is vindicating his apostleship from some acts, of which probably he had no witnesses at hand to produce; but they may be understood (by the supplement of, I speak, or, I say this) only as a form of serious assertion, to confirm the truth of what he asserted. He minds them, that he was sensible of God's presence in all places, and particular taking notice of the things spoken; as being spoken before him, who knew that what he spake was truth.

i Acts 9. 30. 21 ⁱAfterwards I came into the regions of Syria and Cilicia;

After that I came from Jerusalem, I came into the country of Syria; probably not to Damascus, the chief city of Syria, (where he had so narrow an escape in a basket,) but into the country parts of Syria; for Syria lay in the way betwixt Judea and Cilicia. It appeareth by Acts ix. 30, that Paul was designed for Tarsus, his native place; where we are also told, that the brethren conducted him to Cæsarea, which stood upon the confines of Syria. It is probable that he stayed some time at Tarsus; for there Barnabas found him, Acts xi. 25, 26, and *brought him to Antioch;* so that Paul had but fifteen days at Jerusalem to converse with the apostles, and in that time he saw none of them, but Peter, and James the son of Alpheus.

k 1 Thess. 2.
14.
l Rom. 16. 7.

22 And was unknown by face ^kunto the churches of Judæa which ^lwere in Christ:

To be *in Christ*, signifieth, 1. Their being Christians indeed; they having received Christ by a true and lively faith, and given themselves to the obedience of his precepts. In this sense the apostle saith, *If any man be in Christ he is a new creature.* 2. Their being Christians in name, by baptism and outward profession. These churches are said to be in Christ in this latter sense. We have a parallel text, 1 Thess. ii. 14. They do not judge improperly, who think that by Judea here is not meant the province, but the whole country of Judea; which comprehended not Judea only, but Samaria and Galilee. John Baptist and our Saviour (who both mostly preached in Galilee) had prepared their due matter for gospel churches. Peter, and John, and Philip, preached the gospel in many villages of the Samaritans, Acts viii. 25, 40. Of all these churches Paul speaks, telling us he was personally unknown unto them; so far he was from learning the Christian doctrine from the apostles or them.

23 But they had heard only, That he which persecuted us in times past now preacheth the faith which once he destroyed.

Though those churches in the country of Judea had never seen Paul's person, yet they had heard of him: 1. That he had been a persecutor of those which professed the doctrine of the gospel, which he here calleth *the faith*, it being the object and the means of faith. 2. That there was such a change wrought in him, as that he was now become a preacher of that doctrine, for the profession of which he had formerly wasted and destroyed the churches of Christ.

24 And they glorified God in me.

And they praised God on his behalf, for working so great a change in him.

CHAP. II

Paul showeth for what purpose after many years he went to Jerusalem, 1, 2: *that Titus, who went with him, was not circumcised, and that on purpose to assert the freedom of the Gentile converts from the bondage of the law,* 3—5: *that no new knowledge was added to him in conference with the three chief apostles, but that he received from them a public acknowledgment of his Divine mission to the Gentiles,* 6—10: *that he openly withstood Peter for dissimulation with respect to Gentile communion,* 11—13; *expostulating with him, why he, who believed that justification came by the faith of Christ, acted as though it came by the works of the law,* 14—20; *which was, in effect, to frustrate the grace of God,* 21.

THEN fourteen years after ^aI went up again to Jerusalem with Barnabas, and took Titus with *me* also.

A. D. 52.
a Acts 15. 2.

Fourteen years after; either fourteen years after the three years before mentioned, and the fifteen days; or fourteen years after the conversion of Paul, or fourteen years after the death of Christ. This journey seeming to be that mentioned Acts xv. 2, it seems rather to be understood of fourteen years after the death of Christ. *I went up again to Jerusalem:* motions to Jerusalem are usually in Scripture called ascendings or goings up; either because of the mountains round about it, or in respect of the famousness of the place: see Acts xv. 2; xxi. 4. The occasion of this journey we have, Acts xv. 1, 2. It was to advise with the apostles and elders, about the necessity of circumcision; some that came from Judea having taught the disciples at Antioch, that except they were circumcised they could not be saved. *With Barnabas, and took Titus with me also;* Barnabas was chosen to go with Paul, Acts xv. 2, and some others, whom Luke nameth not, but it is plain by this text Titus was one.

2 And I went up by revelation, ^b and communicated unto them that Gospel which I preach among the Gentiles, but || privately to them which were of reputation, lest by any means ^cI should run, or had run, in vain.

b Acts 15.12.

|| Or, *severally.*
c Phil. 2. 16.
1 Thess. 3.5.

And I went up by revelation; revelation signifieth God's immediate declaration of his will to him, that he would have him take this journey; which is not at all contradicted by Luke, saying, Acts xv. 2, 3, that their journey was determined by the Christians at Antioch. God, to encourage Paul, had let him know it was his will he should go; and also put it into the Christians' hearts at Antioch, to choose him to the journey. His motions from one place to another were much by revelation, or immediate order and command from God, Acts xvi. 9; xxii. 18; xxiii. 11. *And communicated unto them that gospel which I preach among the Gentiles;* he saith, he communicated, or made a report or relation of, (in which sense the word is used, Acts xxv. 14,) that doctrine of the gospel which he had preached amongst the Gentiles; he, doubtless, more particularly means, the abolition of circumcision, and no necessity of the observance of the law of Moses contained in ordinances. *But privately to them which were of reputation;* but he saith that he did it *privately*, and to men of *reputation;* by which he meaneth the apostles, or some other Christians of greatest eminency. *Lest by any means I should run, or had run, in vain;* lest he should have prejudiced himself, as to the course of the gospel, which he metaphorically compareth to a race: see 1 Cor. ix. 26. *Object.* If any ask how this influenced Paul, so as to make him privately to communicate the doctrine which he had amongst the Gentiles preached publicly? It is easily answered, 1. That the consent of those who were apostles before him to the doctrine which he preached, was of great moment to persuade all Christians to embrace it; and by this means he obviated the scandal of being singular in the doctrine which he preached. 2. Besides that Paul was now at Jerusalem, which was the chief place of the Jews' residence, to whom God indulged a greater liberty for the ceremonial usages, than to the churches of the Gentiles, who had not been educated in that religion. And had Paul openly there declared the liberty of Christians from circumcision, and the ceremonial usages, he had both enraged those who as yet continued in the Jewish religion, and possibly given no small offence to those who had been educated in that religion, though they were converted to the faith of the gospel, they not fully yet understanding the liberty of Christians from that yoke. By one or both of which ways, had Paul openly at Jerusalem published the doctrine which he had publicly preached in Damascus and Arabia, and other places of the Gentiles, his labours might have been rendered useless, and he might also have been less successful in his further course of preaching it.

3 But neither Titus, who was with me, being a Greek, was compelled to be circumcised:

The apostle brings this as an instance of the apostles at Jerusalem agreeing with him in his doctrine, as to the non-necessity of circumcision; for though Titus was with him, who was a native Gentile, being a Greek, and a minister of the gospel, (and possibly Paul carried him with him for an instance,) yet the apostles at Jerusalem did not think fit to impose upon him circumcision; no, not upon a solemn debate of that question. If any shall object that Paul himself circumcised Timothy, who was a Greek, Acts xvi. 1, 3; the answer is easy, the same text letting us know that his mother *was a Jewess*, and that he did it *because of the Jews in those quarters*. As to the Jews, it was matter of liberty at this time, they might or might not be circumcised. Now in matters of this nature, where men have a liberty, they ought to have regard to circumstances, and to do that which they, from a view of circumstances, judge will be most for the glory of God, the good of others, and give least offence, 1 Cor. x. 28—31.

d Acts 15. 1, 24. 2 Cor. 11. 26.
e ch. 3. 25. & 5 1, 13.
f 2 Cor.11.30. ch. 4. 3, 9.

4 And that because of ᵈ false brethren unawares brought in, who came in privily to spy out our ᵉ liberty which we have in Christ Jesus, ᶠ that they might bring us into bondage:

He gives the reason why circumcision was not urged upon Titus, viz. because there were some got into that meeting, where Paul debated these things with the apostles that were at Jerusalem, who, though they had embraced the Christian religion, (and upon that account were *brethren*,) yet were soured with the Jewish leaven, and were very zealous for all Christians to observe the Jewish rites of circumcision, &c.; upon which account it is that he calleth them *false brethren*. These (he saith) *came in privily, to spy out* that liberty which all Christians had, and Paul had preached and used, as to these Jewish ceremonies; who, could they have obtained to have had Titus circumcised, they had had a great advantage to have defamed Paul, as teaching one thing to the Gentile churches, and practising the contrary when he came to Jerusalem to the apostles, and amongst the Jews. And this being a liberty which he and all Christians had, in and from Jesus Christ, he would not part with it, for they aimed at nothing but the bringing of Christians again under the *bondage* of the ceremonial law. Some may say, It being a thing wherein Christians had a liberty, why did not St. Paul yield to avoid their offence; becoming all things to all men to gain some? *Answ.* In the use of our liberty, all circumstances are to be considered, as well as that of scandal and offence. The valuable opposite circumstance in this case, seemeth to be the validity and success of the apostle's ministry, the efficacy of which would have been much weakened, if his enemies had from hence gained an advantage to represent him, as doing one thing in one place and the quite contrary in another. Besides, though at this time the use or not use of the ceremonial rites, by the Jews, was a matter of liberty, by reason of God's indulgence to them for the prejudices of their education, yet whether they were at all so to the Gentile churches, may be doubted: see chap. v. 2, 3. Further yet, these brethren urged the observation of these rites, as necessary to salvation, (as appears from Acts xv. 1,) for they were of the sect of the Pharisees, ver. 5. And to use them under that notion, was no matter of liberty.

5 To whom we gave place by subjection, no, not for an hour; that ᵍ the truth of the Gospel might continue with you.

g ver. 14. ch. 3. 1. & 4. 16.

To these Judaizing Christians the apostle did not think fit to yield one jot, not for the least time, nor in so much as one precedent; having a desire that these Gentile churches might not be perverted. Or, (as others think,) to which men *of reputation* we yielded not in the least. It is very probable, that Peter and James, upon their first arguing the case, to avoid the scandal and offence of the Jews, would have had Titus circumcised: St. Paul would not yield to it, that he might preserve the doctrine of the gospel, which he had planted amongst the Galatians, and other Gentiles, pure, and not encumber those churches with the Mosaical rites. But the most and best interpreters rather judge the persons here mentioned, to whom Paul would not yield, to be some Judaizing Christians, rather than the persons *of reputation*, mentioned ver. 2.

6 But of those ʰ who seemed to be somewhat, whatsoever they were, it maketh no matter to me: ⁱ God accepteth no man's person: for they who seemed *to be somewhat* ᵏ in conference added nothing to me:

h ch. 6. 3.
i Acts 10. 34. Rom. 2. 11.
k 2 Cor. 12. 11.

But of those who seemed to be somewhat: the word translated *seemed*, is the same with that ver. 2, which we there translate *of reputation*. The apostle meaneth the same persons that were of the greatest reputation, and so the following words, *to be somewhat*, do import, Acts v. 36; viii. 9. We must not understand the apostle, by this expression, to detract from the just reputation that the apostles, and these eminent Christians at Jerusalem, had; he only taketh notice here of them, as magnified by the false teachers of this church, to the lessening of himself; and as *those who seemed to be somewhat*, must be interpreted as relating to these men's estimation of them; that seemed to you to be somewhat, though I seem nothing to you. *Whatsoever they were, it maketh no matter to me;* whatsoever they were formerly, suppose (as probably some of these Galatians had said) that they saw Christ in the flesh, when I was a Pharisee, &c. *God accepteth no man's person;* hath no regard to what a man hath been, but to what he is. *For they who seemed to be somewhat in conference added nothing to me;* when I came to confer and discourse with them, about the doctrine which I and they had taught, I learned no new doctrine from them, different from what I had before taught, neither did they reprove or correct me, for any thing which I had taught amiss; we were all of the same mind.

7 But contrariwise, ˡ when they saw that the Gospel of the uncircumcision ᵐ was committed unto me, as *the Gospel* of the circumcision *was* unto Peter;

l Acts 13. 46. Rom. 1. 5. & 11. 13.
1 Tim. 2. 7.
2 Tim. 1. 11.
m 1 Thess. 2. 4.

But contrariwise, when they saw; they were so far from contradicting any thing that I had preached, that when they understood from me, and Barnabas, (who, Acts xv. 12, declared in the council *what miracles and wonders God had wrought among the Gentiles by them,*) *that the gospel of the uncircumcision*, that the business of preaching the gospel to those who were no Jews, (for that is meant by *uncircumcision;* not simply those that were not circumcised, for some of the heathens were circumcised, yet all go in Scripture under the name of uncircumcised,) *was committed unto me, as the gospel of the circumcision was unto Peter;* as the preaching of the gospel to the Jews was committed to Peter, and not to him only, but to James and

GALATIANS II

John. It must not be so understood, as if Paul might not preach to the Jews, or Peter might not preach to the Gentiles, (for the contrary is evident from Acts ix. 15, as to Paul, and from Peter's preaching to Cornelius, Acts x.,) but because God designed the Gentiles to be more especially the province for Paul to exercise his ministry in, Acts xxvi. 17, (and accordingly he was specially sent out by the church, Acts xiii. 3,) as Peter's chief work was among the Jews.

n Acts 9. 15.
& 13. 2. &
22. 21. & 26.
17, 18. 1 Cor.
15. 10. ch. 1.
16. Col. 1.29.
o ch. 3. 5.

8 (For he that wrought effectually in Peter to the apostleship of the circumcision, ⁿthe same was °mighty in me toward the Gentiles:)

As Paul's call was equal to that of Peter. both of them being Divine, so, saith the apostle, my ability and success was equal; as God *wrought effectually in* and by *Peter* in the discharge of his apostleship in the province intrusted to him, (which was preaching to the Jews,) so he wrought effectually and mightily in me, or by me, in the province wherein I was employed, viz. carrying the gospel to the Gentiles. This efficacious working of God, both by Paul and Peter, was seen in the conversion of multitudes by their ministry, as well as in their miraculous operations, by which they confirmed the doctrine of the gospel which they preached.

p Mat. 16.18.
Eph. 2, 20.
Rev. 21. 14.
q Rom. 1. 5.
& 12. 3, 6.
& 15. 15.
1 Cor. 15. 10.
Eph. 3. 8.

9 And when James, Cephas, and John, who seemed to be ᵖpillars, perceived ᑫthe grace that was given unto me, they gave to me and Barnabas the right hands of fellowship; that we *should go* unto the heathen, and they unto the circumcision.

James, (called, the less,) the son of Alpheus, before called *the Lord's brother,* as is thought, because he was the son of the virgin Mary's sister; whose naming here in the first place spoileth the papists' argument for Peter's primacy, because in some other places he is first named. *Cephas;* that is, Peter, called here *Cephas* in the Syriac, possibly because he is named with others who had Syriac names; in most places he is by this apostle called Peter. *John,* the apostle and evangelist, who is also known by the name of *the beloved disciple. Who seemed to be pillars;* Paul, in saying they *seemed to be pillars,* doth not deny them to be so; being such as God made use of in the first founding and building of the gospel church; as also to bear it up, (in the same sense that the church is called *the pillar and ground of truth.*) and as by them the gospel was carried out into the world; but he useth the word *seemed,* because the false teachers had magnified their ministry, but disparaged his. When these, he saith, *perceived the grace that was given to me;* by which, he either understands his office of apostleship. or the crown and seal of his office in the blessing which God had given to his labours amongst the Gentiles. *They gave to me and Barnabas the right hands of fellowship;* they looked upon him and Barnabas as much pillars as themselves; and in token of it gave them their right hands, (a token of admitting into fellowship, 2 Kings x. 15; Jer. l. 15,) and agreed *that we should go unto the heathen, and they unto the circumcision;* that it should be their special work to go and preach to the Gentiles, as they (viz. James, and John, and Peter) would make it their special work to preach the gospel to the Jews.

r Acts 11. 30.
& 24. 17.
Rom. 15. 25.
1 Cor. 16. 1.
2 Cor. 8, &
9, chapters.

10 Only *they would* that we should remember the poor; ʳthe same which I also was forward to do.

These pillars and apostles, which have among you the greatest reputation, added no new doctrine to us, gave us nothing new in charge; they only desired us that we would be careful, wheresoever we went, to make collection for the poor Christians in Judea, who either by selling all they had to maintain the gospel in its first plantation, or by the sharp persecution which had wasted them, or by reason of the famine, were very low; nor was this any new thing, I had before done it, and was very forward to do it again, had they said nothing to us about it.

s Acts 15. 35.

11 ˢBut when Peter was come to Antioch, I withstood him to the face, because he was to be blamed.

Of this motion of Peter's to Antioch the Scripture saying nothing, hath left interpreters at liberty to guess variously as to the time; some judging it was before, some after, the council held at Jerusalem, of which we read, Acts xv. Those seem to judge best, who think it was after; for it was at Antioch, while Barnabas was with Paul; now Paul and Barnabas came from Jerusalem to Antioch, to bring thither the decrees of that council; and at Antioch Barnabas parted from Paul; after which we never read of them as being together. While Paul and Barnabas were together at Antioch, Peter came thither; where, Paul saith, he was so far from taking instructions from him, that he *withstood him to the face.* Not by any acts of violence, (though the word often expresseth such acts,) but by words reproving and blaming him; for, (saith he) he deserved it, *he was to be blamed.* Though the word signifies, he was condemned, which makes some to interpret it, as if Peter had met with some reprehension for his fact before Paul blamed him, yet there is no ground for it; for though the Greek participle be in the preterperfect tense, yet it is a Hebraism, and put for a noun verbal, which in Latin is sometimes expressed by the future, according to which we translate it; see 1 Cor. i. 18; 2 Cor. ii. 15; 2 Pet. ii. 4: so our interpreters have truly translated it according to the sense of the text.

12 For before that certain came from James, ᵗhe did eat with the Gentiles: but when they were come, he withdrew and separated himself, fearing them which were of the circumcision.

t Acts 10. 28.
& 11. 3.

It should seem that Peter had been at Antioch some time; while he was there, there came down certain Jews from James, who was at Jerusalem: before they came Peter had communion with those Christians at Antioch, which were by birth Gentiles, and at meals eat as they eat, making no difference of meats, as the Jews did in obedience to the ceremonial law; but as soon as these zealots for the Jewish rites (though Christians) were come, Peter withdrew from the communion of the Gentile Christians, and was the head of a separate party; and all through fear of the Jews, lest they should, at their return to Jerusalem, make some report of him to his disadvantage, and expose him to the anger of the Jews.

13 And the other Jews dissembled likewise with him; insomuch that Barnabas also was carried away with their dissimulation.

The fact was the worse. because those Christians which were of the church of Antioch, having been native Jews, followed his example, and made a separate party with him. Nay, *Barnabas,* my fellow labourer, who was joined with me in bringing the decrees of the council in the case, *was carried away with their dissimulation.* So dangerous and exemplary are the warpings and miscarriages of those that are eminent teachers.

14 But when I saw that they walked not uprightly according to ᵘthe truth of the Gospel, I said unto Peter ˣbefore *them* all, ʸIf thou, being a Jew, livest after the manner of Gentiles, and not as do the Jews, why compellest thou the Gentiles to live as do the Jews?

u ver. 5.
x 1 Tim. 5. 20.
y Acts 10. 28.
& 11. 3.

Uprightly, here, is opposed to halting. Peter halted betwixt two opinions, (as Elijah sometime told the Israelites,) when he was with the Gentiles alone, he did as they did, using the liberty of the gospel; but when the Jews came from Jerusalem, he left the Gentile church, and joined with the Jews; this was not according to that plainness and sincerity which the gospel required; he did not (according to the precept he held, Heb. xii. 13) *make straight paths* to his *feet, lest that which is lame be turned out of the way.* Paul not hearing this from the report of others, but being an eye-witness to it, doth not defer the reproof, lest the scandal should grow: nor doth he reprove him privately, because the offence was public, and such a plaster would not have fitted the sore; but he speaketh *unto Peter before them all*, rebuking him openly, because he sinned openly; and by this action had not offended a private person, but the church in the place where he was, who were all eye-witnesses of his halting and prevarication, 1 Tim. v. 20. *If thou, being a Jew, livest after the manner of Gentiles, and not as do the Jews;* if thou, who art a Jew, not by religion only, but by birth and education, hast formerly lived, eat, and drank, and had communion with the Gentiles, in the omission of the observance of circumcision, and other Jewish rites, generally observed by those of their synagogues; (as Peter had done before the Jews came from from Jerusalem to Antioch;) *why compellest thou the Gentiles to live as do the Jews?* why dost thou, by thy example, compel the members of a Gentile church to observe the Jewish rites? for compelling here doth not signify any act of violence, (Peter used none such,) but the example of leaders in the church, who are persons of reputation and authority, is a kind of compulsion to those that are inferiors, and who have a great veneration for such leaders. So the word here used, ἀναγκάζεις, is used in 2 Cor. xii. 11, as also to express the force of exhortations and arguments. Of such a compulsion the word is used, Luke xiv. 23. Peter, by his example, and possibly by some words and arguments he used, potently moved those proselyted Jews, who were in communion with the churches of Galatia, to observe the Jewish rites: so that by this fact he did not only contradict himself, who by his former walking with the Gentile church had practically asserted the gospel liberty; but he also scandalized those Christians in these churches who stood fast in the liberty which Christ had purchased for them, and Paul had taught them; and also drew others away from the truth they had owned and practised. This was the cause of Paul's so open and public reproof of him.

z Acts 15. 10, 11.
a Matt. 9. 11. Eph. 2. 3, 12.

15 [z] We *who are* Jews by nature, and not [a] sinners of the Gentiles,

Jews by nature; born Jews, not only proselyted to the Jewish religion, (and so under an obligation to the observation of the Jewish law,) but of the seed of Abraham, and so under the covenant made with him and his seed, as he was the father of the Jewish nation. *Not sinners of the Gentiles:* the Gentiles were ordinarily called by the Jews *sinners;* though it appeareth that there were divers of them worshippers of the true God, and came up to Jerusalem to worship; for whose sake there was a peculiar court allotted in the temple, called *The court of the Gentiles.* Yet not being under the obligation of the Jewish law, they went under the denomination of sinners by the Jews; and the most of the Gentiles were really sinners, and that eminently, (for such the word here used ordinarily signifieth,) as the apostle describeth their manners, Rom. i. 29—31.

b Acts 13. 38, 39.
c Rom. 1. 17. & 3. 22, 28. & 8. 3. ch. 3. 24. Heb. 7. 18, 19.

16 [b] Knowing that a man is not justified by the works of the law, but [c] by the faith of Jesus Christ, even we have believed in Jesus Christ, that we might be justified by the faith of Christ, and not by the works of the law: for [d] by the works of the law shall no flesh be justified.

d Ps. 143. 2. Rom. 3. 20. ch. 3. 11.

Knowing that a man is not justified; we knowing that a man is not absolved from the guilt of sin, and declared righteous in the sight of God; *by the works of the law;* by any kind of works done in obedience to the law of Moses, whether ceremonial or moral. For it is manifest, that although this question about justification by works began about circumcision and works done in obedience to the ceremonial law, yet the determination of it extended further. For the apostle, by *the law,* understands that law by which *is the knowledge of sin,* Rom. iii. 20. Now the knowledge of sin, is neither only nor chiefly by the ceremonial law; nor did ever any of those, against whom the apostle argueth, think, that men could be justified by obedience only to the law contained in ordinances; nor could boasting be excluded, (which the apostle showeth, Rom. iii. 27, was God's design in fixing the way of a sinner's justification,) if men might be justified by works done in obedience to the moral law; nor was it the ceremonial law only, the violation of which *worketh wrath,* Rom. iv. 15, or disobedience to which brought men *under the curse,* chap. iii. 10. *But by the faith of Jesus Christ;* but we are justified by believing in Christ: not by faith as it is a work of ours, for that was denied before; nor by faith as a principal efficient cause, for in that sense it is God that justifieth; nor as a meritorious cause, for so we are justified by the blood of Christ; but by faith as an instrument apprehending and applying Christ and his righteousness. *Even we have believed in Jesus Christ, that we might be justified by the faith of Christ, and not by the works of the law;* we (saith the apostle) that are Jews, knowing this, have not only assented to the truth of the gospel proposition, and received the Lord Jesus; that we so doing, not trusting to the law, or any obedience of ours to it, might be absolved from the guilt of sin, and declared righteous before God. *For by the works of the law shall no flesh be justified;* for no mortal man shall ever be absolved or declared righteous upon his own personal obedience to the law of God; being in the best imperfect, and much short of what the law requireth.

17 But if, while we seek to be justified by Christ, we ourselves also are found [e] sinners, *is* therefore Christ the minister of sin? God forbid.

e 1 John 3. 8, 9.

Some interpreters think, that the apostle here begins his discourse to the Galatians upon the main argument of his Epistle, viz. justification by faith in Christ; though others think it began, ver. 15. *If, while we seek to be justified by Christ, we ourselves also are found sinners;* if (saith the apostle) you make us grievous offenders in our expectation of being justified by Christ, and not by the works of the law, you make *Christ the minister of sin,* who hath taught us this. But others think that the apostle here obviateth a common objection which was then made, (as it is also in our age,) against the doctrine of justification by faith in Christ; viz. That it opens a door of liberty to the flesh, and so makes Christ a *minister of sin,* as if he relaxed men's obligation to the law of God; which is the same objection which the apostle answered in his Epistle to the Romans, chap. vi. If, while we plead for justification by Christ, we live in a course of notorious disobedience to the law of God, then Christ must be to us a minister of sin, and come into the world to purchase for us a possibility of salvation, though we live in never so much notorious disobedience to the law of God. As if there were no obligation upon men to keep the law, unless by their obedience to it they might obtain pardon of sin and justification. This calumny the apostle disavows, first, by a general aversation, *God forbid!*

18 For if I build again the things which I destroyed, I make myself a transgressor.

By *the things which he destroyed,* some understand the state of sin; and from hence conclude the mutability of a state of justification: but there is no need of that, it may as well be understood of a constant course and voluntary acts of sin. If I teach a doctrine that shall encourage a sinful life, or if I should live in a course of sin, these are *the things which I,* as a minister of Christ, have in my preaching and doctrine *destroyed,* teaching you, that not only the guilt of your sins was removed upon your justification by Christ, but the dominion of sin also destroyed: and they are things which justification destroyeth; God never saying to any soul, *Thy sins are forgiven thee,* without adding, *sin no more.* So as, if a justified state would admit of a going on in a settled course of sin, it would build what it destroyed. *I make myself a transgressor;* now should I, or any one, do any such thing, we should thereby make ourselves great transgressors. So as the apostle's argument here seemeth to be the same with that, Rom. vi. 2, *How shall we, that are dead to sin, live any longer therein?* He strives at the same thing here, viz. to prove that the doctrine of justification by faith in Christ, could not give a liberty to any to sin, because it shows persons made partakers of that grace, that they are freed, not only from the guilt, but also from the power and dominion of sin, so as that none can from it receive any comfort as to the former, nor find the latter wrought in them.

19 For I [f] through the law [g] am dead to the law, that I might [h] live unto God.

f Rom. 8 2. g Rom. 6.14. & 7. 4, 6. h Rom. 6. 11. 2 Cor. 5. 15. 1 Thess. 5. 10. Heb. 9. 14. 1 Pet. 4. 2.

Through the law of Christ, as some say; or rather, through the law of Moses, of which he had been before speaking: that is, say some, through the death of the law; the law itself being dead, as a covenant of works. Rom. vii. 6. Or rather, by means of the law, giving me a knowledge of sin, and condemning me for sin. *Am dead to the law,* as to any expectation of being justified by obedience to it. *That I might live unto God;* not that I might live in disobedience to it, as it is a rule of life, but that I might live more holily unto God: so as my being dead to the law, as a covenant of works, or as to any expectation of being justified from my obedience to it, gives me no liberty to sin at all; for this is the end why God hath freed me from the bondage and rigour of the law, that I might live unto him, and serve him without fear, in holiness and righteousness.

^{i Rom. 6. 6.
ch. 5. 24.
& 6. 14.}
^{k 2 Cor. 5. 15.
l Thes. 5. 10.
1 Pet. 4. 2.
l ch. 1. 4.
Eph. 5. 2.
Tit. 2. 14.}

20 I am ⁱcrucified with Christ: nevertheless I live; yet not I, but Christ liveth in me: and the life which I now live in the flesh ^kI live by the faith of the Son of God, ^lwho loved me, and gave himself for me.

This Epistle is much of the same nature with that to the Romans, and the substance of what the apostle saith in the latter part of this chapter, agreeth much with the 6th chapter of that Epistle; where we find an expression much like to this, ver. 6, *Our old man is crucified with him, that the body of sin might be destroyed, that henceforth we should not serve sin. I am* (saith the apostle) *crucified with Christ;* not only by justification made partaker of the benefits coming by a Christ crucified, but also as having communion with the death of Christ, in the mortification of my lusts. A figure of which (as he informeth us, Rom. vi. 4) we have in baptism, *buried with him by baptism into death. Nevertheless I live;* yet (saith he) I live a holy, spiritual life; though dead to the law, and though crucified with Christ. *Yet not I, but Christ liveth in me;* but I cannot say so properly that it is I, for my motions are not according to my natural propensions and inclinations; *but Christ,* by his Spirit, *liveth in me,* having renewed and changed me, made me a new creature, and begot new motions and inclinations in me. And though I *live in the flesh,* yet *I live by the faith of the Son of God;* all my natural, moral, and civil actions, being principled in faith, and done according to the guidance of the rule of faith in Jesus Christ. *Who loved me, and gave himself for me;* of whom I am persuaded that he loved me, and from that love gave himself to die upon the cross for me.

^{m ch. 3. 21.
Heb. 7. 11.
See Rom. 11.
6. ch. 5. 4.}

21 I do not frustrate the grace of God: for ^mif righteousness *come* by the law, then Christ is dead in vain.

I do not frustrate the grace of God; I do not despise, reject, make void, (for by all these words the word here used is translated, Mark vii. 9; John xii. 48; chap. iii. 15; Heb. x. 28,) the free love of God, in giving his Son to die for our sins: from whence is easily gathered, that those who live a loose life, and take a liberty to sin, from their justification, or from the free grace of God in Christ, they do contemn and despise the grace of God: or rather, (if we refer it to the following words,) those who assert justification by the works of the law, they do reject and despise the free grace of God in the gospel, and (as much as in them lies) make it vain and frustrate. *For if righteousness come by the law;* for if it be possible, that a man by works done in obedience to the law should arrive at a righteousness, in which he may stand before God, *then is Christ dead in vain;* then Christ died to no purpose, or without any just cause: the reason of this must be, because it was the main and principal end of Christ's death, to procure or purchase a righteousness wherein sinners might stand before God, *to bring in* an *everlasting righteousness,* Dan. ix. 24. If the most proper effect of the death of Christ be taken away, then his death is made causeless, and to no purpose. Thus the apostle concludeth his thesis, laid down ver. 16, That none shall be *justified by the works of the law,* from two absurdities that would follow upon the contrary, viz. justification by the works of the law, the rejecting of the grace of God, and the frustration, or making void, of the death of Christ.

CHAP. III

Paul asketh what had moved the Galatians to depend on the law, having already received the Spirit through faith, 1—5. *As Abraham was justified by faith, so they who are of faith inherit his blessing,* 6—9. *The law brought men under a curse, and could not justify,* 10—12. *Christ hath freed us from the curse, and laid open the blessing to all believers,* 13, 14. *Supposing that the law justified, God's covenant with Abraham would be void,* 15—18. *But the law was only a temporary provision against sin till Christ's coming, and in no wise contrary to God's promises,* 19—22; *serving as a schoolmaster to prepare men for Christ,* 23, 24. *But faith being come the law is at an end, and all believers are, without distinction, become children of God, and heirs of the promise,* 25—29.

O FOOLISH Galatians, ^awho hath bewitched you, that ye should not obey ^bthe truth, before whose eyes Jesus Christ hath been evidently set forth, crucified among you? ^{a ch. 5. 7.} ^{b ch. 2. 14.
& 5. 7.}

O foolish Galatians, who hath bewitched you? the apostle beginneth the further pursuit of the argument he was upon, with a smart reprehension of them, as men of no understanding, and bewitched. The word translated *bewitched,* signifies vitiating the eyes, or spoiling the sight, so as that men cannot discern an obvious object in a due position. The meaning is, Who hath seduced you, who hath so corrupted your understanding that your actions are as unaccountable as the effects of witchcraft? *That ye should not obey the truth:* the word translated *obey,* signifies also to believe: in general it signifies to be persuaded; which may refer either to an assent to the truth, or obedience to the precepts of the gospel. *Before whose eyes Jesus Christ hath been evidently set forth, crucified among you;* whenas Christ hath been plainly preached before you, and his death, with the blessed end and effects of it, hath been so made known amongst you, as if you had seen him crucified. Or else Christ may be said to be crucified amongst them, because it was in their time, so as they could not but hear of it, and there was no more reason for them to doubt of the truth of the thing, than if he had been crucified in their country.

2 This only would I learn of you, Received ye ^cthe Spirit by the works of the law, ^dor by the hearing of faith? ^{c Acts 2. 38.
& 8. 15. & 10.
47. & 15. 8.
ver. 14.
Eph. 1. 13.
Heb. 6. 4.} ^{d Rom. 10. 16, 17.}

By *the Spirit* here is understood the gifts of the Spirit, which were either such as were common to all believers, (such as faith, love, &c.,) or else such as were peculiar to some, and those not all believers; such were those abilities for miraculous operations given to some. Some understand this text of the former, some of the latter: it is best to take in both; all the manifestations of the Spirit then given out, either for the sanctification and eternal salvation of those to whom they were given, or for the confirmation of the truth of the gospel. Did you receive the Spirit *by the works of the law?* that he knew they could not say they did; for they were heathens, strangers to the commonwealth of Israel, so as they could pretend to no works of the law. Did you receive this Holy Spirit upon *hearing* the gospel (which is the doctrine *of faith)* preached to you? Men should take heed of vilifying that ministry, or that doctrine, which God hath blessed to the change of their own hearts, or the hearts of others. We also may observe from hence, that the hearing the gospel faithfully preached is a blessed means by which men's hearts are changed, and they receive the Holy Spirit; not enabling them (as it did some, and but some, in the beginning of the gospel) to work signs and wonders, but enabling them to the operations of a spiritual life. The strength of the apostle's argument is this, You have the greatest reason to own that doctrine as the truth, which God hath blessed to your souls to produce spiritual effects there.

3 Are ye so foolish? ^ehaving begun in the Spirit, are ye now made perfect by ^fthe flesh? ^{e ch. 4. 9.} ^{f Heb. 7. 16.
& 9. 10.}

The doctrine of their false teachers was, that to faith in Christ, an obedience also to the law of Moses was necessary to justification; they did not deny Christ, nor the doctrine of the gospel, only they pleaded for the works of the law as necessary to be superadded. The apostle calls this first owning of Christ, and embracing the doctrine of faith, a beginning *in the Spirit;* their adding the necessity of obedience to the law of Moses, a being *made perfect in the flesh;* and argueth the unreasonableness of it, that their justification should be begun by a more noble, and made perfect by a more ignoble cause. He calls the doctrine of the gospel, *Spirit,* because (as he said in the former verse) they had received the Holy Spirit *by the hearing of faith;* that is, by hearing and receiving the gospel. The works of the law he calls *flesh,* because the ordinances of the law were (as the apostle calls them, Heb. ix. 10) *carnal ordinances, imposed on* the Jews *till the time of reformation.* He elsewhere calls them *the rudiments of the world,* Col. ii. 8, 20; and in this Epistle. chap. iv. 9, he calls them *beggarly elements.* For though the ordinances of the law were in their season spiritual, they being commanded by God; yet they being but temporary constitutions, never intended by God to continue longer than the coming of Christ. and the law being but a schoolmaster to lead to Christ; Christ being now come, and having died, and rose again from the dead, they became useless. Besides that God never intended them as other than *rudiments* and first *elements,* the end of which was Christ; and the observance of which, without faith in Christ, was weak and impotent, as to the noble end of justification. It spake great weakness, therefore, in the Galatians, to begin with what was more perfect. (the embracing of the gospel, and Christ there exhibited for the justification of sinners,) and to end in what was more imperfect. thinking by that to be made perfect; or else the apostle here chargeth them with a defection from Christ, as chap. iv. 9—11, and v. 4: and so calleth them foolish, for beginning in the Spirit, (the Holy Spirit inwardly working in them the change of their hearts, and regenerating them.) and then apostatizing from their profession to a carnal life. But I had rather interpret *Spirit* in this text, of the doctrine of the gospel, dictated by the Spirit; and with the receiving of which the Holy Spirit was given. And so their folly is argued from their thinking to be made perfect by the beggarly elements and worldly rudiments of the law, whenas they had first begun their profession of Christianity with embracing the more perfect doctrine of the gospel.

g Heb. 10, 35, 36. 2 John 8. ‖ Or, *so great.*

4 ᵍ Have ye suffered ‖ so many things in vain? if *it be* yet in vain.

There is no doubt but these churches in the regions of Galatia had their share in the sufferings of Christians by the Jews, for their adherence to and profession of the doctrine of the gospel, which they might either wholly, or in a great measure, have avoided, would they have complied with the Jews in the observance of those legal rites. Therefore, (saith the apostle,) to what purpose have you suffered so much for the owning of the Christian religion, if you now bring yourselves under the bondage of circumcision, and other legal observances? *If it be yet in vain;* by which words he either correcteth himself, as if he had said, But I hope better things of you, that I shall find that you did not suffer them in vain; or else he hinteth that their suffering so much would not be in vain, because, by their apostacy from the true faith for which they suffered, they would in effect deny it, as if it had been false, and their former suffering would rise up in judgment against them.

h 2 Cor. 3. 6.

5 He therefore ʰ that ministereth to you the Spirit, and worketh miracles among you, *doeth he it* by the works of the law, or by the hearing of faith?

He had asked them, ver. 2, whether they had received the Spirit by the works of the law, or by hearing the gospel? Some think what he saith here to be a continuation of the same argument, but it rather seems a new one: there he spake of their receiving the Spirit, here he speaks of the ministration of the Spirit. Some understand of God, who gives his Holy Spirit to them that ask him, and who he Author of those miraculous operations wrought by the Spirit. I should rather understand it of the ministers of the gospel, to whom God hath committed the ministration of the Spirit; and to some of whom God, in the primitive times, gave a power to work miracles. *Doeth he it by the works of the law, or by the hearing of faith?* doth God concur with our ministry upon our preaching the law, or upon our preaching the gospel? So that though there be a great cognation betwixt the apostle's arguing, ver. 2, and his arguing in this verse, yet there is some difference; the apostle there arguing from the success of preaching the gospel, here from the ministration itself.

i Gen. 15. 6. Rom. 4. 3, 9, 21, 22. Jam. 2. 23. ‖ Or, *imputed.*

6 Even as ⁱ Abraham believed God, and it was ‖ accounted to him for righteousness.

As Abraham was justified, so must all the children of Abraham; but *Abraham believed God,* (that is, agreed to the truth of all those promises which God gave him, and trusted in God for the fulfilling of them; for both those acts of the mind are included in believing God,) and so was justified alone. *And it was accounted to him for righteousness:* his faith itself was not imputed to him; those that put this sense upon the words, either forget that faith itself is a work, or that the apostle here is arguing for justification by faith in opposition to justification by works, and cannot be imagined to have gone about to prove that justification is not by works, by proving that it is by a work. The meaning is no more than that he was upon it accounted righteous; not that God so honoured the work of faith, but that he so rewarded it, as being the condition annexed to the promise of justification. His faith was not his righteousness, but God so rewarded his exercise of faith, as that upon it he reckoned (or imputed) that to him which was his righteousness, viz. the righteousness of him in whom he believed as revealed unto him in the promise.

k John 8. 39. Rom. 4. 11, 12, 16.

7 Know ye therefore that ᵏ they which are of faith, the same are the children of Abraham.

They which are of faith; those who are believers, and receive Jesus Christ, as exhibited and tendered to them in the gospel, trusting not to any righteousness of their own, arising from their obedience to the works of the law; they *are the children of Abraham,* considered as the father of the faithful, that is, they are justified as Abraham was justified; who was justified, not by his circumcision, but upon his believing in Christ exhibited to him in the promise; not by working, but by imputation. This argument came very close to the Jews, whose great glorying was in having Abraham to their father; for it is in effect a saying, that they were no true children of Abraham, none of that seed to whom the promise was made, if they expected justification from the works of the law, which Abraham never had nor expected.

l See Rom. 9. 17. ver. 22. m Gen. 12. 3. & 18. 18. & 22. 18. Ecclus. 44. 21. Acts 3. 35.

8 And ˡ the Scripture, foreseeing that God would justify the heathen through faith, preached before the Gospel unto Abraham, *saying,* ᵐ In thee shall all nations be blessed.

The Holy Ghost in Scripture (by whose inspiration the Scripture was written) foreseeing, or knowing, the counsels and designs of God, that the heathen (when the fulness of times as to them should come) should be justified through faith in Christ, preached the same doctrine before unto Abraham; so as it is no new doctrine; the gospel which we now preach unto you, was long since revealed unto Abraham, who saw Christ's day, and rejoiced, John viii. 56. To prove which, he quoteth the promise, Gen. xii. 3, where God tells Abraham, that in him all the nations of the earth should be blessed; which quotation of it by the apostle in this place informeth us, that it is to be understood of those spiritual blessings which are in Christ Jesus. For all the nations of the earth were no otherwise blessed in Abraham, than as Christ (who is called *the desire of all nations,* and he in whom *the Gentiles* should *trust,* and *a light to enlighten the Gentiles)* descended from Abraham.

9 So then they which be of faith are blessed with faithful Abraham.

Those that believe in Jesus Christ with such a faith as the gospel doth require, they, and they alone, are blessed

GALATIANS III

with spiritual blessings, justified from the guilt of sin, *with Abraham;* that is, in the same manner that Abraham, the father of the faithful, and who himself was a believer, was justified; which was not (as was before said) by his circumcision, or by any works that he did, but by imputation upon his believing in the Lord Jesus Christ, exhibited and held forth in the promise made to him.

10 For as many as are of the works of the law are under the curse: for it is written, ⁿ Cursed *is* every one that continueth not in all things which are written in the book of the law to do them.

n Deu. 27.26. Jer. 11. 3.

The argument is this: Those that are under a curse cannot be under the blessing of justification: but those that are under the law are under the curse. This he proves out of the law, Deut. xxvii. 26, where those are pronounced *cursed, who continue not in all things written in the book of the law to do them.* To be under the law, is, under the covenant of works, or under the expectation of life and salvation only from obedience to the works of the law. These (he saith) *are under the curse:* the reason of which the apostle gives us, Rom. viii. 3, because it is made *weak through the flesh.* Could man perfectly fulfil the law, he might expect life from it, and salvation from his obedience to it; but the law curseth him that continueth not in all that is written in it: *If a man keep the whole law, and yet offend in one point, he is guilty of all,* James ii. 10, and as liable to the wrath of God as if he had broken it in many things. Hence it necessarily followeth, if no man can keep the law of God perfectly, that all under the law must be under the curse, and consequently cannot be blessed in faithful Abraham.

o ch. 2. 16.

11 But º that no man is justified by the law in the sight of God, *it is* evident: for, ᵖ The just shall live by faith.

p Hab. 2. 4. Rom. 1. 17. Heb. 10. 38.

The apostle, by another argument, proveth that sinners are not justified by works. He grants, they may be justified by their good and blameless living before men, so as that they may have nothing to say against them, but he says they cannot, by such works, be *justified in the sight of God.* His argument is from the opposition that is between faith and works. He proveth, from Hab. ii. 4, that we are justified by faith; where the prophet saith, that *the just* (or righteous man) *shall live by faith;* fetch his life from faith, live his spiritual life by faith, and obtain eternal life by faith, the life of his righteousness shall be by faith.

q Rom. 4. 4, 5. & 10. 5, 6. & 11. 6. r Lev. 18. 5. Neh. 9. 29. Ezek. 20. 11. Rom. 10. 5.

12 And ᵍ the law is not of faith: but, ʳ The man that doeth them shall live in them.

The law saith nothing of faith in the Mediator; though faith in God be commanded in the first precept, yet faith in Christ is not commanded by the law as that by which the soul shall live. For that which the law saith is, *Do this and live: The man that doeth* the things contained in the law, *shall live in them;* life, in the law, is promised to those who do the things which it requireth; not to them who, have failed in their performances, yet accept of the Lord Jesus Christ as the Redeemer which God hath sent, and believe in him who justifieth the ungodly. For that by the life promised to the observation of the law, not a temporal life only is to be understood, but eternal life also, is plain from our Saviour's application of it to the young man, inquiring about the way to eternal life, Matt. xix. 16, 17; Luke x. 28.

s Rom. 8. 3. 2 Cor. 5. 21. ch. 4. 5.

13 ˢ Christ hath redeemed us from the curse of the law, being made a curse for us: for it is written, ᵗ Cursed *is* every one that hangeth on a tree:

t Deu. 21.23.

If the law curseth all those who continue not in all things contained in the law, (as the apostle had said, ver. 10, and proved from Deut. xxvii. 26,) it might be objected, How will believers then escape more than others; for none of them continue in all that is written in the law? The apostle here obviateth this objection, by telling the Galatians, that, as to believers, Christ had *redeemed* them from this curse. The word generally signifies delivering; here it signifies a deliverance by a price paid. This was *by being* himself *made a curse for us,* not only execrable to men, but bearing the wrath and indignation of God due for sin: *for so it* was *written,* Deut. xxi. 23, *He that is hanged is accursed of God;* that is, hath borne the wrath or curse of God due to him for his sin. The apostle applying this to Christ, teacheth us, that Christ also, hanging upon the cross, bare the curse of God due to the sins of believers; in whose stead, as well as for whose good and benefit, he died. And indeed he could no other way redeem believers from the curse of the law, but by being made himself a curse for them. Some think, that under the law he who was hanged was made a curse, not only politically, but typically, as signifying that curse which Christ should be made on the behalf of the elect.

u Rom. 4. 9, 16. x Is. 32. 15. & 44. 3. Jer. 31. 33. & 32. 40. Ezek. 11. 19. & 36. 27. Joel 2. 28, 29, Zech. 12. 10. John 7. 39. Acts 2. 33.

14 ᵘ That the blessing of Abraham might come on the Gentiles through Jesus Christ; that we might receive ˣ the promise of the Spirit through faith.

The apostle, by *the blessing of Abraham,* here, understands those spiritual blessings of justification, reconciliation, and adoption, which came to Abraham upon his believing, and the imputation of righteousness thereupon unto him. *Christ* (he saith) was *made a curse for us,* that all those blessings through him *might come on the Gentiles;* and so all the nations of the earth might be blessed in him. Particularly, that the Gentiles *might receive the promise of the Spirit;* which promise is not to be interpreted so narrowly, as only to signify its miraculous gifts, but to be extended to all those gifts and habits of grace which are the effects of the Holy Spirit in the hearts of believers, whether sanctifying or sealing them; which Holy Spirit is received upon persons' believing: see chap. iv. 6; Rom. viii. 13.

15 Brethren, I speak after the manner of men; ʸ Though *it be* but a man's ‖ covenant, yet *if it be* confirmed, no man disannulleth, or addeth thereto.

y Heb. 9.17. ‖ Or, *testament.*

Though it be but a man's covenant: the word here translated covenant, διαθήκη, is ordinarily translated *testament;* see Matt. xxvi. 28. It signifies in the general, an ordering or disposing of things; more specially, a testament; which is the disposition of the testator's goods after his death. Now, (saith the apostle,) I here argue according to the ordinary methods and doings of men, who have such a respect for a man's testament, as that, *if it be* once *confirmed,* according to the methods of law and civil sanctions of men, or rather by the death of the testator (for a testament is of no force while the testator liveth, Heb. ix. 17); nor will men alter the will or last testament of a deceased person, though it be not as yet confirmed according to the methods of human laws. *No man disannulleth, or addeth thereto; no man,* that is, no just man, will go about to disannul it, or add to it, nor will any just government endure any such violation of it. Hence the apostle argueth both the certainty and unalterableness of the covenant of grace with Abraham, and until the death of Christ it was but a covenant, or a testament not fully confirmed, but yet unalterable, because the covenant of that God who cannot lie, nor repent; but by the death of Christ it became a testament, and a testament ratified and confirmed by the death of the person that was the testator; therefore never to be disannulled, never capable of any additions. Those words, *or addeth thereto,* are fitly added, because these false teachers, though they might pretend not to disannul God's covenant, holding still justification by Christ; yet they added thereto, making circumcision, and other legal observances, necessary to justification; whereas by God's covenant, or testament, confirmed now by the death of Christ, faith in Christ only was necessary.

16 Now ᶻ to Abraham and his seed were the promises made. He saith not, And to seeds, as of many; but as of one, And to thy seed, which is ᵃ Christ.

z Gen. 12. 3, 7. & 17. 7. ver. 8.

a 1 Cor. 12. 12.

Now to Abraham and his seed were the promises made; the promises, Gen. xii. 3; xxii. 18; in the one of which places it is said, *In thee;* in the other, *In thy seed shall all the nations of the earth be blessed.* He saith, *promises,* either because of the repetition of the same promises, or taking in also other promises. *He saith not, And to seeds, as of many; but as of one, And to thy seed, which is Christ:* some may object against the apostle's conclusion, that the promise respected only *one,* and that was Christ; because God said not *seeds, as of many, but seed;* whereas the term *seed* is a noun of multitude, and signifieth more than one; besides that the Hebrew word, which is used Gen. xxii. 18, admitteth not the plural number. But it is answered, that though the word translated *seed* admitteth not the plural number, yet had God intended more than one, he could have expressed it by words signifying children, or generations, &c. 2. That the term *seed,* though a noun of multitude, yet is often applied to a single person; as Gen. iii. 15, where it also signifieth Christ; *Seth* is called *another seed,* Gen. iv. 25; and so in many other places. Some think that by *seed* he meaneth believers, and so interpret it of Christ mystical; and that the scope of the apostle in this place is to prove, that both the Jews and Gentiles were to be justified the same way; because they were justified in force and by virtue of the promise, which was not made to many, but to one church, which was to consist both of Jews and Gentiles, for (according to the prophecy of Caiaphas, John xi. 52) Christ died, that he might *gather together in one the children of God that were scattered abroad.* The promises made to Abraham, were but the exhibition of the eternal covenant of grace, made between the Father and his Son Christ Jesus (who was in it both the Mediator and Surety); which covenant was promulgated, as to Adam and Noah, so to Abraham, in these words, *In thy seed shall all the nations of the earth be called,* that is, in Christ. From whence the apostle proveth, that there is no justification by the works of the law, but in and by Christ, and the exercise of faith in him.

17 And this I say, *that* the covenant, that was confirmed before of God in Christ, the law, [b] which was four hundred and thirty years after, cannot disannul, [c] that it should make the promise of none effect.

[b] Ex. 12. 40, 41.
[c] Rom. 4. 13, 14. ver. 21.

The covenant, that was before confirmed of God in Christ: the word translated *covenant,* is the same as before; ordinarily signifying one's disposal of things in his last will and testament. Which name is given to the covenant of grace, with respect to the death of Christ; for though Christ as yet had not died, yet he was, by virtue of the covenant of redemption, and in God's counsels, *The Lamb slain from the foundation of the world,* Rev. xiii. 8. This (he saith) was *in Christ,* (as Abraham's promised seed,) *confirmed of* God to Abraham, by God's *oath,* Heb. vi. 17, 18; by frequent repetitions of it; by such solemn rites as covenants use to be confirmed by, Gen. xv. 17, 18; by the seals of circumcision, Gen. xvii. 11; Rom. iv. 11; by a long prescription, &c.; though it received indeed its final and ultimate consummation by the death of Christ, yet it was before many ways confirmed. *The law, which was four hundred and thirty years after, cannot disannul:* the law was given four hundred and thirty years after the giving this promise to Abraham: though, Gen. xv. 13, the round number of four hundred years only be mentioned, which are to be counted from the birth of Isaac; yet, Exod. xii. 40, they are reckoned (as here) four hundred and thirty years, from Abraham's going out of Canaan, Gen. xii. 4; from whence to the birth of Isaac were twenty-five years, Gen. xxi. 5, compared with chap. xii. 4; from the birth of Isaac till Jacob was born, sixty years, Gen. xxv. 26; from thence till Jacob went down into Egypt, one hundred and thirty years, Gen. xlvii. 9, where they abode two hundred and fifteen years. Hence the apostle concludes, that it was impossible that the law, which was not given till four hundred and thirty years after the confirmation of the promise, *should make the promise* confirmed *of no effect.*

[d] Rom. 8.17.
[e] Rom. 4.14.

18 For if [d]the inheritance *be* of the law, [e]*it is* no more of promise: but God gave *it* to Abraham by promise.

If the inheritance of the heavenly Canaan, typified by the earthly Canaan, the promise of which was made to Abraham, *be* to be obtained *by* the fulfilling of the *law,* and yielding obedience to it, then *it is no more of* the *promise.* It is much the same with what the apostle said before, Rom. iv. 14; and with what he had said, Rom. xi. 6, *If by grace, then it is no more of works, otherwise grace is no more grace. But if it be of works, then it is no more grace; otherwise work is no more work.* He shows, that there is an opposition betwixt *grace* and *work,* the *law* and the *promise;* that which is of grace, and of the promise, is of free love; that which is of works, and the law, is wages, and a reward of debt. *But* (saith the apostle) *God gave* the inheritance *to Abraham by promise;* he of his free love engaging himself thereunto.

19 Wherefore then *serveth* the law? [f]It was added because of transgressions, till [g]the seed should come to whom the promise was made; *and it was* [h] ordained by angels in the hand [i]of a mediator.

[f] John 15.22. Rom. 4. 15. & 5. 20.
[g] 7. 8, 13. ver. 16.
[h] Acts 7. 53. Heb. 2. 2.
[i] Ex. 20. 19, 21, 22. Deut. 5. 5, 22, 23, 27, 31. John 1. 17. Acts 7. 38. 1 Tim. 2. 5.

Wherefore then serveth the law? some might say, To what purpose was the law given? as if there could be no use of it unless it were available to justification. *It was added because of transgressions;* it was (saith the apostle) given after the promise, not to supply something wanting as to justification, to prescribe some works that must be added; but either to restrain sin, 1 Tim. i. 9, or to show and discover sin, to make men see that they stood in need of Christ: see Rom. vii. 13. *Till the seed should come to whom the promise was made:* till Christ the promised Seed should come, who *is the end of the law for righteousness to every one that believeth,* Rom. x. 4; upon whose coming the law contained in ordinances ceased. That Christ is here to be understood by *the seed,* is plain by the addition, *to whom the promise was made.* Some here understand by *the seed,* Christ and the church, (which both make up Christ mystical,) and interpret this text by Eph. ii. 14, till the Jews and Gentiles should be both made one. This law (he saith) *was ordained by angels.* Luke, Acts vii. 38, speaks of the law as published by one angel: the apostle, Heb. ii. 2, calls it, *the word spoken by angels.* We read of no angels, Exod. xix. xx., nor of any of the saints; yet, Deut. xxxiii. 2, Moses saith God *came from Sinai, with ten thousand saints.* The law was given either by the ministry of an angel, or by God attended with angels. *In the hand of a mediator;* that is, (say some,) under the power of Christ the Mediator; but by *the mediator* is rather to be understood Moses, which agreeth with Deut. v. 5, where Moses telleth the Jews, that he *stood between the Lord and* them *at that time, to show* them *the word of the Lord;* nor is Christ any where called the Mediator of the old, but of the new testament, Heb. viii. 6; xii. 24.

20 Now a mediator is not *a mediator* of one, [k]but God is one.

[k] Rom. 3. 29, 30.

This is a text acknowledged by all interpreters to be very obscure; not so much as considered in itself, (for all know, that a mediator speaks one that goes in the middle betwixt two persons that are at odds, so cannot be of one,) as in regard of the connexion of it with what went before; where he had told us, that the law was given *in the hand of a mediator.* There are various senses given of this verse, and the variety much ariseth from men's different understanding of the mediator in whose hand the law was given. To me the apostle seems to magnify the promise above the law, in that the promise was given to Abraham immediately by God, (who is one in essence,) but the law was given not immediately by God, but by Moses as mediator, who in that action was a type of Christ. And God thereby showed, that the law would bring no man to life and salvation without the one and only Mediator Christ Jesus. Christ, indeed, is the Mediator of the new testament, he mediated for it, he mediateth in it; but it was men's transgression of the law that brought them in need of a Mediator, sin being the only thing that separateth between God and man. *God is one;* and there had been no need of mediating between him and man, but for the law which man had transgressed. Those that by *the mediator,* ver. 19, understand Christ, make this the sense: That as a mediator supposeth two parties at odds, so Christ's being

Mediator speaks him to have respect to Jews and Gentiles. But this interpretation seems to make Christ the Mediator between Jews and Gentiles, whom (the apostle saith) he *made both one*, breaking down the partition-wall, Eph. ii. 14; but we do not find the name of Mediator upon this account any where given unto Christ. Many other senses are given, but the first mentioned seemeth the most probable, viz. that God made use of no mediator in giving the promise, but only in giving the law, which evidenced that justification was not to be by it; nor had there been need of a true Mediator under the gospel, but for the law, men's transgression of which brought in a need of a Mediator; which proved that justification could not be by the law.

l ch. 2. 21.

21 *Is* the law then against the promises of God? God forbid: ¹for if there had been a law given which could have given life, verily righteousness should have been by the law.

Is the law then against the promises of God? God forbid: though it be thus, yet there is no such opposition betwixt the law and the promises, as that either of them make the other useless. Far be it from me (saith the apostle) to assert any such thing! they are not contrary to one another, but subservient to one another. *For if there had been a law given which could have given life;* for if there had been a law which could, by our perfect performance of it, have given us a righteousness, wherein we might have stood righteous before God, then *righteousness should have been by the law;* then men might have hoped to have been justified and accepted of God by me for such obedience; then indeed the law had been against the promises, they holding forth another righteousness, viz. the righteousness of God from faith to faith.

m ver. 8.
n Rom. 3. 9, 19, 23. & 11. 32.
o Rom. 4. 11, 12, 16.

22 But ᵐ the Scripture hath concluded ⁿ all under sin, °that the promise by faith of Jesus Christ might be given to them that believe.

But the Scripture hath concluded all under sin: it pleased God to give a law, which, if Adam had continued in his estate of innocence, might have given life; but considering man in his lapsed state, that now is not possible: Rom. iii. 10, *There is none righteous, no not one:* and Eph. ii. 3, We are all *children of wrath. That the promise by faith of Jesus Christ might be given to them that believe;* that the promises of life and salvation might be given to those who, according to the new covenant of the gospel, should receive and accept of the Mediator, and the terms of salvation which God offers to us in the gospel; where these promises are exhibited upon condition of believing. Though, upon our first reflection upon it, it may seem strange to us, that God, having in his eternal counsels fixed the salvation of man upon a covenant of grace, and his believing in Jesus Christ, should in time first propound a covenant of works, Do this, and live; yet, upon second thoughts, this will appear necessary; for till man was a transgressor by breaking the law, and violating the first covenant, there was no room for a Mediator, no cause for men's applying themselves to a Mediator. God therefore first gave out the covenant of works, and suffered man to break it; and then he revealed the Mediator to lapsed man; that so they who should believe in him might obtain the promise of life, to which by the fall they had forfeited their right.

23 But before faith came, we were kept under the law, shut up unto the faith which should afterwards be revealed.

Before faith came; before the covenant of grace, or the doctrine of the gospel, or Christ himself, was revealed. *We were kept under the law;* the apostle either speaks of all mankind, of whom it is true, that until God's revelation of the covenant of grace, they had no other way of salvation made known to them than by the law of works; or else of the Jews, to whom, though before Christ there was a revelation of the gospel, yet it was more dark and imperfect, so as they *were kept under the law*, but few apprehending any other way of justification than by the works of the law. *Shut up unto the faith which should afterwards be revealed;* but the apostle saith they were but *shut up* under it; God never intended it as that by the observance of which they should be saved; but as even then, to those whom he intended to save, he made a more secret revelation of his gospel, so he had now more fully and plainly revealed the way of salvation which he had from eternity established.

24 Wherefore ᵖthe law was our schoolmaster *to bring us* unto Christ, ᑫthat we might be justified by faith.

p Matt. 5. 17. Rom. 10. 4.
Col. 2. 17. Heb. 9. 9, 10.
q Acts 13. 39. ch. 2. 16.

The law, both the law contained in ordinances and the moral law, *was our schoolmaster;* serving us in the same stead that a schoolmaster in a school doth, who only fitteth children for higher degrees of learning at universities. *To bring us unto Christ:* the ceremonial law showed us Christ in all his types and sacrifices; the moral law showed us the absolute need of a Mediator, as it showed us sin, accused and condemned us for it; and it showed us no help either for the guilt of sin contracted, or against the power of it. *That we might be justified by faith;* so that God's end in giving us the law was, that we might be fitted for Christ, and obtain justification by believing in him.

25 But after that faith is come, we are no longer under a schoolmaster.

After that Christ, the object of saving faith, was in the fulness of time revealed, and the gospel, which is the doctrine of faith, was fully revealed and published, the time of our nonage was over.

26 For ye ʳare all the children of God by faith in Christ Jesus.

r John 1. 12. Rom. 8. 14, 15, 16.
ch. 4. 5. 1 John 3. 1, 2.

All you that believe, whether native Jews or Gentiles, are the children of God by adoption, through faith in Jesus Christ, John i. 12: so that you need not run back to the law to look for help and salvation from that; but only look unto Christ, to whom the law was but a schoolmaster to lead you; who being fully and clearly revealed, you may have immediate recourse to, by faith; and need not to make use of the Jewish schoolmaster, as hoping for justification from the observances of the law.

27 For ˢas many of you as have been baptized into Christ ᵗhave put on Christ.

s Rom. 6. 3.
t Rom. 13. 14.

Baptized into Christ, may either be understood of receiving the sacrament of baptism; which who receiveth, is not only baptized in the name of Christ, and into the profession of Christ; but is sacramentally, or in a sign, baptized into Christ; or else (which, considering what followeth, seemeth much more probably the sense) it may signify a being not only baptized with water, but with the Holy Ghost and fire. Of those thus baptized, he saith, that they *had put on Christ;* they had accepted of and received Christ for their justification, and for their sanctification. We have the like phrase, Rom. xiii. 14.

28 ᵘThere is neither Jew nor Greek, there is neither bond nor free, there is neither male nor female: for ye are all ˣone in Christ Jesus.

u Rom. 10. 12. 1 Cor. 12. 13. ch. 6. 5. Col. 3. 11.
x John 10. 16. & 17. 20, 21. Eph. 2. 14, 15, 16. & 4. 4, 15.

There is neither Jew nor Greek; in the business of justification, the case of Jews and Greeks is the same. This he saith, that the Galatians might not think themselves disadvantaged from their not being under the law, as the schoolmaster that should lead them unto Christ. *There is neither bond nor free;* neither doth Christ consider the qualities and circumstances of persons, whether they be servants or free-men; for though they be servants, Christ hath made them free, 1 Cor. vii. 22; Eph. vi. 8; Col. iii. 11. *There is neither male nor female: for ye are all one in Christ Jesus:* neither hath Christ any respect to sexes: the male children under the law had many privileges; but it is all a case under the gospel, whether persons be males or females, Jews or Gentiles, rich or poor, servants or masters, bond-men or free-men.

29 And ʸif ye *be* Christ's, then are ye Abraham's seed, and ᶻheirs according to the promise.

y Gen. 21. 10, 12. Rom.9.7.
Heb. 11. 18.
z Rom. 8. 17 ch. 4. 7, 28. Eph. 3. 6.

Lest these Galatians should be discouraged, because the promise was made to Abraham and his seed, and they were not the seed of Abraham; he tells them, if they were Christ's, that is, if they truly believed in him, and were implanted into him, that then they were the seed of Abraham, that

CHAP. IV.

The Jews were for a while held under the law, as an heir under his guardian till he be of age, 1—3. *But Christ came to redeem those that were under the law, and to give both to Jew and Gentile the adoption, and consequently the freedom, of sons,* 4—7. *Paul therefore reproveth the Galatians, who from serving idols had been received of God, for falling back to the bondage of legal observances,* 8—10. *He expresseth his fears and tender regard for them, and calleth to mind their former respect and good will to him, from which he admonisheth them not to be seduced in his absence,* 11—20. *He allegorically describeth the Jewish and Christian churches under the types of Agar and Sara, and inferreth that we, being children of the free-woman, are free,* 21—31.

NOW I say, *That* the heir, as long as he is a child, differeth nothing from a servant, though he be lord of all;

The apostle had before determined, that the whole body of such as believed in Jesus Christ, were that seed of Abraham to which the promise was made, and so heirs of the promises made to him; yet so, that, as it is among men, though a child be a great heir, and lord of a great estate, yet while he is under age he is used like a servant; so the time of the law being as it were the time of believers' nonage, those who lived in that time were used like servants.

2 But is under tutors and governors until the time appointed of the father.

The heir, (mentioned in the former verse,) though he be an heir of a great estate, yet is not presently possessed of it; but he is by his father kept under tutors and governors, until the time which he hath appointed when he will be pleased to release him from his pupillage, and settle some part of his inheritance upon him.

[a] ver. 9. ch. 2. 23. & 5. 1. Col. 2. 8, 20. Heb. 9. 10. ‖ Or, *rudiments.*

3 Even so we, when we were children, [a] were in bondage under the ‖ elements of the world:

Such children were all believers, the seed of Abraham; from the first designed to a gospel liberty, but that was not to be fully enjoyed, until the fulness of time should come when God intended to send his Son into the world; and during the time of their nonage they were kept under the law, as a tutor and governor, leading them unto Christ. He chiefly intendeth the ceremonial law, which, Acts xv. 10, Peter calleth *a yoke, which neither they nor their fathers were able to bear.* He calls these ordinances *the elements of the world;* so also Col. ii. 20: he means that discipline by which God instructed, and under which God by Moses at first tutored, the world, that is, the Jews, who were that part of the world to whom God pleased to make his oracles known. He calls those ritual observances, elements, or rudiments, because they were the first instructions God gave believers, leading them to Christ; like the first elements or rudiments in grammar learning.

[b] Gen. 49 10. Dan. 9. 24. Mark 1. 15. Eph. 1. 10. [c] John 1. 14. Rom. 1. 3. Phil. 2. 7. Heb. 2. 14. [d] Gen. 3. 15. Is. 7. 14. Mic. 5. 3. Matt. 1. 23. Luke 1. 31. & 2. 7. [e] Matt. 5. 17. Luke 2. 27.

4 But [b] when the fulness of the time was come, God sent forth his Son, [c] made [d] of a woman, [e] made under the law,

But when the fulness of the time was come; the time, which answered the time appointed of the earthly father, mentioned ver. 2; when that time came in which God had designed to bring his people into the most perfect state of liberty, which in this life they are capable of. *God sent forth his Son,* who was existent before, (being brought forth before the mountains or hills were settled, Prov. viii. 25,) but not *sent forth* until this fulness of time came. And then *made of a woman,* conceived in the womb of the virgin, by the power of the Holy Ghost overshadowing her. *Made under the law;* to which, as God, he was not subject, (being himself the lawmaker,) but he subjected himself. He was born in a nation, and of a parent, under the law; he was circumcised, and submitted to the ceremonial law; he in all things conformed his life to the rule of the law, and subjected himself to the curse of the law, *being made a curse for us.* Nothing of this is questioned, except the last; which yet appears also to have been necessary by what followeth in the next verse, for how else could he have redeemed those who were under the law; and this agreeth with what we had, chap. iii. 13.

5 [f] To redeem them that were under the law, [g] that we might receive the adoption of sons.

[f] Matt. 20. 28. ch. 3. 13. Tit. 2. 14. Heb. 9. 12. Eph. 1. 7. [g] 1 Pet. 1. 18, 19. John 1. 12. ch. 3. 26. Eph. 1. 5.

This makes it appear, that Christ's being *under the law* must be understood as well of the moral as of the ceremonial law, that is, subject to the precepts of it, as well as to the curse of it; for if the end of this being born under the law, was to redeem those that were under it, that he had not reached by being merely under the ceremonial law; for the Gentiles were not under that law, but only under the moral law; and they also were to be redeemed, and to receive the great privilege of *adoption,* or rather, the rights of adopted children; which (some think) is to be understood here, rather than what is strictly to be understood by the term of adoption, viz. a right to be called and to be the sons of God. Others, by *adoption,* understand that full state of liberty of which the apostle had been before speaking, in opposition to that state of childhood and nonage in which believers were until the times of the gospel; for, chap. v. 1, we shall find that that was a *liberty wherewith Christ made us free:* and indeed this last sense seemeth best to agree with what the apostle had before said, ver. 1—3, though the other senses are not to be excluded.

6 And because ye are sons, God hath sent forth [h] the Spirit of his Son into your hearts, crying, Abba, Father.

[h] Rom. 5. 5. & 8. 15.

Lest the Jews should claim the adoption as peculiar to them, the apostle tells them that these Gentiles were also *sons;* and in confirmation of that, he saith, that God had sent *the Spirit of his Son* into their hearts: not that the Holy Spirit is not the Spirit of the Father, as well as of Christ; but he calleth him the Spirit of Christ, because he had made adoption the end and fruit of redemption; and redemption is every where made the work of the Son. The apostle saith, Rom. ix. 4, that the adoption belongeth to the Israelites: the Jews were the first people whom God dignified with the name of his *sons,* his *first-born,* Exod. iv. 22; and so many of them as believed also received the Spirit, Ezek. xxxvi. 27; but the full effusion of the Spirit was reserved to gospel times, and until the time that Christ ascended, John vii. 39; xvi. 7. After which the Spirit was poured out in the days of Pentecost, Acts ii., whose effects were evident, not only in power to work miracles, and speak with divers tongues, (which were not common to all believers,) but also in a variety of spiritual gifts and habits, amongst which this was one, teaching then. to cry, *Abba, Father. Crying,* (it is expounded, Rom. viii. 15, *whereby we cry,* that is, through whose influence and working in us we cry,) *Abba, Father,* that is, Father, Father: which not only signifieth the Spirit's influence upon believers' words in prayer, first conceived in the heart, then uttered by the lips; but chiefly those habits of grace, by which we pray acceptably; faith and holy boldness, by which we call God Father; zeal and fervency, by which we are importunate with God, and say, Father, Father. Which were now not the privileges of Jews only, but of these Galatians also, who were by nature Gentiles, and strangers to God; and a certain evidence of their concern in the redemption of Christ, and that they also might expect salvation from him.

7 Wherefore thou art no more a servant, but a son; [i] and if a son, then an heir of God through Christ.

[i] Rom. 8. 16. 17. ch. 3. 29.

Thou that art a believing Gentile, as well as the believing Israelites, *art no more a servant,* not in that state of servile subjection to the law; *but a son;* but in a more excellent state of liberty, like unto that of sons that have attained to a full and ripe age. Christ told his disciples, John xv. 15, that he did not call them servants, for servants knew not what their lord did; but he had freely communicated to them what he had received from the Father. The apostle here saith, they were sons, sons by adoption; which is the highest notion of freedom and liberty. And this entitled them to an inheritance: *if a son, then an heir of God through Christ:* which agreeth with Rom. viii. 17. And as it is with sons and heirs, though the inheritance cometh not fully to them till the death of the parent, yet while they live they are in a far better condition than servants; so the believing Gentiles, being made sons and heirs of God through Christ, though they were to stay a while for the inheritance reserved for the sons of God in the heavens, yet their state was much better than that of servants; for though they were obliged to serve the Lord, yet they served him without servile fear, and were no otherwise servants than sons are also servants to their father.

8 Howbeit then, ^kwhen ye knew not God, ^lye did service unto them which by nature are no gods.

When ye knew not God, as he is, or as ye ought to have known him, or as, since, you have known him; for even the heathen have some knowledge of God, Rom. i. 21. *Ye did service unto them which by nature are no gods;* you paid religious homages unto idols; which are gods, not by nature and essence, but only in the opinion of idolaters. Which was a more miserable bondage and servitude than the Jews were under, who knew the true God; though in the time when the church was like the heir under age, it was subject to the law contained in ordinances, and under the yoke of the law.

9 But now, ^mafter that ye have known God, or rather are known of God, ⁿhow turn ye ‖ again to ^othe weak and beggarly ‖ elements, whereunto ye desire again to be in bondage?

After that ye have known God; after that you are come to a true and saving knowledge of God in Christ, and know God as he is. *Or rather are known of God;* or rather after you are received of God, approved of him, made through Christ acceptable to him, which is much more than a true comprehension of God in your notion and understanding. *How turn ye again to the weak and beggarly elements, whereunto ye desire again to be in bondage?* how turn you back again to the legal services of the ceremonial law? which he calleth *elements*, or rudiments, because they were God's first instructions given to his church for his worship, to which he intended afterward a more perfect way of worship. He calls them *weak*, because they brought nothing to perfection; and the observance of them was impotent as to the justification of a soul, as all the law is. He calls them *beggarly*, in comparison of the more rational, spiritual way of worship under the gospel. He saith that they desired *to be in bondage* unto these, because they would not see and make use of the liberty from them which Christ had purchased. *Object.* It may be objected, that the Galatians were not educated in Judaism; how then doth the apostle charge them with turning back to them? *Answ.* This hath made some think, that, by *the weak and beggarly elements*, mentioned in this verse, the apostle meaneth their Gentile superstitions and idolatries; but this is not probable, the apostle, all along the Epistle, charging them with no such apostacy. Others think, that he in this verse chiefly reflecteth on the believing Jews, who afterwards returned again to the use of the law. But why may not we rather say, that he calleth their fact a turning back, not so much with reference to their personal practice, as to the state of the church; which was once under those elements, but by the coming of Christ was brought into a more perfect state. So that for them who were called into the church in the time of this its more perfect state, for them to return to the bondage of the law, that was truly to turn back; if not to any practice of their own, which they had cast off, yet to a state of the church which the church of God had now outgrown.

10 ^pYe observe days, and months, and times, and years.

If we had any evidence that these Galatians were relapsed to their former Gentile superstitions, these terms might be understood of such days, &c. as they kept in honour to their idols. But the apostle, throughout the whole Epistle, not reflecting upon them for any such gross apostacy (as returning to the vanities of the heathen in which they formerly lived); but only for Judaizing, and using the ceremonies of the Jewish law, as necessary to be observed, besides their believing in Christ, for their justification; it is much more probable that he meaneth by *days* the Jewish festivals, such as their new moons, &c.; by *months*, the first and the seventh month, when they religiously fasted; by *times*, their more solemn times, such as were their feasts of first-fruits, tabernacles, &c.; and by *years*, their years of jubilee, the seventh and the fiftieth year. His meaning is, that they took themselves to be under a religious obligation to observe these times as still commanded by God.

11 I am afraid of you, ^qlest I have bestowed upon you labour in vain.

Paul knew that, with reference to himself, he had not laboured in vain; he might say with Isaiah, chap. xlix. 5, *Though Israel be not gathered, yet shall I be glorified*. He had told the Corinthians, that he knew he should be a sweet savour to God, as well in them that perished as in them that should be saved, 2 Cor. ii. 15. But he speaks with reference to them. A faithful minister accounteth his labour lost when he seeth no fruits of it upon the souls of his people. Nor was Paul afraid of this as to the sincerer part of this church, who truly believed, and were justified, but he speaketh this with reference to the whole body of this church. That which he feared, was their falling back from their profession of Christianity to Judaism; as judging the observation of the Jewish days necessary by Divine precept to Christians. Nor doth he speak of the observation of such days, as it was their duty in obedience to the moral law to observe, which commandeth the observation of a seventh day for the weekly sabbath, and gives a liberty for setting apart other days, and the commanding the observation of them, to take notice of and acknowledge God in emergent providences. But he only speaks of days imposed by the ceremonial law, and men's religious observation of them, as being tied to it by a Divine precept, by which they made them a part of worship. We have a liberty to set apart any day for God's worship, and magistrates have a liberty to set apart particular days for the acknowledgment of God in emergent providences, whether of mercy or judgment; but none hath a power to make a day holy, so as that it shall be a sin against God for all to labour therein, much less hath any a liberty to keep Jewish holy-days.

12 Brethren, I beseech you, be as I am; for I am as ye are: ^rye have not injured me at all.

Be as I am; for I am as ye are; be as friendly to me as I am to you: see the like phrase, 1 Kings xxii. 4. But how doth the apostle say they had not injured him at all, when it is manifest they had defamed him? *Answ.* He had forgiven, or was ready to forgive, this to them; he had no desire or design to be revenged on them. Or in this particular thing of Judaizing, for which he had been reflecting upon them, they had done him no personal injury; it was only his care and love to their souls, which had drawn out this discourse from him; not any particular prejudice to them, or any desire he had to take any revenge upon them, for any personal injury done to himself.

13 Ye know how ^sthrough infirmity of the flesh I preached the Gospel unto you ^tat the first.

The Scripture having not given us a particular account of Paul's circumstances when he first preached the gospel to the Galatians, we are at a loss to determine what those infirmities were which Paul here speaketh of, more than that he calls them *infirmities of the flesh:* by which may be understood, either the baseness and contemptibleness of his presence, (which the false teachers at Corinth objected to him, 2 Cor. x. 10,) or some bodily sickness which Paul had at that time, (as some of the ancients guess,) or his sufferings for the gospel, which were those infirmities wherein he chose to glory, 2 Cor. xi. 30.

14 And my temptation which was in my flesh ye despised not, nor rejected; but received me

GALATIANS IV

u 2 Sam. 19. 27. Mal. 2. 7. See Zech. 12. 8.
x Matt. 10. 40. Luke 10. 16. John 13. 20. 1 Thess. 2. 13.

^uas an angel of God, ^x*even* as Christ Jesus.

And my temptation which was in my flesh ye despised not, nor rejected; the apostle saith they were so far from injuring him, (as he had said, ver. 12,) that they had expressed great kindness to him : for though, when he first came amongst them to preach the gospel, he was a man of no great presence ; but, in the judgment of some, vile and base ; or was full of bodily weakness and disease, was persecuted by men ; yet they did not reject nor despise him, for those temptations he had in the flesh : by which he means, the same things he before meant by infirmities, for both bodily weaknesses, and sufferings for the gospel, are temptations, or, as the word signifieth, trials. *But received me as an angel of God, even as Christ Jesus;* nay, (saith he,) you were so far from rejecting or despising me upon that account, that (on the contrary) you received me as if I had been an angel ; yea, if Jesus Christ himself had come amongst you, you could not have been more kind to him than you were to me. This he tells them, partly, to let them know, that what he had spoken was not out of any ill will or prejudice to them ; partly, to retain their good will, that they might not show themselves uncertain and inconstant in their judgments and affections ; and partly, (as the following verse testifieth,) to show the levity of some of them, who had too much forgotten their first judgment of him, and value for him.

‖ Or, *What was then?*

15 ‖ Where is then the blessedness ye spake of ? for I bear you record, that, if *it had been* possible, ye would have plucked out your own eyes, and have given them to me.

Some understand the *blessedness* here spoken of in a passive sense ; you were then a blessed and happy people, receiving the doctrine of the gospel in the truth and purity of it ; what is now become of that blessedness ? But both the preceding and the following words seem to rule the sense otherwise, viz. Where is that blessedness which you predicted of me ? you called me then blessed, and showed me such a dear affection that you would, if it would have done me good, have parted with what was dearest to you.

16 Am I therefore become your enemy,
y ch. 2. 5,14.   ^ybecause I tell you the truth ?

What hath now altered your mind, or made you have a worse opinion of me ? wherein have I offended you or done you any harm ? I have done nothing but revealed to you the truth of God ; am I therefore become your enemy ? or do you account me your enemy on that account ?

z Rom. 10. 2. 1 Cor. 11. 2.
‖ Or, *us.*

17 They ^z zealously affect you, *but* not well ; yea, they would exclude ‖ you, that ye might affect them.

They ; the false teachers, that have perverted you as to the faith of the gospel. *Zealously affect you;* pretend a great warmth of affection for you. *But not well;* but in this they do not well, nor for a good end. *They would exclude you* from our good opinion and affection. *That ye might affect them ;* that they might have all your love and respect ; and so, by the ruin of our reputation with you, they might build up their own reputation.

18 But *it is* good to be zealously affected always in *a* good *thing,* and not only when I am present with you.

It is good to be zealously affected always in a good thing : the apostle, in the former verses, had been speaking of a great zeal, or warmth of affection, (for that zeal signifieth,) which these Galatians had for and declared towards him, when he first preached the gospel amongst them ; and also of a great warmth and degree of affection which these false teachers had pretended to this church. These words are so delivered that they are applicable to either of these ; but the latter words seem to make them most properly applicable to the former ; so the term *always* is emphatical : There was a time, when you were very warm in your love to me ; the cause being good, your warmth of affection ought not to have abated, but continued always, *and not only* while you saw me, and I was *present with you.*

19 ^a My little children, of whom I travail in birth again until Christ be formed in you,
a 1 Cor. 4. 15. Philem. 10. Jam. 1. 18.

By calling them *little children,* he both hints to them that he was their spiritual father, and had begotten them to Christ ; and that they were as yet weak in the faith, not grown men, but as yet little children : and also hints to them, the tender affection he had towards them, which was the same as of a mother to her little children : though they did not own and honour him as their spiritual father, yet he loved them as his *little children. Of whom I travail in birth again ;* for whom I am in as great pain, through my earnest desire for the good of your souls, as the woman is that is in travail for the bringing forth of a child. *Until Christ be* fully and perfectly *formed in you ;* that is, till you be brought off from your Judaism, and opinion of the necessity of superadding the works of the law to the faith of Christ in order to your justification, and be rooted in the truth and established in the liberty of the gospel, with which Christ hath made you free.

20 I desire to be present with you now, and to change my voice ; for ‖ I stand in doubt of you.
‖ Or, *I am perplexed for you.*

I desire to be present with you now ; I wish circumstances so concurred that I could be present with you. *And to change my voice;* that I might use my tongue towards you as I saw occasion ; either commending, or reproving, or exhorting, as I saw cause. *For I stand in doubt of you ;* for I do not know what to think of you ; I am afraid of your falling away from the profession of the gospel to Judaism.

21 Tell me, ye that desire to be under the law, do ye not hear the law ?

Tell me, ye that desire to be under the law; you that cannot be content to receive Jesus Christ alone, for justification ; but have a mind to maintain a necessity of obedience to the law of circumcision, and other Judaical rites ; *do ye not hear the law,* that law which curseth every one who continueth not in all that is therein written to do it ? or rather, the story which follows ; which is taken out of one of the books of the law, which the apostle makes a mystical revelation of the Divine will, that there should come a time when circumcision should be cast out.

22 For it is written, that Abraham had two sons, ^b the one by a bondmaid, ^c the other by a freewoman.
b Gen. 16. 15. c Gen. 21. 2.

The substance of this is written, Gen. xvi., where we read of Abraham's having Ishmael by Hagar his bondwoman ; and Gen. xxi. 2, where we read of the birth of Isaac, whom he had by Sarah, who was his wife.

23 But he *who was* of the bondwoman ^d was born after the flesh ; ^e but he of the freewoman *was* by promise.
d Rom. 9. 7, 8. e Gen. 18. 10, 14. & 21. 1, 2. Heb. 11. 11.

They were both (in a sense) *born after the flesh,* viz. in a natural way and course of generation : but *after the flesh* is plainly, in this verse, opposed to *by promise ;* and the meaning is, that Ishmael, the son of Hagar, was not that son of Abraham to whom the promise was made, that *in him all the nations of the earth should be blessed :* see Gen. xv. 4 ; xvii. 19. Isaac is said to have been born after the *promise,* either because God gave Isaac to Abraham, in completion or fulfilling of the promise made to him, that he should have an heir out of his own loins ; or because the mighty and miraculous power of God was seen in his production, enabling Abraham at those years to beget, and Sarah to bear, a child, when both their bodies were as dead.

24 Which things are an allegory : for these are the two ‖ covenants ; the one from the mount †^fSinai, which gendereth to bondage, which is Agar.
‖ Or, *testaments.* † Gr. *Sina.* f Deut. 33. 2.

Which things are an allegory : that is called *an allegory,* when one thing is learned out of another, or something is mystically signified and to be understood further than is expressed. The Scripture hath a peculiar kind of allegories, wherein one thing is signified by and under another thing. The thing here signifying, was Abraham's wife and concubine, Sarah and Hagar. *For these are* the two covenants; the apostle saith, these signified *the two covenants*, for that is the meaning of *are*: so as here we have one text more where the verb substantive is put for signifieth; and it will be hard to assign a reason why it should not be so interpreted in the institution of the Lord's supper, notwithstanding the papists' and Lutherans' so earnest contending to the contrary. The very word is here used, διαθῆκαι, that is used in the institution of the Lord's supper. Here it is, *these are the two covenants* or testaments; there, *this is the new covenant*. The apostle calls them *two covenants*, (whereas they were but one,) with reference to the time of their exhibition, and manner of their administration, in which they much differed. Nor must we understand the apostle as signifying to us by these words, that Moses wrote the history of Sarah and Hagar with such a design and intention; but only that that history is very applicable to the two covenants, and we shall find, ver. 27, the apostle justifying this application from the authority of the prophet Isaiah. And herein he complied with the general sense of the Jews, who judged that there was not only a literal, but a mystical sense also, of those histories of the patriarchs. *The one from the mount Sinai, which gendereth to bondage, which is Agar*: the one covenant was that of the law delivered from mount Sinai, this was like Hagar; for as Hagar was herself a bondwoman, and so her child did partake of the condition of the mother, and Hagar bare a bondman or servant; so the law (which he calls a covenant, because of the stipulation of obedience from the people to the will of God revealed and declared) left those that were under it in a state of bondage or servitude.

25 For this Agar is mount Sinai in Arabia, and ‖ answereth to Jerusalem which now is, and is in bondage with her children.

‖ Or, *is in the same rank with*.

Agar, the bondwoman, fitly represented *Mount Sinai*, the mountain in Arabia, from which the law was given: and *Jerusalem which now is* answereth to Mount Sinai; for as in Mount Sinai the law was given in a terrible manner, so now Jerusalem is the seat of the scribes and Pharisees, who are the doctors of that law, and rigidly press the observation of it, by which the Jews are kept *in bondage*. The apostle speaketh not here of the civil servitude that the Jews were in under the Romans, to whom they were now tributaries, but of that religious servitude in which the scribes and Pharisees kept them to their legal services.

26 But ᵍ Jerusalem which is above is free, which is the mother of us all.

g Is. 2. 2. Heb. 12. 22. Rev. 3. 12. & 21. 2, 10.

The new covenant, or the dispensation of the gospel, or the Christian church, *which is above*, or from above, which answereth to Sarah, and is said to be *above*, because revealed from heaven by Christ, sent out of the bosom of the Father, not as the law was revealed upon earth, upon Mount Sinai. Hence apostates from the doctrine of the gospel, are said to turn from him who *speaketh from heaven*, Heb. xii. 25. Or else it is said to be *above*, because it is the *assembly of the firstborn written in heaven*, ver. 23: hence the gospel church is called *the heavenly Jerusalem*, ver. 22. Of this gospel church the apostle saith, that it is *free*; i. e. free from the yoke and bondage of the ceremonial law, or from the covenant and curse of the law. Which church, he saith, *is the mother of all* believers, they embracing the same faith, and walking in the same steps; from whence it was easy for the Galatians to conclude their freedom and liberty also from the law.

27 For it is written, ʰ Rejoice, *thou* barren that bearest not; break forth and cry, thou that travailest not: for the desolate hath many more children than she which hath an husband.

h Is. 54. 1.

It is written, Isa. liv. 1. Some think that the apostle doth but allude to that of the prophet; and that the sense of the prophet was only to comfort the Jews, whose city, though it should be for a present time barren, thin of inhabitants, during the time of the Babylonish captivity; yet it should be again replenished with people, and be more populous than other cities. But the apostle seemeth rather to interpret that prophecy, than merely to allude to it; so that verse is one of those prophetical passages about the calling of the Gentiles, of which are many in that prophet. In this sense, the Gentiles are to be understood under the notion of the woman that was *barren* and *desolate*. The church of the Jews is represented under the notion of a woman that had a husband and children. The prophet, by the Spirit of prophecy, calleth upon the Gentiles, that brought forth no children to God, and to whom God was not a husband, to rejoice, and to cry out for joy, for there should be more believers, more children brought forth to God, amongst them, than were amongst the Jews: so as the church of the Gentiles are compared to Sarah, who was a long time barren, but then brought forth the child of the promise, the seed in which all the nations of the earth were to be blessed.

28 Now we, brethren, as Isaac was, are ⁱ the children of promise.

i Acts 3. 25. Rom. 9. 8. ch. 3. 29.

Isaac was the promised seed, Gen. xxi. 12; Rom. ix. 7: the apostle tells the Galatians that the believing Gentiles were *(as Isaac) the children of the promise*. Isaac being born, not by virtue of any procreative virtue in his parents, which was now dead in them, Rom. iv. 19, but by virtue of the promise, and by a power above nature, was a type of the believing Gentiles, who are a spiritual seed, and that seed to whom the promise was made, being the members of Christ by faith: so as the Jews had no reason so much to glory as they did, that Abraham was their father, for those amongst them that believed not were but his carnal seed, believers only were the spiritual seed, *the children of the promise;* to which the believing Gentiles had the same claim with the believing Jews, and a much better than those of them that believed not in Christ.

29 But as then ᵏ he that was born after the flesh persecuted him *that was born* after the Spirit, ¹ even so *it is* now.

k Gen. 21. 9.
l ch. 5. 11. & 6. 12.

As it was in Abraham's time, Ishmael, who was born in a mere carnal and ordinary way of generation, persecuted Isaac, by mocking at him, Gen. xxi. 9, who was born by virtue of the promise, and the mighty power of God, enabling Sarah at those years to conceive, and Abraham to beget a child; *even so it is now*, the carnal seed of Abraham, the Jews, persecute the Christians, which are his spiritual seed. From whence we may observe, that the Holy Ghost accounteth mockings of good people for religion, persecution. So Heb. xi. 36, *Others had trial of cruel mockings;* and we know these were one kind of the sufferings of Christ. By this also the apostle doth both confirm what he had before said, in making Hagar a type of the Jews, and Sarah a type of the Gentiles, the Jews persecuting the seed of Christ, as Hagar's seed persecuted Isaac.

30 Nevertheless what saith ᵐ the Scripture? ⁿ Cast out the bondwoman and her son: for ᵒ the son of the bondwoman shall not be heir with the son of the freewoman.

m ch. 3. 8, 22.
n Gen. 21. 10, 12.
o John 8. 35.

We read, Gen. xxi. 10, that when Sarah saw Ishmael mocking at her son Isaac, she was not able to bear it, but speaketh to her husband Abraham, saying, *Cast out this bondwoman and her son; for the son of this bondwoman shall not be heir with my son, even Isaac*. The principal design of the apostle seems to be, by that type of the ejection of Ishmael out of Abraham's family, to let them know the mind and will of God, 1. Concerning the exclusion of the law from a partnership with Christ and the gospel, in the justification of sinners before God. 2. Concerning the rejection of the Jews, upon the calling of the Gentiles. 3. Concerning the total destruction of the Jewish church and nation, for their persecution of Christ and the Christian church.

31 So then, brethren, we are not children of the bondwoman, ᵖ but of the free.

p John 8. 36. ch. 5. 1, 13.

The church of the Gentiles was not typified in Hagar, but in Sarah; from whence the scope of the apostle is to conclude, that we are not under the law, obliged to Judaical observances, but are freed from them, and are justified by faith in Christ alone, not by the works of the law.

By this conclusion the apostle maketh way for the exhortation in the following chapter, pressing them to stand fast in their liberty.

CHAP. V

Paul exhorteth the Galatians to maintain their Christian liberty, 1, *and showeth that by being circumcised they would forfeit their hopes in Christ,* 2—6. *He disclaimeth the preaching of circumcision himself, and condemneth it in others,* 7—12. *He adviseth them not to abuse their liberty, but to serve one another in love, which comprehendeth th whole law,* 13—15. *The opposition between the flesh and the Spirit,* 16—18: *the works of the flesh,* 19—21; *the fruits of the Spirit,* 22—24. *Advice to walk in the Spirit, and not in vain-glorious emulation,* 25, 26.

a John 8. 32.
Rom. 6. 18.
1 Pet. 2. 16.

STAND fast therefore in ᵃthe liberty wherewith Christ hath made us free, and

b Acts 15. 10.
ch. 2. 4. &
4. 9.

be not entangled again ᵇwith the yoke of bondage.

The *liberty* here spoken of, is a right which a person hath to action, that he may do or forbear the doing of things at his pleasure, as he apprehends them suitable or not, without the let or hinderance of another. This is either in things of a civil nature, or of a spiritual nature. The former is not understood here, for it is none of *the liberty wherewith Christ hath made us free*, for subjects to be free from the lawful commands of princes, or children to be free from the laws of their parents, or servants to be free from the commands of masters. There is hardly any book in the New Testament wherein obedience of this nature, in things that are lawful, is not either exemplified as our duty in Christ and the apostles, or urged by very strong arguments. The *liberty* here, is that freedom from the law, of which the apostle hath been speaking all along this Epistle: from the curse of the moral law, and from the coaction of it; and principally from the ceremonial law contained in ordinances. This is the liberty which Christ hath purchased for us, and in which the apostle willeth all believers to *stand fast;* not being *again entangled with* a *yoke,* which God had taken off from their necks. The apostles, in their synod, Acts xv. 10, had called it *a yoke,* which neither they nor their fathers were able to bear.

c Acts 15. 1.
See Acts 16. 3.

2 Behold, I Paul say unto you, that ᶜif ye be circumcised, Christ shall profit you nothing.

It is manifest that the apostle is speaking here concerning circumcision, looked upon as necessary to justification, now under the gospel state. For under the Old Testament undoubtedly Christ profited the fathers, though circumcised; yea, Christ undoubtedly profited Timothy, even under the gospel, though he was circumcised, Acts xvi. 3, that being done to prevent a scandal, and during a time whilst, for the gaining of the Jews to the Christian faith, the Jewish ceremonies, though dead, were (as it were) kept above ground, unburied for a time. But for men, after a sufficient time indulged them for their satisfaction concerning the abolition of the ceremonial law, still to adhere to it, and religiously to observe the rites of it, as in obedience to a Divine precept, and as necessary, over and above faith in Christ for justification, was indeed to deny Christ, and disclaim his sufficiency to save, who *is able to save to the utmost them that come to God by him,* Heb. vii. 25; and besides whom there is no name given under heaven, by which men can be saved, *neither is there salvation in any other,* Acts iv. 10, 12; and who *is the end of the law for righteousness to every one that believeth,* Rom. x. 4. So that to join any thing with Christ, and faith in him, for the justification of the soul before God, is plainly to deny and disclaim him, and to make him insignificant to us. This Paul affirms with an apostolical authority and gravity, *I Paul say unto you.*

3 For I testify again to every man that

d ch. 3. 10.

is circumcised, ᵈthat he is a debtor to do the whole law.

This must be understood either of the Gentiles only, who were never under any obligation to circumcision, or of such as were circumcised, with an opinion that it was necessary at this time to justification and salvation. Of these the apostle saith, that by this they made themselves *debtors to do the whole law;* they were obliged to one part of the law, they must also be obliged to all the other parts of it. Besides that circumcision was an owning and professing subjection to the whole law; as the receiving the sacrament of baptism is a professed subjecting ourselves to the whole gospel. *Object.* But (may some say) ought not then all Christians to observe the law? *Answ.* 1. Not the ceremonial and political law, which were peculiar to the Jewish church and state. 2. It is one thing to be under an obligation to our utmost to fulfil the law, another thing to acknowledge ourselves debtors to the law. *Object.* But did not the fathers, then, by being circumcised, acknowledge themselves debtors to the law? *Answ.* Yes, they did acknowledge themselves bound to the observation of the law, and to endure (upon the breaking it) the curse of it: but they were discharged from this obligation by believing in the Lord Jesus Christ, who was made a curse for them, that he might redeem them from the curse of the law. But if any disclaimed Christ, (which, whosoever added any thing to his righteousness and to faith in him, as to the justification of the soul, did, as the apostle had said in the former verse,) they laid themselves under an obligation to fulfil the whole law of God, if they would be saved.

4 ᵉChrist is become of no effect unto

e Rom. 9. 31, 32. ch. 2. 21.

you, whosoever of you are justified by the law; ᶠye are fallen from grace.

f Heb. 12. 15.

The word here translated *become of no effect,* is used Rom. iii. 3. By those who *are justified by the law,* are to be understood such as seek or desire to be justified by the law, for actually none is so justified. The sense is, Whoever seeketh to be justified by the works of the law, he disclaimeth the righteousness of Christ; to him Christ's death signifieth nothing, nor is of any virtue at all. For he had told us before, chap. ii. 21, *If righteousness come by the law, then Christ is dead in vain:* and Rom. viii. 3, 4, *What the law could not do, in that it was weak through the flesh, God sending his own Son in the likeness of sinful flesh, and for sin, condemned sin in the flesh; that the righteousness of the law might be fulfilled in us,* &c. The very end of Christ's coming and dying was to supply us with a righteousness, which (apprehended by faith) should be reckoned to us as ours, wherein we might stand before God. Which end of Christ's death had been frustrated, if, through our flesh, there had not been such a weakness or impotency in the law as to justification. So as if any still looked for justification by performance of the law, as such made the death of Christ in vain, because if such a thing could have been done that way there had been no need of Christ's dying; so they also made it, which was not in vain in itself, yet in vain and of no effect to their souls, because Christ would not be a partial cause in the justification of a soul. *Ye are fallen from grace;* and they, by this, renounced the grace of God exhibited in the gospel, and fell from the grace of it. For by *grace* here is not to be understood a state of grace, (from which none can fall totally and finally,) but the grace of the gospel; by which is signified the free love of God in it exhibited, offering Christ to sinners for righteousness.

5 For we through the Spirit ᵍwait for

g Rom. 8. 24, 25.
2 Tim. 4. 8.

the hope of righteousness by faith.

For we; we Christians, who have truly embraced Christ; or, (as others think,) we that are turned from Judaism to Christianity, and so are more concerned in the law, which was not given to the Gentiles, but to us Jews: yet, *through the Spirit,* by the guidance and direction of the Spirit, or through the operation of the Spirit in us, we *wait for the hope of righteousness;* that is, we hope for righteousness; that righteousness whereby we shall be made righteous before God; or, (as some will have it,) the crown of righteousness: I had rather understand it of righteousness itself, that having been all along the argument of the apostle's discourse here. *By faith;* not by our observance of the law, but by faith in Jesus Christ.

6 For ʰin Jesus Christ neither circum-

h 1 Cor. 7. 19.
ch. 3. 28. & 6. 15. Col. 3. 11.
i 1 Thess. 1.
3. Jam. 2. 18, 20, 22.

cision availeth any thing, nor uncircumcision; but ⁱfaith which worketh by love.

Under the new testament established in Christ, and confirmed by the death of Christ, there is no difference betwixt

Jew and Gentile; there is but one way of justification, one of salvation, for them both; and that is, by believing in Christ Jesus; which faith is not an idle, inactive, inoperative faith, but such a *faith* as *worketh by love,* both towards God and towards men, in an obedience to all the commandments of God: yet is not the soul justified, nor shall it stand righteous before God, in and for this obedience, which neither is faith, nor goeth before it, but followeth it, as the true, proper, and necessary effect of it.

7 Ye [k] did run well; [l] ‖ who did hinder you that ye should not obey the truth?

This was once your faith, your profession, and according to this you directed the course of your life and actions; who hath hindered you in your course, or turned you out of your way, or given you a check in your race; and hath made you disobedient to, or to swerve from, the truth which you formerly owned and professed.

8 This persuasion *cometh* not of him [m] that calleth you.

This persuasion; this new opinion into which seducers have misled you, which, by embracing it, you have made yours. *Cometh not of him that calleth you;* is not from God, who hath called you out of darkness into marvellous light, unto fellowship with himself, into a state of grace and favour with him, and to the hopes of eternal life; and who yet calleth you by his gospel: it must therefore be from the devil and his instruments, who go about to seduce and pervert you.

9 [n] A little leaven leaveneth the whole lump.

This is a proverbial expression, which (as others of that nature) is applicable in more cases than one. The apostle made use of it, 1 Cor. v. 6, to persuade that church to purge their communion, by casting out the incestuous person: he maketh use of it here to persuade them to take heed of admitting any principles of false doctrine, which he compareth to leaven, (as our Saviour does, Matt. xvi. 6, 12.) and that very fitly, both in regard of the sour and of the diffusive nature of it; the latter of which is here chiefly intended; the truths of God having such dependence one upon another, that he who erreth in any one doctrine of faith, seldom continueth long sound as to other points.

10 [o] I have confidence in you through the Lord, that ye will be none otherwise minded: but [p] he that troubleth you [q] shall bear his judgment, whosoever he be.

I have confidence in you through the Lord, that ye will be none otherwise minded: the apostle (according to his usual method) sweeteneth his sharp reproof of this church for their deviations from the faith of the gospel, with a declaration of his good opinion of them; declaring that he had a confidence in them, that through the grace of God they would be reduced to the truth, or kept from wandering from it, and that in matters of faith they would be all of the same mind. *But he that troubleth you shall bear his judgment, whosoever he be;* and for those who endeavoured to seduce and pervert them, God should reward them according to their works. He seems to aim at some particular false teacher, (whose name he concealeth,) who gave this church this trouble.

11 [r] And I, brethren, if I yet preach circumcision, [s] why do I yet suffer persecution? then is [t] the offence of the cross ceased.

It should seem by what the apostle saith in this verse, that some of these false teachers had quoted the apostle for them, as if he himself had preached circumcision; possibly taking advantage from his circumcising Timothy, not distinguishing betwixt what was done by Paul as of liberty, and to avoid the offence of the Jews, and what they pressed as necessary to be done (besides believing in Christ) for justification. Now, (saith the apostle,) *if I yet preach* up *circumcision* as necessary to be observed, *why do I yet suffer persecution?* why am I then persecuted by the Jews, as one apostatized from their religion? *Then is the offence of the cross ceased:* by *the cross,* he either means the cross of Christ; then the sense is, It is my opposing the observance of their law, that more offendeth them than my preaching of Christ crucified. Or else he meaneth the afflictions which he suffered for the sake of Christ and the gospel; (in which sense the term is used, Matt. xvi. 24; Luke ix. 23; xiv. 27;) then the sense is, that all sufferings for the owning and preaching of Christ are at an end; let us but yield the Jews that point, (that Christians are obliged to the observance of the law of Moses,) the great quarrel between them and us is at an end; but their daily persecuting of me is a sufficient demonstration that I do not preach up circumcision.

12 [u] I would they were even cut off [x] which trouble you.

I wish that God would some way or other put an end to these that trouble you. This Paul speaketh not out of hatred to their persons, but out of a zeal to the glory of God, and a just indignation against these men, who had so much hindered the salvation of the members of this church. And it is not improbable that the apostle here spake by the Spirit of prophecy, as knowing God would cut them off; so that his and the like imprecations of holy men in Scripture are not to be drawn into precedents, or made matters for our imitation, unless we had the same discerning of spirits which they had, or the same Spirit of prophecy and revelations from God as to future things. But how far it is lawful or unlawful for ordinary persons, whether ministers or private Christians, to pray against God's or his church's enemies, is a question for the arguing which this place is too narrow.

13 For, brethren, ye have been called unto liberty; only [y] *use* not liberty for an occasion to the flesh, but [z] by love serve one another.

Ye have been called unto liberty; a liberty from the covenant of the law, and the curse of the law, as chap. iii. 13; from servile fear, as Luke i. 74; and from sin, Rom. vi. 7. *Only use not liberty for an occasion to the flesh;* but you must take heed that you do not abuse this liberty by making it an occasion for sin, so as from thence to conclude, that you may give your flesh more liberty in obeying the lusts of it: you must not think, that the gospel hath set you at liberty from the obedience of the law; the gospel liberty to which you are called, doth not set you free from the duty of love, either to God or men. Therefore *by love serve one another.* Our Christian liberty neither freeth us from the serving of God, nor from our mutual serving each other by love, according to Rom. xiii. 8, *Owe no man any thing, but to love one another.*

14 For [a] all the law is fulfilled in one word, *even* in this; [b] Thou shalt love thy neighbour as thyself.

The whole will of God, containing our duty towards men, is reducible to this one thing, *love;* for whatsoever God hath commanded us to do towards men, is but a branch from this root, and must flow from love as its principle. Or, the whole will of God concerning man is fulfilled in this one thing of love; where love to God is not excluded, but supposed, as the root of our love to our neighbour; for our neighbour is to be loved for God. Thus Rom. xiii. 8, *He that loveth another hath fulfilled the law:* and 1 John iv. 20, the apostle proveth, that a man cannot love God unless he loveth his brother: and 1 Tim. i. 5, *The end of the commandment is charity.* Yet what the papists would conclude from hence, (viz. that it is possible for a man to fulfil the law because it is possible for him to love his neighbour,) doth by no means follow; for the apostle (1 Tim. i. 5) telleth us, this love must proceed *out of a pure heart, and of a good conscience, and of faith unfeigned.* Mr. Calvin observeth well, that the apostle here mentioneth love to men as the fulfilling of the law, in opposition to the false teachers; who made the fulfilling of the law to lie in the observance of the ceremonies of the law, whereas the great thing which the law of God requireth is *love, out of a pure heart, good conscience, and faith unfeigned.* So that he who believeth with a faith unfeigned, and, out of that principle, with a pure heart and a good conscience, loveth his neighbour as himself, shall be by God accounted to have fulfilled the law; for love is the end of the law.

15 But if ye bite and devour one another, take heed that ye be not consumed one of another.

This lets us know, that there were great contentions and divisions amongst the members of this church, whether (which is probable) occasioned by their differences in and about the doctrine of justification, or upon other accounts, we are not told; but upon whatever account they were raised, they were contrary to that serving one another in love, to which the apostle had exhorted them. Nor did they terminate in a mere dislike of and displacency to each other, but broke out into overt acts, more becoming dogs than Christians, and therefore it is expressed under the notion of biting and devouring. The issue of which, the apostle prophesieth, would be a consuming one another; they being actions that had a natural tendency to this end.

16 *This* I say then, [c]Walk in the Spirit, and || ye shall not fulfil the lust of the flesh.

Walk in the Spirit; the apostle having, ver. 13, cautioned them against turning the grace of God into wantonness, by using their liberty as an occasion to the flesh; here he directeth them to the best means for the avoiding thereof, viz. *walking in the Spirit.* Where by *Spirit* he doth not mean our own spirits, or the guide and conduct of our own reason; for the term *Spirit,* set (as here) in opposition to the *flesh,* is in no place of Scripture understood of any other than the Holy Spirit of God, which dwelleth in and influenceth believers, guiding them both by a rule from without, (which is the word of God, given by its inspiration,) and by its inward motions and operations. Walking, signifieth the directing of their whole conversations. The phrases *in the Spirit,* and *after the Spirit,* Rom. viii. 1, seem to be of the same import, unless the alteration of the preposition signifieth, that Christians are not only to look to the word of God dictated by the Holy Spirit as their rule, and to listen to its dictates, but also to look up to the Holy Spirit for its strength and assistance; and implieth a promise of such assistance. The sense is, Let your whole conversation be according to the external rule of the gospel, and the more inward motions, directions, and inclinations of the Spirit of Christ, dwelling and working in you, and moving you to the obedience of that word. *And ye shall not fulfil the lust of the flesh;* this doing, though the flesh be yet in you, and you will find the lustings and warrings of it, yet you shall not fulfil the sinful desires and lustings of it; that is, sin, though it be in you, shall not be in dominion in you; it shall not reign in your mortal bodies: Rom. vi. 12, *Let not sin reign in your mortal body, that ye should obey it in the lusts thereof.*

17 For [d]the flesh lusteth against the Spirit, and the Spirit against the flesh: and these are contrary the one to the other: [e]so that ye cannot do the things that ye would.

By *the flesh* and *the Spirit,* we cannot so much understand the sensitive and rational appetite; for these two appetites are not so contrary, but that in many things they agree well enough; and we are enemies not only in our sensitive part, to spiritual things, but ἐν τῇ διανοίᾳ, in our mind and rational part also, Col. i. 21. And some of the *works of the flesh,* which are afterward mentioned, ver. 19—21, (such as *idolatry, heresies,* &c.,) cannot be referred to the sensitive part. But by these terms are either to be understood the unregenerate part of man; or rather, that carnal concupiscence which we derived from Adam, and is seated in our rational as well as sensitive appetite; which opposeth itself to the Divine rule, and to the dictates and motions of the Spirit of God. *The flesh lusteth against the Spirit;* this concupiscence moveth strongly against the directions of the Spirit. *And the Spirit against the flesh;* and the Holy Spirit of God, dwelling in the saints, moveth us potently against the propensions and inclinations of the flesh. *And these are contrary the one to the other;* for they are two contrary principles, and work contrarily in their motions and inclinations. *So that ye cannot do the things that ye would;* so that even the best of God's people cannot at all times do either what they should do, (according to the precept of the word,) or what they would do, according to the bent of their regenerate part.

18 But [f]if ye be led of the Spirit, ye are not under the law.

To be *led of the Spirit,* and to *walk in the Spirit,* are the same thing; and differ only as the cause and the effect. To be *under the law,* is to be under the curse of it, or coaction of it, and an obligation to the performance of the ceremonial law. The reason is, because the Spirit is a Spirit of adoption and liberty; and where it is, it teacheth to serve the Lord without fear from a principle of freedom and ingenuity.

19 Now [g]the works of the flesh are manifest, which are *these;* Adultery, fornication, uncleanness, lasciviousness,

The works of the flesh; the products of the natural inclinations and propensions in the heart of man. *Are manifest, which are these;* he saith, these are *manifest,* the filthiness of them appears by the light of nature, by the checks of conscience men meet with for them; or else, it is *manifest* that these actions are not from the Spirit of God, (because of their contrariety to the Divine rule,) but are from the corrupt part of man. These (he saith) are *adultery,* or the defiling of our neighbour's bed; *fornication,* which is the uncleanness of single persons each with other; and all other species of *uncleanness,* or unclean conjunctions: *lasciviousness;* whatsoever wanton carriage, gestures, or behaviour lead to these acts.

20 Idolatry, witchcraft, hatred, variance, emulations, wrath, strife, seditions, heresies,

Idolatry; either the worshipping of the creature for God, or the worshipping of God in and by the creature, as by images, &c. *Witchcraft;* the product of compacts with the devil; by virtue of which, the persons so contracting are assisted by the power of evil spirits to produce effects beside the ordinary course and order of nature, and for the most part mischievous to others. And not these gross crimes only are the fruits of the flesh, but also abiding *hatred* of our brethren in our hearts, enmities to others, as the word signifieth. The result of which are, *variance;* men's quarrellings and contendings one with another for little or no cause: *emulations;* people's endeavouring to hinder others of such good things as they see them desirous of: *wrath;* heats and immoderate passions of men one against another: *strife;* a continual readiness and proneness to quarrelling: *seditions;* dividing into parties, which in the state is called sedition, in the church, schism: *heresies;* that is, differing and false opinions in the grand doctrine of religion.

21 Envyings, murders, drunkenness, revellings, and such like: of the which I tell you before, as I have also told *you* in time past, that [h]they which do such things shall not inherit the kingdom of God.

Envyings; repinings at that good which is enjoyed by our brethren: *murders;* unjust taking away the lives of others, with any actions tending or subservient thereunto: *drunkenness;* immoderate drinkings: *revellings, and such like;* immoderate eatings; all abuses of the creatures of God beyond necessity, or a moderate delight. *Of the which I tell you before;* I tell you of it before the day of judgment comes, when you will find that which I tell you to be truth. *As I have also told you in time past;* as you know I have in my preaching to you told you in times past told you. *That they which do such things shall not inherit the kingdom of God;* that they who ordinarily do these things, and do not only live in such practices, but die without repentance for them, shall never be saved; see 1 Cor. vi. 9, 10; Rev. xxi. 7, 8.

22 But [i]the fruit of the Spirit is love, joy, peace, longsuffering, [k]gentleness, [l]goodness, [m]faith,

The fruit of the Spirit; those habits which the Holy Spirit of God produceth in those in whom it dwelleth and worketh, with those acts which flow from them, as naturally as the tree produceth its fruit, are, *love* to God, and to our neighbours: *joy;* the soul's satisfaction in its union with God, as the greatest and highest good; with an actual rejoicing in Christ, and in what is for his honour and glory, called a rejoicing in the truth, 1 Cor. xiii. 6 ; and in the good of our brethren, Rom. xii. 15 : *peace;* quietude of conscience, or peace with God, (of which peace of conscience is a copy,) and a peaceable disposition towards men, opposed to strife, variance, emulations, &c. : *long-suffering;* opposed to a hastiness to revenge, and inclining us patiently to bear injuries: *gentleness;* sweetness and kindness of temper, by which we accommodate ourselves, and become mutually useful to each other : *goodness;* a disposition in us to hurt none, but to do all the good we can to all : *faith;* by *faith* seemeth here to be meant, truth in words, faithfulness in promises, and in dealings one with another.

n 1 Tim. 1. 9.

23 Meekness, temperance : [n] against such there is no law.

Meekness; forbearance of passion, rash anger, and hastiness of spirit : *temperance;* a sober use of meats, drinks, apparel, or any thing wherein our senses are delighted. Many of these are moral virtues, and such as some have attained to by moral discipline, the cultivating of their natures by education, and moral philosophy : yet they are also the fruits of the Spirit of God ; such as it doth always work in the souls wherein it dwelleth (though in different measures and degrees) : only the moral man thus comporteth himself from principles of reason, showing him the beauty and comeliness of such a conversation, and aims no higher in it, than a happiness of converse in this life, his own honour and reputation. But the spiritual man, doing the same things, aimeth at a higher end (the glorifying of God, and saving his own soul) ; and doth these things from a fear of God, out of love to him, and out of faith, as seeing in them the will of God. *Against such* (saith the apostle) *there is no law; no law* to accuse or to condemn them ; for these are things which the law commandeth to be done, and are acts of obedience to the law. So as those who do these things are *led by the Spirit,* and are not under the condemning power or curse of the law.

o Rom. 6. 6. & 13. 14. ch. 2. 20. 1 Pet. 2. 11. ‖ Or, *passions.*

24 And they that are Christ's [o] have crucified the flesh with the ‖ affections and lusts.

They that are Christ's; those who are ingrafted into Christ by faith, united to him, and so his members ; *have crucified the flesh;* by virtue of a power derived from the cross of Christ, have got their unregenerate part in a great measure mortified ; *with the affections and lusts;* with the inordinate desires, affections, and passions of it : not that they have wholly put off these, (they are men still,) but the inordinateness of them is corrected, mortified, and subdued.

p Rom. 8. 4. 5. ver. 16.

25 [p] If we live in the Spirit, let us also walk in the Spirit.

If we live in the Spirit; if (as we profess) there is a union betwixt the Holy Spirit of God and us, so as that Holy Spirit is to us the principle of our life, and we live more from him than from any principle in ourselves ; *let us also walk in the Spirit;* let us manage all our conversation according to the guidance and direction of the same Spirit. Operations naturally follow the principle of life from which they proceed, so that as those who only live in the flesh, walk in and after the flesh, and its inclination ; so those who live in the Spirit ought to produce, and will produce, effects suitable to the cause of them, and the principle from which they flow.

q Phil. 2. 3.

26 [q] Let us not be desirous of vain glory, provoking one another, envying one another.

Let us not be desirous of vain-glory: ambition or vainglory is a natural corruption, disposing us to boast and commend ourselves, and to seek the honour and applause of men. *Provoking one another;* this is an effect of the former, disposing us, out of hope of victory, to challenge others to a contest with us. Or it may be understood of provoking others by injuries and wrongs done them ; which is contrary to the duty of love. *Envying one another;* not repining at the good of others ; either desiring their portion, or being troubled that they fare so well. Possibly this verse might more properly have been made the first of the next chapter, (as Luther maketh it,) where the apostle goeth on, pressing further spiritual duties common to all Christians.

CHAP. VI

Paul adviseth them to reform the faulty with gentleness, 1, *and to bear one another's burdens,* 2. *A caution against vanity,* 3—5. *He exhorteth to be liberal toward spiritual instructors,* 6—8; *and not to be weary in doing good,* 9—11. *He showeth the carnal views of those who preached circumcision,* 12, 13, *and his own professed dependence on Christ only, regardless of the world,* 14—17. *He concludeth with a prayer,* 18.

BRETHREN, [a] ‖ if a man be overtaken in a fault, ye [b] which are spiritual, restore such an one [c] in the spirit of meekness ; considering thyself, [d] lest thou also be tempted.

a Rom. 14. 1. & 15. 1. Heb. 12. 13. Jam. 5. 19. ‖ Or, *although.* b 1 Cor. 2. 15. & 3. 1. c 1 Cor. 4. 21. 2 Thes. 3. 15. 2 Tim. 2. 25. d 1 Cor. 7. 5. & 10. 12.

In the term *brethren,* there is a secret argument persuading the duty which he is pressing, because Christians, particularly members of the same church, are all brethren. By persons *overtaken in a fault,* he means such as do not make a trade of open and scandalous sinning, (for such must be rebuked sharply,) but such as may be sometimes through infirmity overborne, and run down with a temptation to sin. By those *that are spiritual,* he means not only the pastors and governors of the church, (though this care and duty is much incumbent upon them,) but such as have received the Spirit of Christ ; more especially such as were more knowing in the ways of God, and had spiritual habits more confirmed in them ; in which sense *spiritual* is used in 1 Cor. iii. 1. *Restore such an one in the spirit of meekness:* the word translated *restore,* signifies to put again into joint, or into right order and place. Sin is an inordinate action, and putteth the soul that committeth it out of its due order and place. He willeth the brethren that are spiritual to use all due means to put such a member in joint again, but not to do this roughly, and with passion, and severe correption, but meekly, so as may be most probable to win the sinner's soul. *Considering thyself, lest thou also be tempted;* having an eye and respect to themselves, as neither being free from sin, nor from temptations to sin, dealing with others as they would have others deal by them.

2 [e] Bear ye one another's burdens, and so fulfil [f] the law of Christ.

e Rom. 15. 1. ch. 5. 13. 1 Thes. 5. 14. f John 13. 14, 15, 34. & 15. 12. Jam. 2. 8. 1 John 4. 21.

Bear ye one another's burdens; it is a general precept, and may be either understood with reference to what he had said in the former verse, so it hints our duty : though we discern our brethren to have fallen into some sin or error, yet if we discern that they are sensible of their lapse, and their sin is not a pleasure, but a burden to them, though we ought not to bear with them or connive at them in their sins, yet we ought to sympathize with them when we see their sin is become their load and burden, under which they groan and are dejected. Or else more generally, as a new precept commanding us to sympathize with our brethren under any load of trials and affliction which God shall lay upon them. And so it agreeth with that precept, Rom. xii. 15. By *the law of Christ,* he means the will of Christ revealed in the gospel ; particularly the law of love, so much enjoined by Christ, John xiii. 15, 33—35 ; xv. 12. Which is not called the law of Christ because first given by him, (for himself maketh it the sum of the ten commandments,) but because he received it and vindicated it from the corruption of the Pharisees' interpretation, Matt. v. 43, 44 ; because he so often urged it, and so seriously commanded and commended it to his disciples ; and set us the highest precedent and example of it, and hath by his Spirit written it in the hearts of his people.

3 For [g] if a man think himself to be something, when [h] he is nothing, he deceiveth himself.

g Rom. 12. 3. 1 Cor. 8. 2. ch. 2. 6. h 2 Cor. 3. 5. & 12. 11.

It is a general maxim, and the truth of it is obvious to every one that readeth it, for supposing a man to be *nothing* of what he thinks himself to be, he must needs *deceive himself* in nourishing and entertaining such an opinion of himself. For the dependence of it upon what the apostle had said before, it is obvious. Pride, and men's high opinions of themselves above what they ought, are the cause of their censoriousness and morosity in dealing with other offenders; which modesty would not suffer in them, if they apprehended themselves to be as weak, and as much exposed to temptations, as others are. It is pride and overweening opinions of ourselves, that make us despise or neglect others under their burdens, and so forget the law of Christ; the apostle therefore properly addeth this precept for humility and modesty to those former precepts.

<small>i 1 Cor. 11. 28. 2 Cor. 13. 5.
k See Luke 18. 11.</small>
4 But ¹ let every man prove his own work, and then shall he have rejoicing in himself alone, and ᵏ not in another.

Let every man prove his own work: the apostle, by a man's *own work* here, understands his own actions and manners, which he would have every man to busy himself to search, try, and examine by the Divine rule, whether they be conformable to the will of God, yea or no; *and then*, he saith, *shall he have rejoicing in himself alone, and not in another ;* a man shall (if he findeth his work such as is agreeable to the will of God) have a cause to rejoice in himself; not in the merit or perfection of his works, but in his own works; not in others; that is, he shall rejoice in something which God hath wrought in and by him, and not in others. This the apostle wisely propounds, as a means to bring a man to know his own measures; it being a great error for men to measure themselves by the measures of other men, their perfections by others' imperfections.

<small>l Rom. 2. 6.
1 Cor. 3. 8.</small>
5 For ˡ every man shall bear his own burden.

That is, God will judge every man in the last day, according not to what others have done, but to what he himself hath done, 1 Cor. iii. 8. Therefore every one is concerned to *prove his own work;* for at last his eternal joy and rejoicing, or sorrow and mourning, shall be according to what he himself hath wrought, not according to what others have wrought. If ever they enter into the joy of heaven, they shall rejoice in their own work. And if eternal sorrow be their portion, they shall groan under their own burdens; they will not be the sins of others, but their own sins, which will sink them into eternal misery. For though superiors shall answer to God for the sins of their inferiors, yet it shall not properly be for their inferiors' sins, but for their own sins, in neglecting to warn and to reprove them, and to do what in them lay to have hindered them in their sinful courses.

<small>m Rom. 15. 27.
1 Cor. 9. 11, 14.</small>
6 ᵐ Let him that is taught in the word communicate unto him that teacheth in all good things.

Let him that is taught in the word: the word here translated *taught*, signifieth catechised; and is the same word from which that word is derived; but it here signifieth *taught*, catechising being but a mode or species of teaching. *Communicate unto him that teacheth in all good things;* the precept is concerning the maintenance of ministers, which is fitly expressed by the term *communicate*, because as the people distribute to their ministers things temporal, so the ministers distribute things spiritual. The *good things* here mentioned are temporal good things, such as may be useful to the teacher for him to uphold himself and family. The text teacheth us, that it is the will of God that ministers should be maintained at the charge of the church to which they minister, and it is but an act of justice, for they do but communicate temporal things to those who communicate to them much more valuable things.

<small>n 1 Cor. 6. 9. & 15. 33.
o Job 13. 9.
p Luke 16. 25. Rom. 2. 6. 2 Cor. 9. 6.</small>
7 ⁿ Be not deceived; ᵒ God is not mocked: for ᵖ whatsoever a man soweth, that shall he also reap.

Be not deceived; God is not mocked: the apostle addeth this to terrify those who find out vain and false excuses to save their purses; he adviseth them not to cheat themselves, for though they might deceive men, yet they could not deceive the all-seeing and heart-searching God. *For whatsoever a man soweth, that shall he also reap ;* further to encourage them to this communicating, he mindeth them, that what they distributed in this nature, was no more lost than the seed is which the husbandman casteth into the ground; which in its season springs up, and returneth into the husbandman's hand with increase. This metaphor of sowing is made use of also, Prov. xi. 18; 2 Cor. ix. 6, to express men's actions; and lets us know, that our actions, when done, are not done with; but as our bodies shall rise again, so what we have done in the flesh shall be revived and judged; whatsoever, either for quantity or for quality, men sow, the same shall they reap: as to quantity, he had said in 2 Cor. ix. 6, that he who *soweth sparingly should reap sparingly*, and he who *soweth bountifully* should *reap bountifully :* as to quality, he here further addeth,

<small>q Job 4. 8.
Prov. 11. 18. & 22. 8.
Hos. 8. 7. & 10. 12.
Rom. 8. 13.
Jam. 3. 18.</small>
8 ᑫ For he that soweth to his flesh shall of the flesh reap corruption ; but he that soweth to the Spirit shall of the Spirit reap life everlasting.

For he that soweth to his flesh ; he that layeth out his estate, or spendeth his time and talents, for the gratifying of the flesh; *shall of the flesh reap corruption ;* shall or may reap some carnal satisfaction, of a corruptible, dying, perishing nature. *But he that soweth to the Spirit ;* but he who layeth out his estate, or spendeth his time, strength, talents, whatsoever God hath given him, for the glory of God, in obedience to the commands, motions, and dictates of the Spirit, or the revelations of the Divine will; *shall of the Spirit reap life everlasting ;* he shall not of merit, but of grace from the Spirit, reap everlasting life, reward, and satisfaction. So that as in the world, that man doth not suffer loss that layeth out his money, time, or strength about good things of a valuable and enduring nature; but he only who layeth them out about things perishing, and transitory, and of a corruptible nature : so that man shall not lose his estate that layeth it out for the maintenance of the gospel, and upholding the ministry of it ; for he *soweth to the Spirit,* and shall thereof reap eternal life and salvation : he only loseth his estate, &c., who spendeth it to gratify his lusts, and please his flesh, for all the return which he shall have, will be in poor, sensible, perishing good things, which perish with the using, and will be of no significancy to him beyond this life.

<small>r 2 Thess. 3. 13.
1 Cor. 15. 58.
s Mat. 24. 13.
Heb. 3. 6, 14.
& 10. 36. & 12. 3, 5. Rev. 2. 10.</small>
9 And ʳ let us not be weary in well doing : for in due season we shall reap, ˢ if we faint not.

Let us not be weary in well doing : we have the same precept, 2 Thess. iii. 13. As the not executing of judgment speedily imboldens sinners, and encourageth them to go on in courses of sin, so God's delaying the rewards of the righteous, often proveth a temptation to good men to be weary of well doing. Against this the apostle cautioneth us here, by minding us, that there is a *due season* for all things (which is best known to the wise God); and assuring us, that though, as we see not the husbandman presently reaping as soon as he hath sown, but waiting patiently in hope that in a due season he shall reap ; so we, though we be not presently rewarded, yet in God's season shall as certainly reap as he doth. But he also mindeth us, that if we will reap we must not *faint*, but go on and persevere in our course of well doing ; otherwise we can no more expect to reap. than the husbandman can that hath sown well, but out of impatience, before the time cometh for him to reap, shall go and plough up again all that he hath sown : see Ezek. xxxiii. 13.

<small>t John. 9. 4. & 12. 35.
u 1 Thess. 5. 15. 1 Tim. 6. 18. Tit. 3. 8.
x Eph. 2. 19. Heb. 3. 6.</small>
10 ᵗ As we have therefore opportunity, ᵘ let us do good unto all *men*, especially unto them who are of ˣ the household of faith.

As we have therefore opportunity ; as we have objects before us, or as God gives us time and ability. *Let us do good unto all men ;* let it be our business to harm none, but to supply the necessities of all men ; either with our spiritual advice and counsels, with all the assistance we can give them that may any way be of spiritual profit or advantage to them ; or with our worldly goods, ministering to their necessities. *Especially unto them who are of the household of faith ;* but all in an order, preferring Christians before others ; those that belong to the church, (which is called *the house of God*, 1 Tim. iii. 15; 1 Pet. iv. 17, and *the household of God*, Eph. ii. 19,) before such as have no such relation to the church.

11 Ye see how large a letter I have written unto you with mine own hand.

Paul made use of the hands of others in the writing some others of the Epistles, as appears from Rom. xvi. 22, and sometimes he himself only wrote the salutation, 1 Cor. xvi. 21: but he tells them he wrote this Epistle to them wholly with his own hand, that he might thereby more commend his love to them and care over them.

12 As many as desire to make a fair
y ch. 2. 3, 14. shew in the flesh, ʸ they constrain you to
z Phil. 3. 18. be circumcised; ᶻ only lest they should
a ch. 5. 11. ᵃ suffer persecution for the cross of Christ.

The apostle here reflecteth upon those false teachers who had perverted this church, and discovereth their hypocrisy under all their pretences of good will to them. These are those who (he saith) desired *to make a fair show in the flesh*; that is, to make a fair show to the world, as men very devout, which formalists and persons over-zealous for rituals ordinarily do. These would *constrain*, were very urgent to persuade, these believers *to be circumcised*; not out of any love they had to the law of God, or to the souls of these Galatians, but *only* to avoid *persecution*; for as the Jews were more favourable to such Christians, who, together with the doctrine of Christ, observed also their rites and legal ceremonies; so we are told by some of the ancients, that some of the Roman emperors, by their edicts, gave liberty to the Jews, in the provinces subject to them, to use their own religious rites: now all who were circumcised went under that notion, so had more liberty than those who were not circumcised, who were persecuted both by the Jewish and the heathen magistrates. The apostle saith, that these false teachers, who so zealously urged circumcision upon this Gentile church, did it for the avoiding the danger of persecution; which they saw would follow their standing fast in their gospel liberty, and not bringing themselves under the law: which persecution, he tacitly hinteth, ought not to be so industriously shunned and avoided, because it was for Christ's sake, who had endured the cross for them.

13 For neither they themselves who are circumcised keep the law; but desire to have you circumcised, that they may glory in your flesh.

In this the hypocrisy of your false teachers discovereth itself, that whereas, by their being circumcised, they had declared themselves debtors to the whole law, and under an obligation entirely to keep it if they would be saved, yet they themselves did not keep it; only they were very zealous for this one thing, not out of any love they had to the law, but that they might glory of you, as their converts, being by them persuaded to be circumcised.

b Phil. 3. 3, 7, 8. 14 ᵇ But God forbid that I should
glory, save in the cross of our Lord Jesus
|| Or, *whereby*. Christ, || by whom the world is ᶜ crucified
c Rom. 6. 6. ch. 2. 20. unto me, and I unto the world.

For my part I have no such ends, I have no ambition to glory in you as my converts; all that I desire to glory in, is in the doctrine of the gospel, and my sufferings for the propagation of it, and my conformity to Christ in suffering for preaching the gospel. By the cross of Christ *the world is crucified unto me, and I unto the world*; I care no more for the world than it careth for me; the world despiseth and contemneth me, and the doctrine of the cross which I preach and publish in it, and I contemn it, with all its vain pomp and splendour. And this I do through the *cross of Christ*, remembering how the world dealt with Christ, and how little he regarded the world: or, through the grace of Christ, who hath enabled me to it, for the particle translated *by whom*, may be indifferently translated by whom or by which.

d 1 Cor. 7. 19. ch. 5. 6. Col. 3. 11. 15 For ᵈ in Christ Jesus neither circumcision availeth any thing, nor uncircumcision, but ᵉ a new creature.
e 2 Cor. 5. 17.

Under the gospel state as settled by Christ, with reference to salvation, it is of no moment whether a man be a Jew or a Gentile; but whether a man be regenerated or no, and be renewed by the Holy Ghost, so as old things with him be passed away, and all things be become new. He had said the same, chap. iii. 28; v. 6. See also 2 Cor. v. 17. Under the law, indeed, there was something in circumcision, as it was God's covenant in the flesh to that people to whom he gave it, and the uncircumcised were strangers to the covenants of promise, and aliens to the church of God; but under the gospel, circumcision and uncircumcision are of no significancy; God neither regardeth any for the former, nor rejecteth any for the latter, he only looketh at the heart and inward man, whether that be renewed and sanctified, yea or no.

16 ᶠ And as many as walk ᵍ according f Ps. 125. 5. g Phil. 3. 16.
to this rule, peace *be* on them, and mercy, h Rom. 2. 29. & 4. 12. & 9.
and upon ʰ the Israel of God. 6, 7, 8. ch. 3. 7, 9, 29. Phil. 3. 3.

And as many as walk according to this rule; he either meaneth the rule of Scripture, the whole word of God; or the doctrine which he had taught them throughout this Epistle, or what he had said in the words immediately going before, where the apostle had given them this rule, not to regard either circumcision or uncircumcision, or any thing in the flesh, but only the change of their hearts. To these he either prophesieth *peace and mercy*, or he prayeth *peace and mercy* for them; under which large terms he comprehendeth all good things, whether internal or external. *Upon the Israel of God*; upon the true Israelites, whom he calleth *the Israel of God*; hereby intimating and confirming the truth of what he had said, Rom. ii. 28, 29, and what our Saviour had said of Nathanael, John i. 47, calling him *an Israelite indeed*, because in him was *no guile*; and establishing a distinction between such as were so really, and those who were only Israelites in name, because descended from Jacob, to whom God gave the name of Israel. Hereby also checking the vanity of the Jews, who gloried in the name of Israelites, and thought there could no water come out of the fountains of Israel which God would cast away. The apostle doth not promise, or prophesy, mercy and peace to all Israelites, but only to the Israel of God; that is, to believers, that received and embraced Jesus Christ offered in the gospel.

17 From henceforth let no man trouble i 2 Cor. 1. 5.
me: for ⁱ I bear in my body the marks of & 4. 10. & 11. 23. ch. 5. 11.
the Lord Jesus. Col. 1. 24.

Let no man trouble me, either with questions about circumcision, or with imputations as if I were a friend to their opinion, of the necessity of adding to the doctrine of faith, circumcision and other observances of the law. *For I bear in my body the marks of the Lord Jesus*; I sufficiently declare my judgment to the world, suffering for my profession, and preaching the gospel. These sufferings he calls *the marks of the Lord Jesus*, because he endured them in testimony to the gospel, as well against the Jews as against the Gentiles.

18 Brethren, ᵏ the grace of our Lord k 2 Tim. 4. 22. Philem.
Jesus Christ *be* with your spirit. Amen. 25.

The apostle closeth this Epistle with this prayer, as he generally concludeth all his Epistles, with wishing them grace, *the grace of our Lord Jesus Christ*; under which he comprehendeth all the effects of the free love of God upon believers' souls, for the sake, in and in and through the merits, of the Lord Jesus Christ: this he prayeth that they might feel in their hearts, and that it might be in their spirits, to quicken, strengthen, comfort, and establish them, according to the different manifestations of the Spirit of grace.

¶ Unto the Galatians written from Rome.

It hath been said before, that we are not to look upon these dates of apostolical Epistles as part of holy writ, for in some of them there are manifest mistakes; but most think that this Epistle was written from Rome, while Paul was a prisoner there, who are in part guided to it from ver. 17, thinking that it was written at a time when Paul was there suffering imprisonment. But of this there is no certainty.

THE EPISTLE OF PAUL THE APOSTLE

TO THE

EPHESIANS

THE ARGUMENT

EPHESUS was the most considerable city of the lesser Asia; famous, first for sin, witchcraft, Acts xix. 19, idolatry (especially the worship of Diana, ver. 24,) and persecution, 1 Cor. xv. 32; xvi. 9; then for piety, having received the gospel by Paul's preaching, Acts xviii., and showed great zeal, Acts xix. 17, 18, &c.; Rev. ii. 2, 3; but, lastly, it was noted for coolness and declining, Rev. ii. 4, leaving her *first love*. The apostle seems to have foreseen this as like to come to pass among them by means of false teachers, *grievous wolves* that would not spare the flock, Acts xx. 29, and some that would arise from among themselves *speaking perverse things*, ver. 30. Hereupon he not only admonished the elders of the church to look to themselves and all the flock, ver. 28; but afterward, when a prisoner at Rome, out of his care of these Ephesians, and concern for them, he writes this Epistle to them, to confirm and settle them in the faith they had received, and persuade them to a holy conversation, as best suited to a holy gospel. In the Epistle there are two principal parts: 1. Doctrinal, in the first three chapters, where he lays down and commends to them the doctrine of the grace of God in election, redemption, vocation, justification, adoption, chap. i., illustrating it by the deplorable condition in which before their conversion they had been, chap. ii., and assuring them of the truth of their call, by asserting, against all objectors and cavillers, his apostleship with respect to them Gentiles, and his commission from God to *preach among them the unsearchable riches of Christ*, chap. iii. 2. Practical; in which he exhorts them to walk worthy of their calling in the diligent practice of Christian duties, whether more general, and which concern all believers or special, such as belong to them in their several relations, especially economical, chap. v. and vi.

CHAP. I

After saluting the Ephesians, 1, 2, Paul blesseth God for his spiritual blessings on those whom he had chosen in Christ, and predestinated to the adoption of children, 3—6; for our redemption by his grace, according to his revealed purpose of gathering together all in one under Christ, 7—10; for the inheritance already obtained by those who first trusted in Christ, 11, 12; and for the Spirit given to after believers, as an earnest of the same, 13, 14. He declareth his continual thankfulness to God for their faith, and his prayers that God would perfect them in the knowledge of those things which concerned their state in Christ, 15—19; whom God had raised up, and exalted to be the supreme Head of his body the church, 20—23.

A. D. 64.
a 2 Cor. 1. 1.
b Rom. 1. 7.
2 Cor. 1. 1.
c 1 Cor. 4.
17. ch. 6. 21.
Col. 1. 2.

PAUL, an apostle of Jesus Christ [a] by the will of God, [b] to the saints which are at Ephesus, [c] and to the faithful in Christ Jesus:

The faithful; this may be understood either, 1. By way of restriction, of those that are sincere and constant to Christ, and so not only saints by profession, but true to their profession; or rather, 2. By way of explication: he defines those saints he spake of, and calls them *faithful in Christ* here, whom he called saints before. *Christ Jesus;* the Author and Fountain of that holiness which denominates them saints.

d Gal. 1. 3.
Tit. 1. 4.

2 [d] Grace *be* to you, and peace, from God our Father, and *from* the Lord Jesus Christ.

e 2 Cor. 1. 3.
1 Pet. 1. 3.

3 [e] Blessed *be* the God and Father of our Lord Jesus Christ, who hath blessed us with all spiritual blessings in heavenly ‖ *places* in Christ:

‖ Or, things,
ch. 6. 12.

Blessed be; i. e. thanked, praised. We bless God when we praise him for, and acknowledge him in, his excellencies or benefits. *Who hath blessed us;* hath vouchsafed or communicated all spiritual blessings to us. God blesseth us when he doeth good to us: and so the word *blessed* is taken in a different sense from what it was in the former clause. *With all;* of all sorts or kinds. *Spiritual blessings;* in opposition to temporal and worldly, with the carnal Jews principally expected, and the law mostly promised, (Deut. xxviii. 1—14,) and which were but types and shadows of those spiritual blessings which immediately relate to the spiritual life and salvation of believers. *In heavenly places*; Gr. supercelestial, or heavenly: understand either, 1. Things; and then it seems to be the same as spiritual blessings, only in other terms. Or, 2. Places, in opposition to earthly places, particularly the land of Canaan, in which God had formerly promised to bless his people. These spiritual blessings are in heavenly places, because, though they reach us here on earth, yet they are derived to us from God and Christ in heaven, and in heaven only have their full perfection and consummation hereafter. *In Christ;* by or through Christ; upon the account of whose merit, and by whose efficiency, these spiritual blessings are derived from God to us. Or, in Christ as our Head, the repository and seat of all Divine blessings, from whom they flow down upon us as his members, receiving all we have out of his fulness. He seems to have respect to the promise made to Abraham, Gen. xxii. 18, That in his seed all the nations of the earth should be blessed; pointing out Christ as that seed, and those blessings as spiritual. See Acts iii. 25, 26.

4 According as [f] he hath chosen us in him [g] before the foundation of the world, that we should [h] be holy and without blame before him in love:

f Rom. 8. 28.
2 Thes. 2. 13.
2 Tim. 1. 9.
Jam. 2. 5.
1 Pet. 1. 2.
& 2. 9.
g 1 Pet. 1. 20.
h Luke 1. 75.
ch. 2. 10. & 5. 27. Col. 1. 22. 1 Thes. 4. 7. Tit. 2. 12.

God blesseth us with all spiritual blessings *according as he hath chosen us;* election being the fountain from whence those blessings come, so that God doeth nothing for us in carrying on the work of our salvation, but what he had in his eternal counsel before determined. *Chosen us;* separated us in his purpose and decree from others, (whom he left out of that gracious act of his will,) and determined that we should be holy and unblamable, &c. *In him;* either, 1. By and through Christ, (as in the former verse,) for his sake, and upon the account of his merit as the procuring cause, not of our election, but sanctification; q. d. God hath chosen us, that we should be made holy and unblamable by Christ. Or rather, 2. In Christ, as the foundation on which he would build us, (his spiritual house,) and by which both we might be united to God, and he communicate his influence and grace to us; or as our Head, by which he might convey grace, and strength, and life to us as Christ's members. *Before the foundation of the world;* either before God's decree of creating the world, or rather, before his executing that decree in the actual creation of it; i. e. from eternity, when neither we nor the world had a being. *That we should be holy and without blame;* by inherent grace begun in regeneration, and carried on in sanctification and mortification in this life, though not perfected till the other. Holiness in us is declared here to be not the cause, but the effect of our election; we are chosen that we may be holy, not because we are, or God foresees we will be holy. *Before him;* in the sight of God, who is not deceived with an outward appearance, but looks to the heart. *In love;* as a principal part of our sanctification, and the best evidence of the fear of God in us, and our obedience to the whole law.

5 ¹Having predestinated us unto ᵏthe adoption of children by Jesus Christ to himself, ˡaccording to the good pleasure of his will,

Having predestinated us unto the adoption of children; having appointed us unto a state of sonship and right to glory. This seems to be more than the former, a greater thing to be the sons of God, and heirs of heaven, than to be holy. *By Jesus Christ;* as Mediator, and Head of the elect, and the foundation of all spiritual blessings vouchsafed them, and so of this relation into which they are brought, by being united to him. The adopted children come into that state by the intervention of the natural Son. *To himself;* either, 1. In himself, i. e. looking no farther than to himself for the cause of and motive to his adopting them. Or, 2. *To* himself, (according to our translation,) i. e. to God. Or, rather, 3. For himself (as the Syriac renders it); God would have the honour of having many adopted children that shall all call him Father. *According to the good pleasure of his will;* his sovereign grace and good will, as the only spring from which predestination issued, God being moved to it by nothing out of himself.

6 To the praise of the glory of his grace, ᵐ wherein he hath made us accepted in ⁿ the beloved.

To the praise of the glory of his grace: glory of his grace, by a usual Hebraism, for glorious grace, i. e. large, abundant, admirable. The praise of this grace the apostle makes the end of God's choosing and predestinating us to the adoption of children. God hath chosen us, &c, and therein manifested his grace to us, that such as it is in itself, such it may be acknowledged to be; and therefore praised and adored by us. *Wherein;* in, or through, or by the same grace out of which he chose us. *He hath made us accepted in the beloved;* having chosen us in Christ, he likewise favours us, is well pleased with us in Christ, to whom we are united, whose members we are, and in whom God looks upon us. We are hateful in ourselves as sinners, but accepted in Christ as sons.

7 ᵒIn whom we have redemption through his blood, the forgiveness of sins, according to ᵖ the riches of his grace;

In whom; in Christ, God-man, the immediate worker of this redemption; for though the Father and the Spirit concurred to it, yet the redeeming work was peculiarly terminated in the Second Person. The other two Persons have a right of propriety to redeem us; Christ only a right of propinquity, as assuming our nature, and being of kin to us. *We;* we elect, before mentioned. *Have redemption;* freedom from the wrath of God, and curse of the law, to which we are obnoxious, and consequently the power of sin and tyranny of Satan, as the effects of the former. *Through his blood;* i. e. by the sacrifice of his death upon the cross, where his blood was shed. This was the price of redemption paid to God for us, and wherewith his justice being satisfied, we could no longer be detained under the custody of the devil, or the dominion of sin. *Even the forgiveness of sins;* redemption is not formally forgiveness, but causally, forgiveness being the effect of it; and it is mentioned not as the only or adequate, but the prime and principal fruit of redemption, and upon which the other depend. *According to the riches of his grace:* what he called glorious grace, ver. 6, here he calls *riches of grace,* meaning plentiful and superabundant grace, by a phrase frequently used by him elsewhere in the same sense, Rom. ix. 23; chap. ii. 4, 7.

8 Wherein he hath abounded toward us in all wisdom and prudence;

Wherein, in which grace before mentioned, *he hath abounded toward us;* i. e out of abundance of grace in himself, (called *riches of grace,* ver. 7,) he hath bestowed upon us wisdom and prudence. The like expression we have, 1 Tim. i. 14. *In all wisdom;* this denotes either, the perfections or excellency of it, being instead of all other wisdom, and more excellent than all else; or *all* in comparison of what was under the Old Testament. They then had Divine truths revealed but by parts and parcels, and so a more sparing measure of spiritual wisdom; but under the gospel, believers have it more fully and largely, the Spirit of wisdom and revelation being poured out on them. *Wisdom and prudence;* either the doctrine of the gospel, which contains more perfect and higher wisdom than that the Greeks sought after, 1 Cor. i. 22, and for lack of which they counted the gospel *foolishness;* or rather, by *wisdom* is understood that knowledge or faith whereby we receive spiritual truths revealed to us, and to be believed by us, so as to their excellency, and have our hearts affected with them; and by *prudence,* the knowledge of the rule of our duty, with skill to govern ourselves according to it: and so *wisdom* is no other than faith, and *prudence* the same in effect with holiness; the former relates to the things we are to believe, the latter to the things we are to do. In the working these two in the soul, consists inward and effectual calling, which the apostle mentions in this verse, as he doth the outward likewise, by the preaching the word of the gospel, in the next.

9 ᑫHaving made known unto us the mystery of his will, according to his good pleasure ʳwhich he hath purposed in himself:

Having made known unto us; having revealed to us outwardly by the preaching of the gospel; inwardly, by the illumination of the Spirit. *The mystery of his will;* the whole doctrine of grace and salvation by Christ, which is a secret to others, and had still been so to us, had not God discovered it to us in the gospel. *According to his good pleasure;* the good pleasure of God is the fountain of all spiritual blessings which flow out to us, as well as it is of our being first chosen and appointed to be the subjects of them. *Which he hath purposed in himself;* this signifies a firm, settled will in God, either merely of God, and moved by nothing out of himself, or his keeping this purpose in himself till the time appointed for the publication of it.

10 That in the dispensation of ˢthe fulness of times ᵗhe might gather together in one ᵘall things in Christ, both which are in †heaven, and which are on earth; *even* in him:

Some copies join the last clause of the former verse with this, leaving out the relative *which,* and concluding the sentence at *good pleasure,* and then read, He *purposed in himself, that in the dispensation,* &c.; but most read it as our translators have rendered it, only some understand an explicative particle, to wit, in the beginning of this verse, to wit, *that in the dispensation,* &c.; but either way the scope of the words is the same, viz. to give the sum of that *mystery of* God's *will,* mentioned before.

In the dispensation; in that administration or distribution of the good things of God's house, which he had determined should be in the fulness of time. It is a metaphor taken from a steward, who distributes and dispenseth according to his master's order to those that are in the house, Luke xii. 42. The church is the house of God, God himself the Master of the family, Christ the Steward that governs the house; those *spiritual blessings,* mentioned ver. 3, are the good things he gives out. These treasures of God's grace had been opened but to a few, and dispensed sparingly under the Old Testament, the more full communication of them being reserved till the fulness of times, when they were to be dispensed by Christ. *The fulness of times;* the time appointed of the Father for the appearance of Christ in the flesh, (according to former promises,) the promulgation of the gospel, and thereby the gathering together in one all things in Christ. It is spoken in opposition to the times and ages before Christ's coming, which God would have run out till the set time came which he had pitched upon, and believers expected: see Gal. iv. 2, 4. *Gather together in one;* to recapitulate; either to sum up as men do several lesser numbers in one total sum, which is the foot of the account, but called by the Greeks the head of it, and set at the top; or as orators do the several parts of their speeches in fewer words; thus all former prophecies, promises, types, and shadows centred, and were fulfilled, and as it were summed up, in Christ: or rather, to unite unto, and gather together again under, one head things before divided and scattered. *All things;* all intellectual beings, or all persons, as Gal. iii. 22. *In Christ;* as their Head, under which they might be united to God, and to each other. *Which are in heaven;* either saints departed, who have already obtained salvation by Christ, or rather the holy angels, that still keep their first station. *Which are on earth;* the elect of God among men here upon earth in their several generations. The meaning of the whole seems to be, that whereas the order and harmony of God's principal workmanship, intellectual creatures, angels and men, had been disturbed and broken by the entering of sin into the world; all mankind, and many of the angels, having apostatized from him, and the remnant of them being in their own nature labile and mutable; God would, in his appointed time, give Christ (the Heir of all things) the honour of being the repairer of this breach, by gathering together again the disjointed members of his creation in and under Christ as their Head and Governor, confirming the good angels in their good estate, and recovering his elect among men from their apostate condition. Though it be true, that not only believers under the Old Testament were saved, but the elect angels confirmed before Christ's coming, yet both the one and the other was with a respect to Christ as their Head, and the foundation of their union with God; and out of whom, as the one, being lost, could not have been restored, so the fall of the other could not have been prevented, nor their happiness secured.

x Acts 20. 32. & 26. 18. Rom. 8. 17. Col. 1. 12. & 3. 24. Tit. 3. 7. Jam. 2. 5. 1 Pet. 1. 4. y ver. 5. z Is. 46. 10, 11.

11 ˣIn whom also we have obtained an inheritance, ʸ being predestinated according to ᶻ the purpose of him who worketh all things after the counsel of his own will:

In whom we; we apostles and others elect of the Jewish nation, we *who first trusted in Christ,* ver. 12. *Have obtained an inheritance;* are called, or brought into the participation of an inheritance, or have a right given us to it as by lot: in allusion to the twelve tribes having, in the division of the land of Canaan, their inheritances assigned them by lot. He shows that they did not first seek it, much less deserve it, but God cast it upon them: their lot fell in the heavenly inheritance, when others did not. *Being predestinated;* this, as well as the forementioned privileges, was designed to us by eternal predestination, and though it be free, and without our procuring, yet in respect of God it is not casual, but of his ordering. *Who worketh all things,* powerfully and effectually, *after the counsel of his own will;* i. e. that infinite wisdom of God, which is always in conjunction with his will, whereby he acts wisely as well as freely, and though not by deliberation, which falls beneath his infinite perfection, yet with his greatest reason and judgment.

a ver. 6, 14. 2 Thes. 2. 13. b Jam. 1. 18. ‖ Or, *hoped.*

12 ᵃThat we should be to the praise of his glory, ᵇ who first ‖ trusted in Christ.

That we should be to the praise of his glory; either, 1. Passively, that the excellency and greatness of God's wisdom, power, grace, mercy, &c. might be shown forth in us by our being predestinated, called, sanctified, saved: or rather, 2. Actively, that we, by the holiness, obedience, and fruitfulness of our conversations, suitable to such privileges, might manifest and set forth the glory of him that vouchsafed them to us. *Who first trusted in Christ;* who were the fruits of the New Testament church, the gospel having been first preached to the apostles by Christ himself, and by them to the Jews, (their own nation,) and having been first believed by them.

13 In whom ye also *trusted,* after that ye heard ᶜthe word of truth, the Gospel of your salvation: in whom also after that ye believed, ᵈye were sealed with that holy Spirit of promise,

c John 1. 17. 2 Cor. 6. 7.

d 2 Cor. 1. 22. ch. 4. 30.

In whom ye also; here is a defect of the verb in the Greek, which may be supplied either from ver. 11, which seems to be the principal verb in the sentence, and then it must be read, *In whom ye also have obtained an inheritance;* or from ver. 12, *trusted,* which is the nearest verb; so our translation, *In whom ye also trusted;* but neither way makes any difference in the scope of the words. *Ye;* ye Ephesians and other Gentiles. *The word of truth;* the gospel, so called, either, 1. By a usual Hebraism, from the true word; or, 2. By way of eminency, as containing the most excellent and necessary of all truths, the doctrine of righteousness and life by Jesus Christ; or, 3. With respect to the law and its shadows, the truth and substance of which is held forth in the gospel. *The gospel of your salvation:* both in respect of the matter contained in it, the doctrine of salvation, and in respect of its efficiency, as being the means whereby God works faith, and brings to salvation, Rom. i. 12; Heb. ii. 3. *In whom also after that ye believed: in whom* either is to be referred to believers; q. d. After ye believed in Christ: or to sealing; and then it shows by virtue of whom this benefit of sealing is bestowed, viz. by virtue of Christ. *Ye were sealed with that holy Spirit;* ye were secured and ascertained of your right to the inheritance; which we may understand to be done either by the Spirit's impressing upon the soul the image of God in the work of regeneration, or (because that cannot so well be understood to be after believing) rather by his testimony in men's own consciences afterward; whether immediate, by an overpowering light shining into the soul, and filling it with assurance of its interest in Christ and heaven; or mediate, enabling a man to discern that image of God in his soul, by which the Spirit bears witness to his interest in the inheritance, and assures him of it: see chap. iv. 30; Rom. viii. 16; Gal. iv. 6. *Of promise;* because the Spirit's coming was before promised, or because he verifies and confirms the promises in and to the hearts of believers.

14 ᵉWhich is the earnest of our inheritance ᶠuntil the redemption of ᵍ the purchased possession, ʰunto the praise of his glory.

e 2 Cor. 1. 22. & 5. 5. f Luke 21. 28. Rom. 8. 23. ch. 4. 30. g Acts 20. 28. h ver. 6, 12. 1 Pet. 2. 9.

Which is the earnest of our inheritance: the Spirit, given to and dwelling in believers by his gifts and graces, is the earnest or pledge whereby their inheritance is secured to them; as men are secured the payment of a promised sum, by a part given beforehand in earnest for the rest. *Until the redemption of the purchased possession;* either, 1. The redemption of the possession is put for the possessing of the redemption, (by an hypallage,) viz. full and final redemption from sin, and death, and hell, and Satan; which redemption though perfectly wrought by Christ, is but in part applied in this life, and is to be fully enjoyed in the other: or rather, 2. (though to the same sense,) To the full and final redemption in the end of the world, of all God's people, who are here called his *purchased possession:* see the same word so taken, Acts xx. 28; 1 Pet. ii. 9. *Unto the praise of his glory;* the final salvation and complete redemption of God's people, will be especially for the glory of God, 2 Thess. i. 10.

15 Wherefore I also, ⁱafter I heard of your faith in the Lord Jesus, and love unto all the saints,

i Col. 1. 4. Philem. 5.

After I heard; he was an eye-witness of their first believing, but here he speaks of their increase and constancy in the faith since, of which he had heard by others. *Of your faith in the Lord Jesus;* i. e. not barely a belief of Christ's excellencies, but a belief of his being their Saviour, their receiving and relying on him as such, and so a believing in him as the immediate object of their faith, and him by whom they believed in God, 1 Pet. i. 21. *And love unto all the saints;* this is added to show the truth of their faith, which works by love. *Love to the saints* is mentioned, as an evidence of their love to God; and to *all* the saints, to show the sincerity of that love, in its not being partial, but respecting all saints, and therefore saints as saints.

16 [k] Cease not to give thanks for you, making mention of you in my prayers;

Cease not to give thanks for you; for your faith and love, and all the spiritual blessings God hath bestowed upon you. *Making mention of you in my prayers;* I not only acknowledge what ye have received, but pray that what is yet lacking in you may be made up.

17 That [l] the God of our Lord Jesus Christ, the Father of glory, [m] may give unto you the spirit of wisdom and revelation ‖ in the knowledge of him:

That the God of our Lord Jesus Christ; he is the God of Christ not according to Christ's Divine nature, but his human, and as Mediator, in which respect he was subject to the Father. *The Father of glory;* the most glorious Father, and the Author of all glory and glorious things, and to whom all glory is due. *May give unto you the spirit of wisdom;* a greater measure (for some they already had) of faith, (as ver. 8, where it is called *wisdom.*) or of the knowledge of the things of God, whereof the Spirit is the Author. God is said to give or send the Spirit, where the Spirit works effectually; and, so to give the Spirit of wisdom, where the Spirit effectually works that wisdom. *And revelation:* by *revelation* he means not extraordinary, such as the prophets had, but ordinary, such as was common to believers, and expresseth the manner of the Spirit's working this wisdom, that he doth it by removing the covering or veil of natural ignorance, (Psal. cxix. 18; Luke xxiv. 45,) shining into the mind, and making it see what before it saw not; sometimes new objects, sometimes new excellencies in objects before known. Thus the Spirit works not only in the beginning of faith and spiritual knowledge, but in its further progress he lets in new light into the mind, and removes some remaining degree of natural darkness. *In the knowledge*, or acknowledgment, which may imply an owning, approving, and embracing things before known. *Of him;* i. e. God or Christ, or God in Christ : and so either he declares here wherein the wisdom he mentioned consists, viz. the knowledge of God and Christ, in whom are hid all the treasures of wisdom and knowledge : or rather, the end of that wisdom and revelation, viz. the acknowledgment of God or Christ, when we so know him, as to own him as ours, to embrace, and love, and wholly subject ourselves to him, Col. i. 9, 10.

18 [n] The eyes of your understanding being enlightened; that ye may know what is [o] the hope of his calling, and what the riches of the glory of his [p] inheritance in the saints,

The eyes of your understanding being enlightened, viz. by that *spirit of revelation:* and so this clause explains the former. What the eye is to the body, that the understanding is to the soul. He prays for a further degree of illumination for them. *That ye may know what is the hope of his calling;* either, 1. The object of hope, the thing hoped for, as Col. i. 5; Gal. v. 5; and then the meaning is, what it is to the hope of which God hath called you by the gospel. Or, 2. The grace of hope : q. d. That ye may know how great, and sure, and well grounded that hope is, which by the gospel is wrought in you. *And what the riches of the glory;* the glorious riches, or the abundant glory; *riches of glory*, and *riches of grace*, ver. 7, and *riches of glory*, Rom. vi. 23. *Of his;* because he is the Father of it : he gives this glory as the Father of glory. As men give inheritances suitable to their estates, so God, as the God of glory, and Father of glory, gives a glorious inheritance. *Inheritance;* heaven, called an *inheritance* both in respect of believers' title to it by virtue of their adoption, being heirs of God; and in respect of the perpetuity of their enjoying it, on which account it is called an *eternal inheritance,* Heb. ix. 15. *In the saints;* or, among the saints, those, namely, that are perfect, who alone are possessed of the inheritance, which saints on earth have only in hope.

19 And what *is* the exceeding greatness of his power to us-ward who believe, [q] according to the working † of his mighty power,

And what is the exceeding greatness of his power to us-ward who believe; he means that power of God which is put forth in the whole of our salvation, from first to last : not that absolute power whereby he can do whatsoever is possible to be done ; but his ordinate power, or power joined with his will, whereby not only he will work in raising us up at last, and finally saving us, but hath wrought in begetting faith in us, and doth work in still preserving that faith, (1 Pet. i. 5,) and carrying us on in the way of salvation. And this he speaks for the encouragement of the Ephesians, that they should not fear falling short of the riches of the glory of the inheritance mentioned, seeing God, who hath by his power brought them to Christ, is able likewise by the same power to bring them to glory. *According to the working of his mighty power:* some point the words after *us-ward*, and read them, *who believe according to the working of his mighty power,* &c.; and then the meaning must be, that the working faith in believers, is an instance of his mighty power ; he hath shown his power in working faith, and therefore will show it in the remainder of salvation which is to follow. But our translation favours the former sense, and then, as in the preceding clause he shows the greatness of God's power, so in this latter the efficacy of it in its actual operation, particularly the raising up Christ from the dead.

20 Which he wrought in Christ, when [r] he raised him from the dead, and [s] set *him* at his own right hand in the heavenly *places,*

Which he wrought in Christ, when he raised him from the dead; i. e. the power God exerciseth toward believers is such as that was whereby he raised up Christ from the dead. *And set him at his own right hand;* hath invested him with the greatest honour, dignity, and power, as princes set the next in honour and authority to themselves at their right hands : see Matt. xx. 21. *In the heavenly places;* in the highest heaven, called *the third heaven,* 2 Cor. xii. 2, and *paradise,* ver. 4.

21 [t] Far above all [u] principality, and power, and might, and dominion, and every name that is named, not only in this world, but also in that which is to come :

Principality, and power, and might, and dominion: these terms are sometimes applied to magistrates and men in authority here in the world, Tit. iii. 1; Jude 8 : sometimes to angels; to good ones, Col. i. 16; to evil ones, chap. vi. 12; Col. ii. 15; though with allusion to powers in the world, or because by them God puts forth and exerciseth his power and dominion. By these, then, the apostle understands good angels, as chap. iii. 10 ; or, comprehensively, all sorts of powers, both visible and invisible, as Col. i. 16; 1 Pet. iii. 22. *And every name that is named;* lest any might think he had not named all above whom Christ is exalted, he adds this, to take all in. *Every name*, that is, every person, and every thing which hath a name ; whatever hath any dignity or excellency. *Not only in this world, but also in that which is to come;* because, though it hath a being at present, yet it is future to us who are not yet possessed of it. Either this clause relates to Christ's sitting at his Father's right hand, and then it notes the perpetuity of his reign, that his kingdom is an everlasting kingdom, Luke i. 33; or rather, to the words immediately going before: q. d. If there be any name, any dignity, or excellency, not known in this life, and which shall be known in the other; yet, be they what they may, Christ is above them all.

22 And [x] hath put all *things* under his feet, and gave him [y] *to be* the head over all *things* to the Church,

All things; either all his enemies, as Psal. cx. 1, all except the church, which is said to be his body ; or all things more generally, of which he spake before, angels and men ; all are made subject to Christ, 1 Pet. iii. 22. *Hath put all*

things under his feet; put them into a perfect and full subjection to him. *Object.* All things are not yet put under him. *Answ.* 1. All things are so put under him that he can do with them what he please, break all his enemies in pieces when he will, though for many reasons he yet doth it not. 2. They are begun to be subjected to him, and by degrees shall be further subjected, till they be perfectly and absolutely subjected unto him, *de facto*, as already they are *de jure*. *And gave him;* appointed, or constituted, or made him. *To be head;* a mystical head; such a one not only as a king is to his subjects, to rule them externally by his laws, but such as a natural head is to the body, which it governs by way of influence, conveying spirits to it, and so causing and maintaining sense and motion in it, chap. iv. 16; Col. ii. 19. *Over all things;* either, 1. God hath chiefly, and above all before mentioned, given Christ to be the Head of the church; q. d. Though he be King and Lord of all, yet God hath made him the only proper Head to the church only; God hath set him above principalities and powers, but especially hath appointed him to be the Head of the church. Or, 2. *Over all things* may be meant, for the communication of all good things to the church, and performing all offices of a Head to her; a Head to the church, with a power over all things for her good. *To the church;* the catholic church, or whole collection of believers throughout the world, and in all ages of it.

z Rom. 12.5.
1 Cor. 12.12,
27. ch. 4. 12.
& 5. 23, 30.
Col. 1. 18, 24.

23 ᶻ Which is his body, ᵃ the fulness of him ᵇ that filleth all in all.

a Col. 2. 10. b 1 Cor. 12. 6. ch. 4. 10. Col. 3. 11.

Which is his body; i. e. a mystical one, whereof every member is influenced by the Spirit of Christ the Head, as in the natural body the members are influenced by spirits derived from the natural head. *The fulness of him:* the church is called the fulness of Christ, not personally, but relatively considered, and as Head of the church. The head is incomplete without the body; Christ in his relative capacity as a Head, would not be complete without his mystical body the church. *That filleth all in all:* lest Christ should be thought to have any need of the church, because of her being said to be his fulness, it is added, that she herself is filled by Christ. Christ fills all his body, and all the members of it, with the gifts and graces of his Spirit, chap. iv. 10.

CHAP. II

Paul setteth before the Ephesians their former corrupt heathen state, 1—3, and God's rich mercy in their deliverance, 4—7. We are saved by grace, not of works, yet so as to be created in Christ unto good works, 8—10. They who were once strangers, and far from God, are now brought near by Christ's blood; who having abolished the ritual law, the ground of distinction between Jew and Gentile, hath united both in one body, and gained them equal access to the Father, 11—18. So that the Gentiles are henceforth equally privileged with the Jews, and together with them constitute a holy temple for the habitation of God's Spirit, 19—22.

a John 5. 24.
Col. 2. 13.
b ver. 5.
ch. 4. 18.

AND ᵃ you *hath he quickened*, ᵇ who were dead in trespasses and sins;

And you hath he quickened; this verb *quickened* is not in the Greek, but the defect of it may be supplied from chap. i. 19, thus, *The greatness of his power to us-ward, and to you that were dead in trespasses and sins;* the remaining part of that chapter being included in a parenthesis, which, though long, yet is not unusual. Or rather, as our translators and others do, from ver. 5 of this chapter, where we have the word *quickened*. It imports a restoring of spiritual life by the infusion of a vital principle, (in the work of regeneration,) whereby men are enabled to walk with God in newness of life. *Who were dead;* spiritually, not naturally; i. e. destitute of a principle of spiritual life, and so of any ability for, or disposedness to, the operations and motions of such a life. *In trespasses and sins:* the preposition *in* is wanting in the Greek by an ellipsis, but the expression is full, Col. ii. 13; this dative case therefore is to be taken in the sense of the ablative. By these words he means either all sorts of sins, habitual and actual, less or greater; or rather, promiscuously and indifferently, the same thing several ways expressed. Sin is the cause of spiritual death; where sin reigns, there is a privation of spiritual life.

2 ᶜ Wherein in time past ye walked according to the course of this world, according to ᵈ the prince of the power of the air, the spirit that now worketh in ᵉ the children of disobedience:

c 1 Cor. 6. 11.
ch. 4. 22.
Col. 1. 21.
& 3. 7.
d 1 John 5. 19.
d ch. 6. 12.
e ch. 5. 6.
Col. 3. 6.

Wherein in time past ye walked; conversed in a continual course of life. They were alive *to* sin, when dead *in* sin; or by sin dead to spiritual good. *According to the course of this world;* either according to the age of the world that then was, or men then in the world, or according to the custom and mode, the shape and fashion, of the world. The same word here translated *course* is rendered *world*, Rom. xii. 2, *Be not conformed* (configured or fashioned) *to this world*, i. e. to the ways and manners of it. So here, *according to the course*, is, according to the ways of men in the world, both in manners and religion. *According to the prince;* the devil, or, as Matt. xii. 24, 26, *the prince of devils. Of the power; power* for *powers*, as they are called, chap. vi. 12: those devils, or powers of darkness, are marshalled under him as their prince, who sets up a kingdom to himself in opposition to Christ. *Of the air;* that are in the air, this lower region, (by God's permission,) that they may be ready and at hand to tempt men, and do mischief in the world. Or, that work so many effects in the air, raise storms and tempests, &c., as in the case of Job and his children. *The spirit that now;* even at this time, since the coming of the gospel, still continues to work. *Worketh in;* effectually works in; rules, and governs, and acts them, 2 Tim. ii. 26. *The children of disobedience*, by a Hebraism; they that are addicted to disobedience, i. e. obstinate sinners.

3 ᶠ Among whom also we all had our conversation in times past in ᵍ the lusts of our flesh, fulfilling † the desires of the flesh and of the mind; and ʰ were by nature the children of wrath, even as others.

f Tit. 3. 3.
1 Pet. 4. 3.
g Gal. 5. 16
† Gr. the wills.
h Ps. 51. 5.
Rom. 3. 12, 14.

Among whom also we all; we apostles and believers of the Jews. Either Paul by a *cœnosis* reckons himself among them, though not guilty with them; or rather, though he were not an idolater as the Ephesians, yet he had been *a blasphemer, and a persecutor,* 1 Tim. i. 13; and though he were blameless as to the righteousness of the law, Phil. iii. 6, yet that was only as to his outward conversation, and still he might fulfil the desires of a fleshly mind. *Had our conversation;* walked in the same way after the course of the world, &c. *In the lusts of our flesh: flesh* is here taken more generally for depraved natures, the whole principle of corruption in man. *Fulfilling the desires of the flesh;* the inferior and sensitive faculties of the soul, as appears by the opposition of the *flesh* to the *mind*. *And of the mind;* the superior and rational powers, to denote the depravation of the whole man even in his best part, and which seems to have rectitude left in it: to the former belongs the *filthiness of the flesh*, to the latter that of the *spirit*, 2 Cor. vii. 1: see Rom. viii. 7; Gal. v. 19—21. *And were by nature;* not merely by custom or imitation, but by nature as now constituted since the fall. *The children of wrath*, by a Hebraism, for obnoxious to wrath; as sons of death, 1 Sam. xxvi. 16, for worthy of or liable to death.

4 But God, ⁱ who is rich in mercy, for his great love wherewith he loved us,

i Rom. 10. 12. ch. 1. 7.
ver. 7.

Rich in mercy; abundant. Riches of mercy here, as riches of grace, chap. i. 7; see Psal. li. 1; lxxxvi. 5. *For his great love;* the fountain from whence his mercies vouchsafed to us proceed; riches of mercy from great love: God shows mercy to us miserable creatures in time, because he loved us from eternity, viz. with a love of good will. *Wherewith he loved us*, both Jews and Gentiles; there being the same original cause of the salvation of both.

5 ᵏ Even when we were dead in sins, hath ˡ quickened us together with Christ, (‖ by grace ye are saved;)

k Rom. 5. 6, 8, 10. ver. 1.
l Rom. 6. 4, 5. Col. 2. 12, 13. & 3. 1, 3.
‖ Or, by whose *grace*: See Acts 15. 11. ver. 8. Tit. 3. 5.

EPHESIANS II

Hath quickened us; hath raised us up from the death of sin to the life of righteousness, not only in our justification, in which God frees us from our obnoxiousness to eternal death, and gives us a right to eternal life, who before were dead in law, (though this may be included,) but especially in our regeneration, by the infusion of a vital principle. *Together with Christ;* either, 1. God, in quickening Christ, hath also quickened us; Christ's quickening, or receiving his life after death, being not only the type and exemplar of our spiritual enlivening or regeneration, but the cause of it, inasmuch as we are quickened, as meritoriously by his death, so effectively by his life: Christ, as having died and risen again, exerciseth that power the Father gave him of quickening whom he will, John v. 21. Or, 2. In Christ as our Head virtually, and by the power of his resurrection actually. Or, 3. By the same power whereby he raised up Christ from the dead, chap. i. 20. See the like expression, Col. ii. 13. *(By grace are ye saved;)* some read the words without a parenthesis, supplying by whose, and so refer them to Christ, *quickened us together with Christ, by whose grace ye are saved;* but if the parenthesis stand, yet here seems to be a connexion with the foregoing words, at least a reason of the apostle's bringing in these; for having mentioned God's *great love,* ver. 4, as the cause of their spiritual enlivening here, which is the beginning of their salvation, he infers from thence that the whole of their salvation is of grace, i. e. alike free, and as much out of God's great love, as the beginning of it, viz. their quickening, is.

6 And hath raised *us* up together, and made *us* sit together ᵐ in heavenly *places* in Christ Jesus:

m ch. 1. 20.

And hath raised us up together; either this may be understood of a further degree of spiritual life in the progress of sanctification vouchsafed to believers in this world; or rather, of the resurrection of the body, which is said to be raised together with Christ, because it is to be raised by the same power that raised him up, and by virtue of his resurrection, in which we have fellowship with him, as being united to him. *And made us sit together in heavenly places in Christ Jesus,* as our Head, and representative. Our spiritual enlivening (ver. 5) we have not only fundamentally in Christ when restored to life, but actually begun in ourselves in our effectual calling; but the resurrection of our bodies, and our sitting in heaven, we have not as yet actually fulfilled in ourselves, yet have it in Christ our Head, who rose for us and we in him, and sits in heaven for us, and we in him may be said to sit there too, by reason of our union with him, and being members of him.

7 That in the ages to come he might shew the exceeding riches of his grace in ⁿ*his* kindness toward us through Christ Jesus.

n Tit. 3. 4.

That in the ages to come; in all succeeding generations while the world continues. *He might show, &c.;* as in an instance or specimen, 1 Tim. i. 16: q. d. God's *kindness to us* believers in this age, since Christ's coming, is such an instance of *the exceeding riches of his grace,* as may be an encouragement to future generations to embrace the same Christ in whom we have believed. *Through Christ Jesus;* by and through whom God conveys all saving benefits to us.

o ver. 5. Rom. 3. 24. 2 Tim. 1. 9. p Rom. 4. 16. q Mat. 16. 17. John 6. 44. 65. Rom. 10. 14, 15, 17. ch. 1. 19. Phil. 1. 29.

8 ᵒ For by grace are ye saved ᵖ through faith; and that not of yourselves: ᑫ *it is* the gift of God:

For by grace, the free favour of God, as ver. 5, *are ye,* even ye Ephesians, Gentiles, who had not such promises made to you as the Jews had, ver. 12, *saved,* from first to last, from your calling, ver. 5, to your glorification, ver. 6. *Object.* How are believers said to be saved, when they are not yet glorified ? *Answ.* 1. Because Christ their Head is glorified. 2. Because their salvation, begun in their effectual calling, shall be as certainly accomplished in them as it is begun in them, and perfected in their Head, Christ. *Through faith;* by which ye lay hold on the grace offered you in the gospel. Faith is not considered here as a work done by us, but as an instrument or means applying the grace and salvation tendered to us. *And that not of yourselves;* not for your own worth, nor by your own strength. *It is the gift of God;* that ye saved is the gift of God, and therefore free and purely by grace. *God* is opposed to self: *gift* relates not merely to faith immediately preceding, but to the whole sentence.

9 ʳ Not of works, lest any man should boast.

r Rom. 3. 20, 27, 28. & 4. 2. & 9. 11. & 11. 6. 1 Cor. 1. 29, 30, 31. 2 Tim. 1. 9. Tit. 3. 5.

Not of works; any works whatever, and not only works of the ceremonial law: for if they only were excluded, the opposition between God and man, grace and works, were not right, which yet we find so often elsewhere; (see Rom. xi. 6;) men might not be saved by works of the ceremonial law, and yet still be saved by works, and of themselves. *Lest any man should boast;* glory in their own works or worth, as men are apt to do when they think they have any thing of their own which contributes to their salvation · see Rom. iii. 27; iv. 2.

10 For we are ˢ his workmanship, created in Christ Jesus unto good works, ᵗ which God hath before ‖ ordained that we should walk in them.

s Deut. 32. 6. Ps. 100. 3. Is. 19. 25. & 29. 23. & 44. 21. John 3. 3, 5. 1 Cor. 3. 9. 2 Cor. 5. 5, 17. ch. 4. 24. Tit. 2. 14. t ch. 1. 4. ‖ Or, *prepared*.

For we, we believers, both Jews and Gentiles, *are his workmanship;* not only as men, but especially as saints, which is the proper meaning here. The Israelitish people formerly were God's work, Deut. xxxii. 6; Isa. xliii. 21; xliv. 21; so are believers under the gospel, being new creatures, Gal. vi. 15. The apostle confirms what he said before, that *by grace* we *are saved,* and *not of works,* in that we are God's workmanship, and are formed by him ere we can do any good work; and his forming us in our regeneration is a part of the salvation mentioned ver. 8. *Created in Christ Jesus;* who, as our Head, enlivens us, as members united to him by faith. As the first creation was by Christ as the Second Person in the Trinity, John i. 3, so the second creation is by the same Christ as Mediator, the Lord and Head of the new creation, in whom we live, and move, and have our new being, and not in ourselves, 2 Cor. v. 17. *Unto good works;* as the immediate end for which we are new-created. We receive our new being that we may bring forth new works, and have a carriage suitable to our new principle. *Which God hath before ordained;* or rather, as the margin, prepared, i. e. prepared and fitted us for them, by enlightening our minds to know his will, disposing and inclining our wills, purging our affections, &c. *That we should walk in them;* i. e. that we should glorify God in a holy conversation, agreeable to that Divine nature, whereof we are made partakers in our new creation.

11 Wherefore ᵘ remember, that ye *being* in time past Gentiles in the flesh, who are called Uncircumcision by that which is called ˣ the Circumcision in the flesh made by hands;

u 1 Cor. 12. 2. ch. 5. 8. Col. 1. 21. & 2. 13. x Rom. 2. 28, 29. Col. 2. 11.

In the flesh; either, 1. Carnal, unregenerate, as Rom. viii. 8, 9. Or rather, 2. Uncircumcised in the flesh, as well as in heart, Ezek. xliv. 7; such as neither had the grace signified, nor the sign representing it. *Who are called Uncircumcision,* by way of reproach; to be uncircumcised being the badge of them that were not Israelites, and so were not in the number of God's people. *By that which is called the Circumcision in the flesh made by hands;* i. e. by those that are circumcised; the abstract here, as in the former clause, being put for the concrete. He means the carnal Jews, who had the circumcision of the flesh which was made with hands, but not that of the heart, Rom. ii. 29, *made without hands,* Col. ii. 11.

12 ʸ That at that time ye were without Christ, ᶻ being aliens from the commonwealth of Israel, and strangers from ᵃ the covenants of promise, ᵇ having no hope, ᶜ and without God in the world:

y ch. 4. 18. Col. 1. 21. z See Ezek. 13. 9. John 10. 16. a Rom. 9. 4, 8. b 1 Thes. 4. 13. c Gal. 4. 8. 1 Thes. 4. 5.

That at that time ye were without Christ; i. e. without knowledge of him, or interest in him. This is the foundation of all other miseries, as Christ is the foundation of all saving good, and therefore the apostle begins with this. *Being aliens from the commonwealth of Israel;* the church

EPHESIANS III

of God, confined formerly to the Israelites: their church and state was the same body, and God the founder of and lawgiver to them in both respects. *And strangers from the covenants of promise;* those covenants in which the great promise of Christ and salvation by him was made. The covenants were several, as that with Abraham, and that by Moses, and differ in some accidents, but the promise in them was one and the same, which was the substance of each. *Having no hope;* viz. beyond this life; as they could not but be who were without Christ, and without the promises. *And without God;* not without some general knowledge of a God, but without any saving knowledge of him, as not knowing him in Christ: or they lived as without God, neglecting him, and being neglected by him, and suffered to walk in their own ways. *In the world;* which is the congregation of the wicked, and is here opposed to the church.

d Gal. 3. 28.
e Acts 2. 39. ver. 17.

13 [d] But now in Christ Jesus ye who sometimes were [e] far off are made nigh by the blood of Christ.

But now in Christ Jesus: either in the kingdom of Christ, or gospel administration, Gal. v. 6; or, ye being in Christ, united to him by the Spirit and faith. Being *in Christ*, here, is opposed to being *in the world*, ver. 12. *Ye who sometimes were far off;* far from God, from his church, from his promises, &c., having no communion with him by his Spirit. He means a spiritual distance, yet seems to allude to Isa. xlix. 1, 12; those Gentiles there mentioned being estranged from God in their hearts, as well as removed from his people in place. *Are made nigh;* brought into a state of communion with God and his people, and participation of their privileges, and right to the promises. *By the blood of Christ;* the merit of his death expiating sin, (which caused this distance,) and so making way for their approach to God, and enjoyment of gospel blessings.

f Mic. 5. 5.
John 16. 33.
Acts 10. 36.
Rom. 5. 1.
Col. 1. 20.
g John 10 16.
Gal. 3. 28.

14 For [f] he is our peace, [g] who hath made both one, and hath broken down the middle wall of partition *between us ;*

For he is our peace; i. e. Peace-maker, or Mediator of peace, both between God and man, and between Jew and Gentile. He is called *our peace*, as elsewhere our righteousness, redemption, salvation. God is said to reconcile us, 2 Cor. v. 19, but Christ only to be our peace. *Who hath made both one;* i. e. one body, or one people, or *one new man*, ver. 15. *And hath broken down the middle wall of partition between us;* having taken away the ceremonial law, which was as a wall of separation between Jew and Gentile, as appears in the next verse. It seems to be an allusion to that wall of the temple which parted between the court of the people into which the Jews came, and the outmost court, that of the Gentiles, who, when they came to worship, might not come into the other court, and were excluded by this wall.

h Col. 2. 14, 20
i Col. 1. 22.

15 [h] Having abolished [i] in his flesh the enmity, *even* the law of commandments *contained* in ordinances; for to make

k 2 Cor. 5. 17.
Gal. 6. 15.
ch. 4. 24.

in himself of twain one [k] new man, *so* making peace;

Having abolished; abrogated, taken away the power of binding men. *In his flesh;* not the flesh of sacrificed beasts, but his own flesh: before he mentioned his blood, and now his flesh, to imply the whole sacrifice of Christ, comprehending his flesh as well as blood. The ceremonies had their accomplishment in Christ, and so their abolishment by him. *The enmity;* by a metonymy he so calls the ceremonies, which were the cause and the sign of enmity between Jew and Gentile: the Jews hated the Gentiles as uncircumcised, and the Gentiles despised the Jews for being circumcised. *Even the law of commandments contained in ordinances:* either, by *the law of commandments*, the apostle means the law of ceremonial rites, and by the word which we render *ordinances*, he means doctrine, and then (the word *contained* not being in the Greek) the sense is, that Christ, by his doctrine or commandments, abolished those ceremonial rites: the word *commandments* seems thus to be used, Deut. xvi. 12; 1 Kings ii. 3; Ezek. xviii. 21.

Or else (which yet comes to the same) the word rendered *ordinances* signifies such ordinances as depended upon the sole will of the lawgiver; and is, Col. ii. 14, taken for ceremonial ones, and so is to be taken here. This the apostle seems to add, to show what part of the law was abrogated by Christ, viz. nothing of the moral law, but only the ceremonial. *For to make*, or create, or form, in opposition to abolish. *In himself;* by union with himself, as the Head, in which the several members agree. *Of twain;* two bodies, or two people, Jews and Gentiles. *One new man;* i. e. new body, or new (viz. Christian) people. As the body of a commonwealth is one civil person, so the body of the church is in a like sense one person. *So making peace*, between Jew and Gentile, having taken away those ceremonial laws, which were the cause of the difference between them.

l Col. 1. 20;
21, 22.
m Rom. 6.
6. & 8 3.
Col. 2. 14.
|| Or, in himself.

16 And that he might [l] reconcile both unto God in one body by the cross, [m] having slain the enmity || thereby:

And that he might reconcile both unto God; another end of Christ's abolishing the ceremonial law, viz. that he might reconcile both Jew and Gentile (all the elect together) unto God; and in this respect especially he is our peace. *In one body;* either both people united as one mystical body, or rather this *one body* here, is the body of Christ offered up to God as the means of reconciliation, Col. i. 22. *By the cross;* i. e. by the sacrifice of himself upon the cross. *Having slain the enmity thereby;* the enmity between God and man, by the expiation of sin, the cause of it. Of this enmity the ceremonial law was a witness, Col. ii. 14, as well as a sign of that between Jew and Gentile.

n Is. 57. 19.
Zech. 9. 10.
Acts 2. 39.
& 10. 36.
Rom. 5. 1.
ver. 13, 14. o Ps. 148. 14.

17 And came [n] and preached peace to you which were afar off, and to [o] them that were nigh.

And came; partly in his own person, as to the Jews, and partly by his apostles, whom he appointed to preach the gospel to the Gentiles: so 2 Cor. xiii. 3. *And preached peace to you which were afar off;* far from the knowledge of the truth, from Christ, and salvation by him, as ver. 13. *And to them that were nigh;* nigh in comparison of the Gentiles, nigh by the knowledge of God and his law, and the promises of the Messiah: see Isa. lvii. 19.

p John 10. 9.
& 14 6. Rom.
5. 2. ch. 3. 12.
Heb. 4. 16.
& 10. 19, 20. 1 Pet. 3. 18. q 1 Cor. 12. 13. ch. 4. 4.

18 For [p] through him we both have access [q] by one Spirit unto the Father.

For through him, as our Mediator and Peace-maker, who hath reconciled us to God, *we both have access*, are admitted or introduced, *by one Spirit unto the Father;* by the Holy Ghost, who is our Guide to lead us to the Father, as Christ is the way by which we go to him, John xiv. 6. As there is but one Mediator through whom both Jews and Gentiles come to God, so but one and the same Spirit, chap. iv. 4.

r Phil. 3. 20.
Heb. 12. 22,
23.
s Gal. 6. 10.
ch. 3. 15.

19 Now therefore ye are no more strangers and foreigners, but [r] fellow-citizens with the saints, and of [s] the houshold of God;

Now therefore ye are no more strangers and foreigners; such are they that may dwell in a city, but are not free of it. He means the same as ver. 12, they were not now *aliens from the commonwealth of Israel,* &c. *But fellow citizens with the saints;* members of the same spiritual society or corporation with other saints, patriarchs, prophets, &c. The church of God is compared to a city, of which every saint is a member or free-man, Phil. iii. 20. *And of the household of God:* the church is here compared to a house, as 1 Tim. iii. 15. They are said to be of the household that belong to it, but especially the children. Among men, servants are counted domestics; but with God, none but his children.

t 1 Cor. 3. 9,
10. ch. 4. 12.
1 Pet. 2. 4, 5.
u Matt.16.
18. Gal. 2. 9.
Rev. 21. 14.
x 1 Cor. 12.
28. ch. 4. 11. y Ps. 118. 22. Is. 28. 16. Matt. 21. 42.

20 And are [t] built [u] upon the foundation of the [x] apostles and prophets, Jesus Christ himself being [y] the chief corner *stone ;*

And are built upon the foundation of the apostles and prophets; the foundation which the apostles and prophets laid by their preaching, viz. Christ, whom they held forth as the only Mediator between God and man, the only Saviour and head of the church: see 1 Cor. iii. 11. *Foundation*, in the singular number, to imply the unity of their doctrine centring in Christ: *apostles and prophets*, whose office was to preach, not kings and patriarchs. *Jesus Christ himself being the chief corner-stone;* as both supporting the building by his strength, and uniting the several parts of it, Jew and Gentile: see Matt. xxi. 42; Psal. cxviii. 22. They that are of chief authority are called the corners of a people, as sustaining the greatest burden, 1 Sam. xiv. 38; Isa. xix. 13. *Object.* If Christ be the corner-stone, how is he the foundation? *Answ.* The same thing may have different denominations in different respects; Christ is called a *foundation,* 1 Cor. iii. 11, a *corner-stone,* 1 Pet. ii. 6, a *temple,* John ii. 19, a *door,* John x. 7, a builder, Matt. xvi. 18; so here again a *corner-stone,* and yet laid *for a foundation,* Isa. xxviii. 16.

z ch. 4. 15, 16.
a 1 Cor. 3. 17. & 6. 19.
2 Cor. 6. 16.

21 *In whom all the building fitly framed together groweth unto *an holy temple in the Lord:

In whom; or upon whom, viz. Christ the foundation. *All the building;* whatsoever is built on Christ the foundation, and so all particular believers, as the several parts of the building. *Fitly framed together;* joined and united both to Christ the foundation by faith, and to each other by love. *Groweth;* either, 1. Ariseth; the building goeth on till it comes to be a temple. Or, 2. It notes the stones or materials of the house to be living ones, receiving life from Christ, 1 Pet. ii. 5. Growth supposeth life. The verb is in the present tense, to signify that the builders are still at work, and this temple not yet finished. *Unto an holy temple;* in allusion to the temple at Jerusalem; whereas the holy of holies was a type of heaven, so the temple itself was a type of the church, both as it was the place of God's presence, and of his worship. *In the Lord:* either this must be joined to *groweth,* and then it is a pleonasm, the antecedent being here repeated, though the relative had been expressed, and it implies the growth of believers (the materials of this spiritual building) to be from Christ; or it may be joined with *holy,* and then it signifies that they have their holiness from Christ; or it may be read, *holy to the Lord,* and then it expresses the nature of this temple, that it is undefiled, consecrated to the Lord, and meet for him.

b 1 Pet. 2. 5.

22 *In whom ye also are builded together for an habitation of God through the Spirit.

An habitation of God; a temple where God may dwell. Not only the whole collection of believers is called the temple of God, but particular churches and particular saints are so called, because of God's dwelling in them by his Spirit: see 1 Cor. iii. 16, 17; vi. 19. *Through the Spirit:* this may relate either to the words immediately going before, *an habitation of God,* and then the meaning is, an habitation or temple in which God dwells by his Spirit; or to the verb *builded,* and then they import the building of them into a temple to be the operation of the Spirit, working that faith and love in them whereby they are united to Christ the foundation, and to the several parts of the building.

CHAP. III

Paul, in bonds for preaching Christ to the Gentiles, showeth that the mystery of their calling, heretofore hidden, had been revealed to him, 1—6; *that by his ministry God's gracious purpose might be universally known, and the Gentiles be assured of their acceptance by faith,* 7—12. *He desireth his Ephesian converts not to be discouraged at his sufferings on their account,* 13; *and prayeth that God would strengthen their faith and knowledge of the infinite love of Christ,* 14—19. *He giveth glory to God for his power in the church by Christ Jesus,* 20, 21.

a Acts 21. 33. & 28. 17, 20. ch. 4. 1, & 6. 20, Phil. 1. 7, 13, 14, 16. Col. 4. 3, 18. 2 Tim. 1. 8. & 2. 9. Philem. 1, 9. b Gal. 5. 11. Col. 1. 24. 2 Tim. 2. 10.

FOR this cause I Paul, *the prisoner of Jesus Christ b for you Gentiles,

For this cause; i. e. that ye may be further confirmed in the faith of Christ, and more and more built up in him as *an habitation of God,* chap. ii. 22. *The prisoner of Jesus Christ;* for Christ's sake, for asserting his cause and honour: see 2 Tim. i. 8; Philem. 1, 9. *For you Gentiles;* for your cause and salvation; having preached and declared the grace of God to be free, and to belong to you Gentiles as well as to the Jews, (the middle wall of partition being taken away,) and so equalled you with them. There is no small difference among expositors about the connexion of these words: the fairest and easiest seems to be, either, 1. That the substantive verb *am* be here supplied, and the word read, *I Paul am the prisoner of Jesus Christ;* q. d. I have for some time been and still am the prisoner of Jesus Christ. Or, 2. That this verse be joined to the 14th, (all the rest, ver. 2—13, being included in a parenthesis,) where he begins with the same words as here; and so we may read it thus, ver. 1, For this cause I Paul, the prisoner, &c.; and then, ver. 14, I say, *For this cause I bow my knees,* &c., viz. praying that ye may be strengthened with might by his Spirit, &c.; i. e. that they might be more and more built up on Christ, on whom they were founded, and had begun to be built.

2 (If ye have heard of *the dispensation of the grace of God d which is given me to you-ward:

c Rom. 1. 5. & 11. 13. 1 Cor. 4. 1. ch. 4. 7. Col. 1. 25. d Acts 9. 15. & 13. 2. Rom. 12. 3. Gal. 1. 16. ver. 8.

If ye have heard; this doth not imply doubting, but rather the apostle takes the thing for granted; q. d. Seeing ye have heard; and so some render it. See the like, 1 Pet. ii. 3. *Of the dispensation of the grace of God:* either by *grace* he means his apostleship, as Rom. i. 5; Gal. ii. 9; or the free grace of God for salvation revealed in the gospel which he was to preach; and then by *dispensation* we must understand his commission or ordination of God to that work, viz. to publish that grace whereof the ministers of the gospel are the dispensers, 1 Cor. iv. 1. *Which is given me to you-ward;* to you Ephesians and other Gentiles, for whom particularly I am appointed an apostle, Acts ix. 15; xxvi. 17, 18; Gal. ii. 7.

3 *How that f by revelation g he made known unto me the mystery; (h as I wrote || afore in few words,

e Acts 22. 17, 21. & 26. 17, 19. f Gal. 1. 12. g Rom. 16. 25. Col. 1. 26, 27. h ch. 1. 9, 10. || Or, *a little before.*

By revelation; not by man, but immed:ately, Acts ix. 15; Gal. i. 12. *He made known unto me the mystery;* viz. of calling the Gentiles to salvation by faith in Christ, without the works of the law, ver. 6. *As I wrote afore;* in the two former chapters of this Epistle.

4 Whereby, when ye read, ye may understand my knowledge i in the mystery of Christ)

i 1 Cor. 4. 1. ch. 6. 19.

When ye read; or, unto which attending.

5 k Which in other ages was not made known unto the sons of men, l as it is now revealed unto the holy apostles and prophets by the Spirit;

k Acts 10. 28. Rom. 16. 25. ver. 9. l ch. 2. 20.

Which in other ages; in the times before Christ's coming in the flesh. *Was not made known unto the sons of men:* that the Gentiles should be called was formerly known and foretold, but not as since, viz. as to the time and manner of it, and the means whereby it should be effected. *Prophets;* New Testament prophets, chap. iv. 11; Rom. xii. 6; 1 Cor. xiv. 1, 3. *By the Spirit;* either by the Spirit's being poured out on the Gentiles, it was known that they should be co-heirs with the believing Jews; or rather, by the Spirit instructing the apostles and prophets, and immediately acquainting them with this mystery.

6 That the Gentiles m should be fellowheirs, and n of the same body, and o partakers of his promise in Christ by the Gospel:

m Gal. 3. 28, 29. ch. 2. 14. n ch. 2. 15, 16. o Gal. 3. 14.

That the Gentiles should be fellow heirs; i. e. have an equal right to the heavenly inheritance with the believing Jews. *And of the same body;* the same mystical body whereof Christ is the Head. *And partakers of his promise;* the great promise of the covenant, which comprehends all the rest under it. *In Christ;* in whom all the promises have their accomplishment, 2 Cor. i. 20. *By the gospel;* as the means or instrument by which God works faith, whereby they are made partakers of the promise, fellow heirs, &c.

p Rom. 15. 16.
Col. 1. 23, 25.
q Rom. 1. 5.
r Rom. 15. 18. ch. 1. 19.
Col. i. 29.

7 ᵖ Whereof I was made a minister, ᑫ according to the gift of the grace of God given unto me by ʳ the effectual working of his power.

According to the gift of the grace of God; either according to the free gift of God, and which was given merely of grace; or by *gift* he understands all those several gifts (as of knowledge, utterance, &c.) which were the necessary qualifications and furniture of an apostle for the due discharge of his office, all which were freely given to him. *Given unto me by the effectual working of his power;* whereby God made him a preacher of the gospel, who had been a persecutor of believers, and wrought effectually by the Spirit with his preaching for the conversion of thousands, and spreading the gospel in many countries; and likewise wrought miracles for the confirmation of the truth, and conviction of hearers, Acts xix. 12; xxviii. 8.

s 1 Cor. 15. 9.
1 Tim. 1. 13, 15.
t Gal. 1. 16. & 2. 8. 1 Tim. 2. 7. 2 Tim. 1. 11.
u ch. 1. 7.
Col. 1. 27.

8 Unto me, ˢ who am less than the least of all saints, is this grace given, that ᵗ I should preach among the Gentiles ᵘ the unsearchable riches of Christ;

Who am less than the least of all saints; this the apostle speaks considering his former estate in Judaism, when he persecuted the church of Christ: so 1 Cor. xv. 9; 1 Tim. i. 13, 15. Thus modest is the apostle, when speaking of himself, and not of his office. *The unsearchable riches of Christ;* all that grace of Christ which he was to make known to the Gentiles in his preaching, *wisdom, righteousness, sanctification, redemption,* 1 Cor. i. 30.

x ver. 3.
ch. 1. 9.
y Rom. 16. 25. ver. 5.
1 Cor. 2. 7.
Col. 1. 26.
z Ps 33. 6.
John 1. 3.
Col. 1. 16.
Heb. 1. 2.

9 And to make all *men* see what *is* the fellowship of ˣ the mystery, ʸ which from the beginning of the world hath been hid in God, ᶻ who created all things by Jesus Christ:

To make all men; all those to whom the apostle was sent. *See;* or, to enlighten them; i. e. ministerially, Acts xxvi. 18; as to enlighten them principally belongs to Christ, John i. 9. *What is the fellowship of the mystery;* or communication of the mystery, viz. concerning the salvation of the Gentiles without circumcision, or the works of the law, which God now made known by Paul's ministry, contrary to what the Jews believed. *Which from the beginning of the world hath been hid in God;* not revealed to men as to the circumstances and manner of it, but hid in the mind and purpose of God: see the like, chap. i. 9. *Who created all things by Jesus Christ;* this may be understood either of the first creation, or the second, or immediately of the first, and by that of the second; as God created all things at first, (and so both Jews and Gentiles,) and gave them their being, by Christ, John i. 3; so he recreates, regenerates, and gives them a new being, by Christ, that they may be of the same body under him: see the like, 2 Cor. iv. 6.

a 1 Pet. 1. 12.
b Rom. 8. 38.
ch. 1. 21.
Col. 1. 16.
1 Pet. 3. 22.
c 1 Cor. 2. 7.
1 Tim. 3. 16.

10 ᵃ To the intent that now ᵇ unto the principalities and powers in heavenly places ᶜ might be known by the Church the manifold wisdom of God,

Principalities and powers in heavenly places; good angels, Col. i. 16; 1 Pet. iii. 22. *Might be known by the church;* not effectually, as a teacher or instructor of angels present in church assemblies; but objectively, as a mirror in which they might behold and contemplate the manifold wisdom of God. *The manifold wisdom of God;* exceedingly, or many ways, various. The Divine wisdom is in itself one simple thing, but appearing in so great variety of works, it is said to be various. This may be best understood of the whole economy of men's redemption, and God's governing his church in several ages, the several forms of the church, the various ways of revealing the Divine will, the different measures of light let out in different times, the different dispensations of the covenant of grace before the law,

under the law, under the gospel, to the Jews, to the Gentiles, &c.

11 ᵈ According to the eternal purpose which he purposed in Christ Jesus our Lord:

d ch. 1. 9.

According to the eternal purpose: all that God doeth in the work of our redemption, whereby he sets forth his manifold wisdom, he doeth according to what he had from eternity purposed to do, and therein likewise shows his wisdom, to which it belongs to order and determine things before the doing of them, and then to do them as they have been ordered. *Which he purposed in Christ Jesus our Lord;* not only as the eternal Wisdom of the Father, but as designed in God's decree to be the Head of the church, and he by whom God would in time execute his eternal purpose.

12 In whom we have boldness and ᵉ access ᶠ with confidence by the faith of him.

e ch. 2. 18.
f Heb. 4. 16.

In whom; or by, or through whom, or into whom being ingrafted and incorporated. *We have boldness,* or freeness of speech. It signifies that liberty and spiritual security, whereby we come to God as to a Father, in the freedom of children, not the fear of slaves, Rom. viii. 15; Gal. iv. 6; 1 John iii. 21. *And access;* not only in prayer, but all the communion we have with God by faith in Christ, 1 Pet. iii. 18. *With confidence;* either securely without fear, (as before,) or with confidence of acceptance with God, and obtaining what we ask. *By the faith of him;* i. e. faith in him, as Rom. iii. 22: see the like, Mark xi. 22.

13 ᵍ Wherefore I desire that ye faint not at my tribulations ʰ for you, ⁱ which is your glory.

g Acts 14. 22.
Phil. 1. 14.
1 Thes. 3. 3.
h ver. 1.
i 2 Cor. 1. 6.

Wherefore I desire; I pray you. This is an exhortation to the Ephesians, not a prayer to God, for that follows, ver. 14. *That ye faint not at my tribulations for you;* the truth I have preached to you being the cause of my sufferings, and your salvation (to which they tend as a means to confirm your faith) being the end of them. *Which is your glory;* either he means, that their not fainting, or not falling away from Christ, by reason of his sufferings, was their glory; or rather, that his sufferings were their glory, in that he did by them seal the truth of the doctrine he had preached, being still ready to suffer for what he delivered to them.

14 For this cause I bow my knees unto the Father of our Lord Jesus Christ,

For this cause; this may be referred either to the former verse, *For this cause,* viz. *that ye faint not,* &c.; or rather to the 1st verse, the apostle here resuming what he had been beginning there.

15 Of whom ᵏ the whole family in heaven and earth is named,

k ch. 1. 10.
Phil. 2. 9, 10, 11.

Of whom; either of God, or rather of Christ, last mentioned. *The whole family,* or kindred, the church of God being his household, chap. ii. 19. *In heaven and earth;* all the saints, both which are already in glory, and which yet live upon the earth, wherever or whoever they be, Jews or Gentiles. *Is named:* to be named, or called, implies the thing as well as the name. Isa. vii. 14; Luke i. 35. The whole family is named of Christ; i. e. of him they are, as well as are called, Christians, and the church of God. The Jews boasted of Abraham as their father; but now all believers, even Gentiles, are one family of God's people, and upon them the name of Christ is called.

16 That he would grant you, ˡ according to the riches of his glory, ᵐ to be strengthened with might by his Spirit in ⁿ the inner man;

l Rom. 9. 23.
ch. 1. 7.
Phil. 4. 19.
Col. 1. 27.
m ch. 6. 10.
Col. 1. 11.
n Rom. 7. 22.
2 Cor. 4. 16.

The riches of his glory; i. e. the abundance of his power: see Rom. vi. 4. *To be strengthened with might;* further degrees of spiritual strength, proceeding from God's power as the fountain. *By his Spirit;* as the immediate worker of all inherent grace. *In the inner man;* the reasonable powers of the soul as renewed by grace, the same as *heart* in the next verse, and *spirit,* 1 Thess. v. 23: see 2 Cor. iv. 16.

17 ᵒ That Christ may dwell in your

o John 14. 23.
ch. 2. 22.

EPHESIANS III, IV

p Col. 1. 23.
k 2. 7.
hearts by faith; that ye, ᵖbeing rooted and grounded in love,

That Christ; on whom this Spirit (who must strengthen you, as being a *Spirit of might,* Isa. xi. 2) resteth, Isa. lxi. 1. *May dwell in your hearts;* may intimately and continually possess and fill, not your heads only with his doctrine, but your affections with his Spirit : see John xiv. 23. *By faith;* whereby ye not only believe Christ's truth, but receive and apprehend himself, and which is the means by which ye have union and communion with him. *That ye, being rooted and grounded in love :* either he means, 1. Our love to God and our neighbour; and then he prays that their love might not be slight and superficial, but strong and firm. Or, 2. God's love to us; and then he prays that the Ephesians, who had already tasted God's love to them in Christ, might be more fully strengthened in the persuasion of that love.

q ch. 1. 16.
r Rom. 10. 3, 11, 12.
18 ᵠMay be able to comprehend with all saints ʳwhat *is* the breadth, and length, and depth, and height;

May be able to comprehend, more fully and perfectly to perceive and understand, *with all saints,* which are or have been, *what is the breadth, and length, and depth, and height,* the immense vastness, dignity, and perfection; either, 1. Of redemption by Christ, extending both to Jew and Gentile, and so the mystery before mentioned. Or rather, 2. Of the love of Christ, as follows.

s John 1. 16.
ch. 1. 23.
Col. 2. 9, 10.
19 And to know the love of Christ, which passeth knowledge, that ye might be filled ˢwith all the fulness of God.

And to know, sensibly and experimentally to perceive in yourselves, *the love of Christ, which passeth knowledge;* which, though it may in a greater degree than hitherto be known and experienced, yet never can be in this life fully and absolutely understood and comprehended : see ver. 8, and the like expression, Phil. iv. 7. *That ye might be filled with all the fulness of God;* all that fulness of knowledge, faith, love, holiness, and whatsoever it is with which God fills believers gradually here, and perfectly hereafter, when *God* shall *be all in all,* 1 Cor. xv. 28.

t Rom. 16. 25. Jude 24.
u 1 Cor. 2. 9.
20 Now ᵗunto him that is able to do exceeding abundantly ᵘabove all that we ask or think, ˣaccording to the power that worketh in us,

x ver. 7.
Col. 1. 29.

Now unto him; i. e. God the Father. *That is able to do exceeding abundantly above all that we ask or think;* and therefore is able to stablish you to the end, and do all for you that hath been desired. *According to the power that worketh in us; the exceeding greatness of his power,* chap. i. 19; whereby God works faith, and preserves to salvation, 1 Pet. i. 5, and enables to bear afflictions, 2 Tim. i. 8.

y Rom. 11. 36. & 16. 27.
Heb. 13. 21.
21 ʸUnto him *be* glory in the Church by Christ Jesus throughout all ages, world without end. Amen.

Unto him be glory in the church; the whole church of Jews and Gentiles. The church only knows the mystery and partakes of the benefits before mentioned, and therefore the church only can rightly glorify God for them. *By Christ Jesus;* either in Christ, in whom the Father hath displayed all his love to us; or rather *by* (according to our version) Christ, as the Mediator between God and us; by whom we offer up our services to God, praises as well as prayers, Rom. i. 8; vii. 25. *Throughout all ages;* or, through all generations.

CHAP. IV

Paul exhorteth to those virtues which become the Christian calling, particularly to unity, 1—6; *declaring that Christ gave his gifts differently, that his body the church might be built up and perfected in the true faith by the co-operation of the several members with one another, and with him their Head,* 7—16. *He calleth men off from the vain and impure conversation of the heathen world,* 17—21; *to renounce the old, and to put on the new, man,* 22—24; *to discard lying,* 25, *and sinful anger,* 26, 27; *to leave off dishonest practices, and to gain by honest labour what they have occasion for,* 28; *to use no corrupt talk,* 29, *nor grieve God's Spirit,* 30; *to put away all expressions of ill-will, and to practise mutual kindness and forgiveness,* 31, 32.

a ch. 3. 1.
Philem. 1, 9.
‖ Or, *in the Lord.*
b Phil. 1. 27.
Col. 1. 10.
1 Thes. 2, 12.
I THEREFORE, ᵃthe prisoner ‖ of the Lord,) beseech you that ye ᵇwalk worthy of the vocation wherewith ye are called,

The prisoner of the Lord; marg. in the Lord, a Hebraism : it is as much as, for the Lord : see chap. iii. 1. *Beseech you that ye walk worthy;* proceed constantly and perseveringly in such ways as suit with and become your calling, 1 Thess. iv. 7; 1 Pet. i. 15 : see the like expression, Rom. xvi. 2, and in the places in the margin. *Of the vocation wherewith ye are called;* both your general calling, whereby ye are called to be saints, and your particular callings, to which ye are severally called, as chap. v. and vi.

c Acts 20. 19.
Gal. 5. 22, 23. Col. 3. 12, 13.
2 ᶜWith all lowliness and meekness, with longsuffering, forbearing one another in love;

With all lowliness, or humility; submissiveness of mind, whereby we esteem others better than ourselves, Phil. ii. 3. A virtue peculiar to Christians, unknown to philosophers : see Acts xx. 19; Col. iii. 12, 13. *And meekness;* whereby we are not easily provoked, or offended with the infirmities of others : this is opposed to peevishness, as the former to pride. *With long-suffering;* whereby we bear with greater or repeated injuries, 2 Cor. vi. 6. *Forbearing one another;* or supporting, i. e. bearing with the infirmities, frowardness, or moroseness of others, so as not to cease to love them, and do them good. *In love;* not out of any carnal affection, or for our own advantage, but out of love, which is wont to make men patient and long-suffering, 1 Cor. xiii. 4.

3 Endeavouring to keep the unity of the Spirit ᵈin the bond of peace.

d Col. 3. 14.

The unity of the Spirit; either unity of mind, or spiritual unity, as being wrought by the Spirit, and then he means that unity he spoke of, chap. ii. 14—16, and iii. 6, whereby is intended the mystical body of Christ. *In the bond of peace;* i. e. in peace as the bond which keeps the members or parts of the church together, which by dissensions are dissipated and scattered. The first step to this unity is humility, for where that is not, there will be no meekness nor forbearance, without which unity cannot be maintained.

e Rom. 12. 5.
1 Cor. 12. 12, 13. ch. 2. 16.
f 1 Cor. 12. 4, 11.
g ch. 1. 18.
4 ᵉThere is one body, and ᶠone Spirit, even as ye are called in one ᵍhope of your calling;

There is one body; i. e. the church of Christ, chap. i. 23 : see Col. iii. 15. *And one Spirit;* the self-same Spirit of Christ in that body by which all the members live and act, 1 Cor. xii. 11, 13. *Even as ye are called in one hope of your calling;* one inheritance in heaven, to the hope of which ye are called, Col. i. 12. *Hope,* for the thing hoped for, as Col. i. 5 : see 1 Pet. i. 3, 4.

h 1 Cor. 1. 13. & 8. 6.
& 12. 5. 2 Cor. 11. 4. i Jude 3. ver. 13. k Gal. 3. 27, 28. Heb. 6. 6.
5 ʰOne Lord, ⁱone faith, ᵏone baptism,

One Lord; Christ, viz. as Redeemer, Head, and Husband of the church, to whom, by God's appointment, she is immediately subject, 1 Cor. viii. 6; John xiii. 13; Acts ii. 36. *One faith;* i. e. one object of the faith of all believers, viz. the doctrine of salvation, which is but one. *One baptism;* both as to the outward symbol, and the thing signified by it.

l Mal. 2. 10.
1 Cor. 8. 6.
& 12. 6.
m Rom. 11. 36.
6 ˡOne God and Father of all, who *is* above all, and ᵐthrough all, and in you all.

One God; God is here taken personally for the Father, the other two Persons being before mentioned, ver. 4, 5. *And Father of all;* of all believers. *Who is above all;* not only in the excellencies of his nature, but especially in his sovereign dominion over the church. *And through all;* by his special providence, through all the members of the church. *And in you all;* by inhabitation, and the conjunction of believers with him. Though the former two may be applied to God's universal dominion and providence over all the creatures, yet, the apostle speaking of the conjunction of believers in one Father, they are both to be restrained according to this last clause.

7 But ⁿunto every one of us is given grace according to the measure of the gift of Christ.

But unto every one of us is given grace; either by *grace* he means gifts which are not common to all believers, but proper to some, according to their various functions and places in the church, Rom. xii. 6; 1 Cor. xii. 11. Or rather, more generally, it comprehends also those graces which are common to all believers as such, faith, hope, love, zeal, &c.; which, though they are of the same kind in all, and have the same object, yet they are received in different degrees and measures. *According to the measure of the gift of Christ;* in that measure in which it pleaseth Christ to give them, who gives to some one gift, to some another; to some one degree of grace, to some another: all have not the same, but need the help of those that have what they want.

8 Wherefore he saith, °When he ascended up on high, ᵖhe led ∥captivity captive, and gave gifts unto men.

Wherefore he saith; the psalmist. *When he;* Christ, God manifested in the flesh: and then what was spoken by the psalmist prophetically in the second person, is spoken by the apostle historically in the third. *Ascended up on high;* Christ ascended up on high after his death, both as to place, in his human nature, into heaven; and chiefly as to his state, in his being glorified. *He led captivity captive;* either led those captive who had taken us captive, or rather led them captive whom he had taken captive; *captivity* being here put for captives, as elsewhere poverty for poor, 2 Kings xxiv. 14. This Christ did when, having conquered sin, death, Satan, he triumphed gloriously over them in his ascension, Col. ii. 15. It is spoken with allusion to conquering princes or generals, who in their triumphs had their captives attending upon their chariots. *And gave gifts unto men;* he alludes in this likewise to the custom of conquerors casting money among the people that were the spectators of their triumphs, or giving largesses to their soldiers. Christ upon his ascension sent the Holy Ghost on the disciples, Acts ii., and continues ever since to furnish his church with gifts and graces: see on Psal. lxviii. 18.

9 ᵠ(Now that he ascended, what is it but that he also descended first into the lower parts of the earth?

Now that he ascended, what is it but that he also descended first? the apostle interprets the psalmist, and concludes, that David, when he foretold Christ's glorification, or ascending up to heaven, did likewise foresee his humiliation and descent to the earth: q. d. When David speaks of God in the flesh ascending up on high, he doth thereby imply, that he should first descend to the earth. *Into the lower parts of the earth;* either simply the earth, as the lowest part of the visible world, and so opposed to heaven, from whence he came down, John iii. 13; vi. 33, 38, 41, 42, 50, 51; or the grave and state of the dead; or both rather, implying the whole of his humiliation, in opposition to his ascending, taken for the whole of his exaltation.

10 He that descended is the same also ʳthat ascended up far above all heavens, ˢthat he might ∥fill all things.)

He that descended is the same also that ascended: he saith not, he that ascended is the same that descended, lest it should not be thought that Christ brought his body with him from heaven; but, on the contrary, *he that descended is the same that ascended,* to show that the Son of God did not by his descent become other than what he was, nor the assumption of the human nature add any thing to his person, as a man is not made another person by the clothes he puts on. Christ descended without change of place as being God, but ascended by changing place as man, yet, by communication of properties, whole Christ is said to have ascended. *Far above all heavens;* all visible heavens, into the third heaven, or paradise, Acts iii. 21; Heb. ix. 24. *That he might fill all things;* all the members of his church, with gifts and graces. This began to be fulfilled, Acts ii., and still will be fulfilling to the end of the world: see John vii. 39; xvi. 7.

11 ᵗAnd he gave some, apostles; and some, prophets; and some, ᵘevangelists; and some, ˣpastors and ʸteachers;

And he gave; distributed several gifts, (which are spoken of in general, ver. 7,) according to his Father's appointment, who is said to set in the church what Christ is here said to give, 1 Cor. xii. 28. *Object.* Nothing is here said of gifts, but only of offices. *Answ.* Christ never gave offices without suitable furniture; this diversity therefore of offices includes diversity of respective gifts. *Apostles;* extraordinary officers, with an immediate call, universal commission, infallibility in teaching, and power of working miracles, appointed for the first founding the Christian church in all parts of the world, Matt. xxviii. 19; Acts xix. 6. *Object.* The apostles were appointed by Christ before his death. *Answ.* The apostle here speaks not of Christ's first calling them, but, 1. Of his fully supplying them with gifts necessary to the discharge of their office, which was after his resurrection, Acts i. 4; John vii. 39. And, 2. Of their solemn inauguration in their office, by the pouring out of the Holy Ghost upon them in a visible manner, Acts ii. *Prophets;* extraordinary officers who did by immediate revelation interpret the Scriptures, 1 Cor. xiv. 4, 5, and not only such as did foretell things to come, Acts xi. 27; xxi. 10. *Evangelists;* these were likewise extraordinary officers, for the most part chosen by the apostles, as their companions and assistants in preaching the word, and planting churches in the several places where they travelled. Such were Timothy, Titus, Apollos, Silas, &c. *Pastors and teachers;* either two names of the same office, implying the distinct duties of ruling and teaching belonging to it; or two distinct offices, but both ordinary, and of standing use in the church in all times; and then *pastors* are they that are fixed to and preside over particular churches, with the care both of instructing and ruling them, 1 Thess. v. 12; Heb. xiii. 17; called elsewhere *elders,* and *bishops,* Acts xx. 28; Phil. i. 1; 1 Tim. iii. 1; Tit. i. 5, 7; 1 Pet. v. 1, 2. *Teachers;* they whose work is to teach the doctrine of religion, and confute the contrary errors.

12 ᶻFor the perfecting of the saints, for the work of the ministry, ᵃfor the edifying of ᵇthe body of Christ:

For the perfecting of the saints; either for the restoring and bringing them into right order, who had been, as it were, dissipated, and disjointed by sin: or rather the knitting together and compacting them more and more, both in nearer union to Christ their Head by faith, and to their fellow members by love: see 1 Cor. i. 10. *For the work of the ministry;* or, for the work of dispensation, i. e. for dispensing the word, and all those ordinances which it appertains to them to dispense; and so it implies their whole work. But there may be a trajection in the words, and then this clause is to be read before the former, and the meaning plainly is, *For the work of the ministry,* which is to perfect the saints, and edify the body of Christ. *For the edifying of the body of Christ;* the same in effect as *perfecting the saints,* viz. the building up the church, both in bringing in new members to it, and strengthening those that are brought in already, in faith and holiness.

13 Till we all come ∥in the unity of the faith, ᶜand of the knowledge of the Son of God, unto ᵈa perfect man, unto the measure of the ∥stature of the fulness of Christ:

Till we all come, or meet; all we believers, both Jews and Gentiles, (who while in the world not only are dispersed in several places, but have our several degrees of light and knowledge,) meet, or come together, in the unity of, &c. *In the unity of the faith;* either that perfect unity whereof faith is the bond, or rather that perfect uniformity of faith in which we shall all have the same thoughts and apprehensions of spiritual things, to which as yet, by reason of our remaining darkness, we are not arrived. *And of the knowledge of the Son of God;* or acknowledgment, i. e. not a bare speculative knowledge, but such as is joined with appropriation and affection. *Unto a perfect man:* he compares the mystical body of Christ to a man, who hath his several ages and degrees of growth and strength, till he come to the height of both, and then he is a perfect man, or a man simply, in opposition to a child, 1 Cor. xiii. 11. The church of Christ (expressed by a *man*, in the singular number, to show its unity) hath its infancy, its childhood, its youth, and is to have hereafter its perfect manhood and state of consistency in the other life, when, being arrived to its full pitch, it shall be past growing. *Unto the measure of the stature of the fulness of Christ;* either actively, that measure of stature or age which Christ fills up in it, or hath allotted to it, ver. 7 ; or rather passively, that measure which, though it do not equal, yet it shall resemble, being perfectly conformed to the fulness of Christ. As in the 12th verse he showed the end of Christ's appointing officers in his church, so here he shows how long they are to continue, viz. till their work be done, the saints perfected, which will not be till they all come to the unity of the faith, &c.

14 That we *henceforth* be no more ^e children, ^f tossed to and fro, and carried about with every ^g wind of doctrine, by the sleight of men, *and* cunning craftiness, ^h whereby they lie in wait to deceive ;

e Is. 28. 9. 1 Cor. 14. 20. f Heb. 13. 9. g Mat. 11. 7.
h Rom. 16. 18. 2 Cor. 2. 17.

That we henceforth be no more children; i. e. weak in the faith, unstable in judgment, *children in understanding,* 1 Cor. xiv. 20 ; such as need teaching, and strengthening : see Rom. ii. 20 ; 1 Cor. iii. 1 ; Heb. v. 13. *Tossed to and fro;* light and unconstant, like ships without ballast, tossed with every wave. *And carried about with every wind of doctrine;* not only shaken and staggering as to our faith, (as in the former clause,) but carried about to errors for want of judgment, by false doctrines, here compared to violent winds. *By the sleight of men;* their sophistry, whereby they easily seduce those that are unskilful, as men easily cheat children in playing at dice, from whence this metaphor is taken. *Cunning craftiness;* their skilfulness in finding out ways of deceiving, whereby they can make any thing of any thing. *Whereby they lie in wait to deceive,* viz. as in ambush ; the word here used, is translated *wiles,* chap. vi. 11, against which the apostle would have them fenced with *the whole armour of God,* and seems to signify a laying in ambush, or assaulting a man behind his back ; a secret and unseen way of circumventing, a laying wait to draw them that are weak from the truth.

i Zech. 8. 16. 2 Cor. 4. 2. ver. 25. 1 John 3. 18. ‖ Or, *being sincere.* k ch. 1. 22. & 2. 21. 1 Col. 1. 18.

15 But ^i ‖ speaking the truth in love, ^k may grow up into him in all things, ^l which is the head, *even* Christ :

But speaking the truth in love; or, following the truth in love : q. d. Not only let us not be seduced by the craftiness of men, but constantly adhere to, and persevere in, the belief of the truth, joining love with it, in which two the sum of Christianity consists ; and this will be a means of our growing up, and being no more children. *May grow up;* this is opposed to being children ; we are not to stand at a stay, but grow to maturity, Heb. vi. 1. *In all things;* in knowledge, faith, love, and all the parts of the new man. *Into him which is the head, even Christ;* our growth must be with respect to Christ our Head, as the end of it ; we must grow in our acknowledgment of him, and dependence on him, as he by whom we are influenced, and from whom all our proficiency and strength proceeds ; so that whatever increase we make, must tend not to the magnifying ourselves, but exalting our Head.

m Col. 2. 19.

16 ^m From whom the whole body fitly joined together and compacted by that which every joint supplieth, according to the effectual working in the measure of every part, maketh increase of the body unto the edifying of itself in love.

From whom; Christ the Head, ver. 15. *The whole body;* the mystical body, or church of believers, whereof every true saint is a member, Rom. xii. 4, 5. *Fitly joined together;* viz. in the right place and order, both in respect of Christ the Head, and of the members respectively. Some are eyes, some ears, some hands, some feet, 1 Cor. xii. 15, 16. *And compacted;* firmly knit, so as not to be separated. *By that which every joint supplieth;* or, by every joint or juncture of administration ; i. e. whose office is to administer spirits and nourishment to the body. *Bands* are added to joints, Col. ii. 19, which signifies the ligaments by which the joints are tied one to another, as well as the joints in which they touch. *Quest.* What are those joints and bands in the mystical body ? *Answ.* Every thing whereby believers are joined to Christ, or to each other as Christians ; especially the Spirit of Christ, which is the same in the Head and all the members ; the gifts of the Spirit, chiefly faith, whereby they are united to Christ, and love, whereby they are knit to each other ; the sacraments, likewise, church officers, ver. 11, &c. *According to the effectual working;* either the power of Christ, who, as a Head, influenceth and enliveneth every member ; or *the effectual working* of every member, in communicating to others the gifts it hath received. *In the measure of every part;* according to the state, condition, and exigence of every part, nourishment is conveyed to it meet for it ; yet more to one and less to another, according as more is required for one and less for the other, and so to all in their proportion. Or else as each part hath received, so it communicates to others ; all have their use and helpfulness to others, but not all alike, or in the same degree. *Maketh increase of the body :* either *body* here redounds by a Hebraism, and the sense is, the body (mentioned in the beginning of the verse) maketh increase of itself ; or, without that redundancy, *increase of the body* is an increase meet and convenient for the body. *Unto the edifying of itself :* the apostle here changeth the metaphor from that of a body to this of a house, but to the same sense, and shows the end of this nourishment they ministered from one member to another, viz. not its own private good, but the good of the whole body, for the benefit of which each part receives its gifts from Christ the Head. *In love ;* either by the offices of love, or it denotes the impulsive cause, whereby the members are moved thus to promote the common increase of the body, viz. love to the Head and each other.

17 This I say therefore, and testify in the Lord, that ^n ye henceforth walk not as other Gentiles walk, ^o in the vanity of their mind,

n ch. 2. 1, 2, 3. ver. 22. Col. 3. 7. 1 Pet. 4. 3.
o Rom. 1. 21.

This I say therefore, and testify in the Lord; I beseech or adjure you by the Lord : see the like, Rom. xii. 1 ; Phil. ii. 1. *That ye henceforth walk not as other Gentiles walk, in the vanity of their mind;* their minds themselves, and understandings, the highest and noblest faculties in them, being conversant about things empty, transient, and unprofitable, and which deceive their expectations, and therefore vain, viz. their idols, their worldly enjoyments, &c.

18 ^p Having the understanding darkened, ^q being alienated from the life of God through the ignorance that is in them, because of the ^r ‖ blindness of their heart :

p Acts 26. 18. q ch. 2. 12. Gal 4. 8. 1 Thess. 4. 5. r Rom. 1. 21. ‖ Or, *hardness.*

Having the understanding; the mind as reasoning and discoursing, and so their ratiocinations and discourses themselves. *Darkened;* as to spiritual things. *Being alienated from the life of God;* not only strangers to it, (for so are those creatures which are not capable of it,) but estranged from it ; implying, that in Adam originally they were not so. *The life of God;* a spiritual life ; that life which God commands, and approves, and whereby God lives in believers, and they live in him, Gal. ii. 19, 20 ; and that both as to the principle of life, and the operations of it. *Through the ignorance that is in them;* that ignorance which is naturally in them, is the cause of their alienation from the life of God, which begins in light and knowledge. *Because of the blindness of their heart;* or rather hardness : the Greek word signifies a *callum* or brawniness in the flesh, which is usual in the hands of labourers. Either this is set down as another cause of their estrangement from the life of God, or as the cause of their ignorance, which, though in part it be natural to them, yet is increased to further degrees by their own hardness and obstinacy, shutting their eyes voluntarily against the light.

19 ^s Who being past feeling ^t have given themselves over unto lasciviousness, to work all uncleanness with greediness.

s 1 Tim. 4. 2. t Rom. 1. 24, 26. 1 Pet. 4. 3.

Who being past feeling; having lost all sense and conscience of sin: a higher degree or effect of the hardness before mentioned, 1 Tim. iv. 2. *Have given themselves over unto lasciviousness;* voluntarily yielded themselves up to the power of their own sensuality and lasciviousness, so as to be commanded by it, without resisting it. *To work;* not only to burn with inward lusts, but to fulfil them in the outward acts. *All uncleanness;* all sorts of uncleanness, even the most monstrous, Rom. i. 24, 26, 27 ; 1 Cor. vi. 9; Gal. v. 19. *With greediness;* either with covetousness, and then it respects those that prostituted themselves for gain ; or rather with an insatiable desire of still going on in their filthiness.

20 But ye have not so learned Christ ;

But ye have not so learned; so as to walk as other Gentiles walk, in the vanity of your minds, &c. *Christ;* the doctrine of Christ, or rule of life prescribed by him.

u ch. 1. 13. 21 "If so be that ye have heard him, and have been taught by him, as the truth is in Jesus :

If so be that ye have heard him; either heard Christ speaking to you in the gospel, Heb. xii. 25, and then the sense will be the same as in the following clause ; or heard him preached to you, and then it may refer to the outward hearing of the word. *And have been taught by him;* or taught *in* him; *in* for *by*, as Col. i. 16; Heb. i. 2; and then this relates to the power of the word, and the impression made by it upon the heart: q. d. If ye have not only heard of him by the hearing of the ear, but have been effectually taught by the Spirit to know him, and receive his doctrine, Isa. liv. 13 ; John vi. 45. *As the truth is in Jesus;* as it really is, and hath been taught by Christ himself, both in his doctrine and example, viz. what is the true way of a Christian's living ; as in the following verses : see John xvii. 17 ; Tit. i. 1.

x Col. 2. 11. & 3. 8, 9. Heb. 12. 1. 1 Pet. 2. 1. y ch. 2. 2, 3. ver. 17. Col. 3. 7. 1 Pet. 4. 3. z Rom. 6. 6. 22 That ye ˣput off concerning ʸthe former conversation ᶻthe old man, which is corrupt according to the deceitful lusts;

That ye put off; a usual metaphor, taken from garments (implying a total abandoning, and casting away, like a garment not to be put on again) : it is opposed to putting on, ver. 24, and is the same as mortifying, Col. iii. 5, crucifying, Gal. vi. 14. *Concerning the former conversation;* the former heathenish life and manners, chap. ii. 2. He shows how they should put off their old man, viz. by relinquishing their old manners ; the same as putting off *the old man with his deeds,* Col. iii. 9. *The old man;* the pravity of nature, or nature as depraved. *Which is corrupt;* or, which corrupteth, i. e. tends to destruction, Gal. vi. 8; or, which daily grows worse and more corrupt by the fulfilling of its lusts. *According to the deceitful lusts;* i. e. which draw away and entice men, James i. 14; or which put on a show and semblance of some good, or promise pleasure and happiness, but lurch men's hopes, and make them more miserable.

a Rom. 12.2. Col. 3. 10. 23 And ᵃbe renewed in the spirit of your mind ;

And be renewed; viz. more and more, being already renewed in part. *In the spirit of your mind;* i. e. in your mind which is a spirit: see 1 Thess. v. 23 ; 2 Tim. iv. 22. He means the superior powers of the soul, where regeneration begins, and which the philosophers magnified so much, and thought so pure.

b Rom. 6. 4 2 Cor. 5. 17. Gal. 6. 15. ᶜ ch. 6. 11. Col. 3. 10. c ch. 2. 10. ‖ Or, *holiness of truth.* 24 And that ye ᵇput on the new man, which after God ᶜis created in righteousness and ‖true holiness.

And that ye put on; the same metaphor of a garment as before, to show the intimateness of the new man with us, and its being an ornament to us. *The new man;* i. e. a new disposition or constitution of the whole man, called the *new creature,* 2 Cor. v. 17, and a *divine nature,* 2 Pet. i. 4. *Which after God;* after God's image. *Is created in righteousness and true holiness;* either *righteousness* may relate to the second table, and *holiness* to the first, and so both contain our duty to man and to God ; or *righteousness* may imply that Divine principle in us, whereby we perform our whole duty to God and the creature, and *holiness* that which denieth all mixture of corruption in our duty to God and man. *True;* sincere and sound. As *righteousness and holiness* are opposed to *lusts,* ver. 22, so *true* here, to *deceitful* there.

25 Wherefore putting away lying, ᵈspeak every man truth with his neighbour: for ᵉwe are members one of another.
d Zech.8.16. ver. 15. Col. 3. 9. e Rom. 12.5.

Wherefore putting away lying; all fraudulency and dissimulation, and whatever is contrary to truth. *Speak every man truth;* not only speak as things are, but act sincerely and candidly. *For we are members one of another;* i. e. to or for one another, and therefore must be helpful to each other.

26 ᶠBe ye angry, and sin not: let not the sun go down upon your wrath : f Ps. 4. 4. & 37. 8.

Be ye angry and sin not: by way of concession, rather than by way of command : q. d. If the case be such that ye must be angry, yet see it be without sin. *Let not the sun go down upon your wrath ;* if your anger is excessive, (for so this word signifies, being different from the former,) yet let it not be lasting ; be reconciled ere the sun go down.

27 ᵍNeither give place to the devil. g 2 Cor. 2.10, 11. Jam. 4, 7. 1 Pet. 5. 9.

Do not give advantage to the devil to possess your hearts, and put you upon more and greater evils : see Luke xxii. 3; John xiii. 27 ; Acts v. 3.

28 Let him that stole steal no more : but rather ʰlet him labour, working with his hands the thing which is good, that he may have ‖ to give ⁱto him that needeth. h Acts 20.35. 1 Thes. 4.11. 2 Thes. 3, 8, 11, 12. ‖ Or, *to distribute.* i Luke 3. 11.

Let him that stole steal no more; stealing is understood largely for seeking our own gain by any way, defrauding others, whether by taking away, or unjustly detaining what is theirs. *But rather let him labour ;* i. e. diligently and industriously, as the word imports. Idleness is condemned as tending to theft. *Working with his hands,* as the only instrument by which most arts and trades are exercised. *The thing which is good ;* not in any unlawful way, but in an honest calling. *That he may have to give to him that needeth ;* that he may have not only whereupon to live, and prevent stealing, but wherewith to help those that want, Luke xxi. 2.

29 ᵏLet no corrupt communication proceed out of your mouth, but ˡthat which is good ‖to the use of edifying, ᵐthat it may minister grace unto the hearers. k Matt. 12. 36. ch. 5. 4. Col. 3. 8. 1 Col. 4. 6. 1 Thes. 5.11. ‖ Or, *to edify profitably.* m Col. 3. 16.

Let no corrupt communication; unprofitable, unsavoury, not seasoned with the salt of prudence, Col. iv. 6 : see Mark ix. 50. *To the use of edifying ;* Gr. to the edification of use, by an hypallage, for, *to the use of edifying,* as our translators render it, implying, that the great use of speech is to edify those with whom we converse. But the same word translated *use,* signifies likewise profit, and necessity, and, by a Hebraism, this (as the latter substantive) may be instead of an adjective, and the words translated, to useful, or profitable, edifying, or, (according to the marginal reading,) *to edify profitably,* with little difference of sense from the former : or, to necessary edifying ; and then it respects the condition and necessities of the hearers, to which our discourse must be suited by way of instruction, reprehension, exhortation, or consolation, as their case requires. *That it may minister grace to the hearers ;* by which some grace may be communicated to or increased in them, by instruction, reprehension, exhortation, &c.

30 And ⁿgrieve not the holy Spirit of God, ᵒwhereby ye are sealed unto the day of ᵖredemption. n Is. 7. 13. & 63. 10. Ezek. 16. 43. 1 Thes. 5. 19. o ch. 1. 13. p Luke 21. 28. Rom. 8. 23. ch. 1. 14.

And grieve not the holy Spirit of God ; viz. by corrupt communication. The Spirit is said to be grieved when any thing is done by us, which, were he capable of such passions, might be matter of grief to him ; or when we so offend him as to make him withdraw his comfortable presence from us : see Isa. lxiii. 10. *Whereby ye are sealed ;* set apart or marked for, and secured unto the day of redemp-

31 ᵃLet all bitterness, and wrath, and anger, and clamour, and ʳevil speaking, be put away from you, ˢwith all malice:

Let all bitterness, and wrath, and anger; these all seem to relate to the inward affection, as the two following to the effects of it in the words. *Bitterness* may imply a secret lurking displeasure at another, or rather a confirmed and permanent one; *wrath,* the first boiling up of the passion, which affects the body in the commotion of the blood and spirits; and *anger,* a greater height and paroxysm of the same passion, or an eager desire of revenge: see Col. iii. 8. *And clamour;* such inordinate loudness as men in anger are wont to break out into in their words. *And evil speaking;* either with respect to God or man, though the latter seems particularly meant here; railing, reviling, reproaching, &c., the ordinary effects of immoderate anger. *With all malice;* maliciousness, or malignity of heart, in opposition to kindness and tenderness, ver. 32: see Rom. i. 29; 1 Cor. v. 8; xiv. 20; Tit. iii. 3.

32 And ᵗbe ye kind one to another, tenderhearted, ᵘforgiving one another, even as God for Christ's sake hath forgiven you.

And be ye kind; sweet, amiable, facile in words and conversation, Luke vi. 35. *Tender-hearted;* merciful, quickly moved to compassion: so we have *bowels of mercies,* Col. iii. 12. *Forgiving one another, even as God for Christ's sake hath forgiven you;* be placable, and ready to forgive, therein resembling God, who for Christ's sake hath forgiven you more than you can forgive to one another.

CHAP. V

Paul exhorteth to the imitation of God, and of the love of Christ, 1, 2: *to avoid fornication and all uncleanness,* 3, 4; *which exclude from the kingdom of God, and draw down God's wrath on unbelievers,* 5, 6; *with whose works of darkness Christians, that have better light to inform and influence them, should have no fellowship,* 7—14: *to walk with prudence and circumspection,* 15—17: *not to drink wine to excess, but to be filled with the Spirit, singing psalms, and giving thanks to God,* 18—20; *and being in due subordination to one another,* 21. *The duty of wives toward their husbands,* 22—24; *and of husbands toward their wives, enforced by the example of Christ and his church,* 25—33.

BE ᵃye therefore followers of God, as dear children;

Be ye therefore followers of God; particularly in being kind, and forgiving injuries, Matt. v. 45, 48; so that this relates to the last verse of the former chapter. *As dear children;* viz. of God. Children should imitate their fathers, especially when beloved of them.

2 And ᵇwalk in love, ᶜas Christ also hath loved us, and hath given himself for us an offering and a sacrifice to God ᵈfor a sweetsmelling savour.

And walk in love; let your whole conversation be in love. *As Christ also hath loved us, and hath given himself for us;* viz. to die for us, Gal. ii. 20, as the greatest argument of his love, John xv. 13; Rom. v. 8. *An offering and a sacrifice to God;* either *offering* signifies a meat-offering, which was joined as an appendix with the bloody sacrifice; or rather more generally, all the oblations that were under the law; and the word *sacrifice* either restrains it to those especially in which blood was shed for expiation of sin, or explains the meaning of it: q. d. Christ gave himself an offering, even a sacrifice in the proper sense, i. e. a bloody one. *For a sweet-smelling savour;* i. e. acceptable to God; alluding to the legal sacrifices, (see Gen. viii. 21; Lev. i. 9,) and intimating those other to have been accepted of God, only with respect to that of Christ; and that as Christ dying to reconcile sinners to God was acceptable to him, so our spiritual sacrifices are then only like to be accepted of him, when we are reconciled to our brother, Matt. v. 23, 24.

3 But ᵉfornication, and all uncleanness, or covetousness, ᶠlet it not be once named among you, as becometh saints;

But fornication; folly committed between unmarried persons, especially men's abuse of themselves with common strumpets, a sin not owned as such among the heathen. *And all uncleanness;* all other unlawful lusts whereby men defile themselves. *Or covetousness;* either an insatiable desire of gratifying their lusts, as chap. iv. 19; or rather an immoderate desire of gain, which was usual in cities of great trade, as Ephesus was: see ver. 5. *Let it not be once named among you;* not heard of, or not mentioned without detestation: see Psal. xvi. 4; 1 Cor. v. 1. *As becometh saints,* who should be pure and holy, not in their bodies and minds only, but in their words too.

4 ᵍNeither filthiness, nor foolish talking, nor jesting, ʰwhich are not convenient: but rather giving of thanks.

Neither filthiness; obscenity in discourse, *filthy communication,* Col. iii. 8. *Nor foolish talking;* affectation of foolish, vain speech, (whether jocose or serious,) unprofitable, to the hearers. *Nor jesting;* either the same as the former, as may seem by the disjunctive particle *nor,* which may be by way of explication; or (which is of kin to it) scurrility in discourse, which is many times, by them that are addicted to it, called by the name of urbanity, or jesting: for all that jesting is not here condemned appears by 1 Kings xviii. 27; Isa. xiv. 11. *Which are not convenient;* viz. for saints. *But rather giving of thanks;* i. e. to God for mercies received, which will better cheer up and recreate the mind than foolish talking and jesting can.

5 For this ye know, that ⁱno whoremonger, nor unclean person, nor covetous man, ᵏwho is an idolater, ˡhath any inheritance in the kingdom of Christ and of God.

Nor covetous man, who is an idolater; because he serves Mammon instead of God, loves his riches more than God, and placeth his hope in them. *Hath any inheritance;* without repentance; for he speaks of those that persevere in such sins, whom he calls *children of disobedience,* ver. 6. *In the kingdom of Christ and of God;* not two distinct kingdoms, but one and the same, which belongs to God by nature, to Christ as Mediator. By this phrase he intimates, that there is no coming into the kingdom of God but by Christ.

6 ᵐLet no man deceive you with vain words: for because of these things ⁿcometh the wrath of God ᵒupon the children of ‖disobedience.

Vain words; false and deceitful, which cannot secure to you the impunity they promise you, bearing you in hand, either that those things are not sins, or not so dangerous. *The wrath of God;* viz. in the other world.

7 Be not ye therefore partakers with them.

With those children of disobedience, who continue in the forementioned sins: see Job xxxiv. 8; Psal. l. 18.

8 ᵖFor ye were sometimes darkness, but now ᵍ*are ye* light in the Lord: walk as ʳchildren of light:

For ye were sometimes darkness; the same as *in darkness,* Rom. ii. 19; 1 Thess. v. 4; viz. the darkness of sin, ignorance, unbelief. The abstract being put for the concrete, shows the greatness of that darkness in which they were. *But now are ye light in the Lord;* either now, being in Christ, ye are light, or rather, ye are enlightened or made light by Christ, being furnished with spiritual knowledge, faith, purity, and holiness. *Walk as children of light;* a Hebraism; *children of light,* for those that are in the light, 1 Thess. v. 5 : q. d. Let your conversation be suitable to your condition and privileges : see 1 John i. 7.

a Gal. 5. 22.   9 (For *the fruit of the Spirit *is* in all goodness and righteousness and truth ;)

The fruit of the Spirit; either in the fruit or work of the new nature, or of the Holy Ghost, by whom we are made light in the Lord : see Gal. v. 22. *In all goodness;* either a general virtue in opposition to wickedness, or benignity and bounty. *Righteousness ;* in opposition to injustice, by covetousness, fraud, &c. *Truth ;* in opposition to error, lies, hypocrisy. He shows what it is to *walk as children of light.*

t Rom. 12. 2.
Phil. 1. 10.
1 Thes. 5.21.
1 Tim. 2. 3.   10 *Proving what is acceptable unto the Lord.

Searching what the will of the Lord is, and approving it by your practice as the rule of your walking, Rom. xii. 2.

u 1 Cor. 5. 9,
11. & 10. 20.
2 Cor. 6. 14.
2 Thess. 3.
6, 14.
x Rom. 6.21.
& 13. 12. Gal. 6. 8. y Lev. 19. 17. 1 Tim. 5. 20.

11 And *have no fellowship with *the unfruitful works of darkness, but rather *reprove them.*

Have no fellowship with; not only do not practise them yourselves, but do not join with others in them, by consent, advice, assistance, or any other way whereby ye may be defiled by them. *The unfruitful;* by a meiosis, for bringing forth evil fruit, destructive, pernicious, Rom. vi. 21 ; Gal. vi. 8. *Works of darkness;* wicked works, so called because they proceed from darkness in the mind, the ignorance of God, and men are put upon them by the devil, the prince of darkness, and because they are afraid of the light. *But rather reprove them ;* or convince them, viz. not only by your words, Lev. xix. 17 ; Matt. xviii. 15, but especially by your actions, which being contrary to them, will both evidence them to be, and reprove them as being, works of darkness.

z Rom. 1.24,
26. ver. 3.   12 *For it is a shame even to speak of those things which are done of them in secret.

For it is a shame even to speak of those things; much more to have fellowship with them in them. *Which are done of them in secret;* the darkness adding boldness, as if what men did not see, God did not observe.

a John 3. 20,
21. Heb. 4.
13.
‖ Or, *discovered.*   13 But *all things that are ‖ reproved are made manifest by the light : for whatsoever doth make manifest is light.

But all things ; or all those things, viz. those unfruitful works of darkness, which are to be *reproved. Are made manifest;* i. e. in the minds and consciences of the sinners themselves. *By the light;* the light of doctrine in verbal reproofs, and of a holy life in real and practical ones. *For whatsoever doth make manifest is light;* or, it is the light which manifests every thing, viz. which was before in the dark. The apostle argues from the nature and office of light ; q. d. It is the property of light to discover and manifest what before was not seen, and therefore it becomes you who are light in the Lord to *shine as lights in the world,* Phil. ii. 15, that ye may by your holy conversation convince wicked men of their wickedness, and deeds of darkness, which they did not before perceive in themselves.

‖ Or, *it is,*
b Is. 60. 1.
Rom. 13. 11,
12. 1 Cor.
15. 34.
1 Thes. 5. 6.
c John 5. 25. Rom. 6. 4, 5. ch. 2. 5. Col. 3. 1.

14 Wherefore ‖ he saith, *b*Awake thou that sleepest, and *c*arise from the dead, and Christ shall give thee light.

He saith; either God by the prophets, of whose preaching this is the sum ; it may allude in particular to Isa. lx. 1. Or, Christ by his ministers, in the preaching of the gospel, who daily calls men to arise from the death of sin by repentance, and encourageth them with the promise of eternal life. *Awake thou that sleepest, and arise from the dead ;* the same thing in two different expressions. Sinners in some respects are said to be asleep, in others, to be dead. They are as full of dreams and vain imaginations, and as unfit for any good action, as they that are asleep are for natural ; and they are as full of stench and loathsomeness as they that are dead. Here therefore they are bid to awake from sin as a sleep, and to arise from it as a death. The meaning is, that they should arise by faith and repentance out of that state of spiritual death in which they lie while in their sins. *And Christ shall give thee light ;* the light of peace and joy here, and eternal glory hereafter. The apostle intimates, that what is the way of Christ in the gospel should likewise be the practice of these Ephesians, whom he calls *light in the Lord,* viz. to reprove the unfruitful works of darkness, and awaken sleeping, dead sinners, and bring them to the light of Christ.

15 *d* See then that ye walk circumspectly, not as fools, but as wise,   d Col. 4. 5.

See then that ye walk circumspectly ; being called to reprove the evil conversation of others, see that ye walk exactly and accurately yourselves, avoiding extremes and keeping close to the rule. See the same word rendered *diligently,* Matt. ii. 8, and *perfectly,* 1 Thess. v. 2. *Not as fools ;* who are destitute of spiritual wisdom, and through carelessness fall into sin or error, though in the light of the gospel. *But as wise ;* those that are taught of God, and are endued with wisdom from above.

16 *e*Redeeming the time, *f*because the days are evil.   e Col. 4. 5.
Gal. 6. 10.
f Eccles. 11.
2. & 12. 1. John 12. 35. ch. 6. 15.

Redeeming the time ; or, buying the opportunity : a metaphor taken from merchants, that diligently observe the time for buying and selling, and easily part with their pleasure for gain ; q. d. Deny yourselves in your ease, pleasure, &c. to gain an opportunity of doing good. *Because the days are evil ;* either wicked, by reason of the wickedness of those that live in them, or troublesome, full of difficulties and dangers, by reason of men's hatred of you, and so either depriving you of the opportunity of doing good, or exposing you to hazards for doing it.

17 *g*Wherefore be ye not unwise, but *h*understanding *i*what the will of the Lord *is.*   g Col. 4. 5.
h Rom.12.2.
i Thess. 4.
3. & 5. 18.

Understanding, diligently considering, *what the will of the Lord is,* in the understanding of which your chief wisdom consists.

18 And *k* be not drunk with wine, wherein is excess ; but be filled with the Spirit ;   k Prov. 20.1.
& 23. 29, 20.
Is. 5. 11, 22.
Luke 21. 34.

Wherein, in which drunkenness, *is excess ;* profuseness, lasciviousness, and all manner of lewdness, as the effects of drunkenness, Prov. xxiii. 29, &c. *But be filled with the Spirit;* the Holy Spirit, often compared to water ; or the joy of the Spirit, in opposition to being filled with wine, Acts ii. 13, and that carnal mirth which is caused by it : q. d. Be not satisfied with a little of the Spirit, but seek for a greater measure, so as to be filled with the Spirit. See Psal. xxxvi. 8 ; John iii. 34 ; iv. 14.

19 Speaking to yourselves *l* in psalms and hymns and spiritual songs, singing and making melody in your heart to the Lord ;   l Acts 16.25.
1 Cor. 14. 26.
Col. 3. 16.
Jam. 5. 13.

Speaking, &c. ; in opposition to the vain chaff and lewd talkativeness of drunkards over their cups. *To yourselves;* Gr. in yourselves, i. e. among yourselves, both in church assemblies and families. *In psalms, and hymns, and spiritual songs ;* under these names he comprehends all manner of singing to mutual edification and God's glory. The particular distinction of them is uncertain, but most take *psalms* to be such as anciently were sung with musical instruments ; *hymns,* such as contained only matter of praise ; *spiritual songs,* such as were of various matter, doctrinal, prophetical, historical, &c. : see on Col. iii. 16. *Singing and making melody in your heart ;* not only with your voice, but with inward affection, contrary to the guise of hypocrites. *To the Lord ;* to the glory of God, not for the pleasure of the sense, or for gain, &c.

20 *m*Giving thanks always for all things unto God and the Father *n* in the name of our Lord Jesus Christ ;   m Ps. 34. 1.
Is. 63. 7.
Col. 3. 17.
1 Thes. 5.18.
2 Thess. 1. 3.
n Heb. 13. 15. 1 Pet. 2. 5. & 4. 11.

Giving thanks always : God still by fresh mercies gives fresh occasion for thanksgiving, and we must accordingly continue our thanksgiving through the whole course of our lives without weariness. *For all things ;* all sorts of mercies, among which afflictions may be reckoned, as working for good to them that love God, Rom. viii. 28. *Unto God and the Father;* i. e. unto God even the Father, the Fountain of all our good. *In the name of our Lord Jesus Christ;* in whose name, and by whose merit, all good things are given to us, and by whom we offer up all our prayers, and praises, and spiritual services, that they may be accepted of God.

o Phil. 2. 3.
1 Pet. 5. 5.

21 °Submitting yourselves one to another in the fear of God.

Submitting yourselves one to another, viz. to those to whom ye ought to be subject in natural, civil, or church relations. *In the fear of God;* either for fear of offending God, the Author of all power, who commands this subjection; or so far as is consistent with the fear of God, and so in those things which are not forbidden of him.

p Gen. 3. 16.
1 Cor. 14. 34.
Col. 3. 18.
Tit. 2. 5.
1 Pet. 3. 1.   q ch. 6. 5.

22 ᵖ Wives, submit yourselves unto your own husbands, ᑫ as unto the Lord.

Wives, submit yourselves unto your own husbands; yielding honour and obedience to them. *As unto the Lord;* for the Lord's sake who hath commanded it, so that ye cannot be subject to him without being subject to them : see 1 Tim. ii. 12.

r 1 Cor. 11. 3.

23 ʳ For the husband is the head of the wife, even as ˢ Christ is the head of the Church : and he is the saviour of ᵗ the body.

s ch. 1. 22.
& 4. 15.
Col. 1. 18.
t ch. 1. 23.

For the husband is the head of the wife; superior to her by God's ordination in authority and dignity, as the head in the natural body, being the seat of reason, and the fountain of sense and motion, is more excellent than the rest of the body. *Even as Christ is the head of the church :* see chap. i. 22; Col. i. 18. The particle *as* notes not equality, but likeness, Christ being the Head of the church in a more excellent way than the husband is of the wife. *And he is the saviour of the body;* i. e. Christ is the Saviour of his church, implying that so likewise the husband is given to the wife to be a saviour to her, in maintaining, protecting, and defending her; and therefore the wife, if she regard her own good, should not grudge to be subject to him.

24 Therefore as the Church is subject unto Christ, so *let* the wives *be* to their own husbands ᵘ in every thing.

u Col. 3. 20,
22. Tit. 2. 9.

As the church is subject to Christ, viz. with cheerfulness, chastity, humility, obedience, &c. *So let the wives be to their own husbands;* in imitation of the church's subjection to Christ, as a pattern of their subjection to their husbands. *In every thing;* understand, to which the authority of the husband extends itself.

x Col. 3. 19.
1 Pet. 3. 7.
y Acts 20. 28.
Gal. 1. 4. &
2. 20. ver. 2.

25 ˣ Husbands, love your wives, even as Christ also loved the Church, and ʸgave himself for it;

Husbands, love your wives, even as Christ also loved the church, viz. with a sincere, pure, ardent, and constant affection. As they resemble Christ in the honour they have of being the heads of their wives, so they must likewise in performing the duty of loving them, under which all matrimonial duties are comprehended. *And gave himself for it;* whereby he testified the greatness of his love.

z John 3. 5.
Tit. 3. 5.
Heb. 10. 22.
1 John 5. 6.
a John 15. 3.
& 17. 17.

26 That he might sanctify and cleanse it ᶻ with the washing of water ᵃ by the word,

That he might sanctify; purify from its filth, and consecrate unto God: implying the whole translation of it out of a state of sin and misery into a state of grace and life, consisting in the remission of sin, and renovation of nature. *And cleanse it;* or, cleansing it, importing the means whereby he works the former effect. *With the washing of water,* viz. in baptism, in which the external washing represents seals, and exhibits the internal cleansing from both the guilt and defilement of sin by the blood of Christ, Heb. ix. 14; Rev. i. 5. *By the word;* the word of the gospel, especially the promise of free justification and sanctification by Christ, which received by faith is a means of this sanctification, and without which the external washing is ineffectual; the sign, without the word whereof it is a seal, being no sacrament

27 ᵇ That he might present it to himself a glorious Church, ᶜ not having spot, or wrinkle, or any such thing; ᵈ but that it should be holy and without blemish.

b 2 Cor. 11. 2.
Col. 1. 22.
c Cant. 4. 7.
d ch. 1. 4.

That he might present it to himself; hereafter in heaven; that the whole church of the elect may be present with him, 2 Cor. v. 6, 8; 1 Thess. iv. 17. *A glorious church;* perfect in knowledge and holiness, shining with a heavenly glory, and fully conformed to himself, 1 John iii. 2. *Not having spot;* spot of sin, in allusion to spots in garments. *Or wrinkle;* any relic of old Adam, in allusion to wrinkles in the body, which are signs of old age, and imply deformity. *Or any such thing,* viz. which is contrary to the beauty of the church, and might make her unpleasing to Christ her Husband. *Without blemish;* without any fault to be found in her. He seems to allude to the sacrifices, which were to be without blemish, Lev. i. 3 : see Cant. iv. 7.

28 So ought men to love their wives as their own bodies. He that loveth his wife loveth himself.

So ought men to love their wives as their own bodies; with the same kind of love wherewith they love their own bodies. The woman at first was taken out of the man, and on that account the wife may be said to be a part of her husband. *He that loveth his wife loveth himself;* either this explains the former, and *himself* here is the same as *their own bodies* before; or it adds to it, and is as much as, his own person, the wife being another self, one flesh, the same person (in a civil sense) with her husband.

29 For no man ever yet hated his own flesh; but nourisheth and cherisheth it, even as the Lord the Church :

No man; none in his right senses; or no man hates his flesh absolutely, but the diseases or miseries of it. *His own flesh;* his body. *Nourisheth and cherisheth it;* feeds and clothes it, and supplies it with things necessary for it. *Even as the Lord the church,* which he furnisheth with all things needful to salvation.

30 For ᵉ we are members of his body, of his flesh, and of his bones.

e Gen. 2. 23.
Rom. 12. 5.
1 Cor. 6. 15.
& 12. 27.

We are members of his body; his mystical body. *Of his flesh, and of his bones;* as Eve was of Adam's, Gen. ii. 23; only that was in a carnal way, this in a spiritual, as by the communication of Christ's flesh and blood to us by the Spirit we are united to him, and members of him.

31 ᶠ For this cause shall a man leave his father and mother, and shall be joined unto his wife, and they ᵍ two shall be one flesh.

f Gen. 2. 24.
Matt. 19. 5.
Mark 10. 7, 8.
g 1 Cor. 6. 16.

For this cause; because the woman was formed of the flesh and bones of the man. He refers to Adam's words, Gen. ii. 24. *Shall a man leave his father and mother;* as to cohabitation, and domestic conversation; or, let a man rather leave his father and mother than not cleave to his wife. The apostle doth not cancel the obligations of other relations, but prefers this before them. *They two shall be one flesh;* i. e. one body, or one man, viz. by the marriage bond, whereby each hath power over the other's body, 1 Cor. vii. 4.

32 This is a great mystery : but I speak concerning Christ and the Church.

This is a great mystery; either, this that was spoken before of a marriage union between Christ and the church, and its being of his flesh and of his bones, is a great mystery, and so in the latter part of the verse the apostle explains himself. Or, this that was said of the conjunction of Adam and Eve was a great mystery, (i. e. a great secret in religion,) as being a type of Christ's marriage with his church; though not an instituted type appointed by God to signify this, yet a kind of natural type, as having a resemblance to it.

33 Nevertheless ʰ let every one of you in particular so love his wife even as himself; and the wife *see* that she ⁱ reverence her husband.

h ver. 25.
Col. 3. 19.

i 1 Pet. 3. 6.

Nevertheless; q. d. Setting aside this mystery; or, to return to my former exhortation. *Love his wife even as himself;* as her that is one flesh with him. *Reverence her husband;* or fear, yet not with a servile, but ingenuous fear, and such as proceeds from love.

CHAP. VI

The relative duties of children, 1—3, *and parents,* 4; *of servants,* 5—8, *and masters,* 9. *Paul exhorteth the brethren to resist spiritual enemies by putting on the whole armour of God,* 10—17, *and by perseverance in prayer, which he requireth for all saints, and particularly for himself, that he might preach the gospel with due boldness,* 18—20. *He commendeth Tychicus,* 21, 22; *and concludeth with good wishes to all sincere Christians,* 23, 24.

a Prov. 23. 22. Col. 3.20.

CHILDREN, [a] obey your parents in the Lord: for this is right.

Obey your parents; with inward reverence and promptness, as well as in the outward act. *In the Lord;* either, because the Lord commands it; or, in all things agreeable to his will: see chap. v. 21; Acts v. 29. *For this is right,* or just, every way so, by the law of nature, of nations, and of God.

b Ex. 20. 12. Deut. 5. 16. & 27. 16. Jer. 35. 18. Ezek. 22. 7. Mal. 1. 6. Ecclus. 3. 6. Matt. 15. 4. Mark 7. 10.

2 [b] Honour thy father and mother; which is the first commandment with promise;

i. e. A special promise annexed to the particular duty commanded. There being promises added to only two commandments, viz. the second and this fifth; that which is annexed to the second commandment is a general one, and which relates to the whole law, but this a special one, and which respects this commandment in particular.

3 That it may be well with thee, and thou mayest live long on the earth.

That thou mayest live long and happily. This promise is still fulfilled to believers, either in the thing itself here promised, or in a better way, God's giving them eternal life.

c Col. 3. 21.
d Gen. 18.19. Deut. 4. 9. & 6. 7, 20. & 11. 19. Ps. 78. 4. Prov. 19. 18. & 22. 6. & 29. 17.

4 And, [c] ye fathers, provoke not your children to wrath: but [d] bring them up in the nurture and admonition of the Lord.

Provoke not your children to wrath; viz. by unreasonable severity, moroseness, unrighteous commands, &c. *But bring them up in the nurture;* or correction, as the word signifies, Heb. xii. 6—8. *And admonition;* this denotes the end of the former; instruction in their duty must be, as well as correction to drive them to it. *Of the Lord;* the Lord Jesus Christ; and so it is either that admonition which is commanded by him, or whereby they are brought to be acquainted with him.

e Col. 3. 22.
1 Tim. 6. 1. Tit. 2. 9.
1 Pet. 2. 18.
f 2 Cor.7.15. Phil. 2. 12.
g 1 Chron. 29. 17. Col. 3. 22.

5 [e] Servants, be obedient to them that are *your* masters according to the flesh, [f] with fear and trembling, [g] in singleness of your heart, as unto Christ;

Servants; these servants were generally slaves: Christian liberty doth not take away civil servitude. *Be obedient to them that are your masters;* whether good or bad, as 1 Pet. ii. 18, is expressly said. *According to the flesh;* as to your outward state, not as to your souls and consciences. *With fear and trembling;* either with reverence and fear of offending them, and being punished by them, see Rom. xiii. 4; or rather, with humility, as appears by Psal. ii. 11; 1 Cor. ii. 3; 2 Cor. vii. 15; Phil. ii. 12: compare Rom. xi. 20. *In singleness of your heart;* sincerity, and without guile. *As unto Christ,* who hath commanded this obedience, and whom ye obey in yielding it to your masters.

h Col. 3. 22, 23.

6 [h] Not with eyeservice, as menpleasers; but as the servants of Christ, doing the will of God from the heart;

Not with eyeservice; not merely having respect to your masters' presence, and looking upon you in your work. *As men-pleasers;* such as make it their only business to please their masters, right or wrong, and ingratiate themselves with them, though by offending God. *But as the servants of Christ;* as becomes the servants of Christ, or as those that are the servants of Christ, and seek to please him. *Doing the will of God;* performing obedience to your masters not barely as their will, but God's will, who requires it, as ver. 5.

7 With good will doing service, as to the Lord, and not to men:

With good will doing service; not grudgingly or as of constraint, but freely and cheerfully. *As to the Lord, and not to men;* not only regarding men your masters, but Christ your great Master. That which is done for the worst masters, and in the hardest things, is service done to Christ, when out of love to him servants bear their masters' folly or cruelty.

8 [i] Knowing that whatsoever good thing any man doeth, the same shall he receive of the Lord, [k] whether *he be* bond or free.

i Rom. 2. 6. 2 Cor. 5. 10. Col. 3. 24.
k Gal. 3. 28. Col. 3. 11.

Whatsoever good thing any man doeth; viz. as the servant of Christ and as unto the Lord. *The same shall he receive of the Lord;* the reward of the same, by a metonymy. *Whether he be bond or free:* Christ regards not those differences of men at the present, nor will in the day of judgment, 1 Cor. vii. 22; xii. 13: Gal. iii. 28; Col. iii. 11.

9 And, ye [1]masters, do the same things unto them, ‖ [m] forbearing threatening: knowing that ‖ [n] your Master also is in heaven; [o] neither is there respect of persons with him.

1 Col. 4. 1.
‖ Or, moderating.
m Lev.25.43.
‖ Some read, *both your and their master.*
n John 13.13. 1 Cor. 7. 22.
o Wisd. 6. 7. Ecclus. 35. 12. Rom. 2. 11. Col. 3. 25.

And, ye masters, do the same things unto them; not the same in special, which belong only to servants, but in general, which concern you no less than them, viz. do your duty to them with good will, with an eye to God and Christ, &c.; or rather, do your duty mutually to them, according to your condition and calling, Col. iv. 1. *Forbearing threatening;* or rather, (as in the margin,) moderating, or remitting; i. e. do not carry yourselves angrily to them, (which appears in vehement and frequent threatenings,) when ye may otherwise maintain your authority over them. *Knowing that your Master also is in heaven;* and therefore too strong for you, though you may be too hard for your servants. *Neither is there respect of persons with him;* he is just as well as powerful, and will neither spare you because you are masters, nor punish them because they are servants: see Acts x. 34; Gal. ii. 6; Col. iii. 25.

10 Finally, my brethren, be strong in the Lord, and [p] in the power of his might.

p ch. 1. 19. & 3. 16.
Col. 1. 11.

Be strong; or, strengthen yourselves; i. e. be courageous, and constant in the practice of your duty, against the devil and all his assaults. *In the Lord:* not in yourselves, but in the Lord Jesus Christ, in whom your strength lies, and from whom by faith you may obtain it: see Phil. iv. 13; 2 Tim. ii. 1. *And in the power of his might;* or mighty power, see chap. i. 19: q. d. Though your own strength be but weakness, yet Christ's power is mighty, and he can communicate enough to you.

11 [q] Put on the whole armour of God, that ye may be able to stand against the wiles of the devil.

q Rom. 13. 12. 2 Cor. 6. 7. ver. 13. 1 Thess. 5. 8

Put on the whole armour; get yourselves furnished with every grace, that none be wanting in you, no part naked and exposed to your enemies. *Of God;* i. e. not carnal, but spiritual, and given by God: see 2 Cor. x. 3, 4; 1 Thess. v. 8. *That ye may be able to stand;* either to fight, or rather to overcome. He that loses the victory is said to fall; he that gains it, to stand: see Psal. lxxxix. 43. *Against the wiles of the devil:* the devil useth arts and stratagems, as well as force and violence, and therefore, if any part of your spiritual armour be wanting, he will assault you where he finds you weakest.

12 For we wrestle not against †[r] flesh and blood, but against [s] principalities, against powers, against [t] the rulers of the

† Gr. *blood and flesh.*
r Mat. 16.17. 1 Cor. 15. 50.
s Rom. 8. 38. ch. 1. 21.

Col. 2. 15. † Luke 22. 53. John 12 31. & 14. 30. ch. 2. 2. Col. 1. 13

EPHESIANS VI

‖ Or, *wicked spirits.*
‖ Or, *heavenly,* as ch. 1. 3.

darkness of this world, against ‖spiritual wickedness in ‖high *places.*

We *wrestle not;* not only, or not principally. *Against flesh and blood;* men, consisting of flesh and blood, Matt. xvi. 17; Gal. i. 16. *But against principalities, against powers;* devils, Col. ii. 15: see chap. i. 21. *Against the rulers of the darkness of this world;* either that rule in the dark air, where God permits them to be for the punishment of men; see chap. ii. 2: or rather, that rule in the dark places of the earth, the dark minds of men, and have their rule over them by reason of the darkness that is in them; in which respect the devil is called *the god of this world,* 2 Cor. iv. 4, and *the prince* of it, John xiv. 30. So that the dark world here seems to be opposed to *children of light,* chap. v. 8. *Against spiritual wickedness;* either wicked spirits, or, emphatically, spiritual wickednesses, for wickednesses of the highest kind; implying the intenseness of wickedness in those angelical substances, which are so much the more wicked, by how much the more excellent in themselves their natures are. *In high places;* or heavenly, taking heaven for the whole *expansum,* or spreading out of the air, between the earth and the stars, the air being the place from whence the devils assault us, as chap. ii. 2. Or rather, *in* for about heavenly places or things, in the same sense as the word rendered heavenly is taken four times before in this Epistle, chap. i. 3, 20; ii. 6; iii. 10; being in none of them taken for the air; and then the sense must be, that we wrestle about heavenly places, or things, not with flesh and blood, but with principalities, with powers, &c. *Object.* The Greek preposition will not bear this construction. *Answ.* Let Chrysostom and other Greeks answer for that. They understood their language best, and they give this interpretation.

u 2 Cor. 10. 4. ver. 11.

13 ᵘWherefore take unto you the whole armour of God, that ye may be able to withstand ˣin the evil day, and ‖ having done all, to stand.

x ch. 5. 16.
‖ Or, *having overcome all.*

In the evil day; times of temptation, and Satan's greatest rage: see chap. v. 16. *Having done all;* all that belongs to good soldiers of Jesus Christ, all that we can do being little enough to secure our standing. *To stand;* as conquerors do that keep the field, not being beaten down, nor giving way.

y Is. 11. 5. Luke 12. 35.
1 Pet. 1. 13.
z Is. 59. 17.
2 Cor. 6. 7.
1 Thess. 5. 8.

14 Stand therefore, ʸhaving your loins girt about with truth, and ᶻhaving on the breastplate of righteousness;

Stand therefore: standing here (in a different sense from what it was taken in before) seems to imply watchfulness, readiness for the combat, and keeping our places, both as to our general and particular callings: if soldiers leave their ranks they endanger themselves. *Having your loins girt about with truth:* having exhorted to put on the whole armour of God, he descends to the particulars of it, both defensive and offensive. We need not be over-curious in inquiring into the reason of the names here given to the several parts of a Christian's armour, and the analogy between them and corporal arms, the apostle using these terms promiscuously, 1 Thess. v. 8, and designing only to show that what bodily arms are to soldiers, that these spiritual arms might be to Christians; yet some reason may be given of these denominations. He begins with the furniture for the loins, the seat of strength, and alludes to the belt or military girdle, which was both for ornament and strength; and so is *truth,* understood either of the truth of doctrine, or rather, (because that comes in afterward under the title of the sword of the Spirit,) of soundness, and sincerity of heart, than which nothing doth more beautify or adorn a Christian. He alludes to Isa. lix. 17: see 2 Cor. i. 12; 1 Tim. i. 5, 19. *And having on the breastplate of righteousness;* righteousness of conversation, consisting both in a resolvedness for good, and repentance for evil done, which is as a breastplate (that piece of armour which covers the whole breast and belly) to a Christian; that resolvedness against sin fencing him against temptation, and the conscience of well-doing against the accusations of men and devils: see 1 Cor. iv. 3, 4; 1 John iii. 7.

a Is. 52. 7.
Rom. 10. 15.

15 ᵃAnd your feet shod with the preparation of the Gospel of peace;

Your feet shod; in allusion to the greaves or military shoes with which soldiers covered their feet and legs. A Christian's way lies through rough places, through briers and thorns, and therefore he needs this piece of armour. He must be prepared to hold the faith, and confess Christ in the most difficult times. *With the preparation of the gospel of peace;* with that furniture which the gospel affords him, which being a *gospel of peace,* and bringing the glad tidings of reconciliation to God by Christ, prepares men best to undergo the troubles of the world: see John xvi. 33.

16 Above all, taking ᵇthe shield of faith, wherewith ye shall be able to quench all the fiery darts of the wicked.

b 1 John 5. 4.

Above all; chiefly, Col. iii. 14: this he sets, as the principal part of the Christian armour, against the greatest temptations, fiery darts, 1 Pet. v. 8, 9; 1 John v. 4. *Taking the shield of faith:* faith, as receiving Christ and the benefits of redemption, is compared to a shield, (under which soldiers were wont to shelter themselves against their enemies' darts,) as being a sort of universal defence covering the whole man, and guarding even the other parts of our spiritual armour. *Fiery darts;* it seems to be an allusion to the poisoned darts some barbarous nations were wont to use, which inflamed the bodies they hit. By them he means all those violent temptations which inflame men's lusts. These fiery darts of temptations faith is said to *quench,* when, by the help of grace obtained of Christ, it overcomes them. *Of the wicked;* the devil, Matt. xiii. 19.

17 And ᶜtake the helmet of salvation, and ᵈthe sword of the Spirit, which is the word of God:

c Is. 59. 17.
1 Thess. 5. 8.
d Heb. 4. 12.
Rev. 1. 16.
& 2. 16.
& 19. 15.

Take the helmet of salvation: salvation, for *the hope of salvation,* 1 Thess. v. 8. This follows faith, and is of kin to it. Soldiers dare not fight without their helmet: despair, to which the devil tempts us, makes us quit our combat; whereas hope of salvation makes us lift up our heads in the midst of temptations and afflictions. This likewise alludes to Isa. lix. 17. *The sword of the Spirit;* either the spiritual sword, the war being spiritual, and the enemy spiritual, or rather the sword which the Spirit of God furnisheth us with, and makes effectual in our hands. *Which is the word of God;* the doctrine of God in the Scripture, called a *two-edged sword,* Rev. i. 16; ii. 12; which enters into the soul, and divides between the most inward affections, Heb. iv. 12, and cuts the sinews of the strongest temptations, Matt. iv. 4, 7, 10; and conquers the devil, while it rescues sinners from under his power. This relates to Isa. xlix. 2.

18 ᵉPraying always with all prayer and supplication in the Spirit, and ᶠwatching thereunto with all perseverance and ᵍsupplication for all saints;

e Luke 18. 1.
Rom. 12. 12.
Col. 4. 2.
1 Thess. 5. 17.
f Mat. 26. 41.
Mark 13. 33.
g ch. 1. 16.
Phil. 1. 4. 1 Tim. 2. 1.

Praying always; i. e. in every opportunity, so often as our own or others' necessities call us to it, 1 Thess. v. 17. *With all prayer and supplication;* prayer, when opposed to supplication, seems to signify petitioning for good things, and supplication the deprecating of evil, 1 Tim. ii. 1. *In the Spirit;* either our own spirit, with which we pray, so as not to draw nigh to God with our mouth only, as Isa. xxix. 13; or rather, the Holy Spirit of God, by whose assistance we pray, Rom. viii. 26, 27; Jude 20. *Watching thereunto;* to prayer, in opposition to sloth and security: see Matt. xxvi. 41; Col. iv. 2; 1 Pet. iv. 7. *With all perseverance;* constancy and continuance in prayer in every condition, adverse as well as prosperous, though prayer be not presently answered, Luke xviii. 1. *And supplication for all saints;* not only for ourselves, but for our brethren in the world, none being in so good a condition but they may need our prayers.

19 ʰAnd for me, that utterance may be given unto me, that I may open my mouth ⁱboldly, to make known the mystery of the Gospel,

h Acts 4. 29.
Co . 4. 3.
2 Thess. 3. 1.
i 2 Cor. 3. 12.

Utterance, or speech, viz. both the things I am to speak, and the faculty of speaking as becomes the matter I deliver. *That I may open my mouth;* or, in or unto the opening of my mouth, i. e. full and free profession of the truth, without shame or fear. *Boldly ;* either, freely and confidently, the same as before in other words ; or, openly and plainly, in opposition to speaking closely and in secret, Mark viii. 32 ; John xi. 14 ; and so it may have respect to the removing of his bonds, which were the present impediment of his so speaking.

k 2 Cor. 5. 20.
l Acts 26. 29.
& 28. 20. ch.
3. 1. Phil. 1.
7, 13, 14.
2 Tim. 1. 16.
& 2. 9. Philem. 10. ¶ *Or, in a chain.* ¶ *Or, thereof.* m Acts 28. 31. Phil. 1. 20.
1 Thess. 2. 2.

20 For which [k] I am an ambassador [l] ∥ in bonds : that ∥ therein [m] I may speak boldly, as I ought to speak.

For which I am an ambassador in bonds ; for which gospel I still continue, though a prisoner, in the embassy committed to me by Christ. *That therein I may speak boldly ;* this may imply not only free speaking, but free acting in all things whereby the gospel may be propagated.

n Col. 4. 7.
o Acts 20. 4.
2 Tim. 4. 12.
Tit. 3. 12.

21 But [n] that ye also may know my affairs, *and* how I do, [o] Tychicus, a beloved brother and faithful minister in the Lord, shall make known to you all things:

But that ye also, as well as other churches, *may know my affairs,* how I am used by the Romans in my bonds. *How I do,* or rather, what I do, i. e. how I behave myself: see Acts xxviii. 30, 31. *Faithful minister : minister* is here taken in a large sense, for any that labour in the gospel, such as were not only ordinary pastors, but evangelists and apostles themselves.

22 [p] Whom I have sent unto you for   p Col. 4. 8.
the same purpose, that ye might know our affairs, and *that* he might comfort your hearts.

That ye might not *faint at my tribulations,* chap. iii 13. It might be a comfort to them to hear that Paul was well used, (setting aside his bonds,) and had liberty to preach to those that came to him.

23 [q] Peace *be* to the brethren, and love q 1 Pet. 5. 14.
with faith, from God the Father and the Lord Jesus Christ.

He prays for their continuance and increase in these graces, which already were begun in them.

24 Grace *be* with all them that love our r Tit. 2. 7.
Lord Jesus Christ [r] ∥ in sincerity. Amen.   ∥ *Or, with incorruption.*

This is more extensive than the former, he prays here for all true believers every where. *In sincerity ;* or, as the margin, with incorruption, i. e. so as that nothing can draw them off from the love of Christ, and so it implies constancy as well as sincerity.

¶ Written from Rome unto the Ephesians by Tychicus.

THE EPISTLE OF PAUL THE APOSTLE

TO THE

PHILIPPIANS

THE ARGUMENT

PAUL, being called of the Lord to preach the gospel in Macedonia, having touched at Neapolis of Greece, came to Philippi, the first city, in regard of its situation, within that part of Macedonia, on his way from *Samothracia* (Acts xvi. 11, 12) into that country, through Amphipolis and Apollonia, to Thessalonica. Appian describes this Philippi to be seated on a little hill near the foot of the Pangæan mountain, in old time called Crenides, from the fountains and gold mines adjoining, and Datus or Dathus, from the treasure, agreeing with the island Thasus near it ; afterwards enlarged and fortified by Philip king of Macedon, who therefore gave it the name of Philippi, as a frontier town within his dominions on the confines of Thracia. Yet afterwards it fell into the hands of the Romans, and became memorable for the victory which Augustus and Antony obtained there over Brutus and Cassius ; and in Paul's time it was *a colony,* Acts xvi. 12, 21. But there is no evidence from Scripture, or the most authentic civil history, that it was (as a learned man would have it) the metropolis of Macedonia when this Epistle was written to it. For it doth not appear that it had so much as a proconsul, or deputy, (as in some other colonies of Macedonia,) Acts xvi. 12, but rather that the magistrates and military officers (ver. 20, 22, 35, 36, 38) show themselves to be of an under city, which (some affirm) did depend on the great mother city Thessalonica, in a civil sense, and some centuries after (say others) in an ecclesiastical. However, it received Paul, who planted the gospel here ; who now being prisoner at Rome, (probably the first, not second time,) chap. i. 7, 13, 14, 16, with 2 Tim. iv. 6, and having received by *Epaphroditus,* their *messenger,* chap. ii. 25, their acceptable and liberal present, chap. iv. 18, and understood from him their constancy in the doctrine they had received, (though it seems some affecting pre-eminencies did trouble them,) he writes back most pathetically, as full of paternal affections towards them his dear children, move them to persevere in faith and godliness ; and not to be at all discouraged by his present sufferings, but to live as becomes the gospel, in humility and unity ; intimating his tender love and care of them in designing to send Timothy to them, and then to come and visit them ; whom he cautions to beware of seducers, who might else pervert them in mingling the law and gospel : whereupon he quickens them to a heavenly conversation in the exercise of several graces ; and, expressing his thankfulness for their repeated bounty, concludes with his salutations and apostolical blessing.

CHAP. I

Paul saluteth the Philippians, 1, 2 ; *and testifieth his thankfulness to God for their uninterrupted fellowship in the gospel,* 3—7 ; *his affection for them,* 8, *and prayers for their spiritual improvement,* 9—11. *He informeth them that his bonds at Rome had turned out to the advancement of the gospel, which many were thereby induced to preach, though with different views,* 12—20 ; *that, considering how serviceable his life might be to the cause of Christ, though for himself it were happier to die, he was doubtful in his choice,* 21—24 ; *but that he knew he should soon be at liberty to visit them again for their comfort,* 25, 26. *He exhorteth them to walk worthy of their profession, and to be steady and unanimous in the faith, for which they had already been fellow sufferers with him,* 25—30.

PHILIPPIANS I

A. D. 64.
a 1 Cor. 1. 2.

PAUL and Timotheus, the servants of Jesus Christ, to all the saints ^a in Christ Jesus which are at Philippi, with the Bishops and Deacons:

Paul and Timotheus; i. e. the author and approver, intimating the good agreement betwixt Paul and Timothy, whom they well knew, to gain their fuller assent to what should be written, Matt. xviii. 16 : see 1 Cor. i. 1 ; 2 Cor. i. 1. *The servants of Jesus Christ;* in a special manner, being wholly and perpetually dedicated to his more immediate service in the ministry of reconciliation, Acts xiii. 2 ; Rom. i. 1 ; 1 Cor. iv. 1 ; 2 Cor. v. 18 ; Gal. i. 1 ; James i. 1. *To all the saints in Christ Jesus;* i. e. all the community of church members at Philippi, called out of the world to Christ, sanctified, separated, and dedicated to him, by a credible profession of faith in him and obedience to him, 1 Cor. i. 2 ; Eph. i. 1 ; Col. i. 2 ; the apostle now being well persuaded of their perseverance, ver. 6. 7. *With the bishops and deacons:* from the Syriac version it is rendered presbyters and ministers. And there appears no cogent reason why we should not adhere to the exposition of ancient and modern interpreters, who understand the apostle writing in the plural number, particularly, to the church and her officers living in this city, as meaning the two orders of ordinary standing officers, which are appointed for the church, and not the church for the officers. By the former of which are meant such pastors and teachers as did agree in name, office, and power with the bishops during the apostles' times, as they collect from several other scriptures besides this, compared together, viz. Acts xx. 17, 20, 25, 28, with xi. 30; 1 Cor. iv. 1 ; xii. 28 ; 1 Thess. v. 12, 13; 1 Tim. iii. 1—8 ; v. 17; Tit. i. 5, 7 ; Heb. xiii. 17 ; James v. 14 ; 1 Pet. v. 1, 3 ; 3 John 1, 9 : these, whether bishops or elders, having the oversight, rule, guidance, feeding of the people, preaching of the word, and administration of the sacraments or mystical ordinances of the gospel, committed to them in common. By the latter, those to whom the special care was committed for serving of tables, the Lord's table and the poor's, together with a receiving and orderly disposing and distributing the collected alms and other goods of the church given to pious uses, according to their own discretion, taking advice of the pastors, for the support and benefit of the poor members of the church who needed as to this temporal life, to orphans, widows, yea, and strangers, especially of the household of faith, that their bodily necessities might be supplied, Acts vi. 2, &c. with Rom. xii. 7, 8 ; xv. 25—27 ; xvi. 1 ; 1 Cor. xii. 28 ; 2 Cor. ix. 1, 2, 12 ; 1 Tim. iii. 8, with 1 Pet. iv. 11 ; Gal. vi. 10, 11 ; chap. ii. 1, 25, 30, with iv. 18; Jude 12. " But two learned doctors amongst us have opposed this and made it difficult, the one by restraining the word *bishops* to diocesans, and the other by enlarging the word *deacons* to note their presbyters. He would have no such order of presbyters as now in the apostles' days ; this would have deacons then to be only temporary, not standing officers in the church; and so they agree not. The former finding Clement and Polycarp agreed with the apostle here, as to two distinct orders of bishops and deacons, going upon an unproved supposition that Philippi was then a metropolis, he would, without any satisfactory evidence to one that doubted, infer the bishops here were diocesans ; however, the forementioned scriptures compared, all prove the words *bishop* and *elder* in the apostles' days, to be used promiscuously, only the word elders, or presbyters, more frequently than that of bishops ; conceiving that the office of presbyters was not in use till after-ages, though he assigns not the time how and when it came in. So that in effect he would have Philippi to be a mother church (that then had several daughter churches) in her infancy. Whereas the apostle writes to those who were church officers in that city, yet he would have them none of that order which we now call presbyters ; thinking, whatever the apostle writes of laying on the hands of the presbytery, there were then no presbyters ordained in the church : which is a singular opinion, of holding all the places in the New Testament where presbyters are named, precisely to intend diocesan bishops in distinction from them who are only deacons, allowing the office of deacons, and the continuance of it, to be appointed therein, when that of elders (acknowledged to be superior) is not. But if, according to this novel tenet, there were not then preaching presbyters, that were not metropolitans or diocesans, how could diocesans have presbyters under them? and if they had none, what should denominate them properly diocesans ? when it seems to be of the formal reason of a diocesan, to be chosen out of presbyters, or to have them to govern. And if the diocesan bishops were then as the apostles, who must the pastors and teachers be? 1 Cor. xii. 28, 29; Eph. iv. 11, 12. Exhorting, teaching, ruling were then present offices, which the apostles *ordained in every church,* Acts xiv. 23. Cenchrea was no diocess or metropolis, neither was Aquila's and Priscilla's house, Rom. xvi. 3. 4 ; 1 Cor. xvi. 19, yet are said to be *churches*, in the plural number, 1 Cor. xiv. 33. 34. If metropolitical or diocesan, how hath not the Scripture the name or thing ? This appears not to be agreeable to the apostle's way, who writes particularly to churches in cities, towns, and countries, as to the Hebrews. He distinguisheth Thessalonica, in directions from Macedonia and Achaia, 1 Thess. i. 7, 8 ; Colosse and Laodicea, Col. iv. 13. And as there were bishops, plural, in this city of Philippi, so more doing the office in Thessalonica, 1 Thess. v. 12, which was in Macedonia too. And would it not look oddly, Ye Christians of Macedonia are examples to all the Christians of Macedonia? In Colosse were more bishops or presbyters, because there is mention made of Epaphras and Archippus, Col. iv. 12, 17. And would it not appear strange, when they were charged, upon persons being sick, to send for the elders of the church, to conclude the intent of the injunction was to send for all the diocesans of the metropolis ? James v. 14. If so, he would likely have enjoined them to have called the elders of the churches, not of the *church*, of which, in the singular, at Jerusalem Paul and Barnabas were received, *and of the apostles and elders,* Acts xv. 4, who were all present at Jerusalem, Acts xxi. 18, which, under the Roman power, was not the metropolis of Palestine, but Cæsarea was chief. The latter, contradictory to the former doctor, and to the office of the Church of England for ordaining of deacons, would have the term *deacons* to note the order of presbyters, looking upon deacons only as temporary and occasional trustees, whose office Paul in his Epistle did not so much as hint, thinking it unreasonable by *deacon* in those Epistles to understand any other office than that of presbyters as now used. Whereas the word *deacons* being analogous and put absolutely here, in contradistinction to *bishops*, should, according to right reason, be expounded in the most famous and distinctive signification, wherein, no doubt, Luke, a good Grecian, and Paul's companion at Philippi, used it in the Acts, (chap. vi. 3, 4, &c.,) written after this Epistle ; unto which special import we should rather understand Paul using it here, for those who were not mere occasional and prudential temporary officers, but such as were to abide in the church : wherein, upon the multiplying of disciples, the bodily necessities of the poor saints, always with us, John xii. 8, did require such who should have the peculiar care of these committed to them, Acts xx. 34, 35. We find the apostle in his Epistles evidently enough appointing and describing such a special ministry, yea, and giving directions about it as a distinct branch from prophecy and teaching, if we compare places, Rom. xii. 6—8, with xv. 26, 27 ; xvi. 1 ; 2 Cor. viii. 19 ; ix. 1, 2, 12 ; and what is said in this Epistle, chap. ii. 25, 30; iv. 18; answerable to Luke's history of the Acts, and to what is written by Peter, 1 Pet. iv. 11 ; taking in what Paul wrote to Timothy about this office, in distinction from his who was to be apt to teach, that he should be grave, temperate, giving proof of freedom from covetousness, of conversation blameless, having a faithful wife, and governing his family (that he may be hospitable) orderly, 1 Tim. iii. 8—13, qualified to distribute, as in the texts forementioned, &c. The Church of England, in her ordination, hath reference to this special office, when yet it calls deacons, ministers ; declaring there, ' It appertains to the deacon's office to assist the presbyter in distribution of the elements, gladly and willingly to search for the poor, sick, and impotent, that they may be relieved. Praying that they may be modest, humble, and constant in their ministration.' "

2 ^b Grace *be* unto you, and peace, from God our Father, and *from* the Lord Jesus Christ.

b Rom. 1. 7.
2 Cor. 1. 2.
1 Pet. 1. 2

The evangelical salutation, as Rom. i. 7; Eph. i. 2; 2 Pet. i. 2; praying for the free and undeserved favour of God the Father to them, as the fountain, James i. 17; together with all inward and outward blessings, flowing thence through Christ the procurer of them.

3 ^cI thank my God upon every ‖ remembrance of you,

c Rom. 1. 8, 9. 1 Cor. 1. 4. Eph. 1. 15, 16. Col. 1. 3. 1 Thess. 1. 2. 2 Thess. 1. 3. ‖ Or, *mention.*

As in most of his Epistles, (viz. Rom. i. 8; 1 Cor. i. 4; 2 Cor. i. 3; Eph. i. 3; Col. i. 3; 1 Thess. i. 2; 2 Thess. i. 3; 2 Tim. i. 3,) he begins with thanks to God; and here, *my God,* i. e. *whose I am, and whom I serve in the gospel of his Son,* Acts xxvii. 23, with Rom. i. 9, whom the Jews and Gentiles do not so acknowledge. *Upon every remembrance of you;* intimating that he ever bore them upon his heart to God with delight.

4 Always in every prayer of mine for you all making request with joy,

As in praising of God, the Author of all that grace they had received, in every solemn prayer, so in continuing his fervent and assiduous requests unto God always, 1 Thess. v. 17, for them all: the term *all* being used three times emphatically: compare Luke ii. 37; Rom. i. 9.

5 ^dFor your fellowship in the Gospel from the first day until now;

d Rom. 12. 13. & 15. 26. 2 Cor. 8. 1. ch. 4. 14, 15.

Your being joined with us and other Christians in the communion of Christ, and glad tidings of salvation by him, 1 Cor. x. 16, 17; 1 Pet. iv. 13; 1 John i. 3, 7; evidenced by the communication of your bounty, Gal. vi. 6; Heb. xiii. 16; your stedfastness and perseverance in all Christian duties from the first time of your receiving the gospel.

6 Being confident of this very thing, that he which hath begun ^ea good work in you ‖ will perform *it* ^funtil the day of Jesus Christ:

e John 6. 29. 1 Thess. 1. 3. ‖ Or, *will finish it.* f ver. 10.

Being confident of this very thing; i. e. having thanked God for what he had done and did for them, he expresseth his firm persuasion and charitable hope of their perseverance for the future. *That he which hath begun a good work in you will perform it;* not from any thing in themselves more than others, but because God the Father, (who is not weary of well-doing,) having begun the work of faith in them, chap. ii. 13, with John vi. 29, who else were dead in sins, as the Ephesians, chap. ii. 1, he would preserve and carry on that internal and spiritual work in the fruits of real Christians, and not leave it imperfect, Psal. cxxxviii. 8; Isa. lxiv. 8; but would make it perfect, or perfect, stablish, strengthen, and settle them in it, those words being of the same import in Scripture with *perform it,* connoting the difficulty of it. *Until the day of Jesus Christ;* i. e. either until the day of their death, when the spirits of just men are made perfect, and Christ appears to their particular judgment, Heb. xii. 23, not as being perfect while here in this state, chap. iii. 12; or rather, until the day of Christ, or latter day, at judgment, 1 Cor. i. 8; 1 Thess. iv. 15; when they shall be acknowledged to be blameless, to the glory of Christ, who hath carried them through all, and fulfilled the work of faith in them, and glorified them, 2 Thess. i. 11, and who are his glory, 2 Cor. viii. 23.

7 Even as it is meet for me to think this of you all, because ‖ I have you ^gin my heart; inasmuch as both in ^hmy bonds, and in ⁱthe defence and confirmation of the Gospel, ^kye all are ‖ partakers of my grace.

‖ Or, *ye have me in your heart.* g 2 Cor. 3. 2. & 7. 3. h Eph. 3. 1. & 6. 20. i Col. 4. 3, 18. 2 Tim. 1. 8. i ver. 17. k ch. 4. 14. ‖ Or, *partakers with me of grace.*

Even as it is meet for me to think this of you all; i. e. consonant to the law of equity and charity, Acts iv. 19; 1 Cor. xiii. 7; Col. iv. 1, with 2 Pet. i. 13. It behoves me to pass this judgment on you all, upon good grounds. *Because I have you in my heart;* not barely in that he had them as it were engraved upon his heart, 2 Cor. iii. 2, 3; vii. 3; for he could live and die with them, whom he did continually present unto God (as before). *Inasmuch as both in my bonds, and in the defence and confirmation of the gospel, ye all are partakers of my grace;* but in that (for which they had gotten so much of his cordial affection)

they were co-partners with him in the *like precious faith,* 2 Pet. i. 1; and *holy brethren, partakers of the heavenly calling,* Heb. iii. 1; as *children of light,* 1 Thess. v. 5; walking in faith and love, 2 Thess. i. 3; maintaining the communion of saints, in showing the reality of the same grace with him, in that, as ver. 29, it was given to them *in the behalf of Christ, not only to believe on him, but also to suffer for his sake.* Which he reckoned they did in compassionately and seasonably supporting and relieving of him in his imprisonment, whereby the gospel was defended, and what he had preached of it was confirmed, by his becoming a real patron of it, in holding fast the profession and ratifying the confession of his faith, in glorying that he was counted worthy to suffer them for the name of Christ, Acts v. 41; 1 Pet. iv. 15, 16; wherein they did by all honest means succour him, and showed themselves companions with him, chap. iv. 14; Heb. x. 33.

8 For ^lGod is my record, ^mhow greatly I long after you all in the bowels of Jesus Christ.

l Rom. 1. 9. & 9. 1. Gal. 1. 20. 1 Thess. 2. 5. m ch. 2. 26. & 4. 1.

Confirming what he had before written, he appeals to God in the heavens, who searcheth the heart and trieth the reins, as in some other Epistles, Rom. i. 9; 2 Cor. i. 23, with xi. 31; Gal. i. 20; 1 Thess. ii. 5, 10; and as Job, chap. xvi. 19; by making a solemn protestation, or oath, to put the matter out of doubt, Heb. vi. 16, and giving them assurance, (as he lawfully might in this way for God's glory, and their good, Deut. vi. 13,) of the sincerity and intenseness of his hearty affections towards every one of them, chap. ii. 26; iv. 1; with 2 Cor. ix. 14. *In the bowels of Jesus Christ;* not out of any carnal, selfish, or worldly respects; but a really Christian, spiritual, and tender love, seated in the inward parts of this sanctified apostle, Jer. xxxi. 33; by the same Spirit that united him unto Christ, who loves his spouse with no common love, but is the spring and procurer, and great exemplar, of that affectionate Christian love, which, like him, they are to exert from the very root of their hearts, purely, unfeignedly, and fervently, *without dissimulation,* Rom. xii. 9; 1 Pet. i. 22; imitating God and Christ, (Luke i. 78,) as Paul here, in the highest degree of dearest affection, did love the Philippians, and elsewhere the Thessalonians, 1 Thess. ii. 7, 8, 11.

9 And this I pray, ⁿthat your love may abound yet more and more in knowledge and *in* all ‖judgment;

n 1 Thess. 3. 12. Philem. 6. ‖ Or, *sense.*

And this I pray: having praised God for their attainments, he returns, (as ver. 4,) in token of his love, to his great petition for them. *That your love may abound;* viz. that their love both to God and man, showed in their bounty to him, might, as a rising stream from its springing fountain, yet further flow out, and more abundantly communicate itself in all Christian offices, and not abate, (as it seems it afterwards did among the Ephesians, Rev. ii. 4,) as our Saviour foretold it would do in some, Matt. xxiv. 12, (see 2 Tim. i. 13; iv. 10,) but continue increasing to the end, 1 Thess. iii. 12. *Yet more and more in knowledge;* being founded on a sound and saving understanding of the things of God, and ourselves, John xvii. 3; Rom. iii. 20; Eph. i. 17, with iv. 13; 2 Pet. iii. 18; and an acknowledgment *of the truth which is after godliness,* Tit. i. 1. *And in all judgment;* in the practical judgment, or internal sense, and particular experience, taste, and feeling the testimony of the Spirit in the heart concerning the grace of God, and adoption, Rom. v. 1, 5; viii. 16, 17; xiv. 17; when there is not only a right notion in the head, but a true sense and savour of spiritual things in the heart, Heb. v. 14; which is when knowledge is not only an empty cloud in the air, but becomes effectual by falling down in a kindly shower upon the heart, warmed with the love of God, and the virtue of Christ's resurrection, as he after gives his own experience, chap. iii. 10, like David's, Psal. xxxiv. 8.

10 That ^oye may ‖approve things that ‖are excellent; ^pthat ye may be sincere and without offence ^qtill the day of Christ;

o Rom. 2. 18, & 12. 2. Eph. 5. 10. ‖ Or, *try,* ‖ Or, *differ.* p Acts 24. 16. 1 Thess. 3. 13. & 5. 23. q 1 Cor. 1. 8.

i. e. To the ends he subjoins, namely, *that ye may*

approve things that are excellent; that upon a due expense of circumstances in a judicious trial, upon rightly discerning the differences of things not obvious to every eye, so as to choose and approve those things that are really to be preferred, being the best, Rom. ii. 18; 1 Thess. v. 21; surpassing all desirable things besides, Eph. iii. 19, as being most acceptable unto God, Rom. xii. 2. *That ye may be sincere;* and be upright, Prov. xi. 20. It is an emphatical word in the original here, being borrowed either from such things as are tried by being held up at the beams of the sun to see what faults or flaws are in them, whether without fraud, or else from such as are clarified by the heat of the sun; and notes here, that Paul would have them to be uncorrupt and impartial in heart and life, in faith and manners; free from prevailing corruptions, of *pure minds*, 2 Pet. iii. 1; purged from the old leaven, 1 Cor. v. 6—8; not suffering the knowledge of Christ to be mixed with traditions and human inventions, but endowed with evangelical simplicity in the sight of God, 2 Cor. i. 12; 1 Tim. i. 5; v. 22. *And without offence;* not erring from the main scope and design of Christianity, or stumbling, so as either actively or passively to trouble and offend either themselves or others in the heavenly course, but working so prudently, as to give no just occasion of scandal, or laying a snare for one or other, Matt. xviii. 7; Acts xxiv. 16; 1 Cor. x. 32; abiding blameless to the coming of Christ, 1 Thess. v. 23. *Till the day of Christ:* see on ver. 6; repeated here to engage them unto serious thoughtfulness of that day.

r John 15. 4,
5. Eph. 2. 10.
Col. 1. 6.
s John 15. 8.
Eph. 1. 12, 14.

11 Being filled with the fruits of righteousness, ʳ which are by Jesus Christ, ˢ unto the glory and praise of God.

Being filled with the fruits of righteousness; i. e. not only bringing forth some single, yea, or singular fruit, but replenished, plurally, with the fruits of righteousness, Acts ix. 36; Col. i. 10; elsewhere called the *fruits of the Spirit*, Gal. v. 22; Eph. v. 9; in all goodness and truth, as well as righteousness. These are such good works as are not (whatever the papists conceive) causal of righteousness, but are, through the Spirit, (who regenerates the persons, and directs the internal and external actions of those who walk in the steps of the faith of their father Abraham, Rom. iv. 12,) wrought by supernatural grace in the heart *joined unto the Lord,* with whom they are *one spirit*, 1 Cor. vi. 17. *Which are by Jesus Christ;* and without whom, from their own stock and strength, till they be ingrafted into him, John xv. 1, 5, *trees of righteousness*, of the Lord's planting, Isa. lxi. 3, and *his workmanship, created unto good works*, Eph. ii. 10, they cannot bring forth fruits, and do such good works as are acceptable unto God, 2 Cor. xiii. 5; but Christ living and dwelling in them by faith, Gal. ii. 20; Eph. iii. 17, and God working in them *both to will and to do*, chap. ii. 13, they *can do all through Christ,* chap. iv. 13, so that they shall be accepted in him. *Unto the glory and praise of God;* not being empty vines, bringing forth fruit to themselves, Hos. x. 1, but to the eternal honour of him who hath called them, Matt. v. 16; 1 Cor. x. 31; Eph. i. 6, 12, 14; 1 Pet. ii. 12; iv. 11; Rev. v. 13.

12 But I would ye should understand, brethren, that the things *which happened* unto me have fallen out rather unto the furtherance of the Gospel;

But I would ye should understand, brethren: to obviate the insinuations which false teachers and others might make use of from Paul's sufferings, to obstruct the cordial entertainment of those glad tidings he had brought, and to discourage those who did obey the truth, he doth by this friendly compellation (which he often useth) kindly entreat them to consider well, *that the things which happened unto me have fallen out rather unto the furtherance of the gospel;* that his imprisonment, and what other troubles from without did befall him in his apostolical office, whereby the overruling providence of God so ordered, that they did (contrary to the intention of his persecutors) rather advantage than hinder the progress of the gospel, increase than decrease the church, since he had opportunity two years, in his own hired house, of teaching with freedom the things of Christ, Acts xxviii. 30, 31; whereupon he would not have the Philippians discouraged, but rather comforted, as the Corinthians, 2 Cor. i. 5—7: for, 1. His iron chain in the cause of Christ was more an honour to him, even in the emperor's court, chap. iv. 22, or guard chamber, Acts xxviii. 16, or judgment hall, Matt. xxvii. 27; Mark xv. 16; John xviii. 28, 33; than those glittering golden ones which others were ambitious to wear, Acts v. 41; James ii. 2; it being apparent there, and elsewhere, to courtiers, citizens, Jews, and foreigners, that he did not suffer as an evil-doer, 1 Pet. ii. 19, 20; iii. 14; only for the Lord's sake, Eph. iii. 1; iv. 1; whose power in his confinement did work in and by him, who approved himself faithful, which, when inquiry was made concerning his suffering, gave occasion to communicate some notions of Christ, and glad tidings of salvation by him.

13 So that my bonds ‖ in Christ are manifest ᵗ in all ‖ the palace, and ‖ in all other *places*;

‖ Or, *for Christ.*
t ch. 4. 22.
‖ Or, *Cæsar's court.*
‖ Or, *to all others.*

14 And many of the brethren in the Lord, waxing confident by my bonds, are much more bold to speak the word without fear.

And many of the brethren in the Lord, waxing confident by my bonds; and here again, contrary to the expectation of those persecutors, who designed to make havoc of the church, his innocent carriage and constancy in bearing the cross, had an influence upon the greater part of *the brethren* (not *according to the flesh*, Rom. ix. 3, but) in the service of Christ. *Are much more bold to speak the word without fear;* pastors, and teachers, who had been timorous at the first, were greatly imboldened to shake of carnal fear, and to profess and preach Christ crucified, or the cross of Christ, 1 Cor. i. 18, 23, which is *the power of God to salvation,* Rom. i. 16, more confidently than ever; as he and Barnabas had done elsewhere, Acts xiii. 46; and as Joseph of Arimathea and Nicodemus, who were but secret disciples before Christ's sufferings, upon his death owned him openly for their Lord, Matt. xxvii. 57, with John xix. 39.

15 Some indeed preach Christ even of envy and ᵘ strife; and some also of good will: u ch. 2. 3.

He doth here tacitly answer an exception which might be made; It were better some of them were silent, than preach so boldly as to procure him hatred, and lessen his reputation; 1. By granting there was somewhat in the allegation, yet it did not conclude against this, that his suffering was advantageous to promote the gospel. 2. By distinguishing of those who were hollow-hearted and false, from an envious principle, designing to disparage this excellent person, who having done much in the lesser Asia and Greece, did now, in the head city of the world, when in prison, also gain proselytes, courtiers and others, for the receiving of Christ; and those were sincere and true-hearted brethren. joining with him in the cause of Christ, and assisting him from true love to Christ, and him his apostle, to get the truth of Christianity entertained in the love of it. The former were evil works, both as to their principle and end, chap. iii. 2; the latter acted sincerely in both respects, 2 Cor. ii. 17.

16 The one preach Christ of contention, not sincerely, supposing to add affliction to my bonds:

This distinction he did amplify and explain here, by particularly showing the ill motive, manners, and end of the worst sort of preachers, from an ill affection of hatred, emulation, and wrath, 2 Cor. xii. 20; Gal. v. 20; with an intemperate zeal to render Paul suspected and despicable in the eyes of the church; and to occasion in the emperor a more severe persecution, and heighten the accusers' rage against Paul, and to gain applause to themselves, and vex his soul under outward troubles.

17 But the other of love, knowing that I am set for ˣ the defence of the Gospel. x ver. 7.

Then intimating the genuine principle and good end of the better sort, who were moved from a prevailing affection to God, the edification and salvation of souls; cordially joining with Paul in carrying on the same design that he did, who was appointed of God, Acts xxiii. 11; 1 Thess. iii. 3; both by doctrine and obedience, active and passive, to defend the gospel, unto which he was admirably called to be a minister, yea, and here a patron, Rom. i. 1; Eph. iii. 7; with 1 Cor. i. 1; and, as it were, to tread the devil under foot (as Tertullian speaks) in his own house. Intimating from all this, that however the former did with an ill mind, in man's judgment, as circumstances then were with Paul, (some of which we are ignorant of,) the latter with a pious desire, preach the gospel; yet the event proved, by the good hand of God, beneficial to promote the gospel: and so it may happen still, when some false brethren, moved by blind ambition and intemperate zeal, may snatch a weapon out of the gospel to vex good and godly pastors in their promulgation of it.

18 What then? notwithstanding, every way, whether in pretence, or in truth, Christ is preached; and I therein do rejoice, yea, and will rejoice.

What then? notwithstanding, every way, whether in pretence, or in truth, Christ is preached: q. d. It doth not follow, that these different intentions of the preachers should hinder the spreading of the gospel, and therefore it should not abate either your confidence or mine in the cause of Christ, since, by the overruling providence of God, that is carried on, both by the one and the other; not only by those who in truth preach the word faithfully, Jer. xxiii. 28; Matt. xxii. 16, from a principle of love, (as before,) to the same good intent with myself; but also by those who, though they act (as in ver. 15) out of envy and ill-will to me, for base ends under a fair show, 1 Thess. ii. 5, yet they occasionally and accidentally, not by any direct causality, do promote the interest of Christ. *And I therein do rejoice;* and upon this account, that there is so good an effect, as the making known of Christ for the salvation of sinners, I have matter of present joy. *Yea, and will rejoice;* yea, and hereupon for the future, though some should continue to do that in itself which might aggravate his affliction, yet it should not take his joy from him eventually; however directly and of itself it tend to it, yet indirectly and by accident, God disposing, it should issue well for the furtherance of the gospel.

19 For I know that this shall turn to my salvation [y] through your prayer, and the supply of [z] the Spirit of Jesus Christ,

[y] 2 Cor. 1. 11.
[z] Rom. 8. 9.

For I know that this shall turn to my salvation: rendering a reason of what went before, (as the causal particle notes,) he doth here oppose his knowledge to the envious preachers' opinion, and his salvation to the affliction they did exercise him with; so that he was fully persuaded, that the trouble they had given, or should give to him, (though in the nature of the thing it had a tendency to take him off from the defence of the gospel, and so to hazard his soul, or, if he stood in defence of it, Nero would persecute him to death,) would, upon sure ground, work for his good, Rom. viii. 28, even the great good, the salvation of his soul; yea, and for some time, (compare ver. 25,) the safety of his life here, Acts xxvii. 34; Heb. xi. 7. His prison should be an ark to him resting on God's promise, so that he could go on boldly and cheerfully in bearing his testimony to Christ with *the helmet of salvation,* Eph. vi. 17. *Through your prayer;* having an interest in their prayers as a means of support, which he intimates they would continue to help him with, 2 Cor. i. 11, as much as if he had downright asked an interest in them, Heb. xiii. 18. *And the supply of the Spirit of Jesus Christ;* yea, in the use hereof, that he might have a great measure of the Spirit, promised to those that ask him, Luke xi. 13, he looks higher, not doubting but he shall have a renewed subsidy of grace continued to him from the same Spirit, which is in Christ Jesus his Head, Rom. viii. 9; Gal. iv. 6; thereby he should be helped in his infirmities, Rom. viii. 26; 1 Cor. xii. 11; and receive *grace for grace,* John i. 16, out of his fulness, who had not *the Spirit by measure,* John iii. 34; whereupon, whatever his enemies conceited, he should have undersupplies secretly communicated, like those from the head to the members, which would be effectual and victorious to deliver him from every evil work, and preserve him to the heavenly kingdom, 2 Tim. iv. 18.

20 According to my [a] earnest expectation and *my* hope, that [b] in nothing I shall be ashamed, but *that* [c] with all bold-

[a] Rom. 8. 19.
[b] Rom. 5. 5.
[c] Eph. 6. 19, 20.

ness, as always, *so* now also Christ shall be magnified in my body, whether *it be* by life, or by death.

According to my earnest expectation and my hope; he allegeth and explaineth the ground and certainty of his knowledge and persuasion of his enemies' disappointment, and all succeeding well with him, trusting *in the living God,* 1 Tim. iv. 10, who in all death-threatening afflictions hath upon his word engaged himself to support all those that hope in his mercies, Psal. xxxiii. 18, 19; xxxvii. 7, 9; cxlvii. 11. Then be sure, when his sincere servants, assisted by his Spirit, wait for his deliverance with their necks stretched out, (as the word here notes,) being raised from past experience, intensely and wistly looking for his appearance, shall be able each to say as the apostle intimates. *That in nothing I shall be ashamed;* negatively, he shall not be left to do any thing which may justly bring him under reproach. His well-grounded hope would not make him ashamed. Rom. v. 5, with viii. 25; but upon this account he shall have wherewith to answer him that should reproach him, Psal. cxix. 41, 42, 46; Luke ix. 26; 2 Tim. i. 12. *But that with all boldness;* positively, that he should continue constant in a courageous owning of the truth, and acknowledging of his Lord every way, whether he was delivered from or to death. *As always, so now also Christ shall be magnified in my body, whether it be by life, or by death;* as in the former years of his ministry he had been supported, yea, and victorious, in freely speaking for Christ, preaching and defending of his gospel, Acts ix. 27; xiv. 3, with as much courage as any other, Acts iv. 13, 29, 31, with 2 Cor. xi. 21; Gal. vi. 17: so now he was humbly confident, in his present sad circumstances, Christ should be magnified. (not that himself can become greater,) i. e. before men, his glory should be rendered greater and more illustrious, and acknowledged with praise, whether he lived or died, Rom. xiv. 8; yea, in the earthen vessel of his body, 2 Cor. iv. 11, (about which he was not solicitous, having resigned it entirely to Christ,) either in his enlargement and preaching of the doctrine of Christ, or in his being offered up and sealing it by his martyrdom.

21 For to me to live *is* Christ, and to die *is* gain.

Some read it, For Christ is my gain in life and in death; or, For Christ is to me both in life and in death advantage. Both acknowledge it to be brought in as a reason of Paul's hope in life and death; and of his indifferency, in submission to God's pleasure, in life and death, intimating it was all one to him, so Christ was magnified in his body, whether it were by life or by death. They who follow our translation, do expound the proposition disjunctively; the former referring to the honour of Christ, and the latter to the salvation of Paul, which is understood by the name of *gain.* Some understand the former branch efficiently, q. d. I derive myself from Christ, unto whom I am united, he being the principle of it, as Gal. ii. 20; but others rather objectively and finally, q. d. As I have hitherto made it the business of life to serve Christ in preaching his gospel, so, if he continues my life, I purpose that in my living body, by preaching his gospel, and suffering for his name, as he requireth, he shall be glorified. Then, for the latter branch, if I die, in bearing testimony to Christ, it will be gain to myself, in that I shall be with Christ, which is better for me, ver. 23, being *present with the Lord,* 2 Cor. v. 8, in whom my *life is hid,* Col. iii. 3. So that death would not impoverish, but enrich him. They who choose the latter reading, take the proposition conjunctively, to the sense that he accounted gain to him, to have the honour of Christ magnified in his body, whether it happened to him to live or die, since he faithfully served him living or dying, and owned himself to be his both ways, Rom. xiv. 8. He was not (as he saith elsewhere, Acts xx. 24) moved with accidentals; neither counted he his *life dear* to him *to testify the gospel of the grace of God;* reckoning he had no life, but from Christ, whom he made it his business to serve and enjoy; so that if he continued in the body, Christ would gain, in that he designed to spend his life for the edification of his church; and if he died in that cause, Christ would gain by his death, in that his truth would, by the blood of him, who was a martyr, be further sealed, and his interest promoted, and his glory advanced; and he himself would gain, since upon his departure he should be advanced *to be with Christ,* ver. 23, who alone makes his faithful servants happy in life and death.

22 But if I live in the flesh, this *is* the fruit of my labour: yet what I shall choose I wot not.

But if I live in the flesh, this is the fruit of my labour: some, from the various use of the Greek particles, render this first clause interrogatively; But whether to live in the flesh were worth the while? or more profitable? (understand, than to die). The apostle having intimated the equality and indifferency of his mind in an entire submission to the will of God, whether that glorifying of Christ by his life or that by his death were more eligible, is upon deliberation, finding the advantage to Christ and himself, upon expense of circumstances either way, in an equal balance, weighing one thing with another: living in the flesh, i. e. abiding here in this mortal body, which he thus expresseth by way of diminution, Gal. ii. 20; 1 Pet. iv. 1; in opposition to, and comparison of, dying for and in the Lord, and so being with him, ver. 23. *Yet what I shall choose I wot not;* he seems, loving the Philippians as himself, to be at a loss what to determine, if God should permit him his choice, whether by labouring in his ministry for the good of their souls he should bring more fruit to Christ, or by suffering, that which would arise from the blood of a martyr, who himself should receive a crown, 2 Tim. iv. 8.

d 2 Cor. 5. 8.
e 2 Tim. 4. 6.

23 For ^d I am in a strait betwixt two, having a desire to ^e depart, and to be with Christ; which is far better:

For I am in a strait betwixt two; because he knew not what to choose for the best, he was held in suspense, Luke xii. 50; Acts xviii. 5, as one drawn both ways with weighty reasons, which he amplifies with respect to himself and the church, that Christ might be honoured in both: his love to the enjoyment of Christ and the edification of his members constraining him on each hand; the former was more delightful to him, and the latter more profitable for them. *Having a desire to depart;* being held not only with a bare inclination, but an ardent and perpetually active desire, to loose from this clayey tabernacle, Psal. xlii. 1, 2; Eccles. xii. 7; Luke ii. 29; xii. 36; 2 Cor. v. 1, 4; 2 Tim. iv. 6: so to depart as to abide in a better place. *And to be with Christ; which is far better;* upon being absent from the body to be present with Christ, 2 Cor. v. 8, in paradise, Luke xxiii. 43; 1 Thess. iv. 17; so to leave the body as to live with and enjoy him in heaven, is by far much better for me.

24 Nevertheless to abide in the flesh *is* more needful for you.

However, with respect to the church, by his staying here in this mortal body he persuades himself, knowing the subtlety of false apostles, who would enter in as *grievous wolves,* Acts xx. 29, it was necessary to strengthen them and other churches in the faith of Christ.

f ch. 2. 24.

25 And ^f having this confidence, I know that I shall abide and continue with you all for your furtherance and joy of faith;

And having this confidence; viz. being persuaded of what went immediately before, how useful the continuance of his life, for a further time in this world, would be to the church of Christ, and particularly to them, he determines (as should seem) with more than probable conjecture; though, upon supposition it should be otherwise, he gives them abundant satisfaction in their adhering to Christ, ver. 27; chap. ii. 17. *I know;* even with a well-grounded knowledge, either by a prophetic Spirit, from a particular revelation such as he had sometimes before had, Acts xvi. 9, 10; xxiii. 11, or the sanctifying Spirit witnessing with his spirit, Rom. viii. 16, strengthening his faith and persuasion, helped by their faith and prayer, ver. 19, compared with 1 Pet. i. 8. *I shall abide and continue with you all for your furtherance and joy of faith;* to these ends, that, by his personal presence with them, he might by his ministry further their faith in Christ, their joy in the Holy Ghost, and more abundant glorying in the power of Jesus Christ, for his safety, and being restored to them, as we see in what follows; and Eph. iv. 1, with 2 Tim. iv. 17, we find, from his first imprisonment at Rome, (when likely this Epistle was written,) he was delivered, and for some years restored to the churches which he had planted.

26 That ^g your rejoicing may be more abundant in Jesus Christ for me by my coming to you again.

g 2 Cor. 1. 14. & 5. 12.

Here, in confidence of being again with them, and staying with them, he expresseth an admirable affection to them, that he can be content for a time to be deprived of the glorious sight of Christ, that he might see and serve them, and that under persecution; that they might, upon his return to them, more abundantly glory together, not in themselves, but, Christian-like, in Christ Jesus, the author of that doctrine he had preached to them, the Captain of their salvation, and the common Head of Christianity.

27 Only ^h let your conversation be as it becometh the Gospel of Christ: that whether I come and see you, or else be absent, I may hear of your affairs, ⁱ that ye stand fast in one spirit, ^k with one mind ^l striving together for the faith of the Gospel;

h Eph. 4. 1. Col. 1. 10. 1 Thess. 2. 12. & 4. 1.
i ch. 4. 1.
k 1 Cor. 1. 10.
l Jude 3.

Only let your conversation be as it becometh the gospel of Christ: q. d. In the mean time, whatever becomes of me, that which is for your part solely incumbent on you, who are brought into the fellowship of the gospel, is to demean yourselves truly agreeable to that state. The original phrase, as afterwards in this Epistle, chap. iii. 20; iv. 8, and elsewhere, Acts xxiii. 1, imports, that their deportment should be answerable to their citizenship, that they should behave themselves as might be most to the public good of the society to which they do relate, not being of the world here, any more than their Head, John xv. 19; xvii. 16. Their course of life should be every way answerable to their high calling, Eph. iv. 1; Col. i. 10; 1 Thess. ii. 12; bringing forth fruit meet for repentance. *That whether I come and see you, or else be absent, I may hear of your affairs;* intimating, that it did behove them constantly to adorn the gospel, in the exercise of Christian courage, unanimity, and patience, as well when he was distant from them, as when among them to oversee them : not as if he doubted of returning to them for their greater edification, but further to satisfy them as to his entire submission unto God's pleasure on his journey, or at home, 2 Cor. v. 6, 8; and to excite them to shake off sloth, and to discharge their duty with all diligence, which would greatly cheer his heart. *That ye stand fast in one spirit, with one mind striving together for the faith of the gospel:* 1. By their stedfast endeavour after a sweet, close, holy, lasting union amongst themselves. For *one spirit,* one soul or mind, here seem to imply one understanding enlightened by the sanctifying Spirit, and one heart, as an inward, uniting principle, which must upon no temptation be changed : compare chap. ii. 2; iii. 16; iv. 2; with Rom. xii. 16; 1 Cor. i. 10; 2 Cor. xiii. 11; Eph. iv. 2, 3; 1 Pet. iii. 8; according to our Saviour's prayer, John xvii. 11, 20—23, which was heard, Acts i. 14; ii. 46; iv. 32; v. 12. Nor only by their union in heart and mind, but, 2. Their mutual helpfulness in action, as spiritual champions joining their forces together, for the defence of their royal charter, the maintenance of the main principles of Christianity, against all troublers of the church, and subverters of the evangelical faith, 1 Cor. ix. 24, 25; Gal. v. 13; Eph. vi. 14, with 2 Tim. iv. 7. 3. A courageous spirit under sufferings from their most malignant gainsayers and persecutors, who do wittingly and willingly oppose the truth, and them professing of it, as Simon Magus and others did, Acts viii. 18—21; 1 Tim. i. 20; 2 Tim. i. 15.

28 And in nothing terrified by your adversaries: ^m which is to them an evident token of perdition, ⁿ but to you of salvation, and that of God.

m 2 Thess. 1. 5.
n Rom. 8. 17. 2 Tim. 2. 11.

And in nothing terrified by your adversaries: the original word which the apostle useth, imports, they should not be appalled or affrighted, as men and horses are apt to be when furiously charged by their deadly enemies, but stoutly receive them, keeping their ground, Matt. x. 28; Luke xii. 32. *Which is to them an evident token of perdition;* considering, on the one hand, their most pertinacious rage, it is no other than an evident and convincing argument, or certain forerunner, of the adversaries' utter ruin, Exod. xxii. 22—24; Rom. ii. 8, 9; 2 Thess. i. 5—9. *But to you of salvation;* but, on the other hand, to sound believers, who behave themselves as becomes the gospel, a manifest demonstration of their everlasting welfare and glory, Matt. v. 10; x. 32, 39; Rom. ii. 7, 10; Eph. iii. 13; 2 Thess. i. 6, 7. *And that of God;* by the disposal of the all-wise and righteous Governor, who may for a time permit his or his people's adversaries to domineer, Job i. 12; Prov. xvi. 4; but being *a rewarder of them that diligently seek him,* Heb. xi. 6, will of his grace lenify the sharpness of the cross, enable believers to hold out against all the opposition of their enemies, make them *partakers of his holiness,* and bring them to glory, Heb. xii. 10, 11; 2 Tim. ii. 11, 12: which might abundantly comfort the Philippians, as others, Gal. vi. 17.

o Acts 5. 41.
Rom. 5. 3.
p Eph. 2. 8.

29 For unto you °it is given in the behalf of Christ, ᵖnot only to believe on him, but also to suffer for his sake;

For unto you it is given; he adds a further argument to move them unto that he had exhorted, from God's freely bestowing, of his mere grace, what he had required of them. *In the behalf of Christ;* upon the account of Christ's merit and mediation; not that they could have either evangelical faith, or patience, by virtue of their own strength, chap. iv. 13. *Not only to believe on him;* that they did not only believe Christ, but believe on him, was not from any power of their own, John vi. 37, 44, but of God's free gift, Eph. ii. 8, as they had an instance amongst them in Lydia, Acts xvi. 14; unto her and others was this victorious grace of faith freely given by the hearing of the word, which was not unto many others that heard, Matt. xiii. 11; 2 Thess. iii. 2; Tit. i. 1; and as the grace itself was given, so was the exercise of it. *But also to suffer for his sake;* upon the account of Christ, patience was given; so that *to suffer,* here, doth not only import a power to suffer, but actual suffering; not only the habit of faith, but the act of believing, even as the fruits of trees at the first creation were produced, as well as the trees which had a power to bear them: wherefore, if, by the grace of God, and Spirit of faith, they were empowered actually to believe, Mark ix. 24; 1 Cor. xv. 10; 2 Cor. iv. 13, having *trust through Christ God-ward,* 2 Cor. iii. 4; and upon the same account they were continually enabled to suffer, not simply, but in bearing testimony to Christ, Acts v. 41; 1 Pet. iii. 14; iv. 16; they might be of good comfort and courage, to the daunting of their adversaries.

q Col. 2. 1.
r Acts 16. 19,
&c. 1 Thess.
2. 2.

30 ᑫHaving the same conflict ʳwhich ye saw in me, *and* now hear *to be* in me.

And be heartened to partake with him in the like trials he sustained when amongst them, Acts xvi. 19—24, and which he now was enduring at Rome, ver. 13; an example of suffering unto them, if they would but await the blessed issue of his agony.

CHAP. II.

Paul earnestly recommendeth to the Philippians mutual love and union, 1, 2; *lowliness of mind,* 3; *and that charitable condescension for the good of others, exemplified in the life and death of Christ,* 4—8, *for which God had exalted him to be Lord of all,* 9—11. *He exhorteth them to carefulness in working out their own salvation,* 12, 13; *to obey the will of God cheerfully and universally, that so they might distinguish themselves from the rest of the world by a bright example of virtue,* 14, 15; *and by their steadiness give him cause to rejoice in the success of his labours, who would gladly lay down his life to serve them,* 16—18. *He hopeth to send Timothy to them shortly, whom he greatly commendeth,* 19, 20; *as he doth the affection and zeal of Epaphroditus, whom he sendeth with this Epistle,* 21—30.

IF *there be* therefore any consolation in Christ, if any comfort of love, ᵃif any fellowship of the Spirit, if any ᵇbowels and mercies,

a 2 Cor. 13. 14.
b Col. 3. 12.

The apostle, reassuming his exhortation in the former chapter to unanimity, ver. 27, doth here, by way of inference from what went immediately before, press them in a very affectionate manner, with a kind of rhetorical relation, and obtestation, as it were, adjure them. *If there be therefore any consolation in Christ;* if any such exhortation, (as the word is rendered, Acts xiii. 15; 1 Thess. ii. 3; 1 Tim. iv. 13,) in the name of Christ, might avail with them to cheer him and one another by their loving concord and being unanimous. Or as we, rendering it *consolation;* (so Rom. xv. 4; 2 Cor. i. 4;) *If,* which he may well suppose, and strongly affirm that he took it for granted, the main body of them had in some measure found by his ministry, what he here moves them to complete, (compare chap. i. 6, 7, 27,) in expectation to find more of what they had experimented, whatever indisposition might have crept upon some by the insinuations of the false apostles; yet, this *consolation in Christ* may be considered either, 1. Actively: q. d. If ye would comfort me afflicted, in the concerns of Christ, or if ye have any Christian comfort which doth only proceed from those that are in Christ, (not from moral philosophy,) or which is wont to be in those who worship the same Christ, let me his apostle be a partaker thereof. Or, 2. Passively, 2 Cor. vii. 4. 6; Philem. 7: If you, being in Christ, find any consolation against your afflictions, forasmuch as you have received it by my ministry, we, being both in suffering circumstances, should be further comforted by a sweet agreement. *If any comfort of love;* the Syriac renders it, any speaking to the heart, any solace from good and comfortable words did reach your hearts, John xi. 19, 31; 1 Cor. xiv. 3; 1 Thess. ii. 11; v. 14, cheered with the love of God or Christ, or the brethren: or refreshed with my love to you, chap. i. 8, 9; or would that I should be comforted with your love to me, (as he himself and others were with the gracious affections of the Corinthians, 2 Cor. vii. 7,) which ye ought unfeignedly. *If any fellowship of the Spirit;* if ye have any communion with me in the graces of the Spirit, and *stand fast in one spirit,* chap. i. 27, and would show that you do persevere in *the same Spirit,* 1 Cor. xii. 4, which acts in all the members of the mystical body of Christ, that do in him their Head partake of it. *If any bowels and mercies;* if ye are duly affected with any real sympathy and commiseration towards me in my bonds for Christ, such inward affections as were moving in him towards them; chap. i. 8, with Luke i. 78; 2 Cor. vii. 15; Col. iii. 12; the latter word emphatically expressing the sense of the metaphor in the former. Then he, having thus pathetically urged these arguments, and closely followed them to embrace the matter proposed, puts them upon.

2 ᶜFulfil ye my joy, ᵈthat ye be likeminded, having the same love, *being* of one accord, of one mind.

c John 3. 29.
d Rom. 12. 16. & 15. 5.
1 Cor. 1. 10.
2 Cor. 13. 11.
ch. 1. 27. & 3. 16. & 4. 2. 1 Pet. 3. 8.

Fulfil ye my joy; viz. the exercise of those graces he had been joyful for, which would be an addition to that joy he had for them, and the making of it much more abundant, contributing as much as the friends of the Bridegroom here can to the completing of it, John iii. 29. *That ye be likeminded;* which is when they believe and affect the same things, agreeable to the mind of God, chap. iii. 15; Acts iv. 32; Rom. xii. 16; 2 Cor. xiii. 11. *Having the same love;* having the same mutual sincere charity, Eph. iv. 2; Col. iii. 14. *Being of one accord;* being unanimous in their honest designs, John xvii. 22; 1 Pet. iii. 8. *Of one mind;* agreeing as to the main in the same judgment and opinion, to promote the interest of Christ, 1 Cor. i. 10; Gal. v. 7, 10.

3 ᵉLet nothing *be done* through strife or vainglory; but ᶠin lowliness of mind let each esteem other better than themselves.

e Gal. 5. 26.
ch. 1. 15, 16.
Jam. 3. 14.
f Rom. 12. 10. Eph. 3. 21. 1 Pet.. 5. 5.

Here, the better to engage them to embrace what he had so pathetically exhorted them to, he doth dissuade them from animosity, an affectation of applause, and self-seeking; and direct them to modesty and self-denial. *Let nothing be done through strife or vain-glory;* intimating, they should by no means indulge an inordinate affection to strive and quarrel with one another, provoking each other by an ambitious emulation to cross or excel others; this arguing a carnal temper, opposite to true Christianity, ver. 14; Rom. ii. 8; Gal. v. 16, 24, 26, being the very bane of true Christian concord, Rom. xiii. 13; James iii. 16, and destructive to faith, John v. 44; 2 Cor. xii. 20. *But in lowliness of mind let each esteem other better than themselves;* but cherish and exercise true Christian modesty and meekness, (which is of another kind than that the heathen philosophers did prescribe,) in a due preference of each other, Matt. xi. 29; Rom. xii. 10; Eph. iv. 2; v. 21; 1 Pet. v. 5; as the apostle himself gave example, 1 Cor. xv. 8, 9. *Quest.* If any say, How is this consistent with what the apostle writes to them to think of *praise* and *good report,* chap. iv. 8, and of himself, *not a whit,* and *nothing, behind the very chiefest apostles?* 2 Cor. xi. 5; xii. 11; and further, how can some think others better than themselves in truth, unless they reckon good evil and evil good? I answer, 1. Be sure Christian modesty and real humility, with prudence and mildness, are very commendable graces, and *in the sight of God of great price,* 1 Pet. iii. 4. And therefore what he doth afterwards exhort to in this Epistle, doth very well agree with what he doth write here; where, 2. He is treating of grace and godliness, whereas in those places to the Corinthians he writes of some certain gifts, which, by reason of the insinuations of false apostles against him, he was necessitated, in magnifying of his apostolical office and authority, 2 Cor. x. 8, to mention, being as it were compelled to it by the ingratitude of some of them at Corinth who had been influenced by the false apostles, 2 Cor. xii. 5, 6; yet you may see there, he doth not glory of himself, or his person, but acknowledges his infirmities, 2 Cor. xi. 30, and that unfeignedly, speaking the truth every where, 2 Cor. xii. 6, which he makes evident to them from the nature of the thing itself, 2 Cor. x. 12, 13, 15, 16; xii. 12; appealing to God, as witness in the case, 2 Cor. xi. 31, referring all the glorying they put him upon, to the grace of God through Christ, 1 Cor. xv. 10; 2 Cor. xi. 31, when they had cast contempt on his ministry, 2 Cor. x. 10—13, 18. So that in respect of gifts and external privileges, wherein are distinctions of superiors and inferiors, chap. iii. 4, he doth not urge that every Christian should prefer every other to himself, wherein it is evident there is a real difference; but in respect of the persons, the honesty and piety of others in God's sight, (lest a man, by thinking himself something when he is nothing, should deceive himself, Gal. vi. 3,) since in his judgment they may be endowed with some hidden quality we know not of, and be accepted with him. Hence, 3. Our estimation and preference of others to ourselves, who as Christian brethren are obliged to serve one another, Gal. v. 13, is not taken simply, and with an absolute judgment, as if it were necessary to give them the pre-eminence in all things: but, as to this, that a man may think there is some defect in himself, which it may be is not in another; or with a suspense; Perhaps he is not better in truth, but considering my heart is deceitful, and possibly he may be more without guile, I judge it not meet to prefer myself to him God-ward; but seeing mine own black legs, and being bound in love to confess mine own and cover the infirmities of my brother, who labours to walk answerably to his profession, it is safe for me to prefer him, who may have some good latent which I have not, and whereupon he is to be esteemed by me. Wherefore, 4. The right management of the duty which the apostle calls for to preserve unanimity, depends upon a right and due estimation of God's divers gifts and graces which flow from *the same Spirit,* 1 Cor. xii. 4, and a humble sense of our own infirmities: so that however one Christian may excel with some singular endowments, yet he ought to think they were not bestowed upon him that he should be puffed up, or value himself above what is meet upon that account before God, being he hath received them of God, 1 Cor. iv. 7, but judge himself for his own defectiveness and faultiness, which will afford himself matter of abasement and humility; when yet with respect to others, whose hearts he knows not, he in charity thinketh the best, 1 Cor. xiii. 4, 5; and if in this case he should be mistaken, his modest apprehensions would be acceptable to God (designing to approve that which he doth) and profitable to himself. To engage them further unto Christian concord, he here directs them as to their aim and scope, (according to the import of the word,) that it should not be their own private interest, but the common good of Christianity, becoming those who have true Christian love, 1 Cor. x. 24; xiii. 5; not as if he did disallow providing for their own, 1 Tim. v. 8, or studying to be quiet, and doing their own business, 1 Thess. iv. 11; but that every member of Christ, while he considers his own gifts, graces, honour, and advantage, would remember that he is not born only to serve himself or Pharisaically to conceit well of himself in the contempt of others, Luke xviii. 11; but also, and that much rather, he should consider his relation to the Head, and every other member of the body, and so consult the gifts, graces, honour, and edification of others, especially when more eminently useful, knowing that members should have the same care one for another, 1 Cor. xii. 24—28.

4 ᵍ Look not every man on his own things, but every man also on the things of others. ^{g 1 Cor. 10. 24, 33. & 13. 5.}

5 ʰ Let this mind be in you, which was also in Christ Jesus: ^{h Mat. 11.29. John 13. 15. 1 Pet. 2. 21. 1 John 2. 6.}

Let; most translations do express the causal or rather illative Greek particle, which ours doth here omit as an expletive. However, the apostle doth urge them to the exercise of self-denial, mutual love, and a hearty condescension to one another, from the great example of Jesus Christ, 2 Cor. viii. 9: that so the mind which was in Christ may be perceived in us, who, if spiritual, judge all things and have the mind of Christ; being enlightened by the same Spirit, we do judge as he coming in the flesh did: or, Let the same affection be found in you that was really in him, Matt. xi. 28; John xiii. 15.

6 Who, ⁱbeing in the form of God, ᵏthought it not robbery to be equal with God: ^{i John 1. 1, 2. & 17. 5. k 2 Cor. 4. 4. Col. 1. 15. Heb. 1. 3. k John 5. 18. & 10. 33.}

Who, i. e. relative to Christ Jesus, the eternal Son of God by nature, very God extant with his Father before the beginning, John i. 1; Gal. iv. 4; 1 Tim. iii. 16; vi. 14—16; Tit. ii. 13; the express image and character of his Father's person, which implies a peculiar subsistence distinct from the subsistence of his Father, John viii. 42; 2 Cor. iv. 4; Col. i. 15; Heb. i. 3; concerning whom, every word that follows, by reason of the Socinians, and some Lutherans, is to be well weighed. *Being;* i. e. subsisting, in opposition to taking or assuming, ver. 7; and therefore doth firmly prove Christ pre-existing in another nature to his so doing, namely, his actual existing of himself in the same essence and glory he had from eternity with the Father, John i. 1, 2; xvii. 5; 2 Cor. viii. 9; Rev. i. 4, 8, 11. *In the form of God;* to understand which clearly, 1. The word *form,* though it may sometimes note somewhat outward, and so infer the glory of Christ's miracles, yet we do not find it any where so used in Scripture: it is true it is once used there for the outward visage, Mark xvi. 12, which had excelling splendour and beauty, giving occasion to conceive majesty in the person, Matt. xvii. 2; 2 Pet. i. 16, (however, his resplendent garments could not be accounted *the form of God,*) yet being, Luke saith, chap. xxiv. 16, the eyes of the persons which saw were holden, that for a time they could not acknowledge him, it argues that the appearance Mark speaks of noted only an accidental form. Whereas the *being* or subsisting Paul here speaks of, respects (what the best philosophers in their most usual way of speaking do) the essential form, with the glory of it, since the verbs, in other scriptures of the same origin, signify somewhat inward and not conspicuous, Rom. xii. 2; 2 Cor. iii. 18; Gal. iv. 19; especially when there is a cogent reason for it here, considering *the form of God,* in opposition to *the form of a servant* afterward, and in conjunction with equality to God, which implies the same essence and nature, Isa. xl. 25; xlvi. 5, it being impossible there should be any proportion or equality betwixt infinite and finite, eternal and temporal, uncreate and create, by nature God and by nature not God, Gal. iv. 4, 8, unto which the only living and true God will not suffer his glory to be given. Neither indeed can he *deny himself* who is *one,* and besides whom there is no other true God, or God by nature, Deut. iv. 35; vi. 4; 2 Tim. ii. 13; *who only doeth wondrous things*, Psal. lxxii. 18 : for to all Divine operations a Divine power is requisite, which is inseparable from the most simple essence and its properties. *Being*, or subsisting, *in the form of God*, imports not Christ's appearance in exerting of God's power, but his real and actual existence in the Divine essence, not in accidents, wherein nothing doth subsist : neither the vulgar nor learned do use to say any one doth subsist, but appear, in an outward habit; why then should any conceit the apostle means so ? The Gentiles might speak of their gods appearing; but then, even they thought the Deity was one thing, and the habit or figure under which, or in which, it appeared was another, Acts xiv. 11 : so that *subsisting in the form* intimates in the nature and essence of God, not barely, but as it were clothed with properties and glory. For the apostle here treats of Christ's condescension, proceeding from his actual existence, as the term wherein he is co-eternal and co-equal to God the Father, before he abated himself with respect unto us. For he says not the form of God was in Christ, (however that might be truly said,) that the adversaries might not have occasion to say only there was somewhat in Christ like unto God; but he speaks of that wherein Christ was, viz. *in the form of God*, and so that form is predicated of God, as his essence and nature, and can be no other thing. None can rationally imagine that God was an external figure, wherein Christ was subsisting. For subsistence implies some peculiarity relating to the substance of a certain thing, whence we may conclude the Son to be of the same (not only of like) substance with the Father, considering what significantly follows. He *thought it not*, esteemed, counted, held (so the word is used, ver. 3; chap. iii. 7, 8; 1 Thess. v. 13; 2 Thess. iii. 15; 1 Tim. i. 12; vi. 1; Heb. x. 29; xi. 26,) it not *robbery*, it being his right by eternal generation; i. e. he did not judge it any wrong or usurpation, on that account of his *being in the form of God*, to be equal to his Father, being a subsistent in the same nature and essence with him. From openly showing equal majesty with whom he did not for a time abstain, in that he could reckon this robbery, as if such majesty were that which did not agree to his nature, ever presupposing this inherent right, to his great condescension, or abasing himself, which follows as the term to which : or, he resolved for a time not to show himself in that glory which was his own right, but freely condescended to the veiling of it. He did not really forego (neither was it possible he should) any thing of his Divine glory, being the Son of God still, without any robbery or rapine, equal to his Father in power and glory, John x. 33 ; 1 John v. 7, 20. *Thought it not robbery ;* Paul doth not say, (as the Arians of old would pervert his sense,) he robbed not, or snatched not, held not fast equality with God ; or, (as the Socinians since,) Christ thought not to do this robbery to God, or commit this rape upon God, so as that he should be equal to him, but acknowledged he had it of the free gift of God, chopping in the adversative particle, *but*, where it really is not : whereas we read not in the sacred text, he thought not to do this robbery, but, he *thought it not robbery* to be equal to God ; which two are vastly different, even as much as to have the Godhead by usurpation, and to have it by nature. In the former it is, q. d. Christ did not rob or snatch away the equality ; in the latter, the equality which Christ had with God, he thought it no robbery ; he reputed not the empire he might have always continued in the exercise of, equal with the Father, as a thing usurped, or taken by force (as one doth hold that he hath taken by spoil, making show of it). For when he had said he had subsisted in the form of God, he could (before he condescended) say also, he was equal to God, i. e. the Father, without any robbery, rapine, or usurpation. And if Socinus urge that it is absurd and false in any sense to say, God thought he had robbed, or taken by robbery, the Divine essence; then this contradictory, God thought not he took by robbery the Divine essence, is rational and true; as when it is said, God cannot lie, or God changeth not, as 1 Sam. xv. 29; Isa. lv. 8; Mal. iii. 6. What things are denied of God, do not imply the opposites are affirmed of him. The particle *but*, which follows in its proper place before *made himself of no reputation*, may be fairly joined with this sense. For if Christ should know that by rapine and unjust usurpation he was equal to God, (as likely the attempt to be so was the sin of our first parents, which robbery of theirs Christ came to expiate,) he had not emptied himself, nor vouchsafed to abase himself. *To be equal with God;* neither is Christ said to be equal to God only in respect of his works, (which yet argue the same cause and principle, John v. 19, 21, 23, 26, 27 ; x. 37,) but absolutely, he thought it not robbery to be altogether equal with God, as subsisting in the same nature and essence, the original phrase connoting an exact parity. All the things of Christ (though he chose to have some of them veiled for a time) are equal to God ; so some expound the neuter plural emphatically, (as usual amongst the Greeks,) to answer the masculine singular foregoing, to express the ineffable sameness of the nature and essence of the Divine subsistents. It may be read, He counted it no robbery that those things which are his own should be equal to God, i. e. the Father ; or rather, that he himself should in all things be equal or peer to God. For had Christ been only equal by a delegated power from God, why should the Jews have consulted to kill him, for making himself equal with God ? which with them was all one as to make himself God, John v. 18 ; x. 33. But that he spake of his eternal generation, as owning him for his own Father, with whom he did work miracles, even as the Father did in his own name, by his own power, of himself, for his own glory : neither will the evangelist's saying, *The Son can do nothing of himself*, John v. 19, infer an inequality with the Father, when what he doth is equally perfect in power and glory with the Father's, whence, as son, he hath it by nature. For (looking lower) though every son receives from his father human nature, yet he is not less a man than his father, or his father more a man than he ; the son having a being of the same perfection which is naturally in both. However the Father, to whom Christ is in subordination as the Son, and in office a servant, undertaking the work of mediation, may be said to be greater than the Son, that can only be understood with respect to the order of their working, if we compare texts, John xiv. 28 ; xvi. 13—15. Neither, when Christ accounted it not robbery to be equal with God, is he said (as the adversaries urge) to be equal to himself, but to another person, viz. God the Father. Things may be equal which are so diverse, that yet they may be one in some common respect wherein they agree : wherefore when Christ is said to be equal with the Father, he is distinguished from him in person and subsistence, yet not in essence, wherein it is his due to be his equal, and therefore one.

7 ¹But made himself of no reputation, and took upon him the form ᵐ of a servant, and ⁿ was made in the ‖ likeness of men.

l Ps. 22. 6. Is. 53. 3. Dan. 9. 26. Mark 9. 12. Rom. 15. 3. m Is. 42. 1. & 49. 3, 6. & 52. 13. & 53. 11. Ezek. 34. 23, 24. Zech. 3. 8. Matt. 20. 28. Luke 22. 27. n John 1. 14. Rom. 1. 3. & 8. 3. Gal. 4. 4. Heb. 2. 14, 17. ‖ Or, *habit*.

But ; some expound this particle as a discretive, others an adversative, or redditive. *Made himself of no reputation ;* i. e. most wittingly emptied himself, or abated himself, of the all-fulness of glory he had equally with God the Father, that, considering the disproportion betwixt the creature and the Creator, he, in the eyes of those amongst whom he tabernacled, appeared to have nothing of reputation left him, Dan. ix. 26. It is not said the *form of God* was cut off, or did empty itself; but he who did suffer *in* the form of God, made himself of no account, did empty, abate, or abase himself, (so the apostle elsewhere actively and passively useth the word, 1 Cor. ix. 15, with 2 Cor. ix. 3,) and that indeed while subsisting in the form of God, (according to agreement, Zech. vi. 15 ; xiii. 7,) not by laying aside the nature of God, but in some other way, i. e. his own way, kept secret till he was pleased to manifest it, Rom. xvi. 25 ; Col. i. 26 ; by freely coming in the flesh, 1 Tim. iii. 16; Heb. x. 7; which is such an astonishing wonder, and mysterious abasement, as gains the greatest veneration from his saints. Thus for a little time laying aside, at his own pleasure withdrawing, and going aside from his glorious majesty, he lessened himself for the salvation of his people. He had a liberty not to show his majesty, fulness, and glory during his pleasure, so that he could (as to our eyes) contract and shadow it, John i. 14 ; Col. ii. 9. His condescension was free, and unconstrained with the consent of his Father, John iii. 13 ; so that though the Scripture saith, *The Most High dwelleth not in temples made with hands*, 1 Kings viii. 27 ; Isa. lxvi. 1 ; Mark v. 7 ; Acts vii. 48, yet the Son of the Highest can, at his own pleasure, show or eclipse his own glorious brightness, abate or let out his fulness, exalt or abase himself in respect of us. However, in his own simple and absolute nature, he be without *variableness* or *shadow of turning*, James i. 17, being his Father's equal, and so abides most simple and immutable; yet respectively to his state, and what he had to manage for the redemption of lost man, with regard to the discovery he made of himself in the revelation of his Divine properties, the acknowledgment and celebration of them by the creatures, he emptied himself, not by ceasing to be what he was before, equal with his Father, or laying down the essential form of God, according to which he was equal to God; but by taking *the form of a servant*, wherein he was like to men, i. e. assuming something to himself he had not before, viz. the human nature; veiling himself, as the sun is said to be veiled, not in itself, but in regard of the intervening cloud, Matt. xxvii. 39—45; what could hinder that he should not manifest his excellency now more, then less clearly; men one while acknowledging and praising it, another while neither acknowledging nor praising of it, then again praising of it, yet more sparingly? He, by taking the form of a mean man, might so obscure the dignity of his person, as to the acknowledgment of him to be the Son of God, equal with his Father, that in vouching himself to be so he might be accounted a blasphemer, John x. 36; and, during that appearance, not seem to be the Most High; even as a king, by laying aside the tokens of his royalty, and putting on the habit of a merchant, when all the while he ceaseth not to be king, or the highest in his own dominions. Hence the Most High may be considered, either in regard of his nature, wherein he holdeth the highest degree of perfection, or in regard of those personal acts he performs in the business of our salvation. In the former, Christ is the Most High; in the latter, our Mediator. So *the form of God* was the term from which, and *the form of a servant* the term to which, he moved in his demission, or abasement; which did not simply lie in an assumption or union of the human nature to the Divine, for this doth abide still in Christ highly exalted, but in taking the form of a servant, which with the human nature he took, by being *sent forth, made of a woman, under the law*, Gal. iv. 4, but by his resurrection and glorification, lest that relation or habit of a servant, (being such a one who was also a Son, and a Lord, Heb. i. 2, with iii. 6,) when yet he retains the human nature still. As therefore he was *of the seed of David according to the flesh*, Rom. i. 3, though before he had not flesh; so he took the form of a servant in the likeness of man, according to his human nature, although before he took that form he could not have human nature: he did not annihilate any thing he was before, only, of his own accord, bowed down himself, and veiled his own glory, in taking our nature, therein to be a servant unto death. *And took upon him the form of a servant;* taking, (in the Greek, without any copulative *and* before it,) in opposition to being, or subsisting; he *was* in the form of God, which he had before, and *took* this, which he had not then, into the unity of his subsistence, by a personal union, Heb. ii. 16. He was the servant of God, Isa. xlii. 1; Matt. xx. 28, in the whole work of his condescension, which was gradual, else the apostle's art to engage the Philippians to condescension had not been cogent from Christ's example. For, 1. He being increate, did assume to himself a created (not angelical, but) human nature with no reputation, in that regard taking *the form of a servant*, wherein he was like a man, as the next clause explains this. It was an infinite, inconceivable condescension of the Son of God, to take our nature into union with himself, whereby he who was very God, in all things like unto his Father, became like unto us in all things, sin only excepted, Rom. viii. 3; Heb. ii. 17. Hence, 2. He did not immediately advance the nature he took into glory, but became a servant in it to his Father, to perform the most difficult service that ever God had to do in the world; he was not only *in the likeness of sinful flesh*, as soon as he was a man, Rom. viii. 3, of the seed of Abraham, Heb. ii. 11—16; but subject to the law, Luke ii. 42, 51; Gal. iv. 4, in a mean condition from his birth, despicable in the judgment of the world, his mother poor, &c., Isa. liii. 2, 3; Matt. ii. 14; viii. 20; xiii. 55; Mark vi. 3; Luke ii. 7, 22, 24; xxii. 27; so that in finishing his work he was exposed to scorn, Psal. xxii. 6, 7; Isa. liii. 1, 2; however, all the relation of his service was to God the Father, as his antecedent correlate. To the further clearing of what went before, the apostle adds, *in the likeness*, or habit, *of men*, without any copulative particle, by apposition for fuller explication, (compare forecited parallel places,) connoting his employment, (rather than condition,) having a true body and a reasonable soul for this purpose, according to the prophecy, to be servant to his Father, Isa. xlii. 1. And if the adversaries say, He only took on him the form of a servant, when he suffered himself to be beaten, &c.; it is easily answered, These were only consequents upon the form of a servant; one may be a servant, and yet not beaten; and when they so treated our Saviour, he accounted it dealing with him as a malefactor, Luke xxii. 52. Christ obeyed not men, but God the Father, to whom alone he was servant, when made man, Psal. xl. 6—8. It is the nature of lord and servant, to relate to each other. Every servant is a man (brutes are not servants). Labouring in service accompanies the human nature, which is common to Christ with other men, on whom it crept by the fall: Christ regards none others' will but the will of his Father, how hard soever it was, even to the laying down of his life for the reconciling of his church to him. And be sure he died as a man, and not only in the habit of a servant. Only in human nature could he (as it follows without a particle in the Greek) be made like unto men, or in the likeness and habit of men. The Hellenists do use words of similitude, when they design sameness, or the thing itself, and that indeed essentially. For however it be urged, that likeness be opposed to the same, and that which is true, John ix. 9, yet not always; as one egg is like to another, there is convenience in quality, and that in substance is included. Christ is like to other men in human properties, and an afflicted state, so that sameness of nature cannot be denied, Rom. viii. 3; Heb. ii. 16, 17; or rather sameness of kind, though not of number, it being by a synecdoche to be understood generally, Gen. l. 3; Matt. i. 16; John i. 14; Heb. iv. 15; 1 John i. 1; iv. 2, 3. The properties of human nature are of the essence he took, who was found in habit as a man, when yet he was separate from sinners, 2 Cor. v. 21, with Heb. vii. 26; yet the apostle's business here, is not of Christ's sinlessness in that condition, but of his condescending love, in taking on him that condition, being sent in the likeness of sinful flesh, yet without sin. It is a likeness of nature to all men, and not a likeness of innocency only to the first, Gen. v. 1, that Paul here speaks of. And as it is said, John i. 14, *The Word was made flesh;* so here, Christ is *made in the likeness of men*, that we may understand it is the same numerical person, who was *in the form of God*, that was made man; the abasement of God-man being so great, that he was made like to man, i. e. to mere and bare man, though he was more. Nor only did he appear in many forms, (as might be under the Old Testament,) or was joined to man, but personally assumed a true body and a reasonable soul, and so was very man, as well as very God. For when it is not said simply made man, but with that addition, *in the likeness*, it is done to a notable limitation of his station on each part; on God's part it imports, Christ did not lay aside the Divine nature, but only (veiled) his majesty and power; on man's, to exclude sin, viz. that he was true man, yet only like to all other men. But what is now the natural affection of all men from the fall of Adam, and is an infirmity and abatement, as to that, he was without sin, and only in the likeness of sinful flesh.

8 And being found in fashion as a man, he humbled himself, and °became obedient unto death, even the death of the cross.

o Mat. 26.39, 42. John 10. 18. Heb. 5. 8. & 12. 2.

To be *found* is a mere Hebraism, not unusual in the New Testament, not importing any question of the thing, but only the thing certainly happening beyond expectation. It notes here, not his being apprehended of the soldiers when betrayed by Judas, being before his humble obedience, but his being, and really appearing to be, (as the Greek word is elsewhere used, chap. iii. 9; Gen. v. 24; 2 Cor. v. 3; Gal. ii. 17; Heb. xi. 5, with 1 Pet. i. 7,) as a man, simply considered, among men, which was before his being scourged, &c. consequent upon his apprehension. Now being made man, not reserved for a time, like the angels, for heaven itself and the view of angels; neither, from the privilege of the first man, (which Adam could not keep,) did he reserve himself for the inhabiting of Paradise only: but, after the manner of men, he stayed in this earth amongst and conversed with them, and therefore is said to be *in the fashion* of men, or *as a man;* whereby his habit and deportment is more especially expressed, as his essence in the foregoing phrase. *Man,* here, is considered according to what is proper unto human nature, not having the article prefixed, as if it connoted the first man, Adam, only *man* as man; the particle *as,* here, not intimating only likeness, without reality of nature, (as the Marcionites conceited,) but as a confirming and assuring particle, noting certainty, John i. 14. Some indeed take *fashion* more strictly, as noting only the external figure of Christ's body; others, more largely and commodiously, for the whole outward species of human nature: whence the truth of the human nature shined out, not only in the figure and matter of the body, with true flesh and bones, the habit of his members, mouth, eyes, &c., that he might be seen and touched, 1 John i. 1, as he himself allegeth, Luke xxiv. 39; John xx. 20, 27, growing *in wisdom and stature,* Luke ii. 52; but his labouring with hunger, thirst, and weariness, eating, drinking, sleeping, watching, speaking, gestures, being moved with pity, sorrow, joy, weeping, in all which his human nature was evidenced of God, and easily found of men who conversed with him, John iv. 29; ix. 11; xviii. 22. What the Socinians urge, that this gainsays his being incarnate, from Samson's saying, *I shall be weak, and be as another man,* Judg. xvi. 7, 11; there is no strength in the allegation, that Samson, of Dan's tribe, Judg. xiii. 2, should be compared with Christ coming from heaven, (as they themselves do not deny,) *found in fashion as a man:* because Samson, being stronger than a hundred men, if he were dealt so and so withal would become as other men, (for that is the import of the words,) no stronger than any other man, Judg. xvi. 17; whereas here, it is not said as one, any, or every, but simply *as a man:* and from those in power dying as other men, Psal. lxxxii. 7. When they scoffingly ask, Doth it evidence these to be incarnate? it *is* answered, Though he who was strong as many became weak as any one man; they who live in power die in weakness, as other men do, and are not said to be incarnate: yet he who, being equal with God, took on him the form of a servant, and was in this world a very man, may very well be said to be incarnate. 1 Tim. iii. 16. *He humbled himself;* he doth not say he was humbled or depressed by the just judgment of God, but of *himself,* voluntarily, on his own accord, without any constraint. He did really submit himself to the will of his Father, unto whom he was a servant, both in regard of the Divine nature, which he veiled, and also the human in his whole life, Luke i. 48, both outwardly and inwardly, ver. 5, in thoughts and affections, as well as actions and passions: wholly yielding his own will and appetite to God, by a patient subjection to affliction, not in showing humility only, but really undergoing it. For we find this low degree of his humiliation opposed to his super-exaltation, in the following verse, and agreeing with what Isaiah prophesied of him, Isa. liii. 7, expounded by Philip, Acts viii. 32. *And became obedient unto death;* without the copulative in the Greek, and expressing the manner of his humiliation, being of his own free will, and not by any force; made *obedient,* i. e. to God, *(Not my will, but thine be done,)* to others, parents and magistrates, for God, according to the prescript of his law and will, in his life-time *unto death,* and in death; *unto* being taken here, not exclusively, but inclusively, for the further amplification of the obedience, Matt. xxvi. 42; John iv. 34; viii. 29, 46; Heb. x. 9. Had he staid in his life for degrees of obedience, his condescension had been admirable, but that he should submit to a penal and painful death, (taking in his burial, and abiding in a separate state till the third day,) this is stupendous: aggravated by the shame of dying on *the cross,* willingly and meekly yielding himself, though a Son, to that ignominious, cursed death, Deut. xxi. 23; Acts v. 30; Gal. iii. 10, 13; Heb. xii. 2; far more reproachful than beheading, hanging, or burning; out of unspeakable love, to bring us nigh unto God, Rom. v. 19; Col. ii. 14; 1 Pet. ii. 24; iii. 18. Upon these considerations, how should Christians in mutual love condescend to each other!

9 Wherefore God also ᵖhath highly exalted him, and ᵍgiven him a name which is above every name:

ᵖ John 17. 1, 2, 5.
ᵍ Acts 2. 33. Heb. 2. 9.
ᵍ Eph. 1. 20, 21. Heb. 1. 4.

Wherefore; some take this particle illatively, connoting the consequent of Christ's exaltation, upon his antecedent humiliation, as elsewhere, John x. 17; Acts xx. 26; Heb. iii. 7; 2 Pet. i. 10; the apostle showing the sequel of his sufferings to be glory, according to that of Luke xxiv. 26. This the Ethiopic version favours. Christ respecting not himself, but us, and our good, the glory that he had eternally, but veiled for a time, emerging (as the sun out of a cloud) upon his finishing the work his Father gave him to do, John xvii. 5; Rom. ix. 5. Others take the particle causally, intimating Christ's meriting his own exaltation and our salvation, and his accepting of superexcellent glory as a reward of his unparalleled obedience, though he might have challenged it by virtue of the personal union, Heb. xiii. 20, with xii. 2: obedience superior to angels' required a recompence superior to their glory, and Christ might, upon his exquisite obedience, demand his own mediatory glory, as being our Head, and that being the beginning and cause of ours. However, whether the particle of order note that of consequence, or causality, or both, there is no need of controversy, (because of the communication of properties,) since the person of Christ, as God-man, was glorified. *God also hath highly exalted him;* the Greek elegancy imports superexalted, or exalted with all exaltation, answering to his gradual humiliation; above the grave in his resurrection, the earth in his ascension, and above the heavens, at his Father's right hand, upon the throne of his glory, to judge the world, Eph. i. 20—22; iv. 10. *And given him a name:* some take *name* literally, restraining it to *Jesus,* but those letters and syllables are not above every name, it being common to others, Ezra ii. 2; x. 18; Hag. i. 1; Acts vii. 45; Col. iv. 11; Heb. iv. 8, though upon a different account it was to Christ, even before his incarnation, Luke i. 31. Others, for the name of the only begotten Son of God the Father, John i. 14, (with Heb. i. 4, and v. 8,) who was more eminently manifested in his exaltation, to angels and to men, than before. Others, not for any title, but the thing consequent upon his humiliation, surpassing that of all creatures, potentates on earth, and angels in heaven, Eph. i. 20, 21. Name imports power, Acts iii. 6; iv. 7; Rev. v. 12; of the Christ, the Saviour, Matt. xii. 21; John iv. 42; Acts iv. 11, 12; x. 43, at God's right hand, where he living to intercede, makes all comfortable to us, who in his name alone do believe, pray, praise, and do all that shall find acceptance, Matt. xviii. 20; xxviii. 19; John i. 12; iii. 18; xiv. 13; Rom. x. 13, 14; Col. iii. 17. Power to confer all for the good of his church being given him upon his death, when with respect to the creatures he received a glory, not in regard of himself, and in itself, but in regard of its patefaction to others; from which glory, during the time of his humiliation, he had by a voluntary dispensation abstained; and the exercise of that authority conferred upon him as Mediator in that human nature, he had so obediently subjected himself to the cross. Though as God there was a manifestation, yet there was no intrinsical addition of glory; he did as man receive the name, or glory, he had from all eternity as God. So that the name or glory given relates to him according to both natures, as Mediator, God-man: not as God, so he could not be exalted at all, being the Most High; not as mere man, so a creature is not capable of Divine worship, which in what follows is expressly required to be given to him, who is superexalted by God's right hand, above every name, and every thing known by any name, Acts ii. 24, 33, 36; v. 31; 1 Cor. xv. 25; Rev. xvii. 14, with xix. 16.

10 ʳThat at the name of Jesus every knee should bow, of *things* in heaven, and *things* in earth, and *things* under the earth;

ʳ Is. 45. 23.
Mat. 28. 18.
Rom. 14. 11.
Rev. 5. 13.

At the name of Jesus; in the old translation by bishops in Queen Elizabeth's time, (and some say in the manuscripts of this,) it is *in* the name. However, in ours now, it is not appositively, *at* the name Jesus; but constructively, *of* Jesus, intimating, that the power, glory, and majesty of him who hath that name, unto which every knee is bowed, is that name which is above every name; which would not hold true, if the name were taken for the very word *Jesus*, that (as before) being common to others in Hebrew, Greek, and Latin, yea, and English. Besides, neither in letters, nor syllables, nor sound, nor time, hath that word any thing above other words. *Every knee should bow*: bowing of the knee is meant metonymically, and metaphorically, because some of those hereafter named, from whom the homage is due, have neither knees nor tongues, yet must, either willingly or by constraint, yield subjection and obedience to the sovereign authority of Christ, here and hereafter, Matt. xi. 27; xxviii. 18; John v. 22, 23; Acts iii. 15; all creatures being made subject to him, Heb. ii. 8. Some of the papists, searching for their subterraneous, fictitious purgatory, would restrain it to men, but that would straiten and diminish the august glory of Christ, exalted above every name, who had, even here in his humiliation, homage from unclean spirits, Mark v. 6, 7, 10, 12; Luke viii. 31; James ii. 19; how much more when at his tribunal his consummate glory shall be manifest to all! which the apostle hath ultimately a reference to, according to the evangelist, Matt. xvi. 27; xxiv. 30. Then shall his equality with his Father, and his superlative glory as Mediator, be manifested to all, good and bad, angels as well as men, who shall be subjected to his sovereign Majesty, as the Lord God omnipotent; the good willingly, and the bad by constraint, Isa. xlv. 23; Acts xvii. 31; Rom. ii. 16; xiv. 10, 11; 2 Cor. v. 10. *Of things in heaven;* good angels, from whom he had homage and service here, Psal. xcvii. 7; Matt. ii. 13; iv. 11; Luke i. 30, 31; ii. 13; Heb. i. 6; at his resurrection, and ascension, Matt. xxviii. 6; Acts i. 11; much more in his glory, Matt. xxiv. 31; xxv. 31; Eph. i. 21, 22; Col. i. 16; ii. 10; 2 Thess. i. 7: and the spirits of just men made perfect, Heb. xii. 22, 23; Rev. iv. 6, &c.; v. 9, 10. *And things in earth;* good men willingly, Psal. cx. 3; Acts x. 33; 1 John v. 3; and bad by force, Psal. ii. 9; Luke xix. 27; Heb. ii. 14. *And things under the earth;* either the dead, who are hid in the earth, and shall be raised by the power of Christ, in, or upon them, Acts xxiv. 15: or, devils, and wicked souls; for though devils move in the air by God's permission, Eph. ii. 2; yet hell is the place prepared for them, and the wicked, Matt. vii. 23; xxv. 41; Luke viii. 31; 2 Pet. ii. 4; Jude 6. Upon Christ's exaltation, all things above, and in the world, are subjected to his dominion. If it be said, On the earth, and under it, they rebel; I answer, They are bound to obey, Matt. iv. 9, 10, and will be forced to submit to the penalty for disobedience. Christ doth at present exercise a sovereignty over bad men and devils, in limiting and punishing them as he pleaseth, Job i. 11, 12; Luke iv. 34, 35; viii. 32; xix. 27; 2 Pet. ii. 6; Rev. ii. 10.

s John 13.13.
Acts 2. 36.
Rom. 14. 9.
1 Cor. 8. 6.
& 12. 3.

11 And *that* every tongue should confess that Jesus Christ *is* Lord, to the glory of God the Father.

By *tongue*, not only every language, people, and nation is meant; because it is to be understood, as before particularized, of angels as well as men, for though angels properly, and by nature, want tongues, (as well as knees, which are both here joined, and must not be severed, in the worship given to Christ,) yet in their manner of speaking to men, under an extraordinary dispensation, they may use them, (or that which is equivalent,) 1 Cor. xiii. 1; and, in a way proper to them, can *confess*, or express, their adoration of Christ, Rev. vii. 9—12, either with delight, or by a forced subjection, Rev. vi. 16, and acknowledge that he is Lord, i. e. of glory, Rom. xi. 36; 1 Cor. ii. 8; viii. 6, the Son of God, 2 Cor. iv, 5; Heb. i. 2, 4, having only power to command the soul and conscience, James iv. 12, and to save, Heb. vii. 27, being *Lord both of the dead and of the living*, Rom. xiv. 9. *To the glory of God the Father;* some render, in the glory of the Father. Either in that the honour of Christ redoundeth to the honour of the Father, Prov. x. 1, with John v. 23; Eph. i. 6; or the Father doth most glorify the Son in his exaltation, who had most glorified him in his humiliation, John xii. 28, with xvii. 5, 6.

t ch. 1. 5.

12 Wherefore, my beloved, *as ye have always obeyed, not as in my presence only but now much more in my absence, work out your own salvation with "fear and trembling. u Eph. 6. 5.

Wherefore, my beloved, as ye have always obeyed: having confirmed the example of Christ's admirable condescension and affection from the glorious issue of it, he doth here reassume his exhortation, with a friendly compellation, commending their former sincere endeavours to obey the gospel (so chap. i. 5, and ver. 15 of this) in following Christ, Matt. xi. 28, and moving them to persevere in obedience and love to God and man. *Not as in my presence only, but now much more in my absence;* that it might be evident, whether the eye of their pastor were upon them or no, a prevailing love to Christ, and their own souls' welfare, was prevalent with them; but especially, being he was now detained from them, and might be jealous of some defects in them, James iii. 2; 1 John i. 8, did engage them more than any thing to embrace his exhortation, which he enlargeth in other words. *Work out your own salvation:* he moves them as saints, chap. i. 1, in whom God would perfect his work begun, ver. 6, having given them to believe and suffer, ver. 29, that they would seriously and earnestly busy themselves in those things, which on their parts are necessary to salvation, as John vi. 27; Heb. vi. 9, and without which it cannot be had, as chap. i. 10; Matt. xxiv. 13; Col. iii. 10, 12, &c.; 1 Tim. i. 18, 19; vi. 19; 2 Tim. i. 5; iv. 7, 8; 2 Pet. iii. 17; yea, press on in the way to their own salvation, as he moved, 1 Tim. iv. 16, not that they should not be solicitous about others, for that mutual care is implied, as elsewhere required, Heb. iii. 13; x. 24; but that every one should strenuously go on towards the mark with a special regard to himself, and the temptations he may meet with, knowing he must bear his own burden, Gal. vi. 1, 5, and therefore should take heed lest he fall. The papists' arguings hence that our actions are sufficient and meritorious causes of salvation, are altogether inconsequent. For the apostle doth not say our actions work out salvation, but, *Work out your own salvation*, which is much different. It were absurd to say, because the Jews were enjoined to eat the passover with loins girt, that loins girt were eating of the passover. Indeed, what the papists urge is contrary to this doctrine of Paul, who doth elsewhere place blessedness in remission of sins, and shows eternal life is the gift of God, Rom. iv. 6, 7; vi. 23; and we are saved by grace, not of works, Rom. iii. 20, 24, 25; iv. 16; Eph. ii. 8; Tit. iii. 5; and contrary to the main scope of the apostle, which is to beat down pride and conceit of deserving, and persuade to humility. He drives at this, that we should not be idle or lazy in the business of salvation, but work together with God, (yet as instruments, in whom there is no strength which is not derived from him,) that we may evidence we do not receive his grace in vain, 2 Cor. vi. 1, 2. But this co-operation doth not respect the acquiring or meriting of salvation, which is proper to Christ alone, and incommunicable to any others, Acts iv. 12, who cannot be said to be their own saviours: this co-operation, or working out, respects only the application, not the performing of the payment, which Christ hath abundantly perfected: but the embracing of the perfect payment, is not that which can be the cause and foundation of right for which it is deservedly conferred; but only the way and means by which we come to partake of salvation. *With fear and trembling;* i. e. with a holy care to do all acceptably: he doth by these two words mean not any servile fear and slavish despondency, arising from doubting, chap. iv. 4, but only a serious, filial fear, implying a deep humility and submissiveness of mind, with a reverential awe of the Divine Majesty, and a solicitude to avoid that evil which is offensive to him and separates from him. We find these words used to the like import, Psal. ii. 11; Dan. v. 19; vi. 26; Rom. xi. 20; with 1 Cor. ii. 3; 2 Cor. vii. 5; Eph. vi. 5; connoting that, after the example of Christ, we should be humble, and though we distrust ourselves, yet we are to trust solely to God, (as an infant may be afraid, and yet cling fast to and depend upon, begging help of, the parent, going over a dangerous precipice,) for the accomplishment of our salvation.

13 For *it is God which worketh in you both to will and to do of *his* good pleasure. x 2 Cor. 3. 5. Heb. 13. 21.

That they might not be negligent in working out their

salvation with humility, from any conceit or carnal confidence any might have that they could believe and repent when they pleased, imagining their wills to be as pliable to good as evil; the apostle urgeth the effectual grace of God, as a powerful inducement and encouragement to embrace his exhortation. *For it is God which worketh in you:* they should not despond of any attaining salvation, or think they did labour in vain in the diligent use of means, and should altogether fall under the dominion of sin, considering, though they were free agents, yet the efficiency and sufficiency was of God, Rom. vi. 13, 14; 1 Cor. iv. 7; 2 Cor. iii. 5; who worketh within them powerfully and effectually, carrying on the work through all difficulties and obstacles, with victorious efficacy, till it be wrought, chap. i. 6; Isa. xli. 4; Heb. xiii. 20, 21: God worketh not only by suasion to gain assent, but by a special energy effecting what he would have us to do. *Both to will:* and not only in a general way, Acts xvii. 28, but in a special way, making us willing, Psal. cx. 3, remotely in regard of the principle, nextly in regard of the act: circumcising the heart, Deut. xxx. 6; taking away the heart of stone, and giving a heart of flesh, Ezek. xi. 19; xxxvi. 26, 27; causing light to shine out of darkness, 2 Cor. iv. 6; and so renewing the will, to choose that which is savingly good, the natural bent of which, before the influence of this insuperable grace, stands another way, John viii. 44, viz. to will and do contrary: yet he doth not necessitate by any compulsion, but powerfully, yet sweetly, and suitably to man's free faculty, incline the will to that which is good, John vi. 37, 44, i. e. to a certain effect. For the will influenced to will that it doth perform, it undoubtedly wills somewhat that is certain, and so is determined by God. *And to do;* to do that which is savingly good. Whereupon being made willing, it hath not only an inclination, and doth not only exert a woulding, but, being moved by God's insuperable grace, 1 Cor. iii. 7, that will is effectual, and is the very deed, where the command of the will is executed to the glory of God, as the author. As in alms, not only doth God incline the will to relieve the poor, but further contributes special gracious aids to perform what was deliberated, which evinceth that it is from another principle than ourselves. It is not, that ye may be able to will, and may be able to do; but he worketh *both to will and to do:* which connotes the very act itself; that ye will to believe, obey, pray, persevere, and that ye do believe, obey, pray, persevere: of unwilling, he makes willing; and further, *to will and to do.* It is true, to will, as it is an act of the will, is ours by creation; and to will well is so far ours, we being made effectually willing by God's grace: yet not ours, as though of ourselves we begin to will, or go on, but it is of him who worketh in us. Not that we cannot will well, but that of ourselves we cannot will well. The precept therefore requiring our obedience does not show what we can or will of ourselves, but what we ought to will and to do by God's special help. But though God work in us obedience, yet we obey, we ourselves act, being acted of God. *Of his good pleasure;* not for any previous disposition in any of us, but of, or according to, his own good pleasure, Luke x. 21; Eph. i. 5, 9, 11; ii. 8; 2 Thess. i. 11, with 2 Tim. i. 9. In working out our own salvation, the very beginning in the will, as well as the perfection, is ascribed to the efficacy of God; his good pleasure is the procreating and helping cause of this work on the will, and not the will's good pleasure.

14 Do all things ʸwithout murmurings and ᶻdisputings:
_{y 1 Cor. 10. 10. 1 Pet. 4. 9.}
_{z Rom. 14. 1.}

Do all things without murmurings; the apostle here subjoins to his exhortation to condescension and humility, a dissuasive from the opposite vices, moving them to do all that was incumbent on them as Christians without private mutterings, secret whisperings, and complainings, which might argue their impatience under the yoke of Christ, while put upon doing or suffering such things; either reflecting on God's providence, as the Israelites of old, Numb. xi. 1, &c.; 1 Cor. x. 10; reckoning they had hard measure: or rather, (here considering the context,) grudging at others, as the Greeks and Jews had done, Luke v. 30; John vi. 41, 42; Acts vi. 1; yea, and some of the disciples were found guilty of this ill temper against their Master, John vi. 61. Christian charity disallows grudgings, 1 Pet. iv. 9; Jude 10; and also *disputings;* hot and eager contests and quarrellings about those things wherein the life and main business of religion is not concerned, but the unity of the Spirit of holiness is opposed, Matt. xviii. 1; Mark ix. 33; Luke ix. 46; Rom. xiv. 1; 2 Cor. xii. 20, with 1 Tim. i. 6; ii. 8.

15 That ye may be blameless and ‖ harmless, ᵃthe sons of God, without rebuke, ᵇin the midst of ᶜa crooked and perverse nation, among whom ‖ ᵈye shine as lights in the world;
_{‖ Or, sincere. a Matt. 5.45. Eph. 5. 1. b 1 Pet. 2.12. c Deut. 32. 5. ‖ Or, shine ye. d Matt. 5. 14, 16. Eph. 5. 8.}

That ye may be blameless and harmless; that ye behave yourselves so that none can justly reproach you, Luke i. 6; and though you cannot altogether put to silence foolish men, John xv. 25; 1 Pet. ii. 15. yet they cannot have any just cause to stain your reputation; but you may be found sincere, simple, void of guile, Matt. x. 16; John i. 47; Rom. xvi. 19; 1 Pet. ii. 1, with i. 14. *The sons of God, without rebuke;* without such spots and blemishes as are inconsistent with your adoption, or sonship, Eph. v. 27. Sons of God, in regard of their relation, should be careful, as much as may be, that they do not expose themselves to the biting reproofs of those carping neighbours who are not of their Father's family, Cant. iv. 7; Matt. v. 48; Eph. i. 4; Jude xxiv. *In the midst of a crooked and perverse nation;* who show by their lying in wickedness, 1 John v. 19, and the uncured spots, yea, even plague sores, upon them who have notoriously corrupted themselves, that they are a perverse, crooked, untoward, and adulterous generation, Deut. xxxii. 5; Psal. cxxv. 5; Matt. xii. 39; Acts xiii. 8, 10. *Among whom ye shine as lights in the world;* in conversing with such a sort of men, ye either do, or ought, unanimously to show yourselves to be light in the Lord, Matt. v. 14, 16; Eph. v. 8, 15; enlightened by the Sun of righteousness, Mal. iv. 2, to give a more clear light, that however the uncivil wicked would bespatter you, and cast reproach upon you in the necessary exercises of religion; yet, you not suffering as murderers, thieves, busybodies, &c., 1 Pet. iv. 4, 15, 16, you will then, especially if Christ's faithful ambassadors, show yourselves to be not such lantern or torchbearers as accompanied treacherous Judas, John xviii. 3, (however the ill men you live among may reckon you no better,) but such light-bearers under Christ, (the Seventy use the word for stars, Gen. i. 16; Dan. xii. 3; Rev. i. 16, 20,) as irradiate the world; not a house, as a candle doth, but the world, as stars do, Rev. xii. 1.

16 Holding forth the word of life; that ᵉI may rejoice in the day of Christ, that ᶠI have not run in vain, neither laboured in vain.
_{e 2 Cor. 1. 14. 1 Thess. 2. 19. f Gal. 2. 2. 1 Thess. 3. 5.}

Holding forth the word of life; carefully bearing before you, and stedfastly showing, not only by your profession, but conversation, the Lord Jesus Christ, 1 John i. 1, whose gospel is the word of life, in that *it is the power of God to salvation,* Acts xiii. 26; Rom. i. 16. He doth not say, holding forth carnal institutions, nor human traditions; but that word, wherein is to be had *eternal life,* John v. 39; vi. 68. *That I may rejoice in the day of Christ:* he quickens them from the consideration of the glorious joy he should have in their salvation, at the day of Christ, (see chap. i. 6,) when he and they should, of God's free grace, receive an abundant reward, viz. of his ministry and exhortation, and of their embracing it, and working out their salvation by God's special assistance. *That I have not run in vain, neither laboured in vain;* for it would be evident to his, as well as their, everlasting comfort, when he should see them, that his laborious ministry amongst them had not been frustrate, or fruitless in the Lord, Matt. xxv. 21; 1 Cor. iii. 8, 9; xv. 58. Then, in a more glorious way they would be his *joy and crown,* than they were at present, chap. iv. 1.

17 Yea, and if ᵍI be † offered upon the sacrifice ʰand service of your faith, ⁱI joy, and rejoice with you all.
_{g 2 Tim. 4.6. † Gr. poured forth. h Rom. 15. 16. i 2 Cor. 7. 4. Col. 1. 24.}

Yea, and if I be offered: that he might further confirm and encourage them in their duty, he doth not here conclude the certainty of his death, at his first imprisonment, having expressed before some confidence of his surviving it, chap. i. 19, 25; but, in imitation of Christ, *the good Shepherd*, John x. 11, to demonstrate his constant affection to them, (as he doth to others, 2 Cor. xii. 15; 1 Thess. ii. 8,) he argues upon supposition of his own death, which might afterwards happen, 2 Tim. iv. 6; using an elegant allegory, borrowed from legal offerings, Lev. ii. 6; Numb. xv. 5, 7; xxiii. 4; Judg. ix. 13; to show that he could cheerfully lay down his life for their salvation; not for reconciling them to God, for that was done before by Christ's own offering up himself, Heb. vii. 27, a sacrifice of a sweet smell unto God, Eph. v. 2; but whereby they might be confirmed in the faith sealed with his blood, for bearing witness to Christ, precious to God, Psa. cxvi. 15. The Greek word he hath here, is borrowed from the usage in sacrificing, of pouring wine or oil upon the victim, Exod. xxx. 9; 2 Kings xvi. 13; Jer. xix. 13, when that which was poured forth was called the drink-offering, to the confirming of covenants. *Upon the sacrifice;* by *sacrifice*, he means either specially their alms, prepared by them, and presented by Epaphroditus, for supporting him in his sufferings, and in the person of the apostle offered up unto God, chap. iv. 18; 2 Cor. ix. 12; or, more generally, the Philippians' conversion, because sanctified by a principle of faith, and so made a sacrifice. For he doth more than once write of believers being offered, and resigned to God, under the notion of a sacrifice, Rom. xii. 1; xv. 16; and so doth another, 1 Pet. ii. 5. *And service of your faith;* to bring them unto which by his ministration, was a very pleasing service to him, who by pouring out his blood in this martyrdom, would confirm the doctrine of the gospel, or new covenant, and fix it more strongly in the hearts of them and others of God's chosen people. *I joy;* whereupon he expresseth his joy and delight in that, which, upon this supposition, would in the issue be so much to their honour and advantage, when it should seem good to the Lord. They would reckon it no small honour, to have him, the apostle that planted the gospel amongst them, satisfied in their vouching of the truth, which therefore could not but be profitable to the establishing of them in it, who had cordially embraced it. *And rejoice with you all;* whereupon he doth heartily congratulate with each of them, the meanest as well as the greatest of them, who would be so privileged.

18 For the same cause also do ye joy, and rejoice with me.

For the same cause also do ye joy; he expects the like affection and sympathy in every one of them, that upon the account of his sufferings they would the more readily, cheerfully, and courageously believe in and suffer for Christ: considering the difference betwixt death threatened by man, for our sticking close to God, Matt. x. 28, and denounced for slipping aside from God, in whole or in part, 2 Thess. i. 5. *And rejoice with me;* and that would be a congratulation of him, who should account their being established in the faith with mutual love and unity, a fulfilling of his faith, as before, ver. 2.

|| Or, *Moreover*.
k Rom. 16. 21. 1 Thess. 3. 2.

19 || But I trust in the Lord Jesus to send ᵏTimotheus shortly unto you, that I also may be of good comfort, when I know your state.

But I trust in the Lord Jesus; diverting from his former exhortation, the more to comfort them, he expresseth his good hope (which in respect of the object we translate *trust*) in the Lord Jesus, exalted above every name, that he would be pleased, some way or other, to afford him such liberty, notwithstanding his restraint. *To send Timotheus shortly unto you;* that he should, within a little while after the arrival of Epaphroditus, now upon his return, despatch Timothy to them. *That I also may be of good comfort;* not for their further benevolence, but for the composing of their spirits, and settling of their affairs, which to him, solicitous of their souls' welfare, (as in a like case for others, 1 Thess. ii. 19, with iii. 5,) would be great satisfaction. *When I know your state;* when he should be certainly acquainted how things went with them; who might justly expect his sympathy, Rom. xii. 15; 1 Cor. xii. 26; 2 Cor. xi. 28, 29.

20 For I have no man ¹ || likeminded, who will naturally care for your state.

l Ps. 55. 13.
|| Or, *so dear unto me*.

For I have no man likeminded; for which purpose I have designed Timothy, who joins with me in this Epistle, and is most of the same mind with myself, endued with the same Spirit, faith, and love; finding none of like soul to him with myself, in desiring your prosperity, and so have pitched upon him. *Who will naturally care for your state;* who, being cordial to me and you, will, without regard to lucre, ingenuously and sincerely, above all the rest I have here, propagate the kingdom of Christ amongst you, and promote your salvation in watching for your souls, as one that must give an account, that he may do it with joy, Heb. xiii. 17.

21 For all ᵐseek their own, not the things which are Jesus Christ's.

m 1 Cor. 10. 24, 33. & 13. 5. 2 Tim. 4. 10, 16.

He doth here further commend Timothy, compared with the generality of those who with him did attend the ministry of the gospel at Rome, where it seems (whatever the papists pretend) Peter did not then preside as metropolitan. When he saith *all*, he doth not necessarily imply every individual besides Timothy, (though, as before, he knew not one like-minded as he was,) but almost all, (as the universal sign is elsewhere synecdochically taken, Jer. vi. 3; Matt. x. 22; Mark i. 5,) or the most part of those then employed in the ministry, who were then at liberty, and whose inclinations, probably, he had inquired into. *Seek their own;* did, though not simply and absolutely, yet after a sort, seek their own profit, ease, safety, pleasure, and satisfaction; called *their own*, in regard of their civil right, and the world's opinion, but yet at God's disposal, Hag. ii. 8. These they did (as John Mark in another case) prefer to a long and tedious journey, for the service of Christ, unto Philippi. *Not the things which are Jesus Christ's;* so that they did postpone the glory of Christ, the safety and edification of the church there, to their own things. Wherefore he doth not mean it absolutely, that they did not seek the things of Christ, or that they did deny Christ, for it is apparent, even when he penned this Epistle, chap. i. 13, 14, with Acts xxviii. 14, 15, and Rom. i. 8, there were many that did seriously seek Christ; but comparatively, and in a sort, they did not seek the things of Christ so intently as they should, 1 Cor. x. 24, 33, but failed as others did in other cases, Matt. xxvi. 58; 2 Tim. iv. 16: not as if all minding of their own things were denied to Christ's ministers, 1 Tim. iii. 4, 5; v. 8; but they did slip their necks from under the yoke, and did not mind the glory of Christ in the church of Philippi, as he did.

22 But ye know the proof of him, ⁿthat, as a son with the father, he hath served with me in the Gospel.

n 1 Cor. 4. 17. 1 Tim. 1. 2. 2 Tim. 1. 2.

However others were found in some respects defective to the service of Christ, yet he appeals to their experience of the integrity and fidelity of Timothy in conjunction with himself, when he preached the gospel amongst them, and afterwards, Acts xvi. 1; xvii. 15; xviii. 5; xix. 22; xx. 4; which he amplifies and illustrates by a simile, when he saith, *as a son with the father;* q. d. Just as a genuine and obedient son is wont to retain the spirit of his father that begat him: and Paul doth metaphorically call Timothy his *own son*, begotten by the gospel, 1 Tim. i. 2, his *dearly beloved Son*, 2 Tim. i. 2, and *faithful in the Lord*, 1 Cor. iv. 17, *likeminded* with himself, ver. 20; with whom he had not only preached, but *served in the gospel*, chap. i. 1, given himself wholly to the thing. He doth not say, served me, or under me, but *with me* in the gospel, i. e. to advance the glory of Christ in promoting the gospel, by helping with Paul, and labouring, working the work of the Lord, as Paul also did, and being sometime a sufferer under restraint for that service, as Paul himself, Heb. xiii. 23, for the gospel, which is not a domination, but ministration, wherein this great apostle owns Timothy as his fellow minister.

23 Him therefore I hope to send presently, so soon as I shall see how it will go with me.

Him therefore I hope to send presently; seeing the matter was thus, he thought not of any other to employ in the service of their faith, but hoped, i. e. *in the Lord Jesus* as ver. 19, in a short time after his present writing, to send this excellent, humble, and approved young man, who would naturally care for their concerns, ver. 20. *So soon as I shall see how it will go with me;* even without any delay, (though as yet, to accompany Epaphroditus, he could not spare him, who was so useful to him in his bonds, to take care for things necessary to the propagation of the gospel, in the ample city of Rome,) from the hour he should come to a certainty what would be the issue of his present imprisonment, which if it should end in his being offered up, he had satisfied them before, as it would be for his own advantage, chap. i. 21, so, by the providence of God, no disservice to their faith, ver. 17, 18; from which, with ready submission to God's will, whatever occurred, it seems he had a greater inclination to conceive a good hope of freedom.

o ch. 1. 25.
Philem. 22.
24 But °I trust in the Lord that I also myself shall come shortly.

But I trust in the Lord; so he expresseth his strong persuasion, as the word we translate *trust,* being seldom used, but when the thing trusted imports the object. *In the Lord;* i. e. Jesus, whom he doth absolutely and eminently call Lord, being so *highly exalted* above all others, ver. 9, not only here, but elsewhere, ver. 29; chap. iii. 1; iv. 1, 4, 10; on whom he doth wholly depend, and to whom he doth submit for the issue. *That I also myself shall come shortly :* before he had suggested his persuasion of abiding with them, chap. i. 25, and here, that he might satisfy them he had not changed his mind, he adds for their comfort, that they might not be discouraged in their sufferings, what apprehensions he had, after a while, of being set at liberty (if God pleased) ; and if so, he would have them conceive, soon after he had done what was necessary at Rome, (for him who had care of all the churches,) he designed to follow Timothy to them.

p ch. 4. 18.
q Philem. 2.
r 2 Cor. 8. 23.
s 2 Cor. 11.9.
ch. 4. 18.
25 Yet I supposed it necessary to send to you ᵖEpaphroditus, my brother, and companion in labour, and ᵠfellowsoldier, ʳbut your messenger, and ˢhe that ministered to my wants.

Yet I supposed it necessary to send to you Epaphroditus; in the mean time he gives them an account why he esteemed it needful to send back Epaphroditus (whom some, but without sufficient warrant, would have to be the same with Epaphras, Col. i. 7; iv. 12; Philem. 23) unto them, not as if he had failed in doing what he was intrusted with, but for other weighty reasons. *My brother and companion in labour ;* he would have them to know he had nothing to blame him for, but all in his commendation, whom in the common faith he owned to be his Christian brother, and fellow helper, or fellow worker in the business of the gospel, as he calls others in the like circumstances, Rom. xvi. 3, 21 ; 2 Cor. viii. 23 ; Col. iv. 11 ; 1 Thess. iii. 2 ; Philem. 24. *And fellow soldier ;* and a faithful and a constant associate with him in the Christian warfare, 2 Cor. x. 4 ; 1 Tim. i. 18; Philem. 2, under Christ their Captain, against all the assaults of the devil, and the carnal world, which are continually warring to destroy real Christianity. *But your messenger ;* but your apostle, which must be understood largely, as it is sometimes put for any evangelist, deacon, or minister of the gospel, Rom. xvi. 7, 9, well rendered by us in this place *messenger,* compared with chap. iv. 18; 2 Cor. viii. 22, 23 ; not being a special apostle of Christ, Matt. x. 2, but an officer of the church at Philippi, delegated by them to carry relief to Paul. *And he that ministered to my wants ;* unto whom, it seems, he did not only deliver the present for his support according to his trust and commission, wherein he faithfully served the church, but also, as their public minister, greatly help Paul the prisoner in what he stood most in need of, which Paul could not but value, being the Romans were so mild as to permit him, a captive, so good attendance and assistance ; yet, to declare his affections to the church at Philippi, he chose rather to deny himself his necessaries, than not to comfort them in remitting their faithful messenger, so greatly desiring their welfare, with this letter to them.

t ch. 1. 3.
26 ᵗFor he longed after you all, and was full of heaviness, because that ye had heard that he had been sick.

For he longed after you all ; he gives them the first reason of his present sending, not that Epaphroditus was unwilling to stay longer with him, but because he was greatly concerned for all of them of the church at Philippi, who had his heart, as they had Paul's, chap. i. 8 ; iv. 1 ; Rom. i. 11 ; solicitous to be with them to do their souls good. *And was full of heaviness ;* especially, considering their great affection to him, whom they had intrusted in this service, he was in such distress for them, that his spirits were even ready to fail him (as Matt. xxvi. 37) from sympathy, 2 Cor. xi. 29. *Because that ye had heard that he had been sick ;* knowing how much the certain report of his dangerous sickness in those circumstances, when they could understand nothing of his recovery, would affect them.

27 For indeed he was sick nigh unto death : but God had mercy on him; and not on him only, but on me also, lest I should have sorrow upon sorrow.

For indeed he was sick nigh unto death ; by reason he was really taken with such a disease, as in its own nature was mortal, and in its tendency brought him even to death's door, as Isa. xxxviii. 1. *But God had mercy on him ;* but God, who is the great Physician, and unto whom it belongs to show mercy unto those who address to him, (without whom bodily physicians can do nothing,) by compassionating of him in his misery, was pleased to restore him to health, as 2 Kings xx. 5, 6. But if any say, Would it not have been great mercy to have taken him from the miseries of this life, which are here prolonged ? consider chap. i. 21. It may be answered, 1. Death itself, as it is a privation of life, and opposite to nature, was not desirable by Paul any more than by our Saviour, but might be looked upon as a kind of misery, not to be preferred to life looked upon in itself, but with respect to another, viz. as it is a passage to eternal life ; so it is desirable for that life into which it leads the godly, and so is to be preferred to the miserable condition of this life. Paul speaks here of mercy respecting the former, considering that this life itself is a favour of God, for the service of him, and our neighbour. Further, 2. God's mercy here respects not only the grievous sickness of Epaphroditus, but the joint affliction that the loss of him would be both to the Philippians and to Paul, in thus juncture, as we may see from what follows. *And not on him only, but on me also ;* what power had Paul for working of miracles, was chiefly to convince infidels, and he could only exert it when God saw good for his own glory. Therefore he magnifies God's mercy here in a more ordinary way, as a return to prayer, when he was so afflicted for his colleague's illness ; being upon an office of kindness and compassion, his loss would be in its tendency a ground of so much sorrow to the church, as well as to himself. *Lest I should have sorrow upon sorrow ;* his Christianity had not extinguished his natural affections, but if the church had then been bereft of Epaphroditus, it would have added the affliction for his loss to his affliction by his suffering for Christ, it would have doubled his affliction, (yet somewhat in a different sense from that, chap. i. 16,) it being an ill temper not to be grieved for the affliction of the church, Amos vi. 6 ; yet all our affections are to be moderated according to the will of God.

28 I sent him therefore the more carefully, that, when ye see him again, ye may rejoice, and that I may be the less sorrowful.

I sent him therefore the more carefully ; after his recovery, without delay, denying myself the comfort of his society, I have despatched him away to you. *That, when ye see him again, ye may rejoice ;* to the end that he whom you looked upon as dead might seasonably appear among you in person, and cheer you up in your troubles for him and me. *And that I may be the less sorrowful ;* and that I, who, by reason of your kindness to me, have occasioned his absence from you, might upon his safe return to you have somewhat to alleviate my grief, 2 Cor. vi. 10.

29 Receive him therefore in the Lord with all gladness; and ∥ ᵘhold such in reputation :

1 Or, honour such.
u 1 Cor. 16. 18. 1 Thess. 5. 12. 1 Tim. 5. 17.

Receive him therefore in the Lord with all gladness :

hereupon, having given his due character, he chargeth them all, officers and people, to entertain him as a servant of the Lord, (as Christ would have them receive his servants, Matt. x. 40, 41, even with all spiritual joy,) as sometimes the Galatians had received him, Gal. iv. 14. *And hold such in reputation;* yea, as it becometh saints, Rom. xvi. 2, to have such in esteem very highly for their work's sake, 1 Thess. v. 13.

30 Because for the work of Christ he was nigh unto death, not regarding his life, ˣto supply your lack of service toward me.

x 1 Cor. 16. 17. ch. 4. 10.

Because for the work of Christ he was nigh unto death; by reason he was so zealous about the work of the ministry in the general, or in special to carry on that service, as the church's messenger, he was intrusted with, chap. iv. 18, not only in conveying their benevolence on so long and hazardous a journey, for the relief of the Lord's prisoner, which Christ would own and reward as his work, Matt. xxv. 39, 40, but in attending him (whom he was sent to visit) in his confinement, both within doors and abroad, as occasion required, (for it seems the Romans were so generous as to give free egress and regress to his visitants, Acts xxviii. 30,) whereby he contracted that forementioned disease that hazarded his life. *Not regarding his life;* the preservation of which with respect to the work he was about, he did not consult, (John xii. 25, 26,) but made little account of it, (as Esth. iv. 16,) yea, did even despise it in the service of Christ, as the original word doth import, being borrowed from those whose lives are hazarded in being cast to be devoured by beasts in the theatre, which he himself, by sad experience, sometime knew the meaning of, 1 Cor. xv. 32. *To supply your lack of service toward me;* so faithful was he to his trust for the honour of his Lord, that to the very utmost of his strength, yea, and beyond it, that which he reckoned those who sent would have done themselves had they been present, (considering what the gospel requires, Gal. vi. 2; Heb. xiii. 3,) that he, Onisephorus-like, 2 Tim. i. 16, according to his measure made supply of in their absence.

CHAP. III

Paul exhorteth to rejoice in the Lord, and to beware of the false teachers of the circumcision, 1—3 : *showing that as a Jew he had better grounds of confidence than they,* 4—6 ; *but that he disclaimed them all, trusting only to the justification which is of God by faith, and hoping to partake of the resurrection through Christ,* 7—11. *He acknowledgeth his present imperfection, and that he was still anxiously striving for the prize,* 12—14 : *exhorteth others to be like-minded,* 15, 16, *and to follow his example,* 17 ; *for many were enemies to the gospel, being earthly-minded,* 18, 19 ; *but his conversation and views were heavenly,* 20, 21.

FINALLY, my brethren, ᵃrejoice in the Lord. To write the same things to you, to me indeed *is* not grievous, but for you *it is* safe.

a 2 Cor. 13. 11. ch. 4. 4. 1 Thess. 5. 16.

Finally; moreover, or as to what remains, i. e. by way of conclusion to the antecedent matter, and transition to the general exhortation, he here premiseth to the subsequent admonition. *My brethren;* willingly repeating the title of *brethren,* to show the respect he had for them, and to sweeten that he was about to subjoin. *Rejoice in the Lord;* he moves them (as we, with almost all, do translate it) not as saluting or bidding them farewell, Luke i. 28 ; 2 Cor. xiii. 11 ; but to rejoice in the Lord, as chap. iv. 4, either connoting the object matter of their joy, compared with ver. 3, or rather the efficient, importing for and according to the will of the Lord, in a manner agreeable to the pleasure of him who affords a ground of rejoicing in the midst of your tribulations and afflictions ; considering his mercy, chap. ii. 18, 27, 29, they might taste how good the Lord is, as elsewhere, Psal. xxxvii. 4 ; Jer. ix. 24, with Rom. v. 11 ; 2 Cor. x. 17 ; 1 Thess. v. 16 ; 1 Pet. i. 8 ; and so not after a carnal and worldly, but spiritual and Christian manner, to cheer up themselves in him, when the world frowns most, Psal. iv. 6, 7. *To write the same things to you;* writing of the same things cannot be referred to any other epistles which he wrote to the Philippians, but to those things which, while present with them, he had delivered to them by word of mouth, as chap. iv. 9 : compare Isa. xxviii. 10 ; Rom. xv. 15 ; 2 Pet. i. 12 ; 1 John ii. 21. *To me indeed is not grievous;* for my part, I do not do it with regret, nor account it tedious, (as some teachers do,) as if I were ashamed of it, that I should do any thing superfluous, or not necessary, in writing again the same things for the matter of them, that I had before preached to preserve you from falling, as others have done, ver. 18. *But for you it is safe;* because this repetition of the same doctrine, though in another way, is pertinent to your edification, (yea, as some read, it is necessary,) it is greatly advantageous for your stability in the faith, and to caution and keep you in safety, from the insinuations of false teachers, that I now give you a brief memorial in writing of those things, that you may be cautioned, and they may not, especially in this day of adversity, slip out of your memories, or be lost.

2 ᵇBeware of dogs, beware of ᶜevil workers, ᵈbeware of the concision.

b Is. 56. 10. Gal. 5. 15. c 2Cor. 11. 13. d Rom. 2. 28. Gal. 5. 2.

Beware; he cautions all, both officers and people : and though the original word doth signify to look with mind and eye, yet it is also frequently rendered, to take heed, Mark viii. 15 ; xii. 38 ; xiii. 9, 23, 33 ; 1 Cor. xvi. 10 ; 2 John 8. *Of dogs;* of those dogs, (with the article emphatically proposed,) a metaphor borrowed from those voracious, fierce, impure animals, whose price was not brought into the Lord's house, Deut. xxiii. 18 ; Prov. xxvi. 11 ; Isa. lxvi. 3 ; 2 Pet. ii. 22 ; to connote the false apostles, who endeavoured to corrupt the gospel with Judaism and profaneness, even antichristianism ; compare Psal. xxii. 16, 20 ; Matt. vii. 6 ; xv. 26 ; Rev. xxii. 15. Some think the apostle may allude unto the proverbial speech, Take heed of a mad dog, forasmuch as false teachers, being acted as with a certain madness, would bite Christ and his apostles, and tear his body ; and these mad dogs were the more dangerous, in that they did not bark so much as bite. Hence they say, Take heed of a dumb dog and still watcher. There were of several sorts, enemies to the cross of Christ, Gal. v. 12 ; 1 Thess. ii. 14, 15 ; some more secret, as Absalom against Amnon, 2 Sam. xiii. 22, pretending contrary to their practice, 2 Kings viii. 13 ; xiii. 22. Our Saviour bade his disciples beware of such, Matt. x. 17, which he found to be of this temper, Psal. xxii. 16, 20 ; lv. 15 ; though some of them were but dumb dogs, Isa. lvi. 10 : some such there were amongst the Philippians, who, notwithstanding their fair pretext, were enemies to the cross of Christ, did secretly disparage his true apostle, and tear his flock : see ver. 18 of this chapter, with chap. i. 15, 16. *Beware of evil workers;* such as pretended to labour in promoting the gospel of Christ, but secretly were doing mischief amongst Christians, not serving the glory of Christ, but their own bellies, ver. 18, 19 ; being, as he elsewhere calls them, *deceitful workers,* 2 Cor. xi. 13, glorying in the flesh, Gal. vi. 13. *Beware of the concision;* by an elegant allusion to the name circumcision, which rite the Jews did glory in, and some false teachers of Christianity, after the time of reformation, did urge as necessary to salvation, and require it from others, Acts xv. 1 ; Gal. v. 2, 4 ; vi. 12. These Paul here, in a holy sarcasm, charges the Philippians to take heed of, under the contemptible name of *the concision,* or cutting off, intimating that the exterior part of that typical work, which was done in the cutting off the foreskin, was now, from the coming of Christ, altogether made a mere cutting off the skin, condemned by God in the heathens, as a profane incision, Lev. xix. 28 ; xxi. 5, where the LXX. use the same preposition in the compound word, the apostle here doth in contempt of the thing ; which could now bring nothing of profit, nothing of holiness, nothing of honour to any Christian, could no more avail or advantage a man now, than if it were conferred on a beast, being no seal of the covenant now, but a stickling for that rite (when abolished by Christ) which was a mere rending of the church, and in that effect a cutting off from it, Gal. v. 10, 12. And the apostle doth three times significantly repeat this word, *beware* of these enemies to Christian purity and unity, to show how necessary it was to avoid their insinua-

PHILIPPIANS III

tions, against which he is more sharp in his Epistle to the Galatians.

e Deut. 10. 16. & 30. 6.
Jer. 4. 4.
Rom. 2. 29. & 4. 11, 12.
Col. 2. 11.
f John 4. 23, 24. Rom. 7. 6.
g Gal. 6. 14.

3 For we are ᵉthe circumcision, ᶠwhich worship God in the spirit, and ᵍrejoice in Christ Jesus, and have no confidence in the flesh.

In opposition to and confutation of *the concision*, he speaks of himself, and all true believers in the fellowship of the gospel, partakers of the same grace and Spirit with him, chap. i. 5, 7; ii. 1; and saith, *we*. *Are the circumcision;* using a metonymy, are the circumcision now acceptable, and not displeasing to God, i. e. we are what is really signified by it, and therefore as to the main intent of it are the circumcised (it being usual to put circumcision for circumcised, Acts xi. 2; Rom. iii. 30; iv. 12; xv. 8; Gal. ii. 7, 8, 9, 12; Col. iv. 11; Tit. i. 10): he doth not mean with respect to carnal circumcision, i. e. which is outward in the flesh, but which is inward in the Spirit, Rom. ii. 28, 29, made without hands by the circumcision of Christ, with whom we are buried in baptism, Col. ii. 11, 12; and being Christ's are Abraham's spiritual seed, and heirs of the promise, Gal. iii. 29. *Which worship God in the spirit;* i. e. who have cut off all carnal confidence of salvation in any external services, (which they of the concision contend for,) and do worship God, not with carnal, but spiritual worship, such as now under the gospel he doth require, John iv. 23, 24; Rom. i. 9; from a renewed heart, John iii. 8; 1 Pet. iii. 15; yielding peculiar adoration to the Lord our God, with a sincere mind, and by the assistance of his Spirit in the exercise of faith and love, Rom. viii. 5, 6, 26, 27; Eph. iii. 16, 17; vi. 18; Heb. x. 22; according to the same rule he hath prescribed, ver. 16, with Rom. xii. 1, 2; Gal. vi. 16, in and through Christ, Heb. xiii. 15. *And rejoice in Christ Jesus;* in whom alone (not in Moses also, as false teachers would join them) glorying we trust for acceptance with God, 2 Cor. v. 9; Gal. vi. 14; in communion with whom is ground of rejoicing through Christ, who is the substance or body of Mosaic shadows, ver. 9. *And have no confidence in the flesh;* and not rest, or trust, or place our hope in any carnal or external privilege or performance, or any other besides Jesus Christ, to commend us to God, Gal. iii. 2, 11—13.

h 2 Cor. 11. 18, 21.

4 Though ʰI might also have confidence in the flesh. If any other man thinketh that he hath whereof he might trust in the flesh, I more:

Though I might also have confidence in the flesh: to prevent any cavil about what he said, as if he did magnify Christ, and forbear glorying in those external privileges they did so much bear themselves upon, out of envy to them for what they had; he here argues upon supposition, (as elsewhere, to cut off occasion from boasters, 2 Cor. xi. 12, 18, 21, 22,) that, if it were lawful, and would turn to any good account, to confide in the flesh, he had the same ground the impostors had, and might build up that in himself which he had destroyed in others, Gal. ii. 18. *If any other man thinketh that he hath whereof he might trust in the flesh, I more:* yea, and to compare things by a just balance, if any of those he had justly taxed, or any other in conceit might hold his head higher in that way, he could produce not only as much, but much more ground of trust in those external rites, &c. as he that was most excellent; only that it was in vain, and of no value, ver. 7.

i Gen. 17. 12.
k 2 Cor. 11. 22.
l Rom. 11. 1.
m 2 Cor. 11. 22.
n Acts 23. 6. & 26. 4, 5.

5 ⁱCircumcised the eighth day, ᵏof the stock of Israel, ˡ*of* the tribe of Benjamin, ᵐan Hebrew of the Hebrews; as touching the law, ⁿa Pharisee;

Circumcised the eighth day; or, there was, or I had, the eighth day circumcision; so it may by a usual supply of the verb be read, (as also what follows,) without a metonymy. He begins with his birth privilege, intimating that he was not proselyted, but born within the pale of the church, and dedicated to God under the seal of the covenant at the day of God's appointment, Gen. xvii. 12. *Of the stock of Israel;* not sprung from ethnic parents, not an Ishmaelite, or Edomite, but a genuine Israelite, Rom. xi. 1; 2 Cor. xi. 22. *Of the tribe of Benjamin;* of that more

honest division where the temple stood, Josh. xviii. 28, of the tribe of Benjamin, the son of beloved Rachel, and his father's darling, Gen. xliv. 20; under God's special protection, Deut. xxxiii. 12, forward in the reformation, Ezra i. 5. *An Hebrew of the Hebrews;* a true descendant by Jacob from Abraham the father of the faithful, called an Hebrew, (Eber joined not in building Babel,) Gen. x. 21, 25; xiv. 13; 1 Sam. iv. 6; signifying that he was of the truly ancient lineage which retained the Hebrew tongue, John viii. 33, 39; Acts xxii. 2; Rom. iv. 12; 2 Cor. xi. 22. *As touching the law, a Pharisee;* by religion and stricter observation of the law, according to the prescript most in vogue, of that sect which for learning, knowledge of the Scripture, and reputation for holiness, was the most eminent, Acts xxvi. 5; yea, and his father was of this order before him, Acts xxiii. 6.

o Acts 22. 3. Gal. 1. 13, 14.
p Acts 8. 3. & 9. 1.
q Rom. 10. 5.
r Luke 1. 6.

6 ᵒConcerning zeal, ᵖpersecuting the Church; ᑫtouching the righteousness which is in the law, ʳblameless.

Concerning zeal; not lukewarm, but exceedingly fervent in the strictest observances of the Pharisaic order, which was much in external devotion, Luke xviii. 12, very solicitous for proselytes, Matt. xxiii. 15, 25. Herein he was above his equals for years, being exceedingly zealous of the traditions of the fathers, Gal. i. 14, (and his zeal had been very commendable had it been in a good matter, Gal. iv. 18,) that which the false apostles contended much for. *Persecuting the church;* which he showed all manner of ways in his rage against the church of Christ, conceived by the Pharisees to be opposite to the law of Moses, Acts ix. 1; xxii. 3, 4; xxvi. 9—12; Gal. i. 13. *Touching the righteousness which is in the law, blameless;* he rises higher yet in his personal obedience; he might have been a zealot in his sect, and yet a hypocrite, if not of a scandalous life; but it seems, in the external observation of those things which the ceremonial or moral law did prescribe, he was, in the eye of man, of a blameless conversation, resembling Zacharias and Elisabeth, Luke i. 6. Men could not tax him, he had behaved himself so conscientiously, Acts xxiii. 1; yet when he had his eyes opened, he found here was no such matter of confidence for him before God, 1 Sam. xvi. 7; 1 Cor. iv. 4. This external performance he found, when enlightened, was far short of internal and perfect obedience, Rom. vii. 7; and therefore he saw it necessary to change the ground and foundation of his confidence, all that he before rested on, unto Christ alone, 1 Cor. iii. 11; 2 Cor. v. 17; not seeking to receive honour from men, but that from Christ only, John v. 44.

s Mat. 13. 44.

7 But ˢwhat things were gain to me, those I counted loss for Christ.

Having argued how he might have had as great a plea for confidence of his acceptance with God as any, if it would have held from the recited particulars, he now shows, how advantageous soever they had, in the judgment of others as well as himself, been reckoned to be, before he was effectually called, yet, since the scales fell off his eyes, that he could discern the truth, he was so far from accounting them profitable, that indeed he accounted them prejudicial; so far from an advantage, that they were a damage to him, looking for salvation by Christ alone, Matt. xxi. 31; Rom. ix. 30. They were but as pebbles that hide the Pearl of price, Matt. xiii. 46; as ciphers to this figure, that can make any thing valuable, therefore by Paul preferred to all before.

t Is. 53. 11.
Jer. 9. 23, 24.
John 17. 3.
1 Cor. 2. 2.
Col. 2. 2.

8 Yea doubtless, and I count all things *but* loss ᵗ for the excellency of the knowledge of Christ Jesus my Lord: for whom I have suffered the loss of all things, and do count them *but* dung, that I may win Christ,

Yea doubtless; he very emphatically, in the Greek, expresseth his stronger resolution upon further deliberation. *And I count all things;* as he had reckoned and rated when he was first wrought upon to entertain Christ, so at present he did not alter his judgment, in the valuation of any thing he had rejected; yea, he speaks universally, what he did but indefinitely, using the present tense with a discretive particle: he disesteemed, not only his

Jewish privileges and exercises before, but his Christian after conversion, as of any worth to commend him to God, or as any matter to be rested on for his justification before God; showing he did not ascribe his being accepted to eternal life, unto his own works after he was renewed, and now had so many years served God in his apostolical ministry, performed such excellent works, planted so many churches, gained so many souls to Christ, passed through perils for the name of Christ. He remarkably puts in *all*, not only which he had before recited, but to all works as such whatsoever, yea, and to all whatsoever could be thought on besides Christ. *But loss;* whatever they be in themselves, they are but loss or damage, of no worth to me, as to any dependence on them for acceptance with God. *For the excellency of the knowledge of Christ Jesus my Lord;* compared with the surpassing worth and excellency in the fiducial, experimental (as is plain from what follows) knowledge of Jesus Christ, in his person, offices, and benefits, wherein an eye of faith can discern transcendent mysteries, Isa. liii. 11; John xvii. 3; 1 John v. 20; 1 Tim. iii. 16; 1 Pet. i. 12; to be adored by the sincere servants of so excellent a Lord, Mark v. 30, 33; to have an interest in whom, and to enjoy whom, every thing besides is despicable. *For whom I have suffered the loss of all things;* for whom (he adds) he did not only account them loss, (as ver. 7,) in his judgment and readiness to lose them, but he actually sustained the loss of them, Acts xx. 23; 1 Cor. iv. 13; 2 Cor. xi. 23, &c.: as to any plea for his acceptance, he suffered them all to go in this case, which he could not do till God, of his rich and insuperable grace, wrought this resolution in him, by his Holy Spirit; then he willingly did it. *And do count them but dung;* yea, and upon a right stating of the accounts he reckoned he was no loser by the exchange, in that he did esteem them, in a just balance, *comparing spiritual things with spiritual*, 1 Cor. ii. 13, in point of trust, those excellent things with an excellent Christ, to be no better than dung, as we with the Syriac and others translate the word; or dogs' meat, refuse cast to the dogs, with others; and might agree with the gust of those, ver. 2, whom he calls *dogs*, Matt. xv. 26; Mark vii. 27. Those much conversant in Greek authors do criticise largely upon the word, which is acknowledged on all hands to import things, if not loathsome, yet vile and contemptible, as chaff, &c.; and so not absolutely, but in their respect, did Paul account all things in comparison of Christ, even our good works proceeding from a heart sanctified but in part; he doth not mean of the substance, but quality of the trust or merit placed in them; not in themselves, but in regard of confidence in them, as to pardon and acceptance with God: not in point of sanctification, but justification, the apostle is here speaking to. So to rely upon them would not only comparatively, but positively, be greatest loss, as keeping from Christ, who is the greatest gain, for which the loss of all besides was to be sustained. *That I may win Christ;* that he might gain him, and be assured of an interest in him, whom he had above described in his state of humiliation and exaltation, and enjoy communion with him, Matt. xi. 28; Luke xiv. 26, 33; 2 Cor. iv. 6; 1 John v. 12; of whom he would receive more, and for whom he would do more, aiming at the making of Christ himself his own, by some kind of propriety, 1 Cor. i. 30.

9 And be found in him, not having [u] mine own righteousness, which is of the law, but [x] that which is through the faith of Christ, the righteousness which is of God by faith:

u Rom. 10. 3, 5.
x Rom. 1. 17. & 3. 21, 22. & 9. 30. & 10. 3, 6. Gal. 2. 16.

And be found in him; a learned interpreter reads it actively, and may find, or recover, in him, all my losses. But following our own translation: by winning of Christ, the apostle doth not only mean the profession of the faith of the gospel, but his union with Christ, and participation of him, which, in the judgment of the all-seeing God, will answer all damages, when a man comes to stand in judgment at his tribunal here or hereafter, Rom. viii. 1; this being the only course can be taken to be *found of him in peace* at the last, 2 Pet. iii. 14, for out of him is to be *under the curse*, Gal. iii. 10; Eph. ii. 3, 12, 13. It is necessary, therefore, that a man be implanted into him, who in his priestly office acted in our name towards God, Heb. v. 1;

x. 7; and that he abide in him, our Head, John vi. 56; xv. 4; Eph. v. 30; Col. ii. 6, 7; 1 John v. 12, and not be found in himself. *Not having mine own righteousness;* that we might more fully understand his meaning of being found in Christ, he defines it negatively and positively, by distinguishing of a twofold righteousness, supposing one necessary to his acceptance with God: 1. Inherent, within him, which he called his *own*, as being personally performed by him. *Which is of the law*· he describes it to be in a conformity to the law, and the righteousness which the law requires, and those works of it, which if a man do, loving God with all his heart, he shall live in them, Rom. ii. 13; iii. 27, 28; x. 5. He makes no distinction of any works done by him before or after conversion, but declares he dare not adventure to be found in any personal inherent righteousness of his own, as to the special end of his justification before God, Gal. iii. 10—12. He doth not say, not having good works, unto which he was created in Christ Jesus to walk in them, Eph. ii. 10; but, *not having mine own righteousness;* he could not trust to any thing within him, as to his standing before God; however he was now enlightened, and acted by a better principle, having a better end than while a Pharisee, he could not upon that account have confidence towards God, no more than Noah, who was a prophet and preacher of righteousness, and in his generation, as to his inherent righteousness, the most perfect and just man; or Abraham, Gen. xv. 6; Rom. iv. 3; or David, Psal. cxxx. 3; cxliii. 2. But, 2. He stays upon a righteousness without him, which is not his own by any acquisition of his, but the righteousness of another, Tit. iii. 5—7, viz. of Christ, without which he would not be found, and in which he would be found, i. e. *that which is through the faith of Christ*, having him for its object; which he doth elsewhere oppose to the deeds of the law, or works of righteousness that he had done. Rom. iii. 28; Gal. ii. 16; Tit. iii. 5; as he doth believing unto doing, which describe these two sorts of righteousness, in the one of which he would be found at his trial for justification, in the other he would not, Rom. i. 17; x. 5, 10, 11. Hence, he doth by the following expression signify more clearly the righteousness he stays himself upon, and wherein he would be found at God's tribunal, viz. the same righteousness which Noah had an eye upon (typified by the ark) when, by preparing an ark, he became *heir of the righteousness which is by faith*, Heb. xi. 7: *the righteousness which is of God by faith;* not his own, but counted unto him for righteousness; as unto Abraham, who *believed God*, Rom. iv. 3; as unto David, unto whom God imputed righteousness without works, Rom. iv. 6. This righteousness of God which he imputes upon believing, is not originally the believers' own inherent righteousness, but the righteousness of another in another, and theirs only derivatively from him, in whom believers are *made the righteousness of God*, 2 Cor. v. 21 (who are not said to have the mercy of God): unto them, being *in Christ Jesus*, he is *made righteousness*, 1 Cor. i. 30, yea, *the righteousness of God*, Rom. i. 17, (these are spoken of by the apostle distinctly, as here, so elsewhere, Rom. x. 3, with ix. 30, 31,) as not only freely given and imputed of God, but as being only of value in the judgment of God to justify, because performed by him, who is not only man but God, Acts xx. 28; Rom. iii. 21, 24, 25; x. 3. Not that it can be meant of the essential righteousness of God; for the righteousness by the faith of Christ, Rom. iii. 22, or that which constitutes them righteous in God's sight, upon their receiving of Christ and being implanted into him, was that obedience which he yielded unto God for them, voluntarily doing and suffering his will, John xv. 13; Rom. v. 6—8; Phil. ii. 8; 1 Tim. vi. 13; Heb. ix. 14. For this obedience in their stead being fully performed by him who had the Divine and human nature conjoined in himself, was of infinite value, so that his mediatorial righteousness being some way imputed to those who are found in him, they are found righteous before God in his just judgment, as living members of Christ, to whom they are united by the Spirit and faith, John vi. 56; xv. 4; Eph. v. 30, 32; Col. i. 27. This mystical head and body making but one Christ, and thereupon his righteousness is reputed theirs (and thereby they are set right with God) in such a measure as is meet for it to be communicated from Head to members, who partake of the thing imputed, the righteousness which satisfied the law, and therefore most proper to justify against it, and answer the demands of it. And in that it is said to be *the righteousness of God by faith*, we consider faith as the means whereby we came to be interested in it. Faith itself is not the righteousness, which is *upon*, not in the believer, Rom. iii. 22, entering into judgment with God; but the righteousness which believers find in Christ, which was ordained of God to denominate them righteous. The law (which requires obedience) having its end in nothing but the righteousness which satisfied it, called the righteousness of Christ, Rom. x. 4, with Tit. ii. 13; 2 Pet. i. 1; wherein the law is established, Rom. iii. 31, and its righteousness fulfilled, Rom. viii. 4; inherent graces are not called the righteousness, but our own, Matt. v. 20; Luke xxi. 19; Rom. x. 8; 2 Cor. viii. 8; Col. i. 4; 1 Pet. i. 21. Christ is so far righteousness as he is the end of the law, and that he is in the satisfaction itself, not in remission, which is an effect of it.

y Rom. 6. 3, 4, 5. & 8. 17.
z Cor. 4. 10, 11. 2 Tim. 2. 11, 12.
1 Pet. 4. 13.

10 That I may know him, and the power of his resurrection, and ʸthe fellowship of his sufferings, being made conformable unto his death;

That I may know him; as consequent upon the former he had by winning of Christ, he doth here insist upon sanctification, which would result from faith's exerting itself in a further saving, experimental knowledge of Christ, to be found in whom, he undervalued all besides conformity to Christ in holiness, being to have communion with him in righteousness, 1 Cor. i. 30; God having appointed those who are found in Christ, to be conformed to his image in holiness, Rom. viii. 29; 2 Cor. iii. 18. This saving knowledge is expressed elsewhere in Scripture by the senses, John x. 4; 2 Cor. ii. 14; iv. 6; Eph. i. 18; 1 Pet. ii. 3. All and only those found in Christ, do so know him, John v. 20; vi. 46, 69; Heb. viii. 11; and desire so to know him, chap. i. 9, that they may have a lively sense of his power, communion, and conformity. *The power of his resurrection;* the power of his resurrection in us; i. e. from the death of the soul, under a privation of spiritual life, and the image of God, unto newness of life, by the effectual working of the same Spirit which raised Christ himself from the dead, Rom. vi. 4, 10; Eph. i. 20; ii. 5, 6; called *the first resurrection,* Rev. xx. 5; when the soul is raised from under the dominion of sin where it lay. *The fellowship of his sufferings;* by communion of Christ's sufferings, is not meant of bearing a part in the merit of his personal sufferings, but of being partaker of his sufferings in his members, or mystical body, whether inward or outward, (though this chiefly,) Matt. xx. 23; Acts ix. 4; Rom. viii. 17; 2 Cor. i. 7; iv. 10, 11; Gal. v. 24; Col. i. 24; 2 Tim. ii. 11, 12. *Being made conformable unto his death;* some read, while made conformable to his death, not only in dying to sin, Rom. vi. 5, 6, but in being conformed to his image in suffering, Rom. viii. 29; dying daily, or always living ready to be delivered to death for Jesus' sake upon his call, Rom. viii. 18; 2 Cor. iv. 11. Such was his Christian temper, that he could cheerfully go through sufferings by reason of some communion and conformity he had in them with Jesus Christ.

z Acts 26. 7.

11 If by any means I might ᶻattain unto the resurrection of the dead.

Being found in whom, after justification and sanctification, he doubts not to be glorified, (by a figure of a part, resurrection of the body, for the whole,) though he expresseth himself as one that must pass through difficulties ere he attain not only to a spiritual resurrection from sin, but a glorious one of the body from the grave, even such a one as will be an elevation or ascension of the body united to the soul, not only exempted from the grave, but exalted into the air, to be for ever with the Lord, 1 Thess. iv. 14, 17; from whom he was assured no death should separate him, Rom. viii. 38, 39; 2 Tim. iv. 8; who lived by faith in expectation of the time and the manner of it, 1 Cor. xv. 14, 19, 30, 32; 1 Pet. i. 6, 7, that he should be then completely holy in his measure as Christ himself is.

a 1 Tim. 6. 12.
b Heb. 12. 23.

12 Not as though I had already ᵃattained, either were already ᵇperfect: but I follow after, if that I may apprehend that for which also I am apprehended of Christ Jesus.

Not as though I had already attained, either were already perfect: by an elegant anticipation and correction, lest any should conclude from what he had written, as if he were now arrived at the height he aimed at in the excellency of the knowledge of Christ, and a full and perfect stature in that body, or almost at the very pitch, he doth here make a modest confession of his not attainment, (whatever false apostles might pretend to,) 2 Cor. x. 12; xii. 6, 7; but of his earnest desire and utmost endeavour to be raised to the complete holiness he was designed to, *in heavenly places in Christ Jesus,* Eph. ii. 6. *But I follow after;* he did pursue with all vigour, as those labouring in the agonistics, with all his might and main, not desponding of obtaining the goal, 1 Cor. ix. 26, with 2 Cor. iv. 8; with groanings and longings after utmost perfection, 2 Cor. v. 4, 6, 7; 2 Pet. iii. 12; as those perfected in glory, Heb. xii. 23. *If that I may apprehend that; if that,* or whether that, (not as intimating any uncertainty, but his more earnest contending for holiness in the Christian race,) I may lay hold on that attainment to be as holy as men shall be at the resurrection. *For which;* even as, or *for which,* (as we render it well so, chap. iv. 10,) i. e. for which end, or for this purpose, to be perfectly sanctified and glorified at the resurrection. *I am apprehended of Christ Jesus;* he was at his effectual calling laid hold on by Christ, being found in whom, he was striving after perfection. This *apprehended* is a metaphor borrowed from those that run in a race, one taking hold of another to draw him after to win the prize as well as himself. He eyed Christ having taken him into his hand, as one that would not suffer him to be plucked out by any opposers, John x. 28. He knew that Christ, having brought him nigh unto God, and undertook to work such a measure of holiness in him, one day would completely glorify him, so that, whatever he passed through, nothing should be lost, John vi. 39.

13 Brethren, I count not myself to have apprehended: but *this* one thing *I do,* ᶜforgetting those things which are behind, and ᵈreaching forth unto those things which are before,

c Ps. 45. 10.
Luke 9. 62.
2 Cor. 5. 16.
d 1 Cor. 9. 24, 26.
Heb. 6. 1.

Brethren, I count not myself to have apprehended; he repeats, in somewhat a different manner of expression, what he had written in the former verse, with a friendly compellation, gently and kindly to insinuate a caution against the false teachers' suggestion about perfection in this state, from the instance of himself, so eminently called to be an apostle of Christ, (1 Cor. x. 12,) who, after all his labours and sufferings for his sake, did reckon he had not yet arrived to the height of what he was called to. *But this one thing I do;* but he would have them to understand that he was so intent upon this one thing, for which he was brought by the Spirit into communion with Christ, as if there were not any thing else worthy of his thoughts: as Psal. xxvii. 4; Luke x. 43. *Forgetting those things which are behind;* like a true spiritual racer, not minding what he had received by grace from him who had took hold of him, or how much he had run of his Christian race, reckoning it was much short of the whole, or the main intended by Christ in taking hold of him. *And reaching forth unto those things which are before;* but straining forward, as it were, with all his force and skill, casting himself like a dart towards the mark, so running that he might obtain (1 Cor. ix. 24) all and the whole, that was his particular portion for ever, to be received from God, as the purchase of Christ, even the total that God had in and by Jesus Christ designed him, and in Christ bestowed upon him, out of his rich grace, as his special allotment.

14 ᵉI press toward the mark for the prize of ᶠthe high calling of God in Christ Jesus.

e 2 Tim. 4. 7, 8. Heb. 12. 1.
f Heb. 3. 1.

I press toward the mark; he did not look back, Luke ix. 62, nor was lazy, but did follow hard, with an eager pursuit, (Matt. xi. 12,) after the perfection that was in his eye; not erring from his main scope; considering what he had received was but in part, he did still press for more, upon that ground that Christ had apprehended him for more, as if he were stretching out his hands to lay hold of it. *For the prize of the high calling of God in Christ Jesus;* trusting he should, through grace, be kept all along, maugre all difficulties, in the hand of Christ, till upon his account he should be fully possessed of all that was aimed at, even that which is styled the prize, or victorious palm of our high calling; and the Christians' may well be termed a high calling, considering their heavenly birth when called, and laid hold of by Christ, John i. 13, and the purchased inheritance eternally settled upon such spiritual, high-born princes, Eph. i. 14; Rev. i. 6; who are by one oblation *perfected for ever*, Heb. x. 14; which will appear most glorious when they are raised up in Christ, who will then give out all the salvation he hath called us unto.

15 Let us therefore, as many as be ^gperfect, ^hbe thus minded: and if in any thing ye be otherwise minded, God shall reveal even this unto you.

g 1 Cor. 2. 6. & 14. 20.
h Gal. 5. 10.

A learned man reads it from the Greek to this purpose : As many therefore as are perfect, let us think this; and if ye think any thing otherwise, even this also God will, or may, reveal to you, (besides what we have attained to,) to walk by the same rule, to think the same thing : conceiving it not congruous to the sense, or syntax, but alien from all manner of speaking, to translate it imperatively, *Let us walk by the same rule.* But following our own translation : *Let us therefore, as many as be perfect;* from the instance of himself, imitating Christ, in loving condescension and lowliness of mind, chap. ii. 3, 5, worshipping God in the spirit, and not having confidence in the flesh, chap. iii. 3, in the fellowship of Christ's sufferings, ver. 10, pressing forward to absolute perfection, he here doth with himself encourage as many rulers and ruled who were settled in the fundamentals of Christianity, and who had made progress in holiness, to mind that main business of religion, for the prevention of what might ensue upon exasperating differences ; whereupon he styles them comparatively perfect in the way, not in the heavenly country, 1 Cor. xiii. 10; which doth not disagree with what he said before, if we further distinguish of a perfection, 1. Of integrity and sincerity, which some call of parts ; as a perfect living child, that hath all the parts of the parent, so, upon the new birth, every real believer receiving *grace for grace,* John i. 13, 16. 2. Of maturity, proficiency or degrees where grown to a full stature in Christ; here relatively and comparatively to others, who are more rude, ignorant, and weak brethren, since, in regard of their progress in godliness, they are not taken up with childish things, 1 Cor. xiii. 9—11, with xiv. 20; but are grown more adult, and no more children, 1 Cor. ii. 6; Eph. iv. 13, 14; Heb. v. 13, 14; vi. 1; which he doth elsewhere, in regard of their experimental knowledge, call *spiritual,* Gal. vi. 1, who here *worship God in the spirit,* ver. 3 : as many as are sincere, of whatsoever stature, whether bishops, deacons, or private Christians. *Be thus minded;* he would have them to be so minded as he himself was, in renouncing all carnal confidence, acknowledging their gradual imperfection, and still to be striving and contending to a fuller measure of holiness, till they come to be consummate in Christ. *And if in any thing ye be otherwise minded;* and if any, through ignorance of Christ and themselves, conversing with those ready to mislead them, should be of any other persuasion in some things only, considering the different attainments of the strong and weak, and thereupon the variety of sentiments, whence would spring some differences not only in opinions but practices amongst them, (which yet hindered not their agreement in what they were attained to,) *God shall reveal even this unto you;* he hoped Christ, who had already called or apprehended those sincere ones, would in due time rescue them from so dangerous an error, 1 John ii. 20, 27, if they would attend upon him in the use of means to come to the knowledge of the truth, with faith and prayer, yielding up themselves to be taught of him.

16 Nevertheless, whereto we have already attained, ⁱlet us walk ^kby the same rule, ^llet us mind the same thing.

j Rom. 12. 16. & 15. 5.
k Gal. 6. 16.
l ch. 2. 2.

Nevertheless, whereto we have already attained; however, let us, or we ought to, walk in obedience to Christ, love to him and each other, according to the light we have already received, trusting he would make known his mind more clearly to us. Our using the light we have well, is the ready way to have more : it behoves us, then, to live suitably to that degree of the knowledge of Christ we have attained, 1 John. ii. 3—5 but still within our lines, with regard to the same rule. *Let us walk by the same rule :* whether in this metaphorical allusion the apostle do borrow his phrase from architects, soldiers, or racers, is not much material. Be sure he had an eye to that *same rule* which was well known to them, and by which he regulated himself, and therefore it was such a canon as really had a Divine stamp upon it, that very canon in exact conformity whereunto God's Israel might be sure of the best peace, Gal. vi. 16; Phil. iv. 7. The unerring word of God, exemplified in the condescending love of Christ, whom he had proposed to their imitation, in whom he was found, and the fellowship of whose sufferings he desired to know more perfectly, being heavenly-minded, in opposition to those who became enemies to his cross, ver. 18, 19, with Gal. vi. 14, 15; the rule of faith, love, and a Christian life, or heavenly conversation, which he doth elsewhere call a walking in the Spirit, and according to the Spirit, in opposition to walking in and after the flesh, Rom. viii. 1, 5 ; Gal. v. 16. *Let us mind the same thing :* in like manner, all of us who are spiritual, grown Christians, should be so affected, being of one accord, one mind, and one judgment, in imitation of Christ ; so far that the adult, or better grown Christians, should not despise the weak or less grown, neither should they judge the adult ; but in the fundamental articles, those main principles of the Christian institution wherein we all agree, in that common salvation towards which we all press, agreeable to the analogy of faith, we should still be perfecting holiness in the fear of God, by the same rule of faith, and loving and mutual condescension, by the unity of our judgments in the main business of religion, the concord of our affections, the concurrence of our ends, our consent and delight in the same truth : we should declare to the church of God, in our differences Christ is not divided, but in the variety of persuasions in lesser matters, (not fundamental,) the purity, holiness, and peace of the church is still preserved, chap. ii. 14. The main principles attained wherein dissenting parties agree, being the measure of all other doctrines, to hold nothing inconsistent with the majesty or truth of the foundation ; to walk circumspectly, and in order, according to that wherein is a harmony ; not to break our rank, or leave our station, contrary to received prescripts ; wherein every Christian is to exercise a judgment of discerning for himself, Rom. xiv. 23, and not impose on each other, (as that sort of Christian Jews who did compel the Christian Gentiles, Gal. ii. 14, 15, &c.) superadding no preter-evangelical doctrine, Gal. i. 8, 9 ; to live godly, agreeably to known truths ; to serve God soberly and prudently, (with due moderation,) in our places, consonantly to *the measure of the rule God hath distributed to us,* 2 Cor. x. 13, holding the truths wherein we agree in love, unity, and constancy. It being more reasonable that the many truths wherein we agree, should cause us to join in love, which is a Christian duty, rather than the few opinions wherein we disagree, should cause a breach in affection, which is a human infirmity.

17 Brethren, ^mbe followers together of me, and mark them which walk so as ⁿye have us for an ensample.

m 1 Cor. 4. 16. & 11. 1.
ch. 4. 9.
1 Thess. 1. 6.
n 1 Pet. 5. 3.

Brethren, be followers together of me; he doth here not only propound his own single example to the brethren at Philippi, as he doth to others elsewhere, 1 Cor. iv. 16, implying the limitation there expressed, viz. as he and others were followers of God and Christ, 1 Cor. xi. 1 ; Eph. v. 1 ; 1 Thess. i. 6 ; ii. 14 ; but, by a word expressing joint consent, he would have them to be fellow imitators or fellow followers of him and others in what he had exhorted them to, yea, with one heart. *And mark them which walk so as ye have us for an ensample ;* so they would be like other churches which he had planted, that had an eye upon his example ; whom he would have them accurately to observe, following their faith, and *considering the end of their conversation,* Heb. xiii. 7, agreeing with his, and Timothy's, (who joined with him in this Epistle,) and other's, in opposition to those who were causal of division, Rom. xvi. 17 ; 1 Cor. i. 12, even such as he describes, ver. 18, 19; who did not lord it over God's heritage, but were ensamples (in faith, love, and humility) to the flock, 2 Cor. i. 24 ; 1 Tim. iv. 12 ; Tit. ii. 7, 8 ; 1 Pet. v. 3.

18 (For many walk, of whom I have told you often, and now tell you even weeping,

that they are °the enemies of the cross of Christ:

He doth, as in a parenthesis, according to our Bibles, allege reasons for his proposals. *For many walk;* there were not a few who did at present walk otherwise, being *evil workers,* ver. 2, not to be imitated or followed, Matt. vii. 22, 23. *Of whom I have told you often;* of which, as a faithful watchman, he had again and again given them warning. *And now tell you even weeping;* and now also by this present writing, out of great compassion to their immortal souls, he did repeat it again with tears in his eyes. *That they are the enemies of the cross of Christ;* they were such who did in the general (whatever they might under a fair show pretend) oppose the gospel of Christ, yea, did in effect under the cloak of profession, that which was in a tendency to evert the true Christian doctrine, discipline, and holiness. They did go about to mingle the law and the gospel, to join Moses with Christ for justification, as ver. 4, &c.; Gal. ii. 21, and so undervalue redemption from the curse, Gal. iii. 13; v. 2, 4. In special, these Epicureans (as it should seem they were by the following character, rather than real Christians) might rightly be called enemies, because they did seem by their sensuality to restore the kingdom to those whom Christ had on his cross openly spoiled of it, Col. ii. 15, that they might gratify the Jews in urging the necessity of circumcision; so undermining the virtue and merit of Christ's passion, defaming the end of it, as the Jews did him in it, and in times of trial avoid persecution, Gal. vi. 12, 14, they showed themselves by interpretation really to be enemies to Christ crucified, 1 Cor. i. 23, 24; ii. 2.

19 ᵖWhose end *is* destruction, ᵠ whose God *is their* belly, and ʳ *whose* glory *is* in their shame, ˢ who mind earthly things.)

Whose end is destruction; their condition will at last be miserable, as he had limited above, chap. i. 28, of their being under the dismal *token of perdition;* their end will be *according to their works,* 2 Cor. xi. 15. However they may live delicately at present, in gratifying their sensual appetites, be free from persecution, admired and respected by many, and please themselves in their present course, yet their fruit and wages at the last cast will be dreadful, Rom. vi. 21, 24; Gal. vi. 8; Rev. xviii. 8; xix. 20, 21. *Whose God is their belly;* the great business of these is, their sensuality, their good eating and drinking; they mind the pleasing of their carnal appetite, as if it were their God, 2 Pet. ii. 13, 18; iii. 3; instead of our Lord Jesus Christ, really they serve their own belly, Rom. xvi. 18, love their pleasures indeed more than God, 2 Tim. iii. 4. *And whose glory is in their shame;* yea, they boast of those things whereof they ought to be ashamed, thinking it reputation they have got many to imitate them, John v. 44; xii. 43; they are puffed up with that which should rather make them to blush, 1 Cor. v. 2, as being attended at last with confusion. *Who mind earthly things;* however under the colour of Christianity, they at present are taken up in the pursuit of their sensual and earthly enjoyments. The Greek word comprehends the actions and operations of the mind, will, and affections, importing they did inordinately mind, favour, and relish sublunary accommodations, Rom. viii. 5, the profits, ease, bounty, pleasure, and glory of this world, preferring them in their hearts to the things of Christ.

20 For ᵗour conversation is in heaven; ᵘfrom whence also we ˣlook for the Saviour, the Lord Jesus Christ:

For our conversation is in heaven; he here adds a further reason why he would have them to be fellow followers of him, and such-like as he, because though they were not already in heaven, yet their citizenship was there, the privileges of that city did belong to them, who, according to the municipal laws of that corporation (which cannot lose its charter or be discorporated) whereof they were free denizens, made it their business to demean themselves with minds above the earth, chap. i. 27; 2 Cor. iv. 18; Eph. ii. 6; Col. iii. 1; accounting nothing inconvenient to any one of them, which was for the advantage of the whole community; they set their affections on things above, John xiv. 2; 2 Cor. xii. 25; Heb. xiii. 14. *From whence also we look for the Saviour, the Lord Jesus Christ;* and reason good, for from thence, or from that place, in the heavens, or heaven, they stedfastly expect him who is both Lord and Christ, Acts i. 11; 1 Cor. i. 7; 1 Thess. i. 10; 2 Tim. iv. 8; Tit. ii. 13, to come not only as their judge, 2 Tim. iv. 8, but as their heart-comforting Saviour, Heb. ix. 28.

21 ʸWho shall change our vile body, that it may be fashioned like unto his glorious body, ᶻaccording to the working whereby he is able ᵃeven to subdue all things unto himself.

Who shall change our vile body; who shall transform the body of our humility, or our lowliness, i. e. our low-brought body, the singular for the plural, our humble and mean bodies, which depend upon and are beholden to our eating and drinking, and the actions which follow thereupon, that do humble and lower them, Luke i. 48; now, it may be, languishing with pains, sickness, and many infirmities, perhaps cooped up in a noisome prison, and it may be, an unclean dungeon, sown in dishonour and weakness in the grave, 1 Cor. xv. 43. *That it may be fashioned like unto his glorious body;* that they may be conformed to Christ's incorruptible, impassible, and immortal body, and so glorious, 1 Cor. xv. 51—53, in their proportion agreeing with the blessed body of our Lord when he shall appear, 1 John iii. 1—3, and they shall see him with the eyes of their bodies, made like unto his, Job xix. 26, 27; Col. iii. 4, not in equality, but only in respect of the same qualities that his body hath, 1 Cor. xv. 51, 52; 1 Thess. iv. 17. A conformity agreeable to that of head and members, that like as the sun is the fountain of all that glory which the stars have, so shall our Lord and Saviour Christ's glory be of all our glory, Dan. xii. 3; Matt. xvi. 27; 1 Cor. xv. 40, 41; 2 Cor. iv. 14; Rev. xxi. 11, 23. But we must not imagine that our bodies shall be raised to the same height and degree of glory that his is: and therefore in regard of that power and majesty which is included in the body of Christ from the hypostatical union, our bodies will not be conformable, or made like to his; but in glory which he obtained from his resurrection. For the body of Christ may be considered either, 1. In its nature, and so there will be an agreement betwixt the bodies of saints and Christ's body; or, 2. In regard of its subsistence in the person of the Word, and so there will be none. For it is impossible that the saints should be raised up to the same union with the Godhead which Christ hath. But however their bodies may be tormented here, by unreasonable persecutors, then they shall be like to his glorious body. *According to the working whereby he is able even to subdue all things unto himself:* how incredible soever this may appear to be unto carnal reason, Acts xvii. 32; xxvi. 8, yet he who thought it no robbery to be equal with God the Father, and therefore can do what he pleaseth, Luke xviii. 27, can, by the same Divine power whereby he himself was raised from the grave, John v. 21, 26, 29; Eph. i. 19, 20, subject all things to himself, destroy death and the grave, 1 Cor. xv. 24—27; Heb. ii. 8, 14, raise them up to the throne of his glory, Matt. xix. 28, and make them like the angels in glory.

CHAP. IV

Paul exciteth to stedfastness in Christ, 1; *and after some particular admonitions,* 2, *exhorteth generally to religious joy,* 3, 4, *moderation,* 5, *trust in God with prayer,* 6, 7, *and to every branch of moral goodness,* 8, 9. *He testifieth his joy in the care shown by the Philippians for his supply in prison, though being always content he was above want,* 10—14; *and commendeth their former liberality to him, not for his own sake, but for the good that would redound to them from it,* 15—17. *He acknowledgeth the receipt of their late bounty, assuring them that God would both accept and reward it,* 18, 19. *He giveth glory to God, and concludeth with salutations, and a blessing,* 20—23.

THEREFORE, my brethren dearly beloved and ᵃlonged for, ᵇmy joy and ns c ch. 1. 27. crown, so ᵉstand fast in the Lord, *my dearly beloved.*

Therefore; this particle connotes that which follows to be inferred by way of conclusion from what he had premised in the close of the former chapter, in opposition to the shame of the earthly-minded, concerning the glory of the heavenly-minded. *My brethren;* he affectionately owns them to be his brethren in *the common faith,* Tit. i. 4. *Dearly beloved;* those who, not being enticed by the insinuations of seducers, did adhere to him, had his sincere affections, chap. ii. 12. *And longed for;* whose safety and felicity every way he most heartily desired, chap. i. 8; ii. 26; with Rom. i. 11; 1 Thess. iii. 6. *My joy;* intimating how their faith and holiness did at present afford matter of rejoicing to him, chap. i. 4, 7, 8, with 1 Thess. ii. 19, 20. *And crown;* he was not ambitious of man's applause, but accounted them his honour and glory, the great ornament of his ministry, whereby they were converted to Christ, (as elsewhere in Scripture a crown is taken figuratively, Prov. xii. 4; xiv. 24; xvi. 31; xvii. 6,) 1 Thess. ii. 19; the reward which had some similitude with the honour they had who were victorious in a race, chap. ii. 16, 17: as James i. 12; 1 Pet. v. 4; Rev. ii. 10; iii. 11. *So stand fast;* he exhorteth them not barely to stand, but so to stand that they did not fall, 1 Cor. x. 12. Hereupon he adds, *in the Lord;* i. e. considering their relation unto Christ, they would derive power and virtue from him, into whom they were implanted, to persevere, conformably to his will, in Christian concord, till they were made like to him, chap. iii. 21, with i. 27; John xv. 4, 7; 1 Cor. xv. 58; xvi. 13; Gal. v. 7; Eph. vi. 11, 14. *My dearly beloved;* in whom looking upon them, (the more to fix them,) he pathetically and rhetorically repeats his endearing compellation *beloved.*

d ch. 2. 2. & 3. 16. 2 I beseech Euodias, and beseech Syntyche, ᵈthat they be of the same mind in the Lord.

I beseech Euodias, and beseech Syntyche: after his general persuasive to perseverance, he doth here particularly by name with great affectionateness importune two women, who had been very useful in that church for the furtherance of the gospel, that they would come to a better understanding of each other, and the interest of religion amongst them, who received the gospel upon Paul's preaching, Acts xvi. 13. *That they be of the same mind in the Lord;* as he had moved all to love, unity, and amity, (as it became disciples of Christ,) chap. ii. 2; so he doth here especially move them unto unanimity, according to the mind of the Lord, and his way, for the sake of him whose honour is to be preferred to all private concerns, Rom. xv. 5.

e Rom. 16.3.
ch. 1. 27.
f Ex. 32. 32.
Ps. 69. 28.
Dan. 12. 1.
Luke 10. 20.
Rev. 3. 5. &
13. 8. & 20.
12. & 21. 27. 3 And I intreat thee also, true yokefellow, help those women which ᵉlaboured with me in the Gospel, with Clement also, and *with* other my fellowlabourers, whose names *are* in ᶠthe book of life.

And I entreat thee also, true yoke-fellow; he subjoins his most importunate request to some eminent person who did faithfully and sincerely draw in the same yoke of Christ with him, even such another in that church at Philippi, (whom they well knew from the freedom he used when he planted the gospel amongst them, or might more distinctly know from Epaphroditus,) as he had represented Timothy to be, chap. ii. 20. Some, both ancient and modern, would have this to be Paul's own wife, whom he left behind; but seeing it doth not appear that when he wrote this Epistle he had ever staid above two months at Philippi, he elsewhere reckons himself amongst the unmarried, 1 Cor. vii. 8, and wished those who had the gift of continency to continue so, under the sharp persecution of the church, for which he was frequent in journeyings, labours, and prisons, 2 Cor. xi. 23, there is no cogent argument to evince that he was then married, however he had liberty to have had a wife, as well as Peter and others: see Matt. xix. 29; xxii. 28, with 1 Cor. ix. 5. Some conceive by *yoke-fellow* here is meant the lawful husband of one of the forenamed honourable matrons: others, one called by that proper name in Greek; but the epithet annexed doth not so well suit. It may suffice to say it was an intimate colleague and sincere companion of Paul's, who was alike affected with him, drawing in the same yoke, for the furtherance of the gospel, his genuine helper; whose special aid, by advice, prayer, and otherwise, he solicited on the behalf of those pious women, who aforetime (though not by public preaching in the church, which he elsewhere disallowed, 1 Cor. xiv. 34, 35; 1 Tim. ii. 12, but privately) had not only wrought, but earnestly striven together with him, by teaching youth, and other women, good things, Tit. ii. 3, 4; putting themselves in hazard with him, in that difficult work he had amongst them, and enduring troubles with him for the propagation of the gospel, chap. i. 27; Acts xvi. 13; as Phebe, and Priscilla, and Mary, elsewhere, Acts xviii. 2, 3, 26; Rom. xvi. 1—3; 1 Tim. v. 10; 2 Tim. iv. 19; in offices proper to their sex. *Clement,* probably, was some church officer of Roman extract in that colony at Philippi; whether he, about whose order in the catalogue of Roman bishops historians dispute, there is no certainty. *And with other my fellow labourers;* the rest, whom he doth not name, but only describe by the assistance they gave him in the holy work of the gospel, probably were other church officers. *Whose names are in the book of life;* whose names he did in charity apprehend to be enrolled in heaven, as our Saviour speaks to the rejoicing of his seventy disciples, Luke x. 20. We are not to think there is any material book wherein their names were written, but that he useth it as a borrowed speech, intimating his persuasion of them, (as of the election of others, 1 Thess. i. 4, with 1 Pet. i. 2,) that their life was as certainly sealed up with God, as if their names had been written in a book for that purpose; looking upon them by their fruit as truly gracious persons, whom God had effectually called according to his purpose, Rom. viii. 28, 29, 33, which is a book written, Exod. xxxii. 32; Isa. iv. 3; Ezek. xiii. 9; Dan. xii. 1; Rev. iii. 5; xiii. 8; xx. 12; xxi. 27; wherein the Lord knows who are his, 2 Tim. ii. 19.

4 ᵍRejoice in the Lord alway: *and* again I say, Rejoice. g Rom. 12. 12. ch. 3. 1.
1 Thess. 5.16.
1 Pet. 4. 13.

He doth here, considering the importance of Christian cheerfulness, which he had twice before put them upon, chap. ii. 18; iii. 1, stir them up to true rejoicing, not only by repetition of the injunction, but by extending the duty to all times, and under all conditions. For though there be woe to the enemies of Christ's cross, who laugh at his followers, Luke vi. 25; yet they who are really found in him, have evermore ground of rejoicing, for all the benefits of God they have through him, and the far more excellent they do expect to receive upon his account, John xvi. 33; 1 Cor. i. 31; 1 Thess. v 16; 1 Pet. i. 8.

5 Let your moderation be known unto all men. ʰThe Lord *is* at hand. h Heb. 10. 25. Jam. 5.
8, 9. 1 Pet.
4. 7. 2 Pet.
3. 8, 9. See 2 Thess. 2. 2.

Let your moderation be known; exercising an even temper of mind, in governing the sensual appetite, with modesty, patience, and meekness, in opposition to all impetuousness and inordinacy of affections, yea, to all excess and exorbitances in words and actions. *Unto all men;* both in the eye of the church, and those without, according to our Saviour's sermon and example, Matt. v. 16, 39—41; xvii. 27; not rigorously insisting upon our own rights, but with due self-denial putting the best construction upon the words and deeds of others; not troubling our hearts, John xiv. 1; banishing that solicitude about the good things of this life, which he doth in the next verse caution against: so 1 Cor. vii. 29—32. *The Lord is at hand;* considering the cogent motive of the Lord's approach, as Heb. x. 25; James v. 8; not only in regard of his Deity, whereby he reigns amongst his enemies, Acts xvii. 27; Jer. xxiii. 29; nor in regard of his special aids to his servants, Psal. xiv. 5; but in regard of his coming to judgment, and setting all things right in a just distribution of rewards and punishments, to comfort his children, and confound those that disobey him, Matt. xviii. 34, 35; Mark x. 29, 30; Col. iii. 24; iv. 1; Heb. x. 37; 1 Pet. iii. 8, 9; Rev. xxii. 20. But still we must remember, when we conceive of the Lord's being at hand in regard of death and judgment, we must not take our own but God's measures, in waiting our appointed time during his pleasure, Matt. xxiv. 36; Acts i. 7.

PHILIPPIANS IV

^{i Ps. 55. 22.}
^{Prov. 16. 3.}
^{Matt. 6. 25.}
^{Luke 12. 22.}
^{1 Pet. 5. 7.}

6 ¹ Be careful for nothing; but in every thing by prayer and supplication with thanksgiving let your requests be made known unto God.

Be careful for nothing; he dissuades not from a spiritual care, arising from a good principle, according to a right rule, for a good end; this care of diligence, in a due manner, within our own sphere, is incumbent on us, both for spirituals and temporals; as chap. ii. 20; with Rom. xii. 11; 2 Cor. xi. 28; xii. 14; 2 Thess. iii. 10; 1 Tim. v. 8; 2 Tim. ii. 15: yet he earnestly dissuades from and prohibits all carnal solicitude, or carking, distrustful, worldly care, which doth divide and, as it were, split the heart in pieces; that anxious solicitude which doth torture the mind with such thoughts as our blessed Lord will not allow so much as one of them to be predominant in his real disciples, Matt. vi. 25, because such immoderate, distracting care, is on our part a disparagement to our heavenly Father's good providence, Matt. vi. 32; with Psal. lv. 22; cxxvii. 1, 2; Matt. iv. 18, 19; 1 Pet. v. 7. The remedy against which he doth here subjoin. *But in every thing;* but in all things, or in every occurring necessity, whether prosperous or adverse; sacred or civil, public or private: some render it, every time, in every condition, on every occasion. *By prayer;* by petition or apprecation of good to ourselves or others; mercies, or blessings, temporal, spiritual, and eternal. *And supplication;* and by a deprecation of evils felt or feared, wrath and judgments deserved. *With thanksgiving;* with a grateful acknowledgment of mercies received, benefits conferred, and deliverances vouchsafed; implying that no prayer is acceptable to God, without this ingredient of thankful resentment of his favours. *Let your requests be made known unto God:* our affectionate desires should be opened to God, and poured forth before him; not that he is ignorant of us or our wants in any circumstances, but that he accounts himself glorified by our addresses to him, in seeking to be approved and assisted of him in every condition.

^{k John14.27.}
^{Rom. 5. 1.}
^{Col. 3. 15.}

7 And ᵏ the peace of God, which passeth all understanding, shall keep your hearts and minds through Christ Jesus.

He adds, as an encouragement to prayer, *the peace of God,* who was in Christ reconciling the world unto himself, so that upon believing and obeying the gospel, they who really do so are reconciled to him, 2 Cor. v. 19, 20, and at peace with him, Rom. v. 1, through Christ, who leaves and gives peace to his, John xiv. 27. It is then *the peace of God,* in that he is the object, the donor, the author of it, by his Spirit, to those who persevere in the communion of Christ, as in ver. 9, have the God of peace with them, and a sense thereof in their own spirits. *Which passeth all understanding:* how it transcends a finite understanding, may be answered, 1. In that he who hath perceived it, before he had done so, could not sufficiently conceive in his own mind what at length it might be, 1 Cor. ii. 9: hence, 2. After it is perceived, it cannot be that any one should esteem and express the power and virtue of it, according to the worth and excellency of the matter. Not that the peace should affect the heart, the will without the intervention of the understanding; since it is said to keep the heart and mind; and, Rev. ii. 17, the *white stone* given to believers (whereby this peace is signified) is of that kind, *which no man knoweth save he that receiveth it;* and it is no new thing in Scripture, to say that doth exceed all understanding, which human understanding doth not so distinctly conceive as to be able to express it, as Eph. iii. 19. No man's mind doth receive that which is taken into admiration, that it perceives something always to remain, which it hath notice of, yet cannot so perceive as to express the whole of it. *Shall keep your hearts and minds through Christ Jesus;* wherefore they who are really interested in this peace shall be kept as in a garrison, 1 Pet. i. 5. So their whole souls shall be in safety against the assaults of Satan, their affections and reasoning shall be so kept in order, that, through Christ, they shall not finally fall.

8 Finally, brethren, whatsoever things are true, whatsoever things *are* ‖ honest, whatsoever things *are* just, whatsoever

‖ Or, *venerable.*

things *are* pure, whatsoever things *are* lovely, ¹ whatsoever things *are* of good report; if *there be* any virtue, and if *there be* any praise, think on these things.

^{l 1 Thess. 5. 22.}

As to what remains, he doth, with the fair compellation of *brethren,* furthermore propose to their serious consideration, living in the neighbourhood of the Gentiles, what he doth here, hastening to a conclusion, heap up and hold together: especially, *whatsoever things are true,* agree with truth and doctrine, in word and conversation, which show candour and sincerity of conscience, both with reference to believers and to infidels, Psal. xv. 2; Eph. iv. 14, 15, 25. *Honest;* venerable and grave, as *becometh the gospel,* chap. i. 27, to adorn the gospel of God our Saviour, Rom. xii. 17; xiii. 13; Tit. ii. 10; avoiding what may argue levity or dishonesty in gesture, apparel, words, and deeds, 2 Cor. vii. 2. *Just;* giving what is due to every one by the law of nature, or nations, or the country, without guile, and not injuring any one, Ruth iii. 13; Neh. v. 11; Matt. xxii. 21; Rom. xiii. 7, 8; Col. iv. 1; 1 Tim. v. 8; Tit. i. 8; ii. 12. *Pure;* keeping themselves *undefiled in the way,* Psal. cxix. 1, from the pollution of sin, 1 John iii. 3, and the blemishes of filthy words and deeds, Eph. iv. 29; v. 3—5. *Lovely;* whatsoever may gain the real respect of, and be grateful to, good men, in an affable deportment acceptable to God, Tit. iii. 2. *Of good report;* whatsoever is in a tendency to maintain a good name; not to court vain-glory or popular applause, Gal. i. 10, but that which may be for the honour of Christ, and the reputation of the gospel among the Gentiles, Rom. xv. 2; 1 Pet. ii. 12; in agreement with the word of God; otherwise we must pass through evil as well as good report, Luke xvi. 15; 2 Cor. vi. 8. *If there be any virtue, and if there be any praise;* and upon supposition there be really any other commendable practice amongst any, any praiseworthy deportment. *Think on these things;* diligently consider and prosecute these things.

9 ᵐ Those things, which ye have both learned, and received, and heard, and seen in me, do: and ⁿ the God of peace shall be with you.

^{m ch. 3. 17.}
^{n Rom. 15. 33. & 16. 20.}
^{1 Cor. 14. 33.}
^{2 Cor. 13. 11.}
^{1 Thess. 5.23.}
^{Heb. 13. 20.}

Those things, which ye have both learned; he recommends to their serious practice not new things, but those weighty matters which they had before learned of him when preaching amongst them. *And received, and heard;* yea, and approved as worthy to be kept. *And seen in me;* and that all things might be more lively and affecting, with an increase of words, he moves with this, that his doctrine was exemplified by his own practice when amongst them, (as he had hinted before, chap. iii. 17,) expressing the same thing by his life which he did by his word, 1 Tim. iv. 12; 1 Pet. v. 3. *Do;* whereupon he would have them to be doers also of the same things, 1 Thess. i. 6; ii. 13; Heb. xiii. 7; James i. 22. *And the God of peace shall be with you;* and in this practice you have comfort from the presence of the God of peace, (as above, ver. 7,) who will embrace and prosper you, being reconciled to you in Christ, and at peace with you: so Rom. xv. 5, 33; xvi. 20; 2 Cor. xiii. 11; 1 Thess. v. 23.

10 But I rejoiced in the Lord greatly, that now at the last °your care of me ‖ hath flourished again; wherein ye were also careful, but ye lacked opportunity.

^{o 2 Cor. 11.9.}
‖ Or, *is revived.*

But I rejoiced in the Lord greatly; he signifies that he had been much raised in true spiritual (not carnal) joy, that the Lord had by his Spirit wrought in them such enlargedness of heart, as did show itself in their care of him for the sake of Christ. What follows, a learned man writes, may be rendered, that now at last, ye could bring to maturity the care of me; for whom indeed ye had been careful, but had not the ability. The apostle's phrase is borrowed from trees, which in the winter season keep their sap within the bark, in the spring and summer grow green, and yield their fruit: so was the Philippians' care of Paul, suffering in Christ's cause; for the Greek word we translate *flourished again,* or revived, is sometimes used actively, and transitively. So in the Seventy, Ezek. xvii. 24; with the apocryphal writer, Ecclus. i. 18: xi. 22; l. 11: and so it may be expounded here, not only of reviving, growing green, and budding again, (which is less than the thing is,) but of bringing forth fruit. For their care of Paul was in their heart, but by reason of troubles it could not exert itself, or yield fruit, but only in the season, (as Matt. xxi. 34,) which the apostle, softening his speech, allegeth as an apology for them: he doth not say there was not any opportunity in respect of himself, but a seasonableness in respect of them; they being destitute of a faculty of bringing forth fruit, ver. 17, (which yet they always nourished in their most intimate affections towards him,) till the present, when at length they had a seasonableness and an ability given them of God, to the perfecting of that fruit for the apostle. For what we translate *wherein*, may, as chap. iii. 12, be translated, for where: compare the use of the particle and article, Matt. xviii. 4, with xxvi. 50; Rom. v. 12.

11 Not that I speak in respect of want: for I have learned, in whatsoever state I am, ᵖ*therewith* to be content.

p 1 Tim. 6. 6, 8.

Not that I speak in respect of want: he doth anticipate any conceit they might have, as if he had a mean soul, and his joy were solely for the fruit of their care he had received in the supply of his want, as the same word is elsewhere used, Matt. xii. 44. *For I have learned, in whatsoever state I am, therewith to be content;* because he knew better things; being instructed at a higher rate, he had practically learned to rest satisfied with his own lot, 2 Cor. xi. 27, accounting God's allowance a sufficiency to him in any condition, 1 Tim. vi. 6, 8. How adverse soever his state was, he had attained to such equanimity that he could be content with such things as he had, Heb. xiii. 5, and cheerfully and patiently submit to God's most wise disposal of him, knowing his most righteous and tenderhearted Father would never leave nor forsake him, having already given him greater things than any of these sublunary ones he could stand in need of, Rom. viii. 32.

q 1 Cor. 4. 11. 2 Cor. 6. 10. & 11. 27.

12 ᑫI know both how to be abased, and I know how to abound: every where and in all things I am instructed both to be full and to be hungry, both to abound and to suffer need.

He explains the equality of his mind he had through grace attained to, in a free submission to God, either in the absence or affluence of external good things. *I know both how to be abased;* in a mean and ignominious state, he had spiritual skill to exercise suitable graces without murmuring, or repining when trampled on, 1 Cor. iv. 11; 2 Cor. xi. 27; having entirely resigned his will to the will of God. *And I know how to abound;* in a higher state, had in much esteem, and well accommodated. *Every where and in all things I am instructed;* yea, in all circumstances religiously initiated and taught, fortified against temptations on all hands. *Both to be full and to be hungry, both to abound and to suffer need;* when faring well, and having a large revenue, to be temperate, 1 Cor. ix. 25, humble, and communicative, 1 Tim. vi. 18. When hungry and poor, not to be distressed, but confident our heavenly Father will provide enough in his season, Matt. vi. 32; vii. 11; 2 Cor. iv. 8, giving an elixir at present that will turn all into gold.

r John 15. 5. 2 Cor. 12. 9.

13 I can do all things ʳthrough Christ which strengtheneth me.

Having written of the great things he had learned, that it might not be attributed to his proud conceit, or give occasion to any others' vanity to boast, (as he had recourse before to the Divine efficiency to will and do, chap. ii. 13,) he rests solely for power upon Christ, being found in whom, when he saith he *can do all things*, we are not to understand it absolutely, but restrictively to the subject matter he had before mentioned in the precedent verses, intimating he could by the Lord's help use well both prosperity and adversity: or, all those things the Lord called him to and put him upon. Not, as the papists urge, that any mere man since the fall is able in this life perfectly to keep the commandments of God; but that he by faith being united to Christ, by the power of his Spirit dwelling in him, hath in the Lord righteousness and strength, Isa. xlv. 24; and thereupon hath a sincere respect to all God's commands, as David had, Psal. cxix. 6; so also had Zacharias and Elisabeth, Luke i. 6; in opposition to Pharisaical obedience: not by any power he had of himself, but through Christ strengthening of him, so that God would accept of his sincere performance (though not every way perfect) of what was incumbent on him.

14 Notwithstanding ye have well done, that ˢye did communicate with my affliction.

s ch. 1. 7.

Lest any should suspect, from what he had suggested of his contentment, that he was not much affected with their liberality, but might have done as well without as with it, and they might have spared their bounty and labour, he doth prudently commend their Christian commiseration, (as the phrase is, Acts x. 33,) and give them to understand how acceptable their seasonable supply was to him, who did so joyfully resent their kindness to him, in that it was well-pleasing to God, Rom. xii. 15; they did so effectually sympathize and take a share in the oppression he sustained for the cause of Christ, 2 Cor. i. 7, and remember him in his bonds as if it were their own case, Heb. xiii. 3; Rev. i. 9.

15 Now, ye Philippians, know also, that in the beginning of the Gospel, when I departed from Macedonia, ᵗno church communicated with me as concerning giving and receiving, but ye only.

t 2 Cor. 11. 8, 9.

He amplifies the present favour the Christians at Philippi had vouchsafed to him, by a thankful recollection of their former liberality. *In the beginning of the gospel;* soon after he had preached and planted the good things of salvation amongst them, chap. ii. 22; Acts xvi. 12, 13, 40. *When I departed from Macedonia;* comparing their first benevolence with other churches, when leaving of Macedonia, Acts xviii. 5; 2 Cor. xi. 9. *No church communicated with me as concerning giving and receiving, but ye only;* none of the rest of the churches had, for the spiritual things received of him in his ministration, distributed of their carnal or temporal, (though that was their duty beyond dispute, 1 Cor. ix. 7, 11, 13, 14; Gal. vi. 6; 1 Tim. v. 17, 18,) but they alone: which might at once commend their Christian liberality, and evince that he in preaching of the gospel was not mercenary, not having exacted a reward from others, but preached the gospel freely, 2 Cor. xi. 7.

16 For even in Thessalonica ye sent once and again unto my necessity.

They, for their parts, were most commendable in this matter, that when he was in Thessalonica, the mother city, (not above twenty-five miles distant,) their care for his comfortable livelihood was more than once manifested, he passing again and again through Macedonia, 1 Cor. xvi. 5; 2 Cor. i. 16; which argues his thankful resentment of the constant purpose of their mind to succour him upon all occasions.

17 Not because I desire a gift: but I desire ᵘfruit that may abound to your account.

u Rom. 15. 28. Tit. 3. 14.

Neither would he have any of them to think, as if his commendation of them were any oblique insinuations, with design to draw something more from them; he would have them to understand he did not seek himself, or theirs for his use, (as elsewhere, 1 Cor. x. 33; 2 Cor. xii. 14,) but his great intent was, that they themselves might of God's grace have the fruit of their charity they had showed to him, chap. i. 11; iv. 10; which, in the balancing of the accounts, (by accepting as it were of Christ's will, Prov. xix. 17; Matt. x. 42; xxv. 35, 36, 40,) will turn to their best advantage.

18 But ‖ I have all, and abound: I am full, having received ˣof Epaphroditus the things *which were sent* from you, ʸan odour of a sweet smell, ᶻa sacrifice acceptable, wellpleasing to God.

‖ Or, *I have received all*. x ch. 2. 25. y Heb. 13. 16. z 2 Cor. 9. 12.

He further testifies his thankfulness from the effect their gratuity had upon him, by three words here which declare the same thing, viz. that he was abundantly satisfied, having all that he could wish, even enough and more; so that he did not expect any thing more than what he had already received by their faithful messenger Epaphroditus; which he further commends from its great acceptableness to God, in allusion to the sweet odours in the sacrifices that God himself took pleasure in, Lev. ii. 1, 2; iii. 16; Heb. xiii. 16; so that that present God himself would accept through Christ, as if it had been offered to himself, 1 Pet. ii. 5. It is true, the Socinians, to lessen the meritoriousness of Christ's sacrifice of himself, which the apostle mentions, Eph. v. 2, with respect to Gen. viii. 21, would by this text corrupt that: but the truth is, it hath nothing like with that, for the benevolence and gratuity of the Philippians is said by Paul to be *an odour of a sweet smell, a sacrifice acceptable,* &c.; but it is not said that the Philippians themselves did give themselves and dour of a sweet smell, as it is said Christ gave himself *for us an offering and a sacrifice to God for a sweet-smelling savour;* which being once offered for all, was sufficient to take away sin, Heb. x. 10, 12. And therefore their reasoning is fallacious from that parity they suggest. It is true, believers and their good works are as sweet odours, Rom. xii. 1, acceptable, but in Christ, 1 Pet. ii. 5, because they please God only for him, for his sake and merit. But Christ, because he doth appease God himself, who smells a savour of rest in his sacrifice, which all others under the law did but shadow, receiving their efficacy from his: Christ did it by himself, believers and their services are only acceptable in him.

a Ps. 23. 1.
2 Cor. 9. 8.
b Eph. 1. 7.
& 3. 16.

19 But my God *a* shall supply all your need *b* according to his riches in glory by Christ Jesus.

But my God: see ver. 3: he saith *my God,* because he imputeth and owneth that to be done to himself which is done according to his mind unto any of his ambassadors, he having received the gift from their hand by Paul. *Shall supply all your need;* will, in a gracious return to Paul's prayer, abundantly answer (yea, above all he could ask or think) all their expectations, Psal. xli. 1—3, with 2 Cor. ix. 8, 10. *According to his riches in glory;* agreeably to his own fulness and rich mercy, Psal. xxiv. 1; 1 Cor. x. 26; Eph. ii. 4; gloriously, or *riches of his glory,* Eph. iii. 16, and goodness, Rom. ii. 4; ix. 23; sustaining and defending them liberally and powerfully here, to his own glory, and taking them hereafter into everlasting glory. *By Christ Jesus;* through the mediation of, and by virtue of their communion with, Christ Jesus.

c Rom. 16. 27. Gal. 1. 5.

20 *c* Now unto God and our Father *be* glory for ever and ever. Amen.

From thanking of the Philippians, the holy man passeth to a giving of thanks unto God, the first cause, that they might not be elated. He had *my God,* ver. 19; now, *our Father;* not only adoring him as Maker of all, but as Father of all the faithful as well as of Paul, being born of him in Christ, John i. 12, 13, through whom he takes a fatherly care of them, Matt. vi. 32. Christ saith, *my Father,* John xx. 17, as being his only Son by eternal generation; and he allows believers to say *our Father,* as being his children by adoption. Unto whom they are obliged to ascribe praise, and always to give thanks in the name of our Lord Jesus Christ, Eph. v. 20. And this indeed hath been their practice, which should be ours, Rom. i. 25; ix. 5; xi. 33, 36; xvi. 25, 27; Eph. iii. 21; 1 Tim. i. 17; 1 Pet. iv. 11; v. 11; 2 Pet. iii. 18; Jude 25; Rev. i. 6, &c. It intimates, their hearts being full with the glory of God, their pens and mouths were enlarged accordingly, exciting others to the like doxologies. To almost all which in the forecited places (as here) *ever and ever* is added, connoting absolute eternity, and joining past, present, and future ages together. This form of *Amen,* affixed in the close, doth signify how his heart did give, and rejoiced to give, all blessedness to our Father in Christ, as rejoicing that he is so blessed a God.

21 Salute every saint in Christ Jesus. The brethren *d* which are with me greet you.

d Gal. 1. 2.

He doth friendly embrace and wish happiness to all and every sanctified one who is a member of Christ, hath entirely resigned up to him, and doth abide in him. Then shows, that most probably his colleagues and fellow labourers in the Christian church at Rome, (calling such elsewhere *brethren,* 1 Cor. i. 1; Col. i. 1; iv. 7; Philem. 1, 7, 20,) chap. i. 14; ii. 25; 1 Cor. xvi. 20, do so likewise.

22 All the saints salute you, *e* chiefly they that are of Cæsar's houshold.

e ch. 1. 13.

The rest of the Christians at Rome do the same; more especially they of Nero the emperor's own family and court, his domestics, chap. i. 13. It seems there were some there truly pious and Christian: but however some conceit, there is no real evidence that Seneca was of that number; he being not a courtier, but a senator, who left no real token (we know of) that he was a Christian.

23 *f* The grace of our Lord Jesus Christ *be* with you all. Amen.

f Rom. 16. 24.

He concludes this (like his other Epistles) much as he began, (see on chap. i. 2,) praying the same grace of the Lord might abide with them, which he had prayed to them all, chap. i. 1. *Amen;* not at all doubting, but with full confidence trusting, all should be firm, as he had prayed.

¶ It was written to the Philippians from Rome by Epaphroditus.

THE EPISTLE OF PAUL THE APOSTLE

TO THE

COLOSSIANS

THE ARGUMENT

GOD having a church planted in the city of Colosse, (by some since called Chone,) situated at the conflux of the rivers Meander and Lycus, in the neighbourhood of Laodicea and Hierapolis, chap. iv. 13, in Phrygia of the lesser Asia; whether at first only by the preaching of Epaphras, one of them who was *a servant of Christ,* and *faithful minister,* chap. i. 7; iv. 12; or by Paul himself, who (we learn from Luke that accompanied him) *had gone throughout Phrygia,* Acts xvi. 6, and again, *over all the country of Phrygia in order,* Acts xviii. 23, having staid for a season in Asia, where he wrought miracles, and was complained of for turning away much people from idolatry *almost throughout all Asia,* Acts xix. 11, 22, 26; we may leave undetermined. But whoever was God's prime instrument in planting the gospel here, upon Paul's being advertised by Epaphras, (chap. i. 8; iv. 12; Philem. 23,) that weeds sprang up to choke the good seed; as he was careful for the Philippians during his imprisonment, so for the Colossians, that they might not be perverted by those Judaizing false teachers who mingled Moses with Christ, stickling for the necessity of abrogated ceremonies to salvation, chap. ii. 4, 8, &c., varnishing their doctrines with notions of vain or abused philosophy, did seek to introduce a superstitious worship grounded on human traditions, chap. ii. 8, 18, &c.; but, reposing all their hope of salvation in Christ alone, persevere in that doctrine they had received according to his mind, and in the practice of real holiness with heavenly affections, both personally and relatively in heart and life, craving help of God; unto whom, having blessed God for the grace wrought in them, he doth recommend them in his own and brethren's salutations, contracting as it were the matter he had more fully written to the Ephesians, that Epistle and this, as the Evangelists, explaining each other.

CHAP. I

After saluting the saints at Colosse, 1, 2, Paul testifieth his thankfulness to God for the good account he had heard of their faith and love, 3—8; and his continual prayers for their improvement in spiritual knowledge, right practice, and thanksgiving to God for the benefits of redemption by his Son, 9—14. He showeth them the exalted nature and mediatorial office of Christ, 15—20, by whom they, who were once enemies, were now reconciled, if they continued true to the gospel, 21, 22, whereof he Paul was made a minister to preach to the Gentiles, 23—29.

A. D. 64. PAUL, ^aan apostle of Jesus Christ by
a Eph. 1. 1. the will of God, and Timotheus *our* brother,

Paul; he who of a persecutor was become a preacher, and that amongst the Gentiles laid aside his Hebrew name Saul, and made use of this, which was more familiar amongst the Gentiles, viz. *Paul*, Acts xiii. 2, 3, 9. *An apostle of Jesus Christ by the will of God;* one of those extraordinary persons immediately deputed by the special command of our Lord himself, with sovereign authority to preach the gospel, and establish his church, which is the highest charge God ever gave to men, Matt. x. 2; Luke vi. 13; 1 Cor. xii. 28; Gal. i. 12: see on Eph. i. 1; iv. 11. *And Timotheus our brother;* he joins Timothy, as elsewhere Sosthenes, 1 Cor. i. 1, by the title of *brother*, as being of the same faith, labouring in one and the same work, which might be more for their satisfaction.

b 1 Cor. 4. 17. 2 To the saints ^band faithful brethren
Eph. 6. 21.
c Gal. 1. 3. in Christ which are at Colosse: ^cGrace *be* unto you, and peace, from God our Father and the Lord Jesus Christ.

To the saints: see on Phil. i. 1. *And faithful brethren in Christ:* see on Phil. iv. 21. *Which are at Colosse:* see the Argument. *Grace be unto you, and peace, from God our Father and the Lord Jesus Christ:* see on Eph. i. 2, and Phil. i. 2.

d 1 Cor. 1. 4. 3 ^dWe give thanks to God and the
Eph. 1. 16.
Phil. 1. 3. Father of our Lord Jesus Christ, praying
& 4. 6. always for you,

We give thanks to God: see on Phil. i. 3. He doth here take in Timothy and others, in acknowledging of God's grace to them, which might express his great good-will to them. *And the Father of our Lord Jesus Christ;* describing God, to whom they render thanks both absolutely and relatively, as the Father of Jesus Christ, according to both natures: see on 2 Cor. i. 3, with Eph. i. 3. *Praying always for you;* always when they did address themselves to God by prayer making mention of them, as he also wrote to the Philippians: see on Phil. i. 3, 4.

e ver. 9. 4 ^eSince we heard of your faith in
Eph. 1. 15.
Philem. 5. Christ Jesus, and of ^fthe love *which ye*
f Heb. 6. 10. *have* to all the saints,

He instanceth in principal graces, as the matter of his thanksgiving, beginning with *faith*, described and differenced from the special object of it, *Christ Jesus*, implying not a bare knowledge or assent, but a trust in him alone for salvation; so Rom. i. 8. Understanding this saving grace with the consequent was wrought in them, as he heard it was in the Ephesians, and Philemon, it was a cogent motive to engage them in solemn thankfulness to God: see on Eph. i. 15, compared with Philem. 5. He joins *love*, or charity, *to all the saints*, with faith to our Saviour, because they are in effect inseparable, there being no real embracing of Christ without loving of him, and all his members for his sake, Gal. v. 6; 2 Tim. i. 13: not as if believers were not to show love or charity to others, who are of the same nature, and so bear the image of God, for this Christ requires of them, Matt. v. 44, 45; but by how much the nearer any are brought to God by sanctification, by so much the more a special love is to be showed to them, as fellow citizens, of the household of God, and the household of faith, Rom. xv. 26, with Gal. vi. 10; Eph. ii. 19.

5 For the hope ^gwhich is laid up for g 2 Tim. 4. 8.
you in heaven, whereof ye heard before 1 Pet. 1. 4.
in the word of the truth of the Gospel;

For the hope which is laid up for you in heaven: hope here, in this description of it, seems chiefly by a metonymy to be put for the glorious eternal salvation hoped for, Rom. viii. 24; Eph. i. 18; which may also include that lively grace whereby we lay hold of eternal life contained in the promise, Tit. i. 2. This indeed is set before believers here to encourage them to fly unto Christ for refuge, Heb. vi. 18, and reserved in heaven for them, 1 Pet. i. 4; which may well quicken in Christian love all the members of Christ in every condition; yet not with a mercenary affection, 2 Cor. v. 14, as if any by offices of Christian love to brethren could merit what is laid up for those who exercise faith, love, and hope, but that God of his mere grace and undeserved love is pleased to reward such as diligently seek him, and thereby gives an exact evidence of his admirable liberality, Heb. xi. 6, which will abundantly weigh down those light afflictions they sustain here, 2 Cor. iv. 17. *Whereof ye heard before in the word of the truth of the gospel;* hereupon he puts them in mind of the means whereby they attained to this good hope when they first embraced the gospel, viz. by hearing, Rom. x. 14, *the word of truth*, eminently, 2 Cor. vi. 7; Eph. i. 13; not only because it is the word of Jesus Christ, who is *the truth*, and *the life*, John xiv. 6, but because the gospel (which is here put appositively) is the most excellent of all truths, surpassing all in philosophy, and the law, John i. 17.

6 Which is come unto you, ^h as *it is* h Mat. 24. 14.
Mark 16. 15.
in all the world; and ⁱbringeth forth fruit, Rom. 10. 18.
ver. 23.
as *it doth* also in you, since the day ye i Mark 4. 8.
John 15. 16.
heard *of it*, and knew ^kthe grace of God k 2 Cor. 6. 1.
Phil. 1. 11.
in truth: Eph. 3. 2.
Tit. 2. 11. 1 Pet. 5. 12.

Which is come unto you, as it is in all the world; and passing the narrow bounds of Judea, unto all or most of the regions of the world, ver. 23; Matt. xxiv. 14; Acts ii. 5; Rom. i. 8; x. 18. So admirable was the progress of it east, west, north, and south, well nigh over the world as it was then known to the Greeks and Romans; whereupon the apostle might well write, Christ was *believed on in the world*, 1 Tim. iii. 16: as Christ had said he was the light of the world, and, by a figure of part for the whole, would upon his death draw all men to him, John xii. 32, 46. Yet let not the Rhemists, or any other Romanist, think that the promulgation of the mysteries of the gospel then is any proof of the verity of the Romish religion in these latter ages, when by tyranny they impose for doctrines the traditions of men: they do not bring forth that genuine fruit which the Colossians did. *And bringeth forth fruit;* viz. becoming the gospel, (as the Philippians did, chap. i. 27,) and true repentance, Matt. iii. 8; xiii. 23; John xv. 16; and real holiness, abiding in the hearts and lives of men, and effectually working in them that believe it, Isa. lv. 10; Acts v. 14; vi. 7; xii. 24; xvi.; xvii.; xix.; xx.; 1 Thess. ii. 13; which the practical religion of the papists generally bears no proportion to, being contrary to that. *As it doth also in you, since the day ye heard of it;* which from the first receiving of the gospel, was found growing amongst the true converts at Colosse, though it should seem false teachers crept in to choke the good fruit with their tares. *And knew the grace of God in truth;* however, they who had real experience of the grace of God and the excellency of the knowledge of Christ, Psal. iii. 8, did hold, bringing forth fruit in old age, Psal. xcii. 14.

l ch. 4. 12.
Philem. 23.
m 2 Cor. 11.
23. 1 Tim. 4.
6.

7 As ye also learned of [l]**Epaphras our dear fellowservant, who is for you** [m] **a faithful minister of Christ;**

As ye also learned of Epaphras: to maintain the truth, it did much concern them to have a good opinion of him, who was an eminent instrument in communicating it to them, and therefore Paul doth here very opportunely commend Epaphras, in opposition to those false teachers, who likely might insinuate somewhat to his disparagement. *Our dear fellow servant;* the respect they bare, and relation he stood in to them, being dearly beloved of him for his sincerity in promulgating the gospel; and being engaged with them in the service of the same Master, chap. iv. 7; Rev. vi. 11. *Who is for you a faithful minister of Christ;* his office, which he discharged with fidelity and affection unto them. He did with all honesty and integrity, as became one intrusted by his Master Christ, discharge what was incumbent on him for their good, chap. iv. 13; John xii. 26; 1 Cor. iv. 1, 2; Eph. iv. 12; 1 Tim. iv. 6; Heb. xiii. 17.

n Rom. 15. 30.

8 Who also declared unto us your [n]**love in the Spirit.**

Having with kindness and delight reported to Paul and Timothy, &c., what a spiritually fervent affection, not moved by carnal considerations, but inwrought by the Spirit, Gal. v. 6, 22, arising from a renewed heart, 1 Tim. i. 5; 2 Tim. i. 7, they had for Christ, for the gospel, the apostle, and all that did love the Lord Jesus in sincerity, Gal. vi. 10; 1 Pet. i. 22, 23.

o Eph. 1. 15, 16. ver. 3, 4.
p 1 Cor. 1. 5.
q Rom. 12.2.
Eph. 5. 10, 17.
r Eph. 1. 8.

9 [o] **For this cause we also, since the day we heard** *it,* **do not cease to pray for you, and to desire** [p]**that ye might be filled with** [q]**the knowledge of his will** [r]**in all wisdom and spiritual understanding;**

For this cause we also; he doth here suggest the motive mentioned in the precedent verses, viz. their faith and love, ver. 4, 5, and their special love to him, ver. 8, why he and his brethren had them so much upon their hearts: see on Eph. i. 15—17. *Since the day we heard it, do not cease to pray for you:* it seems, from the time they were refreshed with these tidings they did (as he exhorts the Colossians here, chap. iv. 2) always upon all solemn occasions wait upon God for the Colossians' spiritual prosperity, as Paul himself did for the Philippians : see on Luke xviii. 1; Rom. xii. 12; Phil. i. 4, 9; with 1 Thess. v. 17. *And to desire that ye might be filled with the knowledge of his will;* and the subject matter of their instant prayer was, that they might attain to a more distinct, clear, and practical knowledge of the mind of God in Christ, and a greater measure of conformity to what he requires in the gospel, ver. 6; Eph. v. 15—17. *In all wisdom;* in (rather than with) all necessary knowledge of the things of faith and manners, according to the prescript of the gospel: for sapience or wisdom doth properly respect the most excellent things, and such we learn most distinctly and satisfactorily from the revealed will of God, which we have in the Bible: this is that which Paul and other holy men spake as taught of God amongst the perfect or grown Christians, in opposition both to the wisdom of man and of the world, 1 Cor. ii. 4, 6, being agreeable to the will of God, Job xxviii. 28; Prov. xxviii. 7; John vi. 40; 1 Thess. iv. 3. And with this Christian wisdom some would render the following words, in *spiritual prudence,* but if we render it *understanding,* or intelligence, it may be expounded to the same sense; for which there may be very good reason, for the philosopher doth sometimes by the Greek word mean that power or habit whereby men judge aright of things presented conducing to happiness, so as upon a due expense of circumstances to discern the good from the evil, the true from the false, and the real from the apparent: such a gift as Paul prays the Lord would give unto Timothy, 2 Tim. ii. 7, compared with 1 Cor. i. 5, that they might rightly distinguish betwixt the simplicity and purity of the gospel, and those false glosses and colours that false teachers went about to sophisticate it with; not be without understanding (as some who followed our Saviour, Matt. xv. 16) what course they should take in the practice of piety, but be able to discern the times, 1 Chron. xii. 32, and other circumstances, Psal. xxxix. 1; l. 23; Eccles. v. 1; Luke viii. 18; for the ordering their actions aright, so as they may adorn the doctrine of God our Saviour in all things, as becomes the good, Eph. i. 8, with Phil. i. 10, 27; Col. iv. 5; Tit. ii. 10. Ignorance then can be no mother of true devotion, nor the inventions of men acceptable service to the living God, whose will alone is the rule of his worship.

s Eph. 4. 1.
Phil. 1. 27.
t 1 Thes. 2. 12.
t 1 Thes. 4.1.
u John 15.16.
2 Cor. 9. 8.
Phil. 1. 11.
Tit. 3. 1. Heb. 13. 21.

10 [s]**That ye might walk worthy of the Lord** [t]**unto all pleasing,** [u]**being fruitful in every good work, and increasing in the knowledge of God;**

That ye might walk worthy of the Lord: they prayed for the above-mentioned gracious habits, that the Colossians might exercise them in a course of life as it becomes those who are effectually called by the gospel to be the sons of God, and the servants of Christ; suitable to the members of the body of Christ: see on Eph. iv. 1; Phil. i. 27; compared with Rom. xvi. 2; 1 Thess. ii. 12; 2 Thess. i. 11. As the word God alone ordinary connotes the Father, so Lord doth Christ; answerable to whose wisdom, holiness, and example, Christians professing a relation to him, and expecting benefit by his purchase, should behave themselves; so that the papists cannot from this walking *worthy of the Lord* justly infer a merit of condignity, behaving ourselves as Christians being so far from any merit or desert of ours, that it is a debt, we being indispensably obliged to do so, practice being the end of our knowledge. And this end we are to respect *unto all pleasing,* i. e. designing and endeavouring not in one thing only, or in few things, but in all things whatsoever are incumbent on us, we may find acceptance with our Lord and Master, chap. iii. 20; 1 Cor. vii. 32; x. 31; 1 Thess. ii. 4; Heb. xii. 28: all should be great and generous, such as may best like our Lord, keeping themselves from the defilements of the age, Rev. iii. 4. *Being fruitful in every good work;* particularly fructifying, which in the sense may be joined with being *filled,* ver. 8: *being fruitful* is a metaphorical expression borrowed from fruit-bearing trees, unto which godly men and real Christians are compared, Psal. i. 3; John xv. 8; and *every good work* is the fruit which these plants of the Lord, having his Spirit as the seed remaining in them, 1 John ix. 9, do bring forth of every sort from a right principle, 1 Tim. i. 5, according to rule warranted by God, Isa. xxix. 13; Gal. vi. 16; or having a call from him, for his glory: see 2 Cor. ix. 8; Phil. i. 11; 2 Thess. ii. 17; Heb. xiii. 21. *And increasing in the knowledge of God:* the Colossians were not yet perfect in knowledge, and therefore they prayed that they might go on, and grow in grace and knowledge of God and Christ, 2 Pet. iii. 18, the best here knowing but in part, 1 Cor. xiii. 9; therefore they desired these Christians, as the Philippians, Phil. iii. 10, 12, and the Ephesians, Eph. iv. 13, might come to their stature: see on the texts.

x Eph. 3. 16. & 6. 10.
y Eph. 4. 2.
z Acts 5. 41.
Rom. 5. 3.

11 [x]**Strengthened with all might, according to his glorious power,** [y]**unto all patience and longsuffering** [z]**with joyfulness;**

Strengthened with all might, according to his glorious power: whereunto that they might be enabled, it was needful to pray for a power from above, for the best Christians here below are but infirm as well as imperfect, not able to perform what is required of them for doing and suffering the will of God till strengthened: see on Phil. iv. 13, compared with Rev. vii. 17. We have here great need of *all might,* special aids of God, to discharge difficult duties, to mortify strong corruptions, to contemn worldly allurements, to repulse frequent temptations, to bear manifold crosses, and to improve daily mercies, derived from exceeding great and mighty power; see on Eph. i. 19, 20, with iii. 16; an excellent glorious power, 2 Cor. iv. 7, 13, needful to consummate and complete, as well as begin, the work of grace, 2 Thess. i. 11; a great reality (and not a metaphor) to sincere converts and sound believers. *Unto all patience;* every way to bear the things which come hard upon them or continue long. Philosophy, with all its prescriptions, is ineffectual to form the soul to true patience and contentment under sufferings, it must be given on the behalf of Christ, Phil. i. 29, to a believer, to suffer patiently in tongue and heart, without a prevailing mixture of passion, so that evils do not make an impression upon him, but he doth possess his soul with patience to the end. *And long-suffering with joyfulness;* which he could not do with a becoming Christian cheerfulness, when, surcharged with a weight of troubles, he finds himself sinking, if he were not supported with the hands of Heaven, which relieve with present comfort, and raise up to believe a future reward, Matt. v. 12; Acts v. 41; Rom. v. 3; 1 Cor. xi. 32; 2 Cor. i. 5; Heb. xi. 27; xii. 10, 12; James i. 2, 4.

a Eph. 5. 20. ch. 3. 15.
12 ^aGiving thanks unto the Father, which hath made us meet to be partakers of ^bthe inheritance of the saints in light:
b Acts 26. 18. Eph. 1. 11.

Giving thanks unto the Father; he passeth from petitioning, ver. 9, to thanksgiving to God the Father, upon the consideration of his grace manifested in his Son for our redemption. In the Ephesians, chap. i. 3, 4, he began with election, here with effectual vocation; he acknowledgeth God the Father to be the object and author of what was wrought for us by his Son, and in us by his Spirit. *Which hath made us meet;* who hath made us capable of communion with himself, or ready and fit, which implies that by nature we are unready and unfit; so that merit cannot be drawn hence, and the Rhemists have done ill, contrary to the translation of the Syriac, to translate it, made us worthy: one copy hath, who hath called us. The original word, in that we follow, seems to be an idiom of the apostle (as the learned think) borrowed from the Hebrew; we find it used only in one other text by the apostle, 2 Cor. iii. 5, 6; and there he shows we are insufficient for, and incapable of, saying good things, till God do capacitate us by making us *accepted in the beloved,* Eph. i. 6; we cannot understand things of the Spirit of God, nor affect God, John xii. 39; Rom. viii. 5; 1 Cor. ii. 14, till God do draw and capacitate us, John vi. 44, 45; Phil. ii. 13, and form and work us by his Spirit unto this selfsame thing, Rom. iv. 17; 2 Cor. v. 5. *To be partakers of the inheritance of the saints in light;* to have a part in the lot of the purchased inheritance with them that are sanctified, Acts xxvi. 18; Eph. i. 14. The apostle seems to allude to the land of Canaan, wherein a portion was assigned to every one by lot for his inheritance, that being a type of the rest which remaineth to the people of God, Heb. iv. 9; and this is here said to be *of the saints in light,* as allegorically connoting the joy and glory of that state and place, in opposition to the power of darkness.

c Eph. 6. 12. Heb. 2. 14. 1 Pet. 2. 9. d 1 Thess. 2. 12. 2 Pet. 1. 11.
13 Who hath delivered us from ^c the power of darkness, ^d and hath translated us into the kingdom of †his dear Son:
† Gr. *the Son of his love.* Matt. 3. 17. Eph. 1. 6.

The power of darkness, which signifies the sadness and despair of the damned, Eph. vi. 12; Jude 8, that they who are made meet to walk in the light *as children of the light,* Eph. v. 8, are eternally freed from. The word which the apostle useth to express God's delivering of believers from the power of sin and Satan is very emphatical, signifying a gratuitous freedom, where a stranger hath delivered him from slavery who did not deserve it, nor then desire it, Mark iii. 27; Luke i. 74, 79; Eph. ii. 2, 5, 6; Heb. ii. 14, 15, though he was held fast as in fetters of iron. And which is more, he adds another word, *hath translated us into the kingdom of his dear Son;* intimating he did not leave us as Adam was before the fall, but transport us without any precedent will of ours, by the effectual call of his insuperable grace, John vi. 44; 1 Thess. ii. 12; 1 Pet. ii. 9, from the dominion of Satan, into that of his own Son. the Son of his love, Matt. iii. 17; xvii. 5; Eph. i. 6, amongst his subjects and servants, where he reigns, in his kingdom of grace, Matt. xiii. 11, where Christ dwells in the heart by his Spirit, that is united to him by faith, Eph. iii. 17; iv. 12, 13; Heb. xii. 22, 23; and of glory indeed in our Head, ver. 24, with Eph. ii. 6, by right of adoption, Rom. viii. 17, and hope of salvation through him promised by the omnipotent and true God, Rom. viii. 24; 1 Thess. v. 23, 24; Tit. i. 2; who may well call it *the kingdom of his dear Son,* in that he admits none into it but by the mediation of his Son, who makes his subjects willing, Psal. cx. 3, and received this government of his Father, Matt. xxviii. 18; Luke xxii. 29; Eph. i. 6, 7; of whose dear Son Paul hath more to say, to the comfort of his faithful subjects at Colosse, and every where.

14 ^eIn whom we have redemption through his blood, *even* the forgiveness of sins: e Eph. 1. 7.

In whom; i. e. in the person of Christ alone God-man, deputed of his Father to die for our salvation, Acts iv. 12; xx. 28. *We;* as we are in him, made meet, ver. 12. *Have redemption;* we have eternal deliverance, Heb. ix. 12, effected by a full ransom paid, 1 Cor. vi. 20; vii. 23; 1 Pet. i. 18, 19, for the freeing us indeed out of a state of sin and misery, John viii. 36, or eternal death the wages of sin, Rom. vi. 23; xvi. 20; so that by redemption here is not meant barely laying down the price, Luke ii. 38, nor consummate redemption at the last, Eph. i. 14; iv. 30, but efficacious redemption. *Through his blood;* upon the account of Christ's offering himself an expiatory sacrifice to God, without which *is no remission,* Heb. ix. 22; Rev. v. 9; effusion of his blood, by a synecdoche, takes in his humiliation to the death of the cross, and the pains of the second death he underwent for us, Isa. liii. 5, 6; Acts ii. 24; Gal. iii. 13; Phil. ii. 8. *Even the forgiveness of sins;* plenary remission of offences is by apposition to, or follows, redemption as a necessary effect, chap. ii. 13; Luke i. 77; Acts x. 43, by a metonymy transferring the cause to the effect: see more on Eph. i. 7.

15 Who is ^fthe image of the invisible God, ^gthe firstborn of every creature: f 2 Cor. 4. 4. Heb. 1. 3. g Rev. 3. 14.

Having touched on the benefit of Christ's sacrifice, which implies his human nature, he doth here rise higher, to set forth the dignity of his person, (which made it satisfactory,) both with respect to his Father and the creature. As to the former, he styles him his *image,* which is not to be understood of an artificial, accidental, or imperfect image, as that of the king on his coin, or as man was the feeble image of God, Gen. ix. 6; 1 Cor. xi. 7; Col. iii. 10; for the apostle's arguing Christ's dignity to redeem, would have no force in it, if Christ were no more than a mere man; but of a natural, substantial, and perfect image: as Seth was the natural image of his father Adam, of the same substance with him, Gen. v. 3; so Christ, the eternal Word, the only begotten Son of God by nature, John i. 1, 18, (see on Phil. ii. 6,) very God of very God, John xvii. 3, 5, doth exactly resemble, perfectly and adequately represent, his Father, of whose person he is the express character, or perfect image, Heb. i. 3. Yet more distinctly Christ is the image of God, either, 1. As he is the Second Person in the blessed Trinity, from an intrinsical relation to the Father, in regard of the same essence with him by eternal generation before the world was made. He being eternally in the Father, and the Father in him, John xiv. 10; so he is in respect of his Father his essential image, and in regard to us as invisible as the Father himself; no creature could be the eternal image of the Creator, as that Son of the only true God, *the living God,* was, and is, Matt. xvi. 16; John vi. 69, in respect of his Father. 2. As he is God-man, in whom the fulness of the Godhead dwells bodily, chap. ii. 9, whereby he doth infinitely exceed and surpass angels and men at first, Heb. i. 5, 6; ii. 5. The apostle in this place doth not say simply Christ the image of God, but *of the invisible God,* (considered personally,) i. e. the Father; because the Father cannot be known to us but in his Son, as in an image, in which he would represent or manifest himself to be seen or known, John i. 14, 18; xiv. 8, 9; 2 Cor. iv. 4. And in this latter respect (which imports the manifestative, not essential image) is Christ the image of his invisible Father unto us; unto whom, in all his offices and works of mediation, the attributes, affections, and excellencies of God clearly shine forth, they being otherwise incomprehensible and invisible by a creature: but Christ is the complete image of them, in a transcendent way; for as they are in him, they are incommunicable to any mere creature, and therefore he is the image of *the invisible God*, in that he makes him visible unto us. God is a pure Spirit, without body, or bodily parts, but yet was clearly manifested in Christ tabernacling amongst us, John i. 14 ; 1 Tim. iii. 16 : he represents him to us in his understanding and wisdom, Prov. viii. 14, 15; almightiness and eternity, Isa. ix. 6 ; John i. 1 : viii. 58, permanency and unchangeableness, Heb. i. 11, 12 ; xiii. 8, omnipresence and omnisciency, John ii. 24, 25 ; xiii. 18; Rev. ii. 13. Not (as the Lutherans strangely imagine) that Christ is omnipotent with the omnipotency of the Divine nature, or omniscient with that omnisciency, as if the manhood did instrumentally use the attributes of the Godhead ; but such perfections are really inherent in and appertaining to the manhood, by virtue of its union with the Divine nature in the Second Person of the Trinity, that though they are vastly short of the attributes which are essential to the Godhead, yet they are the completest image of them, and such as no mere creature is capable of. Hence it is said, *we beheld his glory, the glory of the only begotten Son of God*, who did further represent and manifest his Father to us, in the works of creation and preservation which he did, John i. 3; v. 19; Heb. i. 10. Hence the apostle in this verse considers the dignity of Christ, with respect to the creature, adding to the forementioned intrinsic, an extrinsic royalty. *the first-born of every creature*, which a learned man would render, begotten before all the creation, or born before every creature, which is a Hebrew phrase. The Greek scholiast and several of the Greek fathers go this way ; not as if the ineffable generation of Christ had any beginning, as some falsely conceited Christ to be made in time, just in the beginning before the world, by whom as an instrument all the rest were created ; but the apostle doth not say he was first made, or first created ; but, ver. 17, was, or did exist, *before all things* besides ; (as John Baptist said, *he was before me*, John i. 15 ;) and therefore none of the rank of all them, but of another. viz. equal with his Father, whose image he was, above all that was made or created : he was not created at all. though first-born, or first-begotten, yet not first-created. (being distinguished here from created, as the cause from the effect.) as it refers to him that begets, so it may to only begotten, Christ being so begotten as no other was or could be, Prov. viii. 22 ; Micah v. 2 ; Heb. i. 5, 6, even from eternity. The word *first* may either respect what follows, and so notes order in the things spoken of, he who is first being one of them, 1 Cor. xv. 47 ; or things going before, in which sense it denies all order or series of things in the same kind : as God is first before whom none, Isa. xli. 4 ; xliii. 11 ; Rev. xxi. 6 ; so Christ may be said to be first-born because the only begotten Son of his Father, John i. 14 : so the apostle may consider him here, in order to establish the consideration of him as Mediator and Head of his church, ver. 18 ; he speaking before, ver. 16, of those things more generally whose creation are assigned to him, in contradistinction to those of the church or new creation, ver. 18. Agreeably to our translation, *first-born of every creature*, (note, here is a difference in the Greek, betwixt first-born *of* and *for*, ver. 18,) we may consider, 1. Negatively. It is not to be understood properly for the first in order, so as to be one of them. in reference to whom he is said to be the first-born. But, 2. Positively, yet figuratively in a borrowed speech : so primacy and primogeniture may be attributed to him in regard of the creatures, (1.) By a metonymy of the antecedent for the consequent ; he who hath the privileges of enjoying and disposing of his father's goods and inheritance, is accounted the first-born, Gen. xxvii. 29 ; Gal. iv. 1 ; so is Christ, being Owner, Lord, and Prince of every creature, as he is God-man, or ordained to human nature, he hath the preeminence of the whole creation, and is the chief, Psal. ii. 7, 8 ; Heb. i. 2, 6. The heir amongst the Hebrews was reckoned the prince of the family, and so amongst the Romans the heir was taken for the lord : so God said he would make David his *first-born*, Psal. lxxxix. 27, compared with Job xviii. 13; Isa. xiv. 30; Jer. xxxi. 9. This sovereign empire which Christ hath over all the creation, and the parts of it, is by his primogeniture, or that he is first-born, since there is left nothing that is not under him, Heb. ii. 8, (as Adam in this lower world, in regard of his dominion, the state of innocency, might be first-born of them created for him,) for the apostle brings in the next verse as the fundamental reason of this assertion. (2.) By a consideration of Christ in God's eternal decree and purpose, as the common womb of him who is God-man, and all creatures ; being *fore-ordained before the foundation of the world*, 1 Pet. i. 20, he may be looked upon as the first-born amongst those who are predestinated to be conformed to his image, Rom. viii. 29, with Eph. i. 4, 5 ; for upon this account he is the first-born of the first-born creatures or church, (but this, as hinted before, is considered more specially, ver. 18,) Heb. xii. 23, therefore the firstborn of all others : and this may be one respect in which he is before them, ver. 17, with Prov. viii. 22 ; yea, all of them of the old, as well as the new creation. The Socinians are so daringly bold as to restrain this extensive expression of *every creature*, or all the creation, to the new creation of men or the faithful only, by perverting some texts of Scripture to strain them that way ; when it is plain by what follows, the Spirit of God means all created beings, either in the first or second world, Christ being the principal cause both of the one and the other ; the apostle, by the general term *every creature* simply, without any additament, doth import all created things, viz. the heavens and the earth, with all that is made in them : neither angels, nor inanimate and irrational creatures, are excluded ; as in the apostle's reason immediately following this expression.

16 For [h] by him were all things created, that are in heaven, and that are in earth, visible and invisible, whether *they be* thrones, or [i] dominions, or principalities, or powers : all things were created [k] by him, and for him :

[h] John 1. 3. 1 Cor. 8. 6. Eph. 3. 9. Heb. 1. 2. [i] Rom. 8.38. Eph. 1. 21, ch. 2. 10, 15. 1 Pet. 3. 22. [k] Rom. 11. 36. Heb. 2. 10.

For by him were all things created : he proves Christ to be before and Lord over every creature, more excellent than them all, with a prerogative other princes want, for none of them is a creator of his subjects, who were not made by him or for him, as all creatures without exception were made by and for Christ. The apostle here is as cautious as may be, lest by speaking of Christ as *the firstborn of every creature*, he should seem to put him in the order of creatures, which he shows do depend upon him for their creation and preservation, since he brought them out of nothing into being, and therein doth sustain them. *By him ;* in whom they have their beings, live and move, Acts xvii. 28. Some render the particle *in*, rather than *by*. But they disclaim the philosophical notions about Platonic ideas, only conceive all to be made *in* Christ, as the exemplary cause, whom God had in his eternal decree set up as the pattern of all perfections, being his image, according to which it was agreed, in the council of the Trinity, man should be made, Gen. i. 26. But the most do, according to our translation, render it (as a Hebrew phrase) *by*, (being of the same import with that in the end of the verse,) or through, which is expressive of the principal efficient, not the instrumental cause, for all the things made were produced out of nothing into being immediately by him, John i. 3, 10 ; Heb. i. 8, 10 : he might well be Lord over them all, who was the first founder of them, Acts x. 36 ; 1 Cor. viii. 6 ; and whatever the adversaries allege, it is plain in Scripture that *by* is used of the principal cause, ver. 1 ; Rom. xi. 31, 36 ; 1 Cor. i. 1 ; xii. 8, 9 ; 2 Cor. i. 1 ; Gal. i. 1 ; 1 Thess. iv. 2 ; 2 Thess. iii. 12. *Were all things created :* creation is simply, universally, and absolutely attributed to him ; for whatever subtilties some would suggest, *all things created by him* is equivalent to he created all things ; compare Psal. xcvi. 5; cii. 25, with Isa. xliv. 24 ; xlviii. 13 ; Jer. x. 12 ; Acts xvii. 24, with Rom. xi. 36 : (like 1 Cor. i. 9, with 1 Thess. ii. 12.) *That are in heaven, and that are in earth :* the apostle speaks extensively of all proceeding from not being into being, both generally and distributively, agreeably to the common expression of *all things* that were made at the beginning, Acts iv. 24 : though in Scripture, where mention is made of the creation, heaven and earth be not always expressed, Isa. xl. 26 ; Mark x. 6 ; xiii. 19 ; Acts xvii. 24 ; Rom. i. 20 ; 2 Pet. iii. 4 ; Rev. iv. 11 ; but here, where all things in heaven and earth, visible and invisible, are expressed, it is evident that heaven and earth are together comprehended. *Visible and invisible :* these two adjuncts of *visible and invisible* do divide all creatures whatsoever, there being nothing made that is not one or the other. *Whether they be;* an enumeration is particularly made of the latter, which for their excellency (if any) might seem to be exempted (by those in danger of being beguiled to the worshipping of angels) from the state and condition of being created by Jesus Christ; particularly, *thrones, or dominions, or principalities, or powers;* those he here names, as elsewhere, Rom. viii. 38; Eph. i. 20, 21; iii. 10; vi. 12, in the abstracts for the concretes, the invisible inhabitants of the world. I know some would have dignities in human policy to be meant, as Tit. iii. 1; 2 Pet. ii. 10; Jude 8; but it is more rational, with the generality of ancient and modern interpreters, as chap. ii. 15, to expound these titles of incorporeal and angelical creatures, whether by an emphatical synonymy, angels generally, by a metonymy, being ministers of the heavenly state; or more probably, as should seem from the scope of the place, by such a subdivision of invisibles as the apostle did conceive there was, according to the properties wherein they were eminent, and the offices whereunto they were delegated of God, which he expresseth disjunctively by borrowed titles from the distinctions of men in dignities and offices here below, as dukes, earls, lords, and other magistrates; the Scriptures elsewhere intimating distinctions amongst the spiritual ministers attending the commands of the heavenly Majesty upon his throne, represented shadowed by the cherubims, Gen. iii. 24; Exod. xxv. 18. 22; 1 Sam. iv. 4; 2 Sam. vi. 2; 1 Chron. xxviii. 18; Psal. lxxx. 1; Isa. xxxvii. 16; Ezek. i. 13; denominated archangels and princes, Dan. x. 13, 21; 1 Thess. iv. 16; Jude 9; which imply some distinctions and orders amongst angelical beings, but what that is we know not, (whatever is disputed in the Roman schools from the spurious Denys,) and therefore having no ground from Scripture, account it no better than curiosity to inquire, and rashness to determine. *All things were created by him:* after his enumeration and distribution of things created, the apostle doth, for further confirmation, repeat the universal proposition or assumption, with a preposition expressive of the same absolute efficiency of causality that is attributed to God the Father and the Holy Ghost; all created things being made *by* him, i. e. by Christ, whose works without are undivided from those of the other Persons in the Trinity; they were all brought out of nothing into being by him, not by angels. *And for him;* which is more fully proved from his being the final (as well as efficient) cause of them; they all had their being in respect of him or *for* him, i. e. his glory, Rom. xi. 36, to manifest his Divine power and infinite goodness, John v. 17, 23; xvii. 5; he is their end as well as founder, Rev. v. 13; the apostle affirms the same of him that is affirmed of the Father, Job ix. 8; Prov. xvi. 4; Isa. xliv. 24; he made them all for his own sake. The Socinians, in derogation to Christ's Divinity, would restrain, limit, and narrow what Christ saith here in this verse to the new creation, or reparation, but against manifest reason. For, 1. The words *creature* and *creation* in the foregoing verse and this, are used absolutely, as was before suggested, and so *created*, here repeated twice, and joined with the word *all*, and therefore to be understood, as elsewhere, absolutely of the old or first creation, Mark x. 6; xiii. 19; xvi. 15; Rom. i. 20, 25; 1 Cor. xi. 9; 1 Tim. iv. 3; Heb. iv. 13; 2 Pet. iii. 4; Rev. x. 6; for when it is used of the second creation, or restoration, the restrictive additament of *new* is joined with it, Isa. lxv. 17, 18; 2 Cor. v. 17; Gal. vi. 15; Eph. ii. 15; iv. 24, not left indefinitely as here. 2. In parallel places, the making and founding of the old creation is ascribed to Christ, both negatively and positively, John i. 3; Heb. i. 3, 10; not one thing is excepted, and therefore should not be restrained to men. 3. It is most evident from the context the apostle doth in this verse discourse of creation, in contradistinction to what he speaks of afterwards in the 18th and 20th verses, when he comes to treat of Christ as Head of his church, and we have no reason to charge the apostle with a useless repetition further. 4. The apostle's significant enumeration and distinction of things created, doth evidence that he understood the subject, the creation, in the most extensive and unlimited consideration of it. He reckons up material as well as immaterial things, and those in heaven, which needed no restoration, as well as those on earth, which did, being polluted with sin. Those angels who had not put off the honour of the first, did not belong to the new creation; having not divested themselves of their original integrity, they needed not to be reinvested with that they never lost: and devils cannot be ranked among new creatures, neither can wicked souls, Matt. xxv. 41; Rev. xxii. 15; neither are there new and old orders of angels; so that the dominion Christ is here (as elsewhere) asserted as founder of, is the whole, not only the new creation, Rev. v. 13.

17 ¹And he is before all things, and by him all things consist. _{1 John 1. 1, 3. & 17. 5. 1 Cor. 8. 6.}

And he is before all things: to obviate all exceptions to what he had said before, the apostle doth expressly assert (what was implied before) Christ's pre-existence to all the things that were created, and therefore that he himself was not made, but eternally begotten, and so did exist, and was actually before all creatures in causality, dignity, and time; which proves his eternity, (consonant to other scriptures, Prov. viii. 22; Isa. xliv. 6; Micah v. 2; John i. 1; xvii. 5; Rev. i. 8, 11, 17; xxii. 13,) because before all things there was nothing but proper eternity, Psal. xc. 2. *And by him all things consist:* then follows this further argument of Christ's excellency and perfection, that he is not only the Creator or Founder, but likewise the Supporter or Upholder, of all things whatsoever are created, yea, even of the most excellent and useful of them, who in him do live and move, Acts xvii. 28; Heb. i. 3: he being the conservant as well as procreant cause of the heavens and earth, with all things therein, because in respect of God it is the same action which is continued in conservation and providence which was in creation, not breaking off the same influence which was exerted in producing them out of nothing into being, Isa. xlvi. 4; John v. 19.

18 And ᵐhe is the head of the body, the Church: who is the beginning, ⁿthe firstborn from the dead; that ‖ in all *things* he might have the preeminence. _{m Eph. 1. 10, 22. & 4. 15. & 5. 23. 1 Cor. 11. 3. n Acts 26. 23. 1 Cor. 15. 20, 23. Rev. 1. 5. ‖ Or, *among all.*}

And he is the head of the body, the church: having spoken of Christ in reference to the creatures in general, or old creation, showing how he is the Creator, Preserver, and Governor thereof, the apostle doth here speak of him with a special reference to his church, or the new creation, whereof he shows here, (as elsewhere, see on Eph. i. 22, 23, with iv. 15, and v. 23,) that he is the Head and Governor, his chosen and called being the proper subjects of his special kingdom, the choice body, unto which he doth more peculiarly relate, ver. 24, for the guiding and governing of it, he being that to it which the head is to the natural body, and more especially in the two former respects : 1. Of their union to God, which was chiefly designed and expressed in those words, *who is the beginning*, i. e. the first foundation or principle of their union to God, whereupon the first corner-stone of the church's happiness is laid, he being the beginning of the second creation, as of the first, Rev. iii. 14. And, 2. Of their restoration from sin and death, being brought into that first-designed happiness, which is the great intention of that union, as appears from the following expression, *the firstborn from the dead*, in a special distinction from the dead, here too of the *creature*, ver. 15. The apostle doth not tautologize, but what he spoke of Christ there with respect to the creature, he doth here speak of him with respect to his church, as 1 Cor. xv. 20, 23; Rev. i. 5. By the particle *from* is implied not only that he was before the dead, but that he was numbered amongst the dead in respect of that nature wherein he was once dead; from which he was demonstrated to be firstborn; his resurrection with a glorious body (Phil. iii. 21) being a kind of new birth, whereby upon the reunion of his holy soul and body he was born from the womb of the grave, the Head in regard of the members: resurrection is called a *regeneration*, Matt. xix. 28; and as there is a gracious resurrection of the soul upon effectual calling in conversion, so there is a glorious regeneration of the body in the resurrection, Luke xx. 36, in contradistinction to ver. 34. Christ is the first-born of these, in reference to God, Acts xxvi. 23; 1 Cor. xv. 20, 23; as the first-fruits, or first ear of this blessed harvest, that was carried up into the sanctuary, and offered in due season to the eternal

Father, until the rest do become ripe: and in reference to the dead, i. e. in the Lord, 1 Cor. xv. 18; 1 Thess. iv. 14; Rev. xiv. 13; from whom he first rose in regard of time fully and perfectly; and of whom, in regard of dignity and dominion, Psal. lxxxix. 27; Gal. iv. 1, he is chief, and Lord, (hath the pre-eminence, as it follows,) and is first in regard of causality of those dead in him, standing in relation to him their Head, Rom. xi. 15, with 1 Cor. xv. 20, who shall be perfectly raised by virtue of his resurrection. And however it be said, both in the Old and New Testament, some were before raised; yet he was the cause of his own resurrection, as none others were, or can be. He properly rose, and that by his own power, Psal. cx. 7; John x. 17, 18; others were and will be raised by his. In regard of the sort and kind of resurrection, he it was first which was not imperfect, as others, or Lazarus, who was raised but to return to his former state of mortality; but perfect, Christ rose to die no more, Rom. vi. 9; Heb. ix. 28. He was the first that rose as a public person, Head of his church, the Second Adam, representing all his members, 1 Cor. xv. 21, 22, who are raised together with him spiritually, virtually, and representatively, Eph. ii. 6; 1 Pet. iii. 21: those actually raised before in another sort were like singular ears of corn, by occasion more timely gathered for a special instance of Divine power, but Christ was the first that ever rose in the nature and quality of the first-fruits duly gathered, to sanctify and consecrate the whole harvest of the dead in him, who shall one day be raised to a conformity unto him, Phil. iii. 21. The Socinians, from this metaphorical expression of Christ's being *the first-born from the dead*, and fetching in that passage where it is said, *Thou art my Son, this day have I begotten thee*, Acts xiii. 33, do oppose Christ's natural and eternal Sonship, but very inconsequently and absurdly; for, 1. Christ was properly the Son of God before his resurrection from the dead, he did not then receive that relation by it, as other texts clearly prove, Psal. ii. 7; Prov. xxx. 4; Micah v. 2; John i. 1; xvii. 5. 2. If his resurrection had been a begetting of him, then would he have begotten himself, so been Father and Son to himself, because he raised himself. As to that other text they allege, things are sometimes said to be done then, when only manifested and declared to be done: then was Christ the first of all the dead that was born, and raised again in incorruption, *declared to be the Son of God with power*, Rom. i. 4, according to the prophecy: q. d. This day I have manifested thee by raising of thyself to be my natural Son, whom I begat from everlasting. Be sure he hath the primacy and pre-eminence, as it follows. *That in all things he might have the pre-eminence;* which some expound as the end and intention of Christ the agent, that he might obtain the primacy, Rom. xiv. 9; 2 Cor. v. 15, or hold the first place in all things; whether more generally, according with the common scope of the apostle in the precedent verses, compared with chap. ii. 10; John v. 25, 29; Eph. i. 22; or more specially, amongst his brethren and all the members of his mystical body, Rom. viii. 29, with 2 Cor. v. 17, 18; but this is not material, because all things are brought under his empire. Others, because the primacy doth belong to him by undoubted right, and that he, being Head of his church, did ultimately design to save it, and so to glorify his Father, do expound it rather as the event, consequent, and conclusion from the antecedent, which is the end of the work, so as that, or in such a sort as, he actually is declared to be the first, or he holds the primacy in the old and new creation. According to the agreement with his Father, he is such a one as not only hath all manner of privileges, that any in this or the other world do, or may be supposed to, excel in; but also with a pre-eminence, a primacy in all, above what any one hath in any thing he may glory of.

o John 1. 16.
& 3. 34.
ch. 2. 9.
& 3. 11.

19 For it pleased *the Father* that °in him should all fulness dwell;

A learned man reads it, For all fulness pleased to dwell in him. Others, He liked, or approved, that all fulness should dwell in him, bringing instances for that construction of the word *it pleased*. *For it pleased the Father;* it is true the word *Father* is not in the Greek text, nor in the oriental versions, but is well understood and supplied from the context, ver. 12, where the apostle gives thanks to the Father, and then describes his dear Son in the following verses, and here in this adds a cogent reason why he should be the Head of his church. since the Son of his love, (in whom he is well pleased, Matt. iii. 17.) is he alone in whom he likes to dwell with all fulness. or all fulness doth will to abide. *That in him should all fulness;* here is another *all.* and a *fulness* added to that *all;* an *all* for parts, a *fulness* for degrees; a transcendency in all, above all. It is of the Father's good pleasure that Christ, not here considered simply, as the Son of God, but respectively, as Head of his church, and Mediator, should be the subject of this *all fulness*, which is not directly that of his body mystical, Eph. i. 23. But, 1. Originally, the fulness of the Godhead, whereby he hath an all-sufficiency of perfections for his mediatory office upon the mystical union, which none other hath or can have, chap. ii. 9; John i. 14: of which more distinctly in the next chapter. 2. Derivatively, a fulness of the Spirit and habitual grace, Luke i. 80, with John i. 16, 33; iii. 34; holiness, wisdom, power, perfectly to finish his work, John xvii. 4; xix. 30, and other excellencies for the reconciling (as it follows) and actual influencing of his body, Psal. cxxx. 7, 8; Matt. xxviii. 18; John v. 20; Rom. i. 4; 1 Cor. v. 4; with 2 Cor. xii. 9; Eph. i. 20—22; Heb. vii. 25, 26; Rev. v. 6, 12. *Dwell;* and this *all fulness* doth not only lodge in him for a time, but resideth and abideth in him; it is not in him as the Divine glory was awhile in the tabernacle of Moses, and the temple of Solomon, but dwells constantly in him, not as a private person, but a universal principle; as Head of the body, (as well as reconciler,) to fill up the emptiness of man with the abundant grace that perpetually resideth in him.

20 And, ||ᵖ having made peace through the blood of his cross, ᵍ by him to reconcile ʳ all things unto himself; by him, *I say*, whether *they be* things in earth, or things in heaven.

|| Or, making peace.
p Eph. 2. 14, 15. 16.
q 2 Cor. 5. 18.
r Eph. 1. 10.

Some, from the Greek, would (not have that clause we read in a parenthesis to come next the copulative *and,* but) have it, And by himself he should reconcile unto himself (in or to himself) all things, (having made or obtained peace through the blood of his cross,) I say, &c. But the reading of that sentence in the parenthesis after, or before the reconciliation of *all things*, as we do, because of the next following distribution, is not very material as to the sense of the thing, redemption, ver. 14, or rather, the manner or means of reconciliation unto God by Christ, in whom the fulness of all Divine and human perfections were seated for the bringing of heaven and earth together. *Having made peace through the blood of his cross:* God the Father, for bringing enemies nigh unto himself in *the kingdom of his dear Son*, ver. 13, 19, 21, was in him, 2 Cor. v. 18, 19, who having took on him the seed of Abraham, Heb. ii. 16, and because without shedding of blood there could be no remission, or being brought nigh, Eph. ii. 13; Heb. ix. 12, 22, 23, according to his Father's ordination and agreement with him for the expiation of sin, became obedient unto death, that cursed death of the cross, Isa. liii. 5; Gal. iii. 13; Phil. ii. 8; and by that bloody sacrifice of himself, there once perfected, Heb. ix. 14; x. 10, 14, obtained peace: that by a figure being put to express his most perfect merit, as being the finishing of his obedience and passion, chap. ii. 14; Rom. iii. 25; v. 10; Eph. ii. 16; Heb. ix. 12. *By him;* which alone could satisfy his offended Father's demands: angels could not shed blood which was necessary to make peace and reconcile enemies; and though some false apostles might seduce to the worshipping of them, their obedience could not be meritorious. *To reconcile all things unto himself;* God designing an atonement to himself, i. e. God the Father, (and, by consequence, to the whole Trinity,) did it by Christ, in whom all fulness dwelling there was a proper fitness upon his Father's call, Isa. xlii. 1, 4, 6, with Heb. ix., for so perfect a work as to take away the enmity of those alienated from God, and to bring them into favour again. The great inquiry is about the extent of this reconciliation, because the apostle mentions *all things* (rather than all persons); and then, having emphatically repeated *by him*, viz. Christ as God-man, and none other, Acts iv. 12, he adds a distribution of *all things, whether they be things in earth, or things in heaven.* To answer which, *all things* may be understood, either, 1. Restrictively to the subject, the universal church of which Christ is the Head; so he doth not mean all things whatsoever, unlimitedly, but with respect to the subject matter, as, ver. 21, all things which being alienated from God are reconciled to him; i. e. whatsoever things are reconciled, are by him reconciled, all relating to the subject matter of reconciliation, (as all made to creation, ver. 16.) all the real subjects of his kingdom, whether gathered and gone to heaven before in hope of the Messiah to come, or now and hereafter shall be gathered, Acts xv. 11; Rom. iii. 25; Eph. iii. 15; Heb. xi. 39, 40; xii. 23: yet this doth not altogether satisfy some, by reason of the sublimity of the apostle's word in the distribution; and ordinarily in Scripture, by things in heaven are meant the angels, whose natural seat it is, spirits of just men made perfect being advanced thither only by God's gracious vouchsafement. Or, 2. Largely, as comprehending the good angels, especially if upon the foundation of reconciliation considered strictly, we take reconciliation here more generally, (as the apostle doth in his Epistle to the Ephesians, expatiating more upon this matter there than he doth here, writing more concisely and contractedly,) for recapitulation, (or analogical reconciliation,) bringing all under one head, the recomposing or reuniting of creatures terrestrial or celestial, upon the atonement for sinners by Christ; so that all his subjects, those that divide the state of his kingdom, are at an agreement amongst themselves and with each other; God did so by Christ conjoin miserable men with himself, that now also the holy angels are conjoined, they come under the same Head, Christ, chap. ii. 10; Eph. i. 22, whom they worship as at his first, so second coming, Luke ii. 13, 14; Heb. i. 6. As men cleave to him by faith, so the angels by vision (1 Tim. iii. 16) look upon him their Head; yet is he not their Redeemer, ver. 14; Eph. i. 3; not partaking of their nature, they are not his members as believers are (as God is the Head of Christ, yet is not he a member of God, 1 Cor. xi. 3); Christ beareth a more special relation to them, than he doth unto those principalities and powers, Eph. v. 23, 30, 31; however, they, being under a hypothetical possibility of falling, should seem to have need of a preventive kind of reconciliation, upon that account, if their standing is otherwise secured to them, they abiding in their purity could not be friends to impure creatures, Gen. iii. 24; but upon the satisfaction of their Lord, their distaste and dissatisfaction is removed, they being reduced into a corporation, under Christ, with those whom he hath reconciled, Eph. i. 10. As they, to the glory of the supreme Majesty, rejoiced when Christ came to seek these lost ones, so they are ministers to them that he hath made willing, Heb. i. 14; they delight in the ministry of reconciliation, Eph. iii. 10; 1 Pet. i. 12, attend the service with their brethren, (in doing their office,) Rev. xix. 10; xxii. 9, further the work, Acts viii. 26, rejoice when it takes effect, Luke xv. 10, and carry those that are perfected to the place of their own residence, Luke xvi. 22, to their own innumerable assembly in the heavenly Jerusalem, Heb. xii. 22; waiting on Christ, (according to the typical representatives, Exod. xxv. 19; xxvi. 1; 1 Kings vi. 23, 29,) with those that are with him, and made like to him at his throne, Matt. xxii. 30; Mark xii. 25, where he sits as the Son of man, and the holy angels (as he saith) are continually ascending and descending upon him, John i. 51: he fills them, as the rest of his subjects, *all in all*, Eph. i. 21, 23; they have grace by way of participation, having it from him their Head, who hath it of himself, John v. 26. So that upon the matter, this reconciliation of things in heaven, seems most to accord with Eph. i. 9, 10, and is not much unlike that in Eph. ii. 13, 16; that which is separately said there *by his blood*, ver. 13, and *by the cross*, ver. 16, is here conjoined by *the blood of his cross*. There is *making peace* in one simple word; here, (in the Greek,) in a compounded one. There, *that he might reconcile both unto God*; here, that he might *reconcile all things unto himself*, i. e. God. There he speaks only of men on earth being reconciled amongst themselves, because they had also been reconciled to God; if we take in angels also under those *all*, we have an allowance from that foreciied Eph. i. 10; yea, and in favour of the larger acceptation of reconciliation here, it may be considered that the whole creation which was put into disorder and subjected unto vanity, is in earnest expectation of the fruits of this gracious reconciliation, in being brought to a perfect harmony, to the glory of him who is all in all, Rom. viii. 19—23, with 1 Cor. xv. 58.

21 And you, ˢthat were sometime alienated and enemies ∥ in *your* mind ᵗby wicked works, yet now hath he reconciled.

s Eph. 2. 1, 2, 12, 19. & 4. 18. ∥ Or, *by your mind in wicked works*. t Tit. 1. 15, 16.

And you, that were sometime alienated: the particle *and*, by a Hebraism, is put for therefore, or wherefore, leading the Colossians from the doctrines he had proposed, to consider their own estrangement from God and the things that please him, before they were effectually called by the gospel, being then in such a miserable condition as others were in a state of corrupted nature. See Psal. v. 9; Rom. vi. 19; 1 Cor. vi. 11; Eph. ii. 1, 3, 11, 12. *And enemies;* not only in their outward deportment had they no communion with the true God, but inwardly they hated God as an enemy, and they were hated of him as his enemies; by their willing and nilling that which was contrary to him and his pleasure, in opposing his revealed will, John xv. 18, 24; Rom. i. 29, 30; v. 10; viii. 7; James iv. 4. *In your mind by wicked works;* this enmity was predominant in their mind, or cogitation, or carnal reasoning, not receiving or comprehending the things of the Spirit of God, 1 Cor. ii. 14; that leading power of their souls being darkened, Eph. iv. 18, there was an enmity against God, so that they neither could be subject to God's law, Rom. viii. 7, under the prevalency of that corrupt reasoning which was so intent upon their corrupt courses, Gen. vi. 5, that then they thought not of peace with God. *Yet now hath he reconciled;* yet such was the unconstrained compassion of God, that *now* while sinners, (in a divided sense,) Rom. v. 10, they were actually reconciled; now, not before, not from eternity in his decree, nor meritoriously when upon the cross, 2 Cor. v. 19: he doth not mean simply the action, of such virtue, necessary and efficacious to make reconciliation, and the appeasing of God's displeasure; but compriseth the effect of it also when it is wrought in time, 2 Cor. v. 20, and the enmity in the subject is actually removed.

22 ᵘIn the body of his flesh through death, ˣto present you holy and unblameable and unreproveable in his sight:

u Eph. 2. 15, 16. x Luke 1. 75. Eph. 1. 4. & 5. 27. 1 Thess. 4. 7. Tit. 2. 14. Jude 24.

In the body of his flesh through death; the means whereby their reconciliation to God was purchased, (which they had particularly applied by faith, ver. 4,) was the sacrifice of that fleshy (not fantastical) body which Christ had assumed, subject to the condition of an animal life, being capable of suffering and mortal, (not refined and immortal, as after his resurrection, Rom. v. 10; 1 Cor. xv. 44, 53,) 2 Cor. v. 14; Eph. ii. 16, with Heb. x. 5, 10; 1 Pet. ii. 24; iii. 18. Christ's death was not only for our good, but in our stead thereby offering himself to God, he satisfied Divine justice, and his sacrifice, giving himself for us, was a sacrifice of a sweet smell to God, Eph. v. 2. *To present you holy and unblamable and unreprovable in his sight;* before whom believers cannot make themselves to stand holy, but Christ doth upon the account of his sacrifice for them; so that through the veil of his flesh, Heb. x. 19, 20, God doth look upon such as having neither spot nor wrinkle, without blame or blemish: see Eph. i. 4; v. 27. Unto whom Christ is made righteousness, he is also made sanctification, 1 Cor. i. 30. Those who are washed are sanctified, 1 Cor. vi. 11. The end of reconciliation is restoration or sanctification, Luke i. 74, 75; 2 Cor. v. 15; Tit. ii. 14; 1 Pet. ii. 21; inchoatively here, with a perfection of parts, Heb. xiii. 21, and consummatively hereafter, with a perfection of degrees, 1 Cor. xiii. 10; Eph. iv. 13; Phil. iii. 11, 12.

23 If ye continue in the faith ʸgrounded and settled, and *be* ᶻnot moved away from the hope of the Gospel, which ye have heard, ᵃ*and* which was preached ᵇto every creature which is under heaven; ᶜwhereof I Paul am made a minister;

y Eph. 3. 17. ch. 2. 7. z John 15. 6. a Rom. 10. 18. b ver. 6. c Acts 1. 17. 2 Cor. 3. 6. & 4. 1. & 5. 18. Eph. 3. 7. ver. 25. 1 Tim. 2. 7.

If ye continue in the faith grounded and settled: this *if* doth not import the believers' continuance in faith to depend merely upon their own free-will, or a carnal doubting of being kept to salvation, 1 Pet. i. 5, but infers that they are then reconciled to God when they do indeed persevere in the faith; implying that by reason of the seducers amongst them all and every one might not really have that sound faith they would be thought to have. Wherefore the apostle engageth them to prove their faith, whereby only they can have peace with God, Rom. v. 1, to be real, by taking care it be well founded and firm, Matt. xiii. 23, as a house built on a sure foundation, a tree well rooted, Eph. iii. 17, 18; Heb. xiii. 9. *And be not moved away from the hope of the gospel;* and be not as temporary believers which have no root, Luke viii. 13, or as those who want anchor-hold are *tossed to and fro*, Eph. iv. 14, and put off from that hope of eternal life, set before us in the gospel, which is sure and certain, Heb. vi. 18, 19, *built upon the foundation of the prophets and apostles*, Eph. ii. 20, the sweet promises of eternal life. *Which ye have heard;* not the works of vain philosophy which leave the minds of men unsettled, but the plain and solid doctrines of Christ, wherein the believers at Colosse had been instructed, ver. 7. *And which was preached to every creature which is under heaven;* and which the faithful apostles, according to the commission of Christ, had promulgated to every creature beneath the heavens, i. e. every rational creature here below, i. c. to all men, collectively, or nations in the world, as ver. 6; Matt. xxviii. 19; Mark xvi. 15. *Creature* with the Hebrews doth eminently signify man, by an antonomasia, or a synecdoche, putting the general for a particular. In the original it *is*, in all the creature; and so it may be, in all the world, *(creature* being sometimes used for the system of the world, Rom. viii. 19—21,) in opposition to Judea, i. e. in those other parts of the earth which the Greeks and Romans knew to be then inhabited: *under heaven*, which is a pleonasm, but of the greatest emphasis, as Acts iv. 12. *Whereof I Paul am made a minister;* and the more to confirm them in what he had said, he adds, of this gospel of reconciliation so spread, he was immediately called, Gal. i. 1, and constituted to be a minister for the promulgation of it amongst the Gentiles, it being, with others, most notably committed to him, 2 Cor. v. 19; 1 Tim. i. 11.

d Rom. 5. 3.
2 Cor. 7. 4.
e Eph. 3. 1, 13.
f 2 Cor. 1.5,6. Phil. 3. 10.
2 Tim. 1. 8.
& 2. 10.
g Eph. 1. 23.

24 ᵈ Who now rejoice in my sufferings ᵉ for you, and fill up ᶠ that which is behind of the afflictions of Christ in my flesh for ᵍ his body's sake, which is the Church:

Who now rejoice in my sufferings for you; he confirms his call to the ministry of the gospel from his cheerfulness in his present sufferings, so that they should not be discouraged, being it highly contented him to witness and seal his doctrine by bearing his cross for them, Rom. v. 2, 3; 2 Cor. vii. 4: see Phil. i. 14, 20; ii. 17. The Jews hated him and persecuted him because of his communion with the Greeks and other Gentiles, which occasioned his imprisonment at Rome, chap. ii. 1; iv. 3, 18; Acts xxi. 28, 29; xxvi. 17, 18; Eph. iii. 1; yet this did not deter him from his office, but he took pleasure in doing his duty. Acts v. 41; 2 Tim. ii. 10, gladly spending himself and being spent for their souls, 2 Cor. xii. 15, for their edification and consolation, 2 Cor. i. 6, 7; Phil. i. 13, 14. *And fill up; and,* the copulative, is used as causal; *fill up*, not simply, but in one's turn, implying a contradistinction betwixt what Christ suffered for the apostle, and what the apostle suffered for Christ. Christ in his rank suffered what was necessary for my redemption; now I, in my turn, (by his gift, Phil. i. 29,) undergo what afflictions are useful for his glory. He purchased salvation by his cross, I advance his kingdom and cause by my combats. *That which is behind of the afflictions of Christ in my flesh:* one learned man renders this clause, what remains concerning the afflictions for Christ in my flesh; however, if we conceive of things distinctly, we may retain our own translation, considering Paul's filling up is either, 1. With respect to Christ; so he doth not mean what Christ suffered in his own proper person during his tabernacling here; for neither Paul nor any other penman of the New Testament doth use the term *affliction*, to express the sufferings of Christ whereby he appeased God's wrath and satisfied his justice: that he finished in his own person when he gave up the ghost, John xix. 30, he perfected all completely, ver. 14, 22; nothing will be required from any believer upon that account, Rom. vi. 9, 10; Heb. x. 14; there be no remains upon that account, all was filled up by Christ himself. All can be imagined that Paul should mean in this respect, would be only from Christ's leaving an example, 1 Pet. ii. 21: q. d. As Christ hath suffered *for my* salvation, so in like manner, following him, I bear his cross, suffering for his gospel and glory. Or, 2. With respect to Paul himself: the sense is, q. d. As I have borne a great part of afflictions for the name of Christ, and in his glorious communion, 2 Cor. i. 5; Gal. vi. 17; 2 Tim. i. 8, 10; so in like manner I fill up the remains of them assigned to me a member of the mystical body, in conformity to the image of him who is the Head, Rom. viii. 18; 1 Pet. iv. 13. I do by little and little accomplish in my present sufferings (which make a part of it) the portion allotted to me in the same afflictions, which are accomplished and accomplishing in our *brethren that are in the world*, 1 Pet. v. 9, in time and degree according to God's counsel, (whereby the Head was preordained to suffer, Acts iv. 28; 1 Pet. i. 20.) which apportioned to every member what share it is to bear, till it be perfectly conformed to Christ, Phil. iii. 10, 12, 21. These sufferings as Christians, 1 Pet. iv. 13, 14, 16, (which the members undergo in their causes,) may be said to be the afflictions of Christ: (1.) Being for his cause and glory, the troubles they receive upon his account may be called his, the badges of his family and followers, Gal. vi. 17; Heb. xi. 26. (2.) Because of the union betwixt Head and members, 1 Cor. xii. 12; they being given to the whole body, the wounds of his members are his, Acts ix. 4, 16, he doth sympathize with them; but as he finished his work of proper sufferings while in the flesh, so the apostle's expression intimates here, their sufferings shall not last longer than they are in the body, they need not fear any purgatory afterwards. *For his body's sake, which is the church:* and while Paul suffered here, he adds another reason for the supporting and cheering of him, viz. the usefulness of his sufferings for the whole church, the mystical body of Christ, as ver. 18; which consideration might sweeten his bitterest afflictions, not only because it was in their service, to further their faith, that he was so persecuted, but for their edification and consolation; this was the scope of his patience, Phil. i. 12—14, to encourage those who knew his testimony to embrace the truth, 2 Tim. ii. 10. What the Rhemists and other papists infer hence, that the apostle satisfied for the sins of other believers by his sufferings, contributing to the church's treasury of satisfactions for temporary punishments, is altogether groundless. It is brutish to conclude, because he sustained afflictions for the edification of the church, that therefore he satisfied for the sins of the church; because he was spent for the Corinthians, that he answered for their faults, 2 Cor. xii. 15: he was not crucified for any, 1 Cor. i. 13. To make Paul's sufferings satisfactory is to derogate from Christ's merit; none is without sin as Christ was, and as it is necessary for him that satisfieth, Prov. xx. 9. Christ's sacrifice became expiatory, being offered by *the eternal Spirit,* Heb. ix. 14; he having borne the sins of believers in his own natural body upon the cross, and that by himself, there needs no supplements (could any be found) from others, John i. 29; Heb. i. 3, 8; 1 Pet. ii. 24; 1 John ii. 2. To conceit there is any need of human satisfactions as supplies to Christ's sufferings, is to cross the apostle's main drift here, ver. 12—14, 20—22; he was far from satisfying for himself, Phil. iii. 9, 12, and shows that *every man shall bear his own burden.* Gal. vi. 5, however he should endeavour to honour Christ, and edify his church, 2 Cor. xii. 10.

25 Whereof I am made a minister, according to ʰ the dispensation of God which is given to me for you, ‖ to fulfil the word of God;

h 1 Cor.9.17.
Gal. 2. 7.
Eph. 3. 2.
ver. 23.
‖ Or, *fully to preach the word of God,* Rom. 15. 19.

Whereof I am made a minister; see under what title he suffers for the church, because *a minister,* (in the more general acceptation of the word,) as ver. 23, not (as one of the ancients saith) to give the price of redemption, but to preach. He looked not on his apostleship as a domination, but ministration, 2 Cor. v. 18; and though in regard of his call he was an extraordinary apostle, yet he, (remembering his Master's injunction, Matt. xx. 26.) no more than Peter, did affect dominion or a lordship over Christ's heritage, 2 Cor. i. 24; 1 Pet. v. 1—3, according to his singular and eminent call to be a minister and a witness, Acts xxvi. 16. As he doth elsewhere make mention of the *minister of God*, 2 Cor. vi. 4; 1 Thess. iii. 2; of the New Testament, gospel, word, reconciliation, Acts vi. 4; 2 Cor. iii. 6; v. 18, 19; Eph. iii. 7; of Jesus Christ and of the Lord, Rom. xv. 8; 1 Cor. iv. 1; Eph. vi. 20; 1 Tim. iv. 6; so he doth here, by reason of the union betwixt the Head and the body, own himself to be constituted a minister of the church, which some, of a lower rank, like not now to be called. *According to the dispensation of God;* and that by Divine vouchsafement and commandment, being called from persecution of the church to this ministry, Acts ix. 15, 16; 1 Cor. iv. 1; 2 Cor. v. 19; Eph. i. 1. Yea, and also for them at Colosse, who, being of the Gentiles, were in his commission, according to the gift of the grace of God given to him, Eph. iii. 7. *Which is given to me for you, to fulfil the word of God;* fully to preach the word of God amongst them, as well as to the Romans and others, Rom. xv. 19, and so to fulfil the prophecy, Zech. ii. 11, for the calling of the Gentiles by the promulgation of the gospel amongst them, Acts xxii. 21; Rom. i. 5; xi. 13; 1 Tim. ii. 7; and so fulfilling God's word, by fully expounding the whole doctrine of salvation amongst them, and promoting of it to the end of his life.

26 Even *i* the mystery which hath been hid from ages and from generations, *k* but now is made manifest to his saints:

i Rom. 16.25. 1 Cor. 2. 7. Eph. 3. 9.
k Mat.13.11. 2 Tim. 1. 10.

Even the mystery which hath been hid from ages and from generations; viz. that holy secret of godliness, chap. ii. 2, 3; iv. 3; Matt. xiii. 11; Rom. xvi. 25, 26; 1 Cor. ii. 7; Eph. iii. 3, 4, 6, 8. 9, 10; see 1 Tim. iii. 16; Rev. xiv. 6; which doth not consist in *beggarly elements*, Gal. iv. 9, or vain speculations, which these Colossians are cautioned to avoid, chap. ii. 8, however varnished; but is to them who are saved, *the power of God*, Rom. i. 16; 1 Cor. i. 18, 19, and *the wisdom of God*, 1 Cor. i. 24, which lay hid in God before the world, 1 Cor. ii. 7; 2 Tim. i. 9; Tit. i. 2; 1 Pet. i. 20: yea, and after God had to our first parents, and so to his people the Jews, given some glimpse of this mystery, which yet the Gentiles of several ages were ignorant of, and many of the Jews, yea, the most knowing of them did not, for many generations, know that the Gentiles without circumcision, &c. were to be admitted into the church, Acts x. 28: the prophets were very inquisitive to know the meaning of it, but yet they also were much in the dark, 1 Cor. ii. 9; 1 Pet. i. 10, 11; yea, the angels did not know this hidden mystery, till revealed by the church, Eph. i. 10. *But now is made manifest to his saints;* but now God *that revealeth secrets*, Dan. ii. 28, hath opened his bosom counsel about this affair most clearly, so that his glory, by those that really fear him, may be seen with open face as in a glass through Christ, Matt. xiii. 11; Mark iv. 11; John viii. 47; xv. 15; Acts xvi. 14; 1 Cor. ii. 10, 16; 2 Cor. iii. 18; all necessary to salvation being made conspicuous and clear to them, 1 Pet. i. 9.

27 *l* To whom God would make known what *is* *m* the riches of the glory of this mystery among the Gentiles; which is Christ ||in you, *n* the hope of glory:

l 2 Cor. 2.14.
m Rom. 9. 23. Eph.1.7. & 3. 8.
|| Or, *among you*.
n 1 Tim.1.1.

To whom God would make known; he refers the manifestation purely to God's good will and pleasure, as Christ himself doth, Matt. xi. 26, 27; Luke x. 21; so in the like case, Rom. ix. 18; that having mentioned saints, none might conceit it was for foreseen faith, but the Colossians might value their privilege, reverently receive that grace which was not given to all: in short, to restrain curiosity why God would not do it otherwise or sooner, he cuts the knots of all questions, only by signifying his sovereign pleasure, he would make it known to them; elsewhere, this *mystery of his will, according to his good pleasure*, Eph. i. 9, which was not to be touched till he thought meet to make it known. *What is the riches of the glory of this mystery among the Gentiles:* some refer *the glory* to *mystery*, as glorious mystery, because it lets forth Divine glory, and promiseth it to believers, Luke ii. 14; others, and the most, rather to *riches*, and that either as its epithet, (ver. 11,) the glorious riches of this mystery, or noting the subject, for salvation of the church amongst the Gentiles, Eph. i. 18; iii. 7, 8. It is usual with the apostle to use the word *riches* to set forth abundance, Rom. ii. 4; xi. 33; Eph. i. 7: here, for the praise of the gospel, he would signify a very great and most abundant glory, far surpassing any former ministration, 2 Cor. iii. 8, 18. In the law those riches (Eph. ii. 7) were not only imperfectly and obscurely discovered, but scatteredly with broken beams, as the sun in water when the water is disturbed; one attribute shining out in one work, another in another; but now the harmony of the Divine attributes in man's redemption shines out most fully, clearly, and gloriously, contracted in Christ, who is the object and revealer of the mystery by his Spirit, the glory whereof breaks forth with much more splendour amongst the Gentiles, Rom. xv. 7—9; 1 Cor. ii. 10; 2 Cor. iii. 9, 18; all glory before was but a shadow to this, chap. ii. 17; 2 Cor. iii. 18; Gal. iii. 1; Heb. x. 1. *Which is Christ in you;* which is Christ, amongst, for, or *in* them, i. e. who not only was preached amongst them, but whom they possessed, and who dwelt in them by faith, Eph. iii. 17; the revelation being accompanied with the power of the Spirit in the translating them by his glorious power from the kingdom of darkness into his kingdom, ver. 13; Luke xvii. 21; Gal. ii. 20; iv. 19; Eph. iii. 5, 7. *The hope of glory;* so is not only the object, 1 Tim. i. 1, but the ground of their expectation of glory, he in whom the mystery begins and ends, 1 Tim. iii. 16; out of whom all are hopeless of being happy, Eph. ii. 12, and in whom all have *strong consolation*, Heb. vi. 18.

28 Whom we preach, *o* warning every man, and teaching every man in all wisdom; *p* that we may present every man perfect in Christ Jesus:

o Acts 20.30, 27, 31.
p 2 Cor. 11.2. Eph. 5. 27. ver. 22.

Whom we preach: here he shows that the subject of his and other ministers' preaching was Christ, (as he had before described him,) in whom alone hope of glory was to be had, Acts iv. 12; 1 Cor. ii. 2; Gal. v. 4; 1 John i. 3. *Warning every man, and teaching every man in all wisdom;* the manner of it was by admonishing and instructing all, in all the Christian wisdom that Christ required, that they might avoid sin and do their duty. He means *all* collectively, not distributively; of the generals of each, not each one of those generals; excluding none from the communion of so great a benefit, having no acceptation of nations or persons, making no exception of any condition, but inviting all men to Christ, holding forth this light of the gospel to whosoever would receive it, while God did vouchsafe life and strength to them, in the most taking way, Acts xx. 21, 27, 31; Rom. i. 14—16; 1 Tim. iii. 2; 2 Tim. ii. 24; iii. 16; iv. 2; Tit. i. 9. *That we may present every man perfect in Christ Jesus;* and the end and aim he and others of his mind had in preaching of this matter in such a manner was the same with Christ's, ver. 22, to put them into such an estate by their labours that they might, through Christ, appear at a throne of grace without confusion, 2 Cor. xi. 2; Phil. iii. 12, 15; Heb. v. 14.

29 *q* Whereunto I also labour, *r* striving *s* according to his working, which worketh in me mightily.

q 1Cor.15.10.
r ch. 2. 1.
s Eph. 1. 19. & 3. 7, 20.

To perform which, saith he, I earnestly endeavour and take pains to weariness, as a husbandman, 2 Tim. ii. 6, contending as one in an agony, 1 Thess. v. 12, by his grace which was with me (1 Cor. xv. 10) in power; not by my own strength or wisdom to do or suffer, but by his effectual aids, enabling me for his service with might, ver. 11; Rom. xv. 15—21; 1 Cor. ix. 25—27; Eph. i. 19, 20; iii. 7; Phil. iv. 13.

CHAP. II

Paul testifieth his solicitude for the churches which had not seen him, that they might be united in love, and attain a perfect knowledge of the Christian revelation, 1—3, *not being seduced from their stedfastness in the faith,* 4—7, *nor corrupted through philosophy and human traditions,* 8. *He showeth that they were already complete in Christ, having attained the true circumcision figured in baptism,* 9—12; *that God had quickened them with Christ, and both abolished the law of ordinances, that was against them,* 13, 14, *and also spoiled principalities and powers,* 15. *He therefore urgeth them not to submit to legal ordinances, which were but a shadow of Christ; nor to the worship of angels, and other vain practices of human devising,* 16—23.

FOR I would that ye knew what great ∥ ᵃ conflict I have for you, and *for* them at Laodicea, and *for* as many as have not seen my face in the flesh;

∥ Or, *fear,* or, *care.*
a ch. 1. 29.
Phil. 1. 30.
1 Thess. 2. 2.

For; this causal particle refers to what he had said just before in the former chapter. *I would that ye knew what great conflict I have for you;* the certainty of which truth, for the evidence of his unfeigned affection to them, he heartily wishes they might be certified what a combat he sustained for them, by reason of that opposition he met with in his ministerial labours. This filled him with inward fears and cares, and encompassed him with outward troubles, as 2 Cor. xi. 23—30; 2 Tim. ii. 10, wherein he addressed himself to God for them by earnest prayers, as chap. iv. 12; 2 Thess. i. 11, desiring the assistance of their prayers, Rom. xv. 30; Heb. xiii. 18: these, with his travels, writings, &c., might well be called a *conflict,* Phil. i. 30. *And for them at Laodicea;* which he had not only for the saints at Colosse, but for their neighbours, liable also to the impression of the same or the like seducers, at Laodicea, definitely, to whom he designed this Epistle might be imparted, chap. iv. 16. *And for as many as have not seen my face in the flesh;* and indefinitely, for as many Christians, especially in Phrygia, as had not seen him bodily present amongst them, or heard him preach with a lively voice; whether, because it is said he twice passed through all Phrygia, where Colosse and Laodicea were situate, Acts xvi. 6; xviii. 23, he had been personally at these cities, is not determinable from the copulative here, (which possibly may be used as a particle to separate these from those who had not conversed with him,) neither is it of much importance. It should seem Paul was acquainted with Philemon, (a Colossian or Laodicean,) his wife and family, Philem. 1, 2.

b 2 Cor. 1. 6.
c ch. 3. 14.

2 ᵇ That their hearts might be comforted, ᶜ being knit together in love, and unto all riches of the full assurance of understanding, ᵈ to the acknowledgement of the mystery of God, and of the Father, and of Christ;

d Phil. 3. 8.
ch. 1. 9.

That their hearts might be comforted: whereas false teachers did endeavour to adulterate the Christian institution, the striving of the apostle's holy soul here was, as in the former chapter, ver. 28, to this end, that they might be complete and established Christians to the last. *Being knit together in love;* and as a proper means conducible to this good purpose, he would have them be joined or compacted together, be all of a piece, in the affection and exercise of love. *And unto all riches of the full assurance of understanding;* and to attain to a well-grounded, powerful, evangelical faith, which he sets forth livelily by an elegant increase of words, both in regard of the acts and the object of it, which is called a mystery to be believed, 1 Tim. iii. 9, upon its being revealed. The sense of that which he heartily desires is that they might have, 1. All abundance of understanding with full satisfaction in these main principles of the gospel they are called to assent to. Signifying faith is no blind, but a certain intelligent persuasion; to distinguish it from uncertain opinion, John vi. 69; Rom. iv. 21; 1 Thess. i. 5; Heb. vi. 11; x. 22. *To the acknowledgment:* 2. An inward consent, and vital owning, a cordial embracing of the fundamental truths of the gospel, Eph. iv. 13, 14; Heb. vi. 1, in opposition to those vain speculations and traditions which deluded many. He calls this *the mystery of God,* or a Divine mystery, (no human invention,) as before, chap. i. 26, 27; and so vindicates the dignity of faith and the excellency of the gospel, asserting it to be a mystery of God, not only as the object, but revealer of it; for the Father reveals Christ, chap. i. 27; Matt. xvi. 17; Eph. iii. 3, as Christ doth the Father, Matt. xi. 27; John i. 18. Whereas it is said, *and of the Father, and of Christ;* this first *and* here needs not be rendered as a copulative, but as exegetical, or as expletive, and may be read, even, or to wit, or both, as (a learned man observes) the Greeks and Latins usually do when the copulative is to be repeated, the name of God referring commonly to the Father and the Son; as elsewhere, *God, even the Father,* chap. i. 3; 1 Cor. xv. 24; 2 Cor. xi. 31; Eph. i. 3; Phil. iv. 20. So the former *and* here may be read; q. d. The mystery not of God, abstractedly considered; but, I would have you be united and all one, in the acknowledging of the whole mystery of God, i. e. both of the Father and of Christ.

3 ∥ ᵉ In whom are hid all the treasures of wisdom and knowledge.

∥ Or, *Wherein.*
e 1 Cor. 1. 24.
& 2. 6, 7. Eph. 1. 8. ch. 1. 9.

In whom: this may relate either to the Divine mystery, wherein are in abundance all necessary doctrines to consolation and salvation stored up, respecting the foregoing verse; compare 1 Cor. ii. 7; Eph. iii. 3, 4; in opposition to the vain show of wisdom seducers did boast of; or, (as the most ancient and modern take it,) to Christ, the immediate antecedent: *in whom,* (as we render it,) i. e. in Christ, considered either, 1. As the object, which being rightly known, we may have all wisdom and perfect knowledge to salvation: he speaks not here of all that Christ knoweth, he reveals not all that in the gospel to us, but what we must know of him that we may be saved. Or, 2. As the subject, because *all the treasures of wisdom* in order to salvation, are not only known and found out in Christ, but also *are hid,* do dwell and abide in him as the fountain, what he can give to us for our consolation and perfection. It had been little pertinent for Paul to have said that all these *deep things of God* (1 Cor. ii. 10) were known to our Lord; but that they are found in him, do dwell in him, are all stored up, displayed, and set forth in him, to be seen *through the veil, that is to say, his flesh,* Heb. x. 20, or the infirmity of his cross. The series of the apostle's discourse, comparing ver. 8 and 9, shows it to be thus understood of Christ as the subject and fountain of all saving wisdom, in opposition to the comments of human wisdom which the false doctors did boast of. Continuing the metaphor, he shows from what fund the treasures of saving knowledge may be drawn: by *treasures* intimating the excellency and abundance thereof; there was some store in the tabernacle of Moses, but very small compared to the abundance certainly to be found in Christ, all else of no worth to the excellency of the knowledge of Christ for consolation, ver. 2; Phil. iii. 8: things to be believed and practised are, by way of eminency, Christian *wisdom and knowledge.* The *treasures* of which, how and when hid, is to be well considered, because in our translation, and in almost all others, the Greek word we render *hid* is by trajection put next to the relative *whom,* whereas it is indeed in the original the last word in the verse, and seems to be expressive rather of what was hid before Christ than what is hid in him. For, as a learned man saith, hidden treasures, as such, seem to be like hidden music, of no regard; or like the hidden talent, Luke xix. 20. It not being so easy to think that the apostle in this Epistle teaches, that the secrets which had lain hid from the wise men of the world, in the ages past, now were made bare, brought into light, and made known even to babes by Christ, chap. i. 26, 27, with Luke x. 21; and having just before, ver. 2, spoken of the understanding and acknowledgment of the mystery of the Father and the Son, what should the riches of glory to the knowledge of the mystery be, but the treasures of wisdom now revealed, heretofore hid, of which continuedly a little after he says that all the fulness of the Godhead dwells in him bodily, i. e. personally, not in a shadow, as it were hid in a cloud, but in flesh that may be really seen and touched? So that it should seem best to retain *hid* as it is placed in the Greek, to this sense; q. d. In Christ are, and dwell in the greatest fulness, all the treasures of wisdom, hid under the law, which are therefore called a mystery, secret, or hidden thing from ages and generations, chap. i. 26, 27, now made manifest to his saints, they are now not hid in Christ, but made known amongst the Gentiles as God willed. Not then hidden riches, i. e. treasures of wisdom and knowledge of this mystery as of hid treasure, but out of Christ, and before Christ amongst the Jews: for

Christ himself is that mystery, chap. iv. 3, not hid after his appearance, but manifested, and manifesting the Father, John i. 18. However, if any will rather choose to read, as if in Christ were at present hid all treasures, it is to be understood, stored up, not exposed to the view of every eye, being as in a rich cabinet, not to keep them from being known to men, but rather to make them more precious and desirable. For Christ came when sent of his Father to spread this heavenly wealth. He is the Sun of righteousness, John i. 9: the unbelieving must thank themselves if, where he is truly preached, he be hid to them, and his arm be revealed but to a few, Isa. liii. 1; 2 Cor. iv. 3, 4: it is their own blinding that they do not savingly discern what is displayed in Christ. Wherefore both may be true in divers respects: 1. Consider the thing in itself, objectively; so treasures of wisdom are evidently laid up in Jesus Christ, and manifested upon his appearance, 1 Tim. iii. 16; Tit. ii. 11. But, 2. With respect to the eyes and perceptions of men, subjectively, as naturally obscured and corrupted by sin; so natural men, or mere animal men, perceive not in Christ the riches of wisdom and knowledge which are in him as our Mediator, when they look upon him as having no beauty or comeliness for which they should desire him, Isa. liii. 2; he, as crucified, being to the Jews *a stumbling-block* and to the Gentiles *foolishness*, when he is to those of them who are called, *the power of God, and the wisdom of God*, 1 Cor. i. 23, 24. The Lutherans' inference hence, that omniscience agrees to Christ's human nature, is altogether inconsequent; both (as before) because the apostle's business here is not to acquaint us what Christ himself knoweth, but what is to be known by us, which may be found treasured up in him. *Treasures* here in him not being considered absolutely, but comparatively to all the knowledge of men and angels. Yet, from a supposal of an infinite knowledge in Christ, who is God-man in one person, it followeth not that the soul of his human nature knoweth all things.

f Rom. 16. 18. 2 Cor. 11. 13. Eph. 4. 14. & 5. 6. ver. 8, 18.

4 And this I say, ᶠlest any man should beguile you with enticing words.

And this I say; here he suggests the ground of his insisting upon the excellent treasures of the saving knowledge of Christ, and the ample description of him. *Lest any man should beguile you;* to this end, that he might fortify them against delusion by paralogisms, or sophistical and false reasonings, fallacious arguing, (as the word notes, James i. 22,) under a colourable pretence and *show of wisdom*, ver. 8, 18, 23. *With enticing words;* set off with rhetorical suasions and embellishments, intimating the prevalency of such blandishments, with fair words and good speeches to seduce the simple, if the heart were not established with grace, Rom. xvi. 18; Eph. iv. 14; v. 6; Heb. xiii. 9; and therefore, esteeming the excellent knowledge of Christ, and being found in him, Phil. iii. 8, 9, they should beware of whatever, under a show of religion, is introduced to seduce them from *the simplicity that is in Christ*, 2 Cor. xi. 3.

g 1 Cor. 5. 3. 1 Thes. 2. 17.

5 For ᵍ though I be absent in the flesh, yet am I with you in the spirit, joying

h 1 Cor. 14. 40. i 1 Pet. 5. 9.

and beholding ʰyour order, and the ⁱstedfastness of your faith in Christ.

For though I be absent in the flesh, yet am I with you in the spirit: to prevent any surmise that his distance at Rome might take him off from minding of them at Colosse, he shows that the great affection he bare to them did oblige him to interest himself in all their concerns, *(the care of all the churches* being incumbent on him, 2 Cor. xi. 28,) and therefore that his bodily confinement at Rome did not hinder his presence with them in spirit. Not that we can conclude, that by some extraordinary operation of the Holy Ghost God gave him now and then a clear prospect of what they did, as he did to Elisha of Gehazi's behaviour, 2 Kings v. 26; and to Ezekiel in Babylon of the secret actions of the Jews in Jerusalem; but that he was with them as with the Corinthians, 1 Cor. v. 3, when distant in body his thoughts and affections were exercised about them. *Joying and beholding your order;* as it follows there is moving of fears lest they should be insnared, so of joy understanding their *order*, i. e. their good estate, constitution, and consent in orderly walking and discipline, 1 Cor. xiv.

40; 1 Thess. iv. 1; v. 14. *And the stedfastness of your faith in Christ;* and the firmament of their faith in Christ, it being (if genuine) as firm as the firmament itself; stable as the heavens and heavenly bodies, keeping their constant stations and regular courses, and admitting nothing heterogeneous into them: all heavenly truths are as fixed stars in this orb. Seeing all grace, because Divine, hath an establishing property; so faith coming from the eternal mountains, all graces being connected in faith, which is a kind of firmament to them all, it comes to pass that faith, in actuating any one grace, gives a strength and further growth to every other grace.

6 ᵏ As ye have therefore received Christ Jesus the Lord, *so* walk ye in him:

k 1 Thess. 4.1. Jude 3.

Having cautioned them against sophistical seducers, and commended them for that order and sound faith he understood to be amongst them, he here infers an exhortation to continuance in both, especially in the latter, with respect to the person of Christ, according as he had before described him; for he doth not say, As ye have received the doctrine of Christ, or concerning Christ, but, *As ye have received Christ* himself, as John i. 11, 12; 1 John v. 11, 12, in whom is all treasured up for salvation. He adds not only *Jesus*, (who came to save his people from their sins,) but *the Lord*, intimating they should not therefore suffer any rules of faith or life to be imposed upon them by any other whatsoever, but should be persuaded to abide *in him*, whom they had embraced, and order their conversation according to his mind, 1 Thess. iv. 1, knowing that he is *the way, the truth, and the life*, John xiv. 6; being led by his Spirit, and deriving virtue to go on in this orderly walk and persevere in the faith.

7 ˡRooted and built up in him, and stablished in the faith, as ye have been taught, abounding therein with thanksgiving.

l Eph. 2. 21, 22. & 3. 17. ch. 1. 23.

Rooted and built up in him; showing how they should abide and persevere in the faith, by continuing in him as branches do in the root, John xv. 4, and resting upon him as a building upon the foundation, Isa. xxviii. 16; 1 Cor. iii. 11; Eph. ii. 22. *And stablished in the faith;* and being firm and settled in the faith, as 1 Pet. v. 10: he adds this, not only to clear the metaphorical expressions before, but to show that they should be growing stronger as to the internal habit, Psal. xcii. 13, 14. He repeats as it were in a parenthesis, *as ye have been taught;* upon the matter, the same with *as ye have received Christ* in the former verse; for greater caution to them, who might be apt to have itching ears, that they should not be listening to any novel doctrines, but abide in the faith of Christ. *Abounding therein with thanksgiving;* setting down with themselves, according to the superabounding grace they had, Rom. v. 20, with 1 Cor. iv. 8, to abound and increase therein, 1 Cor. xv. 58; 2 Pet. i. 8; having herein all the saving knowledge desirable, without need of the addition of aught any other way; being thankful to God that he had revealed such a Christ, his Christ, to them, for they could not have a better or another.

8 ᵐ Beware lest any man spoil you through philosophy and vain deceit, after ⁿthe tradition of men, after the ‖ ᵒ rudiments of the world, and not after Christ.

m Jer. 29. 8. Rom. 16. 17. Eph. 5. 6. ver. 18. Heb. 13. 9. n Matt. 15.2. Gal. 1. 14. ver. 22. ‖ Or, *elements.* o Gal. 4. 3, 9, ver. 20.

Beware: the apostle, after his exhortation, considering their danger from seducing spirits lying in wait to deceive by their sleight and craftiness, 1 Tim. iv. 1, 2, doth here reinforce and enlarge his caution he had before suggested, ver. 4, to engage to a heedful avoidance of all seduction from Christ. *Lest any man spoil you;* lest their souls should be made a prey, and they be carried for a spoil by those worst of robbers that beset Christ's fold, 2 Cor. xi. 20; Gal. vi. 13. *Through philosophy;* either through the abuse of true philosophy in bringing the mystery of Christ under the tribunal of shallow reason, or rather through erroneous, though curious, speculations of some philosophers, as Plato, Pythagoras, Hesiod, &c. then in vogue, which the Gnostics afterwards (who, thinking themselves enriched with the notions of other heretics, would be thought the only knowing persons) dressed up Christ with, not like himself. Their philosophy being a falsely so called science or knowledge, 1 Tim. vi. 20. whatever show of wisdom it might seem to carry along with it, ver. 23. it was not really profitable; but a *vain deceit*, or seduction, as several take the next clause appositively, and the conjunction expositively; yet, if we consider what follows, we may understand another general imposture, viz. superstition, seeing *vain deceit, after the tradition of men*, is so like that superstition our Saviour doth rebuke in the Pharisees, Matt. xv. 9, several branches of which the apostle doth afterward in this chapter dispute against, ver. 16—23: superstition might well be called *deceit*, from the cheat it puts upon men, and the notation of the Greek word, which imports a withdrawing men from the way. Christ, and from his way of worship prescribed in his word; and *vain* it is as well as a deceit, since it is empty and unprofitable, not accompanied with God's blessing, nor conducing to the pleasing of him, but the provoking of him, Psal. cvi. 29, 43. Being led by no other rule than *the tradition of men*, which is the same with the precepts of men, Mark vii. 8. which God likes not, Isa. viii. 20; xxviii. 13; John xx. 31; Acts xxvi. 22; 2 Tim. iii. 15, 16; he would not give place to human traditions in his house, nor to *the rudiments of the world*, (in allusion to grammar, wherein the letters are the elements or rudiments of all literature,) i. e. the ceremonies of the Mosaical law, containing a kind of elementary instruction, for that seems to be the apostle's meaning, comparing this verse with the 20th and 21st of this chapter, and other places, Gal. iii. 24, these being but corporeal, *carnal*, and sensible *ordinances*, suitable to *a worldly sanctuary*. Heb. ix. 1, 10. not to be imposed in that spiritual one which Christ hath set up, John iv. 23, 24; Gal. v. 2. Whatsoever philosophical colours or Pharisaical paint they might appear in, they are *not after Christ*: we say a false picture of a man is not after the man, being not taken from or resembling his person, but clean another; such descriptions of him, as were not taken from the life and truth that was in him. And therefore he who is Head of his church, and likes not to be misshaped or misrepresented, will not accept of homage from those of his own house, in a livery that he hath not given order for, Lev. x. 1; Jer. vii. 31; 2 Cor. v. 9. how specious soever it may be in the wisdom of this world and the princes thereof, 1 Cor. ii. 6, 7.

p John 1. 14. ch. 1. 19. 9 For ᵖin him dwelleth all the fulness of the Godhead bodily.

For; the causal particle induceth this as an argument to enforce the caution immediately foregoing, against those who did seek to draw from Christ by philosophy, as well as urging the ceremonial law; else the apostle's reasoning were not cogent unless against both. *In him;* it is evident that the Lord Jesus Christ himself, whom he had described and but just now named, is the subject, the person of whom he speaks, and in whom is seated, and unto whom he attributes, what followeth, chap. i. 19; John i. 4; 1 Tim. iv. 16. He doth not say, in his doctrine, whatever Socinians cavil, as if they would render the apostle absurd, and not to agree with himself in what he asserts of Christ's person before (as hath been showed) and after in the context. It is plain this relative *him*, respects not only ver. 8, but ver. 11, &c. in whom the believing Colossians are said to be *complete* as their *Head*, both in the former chapter, and soon after in this. Would it not be absurd to say, Christ's doctrine is the head of angels? we are crucified in the doctrine of Christ? buried and quickened together with his doctrine? the hand-writing of ordinances was nailed to the cross of doctrine? Is a doctrine the head of principalities and powers? can a doctrine be buried in baptism? &c. To silence all the earth, that they should not restrain it to Christ's doctrine only, what he asserts of his person, Paul, after Christ had been several years in heaven, put it in the present tense, *dwelleth*, not dwelt, (as 2 Tim. i. 5,) in regard of the person eternally the same, Heb. xiii. 8; for his argument had not been cogent, to contain Christians in the faith of Christ, and their duty to him, to have alleged, in the doctrine of Christ now in heaven hath dwelt all the fulness of the Godhead bodily (could propriety of speech have allowed it); but from the other respect, because in their very flesh (the body of Christ, now an inhabitant of the heavens) the very Godhead, in the whole fulness thereof, personally, from the moment of his incarnation, doth yet dwell. What will not the faithful perform and work out with their utmost faith, that they may never suffer themselves to be rent from spiritual and mystical union with him, in whom they understand that even they themselves shall be also divinely filled, ver. 10, i. e. in their measure be made *partakers of the Divine nature*, 2 Pet. i. 4. *Dwelleth* imports more than a transient stay for a few minutes, or a little while, even abiding in him constantly and for ever, as dwelling most usually notes, 2 Cor. vi. 16. That which doth thus perpetually abide in him, as denominated after the human nature, is *all the fulness of the Godhead*, viz. that rich and incomprehensible abundance of perfections, whereof the supreme and adorable nature is full; so that indeed there is not at all any perfection or excellency in the Divine nature but is found abiding in him. And after no common or ordinary way, but by a hypostatical or personal union of the Godhead with the manhood in Christ; which is not by way of mixture, confusion, conversion, or any other mutation; but *bodily*, to exclude that inhabitation which is only by extrinsical denomination. It being an adverb, doth denote the manner as well as the subject; wherefore when he speaks of the temple of his body, John ii. 21, that doth not fully reach the apostle's meaning here: but it must be expounded personally, since in the Greek that which signifies with us a body, and so our English word *body*, is put for a person, Rom. xii. 1; 2 Cor. v. 10; Rev. xviii. 13: somebody or nobody, i. e. some person or no person. There is a presence of the Godhead general, by essence and power; particular, in the prophets and apostles working miracles: gracious, in all sanctified ones; glorious, in heaven, in *light which no man can approach unto*, 1 Tim. vi. 16; relative, in the church visible and ordinances, typically under the law, and symbolically in the sacraments: but all these dwellings, or being present in the creature, fall short of that in the text, viz. *bodily*, connoting the personal habitation of the *Deity* in, and union of it with, the humanity of Christ, so close, and strait, and intimate, that the Godhead inhabiting and the manhood inhabited make but one and the same person, even as the reasonable soul and body in man make but one man. The way of the presence of the Deity with the humanity of Christ is above all those manners of the presence of God with angels and men. The Godhead dwells in him personally, in them in regard of assistance and energy; Godhead notes the truth of it; Christ was not only partaker of the Divine nature, 2 Pet. i. 4, but the very Godhead dwells in him: it is not only the Divinity (as the Socinians, following the Vulgar Latin in this, would have it) but the Deity, the very nature and essence of God. Now it is observable, though in God himself Divinity and Deity be indeed the same, Rom. i. 20, and may differ only from the manner of our conception and contemplation; yet here. when the enemies to Christ's Deity might by their cavilling make more use of the word Divinity, (as when the soul of man is said to be a divine thing,) to insinuate as if it here noted only the Divine will exclusive to the other attributes, (which exclusion the term *all* doth significantly prevent,) the apostle puts in Deity or *Godhead*. Then lest Christ might (as by the Arians) be deemed a secondary God, or (as some since) a made God, inferior to the Father, he saith *the fulness of the Godhead*, which speaks him perfect God, coequal with the Father: further, connoting a numerical sameness of essence betwixt the Godhead of the Father and the Son, *all* the fulness of the Godhead dwelleth in him. There is not one fulness of the Father and another of the Son. but one and the same singular Godhead in both, John x. 30. The fulness of the manhood in Adam and Eve were not numerically the same, but the Godhead of the Father and the Son is: yet is not the manhood of Christ co-extended and commensurate with the Godhead (as some Lutherans conceit); but where the manhood is, or Christ as man is, or hath his existence, there the fulness of the Godhead dwells bodily: so that this fulness is extended as the manhood only in which it is, and not as far as the Deity in which this derivative fulness is not as in its seat, though it be all originally from it, but inherently or subjectively in Christ.

10 ᑫAnd ye are complete in him, q John 1. 16.

^r^ Eph. 1. 20, 21. 1 Pet. 3. 22.
^s^ ch. 1. 16.

^r^which is the head of all ^s^principality and power :

And ye; ye saints and holy brethren, chap. i. 2, who have received Christ, chap. ii. 6, 7, and so are mystically united to him, in whom dwelleth all fulness (as you have heard); being in him, having one Spirit with him, as members with the head, Rom. viii. 1, 9; Eph. i. 23, *are complete;* are implete, or filled, and so mediately and causally complete from the all-fulness that is in your Head, yet not immediately and properly complete with it (as some have been apt to think). But *in him* ye have that completeness and perfection which is reckoned and made over to you and accepted for you to justification, so that *of his fulness* ye receive, *and grace for grace,* John i. 16; 1 Cor. i. 30; 2 Cor. v. 21; Eph. i. 6; Phil. iii. 9; derive in and from him *all spiritual blessings,* Eph. i. 3; so that every one hath *grace sufficient,* 2 Cor. xii. 9, to do all things incumbent on him, through Christ strengthening him, Phil. iv. 13. It is true there is here in this state no being complete or perfect actually, as to glorification, yet, virtually and seminally, that may in a sort be said of true believers, not only in regard of their Head, but in regard of their certain hope of being saved in Christ, yea, and indeed as to the earnest, the seed and root of it, having already that life which shall never have an end, John iii. 36; iv. 14; Rom. v. 2; Eph. iv. 30; 2 Thess. ii. 13; Heb. ix. 15; x. 14; 1 Pet. i. 3, 4; 1 John v. 12. *Which is the head of all principality and power:* the apostle, for consolation of the saints, and in opposition to those who did endeavour a withdrawing from Christ to the worshipping of angels, ver. 18, doth further infer, from the personal union, the dignity of the human nature of Christ, in regard of the good angels, which are here meant by *principality and power,* by reason of their excellency by nature and grace, and their authority delegated to them by God over other creatures, Matt. xxiv. 36; 2 Cor. xi. 14; 1 Tim. v. 21. Christ having the fulness of the Godhead dwelling in him bodily, is Head unto the good angels in regard of his excellency and eminency above them, who are far below him in perfection, Eph. i. 21; Heb. i. 4; the best of them are *ministering spirits* and *subject to him,* and so under his authority and at his command, Matt. xiii. 41; xvi. 27; xxiv. 31; Eph. iii. 10; Heb. i. 14; 1 Pet. iii. 22; Rev. i. 1; xxii. 16.

^t^ Deut. 10. 16. & 30. 6.
Jer. 4. 4.
Rom. 2. 29.
Phil. 3. 3.
^u^ Rom. 6. 6.
Eph. 4. 22.
ch. 3. 8, 9.

11 In whom also ye are ^t^circumcised with the circumcision made without hands, in ^u^putting off the body of the sins of the flesh by the circumcision of Christ :

In whom also ye are circumcised with the circumcision made without hands: he removes what they who are addicted to superstition might suggest, as if there were somewhat defective to a completeness in Christ, by showing there was no need of any addition to what he required in the gospel; for that they might most plausibly urge of circumcision, as being the seal of the old covenant, and an obligation to the whole law, Gal. v. 3, which some pressed as necessary to salvation, Acts xv. 1, 24, he here shows was altogether needless now, that they were sanctified and had the thing signified by it, the circumcision of the heart, Rom. ii. 28, 29; Phil. iii. 3, and were complete in Christ without it; yea, the urging of that and other ceremonies now, was a pernicious error, tending to annihilate the cross of Christ, and overthrow the whole mystery of his grace. It is true it was appointed to the Jews, a figure of a thing absent; they therefore who retain that figure after the coming of Christ, deny that to be complete which it doth figure, and so abolish the presence of the truth; by stickling for the shadow, they let go the substance, viz. the circumcision not made by the operation of man, but of God; not with the knife of Moses, but the word of Christ, *sharper than any two-edged sword,* Heb. iv. 12 : and if we compare this with the verse following, and Phil. iii. 3, the apostle intimates that baptism is the same to us Christians which circumcision was to the Jews; and that is often ascribed to the external administration, that is only the internal operation of the Spirit, as Rom. vi. 3, 4; Gal. iii. 27, 28; Tit. iii. 5; 1 Pet. iii. 21. Now though there was during the shadow of it, Heb. x. 1, under the Old Testament, the circumcision of the heart, as well as under the New, Deut. x. 16; xxx. 6; Jer. iv. 4; yet under the New Testament Christ the substance (who was only before in the promise) being now exhibited, having abolished the old symbol and instituted baptism in the room of it; that with the hands in the flesh, Eph. ii. 11, which they who *received not the promise,* i. e. the Messiah promised, used, Heb. xi. 39, was to be no more urged, now the benefit by the merit of his obedience unto the death of the cross, whereby he circumciseth from sin, might be enjoyed, as was signified by baptism, appointed to this end, Matt. xxviii. 19 ; Acts ii. 38; Rom. vi. 3, 4; Gal. iii. 27; 1 Pet. iii. 21. *In putting off the body of the sins of the flesh :* hence he doth illustrate this spiritual circumcision by describing the parts of it, beginning with the mortification of the old man, corrupted nature, containing not only the body and senses, but the soul tainted with the defilements of sin, chap. iii. 5; Rom. vi. 6; Gal. v. 19—21, 24; Eph. iv. 22. The body of sins which do mostly exert themselves in the flesh, every member and power while unregenerate being active in the committing of sin, till the new man be put on, Eph. iv. 24, and the dominion of it be subdued; not by any natural part which a man hath of himself for that purpose, but *by the circumcision of Christ,* not properly that whereby he himself was circumcised in the flesh the eighth day, but that which he hath indispensably required to have admission into his kingdom, John iii. 3, and which he himself is the worker of, doth procure by his merit, and effect by his Spirit, which all the suasion of the sublimest philosophers, and devotion of superstitious ones, cannot do.

12 ^x^ Buried with him in baptism, wherein also ^y^ ye are risen with *him* through ^z^the faith of the operation of God, ^a^who hath raised him from the dead.

^x^ Rom. 6. 4.
^y^ ch. 3. 1.
^z^ Eph. 1. 19. & 3. 7.
^a^ Acts 2. 24.

Buried with him in baptism: he shows that in Christ they who are found have not only the thing signified, but right to the outward sign and seal, viz. baptism, in the room of circumcision abolished ; the death and burial of Christ is not only the exemplar, but the cause of the death of the old man, signed and sealed in baptism: or, *by baptism into death,* Rom. vi. 3, 4, analogically, or symbolically, or sacramentally, when the Lord, together with the external sign, conferreth his grace signified by that sign; for even then the sins of such a one are buried with Christ so as they shall appear no more, either to his eternal condemnation, or in their former dominion, Rom. vi. 6, 9, 14. *Wherein also ye are risen with him;* in or by which baptism becoming effectual, having mortified the body of sin, like as Christ was raised from the dead, ye are quickened and raised to *newness of life,* Rom. vi. 4; Gal. iii. 27—29; Eph. iv. 23, 24; v. 14, 26, 27; Col. iii. 10, 11. By virtue of Christ's resurrection, a spiritual and mystical one is produced in you, which hath a resemblance and analogy to his. *Through the faith of the operation of God;* not of yourselves, but *through faith,* Eph. ii. 8, and that wrought in you by the energy or efficacy of God, John vi. 29; Phil. i. 29; ii. 13; Heb. xii. 2. *Who hath raised him from the dead;* who did exert his power in raising up Christ from the dead : compare Rom. iv. 24, with Eph. i. 19, 20. This faith is not only wrought by God, as the circumcision without hands, but it doth respect that wonderful power of God put forth in the raising of Christ, as the subject, which he mentions by way of congruity, speaking of our resurrection, and of Christ's. And he specifieth faith rather than love or other graces which are wrought also by God, because in this grace, which is the constitutive part of the new creature, God comes in with a greater irradiation upon the soul, being it hath not one fragment or point of nature to stand upon; carnal reason and mere moral righteousness being opposite to it, whereas other graces are but as the rectifying of the passions, and setting them upon right objects.

13 ^b^ And you, being dead in your sins and the uncircumcision of your flesh, hath he quickened together with him, having forgiven you all trespasses ;

^b^ Eph. 2. 1, 5, 6, 11.

And you, being dead in your sins : he further shows they had no need of *circumcision in the flesh,* Eph. ii. 11, having all in Christ for justification as well as sanctification, though they (as well as the Ephesians, see Eph. ii. 1, 5) were by nature spiritually *dead in sins,* deprived of the life of grace, and separated from the life of glory. *And the uncircumcision of your flesh ;* and having the foreskin of their flesh in paganism ; which was true literally, but, considering the internal circumcision, ver. 11, the apostle's expression here is to be expounded of the internal corruption of our nature, the uncircumcised heart, original corruption derived unto all by carnal propagation, which is predominant in the unregenerate. These being dead as to the life of grace, Matt. viii. 22 ; John v. 25 ; Rom. viii. 7 ; 1 Cor. ii. 14 ; 1 Tim. v. 6. *Hath he quickened together with him ;* you who were strangers from the life of God, Eph. iv. 18, hath he now quickened or revived to a spiritual life with him here, and hereafter to eternal life, 1 Cor. xv. 22. *Having forgiven you all trespasses ;* having freely pardoned to you (the word noting a free affection to give and forgive, 2 Cor. ii. 10 ; Eph. iv. 32) all your sins, after as well as before baptism, which is the sign and seal of it, Psal. ciii. 3 ; so that the Spirit of Christ doth not only infuse a principle of grace, and implant a living and abiding seed to work out vicious habits, but God, upon the account of Christ's plenary satisfaction, doth freely remove all the guilt that binds over to eternal death, and doth not impute to believers any of their sins in whole or in part, but treateth them as if they had committed none at all, Matt. xxvi. 28 ; Acts x. 43 ; Eph. i. 7 ; Heb. ix. 15, and will remember them no more, so that when they are sought for they shall not be found, Jer. xxxi. 34 ; I. 20 ; Heb. x. 17. What the papists say of the fault being remitted, when the punishment may be exacted either in whole or in part, that they may have a pretence for human satisfactions, (the groundlessness of which was hinted, chap. i. 24,) is a mere figment of the schools, against Scripture and reason.

e Eph. 2. 15, 16. **14** *e* Blotting out the handwriting of ordinances that was against us, which was contrary to us, and took it out of the way, nailing it to his cross ;

Blotting out the handwriting of ordinances that was against us : having just before manifested God's grace in the free forgiveness of all their trespasses, he doth here adjoin the foundation and means of this remission, viz. " Wiping out the bill of decrees," as one reads ; or effacing and cancelling " the hand-writing that was against us, which was contrary to us in traditions," as another, pointing after chirograph or hand-writing : upon the matter in the explanation there will be no difference from our reading of it. Sin, in Scripture, is frequently accounted a debt, and the acquitting, the pardoning of it, Matt. vi. 12 ; Luke xi. 4 ; xiii. 4 : as the debtor is obliged to payment, so the sinner to punishment ; only it is to be remembered, that though a private creditor may forgive his debt, yet unless the conservator of public justice do exempt an offender against the law, he is not acquitted, but is still under an obligation, bond or handwriting, having, as they under the Mosaic law, professed allegiance, Exod. xxiv. 7, which upon default was an evidence of this guilt to avenging justice. The law prescribed by the ministration of Moses was appendaged with many ceremonial ordinances, to the observation of all which circumcision did oblige : this obligation interpretatively was as a hand-writing which did publicly testify a man's native pollution, and was a public confession of his sin and misery, as washings did testify the filth of his sins, and sacrifices, capital guilt to them who lived under it, and did not perform it ; that they were accursed, Gal. iii. 10, 19, under a *ministration of death,* 2 Cor. iii. 7, 9 ; while by laying their hands on the sacrifices, they did as it were sign a bill or bond against themselves, whereby conscience of guilt was retained, Heb. x. 2, 3, and a conscience of sin renewed, so that the heart could not be stablished in any firm peace, Heb. ix. 9 ; x. 1 ; but they did confess sin to remain, and that they did want a removal of the curse by a better sacrifice. Upon the offering up of this, the law of commandments was blotted out, cancelled or abolished, even that *contained in ordinances,* saith the apostle elsewhere ; see Eph. ii. 15, compared with, ver. 16, 20, 21, of this chapter ; and therefore there is no condemnation to them that are circumcised with the circumcision of Christ, being found in him, ver. 11, with Rom. viii. 1 ; vii. 4. *Which was contrary to us ;* so that however the law, which was in itself holy, just, and good, through sin became in some sort contrary, or subcontrary, to us, in that it did serve to convict, and terrify with the curse for our default, Rom. vii. 5, 9, aggravating all by its ceremonies, and shutting the gate of God's house against the Gentiles, of whose number the Colossians were, *strangers from the covenants of promise,* Eph. ii. 12 ; yet this obligation was abrogated and annulled by the death of Christ, as the apostle expresseth it with great elegancy, having not only said that the debt was wiped out, defaced by the blood of Christ being drawn over it, as they used to blot out debts or draw red lines across them ; but he adds, *and took it out of the way ;* taken out of the way, as the debtor's bond or obligation is, being cancelled and torn to pieces, so that there is no memorial or evidence of the debt doth remain, all matter of controversy being altogether removed. Yet, if it may be, to speak more fully and satisfactorily, he annexeth, *nailing it to his cross ;* what could be more significant ? implying that Christ, by once offering himself a sacrifice on the cross, had disarmed the law, and taken away its condemning power, Rom. vii. 4 ; Gal. iii. 13. It being customary (as learned men say) of old, especially in Asia, to pierce cancelled obligations and antiquated writings with nails ; Christ by his plenary satisfaction did not only discharge from the condemnation of the law, Rom. viii. 1, 34, but he did effectually, with the nails with which he himself was crucified, by interpretation, fasten the hand-writing of ordinances to his cross, and abolished the ceremonial law in every regard, since the substance of it was come, and that which it tended to was accomplished, in giving *himself a ransom for all,* 1 Tim. ii. 6, to the putting away of sin, Heb. ix. 26, and obtaining eternal redemption, Heb. ix. 12.

15 *And* *d* having spoiled *e* principalities and powers, he made a shew of them openly, triumphing over them || in it.

d Gen. 3. 15. Ps. 68. 18. Is. 53. 12. Matt. 12. 29. Luke 10. 18. & 11. 22.
John 12. 31. & 16. 11. Eph. 4. 8. Heb. 2. 14. e Eph. 6. 12. || Or, *in himself.*

And having spoiled ; some render it, seeing he hath stripped or made naked, as runners and racers used to put off their clothes. *Principalities and powers ;* hence some of the ancients read putting off his flesh (possibly by the carelessness of some scribes, writing that which signifies flesh instead of that which signifies principalities, in all the authentic copies) ; but besides that Christ hath not put off the human nature, only the infirmities of the flesh, 2 Cor. v. 16 ; Heb. v. 7, it doth not agree with what follows. One conceits that by *principalities and powers* are meant the ceremonies of the law, because of the Divine authority they originally had ; and that Christ unclothed or unveiled them, and showed them to be misty figures that were accomplished in his own person. But I see no reason thus to allegorize, for it is easy to discern the word is borrowed from conquering warriors having put to flight and disarmed their enemies, (as the word may well signify disarming, in opposition to arming, Rom. xiii. 12 ; Eph. vi. 11, 14,) and signifies here, that Christ disarmed and despoiled the devil and his angels, with all the powers of darkness. We have seen that by *principalities and powers* are meant angels, chap. i. 16, with Rom. viii. 37 ; Eph. i. 21 ; and here he means evil ones, in regard of that power they exercise in this world under its present state of subjection to sin and vanity, Luke iv. 6 ; John xii. 31 ; 2 Cor. iv. 4 ; Eph. ii. 2 ; vi. 12 ; 2 Tim. ii. 26 ; whom Christ came to destroy, and effectually did on his cross defeat, Luke xi. 22 ; John xvi. 11 ; 1 Cor. xv. 55 ; Heb. ii. 14 ; 1 John iii. 8 ; delivering his subjects *from the power of darkness,* chap. i. 13, according to the first promise, Gen. iii. 15. *He made a show of them openly ;* yea, and Christ did, as an absolute conqueror, riding as it were in his triumphal chariot, publicly show that he had vanquished Satan and all the powers of darkness, in the view of heaven and earth, Luke x. 17, 18. *Triumphing over them ;* even then and there where Satan thought he should alone have had the day by the death of the innocent Jesus, was he and his adherents triumphed over by the Lord of life, to their everlasting shame and torment. What the papists would gather hence, that Christ did, in this triumphant show upon the cross, carry the souls of the patriarchs out of their Limbus, i. e. their appointment to hell, is a mere unscriptural fiction ; for those that he made show of in his victorious chariot are the

COLOSSIANS II

very same that he spoiled to their eternal ignominy and confusion. *In it:* some render this, (as in the margin,) in himself, or by himself, i. e. by his own power and virtue, and not by the help of any other; the prophet saith he trod the winepress alone, and had not any of the people with him, Isa. lxiii. 3: yet it seems here better to adhere to our own translation, *in it*, considering what went before of *his cross*, that he triumphed over Satan on it or by it, because the death that he there suffered was the true and only cause of his triumphs; there he trod Satan under his feet, there he set his seed at liberty, and they who go about to bereave them of it, and bring them into bondage, do no other than restore to Satan his spoils.

f Rom. 14.3, 10, 13.
‖ Or, *for eating and drinking.*
g Rom. 14. 2, 17.
1 Cor. 8. 8.
‖ Or, *in part.* h Rom. 14. 5. Gal. 4. 10.

16 Let no man therefore ᶠjudge you ‖ ᵍin meat, or in drink, or ‖ in respect ʰof an holyday, or of the new moon, or of the sabbath *days:*

Let no man therefore judge you; he infers none should be condemned: none condemns another for exercising Christian liberty; none hath power to judge and censure herein: q. d. Suffer not any one (he excepts none) to impose upon you that, as necessary in the use and practice of it, which is not *after Christ*, ver. 8, not warranted by his law of liberty, Rom. xiv. 3, 4; Gal. v. 1; James i. 25. Paul himself would not be imposed on, 1 Cor. vi. 12; vii. 23; Gal. ii. 5, 11, 14, &c.; he would not (as one of the words doth note) be domineered over by any, or suffer any to exercise authority over him, who held the Head, and owned Christ to be Lord of the conscience, and sole dictator of what way he will be served in. *In meat, or in drink;* he therefore would not have the practice of ceremonials obtruded, instancing in some, as the difference of meats and drinks, in the use or not use of which (now after Christ had nailed those decrees to his cross) superstitious ones would, from the antiquated rites of the Jews and Pythagorean philosophers, place holiness in, and add them to the Christian institution. *Or in respect of an holy-day, or of the new moon, or of the sabbath days;* or the difference of festivals and sabbaths, whether annual, or monthly, or weekly, from the Levitical institutions.

i Heb. 8. 5. & 9. 9. & 10. 1.

17 ⁱWhich are a shadow of things to come; but the body *is* of Christ.

Which are a shadow of things to come; which, as they were but obscurer representations or shadowy resemblances of future benefits procured by Christ, Heb. viii. 5; ix. 11; x. 1, whatever temporary glory they had from the former institution, *till the time of reformation*, Heb. ix. 10, yet that was done away, and they now had none, in respect of the glory that excelleth and remaineth, 2 Cor. iii. 10, 11. So that this doth no way gainsay the sacraments now of Christ's own institution, which may be called figures and shadows, not of things future, of Christ not yet come, but as already exhibited, whom they manifest to the mind and faith to be present, to those who rightly partake of them: we cannot say he condemns all distinctions of meats and drinks, viz. bread and wine in the Lord's supper; or of days; only the decrees and ordinances of Moses, or any other which the false teachers cried up, that were not after Christ. *But the body is of Christ;* who is really the substance and antitype of all the Old Testament shadows, which have completion or accomplishment in him, John i. 17: Rom. x. 4; Gal. iv. 10—12; as all the promises were in him yea and Amen, Dan. ix. 24; 2 Cor. i. 20; all was consummated in him, John xix. 30, who came in the place of all the shadows. He is *Lord of the sabbath*, Matt. xii. 8, and therefore, having broken the devil's head-plot by his propitiatory sacrifice, and entered into his rest, ceasing from his own works of redemption by price, as God did from his of creation, Heb. iv. 10, he did away (2 Cor. iii. 7, 11) all that was typical and ceremonial of the old sabbath, (as other types of himself,) keeping only that which was substantial, for a holy rest of one day in seven, and appointing that in commemoration of the Father's work and his to be, from his resurrection, observed on the first day of the week, for the edification of his church; which he honoured by his appearance amongst his apostles on that day, and that day sevennight after, which proceeded originally from his instituting of that day (to prevent dissension) for public worship in Christian assemblies. Some have observed that the Jewish doctors did foresay, That the Divine Majesty would be to Israel in a jubilee, freedom, redemption, and finisher of sabbaths: and that four sabbaths did meet together and succeed each other at the death and the resurrection of Christ, viz. 1. The sabbatical year of jubilee, Luke iv. 19. 2. The high sabbath, John xix. 31. 3. The seventh-day sabbath, when his body rested in the grave. 4. The first day of the week, when he rose a victorious conqueror of the devil, and had all put in subjection to him, unto whom all the rest did refer, and therefore they were to disappear, upon his estating his people in a rest which the law could not; whereupon his people are obliged in public adoration and praise to commemorate him on the first day of the week, or the Lord's day, to the end of the world, 1 Cor. xvi. 1, 2; Rev. i. 10.

k ver. 4.
‖ Or, *judge against you.*
† Gr. *being a voluntary in humility.*
ver. 23.
l Ezek. 13. 3.
1 Tim. 1. 7.

18 ᵏLet no man ‖ beguile you of your reward † in a voluntary humility and worshipping of angels, intruding into those things ˡwhich he hath not seen, vainly puffed up by his fleshly mind,

Let no man beguile you of your reward: the original compound word, peculiar in the New Testament to Paul, and that in this Epistle only, (and not very frequent in other authors,) hath occasioned interpreters here to render it variously, some joining the next following word with it, and some (as we read it) to that which follows after. The simple word is, chap. iii. 15, read *rule*, or judge, and it may be rendered intercede. Yet Paul doth not elsewhere use this word simply or in composition where he speaks of judging and condemning, Rom. ii. 1; however, it is borrowed from those who were judges or umpires in their games, the apostle most likely alluding to those who through favour or hatred determined unjustly, to the defrauding those victors of their prize or reward to whom it was due. Hence some would have the import to be agreeable to our translation: Be careful these unjust arbiters do not defraud you of gaining Christ, and *deceive you*, (as Matt. xxiv. 4; Eph. v. 6; 2 Thess. ii. 3,) by prescribing false lists and giving you wrong measures, and so judging against you. One renders it, Let no man deceive you with subtle argument, who pleaseth or delights himself in humility; another, Let no man take your prize; others, Let no man master it or bear rule over you at pleasure; let none take upon himself, or usurp to himself, the parts or office of a governor or umpire over you. The apostle labours to fortify the true followers of Christ against such superstitious subtle ones, who by their artifice did assume a magisterial authority (without any sure warrant from God) to impose their traditionary and invented services upon them, and determine of their state, accordingly as the papists do at this day. One learned man thinks the apostle had not used this word here, but for some notable advantage, viz. because the simple word may signify to intercede as well as to judge; it made wonderfully to his purpose in this composition, (as he uses *concision*, Phil. iii. 2,) to disparage those seducers who did, from some notions of the Platonists, labour to gain credit to that opinion that the angels were intercessors betwixt God and man. *In a voluntary humility, and worshipping of angels;* covering their imperious spirit by being volunteers in humility, or by a pretence of voluntary, uncommanded humility, alleging it would be presumption in them to address themselves immediately to God, and therefore they would pay a religious homage to angels, as of a middle nature betwixt God and them, presuming they would mediate for them: an instance to express all that invented worship, which, how specious soever it may seem to be, hath no warrant from Christ, who alone can procure acceptance of our persons and services. He expects that his disciples should assert his rights, and the liberty with which he hath made them free, against the traditions of self-willed men, and no more to solemnize for worship, than teach for doctrines, the traditions of men, Matt. xv. 2, 6, 9. We must not, under any pretext of humility, presume to know what belongs to our duty and God's service better than Christ doth, showing us that he alone is the true and living way, and we may come boldly by him, Matt. xi. 28; John xiv. 1, 6; Eph. iii. 12; Heb. iv. 16; x. 19, 20. And therefore the adoring and invocating of angels as heavenly courtiers, whatever the papists out of a show of humility do argue, is not after Christ, but against him. *Intruding into those things which he hath not seen:* yea, and for any one to assert it, and the like, is to be a bold intruder upon another's possession, a thrusting a man's self into the knowledge and determination of that which is above his reach, Psal. cxxxi. 1, and he hath no ground at all for, but doth pry or wade into a secret which a man cannot know. The apostle useth a Platonic word against those who did indulge themselves out of curiosity in the opinions of the Platonists about angels, the worshippers of which, amongst those who were professed Christians in Phrygia, were so tenacious of their error that they were not rooted out after the third century, when a canon was made against them under the name of Angelici, in the council of Laodicea near Colosse. *Vainly puffed up by his fleshly mind;* the first rise of such foolish presumption, was a being rashly puffed up with the sense of their flesh, a deluded mind moved by some carnal principle, setting out things with swelling words of vanity, wherewith in truth they have no acquaintance, and whereof they have no experience, 1 Tim. i. 7.

m Eph. 4. 15, 16.
19 And not holding ᵐthe Head, from which all the body by joints and bands having nourishment ministered, and knit together, increaseth with the increase of God.

And not holding the Head: here the apostle suggests, that those things he had before taxed did proceed from hence, that they let go the Lord Christ himself, ver. 8, 9, from whom all truths are to be derived, and consequently he is all truth itself, John xiv. 6; not to adhere to him is the spring of all apostacies, he being the Head: see Eph. iv. 15, 16. *From which all the body;* whence is communicated and distributed such influence to the body, the church, as is necessary to all the sensations and motions thereof. *By joints and bands having nourishment ministered;* being in all its members fitly framed together by the Spirit, Eph. ii. 21, 22, and united by faith, Eph. iii. 17, hath a continual subsidy of life and vigour. *And knit together;* and fastened together in a spiritual union, which joineth all believers to their Head, and each of them to the other in him, 1 Cor. x. 17; xii. 12, 20, 25, 27. *Increaseth with the increase of God;* whereupon, to mutual edification in love, it groweth with a Divine growth and spiritual increase, arising from the efficacy of God, and tending to his glory; being filled with the influences of his grace, 1 Cor. iii. 6, it is established and strengthened by little and little, in light and purity, and all graces, till it attain to the measure of its perfect stature in Christ Jesus our Lord; whereas an increase in the traditions of men, and the inventions of flesh, do only blow it up with wens and imposthumes, to the disfiguring, deforming, and destroying of it.

n Rom. 6. 3, 5. & 7. 4, 6. Gal. 2. 19. Eph. 2. 15. o ver. 8. ‖ Or, *elements.* p Gal. 4. 3, 9.
20 Wherefore if ye be ⁿdead with Christ from ᵒthe ‖ rudiments of the world, ᵖwhy, as though living in the world, are ye subject to ordinances,

Wherefore if ye be dead with Christ from the rudiments of the world: here the apostle doth further argue against all impositions of superstitious observances, obtruded as parts of Divine worship, whether in reviving those abrogated, or setting up new ones, upon supposition of their union with Christ their Head, and their being dead in him as to all beggarly elements from which he had freed them by his death, Rom. vi. 3, 5; vii. 4, 6; Gal. iv. 9, 10, 11, with ii. 19; no uncommanded worship or way of worship being *after Christ,* ver. 8, in whom they were *complete,* ver. 10, being *buried with him in baptism,* ver. 12, having nailed those ritual ordinances to his cross, as antiquated or outdated, ver. 14. *Why, as though living in the world, are ye subject to ordinances?* why should they, who held the Head, ver. 19, as if they lived in the old world with those *children in bondage,* Gal. iv. 3, before Christ came, be subject to ceremonial observances? q. d. It is most injurious that they should impose this yoke upon you, (Acts xv. 10,) ye are most foolish if ye submit your necks; for God would not have a ceremonial worship which he himself instituted to be abrogated, that a new one should be invented by men.

If the Head of the church like not the reviving that worship he hath laid aside, be sure he will not approve of any new one which he never appointed. The apostle is not here speaking of the magistrates' ordinances about things indifferent in their use, for the real good of the civil government, but of the way of worshipping God by religious abstinences, &c.

21 (ᵠTouch not; taste not; handle not;
q 1 Tim. 4. 3.

Which he doth here by way of imitation, upbraiding of them, elegantly recite in the words, phrases, or sense of those imposing dogmatists, whose superstition and lust of domineering over the consciences of Christians is taxed, in the gradation which the well skilled in the Greek judge to be in the original. For though the first, and which we render *touch not,* be sometimes so rendered, yet, considering here the coincidency or tautology will, so rendered, make with the last, the sense of it, as the most judicious and learned have evidenced, seems to be, eat not, as noting they did forbid the eating, i. e. using certain meats at their ordinary meals; (against the reviving of which imposition above, ver. 16, as will bring in a new one of like import, the apostle elsewhere expresseth himself, Rom. xiv. 17; 1 Cor. viii. 8; 1 Tim. iv. 3;) obtaining which, they proceeded to forbid the not tasting, and then the not handling, or touching of them with the hand, as if that would defile. It being more not to taste than not to eat, and likewise more not to touch with the finger than not to taste. Expressing the ingenuity of such superstitious imposers, that they heap up one thing upon another to the burdening of consciences, not knowing where to make an end in their new-invented external devotions and observances, which, as snares, do first bind fast, and in tract of time strangle. He speaks of these as distinct from those, ver. 16, they being for antiquated rites which had been of God's appointment, these for innovations of man's invention, as is apparent from the last verse.

22 Which all are to perish with the using;) ʳafter the commandments and doctrines of men?
r Is. 29. 13. Matt. 15. 9. Tit. 1. 14.

Which all are to perish with the using: he adds his reasons why, under the Christian institution, acceptable worshipping of God doth not consist in such observances, both because meats, drinks, garments, &c. are designed unto the benefit of man, for the preserving of his temporal life, and are consumed in their use. They cannot, in or by themselves, either make a man holy or render him unclean, Matt. xv. 11; Mark vii. 19; Rom. xiv. 17; 1 Cor. vi. 13; 1 Tim. iv. 3; they all come to corruption, or are consumed in doing us service, they cannot otherwise be of use; which may evince that all the benefit we receive from them doth only respect this mortal life, it not being imaginable that what perisheth in our use should be of any force to the life of our soul, which is immortal and incorruptible. And therefore to urge the reviving of antiquated ordinances, or bringing in such-like new ones, is to corrupt or consume the creatures without any spiritual advantage, whereupon such impositions must needs be destructive; and because of the apostle's stronger argument, they are not after Christ, but after the precepts and decrees of men, compare ver. 8, which is our Lord and Master's argument against the innovations of the Pharisees, Matt. xv. 9, agreeing with the prophet, Isa. xxix. 13. To bring in additionals of uncommanded worship, or rites and ways of it, is forbidden of God, Deut. xii. 32; John xiv. 26; xvi. 13; Rev. xxii. 18; who (according to the purport of the second commandment) must be worshipped in a manner peculiar to him and appointed by him; and therefore worship not appointed, i. e. not commanded, is forbidden by him, who will accept of no homage from Christians in the business of religion, unless it be taught by him, and not by men only.

23 ˢWhich things have indeed a shew of wisdom in ᵗwill worship, and humility, and ‖ neglecting of the body; not in any honour to the satisfying of the flesh.
s 1 Tim. 4. 8. t ver. 8. ‖ Or, *punishing,* or, *not sparing.*

Which things have indeed a show of wisdom: by way of concession the apostle here grants that the precepts and doctrines of men about religious abstinences had a *show of wisdom;* and it was but a mere show, a bare pretext, a specious appearance, a fair colour of wisdom, which is of no worth, not the reality and truth of Christian wisdom, however it might beguile those that were taken more with shadows than substance, ver. 3, 4, 8, 17. *In will-worship;* 1. In arbitrary superstition, or human invention, or self-willed religion, rather than Divine institutions; as all the ancients, and almost all the moderns, do interpret that word, it having no good, but an ill character; accounting the compound word here which we render *will-worship,* of no better import, as to the ordainers of worship, than the two simple words of which it is compounded, expressing human arbitrariness and worship, ver. 18, (even as the apostle doth, by a compound word which signifies peace-making, chap. i. 20, understand the very same thing which he expressed by the two simple words of which it is compounded in another Epistle, Eph. ii. 15,) it being rational to conceive, considering the apostle's drift in the context, that by *will-worship* he doth connote the same here, that by willing in worship he doth asunder there. For though a performing those acts of worship willingly, which God himself hath commanded, be necessary, and commendable in his willing people, Psal. cx. 3, and they cannot be acceptable otherwise; yet when the will of man, in contradistinction to the will of God, is considered as constitutive of that worship which is offered to God of a man's own brain and devising, without God's warrant, then that will-worship is hateful to God, and the more voluntary the more abominable. It being most just, that not in what way we will and choose, but only in that way which he willeth and chooseth, we should worship him with acceptance; which should be our greatest care, 2 Cor. v. 9. We know, amongst men, those persons of honour that give liveries to their servants, would discard such of them as should come to attend them in new ones of their own devising, though those servants might be so foolish as to conceit those of their own devising were more expressive of their humble respects. Much more is worship of man's devising distasteful to the all-wise God, who sees through all colours, and though he loves a willing worshipper, yet he hates will-worship. *And humility;* however it be palliated, 2. With a pretended demission of mind, or an affectation of humility, as if more self-abasement were designed in such an arbitrary way of worship; like those hypocrites in their fasts, who put on mortified looks and a neglected garb, with disguised contenances, Matt. vi. 16, showing themselves most submissive to the orders of their superiors in that way of man's devising. *And neglecting of the body;* wherein the more superstitiously devout do labour to outdo others, 3. In punishing, not sparing, neglecting, or afflicting the body; as some monks at this day in the papacy, in denying it that with which nature should be supplied. *Not in any honour,* which a learned man thinks the apostle would have read as included in a parenthesis, as conceiving the series of his discourse requires these to be joined, viz. *neglecting of the body* as to what pertains *to the satisfying of the flesh.* So by *not in any honour,* is not here meant a sparing of the body in order to real sanctification, temperance and continence, in opposition to the dishonouring of the body by luxury, as Rom. i. 26, with 1 Cor. vi. 18—20; 1 Thess. iv. 4; Heb. xiii. 4. That honour of the body the apostle doth elsewhere require, he doth here oppose to the seducers' pretended mortifications. For their religious abstinence was not from that which occasioned luxury, only from some certain sorts of meat, the use of which no way defiles the body, nor violates in any manner the holiness and honour it ought to be kept in. Others read, neglecting the body, which is in no esteem. *To the satisfying of the flesh;* for pampering the flesh. Not in any esteem, i. e. with God, or not in any honour to God, but in a tendency only to make *provision for the flesh,* as Rom. xiii. 14. Others take *honour* for regard; q. d. In no regard to the supplying of nature with that which is due to it. Others take honour for having a care of, 1 Tim. v. 3; q. d. Neglecting the body in taking no care of it, or not at all valuing the things that are requisite to the due nourishment of it: this is somewhat generally received; having no care that the body may have that which will satisfy nature. And if the last phrase, which we translate *to the satisfying of the flesh,* seem not so well to express moderate satiety, we should consider it is said in a good sense, God *filled the hungry with good things,* Luke i. 53, and Christ *filled* the multitude, John vi. 12; yea, the use of the word in authentic Greek authors may be found to note a moderate as well as immoderate filling, i. e. in a good sense, for a satiety (or enough) that is not vicious.

CHAP. III

The apostle exhorteth to be heavenly-minded, 1—4; *to mortify carnal lusts, and to put away all malice and ill dealing in respect of one another, as becometh Christians,* 5—11. *He recommendeth brotherly kindness, charity, and other general duties,* 12—17; *the relative duties of wives,* 18, *and husbands,* 19, *of children,* 20, *and parents,* 21; *and of servants towards their masters,* 22—25.

IF ye then [a] be risen with Christ, seek those things which are above, where [b] Christ sitteth on the right hand of God. a Rom. 6. 5. Eph. 2. 6. ch. 2. 12. b Rom. 8. 34. Eph. 1. 20.

If ye then be risen with Christ: having refuted superstitious observances placed in things earthly and perishing, and called them off from shadows to mind the substance; he doth, upon supposition of what he had asserted before, chap. ii. 12, 13, here infer that, since they were risen again with Christ, it did behove them to set about the duties required of those in that state: not of the proper resurrection of the body, which, while here below, can only be in our Head by virtue of the mystical union, as in regard of right the members of Christ are said to *sit* with him *in heavenly places,* Eph. ii. 6, signified and sealed by baptism: but the metaphorical and spiritual resurrection from spiritual death, which is regeneration, Rom. vi. 4; Tit. iii. 5, wrought by the same Spirit which raised Christ, and whereby renewed Christians live in certain hope of that proper resurrection of their bodies, which Christ hath procured. *Seek those things which are above:* hereupon he urgeth them, (in the same sense our Saviour doth command to seek his kingdom, Matt. vi. 33,) with diligence to pursue heaven and happiness as the end, and holiness as the means to the attaining of it; to have their *conversation in heaven,* Phil. iii. 20. *Where Christ sitteth at the right hand of God:* while the apostle speaks of God after the manner of men, we must take heed of the gross error of the Anthropomorphites, who did imagine God to sit in heaven in the shape of a man. Some indeed, who abhor such a gross imagination, yet conceive that because more generally the heaven is God's throne, and shall be so for ever, Jer. xvii. 12; Lam. v. 19; Matt. v. 34, that he hath a particular throne in heaven, whereon he doth show himself specially present, as in his temple, 1 Kings xxii. 19; Psal. xi. 4; and so, though Christ is set properly on the right hand of this throne, Heb. i. 3; viii. 1; xii. 2; Rev. iii. 21; but because the conception of such a particular material throne, with extension of parts and proper dimensions, may (besides other inconveniences) misguide our apprehensions, and occasion adoration to the creature, which should be terminated on God alone, who is a pure Spirit; and whereas sitting is not taken properly, since Stephen saw Christ *standing,* Acts vii. 55, and is opposed to the ministration of angels, which have no bodies or bodily parts, Heb. i. 13; by most it is taken metaphorically, importing that Christ hath all real power and dominion put into his hands, connoting his authority and security from his enemies, who are put under his feet, Matt. xxviii. 18; 1 Cor. xv. 25, is crowned with majesty, glory, and honour, Heb. i. 3; ii. 9, enjoying all blessedness in a most transcendent way, Psal. xvi. 11; cx. 1; Acts ii. 33, 36; having the human nature filled with abilities to execute all when he entered into glory, Isa. xvi. 5; Luke xxii. 29, 30; xxiv. 26; 1 Cor. xv. 43; Rev. xix. 6; where he resides possessed of all in safety, Acts iii. 21; Rev. iii. 21. It was above whither Christ ascended by a local motion from a certain where here below into a certain where above; so that whatever the Lutherans argue from Christ's glorious ascension and session, to prove Christ's body a ubiquitary, or every where present, is inconsequent, since it is in heaven where he wills that believers should be to behold the glory that his Father hath given him, John xvii. 24: wherefore,

COLOSSIANS III

|| Or, mind.

2 Set your ‖ affection on things above, not on things on the earth.

Set your affection on things above: that the hearts of believers here might be where their treasure is, the apostle here repeats his exhortation, using another word, importing they should intensely mind things above, Rom. viii. 5, viz. the inheritance *reserved in heaven* for us, 1 Pet. i. 4, with heart and affections, together with all that God hath appointed to be a furtherance to the enjoyment of it; not curiously to search the deep things of God, which cannot be found out, but to mind things above with sobriety, Rom. xii. 3. *Not on things on the earth;* taking off the mind and heart from all that is opposite to heavenly things, viz. not only those human, carnal ordinances and ceremonies, chap. ii. 22, with Phil. iii. 18, 19, but also from the eager pursuit of the pleasures, profits, and honours of this world, which the men of it do inordinately desire, ver. 5, with Matt. vi. 33; Gal v. 24, and are carried away with, Tit. ii. 12; James iv. 4; 2 Pet. i. 4; 1 John ii. 17. Christians should not be, to the neglect of things spiritual; however, they are obliged, in a due subordination, to take care of themselves and families for these things below, so far as to put them into a capacity of raising them more heavenward.

c Rom. 6. 2.
Gal. 2. 20.
ch. 2. 20.
d 2 Cor. 5. 7.
ch. 1. 5.

3 ^cFor ye are dead, ^dand your life is hid with Christ in God.

For ye are dead; the apostle adds another reason why the believing Colossians should not be earthly-minded, because they were dead, not absolutely, but in a certain respect, viz. of sin, and the world. 1. In regard of that carnal, corrupted, sin-infected life, received from our first parents by carnal generation, the life of the old man, altogether depraved, the real members of Christ are dead: see chap. ii. 11, 12, 20; Rom. vi. 2, 4, 6—8, 11; vii. 9; 2 Cor. v. 14, 17; Gal. v. 24. 2. In regard of the world, by communion with Christ their Head, Psal. xxii. 15; Isa. xxvi. 19; Gal. vi. 14; 2 Tim. ii. 11; 1 Pet. iv. 1, 2. *And your life is hid with Christ in God;* and their spiritual life, (opposed to the life of sin.) which is received by their receiving of Christ, the life they now live by faith, quickened together with Christ, chap. ii. 13; John xi. 25, 26; xiv. 6; Gal. ii. 20; Heb. x. 38; 1 John v. 11, 12; this is *hid with Christ* by virtue of their union with him, as Christ is in God by union with the Father; Christ in God, and our life in Christ, John xvii. 21, because in him lie the springs of our spiritual life, which in and by our regeneration, renovation, and sanctification is communicated to us; and its progress in fruitfulness till it arrive to perfection, Phil. iii. 10, 14.

e 1 John 3. 2.
f John 11.
25. & 14. 6.
g 1 Cor. 15.
43. Phil. 3.
21.

4 ^eWhen Christ, *who is* ^four life, shall appear, then shall ye also appear with him ^gin glory.

When Christ, who is our life, shall appear; which will be, according to the purpose and promise of God, with whom it is laid up, chap. i. 5, when Christ by whom they live shall so appear that they shall be like him, 1 John iii. 2, and be taken to be with him in the heavenly inheritance, 1 Pet. i. 4; then their conformity to him, began here, partly in holiness and partly in sufferings, Rom. viii. 18, shall be completed at last in glory and felicity, Phil. iii. 21; Heb. xi. 26, 35. *Then shall ye also appear with him in glory;* and then shall these adopted children be brought into glory with him, Heb. ii. 10, out of whose hands none shall be able to pull them, John x. 28; but however the world look upon them as despicable, John xvi. 2, and sometimes they are so in their own eyes, wherein ofttimes there be tears, so that they can see but as *through a glass, darkly,* Psal. xxxi. 22; 1 Cor. xiii. 12; but then they shall see Christ face to face, all tears shall be wiped away from their eyes, Rev. vii. 17, and at the last day they shall shine as the sun in glory, Matt. xiii. 43; 1 Cor. xv. 43, 53; 2 Thess. i. 7, 10, 12.

h Rom. 8. 13.
Gal. 5. 24.
i Rom. 6. 13.
k Eph. 5. 3.
l 1 Thess. 4. 5.
m Eph. 5. 5.

5 ^hMortify therefore ⁱyour members which are upon the earth; ^kfornication, uncleanness, inordinate affection, ^levil concupiscence, and covetousness, ^mwhich is idolatry:

That they might not think he, who had given check to superstitious abstinences, was for the indulging of any carnal affections, he infers here, how the exercise of truly Christian mortification was incumbent on those who were dead to sin and had their life hid in Christ. Neither is it any incongruity, that they who are in a sort already dead should be exhorted to mortification, if we do but distinctly consider of mortification, and what they are to mortify, or endeavour to make dead. 1. As to mortification; which may be considered either as to its inchoation, when, upon effectually calling, a mortal wound is by the Spirit of God given to the old man, or to the habit of sin, which will in the end or consummation be a total privation of its life, though as yet it be but partial. It is not in regard of this inchoative mortification, which was begun upon their effectual calling, that the apostle exhorts the saints at Colosse in this verse to mortify. But mortification may be considered as to its continuation, and the carrying on the life of grace, in the making dead all that is contrary to it; even the renewed person should be continually solicitous to have the old man killed outright without any reprieve. This is it that the apostle put the believing Colossians upon, not to spare any remaining ill dispositions or depraved habits of the old man; but by the assistance of the Spirit, (for it is not a natural, but spiritual work,) Rom. viii. 13; Gal. v. 24, continually to resist to the killing of it, or putting it to death: never to desist in this war. 2. As to the earthly members of it. The apostle expresseth the object of mortification, or what they are to mortify, by their *members upon the earth;* not as if he designed to put them upon a dismembering of their bodies, or a deadening of those bodily natural parts whereby the sex is distinguished, Rom. vi. 13, (though, agreeably to his own practice, he would have the body kept under and brought into subjection, 1 Cor. ix. 27,) but upon subduing inordinate motions and carnal concupiscences, as is evident from the particular vices following, which, taken as collected and heaped up together, may well pass under the notion of a body. He had before in this Epistle mentioned *the body of the sins of the flesh,* chap. ii. 11; this he might say not only metonymically, by reason such lusts do reside in the natural body and members of it, Rom. vi. 6, 12, 19; but (and that chiefly) metaphorically, the mass of corrupt nature dwelling in us is compared to a person, the *old man,* or old Adam, or body of sin, ver. 9; Rom. vi. 6; vii. 24; Eph. iv. 22; and, continuing the metaphor, the parts of this corrupt body are called *members,* and our members, the whole body of the old man being made up of them, which are said to be *upon the earth,* as being inclined to earthly things and employed about them, taking occasion from sensual objects here below to get strength, unless we be continually upon our watch to abolish all that contributes to the life of the old man in the particular members; viz. *fornication:* see the parallel place, Eph. v. 3, with 1 Cor. vi. 9, where he begins with this, as most turbulent, understanding by it not only the outward act, but the inward affection, which the heathens were apt to reckon no fault, though the Spirit of God in the Scripture do greatly condemn it, Matt. v. 28; Rom. i. 29; 1 Cor. v. 1; vi. 18; vii. 2; x. 8; 1 Thess. iv. 3. *Uncleanness:* see Eph. v. 3: impurity which is more unnatural, whereby they dishonour their own bodies, Rom. i. 24, 27; Gal. v. 19; 1 Thess. iv. 7; Rev. xvii. 4. *Inordinate affection;* that passion which some render softness, or easiness to receive any impression to lust, i. e. the filthy disposition of a voluptuous, effeminate heart, delighted with lascivious objects, Psal. xxxii. 9; Rom. i. 26, 27; 1 Cor. vi. 9, with 1 Thess. iv. 3, 5. *Evil concupiscence;* that concupiscence which in nature and measure is excessive, being an irregular appetite, and an undue motion against reason, especially against the Spirit, Gal. v. 17. *And covetousness;* and an immoderate desire after and cleaving to the things of this world, either in progging for them, or possessing of them to the feeding of other lusts, and so estranging the heart from God, Eccles. v. 10; Luke xii. 18; trusting in riches rather than in the living God, Job xxxi. 21; Matt. vi. 24; 1 Tim. vi. 17. *Which is idolatry;* upon which account it may pass under the title of *idolatry,* as the covetous person is an idolater; see Eph. v. 5: and further he might reckon covetousness to be idolatry, because nothing was more execrable in the judgment of the Jews than idolatry was, it being ordinary with the Hebrews to note sins by the names of those most detested; as *rebellion* against God *by witchcraft,* 1 Sam. xv. 23,

6 ⁿ For which things' sake the wrath of God cometh on ᵒ the children of disobedience:

Especially remembering how the indulging or sparing any of them will be of dreadful consequence; see Eph. v. 6; for however they may by carnal men be looked upon as little faults, which God will overlook of course, yet they do certainly incur Divine displeasure, and will bring most inevitable judgments upon those unpersuadable, rebellious, and contumacious ones, who would be thought God's children and yet remain incorrigible, Matt. xxiv. 38, 39; 1 Cor. vi. 9; Gal. v. 21.

7 ᵖ In the which ye also walked some time, when ye lived in them.

In the which; some render it, amongst whom; but, alas! they lived amongst such disobedient ones still; therefore we do better render it *in which,* i. e. sins or vices. *Ye,* the now believing Colossians, *also walked some time;* had heretofore practised and exercised; and had not only been infected with the venom of them, in descending from polluted parents, but *lived in them,* were servants to them, Rom. vi. 17, 19, while in a sensual course of life they were carried away with them, 1 Cor. xii. 2, before their conversion, when they did live and reign in their mortal bodies, chap. i. 21; 1 Cor. vi. 11; Eph. ii. 3, 11, 12; v. 8.

8 ᑫ But now ye also put off all these; anger, wrath, malice, blasphemy, ʳ filthy communication out of your mouth.

But now ye also put off all these: having minded them of their former condition under paganism in a state of sin, while they served various sensual lusts, he doth here in their present circumstances under Christianity in a state of grace, show them that, now they professed to *walk as children of light,* Rom. xiii. 12; Eph. v. 8, with 1 Thess. v. 5, 8, they were more strongly obliged to lay aside those inordinate affections which were more spiritual, Eph. iv. 22; some of which he doth instance in, viz. *anger;* whereby he doth not mean the passion itself, Eph. iv. 26, with 31, but the inordinacy of it, being a vindictive appetite to hurt another unjustly for some affront conceived to be given or occasioned by him. *Wrath; indignation,* Rom. ii. 8, a sudden, hasty, and vehement commotion of the offended mind apprehending an injury, when it shows itself in the countenance in a manner and measure unbecoming a Christian, as in them who with rage thrust Christ out of the city, Luke iv. 28, 29, with Eph. iv. 31. *Malice;* connoting both the evil habit and the vicious act: now though this word be taken oftentimes more generally, for that mischievous vitiosity and venom which runs through all the passions of the soul, reaching to all sins, 1 Cor. v. 8; xiv. 20; yet here it seems to be taken more specially, for a secret malignity of rooted anger and continued wrath, remembering injuries, meditating revenge, and watching for an occasion to vent it, being much the same with that which the apostle in a parallel Epistle calls *bitterness,* Eph. iv. 31, compared with other places, Gen. iv. 5; Rom. i. 29; Tit. iii. 3; 1 Pet. ii. 1. After he had urged the laying aside of heart evils as the cause, he moves to the laying aside those of the tongue, viz. *blasphemy,* which in a like place we render *evil speaking,* Eph. iv. 31; the original word, according to the notation of it, doth signify the hurt of any one's good name, which when it respects God we do more strictly call blasphemy. When it respects our neighbour, though more largely it be so, defamation, Rom. iii. 8; 1 Cor. iv. 13; Tit. iii. 2; yet more strictly, if it be done secretly, it is detraction or backbiting; more openly, reviling or slandering, Matt. xv. 19; Mark vii. 22; 1 Tim. vi. 4. *Filthy communication out of your mouth:* obscene discourse, dishonest talk, should not come into the Christian's mouth, chap. iv. 6; see on Eph. iv. 29; v. 4: wanton, lewd, and unclean speeches should not proceed from a Christian's tongue, 1 Cor. xv. 33.

9 ˢ Lie not one to another, ᵗ seeing that ye have put off the old man with his deeds;

Lie not one to another: here he puts them upon laying aside that vice which violates the ninth commandment, being opposite to truth in word and work: see Eph. iv. 25, where he doth more fully urge the putting away lying, from the same argument that follows here: a lie being no other than that voluntary expression by word or deed, which accords not with the conception of the mind and heart, on purpose to deceive those with whom we do converse; contrary to the principles of a new creature, because God, after whose image he is renewed, hates it more than any vice, since it is contrary to truth, and proceeds from the father of lies, Psal. v. 6; xv. 2; Prov. xii. 22; John viii. 44; Rev. xxi. 8, 27. They who in conversation do most stomach to be told of it, are most ordinarily guilty of it. But the apostle requires Christians indeed to put away all fraud and fallacy in commerce with men and one another, (as well as converse with God,) that there may be in all due circumstances a just representation of that without which is conceived within, Eph. iv. 15; James iii. 14. *Seeing that ye have put off the old man with his deeds:* the apostle subjoins his reason from the parts of regeneration or sanctification, viz. 1. Mortification, which he reassumes under an elegant metaphor, (intimating his solicitude to have the foregoing and the like vices to be wholly laid aside, as much as was possible in this life,) borrowed from the putting off old and worn garments, which did as it were crawl with vermin; intimating that if the old man, as the cause, were put off with loathing, then those inordinate affections and actions which did proceed from it would also be removed; see on Rom. vi. 6, 11, with Eph. iv. 22: if that which is born of the flesh and contrary to the Spirit, John iii. 6, with Gal. v. 17, then inordinate affections and lusts, Gal. v. 24.

10 And have put on the new *man,* which ᵘ is renewed in knowledge ˣ after the image of him that ʸ created him:

And have put on the new man: 2. Vivification, or renovation; this he connecteth with the former, continuing the metaphor. As in natural generation the expulsion of the old form is attended with the introduction of the new, so in spiritual regeneration, having put off the old Adam they had put on the new, i. e. Christ, not only sacramentally, chap. ii. 12, 13; Gal. iii. 27, but really, being new creatures in Christ Jesus, 2 Cor. v. 17; Eph. ii. 10, renewed in the inward man, Rom. vii. 22; 2 Cor. iv. 16; see on Eph. iii. 16; iv. 24; and endowed with a new frame of heart and a new spirit, Ezek. xi. 19; John iii. 5, 6, new qualities and affections. *Which is renewed in knowledge;* the understanding being savingly enlightened, and the will powerfully inclined by the victorious working of the Spirit, Eph. i. 18—20; see on Eph. iv. 23, with Phil. ii. 13; 2 Thess. ii. 13, 14; and brought to more than a speculative, even to a lively and effectual knowledge, 1 John ii. 3. *After the image of him that created him;* agreeable to the impress of him that had new framed or created them in Christ Jesus, 1 Cor. xv. 49; 1 Pet. i. 15, 16, by the *renewing of the Holy Ghost,* Tit. iii. 5: for as the natural image of God consisted in knowledge and righteousness; so it was requisite that the spiritual image restored by grace should consist in the rectifying of the faculties of the soul, the understanding with spiritual knowledge, and the will with a spiritual inclination to embrace the things that please God; in communion with whom sanctified souls do take in hand a new course of life, and move therein, in a spiritually natural way.

11 Where there is neither ᶻGreek nor Jew, circumcision nor uncircumcision, Barbarian, Scythian, bond *nor* free: ᵃ but Christ *is* all, and in all.

He prevents the reasoning of those, who did not neglect regeneration, and place religion in mere externals, showing that in the new man, or true sanctification, and real Christianity, there was sufficient to save us, in communion with Christ, without those external observances false teachers did stickle for as necessary. *Where there is neither Greek nor*

Jew; God, in effectually calling persons into a state of regeneration, had no regard to those known distinctions then in the world, of those who were born of the Gentiles or the seed of Abraham, Matt. iii. 9; John viii. 39; Rom. ii. 11; x. 12; xi. 7, 11, 12: see on Gal. iii. 28. *Circumcision nor uncircumcision;* he works upon those who are not circumcised, as well as on those who are circumcised, now Christ is come, Gal. v. 6; vi. 15, since which the posterity of Japheth, constituting the greater part of the Gentile church, do *dwell in the tents of Shem,* according to Noah's prophecy, Gen. ix. 27, compared with Balaam's, Numb. xxiv. 24. Shem and Ham are not excluded, yet (a learned man observes) the faith of Christ from the ages of the apostles hath flourished most hitherto in Europe, and the parts of Asia where Japheth's lot lay; and as of old some of the latter might, so we know of the former many of late have passed into America. Upon the apostle's adding *Barbarian, Scythian,* without conjunction either copulative or disjunctive, some have inquired whether these two should be balanced in the like opposition with the former? And it may be said, there is no more necessity for such exactness here, than elsewhere in the like form of speech, Rom. viii. 39; 1 Cor. iii. 22: and the most think here is an increase of the oration, understanding by *Scythian* (which is now more strictly the Tartarian) the most barbarous of the Barbarians. Yet, because the Grecians sometime accounted the world, besides themselves, (who were polished with human learning and philosophy,) Barbarians, if any think there ought to be an opposition betwixt the *Barbarian* and *Scythian,* then by *Barbarian* (i. e. in the philosophers' reckoning) may be understood the Jews; by *Scythian,* the Gentiles. So *Jew, circumcision, Barbarian,* as in a parallel, are opposed to *Gentile, uncircumcision, Scythian.* For Scythians being numerous, thereby some used to express the *nations,* (as Symmachus translates Gen. xiv. 9, *Tidal king of the Scythians.*) and so reckon the whole world might be divided into the Jews and Scythians, no otherwise than into circumcised and uncircumcised. *Bond nor free;* as to acceptance with God in Christ, the distinctions of people were abolished with their observances and polities, because, some where they were more free, having milder laws; some where they were more servile, having more severe laws, which was an indifferent thing now as to their being in Christ, concerned to submit to certain honest laws, ordinances of magistrates, 1 Pet. ii. 13, though not Judaic or judicial ones. In every condition, high or low, whether of service or freedom, Acts x. 34, 35; 1 Cor. vii. 20—22, whosoever hath put on the new man in Christ is accepted. Neither the eloquence of the philosopher nor the rudeness of him who is uncultivated, neither the liberty of the freeman nor the bondage of the slave, doth further or obstruct the work of the new creation. *But Christ is all, and in all;* but they that are truly interested in Christ, have really put him on, they are certainly privileged with that which answers all, they are indeed the blessed with faithful Abraham, whether they be of his seed according to the flesh, yea or no, Psal. xxxii. 2; Gal. iii. 7—9; having *put on Christ,* Rom. xiii. 14, they are all *complete in him,* chap. ii. 10. He is all things to and in all those who are renewed, both meritoriously and efficaciously, 1 Cor. i. 30; xv. 10; Gal. ii. 20: being by faith one with him who hath all, they have all, Eph. iii. 17, either for their present support or their eternal happiness, Acts iv. 12.

12 ᵇ Put on therefore, ᶜ as the elect of God, holy and beloved, ᵈ bowels of mercies, kindness, humbleness of mind, meekness, longsuffering;

b Eph. 4. 24.
c 1 Thess. 1.
4. 1 Pet. 1. 2.
2 Pet. 1. 10.
d Gal. 5. 22.
Phil. 2. 1.
Eph. 4. 2, 32.

Put on therefore: as he had mentioned some particular vices of the old man they were to put off, ver. 8, he doth here infer, that they might be complete in Christ, there be particular virtues and graces of the new man they are to put on, or, being new creatures, continually to exercise themselves in. *As the elect of God, holy and beloved;* chosen of God before all time, and effectually called in time from the rest of mankind; see John xv. 16; Rom. viii. 29, 30; Eph. i. 4, 5; 2 Thess. ii. 13: saints not only by obsignation, but renewed by the sanctifying Spirit, chap. i. 2; 1 Pet. i. 2; beloved with a gratuitous and special love of complacency, John xiv. 21; Rom. i. 7; 1 Thess. i. 4. *Bowels of mercies;* he would have us put on, i. e. exercise, (being sanctified by the Spirit,) mercy, not simply, but according to the Hebrew phrase, *bowels of mercies,* i. e. tendernesses of compassions, resenting the miseries of our brethren, as sharing with them in their sufferings, from our very heart: see Luke vi. 36; Rom. xii. 15; Gal. vi. 2; Eph. iv. 32; 1 Pet. iii. 8. *Kindness;* courtesy and goodness, Gal. v. 22; endeavouring to succour one another in all offices of benignity, 2 Cor. vi. 6; 1 Pet. v. 14. *Humbleness of mind;* a sincere (not an affected) lowliness of spirit: see on Eph. iv. 2; Phil. ii. 3. *Meekness;* gentleness and mildness, receiving one another with an open heart and pleasant countenance: see Gal. v. 13, 23; vi. 1; 1 Thess. ii. 7. *Long-suffering;* patience, bearing affronts and outrages, with other vexatious afflictions, without exasperation, abiding sedate after many wrongs offered, chap. i. 11; Acts v. 41; 2 Tim. ii. 10; iv. 2; 1 Pet. iv. 16.

13 ᵉ Forbearing one another, and forgiving one another, if any man have a ‖ quarrel against any: even as Christ forgave you, so also *do* ye.

e Mark 11. 25. Eph. 4. 2, 32.
‖ Or, *complaint.*

Forbearing one another; clemency towards each other, not only in undergoing affronts, but a suspending to take advantage from the infirmities of others, so as not to irritate them to passion, or to take them tripping, so as to aggravate their failings, Prov. xvi. 32; 1 Cor. iv. 12; Gal. vi. 2; Eph. iv. 2; 2 Thess. i. 4. *And forgiving one another, if any man have a quarrel against any;* yea, and if one hath any just complaint against another, mutually passing it by amongst ourselves: we render *forgiving one another,* that which in the Greek is forgiving ourselves; and indeed he that doth see the need he hath of pardon himself, will pass by the fault of his brother, (so ourselves here is put for *one another,*) Mark x. 26; Luke xxiii. 12. *Even as Christ forgave you, so also do ye;* considering the exemplar cause here added as a motive to mutual forgiveness, viz. our Head the Lord Jesus Christ forgiving of us, who are bound to conform to him in forgiving others; see on Matt. vi. 14; xviii. 32, 33; Mark xi. 25, 26; John xiii. 14; Eph. iv. 32, with 1 Pet. ii. 21; yea, the strong to indulge and gratify their weak brethren in smaller matters for their good, Rom. xv. 1—3.

14 ᶠ And above all these things ᵍ put on charity, which is the ʰ bond of perfectness.

f 1 Pet. 4. 8.
g John 13. 34. Rom. 13. 8. 1 Cor. 13.
Eph. 5. 2.
ch. 2. 2.
1 Thess. 4. 9. 1 Tim. 1. 5. 1 John 3. 23. & 4. 21.
h Eph. 4. 3.

And above all these things put on charity: that which we render *above,* as surpassing all, some read upon, or over, and some, for all these things, viz. the graces he exhorted them to be clothed with. Both agree, that mutual Christian love or charity is the chiefest garment the new man can put on, being the livery of Christ's disciples, John. xiii. 35. But in prosecuting the allegory under the former notion, there is some danger of being over fine; and therefore it may be very pertinent to understand the putting on or exercising of charity, for the performance of the other graces and exercises, this being that which sets them on work with reference to their several objects, engaging to sincerity in their actings, without which the motions of the new man are no way acceptable; this links them together, and so is in a sort, as the apostle says elsewhere, a fulfilling of the whole law, Rom. xiii. 8, 9; Gal. v. 14, with Matt. xxii. 39, 40; being the subjects of this hearty and regular affection of love to God and our neighbour, are inclined by it to do good continually, and to avoid the injuring of another in any respect. Not that there is any fulfilling of the law perfectly in this state, as the papists argue impertinently from what follows of charity, that it is *the bond of perfectness,* or, by an hypallage or Hebraism, the most perfect bond, therefore we are justified by it, and so by the works of the law before God. For, 1. Love, or charity, itself is not perfect, and so the very best of the new creatures who have put it on, however they may be perfect with a perfection of integrity or parts, yet not with a perfection of maturity or degrees, absolutely, while in this life; see on Eccles. vii. 20; Rom. vii. 18, 19; Gal. v. 17; Phil. iii. 12, 15, with Jam. iii. 2, &c. 2. Upon supposition that charity in a new creature doth in some sort perfectly fulfil the law, from the time he is endowed with it of God's grace, and a man hath put it on; he could not by it be justified from the breach of God's law before, he being a transgressor of it in time past, 1 John i. 8, 10. 3. That perfection of which charity here is said to be the bond, doth most likely respect the integrity and unity of the members of the church, holding the Head, being knit together in one body; see on chap. ii. 2, 19, with Eph. iv. 16 : the Greek word we translate *bond* here, noting such a collection and colligation of parts whereof a body is composed; and in one Greek copy it is found written, the bond of unity. As a prevailing love to God, and to those who bear his image, for his sake, doth bind up the other graces in every regenerate soul, so it doth the true members of the body of Christ one to another, being the best means for the perfecting of them under Christ their Head, who hath upon that account expressly required mutual love amongst his followers, John xv. 12; 1 John iii. 23; iv. 21 : and the cogent reason hereof is, (as above in that 4th chapter of John's Epistle, ver. 10. 11,) God's loving of us : and then indeed, when we entirely love God and his children, we show our love to be the bond of perfectness in returning love to him and his; when by this reciprocal affection both ends of the band of love do meet and are knit together, we become one with God, and in him, through Christ, as one soul amongst ourselves, walking in love according to his commandment, Acts iv. 32; Eph. v. 2; 1 Thess. iv. 9.

15 And let ⁱthe peace of God rule in your hearts, ᵏto the which also ye are called ˡin one body; ᵐand be ye thankful.

And let the peace of God; he doth not say the peace of the world, but *the peace of God,* or, as some copies, the peace of Christ; be sure, without the mediation of Christ we can have no peace with God; he alone hath *made peace,* chap. i. 20, with ii. 14; he is *our peace,* making it with God and amongst ourselves, to whom he hath preached it, Acts x. 36; Eph. ii. 14—17, and whom he hath brought into the bond of it, Eph. iv. 3; *the Lord of peace* himself, who always gives it where it is enjoyed, John xiv. 27; 2 Thess. iii. 16. It is then the peace of God through Christ; see Phil. iv. 7, 9; by faith in whom we have peace in our own hearts with God, Isa. xxxii. 17; Rom. v. 1, and xiv. 17, and with one another, John xvii. 21; Rom. xv. 6, 7, 13. That the members of Christ may live in this peace, 2 Cor. xiii. 11, the apostle here enjoins, as we render the word, let it *rule in your hearts :* the Greek word (both simple here, and compound, chap. ii. 18) is no where else to be found in the New Testament but in this Epistle, and it may signify either to arbitrate, or to mediate : our translation and the generality of interpreters take it in the former notion, for to arbitrate, or to rule, govern, sway, or moderate by way of arbitration, as he who sat judge, or umpire, to adjudge the reward in the agonistics. So the import of the apostle's injunction is, let it regulate, govern, superintend, or give law to the rest of the affections of the new man; let it be mistress and governess of all your motions, to keep them in due respect, and withhold them from attempting any thing disorderly, and to oversway disinclinations to the Divine pleasure or the good order of Christian community. The Arabic version is, let it be as the centre. Yet one learned man, conceiving the apostle doth here, as before, chap. ii. 18, glance upon the false apostles, (who would insinuate the mediation or intercession of angels,) thinks because the word signifies also to mediate, intercede, or interpose, the apostle's meaning may be, let the peace of God be to you instead of all conceited angelical mediators or intercessors, which would derogate from him that made peace, chap. i. 20, nailing what hindered to his cross, chap. ii. 14; let that preponderate with you in your hearts to overbalance any thing that can be suggested to the contrary. *To the which also ye are called in one body;* considering the Divine vocation, or the call of God, Rom. xii. 18; 1 Cor. vii. 15, and the condition or unity of the body into which ye are called under Christ your Head, 1 Cor. x. 16¶ xii. 12, 13, 25, 26; Eph. iv. 4. He adds, *and be ye thankful;* be ye gracious, or amiable, of an obliging temper (as some render the word, passively); or rather, as we take it, actively, *be ye thankful,* i. e. to God and Christ, and Christians; be mindful of the benefits ye have received, giving thanks to God always for all things, Eph. v. 20, and behaving yourselves as becomes the gospel.

16 Let the word of Christ dwell in you richly in all wisdom; teaching and admonishing one another ⁿin psalms and hymns and spiritual songs, singing ᵒwith grace in your hearts to the Lord.

Let the word of Christ dwell in you richly in all wisdom : one learned man conceives Paul to have written this first clause of the verse as in a parenthesis, joining in the sense what next follows to *be ye thankful* in the foregoing verse; another would have the parenthesis to begin from the 14th verse. The thing here exhorted to, is the plentiful inhabitation of the doctrine of the Bible, more especially of the gospel, that it may take up its residence and abode in our souls, which comes from the spiritual incorporation or mixing of it with faith, Heb. iv. 2; without which it may enter in as a stranger, but will not abide; it may cast a ray, or shine, but is not comprehended and doth not enlighten, John i. 5; 2 Cor. iv. 4; it may afford some present delight, Mark vi. 20, but not lasting. The apostle would have the word to be diligently searched, heartily received, and carefully observed; a child may have it in his memory, that hath it not in his heart : this indwelling of the word imports a regarding, as well as a remembering of it, Psal. i. 2; John v. 39; xx. 31; Acts xvii. 11; 2 Tim. iii. 15—17. If all the saints at Colosse were concerned in this exhortation, the papists oppose the Spirit of God in excluding (those they call) the laity from familiarity with the Scriptures in their mother tongue, being that all Christians are here indispensably obliged to instruct and warn themselves, (according to the original word,) as well as each other mutually, see Eph. v. 19. Then the use of the word, and the manner of expressing their thankfulness to God amongst themselves, is in singing to his praise *psalms, and hymns, and spiritual songs.* He doth not say, *teaching and admonishing* from these, (as elsewhere, Acts viii. 35; xxviii. 23,) but *in* them; implying it is a peculiar ordinance of Christ for Christians to be exercised in holy singing, as James v. 13, with an audible voice musically, Psal. xcv. 1, 2; c. 1, 2; Acts xvi. 25, as foretold, Isa. lii. 8, with Rom. x. 14. Some would distinguish the three words the apostle here useth from the manner of singing, as well as the matter sung; others, from the Hebrew usage of words expressed by the seventy, in the book of Psalms; yet, whoever consults the titles of the Psalms and other places of the Old Testament, they shall find the words used sometimes promiscuously; compare Judg. v. 3; 1 Chron. xvi. 8, 9; 2 Chron. vii. 6; xxiii. 13; xxix. 30; Psal. xxxix. 3; xlv. 1; xlvii. 1; xlviii. 1; lxv. 1; cv. 1, 2; Isa. xii. 2, 4; xlii. 10; or conjunctly to the same matter, Psal. xxx., xlviii., lxv., lxvi., lxxv., lxxxiii., lxxxvii., titles. Hereupon others stand not upon any critical distinction of the three words, yet are inclined here to take *psalms* by way of eminency, Luke xxiv. 44; or more generally, as the genus, noting any holy metre, whether composed by the prophets of old, or others since, assisted by the Spirit extraordinarily or ordinarily, Luke xxiv. 44; Acts xvi. 25; 1 Cor. xiv. 15, 26; James v. 13. Here for clearness' sake two modes of the psalms, viz. hymns, whereby we celebrate the excellencies of God and his benefits to man, Psal. cxiii.: Matt. xxvi. 30; and odes or songs, which word, though ordinarily in its nature and use it be more general, yet here synecdochically, in regard of the circumstances of the conjoined words, it may contain the rest of spiritual songs, of a more ample, artificial, and elaborate composure, besides hymns, Rev. xiv. 2, 3; xv. 2, 3; which may be called *spiritual* or holy *songs* from the efficient matter, or end, viz. that they proceed from the Holy Spirit, or in argument may agree and serve thereto; being convenient they be so called from the argument, as opposed to carnal, sensual, and worldly ditties. *Singing with grace in your hearts;* and then that this holy singing be not only harmonious and tunable to the ear, but acceptable to God, it is requisite it do proceed from a gracious spirit, or grace wrought in the heart by the Holy Spirit, and the inhabitation of the word, Isa. xxix. 13; Matt. xv. 8. *To the Lord;* to the honour of God through Christ our Lord, Luke i. 46, 47; John v. 23; 1 Pet. iv. 11.

17 And [p]whatsoever ye do in word or deed, *do* all in the name of the Lord Jesus, [q]giving thanks to God and the Father by him.

[p 1 Cor. 10. 31.
q Rom. 1. 8. Eph. 5. 20. ch. 1. 12. & 2. 7. 1 Thes. 5. 18. Heb. 13. 15.]

And whatsoever ye do: here the apostle give a universal direction how in every capacity, both personal and relative, in every motion, a Christian may do all so as to find acceptance with God. *In word or deed;* and that is in his expressions and actings, viz. comprehending his internal as well as external operations; his reasonings and resolutions within, as well as his motions without; the thoughts of his heart, as well as the words of his tongue and the works of his hand; to take care as much as possible that all be *in the name of the Lord Jesus:* elsewhere writing the same thing, the apostle adds *Christ,* Eph. v. 20. Plato could say, Not only every word, but every thought, should take its beginning from God; but he understood nothing of the Mediator, of the love of him and the Father: but Christians know, as there is salvation in no other name, Acts iv. 12, so there is no acceptance of their persons and performances in any other name than in his in whom they believe, Phil. ii. 10; Heb. x. 19, 20; 1 John v. 13; and therefore in all their desires they are to respect him, John xiv. 13, 14; xv. 3, 16; xvi. 23, 26; looking for his authority and warrant, Matt. xviii. 18—20; Mark xi. 9; 1 John v. 14; following his example, Matt. xi. 29; xvi. 24; John xiii. 15; 1 Pet. ii. 21—24; 1 John ii. 6; in all they set about, desiring strength from him, Psal. lxxi. 17; Acts iv. 7, 10; 1 Cor. xv. 10; Phil. iv. 13; 2 Tim. ii. 1; living by faith upon him, Gal. ii. 20; Heb. x. 38; 2 Pet. i. 2, 3; waiting upon him, worshipping and serving of him, according to his prescription, Micah iv. 5; Matt. xxviii. 19, 20; Acts ii. 42, 43; 2 Tim. ii. 19; for his sake, Matt. xix. 29; xxiv. 9; Acts ix. 16; Rev. ii. 3, 13; iii. 8; to his honour and glory, Psal. xxxi. 3; 1 Cor. x. 31; Rev. iv. 9, 11; v. 12, 13; xi. 13. Endeavouring to render hearty *thanks unto God and the Father,* i. e. to God the Father: the Syriac and Arabic do omit the conjunction copulative; however, it is to be understood expositively of God the Father of Christ, and our Father, who doth embrace us as his children. *By him;* by or through Christ, Eph. v. 20; Heb. xiii. 15, the only Mediator.

[r Eph. 5. 22. Tit. 2. 5. 1 Pet. 3. 1. s Eph. 5. 3.]

18 [r]Wives, submit yourselves unto your own husbands, [s]as it is fit in the Lord.

The apostle, entering upon an exhortation to relative duties, begins first with that which wives owe to their husbands to whom they are married, by reason this relation is the first in nature, and the fountain whence the rest do flow, Gen. ii. 22; Psal. cxxvii. 3; cxxviii. 3; Prov. v. 15, 16. That which he requires is self-submission in every thing, see Eph. v. 22, expressing a subjection with reverence, ver. 24, 33; 1 Pet. iii. 1. The God of order made the woman inferior, Gen. ii. 18, 22; iii. 16; 1 Cor. xi. 7—9; 1 Tim. ii. 11; Tit. ii. 5; yet her submission is not to be servile, as that of a handmaid, but conjugal, as of a meet companion. *As it is fit in the Lord;* suitable to God's institution, in a becoming manner, agreeable to the mind of Christ, Acts v. 29; 1 Cor. vii. 39; Eph. vi. 1, 5.

[t Eph. 5. 25, 28, 33. 1 Pet. 3. 7. u Eph. 4. 31.]

19 [t]Husbands, love *your* wives, and be not [u]bitter against them.

The husband's duty is *love,* which the apostle doth ever inculcate from the most obliging considerations when he speaks of this relation; see Matt. xix. 6; 1 Cor. vii. 3, with Eph. v. 25, 33; to sweeten on the one hand the subjection of the wife, and to temper on the other hand the authority of the husband. *And be not bitter against them;* who, that upon his authority he may not grow insolent, the apostle forbids him frowardness with his wife, thereby requiring a conversation with her full of sweetness and amity: wrath and bitterness is to be laid aside towards all others. ver. 8, with Eph. iv. 31, much more towards his own wife, in whom he is to joy and delight, Prov. v. 15, 18, 19; 1 Pet. iii. 7.

[x Eph. 6. 1. y Eph. 5. 24. Tit. 2. 9.]

20 [x]Children, obey *your* parents [y]in all things: for this is well pleasing unto the Lord.

By *children* he understands both males and females.

Obey your parents; he requires them to yield humble subjection to those that brought them forth, or have just authority over them; see Exod. xx. 12: Eph. vi. 1; paying reverence to them, Lev. xix. 3; Heb. xii. 9; observing their holy and prudent prescriptions, Luke ii. 51; showing piety and kindness to them in all grateful offices, 1 Tim. v. 4, and submitting to their parental discipline, Jer. xxxv. 6; Heb. xii. 9. *In all things;* in whatsoever is agreeable to the mind of the supreme Governor, who is absolute Sovereign, Acts iv. 19; v. 29. *For this is well pleasing unto the Lord;* and this upon the most cogent reason imaginable, because it is not barely pleasing, but *well pleasing,* or very acceptable, *to the Lord,* who arms parents with authority over their children, Eph. vi. 1—3.

21 [z]Fathers, provoke not your children *to anger,* lest they be discouraged.

[z Eph. 6. 4.]

Fathers, provoke not your children to anger: and to moderate the parental authority, that they may exercise it Christianly, he allows not parents to do that which is in a direct tendency to irritate or move the passions of their children merely for their own pleasure, without a principal regard to God's glory, and their children's profit, Heb. xii. 10. Indeed, he seems here more strictly to guard fathers against mal-administration of their power in this extreme than he doth elsewhere, when writing upon the same subject, Eph. vi. 4, considering the original word he here puts the negative upon, to engage them to lay aside rigour in their government, (as well as unwarrantable indulgence,) and that upon a very weighty reason, drawn from the end, viz. *lest they be discouraged;* lest some children, who might with a moderate hand be reduced to obedience, should be (as it were) dispirited, by the roughness of their father's discipline, and even pine away with grief, or grow desperate.

22 [a]Servants, obey [b]in all things *your* masters [c]according to the flesh; not with eyeservice, as menpleasers; but in singleness of heart, fearing God:

[a Eph. 6. 5, &c. 1 Tim. 6. 1. Tit. 2. 9. 1 Pet. 2. 18. b ver. 20. c Philem. 16.]

Servants: the apostle knowing how hard the condition of servitude was, both under the Jews and Gentiles, lest any believers in that mean condition should disgust so strict a subjection, especially to unbelieving masters, and cast off the yoke by breaking their covenants, to the disturbance of human society, and the disparagement of the Christian institution, he takes a special care to sweeten the harshness of it to all those indefinitely whose lot it was, by recommending the duties of it to them from the consideration of the acceptableness of them to God, who of his unconstrained grace would vouchsafe to them the noblest reward. *Obey in all things your masters according to the flesh:* wherefore Christianity requires that servants of all sorts should readily receive and cheerfully execute all the commands, (see ver. 20,) in things lawful and honest, of those of both sexes, whom God in his wise providence hath given a just authority over them *according to the flesh;* (see also Eph. vi. 5;) which expression is not only for distinction from the Father and Master of spirits, Heb. xii. 9, but for mitigation of their servitude, in that their earthly master's power reacheth only things corporeal and temporal, not the conscience and things that are eternal, which might be some comfort, that the servitude would not last long, and in the mean time they were God's free-men, 1 Cor. vii. 22, whom they might *serve with the spirit in the gospel of his Son,* Rom. i. 9. *Not with eye-service;* yet their masters after the flesh, in those civil things wherein they had power to command, were not lightly to be respected or served to the eye, or only to be observed while their eye was upon them, Eph. vi. 6. *As men-pleasers;* as if regard were to be had to the pleasing of men, and not to the pleasing of God, who searcheth the heart, and by his gospel (which they should adorn) expects they should remember his eye is ever upon them, Tit. ii. 9; 1 Pet. ii. 18. *But in singleness of heart, fearing God;* and expects that, in a holy awe of him, they should do all that is incumbent on them, in the sincerity of their souls, (see Eph. vi. 5, 6,) with more regard to God than man.

23 [d]And whatsoever ye do, do *it* heartily, as to the Lord, and not unto men;

[d Eph. 6. 6, 7.]

Yea, courageously and cheerfully, from the very soul, not constrainedly and murmuringly, though they be froward and their commands harsh; making account it is Jesus Christ, (who hath power over soul and body, Matt. x. 28,) not mortal men only, or in and for themselves, whom you serve, (see Eph. vi. 7,) have an eye unto this Sovereign Lord, in the servile office your masters on earth do employ you.

e Eph. 6. 8.   24 ᵉ Knowing that of the Lord ye shall receive the reward of the inheritance:
f 1 Cor. 7. 22. ᶠ for ye serve the Lord Christ.

Knowing, being fully persuaded of this undoubted truth, *that of the Lord,* who superintends all your services, (not for any merit of yours,) Eph. vi. 8, the recompence which your Master in heaven hath purchased, Eph. i. 14, 18, shall be freely settled upon you whom he hath adopted into his family, Rom. viii. 17; Gal. iv. 7; Eph. i. 5; for in those duties you Christianly perform to masters of the same mould with yourselves, he really looks upon you as his own servants, (see Eph. vi. 6,) yea, and free-men, 1 Cor. vii. 22; so that, as Onesimus, Philem. 10, ye may more cheerfully submit to your masters' yoke, according to the command and for the sake of Christ, who reckons what you do upon that account as done to himself, Matt. xxv. 40, and will instate you in that eternal inheritance, to which neither you nor any mortal man had naturally any right at all.

g Rom. 2. 11.
Eph. 6. 9.
1 Pet. 1. 17.
See Deut. 10. 17.
25 But he that doeth wrong shall receive for the wrong which he hath done: and ᵍ there is no respect of persons.

But he that doeth wrong; but if the reward will not engage to a discharge of these relative duties, the injurious person, *whether he be bond or free,* Eph. vi. 8, an inferior servant or a domineering master, who doth violate the rules of right, agreeing with the law natural and eternal, *shall receive for the wrong which he hath done;* shall have the just recompence of that injury, whereby he wrongs his correlate; the penalty apportioned to his fault, Rom. ii. 6; 2 Cor. v. 10; 2 Pet. ii. 13. *And there is no respect of persons;* from the impartiality of Divine justice, *there is no respect of persons with God,* Rom. ii. 11, or with Christ, in the place parallel to this, Eph. vi. 9, who is so righteous a Judge that he is not swayed by the outward circumstances and qualifications of men, whether potent or poor, Lev. xix. 15; Job xxxiv. 19: he seeth not as man seeth, he looketh not on the outward appearance, but on the heart, 1 Sam. xvi. 7: in the distribution of justice, he will put no difference betwixt the mightiest monarch and the most enslaved peasant; the purloining servant, and oppressing master shall certainly receive answerable to their doings from his impartial hand: the mean one who is at present abused without relief, and the great one who doth tyrannize without control, shall one day have right, and be reckoned with by *the righteous Judge,* 2 Tim. iv. 8, who will show to all the world that he will honour those that honour him, and lightly esteem those that despise him, 1 Sam. ii. 30, and that he is the avenger of all those that are wronged, 1 Thess. iv. 6; 2 Thess. i. 6.

CHAP. IV

The duty of masters towards their servants, 1. *A general exhortation to perseverance in prayer,* 2—4, *discreet conduct,* 5, *and well-ordered speech,* 6. *The apostle commendeth Tychicus and Onesimus, by whom he sent this Epistle,* 7—9; *and concludeth with divers salutations, and a blessing,* 10—18.

a Eph. 6. 9.   MASTERSᵃ, give unto *your* servants that which is just and equal; knowing that ye also have a Master in heaven.

That this verse doth refer to the foregoing chapter, and that it was unadvisedly divided from it, is generally agreed. *Masters:* having put servants upon their duty, he doth here engage all those who have a just right over servants to mind their own duty toward those under their command. *Give unto your servants that which is just;* though your extract or estate hath advanced you above them in human society, yet you have the same nature and infirmities that they have, and (as in the foregoing verse) must appear with them before the same Judge and rewarder at the same tribunal. And the apostle doth elsewhere, Eph. vi. 9, require of masters in their superior relation, what he doth of servants in their inferior one, to *do the same things,* i. e. not the particular offices of their servants, but, according to general rules of right reason, that which, by the law of God, nature, and nations, is common to and incumbent on all relatives, Rom. xiii. 7, 8; Gal. v. 13; Eph. vi. 9. As he doth here require masters to do their servants right, give to them that which is their due for soul and body, Gen. xviii. 19; Exod. xii. 44; with respect to work, that it be neither too much nor too little, Prov. xii. 10; xxix. 21; to food, that it be convenient for nourishment, not luxury, Prov. xxvii. 27; xxxi. 15; Luke xii. 42; xv. 17; wages, Exod. ii. 21; James v. 4; and recompence, Deut. xv. 13. *And equal;* ye are likewise to give them that which is equal, or equitable, as well as just, which implies you should not be cruel to them, or discourage them; as you expect they should serve you with good will, so you should govern them wisely, and be good and gentle to them, Psal. ci. 2; 1 Pet. ii. 18, who are faithful, allowing them seasonable rest and refreshment, Deut. xv. 14, not despising their prudent answers, Job xxxi. 13, 14, but showing them favour in sickness as well as in health, 2 Kings v. 5, 6; Prov. xiv. 35; Matt. viii. 6. *Knowing that ye also have a Master in heaven;* and that upon this weighty reason, intimated before, that the above, whom you serve, will treat you as you do them; this you may be assured of, Eph. vi. 8, 9. If you expect favour at his hands, when he comes to distribute rewards and punishments, show it now to your inferiors, who will then appear as your fellow servants, when you must give an account of your stewardship, Matt. xxiv. 49—51, with Luke xvi. 2.

2 ᵇ Continue in prayer, and watch in the same ᶜ with thanksgiving;
b Luke 18. 1.
Rom. 12. 12.
Eph. 6. 18.
1 Thess. 5. 17, 18.
c ch. 2. 7. & 3. 15.

Continue in prayer; persevere or hold on strongly in prayer with fervency; we are apt to grow sluggish and indisposed, and therefore have need of quickening to this duty, Luke xviii. 1; Eph. vi. 18. *And watch in the same;* endeavouring to keep the heart in all fit seasons unto this, as a help to the precedent and subsequent duties, Psal. v. 3; Mark xiii. 33, &c.; Acts xii. 12; Rom. xii. 12; 1 Thess. v. 17; James v. 16; Rev. iii. 2. *With thanksgiving;* with acknowledgment of thanks for what we have already received, Psal. cxvi. 12, 13; 1 Thess. v. 18.

3 ᵈ Withal praying also for us, that God would ᵉ open unto us a door of utterance, to speak ᶠ the mystery of Christ, ᵍ for which I am also in bonds:
d Eph. 6. 19.
2 Thess. 3. 1.
e 1 Cor. 16. 9. 2 Cor. 2. 12.
f Matt. 13. 11. 1 Cor. 4. 1.
Eph. 6. 19.
ch. 1. 26. & 2. 2. g Eph. 6. 20. Phil. 1. 7.

Withal praying also for us; not only putting up petitions for themselves, but also interceding for Paul, and others with him, especially Timothy, mentioned in the salutation, chap. i. 1, 7; Rom. xv. 30; 2 Cor. i. 11; Phil. i. 19; 2 Thess. iii. 1; Philem. 22. *That God would open unto us a door of utterance;* that God would vouchsafe to us freedom of speech: see on Eph. vi. 19. *To speak the mystery of Christ;* effectually to preach the mystery of Christ: see chap. i. 26, 27; ii. 2; Matt. xiii. 11; 1 Cor. xvi. 9; Eph. i. 9. *For which I am also in bonds: for which I am an ambassador in bonds,* or, in a chain, Eph. vi. 20; i. e. with the soldier that kept him in his own hired dwelling, Acts xxviii. 16, 20, 30, 31.

4 That I may make it manifest, as I ought to speak.

That I may manifest, or open and clear, it in due circumstances, as becomes an able minister of Christ, Rom. i. 15; 1 Cor. ii. 4; ix. 16; with 2 Tim. ii. 15; iv. 2.

5 ʰ Walk in wisdom toward them that are without, ⁱ redeeming the time.
h Eph. 5. 15.
1 Thes. 4. 12.
i Eph. 5. 16.

Walk in wisdom; let your course of life be managed with all Christian prudence, that you may not any way disparage the Christian institution, 2 Sam. xii. 14; Rom. ii. 23, 24, with 1 Tim. vi. 4; with your innocency be *wise as serpents,* Matt. x. 16; see Eph. v. 15: yet, while you become all things to all to gain some, 1 Cor. ix. 20—23, you must take heed of such a compliance, whereby you

COLOSSIANS IV

may wound your consciences, Exod. xxxiv. 15; Eph. v. 11; and, on the other side, of such a contempt of them without just cause as may provoke them to persecute you. Paul was wary in his reasoning with those who were not Christians, and would have others to be so, Acts xvii. 24, 25, &c., with 1 Cor. v. 12, 13; not denying any of them what is due to them by Divine and human rights, Matt. xxii. 21; Rom. xiii. 7; 1 Pet. ii. 13. *Toward them that are without;* considering they are not *of the household of faith*, Gal. vi. 10, as you profess to be, you should be more circumspect, that you do not give occasion of offence to them, 1 Tim. v. 14, as well as take care you be not infected with their practices, 1 Cor. v. 6, but endeavour to *adorn the doctrine of God our Saviour in all things*, Tit. ii. 10. *Redeeming the time;* showing your prudence, say some learned men, in gaining time by honest craft, to secure you from spiritual dangers to your souls, or divert those who have power from persecutions: taking the expression proverbially. And for that purpose cite a passage in the prophet from the Septuagint, Dan. ii. 8. Others, and the most, import of the original words, take time for opportunity, or the fitness it hath for some good; and the participle we render *redeeming*, to import either morally, (not physically, which is impossible,) a recalling or recovery of time past that is lost, by a double diligence in employing what remains; or a buying up the present time, i. e. parting with any thing for the improvement of it to our spiritual advantage; or a buying it out, i. e. a rescuing it, as it were, out of the hands of Satan and the world, which by distracting cares and tempting pleasures do occasion often the misspending of it: see Eph. vi. 16.

k Eccles. 10. 12. ch. 3. 16. 1 Mark 9. 50. m 1 Pet. 3. 15.

6 Let your speech *be* alway [k] with grace, [l] seasoned with salt, [m] that ye may know how ye ought to answer every man.

Let your speech be alway with grace: because discourse is the tenderest part of our converse with men, especially those without, and ought to be managed with the greatest circumspection, upon occasions in every fit season, in imitation of Christ, who entertained those that did converse with him with gracious words, Luke iv. 22, you should endeavour so to speak when called, that the hearers may conceive your discourse doth proceed from a gracious spirit, or grace in the heart, chap. iii. 16, teaching your mouth, Prov. xv. 23, 24, *with meekness of wisdom*, James iii. 13, using knowledge aright, Prov. xv. 2, being in its tendency gracious, Eccles. x. 12; not ungrateful, (as tinctured with gall or venom,) but ministering grace to the hearers, Eph. iv. 29. *Seasoned with salt;* even as meat duly powdered with salt (Matt. v. 13) becomes acceptable to the discerning palate, so to the ear that trieth speech, fitly spoken words (Prov. xxv. 11) are of a grateful savour, cleansed from corruption, Job xxxiii. 3; Mark ix. 50. *That ye may know how ye ought to answer every man;* to this purpose chiefly in the main points of Christianity, that in a gospel-becoming manner, you may be able to give *a reason of the hope that is in you* (to those that ask you) *with meekness and fear*, Matt. vii. 6; 1 Pet. iii. 15, courteousness and sincerity, Eph. iv. 25, free from those evils of speech he had before enjoined them in this Epistle to put away, chap. iii. 8.

n Eph. 6. 21.

7 [n] All my state shall Tychicus declare unto you, *who is* a beloved brother, and a faithful minister and fellowservant in the Lord:

All my state shall Tychicus declare unto you: the apostle drawing to a conclusion, that he at so great distance might certify them of his love to them, and care for them, doth here acquaint them that with this Epistle he was sending two persons of integrity, for their satisfaction and his, viz. Tychicus, an Asiatic, their countryman and his fellow traveller, Acts xx. 4, whom he sometimes sent to others, 2 Tim. iv. 12; Tit. iii. 12, who would give them to understand what circumstances he was in, and all his affairs: see Eph. vi. 21, 22. *Who is a beloved brother;* whom he recommends to them as being a good man, a brother, as Timothy, chap. i. 1, and Epaphroditus, Phil. ii. 25, beloved of the people. *And a faithful minister;* and whom he had experimentally found to be a faithful deacon, in the larger acceptation, or *minister*, i. e. of Jesus Christ, and his messenger. *And fellow servant in the Lord;* and owned as his colleague, or *fellow servant in the Lord*, that they might more kindly receive him.

8 [o] Whom I have sent unto you for the same purpose, that he might know your estate, and comfort your hearts;

o Eph. 6. 22.

Whom I have sent unto you for the same purpose; who was Paul's messenger to them, as to let them know how it was with Paul, so to this end, 1. *That he might know your estate;* that he might clearly understand, how their matters stood, (as Eph. vi. 22,) especially with respect to spirituals, chap. ii. 1, 5. 2. *And comfort your hearts;* and cheer up their spirits, (as Eph. vi. 22,) that under the temptations of Satan, and tyranny of persecutors abroad or at home, they might not be discouraged, 2 Cor. iv. 17.

9 With [p] Onesimus, a faithful and beloved brother, who is *one* of you. They shall make known unto you all things which *are done* here.

p Philem. 10.

With Onesimus, whom he adjoins to Tychicus. Some, because of his following commendation, think him to be another person different from the fugitive servant of Philemon; but the most, comparing the description here with the circumstances in the Epistle to Philemon, ver. 10, 16, &c., conclude him to be the very same, taking Philemon for a Colossian. *A faithful and beloved brother, who is one of you;* there, as here, being expressly called a *beloved brother*, yea, and, which may answer to faithful, Paul's spiritual son, who (whatever he had been) would be profitable and a benefit to Philemon, whom Paul would have to receive him as his own bowels. And that which might commend him to the Colossians was, that he was one of that city, or the same birth with themselves. *They shall make known unto you all things which are done here;* these two persons of credit (upon the apostle's testimony) in their different circumstances, might, as joint witnesses, give them a full and certain account how things went with the church, and particularly with Paul, now a prisoner at Rome.

10 [q] Aristarchus my fellowprisoner saluteth you, and [r] Marcus, sister's son to Barnabas, (touching whom ye received commandments: if he come unto you, receive him;)

q Acts 19. 29. & 20. 4. & 27. 2. Philem. 24. r Acts 15. 37. 2 Tim. 4. 11.

Aristarchus my fellow prisoner saluteth you: here he doth wish prosperity to them, Luke x. 5, in the name of others, beginning with those of the circumcision, viz. *Aristarchus, a Macedonian of Thessalonica*, who had been his fellow traveller, Acts xix. 29; xx. 4; xxvii. 2; yea, and now his fellow prisoner, and fellow labourer, Philem. 24. *And Marcus, sister's son to Barnabas;* and John Mark, who was nephew to Barnabas, Acts xii. 12; xiii. 13; and having sometime displeased Paul by his departure and accompanying his uncle Barnabas, Acts xv. 37, 39, yet afterwards repented, and was reconciled to Paul, 2 Tim. iv. 11; Philem. 24; being profitable to him for the ministry as an evangelist. *Touching whom ye received commandments: if he come unto you, receive him:* concerning this same Mark, Paul had given orders to them, as well as to other churches, (who otherwise, likely, might be prejudiced against him for leaving Paul and his company in Pamphylia, Acts xiii. 13,) that if he came amongst them, they should entertain him kindly, who as Peter's spiritual son, 1 Pet. v. 13. did elsewhere also salute those who were scattered. Some conceive from the *commandments* here they had *received*, that Barnabas had written to the Colossians in commendation of his cousin Mark.

11 And Jesus, which is called Justus, who are of the circumcision. These only *are my* fellowworkers unto the kingdom of God, which have been a comfort unto me.

And Jesus, which is called Justus, who are of the circumcision; a third person of those who had been Jews mentioned in this salutation, is Jesus, surnamed Justus, (probably from his just conversation,) whether the same with him mentioned in Luke's history of the Acts, chap. xviii.

7, is not evident. The Greeks use Jesus for the Hebrew Joshua, Heb. iv. 8, it being common with them to more than one. However, the Christians, since the resurrection of Christ, out of reverence to their Lord and Master, (who is God as well as man,) have forborne to call their children by the name of Jesus. *These only are my fellow workers unto the kingdom of God;* these three alone, i. e. of the Jews, (as for Timothy, his father was a Greek or Gentile, Acts xvi. 1, 3, and others were Gentiles, Acts xxviii. 28,) were assistant to him at Rome (where it seems Peter was not) in expounding and preaching the gospel, enlarging the kingdom of grace in converting of souls, Matt. iv. 23; Mark iv. 11. *Which have been a comfort unto me;* the carrying on of which work did administer matter of great consolation to him in his bonds.

12 [s] Epaphras, who is *one* of you, a servant of Christ, saluteth you, always ‖ [t] labouring fervently for you in prayers, that ye may stand [u] perfect and ‖ complete in all the will of God.

s ch. 1. 7. Philem. 23.
‖ Or, *striving.*
t Rom. 15. 30.
u Mat. 5. 48. 1 Cor. 2. 6. & 14. 20. Phil. 3. 15. Heb. 5. 14. ‖ Or, *filled.*

Epaphras, who is one of you, a servant of Christ, saluteth you: after he had given them the good wishes of some of the Jews, he doth here give the like from some of the Gentiles, beginning with Epaphras, whom he had before commended, chap. i. 7, 8, and doth here recommend him as born and bred amongst them, devoted to their service, in being the servant of Christ, as Paul, separated to the preaching of the gospel, Rom. i. 1, yea, a fellow prisoner with the apostle upon that account, Philem. 23. *Always labouring fervently for you in prayers;* and, as it became such a one, faithful in his office, not diverted by distance of place or length of time, was night and day contending zealously with prayers to God for their spiritual, temporal, and eternal welfare, as Rom. xv. 30. *That ye may stand perfect and complete in all the will of God;* that they might attain a sufficient perfection in all that which God would have them reach to : see on chap. i. 28, 29; Phil. iii. 15. The distance betwixt Colosse and Philippi, &c. render it improbable, whatever a learned man conceits, that Epaphras should be the same with Epaphroditus.

13 For I bear him record, that he hath a great zeal for you, and them *that are* in Laodicea, and them in Hierapolis.

For I bear him record, that he hath a great zeal for you; for, saith the apostle, though I am not privy to his secret prayers, yet I can bear him witness, and do give him mine own testimony, that he hath a most ardent and special affection for you Christians at Colosse. *And them that are in Laodicea, and them in Hierapolis;* yea, and for those also in your neighbour cities; see the argument, and chap. ii. 1 ; viz. Laodicea, the last of the seven churches, to whom excellent epistles were written, recorded by John the divine, Rev. i. 11; iii. 14; and Hierapolis, or the holy city, about six miles distant from the former, say geographers.

14 [x] Luke, the beloved physician, and [y] Demas, greet you.

x 2 Tim. 4. 11.
y 2 Tim. 4. 10. Philem. 24.

Luke, the beloved physician; whether this Luke was the same with him that penned the Gospel and the Acts, because the apostle here gives him no higher a commendation, some doubt. But others, and the most, conclude that as Matthew from a publican became an apostle, and others from fishers of fishes, fishers of men, so Luke from a physician of the body became a physician of souls, and that this was the very person who was Paul's perpetual and individual companion in his travels, 2 Tim. iv. 11; Philem. 24; considering from his style he was an excellent Grecian, (very fit for a physician,) and made use of proper medical terms, Acts xv. 39; xvii. 16 : and here the apostle calls him *beloved,* as he had done Tychicus, ver. 7, and elsewhere his fellow labourer, who only of those that were not prisoners stuck to him, 2 Tim. iv. 11. Some think it to be Luke whose praises are celebrated in the gospel, or evangelical churches, 2 Cor. viii. 18; others would have that to be Barnabas, or some other : his practising of physic was no more inconsistent with being an evangelist than Paul's tent-making with being an apostle, 2 Thess. iii. 8. *And Demas, greet you;* he adds a third in this salutation from others, and that is Demas, who hitherto did persevere, and that as one of his fellow labourers, Philem. 24 ; though it should seem, afterwards, when the persecution grew hotter, he did for some worldly respect leave Paul, and depart unto Thessalonica, 2 Tim. iv. 10.

15 Salute the brethren which are in Laodicea, and Nymphas, and [z] the church which is in his house.

z Rom. 16. 5. 1 Cor. 16. 19.

Salute the brethren which are in Laodicea; having saluted the Colossians, in the names of others, circumcised and uncircumcised, he desires them in his own name to salute the Christians in the church at Laodicea. *And Nymphas;* and some pious man called Nymphas, probably living either in the country near the city of Laodicea, or some eminent Christian of chief note in the city. The masculine article adjoined shows this person to be a male, and not a female, as some have inconsiderately reckoned. *And the church which is in his house;* and the company of believers, either of his own family or neighbourhood, who did, under his protection or inspection, meet to worship God according to his appointment, Rom. xvi. 1, 5 ; 1 Cor. xvi. 15, 19.

16 And when [a] this epistle is read among you, cause that it be read also in the church of the Laodiceans ; and that ye likewise read the *epistle* from Laodicea.

a 1 Thess. 5. 27.

And when this epistle is read among you : the apostle takes it for granted, that, when this Epistle came to their hands, it would be publicly read in a solemn assembly of the church, or brethren, convened to that purpose, as elsewhere usual. For indeed he doth strictly enjoin and adjure the Thessalonians, under the penalty of the Lord's displeasure, that the Epistle or letter which he wrote unto them should be read unto all the brethren, 1 Thess. v. 27 : it being an indispensable duty of Christ's disciples, to search the Scriptures, John v. 39, and there solemnly to read them in the assembly for the edification of all ministers and people, old and young, Deut. xvii. 19 ; Psal. i. 2 ; cxix. 9 ; Mark xiii. 37 ; Acts xiii. 15 ; xvii. 11, 12 ; xviii. 26—28 ; Rom. xv. 4 ; 1 Tim. iv. 13, 15. *Cause that it be read also in the church of the Laodiceans :* hence (as it follows) the apostle (who it is likely had not an opportunity at Rome to have a copy of it transcribed) chargeth them at Colosse, to see or take care after the reading of this same Epistle amongst themselves, that, a copy of it being prepared for that purpose, it might, as from him, be also solemnly read or rehearsed in a public assembly of the Christians at Laodicea. *And that ye likewise read the epistle from Laodicea ;* and he further chargeth those to whom he wrote at Colosse, that they should take care that the Epistle (as we rightly with the generality of ancients and moderns render it) from Laodicea, be read amongst them. The Ethiopic version (as we have it thence in the Latin) reads, send it to Laodicea, that the Laodiceans also may read it, in the house or congregation of Christians there. The Vulgar Latin, that ye likewise may read the Laodicean Epistle, or the Epistle of the Laodiceans. Whence some of old and of late would have it thought, that St. Paul wrote a distinct Epistle to the Laodiceans. In favour of this opinion, some bad man, out of this Epistle to the Colossians, and that to the Ephesians, patched up and forged a short, but gross and trifling, Epistle, and fathered it on the apostle, though very dissonant from his character and style; whereupon it hath been rejected as spurious and apocryphal by the learned fathers, and the second council of Nice ; and since by the learned on all hands, except some few of the papists, and except quakers, who printed a translation of it, and plead for it. Some papists urge this, to argue that the church gives the Scripture authority amongst Christians. But though she is bound to preserve the books of Divine authority, it doth not belong to her to authenticate them, or prescribe them as the rule of faith ; that were no less than to outrage the majesty of the Author. Others allege it, as being lost, and thereupon would infer the canon of Holy Scriptures to be defective. But supposing, yet not granting, that Paul had written an Epistle to the Laodiceans, which had not come down to us, it were altogether inconsequent that the canon of Scriptures we have doth not contain all things necessary to salvation. Some, still harping on the Vulgar translation of the Laodicean Epistle, (though that in common speech might argue they wrote it rather than received it,) would fancy that it was the Epistle Paul wrote to the Ephesians; but Tertullian did brand the impostor Marcian for changing the title of Paul's Epistle to the Ephesians. Others conceit it may be understood of Paul's Epistle to Philemon, whom Paul calls his fellow labourer, likely exercising his ministry in the neighbour city of Laodicea, which was sent by Onesimus, and for the sake of Onesimus, who was a Colossian, was to be read at Colosse. Others, because Luke is mentioned, ver. 14, that it was an Epistle of his to the Laodiceans; but of that there is no evidence. Neither is it probable that Paul would in this Epistle to the Colossians have saluted the Laodiceans, had he written a distinct Epistle to them. Wherefore it is most rational to understand it, not of an Epistle of Paul written to the Laodiceans, but as our Bibles, according to an authentic copy, have, with the Greek fathers, faithfully translated and represented it, writien *from Laodicea*. Some conjecture it to be the First Epistle of John, which they conceive was written from the city of Laodicea. Others think it was the First Epistle to Timothy, from the inscription or subscription of a long time put at the end of it, as if written from Laodicea. But against that it may be excepted, there is no mention of Pacatiana, in the writers of the first age, but only in after-times, dividing the Roman empire into provinces; and some say this was first mentioned in the ecclesiastical records in the fifth synod at Constantinople. Further, there be several passages in the Epistle itself do intimate that it was written from some place in Macedonia, if we consult chap. i. 3, with iii. 14; iv. 13, not from Laodicea. Some think it to be meant of the Epistle from Laodicea, wherein they would answer the Colossians; how probably I determine not. Wherefore it is most probable, that the Epistle was written from Laodicea, to Paul at Rome; either by the church there, or some of her officers, which (likely he in straits of time enclosed, and) he would have read, as helpful to the edification of the Colossians, for the better clearing of some passages in this Epistle to them, wherein he had obviated such errors as he might hear seducers were attempting to disseminate amongst them.

17 And say to [b]Archippus, Take heed to [c]the ministry which thou hast received in the Lord, that thou fulfil it.

b Philem. 2.
c 1 Tim. 4. 6.

He also enjoins them to advise or advertise *Archippus*, whom he doth elsewhere call his *fellow soldier*, i. e. minister in the gospel, Philem. 2, on his and Timothy's behalf, to see to, or be mindful of, the nature of that excellent ministry he had undertaken, Rom. xi. 13; Eph. iii. 7; 1 Tim. iv. 6; yea, and to be more heedful, Acts. xx. 28, 29; 1 Pet. v. 1, 2, considering the authority of the Lord Jesus, in whose name he had been called to it, and intrusted with it, Matt. ix. 38; Phil. i. 17; 1 Tim. v. 1, 21; having been colleague to Epaphras, or in his absence newly received into this sacred charge, to encourage him to a faithful discharge of his duty therein, to fill up all the parts of his office, and leave none of them unperformed: see chap. i. 25; 1 Cor. ix. 16, 17; 1 Tim. iv. 16, with 2 Tim. iv. 5.

18 [d]The salutation by the hand of me Paul. [e]Remember my bonds. [f]Grace *be* with you. Amen.

d 1 Cor. 16. 21. 2 Thess. 3. 17.
e Heb. 13. 3.
f Heb. 13. 25.

The salutation by the hand of me Paul: the apostle having them on his heart, and here (as elsewhere) likely having used an amanuensis to pen the body of his Epistle, to prevent fraud and forgery he doth subscribe his salutation and apostolical benediction with his own hand, which was well known, Rom. xvi. 22; 1 Cor. xvi. 21; Gal. vi. 11; 2 Thess. ii. 2; iii. 17; Philem. 19. *Remember my bonds;* importuning them to be very mindful of his imprisonment in their prayers, ver. 3; Heb. xiii. 3, imitating his constancy and patience if called to suffer; see Phil. i. 14; his sufferings being an excellent seal to the truth of his gospel, and his ardent affection to them and other Gentiles, for whose sake he was in bonds. *Grace be with you;* then earnestly praying that the special grace and favour of God the Father in the Lord Jesus Christ might be ever present with them: see Rom. xvi. 24; 1 Cor. xvi. 23, 24; Phil. iv. 23. In testimony of the reality of his desire, and assurance to be heard, he concludes (as elsewhere) with *Amen.*

¶ Written from Rome to the Colossians by Tychicus and Onesimus.

THE FIRST EPISTLE OF PAUL THE APOSTLE

TO THE

THESSALONIANS

THE ARGUMENT

The apostle Paul, being more especially the minister of the uncircumcision, and preacher of the Gentiles, in his progress through their cities and countries comes to Thessalonica, a chief city in Macedonia, for thither he was called in a vision, Acts xvi. 9, *A man of Macedonia prayed him, saying, Come over into Macedonia, and help us.* In obedience to which he loosed from Troas, and came to Samothracia, from thence to Neapolis, and from thence to Philippi, where he abode certain days, ver. 12; and after passing through *Amphipolis and Apollonia, came to Thessalonica, where was a synagogue of the Jews*, Acts xvii. 1, whither, *as his manner was*, he went, and preached that Jesus was the Christ. Whereupon *some believed, and of the devout Greeks a great multitude, and of the chief women not a few*. But the Jews which believed not raised a persecution against him, whereupon the brethren sent him and Silas away to Berea, ver. 10, where he also went and preached in the Jews' synagogue. But the unbelieving Jews of Thessalonica following him to Berea, he was conducted thence to Athens; and from thence, it is thought by some, he writes this Epistle to the Thessalonians, as is asserted in the postscript. Wherein he gives account of the great success of his preaching among them, for which he gives thanks to God, and makes an honourable mention of them in several places. But because they were new converts, and met with persecution from their own countrymen for the gospel's sake, the apostle was the more solicitous for them, to confirm them in the faith they had received. Whereupon he endeavoured once and again to come to them himself, but some way or other was hindered by Satan, as he tells them, chap. ii. 18. And therefore he sends to them Timothy in his room, to know their faith, and to establish them in it; who bringing an account thereof to him, and of their state, he writes this Epistle to them, according to the account he received by Timothy, and his own observation and knowledge while he was amongst them. Particularly,

I. THESSALONIANS I

1. He gives thanks for the eminency and operation of the graces of God in them, for the special presence of the Holy Ghost in his ministry amongst them, for their exemplary faith and conversation, chap. i.
2. He puts them in mind of his ministerial labours and personal conversation among them, of the malicious carriage of the Jews both against Christ and his apostles, and particularly against himself, whereof he knew they themselves were eye-witnesses; and declares his present rejoicing and glorying in them, chap. ii.
3. He next gives the reason of his sending Timothy to them, and speaks of the good account he gave of them, and the great refreshing and comfort he received thereby; and that he was greatly desirous to see their face; and prays that they might increase in love, and be established in holiness, chap. iii.
4. He then proceeds to exhort them about their personal walking, according to the directions and commandments he had given them from the Lord Jesus. And he instanceth in marriage chastity, righteousness in dealing, brotherly love, peaceable carriage, minding their callings, and diligence therein; and not to mourn inordinately for them that die in Jesus, as knowing that they shall rise from the dead, and meet the Lord in the air, as well and as early as those that shall be found alive at his coming, chap. iv.
5. He next describes the manner of Christ's coming, that it will be sudden and unexpected, whereby many will be surprised in their security; and therefore exhorts these Thessalonians to be watchful, sober, and armed for that day, which will be to them a day of salvation which they had been appointed to. And then he exhorts them to duties belonging to their church state, and communion; to have a high esteem for their guides and teachers; to warn, support, and comfort one another; not to retaliate evil for evil, &c. And so, in the close of the Epistle, recommends them to God in prayer, begging they would also pray for him, and salute one another, and communicate this Epistle to all the brethren; and so concludes with his usual salutation.

This is the substance of the Epistle.

As to the place whence it was written, we need not inquire, whether it was, as is expressed in the postscript, from Athens; or from Corinth, as Grotius and others imagine.

As to the time, it was surely not long after Paul's coming from Thessalonica; for indeed the present state of the Thessalonians did require that he should not long delay it, as his secret affection to them would not suffer it neither.

And as to the order of the Epistle, that that which is called the Second Epistle should be really the first, and by some carelessness misnamed and misplaced, is a bold, groundless conjecture of Grotius, and needs no confutation.

But this is more probable, that it was the first Epistle that the apostle wrote to any church, though other Epistles are in order set before it. The gospel was more early preached here than at Corinth or Rome, as appears in the Acts of the Apostles, and the success of it was more sudden and eminent than in any other city, and their persecutions more, whereby they might obtain an Epistle from the apostle before any other church.

CHAP. I

The salutation, 1. *Paul showeth his thankful remembrance of the Thessalonians in his prayers on account of their faith, charity, and patience,* 2—4; *applauding them for their exemplary reception of the gospel, and improvement under it,* 5—10.

A. D. 54.
a 2 Cor. 1. 19.
2 Thess. 1. 1.
1 Pet. 5. 12.
b Eph. 1. 2.

PAUL, and ªSilvanus, and Timotheus, unto the church of the Thessalonians *which is* in God the Father and *in* the Lord Jesus Christ: ᵇGrace *be* unto you, and peace, from God our Father, and the Lord Jesus Christ.

Paul and Silvanus: why not Paul the apostle, as in some other Epistles? Because his apostleship was not doubted of by them, they had such an eminent seal of it upon their hearts; and there was no false apostles among them to question or deny it. And he joins *Silvanus* with him; whom Peter calls *a faithful brother,* 1 Pet. v. 12, and was a minister of the gospel joining with himself in that work among the Corinthians, 2 Cor. i. 19, as also among these Thessalonians, as appears, Acts xvii. 4, though there called by contraction of his name, or by another name, *Silas;* who is also mentioned, Acts xv. 22, as one *chief among the brethren,* and sent by the church of Jerusalem to accompany Paul and Barnabas to Antioch; and styled a prophet, ver. 32; and chosen by Paul to accompany him rather than Mark, ver. 40. And being an instrument with himself in converting these Thessalonians, and being also in their love and esteem, he joins his name with his own in the Epistle. *And Timotheus;* his name is Greek, for *his father was a Greek,* but his mother *a Jewess,* Acts xvi. 1, whose name was *Eunice,* 2 Tim. i. 5. He was brought up in the Jewish religion, instructed from a child by his parents in the Holy Scriptures of the Old Testament, but instructed by Paul in the faith of Christ, whom therefore he calls his *son in the faith,* 1 Tim. i. 2, *well reported of by the brethren,* Acts xvi. 2; whom Paul laid hands upon with other elders to separate him to the work of the ministry, and the office of an evangelist, and thereby had *a gift of God* bestowed upon him, 2 Tim. i. 6; called by Paul his συνεργὸς, or *workfellow,* Rom. xvi. 21, and particularly in the conversion of these Thessalonians, together with Silvanus, as appears,

Acts xvii. 14. He abode with them when Paul was persecuted from them, as there we find; and was sent to them from Athens afterwards by Paul to know their state, and strengthen their faith, chap. iii. 1, 2. And thereupon, that his Epistle might obtain the greater respect, he joins his name also in it; as he doth also in his Second Epistle to the Corinthians, in his Epistle to the Philippians, and to the Colossians. He being Paul's companion in his ministry among the Gentiles in their first conversion, and a man of great name in the churches, he therefore so frequently joins his name with his own. And also that he might show their consent in the truth they delivered to the churches, which might the more confirm their faith in theirs. *Unto the church of the Thessalonians;* the church inhabiting Thessalonica, which was a chief city in Macedonia, a metropolis, famous for antiquity, largeness, pleasant situation, and commerce. *Plin.* lib. iv. 10. First called Thessalia, and being conquered by king Philip, was called Thessalonica. Philippi was also another great city of Macedonia, where was planted another church, to whom the apostle writes; whereby we may see that God had a great work for Paul here, when he called him in a vision to go to Macedonia. *Which is in God the Father;* not as the Son of God is in the Father, to be one substance and essence with him; nor as the human nature is in the Divine nature of Christ, to be one person with the Father; but it imports either their forsaking false gods and joining themselves to the worship of the true God, as in the 9th verse of this chapter, *ye turned from idols to serve the living and true God;* called therefore in a distinction from them, *God the Father:* or else their worshipping God according to the revelation made of him in the gospel, where he is called Father. But in a sense differing from what Plato or Homer, and other heathens, understood when they called the chief God, Father; either with respect to their inferior deities, of whom they styled him Father, or the works of creation proceeding from him as his offspring. And their being in him may yet imply more than this; which is their being joined to God in covenant, as their God and Father; and so believing in him, established upon him as their foundation, and as their centre resting in him. It may also further imply their union and communion with God through the Spirit, whereby the saints are said to abide in God, and to dwell in him, and he in them, 1 John ii. 27, 28, yea, to be *in him* who is *the true God,* 1 John v. 20. *And in the Lord Jesus Christ;* these two are put together, because there is no access to God the Father, no true worship of him, no union or communion with him, and so no being in him, but through Jesus Christ. And by both they might see the blessed state they were now brought to by the gospel; being before strangers to God the Father and Jesus Christ, but now in them. And though being in God the Father is first mentioned, yet in the order of nature we are first in Christ, and through him in God the Father. And the apostle the rather asserts this of them, because the gospel came to them not in word only, but in power. And hereby he gives them the character of a true church of Christ, what it is, at least what it ought to be; for to be in God the Father and in the Lord Jesus Christ, imports more than literal knowledge, dogmatical faith, or outward profession. *Grace be unto you, and peace;* this the apostle calls his salutation with his own hand, *which is my token,* saith he, *in every epistle, so I write,* 2 Thess. iii. 17. Read 1 Cor. i. 3; 2 Cor. i. 2, &c. And under the Old Testament the Jew's usual salutation was, *Peace be to you;* under the New it is, *Grace and peace.* Peace comprehends all blessings; and grace or favour, the spring out of which they flow. The grace of God is now said to have appeared and to shine forth, Tit. ii. 11, and the church of God to be blest with all spiritual blessings, Eph. i. 3; so that now the apostle Paul salutes the churches with *grace and peace;* and the apostle Peter adds, *Grace and peace be multiplied unto you,* 2 Pet. i. 2. *Mercy unto you, and peace, and love, be multiplied,* Jude 2. Or if we take *grace* for grace inherent in us, as sometimes it is taken; and *peace* for the inward tranquillity of mind, heart, and conscience; the text may bear it. Yet the former rather meant *to you,* to you that are in God the Father, and in Jesus Christ: not to infidels out of the church; grace *to you,* and peace. *From God our Father, and the Lord Jesus Christ;* wherein are showed grace and peace in their original, *from God;* and not from God absolutely considered, but as *our Father:* as a Father he conveys the blessings of grace and peace to his children; but yet not immediately, but through *Jesus Christ,* as merited by his blood, and procured by his intercession. The Holy Ghost is not mentioned, though he must be understood; but he is rather considered as the actual conveyer of these blessings, than the original or procurer of them. And the three Persons work in the same order in the work of redemption as of creation, though more distinctly.

e Rom. 1. 8.
Eph. 1. 16.
Philem. 4.

2 ᶜWe give thanks to God always for you all, making mention of you in our prayers;

We give thanks to God; after his salutation he adds his thanksgiving and prayer for them. He saw in them an eminent seal of his apostleship, and effect of his ministry, and advantage to the gospel in their example, and so gives thanks. And his thanks is to God, because the success of the gospel was more from his blessing than his own ministry. *Always;* πάντοτε, that is, in a constant course; or *affectu,* though not *actu,* by a grateful sense he had of it continually upon his heart. *For you all;* for he had a good report of them all from Timothy, chap. iii. 6, and we find not one reproof in this First Epistle to any one, as in the Second. *Making mention of you in our prayers;* he adds also his prayer for them, wherein he made mention of them by name, as some understand the words, μνείαν ὑμῶν ποιούμενοι. Prayer and thanksgiving ought to go together, especially in the ministers of the gospel, and in the work of their ministry. And thus the apostle practised towards other churches also, as Rom. i. 8; Phil. i. 3, &c.

d ch. 2. 13.
e John 6. 29.
Gal. 5. 6.
ch 3. 6.
2 Thess. 1.
3, 11.
Jam. 2. 17.
f Rom 16. 6.
Heb. 6. 10.

3 ᵈRemembering without ceasing ᵉyour work of faith, ᶠand labour of love, and patience of hope in our Lord Jesus Christ, in the sight of God and our Father;

Remembering without ceasing; the occasion of his constant thanksgivings was his constant remembering of that grace of God that did so abound and work powerfully in them, not as if he had always an actual remembrance of it, but he did not forget it, the habitual sense of it was continually in his mind, and was often actually in his thoughts, especially in his approaches to God; and that is all which is meant in the original word, ἀδιαλείπτως. While the apostle was with them he saw this in them, but being now absent he remembered it; and with such a practical remembrance as stirred up his heart to thanksgiving. That is a good memory where is treasured up matter of prayer and thanksgiving. *Your work of faith;* or the work of the faith of you, that is, their faith and the work of it; whereby he intimates their faith was true and real; a faith *unfeigned,* 2 Tim. i. 5; *the faith of God's elect,* Tit. i. 1; and so distinguished from a dead faith, James ii. 26. They *received the work in much affliction, with joy of the Holy Ghost;* they *turned from idols to the service of the true God;* they waited for the coming of Christ, &c.; here was the work of faith. *And labour of love;* a labour to weariness, as the word imports; laborious love. True faith hath its work, but love hath its labour; and when faith worketh by love it will work laboriously. Whereby the apostle declares the reality of their love, as well as their faith; it was unfeigned love, yea, fervent love, the labour of it went forth towards that true God whom they now worshipped, that Jesus Christ on whom they now believed, and to the saints that were now their fellow brethren, chap. iv. 10; and particularly to the apostle himself, as in other ways, so particularly in the pains and labour that some of them took to conduct and travel along with him from Thessalonica to Athens, Acts xvii. 15. *And patience of hope:* the apostle had mentioned before their *faith* and *love,* and now their *hope;* which are called the three cardinal or theological graces, all mentioned together by him, 1 Cor. xiii. 13; and by which we have all our communion with God on earth. And as their faith had its *work,* and love its *labour,* so their hope had its *patience* as the fruit and product of it. There is a patience with respect to an expected good, and with respect to an incumbent evil; and both produced by hope. The former is more properly called μακροθυμία, or length of mind, consisting in waiting for and expectation of some desired good; the latter is ὑπομονή, consisting in patient suffering, or abiding under some present evil. Their former patience is mentioned in the 10th verse of this chapter, they *waited for his Son from heaven.* The latter in the second chapter, 14th verse, *Ye also have suffered like things of your own countrymen, as they* (i. e. the churches of Judea) *have of the Jews.* This latter is here specially meant in the text; and for which he gives God thanks, 2 Thess. i. 4. And hope produceth the former patience, as it looks upon the expected good as that which will come at last; and the latter patience, as it looks upon the suffered evil as that which will not always continue. And when with respect to both these the mind of man is kept sedate and quiet, this is the *patience of hope.* *In our Lord Jesus Christ;* or, of our Lord Jesus Christ, as the efficient and author of this hope, and of their faith and its work, and love and its labour: or, *in our Lord Jesus Christ,* as here rendered; and so he is the object of this hope, 1 Cor. xv. 19; 1 Tim. i. 1. And by this the Christian's hope is distinguished from all other. All hope worketh patience. The husbandman's hope to receive the former and latter rain, maketh him wait for it with patience, James v. 7; the hope of the merchant, for the return of his adventure; the hope of the heir, for his inheritance; but the Christian's hope worketh patience as fixed upon Christ: other hope resteth upon the things of this lower visible world, but this is as an anchor sure and stedfast, entering within the veil, where Christ is entered as a forerunner, &c., Heb. vi. 19, 20. Faith and love both have Christ for their object; but considered as present; but the patience of hope in Christ respecteth something future, some revelation of him, and salvation by him, which is yet to come. *If we hope for that we see not, then do we with patience wait for it,* Rom. viii. 25. *In the sight of God and our Father:* these words are not in the Syriac or Arabic version. And they respect either the apostle's thanksgiving and prayer for them, and his remembering the grace of God in them when he solemnly approached God's presence; for in all duties of worship we come before God, and present ourselves in his sight, and their graces he before mentioned, he remembered them to God, and presented them to his view: or they respect the omniscience of God, that their work of faith, labour of love, &c. were all in God's sight, and he was a delighted spectator of them: or, lastly, they may respect the sincerity of their hearts in all the actings of their faith, love, and hope; they did all this in the sight of God. As the apostle asserts his sincerity in his ministry by this, *We speak as in the sight* of God, 2 Cor. ii. 17. And thus the apostle mentions their graces, not as the heathen orators, who made great encomiums of virtue to the praise of men, but to the honour and praise of God.

4 Knowing, brethren ‖ beloved, ^gyour election of God.

‖ Or, *beloved of God, your election.*
g Col. 3. 12.
2 Thess. 2. 13.

Another ground of his thanksgiving for them. By the manner of their receiving the gospel, and the evident operation of the graces of God's Spirit, the apostle knew their election of God. We cannot know election as in God's secret decree, but as made manifest in the fruits and effects of it. As there is a knowledge of things *a priori*, when we argue from the cause to the effect, so *a posteriori*, when we argue from the effects to the cause. And thus the apostle came to know their election. Not, we hope it, or conjecture it, but we know it; and not by extraordinary revelation, but by evident outward tokens. And if the apostle knew this, why should we think they themselves might not know it also; and the words may be read, Ye knowing your election of God. And election imports the choosing of some out of others; for election cannot comprehend all. Some deny all eternal election of particular persons, and make it a temporal separation of persons to God in their conversion; but is not this separation from a pre-existing decree, God doing *all things after the counsel of his own will?* Eph. i. 11. Or, they will yield an eternal election of persons, but only conditional; one condition whereof is perseverance to the end. But the apostle asserts their election at present, before he saw their perseverance.

5 For ^hour Gospel came not unto you in word only, but also in power, and ⁱin the Holy Ghost, ^kand in much assurance; as ^lye know what manner of men we were among you for your sake.

h Mark 16. 20. 1 Cor. 2. 4. & 4. 20.
i 2 Cor. 6. 6.
k Col. 2. 2. Heb. 2. 3.
l ch. 2. 1, 5, 10, 11.
2 Thess. 3. 7.

The former part of the verse asserts the reasons on which the apostle built the knowledge of their election, which is the manner of the gospel's coming to them. *Our gospel;* because preached by him and others to them; or intrusted with them ἐγενήθη εἰς ὑμᾶς. *Came not unto you in word only, but also in power;* confirmed by miracles, and had powerful operation upon your hearts. The power of God went along with our ministry, which did not with the false teachers, 1 Cor. iv. 19; and *the kingdom of God is not in word, but in power,* ver. 20. *And in the Holy Ghost;* either in gifts of the Holy Ghost which ye received, or that power which ye felt from the gospel upon your hearts was through the Holy Ghost: that they might not think it was their ministry, or the word alone, that had this power upon them. *And in much assurance;* ye giving full assent to the truth of the gospel, without doubting on your part; or preached to you with much confidence and assurance on our part. The former sense is best. And there is an allusion in the word to a ship riding upon the sea with a full gale, and not turned out of its course by a contrary wind. Your faith triumphed over the waves of all objections, disputes, or hesitations of mind. For doubtings of mind do much hinder the power of the word upon the heart. And this assurance they had from the Holy Ghost. *As ye know what manner of men we were among you for your sake;* we did not carry ourselves among you like ordinary men, but by our laboriousness and zeal in preaching, our patient suffering for the gospel we preached, by our holy conversation, by our denial of ourselves in labouring with our hands amongst you, and by our great tenderness and affection to you, you might perceive that we were men sent of God, and our ministry was from heaven, and that we sought not yours, but you; whereby you had an advantage to entertain the gospel preached by us with greater assurance. And in all these things we had respect to your salvation. And for the truth of all this, he appeals to their own knowledge, and that mighty presence and assistance of God in their ministry among them; as they could not but perceive it, so it was all for their sake.

6 And ^mye became followers of us, and of the Lord, having received the word in much affliction, ⁿwith joy of the Holy Ghost:

m 1 Cor. 4. 16. & 11. 1.
Phil. 3. 17.
ch. 2. 14.
2 Thess. 3. 9.
n Acts 5. 41.
Heb. 10. 24.

VOL. III—24

And ye became followers of us; as you received our gospel in the power of it into your hearts, so you showed it forth in your conversation, becoming followers or imitators of us in our patient and cheerful sufferings, and our holy and self-denying carriage. The doctrine of the gospel which we taught you, we practised it before your eyes, and you followed us therein; though before you walked according to the course of the world, and were followers of the religion and manners of the heathen. The examples of ministers ought to be teaching as well as their doctrine. *And of the Lord;* we have followed the example of Christ, and ye followed us. So that as you believed on Christ as your Saviour, so you followed his commands and examples as your Lord and Master; as he exhorts the Corinthians, *Be ye followers of me, as I also am of Christ,* 1 Cor. xi. 1. *Having received the word in much affliction:* though affliction and persecution attended the word, yet you received it; and this receiving was not only into your heads by knowledge of it, and into your hearts by an effectual believing it, but into your practice by a walking according to it. For receiving the word, in the Scripture phrase, comprehends all this in it. *With joy of the Holy Ghost;* though afflictions attended you, they did not deject your spirits, but you had joy in your hearts by the Holy Ghost; who usually doth give forth his joy most to the saints when under suffering, which is one instance of the gospel's coming to them not in word only, but in the Holy Ghost, as was said before. The glad tidings of the gospel did more comfort them, than all their sufferings did cast them down.

7 So that ye were ensamples to all that believe in Macedonia and Achaia.

As ye followed our example, and of the Lord, so ye were examples yourselves, and such great examples that influenced all the believers both of Macedonia and Achaia. Your example reached beyond the confines of Thessalonica, unto the believers of all Macedonia, yea farther, to the believers of all Achaia. And though the Philippians of Macedonia received the gospel before you, as appears in the story, Acts xvi., yet ye exceeded them, and became examples to them in your faith and patience, &c.

8 For from you ^osounded out the word of the Lord not only in Macedonia and Achaia, but also ^pin every place your faith to God-ward is spread abroad; so that we need not to speak any thing.

o Rom. 10. 18.
p Rom. 1. 8.
2 Thess 1. 4.

How could they be examples to persons so remote, amongst whom they had no converse? The apostle here resolves it. It was by way of report. Things that are eminent, and done in eminent places, such as Thessalonica was, easily spread abroad, either by merchants, travellers, or correspondence by letters. And this report is compared to a sound that is heard afar off, that made an echo, as the word implies. And that which *sounded out from you* was *the word of the Lord.* The word is said to sound by the voice of the preacher, 1 Cor. xiv. 8, 9; Gal. vi. 6, and by the practice of the hearers. The mighty power and efficacy of it was made known abroad, *not only in Macedonia and Achaia, but in every place;* not strictly every where, but here and there, up and down in the world. As it is said of the apostles' ministry, *Their sound went into all the earth, and their words unto the end of the world,* Rom. x. 18; the report of the gospel went farther than the preachers of it, and their receiving the gospel sounded abroad far and near. And not only the word, but *your faith to God-ward is spread abroad,* ἐξελήλυθεν. Your faith being so eminent, it was spoken of far and near. That ye believed so soon at our first entrance, as ver. 9; and though we had been shamefully treated at Philippi a little before our coming to you, and persecution followed us and the gospel we preached to you, yet ye believed, and your faith was eminent in the fruits and operations of it also, as was mentioned before, and is afterwards in the Epistle. And it was faith *God-ward;* it rested not upon men, no, nor only the Man Christ Jesus, whom we preached to you, but upon God himself, though through Christ ye became worshippers of the true God, and believed on him with an exemplary faith. *So that we need not to speak any thing,* either of the manner of our preaching the gospel, or of your manner of receiving it. Where men's deeds speak and commend

9 For they themselves shew of us ^q**what manner of entering in we had unto you,** ^r**and how ye turned to God from idols to serve the living and true God;**

_{q ch. 2. 1.}
_{r 1 Cor. 12. 2. Gal. 4. 8.}

For they themselves show of us, what manner of entering in we had unto you: the believers of Macedonia and Achaia do speak of these things ἀπαγγέλλουσιν, openly, whereby it is evident the word of the Lord sounded forth to them from you, and they, without any information from us, declare the great entertainment you gave us and our gospel at our first entrance among you. *And how ye turned to God from idols;* particularly your forsaking your former idolatry, when you worshipped idols, that were either the images or shapes of the true God, formed by men; or men whom they deified, and set up as gods, and worshipped them and their images; or inanimate creatures, as sun, moon, and stars, or whatever creature they found beneficial to them, the heathens made idols of them. These *ye turned from*: though it was by the power of God and the gospel upon your hearts, yet it was an act of your own. And though it was the worship of these idols you had been trained up in, and was generally practised, yet you turned from it. And as to the manner of it, *how* ye turned from these idols, as in the text; that is, how readily, how sincerely, how speedily, with a holy indignation of them: or, πῶς, *how,* that is, by what means; meaning by our entrance amongst you, and the power of our gospel upon your hearts, according to that prophecy, Isa. ii. 20, 21, which refers to gospel times. *To serve the living and true God;* to serve with religious worship proper to God; though the papists would confine the Greek word δωλεύειν to some lower worship they give to saints or angels; or it may signify the whole service of God. And here the apostle speaks of their religion in the positive part, the former being negative. *The living God,* so called in opposition to idols, which were either images without life, or inanimate creatures, or men that were dead whom they worshipped; or *living,* because God is so eminently, being life essentially, originally, eternally, immutably, and derivatively to all things that live. *As I live, saith the Lord,* as if none had life but himself, Isa. xlix. 18, &c.' And called the *true God* in opposition to false gods. The heathen gods had no deity but what men gave them by worshipping them. They were not gods by nature. Gal. iv. 8, and so not true. And as these things are spoken to show the power of the gospel, so in a way of commendation, that they did not only turn from idols, but did serve the true God; many profess the true God, but serve him not. As also they denote their privilege, that they served a God that could save them, which their idols could not.

10 And ^s**to wait for his Son** ^t**from heaven,** ^u**whom he raised from the dead, even** *Jesus,* **which delivered us** ^x**from the wrath to come.**

_{s Rom. 2. 7. Phil. 3. 20. Tit. 2. 13. 2 Pet. 3. 12.}
_{t Acts 1. 11. ch. 4. 16. 2 Thess. 1. 7.}
_{u Acts 2. 24. x Matt. 3. 7. Rom. 5. 9. ch. 5. 9.}

And to wait for his Son from heaven: this is added to show the further power of the gospel upon them, they had not only faith to God-ward, as was said before, but to Christ-ward. They did not only turn to the true God, in opposition to the heathen, but to the Son of God as the true Christ, in opposition to the unbelieving Jews. For though he was the Son of David after the flesh, yet he was the Son of God also; and not by creation, as the angels are called the sons of God, nor by adoption, as the saints are, but by eternal generation, though the Man Christ Jesus by his personal union is the Son of God. And their faith respecting the Son of God, was their waiting for him from heaven; not that their faith consisted only in this, but it suited their present state of affliction to wait for Christ's coming as a deliverer and rewarder, therefore here mentioned by the apostle; and their faith, hope, love, and patience may all be included in it. They believed that he was gone to heaven, and would come again, which are two great articles of the Christian faith. And though there was nothing in sense or reason, or any tradition, to persuade them of it, yet they believed it upon the apostle's preaching it. And though the time of his coming was unknown to them, yet their faith presently put them upon waiting for it. And the certain time of his coming is kept secret, that the saints in every age may wait for it. Though he will not come till the end of the world, yet the saints ought to be influenced with the expectation of it in all generations that do precede it. It is to their advantage to wait for it, though they live not to see him come. And here the apostle concludes his account of the glorious effects of the gospel upon these Thessalonians; that which follows in the chapter is by way of doctrine concerning the Son of God. *Whom he raised from the dead;* he mentions his resurrection from the dead after his sonship; for he was there *declared to be the Son of God with power,* Rom. i. 4. And, *Thou art my Son, this day have I begotten thee,* applied to Christ's resurrection, Acts xiii. 33. Or the apostle mentions it to confirm their hope of his coming again. Had they heard of his death, and not of his rising again, they could not have expected his coming from heaven. It is used as an argument by Paul to the Athenians, that Christ will come again to judge the world by God's raising him from the dead, Acts xvii. 31. And these believers also might comfortably expect their own resurrection, seeing that he himself is already risen, at his coming; and so be supported under their present sufferings, though they should reach to the killing of the body. *Even Jesus:* he that was before called the Son of God, is here called *Jesus,* or Saviour; a name that might more endear him to them, than by calling him the Son of God. And he mentions a great act of his salvation in the next words, and therefore here properly called Saviour; and when he comes, he will come to his people's salvation, Heb. ix. 28. *Which delivered us from the wrath to come:* if we read the word as our translation hath it, *delivered,* it looks to what Christ hath already done and suffered for our deliverance. If in the present tense, as the Greek now hath it, it implies a continued act: he is delivering us from the wrath to come, either by his intercession, or by supplies of his grace delivering us from the power of sin and temptations, and so preserving us in a state of salvation. Or if we read the word in the future tense, who will deliver us, as we often find the present tense both in the Hebrew and Greek to have a future signification, it refers to his last coming; and therefore the saints need not be afraid of the terror of that day, but wait for it; for though the wrath to come is greater than ever yet brake forth in the world, Rom. ii. 5, yet a drop of it shall not fall upon them. Though they may meet with temporal afflictions and chastisements at present, and may be assaulted by the wrath of men, yet they shall be free from the wrath to come. And this will be done by a powerful rescue of Christ, as the word imports, ῥυόμενον, notwithstanding all the danger and difficulty that may attend it.

CHAP. II

Paul setteth forth in what manner he had preached the gospel to the Thessalonians, 1—12, *and they had received and suffered for it,* 13—16. *He showeth his desire of coming to them, and the cause which had hitherto prevented him,* 17, 18; *testifying his joy and satisfaction in them,* 19, 20.

FOR ^a**yourselves, brethren, know our entrance in unto you, that it was not in vain:**

_{a ch. 1. 5, 9.}

For yourselves; αὐτοί, which some read, they themselves, &c.; and then the words refer to the believers in Macedonia and Achaia, mentioned before, chap. i. 9, 10. Or, if we read, ye yourselves, he appeals to their own experience and knowledge. *Know our entrance in unto you, that it was not in vain;* κένη, was not vain, or empty, without fruit; our very first preaching had great success. Though the gospel is always either the savour of life unto life, or of death unto death, yet if no good fruit spring from a man's ministry, it may be said to be vain; as the prophet complains,

I. THESSALONIANS II

I have laboured in vain, Isa. xlix. 4. Or, as some, our preaching was not about things vain and unprofitable.

2 But even after that we had suffered before, and were shamefully entreated, as ye know, at [b]Philippi, [c]we were bold in our God [d]to speak unto you the Gospel of God [e]with much contention.

[b Acts 16. 22.
c ch. 1. 5.
d Acts 17. 2.
e Phil. 1. 30.
Col. 2. 1.]

Here the apostle begins a new discourse, giving an account more particularly of himself, and of his carriage among them, which he mentions as a subordinate reason why his ministry was so successful; for the evil example of ministers often spoils the success of their ministry. And what he speaks would savour of vain-glory, but that he had therein a holy end; as he excuseth his boasting to the Corinthians and other churches upon the same account. And he first mentions his carriage in the discharge of his ministry among them. A little before his coming to them he had *suffered,* and was *shamefully entreated, at Philippi,* where he and Silas were beaten, thrust into an inner prison, and set in the stocks as a couple of villains, Acts xvi. 23, 24; yet this did not damp their spirits, nor discourage their coming and preaching to them. *We were bold ;* ἐπαρρησιασάμεθα, we used great confidence and liberty of speech, we were not afraid to speak the gospel freely, notwithstanding our sufferings. The same he asserts, 2 Cor. iii. 12. And this becomes the gospel, and will be to the advantage of it, and is most commendable in a time of persecution. *In our God ;* depending upon his protection and help, who is our God, and who sent and called us to the work of the gospel, and particularly in Macedonia: and to show he was not bold beyond his call and duty, or the rules of truth and sobriety. *To speak unto you the gospel of God ;* the glad tidings of salvation by Jesus Christ; which gospel, though we have called it ours because preached by us, yet it is *the gospel of God,* as being the original author and ordainer of it. *With much contention ;* with much agony: which is either to be taken actively, for their great earnestness and zeal in speaking, as Luke xiii. 24; or passively, for the perils they encountered therein, Phil. i. 30: by both which the Thessalonians might be induced, though not enabled, to believe. As he elsewhere calls the ministry *a warfare,* 1 Tim. i. 18, and *a fight,* 2 Tim. iv. 7, (the very word used in the text,) with respect to the difficulties and dangers attending it, or the opposition of false teachers; they contending for the faith, Jude 3.

3 [f]For our exhortation *was* not of deceit, nor of uncleanness, nor in guile :

[f 2 Cor. 7. 2.
ver. 5.
2 Pet. 1. 16.]

Our exhortation ; whereby he means either the whole gospel he preached, by a synecdoche, or particularly that which is hortatory; what was first taught doctrinally was followed with exhortations to faith and practice. The decrees of the council at Jerusalem are called an exhortation, Acts xv. 31; when Paul, and others with him, were desired to preach in the synagogue, the rulers said, *If ye have any word of exhortation for the people, say on,* Acts xiii. 15; but taken more strictly, Rom. xii. 8, in a distinction from prophecy and teaching. *Was not of deceit ;* this refers either to the doctrine taught by them; it was true, not fallacious, not a devised fable, and did not issue out of any error of judgment; and so the apostle gives a reason why they were so bold in preaching it, because they knew it was all truth. Or to their sincerity in preaching ; We did not use any impostures, we designed not to seduce men, as the false apostles did, but we really sought your conversion and salvation. *Nor of uncleanness ;* ἐξ ἀκαθαρσίας. If this refers to the doctrine preached, it denotes the purity of it, which did not tend to gratify the flesh, as that of the Nicolaitanes and Libertines, &c. If we refer it to the manner of their preaching, it denotes the purity of their hearts; they were not acted by any impure lusts in their preaching, as covetousness, pride, or vain-glory. *Nor in guile ;* this seems to be mentioned before, and therefore some expositors refer the two former expressions to the matter that they taught, and this only to the manner, which is most probable. They had no cunning designs upon them, to make merchandise of them, as the false apostles did; but approve their hearts to God, and make themselves manifest to every man's conscience in the sight of God. And the apostle allegeth all this as a further reason of his boldness in preaching, for sincerity breeds boldness; or as some cause also of his great success, for uprightness is usually attended with a blessing; or as an argument to these Thessalonians to continue their affection to him, and to abide in the doctrine preached to them, for suspicion of insincerity in the preacher hinders the efficacy of the word upon the people.

4 But as [g]we were allowed of God [h]to be put in trust with the Gospel, even so we speak ; [i]not as pleasing men, but God, [k]which trieth our hearts.

[g 1 Cor. 7. 25. 1 Tim.
h 1 Cor. 9.
i 17. Gal. 2. 7. Tit. 1. 3.
i Gal. 1. 10.
k Prov. 17. 3. Rom. 8. 27.]

But as we were allowed of God to be put in trust with the gospel : this verse gives the reasons of what the apostle spake in the former about his sincerity. The one is taken from his trust ; God intrusted him with the gospel, to preserve it from corruption by error, therefore his *exhortation* or doctrine *was not of* error or *deceit,* but he preached the gospel in simplicity and purity; he did not, he durst not, adulterate or corrupt it, for it was committed to his trust; as he calls the gospel his trust, 1 Tim. i. 11. And the sense of this great trust kept him also from *uncleanness* and *guile* in the discharge of his ministry. And he had this trust by God's appointment or approbation, God approved of him for this trust, and that upon knowledge and judgment, as the word signifies, δεδοκιμάσμεθα, and as he speaks, 1 Tim. i. 12, *he judged me faithful, putting me into the ministry.* Not so before his conversion, being a *persecutor, blasphemer,* &c.; but God fitted him by extraordinary revelations, gifts, graces, and made him faithful, and then put him into the ministry, and intrusted him with the gospel. And because he speaks in the plural number, *we were allowed of God,* &c., therefore Silvanus and Timotheus, yea, and other apostles and ministers, are to be understood as comprehended with him in this trust. *Even so we speak ;* that is, as men thus approved of by God, and intrusted with the gospel, that we may faithfully discharge our trust, and be able to give a good account of it, as stewards of their trust, 1 Cor. iv. 1, 2. *Not as pleasing men, but God, which trieth our hearts :* this is another reason of their faithfulness and integrity, mentioned in the foregoing verse, which was the sense of God's omniscience, knowing and trying their hearts. Trying imports more than mere knowing, it is a knowledge upon search and proof, as gold and silver are known by the touchstone. And though God trieth the hearts of all men, yet especially such as are intrusted with the gospel. Or these last words may have a more immediate reference to the foregoing; we speak not as pleasing men, because we know God trieth our hearts. And this confirms what he said before concerning his exhortation, that it was not of deceit, uncleanness, or guile. If it had, he would have so preached as to please men ; the opinions, the lusts, the practices of men. In some cases the apostle did seek to please men, 1 Cor. x. 33, *even as I please all men in all things.* But he pleased not men when it stood in competition with his pleasing God ; *we speak, not as pleasing men, but God.* Otherwise the rule takes place with all, Rom. xv. 2, *Let every one of us please his neighbour for his good to edification.* Ministers of the gospel are Christ's servants by office, and, as servants, they are to please their own Master. *If I pleased men,* saith Paul, *I should not be the servant of Christ,* Gal. i. 10. And this made the apostle have regard not only to his doctrine and outward conversation, but the inward aim and intentions of his heart, as knowing God tried his heart. And expecting the reward of his labours more from God than men, he therefore sought to please God rather than men, and approve his heart unto him. And herein he reflects upon those false apostles that sought to please men, preached up the law of Moses to please the Jews; or others, that preached and abused the doctrine of the gospel to gratify the lusts of men.

5 For [l]neither at any time used we flattering words, as ye know, nor a cloke of covetousness ; [m]God *is* witness :

[l Acts 20. 33.
2 Cor. 2. 17.
& 4. 2. & 7.
2. & 12. 17.
m Rom. 1. 9.]

In the former verses the apostle had asserted his integrity more generally; here, and in the next verse, he instanceth in particulars. He vindicates his ministry from the guilt of three vices which too often attend it; flattery, covetousness, and vain-glory. *For neither at any time used we flattering words:* first, flattery, ἐν λόγῳ κολακείας; or, we were not, i. e. conversant, in a word of flattery, as in the Greek; our word was not a word of flattery, as if we sought to please men. When we ascribe to men good things that they have not, or above what they have, or when we applaud or extenuate the evil that is in them, we flatter them. This is reproved often in the false prophets of the Old Testament, Isa. xxx. 10; Ezek. xiii. 10, 18; and in the false teachers in the New. The flattery of ministers is, their preaching of smooth things, rather to please than profit; when they avoid just reproofs, and searching truths, and close applications, that they may not displease; and affect wisdom of words, and rhetorical discourses, that they may please: when they either conceal some part of truth, or pervert it, that people may think their doings better than they are, or their state better than it is. *As ye know:* their words in preaching being an overt act, they themselves could judge of, and therefore the apostle doth appeal to their own knowledge in that. *Nor a cloak of covetousness, God is witness:* in what they could not know, which was their inward aims and designs, he appeals to God, which is a form of swearing; and in all oaths men solemnly do concern God therein; the same in effect that is called protesting, 1 Cor. xv. 31. And that wherein he thus appeals is, that he had no covetous design in his ministry, which he calls *a cloak of covetousness;* which lies either in undue withholding what we have, or inordinate desire of more. The latter is here meant, as the Greek word imports. And the word *cloak* is a metaphor as the word is translated here, and John xv. 22: as that covers the inner garments, so when bad designs are covered with specious pretexts, this we call a cloak. The word in the text, ἐν προφάσει πλεονεξίας, is often used, Matt. xxiii. 14; Mark xii. 40; Luke xx. 47, and sometimes rendered *occasion,* but for the most part *pretence,* and so to be understood here; and in heathen authors sometimes used for accusation. And this is contrary to what is said of false prophets. 2 Pet. ii. 3, *Through covetousness shall they with feigned words make merchandise of you.*

n John 5. 41, 44. & 12. 43.
1 Tim. 5. 17
o 1 Cor. 9.
4, 6, 12, 18.
2 Cor. 10. 1,
2, 10, 11.
& 13. 10.
2 Thess. 3. 9. Philem. 8, 9. ‖ Or, *used authority.* p 2 Cor. 11. 9. & 12. 13, 14. 2 Thess. 3. 8. q 1 Cor. 9. 1, 2, 5.

6 ⁿ Nor of men sought we glory, neither of you, nor *yet* of others, when ᵒ we might have ‖ been ᵖ burdensome, ᵠ as the apostles of Christ.

Nor of men sought we glory: this is the third vice he vindicates his ministry from. The word *glory* first signifies some excellency in any subject; secondly, this excellency as displaying and manifesting itself; thirdly, the opinion and esteem thereof in the minds of men, as the Greek word imports, and so taken in the text: we did not seek men's honour, high esteem, or applause; we sought them not in the inward bent of our thoughts, or the studies of our mind, nor in the outward course of our ministry and conversation, to form them so as to gain glory from men. Though honour and esteem was their due from men, yet they did not seek it. Honour is to follow men, men not to follow it. This Christ reproved in the scribes and Pharisees, that in their prayers, alms, fasting, affected habits, and titles, they sought the praise of men, Matt. vi. *How can ye believe, which receive honour one of another, and seek not the honour that cometh from God only?* John v. 44. Every man ought, with reference to actions honourable and praiseworthy, and a good name is a blessing; but to seek honour, that is the evil. And as the apostle did not seek it himself, so he forbids it to others, Gal. v. 26, *Let us not be desirous of vain-glory,* &c.; and notes some false teachers as guilty of it, 2 Cor. x. 12. It is a vice directly opposite to humility, unbecoming a man as man, and highly dishonourable to God, and contrary to the gospel. The heathens cherished it as the spur to great achievements, it is one of Tully's rules for the institution of princes; but the Christian religion, that gives all glory to God, condemns it. And yet we may seek the vindication of our name, when thereby we may provide for the honour of the name of God, as the apostle Paul often did.

Neither of you, nor yet of others; he adds this to show that this was their general practice among others as well as these Thessalonians; they were not guilty of flattery, covetous designs, or seeking the glory of men among any churches, or in any place; their practice in their ministry was uniform, and in all places upright and sincere. *When we might have been burdensome, as the apostles of Christ;* or, we were able to be in, or for, a burden, a Hebraism. By *burden* some understand authority: q. d. We might have used our ministerial authority more than we did, whereby to get greater honour and respect to our persons among you. And indeed all authority and honour have their weight and burden. Others by *burden* understand maintenance. And then he means, we might have been chargeable to you, according to the power given by Christ to his apostles to reap carnal things from them to whom they sowed spiritual things. And at the first sending them forth in Judea, it was so ordained by Christ, that they should be maintained at the people's charge: see 1 Cor. ix. But they were so far from covetousness, that they took not all that was their due, and what they might of their outward substance, and from seeking their own honour, that they did not use what authority they might to procure it among them; for they laboured with their hands night and day, that they might not be chargeable, ver. 9; though they might have challenged not only maintenance, but honourable maintenance, 1 Tim. v. 17.

7 But ʳ we were gentle among you, even as a nurse cherisheth her children: r 1 Cor. 2. 3. & 9. 22. 2 Cor. 13. 4. 2 Tim. 2. 24.

But we were gentle among you: he next gives account of their carriage more positively: and first he speaks of their gentleness among them; ἤπιοι, the Latin takes it for νήπιοι, infants, we were as infants to you, as nurses are as infants with their infants, and children with children. This is one of the fruits of the Spirit, Gal. v. 22; it stands opposite to moroseness, austerity, and roughness of temper, and is commendable in all, especially in ministers, 2 Tim. ii. 24; and was eminent in Christ, as was prophesied of him, Isa. xl. 11; xlii. 3; and the contrary he reproveth in James and John, Luke ix. 54, 55. It springs from humility, meekness, and patience; as the contraries are pride, passion, and frowardness. In some cases sharpness and severity may be needful; prudence is to direct, therefore, our carriage. The apostle had now to do with young converts, and under the trial of persecution; and not apostates and obstinate sinners, against whom we find he was sometimes severe and sharp, as Jude required. ver. 22, 23. *Even as a nurse cherisheth her children;* and he represents this gentleness by that of a nurse to her children; not of a hired nurse, but a mother nurse, Numb. xi. 12, who useth all tenderness towards them, beareth with their frowardness, condescends to the meanest offices and employments, and draws out her breasts to them, and lays them in her bosom, and all this to cherish them. And she doth this not out of hope of gain, but out of motherly affection. Thus, saith the apostle, were we gentle among you. As he converted them to Christ, he was their spiritual father, but his gentleness was like that of a mother, nursing her own children. He considered their weakness in their first believing, and bore with it; their many infirmities, temptations, afflictions that were upon them, had compassion over them, and supported them under them, and cherished them with the sincere milk of gospel truths; and he did all this not for gain, but out of sincere affection and a willing mind. Some extend the word we render *nurse* to the brute creatures themselves, especially birds, that hatch, and then cherish their young with the warmth of their own body, and care in feeding them: τροφός, the word signifies a feeder, and so may have a more general signification: see Job xxxix. 14.

8 So being affectionately desirous of you, we were willing ˢ to have imparted unto you, not the Gospel of God only, but also ᵗ our own souls, because ye were dear unto us. s Rom. 1. 11. & 15. 29. t 2 Cor. 12. 15.

A further account of their behaviour among them. The former verse showed their great gentleness, this their great love; expressed, first, In their affectionate desire of them; as the Latin phrase, *cupidissimus fui,* imports love to the person. And it was the desire of their salvation, first in their believing, and then perseverance and progress in faith. It was themselves, not their goods, they desired; as Paul elsewhere saith, *We seek not yours, but you.* Secondly, In the effect of it, which was imparting the gospel to them, whereby they might be saved; which is amplified by two things: 1. That they did this willingly, not out of mere necessity, with a backward mind; the word is εὐδοκοῦμεν, we were well-pleased to preach, and with complacence of mind. 2. That they were willing to impart their souls to them; that is, to hazard their lives for them in preaching to them, as Acts xvi.; the same word signifying both the soul and life, and he that dies for another gives his life to them. Or, it may refer to their labours and hardships, whereby they endangered their lives for them, *labouring night and day*, ver. 9. Others understand the words only as an expression of their great affection to them; a man imparts his soul to the person whom he entirely loves, as Isa. lviii. 10; when a man gives relief to a person in want out of love and compassion, he imparts his soul in what he gives. So did they in the gospel thus preached. And the word imparting is used to express relief to the wants of the body, Rom. xii. 8; and the gospel is the bread of life to give relief to the soul, and used in this sense also, Rom. i. 11. The apostle may here further allude to mothers that are nurses, who impart not only other food, but their milk, which is their blood, to cherish their children. *Ye were dear unto us*; or, ye have been beloved of us; wherein the apostle more plainly declares their love to them as the ground of all their labours and perils in preaching to them; yea, it may reach to all that he had said before concerning their carriage among them, all was from love.

9 For ye remember, brethren, our labour and travail: for ᵘlabouring night and day, ˣbecause we would not be chargeable unto any of you, we preached unto you the Gospel of God.

u Acts 20.34. 1 Cor. 4. 12. 2 Cor. 11. 9. 2 Thess. 3. 8. x 2 Cor. 12. 13, 14.

To make good what he had asserted before about their integrity in preaching the gospel, that it was without covetousness, and vain-glory, &c., and about their great affection to them therein, he appeals to their own memory. *Our labour and travail: labour*, in what we suffered, attended with care and solicitude of mind, as the word imports; and *travail*, in what we did, attended with weariness, as some distinguish of the words. *For labouring night and day, because we would not be chargeable unto any of you*; this refers to some bodily labour they used, which I find not mentioned in the story while they were at Thessalonica, though Paul did practise it at Corinth, Acts xviii. 3. To prevent scandal and misconstruction that may arise from receiving maintenance, and in case of the church's poverty, the apostle would refuse it; but without respect to these he pleaded it at his due, 1 Cor. ix. 1, &c. And his refusing was no work of supererogation, as the papists plead hence; for in such cases it was a duty with respect to the honour of his ministry; so that it ought not to pass into a rule, either that ministers in no case may labour with their hands to get their bread, or that they ought so to do always, as some would conclude hence, and preach freely. However, he commends them that they forgot not the labour and travail they underwent for their sake, and that both *night and day*, which implies assiduity and diligence, as chap. iii. 10; Psal. i. 2; Luke ii. 37; and so to be taken here. Though it may signify their spending part of the night as well as the day in some bodily labour, (the same we read 2 Thess. iii. 8.) yet not to be understood as if they spent the whole night and day therein; for how then could they have preached the gospel to them, as he here addeth; and they would take nothing of maintenance from *any* of them, or be chargeable or burdensome to them; not from the poor, to whom it might really be a burden, nor from the rich, who yet might be backward, and account it a burden.

10 ʸYe *are* witnesses, and God *also*, ᶻhow holily and justly and unblameably we behaved ourselves among you that believe:

y ch. 1. 5. z 2 Cor. 7. 2. 2 Thess. 3. 7.

The former verses gave account of their carriage in the ministry, this here of their Christian conversation; *holily*, with respect to God; *justly*, with respect to duties commanded towards men; and *unblamably*, in denying themselves in lawful liberty to avoid all occasion of blame from any of them. And for the truth of this he appeals to themselves; yea, to God himself. There is the witness of men, and the witness of conscience greater than of men, and the witness of God greatest of all, 1 John iii. 20. He appeals to them as witnesses about their external actions, and to God about the integrity of their hearts; and he doth this not in a way of boasting, but to be an example to them, and as a further reason of the great success of his ministry. The conversation of ministers hath great influence upon the success of their labours.

11 As ye know how we exhorted and comforted and charged every one of you, as a father *doth* his children,

Besides his public ministry, he dealt more privately with them, as Acts xx. 20; and that in a way of exhortation and comfort; by exhortation to quicken them, and by comfort to support them under troubles both outward and inward. And he did this as a father to his children, with much earnestness, compassion, and love, yea, and authority also. He was before represented as a mother, ver. 7; and here as a father, whose work and duty is to exhort, counsel, and comfort his children privately at home; so did he as well as publicly, for he was their spiritual father, as he begat them to Christ by the gospel, as he tells the Corinthians also, 1 Cor. iv. 15. As before he represented his gentleness, so here his fatherly care. Or, at their first conversion he carried it with gentleness as a mother, but afterwards used his fatherly authority. And in this he appeals to their own knowledge also, calling their own consciences to bear witness to what he speaks, that it might leave the greater impression upon them.

12 ᵃThat ye would walk worthy of God, ᵇwho hath called you unto his kingdom and glory.

a Eph. 4. 1. Phil. 1. 27. Col. 1. 10. ch. 4. 1. b 1 Cor. 1. 9. 9. ch. 5. 24. 2 Thess. 2. 14. 2 Tim. 1. 9.

In the Greek text the word *charged*, mentioned in the former verse, begins this verse; μαρτυρόμενοι, it signifies testifying: some read it, we obtested, which is as much as beseeching; others, contested, which is a severe charge, containing a threatening, as Exod. xix 21, *Charge the people*, saith God to Moses; in the margin, Contest the people, or wish the people. It is a charge here which the apostle gives solemnly in the name of God to them, calling in the witness of God to it. *That ye would walk worthy of God;* that is, suitably to the nature of that God who is the true and living God. That you may walk like a people who belong to such a God, and express the virtues of this God in your conversation, 1 Pet. ii. 9; or, suitably to the great mercy and glorious privileges you have received from him, which he mentions in the following words. *Who hath called you unto his kingdom and glory;* or, who is calling you; then by God's kingdom and glory we must understand the future state of heaven: though they were not yet possessed of it, yet by the gospel God had called them to it, as Phil. iii. 14; 1 Pet. v. 10. Or, *who hath called you*, as we read it; then he means their present state since they believed and obeyed the call of the gospel, they were brought thereby into God's kingdom and glory; or, his glorious kingdom, wherein the glory of God, especially the glory of his grace, mercy, love, and wisdom, eminently shine forth. Hereupon a Christian's calling is termed a *high calling*, Phil. iii. 14; a *heavenly calling*, Heb. iii. 1. And they being called by God out of Satan's kingdom into this glorious kingdom, the apostle chargeth them to walk worthy of God and this calling, by having a conversation suitable thereunto, Eph. iv. 1; Col. i. 10; to walk according to the laws of this glorious kingdom they were already brought into, and suitably to the glory of heaven that they were called to the hope of.

13 For this cause also thank we God ᶜwithout ceasing, because, when ye received the word of God which ye heard of us, ye received *it* ᵈnot *as* the word of men, but as it is in truth, the word of God, which effectually worketh also in you that believe.

c ch. 1. 3. d Mat. 10 40. Gal. 4. 14. 2 Pet. 3. 2.

The apostle having given the reasons on his part and his fellow ministers', why the gospel had such effect upon them, he next proceeds to show the reason on their part, for which he giveth God thanks. And that is, from their manner of receiving it; though this, as well as the former, are but subordinate reasons. First, they *heard* it; some will not do that; and therefore the apostle here calls it a word of hearing, a Hebraism, as Rom. x. 17, *Faith cometh by hearing.* 2. They *received it:* the word imported a receiving with affection, as Joseph the virgin Mary to his wife, Matt. i. 20. 3. They *received it not as the word of men*, which we receive sometimes doubting, sometimes disputing it; or believing it only with a human faith, upon grounds of reason, as the dictates of philosophy, or on the reports of men, and without the impression of the authority of God upon our minds; or when we receive the word of God because of the eloquence or learning of the preacher, and the affection we bear to him, or admiration of his person; or, as the papists, we believe it because the church believeth it. *But as it is in truth, the word of God;* with a divine faith, ready subjection of our souls to it, and with reverent attention, as a word that is from heaven; which the apostle positively asserts in way of parenthesis. *As it is in truth,* or truly, they believed, so he dispersed the word to them, and so they received it. And for this cause he gave thanks to God. Having mentioned before the subordinate reasons of the efficacy of the word, he now mentions the principal, which is God himself. That any receive the word as the word of God, it is not from the preachers so much as from God. And it is a great cause of thanksgiving to God, when ministers find a people receive the word with a Divine faith, which is not done without Divine grace: then they see the fruit of their ministry, for which they ought to give thanks. *Which effectually worketh also in you that believe:* the powerful working of God is usually expressed by this word, Eph. i. 19; Phil. ii. 13; and the working of Satan also, Eph. ii. 2. Men possessed with the devil are called *energumeni*. And where the word is believed and received as the word of God, there it hath this energy, or worketh effectually, so as to promote love, repentance, self-denial, mortification, comfort, and peace, &c. The apostle had mentioned before their *work of faith, labour of love, patience of hope*, chap. i. 3; and all from hence, their receiving the word as the word of God, and so retaining it.

14 For ye, brethren, became followers ^eof the churches of God which in Judæa ^fare in Christ Jesus: for ^fye also have suffered like things of your own countrymen, ^geven as they *have* of the Jews:

e Gal. 1. 22.
f Acts 17. 5, 13.
g Heb. 10. 33, 34.

This proves the assertion of the foregoing verse, as the illative *for* doth show. They were *followers of the churches in Judea*, which showed the word wrought in them effectually. Though the greatest part of the Jews believed not, yet many did, and hereupon we read of churches in Judea. Though there was before but one national church, yet now in gospel times the churches were many. And believing in Christ they are called churches *in* him, gathered together in his name, into his institutions, and by his Spirit; and these Thessalonians became *followers* or imitators of them, or in the same circumstances with them. The churches among the Jews were the first planted, and the Gentile churches followed them, conforming to the faith, worship, and order that was first in them, yea, and imitating their faith and patience in suffering. *For ye also have suffered like things of your own countrymen;* the Jews that believed suffered from the unbelieving Jews of their own country; so did these Thessalonians. But whether the apostle means only the Gentiles of Thessalonica, or the Jews that dwelt there and were born among them, is uncertain; for the persecution mentioned Acts xvii. was chiefly from the Jewish synagogue, though the Gentiles might also join with them therein. *Even as they have of the Jews:* they suffered *as* the churches of Judea, namely, in the same kind, as Heb. x. 32—34; and in the same cause, and with the same joy, constancy, and courage. And here Christ's words are fulfilled, that a man's enemies shall be those of his own house, Matt. x. 36.

15 ^hWho both killed the Lord Jesus, and ⁱtheir own prophets, and have ∥ persecuted us; and they please not God, ^kand are contrary to all men:

h Acts 2. 23. & 3. 15. & 5. 30. & 7. 52.
i Matt. 5. 12. & 23. 34, 37. Luke 13. 33. 34. Acts 7. 52.
∥ Or, *chased us out.* k Esth. 3. 8.

Who both killed the Lord Jesus; no wonder then though they have persecuted you, and the believing Jews their countrymen. They killed the Lord Jesus by the hands of Pilate, crying, *Crucify him, crucify him*. Though it was by God's determinate counsel, and the Roman power, yet by the Jews' malice they killed him; Matt. xxi. 38, *This is the heir; let us kill him. And their own prophets;* of their own nation, and directed and sent particularly to them of God; so that it was no new thing in them thus to do. Not that these individual Jews who persecuted Paul killed the prophets, but they were of the same nation, the same blood, and of the same spirit with them, and were *the children of them that killed the prophets*, as our Saviour charged them, Matt. xxiii. 31. The spirit of persecution was natural to them, it descended from one generation to another; their kings were guilty of it, their priests, their false prophets, and the common people. And though better things might be expected of the Jews than any other people, yet thus they did. And it was not only because of the new doctrine or worship that the apostle preached, for they killed their own prophets before them; but it was their love to their lusts, hatred of reproof, enmity to holiness, &c., that was the cause. And Christ himself chargeth them with the same things, Matt. xxiii. 37, *O Jerusalem, thou that killest the prophets*, &c.; and foretells it as that which they would yet practise, Matt. xxiii. 34. *And they please not God;* by the figure called meiosis; it is meant they highly displeased God, and were haters of God, and hated, and now rejected, of him. Though they had the advantages and reasons to please God above all other people, having had the law and ordinances of his worship among them, yet they pleased not God, and particularly in their persecutions of the gospel and the apostles, though they might think that therein they did God good service, as John xvi. 2. *And are contrary to all men;* contrary to their worship, laws, and customs. Or rather, *contrary to all men*, in hindering the course of the gospel appointed for men's salvation. And despising all other nations in comparison of themselves, they were apt to be seditious, and raise tumults every where, and to disdain familiarity and common friendship with the Gentiles.

16 ^lForbidding us to speak to the Gentiles that they might be saved, ^mto fill up their sins alway: ⁿfor the wrath is come upon them to the uttermost.

l Luke 11. 52. Acts 13. 50. & 14. 5, 19. & 17. 5, 13. & 18. 12. & 19. 9. & 22. 21, 22.
m Gen. 15. 16. Matt. 23. 32. n Matt. 24. 6, 14.

Forbidding us to speak to the Gentiles that they might be saved: their contrariety to all men is expressed particularly in this instance; they forbade the apostles to preach to the Gentiles, which were the greater number of men; though they opposed also their preaching to the Jewish nation: for the Jews could not endure to hear that the Gentiles should be received into the church, or into special favour with God; as appears by Christ's sermon in the synagogue, Luke iv. 28, and in the apostle's apology for himself at Jerusalem, Acts xxii. 21, 22. And their forbidding them implies, not an act of authority, for they had it not, but their hindering them what they could, and stirring up the people and rulers against them, as Acts xvii. 6. *To fill up their sins alway;* to cause it to rise up to such a measure and degree as will at last bring destruction. Though this was not their intention, yet through the just judgment of God it was the event. They killed the prophets; but killing Christ, and persecuting the apostles, and hindering the salvation of mankind thereby, this filled up their sin. The expression alludes to what is said of the Amorites, Gen. xv. 16, and foretold by Daniel, chap. ix. 27, called *the consummation.* As here is a perfecting of holiness, and filling up of grace, so also of sin. And sin against the gospel ripens sin more than against the law. And because they made a constant progress in sin, they are said to fill it up; *Fill ye up the measure of your fathers*, Matt. xxiii. 32. *For the wrath is come upon them to the uttermost:* first they filled up their sin, and then comes this wrath, or that wrath foretold by Daniel, chap. ix. 27; and by our Saviour, Matt. xxiii. 38. It was their last destruction by the Romans. God's wrath broke forth upon them several times before, but not to the utmost till now. Or, to the end, as in the Greek. In former punishments God removed his wrath and restored them again, but this continues to the end. Or, some, by the end, understand only the perfection

I. THESSALONIANS II, III

and consummation of this wrath. And its coming may be read in the Greek, it hath prevented them; as bringing them to judgment beforehand in this world; as the destruction of the old world, Sodom, and Jerusalem, were figures and forerunners of the last judgment. And yet this doth not contradict what the apostle speaks, Rom. xi., and many of the prophets, concerning their calling into the faith and church of Christ before the end of the world. Also we must understand it with an exception of the remnant of God's election that was amongst them.

17 But we, brethren, being taken from you for a short time °in presence, not in heart, endeavoured the more abundantly P to see your face with great desire.

o 1 Cor. 5. 3. Col. 2. 5.
p ch. 3. 10.

The apostle here makes his apology, for his so soon departing from them, and his continued absence. They were under great sufferings for receiving the gospel he had preached, and for him therefore to leave them so soon as he did, (as appears in the story, Acts xvii.,) and not presently to return, might discourage their hearts and make them question his love. 1. For his leaving them, he tells them it was not voluntary, but forced by the persecution of the Jews, he being sent away in the night by the brethren to Berea, Acts xvii. 10; and therefore he calls it a taking away, rather than a going away from them. And (as the Greek word imports) it was, 2. A thing grievous to him, as children that are bereft of father and mother, and left orphans, are greatly troubled. And he was afflicted as a father bereft of children; so were these Thessalonians to him, having begotten them to Christ by the gospel. 3. It was but *for a short time*, for the time of an hour; when he left them, he intended but a short stay from them, only to avoid the present storm: others think he means by the words his sudden leaving them before he took solemn leave of them. 4. He left them *in presence, quoad faciem*, as to outward sight, not in heart: the proper genius of true lovers, who are present with each other in soul when separated in body. 5. He tells them of his endeavours to see their face; and that the more abundantly, because he came away so suddenly from them. And lastly, he did this with great desire, his endeavours herein were acted with great affection.

18 Wherefore we would have come unto you, even I Paul, once and again; but ^qSatan hindered us.

q Rom. 1.13. & 15. 22.

This he adds further to satisfy them of his real affection to them, that he attempted to come to them *once and again*, that is, often, as Neh. xiii. 20; Phil. iv. 16. And that they might be assured it was not his fellow ministers' desire only to come, therefore he expresseth his own name particularly in a parenthesis *(even I Paul)*. Or by his saying, *even I Paul*, he assures them concerning his own desire to come to them; at least I Paul, though others did not so; as the French Bible reads it. And he had come to them had not *Satan hindered* him, either by raising up disputes against the gospel at Athens by the philosophers there, which he was concerned to stay and answer, Acts xvii. 18; or else by stirring up wicked men to lie in wait for him in the way: or by raising tumults, as the Jews did at Berea, whereby he was constrained *to go as it were to the sea*, Acts xvii. 14; or by sowing dissensions in other churches, which detained him to end them. Or by what way it was, is somewhat uncertain; but being thus hindered it made his desire the more fervent by the opposition. And hereby we see Satan's enmity to the gospel, especially to churches newly planted, that they might not take rooting.

r 2 Cor. 1.14. Phil. 2. 16. & 4. 1.
s Prov. 16. 31.
‖ Or, *glorying*.
t 1 Cor. 15. 23. ch. 3. 13. Rev. 1. 7. & 22. 12.

19 For ^rwhat *is* our hope, or joy, or ^scrown of ‖ rejoicing? *Are* not even ye in the presence of our Lord Jesus Christ ^tat his coming?

Here the apostle gives the reason of his desire to see them. He first calls them his *hope*; that is, the matter of his hope, that among others they should be saved in the day of Christ. Secondly, his *joy*: he at present rejoiced in their ready and sincere receiving the gospel preached by him. Thirdly, his *crown of rejoicing*, which signifies the triumph and height of joy: and seeing he mentions the *presence* and *coming of Jesus Christ*, he looks to the crown that he should receive at that day, which he speaks of, 1 Cor. ix. 25; and these Thessalonians, among others, would help to make up this crown of rejoicing to him. And in the words we may observe an eminent gradation, as also that the crown of ministers will arise not only from Christ, but from their people also.

20 For ye are our glory and joy.

He redoubles the expression, to show his great affection, and complacency of heart in them; or to show that they more than others were this occasion of rejoicing to him. And he mentions *glory* as well as *joy*, for the great success of his ministry among them would redound to his glory in the day of Christ; as Dan. xii. 3, *They that turn many to righteousness shall shine as the stars for ever and ever.* Or, they were his glory at present, a glory to his ministry, and a seal to his apostleship.

CHAP. III

The apostle showeth that out of his great care for the Thessalonians he had sent Timothy to comfort and strengthen them in the faith, 1—5; whose good report of them had been a great consolation to him in his distresses, 6—8. He testifieth his thankfulness to God, and earnest desire to see them, 8—10; praying God to guide him to them, and for their increase in love and holiness unto the end, 11—13.

WHEREFORE ^awhen we could no longer forbear, ^bwe thought it good to be left at Athens alone;

a ver. 5.
b Acts 17. 15.

The apostle proceeds upon the same argument to confirm his love to them, and care of them, that they might not doubt of it because of his long absence from them. Therefore he tells them, that though he could not come himself, yet he sent Timothy to them from Athens; which we find not mentioned in the Acts by Luke: and his love herein is commended the more, 1. Because he sent him out of a strong impulse of affection, he could not *forbear* any *longer*, or bear, it was a heavy burden to him till he had done it, as the word imports. 2. He was content *to be left at Athens alone* by parting with Timothy, though his company was so desirable and useful to him at that time. And he was well pleased so to do for their sakes; εὐδοκήσαμεν, he had a complacence of mind in so doing, so much he preferred their good before his own contentment.

2 And sent ^cTimotheus, our brother, and minister of God, and our fellow-labourer in the Gospel of Christ, to establish you, and to comfort you concerning your faith:

c Rom. 16. 21. 1 Cor. 16. 10. 2 Cor. 1. 19.

3. By the description he gives of him in the text: a man dear to him, and as his right hand in the service of the gospel. And his care of them is commended the more by sending so eminent a person to them. 4. From his end in sending him; which was *to establish* them, that through the fear of suffering, or any temptations, they might not forsake the faith they had received; *and to comfort* them *concerning* their *faith:* the word sometimes signifies to exhort, and the sense is good if we so read it; but because the faith they had embraced presented much matter of comfort to them, therefore our translation well renders the word.

3 ^dThat no man should be moved by these afflictions: for yourselves know that ^ewe are appointed thereunto.

d Eph. 3. 13. e Acts 9. 16. & 14. 22. & 20. 23. & 21. 11. 1 Cor. 4. 9. 2 Tim. 3. 12. 1 Pet. 2. 21.

The apostle had mentioned before his great afflictions, and they knew well what he himself had suffered both at Thessalonica and Berea, Acts xvii., and therefore might fear they might hereupon be shaken in their faith. And Timothy therefore was sent to comfort and establish them: God could do this without him, but the ministry is his ordinance he works by. And when he saith, *that no man should be moved*, it shows what is a Christian's duty, to be unmoved by sufferings for the gospel. The word here used by the apostle answers another word, used 2 Thess. ii. 2, which alludes to the waves of the sea shaken by the winds. Fears, and doubts, or hesitations of mind, do move and shake it, which the apostle sent Timothy to prevent, or remove. And besides, he addeth an argument of his own to confirm them, when he tells them, ye *know that we are appointed thereunto.* The word is used Luke ii. 34; 1 Tim. i. 9. But he means, we suffer afflictions according to the purpose and intention of God; they come not by chance, or merely from men's wrath and enmity, but from the appointment of God. And whether the apostle speaks only of his own sufferings, and other ministers of the gospel, or of all saints in general, as Acts xiv. 22; Rom. viii. 17, 36; 2 Tim. iii. 12, is uncertain; we may well understand it of both; so that he would not have these Thessalonians think it strange, as if some strange thing happened to them, 1 Pet. iv. 12, whereby to be shaken in their minds.

f Acts 20. 24.   4 ᶠFor verily, when we were with you, we told you before that we should suffer tribulation; even as it came to pass, and ye know.

The apostle having said that they knew they were appointed to sufferings, tells them here they knew it because he had told them of it. Paul, by some extraordinary instinct or revelation, often foresaw his sufferings, and God more generally told him of them at his first conversion, Acts ix. 16; and he told them of them that they might reckon upon sufferings. A faithful minister will not only tell the people of the crown, but of the cross of Christ. And what he foretold of his sufferings, he tells them *came to pass;* whereby they might be strengthened further in their faith about the gospel he had preached to them, and not be offended at his sufferings, being foretold to them, as well as appointed of God.

g ver. 1.   5 For this cause, ᵍwhen I could no
h 1 Cor. 7. 5.   longer forbear, I sent to know your faith,
2 Cor. 11. 3.
i Gal. 2. 2.   ʰlest by some means the tempter have
& 4. 11.
Phil. 2. 16.   tempted you, and ⁱour labour be in vain.

The apostle here gives a further account of the reason why he sent Timothy to them, which was *to know* their *faith,* whether it continued stedfast under all their sufferings and temptations. He feared Satan, whom he calls *the tempter,* might have some way or other *tempted* them, either by false teachers to seduce them, or by sufferings to affright them. He was more concerned about the inward state of their souls, than their outward condition; and commonly temptations go along with persecutions. And the apostle, having bestowed great *labour* upon them, feared lest it might *be in vain,* that the tempter had prevailed. Satan's first work is to keep men from believing, his next is to destroy their faith: young converts are commonly most assaulted. Paul's heart was therefore very solicitous for them, so that (as he said before) he could not any longer forbear sending to know how it was with them.

k Acts 18. 1,   6 ᵏBut now when Timotheus came
5.   from you unto us, and brought us good tidings of your faith and charity, and that ye have good remembrance of us always,
l Phil. 1. 8.   desiring greatly to see us, ˡas we also *to see* you:

We had before an account of Timothy's sending, now of his return, wherein we have the message he brought, and the effect thereof upon the apostle. The message may be considered, 1. As to its new-coming, *But now when Timotheus came,* &c.; so that this Epistle seems to be written presently upon his return. 2. As to the good account it brought of them: it *brought good tidings* (the same word is here used that expresseth in the Greek the glad tidings of the gospel) *of* their *faith,* that it continued still stedfast; and of their *charity,* or love, that they had love joined with their faith, and their faith working by love, which showed it was living, and of a right kind. *And that ye have good remembrance of us always;* they forgot him not, though absent some length of time from them; and it waᵃ a *good remembrance,* joined with love and esteem of his person, and of his ministry amongst them; and it was *always,* which implies the constancy of it. *Desiring greatly to see us;* and not satisfied with this good remembrance of him being absent, they greatly desired his presence, to see him and his fellow labourers. And to answer their love on his part, he addeth, *as we also to see you.* By all which he seeks to satisfy them of his continued care and remembrance of them, which was the effect of this message.

7 Therefore, brethren, ᵐwe were com-   m 2 Cor. 1. 4.
forted over you in all our affliction and   & 7. 6, 7, 13.
distress by your faith:

He was *comforted by* this *faith* of theirs *in all* his own *affliction and distress.* The faithfulness and constancy of a people is the great comfort of their teachers. *I have no greater joy than to hear that my children walk in truth,* 3 John 4.

8 For now we live, if ye ⁿstand fast in   n Phil. 4. 1.
the Lord.

The comfort of their faith was so great that it would be as life to him, if they stood fast in it; which he calls a standing *fast in the Lord.* Life is not only the union of soul and body; comfort is the life of the soul, especially that which springs from Divine causes. And on the contrary, the apostacy and degeneracy of a people doth kill the hearts of their faithful teachers.

9 ᵒFor what thanks can we render to   o ch. 1. 2.
God again for you, for all the joy wherewith we joy for your sakes before our God;

This is another effect of the message Timothy brought, it caused in the apostle great thanksgivings to God. First he rejoiced in their faith, and then gives thanks to God for that joy. The matter of his rejoicing was their faith, but the author and upholder of this faith was God; and in giving thanks to God for his joy, he gives thanks also to God for their faith from whence it sprang. The joy that ministers have in their people's faith should break forth into thanksgivings. And the apostle's thanks to God was beyond what he could return or express, as appears by the form of his speech, *For what thanks can we render?* &c.; as Psal. cxvi. 12, *What shall I render unto the Lord?* said David. And his rejoicing *before God* implies both the nature of it, it was divine and spiritual, and his respect to God therein, as *David danced before the Lord with all his might,* 2 Sam. vi. 14; i. e. with a respect to God's goodness then declared. Or the apostle might mean his joy was inward, before God, rather than before men.

10 ᵖNight and day ᵠpraying exceed-   p Acts 26. 7.
                                       2 Tim. 1. 3.
ingly ʳthat we might see your face, ˢand   q Rom. 1 10,
                                          11. & 15. 32.
might perfect that which is lacking in   r ch. 2. 17.
your faith?   s 2 Cor. 13.
                                          9, 11.
                                          Col. 4. 12.

We have here the last effect of Timothy's message upon the apostle, it put him upon prayer for these Thessalonians; expressed by the assiduity of it, *night and day,* &c., that is, in a constant course; as we noted before, chap. ii. 9. And by the fervency of it, *exceedingly,* or excessively. The Greek word cannot well be Englished, yet is often used by the apostle when he would express any thing with an emphasis, as Eph. iii. 20, and in this Epistle, chap. v. 13. And by the matter of it; *that we might see your face, and might perfect that which is lacking in your faith.* Though his Epistles might avail towards it, yet his personal presence would do more. There is a peculiar blessing attends oral preaching, more than reading. The like prayer he made with respect to the Romans, and upon the same account also, Rom. i. 10, 11. Though the apostle had before commended their faith, yet there was something lacking in it. No faith is made perfect at first; yea, the best faith may have some defects. And the word is used elsewhere to signify something that is wanting, or left behind, 1 Cor. xvi. 17; Col. i. 24. And their faith might be defective, 1. As to the matter of it, some mysteries of faith they might not yet understand; as the disciples did not, till after Christ's ascension; and some of the Corinthians a while doubted the doctrine of the resurrection, 1 Cor. xv. 12, &c. 2. As to the clearness of it, with respect to the truths they did already know and believe. ? As to the lively operations and fruits of it. The former defects are removed by doctrine, the last by exhortation and comfort, and the apostle desired to see their face on the account of both: and to *perfect* a thing is to make it complete, both as to parts and degrees. The word here used we find often in the New Testament, 2 Cor. xiii. 11; Gal. vi. 1, &c.; and variously rendered in the several translations, but yet much to the same sense: the apostle being so suddenly driven from them, he left them as a house half built; but his affection to them was so great, that he longed to return to them for the perfecting of their faith, though he had met but a while before with such great perils at Thessalonica.

11 Now God himself and our Father, and our Lord Jesus Christ, ∥ [t]direct our way unto you.

∥ Or, *guide.*
t Mark 1. 3.

Here his prayer is expressed. The person to whom he prays is God himself, personally considered as God the Father, and relatively, when he styles him *our Father*: so ought believers to address themselves to God, not absolutely, but as to their Father. So Christ taught his disciples to pray, *Our Father*; and so the Spirit of adoption doth prompt the saints to pray: we come to God with greater freedom and confidence when we can come to him as a Father. And he prays also to Christ, whom he styles *our Lord Jesus Christ.* Whence we may have an argument that Christ is God, else he could not be the object of Divine worship: not that we are to present our prayers distinctly to the Son without considering his union with the Father, nor to the Father distinctly from the Son, but to the Father in and by the Lord Jesus Christ; for so only we can consider him as our Father in prayer. And he speaks of Christ also in his relation to his people, *our Lord Jesus Christ.* And the thing he prays for is, that God would direct his way unto them; that the hinderances of Satan, whatsoever they were, might be removed, and the providence of God open him a way to come to them: the word *direct* signifies in the Greek to make straight, and, 2 Thess. iii. 5, is applied to the heart, *The Lord direct your hearts,* &c., which is setting the heart straight towards God; answering to the Hebrew word *Jashar*, which signifies to be upright, and is often used in the Old Testament. The French read it, address our way. And hence we learn our duty by the apostle's practice to pray to have our way in all cases directed by God.

12 And the Lord [u]make you to increase and abound in love [x]one toward another, and toward all *men*, even as we *do* toward you:

u ch. 4. 10.
x ch. 4. 9. & 5. 15.
2 Pet. i. 7

Increase and abound; these two words denote an increasing and overflowing abundance. This is another thing he prays for; the former respected himself, this respected them. He desired to come to them to perfect that which was lacking in their faith, and he prays now for the abounding and increase of their love; not only to love one another, but *to increase and abound* in it; to increase the habits and abound in the fruits of love. They were under sore persecutions, and their love to one another was more necessary at such a time. And not only to one another, but to extend their love *towards all men*. Either all men in general; for love is a general duty we owe to all men, *Owe no man any thing but to love one another,* Rom. xiii. 8; and therefore all our duty to men is comprehended under it. And the apostle requires this love to be added to brotherly kindness, 2 Pet. i. 7; yea, love is required to enemies, Matt. v. 44, though not as enemies, yet as men. Or more particularly, believers; as sometimes *all men* is taken under that restriction, Tit. ii. 11. *Even as we do toward you:* and he setteth before them his own love to them, both as a pattern and motive hereunto. Though the love of Christ is especially to be looked at, and is proposed often by the apostle Paul as the great argument of love to men, yet he mentions his own love to them here to show the constancy of his affection to them though absent from them, and to show that he persuaded no duty to them but what he practised himself.

13 To the end he may [y]stablish your hearts unblameable in holiness before God, even our Father, at the coming of our Lord Jesus Christ [z]with all his saints.

y 1 Cor. 1. 8.
Phil. 1. 10.
ch. 5. 23.
2 Thess. 2. 17.
1 John 3. 20, 21.
z Zech. 14. 5.
Jude 14.

These words some refer only to the verse immediately preceding: by increasing and abounding in love, their hearts would be established *unblamable in holiness.* Which is true, for that holiness is justly to be suspected, at least is to be blamed, which is without love to men. And love itself is a great part of holiness; and who will blame holiness when it shines forth in love? yea, it will be unblamable before God and men. And when God doth cause a people to increase in love, he doth hereby establish them in holiness that is unblamable; where love is wanting the heart is not established. The hypocrite will fall off in an hour of temptation, because he wants love; and though he may for a while make a fair show before men, yet he is not unblamable before God, who searcheth the heart: neither will he be found so at the appearance of Jesus Christ; which the apostle prays for here with respect to these Thessalonians, that they might be established *in holiness* until *the coming of Christ*; or that they might be found unblamable in holiness at his coming. Whereby the apostle signifies there is yet another coming of Christ, when there will a strict trial pass upon men, and therefore the saints should labour to be then found unblamable, or without spot and blemish, as 2 Pet. iii. 14. *At the coming of our Lord Jesus Christ with all his saints;* whereof he gives a particular account in the next chapter. Others carry this verse as referring also to the 10th verse, where he desired to see their face to perfect their faith, that both by their faith and love they might be established unblamable in holiness.

CHAP. IV

Paul exhorteth the Thessalonians to proceed in their endeavours to please God by a holy and just conversation, 1—8. He commendeth their love to one another, entreating them to abound in it, 9, 10, and quietly to follow their respective callings, 11, 12. And that they might not sorrow for the dead, as men without hope, he briefly describeth the resurrection of the just, and Christ's second coming, 13—18.

FURTHERMORE then we ∥ beseech you, brethren, and ∥ exhort *you* by the Lord Jesus, [a]that as ye have received of us [b]how ye ought to walk [c]and to please God, *so* ye would abound more and more.

∥ Or, *request.*
∥ Or, *beseech.*
a Phil. 1. 27. Col. 2. 6.
b ch. 2. 12.
c Col. 1. 10.

He descends to some particular duties about their walking, which he ushers in by a general exhortation in this 1st verse; wherein we may observe his style: he calls them *brethren*, and speaks to them with much condescension and earnestness, and in the name of Christ, &c. And the subject he insists on is their walking, the course of their life and conversation, which he describes by the rule of it, *as ye have received of us how ye ought to walk;* he refers them to the directions he had given them about it as the rule; for he did in his ministry not only open gospel mysteries, but explain moral duties. And not only to walk in them, but to *abound more and more*, to press forward to a greater exactness and excellency in their Christian conversation. And he here useth motives: 1. From the Person in whose name he speaks to them, which is *the Lord Jesus Christ;* for he was but Christ's minister and ambassador. 2. From the knowledge they had received of their duty, and therefore they could not plead ignorance. 3. Their walking as they had been instructed by him would *please God*.

2 For ye know what commandments we gave you by the Lord Jesus.

This explains what he said before; what they had received of him about their walking he here calls *commandments*, not so much his own as the Lord's, as the word itself imports here used, and is expressed in the text. *By the Lord Jesus:* though the apostle had authority, yet it was but derivative from Christ; and therefore not to walk as the apostle had commanded would be disobedience to Christ himself. And he minds them of what they knew, that their knowledge might be exemplified in practice; for as faith, so knowledge, is dead which doth not influence the life; and they knew that he commanded them not in his own name, but in the name of Christ.

I. THESSALONIANS IV

^d Rom. 12.2.
Eph. 5. 17.
^e Eph. 5. 27.
^f 1 Cor. 6. 15,
18. Eph. 5. 3.
Col. 3. 5.

3 For this is ^dthe will of God, *even* ^eyour sanctification, ^fthat ye should abstain from fornication:

What in the former verse he called commandments from Christ, he here calls *the will of God;* or he had some further duties to lay before them, which he had not yet given commandments about, which were the will of God. There is the secret and revealed will of God, and his revealed will is about things to be believed or practised. The latter is here meant, so that the will of God is put figuratively here for the things he willeth, or commandeth of us. And that which the apostle first mentions is *sanctification,* which is often taken for holiness in general, which consists in men's conformity to the will of God both in the heart and life. But I think not so taken here, but for chastity, as opposite to the sin of uncleanness, as the apostle explains it in the next words. For to *abstain from fornication* is the will of God. And by it is meant all unchasteness, either of persons married or unmarried; and that either in the heart, or in speech, or in the eye, or lascivious gesture, as well as in the very act itself. It was a sin common among the Gentiles, especially the Grecians, and judged as no sin. And therefore it is particularly mentioned and forbidden to the believing Gentiles by the council of Jerusalem, lest they should apprehend it not to be an evil, Acts xv. 20. For it is not so evident by the light of nature as many other moral evils; and therefore the apostle tells the Thessalonians that it is the will of God they should abstain from it, and that is a sufficient ground either of doing or not doing. This will of God is expressed in the seventh commandment, which though the Jews well knew, yet these new-converted Gentiles might not yet so well understand. And therefore the apostle in his several Epistles to the Gentile churches doth dehort them from it, especially the Corinthians, 1 Cor. vi. 9, and that by many arguments. It is a sin which corrupts and effeminates the mind, captivates the heart, consumes the flesh, and wastes men's estates. So that this will of God that forbids it is a good will, Rom. xii. 2, as all the commandments of God are said to be for our good, Deut. x. 13.

^g Rom. 6. 19.
1 Cor. 6. 15,
18.

4 ^gThat every one of you should know how to possess his vessel in sanctification and honour;

This is added as a means to prevent that sin. By *vessel* some understand the married wife, who is called *the weaker vessel,* 1 Pet. iii. 7; and her husband is to possess her *in sanctification,* in chastity, as the Greek word may signify here. *And honour;* for as marriage is honourable to all men, Heb. iii. 4, so to live chastely in a married estate is honourable also. For by whoredom man gets dishonour, *and his reproach shall not be wiped away,* Prov. vi. 33. Others by *vessel* understand the body, which is the vessel of the soul; the soul carries it up and down, useth it in the several functions of the vegetative, sensitive, and intellectual life. And so some understand the words of David to the priest, 1 Sam. xxi. 5, *The vessels of the young men are holy,* being kept from women; that is, their bodies. Fornication is said above all other sins to be a sin against the body, 1 Cor. vi. 18, and he that keeps his body chaste possesseth his vessel, keeps it under government; whereas by fornication we give it to a harlot, and that which is a member of Christ we make it the member of a harlot, 1 Cor. vi. 15; and though the words are directed properly to the masculine sex, the word ἕκαστον being masculine, yet under that the female is comprehended. And because the practice of this duty requires care, skill, and much watchfulness against temptations, therefore saith the apostle that every man may know *how to possess his vessel in sanctification.* To which is added, *and in honour;* for acts of unclonanness dishonour the body; Rom. i. 24, *God gave them up to uncleanness through the lusts of their own hearts, to dishonour their own bodies,* &c. God hath bestowed much curious workmanship upon the body, it is part of Christ's purchase, and, with the soul, is a member of Christ, a temple of the Holy Ghost, in all true saints, and therefore should be possessed with honour. Or it is to be kept to the honour and glory of God, as 1 Cor. vi. 20, and to be offered up a holy sacrifice to him, Rom. xii. 1.

5 ^hNot in the lust of concupiscence, ⁱeven as the Gentiles ^kwhich know not God:

^h Col. 3. 5.
Rom. 1. 24,
26
ⁱ Eph. 4. 17,
18.
^k 1 Cor. 15. 34. Gal. 4. 8. Eph. 2. 12. & 4. 18. 2 Thess. 1. 8.

Any violence of affection we call passion, whether of love, or anger, or desire, because the soul is passive, or suffers thereby. The Stoics said passions were not incident to a wise man; and. *They that are Christ's,* saith the apostle, *have crucified the flesh with the* passions *and lusts,* Gal. v. 24. And *lust* is usually taken for all inordinate affection, either with respect to the object or degree; though the Greek word doth signify only desire, and is sometimes taken in a good sense, as Phil. i. 23; for, there are good lustings as well as evil, as Gal. v. 17, *the Spirit lusteth against the flesh;* but here the word is taken in a bad sense, for the lust of uncleanness, which the apostle here calls *the lust of concupiscence.* The philosophers distinguish of the affections or passions of the soul, some are irascible, some concupiscible. The former are conversant about evil, to repel it or fly from it; the latter about good, either real or imaginary, to pursue it or embrace it. And the lusts of concupiscence are either of the mind or of the flesh, Eph. ii. 3: here we understand the latter, that fleshly concupiscence that is conversant about women, which if by *vessel* in the former verse is understood man's lawful wife, then he forbids all unchasteness even towards her; if the body, then he forbids all unchaste usage of the body in any kind, or towards any person whatsoever. And, to avoid fornication, he forbids lust that leads to it. *Even as the Gentiles which know not God;* which the apostle useth as an argument to them, Though ye are Gentiles by nation as well as others, yet not in state, such as know not God. There is a natural knowledge of God, which the apostle speaks of, Rom. i. 21, which the Gentiles had; and supernatural, which is by the Scriptures; to know the mind, will, nature, decrees, and counsels of God as they are there revealed: and the knowledge of God in Christ; this is meant in the text, and this the Gentiles had not, and therefore no wonder though they followed the lust of concupiscence, they wanted the rule of God's word to direct them, and that effectual knowledge of God, and presence of his grace, that would have restrained them from such lust. But these Thessalonians now, since their conversion by the gospel, were come to this knowledge of God, which they had not before, and therefore were not to live as before they did. Knowledge ought to influence our hearts and lives, and to sin against knowledge is the great aggravation of sin, and will make men more inexcusable. But yet where knowledge is wanting what wickedness will not men practise! The Gentiles were *alienated from the life of God through the ignorance that was in them,* Eph. iv. 18. The Jews crucified Christ, and Saul persecuted the disciples, through ignorance, 1 Tim. i. 13. Much more are those Christians to be condemned, who, having more knowledge than the Gentiles, yet practise worse than they; as the apostle upbraids the Jews upon this account, Rom. ii. 27.

6 ^lThat no *man* go beyond and ‖ defraud his brother ‖ in *any* matter: because that the Lord ^m*is* the avenger of all such, as we also have forewarned you and testified.

^l Lev. 19. 11, 13. 1 Cor. 6. 8.
‖ Or, *oppress,* or, *overreach.*
‖ Or, *in the matter.*
^m 2 Thess. 1. 8.

This some understand to be another part of sanctification, mentioned before, ver. 3, taking the word *sanctification* in a more general sense. And as before he spake of chastity, so here of commutative justice in commerce and traffic; and the rather because Thessalonica was a city of great trade and merchandise, and it is true that sanctification doth comprehend this righteousness in it, and will restrain men from that which is opposite to it, which, as the apostle speaks, is going beyond and defrauding his brother. To *go beyond,* is that which we call overreaching; when in buying or selling we keep not a just measure, when we observe not a due proportion betwixt the price and the commodity, considering it either in its natural worth, or in such circumstances as make it more or less valuable : or, to take advantage of another's ignorance or necessities, to take unreasonable profit : or, to break covenant with another, answering to the Hebrew word *Gnabhar,* used in this sense, Deut. xvii. 2: the original word signifies to transgress, or go above the due bounds. And to *defraud* is, when, out of a covetous mind, we exact upon another beyond what is meet. Some refer the former word to injustice by force, and the latter by fraud, 2 Cor. vii. 2. And the evil is the greater because done to a *brother*. There is a brother by a common relation, and so all men that partake of human nature are brethren; or by special relation, which is either natural, civil, or spiritual. We may understand the word in all these senses, especially the last, that those that are brethren in Christ and in the faith, should not defraud one another. And when the apostle adds, *in any matter*, the word *any* not being in the Greek, we may better read it, in dealing, or doing; the word is general, and is to be restrained by the subject-matter spoken of. There is another sense of the words, agreeable to the former verses, and the verse that follows, and so some understand the apostle as still speaking of chastity; and so here he forbids the invading another's bed, transgressing the bounds of marriage, whereby men go beyond or defraud their brother, usurping the use of another man's wife, whom he hath no right to. And then *in any matter* we must read, in that matter which he had been speaking of before, or it is a modest expression of the act of adultery. The Hebrew *Bo* is often used in the Old Testament for carnal copulation, and thence the Greek βαίνω and ὑπερβαίνω, here used; and the other word. πλεονεκτεῖν, denotes excessiveness in it, Eph. iv. 19. And the reason he adds is, *because the Lord is the avenger of all such*. *Vengeance is mine; I will repay, saith the Lord,* Deut. xxxii. 35; Rom. xii. 19. Whether we understand it of fraud, or overreaching in dealings, when man cannot right and relieve himself, the righteous God will avenge the unrighteousness of men; or of the fraud of the marriage bed, which is done in secret, and man cannot avenge himself, Heb. xiii. 4. *As we also have forewarned you and testified:* and this the apostle saith he had forewarned them of, and testified. Though the light of nature told the heathen that God was an avenger of wickedness, Acts xxviii. 4, and the heathen could say, "Ἔχει Θεὸς ἐκδικον ὄμμα, God hath a revengeful eye; yet the apostle had in his preaching assured it. He had told them of Christ's coming to judge the world, when he would execute vengeance, Jude 15; and this they were before ignorant of: and though God sometimes takes vengeance in this world, yet he seems to refer to this last vengeance, because he speaks of it as that which he had forewarned them of, and testified in his ministry, and whereof they had not so clear a testimony in natural conscience.

n Lev. 11.44. & 19. 2.
1 Cor. 1. 2.
Heb. 12. 14.
1 Pet. 1. 14, 15.
o Luke 10. 16.
∥ Or, *rejecteth.*
p 1 Cor. 2. 10. & 7. 40. 1 John 3. 24.

7 For God hath not called us unto uncleanness, ⁿ but unto holiness.

8 ᵒ He therefore that ∥ despiseth, despiseth not man, but God, ᵖ who hath also given unto us his holy Spirit.

These two verses are added, as further arguments to persuade to that chastity he had spoken of, called *sanctification*, ver. 3, 4. The first is taken from their Christian calling, which is *not to uncleanness, but to* chastity, called *holiness*. When they were Gentiles in state, they lived in the lust of uncleanness, but they were now called by the power of the gospel, and brought to such a profession that did forbid and condemn it. And the author of their call is *God* himself, though the apostles and other ministers were the instruments. Whence he fetcheth this second argument, ver. 8, that if this chastity be despised, or rejected, as we may read the text, it is not man, but God, that is despised. To despise a minister in a commandment he delivers from God is to despise God himself, Luke x. 16, &c.; and the apostle doth here intimate, not to obey the commandment of God is a despising God. Or, that the apostle was despised by some because of the outward meanness of his person, or questioning his authority. *Who hath also given unto us his holy Spirit:* this he adds as a third argument; so that what he had preached to them, was not from himself, but from the Holy Spirit. Or if by *us* he means these Thessalonians also, as some copies read it, he hath given you, &c., then he argues from the gift of the Holy Spirit they had received against living in the sin of uncleanness. This would be very disagreeable, not only to their holy calling, but the Holy Spirit God had given them. Or else these arguments of the apostle are to persuade to universal holiness, taking sanctification and holiness in a larger sense; and uncleanness, for all sin in general standing opposite thereunto. Sin is often spoken of in Scripture under the notion of filth, defilement, pollution, &c., and so was typed forth under the law, and to be cleansed from sin is a cleansing man from filthiness, 2 Cor. vii. 1; so that to live in sin, as the apostle argues, is to live in uncleanness, to contradict our holy calling, to despise God, and to walk contrary to the nature and dictates of his Holy Spirit.

9 But as touching brotherly love ᑫ ye need not that I write unto you: for ʳ ye yourselves are taught of God ˢ to love one another.

q ch. 5. 1.
r Jer. 31. 34. John 6. 45. & 14. 26.
Heb. 8. 11.
1 John 2. 20, 27.
s Mat. 22. 39.
John 13. 34. & 15. 12. Eph. 5. 2. 1 Pet. 4. 8. 1 John 3. 11, 23. & 4. 21.

But as touching brotherly love ye need not that I write unto you: the apostle proceeds from chastity and justice to speak of brotherly love, which is love upon a spiritual ground; to love the saints as such, with respect to God as a common Father, and so all his children are brethren, chap. ii. 8, 9; so Heb. xiii. 1. And he persuadeth the practice of it by a loving and winning insinuation; Sure you are forward enough of yourselves; as he useth the same artifice, Acts xxvi. 27, 28; 2 Cor. ix. 1; wherein the apostle tacitly commends them, and hereby would engage them to answer the commendation, and good opinion he had of them. *For ye yourselves are taught of God to love one another;* what need I write to teach you that which you have already been taught of God? The saints have this promise, Isa. liv. 13; Jer. xxxi. 34; fulfilled, 1 John ii. 26, 27: and this Divine teaching is always efficacious, for none teacheth like God. Not that all teaching of men is to be laid aside, as some enthusiasts would hence infer, but that the apostle thought he had less need to teach that which God himself had so effectually taught them. Hereby we perceive that God's teaching doth not only enlighten the mind, but reacheth the affections, and especially inclines the heart to love, for God is love; and though they were taught other things of God besides this love, yet he mentions only this as the most proper work of the Spirit of God by the gospel; and though common love of man to man may be found in mere nature.

10 ᵗ And indeed ye do it toward all the brethren which are in all Macedonia: but we beseech you, brethren, ᵘ that ye increase more and more;

t ch. 1. 7.
u ch. 3. 12.

As an evidence of the truth of their love for which he commended them, and that they were taught it of God, he gives a practical instance of it in this verse; else the apostle might have been thought to flatter, or to command a love that was without fruit; and therefore he saith not, ye profess it, but *ye do it:* so 2 Cor. viii. 11, *perform the doing of it. Toward all the brethren which are in all Macedonia;* which was a large province, wherein were planted many churches. Their love was not guided by interests, opinions, civil relations, or self-respects, but it reached to all that were brethren; and that in some real effect of it, in some work of charity, or liberality, or otherwise, not here mentioned, but we read of it, 2 Cor. viii. 1, 2. *But we beseech you, brethren, that ye increase more and more;* but, however, their love was not yet perfect, and therefore he beseecheth them to abound more and more; either meant as to the extent of it, not to confine it only to Macedonia, or as to the degree of it, to excel men in it, as the Greek word may be rendered; and the same word the apostle useth, and upon the same account, 2 Cor. viii. 7. Neither love, nor any other grace, is made perfect at once; even those that are taught of God, are taught by degrees. And love being a grace so suitable to the gospel, and their present suffering state, he therefore especially exhorts to a progress in it.

11 And that ye study to be quiet, and ˣ to do your own business, and ʸ to work with your own hands, as we commanded you;

x 2 Thess. 3. 11. 1 Pet. 4. 15.
y Acts 20. 35. Eph. 4. 28. 2 Thess. 3. 7, 8, 12.

And that ye study to be quiet: he exhorts to quietness, and yet to be diligent; and probably he might see this needful, either by what he himself had observed amongst them, or by what he had heard of them, as appears by what he writes in his Second Epistle, chap. iii. 10, 11. To be quiet is to be of a peaceable temper and carriage, as the Greek word ἡσυχάζειν importeth both; and stands contrary to strife, contention, division, either upon a civil or religious account. And to *study to be quiet*, because the thing may be difficult, especially in some circumstances of times, places, and persons. And the Greek word φιλοτιμεῖσθαι implies an ambitious study. Quietness we should pursue with a holy ambition, as that which is honourable to ourselves and our profession, Prov. xx. 3. The same word is used 2 Cor. v. 9, where it is rendered *we labour*, &c. Study is properly the exercise of the mind, yet it here comprehends any kind of labour. This agrees with what the apostle elsewhere exhorteth to, Heb. xii. 14: see 1 Pet. iii. 11. *And to do your own business :* he next commendeth to them diligence, and that in our own business; and this he prescribeth as a good way for quietness, contentions often arising from meddling in the affairs of other men which concern us not; for which he rebukes some in this church, 2 Thess. iii. 11. But yet only to seek our own things is a great fault, and lamented by the apostle, Phil. ii. 21. We are to concern ourselves in the affairs of others when called to it, and not otherwise; and then we may reckon them among our own things. A Christian's calling is either general or particular, and what falls not within the compass of one of these, is to be accounted not our own business. And our doing and suffering ought to be kept within the sphere of our calling; for to suffer otherwise, is to suffer as busybodies, which the apostle cautions against, 1 Pet. iv. 15; as a bishop intruding himself into another's office, to which the word there alludes. *And to work with your own hands ;* this condemneth idleness, and living out of a calling; we are not only to keep within our own sphere, but to stretch forth our hands to work. The same precept he gives to the Ephesians, chap. iv. 28, not to steal, but to work with their hands, that they may not only *eat their own bread*, 2 Thess. iii. 12, but have to give to him that lacketh. Not that there is no other work but that of the hands; the ministers of the gospel are excused from that, 1 Cor. ix. 6, but not from work; there is the work of the head, and the tongue, and the foot, and the lungs, as well as of the hands; but either under one species he comprehends all, or it may be he fitteth his speech to the condition of the people to whom he writes, who generally had such occupations wherein they wrought with their hands, Thessalonica being a great place of trade. And the apostle speaks of the churches of Macedonia as a poor sort of people, 2 Cor. viii. 2, and liberal beyond their power; though some among them might be tempted to idleness by the charity of others to them, which, as some conceive, was the occasion of the apostle's thus writing. But if men have estates, and upon that account need not work, yet no man is to be idle: men's time, parts, or other talents are to be employed, and account thereof is to be given, Matt. xxv. 19; and the unprofitable servant is cast into outer darkness, ver. 30. Some way or other every man is to work, and may work, for profit to himself and others, unless under some invincible impediment. *As we commanded you ;* he means, when he was with them. He might probably observe some occasion for this commandment. Industry is of good report with all; and by meddling in others' affairs, and unquiet carriage and idleness, they might dishonour their Christian profession among the heathen, which might be the chief reason of this commandment : and the apostle doth not act herein as a civil magistrate, commanding about civil affairs for the public welfare; but as a minister of Christ, with respect to a spiritual end, as appears by what follows.

z Rom. 13.
13. 2 Cor. 8.
21. Col. 4. 5.
1 Pet. 2. 12.
§ Or, *of no man.*

12 ᶻThat ye may walk honestly toward them that are without, and *that* ye may have lack ‖ of nothing.

He enforceth his commands by a twofold reason, the former is *ab honesto*, the other is *ab utili*. First, *That ye may walk honestly*, or decently, as the word is rendered, 1 Cor. xiv. 40. *Toward them that are without ;* that is, Gentiles, infidels, so they are described, 1 Cor. v. 12 ; Col. iv. 5; as those that were received into the church of Christ are said to be *within*. The apostle would have them honour the gospel before the heathen in such moral actions which they did approve of, and were able to judge of, not understanding the higher mysteries of faith and gospel holiness; which he calls walking *in wisdom towards them that are without*, Col. iv. 5. The other reason is *ab utili, That ye may have lack of nothing ;* or, of no man, have no need to beg of any man. It might offend and be a stumblingblock to the Gentiles, to see Christians to beg of any, and especially of themselves, for their necessary relief. Or, of nothing; that you may by your own labour be able to subsist, and not depend upon others, and so not be a burden to friends, or a scandal to strangers. For every man to subsist by his own labour, was the primitive law to Adam, Gen. iii. 19, commended often by Solomon in his Proverbs, and enjoined by the apostle to believing Christians, 2 Thess. iii. 10.

13 But I would not have you to be ignorant, brethren, concerning them which are asleep, that ye sorrow not, ᵃeven as others ᵇ which have no hope.

a See Lev. 19. 28. Deut. 14. 1, 2. 2 Sam. 12. 20.
b Eph. 2. 12.

The apostle now proceeds to a new discourse, about moderating of their sorrow for the dead, not for all, but the dead in Christ. He had either observed their sorrow in this kind excessive, while with them; or else by Timothy, or some other way, he had heard of it. Wherein observe in general, he doth not condemn their sorrow, but the excess of it. Grace destroys not nature, but regulates it; nor reason, but rectifies it; nor takes away the affections, but moderates them; doth not make us Stoics, or stocks. Affections are good when set upon right objects, and kept within due bounds, and this Christianity doth teach, and grace doth effect. And to mourn for the dead, especially the dead in the Lord, is a duty that both nature and grace teach, and God requireth; and the contrary is reproved by God himself, Isa. lvii. 1, and to die unlamented is reckoned as a curse, Jer. xxii. 18, 19. It is only then immoderate sorrow the apostle here means; and to prevent it, or remove it, gives many instructions and arguments. And he supposeth their ignorance might be a great occasion of it, and so instructs them about the doctrine of the resurrection, and Christ's personal coming again, which by the light of nature, while Gentiles, they knew nothing of, or were very uncertain in. And the apostle, because of his short stay among them, had not had opportunity to instruct them about these things, and therefore doth it here distinctly and fully; as he doth the Corinthians, hearing there were some among them, even of the church itself, that said there was no resurrection, 1 Cor. xv. 12. It is such a mystery to reason, that it is hard to believe it; and the most learned of the heathen doubted of it, and some exploded and scoffed at it, as we find, Acts xvii. 18, even such as yet held the immortality of the soul. And hereupon in this verse the apostle doth assert two things in general to relieve them against immoderate sorrow. 1. He calls the death of the saints a *sleep.* (see Dan. xii. 2 ; Luke viii. 52 ; John xi. 11 ; 1 Cor. xv. 20, 51,) whether referring to those that are already dead, or do die, or that shall afterwards die; and why should they then excessively mourn ? After sleep we know there is awaking, and by sleep nature is revived; and so it shall be with the saints in death. Hereupon the grave is called a bed, Isa. lvii. 2; and the burying-place, *cemeterium*, a place of sleep. And, 2. There is hope in their death, as Prov. xiv. 32 ; there is hope concerning their happy state after death, and hope of their resurrection, and seeing them again at Christ's coming; it is not an eternal farewell. This the apostle here intends. And they will be then seen in a more excellent state, and probably so seen then as that their Christian friends may know them; else the apostle's argument would not have so much strength, and so well suit the present case. The heathen and infidels buried their dead without this hope, as they are said to be without hope, Eph. ii. 12 ; and so were excessive in their sorrows, which they expressed by cutting their flesh, making themselves bald, doleful songs, and mourning ejulations, expressed sometimes upon instruments: and which the Jews had learned from them, as appears by God's often reproving it, and Christ's putting out the minstrels, Matt. ix. 23, 24; and as that which he forbade them, Lev. xix. 28 ; Deut. xiv. 1. And the apostle may refer to this in the text, as that which is not only grievous to nature, but dishonourable to a Christian's faith, hope, and profession. We are hereby the betrayers of our faith and hope, and the things we preach will seem false and feigned. *Cypr. de Mortalitate.* And though man is said to die without hope as to a return to his former state of life here, Job xiv. 7—10; yet not with respect to the life at the resurrection, in them that die in Jesus.

e 1 Cor. 15. 13. 14 For *c* if we believe that Jesus died
d 1 Cor. 15. and rose again, even so *d* them also which
18, 23. ch. 3. sleep in Jesus will God bring with him.
13.

As in the former verse the apostle made use of the hope of the resurrection, as an argument against immoderate sorrow, so here he proves the resurrection by Christ's rising again, &c. *For if we believe that Jesus died and rose again;* he supposeth they did believe that Christ died and rose again; it was that which he had taught them, and which they had received, as being the two first and fundamental points of the Christian faith, without which they could not have been a church of Christ. *Quest.* But how doth Christ's resurrection prove the resurrection of the saints? he being the eternal Son of God, might have a privilege above all. *Answ.* This first shows the thing is possible, God hath already done it in Christ. 2. Christ rose for our justification, Rom. iv. 25; and in justification sin is pardoned which brought in death, and which alone by its guilt can keep under the dominion of death. 3. Christ rose not as a private person, but as the Head of the body, his church, Eph. i. 4, 20, &c., and so loosed the bands of death, and conquered the grave, for his people. 4. As *the first-fruits,* 1 Cor. xv. 20, which was a pledge and assurance of the whole harvest to follow. 5. God hath predestinated the elect, whom he foreknew, *to be conformed to the image of his Son,* Rom. viii. 29. 6. He is not complete without them, Eph. i. 23. Lastly, They *sleep in Jesus,* as the text speaks; not only live but die in him, Rev. xiv. 13, their union remains with Christ even in death. *Even so them also which sleep in Jesus;* by which words also the apostle distinguisheth believers from all others; it is only they shall have the privilege of this blessed resurrection who sleep in Jesus. And perseverance in Christ to the end is here also intimated. *Will God bring with him;* and though their resurrection is not expressed in the text, yet it is implied in this saying. By *God* is meant, as some understand here, the Son of God, who is to come from heaven, chap. i. 10, and who will bring the spirits of just men, made perfect in heaven, with him, and unite them to their bodies, which cannot be done without their resurrection: whereby the apostle gives another argument against excessive sorrow for the saints departed, they shall return from heaven again with Christ at his coming. Others understand it of God the Father, who will raise the dead, and then bring them to his Son, and bring them with him to heaven. Those that read the text, those that sleep, or die, for Jesus, and so confine it only to martyrs, restrain it to too narrow a sense.

e 1 Kings 13. 15 For this we say unto you *e* by the
17, 18. & 20. word of the Lord, that *f* we which are
f 1 Cor. 15. alive *and* remain unto the coming of the
51. Lord shall not prevent them which are asleep.

The apostle here sets down particularly the manner of the Lord's coming, the method and order how all the saints shall then meet with him and with one another, which we find not so distinctly in any other scripture; and whereby he further prosecutes the argument he is upon. *For this we say unto you by the word of the Lord;* that they might not think that what he speaks was either by some tradition from others, or an invention of his own; and that is ground enough for faith, to which our judgment and reason ought to be captivated. *That we which are alive and remain unto the coming of the Lord shall not prevent them which are asleep:* that which he saith here about the resurrection, Christ's coming, the ministry of angels, the sound of a trumpet, the voice of Christ at that day, we have it in the evangelists; but the method and order of all the saints meeting together, and meeting the Lord in the air, we find not in any express words before written; the apostle speaks it here by extraordinary revelation, which is the word of the Lord, though not then written. And this order is expressed, 1. Negatively. The saints then living upon earth shall not be with Christ sooner than those that were fallen asleep, and be caught up into the air while the others are in the grave; and the apostle speaks as if he should be one of that number: surely he could not think the coming of Christ should be in the age wherein he lived; he speaks otherwise, 2 Thess. ii. 2; or that his life should be prolonged to that day; for the time of his *departure,* he saith, was *at hand,* 2 Tim. iv. 6. But he looks upon the whole body of saints together, and himself as one of that number, and so speaks, *we which are alive and remain,* &c.; as in 1 Cor. xv. 51, *We shall not all sleep, but we shall all be changed.* 2. Affirmatively. *The dead in Christ shall rise first,* that is, before they that are alive shall be caught up into the air; they shall stay till the rest be risen: as 1 Cor. xv. 51, 52, *We shall not all sleep, but be changed,* and *in a moment;* which the apostle calls *clothed upon,* 2 Cor. v. 2, and which he rather desired than to be *unclothed,* ver. 4: and then they that are dead in Christ shall rise, and be united to these in one visible body.

16 For *g* the Lord himself shall de- g Matt. 24. 30, 31.
scend from heaven with a shout, with Acts 1. 11.
the voice of the archangel, and with *h* the h 1 Cor. 15. 52.
trump of God: *i* and the dead in Christ i 1 Cor. 15. 23, 52.
shall rise first:

For the Lord himself shall descend from heaven with a shout; the means which effect this. The word *shout* in the Greek signifies a command, or word of command; alluding to mariners or soldiers summoned to be ready with their assistance when called upon; and may refer to the angels whom Christ now summons to attend and assist in that day. And the evangelist speaks of the voice of Christ, John v. 28, which is there said to raise the dead. Whether this is an oral shout and voice from the mouth of Christ, or only an expression of his Divine power, whereby he shall awaken them that sleep out of their graves, is a question I shall not be curious about. *With the voice of the archangel:* Christ is said to come with *all the holy angels,* Matt. xxv. 31; and to *send his angels with a great sound of a trumpet,* Matt. xxiv. 31. But here is mentioned only the archangel and his voice, instead of all the rest, they all coming under his conduct. Though there be not such distinct orders of angels as the schoolmen affirm, yet there is order among them, as *archangel* implies. And whether he will put forth an audible voice or not at that day, or whether this archangel be not the same with Christ himself, who is *the Head of all principality and power,* Col. ii. 10, I leave it as doubtful; but, however, it is certain the angels shall be ministering to Christ at that day, especially in the resurrection of the elect, Matt. xxiv. 31, and severing the righteous from the wicked, Matt. xiii. 41. *And with the trump of God;* as 1 Cor. xv. 52. And whether this is to be taken literally, and distinct from the shout and voice before mentioned, or used only to show forth the Divine power of God that shall gather all the elect together out of their graves, as the trumpet in war gathers the scattered army, or as the silver trumpets under the law assembled the congregation of Israel, I shall not be positive. And this is the account of the saints that are raised.

17 *k* Then we which are alive *and* re- k 1 Cor. 15. 51.
main shall be caught up together with
them *l* in the clouds, to meet the Lord in l Acts 1. 9. Rev. 11. 12.
the air: and so *m* shall we ever be with m John 12. 26. & 14. 3.
the Lord. & 17. 24.

Christ will have a church to the end of the world, and some will be found alive at his coming, and will be *caught up,* or snatched up, to denote its suddenness, it may be in the arms of angels, or by some immediate attractive power of Christ; and it will be *together with them* that are now raised from the dead; they shall all ascend in one great body, and it will be *in the clouds;* as Christ himself ascended in a cloud, Acts i. 9, and so will return again, Matt. xxiv. 30, he making the clouds his chariots, Psal. civ. 3. *To meet the Lord in the air:* 1. To congratulate his coming, when others shall flee and tremble. 2. To put honour upon him; as the angels will also attend him for that end. 3. To receive their final discharge. 4. To be visibly joined to their Head. 5. To be assistants with him in judging of the world, and to reign with him upon earth. And whether the last judgment will be upon the earth, or in the air, I shall not determine; but after this Christ and his saints shall never part. Their first meeting shall be in the air, and their continuance will be with him while he is in this lower world, and after that they shall ascend with him into heaven, and so be for ever with him. Augustine imagined that the saints that are found alive shall in their rapture die, and then immediately revive, because *it is appointed to all men once to die;* but the apostle saith expressly, *We shall not all die, but we shall all be changed,* 1 Cor. xv. 51.

n ch. 5. 11.
|| Or, *exhort*.

18 [n]Wherefore || comfort one another with these words.

The apostle makes application of all this discourse to the end he designed, which was to comfort them under their sorrows for departed Christian friends; and he saith not, be ye comforted, but *comfort one another,* to put them upon the great duty of Christian sympathy; though this is a duty we owe to all, yet especially to the saints, and more especially of the same particular congregation. And funeral sorrows are usually most afflictive, and therefore need to be allayed with words of comfort; and not with any words, but, saith the apostle, *with these words,* or these things, as the Hebrew, the things or words that he had before laid before them. The philosophers used many arguments against the fears of death, and for comfort under funeral sorrows, but Christians should fetch their comforts from the Scriptures. These are the best, most solid, most durable, and universal, and therefore the apostle commends them to the believing Romans, Rom. xv. 4, as here to these Thessalonians particularly. These considerations, that those which sleep in Jesus shall rise again, and that we shall meet them again, and we and they shall be for ever with the Lord together, are a great relief against the sorrows of their departure hence. And the comforts arising hence may serve to support under other sorrows as well as these, which the apostle also might intend in the words.

CHAP. V

The apostle proceedeth to show that Christ's coming will be sudden, exhorting Christians to watch and be sober, so as not to be taken by surprise, 1—11. *He beseecheth them to respect their spiritual guides,* 12, 13; *and giveth divers other precepts,* 14—22; *concluding with a prayer and salutations,* 23—28.

a Matt. 24. 3, 36.
Acts 1. 7.
b ch. 4. 9.

BUT of [a]the times and the seasons, brethren, [b]ye have no need that I write unto you.

But when shall these things be? might some say, as the disciples asked Christ, Matt. xxiv. 3, 36; Acts i. 6. He tells them, *It is not for you to know the times or the seasons;* not that they knew them in particular already, but there was no need they should know them. It may be some among them were too curious to inquire. He doth not say they could not be known, as being put into God's own power, as Acts i. 7; but, *ye have no need that I write* of them. The apostle, as in his preaching, so in his writing, had respect to what was most needful and profitable for the people: as when the disciples asked, *Are there few that be saved?* Christ answered them in that which was most needful to them, Luke xiii. 24: and so doth the apostle here; instead of acquainting them with the times and seasons, he puts them upon watchfulness, that they might not be surprised, as in the following verses; and to improve the knowledge they had already, which was this, that Christ's coming would be sudden.

c Matt. 24. 43, 44. & 25. 13. Luke 12. 39, 40.
2 Pet. 3. 10.
Rev. 3. 3. & 16. 15.

2 For yourselves know perfectly that [c]the day of the Lord so cometh as a thief in the night.

By *times and seasons* then, before mentioned, he meant the time of the Lord's coming, or he applies what he spoke in general to this particular, which he here calls *the day of the Lord.* And though they knew not the particular time, yet they did know this, it would be sudden and unexpected, coming *as a thief in the night,* Rev. xvi. 15: the comparison is to be restrained only to the suddenness of it; for his coming will be welcome, and so not as a thief, to all that believe. And it is called *the day of the Lord* here and elsewhere, 1 Cor. iii. 13; Phil. i. 6, 10, and *that day,* 2 Tim. i. 18, not to be taken for a natural day, but a certain period of time. Any eminent manifestation of God, either in works of mercy or judgment, is called his day in Scripture, Isa. ii. 12; Jer. xlvi. 10. And so because Christ will be more eminently manifested now than ever before, therefore his coming is called his day; and that it would be sudden they did not only know, but *know perfectly,* or accurately; Eph. v. 15, *circumspectly:* there could be only conjectures about the particular time: the influence hereof was powerful upon their hearts, and so they may be said to know it *perfectly.* In religion, knowledge is not perfect which is not operative.

3 For when they shall say, Peace and safety; then [d]sudden destruction cometh upon them, [e]as travail upon a woman with child; and they shall not escape.

d Is. 13. 6,—9.
Luke 17. 27, 28, 29. & 21. 34, 35.
2 Thess. 1. 9.
e Jer. 13. 21.
Hos. 13. 13.

For when they shall say, Peace and safety: by these words the apostle proves that the day of the Lord will come unexpected, by the security that will be then found in the world. They say it in their hearts and practice, if not with their tongues. And he useth two words the better to express the greatness of this security, present peace, and no danger of sliding, as the words import. And as the effect of Christ's coming will be *destruction* to such, which will be *salvation* to others, Heb. ix. 28; so through their security it will be *sudden destruction,* which he describes under the similitude of *travail upon a woman with child,* which doth for the most part come of a sudden, and is the most exquisite pains in nature, and is often made use of in Scripture to set forth extremity of misery, Isa. xiii. 8; Jer. xiii. 21. And these pains come upon her unavoidably; so saith the apostle of these men's destruction, *and they shall not escape,* or in no wise escape, expressed in the Greek by two negatives, which do strongly affirm.

4 [f]But ye, brethren, are not in darkness, that that day should overtake you as a thief.

f Rom. 13. 12, 13.
1 John 2. 8.

Lest these believing Thessalonians should be terrified in their minds by this discourse, he adds this by way of comfort to them, that they shall not be surprised as others; though they did not know the particular time of Christ's coming, yet it would not find them unprepared for it as the world would be; and the reason he gives is, because they *are not in darkness. Darkness* is to be taken metaphorically; and so in Scripture it is taken either for sin, ignorance, or misery. The two former are here meant, especially ignorance. These Thessalonians were brought into the light of the gospel; they had the knowledge of Christ, and the way of salvation by him; particularly they knew of his coming, and the manner and ends of his coming, which the infidel world did not; and though Christ's coming would be to others as a thief in the night, yet not to them.

5 Ye are all [g]the children of light, and the children of the day: we are not of the night, nor of darkness.

g Eph. 5. 8.

And because the night is the time of darkness, and the day of light, he therefore hereby describes their present state: 1. Positively, *Ye are all the children of light,* and *the children of the day;* which is a Hebraism: Ye are partakers of a spiritual light, and this light is not the darker light of nature, or the light of prophecy, which the Jews had, compared to a lamp, 2 Pet. i. 19; but ye are *children of the day,* as the time of the gospel is called *day,* Rom. xiii. 12; 2 Cor. vi. 2. 2. Negatively, *We are not of the night, nor of darkness;* your state is exceedingly different from other Gentiles, and from what it once was, as the light is from darkness, and day from night: not as if there was no ignorance remaining in them, for the best men *see* but *through a glass, darkly,* 1 Cor. xiii. 12; but the apostle compares them with their former estate when they were Gentiles, and with the Jews under the law; and with respect to their state in Christ, they were not children of the night, or, as to their state, of the night, but children of light, and of the day.

I. THESSALONIANS V

^h Matt. 25.5.
i Matt. 24.
42. & 25. 13.
Rom. 13. 11,
12, 13. 1 Pet. 5. 8.

6 ^hTherefore let us not sleep, as *do* others; but ⁱlet us watch and be sober.

The apostle draws this inference from the foregoing verses in a twofold duty: 1. Negative; *Let us not sleep, as do others;* sleep is not proper for the children of the day, but of the night. And as the night and darkness are to be taken metaphorically, so the sleep. And though it hath several acceptations in Scripture, yet it is here taken for security. As the natural sleep binds up the senses, and men are not aware of approaching danger, so doth the sleep of the soul: it darkens the mind, stupifies the spiritual sense, that men prepare not for the coming of Christ, nor to avoid the destruction that will then come suddenly upon them. Rom. xiii. 11, 12, is a place parallel to this: *It is high time to awake out of sleep,* &c. *The night is far spent, the day is at hand,* &c. 2. Positive; *Let us watch:* watching stands contrary to sleep; the senses are then in exercise, which were bound up by sleep. When the soul is watching, the faculties are in a spiritual exercise to apprehend both our interest and our duty, to take hold of that which is good, and to avoid the evil, the evil of sin and the evil of suffering. But watching here in the text especially refers to the coming of Christ, to prepare for it, that we may not be surprised as others will, and to be in a readiness to *be found of him in peace, without spot, and blameless,* 2 Pet. iii. 14. *And be sober:* sobriety is reckoned to be one branch of temperance, and one of the fruits of the Spirit, Gal. v. 23, and one link of the chain of grace, 2 Pet. i. 6. It hath its name in the Greek, signifying either soundness of mind, or continency of mind; a mind kept or held within its due bounds. It is usually taken for moderation in meats and drinks, setting bounds to the appetite; but it extends to all earthly things, as honour, riches, pleasures, to have our affections to them, our cares about them, our endeavours after them, kept within due bounds; and all this upon the account of Christ's coming, as a necessary preparation for it: see 1 Cor. vii. 29—31; 1 Pet. iv. 7. Sobriety and watching are here joined together, and so 1 Pet. iv. 7, v. 8. For as intemperance in meats and drinks makes the body dull and sleepy, so without temperance and sobriety the soul will be disenabled to watch.

k Luke 21. 34, 36.
Rom. 13. 13.
1 Cor. 15.34.
Eph. 5. 14.
1 Acts 2. 15.

7 For ^kthey that sleep sleep in the night; and they that be drunken ^lare drunken in the night.

The apostle enforceth the former duties of watchfulness and sobriety from the consideration of their present state. They that sleep choose the night to sleep in, and they that would be drunk choose the night for it: drunkenness being so shameful a vice, especially in the apostles' time, that men were ashamed to be seen drunk in the day-time; see Acts ii. 15; Eph. v. 12, 13; and in ancient times they had their feasts in the night. Ye therefore that are not in the night of your former ignorance, ought neither to be found in the sleep of security, nor in the sin of drunkenness, whereby may be meant also any kind of intemperance; for a man may be drunk, and *not with wine,* Isa. xxix. 9; drunk with pleasure, with cares, with sensual love and desires, with passion, and by spiritual judgments upon the soul, Isa. xxix. 10.

m Is. 59. 17.
Eph. 6. 14,
16, 17.

8 But let us, who are of the day, be sober, ^mputting on the breastplate of faith and love; and for an helmet, the hope of salvation.

The apostle here commands two spiritual duties, and the former is sobriety; which he mentioned before, ver. 6, as a preparation for Christ's coming; but here, as that which was suitable to their present state, and as standing opposite to that drunkenness in the foregoing verse. It is not sufficient to abstain from vice, without practising the contrary virtue. The other duty is, putting on their spiritual armour. The former was to secure them against the good things of the world, the latter against the evil of it, that they be not overcome of either. The armour he mentions is spiritual. Soldiers have their breastplate and helmet for their bodies, so hath the Christian these for his soul. As the breastplate and helmet secure the principal seats of the natural life, the head and the heart, so doth the Christian's armour secure the life of the soul, and therefore these two pieces are only mentioned, as being most necessary. His *breastplate* is *faith and love.* First, *faith;* in Eph. vi. 16, it is called a *shield;* here, a *breastplate.* Great things are ascribed to faith in Scripture; it is that whereby we are justified, adopted, united to Christ, have our hearts purified, &c.; but here it is to be considered as a defensive grace; and it doth defend as it assents to the doctrine of the gospel as true, particularly the doctrine of the resurrection, and the coming of Christ, with the effects and attendants thereof, before mentioned. And as it doth depend upon God's faithfulness and all-sufficiency to perform his promises, and applying them to ourselves for our support and comfort, so faith is a breastplate or defence; and as it is a defence against temptations, so particularly against that sudden destruction that will come upon the secure world, before mentioned. Secondly, *love;* and love is joined with faith to show it to be a true and lively faith, when it *worketh by love,* Gal. v. 6; and love, when it worketh, produceth many blessed effects, and particularly, as faith, it will be a breastplate of defence. It will defend against the persecutions and afflictions of the world: *Many waters cannot quench love, neither can the floods drown it,* Cant. viii. 7. Slavish fear will overcome us if we want love to defend against it, when true religion is under disgrace and persecuted in the world: love will defend against apostacy, and so help us to persevere to the coming of Christ, which the apostle had been speaking of; and love being seated in the heart, is well compared to a breastplate that encompasseth the heart. Secondly, the other piece of armour is the *helmet,* so called in the Greek from encompassing the head; and this helmet is here said to be *the hope of salvation.* In Eph. vi. 17, we read of *the helmet of salvation,* but the hope of it is there to be understood, for salvation is no grace of the Spirit, and so, of itself, no part of a Christian's armour. Hope of salvation is of great use to a Christian many ways: it is a cordial to comfort him, a spur to quicken him, a staff to support him, a bridle to restrain him, and so also a helmet to defend him: and therefore no wonder that the apostle calls true hope *a lively hope,* 1 Pet. i. 3. And as itself is lively, so it is a defence to the life of the soul, as a helmet is to the life of the body. *Hope deferred maketh the heart sick,* saith Solomon; but if quite disappointed and lost, the heart sinks and dies. Let afflictions and distresses break in like a flood, yet hope will keep the head above water; and if Satan assault the soul to drive it into despair, this hope of salvation will be a defence to it. So that the Christian's armour mentioned in this verse are *faith, love,* and *hope,* which divines call the three theological graces, and placed together by the apostle, 1 Cor. xiii. 13. And these the saints, who are children of the day, are to put on, whereby they shall be armed for the coming of Christ with this *armour of light,* Rom. xiii. 12, and against the destruction which will then surprise the children of the night.

n Rom. 9.22.
ch. 1. 10.
1 Pet. 2. 8.
Jude 4.
o 2 Thess. 2.
13, 14.

9 For ⁿ God hath not appointed us to wrath, ^o but to obtain salvation by our Lord Jesus Christ,

For God hath not appointed us to wrath, but to obtain salvation: some expositors make these words an argument to all the duties of holiness mentioned both in this and the foregoing chapters; and it is true, that the knowledge of our being elected, or appointed to salvation, doth not in the elect encourage to sin or sloth, as some affirm, but engage to all holiness: but I had rather restrain the words, and that either to the *hope of salvation,* mentioned immediately before, and then the sense to be this, we may well hope for salvation seeing God hath appointed us to it; or, to his whole discourse about the coming of Christ, and so they may give the reason why the dead in Christ must rise, and must, with the living saints, meet the Lord in the air, and be for ever with him; yea, and why they need not fear the destruction that will come upon others at that day, and why they should be watchful for its coming, because, saith the apostle, *God hath not appointed us to wrath, but to obtain salvation,* &c. Having spoken of two sorts of persons, the children of the day, and children of the night, and the sudden destruction of the one and salvation of the other at the coming of Christ, he here ascends to the first original of both, which is God's appointment, which is an act of God's sovereign will, determining men's final estates;

which seems to be more than mere prescience or foreknowledge, an act of God's mind, as appears by Rom. viii. 29; 1 Pet. i. 2, or more than appointing of the means and way of salvation; but not of persons to be saved, or of persons only materially, as to the number how many, but not formally, or individually, who they are that shall be saved; whereas the apostle writes of some *whose names are in the book of life*, Phil. iv. 3, and that *from the foundation of the world*, Rev. xvii. 8, and *chosen before the foundation of the world*, Eph. i. 4: otherwise, every man's salvation would depend more upon the uncertainty of man's will, than the eternal and immutable will of God; whereas whatever God works in man's salvation, is *according to the counsel of his will*, Eph. i. 11; and God's counsel is certain, immutable, and eternal, extending not only to actions and means, but persons, Rom. viii. 29, 30. Neither is this appointment of God grounded upon the foresight of man's faith; for if faith be the gift of God, this gift proceeds from God's counsel and fore-appointment; else men may say, That I may be saved I must thank God, but that I am saved I must thank myself: and hence there is a possibility for no man to be saved, and all the counsels of God in Christ to be made frustrate. But this is no place for controversy; only where God appoints to salvation, he appoints also to means, and without the means there is no attainment of the end, Eph. i. 4; 1 Pet. i. 2. And the apostle here makes salvation stand opposite to wrath; what before he called *destruction*, ver. 3, he here calleth *wrath*, because God's wrath produceth it, and is manifested in it. And those that are saved are delivered from it; and the supreme reason is, because they were not appointed to it, but to salvation, and none that are appointed to the one are appointed to the other. The *vessels of wrath* and *of mercy* are set in an opposite distinction, Rom. ix. 22, 23, and so in the text, to illustrate the mercy of God the more in them that are saved. And whereas the apostle calls it the obtaining of salvation, it implies man's endeavours for it, though he be appointed of God to it; and speaking positively, not only of himself, but these believing Thessalonians also, he *hath appointed us to obtain salvation*, doth not this also imply that some good assurance of salvation may be obtained in this world. *By our Lord Jesus Christ*; the decrees of salvation are executed in him, and by him; and *there is no salvation in any other*, Acts iv. 12. And he saveth not only by his doctrine and example, as some have affirmed, but by his blood as the meritorious, and his Spirit as the efficient, cause of salvation. Whether the infinite wisdom of God could have found out another way I shall not inquire, but this it hath pitched upon, wherein mercy and justice are admirably glorified together, and the highest engagement imaginable laid upon men to love, serve, and honour their Creator. And as the freeness of God's grace is manifested in his appointing men to salvation, so the exceeding riches of it, in saving them by Jesus Christ. And whereas two things are necessary to it, the reconciling us unto God, and restoring his image in us, the former we have by the merit of his blood, and the latter by the operation of his Spirit; so that we have no ground for that fond opinion, that if men walk honestly and uprightly, they may be saved in any religion.

p Rom. 14. 8, 9. 2 Cor. 5. 15.

10 ᵖWho died for us, that, whether we wake or sleep, we should live together with him.

Some refer these words to the latter end of the foregoing chapter, where the apostle had spoken of the saints' death and resurrection, which is their sleeping and waking, as they are here called. And their being for ever with the Lord, is here called their living together with him. And lest it might be thought that none should be with Christ until they awaked at the resurrection, he therefore speaks of living with Christ even when we sleep. He had spoken of sleep in another sense, ver. 6, as meant of security; but here meant of death, as it is taken chap. iv. 14. And as watching is set opposite to the former sleep, so here waking to the latter, which is a resurrection from death. And we hence gather that the soul doth not sleep with the body, but lives with the Lord when that sleeps in the grave; as the apostle expected to be with the Lord upon the dissolution of his body, Phil. i. 23, and he mentions it as the privilege of other saints as well as his own, 2 Cor. v. 1. When we sleep we are with him only in our souls; when we wake we shall be with him both in body and soul. And both these we have from Christ's death. If he had not died, heaven had been shut against our souls, for our entrance into the holiest of all is by his blood, and the veil of his flesh rent for us, Heb. x. 19, 20; and the grave would have shut up our bodies, and there would have been no resurrection; so that our living with Christ, both when we sleep and when we wake, springs out of his death. Others carry these words no further than the foregoing verse, showing how we are saved by Christ; saith the apostle, he *died for us*. As God appointed persons to be saved, and Christ to be the person to be saved by, so also to be saved by his death; with respect to his Father he is said to be *put to death*, 1 Pet. iii. 18; with respect to his own freedom and willingness, he is said here to die for us. And his dying for us implieth the greatness of our guilt, and expresseth the greatness of his own love, John xv. 13. He loved us, and thereupon would have us live with him; and he died that we and he may live together. And so he may be said to die for our salvation, the substance whereof consisteth in our living with him. To live with so glorious a Person, and a Person that is full of love to us, and shall then be perfectly beloved of us, and that stands in many near relations to us, and whose presence will have such a blessed influence upon us, and in such a place as heaven is, and that for ever, surely carries the substance of our salvation in it. And if this was the end of his death, surely it was more than to be an example of faith, patience, and submission to God, or to confirm to us the doctrine he preached; it was to satisfy Divine justice, and obtain the pardon of our sin, and merit for us the privilege of living with him.

11 ᑫWherefore ‖ comfort yourselves together, and edify one another, even as also ye do.

q ch. 4. 18. ‖ Or, *exhort.*

These words are an exhortation to the whole church of Thessalonica, to comfort and edify one another. Though the ministry is appointed to this by especial office, yet private Christians are to practise it to one another; the former doth it in way of authority, the latter in a way of charity. *Comfort yourselves together*: the apostle had laid before them many comfortable truths, which they were to comfort one another by; and if we read the words, exhort one another, it refers to the necessary duties of religion he had mentioned in this and the foregoing chapter. *And edify one another;* and this follows from both the former, as alluding to a house that is built up by degrees: and so is every church the house of God; and consisting of living stones, every part is to seek the building up of the whole; and by mutual exhortation and comfort the whole may be edified. Christians, then, are to be blamed that only seek to edify themselves, and much more they who pull down, and divide, and destroy, instead of building-up. *Even as also ye do*: and what the apostle exhorted them to, they were already in the practice of; for which he here again commends them, as he had done upon several accounts before, not to flatter, but to encourage them to proceed, and to set before other churches their example for imitation.

12 And we beseech you, brethren, ʳto know them which labour among you, and are over you in the Lord, and admonish you;

r 1 Cor. 16. 18. Phil. 2. 29. 1 Tim. 5. 17. Heb. 13. 7, 17.

13 And to esteem them very highly in love for their work's sake. ˢ*And* be at peace among yourselves.

s Mark 9. 50.

The apostle spake before of their private duties as Christians to one another, now of their duties to their pastors and teachers, lest by what he had said they might think the ministry needless. It seems this church was settled under officers, which is called an organical church. And though the apostle himself was driven from them by persecution, yet they were not without ministers and teachers; and they owed a great duty to them, to which he doth lovingly exhort them. And he describes them not by the name of their office, as pastors, elders, or ministers, but by the work of it. *Them which labour among you;* the word imports diligent labour, causing weariness, as 1 Tim. v. 17, *who labour in the word and doctrine;* which shows both the nature of the work of the ministry, it is laborious; and the duty of ministers therein, not to seek the honour and profit of the office, and refuse the labour of it; they have the work of teaching, and of oversight or government, and admonition, and all require labour. *And are over you in the Lord:* the same word is used 1 Tim. v. 17, and translated *rule;* it signifies that superintendency and precedency, which the elders or ministers have over their respective flocks; and it is said to be *in the Lord,* either to distinguish them from civil officers, or to show both the original, rule, and end of their office; it is from the Lord by institution, and to be managed according to his laws, and directed to his service and glory as its end. *And admonish you:* the word is often used in the New Testament, Acts xx. 31; Rom. xv. 14; Col. i. 28; iii. 16; and signifies either the putting into the mind by way of instruction, or upon the mind by way of counsel, threatening, or reproof; and that either publicly or privately. Now the duty they owed to them is, 1. *To know them,* as in the former words; that is, to own them in their office, to have regard to their teaching, and to submit to their government, and to reward their labours; as knowing is often taken in Scripture to express the acts of the will and affection, and the actions also of the outward man, as well as of the mind; as Psal. i. 6; ci. 4. 2. *To esteem them very highly in love for their work's sake;* ὑπερεκπερισσοῦ· see Rom. v. 20; 2 Cor. vii. 4. The words in the Greek carry such an emphasis as cannot well be expressed in English, importing esteem and love to an hyperbole; their love was to be joined with esteem, and esteem with love, and both these to abound and superabound towards them. We read of a *double honour,* 1 Tim. v. 17, which contains the whole duty of people to their ministers. *For their work's sake;* whether of teaching, ruling, or admonition. Their work is in itself honourable, and work that tends to your salvation, and though their persons be meant, yet to esteem and love them for their work; or if upon any other account they deserve it of you, yet their work is to be the chief reason thereof; especially considering that their work more immediately respected them of this church rather than any others; and their labour was amongst them; or, as some read it, in you, to instruct, edify, and comfort your inward man. *And be at peace among yourselves;* some copies read it, with them, αὐτοῖς for ἑαυτοῖς, by a little alteration of the Greek word; and then it still refers to their teachers, they should be at peace, or live in peace, with them; for oftentimes dissensions arise betwixt ministers and people, whereby their edification is hindered. But I rather follow our own translation; and so it is a new duty of the people towards one another, to preserve mutual peace among themselves, and yet these words may respect the former. For if the people give honour and respect to their ministers, it may be a means to preserve peace among themselves: among the Corinthians, the applauding of some of their teachers, and the contempt of others, made great schisms and divisions amongst them. Our Saviour useth these very words to his disciples, Mark ix. 50, from whence the apostle might take them. And the duty of peace he often presseth in his Epistles, Rom. xiv. 19; 1 Cor. vii. 15; 2 Cor. xiii. 11; Col. iii. 15; Heb. xii. 14; which was to prevent schism, which breaks the bonds of peace, and may make the labours of their teachers less successful.

∥ Or, *beseech.*
t 2 Thess. 3. 11, 12.
∥ Or, *disorderly.*
u Heb. 12.12.
x Rom. 14. 1.
& 15. 1. Gal. 6. 1, 2. y Gal. 5. 22. Eph. 4. 2. Col. 3. 12. 2 Tim. 4. 2.

14 Now we ∥exhort you, brethren, ᵗwarn them that are ∥unruly, ᵘcomfort the feebleminded, ˣsupport the weak, ʸbe patient toward all *men.*

Now we exhort you, brethren: some think the apostle now turns his speech to their teachers, whom he here calls *brethren* in a more peculiar sense, and because the duties here enjoined do more properly belong to the ministry. But others more truly judge he continues his discourse to the whole church, and the several members of it. The same duties are to be performed by both, though under a different obligation: as in the civil state all are to seek the good of the commonwealth, though the magistrates and the governors are more specially obliged by office. *Warn them that are unruly;* or admonish, as the same word is rendered in the former verse, here meant of brotherly, there of ministerial, admonition; wherein great prudence is to be used, as to time, place, persons, manner: and the *unruly* are such as keep not their place, alluding to soldiers that keep not their rank and station, and they are called in the margin *disorderly,* and that, 1. In civil respects, when men live without a calling, or, being in it, neglect it, or intrude into other men's business, and perform not the duties of their civil relations. 2. In natural respects, when men follow not the light of nature, and fulfil not the law of natural relations. 3. In spiritual respects, when men neglect or transgress the rules and order of their walking in their church state, either with respect to their teachers or one another. Admonition belongs to such, and is the first step of church censure when regularly performed. *Comfort the feeble-minded;* ὀλιγοψύχους, or the pusillanimous, men of little souls, as the word imports, such as dare not venture upon hazardous duties, or faint under the fears or feeling of afflictions, or are dejected under the sense of sin, and their own unworthiness, or fears of God's wrath, and assaulted by temptations which endanger their falling. *Support the weak;* ἀντέχεσθε· an allusion to such as lift at one end of the burden, to help to bear it, answering to the word συναντιλαμβάνεται, Rom. viii. 26, *The Spirit helpeth our infirmities:* and the weak are either the weak in knowledge, weak in faith, that understand not their own liberty in the gospel, Rom. xiv. 1; 1 Cor. viii. 9; and hereupon cannot practise as others do; their conscience is weak, 1 Cor. viii. 12; and so were in bondage to some ceremonial rites, when those that were strong stood fast in their liberty. These are to be supported, dealt tenderly with, and not to be despised, or rigorously used. Or, weak in grace, new converts, babes in Christ, tender plants, not well rooted in the gospel. *Be patient toward all men:* this duty is universal; the former concerned only the saints. The word signifies longanimity, or long-suffering, and is often attributed to God, Exod. xxxiv. 6; Rom. ix. 22. It consisteth in the deferring or moderating of anger, to wait without anger when men delay us, and to suffer without undue anger when they deal injuriously with us, whether they be good men or evil, believers or infidels, the strong or the weak, ministers or people.

15 ᶻ See that none render evil for evil unto any *man;* but ever ᵃfollow that which is good, both among yourselves, and to all *men.*

z Lev. 19. 18. Prov. 20. 22. & 24. 29. Matt. 5. 39, 44. Rom. 12. 17. 1 Cor. 6. 7. 1 Pet. 3. 9. a Gal. 6. 10. ch. 3. 12.

These words seem directed to the guides of the church, who are called *overseers,* Acts xx. 28, and therefore the apostle requires them to *see* that none render evil, &c. Or if to the whole church, as before, then it is a solemn charge which they ought to be all circumspect in observing. And the charge is, 1. Negative, not to *render evil for evil;* which is to revenge themselves; and that is forbidden by the apostle, Rom. xii. 17, 19; 1 Pet. iii. 9; and is the resisting of evil forbidden by our Saviour, Matt. v. 39. But it is to be understood of private revenge rising out of malice, not of public censures, either civil or ecclesiastical, or of seeking reparations for injuries received in courts of justice according to law and equity. This private revenge cannot consist with that patience that he required towards all men in the foregoing verse, nor is it conformable to the example of Christ, 1 Pet. ii. 23, nor to the Christian calling and profession, 1 Pet. ii. 21. 2. Positive; good in itself, or that which is good to others, as the word is often taken, Matt. vii. 11; Luke i. 53; Gal. vi. 6; and so stands opposite here to the rendering of evil. And the word *follow* signifies an earnest following, which is sometimes taken in a bad sense, for persecution, Matt. v. 11, and sometimes in a good sense, as Heb. xii. 14; 1 Pet. iii. 11; and to follow good imports more than only to do good, 1 Pet. iii. 11, when the inward bent of the soul and the outward endeavours are towards doing good. And this ought to be *ever,* or always, that is, in all places, times, occasions, company. Man's course of life ought in this to be uniform, though his outward condition vary; sometimes to do good to the souls, sometimes to the bodies of men, and that either in a privative or positive good; preventing evil, or bestowing that which is good. *Both among yourselves, and to all men: Do good unto all men, especially unto them who are of the household of faith,* Gal. vi. 10. As they say of good, the commoner the better; but the contrary of evil. Christians stand in a special relation to one another, but in a common relation to all, and every relation ought to be filled up with good. As love is a common debt to all men, so the fruit of it, which is doing good. Our doing good should not be confined among Christians only of one way, opinion, or congregation; nor to men only under some limiting circumstances; but it should reach all men as we have ability, opportunity, and call, even enemies themselves, as our Saviour requires, Matt. v. 44. This is to act like God, and may commend religion to all men, and is not to be looked upon as commended by way of counsel, as the papists say, but commanded by precept. And it is not enough not to do evil, but we must do good: not to save a man's life when we have power to do it, is to kill him, as Christ argues, Mark iii. 4; so not to save a man's estate when we may, is to steal from him.

b 2 Cor. 6. 10.
Phil. 4. 4.
16 ᵇRejoice evermore.

Here the apostle adds more Christian duties, briefly expressed, and set close one to another; and they seem to have a mutual connexion, but not so relative to others as those before mentioned, but personal to themselves. He begins with the duty of rejoicing. Joy is an affection of the soul springing from the hope or possession of some suitable good. And it is either natural, which is common to men with beasts, arising from that good that is suitable to their several natures; or spiritual, which is joy wrought by the Spirit, and exercised upon spiritual objects. And this the apostle here means, and is called rejoicing *in the Lord*, Phil. iv. 4, and *joy in the Holy Ghost*, Rom. xiv. 17; arising either from what spiritual good we already possess, or hope to possess, *exhibita et promissa*, Bernard; which is thereupon called a *rejoicing in hope*, Rom. v. 2; xii. 12. The apostle speaks here of the duty indefinitely, only requires it to be *evermore;* so Phil. iv. 4. Though God sometimes calls to mourning, yet it is no where said, Mourn evermore, because rejoicing ought to be in a more constant practice, and all spiritual mourning tends to it, and will end in it; and he commends it as seasonable to these Thessalonians, to support them under their present sufferings. The grounds of a Christian's joy always abide, and he is not only to retain it in the habit, but to mix it with all his sorrows and sufferings, as 1 Pet. i. 6, *Ye greatly rejoice, though for a season in heaviness:* whereas carnal mirth is mixed with sadness, Prov. xiv. 13. So that a Christian ought to rejoice in every condition, not only in prosperity but adversity, and especially when called to suffer for righteousness sake; as Matt. v. 12: 1 Pet. iv. 13. It is not only allowed but commanded. This joy is one great part of God's kingdom even in this world, Rom. xiv. 17; much more in the world to come. And therefore the apostle speaks of rejoicing evermore, whereas mourning is but for a time, and ends to the saints in this life.

c Luke 18. 1.
& 21. 36.
Rom. 12. 12. Eph. 6. 18. Col. 4. 2. 1 Pet. 4. 7.
17 ᶜPray without ceasing.

This is a means to maintain our rejoicing, and therefore next mentioned. Prayer is a making known our requests to God, Phil. iv. 6. And it is either mental, in the heart only, as Hannah's was; or vocal, expressed with the voice; or, as some add, vital: so good works have a voice to bring down blessings, as men's sins cry for vengeance. *Without ceasing;* not as the Euchites and Messalians of old, who hence thought no other duties were required, but always praying; but by the word in the text, is either meant a praying without fainting, as in the parable, Luke xviii. 1, and which the apostle calls a perseverance in prayer, Eph. vi. 18; Col. iv. 2; προσκαρτερεῖτε, or praying with strength, as the Greek word there imports, and so not to faint; so Rom. xii. 12. Or a praying in every thing, as Phil. iv. 6, *In every thing let your requests be made known*, &c. Or, in every season, as Eph. vi. 18; to take hold of the seasons of prayer. Or, in all seasons and times, whether good or bad, yet still to pray. And all this is meant by the word in the text, which is also used chap. i. 3; ii. 13; Rom. i. 9; and implies in general no more but a constant course of prayer. so Col. iv. 2, to watch unto prayer, as that the course of it be not interrupted by any diversions. So also to preserve a heart disposed to pray at all times, and to mingle ejaculatory prayers with the several actions of our lives: our wants are continual, and God will be acknowledged in all our supplies, and therefore we ought to pray continually.

18 ᵈIn every thing give thanks: for this is the will of God in Christ Jesus concerning you.
d Eph. 5. 20
Col. 3. 17.

In every thing give thanks: when we have obtained mercy by prayer, then we are to give thanks, and whatever we may pray for, that we ought to give thanks for. And so by that understand and limit the general expression in the text. We are not to give thanks when we fall into sin, for that we ought not to pray for; yet if we have the pardon of it, or get any good by it, we should then give thanks: and so may be said concerning affliction; we are to give thanks in every condition, either of prosperity or adversity. And with all our supplications, we are to join thanksgivings, Phil. iv. 6; Col. iv. 2; and thanksgiving properly refers to some mercy received, whether privative or positive, temporal or spiritual, private or public, and we are in all these to give thanks. Though praising God may reach further, which is to adore the excellencies of his being as they are glorious in themselves, or the excellencies of his works as they are in themselves praiseworthy. And thanksgiving for mercy received is, 1. A taking notice of it as coming from God. 2. Setting a due value upon it. 3. A sense of God's goodness and our own unworthiness. 4. Praising him for it. *For this is the will of God:* some carry this as a motive to all the preceding duties; but rather to this last mentioned: as if this was in special the will of God, being a duty so much to his own glory and our good; and by *will* we must by a metonymy understand the thing willed, Eph. vi. 6; Col. iv. 12. It is required by the law of nature not written, which is part of God's will. The heathen are reproved for not being thankful, Rom. i. 21; and they made laws to punish it, and accounted it the greatest reproach, *ingratum si dixeris omnia dixeris*. And it is required by the law of God that is written. The moral law requires it; and the ceremonial law required offerings by way of thanksgiving, which we call gratulatory. And the gospel requires it, it being one of the gospel sacrifices, Heb. xiii. 15, and pleaseth the Lord better than the greatest of the legal sacrifices, Psal. lxix. 30, 31: and it being said to be the will of God in the text, it must needs be pleasing to him. *In Christ Jesus;* either meant as this will of his is signified to us by him, not only by the law of nature, or of Moses, but by Christ Jesus; and so it may be of greater force upon Christians, and hereby it is to be looked upon as one of the commandments of Christ also. Or we may understand it, upon the account of Christ, and the great love of God in him. Though thanksgiving is due for the least mercy, yet God's will especially requires it with respect to Christ. And so especially of Christians who partake of Christ, and the love of God in him; as the apostle here adds, εἰς ὑμᾶς. *Concerning you;* or towards you in special: the heathens were obliged to thankfulness for rain from heaven, and fruitful seasons, these common blessings; much more are Christians for the special blessings they receive by Christ Jesus.

19 ᵉQuench not the Spirit.
e Eph. 4. 30.
1 Tim. 4. 14.
2 Tim. 1. 6. See 1 Cor. 14. 30.

That ye may be enabled to pray and give thanks, as before, *Quench not the Spirit*. And, by the figure meiosis, he means, cherish the Spirit. The Spirit is compared to fire, Matt. iii. 11; and he came down upon the apostles in the similitude of tongues of fire, Acts ii. 3; but the Spirit himself cannot be quenched; he means it therefore of his gifts and operations; which are either ordinary or extraordinary. Many had extraordinary gifts in the primitive times, of healing, tongues, government, prophecy, &c.; those that had them, without question, should have taken care not, by any fault of their own, to lose them. Especially that of prophecy, which the apostle prefers before all others, 1 Cor. xiv. 1, and mentions here in the following verse; and which the apostle exhorted Timothy to stir up in himself, 2 Tim. i. 6, as we stir up the fire to quicken it, so the word ἀναζωπυρεῖν imports. The like is required of ministers with respect to their ministerial gifts which are now given. But there are ordinary gifts and operations of the Spirit common to all Christians, as enlightening, quickening, sanctifying, comforting the soul: men by sloth, security, earthly encumbrances, inordinate affections, &c., may abate these operations of the Spirit, which the apostle calls the quenching it: the fire upon the altar was kept always burning by the care of the priests. Fire will go out either by neglecting it, or casting water upon it. By not exercising grace in the duties of religion, or by allowing sin in ourselves, we may quench the Spirit; as appears in David, Psal. li. 10—12. Not that the habits of grace may be totally extinguished in the truly regenerate, yet they may be abated as to degree and lively exercise. Yet those common illuminations and convictions of the Spirit which persons unregenerate, especially such that live under the gospel, do often find, may be totally lost, Heb. vi. 4—6; and we read of God's Spirit ceasing to strive with the old world, Gen. vi. 3, and the scribes and Pharisees resisting the Holy Ghost, Acts vii. 51, which were not persons regenerate. He may sometimes strive with men, but not overcome them. And there is a quenching of the Spirit in others as well as ourselves; people may quench it in their ministers by discouraging them, and in one another by bad examples, or reproaching the zeal and forwardness that they see in them.

f 1 Cor. 14. 1, 39. 20 ^fDespise not prophesyings.

Thereby we may quench the Spirit, which usually works upon men's minds and hearts by it. By prophecy is sometimes meant foretelling of things to come, and speaking by extraordinary revelation, 1 Cor. xiv. 29, 30; sometimes the Scriptures are so called, especially the Old Testament, 2 Pet. i. 21; and sometimes the interpretation and applying of Scripture, which is the same that we now call preaching, 1 Cor. xiv. 3. And the duty with respect to it, is not to despise it, to set it at nought as a thing of no worth. The word is often used in the New Testament, Luke xviii. 9; Acts iv. 11; Rom. xiv. 3, 10. But the apostle useth again the figure meiosis before mentioned, and means, prize, value, and highly esteem it, attend upon it, have great regard to it; it being an ordinance of God for instruction and edification, yea, and for conversion also, 1 Cor. xiv. 24, 25. Some despise it because of the outward meanness of the persons which prophesy; some, through a proud conceit of their own knowledge; some, by a contempt of religion itself. These Thessalonians had been commended for their great proficiency, and yet were still to attend upon prophesying in the church; which he calls *prophesyings*, in the plural number, referring either to the several prophets that prophesied, or to the several parts of their prophecy, or the times they prophesied. And the prophets were either such as prophesied only by an extraordinary gift, and immediate revelation, which some private members of the church had in those times, 1 Cor. xiv. 29, 30; or such as prophesied not only by gift, but office also, Eph. iv. 11.

g 1 Cor. 2. 11, 15. 1 John 4. 1. h Phil. 4. 8. 21 ^gProve all things; ^h hold fast that which is good.

Prove all things; this duty relates to the former; as they were to attend upon prophesyings, so to exercise a discerning judgment about what was prophesied; for *all things* is not to be taken here universally, but for doctrines and opinions in religion which were delivered by the prophets. The same which the apostle John requires, *Believe not every spirit, but try the spirits*, &c.; δοκιμάζετε· and it is the same word there which in this text we read *prove;* alluding to gold or other metals, which are tried in the fire, or by a touchstone, as some think. And though there was a peculiar gift of *discerning of spirits*, 1 Cor. xii. 10, yet it is the duty of every Christian to try men's spirits and doctrines whether from God or no. The apostle speaks here to the saints in general, and so doth the apostle John, 1 John iv. 1. And men's doctrines are to be judged by the Scriptures as the standard of truth, as the Bereans were commended for searching the Scriptures about the apostle's doctrine, Acts xvii. 11; and the apostle prays for the Philippians, that they might discern things that differ, Phil. i. 10; and if they had not yet attained it as they ought, yet he prays that they might, and not be always babes, but such as the apostle speaks of, who have their senses exercised in the discerning of good and evil. Heb. v. 13, 14: the people are to look upon them as their guides and leaders, as they are called, Heb. xiii. 7, 17, and such as are to go before them in the searching and dispensing of truth; yet, because the best are but infallible, they ought to try their doctrine by the rule of truth. Which is that judgment of discretion which protestants allow to the people in their disputes with the papists against their doctrine of infallibility and implicit faith, which grounds the people's faith upon the authority of men, which ought to rest upon the authority of God. As we ought not easily to reject the authority and faith of the church, so not to believe with a blind faith, or obey with a blind obedience. *Hold fast that which is good:* the good here meant is truth, which is an intellectual good; the contrary to which is error, which is a mental evil. When we have proved men's doctrines and opinions, what we find agreeable to the Scriptures of truth we ought to hold fast. And though all truth hath a goodness in it, yet especially Divine truth, and the doctrine of the gospel, which the apostle calls, *that good thing* committed to Timothy, 2 Tim. i. 14. It is good with respect to the soul, and so better than any bodily good; and good that refers to eternity, and so better than any temporal good. Now this good we are to *hold fast;* to hold it fast against adversaries and all opposition, as some understand the word; to hold it as with both hands, against seducing doctrine, Satan's temptations, and the world's persecution. The same word is used concerning the good ground that held fast the seed of the word, Luke viii. 15. So 1 Cor. xi. 2, we are to retain the truth, but not detain it, as the heathen are said to do, Rom. i. 18, where we find also the same word as in the text. It is a duty much pressed by the apostles in their Epistles to the saints and churches that had received the gospel, that they would hold it fast, 2 Tim. i. 13; Tit. i. 9; Heb. iv. 14; Rev. ii. 13, 25; iii. 3. And there is holding fast the truth as well in practice as opinion, and which may be the ground of the name given to such as opposed the errors of antichrist before the word *protestant* was known, called *fast-men*.

22 ⁱAbstain from all appearance of evil. i ch. 4. 12.

To make this verse have its connexion with the former, some expositors understand it of doctrines and opinions only; to take heed of opinions that seem erroneous, and not rashly to receive them without due examination. Though this sense is not to be excluded, yet the verse need not be confined to it, but to extend to practice also; as in worship to abstain from the show of idolatry; as to eat meat in an idol's temple was not always gross idolatry, but had some appearance of it, and therefore the apostle forbids it, 1 Cor. x. 14. And so in civil conversation, not only to abstain from vice, but the appearance of it; as of pride, covetousness, drunkenness, whoredom, &c.; and that both with respect to ourselves, lest by venturing upon that which hath some show of evil, we step into the evil itself; and with respect to others, that we may not occasion the taking offence though not justly given, or do that which may any way encourage a real evil in them by that appearance of it which they see in ourselves; yet we ought not upon this account to forbear the discharge of any necessary duty. Some read the words, Abstain from all kind of evil, Ἀπὸ παντὸς εἴδεος πονηροῦ, and the Greek word is so used by logicians: but here to insist on particulars is infinite. And thus the apostle concludes all these positive duties with a general precept which he leaves with them at the close of his Epistle; having dehorted them from many evils, now he exhorts them to abstain from the appearance of evil.

23 And ^k the very God of peace ^l sanctify you wholly; and *I pray God* your whole spirit and soul and body ^m be preserved blameless unto the coming of our Lord Jesus Christ. k Phil. 4. 9. l ch. 3. 13. m 1 Cor. 1.8.

The apostle here concludes all with prayer, as knowing all his exhortations and admonitions before given would not be effectual without God; and he prays for their sanctification and preservation. Though they were sanctified already, yet but in part, so that he prays for further progress in it to perfection. which he means by *wholly;* a word no where used by the apostle but in this place, and variously rendered; some render it throughout, some, perfectly, some, in every part, some, in all things, some, fully, and the French, entirely. It may refer to all the parts of holiness, and the degrees of holiness, and to the whole man in the several faculties of soul and body, expressed in the next words by *spirit, soul, and body*, that their whole man may be entirely separated and consecrated to God, offered up to him as a sacrifice, Rom. xii. 1; and hence we observe that not only the beginning, but progress in grace is from God. The apostle therefore prays for it to God, (whom he calls *the God of peace,* to enforce his exhortation to peace, ver. 3,) which confutes the Pelagians, who thought objective grace sufficient to sanctify, or that man's nature needs only at first to be excited by God, and then can go forward of itself, being only maimed, not totally corrupted by the fall. It is true, our faculties co-operate with God, but not of themselves, but as acted by his inherent grace and indwelling Spirit. And what the apostle prays for, that Christians should endeavour after, which is a progress in sanctification to perfection. We may also note, that true sanctification reacheth to the whole man, spirit, soul, and body. 2. Preservation, which we call perseverance, expressed here both by the subject and term of it. The subject is the whole man, branched into three parts, *spirit, soul, and body,* figured, at least resembled, by the three parts of the temple. Consider man naturally; and then by *spirit* we mean his superior faculties, as the mind, conscience, rational will. By *soul,* his sensitive appetite, with the affections and passions. By *body,* the outward man, the tabernacle and instrument of the soul. The Jewish rabbins and others think all these are expressed in the creation of man, Gen. ii. 7; *God formed man of the dust of the ground,* there is his body; *and breathed into his nostrils the breath of life,* or lives, *Nishmath Chaiim, Nephesh Chaijah,* that is, the faculties of the rational soul; *and man became a living soul,* that is, the animal and sensitive life. Neither is properly meant here the Spirit of God, for he saith, *your spirit;* nor the sanctified part of the soul, for he prays for the preserving of their persons. Only observe, when he speaks of their spirit, he calls it their *whole spirit.* And by the figure zeugma, the word *whole* is to be carried also to *soul and body;* so that as he prayed their whole man might be sanctified, so their whole spirit, their whole soul, their whole body might be preserved; and the same word we find James i. 4, where it is rendered *perfect,* alluding to the perfect possessing of an inheritance or lot that belongs to a man. And by preserving, he means not so much the substance of the spirit, soul, and body, to preserve them in being, as to preserve them in holiness. And they are preserved, partly by being delivered from the sinful distempers that are naturally in them, as ignorance, vanity, impotency, and enmity in the mind, reluctancy and obstinacy in the will, inordinacy and irregularity in the affections, disobedience to the law of God and the regular commands of the soul in the body. If these prevail, they will bring destruction; as diseases prevailing destroy the natural life. And partly also by being supplied with that grace whereby they act regularly towards God, and are serviceable to the end of man's being, as supply of oil preserveth the lamp burning. And hereby we may understand, that not only the inferior faculties are corrupted in man's fall, but the superior and the supreme of all, else the apostle need not have prayed for the spirit to be sanctified and preserved, as well as the soul and body. And elsewhere he prays for a renewing *in the spirit of the mind,* Eph. iv. 23. Next we may consider this preservation with respect to the term of it, *preserved blameless unto the coming of Christ:* the same which the apostle means by being preserved to God's heavenly kingdom, 2 Tim. iv. 18; 2 Pet. iii. 14. And those that are preserved to that day, are preserved to the end, and will be found blameless; and their whole man, spirit, soul, and body, being first sanctified, and then preserved, shall be saved and glorified. And the apostle insinuates in the word ἀμέμπτως, *blameless,* that strict discovery that will be made of persons at that day, wherein some will be blamed, and others be found without blame. And herein the apostle may have respect both to the teachers and ministers in this church, and the private members of it, that with respect to their several duties belonging to them they may be found blameless; and though, according to the strictness of the law of God, none can be without blame, yet, those that have been sincere, and have their sin pardoned, and their persons accepted in Christ, may be found blameless in the day of Christ: however, it is that which we should strive after.

n 1 Cor. i. 9. & 10. 13
2 Thess. 3.3.

24 ⁿFaithful *is* he that calleth you, who also will do *it.*

We had in the former verse the apostle's prayer, here his faith; and he speaks it by way of consolation to them, that what he had prayed for God would effect. What need he then have prayed? Because God's decrees and promises, though immutable and infallible, yet are to be accomplished in a way of prayer. Prayer is our duty, and God's decrees and promises are no dispensation from our duty: besides, duties are more known to us than God's decrees; and God decree the means as well as the end. But what is it he saith God will do? It is not here expressed, and the word *it* is not in the original, but only God *will do,* God will effect. He had prayed God would sanctify them wholly, and preserve them blameless, &c.; and this he would do or effect. And he grounds his confidence partly upon God's calling them. For the apostle knew that God's *gifts and calling are without repentance; and whom he called, them he justified, and glorified,* Rom. viii. 30; xi. 29. And this the apostle saw in these Thessalonians, by that efficacy of the gospel upon their hearts, that they were effectually called and chosen, as chap. i. 4; whence he concluded they should be at last wholly sanctified and finally preserved, which is a strong argument against final apostacy from a state of grace; though many that are outwardly called are never sanctified, much less wholly. But of this call the apostle speaks not here, at least not only. And partly also upon God's faithfulness, who had called them. He doth not say, God is able to do it, though that is true, but he is *faithful,* and *will do it.* Those that are effectually called are brought into God's covenant, where perfection and perseverance are promised, and God's faithfulness obligeth him to make good his covenant. It is an act of grace and mercy to call men; but when called, God's faithfulness is engaged to preserve them, and perfect the work begun; as, 1 Cor. i. 8, the apostle tells the Corinthians, God will confirm them, to the end they might be blameless in the day of Christ; and his argument is, for *God is faithful, by whom ye were called,* &c., ver. 9.

25 Brethren, °pray for us.   o Col. 4. 3. 2 Thess. 3. 1.

The apostle a little before had prayed for them, now he begs prayers of them, as he doth of other churches, Rom. xv. 30; Col. iv. 3. Ministers and people need each others' prayers, and it is a mutual duty they owe to one another. Ministers are obliged by special office, people by common duty, with respect to the success of the gospel in general, 2 Thess. iii. 1, and their own edification by their labours. The apostle, as he did not think it below him to call these Thessalonians brethren, so neither to beg their prayers. Those that stand highest in the church may stand in need of the meanest and lowest; the head cannot say to the foot, I have no need of thee. Those that preach not the gospel, may yet promote it by their prayers; yet this gives no warrant to beg the prayers of saints departed, for which we have no precept, promise, or example, as we have for the other; and what is without faith is sin. It is at the best doubtful whether they know our state below, or can hear us when we pray; and certainly God never required us to pray upon such uncertainties, and it cannot be in faith.

26 ᵖGreet all the brethren with an holy kiss.   p Rom. 16. 16.

The apostle concludes several of his Epistles with greeting, or salutations, as men usually do at this day; sometimes with salutations from himself alone, sometimes from others, either particular persons, or churches which he sometimes names, as Rom. xvi. 6, &c.; 1 Cor. xvi. 19; and sometimes commends to the saints their saluting one another, as Rom. xvi. 16; 1 Cor. xvi. 20; so here in the text. The persons to be saluted are *all the brethren,* that is, all believers incorporated into the gospel church, under one common Head and common Father; more particularly, those of this particular church. We call men brethren, sometimes upon a natural, sometimes a civil account; and why not much more upon a spiritual account? And as their love should reach to the brotherhood, 1 Pet. ii. 17, so their salutation should reach all the brethren, poor and rich, high and low, bond and free. *With an holy kiss;* ἐν φιλήματι ἁγίῳ. The rite or ceremony of men kissing each other was much used among the Jews, and in the Eastern countries, in their salutations, Gen. xxvii. 26; Prov. xxiv. 26; Luke vii. 45; and thence it came to be practised in the churches of Christ as an outward symbol and token of love and friendship; which is not now practised with us amongst men, but is of the same signification with joining of hands; the uniting of lips or hands together denoting the inward conjunction of the heart. The word in the Greek signifies love or friendship, and is called *a kiss of charity*, 1 Pet. v. 14. And though the ceremony is ceased, yet that which it signified is to be preserved in all churches, places, and ages. It was practised in the time of Justin Martyr, *Just. Mar. Apolog.* 2., and Tertullian, *Tertul. de Oratione;* and called *osculum pacis*, a kiss of peace; and used especially at their meeting together at the Lord's supper, their love feasts, and other solemn assemblies. It is called *a holy kiss*, to distinguish it from the treacherous kiss of Judas, or the lustful kiss of the harlot, Prov. vii. 13. And why it is not used among us now, we need say only, as concerning washing of feet also, *We have no such custom, nor the churches of Christ;* or, as the apostle speaks, Phil. iv. 8. *Whatsoever things are lovely, and whatsoever things are of good report, &c.*

|| Or, *adjure*.

27 I || charge you by the Lord that ᵍthis epistle be read unto all the holy brethren.

q Col. 4. 16.
2 Thess. 3. 14.

The apostle having now finished the Epistle, lays a solemn charge upon them all, especially their elders and teachers, to have this Epistle published. He now being himself hindered from preaching to them, he sends this Epistle to them to be read to all. He wrote it for public use, and therefore would have none ignorant of it, whereby they might all understand what he had written about his great love and care of them, and the commendations he had given of them, and the instructions, admonitions, exhortations, and comforts that were contained therein, of great use to them all. And his charge herein is in a way of adjuration, Ὁρκίζω ὑμᾶς τὸν Κύριον, imposing it on them as by an oath; as Abraham did upon his servant in the case of providing a wife for Isaac, Gen. xxiv. 3. And so the high priest said to Christ, *I adjure thee by the living God,* &c., Matt. xxvi. 63; answering to the Hebrew word *Hishbagnti*, I adjure you; Cant. v. 8, *I charge you, O daughters of Jerusalem*, &c. It imports the requiring of a thing in the name and authority of God, with a denunciation of vengeance if it be not done. And all this charge is about the reading of this Epistle; as he commands the Epistle to the Colossians to be read in the church of the Laodiceans, and that from Laodicea to be read to them, Col. iv. 16, but not with that solemn charge as this is. Hence we may gather the duty of reading the Scriptures in the church assemblies, as the law of Moses was read in the synagogues. And very early in the Christian churches there were some appointed to be readers. Julian the Apostate was a reader in the church at Nicomedia. And if this was the first Epistle written by the apostle, as some suppose it, he lays this solemn charge first for the reading of this, to show the duty of the several churches to the rest of the Scriptures, as they should come to their hand. The word of God should dwell richly and plentifully in the people, and therefore reading it is necessary, together with expounding and applying it. And we hence also may prove against the papists, it ought to be made known to the people, even all the holy brethren, and not confined to the clergy; and to be read in their own tongue, for so, without question, was this Epistle read in a language which the people understood. The apostle was not for confining of knowledge, and keeping the people in ignorance, as those are who make it the mother of devotion.

28 ʳThe grace of our Lord Jesus Christ *be* with you. Amen.

r Rom. 16. 20, 24.
2 Thess. 3. 18.

Having exhorted them to salute one another, he now sends them his own salutation; not in a lip compliment, as the mode now is, but in a serious expression of the desire of his soul: and this, or words to the same purpose, are his salutation in every Epistle, which he makes to be his *token*, 2 Thess. iii. 17. And by *grace* here he means favour and good will, rather than inherent grace: and all blessings which spring from grace, as sometimes all are comprehended under the word *peace.* Yet grace and peace are sometimes in his salutations both joined together. And though here Christ is only mentioned, yet in many other places God the Father is mentioned with him, 2 Thess. i. 2; 2 Pet. i. 2; yea, and God the Holy Ghost also, 2 Cor. xiii. 14; and where they are not mentioned, yet are all to be understood, for in all works *ad extra* they co-operate. And because grace is so eminently manifested in the whole work of our salvation, therefore the apostle doth still mention it in all his salutations. And with this he concludes this Epistle, and with this St. John concludes the whole Bible, Rev. xxii. 21. And the seal added, not to shut up, but confirm the whole, is, *Amen;* and is added as the voice of the whole church upon reading the Epistle, as some think, and not by the apostle himself.

¶ The first *epistle* unto the Thessalonians was written from Athens.

These postscripts to the apostle's Epistles are judged to be added by some scribes that copied them out, and not by the apostle himself, as might be made evident; and they are not found in any Epistles but in St. Paul's alone. But as it is usual to date letters from the places where they are written, so is this dated from Athens. Hither he was conducted by some brethren after his persecution at Thessalonica and Berea, Acts xvii. 15, and here we read he stayed for some time; but that from thence he wrote this Epistle, either then, or any time after, is but conjecture; it is more probable he wrote it from Corinth, because he sends it from Timotheus and Silvanus, as well as from himself, and they came to him from Macedonia when he was at Corinth, as Acts xviii. 5.

THE SECOND* EPISTLE OF PAUL THE APOSTLE

TO THE

THESSALONIANS

THE ARGUMENT

THE apostle being yet hindered from coming to them, and understanding some mistake of what he wrote in his former Epistle about the coming of Christ, he thereupon sends this Second Epistle; where, after his usual salutation, he gives thanks for them, and hearing of the continuance of their faith and patience under all their persecutions, he glories in them; and then comforts them by arguments taken from the righteous judgment of God, and the different manner and effect of Christ's coming, both to themselves and all the saints that believe, and to their adversaries, and all that knew not God, nor obeyed the gospel; and then prays for the perfecting of their faith to the glorifying the name of Christ, chap. i.

* Δευτέρα. This is well called the Second or latter Epistle to these Thessalonians, for so it is; though Grotius would have it the first, if not sent, yet first written.

But hearing they were shaken in their minds about the time of Christ's coming, as if it should be presently, in the age wherein they lived, he doth vehemently caution them against such a mistake; and tells them of a great apostacy, and the revelation of the man of sin, which must precede that day, which he doth particularly describe in the manner and effects thereof: but speaks of these Thessalonians with thanksgiving to God, as such as God had chosen, and called to obtain the glory of the Lord Jesus; and then prays for their comfort and establishment, chap. ii. He next proceeds to desire their prayers, both with respect to the success of the ministry, and the safety of the persons who were employed therein; and declares his confidence in them that God would establish them, and that they would obey the commandments they had received from them; and gives them some further commandments about such in the church as did walk disorderly; and so concludes his Epistle with prayers for their peace, and recommending them to the grace of Jesus Christ, chap. iii.

CHAP. I

The salutation 1, 2. Paul certifieth the Thessalonians of the good opinion which he had of their faith, love, and patience. 3—5; of the righteous judgment of God in punishing their enemies, and recompensing their sufferings, 6—10; and of his prayers that God would fulfil his gracious purpose in them, 11, 12.

A. D. 54.
a 2 Cor. 1. 19.
b 1 Thes. 1. 1.

PAUL, [a] and Silvanus, and Timotheus, unto the church of the Thessalonians [b] in God our Father and the Lord Jesus Christ:

e 1 Cor. 1. 3.

2 [e] Grace unto you, and peace, from God our Father and the Lord Jesus Christ.

These two verses are the same as in the former Epistle, and therefore I proceed.

d 1 Thess. 1. 2, 3. & 3, 6, 9. ch. 2. 13.

3 [d] We are bound to thank God always for you, brethren, as it is meet, because that your faith groweth exceedingly, and the charity of every one of you all toward each other aboundeth;

The apostle begins this Epistle as the former, with thanksgiving; only there he gave thanks for their faith, hope, and love, here he only mentions their faith and love; there for the efficacy of their grace, here for the growth of it. There he said only, *We give thanks*, here he addeth *We are bound*, and *as it is meet;* as if he was obliged to give thanks for them now somewhat more than before, perceiving their grace did not only yet abide, notwithstanding all their persecutions, but increase and grow. But the apostle's thanksgiving here respects particularly these Thessalonians' growth. Not only the beginning, but growth of grace is from God; else why doth the apostle give thanks for it? as Phil. i. 6. Hence he is styled *the God of all grace*, 1 Pet. v. 10, weak and strong, first or second. The manner of its growth, whether by infusion of new degrees, as the first grace is infused, or by co-operating only with it, and so it is increased by exercise, is a question I leave to the schoolmen. However, growth is a duty, and commendable in churches. And the apostle mentions particularly, 1. Their growth in faith; and that to a great degree, ὑπεραυξάνει, it *groweth exceedingly*; it grows over and above, above the ordinary rate of growth, or the common pitch of faith. Their progress was from faith to faith, their assent to the doctrine of the gospel grew more firm and rooted, and the persuasion of their happy state in Christ was much confirmed and strengthened, with a more confident reliance on him; or their faith was extended to more objects by the increase of their knowledge. 2. Their increase in love; which he also expresseth by an emphatical word, πλεονάζει, which signifies increasing to more and more; their love grew in the habit, and abounded in the fruits of it. And this love he sets forth by the universality of it, and the reciprocalness of it, it was *the love of all to each other;* they all did love, and were all beloved of one another; there was no schism among them, as in some other churches. Faith and love are two sister graces, and are always more or less together; only in the order of nature, faith is first, and worketh by love; but not first in time; and then afterwards, when it brings forth, love is *fides formata*, faith formed, as the papists speak. Hence some have said, that there was not one hypocrite or false Christian in this whole church. Now the apostle and his fellow ministers hereupon judged themselves bound to give thanks. Christians are obliged to give God thanks for the grace of God in others as well as in themselves; and especially the ministers of the gospel, for the people that have been converted by them, or are committed to them. Hereby the apostle's joy was increased at present, and his future glory might be advanced also.

4 So that [e] we ourselves glory in you in the churches of God [f] for your patience and faith [g] in all your persecutions and tribulations that ye endure:

e 2 Cor. 7. 14. & 9. 2.
f 1 Thess. 2. 19, 20.
f 1 Thes. 1. 3.
g 1 Thess. 2. 14.

In the former verse the apostle gave thanks for them, in this he glories in them; he gave thanks for them to God, and glories in them before men. Wherein Silvanus and Timotheus are to be understood as joined with him herein. Glorying includes in it high estimation of a thing, rejoicing in it, high commendation of it, and applauding ourselves in it; and it must be some great thing, either really or in opinion, and in which some way or other we ourselves are concerned. And glorying is good or evil according to the matter or object of it. To glory in our *wisdom, strength, riches*, Jer. ix. 23; to *glory in men*, 1 Cor. iii. 21, in our own *works*, Rom. iv. 2, in what we have received as if not received, 1 Cor. iv. 7, *after the flesh*, 2 Cor. xi. 18, or in our *shame*, Phil. iii. 19; all this glorying is evil. But to glory in God, Isa. xli. 16, *in his holy name*, 1 Chron. xvi. 10, *with God's inheritance*, Psal. cvi. 5, in the knowledge of the Lord, Jer. ix. 24, *in the cross of Christ*, Gal. vi. 14, *in tribulation*, Rom. v. 3, in Christ Jesus, 1 Cor. i. 31, in hope, Heb. iii. 6, and of the success of the ministry in the church's growth, and their faith and patience, as here in the text; all this glorying is good: as elsewhere he boasted or gloried in the Corinthians' liberality, 2 Cor. ix. 2; but his glorying in them was not to exalt himself, but to magnify the grace of God, and provoke other churches to imitate them. *In the churches of God;* where the excellency of grace is known, and the commendation of it will be received and imitated; and not amongst carnal men, who scoff at true goodness. And it was the apostle himself, and Silvanus and Timotheus, that thus gloried in them. It adds to persons' commendation, when it is by men of great knowledge, wisdom, and goodness. And it was by such as well knew them, and understood their state; and being instruments in their conversion, were more concerned to glory in them than any other apostles or ministers. And their glorying in them, as it respects what he said of them in the former verse, so what he further adds in this, which is their *patience and faith in all* their *persecutions and tribulations*. Persecutions are properly sufferings for righteousness' sake: tribulations, any kind of suffering, as some distinguish. And it seems they had many of both, when he saith *all*, &c. And yet they endured them, that is, not only suffered them because they could not cast them off, but in the sense of the apostle James, chap. v. 11, *Behold, we count them happy which endure;* which is a suffering out of choice, and not mere necessity, as Moses did, Heb. xi. 25, when sufferings stand in competition with sin, or the dishonour of the Christian profession. Sufferings in themselves are not desirable, and the apostle did not glory in their sufferings, but in their *faith and patience*. As he before joined faith and love together, so here faith and patience; and as love springs from faith, so doth Christian patience, whereby it is distinguished from patience as a mere moral virtue found among the heathen, either that of the Stoics, Peripatetics, or Platonists. Faith and patience are well styled the two suffering graces, and therefore here mentioned by the apostle when he mentions their sufferings. Faith, as it depends upon God, and sees love under afflictions, believes his promises, looks at the recompence of reward, &c., so it supports under suffering. And patience, as it keeps down passion, and quiets the soul under its burden, makes it to sit lighter, and gives advantage to the exercise of that grace and reason, whereby a Christian is strengthened under his sufferings. Now hereupon the apostle glories in them, as men are apt to do in the heroic acts of great conquerors ; or the captain of an army, in the valiant performances of his soldiers.

h Phil. 1. 28. i 1 Thess. 2. 14.

5 *Which is* [h] a manifest token of the righteous judgment of God, that ye may be counted worthy of the kingdom of God, [i] for which ye also suffer :

These words seem to follow by way of argument, to comfort these Thessalonians under their sufferings : 1. By what they *manifest,* viz. *the righteous judgment of God ;* they are a plain indication of it, or demonstration, as the word is used by logicians. And by *judgment* we must not here understand the judgments or afflictions God inflicts in this world ; so that when God doth not spare, but chasten his own children, it is a token of his righteous judgment. But rather under understand it of the last judgment: when we see the righteous suffering such wrongs and injuries from wicked men, and they go unpunished, we may argue thence that there is a judgment to come ; we cannot else well vindicate the righteousness, wisdom, goodness, and faithfulness of God in his governing the world : as Solomon so argued, when he saw so much unrighteousness in the very seat of justice ; *I said in my heart, God shall judge the righteous and the wicked : for there is a time for every purpose and work,* Eccles. iii. 16, 17. And this judgment is called here *righteous judgment,* by way of eminency, as it is expressed by one word, δικαιοκρισία, Rom. ii. 5, (for all God's judgments are righteous), (1.) Because the wicked will then meet with justice without mercy, which is not so in any present judgments. (2.) Justice will then be clearly manifested, which now lies obscure, both with respect to the righteous and the unrighteous. And in this sense the words carry an argument of comfort to the saints, under their present unjust sufferings from their enemies. As to the same purpose the apostle speaks to the Philippians, Phil. i. 28. 2. The other argument of comfort is from the result of their sufferings, the great advantage which will arise out of them ; they will be hence *accounted worthy of the kingdom of God :* not by way of merit, as the papists say ; the Greek word in the text, in its usual acceptation, will not favour that opinion, it signifies no more in the active voice, than the Latin word *dignari,* which we English to deign, or vouchsafe ; and yet we may allow the word to signify more here, not only that this kingdom may be vouchsafed, but that ye may be meet or worthy to receive it ; not that all their sufferings could deserve this kingdom, for the apostle saith, Rom. viii. 18, *I reckon the sufferings of this present time not worthy of the glory,* &c. There is no proportion betwixt them. and so they cannot merit it, yet God may account those that suffer for this kingdom worthy of it, according to the grace of the new covenant in Jesus Christ, and as it hath a congruity with the nature of God, and his faithfulness in his promises ; and so our translation renders the word, not that ye may be worthy of the kingdom of God, but *accounted worthy ;* God of his free grace will account them worthy. The kingdom of God is propounded to men in the new covenant upon certain conditions, and those that perform them have a worthiness of right, as Rev. xxii. 14, but not of merit. But God enables men to perform the conditions, so that there is nothing on our part properly meritorious ; yea, when we have performed them, yet our worthiness is to be attributed to Christ, and God's grace, and not to ourselves, else man would have whereof to glory. The Scriptures call *eternal life the gift of God,* Rom. vi. 23, and attributes salvation to grace, Eph. ii. 8. We must allow a worthiness only that is consistent with grace ; but when we have done all we must say, *We are unprofitable servants.* Luke xvii. 10 ; and after all we have done and suffered for the kingdom of God, must pray, as Paul for Onesiphorus, that we *may find mercy of the Lord at that day,* 2 Tim. i. 18. *For which ye also suffer ;* the sense either respects their enemies, that it was upon the account of this kingdom that they persecuted them, having nothing else justly against them ; or else their own aim and intention in suffering, it was for the kingdom of God. And hence we may learn that his kingdom is worth suffering for, and that in some cases it cannot be obtained without suffering : and he that then refuseth to suffer will be accounted unworthy of it ; as he that doth suffer for it, as these Thessalonians, hath, upon the account of God's covenant, and the merits of Christ, not only the grace and mercy, but the justice and faithfulness, of God engaged to bestow it upon him. And also that we may and ought in our sufferings look to the reward, as Moses did, Heb. xi.

6 [k]Seeing *it is* a righteous thing with God to recompense tribulation to them that trouble you ;

k Rev. 6. 10.

By these words the apostle doth illustrate his argument for a judgment to come, taken from the persecutions and tribulations of the saints. It is of necessity that God should be righteous, and recompensing is a necessary act of righteousness ; but we yet see it not, therefore there is a judgment to come. And this recompence is both to the righteous and the wicked, the persecutors and persecuted. The former he here speaks first of : and to recompense tribulation to them that trouble the people of God, is a just recompence ; it is according to the law of retaliation, whereof we have some instances in this world, as in Pharaoh, Adoni-bezek, Haman, &c. ; and many others, whereof we have a large account in the history of the church and her persecutors ; but this will be more fully verified in the judgment to come, called *the revelation of the righteous judgment of God,* Rom. ii. 5. And God's recompence to them is here called *tribulation* ; so Rom. ii. 9. And though in other scriptures the punishment of the wicked is set forth by other names, yet here it is called by this name ; not only for elegancy of speech, by a paranomasia, but to parallel their suffering to their sin ; they brought tribulation upon others, and God will bring it upon them. And under this word is comprehended all the torments of hell, which our Saviour expresseth by *weeping, wailing, and gnashing of teeth,* Matt. viii. 12, which is the extremity of tribulation. And it is said here, God will recompense, &c., which should teach us not to revenge ourselves ; as Psal. xciv. 1 ; Rom. xii. 19. And this the apostle sets before these Thessalonians by way of comfort ; not that we ought to rejoice in men's destruction merely for itself, but in the honour that will thereby arise to God's justice, and in the favour, honour, and salvation God will vouchsafe to his people herein.

7 And to you who are troubled [l]rest with us, when [m]the Lord Jesus shall be revealed from heaven with † his mighty angels,

l Rev. 14. 13.
m 1 Thess. 4. 16. Jude 14.
† Gr. *the angels of his power.*

Having spoken of the recompence of the troublers, here of the *troubled :* and in this we may observe a parallel, as in the former. The recompence to these is expressed by *rest ;* in the Greek, dismission, or cessation from labour or trouble ; as Heb. iv. 9, *There remaineth a rest to the people of God,* where the word is, keeping a sabbath, importing a rest from labour, as this text doth speak of a rest from trouble. And though the word *rest* is properly negative, yet under it the apostle comprehends all the felicity of the future state ; elsewhere called a crown, a kingdom, an inheritance, glory, salvation, eternal life, yea, it contains in it the perfect satisfaction of the soul in the fruition of God, &c. And this is said to be given them by way of recompence, as tribulation is to their troublers ; though there is no parity betwixt their troubles and the rest, that is, their recompence, yet it is a proper recompence ; and therefore the grace and mercy of God will be much manifested therein, though it is said to come from God's righteousness in the text. The righteousness of God dispenseth both these recompences ; but yet the righteousness in both is not alike ; ἀκριβοδίκαιον, strict justice, dispenseth the one, and the punishment of the wicked riseth from the nature of their sin, and the merit of it ; but it is only ἐπιείκεια, equity, that dispenseth the other, and that not so much with respect to the nature of the saints' duties or sufferings, as the promises and ordinance of God, and the merit of Christ for them. And this rest the apostle sets forth before them, under a twofold circumstance : 1. *Rest with us.* Us, the apostles and ministers of Christ, we and you shall rest together ; as we have partaken of troubles together, so we shall of rest. And you shall enjoy the same felicity with the apostles themselves, in the same state of rest. And though now place doth separate us, yet we and you shall rest together, which will the more sweeten this rest to you and us. 2. *When the Lord Jesus shall be revealed from heaven;* the other circumstance. This is the time of their entering into this rest. Christ's coming is sometimes called his ἐπιφάνεια, *appearing*, 2 Tim. iv. 8, or shining forth; sometimes, φανέρωσις, his manifestation, 2 Cor. iv. 2 ; 1 John iii. 2 ; sometimes, ἀποκάλυψις, his revelation, as in the text. Now the heavens contain him, but he will come in person, and his glory shine forth : though before that their souls shall be at rest in heaven, and their bodies in the grave, yet not till then shall their persons be at rest. And as Christ himself is already entered into his rest, Heb. iv. 10, so he will come again to take his people into the same rest with him.

n Heb. 10. 27. & 12. 29.
2 Pet. 3. 7.
Rev. 21. 8.
‖ Or, *yielding.*
o Ps. 79. 6.
1 Thess. 4. 5.
p Rom. 2. 8.

8 ⁿIn flaming fire ‖ taking vengeance on them °that know not God, and ᵖthat obey not the Gospel of our Lord Jesus Christ :

But his coming will be upon another account to many others, which is said here to be to take vengeance, for which purpose he is said to be revealed *with his mighty angels*, or angels of might ; and elsewhere, with all his holy angels. They are said to *excel in strength*, Psal. ciii. 20, or to be mighty in strength, and have the name of *might*, Eph. i. 21. And here called *mighty*, because as the work Christ comes upon is great and difficult, so he will have instruments sufficient for it, and none shall be able to hinder. And though he hath power himself sufficient, yet the angels must attend him to solemnize this great day, and to be serviceable to him in the work thereof, which, as it will respect the saints in their resurrection from the dead, and their gathering from the four winds, and separating them from the ungodly, as tares from the wheat and sheep from the goats, so the taking vengeance also in this day of the Lord's wrath, which the apostle, especially, is in these verses speaking of, is the work they shall be employed in. As also *in flaming fire*, or the fire of flame, a Hebraism. Fire is the most dreadful of all the elements, especially flaming, to denote the great wrath of that day, and its breaking forth, as fire when it flameth. God's wrath is often expressed in Scripture by *fire*, Deut. xxxii. 22 ; Psal. xcvii. 3, &c. ; Jer. xxi. 12 ; Heb. x. 27 ; and as that which attendeth the great day of Christ, Dan. vii. 10 ; 1 Cor. iii. 13 ; 2 Pet. iii. 7, 12. And whether this flaming fire is material, or only metaphorical ; if material, whether the present elementary fire, which shall descend, and be joined with that which shall break forth out of the bowels of the earth, as in Noah's flood the waters were from above and from beneath ; or whether it shall be some new-created fire, and the action of it natural, or supernatural, I shall leave it to the schoolmen. Yet it is generally conceived it is a material fire ; else how can *the elements* be said to *melt with fervent heat*, and the world and the works thereof burnt up, as the apostle Peter speaks, 2 Pet. iii. 10 ; and parallels it with the deluge in Noah's time, which was with material water. But yet it is to be a manifestation of the fire of God's wrath, and an instrument of it also in the destruction of ungodly men, 2 Pet. iii. 7 ; for it is said in the text, Christ is revealed in it to take vengeance. Vengeance is an act of justice ; it is a retribution of evil for evil, the evil of suffering for the evil done : and God claims it as belonging to himself, Psal. xciv. 1 ; Rom. xii. 19 ; Heb. x. 27 ; and it is mentioned in the parable, Luke xviii. 7, 8, as one great work of Christ, at his coming, to avenge the elect. *On them that know not God ;* these are the persons upon whom he will execute vengeance : by whom some think are meant the heathen, who had not the gospel. Those that had not the gospel, yet had means to know God, by the light of nature, and the works of creation and providence, which if they did not improve, but remained ignorant of God, will fall under this vengeance. And by knowledge here is not meant so much a speculative as a practical knowledge of God ; and so such as do not fear, love, and honour God, may be said not to know him. As the Gentiles, who are said to know God, Rom. i. 21, but yet not glorifying him as God, and living in idolatry, are said not to know him, Gal. iv. 8 ; 1 Thess. iv. 5. And as God tells the king of Judah, that to do justice and judgment is to know him, Jer. xxii. 16. And Eli's sons, though priests, yet are said not to know the Lord, 1 Sam. ii. 12. *And that obey not the gospel;* which may be taken in conjunction with the former words, and then such as *obey not the gospel* are the same with *them that know not God*. As God is not known aright but by the gospel, so they only know God aright by the gospel who obey it. Some are ignorant and know not God, though they live under the gospel. Or, such as have knowledge, yet are not obedient. Knowledge and obedience ought to go together. And this obedience is called the obeying of the gospel. The gospel hath not only promises to be believed, but precepts to be obeyed. Yea, faith itself may fall under its precepts, and then those that believe not the gospel do not obey it : as the same word in the Greek signifies to believe and obey. And as the gospel hath some peculiar precepts and institutions, so all the commands of the moral law are comprehended in it ; and the equitable part of the judicial law, yea, and the ceremonial law also, where that which is moral is figured by it ; and so far as the gospel commands, men ought to obey ; and disobedience appears to be a great evil, when it will expose men to this great vengeance. So Rom. ii. 8, 9, *To them that do not obey the truth, indignation and wrath, tribulation and anguish,* &c. Not to obey the law of nature, exposed the heathen to God's wrath, Rom. i. 18 ; and to disobey the law of Moses, the Jew, Rom. ii. 2 ; Heb. ii. 3 ; x. 28 ; xii. 25 ; much more not to obey the gospel. Christ is said here especially to take vengeance of such at his coming. Gospel sins are most heinous and most provoking, and will be most severely punished.

9 ᑫWho shall be punished with everlasting destruction from the presence of the Lord, and ʳfrom the glory of his power;

q Phil. 3. 19.
2 Pet. 3. 7.
r Deut. 33. 2.
Is. 2. 19.
ch. 2. 8.

This is the vengeance before spoken of ; it is here called *destruction*, not an annihilation, and cessation of being, but of all well-being : and elsewhere called *death*, Rom. vi. 23, and *the second death*, Rev. xx. 6, which imports also not all ceasing of life, but all comfort of life. And it is not the body alone, nor the soul alone, but their persons, *who*, &c. ; and as fire is a great destroyer, so Christ's coming in flaming fire brings their destruction. And this destruction is *everlasting* : the fire that destroys them is never quenched, Mark ix. 43, 44. As the fire of the altar, which was a fire of mercy, was not to go out, so the fire of Tophet burns for ever, Isa. xxx. 33, which is the fire of justice ; and God living for ever, and his justice never satisfied, their destruction is for ever. They sinned in their eternity, and will be punished in God's eternity. There was a remedy provided in the gospel for men, but rejecting the gospel, and not obeying it, there remains no hope ; their destruction is everlasting. And this destruction is called punishment, δίκην τίσουσιν, *pœnam luent;* not the chastisement of a Father, as the temporal affliction of God's people. It proceeds from vindictive justice ; it is taking vengeance. And this punishment is twofold, punishment of loss and sense, and from both together proceed perfect destruction. *From the presence of the Lord, and from the glory of his power ;* the preposition *from* in the first expression noting separation, in the second noting efficiency. Others conceive efficiency to be meant in both, their destruction proceeding from the face of Christ frowning on them, frowning them into hell, (which smiling upon others, will bring their salvation,) as well as from his glorious power manifested against them to destroy them, Rom. ix. 22. And yet others interpret the preposition in both places to note separation, both from the face of Christ, which the saints shall behold and rejoice in for ever, and from his glorious power ; which will work in some for their complete salvation in the day of his appearing, as it had done before in their first conversion, and sanctification. The destruction of the wicked will be from or by the power of Christ ; but by this *glory of power* may be meant only that power which will bring glory both to the bodies and souls of the saints, and this the wicked shall have no experience of in that day.

10 ˢWhen he shall come to be glorified in his saints, ᵗand to be admired in all them that believe (because our testimony among you was believed) in that day.

s Ps. 89. 7.
t Ps. 68. 35.

II. THESSALONIANS I

This speaks the different manner of Christ's coming towards the saints and believers; not in flaming fire to destroy them, as in the former verse; but to be *glorified* and *admired* in them. He saith not to be glorified by them, by their adoring and praising of him, but in them. He hath a personal glory, wherein he will appear glorious, and another mystical, in his saints. The Head will be glorified in the members, as they are glorified in and from the Head: as the sun hath a lustre and glory in the moon and stars besides what it hath in its own body, as Col. iii. 4, *When Christ, who is our life, shall appear, we also shall appear with him in glory.* The glory God gave his Son, he hath given it to his saints, John xvii. 22, and will put it upon them, and be glorified in it in the day of his appearing; as God is said to have *glorified himself in Israel*, Isa. xliv. 23. *And to be admired;* and this glory will be so great, that he shall be admired in it, as the word signifies. It will set the saints themselves, and all the angels of heaven, yea, the whole world, a wondering. Small things do not cause admiration, but what is great and we cannot comprehend, that we admire. And Christ will not only be admired by them, but in them; the wonderful love, grace, mercy, wisdom, and faithfulness of Christ towards them will be admired. To raise up such a number of poor, sinful, despicable worms out of the dust into such a sublime state of glory and dignity, will be admirable. *Because our testimony among you was believed;* and that these Thessalonians might have the comfort of this particularly, he having spoken of *saints*, and *those that believe* in general, the apostle applies this therefore to themselves in way of parenthesis: q. d. Christ will be admired in all that believe; and ye are among them that believe; ergo, &c. And the doctrine of the gospel he had preached, he called it his *testimony*, as John iii. 33; 1 Cor. iii. 6; which implies it was not an invention of his own, he did not speak of himself, as the word implies: and this testimony found different entertainment, some believed it not, others believed it and received it; upon which account the Thessalonians are commended and comforted here by the apostle. The Syriac read the words in the future tense, without a parenthesis; Christ will come to be thus glorified and admired in his saints, because our testimony among you concerning it shall be believed or confirmed *in that day;* he means the day of Christ's last coming, which he called *the day of the Lord*, 1 Thess. v. 2; and because it is so great a day, is therefore by way of emphasis called *that day*.

11 Wherefore also we pray always for you, that our God would ‖ ᵘcount you worthy of *this* calling, and fulfil all the good pleasure of *his* goodness, and ˣthe work of faith with power:

‖ Or, *vouchsafe*.
u ver. 5.
x 1 Thes. l. 3.

The apostle here again mentions his praying for these Thessalonians, as he had often mentioned it in the former Epistle. And the reason might be, because he was absent from them; they might the more need his prayer, and by telling them of it, he thereby assures them that he forgot them not. And the prayer he here makes for them hath reference to the discourse he had been upon, as appears by this word Εἰς ὅ, *Wherefore*, or for, or in order to which, *we pray*, &c. *This calling;* which is figuratively to be understood of the blessed state they were called to, for the calling itself they had received already. And so it is the same in effect mentioned before, ver. 5, called there *the kingdom of God;* or to have Christ *glorified and admired in them,* ver. 10. And elsewhere termed *the prize of the high calling of God*, Phil. iii. 14. And that God would *count* them *worthy of* it; as he had used the same expression before; only there it was mentioned with respect to their sufferings, here in a way of prayer. He encouraged them under their sufferings, that they might thereupon be counted worthy of the kingdom of God, and now prays that God would count them worthy; their worthiness arising more from the gracious account of God than their own sufferings. A Christian's calling hath duty annexed to it, whereupon the apostle exhorts the Ephesians to walk worthy of it in discharge of those duties, Eph. iv. 1, 2. And it hath a state of blessedness belonging to it, which is meant here; and none shall partake of it, but those whom God shall count worthy of it. But God's account is not according to the strictness of the law, but the gracious indulgence of the covenant of grace; but yet his prayer implies such a walking according to this covenant, as whereby they might be counted worthy of the blessed state they were called unto. *And fulfil all the good pleasure of his goodness:* the gracious purposes of God towards his people are called often his *good pleasure*, as Matt. xi. 26; Luke xii. 32; Eph. i. 5, 9; and the same is meant Isa. liii. 10, *The pleasure of the Lord shall prosper in his hand;* the Hebrew word *Chephets* being of the same signification with the Greek word here used. Christ shall accomplish the gracious purposes of God towards his people. And called his *good pleasure*, partly because they have no reason out of the sovereign will of God, and they are such also as he hath great complacence and delight in; and though they are executed in time, yet they were in his heart from everlasting, and therefore called *eternal*, Eph. iii. 11. And I find purpose and good pleasure put both together, Eph. i. 9. It is here called *the good pleasure of his goodness*, which is not a tautology, as it may seem to be, but to make his expression of God's grace the more emphatical; or rather, to show that this good pleasure of God towards his people ariseth out of his goodness. God hath purposes of wrath towards some, but such cannot be called the good pleasure of his goodness. Goodness is that excellency in God, whereby he is ready to communicate good to his creature; but by goodness here is meant God's special goodness, which is peculiar to his people whom he hath chosen. To *fulfil all the good pleasure of his goodness*, is to accomplish all those good purposes that were in his heart; some whereof were already fulfilled in their calling, adoption, justification, and sanctification begun, but the whole was not yet fulfilled, which he therefore here prays for; so that as their election, and their first conversion, were not from any worthiness or foresight of faith in them, but the good pleasure of his will, so the progress and perfection of their salvation was also to be from the same good pleasure. *And the work of faith with power:* by *the work of faith* is either meant faith itself, which is the work of God, or else the fruits of faith; and so work is here taken for works or operations of faith. And the apostle addeth this in his prayer, to show that we are not saved only by God's good pleasure without faith, such a faith that worketh. And to perfect their salvation is a fulfilling the work of faith, for perseverance and progress towards perfection is from the work of faith. Or it may particularly refer to their patience and constancy under their sufferings, which he had before spoken of, and which is a peculiar work of faith. But because faith is not sufficient of itself, and the work of faith may fail, he therefore addeth, in power, or *with power;* that is, the power of God, which is his Spirit, so called, Luke i. 35. Our faith and the power of God are here joined together, as 1 Pet. i. 5. The same power that first worketh faith, afterwards co-worketh by it and with it.

12 ʸThat the name of our Lord Jesus Christ may be glorified in you, and ye in him, according to the grace of our God and the Lord Jesus Christ.

y 1 Pet. l. 7.
& 4. 14.

That the name of our Lord Jesus Christ may be glorified in you, and ye in him; ὅπως. All expositors agree that these words contain in them a final cause, as the Greek word imports; and so understand them as the ultimate end of the apostle's prayer for them; he had prayed for things that did concern their salvation, but he looked further, which was, that thereby the name of the Lord Jesus may be glorified in them. The glory of Christ and the saints' salvation are wrapt up together; and though they are to look immediately to the latter, yet ultimately to the former. But whether the apostle means the glorifying Christ in this life, or the life to come, is a question. I rather think the words refer to the life to come, when the name of Christ shall be for ever glorified in the salvation of his people, when all the good pleasure of God's goodness shall be fulfilled upon them, they having been kept in the faith by the power of God unto the end, through Jesus Christ; and then also they shall be glorified not only by him, as we may read the text, but in him, in being received into a participation of the same glory with Jesus Christ, and by their union with him are glorified in him, John xvii. 22; Col. iii. 4; 1 John iii. 2. And when this is done, then have they received the prize of their calling, then is the whole good pleasure of God's goodness fulfilled, then is the work of faith accomplished; which things the apostle saith he prayed for in their behalf. *According to the grace of our God and the Lord Jesus Christ:* what the apostle before called the good pleasure of God's goodness, he here calls his *grace*, and he adds the grace of Christ, because the grace or favour of both are so eminently manifested in these things, whereby not only the name of God, but of Christ also, shall be glorified, as he said before; and that it may be glorified in them according to his grace, that is, greatly glorified; and they glorified in him according to the grace of God and Jesus Christ, that is, greatly glorified, as we may further understand the words; the grace of God being exceeding great towards them in Jesus Christ. And hereby the apostle would exclude all thoughts about their own merit, ver. 11.

CHAP. II

Paul warneth the Thessalonians against the groundless surmise that the day of Christ was near at hand, 1, 2; *showing that it would be preceded by a great apostacy, and that the man of sin would be first revealed, and by his wicked impostures draw many into perdition,* 3—12. *He repeateth his good hopes concerning them,* 13, 14; *exhorting them to stand fast in his doctrine, and praying God to comfort and stablish them in all goodness,* 15—17.

a 1 Thess. 4. 16.
b Matt. 24. 31. Mark 13. 27. 1 Thess. 4. 17.

NOW we beseech you, brethren, [a] by the coming of our Lord Jesus Christ, [b] and by our gathering together unto him,

The apostle now comes to refute the opinion that some at least of these Thessalonians had received, as if the day of Christ was near at hand. He having said, 1 Thess. iv. 17, *We which are alive and remain shall be caught up to meet the Lord in the air,* &c., then some might think his coming would be in the apostle's time, or some other way they might fall into this conceit; and some do conceive this was the chief reason of the apostle's writing this Epistle. And because this mistake might be of dangerous consequence, therefore he is very vehement and particular in refuting it: for hereupon they might be brought to question the truth of the whole gospel when this should not come to pass: they might be unprepared for the sufferings that were to come upon the church; their patience might fail in expecting this day, and their minds be doubting about the coming of Christ at all. This opinion also would much narrow their thoughts about Christ's kingdom, and the enlarging of the gospel among other Gentiles; and the profane might abuse it to sensuality, as 1 Cor. xv. 32, *Let us eat and drink,* &c. That he might the better persuade, he calls them *brethren*, and beseeches them, &c. And next, conjures them, using the form of an oath, *by the coming of our Lord Jesus Christ,* &c. We conjure men either by what they love, or by what they fear; as they would enjoy the one, or avoid the other. The coming of Christ was what they desired and rejoiced in, as that which would bring rest to them, and tribulation to their adversaries; and by this he doth therefore beseech or adjure them: and therefore we must understand this of Christ's last coming, as the word παρυσία, in the text, is still applied to this coming, 1 Thess. ii. 19; iii. 13, &c.; and not of his coming to destroy the Jewish church and state, for that coming was at hand. *And by our gathering together unto him;* at his last coming, when the whole body of Christ shall be gathered to him, to meet him in the air, 1 Thess. iv. 17. And then the sense is, As ye hope ever to see such a blessed meeting, and to be of that number, so take heed of this opinion. Yet some read the text otherwise, because in the Greek it is not διά, but ὑπὲρ τῆς παρυσίας, and so the same with πέρι, not *we beseech you by*, but concerning *the coming of our Lord Jesus Christ, and our gathering together unto him,* as denoting only the subject matter treated of. I prefer the former; and so the apostle conjures them not to be soon shaken in mind, but to stand fast in the truth about the doctrine of Christ's coming, which they had been taught, and very lately taught, and therefore it was the greater evil to be *soon shaken;* as the apostle upbraids the Galatians, Gal. i. 6, and God the Israelites, Psal. cvi. 13.

2 [c] That ye be not soon shaken in mind, or be troubled, neither by spirit, nor by word, nor by letter as from us, as that the day of Christ is at hand.

c Matt. 24. 4. Eph. 5. 6. 1 John 4. 1.

That ye be not soon shaken in mind; σαλευθῆναι· it is an allusion to the waves of the sea that are tossed with the winds, as false doctrines tend to unsettle the mind, as Eph. iv. 14; Heb. xiii. 9; and to be established in the truth is often commanded, 1 Cor. xvi. 13; Phil. iv. 1; Col. i. 23, &c. And by *mind* here is either meant the faculty itself; and then the apostle beseecheth them to keep company with their understanding, not to be removed from their mind: as false doctrine is said to bewitch men, Gal. iii. 1, and to make men foolish, ver. 3; as madness is called *amentia*, or *dementia*, as that which doth as it were unmind men, and corrupt the mind, and pervert the judgment, 2 Tim. iii. 8, 9, as Jannes and Jambres deceived the people by their enchantments, as the apostle there mentions. Or else, the sentence and judgment of the mind; and then he beseecheth them to hold fast the right judgment they had entertained about Christ's coming, and not to hesitate and waver about it; so the word is taken, 1 Cor. ii. 16. *Or be troubled;* ϑροεῖσθαι, alluding to soldiers affrighted with a sudden alarm. We find the word, Matt. xxiv. 6; Mark xiii. 7, used in this allusion. And the opinion of Christ's coming to be at hand might occasion this trouble in them, either lest they might be surprised by it, and unprepared for it, or by judging themselves mistaken in their former apprehensions about it; and those false teachers that broach this opinion, did also perhaps so represent this coming in such terror as to cause this trouble; as false teachers in general are such as are said to cause trouble, Gal. i. 7; v. 12; though the coming of Christ is in itself rather the saints' hope and joy, than ground of trouble, as 1 Thess. i. 10; iv. 18, &c. And it may be some did pretend for this opinion the Spirit, or some letter from the apostle, either the former Epistle to them, or some letter that was forged, or some word he had spoken, or preached. And those words *as from us* may refer to all these: the Spirit, *as from us;* or word, *as from us;* or letter, *as from us. Neither by spirit;* some extraordinary revelation of the Spirit, which the false teachers pretended to, especially in the primitive times, when they were more ordinary; as in the church of Corinth, 1 Cor. xiv. 6, and the churches of Galatia, Gal. iii. 2, 5: some would pretend the Spirit that called Jesus accursed, 1 Cor. xii. 3, and therefore the apostle bids, *Try the spirits,* 1 John iv. 1. Simon Magus pretended to it, and had his Helene, Montanus his Paraclete, Mahomet his Dove: and the man of sin pretends to this Spirit, though it is in truth *the spirit of antichrist,* 1 John iv. 3, and the spirit of Satan, in the next chapter of this Epistle, as was foretold that in the last times there would arise *seducing spirits,* 1 Tim. iv. 1; as there was in the times of the Old Testament false prophets that pretended to the Spirit, as 1 Kings xxii. 24; Micah ii. 11. And the very heathen would pretend to divine oracles, inspirations, and revelations, especially their kings and lawgivers, as Numa Pompilius, Lycurgus, &c.; and still there are enthusiasts who make these pretences. *Nor by word;* διὰ λόγου, whereby some understand calculation by astrological rules, that the day of Christ was at hand; others render the word reasoning; and so from the declining of the vigour of the earth, and the nearer approach of the sun to it, as Ptolemy observed in his time, or some other natural causes, they reasoned the coming of Christ and the dissolution of the world to be nigh at hand: but rather we understand by it some word from the apostle's own mouth, which was pretended he had spoken or preached some where, though not written. As the Church of Rome pretends to traditions, besides the written word, upon which they ground many of their superstitions and idolatries, not warranted by Scripture. As the Jews had a second *Mishneh*, and their *Cabbala*, collected in part from the sayings of Moses, or some other of their prophets, which they did not write. *Nor by letter;* some letter that was sent to them from some other hand, or else by some forged letter as from the apostle himself, or his former Epistle misunderstood. *As that the day of Christ is at hand.* Object. But is it not said that the day of the Lord, or the coming of the Lord, is at hand, 1 Cor. x. 11; Phil. iv. 5; James v. 7, 8;

II. THESSALONIANS II

1 Pet. iv. 2? *Answ.* The word used in those places differs from this in the text; for it signifies either that which is actually present, or very near it, as Rom. viii. 38; Gal. i. 4; as that which is to be done presently is spoken of as done, John xvii. 4; 2 Tim. iv. 7. Or those places mean his coming is at hand, as to God's account of time, though not as to man's. And in that sense Christ saith, *Behold, I come quickly,* Rev. xxii. 7. But the error the apostle warns them of is, as if the coming of Christ would be in the age in which they lived. The apostles all said that the coming of the Lord was at hand, but their right meaning was perverted to a false sense, as seducers usually do.

3 ᵈ Let no man deceive you by any means: for *that day shall not come,* ᵉ except there come a falling away first, and ᶠ that man of sin be revealed, ᵍ the son of perdition;

d Mat. 24. 4.
Eph. 5. 6.
e 1 Tim. 4. 1.
f Dan. 7. 25.
1 John 2. 18.
Rev. 13. 11, &c.
See 1 Mac. 2. 48, 62.
g John 17. 12.

Let no man deceive you: here the apostle urgeth again his charge against this error, though in other words, and begins his arguments to refute it. He had adjured them not to be *shaken,* and here he cautions them against being *deceived,* for the one makes way for the other; so also not to be *troubled,* ver. 2, for troubled minds are apt to be made a prey to seducers. And the caution in the text proves that their shaking and trouble did arise from some deceivers that were amongst them, rather than any misunderstanding of their own of what he wrote in the former Epistle about Christ's coming. To be shaken in mind is bad, but to be deceived is worse, for it is a going out of the path, as the word signifies; and therefore his caution against it is universal, both as to persons and ways: *Let no man deceive you,* though he pretend to revelations, or be of the greatest reputation in the church. *By any means;* either of craft, flattery, pretending love, or plausible arguments, or misrepresenting our words, or forging of letters, or misinterpreting our Epistle to you or any other part of Scripture, or feigned miracles, &c. Then he enters the arguments to confute it, which are, 1. The general apostacy. 2. The revelation of the man of sin. Neither of these are yet, nor will be in this age; and yet *that day shall not come* till these both first come. *For that day shall not come, except there come a falling away first;* there is a supplement in our translation, for in the Greek it is only, *for, except there come a falling away first,* &c., or an apostacy, a recession, a departing, or a standing off, as the word imports; so that apostacy may be either good, when it is from evil to good, or evil, when it is from good to evil: it is always used in this latter sense in Scripture. Again, it is either civil or spiritual: civil, as when people fall off from the civil government they were under, and so some would interpret the text of the defection from the Roman empire, the east part from the west, and the ten kingdoms that arose out of it; which was the opinion of Hierom, Epist. ad Algasiam. But the apostle writing to the church speaks not of civil government, and the affairs of state, and speaks of such an apostacy which would give rise to the man of sin, and the revelation of him. And this man of sin riseth up in the church, not in the civil state; and the consequence of this apostacy is giving men up to strong delusions to believe a lie, and then follows their damnation; and the cause of it is said to be, not receiving the truth in the love of it; so that it is not a civil, but a spiritual apostacy, as the word in Scripture is always (I suppose) so taken. And it is not of a particular person, or of a particular church, but a general apostacy of the church, though not of every individual; that church that is afterwards called *the temple of God,* where the man of sin sitteth, and is exalted above all that is called God; which cannot be in any particular church; and would not the apostle have specified that particular church? Neither is it some lesser apostacy which may befall the best church; but such as would be eminent, called ἡ ἀποστασία, that apostacy, greater than that of some believing Jews to Judaism, or of some Christians to Nicolaitanism, which some think is meant. Much less can it be Caius Cæsar, as Grotius interprets, or any one person, for the apostle saith not apostate, but apostacy; else a man of sin could not rise out of it, and exalt himself above all that is called God, and worshipped. It is an apostacy from sound doctrine, instituted worship, church government, and true holiness of life, as may be further considered afterwards. Neither is the apostacy all at once, but gradual; for out of it ariseth a man of sin, who grows up to this manhood by degrees; and sin and wickedness are not completed at first, as well as holiness. Much less is this apostacy a falling off from the Church of Rome, as some papists affirm, and make the Reformation to be the apostacy, which was a return from it. Doth the man of sin rise out of the Reformation? Did any of the first Reformers oppose and exalt themselves above all that is called God, or is worshipped? or, as God sat in the temple of God, &c.? Was any of their coming with all power, and signs, and lying wonders? or did any of them forbid to marry, and to abstain from meats, &c.? which is the character our apostle gives of this apostacy, 1 Tim. iv. 1—3. Neither is the Mahometan religion this apostacy, for Mahomet sitteth not in the temple of God. Neither is it in the falling of the converted Jews from the Jewish church to the gospel church; the apostle would never call that an apostacy. *And that man of sin be revealed:* the next argument is from the revelation of the man of sin; this is also to precede Christ's last coming: it is a Hebraism. A warlike man is styled a man of war; a bloody man, a man of bloods; a deceitful man, a man of deceit, &c.: so a man eminent in sin is here called a man of sin; not only personally so, but who doth promote sin, propagate it, countenance it, command it. See Platina, Sigebert, Blonetas, Beuno Uspregensis, Matt. Paris. In sins of omission, forbidding what God requireth; in sins of commission, requiring or allowing what God hath forbidden. In sins of the first table; corrupting God's worship by superstition and idolatry, taking God's name in vain by heartless devotion, dissembling piety, dispensing with perjury and false oaths, taking away the second commandment and the morality of the fourth commandment, and making men's faith and obedience to rest upon a human authority, &. In sins of the second table; to dispense with duties belonging to superiors and inferiors; with murder, adultery, fornication, incest, robbery, lying, equivocation, &c. And besides all these, promoting a false religion, and destroying the true, by fines, imprisonments, banishments, tortures, poisons, massacre, fire, and faggot. And this man of sin is not a single person, but a company, order, and succession of men; because all are acted by the same spirit, therefore called a man; as *the man of the earth,* Psal. x. 18, is all men of an earthly spirit, and *a man of the field,* Gen. xxv. 27, is men whose minds and employments are in the field. Or, it is a sinful state. As the civil state of the four monarchies in Daniel is represented by four single beasts, and the antichristian state by a beast rising out of the sea, Rev. xiii. 1; so by *man of sin* is meant a sinful state, which though it consisteth of many people and nations, yet, being under the influence and government of one man, may be also styled *the man of sin* upon that account; *impietatis Coryphæus. Moulin.* And because the sin of the whole community is chiefly centred in him, and springs out from him; a man in whom is the fountain of all sins. *Hierom ad Algasiam.* And the sin of this state is called *a mystery of iniquity,* ver. 7, and so differing from the sin in all other political states; and therefore may well be judged to be the same with the whore sitting on many waters, that hath *mystery* written in her forehead, Rev. xvii. 1, 5. And as no expositor takes the whore to be meant of a single woman, and the true apostolic church is represented by a woman in travail, Rev. xii. 1, 2, why then should we take the man of sin to be a single man, as the papists do? viz. a Jew of the tribe of Dan, that shall erect his kingdom and temple in Jerusalem, seduce the Jews, continue three years and a half, make great havoc of the church, to be opposed by Enoch and Elias, and is to come a little before the end of the world. Ridiculous! Neither can this man of sin be Simon Magus and his followers, for he was revealed in the apostle's time, seeing the mystery of iniquity belonging to this man of sin began to work in the apostle's days, as ver. 7, and he is the same whom St. John calls *antichrist,* 1 John ii. 18; and the *spirit of antichrist* began to be *in the world* in his time, chap. iv. 3; and the nations are to be made drunk with the cup of his fornication, and to serve and obey him, &c., Rev. xiii. 8; xvii. 4; all which requires more time than is allotted by them: but they set him a great way off, that none may suspect him to be among themselves; but he that will compare the Church of Rome in the apostle Paul's times with what it is now, and the doctrine of the council of Trent with that laid down in his Epistle to the Romans, may say, How is the faithful city become a harlot! And this man of sin is to *be revealed* also, which shows that he is not a single person, not yet born: revealing relates not so much to a person, as a thing; in particular to *the mystery of iniquity*, mentioned ver. 7: his revealing is either *quoad existentiam*, or *apparentiam*. The former is meant here, and the latter ver. 8. He grows up into an existence, as the apostacy grows, as vermin grows out of putrefaction. As the church's purity, faith, love, holiness declined, and as pride, ambition, covetousness, luxury prevailed, so he grew up: and which was the direct point and time of his full revelation in this first sense is conjectured by many, but determined by none; it is most generally referred to the time of Boniface the Third, to whom Phocas granted the style of œcumenical bishop, and to the Church of Rome to be the mother church. But as the apostacy brings forth this man of sin, so as he riseth he helps it forward; so that he both causeth it, and is caused by it. As corruption in doctrine, worship, discipline, and manners brought him forth, so he was active in corrupting them more and more. *The son of perdition;* another Hebraism, where sometimes that which any way proceeds from another, as its cause, is called its son, as sparks the sons of the coal, Job v. 7, and branches sons of the tree, Gen. xlix. 22, and the learner the son of the teacher, Prov. iii. 1; and sometimes that which a man is addicted to, as a wicked man is *the son of wickedness*, Psal. lxxxix. 22. Again, that which gives forth what it hath in itself, as the branches of the olive trees giving oil are called the sons of oil, Zech. iv. 14; and in the text, the man of sin is *the son of perdition*, as Judas is called, John xvii. 12: and he is so either actively, as he brings others to destruction, and so may be called *Apollyon*, Rev. ix. 11; or rather passively, as devoted to perdition; as Rev. xix. 20, *the beast and false prophet* are both cast into the lake of fire and brimstone; and *the beast that was, and is not*, is said to go into perdition, Rev. xvii. 11. The destroyer of others both in soul and body will be destroyed himself: first, morally, by the word and Spirit, as ver. 8; and then judicially, by God's revenging justice in this world, and that to come. The apostle, at the very first mentioning him, declares his destiny; at his first rising and revealing, mentions his fall and ruin.

h Is. 14. 13.
Ezek. 28. 2.
6, 9. Dan. 7.
25. & 11. 36.
Rev. 13. 6.
i 1 Cor. 8. 5.

4 Who opposeth and [h] exalteth himself [i] above all that is called God, or that is worshipped; so that he as God sitteth in the temple of God, shewing himself that he is God.

A further description of this man of sin, by his opposition and exaltation. *Who opposeth;* or, ὁ ἀντικείμενος, the opposer; or rather, opposing, expressed in the participle of the present tense, denoting a continued act, or that which he bends himself strongly to. But against what? The same that he exalteth himself above, as some conceive; but the grammar will not well admit that sense, and we should not so restrain it; and therefore we will take the word indefinitely, as expressed in the text. But we may well conceive, it is Christ himself whom he opposeth; as his name given him by the apostle John doth evidence, when he is called *antichrist*, or *the antichrist*, one that is against Christ; not that he openly and professedly opposeth him, but as Judas kissed his Master, and betrayed him: see those that have written of antichrist, as Philip Nicholas, Whitaker, Danæus, Chamier, Moulin, Junius, &c. It is iniquity in a mystery. He serveth Christ, but it is to serve himself upon him. He acknowledgeth him in all his offices, and yet doth virtually deny and oppose him in them all: called antichrist, as opposite to the unction of Christ: Christ signifies anointed, and so he opposeth him in the offices to which he is anointed, while he owns his natures. He professeth himself a "servant of the servants of God," and yet persecutes, curseth, proscribes, and killeth them, opposing Christ in his members. He maketh *war with the saints*, Rev. xiii. 7. He hath two horns like a lamb, and speaks as a dragon, ver. 11; speaks lies in hypocrisy, 1 Tim. iv. 2. And then he is described by his exaltation;

ὑπεραιρόμενος, exalted, which is well supplied, he *exalteth himself:* it is not from God. He *exalteth himself*, or lifteth himself, *above all that is called God*, though not really and essentially God. The apostle well knew that in the Old Testament magistrates were called *gods*, Psal. lxxxii. 1, 6; and 1 Cor. viii. 5, *There be that are called gods, whether in heaven or in earth*. Magistrates and rulers are of several degrees; some inferior, some superior; some supreme, as kings and emperors; but he exalteth himself above them all, and that not only in spirituals, by excommunications, but in civils, by deposing kings, disposing kingdoms, yea, making emperors to wait at his gate, hold his stirrup, prostrate themselves to kiss his toe, and then to tread upon their neck, as Alexander the Third did to Frederic Barbarossa; and this not condemned as the extravagancy of some particular persons, but allowed and justified by the doctrine and doctors of the Romish Church. And Bellarmine, de Rom. Pont. lib. 5. c. 8, gives it as the reason why the pope would not come to the council of Nice, lest if the emperor should come thither he should attempt to sit above him. So that by these two words in the text, the apostle describes him both in his enmity and pride, opposition, and exaltation. Observe, first, He assumeth to himself a higher power than those that are only called gods; theirs is human, his is Divine; theirs on the bodies or estates of men, his over the conscience; theirs only to the living, his to men's souls after death. Next, he makes himself like God, and is *as God*, as the king of old Babylon said, *I will be like the Most High*, Isa. xiv. 14. As God's residence of old was in the temple of Jerusalem, so *he, as God, sitteth in the temple of God:* not that temple that was built by Solomon, and afterwards rebuilt, and to be built again, as the popish doctors speak: for it is now destroyed, and if it be built again by this man of sin, as they say, at his coming, would the apostle call that *the temple of God?* 2 Cor. vi. 16; Rev. iii. 12, &c. But it is a spiritual temple, as the church is called, 1 Cor. iii. 16, 17. So Augustine, Jerome, Hilary, Chrysostom, understand it. And he is said here to sit, to have here his *cathedra*. The apostle speaks of him as a bishop, whose episcopal see is called a seat, or *cathedra;* and here he sitteth *as God:* the popish writers give the pope that and suchlike titles, *Dominus Deus noster Papa, Idem est Dominium Dei et Papæ, Tu es alter Deus in Terra*, "Thou art another God on earth." *Concil. Later. sess.* 4. And as God he maketh laws to bind the conscience, and dispenseth with laws natural and moral; pardons sin as he pleaseth, past, present, and to come; can deliver souls out of purgatory, and translate them to heaven: so that this man of sin is not to be looked for among the Turks, pagans, or infidels. He *sitteth in the temple*, the church, *of God;* not that it can be the true church where he thus sitteth and acteth, but rather the synagogue of Satan; but that which he calleth so, and which beareth that name, and which before the falling away was really so, Rom. i. 8. As Jerusalem is called *the holy city* after it had lost its holiness, Matt. iv. 5; and *the faithful city*, when *become an harlot*, Isa. i. 21; and Mount Tabor a *holy mount*, 2 Pet. i. 18; because once so: or called so according to men's opinion; as idols, that are nothing, are yet called *gods*, 2 Chron. xxviii. 23; 1 Cor. viii. 5. Some read the words, εἰς τὸν ναόν, *in templum Dei*, as we say, *in amicum*, i. e. *velut amicus*, he sitteth for the temple of God, as if he himself was the temple and church of God. So Aug. de Civ. Dei, lib. 20. c. 19. And so some of our protestant writers, applying it to the pope, who, as the head of the church, hath the whole church virtually in himself, and doth exercise all church power. *Showing himself that he is God;* not saying it with his mouth, as Œcumenius saith, but making such a show before men; though Bellarmine interprets it of an open boasting and vaunting himself to be God, which, saith he, the pope doth not; but by pretended miracles, signs, and wonders, by pardons, indulgences, canonizing saints, dominion over princes and kingdoms, he shows himself as a God before men, and claims a power to be judged of no man, and to be judge of all men. *A seculari potestate non solvi posse nec ligari pontificem, quem constat a Constantino Deum appellatum, cum nec Deum ab hominibus judicari manifestum sit. Decret.* distinct. 96. c. 7. Yea, lastly, he exalteth himself above God himself, when he maketh the Scriptures to derive their authority more from the pope's canonizing, than God himself; and without it no man is bound to believe them. *Decret.* lib. 2. tit. 23. Again, If the pope should err by commanding vice and forbidding virtue, the church was bound to believe vice to be good and virtue to be evil. *Bellarm.* lib. 4. *de Summo Pont.* c. 5. And it is frequent among their divines and canonists to say, that the pope can dispense against the apostles and the Old Testament, and the Scriptures are inferior to his decrees, and without the authority of the church are a nose of wax, paper, and parchment, &c.; so that upon the whole, as John's disciples asked concerning Christ, Art thou he that should come, or must we look for another? so, may we not say to the pope concerning antichrist, Art thou he, &c.? I will speak boldly, either there is no antichrist, or the bishop of Rome is he. *Chamier.* l. 16. c. 8.

5 Remember ye not, that, when I was yet with you, I told you these things?

The apostle tacitly upbraids them for their forgetfulness. To forget the things that have been taught us, is a great evil: Solomon often cautions against it, Prov. iii. 1; iv. 5; and it is often reproved, Heb. xii. 5; Jam. i. 24; and the contrary required, Mal. iv. 4; John xvi. 4; Jude 17; Rev. iii. 3. David hid the word in his heart, Psal. cxix. 11, and the virgin Mary kept the angel's sayings, Luke ii. 19. The apostles did take care to tell the churches of the apostacy that would come, and of false prophets and teachers that would arise, as Paul the elders of Ephesus, Acts xx. 29, 30, and Peter, 2 Pet. ii. 1, and St. John of the coming of antichrist, 1 John ii. 18; and more fully, though obscurely, in the book of the Revelation; and the apostle here in this verse minds these Thessalonians that he told them of the coming of the man of sin before the coming of Christ, so that they should not have been shaken in their minds about Christ's coming in that present age. And they told the churches of these things, that they might not be surprised by them, or offended at them, when they came.

‖ Or, *holdeth.*

6 And now ye know what ‖ withholdeth that he might be revealed in his time.

And now ye know what withholdeth. The apostle it seems had told them, as of his coming, so of what at present withheld the revealing of him. And what this was is difficult to know now, though it seems these Thessalonians knew it: there are many conjectures about it. This I shall say in general: 1. It was something that the apostle thought not safe openly to declare in writing; else he would not have written of it so obscurely. 2. It was both a thing, and a person; a thing, τὸ κατέχον, in this verse, *that which withholdeth;* and a person, as in the next verse, ὁ κατέχων, *he who letteth.* 3. It was also such a thing and such a person as were to be removed out of the way, not totally, but as they were hinderances of this revelation. Expositors, both popish and protestant, pitch upon the Roman emperor and empire as most probably meant here by the apostle; and therefore he wrote not plainly, lest by writing of the taking away that empire, which the Romans thought to be eternal, he might stir up their hatred against the Christians. Some understand it of the removing only the seat of the emperor from Rome to Constantinople, whereby the bishop of Rome had opportunity to grow up into greater power. The popish writers understand it of the total destruction of the empire, which because they see not yet done they conclude the man of sin is not yet revealed. Our protestant writers understand it only of such a weakening of the empire and imperial dominion, as gave the bishop and clergy of Rome advantage to rise up into power both spiritual and secular; as some learned writers have given an account thereof. When the empire was broken into ten kingdoms, the imperial power of the emperors was much weakened; and being afterwards united in the pope as an ecclesiastical monarch, he grew up, and the imperial power declined, the grandeur of them both could not stand together. And this is the beast with the ten horns, and ten crowns upon the horns, which is spoken of, Rev. xiii. 1; whereupon this beast is worshipped, and the voice is, *Who is like unto the beast? who is able to make war with him?* ver. 4. Some of the ancient fathers had this sense of the text: see Tertul. de Resurrect. l. 4. c. 24. Chrysost. in locum. Aug. de Civ. Dei, l. 19. c. 20. Jerome, when he heard of the taking of Rome by Alaricus, expected the coming of antichrist not far off. Whereupon the ancient church did pray that the Roman empire might continue long, that his coming might be delayed: *Tertul. Apol.* c. 32, 39. But it is now evident how it is fallen from what once it was. The eastern part is under the dominion of the Turk; the western divided into ten distinct kingdoms under distinct governments; and in Germany, where it is most remaining, the empire is little more than titular; and Italy and Rome wholly in the pope's possession: and hence this man of sin hath been long since revealed. *That he might be revealed in his time:* as God appoints seasons for all his works, so for the revealing of him, as also for his ruin.

7 For [k] the mystery of iniquity doth already work: only he who now letteth *will let*, until he be taken out of the way.

[k] 1 John 2. 18. & 4. 3.

For the mystery of iniquity doth already work; the way was prepared by degrees for the man of sin, before he came actually to be revealed, or constituted in his complete existence; and this was by the working of the mystery of iniquity. A mystery is something in general which is abstruse, intricate, and not easily discerned. And there are mysteries in doctrine, and in practice; mysteries of godliness, and mysteries of iniquity; mysteries of the kingdom of God, and of the devil's kingdom. So there are *the deep things of God,* 1 Cor. ii. 10, and *the depths of Satan,* Rev. ii. 24. The mystery ushering in the man of sin is a mystery of iniquity. It is not open sin and wickedness, but dissembled piety, specious errors, wickedness under a form of godliness cunningly managed, that is here meant: see the book called The Mystery of Jesuitism, or the Provincial Letters. And it is a mystery that worketh; it doth exert and put forth itself, but secretly, as a mole which worketh under ground. And its working is not against the being, providence, and attributes of God, or natural religion; but to undermine Christianity in the peculiar doctrines, worship, and practice of it. In doctrines are brought in *privily damnable heresies,* 2 Pet. ii. 1. In worship, inventions and commandments of men, under pretences of greater reverence, devotion, and humility, Col. ii. 22, 23. In practice, dispensations to moral impieties under colour of service to the catholic church. And this mystery, saith our apostle, already worketh; in the false doctrines of the false teachers of his time, in the traditions and inventions of men obtruding themselves into the worship of God in his time, in the affectation of pre-eminence in the church in his time, and making merchandise of the gospel in his time, and gain godliness; and in mingling philosophical notions with the simplicity of the gospel, and gratifying the flesh under a form of godliness, and pretence of gospel liberty. And it was not among the heathen, or the Jews, but among the professors of Christianity, that this mystery was then working, as I suppose the apostle meaneth. And when the man of sin was fully revealed all these corruptions did centre in him, as sinks in the common sewer; the lesser antichrists in the great antichrist. *Only he who now letteth will let, until he be taken out of the way:* the idolatries and persecutions of the heathen emperors must be taken out of the way, to make way for those that arise under a Christian, or rather antichristian, state, the dragon giving his seat, spirit, and power to the beast. And the power that was in the Roman emperor, whether heathen or Christian, must be taken out of the way to make room for the exaltation of this man of sin. For notwithstanding all corruptions in doctrine, worship, or practice which might be introduced before, yet he is not fully revealed till he hath his jurisdiction and secular power also in his hand. And then this mystery of iniquity is arrived to its height; which St. John saw written in the forehead of the great whore, Rev. xvii. 5, *Mystery, Babylon the great,* &c., and which, some have said, was written anciently in the pope's mitre.

8 And then shall that Wicked be revealed, [1]whom the Lord shall consume [m]with the spirit of his mouth, and shall destroy [n] with the brightness of his coming:

[l] Dan. 7. 10, 11.
[m] Job 4. 9. Is. 11. 4. Hos. 6. 5. Rev. 2. 16. & 19. 15, 20, 21.
[n] ch. 1. 8. 9. Heb. 10 27.

And then shall that Wicked be revealed: this revealing I think differs from that mentioned before, ver. 3; he is first revealed, as I said, *quoad existentiam,* when he comes forth into being, and then *quoad apparentiam,* when he comes to be discovered. And this I suppose is meant here, because his destruction is mentioned as following upon it; for the discovering of him is the first step to his ruin, and here is called by another name. At his first rising he is a man of sin; but after he hath violated the laws of God and the laws of Christ by setting up his own, he is well called ἄνομος, that lawless one; and now he that pretended so highly for Christ is discovered to be antichrist. The mystery of iniquity that before lay hid comes to be revealed, God enlightening the eyes of many learned ministers and princes, yea, and of multitudes of people herein; the Scriptures, before shut up in an unknown tongue, being now translated to the understanding of the common people; those that were *made drunk with the wine of her fornication*, Rev. xvii. 2, now put away their wine from them, as Eli said to Hannah; and the kings and kingdoms that gave their power to the beast, now come to *hate the whore*, &c., the time being come for the fulfilling the words of God herein, Rev. xvii. 17. And this revelation is signified and foretold when the angel said to John, *I will tell thee the mystery of the woman, and of the beast that carrieth her,* Rev. xvii. 7. There is need of a Divine revelation to know the mystery of iniquity, as well as the mystery of godliness. And the woman is the same with the man of sin mentioned before, once the spouse of Christ, but now by her idolatry become a whore, and divorced from him; said to be also *that great city, which reigneth over the kings of the earth,* Rev. xvii. 18. By the understanding these things this wicked one comes to be revealed. *Whom the Lord shall consume;* which is not done all at once; his consumption goes before his destruction. As Jezebel, the prophetess who seduced the servants of God to commit fornication, is said to be cast into a bed of languishing, Rev. ii. 20, 22; as he rose up by degrees, so shall he be consumed gradually. His power declines by degrees, both civil and ecclesiastical, and the authority he had got both in and over the consciences of men. The seven vials are the seven last plagues, which do gradually consume him. And this is said to be done by the Lord himself, which is the Lord Jesus. He that made war with the Lamb is overcome by the Lamb, Rev. xvii. 14; though many instruments may be employed herein; for he is said to have those with him who are called *chosen and faithful;* and it belongs to him, as all power of heaven and earth is given to him, to save his people, and to destroy his adversaries; as it is said of him, Psal. xcvii. 3, *A fire goeth before him, and burneth up his enemies round about.* As he is a refreshing, directing light to his people, so a consuming fire to his adversaries. The stone cut out of the mountain without hands, Dan. ii. 34, smites the image in the time of the fourth monarchy, when Christ came into the world, and in the latter end of it, under the antichristian state, it is broken in pieces. *With the spirit of his mouth;* as was prophesied of him, Isa. xi. 4, *With the breath of his lips shall he slay the wicked,* even this wicked one here in the text, Rev. xviii. 8; xix. 15. And this, as some interpret, he shall do with ease, as by a word speaking; or by a word of command, saying, Let it be done, and it shall be done. Or, as we may read it, with the spirit of his lips, because of the power or spirit that goes along with his word. But this breath of Christ's mouth Cajetane and others understand of the word of the gospel, which is the breath of Christ's mouth in the mouths of his ministers, called *the everlasting gospel*, Rev. xiv. 6, which an angel flying through the midst of heaven is said to have, to preach to them that dwell upon the earth; and then followed by another angel, saying, *Babylon is fallen, is fallen*, ver. 8. The mystery of iniquity will be unveiled by the clear preaching of the word; and the primitive pure institutions of worship, and doctrines of the gospel, will be vindicated from the antichristian corruptions and innovations. And the spirit of Christ going forth with the gospel, will make it effectual hereunto. These are the rod of his strength, whereby he rules in the midst of his enemies, Psal. cx. 2, and whereby he shall consume this man of sin. Nations and people will fall off from him as they come to understand the truth by the word preached. *And shall destroy;* after his consuming follows his destruction, καταργήσει· the word *destroy* here signifies to abolish, enervate, to make of no force; and so used often in the New Testament: sometimes applied to the law, Rom. iii. 31, sometimes to the body of sin, Rom. vi. 6, sometimes to persons to whom Christ will not be effectual, Gal. v. 4; here to the man of sin; so that whatever remains there may be of him in the world, they shall be without any efficacy or power: his jurisdiction shall be abolished, his keys shall not be able to open or shut, the edge of both his swords shall be quite blunted, his triple crown shall fall off his head, his purgatory fire shall be put out, his images shall lose their veneration; the spell of the cross shall be detected, the intercession of saints shall be found to be a fiction, infallibility shall be found to be a deceit, supremacy of the church shall fall to the ground; the rivers of his large revenues shall be dried up, &c., and *the beast that was, and is not, and yet is,* Rev. xvii. 8, shall now utterly cease to be. *With the brightness of his coming:* the breath of his mouth wasted him, and the brightness of his coming destroys him. Some interpret this of Christ's personal coming to judgment, which will be with great brightness, as Matt. xxiv. 27. *As the lightning cometh out of the east, and shineth even unto the west, so shall the coming of the Son of man be;* coming in the glory of heaven, and every eye shall see him; and of his coming he spake 1 Thess. iv., and in this chapter also, as that which was not so near at hand as some imagined. And without question this coming will destroy him, if not destroyed before, as well as the rest of the wicked, chap. i. 9; but whether judgment may not first proceed against the antichristian state, and those that have sinned under the gospel, is a question. It is sometimes mentioned particularly with respect to them: as in the parable of the tares and wheat, Matt. xiii., of the ten virgins, and the talents, Matt. xxv. And the beast and false prophet are cast into the lake of fire, Rev. xix. 20, before the general judgment, mentioned Rev. xx. 12. So that at Christ's personal coming his judgment will, as some conceive, begin here, and then proceed to the rest of the world; whereupon many assign some great length of time to Christ's stay upon earth, and judging the world. Others take *the brightness of his coming* in a spiritual sense, for a clearer manifestation of Christ in the world. As the kingdom of antichrist, or of this man of sin, is founded in darkness, so the brightness of this coming will dispel and destroy it. With respect to his eternal generation, Christ is said to be *the brightness of his Father's glory*, Heb. i. 2; but this is a brightness with respect to men. And though he hath come in his Spirit to enlighten his church from the beginning of the world, and more eminently after his ascension, yet this will exceed all the former, and is peculiarly styled *the brightness of his coming.* And so they expect this destruction of this man of sin before Christ's coming to judgment; for if it be the same with the fall of Babylon, mentioned in the Revelation, many things are to be done here upon earth after that, before Christ's last coming, and they mention the calling of the Jews, the destruction of those enemies called Gog and Magog, the coming down of the new Jerusalem from heaven, which is some glorious state of the church here upon earth. However, the apostle here mentions nothing of a destruction by the material sword; what princes may do of different religions upon a civil account, I do not know, but as this man of sin rose out of the apostacy of the church, so he will not be consumed and destroyed but by a return from it, which is done by the breath of Christ's mouth, and the brightness of his coming. But yet, by some instruments or other, God will avenge the blood of his servants upon this man of sin in the time and way appointed of him.

9 *Even him,* whose coming is [o] after the working of Satan with all power and [p] signs and lying wonders,

[o] John 8. 41. Eph. 2. 2. Rev. 18. 23. p See Deut. 13. 1.
Mat. 24. 24. Rev. 13. 13. & 19. 21.

The apostle still continues his discourse about this man of sin. He had declared whence he arose, and to what height of power, and the manner and place of his exercising it, and what opened him the way to it, and also his destruction, with the means of it. But he thought it needful to explain particularly the manner of his rising into all this power, and preserving himself in it, and the persons over whom he doth exercise it. *Whose coming is after the working of Satan;* Κατ' ἐνέργειαν. Christ's coming is in power, and so is his: Christ comes with the Spirit of God, and his is with a spirit also, but it is of Satan: and the Spirit of God worketh with Christ in his coming, and the spirit of Satan with the man of sin in his coming; which implies either the principle of this working in his

II. THESSALONIANS II

coming, it is the devil; or the similitude of it, it is like the working of Satan. If in the first sense, it shows by what spirit the antichristian church was first formed, and by which it is still informed and acted; as in natural bodies the matter is formed and informed by the spirit within it. The true church hath the Holy Spirit, that forms it into a spiritual temple, Eph. ii. 21, 22; the false church hath the spirit of the devil, forming it into the synagogue of Satan, Rev. ii. 9. The dragon is said to give the beast his *power, seat, and great authority*, Rev. xiii. 2; and this dragon is the devil in the heathen empire, who being cast out of his seat and power when the emperor became Christian, found the antichristian church, and here exercised that power and authority which he did formerly in the imperial seat of the heathen emperors; whence we may see whence all the furious zeal and bloody cruelties appearing in the popish church do spring, notwithstanding all their outward shows of devotion. If we take the words in the latter sense, then his coming is like the working of Satan; either with great power and energy, as the word imports: the Greek word is often used in a good sense; for God's working in the heart, Phil. ii. 13, for the working of the word, 1 Thess. ii. 13, for the working of the heart in prayer, James v. 17: or by the same methods; by pretences of piety and devotion, as Satan transforms himself into an angel of light; or by keeping men in blindness and ignorance, so doth Satan by setting before men secular grandeur, and the pomp of the world, as thus Satan dealt with our Saviour, Matt. iv.; or by suggesting lies instead of truth, so he dealt with our first parents, and is called a liar from the beginning. *With all power; ἐν πάσῃ δυνάμει.* Besides that energy of Satan that works inwardly in this man of sin, which was mentioned before, he hath outward strength or power wherein he comes; which may be here meant. He hath the secular power to assist him, the kings of the earth giving their power to the beast; and we read of ten horns upon his head, which are the emblems of strength and power, Rev. xiii. 1; whereupon it is said, *Who is like unto the beast? who is able to make war with him?* ver. 4. *And signs, and lying wonders:* some, by the figure called hendyadis, read it, by the power of signs and lying wonders; but not properly. Observe how Satan is God's ape; God confirmed the gospel with *signs and wonders*, Rom. xv. 19; *God bearing them witness, with signs and wonders*, &c. Heb. ii. 4; and Satan brings this man of sin into the world in the same manner: God did it to confirm the truth, but Satan to countenance a falsehood. But though he comes with signs and wonders, yet not properly with *miracles*, as the Greek word is rendered in Heb. ii. 4; because though the devil can work the one, he cannot the other: he can by his great natural knowledge and experience improve natural causes to their utmost, but he cannot effect things above all possibility of nature, which is the same power as creating. The schoolmen give their distinction between wonders and miracles, which is not needful here to insert: all miracles are wonders, but all wonders are not miracles; and yet are esteemed miracles when their cause is not known. The Romish legends are full of stories of miracles wrought to confirm their false doctrines of purgatory, of relics, invocation of saints, &c.; which might be wonders really wrought by the devil; such as were wrought by Jannes and Jambres in Egypt, and by Simon Magus, and Apollonius Tyaneus, &c.; who used magic arts, and the people, not knowing them in their causes, might judge them miracles. And being wrought for such ends, they are termed signs, for a sign is any thing that is used to make signification, whether it be a natural or artificial, an ordinary or extraordinary sign; used either for a good end, as those shown by Christ and the apostles, or for a bad end, as those used by this man of sin. People are apt to be affected with signs. *The Jews*, saith the apostle, *require a sign*, 1 Cor. i. 22, as they often desired Christ to show them a sign, and therefore this man of sin comes with signs. Some signs are only for representation, as the sign of the cross, and the images of Christ, and of his death and resurrection, &c.; and he comes in these: others are for confirmation, which are either real miracles, or such as seem so; and he comes in these latter also, which are here called τέρασι ψεύδους, *lying wonders*, or wonders of a lie, Hebrew. Though the Greek word is oft used for a real miracle, yet not so here; for miracles are the effects of a Divine power only, Rom. xv. 19; Heb. ii. 4, and not diabolical. And called *lying wonders*, either because they are used to confirm a lie, or because they are not real, but feigned wonders; impostures, to cheat the people, and make them wonder; whereof we have account in Gregory's Dialogues, and in Paulus Diaconus, and others; and yet such miracles as these the papists boast of as marks of their church to be true, though they are here by the apostle made the marks of the man of sin. And Christ foretells of false prophets that should *show great signs and wonders*, to *deceive, if possible, the very elect*, Matt. xxiv. 24. See Deut. xiii. 1; Rev. xiii. 13, 14.

10 And with all deceivableness of unrighteousness in ^q them that perish; because they received not the love of the truth, that they might be saved.

^q 2 Cor. 2. 15. & 4. 3.

And with all deceivableness of unrighteousness; or, deceit of unrighteousness, unrighteous deceit, or deceitful unrighteousness. And it is universal, *all*. It is unrighteousness managed with great subtlety to deceive; and so the same with the mystery of iniquity, mentioned before, or the mystery of unrighteousness, as we may read it. All sin is unrighteousness, whether against God or man, as all virtue is comprehended in righteousness. The apostle here means unrighteousness so cloaked and covered, that men discern it not, but are deceived by it: as the Pharisees, who devoured widows' houses, and for pretence made long prayers; and so also they tithed mint and cummin as exactly religious, built the sepulchres of the prophets, made broad their phylacteries, would not eat with unwashen hands, &c. The like we find in the Church of Rome, as I mentioned before, where men are ambitious, covetous, cruel, superstitious, &c., and all under a pretence of righteousness, and for honour to Christ and the church: make use of Peter's keys to open rich men's coffers; and for a sum of money, to absolve men in this world, or to redeem them out of purgatory in the other world; which is a mere cheat, &c. Thus comes this man of sin, and by such ways he hath advanced himself. *In them that perish:* this shows who they are that are deceived by him. Reprobates are often so described, 2 Cor. ii. 15; iv. 3; and it is the same as elsewhere signifies damnation. The word signifies men that are *lost*, so used Matt. xviii. 11, or *destroyed*, 2 Cor. iv. 9. They are such as have not their *names written in the book of life*, Rev. xiii. 8; and who *shall drink of the wine of the wrath of God, and the smoke of their torment ascendeth for ever*, Rev. xiv. 10, 11. *Because they received not the love of the truth:* and the apostle gives the reason why they are thus deceived. He saith not they had not received the truth, but the love of it, and so hold it not fast, but are carried away with the general apostacy. Truth is either natural, which the heathen had, and detained in unrighteousness, Rom. i. 18; or supernatural, from Divine revelation. This is meant, for he speaks not of heathens, but Christians; not the world, but the church. *That they might be saved:* and the truth here meant is saving truth, as the gospel is called *the word of truth*, Eph. i. 13; Col. i. 5; for had they received it in love they might have been saved, but for want of that they perish; so that it is unsound, notional professors that are carried away by the man of sin, and deceived by him. Truth, if it be not received into the heart as well as the head, will not secure against apostacy or popery, nor prevent perishing. And the amiableness that is in gospel truth calls for love, as the certainty of its revelation calls for faith; and had they so received the truth they might have been saved.

11 And ^r for this cause God shall send them strong delusion, ^s that they should believe a lie:

^r Rom. 1, 24. &c. See 1 Kings 22. 22. Ezek. 14. 9. ^s Matt. 24. 5, 11. 1 Tim. 4. 1.

And for this cause God shall send them strong delusion: we had account in the former verse of such as are deceived by the man of sin, of their sin, and here of their punishment. They were first deluded, which was their sin; and God sends them strong delusion, and that is their punishment. They did not receive the truth in the love of it, which was their sin; and therefore are given up to believe a lie, which is their punishment. Had they received the truth aright, they might have been saved; but not receiving it, they are damned. And they were said to be such as perish, and their perishing is here called damnation. So that though God is not the author of sin or falsehood, *Deus*

II. THESSALONIANS II

non est auctor cujus est ultor, Fulgent.; yet he may in justice give men up to them, which the apostle here calls God's sending, &c.; which imports either, 1. Tradition, delivering men to Satan to tempt and deceive. 2. Desertion, withholding or withdrawing that grace that might preserve them. 3. A judicial permission, God purposing not to hinder men to fall into that sin or delusion which he seeth their own hearts incline them to. God concurs to evil, not *positive*, but *privative*; not *efficienter*, but *deficienter*; Schoolmen. God in Scripture is often said to do that which he permits to be done; as in the case of Joseph's selling into Egypt, Gen. xlv. 7, David's numbering the people, 2 Sam. xxiv. 1, compared with 1 Chron. xxi. 1; and the ten kings giving their power to the beast, by God's putting it into their hearts, Rev. xvii. 17: and it is not a bare permission, for what evil God permits, he decreed to permit it; and he decreed the circumstances attending it, and the end to which he would order and dispose it, and the degree to which it should break forth. They were deceived into error, and God gave them up to it. And it did work with great efficacy; which either relates to the man of sin, that did lead them strongly into it, or to them that were led by him. When error doth vitiate the life, and one error begets another, and makes men violent against the truth, then it is the efficacy of error. And thus God doth judicially punish sin with sin, and delusion with delusion; and then they are always most operative, and most incurable. But men fall not presently under these judicial acts; men first refuse to see, before God sends blindness, and first harden their own hearts, before God hardens them. These in the text first refused to receive the truth, before they were given up to believe a lie: see Rom. i. 24. So that both God and this man of sin, and themselves also, are concerned in these evils; but they sinfully and unrighteously, but God judicially and in righteousness. *That they should believe a lie*: and the lie they were given up to believe, is a doctrinal lie: false speaking is a lie in words, hypocrisy is a lie in fact, and error is a lie in doctrine, Hos. xi. 12; Acts v. 3. Some by *lie* here suppose is meant the lying wonders before mentioned; and this sense need not be excluded, but I rather interpret it of false doctrine, as that which stands opposite to the truth before mentioned, and again mentioned in this verse. Sometimes idols are called *lies*, Isa. xliv. 20; sometimes, the things of the world, Psal. iv. 2; sometimes, the great men of the world, Psal. lxii. 9; sometimes, false divinations, Ezek. xxii. 28; Zech. x. 2; sometimes, false prophesyings and predictions, Jer. xiv. 14; xxiii. 25, 26; and sometimes, false doctrines, as 1 Tim. iv. 1, 2, where we read of false prophets, who shall arise in the last time, and speak *lies in hypocrisy*, &c. And false apostles are said to be *liars* upon that account, Rev. ii. 2. And such are many popish doctrines, which the apostle here probably refers to. What is transubstantiation but a lie? purgatory, infallibility of the church, mediation of saints, their *opus operatum*, &c.? Men must be strongly deluded to believe such doctrines, and it is mentioned as a great judgment of God upon them to believe such lies, as it is a great mercy to believe the truth, especially if we consider what follows upon it.

12 That they all might be damned who
t Rom. 1.32. believed not the truth, but ᵗhad pleasure in unrighteousness.

That they all might be damned, or condemned. The Greek is, judged, but often translated as in the text; the simple verb being taken for the compound: so John iii. 17; 1 Cor. xi. 29; Jude 4. It is true a man may be judged and not condemned, but the judgment of the wicked is condemnation; and damnation is here mentioned either as the event, or the effect of their believing lies, or as the purpose of God in sending them strong delusions. They are first justly punished with spiritual judgment, and then eternal, and God is just in both; whence we see that there are some errors in judgment which are damnable. As we read of *damnable heresies*, 2 Pet. ii. 1, or heresies of destruction; such are many in the Romish Church; and the apostle speaks of such, Col. ii. 19, *not holding the Head*, &c.; not meant of a total rejection of Christ, but of voluntary humility, and worshipping of angels, mingled with the true worship of the gospel; and such cannot be saved. *Who believed not the truth*: where we have a further description of these persons who are to be damned, which is added by the apostle, either to clear God's justice, as in sending them strong delusions to believe a lie, so also in their condemnation; or to assign the cause why they believed a lie, because they *believed not the truth*. Those will easily be brought to believe a lie who believe not the truth; and the belief here mentioned is that of assent, yet such an assent as is operative and practical, which they had not; for it was said before, they received not the truth in the love of it. *But had pleasure in unrighteousness*; did not only practise, but had great complacence and contentment of mind in it, as the Greek word imports, and so had rather believe a false doctrine which will countenance their practice, than the truth which doth condemn it: see Prov. x. 23; Rom. i. 32. By *unrighteousness* some expositors understand false doctrine, or error, because it is set in opposition here to truth, as sin is set in opposition to it, John viii. 46; and that the apostle hath peculiar reference to the corrupt doctrines of Simon Magus and the Nicolaitanes, that gave liberty to the lusts of the flesh. But why not rather to the doctrines of the man of sin, which he had been before speaking of? I rather take the word in the largest sense, so all sin is unrighteousness; and the apostle St. John saith, *all unrighteousness is sin*, 1 John v. 17, where *unrighteousness* is expressed by ἀνομία, a word which imports transgression of the law, as in this text by ἀδικία, a word which signifies injustice. So that we see here an erroneous mind and a vicious life going together. And when sin is come to this height, that men take pleasure in it, it makes them ripe for damnation. And how well these things agree to the antichristian church, let men consider and judge.

13 But ᵘwe are bound to give thanks u ch. 1. 3.
alway to God for you, brethren beloved
of the Lord, because God ˣhath ʸfrom x 1 Thess. 1.4.
the beginning chosen you to salvation y Eph. 1. 4.
ᶻthrough sanctification of the Spirit and z Luke 1.75.
belief of the truth: 1 Pet. 1.2.

The apostle here exempts these Thessalonians out of the number of those reprobates that he had before spoken of, and speaks of them as such as should be preserved from apostacy in faith or practice, and obtain salvation. And this he mentions for comfort to them, and with thanksgivings to God. He had often before given thanks for them, 1 Thess. i. 2; ii. 13; iii. 9; and in the 1st chapter of this Epistle, ver. 3; and both here and there mentions it as a debt he was bound unto, or a duty he owed, we ought to give thanks, as in the Greek. And here he styles them, not only *brethren*, as often before, but *beloved of the Lord*, such as have been and are beloved; and therefore not in the number of them that should be damned, mentioned in the former verse. *Because God hath from the beginning chosen you to salvation*: which words are either to give the reason of the apostle's thanksgivings, or rather all arguments to evidence they were beloved of the Lord. And he instanceth in their election as a proof of it. There is an election to office, as David to be king, 2 Sam. vi. 21, and Judas to be an apostle, John vi. 70; and election to a visible church, and means of salvation, and thus the seed of Abraham were chosen, Deut. xxvi. 18; Psal. cxxxv. 4; cxlvii. 19; and election to salvation, as in the text; which is either that which follows faith, as some understand that place, Matt. xxii. 14, or rather that which goes before it, said here to be *from the beginning*: not from the beginning of the gospel, as some say; nor from the beginning of our preaching to you, or of your effectual calling, as others say; no, nor yet is it meant from the beginning of the world, which was the beginning of time; or immediately upon Adam's fall: but by *beginning* is here meant eternity itself, as election is said to be from *before the foundation of the world*, Eph. i. 4, which is from eternity. Though *beginning* seems to relate to time, yet the Scriptures often express eternity by such words as relate to time: as when God is called *the Ancient of days*, Dan. vii. 9, it signifies his eternity; and Jude speaks of some that were of old ordained to condemnation, Jude 4, πάλαι προγεγραμμένοι, God's eternal decrees being compared to a book wherein names are written. When was their ordaining but from eternity? And it is election to salvation, complete salvation, which is here meant, in the full fruition of it; not in the title to it by faith, or the first-fruits of it in sanctification, because they are here mentioned as the means that tend to it. *Through sanctification of the Spirit:* election is to the means as well as the end, as Eph. i. 4. Holiness is not the cause of God's election, but God hath decreed it to be the way to salvation; without holiness none shall ever see the Lord, Heb. xii. 14. *And belief of the truth:* and therefore those were spoken of as persons to be damned who believed not the truth, in the former verse. And so it is evident, election is not upon the foresight of faith, it is through it we have salvation, but not election : but of this before, 1 Thess. iv. And the apostle joins sanctification and faith together, for they are not and cannot be put asunder. Now by all this the apostle proves they were beloved of the Lord. He saw the fruits of election in their sanctification and belief of the truth, thence concludes they were elected, and therefore loved.

14 Whereunto he called you by our Gospel, to ªthe obtaining of the glory of our Lord Jesus Christ.

a John 17. 22. 1 Thess. 2. 12. 1 Pet. 5. 10.

Whereunto he called you by our gospel: before, the apostle mentioned their election, now their calling ; which are often in Scripture put together, Rom. viii. 30 ; 2 Pet. i. 10 ; and are both applied to Christ himself, Isa. xlii. 1, 6. They are those two sovereign acts of God, prerequisite to a state of salvation ; the one eternal, the other in time ; the one immanent in God, the other transient upon the creature ; and it is the first transient act that flows from election. And because there is an outward and inward call mentioned in Scripture, we must here understand the apostle of both: for Εἰς ὅ, *Whereunto,* or to which thing, mentioned in the beginning of this verse, refers to all that he said in the former verse, which is, *salvation, sanctification, belief of the truth,* which they could not attain with a mere outward call, though they had that also ; for the apostle mentions here the gospel, which he calls *our gospel,* because preached by them, and intrusted to them, though the original of it is from God, and the matter of it from Jesus Christ. And he puts them in mind of the great mercy they had received in their preaching the gospel to them, for thereby they were called into a state of salvation ; as also of the way wherein they are to obtain this salvation, which is *through sanctification of the Spirit, and the belief of the truth,* that they might be careful to persevere both in faith and holiness ; and not to expect it from the law, or the speculations of philosophy, which some false teachers might suggest, for as *faith cometh by hearing* the gospel, Rom. x. 17, so it is that only which is *the power of God unto salvation,* Rom. i. 16. And by this he confirms to them also their election, because they had been thus effectually called by the gospel : for no man can conclude his salvation from election, if he hath not been also thus called, which is by feeling the power of the gospel in the heart, and yielding obedience to it in his life. What the apostle before called *salvation,* he here styles *the obtaining of the glory of our Lord Jesus Christ.* Though in 1 Thess. v. 9, he had there also called it obtaining salvation, and by the same word here used in the text : yea, the word περιποίησις, here rendered obtaining, sometimes signifies salvation itself, Heb. x. 39, and, which is equivalent, *the purchased possession,* Eph. i. 14 ; and it may signify in the text, the obtaining the glory of Christ in a way of purchase, as also by diligent endeavours after it, by way of acquisition, as the word seems to signify. And by *the glory of Christ* is not meant the glory we give to him, as some would strain the words to that sense ; but rather, the glory we shall receive from him, which is the same which the Father hath given to him, and which he hath given to his people, John xvii. 22, whereby they are co-heirs with him, Rom. viii. 17. And so the apostle sets forth the greatness of this salvation, to which these believers were called, it is to the obtaining the same glory with Christ, in kind at least ; and shows their different state from those that perish, and will be damned, mentioned in the former verses. Or if we read the words, ye are called to be a peculiar people, as the Greek word is so rendered, 1 Pet. ii. 9, λαὸς εἰς περιποίησιν, *a peculiar people,* and understand by *the glory of Christ,* that glory of his grace he hath manifested herein, it shows also how God hath distinguished them from those before mentioned.

15 Therefore, brethren, ᵇstand fast, and hold ᶜthe traditions which ye have been taught, whether by word, or our epistle.

b 1 Cor. 16. 13. Phil. 4. 1. c 1 Cor. 11. 2. ch. 3. 6.

The former verses contained consolation, this is an exhortation : the apostle had assured them of their being elected and called, yet exhorts them to their duty. Assurance of salvation doth not encourage negligence ; the apostle takes his argument from thence to quicken them, *Therefore,* &c. And that which he exhorts them to is, 1. To *stand fast ;* a military word, speaking as a captain to his soldiers ; so 1 Cor. xvi. 13 ; Eph. vi. 14 ; having before foretold a great apostacy that would come. Or because he had told them of the great glory they had been called to the obtaining of by the gospel, he exhorts them to *stand fast,* which implies a firm persuasion of mind and constant purpose of will, and stands opposite to hesitation and despondency. 2. To *hold the traditions which* they had *been taught.* The word *tradition* signifies any thing delivered to another ; especially meant of doctrines. The Pharisees' doctrine is called *tradition,* Matt. xv. 3 ; and so the true doctrines of the gospel, being such as the apostles delivered to the people ; as the doctrine of the Lord's supper is said to be *delivered,* 1 Cor. xi. 23 ; and so Rom. vi. 13. *Whether by word, or our epistle ;* by word of mouth in public preaching, or private instruction. The apostle had both preached and written to these Thessalonians, before he wrote this Second Epistle. And that the papists should hence infer that there are matters of necessary consequence in religion, not contained in the Scriptures, is without ground. These they call traditions, some whereof are concerning faith, others concerning manners, others ritual, with respect to the worship of God, or the external polity of the church. But who can assure us what these are ? What a door is here opened to introduce what men please into the church, under pretence of tradition ! Who were the persons the apostle intrusted to keep these traditions ? why should he not declare the whole system of gospel truths he had received from Christ in writing, as well as part ? why should he conceal some things, when he wrote others ? And doth not the apostle assure Timothy that *All Scripture is given by inspiration of God, and is profitable for doctrine, for reproof, for correction, for instruction ; that the man of God may be perfect, throughly furnished unto all good works ?* 2 Tim. iii. 16, 17. What need them traditions ? And how can we know that they are by Divine inspiration, as we are assured all Scripture is ? Our Saviour reproved the Pharisees about their traditions, when from hence they would observe and impose ceremonies of washing hands, cups, and platters, Matt. xv. 2—6, yea, and by them make the commandments of God of none effect ; which the apostle cautions the Colossians about, Col. ii. 8 ; and whereof Paul declares his zeal before his conversion, Gal. i. 14 : and we find men's zeal still more about them than moral duties, and express institutions of God's worship. All the apostle's doctrine, *whether by word or epistle,* he calls by the name of *traditions* in the text here, and he commends the Corinthians, 1 Cor. xi. 2, that they kept the traditions delivered to them ; but were not they all committed to writing in some place or other of his Epistles ? and which were, and which were not, who can be certain ? And why should *traditions* be confined only to those things which the apostle did not write ? He exhorts the Thessalonians to hold the traditions which they had been taught, *whether by word or epistle.* And if they hold them with strength, as the word is, by this means they would stand fast.

16 ᵈNow our Lord Jesus Christ himself, and God, even our Father, ᵉwhich hath loved us, and hath given *us* everlasting consolation and ᶠgood hope through grace,

d ch. 1. 1, 2. e 1 John 4. 10 Rev. 1. 5. f 1 Pet. 1. 3.

The apostle here addeth prayer to his exhortation : the word and prayer are to go together, whether it be written or preached ; as the twelve told the disciples, Acts vi. 4, We will give ourselves to the word and prayer. He had planted them a church, but he knew *God gave the increase,* 1 Cor. iii. 6. The persons he prays to are here, first, *our Lord Jesus Christ ;* which was a good argument in Athana-

VOL. III—25

sius's time, for the dignity of Christ, against the Arians; and so it is still, and now against the Socinians: for God alone is the object of worship, and the bestower of those gifts which he here prays for. Only the apostle, when he mentions Christ, delights to mention him in his relation to his people; so he doth for the most part in all his Epistles, and so in this text. He useth a pronoun possessive, *our*, for it is relation and interest which commendeth and sweeteneth any good to us. And the other person is *God the Father*, who is *the Father of lights*, from whom *cometh every good and perfect gift*, James i. 17; and whom in his prayer he mentions together with Christ, because no access can be to God but through Christ, and no good gift descends to us but through him. And so God the Father is mentioned in his relation to his people also, *God, even our Father;* and when Christ is ours, in him God is ours also. And the apostle thus looking, and thus speaking of Christ and of God, strengthens his own and their faith, for the obtaining of the gifts he prays for. *Which hath loved us:* another argument is from God's love: our doubts in prayer arise more from unbelief in God's will, than his power, which will vanish when we look upon him in his love to us; for the nature of love is *velle bonum*, to will good to whom we love. Another is, from gifts already received, which are, first, *everlasting consolation;* whereby it appears, that God's love is communicative, and that it is not common, but his special love he spake of. Outward comforts are common gifts, but these the apostle means not here, because they are not everlasting; they continue not beyond death; they begin in time and end with time: but this consolation begins in time, and abides to eternity; and this man cannot give, the world cannot give, nor we give it ourselves, God giveth it only; and he gives it to whom he loveth, as every man seeks to comfort those whom he loves: and though some whom God loves may not feel his consolation, yet they have a right, and God hath it in reserve for them: *Light is sown for the righteous, and gladness for the upright in heart*, Psal. xcvii. 11. And though sometimes it may be interrupted where it is felt, yet not so as to be destroyed in its foundation, or to hinder its return, either in the temporal or eternal world, where it will be everlasting; so that as God is styled *the God of all grace*, 1 Pet. v. 10; so, *the God of all comfort*, 2 Cor. i. 3. And by *us* in the text he means these Thessalonians as well as himself, for he had spoken before of their *joy in the Holy Ghost*, 1 Thess. i. 6. And the other gift is, *good hope*. Hope, as a natural affection, is the expectation of the soul; and the object of it is *bonum futurum, arduum, possibile;* good, future good, difficult, and possible. But, as a grace, it is the expectation of the good things God hath promised, and not yet exhibited. And it is called *good hope*, good by way of eminency; with respect to the objects of it, which are eminently good; the certainty of it, it will not make ashamed, Rom. v. 5; compared to *an anchor sure and stedfast*, Heb. vi. 19: the regularness of it; things promised only, and as they are promised; else it is presumption, and not hope: the fruits of it; peace, purity, industry, and consolation also, and therefore joined with it here in the text: as the apostle speaks elsewhere of *rejoicing in hope*, Rom. v. 2; xii. 12; Heb. iii. 6. Or, as some, it is called *good hope*, with respect to the degree they had attained of it in their hearts; though they had not yet the good things promised, yet they had good hope of enjoying them. And by this epithet he distinguisheth this hope from the carnal vain hope of the men of the world, and the false hope of hypocrites, Job viii. 13; and themselves also from the state they were in when Gentiles, without hope, Eph. ii. 12. And this also is God's gift, as he is called *the God of hope*, Rom. xv. 13, not only as the object, but the author of it. And both these gifts are here said to be *through grace;* for else we could have had no ground either of hope or comfort. Sin had shut up our way to both, it is only grace that hath opened it to us. What we enjoy at present, and what we hope to enjoy, is all through grace. And from these gifts already received the apostle strengthens his faith about the other things he here prays for.

[g 1 Cor. 1. 8. 1 Thess. 3. 13. 1 Pet. 5. 10.] 17 Comfort your hearts, ᵍ and stablish you in every good word and work.

Next, we have the things prayed for: *Comfort your hearts;* though he said before, *who hath given us everlasting consolation*. The apostle means, either actual possession of what God had given title to, or a continued supply and increase of comfort already received. And he prays for this either in respect of the afflictions they suffered, that they might not faint; or to enable them the better to stand fast in the faith, and not fall away, as others. And so it agrees with the next petition for them. *And stablish you in every good word and work: the word of truth* is this *good word*, Prov. iv. 2, as the gospel is called, 2 Cor. vi. 7. And the doctrines of it are all *good*, 1 Tim. iv. 6; they are good *for instruction, for correction, for reproof, for doctrine*, 2 Tim. iii. 16. All truth is an intellectual good, whether natural or moral; but evangelical truth is by way of eminence good. It is a good word which is a *word of salvation*, Acts xiii. 26; and to be established in it, is firmly to believe it, and to hold it fast against seducing opinion, or persecutions; and by *every good word* he means all Divine truth, especially the greater truths; not to hold some truths and let others go. And to *word* the apostle adds *work*, that there may be a harmony betwixt faith and practice. As the doctrines of the gospel are true, so the works they require are good. And good works are manifold, respecting God, our neighbour, and ourselves. A Christian should not only practise them all, but be established in them, which implies constancy, perseverance, and resolution. True religion is not word only, but work; it is not only speculative, but practical. A sound mind ought to be joined with a holy life. And to make a work good, the principle, rule, manner, and end must all be good.

CHAP. III

The apostle desireth the Thessalonians to pray for him, 1, 2, *testifying his confidence in them,* 3, 4, *and praying God to direct them,* 5. *He censureth the idle and disorderly, and requireth others to abstain from their company,* 6—15: *concluding with prayer and salutation,* 16—18.

FINALLY, brethren, ᵃ pray for us, that the word of the Lord † may have *free* course, and be glorified, even as *it is* with you: [a Eph. 6. 19. Col. 4. 3. 1 Thes. 5. 25. † Gr. *may run.*]

The apostle now draws towards the close of his Epistle, as appears by the word *finally*, which he also useth in the close of other Epistles, as 2 Cor. xiii. 11; Eph. vi. 10; Phil. iv. 8: τὸ λοιπόν. It imports the adding of something that remains. And that which he first addeth, is the desire of their prayers; as he had desired them in the former Epistle, chap. v. 25; and so of other churches, 2 Cor. i. 11; Eph. vi. 19; Heb. xiii. 18, &c. He had prayed for them in the foregoing chapter, and now he begs their prayers. It is a mutual duty that ministers and people owe to one another. Though the apostle gave himself to the word, and prayer also, Acts vi. 4, yet the prayers of many may be more prevalent than of one, though an apostle: and they being concerned for the advancing of Christ's interest in the world, as they were Christians, were therefore engaged to pray for him. And the apostle was sensible of the greatness of the work which was in his hand, and his own insufficiency, without God, therefore he desires prayer; and it is of them whom he here calls *brethren:* he knew the prayers of the wicked and unbelievers would avail nothing; and though he was a great apostle, yet the greatest in the church may stand in need of, and be helped by, the prayers of the meanest brethren. And their prayers he desires are, first, with respect to his ministry, *that the word of the Lord may have free course*, or may run; that the course of it may not be stopped, it being as a river of the water of life. The apostle was to teach all nations, and so desires the word may pass from one nation to another, yea, and run down from one generation to another, that it may spread and diffuse itself, and disciples might be multiplied. This is called the increasing of it, Acts vi. 7; the growing and multiplying of it, Acts xii. 24; the growing and prevailing of it, Acts xix. 20: which Christ sets forth by the parable of the mustard-seed, which grew and spread; and of the leaven, that diffused its virtue in the meal, Matt. xiii. 31—33: the apostle referring here to the external course of the word, rather than its inward efficacy in the soul, as also Christ seems chiefly to do in those parables. There are many things that hinder the course of the gospel; sometimes wicked rulers make laws against it, sometimes great persecutions have been raised, sometimes false teachers oppose it, sometimes professors prove apostates and scandalize the world against it, sometimes reproaches are thrown in the way of it. And to the free course of it is required, on the contrary, a provision of suitable help herein, both of magistracy and ministry, and the bestowing of the Spirit, and the blessing of endeavours used herein. All these are to be prayed for, as the former to be prayed against. *And be glorified:* he means, that it might have honour, reputation, and high esteem in the world, and not lie under reproach; as the Jews accounted it heresy, and the Gentiles foolishness: as it is said of those Gentiles, Acts xiii. 48, they *glorified the word of the Lord,* by their honourable respect to it, and joy in it. As also that it might produce glorious effects in the world, in subduing people to God, and making men new creatures, and bringing them out of the devil's into Christ's kingdom, &c.; that it may evidence itself to be from heaven, and the power of God to men's salvation, and not an invention of man; to which we may add, that it may be honoured in the unblamable and exemplary walking of the professors of it. *Even as it is with you:* the glorious success of it with them he had largely shown before in both these Epistles; and he would have them pray for the like with others. Those that have felt the power of the gospel themselves to their conversion and salvation, should pray that others may partake of it with them. Herein they show their charity to men, and love to God, which the apostle here puts them upon, as that which would be acceptable to God; and the rather, because their own experience might teach them what God was able to do for others. Or else the apostle in these words sets forth these Thessalonians as a pattern of the mighty success of the word: it had its free course and was glorified among them; they received it as the word of God, and not of men. As if the apostle should say, They that would know the glorious success of the word of the Lord, let them go to Thessalonica.

b Rom. 15. 31.
† Gr *absurd.*
c Acts 28. 24. Rom. 10. 16.

2 And ^bthat we may be delivered from †unreasonable and wicked men: ^cfor all *men* have not faith.

Their prayers are here desired by the apostle with respect to their persons, which relates to the prayer desired before with respect to the word; for the apostle and his fellow labourers met with such men that did oppose them, and by that means were hindered in their work of the ministry, and the free course of the word obstructed. What were these men? were they the persecuting Gentiles? they met with such: or the envious, malicious Jews? they met with such also; and here at Thessalonica in particular, and which followed Paul to Berea, Acts xvii. Or were they false brethren crept into the church? as he complains of his perils by them, 2 Cor. xi. 26; which some think most probable, by what he adds, *for all men have not faith,* even of those that make profession. Why may not we take in all these? But whoever they were, he styles them, first, *unreasonable men,* men out of place, as the word imports; taken either literally, for vagrants, wanderers, not keepers at home; or such as follow the apostle from place to place, to hinder his ministry. Or logically, for men that argued absurdly, and kept to no sound topics in reasoning; either false teachers among the Jews, or the heathen philosophers, such as he met with at Athens, whom he disputed with, Acts xvii. Or morally, for men that had corrupt principles and practices, that kept not to the duty of their place and station, *(desordonnez,* French translation,) and wandered out of the path of righteousness. We render it *unreasonable men;* men transported with fury and passion against all reason, as we read of the Jews, Acts xvii. 5. Or such as acted contrary to reason, as the apostle speaks of such Jews in the former Epistle, who were *contrary to all men, forbidding* them *to preach to the Gentiles, that they might be saved,* 1 Thess. ii. 15, 16. Or men of sensual lives, living more like brutes than reasonable creatures. Secondly, *wicked men;* so that whoever they were, whether Jews or Gentiles, teachers or the common people, learned or unlearned, they were wicked; and whatever was meant by the former word, yet this is plain; and the word imports either men that are laborious in wickedness, or that by their wickedness create labour and trouble to others. And such the apostle met with at Thessalonica, Jews who took to them *certain lewd fellows of the baser sort,* and drew Jason and others before the rulers, assaulting his house, Acts xvii. 5, 6: and indeed wherever they came, they met with such kind of men. Through the lusts of men's hearts, and the enmity and malice of the devil, faithful ministers will meet with opposition, and such as will hinder what they can the free course of the word. And therefore the apostle desires prayer to be *delivered from* them, ἵνα ῥυσθῶμεν, the word signifies a rescue by strength from some impending or incumbent evil, oft used, Luke i. 74; Col. i. 13; 1 Thess. i. 10. And he desires deliverance rather for the gospel's sake than his own. And though it is honourable to suffer for the gospel, yet it is desirable to be kept out of the hands of such men as these. The apostle subjoins the reason why men are thus, *for all men have not faith.* He needed not say this of infidels, which all men know to be without it, and therefore it is thought the apostle here means professors. There may be true faith wanting where faith is professed. Faith is sometimes taken for fidelity, a moral virtue, and some think is meant here, because it follows in the next verse by way of antithesis, *But the Lord is faithful.* But rather, I take it for a theological grace; for that true evangelical faith which purifies the heart, and worketh by love, and brings forth the acts of obedience to all God's commandments. Had they this faith they would not be unreasonable and wicked. But can we suppose such to be in the church? As well as those, 2 Tim. iii. 5, whom the apostle describes to have a *form of godliness* under all that wickedness he there mentions. But let men have civility, sobriety, external devotion, and profession, yet if they oppose the gospel, in the power, purity, and progress of it, they may be styled unreasonable and wicked men; and from such men we may pray, as the apostle desired here, Good Lord, deliver us. And it is the duty of people with respect to their faithful ministers, and the work of the gospel in their hands, to pray that they may be delivered from such men.

3 But ^dthe Lord is faithful, who shall stablish you, and ^ekeep *you* from evil.

d 1 Cor. 1. 9. 1 Thess. 5. 24.
e John 17.15. 2 Pet. 2. 9.

These words are added by way of consolation: 1. With respect to their establishment, which the apostle had before prayed for, chap. ii. 17, and here he assures them of it. What God hath promised, yet we may and ought to pray for; and ministers should exhort people to seek that grace which they may be sure beforehand God will give. And this establishment respects either their mind, in the belief of the gospel against false doctrine; or their hearts, against inordinate fears of men; or their practice, against departing from the way of holiness. The apostle well knew the tenure of the new covenant, which contains promises of perseverance and establishment, as well as of pardoning mercy and sanctifying grace, Jer. xxxii. 40; and he grounds his confidence of their establishment upon God's faithfulness, as upon the same account he comforts the Corinthians, 1 Cor. x. 13, and these Thessalonians. 1 Thess. v. 24, and it may be the apostle hath here reference to what he had said before; Though we shall meet with wicked and unreasonable men, yet fear not, God will establish you, for he is faithful. As God's promises are according to his purposes, so his performances will be according to his promises, which is his faithfulness. 2. As God would *establish* them, so *keep* them *from evil.* There is moral and penal evil, of sin and suffering; the Greek word imports the former; never used but for sinful evil, or sometimes for the devil, with respect to the sin that dwells in him, and occasioned by him, Eph. vi. 16; 1 John v. 18. And it is true, that God will keep his people from the devil, as some read the word. But I suppose the apostle means here by *evil,* evil work; as he speaks, 2 Tim. iv. 18, *The Lord shall deliver me from every evil work.* But whether the evil work of others, or their own? the latter I incline to, for he could not well assure them of the former. But how could he assure them of the latter? did he think God would keep them from all sin? The apostle doth not mean so, nor say so; God keeps his people from much evil and sin which others fall into, though not from all. And he keeps them

II. THESSALONIANS III

from falling under the power of it. Though they may be tempted by Satan, the world, or their own hearts, yet not so as finally to be overcome. However, the more God doth establish his people, the more will they be kept from evil. And the apostle doth also comfort them in this from the consideration of God's faithfulness. But these promises of God's keeping us do not exclude our endeavours of keeping ourselves: *He that is begotten of God keepeth himself, and that wicked one toucheth him not,* 1 John v. 18. Hence those exhortations, *Keep thy heart with all diligence,* Prov. iv. 23, and *Keep yourselves in the love of God,* Jude 21, &c. And our keeping is ascribed to our own faith with the power of God, 1 Pet. i. 5.

f 2 Cor. 7. 16.
Gal. 5. 10.

4 And ᶠwe have confidence in the Lord touching you, that ye both do and will do the things which we command you.

The apostle had before declared his confidence that God would establish them and keep them from evil, and now here declares his confidence in them concerning their obedience; for he knew well that this is the way of God's keeping men; and hereby he shows that he built his confidence concerning what he had before declared about their election, calling, establishment, and preservation upon some good ground. And he describes their obedience by doing what the apostle and his fellow labourers in the gospel among them commanded them, whether they were commandments about the duties of the law of the first or second tables, or the doctrine, order, worship, or discipline of the gospel; so that their commandments were no other but the commandments of the Lord himself, Matt. xxviii. 20; 1 Cor. xiv. 37. Ministers are not arbitrary commanders in the church; not *lords over God's heritage,* 1 Pet. v. 3, or have dominion over the people's *faith,* 2 Cor. i. 24; nor may they, as the Pharisees, teach *for doctrines the commandments of men,* Matt. xv. 9. And he speaks before of these Thessalonians, that they received the word preached by them, *not as the word of men, but of God,* 1 Thess. ii. 13. Both our faith and practice in religion are to be built upon Divine authority; either upon what God hath expressly declared, or what by clear consequence may be derived from it. So that what they command the people is from the Lord, and not themselves. Their work is to search out the mind and will of Christ, as revealed in the Scripture, seeing they have not that immediate infallible inspiration that the apostles had, who were called to lay the foundation which others were to build upon. And as to those things that are but appendices, and not of the substance of religion, and for which no particular rule is or can be laid down, Christian prudence is to regulate them according to general rules, wherein the advice, appointment, and authority of the minister is to be regarded in every church. Yet nothing ought to be enjoined in these things that is uncomely, that is not for edification, that is not of good report, that hath an appearance of evil, that gives just occasion of offence, that transgresseth the general rule of mercy, that is a direction of superstition, whereby many of the commandments of the Romish Church are justly condemned. And obedience to these commandments of the apostle he describes by the universality of it, *the things that we command you;* that is, all things; the indefinite being equivalent to the universal. And by the constancy of it, *that ye both do and will do,* &c.; ye will persevere to do what commandments ye have already received, or any new commandments we shall further give you; some whereof are probably such as are mentioned in the following part of this chapter. And their present obedience gave the apostle confidence about that which was future; at least he declares to them this confidence, as an insinuating argument to persuade them thereunto.

g 1 Chron. 29. 18.
‖ Or, *the patience of Christ.*
1 Thess. 1. 3.

5 And ᵍthe Lord direct your hearts into the love of God, and ‖ into the patient waiting for Christ.

Here the apostle prays for them again, as he had done a little before, chap. ii. 17; and as this shows how much they were in his heart, so the frequent mingling of prayers with his exhortations shows they could not be effectual without God. And he prays for two things: 1. To have their hearts directed *into the love of God;* which is either meant passively, for God's love to them, to have their hearts, that is,

their whole soul, engaged in the study, contemplation, and admiration of this love; or rather actively, for their love to God, to have their hearts set straight into the love of God, as the Greek word imports; drawn out towards him as a straight line to its centre, or as an arrow directed to the mark. Till man's love is set upon God, the motions of the heart are crooked and irregular; as the ways of sin are called *crooked ways,* Psal. cxxv. 5; and John Baptist's ministry was to make crooked things straight, Isa. xl. 4. The turning man's heart and ways towards God makes them straight. David prays, Psal. cxix. 36, *Incline my heart unto thy testimonies;* השׂמי or, bend my heart; as we bend a crooked stick to make it straight. Or as he prays God to unite his heart to his fear, Psal. lxxxvi. 11; so here Paul, to direct theirs to his love, by which some understand all religion. We learn hence, that to direct man's heart to the love of God is the work of God, and beyond our power. And the hearts of the best saints stand in need of a more perfect and constant direction unto the love of God. Patient sufferings for Christ's sake; as the apostle calls his sufferings for Christ's sake, *the sufferings of Christ,* often, 2 Cor. i. 5; Phil. iii. 10, &c.; and patience for his sake, is called the *patience of Christ,* Rev. i. 9. In this sense, the apostle prays they may have hearts ready to suffer, and patiently to suffer for Christ's sake, Heb. x. 36; James v. 10; and suited to a suffering state, which the heart is naturally averse and disinclined unto. And the word is often used in this sense for patience under the cross. And so the apostle hath his eye in his prayer upon the suffering state these believers were in for Christ's sake. If the sense be rendered as in our translation, he prays for their hearts to be fixed upon the coming of Christ, to look towards it, and patiently to wait for it; the Greek word being often taken for the patience of expectation as well as of suffering, Rom. viii. 25; Heb. x. 36: and so it is the same as waiting for the Son of God from heaven, mentioned 1 Thess. i. 10, and looking for the Saviour, Phil. iii. 20; that hereby they might not faint under his sufferings, nor be surprised by his coming. And because the hearts of the best are apt either to be remiss or secure upon the delay of Christ's coming, he therefore prays their hearts might be directed to a patient waiting for it, as the apostle Peter upon the same account exhorts believers to the girding up the loins of their mind, 1 Pet. i. 13.

h Rom. 16. 17. ver. 14.
1 Tim. 6. 5.
2 John 10.
1 Cor. 5. 11, 13.
k 1 Thess. 4. 11. & 5. 14, ver. 11, 12, 14.
1 ch. 2. 15.

6 Now we command you, brethren, in the name of our Lord Jesus Christ, ʰthat ye withdraw yourselves ⁱfrom every brother that walketh ᵏdisorderly, and not after ˡthe tradition which he received of us.

Here the apostle proceeds to a discourse of another kind, which is about their carriage to disorderly members in the church. And having before declared his confidence, ver. 4, that they did and would do the things he commanded them, he now tells them what he commands; and because either it is a matter of great importance, or that which they would be backward in, he therefore speaks with great vehemence. When he spake in the former Epistle, chap. v. 14, of warning the unruly, he then spake with greater mildness, *We exhort you, brethren,* &c.; but now to withdraw from them is a harsher duty; or they having first warned them, if they reform not, next they are to proceed to withdraw from them. And this he now commands as that which he supposeth they might be backward to. Παραγγέλλομεν, the word properly signifies a command conveyed from another, so the apostle commands here *in the name of the Lord Jesus Christ.* Though he had authority to command as an apostle, yet it was derived to him from Christ, and therefore he usually conjoins Christ with his exhortations and commands. *That ye withdraw yourselves from every brother;* or avoid, as the word signifies, and is so rendered, 2 Cor. viii. 20. The word is used also, Gal. ii. 12, of Peter's withdrawing himself from eating with the Gentiles; and rendered drawing back, Heb. x. 38, alluding, as some think, there to a soldier that draws back from the battle; but here in the text to a mariner that steers his ship from the rocks; and so it implies the danger of not withdrawing, which may be the reason of the apostle's so solemn command about it. And it is not from a heathen man, but a *brother*, one that is of the church; and it is *every brother*, let him be rich or poor, high or low, &c.; as he writes to the Corinthians, 1 Cor. v. 11, *If any man that is called a brother be a fornicator*, &c. *That walketh disorderly*: alluding, as some think, to soldiers who keep not their rank, not walking according to rule, or, as he expresseth it, *not after the tradition which he received of us*. What is to be meant by *tradition*, is explained in the former chapter. And he cannot be understood to speak here of rites and ceremonies relating to church worship or order, as some imagine; the apostle doth in the following verses explain himself otherwise. But what is this withdrawing? Is it excommunication, the greater or the less? In a general sense it may be so called, for it is an abstaining from communion; but it is not so properly, for that is called putting away a person, a purging out the old leaven, 1 Cor. v. 7, this is only a withdrawing from him; much less is it a delivering up to Satan, which the apostle required, 1 Cor. v. 5, and himself inflicted upon Hymeneus and Alexander, 1 Tim. i. 20. The nature of the crime here mentioned will not bear that. It was not incest or blasphemy, as in the former instances, but only disorderly walking, which he specifies afterwards. And with respect to such the apostle required in the former Epistle warning only, *Warn the unruly*. And though this is something more, yet it implies not a casting a man out of the church, which is Christ's visible kingdom, into Satan's kingdom, for he is still to be admonished *as a brother*, as ver. 15. And excommunication is the exerting an act of church power, as 1 Cor. v. 4, whereof no mention is made here; or of an absolute rejection, which is elsewhere required, Tit. iii. 10. It seems then to be only a withdrawing from familiar converse and society, as 1 Cor. v. 11, *If any man that is called a brother be a fornicator, covetous*, &c.; *with such an one no not to eat;* alluding to the custom of the Jews, who would not eat with the Gentiles; and by eating is expressed communion in Scripture, and profane writers also. And such communion is forbidden to such a brother, which the apostle allowed them to have with such sinners that were of the world, and not of the church, as ver. 10, which cannot be meant of sacred communion. And familiarity with such a brother would harden him in his sins, and reflect dishonour upon religion, and endanger their infection, more than with a pagan, or infidel: which therefore the apostle forbids them to a brother, as he did the Corinthians mentioned before, as also the Romans, chap. xvi. 17. And which may be a step towards excommunication from spiritual communion, which is the greater punishment, especially if the brother be not hereby made ashamed, and reform his course, and doth not only now and then do a disorderly action, but *walketh disorderly*, and that after warning also. Others think it is meant of excommunication, and judge not the reason against it to be cogent.

^{m 1 Cor. 4. 16. & 11. 1. 1 Thess. 1. 6, 7. n 1 Thess. 2. 10.}
7 For yourselves know ^m how ye ought to follow us: for ⁿ we behaved not ourselves disorderly among you;

Whereby the apostle intimates the aggravation of their crime who did walk disorderly, and so justifies the withdrawing from them. For they would be reproved not only by his doctrine, but example: what he required of others he practised himself, and that in some cases for this end alone, that he might be an example; examples teaching more than precepts, especially in ministers. And they did not only know how the apostle and his fellow ministers walked among them, but their end therein, whereby they knew they ought to follow them, and how to follow them; being guided as well as excited by their example. And this is expressed more generally. First, negatively, *We behaved not ourselves disorderly among you*, which he speaks not in a way of self-commendation, but for their imitation; and he useth here the same word to express his own practice which he did in theirs, being properly a military word, as was said before. He went before them as a captain before the army, and taught them order by his own example; for in the negative the positive is included.

^{o Acts 18 3. & 20. 34. 2 Cor. 11. 9. 1 Thess. 2. 9.}
8 Neither did we eat any man's bread for nought; but ^o wrought with labour and travail night and day, that we might not be chargeable to any of you:

Neither did we eat any man's bread for nought: the apostle here gives a particular positive instance of what before he speaks negatively, and in general; and brings his discourse home to the present case, and declares his orderly working in this, that he wrought for his own bread, and did not eat for nought, or live upon that which was freely given. Δωρεὰν· the word is sometimes taken for that which is without effect, as Gal. ii. 21, answering to the Hebrew word *Chinnam*, oft used, Psal. vii. 4; xxv. 3; lxix. 4; cxix. 61. Or, that which is without cause; and that either with respect to injury received, as John xv. 25, or benefit bestowed, as Rom. iii. 24, when it is freely given without merit. The apostle means that he preached the gospel to them freely, as he tells the Corinthians, 2 Cor. xi. 7. Though if he had received maintenance for his labour in the gospel among them, it was that which he well deserved, and he had not eaten their bread for nought; but he wrought with his own hands to maintain himself, as he did at Corinth, Acts xviii. 3. *But wrought with labour and travail;* and he wrought laboriously, with wearisome and toilsome labour, as the words import; and that *night and day;* as he had told them in the former Epistle, chap. ii. 9; only he speaks of it here upon a different account; there, to clear his ministry from suspicion of covetousness, and to evidence his sincere affection to them; here, to set before them an example of industry against such who lived idly, and did eat others' bread. Had he not wrought with his hands, he had not walked disorderly; but lest any should think so, he would do it to take away all occasion of evil. For though the labour of the ministry in the exercise of the mind and study may be reckoned as the greatest, yet most people cannot judge of it, and think it such; and though he had *power to forbear working*, as he tells the Corinthians, 1 Cor. ix. 6, yet he would do it rather than any good should be hindered, or any evil furthered thereby.

9 ^pNot because we have not power, but to make ^qourselves an ensample unto you to follow us. ^{p 1 Cor. 9. 6. 1 Thess. 2. 6. q ver. 7.}

The contents of this verse are already spoken to in the former, only the apostle asserts the right of maintenance due to the ministry by the name of *power*. It may be claimed by authority from Christ, though it should not be commanded by any laws from men. As the priests under the law had their maintenance settled upon them by the law of God; *so hath the Lord ordained that they which preach the gospel should live of the gospel*, 1 Cor. ix. 14; Gal. vi. 6. And though this power may be claimed, yet in some cases it is to be denied, as the apostle did, 1 Cor. ix. 12, *We have not used this power; lest we should hinder the gospel of Christ*. And so he did here, to make himself an example, τύπον, which signifies any mark that is cut or engraven to stamp things into its own likeness; oft used in the New Testament, and variously applied. *But to make ourselves an ensample unto you to follow us*: it is desirable to follow good examples, but more to become a good example: and as the old verse is true, *Regis ad exemplum*, &c., so the old proverb, "Like priests, like people;" and to follow them is to imitate them, as 1 Cor. xi. 1, *Be ye followers of me, even as I also am of Christ*. He is the first pattern, and others are to be regulated by it; and so far, and no further, to be imitated. As ministers ought to be patterns, Tit. ii. 7; 1 Pet. v. 3; so the people ought to be followers, and their sin will be the greater if they follow not their doctrine, when it is exemplified in their practice.

10 For even when we were with you, this we commanded you, ^rthat if any would not work, neither should he eat. ^{r Gen. 3. 19. 1 Thess. 4. 11.}

The words contain a reason, as the illative *for* imports; but what it refers to is uncertain; most probably a further reason of the apostle's working with his hands, because when with them he left this command, *that if any would not work, neither should he eat;* he would therefore practise himself what he commanded them, and not be thought to be as the Pharisees, binding heavy burdens upon others, and he not touch them himself. And this is another of the commandments which the apostle gave them, which he declared his confidence that they would do, ver. 4. And this command seems grounded upon the law given to Adam,

In the sweat of thy face shalt thou eat bread, Gen. iii. 19. For when he recommends a practice not directly grounded upon some word of God, or of Christ, or from infallible inspiration, he calls it a *permission,* as 1 Cor. vii. 6; but when otherwise, he saith, *I command, yet not I, but the Lord,* ver. 10; and calls it *the commandment of the Lord,* 1 Cor. xiv. 37. And this in the text is not his alone, but the Lord's, and is elsewhere mentioned, as Eph. iv. 28, *Let him that stole steal no more, but work with his hands,* &c.: see 1 Cor. vii. 20. God requires it of us as men, that we may be profitable in the commonwealth, supply our own wants and of those that depend upon us, and have wherewith also to supply the wants of the poor. Eph. iv. 28, to be kept from the temptations of idleness. Christianity doth not extinguish the profitable laws of nature or nations. Yet this general command admits limitations; if men have ability and opportunity to work, or if the ends of working are not otherwise supplied. For he that lives out of the reason of the law seems not bound by the law; or if the work be mental, and not manual, the law is fulfilled; and the equity of the law reacheth all men so far, as that none ought to be idle and useless in the world. And the apostle's argument for it in the text is cogent from nature itself; agreeably to that of Solomon, Prov. xvi. 26, *He that laboureth laboureth for himself, for his mouth craveth it of him.* Whereupon some judge these believing Thessalonians to be generally a people that lived by some handicraft trade, or some other manual labour. And the eating here intended is meant of relief from the stock and charge of the church: such should not be relieved *who would not work,* as it is in the text; who could, but would not, the fault being in the will.

11 For we hear that there are some ⁸which walk among you disorderly, ᵗworking not at all, but are busybodies.

For we hear : the apostle gives the reason of this discourse he fell into about disorder, and commends, yea, commands, a remedy against it. He had heard of this disorderly walking, else his discourse might have been esteemed vain and needless. Reports are to obtain credit according to the quality of the person that makes them, his end therein, and probability of truth. He took notice of reports brought to him about the divisions that were at Corinth, 1 Cor. xi. 18. *That there are some among you :* and the persons that he here chargeth the report upon, are not all, but some only, and he nameth none; for as to the body of the church, he had confidence they did, and would do, the things he commanded, ver. 4. And he requires them to withdraw from the disorderly. *Which walk among you disorderly, working not at all :* and the disorder he chargeth upon these *some* is, 1. Μηδὲν ἐργαζομένους, that they worked not at all, at least not the work of their own place, as it follows. 2. *But are busybodies ;* busy, and yet idle, and not working; περιεργαζομένους· *curieusement,* French Bible; as the *curious arts* of sorcerers are called περίεργα, Acts xix. 19. The word signifies working about, and denotes either vain curiosity, meddling in matters that they ought not, or going round their proper work, but not falling or fixing upon it. The same the apostle speaks of younger widows, 1 Tim. v. 13, who learnt *to be idle,* and yet were *busybodies ;* and such are called ἀλλοτριοεπίσκοποι, 1 Pet. iv. 15. And the one follows from the other; for they that are idle and neglect their own business will be apt to intermeddle in another's : and they that are not keepers at home, will be gadders abroad, and so not eat their own, but others' bread, which the apostle here reproves, as dishonourable to the Christian profession; and, as a further remedy, doth with much earnestness address his speech particularly to them.

12 ᵘNow them that are such we command and exhort by our Lord Jesus Christ, ˣthat with quietness they work, and eat their own bread.

Now them that are such we command and exhort by our Lord Jesus Christ : he had before given command to the church to withdraw from them, ver. 6; and now he lays he commandment upon themselves, and that in the name of Christ. *That with quietness they work :* working is set opposite to their idleness, and quietness to their busy meddling where they ought not, whereby they might occasion strife. The apostle here, and in many other places, requires Christians to live peaceably, as 2 Cor. xiii. 11; Col. iii. 15; 1 Thess. v. 13; Heb. xii. 14. *And eat their own bread ;* not to live as drones, upon another's labours; yet he forbids not dealing their bread to the hungry, nor requires this of the poor that are necessitated to live upon alms. And by eating *their own bread* the apostle means, maintaining themselves and families, for bread is taken in Scripture for all things that maintain the natural life : and the apostle here insinuates a blessing upon honest labour, that thereby men shall have bread of their own; and doth assert property against that community which some have pleaded for, the civil right that men have to what they honestly get and possess; but hereby condemns oppressors, pirates, robbers, cheaters, usurpers, yea, and tyrannical princes, who maintain themselves upon the spoil of others, and take their bread out of others' mouths; and why not also such as are not quiet and contented with their own portion, but either envy others, or murmur against providence?

13 But ye, brethren, ʸ‖be not weary in well doing.

But ye, brethren : the apostle now directs his speech to those of the church that were not guilty of the disorders before mentioned, to whom he speaks in mild and familiar language, as if the others deserved not to be so called. *Be not weary in well doing :* and that which he speaks to them is, not to be weary of well doing. The Greek word is often used about sufferings, as 2 Cor. iv. 1; Eph. iii. 13; and then usually translated fainting, and which seems to be its most proper use, to shrink or faint as cowards in war; Μὴ ἐκκακήσητε, *Ne segnescite, definite, defatigamini;* it signifies a receding or fainting, or tiring in our duty, because of the evil that attends it. Sometimes it is used of prayer, Luke xviii. 1; and sometimes generally of all duties of religion, which are generally called *well doing,* Gal. vi. 9, and signifies either a slothfulness in them, or weariness of them : as those whom the prophets complain of, Amos viii. 5; Mal. i. 13. The apostle useth the same word in this sense, Gal. vi. 9, *Let us not be weary in well doing;* and in the text, those that did walk orderly, he exhorts them to hold on their course, either more peculiarly to the works of charity, which are called well doing, Phil. iv. 14; though those that worked not did not deserve them, or enjoy them, yet this should not discourage them from practising them towards others : or the word may extend more generally to all good works; we should persevere in them without fainting or weariness, notwithstanding the evils that may threaten us therein.

14 And if any man obey not our word ‖ by this epistle, note that man, and ᶻhave no company with him, that he may be ashamed.

Here we have further commandments given concerning the disorderly; in case of obstinacy, to proceed further against them. The apostle had given commandments about their walking in his first preaching to them, after that he repeats them in his First Epistle, and again in this Second. *And now if any man obey not our word by this epistle,* saith he, *note that man ;* and he would have none excepted, either through fear or favour, and nothing done by partiality, 1 Tim. v. 21. What is meant by noting is disputed among expositors; more seems to be meant than marking them, Rom. xvi. 17. Some take it for what we call excommunication; so Aug. lib. 3, Cont. Epist. Parmen. cap. 4. Theophyl. in locum; either the casting him out of the church, which is the greater, or suspension from the Lord's supper, which is the lesser. As there were degrees of church censure among the Jews, so also we read practised in the gospel church, as is evident in the councils. Others think it is no more than a withdrawing from him, as was mentioned before, ver. 6; but then the apostle saith the same thing over again, which seemeth needless. And he speaks here of some greater contumacy than before, when his word in this Second Epistle is not obeyed. We may suppose the apostle may mean not only a withdrawing from familiarity with him, but exposing his name to some public notice in the church, that both his crime and his name should be publicly noticed; as the apostle speaks of Hymeneus and Alexander, and Philetus, by name in his Epistles that were made public. Σημειοῦσθε, note him by a sign, as the word signifies, which cannot well be done by a mere withdrawing. And seeing he speaks here of one that is not only disorderly, but obstinate, some further and more signal act of discipline is to be inflicted on him. And what word the apostle refers to in this Epistle as not obeyed is not expressed, neither need we limit it, but it may be meant of all his commandments herein, to which obedience was required. And the word, as written, is the word of God, and is to be obeyed as well as that which is preached. I know there is another reading of the text, If any man obey not our word, note that man by an epistle; and so it is in our margins. But this is not probable. By an epistle? to whom? to the apostle himself? And for what? to know how to proceed towards such a one? What need that, when he here gives direction about it to them; which follows. *And have no company with him;* or be not mingled with him, which refers either to his crime, as the Greek word is so applied, Eph. v. 11, or to his person also, as the word is used, 1 Cor. v. 9. And yet some think the apostle here forbids only civil communion, not sacred, because the word in the text is generally so used, and so rendered by expositors; but sacred communion is expressed in the New Testament by another word, 1 John i. 3. And if meant of sacred, it is then casting him out of the church, which is a delivering him up to Satan: see Estius in loc. And that seems not to agree with what follows, *Admonish him as a brother;* and so not to be accounted as a heathen or a publican, Matt. xviii. 17. And we know admonition goes before casting out. But to be thrust out of the company of the people of God in all civil, friendly society, is a great punishment and affliction. And some think, that the noting of him was to be done by the governors of the church, and the renouncing his company, by all the people: let the reader judge. *That he may be ashamed:* the end of both is here expressed. This is not added before as a reason of withdrawing, and therefore some think the apostle required that only to avoid the infection of sin by familiar society; but this further proceeding here mentioned is to make the man ashamed that is obstinate in disobedience; but we need not so limit it. And this making him ashamed is not to be out of hatred to his person, but for his good, as all church censures ought to be so intended, to bring him to that shame that may be the first step to true repentance. There is a shamefulness in sin; and when sinners repent, they see it, and are ashamed, Isa. i. 29; Ezek. xvi. 61; Rom. vi. 21; and God complains of sinners when not ashamed, Jer. iii. 3. Shame is a natural affection in men, and is not in the nature of beasts, neither was it in man before the fall; and though in itself it is no virtue, being the proper effect of sin, yet it is of use to restrain much open wickedness, and to keep decorum in men's outward actions: and God makes use of it also in leading men to true repentance. To shame men out of envy or hatred is sinful, and against the law of charity; but to do it to bring them to repentance, is better than by flattery or familiar society to harden them in sin.

a Lev. 19.17.
1 Thes. 5. 14.
b Tit. 3. 10.
15 ªYet count *him* not as an enemy, ᵇbut admonish *him* as a brother.

They having thus proceeded against the disorderly and disobedient, the apostle directs them about their after-carriage, which either respects their inward opinion of the mind, or outward action. *Yet count him not as an enemy;* they should not count him an enemy, putting a great difference betwixt an offending brother and a professed enemy. They ought not to hate him as an enemy, nor look upon him as upon such who out of enmity to the gospel persecute Christianity, nor to have an unreconcilable mind towards him. *But admonish him as a brother;* and as to outward action, should admonish him as a brother. It is either private or public, ministerial or fraternal, gentle or severe, joined with commination. The Greeks express it in the degrees of it by three words, νουθεσία, ἐπιτιμία, ἐπίπληξις. The word in the text signifies a putting in mind: they were to put the offender in mind of his sin, and in mind of his duty. Though they were to have no company with him in a way of familiarity, yet to be in his company so as to admonish him; and the admonition here meant is either public, in the church, or private; or first private, then public, as our Saviour gives the rule, Matt. xviii. 15—17. So that his repentance is to be endeavoured not only by abstaining his company, but by admonition. And it is to be performed to him *as a brother*, which either respects the state of the person admonished: he is not an enemy, or pagan, or one out of the visible church, but a brother, whereby some conceive that the apostle had not before spoken of his excommunication. Or it respects the way of admonition: it is to be performed with love, tenderness, and compassion, as to a brother, not to upbraid him, but to gain him; as Matt. xviii. 15, *If he shall hear thee, thou hast gained thy brother.* And for that end great prudence is to be used. The temper of the offenders, the quality of the sin, their outward condition in the world, their age, yea, the circumstances of time and place, are to be considered.

16 Now ᶜthe Lord of peace himself give you peace always by all means. The Lord *be* with you all.

c Rom. 15. 33. & 16. 20.
1 Cor. 14. 33.
2 Cor. 13. 11.
1 Thes. 5. 23.

Now the Lord of peace himself give you peace: the apostle is now taking his leave, and closing up his Epistle; and this he doth with prayer; and what he prays for is peace: and though the word peace hath various acceptations, and is of comprehensive signification, yet here it is to be understood of brotherly peace and unity. Whether it was occasioned by any dissensions that were actually among them, or his fears of such to arise upon the practice of their duties to the disorderly among them, that he thus prays, is uncertain. And it is that which he much presseth and prays for in his several Epistles to the churches, as being that wherein the honour of the gospel, and their own comfort and edification, were so much concerned. And the person he prays to he styles *the Lord of peace*, whereby I suppose he means Jesus Christ, who is sometimes called *the Prince of Peace*, Isa. ix. 6; as God is called *the God of peace*, 1 Thess. v. 23. It is he that hath made peace betwixt God and us, betwixt the Jew and Gentile, and it is one of the fruits of his Spirit in the hearts of Christians, Gal. v. 22. True Christian peace is the gift of Christ, and therefore the apostle prays the Lord to give it, and saith, *the Lord himself*, as intimating none but he can give it, and that it is a singular blessing to enjoy it, as we must so interpret the phrase when at any other time we find it, as 1 Thess. v. 23. *Always by all means:* he shows both the desirableness and difficulty of peace. It is worth the using all endeavours for it, and without such we shall hardly attain it, as Rom. xii. 18, *If it be possible, as much as lieth in you, live peaceably with all men;* quite contrary to the temper and practice of some men, who will live peaceably with no man: and elsewhere we read of following peace; Heb. xii. 14, and seeking peace and pursuing it, 1 Pet. iii. 11, and *endeavouring to keep the unity of the Spirit in the bond of peace*, Eph. iv. 3. And the apostle prays for it in the text with much earnestness, and that they might enjoy it without interruption, *always;* that there might be no schism rise up among them at any time. And if we read the next words, in every thing, he prays that their peace might be universal with respect to opinions, words, and actions. And as a final farewell he addeth, *The Lord be with you all;* which shows his affection to them all, though he had reproved sharply the disorders that some were guilty of. And a greater thing he could not desire for them, it comprehends all blessings in it, and the very blessedness of heaven itself; as a usual farewell word, Adieu, is a recommending a person to God.

17 ᵈThe salutation of Paul with mine own hand, which is the token in every epistle: so I write.

d 1 Cor. 16. 21. Col. 4. 18.

This the apostle addeth after he had finished his Epistle, and taken his farewell, as a proof that the Epistle was genuine, and came from himself; because it may be there were some then who did counterfeit his Epistles, as there have been many since who have counterfeited creeds, liturgies, gospels, writings of the fathers, &c., and he knew it might be of dangerous consequence to the churches, to have his writings counterfeited. Heretics in several ages, and the Church of Rome particularly, have herein been deeply guilty. And though it is probable the body of this Epistle was written by some amanuensis, as is evident of the Epistle to the Romans, that it was written by one Tertius, Rom. xvi. 22; and when he tells the Galatians, Gal. vi. 11, he wrote their Epistle with his own hand, so Philem. 19, it implies sometimes he did not so; yet this salutation he wrote with his own hand, which he practised not only in this, but in all his other Epistles, as he here affirmed. And he wrote it in such characters whereby his own hand might be known; else it was an easy matter for any impostor to write the same words. And the words of it are here set down, but elsewhere explained, and therefore nothing is further needful here.

18 ^eThe grace of our Lord Jesus Christ be with you all. Amen.   e Rom. 16. 24.

¶ The second *epistle* to the Thessalonians was written from Athens.

THE FIRST EPISTLE OF PAUL THE APOSTLE
TO
TIMOTHY

THE ARGUMENT

TIMOTHY is thought to have been a native of Lystra in Lycaonia, Acts xvi. 1. His mother, Eunice, was a Jewess, Acts xvi. 1; a believer, 2 Tim. i. 5. His father a Greek, Acts xvi. 1, but (possibly) proselyted to the Jewish religion. They gave Timothy his name, signifying thereby their pious desire that their son should fear and honour God, and be put in mind of his duty by his name. They bred him up in the knowledge of the Scriptures from a child. When it was he first became a disciple to Paul doth not appear; but it appears from 2 Tim. iii. 11, that he was with Paul at Antioch and Iconium, which was before he came to Lystra, Acts xvi. 1, where Paul circumcised him. After this Paul made him his companion, and sent him upon several messages. He was a sickly person, 1 Tim. v. 23, but eminent in gifts and graces, 2 Tim. i. 5; iii. 15; 1 Cor. iv. 17. After this he was ordained a minister by Paul and the presbytery, 2 Tim. i. 6. He became very dear to Paul for his faithfulness, Phil. ii. 19—21; so as he calls him his *beloved son, and faithful*, 1 Cor. iv. 17, his *son in the faith*, 1 Tim. i. 2, his *dearly beloved son*, his *fellow worker, fellow labourer*, &c. Paul left him a time at Thessalonica and Berea, Acts xvii. 13, 14; then sent for him to Athens, ver. 15. He came to him at Corinth, Acts xviii. 5. Thence he sent him into Macedonia, Acts xix. 22. From thence he came to Corinth, and goes with Paul into Asia, Acts xx. 4; where Paul entreats him to stay some time at Ephesus, as an evangelist, to settle the churches there, 2 Tim. iv. 5. From thence he sends for him to Rome, 2 Tim. iv. 9, and sends Tychicus in his room to Ephesus, ver. 12. Paul having left Timothy, a young man, in this great trust, being himself to be absent, writes this Epistle to him, to encourage him against all dangers, and to direct him in the management of his office. The scope of the Epistle is to direct Timothy in the first place, and then all ministers of the gospel, how to behave themselves in the ministerial work, as to preaching, praying, government, opposing gainsayers, &c.; so as it is the most perfect direction we have in all Scripture for the discharge of the ministerial office. The time when Paul wrote this Epistle is uncertainly judged, but guessed to be the one and twentieth year after Christ's death, and about the nineteenth after Paul's conversion; it is certain it was when he was in Macedonia, and before he returned to Ephesus, Acts xix. 1.

CHAP. I

The salutation, 1, 2. *Timothy is put in mind of the charge before given him by Paul*, 3, 4. *The end of the commandment is charity, from which some had turned aside to teach the law, which they understood not*, 5—7. *The scope of the law was to condemn wickedness, which is the design of the gospel also*, 8—11. *Paul blesseth God for calling him to the ministry notwithstanding his great demerit, whereby all penitent sinners that believe are assured of mercy through Christ*, 12—17. *He urgeth Timothy to a due discharge of his trust, warning him of some who had deserted the truth, of whom Hymeneus and Alexander had been delivered by him unto Satan*, 18—20.

A. D. 65.   PAUL, an apostle of Jesus Christ ^aby the commandment ^b of God our Saviour, and Lord Jesus Christ, ^c*which is* our hope;
a Acts 9. 15. Gal. 1. 1, 11.
b ch. 2. 3. & 4. 10. Tit. 1. 3. & 2. 10. & 3. 4. Jude 25.   c Col. 1. 27.

Paul, an apostle of Jesus Christ; one immediately sent by Jesus Christ, by his voice from heaven, Acts ix. 15, though not by his voice upon earth, as those, Matt. x. *By the commandment of God our Saviour, and Lord Jesus Christ: through the will of God,* 1 Cor. i. 1, not his permissive, but preceptive will; and this is the same with his being *called to be an apostle,* Rom. i. 1; 1 Cor. i. 1. But our *Lord Jesus Christ,* the Father not being excluded, but the Son only being named, to whom the mediatory kingdom was committed. *Which is our hope:* our *hope*, there is no more in the Greek, that is, the object of our hope: as when it is said, Gen. xxxi. 53, that *Jacob sware by the fear of his father Isaac,* that is, by the Deity whom his father feared. This glorious eulogy belongs to our Saviour, in whom there is a concurrence of all that is requisite to free us from destructive evils, and to make us everlastingly happy: for he is *wisdom, righteousness, sanctification, and redemption.* Hence the Gentiles without Christ are said to be without hope, Eph. ii. 12. And from hence it is evident that Jesus Christ is the eternal God, for if he were only a man, though in excellence above all others, he could not be our hope, for *cursed is he that trusteth in man,* Jer. xvii. 5.

2 Unto ^dTimothy, ^e*my* own son in the faith: ^fGrace, mercy, *and* peace, from God our Father and Jesus Christ our Lord.
d Acts 16. 1. 1 Cor. 4. 17. Phil. 2. 19. 1 Thess. 3. 2.
e Tit. 1. 4. f Gal. 1. 3. 2 Tim. 1. 2. 1 Pet. 1. 2.

He dignifies Timothy with the title of his *son in the faith;* that is, being converted to Christianity, and begat to the Divine life: and by styling Timothy his *own son,* he signifies his piety and virtue, that rendered him a worthy son of such a father, whom he imitated and honoured, and with whom he corresponded in a grateful, obedient affection. Having thus designated the person to whom he writes, he expresses his ardent desires of his complete felicity; which is included in *grace, mercy, and peace.* By *grace* he means the free favour and good will of God, with all the spiritual gifts that proceed from it, either requisite for salvation, or the great work of the evangelical ministry. By *mercy*, his compassionate tender love. pardoning, relieving, supporting, and assisting us in our Christian course. By *peace* he signifies. principally, the peace of God, that divine calm of conscience, that tranquillity and rest of soul, which proceeds from the assurance that God is reconciled to us in Christ, and our freedom by the sanctifying Spirit from the tyranny of carnal lusts: this peace can never be to the wicked. And besides this principal peace, we may understand peace with man, that is, a quiet state, exempt from hatred and persecutions, that Timothy might more comfortably and successfully perform the work of his ministry. He prays for these blessings *from God*, who is the original Fountain of all good : and from *Jesus Christ* as the channel, by which all the gifts of God are conveyed to us; for without his mediation the Deity is as a sealed fountain, no grace would flow to us. He styles God *our Father*, because he has adopted us in his Son, and in that quality he communicates his *grace, mercy, and peace* to us: he styles Christ *our Lord*, who hath supreme power over us, as well by the right of creation as of redemption.

3 As I besought thee to abide still at Ephesus, ^gwhen I went into Macedonia, that thou mightest charge some ^hthat they teach no other doctrine,

g Acts 20. 1,
3. Phil. 2.
24.
h Gal. 1. 6, 7.
ch. 6. 3, 10.

Ephesus was a great city in Asia the Less, whither Paul came, Acts xix. 1; where Demetrius raised a tumult against him, which the town clerk appeased, as we read there. From thence he *went into Macedonia*, Acts xx. 1—3. Upon this his motion into Macedonia (as divines judge) he left Timothy at Ephesus. The end of leaving him at Ephesus was, that he might *charge some that they* preached *no other doctrine*, that is, none contrary to what he had preached, none contrary to the doctrine of the gospel, Gal. i. 8, 9. What power was here committed to Timothy is by some questioned; supposing (which is very probable) there were a greater number of disciples than could meet in one assembly, his power was more than pastoral, for he had a power over the teachers. Whether this power was extraordinary, or ordinary, and what God intended ever to continue in the church, is the question. Those who make it to be such, make it to be episcopal; those that make it extraordinary, say it was the work of an evangelist, 2 Tim. iv. 5. That there was such an officer in the primitive church appears from Acts xxi. 8; Eph. iv. 11. That this was Timothy's work appears from 2 Tim. iv. 5. Nor is it a new thing, but very common in the settlement of all new governments, to authorize some special commissioners, and to give them an extraordinary power for a time, till the government can be settled and things brought into a fixed order. If we consider the words without prejudice, *I besought thee to abide still at Ephesus*, they seem to signify that Timothy was not the established bishop of Ephesus; for to what end should the apostle desire a bishop to reside in his own diocess, which he could not forsake without neglecting his duty, and the offence of God? This were a tacit reflection, as if he were careless of his duty. And the word *abide*, προσμεῖναι, does not necessarily import his constant residence there; for it is used to signify continuance for some time only; as it is said of the apostle, that he remained many days at Corinth, Acts xviii. 18, when his stay there was only for some months. The intention of the apostle seems to be that Timothy should continue for a while at Ephesus, and not accompany him in his voyage to Macedonia, as he was wont to do upon other occasions. And it is evident by the sacred history, that about six months after Timothy was with the apostle in Greece, that he went with him to Macedonia, and Troas, and Miletus, Acts xx. 1, 4, where the apostle sent for the elders or bishops of Ephesus, to leave his last solemn charge with them. In short, if Timothy had been appointed the bishop of Ephesus, the apostle would probably have given this title of honour to him in the inscription of his Epistle. Upon the impartial considering of the whole matter, though the passion of prelacy is so ingenious as to discover so many mysteries and mitres in a few plain words, (viz. that Timothy was bishop of that city, metropolitan of the province, and primate of all Asia,) yet it is most likely that Timothy was left only for some time with a kind of apostolical power in the church of Ephesus: of which power this was one branch, authoritatively to command seducers not to teach another doctrine than what was taught by the apostles, who were Divinely illuminated: a Divine rule, and most worthy of perpetual observation by all in the office of the ministry. And this showeth the mighty proneness of men, as to deviate in their conversations from the right ways, so in their judgments from the truths of God, otherwise Paul had no need to have left Timothy for that end in this church so newly planted.

4 ⁱNeither give heed to fables and endless genealogies, ^kwhich minister questions, rather than godly edifying which is in faith: *so do.*

i ch. 4. 7.
& 6. 4, 20.
2 Tim. 2. 14,
16, 23. Tit.
1. 14. & 3. 9.
k ch. 6. 4.

Neither give heed to fables : by *fables* he probably meaneth the *Jewish fables, and commandments of men*, mentioned Tit. i. 14; or more generally, all vain and idol speculations. *And endless genealogies, which minister questions, rather than godly edifying;* whatsoever tendeth not to build men up in godliness, which is the end of preaching. The Jews had many unwritten fables, about what God did before he made the world, &c., and many unwritten *endless genealogies*, which were as so many labyrinths, intricate, without an issue out of them: and it is probable that some of them (converted to the Christian faith) still busied their heads about them, according to their education and the practice of the Jewish doctors, and made the subject of their sermons and discourses to the assemblies of Christians; which is the thing the apostle here declareth a corruption of the ordinances of preaching, and inveigheth against, chap. vi. 4; 2 Tim. ii. 23; Tit. i. 14; iii. 9; and willeth preachers to avoid, and people to give no heed to them, as nothing tending to the building Christians up in holiness, which he here calleth οἰκοδομίαν Θεᾶ, the building up of God, either so objectively, or efficiently, or by his command, because it is in God, viz. in the knowledge of God, and an increase in the love of God, and other spiritual habits; or from God, being wrought by him, and serving for his honour and glory, or according to his will. *Which is in faith :* he tells us this edifying can be no otherwise than *in faith*, preaching the doctrine of the gospel, and embracing that which is the doctrine of faith, a doctrine of Divine revelation, to which men must give their assent, because of the authority of God revealing it. So as no discourses which are not founded in a Divine revelation, and to be proved from thence, can possibly tend to any building of God, which cannot stand in the wisdom of men, but must stand in the power of God. From this text we may observe the vanity and proneness of some persons, even from the infancy of the church, to make up what they call sermons of discourses about fables, idle questions, and speculations, and genealogies of which there is no end; the teachers being able to bring the minds of hearers to no rest about them, nor they tending to any good and saving use, but merely to show men's wit and parts; and we may also learn, that this is no religious preaching or hearing, it being impossible men should be under any religious obligations to hear any but prophets, that is, such as reveal the Divine will. For other discourses, men in their seasons may hear them, or let them alone, and credit or not credit them as they see reason.

5 Now ^lthe end of the commandment is charity ^m out of a pure heart, and *of* a good conscience, and *of* faith unfeigned:

l Rom. 13.
8, 10.
Gal. 5. 14.
m 2 Tim. 2.
22.

Now the end of the commandment is charity : the word translated *commandment* here is παραγγελία, which rather signifies a particular charge given by superiors as to some thing, than a general law, Acts v. 28; xvi. 24; and so in this chapter, ver. 18; which inclineth me to think, that though the proposition be true of the whole law of God, (for *love is the fulfilling of the law,*) and more eminently of the Divine doctrine in the gospel, for the end and perfection it aims at and produces is a pure, ardent love of God, and of men for his sake, and of the gospel, yet it is rather here to be restrained to the commandment relating to preaching, or discoursing the revealed will of God relating to men's salvation, *the end* of which is doubtless *charity*, which ought to be *finis operantis*, the end of the workman, what he ought to intend and aim at; and is *finis operis*, the effect of the work, viz. the begetting in the souls of people love to God and their neighbour, neither of which can rationally be obtained by preachers telling people idle stories, and filling their heads with idle questions and speculations. *Out of a pure heart:* which love to God and men must proceed from a clean, and holy, and sincere heart. *And of a good conscience;* and a good and holy life, when conscience doth not sourly reflect upon men for presumptuous miscarriages. *And of faith unfeigned;* which must all be rooted in and attended with a *faith unfeigned;* rooted in it, as faith signifies a steady assent to Divine revelation; attended with it, as it signifies the soul's repose and rest upon Christ for the fulfilling of the promises annexed to him that believes and liveth up to such propositions. These are the noble ends of the whole law of God, and particularly of the charge or command God hath given ministers as to preaching, which can by no means be attained by teachers' discoursing fables and endless genealogies to people, nor by people's attendance to such discourses, for they can only fill people's heads with notions and unprofitable questions, which serve to gender strife and contention amongst people, instead of love either to God or men, and so to defile instead of purifying the heart, and have no influence at all upon a holy life, all which can grow out of no root but an unfeigned faith.

l Or, *not aiming at.* n ch. 6. 4. 20.

6 From which some ‖ having swerved have turned aside unto ⁿ vain jangling;

From which; from which things (for the article is plural, ὦν); from which commandment, and from the end of which commandment, from which pure heart, good conscience, and faith unfeigned. *Some having swerved:* ἀστοχήσαντες, the word signifies to wander from a scope or mark. Some men either propounding to themselves ends in their discourses to people different from the command concerning preaching, and the true end of that, or at least wandering from that true end, they have turned aside. To do an action well, two things are necessary: 1. The propounding to ourselves a right end; 2. A moving to it by due means and in right order: whoso faileth in either of these, can no more do an action well, than he can shoot an arrow well, that either eyeth no mark, or levelleth his arrow quite beside it. The preachers reflected on by the apostle, either never considered the true end of preaching, or never regarded it in their action; this made them turn aside from theology to mataeology, from preaching to *vain jangling;* so we translate it, but the word signifieth foolish talking; so we translate the adjective, Tit. i. 10, and so the word properly signifieth, any kind of foolish, impertinent discourse, either serving to no good end, or at least not that which the discourse pretendeth to. And indeed all discourses of fables, and unprofitable, idle questions, tending not to edifying, is no better than foolish talking.

c ch. 6. 4.

7 Desiring to be teachers of the law; ᵒunderstanding neither what they say, nor whereof they affirm.

Desiring to be teachers of the law; Νομοδιδάσκαλοι. This term lets us know, that the apostle reflecteth upon some who were or had been Jews, who either pressed the observance of the law in order to justification, or spent their time in pressing the traditions of the elders, and constitutions of the scribes, as *sepimenta legis,* hedges (as they called them) to the Divine law, though not of the letter of it; upon which there arose a great many questions as insignificant as their traditions themselves, which these vain preachers spent their time in speaking to. *Understanding neither what they say, nor whereof they affirm;* neither understanding the Divine law, nor the questions themselves started and spoke unto, yet ambitious to be accounted *teachers of the law.* This vain desire of reputation, as persons of excellent skill in the land, was the cause of their erroneous, idle sermons: and their ignorance is aggravated and inexcusable, in that they with presumptuous boldness assert the things of which they are ignorant.

p Rom. 7. 12.

8 But we know that ᵖ the law *is* good, if a man use it lawfully;

But we know that the law is good: not that I speak against the law of God, I know that it is *holy, and spiritual, and just, and good,* Rom. vii. 12, 14. It is good, though not for justification, yet for conviction, to convince men of sin, and as a schoolmaster to lead men unto Christ, and to direct us in our walking with God; the equity and sanctity of its precepts are evident to the sincere and purified mind. *If a man use it lawfully:* and as the law has an intrinsic goodness in its nature, so it is good to men when it is used for the end to which God gave it.

q Gal. 3. 19. & 5. 23.

9 ᑫKnowing this, that the law is not made for a righteous man, but for the lawless and disobedient, for the ungodly and for sinners, for unholy and profane, for murderers of fathers and murderers of mothers, for manslayers,

By *the law* is to be understood the moral law, (though possibly not excluding the law of Moses, consisting in many ordinances,) as it is armed with stings and terrors, to restrain rebellious sinners; by the *righteous man,* one in whom a principle of Divine grace is planted, and, from the knowledge and love of God, chooses the things that are pleasing to him, and is ardent and active to do his will. Now it is true, the holiness commanded in the law, that consists in the love of God and our neighbour, obliges every reasonable creature indispensably and eternally; but as the law was delivered in so terrible a manner, as it has annexed so many severe threatenings to the transgressors of it, it is evident that it is directed to the wicked, who will only be compelled by fear from an outrageous breaking of it. And this may be emphatically signified in the word here used, κεῖται, for it signifies to be laid, as well as to be made. The law *non objicitur* is not laid against a righteous man. Thus we translate it, Matt. iii. 10, *The axe is laid unto the root of the trees:* there is some difference in the construction; here it is immediately joined with the dative case, there with an accusative case, with the preposition πρός betwixt the verb and the case; but that must be the sense. It is very probable, that these false teachers had been terrifying the Christians with the law, in opposition to whom the apostle saith, the law was not made for a righteous man, as to its condemning office; it was never intended against a righteous man, but against men that committed and lived in gross sin and wickedness. These sinners are first mentioned in general terms, then the apostle proceedeth to a more particular enumeration of them; whether in them (as some think) the apostle hath respect to the several precepts of the decalogue, I cannot determine. By *the lawless* he meaneth persons living without any respect to the laws of God or men. By the *disobedient* he meaneth such as will live in subjection to no government. The word by us translated *ungodly,* signifieth such as live without any religion, having no regard to the worship of God, ἀσεβέσι. The word translated *sinners* signifies infamous, scandalous sinners. *Unholy and profane* are also general terms, signifying persons that have no piety, but lewdly talk of things sacred, and live as lewdly. *Murderers of fathers and murderers of mothers:* the words signify such as strike or beat their parents, though they do not give them mortal wounds, and well expresseth violaters of the fifth commandment. *Manslayers,* ἀνδροφόνοις, signifies such as kill men, whether maliciously or passionately, violaters of the sixth commandment.

10 For whoremongers, for them that defile themselves with mankind, for menstealers, for liars, for perjured persons, and if there be any other thing that is contrary ʳ to sound doctrine;

r ch. 6. 3. 2 Tim. 4. 3. Tit. I. 9. & 2. 1.

The two next terms express violaters of the seventh commandment, whether by fornication, adultery, incest, sodomy, or any beastly lusts. *Men-stealers;* the word signifieth such as carry men into captivity, or make slaves of them in the first place; it signifies also any stealing of men. It is probable the first of these is the man-stealing principally intended, being the most common sin by pirates at sea, and soldiers at land; yet not excluding any other stealing of men from their relations, which he instanceth in, as one of the highest violations of the eighth commandment. By *liars* he meaneth such as knowingly speak what is false, especially to the prejudice of others. By *perjured persons* he means such as swear falsely. And be-

11 According to the glorious Gospel of ^sthe blessed God, ^twhich was committed to my trust.

<small>s ch. 6. 15. t 1 Cor. 9. 17. Gal. 2. 7. Col. 1. 25. 1 Thes. 2. 4. ch. 2. 7. 2 Tim. 1. 11. Tit. 1. 3.</small>

Here the apostle specifies the sound doctrine of which he spake; that it is contained in the gospel, the perfect rule of righteousness, which he styles *the glorious gospel of the blessed God*, it being a doctrine revealed from heaven, wherein the concurrence and command of the Divine attributes, wisdom, power, mercy, and justice, do most clearly shine to the glory of God, 2 Cor. iv. 6; Eph. i. 6, 12: and he gives the title of *blessed* to God, thereby to signify his transcendent goodness, in that, being infinitely happy in the possession of his own excellencies, without any possible advantage and profit from any creature, yet he was pleased to give his Son to be our ransom, and with him grace and glory to us. The apostle adds, *which was committed to my trust*, to distinguish it from the false doctrine which seducers published under the name of the gospel.

12 And I thank Christ Jesus our Lord, ^uwho hath enabled me, ^xfor that he counted me faithful, ^yputting me into the ministry;

<small>u 2 Cor. 12. 9. x 1 Cor. 7. 25. y 2 Cor. 3. 5, 6. & 4. 1. Col. 1. 25.</small>

Here St. Paul expresses his most humble and solemn thanks to Christ for his rich favour in calling him to the high office of an apostle, for by *the ministry* that is to be understood; and it is so called by way of excellence, it being the most glorious and Divine ministry that ever was established in the church: and he ascribes to our Saviour the praise of all that he performed in the faithful discharge of it. He saith, *Christ enabled me*, that is, endowed him with fidelity, zeal, courage, and all other qualifications requisite for that honourable and difficult ministry, 2 Cor. iii. 5, 6. The end of that sacred ministry was, to enlighten and reform the world from superstition, and that vicious and vain conversation that was so pleasing to carnal men, to abolish those corrupt customs that had taken such deep root, and to plant the truth that comes from above, and to publish a holy law so opposite to corrupt nature. This work was opposed by the craft and cruelty, the artifice and violence, of the powers of darkness, in conjunction with the perverted world; and the glory of the apostle's resisting such enemies is entirely due to Christ. He adds, as a motive of his thankfulness, that Jesus Christ *counted* him *faithful*, which is an evident proof that he intends that he made him faithful. His faithfulness was not the cause or motive, but the fruit and effect, of the grace of God in calling him to the ministry. This he expressly declares, 1 Cor. vii. 25, *hath obtained mercy to be faithful*. If our Saviour had only discovered his fidelity, without bestowing that grace upon him, there had not been a reason of such affectionate thanksgiving; for that always supposes some favour and benefit received.

13 ^zWho was before a blasphemer, and a persecutor, and injurious: but I obtained mercy, because ^aI did *it* ignorantly in unbelief.

<small>z Acts 8. 3. & 9. 1. 1 Cor. 15. 9. Phil 3. 6. a Luke 23. 34. John 9. 39, 41. Acts 3. 17. & 26. 9.</small>

The kindness of God in putting me into so noble a service was the greater and more thankworthy, because *before* that time I *was a blasphemer*, one who spake of Christ reproachfully, for that blasphemy signifieth. Paul was a zealous man in the Jewish religion, his blasphemy therefore only respected the Second Person in the Trinity, which the Jews owned not. Paul *compelled* others *to blaspheme*, Acts xxvi. 11. *And a persecutor:* of his persecution, see Acts viii. 3: he entered houses, haled men and women to prison; he breathed *threatenings and slaughter against the disciples of the Lord*, Acts ix. 1; he persecuted Christianity even to death, Acts xxii. 4, 5. Thus he was *injurious*, for in other things he was, as to *the law, blameless*, Phil. iii. 6, bred up a Pharisee according to the strictest sect of the Jewish religion, Acts xxvi. 5; but he *verily thought* with himself that he *ought to do many things contrary to the name of Jesus of Nazareth*, ver. 9; so as he went according to his conscience, (such a one as he had,) and, ver. 10, he had also *authority from the chief priests*. But neither the dictates of his own erroneous conscience, nor yet the command of his superiors, could (according to Paul's divinity) excuse him from being a *persecutor*, and *injurious*, and standing in need of the free pardoning *mercy* of God, which he saith he *obtained* of God's free grace, because *he did it ignorantly*. We cannot reasonably think that ignorance of the Divine law (once published) should excuse any transgressor of it, we see men will not allow it as to their laws, after promulgation; so that although Paul persecuted Christians *ignorantly*, yet he stood in need of *mercy*. Ignorance excuseth not *a toto*, but *a tanto*, not in whole, but in part, and makes the sinner's sin not to be so exceeding sinful, especially where it is not vincible. Paul's ignorance here mentioned was vincible; he lived in Judea, where the gospel had been preached some years before he persecuted the professors; he might have heard the sermons preached, and seen the miracles wrought, by Christ and the apostles; but he was bred a Pharisee, and under the prejudices of that sect which were implacable enemies to Christ, this kept him in ignorance. Christ allows something for the prejudices of men's education. He did what he did also while he was in a state of *unbelief*. He believed one true and living God, (all the Jews did so,) and worshipped him according to the Jewish manner, yet styles himself an unbeliever. Every man is *an unbeliever* (in a gospel sense) that receiveth not Jesus Christ as the Son of God and his Saviour, though he believes there is one God, &c. Paul addeth this circumstance of his ignorant blaspheming and persecuting the truth, partly to justify the Divine mercy that pardoned and preserved him; for the gospel peremptorily excludes from pardon all that sin against the Holy Ghost, such who, being enlightened by the knowledge of the saving truth, yet for carnal reasons deliberately and maliciously oppose it; now the showing mercy to Paul was no contradiction to this most wise law of God: and partly he mentions his ignorance to prevent the abuse of the Divine mercy by men; as if from his example they might securely imitate his persecuting the saints, or live in a course of sin, though convinced of their wickedness, and hope for mercy at the last.

14 ^bAnd the grace of our Lord was exceeding abundant ^cwith faith ^dand love which is in Christ Jesus.

<small>b Rom. 5. 20. 1 Cor. 15. 10. c 2 Tim. 1. 13. d Luke 7. 47.</small>

And the grace of our Lord was exceeding abundant; the free love of God towards me, in justifying such a guilty creature, and sanctifying such an unholy creature, and afterwards calling me to the office of an apostle, fitting me for it, and trusting me with that great work and employment, abounded beyond all measure and possibility of expression. *With faith and love which is in Christ Jesus:* Christ working faith in me, enabling me to receive him as the Son of God, and my Lord and Saviour; and to love him, whom I formerly thought I ought to do much against, and his disciples, whom I formerly haled to death, of whom I made havoc, persecuting them to death. He mentions *faith and love*, the two principal graces, in opposition to the reigning sins in his unconverted state: faith in the doctrine of the gospel, in opposition to his former ignorance and infidelity; and love to Christ and believers, in opposition to his former rage and cruelty against them. And these graces were from Christ, the fruits of his merit, and Holy Spirit.

15 ^eThis *is* a faithful saying, and worthy of all acceptation, that ^fChrist Jesus came into the world to save sinners; of whom I am chief.

<small>e ch. 3. 1. & 4. 9. 2 Tim. 2. 11. Tit. 3. 8. f Matt. 9. 13. Mark 2. 17. Luke 5. 32. & 19. 10. Rom. 5. 8. 1 John 3. 5.</small>

This is a faithful saying; the following saying, which is the great proposition of the gospel, is a saying that is in itself true, and wherein God hath declared his truth. *And worthy of all acceptation;* and worthy to be with all thankfulness received, believed, and accepted. *That Christ Jesus came into the world to save sinners;* that Jesus Christ, being sent of the Father, in the fulness of time, was incarnate, lived, and died in the world; not only to set sinners an example of a better life, nor only to make God placable towards men, that if they would they might be saved; but to purchase a certain salvation for sinners, satisfying Divine justice, and meriting all grace necessary to bring them to salvation, to carry the lost sheep home upon his shoulders; yea, though they had been great wanderers, ἁμαρτωλῶν. *Of whom I am chief;* and I was as great a one as any other, yea, the chief. Paul, though converted, had his former sin of persecution before his eyes. Persecutors are some of the chief sinners. Some will have the relative *of whom* to refer to the saving mentioned: of which sinners brought to salvation I am the great president, having been so great a sinner as I have been and yet received to mercy.

g 2 Cor. 4. 1.

16 Howbeit for this cause ᵍI obtained mercy, that in me first Jesus Christ might shew forth all longsuffering, ʰfor a pattern to them which should hereafter believe on him to life everlasting.

h Acts 13.39.

'Ἀλλὰ, the word we translate *howbeit*, is as well to be translated *but*, and ordinarily is so. *For this cause*, that is, for this end, God showed me mercy. *That in me first;* that in me, the first, (so it is in the Greek, for it is an adjective,) that is, as he said before, the chiefest or greatest sinner, *Christ might show forth all long-suffering*, bearing with me while I was in my rage against his gospel and saints, and then changing my heart to embrace him and to love him. Or, *that in me first*, may respect the design of our Saviour in sending Paul to convert the Gentiles: for such a conspicuous example of his clemency and grace towards so great a sinner, whom he not only pardoned but preferred to the dignity of an apostle, would be a strong persuasive to them to receive the gospel with faith and obedience. For it follows, *for a pattern* of God's patience and free grace to other sinners, from whence they might learn, that if they also shall receive and believe in him, their past sins need not be to them any reason to despair in his mercy. *To life everlasting:* there being a certain connexion betwixt true believing in Christ and eternal life.

i Ps. 10. 16.
& 145. 13.
Dan. 7. 14.
ch. 6. 15, 16.
k Rom. 1.23.
l John 1. 18.
Heb. 11. 27.
l John 4. 12.

17 Now unto ⁱthe King eternal, ᵏimmortal, ˡinvisible, ᵐthe only wise God, ⁿbe honour and glory for ever and ever. Amen.

m Rom. 16. 27. Jude 25. n 1 Chron. 29. 11.

The apostle falleth out of this discourse with a doxology, or sentence giving glory to God, whom he calls *the King*, that is, the Moderator and Governor of all things. *Eternal;* without beginning of days or end of life. *Immortal;* not subject, as creatures, to any passion, or determination of being. *Invisible;* not obvious to our senses, whom no mortal eye ever saw. *Only wise.* primitively and originally, and eminently, from whom all wisdom is derived. *Be honour and glory for ever and ever;* be given all praises, homage, and acknowledgments, by which he can be made glorious for ever.

o ch. 6. 13, 14, 20.
2 Tim. 2. 2.
p Ecclus. 46. 1.
ch. 4. 14.
q ch. 6. 12.
2 Tim. 2, 3.
& 4. 7.

18 This charge ᵒI commit unto thee, son Timothy, ᵖaccording to the prophecies which went before on thee, that thou by them mightest ᵍwar a good warfare;

This charge I commit unto thee, son Timothy: the term *son*, here applied to Timothy, whom he elsewhere calls his brother, is not a term of natural relation, but of spiritual relation, and of affectionate friendship and endearment. By *the charge* mentioned he probably means that before mentioned, ver. 3, 4, to charge the false teachers to *teach no other doctrine, nor give heed to fables*, &c. *According to the prophecies which went before on thee:* these *prophecies* were either the judgments of good men before concerning him, or (which possibly is more probable) some Divine revelations Paul, or some believers, had received concerning this young man. *That thou by them mightest war a good warfare;* that thou, having heard of them, or remembering them, (though thou meetest with opposition as a minister and as a Christian, yet) mightest not be discouraged, but preach and hold the faith, against all opposers. So the apostle expoundeth himself.

19 ʳHolding faith, and a good conscience; which some having put away concerning faith ˢhave made shipwreck:

r ch. 3. 9.
s ch. 6. 9.

By *faith* here is meant, the doctrine of faith, and the *holding* of it signifies a steadiness of the mind's assent unto it, without wavering or fluctuation, much less deserting or denying it. By *a good conscience* is here to be understood what the Scripture elsewhere calls *a conscience void of offence toward God, and toward men*, Acts xxiv. 16, opposed to the *evil conscience*, mentioned Heb. x. 22; so as a good conscience here signifies a pure conscience, which necessarily implieth a holy life; for our actions are presently copied out into our consciences, and make either blots or good copies there. *Which some having put away;* which some taking no care in, viz. to live holily, so keeping a good conscience; *concerning faith have made shipwreck;* have made shipwreck concerning faith, suffered loss as to it, falling from the truths of the gospel. Error seldom goes along with a holy life. The truths of the gospel have such an influence upon men's conversation, that ordinarily men's holiness is proportioned to their soundness in the faith, and usually the love of some lust is what betrayeth men into erroneous judgments and opinions.

20 Of whom is ᵗHymenæus and ᵘAlexander; whom I have ˣdelivered unto Satan, that they may learn not to ʸblaspheme.

t 2 Tim. 2. 17.
u 2 Tim. 2. 14.
x 1 Cor. 5. 5.
y Acts 13. 45.

Of which men who have made shipwreck of a good conscience and concerning faith, *Hymenæus and Alexander* are two persons. Of Hymenæus we read, 2 Tim. ii. 17, 18; he affirmed the resurrection was past, and overthrew the faith of many. Of Alexander we read, 2 Tim. iv. 14; he was a great enemy to Paul, the same person, as some judge, mentioned Acts xix. 33, then a friend to Paul, but afterwards one who did him much harm. *Whom I have delivered unto Satan:* we meet with the same phrase, 1 Cor. v. 5: see the notes there. Some think by it is signified a peculiar power granted the apostles, God in those primitive times confirming regular excommunications, by letting Satan loose upon persons excommunicated to torture them; but we find nothing of this in Scripture. I rather think the sense is no more than, whom I excommunicated and cast out of the church, making them of the world again, (as the world is opposed to the church, and kingdom of Christ,) which, for the greater terror, the apostle expresseth by this notion of being delivered to Satan, who is called *the god of this world*, &c. *That they may learn not to blaspheme:* not that I might ruin and undo them, but that I might amend them by this exercise of discipline, teaching them to take heed of spreading damnable and pernicious errors to the reproach of God. Or, perhaps, with their perverse opinions (which is very ordinary) they mingled reproachful speeches concerning God.

CHAP. II

Paul exhorteth to pray and give thanks for all men, for kings and magistrates especially, 1—3. *God willeth the salvation of all men,* 4—6. *Paul's commission to teach the Gentiles,* 7. *He directeth how women should be attired,* 8—10; *permitteth them not to teach,* 11—14; *promiseth that they shall be saved in child-bearing on certain conditions,* 15.

I ∥ EXHORT therefore, that, first of all, supplications, prayers, intercessions, *and* giving of thanks, be made for all men;

∥ Or, *desire*.

Timothy (as was said before) was left at Ephesus to manage the affairs of the church there in the absence of Paul, who in this Epistle directs him as to this management. First he exhorts him to see that prayers should be made for all men. *Supplications*, δεήσεις, for supply of wants. *Prayers*, προσευχὰς, signifieth much the same; some will have it to signify petitions for the conservation or increase of what good things we have. *Intercessions*, ἐντεύξεις, prayers for others, whether for the averting of evils from them, or the collation of good things upon them. *And giving of thanks;* and blessings of God for good things bestowed upon ourselves or others. These Paul wills should *be made* ὑπὲρ πάντων, which may be of all men, or *for all men*, but the next verse plainly shows that it is here rightly rendered *for all men*, for there were at this time no *kings* in the church. Paul here establisheth prayers as a piece of the public ministry in the church of God, and a primary piece; therefore he saith, he exhorts *that first of all;* not in respect of time so much as, principally, intimating it a great piece of the public ministry, which he would by no means have neglected. And he would have these prayers put up for all orders and sorts of men, such only excepted of whom St. John speaks, 1 John v. 16, who had sinned that sin, for which he would not say Christians should pray.

^{a Ezra 6. 10.
Jer. 29. 7.
b Rom. 13. 1.
‖ Or, eminent place.}

2 ^aFor kings, and ^b*for* all that are in ‖ authority; that we may lead a quiet and peaceable life in all godliness and honesty.

For kings, and for all that are in authority: the kings of the earth at that time were all heathens, and enemies to the Christian religion, so (generally) were those who were in a subordinate authority to them, yet the apostle commands that prayers should be made in the Christian congregations for them. What the matter of their petitions was to be is not expressed, but doubtless not to be limited by the next words, for that were not to have prayed for them but for themselves. Prayers for magistrates ought to be directed by their circumstances. If magistrates were idolaters and persecutors, they were to pray for their conversion, and the change of their hearts. However, they were to pray for their life and health so far forth as might be for God's glory, and for God's guidance of them in the administration of their government, and their success in their lawful counsels and undertakings, &c. The latter words, *that we may lead a quiet and peaceable life in all godliness and honesty*, contain the reason why prayers should be made for governors, and the good effect of them. For it is for this end that the supreme Lord hath ordained the office and dignity of kings and governors, that, being armed with authority and power, they may perserve public order and peace, by punishing evil-doers, and protecting and encouraging those that do well. Thus, under the Old Testament, the Jews were commanded to pray for the peace of the nation or city whither they should be carried captives, for in their peace they should have peace, Jer. xxix. 7.

^{c Rom. 12. 2.
ch. 5. 4.
d ch. 1. 1.
2 Tim. 1. 9.}

3 For this *is* ^cgood and acceptable in the sight ^dof God our Saviour;

To pray for all, as well our enemies as our friends, especially for princes, and such as are in places of magistracy and authority, is *good*, being according to the will and commandment of God, and *acceptable* to God, as all acts of obedience to his will are. The word *Saviour* may either be understood with reference to the Divine Being, God being our Preserver, who maketh his sun to shine and his rain to fall upon the just and unjust, Matt. v. 45, which our Saviour brings as an argument to enforce his precept of love to our enemies; or with a special reference to Christ, to whom the title of *Saviour*, with reference to eternal salvation, more strictly belongs, who also by his death, when we were enemies, reconciled us to God: so that such a charitable office must be acceptable to God, because in doing it we both show ourselves the children of our heavenly Father, and also the followers of Christ.

^{e Ezek. 18.
23. John 3.
16, 17.
Tit. 2. 11.
2 Pet. 3. 9.
f John 17. 3.
2 Tim. 2. 25.}

4 ^eWho will have all men to be saved, ^fand to come unto the knowledge of the truth.

The apostle produces a clear, convincing reason, that the duty of charity in praying for all men is pleasing to God, from his love extended to all, in his willing their salvation, and their knowledge and belief of the gospel, which is the only way of salvation. From hence our Saviour's commission and command to the apostles was universal, *Go and teach all nations*, Matt. xxviii. 19; *Preach the gospel to every creature*, that is, to every man, Mark xvi. 15; he excludes no people, no person. And accordingly the apostles discharged their office to their utmost capacity, Col. i. 24. But a question arises, how it can be said that God would *have all men saved*, when that the most of men perish? For the resolving this difficulty, we must observe, that in the style of Scripture the will of God sometimes signifies his eternal counsel and decree; that things should be done either by his immediate efficiency, or by the intervention of means: or, secondly, his commands and invitations to men to do such things as are pleasing to him. The will of God in the first sense always infallibly obtains its effect, Psal. cxv. 3; thus he declares, *My counsel shall stand, I will do all my pleasure*, Isa. xlvi. 10; for otherwise there must be a change of God's will and counsel, or a defect of power, both which assertions are impious blasphemy. But those things which he commands and are pleasing to him, are often not performed without any reflection upon him, either as mutable or impotent. Thus he declares, that he wills things that are pleasing to him; as, I will not the death of a sinner, but that he should turn and live, Ezek. xxxiii. 11; and sometimes that he will not those things that are displeasing to him, as contrary to holiness, though he did not decree the hindering of them: thus he complains in Isa. lxv. 12, *Ye did evil before mine eyes, and did choose that wherein I delighted not*. This distinction of the Divine will being clearly set down in Scripture, answers the objection; for when it is said in the text, that God *will have all men to be saved, and to come to the knowledge of the truth;* and in the same sense by St. Peter, that God will have none perish, but come to repentance, 2 Pet. iii. 9; we must understand it, not with respect to his decretive will, but his complacential will, that is, the repentance and life of a sinner is very pleasing to his holiness and mercy. And this love of God to men has been declared in opening the way of salvation to them by the Mediator, and by all the instructions, invitations, commands, and promises of the gospel, assuring them that whoever comes to Christ upon the terms of the gospel shall in no wise be cast off; that no repenting believer shall be excluded from saving mercy.

5 ^gFor *there is* one God, and ^hone mediator between God and men, the man Christ Jesus; ^{g Rom. 3. 29, 30. & 10. 12.
Gal. 3. 20.
h Heb. 8. 6.
& 9. 15.}

The apostle proves the universal love of God to men by two reasons, the unity of God, and the unity of the Mediator: though there are divers societies and vast numbers of men, yet there is but one God, the Creator and Preserver of all. If there were many gods in nature, it were conceivable that the God of Christians were not the God of other men, and consequently that his good will were confined to his own portion, leaving the rest to their several deities; but since there is but one true God of the world, who has revealed himself in the gospel, it necessarily follows that he is the God of all men in the relation of Creator and Preserver. And from hence he concludes, *God will have all men to be saved*. He argues in the same manner that salvation by faith in Christ belongs to the Gentiles as well as the Jews, Rom. iii. 29, 30. The apostle adds, for the clearest assurance of his good will of God to save men, that there is *one mediator between God and men, the man Christ Jesus*. When the sin of man had provoked Divine justice, and the guilt could not be expiated without satisfaction, God appointed his Son incarnate to mediate between his offended Majesty and his rebellious subjects. And it is observable, the parallel between the unity of God and the unity of the Mediator; as there is one God of all nations, so there is one Mediator of all. The strength of the apostle's argument from the unity of the Mediator is this: If there were many mediators, according to the numbers of nations in the world, there might be a suspicion whether they were so worthy and so prevalent as to obtain the grace of God, every one for those in whose behalf they did mediate. But since there is but one, and that he is *able to save to the uttermost all that come to God by him*, it is evident that all men have the same Mediator, and that every one may be assured that God is willing he should be saved, and, for that blessed end, should by faith and repentance accept the covenant of grace. The apostle for the stronger confirmation specifies the Mediator, *the man Christ Jesus*, to encourage the hopes of all men, from the communion they have with him in nature, that they may partake of

I. TIMOTHY II

his salvation, and that this great Mediator, having come from heaven and assumed the infirmity of our nature, Heb. iv. 15, will be inclined compassionately to assist them, and raise them to his heavenly kingdom.

i Mat. 20, 28. Mark 10. 45.
Eph. 1. 7.   k ||
Tit. 2. 14.
k 1 Cor. 1. 6. 2 Thess. 1. 10. 2 Tim. 1. 8. || Or, *a testimony*.   1 Rom. 5. 6. Gal. 4. 4. Eph. 1. 9. & 3. 5. Tit. 1. 3.

6 ⁱWho gave himself a ransom for all, ᵏ‖ to be testified ¹in due time.

'Ἀντίλυτρον, the word here translated *ransom*, is very emphatical; it signifies the exchanging of condition with another, the laying down of one's life to save another's. This our Saviour has done for us. The Scripture discovers to us, that *by nature we are the children of wrath*, and guilty of many rebellious sins, and devoted to eternal death: being in this deplorable state, the Son of God, moved by his Divine love, undertook our restoring to the favour of God; and voluntarily endured the punishment due to our sins, and gave his most precious blood and life the price of our redemption, Matt. xx. 28. If it be objected, How is it consistent with Christ giving *himself a ransom for all*, that so many perish in their sins? the answer is clear: We must distinguish between the sufficiency of his ransom and the efficacy of it; he paid a ransom worthy to obtain the salvation of all men, and has done whatever was requisite to reconcile God, and make men capable of salvation; but only those who by a lively faith depend upon him, and obey him, are actual partakers of salvation: that is, no person but may be saved in believing; and if men perish, it is not from a defect of righteousness in the Mediator, but from the love of their lusts, and their obstinate rejecting their own mercies. And it is unjust that the glory of his Divine compassion and love should be obscured or lessened for their ungrateful neglect of it.

m Eph. 3. 7, 8. 2 Tim. 1. 11.
n Rom. 9. 1.
o Rom. 11. 13. & 15. 16. Gal. 1. 16.

7 ᵐWhereunto I am ordained a preacher, and an apostle, (ⁿI speak the truth in Christ, *and* lie not;) ᵒa teacher of the Gentiles in faith and verity.

Whereunto I am ordained a preacher; for the publishing and making known of which testimony of the Divine goodness and truth I am set, or *appointed*, 2 Tim. i. 11, ἐτέθην, *a preacher*, or a public officer to proclaim and make it known. *And an apostle*; and am immediately called by Christ, and sent out upon that employment. *I speak the truth in Christ, and lie not;* I call Christ to witness that I speak nothing but what I know to be true. It is a phrase which hath, if not the form, yet the force of an oath; and was necessary in this case, for it was not easy to persuade the Jews that God had sent any to reveal the way of salvation to the Gentiles. *A teacher of the Gentiles in faith and verity*; and my special province was to teach the Gentiles, Acts ix. 15; xxvi. 17; Gal. ii. 7—9; and to instruct them in the doctrine of faith and truth: or, I was set faithfully and truly to instruct the Gentiles.

p Mat. 1. 11. John 4. 21.
q Ps. 134. 2. Is. 1. 15.

8 I will therefore that men pray ᵖevery where, ᑫlifting up holy hands, without wrath and doubting.

I will therefore that men pray every where; this is one precept that I give thee in charge as to the management of the affairs of the church, that wherever men meet together to worship God, whether in houses built for that purpose, or in more common houses, or any other place, (for the time is now come when there is no special command for one place more than another, no special promise made to men's prayers in one place more than another, as there was to and concerning the temple of old, John iv. 21,) they should pray, either ministering to others in the duty of prayer, or joining with him who doth so minister. *Lifting up holy hands;* but let them take heed how they pray, for *God heareth not sinners*, John ix. 31; let them therefore lift up holy hands, not regarding iniquity in their hearts. *Without wrath;* and let them take heed of carrying malice, or inveterate anger, in their hearts when they go to God in prayer, for they must pray, Father, *forgive us our trespasses, as we forgive them that trespass against us;* and, Matt. vi. 15, *If ye forgive not men their trespasses, neither will your heavenly Father forgive your trespasses. And doubting;* and let them also take heed of doubting in prayer of the goodness, truth, or power of God to fulfil his wishes; but, James i. 6, 7, *let them ask in faith, nothing wavering.* For *let not that man think that he shall receive any thing of the Lord.*

9 In like manner also, that ʳwomen adorn themselves in modest apparel, with shamefacedness and sobriety; not with ‖ broidered hair, or gold, or pearls, or costly array;

r 1 Pet. 3. 3.

‖ Or, *plaited*.

The apostle's next precept to be urged by Timothy, is concerning the habits of women, especially when they come to worship God in the public assemblies; for to such assemblies the precepts in this chapter, both before and after this, chiefly relate. Concerning these he commands, that they should *adorn themselves in modest apparel*, observe a decency, with respect to the modesty of their sex, the purity of religion, the quality of their condition, and their age. Religion has no other interest in our habits, but to regulate them according to a modest comeliness; for they are indifferent in their nature, and neither add nor detract from the acceptance of our religious services. *Shamefacedness and sobriety*, or modesty; a moderation of mind showed both in the habit of the body, and the manners and behaviour, both with these inward habits, and in an outward habit that may speak souls possessed of these inward habits. *Not with broidered hair, or gold, or pearls, or costly array;* not with hair plaited or curled, not adorned with ornaments of gold, or pearls, or costly array. The apostle condemneth not these ornaments where they are suited to the quality of women, and ask not too much time to put on, and in order; but where they are too excessive with respect to the purse of those that wear them, or take up more time to be spent in putting them on than is fit to be so spent, especially on a sabbath day, or where they are put on out of pride, or to make a vain show, or are of that nature and fashion as they speak an unchaste or an immodest heart, or may cause scandal to others. The apostle Peter, 1 Pet. iii. 3, hath much the same precept, where he is not speaking of women's habits, but to their ordinary conversation; but it ought to be more specially avoided when people come to worship God. They should not so habit themselves when they go to pray, as if they were going to a dancing school, as Chrysostom in his time complained of some that did.

10 ˢBut (which becometh women professing godliness) with good works.

s 1 Pet. 3. 4.

They ought to look at the ornament of good works; for those are the ornaments which best become women professing godliness, whose hearts should despise the ornament of the figure of excrementitious hair, or a little yellow earth, or a stone, or the work of a pitiful silkworm.

11 Let the woman learn in silence with all subjection.

That is, in the public assemblies for worship, it is the woman's part silently to learn, showing thereby a subjection to the man, who is the head of the woman.

12 But ᵗI suffer not a woman to teach, ᵘnor to usurp authority over the man, but to be in silence.

t 1 Cor. 14. 34.
u Eph. 5. 24.

But I suffer not a woman to teach; not to teach in the public congregation, except she be a prophetess, endued with extraordinary gifts of the Spirit, as Mary, and Anna, and Huldah, and Deborah, and some women in the primitive church, concerning whom we read, 1 Cor. xi. 5, that they prophesied. *Nor to usurp authority over the man:* ordinary teaching of the woman was a usurpation of authority over the man, who is the head, which the apostle also forbade in 1 Cor. xi. 3, and here repeateth. It is probable that the speaking of some women in the church who had extraordinary revelations, imboldened others also to aim at the like, which the apostle here directs his speech against. Nevertheless women may, and it is their duty to instruct their children and families at home, especially in the absence of their husbands.

13 For ˣAdam was first formed, then Eve.

x Gen. 1. 27. & 2. 18, 22.
1 Cor. 11. 8, 9.

The man had the priority of the woman in his creation, he was not made for her, but she was made for a helpmate for him; therefore she, being made for him, ought to usurp no authority over him.

^y Gen. 3. 6.
2 Cor. 11. 3.
14 And ^y Adam was not deceived, but the woman being deceived was in the transgression.

Besides, Adam was not first deceived, nor indeed at all deceived immediately by the serpent, but only enticed, and deceived by the woman, who was the tempter's agent; so as that she was both first in the transgression in order of time, and also principal in it, contributing to the seduction or transgression of the man; which ought to be a consideration to keep the woman humble, in a low opinion of herself, and that lower order wherein God hath fixed her.

15 Notwithstanding she shall be saved in childbearing, if they continue in faith and charity and holiness with sobriety.

Though the woman was so unhappy as to be deceived by the serpent, and to be the first in taking the forbidden fruit, and an instrument to entice her husband to do the like, which may give all of that sex a cause of humiliation, and show them the reasonableness of God's order in putting them in subjection to man, and prohibiting them to break God's order in usurping authority over the man; yet through the gracious interposition of the Mediator, (afterward born of a woman,) she hath no reason to despair, either of a temporal salvation, from the peril and danger of child-birth, or, much less, of an eternal salvation, for *she shall be saved*; she stands upon equal ground with the man as to eternal salvation, who cannot be saved without faith and holiness, and a discharge of the duties incumbent upon him, and patient enduring the crosses and trials God exerciseth him with; and the woman also shall be saved, by faithful performance of her duty, and patiently enduring her crosses and trials, in the pains and peril of *child-bearing*; notwithstanding they are the sensible marks of God's displeasure for sin, yet the sufferings of Christ has taken away the said bitterness. *If they continue in faith and charity and holiness with sobriety*; if she also liveth in the exercise of faith in Christ, and love to God, and her husband, and all saints, and in all exercises of holiness with sobriety. Some refer the pronoun *they* to the children, because the apostle had been before speaking of the woman in the singular number; but there is nothing more ordinary than that change of the number, especially where collective words are used, that signify a whole species or sex; and it is unreasonable to think the apostle should suspend the salvation of the mother upon the faith and holiness of the child, and to interpret it of the mother's endeavours towards it, seemeth hardly a sufficient interpretation of the term *continue*.

CHAP. III

The office of a bishop is to be esteemed a good work, 1. *The qualifications requisite in a bishop*, 2—7, *and in deacons*, 8—13. *Why Paul wrote these instructions to Timothy*, 14, 15. *The important truths of the Christian revelation*, 16.

^a ch. 1. 15.
^b Acts 20.28.
Phil. 1. 1.
^c Eph. 4. 12.
THIS ^a *is* a true saying, If a man desire the office of a ^b Bishop, he desireth a good ^c work.

This is a true saying; πιστὸς, a faithful saying, that which none can dispute, of which none ought to doubt. *If a man desire the office of a bishop*; if a man desire any office to which belongs an oversight of the church of God. The Greek word ἐπισκοπή signifies in the general an oversight of others; here the following discourse restrains it to an oversight of persons and affairs in the church. The apostle by this phrase determines this employment lawful, and under due circumstances to be desired, and saith of it, that he who desireth it *desireth* καλὸν ἔργον, *a good work*, a noble employment; it is a *work*, the office of the ministry in the church is and ought to be a work. The titles of gospel ministers are not mere titles of honour, and of all works or employments, the ministry is the most noble employment. We (saith the apostle) are *stewards of the mysteries of God, ministers of Christ*, 1 Cor. iv. 1; ambas-*sadors for Christ, in Christ's stead*, 2 Cor. v. 20; God's angels or messengers to churches, Rev. ii. 1. It being so good, so great, and noble an employment, it is no wonder that God hath restrained women, the weaker and more ignoble sex, from invading it, for all men are not fit for it, but only such as are hereafter described.

2 ^d A Bishop then must be blameless, ^e the husband of one wife, vigilant, sober, ‖ of good behaviour, given to hospitality, ^f apt to teach;

^d Tit. 1. 6, &c.
^e ch. 5. 9.
‖ Or, *modest*.
^f 2 Tim. 2. 24.

In the following description there is the complete character of an evangelical bishop, with respect to the virtues wherewith he must be adorned, and the vices from which he must be exempt, and as to the conduct of his person, and the government of his family, and his carriage to the church, and to those that are without. *A bishop*, whoever hath the office of oversight in the church of God, *must be blameless*, such a person as none can truly blame for any notorious or conspicuous errors in his life. *The husband of one wife*; none who at the same time hath more wives than one, as many of the Jews had; nor was polygamy only common amongst the Jews, but amongst the other Eastern nations; but this was contrary to the institution of marriage. Some interpret this of successive marriage, as if it were a scandalous thing for a minister to marry a second time; but for this they have no pretence from holy writ, or reason, or the practice and custom of nations. Many persons lose their first wives so soon after marriage, that, were not second marriages lawful, all the ends of marriage must be frustrate as to them. The apostle commanding ministers to be the husbands but of *one wife*, doth not oblige them to marry, if God hath given them the gift of continency, but it establisheth the lawfulness of their marrying, against the doctrine of devils in this particular, which the Church of Rome teacheth. *Vigilant*: the word here translated *vigilant* signifieth also *sober*, but for that σώφρονα is after used. He must be one that watcheth his flock, and is attentive to his work; one that will neither be long absent from his flock, nor yet sluggish while he is with them. *Sober*; one that is prudent, modest, temperate, that can govern his affections and passions. *Of good behaviour*; a man of a comely, decent behaviour, κόσμιος, no proud, supercilious man, that despiseth others, nor a morose man, who cannot accommodate himself to others. *Given to hospitality*; one that loveth strangers, that is, who is ready to express his love to strangers (especially such as for the truth have left their country) by all courteous offices. *Apt to teach*; one that is able to instruct others, and who hath a facility or aptness to it, neither an ignorant nor yet a lazy man.

3 ^g ‖ Not given to wine, ^h no striker, ⁱ not greedy of filthy lucre; but ^k patient, not a brawler, not covetous;

^g ver. 8.
Tit. 1. 7.
‖ Or, *Not ready to quarrel, and offer wrong, as one in wine.*
h 2 Tim. 2. 24. i 1 Pet. 5. 2. k 2 Tim. 2. 24.

Not given to wine; the word signifieth a common tippler, whether he drinks to the loss of his reason or no; a wine-bibber, that makes bibbing at a tavern his trade: no sitter at wine. *No striker*; no quarreller, that cannot keep his fists off him that provoketh him. *Not greedy of filthy lucre*; one that abhors all filthy and dishonest gain, any kind of way. *But patient*; ἐπιεικῆ, a fair, equal man, who will not exact the rigour of what he might; a patient, gentle, courteous man, so far from contention, that he will rather part with what is his right. *Not a brawler*; ἄμαχον, one that will not fight, whether it be with his hand or tongue. *Not covetous*; one that doth not love silver, that is, not with an immoderate, sinful love, so as to get it any way.

4 One that ruleth well his own house, ^l having his children in subjection with all gravity;

l Tit. 1. 6.

One that ruleth well his own house; if he be one to whom God hath given a family, one who hath given an experiment of his conversation and ability to take care of a church, by the care that he hath taken of his family, and his ruling in that lesser society. *Having his children in subjection with all gravity*; one that hath not let his children behave themselves rudely, and indecently, and rebelliously, but kept them in order by a grave demeanour towards them.

5 (For if a man know not how to rule his own house, how shall he take care of the Church of God?)

For if a man hath a family, and hath showed that he neither hath wit nor honesty enough to govern that little society, which hath his constant presence with it, with what reason can any one presume, that he should be fit to be trusted with the care of the church of God? which is a larger society, with all the members of which he is not so constantly present, and over whom he hath not such a coercive power, and as to whom a far greater care must be taken.

‖ Or, one newly come to the faith.
m Is. 14. 12.

6 Not ‖ a novice, lest being lifted up with pride ᵐ he fall into the condemnation of the devil.

Not a novice; not a young plant, that is, one that is newly made a member of the church of Christ; such persons are apt to swell in the opinion of their newly acquired knowledge, state, or dignity; and being so lifted up, they will be in danger of such a punishment as the devil for his pride met with, or to be guilty of some ill or indecent behaviour, which may give the devil occasion to accuse them. Others here interpret διαβόλῳ more appellatively, and understand by it a man that is an accuser, making the sense this,—and fall into the judgment, censure, or condemnation of men, accusing them for such behaviour.

n Acts 22. 12.
1 Cor. 5. 12.
1 Thes. 4. 12.
o ch. 6. 9.
2 Tim. 2. 26.

7 Moreover he must have a good report ⁿ of them which are without; lest he fall into reproach ᵒ and the snare of the devil.

Moreover he must have a good report of them which are without: the apostle would have ministers men of good reputation amongst such as were without the pale of the church, for that is the meaning of that term, *which are without;* see 1 Cor. v. 12; 1 Thess. iv. 12: others might be admitted as members of the church, but not as rulers in it, because the glory of God was much concerned in the reputation of such persons, they were as lights set upon a hill. *Lest he fall into reproach;* lest men reproach such persons for their former infamous life, and so prejudice others against the doctrine they bring. *And the snare of the devil;* and the snare, either of some accuser, or of the devil, who hath this name from his accusing of the brethren; or lest he fall into some temptation to revenge, hatred, undue anger, or to be cowardly in the discharge of his duty, lest he should by faithfulness provoke others to reproach him for his former course of life.

p Acts 6. 3.
q ver. 3.
Lev. 10. 9.
Ezek. 44. 21.

8 Likewise must ᵖ the Deacons be grave, not doubletongued, ᑫ not given to much wine, not greedy of filthy lucre;

Likewise must the deacons be grave: the term *deacon* signifies the same with one that ministereth, and is applicable to any that have any service in the church. But it is also a term peculiar to the office of those who *serve tables,* that is, took care of the poor, for which purpose these officers were first instituted, Acts vi. 3; and thus the term is taken, Rom. xii. 7, 8; Phil. i. 1; and so it here must be interpreted, being distinctly mentioned from the other officers, whose qualifications were before expressed, nor is it required of these officers that they should be διδακτικοί, apt to teach. Indeed both Stephen and Philip did preach, but the latter was an evangelist, and it was a time of persecution, when even the more private brethren went every where preaching the gospel. Of these officers he requires, that they should be persons not of light, airy tempers, but serious and composed, men of a modest, seemly carriage. *Not double-tongued;* not excessive talkers, or men that regarded not what they said, but talked any thing, according to the place or company they were in or with. *Not given to much wine;* not too much attending taverns, and places where wine was sold or drank. *Not greedy of filthy lucre;* not greedy of gain, any sordid, base way.

r ch. 1. 19.

9 ʳ Holding the mystery of the faith in a pure conscience.

Not ignorant or inconstant persons, but such as were acquainted with the mysteries of the gospel, and believed them, and held to them; and men of a holy life.

10 And let these also first be proved; then let them use the office of a Deacon, being *found* blameless.

The higher officers ought to *be proved,* (as well as these of a lower order,) as by examination or conference, so (which possibly is here more intended) by an observation of their lives and conversation, for some time before they were admitted into this employment. Then, *being found blameless,* they were to be admitted into this employment.

11 ˢ Even so *must their* wives *be* grave,
s Tit. 2. 3.
not slanderers, sober, faithful in all things.

Even so must their wives be grave: must *their* is not in the Greek, but supplied by our interpreters, and, as some think, ill, judging that he speaks here not of deacons' wives, but of deaconesses, of such women as had the deacon's office conferred on them, such a one was Phebe, Rom. xvi. 1; but it may be understood of either, both ought to be not light, airy, tattling persons, but composed, serious, grave people. *Not slanderers;* not devils, (so it is in the Greek,) that is, persons given to railing and accusing others. *Sober:* see the sense of that word, ver. 2. *Faithful in all things;* who have approved themselves every way honest, and such persons as may be trusted.

12 Let the Deacons be the husbands of one wife, ruling their children and their own houses well.

See the sense of these words, ver. 2, 4, being the qualifications also of a bishop.

13 For ᵗ they that have ‖ used the office of a Deacon well purchase to themselves a good degree, and great boldness in the faith which is in Christ Jesus.
t See Matt. 25. 21.
‖ Or, ministered.

Purchase to themselves a good degree; a good degree of honour, so that none hath reason to decline or to despise that office. This seems rather to be the sense, than what pleaseth some better, viz. that they purchase to themselves a higher degree in the ministry of the church; for though it be very probably true, and but rational, that the primitive church did out of their deacons choose their higher officers for the church, yet neither was this done universally as to all persons chosen into those high employments, nor as to all those that used the office of a deacon well, there doubtless being many who had done so, who yet were not διδακτικοί, fitted with an ability sufficient to be preachers, without which fitness the primitive church would not choose any to such employment. *And great boldness in the faith which is in Christ Jesus;* by the well performance also of the office of a deacon, many obtained a great liberty, or freedom of speech, παρρησίαν, as to the doctrine of the faith of Christ. For by the exercise of the deacon's office, they had much converse both with the pastors and members of the church; which converse did not only improve their knowledge in the doctrine of faith, but took off that excessive bashfulness which possesseth many till they come to be fully acquainted with the thing of which, and the persons before which, they are to speak, which we see by daily experience. Or, the apostle intends that courage that arises from a good conscience. Those that are careless and unfaithful in the discharge of their duty, guilt makes them timorous; but the good and faithful servant of God enjoys that liberty and courage which faith in the Lord Jesus gives, and without fear discharges all the parts of his office.

14 These things write I unto thee, hoping to come unto thee shortly:

I being now in Macedonia, or at Athens, or some parts thereabouts, have wrote to thee whom I left at Ephesus these precepts about the officers of churches, not being sure I shall, but hoping myself soon to come to Ephesus unto thee; which yet he did not, as we read, for he met Timothy at Troas, Acts xx. 5.

15 But if I tarry long, that thou mayest know how thou oughtest to behave thyself ᵘ in the house of God, which is
u Eph. 2. 21, 22. 2 Tim. 2. 20.

I. TIMOTHY III, IV

Or, *stay.* the Church of the living God, the pillar and ||ground of the truth.

I do not know how God will dispose of me, though I hope shortly to see thee, and therefore I have written to direct thee how in the mean time thou shouldst carry thyself in the affairs of the church, which I have committed to thee, which is a matter of great moment; for the people which constitute the church of him who is not like the gods of the heathens, a dead man consecrated and made a god, nor a being without life, like their images, but one who hath life in himself and from himself, is *the house of God,* a people in and amongst whom he dwelleth, and amongst whom he is worshipped; and of whom he hath a great care, and for which he hath a great love, Christ having died for it, *that he might sanctify and cleanse it with the washing of water by the word,* Eph. v. 26; and which (as a man doth by his house) he is daily enlarging, beautifying, and adorning with the graces of his Holy Spirit, *that* (as there, ver. 27) *he might present it to himself, a glorious church, not having spot or wrinkle, or any such thing; but that it should be holy and without blemish.* Which church is *the pillar and ground of the truth,* τύλος καὶ ἑδραίωμα. We want a good English word whereby to translate the latter of the two words in the Greek, which possibly hath advantaged the great contests about the sense of this text. It comes from ἕδρα, which signifieth a star, and a thing to support, and a seat, the place (say some) in which the idol was set in the pagan temples. Thence this word ἑδραίωμα is translated, the underpropper, the establisher, any firm basis upon which a thing standeth or leaneth; so that it is much of the same significancy with the former word, which we rightly translate a pillar, the two things signifying in use the same thing, that which underproppeth and holdeth up another thing, as the pillars do the building, and the basis of the image or statue doth the statue. Pillars also were of ancient use to fasten upon them any public edicts, which princes or courts would have published, and exposed to the view of all; hence the church is called, *the pillar* and basis, or seal, *of truth,* because by it the truths of God are published, supported, and defended, and in it they are only to be found as in their proper seat and place; for to it the oracles and mysteries of God are committed, and in it they are exposed to the notice and knowledge of all, as public edicts are upon pillars. But neither that saving truth, nor the faith which we give to it, is established upon the authority of the church, (as the Romanists vainly pretend,) but upon the authority of God the author of it. The church discovers and recommends the truth, but the testimony it gives is not the foundation of its credibility. The universal church (of which the church of Ephesus, over which Timothy had a charge, was a genuine part) is, in the sense before expressed, the pillar and supporter, or seat, of truth.

x John 1. 14.
1 John 1. 2.
† Gr. *manifested.*
y Matt. 3.16.
John 1. 32, 33. & 15. 26.
& 16. 8, 9.
Rom. 1. 4.
1 Pet. 3. 18.
1 John 5. 6, &c.

16 And without controversy great is the mystery of godliness: ˣGod was † manifest in the flesh, ʸjustified in the Spirit, ᶻseen of angels, ᵃpreached unto the Gentiles, ᵇbelieved on in the world, ᶜreceived up into glory.

z Matt. 28. 2. Mark 16. 5. Luke 2. 13. & 24. 4. John 20. 12. Eph. 3. 10. 1 Pet. 1. 12.
a Acts 10. 34. & 13. 46, 48. Gal. 2. 8. Eph. 3. 5, 6, 8. Rom. 10. 18. Col. 1. 27, 28. ch. 2. 7. b Col. 1. 6, 23. c Luke 24. 51. Acts 1. 19. 1 Pet. 3. 22.

And without controversy great is the mystery of godliness: the various use of the particle καί in the Greek, which we translate *and,* maketh it doubtful what is the force of it here, whether it relates to the *truth* mentioned in the latter part of the former verse, or shows another reason why Timothy should have a care how he behaved himself in the house of God. If to the former, it is exegetical, and opens what he meant by truth, viz., *the mystery of godliness,* by which he means the gospel, which is the doctrine of godliness, being that which teacheth how aright to worship God, and walk before him; this he first calls, then proves to be, a *mystery,* a great mystery. The word is derived from the heathens, who had mysteries of their superstition and idolatrous religion. A mystery signifies a thing sacred and secret. The heathens also had their greater and lesser gods, and their greater and lesser mysteries. Paul calls the gospel, the doctrine of godliness, a *great mystery,* and says it is confessedly so, or such *without controversy;* then he proveth it by telling us what it is, and giving us the sum of it. It teacheth us that he who was truly God, *God over all, blessed for ever,* (as the apostle saith,) was *manifested in the flesh;* John i. 14, *The Word was made flesh.* How an infinite nature could be personally united to a finite nature, so as to make one person, is a mystery, and a great mystery. And this God thus manifested in the flesh was *justified in the Spirit;* either by his Divine nature, (which is here as some think called *the Spirit,*) by virtue of which he in the flesh wrought many miraculous operations, and when he was buried he rose again from the dead, by which he was justified, that is, undoubtedly proved to be the Son of God. Or, by the Holy Spirit of God, (the Third Person in the holy Trinity,) by whom he was conceived in the womb of the virgin, Luke i. 35. *Seen of angels,* who declared his conception, Luke i. 32, 33; sang and glorified God when he was born, Luke ii. 10, 11; ministered to him when he was tempted, Matt. iv. 11: who comforted him in his passion, declared his resurrection, Matt. xxviii., and attended his ascension, Acts i. 10. *Preached unto the Gentiles:* Christ's being preached to the Gentiles was also a mystery, so great, that Peter would not believe it to be the will of God, till he was confirmed in it by a vision, Acts x. This some think is spoken with some reference to the Gentile superstition, who also, (as was said before,) had their greater and lesser mysteries, and to the former would admit no strangers. *Believed on in the world:* that Christ should, upon the ministry of a few fishermen, and the report the world had received of what Christ did in Judea, be received and embraced by the world as their Saviour, was as great a mystery as any other, especially considering that the doctrine of Christ was as incomprehensible by human reason, as ungrateful to the propensions and inclinations of human nature. *Received up into glory:* the resurrection of Christ is not mentioned, because necessarily supposed to his ascension, which he mentioneth as the last thing whereby Christ was declared to be *God manifested in the flesh.*

CHAP. IV

Paul foretelleth and describeth a great apostacy to happen in the latter times, 1—5. *He directeth Timothy what doctrines to teach,* 6—11; *and by what rules to regulate his conduct, so as to save both himself and his hearers,* 12—16.

NOW the Spirit ᵃspeaketh expressly, that ᵇin the latter times some shall depart from the faith, giving heed ᶜto seducing spirits, ᵈand doctrines of devils;

a John 16. 13.
2 Thess. 2. 3.
2 Tim. 3. 1, &c.
e 2 Pet. 3. 3.
1 John 2. 18.
Jude 4. 18.
b 1 Pet. 1. 20.
c 2 Tim. 3. 13. 2 Pet. 2. 1. Rev. 16. 14.   d Dan. 11. 35, 37, 38. Rev. 9. 20.

It was usual with the prophets, when they declared the oracles of God, to assert in the beginning of their revelations, that *the Lord hath spoken,* Isa. i. 2; Jer. i. 2; Joel i. 1. The apostle in the same manner, in the beginning of his prediction of things future, declares *the Spirit speaketh expressly,* that is, either clearly revealed it to me, as Acts x. 19, and xiii. 2, thus *expressly* is opposed to obscurely; for sometimes the revelations given to the prophets were under shadows and figures in divers manners, but the Spirit discovered in a most intelligible manner what seducers should come in the church, &c. *Now the Spirit speaketh expressly;* either hath inwardly revealed it to my Spirit, as Acts x. 19; xiii. 2, or, (which is more probable,) because the verb is in the present tense, λέγει, it saith it in the written word, which must be in the Old Testament, for the New was not at this time written: but then the question is, where the Holy Ghost hath expressly in the Old Testament spoken of the apostacy of the latter times. Our famous Mede answers, in Dan. xi., where from ver. 30 is a plain prophecy of the Roman empire, and ver. 35—39, of antichrist, where it is said, *Some of them of understanding shall fall, to try them, and to purge,* &c.; and he speaks of a *king,* that *shall do according to his will, and shall exalt himself, and magnify himself above every god, and shall speak marvellous things against the God of gods.—Neither shall he regard the God of his fathers, nor the desire of women, nor regard any god,* but *magnify himself above all.* Where that learned man thinks is an excellent description of the Roman empire, their various victories, successes, declinations, and mutations, and amongst other things, ver. 36, that they should cast off their old pagan idolatry, and after that make a defection from the Christian faith, and not regard marriage, (called there *the desire of women.*) nor indeed truly regard any god. This the apostle saith should be in the *latter times.* The last times (saith the afore-mentioned famous author) are the times of Christ's kingdom, which began in the time of the Roman empire; during which time this Epistle was written, where the apostle speaking of time yet to come, the *latter times* by him mentioned must needs be the latter part of the last times, which he saith began in the ruin of the Roman empire, upon which followed the revealing of antichrist, that wicked one, mentioned 2 Thess. ii. 7. Concerning these times, the Spirit said expressly, *that some should in them depart from the faith, giving heed to seducing spirits;* by which some understand the devils themselves; others, false teachers, or false doctrines, which are afterwards mentioned, called *doctrines of devils,* by which some understand doctrines suggested by devils, or published by the cunning and art of devils. But others think that by *doctrines of devils* here are not to be understood doctrines so published, but doctrines concerning devils; and that the meaning is, that in the last times the pagan doctrine concerning demons should be restored. The pagan demons were an inferior sort of gods, a kind of middle beings between their highest gods and men, whose office was to be advocates and mediators between men and the highest gods, because they judged it was not lawful for men to come to the highest gods immediately; these they worshipped by images, even as the papists at this day make use of and worship angels and saints. See more fully what Mr. Mede saith upon this argument in his own book, and in Mr. Pool's Latin Synopsis upon this text; and what he saith seems very probably the sense of this text, especially considering the two doctrines mentioned ver. 3.

e Matt. 7. 15.
Rom. 16. 18.
2 Pet. 2. 3.
f Eph. 4. 19.

2 ᵉSpeaking lies in hypocrisy; ᶠhaving their conscience seared with a hot iron;

The words, as translated by us, are very difficult; for the word which we translate *speaking lies,* being the genitive case, will neither agree with *spirits* nor *doctrines,* in the former verse, they being both the dative: but neither is our translation agreeable to the Greek, which is thus, In or through the hypocrisy of such as speak lies, and of such as have a conscience seared with a hot iron; which doubtless is the sense; so the words explain the manner how they were seduced to apostasy, viz. through the hypocrisy or dissimulation of men that speak lies, and had consciences benumbed, and mortified, as it were cauterized and seared with a hot iron. By their hypocrisy he characterizes seducers, uncertain, false men, that regarded not what they said, but made a show and appearance of piety, when indeed they had no sense of piety in them. By men whose *consciences* were *seared with a hot iron,* he means persons so far from any sense of piety, that they were hardened to any degree of iniquity: and indeed by both terms he excellently expresseth such persons as generally they are who seduce others to false doctrine, they could not do it without some show or pretence of piety, they would not do it if they had any true sense of it; and by both terms he too well expresseth those that in our days seduce men to the doctrines concerning demons, and abstaining from marriage and meats, which are those doctrines he alone instanceth in.

g 1 Cor. 7.
28, 36, 38.
Col. 2. 20, 21.
Heb. 13. 4.
h Rom. 14.
3, 17.
1 Cor. 8. 8.
i Gen. 1. 29.
& 9. 3.
k Rom. 14. 6.
1 Cor. 10. 30.

3 ᵍForbidding to marry, ʰ*and commanding* to abstain from meats, which God hath created ⁱto be received ᵏwith thanksgiving of them which believe and know the truth.

Forbidding to marry: the Greek is, hindering to marry, but that might be by forbidding it by a law under a severe penalty. There are great disputes whom the apostle speaketh of, to find out which it is considerable, 1. That the apostle speaketh of a time that was then to come; 2. Of some who had it in their power to hinder it: which will make the prophecy hardly applicable to any but the Romish synagogue, to be sure, not so applicable; for though there were some persons before them that condemned marriages, yet as they were but a small, inconsiderable party, so they were persons that had no power to hinder marriage by any penal laws, nor any that did it in such hypocrisy under a pretence of piety, when he who runs may read that they do it to maintain the grandeur of their ecclesiastical hierarchy. How applicable therefore soever this might be to the Ebionites, and those that followed Saturninus and Marcion, and the Encratitæ, (which the papists contend for,) it certainly more nearly concerns the papists themselves, who more universally forbade them to their clergy, and were the first that had a power to hinder them, and fell into much later times than any of the others. *And commanding to abstain from meats;* to abstain from some meats; and this also they should teach in hypocrisy, i. e. under a pretence of piety. This every whit as well agrees to the Romish synagogue as the other, whose prohibitions of flesh are sufficiently known. Mr. Mede is very confident that the Holy Ghost doth here describe the popish monks, and those that gave rules to those orders. *Which God hath created to be received with thanksgiving;* which meats, as well as other, God hath created for the use of man, giving him a liberty to kill and eat, only we ought to receive them with *thanksgiving;* which confirmeth our religious custom both of begging a blessing upon our meat before we eat, and returning thanks to God when we have eaten, for which also we have our Saviour's example, Matt. xiv. 19; xv. 36. *Of them which believe and know the truth:* not that such as believe not and are ignorant of the truth may not eat, but they have not so good and comfortable a right to the creatures as believers, Tit. i. 15; and they know and understand their liberty to eat of those things, which others deprive themselves of by their superstitious opinions and constitutions.

4 For ˡevery creature of God *is* good, and nothing to be refused, if it be received with thanksgiving:

l Rom. 14. 14, 20. 1 Cor. 10. 25. Tit. i. 15.

For every creature of God is good; not only good in itself, as all was which God made, Gen. i., but lawful to be used, pure, Tit. i. 15, there is no uncleanness in it. *And nothing to be refused;* and therefore nothing upon that account is to be refused, as unclean and defiling. *If it be received with thanksgiving;* only it must be made use of in such a manner as in and by the use of it we may glorify, and express our thankfulness to, God.

5 For it is sanctified by the word of God and prayer.

For it is sanctified: sanctified in this place signifies made pure, or lawful to be used. *By the word of God;* by the gospel, which declares it so, Acts x. 15; or by God's ordination, which hath so determined it. *And prayer;* and prayer to God for a blessing upon it.

6 If thou put the brethren in remembrance of these things, thou shalt be a good minister of Jesus Christ, ᵐnourished up in the words of faith and of good doctrine, whereunto thou hast attained.

m 2 Tim. 3. 14, 15.

If thou put the brethren in remembrance of these things; if by thy preaching publicly, and by thy more private instructions of Christians at Ephesus, thou teachest them these things. *Thou shalt be a good minister of Jesus Christ;* thou shalt faithfully discharge the office of him who is a servant of Jesus Christ, not of men merely. The ministers of the gospel are in the first place ministers or servants to Christ. Secondarily, ministers (that is, servants) of the church; as a nobleman's servant employed to distribute wages or meat to inferior servants, is a minister to those to whom he so distributeth food or wages, but in the first place a servant to his lord. *Nourished up in the words of faith and of good doctrine;* such a minister of the gospel ought to be one bred up in the true faith, and persevering in it. *Whereunto thou hast attained;* whereto thou art not a stranger, only I would have thee go on and persevere in it.

7 But ⁿrefuse profane and old wives' fables, and ᵒexercise thyself *rather* unto godliness.

n ch. 1. 4.
& 6. 20.
2 Tim. 2. 16, 23. & 4. 4.
Tit. 1. 14.
o Heb. 5. 14.

But refuse profane and old wives' fables; all impertinent

I. TIMOTHY IV.

discourses, which tend nothing to promote either faith or holiness, which he disdainfully calls *old wives' fables*, tales of a tub, as we say, discourses having no bottom in the word of God, are not fit for pulpits. *And exercise thyself rather unto godliness ;* let thy constant study be things that may promote godliness, impart those things unto people, and live up to them in thy conversation.

p 1 Cor. 8. 8.
Col. 2. 23.
∥ Or, *for a little time.*
q ch. 6. 6.
r Ps. 37. 4. & 84. 11. & 112. 2, 3. & 145. 19. Matt. 6. 33. & 19. 29. Mark 10. 30. Rom. 8. 28.

8 For ᵖ bodily exercise profiteth ∥ little: ᑫ but godliness is profitable unto all things, ʳ having promise of the life that now is, and of that which is to come.

For bodily exercise profiteth little ; bodily discipline, lying in abstaining from certain meats, keeping set fasts, watchings, lying upon the ground, going barefoot, wearing sackcloth or haircloth, abstaining from wine or marriage, is of little advantage, the mind and soul of man is not bettered by them : the apostle doth not altogether despise these things, some of which may be useful (moderately used) to make us more fit for prayer, especially upon solemn occasions ; but these are not things wherein religion is to be put, and alone they are of no avail. *But godliness is profitable unto all things ;* but godliness, which lieth in the true worship and service of God, out of a true principle of the fear of God and faith in him ; or (more generally) holiness of life in obedience to God's commandments, is of universal advantage ; *having promise of the life that now is, and of that which is to come ;* not from any meritoriousness in it, but from the free grace of God, which hath annexed to it not only the promises of health, peace, and prosperity, and all good things while we live here upon the earth, but also the promises of salvation and eternal happiness when this life shall be determined.

s ch. 1. 15.

9 ˢ This *is* a faithful saying and worthy of all acceptation.

This saying about the advantage of godliness is true, and worthy to be received of all men. See the notes on chap. i. 15, where the same words are applied to the great proposition of the gospel, *That Christ came into the world to save sinners.* That Christ came into the world to save sinners, and that such sinners as from ungodly will become godly, and persevere in the practice of godliness, shall be happy in this life, and saved in the life to come, are two faithful and remarkable sayings, worthy the acceptation of all reasonable creatures.

t 1 Cor. 4. 11, 12.
u ch. 6. 17.
x Ps. 36. 6. & 107. 2, 6, &c.

10 For therefore ᵗ we both labour and suffer reproach, because we ᵘ trust in the living God, ˣ who is the saviour of all men, specially of those that believe.

If we did not believe this as *a faithful saying*, that *godliness is profitable for all things*, and *trust in God*, who liveth for ever, to see to the fulfilling of it, to what purpose should *we labour and suffer reproach* as we do ; labouring in the work of God, suffering reproach in the cause of God, and for living godly lives, worshipping God according to his will, and denying ourselves in sensual satisfactions and sensible enjoyments, that we might fulfil the law of Christ ? *Object.* But, will some say, how then is godliness profitable for all things, how doth the faithfulness of the promises for this life annexed to godliness appear, if those that profess it must labour and suffer reproach ? *Solut.* Labour for God is a reward to itself, our honour, not our burden, his service is perfect freedom : the promises of this life, annexed to godliness, are not promises of sensual rest and ease, but of inward peace, satisfaction, and support of other things, only with a reserve to the Divine wisdom and judgment, so far forth as our heavenly Father shall see it fit for his glory and our good ; yet they are not vain, for God, *who is the Saviour*, that is, the Preserver, *of all men*, the Preserver of man and beast, as the psalmist speaketh, is in a more especial manner the Saviour *of those that believe*, Psal. xxxiii. 18, 19. This seemeth rather to be the sense of the text, than to understand it of eternal salvation, for so God is not the actual Saviour of all ; besides that the text seemeth to speak of a work proper to the Father, rather than to the Son.

y ch. 6. 2.

11 ʸ These things command and teach.

All the things before mentioned, in this or the former parts of this Epistle, he willeth Timothy to make the matter of his sermons and other discourses.

12 ᶻ Let no man despise thy youth ; but ᵃ be thou an example of the believers, in word, in conversation, in charity, in spirit, in faith, in purity.

z 1 Cor. 16. 11. Tit. 2. 15.
a Tit. 2. 7. 1 Pet. 5. 3.

Let no man despise thy youth ; so carry thyself in thy office, as not to give occasion to any to despise thee because thou art but a young man. *But be thou an example of the believers :* which thou wilt do if thou so livest as to be a just pattern unto Christians, imitable by them *in word*, in thy common and ordinary discourse, (for he speaks not of his being a pattern only to other ministers, but *to believers* in the generality,) not talking frothily or profanely, or idly and impertinently, but seriously and gravely, of *things that are good, to the use of edifying, that it may administer grace to the hearers. In conversation ;* and in all thy converse with men behaving thyself justly, and comelily, and gravely. *In charity ;* performing also to all, all offices of charity and brotherly love. *In spirit ;* in zeal, and warmth of spirit, truly inflamed with the love of Christ, and for his glory. *In faith ;* in a steady confession and profession of the doctrine of the gospel ; and *in purity ;* in all cleanness and holiness of life and conversation. This is the way for the ministers of the gospel not to be despised : let them use what other methods they will, they will find what God said of Hophni and Phinehas will be made good, 1 Sam. ii. 30, *Them that honour me I will honour, and they that despise me shall be lightly esteemed ;* nor will any titles, or habits, or severities secure them from that curse, which will cleave to them.

13 Till I come, give attendance to reading, to exhortation, to doctrine.

Till I come, and after that time too, but then I will further instruct thee. *Give attendance to reading ;* be diligent in reading the Holy Scriptures, both for thine own instruction and for the edification of others. *To exhortation ;* to exhort others to their duty there described, or to comfort others from arguments fetched thence. *To doctrine ;* to instruct others in the principles of religion.

14 ᵇ Neglect not the gift that is in thee, which was given thee ᶜ by prophecy, ᵈ with the laying on of the hands of the presbytery.

b 2 Tim. 1. 6.
c ch. 1. 18.
d Acts 6. 6. & 8. 17. & 13. 3. & 19. 6.
ch. 5. 22.
2 Tim. 1. 6.

Neglect not the gift that is in thee ; neglect neither the ability which God hath given thee for the discharge of the office of the ministry, nor the office to which God hath called thee ; neither the improvement of them, nor the use, exercise, and discharge of them or it. *Which was given thee by prophecy ;* remember that they were given thee by the revelation of the Divine will, or by the extraordinary influence of the Spirit of God ; and *the laying on of the hands of the presbytery* was a declaration of it ; God also (as usually when he calls any to any special work) calling thee to the work of the ministry then also, fitting and enabling thee for the discharge of it.

15 Meditate upon these things ; give thyself wholly to them ; that thy profiting may appear ∥ to all.

∥ Or, *in all things.*

Meditate upon these things ; Μελίτα, let these things be the business of thy thoughts, and take care of them. *Give thyself wholly to them ;* be in them, (so it is in the Greek,) let them be thy whole work, not thy work by the by, but thy chief and principal business. *That thy profiting may appear to all ;* that so, as all men's gifts improve by study and exercise, thine also may so improve, that all men may take notice of the improvement of them.

16 ᵉ Take heed unto thyself, and unto the doctrine ; continue in them : for in doing this thou shalt both ᶠ save thyself, and ᵍ them that hear thee.

e Acts 20. 28.
f Ezek. 33. 9. g Rom. 11. 14. 1 Cor. 9. 22. Jam. 5. 20.

Take heed unto thyself ; take heed how thou livest, and orderest thy life, that it may be exemplary. *And unto the doctrine ;* and take heed also both that thou teachest, and what thou teachest. *Continue in them ;* and do both these things not for a time, but constantly. *For in doing this thou* shalt both save thyself, and them that hear thee; thus thou shalt do what in thee lieth to save thine own soul, and also to save the souls of others to whom thou preachest, or among whom thou conversest.

CHAP. V

Directions to Timothy how to admonish persons of different conditions, 1, 2. *Concerning widows*, 3—16. *Elders, if they do well, are to be doubly honoured*, 17, 18; *and are not to be censured without full proof, and then openly and impartially*, 19—21. *A caution not to ordain any one precipitately*, 22. *Advice respecting Timothy's health*, 23. *Some men's characters are more easily discerned that those of others*, 24, 25.

a Lev. 19.32. REBUKE [a] not an elder, but intreat *him* as a father; *and* the younger men as brethren;

Rebuke not an elder: it appeareth by the next verse, that the apostle by *elder* here understandeth not a church officer, but an ancient man. The word translated *rebuke* is translated too softly; it should be, Rebuke not too roughly, as appears by the opposite phrase, and indeed the word properly signifies to beat or lash. Rebuke him not but with a decent respect to his age. *But entreat him as a father;* so that thy reproofs may look more like counsels and exhortations than rebukes. *And the younger men as brethren;* prudence also must be used as to the younger men, ministers in rebuking them should remember that they are *brethren*, and treat them accordingly, not too imperiously.

2 The elder women as mothers; the younger as sisters, with all purity.

The elder women as mothers; the same prudence also is to be used to matrons and aged women. *The younger as sisters;* yea, and to younger women too, considering our relation and equality in Christ. *With all purity;* only as to them, (considering their sex,) a further gravity and prudence is to be used, that we give no occasion to lust, or unclean motions.

b ver. 5, 16. 3 Honour widows [b] that are widows indeed.

Honour widows; give a respect to such as have lost their husbands, with a regard to that honourable estate of marriage in which they have been formerly, and do not only pay them a due respect, but afford them a maintenance, Acts vi. 1. *That are widows indeed:* who are widows indeed he openeth further, ver. 5; such as are not only pious, but desolate, as the Greek word for a widow implies, according to its derivation.

4 But if any widow have children or nephews, let them learn first to shew
‖ Or, kindness.
c See Gen. 45. 10, 11.
Matt. 15. 4.
Eph. 6. 1, 2.
d ch. 2. 3.
‖ piety at home, and [c] to requite their parents: [d] for that is good and acceptable before God.

But if any widow have children or nephews: by the *widows indeed*, mentioned by the apostle, ver. 3, he here showeth that he meant women that not only wanted husbands, but children, or grandchildren, or any near kindred that were Christians, and in a capacity to relieve them; but if any widows had any such near relations, the apostle willeth that they should be taught *to show piety at home;* τον ἰδιον οἰκον εὐσεβεῖν, word for word, to worship their own house, or to be religious or godly toward their own house; that is, to show a respect or pagan homage to their own house. For worship is nothing but a respect, honour, or homage paid to another in consideration of his or her excellency and superiority; only the use of this word, which is the Greek word generally used to express religion and godliness by, lets us know that religion and godliness is vainly pretended to any that have of this world's goods, and relieve not those from whom they are descended, (for the word ἔκγονα signifies persons descended from another, whether in the first generation or no,) if they be in want, and stand in need of their assistance. *And to requite their parents:* nor is this an act of charity, but justice, a just requital of our parents for their care of us, and pains with

us in our education. *For that is good and acceptable before God;* and this is good, just, decent, and commanded by God, and acceptable in the sight of God, for the precept, Honour thy father and mother, is the first commandment with promise, Eph. vi. 2. By the way, that precept is excellently expounded by this text, both as to the act commanded, which this text teacheth is to be extended to maintenance as well as compliments; and as to the object, viz. all those as to whom we are ἔκγονα, descended from, whether immediate parents, yea or no.

5 [e] Now she that is a widow indeed, e 1 Cor. 7. 32.
and desolate, trusteth in God, and [f] con- f Luke 2. 37. & 18. 1.
tinueth in supplications and prayers [g] night g Acts 26. 7.
and day.

Now she that is a widow indeed, and desolate: the apostle here opens the term of *widow indeed*, ver. 3; one that is μεμονωμένη one that is made alone, destitute of such as ought to help her, a husband, or children; and being so, *trusteth in God;* is a believer, reposing her trust and confidence in God; *and continueth in supplications and prayers night and day;* spendeth her time religiously in prayer and acts of devotion. Not that other persons that are poor and desolate should not be regarded and taken care for, but the church is not so concerned in them, at least as a church; the magistrate ought to take care of them, and all good Christians, being men as well as Christians, ought to consider them; but in the first place, and principally, they are to take care of such widows, such desolate persons.

6 [h] But she that liveth ‖ in pleasure is h Jam. 5. 5.
dead while she liveth. ‖ Or, delicately.

Ἡ δὲ σπαταλῶσα, she that is wanton, James v. 5, she that spends her money in needless costs, as to meat, drink, or apparel, is spiritually dead, dead in sin, while she liveth a temporary voluptuous life, in vanity, and luxury, and impurity of flesh and spirit.

7 [i] And these things give in charge, i ch. 1. 3. & 4. 11. & 6. 17.
that they may be blameless.

In the discharge of thy ministry declare these things, that all Christians, women especially, may be blameless.

8 But if any provide not for his own, k Is. 58. 7. Gal. 6. 10.
[k] and specially for those of his own ‖ house, ‖ Or, kindred.
[l] he hath denied the faith, [m] and is worse l 2 Tim. 3. 5. Tit. 1. 16.
than an infidel. m Mat.18.17.

But if any provide not for his own, and specially for those of his own house: here is a manifest distinction betwixt *his own,* ἰδίων, and *his own household,* οἰκείων, they are distinguished by terms in the Greek, and as to the care which men and women ought to extend to them. By *his own* he means his relations, all of a man's family or stock; by *his own household,* he seemeth to mean those who cohabit with him. The apostle saith that he who is careless of providing for the former, (so far as he is able,) but especially for the latter, *hath denied* the Christian *faith,* that is, in the practice of it, though in words he professeth it; he liveth not up to the rule of the gospel, which directeth other things. *And is worse than an infidel;* and is worse than a heathen, that believeth not; because many good-natured heathens do this by the light of nature, and those who do it not, yet are more excusable, being strangers to the obligation of the revealed law of God in the case.

9 Let not a widow be ‖ taken into the ‖ Or, chosen.
number under threescore years old, [n] hav- n Luke 2.36. ch. 3. 2.
ing been the wife of one man,

Let not a widow be taken into the number under threescore years old; what number he meaneth is very doubtful, whether he means the number of deaconesses, or the number of such as should receive alms from the church. Those who translate καταλεγέσθω here *chosen* seem to favour the former. They say, that in the primitive church there being a want of hospitals and public places for the reception of people deceased in their estates, &c., they chose some old widows to take care of the poorer sort of women when they were sick, and these also were themselves maintained by the church, and served the church in that charitable employment. Whether this number, or the more general number of widows relieved by the church, be meant, the caution of their age was very prudent: 1. Because younger widows could work for their living, and needed not to burden the church. 2. Because under those years they probably might marry again, and so become useless to the church. 3. Because after those years there could be no great fear of scandal from their wantonness and incontinency. *Having been the wife of one man:* this condition seems harder to be understood; for though in former times, amongst the Jews and pagans, men were allowed more wives than one at the same time, yet no laws ever allowed the woman liberty of more husbands. 2. To understand it of women that had not been twice married, their first husbands being dead, seems hard, no law of God forbidding the second marriages of men and women successively. 3. Some therefore rather understand it of such widows as were become wives to second husbands, the first not being dead, but parted from them legally, either through their own fault, or through their voluntary desertion. This the apostle seems to forbid, to avoid reproach and scandal to the church.

10 Well reported of for good works; if she have brought up children, if she have °lodged strangers, if she have ᵖwashed the saints' feet, if she have relieved the afflicted, if she have diligently followed every good work.

o Acts 16.15.
Heb. 13. 2.
1 Pet. 4. 9.
p Gen. 18. 4.
& 19. 2.
Luke 7. 38,
44. John 13.
5, 14.

Well reported of for good works; if she be a person of repute for actions concerning others which are consonant to the will and commandment of God. *If she have brought up children* well, in the nurture and admonition of the Lord. *If she have lodged strangers;* if when persons that are Christians have come from other places, either driven from them, or upon their occasion, and could not amongst pagans find a convenient inn, her house have been open to them. *If she have washed the saints' feet;* if she have been ready to do the meanest offices for the servants of God, of which this washing of feet was one in great use in those hot countries, where they had not the benefit of shoes, either to cool, or refresh, or cleanse them. *If she have relieved the afflicted;* if to her ability she have relieved such as have been in any kind of distress. *If she have diligently followed every good work;* if though it may be she have not had ability, or opportunity, to do all the good works she would, yet she have diligently followed them, doing what she could;—let such a one be put into the catalogue of those whom the church will relieve, and honour, and employ.

11 But the younger widows refuse: for when they have begun to wax wanton against Christ, they will marry;

But the younger widows refuse: by *the younger widows* the apostle means (by the last words of this verse) not to mean those that were under threescore, but the younger sort of widows, not past child-bearing; he would not have those (that is, being under no extraordinary circumstances of sickness, or lameness, or the want of their senses) be maintained at the charge of the church, because they were able to labour; nor yet to be taken into any employment relating to the church. *For when they have begun to wax wanton against Christ;* καταστρηνιάσωσι τῦ Χριστῦ. How the Vulgar Latin comes to translate this, *wax wanton in Christ,* I neither understand whether with respect to grammar or sense. Erasmus translates the verb, *when they have committed whoredom;* but Rev. xviii. 9 confuteth this sense, where we translate it, *lived deliciously,* (being without the preposition κατὰ,) which certainly better expresseth the sense, as also doth our translation, *wax wanton;* it properly signifies either the lustiness, or the headstrong temper, of beasts, that wax fat. *Against Christ,* is against the rule of the gospel, and their profession of Christ; or they disdain the office of serving the saints, as too mean, and laborious, and sin against Christ, in whose name, and for whose glory, and to whose members, the service was to be performed. And then *they will marry,* and so put themselves into an incapacity to serve the church in the place of widows.

12 Having damnation, because they have cast off their first faith.

This sentence is not without its difficulties: here are two questions: 1. What is meant by κρίμα, which we both here and elsewhere translate *damnation.* 2. How they *cast off their first faith.* Many think the Greek word by us translated *damnation,* ought to have had a softer sense, it being certainly capable of it. Some think it signifies here no more than guilt, or a blot; others, a public infamy; others, the judgment of good men against them. But it may be we cannot so well determine this without understanding what is meant by *their first faith,* which they are here said to *have cast off:* by which some understand their profession of Christianity; others, their promise or engagement to the church, not to marry. The latter sense supposeth that all those widows that were taken into the ministry of the church before mentioned, promised that they would keep themselves unmarried, which is a most groundless supposition. I do rather think that by *their first faith,* he means their first or former profession of Christianity; which was a crime that did expose them not only to the judgment and censure of sober Christians, but to eternal damnation. I shall offer my own sense of this text thus: it is certain these Christians were lilies among thorns, a small handful amongst a far greater number of pagans; and it is not improbable, that some younger widows, out of a desire to marry, might marry to pagans, and be by them tempted to apostacy from the Christian profession; upon which the apostle orders, that none under sixty years of age should be henceforth taken into the ministry of the church, lest doing such a thing when they were under that character, it should be a greater scandal. This seems the more probable from ver. 15, where the apostle adds, *for some are already turned aside after Satan.*

13 ᑫAnd withal they learn to be idle, wandering about from house to house; and not only idle, but tattlers also and busybodies, speaking things which they ought not.

q 2 Thess. 3. 11.

The apostle here gives some other reasons, why he would not have widows too young taken into the ministry of the church. *And withal they learn to be idle, wandering about from house to house;* they being young, and having no business at home, nor any husbands to conduct and govern them, are subject to be gadding up and down; *and not only idle, but tattlers also;* and to be tattling idly and impertinently, and that not only of their own, but others' concerns; *and busybodies,* interesting themselves in the matters of other persons and families; *speaking things which they ought not,* and in the multitude of words, folly being never wanting, they are prone to speak things which they ought not: from whence we may observe, that nothing more becometh Christians than a gravity and composedness of behaviour and speech, a government of their tongues, and considering aforehand well what they speak.

14 ʳI will therefore that the younger women marry, bear children, guide the house, ˢgive none occasion to the adversary † to speak reproachfully.

r 1 Cor. 7. 9
s ch. 6. 1.
Tit. 2. 8.
† Gr. *for their railing.*

I will therefore that the younger women marry: I will, here, must not be interpreted into an absolute precept, (for the apostle would never have made that necessary by his precept which God had left indifferent,) but in a limited sense, viz. if they have not the gift of continency, if they cannot restrain themselves from such scandalous courses, let them marry; *bear children,* and not only bring forth children, but take care of their education; *guide the house,* and take care of the government of families within doors (which is the woman's proper province); *give none occasion to the adversary to speak reproachfully;* and give no occasion to Jews or pagans (the adversaries of Christian religion) to speak of the church, or any particular members of it, reproachfully, as living beneath the rules of morality and decency.

15 For some are already turned aside after Satan.

We have scandals enough already, we had need take as good heed as we can that we have no more; some young women already are apostatized (and, possibly, for the sake or by the occasion of such marriages) to Judaism or paganism; or, it may be, to a loose and lewd course of life, not suiting the profession of Christianity.

I. TIMOTHY V

16 If any man or woman that believeth have widows, let them relieve them, and let not the Church be charged; that it may relieve ᵗthem that are widows indeed.

ᵗver. 3, 5.

If any man or woman that believeth have widows; if any men or women that are Christians have any widows that are nearly related to them, if themselves be able, *let them relieve them, and let not the church be charged;* and not turn off that natural duty which they owe to their parents, or near relations, to relieve them, to the church, which hath others enough to look after, and upon which there lies only a moral and Christian obligation. *That it may relieve them that are widows indeed;* that so the alms of the church may go to relieve those only who are perfectly desolate, having neither husbands nor any other near relations to provide for them.

17 ᵘLet the elders that rule well ˣbe counted worthy of double honour, especially they who labour in the word and doctrine.

ᵘ Rom. 12. 8. 1 Cor. 9. 10. 14. Gal. 6. 6. Phil. 2. 29. 1 Thess. 5. 12, 13. Heb. 13. 7, 17.
ˣ Acts 28. 10.

Who these *elders* are here intended hath been a great question: it is plain they are not such only as are preachers. They are such as are *worthy of double honour*. The learned Mr. Pool, in his Latin Synopsis, giveth us an account of the most opinions about it: 1. Some judging them some of the elder sort of the members of the church, joining with the ministers in the government of the church, but not meddling with preaching, or administering sacraments. 2. Some judging by elders here are meant such as had been ministers, but being aged were superannuated. 3. Others understanding by it the civil magistrates; which seemeth of all other opinions least probable, because at this time there were no such members of the Christian church. 4. Others think that deacons are here by that term understood, who being church officers have the name of *elders* given to them. 5. Others understand by *elders* the ordinary pastors of churches, that resided with their flocks, in opposition to apostles and evangelists: this seemeth less probable, because there were no such in the primitive church but did labour in the word and doctrine. 6. Others think that some such are meant, as were not so fit for preaching, but yet administered the sacraments, prayed with the church, and privately admonished exorbitant members; but we shall want a good proof, either from Scripture or other authority, of any such officers in the primitive church. I shall not determine which of these opinions is rightest, but leave the reader to his own judgment. Whoever are here meant by elders are declared *worthy of double honour;* by which is understood either abundant honour, or else (as some say) respect and reverence, and also maintenance. *Especially they who labour in the word and doctrine;* but especially such as take pains in preaching the gospel.

18 For the Scripture saith, ʸThou shalt not muzzle the ox that treadeth out the corn. And, ᶻThe labourer is worthy of his reward.

ʸ Deut. 25. 4. 1 Cor. 9. 9.
ᶻ Lev. 19. 13. Deut. 24. 14, 15. Matt. 10. 10. Luke 10. 7.

This verse maketh it evident that maintenance is part of the *double honour* that is due to such as labour in the word and doctrine in the first place; and not to them alone, but to any such as are employed in the rule and government of the church. The apostle had made use of Deut. xxv. 4 to the same purpose, 1 Cor. ix. 9: neither of these texts conclude the duty of elders to take maintenance, but the duty of those who are members of churches to give it them, which yet they may refuse, as Paul himself did, if either the people's or minister's circumstances call for or will allow such a thing.

19 Against an elder receive not an accusation, but ‖ ᵃbefore two or three witnesses.

‖ Or, *under.*
ᵃ Deut. 19. 15.

Against an elder; whether an elder in years or in office, though the latter being the persons formerly spoken of, seem here principally intended. *Receive not an accusation, but before two or three witnesses;* that is, not to proceed to any judicial inquiry upon it, Deut. xvii. 6. This was a law concerning all elders or younger persons, especially in capital causes, but the apostle willeth this to be more specially observed as to officers in the church, whose faithful discharge of their trusts usually more exposeth them to people's querulous tongues.

20 ᵇThem that sin rebuke before all, ᶜthat others also may fear.

ᵇ Gal. 2. 11, 14. Tit. 1. 13.
ᶜ Deut. 13. 11.

Them that sin; that is, that sin publicly and scandalously, so as others have taken notice of it. *Rebuke before all;* rebuke not privately, by a ministerial correption, but by a public ecclesiastical correption before the whole church. *That others also may fear;* that the salve may answer the sore, and the plaster be as broad as the wound; and that others may be afraid to do the like. This end of the punishment agreeth with that mentioned Deut. xiii. 11.

21 ᵈI charge thee before God, and the Lord Jesus Christ, and the elect angels, that thou observe these things ‖ without preferring one before another, doing nothing by partiality.

ᵈ ch. 6. 13. 2 Tim. 2. 14. & 4. 1.
‖ Or, *without prejudice.*

I charge thee before God, and the Lord Jesus Christ, and the elect angels, that thou observe these things: by *these things* may be understood the whole of what went before, or what followeth. I judge it most proper to refer it to all the precepts foregoing in this Epistle, which evidenceth them to be things which he had received from the Lord, not what he directed without any express notice of the will of God as to them. This is evident by his grave and severe charge to Timothy to observe them, for he chargeth him to observe them as in the presence of God and Christ, and calleth the good angels to be witnesses, both of his faithfulness, in giving him this charge, and of Timothy's faithfulness or unfaithfulness, according as he should observe or neglect the things given him in charge: he calls the angels *elect,* unquestionably in opposition to the evil and reprobate angels. *Without preferring one before another, doing nothing by partiality:* he requires the doing of them without respect to any persons, rich or poor, friends or foes; *partiality* no way becoming a judge in any cause, who ought to hold the balance even, not inclining it any way, but judging things and not persons. Some of the things before mentioned may seem of too minute a consideration for the apostle to lay such a stress upon, or God to give him particular direction in; but the things are not so much to be considered as the end of the precepts, which was the upholding the true honour and reputation of the church, which is a very great thing; and supposing the things given in charge to have any tendency of that nature, they must not be judged small.

22 ᵉLay hands suddenly on no man, ᶠneither be partaker of other men's sins: keep thyself pure.

ᵉ Acts 6. 6. & 13. 3. ch. 4. 14. 2 Tim. 1. 6.
ᶠ 2 John 11.

By *Lay hands suddenly on no man,* is certainly to be understood, Do thou suddenly set no man apart to any ecclesiastical employment. Laying on of hands was but an external ceremony used in blessing, Gen. xlviii. 14, 15, and in the conferring of power upon persons, Numb. xxvii. 18; Deut. xxxiv. 9. In the New Testament we find this rite used: in prayer upon healing the sick, Mark xvi. 18; Acts xxviii. 8; in blessing, Mark x. 16; in conferring the gifts of the Holy Ghost, Acts xix. 6; in ordination, or setting persons apart to some ecclesiastical employment, chap. iv. 14; Acts vi. 6; and being so used, it is sometimes put for the whole action. This the apostle forbids Timothy to do *suddenly,* that is, without a first proof of the person's fitness for his work, chap. iii. 10, both with respect to his knowledge, and to his holiness of conversation. *Neither be partaker of other men's sins:* this participation of other men's sin ought to be taken heed of in the whole course of our conversation, but it seemeth here to be especially forbidden with reference to what was before spoken of, viz. the setting men apart for or putting them into any ecclesiastical employment; he who puts into the ministry any erroneous or ignorant persons, or any persons of a lewd conversation, makes himself guilty of all the harm they do, if he hath not first taken a due and reasonable proof of them, but hath laid hands upon them suddenly. Amongst other ways by which we interest ourselves in others' guilt, one is, by not hindering it, having power so to do. He, or they, whom it lies upon to admit, or not admit, men into the ministry, have a power to refuse them in case upon proof of them they do not find them apt to teach, or fit for the ministration they are to undertake, or such for holiness of life as God requireth : God by his word declaring what such persons ought to be, and commanding him or them first to prove such persons, and to lay hands on none suddenly, hath invested him or them with such a power, of which man cannot deprive them. *Keep thyself pure :* the purity here mentioned, is comprehensive of that chastity which some would have the word here signify, but it is most reasonable to understand it here with relation to what went before, viz. partaking of other men's sins ; If thou canst not keep the church pure, but ignorant or erroneous persons, or sots, will get into the church, yet let them not get in through thy hands, *keep thyself pure.*

23 Drink no longer water, but use a little wine ^g for thy stomach's sake and thine often infirmities.

g Ps. 104. 15.

Drink no longer water ; not wholly, as many did in those countries, and Timothy probably did, not because he was not able to buy wine, but religiously, as a piece of discipline to keep under the flesh. *But use a little wine ;* but mix some wine with the water. *For thy stomach's sake ;* to help thy digestion. *And thine often infirmities ;* in regard of thy weakness and frequent infirmities.

h Gal. 5. 19.

24 ^h Some men's sins are open beforehand, going before to judgment ; and some *men* they follow after.

The sense of this verse depends upon the term κρίσιν, which we translate *judgment,* it being doubtful whether it is to be understood of the judgment of God, or the judgment of men in ecclesiastical judicatories. If we understand the words of the judgment of God, the sense is this : Some men's sins are punished in this life, before their persons come before God's judgment-seat ; others are more private and concealed, the punishment of which follows after. But this interpretation must suppose Paul here to run into another argument, differing from what he had before spoken upon, which though it be not unusual with the apostle, yet there being no need we should say he doth so in this place, I rather incline to think, that by judgment is in this place meant the judgment of the church, as to persons fit to be trusted with any part of the ministry of it: Some men (saith the apostle) are open, lewd, scandalous persons, whose erroneousness, or sottish life, hath been manifest before they offer themselves to the church's judgment, to be put into the office of elders or deacons ; concerning these thy way is plain, admit them not. Others discover not the erroneousness of their principles, nor the impetuousness of their lusts, before they have obtained what they aim at, and are got into office ; for these, they must fall under thy judgment, when they do discover what they are, and turn them out again.

25 Likewise also the good works *of some* are manifest beforehand ; and they that are otherwise cannot be hid.

In like manner some men's holy life and conversation hath been so evident, that there needs little judgment concerning them ; and for others, under a due government they cannot be long concealed, but by thy due management of and vigilance in thy office they will soon be discovered, by their publishing their erroneous principles, and the breaking out of their lusts into enormous acts, so as they will soon fall under thy censure. Or else thus : The good works of some whose life hath not been so exemplary, but yet such as in charity thou mayst judge them to have the root of the matter in them, (if thou be not mistaken,) cannot be long hid, so as thou shalt soon see what they are, and accordingly know how to behave thyself to them. Thus I should choose rather to interpret this text than concerning the judgment of God, who sometimes rewards good works presently, and always rewards them certainly, either in this life or that which is come.

CHAP. VI

The duty of servants, 1, 2. *Those who teach not according to the apostle's doctrine are to be avoided, as corrupters of Christianity,* 3—5. *The gain of godliness with content,* 6—8. *The evil of covetousness,* 9, 10. *What Timothy is to flee, and what to follow and perform,* 11—16. *A charge to the rich not to be proud and confident in their riches, but to be beneficent and liberal,* 17—19. *Timothy is enjoined to adhere to the true faith, and to shun profane and vain controversies,* 20, 21.

LET as many ^a servants as are under the yoke count their own masters worthy of all honour, ^b that the name of God and *his* doctrine be not blasphemed.

a Eph. 6. 5. Col. 3. 22. Tit. 2. 9. 1 Pet. 2. 18. b Is. 52. 5. Rom. 2. 24. Tit. 2. 5, 8.

Let as many servants as are under the yoke ; under the yoke of servitude, not being manumised, or made free. *Count their own masters worthy of all honour ;* abundant honour : let Christian servants give their masters, instead of less, double the honour which pagan servants do. *That the name of God and his doctrine be not blasphemed ;* for the credit of the gospel, and for the honour of God ; that none may say that religion teacheth servants any disobedience, or breaketh the bands of civil relations : but on the contrary, that it obligeth professors to a more faithful and full discharge of such duties, servants to be the best of servants, &c.

2 And they that have believing masters, let them not despise *them,* ^c because they are brethren ; but rather do *them* service, because they are ‖ faithful and beloved, partakers of the benefit. ^d These things teach and exhort.

c Col. 4. 1.

‖ Or, *believing.* d ch. 4. 11.

Some Christians were servants to Jews or pagans, who both came under the gospel notion of believers ; as to these the apostle had given directions in ver. 1. Others served masters and mistresses that were Christians. The apostle, not ignorant of Satan's devices, foresaw that the former would be under a temptation to neglect and despise their masters or mistresses, because they were idolaters, or of a false religion, enemies to the gospel ; and the latter under a temptation not to be so diligent and serviceable as they should be, because their governors in a spiritual sense were their equals, their brethren and sisters. The apostle here declares, that the rules of the gospel neither allow the one nor the other : as to the former he had spoken ; nor, saith he, let those that have masters or mistresses that are Christians *despise them,* by which he means, not be equally obedient or serviceable to them, because there is a spiritual equality or relation betwixt them. *But rather do them service,* looking upon this as a further obligation upon them. *Because they are faithful and beloved, partakers of the benefit ;* because they are believers, such as love our common Lord, and are beloved of him, and such as all good Christians ought to love, being partakers of the gift of God, Christ Jesus, and the great benefit of redemption through his blood. *These things teach and exhort ;* and he willeth Timothy to teach the Christians at Ephesus, that this was the will of God, and accordingly to call upon them for an obedience to it.

3 If any man ^e teach otherwise, and consent ^f not to wholesome words, *even* the words of our Lord Jesus Christ, ^g and to the doctrine which is according to godliness ;

e ch. 1. 3. f ch. 1. 10. 2 Tim. 1. 13. & 4. 3. Tit. 1. 9. g Tit. 1. 1.

If any man teach otherwise ; if there be any person who either more publicly or more privately shall take upon him to instruct people otherwise. *And consent not to wholesome words :* what he means by *wholesome words* his next words show ; they are called wholesome because they tend to prevent the sickness of sin, or to cure the soul of its spiritual distempers. *Even the words of our Lord Jesus Christ, and to the doctrine which is according to godliness ;* words either spoken by Christ, or from Christ, or tending to his honour and glory, or to the promoting of piety and godliness, or which are according to the rule of godliness.

4 He is ‖ proud, [h]knowing nothing, but ‖ doting about [i]questions and strifes of words, whereof cometh envy, strife, railings, evil surmisings,

He is proud; τετύφωται, he is swelled or blown up, i. e. with pride swelling in opinion and conceit of himself, he is a fanatic. *Knowing nothing* solidly and truly, *but doting about questions and strifes of words;* is brain-sick about questions of no use, but to make a contention about words. *Whereof cometh envy;* when he once comes to perceive that others are wiser than he. *Strife;* for an ignorant person, if proud, can never yield that another knows more than he doth. *Railings* are commonly the revenges of ignorant sciolists, that would be thought something and are nothing; when they perceive they are outdone by others, then they rail. *Evil surmisings,* ὑπόνοιαι· when they can in truth say no evil of others, they will uncharitably surmise and suspect evil of them.

5 [k]‖ Perverse disputings of [l]men of corrupt minds, and destitute of the truth, [m]supposing that gain is godliness: [n]from such withdraw thyself.

Perverse disputings of men of corrupt minds, and destitute of the truth; Παραδιατριβαί, mutual tearings, and gallings of or interferings with one another. The word is applied to horses knocking one foot against another. The word without the preposition παρά signifies school-conflicts by disputations; the preposition added makes it to signify, in an evil sense, disputations of sophisters, not candid for the finding out of truth, but perverse and litigious merely for masteries; which he saith proceeds from men corrupted as to their understanding and judgment. *Supposing that gain is godliness;* all whose religion is gain of riches or reputation. *From such withdraw thyself;* with such men have nothing to do, avoid them in thy private converse, and cast them out of the church if their faults be public scandals, and they be contumacious.

6 But [o]godliness with contentment is great gain.

Godliness, the exercise of a true faith in Christ, conjoined with a holy life, is a good revenue of itself, having in it αὐταρκείας, a self-sufficiency. He doth not here suppose that godliness can be separated from a contented frame of spirit with that lot which God hath chosen for us, for that cannot be; but as being always attended with a contentation of mind, in which alone lieth true riches, for such men never want enough. *A good man,* Solomon saith, *is satisfied from himself,* Prov. xiv. 14; for which reason alone godliness is πορισμὸς μέγας, a great annual revenue.

7 For [p]we brought nothing into this world, *and it is* certain we can carry nothing out.

This agreeth with Job i. 21, and with experience, and is a potent argument against immoderate desires of having much of this world's goods, or using extravagant actions to obtain them; for when we have got all we can, we have got but a *viaticum,* something to serve us in our journey, which we must leave when we die, and whether to a wise man or a fool none knoweth, Eccles. ii. 19.

8 And [q]having food and raiment let us be therewith content.

If therefore God gives us any thing more than is necessary for us, let us take it thankfully, and use it for God's glory; but if we have no more than is just necessary for us, let us not repine, or murmur, but be content, without murmuring against God, or using any undue means, out of an inordinate desire to get more.

9 But [r]they that will be rich fall into temptation [s]and a snare, and *into* many foolish and hurtful lusts, [t]which drown men in destruction and perdition.

But; or, for. *They that will be rich;* they who, out of a covetous and immoderate desire of being rich in this world's goods, will use any arts, and do any unlawful thing, without any just regard to the law of God. *Fall into temptation and a snare;* fall into many temptations and snares, are exposed to impetuous inclinations and motions to that which is evil, and may and will be snares to their souls. *And into many foolish and hurtful lusts;* kindling in them many foolish and pernicious desires, contrary to the law of God. *Which drown men in destruction and perdition;* have a direct tendency to the eternal ruin of their souls, not to be prevented but by the force and powerful grace of God.

10 [u]For the love of money is the root of all evil: which while some coveted after, they have ‖ erred from the faith, and pierced themselves through with many sorrows.

For the love of money is the root of all evil: money itself is not evil, but the immoderate love of it, whether discerned in an over-eager desire after it, or an excessive delight in it, is the cause of much evil, both of sin and punishment. *Which while some coveted after, they have erred from the faith;* which money while some too greedily thirsted after, (for though the article be feminine and cannot grammatically agree with ἀργύριον, which is neuter, yet that doth agree with it as to the sense, being understood in φιλαργυρία, with which the subjunctive article grammatically agreeth,) *they have erred,* or been seduced, *from the faith,* that is, the doctrine of the gospel, or profession of Christianity. *And pierced themselves through with many sorrows;* and exposed themselves to a great many sorrows, which have pierced their very souls, such as cares, troubles for the loss of their estates, &c.

11 [x]But thou, [y]O man of God, flee these things; and follow after righteousness, godliness, faith, love, patience, meekness.

O man of God; that is, O thou minister of God, whose service is not the service of the world. It is a compellation borrowed from the Old Testament, where we find it often applied to such whose work was to reveal the Divine will, 2 Kings i. 9; iv. 40, 42. By giving Timothy this compellation, he mindeth him how much he was concerned to contemn the world. *Flee these things;* flee this eager pursuit of riches. *And follow after righteousness;* and follow after justice, or the business of a righteous life, in thy conversation with men. *Godliness;* piety toward God. *Faith;* the exercise and life of faith. *Love;* love to God and thy neighbour. *Patience;* a quiet bearing of injuries. *Meekness;* a gentleness of spirit, opposed to all rash anger.

12 [z]Fight the good fight of faith, [a]lay hold on eternal life, whereunto thou art also called, [b]and hast professed a good profession before many witnesses.

The *fight of faith* is our encountering that opposition which we meet with from the world, the flesh, or the devil, for a strenuous defending the doctrine of faith, or making it good by a life suitable to the rule of faith. This is called a *good fight,* either in opposition to the bad fights of the men of the world in maintenance of their lusts, or the ludicrous fights usual in their public games, or of the intrinsic nobleness and exercise of it, or the good event or issue of it; and Timothy is bid to *fight* it, by a metaphor either drawn from soldiers, or such as exercise themselves in their games. *Lay hold on eternal life;* by *eternal life* is meant a right and title to it, which he calls to him to *lay hold on,* as is thought, by a metaphor from those that were exercised in their games, and did what they could first to lay hold of the prize proposed to conquerors. *Whereunto thou art also called;* to which *eternal life,* or rather to which *good fight,* thou art called, both by the internal call of God's Spirit, and by thy more external call to the ministry. *And hast professed a good profession before many witnesses;* and to which thou hast obliged thyself by covenant or promise, made either in thy baptism, or when thou wert set apart to thy ministry, or of which thou hast given a pledge, by thy profession and practice, in the sight of the Christians in Ephesus.

13 [c]I give thee charge in the sight of

I. TIMOTHY VI

God, ^dwho quickeneth all things, and *before* Christ Jesus, ^ewho before Pontius Pilate witnessed a good || confession;

a Deut. 32. 39. 1 Sam. 2. 6. John 5. 21.
e Mat. 27. 11. John 18. 37.
Rev. 1. 5. & 3. 14. || *Or, profession.*

The apostle's care of the church showeth itself in these severe charges laid upon Timothy; though one whom he knew to be a faithful minister, he chargeth him, calling God to witness that he had fulfilled his part in laying this charge upon him. The name he here giveth unto God may possibly have a particular reference to the state of the gospel at that time, the doctrine and profession of which had many enemies, and so it is made use of here to comfort and encourage Timothy. God is called he *who quickeneth the dead*, Rom. iv. 17; here, he *who quickeneth all things*. *And before Christ Jesus, who before Pontius Pilate witnessed a good confession;* he proposeth the example of Christ to Timothy, as being the Head of those that witness a good confession.

14 That thou keep *this* commandment without spot, unrebukeable, ^funtil the appearing of our Lord Jesus Christ:

f Phil. 1. 6, 10. 1 Thess. 3. 13. & 5. 23.

The charge is, that he faithfully perform all the duties belonging to him as a Christian and a minister, commissioned from God, in the whole course of his life, that he may not be liable to a just accusation for the neglect of any part of his office. This is enforced by the consideration of the appearance of our Lord Jesus Christ, that is, in the day of judgment, as the following words make evident. Yet the apostle seems to speak of it, as if Timothy should continue in his ministry till that appearance. But it is manifest by his cautioning the Thessalonians against that false conceit, 2 Thess. ii. 2, 3, that the apostle knew the contrary; for he assures them that that day should not come till many great things enumerated by him should be accomplished. The meaning therefore of the words *until the appearing of our Lord Jesus Christ*, is the same with our Saviour's command to the angel of the church of Smyrna, *Be thou faithful unto death*, Rev. ii. 10; for the whole flux of time from the death of any person till the day of judgment makes no alteration in his life; and consequently, whoever is faithful unto the death is so till the appearing of Christ. And there is no motive more powerful to a zealous and faithful discharge of our duty, no excitation more rousing from the security and carelessness of the flesh, than the serious believing consideration of the glorious reward to be dispersed by our Saviour to his faithful servants in that day, and the dreadful condemnation that shall pass upon those who have been careless and negligent in the sacred ministry.

15 Which in his times he shall shew, ^g*who is* ^g the blessed and only Potentate, ^h the King of kings, and Lord of lords;

g ch.1.11,17.
h Rev. 17. 14. & 19. 16.

Which in his times he shall show; ὅν· Which Christ coming the second time, God in his time, his proper seasons, (so it is in the Greek.) will show. Or, Which appearing of our Lord Jesus God in his time will show; for some Greek copies read the article in the feminine termination, to distinguish the order of the Trinity's working; as the first coming of Christ is made to be from the Father's sending, so is also the second coming. *Who is the blessed and only Potentate:* God is said to be the *only Potentate*, because he only hath power in and from himself, by him kings reign; and he is called the *blessed Potentate*, because he is the fountain of all felicity and happiness. *The King of kings, and Lord of lords;* that is, the most mighty King and Lord, to whom all other princes are subjects, all other lords are vassals, Rev. xvii. 14; xix. 16. These terms seem here to be applied to the Father, though they agree also to the Son and the Spirit. They are applied to Christ, Rev. xvii. 14; xix. 16.

16 ⁱ Who only hath immortality, dwelling in the light which no man can approach unto; ^k whom no man hath seen, nor can see; ^l to whom *be* honour and power everlasting. Amen.

i ch. 1. 17.
k Ex. 33. 20. John 6. 46. 1 Eph. 3. 21. Phil. 4. 20. Jude 25. Rev. 1. 6. & 4. 11. & 7. 12.

Who only hath immortality; of himself; our souls and angels are immortal from the gift of God: or *immortality* signifies here the same with eternity, or immutability. *Dwelling in the light;* continually encompassed with a glory that is unspeakable, 1 John i. 5. *Which no man can approach unto;* to which no man can in this life come nigh. *Whom no man hath seen;* nor did Moses, or Stephen, or any other, ever see his glory so as to comprehend it, or in the full perfection of it. *Nor can see;* nor can the sons of men see him with their bodily eyes, or so as to comprehend him in his perfection, though some have with their bodily eyes seen his back parts and appearances, and with their souls have, through his grace, been enabled spiritually to behold him. *To whom be honour and power everlasting. Amen:* to which immortal, glorious, invisible God belongs, and let there for ever be given, honour and power.

17 Charge them that are rich in this world, that they be not highminded, ^m nor trust in †ⁿ uncertain riches, but in ^o the living God, ^p who giveth us richly all things to enjoy;

m Job 31. 24. Ps. 52. 7. & 62. 10. Mark 10. 24.
Luke 12. 21. † Gr. *the uncertainty of riches.*
n Prov. 23. 5.
o 1 Thess. 1. 9. ch. 3. 15. & 4. 10. *p* Acts 14. 17. & 17. 25.

Charge them that are rich in this world: those that are rich in grace, and the good things of another life, need not this charge; but there are divers at Ephesus who have great estates in goods, or houses, or lands, and but poor in gracious habits, charge them. *That they be not highminded;* that their riches do not lift them up into a high conceit or opinion of themselves, which worldly riches often do. *Nor trust in uncertain riches;* and that they repose no confidence in them, making them their *strong city*, Prov. x. 15, as if they could secure them from evil, or make them happy. *But in the living God;* but let them repose their trust in God, who hath life in himself, giveth life unto all other things, and liveth for ever. *Who giveth us richly all things to enjoy;* and is he who gives us all we have, though it be bought with our penny.

18 That they do good, that ^q they be rich in good works, ^r ready to distribute, || ^s willing to communicate;

q Luke 12. 21. ch. 5. 10.
Tit. 3. 8.
Jam. 2 5.
r Rom. 12. 13.
|| Or, *sociable.* *s* Gal. 6. 6. Heb. 13. 16.

That they do good; that is, to others, as they have opportunity. *That they be rich in good works;* be plentiful in alms-deeds, or more generally in all good works of piety or charity. *Ready to distribute;* that they be not backward to distribute that of which God hath made them stewards, to those that want. *Willing to communicate;* but give freely and without grudging, according to their Master's order, as becometh those who are but stewards as to the riches which they have.

19 ^t Laying up in store for themselves a good foundation against the time to come, that they may ^u lay hold on eternal life.

t Mat. 6. 20. & 19. 21.
Luke 12. 33. & 16. 9.
u ver. 12.

Riches in themselves are but for the present, but there is a use may be made of them *for the time to come*, if we employ them for the better enabling us to do what God hath commanded us to do, Matt. vi. 20; Luke xii. 33: those acts of obedience to the command of God for the use of our estates, though they can merit nothing, (for what proportion can there be betwixt a few shillings and eternal life?) yet will be a good bottom for us to hope for the time to come. *That they may lay hold on eternal life;* that God will give us an eternal happiness, not as a reward of debt, but of free grace.

20 O Timothy, ^x keep that which is committed to thy trust, ^y avoiding profane *and* vain babblings, and oppositions of science falsely so called:

x 2 Tim. 1. 14. Tit. 1. 9.
Rev. 3. 3.
y ch. 1. 4, 6. & 4. 7.
2 Tim. 2. 14, 16, 23. Tit 1. 14. & 3. 9.

O Timothy, keep that which is committed to thy trust; either the doctrine of the gospel, which ministers ought to keep pure, and without mixture, or the ministerial office; be true and faithful in the discharge of it, preaching Christ and the doctrine of Christ. *Avoiding profane and vain babblings;* avoid all impertinent discoursings under the notion of preaching, which in thy discharge of that work are the best of them but profane babblings. *And oppositions of science falsely so called;* avoid also all idle speculations, and disputations, no way serving to the end of preaching, and falsely called science.

z ch. 1. 6, 19.
2 Tim. 2. 18.
21 Which some professing ᶻ have erred concerning the faith. Grace *be* with thee. Amen.

Which some professing have erred concerning the faith; which kind of science, some pretending and boasting of, studying to show themselves learned and subtle men, they have been led into errors in Christianity, apostatizing from the doctrine of faith. *Grace be with thee;* viz. the *grace, mercy, and peace, from God the Father and Christ Jesus our Lord,* mentioned 2 Tim. i. 2.

¶ The first to Timothy was written from Laodicea, which is the chiefest city of Phrygia Pacatiana.

THE SECOND EPISTLE OF PAUL THE APOSTLE

TO

TIMOTHY

THE ARGUMENT

This Second Epistle to Timothy was most certainly written from Rome, when Paul was a prisoner there, chap. i. 8, and, as most judge, a very little while before his death, for he tells us, chap. iv. 7, 8, that he was *ready to be offered,* he had *finished* his *course, the time of* his *departure was at hand.* He is said to have died Anno Christi 68, and in the five and thirtieth after his conversion; so this Epistle was written about sixteen years after the writing of the former. The scope of it is much the same as of the former : to exhort and encourage him to faithfulness in his ministry, to keep stedfast in the faith, to be diligent in his work; to avoid all strifes of words, perverse disputings, &c. He also in it admonisheth him, that the latter times were like to be yet more dangerous, and therefore adviseth him to prepare for hardship and persecutions, propounding his own example to him, both as to doctrine and as to suffering.

CHAP. I.

Paul affectionately saluteth Timothy, 1, 2, *assuring him of his constant prayers for him, and remembrance of that sincere faith which had been derived to Timothy from his mother and grandmother,* 3—5. *He exhorteth him to stir up the gift of God which was in him,* 6, 7; *and not to be ashamed of the testimony of the gospel, but to be ready to suffer for it, according to his example,* 8—12; *and to hold fast the form of sound words which he had learned,* 13, 14. *He putteth him in mind of the general defection of the converts in Asia,* 15, *and commendeth Onesiphorus for his repeated kindness toward him,* 16—18.

A. D. 66.
a 2 Cor. 1. 1.
b Eph. 3. 6.
Tit. 1. 2.
Heb. 9. 15.
PAUL, ᵃan apostle of Jesus Christ by the will of God, according to ᵇthe promise of life which is in Christ Jesus,

Paul, an apostle of Jesus Christ by the will of God: see the notes on 1 Tim. i. 1. *According to the promise of life:* it is much the same with Rom. i. 1, 2, according to *the gospel, which he had promised afore by his prophets.* These words either signify the end of his apostleship, to declare the gospel in which is *the promise of life,* or the matter of his preaching. *Which is in Christ Jesus;* which eternal life was promised of old, but is not to be had but in Christ Jesus, and in him is the promise fulfilled.

c 1 Tim. 1. 2.
2 ᶜTo Timothy, *my* dearly beloved son: Grace, mercy, *and* peace, from God the Father and Christ Jesus our Lord.

See the notes on 1 Tim. i. 2; there he calls him his *own son,* testifying his relation, here his *beloved son,* to testify his affection to him. The salutation is the same with that 1 Tim. i. 2 : see the notes there.

d Rom. 1. 8.
Eph. 1. 16.
e Acts 22. 3.
& 23. 1. & 24.
14. & 27. 23.
Rom. 1. 9.
Gal. 1. 14
f 1 Thess. 1.
2. & 3. 10.
3 ᵈI thank God, ᵉwhom I serve from my forefathers with pure conscience, that ᶠwithout ceasing I have remembrance of thee in my prayers night and day;

Paul here by his *forefathers* either intends his immediate parents, or Abraham, Isaac, and Jacob; for he served the same God whom they served. But how did Paul from his forefathers serve God *with pure conscience,* who was a native Jew, and zealous in that religion, in opposition to the faith of the gospel, which alone purifieth the heart? Acts xv. 9. *Solut.* A pure conscience seemeth here to signify the same with Phil. iii. 6, *touching the righteousness which is in the law, blameless.* Paul was strict to the rules of that religion which he professed, though that religion was not that which universally purifieth the heart. Or else his meaning is, that he at this time served that God who was the God of his forefathers, with a pure conscience. *That without ceasing I have remembrance of thee in my prayers night and day:* he either thanketh God on the behalf of Timothy for his gifts and graces, or else he blesseth God, that had put it into his heart daily to remember Timothy in his prayers, Philem. 4; by which expression he both lets us know the mutual duty of Christians to pray one for another, and also that when we find any inclinations to do our duty, we ought to acknowledge them to God, being not of ourselves sufficient to one good thought.

g ch. 4. 9, 21.
4 ᵍGreatly desiring to see thee, being mindful of thy tears, that I may be filled with joy;

There was a great brotherly love amongst primitive Christians, so as the apostle often expresseth his desire to see such Christians as were at a distance from him, Rom. i. 11; 1 Thess. ii. 17; but he expresseth a particular reason of his desire to see Timothy, remembering the *tears* he shed at his parting from him and the rest, Acts xx. 37, 38; besides the desire he had by his presence to satisfy him, and give him occasion of *joy,* with which he also should *be filled;* unless he speaketh of the joy he promised himself when he saw Timothy, upon his seeing the improvement he had made both of his graces and gifts in the ministerial office.

h 1 Tim. 1.
5. & 4. 6.
5 When I call to remembrance ʰthe unfeigned faith that is in thee, which dwelt first in thy grandmother Lois, and
i Acts 16. 1.
ⁱthy mother Eunice; and I am persuaded that in thee also.

The apostle expresseth another cause of his affection to

Timothy, viz. his sincere owning and adhering to the profession of the gospel; as his *grandmother Lois* and his *mother Eunice* had done before him (he saith nothing of his father, for he was a Jew proselyted, or a heathen, Acts xvi. 1); and though he could not infallibly determine, yet he was verily persuaded of his sincerity also.

6 Wherefore I put thee in remembrance [k] that thou stir up the gift of God, which is in thee by the putting on of my hands.

k 1 Thess. 5. 19. 1 Tim. 4. 14.

Wherefore I put thee in remembrance: Paul's affection to Timothy was so far from abating his faithfulness to him, that it quickened him to admonish him to be faithful in his ministry. *That thou stir up the gift of God which is in thee;* and to that end, he adviseth him to put new life unto that holy fire (the word signifies the recovering of fire choked with ashes or decaying) which God had kindled in him, by daily prayer, and meditating on the things of God and use of his gifts, improving those spiritual abilities which God had given him. *By the putting on of my hands;* upon the prayers of Paul and the presbytery, when he was by them set apart to the work of an evangelist, for the end for which God had given them to him.

7 For [l] God hath not given us the spirit of fear; [m] but of power, and of love, and of a sound mind.

l Rom. 8. 15.
m Luke 24. 49. Acts 1. 8.

For God hath not given us the spirit of fear: fear in this place signifieth fearfulness, or cowardice, or poorness of spirit, in opposition to that holy fortitude which becomes ministers; this, he saith, is none of the gifts of the Holy Spirit, and proceedeth not from God. *But of power:* by *power* he means Christian courage and fortitude, not declining duty because of danger threatening us in the performance, but enabling us to encounter the greatest dangers and difficulties. *And of love;* love to God, and to the souls of his people; love so strong as to constrain us to be willing to lay down our lives for Christ, and for his church and people. *And of a sound mind;* σωφρονισμε· we translate it *a sound mind;* others, sobriety; others, a calm and quiet mind. A sound mind, in the ordinary notion of it, for a judgment sound in the faith, is requisite to a minister of the gospel. Sobriety is the gift of the Spirit: sobriety is a very general term, and signifies the moderation and government of our passions; that which seems to be here meant is such a government, and composure of spirit, that nothing shall deter us from the discharge of our duty; and the term sound mind, opposed to a weak and sickly mind, staggering at every danger, may well enough express the apostle's sense.

8 [n] Be not thou therefore ashamed of [o] the testimony of our Lord, nor of me [p] his prisoner: [q] but be thou partaker of the afflictions of the Gospel according to the power of God;

n Rom. 1.16.
o 1 Tim. 2. 6. Rev. 1. 2.
p Eph. 3. 1. Phil. 1. 7.
q Col. 1. 24. ch. 4. 5.

Be not thou therefore ashamed of the testimony of our Lord; either the testimony of Christ himself, *who before Pontius Pilate witnessed a good confession;* or that testimony which thou art obliged to give, for the ministers of Christ are to be witnesses unto him, Acts i. 8. *Nor of me his prisoner:* by this it appears that Paul was a prisoner at Rome when he wrote this; he would not have Timothy ashamed to own him, and the doctrine he had taught, because of that circumstance. *But be thou partaker of the afflictions of the gospel;* that is, be thou content, if God calls thee to it, to take a share with me in those afflictions which I suffer for preaching and professing the gospel, or those afflictions which are inseparable from the gospel. *According to the power of God;* through the power of God, for it is given to us on the behalf of Christ, as to believe, so to suffer for Christ's sake, Phil. i. 29.

9 [r] Who hath saved us, and [s] called *us* with an holy calling, [t] not according to our works, but [u] according to his own purpose and grace, which was given us in Christ Jesus [x] before the world began;

r 1 Tim. 1.1. Tit. 3. 4.
s 1 Thess. 4. 7. Heb. 3. 1.
t Rom. 3. 20. & 9. 11.
u Tit. 3. 5. Rom. 8. 28.
x Rom. 16. 25. Eph. 1. 4. & 3. 11. Tit. 1. 2. 1 Pet. 1. 20.

Who hath saved us; that is, brought us into a state of salvation, and given us a right to it. *And called us with an holy calling;* and, in order to our obtaining it, hath effectually called, renewed, and sanctified us. *Not according to our works;* not for any merits of ours. *But according to his own purpose and grace;* but from his own free love purposing and decreeing eternal salvation to us, with the means adequate to it. *Which was given us in Christ Jesus;* to be obtained through the merits and mediation of Jesus Christ. *Before the world began;* which purpose of his was before the foundation of the world was laid, and therefore could not be according to our works, but must be of his own grace, Eph. i. 4; Tit. iii. 5.

10 But [y] is now made manifest by the appearing of our Saviour Jesus Christ, [z] who hath abolished death, and hath brought life and immortality to light through the Gospel.

y Rom. 16. 26. Eph. 1. 9. Col. 1. 26. Tit. 1. 3.
1 Pet. 1. 20.
z 1 Cor. 15. 54, 55. Heb. 2. 14.

But is now made manifest by the appearing of our Saviour Jesus Christ; which purpose of God in Christ Jesus was in a great measure hidden under the Old Testament, but by the coming of Christ is made evident. *Who hath abolished death;* by his death he hath taken away the sting and power of death, delivering us from that which is the second death. *And hath brought life and immortality to light through the gospel;* and through the doctrine of the gospel he hath made the promises of eternal life plain and clear; which though existent under the law, yet were very obscurely revealed, so as they lay out of the sight of most men and women, but are now brought to light, so as he who runneth may read them.

11 [a] Whereunto I am appointed a preacher, and an apostle, and a teacher of the Gentiles.

a Acts 9. 15. Eph. 3. 7, 8. 1 Tim. 2. 7. ch. 4. 17.

Whereunto I am appointed a preacher; for the publication of which gracious counsel and purpose of God thus made manifest by Christ's coming, and of that life and immortality thus by the gospel brought to light, God hath appointed me as his crier; *and an apostle;* and sent me immediately as his messenger to make publication of it; *and a teacher of the Gentiles;* and hath made the instructing of the heathen my peculiar province, 1 Tim. ii. 7.

12 [b] For the which cause I also suffer these things: nevertheless I am not ashamed: [c] for I know whom I have ‖ believed, and am persuaded that he is able to [d] keep that which I have committed unto him [e] against that day.

b Eph. 3. 1. ch. 2. 9.
c 1 Pet. 4.19. ‖ Or, *trusted.*
d 1 Tim. 6. 20.
e ver. 18. ch. 4. 8.

For the which cause I also suffer these things; for the preaching and publishing of which gospel, or for the teaching of the Gentiles, I suffer these things, being accused by the Jews as a seditious person stirring up the people, and by them delivered to the Romans, and by them imprisoned. *Nevertheless I am not ashamed;* yet I am not ashamed of my chains. *For I know whom I have believed,* I have committed myself to God, *and am persuaded that he is able to keep that which I have committed unto him against that day;* and I am out of doubt concerning God's ability to keep until the day of judgment my soul, or my whole concerns both for this life and another, which I have by faith committed to him. Some, by *that which I have committed unto him,* in this text, understand the church or body of believers; others understand the fruit and reward of his labours and suffering. Mr. Calvin would have life eternal here meant; our eternal salvation is in Christ's keeping. I rather incline to the first notion; so it agreeth with 1 Pet. iv. 19. God commits his gospel to our trust who are ministers, 1 Tim. vi. 20; we, according to the phrase of Scripture, are said to commit our souls to him, Luke xxiii. 46; Acts vii. 59. I am, saith Paul, unconcerned as to my sufferings, I have intrusted God with all my concerns in order to this life and that which is to come, and I know he is able to secure them.

13 [f] Hold fast [g] the form of [h] sound words, [i] which thou hast heard of me, [k] in faith and love which is in Christ Jesus.

f ch. 3. 14. Tit. 1. 9. Heb. 10. 23. Rev. 2. 25.
g Rom. 2.20. & 6. 17.
h 1 Tim. 1. 10. & 6. 3.
i ch. 2. 2.
k 1 Tim. 1. 14.

By *sound words* which he had heard from Paul, can be

meant nothing but the doctrine of the gospel, which, as it is itself pure, and consistent with itself, not rotten, one piece of which will not hold with the other, so it tends to make souls sound as to their spiritual health: this doctrine Timothy had been instructed in by Paul; whether he had given him a written form of them or no is not much material, for this (if he did) was not that which he would have him *hold fast*, but to keep the idea or pattern of that doctrine in his mind, written in his heart, making his discourses conform to it. The sum of which form of sound words he declareth to be *faith and love*, for all that the gospel teacheth is either believing in the Lord Jesus Christ, or keeping his commandments, which is the demonstration of love, John xiv. 15: or else the sense may be this, Keep thyself sound in the principles of religion, which thou hast learned of me. *Which is in Christ Jesus;* but do not think this enough without exercising a faith in Christ as thy Redeemer, and living in obedience to his commandments. Many an orthodox man may go to hell, notwithstanding his orthodoxy.

l 1 Tim. 6. 20.   14 ¹That good thing which was committed unto thee keep by the Holy
m Rom. 8. 11.   Ghost ᵐ which dwelleth in us.

That good thing which was committed unto thee keep: this is expounded by 1 Tim. vi. 20; he means the doctrine of the gospel, or his office in the publication of it: Be faithful in thy ministerial work. *By the Holy Ghost which dwelleth in us;* to which purpose beg the assistance and operation of the Holy Spirit, which dwelleth both in all believers. and more particularly assisteth the ministers of the gospel. We can neither keep our minds sound in the faith, as to the doctrine of it, nor our souls steady in the exercises of faith or love, without the assistance of the Holy Spirit; which yet the Lord giveth to them that ask him, and it abides in them who do not vex, quench, grieve, or resist it.

n Acts 19. 10.   15 This thou knowest, that ⁿall they
o ch. 4. 10, 16.   which are in Asia be ᵒturned away from me; of whom are Phygellus and Hermogenes.

This thou knowest: probably as to some he had a personal knowledge of their apostacy, as to others he knew it by information, which Paul confirmeth. *That all they which are in Asia be turned away from me:* it seemeth unreasonable to interpret *all* here of every individual, but many, as all oft signifieth in holy writ. Some interpret it of all the Jewish proselytes; others, of those of Asia who accompanied Paul to Rome, and there, seeing his sufferings, apostatized; others, of many who still abode in Asia, where Timothy now was: these all, or many of them, deserted Paul, either wholly casting off the Christian profession, or withdrawing themselves from communion with Paul, when they saw him a prisoner. *Of whom are Phygellus and Hermogenes;* of these two we have no more said in holy writ, and therefore can assert nothing of them with any certainty.

p Matt. 5. 7.   16 The Lord ᵖgive mercy unto ᑫthe
q ch. 4. 19.
r Philem. 7.   house of Onesiphorus; ʳfor he oft re-
s ver. 8.   freshed me, and ˢwas not ashamed of
t Acts 28. 20.
Eph. 6. 20.   ᵗmy chain:

The Lord give mercy unto the house of Onesiphorus; whether Onesiphorus was at this time alive, or no, is very doubtful, for he only prays for his family in this text, and saluteth them only, chap. iv. 19. *For he oft refreshed me;* either when he was in Asia, or (which is more probable by reason of what followeth) at Rome, whither he might attend him, or follow him. *And was not ashamed of my chain;* and showed kindness to him when he was a prisoner; for which Paul prayeth mercy for his whole family.

17 But, when he was in Rome, he sought me out very diligently, and found *me*.

But when he was in Rome, whither he might go upon his private occasions, and, being there, *he sought me out very diligently and found me;* he made it his business to find out Paul, and rested not until he found him, either at his inn, or in the prison where he was put.

u Matt. 25. 34—40.   18 The Lord grant unto him ᵘthat he
x 2 Thess. 1. 10. ver. 12.   may find mercy of the Lord ˣin that day:

and in how many things he ʸministered   y Heb. 6. 10.
unto me at Ephesus, thou knowest very
well.

This would incline us to think that Onesiphorus was yet alive. The term *mercy* he here prays that he may *find of the Lord,* is comprehensive of all good, both corporal and spiritual, which he prays God the Father to grant to this good man, to find from the Lord Jesus Christ in that day when he shall come to judge the quick and the dead; for he had not only ministered to the apostle while he was a prisoner at Rome, but many ways at Ephesus, (where probably this Onesiphorus lived,) which Timothy, being there, well knew.

CHAP. II

Timothy is exhorted to constancy and perseverance in the discharge of his duty, as a good soldier of Christ, looking for a certain reward of his fatigues and sufferings, 1— 14; *to divide the word of truth rightly, and to shun profane and vain babblings,* 15, 16. *The dangerous error of Hymenæus and Philetus,* 17, 18. *The foundation of God standeth sure,* 19. *Of vessels honourable and dishonourable,* 20, 21. *Timothy is taught what to flee, and what to follow, and how the servant of Christ must behave toward all men,* 22—26.

THOU therefore, ᵃmy son, ᵇbe strong   a 1 Tim. 1. 2.
in the grace that is in Christ Jesus.   ch. 1. 2.
                                       b Eph. 6. 10.

The sense is either, Show thyself a stout and valiant man, not being affrighted at the dangers that threaten thee in the publishing and defence of the gospel which brings the glad tidings of the grace of Jesus Christ: or, Be thou strong through the gracious influence of Christ Jesus, without which thou canst do nothing.

2 ᶜAnd the things that thou hast heard   c ch. 1. 13.
of me ‖among many witnesses, ᵈthe same   & 3. 10, 14.
                                         ‖ Or, by.
commit thou to faithful men, who shall   d 1 Tim. 1.
                                         18.
be ᵉable to teach others also.   e 1 Tim. 3.
                                         2. Tit. 1. 9.

And the things that thou hast heard of me among many witnesses; the doctrine of the gospel which thou hast heard from me, confirmed by the testimony of many of the prophets of old, or, which thou heardest from me committed to thy trust, there being many witnesses present, when thou wert ordained, or set apart to that office. *The same commit thou to faithful men, who shall be able to teach others also;* commit unto others that shall be set apart for the ministry; but let them be such as have an ability to communicate their knowledge to others, and such as thou shalt judge will be faithful to their trust.

3 ᶠThou therefore endure hardness,   f ch. 1. 8.
                                     & 4. 5.
ᵍas a good soldier of Jesus Christ. g 1 Tim. 1.
                                     18.

Endure hardness; in the Greek it is, suffer evils, sc. evils of affliction, expect them, and encounter and patiently endure them. *As a good soldier of Jesus Christ;* remembering that the life of a minister is not a life of ease and pleasure, but the life of a soldier, whose life is a life of hardship, exposed to numberless hazards and dangers.

4 ʰNo man that warreth entangleth   h 1 Cor. 9.
himself with the affairs of *this* life; that   25.
he may please him who hath chosen him
to be a soldier.

Having told Timothy that his life was to be the life of a soldier, in which he would be exposed to many difficulties, and dangers, and hazards, he here mindeth him of the law and custom of soldiers, who being once entered in the muster-roll, use to sequester themselves from other employments in trading, husbandry, or the like, that thereby they might be at the command of their general, or captain, to be called out upon what service he pleaseth. So he who is a minister of the gospel ought not voluntarily and of choice engage himself in secular employments, but give up himself wholly to the ministerial work, that so he might please the Lord Jesus Christ, who hath chosen him to be his soldier.

5 And ⁱif a man also strive for mas-   i 1 Cor. 9.
teries, *yet* is he not crowned, except he   25, 26.
strive lawfully.

And look as it is in the public games in use amongst you, where divers strive by wrestling, fighting, racing, where there is a crown proposed as the prize for those who are the conquerors in the game; they have not that crown set upon their heads, unless they keep to the laws of that game wherein they are exercised. So it is in the spiritual warfare, or contest; there is a far greater reward, even a crown of glory, proposed for such as overcome; but none shall have it, unless those who keep to the laws which God hath made for those who exercise themselves in that spiritual combat.

6 ᵏ‖ The husbandman that laboureth must be first partaker of the fruits.

man, labouring first, must be partaker of the fruits.

As the apostle had before compared the minister of the gospel to a soldier, and from thence concluded his duty not to entangle himself unnecessarily in secular employments; and to those that exercised themselves in their public games, and from thence concluded the obligation upon him to keep to the Divine rule in the management of his office, and of himself under the opposition he should meet with; so here he compares him to a husbandman, (as Christ himself had done, Matt. xiii. 1, &c..) either to mind him of his duty, first to look to save his own soul, then the souls of others, or of his advantage, it being the privilege of a husbandman, being the proprietor of the fruits, (if he will,) first to eat thereof, thereby intimating the privilege of those who turn many to righteousness, Dan. xii. 3.

7 Consider what I say; and the Lord give thee understanding in all things.

Consider what I say; weigh these things with thyself in thy own thoughts. *And the Lord give thee understanding in all things;* but thou wilt not effectually understand them without a Divine influence, opening thy mind to a comprehension of them, and thy heart to a reception of all these things, and all other things which it is reasonable for thee to know and understand.

8 Remember that Jesus Christ ˡof the seed of David ᵐwas raised from the dead ⁿaccording to my Gospel:

The apostle passeth from his former discourse, wherein he had armed Timothy against the afflictions of the gospel, to a discourse about the doctrine of the gospel; and here mentioneth two principal heads of that doctrine, the incarnation of Christ, and his resurrection, which he instanceth in, as more particularly to be remembered and pressed upon Christians, in regard they were those two points of the gospel which were either at that time denied, as that of the incarnation was by the Jews, or he knew would first be opposed; and the latter that which *declared Christ to be the Son of God with power,* Rom. i. 4, and upon a faith in which Christians' salvation and consolation much depended, Rom. iv. 25; viii. 34; he therefore calls to him especially to *remember that Jesus Christ was of the seed of David,* truly man, and the true Messiah, who was to be the seed of David, (as the Jews themselves confessed): the manhood of Christ, soon after the apostle's times, was denied by the Marcionites and Manichees, &c. And that he *was raised from the dead* deserved Timothy's remembrance, both because upon that depended the great evidence of Christ's Divine nature, and the salvation and consolation of believers. *According to my gospel;* this, he saith, was suitable to the doctrine of the gospel which he had preached to them: he calls it his gospel, because committed to his trust to publish; so Rom. ii. 16, and xvi. 25, which he expoundeth, Gal. i. 11, *the gospel preached of me:* he speaks in the plural number, 1 Thess. i. 5; 2 Thess. ii. 14; declaring that the gospel was no more his than others' also who were ministers of it.

9 ᵒWherein I suffer trouble, as an evil doer, ᵖ*even* unto bonds; ᵠbut the word of God is not bound.

Wherein I suffer trouble, as an evil-doer, even unto bonds; that is, for which I suffer affliction, as if I were an evildoer, to that degree that I am put in chains. *But the word of God is not bound;* but yet I preach the gospel, or the gospel is preached; though they have restrained me, they are not able to restrain that.

10 Therefore ʳI endure all things for the elect's sakes, ˢthat they may also obtain the salvation which is in Christ Jesus with eternal glory.

Therefore I endure all things; that is, all things which I do endure, reproach, imprisonment, &c., for he had not yet resisted to blood. *For the elect's sakes;* as for Christ's sake, to imitate his example, and testify my love to him; so for the sake of those whom God hath chosen to eternal life, that they, seeing my patience and constancy, may be confirmed in the faith of the gospel, and by that means may obtain eternal life, *salvation, with eternal glory, which is* to be had *in Christ.*

11 ᵗ*It is* a faithful saying: For ᵘif we be dead with *him,* we shall also live with *him:*

It is a faithful saying: see the notes on 1 Tim. i. 15, and iv. 9, where we had the same phrase. *For if we be dead with him:* we are said to be dead with Christ two ways: 1. By our dying to sin, as he died for sin, Rom. vi. 5. 2. By our suffering in testimony of the truth, 2 Cor. iv. 10, which is that being dead with him which is here mentioned. *We shall also live with him:* there is also a twofold living with him, by a rising again to a *newness of life,* Rom. vi. 5, and hereafter in glory, which latter is here intended.

12 ˣIf we suffer, we shall also reign with *him:* ʸif we deny *him,* he also will deny us:

If we suffer, we shall also reign with him; that is, if we suffer for his name's sake, for a constant owning and adherence to his doctrine of faith, or discharge of any trust he hath reposed in us, we shall reign with him in glory. *If we deny him, he also will deny us;* but if we, upon prospect of danger, deny his truth, or desert the profession of him, he in the day of judgment will not own us before his Father and the holy angels, Matt. x. 33; Mark viii. 38; Rom. viii. 17.

13 ᶻIf we believe not, *yet* he abideth faithful: ᵃhe cannot deny himself.

If we believe not, yet he abideth faithful; whether we believe or believe not, or whether we be faithful to our trust or be not, yet God will show himself faithful, either to his promises made to them that believe, or to his threatenings denounced against those that believe not. *He cannot deny himself;* for it is impossible that he who is truth itself should be otherwise, that were for him to deny himself.

14 Of these things put *them* in remembrance, ᵇcharging *them* before the Lord ᶜthat they strive not about words to no profit, *but* to the subverting of the hearers.

Of these things put them in remembrance; that is, put other teachers in remembrance of all these things which I have given thee in charge. *Charging them before the Lord;* charging them as in the sight of God, who most certainly observeth and taketh notice of them, and will call them to an account. *That they strive not about words to no profit;* that they spend not their time in their pulpits in contests about words which tend to no solid advantage of their hearers. *But to the subverting of the hearers;* but may tend to the subversion of them, and the destroying their steadiness in the faith, drawing them into parties and factions, the fruit of which is nothing but envy, and contentions, and different opinions in matters of faith; as to which it hath been always observed, that the affectation of new phrases hath been introductive of a novelty in opinion.

15 Study to shew thyself approved unto God, a workman that needeth not to be ashamed, rightly dividing the word of truth.

Study to show thyself approved unto God; let it be thy study, not to please men, to get their hum and applause for speaking quaintly, learnedly, or smoothly, but to approve thyself to God, who is thy Master in this work, and whom thou oughtest to serve. *A workman that needeth not to be ashamed;* a workman that doth his work so well, and faithfully, that he need not be ashamed, whoever looketh and judgeth upon it. *Rightly dividing the word of truth;* ὀρθοτομοῦντα, rightly cutting out; we translate it *rightly dividing:* it is not material whether the metaphor be drawn from the priests right cutting out their sacrifices, so as all had their shares in them; or from carpenters cutting out their timber, cutting off the sappy part, and by a right line dividing the other parts; or from cooks, or carvers, or parents rightly dividing a dish of meat among several guests or children; or from those that use to cut out ways; or from husbandmen cutting out furrows, &c. The sense is, rightly handling the word of God, and giving to all their portion. For their notion who would make the sense of it, cutting out a right way for others by thy example, because the word ὀρθοτομεῖν sometimes signifies to cut a right way, it no way agreeth to the text, for whatever the verb signifies alone, he is meanly skilled in the Greek that knows not it cannot have that sense, being joined (as here) with τὸν λόγον τῆς ἀληθείας, the word of truth.

16 But [d] shun profane *and* vain babblings: for they will increase unto more ungodliness.

[d 1 Tim. 4. 7. & 6. 20. Tit. 1. 14.]

But shun profane and vain babblings; by these dishonourable terms the apostle defameth all impertinent discourses in discharge of the ministerial office, such as he had called *fables and endless genealogies, which minister questions,* 1 Tim. i. 4; *profane and old wives' fables,* chap. iv. 7: here he calls them κενοφωνίας, empty, vain, and unprofitable discourses, which though possibly not profane in themselves, yet were profane as used in the discharge of the ministerial office, where nothing ought to be discoursed but the solid, useful truths of the gospel. *For they will increase unto more ungodliness;* these, he saith, will issue at last in errors and ungodliness of life.

17 And their word will eat as doth a ‖ canker: of whom is [e] Hymenæus and Philetus;

[‖ Or, *gangrene*. e 1 Tim. 1. 20.]

And their word will eat as doth a canker; in the Greek it is, And their word will have pasture (or place to feed upon) as a gangrene: we have ill translated the word *a canker,* for it signifieth a gangrene; both our English word gangrene and the Latin word are derived from the Greek. There is a great difference between a canker and a gangrene, in the causes of those two diseases, and the nature of them, and the time in which they destroy the body of a man; only they both agree in their infecting the parts contiguous, the canker eating them, the gangrene mortifying them; and for this, the words of erroneous persons are here compared to this disease, because either of them will have something to feed upon; so νομήν signifieth, John x. 9. Most errors in matters of faith are contagious and infectious; the reason is, because ordinarily an error is broached by some, and entertained by others, in satisfaction to some lust, as favouring some evil desire and inclination of our minds, and so naturally pleaseth those who have the same evil propensions. *Of whom is Hymenæus and Philetus:* of *Hymenæus* we read before, 1 Tim. i. 20, there he is joined with Alexander; but not of *Philetus,* nor do we find him further mentioned in holy writ.

18 Who [f] concerning the truth have erred, [g] saying that the resurrection is past already; and overthrow the faith of some.

[f 1 Tim. 6. 21. g 1 Cor. 15. 12.]

Who concerning the truth have erred; these two he saith had already erred as to the doctrine of faith, giving heed to profane and vain babblings. *Saying that the resurrection is past already;* their particular error was in the business of the resurrection, which they said was past. That there shall be no resurrection is a very pleasing doctrine to men that have lived sensual lives; those whose lives have been nothing but eating and drinking, do very unwillingly think of dying, but seeing they cannot avoid that, they would gladly there should be no resurrection: so that it was no wonder if such an error as this did spread and mortify like a gangrene. Upon what pretence these men denied the resurrection, we are neither told in holy writ, nor with any certainty by any other authors. Some say, that they held that it was past in the resurrection of Christ, and those mentioned Matt. xxvii. 52. Others think they confounded the resurrection with regeneration, and glorification, which they allowed only as to the souls of believers. Others say they maintained no other resurrection than what men have in the procreation of children. Others, that they denied any resurrection but that in baptism. The resurrection of the body was denied by the Sadducees, by these in Paul's time, and afterwards by those that followed, Marcion, Basilides, Valentinus and Apelles, and others. Some in our times also have trodden in their steps, and are still treading (unless they think God will be more kind to those infinite numbers of heathens in the country of the Great Mogul than to Christians; for as to them, they tell us they cannot believe any such thing). Two sorts of men have been guilty of this: 1. The philosophers of the world, that think they must be able with their reason to span all articles of faith. 2. Men of sensual and sottish lives, who having lived like beasts, are willing to believe they shall also die like brutes. *And overthrow the faith of some;* those who are tainted with this error do both themselves deny the faith, divers principal articles of which depend upon it, such as the resurrection of Christ, 1 Cor. xv., and eternal life, &c., and also subvert the faith of others; for whoso can persuade another that there shall be no resurrection, makes him an infidel. Such heretics therefore were never endured to keep any station in the Christian church, it being always judged reasonable, that those who were turned infidels should be turned out of the flock of Christ to their proper herd.

19 Nevertheless [h] the foundation of God standeth ‖ sure, having this seal, The Lord [i] knoweth them that are his. And, Let every one that nameth the name of Christ depart from iniquity.

[h Mat. 24. 24. Rom. 8. 35. 1 John 2. 19. ‖ Or, *steady*. i Nah. 1. 7. John 10. 14, 27. See Num. 16. 5.]

Nevertheless the foundation of God standeth sure; notwithstanding that these two men (possibly of some note in the church of Ephesus) have fallen from the faith, and have been ill instruments to subvert the faith of others, yet God hath a number in the world, who are built upon the rock Christ Jesus, Matt. vii. 25; these are founded surely, *having this seal, The Lord knoweth them that are his;* sealed, and confirmed in their state by the eternal decree and counsel of God, who hath foreknown his elect, both as to their number and perseverance; but God hath from eternity known who are his, and therefore such as truly are so must be kept through faith by his power to salvation, and it is not possible that these should be totally and finally deceived. *And, Let every one that nameth the name of Christ depart from iniquity;* and every one that nameth the name of the Lord must depart from the tents of wicked men, who have made shipwreck both of faith and a good conscience. Therefore let not the apostacy of these men be a temptation to thee to think that the church of God may or shall fail; that cannot be, there can be no more lost than the sons of perdition, such as God never knew as his, though they put on a mark of Christianity and godliness, and deceived many. Those who have God's seal upon them, and are of his foundation, shall stand and keep themselves from those damnable errors. Only, to let us know that neither the certainty of God's decree or promise doth excuse our endeavours and using means for obtaining the thing decreed or promised, the apostle puts the verb in the imperative mood, Let him depart, &c.

20 [k] But in a great house there are not only vessels of gold and of silver, but also of wood and of earth; [l] and some to honour, and some to dishonour.

[k 1 Tim. 3. 15. l Rom. 9. 21.]

Look as it is in a great house, there are several vessels, made of several materials, and for several ends and uses; some are made of gold, some of silver, some of wood, some of earth; some made and bought for more noble and honourable uses, others for more vile, base, and dishonourable uses: so it is in the church of God, which is large, and like a great house. In it are many members; some have obtained like precious faith with us, who are as gold tried in the fire, or like silver purified seven times, by the word of God, and his Spirit sitting as a refiner upon their hearts. But all they are not gold or silver who glitter in an outward profession; some of them have earthy, wooden souls, savouring only sensual things, having nothing of precious faith in them, and are not yet purged from their filthiness, wanting all truth of grace, or sincerity of love. Some, whose work is to honour God, being created to good works, and whose reward will be to be honoured and glorified by him: others, who, by their apostacy from their faith and profession, and by their wicked lives, will dishonour him, and will be eternally rejected by him, as reprobate silver, and sons of perdition.

21 ^m If a man therefore purge himself from these, he shall be a vessel unto honour, sanctified, and meet for the master's use, *and* ⁿ prepared unto every good work.

If a man therefore purge himself from these; from these wicked men that subvert the faith of others, or from their wicked opinions and courses. *He shall be a vessel unto honour, sanctified, and meet for the master's use;* God will honour him; and he will by it be set apart, and made fit for Christ's use in his church. *And prepared unto every good work;* and made fit for every good work; which men are not, while they are either tainted with pernicious, damnable errors relating to the doctrine of faith, or the companions of those fools.

22 Flee also youthful lusts: but ^o follow righteousness, faith, charity, peace, with them that ^p call on the Lord ^q out of a pure heart.

Flee also youthful lusts: by *youthful lusts* he means such sinful desires, propensities, and inclinations of mind as are most incident to youth, whether they be lusts of the flesh, or spiritual lusts, such as are the vices of the mind, ambition, ostentation, pride, vain-glory, contempt of others, &c. *But follow righteousness;* follow justice, or innocency, which wrongeth none, but rendereth to every one his due; or, the righteousness of a holy life. *Faith, which teacheth* a soul to receive Divine revelations steadily, without perverse disputings. *Charity,* which *is kind, envieth not, vaunteth not itself, is not puffed up, doth not behave itself unseemly, seeketh not her own,* 1 Cor. xiii. 4—6. *Peace, with them that call on the Lord out of a pure heart;* a union, not with men of corrupt minds and practices, but with all such as serve and worship God purely and sincerely.

23 But ^r foolish and unlearned questions avoid, knowing that they do gender strifes.

It is a precept or caution of the same nature with those, 1 Tim. i. 4; iv. 7; and ver. 16 of this chapter. The repetition of this precept of the apostle four times in these two short Epistles, lets us know how important a thing he judged it, that ministers of the gospel should not spend their time in their discourses to their congregations, in things that tend nothing to the building up of their hearers in faith or holiness, being either old wives' fables, like the stories in the popish legends, or the apocryphal stories of Bel and the Dragon, Tobit and his dog, and the swallows dunging in his eye, &c.; or sifting out genealogies, or vain and impertinent discourses, or idle, fruitless questions, which tend not to edifying, but to satisfy curiosity, and increase strife and ungodliness; which kind of preaching the apostle also had defamed, 1 Tim. vi. 4, as the issue of pride, and ignorance, and dotage, and here he calls such questions *unlearned* in the same sense, because impertinent to the end of preaching. The vanity of human nature, and their non-subjection to the will of God, appeareth much in this, that notwithstanding the unreasonableness of such preaching, and the direct opposition of it to the so often repeated precepts of the apostle, and to Titus, chap. iii. 9, and Paul's proposing of his own example to the contrary, 1 Cor. ii. 1—4; yet for many years in the times of popery the people were fed with little besides these husks; and too many yet, either out of pride, to show their parts and reading, or ignorance of the mysteries of godliness, and the true end of preaching, or dotage about unprofitable speculations and niceties, can find little better food than these husks for poor people's souls.

24 And ^s the servant of the Lord must not strive; but be gentle unto all *men,* ^t apt to teach, ‖ patient,

He that is *the servant of the Lord* in the work of the ministry, *must not μάχεσθαι,* fight or *strive;* he must neither be a striker nor a brawler, neither fight with his hands nor his tongue. *But be gentle unto all men;* but show himself to all courteous, of a soft temper, meek and gentle. *Apt to teach, patient:* see the notes on 1 Tim. iii. 2, 3.

25 ^u In meekness instructing those that oppose themselves; ^x if God peradventure will give them repentance ^y to the acknowledging of the truth;

In meekness instructing those that oppose themselves; without passion better informing such as have sucked in an error, not reviling them, but gently instructing them, and labouring to convince them of their mistake; for all those who for a time may oppose the truth, are not such as never repent, nor do it out of malice or hatred, they may do it out of ignorance and weakness. *If God peradventure will give them repentance to the acknowledging of the truth;* and God may give them a power, and a heart to repent, and to acknowledge that truth, which they at present oppose; and although this must be God's work, yet he doth it by ministers as his means and instruments, who are to use probable means in order to it; such are not railing and reviling, but meek instructions, and a kind and gentle behaviour to them. A foul-mouthed minister is seldom an instrument to cleanse another's heart.

26 And *that* they may † recover themselves ^z out of the snare of the devil, who are † taken captive by him at his will.

And that they may recover themselves; the Greek word ἀνανήψωσιν properly signifieth to awake out of a drunken sleep. A state of sin is a kind of drunkenness, in which men have lost the use of their reason. *Out of the snare of the devil;* by *the snare of the devil* he means his temptations, which like snares are set covertly to catch souls. *Who are taken captive by him;* ἐζωγρημένοι signifies persons taken captive in war; in such a miserable captivity are sinners. *At his will;* εἰς τὸ ἐκείνου θέλημα, which we translate *at his will,* may be as well translated to his will; and so the will of God may be meant, and the whole referred to the first sentence thus, may recover themselves out of the snare of the devil to the will of God, that is, to embrace and do the will of God; and this is the sense some make of it: but it seems more proper to refer it to the participle, *taken captive,* for that is next it; and so it signifieth the miserable state of sinners, who are captives at the devil's command and will, that if he saith to them, Go, they go; if he saith, Come, they come; if he saith, Do this, they do it.

CHAP. III

The apostle foretelleth the evil characters that should appear in the last days, 1—5. *He describeth the enemies of the truth,* 6—9; *propoundeth unto Timothy his own example,* 10—13; *and exhorteth him to abide in the doctrine he had learned, commending unto him the manifold use of the Holy Scriptures,* 14—17.

THIS know also, that ^a in the last days perilous times shall come.

We met with this term, *last days,* 1 Tim. iv. 1, and there said that the Scripture by that term understands all the time from Christ's ascension to the end of the world. We meet with the term, Gen. xlix. 1; Isa. ii. 2; Micah iv. 1; Acts ii. 17; Heb. i. 2; James v. 3; 2 Pet. iii. 3. Of these days some are later than others, but it appears by Acts ii. 17; Heb. i. 2, that that whole period of time is so called. *Perilous times shall come;* in the Greek it is, difficult times, that is, times when it will be difficult for Christians to keep their lives or estates, or any happy station in the world, with a good conscience, by reason of the plenty of ill men that should live in those times, and make them so difficult.

2 For men shall be ^b lovers of their own selves, ^c covetous, ^d boasters, ^e proud,

II. TIMOTHY III

f 1 Tim. 1. 20. 2 Pet. 2. 12. Jude 10. g Rom. 1.30.

[f] blasphemers, [g] disobedient to parents, unthankful, unholy,

For men shall be lovers of their own selves; that is, the generality of men shall be persons that will neither love God nor men, in comparison with themselves; charity, which seeketh not her own, shall wax cold, men shall be wholly for themselves. *Covetous;* lovers of silver immoderately, so as they will get it any way, and when they have it will be as sordidly tenacious of it. *Boasters;* vaunting of themselves, vain-glorious, boasting of what they have not. *Proud;* lifted up in an opinion of themselves. *Blasphemers;* speaking evil of God and men. *Disobedient to parents;* stubborn and rebellious against those that bare them. *Unthankful,* both to God and men, for kindnesses received from either. *Unholy;* profane and impure.

h Rom. 1.31. i Rom. 1.31. ‖ Or, *makebates.* Tit. 2. 3. k 2 Pet. 3. 3.

3 [h] Without natural affection, [i] trucebreakers, ‖ false accusers, [k] incontinent, fierce, despisers of those that are good,

Without natural affection; having no kindness for such as nature obligeth them to love and honour. *Truce-breakers;* men that will be held by no bonds or leagues. Or rather, implacable; so we translate the same Greek word, Rom. i. 31; men so full of malice that they will admit no terms or covenants of peace. *False accusers;* Greek, devils, venting their malice by informing against and accusing others, without any regard to truth. *Incontinent;* intemperate, drunkards, gluttons, unclean persons, &c. *Fierce;* men without any gentleness, cruel. *Despisers of those that are good;* men that have no kindness for any good men, haters of them.

l 2 Pet. 2. 10. m Phil.3.19. 2 Pet. 2. 13, &c. Jude 4, 19.

4 [l] Traitors, heady, highminded, [m] lovers of pleasures more than lovers of God;

Traitors; προδόται signifies the betraying of any trust, or a falsehood to any person to whom we are obliged. It is in Scripture applied to Judas, Luke vi. 16, and to the Jews that crucified Christ, Acts vii. 52. The verb whence it derives is by authors applied to persons, places, and causes; it signifies that in the latter times there should be a general falsehood amongst men; see Matt. x. 21; falsehood towards their superiors, their relation, profession, &c. *Heady;* rash, inconsiderate. *High-minded;* blown up as bladders with an opinion of their own deserts. *Lovers of pleasures more than lovers of God;* voluptuous men, not using what God hath given them with a moderate satisfaction and delight in them, but contrary to God's commandments, and thereby showing that they have more love for the gratification of their sensitive appetite than the pleasing of God.

n 1 Tim. 5. 8. Tit. 1. 16. o 2 Thess. 3. 6. 1 Tim. 6. 5.

5 Having a form of godliness, but [n] denying the power thereof: [o] from such turn away.

Having a form of godliness: a form here is the same with a mask, or vizor, or appearance, an accidental form, opposed to substance and reality. It signifieth that in the latter times there should be many such as owned themselves Christians, and pretended to a right way of worshipping God, to be the church, the only church of God. *But denying the power thereof;* but in practice, though not in words, denying all substantial godliness, which lieth not in assuming the empty name of Christians, and making a profession, but lies in truth, righteousness, love and peace, self-denial, mortifying our members; it being a thing attended with life and power, a man being no more a Christian than he acts and lives like a Christian. *From such turn away;* from such kind of professors as we're before described, the apostle willeth Timothy to *turn away,* both as to having any church fellowship or communion, or any intimacy of converse with them.

p Matt. 23. 14. Tit. 1. 11.

6 For [p] of this sort are they which creep into houses, and lead captive silly women laden with sins, led away with divers lusts,

For of this sort are they which creep into houses; who do not only privily enter in at the doors of houses, but pierce into the secrets of them, making it their business to pry into all families, *and lead captive silly women,* and take their advantages upon women, (the weaker sex,) and not the wisest of them, but γυναικάρια, the diminutive word, is used to vilify; the little despicable women, of no judgment in sound religion, whom they by their tongues and pleasing errors make their captives. *Laden with sins;* nor do they deal with the most pious and honest women, but such as are laden with the guilt of much sin; *led away with divers lusts;* and who, being possessed of divers sinful inclinations, not only lusts of the flesh, but any other, such as pride, &c., are easily led away; lust always smoothing the way for such errors as will be principles to justify it against the reflections of conscience. Their vices, rather than sex, made them easily seduced.

7 Ever learning, and never able [q] to come to the knowledge of the truth. q 1 Tim. 2. 4.

Women that pretend to be ever learning the truth, but cannot obtain of their lusts a leave to acknowledge the truth in their practice. The word is ἐπίγνωσιν, which rather signifies a practical acknowledgment than a notional knowledge.

8 [r] Now as Jannes and Jambres withstood Moses, so do these also resist the truth: [s] men of corrupt minds, [t] ‖ reprobate concerning the faith.

r Ex. 7. 11. s 1 Tim. 6.5. t Rom. 1. 28. 2 Cor. 13. 5. Tit. 1. 16. ‖ Or, *of no judgment.*

Concerning this resistance of Moses by *Jannes and Jambres,* the Holy Scripture saith nothing but in this text. It is said by interpreters, that they were two brethren, the chief of Pharaoh's magicians, who opposed Moses in the miracles he wrought, Exod. vii. 11, whose names might be known in Paul's time by tradition, or the public writings of the Jews. *So do these also resist the truth;* so will corrupt teachers under the gospel resist the truth of the gospel published by Christ's ministers. *Men of corrupt minds;* men whose hearts are corrupted with sordid lusts. *Reprobate concerning the faith;* ἀδόκιμοι, of no sound judgment as to the doctrine of faith, or not approved of God, or good men, as to their sentiments about our faith.

9 But they shall proceed no further: for their folly shall be manifest unto all men, [u] as their's also was.

u Ex. 7. 12. & 8. 18. & 9. 11.

But they shall proceed no further; God will preserve those in his church that are sincere; though they may captivate a few poor, ignorant women, they shall have no great success. *For their folly shall be made manifest unto all men;* for God will in his providence so order it, that their folly or madness shall appear to all, and their party shall decline. The Divine Providence, that governs all things by the invincible light of truth, discovers and confounds the most specious and subtle seducers in his own time. And this prediction of the apostle was exactly fulfilled with respect to those primitive seducers. *As theirs also was;* as God by his providence laid open Jannes and Jambres.

10 [x] But ‖ thou hast fully known my doctrine, manner of life, purpose, faith, longsuffering, charity, patience,

x Phil. 2. 22. 1 Tim. 4. 6. ‖ Or, *thou hast been a diligent follower of.*

But thou hast fully known my doctrine: our translation here seemeth a little strange, for the Greek is, Thou hast diligently followed me in doctrine, Σὺ δὲ παρηκολέθηκάς μυ τῇ διδασκαλίᾳ· that is, Thou wert in my company, thou wert a follower of me, and so must know what doctrine I preached; what *manner of life* I lived; what my *purpose,* whole scope and design, was; what *faith* I taught and professed; what *long-suffering* I used, both towards my malicious adversaries and my weaker brethren; what *charity* or love I showed towards all men, whether friends or foes; what *patience* I showed in bearing injuries.

11 Persecutions, afflictions, which came unto me [y] at Antioch, [z] at Iconium, [a] at Lystra; what persecutions I endured: but [b] out of *them* all the Lord delivered me.

y Acts 13. 45, 50. z Acts 14. 2, 5. a Acts 14. 19, &c. b Ps. 34. 19. 2 Cor. 1. 10. ch. 4. 7.

What persecutions for the preaching of the gospel I was under; what *afflictions* I met with *at Antioch* in Pisidia, Acts xiii. 14, 45, 50; *at Iconium,* whither he went from Pisidia; of the afflictions he met with there also, read Acts xiv. *At Lystra; what persecutions I endured:* the apostle went from Iconium to Lystra, Acts xiv. 6, there also he was persecuted, Acts xiv. 19. Now it seemeth that in all these motions Timothy was in Paul's company and a follower of him, so as he was a witness to all; which assureth us that though we first read of Timothy, Acts xvi. 3, when he was circumcised, yet Paul knew him before. *But out of them all the Lord delivered me;* yet God delivered Paul from all these, and that Timothy, being all that time in company with Paul, knew; from whence the apostle would have him take courage, exercise patience under suffering for such preaching and such living, being assured that God would deliver him also, preaching the same truth, and living the same holy life, though he met with the same troubles, persecutions, and afflictions.

c Ps. 34. 19.
Acts 14. 22.
Matt. 16. 24.
John 17. 14.
1 Cor. 15. 19. 1 Thess. 3. 3.

12 Yea, and ^call that will live godly in Christ Jesus shall suffer persecution.

Such is the disposal of Divine Providence, such the malice of the men in the world, that though not every individual person, yet it is the usual lot of them who will keep a pure faith and a good conscience, to suffer persecution in some kind or other, either in their persons, or reputation, or estates. Men may live profanely, or may be morally honest men, and be safe enough; but if they will profess faith in Christ, or love to him in keeping his commandments, they will be exposed to troubles: the world will not endure men to live in peace, that will not live as they live, and believe as they believe.

d 2 Thess. 2. 11. 1 Tim. 4. 1. ch. 2. 16.

13 ^dBut evil men and seducers shall wax worse and worse, deceiving, and being deceived.

Neither do thou expect that the times should mend, for men that are given up to their lusts and γόητες, such as go about to deceive others, will grow *worse and worse,* as the world groweth older, both in their endeavours to deceive, and in their malice and hatred to those that oppose them. *Deceiving, and being deceived;* deceiving others, and being left by the just judgment of God to deceive and ruin their own souls.

e ch. 1. 13.
& 2. 2.

14 But ^econtinue thou in the things which thou hast learned and hast been assured of, knowing of whom thou hast learned *them;*

But continue thou in the things which thou hast learned; in the doctrines relating to faith, and the precepts relating to thy life as a minister, or as a Christian. *And hast been assured of;* and hast assented to steadily, hitherto believing them. *Knowing of whom thou hast learned them;* remembering that thou hast learned them of me the apostle of our Lord Jesus Christ, which is the same as from Christ himself.

f John 5. 39.

15 And that from a child thou hast known ^fthe holy Scriptures, which are able to make thee wise unto salvation through faith which is in Christ Jesus.

And that from a child; from thy infancy, by the instruction of thy mother Eunice, and thy grandmother Lois, chap. i. 5. *Thou hast known the Holy Scriptures;* thou hast had a notion of the writings of Moses and the prophets, the Holy Scriptures of the Old Testament, for at this time no others were written. *Which are able to make thee wise unto salvation;* which Holy Scriptures (without the help of the writings of Plato or Pythagoras, or any other pagan philosophers) have in them a sufficiency of doctrine to make thee, or any other, wise enough to get to heaven. *Through faith which is in Christ Jesus;* but not without a faith in Christ Jesus, receiving him as thy and their Saviour, besides a faith assenting and agreeing to those holy writings as the revelation of the Divine will.

g 2 Pet. 1. 20, 21.
h Rom. 15. 4.

16 ^gAll Scripture *is* given by inspiration of God, ^hand *is* profitable for doctrine, for reproof, for correction, for instruction in righteousness:

All Scripture is given by inspiration of God: Scripture signifies no more than writing; some therefore translate this text thus: All Scripture which is inspired of God; not all writings, but all the books of the Old Testament, is θεόπνευστος. This is expounded by Peter, 2 Pet. i. 21,

For the prophecy came not in old time by the will of man; but holy men of God spake as they were moved by the Holy Ghost. And is profitable for doctrine; and it is profitable to instruct us in all propositions of truth which we need believe in order to salvation. *For reproof;* ἐλεγχον, to convince us either of any truth, that we may believe it without any hesitation, or of any sin, that we may be humbled for it, without any extenuation. *For correction;* for reproof, or correction, or reformation, to reprove us in what we are to be reproved, to correct us in any error, to show us the way to bring us to rights and to reform us. *For instruction in righteousness;* to instruct us in the true righteousness, in which we must appear before God; for in it *the righteousness of God is revealed from faith to faith,* Rom. i. 17.

17 ⁱThat the man of God may be perfect, || ^kthroughly furnished unto all good works.

i 1 Tim. 6. 11.
|| Or, *perfected.*
k ch. 2. 21.

That the man of God may be perfect; that both ministers and all godly men may be as perfect as they can be in the state of mortality, fitted for the duties of their several callings and places. *Throughly furnished unto all good works;* and be prepared to every work which is good, acceptable and well-pleasing unto God, whether it be a work of piety, or justice and charity. The Scripture, as to all, is so full a direction, that Christians need not go down to the Philistines to whet their tools, nor be beholden to unwritten traditions, or to the writings of pagan philosophers, for directions what to do, how to worship God, or manage any part of their conversation, either as to their general calling, or as to their particular relations.

CHAP. IV

Paul giveth Timothy a solemn charge to do his duty with all care and diligence, 1—5: *certifieth him of his approaching end, and of the glorious prospect he had in view,* 6—8. *He desireth him to hasten his coming, and to bring Mark with him, and certain other things,* 9—13: *warneth him to beware of Alexander,* 14, 15: *informeth him what had befallen him at his first apology,* 16—18: *and concludeth with salutations, and a benediction,* 19—22.

I ^aCHARGE *thee* therefore before God, and the Lord Jesus Christ, ^bwho shall judge the quick and the dead at his appearing and his kingdom;

a 1 Tim. 5. 21. & 6. 13.
ch. 2. 14.
b Acts 10.42.

I charge thee therefore before God, who seeth and observeth what thou doest, and will one day call thee to account for thy discharge of thy ministry. *And the Lord Jesus Christ, who shall judge the quick and the dead;* and before the Son of God, the Lord Jesus Christ, whom thou hast more reason to regard, not only because he is thy Master, and thou his servant, in a special sense, but because he is to be thy Judge also, for he shall be the Judge, as of those that are dead before his coming, so of those also who shall be alive at his coming, 1 Cor. xv. 52 ; 1 Thess. iv. 15, 17. *At his appearing and his kingdom;* when he shall appear the second time, and set up his kingdom of glory, delivering up his mediatory kingdom to this Father. I charge thee, as in the presence of God and this Christ, or as thou hast a regard to God and to this Christ, and fearest the angry face of this Judge, or believest his second coming, or expectest a share in his kingdom of glory : a most severe obtestation, charge, or adjuration. What is that duty which is ushered in in so solemn a manner? It followeth.

2 Preach the word ; be instant in season, out of season ; reprove, ^crebuke, ^dexhort with all longsuffering and doctrine.

c 1 Tim. 5. 20. Tit. 1. 13. & 2. 15.
d 1 Tim. 4. 13.

Preach; proclaim like a herald, cry like a common crier in the hearing of a multitude. Thus God to Isaiah, chap. lviii. 1, Cry aloud, spare not, lift up thy voice like a trumpet. *The word;* the word of truth, chap. ii. 15, or the gospel, called *the word* by way of emphasis : see Matt. xxiv. 23 ; xxiv. 14; Mark i. 14; xiii. 10; xvi. 15. The word of God, not old wives' fables, endless genealogies, perverse disputings, unedifying questions, &c. This precept reflects upon unpreaching ministers, and impertinent, vain preachers. *Be instant;* be earnest and diligent. This reflects upon a cold and perfunctory preaching. God bid Isaiah *cry aloud, lift up* his *voice like a trumpet.* Sinners are like deaf adders. *In season, out of season;* that is, at all times, not on the Lord's days only, but any other time when thou hast opportunity; not in times when thou mayst do it with safety, but when the wisdom of the flesh tells thee it is *out of season.* This reflects upon such as preach rarely, and consult their flesh, whether they should perform it at all, or no. *Reprove;* ἔλεγξον, convince such as gainsay the truth. *Rebuke* all sinners, all that live an ill life. This reflects upon those effeminate preachers, against whom Ezekiel denounced the *woe,* Ezek. xiii. 18, *that sew pillows to all armholes;* that prophesy smooth things instead of the right things of the word. *Exhort;* persuade or comfort, (the word signifies both,) as thou seest occasion. *With all longsuffering;* but do what thou doest prudently, with meekness. God needeth not thy passion, though he makes use of thy art in instruction. *And doctrine;* do it so as to join instruction with thy reproof. This reflects upon flattering, fawning, unfaithful preachers, and such as vent their own passion, rather than pursue their due end for instruction and reformation of souls.

e ch. 3. 1.
f 1 Tim. 1. 10.
g ch. 3. 6.

3 ᵉFor the time will come when they will not endure ᶠsound doctrine; ᵍbut after their own lusts shall they heap to themselves teachers, having itching ears;

For the time will come; this time always was, (as appears by the writings of the prophets,) but it will come more and more; as the world grows older, it will grow more mad. *When they,* very many that shall live in the world, yea, in the bosom of the church, *will not endure sound doctrine,* will not endure that preaching which hath any soundness in it, or is of any tendency, life, power, or efficacy, to recover their souls from the diseases of sin and lusts. *But after their own lusts,* but in favour of their own lusts, and to secure their satisfaction in them, *shall they heap to themselves teachers,* will be finding out teachers, not according to God's, but to their own hearts; and there will be plenty of them to be found, they shall *heap* them up, choosing them without any judgment, regarding nothing but whether they will not be smart upon their lusts. *Having itching ears;* for their ears itch, and they must have those that will scratch them. The disease of lust in their souls brings forth an itch in their ears, that they will have a mind to hear only such as will by scratching please them.

h 1 Tim. 1. 4. & 4. 7.
Tit. 1. 14.

4 And they shall turn away *their* ears from the truth, and ʰshall be turned unto fables.

And they shall turn away their ears from the truth; either in contempt, or scorn of it, as being delivered in too plain notions or style; or through impatience, not enduring their lusts should be touched, and the evil of their ways showed them. *And shall be turned unto fables;* delighting to hear fables, any idle stories, or impertinent discourses, provided they touch not their lusts. *Missa non mordet,* The mass will not bite, was an old saying of the popish faction.

i ch. 1. 8. & 2. 3.
k Acts 21. 8. Eph. 4. 11.
l Or, *fulfil,* Rom. 15. 19. Col. 1. 25. & 4. 17.

5 But watch thou in all things, ⁱendure afflictions, do the work of ᵏan evangelist, ‖ make full proof of thy ministry.

But watch thou in all things, endure afflictions: watching implieth, 1. A negation of sleep. 2. An industrious keeping ourselves awake for some end. Keep thyself from all sin, and from all idleness and laziness, and do this industriously, that thou mayst honour God in thy work. *Do the work of an evangelist;* for thy work is a great work, the work of one who is to publish the gospel; or of one who is left by me the apostle of Christ to settle the church which I have laid the foundation of, Acts xxi. 8; Eph. iv. 11. *Make full proof of thy ministry;* make a full proof unto others of thy faithfulness in thy ministerial office and employment.

l Phil. 2. 17.
m Phil. 1. 23. See
2 Pet. 1. 14.

6 For ˡI am now ready to be offered, and the time of ᵐmy departure is at hand.

For I am now ready to be offered; σπένδομαι, the word properly signifieth to be offered as a drink-offering, which was offered by being poured out. Some say that σπένδομαι is only used to signify such offerings whereby some covenant was confirmed; so as it not only signifieth that Paul was sensible that he should die a violent death, but that his death should be an establishment and confirmation of the doctrine of the gospel which he had preached, that he should be *offered upon the sacrifice and service of* their *faith,* as he speaketh, Phil. ii. 17, where the same word is used. A learned author thinks it is there used in a little different sense, there as an accession to the sacrifice, here as a preparation to it, they being wont to prepare their sacrifice by pouring wine upon it; which possibly guided our translators to translate it here, *I am ready to be offered. And the time of my departure is at hand;* ἀναλύσεως we translate it *departure,* it properly signifieth resolution, because in death we are resolved into dust, from whence we are. If any ask how Paul knew that the time of his death was so near; *Answ.* He might know it by revelation from God, or from his observation of Nero's temper, malice, or behaviour toward him.

n 1 Cor. 9. 24, 25.
Phil. 3. 14.
1 Tim. 6. 12.
Heb. 12. 1.

7 ⁿI have fought a good fight, I have finished *my* course, I have kept the faith:

I have fought a good fight; my life hath been a military life, but I have not fought the evil fights of ambitious or quarrelsome men: my fighting hath been the good and noble fight of faith, a fight with the world, the flesh, and the devil, a contending for the faith delivered to the saints, a maintaining the lustings of the Spirit against the flesh, a warring with spiritual wickednesses in high places. *I have finished my course;* God appointed me a race to run, as a Christian, as an apostle and minister of Christ; I have now finished it. *I have kept the faith;* I have kept the doctrine of faith, upholding and maintaining it in and by my ministry; and I have lived in the exercise of the grace of faith

o 1 Cor. 9. 25. Jam. 1. 12. 1 Pet. 5. 4. Rev. 2. 10.
p ch. 1. 12.

8 Henceforth there is laid up for me ᵒa crown of righteousness, which the Lord, the righteous judge, shall give me ᵖat that day: and not to me only, but unto all them also that love his appearing.

Henceforth there is laid up for me; as to what remains for me, (so the word λοιπόν signifies, not *henceforth,* as we translate it,) there is prepared, and in safe keeping for me, Col. i. 5; or, there is appointed for me: see Heb. ix. 27. *A crown;* another kind of crown than what the conquerors used to have in the Grecian games; a high and great reward, a glory with which my whole man shall be encompassed, as a man's head is with a crown. *Of righteousness;* the purchase of Christ's righteousness, and an ample reward of mine also, the giving out of which also will be the effect of God's truth and justice, 1 John i. 9. *Which the Lord, the righteous judge;* and Jesus Christ, who in this shall show himself a righteous judge, *shall give* it *me* of his free mercy, for all I have done hath not merited it, *at that day,* at the day of judgment; my soul shall have it at my dissolution, my whole man in the resurrection. *And not to me only, but unto all them also that love his appearing;* nor is this crown my particular reward, but if any persons so lead their lives in this world, as that they can desire and be pleased with the thoughts and hopes of the second coming of Christ to judgment, Christ will give them also the same reward.

9 Do thy diligence to come shortly unto me:

To Rome, where Paul was at this time a prisoner. It appears from Phil. ii. 19, that Timothy did go to Paul at Rome, according to this desire of his, and was with him while a prisoner there.

q Col. 4. 15. Philem. 24.
r 1 John 2. 15.

10 For ᵠDemas hath forsaken me, ʳhaving loved this present world, and is departed unto Thessalonica; Crescens to Galatia, Titus unto Dalmatia.

He showeth the reason why he desired Timothy to come to him, because most of those who were with him were gone. *For Demas hath forsaken me;* some think this *Demas* is Demetrius, mentioned 3 John 12, the name being only shortened. He was at Rome with Paul some time, Col. iv. 14. Some make a question, whether Demas wholly apostatized, or only left Paul for a time, and went to Thessalonica about some secular business, afterward returning. *Having loved this present world;* some make the sense of this phrase no more than minding his worldly business. Others think that he, being frighted with Paul's danger, wholly left him, and went *to Thessalonica,* possibly his own country, however, at a great distance from the danger of Nero's court. *Crescens to Galatia,* a province in the Lesser Asia, whither probably Crescens went to preach the gospel. *Titus unto Dalmatia;* Dalmatia is in Sclavonia; Titus went thither (without all doubt) to preach the gospel.

11 *Only* *Luke is with me. Take Mark, and bring him with thee: for he is profitable to me for the ministry.

Only Luke is with me; of whom we also read Col. iv. 14. He was a physician, Paul's *fellow labourer,* Philem. 24. *Take Mark, and bring him with thee;* of Mark we read Acts xii. 12, and xv. 37. He was kinsman to Barnabas, Col. iv. 10. It appears by that text that he was at Rome with Paul, and his *fellow labourer,* Philem. 24. *For he is profitable to me for the ministry;* the ministry of the gospel. Paul's care was more for that, than for a ministering to himself, though he was a prisoner.

12 And *Tychicus have I sent to Ephesus.

I have given order to Tychicus to come to Ephesus in thy absence.

13 The cloke that I left at Troas with Carpus, when thou comest, bring *with thee,* and the books, *but* especially the parchments.

Troas was a city in Asia, where we find Paul more than once, Acts xvi. 8; xx. 5; he preached Christ there, 2 Cor. ii. 12. There Paul left an upper garment with one *Carpus,* which probably (having no great wardrobe) he might want, being a prisoner. *And the books, but especially the parchments:* interpreters idly busy themselves in inquiring after what they can never find out, what these books were, or what was written in these parchments.

14 *Alexander the coppersmith did me much evil: *the Lord reward him according to his works:

Alexander the coppersmith did me much evil: we read of three Alexanders; one, Mark xv. 21, the son of him that bare Christ's cross; another, Acts iv. 6, akin to Annas the High Priest; a third, Acts xix. 33, probably the person here meant, for he was an Ephesian; but he at that time was a disciple of Paul's, as appears there; probably afterward he apostatized, and was excommunicated by Paul, 1 Tim. i. 20, which might possibly provoke him: what harm he did him, and where, whether at Ephesus or Rome, it is not said. *The Lord reward him according to his works:* how far it is lawful to pray against our enemies, (as Paul did here against Alexander,) see the notes on Psal. cix. 6, &c.; Jer. xi. 20; xii. 3, &c.

15 Of whom be thou ware also; for he hath greatly withstood ‖ our words.

16 At my first answer no man stood with me, *but all *men* forsook me: *b* *I pray God that it may not be laid to their charge.

At my first answer, at my first appearing before Nero, and the court of Rome, *no man stood with me;* none of the Christians stood by me, or owned me; *but all men forsook me;* but all, being frighted at my danger, left me alone to speak for myself. *I pray God that it may not be laid to their charge;* they sinned through weakness and human frailty, and the Lord, I hope, will pardon it; God grant them remission.

17 *Notwithstanding the Lord stood with me, and strengthened me; *that by me the preaching might be fully known, and *that* all the Gentiles might hear: and I was delivered *out of the mouth of the lion.

Notwithstanding the Lord stood with me; that is, did not leave me. It is opened by the next word, *and strengthened me;* he gave me courage and inward ability, so as I was able to plead, and to defend my cause. *That by me the preaching might be fully known;* that all men that heard me might fully know by God's presence with me, seen in my courage, that my preaching was not from myself, or from men, but from God, the message of God by one to the sons of men. *And that all the Gentiles might hear;* and that all the heathen present in the court of Rome might hear and believe. *And I was delivered out of the mouth of the lion;* and I was for the present delivered out of my great danger: or possibly he calls Nero (the Roman emperor at that time) a *lion* for his barbarous cruelties.

18 *And the Lord shall deliver me from every evil work, and will preserve *me* unto his heavenly kingdom: *g* to whom *be* glory for ever and ever. Amen.

And the Lord shall deliver me from every evil work: faith riseth upon experience, 1 Sam. xvii. 37, 46; 2 Cor. i. 10. By *evil work* may be understood any sin into which Paul might fall through temptation; or the evil works of others, designing mischief to the apostle. He expresseth his faith in this term of various signification, to learn us how to exercise our faith in God in an evil time, viz. believing that God will either deliver us from our danger, or from sinning by reason of our danger, for we have no foundation for our faith to believe that God will at all times keep us from evils of suffering. *And will preserve me unto his heavenly kingdom;* and that he will save us, and preserve us, if not as to a temporal life, yet to a celestial, honourable, glorious inheritance. *To whom be glory for ever and ever. Amen:* this is a usual form of giving praise to God, desiring all honour might be given to him.

19 Salute *Prisca and Aquila, and *the houshold of Onesiphorus.

Salute Prisca and Aquila; by this *Prisca and Aquila* it is more than probable he means that Priscilla and Aquila mentioned 1 Cor. xvi. 19. *And the household of Onesiphorus;* it cannot be concluded from hence that Onesiphorus was now dead, but probably he was. It is the same man mentioned chap. i. 16.

20 *Erastus abode at Corinth: but *Trophimus have I left at Miletum sick.

Erastus abode at Corinth: of this Erastus see Rom. xvi. 23. He was the chamberlain of Corinth, so he abode there. Paul sent him into Macedonia, Acts xix. 22. *But Trophimus have I left at Miletus sick;* Trophimus was an Ephesian, Acts xxi. 29, one of Paul's companions, Acts xx. 4; he was left at Miletum, a city in Asia, not far from Ephesus.

21 *Do thy diligence to come before winter. Eubulus greeteth thee, and Pudens, and Linus, and Claudia, and all the brethren.

Do thy diligence to come before winter; that is, to come to Rome no more before winter, either because sailing in the winter time would be more dangerous, or because in the winter time he might have more need of his assistance. *Eubulus greeteth thee, and Pudens, and Linus, and Claudia, and all the brethren:* we have no further account of these persons in holy writ; the first is a Greek name, the rest Latin, Claudia is a woman's name. Paul sends the respects of these persons, and all the other Christians that at that time were in Rome, to Timothy.

22 *The Lord Jesus Christ *be* with thy spirit. Grace *be* with you. Amen.

The Lord Jesus Christ be with thy spirit: see the like, Gal. vi. 18; Philem. 25. *Grace be with you;* the free grace of God, in its various emanations, suited to all your necessities, be with you. *Amen.*

¶ The second *epistle* unto Timotheus, ordained the first Bishop of the church of the Ephesians, was written from Rome, when Paul was brought before † Nero the second time.

THE EPISTLE OF PAUL
TO
TITUS

THE ARGUMENT

As a general of an army, who hath a large country to conquer, cannot himself stay long in a conquered city, but leaving it with a garrison, under commanders, himself still goes forward in his conquests, and by his letters directs those whom he hath left governors in his conquered places how to behave themselves; so the apostle of the Gentiles, having a large field to run over, before he could finish his course, Acts xxvi. 17, 18. could not himself stay long in places where he had brought people into a subjection to the gospel, but after a time, leaving them as a garrison to keep Christ's possession in the place, left them under the conduct of some eminent disciple and minister, to whom he afterwards wrote letters directive of such minister, to settle the church in such a place, what and how to preach, and behave himself; thus he left Timothy at Ephesus, Titus at Crete. Crete is a great island belonging to Grecia, which on the north hath the Ægean Sea, the African Sea on the south. It was anciently called Cures; the inhabitants of it were called Cretes, Acts ii. 11. We read of the island, Acts xxvii., as Paul sailed by it to Rome. It had formerly in it one hundred cities, being in length two hundred and seventy miles, in breadth fifty, in compass eight hundred and nine miles; Cortina, Cydon, Gnossus, Minois, (the country of the famous geographer Strabo,) were some of the cities famous in it. It is now called Candia. It was lately taken from the Venetians, and is now in the possession of the Turks. It was a very rich place, famous for wines, and the place where brass was first found out. When the first plantation of the gospel was made there, the Scripture doth not say: it was made by Paul, as appears by his leaving Titus there. Titus was a Greek, Gal. ii. 3; converted by Paul, as appears by chap. i. 4; afterwards made a minister, for he was Paul's *partner and fellow helper*, 2 Cor. viii. 23, and called his *brother*, 2 Cor. ii. 13, used as his messenger, 2 Cor. viii. 6. He was left by Paul in Candia, or Crete, to settle the church there, and to *ordain elders in every city*, chap. i. 5. He writes this Epistle to him from Nicopolis, chap. iii. 12. There were four cities of that name. The scope of it appears, to any that read it, to be, to direct him, what persons he should ordain as ministers, how to deal with false teachers, and how to behave himself, both as to preaching and living, towards all sorts of persons.

CHAP. I

The salutation, 1—4. For what end Titus was left in Crete, 5. How they should be qualified who are ordained to the ministry, 6—9. The mouths of evil teachers must be stopped, 10, 11. The bad character of the Cretians, 12—16.

A. D. 65.

PAUL, a servant of God, and an apostle of Jesus Christ, according to the faith of God's elect, and ªthe acknowledging of the truth ᵇwhich is after godliness;

a 2 Tim. 2. 25.
b 1 Tim. 3. 16. & 6. 3.

Paul, a servant of God; that is, in the work of the ministry. *And an apostle of Jesus Christ;* who glory in this as my greatest honour and dignity, that I was one immediately sent by Jesus Christ to preach the gospel. *According to the faith of God's elect;* κατὰ πίστιν, according to what the elect, or chosen of God from the beginning of the world, have believed; so as it is no new doctrine which I bring: or else κατὰ here should be translated for, denoting the final cause, as some judge it signifieth, 2 Tim. i. 1, and in ver. 9 of this chapter; then the sense is, that he was sent to be an instrument to beget faith in such as God had chosen unto life, Acts xxvi. 18, for those only *ordained to eternal life* believe, Acts xiii. 48, and Paul was sent to be a helper of their faith. Some think the apostle by this phrase only distinguisheth himself from the ministers of the law. *And the acknowledging of the truth which is after godliness;* to which faith men are brought by the knowledge of the truth, and it worketh by the owning, profession, and acknowledgment of the truth; not all propositions of truth, but that which is productive of a godly life, lying in the true worship of God, and a universal obedience to the Divine will.

2 ‖ ᶜIn hope of eternal life, which God, ᵈthat cannot lie, promised ᵉbefore the world began;

‖ Or, *For.*
c 2 Tim. 1.1.
d Num. 23. 19. 1 Tim. 2. 13.
e Rom. 16. 25. 2 Tim. 1. 9. 1 Pet. 1. 20.

In hope of eternal life; which faith also, producing the acknowledgment, profession, and obedience to the truth, according to godliness, produceth in the soul a *hope*, or certain expectation, of eternal salvation or happiness. *Which God, that cannot lie, promised;* nor doth this hope grow up as a rush without mire, or a flag without water, but is bottomed in God's declaration of his will to that purpose; and it is impossible that the God of truth should lie, or speak what he never intended to effect. Ἐπηγγείλατο might as well here have been translated purposed, and must be so interpreted, if we interpret the next words, before the beginning of time. unless we say it was promised to the Head of the elect, Christ, on their behalf. *Before the world began;* before the beginning of time, or rather, many ages since, as Rom. xvi. 25. Thus eternal life was promised, though more obscurely, Gen. xv. 1; xvii. 7; xxii. 18.

3 ᶠBut hath in due times manifested his word through preaching, ᵍwhich is committed unto me ʰaccording to the commandment of God our Saviour;

f 2 Tim. 1 10.
g 1 Thes. 2.4. 1 Tim 1.11.
h 1 Tim. 1.1. & 2.3. & 4.10.

But hath in due times; in proper time, (saith the Greek,) in such time as God had eternally purposed, and as seemed good to the Divine wisdom. *Manifested his word through preaching;* he hath by setting up the ordinance of preaching, or publishing the gospel, by men sent by him, manifested this promise of eternal life, which lay much obscured under the veil of temporal promises under the Old Testament. *Which is committed unto me according to the commandment of God our Saviour;* which office of preaching, or which word, was committed to me, by the will of God, or immediate command of God: as to which, see Acts xxvi. 17, 18.

4 To ⁱTitus, ᵏ*mine own son after* ˡthe common faith : ᵐ Grace, mercy, *and* peace, from God the Father and the Lord Jesus Christ our Saviour.

i 2 Cor. 2.13. & 7. 13. & 8. 6, 16, 23. & 12. 18.
k Gal. 2. 3.
l 1 Tim. 1.2.
1 Rom. 1. 12. 2 Cor. 4. 13.
2 Pet. 1. 1. m Eph. 1. 2. Col. 1. 2. 1 Tim. 1. 2. 2 Tim. 1. 2.

TITUS I

Mine own son after the common faith; from hence we learn that Titus was converted to Christianity by Paul. Timothy was so called, 1 Tim. i. 2. The salutation is the same with that to Timothy, 1 Tim. i. 2; 2 Tim. i. 2, and in most of the Epistles, with small variation: see the notes there, and in the beginning of most of the Epistles.

n 1 Cor. 11. 34.
‖ Or, *left undone.*
o Acts 14. 23.
2 Tim. 2. 2.

5 For this cause left I thee in Crete, that thou shouldest ⁿset in order the things that are ‖ wanting, and ᵒordain elders in every city, as I had appointed thee:

In Crete; in Candia, as it is now called: see the Argument to this Epistle. *Set in order the things that are wanting;* set to rights things which I left undone, being hastened away to other places. *And ordain elders in every city, as I had appointed thee:* in this island we are told there were a hundred cities, in how many of them the gospel had taken place we are not told. Paul left Titus in this place for this end, to regulate the churches, and constitute officers for the holy ministry, to execute the office of an evangelist; doing what the apostle should have done there could he have stayed.

p 1 Tim. 3. 2, &c.
q 1 Tim. 3. 12.
r 1 Tim. 3. 4, 12.

6 ᵖIf any be blameless, ᑫthe husband of one wife, ʳhaving faithful children, not accused of riot, or unruly.

If any be blameless: the apostle now directs what kind of persons should be made elders or officers in the church. It is an elliptic speech, where must be something understood to perfect the sense. Do not make every one an elder, but if any be ἀνέγκλητος, see the notes on 1 Tim. iii. 10, such a one, as though possibly he may be clamoured on by ill men, yet cannot be justly charged with or accused of any notorious crime. *The husband of one wife;* one that doth not take the sinful liberty, taken by the Jews and heathens, (but contrary to the rule of Christ,) to have at the same time more than one wife: see the notes on 1 Tim. iii. 2. *Having faithful children;* having also a religious family, children that are believers, or at least honest in a moral sense (so then ministers in those days might marry). *Not accused of riot;* the Greek is, under an accusation of ἀσωτίας· we translate it by a general word, *riot,* and undoubtedly our English words, sots and sottishness, comes from this word. The word signifieth any kind of luxury, drunkenness, whoredom, prodigality. *Unruly;* sons of Belial, ungoverned, disorderly persons, like soldiers that will not keep their ranks, or rather, like cattle untamed, that will not endure any yoke. *Object.* But why must none be put into the ministry that have such children? the fathers may be good men, though the children be bad. *Solut.* 1. Because the honour and repute of the church is more to be regarded than the interest of any private person. 2. Because it is an ill sign that the parents of such children have not ruled their own houses well, keeping their children in all subjection and gravity under authority, and are therefore very unfit to rule the greater society of a church.

s Mat. 24. 45.
1 Cor. 4. 1, 2.
t Lev. 10. 9.
1 Tim. 3. 3.
8. Eph. 5. 18.
u 1 Tim. 3. 3, 8. 1 Pet. 5. 2.

7 For a Bishop must be blameless, as ˢthe steward of God; not self-willed, not soon angry, ᵗnot given to wine, no striker, ᵘnot given to filthy lucre;

For a bishop must be blameless; one that hath an oversight of the church of God, ought to be one whom none can truly tax with any scandalous sin. *As the steward of God;* as a chief servant in God's house, intrusted to dispense his mysteries, 1 Cor. iv. 1, one that should set an example to the under-servants in the house of God. *Not self-willed;* not αὐθάδη, one that pleaseth himself, proud, stubborn, pertinacious, confident, &c., having a high opinion of his own person, parts, judgment, or humour; for all this the word signifies. *Not soon angry;* ὀργίλον, not too quick and subject to passion; how then shall he in meekness instruct those that are without? *Not given to wine:* see the notes on 1 Tim. iii. 3, where the same word is used. *No striker, not given to filthy lucre:* see the notes on 1 Tim. iii. 3, where both these qualifications are mentioned, and opened.

x 1 Tim. 3. 2.
‖ Or, *good things.*

8 ˣBut a lover of hospitality, a lover of ‖ good men, sober, just, holy, temperate;

But a lover of hospitality; a lover of strangers: see the notes on 1 Tim. iii. 2. *A lover of good men;* one that hath a kindness for good men, or who loves all good things. *Sober:* see the notes on 1 Tim. iii. 2. *Just;* just in his dealings betwixt man and man, giving to all their due. *Holy;* one that reverenceth and worshippeth God, and is heavenly and spiritual in his conversation. *Temperate;* one that restraineth all his evil inclinations and propensions, that hath brought his sensitive appetite under the dominion and government of his reason.

y 2 Thess. 2. 15. 2 Tim. 1. 13.
z 1 Tim. 1. 15. & 4. 6.
6. 3. 2 Tim. 2. 2.
‖ Or, *in teaching.*
a 1 Tim. 1. 10. & 6. 3. 2 Tim. 4. 3. ch. 2. 1.

9 ʸHolding fast ᶻthe faithful word ‖ as he hath been taught, that he may be able ᵃby sound doctrine both to exhort and to convince the gainsayers.

Holding fast the faithful word, as he hath been taught; no airy, uncertain man, that is of that opinion which his company is of, or his age favours, but holding steady the word of faith, as he hath learned it from me, and the rest of the apostles. *That he may be able by sound doctrine, both to exhort,* his work is to persuade others to the faith, *and to convince the gainsayers;* by sound arguments to convince those that speak contrary to it; and if he himself be ignorant of, or uncertain, as to that, how can he ever discharge this employment?

b 1 Tim. 1. 6.
c Rom. 16. 18.
d Acts 15. 1.

10 For ᵇthere are many unruly and vain talkers and ᶜdeceivers, ᵈspecially they of the circumcision:

For there are many unruly and vain talkers: we have had both of these words before; the first signifieth stubborn, unruly men; the second, idle, foolish, vain talkers: the apostle saith, that in that age there were many of these. *And deceivers;* and such who were deceivers of other men's souls, or had their own souls deceived. *Specially they of the circumcision;* especially (he saith) the Jews, who mixed the law with the gospel; pressed the necessary observance of their ceremonies, and taught that all the Jews should be saved: of these there were many in Crete, they at this time being scattered abroad over the face of the whole earth.

e Matt. 23. 14. 2 Tim. 3. 6.
f 1 Tim. 6. 5.

11 Whose mouths must be stopped, ᵉwho subvert whole houses, teaching things which they ought not, ᶠfor filthy lucre's sake.

Whose mouths must be stopped; the word is active; such ministers ought to be placed in cities as shall be able and fit to stop such persons' mouths, by sound doctrine and arguments fit to convince them: or, thou oughtest to stop their mouths by silencing them; though I do not see how this was practicable in a pagan country, otherwise than by persuading Christians not to hear them. *Who subvert whole houses;* who, as to the foundation of faith and its building, overturn whole families of Christians. *Teaching things which they ought not;* infusing false doctrine into them. *For filthy lucre's sake;* and all for filthy gain: and all gain is so, that is got by deceiving and ruining of people's souls, as to their faith and salvation.

g Acts 17. 28.

12 ᵍOne of themselves, *even* a prophet of their own, said, The Cretians *are* alway liars, evil beasts, slow bellies.

One of themselves, even a prophet of their own; Epimenides, a Greek poet, thus spake of the people of this country, whom he calls a prophet, because he was a poet, and wrote something about such divine oracles as they had. *Said, The Cretians are alway liars:* the Cretians were famous for lying and falsehood, so as it became a proverb. He called them *evil beasts,* either for their cruelty or treachery. *Slow bellies;* a lazy, idle people, that had much more inclination to eat and drink than they had to work in any honest labour. From all this the apostle would infer, that Titus had the more need be watchful in his place, and faithful in the discharge of his office, being amongst such a people.

h 2 Cor. 13. 10. 2 Tim. 4. 2.
i ch. 2. 2.

13 This witness is true. ʰWherefore rebuke them sharply, that they may be ⁱsound in the faith;

This witness is true; this testimony of Epimenides is true, what I have found by experience, and those of them that in profession have embraced the Christian faith may have some tincture of their nation's vices. *Wherefore rebuke them sharply;* if thou meetest with any such, reprove or convince them ἀποτόμως, cuttingly, that is, sharply, severely: the metaphor possibly is fetched from surgeons, who cut out dead flesh to the quick. *That they may be sound in the faith;* that they may be sound in the doctrine of the gospel, or in their minds, not infected with any vice.

14 ᵏ Not giving heed to Jewish fables, and ¹ commandments of men, that turn from the truth.

Not giving heed to Jewish fables: by his calling them *Jewish fables,* (not *old wives' fables,* as in the Epistle to Timothy,) he lets us know that he reflects upon those Jews that seemed to be proselyted, but yet had a tincture of their Jewish education, and spent their discourse about such fabulous traditions as the Jews had. *And commandments of men;* and the traditions and constitutions of the scribes and Pharisees. *That turn from the truth;* abhorring the gospel, and the doctrine of truth in it.

15 ᵐ Unto the pure all things *are* pure: but ⁿ unto them that are defiled and unbelieving *is* nothing pure; but even their mind and conscience is defiled.

Unto the pure all things are pure: by *the pure* here (as appeareth by the terms opposed to it) are meant all those whose hearts are purified by faith, working by love in a holy life. To these he saith *all things,* that is, all the creatures of God, all meats and drinks, *are pure. What God hath cleansed* none ought to *call common* or impure, Acts x. 14; so as, notwithstanding any law of God to the contrary, any believers under the gospel may eat of any meats. *But unto them that are defiled and unbelieving is nothing pure;* but if men be unbelievers, and so defiled, having not their hearts purified by faith, Acts xv. 9, nothing is pure to them. *But even their mind and conscience is defiled;* their mind, their notion and understanding, is defiled; and their conscience, which is the practical judgment they make up about things, is defiled: if they forbear to eat, they are defiled through superstition; if they do eat, they sin by acting against the dictate of their conscience, which is the proximate rule of men's actions.

16 They profess that they know God; but ᵒ in works they deny *him,* being abominable, and disobedient, ᵖ and unto every good work ‖ reprobate.

They profess that they know God; he is speaking of the Jews, who (all of them) professed to know and to believe one living and true God. *But in works they deny him;* but they lived like atheists, as if there were no God in the world, Rom. ii. 17—24. *Being abominable, and disobedient, and unto every good work reprobate;* they are persons justly to be abominated of all good men, ἀπειθεῖς, unbelieving in the gospel, disobedient to the rule of the law, and awkward to, and averse from, any good work.

CHAP. II

Directions given to Titus both for his doctrine and life, 1—8. *The duty of servants,* 9, 10. *The gospel teacheth all men to renounce wickedness, and to lead sober, righteous, and godly lives,* 11—15.

BUT speak thou the things which become ᵃ sound doctrine:

That is, preach those things which agree with that doctrine which is sound, and which tendeth to make others sound in the faith, and in a holy life. Be not thou led by the example of those triflers in preaching, but let the subjects of thy discourse be what may tend to edifying; nor is there any more effectual way to stop the mouths of those fablers. Dagon will fall down before the ark of God.

2 That the aged men be ‖ sober, grave, temperate, ᵇ sound in faith, in charity, in patience.

That the aged men be sober: by the word πρεσβύτας seems here to be signified elders in age; he would have Timothy preach that these should be νηφάλιοι, sober, both as to body and mind: we met with the word before, 1 Tim. iii. 2, 11. *Grave;* of a modest, composed behaviour, not light and airy. *Temperate;* that is, able to govern their passions and inclinations. *Sound in faith;* we have met with the phrase before, chap. i. 13; see the notes; neither rotten through error, nor sick through fluctuation or scepticism. *In charity,* that is, love. *In patience;* a patient bearing of evils.

3 ᶜ The aged women likewise, that *they be* in behaviour as becometh ‖ holiness, not ‖ false accusers, not given to much wine, teachers of good things;

The aged women likewise; that is, do thou also teach the women that in age exceed others. *That they be in behaviour as becometh holiness;* ἐν καταστήματι ἱεροπρεπεῖς· to be in their habit becoming holiness. The word is of a very large signification, it signifies state, gesture, and habit; we have well translated it by as general a word, *behaviour;* it signifies clothes, converse, one's whole carriage. *Not false accusers;* not devils. That name is given to the devil, because he is *the accuser of the brethren,* and he was a liar from the beginning; it is applied to any persons that charge others falsely. *Not given to much wine:* Greek, not serving much wine; for those that frequent the tap too much, are ordinarily enslaved to it. *Teachers of good things;* privately instructing others in what is good, both by their discourse and example.

4 That they may teach the young women to be ‖ sober, ᵈ to love their husbands, to love their children,

That they may teach the young women to be sober: young women, especially conversing amongst heathens, are prone to be light and airy, and over frolicsome, following the heat of their youthful temper, and forming their converse after the manner of others; which is a behaviour, though it may suit their youth, yet if they be Christians it will not suit their profession, which calls to them for more gravity: speak to them that are aged to mind them to be sober. *To love their husbands, to love their children:* it being natural for young women to love their husbands and children, these precepts seem not so much to concern the things, as the manner of it, to love them as they ought to love them.

5 *To be* discreet, chaste, keepers at at home, good, ᵉ obedient to their own husbands, ᶠ that the word of God be not blasphemed.

To be discreet; σώφρονας· the word signifies temperate, and imports an ability to govern all our affections and passions. Discretion is but one piece of the fruit. *Chaste;* the word signifieth pure as well as chaste, and chastity only as it is a species of purity. *Keepers at home;* housewives, not spending their time in gadding abroad, but in looking to the affairs of their own families. *Obedient to their own husbands:* the same is required of wives, Eph. v. 22, and is due from them to their husbands, as being their head. *That the word of God be not blasphemed:* as for the discharge of their duty towards God, so for the credit and reputation of the gospel, that for their carriage contrary to the rules of nature and morality, as well as of religion, the gospel may not be evil spoken of, as if from that they had learned their ill and indecent behaviour.

6 Young men likewise exhort to be ‖ sober minded.

The word signifieth to be temperate, sober, wise, discreet, to govern their passions; an exhortation more specially necessary for young men, whose natural heat inclineth them to passion and rashness.

7 ᵍ In all things shewing thyself a pattern of good works: in doctrine *shewing* uncorruptness, gravity, ʰ sincerity,

In all things showing thyself a pattern of good works: he is an ill teacher of others who teacheth them not by his own example, as well as by his doctrine; for that physician proves ordinarily little valued in his prescriptions to his patients, whom they know to be in the same danger, and sick of the same disease, and yet refuseth himself to use what he prescribeth others : the patients will surely say to him, *Physician, heal thyself.* The apostle therefore requires of Titus that he should be himself a pattern of holiness ; and those ministers who are not so, vainly persuade others to be such. People (let ministers say what they will) will believe little danger to be in those courses in which their leader himself walks. *In doctrine showing uncorruptness ;* preaching not rotten, but sound doctrine ; and doing it with authority, and *gravity,* and *sincerity ;* the word is ἀφθαρσίαν, incorruptibility. It is not read in many copies, nor translated by many interpreters; and is much of the same sense with ἀδιαφθορίαν, which is the first word, by our translation interpreted *uncorruptness.*

i 1 Tim. 6. 3.
k Neh. 5. 9.
1 Tim. 5. 14.
1 Pet. 2. 12, 15. & 3. 16.
l 2 Thess. 3. 14.

8 ⁱSound speech, that cannot be condemned ; ᵏthat he that is of the contrary part ˡmay be ashamed, having no evil thing to say of you.

Sound speech, that cannot be condemned : Paul (as yet) seemeth to be directing Titus as a minister, and the rest of the ministers in Crete, how to behave themselves in the ministry, for the last word being plural, *you,* signifieth either the ministry, or else is put for thee ; he would have Titus not only preach sound doctrine, not corrupt, and do it gravely, but also preach profitable doctrine, tending to make the souls of others sound and healthy ; unless perhaps by λόγον be here meant his style and phrase, which he would have such as none could justly condemn. What was said of Cæsar's wife, that she ought not only to be chaste, but so to behave herself as not to be suspected otherwise, is applicable to ministers ; their doctrine, and phrase used in their ministry, ought not only to be sound and grave, but such as none should judge or censure for other. *That he that is of the contrary part may be ashamed ;* that the adversaries of the truth may be ashamed of their aspersing them or it. *Having no evil thing to say of you ;* and may have no evil thing to charge them with.

m Eph. 6. 5.
Col. 3. 23.
1 Tim. 6. 1, 2.
1 Pet. 2. 18.
n Eph. 5. 24.
∥ Or, *gainsaying.*

9 Exhort ᵐservants to be obedient unto their own masters, *and* to please *them* well ⁿin all *things ;* not ∥ answering again ;

Exhort servants to be obedient unto their own masters ; the apostle directeth as to servants of all sorts, whether bond or free, otherwise than that by covenant they have obliged themselves to men, he willeth they should be obedient to the commands of those who were their legal masters, neither thinking themselves free from them by their Christianity, if their masters were pagans, nor that they had a greater liberty to be saucy with them, or less obedient to them, because they were Christians, and upon that account brethren, 1 Tim. vi. 2. *And to please them well in all things ;* that is, in civil things, wherein alone they were servants. *Not answering again ;* not saucily replying when they were reproved, nor contradicting the commands of their masters.

o Matt. 5. 16.
Phil. 2. 15.

10 Not purloining, but shewing all good fidelity ; ᵒthat they may adorn the doctrine of God our Saviour in all things.

Not purloining ; Νοσφιζομένυς· the word signifieth taking something away from others to our own use, and it signifies properly the taking not the whole, but a part of a thing; it is used to signify the sin of Ananias and Sapphira, who kept back part of what they sold their estate for, Acts v. 2, 3. *But shewing all good fidelity ;* honesty, and truth, and diligence. *That they may adorn the doctrine of God our Saviour in all things ;* that they may not be a scandal or reproach to the gospel to which they make a profession, but may be an ornament to it in all things, as remembering that it is the doctrine of God our great Preserver, and of Jesus Christ our blessed Saviour.

p Rom. 5. 15. ch. 3. 4, 5.
1 Pet. 5. 12.
∥ Or, *that bringeth salvation to all men, hath appeared.*

11 For ᵖthe grace of God ∥ that bringeth salvation ᑫhath appeared to all men,
q Luke 3. 6. John 1. 9. 1 Tim. 2. 4.

The gospel of our Lord Jesus, which containeth the glad tidings of salvation, is not now hidden, and obscurely delivered, as in the times of the Old Testament ; but is risen up as the sun, or some bright star, directing all men their duties in their several stations, that is, all sorts of men amongst whom it cometh.

12 Teaching us ʳthat, denying ungodliness ˢand worldly lusts, we should live soberly, righteously, and godly, in this present world ;

r Luke 1. 75.
Rom. 6. 19.
Eph. 1. 4.
Col. 1. 22.
s 1 Thess. 4. 7.
a 1 Pet. 4. 2.
1 John 2. 16.

Teaching us that, denying ungodliness ; all atheism or false religion, living without regard to any Divine Being, or according to our own erroneous and superstitious conceits and opinions of him. *And worldly lusts ;* and such inclinations, and unlawful desires, and lustings after secular things, as are commonly found in men of the world. *We should live soberly ;* we should live, with respect to ourselves, in a just government of our affections and passions. *Righteously ;* and with respect to others, giving to every one their due. *And godly ;* and with respect to God, piously discharging the duties and paying the homage we owe unto him. *In this present world ;* so long as we live in this world, where we have temptations to the contrary.

13 ᵗLooking for that blessed ᵘhope, and the glorious ˣappearing of the great God and our Saviour Jesus Christ ;

t 1 Cor. 1. 7.
Phil. 3. 20.
2 Pet. 3. 12.
u Acts 24. 15.
Col. 1. 5, 23.
ch. 1. 2. &
3. 7. x Col. 3. 4. 2 Tim. 4. 1, 8. Heb. 9. 28. 1 Pet. 1. 7. 1 John 3. 2.

Looking for that blessed hope ; the object or end of our hope, the salvation of our souls, Gal. v. 5 ; Col. i. 5. *And the glorious appearing of the great God and our Saviour Jesus Christ ;* and in order thereunto, looking for the coming of the great God, and our Saviour Jesus Christ, to the last judgment. The same person is here meant by *the great God and our Saviour Jesus Christ.* 1. It is he whom God hath appointed to be the judge of the quick and dead. 2. Ἐπιφάνεια, by us translated *appearing,* is attributed only to the Second Person in the Blessed Trinity, 2 Thess. ii. 8 ; 1 Tim. vi. 14 ; 2 Tim. iv. 1, 8. From this text the Divine nature of Christ is irrefragably concluded ; he is not only called *God,* but μέγας Θεός, *the great God,* which cannot be understood of a made God.

14 ʸWho gave himself for us, that he might redeem us from all iniquity, ᶻand purify unto himself ᵃa peculiar people, ᵇzealous of good works.

y Gal. 1. 4.
& 2. 20.
Eph. 5. 2.
1 Tim. 2. 6.
z Heb. 9. 14.
a Ex. 15. 16.
& 19. 5.
Deut. 7. 6.
& 14. 2. & 26. 18. 1 Pet. 2. 9. b Eph. 1. 10. ch. 3. 8.

Who gave himself for us; which great God and Saviour Jesus Christ was not only sent and given by the Father, John iii. 16, but freely gave up himself to be incarnate, and to die for us, ὑπὲρ ἡμῶν, in our stead to die. *That he might redeem us from all iniquity ;* that by that price he might purchase salvation for us, delivering us both from the guilt and power of sin, who were slaves and captives to our lusts. *And* that he might *purify unto himself* λαὸν περιέσιον, we translate it *a peculiar people ;* some translate it an egregious, famous, principal people ; others say it signifieth something got by our own labour and industry, and laid up for our own use ; others say it signifieth something we have set our hearts and affections upon, in a special, peculiar manner. *Zealous of good works ;* studious to do, and warmly pursuing, all such works as are acceptable to God, and profitable to ourselves and others.

15 These things speak, and ᶜexhort, and rebuke with all authority. ᵈ Let no man despise thee.

c 2 Tim. 4. 2.
d 1 Tim. 4. 12.

These things speak, and exhort ; whatsoever I have in this Epistle said unto thee, I have therefore spoke, that thou mightest speak to the same sense to others, and persuade them to the practice of them. *And rebuke with all authority ;* when thou hast occasion to reprove any for their errors, do not do it imperiously, but with meekness ; nor yet slightly and cursorily, but showing all gravity and authority. *Let no man despise thee ;* and do not so demean thyself, as to give any persons occasion to despise thee.

CHAP. III

Christians are admonished to be subject to civil powers, and of a peaceable and quiet demeanour, 1, 2. *They are saved from their sins by God's mercy through Christ, but must maintain good works,* 3—8. *Genealogies and contentions about the law are to be avoided,* 9; *and obstinate heretics to be rejected,* 10, 11. *Paul appointeth Titus when and where to come to him,* 12, 13; *recommendeth acts of mercy to Christians,* 14; *and concludeth with salutations and a benediction,* 15.

a Rom. 13. 1.
1 Pet. 2. 13.

PUT them in mind ᵃ to be subject to principalities and powers, to obey magistrates, ᵇ to be ready to every good work,

b Col. 1. 10.
2 Tim. 2. 21.
Heb. 13. 21.

Put them in mind to be subject to principalities and powers: all the supreme secular powers at this time were pagans, and no friends to the Christians in their dominions, which might be a temptation to the Christians to rebel against them, or at least not to yield them so free, universal, and cheerful an obedience as they ought; therefore the apostle presseth this duty upon them, and that not here only, but Rom. xiii. 1: see 1 Pet. ii. 13. *To obey magistrates:* by the former term he might understand the supreme magistrates, by the latter, those inferior ranks; as the apostle Peter expresseth himself more particularly, 1 Pet. ii. 13, 14. *To be ready to every good work;* to be free, and prepared to every work which is acceptable to God and honourable in itself.

c Eph. 4. 31.
d 2 Tim. 2. 24, 25.
e Phil. 4. 5.
f Eph. 4. 2.
Col. 3. 12.

2 ᶜTo speak evil of no man, ᵈto be no brawlers, *but* ᵉgentle, shewing all ᶠmeekness unto all men.

To speak evil of no man; Greek, to blaspheme no man. Blasphemy is a speaking evil, whether it be applied to God or man, though use hath so obtained, that we only in common discourse speak of blaspheming God. *To be no brawlers;* to be no fighters, (ἀμάχους,) neither with hands nor tongues. *But gentle;* to be modest, fair, equitable men. *Showing all meekness unto all men;* forbearing wrath and passion in their converse with all.

g 1 Cor. 6. 11. Eph. 2. 1.
Col. 1, 21.
& 3. 7.
1 Pet. 4. 3.

3 For ᵍ we ourselves also were sometimes foolish, disobedient, deceived, serving divers lusts and pleasures, living in malice and envy, hateful, *and* hating one another.

For we ourselves also were sometimes foolish; without any knowledge, wisdom, or spiritual understanding. *Disobedient:* the word signifieth as well unbelieving as disobedient, neither persuaded to assent to the truth, nor yet to live up to the rule of the gospel. *Deceived* by the deceitfulness of sin. *Serving divers lusts and pleasures;* being slaves to our sensitive appetite. *Living in malice and envy;* suffering wrath to rest in our bosoms, till it boiled up to a desire of revenge, and showed itself in actions of that nature, and pining at the good and prosperity of others. *Hateful;* deserving to be abominated by good men. *And hating one another;* and hating good men, or such as were our neighbours: and having been so ourselves formerly, we ought to pity such as still are so.

h ch. 2. 11.
‖ Or, *pity.*
i 1 Tim. 2. 3.

4 But after that ʰthe kindness and ‖love of ⁱGod our Saviour toward man appeared,

Kindness; χρηστότης· the word signifies one's easiness to do good to another; that native goodness that is in God, rendering him inclinable to love, and prone to do good unto the sons of men. This was in God from eternity, but *appeared* in his sending Christ, and then his Spirit, and in the application of Christ's redemption to particular souls.

k Rom. 3. 20. & 9. 11. & 11. 6. Gal. 2. 16.
Eph. 2. 4, 8, 9. 2 Tim. 1. 9.
l John 3. 3, 5.
Eph. 5. 26.
1 Pet. 3. 21.

5 ᵏNot by works of righteousness which we have done, but according to his mercy he saved us, by ˡthe washing of regeneration, and renewing of the Holy Ghost;

Not by works of righteousness which we have done; not according to our works, 2 Tim. i. 9, whether ceremonial or moral. *But according to his mercy;* but *from* his own bowels freely yearning upon persons in misery. *He saved us;* he hath put us into a state of. and given us a right to, eternal salvation. *By the washing of regeneration;* washing us by regeneration. as in a laver, the pledge and sign of which is in baptism. *And renewing of the Holy Ghost;* the Holy Spirit changing and renewing our natures.

m Ezek. 36. 25. Joel 2. 28. John 1. 16. Acts 2. 33. & 10. 45. Rom. 5. 5.
† Gr. *richly.*

6 ᵐWhich he shed on us †abundantly through Jesus Christ our Saviour;

Which Holy Spirit, as well for the renewing of us, as for the collation of more common or extraordinary gifts, God poured out upon us *abundantly, through* the merits and mediation of *Jesus Christ our Saviour.*

n Rom. 3. 24.
Gal. 2. 16.
ch. 2. 11.
o Rom. 8. 23, 24.
p ch. 1. 2.

7 ⁿThat being justified by his grace, ᵒwe should be made heirs ᵖaccording to the hope of eternal life.

That being justified by his grace; that, through the free love of God, having the guilt of our sins removed, and the righteousness of Christ reckoned to us for righteousness, *we should be made heirs;* should, through adoption, be made *children, then heirs; heirs of God, and joint-heirs with Christ,* Rom. viii. 17. *According to the hope of eternal life:* some think that the words should be read thus, That we, according to hope, should be made heirs of eternal life; because otherwise, the text hath no object to relate to heirs. But what should we be heirs of, but the kingdom mentioned Matt. xxv. 34? Though it be true, we are no more than heirs according to hope, nor is any man otherwise an heir of an inheritance, as heir stands distinguished from an owner or proprietor.

q 1 Tim. 1. 15. ch. 1. 9.

8 ᑫ*This is* a faithful saying, and these things I will that thou affirm constantly, that they which have believed in God might be careful ʳto maintain good works. These things are good and profitable unto men.

r ver. 1, 14.
ch. 2. 14.

This is a faithful saying: we had this phrase before, 1 Tim. i. 15; iii. 1; iv. 9; 2 Tim. ii. 11. It may be applied to what went before, or what follows. *And these things I will that thou affirm constantly;* this is the doctrine I would have thee preach, maintain, and stand to. *That they which have believed in God might be careful to maintain good works;* that those who assent to these things as true, and have cast their souls upon God and Jesus Christ for the fulfilling of them, may (considering good works are the condition annexed to the promise of this eternal life and salvation) be careful to practise all that God hath commanded them in all their relations. *These things are good and profitable unto men;* all these things are true in themselves, and profitable for men to know and understand.

s 1 Tim. 1. 4.
2 Tim. 2. 23.
ch. 1. 14.

9 But ˢavoid foolish questions, and genealogies, and contentions, and strivings about the law; ᵗfor they are unprofitable and vain.

t 2 Tim. 2. 16.

But avoid foolish questions; in the discharge of thy ministry meddle not with idle questions, 2 Tim. ii. 23, tending to no godly edifying. *And genealogies;* and sifting out genealogies, 1 Tim. i. 4. *And contentions;* and strifes about words, or things unprofitable; *perverse disputings,* and *oppositions of science falsely so called,* 1 Tim. vi. 4, 5, 20. *And strivings about the law;* particularly questions about the law, the traditions and constitutions of the elders about it. *For they are unprofitable and vain;* these things are to no purpose or advantage.

u 2 Cor. 13. 2.
x Matt. 18. 17. Rom. 16. 17. 2 Thess. 3. 6, 14. 2 Tim. 3. 5. 2 John 10.

10 A man that is an heretick ᵘafter the first and second admonition ˣreject:

A man that is an heretic: two things make up a heretic according to the common acceptation of the term now: 1. an error in some matters of faith. 2. Stubbornness and contumacy in the holding and maintaining of it. Whether it so signified so early I cannot tell; it seems to refer to the former verse, supposing some that, notwithstanding all the endeavours of Titus, would be striving and contending for niceties about questions, genealogies, &c. *After the first and second admonition reject:* for such, saith the apostle, admonish them once and again; if they will not have done, refuse them, reject them. Whether excommunication can be certainly built upon this text, may be doubted; παραιτέομαι signifies no more than to avoid, reject, or refuse.

11 Knowing that he that is such is subverted,

PHILEMON 805

y Acts 13.46. and sinneth, ʸbeing condemned of himself.

Is subverted; ἐξέςραπται, is turned out of the true and right way and road; *and sinneth*, and is a transgressor, *being condemned of himself*, condemned of his own conscience; for he who spends his time about questions and genealogies, and strifes of words, and little questions about the law, instead of preaching Christ, is told by his own conscience that he doth not do his duty.

z Acts 20. 4.
2 Tim. 4. 12.
12 When I shall send Artemas unto thee, or ᶻTychicus, be diligent to come unto me to Nicopolis: for I have determined there to winter.

Of *Artemas* we read in no other place, but of *Tychicus* often; they were both ministers, one of which Paul intended to send to take care of the church in Crete, in the absence of Titus, whom he would have come to him to Nicopolis, where he designed to take up his winter quarters; but being very loth that the flock at Crete should for a little time be without a shepherd, he limits the time of Titus's setting out towards him, till one of them should come into Crete.

a Acts 18. 24. 13 Bring Zenas the Lawyer and ᵃApollos on their journey diligently, that nothing be wanting unto them.

Of this *Zenas* we read no more in holy writ, but of *Apollos* we read both in the Acts, and 1 Cor. iii. 4, 5, 22: it seemeth they were about to go to Paul to Nicopolis. *That nothing be wanting unto them;* the apostle would have Titus take care that they might want no necessaries that might accommodate them in their journey.

14 And let our's also learn ᵇto ∥ maintain good works for necessary uses, that they be ᶜnot unfruitful.

b ver. 8.
∥ Or, *profess honest trades.*
Eph. 4. 28.
c Rom. 15. 28. Phil. 1. 11. & 4. 17. Col. 1. 10. 2 Pet. 1. 8.

And let ours also; either those of our order, ministers of the gospel, or those that are Christians. *Learn to maintain good works;* in the Greek it is, to excel, or to be in the front, or to show forth, or maintain, and each sense hath its patrons of note. *For necessary uses;* for the necessary uses of the church, or of others, or for their own necessary uses. I take their sense who would expound the phrase, *maintain good works*, by learning some honest trade, to be foreign to the true sense of the phrase.

15 All that are with me salute thee. Greet them that love us in the faith. Grace be with you all. Amen.

Greet them that love us in the faith; that love us as we are Christians, in and for the gospel. *Grace be with you all. Amen:* the free love of God be thy portion, and the portion of all the Christians in Crete.

¶ It was written to Titus, ordained the first Bishop of the church of the Cretians, from Nicopolis of Macedonia.

THE EPISTLE OF PAUL

TO

PHILEMON

THE ARGUMENT

This Epistle is different from the other Epistles, because it is written upon a particular subject, of more special concernment: that it was written by Paul it is not doubted, it hath what he calleth his *token in every Epistle*, 2 Thess. iii. 17. Who this Philemon was is not so easily determined. Some have judged him a Phrygian, and of Colosse: see Col. iv. 9. He appeareth to have been a minister by Paul's calling him his *fellow labourer*, ver. 1, his *brother*, ver. 7, his *partner*, ver. 17. It is conjectured that he was one in the conversion of whom God made use of Paul as an instrument, from ver. 19, where Paul tells him, that he would not say that he owed unto him his own self. He seems to have been a man of some estate, for he kept a servant, and *refreshed the bowels of the saints*, ver. 7. He had a company of Christians in his house, ver. 2. The time when Paul wrote this Epistle is not certain; it was when he was *aged* and a *prisoner*, ver. 9, from whence it is evident that it was written from Rome. Some think it was written before the Second Epistle to Timothy, because he speaks of hopes that he had of being restored to his liberty, ver. 22, and in his Epistle to Timothy, 2 Tim. iv. 7, he seems to have no such hopes. He also here, ver. 24, sends him the salutation of Demas, who he saith, 2 Tim. iv. 10, had forsaken him. Others think it was written after that, when Demas was again returned to him; but it is not so clear that he ever returned. It is very probable that it was written much about the same time with the Epistle to the Colossians, for mention is made of *Onesimus* as *a faithful brother*, Col. iv. 9; there is also mention made of *Marcus, Aristarchus, Epaphras, Lucas*, and *Demas*, and *Archippus*, who are all named in this Epistle, and no more are here named, but *Apphia*. The scope of the Epistle is evident, to reconcile Onesimus to Philemon. Onesimus had been a servant to Philemon, and it should seem had wronged him by purloining some of his goods. He came to Rome, and was there converted by Paul, being a prisoner, ver. 10. The apostle would not detain him, being another man's servant, but sends him back with this recommendatory letter to his master. This recommendation was the occasion and is the matter of this Epistle; in the penning of which the apostle showeth himself as much an orator, as he had in his Epistle to the Romans, and some other of his Epistles, showed his skill at an argument; for the Epistle is penned with great art, and many topics are used to persuade Philemon again to receive him into his service; some such, as would incline one to think, that Paul knew this Philemon was something covetous, and would be a little difficult to grant his request.

The salutation, 1—3. *Paul declareth his joy in hearing of the love and faith of Philemon*, 4—7; *earnestly entreating him to receive into his favour his once fugitive servant Onesimus, now become a faithful Christian*, 8—21. *He desireth him to provide a lodging for himself, who was in expectation of a speedy release,* 22; *and concludeth with salutations and a benediction*, 23—25.

PAUL, ᵃa prisoner of Jesus Christ, and Timothy *our* brother, unto Philemon our dearly beloved, ᵇand fellowlabourer,

A. D. 64.
a Eph. 3. 1.
& 4. 1.
2 Tim. 1. 8.
ver. 9.
b Phil. 2. 25.

Paul, a prisoner of Jesus Christ; that is, for the sake of Christ, for the gospel, and for preaching of Jesus Christ. *And Timothy our brother;* from whence it is evident that

Timothy was come to Paul at Rome, according to his desire, 2 Tim. iv. 9, 21, before this Epistle was written, which manifesteth that Second Epistle not to have been the last he wrote. The apostle useth to join some others with himself in his salutation; Sosthenes, 1 Cor. i. 1; Timothy, 2 Cor. i. 1; Phil. i. 1; Col. i. 1; 1 Thess. i. 1, where Silvanus also is added; from whence it appeareth that Timothy was Paul's ordinary companion, and the apostle showeth his humility in joining the name of so young a man with his own. *Fellow labourer;* whence we gather that Philemon was not a Christian only, but a minister, probably one of the ministers in Colosse in Phrygia, for it appeareth that Onesimus his servant was a Colossian, Col. iv. 9.

2 And to *our* beloved Apphia, and ^cArchippus ^dour fellowsoldier, and to ^ethe church in thy house:

c Col. 4. 17.
d Phil. 2. 25.
e Rom. 16. 5.
1 Cor. 16. 19.

Apphia was the Roman name of a woman; the naming of her before Archippus, a minister, makes it probable she was Philemon's wife. It appears this *Archippus* was a minister, from Col. iv. 17. He calleth him his *fellow soldier,* because he was engaged in some of those many dangers Paul encountered, but we are not told in Scripture which. *And to the church in thy house;* all those Christians that live in thy family: we have the like expression, Rom. xvi. 5; 1 Cor. xvi. 19; Col. iv. 15. The apostle doth not always by the term *church* signify a body under ecclesiastical discipline, but sometimes calleth a company of Christians ordinarily conversing together by that name. Those who think the body of the church were wont constantly to meet in Philemon's house, seem not to consider how the dangers of those times made such a thing hardly practicable.

3 ^fGrace to you, and peace, from God our Father and the Lord Jesus Christ.

f Eph. 1. 2.

The common salutation: see the notes on Rom. i. 7; 1 Cor. i. 3; 2 Cor. i. 2, &c.

4 ^gI thank my God, making mention of thee always in my prayers,

g Eph. 1. 16.
1 Thess. 1. 2.
2 Thess. 1. 3.

See the notes on 2 Tim. i. 3.

5 ^hHearing of thy love and faith, which thou hast toward the Lord Jesus, and toward all saints;

h Eph. 1. 15.
Col. 1. 4.

Hearing of thy love; thy love to God and to the saints, ver. 7. The apostle putteth love here before faith, contrary to the true order of those spiritual habits, for love must be the fruit of faith, *which worketh by love,* and to his own order in other places, 1 Tim. ii. 7; 2 Tim. i. 13; possibly to show us that he spake of that love which is conjoined with faith, and of that faith which showeth its truth by love. *And faith;* faith in Christ. *Which thou hast towards the Lord Jesus;* that faith which thou hast in Christ, reposing thy confidence in him for salvation, and that love which worketh in thee towards Christ. *And toward all saints;* and is seen in thy readiness to do good to all Christians, such especially as are saints indeed; because thy *goodness extendeth not to God,* thou showest it to *the saints that are in the earth, and to the excellent,* like David, Psal. xvi. 2, 3.

6 That the communication of thy faith may become effectual ⁱby the acknowledging of every good thing which is in you in Christ Jesus.

i Phil. 1. 9, 11.

That the communication of thy faith: the word sometime signifieth communion, in all which there is a mutual communication betwixt those with whom the communion is. That thou mayst declare that thou hast the same common faith with us, thou communicatest the fruits of it. *May become effectual;* and showest that it is not a dead, inoperative faith, but the true *faith of God's elect,* Tit. i. 1, working *by love,* Gal. v. 6, and showing itself by good works, James ii. 18. *By the acknowledging of every good thing which is in you in Christ Jesus;* that every *good thing,* every good habit of grace which Jesus Christ hath wrought in thy soul, might be acknowledged by others, (the servants of Christ,) to whom thou declarest thy love and goodness.

7 For we have great joy and consolation in thy love, because the bowels of the saints ^kare refreshed by thee, brother.

k 2 Cor. 7. 13.
2 Tim. 1. 16.
ver. 20.

For we have great joy and consolation in thy love; thy love doth not extend only to the poor distressed saints helped and relieved by thee, but it hath its effect upon others together with myself; it is a wonderful joy and comfort to us to hear that God hath so opened and enlarged thy heart: the fruits of grace in one, are a true cause of joy and thanksgiving to all Christians, because God by them is glorified. *Because the bowels of the saints are refreshed by thee, brother;* the saints, or the bowels of the saints, ἀναπέπαυται, are brought to a rest, as travellers after their journey, or labourers after their day's labour, when they come to sit still.

8 Wherefore, ^lthough I might be much bold in Christ to injoin thee that which is convenient,

l 1 Thess. 2. 6.

Wherefore, though I might be much bold in Christ; in the Greek it is, Wherefore, having much παρρησίαν, boldness, liberty or freedom of speech, or much power and authority, or right, as Heb. x. 19, for Christ's sake, being Christ's apostle, or speaking for the sake of Christ. *To enjoin thee;* to command thee, authoritatively. *That which is convenient;* τὸ ἀνῆκον, things that are expedient, or convenient, fit for thee to do. My office authorizeth me in such cases.

9 Yet for love's sake I rather beseech *thee,* being such an one as Paul the aged, ^mand now also a prisoner of Jesus Christ.

m ver. 1.

Yet for love's sake; writing to thee in a cause of love, where so good and charitable a man may have an opportunity to express his charity. Or rather, out of my love and kindness to thee, persuading me that I need not use my apostolical authority to such a brother and friend, *I beseech thee. Being such an one as Paul the aged;* being such a one as Paul now much in years, and not like to trouble thee long with any request. Or, Paul the elder by office, one who is thy brother in the ministry. *And now also a prisoner of Jesus Christ;* and now a prisoner for Christ's sake, and so cannot personally speak to thee; and I know such is thy piety, that my being a sufferer for the sake of Christ will not render my petition to thee less acceptable, or to be regarded less.

10 I beseech thee for my son ⁿOnesimus, ^owhom I have begotten in my bonds:

n Col. 4. 9.
o 1 Cor. 4. 15.
Gal. 4. 19.

I beseech thee for my son Onesimus; Onesimus, lately thy servant, (the same mentioned Col. iv. 9.) but my son. *Whom I have begotten in my bonds;* not naturally, but spiritually, to whom I have been a spiritual father, and begotten him to Christ in my old age, and while I have been here suffering as a prisoner.

11 Which in time past was to thee unprofitable, but now profitable to thee and to me:

Which in time past was to thee unprofitable; ἄχρηστον· he useth a soft word, for it appears, ver. 18, he had *wronged* him, taking away some of his goods, and running away with them, without Philemon's knowledge, which made him doubly criminal. *But now profitable to thee and to me;* but now εὔχρηστον, *profitable,* one that may be profitable to thee, having learned Christ, and to me, who have used him in my service, and whose conversion will add to my crown.

12 Whom I have sent again: thou therefore receive him, that is, mine own bowels:

Whom I have sent again; he comes not of his own head, but upon my persuasion, and upon my errand. *Thou therefore receive him;* I therefore beseech thee to receive him kindly, and entertain him in thy house. *That is, mine own bowels;* whom I love as I love my own soul; thou canst not therefore be unkind to him, but it will reflect upon me.

13 Whom I would have retained with me, ^pthat in thy stead he might have ministered unto me in the bonds of the Gospel:

p 1 Cor. 16. 17. Phil. 2. 30.

I have such an opinion of his sincerity, that I would willingly have kept him with me, that he might, while I am a prisoner for the gospel of Christ, have done those

PHILEMON

offices for me, which thou wouldst have done hadst thou been here.

14 But without thy mind would I do nothing; ^qthat thy benefit should not be as it were of necessity, but willingly.

q 2 Cor. 9. 7.

But without thy mind would I do nothing; but he was thy servant, and I would not do it without thy knowledge and consent, that it might not be thought that thou hadst done me a kindness necessarily, but that thou mightest do it freely. *That thy benefit should not be as it were of necessity, but willingly:* which seems to argue that St. Paul expected that he, being reconciled to Onesimus, should send him back to Paul; unless he means the benefit done to Onesimus, in not revenging the wrong he had done him, should not be of necessity, because he was out of his reach, but freely, having him first in his power.

r So Gen. 45. 5, 8.

15 ^rFor perhaps he therefore departed for a season, that thou shouldest receive him for ever;

Onesimus in departing designed no such thing, but possibly God, in the wisdom of his providence, suffered him to depart from thee, and to fall into theft, that he might upon that occasion come to a quicker sense and conviction of sin, and see a need of a Saviour; that, being turned from sin unto God, and having embraced Christ our common Saviour, thou mightest receive, love, and embrace him αἰώνιον, *for ever,* this ever, in this life, that is, so long as you both should live.

16 Not now as a servant, but above a servant, ^s a brother beloved, specially to me, but how much more unto thee, ^tboth in the flesh, and in the Lord?

s Matt. 23. 8.
1 Tim. 6. 2.
t Col. 3. 22.

Not now as a servant; not now merely as a servant. *But above a servant;* but as one that deserveth much more kindness than a servant. *A brother beloved;* being a Christian deservedly to be loved. *Specially to me;* especially of me, who have a spiritual relation to him, as the instrument of his conversion, and as he hath been useful in ministering to me in prison. *But how much more unto thee, both in the flesh, and in the Lord?* but how much more to thee, to whom he stands not only in the relation of a brother, being converted to the Christian faith, but *in the flesh,* as thy kinsman, or thy servant, or one of thy family, or thy countryman, one of the same town and place!

u 2 Cor 8. 23.

17 If thou count me therefore ^ua partner, receive him as myself.

If thou count me therefore a partner, κοινωνὸν, one with whom thou hast communion, a partner in the same grace of the gospel, and in the same trials and afflictions of the gospel. *Receive him as myself;* do not only forgive him, but kindly entertain him, who is my friend, as thou wouldst do myself.

18 If he hath wronged thee, or oweth *thee* ought, put that on mine account;

If he hath any way been unfaithful, if he hath taken any thing from thee, or be in my debt, charge that upon me, let me be accountable to thee for it.

19 I Paul have written *it* with mine own hand, I will repay *it:* albeit I do not say to thee how thou owest unto me even thine own self besides.

Thou hast it here under my hand, I take upon me to satisfy the Onesimus's debt; yet I could tell thee, that thou owest me more than it can be, even thy own self, God having made use of me as an instrument to convert and turn thee unto God. Such persons are great debtors to their spiritual fathers, Rom. xv. 27.

20 Yea, brother, let me have joy of thee in the Lord: ^xrefresh my bowels in the Lord.

x ver. 7.

Yea, brother: the particle ναὶ is used in swearing, affirming, persuading, entreating, the latter seemeth here most proper; as much as, of all love, brother. *Let me have joy of thee in the Lord;* it will rejoice my heart to see thee charitable and obedient to my monitions, let me have a spiritual joy from thy satisfying of me in what I desire. *Refresh my bowels in the Lord;* either Onesimus, whom he had called his *bowels,* ver. 12; or, my inward man.

21 ^yHaving confidence in thy obedience I wrote unto thee, knowing that thou wilt also do more than I say.

y 2 Cor. 7. 16.

I have not written this without a confidence that thou in this thing wilt do what I desire of thee, but I write it out of my affection to poor Onesimus, and desire to help him, not doubting of thy readiness to do the thing.

22 But withal prepare me also a lodging: for ^zI trust that ^athrough your prayers I shall be given unto you.

z Phil. 1. 25. & 2. 24.
a 2 Cor. 1. 11.

This would incline one to think that this Epistle was written before the Second Epistle to Timothy, for there, chap. iv. 6—8, he seems to have other apprehensions; yet it is plain Timothy was with Paul when he wrote this, which he was not when that Second Epistle was written, as appears from chap. iv. 9, 21. Here, upon a confidence that through the help of the church's prayers he should again come to them, he writeth to Philemon to prepare him a lodging.

23 There salute thee ^bEpaphras, my fellowprisoner in Christ Jesus;

b Col. 1. 7. & 4. 12.

We read of this *Epaphras,* Col. i. 7, where he is called Paul's *fellow servant,* and *a faithful minister of Christ:* he was with Paul at Rome, Col. iv. 12, but there is no mention of him as a prisoner; but now he was a *fellow prisoner* with Paul, either in the same place, or upon the same account.

24 ^cMarcus, ^dAristarchus, ^eDemas, ^fLucas, my fellowlabourers.

c Acts 12. 12, 25.
d Acts 19. 29. & 27. 2.
Col. 4. 10. e Col. 4. 14. f 2 Tim. 4. 11.

All ministers of the gospel: they are also named, Col. iv. 10, 12, 14: they were all at this time at Rome with Paul: see Acts xii. 12, 25; xv. 37, 39; xix. 29; xx. 4; xxvii. 2; 2 Tim. iv. 10.

25 ^gThe grace of our Lord Jesus Christ *be* with your spirit. Amen.

g 2 Tim. 4. 22.

See the notes on Gal. vi. 18: see also Rom. xvi. 24; 1 Cor. xvi. 23; Phil. iv. 23; 2 Thess. iii. 18. *With your spirit* is the same as with you. By *the grace of our Lord Jesus Christ,* he means the Spirit of Christ in all its gracious emanations: we have his meaning fully, 2 Cor. xiii. 14, *The grace of our Lord Jesus Christ, and the love of God, and the communion of the Holy Ghost, be with you all. Amen* is a particle of praying and affirming, by which he declareth his earnest desire it might be so, and also his faith that it should be so. Nor doth he pray for Philemon alone, (though the Epistle chiefly concerned him,) but for all those who at Colosse had with him obtained like precious faith.

¶ Written from Rome to Philemon, by Onesimus a servant.

THE EPISTLE OF PAUL THE APOSTLE

TO THE

HEBREWS

THE ARGUMENT

Some few Greek copies not having the name of the apostle Paul prefixed to this Epistle, though most of them have, hath made many doubt concerning the writer of it, as others, especially heretics, of its authority. The conjectures of those who ascribe it to Barnabas, Luke, or Clemens, &c. seem groundless; since the character the Holy Ghost gives of its penman, and his state, in chap. x. 34, and chap. xiii. 19, 23, is not agreeable to any of them. This is most certain, that the apostle Paul did write such an Epistle; that it was well known to the dispersed churches of Christ then; that it was abused by men of corrupt minds, as it is at this day, since the Spirit gives us undeniable testimony of it in 2 Pet. iii. 15, 16. That this Epistle should be it, (when it is so like the rest of his writings; when it is strongly confirming the truth the apostle Peter had written to them, chap. vi. 2; x. 26, 27; when it is so expressive of his condition in bonds, chap. x. 34; xiii. 19; Col. iv. 18, of his known companion Timothy, chap. xiii. 23; Col. i. 1, of his love to, and concern for, those to whom he writes, Rom. ix. 1—3; x. 1, and of his known doctrine, that Judaism had its completion in Christianity; that the veil was rent asunder, that they might discern the temple or church to be laid open to Gentiles as well as Jews, as at Antioch, Galatia, &c., he taught them; besides, that it hath the signal by which he declareth all his Epistles are to be known, chap. xiii. 25, compare 2 Thess. iii. 17, 18, and the general consent of the church through the successive ages of it, entitling of him to it,) I say, that this Epistle should be it, seems not difficult to determine. It is conjectured that the reason why he prefixed not his name to it, as to the rest of his Epistles, was, lest the great prejudice the Jews had causelessly taken up against him, as an enemy to the Mosaical law, would prevent their reading or weighing of it as they ought. It is directed by him to the dispersed tribes of believing Israel, under the name of *Hebrews*, being the common one of all the posterity of Heber by Abraham, both which patriarchs were great separatists from the idolatrous world in their respective ages, and in whose families the church of God was continued; a name grateful to them, because the Lord honoured it by adding it to his title, Exod. iii. 18, and ascribed it to their progenitor, Gen. xiv. 13, of a natural descent from whom they were most fond, John viii. 33; 2 Cor. xi. 22. And the apostle Peter confirmeth these to be the persons, 1 Pet. i. 1, 2; compare 2 Pet. i. 1; iii. 15. Written this was in the Greek language, as his other Epistles, it being then the most diffusive dialect in the world, and especially the common one of these Hebrews, Acts vi. 1, as Josephus himself testifieth; though the Greek idioms themselves, and the translation of other words in the Epistle, show it abundantly. For the time of his writing it to them, most likely it was after his appearing before the emperor Nero at Rome, 2 Tim. iv. 16, 17, during his liberty, Acts xxviii. 30, upon Timothy's dismission to him, chap. xiii. 23, and before the first of the ten bloody persecutions, chap. xii. 4, about the same year wherein he despatched other of his Epistles to the churches.

The design of the apostle in this Epistle, is fully to discover to the believing Hebrews, that they had not lost by renouncing Judaism and turning Christians, since the whole economy of Moses was designed but to lead them to the Lord Jesus Christ, and to be perfected in him, he being the truth and substance of all those shadows. To confirm them in the faith of this, and to encourage them more cheerfully to undergo those cruel persecutions, in loss of goods, liberty, relations, estates, country, and life itself, which their enemies would pursue them with for it; he shows them, that it was never God's purpose to have the earthly Mosaical church-frame continue in the world, it being weak and insufficient for priesthood, sacrifice, ordinances, ceremonies, to purge their conscience, and to bring them unto God; but to be a type of, and a guide to, a better, which he did resolve to pitch by his own Son, even that heavenly one, in which both Jew and Gentile should acquiesce, and which should continue immovable to the end of the world. In handling which, first, He instructs them in the transcendent excellency of his person and offices; in respect of his Deity, chap. i.; of his humanity exceeding angels, chap. ii.; as a Prophet exceeding Moses, chap. iii. 1, to iv. 13; as a Priest exceeding Aaron, chap. iv. 14, to v. 9; as a King and Priest exceeding Melchisedec, chap. v. 10, to vii. 28. Secondly, He instructs them in the doctrine of the heavenly church-frame pitched by him, with its appurtenances, which exceeded the earthly Mosaical one; in respect of covenant most excellent, chap. viii.; of gospel sacrifice, ordinances, and administrations, for efficacy exceeding all the Levitical ones, chap. ix. 1, to x. 18; where he proceedeth to improve and apply his former doctrine, that they might answer their high privileges by the performance of proportionable duties, becoming this great gospel Minister and his heavenly church-frame, from chap. x. 19, to xiii. 20; concluding the whole with solemn prayer to God, for his enabling of them to the performance of these duties, ver. 20, 21: adding his desire of their candid acceptance of this Epistle from him; comforting them with Timothy's despatch to them, and his own hopes of seeing them; giving them the church's usual salutations, and his own valediction, whereby he discriminateth and closeth all his Epistles.

CHAP. I

The essential dignity of the Son, by whom God hath revealed himself in these last days, 1—3. His pre-eminence above the angels in office, 4—14.

A. D. 64.
a Num. 12. 6, 8.

GOD, who at sundry times and ^ain divers manners spake in time past unto the fathers by the prophets,

God: the apostle designing the conviction of these Hebrews by this discourse, enters on it solemnly, that if a God can awe them, the consideration of Him should gain credit to his doctrine. The God he speaks of is to be apprehended here personally, as well as essentially; God the Father, the one admirable sovereign, immutable Being, the Author of first and second revelation: order is kept here in the subsistence of the relations, as in their works. *Who at sundry times;* πολυμερῶς, by many parts, turns and changes of time, seasons and opportunities, and by many parcels of revelation. God's will was discovered by piecemeal, and not all at once. He vouchsafed one promise to Adam, and so gradually opened further to Enoch, Noah, Abraham, David, pointing out a Christ to come, to come of Abraham's seed in David's family: he discovered *here a little, and there a little*, Isa. xxviii. 13. *And in divers manners;* πολυτρόπως, suitable to the manifold wisdom of God, in divers forms and manners, was his revelation to them; sometimes by sensible representations to them waking, as by angels, fire in the bush, the pillar of fire and cloud: terribly, as at Mount Sinai, chap. xii. 18—21. Sometimes by dreams and visions, Numb. xii. 6; by Urim and Thummim, by voice from the ark, by types and signs from heaven, by riddles, and dark speeches, and Levitical ceremonies; sometimes by immediate illapses on the soul, powerfully influencing it with a Divine light. *Spake;* revealed and declared infallibly his mind and will concerning the way of man's salvation, which his wisdom contrived and his will decreed. *In time past;* all that time past between Adam and Christ, about 4000 years before. *Unto the fathers;* the holy ancestors of these Hebrews, from Adam, down along the Old Testament church of God; the believers of old, such as are registered, chap. xi., and all like them to the times of Christ, from Gen. iii. 15, to that time. *By the prophets;* all those holy men to whom and by whom God revealed his will to his church throughout the successive ages of the Old Testament day; such as were but God's servants, chap. ii. 4, and had his will and mind by measure; who as they preached God's will were God's mouth, as they wrote it were God's scribes; as Abel, Enoch, &c. before the flood; Noah before and after; Abraham, Isaac, Jacob, Joseph, Moses, David, &c.; to these did God infallibly declare it, and they did infallibly deliver it to the church by word and writing; God was by gracious inhabitation in them, in their hearts, tongues, and hands, 2 Pet. i. 21.

b Deut. 4. 30. Gal. 4. 4.
Eph. 1. 10.
c John 1. 17.
& 15. 15.
ch. 2. 3.
d Ps. 2. 8.
Matt. 21. 38.
& 28. 18. John 3. 35. Rom. 8. 17. e John 1. 3. 1 Cor. 8. 6. Col. 1. 16.

2 Hath ᵇin these last days ᶜspoken unto us by *his* Son, ᵈwhom he hath appointed heir of all things, ᵉby whom also he made the worlds:

Hath in these last days; the gospel day, *last,* as after the days of the old world, and after the law given to Israel by Moses; the days of the fourth kingdom of the Roman empire, in the height of which Christ came into the world, and at the end of it shall accomplish his kingdom, Dan. ii. 40, 41. The *last,* because the perfection of those types which went before, when Christ settled in the church that religion which must remain unalterable to the end of the world, chap. xii. 25—28: the best days for clearest light and greatest mercies. *Spoken;* revealed his will to us once and entirely, John i. 17, 18; Jude 3, 4; discovering the excellent things of God more clearly than they were before, Eph. iii. 3—11; 1 Pet. i. 10—12. *To us:* the believing Hebrews were so favoured beyond their fathers, to have the best revelation of God in Christ made to them, Matt. xiii. 16, 17; Luke x. 23, 24. *By his Son;* our Lord Jesus Christ, who cometh out of the Father as a Son, John i. 14; xvi. 28. He is his bosom Son, nearest his heart, John i. 18; the complete Word of him, creating the new world as well as the old, John i. 1; his wisdom, who teacheth without any mistake, declaring all of God, being truth itself, and exhibiting of it, what he hath seen as well as heard, John iii. 11. *Whom;* this Son, who naturally issueth from his Father by a Divine and an unutterable generation, Prov. viii. 22—31; xxx. 4. On him all the Father's love doth terminate, Col. i. 13. He is to be the Founder and Builder of God's family, propagating being to a holy seed for him, chap. iii. 3—6. *He hath appointed;* the Father hath chosen and ordained him as God-man to heirship by an inviolable ordinance of his decree, as 1 Pet. i. 20; compare Eph. i. 10; giving him thereby right and title to all things; appointing to him his nature, chap. ii. 16, compare chap. x. 5; his offices in this nature, his kingly, Psal. ii. 6, 7, his priestly, chap. iii. 1, 2, his prophetical, Acts iii. 22; being heir by nature, as God the Son, and heir by an irresistible ordinance, as God-man Mediator: so as he had a superadded right from the Father, which right he was able to make over to us, but his natural right he could not, Rom. viii. 17. And he was by solemn investiture put in possession of it at his ascension, when he sat down on the Father's right hand, chap. xii. 2; Matt. xxviii. 18; Eph. i. 20—22; Phil. ii. 9—11. *Heir;* Lord Proprietor, who hath sovereign and universal power over all, being the *firstborn,* and receiving the right of it in the whole inheritance, Psal. lxxxix. 27; Rom. viii. 29; Col. i. 15, 18. The lot and portion is fallen to him by God's law, the heir being *Lord of all,* Gal. iv. 1; being heir of his brethren, Psal. ii. 8, and the builder and purchaser of his inheritance, Rev. v. 9—14; compare 1 Pet. i. 3, 4, 18, 19; possessing the inheritance during his Father's life, and making all his brethren heirs of it with him. *Of all things;* of all things within the compass of God, all that God is, all that God hath, all that God can or will do. All dominions of God, heaven, earth, and hell, are his. He is Lord of angels, Eph. i. 21; Col. i. 18, and hath made them fellow servants with us, to himself, and ministering guards to us, ver. 14; Rev. v. 11; xix. 10: of devils, to overrule them, who cannot go or come but as he permits them, Matt. viii. 31; Col. ii. 15: of saints, John xvii. 13; Rom. viii. 29: of wicked men, his enemies, 2 Thess. i. 8, 9: of all creatures, Col. i. 15—17: of all God's works, spiritual, temporal, past, present, or to come; pardon, peace, righteousness, life, glory; all blessings of all sorts, for time and for eternity. This Son-prophet hath right to, actual possession of, and free and full disposal of them. All, both in law and gospel, his, Moses himself, and all his work, to order, change, and do his pleasure with. *By whom;* his Son God-man, a joint cause, a primary and principal agent with the Father, and not a mere instrument, second in working as in relation; by this Word and Wisdom of God, who was the rule and idea of all things, all things were modelled, received their shapes, forms, and distinct beings, John i. 1—3; v. 19, 20; Col. i. 16. In the works of the Trinity, what one relation is said to do the other do, but in their order, answerable to the three principles in every action, wisdom, will, and power. *He made;* created and framed, giving being where there was none, causing to subsist; suggesting herein his ability for redemption work. He who made the world can remove it, chap. xi. 3. *The worlds;* τοὺς αἰῶνας, scarce to be met with in any part of Scripture but this Epistle; strictly it signifieth ages, and things measured by time; answer it doth to the Hebrew עולם which imports both an age and the world: so ages are here well translated *worlds,* all creatures and things measured by them. The Scriptures acquaint us with an upper world, and the inhabitants thereof, angels and glorified saints; the heavenly world, ver. 10, where *the morning stars sang together,* Job xxxviii. 7; compare Gen. i. 1. There is a lower earthly world, with its inhabitants, men, who live on the things in it, Psal. xxiv. 1. And there is a regenerate world, the new heavens and new earth made by Christ, and a new sabbath for them, chap. xii. 26—28; compare 2 Pet. iii. 13. There is Adam's world that now is, this present world, Eph. i. 21; and the world to come, which as it is made by, so for, the Second Adam, the Lord from heaven, in which he eminently is to reign, Psal. viii. 5—8; of which see chap. ii. 5.

3 ᶠWho being the brightness of *his* glory, and the express image of his person, and ᵍupholding all things by the word of his power, ʰwhen he had by himself purged our sins, ⁱsat down on the right hand of the Majesty on high;

f Wisd. 7. 26. John 1. 14. & 14. 9. 2 Cor. 4. 4. Col. 1. 15. g John 1. 4. Rev. 4. 11. h ch. 7. 27. & 9. 12, 14, 16. i Ps. 110. 1. Eph. 1. 20. ch. 8. 1. & 10. 12. & 12. 2. 1 Pet. 3. 22.

Who being the brightness; the same gospel minister, God's Son, was, as to his person, ἀπαύγασμα, a brightness shining out: which word sets forth the natural eternal generation of God the Son, discovering both the rise and flux of his being, and the beauteous and glorious excellency of it. It is the same in the sight of it with the Father's, the brightness of glory, light of light, glory of glory to perfection, streaming from his Father incessantly; as beams issue from the sun, or the mental word is the invisible brightness of that spiritual light the intellect. *Of his glory;* essential glory. Light is a faint, visible resemblance of God's essence, his manifestation of himself in glory hath been by light; to Moses, Exod. xxxiii. 18—23; xxxiv. 5, 29—31; to Isaiah, chap. vi. 1—4; to Ezekiel, chap. i. 4—28, and x.; to Daniel, chap. x. 5, 6, 8, 16—19; to John, Rev. i., iv., and v. And so Christ represented that of his person at his transfiguration, Matt. xvii. 1—7. If created light be glorious in the sun, in angels; how much more God's essential glory! Purity, beauty, light, how pleasant!

but what are these to God? However the being of God be conceived, as wisdom, holiness, goodness, justice, power, the excellency of these above all created beings is this glory. No being is glory but God's; this fundamental excellency shines no where as in this Son, John i. 14. By this are Father and Son declared distinct relations, subsisting together and co-eternal. *And the express image*; as the beams are with the sun the same in time, yet are weaker, therefore the Holy Ghost adds, he is his very *image*; χαρακτήρ is an engraven image of the Father, every way like him; the word signifieth a sculpture, print, engraving, or seal; intimating its distinction from what impressed it, and its likeness or parity to it: so is the Son's a distinct relation, yet naturally and integrally having all that might liken him to his Father, Col. i. 15. *Of his person*; τῆς ὑποστάσεως αὐτῦ, of his subsistence. He is not the character of the Godhead, or of the Divine essence, but of the Father, the personal subsistence in the Deity. He is one and the same God with the Father, but his character as God is a Father, so that who seeth him seeth his Father, John xiv. 9; he is the visible representation of him, Col. ii. 9. *And upholding*; the whole work of Providence is set out by *upholding*; φέρων imports sustaining, feeding, preserving, governing, throwing down, raising up, comforting, and punishing, &c. All would have fallen in pieces on man's sin, had not he interposed, and stopped the world when it was reeling back into nothing, Col. i. 17; and to this instant he preserveth and ruleth all, Isa. ix. 6; John v. 22. *All things*; τὰ πάντα, a full, universal, comprehensive *all*, persons and things, angels, men, creatures good and bad, small and great, with all events, Acts xvii. 24—31. *By the word of his power*; not by an articulate voice, but his beck, will, or powerful command, whereby he doth whatsoever he pleaseth; his absolute, powerful, irresistible word; he acts as easily as others speak; there is no distinguishing between this word and power, they went together in the creation, Gen. i. 3, 6, 7, and do so in his providence, Psal. xxxiii. 9; cxlviii. 8. *When he had by himself*; when this God-man, as the great gospel High Priest, so styled, chap. ii. 17, had by himself alone, being altar and sacrifice, as well as Priest, the sole efficient of this work without any assistance. He, by his eternal Spirit, offered up a sacrifice propitiatory to God, his human nature hypostatically united to his Divine, and expiring his soul, he immediately entered with the blood of the covenant the holy of holiest in heaven, and presenting it before the eternal Judge, made full satisfaction and expiation for sins, chap. vii. 17; ix. 11, 12, 14, 24, 26; x. 10, 12, 14. *Purged*; by his satisfaction and merit, removing both the guilt and stain of sin; so as God, the injured Lawgiver, could be just as well as merciful in pardoning it; and justifying those who believe and plead it from the condemnation they were liable to for it, Rom. iii. 24—26; 1 John i. 7, 9; and mortifying and killing sin in them by his purchased Spirit, chap. x. 10, 12, 14, 18; compare 1 Cor. vi. 11; Eph. v. 25—27. *Our sins*; the sins of men, and not of angels; and the consequents of them, removing guilt, stain, and punishment, which they would fasten on us by his self-sacrifice, chap. ii. 16. *Sat down*; after his atoning for sinners, at the forty days' end he ascended in his human nature, immortal in body and soul, and entered the second time the holy of holiest in heaven; and then ἐκάθισεν, made himself to sit as High Priest in the most honourable and immovable state and condition. He did not stand, as the typical high priest before God's ark, but *sat*; and in this co-operated with his Father, and obeyed him, Psal. cx. 1; angels, and men, and creatures, all subjected to him, Eph. i. 20—22. He doth sit quietly, Acts iii. 21, and surely; there is no shaking him from his ever-interceding for his, chap. vii. 25. *On the right hand*; a similitude expressing the height of glory that this God-man is advanced to; alluding to the state of the greatest king on his throne in his majesty, Ezek. i. 4, 26—28; Dan. vii. 9—14; 1 Tim. i. 17. He is exalted by the royal Father as his eldest Son, invested with Godlike power, majesty, and glory, as chap. viii. 1; x. 12; xii. 2; there enjoying all that happiness, blessedness, all those dignities and pleasures, Psal. xvi. 11; fulness of honour and glory, chap. ii. 7; of government, rule, and dominion, Matt. xxviii. 18; of all royal and glorious abilities and endowments for the managing all things; he enjoyeth all these as the Father himself doth, who ordereth all by him, so as no creature is capable of it, ver. 13. All the power of doing all things in all worlds is lodged in his hands. *Of the Majesty on high*; in the highest heaven is this possessed by him, and there is he to display his glory in ordering all, chap. vii. 26; viii. 1; Eph. iv. 10: as in the happiest, so in the highest place is he to rule for ever; our advantage is by it, Eph. ii. 6, as to best of places and states.

4 Being made so much better than the angels, as ᵏhe hath by inheritance obtained a more excellent name than they.

k Eph. 1. 21. Phil. 2. 9,10.

Being made so much better than the angels: this Godman, the great gospel Minister, is more excellent than angels, and so must surpass all the prophets. He became thus by being surety constituted and declared, as ordained by God's decree from eternity, in eminency above them by actual investiture on his ascension, Eph. i. 20, 21. A more excellent person he is beyond any comparison for his Divine nature, and in his human transcending the angelical, on the account of the hypostatical union: see ver. 6. *Angels*; these were spirits likest God, and called *Elohims*, or gods, ver. 7; Psal. civ. 4; being most pure, glorious, powerful, and heavenly creatures, Mark viii. 38; xiii. 32; 2 Thess. i. 7; of various ranks, orders, and degrees, Eph. i. 21; Col. i. 16; used by Christ as his ministers in the delivering of his law on Mount Sinai to Israel, chap. ii. 2; Acts vii. 53; Gal. iii. 19. The measure of his transcendency over these, for person, office, and name, is infinitely beyond expression. *As he hath by inheritance obtained a more excellent name*; this was his peculiar, hereditary lot, due to him by natural right, as the heir and first-born of God, justly acquired by him, and actually possessed of him, not as a mere title, but a name descriptive of his person, distinguishing him from, and setting him above, all others: God the Son incarnate, Isa. vii. 14; ix. 6; Lord over all creatures in heaven and in earth, and under it, Phil. ii. 9—11; not a simple messenger, but a *Son*, Matt. xvii. 5; John i. 18; the Redeemer, Justifier, and Saviour of his people, Luke i. 31, 32. He is a person of name famous for power, glory, and dignity above all others, Eph. i. 21; Phil. ii. 9—11. *A more excellent name than they*; διαφορώτερον, differencing from, and setting above, all the names of angels for eminency, the archangel himself being a servant and attendant on him, 1 Thess. iv. 16. His is more differencing and transcending in his kind than the name of angels is in their kind; he is above whatever they can pretend to, and so a more excellent Prophet than they. He hath in all things, as well as name, over them the pre-eminency.

5 For unto which of the angels said he at any time, ˡThou art my Son, this day have I begotten thee? And again, ᵐI will be to him a Father, and he shall be to me a Son?

l Ps. 2. 7. Acts 13. 33. ch. 5. 5.
m 2 Sam. 7. 14. 1 Chron. 22. 10, & 28. 6. Ps. 89. 26, 27.

The apostle here proves that Christ hath a more excellent name, and pre-eminency over angels, by Scripture texts owned by these Hebrews. He had the name of Son of God, and so had not angels; for God the Father, who hath absolute power to give and state all excellency, never said to any angel, so as to constitute him his only Son by an ordinance or word of power. *Sons* he may style them, as Job ii. 1; Psal. lxxxix. 6; as he doth members of his church, Gen. vi. 2, and princes and magistrates, Psal. lxxxii. 1, 6; but always in the plural number, as he doth the angels, Job xxxviii. 7, noting out their power, place, and ministry. But *Son* is singular to Christ, and incommunicable to any other. *Thou art my Son*: this is quoted out of Psal. ii. 7. *Thou* God-man, thou thyself, thou, and thou alone, (that this was spoken of Christ truly, and of David only as a type of him, the Spirit asserts, Acts xiii. 33,) art my own Son, my ever-being Son, my Son by nature, Rom. viii. 32. Singularity sets out his eminency above all, and his propriety by nature in him. *This day have I begotten thee*: at the day of his incarnation, Isa. ix. 6; Luke i. 31, 32, 35, but eminently at the day of his resurrection, was he declared and published to be his only begotten Son with power, Rom. i. 4; and at his ascension inaugurated the supreme, universal King and Priest in heaven and earth, chap. v. 5, possessed of a better name, place, and power than angels, Eph. i. 20, 21. What men enjoy in this kind attributed to them, is with a vast disproportion to this; born, or begotten, they are said to be, in respect of God's operation on them, infusing Divine qualities into their souls, but this *Son* by a generation proper to a substantial person. *And again, I will be to him a Father, and he shall be to me a Son:* in another Scripture, as 2 Sam. vii. 14; 1 Chron. xvii. 13; xxii. 10, it is declared, I his natural Father, and he my natural Son; so as they are not related to any other as they are to each other. This in the type was spoken of Solomon, but fulfilled in Christ, who was universal King and Priest over his church for ever; so David understood it, Psal. cx. 1; compare lxxxix. 19, 26—29. He was the first-born Son, born a King; the Son of the universal and supreme King, the Heir and Lord of all.

|| Or, *When he bringeth again.*
n Rom. 8. 29. Col. 1. 18. Rev. i. 5.
o Deut. 32. 43, LXX. Ps. 97. 7. 1 Pet. 3. 22.

6 || And again, when he bringeth in ⁿthe firstbegotten into the world, he saith, ᵒAnd let all the angels of God worship him.

This is a further proof of the great gospel Minister being more excellent than angels, by God's command to them to worship him. *And again, when he bringeth in the firstbegotten into the world:* Πάλιν some refer to God the Father's speech, as, *Again he saith:* others think it too gross a transposition, and unusual in the Scripture, and so read it as it stands in the Greek text, He again, or a second time, bringeth, &c. This hath started a query about what time it is that the Father saith this, and that he brought in the First-born into the world? Some say it was at his incarnation; others, at his coming to judgment. Considering the former proofs brought out of Psal. ii. 7, and 2 Sam. vii. 14, it seems most fairly to be at his resurrection and ascension, when the decree was proclaimed of his being the great King; and he was actually exalted far above all gods, whether angels or men: compare Psal. ii. 7, with xcvii. 1, 9, and Acts xiii. 33, to which agrees Col. i. 15, 18. Then was the demonstration of what a royal Head he was to be, and how acknowledged by all, Phil. ii. 9—11. *He saith, And let all the angels of God worship him;* he powerfully and effectually publisheth his command unto his angels, as recorded by his prophet in his word, Psal. xcvii. 7, where the sense of the Hebrew text is full, Bow down to him all ye Elohim, or *gods;* which the Septuagint renders *angels,* and is so quoted by Paul here; and the Spirit warrants it: so is it rendered, Deut. xxxii. 43. That translation was commonly used by the dispersed Græcising Hebrews. This title is attributed to angels, Psal. viii. 5. By their worship they do obey the Father, and own their subjection to his Son at his resurrection, Matt. xxviii. 2; Luke xxiv. 4; John xx. 12; and at his ascension, Acts i. 9, 10; Rev. v. 11, 12: so that the worshipped is more excellent than the worshippers.

† Gr. *unto.*
p Ps. 104. 4.

7 And † of the angels he saith, ᵖWho maketh his angels spirits, and his ministers a flame of fire.

He adds another demonstration of the gospel Minister's exceeding angels, because he hath the name of *God,* and angels are called only God's *ministers:* for the Creator of angels, who best understandeth their nature and office, by his Spirit testifieth what they are, Psal. civ. 4. *Who maketh his angels spirits;* he created them such as they are, spiritual, intellectual, and immortal substances, the highest in this sort and kind of creatures. Πνεύματα do not here signify winds, as if the Spirit compared angels to them for their swiftness and power, but spiritual, intellectual beings, as the Son of man is; and in this it is the attribute, and not the subject. that which is predicated or spoken of angels. *And his ministers a flame of fire;* they are but ministers and servants, who reveal or perform his will to those to whom God sends them; honourable officers of the great King, fulfilling his pleasure, ver. 14, executing all his commands, and going and coming at his beck, Psal. ciii. 20, 21. Though they are seraphims, bright, glorious, and excellent creatures, they are but the grand officers of state in heaven. encompassing God's throne, waiting for his commands, which they obey and fulfil as swiftly as the winds or flashes of lightning could despatch them. Though they are styled by the Spirit *cherubims,* Gen. iii. 24; compare Ezek. i. 5; x. 1—15; and *seraphims,* Isa. vi. 6; for their light, glory, and excellency; yet still are they creatures, and below the Son, because his servants.

8 But unto the Son *he saith,* ᵠThy throne, O God, *is* for ever and ever: a sceptre of † righteousness *is* the sceptre of thy kingdom.

q Ps. 45. 6, 7.
+ Gr. *rightness, or, straightness.*

In the Father's apostrophe to the Son, he giveth him the name of *God,* and thereby is he proved to have a better one than angels, made by, and servants to, him; and as the great gospel Minister hath a kingdom, in which they are his ministers and servants: this proof is quoted out of Psal. xlv. 6, 7. It was not to Solomon or David, but to the Son God-man, spoken by the Father. The whole Psalm is written of him, and incompatible to any other is the matter of it. It represents him and his mystical marriage to the church; compare Eph. v. 23—33; Rev. xix. 7, 8; xxii. 17. *Thy throne, O God:* some heretics, to elude this proof of Christ's Deity, would make *God* the genitive case in the proposition, as, Thy throne of God, expressly contrary to the grammar, both in Hebrew and Greek: others gloss it, that ὁ Θεὸς is the nominative case, as, God is thy throne for ever, &c. i. e. He doth and will establish it: but this is cavilling, since it is the Father's speech to and of his Son, describing his nature in opposition to the angels before. They were created *spirits,* but he was *God;* they were *ministers* and servants in his kingdom, where he was King; therefore his name and person is better than theirs. *God,* in the singular, was a name never given to any creature, but is expressive of his Divine nature, and his relation in the Deity, being God the Son. *Is for ever and ever:* his office as God-man, and great gospel Minister, is a royal one. He is a great King, angels are subjects of his kingdom as well as men, which royalty is set out by the ensigns of it; as here, by a throne, which is an emblem of royal authority, dominion, and power, whence he displayeth himself in his kingdom. It is a heavenly one, of a perfect constitution and administration, and of eternal continuance. His it was by natural inheritance, as God the Son; and as man united to the Godhead, he inheriteth the privileges of that person. This natural dominion over all things remaineth for ever, Col. i. 16. *A sceptre of righteousness is a sceptre of thy kingdom:* another ensign of his royal dominion and kingdom is his *sceptre,* which is his Spirit put out in his government of the world, and in his special work of grace, guiding and conforming, through his word and ordinances, the hearts of his chosen to the will of his Father. This sceptre is subjectively right in itself, and efficiently, making all under its power to be rectified according to the right and pure mind and will of God: compare Psal. cx. 1—3.

9 Thou hast loved righteousness, and hated iniquity; therefore God, *even* thy God, ʳhath anointed thee with the oil of gladness above thy fellows.

r Is. 61. 1. Acts 4. 27. & 10. 38.

Thou hast loved righteousness, and hated iniquity: the administration of this King in his kingdom is suitable to his throne and sceptre, it is all goodness; for he so loved righteousness, and hated iniquity, being righteous and holy in himself, in life and death, expiating sin, and sanctifying believers. So that he acts as to both of these properly from himself, perfectly and for ever. *Therefore God:* it may be a reason why he so loved righteousness, being anointed, or of his unction, because he loved the one, and hated the other; therefore God the Son is the person to whom the Father speaketh this. *Even thy God;* God the Father, his God in respect of the human nature, Luke i. 35; formed by him, Gal. iv. 4, as Mediator between God and sinners, John xx. 17; the Head of the church, in covenant with God, his great gospel Minister. *Hath anointed thee with the oil of gladness;* so his Father *anointed* him *with the Holy Ghost and with power,* John iii. 34; Acts x. 38; and thereby as endowed, so exalted him above all kings and prophets who were literally anointed, and above all angels, having Divine power and authority supereminent to all communicated to him; enjoying the best and highest joy in all his transactions with the Father for us, and which may perfect joy in us, John xv. 11; xvii. 13. *Above thy fellows*, the coheirs of his kingdom, beyond whatever God communicated to saints or angels. He had not the Spirit by measure, John iii. 34. What others enjoy, it is from his fulness, John i. 16; Luke iv. 18—21.

^{s Ps. 102. 25, &c.} 10 And, ^s Thou, Lord, in the beginning hast laid the foundation of the earth; and the heavens are the works of thine hands:

And, Thou, Lord : this connective particle joins this to the former proof, that Christ had a more excellent name than angels, even that of God. That he was God, he proved out of Psal. xlv. 6, 7. He seconds it in this and the two following verses, which he quotes out of Psal. cii. 25—27. The strength of which lieth thus : He who was Jehovah, and the great Creator of the world, is God ; such is Christ, the great gospel Prophet. This is evident in the prayer recorded in the Psalm made to him, compared with the Spirit's testimony, ver. 8 ; the very works appropriated to Jehovah there, are the acknowledged works of God the Son, as redemption, Psal. cii. 20, 21, vocation of the Gentiles, ver. 15, 18, 22. *In the beginning ;* in the beginning of time, when that came to be the measure and limit of things, as Gen. i. 1. Before there were any such creatures as angels, he was Jehovah, John i. 1 ; and then manifested himself to be Jehovah. The enemies of Christ's Deity say that the name Jehovah is not in the verse of the Psalm quoted by the Spirit; yet *thou*, the relative used in all those verses, refers to *God*, the antecedent, prayed to in ver. 24, and to Jehovah, the name given him in ver. 1, 12, 15, 16, 18, 19, 21, 22, of that Psalm ; all importing one and the same person. And it is well known that Κυριος, Lord, doth eminently decipher the Redeemer in the New Testament ; he is not an instrument of Jehovah to create by, but the fountain of all being, Jehovah himself. *Hast laid the foundation of the earth ; and the heavens are the works of thine hands :* by founding the earth, and the heavens being the work of his hands, is meant the whole work of creation throughout the space of six days: he was the true, full, sole, and self-causality of the earth's being, and all creatures in it, and of the heavens, and all beings which are in them; he was the great Architect and Founder of them all ; they were his peculiar workmanship, possession, and dominion, 1 Cor. viii. 6 : compare John i. 3 ; Col. i. 16. If the heavens were the works of his hands, and all in them, then he was the Creator of angels, and therefore must be, for person, name, and office, more excellent than they.

^{t Is. 34. 4. & 51. 6. Mat. 24. 35. 2 Pet. 3. 7. 10. Rev. 21. 1.} 11 ^t They shall perish ; but thou remainest ; and they all shall wax old as doth a garment ;

They shall perish ; the heavens themselves instanced in, as containing the most excellent part of the creation, (such as the Gentile philosophy esteemed incorruptible,) are mutable, as by the various changes, not only in the airy part of it, but in the ethereal, doth appear : the glorious lights in it have their spots and rusts, as the sun itself, both increasing and diminishing upon them, and so as to their present, natural frame, are changeable, perishable, and dissolvable, Isa. li. 6 ; Matt. xxiv. 35. *But thou remainest ;* but the Son Jehovah is unchangeable, hath a stedfast being, such as never loseth its state, no term is set for the ending of him. His immutability proves his Deity. *Remainest* is an expression of present time, denoting constant abiding. He was before, in, and after all ages immutable, Lam. v. 19. *Jesus Christ the same yesterday, and to-day, and for ever*, chap. xiii. 8. *And they all shall wax old as doth a garment :* the antiquation of a garment is a metaphor borrowed, to show the corruptibility of the heavens. A garment wears and decayeth with use in tract of time, it changeth its fashion, is another thing as to its matter and form : so will the heavens, as to their form and face, decay, they are gradually coming to an end as to what they are now, 2 Pet. iii. 7, 10. *That which decayeth and waxeth old is ready to vanish away*, chap. viii. 13 ; so these heavens do.

12 And as a vesture shalt thou fold them up, and they shall be changed : but thou art the same, and thy years shall not fail.

And as a vesture shalt thou fold them up : περιβόλαιον is an upper garment, cloak, or coat, which a man puts on or casts off at his pleasure ; when it is of no more use it is folded up and laid by : so the great gospel Minister, God the Son incarnate, shall roll up the natural heavens when useless, and lay them by. *And they shall be changed ;* by him they shall be altered, and made more glorious by new modelling them, changing of them into a better state, Isa. xxxiv. 4 ; lxv. 17 ; lxvi. 22 : compare 2 Pet. iii. 10—13. *But thou art the same :* the identity of this Person is opposed to the changeableness of excellent creatures, and showeth him to be what he is here entitled, Jehovah, chap. xiii. 8. His assumption of the humanity to his person made no alteration in him, being still the same most excellent person as ever, Mal. iii. 1, 6 ; 1 Cor. xii. 5. *And thy years shall not fail ;* as the being of God the Son is not measured nor terminated by years or time, so, in respect of his humanity, the years which were the measure of it shall never fail ; for being raised from the dead, he shall die no more, but *abideth for ever*, John xii. 34, and ruleth, as foretold, Luke i. 33 ; 1 Pet. iv. 11. How transcendently excellent is He, who is immutable and eternal, for state and name above angels !

13 But to which of the angels said he ^{u Ps. 110. 1. Matt. 22. 44.} at any time, "Sit on my right hand, until ^{Mark 12. 36. Luke 20. 42.} I make thine enemies thy footstool ? ^{ch. 10. 12. ver. 3.}

But to which of the angels said he at any time? this introduceth the last demonstration of the gospel Minister's pre-eminency for state, office, and name, above angels. The form is thus ; He that is God's fellow, and right-hand man, is more excellent, and hath a better name, than those who are only ministers to his saints. This is to be the state of Christ he proves here ; for to none of the angels did Jehovah ever say this, he never gave them that honour by his word. It is an interrogatory challenge to the Hebrews to produce that text in Scripture, which doth assert, that at any time, in any place, God gave such an honorary word to angels : this was impossible for them to do. Though God the Father never said this to any angel, yet did he say this, and records it in the Scripture, to the Lord Christ. And it was a word to him *constitutivum rei*, fixing the very thing. This is recorded in Psal. cx. 1, where God's powerful word settled Christ in the honour, glory, and dignity of universal lordship over angels and men, so as to reign over them, 1 Cor. xv. 25 ; which administration he is now in the flesh solemnly managing at the right hand of his Father, ver. 3, ever since his ascension, and so is to continue. *Sit on my right hand, until I make thine enemies thy footstool ;* during all the time of this world, until by his power he reduce, subdue, and subjugate all to him, even every thing and person that should be adverse to his sovereign person and kingdom, all devils and men, subjugating of them to the basest condition, to be trod under his feet, as mire in the street, utterly destroying them, when he glorifieth his saints, 2 Thess. i. 7—10. The term of this word *until* doth not denote the end of his reign, as if after this he should not reign, but is declarative of his reign all the time before : though his enemies were many and strong, yet it is said, 1 Cor. xv. 24, 28, that then he shall deliver up the kingdom to his Father. As to his natural kingdom, which is his as God the Son, that is, equally enjoyed with the Father, and that for ever, there is no end of it ; but as to his mediatory kingdom, given him by choice, and in a special manner appropriated to him as God-man for his season, this, when his work is done, and all his enemies subdued, he will resign unto the Father, that God may be all in all.

14 ^x Are they not all ministering spirits, ^{x Gen. 19. 16. & 32. 1, 2, 24. Ps. 34. 7. & 91. 11. & 103. 20, 21. Dan. 3. 28.} sent forth to minister for them who shall be ^y heirs of salvation ?
^{& 7. 10. & 10. 11. Matt. 18. 10. Luke 1. 19. & 2. 9, 13. Acts 12. 7, &c. & 27. 23. y Rom. 8. 17. Tit. 3. 7. Jam. 2. 5. 1 Pet. 3. 7.}

Are they not all ministering spirits? the apostle here proves, that angels are but ministers to the great gospel Minister, and to the members of his body the church, and so must be meaner than him for state, nature, and name. This negative interrogation is a vehement assertion. The nature, dignity, and office of angels were well known to these Hebrews out of the Old Testament, and which he repeats : they were for nature *spirits*, intellectual, active, incorporeal, and incorruptible creatures ; yet though so ex-

HEBREWS II

cellent, were still creatures; whereas Christ was an uncreated Spirit, and they were but servants to him their Lord; and though there be degrees and orders among them from the archangel to the lowest angel, they are every one of them single, and all of them together, servants to Christ, and so they own themselves to be, Rev. xix. 10; xxii. 9. *Sent forth to minister for them;* and so they move all at his order, and go and come at his command. Their employment directed by him; he sends them forth to deliver his errands, Acts v. 19, and xii. 7, 11, to reveal his will to them, Rev. i. 1; Psal. ciii. 21, &c. All the parts of ministry to which he appointeth them, they cheerfully, swiftly, and effectually perform. *Who shall be heirs of salvation;* such as God hath chosen and called to be children to himself, and joint-heirs with his only Son, as have a right to, are fitting for, and shall be at last possessed of, eternal glory; these angels are to serve and help them on for to attain it, they themselves being elect in and by Christ unto this end, 1 Tim. v. 21; 2 Tim. ii. 10. All which demonstrate him to be a more excellent person, and to have a more excellent name, than they.

CHAP. II

The obligation we are under to give more earnest heed to the gospel doctrine, 1—4. *The dominion of the world to come was not granted to angels, but to the Son of man, whom it behoved to undergo a previous course of humiliation and suffering,* 5—18.

THEREFORE we ought to give the more earnest heed to the things which we have heard, lest at any time we should † let *them* slip.

† Gr. run out as leaking vessels.

In this and the three following verses the apostle applieth the doctrine of the great gospel Prophet's being more excellent for nature and person than any of the angels in respect of his Deity; and from thence inferreth the duty, that since God speaking by the prophets is to be heard by those to whom he sends them; how much more when speaking to them by his Son-prophet, who so infinitely excelleth not only all prophets, but angels too! *We ought to give the more earnest heed;* we believers, who know the things spoken to be good for us, whether apostles, ministers, or Christian members, by the indispensable necessity laid on us by God's precept, are obliged more abundantly, exceeding abundantly, than formerly they had; more than they gave to Moses and the legal ministry, excessively beyond that, 2 Cor. xi. 23; Eph. iii. 20; to give heed with an attentive and intent mind, so as to have hearts fastened to what was diligently considered of before, received, believed; heeding them so as to retain and practise them; so to believe, profess, be, keep, and do what he speaks from the Father to them, having souls knit and cleaving to them, James i. 22, 25. *To the things which we have heard;* all that mind and will of God which his Son revealeth to us fully, the whole gospel doctrine which by himself, and by his Spirit in the apostles, he had preached and written to them, Rom. x. 14—16. *Lest at any time we should let them slip;* an act opposite to the former giving heed, which is by them to be denied, viz. their being like leaking vessels, or having chinks open in their souls, letting by them slide out the most precious gospel of Christ, as water out of a cracked, leaky, broken vessel, or spilt on the ground. All forgetfulness of memory, all apostasy in heart or profession, is that which the Spirit forbiddeth in this metaphor, παραῤῥυῶμεν. Their danger as to their persons is made a motive to this duty, ver. 3, and is not therefore so immediately concerned in this, though it may be implied, for none will let the gospel of Christ slide from them who will not, as to their persons, slide from him at last.

a Deut. 33. 2.
Ps. 68. 17.
Acts 7. 53.
Gal. 3. 19.
b Num. 15.
30, 31.
Deut. 4. 2.
& 17. 2, 5, 12.
& 27. 26.

2 For if the word ª spoken by angels was stedfast, and ᵇ every transgression and disobedience received a just recompence of reward;

This and the following verse is a rational motive used by the Spirit to enforce the foregoing duty, and shows the danger of their persons by the neglect of it. *For if the word spoken by angels;* for if the law of God delivered by the ministry of angels to these Hebrews' forefathers at Mount Sinai, Deut. xxxiii. 2, as ministers and servants of Christ there, Acts vii. 38, 53, compare Gal. iii. 19, and all other revelations of God's will to Moses and the prophets by angels, consisting of precepts, prohibitions, promises, and comminations, the whole body of God's laws contained in the Old Testament. The term by which law is expressed, λόγος, signifies in most of the Eastern languages a command as well as a word; and λεγεῖν, to command, as well as to speak. The force or obligation of this law or word was from God the Redeemer, whose word it was, though published and promulgated to the church by angels. *Was stedfast;* made firm by the solemn sanction of God, with a penalty, if any durst use it arbitrarily, or despise it; there was no violating it by commission or omission without being punished for it; God establishing it by fulfilling promises and executing judgments, chap. x. 28. Not a contumacious transgressor of it could escape his punishment; which made the law firm and valid; see Deut. xvii. 10, &c.; and this not only as the law of a Creator, but of a Redeemer, stablishing of it by entering into a covenant with them by it, and they confirming it, Josh. xxiv. 22, 24. *And every transgression and disobedience;* every contumacious going beside the law, or casting it aside by commission of evil, or rejecting prohibitions, or disobedience to positive laws by omission of what they required. And by a metonymy is understood transgressors by either of these ways. *Received a just recompence of reward;* a just retribution, a righteous proportionable rendering of punishment to them for their sin; evil for evil, and death for sin, executed either immediately by God, or mediately by his instruments of government, according to the exact grains of justice, Rom. ii. 5—13. This punishment was either inflicted on, or received certainly by, the offender in his own person if capital, or in his representative sacrifice for lesser crimes, chap. x. 28; Rom. i. 32; 1 Cor. x. 5—11.

3 ᶜ How shall we escape, if we neglect so great salvation; ᵈ which at the first began to be spoken by the Lord, and was ᵉ confirmed unto us by them that heard him:

c ch. 10. 28,
29, & 12. 25.
d Matt.4.17.
Mark 1. 14.
ch. 1. 2.
e Luke 1. 2.

How shall we escape? this consequent answereth the antecedent in ver. 2, but in one part of it, that which concerns the punishment of the transgressors of the law, thus: If the word by angels, much more the word by the Son; and if sins against that were punished, much more sins against this: the Spirit including the sanction of the gospel's power in the judgment which it pronounceth upon its despisers, which it could not do if it were not established. The interrogative *how,* introducing the consequent, is vehemently negative; by no means, or there is no possibility of our escaping in the case proposed: compare the close of Isa. xx. 6. There is no avoiding the righteous punishment which the just God doth threaten gospel sinners with, such as is recorded in Matt. x. 15; xi. 22, 24; 2 Thess. i. 7—9; chap. x. 28, 29; none can escape it, neither I nor you, if such transgressors; external offices, or church privileges, will not excuse any one from the just punishment and retribution of God. *If we neglect so great salvation;* if being careless, so as to despise and make light of the gospel, or to reject it, chap. viii. 9; Matt. xxii. 5. Opposed this is to the sins of commission and omission about the law; any denial of receiving it, or of a progress into the necessary duties it requires, so to neglect them as to end in apostasy. For the gospel law of Christ revealing and promising salvation to believers, opposed here to the law given by angels, will make safe all spiritual good both for time and eternity to the sincere believers and obeyers of it. The gospel is called *salvation* metonymically, because the subject matter of it is salvation, Eph. i. 13, and it hath a causal power and virtue to save, Acts xiii. 26; Rom. i. 16; opposed to the law, which was the ministration of death and condemnation, 2 Cor. iii. 7, 9, being revealed by angels under carnal types and temporal promises, and, by reason of the veil on their hearts, became killing to them. The word by the Son is salvation, because a full and clear discovery to it. This salvation is transcendent, being not a terrene or temporary, but a heavenly, eternal salvation, delivering those who truly obey it from the worst of enemies, the sorest and most lasting punishment, and instating them in eternal happiness and blessedness in heaven. This was *great* for clearness of light, 2 Cor. iv. 4, and diffusive efficacy and success. *Which at the first began to be spoken by the Lord;* an aggravation of the neglect of this salvation from *the Lord* publishing it. It had its rise and beginning from the Fountain of all truth, and was first by voice and preaching made known to the Hebrews, and such Gentiles as came to hear the promulgation of it, Matt. iv. 17, at Christ's solemn entering on his ministry, above three years before his death and resurrection. And it may refer higher; for as it was most clearly, plainly, sweetly, and eminently preached by himself, beyond what was taught by the prophets in the Old Testament, or John; yet he first preached it himself *in the beginning* to our apostate parents in Paradise, Gen. iii. 15, and he preached it in all the prophets publishing of it since: yet this priority may be in respect of the ministry which he ordained to follow him, and not of that which went before. It was so preached *by the Lord* himself, the Mediator, Lord of life and death, Head of angels and all principalities and powers, the great Prophet, swaying all things by the word of his power. The law was preached by angels, the gospel by God the Son himself, chap. i. 2; and so is preferred before the law, in respect of its ministration by the Head, not of its authority. *And was confirmed unto us by them that heard him;* settled it was, made firm and authentical, by himself. The Trinity bear witness to it in heaven, confirm it on earth by miracles, signs, and wonders, and mighty deeds, by Christ, John v. 36, by his apostles, 2 Cor. xii. 12, and by the gifts of the Holy Ghost in great variety distributed to his apostles and publishers of this gospel, which made their ministration of it effectual, Acts ii. 1—3; compare 1 Cor. xii. 9—11; even to the apostles and Hebrews, and to all who believe, it is so confirmed. Nor is Paul less the writer of this Epistle for that he joins himself with them, since he did hear both the Lord and the apostles, and was confirming those of them with whom he had fellowship, and was confirmed by them, Acts ix. 17, 19; Gal. ii. 9. Christ's disciples and apostles heard this gospel from him, and did witness it by preaching, writing, and sealing it with their blood, Phil. i. 12; 2 Pet. i. 16, 17; which confirmation by their sufferings was instrumental, mediate, and subservient to the miracles and gifts of the Holy Ghost enjoyed of them and wrought by them.

f Mark 16.20.
Acts 14. 3. &
19. 11. Rom.
15. 18, 19.
1 Cor. 2. 4.
g Acts 2. 22,
43.
‖ Or, *distributions.* h 1 Cor. 12. 4, 7, 11. i Eph. 1. 5, 9.

4 ᶠGod also bearing *them* witness, ᵍboth with signs and wonders, and with divers miracles, and ‖ ʰgifts of the Holy Ghost, ⁱaccording to his own will?

God also bearing them witness: here is a further aggravation of the neglect of the gospel of salvation, from God's testifying to it by the works and gifts of his Holy Spirit: such sin grievously, and will receive a proportionable punishment; for God, the Father, Son, and Holy Spirit, co-testify with all those instruments confirming the gospel of salvation, with a testimony peculiarly fitted to it; yet in this joint-witnessing God is the highest, and αὐτος πιςος, only to be believed for himself. *Both with signs and wonders;* by works above nature's reach, signifying God's being in and approving the gospel law, which they attend, Mark xvi. 17. More numerous and glorious were these than they which confirmed the law, Acts ii. 22, 43; iv. 30; such strange works as raised admiration in all that saw them, and are prodigious to those that hear of them, or read them, Rom. xv. 19. *And with divers miracles;* miraculous works, such as are compassed only by a Divine, supernatural power; and variety of these, as healing all diseases, raising the dead, ejecting devils, Mark xvi. 17, 18; works of as great mercy, as wisdom or power. *And gifts of the Holy Ghost, according to his own will;* as gifts of tongues, prophecies, &c., Rom. xii. 6—8; compare 1 Cor. xii. 7—10; such as nature could not furnish any with, but the Redeemer did by his Spirit, communicating them to various persons of divers kinds and indifferent degrees. From, by, and for himself he giveth out these wonderful works; his will the only rule for time, persons, manner, and measure of their distribution, allotting all their portion, Rom. xii. 3; 1 Cor. vii. 17; xii. 4, 7, 11, 18; Eph. iv. 7.

5 For unto the angels hath he not put in subjection ᵏthe world to come, whereof we speak.

k ch. 6. 5.
2 Pet. 3. 13.

For unto the angels: the Spirit having applied the doctrine of the great gospel Minister, exceeding the prophets of old, and having a more excellent name and office than angels, in respect of his Deity, pursues to show these Hebrews, that he is so likewise in respect of his humanity, the other nature in his person. This he proves negatively in this verse. The rational particle introducing, shows it to be a demonstration of his excelling angels, having a world to come subjected to him, which they have not; for so none of these incorporeal, intellectual, spiritual substances, so often diminished before, have; because those Hebrews were more addicted to esteem of them, and the law ministered by them, than of God the Son incarnate and his gospel. *Hath he not put in subjection;* this God the Father, Son, and Spirit, the Creator who formed all things, and had right of disposing all things under their proper Lord, hath not put under their ordering or government; he never decreed, foretold, or promised that it should be under their authority. *The world to come,* must be interpreted by that scripture, where it is asserted and proved that it was subjected to the great gospel Minister, and that is in Psal. viii. 5—8. It is a world that must consist of heaven and earth; compare ver. 3, 6, 7. It was a world not come when Paul wrote this Epistle to the Hebrews, see ver. 8. It is a world distinct from this present world, Eph. i. 21, in which God-man must eminently reign; a world between this world and a heavenly one which is to come, in respect of us, Luke xviii. 30; 1 Tim. iv. 8. A world to come, which the angels have nothing to do with, as they have with this, which is greatly under their administration; such as consists of a *new heaven and a new earth, in which dwelleth righteousness,* 2 Pet. iii. 13; for Peter asserts, that Paul, according to the revelation given him of it, had written to those Hebrews, and eminently in this text. And unto this do the prophets give witness, Isa. lxv. 17, 18; lxvi. 22; and of his day of rest and sabbath in it, as chap. iv. 7, 9, 10; so Isa. lxvi. 23. And for their restitution in this world to come do the creatures groan, Rom. viii. 19—23, that they may be therein under the happy administration of the Second Adam, the Lord from heaven. And of this the 8th Psalm doth assure us; for it is not, as some have imagined, a representation of the state of the first Adam, but of God-man, the Second Adam, and his world; for Christ applieth it to himself, and testifieth it was written of him, and it is not compatible in itself to any other, Matt. xxi. 16. This world to come is a heavenly world, begun by Christ to be created when he commenced to preach the gospel covenant, which angels were not to meddle with, as they did the law, but was only to be ministered by men, Psal. viii. 2; through whose ministry of the word by the Spirit, is ingrafted into the sinful nature of the elect a new creature, whereby they are delivered *from this present evil world,* Gal. i. 4, and fitted for being inhabitants of this new one, 2 Cor. iv. 6; v. 17; compare Eph. iv. 22—24; which hath been preparing by Christ's casting down heathenism and Judaism by the gospel, Luke x. 18; Heb. xii. 26, and bringing them into a new world of ordinances and church privileges, fitted for them, and called by the Spirit, the kingdom of heaven, it surpassing the Sinai church state as much as heaven doth earth. And he is now proceeding to cast down papism, or Roman Christian paganism, and Mahometism, Rev. xix. 19—21, and to subdue the generality of men, both Jews and Gentiles, to himself, Zech. xiv. 9; Rom. xi. 25, 26; when this Christian heavenly frame shall be advanced to a higher degree by the descent of the new Jerusalem from God out of heaven, Rev. xxi. 1, 2; xxii. 1—5; in the which the kingdom of Christ shall be most peaceable, glorious, and prosperous. And to the rendering of it eminently so, Scripture seems to intimate, that the bodies of the martyrs of Jesus shall be raised, and their souls united to them, and so be made conformable to Christ's glorified person, Phil. iii. 21; compare Rev. xx. 4—6. These will their Lord send down into this new world, and to have the same state in it, and to perform the same offices to the saints, as the angels had and did in the world past, Mark xii. 25; there to be kings, and reign as the angelical thrones and principalities did before, Rev. v. 10; xx. 4. As priests, help on the saints' duties, and instruct them in the matters of the kingdom of God, and so answer in conformity to their Head, as he was forty days after his resurrection; during whose reign in this new world the devil shall be chained up, so as they shall not be infested, nor the nations deceived, as formerly they were by him, Rev. xx. 1—3, so as there shall be no need of good angels to oppose or restrain him. At the close of which thousand years the devil will be loosed for a little while, as ver. 3, 7, 8, and infest the world, when the great Lord and King of it shall in the greatest solemnity descend into the air with all his hosts of angels; and by the trumpet of God sounded by the archangel, the dead in Christ shall first be raised, and the living changed in the twinkling of an eye; and being openly owned and acknowledged by the Supreme Judge, shall be assessors with him; when the judgment shall proceed by the angels bringing devils and all impenitent mankind to the bar of Christ, where the vast accounts of them shall be cast up and audited, and on the charge against them they shall be found speechless and convict, so as the great Judge shall solemnly sentence them, and it be assented to and applauded by all the saints, Rev. xx. 2, 11, 12, 15, compare 1 Cor. vi. 2, 3, and be as gloriously executed by the ministering angels, Matt. xiii. 41—43. And so this great King and Lord, having thus shut up the scene of this world, shall return in triumph into the heaven of heavens, and there in the height of his glory deliver up his kingdom to the Father, that God may be all in all, 1 Cor. xv. 22—28. *Whereof we speak;* we describe it further in the following testimony, and in this Epistle, as to some part of it.

6 But one in a certain place testified, saying, ¹What is man, that thou art mindful of him? or the son of man, that thou visitest him?

But one in a certain place testified: the Spirit proves affirmatively out of one of the prophets, that with these Hebrews it might have the more weight and authority, by an elliptical speech, that this world to come was subject to the great gospel Minister: But to Jesus he put in subjection the world to come, as one testifieth. This *one* was the king and prophet David, a Lord and Son to whom was this Jesus; the title of the 8th Psalm ascribes it to him: he is not particularly named, because these Hebrews well knew it, yet he διεμαρτύρατο, thoroughly *testified*, or most expressly, giving a full confirmation of what is asserted, that Jesus is the Lord of the world to come: and this *certain place* was a well-known place, and very ready with those, even Psal. viii. *Saying;* making it known by word and writing there beyond any contradiction. *What is man?* the subject of David's admiration is not the first Adam, nor any mere man, but the gospel Prophet, God-man, a most eminent One, the Messiah of these Hebrews, *the man Christ Jesus,* 1 Tim. ii. 5; and to him only are the privileges vouchsafed agreeable, and by him only enjoyed. For Adam had now lost his dominion when this Psalm was penned, and was never so honoured as to have all things under his feet, even principalities and powers, which Christ had, ver. 8; Eph. i. 20—22; and Christ interprets it of himself, Matt. xxi. 16. The expostulation is resolvable: Man is nothing in himself, that such royalty should be assigned to him. *That thou art mindful of him;* that God should respect him, should remember and design such a worm as man for so great preferment, as union to the Deity and universal dominion. *Or the Son of man:* this is the peculiar title of the *Second Adam.* Adam was a man, but not the son of man, but of God by creation, Luke iii. 38; but the Spirit testifieth this of Christ, Dan. vii. 13; *Lord of the sabbath,* Luke vi. 5; God-man, John iii. 13; v. 27. *That thou visitest him;* ἐπισκέπτῃ, to be peculiarly inspected; and with a special care concerned for him, so industriously and with so great a providence to afford him suitable succour. The form of it is an expostulation with admiration: it is an amazement at the discovery of so stupendous love to man. How emptied he himself for sinners! This work of Christ is the greatest wonder and astonishment to angels.

|| Or, *a little while inferior to.*

7 Thou madest him ||*a little lower than the angels;* thou crownedst him with glory and honour, and didst set him over the works of thy hands:

Thou madest him: Ἡλάττωσας, so diminished, as it supposed the subject to be in a higher condition before: this no man ever was, but the man Christ Jesus: see Phil. ii. 7, 8. *A little lower than the angels:* βραχύ τι, may refer to his condition, and to the duration of it. He was lower a little in his nature, being a man and servant; in his condition, suffering and dying; yet this was but for a little while, being about thirty-three years in the form of a servant, and three days in the grave, Eph. iv. 9: so he was lesser than the angels, in the Psalm styled היים אל God's sons, Psal. xcvii. 7, to whom he is here compared; though it be a truth he is lesser than God in the human nature. *Thou crownedst him with glory and honour;* an allusion to the crowning of kings at their inauguration; so God visibly took him up to heaven, set him down on his right hand on his throne, and conferred on him the highest royal dignity, honour, and glory, though the Hebrews disesteemed him, Eph. i. 20, 21; iv. 9, 10; Phil. ii. 9. *And didst set him over the works of thy hands;* his institution to his mediatory sovereignty and dominion, as the supreme Lord of all that God made in heaven and in earth, to order, rule, command, and dispose of them as he will, Psal. viii. 6: compare Phil. ii. 10, 11.

8 ᵐThou hast put all things in subjection under his feet. For in that he put all in subjection under him, he left nothing *that is* not put under him. But now ⁿ we see not yet all things put under him.

m Matt. 28. 18. 1 Cor. 15. 27. Eph. 1. 22. ch. 1. 13.

n 1 Cor. 15. 25.

Thou hast put all things in subjection under his feet; the impartial, righteous Jehovah the Father, is the relation in the Trinity, spoken of in the relative *Thou,* throughout these verses. He is God's King¦ for his personal worth and excellencies, preferred before principalities and powers, and every name; before all persons, things, and places, the world to come as well as this: all angels, as well as men; all creatures wherever, in heaven, earth, sea, or hell; are under his sovereign dominion, they all lie at his feet, to dispose of as he pleaseth; they are all set in subjection to him by the ordination of his Father: see Psal. viii. 6—8; 1 Cor. xv. 24—29; Eph. i. 20—22; Phil. ii. 9, 10; Col. ii. 10. According to the Eastern custom, as subjects lie prostrate at the feet of their sovereign, so do all creatures to him who is Lord of lords, and King of kings, as Exod. xi. 8, see the margin; Isa. xlix. 23. They bow down and worship him as their own Lord; but as being *under his feet* signifies the utmost subjection of them to him, and his triumph over them, it especially refers to his enemies, sin, devils, sinners, and death; as Joshua, a type of him, did, Josh. x. 23, 24; showing thereby what God would do with all the rest. Allusive to this is Isa. li. 23, especially to all the enemies of his Son, as Psal. cx. 1; 1 Cor. xv. 25, 27. As to his church, it is his body, and though distant from him as creatures, and so worshipping and honouring of him as elect angels, yet being his queen too, she loves and honoureth him as a wife, Psal. xlv. 9, 11; Eph. i. 22, 23; v. 23, 24: she hath her subjection as well as her dignity; she is not a peer to him before marriage: but as Eastern emperors marry slaves born or captivated, because they acknowledge no king greater than they, or equal to them; so Christ takes sinners and makes them his body, his church, his queen, who though for condition are under his feet, yet he so dearly loves them, that he takes them friends, and sets them at his right hand. *For in that he put all in subjection under him, he left nothing that is not put under him:* if nothing is left unsubjected, then angels and the world to come are subjected to him; and it is evident they are so, by their ministering to him at his conception, birth, danger from Herod, temptations by the devil, at his entrance on his ministry, at his passion, at his resurrection, ascension, and since his session on his throne, obeying his commands, and performing his errands, Psal. viii. 8. *But now we see not yet all things put under him;* it is evident to our sense and experience, that though he hath obtained this sovereign dominion over all on his ascension, yet he hath not exerted his power in utterly subjecting and triumphing over his enemies at present, nor in reducing all his own people to subjection to him; yet this shall be gradually done in every age, and completely when he shall come to be glorified in his saints, to punish his enemies with everlasting destruction, 1 Cor. xv. 24, 26; 2 Thess. i. 7—10; Rev. xx. 11—15.

o Phil. 2. 7, 8, 9.
|| Or, *by*.
p Acts 2. 33.
q John 3. 16. & 12. 32.
Rom. 5. 18. & 8. 32.
2 Cor. 5. 15.
1 Tim. 2. 6.
1 John 2. 2. Rev. 5. 9.

9 But we see Jesus, °who was made a little lower than the angels || for the suffering of death, ᵖ crowned with glory and honour; that he by the grace of God should taste death ᑫ for every man.

But we see Jesus, who was made a little lower than the angels: this second application of the psalmist's words demonstrates Jesus, the gospel Prophet, to be the man or Adam intended by the Spirit there; and his humiliation and exaltation to be the matter asserted of him: see ver. 7. *For the suffering of death. crowned with glory and honour:* the reason or end of his diminution, in respect of angels, for a little while, and of the necessity of his being man, was, that he might be crucified and die, Phil. ii. 7—11, and thereby merit for himself a crown of honour and glory. This was given him for his giving himself to be a sacrifice for sin, and by his own blood to expiate it. *That he by the grace of God;* the principle determining, which was God's good pleasure; he alone, out of his free love and favour to sinners, ordered this, as John iii. 16; 1 John iv. 9. Therefore the Hebrews had no reason of being offended with him as they were, 1 Cor. i. 23. *Should taste death;* a metaphor to express to die as a sacrifice, making satisfaction to Divine justice, and expiating sins, Isa. liii. 10. All his sufferings in body and soul, which were many and bitter, are here intended, and their completion by death, Matt. xxvi. 39, 42, intimating by his taste of this deadly cup, his sipping of it, but not having swallowed it: and it is a metaphor allusive to the Grecian customs, who put men to death by giving them a cup of poison, as the Athenians executed Socrates. *For every man;* to render sin remissible to all persons, and them salvable, God punishing man's sin in him, and laying on him the iniquities of us all, Isa. liii. 4—6; 1 John ii. 2; and so God became propitious and pleasable to all; and if all are not saved by it, it is because they do not repent and believe in him, 2 Cor. v. 19—21: compare John x. 15. This was evident to and well known by these Hebrews, as if they saw it, the work, concomitants, and effects of it demonstrating it. And this now in the gospel is evident to faith: it was so certainly visible and evidently true, as not to be denied but by infidels.

r Luke 24. 46.
s Rom. 11. 36.
t Acts 3. 15. & 5. 31. ch. 12. 2.
u Luke 13. 32. ch. 5. 9.

10 ʳ For it became him, ˢ for whom *are* all things, and by whom *are* all things, in bringing many sons unto glory, to make ᵗ the captain of their salvation ᵘ perfect through sufferings.

For it became him: a further reason of Christ's humiliation and sufferings is added, to show the necessity of his being lower than the angels for a while; in which the Spirit prevents what these Hebrews were apt to question, why God would have Christ thus to die, &c., by adding, Therefore it became him so to do; it was agreeable to him, and had a meetness in it to his excellent perfection; by it displaying together his Divine wisdom, justice, mercy, and power. Amongst all his methods, he pitched upon this as the best, and did by it what was befitting and becoming a God to do. He likewise revealed this so becoming decree of his by the prophets to the church, and it was meet to and becoming his truth to fulfil it, Isa. liii.; Luke xxiv. 25—27. *For whom are all things, and by whom are all things;* for the manifestation of God the Father's glory, whose grace gave Christ to die for us, are all things which have a being; and by him are all things, as the Efficient and Creator of them, by his powerful word they are: this being likewise attributed to the gospel Prophet, God-man, John i. 3; Col. i. 16. *By whom;* it shows he is no more an instrument in this work than the Father, and equally efficient with him, Rom. iii. 26. *In bringing many sons unto glory:* ἀγαγόντα cannot agree with αὐτῷ, him, for that is the dative case, but with what follows, Ἀρχηγὸν, the Leader of their salvation bringing many sons to glory: so that though the Father indeed glorify, yet it is most properly spoken of the Leader, to lead or bring his company thither; and so it is written, Eph. ii. 18; iii. 12. He showed and led them the way wherein they were to reach it, 1 Pet. iii. 18, who though for state were sinners, yet made fit by regeneration and adoption, and have their title from their Leader, John i. 12, 13. He merited by his sufferings both the relation and inheritance for them, Rom. viii. 14—18; 1 Pet. i. 2—5; and so as to bring them to that glorious state and condition, for persons and enjoyments, in the heavenly Canaan prepared for them, Matt. xxv. 34; 1 Pet. v. 10; 1 John iii. 1, 2. *To make the captain of their salvation perfect through sufferings:* so their Ἀρχηγὸν, a prime Leader of many, a person eminent for priority and dignity, directing and ordering all under his power, who is the prime of the creation of God, Col. i. 18, having the pre-eminency of all angels and men: he was perfected; τελειῶσαι signifieth the consecrating or accomplishing of a person for office by sacrifice; so Christ useth it, Luke xiii. 32, *I shall be perfected*, i. e. sacrificed and completed in my office by death: so John xix. 30. By his sufferings of all sorts accomplished in death, and by the blood of that sacrifice, was this great gospel Prophet made a perfect Mediator, and fitted for his officiating and ministering in heaven for ever, herein fulfilling his types, chap. ix. 11, 12, 14, 15, 22—24: compare Exod. xxix. He, in respect of saving his, is the author, purchaser, and perfecter of it to them: he by his sufferings and death merited salvation for them, by his word and Spirit fits them for it, by his intercession increaseth and applieth it; he vanquishes all opposers of it, and puts them finally into the actual possession of it in glory in heaven.

11 For ˣ both he that sanctifieth and they who are sanctified ʸ *are* all of one: for which cause ᶻ he is not ashamed to call them brethren,

x ch. 10. 10, 14.
y Acts 17. 26.
z Mat. 28. 10. John 20. 17. Rom. 8. 29.

For both he that sanctifieth: for shows the reason of the Son's incarnation, viz. the necessity of union in nature between the sanctifying Mediator and the sanctified sinner. The great gospel Minister was to bring many sons to glory by suffering, which he was not capable of, but by being united to one and the same nature with them to whom the penalty was due, and so he must be Head of them. This God-man is separating and consecrating of penitent believing sinners from the common mass to God, meriting by his death for them remission of their sins, and sanctifying their persons by his Spirit from their pollutions by them, 1 Cor. vi. 11; Tit. iii. 4—7; Heb. ix. 14; x. 10, 14. *And they who are sanctified;* penitent believing sinners, justified by his blood, and sanctified by his Spirit, Eph. v. 25—27. *Are all of one:* this is an attribute of the unity of the principle of both these; such an one as is proper to man with himself, whom he sanctifieth, and not competent to angels; it must therefore be the principle of humanity. He took a human soul and body united to his person, and so became of one nature with us, (compare ver. 14,) of one human mass, alluding to the first-fruits offered at the Passover, or the loaves at Pentecost, whereby all the rest were sanctified: so Christ assumed the same human nature, that he might be the Head and leading Representative of a body of mankind, differenced from them by his being holy, and they sinful, and personally united to the Word. *For which cause he is not ashamed to call them brethren;* the unity of him and them in the human nature, is the cause why he calls them *brethren*, therefore they must be one: considering him in the holiness of his Deity, and them in the filthiness of sin, he might have been ashamed of such a brotherhood; but by his effectual word he adopted them into a state of childship and heirship to God with himself; and in the flesh to give them that glory, that they might be one with God, as he and the Father are one, John xvii. 22.

12 Saying, ᵃ I will declare thy name unto my brethren, in the midst of the Church will I sing praise unto thee.

a Ps. 22. 22, 25.

Saying; this brings in the proof, that the great gospel Minister, Christ, God-man, did call his sanctified ones *brethren;* and was by the same nature so related to them. The proof is in Psal. xxii. 22, where the apostle asserts, Christ spoke what was said by the prophet there; and that this Psalm concerneth him, is evident by the application of other passages in it to him, both by himself and the Spirit; and who reads it, may see him crucified afresh there. *I will declare thy name unto my brethren:* I, as the gospel Prophet, who have seen thee, and am of thee, John i. 18, and who only understand *thy name*, will teach, and make it to be known and admired, as that whereby thou art described, distinguished, and set above all other beings and relations to them; a name suitable to their state and relation unto thee and me. Thee in all thy glorious attributes, related to them as to Moses, Exod. xxxiv. 5—7, especially thy name of Father, whereby thou standest related to me and them as brethren, fulfilled, John xx. 17, *My Father, and your Father; my God, and your God;* when he sent this message by Mary Magdalene to his apostles and disciples, to whom he was related as a brother in his humanity, sonship and heirship, family and household, and amongst whom he is the First-begotten and elder Brother. Brethren are one, and as one; and so is he and his sanctified ones, ver. 14; Luke i. 31, 35; John xvii. 22, 23; Rom. viii. 14; so ver. 17, 29; Gal. iv. 5—7; Eph. iii. 14, 15. *In the midst of the church will I sing praise unto thee;* in the respective parts and congregations of his mystical body, implicitly his brethren. Christ and they are from one Father divine, he by nature, they by grace; and from one human parent, Luke iii. 23, 38, and both of one flesh: he solemnly sung and praised his Father with them at his supper, in that representative church, Matt. xxvi. 30; Mark xiv. 26.

^{b Ps. 18. 2.} ^{Is. 12. 2.} ^{c Is. 8. 18.} ^{d John 20.} ^{29. & 17. 6,} ^{9, 11, 12.} 13 And again, [b]I will put my trust in him. And again, [c]Behold I and the children [d]which God hath given me.

And again, I will put my trust in him: this is a further proof, that Christ's sanctified ones are his brethren, his exercising himself in a necessary work proper to that brotherhood only. They are all *of the household of faith*, Gal. vi. 10; their business is to believe in God. All who do so, are brethren; Christ doth so, and so is a Brother to them; he and they rely on one and the same God and Father to both: he did believe, confide, and rest on God, that he would help his humanity to go through all his works and sufferings to the perfecting of that of redemption. Some say he spake this in the person of David in Psal. xviii. 2, because the 49th verse of it is applied to Christ by the Spirit in Rom. xv. 9. But others think that Psalm is not so properly understood of Christ, and that these words are not found in the Septuagint, which the apostle frequently useth, as being most familiar with these Hebrews; but that these words of his trusting in God, and of his *children*, are to be found near together in Isa. viii. 17, 18, which chapter is a clear prophecy of this God-man the Redeemer, and punctually fulfilled by him on earth. This seems most rationally to be the place the apostle refers as to both these texts. *And again, Behold I and the children which God hath given me:* this is the third proof, which, though it be literally Isaiah's words, who complained how himself and the children of God in his days were scorned by the world for cleaving to him, yet herein was he a type of Christ, and in him was it eminently fulfilled. This the word *Behold* intimates, it being a matter of great weight and importance, to be attended, to be considered and unstood, by the church. *I and the children which God hath given me;* I and my brethren, children of the same heavenly Father, John xi. 52; xx. 17; 1 John iii. 1; which my Father of free grace chose and delivered on my purchase, and whom he had fitted and wrought by his Spirit, to be brought home by him unto glory, though they were the wonder and contempt of this world, John xvii. 2, 6, 8, 9, 11, 19, 22, 24.

^{e John 1. 14.} ^{Rom. 8. 3.} ^{Phil. 2. 7.} ^{f 1 Cor. 15.} ^{54, 55.} ^{Col. 2. 15.} ^{2 Tim. 1. 10.} 14 Forasmuch then as the children are partakers of flesh and blood, he [e]also himself likewise took part of the same; [f]that through death he might destroy him that had the power of death, that is, the devil;

Forasmuch then as the children are partakers of flesh and blood: the Spirit having proved the children and brethren sanctified by Christ to be men, proceeds to prove, that the Sanctifier of them was of the same nature with themselves; and so confirms what he asserted, ver. 11, that they were *of one:* forasmuch as those were chosen, born of God, and given to him, adopted into his sonship and heirship, and by this, as well as by their humanity, derived jointly with his own from Adam, his brethren, κεκοινώνηκε, these having it in common. The word imports the reality, integrity, unity, and community they all have of the human nature; they are all truly, only, and fully men, and every individual person hath this humanity. These *flesh and blood* metonymically set out the whole human nature, though the body only be literally expressed by it, a body subject to many infirmities. *He also himself likewise took part of the same;* God the Son himself παραπλησίως, had the next and nearest correspondent condition with theirs, even the same as to the kind of it, as like as blood is to blood, properly and truly, only freed from our sinful infirmities, as ver. 17; chap. iv. 15; this word diminisheth him not, but showeth his identity: μετέσχε, *took part*, he became a partner with the children, and took their nature. It is not the same word as before, κεκοινώνεκε, as the Marcionites and Manichees corrupt it, as if he had this nature only in common with them, making him only man. But being God, besides his Divine nature, &c., to it he took the human, even their true and full nature, consisting of a body and a soul, and so united them, that in him they became one person; so that hence results a double union of Christ with man. By his incarnation he is of one nature with all the human race, and so is the Head of them: and by his dying for them all the human race are made salvable, which angels are not; and those who repent and believe on him, are actually sanctified and united to him, as his elect and chosen body, and shall be saved by him. *That through death he might destroy him that had the power of death:* by his dying on the cross as testator of God's covenant, and not by his power as a God, (which was most glorious to himself, but most ignominious to the devil, according to the promise, Gen. iii. 15,) did he abolish, or bring to nought, and render powerless without any recovery, not by taking away the immortal life and being, but the κρατος, the strength and power to kill. For the ἐξουσία, the authority, right, and command, the keys of death, are in Christ's hand only, and he useth the strength of this execution in it, as to his enemies; when sinners become penitent believers, then his death satisfying God's justice for their sin, hath executed the power as to death, which the devil had by law against them: 1 Cor. xv. 56, 57, *The sting of death is sin*, that gives him power; *and the strength of sin is the law*, that, unless satisfied for, takes part with sin; but Christ by dying takes away the law's enmity, removes sin, as to guilt, stain, and power, and so brings to nought this power. *That is, the devil;* the prince himself, set here collectively for all the rest of his evil spirits, Matt. xxv. 41, who by his lies drew man into sin, and by sin stings him to death; having therefore such power to seduce to sin, he powerfully renders men obnoxious to death; and then, as executioner, having them by the law delivered into his hands, putteth forth his strength to torment and destroy them. Christ by his death doth with price and power redeem them out of his hand, and destroys all his works, takes possession of them, and brings them through death to eternal life.

15 And deliver them who [g]through fear of death were all their lifetime subject to bondage. ^{g Luke 1. 74.} ^{Rom. 8. 15.} ^{2 Tim. 1. 7.}

The effect of the former destruction of the devil is laid down in this verse, viz. the children's freedom from the fear of death, to which, being slaves to the devil, they were once in bondage. *And deliver them;* he, by breaking and disannulling the devil's power, doth really, fully, and justly exempt them from the concomitant evil. *Who through fear of death;* a painful and wasting horror, working the saddest apprehensions and tumultuous workings of soul, from its apprehended danger of death spiritual, temporal, and eternal, when the wrath of God doth not only dissolve the natural frame, but makes an everlasting separation from himself, shutting them up with the worst company, in the worst place and state that is possible for the human mind to imagine, and that for ever, Job xviii. 11, 14; xxiv. 17; Psal. lv. 4, 5; lxxiii. 19; lxxxviii. 14—18. *Were all their lifetime subject to bondage:* when they come to the exercise of the reasonable life of man, and under convictions of sin, then these terrors arise, and never leave affrighting or tormenting them, but make them pass as many deaths as moments, as is evident in Cain and Judas; for they are enslaved, and in such a state of drudgery and vassalage to the devil, the most cruel tyrant, by their own guilt, and so are justly, invincibly, and miserably held in it. Christ by his death rescueth them from this woeful, intolerable vassalage to the devil and hell, and brings them into the glorious liberty of the children of God, Rom. viii. 21; Col. i. 12, 13.

† Gr. *he taketh not hold of angels, but of the seed of Abraham he taketh hold.* 16 For verily † he took not on *him the nature of* angels; but he took on *him* the seed of Abraham.

For verily he took not on him the nature of angels: the Spirit having asserted the deliverance of the children from their slavery to the devil, shows here the means by which it was effected, even by the gospel Prophet, being a man, and not an angel; he took their nature to himself, that by death he might deliver them: οὐ δήπου may signify no where, or in no wise; ἐπιλαμβάνεται is read by some, to take hold of, and so make this work denied of God the Son, that he did not take hold of the falling angels, to save or recover them: but the Spirit speaks not one word of lapsed angels in either this or the foregoing chapter, and so it cannot refer to them; and for good angels, they never departed or fell, that he should stretch out his hand to save them. And it cannot be understood otherwise than affirmatively here, which must needs have another sense, because the same act is denied and affirmed. The word therefore signifieth to assume, or to take to one, to assume or take into union. He united not to his person the angelical nature, the individual substance of an angel, so as to redeem those sinning lapsed spirits. *But he took on him the seed of Abraham;* but he assumed into union with his person the seed of Abraham; which seed is not to be understood here collectively, for either his carnal or believing seed; but it is the one singular, eminent Seed of Abraham, in and by whom, himself, his seed, and all nations were to be blessed, Gen. xxii. 18, compare Gal. iii. 16, the man Christ Jesus. This man, God the Son took of the virgin Mary, the offspring of Abraham, and united him to his person, and of God and this Seed united into one person, became our Lord Jesus Christ, so as he might bring the blessing of salvation to the chosen of God in all nations. The assumption of this eminent Seed into the unity of his own person, is here asserted by the Spirit, and denied concerning any angel, there being no promise ever made to them for it, Zech. xiii. 7; Luke i. 31, 35; Gal. iv. 4; 1 Tim. ii. 5. If the verb signify no such assumption in human authors, as some cavil, it is because the matter to which it is here applied was never treated on among them; and it is common with the Spirit to make words which are ordinary with men, transcendent, when he applieth them to the great mysteries of God, as Trinity, Son, adoption, &c.

h Phil. 2. 7.
i ch. 4. 15. & 5. 1, 2.

17 Wherefore in all things it behoved him ʰto be made like unto *his* brethren, that he might be ⁱa merciful and faithful High Priest in things *pertaining* to God, to make reconciliation for the sins of the people.

It behoved him: the last reason why God the Son assumed and united the human nature in the seed of Abraham to his person, and was by it made like his brethren, and for a little while lower than the angels, was, that he might be capable to receive and execute the office of priesthood, by which reconciliation of sinners to God was to be effected; for he could neither be a sacrifice nor priest without it. Ὠφειλε signifies not only its being necessary, but becoming, meet, convenient, and right, both on the account of his mediatorship, suretiship, priesthood, and of his very work, considering the two parties whose cause he was to manage. It was fit this Person should be God, that he might be just to God, and satisfy him; Adam had betrayed God's interest before, he would not therefore rely on a mere man: and man, that he might feelingly understand the state of that nature, and be a complete Saviour of it, Zech. xiii. 7. By this Person God had no unfitness nor disparagement in treating with sinners, which in a mere creature he would. For what creature could have mediated with him? Who durst undertake it, but this Son of his in their nature, whose heart he engaged to it? Jer. xxx. 21. And fittest for man, he being near in nature to us, and coming out of the midst of us, and by it communicating the benefit of his mediation to us. The intention of Christ's merits arise from his sufficiency, but the extension of them from his proper personal fitness, and so reneweth men of the same nature with him, and not angels. *To be made like unto his brethren;* a man having a true body and soul like them in every thing, which was necessary to make him a complete Redeemer; agreeable to them in all things necessary to their nature, qualities, conditions, and affections; like them in sorrows, griefs, pains, death. *Merciful;* knowing and sensible of the misery of sinners on the account of sin, pain, and loss, and so inwardly touched with them, as compassionately and effectually to relieve them. How transcendent are his bowels of mercy, pity, and compassion to them! Alas, man and angels cannot reach it! Isa. liii. 3, 4; lxiii. 9. If he should be otherwise the least moved, and desert their cause, or accuse or plead against them, what a world of them must perish for ever! He tells the Jews so much, chap. viii. 12; compare John v. 45. A Moses may miscarry in his mediatorship, and did so, Exod. xxxii. 19; but he can never, he is always merciful. *And faithful;* he is faithful also to penitent believers, as well as to God. They may safely trust themselves and their cause with him, and depend on him, he will never deceive them. He will satisfy God fully, and give him his due, and discharge that trust reposed on him. And to souls relying on him, he will go through his work, performing all, till they reach that for which they trusted him, Isa. xi. 5; 1 Cor. x. 13; 1 Thess. v. 23, 24. *High Priest;* an officer that was to order sacrifice, and all matters wherein God was concerned, according to his written law and rule. This priest must be a man; and a partnership in our conditions, both of temptations and miseries, must qualify him for it. Of this office he treats largely in chap. vii., viii., ix., and x. Amongst the officers of this kind he is the prime, chief, and head of all that ever God had, and hath in his person performed and fulfilled what all of them in theirs did but weakly shadow forth. He was actually in the flesh installed in it, of which hereafter. *In things pertaining to God, to make reconciliation for the sins of the people:* the compass of his business lieth in all Divine matters, all those wherein sinners are concerned with God, chap. v. 1; satisfaction, intercession, and blessing, are his great concerns. His principal work is to bring God and sinners together; ἱλάσκεσθαι properly signifieth to make one propitious or gracious to another by sacrifice. This High Priest, by the sacrifice of himself, satisfied God's justice, removed his wrath, procured his pardon as to all sins of omission or commission, however aggravated, for penitent, believing sinners; and so makes God and them friends, and fits them for communion with him here, and for the enjoyment of him for ever, 2 Cor. v. 19, 21.

k ch. 4. 15, 16. & 5. 2. & 7. 25.

18 ᵏFor in that he himself hath suffered being tempted, he is able to succour them that are tempted.

For in that he himself hath suffered: the reason foregoing the Spirit illustrates in this verse; he is such a merciful and faithful High Priest, by being a sufferer himself, which he could not have been feelingly, but by his being incarnate. So many, great, and afflictive sufferings never any endured but himself; he felt what sin deserved, and would fasten on sinners without his interposing; though he were sinless, what terrors from God within, what pains in his body without, did he suffer and undergo! such as are unparalleled, chap. xii. 3. *Being tempted;* not from any corruption or sin within him, chap. iv. 15; John xiv. 30; but from an inveterate enemy, the devil, without him, and all the instruments he used of his associated spirits and men. How early on the entrance on his office did the devil begin with him, and thought to have foiled him as he did the first Adam! and how did his children tempt him, with the which the gospel is filled in so many pages! By these he felt what temptations were, how difficult to avoid sin under them, how fearful it was to be exercised by them, chap. v. 7, how much such as miscarry under them are to be pitied; what sore evils sin brings on the committers of it; what succour, strength, stablishing, settlement his brethren need under it, Luke xxii. 43, 44; and how easily without his assistance his tempted ones may be foiled by it. *He is able to succour them that are tempted:* now sensibly made fit by his own sorrows, temptations, and sufferings, he is powerfully inclined to help his; subjected he was to all of them, to make him feelingly, tenderly pitying of us. He had the mercies of God before, and as if that were not enough, the tempted nature of a man, to soften his heart to pity his brethren in their sufferings and temptations. These sufferings of his had a purchasing power and ability in them for us, he thereby buying help and succour for us as to all ours, that should be correspondent unto his; so as by his bloody death under temptation he bought off ours, either not to overtake us, or if under them, he is habitually and meritoriously thereby to succour his; most compassionately and readily giving forth all reasonable, suitable, and sufficient support under and remedy against all these temptations, which for sin, or from it, his brethren are afflicted with, and come to him for help. This is the most powerful preservative against despair, and the firmest ground of hope and comfort, that ever believing, penitent sinners could desire or have. From all which these Hebrews might have been convinced what little reason they had to be offended with his humiliation or death, who was their Messiah; and though for state and time a little lower than the angels, yet in the human nature was thereby exalted to be the Lord and Head above them all.

CHAP. III

Christ is showed to be more worthy than Moses, 1—6: *we must be careful therefore not to follow the example of the obstinate and unbelieving Israelites in the wilderness,* 7—19.

a Rom. 1. 7.
1 Cor. 1. 2.
Eph. 4. 1.
Phil. 3. 14.
2 Thess. 1.
11. 2 Tim.
1. 9. 2 Pet.
1. 10.
b Rom. 15. 8. ch. 2. 17. & 4. 14. & 5. 5. & 6. 20. & 8. 1. & 9. 11. & 10. 21.

WHEREFORE, holy brethren, partakers of ᵃthe heavenly calling, consider ᵇthe Apostle and High Priest of our profession, Christ Jesus;

Several uses the Holy Ghost makes, from the beginning of this chapter to the end of chap. iv., of the gospel doctrine of God the Son incarnate, set by the Father in office, to deal for sinners towards God as their great Prophet. The counsel he giveth is comprehended in the first six verses of this chapter; and as directing these Hebrews to their duty, so further explaining and confirming his office to them, by comparing of him with Moses, and setting him as above angels, so above him; and to be so valued, esteemed, and preferred by these Hebrews: seeing this great gospel Prophet was for a little while made lower than the angels in his humanity, and it was infinitely beneficial to us upon the account of what he suffered in it in our stead, and purchased by it for our good; therefore should those who are partakers of it, being related in the flesh to him as Hebrews, descending with them from Abraham, consider, but much more as Christians, believing and adopted in him to be God's children, and sanctified by his Spirit, 1 Pet. i. 1—5; 2 Pet. i. 1. *Partakers of the heavenly calling;* and made thus a Christian fraternity by the heavenly calling of them out of the world by the gospel; when by his Spirit he enlightened their minds, and renewed their wills, and made them obedient to it, so as for the temper of their souls they are made holy, and for their condition happy; the work of God's power and mercy eminently appearing in it: God therein preventing man, so as he influenceth him to hear him from heaven, walk worthy of heaven, and at last to rest in heaven for ever. *Consider;* κατανοήσατε imports not a bare single act of the mind, to think on, or understand, but a repeated one, to think again and again, expressed by that periphrasis of laying it to heart, pressing on their spirits the due effort of faith and obedience arising out of this observation, Isa. lii. 15. *The Apostle;* God's Messenger, his own Son sent from heaven to be incarnate, with authority to execute in his human nature his prophetical, as all his offices, and with authority to send forth his apostles to do their part, John xx. 21; which is no more than is intimated in that title, *the Messenger of the covenant,* Isa. xlii. 19; Mal. iii. 1; that was, to propose it to and confirm it with them. This was he by whom Moses desired God's message might be sent to them, Exod. iv. 13; and whom he foretold should bring it, Deut. xviii. 15; Acts iii. 22, 23. *And High Priest of our profession, Christ Jesus:* the Son is the great gospel High Priest, to deal in all matters with God for them, chap. ii. 17. The offices divided among other persons in the Old Testament church were all united in his person, he doth transcend them all, being a High Priest peculiar to the called and sanctified ones of God, of which all preceding were faint resemblances and types; he, the most excellent Minister of the Christian faith and religion professed by them, being anointed with all these offices in the flesh by the Father with the Holy Ghost, chap. i. 2; and being Jesus a Saviour, our Emmanuel, God on our side, saving his people from their sins, and re-uniting them to God, Matt. i. 21, 23; John xvii. 21—23.

2 Who was faithful to him that † appointed him, as also ᶜMoses *was faithful* in all his house.

† Gr. *made,*
1 Sam. 12. 6.
c Num. 12. 7. ver. 5.

The Spirit enforceth the duty counselled on them from the fidelity of that grand gospel Minister in his offices; exemplified in a parallel with Moses, whom he did exceed. *Who was faithful to him that appointed him;* he did most exactly perform all he was intrusted with, according to the intention and end of his commission. He did most faithfully reveal God, John i. 18, and his whole saving will, to whom God sent him, John iii. 31—34; v. 34; viii. 28, 38; as his great Prophet, Acts iii. 22. He as faithfully discharged the office of his priesthood in sacrificing himself to atone God for sinners, and as faithfully intercedes for all with him unto this day, and will do so for ever, with all truth and fidelity discharging his trust, chap. vii. 24—28; ix. 11, 12, 14, 24, 26. He was faithful in fulfilling all his types, and in changing and finishing all the ceremonial constitutions, and filling them up with gospel ones, according to God's will revealed to him about it. He was true to his Father, who appointed and constituted him to these offices, and solemnly invested him in them; ποιήσαντι here not signifying the making of a creature, but the making of an officer, the person existing before; he puts him into this special charge and office by anointing him for it, Acts ii. 36. *As also Moses was faithful in all his house:* Moses was the Jewish mediator, and brought them the law moral, judicial, and ceremonial from God; as he was highly esteemed by them, so God testifieth of his fidelity. Christ was not only like to him in fidelity, but, as to both the truth and degree of it, exceeding him. Moses kept to his pattern shown him in the mount, and Christ fulfilled entirely his Father's will, John v. 30; vi. 38, and is preferred to him. Moses was so in the whole church of Israel, set out by this metaphor of a *house;* but Christ in all God's house and family both in heaven and in earth; not the least thing that concerned the family, but Christ fulfilled; not the meanest person in it, but he careth for and saveth.

3 For this *man* was counted worthy of more glory than Moses, inasmuch as ᵈhe who hath builded the house hath more honour than the house.

d Zech. 6.12.
Mat. 16. 18.

For this man was counted worthy of more glory than Moses: the Spirit proves to the Hebrews, that the gospel Prophet was not only like to, but more excellent than, their greatest prophet, and who had familiarity with God beyond others, as God testifieth, Numb. xii. 6—8. This he proves by an undeniable supposition, that God is better than man; such is Christ; which he demonstrates by a work of God, his making the church and all things. If he made the church, then he is better than the whole church, and worthy of more honour than Moses, who is but a member of it. For this, *man* is not in the original, this gospel Prophet, who was God as well as man, the apostle and High Priest of Christians, was esteemed and accounted by God the Father, the best judge of worth, and who appointed him to his offices: he treated him more honourably than Moses, as he deserved it, having real excellency and worth in himself. He was God's Son, Moses his servant. He lay in God's bosom, saw his face, was his *fellow,* Zech. xiii. 7; John i. 14, 18; Moses only heard his voice, and saw his *back parts,* Exod. xxxiii. 19, 20, 23; xxxiv. 5—7. Moses's face only shined, but Christ's person was entirely glorious, Exod. xxxiv. 29, 30 ; 2 Cor. iii. 7 : compare Matt. xvii. 2—6 ; 2 Pet. i. 17. *Inasmuch as he who hath builded the house hath more honour than the house ;* he is the cause, principal, efficient, and architect of this building, not a stone is laid in it without him. By this metaphor of *house* to which it relateth, is meant God's spiritual building and temple, 1 Cor. iii. 10, 16, 17 ; styled God's household or family, Eph. ii. 19—22 : in sum, God's church, built by and on Christ, of which Moses was but one living stone or member, 1 Pet. ii. 4—8. Therefore this builder ought to be esteemed and honoured above the church, or Moses, a member of it.

e Eph. 2. 10. & 3. 9. ch. 1. 2. **4 For every house is builded by some man; but** e **he that built all things** *is* **God.**

The excellency of this builder is evinced by his nature and preference beyond his building, as any man is beyond his. *For every house is builded by some man ;* for every earthly artificial building, a material house built for habitation, though it may metaphorically and analogically be understood of a commonwealth, or political one, which is contrived, framed, and raised by some man ; yet an effect cannot produce itself, nor a house raise itself ; both must have a cause, both the house wherein Moses was faithful, and Christ's house. *But he that built all things is God;* but he who built his church in all ages, whether the Israelitish or Christian, and all things about it of which we speak, and all things else, Matt. xvi. 18 ; John i. 1, 3 ; Col. i. 20 ; he *is God* essentially ; and Christ, doing God's work and building all things, is not by name only, but by nature, God. The whole world is his workmanship, but the church is the most rare, curious, and excellent piece of it. Christ is not part of the house, as Moses is, but the builder of it ; he is the Creator and builder both of the church and him, and so infinitely above him.

f ver. 2. g Ex. 14. 31. Num. 12. 7. Deut. 3. 24. Josh. 1. 2. & 8. 31. h Deut. 18. 15, 18, 19. **5** f **And Moses verily** *was* **faithful in all his house, as** g **a servant,** h **for a testimony of those things which were to be spoken after ;**

The gospel Minister doth not only excel Moses as much as a builder doth his work, but as a son doth a servant, proved in this and ver. 6. *And Moses verily was faithful in all his house, as a servant;* your great legal prophet, in whom many of you Hebrews trust, John v. 45, did truly and fully reveal and do what God charged him, in ministering his will to his church, Exod. xl. 16—33 ; he did not diminish from, nor add the least to, God's charge, θεράπων, Numb. xii. 7. As a minister, Moses was as faithful as any God had ; not a slave or a drudge, but a free, willing, ingenuous servant, most entirely and obsequiously addicting himself in that honourable place and office of great trust, to which God called him ; a stewardly servant, a prophet and a prince, inspecting and ordering all according to God's will ; in all Christ's house and family, his church, he is but a servant. *For a testimony of those things which were to be spoken after :* his faithfulness was evident in his bearing true witness to the church, of all God made known to him, that they might not be uncertain of the truth ; even all that truth, which was more fully and clearly to be spoken by the prophets after him, and by Christ and his apostles ; but which the Spirit shall speak to them further concerning Christ and his church in this Epistle, John v. 46. In which is insinuated, that Christ was the truth himself witnessed to by Moses, who was a witness of an inferior degree, though in his work faithful, and conformed unto Christ.

i ch. 1. 2. k 1 Cor. 3. 16. & 6. 19. 2 Cor. 6. 16. Eph. 2. 21, 22. 1 Tim. 3. 15. 1 Pet. 2. 5. **6 But Christ as** i **a son over his own house ;** k **whose house are we,** l **if we hold fast the confidence and the rejoicing of the hope firm unto the end.**

l ver. 14. Mat. 10. 22. & 24. 13. Rom. 5. 2. Col. 1. 23. ch. 6. 11. & 10. 35.

But Christ as a son over his own house ; the anointed gospel Prophet by God the Father, chap. i. 9, who was eminently faithful and true to his trust, who is Heir and Lord of all, and therefore by the law of nature and nations is above the best servant, Gal. iv. 1. Who is the Head and Lord over his own church, which he purchased by his own blood, Acts xx. 28, and built for himself. Moses was in it but a servant, fulfilling his Master's will and pleasure, and ordering all in it agreeable to it. *Whose house are we;* the Hebrews' personal privilege, as well as the Prophet's excellency, persuading and obliging them to know by consideration what is represented to them, and to influence their hearts to a perseverance under his teaching and government in their Christian course, because they are parts of his house, and members of his church ; a particular house, and body, and church to him, and members of the catholic one. A temple, wherein God doth inhabit and dwell by his Spirit, 1 Cor. iii. 16, 17 : compare Eph. ii. 21 ; iii. 17 ; 1 Tim. iii. 15. A house he will glorify and perfect with his own presence, and which he will fill with transcendently more glory than he did the literal temple, Exod. xl. 34, 35 ; 2 Chron. vii. 1, 2 ; Isa. vi. 1, 5 : compare Hag. ii. 6. But how completely shall it be filled with his glory in heaven ! Phil. iii. 21. How should such a glorious state influence them to a sincere perseverance in his religion ! *If we hold fast the confidence ;* a tenacious holding, as with both hands, with our utmost strength, against all insinuations and temptations of all adversaries whatsoever, which would either entice or force them from it. Παρρησίαν τῆς ἐλπίδος, is an ingenuous, bold, and confident profession of our hope before all the world, without doubting, wavering, or fearful shaking about what is the true object of it, let the persecutions or sufferings for it be what they will. *And the rejoicing of the hope :* hope here is a firm expectation of salvation in eternal glory by Jesus Christ. It necessarily includes in it faith, for we cannot hope for that we do not believe ; and faith representing to the soul from the gospel, Christ purchasing, and the Father in him covenanting and promising to give it to us, if we truly believe in and sincerely obey him, so as we may on the surest and best grounds look out for it, and expect it, ver. 14 ; chap. vi. 11 ; Acts xxvi. 6, 7 : compare Col. i. 5, 23 ; Tit. ii. 13 ; 1 Pet. i. 3. This *hope* keeps up the soul in a joyous and glorious condition under all threatening evil ; it makes Christians glory in tribulation, Rom. v. 2, 3 ; xii. 12 ; rejoicing in want of sensible good, 2 Cor. vi. 10 ; compare 1 Pet. v. 10. *Firm unto the end;* both this confidence and glorying of hope must be retained firm to the end. Persevere they must in the exercise of them with stability and constancy, till they reach the salvation of their souls, Col. i. 23 ; 1 Pet. i. 5—10 ; which Christians are not to trust to their own power to compass, but on the continued assistance of God in the use of those means that he hath appointed thereunto, who will never be wanting to such who do so rely on him, and constantly seek it from him, 1 Cor. i. 8, 9.

7 Wherefore (as m **the Holy Ghost saith,** n **To day if ye will hear his voice,**

m 2 Sam. 23. 2. Acts 1. 16. n ver. 15. Ps. 95. 7.

The Spirit enforceth his counsel for those Hebrews' improvement of his doctrine about the gospel Prophet, by alleging a sad example of their fathers refusing to hear and obey him, from ver. 7—11. The allegation might be best placed in parenthesis, and the introductive illative particle *Wherefore,* may refer to ver. 12, *Take heed, brethren.* *As the Holy Ghost saith ;* as the Spirit, the Holy One, that third relation in the Trinity, whose essence is holiness, is the author of what the psalmist doth write, and is here quoted by him, Psal. xcv. 7—12. So that the example registered is true and infallible, and should suitably affect them, reading it. *To-day if ye will hear his voice ;* every present time, wherein the great Builder and Lord of God's church speaketh to them ; God would not have a hearer of his Prophet to procrastinate a day, but to be exercising all those internal acts, which this word of sense *hear* doth comprehend, such as reacheth the heart as well as the ear ; if you will attend, intend, believe, love, and obey ; a hearing better than all external sacrifices, 1 Sam. xv. 22. The angel of the covenant speaking his mind and will to them by Moses and the prophets, which was for the matter of it faith in God's covenant, made with them in and through Christ, Psal. xcv. 7 : compare Exod. xxiii. 20—23.

8 Harden not your hearts, as in the provocation, in the day of temptation in the wilderness :

Harden not your hearts : to help in the former duty the Spirit subjoins this negative counsel. That is styled hard, which will not yield to any impression : make not your heart a stone, so as not to understand, believe, or obey God's voice to it, Deut. xv. 17 ; 1 Sam. vi. 6 ; for God requires them to be fleshy tables, to write his will on, 2 Cor. iii. 3.

The hardening of this part is the hardening of the whole person, and when hardened by themselves, is provoking God's judicial hardening of them to their destruction. *As in the provocation;* ἐν τῷ παραπικρασμῷ, in the bitter contention, comprehending in it both work, season, and place; called Meribah, Numb. xx. 13, 14; names of places and persons by words of the same signification, though not of the same sound. *In the day of temptation in the wilderness;* in the day of Massah, when Israel in the wilderness did murmur, and strive against, and vexed God, (after he had divided the sea for them,) for their want of water, Exod. xvii. 2. 7; Deut. vi. 16; xxxiii. 8; that bitter contest of unbelief after the sight of so many miracles, when they cried out, *Is the Lord among us?* Psal. xcv. 8. It may also refer to the whole forty years' time of their murmuring and tempting him in the wilderness.

9 When your fathers tempted me, proved me, and saw my works forty years.

When your fathers tempted me; in the time and place forementioned, the fathers from whom you derive your being and corruption, yet glory in them and their traditions, whose state is aggravated from your line of successive rebellion, Acts vii. 51—53. They have imbittered my Spirit by their unbelief; for upon the want of water, they questioned his power, wisdom, truth, and providence, to the denial of all, and sometimes multiplied it, Numb. xvi., &c. *Proved me;* a discontented quarrel with, and scrutiny of, Christ the Redeemer, that if he would not serve their lust, they would deny him, and apostatize from him, and return to Egypt; notwithstanding their having sufficient proof of him, yet they would contend with him, 1 Cor. x. 9. *And saw my works forty years;* all the Redeemer's miracles, which he wrought for them in Egypt and the wilderness, they saw them plainly and presently on their tempting him; miracles of mercy and of punishments, by fire, by the earth opening, by fiery serpents, by the sword, by consuming six hundred thousand of them; all which were evidences sufficient to convince any of the wickedness of mistrusting him, Deut. xxix. 2—4. This hardening of their hearts yet continued *forty years,* till all but two of them, Joshua and Caleb, were consumed; God by their sin was so grieved with them after such experience of his power for so long a time: see Exod. xxxii. 10; Numb. xiv. 22.

10 Wherefore I was grieved with that generation, and said, They do alway err in *their* heart; and they have not known my ways.

Wherefore I was grieved with that generation; because they thus tempted and proved him by hardening their hearts in unbelief forty years, God the Redeemer, Isa. lxiii. 16; 1 Cor. x. 9, *was grieved;* which is attributed to him improperly, who is not subject to passions; but as men grown impatient with grievous and oppressive burdens, so he expresseth his dislike, disdain of them, and resolution to bear no longer, as Amos ii. 13. They split on him, as a ship on a sharp point of a rock, so as God hath loss, offence, and trouble by it; and all of them did so carry it to him, the whole age of them but Caleb and Joshua, Psal. xcv. 10. *And said, They do alway err in their heart;* they follow deceit and lying in their doctrine and worship with all their heart, so that it is diffused through their persons, and that seat of truth is made a depth of error, to the stupifying of their hearts even to very madness; and this was their state all their time. *And they have not known my ways;* notwithstanding God's works were among them, and his word, yet they would not know his mind, so as to approve, love, and walk in God's ways; his law, doctrine, revealed truth, and commands were all cast behind their back, Ezek. xxiii. 35.

† Gr. *If they shall enter.*

11 So I sware in my wrath, †They shall not enter into my rest.)

So I sware in my wrath: such were their provocations and temptations of their Redeemer, that he determined their punishment; the certainty of which he fixed by an irreversible oath, which is the highest confirmation of vengeance when it cometh from wrath; as of his promise, when it issueth from grace, Numb. xiv. 27—36; Psal. xcv. 11: compare chap. vi. 17, 18. And the spring of it here is *wrath,* enraged by their murmurings and unbelief. *They shall not enter into my rest:* the punishment is expressed in an expostulatory form, which is vehemently asserting the negative of the question; They shall never enter into my rest. If they enter in, then I am neither true nor God. The rest literal was the land of Canaan, Deut. xii. 9; in the truth of type, heaven. It is the Redeemer who speaks this, whose rest is by way of efficiency, purchase, and donation; he gives entrance into it, and shuts out-of it, Matt. vii. 21—23. This is a shutting them out of all peace, into eternal sorrow, anguish, distress, and trouble, and every other evil contrary unto this rest.

12 Take heed, brethren, lest there be in any of you an evil heart of unbelief, in departing from the living God.

Here the Spirit applieth the former dreadful example of sin and judgment to the Hebrews, to forewarn them how they sinned as these did, lest they partake of the like vengeance; and so enters his caution against unbelief. *Take heed, brethren:* Βλέπετε signifies not an act of sight, but of the mind, circumspection, watchfulness, and heed, taking exactest caution of the evil forbidden, chap. xii. 15, 25; 1 Cor. viii. 9. *Brethren* they were to Paul in the flesh, and more so as true believers in Christ; he cautions them particularly, one by one, lest any root of bitterness should be amongst them, chap. xii. 15. *Lest there be in any of you an evil heart of unbelief:* the heart is the first, and proper, and chief subject, wherein all sin riseth, and from thence issueth into words and works, Matt. xv. 18, 19; compare James i. 14, 15. This comprehendeth the mind, will, and affections, the whole inward man: and this heart in every man is naturally and habitually evil, continually forging and framing of it, Gen. vi. 5; compare Jer. xvii. 9. Almighty grace only can change this heart; yet it works by counsel, and makes the soul willing to use the means appointed to effect it. *Unbelief,* though but in itself, is but a denial to assent to or rely on the will of God revealed to it, yet is the spring and fountain of all other sin, the teeming womb from whence all issueth, as uncleanness, idolatry, unrighteousness, superstition, &c. It was the hardening sin of their forefathers, they would not believe, and then did murmur and rebel. It is the root of apostasy; men breaking their covenant with God in Christ, do then desert him. Against this perfidious, impious, perverted temper doth he caution them to watch, that neither for measure, nor season they ever do admit or allow it; that there be not at all in the least degree, or at any time, such a base, malignant quality in their hearts, Rom. xi. 20, 21. *In departing from the living God;* turning away, standing off, and separating the heart; it implies in it a real, total, final defection; actual and formal apostacy from him whom they had owned and received; and is actual rebellion against their lawful Sovereign, by turning either Jews or heathens, and renouncing the Christian religion and its Author, who is the living God, not only formally, as opposed to dead idols, but efficiently the Author and Fountain of all sorts of life, but especially of spiritual and eternal life, John v. 19—21, 25, 26: which living God is our Lord Jesus Christ, ver. 7, whose voice they were to hear, who was tempted by their unbelief in the wilderness, 1 Cor. x. 9, who gave the law to them at Sinai, chap. xii. 26. So that to apostatize from him and his religion, is to apostatize from God, and to renounce eternal life, and to subject themselves to eternal punishments, which he ever liveth to inflict on them. Unless they took heed to avoid this unbelief, it was impossible for them to persevere in Christianity, when threatened with persecutions, and the loss of peace, liberty, safety, estates, honours, relations, and life itself for it.

13 But exhort one another daily, while it is called To day; lest any of you be hardened through the deceitfulness of sin.

But exhort one another daily, while it is called To-day: the means to avoid the former evil is, to *exhort;* which, as a private duty, is an earnest, frequent calling on, stirring up, or persuading, encouraging to perseverance in the Christian religion, and to put away all heart evil, especially unbelief, which traineth to apostacy; to which are subservient God's precepts, promises, threatenings suitably applied by them. And this is not only privately, but especially publicly, by the regular ministration of the word and ordinances to the whole society of Christians, as they are personally obliged to it, being members one of another, 1 Cor. xii. 25, 27. And this they are to do instantly, for no man is sure what may be on the morrow, he being but a days-man, living, and supplied, as working by the day: Sufficient to the day is the duty as well as the evil in it, Matt. vi. 11, 34. Whilst then the day of grace and repentance lasts, in which God calls and entreats, and will hear and help, the opportune time of exhorting, the very instant wherein God expecteth it, ver. 7; Psal. xcv. 7. And every one, as thus to look to another, must begin with himself, lest any miscarry; charity, especially as to this, should begin in every Christian at home. *Lest any of you be hardened through the deceitfulness of sin;* lest themselves or others refuse the gospel tendered, or reject and apostatize from it after professing it, so as to become not only obstinate, but rebellious, by unbelief, and an habitual hardened heart; so as the sinful, natural habit of our soul, James i. 12, 15, so horribly vile in itself, that were it not masked nature would abhor it, might be drawn forth by the false colours, as the devil blinds sin with, to delude the understanding, and to catch and insnare the malignant will, that it swallows it more and more, to the hardening of the heart; that Divine promises, threatenings, nor admonitions, can make any impression; it being unmoved under the application of all these, disregards the Christian faith, and hath its issue in a total apostasy, Jer. xvii. 9; Eph. iv. 22; 1 Tim. i. 19.

14 For we are made partakers of Christ, °if we hold the beginning of our confidence stedfast unto the end:

o ver. 6.

For we are made partakers of Christ: for shows this to be a rational motive, urging home the former counsel, unto which the following condition doth agree; for we believing Christians and brethren are made μέτοχοι, partners with the primitive Proprietor supposed in it, even Christ, who hath of his own the fulness of God, life, grace, glory, and all good; in all which fulness of his we share, by virtue of our union with him, John i. 16; Eph. i. 22, 23; Col. i. 19; ii. 9, 10; and he by his Spirit will free us from the deceitfulness of sin, and hardening by it. *If we hold the beginning of our confidence;* if by a spiritual tenaciousness, and firm fixing in our hearts, we hold ἀρχήν, either the principal or fundamental truth, as the word signifieth in sciences; or, the entrance or beginning of our course, as used in things, so as the first step in Christianity is styled a beginning of grace. *Stedfast unto the end:* ὑποστάσεως, in personal relations, is, a real subsistence, as of the Son in the Trinity, chap. i. 3; in things, the basis and foundation upholding others; and this in Christianity is Christ principally, who bears up his church, Eph. ii. 20—22. And faith, the instrument whereby we receive Christ, is so called, chap. xi. 1, that which renders present and subsisting what is hoped for to the soul; so that here it imports the retaining firm that principle of truth, upon which Christians are bottomed and supported to life, that is, Christ himself, and the true doctrine of him; as also, that we must firmly stand in the first beginnings of faith, and increase in them, so as they may be firmly fixed in our hearts, and our hearts on them, so as never to be removed as long as we live. Our retaining firmly of this, makes us partners in Christ; both instrumentally helping in it, and evidentially; it being the infallible consequence of true grace, holding us to this communion with Christ. How ought these conditions to quicken the activity of believers!

p ver. 7. 15 While it is said, ᵖTo day if ye will hear his voice, harden not your hearts, as in the provocation.

This is another circumstance of the example of the Jews applied to them: That since now Christ is speaking to you, as he did to your forefathers then; the same voice concerneth you both, so as, not to-morrow, or when you will, but *To-day,* if you will believe what God speaketh to you by him, and hath recorded in his word concerning his being the Messiah, and render not yourselves deaf to God's voice, or obdurate through unbelief, as your forefathers did, when their unbelief and hardness of heart imbittered God's Spirit against them, because acting in it against their solemn vows and engagements to him, so as to apostatize from him.

16 ᑫFor some, when they had heard, did provoke: howbeit not all that came out of Egypt by Moses.

q Num. 14. 2, 4, 11, 24, 30. Deut. 1. 34, 36, 38.

For some, when they had heard, did provoke: this is a rational enforcement of the former duty pressed; it being as possible for them to provoke Christ as others, they should look to it, and not harden their hearts; for the greater *some,* the most of the congregation of Israel, imbittered God's Spirit by their unbelief and hardness of heart; though Christ spake to them from heaven, as never was before done, and daily by Moses they were hearing counsels by which they might live, yet provoked they him, and would not believe. *Howbeit not all that came out of Egypt by Moses:* this rightly interprets the psalmist, and sets a better example of their fathers for them to follow. Let Caleb and Joshua, believers, and obedient to God, be your patterns to imitate. He aggravates the disobedience of the one, and the obedience of the other. They all had equally a clear exemption and deliverance from the place of bondage, and that by Moses, by whom God wrought such miracles as might command faith from any; yet these *some,* by murmuring and striving with the Redeemer, provoked him: how great is their sin! how suitable and pleasing the obedience of the others to him!

17 But with whom was he grieved forty years? *was it* not with them that had sinned, ʳwhose carcases fell in the wilderness?

r Num. 14. 22, 29, &c. & 26. 65. Ps. 106. 26. 1 Cor. 10. 5. Jude 5.

By these questions the Spirit makes a more lively representation of these unbelieving provokers of God, that his reason may have the more force with them. Do ye observe with whom God was grieved? the form puts them on more exact notice for their caution: God suffers not by passion, but these redeemed out of Egypt carried it contrary to him, and crossed his will, that which usually grieveth us. Concerning the word, see ver. 10. It is used by the Septuagint, Deut. vii. 26, to express that detestation and abhorrence which Israel was to show against idols, that they should be a grief to their soul not to be endured: idols are called grievances. He was displeased and grieved with their covenant-breaking with him forty years together. These sinners, by their unbelief, murmuring, idolatry, rebellion against his officers and ordinances, and their other lusts, so imbittered his Spirit, that he by various judgments destroyed them, and turned them into the grave and hell together, 1 Cor. x. 5—11. Moses and others of God's own cannot be numbered among these sinners, for their sins were pardoned and persons accepted; and though they came short of the literal, had a much more abundant entrance administered to them into the heavenly Canaan.

18 And ˢto whom sware he that they should not enter into his rest, but to them that believed not?

s Num. 14. 30. Deut. 1. 34, 35.

To prevent these Hebrews falling, the Spirit repeats the direful oath of God to apostates in the wilderness; the form of which was opened, ver. 11: compare Numb. xiv. 30. The matter sworn was, that they should be so far from possessing, that they should not so much as enter into the land of promise, Canaan, which was God's property, as the whole earth is; he promised it to them, could only dispossess their enemies, did give it in possession to their seed, and made it a type of heaven, and of his rest there; he swore this in his severe vindictive justice, so as his sentence was irreversible; which oath stands good against all total and final apostates from him, who have thereby forfeited any title to God's eternal rest. *Them that believed not;* those who were unbelieving under all God's miracles of mercies and judgments, which they saw, and so became obstinately disobedient to God's commands, and broke his covenant, chap. viii. 9; Jer. xxxi. 32, and apostatized from him, and so perished in their gainsaying.

19 ᵗSo we see that they could not enter in because of unbelief.

t ch. 4. 6.

The execution of the matter sworn was felt by these Hebrews, which should make them and all that read it to dread both their sin and punishment, which the gospel would as justly inflict on them, if unbelievers. It is to be seen in God's written record of it, and the experienced downfal of such, that God's oath had shut the door as to their entrance there, and his judgments consumed them in the wilderness, because of their denial of resting on God's word, and the impious practices that issued from it, in their rejecting promises, rebelling against precepts, and murmuring against providence. God is no respecter of persons; if we sin so against his Son and gospel, how much sorer punishment will overtake us! chap. x. 27, 29.

CHAP. IV

The rest of Christians to be attained by faith, 1—11. The power of God's word, 12, 13. Having Jesus the Son of God for our High Priest, we must hold fast our profession, and come boldly unto the throne of grace, 14—16.

a ch. 12. 15. LET ᵃ us therefore fear, lest, a promise being left *us* of entering into his rest, any of you should seem to come short of it.

Let us therefore fear: the Spirit draws this counsel from the former sad event of unbelief in the progenitors of these Hebrews, who were shut out of an earthly Canaan by it, which was promised to them: hereon he adviseth them to avoid that sin which will have now as fearful a punishment, viz. the shutting them out of the heavenly Canaan, tendered and promised to believers in the gospel. Fear is that affection of the soul, by which it avoideth and shunneth what is hurtful to it, and here carrieth it in a gracious and child-like care and jealousy of slighting the Father's promise, and coming short of heaven; it is a fear issuing from faith, Phil. ii. 12. *Lest, a promise being left us;* lest the promise of God to men, who sware some should not enter, but promised others should, as Numb. xiv. 23, 24, 30, 31; a promise of the most excellent, glorious, and heavenly rest made to believers, Isa. xi. 10. This was graciously *left* or made to them by God; but καταλειπομένης here is an act of sin, lest we by sin should leave or reject God's promise of the better, as the Hebrews did of the literal, rest, by their unbelief and disobedience to God's law; and so is the proper object of fear, and therefore ought to have been read, lest the promise being left behind. *Of entering into his rest;* of a free entrance into heaven, and enjoying a glorious rest with God there. *Any of you should seem to come short of it:* he would have it the fear of all, that not one soul might be endangered by it; so as not in any measure to slight such a promise, nor as much as to seem so, flying from the very appearance of evil, 1 Thess. v. 22; ὑστερηκέναι, a metaphor taken from racers, where any are outrun and left behind; noting the miserable state of such Christians who profess to run to heaven, but never do so as to obtain it, 1 Cor. ix. 24—26. Alas, he that falleth short of heaven, reacheth home to hell!

† Gr. *the word of hearing.* ‖ Or, *because they were not united by faith to.*

2 For unto us was the Gospel preached, as well as unto them: but †the word preached did not profit them, ‖ not being mixed with faith in them that heard *it*.

For unto us was the gospel preached, as well as unto them: the reason enforcing the former counsel is, their having mutually the same means, the one as the other, and if they fear not, may be guilty of the same sin; for the Hebrews and the whole church were evangelized by the outward publishing to them, and their professed reception of the, glad tidings of salvation by God the Son incarnate, who was to lead them in the way to God's eternal rest; which if they had been truly evangelized and transformed by, they could never have been shut out of God's rest; the same gospel being preached to both their forefathers and them, though more gloriously revealed to the latter, 2 Cor. iii. 10, 11. For the gospel was preached to Abraham and to his offspring, that in his eminent Seed, the Lord Jesus Christ, all nations should be blessed, Gen. xxii. 18; compare John viii. 56. He was the Angel of the covenant that was Lord of God's hosts, and was to lead them into the literal and heavenly Canaan, Exod. xxiii. 20; Josh. v. 13—15; Isa. xi. 10. So that none entered into either of God's rests but by him alone, who so testifieth by himself, John v. 39, 46, and by his Spirit, Acts xv. 11. *But the word preached did not profit them:* the gospel was so preached to them, that they did or might hear it, Rom. x. 14, 15; compare Psal. xcii. 4; Isa. lii. 7; yet did it not prove effectual to many of those Hebrews, to bring them either into the literal or heavenly Canaan, but they came short of God's rest in both; they not performing what he required, he by an irreversible sentence excluded them: see chap. iii. 17, 19. *Not being mixed with faith in them that heard it;* συγκεκραμένος· a metaphor taking from mixing things in the stomach, as meat and drink, without the concoction of which there can be no nourishing the body; setting forth the sin of these Hebrews, who never received nor mixed this gospel which they heard with a sincere faith in their souls, so as, being digested thereby, it might be united with it. Thus that which was the mighty power and wisdom of God to salvation to those who believed, was a word of condemnation and eternal death to unbelievers, 1 Cor. i. 18; 1 Pet. ii. 2, 3.

3 ᵇ For we which have believed do enter into rest, as he said, ᶜ As I have sworn in my wrath, if they shall enter into my rest: although the works were finished from the foundation of the world.

b ch. 3. 14.
c Ps. 95. 11. ch. 3. 11.

For we which have believed do enter into rest: a further reason setting home this counsel, was the certain benefit of our care in believing; for that the community of real Christians, partakers and exercisers of the same precious faith, as Paul himself, 2 Pet. i. 1, have the same privilege as believing Caleb and Joshua had, Numb. xiv. 24, 30, to enter into God's rest; initially having peace with God now, and his love shed abroad in their hearts by the Holy Ghost, witnessing their reconciliation, justification, renovation, adoption, so as they rejoice in hope of the glory of God, Rom. v. 1, 2, 5; and are by believing and obedience making out to the attainment of the final and complete rest of God in heaven, of which they are afraid to fall short. *As he said, As I have sworn in my wrath:* God himself confirms this by his oath, chap. iii. 11, 18; Psal. xcv. 11. At the same time that he excludeth all unbelievers from entering in, he inclusively and by consequence sweareth that all believers do and shall enter in. *If they shall enter into my rest:* that rest which David there speaks of was not God's rest on the seventh day from the creation after the finishing of God's works, nor the temporal rest in the land of Canaan which the Jews had, and were past, as these Hebrews might suggest; but another rest to come, either in the world to come, chap. ii. 5, or in the heavenly rest in glory, which he takes occasion further to explain to them. *Although the works were finished from the foundation of the world:* καί τοι some render as a particle of exception, *although,* as if it intended, although God's rest is some where meant of his rest after the finishing of the works of creation, yet here God speaks of the rest of Canaan, a type of the heavenly one: others, that God sware they should not enter into his rest, although God's works were done, and the rest were ready, because of their unbelief. Others render it, and indeed he said and spake of the same heavenly rest, long before he spake of the rest of Canaan, even upon the finishing of his works from the foundation of the world: which seems most agreeable to the Spirit's design here.

4 For he spake in a certain place of the seventh *day* on this wise, ᵈ And God did rest the seventh day from all his works.

d Gen. 2. 2. Ex. 20. 11. & 31. 17.

For he spake in a certain place of the seventh day on this wise: the Spirit proves, that the rest mentioned by David, Psal. xcv. 11, is not meant the seventh day's rest, because spoken three thousand years after that rest was past; but this rest of which he speaks was to come, though spoken of and known then: for Moses had spoken of it in a wellknown place to them, Gen. ii. 1—3, and this when he wrote of the seventh day, which was eminently noting the sabbath, and a type of God's most excellent rest which he sware unto believers. *And God did rest the seventh day from all his works:* God doth not here rest as if he were weary, Isa. xl. 28, but ceased from the creation of all kind of things he purposed to make, but not from their propagation and his providence about them, Acts xvii. 25. And this he did on the seventh day, which he instituted a sabbath for his people, Gen. ii. 3; which resting day may type out the eternal rest of angels and men, when their work of obedience is finished : and yet was not God's rest spoken of in the Psalm, nor promised in the gospel to believers, for this was yet to come; whereas the seventh day's rest was entered into from the foundation of the world.

5 And in this *place* again, If they shall enter into my rest.

And in this place again: καὶ here is not so much copulative, connecting an instance of David to the same purpose of that of Moses about the seventh day's rest from the creation ; but discretive, joining an instance of another rest of God different from the seventh day's rest. Moses spake of this, but David here of a further rest ; for in Psal. xcv. 11, David spake not of the seventh day, but of God's last and eternal rest. *If they shall enter into my rest ;* εἰ here is affirmative, as appears by comparing ver. 3 and 6, that these shall have a real and full possession in the future after David's time of this rest, and therefore different from Moses's rest so long past before. The word *rest* in the Hebrew is not the same in the text of Moses and David ; Gen. ii. 2, 3, it is שבת in Psal. xcv. 11, מנוחתי this of David noting the full, eternal, comfortable rest of souls in glory, sworn by God to believers in the gospel.

6 Seeing therefore it remaineth that some must enter therein, ᵉand they to whom ‖ it was first preached entered not in because of unbelief :

c ch. 3. 19.
‖ Or, *the Gospel was first preached.*

The Spirit having demonstrated, that God's rest sworn to believers in the gospel, and mentioned by David, could not be the seventh day's rest ; proceeds to prove likewise, that it could not be the rest of Israel in the land of Canaan, since that was entered into four hundred years before he wrote by the Spirit of this better rest, since those unbelieving Israel that entered into Canaan never entered into this rest. *Seeing therefore it remaineth that some must enter therein;* forasmuch then as a rest to come is spoken of, and that some believers must have a real and full possession of the glorious rest offered to them in the gospel, as David foretold : see ver. 9—11. *And they to whom it was first preached entered not in because of unbelief;* the unbelieving Israel, who had the glad tidings of this rest preached unto them by Moses and by David, &c., yet entered not into it, though they entered into and lived in Canaan, because of their disobedience and unbelief. Then it follows Canaan's rest and this cannot be all one, and the latter only is intended by David here.

7 (Again, he limiteth a certain day, saying in David, To day, after so long a time; as it is said, ᶠTo day if ye will hear his voice, harden not your hearts.

f Ps. 95. 7. ch. 3. 7.

Again, he limiteth a certain day, saying in David : this is a further proof, that David did not mean or intend the rest of the Jews in Canaan, in the 95th Psalm, from the determined time of it ; as if the Spirit had said, Besides what I have proved, take another argument ; Again I argue. God by the prophet setteth out, and severeth from all other time, a certain stated day, from which the rest spoken of is cleared, and of it testifieth by him. Psal. xcv. 7, 8. *To-day, after so long a time;* after four hundred years past of Israel's rest in Canaan, which was a long time, doth David say of to-day, a time present, then and further to be extended, even the gospel day, in David's time, and after it ; not in Joshua's, for that was past long before. *As it is said, To-day if ye will hear his voice, harden not your hearts ;* ye ought to-day to hear, receive, and believe the gospel of God's rest, and not by unbelief to turn your hearts from the voice of God in the gospel.

8 For if ‖ Jesus had given them rest, then would he not afterward have spoken of another day.

‖ That is, *Joshua.*

This is the improvement of the former instance, ver. 7. If Joshua, by bringing Israel into Canaan, had given rest to all believers, then God would not by David have spoken of another day and state of rest to come. Joshua was a type of Jesus bringing believers into the true rest of the heavenly Canaan, as he did Israel into a literal one, Acts vii. 45. *For if Jesus had given them rest;* if that of Canaan was the full and perfect rest of believers, which was given them by him. *Then would he not afterward have spoken of another day ;* then God himself would not have spoken by David of a better and heavenly rest promised believers in the gospel ; of which spiritual and eternal one, both God's seventh-day sabbath, and the rest of Canaan, were but fainter shadows and types. The expostulation is vehemently denying it.

9 There remaineth therefore a ‖ rest to the people of God.

‖ Or, *keeping of a sabbath.*

Here the Spirit concludes from his former proofs, tha: there is a more excellent rest revealed to faith in the gospel, which is remaining, future, and to come, and will surely and most certainly do so ; though it be behind, yet it will be enjoyed. A sabbatism, which is a state and season of a most glorious rest, (see ver. 10,) shall be enjoyed by sincere believers, the true Israel of God, of whom he is the Proprietor, and who are for their eternal state so excellently holy, and of so Divine a nature, that he is not ashamed to be called their God. They have an entrance here into the initials of this sabbatism in internal peace, and the glorious liberty of the children of God ; and by it are secured of their full possession of it in the eternal inheritance of the saints in light, Col. i. 12, 13 ; 1 Pet. i. 3—5 ; Rev. xiv. 13.

10 For he that is entered into his rest, he also hath ceased from his own works, as God *did* from his.)

This proveth the foregoing consequence of a rest remaining. from the nature of a true rest, which is a resting from all labours, which the Israelites did not in Canaan, therefore it is yet to come. For every true believer who hath full possession of God's rest, where God is satisfying of them in bliss, they rest in his loves, of which the sabbath and Canaan were but types. *He also hath ceased from his own works;* such true Christians have ceased and rested from all their sinful works and labours, as works of callings, miseries, anxieties, and sufferings of any kind, resting from them perfectly and perpetually, having finished all his work of evangelical obedience through them. *As God did from his;* they have rested not in a parity of rest, or work in kind, but as God from his own in likeness of order, his work going before rest, and of rest fitted for believers by him conformable to his own. Some refer these words and the relative *he* to our Lord Jesus Christ, as Head of his body, the church of true believers; and that the parallel runs between God the Father and him in the works of the old and new creation, which works were good and complete in their different kinds, in their cessation from them, and their rest in their respective sabbaths, both days being founded thereon ; and that believers shall be conformable to their Head, treading in his steps in doing and suffering, and then in rest.

11 Let us labour therefore to enter into that rest, lest any man fall ᵍ after the same example of ‖ unbelief.

g ch. 3. 12, 18, 19.
‖ Or, *disobedience.*

Let us labour therefore to enter into that rest : this is the use of the former doctrine, that since many through unbelief fall short of God's rest, therefore let us labour : σπουδάσωμεν imports study of mind, earnestness of affection, diligence of endeavour, with all the powers of soul and body to intend this work : so is it used, 2 Pet. i. 10. This is the most necessary, excellent, and important one to us in this world, our single great business in it ; and therefore, as students, our minds must be bent on it, and our wills fixed and resolved about it, and the operations of all the executive powers of our persons put forth to the utmost degree, so as all the duties necessary thereunto, as attendance on all ordinances, and the constant exercise of faith and obedience, must be fitting us for, and bringing us into, the full possession of the eternally blessed and glorious rest of God, 2 Pet. i. 5—11. *Lest any man fall after the same example of unbelief;* that not any particular person may fall into sin and the consequences of it. The particle ἐν may be read, into, and then it implies, lest any of you prove rebels and apostates. Or it is read, by, or after, and then it is a fall to destruction and hell, with all the miseries that those feel who are shut out of God's rest, as their unbelieving forefathers were. God spared neither apostate men nor angels, and will not spare others if they sin as those did. Our judgments may be rather sorer, being warned by their example, 1 Cor. x. 11; compare Heb. x. 26, 27, 29. They were contumacious and disobeyed the gospel of God's rest, therefore he destroyed them in the wilderness, and thrust them down to hell for ever: avoid you their sin, as you would labour to avoid their punishment.

12 For the word of God *is* [h] quick, and powerful, and [i] sharper than any [k] two-edged sword, piercing even to the dividing asunder of soul and spirit, and of the joints and marrow, and *is* [l] a discerner of the thoughts and intents of the heart.

For the word of God: the efficacy of the word of God is a further enforcement of their studious labour to enter into God's rest, for that calleth us thereunto; even the law and doctrine of the gospel brought by the incarnate Word from heaven, preached by him to the world, dictated and inspired into the holy penmen both of the Old and New Testament by the Holy Ghost, and written by them at his call and order, 2 Pet. i. 19—21; representing all those precepts and prohibitions, promises and threatenings, by which God will judge to whom this gospel hath been preached in that man whom he hath appointed: compare chap. ii. 1, 2, and ver. 1, 2 of this. And this word was written by David, Psal. xcv., even a word of exhortation, promise, and threatening, as opened before, and shows the perfection of this gospel law in its administration by Christ. *Is quick;* this word, like the incarnate Word, is ζῶν, not only a living word, but a quickening word, making dead sinners living Christians; souls dead in sins and trespasses, alive to God. This word, the breath of God, conveyeth spirit and life to them, 2 Tim. iii. 16; 1 Pet. i. 23: so David experienced it, preserving the life it breathed into him, Psal. cxix. 50; and the members of the church, 1 Cor. iv. 15; compare 2 Cor. iii. 6, 17, 18; and as a rule it guideth and directeth them through Christ unto eternal life, John vi. 68. *And powerful;* ἐνεργής· it is an active word, powerful in its effects, the very ministration of the Spirit, 2 Cor. iii. 8, most efficacious and energetical for convincing, converting, comforting; and for condemning, killing: it acts like the power of God; so Rom. i. 16, 18. *And sharper than any two-edged sword;* τομώτερος signifieth a cutting sharpness, as becometh several uses, as searching, letting out corruption, or for killing; all which agree to this Divine word; sharper than any sword with two mouths. The Hebrews style the edge the mouth, that which bites, teareth, or woundeth; as Rev. i. 16, and ii. 12. The word for spiritual execution upon souls is more sharp, and above every other sword; there is none so piercing for cutting the heart, or killing sin in it. So is it used, Eph. vi. 17; compare Acts ii. 37; vii. 54. It is Christ's weapon of offence and defence for his people, and it cuts without resistance; with it he is defending his truth, and smiting his enemies, Isa. xi. 4; compare Rev. xix. 13, 15, 21. *Piercing even to the dividing asunder;* διϊκνύμενος, piercing, or going through what is smitten with it; which way soever it is turned it forceth its way through all opposition, to a dividing into parts, and separating the most nearly united and closely joined things, laying open the very entrails, the most inward in a man; where the metaphors taken from the closest parts of the person are applied to the soul. *Of soul:* ψυχή may denote not so much the natural life and the faculties of that, but that which is styled the rational soul as unregenerate: see 1 Cor. ii. 14. Such an animal, carnal soul as is purely human, 1 Cor. iii. 3, which wants both a principle, light, and faculty to discern the things of God, as no natural eye can see a spirit, Rom. viii. 5—8. *And spirit;* πνεύματος, the soul of man regenerate and spiritualized, called *spirit,* 1 Thess. v. 23. The soul enlightened, renewed, and governed by the Holy Ghost; not altered as to its substance, but as to its qualities; whose understanding, will, and affections are spiritualized, manifested in its actions, agreeable to the spiritual will of God, 1 Cor. ii. 10, 12, 14, 15. These are both of them under the piercing power of the word, and the Spirit can reach them by it as he pleaseth. *And of the joints and marrow:* ἁρμῶν are not the members, but the nerves, membranes, muscles, whereby the members or limbs are joined one to another, so as not without incision to be discovered; and *the marrow* within the bones, there must be a breaking or perforating them to reach it. By which metaphors are set out the hardest, compactest, and most intimate parts of a sinner, the most secret hidden ones, which no natural reason can reach; yet the word of God pierceth them, to discover either the evil or good of them, and to inflict wrath, or communicate comfort, according to their conditions. *And is a discerner of the thoughts and intents of the heart:* the word of God is a most nice, exact, and critical judge, discerning the gravity and rectitude of them; it discovers and distinguisheth them as they are, or not, agreeable to itself, the fundamental truth; and is capable, as a judge, to charge or discharge, as its author will, by it, Rom. ii. 12, 15, 16; compare 1 Cor. xiv. 24, 25. It discovers the most inward, close, secret, and constant motions, both speculative and practical, of the soul of man inseparably united to the heart; and one with another, whether they are opinions, conceptions, resolutions, or decrees, so subtile and so secret, as who can know them, but he who made the heart? Gen. vi. 5; Jer. xvii. 9.

13 [m] Neither is there any creature that is not manifest in his sight: but all things *are* naked [n] and opened unto the eyes of him with whom we have to do.

Neither is there any creature that is not manifest in his sight: καί is not only copulative, but rational, showing the ground of the former efficacy of the gospel word, because its Author seeth and knoweth all persons and things, and filleth it with this power and force. For every creature which God the Son created, angel, or man, or any other, from the greatest to the least, from the leviathan to a mite, and all parts of every creature, especially of every creature to whom the gospel is preached, Mark xvi. 15; not any one is ἀφανής, without light, invisible, unapparent, obscure, or possible to be covered, or hid, or concealed from his view or face: where the relative αὐτοῦ agreeth with Θεοῦ, God in Christ, and not with λόγος, or the word, ver. 12, as the following relative evinceth. To this God-man no spirit nor thought can be hid; it shall not be so from the efficacious power of his word; much less shall infidelity or hypocrisy be hid from it, or his most piercing eye. *But all things are naked and opened;* but all things in general and particular, not any one excepted, are bare, naked, unclothed, the covering is removed, all secrets are open and manifest to view, God the Son seeth within and without, all are unveiled to him, and laid open as by dissection, τετραχηλισμένα· a metaphor taken from the sacrificed beasts, which being skinned, were cut open from the neck, and so divided by the chine to the rump, or by the throat downward embowelled by the priests, so as every part within may be clearly seen whether clean or unclean. The truth of which is, that every thing in the world, even the most secret and inward thoughts of the heart of a sinner, which is a great deep, is opened and laid forth to every scruple unto God in Christ; every secret unbelief, apostatizing principle, or hypocrisy, he discerneth clearly and fully, Jer. xvii. 9, 10: he that made the eye, must see best. *Unto the eyes of him with whom we have to do;* his eyes who pierceth beyond the vulture's, into things and places that no eye can discern, the souls of men, Job xxviii. 7, 10; Psal. xciv. 9; Prov. xx. 12. All this is asserted concerning the person of whom Paul writes, Christ, God-man, the great gospel Minister, whose word is so powerfully piercing: of him and his word is all this speech and discourse; he it is who is the all-knowing and impartial Judge, and makes his gospel word of counsel, promise, and threatenings to cut so deeply, and search the secrets of the hearts of all.

14 Seeing then that we have [o] a great High Priest, [p] that is passed into the heavens, Jesus the Son of God, [q] let us hold fast *our* profession.

The excellency of the great gospel Minister beyond all others in respect of his priestly office, especially beyond Aaron and the Levitical priesthood, is shown by the Holy Ghost from this verse to chap. v. 11. It is introduced as the Spirit's counsel to these Hebrews, from the premises, for their using of this High Priest, in order to their reaching home to the rest of God, to whom and whose profession they ought to adhere, since he is so fit and so willing to give them an entrance into it: compare chap. ii. 17, 18; iii. 1, 6. *Seeing then that we have a great High Priest;* being therefore by the Spirit through faith not only interested by a common relation in him, but by a real union to, and communion with him, as here described, a High Priest (chap. ii. 11, and iii. 1) so great as none was, or can equal him : all the high priests on earth but imperfect types of him ; above Aaron and all others ; the grand presider over all God's worship, who had work peculiar to himself above all ; the supreme and universal Priest in heaven and earth, whose title the Roman antichrist usurpeth, to him only due, *Pontifex optimus maximus;* yet officiating always for us. *That is passed into the heavens;* he hath fulfilled his type, entering into the holy of holiest in heaven, taking possession of God's rest, and purchasing an entrance for us into it, and this after the removal of the curse, satisfaction of the Divine justice for our sins, victory over all enemies that would oppose his or our entrance by him, as sin, wrath, death, and the devil, and keeping possession of this rest for us, chap. ix. 23, 24, 28. *Jesus the Son of God;* Jesus the Saviour of his people from all their sins, their Emmanuel, Matt. i. 20, 21, 23, who being God the Son by eternal generation, was incarnate by taking to himself and uniting a true body and a reasonable soul, being conceived miraculously by the virgin Mary from the overshadowing of the Holy Ghost : in which nature, inseparably united to his person, he fulfilled all righteousness, and died a sacrifice for our sins, and rose in our nature, and ascended and entered into the holy of holiest in heaven, and made atonement, and laid open the way to believers to enter God's rest there. *Let us hold fast our profession;* the entire religion of which Jesus is the author, as opposite to that of the Jews in its principles and practical part of it, chap. iii. 1, is powerfully, strongly, and perseveringly to be held by his without relaxation ; in which if we follow him, cleave to him, and by him labour to enter, we shall not come short of God's rest, chap. vii. 24, 25 : where the Head is, there shall the body be also, John xiv. 2, 3 ; xvii. 24.

r Is. 53. 3. ch. 2. 18. s Luke 22. 28. t 2 Cor. 5. 21. ch. 7. 26. 1 Pet. 2. 22. 1 John 3. 5. 15 For ʳ we have not an High Priest which cannot be touched with the feeling of our infirmities ; but ˢ was in all points tempted like as *we are,* ᵗ *yet* without sin.

For we have not an High Priest which cannot be touched with the feeling of our infirmities : this duty of perseverance in the Christian religion, is enforced by the consideration of the sympathy of this High Priest, with the states of all who will enter into God's rest by him. He is worthy that we should hold it fast, being without impotency. It is impossible he should be pitiless to penitent sinners, though he be glorious, there being nothing in himself, or out of himself, indisposing him to it. Συμπαθῆσαι imports such a sympathy or fellow feeling, as makes him like affected as if he were in the same case with them. He cannot but be compassionate, since inwardly affected and moved with the sufferings of his, Acts ix. 5 ; compare Isa. lxiii. 9. As God, he is infinitely merciful ; as man, inwardly feeling them, even all the miseries they were liable to, but sinful ones. He wants no bowels, but he hath, as a fellow feeling, so a fellow grieving, and fellow caring for the redress of them, even all such as are fit for his pity ; and works on affections, a sense of guilt, fears, doubts, tremblings, weak-workings to God, the concomitant infirmities of sinful souls ; all the weaknesses of grace in us, all troubles, distresses, anguishes in the flesh, the fruits of sin. He knows these sensibly as man, which as God singly he could not. These sinful weaknesses of soul inclining to sin, and disabling from resisting temptations, by which the subtle, powerful enemy of our soul prevaileth over us to the accumulating of sin and guilt daily, and so need this sympathy of his to us-ward : see chap. v. 2 ; 1 Cor. ii. 3 ; 2 Cor. xi. 23—31 ; xii. 5, 9, 10. *But was in all points tempted like as we are, yet without sin ;* but πεπειρασμένον, was pierced and tried by all sorts of sufferings, being outwardly tempted by the devil to sin ; inwardly he could not, being perfectly holy, John xiv. 30 ; but was outwardly with violence assaulted by him, Matt. iv. 1—11 : and tried by men beyond any man, and tempted to the same sins whereby Adam fell, and others miscarry every day. He felt the curse of sin,

the wrath of God, agonies in his soul, violent pains in his body, sorrows to the death from the cradle to the cross : and in every matter of grief and suffering in soul, in body, from the world, from Satan, from God, in all kinds of temptations spiritual and temporal ; experiencing the evils of this life. hunger, thirst, weariness, grief, Isa. liii. 3—10, even such as we are liable to, all of them really and truly like ours, and more powerfully than ours ; they were for similitude like, but for degree exceeding them ; ours, for exquisiteness of sense, but a shadow of his. Yet under all these temptations he was sinless, as the Holy One of God ; never did temptation prevail over him, he overcame all. Nothing was out of place or order by his sufferings in him : all his affections and passions under these, regular, showing his innocency under variety of sufferings, and eminency of compassions. Sin hardens bowels, but he is compassionate without any mixture with or hinderance by corruption ; and his intercession is the more effectual with God for us. What Christian under his conduct would not follow his great example, so to resist and conquer by him ?

16 ᵘ Let us therefore come boldly unto the throne of grace, that we may obtain mercy, and find grace to help in time of need. u Eph. 2. 18. & 3. 12. ch. 10. 19, 21, 22.

Let us therefore come boldly unto the throne of grace : since our High Priest hath a sense of our infirmities, hath experienced our trials, and no sin is in him to shut up his bowels of compassion, therefore haste we to him, as those who desire to reach favours from our Sovereign, as our poor, guilty, needy souls want them. It is a soul-motion by faith and love, breathed forth in strong cries to his God and Father and ours, constantly approaching God in every duty by him ; compare chap. x. 19—22 ; and that with open face, boldness, and assurance, without any shame or dismay, coming in the name and with the person of our great High Priest, who takes our duties and persons, and presents them, perfumed with the incense of his merits, to him. Away now with all unbelief, doubtings, or fears in our approach to him ; admission to him, and hearing by him, is now certain unto the believer, Rom. v. 1, 2 ; Eph. ii. 18 ; iii. 12 ; 1 John iii. 21, 22 ; v. 14, 15. For his throne, now the Father is propitiated by him, is from a throne of strict justice made a throne of grace, of which the propitiatory seat over the ark of the covenant in the holy of holiest, both in the tabernacle and temple, was a type. All the terror and dread of it is now done away by Christ. Thunderings, and lightnings, and voices, and the sound of a trumpet are now ceased ; the still voice of pardon, peace, purging and saving sinners, proceeds from it ; grace, in reference to believers, sits in all its glory, and majesty, and power only, Rev. v. 1. 6. 13 ; compare chap. viii. 1 ; xii. 2 ; Eph. i. 20. Christ now takes us by the hand, brings us thither, and pleads by his own blood for us, so as we may approach to it with greatest confidence. *That we may obtain mercy, and find grace to help in time of need;* that we may actually partake of the fruits of Christ's purchase and intercession from the Father of mercy ; pity suitable to our misery, pardon for our guilty souls, and relief for us under all our afflictions, Isa. lxiii. 7—9, and all grace necessary for us at all times for a seasonable help, but especially in times of greatest need. It is most opportune, when most helpful : when infirmities, afflictions, temptations, and the snares of sin, beset us with grievous persecutions, then may we by prayer, through our High Priest, have recourse to this throne of grace for our suitable and sufficient supply, without which there is no holding fast our profession, or possibility of entrance into God's rest.

CHAP. V

Concerning the office of high priests taken from among men, 1—4; *wherewith Christ's priesthood is compared, and its privileges set forth,* 5—10. *A further account of which is deferred, and for what reason,* 11—14.

FOR every High Priest taken from among men ᵃ is ordained for men ᵇ in things *pertaining* to God, ᶜ that he may offer both gifts and sacrifices for sins :

a ch. 8. 3. b ch. 2. 17. c ch. 8. 3, 4. & 9. 9. & 10. 11. & 11. 4.

HEBREWS V

For every high priest taken from among men: for is a rational particle, enforcing the truth of what was asserted concerning the gospel High Priest before, that he was the most sensible and tender-hearted of all other, beyond what all his types were, even Aaron himself: how did it therefore behove those Hebrews to cleave to him and his religion, as to desert the Levitical priesthood which he had perfected in himself; he being more excellent for rise, qualities, office, call, than his preceding types, and the permanent truth of them all! For every one of that order in God's institution, and according to his law, ought to be selected out of the numbers of men for whom he was to minister, and therefore to be a man. He was not to be an angel, nor to minister for them; and being separated from men, is to be put into another and higher rank and order, Exod. xxviii. 1, than he was in before: no person was to usurp it, but to be designed to it according to the Divine law settled in that behalf. This was accomplished in Christ's person, and he hath not since selected out of men any such order of priests properly so called in the Christian church. His officers being so far from being high priests, that they are not so much as in the enumeration of their titles styled ἱερεῖς, priests; and as far is it from truth, that there are now as priests, so altars, sacrifices, temples in the Christian church properly so called; since it is expressly against the New Testament, and if so spoken of by the fathers, it must be understood figuratively and metaphorically, or else it is untrue. *Is ordained for men in things pertaining to God;* καθίσταται, the designed person, is constituted and set over others for their good, to seek either temporal or spiritual good, as the office is: compare chap. viii. 3. By this ordination is power conveyed to this officer, and an obligation laid on him by a charge to exert it about things wherein men are concerned with God: he is a religious officer. Τὰ is imperfect, as chap. ii. 7, for ἐν τοῖς, in things, or κατὰ τὰ, about things. A sinner can undertake to manage nothing towards God immediately, or by himself, but with a mediating priest, who must know God's mind and perform it; and it was infinite mercy for God to institute such a help to sinners. The common sense of mankind about it since the fall doth evince it; no nation being without a religion, a temple, a place of worship, or a priest. *That he may offer both gifts and sacrifices for sins;* who may bring home to God, the supreme Lord and King of all, gifts, which were those free-will offerings, as of things inanimate, the first-fruits of corn, wine, and oil, &c., or of sacrifices, such whereby they were to atone and propitiate God for their sins, they being guilty, and he just; those were necessary to satisfy his justice, remove his wrath, and procure his blessing. What those sacrifices were which would please him, God only could reveal, as who should offer them both for himself and others; and this he did reveal to Adam, Noah, and Abraham, and to Moses fully in his law given him about them on the mount, and of which he hath written in his last four books.

2 ᵈWho ‖ can have compassion on the ignorant, and on them that are out of the way; for that ᵉhe himself also is compassed with infirmity.

ᵈ ch. 2. 18. & 4. 15.
‖ Or, *can reasonably bear with.*
ᵉ ch. 7. 28.

Who can have compassion on the ignorant: the melting quality of the typical high priest is eminently to be fulfilled in the gospel one; each is to have an aptness, disposition, and a sufficiency of it, by the institution of God, for his ministrations, for manner as well as for matter, chap. ii. 18; iv. 15. Μετριοπαθεῖν, strictly, is to bear, suffer, or be affected in measure, or suffer moderately, with the failings of others, in such a degree as is necessary to incline, as far as he is able, to succour, help, and comfort those who are in misery. It notes sympathy, chap. ii. 18; Rom. xii. 15; and a suffering with them, yet so regulated by the Divine rule, as not to extend it unto unfit subjects, nor in an undue measure, lest it unfits him for ministering for them. But the great High Priest excelleth in this, and is not bound to our measures, but sinlessly overabounds in it, to such as sin for want of knowledge of their duty, unwittingly, and without any forecast, for which the law provided a sacrifice, Lev. iv. 2; Numb. xv. 24—29. *And on them that are out of the way;* πλανωμένοις· a metaphor borrowed from travellers gone out of their way; by which are understood such sinners as are misled by infirmity or violence of temptation, and so offend God by their opinions or practices; for the expiation of such were those sacrifices appointed, Lev. v. 6, 7; but then they were such as were sensible of their sins, confessed them, and begged for pardon, of whom the High Priest was to be compassionate; but not of presumptuous and capital sinners, who were unfit subjects of God's mercy or man's: there being no sacrifices provided for such, but they were to die without mercy, Numb. xv. 30, 31; compare Exod. xxii. 14. God's altar itself is no protection to them, 1 Kings ii. 28, 31. Such sins of infirmity which the Levitical high priest was liable to himself, was he to be compassionate of. *For that he himself also is compassed with infirmity;* for that he was beset with infirmity, sin, ignorance, error, and disobedience; infirm in respect of duty and sacrifice, which was by reason of its weakness to be repeated yearly, chap. x. 1, 11; and of the same infirm nature, liable to the griefs and miseries of his brethren both in soul and body. All these did surround and lie about him; he was sin and weakness all over, and therefore should be the more feeling of his brethren's states, and more careful and ready to sacrifice and intercede for himself and them. But our great High Priest hath all the sense of these, but no sin, chap. iv. 15.

3 And ᶠby reason hereof he ought, as for the people, so also for himself, to offer for sins.

ᶠ Lev. 4. 3. & 9. 7. & 16. 6, 15, 16, 17. ch. 7. 27. & 9. 7.

This connexion demonstrates the infirmity of the legal high priest: for this their infirmity, sins of ignorance and error. *And by reason hereof he ought, as for the people;* he was obliged to his work by the express law of God, Lev. i. It is a rule for what the priests ought to do, and so is the whole book, to which they are to be punctually obedient, even to sacrifice for particular sinners in the church, as they were guilty and brought their sacrifice, Lev. iv., and for the whole church of Israel on the atonement day, Lev. xvi. 15—34. *So also for himself, to offer for sins;* he had also his proper sacrifice for his own sins commonly, Lev. iv. 3, extraordinarily on the day of atonement annually, Lev. xvi. 6—14. It is not necessary to a priest to be a sinner, but it is to be merciful. Adam offered prayers and praises to his Creator for himself and Eve in innocency; but since the fall our Lord Jesus Christ is the only High Priest without sin, and yet most merciful, as well as most sensible of the sins and miseries of penitent believing sinners. He offers up the sacrifice to God truly propitiatory, as his types did the typical ones, and procured the pardon which God promised to give upon his so sacrificing to him.

4 ᵍAnd no man taketh this honour unto himself, but he that is called of God, as ʰwas Aaron.

ᵍ 2 Chron. 26. 18.
John 3. 27.
ʰ Ex. 28. 1.
Num. 16. 5, 40. 1 Chron. 23. 13.

This connecteth the last thing describing the typical Levitical priesthood, their call to it. *And no man taketh this honour unto himself;* not any person whatsoever hath or can lawfully take to himself the honourable office of a high priest, so as to be the author or end of it. Many have usurped this office, and others have distributed it contrary to God's law, whose priesthood, offerings, and ministry are no true ones, especially where men are self-officiating, corruptly managing of it, as Eli's sons and Jeroboam's priests, or self-benefiting by it, 1 Sam. ii. 13, &c.; Micah iii. 11. This was so honourable an office as it was united to the princedom in Melchisedec and Jethro. *But he that is called of God, as was Aaron;* he that is according to God's law, (the Author of this priesthood, its work and success,) qualified in himself, separated from others, and actually honoured by God with it, he ought to take this office and execute his work in it to God's glory, depending on him for his blessing. Aaron is the particular instance of the Divine call to this office. God separated his tribe, family, and person for his service in the room of the first-born: God qualified him for it, entailed the high priesthood to his seed and offspring with the subordinate priesthood. He solemnly consecrated him by Moses, confirmed him in his work by fire from heaven at his first sacrifice, and vindicates his own call of him to it by the blossoming rod, and destroying the rivals with him for it, Exod. xxviii. 29, 30; Numb. xvi. 35; xvii. 5.

5 ⁱSo also Christ glorified not himself to be made an High Priest; but he that

ⁱ John 8. 54.

said unto him, *Thou art my Son, to day have I begotten thee.*

The Spirit now draws the parallel, and shows, that whatsoever is requisite in God's high priest, is transcendently fulfilled in the Lord Jesus Christ, the infirmities of his types, which were accidental to the office, excepted. *So also Christ glorified not himself to be made an High Priest:* he begins the parallel in his call to it: God-man, the great gospel High Priest, anointed to this office in the flesh with the Holy Ghost, was not tainted with ambition, neither did usurp this honour and dignity, John viii. 54, though there never was person qualified for it, or deserved it, like him. He never did intrude himself upon the office, or take the sacerdotal power to him, whatever others have done, and usurped it. *But he that said unto him;* but God the Father bespeaketh him, and calleth him to this high office, as he did Aaron: he chose him, separated, sent, and anointed him for it. No less person than the eternal Jehovah could constitute and invest him in what was so high for dignity, so glorious for power; he did by speaking commission him for it, and did publish and testify the constitution, glorifying him in it, as is testified, Psal. ii. 7. *Thou art my Son: Thou,* is not David, but Christ, as is interpreted, chap. i. 5; Acts xiii. 33. Art my only begotten Son, my natural Son, John i. 14, 18; the first-born of God, Psal. lxxxix. 27; compare Rom. viii. 29; Col. i. 18. As his Son, the Father could appoint him to what calling he pleased. By his primogeniture he had right to the priesthood and kingship; and to these doth the Father call him, as who would not be denied by him. *To-day have I begotten thee;* from eternity he had a right and title to this office, but his solemn investiture in it was on the resurrection day, then was he begotten to it; not only dedicated, as Hannah did Samuel to the priesthood, but solemnly, after his consecration by his own blood to it, chap. ix. 10—12, 23, 24, compare Rom. i. 4, was he by the Father proclaimed to be the Son-mediator, King, Priest, and Prophet, and made to enter the holy of holiest in heaven, and to sit down there on his Father's right hand, invested with glory and power for the execution of his offices, and this of his priesthood in special, which he is daily fulfilling with him by his intercession: see chap. vii. 25, 28; ix. 24; compare Psal. ii. 8.

6 As he saith also in another *place,* ¹Thou *art* a Priest for ever after the order of Melchisedec.

As he saith also in another place, Thou art a Priest for ever: the Spirit proves his call and investiture into this office, its confirmation to him for ever, by another testimony of the Father about it, penned by David, Psal. cx. 4, and ratified to be so by the Lord himself, Matt. xxii. 41—45; that he as man was David's Son: as God-man, David's Lord, and the grand officer to atone God by his sacrifice for sinners, and to intercede for them. By this word of God to him was he invested with the most glorious priesthood, and settled in that which he must execute for ever, chap. vii. 24, having no successor in it. *After the order of Melchisedec;* which order was a singular and most excellent one, such as Aaron's did but imperfectly shadow to us. It was a royal priesthood God installed him in, such as was Melchisedec's, largely described, chap. vii. This was by God the Father revealed to David, and prophesied by him to the church, but actually fulfilled as to proclamation and inauguration at his ascension into the holy of holiest in heaven, where he actually in the flesh doth officiate and minister in it.

7 Who in the days of his flesh, when he had ᵐ offered up prayers and supplications ⁿ with strong crying and tears unto him °that was able to save him from death, and was heard ‖ᵖ in that he feared;

Here Christ is paralleled in his nature, work, and compassions, to his types, and is set above them. *Who in the days of his flesh:* he was taken out of men, as his type was, ver. 1. He was made flesh, and dwelt among us in the human nature, John i. 14. He had his days numbered, and his time set for his being and ministry beneath, doing and suffering the will of God here in a state of humiliation, frailty, and mortality; which infirmities attending his flesh, are now put off for ever, chap. ii. 14. *When he had offered up prayers and supplications:* he performed his service and offering to God, as his types, for the men for whom he was ordained, such as he delighted in; his prayers represented his inward desires to God for what he needed, and was necessary in our behalf to be obtained, a sacrifice fit to be offered by him, chap. xiii. 15; compare 1 Pet. ii. 5. Ἱκετηρίας, a word but this once used in the New Testament; its root signifieth an olive branch, which petitioners carried in their hands; an emblem of the vehement desire of such supplicants of a peaceful answer or return to their prayers. These of Christ were the most fervent supplications, flowing from a deeply afflicted soul in a prostrate body, when he was preparing for the offering up his soul a sacrifice for sin, when he was in the garden, Luke xxii. 40, 46, in his agony, and when actually offering it on the cross, Matt. xxvii. 46. These were the prayers of God-man, the gospel High Priest. *With strong crying and tears,* put up by him unto God the Father, who is essentially good and powerful, willing and able to hear and answer his supplications, the fountain of all mercy, blessing, and help, who could deliver him from, and save him in, the greatest dangers, so as none of those which encompassed him should hurt him, no, not death; for he was delivered from the evils which were far more dreadful to him than death itself, and which were to exercise him both before and at the hour of death. Those deadly temptations which he underwent in his agony and on the cross, and from which he chargeth the disciples to pray, that both he and they might be kept, Matt. xxvi. 37, 38. Those deadly stings in his soul, ver. 41; Mark xiv. 38; Luke xxii. 40, 46; such conflicts as his Father supported him under, carried him through, and gave him the victory over all that curse and power that might do him or his mystical body hurt. It was this death of deaths that did terrify him. As for the other, he cheerfully underwent it, resigned his spirit to his Father, trusted his body in his treasury, and was so far from being swallowed up by it, that he was gloriously risen from it. *Unto him that was able to save him from death;* evident in his agony, in the mighty groans that his soul poured out then when *he prayed more earnestly,* Luke xxii. 44; that which made him sweat through his flesh congealed clots of blood, squeezed by his agony out of his body, which made him weep and cry loudly; his voice as well as his soul was stretched out in prayer: the like was exercised by him in his conflict on the cross, Matt. xxvii. 46. How bitter was his passion to him! How fervent, importunate, and loud his prayers! How did it break through the cloud wherewith God covered his face then! Psal. xxii. represents in prophecy what was now fulfilled, Mark xv. 34, 37; Luke xxiii. 46: It was in making satisfaction to the justice of God for us that these were exercised, to show his inward compassions to us, and to secure sustentation for us in our sufferings by temptations, chap. ii. 17, 18; iv. 15, 16. *And was heard in that he feared;* the efficacy of these mighty prayers and supplications is evident by their reaching God's ear, and procuring his help for him. He was helped, delivered, saved; so the Septuagint use this word in the Old Testament, putting hearing for helping and saving, as in Psal. lv. 16—18; 2 Chron. xviii. 31: ἀπὸ τῆς εὐλαβείας, this is the right acceptation strictly read; for as a thing is truly apprehended, it stirreth up fear. This word hath in Scripture use two senses: 1. From the thing feared, by a metonymy, fear being put for that which works it, which was not here death simply, for that he suffered, but what he was more afraid of than death, viz. from the fear of being by his temptations hurried into diffidence of his Father, impatience in his agony, or despair at the eclipse in his death, which the devil designed. As to this his Father did hear, answer, and help him; in his agony sent his angel to strengthen him, Luke xxii. 43; and which he perfected for him at the end of his passion, when he breathed out his soul triumphantly into his Father's hands, Matt. xxvii. 46, 50; Mark xv. 37, 39; John xix. 28—30. Or, 2. From the fear, that godly fear and care in him not to displease God in any thing he did or suffered; this was a proper cause of his acceptance, and his prayer being heard, and his deliverance, which is becoming the Mediator. This is a truth, and may be admitted; but it seemeth especially to refer to the former by his prevalency, against which by prayer he defeated the devil, was made feelingly sensible of his temptations, showed himself compassed with infirmities, though not with sinful ones, and as our High Priest was rendered pitiful and compassionate to us under our temptations, so as to intercede for us above, as he did pray for himself on earth, and to procure for us succour under and deliverance from them.

q ch. 3. 6.
r Phil. 2. 8.

8 *Though he were a Son, yet learned he ʳobedience by the things which he suffered;

He fulfilled his type in the end; for though he were God the Son incarnate, in a nearer and more excellent relation to the Father than any angel, or any high priest among men his types, being all servants to his Father and him; God's Son by eternal generation as to his Deity, by conception from the Holy Ghost by the virgin as to his humanity, who for his worth might have been exempted from such burdens; yet did God teach him (not as if he wanted it at any time) by what he imposed and commanded him, and he learnt by what he did agree and covenant to perform, active obedience to God's will, fulfilling all righteousness, being for his person, and doing for his work to a tittle what God required from him; but especially passive obedience, by his experience knowing what it meant, freely subjecting himself to his state of humiliation, Phil. ii. 6—8, enduring all the indignities and sufferings for sinners from his birth to his death, even the most vile and cursed. This the Father enjoined and commanded him, and he did obey it: read Isa. liii. He who offered prayers for himself, as a high priest offered himself a sacrifice for us, as ours. By this did he finish his Father's will entirely, experimentally, feelingly, knowing how difficult patience under the cross is, and how to pity us under all our sufferings.

s ch. 2. 10.
& 11. 40.

9 And ˢbeing made perfect, he became the author of eternal salvation unto all them that obey him;

And being made perfect: as to the powerful execution of his office, this God-man exceeds his types; for having consummated all the work to which he was designed, by his doing, suffering, dying, rising, and ascending into heaven in the human nature, he perfected the work of redemption, and consecrated himself to his office. *He became the author of eternal salvation unto all them that obey him:* by this was he constituted, made, and declared by his Father to be, not an instrument, as all his types were, but the cause efficient, meritorious, and exemplar of salvation; by his sacrifice satisfying God's justice, meriting and effecting reconciliation and justification for sinners; and on his ascension sends forth the Holy Ghost, to qualify them for the reception of his benefits, by working in them what he requires; and on their application to him, he, as their High Priest, pleads the merit of his blood, and intercedes for their justification and salvation, which is the freeing them from all evil, criminal and penal, sin, and whatever it subjecteth them to in this world, or that which is to come; and instating them into all the heavenly privileges promised in the covenant of grace, righteousness, holiness, heirship to, and life and glory with, God, and to be safe in the possession of them all, not for time only, but for eternity. This efficient cause produceth this only to the duly qualified subject: mankind is rendered salvable by the obedience and sacrifice of this High Priest; but it is only to penitent believing sinners that he doth communicate this, and for whom he effects it; those who will entirely submit themselves to Christ as a Lord and King, and be loyal to him and obey him, as well as to a Priest or a Saviour, continuing his faithful subjects to the end, John iii. 16, 18, 36; compare Matt. x. 22.

t ver. 6.
ch. 6. 20.

10 Called of God an High Priest ᵗafter the order of Melchisedec.

His constitution by God the Father in his office, maketh it so effectual; he was solemnly proclaimed and declared to be what God had constituted him. God nameth or calleth things as they are, and as he hath made them; and this was done openly, and with the most illustrious solemnity, at his ascension into heaven, when God set him down on his right hand in the presence of all the surrounding angels, who did all submit to him as their Head and King, and acknowledge him as the great royal High Priest of God, as was foretold, Psal. cx. 1, 2; which words of the psalmist the Spirit further explaineth in chap. vii., where he proves this gospel High Priest to be of a more excellent order than Aaron's, even like that of Melchisedec, which it exceedeth, and which must last for ever.

11 Of whom ᵘwe have many things to say, and hard to be uttered, seeing ye are ˣdull of hearing.

u John 16. 12.
2 Pet. 3. 16.
x Mat. 13. 15.

The Spirit here digresseth from discoursing further of the priesthood of Christ, that he may fit these Hebrews to apprehend and improve it when he shall return to it, chap. vii. He beginneth with a reproof, which takes up the remainder of the chapter, and enters on it artificially from the doctrine delivered of Christ's priesthood, insinuating the difficulty of its reception by them. *Of whom we have many things to say, and hard to be uttered:* οὗ, *of whom,* some would make to refer to Melchisedec, but by what followeth in this and chap. vii., it can be spoken of none but of Christ the truth of that type, who was made a High Priest after that order. And of him the apostle was filled by the Spirit with the matter, as Elihu speaks, Job xxxii. 18. Much he had to say of this mystery, which was most excellent and weighty, and which a few words could not express; for it was δυσερμήνευτος, not unutterable in itself, or difficult for him to open and interpret, but for them to understand. *Seeing ye are dull of hearing;* because the ears of their mind were not created nor proportioned to it: they were babes and children in understanding; the difficulty was in themselves, not in the word or mystery; their intellectual faculty was slow to discern, perceive, and judge of this doctrine, and their hearts were averse to it, being so conceited concerning the Levitical priesthood: such were the apostles at the first, John xvi. 12.

12 For when for the time ye ought to be teachers, ye have need that one teach you again which *be* ʸthe first principles of the oracles of God; and are become such as have need of ᶻmilk, and not of strong meat.

y ch. 6. 1.
z 1 Cor. 3. 1, 2, 3.

For when for the time ye ought to be teachers: the conviction of this fault in their understanding and will, is by the Spirit demonstrated; for their dulness proceeded from their neglect of God's means of knowledge, and so was inexcusable; they had time and means enough of improving in the knowledge of this gospel doctrine of Christ's priesthood, and to have gained in them the abilities of teachers of their families, fellow Christians, and neighbours, both from the law of Moses, and the other Scriptures, and by the teaching of Christ and his apostles. *Ye have need that one teach you again which be the first principles;* yet such was their negligence and idleness, that their knowledge was diminished and lost, and they fallen off to the old Mosaical economy of priesthood, ceremonies and services, so as they had need again to be taught and instructed by others which are the στοιχεῖα of God's oracles in the Scriptures, such things as are the first in order, and first to be taught and learnt, the very fundamental principles of Christianity, without the knowledge of which none can be saved, and on which all others do depend. They are so styled by a metaphor, signifying such a state of this in the Scripture, as the elements have in natural bodies which they compound; or, like elements of speech, which must be first attained before there can be either an understanding, speaking, or writing of a language; they are the foundation upon which a system of the Christian religion is raised; see chap. vi. 1: which principles lie dispersed in the New Testament, and are summed up in those ancient creeds which are agreeable to our Saviour's words. *Of the oracles of God:* λογιῶν τῷ Θεῷ, such oracles or revelations of God's mind about the way of our salvation, which he hath made to us by his Son our High Priest, and which he brought from heaven with him, and taught himself, as chap. i. 1, 2; and hath by the inspiration of his Spirit of persons chosen on purpose by him, penned them eminently in the Scriptures of the New Testament, not excluding those of the Old Testament, which are unveiled, opened, and made glorious in them, Rom. iii. 2. *And are become such as have need of milk, and not of strong meat:* these Hebrews had so greatly forgotten these first principles, that they were become mere babes and infants in knowledge, they needed the first and weakest spiritual food, metaphorically styled *milk;* the most plain and easy truths of the gospel, such as they may understand, and give light to others; not the beggarly elements of Judaism, as they are styled, Gal. iv. 3, 9, and Col. ii. 8, 20, which would keep them ignorant babes in the word of righteousness, and unfit them for the understanding and digesting the stronger food of the higher and more excellent doctrines of the gospel concerning Christ's priesthood. Such a babe was Nicodemus, though a master in Israel, John iii. 10, 12.

† Gr. *hath no experience.*
a 1 Cor. 13.
11. & 14. 20.
Eph. 4. 14.
1 Pet. 2. 2.

13 For every one that useth milk † *is* unskilful in the word of righteousness: for he is ᵃa babe.

The Spirit proves these Hebrews such infants by describing the state of them, and of their contrary, and tacitly applying it to them under a metaphor or allegory started by him before. *For every one that useth milk;* for, saith he, every one of you who take in nothing but the elements and weakest kind of doctrines, and can bear no other, have not digested the first principles of the oracles of God. *Is unskilful in the word of righteousness;* are ἄπειρος, not truly knowing, not proving nor experiencing, never exercised or practised in, *the word of righteousness,* the gospel doctrine, which is in itself an eternal certain truth, the revelation of the righteousness of God to faith, Rom. i. 16, 17, and the instrumental conveyer of it to faith; a perfect rule of righteousness, making Christians conform exactly to the mind and will of God, and so reaching the state of strong and perfect ones, Col. i. 25—29. *For he is a babe;* he is but a new-born Christian, a child in Christ's school, one that cannot be experienced in the perfections of God's word, because he is weak in knowledge, ignorant and unconstant like an infant, 1 Cor. xiv. 20; compare Eph. iv. 13.

‖ Or, *perfect.*
1 Cor. 2. 6.
Eph. 4. 13.
Phil. 3. 15.
‖ Or, *of an habit,* or, *perfection.*
b Is. 7. 15.
1 Cor. 2. 14, 15.

14 But strong meat belongeth to them that are ‖of full age, *even* those who by reason ‖of use have their senses exercised ᵇ to discern both good and evil.

But strong meat belongeth to them that are of full age; but those great, deep, and high mysteries of the gospel concerning Christ's natures, their hypostatical union, his offices, his actual fulfilling all his types in the Old Testament both personal and mystical, with the prophecies of his gospel church state, and his mediatory kingdom, &c., these are the strong meat and food of grown Christians, who have reached some maturity in the knowledge of these gospel mysteries, and are of a full age in understanding, 1 Cor. ii. 6; xiv. 20; Phil. iii. 15; reaching on to the measure of the stature of the fulness of Christ in knowledge and grace, Eph. iv. 13. *Even those who by reason of use;* even those who διὰ τὴν ἕξιν, by a gracious habit of wisdom and knowledge infused and perfected by long study, practice, and exercise of themselves in the word of righteousness, by which they are able to apprehend and improve the highest doctrines of the mystery of Christ. *Have their senses:* τὰ αἰσθητήρια are, strictly, organs or instruments of sense, as the eye, the tongue, and the hand, by a metonymy, express seeing, tasting, and feeling; and so is by analogy applied to the inward senses and faculties of the soul, whereby they discern and relish gospel doctrines. *Exercised:* γεγυμνασμένα strictly notes such an exercise as wrestlers use for a victory with all their might and strength, being trained up to it by long exercise. The spiritual organs or faculties of Christians are well instructed, practised, made apt and ready, as the external ones are, for their proper work. *To discern both good and evil:* πρὸς διάκρισιν, for the discerning and differencing things, so as the mind discerns what doctrine is true and what is false by the word of righteousness, and the will chooseth what is good and refuseth what is evil, the affections love good and hate evil. As the senses external can by exercise discern what food is gustful, pleasing, and wholesome for the person, and what is nauseous and unwholesome; so the grown Christian is improved by the exercise of his spiritual senses, that can by his enlightened mind discern higher gospel doctrines, and by his renewed will relish the sublimer mysteries of Christ as they are revealed to him. Such the Christian Hebrews ought to have been, so able proficients in the school of Christ.

CHAP. VI

The higher doctrines of Christianity are proposed to be treated of, 1—3. *The guilt and danger of apostacy,* 4—9. *Charitable deeds will not be forgotten of God,* 10. *An exhortation diligently to imitate the faith and patience of those who inherit the promises,* 11, 12. *The promise of God to Abraham a sure ground of hope,* 13—20.

THEREFORE ᵃleaving ‖the principles of the doctrine of Christ, let us go on unto perfection; not laying again the foundation of repentance ᵇfrom dead works, and of faith toward God,

a Phil. 3. 12, 13, 14.
ch. 5. 12.
‖ Or, *the word of the beginning of Christ.*
b ch. 9. 14.

The Spirit having reproved these Hebrews for their fault, doth now counsel and direct them to amend it. *Therefore leaving the principles of the doctrine of Christ;* seeing ye have lost so much time already, and made so little progress in learning Christ, let us not therefore stay any longer in the principles of it, but proceed to some higher degree: pursuant to which he layeth down the principles of Christian doctrine in which these Hebrews had been initiated, and the doctrine of perfection which they were to pursue. *Leaving* is an omitting or letting go, as to any sticking or standing in, so as to make no further progress, but to gain higher degrees of knowledge in the doctrine of the gospel, which enters novices into Christ, having attained the beginning, the matter or work of entrance into the Christian religion, now not to stick at this first and imperfect inchoation in this doctrine. *Let us go on unto perfection;* a regular motion must succeed, according to the great Mover, incessantly, for our attaining the perfection of the doctrine of Christ. This *perfection* notes height of knowledge, faith, utmost repentance and spiritual change, greatest strength of understanding, and the fullest operation, according to the doctrine of Christ, in doing and forbearing, the fullest perseverance of the mind in the knowledge of it, and of the will in cleaving to it. *Not laying again the foundation:* that which would hinder this was reiterating foundation work, which the apostle laid with them by initiating of them into the first principles of Christianity, the knowledge and faith of which they professed to receive, 1 Cor. iii. 11; Eph. ii. 20, and were therefore obliged to proceed in the building both of persons and truths on it; and lest they had forgot, or others were ignorant, what those fundamental principles and doctrines of the gospel were, he layeth down six heads of them in this and ver. 2, which was the common method of teaching either the children of Christians or infidels, that they might be Christians, at least professedly, or upon their lapse to restore them. *Of repentance from dead works:* the first Christian principle or doctrine to be learnt, was that of *repentance,* which is the fundamental change of a sinner's mind, and, in that, of himself; it carrieth in it knowledge, conviction of sin by God's law, bitter sorrow for it, and full conversion of the soul to God from it, as it is described, 2 Cor. vii. 9—11; as from all sinful works flowing from it while lapsed from God; dead in sins, which would have eaten out and destroyed their souls for ever, Rom. vi. 23; Eph. ii. 1, 2. It supposeth the knowledge of other truths preceding it, as their creation in God's image, their apostacy from it, the misery consequent, &c. These Hebrews were to proceed and advance daily in the exercise of this grace. *And of faith towards God:* the second Christian principle or doctrine is of *faith on God,* comprehending the habit and acts of that Divine grace, of evidence, subsistence, assent, and affiance, chap. xi. 1, all the effects of it; and this exercised on God in his essence, relations, especially in his gracious contrivance and execution of the work of redemption for sinners; as giving reconciliation, righteousness, holiness, adoption, and eternal salvation, through Christ, fulfilling all righteousness by his death, as a sacrifice satisfying his justice, and meriting, as purchasing, all these blessings for believers, and effectually from heaven is dispensing them to them.

2 ᶜOf the doctrine of baptisms, ᵈand of laying on of hands, ᵉand of resurrection of the dead, ᶠand of eternal judgment.

Of the doctrine of baptisms: the third fundamental doctrine in which these Hebrews were initiated was, the *doctrine of baptisms;* containing in it the doctrine which baptism teacheth, as that of the covenant of grace, of which it is a sign and seal, and of their entering into it who partake of it, which, as to its duties and privileges, is sealed and confirmed: and the doctrine in which baptisms are taught, as that of Christ by water and by the Spirit, Matt. iii. 6; John iii. 5; and containing in it the doctrine of the seals of God's testament, distinct from the other doctrines of faith; by the use of which, such who had solemnly professed their repentance, and faith and obedience to the gospel, were sealed and confirmed. *Baptisms*, in the plural, raiseth the doubt, whether it immediately concern the initial seal of the covenant, which some say is so styled as a Hebraism, the plural number being put for the singular; or, from the numerous partakers of it at set times, which were called days of baptisms, or from divers administrators, and the baptisms of believers and their seed, and that so they were many. Others would make these to be Jewish baptisms, frequently used by these Hebrews, as elements to teach faith and repentance, and leading them to the further knowledge of Christ. And the more they suspect this, because these baptisms are used but four times in the New Testament, and always signifying Jewish ones, as chap. ix. 10, and Mark vii. 4, 8. *And of laying on of hands:* the fourth fundamental doctrine, or principle, was, *the imposition of hands*, which by Christ and his apostles were used either for healing diseases, Mark vi. 5; Luke iv. 40; Acts xxviii. 8, or communication of blessing, Matt. xix. 13, 15, or for the communication of the extraordinary gifts of the Holy Ghost, to such who were separated for Christ's service in his church, Acts vi. 6; viii. 17; xiii. 3; xix. 5, 6; and so take in all the saving fruits of the Holy Ghost, by which they are renewed, increased, strengthened, and built up into everlasting life. Others would make this a primitive rite of confirming the baptized grown up, on the confession of their faith, and renewing their covenant with God, which was made for and with them in their infancy, and so was a preparatory admission of them to communicate with the church in the Lord's supper. If other places of Scripture did concur with it, it would be more clear and satisfactory. Some look on them, as *baptisms* before, to be Jewish rites, which should here lead them to Christ; but, on their neglect of him, became beggarly elements, and such as they are called from here unto higher attainments in Christ. *And of resurrection of the dead:* the fifth fundamental principle and doctrine of Christianity, in which they were initiated, is, the doctrine of *resurrection from the dead*. This, as to the propriety and fulness of it, is at the last day; yet the entrance into this is begun in a new life effected by the resurrection of Jesus Christ, John v. 25—29; Rom. vi. 3—13. From this entrance are they called to make out to the full resurrection of the just, as the apostle did himself, Phil. iii. 10—12. This article of the gospel doctrine all Christians were to be founded in, and especially these Hebrews, because it was denied by the Sadducees among them, Matt. xxii. 23; Acts xxiii. 6—8, derided by the Athenian philosophers, Acts xvii. 18, 31, 32, and perverted by heretics, 2 Tim. ii. 17, 18; and is therefore particularly asserted, as described by this apostle, 1 Cor. xv. *And of eternal judgment;* the sixth fundamental doctrine and principle of Christianity, into which they were to be initiated, was that of the general *judgment,* finally determining the believers of it to their rewards, the deniers of it to their eternal punishment, because the one hath observed, the other violated, the covenant of grace. These Hebrews had begun to reach this truth, by being reconciled to their Judge, and therefore are to proceed to perfect their work to the Lord's glorious appearance, chap. ix. 27, 28; Acts xvii. 31; 2 Pet. iii. 7, 10, 15; Jude 6, 14, 15; Rev. xx. 11—15.

3 And this will we do, ᵍif God permit.

This connects the prime cause promoting this progress, and by whom alone it can be effected, as well as his resolution of finishing his discourse of the ministry of Christ's priesthood. *And this will we do;* we will really, certainly, and constantly, leave our entrance into these Christian, fundamental principles, and proceed unto perfection in them; all of us real Christians will do this. Others make it a purpose of the apostle to handle these doctrines at another season, and that he will now proceed to instruct them in the higher mysteries of Christ and the gospel, and so finish his designed discourse about them. *If God permit;* whether it refers to their proceeding from the knowledge of the Christian principles to the perfection of knowledge, or of growth in Christian graces, or of the apostle's proceeding to open to them the higher mysteries of the gospel, it is not a kind of passive letting things to be done, or giving leave only; God is not subject to so weak a condition: but it is all act, noting God's assistance as well as permission; for all persons and things are in his power, who worketh to will and to do, Phil. ii. 13. But as to a progress in Christianity and reaching the perfect man, &c., Eph. iv. 13, if he, the Lord of all knowledge and grace, hath delight in us, and will work this grace in us, then we shall do this, even go on unto perfection, chap. xii. 2; Hos. xiv. 5; Mal. iv. 9; 1 Cor. iii. 6.

4 For ʰ*it is* impossible for those ⁱwho were once enlightened, and have tasted of ᵏthe heavenly gift, and ˡwere made partakers of the Holy Ghost,

The foregoing counsel the Spirit enforceth on these Hebrews, from the danger of apostacy, to which the neglect of it doth dispose them, and the terrifying consequents of it, from ver. 4—8. We must go on to perfection, unless we will draw back to perdition; so that he bespeaks them, You have been sluggish and dull, and going backward already; lest you grow worse, stir up yourselves; if you neglect it you are in danger of utter falling away: *for it is impossible*, not in respect of God's absolute and almighty power, but in respect of any created power in others or themselves, justly, and by right, it is impossible, because contrary to God's declared will and resolution in his church, by which his power is limited, so as he will never do it, nor suffer it to be done; in this he will not, cannot deny himself, ver. 11; chap. xi. 6; compare Matt. vii. 18; xix. 24, 26; 2 Tim. ii. 13. *For those who were once enlightened:* φωτισθέντας, several interpreters render, the baptized, who were illuminated with the beams of Divine light; others, the penitent, such who had been initiated into repentance, as ver. 1, and think the term *once* may be limited to baptisms, whereas it refers to all the other particulars. These are such who are instructed in the principles of the Christian religion, and brought out of the darkness and ignorance of Judaism and heathenism, so that they were other persons for the knowledge of gospel truths than before: they see with a new light spiritual things, and have the mind raised up to such objects as they knew not before; but they have no new eyes or understandings given them, and so are but as devils like angels of light, whereas the light of a real Christian is the light of life, John viii. 12: see 2 Tim. i. 10; 2 Pet. i. 19. Such some Hebrews professed themselves to be, Rom. ii. 17—19; and as Balaam was, Numb. xxiv. 2, 3. *And have tasted of the heavenly gift;* an act of sense in the body, put metaphorically for an act of the mind. Tasting in the soul, is an apprehension and reception by it, and but merely such, and no more; a taste, and not a digestion, of Christ and his benefits as revealed to them in the gospel, John iv. 39, 40, followed with the superficial relishes of their joy and peace on their temporary believing in them, as it was with the stony ground, Matt. xiii. 20. A sinner enlightened so as to see Christ and the glorious promises made to believers in him, it being agreeable to his natural principles, and being not much humbled, runs away with them with joy, having good desires and affections, but a stony heart still: such was Herod, Mark vi. 20. *And were made partakers of the Holy Ghost;* not by an inhabitation of his person in them, but by his operations in them, whereby he is trying how far a natural man may be raised, and not have his nature changed: as is evident in Socrates, who died for owning the unity of the Deity; and as the scribe near the kingdom of heaven, Mark xii. 34. He is proving by his gifts to them how much supernatural good, and workings towards salvation, they are capable of, without the putting forth of the exceeding greatness of his power to make them new creatures, as Gen. vi. 3; compare 1 Cor. i. 21; 1 Pet. iii. 18—20. These did partake of from the Holy Ghost, the light of nature, of the law, of the gospel, with some spiritual power accompanying all these; which as they are trials of lapsed nature, so are lessening many punishments by keeping men off from many sins, as 2 Pet. ii. 20. These professors had escaped the gross and outward pollutions and defilements that many were drenched with in their lives, but have lusts abiding unmortified, from whence these would arise in them still; but here is no pure heart or divine nature wrought in them, and the lusting principle is unmortified still; this God accepts according to its kind: compare Mark x. 21, 22.

5 And have tasted the good word of God, and the powers of ᵐthe world to come,

m ch. 2. 5.

And have tasted the good word of God; so as to relish comfort and sweetness in the doctrine and promises of the gospel through self-flattery; for these hearing of pardon of sin, and crediting it, are filled with joy by it; as a condemned malefactor, hearing of a general pardon, believeth himself to be one of the pardoned, and rejoiceth in it: see Matt. xiii. 20, 21; Luke viii. 13. So did many of the Jews rejoice in John's doctrine, John v. 35. *And the powers of the world to come;* thus some of them were affected with the powerful doctrines of the gospel, concerning the final judgment, as their natural conscience was wrought on by the Spirit in the word, that they feel it as it were begun in them, the sparks of the wrath of God having set their consciences in a light flame for their sins, as in a Felix, Acts xxiv. 25. As on the other hand, being acquainted by the Spirit in the word, of Christ's being a Redeemer, to save them from the wrath to come, and to instate them into happiness, beyond what is attainable on earth; self-love doth externally close with the revelation and apply it to itself, as Balaam did, Numb. xxiii. 10. All these five instances are the workings of the Holy Spirit on corrupt nature for its improvement, and in their falling from these supernatural operations, they do sin *in tanto* against the Holy Ghost.

6 If they shall fall away, to renew them again unto repentance; ⁿseeing they crucify to themselves the Son of God afresh, and put *him* to an open shame.

n ch. 10. 29.

If they shall fall away; a falling away, or apostatizing, in proportion like Adam, such a παράπτωμα as his was, Rom. v. 15—17, whereby they are totally unchristianed, as he was turned into a sinner; perfidiously revolting from all those supernatural workings of the Holy Ghost, whereby their natural spirit was elevated, but not changed, unto their old swinish and canine temper of spirit and course of life that they led before they professed themselves Christians, as 2 Pet. ii. 18—22. They freely forsake their professed Christian state, and make shipwreck of all, Jude 4, 10, 16, 18, 19. Whether πάλιν, *again,* ought to be referred to falling away, so as to denominate the apostate no Christian, as he was at first, before his profession, or to renewing following, it makes no difficulty, for it is a real truth in both parts; only interpreters generally refer it to the latter, as do ours, and so we shall consider it. *To renew them again unto repentance;* they cannot renew and bring themselves to the same state they enjoyed, and from which they fell; nor can the Christian ministry do it by their exhortations or counsels, thunders or comforts; the offended, wronged Spirit withdraws, and will not assist or elevate theirs to act above nature again, Gen. vi. 33; Isa. lxiii. 10; but leaves them justly to themselves, so as he will neither by himself, nor by others, suffer it to be done, having limited his power by his will in it. They shall neither have a new principle infused into them, nor their minds or hearts changed by him to repentance, because they have undervalued his lower operations and motions on their souls, revealing Christ to them through the gospel, and have by their sinful negligence not improved them to seek from him the better and higher ones which he mentions, ver. 9, 10, and were to be effected by the exceeding greatness of his power. *Seeing they crucify to themselves the Son of God afresh :* that which renders this renovation of them impossible, is their ill treatment, by their apostacy, of their Redeemer, who was to bring them as children to glory, which they by the gospel knew, and by profession owned him ascended and sat down on the right hand of God, and who had, by the operation of his Spirit, elevated their natural principles so to discern him, and to confess him: by this their apostacy they look on him as an impostor and deceiver, as 2 Pet. ii. 1; Jude 4, and deny him to be a Saviour to them, rejecting his sacrifice, and would, as much as in them lieth, dethrone him, and, if he were within their reach, would crucify him again, and tread him under their feet, as chap. x. 29, and actually do it to him in his members; as the apostate Julian did in former ages, and the papists do at this day. *And put him to an open shame;* παραδειγματίζοντας, making him a public shameful example, as the Jews did by the most cruel and ignominious death, with all their reproachful carriages to him then, which he despised, chap. xii. 2, and in which his are to imitate him, chap. xiii. 13: so do these apostates verbally and practically blaspheme and disgrace him; in their esteem vilifying him, and by their apostacy put him to an open and public ignominy, and make him a spectacle of the vilest reproach, as if they could find no good in him, and therefore renounced him; and this to the condemning and destroying of themselves, since they cannot repent, Christ having not purchased it for, nor God promised it to, any such: so as by the law of his kingdom their sin is irremissible, the blood of Christ, that could only remove it, being profaned and trampled on by it, and so their final destruction unavoidable.

7 For the earth which drinketh in the rain that cometh oft upon it, and bringeth forth herbs meet for them ∥ by whom it is dressed, ᵒreceiveth blessing from God:

∣ Or, *for.*
o Ps. 65. 10.

For the earth which drinketh in the rain that cometh oft upon it : for is narrative here, and not rational, introducing a parabolical illustration of the states and ends of truly regenerate Christians, and unregenerate apostates; as if he said, You have heard the good of true perfect Christians, and the evil of apostates, you need not to be offended at it, or wonder, for it is with them even as with the earth, which is the *good ground* in Christ's parable, Matt. xiii. 8; Luke viii. 8, and which he interpreteth to be *a good and an honest heart,* Luke viii. 15, renewed in a sinner by the Holy Ghost, naturally of the same mould with all others, Ezek. xi. 19; xxxvi. 26, 27. As the earth drinks up the showers moistening and fructifying it, Psal. lxv. 9, 10; so this good and honest heart receiveth the spiritual dews and rain descending from heaven on it in the word and ordinances, as Deut. xxxii. 2. *And bringeth forth herbs meet for them by whom it is dressed ;* it bringeth forth all sorts of fruit for those who dress it, according to God's institution, Gen. i. 11, 12; ii. 5, 6. So these good souls bring forth fruit which God relisheth and delighteth in as suitable to his husbandry, Matt. xiii. 23; compare 2 Pet. i. 5—8; 2 Cor. ix. 10; Gal. v. 22, 23; and such as the great manurer of souls expects from them, 1 Cor. iii. 6, 7, 9. *Receiveth blessing from God;* this good ground is made fruitful by God's blessing, and the more fruitful it is the more blessing it receiveth, Gen. xxvii. 27. This fruitfulness is not the meritorious cause of this blessing, for that issueth from grace; but it qualifieth these good hearts for it, i. e. the continuance to such souls of the means of grace, and their increase in spiritual comforts, till they reach the perfection of blessing from God in eternal life, ver. 9.

8 ᵖBut that which beareth thorns and briers *is* rejected, and *is* nigh unto cursing; whose end *is* to be burned.

p Is. 5. 6.

But that which beareth thorns and briers : δὲ, *but,* introduceth the state and end of a sinful apostate, that ill earth, showered upon as well as the good; the unregenerate soul, that had gospel dews and spiritual rain by the word and ordinances dropped down on it from heaven; yet bringeth forth, or out of it, not herbs or fruits fit for its owner or dresser, but briers, thorns, and thistles: so apostates, under all enlightenings and tasting of these supernatural dews of

HEBREWS VI

the Spirit, bring forth from a stony, unregenerate soul, nothing but corruptions and evils, their rooted lusts thrust out and sprung together with their common gifts, Luke viii. 7, 13, 14; the words and deeds of whom are pernicious, dishonouring God and hurting men, as unbelief, hypocrisy, apostacy, described, 2 Pet. ii. 1—3, 12, 14, 18—22; Jude 4, 8, 10, 12, 16, 19. *Is rejected;* ἀδόκιμος· it is refuse land, neglected by the owner, he takes no care of it; such are these apostates, of a reprobate mind, approving evil, rejecting good, and are so rejected of God, who withdraws his spiritual dews and ordinances, and the concurrence of his Spirit with them, as unworthy of them, and useless as to any good fruit to be produced there. *And is nigh unto cursing;* such are looked upon as the mountains of Gilboa, accursed, 2 Sam. i. 21; and to be dealt with by the owner as the fruitless fig tree by Christ, Matt. xxi. 19; Mark xi. 21. So these apostates are under the curse, 2 Pet. ii. 14; delivered up judicially by Christ to blindness of mind, and hardness of heart, and even to Satan himself, as the unbelieving Jews were, John xii. 40, and those apostates, 1 Tim. i. 19, 20. *Whose end is to be burned;* the end of briers and thorns is the fire, they are to be burnt up by it; and this will be the final issue with apostates, to be destroyed by a Christ whom they have rejected, with eternal fire, chap. x. 27; xii. 29; Matt. iii. 12; xxv. 41; 2 Thess. i. 7—9.

9 But, beloved, we are persuaded better things of you, and things that accompany salvation, though we thus speak.

For preventing of the application of this discourse unto themselves, the apostle subjoins his judgment concerning these Hebrews in this verse, and his reason for it in the next. *But, beloved, we are persuaded better things of you;* although we have spoken of the attainments, states, and ends of apostates, we reflect not on you by it; *but,* or notwithstanding, *we are persuaded,* which word imports not a simple conjecture, for he had the gift of discerning of spirits, and the Holy Ghost, who indites it, did very well know them, so as he was confident of their good state and condition in Christianity, and the Spirit testified so of them by the Epistles of the other apostles directed to them; they were well assured of this, and certain, not only because they were such whom he dearly loved, as if it were only a good or charitable opinion in him, but because of their relation to him as true Christians, and members of the one body of Christ; and so they were very dear to him, whatever they might fear, because of what he wrote before of apostates, for they had better things in them than enlightenings, &c., which he said were in apostates before, ver. 4, 5, even the saving work of the Spirit on their souls, not by giving them light only, or raising their affections, but by giving them a new eye of understanding, as well as new light, and with it a renewed heart; Christ having by the exceeding greatness of his power made them new creatures, as well as professing Christians; their minds, wills, and affections being all changed, and made truly spiritual by the Spirit of Christ; and which they manifest by the exercise of real graces, and that their light, state, and end is better, more excellent, and of another kind, than that of apostates, evinced ver. 10. *And things that accompany salvation;* such things as have salvation in them, even the spiritual mind, which hath eternal life in the root of it, Rom. viii. 6, 10, 11, 16, 17. That Divine nature, which the apostle saith was in the same persons, 1 Pet. i. 1—5; 2 Pet. i. 1—4; which shows the state of their spirits to be a state of grace, which had salvation in it, secured by promises to it, so as they are inseparable, and their union not to be dissolved.

q Prov. 14. 31. Matt. 10. 42. & 25. 40. John 13. 20. r Rom. 3. 4. 2 Thess. 1. 6, 7. s 1 Thess. 1. 3. t Rom. 15. 25. 2 Cor. 8. 4. & 9. 1, 12. 2 Tim. 1. 18.

10 *q* For *r* God *is* not unrighteous to forget *s* your work and labour of love, which ye have shewed toward his name, in that ye have *t* ministered to the saints, and do minister.

For introduceth the reason of the apostle's former persuasion concerning them, which was the real graces of faith and love to God wrought in their hearts, and shown in their work, which was better than all enlightenings. *God is not unrighteous;* the affirmative is implied, God is just, and faithful, and true, in performing what he promiseth, as well as *not unrighteous:* the certain truth is asserted in this emphatical negative; compare 2 Thess. i. 6, 7, with 1 John i. 9: should he not perform he would be unjust. *To forget your work:* God always remembers all things, because his knowledge is perfect; and he will take notice of grace in these Hebrews manifested by their works, so as to recompense and reward them for it, by perfecting his gracious work in them; which having promised, the apostle is confident of the good estate of them through grace, Phil. i. 6. He will never forget the work of your faith in his name, your courageous profession of the gospel, Gal. v. 6; Col. i. 4; 1 Thess. i. 3: a grace of God in them which made their souls delight in him, such as was purely Divine, beginning and ending in God, carried out in the labour and exercise of it to his glory, showing it in all the supplies they give his in his name, to Christians as they are his, Mark ix. 41. *And labour of love, which ye have shewed toward his name, in that ye have ministered to the saints, and do minister:* their *labour of love* was evidenced by what they had done, and were doing, for Christ, in their using all effectual means for supplying, comforting, preserving, and delivering his members, giving their goods to them, and their lives for them, 1 John iii. 10—18. So the apostle asserts these did, chap. x. 32—34. So did Aquila and Priscilla love Paul, Rom. xvi. 3, 4. And this they did show to such as were God's children, and bore his name, the present suffering Christians, who endured rifling, plundering, banishing, imprisonment, and death for their faith in Christ's name: those brethren who, being loved in and for God, do evidence to these Hebrews that they are passed from death to life, 1 John iii. 14.

11 And we desire that *u* every one of you do shew the same diligence *x* to the full assurance of hope unto the end: u ch. 3. 6, 14. x Col. 2. 2.

And we desire that every one of you do show the same diligence: having thus commended them, to show he did not flatter him in it, he discovereth what was wanting in them, and introduceth it with the particle But, we desire you; ἐπιθυμῶμεν properly signifieth the inward affection and strong desire of heart that the apostle had of their further profit. The Spirit lusted in him for this, Gal. v. 17, which was not only convenient for them, but necessary for their perfection. And this desire of his was not for all promiscuously, but that each single person who was a lover of God and his saints, should use all means diligently, as they had in degree done before, to have this perfected to the end of their life, 2 Pet. i. 5—10. It is an earnest agitation and hastening of spirit within, and a demonstrative discovery of the same without it to the utmost, Rom. ii. 7. *To the full assurance of hope unto the end;* their souls with full sails constantly making out after this most certain and full assurance of faith, to the excluding of every doubtful thought of the truth of God and his promises, and of hope, shutting out all wavering, unsettledness, or impatience in waiting for the accomplishment of the good, which is secured by the merit and intercession of Christ, the purpose, promise, and oath of God to them, chap. x. 22, 23; compare Rom. iv. 21; Col. i. 24. *Hope* here is not synonymous with faith, yet its certain concomitant; and is a vehement desire and longing after, with a patient expectation of, what is possible and sure to be enjoyed, because God hath promised and sworn it; though it be at never so great a distance, yet to be communicated by him to his in his best time, chap. xi. 1; compare Rom. iv. 13; Tit. i. 2; 1 Pet. i. 3, 13, 21. This Christian diligence must continue to the end of their own days, and the perfection of their grace in glory, until they come unto the entire possession of what they believed, hoped for, and were fully assured of, Rom. vi. 22; 1 Pet. i. 9, 13.

12 That ye be not slothful, but followers of them who through faith and patience *y* inherit the promises. y ch. 13. 36.

That ye be not slothful: if you will be diligent, away with sloth: you are inclined to it, chap. v. 11, and though you be quick in affection, yet slow in understanding the mysteries of God; and though you have laboured, yet not with that intense labour to which he here presseth them, even to an utter abolition of all the degrees of sloth. *But followers of them ;* μιμηταί, strictly, imitators, in diligence and pains-taking, of the believers who have performed this duty before you. *Who through faith and patience inherit the promises :* in their graces imitate them, as in faith, by which they rested on, as credited, God's promises revealed to them of things invisible, excellent, and distant, and which by no creature power but only God's could be attained, chap. xi. 1, 9, 10, 16 ; xiii. 7. In *patience,* because the things promised are future, and at a great distance from them, waiting for them, suffering many evils from many, passing through fire and water. Isa. xliii. 2, and staying God's leisure to obtain them, chap. x. 36 ; xii. 1 ; Rom. xv. 4, 5 ; James i. 3. Those they were to imitate, were heirs of blessed promises, ver. 14, of spiritual blessings in Christ, the blessed Seed, in whom themselves and all nations were to be blessed, Gen. xxii. 18. It may be queried, How did Abraham inherit the promises, when he did not receive them, as is testified, chap. xi. 13 ? This is certain as to the promises of spiritual saving, and universal concernment to them, as of justification, sanctification, adoption, and salvation by Jesus Christ; these they received, as is evident, chap. xi. 10, 14, 16 ; Rom. iv. 8—26 : such promises as were of special consideration and reserved to a set time, as the possession of Canaan, and Christ's incarnation, John viii. 56. These they did not receive, though they saw them sure to their seed by faith, but for salvation, and glory, and heaven, carried in the covenant of grace, they did personally enjoy ; of the others they were heirs as given by God to them.

z Gen. 22. 16, 17. Ps. 105. 9. Luke 1. 73.

13 For when God made promise to Abraham, because he could swear by no greater, ᶻhe sware by himself,

For when God made promise to Abraham : for is a confirmation by instance, that faith and patience had made some to inherit the promises, as Abraham, and what was influencing of him in the exercising them, viz. God's promise and oath. God Almighty, who was as able to perform as to make a promise, Gen. xvii. 1, having made a promise to Abraham the father of believers, that he would communicate some temporal and spiritual good, which by it he gave him a right to, and bound himself to perform, which summarily was Christ the Redeemer to be of his seed, and Isaac his immediate seed to be a type of him ; this promise at the offering up of his son Isaac God confirms to him by oath. *Because he could swear by no greater :* an oath is to be made by the greatest, who is able to make good all, and to judge after his will ; by nothing under or beneath God must there be any swearing. *He sware by himself,* as the best and greatest, Jehovah himself confirming that which was evident and certain by that which was most so : a strange condescension of God the Son, the Angel of the covenant, to a creature, to lift up his hand to eternity, and to lay it on the altar of his infinite and unchangeable being, to pawn and pledge his Deity, that he might give the highest assurance ; and is willing that it shall be forfeited and lost, if Abraham fall short of what he hath promised to him : see the oath, Gen. xxii. 15—18 ; an oath confirming the covenant of grace to all believers as firmly as to Abraham.

14 Saying, Surely blessing I will bless thee, and multiplying I will multiply thee.

Here is laid down the form and matter of God's oath: the form, in Gen. xxii. 16, is implied in the particle כּי in this text well rendered *surely,* chap. iii. 11. The other defective expressions are forms of swearing, as if, except, unless ; but here it is positive, *surely,* or verily, which Christ frequently useth ; it is a vehement assertion of what he saith. The whole matter of God's oath is not repeated, but the substance and comprehensive part of it, which made for the apostle's purpose here. By *blessing,* in the Hebrew manner of expressing, is carried the abundance and certainty of all that temporal and spiritual good, which he would convey unto him in and through the blessed and promised Seed, our Lord Jesus Christ, with the multiplicity, abundance, and certainty of the seed natural, and believing, to whom he should be related as a Father through Christ, as is evident, Gen. xxii. 16—18 ; and all this so uttered, as if God could not express how much he loved him.

15 And so, after he had patiently endured, he obtained the promise.

And so, after he had patiently endured : Abraham's carriage was suitable to this sworn promise, his soul did patiently wait for it full thirty years, enduring and suffering many temptations about it ; yet he overcame all, and continued firm in the covenant to the end ; his faith extended his soul in a patient expectation of its accomplishment, without doubting or murmuring, knowing God would fulfil it in the best time : he was a long-breathed believer, John viii. 56 ; Rom. iv. 20, 21 ; James i. 2, 3. *He obtained the promise ;* he did not fall short of any piece of the promise, but fully possessed it at last, both in Isaac, the type of the blessed Seed, and the Messiah himself, as to all the spiritual and eternal good promised in him and by him in the heavenly Canaan, Matt. xxii. 32.

16 For men verily swear by the greater : and ᵃan oath for confirmation *is* to them an end of all strife. a Ex. 22. 11.

For men verily swear by the greater : for here is only narrative, introducing the amplification of the argument drawn from God's promise and oath, for the quickening those and all believers to make out after the full assurance of hope, the promise and oath of God concerning them as well as Abraham. That since men's oaths procure credit, and put an end to doubts, strife, and contradiction amongst them ; much more should God's oath put an end to doubts and gainsayings of creatures, and make them to give faith to him : men are not inventors and authors of this ordinance of swearing, but subject to God's precept requiring this from them, and in this special part of God's worship instituted by him, they ought to swear justly and according to his will ; and swear they must by God only, who knows the intentions and secrets of the heart, and who is absolutely greater than all ; the omniscient, omnipresent, omnipotent, and sovereign Lord of all persons, who knows false swearers, and inflicts on them not only temporal but eternal punishments. The swearing by any other, God rebukes, Deut. vi. 13 ; Jer. iv. 2. *And an oath for confirmation is to them an end of all strife :* and in this special part of God's worship, God is called in as a co-witness of the truth of what is sworn, and as a judge and avenger of it, if it be otherwise : and so the oath becomes a confirmation of faith and confidence of men one in another, and of love accompanying the same ; so that if strife, doubt, suspicion, or jealousy arise among them about either words or deeds, which are not known to those who doubt, and cannot be cleared by sense or reason, or any other way but by a testimony of some person who knows them, which being insufficient of itself, he calls in God by an oath as co-witness, with whom it is supposed he would not break his interest, nor invocate him against himself, by declaring what is false : on this all strife and contradiction is to be decided among men, and to cease, and so the controversy to be determined.

17 Wherein God, willing more abundantly to shew unto ᵇ the heirs of promise ᶜ the immutability of his counsel, †confirmed *it* by an oath :

b c h. 11. 9. c Rom. 11. 9. † Gr. *interposed himself by an oath.*

The apostle having stated the nature of an oath in the antecedent, subjoins and applies it in a consequent, in which he shows that God sware to this end, that his own counsel might appear to be immutable, and the consolation of believers greater. *Wherein God, willing more abundantly to show ;* Ἐν ᾧ, in which matter or case, viz. God's act of promise and oath to Abraham, it was not limited to his person, but to all his believing seed, Rom. iv. 23, 24. Out of his own mere grace and free-will, his goodness and affection to them, without any consideration in them moving him ; but his free, unexpected, as undeserved mercy, did first reveal, then promise, then swear. What more could he do ? How liberal and abundant is his love in these overflowing discoveries of it ! so to reveal and make known his gracious thoughts, making them manifest, perspicuous, and glorious, when none was privy to them, nor could reveal them, but himself. *Unto the heirs of promise ;* the seed of Abraham's faith, all true believers, whom God had made children and heirs by promise, as Isaac, Gal. iii. 22, 26, 29 ; iv. 26—28 ; *joint-heirs with Christ,*

Rom. viii. 17. These alone did God intend to secure, and make certain of their salvation. *The immutability of his counsel:* God's unchangeableness in his will and decree, as in himself, excludes all hesitation, alteration, or transposition of what it was from eternity; God did never, will never, change one iota or tittle of his eternal will and decree of saving, perfecting, and gathering into one penitent believers, by the promised Seed Jesus Christ; which he did reveal to the world, and without which manifestation a believer could have no comfort, and without its immutability, not any lasting and permanent comfort. *Confirmed it by an oath:* ἐμεσίτευσεν is proper for a mediator, one who cometh in between two parties as a surety; and so is justly applicable to God the Son, who interposeth betwixt God the Father promising, and believers to whom the promise is made as heirs, as a Surety engaging to see his Father's promise made good to his seed; and therefore confirms it to them with an oath, that they might know the promise was immutable, and should be punctually fulfilled; by which means he removes all doubts, fears, and jealousies about it from them. If they will believe men who swear, how much more ought they to do so, and rest satisfied, with the oath of the Mediator!

18 That by two immutable things, in which *it was* impossible for God to lie, we might have a strong consolation, who have fled for refuge to lay hold upon the hope ᵈset before us:

ᵈ ch. 12. 1.

That by two immutable things: another end of the Mediator's oath is here added, God's oath and a promise spoken to before, which are firm and stedfast to eternity; heaven and earth may pass away, but they cannot. *In which it was impossible for God to lie,* i. e. to cease to be himself, for essential truth to become a lie is impossible, it is utterly inconsistent with his nature. He is incapable to deceive, or speak against his mind, Numb. xxiii. 19; 1 Sam. xv. 29; Psal. lxxxix. 35; Tit. i. 2; and it is as impossible for him to violate his promise or oath. *We might have a strong consolation;* such as will vanquish all doubts, fears, jealousies, sorrows, distractions, putting the heart into a quiet, peaceful, settled frame, and stablishing it in it, whatsoever temptations, trials, or persecutions it may meet with from without or within to perplex it. *Who have fled for refuge to lay hold upon the hope set before us:* but it is the heart of a persevering believer, not of common professors, which is so strongly settled and comforted by them; such who flee to take hold of them; having cleared their right to them, and possessing their souls of them by faith, so to hold fast, as who would no more leave, than Joab would the horns of the altar, being a far greater security than it, or any city of refuge whatsoever; retreating to, and keeping in, this strong hold, nothing can interrupt their comfort, or hurt them, Job xiii. 15, 16; Prov. xviii. 10. *The hope set before* them is that eternal, good, and blessed state which is reserved in heaven for believers, the object of their hope set out to their view and prosecution as a prize in the promise, 1 Pet. i. 3, 4; by a metonymy of the effect for the cause, hope and good hoped for are joined together for our pursuit.

19 Which *hope* we have as an anchor of the soul, both sure and stedfast, ᵉand which entereth into that within the veil;

ᵉ Lev. 16. 15. ch. 9. 7.

Which hope we have as an anchor of the soul, both sure and stedfast: which, taketh in both the good hoped for, and the grace and act itself of hope exercised about it; which grace is by a metaphor set out to be to the soul what an anchor is to ships in a tempest, when tossed with gusts, and storms, and billows of thoughts rolling one upon another to the oversetting of it; this hope stayeth, strengthens, settleth it, even the hope and certainty of eternal rest and happiness secured to them by the promise and oath of God. This hope is safe and firm efficiently, and makes the soul, in the midst of all the threatening temptations from a tempestuous world, safe, because fastened on God's promise; and firm, because strengthened by God's oath, which will hold out all tempests. *And which entereth into that within the veil:* this *hope,* like an *anchor,* is firmly placed, hath wrought itself into the best holdfast, even the innermost part of the veil. *The veil* was that in the tabernacle and temple which separated the holy place from the holy of holiest. This typical veil was rent at the death of Christ, and the holy of holiest in heaven, the truth of that type, was then laid open unto all believers, whether Jews or Gentiles: compare chap. ix. 24; x. 19—21. Here it is that the anchor of the Christian's hope is fastened; this sure harbour, where no tempest can reach or loosen it, but into which there souls, after all their tossings in the tempestuous ocean of this world, by the hurricanes of temptations, which made them quiver again, shall be over, will enter with a full gale, and enjoy that rest and blessedness for ever, which they had by God's promise and oath, on which they relied, secured to them: see Col. i. 5; 1 Pet. i. 3—9.

20 ᶠWhither the forerunner is for us entered, *even* Jesus, ᵍmade an High Priest for ever after the order of Melchisedec.

ᶠ ch. 4. 14. & 8. 1. & 9. 24.
ᵍ ch. 3. 1. & 5. 6, 10. & 7. 17.

Whither the forerunner is for us entered: this heaven is actually possessed for us already by a harbinger, who came at his Father's word to fit and prepare us for it, and then again returned in our nature, and as our Head and Representative he hath entered, made the way open, and paved the coast for us thither, and made it plain and safe; and having taken real and full possession, is making ready our mansions; and when he hath completed his work in us. will come and take and carry us thither, and put us into the full possession of it in our persons, chap. ix. 24; John xiv. 2—4. *Even Jesus, made an High Priest for ever after the order of Melchisedec:* he describeth the forerunner to be God the Son incarnate, the Saviour of believers, he that will keep them safe for it, and set them safe in it. Their Jesus, who as to his office is the great gospel High Priest, had fulfilled his type, and put an end to it by his entering within the veil into the holy of holiest in heaven, being constituted by his Father a royal High Priest, superior to all other orders and persons, *a High Priest for ever after the order of Melchisedec,* mentioned before, chap. v. 10, where the Spirit begun a digression, and having here ended it, repeats the description of it again, as the thing to be immediately handled and pursued, as he doth in the next chapter.

CHAP. VII

Christ, a Priest after the order of Melchisedec, is proved to be of a more excellent order than that of Aaron, from the character of Melchisedec, and his confessed superiority to Abraham and Levi, 1—10; *from the imperfection of the Levitical priesthood, which induced the necessity of a change to one more perfect,* 11—19; *from the confirmation of Christ's priesthood by an oath,* 20—22; *from the unchangeableness,* 23—25, *and spotless innocence, of the person,* 26—28.

FOR this ᵃMelchisedec, king of Salem, Priest of the most high God, who met Abraham returning from the slaughter of the kings, and blessed him;

ᵃ Gen. 14. 18, &c.

The Spirit now proceedeth to prove, that the gospel High Priest is of a far more excellent order than that of Aaron's, by his being of the order of Melchisedec, of whom they had read, and whom they had in great esteem, and after whose order they were assured, by the prophet David, another Priest was to rise up in the church, rendering Aaron's priesthood useless, and continuing the only means of reconciling sinners, and bringing them to eternal life, to whom they must cleave. He initiates it with a description of the state of Melchisedec's order, from ver. 1—10; and then proceeds to apply it to Christ, from ver. 11—28. Having asserted, chap. vi. 20, that Jesus was made from eternity *a High Priest after the order of Melchisedec,* and declared to be so by his entrance within the veil in heaven at his ascension, he reasoneth it out by showing what this Melchisedec was. The person pointed at by this name, is mentioned only once by Moses, and that in Gen. xiv. 18—20. It is certain he was a man who lived by bread and wine, as well as Abraham, and received tithes from him becoming a man. His place of residence was Salem, afterwards called

Jerusalem, in the land of Canaan, Josh. x. 1. The Jews conceived him to be Shem, the second son of Noah, which this scripture denieth, for his genealogy is well known in it. That he descended from Ham, third son of Noah, because an inhabitant in Canaan, and that his name, Melchisedec, was the common name of the princes of that country, whose metropolis was first called Tsedec, then Salem, then Jerusalem, because the king of it in Joshua's time was named Adoni-zedec, which is synonymous with this, is all conjectural. This is certain, he was *king of Salem*, endowed with royal power, such as the other kings in Canaan had. The capital seat in his kingdom was Salem, the name likely of both his city and territory; not that Salem of the Sichemites, Gen. xxxiii. 18, afterwards called Shechem, demolished and sown with salt by Abimelech, Judg. ix. 34. 45; in John the Baptist's time raised again, and called Salem, John iii. 23. But Salem mentioned Psal. lxxvi. 2, more known by its famous appellation, Jerusalem. This shows him to be a man, as doth his next title. *Priest of the most high God:* his authority in matters of religion, as a prime minister about holy things between God and men, and therefore a man, as chap. v. 1, set up by the most high God for himself, and consecrated in his order of priesthood by him, which should most illustriously set out that of his own Son. He managed all as a priest betwixt his own people and the great God, ruling of them in all matters civil, and teaching and ordering them in all sacred things. *Who met Abraham returning from the slaughter of the kings:* he went from Jerusalem with necessary refreshings to meet Abraham, the friend of God, the father of believers, a prince and a priest himself, and of whose posterity was to come the Messiah, now returning from his victory over Chedorlaomer and his confederate kings, with the rescue of his nephew, and all his, to his tents at Mamre. As he was passing near Salem, Melchisedec meets him, and entertains him, Gen. xiv. 13—20. *And blessed him:* it was an act of his sacerdotal office, such as God enjoined on such officers afterwards in Numb. vi. 23—27, and not a common wish and desire only. The matter of blessing is laid down, Gen. xiv. 19. It was in God's name, by his commission, effectually denounced on Abraham by virtue of his office and God's institution; the height of God and all the good in heaven and in earth within God's possession is conveyed to him, Gen. xv. 1.

2 To whom also Abraham gave a tenth part of all; first being by interpretation King of righteousness, and after that also King of Salem, which is, King of peace;

To whom also Abraham gave a tenth part of all; by which tithing to him, Abraham owns him to be God's priest. As he had received blessing from God by him, so he returns to God, through him, his acknowledgments; he divided, shared, and gave out his part to him, even *the tenth* part of all *the spoils*, ver. 4. This is the first scripture, Gen. xiv. 20. that gives us any account of paying the tenths of goods to God in his priests; which custom afterwards obtained among most nations, to give the tenths of the spoils after victory to God. And this Abraham did, as due to the office by Divine institution, having received a blessing from it. *First being by interpretation King of righteousness:* the mystery of his name, title, and descent, the Holy Ghost now opens to them. His name is a compound of מֶלֶךְ or מַלְכִּי which signifieth a *king* or governor, or my king, and צֶדֶק *righteousness*. A supreme governor, not only formally righteous in his own disposition, but efficiently by just and excellent laws making his subjects righteous; a king working righteousness in a Canaan, and in such a time of universal degeneracy from it. This God ordered for some special use, viz. to type out his own Son, God-man, the great gospel minister, to be the *King of righteousness*, who purchased it for, imputeth it to, and infuseth it into, sinners; who is so fully *the Lord our righteousness*, that we are *made the righteousness of God in him*, Isa. xxxii. 1; Jer. xxiii. 6; xxxiii. 16; Zech. ix. 9; 2 Cor. v. 21. *And after that also King of Salem, which is, King of peace:* the mystery of his title of office, *King of Salem.* The due order of this is observable; he is first *King of righteousness*, and after that he is *King of Salem*, that is, of peace; the fruit of whose righteous government was peace. He kept this among his people, and round about him, while others were wasting and destroying their kingdoms by lusts and wars. This is eminently true of Christ *The Prince of Peace,* Isa. ix. 6, 7, who gave some signal of his government, and begun his priesthood, in the same Salem, or Jerusalem, where Melchisedec reigned, Matt. xxi. 5, 9, 10. He is eminently the royal purchaser, maker, and distributer of peace, reconciling all things to God, angels and men in heaven and in earth, and all persons, Jews and Gentiles, and the creation itself to recovered man, Col. i. 20, 21; compare Eph. ii. 13—17. The Prince and price of our peace, setting peace within souls, giving it to them without, peace spiritual, temporal, and eternal: his kingdom aboundeth in it, Psal. lxxii. 1, 3, 7; Isa. liv. 10, 13; John xiv. 27; James iii. 18.

3 Without father, without mother, † without descent, having neither beginning of days, nor end of life; but made like unto the Son of God; abideth a priest continually. †Gr. without pedigree.

In this verse is a mystical description of the eternity of Christ's person and priesthood, set out by the Spirit in the silence and omission of things that concerned Melchisedec and his glory; so that what here is represented to be typically and in shadow, that was Christ really and substantially; for he gives no account of his father, mother, genealogy, birth, or death; the Spirit either not revealing it to him, or ordering him to leave it out, that he might appear the more lively and perfect type of Christ, being represented in all things different from all the men that ever were, or shall be: such a priest therefore as he was, was Christ to be; not deriving his priesthood from any by birth, nor leaving it to any after him. As Melchisedec was *without father,* that was a priest before him, or is recorded, from whom he should derive, as the Levitical priesthood had; so Christ, as to his humanity, was without any human father, conceived only by the power of the Holy Ghost. *Without mother:* as to any Scripture records of it, or to any title of the priesthood by her, as those of Aaron's family had: so Christ, as to his Deity, was without a mother, being the eternal Son of the Father only, and without any title in his humanity to the priesthood from the virgin, she being of David's family, and not of Aaron's. *Without descent;* there is no line of him described in the Scripture, mentioning from whence he descended, or by what genealogy he came to the priesthood, as the Aaronites did clear their right, Neh. vii. 64. As to Christ, *who shall declare his generation,* or produce the lineal roll by which he claimeth the priesthood? Isa. liii. 8; compare ver. 12, 15. *Having neither beginning of days, nor end of life:* there is no record of his birth or death, though he had a father or mother, as there is of Adam's beginning and end, who had neither: so Christ, as to his priesthood, had no predecessor, nor shall have any successor, ver. 16, 24, 28. As a sacrifice and the Lamb of God, he had his time of entrance into the world, and of his leaving it; yet, as God's Priest, he had neither beginning nor end of days. Pure eternity is its rise, and its end shall not be till God be all in all. *But made like unto the Son of God;* ἀφωμοιωμένος· he was in these things the shadow, picture, and resemblance of what Christ should be in his royal priesthood; in these singular prerogatives a visible type of God-man; he was the sign likening, and Christ was the truth and substance of it. *Abideth a priest continually:* these words are the key to all the description before. God made many other persons eminent types of his Son, but Melchisedec was the only type of the eternity of his royal priesthood; for which the Holy Ghost singled him out, dropped him down, as it were, from above, and then took him up again, without any further account of him in the Scripture, that he might convey this mystery to us. That which hath no beginning nor end of it recorded, is as abiding for ever; which this type had not, and so fully sets out the truth designed to be conveyed by it.

4 Now consider how great this man was, ᵇunto whom even the patriarch Abraham gave the tenth of the spoils. ᵇGen. 14. 20.

Now consider how great this man was: the Spirit compares with, and prefers, Melchisedec before Abraham, as he was God's high priest; he introduces it with pressing these Hebrews to exercise an act of judgment under the metaphor of seeing, denoting it to be such a serious and intent act, as calls for the utmost exercise of the discerning faculty; a carelessness in it, or an oversight, might make the proposal to be to no purpose. The greatness of this high priest is what he sets in their view, and that indefinitely, How great is this officer! intimating him to be somewhat excessive to other great ones: and how much greater then must be Christ, if his type be so great! beyond not only Abraham, Levi, and his posterity, but this great Melchisedec, as to his sacerdotal power and dignity. *Unto whom even the patriarch Abraham gave the tenth of the spoils:* this greatness is evinced by Abraham's (the patriarch, chief of all the fathers of Israel, whom the Hebrews esteemed above all others, John viii. 53, and God owns as his friend, and sets all believers under his fatherhood) giving, as a due to Melchisedec, being the greater person in office, the tenth of all the spoils, that which was due to God, and paid to him as God's high priest: ἀκροθινίων notes either the first or choicest of the heaps of grains, especially the first-fruits dedicated to God; but here signifieth that part of the spoils which, according to the custom of war in most nations, after the victory, were offered to God as his part, whether they did consist of persons or things: the tenth part of these were given by him to Melchisedec, as the greatest priest of God in the world, and superior to himself.

c Num. 18.
21, 26.
5 And verily ^cthey that are of the sons of Levi, who receive the office of the priesthood, have a commandment to take tithes of the people according to the law, that is, of their brethren, though they come out of the loins of Abraham:

This is a proof by instance out of the Levitical law, that he who receiveth is greater than he who giveth. *And verily they that are of the sons of Levi, who receive the office of the priesthood:* the seed of Levi the son of Jacob, son of Isaac, son of Abraham, Numb. i. 48—50; iii. 1—5, and not all of them neither, but the sons of Levi descending from Aaron, were separated and consecrated in the priesthood by God's precept, and vindicated from those who would usurp it, Numb. xvi., xvii., and confirmed in it by miracle. *Have a commandment to take tithes of the people according to the law:* God himself gave them a law from heaven to tithe by, and a charge to observe this law, as to all parts of tithes, such as were due to all Levites, Numb. xviii. 24, to the high priest only as God's substitute, Numb. xviii. 8—19, 25—29; to the Levites, widows, and poor together, Deut. xiv. 22—29. These the same law obliged all the Israelites to pay to these Levites as a homage due from them to God, and so delivered to his substitutes superior unto them, as his priests and ministers, and due to them by his own constitution, being the first-fruits of his own blessing. *That is, of their brethren, though they come out of the loins of Abraham:* yet these Israelites who were to pay those tithes to these as superior to them in office, were their own brethren by nature, of the same rank, coming out of the same loins of Abraham, but subjected to these priests, who, by God's ordinance, were set above them in their office; and their receiving tithes was an inseparable property of that superiority.

| Or,
pedigree.
6 But he whose ||descent is not counted from them received tithes of Abraham, ^dand blessed ^ehim that had the promises.

d Gen. 14.19.
e Rom. 4. 13.
Gal. 3. 16.

The proof is here applied, showing Melchisedec to be greater, not than the Levitical priest only, but than Abraham himself. *But he whose descent is not counted from them;* he drew not his genealogy from any priests before him, but is greater than those priests, who by genealogy and succession were made such, and set above their brethren by God himself: he being independent, having no progenitor, priest, or successor, is greater than whom he decimateth. *Received tithes of Abraham, and blessed him that had the promises;* he decimated Abraham, the father of the Levitical priests, and by the Most High's order blessed him, by assuring him of his peace with God, grace continually from him, and multiplying temporal and spiritual blessings to him, according as God promised, Gen. xv. 1, &c. And this he did to him, though Abraham was a patriarch, and privileged with promises above any other; yet though God were made over to him in all his fulness, the blessing given him of fatherhood to a numerous nation, even the visible church of God among Israel, as to all believing Gentiles, who had Canaan literally promised to his posterity, and even this Salem, among the rest, of which Melchisedec was king, and the heavenly Canaan to himself; and above all, the promised Messiah to descend from him, in whom himself and all nations were to be blessed; he, so great in promises, is tithed and blessed by a greater Melchisedec.

7 And without all contradiction the less is blessed of the better.

This principle is commonly acknowledged, it is a most apparent truth, you Hebrews cannot deny it; it is your common judgment, that a priest blessing, as God's officer, is greater than those blessed by him. He that is in a lower state in God's church, is blessed by one set above him in office by God himself, better and greater than he for his place and dignity in office. He must have the pre-eminency for his blessing, which he authoritatively, powerfully, and effectually conveyeth from God to those he blesseth, representing therein God communicating by him the good he wanteth in his benediction.

8 And here men that die receive tithes; but there he *receiveth them,* ^fof whom it is witnessed that he liveth.

f ch. 5. 6.
& 6. 20.

His greatness as to his priesthood above the Levitical, is proved from its immortality. Immortal is greater and better than mortal; such is his order of priesthood. This argument he brings in to heighten the former, and so connects it to it. *And here men that die receive tithes:* the particle ὧδε, *here,* if referred to time, notes during Moses's economy, while the Levitical law lasted; if it refer to place, it notes Jerusalem in the land of Canaan, where the temple was: in that habitation of the Israelitish church the Levitical priests were not only as to their nature and persons withering and decaying, ceasing to be on earth, though they had the honour to decimate their brethren, but as to their order and office, mortal, they were no better than the tithed and blessed by them, in prospect of death. Aaron himself, the first of the order, died, and so did all his successors, as well as Israel. *But there he receiveth them, of whom it is witnessed that he liveth:* but how much better is Melchisedec and his order! ἐκεῖ, *there,* may refer either to the place where his business was transacted with Abraham, near Salem; or to the place of Scripture record concerning him, either Gen. xiv. 18—20, where there is no account of his death, or in Psal. cx. 4. By the prophet David is the testimony borne, that his order is for ever; that Melchisedec, as to his order and office of priesthood, now liveth and subsisteth in the Son of God incarnate, and continueth for ever. It is suggested by a great light in the church, as if Melchisedec was translated as Enoch was, and so continued a priest to the very moment of his translation; and that neither his person nor priesthood died, but liveth for ever: but in this the Scripture is silent. Another refers it immediately to Christ, reading it thus: Here, i. e. in this world, they receive tenths, or are priests; but there, i. e. *within* the innermost of *the veil, whither the forerunner is for us entered, Jesus;* supplying this out of chap. vi. 19, 20. Here, is to be understood, not who receiveth tithes, but who is, *of whom it is witnessed that he liveth.* He saith this sense is to be found in so many words in ver. 23—25, where those who receive tenths, and die, are no other men than those many priests who were not suffered to continue by reason of death, ver. 23. Nor can *he, of whom it is witnessed that he liveth,* be any other than Jesus, who, ver. 24, is the *man* that *continueth* for *ever;* and, ver. 25, is ever-living.

9 And as I may so say, Levi also, who receiveth tithes, payed tithes in Abraham.

And as I may so say: the Spirit now sets this priesthood above the Levitical by instance, which instance being not so proper or direct, his form of introducing it is considerable, as ὡς ἔπος εἰπεῖν, as to say the word, which is a Greek elegancy of speech, when that is uttered which is remarkable, and yet hard to be understood; and it is not only conclusive to what was spoken before, I will speak a word more, and then end the discourse, but interpretative of what he was about to say concerning Levi, born a hundred and sixty-two years after this transaction ; *As I may so say*, or, in some sense it may be said. *Levi also;* Levi, not so much taken personally as collectively, for the tribe that sprung of him, who were priests or ministers to Israel, which Levi personally was not. He was the third son of Jacob, and his seed God separated for, and consecrated to, his service, settling the priesthood in Aaron's family, which was a branch of that tribe, and making all the rest servants to them. *Who received tithes, paid tithes in Abraham;* these did receive these tenths by God's law from their brethren, and these paid tenths by or in Abraham, and so showed them to be inferior in office to Melchisedec, who received this homage from them as due to God, and to him as his high priest. This was not properly, but figuratively; true parents and children being accounted here as one person before they exist, as well as after; Levi, not actually existing then, but virtually in his parent. Christ was in his loins virtually too, as to his humanity, but not to descend of him by natural propagation, but by miracle ; and in him as an antitype to this Melchisedec, and one to be set above him, in whom Melchisedec himself was to be blessed, and therefore could not pay tenths to him in Abraham.

10 For he was yet in the loins of his father, when Melchisedec met him.

For, introduceth the proof, that Levi tithed in Abraham, being virtually in him, as his productive cause ; so near is the unity and identity of descending children ; and as truly were the posterity of Adam in him when he ate, sinned, and fell, Rom. v. 12. To remove all question of the truth of it, the time is annexed to it, when Melchisedec met Abraham, and blessed him, then did Levi pay tenths in him ; so as Melchisedec was greater than the Levitical priest : Christ, typified by him, being greater than himself, must be greater than them also.

g Gal. 2. 21.
ver. 18, 19.
ch. 8. 7.

11 ᵍ If therefore perfection were by the Levitical priesthood, (for under it the people received the law,) what further need *was there* that another Priest should rise after the order of Melchisedec, and not be called after the order of Aaron ?

If therefore perfection were by the Levitical priesthood : now the Spirit infers from the doctrine of Melchisedec's priesthood, the dignity and perpetuity of Christ's, typified by it : so that it is not Aaron's priesthood, but Christ's, which the Hebrews were to use for their salvation after Aaron's was expired. For perfection was not to be had by Aaron's priesthood or law, but by a better, of another order, even Christ and his law. The form of these words are interrogative, implying a vehement denial of what is queried in them. A perfecting of persons to life eternal by expiation, justification, renovation, &c. ; see chap. ix. 9 ; x. 1 ; freeing sinners from the guilt, stain, filth, and consequents of their sins by an expiatory, satisfactory sacrifice to God, and fitting of them for an eternal enjoying him ; a self-efficiency to these things without Christ, is, as to the Aaronical priesthood, vehemently denied ; as to this, that is defective. *For under it the people received the law ;* for with the priesthood, about the time of its institution by God, the Iraelitish church, God's covenanted people, *received the law ;* by which, as well as by its priesthood, there is no expiation, remission, nor eternal life to be obtained, Gal. iii. 17—19 ; compare Mal. ii. 4—8. This law and priesthood being types of far better to succeed them, they were but leading to them, which in the fulness of time were to be revealed, and which should perfect what they could not, Gal. iii. 23, 24 ; iv. 3—5. *What further need was there, &c. ?* it was needful, since the Levitical priesthood and law could not perfect sinners, that another should take place which could perfect them. David therefore, who lived above four hundred years after their institution, and feeling their imperfection, did by the Spirit foresee and tell of a royal priesthood and law to take place after this, that should perfect sinners, which could not be done by any called after Aaron's imperfect order. This was the Lord Christ the Messiah, who must be after the order of Melchisedec, Psal. cx. 4, and who by his priesthood and law should abundantly effect it ; which was far more excellent for both, than any of the Levitical family can pretend to.

12 For the priesthood being changed, there is made of necessity a change also of the law.

For the priesthood being changed : for refers to the expiration of the Aaronical order, to which these Hebrews now were not bound, for that a better priesthood and law were to fill up their room in the church. The Levitical priesthood was changed and abolished to make way for this; God designing that to continue for a time, and then to expire, when the truth perfecting it should take place. *There is made of necessity a change also of the law ;* the mutation of the priesthood indispensably requireth the change of the law, i. e. the legal dispensation of the covenant of grace, and the bringing in with another priesthood a better hope, Gal. iii. 17—27 ; compare ver. 18, 19 of this chapter ; even the covenant of grace in the gospel dispensation of it. This was made necessary by the decree of God, who determined, that both priesthood and law should expire together, and accordingly hath fulfilled it. For when Christ, the gospel High Priest, had in his person and work perfected all of it in heaven, he roots out that order of priesthood, abolisheth the law, scatters the people which would cleave to it ; demolisheth the temple and city to which he confined the administration, so as all designs and endeavours of Jews, or of apostate Christians, to repair, or to restore it, have been ineffectual to this day.

13 For he of whom these things are spoken pertaineth to another tribe, of which no man gave attendance at the altar.

For he of whom these things are spoken pertaineth to another tribe : that this priesthood was so altered, he proves by Christ's being of another tribe than Levi. This is a periphrasis, describing the priest after Melchisedec's order. Of whom was this said in Psal. cx. 4, but of Christ, God-man, the royal High Priest of God ? Matt. xxi. 42. He, as to his human nature, descended of the tribe of Judah, and not of Levi ; and so the Aaronical priesthood was ended by him, chap. ii. 14 ; Gen. xlix. 10. *Of which no man gave attendance at the altar ;* of which tribe none was a priest, whose work was to attend the altar, and offer sacrifice ; if any of another tribe pretended to, or would usurp it, God either smote them, as Uzziah, 2 Chron. xxvi. 18, or destroyed them, as those rebels, Numb. xvi. 1—3, 28—35 ; neither was the priesthood hereby made tribual, or continued in any such tribe as in Levi, but confined to our Lord only, not because he descended of Judah, but extraordinarily selected of God out of it to discharge it.

14 For *it is* evident that ʰ our Lord sprang out of Juda ; of which tribe Moses spake nothing concerning priesthood.

h Is. 11. 1.
Mat. 1. 3.
Luke 3. 33.
Rom. 1. 3.
Rev. 5. 5.

For it is evident that our Lord sprang out of Juda ; the proof of this change of the tribe, and of what tribe he was, was undeniably evident to these Hebrews from their own genealogies, and the Roman census and enrolment of him ; the providence of God ordering this, that it might be universally known that he was David's seed, as well as Abraham's, and as called by his name, Ezek. xxxiv. 23, 24 ; xxxvii. 24, 25. Our Lord was God-man, Lord-mediator, Psal. cx. 1, 4 ; Matt. xxii. 42, 46. He was, as to his humanity, born of the tribe of Judah, as his genealogy by his mother doth evince, Luke iii. 33, and the concomitant evidence of the Roman rolls, in which his name was registered and kept in their archives above an age after his ascension. *Of which tribe Moses spake nothing concerning priesthood :* no man of which tribe was so designed by God, or so revealed to have the royal priesthood, but himself ; none of them having any right to it, as they could prove out of Moses's writing ; and the rule of priesthood is to be found there, and no where else : so that a negative argument taken from Scripture in matters of religion is valid, though never so much puffed at in this age.

15 And it is yet far more evident : for that after the similitude of Melchisedec there ariseth another Priest,

And it is yet far more evident : the change and abolition of the Levitical priesthood, and law, that the perfecting of Christ might succeed, is not only clearly represented to the

HEBREWS VII

understanding of all, that they assent to it, but *it is far more evident* from the eternity of this priesthood's constitution, as is proved, ver. 16. *For that;* εἰ, if, is a particle vehemently asserting, as in form of swearing, and not doubting, and therefore rendered *for that. After the similitude of Melchisedec;* like and parallel in order to him, and in all the properties foretold, which make him a most excellent priest; a priesthood far above that of Aaron, upon the account of the law and covenant to which it is related, which was not only the law of nature, serving God as Creator, but the law of grace, as he was Redeemer in Christ, who with the patriarchs worshipped God by, as believed in, a Christ to come. *There ariseth another priest;* not only of another tribe than Aaron, but of a different order from his; is constituted, manifested, and beginneth the exercise of his office with the abolition of Aaron's.

16 Who is made, not after the law of a carnal commandment, but after the power of an endless life.

Who is made, not after the law of a carnal commandment; the gospel High Priest, the Lord Jesus Christ, was not constituted nor consecrated after that order and rule of God which did bind the Aaronical priesthood, and regulate it as to their consecrations and ministrations, obliging them by annexed temporal promises and comminations, which could not reach an immortal soul. The Mosaical rites and ceremonies were bodily, fleshly, only external. He was not made a priest by legal purifying with water, nor anointed with oil, nor sprinkled with blood, nor clothed with priestly garments, as Aaron and his order was, Exod. xxxix.; xl. 13—15, 31, 32; nor initiated with sacrifices of bulls, goats, &c. He was not to minister in a tabernacle or temple, as they did, which was carnal, and reached only the flesh, could not expiate sins, nor procure spiritual and eternal blessings, chap. ix. 1—12, 19—26. *But after the power of an endless life;* but was constituted and consecrated by God according to his powerful law. He was anointed with the Holy Ghost and power, Acts x. 38, which mighty influence enabled him to execute his office effectually for saving sinners; and by it he receiveth life peculiar to his priesthood, opposed to the dead letter of the commandment, by which, and under which, souls perished by multitudes. But this High Priest hath by this law life in himself, and the best of life to give out to those who wait on his ministry, John v. 21, 24—26, and such life as is indissoluble, opposite to carnal and bodily, which corrupts and perisheth; but the powerful life of this priest is not to be destroyed, neither in himself, nor his people. He by his death and life makes eternal expiation, and procureth eternal blessings for them: see ver. 25, and chap. ix. 11, 12, 28.

i Ps. 110. 4.
ch. 5. 6, 10.
& 6. 20.

17 For he testifieth, ⁱThou *art* a Priest for ever after the order of Melchisedec.

For he testifieth: this is proved by infallible testimony in Psal. cx. 4, God the Father himself solemnly declared him to be so before the angels in heaven, and revealed it to men on earth by the prophet David. *Thou art a Priest for ever after the order of Melchisedec:* that as Melchisedec had no end of days recorded, so this is repeated again to prove, that the Priest after his similitude, i. e. after his order, (the words being here synonymous,) must continue for ever. Christ was not a temporary Priest by a carnal law, but was made a Priest for ever, with everlasting power endowed to save all his people: see ver. 24, 25, 28, and Matt. i. 21.

18 For there is verily a disannulling of
k Rom. 8. 3.
Gal. 4. 9.
the commandment going before for ᵏthe weakness and unprofitableness thereof.

For there is verily a disannulling of the commandment going before: the Spirit having proved the disannulling of the Aaronical priesthood for its imperfection, proceeds to prove the abolishing of the law or covenant annexed to it, like it for weakness and unprofitableness; ἀθέτησις is a displacing, deposing, or laying it aside as to its binding force, so as there is no obligation from it on any as to obedience or penalty; and this is so disannulled of the Law-maker, God himself, by setting up the gospel by his Son-priest, which is most certainly true. *For the weakness and unprofitableness thereof;* for the Mosaical covenant and law wanted strength to bring about what the Jews sought by it, and wanted good fruit to them who made their boast of it; both which weakness and unprofitableness arose from the Hebrews' abuse of it, expecting expiation and sanctification by it, without minding the promise which preceded it four hundred and thirty years, to which it should have led them, and by its neglect proved so fatal to them. For they would be justified and saved by an external obedience to this law, without any regard to Christ and his sacrifice, by whom alone it could be attained, Gal. iii. 17—27. It was strong and profitable to the end for which God made it, to lead to Christ; but weak and unprofitable to justify or sanctify them without him, which was the end they used it for, or rather abused it.

19 For ˡthe law made nothing perfect, ∥but the bringing in of ᵐa better hope *did;* by the which ⁿwe draw nigh unto God.

l Acts 13. 39.
Rom. 3. 20,
21, 28. & 8. 3.
Gal. 2. 16.
ch. 9. 9.
∥ Or, *but it was the bringing in,* Gal. 3. 24. m ch. 6. 18. & 8. 6. n Rom. 5. 2. Eph. 2. 18. & 3. 12. ch. 4. 16. & 10. 19.

For the law made nothing perfect: the proof of this weakness and unprofitableness of the law is its imperfection; it had no supernatural moral power to justify or sanctify any person, or to bring him to perfection; neither did it perfect any person of itself, so as to reconcile him to God, or bring him to salvation, whatever was expected by it, chap. ix. 9; x. 1, 2. *But the bringing in of a better hope did:* δὲ, *but,* shows the opposition of *hope* to the *law;* though *the law* could not perfect any, yet the *better hope,* the gospel, promulgated to and received by them, could perfect them. Ἐπεισαγωγὴ, superinduction, i. e. it was brought in, and put in force, after the legal covenant expired; and brought in to abolish that, so as by it it was repealed and abrogated. The gospel law is styled *a better hope,* because it is conveying better promises, chap. viii. 6, which gives firm and certain hope of sinners' perfection by it, viz. their enjoyment of justification, sanctification, and eternal life. This hope wrought by the Holy Ghost in their hearts, enableth them to obey the gospel, and seals the promises to them. *By the which we draw nigh unto God;* and by this they have free access to God, as chap. iv. 14, 16; compare chap. x. 19—22; Rom. v. 1, 2; not only to worship him, but to receive the blessings of the covenant from him, without fear of displeasing him, or being consumed by him, as under the law, but in the greatest confidence of pleasing him in Jesus Christ, of having communion with him, and of being blessed in the enjoyment of him for ever: see chap. xii. 18—22, and compare ver. 22—25 with them.

20 And inasmuch as not without an oath *he was made Priest:*

This is a further proof of the excellency of Christ's priesthood above Aaron's, taken from his constitution in it by oath. He who is made a priest by oath, is a better and a greater priest than any made so without it; but so is Christ. Καθ' ὅσον is a comparative, answered ver. 22, insinuating by how much the cause constituting or confirming an office of priesthood is more excellent, by so much the effect and office must excel, receiving greater power for some more excellent end. This ὁρκωμοσία is as much as a double oath, ἀπὸ τε ὀμνυεῖν ὅρκον. By the swearing of an oath by God the Father was the gospel High Priest constituted an eternal one after Melchisedec's order; and it addeth so much the more strength and glory to the sanction. This is testified by David, Psal. cx. 4. The Levitical priests were made by a Divine designation, and with external rites were consecrated; but Christ was constituted a Priest by oath, as our translators well supply it out of the following verse.

21 (For those Priests were made ∥without an oath; but this with an oath by him that said unto him, ᵒThe Lord sware and will not repent, Thou *art* a Priest for ever after the order of Melchisedec:)

∥ Or, *without swearing of an oath.*
o Ps. 110. 4.

For those priests were made without an oath; those priests of Aaron's order were selected, instituted, consecrated, without any oath mentioned by Moses, who did all exactly as the Lord commanded him, Exod. xl. 16. God gave only command for it, and made their priesthood but a temporary and passing honour and office, which he might alter when he would. *But this with an oath by him that said unto him, The Lord sware and will not repent:* but he, or Jesus, was made a Priest after Melchisedec's order, by an oath of God his Father, speaking to him, as is recorded by David, Psal. cx. 4. The Lord Jehovah the Father, sware unto his Son the Lord Messiah, lifting his hand, and saying, *I live for ever,* Deut. xxxii. 40, when he ascended and sat down on the right hand of the Majesty in the heavens, solemnly by this oath ratifying and confirming him in this office; and that he would not repent, i. e. change, or alter, or retract what he swore to him, there being no need of any other, he so effectually performing the work of it, that all that God bestows upon his by him, are gifts not to be repented of, even eternal life and salvation. *Thou art a Priest for ever after the order of Melchisedec:* that which the oath ratified was, that Christ should be God's only and eternal Priest, who was to have no sharer with him in the priesthood, and no end of it; taking away from himself by oath any power to make Christ no priest, or take away his office at will and pleasure, as he did Aaron's; hereby honouring his Son, and highly gratifying sinners by giving them such a royal High Priest, who should effectually manage all their concernments with him for ever.

p ch. 8. 6. & 9.15.& 12.24.

22 By so much ᵖwas Jesus made a surety of a better testament.

This brings in the consequent on ver. 20. *As much* excellency as was in God's oath constituting, *so much* there must be in the office constituted. The Aaronical priesthood, by God's constitution, was excellent; but Christ's is much more so, being by God's oath made personal and everlasting, relating to the best covenant; so as the Hebrews had the greatest reason to renounce Aaron's, and to cleave to Christ's for salvation. He being God-man, is a Surety, one that bindeth himself for another, to see something paid or performed, to give security for another; and is proper to him as a Priest, Job xvii. 3; Psal. cxix. 122: Prov. vi. 1. In the Mosaical economy the priests were typical sureties, or undertakers for the people; so Aaron, as a surety, was sent by Moses to stand between the living and the dead, when God was cutting off those sinners, Numb. xvi. 46, 48. The Spirit interprets this *Surety* to be a *Mediator,* chap. viii. 6, which is the general comprehensive name of all his offices: as he gives all from God to us in and by his promises, he is *the Testator* fulfilling them, chap. ix. 15, 16; as he gives satisfaction to God for us, and returns our duty performed with the incense of his merits, he is our *Surety;* which merit of his resulted from his perfect obedience to the whole law and will of God, and from the full satisfaction he made to God by his death for our sins, Rom. v. 19; 2 Cor. v. 21; Gal. iii. 13. *A better testament;* the gospel covenant, described chap. viii. 10—12, and referreth to what the Lord foretold of it, Jer. xxxi. 33, 34, which is better than the Mosaical for perspicuity, freeness, fulness, spirituality, and the Spirit promised in it for its ratification by the death of Christ, and its perpetuity: see chap. viii. 8, 9, 11.

23 And they truly were many Priests, because they were not suffered to continue by reason of death:

And they truly were many priests: this further demonstrates the excellency of Christ's priesthood above the Aaronical for its singularity and self-sufficiency; whereas theirs was, for the multiplicity of it, weak, vanishing, and mortal, like themselves. They had multitude of priests together under the high priest, to manage the service, and above seventy high priests, beside their sagans, such as were to officiate for them if at any time they were legally disabled from the institution of the Aaronical order, to the destruction of the temple, and were made according to the law successively. *Because they were not suffered to continue by reason of death;* death cut them off one after another; they were all mortal, and could not abide, neither in their priesthood or life, Exod. xxviii. 43. Death transmitted that priesthood from one unto another, till the priesthood itself, by the succession of a better, was abolished, and did expire; so frail, passing, and imperfect were both their persons and office.

∥ *Or, which passeth not from one to another.*

24 But this *man,* because he continueth ever, hath ∥ an unchangeable priesthood.

But this man, because he continueth ever; this Priest, Jesus, ver. 22, is opposed to the Aaronical multitude; this excellent one, 1 Tim. ii. 5, after his resurrection abideth immortal. He is eternal and permanent for person and office: see ver. 25; Rom. vi. 9. They are vanished, but he continues for ever, Rev. i. 17, 18. *Hath an unchangeable priesthood;* ἀπαράβατον, a priesthood that cannot pass from him to any other, as Aaron's did to his successors: no person is to be a sharer in it, nor a successor to it: it is reciprocal with himself; his individual person terminateth it for ever; he hath no vicars nor successors of his priesthood. whatever the pope pretends to in it.

25 Wherefore he is able also to save them ∥ to the uttermost that come unto God by him, seeing he ever liveth ᵠto make intercession for them.

∥ *Or, evermore.*
q Rom. 8 34.
1 Tim. 2. 5.
ch. 9. 24.
1 John 2. 1.

Wherefore he is able also to save them to the uttermost: this inference proves his eminency in office above Aaron's order by the efficacy of it; for he is possessor of a supernatural Divine power, which is able to save to perfection, to the full, to all ends, from sin, in its guilt, stain, and power; from its consequents, the curse, and wrath, and eternal death. What neither ourselves nor others could do for us, he is only able, and as willing as able, to set us in a safe, happy, blessed, and glorious state for ever, Rom. v. 9—11, 17. *That come unto God by him;* all such who will come to God by him as their High Priest, and no other, praying for remission of sins for his sake and merit, by faith in his blood, renouncing self, expecting the mercy of God to flow in him to them, subjecting themselves entirely to him, and depending on him to present them unto God their end, without spot or blemish, or any such thing, and to make them blessed in the enjoyment of him for ever. This is his work, John vi. 35—40; 1 Pet. iii. 18. *Seeing he ever liveth to make intercession for them;* since he always exists and lives a High Priest for the good of those who wait on him, having life in himself, and quickening them; compare Rom. viii. 6; and, as their Advocate, 1 John ii. 1, 2, answereth all charges against them, suing for those penitent believers, and pleading for all promised them by the Father in him. He sitting at God's right hand must ever be in his presence: and appears as the general Representative of his, and useth all his interest with the supreme Lawgiver, Judge, and Governor, for them, (see chap. ix. 24,) as it was foretold he should, Isa. liii. 12, even for them who cannot plead their own cause through guiltiness or weakness; he will manage it for all of them who believe in him, and apply themselves to God by him, atoning him for their sins by his sacrifice, perfuming their duties and person by the incense of his merits, and presenting them to God, answering in heaven his type on earth, Exod. xxx. 1—10: compare Rev. viii. 3, 4; Rom. viii. 31—36.

26 For such an High Priest became us, ʳ*who is* holy, harmless, undefiled, separate from sinners, ˢand made higher than the heavens;

r ch. 4. 15.
s Eph. 1. 20, & 4. 10.
ch. 8. 1.

The last excellency of the gospel High Priest, preferring him to Aaron's order, is the qualification of his person, by which he is described in himself, distinguished from and set above all others, and is that which remained out of David's proof to be cleared, who this person was, who was different from Melchisedec, though after his order, to take place after Aaron's was expired, who was immortal, and constituted an everlasting Priest by God's oath. *For such an High Priest became us, who is holy:* this was God-man, the Messiah, and gospel High Priest, who was convenient, congruous, suitable, useful, and necessary, for us guilty, filthy, miserable sinners, in respect of ourselves hopeless and helpless, and cannot approach God without consumption; and, unless we have a person who can manage our cause with God, are lost for ever. To such is he agreeable and necessary, who only can help and save us. This the titles given him evince, showing all the perfections of a priest, of which others were dark shadows and types; as he was not only externally and relatively by office, but internally and morally holy. His essence as God was holiness; as man his nature was entirely agreeable to God's will; he was *that holy thing,* Luke i. 35; not having holiness engraven on a mitre, as Aaron, Exod. xxxix. 30, 31, but in his person; holy in his conception, birth, life, and death. The devil could find nothing but holiness in him, John xiv. 30. Pure in his soul, in his body, transcendently beyond his type, Lev. xxi. 17—23; not a creature, angel or man, so holy as he, the most like to God of any, John i. 14. *Harmless; ἄκακος*, void of all natural evil in his spirit and flesh, no lust, no disposition to evil, not injurious to any, having no guile, an Israelite indeed beyond a Nathanael, of the most simple, pure, and innocent nature; he was good, and all his work was good, Acts x. 38. *Undefiled; ἀμίαντος*, without any spot, not soiled or stained without or within; the angels and heavens are not so clean in God's sight, as this Priest of his; he was never tainted with the appearance of sin : if his church be so pure, what must himself be! Eph. v. 27. *Separate from sinners*; free from all vicious habit, quality, act, or stain, by what was in sinners, or by his converse with them; as separate from guilt or stain, as if he had never been with them; conjoined with God in being and fulness of righteousness, making sinners righteous, but contracting nothing from them. *And made higher than the heavens*; by the constitution of God, after his sacrifice, mentioned ver. 27, he ascended far above all heavens, Eph. iv. 10, and is settled on God's throne at his right hand, having all principalities, powers, might and dominion, and every name, subjected to him, and all things put under his feet, Eph. i. 21, 22. Never priest can reach where he is; this is his supereminent excellency, chap. iv. 14; viii. 1; ix. 11. How able, mighty, and successful is he for managing all for his clients there! His work now is intercession.

t Lev. 9. 7. & 16. 6, 11. ch. 5. 3. & 9. 7. u Lev. 16. 15. x Rom. 6. 10. ch. 9. 12, 28. & 10. 12.

27 Who needeth not daily, as those High Priests, to offer up sacrifice, ᵗfirst for his own sins, ᵘand then for the people's: for ˣthis he did once, when he offered up himself.

In this verse the Spirit shows the ground of his intercession-work in heaven, and why he doth not sacrifice as a High Priest there; therein setting his far above the Aaronical priesthood. *Who needeth not daily, as those high priests, to offer up sacrifice*; he had no necessity, being so holy as he was, to multiply sacrifices. *First for his own sins, and then for the people's*; for himself, being sinless, and having no infirmity to atone for, as the Aaronical priesthood had, who annually on the day of atonement did offer sacrifice for themselves, being sinners, and needing pardon as well as the people, Lev. ix. 7. And he had no need annually on a day to offer for the people's sins, as Aaron and his successors had, and did continue to do, till his sacrifice took place and abolished them; he having once offered a sacrifice for the sins of the people, which outweighed all their multiplied sacrifices. *For this he did once, when he offered up himself*; and this he did once when he himself died a sacrifice for sins, when he offered up the human nature by the eternal Spirit without spot, a propitiatory sacrifice to God, when his body hung on the cross, and his soul ascended and entered into the throne of God in the holy of holiest in heaven, with the blood of the testament, and atoned him for all his people. How transcendent was this sacrifice to all the Aaronical ones, whereby sinners were reconciled unto God for ever! chap. ix. 11, 12, 14, 24—26. On this offering was he exalted by God far above all heavens, confirmed by oath in his office, and his intercession became so powerful and effectual to save all his people from their sins, and the consequents of them.

y ch. 5. 1, 2.

28 For the law maketh ʸmen High Priests which have infirmity; but the word of the oath, which was since the law, *maketh* the Son, ᶻwho is †consecrated for evermore.

z ch. 2. 10. & 5. 9.
† Gr. *perfected*.

This is the reason why the Aaronical priests had need to sacrifice for themselves, and the gospel High Priest had not, and is finally describing him who is so. *For the law maketh men high priests which have infirmity*; for the law which God gave to Moses, the ceremonial law, constituteth, sets up, and puts into this Aaronical order and office of priesthood, such as are not only liable to bodily infirmities, but to moral ones, sins. Aaron and all his sons had their spiritual sinful infirmities, chap. v. 2, for which they were to offer their propitiatory sacrifices to God, as well as for those of the people; they were sinful, dying men, ver. 26. *But the word of the oath, which was since the law*; but God the Father's promise to his Son, ratified with an oath, that he should be the great High Priest perfecting of souls for God, as David testifieth, Psal. cx. 4, to be revealed to him; and this four hundred years after the law was given which constituted the Aaronical priesthood. The word revealed God's promise to him, the *oath* made it irreversible; yet this promise was not actually performed to him till his ascension in the human nature higher than the heavens, Psal. cx. 1. *Maketh the Son, who is consecrated for evermore*; God the Son incarnate, the man Christ God's fellow, the glorious only begotten and bosom Son of the Father, Zech. xiii. 7; John i. 14, 18; 1 Tim. ii. 5, is made by this ratified word the only single everlasting High Priest, who is not only completely and perfectly holy, as opposed to the infirmities of the Aaronical priests, but ever able and fit for his work, as successful in it. Who would not therefore leave that abolished priesthood, and cleave to this which must abide for ever?

CHAP. VIII

Christ, our great High Priest in the heavens, hath a more excellent ministry than the priests on earth, 1—5; as he is also the Mediator of a better covenant than that which was given to Moses, 6—13.

NOW of the things which we have spoken *this is* the sum : We have such an High Priest, ᵃwho is set on the right hand of the throne of the Majesty in the heavens;

a Eph. 1. 20. Col. 3. 1. ch. 1. 3. & 10. 12. & 12. 2.

The Spirit having cleared the doctrine of the priesthood of the great gospel Minister, now proceeds to show how he executed that office; and that therein as he far excelled, so he was to be valued and used before, the Aaronical priests. He introduceth it with a reflection on his foregoing discourse. *Now of the things which we have spoken this is the sum*; the sum then of the things spoken, is κεφάλαιον· some read, the head, i. e. the scope in a discourse driven at; others, the chief of all the excellencies of the priesthood hitherto held forth; as if it were *palmarium argumentum*, the highest and choicest of all that hitherto had been spoken; and it is proportionably true, as will be seen in what followeth : but it must necessarily join the foregoing and following discourse together, and so it notes a sum, contract, or epitome; a breviate of the heads formerly discoursed on and largely, chap. vii.; and so shows the dependence of the matter remaining to be handled on what went before, when many things are summed up in a few words; as Christ's priesthood, largely opened before from Psal. cx. 4, is, as to the substance of it, briefly handled in this verse. *We have such an High Priest, who is set on the right hand of the throne of the Majesty in the heavens*; we Paul, and believing Hebrews, opposed to the infidel Jews, have not only a right to, and interest in, but actual possession of, Christ, God-man, as our High Priest, while their infidel brethren had only a sinful man : He who hath eminent power above, and though crucified by men, yet thereby became victorious over sin, death, and hell, and the lord of them the devil, led principalities and powers in triumph, when he passed through their kingdom in the air, Col. ii. 15, entered into the heaven of heavens, and there sat him down and settled himself, as was his right, on the right hand of God, as he sat on his throne, invested with all power and dignity, as God's royal Priest, near to him, and the great manager of all our concerns with him; while the sinful priest at Jerusalem stood trembling before the shadow of this heavenly temple on earth, chap. i. 3.

2 A minister ‖of ᵇthe sanctuary, and of ᶜthe true tabernacle, which the Lord pitched, and not man.

‖ Or, *of holy things*.
b ch. 9. 8, 12, 24.
c ch. 9. 11.

A minister; this is spoken of the High Priest sat down on the right hand of the Majesty in the heavens, and relates to that work of his whereby he was constituted λειτουργός, which, according to Suidas, is compounded of two words, παρὰ τὸ λήιον vel λήιτον ἔργον, public work; so as it might be rendered administrator, and notes any public officer from the highest to the lowest. The Spirit of God in the New Testament hath applied it to the highest and subordinate ministry; in this verse to Christ himself in his exalted state, and so notes a ruler, as he was now God's published, settled King. the Lord Administrator of all things in his kingdom, agreeably to what he foretold, Psal. ii. 6, 7; cx. 1; compare Acts xiii. 33. And here properly it notes him in all his offices, his royal, sacerdotal, and prophetical ministry in the heavens and earth, administering and governing all things in them. *Of the sanctuary:* the things about which his administration is concerned are τῶν ἁγίων, of holies. Some refer this to persons, as noting saints, of whom he is the Ruler and Governor, Rev. xv. 3; others, to things, graces and endowments bestowed by him upon his: but most properly here, in the neuter gender, it notes the place, the sanctuary in heaven, the holy of holiest, where he is administering and governing all, though it may be applied to all of these. For heaven is the place, the sanctuary, wherein saints the persons for whom, and all holy endowments the matter about which, he administers, do descend. But the holy house, or *sanctuary*, is the proper import of it; and so, though expressed in the plural number, to all the holy parts of its types, the temple and tabernacle. *And of the true tabernacle:* some, because of the connexion of this to the former word, *sanctuary*, would have it import the same thing, even heaven; but the Spirit distinguisheth these from each other, chap. ix. 1, 2. Some would understand it of the body of Christ, but here not so properly and agreeably to what the Spirit is speaking of. But by *tabernacle*, here, is meant Christ mystical, the true temple, church, and habitation of God on earth. For as Christ was the body and truth by all the shadows and types of the tabernacle, Col. ii. 17, so not all one way. Some of the types were single, and terminated on his person, as priesthood, sacrifice, altar, shew-bread, incense, ark of the covenant, &c. Other types were aggregate, and compounded of many things, as tent, sanctuary, and tabernacle here; parallel to this, there must be a truth in Christ complex, that is, Christ the church, so framed and pitched a house by God, that he may dwell in it. The apostle so interprets it, 1 Cor. iii. 16, 17; 2 Cor. vi. 16; compare Eph. ii. 20, 21; 1 Pet. ii. 4, 5. Christ in person is its foundation; saints are the several living materials, of which the house and tabernacle is made; their dispositions, graces, and endowments, the ornaments of it; the laws, rules, orders, ordinances, are the cement, the cords and stakes that join them together; and the glory of God fills it, as it did the tabernacle and temple, Hag. ii. 7, 9; Rev. xxi. 23. It is styled, *the true tabernacle* of God, because of it the literal tabernacle was but an imperfect shadow and type; in this God dwells truly and personally, therefore to be entered into by the Hebrews; the old one, the type, being abolished and vanished by the appearance of this the truth. For now was that word fulfilled, Jer. iii. 16; the days were come that men should mention no more *the ark of the covenant of the Lord;* so no more the tabernacle of the witness; but the truth of God in Christ should be acknowledged by them. The reason of this interpretation is evident. A tabernacle is God's habitation; the Christian church is such, it answers in all parts, and bears its proportion to the complex type, and cannot fully be matched by any other things: it is congruous to Christ's session in glory; for thence he doth, as the honourable and glorious Administrator of God's church, order and manage all on it according to his will, having settled in his true tabernacle a ministry, Eph. iv. 8—13, covenant, as below, ver. 6—13, service, ver. 3, 5, and privileges, far exceeding its type: all which this grand officer, as the only royal High Priest and Head of his church, Prophet of his people, orders by his Spirit, the only Vicar he useth in it. Of this true tabernacle, church, or house of God, the sovereign, independent, omnipotent, infinitely wise and holy, the eternal Lord, was the author; and such is his work as no other can question it, can add to or alter it, can reach it, so proportioned is it to its Framer. *Which the Lord pitched;* ἐπηξεν he framed and prepared every piece that constituteth this tabernacle himself, as the materials of the first were wrought by his pattern and order. He compacted and joined all the parts of it together, to make it his tabernacle; and especially reared, pitched, and firmly constituted this his own habitation.

This he doth for ever so pitch, as hell and earth, with all their arts and force, can never remove it, Matt. xvi. 16, 18. It is his rest for ever, here he will dwell, for he hath desired it, and will make it glorious, chap. xii. 26—28; Psal. cxxxii. 14; Isa. xi. 10; Rev. xxi. *And not man;* this is denied because man is weak, sinful, and mortal, no such hands intermeddle with the work of God's tabernacle, for his work would be like him, weak, faulty, and perishing, which could not long survive its author.

3 For ^devery High Priest is ordained to offer gifts and sacrifices: wherefore ^e*it is* of necessity that this man have somewhat also to offer. d ch. 5. 1.
e Eph. 5. 2.
ch. 9. 14.

For every High Priest is ordained to offer gifts and sacrifices: in Christ's administration for his in heaven, as he is a King, so he is a High Priest; and as such must have service and ministration suitable to himself there, as the Aaronical high priests had on earth; every of which was constituted to stand and minister at God's altar, and were to offer sacrifices and gifts, as cleared before, chap. v. 1. *Wherefore it is of necessity that this man have somewhat also to offer;* seeing these earthly priests had such service, it would follow thence, if he were earthly and of their order, he should need such too. Ἀναγκαῖον having no verb expressly joined to it, is variously supplied: some, by *it is;* but those who would make the tabernacle his body, do not allow it, that being offered before this, and therefore add, it was, or hath been: but it is best supplied potentially, it would be necessary for this High Priest, if he were so low as those priests, to have something of the like nature or kind of gifts and sacrifices, that he might offer as they did. Now such he needed not, as being utterly inconsistent with his priesthood, as is proved after.

4 For if he were on earth, he should not be a Priest, seeing that ‖ there are Priests that offer gifts according to the law: ‖ Or, they are Priests.

For if he were on earth, he should not be a priest: this gives the reason why the Levitcal gifts and offerings were inconsistent with Christ's priesthood: for if he were earthly for person or office, or was existing on earth, or in an earthly sanctuary or tabernacle proper to the law, he could not by Divine ordination be an offering priest, being not of Aaron's family, nor of the tribe of Levi, nor such a priest as he was made by God's oath after Melchisedec's order, if he were for temper, office, or place of ministry earthly. *Seeing that there are priests that offer gifts according to the law:* this earthly office, state, and work, was by the law settled on Aaron's family, and none could legally offer sacrifices or gifts in God's earthly tabernacle or temple, but his sons alone. Christ, as he was not of that tribe, so he never was either in the court of the priests, or in the holy place in the temple, neither did minister in them as a priest at all; this was proper and peculiar only to his types.

5 Who serve unto the example and ^fshadow of heavenly things, as Moses was admonished of God when he was about to make the tabernacle: ^gfor, See, saith he, *that* thou make all things according to the pattern shewed to thee in the mount. f Col. 2. 17.
ch. 9. 23.
& 10. 1.
g Ex. 25. 40.
& 26. 30.
& 27. 8.
Num. 8. 4.
Acts 7. 44.

Who serve unto the example and shadow of heavenly things; these Aaronical priests and their service in the literal tabernacle, were only subservient, as the model in the mind, to represent the truth, as the platform of a tabernacle serves toward the making and pitching of it. Ὑποδείγματι is an obscure and underhand resemblance, the first draught, that which is the rough part of what is to be represented, chap. xi. 23, such as the shadow is to the natural body, a dark resemblance of it: such were these of Christ's person, ministry, and those heavenly things performed by him; they were leading them to, and instructing them in, Christ and his work, though the veil on their mind and hearts hindered them from discerning it. So true is that, John i. 17. Moses's law was the shadow, Christ the truth of all; compare chap. ix. 6, 23; x. 11. And it is not

HEBREWS VIII

unlikely, that both the literal tabernacle and temple economy are but grosser and obscurer discoveries of that form and manner of the manifestation of God in glory, and the most excellently regulated service and ministry in the economy there. *As Moses was admonished of God when he was about to make the tabernacle;* κεχρημάτισαι· Moses was in the mount, from God's own mouth, (the best of oracles,) charged and admonished about, and infallibly guided in, his duty, Exod. xxv., confirmed by the Spirit in Acts vii. 44: when he had his commission for the work, resolved to enter on and perfect it according to God's charge, then was this oracle given out about the earthly tabernacle, priesthood, and service. *For, See, saith he;* look you to it, observe this, take heed and beware, saith he, who is Jehovah, the Sovereign Lord of him and Israel, a Being of power to enjoy, and command, and to require any neglect, Exod. xxv. *That thou make all things according to the pattern showed to thee in the mount;* thou shalt make, frame, and work, by enjoining Israel what they are to make, and perfect what thou art to do, all those things of the vessels, parts, and structure of the tabernacle for officers and service, for conjoining, rearing, and pitching of it, Exod. xxv. to xl.; all after the type, copy, pattern, exemplar, showed thee by me, and seen and viewed by thee, when thou wert with me in the top of the Mount Sinai forty days and forty nights. This tabernacle was framed by its type, and was to be an ordinance resembling, figuring, and typifying a spiritual tabernacle and ministry of Christ that was to succeed and fulfil it, being different in the whole kind from this type; it being spiritual and heavenly, this a gross, material, earthly fabric. Moses was most exact in framing all as God commanded, after his own pattern; he did not add, diminish, nor alter any thing in it, Exod. xl.

h 2 Cor. 3. 6, 8, 9. ch. 7. 22.
¶ Or, *testament*.

6 But now ʰhath he obtained a more excellent ministry, by how much also he is the mediator of a better ∥ covenant, which was established upon better promises.

But now hath he obtained a more excellent ministry: but is here adversative, setting this High Priest over against and above the Aaronical, on the account both of his ministry and covenant, of which theirs were but types and shadows. The Lord Christ hath now really and fully obtained, and doth possess as the gospel High Priest, a public ministration, which, as to its glorious effects, transcendently excels the Levitical, chap. ix. 11, 12, 14; x. 12, 14, 18. *By how much also he is the mediator;* by how much he is Mediator of a better covenant, by so much he hath a more excellent ministry, so that this is a proof of the former. Μεσίτης is a middler, one that interposeth, not only between persons at distance, but at enmity: his parleying between God and sinners could profit little, God being so highly injured by and offended with them; and therefore he mediates here as a Surety, as chap. vii. 22, and so undertakes for sinners to satisfy God, wronged by them, by sacrificing himself for them, and so secure the performance of his covenant mercy to them. By which sacrifice he purchaseth and merits the Holy Spirit, to enable man to perform the conditions which God requireth from him; to repent, and believe, and obey the Redeemer, and wholly to rely upon his sacrifice for God's favour; as by his intercession he secures to them all the blessings of God's covenant for time and eternity, as proved, chap. ix. *Of a better covenant;* the gospel covenant, which was a solemn agreement between an offended God and sinners; wherein he binds himself to give forth pardon and life to them upon certain conditions; and they bind themselves to perform, in order to the obtaining these. Which covenant was brought about by the intercession of Christ the Mediator between them, who became a Surety for the performance of it, and solemnly ratified and confirmed it by the sacrifice of himself; as other covenants were by the blood of federal sacrifices, of which we have frequent mention in the Scripture; called *better* than the Mosaical covenant, not for the matter of it, but for the manner of exhibition, chap. vii. 22, being comparatively a greater good than that which was less, Gal. iii. 17. *Which was established upon better promises;* which gospel covenant was νενομοθέτηται, as the Mosaical one, confirmed, ratified, and established by the blood of the sacrifice according to the law, chap. ix. 18—21. This was its sanction, it was by it settled unchangeable, attended with and founded on the best promises, such as were more spiritual, clear, extensive, and universal, than those in the Mosaical covenant were.

7 ⁱFor if that first *covenant* had been faultless, then should no place have been sought for the second.

i ch. 7. 11, 18.

This proves the gospel covenant better than the Mosaical, for if it had not, there would have been no second. *For if that first covenant had been faultless:* that first covenant, of which Moses was the mediator, as to the administration of it, (as to the matter of it, it was the same from Adam throughout all ages,) was faulty; not because God made it, though it was a less perfect good than what succeeded it; it was able to save those who would rightly use it, and come unto Christ by it, Gal. iii. 24; but accidentally, by reason of the priests' faults, and people's sinfulness, it became wholly ineffectual to them for saving them; therefore the blame and fault of it is charged on them, ver. 8. *Then should no place have been sought for the second:* the question here is vehemently assertive; if that covenant in its Mosaical administration had reached effectually its end, brought all that were under it to Christ, to be saved by him, no place nor room was there, that then being so perfect, for another to succeed it, God would have rested there; but his excellent wisdom and counsel determined to put in being the second, and to set it in the place of the first, that was faulty, and which was to be abrogated by it, Gal. iii. 21.

8 For finding fault with them, he saith, ᵏBehold, the days come, saith the Lord, when I will make a new covenant with the house of Israel and with the house of Judah:

k Jer. 31. 31, 32, 33, 34.

This is the proof of the faultiness of the Mosaical covenant, from the right cause of it, those who did abuse it. *For finding fault with them:* the Lord, by the prophet Jeremiah, being distasted and offended, accuseth, and with complaints and aggravations chargeth the houses of Israel and Judah, both priests and people, for frustrating God's covenant with them by their unbelief, mistaking God's mind in it, and using it to justify them, and not bring them unto Christ, who justifieth the ungodly. That the covenant was not faulty in itself, but only accidentally, is evident; for it was given to change hearts, though its spiritual efficacy was not so fully revealed, Deut. x. 16; xxx. 6; for Moses, Joshua, Samuel, David, were saved by the right use of it. It did not bind them by works to obtain justification, for it was delivered with blood, which taught them it was to be had only by faith in Christ's blood. But when they would not be led to Christ by it, they were faulty, and not the covenant, and so they perished in their gainsaying. The administration of this covenant by men being so defective, he finds fault with them, and resolves on the change of the administration. *Behold, the days come: Behold,* imports attention to and observation of the rare, excellent, and important thing proposed in the word to the eye and mind of those for whom it was written, and to whom it is sent: so is this here, in Jer. xxxi. 31; the days of the Messiah's coming in the flesh, when *a woman shall compass a man*, as Jer. xxxi. 22; the known times of grace, Jer. xxiii. 5, 6. A time to come when the prophet wrote it, past when the apostle quotes it here; so ordered by God to teach those there the imperfection of that covenant administration, so as they might make out to Christ by it, and not rest in it, as he had revealed him to them in the prophecy; and to strengthen believers in their faith in Christ when come, and to convince and leave inexcusable such Jews as would not believe in him, and further to confirm his priesthood. *Saith the Lord:* this is not an invention of the prophet, but a revelation of the Supreme Lord to him. It is his certain, true, and infallible speech, illuminating his mind by it, and directing him in his words and writings for to convey it to those to whom he sent him; so that the word is firm, and worthy of all acceptation; and the more of the Hebrews, because sent by Jeremiah, a Levitical priest, to them. *I will make a new covenant with the house of Israel and with the house of Judah:* I will make perfect and complete. In the prophet it is וכרתי I will strike or cut, because in covenant-making the sacrifices were cut asunder; and thence is it transferred figuratively, to signify covenant-making. A covenant, for form and manner of administration, second, later, better, stronger, and more excellent than the Mosaical; such as should be effectual to God's saving ends in the ministry of Christ, with the whole seed of Jacob, the visible church of God, when the prophet wrote this, divided into two kingdoms of Israel and Judah, and that of Israel removed afar off by the Assyrian, and seemingly lost, but by this covenant to be made one people again, and to be saved by Christ, David their King, Jer. xxiii. 5, 6; Ezek. xxxvii. 21—28.

9 Not according to the covenant that I made with their fathers in the day when I took them by the hand to lead them out of the land of Egypt; because they continued not in my covenant, and I regarded them not, saith the Lord.

The Spirit proceedeth to show the form of the covenant denied. *Not according to the covenant that I made with their fathers;* not the same covenant for habit or form, nor any like unto the same for the manner of its administration, as was made by the Lord with the Hebrews their progenitors, when they were strangers in Egypt, and under great bondage there. *In the day when I took them by the hand;* the day that I laid my hand on them, and took hold of theirs, even the last day of the four hundred and thirty years foretold to Abraham. Gen. xv. 13, 16; compare Exod. xii. 40, 41; as a father takes hold of his child to pluck it out of danger. It is a metaphor setting out God's special act of providence, in their miraculous deliverance out of Egypt, keeping them in his hand, while he was smiting their enemies; setting them at liberty, and then striking covenant with them, and binding them by it to be his obedient people, as such redemption mercy did deserve. At which time the covenant was unlike, the promise or gospel one for external habit and form only, as carried on by a ceremonial law and priesthood, over which Christ's was to have the pre-eminency for power and efficacy of administration. *Because they continued not in my covenant;* these unbelieving Hebrews, under that administration of the covenant, continued not faithful to it, as by their own word and consent they bound themselves to it, but apostatized from God and his truth, Deut. v. 27. The word used by the prophet הֵפֵרוּ signifieth the breaking and making void the covenant. The administration of it did not hold them in close to God, but they frustrated all God's ordinances, turned idolaters, forsook the Lord, and worshipped the gods of the nations round about. *And I regarded them not;* ἠμέλησα, I took no care of them, I did neither esteem nor regard them, but cast them off from being my people for their lewd, treacherous covenant-breaking with me; they would not return unto me, and I rejected them from being my people, or a people as they were before. Who knows where the nine tribes and the half are? and in what a dispersed, shattered condition, are the remaining Jews to this day! The apostle in this follows the Septuagint, who read the effect of their sin, their rejection, for what was their sin itself, which by the prophet is expressed וְאָנֹכִי בָּעַלְתִּי should I be a Lord or Husband to them; which is an aggravation of their sin from God's dominion over them or marriage-relation to them; yet did they break his marriage-covenant with them according to their lewd and whorish heart: see Ezek. xvi., xxiii. But in this quotation by the apostle, and translation of the Septuagint, it is a metonymy of the effect for the cause, to reject, cast off, or neglect them for their treachery to him in their marriage-covenant, which was the true cause of it. The verb itself בָּעַל may signify to neglect or despise; and so Kimchi reads it, Jer. iii. 1, and is so rendered in this place by other rabbies, and so it signifieth in other languages. *Saith the Lord:* this is God's irrevocable word, used four times by the prophet, Jer. xxxi. 31—34, and three times repeated by the apostle here, as proper only to the Lord; none can speak so truly, certainly, infallibly, as he.

1 ch. 10. 16.

10 For ¹this *is* the covenant that I will make with the house of Israel after those days, saith the Lord; I will †put my laws into their mind, and write them ‖ in their hearts: and ᵐI will be to them a God, and they shall be to me a people:

† Gr. *give.*
‖ Or, *up on.*
ᵐ Zech. 8. 8.

For this is the covenant that I will make: for, showeth it should not be such a covenant-form as was given on Mount Sinai, it being wholly different, and that denied before, being carnal and ceremonious, full of types and shadows, and through their sin ineffectual to them. This is the firm administration of the covenant which I will strike. To which three words answer is in this scripture, I will perfect, make, and dispose; which last is the root from whence the notion of a covenant in the Greek is derived, διαθήσομαι. *With the house of Israel:* Israel is the comprehensive name of all the twelve tribes, as ver. 8; compare Exod. xvi. 31; xl. 38; and is so used by the Lord himself, Matt. x. 6, and by Peter, Acts ii. 36. *After those days;* in the prophet it is, after those days of their delivery from Babylon, Jer. xxxi. 1, 8, 11, 16, 21, but especially when those days of the first administration of the covenant are accomplished, when the fulness of time for the Messiah's revelation is come, Gal. iv. 4. To this God again puts his seal, he saith it. *I will put my laws into their mind;* the great God, the Redeemer himself, the infinitely wise, and good, and powerful Spirit, who only can reach the soul, will make impressions, and write clear characters of Divine truth on it, 2 Cor. iii. 3. None can alter, new-mould, frame, and temper a spirit, but him, who hath a true original right of all the good he promiseth, which he will freely, graciously dispense from himself, John iv. 10, 14. All the doctrines of the gospel, which include in them the moral law, as now managed by Christ, all the will of God concerning our salvation, promises, and commands; and these in their spirit and power, which God not only ratified in, but conveyed to the world by, Jesus Christ, and especially into the mind. Διάνοιαν renders the Hebrew בְּקִרְבָּם the inward parts, in the prophet's text. The mind or understanding being the innermost part of the soul, is capable of receiving impresses of Divine truth, and its characters are by it made legible to the soul; which as promised here, is so prayed for by the apostle, Eph. i. 17, 18. *And write them in their hearts:* ἐπιγράψω is a metaphor setting out a real, actual, powerful work of the Spirit of Christ, which leaveth the express characters of all God's saving mind and will upon the heart or soul as plain as writing upon paper, or engraving upon stones; such an operation of the Spirit of Christ on the souls of them, as whereby is conveyed into them a new light, life, power, so that they are made by it partakers of a Divine nature; and though they are not other faculties, yet they are quite other things than they were for qualities and operations, so as they are enabled to know, observe, and keep his laws, which are set up in authority and dominion in their souls, ruling and ordering all there, Ezek. xi. 19, 20; xxxvi. 26, 27; 2 Cor. iii. 3, 8, 9, 10, 18. *And I will be to them a God:* as in the former word was the promise of conversion, regeneration, and renovation, so joined with it is the promise of adoption. In which God engageth in Christ to be to penitent believers, Rom. ix. 6, 8, *a God,* i. e. the cause and author of all good, Gen. xv.; xvii. 1, 7; what he is, hath, or can do for them of good, is all theirs, and himself terminating all the knowledge, faith, and worship of them. He will exercise all his wisdom, power, and goodness to deliver them from all evil, and to make them eternally happy and blessed in himself. *And they shall be to me a people;* and to him this true Israel shall be a true, spiritual, eternal, adopted seed and people, partakers of all that he hath promised to them or they can desire of him; so as their name is better than the name of sons or daughters, an everlasting one, not to be cut off, Isa. lvi. 5. They, as his people, attend on, witness to, and contend for, him and his glory, are always at his beck, being purchased, made, and covenanted so for his use and service, that they are not their own, but wholly at his disposal, Jer. xxiii. 7; xxxii. 20; Ezek. xi. 20; xxxvii. 23, 27; Zech. viii. 8; 2 Cor. vi. 16.

11 And ⁿthey shall not teach every man his neighbour, and every man his brother, saying, Know the Lord: for all shall know me, from the least to the greatest.

ⁿ Isa. 54. 13.
John 6. 45.
1 John 2. 27.

And they shall not teach: the subject implied in the

plural verb, and by a partitive particle expressed, *they,* and *every man,* is in Jeremiah's text אִישׁ a man, even every truly covenanted one who hath the knowledge of the Lord. *And they shall teach no more,* in Jer. xxxi. 34. A double negative supplieth it in this verse, ὰ μή· denying that weak and fruitless kind of teaching which was under the Mosaical covenant administration, whereby souls were not savingly edified in the knowledge of God, there was imperfection both in their knowledge and teaching, which should not be under the gospel. *Every man his neighbour;* such as are nearer to each other in society or commerce, a fellow citizen; or are near by relation, by nature or alliance, by consanguinity or affinity, one near at hand, ignorant of the Lord; and that needs instruction, one capable and possible to be taught. *Saying, Know the Lord :* this intimates the manner of teaching denied, a formal, customary way of teaching, *saying;* it was proverbial with them; and so was the matter of it, *Know the Lord;* as they used to say, *The temple of the Lord,* Jer. vii. 4, *The burden of the Lord,* Jer. xxiii. 34, *The day of the Lord,* Amos v. 18: or otherwise, not to teach them to know the Lord notionally only, without any influence on their heart, without believing, loving, fearing, or obeying him, 1 John ii. 3, 4; or to teach them to know the Lord, as redeeming and delivering of them out of Egypt, or out of the land of the north, that is, bringing them back from their captivity in Babylon, as they were taught, Exod. xx. 2; Jer. xxiii. 7, 8; but as delivering them from sin, the curse, wrath, and hell. Or, they shall not teach one another so darkly, slenderly, and imperfectly in the meaning of types, shadows, and ceremonies, that they might know the Lord in truth, and worship him according to his mind; or to take so much pains to instruct them concerning the Lord and his worship, as they took with the Gentiles when they proselyted them. *For all shall know me, from the least to the greatest;* for under the gospel administration all the covenanted ones, the infant in the church and the aged, Isa. lxv. 20, all ages in Christ, children, fathers, and young men, as 1 John ii. 12—14, young and old, shall have his laws put into their minds, and written on their hearts, the true saving knowledge of him in Christ in the fulness of it, as Isa. xi. 9: they shall so perfectly know him, as not to depart from him; he shall be theirs and they his by an everlasting covenant, ordered in all things and sure; by the plentiful effusion of his Spirit in all the gifts and graces of it through his gospel institutions on them; they shall be so enlightened in gospel truths, that they shall know their duties, and perform them, as if they were immediately enlightened from above, rather than by the common methods of teaching by his word; that they shall not need so much cautioning, threatening, correcting as they did under the law; but shall entirely cleave to him, without a disposition to revolt.

o Rom. 11. 27.
ch. 10. 17.
12 For I will be merciful to their unrighteousness, °and their sins and their iniquities will I remember no more.

For I will be merciful to their unrighteousness: this *for* states the cause of all the former acts promised in the gospel covenant, as regenerating, illuminating, adopting, and God's gracious removing all sins that might hinder the communication of these and all other good to his covenanted ones; God, in and by the administration of this covenant, ratified by his blood, propitiating him, will of his free mercy pardon, blot out, and take away, chap. ii. 17, and thereby free them from the guilt, power, and punishment of their original and actual unrighteousness; implying his reconciliation to, and free acceptance of, their persons in Jesus Christ, on whose account it is he dealeth so graciously with them in all things, Isa. lv. 7—9; 1 John iv. 9. *And their sins and their iniquities will I remember no more;* all the breaches of God's law by commissions or omissions, whatever they may be for number or for aggravation, he will always through Christ save his covenanted ones from them all, Matt. i, 21; Rom. iii. 21—26. All of these shall not only be for the present blotted out, but his mercy will be so great and certain through Christ, that he will neither punish them for them, nor charge them to them; he will abundantly pardon, and for ever take them away, so as if they be sought for they shall not be found, chap. x. 3, 14; Isa. xliii. 25; Micah vii. 18 19. And when he forgets their sins, he will have their persons in everlasting remembrance, Psal. cxii. 6.

p 2 Cor. 5. 17.
13 ᵖIn that he saith, A new *covenant,* he hath made the first old. Now that which decayeth and waxeth old *is* ready to vanish away.

In that he saith, A new covenant, he hath made the first old : the inference from what was before said, ver. 8, (in the Lord's saying this by the prophet Jeremiah, that he would make a new covenant, for form and manner of administration later and better, even the last and best he will make, and in which he will have penitent, believing sinners to acquiesce,) is this, That the Mosaical one, though first in respect of the gospel, hath lost its power, strength, and vigour, its binding force; and so, by God's instituting another, is abrogated, as useless, needless, and imperfect. *Now that which decayeth and waxeth old is ready to vanish away;* this Mosaical one, thus grown old, weak, and decrepit, and by the institution of the new gospel covenant abrogated, may continue for a while, but in no force; and so gradually moulder and decay by little and little, till it at last vanish and totally cease. It was near to it upon finishing of the ministry of the gospel High Priest on earth, when by his death he fulfilled the truth of this typical one, and so virtually nulled it; and, as to its binding force, vanished, when the gospel was published throughout the world, Rom. x. 16—18; compare 2 Cor. v. 17; as is owned by the apostolical synod, Acts xv. It was high time for these Hebrews to cease from that vanishing Mosaical one, and effectually to close with the gospel priesthood and covenant, which must remain and continue for ever; see Dan. ix. 24, 26, 27; which if they did not, must end in the total destruction of them, their temple and city, which came to pass not many years after the apostle wrote this Epistle

---

CHAP. IX.

The service and sacrifices of the first tabernacle were far less perfect and efficacious to purge the conscience than the blood of Christ, 1—14. *The necessity of Christ's death for the confirmation of the new covenant,* 15—22; *and of better sacrifices than those legal ones to purify the heavenly things,* 23, 24. *Christ was offered once for all,* 25—28.

‖ Or, ceremonies.
a Ex. 25. 8.
THEN verily the first *covenant* had also ‖ordinances of divine service, and ᵃa worldly sanctuary.

The Holy Spirit, from ver. 1 of this chapter, to ver. 18 of chap. x., is illustrating his two last arguments taken from the tabernacle and covenant administrations, about which both the Aaronical priests and the gospel High Priest did minister; in both which Christ hath beyond all comparison the pre-eminence, which the Spirit proves by an argument drawn *a comparatis*, of the tabernacle and service of the Aaronical priests, and the tabernacle and work of Christ. He beginneth with a proposition of the adjuncts of the first covenant from ver. 1—10. The three particles introducing it, μὲν, ὠν, and καὶ, agree, the one in connecting, the other demonstrating, and the last in asserting, that which followeth to depend on what went before, as, And then truly the first. *The first covenant:* ἡ πρώτη is an ellipsis, nothing is in the Greek text joined with it, though some Greek copies add σκηνὴ, the first tabernacle; but this is to make the same thing a property of itself, and it is absurd to read, the first tabernacle had a tabernacle; it is therefore better supplied from that which *first* relates to in ver. 7, 13 of chap. viii., viz. the Mosaical covenant administration, which had or possessed, as its proper adjuncts, even those three distinct ones following. *Had also ordinances;* δικαιώματα, we read *ordinances;* others, ceremonies or rites. It is derived from a passive verb, and may signify, a righteous sentence or ordinance of God, or a righteous event that answers that law or decree, as Rom. viii. 4. In the plural it notes *jura,* the laws of God, but especially here the ceremonial laws, those just constitutions for ministry which God gave by Moses to the Aaronical priesthood. *Of divine service;* λατρείας, which our translators make of the genitive case singular; but this is repugnant to the next words connected to it, which should strictly be of the same case; it is therefore best rendered in the accusative case plural, and by apposition to ordinances, and so is read services or worship, which because it refers to God, our translators have added to it the word *Divine.* How various this worship was in the ministry of the high priest and ordinary priests, the apostle showeth afterward, and therefore most properly to be rendered services. *And a worldly sanctuary:* τὸ ἅγιον was the sanctuary where these services were performed, called the holy, from its relation to God and his service. It consisted of two tabernacles, as is described, ver. 2, 3. It is styled κοσμικὸν, being externally decent, beautiful, and glorious, as is evident by its description, Exod. xxvi. Made it was after God's own model, a mystical structure, and a type of a better; yet though that were so pleasing to the eye of the world, its materials were, like it, frail, brittle, and passing away, as things made with hands make way for better, ver. 24.

b Ex. 26. 1.
c Ex. 26. 35.
& 40. 4.
d Ex. 25. 31.
e Ex. 25. 23, 30.
Lev. 24. 5, 6.
|| Or, *holy.*

2 [b]For there was a tabernacle made; the first, [c]wherein *was* [d]the candlestick, and [e]the table, and the shewbread; which is called || the sanctuary.

For there was a tabernacle made: the Spirit descends to a particular account of the three former adjuncts to the covenant, beginning with the last, the *sanctuary;* which being glorious, he advanceth the glory of Christ from the place of his ministry above it. *For* is demonstrative of what was asserted ver. 1, the first visible habitation that God had amongst men, 2 Sam. vii. 6, as a token of his gracious presence with them. This tabernacle consisted of three parts, of the court where stood the brazen altar of burnt offerings, the brazen laver for the priests to wash the sacrifices in, and to purify themselves when they came and offered them upon the altar, Exod. xxvii. 1, &c.; xxx. 17—21; xxxviii. 1—20; xl. 28—33. This court the Holy Ghost here leaves out. Separated from this court by a veil was the first tent or tabernacle, called the sanctuary, or holy place, where the priest did the daily service, which is called the first, Exod. xxvi. 36; xl. 22—29. Inward of this, and separated by a veil, was the holy of holiest, where the ark was, and where the high priest only entered once a year, Exod. xxv. 10, 22; xl. 20, 21. This tabernacle was according to God's pattern and command, prepared, finished, and reared up by Moses, Exod. xl. *The first;* the sanctuary, or holy place, separated by one veil from the holy of holiest, and from the court by another, had in it the following sacred utensils. *The candlestick;* for matter and form answering God's pattern, as Exod. xxv. 31, 40; xxxvii. 17, 25; xl. 24, 25. It was of pure gold, and of six branches artificially wrought, by which was typified that Spirit of light which Christ giveth to the true tabernacle, his body mystical, the church wherein God dwelleth, not unusually set out by lamps, Rev. iv. 5. And by reason of that light is the church set out by the emblem of candlesticks, Rev. i. 4, 12, 13, 20. *The table;* for matter, of plates of pure gold covering the shittim wood, and a crowning verge of gold round it, Exod. xxv. 23—30; xxxvii. 10—16; xl. 22, 23. Most excellent for its spiritual use, setting out Christ in all his excellencies, well stored and furnished for his; which the Jews by their unbelief and profaneness made contemptible, Mal. i. 7. *The shewbread* was twelve cakes made and set on the table, new every sabbath day in the morning, and when taken away were to be eaten by the priests only, Exod. xxv. 30; xl. 23; Lev. xxiv. 5—9. However, on David's necessity God dispensed with that law, and allowed him to eat of it, Mark ii. 26. This was an emblem of God's provision for the twelve tribes, the type of his church; and the bestowing on them the bread of life from heaven, the all-sufficient food for them, John vi. 32—58; compare Col. ii. 16, 17. *Which is called the sanctuary;* which first tabernacle was called the holy place or sanctuary, being relatively so, as God's tent, and no otherwise, so is it styled by the Spirit, Exod. xxvi. 33.

f Ex. 26. 31, 33. & 40. 3, 21. ch. 6. 19.

3 [f]And after the second veil, the tabernacle which is called the Holiest of all;

And after the second veil: this distinguisheth the second tabernacle from the first; for, passing through it to the end of it, there hung up a curious veil made of blue, purple, scarlet, and fine twined linen, with figures of cherubims, Exod. xxvi. 31, 32; xxxvi. 35, 36: xl. 21. The mystery of which is interpreted after, ver. 8: see chap. vi. 19. A veil noteth distance and obscurity; or, covering, opposite to that which is open and free. *The tabernacle which is called the holiest of all:* behind this veil was the second tabernacle, called the holy of holiest, Exod. xxvi. 33, by God himself, which did really, though typically, hold out the place of God's special appearance for propitiation and gracious answers of peace to the desires of his people in the Lord Jesus; applied afterwards to heaven itself, the holiest of all, where the High Priest is entered for us, and sits at the right hand of his Father, making intercession for us, chap. vi. 19, 20; vii. 25; ix. 24; x. 19.

g Ex. 25. 10. & 26. 33. & 40. 3, 21.
h Ex. 16. 33, 34.
i Num. 17. 10.
k Ex. 25. 16, 21. & 34. 29. & 40. 20.
Deu. 10. 2, 5.

4 Which had the golden censer, and [g]the ark of the covenant overlaid round about with gold, wherein *was* [h]the golden pot that had manna, and [i]Aaron's rod that budded, and [k]the tables of the covenant;

1 Kings 8. 9, 2 Chron. 5. 10.

Which had the golden censer; in the holy of holiest was reserved the golden censer, on which the high priest put the incense when annually he entered there, (see Lev. xvi. 12, 13,) that the cloud of it might cover the mercy-seat, and so was kept for that service in it: see Joseph. Antiq. lib. 3. 7. Many would refer this to the golden altar of incense that stood before the veil in the holy place, Exod. xxx. 6—8; and so they read it, having the golden altar of incense before it for its service, and not within it; signifying the Godhead, by which Christ maketh his intercession, sanctifying and perfuming his own, and all offerings made in his name. *And the ark of the covenant;* it was a coffer or chest of shittim wood, plated all over with gold, Exod. xxv. 10—22; xxxvii. 1, 6; xl. 20, 21. This chest had for its cover a mercy-seat, listed or verged with a crown of gold round it; and is called *the ark of the covenant,* because the tables of testimony were laid up in it, Exod. xxv. 16; xl. 20; those two stone tables wrought by Moses, and carried up into the mount, (after he had on the idolatry of Israel broken those of God's own making, and on which God had written the ten laws, the terms of his covenant with them,) on which God wrote afresh his laws, and renewed his covenant with them, Exod. xxxiv. 1, 2, 28, 29; compare chap. xxxi. 18. This ark was a type of Christ interposing between God and us, who had broken the covenant of his laws. *Wherein was the golden pot that had manna;* ἐν ᾗ, *wherein,* refers not to the ark mentioned just before, for in it was nothing put but the two tables of the covenant; but the tabernacle, called the holy of holiest, in which was reserved the golden censer, pot of manna, provided by God's charge before the giving of the law, and laid up afterwards in that archive by God's order, Exod. xvi. 32—34. This manna was the bread God fed Israel in his church with forty years in the wilderness, and is called *angels' food,* Psal. lxxviii. 25; a type of Christ *the true bread,* that God gave from heaven to his church, John vi. 31—58. *And Aaron's rod that budded;* which was by God's order put before the testimony in the holy of holiest, and not into the ark, for it was to be in view there as a token of the true priesthood, the type of Christ's, against all after-murmurers and usurpers: see Numb. xvii. 1—11. *And the tables of the covenant;* and as these, the urn of manna and rod of Aaron, were in the holy of holiest; so especially the two tables of the covenant were there too, but laid up in the ark which was in that place: see 1 Kings viii. 9; 2 Chron. v. 10. Others think the preposition ἐν is to be read, by which, or about, near which ark, as it is used of Christ's sitting ἐν δεξιᾷ, chap. i. 3; and so notes, as to the pot of manna and Aaron's rod, an apposition of them to or by the ark, when the tables of the covenant were undeniably put into it.

l Ex. 25. 18, 22. Lev. 16.
2. 1 Kings 8. 6, 7.

5 And [l]over it the cherubims of glory shadowing the mercyseat; of which we cannot now speak particularly.

And over it the cherubims of glory shadowing the mercyseat; on the cover of the ark at each end was a cherub of beaten gold; these and the cover of the ark were all of one piece, they had their feet on the ledge of the cover, or its crown, at each end; their faces looked towards each other, and their wings touched each other in the extreme part of them, and so on the cover formed the mercy-seat; see Exod. xxv. 17—22; and xxxvii. 6—9; xl. 20. Their form is described by Ezekiel, chap. i. and x. They were glorious for matter and service, God in his glory manifesting himself over them, gave propitious answers unto Moses about his church, Exod. xxv. 22; Lev. xvi. 2. These cherubims typified the ministry of angels to our Lord Jesus, especially in his great work of rendering God propitious to his church, and saving it, chap. i. 14. Standing on the two ends of the ark's cover, they showed Christ to be the basis of their own standing, when others fell: they spread out their wings, to show their readiness for serving him in all; with their faces opposite to each other, and looking down on the mercy-seat and ark, typifying what the apostle saith of them, 1 Pet. i. 10—12, desirous to pry into the mystery of this great Propitiator, the Surety and Mediator of God's testament, and on his propitiation and its effects, which is admirable and astonishing, not to sinners only, but to angels, Eph. iii. 10. *Of which we cannot now speak particularly;* the apostle apologizeth for his but mentioning these mysterious things now, that it was not to eclipse the glory of that administration, but because the matters were well known to them already, only in this they were defective, that they reached not after Christ, the truth and substance of all these types; and therefore he proceeds from the places, to treat of the services to be performed by the Aaronical priesthood in them.

6 Now when these things were thus ordained, ᵐthe Priests went always into the first tabernacle, accomplishing the service *of God.*

m Num. 28. 3. Dan. 8. 11.

The Spirit now proceeds to the second adjunct of the Mosaical administration, having stated the places of them, even the Aaronical priests' services in them. *Now when these things were thus ordained;* when the tabernacles were made and reared, and the utensils rightly disposed in them, and all things set in God's own order, now *the priests went always into the first tabernacle, accomplishing the service of God;* into the holy place or sanctuary within the first veil, described, ver. 2. Not only the high priest, but all the common priests, consecrated by God's order to their work; every one in his daily course, constantly performing, and completely acting, all the services enjoined on them by God to be done there, as to put on the shew-bread, and to eat what they took off, Exod. xxv. 30; Lev. xxiv. 5—9; to keep the lights in the candlestick, supplying it with oil, and clearing the lights, Exod. xxv. 37, 38; xxvii. 20, 21; xxx. 7, 8; Numb. viii. 2, 3; to burn incense on the golden altar before the ark: the priests took a censer, and filled it with fire from the altar of burnt sacrifice, and then came to the altar of incense before the veil, and there put the incense on the fire in the censer; during the evaporating of which, the people in the court were pouring out their prayers for pardon, each person by himself; see Exod. xxx. 1—9, 34—36; xl. 26, 27; Luke i. 9, 10; even all the ordinances of worship commanded by God, did the priests perform in it. All which services in the holy place do but typify the true services in the gospel church, of all made priests by the blood of Christ, 1 Pet. ii. 5, 9; Rev. i. 5, 6; v. 9, 10; offering prayers and praises to God continually in the name of Christ, perfumed with the incense of his merits, Mal. i. 11; compare Rev. viii. 3; obtaining thereby the light of his grace through his Spirit, and the bread of life, till they are perfected by their great High Priest, and carried into the holy of holiest, there to be praising and enjoying God in him for ever, as he hath prayed for them, and promised to them, John xiv. 2, 3; xvii. 20, 21.

7 But into the second ʷᵉⁿᵗ the High Priest alone ⁿonce every year, not without blood, ᵒwhich he offered for himself, and *for* the errors of the people:

n Ex. 30. 10. Lev. 16. 2. 11,12,15,34. ver 25. o ch. 5. 3. & 7. 27.

This verse contains the special anniversary of the high priest alone in the inward tabernacle, the holy of holiest, of which you have the law, Exod. xxx. 14; Lev. xvi. 2, &c. *But into the second went the high priest alone once every year;* into this place the high priest was to enter once a year only, and every year to repeat it, as Exod. xxx. 10, upon the atonement day, being the tenth day of the month Tisri, the seventh month in their ecclesiastical year, and the first of their civil; that day was he to enter several times into that place, first for himself, Lev. xvi. 11—14, and then for the people, ver. 15, 16, &c., carrying in the blood first within the veil, and then coming out again, and carrying in the incense on the golden censer: none of the other priests were to enter into the holy place while he was ministering, but him alone, as Lev. xvi. 17. *Not without blood:* when he first entered into the holiest of all, it was with the blood of a young bull, of a ram, Lev. xvi. 3, 14, with the blood of the he-goat, ver. 15, 27. After he had offered the incense on his golden censer, ver. 4, he must sprinkle the blood upon the mercy-seat and before it, by which expiatory blood there was made an atonement, ver. 12—14. *Which he offered for himself, and for the errors of the people;* first, for his sinful self and family, Lev. xvi. 11, and then for the ignorances, incogitancies, errors, and all sorts of sins committed by the people, ver. 16; chap. vii. 27; all of them being committed with some error of the understanding. Which type, in all its parts, was perfectly fulfilled in Christ, the gospel High Priest, as is shown in the following verses; whereby not only his office, but his services, are transcendently set above, and preferred to, all the Aaronical ones.

8 ᵖThe Holy Ghost this signifying, that ᑫthe way into the holiest of all was not yet made manifest, while as the first tabernacle was yet standing:

p ch. 10. 19, 20. q John 14. 6.

The Holy Ghost this signifying; God the Spirit himself, the third relation in the Deity, the author of all the Mosaical institutions, who commanded all these ritual, ceremonial services in this tabernacle to be performed, who revealed all this to Moses, and who inspired him with it, Lev. xvi. 1, 2, the most infallible interpreter of his own institutions, declared by these signals and types, and demonstrated by the frame of ordinances, then given to the church, in these expressions, Exod. xxx. 10; Lev. xvi. 2, 12—15, 17: the veil ever covering the holy of holiest, but only on the day of expiation, when it was drawn aside, and that laid open. *That the way into the holiest of all was not yet made manifest;* the true and very means to God's presence in heaven itself, which is only by Christ the great High Priest, through whose blood we can come to the throne of his grace there boldly, chap. x. 19—22, and by the perfect work of his Spirit on us, can enter with him into the holy of holiest in heaven; this was not so plainly, clearly, fully, universally known as afterwards by the shedding of Christ's blood, and the revelation of it in the gospel to all the world. Christ was revealed to the Hebrews, and all these ceremonial ordinances did hold him out, and by him only the saints under that covenant administration got to heaven; yet the manifestation of it was obscure in comparison of what it is since. *While as the first tabernacle was yet standing;* while the Mosaical covenant administration was to continue, till the coming of Christ in the flesh, and perfecting the work by his death, for the space of near one thousand five hundred years, was the true, right, and proper way for entering into heaven, darkly, and obscurely, and typically revealed unto the church; when by the death of Christ the veil of the holy of holiest was rent asunder, heaven laid open to be seen, and entered into by all penitent believing sinners through Christ, every day in their duties, and then in their persons, Matt. xxvii. 51.

9 Which *was* a figure for the time then present, in which were offered both gifts and sacrifices, ʳthat could not make him that did the service perfect, as pertaining to the conscience;

r Gal. 3. 21. ch. 7. 18, 19. & 10. 1, 11.

Which was a figure for the time then present: the tabernacle in all its parts, and the whole economy of it, was παραβολή, which signifieth the translation of a word or thing from its own natural signification to signify another, which thing so signified by it is commonly more excellent than itself, as the substance exceeds the shadow; equivalent it is to those terms of types, examples, figures of things to come: such are the tabernacle and its services, representations of things spiritual and Divine, and very imperfect shadows of them, serving only for that infant state of the church; and when its nonage was to expire by the coming of the truths themselves, then were they to expire too. The only time when the tabernacle administration was present, and no longer. *In which were offered both gifts and sacrifices;* in which tabernacle were performed services to the great God, whose tent it was, suitable to his person, and agreeable to his will, even gifts and sacrifices, as before described, chap. v. 1; viii. 3. *That could not make him that did the service perfect, as pertaining to the conscience;* they were all impotent as to the restoring of a sinner to God's favour by themselves; they could not reconcile him to God, preserve communion with him, nor bring them to happiness in him, chap. x. 3, 4; no perfect justifying, sanctifying could be had by any of them, though never so often repeated. They might do all to the letter which God required, absolving the worshipper as to the external part, but not at all according to the conscience; or they could not take the guilt of sin from the conscience as to themselves, but it would cry guilty still; neither could they remove the power of it, for it was under bondage to it still; neither could they take away the fears and terrors of it, but left it shaking under them and unquiet still, being abused by them as a veil to keep them from Christ the true Priest and sacrifice, when as types and shadows they should have led these worshippers to him.

s Lev. 11. 2. Col. 2. 16.
t Num. 19. 7, &c.
u Eph. 2. 15. Col. 2. 20.
ch. 7. 16.
‖ Or, *rites, or, ceremonies.*

10 *Which stood* only in ˢmeats and drinks, and ᵗdivers washings, ᵘand carnal ‖ ordinances, imposed *on them* until the time of reformation.

Having shown the typicalness, weakness of the Mosaical covenant administration, in respect of the tabernacles, services, and ordinances, he closeth his description of them in this verse, by showing their carnality and mortality. As they were external things, they could reach no further than the flesh only, as appears by particular instances, and therefore could not quiet the conscience, considered without Christ, nor justify, sanctify, or save the sinner. For meat and drink offerings, and meats clean and unclean, and drinks prohibited by God, in which the Jews placed much of their religion, separate from what they signified, commended no man unto God, 1 Cor. viii. 8. *Which stood only in meats and drinks:* as to *meats,* see Lev. xi.; Deut. xiv. 3—21. As to *drinks,* forbidden the priests, Lev. x. 9, and the Nazarites, Numb. vi. 2, 3; the jealousy water, Numb. v. 24, and the paschal cup, Psal. cxvi. 13, and cup of thank-offerings; see Lev. i. and ii. *And divers washings,* which were many for the priests in their services, and for others in performing theirs by them; some by sprinkling with blood, Exod. xxix. 20, 21, with water, Numb. viii. 7; xix. 9—19; some by washing at the brazen laver, as the priests, Exod. xxix. 4; xxx. 17—21; so the sprinkling of healed lepers, Lev. xiv. 4—9, and the purification of the unclean. All these were of God's own instituting, but still reach no further than the flesh or body of the sinner: see ver. 13. *And carnal ordinances:* other carnal rites and ceremonies, such as could not reach the conscience, as they used them, yet were to be used by them in obedience to God's will, and to discriminate them from others, which were various in the ceremonial law. *Imposed on them; ἐπικείμενα,* imposed, may agree with δῶρά, ver. 9, *gifts imposed;* or may have the whole sentence for its substantive, as, being matters imposed or settled in meats and drinks. All these things were not the inventions of Moses, but God's own institutions, enjoined by his own authority on the Jewish church, to lead them by a regular use of them to life by Christ, but by their own corruptions were made burdens to them. The Divine precept obliged them to an observation of them, and to the serving God in, by, and through them. *Until the time;* as they were outward, bodily, and carnal things, so they were mortal; as to their being and continuance enjoined by God, they were μέχρι καιροῦ· *until* is a term settled and limited, and not indefinite, and its limit is a singular time, even that point of time wherein Christ, having finished the work of redemption, ascended and sat down on the right hand of God, and powerfully thence breathed forth the Spirit of infallibility on his apostles, for guiding them in laying the foundation of his church, by preaching the gospel throughout the world, and perfecting of it, and no other. This the Jews and others expected from the Messiah, John iv. 25, in his time. All the New Testament perfecting was by them, and therefore they give a charge against the least alteration of the gospel, truth, and law, which they left as a rule for ordering of Christ's church to his last coming: see Matt. xxviii. 20. *Of reformation; διορθώσεως,* of putting things to rights by the law, rule, and ordinance of Christ, the work of this special point of time. He, the great church reformer, thoroughly righteth things to God-ward, by removing and taking away what was faulty, not in itself, but by man's abuse of it, even all the Mosaical economy and church-frame, which carried men about to God, by opening and making that to be seen with open face, which was well veiled, and so mistaken, even the mystery of Christ hid from ages, by manifesting and establishing that which was the truth itself, instead of the shadows that did but represent it; even that true church-frame intended first by God, and now fully revealed and settled by his Son as a standing rule and pattern to all for ever; which unmovable kingdom of his is described further, chap. xii. 22—28.

11 But Christ being come ˣan High Priest ʸ of good things to come, ᶻby a greater and more perfect tabernacle, not made with hands, that is to say, not of this building;

x ch. 3. 1.
y ch. 10. 1.
z ch. 8. 2.

But; the Spirit, by this adversative *But,* opposeth and applieth the truth to the type, and brings in view the antitype, the office, tabernacle, sacrifice, and ministration of Christ, which vastly exceedeth the Mosaical one. *Christ being come an High Priest of good things to come;* the High Priest preferred is no less person than God the Son manifested in the flesh, and anointed to his office with the Holy Ghost and power, Acts x. 38. In the fulness of time, before the antiquating and removing the former order, was he exhibited and consecrated the true High Priest, of which all the other were but types, and bringing with him all those good things which were figured and promised under that economy, all pardon, reconciliation, righteousness, holiness, adoption, and glorious salvation, which were under that dispensation to come, being present and exhibited with, as effected by, this High Priest at his first coming, but to be completed and perfected at his second, which is intimated, ver. 26, 28. *By a greater and more perfect tabernacle;* the anti-type of the Mosaical sanctuary and tabernacle, where there was the holy place, and the holy of holiest, correspondent to, and figured out by, these, was the more glorious sanctuary of this High Priest; he passeth through the tabernacle of his church on earth, of which he is the minister, as hath been cleared, ver. 10, and chap. viii. 2, and so enters into the heaven of heavens, the holiest of all, ver. 24, where God sits on his throne of grace. *Tabernacle* here cannot signify the body of Christ, for that is the sacrifice that answereth to the legal ones offered in the court, and without the gate, chap. xiii. 11—13, and with the blood of which he enters the holy of holiest as the high priest did, and he doth not pass through his flesh there, but carrieth it with him. The word ἐσκήνωσεν, John i. 14, may not only refer to the Godhead's tabernacling in flesh, but that God the Son incarnate tabernacled in his church; those with whom Christ dwelt while on earth, for his human nature dwelt or had a tabernacle in this world as well as his Deity; and this is such a tabernacle where he in his whole person and his church may meet and communicate together. This tabernacle is greater than the Mosaical for quantity, as it refers to earth the place, even the whole world, where his church is dispersed, beyond all comparison larger than its type, which was a little limited and confined place; and more perfect than that, which was only made of boards, gold, silver, brass, silk, linen, skins, &c. This being a spiritual temple and tent, in which God will inhabit and dwell for ever, 1 Cor. iii. 9, 16, 17; 2 Cor. vi. 16; Eph. ii. 12, 20—22; 1 Pet. ii. 5; it is far more glorious than that tabernacle, Hag. ii. 7—9. *Not made with hands;* what is hand-wrought, or made by men, is at the best mouldering and decaying; but this was wrought by the Spirit of God himself, most excellent for the quality, permanency of the materials, and work, Eph. ii. 22. Man had neither power nor skill to form, polish, frame, or pitch this, chap. viii. 2. Creation-work is God's work, as to the old and new creation. Hands may frame and pitch the other, and pluck it up; but he that worketh, frameth, raiseth, createth this, is God, 2 Cor. v. 5; Eph. ii. 20.

a ch. 10. 4.
b Acts 20. 28.
Eph. 1. 7.
Col. 1. 14.
1 Pet. 1. 19.
Rev. 1. 5.
& 5. 9.
c Zech. 3. 9.
ver. 26, 28. ch. 10. 10. d Dan. 9. 24.

12 Neither [a] by the blood of goats and calves, but [b] by his own blood he entered in [c] once into the holy place, [d] having obtained eternal redemption *for us.*

From his office and sanctuary he proceeds to clear up his service. *Neither by the blood of goats and calves;* it was not about weak, typical, vanishing sacrifices, the blood of goats or young bulls, that he was concerned, as the Aaronical priests were, Lev. xvi. 14, 15, opened before, ver. 7; and this annually on the expiatory day, Lev. xvi. 29, 34; which could not satisfy injured justice, nor expiate sin, nor purge nor quiet the conscience of the offender, chap. x. 1—5. *But by his own blood;* but with his own pure, precious, and unspotted blood, 1 Pet. i. 19. Not a drop or few drops must go for it; then what dropped from his body in his agony, from his head pierced by thorns, from his back when whipped, from his hands and feet when nailed on the cross, might have done; but it must be his own life-blood, the blood of the Second Adam dying by it for the first, Rom. v. 8—20; Phil. ii. 6, 8. And as it is the blood of Adam, that it may have value enough and worth, it must be the blood of him who is God too, *with his own blood,* Acts xx. 28. This price surmounts all treasures, John vi. 51; x. 11, 15. *He entered in once into the holy place;* with this blood of the covenant he entered, immediately upon the breathing out of his soul on the cross, (the veil of the temple being rent asunder, and room made for the great High Priest to fulfil his type,) into the holy of holiest in heaven, where never angel came, nor any but himself, till his now piercing through, rending the veil, and laying it open, chap. x. 19; compare Isa. lvii. 15; and came with it to God's throne of justice there, and made the everlasting atonement for sin, and so turned it into a throne of grace, fulfilling his type, and as the high priest did before the sacrifice was burnt or consumed, Lev. xvi. For the expiation of sin was not deferred by Christ to his ascension, forty-five days after his death, but was immediately on his giving up the Ghost by him performed; and in this he fulfilled *all righteousness,* Matt. iii. 15. This is the *once* that he entered heaven for expiation, satisfying the injured justice of God by sin, fulfilled the law, and then publicly appeared at God's throne, to show all was complete, Luke xxiii. 43, 45, 46; John xix. 30. This *once* he did that which the high priest did annually typify, but could never accomplish for so many hundred years together, ver. 26, 28; chap. x. 10, 12, 14. By which it is evident that *one,* and *once,* refers to the shedding of his blood as a sacrifice, and presenting of it to the Father, as completing propitiation work at that once for ever. *Having obtained eternal redemption for us;* when he with the incense of his merit and prayer to the just and merciful Judge, even God his Father, sued for, found, obtained, and fully received eternal redemption for sinners; i. e. deliverance of their guilty persons from eternal death, full remission of all their sins, Rom. iii. 25, 26, full reconciliation to God, 2 Cor. v. 18, 19, 21, with an instating them into all spiritual good. This work is styled *eternal,* because its virtue is of perpetual continuance, which freeth the duly qualified subjects (Col. i. 21, 23) from the guilt and punishment of all sins for ever.

e Lev. 16.
14, 16.
f Num. 19.
2, 17, &c.

13 For if [e] the blood of bulls and of goats, and [f] the ashes of an heifer sprinkling the unclean, sanctifieth to the purifying of the flesh:

This service of Christ in his sanctuary exceeds the Aaronical, not only for reconciling souls to God, but purifying of them, as cleared in this and the 14th verse. *For if the blood of bulls and of goats:* the blood is the same as spoken of ver. 12. *Bulls,* here put for calves, are but to distinguish the sex; and it is to be noted, where our translators read oxen, as to sacrifices in the Old Testament, as particularly Numb. vii. 87, they mean bulls, for no oxen were by the law to be offered to God at all as sacrifices; see Lev. xxii. 17—23; because they could not be true types of the true sacrifice, which was to perfect them. This blood was sprinkled on the mercy-seat and before it, and on the altar, Lev. xvi. 14, 19, &c., expiating sins, and taking away the guilt and legal punishment. *And the ashes of an heifer sprinkling the unclean:* the rite of preparing it, read in Numb. xix. 1—10. A red heifer was by the people given to the priest; he was to bring her without the camp, and order her to be slain, and then take the blood with his finger, and sprinkle it towards the tabernacle seven times; after which she was to be wholly burnt in his sight, with cedar wood, hyssop, and scarlet, the ashes of which were reserved; when they used them, they took them in a vessel, and put running water to them, and then sprinkled them with a bunch of hyssop on persons legally unclean, ver. 18—20, and so they purified them from their ceremonial filth and pollution; but none of these could purify an unclean soul, that was left unholy and unclean still. *Sanctifieth to the purifying of the flesh;* these sprinklings did sanctify those who were legally unclean, and did procure a legal purity and acceptance of them in the service of the sanctuary, from which else they were excluded; by this they were looked on as externally holy with the congregation, their flesh and outward man being made pure by it for their external worship.

g 1 Pet. 1. 19.
1 John 1. 7.
Rev. 1. 5.
h Rom. 1. 4.
i Eph. 2. 5.
1 Pet. 3. 18.
Tit. 2. 14.
ch. 7. 27.
‖ Or, *fault.*
k ch. i. 3.

14 How much more [g] shall the blood of Christ, [h] who through the eternal Spirit [i] offered himself without ‖ spot to God, [k] purge your conscience from [l] dead works [m] to serve the living God?

& 10. 22. 1 ch. 6. 1. m Luke 1. 74. Rom. 6. 13, 22. 1 Pet. 4. 2.

How much more shall the blood of Christ? the question supposeth an unexpressible difference between Christ's purifying and the legal sacrifices. The blood with which he pierced within the veil to the throne in the highest heavens, on which sat the just God, the proper, precious, powerful blood of God the Son incarnate. *Who through the eternal Spirit;* who in his immortal soul obeying all God's will in suffering, did, through his own eternal Godhead, to which both body and soul were united, and which sanctified the body offered, as the altar the sacrifice, Matt. xxiii. 19, which is called *the spirit of holiness,* Rom. i. 4, and gave value and virtue to the sacrifice, offer up his body a sacrifice for sin, when he died on the cross. Not sheep, bulls, goats, turtles, pigeons, &c., not man, nor the life of angels, were his sacrifice; but himself, pure, holy, and unpolluted, an innocent, harmless person, 2 Cor. v. 21. How much beyond his types for innocency and purity! Lev. xxii. 20, 21; Numb. xix. 2. *Offered himself without spot to God:* the offended, injured Creator and Judge of sinners, who constituted him to this whole work; and was by this most perfect sacrifice propitiated; his justice was satisfied, his law obeyed, and himself set fully free to pardon and forgive sinners without injustice; and to be just, as well as gracious and merciful, in doing of it, Rom. iii. 25, 26; and they might be put in possession of his favour, presence, and person again, as their own God, 1 Pet. iii. 18. *Purge your conscience;* though the sacrifice be over, the virtue and excellent causality of it doth abide, purging now as ever, not only justifying and absolving of a penitent believing sinner, but purifying and sanctifying the soul, procuring the Holy Spirit to renew it, and take away inherent corruption and infuse holiness into it, Eph. iv. 24, and making willing in the beauties of it, Psal. cx. 3; 1 Cor. vi. 11; Tit. iii. 5, 6; making body, soul, and spirit one frame of holiness to God, 1 Thess. v. 23. So as the most quick, lively, and sensible part of the immortal soul, conscious of sin, is freed from the guilt, filth, and fears of sin that did cleave to it; this thus purged, no consciousness of guilt remains, nor fear of punishment, but it is filled, from the interest it ha h in this blood, and the work on it of this Spirit, full of joy and peace and righteousness by believing, Rom. v. 1, 2, 5, 11. *From dead works;* all operations of sin, which come from spiritually dead souls, and work eternal death, Eph. ii. 1, of which they are as insensible as dead men; all sorts of sin which do taint, pollute, and defile the soul, much more contagious, pestilent, and polluting the soul, than any of those things forbidden to be touched by Moses's law could the flesh, Numb. xix. 18: they are as offensive to God, and more, than carcasses are to us, and pestilential things, though themselves keeping souls from any communion with him. *To serve the living God;*

HEBREWS IX

as under the law there was no coming to the congregation of the tabernacle without legal purifying, Numb. xix. 13, 20; so by this purifying correspondent to the type, souls are quickened, have boldness and confidence God-ward in point of duty, present themselves living sacrifices, Rom. xii. 1, aim at him through their whole life; that he delights to keep up communion with them proportioned to himself, till he fit them for their complete serving and enjoying of him in the holy of holiest in heaven.

n 1 Tim. 2. 5.
o ch. 7. 22. & 8. 6. & 12. 24.
p Rom. 3. 25. & 5. 6.
1 Pet. 3. 18.
q ch. 3. 1.

15 ⁿAnd for this cause ᵒhe is the mediator of the new testament, ᵖthat by means of death, for the redemption of the transgressions *that were* under the first testament, ᵠthey which are called might receive the promise of eternal inheritance.

And for this cause he is the Mediator of the new testament: as Christ's priesthood and service, his sacrifice and purifying, so the testamental covenant, and his administration of it, did incomparably exceed all those of Aaron's; so that for what was spoken, ver. 14, even the effects of his sacrifice, the justification and sanctification of sinners, is he the great gospel High Priest, the mediating person between God and sinners, confirming and making effectual by his death God's testamental covenant to them, which is for the administration of it the very best and last, in which God bequeatheth pardon, reconciliation, righteousness, holiness, adoption, and heirship to an eternal inheritance to penitent, believing sinners. *That by means of death;* the death of Christ himself, God-man, the most excellent sacrifice, without which there could be no remission, ver. 22, nor the testament of God about it put in force; for which cause he was the Mediator of it, that they should value him so much the more for his death, fulfilling therein all his types, and reach that which was unattainable by these, both for their fathers and themselves. *For the redemption of the transgressions that were under the first testament;* for the satisfying the justice of God for the wrong their sins had done it, paying that price without which they could not be expiated, by which they were remissible, and to the duty qualified, actually forgiven, even the sins of those who were under the Mosaical administration of the covenant. Aaron, Samuel, David, and the saints, believers in that time, had their transgressions pardoned by virtue of the death of Christ to come, shadowed by these sacrifices typifying him and his death in their own times. What the death of beasts or birds could do for them, his did, delivering them from the guilt and punishment of their transgressions, under which otherwise they must have perished for ever: this Peter publisheth, Acts xv. 11. This virtue of Christ's death is not mentioned exclusive of New Testament sins being remitted by it; but if it did expiate those old ones, reaching so much backward, even to Aaron, it will much more expiate those under the New Testament to penitent, believing, praying sinners for it, as those Old Testament transgressors were. *They which were called might receive the promise of eternal inheritance:* such as on God's call repent and believe on the Lord Jesus, that Angel of the covenant then revealed to them, and enter into covenant with him, Exod. xxiii. 20—23; compare 1 Cor. x. 3, 4, 9; John v. 45—47; such as by it have sins expiated, consciences purged, so as to have a title to and fitness by the work of the Spirit for the heavenly Canaan, Rom. iv. 16, 24, 25; may be put into the possession of that eternal inheritance made over to them by promise, and which the Spirit gave them an earnest of here, chap. xii. 10, 14, 16; compare Eph. i. 13, 14; 1 Pet. i. 3, 4. All this is confirmed to these by Christ's death.

16 For where a testament *is*, there
‡ Or, *be brought in.*
must also of necessity ∥ be the death of the testator.

For where a testament is: for gives the reason of the Mediator's death, even the putting the called into the possession of the bequeathed inheritance, demonstrated by a common, natural law in all nations of the testament's effect on the testator's death; a testament being a disposition by will nuncupative, or written, of either goods or lands, which are the person's own, to be the right and possession of others after his death, whom he nominateth in it: such in proportion is the new covenant, where God gives freely all spiritual good things with a heavenly inheritance, as legacies to all his called ones in Christ, by this last and best will and testament of his, written in his Scripture instrument, witnessed by the prophets and apostles, sealed by the two sacraments, especially the Lord's supper, Luke xxii. 20. *There must also of necessity be the death of the testator;* he who maketh a testament by the law of nature, as of nations, must die before the legatees have any profit by the will; the son and heir inherits not but on the father's death; then is the testament firm and valid, the time being come for the heir's inheriting, and for the will's execution, it being now unalterable; the necessity of which is cleared, ver. 17.

17 For ʳa testament *is* of force after   ʳ Gal. 3. 15.
men are dead: otherwise it is of no strength at all while the testator liveth.

For a testament is of force after men are dead: the testator being by death disseised of his goods and lands, the right takes place of the legatees, and the time of their challenging it; such a sacred tie there is upon the surviving, that none can of right add to it, alter, or disannul it. *Otherwise it is of no strength at all while the testator liveth;* it is of no force while the maker of it liveth, because they have need of the things bequeathed; they can alter and change it, and by the will itself it is declared none shall have any right to the things bequeathed in it till the testator be dead. The consequent of all this is, that the Testator of the new testament must put it in force by death; and his death is of greater force to confirm his testament than that of men, because his will can never be violated, it being a Divine constitution, but the human testament may. Christ, God-man, after dieth, as Testator, and puts the testament in force; and by breaking the bonds of death, doth gloriously effect that the legatees perform the conditions required in the will, to fit them for receiving their legacies; and then faithfully distributeth them to them by his grand executor the Holy Spirit, who applieth the virtue of it to the legatees under the Old Testament, as well as these under the New; he being the Testator, as well as the Lamb slain from the beginning of the world.

18 ˢWhereupon neither the first *testament* was ∥ dedicated without blood.
s Ex. 24. 6, &c.
∥ Or, *purified.*

Forasmuch as all testaments are put in force by the death of the testator, and all covenants are most strongly confirmed by death and blood in God's own judgment, thence it is that the Mosaical covenant was confirmed by them. *Dedicated;* ἐγκεκαίνισται, strictly taken, signifieth made new, or renewed. It is not used in the New Testament but in this place, and chap. x. 20: the Syriac translate it here confirmed, or ratified. In the Old Testament the Septuagint use it to express the Hebrew חנך Deut. xx. 5. In which law, for a man who had built a house, and was called out to the wars, to return and dedicate it, was to take possession of it, and secure it from the claim of another. Here it is properly used to make sure, firm, and inviolable; and that by blood, typical of Christ's, which is the highest and most solemn ratification. So were the covenants before ratified, but especially under the law, and the Mosaical covenant itself, as appears by instance, Gen. xv. 9, 10, 17, 18; xxxi. 44, 54; compare Exod. xxiv. 5, 7, 8.

19 For when Moses had spoken every precept to all the people according to the law, ᵗhe took the blood of calves and of   t Ex. 24. 5, 6, 8. Lev.
goats, ᵘwith water, and ∥ scarlet wool,   16. 14, 15, 18.
and hyssop, and sprinkled both the book,   u Lev. 14. 4, 6, 7, 49, 51, 52.
and all the people,   ∥ Or, *purple.*

For when Moses had spoken every precept to all the people according to the law: that the Old Testament was ratified by blood the Spirit proveth by instance, Moses as mediator having spoken every command, promise, and article of the covenant to all Israel, who came out of Egypt, according to God's charge, reading all to them out of the book, wherein by God's order he had written it; and the people declaring their assent and consent unto this covenant, as Exod. xxiv. 3, 4, 7, as God covenanted and bound himself to his part of it. *He took the blood of calves, &c.:* the Mediator then took, according to the common rite in such ratifying acts, a sprinkling bush made of scarlet wool, cedar wood, and hyssop, Lev. xiv. 4, 6; Numb. xix. 6, 18; to which David alludeth, Psal. li. 7; and with this bunch sprinkles the blood and water (which he had received into basons from the sacrifices, killed by the first-born, for burnt-offerings and peace-offerings, and there mixed, Exod. xxiv. 5, 6; Lev. ix. 3, 4; xiv. 51) on the altar, book of the covenant, and all Israel, Exod. xxiv. 6—8, confirming and ratifying the covenant on God's part and theirs, as the words annexed, ver. 20, and Exod. xxiv. 8, affirm, Behold the blood by which this covenant is made firm and inviolable. All this is but a shadow and type of the ratification of the new covenant with sinners by the death of Christ; he is the Mediator that brings God's testamental covenant to them; he dieth and puts it in force; by his blood ratifieth it on God's part and theirs, by his Spirit applying it to them, and sprinkling it on them; he brings home the testamental blessings to them, chap. x. 22; xi. 28; xii. 24; Isa. lii. 15; Ezek. xxxvi. 25; 1 Pet. i. 2.

x Ex. 24. 8. Mat. 26. 28. 20 Saying, ˣThis *is* the blood of the testament which God hath injoined unto you.

Moses, after his sprinkling the altar, book of the covenant, and all Israel, taught them the meaning of it; saying, This that is the blood wherewith I have sprinkled you, is a sign or a seal of the testament, the blood by which it is ratified and confirmed. The blood typified and represented by it, was that of Christ the Testator, by which all the new testament is ratified to all penitent, believing sinners that look to it, without which it could never have been made good. The blood of Christ is the immovable foundation of this testament, Exod. xxiv. 8; compare 1 Cor. xi. 25; even the testamental covenant which Jehovah had made with them, and which he enjoined them by such a rite as this to ratify and confirm.

y Ex. 29. 12, 36. Lev. 8. 15, 19. & 16. 14, 15, 16, 18, 19. 21 Moreover ʸhe sprinkled with blood both the tabernacle, and all the vessels of the ministry.

Moses did not only sprinkle the book of the covenant with blood, but the tabernacle itself, yearly, on the atonement day, as is charged, Lev. xvi. 14, 16, 17. For as the altar and persons were to be atoned for, so was the tabernacle itself, ver. 18, 20. First they were sprinkled, and then anointed, Lev. viii. 10, 11, as the gospel tabernacle was in the truth of it, 1 Cor. vi. 11. All the garments and vessels of that priesthood were thus to be purified, typifying how unclean all the persons ministering with them, and atoned for in and by them, were; and how polluting all things, and polluted by them, till they were purified by the blood of Christ.

z Lev. 17. 11. 22 And almost all things are by the law purged with blood; and ᶻwithout shedding of blood is no remission.

And almost all things are by the law purged with blood; all such things as are capable of purifying, and which were not to be so by the water of separation, or by fire, as Lev. xvi. 28; Numb. xxxi. 23, were ceremonially purged by blood. *And without shedding of blood is no remission;* and without the death of some living creature as a sacrifice, and the blood of it not only shed, but sprinkled, there could be neither legal pardon of guilt, nor purging of ceremonial filth. By this God signified to Israel, that without the blood of Christ his Son, and the Testator of his testament, shed as a sacrifice, to purchase and procure both remission and the Spirit, there could be neither pardon of the guilt of sin, and removal of the punishment, nor purging the filth, or renewing the nature of the sinner, his blood being the inestimable price purchasing both for them.

a ch. 8. 5. 23 *It was* therefore necessary that ᵃthe patterns of things in the heavens should be purified with these; but the heavenly things themselves with better sacrifices than these.

It was therefore necessary: this conclusion the Spirit draweth from the antecedent, ver. 18, proved in the following verses, therefore is it here rehearsed. The illative particle *therefore*, is but to sum up the use of blood about the first tabernacle, and that Testament dispensation. It is positively *necessary* by the will of God, expressively enjoining them, to point out better, and that there might be an agreement of the type with the truth. *That the patterns of things in the heavens should be* purified *with these:* the tabernacles in all their parts, the book of the covenant, vessels, services, &c., being types, signs, examples, shadows of things in heaven, must be ceremonially purged and separated from common use to Divine, by those external, ritual sprinklings and lustrations, especially with beasts' blood, mystically representing better blood and purifications of persons and things than these. *But the heavenly things themselves with better sacrifices than these;* but things more excellent and glorious than earthly ones, the gospel tabernacle in its parts, testament, and services, about which Christ ministereth, which are heavenly for their descent, agreeableness with, and tendency to it; they are spiritual and incorruptible, ver. 11, 12; chap. viii. 2; xii. 22; Gal. iv. 26; Rev. xxi.; are to be dedicated, set apart, put in force, and sanctified to God by the one sacrifice of Christ, of more value, worth, and virtue than all the legal sacrifices together. It is expressed plurally, to answer the opposite term, and to set out its excellency, being far above all others; the blood of it being that of God by personal union, and which is only efficacious for eternal good, and available with him; so ought it to be esteemed as it was in truth, and not quarrelled with by these Hebrews.

24 For ᵇChrist is not entered into the holy places made with hands, *which are* the figures of ᶜthe true; but into heaven itself, now ᵈto appear in the presence of God for us: b ch. 6. 20. c ch. 8. 2. d Rom. 8.34. ch. 7. 25. 1 John 2. 1.

For Christ is not entered into the holy places made with hands: for shows this to be a rational proof of the transcendency of Christ's death and sacrifice; and this he demonstrates from the place of his ministry, far exceeding that of his type. The gospel High Priest did not, like Aaron, enter with his blood into the holy of holiest of an earthly tabernacle, frail and movable, and appear before the mercy-seat on the ark there, ver. 9. *Which are the figures of the true;* all these were but like and correspondent figures and resemblances of the true, holy, and glorious place of God's residence. *But into heaven itself;* but he, as our High Priest, did enter with his atoning blood, after the sacrificing of himself on the cross, into the heaven of heavens, and approached the throne of justice, and propitiated it, making it a mercy-seat and true throne of grace unto penitent, believing sinners; and then perfected the work of propitiation and redemption: afterwards at his triumphant ascension, he entered in his whole person immortal, and laid open a way for our entering there. *Now to appear in the presence of God for us;* where he now appears as our advocating Mediator, pleading his merit for the remission of our sins, and rendering of God's face smiling on and favouring his clients, which was terrifying and affrighting to guilty Adam before: see chap. vii. 25; x. 19; Rom. viii. 34; 1 John ii. 1, 2; Rev. v. 6. Here he represents our persons to God's face, fitting in the mean while us beneath for our seeing him face to face, and being blessed in the enjoyment of that prospect for ever.

25 Nor yet that he should offer himself often, as ᵉthe High Priest entereth into the holy place every year with blood of others; e ver. 7.

The excellency of Christ's sacrifice beyond the Aaronical is argued here from its singularity; it needs no repetition, as their multiplied sacrifices did. *Nor;* οὐδὲ, introducing it, is but inferring this excellency of Christ's sacrifice, by denying in it that weakness which was annexed to the legal ones; there was no need that he should die yearly, to fulfil the type of the often yearly sacrifices of the legal high priest, who entered with the blood of bulls and goats, strange blood to him, and not his own, into the holy of holiest in the tabernacle, and entered so every year once, to show the virtue of his sacrifice to be only signal, typical, and passing, to make room for a better, that single, individual one of Christ, in respect of sacrifice and oblation.

26 For then must he often have suffered since the foundation of the world: but now *once* ᵍin the end of the world hath he appeared to put away sin by the sacrifice of himself.

f ver. 12.
ch. 7. 27.
& 10. 10.
1 Pet. 3. 18.
g 1 Cor. 10.
11. Gal. 4. 4.
Eph. 1. 10.

For then must he often have suffered; ἐπεί· the consequent is drawn *ab impossibili;* if he had often offered himself, he must have often suffered, but he could not suffer often. For where there was offering, there must be a sacrifice, and so suffering. Now that Christ should do so in his own person, was impossible and absurd, for God to have put his Son on suffering so cruel a death so often. *Since the foundation of the world;* from the fall of Adam at the beginning of the world, ever since sin needed a sacrifice: but his once suffering as a sacrifice for it was of eternal virtue in God's purpose, answering and satisfying God's justice; one death of the Second Adam for the sin and penalty of the first, in the efficacy and virtue of his death, which was everlasting. The often and annual sacrificing of the Aaronical priests, and entering of the holy of holiest with the blood of beasts, was to show the Jews their weakness, and to instruct them in, and lead them to, this one sacrifice once to be offered, of eternal vaid, as is subjoined. *But now:* but Christ the gospel High Priest was not only God-man, manifested to be so, and exhibited as such an officer by his work, but was manifested to be such by promise, and in types and figures from Adam's fall; but now showed it clearly in his suffering work, 1 Tim. iii. 16. *Once in the end of the world;* the days of Christ's ministry on earth under the fourth monarchy, called *the last time,* 1 John ii. 18, *the ends of the world,* 1 Cor. x. 11, *the fulness of the time,* Gal. iv. 4, God's set and best time for his appearance; and it was but once that he appeared in these days, performing this work. *Hath he appeared to put away sin by the sacrifice of himself;* then he sacrificed himself, offered up his blood to God within the veil, taking away by his own blood, which God required, the guilt, stain, and power of all sin, justifying believers from any condemnation by it, by what he did and suffered in their stead for their good, who fly from it for refuge to him, Isa. liii.; Dan. ix. 24; Rom. vii. 24, 25; 1 John iii. 5.

h Gen. 3. 19.
Eccles. 3. 20.
i 2 Cor. 5. 10.
Rev. 20. 12, 13.

27 ʰ And as it is appointed unto men once to die, ⁱbut after this the judgment:

And as it is appointed unto men once to die: the proof of the necessity of Christ's suffering death but once, is introduced in this verse by the conjunction *And.* It was according to God's decreed and published statute of men's but once dying; for God the Supreme Lord, Governor, and Judge of them, set, constituted, and appointed by an unalterable and irrevocable decree, as Lawgiver, and sentence, as Judge, to all of the sinful human race, the corrupt seed of apostate Adam, their grand representative, whom God threatened with this penalty upon his sinning and transgressing his law, Gen. ii. 17; which sentence was denounced upon him, Gen. iii. 19; compare Rom. v. 12, 14; vi. 23. This sentence was but *once* to be undergone by himself and all his sinful offspring, and by their Surety, and no more; so that the Second Adam needed but once to die by this statute. No man can keep himself from this, it being the general rule of God's proceeding with all persons. The Supreme Legislator may make what exceptions and provisos to his law he pleaseth. Those that were translated by him, did suffer a change proportionable to death, as Enoch, chap. xi. 5; Gen. v. 24, and Elijah, 2 Kings ii. 11, 12; and those that shall be changed at Christ's coming must undergo the like, as 1 Cor. xv. 51—54; 1 Thess. iv. 17. Those that were raised from death by Christ, Peter and Paul, &c., God might glorify his name by reiterating it; but whether they did die again, is not certain. This is to be the general settled law and rule of God. *But after this the judgment:* in order, after souls by death are separated from their bodies, they come to *judgment:* and thus every particular one is handed over by death to the bar of God, the great Judge, and so is despatched by his sentence to its particular state and place with its respective people, Rom. xiv. 12. At the great and general assize, the day of judgment, shall the general and universal one take place, Acts xvii. 31, when all sinners in their entire persons, bodies and souls united, shall be adjudged to their final, unalterable, and eternal state, Rom. xiv. 10; 2 Cor. v. 10; Jude 6; Rev. xx. 11—15.

28 So ᵏ Christ was once ˡoffered to bear the sins ᵐ of many; and unto them that ⁿ look for him shall he appear the second time without sin unto salvation.

k Rom. 6. 10.
1 Pet. 3. 18.
l 1 Pet. 2. 24.
l 1 John 3. 5.
m Matt. 26. 28. Rom. 5. 15.
n Tit. 2. 13.
2 Pet. 5. 12.

So Christ was once offered to bear the sins of many: οὕτως· καί is an illative connexion between the antecedent, ver. 27, and this consequent; As it was appointed to men once to die, so it was appointed to Christ once to offer himself. God's statute determineth both of these; Christ the High Priest, opposed to *men,* ver. 27, having died once as a sacrifice for sins, and offered his blood to God to expiate them, bearing their punishment which God laid on him, Isa. liii. 6; and so took away sins, guilt, filth, power and condemnation from *many,* whom the Father gave to him, and he undertook for, in it, Matt. xx. 28; xxvi. 28; John x. 15, 16. *And unto them that look for him shall he appear the second time without sin;* and to his believing, penitent expectants, such as long for his coming, Phil. iii. 20; Tit. ii. 13, stretching out their heads, as the mother of Sisera, Judg. v. 28, with a holy impatience of seeing him, such as by faith and prayer are hastening it, Rom. viii. 23; 2 Cor. v. 1—10; 1 Pet. i. 3—9, shall he once more visibly appear to them and the world, Acts i. 11; Rev. i. 7, gloriously, without need to suffer or die again for them, having at his departure after his first coming, carried all their sins into the land of forgetfulness. *Unto salvation;* and to their persons will he bring entire and complete salvation, raising and uniting bodies and souls together, Phil. iii. 21; and then take them as assistants to himself in the judgment-work on men and angels in the air; and having despatched that work, return with them to the holy of holiest in heaven, there to be completely blessed, in praising, serving, glorifying, and enjoying God in Christ, and the blessedness that attends that state, for ever and ever, as 1 Cor. vi. 2, 3; 1 Thess. iv. 17.

CHAP. X

The sacrifices of the law, being often repeated, could not take away sins, 1—4. *The abolition of them, and substitution of Christ's body in their stead, foretold by the psalmist,* 5—9: *by the offering of which body once for all we obtain perfect remission,* 10—18. *An exhortation to stedfastness in the faith, and to love and good works,* 19—25. *The danger of a wilful relapse after having received the knowledge of the truth,* 26—31; *and of forfeiting the reward of a good beginning for want of perseverance,* 32—39.

FOR the law having ᵃa shadow ᵇof good things to come, *and* not the very image of the things, ᶜcan never with those sacrifices which they offered year by year continually make the comers thereunto ᵈperfect.

a Col. 2. 17.
ch. 8. 5.
& 9. 23.
b ch. 9. 11.
c ch. 9. 9.

d ver. 14.

For: this *for* is connecting this to the foregoing discourse, and is a further improvement of the argument laid down, chap. ix., proving the necessity and excellency of the one sacrifice offered by Christ for sinners unto God, from the weakness of all the legal ones. For if all the multitude of them were not able to take away sins, and Christ's one offering is mighty to abolish them, and to perfect all who use it, then not these legal ones, but his is necessary to be valued by the Hebrews, and preferred to that end; the demonstration of which takes up from ver. 1—18 of this chapter. *The law;* the whole Mosaical economy given from God to Israel by him in the wilderness of Sinai; priesthood, covenant, sacrifices, and services, which that did contain. *Having a shadow of good things to come:* see chap. viii. 5. A *shadow* is lower than an *image,* and of another kind from the reality or substance; a dark, obscure representation of what was to fulfil them, viz. of Christ, with all his ministry and privileges attending his covenant, both for time and eternity; this the Mosaical law-real comprehended, but all in shadow-work. *And not the very image of the things;* they are not the very essence and substance themselves of those things, the pattern, or real sampler, but a shadowy representation; they lead their users to Christ and his matters, which they represented, but were not the substantial good things themselves. So *image* is read, 1 Cor. xv. 49, *we have borne the image of the earthy* Adam, that is, his nature. *Can never with those sacrifices which they offered year by year continually make the comers thereunto perfect:* the legal sacrifices are not only impotent in respect of their constitution, but of their very nature, being only shadows, so as they cannot render a soul complete, either in respect of justification or sanctification; they could not free any either from the guilt or punishment of sin at present, much less eternally: with all the renovation of them either on the day of atonement yearly, or those daily offered by them, though they should continue to be offered for ever, yet could they not perfect either the priests ministering, or those for whom they ministered, who were externally humbling themselves on the expiation day; they being designed only to point the people to this better sacrifice of Christ, which was to perfect them, that work being so noble, and above the power of shadows to perform.

| Or, *they would have ceased to be offered, because, &c.*

2 For then ‖ would they not have ceased to be offered? because that the worshippers once purged should have had no more conscience of sins.

For then would they not have ceased to be offered? for proves the weakness of that shadowy service under the law, because it never ceased, which it would if it had perfected its users; and having reached its end, and done that work, have ceased; for these sacrifices would not of right have been repeated, neither needed they, if they could have justified and sanctified souls for ever. *Because that the worshippers once purged should have had no more conscience of sins:* for then this effect would have followed, the worshippers who were to be atoned for or expiated by these sacrifices, if they had perfected them, i. e. pardoned, justified, and acquitted them from guilt of sin and punishment, there would have nothing remained to have troubled, vexed, or tormented their souls, they being no further accused or condemned by their conscience about sin, God having justified and sanctified them, chap. ix. 14, 26, 28; compare Rom. v. 1, 2, 11.

e Lev. 16. 21. ch. 9. 7.

3 ᵉ But in those *sacrifices there is* a remembrance again *made* of sins every year.

If the legal sacrifices could have perfected their offerers, there would have been no remembrance of sins; *but* there is a remembrance of sins yearly, therefore they are weak and cannot perfect. These shadowy sacrifices yearly reiterated, still left sins in their guilt and killing power, loading and grinding the conscience by accusation and condemnation for them, as well as setting them in the light of God's countenance. For in the expiation day Aaron was to remember and to confess over the head of the scape-goat, laying his hands on it, all the church's sins of the past year and life, notwithstanding former expiatory sacrifices offered for them, Lev. xvi. 22. For as soon as that was done, their expiating virtue vanished, and so they renewed sacrifices without any spiritual profit by them, the guilt of past and present sins remaining still: whereas Christians now renewing sin, do renew their faith and repentance, but not their sacrifice for it; the virtue of which, in a full and final absolution, applied to them by the Spirit, makes them to have, upon their final accounts, no conscience of sin for ever.

f Mic. 6. 6, 7. ch. 9. 13. ver. 11.

4 For ᶠ*it is* not possible that the blood of bulls and of goats should take away sins.

For gives a reason of the precedent proof, that the legal sacrifices did keep sins in remembrance; for they were of such matter as could not have any causal power to take them away. *It is not possible:* this is equivalent to a universal negative, the impossibility being absolute as to the things themselves in their very nature; they being corporeal, can have no influence upon a spiritual evil in the soul, Micah vi. 6, 7; and by God's constitution they were to lead them to better things, God being not pleased with flesh and blood, Psal. l. 13; Isa. i. 11. *That the blood of bulls and of goats should take away sins;* the blood of these were only carried into the holy of holiest on the atonement day, yearly, Lev. xvi., to which this is chiefly applied; nor could the blood of all the other sacrifices by expiation pardon their offerers, nor by sanctification cleanse them, nor by removing the sense of them comfort the soul; they could neither pacify God, nor the sinner's conscience, having no virtue or power to satisfy God's justice, or merit his grace, only it had by his constitution a power to typify that blood which could do both.

5 Wherefore when he cometh into the world, he saith, ᵍ Sacrifice and offering thou wouldest not, but a body ‖ hast thou prepared me:

g Ps. 40. 6, &c. & 50. 8. Isa. 1. 11. Jer. 6. 20. Amos 5. 21, 22.
‖ Or, *thou hast fitted me.*

Wherefore, Διὸ, introduceth the proof of the invalidity of legal sacrifices, and the efficacy of the one sacrifice of Christ, from Divine testimony about both of them. *He saith;* God the Son, who existed before his incarnation, bespeaketh God the Father, when he was coming into this world, to become a part of it, by uniting a holy human nature to the Divine, as David voucheth by the Spirit of God, Psal. xl. 6. *Sacrifice and offering thou wouldest not:* the bloody atoning sacrifices of bulls and goats, the peace-offerings, and thank-offerings, Lev. vii. 16, and offerings of every sort without blood, required by the law of Moses, God did neither desire, require, nor delight in, as in themselves propitiatory; for he never intended them to take away sins, or perfect the worshippers: see 1 Sam. xv. 22; Isa. i. 11—15; Jer. vi. 20; Amos v. 21, 22. *But a body hast thou prepared me:* but, the Hebrew text reads, the ears hast thou bored for me. The apostle makes use here of the Greek paraphrase, *a body hast thou fitted me;* as giving in proper terms the sense of the former figurative expression, discovering thereby Christ's entire willingness to become God's servant for ever, Exod. xxi. 6; and that he might be so, which he could not as God the Son, simply, the Father by his Spirit did articulate him, and formed him joint by joint a body; that is, furnished him with a human nature, so as that he might perform that piece of service which God required, offering up himself a bloody sacrifice for sin, to which he was obedient, Phil. ii. 8. Thus were his ears bored, which could not be if he had not been clothed with a body.

6 In burnt offerings and *sacrifices* for sin thou hast had no pleasure.

Two other sorts of sacrifices are added to the former, as whole *burnt-offerings,* which were all devoured by fire on God's altar, and no part of them came to the priests, Lev. i. 3, 9, 10, 13, 14, 17; and peace-offerings, which were not totally consumed, but part of them was the priests' portion, Exod. xxix. 27, 28. These four sorts of sacrifices comprehend all the Aaronical offerings for expiation. God did not require or desire any of these for themselves, or for the perfecting of sinners; he did not as to such an end approve them, or take any pleasure in them.

7 Then said I, Lo, I come (in the volume of the book it is written of me,) to do thy will, O God.

Then said I, Lo, I come: when the Father declared the sacrifices of beasts and birds would not please him, nor be accepted for expiating sins, then I said, I appeared in person, and declared, Lo, I come with a fit and proper sacrifice; I approach myself with my human nature, fully resolved to offer that to thee as a propitiatory sacrifice, John xii. 27; compare Psal. xl. 7. *In the volume of the book it is written of me:* κεφαλίς, the head; our translators keep to the Hebrew, במגילת ספר *the volume of the book,* Psal. xl. 7. Books, with the Hebrews, were rolls of parchment stitched at the top, and so rolled up. In this book was Christ every where written and spoken of, as he testifieth himself before his death, John v. 39, after his resurrection, Luke xxiv. 44—46. The Septuagint render it, *the head,* as being in the top and beginning of the whole roll, to wit, in the books of Moses; compare Luke xxiv. 27. And in the entrance of them the Spirit testifieth of his Deity, and of his union to the humanity, being to be conceived and born of a virgin, and offering himself a sacrifice to expiate sin, and reconcile sinners, Gen. iii. 15; compare John v. 46, 47. *To do thy will, O God;* to obey his Father's command, of dying an expiatory sacrifice for sinners. It was his Father's will that he should so offer himself for satisfying his justice, making way for his mercy, and so redeeming and recovering lost souls. This will of God was in his heart, he delighted to obey it, Psal. xl. 8; and his own natural will that would regret it, he would deny, and would not use his Divine power to deliver himself from it, Matt. xxvi. 39, 46; John xviii. 11.

8 Above when he said, Sacrifice and offering and burnt offerings and *offering* for sin thou wouldest not, neither hadst pleasure *therein;* which are offered by the law;

In this verse the apostle repeats the whole testimony, produced out of the Psalm, only with a specification in a parenthesis, *which are offered by the law,* viz. such sacrifices, against which the apostle argueth, which could not purge away sin, nor procure righteousness, nor make no more conscience of sins. He observes from the Psalm, that the will of God was plainly signified by his Spirit to David under the law, about the nature, state, and design of his institution of sacrifices, that they were typical of, and leading to, a better sacrifice than themselves; and that for their own sake only they were no way acceptable to God, and so rejected by him.

9 Then said he, Lo, I come to do thy will, O God. He taketh away the first, that he may establish the second.

In this verse the apostle collects the psalmist's assertion of God the Father's accepting his sacrifice, the offering whereof was so exactly agreeable to his will, when he was displeased with the legal ones; and this revealed to David when he was punctually using them according to the law. *He taketh away the first, that he may establish the second:* God therefore abolished all the legal sacrifices, which he commanded to be used as types of the better sacrifice he had provided, because of their insufficiency and weakness as to expiate sin, or pacify conscience, that he might establish that sacrifice of the body of Christ for abolishing sin, and bringing in everlasting righteousness, which was effectual, and an actual obedience agreeable to his will and command, Phil. ii. 7, 8. This being thus proved, he concludes from it,

h John 17.19. ch. 13. 12.
i ch. 9. 12.

10 h By the which will we are sanctified i through the offering of the body of Jesus Christ once *for all.*

By the which will; that spoken of Psal. xl. 8, that will and command of God given to Christ, God-man, that he should once offer up his body a sacrifice for sin, which he willingly and heartily obeyed, Phil. ii. 8. *We are sanctified:* sanctified is to be taken largely, for a communication to us of all the benefits of redemption, as pardon, reconciliation, absolution from punishment, renovation of God's image, and such a discharge of sin at last, as never to be guilty of it more, perfection of grace in glory. *Through the offering;* the voluntarily and heartily yielding it up, and presenting the blood of it to the Father within the veil in heaven to atone him, according to his own command and will, without which it would not have been accepted by him, Luke xxiii. 46; compare John xx. 15, 17, 18; xix. 28, 30. *Of the body of Jesus Christ once for all:* it was that part of Christ's person that was to die a sacrifice, and the blood of it that was to be shed for purchasing the remission of sins, as appears in the memorial of it, Luke xxii. 19, 20; the very body of God-man, Acts xx. 28. The *once* offering of which was eternally available to take away sin from sinners, and perfect them to glory. So that God's end being once reached in it, it is of perpetual virtue to apply its fruits to believing penitents, and needs not any repetition.

k Num. 28. 3. ch. 7. 27.

11 And every Priest standeth k daily ministering and offering oftentimes the same sacrifices, l which can never take away sins:

l ver. 4.

Having proved, that not the yearly repeated legal sacrifices could perfect a sinner, but only the sacrifice of Christ, the Spirit proceeds to prove, that the daily legal sacrifices can do as little for this work as the annual; and therefore these Hebrews ought to desert all these, and depend only upon Christ's, ver. 11—18. *And every priest standeth daily ministering and offering oftentimes the same sacrifices:* every priest in Aaron's family in his course daily ministering, stood at the altar, and performed the service appointed him by God, offering often the same bloody sacrifices to God, of bulls, goats, sheep, fowl, many times in one day, and for many days together, chap. vii. 27. *Which can never take away sins;* these were not available either to the priests offering, or those who brought them to be offered, for the spiritual and eternal expiation of their sins, as to their guilt, stain, power, or punishment, not any, nor all of these, none could do it at any time: see ver. 4.

12 m But this man, after he had offered one sacrifice for sins, for ever sat down on the right hand of God;

m ch. 1. 3. Col. 3. 1.

But this man, after he had offered one sacrifice for sins: opposed to the legal priests is this Priest, God-man, an almighty Minister, having once offered, and no more, one sacrifice of his body for the sins of others, (he had none of his own, as every other priest had,) that they might be pardoned and remembered no more, it being of eternal virtue and efficacy. *For ever* must be joined to the sacrifice to complete the opposition, ver. 11. The legal one could *never take away sins,* but his *one sacrifice* could take them away *for ever. Sat down on the right hand of God;* he ceased from sacrificing any more, and ascended up to heaven, and there he sat himself down (having abolished sin, and finished his work as a servant for ever) in the highest place of dominion and power at God's right hand, while the Aaronites stood trembling and waiting at God's footstool: and thence he powerfully and efficaciously commands the blotting out of sins, applieth his merits, and dispenseth to his servants the covenant mercies which he purchased by his own blood for them, chap. i. 3; ii. 9; viii. 2.

13 From henceforth expecting n till his enemies be made his footstool.

n Ps. 110. 1. Acts 2. 35. 1 Cor. 15. 25. ch. 1. 13.

That which remaineth he expecteth, even the fulfilling of his Father's promise to him, Psal. cx. 1, patiently waiting, earnestly looking, for what is most certain, and wherein he cannot be disappointed; for in respect of himself, his enemies cannot infest him more, being entirely vanquished already; but in respect of his administration, he waits till all that oppose his royal priesthood, as the devil and his angels, sin, the curse, death, and the world, with which he conflicts as a Priest to destroy them with his own blood, as his members do by it, Rev. xii. 11. Having given them their death's wound by his own death, he sits down, and waits in the successive ages of his church, until upon his elect it be made good, putting all under his own and church's feet, so to overcome and trample on them, as men on their footstools: see chap. ii. 8; 1 Cor. xv. 26.

14 For by one offering o he hath perfected for ever them that are sanctified.

o ver. 1.

For by one offering: for here gives the reason of the precedent effect, and it is opposed to the reason of the legal offerings' defect; their sacrifices multiplied could not perfect sinners, but this one doth it fully. *He hath perfected for ever:* Christ, God-man, the gospel High Priest, by the *one offering* of himself a sacrifice for sin to God his Father, and once performed by him, hath secured perfection of justification, sanctification, and blessedness, perpetually to be continued, whereby the persons interested in it are qualified and consecrated to be priests to God and his Father, (as the Aaronical priests were by the sacrifice of the ram of consecration, Exod. xxix. 22, 24,) to serve in their proportion here, but especially after the completion of it by their resurrection, they shall perfectly serve him before his throne in the holy of holiest for ever, 1 Pet. ii. 9; Rev. i. 6; v. 10; xx. 6. *Them that are sanctified;* the renewed souls by the Holy Ghost, such whose consciences he hath sprinkled with the blood of Jesus, and by it freed them from the guilt of sin and its punishment, and whose natures he regenerates and sanctifieth, freeing them from their evil habits, and making them inherently holiness unto the Lord, Psal. cx. 3; 1 Cor. vi. 11.

15 *Whereof* the Holy Ghost also is a witness to us: for after that he had said before,

The assumption cleared before, the apostle now proceedeth to prove out of the Old Testament, viz. that God's purpose was, by Christ's one sacrifice to take away all sins for ever; therefore there was no need of the repetition of the legal sacrifices. *Whereof the Holy Ghost also is a witness to us:* the authority avouched, is the testimony of the Holy Spirit of truth, that cannot deceive nor be deceived in what it witnesseth, but confirms the truth beyond all just ground of doubting, by his amanuensis the prophet Jeremiah, chap. xxxi. 31, 33, 34; where the person that the prophet styleth Jehovah, is by the apostle declared to be *the Holy Ghost;* and by it is proved to be the eternal God. He testifieth *to us,* the church of God, in the prophet's time, and to us all called to be members of it to this day. *For after that he had said before:* this contains the preface of the Spirit's testimony, that which he spake before, the covenant, which is his evidence; and this preface is laid down, Jer. xxxi. 31. Here they are all the apostle's words.

p Jer. 31. 33, 34. ch. 8. 10, 12.
16 ^pThis *is* the covenant that I will make with them after those days, saith the Lord, I will put my laws into their hearts, and in their minds will I write them;

God promiseth his true Israel his entering with them into a new testamental covenant; after the days that the covenant administration at Sinai was expired, then the Lord saith, Jer. xxxi. 33, that he will renew minds and hearts by his Spirit, and conform them to his will, that they shall be living, walking exemplars of his law; of both which see chap. viii. 10. This work of sanctification of souls is properly inferred here, to prove that such as enjoy it are perfected by Christ, because the promise of holiness is joined with that of perfect righteousness. Formerly it was urged from the text to another purpose, to prove God's will of changing the Aaronical administration of the covenant, because this was better. Here it is urged to prove the perfect effect of the sacrifice of Christ once offered to God, without which these promises of the covenant of justifying and sanctifying sinners had neither been made nor effected.

+ Some copies have, Then he said, And their.
17 †And their sins and iniquities will I remember no more.

God covenanteth to give not only sanctification, but justification to his believing Israel, so as their sins shall be remitted, and God will solemnly absolve them from the punishment they merit; see chap. viii. 12; promised, Jer. xxxi. 34. In which proof, though there be no express mention of the sacrifice of Christ, yet is it implied, for it is urged by the Spirit to that purpose; and in other scriptures, speaking of the same thing here promised, it is expressed, as hath been shown, chap. viii. 6, (compare Isa. liii..) that the death of Christ confirms this covenant, of which he is Mediator, and secures remission of sin for ever to the duly-qualified subject for it.

18 Now where remission of these *is, there is* no more offering for sin.

The Spirit having cleared his assumption before, now concludes; Whereas perfect forgiveness of sins is from God's grace, by the one sacrifice of his Son once offered, acquired and effected for penitent believers for ever, as the promise voucheth, Jer. xxxi. 34, For he will in no wise remember their sins, but will forgive them for ever; therefore there needs no repetition of that sacrifice again, or of any other for sin. But the Hebrews had the highest reason now to desert the legal sacrifices, and to rest upon and to cleave to his alone, any being, use, or consistency of such, after the effect of Christ's one sacrifice, being vain; for all being completed in his, it is but just theirs should cease from them.

q Rom. 5. 2. Eph. 2. 18. & 3. 12. ‖ Or, *liberty.* r ch. 9. 8, 12.
19 Having therefore, brethren, ^q ‖ boldness to enter ^r into the holiest by the blood of Jesus,

At this verse the Spirit applieth and maketh use of the doctrine of the great gospel High Priest, and his one all-sufficient sacrifice, and continueth it through part of the 13th chapter. The transition to it is made by the particle οὖν, *therefore*, which refers to the whole of his doctrinal discourse before of the excellency of the gospel High Priest, for his person, as to both his natures, being God-man, and his sacrifice, with its effects. Seeing these things are so, *therefore, brethren;* see chap. iii. 1, 12; inviting them with this endearing term of relation, to receive what his brotherly love imparted to them for their salvation. *Boldness to enter into the holiest;* freedom granted us of God for this motion, and confidence and freeness of Spirit in ourselves to move, so as not only to look into the holy of holiest, but of spiritual and real access for supplication and conversation, while we are personally upon earth; and others are denied such an entrance and approach to him on his throne of grace there, while they have their petitions received, Eph. iii. 12, and thence their persons blessed, chap. iv. 16. *By the blood of Jesus:* and this only vouchsafed them *by the blood of Jesus,* which atoned him, who sits on the throne, for us, and made it accessible to us. How much greater is this gospel privilege than that under the law! Aaron alone, and not the Israelites, could enter into the holy of holiest, and that but once a year, and then with the blood of beasts sacrificed for himself and them; whereas every penitent believing sinner can now by faith in Christ's blood and prayer, enter into the holiest of all in heaven, and there converse with God every day, while sin hath made him inaccessible to others.

s John 10. 9. & 14. 6. ‖ Or, *new made.* t ch. 9. 2.
20 By ^sa new and living way, which he hath ‖ consecrated for us, ^tthrough the veil, that is to say, his flesh;

By a new and living way; which *way* is figuratively setting out the means of entering into the holiest in heaven by the blood of Christ. By *way* is understood that by which approach to God in heaven is made, and wherein we must have our access to him, even Christ himself, John xiv. 6: πρόσφατον, a way newly made manifest by Christ's sacrifice newly slain and offered, rending the veil that hid heaven from them, so as they could not so clearly discern the throne of grace then, as now; and the way is not only *new*, but ζῶσαν, a quickening way, giving life and ability for motion and refreshment to those who walk in it, John xiv. 6, such as is everlasting, and is opened, not as the legal way, only to the high priest, but to all true Israelites to enter into it, and that not once a year, but continually. This is the way of life permanent and safe, Isa. xxxv. 8—10. *Which he hath consecrated for us;* this way Christ himself hath newly made, finished and opened unto them that they might walk therein, and reach home to God; nothing could obstruct or hinder them in it, he having perfected it unto this end. *Through the veil, that is to say, his flesh:* the inner veil, that separated the holiest of all from the holy place, was a type of the flesh of Christ, veiling his Deity; through the breaking and rending of which by death, he opens the way to the throne of grace in the holy of holiest in heaven, and so made God accessible to believers there, chap. ix. 12; compare Matt. xxvii. 51.

u ch. 4. 14. x 1 Tim. 3. 15.
21 And *having* ^uan High Priest over ^xthe house of God;

Christians have not only a liberty of coming, but a way wherein, and a help whereby, to reach home to God; which help is a surpassing Priest to all others, the great and eminent one for real worth and dignity, Christ himself, God-man, exalted to the right hand of the Majesty on high, after he had fulfilled his work here; where he was invested with all authority and power, and set over the church of the living God, consisting both of Hebrew and Gentile Israelites, chap. iii. 6; Acts xx. 28; whose sacrifices of praise and prayer offered up to God, he presenteth, perfumed with the incense of his own merits, before the throne, representing their persons, pleading their cause, and continually interceding for their good, making all they are and perform acceptable to his Father by his own blood, chap. viii. 2.

y ch. 4. 16. z Eph. 3. 12. Jam. 1. 6. 1 John 3. 21. a ch. 9. 14. b Ezek. 36. 25. 2 Cor. 7. 1.
22 ^yLet us draw near with a true heart ^zin full assurance of faith, having our hearts sprinkled ^a from an evil conscience, and ^bour bodies washed with pure water.

Let us draw near ; this contains the duty grounded on, and encouraged to, by the former privileges, viz. the spiritual motion of his church, using Christ for their coming home to God, in prayer, and all parts of worship and conversation: see chap. iv. 16; vii. 25. *With a true heart ;* with sincerity and integrity of heart, both as it is the subject of actions, and exercising them as such in all acts of worship and service unto God, when the mind and heart is fixed to perform all strictly, according to God's will, for matter and manner, so as to reach him glory, and to obtain from him a blessing, Psal. xxxvii. 31. *In full assurance of faith ;* believing in, an dbeing fully assured and confident of, Christ's merits and God's promise, which is true, faithful, and immutable, to all who perform the duty required by it, chap. vi. 11; Col. ii. 2; James i. 5—7. *Having our hearts sprinkled from an evil conscience ;* having the soul in all its rational faculties, the inward man, the prime efficient of all actions, and here under bond to the law of God, purged and cleansed ; alluding to the Aaronical rite of purifying by sprinkling of blood, as souls are to be now by the blood of Christ when they are justified, Rom. iii. 23—26, that God may admit them into his presence, hear them when they worship him, ver. 19, 20 ; so as they may be free from an accusing or condemning conscience, on the account of the guilt of sin gnawing them, and making them obnoxious to punishment; as also of the stain and pollution of sin, making them unfit for any communion with God, chap. ix. 14. *And our bodies washed with pure water ;* the body (as the priests were under the law washed before their service) is the outward man, which is, as well as the soul, to be sanctified by the Holy Spirit, and cleansed from all filthiness of flesh : these corrupt members of the old man must be put off, and mortified by the Spirit of God, before they can be fit to approach to worship him, Ezek. xxxvi. 25 ; 1 Cor. vi. 11, 19, 20; 2 Cor. vii. 1 ; 1 John iii. 3.

23 ᶜLet us hold fast the profession of our faith without wavering ; (for ᵈhe *is* faithful that promised ;)

Let us hold fast ; this duty is inferred from the doctrine of the gospel High Priest, and the perfect work he wrought in taking away sin, and bringing in everlasting righteousness : let us therefore persevere in the faith and hope of him, really, actually, stedfastly, retaining it with all our might and power ; whatsoever insinuations may be used to entice us, or violence by persecutions to force us, from it, retaining it still in mind, will, affection, and operation. *The profession of our faith ;* an outward exhibition to the world both in word and deed, as we have it sincerely in our hearts, solemnly owning it in the ordinances of God in his church, of the hope we have in Christ our High Priest, and of all that he hath purchased for us, and promised to perform in us and to us, chap. iii. 1, 6 ; iv. 14 ; vi. 11 ; Rom. x. 9, 10; 1 Pet. i. 3, 21. *Without wavering ; ἀκλινῆ,* without any declining from it, either to the right or left, from the first and due state of it ; not warping or wavering from the revelation of God about it, when others weakly made a defection from it, chap. vi. 6, 9. And good reason for this unbiassed retention of it, while others declined. *For he is faithful that promised ;* for God, who covenanted with them what he will be to and do for them, is only primitively, eminently, and reciprocally faithful and unchangeable for his person and purpose ; all is sure on God's side, Numb. xxiii. 19, and his power is irresistible. He hath promised to reward those who persevere and continue to the end true to the Redeemer, and to give them grace and assistance that they may so continue, so as they need not fear the power of their enemies, nor their own weakness, for he will enable them to perform the duty, endure the afflictions for it, and then to reach the blessing, 1 Cor. x. 13 ; 1 Thess. v. 23, 24 ; 2 Thess. iii. 3.

24 And let us consider one another to provoke unto love and to good works :

Having urged from the gospel doctrine of our High Priest our duty to God, the Spirit proceeds to show what influence it should have on Christians for performing their duty one to another, in their inspection and observation of the whole body of Christ, consisting of Jew and Gentile, who have equally shared in Christ's sacrifice, and are interested in and related to his person ; and by the apprehensive and judicial faculty so to discern the spiritual state and condition of each other, and the whole, as every particular member of it may be capable to animadvert, exhort, reprove, counsel, or comfort, and act suitably and seasonably in the discharge of their mutual duty, chap. iii. 13 ; Rom. xiv. 19 ; xv. 7, 14 ; Col. iii. 16 ; 1 Thess. v. 11, 15. *To provoke unto love ; εἰς παροξυσμὸν·* it is a word borrowed from physicians, who use it to set out the violent incursion of a fever, when the fit is so strong as to make the body tremble and bed shake with the horror and rigour of it. In this place it is used to set out the vehemency of affection to which the sacrifice of Christ obligeth Christians, as those who had their whole persons acted by love to each other, with all vehemency, to the highest and fullest pitch of it ; as who should exceed in benevolence, beneficence, and complacency in each other, such as is conscientious, pure, and extensive to the very end, chap. xiii. 1 ; Rom. xii. 9, 20 ; 1 Thess. iv. 9 ; 1 Pet. i. 22 ; and manifesting itself in good works to them, especially merciful ones, pitying, counselling, succouring, supplying, and comforting them, James ii. 13, 15, 16 ; 1 John iii. 14, 16—18 ; and this freely, cheerfully, and constantly, Eph. ii. 10 ; iv. 32 ; 1 Tim. vi. 18.

25 ᵉNot forsaking the assembling of ourselves together, as the manner of some *is ;* but exhorting *one another ;* and ᶠso much the more, as ye see ᵍthe day approaching.

Helps to the performance of both the former duties, to God and fellow Christians, with their respective motives, are laid down in the following part of the chapter. The first is couched in this verse ; neither slighting in thought, nor vilifying in word, nor separating, nor leaving by dissociation. *Not forsaking : ἐγκαταλείποντες* imports such a desertion, as leaves destitute in deep trouble or distress, when they should be helping. *The assembling of ourselves together : ἐπισυναγωγὴν* strictly notes an addition to this synagogue of the Jews ; an accession of new members to the former church assembly, even the Gentiles, becoming Abraham's seed by their conversion to, and confession of, the faith of Christ. This some of the Jews, from the self-conceit of their being the only people of God, disdained, and continued in a separation from them, and all communion with them. This the Spirit reproves, and adviseth not to leave the assembly thus augmented, lest in doing it they forsook God and Christ, as well as ordinances of worship and duties attending such church meetings, and promoting their salvation. *As the manner of some is ;* such desertion of those assemblies in the worshipping and serving of God, was the common custom among some of these Hebrews ; a usual, frequent mode of them to do it ; some idolizing their own nation ; others, their own selves, thinking them holier than others, Gal. ii. 12—14 ; others, that valued honours, riches, and ease more than Christ or their souls ; some for fear of persecution, as foretold, Luke viii. 13, 14, fulfilled, Gal. vi. 12. *But exhorting one another ; παρακαλοῦντες* supposeth assembling, in opposition to the former desertion, and the duty of the assembled ; and signifieth, counselling, reproving, encouraging, and comforting one another, so as they might persevere in performing the duties for which they assembled, according to Christ's mind and will ; so as to strengthen each other's hearts and hands in the faith, and in the other duties instanced in before. *And so much the more, as ye see the day approaching ;* they have so much the more reason to do it, and intend the work, as they did not conjecture, but certainly know, that the day of their own death, and particular account to be given of themselves to God ; the day of God's executing his judgments on Jerusalem, as Christ foretold, Matt. xxiv. 1—28, prophesied by Daniel before, chap. ix. 26, 27, when the temple should be burnt, the city destroyed, and the people dispersed through the world ; or, the day of the general judgment, testified by the gospel to the world, Acts xvii. 31 : all these were every day nearer to them than other, and they believed them to approach ; therefore ought they to be more exercised in denying evil and doing good, not forsaking church communion, but keeping close to Christ and his assemblies, that they might better stand together in that day.

HEBREWS X

h Num. 15. 20. ch. 6. 4. i 2 Pet. 2. 20, 21.

26 For ^hif we sin wilfully ⁱafter that we have received the knowledge of the truth, there remaineth no more sacrifice for sins,

If we sin wilfully: the severe exaction which God will take upon such as apostatize from him, is further enforcing the former duty, and is introduced by the particle *for*, to that end; if we by a free and spontaneous desertion of Christ, and his ordinances, without a coercion by threats and persecutions; and this after we had professedly in our judgments, wills, and affections, with faith and reverence, acknowledged a love and subjection to the true gospel doctrine of the way of bringing sinners to God by Christ our great High Priest, John viii. 31; xiv. 6, which was made known to them by Christ and his apostles, and confirmed by miracles and the gifts of the Holy Ghost, so as to profess a full conviction of this truth, so as to assent and consent to it. *After that we have received the knowledge of the truth*; after all this, to renounce the profession of it, and to forsake the assemblies where it is held forth; this is the spontaneous and wilful sinning: see chap. vi. 6. *There remaineth no more sacrifice for sins*: this is unpardonable by the just constitution of God in the gospel, because no sacrifice can atone God for them, without which they cannot be pardoned; and the sacrifice of Christ, which only could do it, they renounce and desert; and so this, nor any other they can bring, can procure pardon for them, so that their sins remain in guilt and power on them, and between them and God's wrath are they like irrecoverably to be ground to perdition.

k Ezek. 36.5. Zeph. 1. 18. & 3. 8. 2 Thess. 1. 8. ch. 12. 29.

27 But a certain fearful looking for of judgment and ^kfiery indignation, which shall devour the adversaries.

But a certain fearful looking for of judgment: But, is introducing the terrible evil asserted to be expected when sacrifice cannot help such sinners, especial and certain, terrible and dreadful (such as fills the soul with fears and horrors) expectation of judgment by their awakened consciences, not knowing how soon it may come; as a malefactor under sentence, in daily expectation of execution, how doth he suffer it over and over! so will this worm gnaw them: to which is synonymous, Mark ix. 44. How must the execution of the sentence of the just Judge terrify them! *And fiery indignation*; when it must be by burning, or heat of fire; wrath of fire proceeding from an injured and wronged God, Ezek. xxxvi. 5; xxxviii. 19; Zeph. i. 18; iii. 8. As in execution of just vengeance, which like fire devours and eateth them up, not putting an end to their being by consumption, but perpetual piercing, searching, torturing, and this for eternity. *Which shall devour the adversaries*; these underhand adversaries, ὑπεναντίυς, who are the most bitter enemies of Christ and his church, because secret ones, and seem to be by profession otherwise, Matt. xxv. 41; Mark ix. 43, 44; 2 Thess. i. 8, 9.

l ch. 2. 2. m Deut. 17. 2. 6. & 19. 15. Matt. 18. 16. John 8. 17. 2 Cor. 13. 1.

28 ^lHe that despised Moses' law died without mercy ^munder two or three witnesses:

The punishment threatened on such sinners is illustrated by an instance proper to the Hebrews; For if the lesser sin against Moses's law was punished by death, the greater sin against the gospel of Christ shall be more punished. *He that despised Moses's law*; any person, whoever he were, none excepted, contemning, rejecting, nullifying, or making to have no place or force, (suitable to forsaking, before prohibited,) the law of God, given by the mediation of Moses, so as to have no power on the conscience by apostacy from it, and to do it openly, proudly, and presumptuously, in the face of the church. Numb. xv. 30, 31. *Died without mercy under two or three witnesses*; was to be sentenced to death without any compassion or mercy, and indispensably executed without any pity, by stoning of the offender by two or three witnesses, which did evidence the fact, and convict him of it, according to the law, as Deut. xiii. 6—11; xvii. 2—7.

n ch. 2. 3. & 12. 25.

29 ⁿOf how much sorer punishment, suppose ye, shall he be thought worthy, who hath trodden under foot the Son of God, and ^ohath counted the blood of the covenant, wherewith he was sanctified, an unholy thing, ^pand hath done despite unto the Spirit of grace?

o 1 Cor. 11. 29. ch. 13. 20. p Matt.12. 31, 32. Eph. 4. 30.

Of how much sorer punishment: the expostulation aggravates both the sin and the punishment in the consequent on the former assertion; a punishment heavier, bitterer, sorer, more grievous, and unexpressibly greater, than death. *Suppose ye*; you yourselves being judges, to whom I appeal about it; what can you suppose, think, or determine of it? *Shall he be thought worthy*; doth he fully deserve, and is liable to, by the judgment of man, but much more by the righteous and inexorable judgment of God? *Who hath trodden under foot the Son of God*; who sinneth at a higher rate than a Jew against Moses's law, being an apostate from the gospel, a revolter from and a rebel against it, discovering it by as much as in him lieth, tearing from his throne God the Son incarnate, and treading him under his feet, wickedly undervaluing and horribly vilifying him, treating him with the greatest contempt that can be expressed by such an action, as if he were the vilest malefactor. A person so much greater and more excellent than Moses, to be so used; so as, if he were here on earth, he would tread him (who is higher than the heavens, and had done and suffered so much for him) as the dust and dirt under his feet; and this by a contemptuous forsaking his church assemblies, wherein he was set out in all his excellencies. *And hath counted the blood of the covenant an unholy thing*; accounting and so deserting the blood of Christ, (which ratified the everlasting covenant of grace, by whose virtue it was made unalterable, firm, and effectual in all the promises of it of pardon, righteousness, holiness, grace, and glory, unto penitent believing sinners,) as either the common blood of men, or the blood of a malefactor, to have not so much excellency in it as the blood of bulls, or goats, or rams, or birds, under the law; as not sanctifying souls, but polluted. *Wherewith he was sanctified*; ἐν ᾧ ἡγιάσθη, in or by which he was sanctified, is by most interpreters referred to the apostate, as aggravating his sin, to despise that blood by which he thought he was so, and boasted of it, and was so reputed by the church upon his baptism and profession of his faith, and, as a member of the church, had a visible relation to it, partaking of those ordinances wherein its fruits were conveyed, and enjoying the external privileges purchased by it. Others refer it unto Christ himself, the blood whereby he was consecrated to God as a holy sacrifice, John xvii. 19. All this was discovered by his forsaking the church assembly, wherein this was declared to be the only way and means to justification of life and salvation. *And hath done despite unto the Spirit of grace*; injuring, wronging, despising, greatly grieving, not a creature, but God the Spirit, the quickening Spirit of dead sinners, who fits them for union to God, and in order to it, uniteth him to Christ and his God, animateth it; who graciously communicated to these apostates the knowledge natural and supernatural which they had and abused, chap. vi. 5, by the desertion of the assemblies, where he manifested his gifts and graces. They reject him with them, and treat his gifts and motions as if they were the delusions and impostures of an evil spirit; and this wilfully done out of malice to Christ, and abhorrence of his church and religion. A sin like the devil's, for them to forsake God loving, Christ redeeming, his blood justifying, his Spirit renewing, and so wilfully refuse to be saved, and expose themselves to the severest punishment God can inflict on such sinners, and they do deserve.

30 For we know him that hath said, ^qVengeance *belongeth* unto me, I will recompense, saith the Lord. And again, ^rThe Lord shall judge his people.

q Deut. 32. 35. Rom. 12. 19. r Deut. 32. 36. Ps. 50. 4. & 135. 14.

For we know him that hath said: For brings in the proof of the soreness of God's punishment to be inflicted on apostates, from God's own testimony about it; which we, who are conversant with the Scriptures, are well acquainted with; we know what God hath spoken, and by whom he hath spoken it, John ix. 29. Their knowledge of it was clear and certain, it being spoken to them by Moses, and written for them, Deut. xxxii. 35, 36. *Vengeance belongeth unto me, I will recompense*; to me is vengeance and recompence; which are the words of the Hebrew text. To me, the sovereign Being, the supreme and universal Law-giver and Judge, doth belong the universal right and power of vindictive justice. It is his propriety, as he will avenge all injuries against his people, he will much more avenge the sins and injuries against his Son; and will actually return to evil-doers, as a recompence for their sins, the evil of punishment. He is not only just and powerful, but actually manifesting both in his retribution on them, Deut. xxxii. 41, 43; Psal. xciv. 1; Rom. xii. 19; 2 Thess. i. 8. *Saith the Lord;* Jehovah saith it, who is faithful and true, powerful, and constant to his threatenings, as well as his promises. This he saith to, and threatens apostate Jeshurun with, who revolted from God, and served idols, Deut. xxxii. 15—17. *And again, The Lord shall judge his people:* a further testimony is urged from God's vindication of his people, when he hath punished apostates, taken from Deut. xxxii. 6, and Psal. cxxxv. 14. The sovereign Being of righteousness, the same Jehovah as before, will rule, justify, save, deliver, and vindicate his covenant people from the contempt and vilifying of his Son and them, by punishing severely such who, by their apostacy from him and them, are guilty of it. He will certainly take vengeance on them, and thereby clear the innocency, truth, and goodness of his, who are trampled on by them.

a Luke 12. 5.

31 *a It is* a fearful thing to fall into the hands of the living God.

The punishment of these apostates is further aggravated from the inflicter of it, the knowledge of which should make them tremble; the thoughts of it might affect them, as the hand-writing on the wall did Belshazzar, Dan. v. 6. It should strike horror into their heart, trembling into their persons, Deut. xxviii. 65, 66, by apostacy from him as a Father, to be subjected to him as a Judge, and as obnoxious to his severest judgment. Him in whose hand is power inexpressible, 1 Chron. xxix. 12, to avenge himself on his enemies, Psal. xc. 11, who have renounced him as their God, and provoked him to fury by it. A God that will not repent of vengeance, and who liveth ever to inflict it; who lifts up his hand to heaven, and saith, *I live for ever,* Deut. xxxii. 39, 40; to punish with everlasting burning, and a devouring fire, such traitors to himself. So is he described, Isa. xxxiii. 14; Matt. x. 28. His vengeance on these apostates is like himself, everlasting.

t Gal. 3. 4.
2 John 8.
u ch. 6. 4.
x Phil. 1. 29,
30. Col. 2. 1.

32 But *t* call to remembrance the former days, in which, *u* after ye were illuminated, ye endured *x* a great fight of afflictions;

But call to remembrance the former days: But is not so much adversative as copulative, adding another direction for their persevering in Christianity, even the revolving in their minds, and bringing again to thought, what was past, carrying in it both the act and the end of it. It is a practical remembrance which bettereth them, while recollecting their own days, and the time that was past. *In which, after ye were illuminated;* in which they were convinced of the truth of the gospel, and received it in the love of it, and externally professed it, by being baptized into Christ, and by it made members of his church, chap. vi. 4, and testified the truth of their being Christ's. *Ye endured a great fight of afflictions;* by their sufferings for him with patience and divine fortitude, willingly, cheerfully, valiantly: Ye have borne, and overcome by bearing, preserving your integrity, so as your faith was immovable, and strengthened you to endure the many and most violent assaults of the devil and his instruments, both within and without the church; who thought to force them from the faith, by the many evils which they inflicted. If they were patient in the enduring these at the first, how much more now, after so long a continuance in it! Rom. viii. 18; 2 Cor. i. 6—8; 2 Tim. i. 8; 1 Pet. v. 9.

y 1 Cor. 4. 9.
z Phil. 1. 7.
& 4. 14.
1 Thess. 2. 14.

33 Partly, whilst ye were made *y* a gazingstock both by reproaches and afflictions; and partly, whilst *z* ye became companions of them that were so used.

Partly, whilst ye were made a gazingstock both by reproaches and afflictions; their sufferings personal in this famous instance, θεατριζόμενοι. They were so publicly exposed as on a stage or theatre, so as multitudes might sport themselves with them, 1 Cor. iv. 9; as many were exposed to be devoured by beasts in their public shows, 1 Cor. xv. 32. Or, to destroy them, exposed in their public courts of justice, and there taunted and reviled, as Christ foretold them, Matt. x. 17, 18. They were suffering reproaches and afflictions publicly both in word and deed. What nick-names imposed on them, what crimes imputed to them which they abhorred, what buffeting, scourging, tormenting, shackling, imprisoning, banishing, were they not exercised with, as their fellow Christians are to this day? *And partly, whilst ye became companions of them that were so used;* their sufferings by participation, in presence and sympathy with their fellow Christians. This is another kind of it; they were consorts and sharers of all those members of Christ, who were so abused by the devil and his instruments, and they bore their burdens with them, were inwardly grieved for them, publicly owned and comforted them, supplied and supported them as they could, as ver. 34; 2 Cor. xi. 25, 26.

34 For ye had compassion of me *a* in my bonds, and *b* took joyfully the spoiling of your goods, knowing ‖ in yourselves that *c* ye have in heaven a better and an enduring substance.

a Phil. 1. 7.
2 Tim. 1. 16.
b Matt. 5. 12.
Acts 5. 41.
Jam. 1. 2.
‖ Or, *that ye have in yourselves, or, for yourselves.*
c Matt. 6. 20. & 19. 21. Luke 12. 33. 1 Tim. 6. 19.

For ye had compassion of me in my bonds; for ye sympathized in my bonds, &c., is a proof of both kinds of their sufferings forementioned. As to their suffering with others, he instanceth in himself, as a witness of it; for when he was in bonds for preaching the gospel, both at Jerusalem, Acts xxi. 33, 37; xxii. 24, 25, at Cesarea, Acts xxiii., xxiv., at Rome, Acts xxviii., they forewarned him of his danger, bore his burden with him, supplied, relieved him, and endeavoured, what in them lay, his release. *And took joyfully the spoiling of your goods;* and in their own sufferings, by being rifled for the gospel; their goods, estates, and means of subsistence, were either by fines, confiscations, or violence, ravished from them; their enemies, like so many harpies, preying on them, 1 Thess. ii. 14. So as these Christian Hebrews at this time had their respective properties, and all was not levelled among them. Though they were so impoverished to make them comply with the Gentile superstition and idolatry, yet they cheerfully bore it, esteeming it their honour and privilege thus to suffer for Christ, and herein obeyed him, as Matt. v. 11, 12, and as the apostles did before them. in Acts v. 41. *Knowing in yourselves that ye have in heaven a better and an enduring substance;* they were fully assured of this by faith in God's promise, and by God's work on their own hearts, qualifying and fitting them for it, Rom. viii. 15—17. That they have by promise given them as theirs, as fitted for them, a spiritual substance, an estate beyond what this world could afford them; riches, honours, and pleasures, better for their quality than all terrene ones; spiritual ones, proper for their souls, 1 Pet. i. 3, 4. The sum of which is God in Christ, their exceeding great reward, Gen. xv. 1, and all he can be to or do for them. He is their portion and their inheritance, the most excellent in itself, and the most enduring, out of the reach of men or devils, who can neither take it from them, nor them from it, it is safe enough in the heavens, Matt. vi. 19, 20; xix. 28, 29; Psal. xvi. 5; 2 Cor. v. 1; 2 Thess. i. 4, 5.

35 Cast not away therefore your confidence, *d* which hath great recompence of reward.

d Matt. 5. 12.
& 10. 32.

Cast not away therefore your confidence: this introduceth the last direction for helping on their perseverance in Christianity. Μὴ ἀποβάλλητε denieth all degrees of apostacy, from secret undervaluing to an utter renouncing, not to slight, despise, or reject; they had endured already so much as might steel and fortify them against what remained, and implieth the bold, resolute, and courageous retention, Eph. vi. 10, 16, of the boldness of their confession of the Christian faith. It is an ingenuous, free, bold, and daring profession of it, which no brow-beating nor violence can dash out of countenance, the fruit of a mighty, invincible faith, and hope of eternal life. This makes them persevere courageously in their religion, notwithstanding their being laden with reproaches and sufferings for it, as Christ himself gave them a pattern, Mark viii. 31, 32; Acts iv. 13, 29, 31. *Which hath great recompence of reward:* what greater encouragement can there be to the retaining this confidence, than the great remuneration secured in the New Testament to them : God himself, in all his fulness, to be their exceeding great reward, seen and enjoyed by them; and which for quality and quantity is inexpressible, Gen. xv. 1 ; Matt. v. 12 ; x. 32.

e Luke 21.
19. Gal. 6. 9.
ch. 12. 1.
f Col. 3. 24.
ch. 9. 15.
1 Pet. 1. 9.

36 ᵉFor ye have need of patience, that, after ye have done the will of God, ᶠye might receive the promise.

For ye have need of patience: for shows this to be an enforcement of the former direction: Cast not away your confidence, for you have need of grace, which that must maintain in order to carry back your reward. It is therefore absolutely necessary, as well as useful to you, for the bearing of your burdens, persevering in all duty, and waiting for your reward, notwithstanding your reproaches, afflictions, and fiery trials, that you preserve your confidence in maintaining this patience, chap. vi. 12 ; Rom. ii. 7 ; James i. 4. *That, after ye have done the will of God;* that having believed God's promises, obeyed his precepts, endured his trials, and persevered in all, according to the good, acceptable, and perfect will of God; and so exercised our patience, and evidenced our confidence, and finished our work ; *ye might receive the promise;* you may carry back, as your full prize, after your race. It is a necessary and true reportation from God, after his will is done, 1 Pet. i. 9 ; v. 4 ; the reward promised metonymically expressed by *the promise*, chap. v. 15 ; ix. 15 ; all that life and glorious inheritance in the reality and fulness of it, called *a crown of glory that fadeth not away*, 1 Tim. iv. 8 ; 2 Tim. i. 1.

g Luke 18. 8.
2 Pet. 3. 9.
h Hab. 2. 3, 4.

37 For ᵍyet a little while, and ʰhe that shall come will come, and will not tarry.

The reason of their retaining their confidence to the end, is the shortness of his coming, who will reward them for it, proved out of God's promise written to and for the church, by Habakkuk, chap. ii. 3. A truth sufficiently known to these Hebrews, as brought them by their own prophet; and though spoken for the comfort of the captives in Babylon then, yet it is extended to the suffering church in all ages, and so to these Hebrews, and to us also, *upon whom the ends of the world are come*, 1 Cor. x. 11. And though the prophet speaks it of a vision of grace, in promise to be despatched, yet the Septuagint refers it to a person; and in this the apostle follows them, because the promise cannot be made good without the coming of its Author to fulfil it. *For yet a little while;* in which promise there is the celerity or speed of it ; as little, little as it may be, as is fit for Christ and them. How little is this time! a very short moment, as he speaks himself, Rev. xxii. 7, 12, 20. *And he that shall come will come;* he that hath promised to come and save you, and reckon with your persecutors, he will certainly come, he and his promise together, will despatch and put an end to the suffering of his, and put on their crowns. Metonymically, his coming is his saving, full refreshing, and rewarding his believing and patient sufferers. *And will not tarry;* he will not spin out time to delay deliverance, beyond the set point; he will not come behind the last moment, the hour fixed and appointed, which is pitched in infinite wisdom and goodness, for the best comfort of Christ's suffering members, Isa. xlvi. 13.

i Rom. 1. 17.
Gal. 3. 11.

38 Now ⁱthe just shall live by faith: but if *any man* draw back, my soul shall have no pleasure in him.

These are, as the former, the words of the Prophet Habakkuk, chap. ii. 4, enforcing the former duty pressed from the gain of perseverance, and the loss by withdrawing, when Christ shall come. They are used by this apostle Paul to several purposes, as to prove, that righteousness is only obtained by faith from God, and not by man's own works, Rom. i. 17 ; Gal. iii. 11 ; that whoever is righteous by faith, shall live for ever, by holding that righteousness in faith, as here. *Now the just shall live by faith ;* the justified, according to the terms of the new covenant, who hath obtained the righteousness of God in Christ by believing, and is renewed and sanctified by the Spirit, shall really, spiritually, happily, eternally live ; and no end shall be to that life of his, till it be perfected by Christ in glory. And this he shall live by a real and spiritual assent to the gospel, and reliance on God's promises in it, especially by an affiance to Christ, God-man, as the Lord their Righteousness, by which we have him ours, and so we live. This faith increased, continued in, and held fast amidst all reproaches, sufferings, and persecutions; by this only is the life, due to righteousness, made sure to sinners, drawing from Christ daily, and making real and present the fulness of it promised to and hoped for by it, Mark xiii. 13 ; John vi. 47 ; Gal. ii. 20 ; Col. iii. 4. *But if any man draw back:* see Hab. ii. 4, where נעפלה translated here ὑποστείληται, is variously rendered, as, elated like a bubble, lifted up ; making pride and unbelief to be the sins threatened there ; and the proper sense of the word here used, is, for fear, or sloth, to withdraw, or leave their understanding: so that the meaning in both amounts to this, If any, out of the pride of their heart, will not depend on Christ's righteousness, as the Jews would not, or, out of fear and sluggishness, will not hold out, but withdraw themselves, in time of persecution, from their faith and confidence in Christ, professed ; shrinking through fear, or losing it through sloth, or forsaking it by treachery, either gradually or totally, confiding in themselves, and so despising God ; reject him, and draw away from him. *My soul shall have no pleasure in him ;* God himself will be so far from taking any pleasure or delight in such a soul, or vouchsafe it any joy or life, that his very soul abhors it, is highly displeased with its sin, and abominates its person. In his displeasure is misery, death, and eternal perdition : see Deut. xxxii. 15, 18—21.

k 2 Pet. 2. 20, 21.
l Acts 16. 30, 31. 1 Thess. 5. 9. 2 Thes. 2. 14.

39 But we are not of them ᵏwho draw back unto perdition ; but of them that ˡbelieve to the saving of the soul.

The conclusion is a hopeful assertion of their condition, or a sweet intimation of what they ought to be, even like himself ; and so the apostle removes all jealousy of his reflecting on them, as chap. vi. 9. *But we are not of them who draw back unto perdition;* the adversative, *but,* is an exception of them to whom he writes from the apostate state, and so joins himself with them, hoping they were such *de facto* as he was, and as they ought to be *de jure;* and so intimates their duty, and that of all Christians : We are not sons of defection, persons withdrawing and backsliding from Christ, his gospel, or duties ; apostates from the truth, whose end is destruction, an utter separation from all good, life, and glory, and full subjection of body and soul to eternal torments in hell, by the righteous sentence of God, Matt. x. 28 : who are sons of defection, are sons of perdition, John xvii. 12 ; 2 Thess. ii. 3. *But of them that believe to the saving of the soul;* sons of faith, true and sincere believers, cleaving to Christ and his body, rooted in his faith, and persevering in it to the end, Eph. iii. 17 ; Col. ii. 7 : which faith acquiring, purchasing, or obtaining, according to the gospel covenant, the soul for salvation, and glory for the soul, John iii. 15, 16, 36 ; v. 40 ; 2 Thess. ii. 14. Faith realizing, applying, and keeping fast the price which Christ himself paid to God for the purchasing of these for them on their souls.

CHAP. XI

The nature of faith, and its acceptableness with God, set forth in the examples of many excellent persons of old time.

NOW faith is the ‖substance of things hoped for, the evidence ᵃof things not seen.

‖ Or, *ground*, or, *confidence*.
a Rom. 8. 24, 25. 2 Cor. 4. 18. & 5. 7.

Now faith: the Holy Spirit proceeds in this chapter to strengthen the counsel he had given these Hebrews to continue stedfast in the faith of Christ, to the end that they may receive their reward, the salvation of their souls, chap. x. 39 ; 1 Pet. i. 9 ; and so beginneth with a description of that faith, and proves it to be effectual to this end, by instances out of all ages of the world before them, wherein the Old Testament believers had found it to be so. The description of it is laid down, ver. 1; the proof of it in both parts, ver. 2, 3; and the illustration of its power by examples, ver. 4—40. The particle δὲ shows this is inferred as a discovery of that faith, which is saving or purchasing the soul; which that none of these.Hebrews may be mistaken in, he describeth from its effect, and not from its form and essence. Faith is here a Divine fruit of the Spirit, given and wrought by it in his elect, and is justifying and purchasing the soul to glory, John xii. 38; Rom. v. 1; 2 Cor. xii. 9; Eph. i. 19, 20; ii. 8. *Is the substance of things hoped for:* ὑπόστασις, in 2 Cor. ix. 4, notes confidence of boasting; Heb. i. 3, personal subsistence; and chap. iii. 14, confidence of faith. Here it is a real, present, confident assent of the soul of a believer to the promise of God, (which is the basis or foundation of it,) by which the spiritual good things to come, and which fall not under sense, yet with a most vehement and intense desire urged for, are made to have a mental, intellectual existence and subsistence in the soul which exerciseth it, Rom. viii. 18, 26; John iii. 36. *The evidence of things not seen:* ἔλεγχοι is a demonstrative discovery of that which falleth not under sense, such as is scientifical, and puts matters out of question to a man; and therefore is styled by logicians a demonstration: here it notes faith to be that spiritual space which by God's revelation demonstrates or makes evident all things not seen by sense, or natural reason, without it, as matters of spiritual truth, good and evil in their several kinds, both past, present, and to come, John xvii. 6, 8; Eph. i. 17, 18.

b ver. 39.

2 For ᵇby it the elders obtained a good report.

This is a proof of the first part of faith's description, that it *is the substance of things hoped for;* for all the fathers were testified of to have this work of faith in realizing their hopes. Πρεσβύτεροι were the fathers and ancestors of these Hebrews, run up through their genealogies to Adam, the special instances of whom follow. These received a testimony or witness, truly and fully from God himself, in some signal acceptance of them, eminent appearances and providences to them, with a Scripture record of them, that through this grace of our Lord Jesus Christ they walked with, worshipped, and pleased God, and were saved by him, even as these Christians; and all this by the same grace of faith, Acts xv. 17, which wrought kindly in them, and made the invisible things of God to subsist with them.

c Gen. 1. 1.
Ps. 33. 6.
John 1. 3.
ch. 1. 2.
2 Pet. 3. 5.

3 Through faith we understand that ᶜthe worlds were framed by the word of God, so that things which are seen were not made of things which do appear.

This proves the second part of faith's description, ver. 1, that it is *the evidence of things not seen;* for by it only we understand the creation, which no eye saw. It is the same Divine faith as described before, but as evidencing invisible truths, it communicates a marvellous light to the understanding, and leaves real impressions of it from the word of God, whereby it arriveth unto a most certain knowledge of what is above the power of natural reason to convey, and gives a divine assent to it, such as is real, clear, sure, and fruitful, different from that of the Gentiles, Rom. i. 19—23. *The worlds;* τῶς αἰώνας the word noteth sometimes ages, Luke xvi. 8; the garb and corrupt habit of men who live in them, Eph. ii. 2; eternity: but there, as chap. i. 2, it is a word of aggregation, signifying all kinds of creatures, with their several places, times, and periods; things celestial, terrestrial, and subterrestrial; angels, men, and all sorts of creatures, together with all the states and conditions in which they were made. *Were framed by the word of God;* heaven, earth, and seas, with all their hosts of creatures, the visible creation and the invisible world, were put into being and existence, placed in their proper order, disposed and fitted to their end, by the mighty word of God: Trinity in Unity the Creator, his powerful fiat, without any pain, or trouble, or assisting causes, instantly effected this miraculous, glorious work; *He spake, and it was done,* Gen. i. 3, 6, 9, 11, 14, &c.; Psal. xxxiii. 6, 9. *So that things which are seen were not made of things which do appear;* the visible world, and all visible in it, were made all of nothing; this reason could never digest. All was produced of that formless, void, dark chaos which was invisible, Gen. i. 2; which void, formless, dark mass itself, was made of no pre-existent stuff, matter or atoms, but of nothing; which differenceth the operative power of God from that of all other agents. See Gen. i. 1; Psal. lxxxix. 11, 12; cxlviii. 5, 6, &c.; Isa. xlii. 5; xlv. 12, 18.

4 By faith ᵈAbel offered unto God a more excellent sacrifice than Cain, by which he obtained witness that he was righteous, God testifying of his gifts: and by it he being dead ᵉ‖yet speaketh.

d Gen. 4. 4.
1 John 3. 12.

e Gen. 4. 10.
Mat. 23. 35.
ch. 12. 24.
‖ *or, is yet spoken of.*

The Spirit beginneth here to illustrate his description of faith, by induction of instances throughout the former ages of the church to the time of these Hebrews; and he begins with believers in the old world before the flood. Faith is the same Divine grace as described before, only here to be considered as fully receiving of God's will in Christ as to sacrificing work, and remitting such affections and operations to God in it as were agreeable thereunto. *By faith Abel offered unto God a more excellent sacrifice than Cain:* Abel, the younger son of Adam, an eminent believer, whose faith orders him and his worship, the first martyr for religion in the world, Luke xi. 51, who sealed the truth of God with his blood; he, in the end of days, that is, the sabbath, Gen. iv. 3, 4, brought a bloody sacrifice of the fattest and best of the flock, and offered up to the Divine Majesty, the true and living God, his Creator and Redeemer, to atone him for his sin; having a regard to, and faith in, the great sacrifice of the Seed of the woman, for him in fulness of time to be offered up, and of which his was but a type. This sacrifice was fuller of what God required in offerings, than Cain his elder brother's, not, it may be, for external price, but internal worth. Cain offered the fruits of the ground, such as God afterwards required in the ceremonial law, but he was not sensible of the guilt and filth of sin, and of its demerits, nor desirous to remove it in the due way and order appointed, as appears by his murdering of his brother after: Abel's sacrifice was better, more excellent, because more fully agreeable to God's will for purging and pardoning sin, full of self-denial and abasement for sin, and faith in Christ's sacrifice. *By which he obtained witness that he was righteous;* by which sacrifice of faith he had testimony that he acknowledged himself a sinner, that had need of the blood of Christ to sprinkle him; yet *he was righteous* by the righteousness of faith, Rom. iii. 22, 25, 26, which is upon Abel, as all other believers, Phil. iii. 9. And this testified to his soul, by God's Spirit, that he was justified and sanctified, and so eminently righteous; and it was manifested to others, Christ himself, God-man, witnessing of it, Matt. xxiii. 35. *God testifying of his gifts;* God himself witnessed from heaven to the truth of his state, by accepting of his person and sacrifice, and giving a visible sign of it, so as Cain could observe it, and be displeased at the difference God made between him and his brother, Gen. iv. 4, 5, 7; likely it was by sending fire from heaven, and consuming Abel's sacrifice, as he did others afterwards, Lev. ix. 24; Judg. vi. 19, 21; 1 Kings xviii. 38; 2 Chron. vii. 1; and by it testified him to be righteous. *And by it he being dead yet speaketh;* by his faith, though murdered out of this world, and his place here knows him no more, and with a design that he should never speak nor be spoken of more, yet he now *speaketh*, i. e. liveth, Matt. xxii. 32, and testifieth to God that he is true, and the only true God to make souls happy. He, in his example, and his record in Scripture, bespeaketh all that read his story to imitate him in his faith and worshipping of God, and his patient martyrdom for God and his gospel worship through Christ. And by his blood he crieth for justice against his murderer, as Gen. iv. 10; see chap. xii. 24; and as joined with the rest of the martyrs of Jesus, impleads God's righteous vengeance to be executed on their bloody persecutors, Luke xi. 51; Rev. vi. 10, 11. By reason of his faith he is spoken of throughout all generations, recorded among the excellent sons of God, and renowned in the church to this day. Such a force hath faith to eternize the persons of believers in acceptance with God through Christ, their wrongs, injuries, and blood on God's remembrance, and their names in heaven and the church below.

f Gen. 5. 22,
24. Wisd. 4.
10. Ecclus.
44. 16. & 49.
14.

5 By faith ᶠEnoch was translated that he should not see death; and was not found, because God had translated him: for before his translation he had this testimony, that he pleased God.

By faith Enoch was translated that he should not see death: by the Divine faith before described, that which reacheth home to God by Christ, Enoch, the seventh patriarch in a descent from Adam of the church's line, Gen. v. 21, an eminent prophet and *Boanerges*, denouncing judgment against the ungodly ones of his time, so as to awaken them to repentance, Jude 14, 15, was taken by God, Gen. v. 24. The apostle keeps to the Septuagint translation of the text. He was miraculously changed in his body from a mortal to an immortal state, and this without any separation of his soul from it. God, out of an extraordinary grace and favour to him, dispensed with the common sentence passed on the human seed in Adam, as he did many ages after this to Elijah. He died not: all the rest of the fathers of the church, Gen. v. 5, 8, 27, the longest liver of them, died. *And was not found; he was not*, Gen. v. 24, neither among men, nor in their sepulchres, as others were, but had changed his habitation and society. If any went to seek him, as others did Elijah, he was far out of their finding, 2 Kings ii. 17. *Because God had translated him;* for God had taken him to himself in heaven, the place of his residence, and in the very act changed his body into a spiritual, powerful, glorious, and incorruptible one; as all ours, who are true believers, shall be at last, 1 Cor. xv. 51; 1 Thess. iv. 15; and so made fit for the place to which he was taken, made like an angel in person, and to be with those spirits in company; now did he fully see and enjoy him whom by faith he walked with beneath. *For before his translation he had this testimony, that he pleased God;* in the time of his life, and walking with God in this sinful world, all the time of his witnessing for God in it, God witnessed by his work on his soul to himself, by his ministry and life to the world, and by the prophet Moses's record of it to all generations to come in the church once and again, Gen. v. 22, 24, that in his walking with God he *pleased* him. He was not only justified, graciously accepted, and beloved of him, but he did that which was pleasing to God, putting out in thought, word, and deed all the power of grace to act for God; preserving constant converse and communion with him; and had no fellowship with the unfruitful works of darkness, but reproved them. By this he pleased God, and God testified to all the world he did so, by a miraculous translation of him from the world to himself. God cares not for, nor will take to him, such who please him not.

6 But without faith *it is* impossible to please *him:* for he that cometh to God must believe that he is, and *that* he is a rewarder of them that diligently seek him.

The Spirit here proveth that Enoch pleased God by faith, though it was not expressly written in his text by Moses, because of the impossibility of pleasing God without faith. *But without faith it is impossible to please him;* but without faith upon God in Christ, whom Enoch pleased, it is absolutely impossible to do any thing acceptable to God, so as to be justified by him; for infidelity, or want of faith, makes God a liar, 1 John v. 10, Christ a vanity, John v. 40, and God's will a deceit, which peremptorily saith, there is no pleasing of him but by faith in Christ, John xiv. 6. The effect cannot exist without its cause, as is proved in the next words. *For he that cometh to God:* for whoever he be, every particular soul, that cometh off from sin to God, so as to be under his conduct and influence; makes out by spiritual motions of his mind, will, affections, and members, in thoughts, desires, resolutions, and operations, to enjoy God, so as to be accepted with, justified by, and blessed of him; and at present makes his access to him with liberty and boldness in prayer, or any other duty, through Christ. *Must believe that he is;* he must really, fully, and supernaturally receive all that which God revealeth in his word is pleasing to him, especially concerning himself; as, that he is the primitive, perfect Being, and the Cause of all; that he is three in relations and one in essence, most excellent in all his attributes, infinitely wise, powerful, just, good, and eternal, &c., the supreme Creator and Governor of, and Lawgiver to, all. *And that he is a rewarder of them that diligently seek him;* and that he will recompense all men according to their works, but will eminently and freely give himself to be the reward of his, and whatever he can be to or do for them for their good, Gen. xv. 1; but to those only, who with an intent heart and spirit pursue him by faith, love, and longing after him as their supremest good, Isa. xlv. 22; Rom. ii. 6, 12; Rev. xxii. 12.

7 By faith Noah, being warned of God of things not seen as yet, ‖ moved with fear, ʰprepared an ark to the saving of his house; by the which he condemned the world, and became heir of ⁱthe righteousness which is by faith.

g Gen. 6.13,
22. Ecclus.
4. 17.
‖ Or, *being weary.*
h 1 Pet.3.20.

i Rom. 3.22.
& 4. 13.
Phil. 3. 9.

By faith Noah, being warned of God; by the same Divine faith Noah, the last example of it in the old world, and the father of the new world, being warned by an immediate revelation from God, Gen. vi. 13, 21, largely rehearsed by Moses: so that God's word is the ground or foundation of Divine faith in all ages of the world. *Of things not seen as yet;* of things not yet seen, but only by faith in God's revelation: which things were the perishing of the world by a deluge of waters above one hundred years after; and that himself and family, with some creatures, should be saved from that deluge, to repeople the world, and to replenish the air and earth; none of which things did fall under Noah's sense then. *Moved with fear;* εὐλαβηθεὶς imports in it a right reception of God's revelation, which made him afraid, and careful not to offend God; and a godly carriage to him who had revealed the imminent danger of the sinful world, and his own deliverance from it: see chap. v. 7. *Prepared an ark to the saving of his house;* hereon he obeyeth God's precept, and prepared and perfected the vessel, both for matter and form, according to God's word; so as to be ready against the time of the deluge, for the preservation of himself and family by it, Gen. vi. 14—16, 22; compare 1 Pet. iii. 20. By virtue of this ark, that water which drowned the world saved them. So that flood was a full type of the water of baptism: his ark, of Christ our ark; his family, of Christ's small family in comparison of the world; their salvation from water, of the eternal salvation of these from the deluge of fire, 2 Pet. iii. 6, 7, 11, 14. The same Divine faith in Noah and in Christians, maketh them to obey God's precept, retire to and enter God's ark, and so enjoy his salvation. *By the which he condemned the world;* by this faith discovered in his work about the ark, he testified against the sinful world of mankind for their unbelief and disobedience, who for one hundred and twenty years together, being by Noah's preaching and building the ark called to repentance, 2 Pet. ii. 5, and to prevent the judgment God threatened on them; and so condemned them virtually by his word and doctrine, judicially by declaring God's sentence on them: see Matt. xii. 41, 42; John xii. 48. *And became heir of the righteousness which is by faith;* by this faith he received the promise of righteousness, which made him an heir of it, and of that eternal life and salvation for which it fitted him, as well as to which it entitled him; and by it he sent out all the fruits of righteousness that are to the praise and glory of God, Rom. v. 1; John i. 12.

8 By faith ᵏAbraham, when he was called to go out into a place which he should after receive for an inheritance, obeyed; and he went out, not knowing whither he went.

k Gen. 12. 1,
4. Acts 7. 2,
3,4.

Here begin instances of this Divine faith after the flood from Abraham to Moses's time, ver. 8—22. The first is the father of believers, so entitled by God, eminent in the exercise of this grace, of whose ancestry, and their descent from him, these Hebrews did greatly glory. He had an express discovery of the will of God unto him, that he should leave the idolatrous place where he lived, Gen. xi. 31; xii. 1—3; compare Josh. xxiv. 2; Acts vii. 2, 3; and with his family should travel to a land which God would show him, and which he would give him as an inheritance for him and his, which was the land of Canaan, as described, Gen. xiii. 14—17; xxv. 18, 19, 21. This command of God, strengthened by a promise, he obeyed, Gen. xii. 4; Acts vii. 4: through faith, really, freely, and fully resigning up himself and his to God's disposal. *And he went out not knowing whither he went;* he went forth with his father Terah from his country, kindred, and friends, in Ur of the Chaldees, to Charran, and there they dwelt till Terah died, Gen. xi. 31; Acts vii. 4. After which, he pursued God's orders in his motion from place to place, though he knew neither the way, nor the place in which and whither he was to move, resting himself on God's word and guidance, and relying wholly on his provision for him, and protection of him in all his ways.

9 By faith he sojourned in the land of promise, as *in* a strange country, ¹dwelling in tabernacles with Isaac and Jacob, ᵐ the heirs with him of the same promise:

l Gen. 12. 8. & 13. 3, 18. & 18. 1, 9.
m ch. 6. 17.

By faith he sojourned in the land of promise, as in a strange country; by the same Divine faith he passed from tent to tent, moving it from place to place, as God ordered; so as he rather sojourned than dwelt in any. His journal is legible in Moses's history, moving from Charran to Shechem, from thence to Beth-el, and then more southward, and thence to Egypt; see Gen. xii.: so that he sojourned in Canaan, and the adjoining countries, which God had covenanted to give for an inheritance to him and his seed, Gen. xv. 18—21; yet by faith he would stay God's time for it, but lived in it as a stranger, not having in possession one foot of ground, but what he bought for a burying-place, Gen. xxv. 9, 10; Acts vii. 5. *Dwelling in tabernacles with Isaac and Jacob, the heirs with him of the same promise:* here he, with his son Isaac, and grandson, and their seed, coheirs with him of Canaan, built no houses, but lived in tents, which they might pitch or remove at God's pleasure, and as he called them, as who were strangers to this country, and to the inhabitants of it, with whom they were to have no spiritual society, as travelling to a better; being in this world, but neither citizens nor inhabitants of it, but as denizens of a more excellent one, Gen. xxvi. 3; xxviii. 13, 14.

10 For he looked for ⁿ a city which hath foundations, ᵒ whose builder and maker *is* God.

n ch. 12. 22. & 13. 14.
o ch. 3. 4. Rev. 21. 2, 10.

The reason of this contented pilgrimage was the excellent end of it, the place and state to which it brought him; he did really discern by the Spirit's work in him, and promise to him, his title to it, and vehemently did desire and long for, and yet patiently waited for, a better place and state than this earthly; and was daily making his approaches to it, Rom. viii. 19; 2 Cor. v. 1, 2, 8, 9. *For he looked for a city which hath foundations:* πόλις notes both a place made up and constituted of buildings and houses, such was the earthly Jerusalem; and a state, polity, or community. Here it must be understood spiritually, for such a place and state as is not to be shadowed out by any in this world; it being for nature, mansions, society, condition, such as no earthly can decipher, or set out. This city is heaven itself, often so styled in this Epistle, as ver. 16; chap. xii. 22; xiii. 14; Rev. iii. 12. It is not movable, as a tent fastened by stakes and cords; nor as creature-buildings, perishable. Histories tell us of the rise and fall of the best earthly cities; this city is built on the Rock of ages, as well as by him, whose immutability, almightiness, and eternity hath laid and settled its foundations, the basis and ground-work, firm and incorruptible, 1 Pet. i. 4. *Whose builder and maker is God;* the happy fabric, with persons and state, endures for ever, because of its Raiser and Founder. The great Architect, that cast the plot and model of it in his own mind, and the publicly-declared Operator and Raiser of it, who laid the foundations, reared the mansions, and finished the whole, is no less person than the infinitely wise, almighty, and eternal God. It all became him alone, and doth as far exceed other cities as God doth men. No human art or power was fit or capable for such a work, but only God.

11 Through faith also ᵖ Sara herself

p Gen. 17. 19. & 18. 11, 14. & 21. 2.

received strength to conceive seed, and ᑫ was delivered of a child when she was past age, because she judged him ʳ faithful who had promised.

q See Luke 1. 36.
r Rom. 4. 21. ch. 10. 23.

Through faith also Sara herself received strength to conceive seed; by the same Divine faith in Abraham and Sarah was brought forth the child of promise. For though the instance be expressly in Sarah, yet it is inclusive of Abraham also, who was eminent for his faith in this thing, acquiring an eminent title by it, even of the Father of believers, as the apostle declareth, Rom. iv. 17—22, and therefore jointly to be considered with Sarah. She, who first through unbelief laughed at the promise, yet being reproved by Christ, the Angel of the covenant, for it, believed on the repetition of it, Gen. xviii. 9—16, and gave testimony of it by her waiting for the promised mercy. As barren as she was, yet faith made her fruitful; when it was impossible of herself to expect it for nature or years, yet received she power and strength from God, by believing, to conceive seed, that is, laying the foundation of it, conceiving in her dead womb, and bearing a son. *And was delivered of a child when she was past age;* she was not only naturally barren, but of ninety years of age at this time, when the most fruitful were past such work; yet was she delivered of a son, and became the mother of Isaac by faith, as he was the son of promise, Gen. xv. 4; xviii. 11; compare Rom. iv. 17—19. *Because she judged him faithful who had promised;* she gave glory to God by a firm and hearty closure with his promise, accounting God faithful to his word, and able to perform it, and so rested on it, and waited for him, as Abraham did, Rom. iv. 18, 20, 21. The promise which he made was, That they in their old age should have a son, Gen. xii. 2; made in general, chap. xiii. 15, 16; in particular, chap. xv. 4, 5; to both, chap. xvii. 15—17; xviii. 10, 14; xxi. 1—3, 12.

12 Therefore sprang there even of one, and ˢ him as good as dead, ᵗ *so many* as the stars of the sky in multitude, and as the sand which is by the sea shore innumerable.

s Rom. 4. 19. t Gen. 22. 17. Rom. 4. 18.

Because of this faith of Abraham and Sarah, and the fruit of it in conceiving and bringing forth Isaac, was laid the foundation of a numerous seed by God's promise; from Abraham, a hundred, and Sarah, ninety years old, and barren, and both dead as to procreation, Rom. iv. 19, there were begotten a vast and unbounded seed, as the stars in the firmament, or the sand on the sea shore; and amongst them the teeming blessing, the one eminent Seed of Abraham, the Messiah, in whom all nations were to be blessed. Within four hundred years from the birth of Isaac, this seed increased to above six hundred thousand fighting men, besides women and children, and after increased to a stupendous greatness, according to the promise, Gen. xiii. 16; xv. 5; Exod. xii. 47; 1 Chron. xxi. 5, 6.

13 These all died † in faith, ᵘ not having received the promises, but ˣ having seen them afar off, and were persuaded of *them*, and embraced *them*, and ʸ confessed that they were strangers and pilgrims on the earth.

† Gr. *according to faith.*
u ver. 39.
x ver. 27. John 8. 56.
y Gen. 23. 4. & 47. 9. 1 Chron. 29. 15. Ps. 39. 12. & 119. 19. 1 Pet. i. 17. & 2. 11.

These all died in faith; all these, Abraham, Sarah, Isaac, and Jacob, &c., who were heirs of the same promises, and who had opportunity to return to the same country from which they came forth, as ver. 15: they did not only live according to faith, walking with, worshipping of, and waiting on God, testifying against sin, but finished their course by dying according to faith; by faith, as the instrumental efficient of it; in faith, as the regulating cause of it; according to faith, as in the state of believing. Faith was immortal in them as their souls, making their death a covenant dissolution, Luke ii. 29, a voluntary, hopeful, blessed death, as 2 Cor. v. 8; 1 Thess. iv. 13. *Not having received the promises;* not receiving actually, and in sense, the things promised, which were a numerous offspring, the literal Canaan, the Messiah in the flesh, and a glorious resurrection; but departed triumphing, and in the faith of all, and that they would be made good to theirs; and this

HEBREWS XI

they discovered by the blessings they left on each other, as Isaac on Jacob, and Jacob on the patriarchs. *But having seen them afar off;* but faith brought all these promises into their view, though so far off; so did Abraham see by it the Messiah, John viii. 56. They all had a real, clear, and strong prospect of them, the inheritance temporal in its time to come, and the heavenly rest beyond the grave, seeing the resurrection, heaven, and glory, by faith, when they died, Gen. xlix. 18. *And were persuaded of them, and embraced them;* by a powerful impression of faith on their souls, of the truth, goodness, and certainty of the things promised, on their minds, with a mighty apprehension of and assent to them in their wills, to the choosing of and closing with them in their affections; cleaving to them in love, desire, and delight, as surely to be accomplished; having their souls thankfully receiving them, graciously returning to God for them, with the greatest satisfaction embracing them, as are welcome friends or relations long absent from us; hugging Christ. saluting heaven, and embracing glory in the promises by faith, when dying. *And confessed that they were strangers and pilgrims on the earth;* in word and deed; while they lived they published it to the world, as Abraham, Gen. xxiii. 4, and Jacob, Gen. xlvii. 9; keeping themselves free from all entanglements of this earth, as became those who are strangers, having no possession of, nor intimacy with this earth; incorporating with no other people, but as pilgrims wandered from place to place, took up and pitched their tents when and where God would have them, unpeopled as to this world, and desiring to be peopled with the Lord, Psal. xxxix. 12; cv. 12, 13; compare 2 Cor. v. 6, 8. They were all of the same mind, loose from and above this world, and longing to remove to their own country and be with God.

z ch. 13. 14.

14 For they that say such things [z] declare plainly that they seek a country.

The reason of faith's effect in their dying, is the bringing in view a better life, state, and place than any earthly one. For these believers, by word and life professing themselves to be strangers and pilgrims on this earth, and seeing God's promises, and embracing them, *declare* and show *plainly* to all who see them, or converse with them, *that they seek a country*, and a place of rest, which they were not possessed of. For no person is a stranger or pilgrim in his own country; but these inquired the way, and walked in it, which led them to a better than any this earth afforded them : and so the apostle brings us back to that which he had declared before, ver. 10, and immediately prevents the suggestion, that this country should be their former country, and clears it to be a better.

15 And truly, if they had been mindful of that *country* from whence they came out, they might have had opportunity to have returned.

Though they were strangers in Canaan, yet they might seek an earthly country, even Ur of the Chaldees, from whence they came forth, and which was their native country, and so might be dearer to them than any other; but it was not that, but a better country, they were mindful of, which they viewed by faith; whereas the other they might have seen with their eyes. If that had been all they desired, they wanted neither means nor opportunity of returning to it, but they remained fixed in obedience to the heavenly call; and when Jacob returned to it for a wife, yet he left it again when God summoned him, as appears, Gen. xxix., xxx., xxxi. They did willingly leave it, and kept from it, and never looked back there, but looked for a better.

a Ex. 3.6,15.
Matt. 22. 32.
Acts 7. 32.
b Phil. 3. 20.
ch. 13. 14.

16 But now they desire a better *country*, that is, an heavenly: wherefore God is not ashamed [a] to be called their God: for [b] he hath prepared for them a city.

But now they desire a better country, that is, an heavenly: having deserted this world, as strangers in it, they sought, desired, and hoped for with the greatest earnestness and fervency, a city in the country of heaven, ver. 10, in comparison with which they contemned and despised all others; a country where there is perfection of life, and fulness of glory: it excelleth all others as far as heaven doth earth, 2 Tim. iv. 18; 1 Pet. i. 4. The state, society, enjoyments, and place, they longed for, were all heavenly, Phil. iii. 20,

21; nothing lower than this world would satisfy them. *Wherefore God is not ashamed to be called their God:* faith having carried them thus estranged from this world to the grave, endearing to them the promises, and engaging of them for heaven only, therefore God did not disdain them, he did not think it any disrepute to him to own them his, but esteemed it an honour and reputation to him, took up his joy and delight in them: see him owning them when dead, Exod. iii. 6, 15; Matt. xxii. 31, 32; surnaming himself by them, and adopting them as his own, as Jacob did Joseph's sons, Gen. xlviii. 56; so that though they are dead as to their bodies, yet they are alive as to their souls, and are owned by God in his name and title, and are assured, as to their dust, of a resurrection; for he will do it, giving them that rest that they never had in their pilgrimage. *For he hath prepared for them a city;* that heavenly state and place which they sought for, ver. 10, which infinitely transcended Canaan, and the Jerusalem in it, of which they were denizens while here, Eph. ii. 19; Phil. iii. 20; the pleasant, peaceful, rich, and glorious metropolis of the living God, chap. xii. 22; xiii. 14; which shall make abundant amends for all their sorrows, sufferings, and restless wanderings on earth, where they shall enjoy pleasures, riches, honours, and rest for evermore, 1 Pet. i. 4.

c Gen. 22. 1, 9.
d Jam. 2. 21.

17 By faith [c] Abraham, when he was tried, offered up Isaac: and he that had received the promises [d] offered up his only begotten *son*,

By faith Abraham, when he was tried, offered up Isaac; by the same excellent faith Abraham alone, and by himself considered, being tried by God, in a rare way, to give proof of the truth of his faith in and love to him above all, was to take his only son, his darling, and to offer him for a whole burnt offering on Mount Moriah, to himself, Gen. xxii. 2. Which command of God was not unjust, he having absolute sovereignty and dominion over all persons and their lives, having power to kill, and to make alive, Deut. xxxii. 39. This son of his he offered up as God commanded; for in his heart he had fully parted with him to God, and proceeded so far in execution, as, if God had not dispensed with it, it had been actually done, he would have killed him and burnt him to ashes on the altar, Gen. xxii. 3, 6—13. *And he that had received the promises offered up his only begotten son:* this mighty faith enabled him to do this, though he was his only begotten son by promise, and in the church's line, concerning whom he had received so many promises, and in whom only they were to be fulfilled, as that a numerous seed should descend from him, who should inherit Canaan, and through whom Christ was to descend into the world, in whom himself and all nations were to be blessed. Yet faith silenceth reason and natural affection, assureth him God could fulfil his promises by him though he should offer him, as he raised him from a dead body and womb at first, and gave him to him: so he obeyeth God's word, and offereth him.

∥ Or, *To.*
e Gen. 21.12.
Rom. 9. 7.

18 ∥ Of whom it was said, [e] That in Isaac shall thy seed be called:

This did greaten Abraham's trial, that unto him it was promised by God himself, That in this only begotten son Isaac, the eminently blessed and blessing Seed, with all his mystical body, should be called; that is, put in being, propagated and made known as by name in Isaac, Gal. iv. 28. This God revealed to Abraham, Gen. xvii. 19, 21, and hereby was his faith put to it to reconcile contradictions, as to believe this special promise, and yet execute this special command to sacrifice Isaac, yet to believe in him his seed should be called.

f Rom. 4. 17, 19, 21.

19 Accounting that God [f] *was* able to raise *him* up, even from the dead; from whence also he received him in a figure.

Accounting that God was able to raise him up, even from the dead: faith put this into Abraham's thoughts in his reasonings about this trial between the temptation and God's power, and influenced him to conclude and determine under it. That since God could raise him from the dead to perform his promises, he would sacrifice him to obey God's command. This faith grew from what God had done, in giving him Isaac from his own dead body, and Sarah's dead womb, Rom. iv. 17—22. God's almighty power to raise from the dead answered all the difficulties in the trial. If God command it, who can raise from the dead, this can be no murder; for he can either prevent or recover. Promises should not fail, though Isaac was sacrificed; for God would raise him up and accomplish them. As to arguments from natural affection: Shall a child be dearer to me than a God, who quickens me, and can raise him from the dead? Since God can do this, what difficulties can he not overcome? Hence is this principle so often revealed and repeated to be a sure prop to a Christian's faith throughout the gospel. *From whence also he received him in a figure:* his generation was a kind of resurrection from the dead, and so was his restitution to Abraham, for in Abraham's account he was dead, his hand being lifted up to kill him, when the angel stops the execution, Gen. xxii. 11, 12. From the altar he carrieth him back as a trophy and reward of the victory of his faith, in such a manner as one risen from the dead, and an eminent signal of his victory over this temptation. Abraham had a figure of the resurrection in his son, and an earnest of a far more glorious resurrection in Christ.

g Gen. 27. 27, 39.
20 By faith ᵍIsaac blessed Jacob and Esau concerning things to come.

Isaac is the next example instanced in of the same Divine faith, described, ver. 1; only here exercised on the special revelation of God to him concerning his seed. By this faith he did not only wish and pray blessings, but prophetically applied them to his two sons, to Jacob and Israel his seed the covenant blessings, and to Esau and the Edomites his seed the temporary blessings, God designed them, Gen. xxvii. 27, 39. Both these were things to come, and to be communicated to their seeds hundreds of years after. As the things to come that concerned Jacob, which were not seen, but hoped for from God's revelation of them, were, plenty, dominion over brethren, blessings above the power of a curse, even the spiritual and covenanted ones of Abraham and Isaac with him, Gen. xxvii. 28, 29. The things to come concerning Esau and his seed, were only earthly, temporal blessings, escape out of servitude in time, common good things at the highest, Gen. xxvii. 39. 40. By faith Isaac foresaw all these future events, foretold them, and applied their several portions to them from the mouth of God, and they were to a tittle fulfilled, 2 Sam. viii. 14, and 2 Kings viii. 20, as to the Edomites; as in the whole Old Testament unto Jacob, and to his seed literal and spiritual.

21 By faith Jacob, when he was a dying, ʰblessed both the sons of Joseph; and ⁱworshipped, *leaning* upon the top of his staff.

h Gen. 48. 5, 16, 20.
i Gen. 47. 31.

By faith Jacob, when he was a dying, blessed both the sons of Joseph: Jacob did not degenerate from his progenitors, but by the same excellent faith (being heir to the birthright and blessing, by God's appointment, and his father's confirmation, as Gen. xxviii. 1, 3, 4) doth, as a grandfather and a prophet, near expiring, weak in body, but strong in faith, bless Joseph, and each of his sons, Gen. xlviii. 15—20, preferring Ephraim the younger before Manasseh the elder, by laying his right hand on his head, and his left on the other's; and so adopts them to be his children, gives them the blessing of the covenant, as to their persons, and the inheritance of two tribes amongst his sons, as belonging to Joseph, as his birthright, Gen. xlix. 22—26. These by faith he foretold, and applied particularly to each of them from God himself through prayer. *And worshipped, leaning upon the top of his staff:* another effect of his faith, is his worshipping God, having bequeathed his body to the burial in a firm expectation of the promised inheritance, as the history clears, Gen. xlvii. 29—31; xlviii. 21, 22. For having sent for Joseph, he raiseth up himself on the pillow at the bed's head, and for his support used his staff, leaning on the head of it, when in faith he declares his will to his son Joseph, and binds him by an oath to bury him in Machpelah in Canaan, with Abraham and Isaac, heirs of the same promise, as an earnest and handsel of the twelve tribes' possessing it; which Joseph having solemnly sworn to him, Jacob bowed himself and worshipped, lifting up his heart to God in thankfulness for his continual providence in the gradual accomplishment of his promise to the seed of Abraham, Isaac, and Jacob. This he did *by faith*, adoring his sovereign Lord and Saviour by his humbly bowing before him. There was no need of faith to bow to Joseph, who was inferior to Jacob, and blessed by him.

22 By faith ᵏJoseph, when he died, ‖ made mention of the departing of the children of Israel; and gave commandment concerning his bones.

k Gen. 50. 24, 25.
Ex. 13. 19.
‖ Or, remembered.

By faith Joseph, when he died, made mention of the departing of the children of Israel: Joseph, the first son of Jacob by Rachel. whom God preferred before his brethren, envied and sold by them, but advanced by him to be lord of Egypt, and a saviour to them, heir of the birthright, and of his father's grace, a patriarch and prophet like him; drawing near to the end of his pilgrimage on earth, and dying, he *made mention*, and brought to the mind of the Israelites his children, brethren, and nephews, and, likely, with a charge to convey it down to their posterity, as it might be remembered by them, that this he did with willingness and choice, looking for a better place and state than any in Egypt, and that his death should not obstruct the issues of providence to them for good; for God lived, and would surely visit them in their posterity, Israel living when he sent Moses to them, and would make them go up gloriously out of Egypt, and bring them into the Land of Promise, and give it to them for their inheritance. This testimony he gives them of it *by faith*, Gen. l. 24; and God fulfilled it one hundred and sixty years after his death, as he had sworn to Abraham, Isaac, and Jacob. *And gave commandment concerning his bones: by faith* likewise he charged them about carrying his embalmed body with them and burying it in Canaan, and obliged the Israelites to it by an oath, Gen. l. 25, making it an earnest and signal to them of the promise and oath of God for their deliverance, that as he desired his bones might be buried in Canaan, being heir together with Jacob of the same promised inheritance, it might be a visible token of, and encouragement in, the appointed time, to their return. And this Israel fulfilled, Exod. xiii. 19, carrying them away with them, and afterwards burying them in Shechem, the lot of Ephraim, Josh. xxiv. 32.

23 By faith ˡMoses, when he was born, was hid three months of his parents, because they saw *he was* a proper child; and they were not afraid of the king's ᵐ commandment.

l Ex. 2. 2.
Acts 7. 20.
m Ex. 1. 16, 22.

By faith Moses, when he was born, was hid three months of his parents: the parents of Moses were as eminent in this faith as their progenitors; for by it Amram and Jochebed, both of them of the tribe of Levi, Exod. vi. 20, ($\pi\alpha\tau\acute{\epsilon}\rho\omega\nu$ here put by a metaphrase for $\gamma o\nu\epsilon\~{\iota}\varsigma$, and though in the history ascribed to the mother only, yet it was by the father's direction, as Exod. ii. 2; compare Acts vii. 20.) hid Moses, born under the bloody edict of a tyrant for drowning all the Hebrew males in the Nile. He was born three years after Aaron, and sixty-five after Joseph's death. They kept him three months from the destroyers, and they adventured the penalties threatened by the edict, Exod. ii. 2, 3; faith overcoming their fears and difficulties about it, and, in all probability, ordered their fitting the ark, and disposal of it for his preservation, with the other acts attending it. *Because they saw he was a proper child:* the reason of faith's work was their seeing of him to be $\dot{\alpha}\sigma\epsilon\~{\iota}o\nu$, fair, beautiful, proper; and this not in himself only, but, as Stephen interprets it, $\dot{\alpha}\sigma\epsilon\~{\iota}o\nu\ \tau\tilde{\omega}\ \Theta\epsilon\tilde{\omega}$, fair to God, Acts vii. 20. Some glorious aspect was by God put upon him as a signal of some great person, and of great use in God's design to his church; some extraordinary stamp of God on his countenance, which faith could discern there, and so influence them to conceal and preserve him. *And they were not afraid of the king's commandment;* faith made them fearless; for they were not afraid that the king's edict should frustrate God's purpose concerning the child, or keep him from its service to the church, wherein God would employ him, and of which he had given them a signal in that lustre cast on his person; and therefore they used means to preserve him, even when they exposed him, and which had a suitable success, Exod. ii. 3—10.

24 By faith [n] Moses, when he was come to years, refused to be called the son of Pharaoh's daughter;

[n Ex. 2. 10, 11.]

Moses himself was as eminent a believer as his parents, and a mighty instance of Divine faith. He who was so named and saved by the enemies of the church, and adopted as a son to a notorious one of them, yet being great in age and stature, full forty, Exod. iii. 11 ; Acts vii. 23, past the folly of childhood and rashness of youth, upon manly deliberation and a rational exercise of faith, notwithstanding he was by birth a poor Israelite, and saved from perishing by a princess, the daughter of a potent king; nourished through her indulgence by his own mother, adopted as her own son, educated by her in all the wisdom of the Egyptians, preferred, owned, and honoured as her son, and might have been in a fair way to have succeeded to the kingdom; yet, not out of any disingenuity, or base ingratitude to his eminent preserver, but out of a Divine faith, he layeth down all his titles and honours, and renounceth his relation, for the enjoyment of a better title with, and a greater good in, God; and this he manifested by word and deed in his after-transactions, ver. 25.

25 [o] Choosing rather to suffer affliction with the people of God, than to enjoy the pleasures of sin for a season;

[o Ps. 84. 10.]

Choosing rather to suffer affliction with the people of God : the same faith influenced his will, the cause of his former renunciation ; for being in the present fruition of all court favours, and under the offers of all worldly delights by Egypt, and of all worldly discontents by God, faith determined his choice, made him a fellow sufferer in all the oppressions, afflictions, persecutions of his natural brethren the people of God, the most privileged society in the world for hope, as the most exercised by trials for God's sake : he knew there would be eternal rest and glory into which they would issue him, besides glorious effects they would have on his soul while he was enduring them; and that they were but passing, and would quickly have an end, Rom. viii. 18; 2 Cor. iv. 17, 18. Than to enjoy the pleasures of sin for a season : the same faith made him to reject the enticing pleasures of sin, which could not be avoided by his continuance in Pharaoh's court, either in dissembling himself to be no Israelite, professing himself to be an Egyptian, taking part with them in their cruel carriage to his brethren, living after their vicious course in all manner of voluptuousness; and the pleasures which he was to enjoy were sinful, transitory, and momentaneous, neither satisfying nor enduring, and must be attended with a sting in the end of them, even eternal anguish and torment, whereas his afflictions would end in eternal joys and pleasures, Mark ix. 43, 44, 47 ; Luke xvi. 25.

26 Esteeming [p] the reproach ‖ of Christ greater riches than the treasures in Egypt: for he had respect unto [q] the recompence of the reward.

[p ch. 13. 13. ‖ Or, for Christ.]
[q ch. 10. 35.]

Esteeming the reproach of Christ greater riches than the treasures in Egypt : faith influenced and determined his former choice from the most excellent ground of it, the representation of these by the Divine inspired truth to him ; it made him weigh and deliberate about the matters proposed, and then to judge, and positively determine about them, That the reproachful suffering of all sorts of afflictions, poverty, distresses, tortures, most ignominiously inflicted on them by their enemies for their faith in Christ, and expectation of him according to God's promise, and who was now the Angel of the covenant that protected them, as well as their ancestor Jacob, Gen. xlviii. 15, 16 : these Moses chose to suffer patiently, out of faith in and love to Christ ; these, with what excellent things were to follow by virtue of God's promise, he preferred as a better and richer estate, and infinitely more desirable, than all the treasures of honours and riches, which either Egypt or its king could oblige him with, the whole of them founded in the dust, disposed by flesh, fading in enjoyment, and ending in vanity. What are these treasures, compared to those laid up in store by Christ for his in heaven ? For he had respect unto the recompence of the reward : these were the things Moses had in his eye, the end of Christ's reproach, and Egypt's glory ; this made him turn his eye and heart away from Egypt, and intently to look on the excellent issue of his reproachful sufferings for Christ, even Christ rendering to him his unexpressibly glorious and eternal reward for it, 2 Cor. iv. 17, 18. This God had promised to, Christ had purchased for, such, who were by faith bearing his reproach, and qualified for the enjoying of it, Rom. viii. 17, 18; 2 Tim. ii. 12 ; 1 Pet. iv. 13, 14.

27 By faith [r] he forsook Egypt, not fearing the wrath of the king : for he endured, as [s] seeing him who is invisible.

[r Ex. 10. 28, 29. & 12. 37. & 13. 17, 18.]
[s ver. 13.]

By faith he forsook Egypt, not fearing the wrath of the king : by the same excellent faith, after his demand from Pharaoh of liberty for Israel to leave Egypt, and he had brought on him and his people the ten plagues God threatened them with, then he brake the bands of captivity, and took up Israel, and left Egypt subdued, wasted by plagues, and a place to be abhorred ; triumphing over it, he forsakes it as a conqueror, and carrieth away the spoils of it. The wrath and rage of Pharaoh at him and his work for Israel, did not appal him ; he was not afraid of his threatening to kill him, Exod. x. 28, 29 ; yet he defied him, even when his rage made him to pursue him and Israel with his host to destroy them. For he endured, as seeing him who is invisible ; ἐκαρτέρησε, he was of a bold, undaunted spirit, so as nothing was too hard for him, either to suffer or do : magnanimity expelled his fear, so as he would stand or march according to God's order, faith presenting to his view at all times the great Angel of the covenant, God the Son, the Redeemer of him and Israel, the only Potentate, the invisible King of kings, and Lord of lords, 1 Tim. vi. 14—16 ; with him, and for him, against Pharaoh, leading, covering, and guarding him and Israel in all the way, and fulfilling his promise of delivering of his church from Egypt ; this makes him to march undauntedly with God's host.

28 Through faith [t] he kept the Passover, and the sprinkling of blood, lest he that destroyed the firstborn should touch them.

[t Ex. 12. 21, &c.]

Through faith he kept the Passover, and the sprinkling of blood : this Divine faith influenced him in all his work about God's ordinances, receiving the law about them from God's mouth, and obeying it. By it he made the Passover, i. e. as God's instrument, he instituted it, and put it into being, Exod. xii. 21 ; he celebrated and solemnly managed in each particular, and finished it, reaching the end of it according to God's law in that behalf, 1 Cor. v. 7. Here he saw Christ, and testified of him, the true paschal Lamb of God ; by whom God's wrath passed over the children of Israel, when it rested upon the Egyptians, Exod. xii. 21, &c. By faith he took a bunch of hyssop, and dipped it in the blood of the paschal lamb, and struck the lintel and two side-posts of the doors with the blood, Exod. xii. 22. He used it as a signal of God's sparing Israel, and passing over their houses by his angel, ver. 23 ; and he saw in it the true blood of sprinkling, of Christ our Passover, which saveth souls from the destroyer, John v. 46, and brings them out of the Egypt of this world into the heavenly Canaan. Lest he that destroyed the first-born should touch them : the end of both these was, that the destroying angel, who slew the first-born of the Egyptians, might not touch an Israelite, Exod. xii. 29, 30. Under all this, faith evidenced to Moses God's faithfulness in his promise, it ordered all his duty, and it realized to their hope in that time of danger, that God would save them, who were under that blood, working the assurance of it.

29 By faith [u] they passed through the Red sea as by dry *land* : which the Egyptians assaying to do were drowned.

[u Ex. 14. 22, 29.]

By faith they passed through the Red sea as by dry land : the same faith enabled Moses eminently, and those other believers, as Aaron, Caleb, Joshua, &c. ; for all Israel believed not, 1 Cor. x. 5. yet for the faithful's sake were they kept from drowning, after Moses had, at God's command, (when the Israelites were ready to be fallen on by the Egyptians,) lifted up his rod, and stretched his hand over the Red Sea, when God immediately, by an east wind, divided it, made the waters to stand up on each side like

HEBREWS XI

walls of crystal, and the bottom of it to be dry; then entered Moses and Israel into the empty and dry space, and walked through it on dry ground, and not a soul of Israel miscarried, but might see astonishing power and mercy in it, Exod. xiv. 22. *Which the Egyptians assaying to do were drowned:* in the mean time the Egyptians, with their king, pursuing Israel for their ruin, find their own; for presumptuously adventuring to pursue them through this miraculous space, guided by sense, and not by faith, and thinking to pass as safe as Israel, when they had no word for it, God troubles them by his angels in their motion, makes them drive heavily; and having brought them into his pit in the midst of the channel, the crystal walls dissolve, and the waters, returning to their fluid nature, quickly overwhelmed and swallowed up all that host, so as not one of these unbelieving, presumptuous, persecuting wretches escaped. God's great work in this, as to Israel, had a double meaning; literal, their salvation from the Egyptians; mystical, their baptismal initiation into the covenant of God by Moses: though all of them had not faith unfeigned, yet they professed faith in God; and the doctrine Moses brought from him, was accounted sufficient to attain both, 1 Cor. x. 2.

30 By faith ˣthe walls of Jericho fell down, after they were compassed about seven days.

This Divine faith, exercised by Joshua and Israel after their entrance into the Land of Promise, (who did, on God's word and command, compass the impregnable walls of Jericho once every day for six days together, and on the seventh day seven times, sounding with trumpets of rams' horns, and at last giving a shout,) brought down these walls flat to the ground by the almighty power of God, to whom they were as nothing, Josh. vi. 20. Faith in all this, realized God's promise to them, reached forth their love to him, and obedience in all particulars required by him, glorifying God, as the great Captain of their hosts, as he revealed himself, Josh. v. 13—15; committing the work and event to him, who, by the breath of faith, doth crumble down these walls before them.

31 By faith ʸ the harlot Rahab perished not with them ‖that believed not, when ᶻshe had received the spies with peace.

By faith the harlot Rahab perished not with them that believed not; by the same gospel faith Rahab, who, as the Jews read the word, Josh. ii. 1, זונה was an hostess, and kept a house of entertainment, and so came to lodge the spies; or, as the Septuagint read it, and the Holy Ghost confirms it here, and James ii. 25, was a public harlot, who gat her livelihood by the prostitution of her body, as well as the sale of meat and drink: so notorious a sinner as she, and a Canaanite too, was preserved from the destruction that was inflicted by the Israelites on the unbelieving and disobedient inhabitants of Jericho, being, after her exclusion out of the camp, in order to a legal purifying, admitted into God's church, and honoured by him to be a mother in Israel, from whom the Messiah should descend, Josh. vi. 23, 25. *When she had received the spies with peace:* the full proof of her being a believer, was her entertaining of the spies sent from Joshua to Jericho, preserving them when sought for, and dismissing them, advising them what they were to do in order to their safety, Josh. ii. 3, 10, to the end. The ground of all this, was her faith in God's promise of giving Canaan to Israel, confirmed by the great works she heard God had done for them, and her own expectation of good only in the portion of God's people, to whom she desired to be united, which was afterwards accomplished. Neither doth Paul and James contradict each other concerning her faith and works, James ii. 25; for she was exempted from destruction by the same faith by which she was justified; and her faith was justified to be sound and true, by her carriage to the spies, for it was a full demonstration of her faith in God.

32 And what shall I more say? for the time would fail me to tell of ᵃGedeon, and *of* ᵇBarak, and *of* ᶜSamson, and *of* ᵈJephthae; *of* ᵉDavid also, and ᶠSamuel, and *of* the prophets:

And what shall I more say? here the Spirit puts a period to the induction by an expostulation, as if he had said, Why do I speak of so many examples of faith? the Old Testament is full of them; but here is proof enough, I will say no more. *For the time would fail me to tell, &c.;* for time of life and writing would be sooner gone, than a full account can be given of all the notable effects of faith by all these worthies who might be named; yet he would give some general hints of persons, and of the works of faith, which he judgeth sufficient, and so nameth promiscuously, and not in order of time wherein they existed. He nameth four judges, one king, and one prophet, and extraordinary prophets in a bulk, whose histories you have; of *Gideon,* Judg. vi. 11, &c., *Barak,* Judg. iv. 5, &c., *Samson,* Judg. xiii.—xvi., *Jephthah,* Judg. xi., xii., *David's* history and *Samuel's* in the First and Second Books of Samuel, and the First of Chronicles; the excellent exploits of whose faith are, as their names, enumerated promiscuously; some of them agreeing to particular persons, others to them all.

33 Who through faith subdued kingdoms, wrought righteousness, ᵍobtained promises, ʰstopped the mouths of lions,

These, by the same gospel faith, *subdued kingdoms,* defeating the mighty enemies of the church; and eminently amongst them, David, who conquered Edom, Moab, Ammon, and the Syrian kingdoms, and extended his conquests to the Euphrates. This he and they did in obedience to God's call, in dependence on God's promise both of conduct and victory. All was done by God's arm at the instance of faith and prayer, Psal. xviii. 29—42; xx. 5, 9. *Wrought righteousness;* they were all of them eminently righteous in their persons, and in their administration of justice to others; the utmost of their abilities were laid out in it, as became righteous judges, as to all matters of God and men, Judg. vi.; 1 Sam. vii. 15, 17; xii. 2, 6. *Obtained promises;* a real and actual possession of all those good things which God secured to them by promise; especially as to Gideon and Barak, victory and success over the Canaanites and Midianites, Judg. iv., vi.; Samson, victory over the Philistines; David, victory over the church's enemies. All which they first obtained in the promise, and then in the execution. Faith secured all, giving a real enjoyment of all the good made theirs in the promise, and then in the event; and will give the fulness of all good in general promises made to the church and them in the end. *Stopped the mouths of lions:* Daniel, an eminent prophet of God, believed in him, and for his testimony to him was cast into the den of lions to be devoured, where God stops the mouths of them on his faith and prayer, and opens them to destroy their adversaries, Dan. vi. 22. By the power and strength of God, both Samson and David slew those lions which would have preyed both on them and others, Judg. xiv. 6; 1 Sam. xvii. 34—36. Faith obtained this success for them.

34 ⁱQuenched the violence of fire, ᵏescaped the edge of the sword, ˡout of weakness were made strong, waxed valiant in fight, ᵐturned to flight the armies of the aliens.

Quenched the violence of fire: by the same faith others of the prophets, ver. 32, eminently acquainted with God, and partakers of his secret, who defying idolatry, and the threatenings of a tyrant, became confessors of the true God and his worship, and were adjudged to the fiery furnace, Dan. iii. 19, 23, and by faith were secured from being consumed by those flames, which in an instant destroyed those which threw them in, ver. 22—28. How did this fetch down the Son of God himself to accompany them, and to suspend the consuming power of the fire, so as it did not singe either their persons or garments, or to leave any scent of it upon them! And how did Moses's and Aaron's prayers extinguish the fire at Kibroth-hattaavah, and at Taberah! Numb. xi. 1, 3; xvi. 22—45. *Escaped the edge of the sword:* by faith these worthies, forementioned 32, were delivered, when others fell by the devouring sword, and all those instruments of war which were destructive to others. Their enemies fell by their swords in those many battles wherein they were engaged, fulfilling at that time God's will, and trusting on his promise. And how many of the prophets hath God delivered from the swords of those who would have killed them! *Out of weakness were made strong;* by faith many of those who had many natural infirmities, both of body and mind, had their tremblings and faintings of spirit, and were, in respect of their enemies, weak, few in number, short of them, as to force, power, and policy, yet by faith in God were made bold as lions, and had wonderful success against numerous and potent enemies, Judg. iv. 8; vi. 15, 16; vii. 5, 7, 10; xi. 29; xv. 11, 19; 1 Sam. vii. 9, 10, &c. *Waxed valiant in fight;* faith made those who were called to the war by God, mighty for that service, 2 Sam. xxii. 30—38, so as no perils could daunt them, no service was too hard for them. How victorious in the most desperate attempts, as to sense, did faith make them! Psal. xxvii. 1, 3. *Turned to flight the armies of the aliens;* they overthrew the camps of adversaries. Παρεμβολή notes a single castle or tower, Acts xxi. 34, or a whole camp or place where an army is pitched, chap. xiii. 11, 13; in the plural, many such tents where soldiers lie; and is metonymically read *armies*. Τὸ κλινεῖν, actively taken, is to make to lie down, or to throw down, as applied to tents and camps; to put to flight, as applied to armies; all which were those of the idolatrous enemies of the church, strangers to their country, and more to their God, as the army and camp of Midian, Judg. vii. 13—23, which were overturned, routed, and destroyed by them.

[n 1 Kings 17. 22. 2 Kings 4. 35. o 2 Mac. 6. 19, 28. & 7. 7, &c. Acts 22. 25.] 35 ⁿ Women received their dead raised to life again: and others were ᵒ tortured, not accepting deliverance; that they might obtain a better resurrection:

Women received their dead raised to life again: through this Divine faith, both the prophets Elijah and Elisha did raise and restore, the one to the widow of Sarepta, 1 Kings xvii. 22, 23, the other to the Shunammite, 2 Kings iv. 35, 36, their sons from the dead; and these women and mothers did by faith receive them from the prophets alive again, who by faith and prayer procured this mercy from the quickening Lord, for them. In the general resurrection all shall be raised by the power of God, and the effect of faith therein is only receptive; we shall enjoy life again, and receive others from the dead also. *And others were tortured, not accepting deliverance;* others also, besides the prophets forementioned, ver. 32, ἐτυμπανίσθεσαν, were tympanized; what manner of torturing death this was, is not so certain, whether by excoriation, and making drum-heads of their skins, or extending them on the rack, as the skin or parchment is on the drum-head, and then with clubs, or other instruments, beating them to death; of which sort of sufferers seems Eleazer to be under Antiochus Epiphanes, 2 Macc. vi. 19, 30, for his not turning heathen, when urged to it by that torture; and though his deliverance from torture and death were offered to him by his tormentors on compliance with them, and renouncing his religion, yet he refused it, as others did, 2 Macc. vii. 24, resolving to endure the utmost extremity rather than turn idolater, and disobey God. *That they might obtain a better resurrection:* that which influenced them to suffer, was their faith in God's promise of obtaining thereby a resurrection to an incomparable better life than they could have enjoyed on earth; for though they might have been spared from death now threatened them, which was a kind of resurrection, yet was it not to be compared with the resurrection to eternal life, glory, bliss, and pleasure, to be enjoyed by them with God in heaven. See what influenced them, 2 Cor. iv. 17, 18.

[p 2 Mac. 7. 1, 7. q Gen. 39. 20. Jer. 20. 2. & 37. 15.] 36 ᵖ And others had trial of *cruel* mockings and scourgings, yea, moreover ᵍ of bonds and imprisonment:

And others had trial of cruel mockings; the same gospel faith enabled others than those mentioned before, prophets and saints, as Micaiah, 1 Kings xxii. 24, Elisha, 2 Kings ii. 23; Isa. viii. 18; Amos, chap. vii. 10, readily, cheerfully, and patiently to accept and receive the experience and trials of mocking, from the insulting, cruel enemies of God and his church, both national and aliens; being exposed and made a laughing-stock by reproaches, sarcasms, and nick-names, to aggravate their afflictions; and these inflicted on them by words and external signs, trials which, to an ingenuous spirit, bears harder than external torments, and which they more deeply sense and resent; yet faith makes them to receive all humbly, and carrieth them above them, as Psal. xxxi. 20; lii. 1—5; cxx. 3, 4; cxl. 3. *And scourgings;* they felt the scourges and whips of their enemies smart on them, such as were excessively shameful and painful, being inflicted on the vilest persons, as slaves; such as was the matter of these scourges, such their smartings, whether of thongs, cords, or wires, Jer. xx. 2; xxxvii. 15. This torment was commonly inflicted on them, not in Antiochus's time only, and those before, but commonly in Christ's and the apostles' days, 2 Cor. vi. 5; xi. 23. *Yea, moreover of bonds and imprisonment:* they cheerfully and patiently submitted to the cruel treating of their persecutors, who put them in the stocks, places of little ease, dungeons, loading them with iron shackles and fetters, which the wickedness of man had invented to torment them with; stern and cruel usage by their gaolers, restraining society from them, and of comfortable relief, feeding them with the bread and water of affliction, 2 Chron. xviii. 26; Acts xvi. 24.

37 ʳ They were stoned, they were sawn asunder, were tempted, were slain with the sword: ˢ they wandered about ᵗ in sheepskins and goatskins; being destitute, afflicted, tormented; [r 1 Kings 21. 13. 2 Chron. 24. 21. Acts 7. 58. & 14. 19. s 2 Kings 1. 8. Matt. 3. 4. t Zech. 13. 4.]

They were stoned; by the same faith were several of the prophets and believing worthies of old carried through cruel deaths, the just punishment of malefactors, but the wicked tortures of these innocent saints, some being stoned to death, as Zechariah the son of Jehoiada, 2 Chron. xxiv. 21, and others, Matt. xxi. 35; xxiii. 37; Luke xiii. 34. *They were sawn asunder;* as Isaiah was, which is a known tradition among the Hebrews, a punishment common among the bordering nations of them, 2 Sam. xii. 31; Amos i. 3, and exercised on these innocents, to which Christ himself alludeth, Matt. xxiv. 51. *Were tempted:* whether ἐπειράσθησαν should not be ἐπυράσθησαν, is much doubted, temptation being no manner of death; and the Spirit had instanced in it before, ver. 35. It may therefore be a slip of the transcriber, and that burning was the cruel death that should fill this place among the rest, a common punishment with them, Jer. xxix. 22; 2 Macc. vii. 5. Or, it may note a death with several trials of racks and torments gradually inflicted, with a design to tempt them by their pains to renounce their religion. *Were slain with the sword;* others were killed by the sword, either by beheading, or cutting in pieces, Mark vi. 16, 17; a kind of death foretold to be attending the martyrs of Jesus Christ, Rev. xx. 4. All these sorts of death were most unjustly and cruelly inflicted on them by their persecutors, and as patiently received and cheerfully undergone by them. *They wandered about in sheepskins and goatskins:* as faith carried these believers through variety of deaths, so it managed others comfortably under their banishments and lingering sufferings, which were in proportion as cruel as death itself; they circuited up and down to preserve themselves from their destroyers, either voluntarily returning themselves into desolate places to keep a good conscience, or were unjustly and violently banished and forced away from their own habitations, to live as vagabonds, clothed only with goatskins and sheepskins, the common apparel of the prophets, as of Elijah, 2 Kings i. 8; Zech. xiii. 4, which they wore as they came from the beasts' backs, without dressing. *Being destitute, afflicted, tormented;* wandering in this forlorn state, stripped of money and necessaries of life, and not supplied by others in their poverty, 1 Kings xvii. 4, grievously pressed within, pained without, and afflicted beyond what can be sensed by any but in the like states, and evilly entreated by all; many miseries attending them by their pursuers, hardship in travels, and all sorts of evils, which multiplied their griefs: through all this faith carried them comfortably, and kept God with them.

38 (Of whom the world was not worthy:) they wandered in deserts, and *in* mountains, and ᵘ *in* dens and caves of the earth. [u 1 Kings 18. 4. & 19. 9.]

Of whom the world was not worthy: the Spirit intermixeth an account of what these persons were who were so treated, lest the reader or hearer of these things might be mistaken of them, judging them to be some heinous malefactors, who were thus hurried in and destroyed by the world. Would you know what manner of persons they were? Be it known to you in the judgment of God, the best judge of their persons and states, they were such as the world did not deserve they should live among them, but were unworthy of their society, and the blessings which did attend it; and were it not for their sakes, God would quickly put an end to the sinful world, and burn it up. Such were these as did more for the preservation of the world, when thus brutishly treated by it, than it would or could do for itself. *They wandered in deserts, and in mountains, and in dens and caves of the earth:* yet were they wandering over the desolate parts of this earth, being forced from all society with men, to the retirements of wild beasts in deserts, and climbing up mountains and rocks from their persecutors, lodging themselves in the natural or artificial dens and caves of the earth, the only receptacles for these worthies, faith giving them the best company, God and his comforts, there: see 1 Sam. xxii. 23, 24; 1 Kings xvii. 3; xviii. 13; 1 Macc. i. 53; ii. 28—30.

x ver. 2, 13.

39 And these all, ˣhaving obtained a good report through faith, received not the promise:

The apostle returns in this verse to the proposition laid down in the second verse, which he had been proving by all these examples, and with it shuts up the history of them. *And these all;* all these elders, mentioned from ver. 2 to this verse. *Having obtained a good report through faith:* μαρτυρηθέντες, strictly, is having been martyred, or made martyrs; specially witnessing to the death for Christ, have a testimony given them, by way of eminency, by God himself in his Scripture record, that through faith they pleased him in their glorious achievements and sufferings, and were God's faithful witnesses to the world, glorifying him in it; though reproached and ruined by the world, yet they were too good to live in it, and were fit to live with him in heaven, as ver. 2, 5, 16, 35. *Received not the promise;* yet these worthies, as Abraham and his believing seed, did not possess the land of Canaan, though they had the promise of it in their time, ver. 13; others did obtain the grace and good things promised for their time, ver. 33, but none of these had fulfilled to them in their day the manifestation of the Messiah in the flesh; though they saw his day and coming by faith, and did rejoice in it, yet none saw him so come as Simeon did, Luke ii. 26, 29; though, as to the eternal benefits by Christ, they did as actually receive them, as those since his perfecting the work of redemption have received them, even eternal blessedness and glory by him, Acts xv. 11.

‖ Or, *foreseen.*
y ch. 7. 22.
& 8. 6.
z ch. 5. 9.
& 12. 23.
Rev. 6. 11.

40 God having ‖ provided ʸ some better thing for us, that they without us should not be ᶻ made perfect.

God having provided some better thing for us: the causes of their not receiving the promise, are summed up in this verse; the efficient of it is God's providence unto believers before and after the incarnation of the Messiah. God having from eternity foreknowledge of those who would believe in God the Son incarnate, Rom. viii. 29, predestinated them to be called to the faith in him, and provided better for New Testament believers than for the Old ones, that what they had of Christ in types and veils, these should have in truth; what they had in promise, these should have in sight and possession; what they had in hope, as to his first coming, these should have it past, and as an earnest of his second coming; what they had by measure of his Spirit and grace, these should have in fulness, Luke x. 23, 24; John i. 14, 16; vii. 39; 2 Cor. iii. 8; Eph. iii. 8—11; Tit. ii. 13; 1 Pet. i. 12. *That they without us should not be made perfect;* the final cause of this gracious providence was, that the former and later believers might be completed together; they shall not reach that perfect state of grace and glory by a re-union of their bodies and souls until the general resurrection, when they shall not prevent us, nor we them; but as soon as the trumpet alarms the dead to rise, in the same moment, and twinkling of an eye, shall the living be changed, and all be caught up together *in the clouds, to meet the Lord in the air; and so shall be ever with the Lord,* 1 Thess. iv. 15—17. The ground of which perfection of all believers in all ages being in the last time, is from his choosing them all to be but one body of Christ, and him their Head; so as one member cannot be perfected but in the perfection of the whole, Matt. viii. 11; Eph. iv. 4. In which perfection of it, God is resolved to be all in all; not in one, or in some, but when Christ hath subdued all his enemies, and gathered all his members, then shall his body and kingdom be perfected, and God be all in all, 1 Cor. xv. 28.

CHAP. XII

An exhortation to patience and constancy enforced by the example of Christ, 1—4. *The benefit of God's chastisements,* 5—13. *Exhortation to peace and holiness,* 14—17. *The dispensation of the law compared with the privileges of the gospel,* 18—24. *The danger of refusing the word from heaven,* 25—29.

WHEREFORE seeing we also are compassed about with so great a cloud of witnesses, ᵃ let us lay aside every weight, and the sin which doth so easily beset *us,* and ᵇ let us run ᶜ with patience the race that is set before us,

a Col. 3. 8.
1 Pet. 2. 1.
b 1 Cor. 9. 24. Phil. 3. 13, 14.
c Rom. 12. 12. ch. 10. 36.

The Spirit proceeds in this chapter in his exhortation or counsel unto duties worthy of the former doctrine of Christ, and suitable to the foregoing examples, enumerated chap. xi. *Wherefore seeing;* he introduceth it with an illative particle, τοιγαροῦν seeing all those worthies finished their course through faith, and received not the promise since made good to us, therefore is there something to be inferred. *We also are compassed about with so great a cloud of witnesses;* we, I Paul, and you Hebrews, having enjoyed the better things provided by God for us, we are so much the more obliged; as also having such a multitude of witnesses of so vast worth and dignity, as all the Old Testament believers were, distilling, like a cloud, abundant influences, from their example, in doing and suffering for God, through faith, on our souls, to make us persevering in the faith to the end, as they did; and so compassing us about, as we cannot want either direction or encouragement to it, whenever we look into their histories for it. *Let us lay aside every weight;* like the Grecian and Roman racers, who laid aside their cumbersome garments, so as they might more easily and lightly run their race; in allusion to which, it is the concern of every Christian to *lay aside,* or put away, all his worldly cumbrances, which would clog him in his race, his corrupt self, the world, &c., Matt. xvi. 24; Luke xxi. 34; 1 Tim. vi. 9—11; 2 Tim. ii. 4. *And the sin which doth so easily beset us:* the evil weight inward is the old man, the corrupt nature, which remaineth in every Christian, styled by Paul, *the body of death,* Rom. vii. 24; but especially each Christian's own personal iniquity, which sticks and cleaves nearer to him than his garments, and which made David so careful about it, in Psal. xviii. 23; that which is so compassing and clasping him about, that he is so far from running, he cannot move for it, 1 Cor. ix. 27; Col. iii. 5. This they are to mortify in them. *And let us run with patience the race that is set before us;* how distant soever the goal is, which finisheth the race of a Christian's life, yet the way passing to it, though it be troublesome and long, and being set to us by God himself, must be patiently, strenuously, and constantly run, that they may obtain it, Psal. cxix. 32, 33; Luke xiii. 24; 1 Cor. ix. 24—27; Gal. v. 7; Phil. iii. 13, 14; 2 Tim. iv. 7. The cloud of witnesses have so run it before them for their direction and encouragement.

2 Looking unto Jesus the ‖ author and finisher of *our* faith; ᵈ who for the joy that was set before him endured the cross, despising the shame, and ᵉ is set down at the right hand of the throne of God.

‖ Or, *beginner.*
d Luke 24. 26. Phil. 2. 8, &c. 1 Pet. 1. 11.
e Ps. 110. 1. ch. 1. 3, 13. & 8. 1. 1 Pet. 3. 22.

HEBREWS XII

Looking unto Jesus the author and finisher of our faith: as if all the former witnesses were not enough, he adds a more excellent one than them all, even our Lord Jesus Christ, who is not only a pattern to them in their race and running of it, but a help, and for which end they were looking to him: the word ἀφορῶντες is only here used in all the New Testament, and signifieth a looking off from whatever would distract us from earnestly looking on the proposed object alone; and though a word of sense, yet here noteth an act of the mind. It is borrowed from racers, the similitude of whom the apostle further improves: they fixedly eye their guides or leaders, to help them on in their course; so must a Christian in his race look off from all things else, and singly and intently look on Jesus to help him through it; ἀρχηγὸν· see chap. ii. 10; here it denotes Jesus to be the great institutor of, and chief leader in, the Christian race, and perfecter of them in running it. The disposition, grace, ability, and success which they have for running, it is all from him; from the beginning of the work of faith unto the end of it, to the finishing of the course, he doth infuse, assist, strengthen, and accomplish the work of it to the last, John vi. 29, 30; Phil. iv. 13; 2 Tim. iv. 7; 1 John v. 4, 5. *Who for the joy that was set before him;* who for that joyful and glorious state which was clearly represented and faithfully promised to him by his Father to succeed his sufferings, that he should immediately attain himself, and successively communicate to all who believe in him, Luke xxiv. 26; John xvii. 1, 5, 24; 1 Pet. i. 11. This did so cheer and strengthen him, that with unexpressible patience he cheerfully *endured the cross,* with all the concomitants of it, the sorrows in his soul, the torturing pains in his body, of buffetings, smitings, piercings of thorns, tearing his flesh with scourges, boring of his hands and feet with nails, with all the evils that either the malice or rage of devils or men could inflict on him; he was neither weary of his burden, nor shrinking from nor fainting under it. With what invincible meekness and passive fortitude did he undergo all that was foretold of him! Isa. liii. *Despising the shame;* at the same time slighting and casting out of his thoughts all the disgrace poured on him by his enemies, both in his mind and action, contemning all the blasphemies, taunts, reproaches, and shameful carriages of sinners to him, suffering without any emotion all their indignities, even in the most shameful death itself, Phil. ii. 6—8, though he were the most innocent as well as excellent person in all the world. *And is set down at the right hand of the throne of God;* the issue of all which was, his exaltation by God for his abasement by man; he riseth from the dead, ascendeth to heaven, sets himself down as a triumphing conqueror over sin, the prince of the powers in the air, death, and hell, *at the right hand of the throne of God;* and thence discovers himself in his state and glory, as the great Ruler of the world, King of kings, and Lord of lords, Phil. ii. 9, 10, (see chap. viii. 1,) and the glorious rewarder of those who serve him, and suffer for him.

f Mat. 10. 24, 25.
John 15. 20.
g Gal. 6. 9.

3 ᶠFor consider him that endured such contradiction of sinners against himself, ᵍ lest ye be wearied and faint in your minds.

For consider him; the connexion is rational, that they ought to regard this example, for that there were greater sufferings behind than any yet they had endured, which would enforce it, as ver. 4: ἀναλογίσασθε signifieth the use of a proportionable consideration, thinking on or reasoning about this example within a man's self, such as may make the considerer bear a proportion to the subject considered. *That endured such contradiction of sinners against himself;* this Jesus spoken of before, who most patiently submitted to, and perseveringly bore up under, such opposition and contradiction by the words and works of the most wicked and vilest men against himself, who was the most innocent and best of men, always going about doing good to them, so as their sin and his patience were without parallel: none was ever so scorned, taunted, reviled, blasphemed, spit on, and ignominiously treated like him; and never any so invincibly endured it, Rom. xv. 3. *Lest ye be wearied and faint in your minds;* the reason of this consideration is, lest faintness, languishing, or deficiency of soul, that is, of vigour, strength, and activity of heart in grace, should befall them; and so they should lie down and cease to run the Christian race, which the devil designed to oblige them to, as he would Christ, by the multitude and soreness of the contradictions they should suffer from sinners in it, so greatly as would not end but by broaching their life-blood, as they did Christ's, and these must expect from them.

4 ʰ Ye have not yet resisted unto blood, striving against sin.

h 1 Cor. 10. 13. ch. 10. 32, 33, 34.

Ye have suffered much for Christ already, but there is more that he requires from you, and is yet behind, chap. x. 32—34; the condition he fixed with you as his disciples, in Luke xiv. 26, to lay down your life as well as your relations and goods for him. You may yet be called to testify to him, by suffering a violent and bloody death from his and your enemies, as other martyrs had done for him: consider him who hath suffered a worse death for you, to sweeten yours to you, that you do not faint, fail, or turn apostates from him and his truth; resisting with agonies whatsoever men or devils use to entice or force us to apostatize from Christ, since there will be neither arts nor powers wanting to it. Watch you, pray, and strive to the utmost against them, Luke xxii. 31, 32; 1 Pet. v. 9.

5 And ye have forgotten the exhortation which speaketh unto you as unto children, ⁱMy son, despise not thou the chastening of the Lord, nor faint when thou art rebuked of him:

i Job 5. 17.
Prov. 3. 11.

And ye have forgotten; ἐκλέλησθε, whether rendered interrogatively, have ye forgotten? or positively, ye have forgotten; either way it carrieth a check upon their forgetfulness of what was of the greatest importance for them to remember in the time of persecutions, and implieth a direction of them to their duty, that they ought to remember the counsel or command given by God to them, how to interpret these persecutions for Christ and the gospel, and how to improve them; and so introduceth a further help to their running of the race of God with patience. *The exhortation;* παρακλήσεως notes properly consolation, and is here a consolatory exhortation to the management of a duty which would be highly such to them, and a dehortation from an evil which would greatly prejudice them; when it is said to speak, it is a metonymy of the effect for the efficient; the Lord in the exhortation speaking this to them. *Which speaketh unto you as unto children:* these words were written by Solomon, from God unto his children in that time; and God speaks no less by him to these Hebrews, who were his children now, as to all others who are such, or should be such, children to him. And whereas it is spoken singularly, *My son,* it is to every child of God in Christ Jesus, and so collectively includeth all of them. *Despise not thou the chastening of the Lord:* the dehortation is written in Prov. iii. 11, that not one of these children should care little for, or set light by, denying all regardlessness, senselessness of, and incorrigibleness under, such smart correction as a parent gives to a child, either by himself, or by any other to whose care it is committed; but this chastening is from the Lord, the most gracious and tender Father, who can do them no evil, and will profit and benefit them by it. As they come from their persecutors for the sake of Christ, they are injuries; but as ordered by God their Father, they are so many favours to them, preventing sin, preserving in duty, and preparing them for blessedness. *Nor faint when thou art rebuked of him;* nor to nauseate his rebukes, or to faint under them; neither to let our faith or hope in our Father fail, nor to sink in our love to him, his way, or truth, or religion; nor to be weary, and give over our course, because of persecutions, but continuing faithful to him to the end, ver. 14, 15; Matt. x. 22; Luke xxii. 28, 29.

6 For ᵏ whom the Lord loveth he chasteneth, and scourgeth every son whom he receiveth.

k Ps. 94. 12. & 119. 75.
Prov. 3. 12.
Jam. 1. 12.
Rev. 3. 19.

For whom the Lord loveth he chasteneth: for showeth this to be a suasory reason against fainting under God's rebukes, and enforcing the foregoing duty; since whomsoever, son or daughter, every child, that God the Father choicely loveth, taketh into his bosom, tendereth as a parent doth a child, Eph. v. 1, he nurtureth, instructs, corrects by his word and rod in its respective measure, for their spiritual profit and advantage, 1 Cor. xi. 32. *And scourgeth every son whom he receiveth: scourgeth* noteth the highest degree of chastening, even with the sharpest and most smarting punishment, wherein God proceedeth with all and every son or child, not any excepted, whom he hath adopted and received into his bosom with complacency and delight, chap. v. 8: compare Prov. iii. 12; Matt. xvii. 5; Rev. iii. 19, where, though the words do vary, yet the sense is one and the same; God correcting, as a Father, the son in whom he delighteth.

<small>1 Deut. 8. 5.
2 Sam. 7. 14.
Prov. 13. 24.
& 19. 18. &
23. 13.</small>
7 ¹If ye endure chastening, God dealeth with you as with sons; for what son is he whom the father chasteneth not?

If ye endure chastening, God dealeth with you as with sons: his reason he illustrateth from the convertibility of suffering affliction and chastening from God the Father, and being his child; If ye have a child-like sense of chastening, such afflictions and sufferings from him as the Father orderoth to you, so as quietly and patiently to bear them, and by faith expecting a saving issue from them; God the Father in love chastening you, beareth, carrieth, and offereth himself to you as a father to his son, full of grace and love, Lev. xxvi. 41; Job xiii. 15; Psal. lxxxix. 30; Micah vii. 9. *For what son is he whom the father chasteneth not?* no son or child of God can be instanced in, who was capable of chastening, but more or less have felt it; even God's only and best beloved One, chap. v. 8, for our sakes felt it, Isa. liii. 5. The interrogation is a vehement assertion, and so to be resolved.

8 But if ye be without chastisement, <small>m Ps. 73. 1.
1 Pet. 5. 9.</small> ᵐ whereof all are partakers, then are ye bastards, and not sons.

But if God chasten you not, or if he do, and ye have not grace, or do not rightly endure it, are not managing yourselves well under it, nor are profited by it, when all and every one of his children are partakers of it, then are ye a false and spurious seed, and not God's genuine offspring, *bastards* in his account; and indeed so the most forlorn, wretched persons of all others, left under the power and dominion of sin, hurrying them on to their utter destruction, John viii. 41. These visible church members have a bastardly disposition, hearts alienated from God and his law, and inclined to the will and works of the flesh, expressing it in their conversation, running into the excess of sin, having no chastening to restrain them, and are deserted by God for it, Isa. i. 4—6; Hos. iv. 14, 17.

<small>n Num. 16.
22. & 27. 16.
Job 12. 10.
Eccles. 12. 7.
Is. 42. 5.
& 57. 16.
Zech. 12. 1.</small>
9 Furthermore we have had fathers of our flesh which corrected *us*, and we gave *them* reverence: shall we not much rather be in subjection unto ⁿ the Father of spirits, and live?

Furthermore we have had fathers of our flesh which corrected us: he enforceth the duty of not despising nor fainting under the Lord's chastening, from the consideration of his being our Father, and better than any earthly one, and from his goodness in that relation, and therefore we ought to submit to it: We have had our natural parents, as we are children, and who were the subordinate cause of our being as to our bodies, chap. vii. 5, 10, and they were instructors and correctors of us, made use of the rod as well as the word for our nurture; they have whipped and chastised us, putting us to smart and pain, 2 Sam. vii. 14; Prov. xxii. 15. *And we gave them reverence;* ἐνετρεπόμεθα imports a turning of bowels and spirits within them towards their fathers, covered with shame and blushing for their faults, and afraid to look them, when offended, in the face; reverencing them chastening, and submitting to the penalty, so as to reform and turn from the faults for which they were corrected. *Shall we not much rather be in subjection unto the Father of spirits?* the expostulation shows the vehemency of the argument more than a simple position. It is the highest reason, of all right we must and ought (being as much our privilege as duty) to deny ourselves, and be in in that subjection, the free and willing subordination of our spirits to God, as the rod calls for it, receiving the correction, reforming under it, and resigning our souls to him who is the Creator of them as to their natural and spiritual being, and the Sovereign, Guardian, Protector, and Disposer of them; men nor angels have any power over them, but this Father of them only, and his great work and concern is about them, Gen. ii. 7; Numb. xxvii. 16; Eccles. xii. 7; Zech. xii. 1. *And live;* by his chastening of our spirits, our immortal souls, John iii. 6; Rom. viii. 5, 6, he is furnishing them with more spiritual life, whereby they are enabled to live and move wholly to God, from grace to glory. He makes them live more the life of God, which God in flesh lived on earth, Gal. ii. 20; Eph. iv. 18; Phil. i. 21; 1 Pet. iv. 6; 1 John iii. 9. This chastening promotes this honourable life as an instrument and means in God's hand, and advanceth it daily, till it is perfected in eternal life, Acts xiv. 22; Rom, v. 3—5; viii. 18; 2 Cor. iv. 17, 18; James i. 12; Jude 22.

10 For they verily for a few days chastened *us* ‖ after their own pleasure; but he for *our* profit, ° that *we* might be partakers of his holiness. <small>‖ Or, as seemed good, or, meet to them.
o Lev. 11. 44. & 19. 2.
1 Pet. i. 15, 16.</small>

For they verily for a few days chastened us after their own pleasure: as God hath his prerogative in paternity, so he hath the transcendency in the end of chastening his children; for our natural parents, fathers of our bodies, nurtured us by the word and rod for a little time, the days of childhood and youth, as they would and thought good, as they apprehended their power over them, arbitrarily, passionately, without reaching what is best for them by it; their own thoughts, whether good or bad, were the rule of their chastening, and such as their thoughts are, such is their end; how imperfect and defective must that be! *But he for our profit, that we might be partakers of his holiness;* but God, the Father of our spirits, corrects us ἐπὶ τὸ συμφέρον, which strictly notes comportation, intimating, that in his chastening his children he brings in his help, puts as it were his shoulder to it, brings in his stock of grace, and so bears together with them unto their advantage and profit in spiritual life, and this during our whole lives. That which he bears home to them, and puts in them by his chastening, is *his holiness;* of which being made partakers, they thrive mightily as to their spiritual life, and increase in the Divine nature with all the increases of God, Eph. iii. 13, 19; Col. ii. 19.

11 Now no chastening for the present seemeth to be joyous, but grievous: nevertheless afterward it yieldeth ᵖ the peaceable fruit of righteousness unto them which are exercised thereby. <small>p Jam. 3. 18.</small>

Now no chastening for the present seemeth to be joyous, but grievous: a further argument to persuade Christians not to despise nor faint under the Lord's chastenings, is the good issue of them, subjoined to fortify them against the suggestions of flesh and blood, as if they could not be from love, nor for good, because they are smarting and grievous; therefore the Spirit asserts the truth as to both: All these chastenings and rebukes that the Father of spirits inflicts on his children, not one excepted, are, for all the time they are so inflicted, sensed by his children to be as they are; they feel them to have no joy in them, but a great deal of grief, pain, and smart; they are not pleasing of themselves, and God would not have them to be so, but his to feel the smart of his rod, when he corrects them with it. *Nevertheless afterward it yieldeth the peaceable fruit of righteousness unto them which are exercised thereby;* yet have not his children any reason to despond or faint under them; for they are not always to continue, and there accrueth after them a benefit to them, that will make amends for them all the afterward following to eternity: this chastening rendereth and bringeth forth to all the corrected children, who labour to improve the smart, under God's direction and blessing, a righteous compliance with the whole will of God, and a purging out of all sin, Isa. xxvii. 9; filling the soul full of joy and peace, and securing to the chastened a confluence of all that good that will abundantly reward them for their sufferings, setting them above them, and making them blessed, Isa. xxxii. 17; Rom. v. 1—5; James i. 2—4.

12 Wherefore ᵠ lift up the hands which hang down, and the feeble knees; <small>q Job 4. 3, 4.
Is. 35. 3.
See Ecclus. 25. 23.</small>

This introduceth the use of the doctrine of God's chastening providences, stated before. *Wherefore* concludes the rationality and necessity of the duty subjoined, as consequent from the truth asserted before. *Lift up; ἀνορθώσατε* notes the making, or setting aright, that which was out of its proper place and posture, as disordered members into their right frame and composure, that there be not any let in our Christian race, nor fainting by our course in it. *The hands which hang down, and the feeble knees;* by hanging down hands, and palsied knees, are metaphorically represented the hearts, spirits, and souls of these children, such as droop, despond, and are ready to faint and die away under chastening, Isa. xxxv. 3–6. The sum of the counsel is, rightly to compose our thoughts, affections, and members, under trials from notorious enemies, and unbelieving brethren, so as to perfect our Christian course in the fear and strength of God, continuing stedfast in prayer, 1 Tim. ii. 8, walking constantly in God's ways, and obeying all his commandments, Psal. cxix. 48, 100, patiently bearing all God's corrections, and bringing forth the peaceful fruit of them. This is the truth of the metaphor.

r Prov. 4. 26, 27.
∥ Or, *even.*
s Gal. 6. 1.

13 ʳAnd make ∥ straight paths for your feet, lest that which is lame be turned out of the way; ˢbut let it rather be healed.

Make straight, smooth ways, such as have all stones of stumbling and rocks of offence removed, so as themselves may be set right in comfort, and duty, and walking; lest being lame or halting in their minds between Judaism and Christianity, because of the violent persecution of them by their infidel brethren, they should be turned aside out of God's way, erring, and deviating from the truth of the gospel; but that they be restored to it, so as no sufferings upon that account, under God's hand, might make them suppress the truth, or expose them to apostacy, or to walk as stumbling-blocks to others, and wounding their own souls, Acts xv. 1; Gal. ii. 11—15; vi. 12.

t Ps. 34. 14.
Rom. 12. 18. & 14. 9.
2 Tim. 2. 22.
u Matt. 5. 8.
2 Cor. 7. 1.
Eph. 5. 5.

14 ᵗFollow peace with all *men*, and holiness, ᵘwithout which no man shall see the Lord:

Here begins the second head of counsel in this chapter. That seeing the gospel church Officer, the great Reconciler of sinners to, and Sanctifier of them for, God, was fully revealed to them, it did now concern them to promote peace with men, and perfect holiness towards God: this is pursued to the end of the chapter. *Follow peace with all men:* διώκετε imports such a fierce, unwearied, unsatisfied pursuit, as persecutors make after the innocent servants of Christ, till they have their purposes on them; and so sets out the real, earnest, violent, unwearied, constant pursuit and labour after peace, i. e. concord, unanimity, and comfortable consociation in all things, good and lawful, to all sorts of persons, in thought, word, and deed, as far as it is possible for us, Psal. xxxiv. 14; 1 Cor. x. 32; xiii. 4, 5, 7; 1 Pet. iii. 10, 11. *And holiness:* ἁγιασμὸν is all that habit and frame of heart, which becometh souls to have towards God, enjoying all purity from spiritual uncleanness, and a conformity to the holiness peculiar to God, Eph. iv. 24. The result and quintessence of all the graces of the Spirit, is holiness, 1 Pet. i. 15, 16; 1 John iii. 2, 3: labouring to the perfection of this within our kind, Psal. xv. 3; 2 Cor. vii. 1. *Without which no man shall see the Lord:* a soul destitute of holiness is in no capacity, either of faith or sight, to *see the Lord;* they can have no union to, communion with, or fruition of, God in Christ, neither in grace nor glory; implying and assuring them, that with holiness they may see and enjoy him, Matt. v. 8; 1 Cor. vi. 9, 10; xii. 13; Gal. v. 21; 1 John iii. 2, 3.

x 2 Cor. 6. 1.
y Gal. 5. 4.
∥ Or, *fall from.*
z Deut. 29. 18. ch. 3. 12.

15 ˣLooking diligently ʸlest any man ∥ fail of the grace of God; ᶻlest any root of bitterness springing up trouble *you*, and thereby many be defiled;

To further their pursuit of peace and holiness, he metaphorically proposeth a caution against what might stop them in it, which he properly specifieth and exemplifieth in Esau, ver. 15–17. *Looking diligently:* ἐπισκοποῦντες notes a very strict and severe inspecting themselves; its primitive, σκοπεῖν, signifieth such a looking to a thing, as those who, in shooting, aim at the mark; and the preposition adds intention to the action, signifying a most earnest care in Christians over themselves, in them over others, and in ministers over them all. *Lest any man fail of the grace of God;* lest any person among them should fail of grace offered in the gospel to it, and never have it, Tit. ii. 11, 12; or apostatize from the profession of it, by seduction or persecution, chap. iv. 1; x. 38; 2 Cor. vi. 1: compare Gal. i. 6; iii. 3. *Lest any root of bitterness springing up trouble you;* a metaphor borrowed from plants, to which roots are proper, and which was used by Moses before, Deut. xxix. 18: a root bearing a poisonous herb; intending by it such persons, whose nature, words, and works, are so bitter unto God, as gall and wormwood are to men; such as apostatized from God to idols. The apostle intending hereby the hindering the springing up and growing of errors, heresies, or immoralities, as profaneness, filthiness, &c., which are apt to infect churches, and, aˢ they spread, to molest, trouble, and disturb them, and to keep them from pursuing holiness, chap. iii. 8; Hos. xii. 14; Gal. i. 7; James iii. 14. *And thereby many be defiled;* lest by but one such poisonous root, a whole church of Christians may be infected and poisoned, their sin being as apt to spread and diffuse itself, as leaven, 1 Cor. v. 6, to taint the whole lump, Gal. v. 9: and how early, even in the apostles' time, for want of obeying this caution, were the primitive churches corrupted, both in doctrine and morals, by loose, filthy heretics among them!

16 ᵃLest there *be* any fornicator, or profane person, as Esau, ᵇwho for one morsel of meat sold his birthright.

a Eph. 5. 3.
Col. 3. 5.
1 Thess. 4. 3.
b Gen. 25. 33.

This properly interprets the *root of bitterness* before, by two special fruits of it. *Lest there be any fornicator:* uncleanness, πόρνος, is not to be taken so strictly, as only to note fornication, uncleanness committed by unmarried persons, but all sorts of pollution and filthiness, as it is used in the general decree, Acts xv. 29; such defilements as had crept in among them already, to which many were propense and inclined, whence warned of and charged against it by James, Peter, and Jude, in their Epistles. *Or profane person:* βέβηλος imports one who had a bitter frame of spirit against the first table, one of an impure mind to God-ward, opposite to godliness, who neglects and spurns at holy things, rolling itself in its own pleasures, riches, honours, with a despising of God, his grace, and glory, 1 Tim. i. 9; iv. 7, 20; 2 Tim. ii. 16. *As Esau, who for one morsel of meat sold his birth-right:* Esau, the best example to these Hebrews, he being Jacob's brother, who was most notoriously profane, who irreligiously undervalued and despised the blessing of the birthright, to which was entailed by God the double portion, the priesthood and dominion over the family, the blessings of the covenant, and the being a type of Christ; he basely and impiously gave it away to his younger brother, slighting it, and freely and fully making it over to him, and all for one eating, the base gratifying of his sensual appetite but once, Gen. xxv. 32, 34. Like to whom were those, Phil. iii. 18; 2 Pet. ii. 10—19; Jude 4—19. In these is his filthy, profane spirit improved.

17 For ye know how that afterward, ᶜwhen he would have inherited the blessing, he was rejected: ᵈfor he found no ∥ place of repentance, though he sought it carefully with tears.

c Gen. 27. 34, 36, 38.
d ch. 6. 6.
∥ Or, *way to change his mind.*

For ye know how that afterward, when he would have inherited the blessing, he was rejected: as Esau's sin was, such was his penalty; for they knew, and were well acquainted with this in Moses's history of him, that after he had despised his birthright, and sold it, being at man's estate, Gen. xxvii., and was desirous to inherit that blessing, he was rejected by his father, as well as by God, and could not obtain it, being unalterably settled on Jacob by both. *He found no place of repentance,* as to the giving it, with God, who gave it, and would not alter it, Rom. xi. 29; nor with his father, who did not repent of giving it to Jacob, but confirmed it, Gen. xxvii. 33, 40; xxviii. 1, 3, 4. *Though he sought it carefully with tears;* and this, although he sought the blessing from his father with cries and tears,

HEBREWS XII

Gen. xxvii. 34, 38. How therefore should these Hebrews, knowing all this, root out such a root springing up in themselves, or others, that they might not be guilty of such sin ; lest having despised God's blessing for their own ease, honours, or profits in this world, when they may desire to seek with tears the blessing of the eternal inheritance from God, he should irreversibly reject them. See Matt. vii. 22, 23.

e Ex. 19. 12, 18, 19. & 20. 18. Deut. 4. 11. & 5. 22. Rom. 6. 14. & 8. 15. 2 Tim. i. 7.

18 For ye are not come unto [e] the mount that might be touched, and that burned with fire, nor unto blackness, and darkness, and tempest,

For showeth, from this verse to the 24th, the apostle enforcing on these Hebrews, and with them on all Christians, the pursuit of holiness and peace, by subjoining the great helps they have for it, beyond what the Old Testament church had, they being freed from the legal dispensation, which was less helpful to it, and admitted to that of the gospel, most promoting it. The first he layeth down, ver. 18—21 ; and the other, ver. 22—24. They are freed from the covenant dispensation at Mount Sinai. *Ye are not come unto the mount that might be touched;* you have not been called, as to your body, to journey it to Sinai, or as to your faith, to close with that covenant administration, to depend on, or have any expectation from it, as delivered by Moses at Mount Sinai in Arabia ; a mountain visible, tactible, sensible, on earth, signifying the covenant dispensation from this mount to be low and earthy, occasioning earthy thoughts of God and carriage to him, sticking in an earthly altar sacrifice, and carnal and sensual religion ; to the law written in stones, without minding the spirituality of it, or having it in their hearts ; walking wisely in this wilderness state, yet, by the charge of God, not touchable by Israel at that time, though they came near to it in the third month after their coming out of Egypt, Exod. xix. 1, 12, 13, 23. *And that burned with fire;* to the fire, in the which the Lord descended on the mount, Exod. xix. 18 ; which burnt unto the midst of heaven, Deut. iv. 11 ; v. 23, 24, and would consume them that broke that law which he spake to them out of it, Deut. xxxiii. 2. *Nor unto blackness, and darkness, and tempest;* to the black, thick smoke that ascended as the smoke of a furnace, Exod. xix. 18 ; to *darkness,* occasioned by the thick clouds enveloping the mount, Deut. iv. 11 ; v. 23 ; to *tempest,* the storm of thundering, and lightnings, and earthquake, the terrible attendants of this solemnity, Exod. xix. 16, 18 ; xx. 18. All these shadowing forth the fiery and terrible storms of wrath and indignation, which should pursue the breakers of this covenant to the lowest hell ; giving them, in this delivery of the law, a visible type of what should be the issue of their breaking it, Exod. xix. 22, 24. These terrors of the Almighty did so fright them, that they ran from God, and set not themselves to the serious pursuit of holiness, Isa. xxxiii. 14.

19 And the sound of a trumpet, and the voice of words ; which *voice* they that heard [f] intreated that the word should not be spoken to them any more :

f Ex. 20. 19. Deut. 5. 5, 25. & 18. 16.

And the sound of a trumpet; which was most shrill and dreadful, it sounded long, and waxed louder and louder, giving a fearful alarm unto Israel to draw near to the Lord to hear his law to them, and covenant with them, and to see a type of their doom, if they transgressed it, in an obscure representation of the general judgment, Exod. xix. 16, 19 ; xx. 18 ; compare 1 Thess. iv. 16 ; 2 Thess. i. 7—9. *And the voice of words:* after which alarm, the Angel of the covenant uttered his voice out of the fire most majestically, distinctly, and loudly, and spake to Israel in their own language the ten words, or *commandments,* that they might hear and understand them, so as they sensed them to be dreadful for their sound and matter, Exod. xx. 1—20 ; Deut. iv. 10, 12, 13 ; v. 1—27. *Which voice they that heard entreated that the word should not be spoken to them any more;* the people, being overwhelmed with the majesty and dreadfulness of that voice, deprecated any more such for matter or manner of manifestation to them, Exod. xx. 19 ; Deut. v. 23—26 ; xviii. 16. And therefore desired Moses to speak to them God's law, and that God might speak no more.

20 (For they could not endure that which was commanded, [g] And if so much as a beast touch the mountain, it shall be stoned, or thrust through with a dart :

g Ex. 19. 13.

The reason of the foregoing deprecation, and which adds to the terribleness of this covenant dispensation ; *for* the voice surpassed their strength and capacity, that they must die if they heard it any more, so dreadful was the sound and matter of it ; for the commandment and threatening was, That if any man or beast did but so much as touch the mountain, they should die for it, Exod. xix. 12, 13, 21, 23, 24. Therefore was Moses so strictly charged to look to it, and to provide against it, showing the dreadfulness of that covenant dispensation, that if men did not keep their beasts from coming near, they should be stoned or darted to death ; how much more themselves, if they should transgress the law, which, though it was designed to lead them unto Christ, yet was not generally so discerned or used by them ! So that if the publication of it be so terrible, how much more the punishment for breaking it ! Exod. xx. 20.

21 [h] And so terrible was the sight, *that* Moses said, I exceedingly fear and quake :)

h Ex. 19. 16.

It must needs be a dreadful, fearful, horrid, and astonishing apparition, and exhibition of the great Lawgiver here, that such a person as Moses, so sanctified by him, so favoured with familiarity with him, so constituted mediator between the people and God in this work for their good and comfort, so called and ordered by God to manage it, yet should cry to God to succour him, while he did quake and tremble at it ; and was comforted and strengthened by God's voice to him again, Exod. xix. 19. Christians now have no call nor access to so terrible a dispensation of the covenant, but have immunity, exemption, and freedom from it, which was not so helpful to holiness as the gospel dispensation, to which now they have actual admission, having freed them from all the terrors and curses of the Mosaical one.

22 But ye are come [i] unto mount Sion, [k] and unto the city of the living God, the heavenly Jerusalem, [l] and to an innumerable company of angels,

i Gal. 4. 26. Rev. 3. 12. & 21. 2, 10. k Phil. 3. 20. l Deut. 33, 2. Ps. 68. 17. Jude 14.

The Spirit now adds the privilege of Christians in the better state to which they have access by the gospel dispensation, from this verse to the 24th ; Ye have left those hinderances and disadvantages instanced in before, but are come to these helps for your furtherance in holiness ; ye have an access to all those most excellent, though invisible, things, by faith, and by it attain them, and are incorporated into them, as they follow. *But ye are come unto mount Sion:* this is not literally to be understood for the mount on which the city of David was built, for that was as visible and touchable as Mount Sinai, to which it is opposed ; but that mount which is higher than the highest, as high as heaven itself, ver. 25 ; chap. ix. 24 ; John iii. 13 ; where is the most orderly government of God for holiness, Micah iv. 7 ; whence all good gifts and gospel blessings are conveyed to the church, of which these believers were members, Isa. viii. 18 ; xxviii. 16 ; lix. 20 ; Rev. xiv. 1. *And unto the city of the living God;* of which the living God is the Builder and Maker, and wherein he dwelleth, where nothing but life is, and whence Christ's voice giveth life to dead souls, enabling them to live a life of holiness to God, as Psal. xlvi. 4, 5 ; xlviii. 1, 8 ; lxxxvii. 3 ; Isa. lx. 14 ; John v. 25. To distinguish this from any earthly city or corporation, it is said to be *the heavenly Jerusalem,* its original, nature, and end being all heavenly ; a fruitful place, whence believers are made partakers of the most spiritual influences for holiness ; where there is nothing carnal, terrible, deadly, barren, but all causal and productive of holiness issueth thence, Isa. lxii. ; lxv. 17—19 ; lxvi. 10 ; John xvii. 24 ; Gal. iv. 26 ; Rev. iii. 12 ; xxi. 2, 10. *And to an innumerable company of angels;* in which city are many excellent inhabitants with whom believers are incorporated, and to whom they have relation, as myriads of angels, who are ministering spirits under the gospel, as under the law, full of holiness, power, agility, and endowments, fit for their work and end ; who, though for number are thousands and millions of them, Psal. lxviii. 17; ciii. 20; civ. 4; Acts vii. 53; Gal. iii. 19; Rev. v. 11, yet are all fulfilling their Lord's pleasure in every place, as ordered by him. Their ministration of the law was terrible in flaming fire, but of the gospel, most sweet and gracious, Luke ii. 13, 14. At Sinai they ministered externally and sensibly, affecting senses; but from Sion they minister spiritually, to hearts, Matt. iv. 11; Luke xxii. 43; Psal. xci. 11, resisting evil spirits ministering wickedly. Their ministry little effectual under the law; but under the gospel, saving, Acts vii. 53; Heb. i. 14; Rev. xix. 10. Their former ministration temporary and ceasing, but this everlasting, till they bring all their trust into Abraham's bosom, Luke xvi. 22. They are promoting holiness by God's sending things to us by them, and by their observing the goings and doings of Christians, whether holy or not, 1 Cor. xi. 10, and giving an account of the success of their ministry towards them, as to this end, Matt. xviii. 10. And the neglect of this means to help our pursuing holiness, will God require, Heb. ii. 2.

m Ex. 4. 22.
Jam. 1. 18.
Rev. 14. 4.
n Luke 10.
20. Phil. 4. 3.
Rev. 13. 8.
‖ Or, *enrolled.*
o Gen. 18.
25. Ps. 94. 2.
p Phil. 3. 12. ch. 11. 40.

23 To the general assembly and Church of ᵐthe firstborn, ⁿwhich are ‖ written in heaven, and to God ᵒthe Judge of all, and to the spirits of just men ᵖmade perfect,

To the general assembly: other inhabitants of this heavenly city and polity with whom believers are incorporated, are such, into whose communion they have admittance here below, viz. to the catholic assembly of Christ, his whole body, the fulness of him who filleth all in all; an assembly gathered out of all nations, Rev. v. 9; vii. 9, throughout the world, extended to all times and ages, especially to that part of it which is on earth, sojourning here, fitting for heaven; the other part is triumphing in it. They are not called or incorporated only into a particular national assembly, a straitened society, as the Old Testament church was; the general assembly of saints are more helpful to holiness than a lesser, Psal. xxii. 27, 28; Gal. iv. 25—27. *And church of the firstborn:* this *general assembly* is not a rout, but a *church*, such as are called out of the world with a holy calling, subjecting themselves to Christ as their Head, and are, as quickened, so ordered and ruled by him: it is not a weak or an infant church, but strong and perfect, come unto maturity, in respect of the great discoveries of the mysteries of God made by Christ to them, chap. v. 12, 13; vi. 1; Gal. iv. 1, 3, 4. This chosen, called, and well-ordered society, were only of such persons who were *the first-born* of God, and partners of Christ's sonship and primogeniture, being regenerated by him, and dignified with his birthright privileges, Rom. viii. 17, 29. They are the might and excellency of Christ; whereas the church at Sinai, for the body of them, were but typically, literally, and externally so, Exod. iv. 22; Col. i. 15, 18, and did not universally enjoy, as those do, the strength and fulness of grace from God, John i. 16; Gal. iii. 26, 29; are *joint-heirs with Christ,* Rom. viii. 17, and made by him *kings and priests to God and his Father,* 1 Pet. ii. 5; Rev. i. 6. *Which are written in heaven:* they were not, as the church at Sinai, of an earthly enrolment, registered here to know their families and descent, whether right Jews and priests or no, whose genealogy was preserved to that end, Ezra ii. 43, &c.; but had their register in heaven, were written in the Lamb's book of life, to be of heavenly descent, born of God, partakers of the Divine nature, and who had a right and title by faith in Christ to the heavenly inheritance, and were free denizens of it, Luke x. 20. and have all heavenly privileges derived to them, Rev. xx. 12, 19; xxi. 27. How obliging, influencing, and promoting are these privileges of every Christian's pursuit of holiness! *And to God the Judge of all;* they were as Christians privileged with an access, not as Israel had at Sinai, with fear, and terror, and trembling, so as to fly from the great Author, Lord, and Judge of the covenant, lest they died, as Exod. xx. 18; but with liberty and boldness of faith, in the strength of love and with firmness of hope, they come now in Sion, Isa. lix. 20; Heb. x. 19, unto God in his being and sovereignty, who ruleth all, and who giveth to all according to their works, and in a most eminent manner ruleth them; who, as he is their Judge, hath not, as at Sinai, any bars to keep them from him, Exod. xix. 12; Eph. ii. 18, nor is terrifying and consuming, as then, Deut. v. 24, 25, but justifying them; full of grace and love to all approaching him in Christ, his throne is a throne of grace to them, he comforting and encouraging them to make home to him, John v. 22; Acts x. 22; Rom. iii. 6. So as they have boldness in the day of judgment, and stand unshaken before their Judge, and are strengthened by him, Rom. viii. 1, 33, 54; 1 John iv. 17. He rewards them gloriously, 2 Tim. ii. 8, perfecting holiness in them beneath, and crowning them with glory above. What a help is this to pursue holiness! *And to the spirits of just men made perfect:* the perfect state to which the gospel covenant leadeth is promoting holiness, for they have an access to the same lot, and are come into the same way of being perfected in holiness, which the spirits of the righteous, separated from their bodies, enjoy in heaven; and have a right unto, and shall have the certain enjoyment of, the same privilege, which carrieth through all difficulties in the pursuit of it, expecting themselves by death to be put in possession with them of the same state, Rom. viii. 22, 23; 2 Cor. v. 1, 2, 8; compare Phil. iii. 12—14.

q ch. 8. 6.
& 9. 15.
‖ Or,
testament.
r Ex. 24. 8.
ch. 10. 22.
1 Pet. 1. 2.
s Gen. 4. 10. ch. 11. 4.

24 And to Jesus ᑫthe mediator of the new ‖ covenant, and to ʳthe blood of sprinkling, that speaketh better things ˢthan *that of* Abel.

And to Jesus the mediator of the new covenant: the Mediator of the Sion covenant is better than the mediator at Sinai, and more able to promote the holiness required by it. Believers have not now access unto, or dependence on, a Moses, a mere man, and a servant, declaring God's will, only a sinner himself, trembling in his office, and weary of his clients, and whose ministry is vanishing, as his person dying; but unto God the Son himself incarnate, a Son-mediator, making sons, and bringing them nearer to God, satisfying the law for them, and writing it on their hearts; above all sin himself, though a sacrifice for it, who is able to save to the uttermost, for that he ever liveth to intercede for them, chap. i. 1—3; iii. 6; vii, 26; Rev. i. 13. He is the Mediator, not of a literal, dark, terrible, charging and condemning, temporary and vanishing, covenant; but of the most spiritual, lightsome, gracious, justifying, sanctifying, and everlasting testamental dispensation of God, more effectually influencing souls to holiness than the old, chap. viii. 10, 11; 2 Cor. iii. 6; v. 19. *And to the blood of sprinkling, that speaketh better things than that of Abel:* the sacrifice ratifying the Sion covenant is unexpressibly better than all the typical sacrifices confirming that at Sinai, it eminently purchasing and securing holiness to those interested in it. The blood of the immaculate Lamb of God, sprinkled on penitent, believing sinners, which hath purchased pardon for them, and, as follows, the Spirit, to sanctify them throughout, and perfect holiness in them, chap. ix. 12; 1 Pet. i. 18; 1 John i. 7, 9; and so they are freed from access to the sprinkling of the blood of sacrificed beasts, which was only typical and weak to purge the conscience, calling sin to remembrance yearly and daily, which was now forbidden and rejected as of no worth, and which, like Abel's, crieth for revenge and condemnation, Gen. iv. 10; since their blood now offered when Christ had spilt his, was accounted of God as the blood of innocents slain, as Isa. lxvi. 3. Others render the blood of Abel, for the blood of sprinkling of the sacrifice that Abel offered unto God, Gen. iv. 4, which was sprinkled upon him; and so prefer Christ's sacrifice, not only to the Mosaical sacrifices, but to all that have been from the beginning of the world, which though accepted by God, yet not like Christ, of which they were the types. The sum of all these comparisons, is to show the greater helps, motives, and encouragements that Christians have to pursue and perfect holiness than all the Old Testament church had before them.

t ch. 2. 2, 3.
& 3. 17. &
10. 28, 29.

25 See that ye refuse not him that speaketh. For ᵗif they escaped not who refused him that spake on earth, much more *shall not* we *escape,* if we turn away from him that *speaketh* from heaven:

Here the Spirit closely applieth his former arguments

for their pursuit of holiness, especially that of Christ's speaking by his blood to them; by caution, ver. 25—27; by counsel, ver. 28, 29. *See that ye refuse not him that speaketh:* he introduceth this caution with, Look ye, or take ye heed; a term expressing the things said to be great and weighty, intimating that fear, solicitude, and watchfulness about this great and important concernment of their souls, Luke xii. 15; that they see to it there be no aversion in their spirits to, no undervaluing or despising of, no dislike or apostacy from, but a hearing, believing, and obeying Jesus speaking by his blood all the gospel covenant to us; convincing them of sin and guilt that needed his blood, calling them to repentance and faith in his blood and satisfaction, declaring his intercession with God for pardon, holiness, and glory by it, and so importunes them to follow holiness, which would evidence all this to them. *For if they escaped not who refused him that spake on earth:* he enforceth his caution by a rational motive of the danger of their refusal, arguing from the less to the greater; that is, their ancestors escaped not the vengeance of God when they refused to hear, believe, and obey the legal covenant, which he spake on earth from Mount Sinai, and wrote on tables of stones, and delivered to Moses on the mount, and by him communicated it to them, chap. ii. 2; x. 28, 30, 31; Deut. xxxiii. 1, 4; Acts vii. 51, 53; 1 Cor. x. 1—10. *Much more shall not we escape, if we turn away from him that speaketh from heaven;* much more and greater sinners are all such who turn aside scornfully from Jesus, and receive not his voice and the revelation of God's gospel covenant by it, who is God's only begotten Son, and brought it down from the Father's bosom in heaven, chap. i. 2; John i. 14, 16—18; iii. 13, and ratified it with his own blood on earth: and as the sin is beyond compare greater, so will the punishment be, and the certainty of its infliction both for time and eternity, Matt. xi. 24; 2 Thess. i. 7—9; Heb. x. 26—31; there remaining no more sacrifice for such sin and sinners.

26 ᵘ Whose voice then shook the earth: but now he hath promised, saying, ˣ Yet once more I shake not the earth only, but also heaven.

ᵘ Ex. 19. 18.
ˣ Hag. 2. 6.

Whose voice then shook the earth: the sin and punishment of gospel despisers and rejecters, is aggravated by the Person concerned in both. It is that Jesus, the great Angel of the covenant, speaking now by his blood, whose voice at the delivery of the law on Mount Sinai, and selling Israel in a church state under that covenant dispensation, Exod. xx. 1, 19; Deut. iv. 12; v. 2, 4, 22, did shake the mount, Exod. xix. 18; Psal. lxviii. 7, 8; cxiv. 4, 7; and not only the literal Sinai, but that low, earthly condition and state of Israel coming out of Egypt, and bearing its reproach as a common people of the earth, together with other nations, Josh. v. 9. This he removed away, and brought them then into a church state with himself by covenant, which church state obtained the name or title of heaven, Matt. xxi. 43, and is by the prophet styled the old heaven, Isa. lxv. 17, which was to be shaken and removed also. *But now he hath promised, saying, Yet once more I shake not the earth only, but also heaven:* but now the same Jesus so shaking them had promised, and had at this time in part fulfilled what he spake, Hag. ii. 6, 7, even after the prophet's little while was expired, and Christ the desire of all nations was come; that yet *once more* he would shake the Israelitish church state, pitched till the time of reformation; not the earthly one only, as he did at Mount Sinai, which yet Jesus literally did at his death and resurrection, Matt. xxvii. 51, 54; xxviii. 2, and the heavens also by his star, Matt. ii. 2, light to the shepherds, Luke ii. 9, his baptism, Matt. iii. 17, transfiguration, Matt. xvii. 5; his prayer, John xii. 28—30, his passion, Matt. xxvii. 51; Luke xxiii. 44, 45, effusion of the Holy Ghost, Acts ii. 2—4: but this is also a powerful, moral shaking, so as to change and remove that heavenly church frame pitched in the Jewish tabernacle; that he might pitch a tabernacle himself more heavenly and spiritual, whereof Jesus should be the Lord High Priest and Ruler, as well as Minister, chap. iii. 1, 2.

27 And this *word*, Yet once more, signifieth ʸ the removing of those things

ʸ Ps. 102. 26.
Matt. 24. 35.
2 Pet. 3. 10.
Rev. 21. 1.

that ‖ are shaken, as of things that are made, that those things which cannot be shaken may remain.

‖ Or, *may be shaken.*

The interpretation of the former matter in this verse, is introduced by reassuming, And this, Yet once more; as if he said, I told you that God promised, Yet once more, &c.; what he meaneth by it I now declare to you: this shaking of God intends not a small alteration, but a total removal and abolition of the Israelitish heaven and earth, forementioned, an alteration of their church, religion, and administration, and a total abrogating of them, because they are hand-work, chap. ix. 24. Such as were at God's direction made by men, as tabernacle, altar, and that typical service, not reaching the spiritual design of God, and but types of far better to succeed them; and which settled, did make the others to be finished, past, and never to return again. *That those things which cannot be shaken may remain:* these better things are the administration of Christ's kingdom unshakeable, his church state which is heavenly, settled by his own evangelical laws and ordinances, which he hath so fixed by promise, as never to be removed till the whole church of Christ be completed with him in heaven, Hag. ii. 7; Matt. xvii. 5; xxviii. 18—20.

28 Wherefore we receiving a kingdom which cannot be moved, ‖ let us have grace, whereby we may serve God acceptably with reverence and godly fear:

‖ Or, *let us hold fast.*

Wherefore we receiving a kingdom which cannot be moved: in this verse the apostle follows his doctrine with counsel to several duties; such as concern the first table, and terminate on God, in this and the following verse; such as concern the second table, chap. xiii. 1, &c. In this verse he begins with the Christians' privilege, and then directs their duty. These Hebrews having received by faith the privileges, and submitted themselves unto the laws and government, of the unmoveable kingdom of Christ, that gospel church state of which God is the author, Christ the King, his spiritual under-officers ministers, penitent believing sinners the subject; the gospel laws by which the government is administered perfectly holy, just, and good; the privileges of it all grace here, and glory above; the descent of all from heaven: all which are to endure for ever unshaken, and against them the gates of hell shall not prevail, Zech. ix. 9; 1 Cor. xv. 24—28; Eph. iv. 11—16; Col. i. 13; ii. 3. *Let us have grace, whereby we may serve God acceptably with reverence and godly fear;* let us get and hold fast that gracious temper of soul, whereby they are made true, wise, believing, loving, humble, and obedient subjects to the laws of this kingdom, and manifest it by worshipping, and serving of, and walking with, God in this world, so as our persons and duties may be all well-pleasing to him in Christ, Eph. i. 6, and constantly conformable to his holy will, chap. xi. 4, 5: and out of a sense of their own lowliness, with a self-abasing heart, and a reverential carriage, as Gen. xviii. 27; Luke xviii. 13, approaching God in all his service with a holy jealousy over itself, that it do not offend him in what it is or doth, but rightly receiving law from him for all his service, and rightly returning all conformable thereunto to him again, John xii. 49, 50.

29 For ᶻ our God *is* a consuming fire.

ᶻ Ex. 24. 17.
Deut. 4. 24.
& 9. 3. Ps. 50. 3. & 97. 3. Is. 66. 15. 2 Thess. 1. 8. ch. 10. 27.

The motive enforcing this duty is no less terrible than that given to Israel under the law, obliging their obedience to that covenant dispensation, Deut. iv. 23, 24, *The Lord thy God is a consuming fire, even a jealous God.* He that was so respecting the transgression of the legal, will much more be so as to this gospel covenant. God Almighty, the most gracious, and yet the most just Being, their own God by covenant obtestation; yet will be to them, if they break his covenant, and do not, through Christ, acceptably serve him with reverence and godly fear, as fire consuming them. His gospel law, in the contempt of it, will be as the fiery law at Sinai, adjudging such sinners unto fire unquenchable, chap. x. 27—31; compare Matt. iii. 12; xxv. 41; 2 Thess. i. 7—9.

CHAP. XIII

Exhortations to charity, 1; *hospitality,* 2; *pity for the afflicted,* 3; *chastity,* 4; *contentment,* 5, 6: *to regard the*

HEBREWS XIII

preachers of God's word, 7, 8; to avoid strange doctrines, 9; to confess Christ, 10—14; to offer up our praises to God by him, 15; to do good and to communicate, 16; to obey spiritual rulers, 17; and to pray for the apostle, 18, 19. The Epistle endeth with a prayer and salutations, 20—25.

^a Rom. 12. 10. 1 Thess. 4. 9. 1 Pet. 1. 22. & 2. 17. & 3. 8. & 4. 8. 2 Pet. 1. 7. 1 John 3. 11, &c. & 4. 7, 20, 21.

LET ^abrotherly love continue.

The apostle in this chapter pursueth his counsel to the subjects of the unmoveable kingdom of Christ, for their performing suitable duties to such a privilege, and especially such as more immediately terminate on their neighbour, and are contained in the second table of the Redeemer's laws; as the chief and fundamental one, *brotherly love.* Let love, a fruit of the Spirit, show forth itself and its existence in you, in pre-eminence, and in duration, by disposing always the inward man, mind, will, and affections, to seek the good, to speak all the good to and of, and to do all good to their Christian brethren, to all true Christians, eminently styled by the Spirit the brotherhood, Matt. xii. 50; xxviii. 10; John xiii. 34, 35; xx. 17; 1 Cor. xiii.; Eph. iv. 32; 1 Thess. iv. 9; 1 John iii. 14, 16.

^b Mat. 25. 35. Rom. 12. 13. 1 Tim. 3. 2. 1 Pet. 4. 9. ^c Gen. 18. 3. & 19. 2.

2 ^bBe not forgetful to entertain strangers: for thereby ^csome have entertained angels unawares.

The next duty suitable to Christ's kingdom, is hospitality to Christian strangers. *Be not forgetful to entertain strangers;* be neither ignorant nor unmindful: by which charge they are bound strongly and always not to have this out of mind, though it may be out of hand; and the negative confirms the positive duty, removing hinderances, and enjoining it strictly, that they have a love and desire to the duty, bearing affection to the person of a Christian brother though a stranger, unknown and brought by Providence to them, Matt. xxii. 39; xxv. 35; and to the work of being an host, of entertaining such Christians; ξενὸς signifying an host as well as a stranger or guest. It is a love to be an hospitable person that is here required, Tit. i. 8; (such was Gaius to Paul and the church, Rom. xvi. 23;) importing a kind, courteous reception of Christians into their houses, being harbourless, which Christ promiseth them, Luke xviii. 29; 1 Tim. v. 10; a free and cheerful provision for their necessary refreshing, Gen. xviii. 4—6; with a careful furtherance and assistance of them in the work of God, and helping them to persevere in the same, 3 John 6—8. *For thereby some have entertained angels unawares;* the advantage that accrues to such hosts of the Christian church and its members is great; for in the exercise of this duty, Abraham and Lot, being strangers, and waiting to entertain such, received angels into their tabernacle and house, Gen. xviii. 2, 3, and had sweet discoveries of God in the Messiah made to them; were delivered by them from judgment, as Lot, Gen. xix. 10, 15—17. And now the general guard of angels goeth along with the saints, and are entertained in them, who never come without a blessing, they attending them in their way, defending them against evil spirits, and offensive ones and places where they are, though their ministry be little observed or acknowledged as it ought, chap. i. 14. Not only angels, but Christ himself accompanieth his pilgrim members, and is entertained, fed, comforted, and lodged in and with them, Matt. x. 40—42; xxv. 34—36; and for this will he reward them in both worlds.

^d Matt. 25. 36. Rom. 12. 15. 1 Cor. 12. 26. Col. 4. 18. 1 Pet. 3. 8.

3 ^dRemember them that are in bonds, as bound with them; *and* them which suffer adversity, as being yourselves also in the body.

Remember them that are in bonds, as bound with them: a further duty of the subjects of Christ's kingdom, is sympathy with their Christian brethren, to remember to pray for, visit, and minister all necessary refreshment to those in bonds, fettered, manacled, and imprisoned for Christ's sake and the gospel; being straitened for them, and partaking of their bonds, bearing them with them, and seeking their deliverance out of them by all just means, Matt. xxv. 36; Eph. vi. 19, 20; Col. iv. 18; 2 Tim. i. 16 —18. *And them which suffer adversity, as being yourselves also in the body;* be mindful of those suffering any evil for Christ's sake and the gospel, persecuted, oppressed, or afflicted, who have not deserved any of this from man, so as to carry it suitably to them in these conditions, chap. xi. 36— 38; so feelingly, as if we were the persons in their conditions; carefully, knowing we are in bodies capable and liable to the same, and are ignorant how soon it may be our own case; conscientiously, as knowing we are members in the same body of Christ with them, and of them in particular, 1 Cor. xii. 25—27.

4 Marriage *is* honourable in all, and the bed undefiled: ^ebut whoremongers and adulterers God will judge.

^e 1 Cor. 6. 9. Gal. 5. 19, 21. Eph. 5. 5. Col. 3. 5, 6. Rev. 22. 15.

Marriage is honourable in all: the next duty charged on the subjects of Christ's kingdom, is chastity; the commendation of it is a precept to it. Marriage is that state which God instituted at the beginning, after the creation of Adam and Eve, which was by his law the making of them two to become one flesh, Gen. ii. 24; confirmed by Christ, Matt. xix. 5. On this state God, the fountain of all honour, hath stamped his own name and excellence, and hath made it, by an irreversible law, a glorious and honourable state. The connexion is present, real, and necessary; God saith it, therefore it is so, and must be so; and this after God's institution in all its concomitants every where, and in all times; but especially in all persons in the kingdom of Christ, true Christians of all sorts and degrees, of what state or calling soever, qualified for and called to it, whether magistrates, ministers, or church members; God by it preventing sin, preserving holy and pure communion between the married, propagating his church, and accomplishing the number of his chosen by it, Psal. cxi. 3; Mal. ii. 15; 1 Cor. vii. 9; 1 Thess. iv. 3, 4; 1 Pet. iii. 1, 7. *And the bed undefiled;* a good, moral use of the marriage bed, the natural and lawful use of the wife by the husband, and of the husband by the wife, according to the law of God; which is so far from being unclean, filthy, and inconsistent with the purity of Christ, as papists, apostates from the faith, assert, 1 Tim. iv. 1—4, that it is holy, pure, and chaste in itself, and a most excellent means of preserving chastity among the subjects of Christ's kingdom, 1 Thess. iv. 4; Tit. ii. 5; 1 Pet. iii. 2; by this they are kept in their bodies from being polluted or dishonoured by fornication or adultery. Marriage is thus honourable in all husbands and wives, of what degree or order soever, whilst they are such; and must be undefiled in all, because their bodies are the members of Christ, and temples of the Holy Ghost, 1 Cor. vi. 15, 17—20. *But whoremongers and adulterers God will judge;* but God hates unclean societies of all men and women, but especially of Christians; and as he will certainly judge, and inflict eternal punishment upon, all kind of unclean persons, so especially upon whoremongers and adulterers who profess themselves subjects of Christ's pure kingdom, 2 Pet. ii. 6; Jude 4, 7; Rev. ii. 21.

5 *Let your* conversation *be* without covetousness; *and* ^f*be* content with such things as ye have: for he hath said, ^gI will never leave thee, nor forsake thee.

^f Matt. 6. 25, 34. Phil. 4. 11, 12. 1 Tim. 6. 6, 8. ^g Gen. 28. 15. Deut. 31. 6, 8. Josh. 1. 5. 1 Chr. 28. 20. Ps. 37. 25.

Contentation with our state and condition is a fifth duty charged on the subjects of Christ's kingdom, and this is expressed privatively and positively, yet both propositions without a verb, which is best supplied by an imperative. *Let your conversation be without covetousness:* Ὁ τρόπος strictly signifieth a turning, but here it sets out the motion or turning of a man up and down in the actions of this life, which in common speech is called conversation; not any motion of the heart, nor turn of the eye, nor action of any member, after money or riches, with a sinful, inordinate love to them, or pursuit of them; forbidden, Matt. vi. 25, 31; 1 Tim. vi. 9, 10; James iv. 13; 1 John iv. 15. The studious endeavour and labour night and day, turning and winding every way, to be scraping together and hoarding up worldly wealth, and lading themselves with thick clay, Eccles. iv. 7, 8; Hab. ii. 6, 9, must not be the case or condition of any Christian, Eph. v. 3, 5; Col. iii. 5; 2 Pet. ii. 3—15. *And be content with such things as ye have;* but having a heart-acquiescence and satisfaction with that portion or pittance of earthly things which God at present doth allot us, whether more or less, and not with that only which we may think enough to serve our turn, Phil. iv. 11, 12; 1 Tim. vi. 8. *For he hath said, I will never leave thee, nor forsake thee :* the reason enforcing it is, God's giving by promise a special engagement to provide for them. This God solemnly made to Jacob, Gen. xxviii. 15, then to Israel, Deut. xxxi. 6, 8, then to Joshua, chap. i. 5, and to all believers as well as them ; for God will not let any such see the miseries of his absence, but will vouchsafe to them his presence, with all the blessings which attend it, Psal. xlvi. 1, 5 ; Isa. xli. 10 ; xliii. 2 ; lxiii. 9.

h Ps. 27. 1. & 56. 4, 11, 12. & 118. 6.

6 So that we may boldly say, [h] The Lord *is* my helper, and I will not fear what man shall do unto me.

So that we may boldly say ; upon the account of which promise of God all the true subjects of Christ's kingdom, together with the apostle, may with an undaunted boldness of heart, above all fears and doubtings, and with a daring confidence, professing that which they believe, nor staggering, nor shrinking, nor being ashamed of their faith, but openly owning it to all the world, own that *The Lord is my helper ;* the Lord in the infiniteness of his power, wisdom, and goodness, is a real, present, universal, and permanent help against all trouble, and for all supplies in all cases, and at all times, to every one of them. They may say as Moses, Exod. xviii. 4 ; as David, Psal. xxvii. 9 ; xl. 17 ; lvi. 4, 11 ; cxviii. 6. *And I will not fear what man shall do unto me :* and therefore faith expelleth fearfulness of, and introduceth fearlessness of, any created evils incident to a believer ; and of which man may be an instrument inflicting, Psal. xlvi. 2, 3. Implying in it an unshaken settledness of mind, judgment, and thoughts on God's help, a fixed frame of heart, without tumultuous passions or perturbations, with an unmovable resolution to keep close to God and his word both in word and deed, amidst all oppositions and persecutions of men for it.

i ver. 17.
‖ Or, *are the guides.*
k ch. 6. 12.

7 [i] Remember them which ‖ have the rule over you, who have spoken unto you the word of God : [k] whose faith follow, considering the end of *their* conversation :

Imitation of their godly ministers, is another duty that Christ's law chargeth on his subjects, both here and ver. 17. *Remember them which have the rule over you, who have spoken unto you the word of God ;* be mindful of your spiritual guides and rulers, firmly and constantly to retain their excellencies in memory, esteeming of them, and thanking God for them, which were sent to them and set over them by the Holy Ghost, who were guiding of them by Christ to God, and enjoyment of eternal life with him, which they did by preaching to them, and writing the gospel of Christ for their edification, by the inspiration of the Spirit. Some of which guides were removed by death, slain and martyred for the truth of Jesus, and ascended unto heaven, and others were alive among them ; they were to remember all of them, but especially their spiritual fathers that had begotten them to God by the gospel, 1 Cor. iv. 15 ; 2 Cor. ii. 17 ; 1 Tim. v. 17 ; 2 Tim. iii. 14—17 ; 1 Pet. iv. 11 ; v. 2, 3. *Whose faith follow ;* the best way of remembering such is by imitating them, to believe the doctrine which they taught and practised, and to be as stedfast in the faith as were they, and holding of it out to others, how eminent believers they were, 1 Tim. iv. 12 ; vi. 11 ; 2 Tim. ii. 22. *Considering the end of their conversation ;* such as their doctrine was, such was their life, conformable to Christ's, 1 Cor. xi. 1. It was honest, upright, and blameless, much in heaven, 2 Cor. x. 3 ; Phil. iii. 20. All their turnings and motions in the world, their very life, was hid with Christ in God ; all agreeable to, as ordered by, his will. And such was the issue and egress of this life, which it is their concernment to review, they having by it an outlet from the remainders of sin and misery, which did defile and oppress them, Rev. xiv. 13, and a victory over the world and all its oppositions to them, sealing the truth with their blood which they had preached and practised among them, and were more than conquerors over all by death, having an inlet into life, and peace, and eternal glory, in the inheritance incorruptible, undefiled, and which fadeth not away, reserved for them in heaven, Rom. viii. 37 ; 2 Tim. iv. 8 ; 1 Pet. i. 4 ; iii. 4.

8 Jesus Christ [1] the same yesterday, and to day, and for ever.

1 John 8. 58.
ch. 1. 12.
Rev. 1. 4.

Though this hath no term of connexion, yet it may be referred either to what precedeth or followeth it ; for the apostle is not here dropping aphorisms, but pressing on the subjects of Christ's kingdom known duties. It is here interposed as a weighty reason of the duty foregoing, to remember their guides, imitate their faith, and consider the end of their conversation, for they taught, believed in, conversed with, and at last were perfected by, Jesus Christ ; so that they might be saved by him as their guides were, there being no other way to blessedness, but by *Jesus Christ the same,* &c., John xiv. 6. Or a reason enforcing what followeth, that since Jesus Christ is the same, as in his person, so in his doctrine, faith, and conversation, which he enjoineth on his subjects, they should not be carried about with divers and strange doctrines. Jesus Christ personal is immutable in his care and love to his mystical body, and all the members of it, throughout all times and ages, he never leaves nor forsakes them ; so Christ doctrinal, in his faith, law, and rule of conversation, Eph. iv. 20, 21. The pure, full, and entire religion of Christ is unchangeable, being simply, indivisibly, and constantly the same throughout all measures of time, Matt. v. 18 ; 2 Cor. xi. 3, 4 ; Gal. i. 6, 7 ; Eph. iv. 4, 5 ; 1 Pet. i. 23, 25.

9 [m] Be not carried about with divers and strange doctrines. For *it is a* good thing that the heart be established with grace ; [n] not with meats, which have not profited them that have been occupied therein.

m Eph. 4. 14. & 5. 6.
Col. 2. 4, 8.
1 John 4. 1.
n Rom. 14. 17. Col. 2. 16. 1 Tim. 4. 3.

Be not carried about with divers and strange doctrines : the doctrine of Christ being immutable, it is but necessary to dehort his subjects from deserting it, which the apostle doth here ; that they should not be wheeling or whirling about with an unstable and inconstant motion of judgment, faith, and practice, about such human doctrines which are vain rules to lead to God, such as are different in nature from Christ, one and the same rule, and those very numerous and various, strange and untrue, taught by false apostles and teachers, taken out of Gentilism and Judaism, and added to the Gospel by them, as necessary, together with Christ, to justification and salvation, Matt. v. 9 ; 2 Cor. xi. 3 ; Eph. iv. 14 ; 2 Thess. ii. 10, 12 ; 1 Tim. iv. 1—3 ; 2 Tim. iv. 3, 4 ; 2 Pet. ii. 1, 18, 19 ; Jude 12. *For it is a good thing that the heart be established with grace ;* for the goodness of heart-establishment unto God is no less than full and complete salvation of the soul, 1 Cor. xv. 58 ; 2 Pet. iii. 17, 18. And this is only wrought by grace, the free love of God put out in Christ, for regeneration and preservation of souls unto life eternal, carried in the simple doctrine of Christ, which is always the same, 2 Thess. ii. 16, 17 ; 1 Pet. v. 10. *Not with meats ;* doctrines of meats and ceremonies, which are divers, and strange from Christ's, cannot make the heart agreeable to God, but only distract and divide it from him ; for whatsoever is not in and from Christ, is strange to God, and abhorred by him, Gal. v. 2 ; Col. ii. 18, 19, 23 ; 2 Tim. ii. 16 ; James i. 8. *Which have not profited them that have been occupied therein :* those who did converse in these various and strange doctrines, professing and constantly practising them, observed times, and meats, and ceremonies, have not been profited by them ; for being carnal and earthly, they could not justify them as to their state God-ward, nor could they renew or sanctify their souls, nor yield any advantage to their spiritual life ; and being perishing, could not profit to the attaining of eternal life, Rom. xiv. 17, 18 ; compare 1 Cor. vi. 13.

10 [o] We have an altar, whereof they have no right to eat which serve the tabernacle.

o 1 Cor. 9. 13. & 10. 18.

We have an altar : these strange doctrines are not only unprofitable, but perilous to Christians, since they disinterest all that entertain them, as to any participation of Christ ; since his subjects, adhering to his simple and immutable doctrine, have a right and just claim to, and an actual use of, Christ, as their altar, in opposition to the Mosaical ; and from whom they have altar sustenance for their souls, in opposition to the Jewish meats, while they attend on him; all the quickening benefits issuing from the sacrifice of his human nature on the altar of his Godhead, as reconciliation and adoption to God, justification of our persons, renovation of our nature, growth in grace, and perseverance therein, to the perfecting of it in glory, John vi. 55—57; 1 Cor. ix. 13; x. 16—18. We have altar sanctification of our persons and offerings in our access to God from him, ver. 15; Matt. xxiii. 19; Eph. v. 20; Col. iii. 17; so as all is accepted with the Father. We have altar protection and salvation, keeping us who attend on him unto the revelation of God in glory, Exod. xxi. 14; Rev. vi. 9, 11. This is altar individuation to all Christians; God had but one altar under the law, and he prohibited all others, and complained of and threatened the increase of them, Exod. xx. 24—26; xxvii. 1, 2; 2 Chron. iv. 1; Hos. viii. 11; x. 1. This one altar did type out that true one of Christ, by which only sinners can come to God, and find acceptance. *Whereof they have no right to eat which serve the tabernacle;* of this altar privilege all Jews or Judaizing Christians, who adhered to the Mosaical administration of the covenant in meats and ceremonies, have no lawful right or title to partake; they cannot have this honour while they cleave to them, because they thereby deny this altar, reject the Son of God, and are in it rejected by him.

p Ex. 29. 14.
Lev. 4. 11, 12, 21. & 6. 30. & 9. 11. & 16. 27.
Num. 19. 3.

11 For ᵖ the bodies of those beasts, whose blood is brought into the sanctuary by the High Priest for sin, are burned without the camp.

The illustration of the legal and gospel altar service is added as a typical proof of the foregoing reason; *for* annexing it to it; that the Jews and Judaizing Christians had no right to eat of the Christian altar, for a law of their own excludes them from it, which is written, Lev. vi. 30; xvi. 27: That the bodies of those living creatures, which were yearly sacrificed as a sin-offering for priests and people, both of the bull and the he-goat, with their skins, &c., were burnt wholly without the camp; so as neither the priests nor any of the people had any part of this bull or goat allowed them to eat, having no right to it by the law of God, which otherwise ordered it. This is the literal sense, yet the use of it is anagogical, leading us to higher things; as that the high priest signified Christ, God-man; the altar, his Godhead; the sanctuary, heaven itself; the sacrifice, his human nature, the true sin-offering, of which neither priest nor people serving the tabernacle ought to eat.

q John 19. 17, 18.
Acts 7. 58.

12 Wherefore Jesus also, that he might sanctify the people with his own blood, ᑫsuffered without the gate.

Because that sacrifice for sin was *burnt without the camp, therefore Jesus,* to fulfil the type, *suffered without the gate;* and as they might not eat of that expiatory sacrifice, so neither of this. Jesus, therefore, to fulfil this type, suffered without the gates of Jerusalem, upon Mount Calvary, where skulls and bones of cursed creatures were scattered; as the expiatory sacrifices were burnt without the camp, when Israel was tabernacling within it; without the gates, when Israel dwelt in cities. As the high priest carried the expiatory blood into the holiest of all, on the day of atonement; so Christ with his own blood entered the holiest in heaven, and by it obtained pardon of sin, peace of conscience, and renewing by the Holy Ghost, for all people who repent, believe, and will come unto God by him. Therefore those who will still Judaize, have no right to eat of his sacrifice, no more than of the expiatory one, which was wholly burnt: so that they were not to be justified by meats and ceremonies, but by the blood of Christ alone, the truth of all the sacrifices, Rom. iii. 25; v. 9; John i. 29.

r ch. 11. 26.
1 Pet. 4. 14.

13 Let us go forth therefore unto him without the camp, bearing ʳhis reproach.

Therefore shows this to be a necessary duty, inferred from the former privilege; That since we have such an altar and sacrifice as Jesus, sanctifying us by his own blood, which he entered with to God, when he *suffered without the gate;* we ought and must *go forth* (from tabernacle service, consisting of meats and ceremonies, from Judaism, in all its parts abolished, and all erroneous doctrines, how numerous and strange soever, and all worldly things) unto Jesus, who was cursed for us, that we might be blessed, Gal. iii. 13, in faith and love; not ashamed of, but glorying in his sufferings, and following and imitating of him, patiently and boldly bearing mockings, revilings, scourgings, crucifyings, and all other persecutions, which are parts of his cross, for his sake, chap. xi. 9; Rom. vi. 5, 6; 1 Cor. i. 30; Gal. ii. 20; Phil. iii. 8—10; making him in all our example, 1 Pet. ii. 21; iv. 12—19.

14 ˢFor here have we no continuing city, but we seek one to come.

s Mic. 2. 10.
Phil. 3. 20.
ch. 11. 10.
16. & 12. 22.

This is an enforcement of the foregoing duty, as the particle *for* cleareth; That they have no reason to be discouraged from going forth from Judaism, and those erroneous doctrines, and the world, to him, though it should cost them their lives for it; *for* at the best this world is not a place fit for us, nor can our state in it be desirable, since it is imperfect, fleeting, and vanishing, and we must die out of it; we may well then go forth, and die with him, and for him. And we have reason to go forth and suffer with him, since it will instantly bring us to that heavenly city, which we profess that we only live to fit ourselves for, and then to enter in and possess it, chap. xi. 10, 16; xii. 22; Phil. iii. 20, 21.

15 ᵗBy him therefore let us offer ᵘthe sacrifice of praise to God continually, that is, ˣthe fruit of *our* lips †giving thanks to his name.

t Eph. 5. 20.
1 Pet. 2. 5.
u Lev. 7. 12.
Ps. 50. 14,
23. & 69. 30, 31. & 107. 22.
& 116. 17.
x Hos. 14. 2. † Gr. *confessing to.*

Therefore, introducing this duty, shows it not only to issue from the former privilege of having Christ our altar and sacrifice, *therefore* we should use him, and sacrifice by him; and it is inferred as anticipating an objection of these Hebrews, That if the tabernacle service ceased, then they should have no sacrifice to offer unto God. Yea, saith the apostle, *let us offer,* which is not hand-work, but heartwork, by a spirit of faith on this altar, *the sacrifice of praise,* 1 Pet. ii. 5, such as God requireth and accepts above all the sacrifices of beasts, &c., Psal. l. 23; praise for the grace-privilege and honour of being denizens of his city, and of being brought home to it by suffering, Col. i. 11, 12; and this always throughout our life, to the God that is the author and distributer of all these blessings to us. This sacrifice of praise the Spirit interprets to be *the fruit of our lips,* which the prophet styleth, *calves of our lips,* in Hos. xiv. 2. By both these must synecdochically be understood the Spirit and heart guiding the whole man in this matter, Rom. xii. 1, confessing that all it is capable of rendering is due from it to God, even all of love, praise, thanksgiving honour, for its redemption through Jesus Christ, whether continually expressed either by lip or life, as Psal. l. 23; 1 Cor. vi. 20; Eph. v. 20; Phil. iv. 6, 7; Col. iii. 17; 1 Thess. v. 17, 18.

16 ʸBut to do good and to communicate forget not: for ᶻwith such sacrifices God is well pleased.

y Rom. 12. 13.
z 2 Cor. 9. 12. Phil. 4. 18. ch. 6. 10.

But to do good and to communicate forget not: the last duty which Christ sufferings without the gate for his subjects obligeth them to, is liberality and beneficence to others. In which is explicitly denied any carelessness of mind, aversation of affection, or omission of the duty; in which is implicitly enjoined, inclination to, retention in memory of, and constant practice of beneficence and liberality, both as to spiritual and temporal good, vigorously and cheerfully edifying the souls and cherishing the bodies of all necessitous ones, but especially of their poor brethren of the household of faith, Gal. vi. 10; 1 John iii. 17; glorifying God by obeying his law and rule about it, Matt. vi. 1—4; Eph. vi. 5—9. *For with such sacrifices God is well pleased;* such doing of good, and communicating to the necessities of poor saints, are part of our evangelical sacrifices, which God requireth of us, instead of the numerous legal ones; and are attending on, concomitant with, and sanctified by, the one true sacrifice of Christ; and being duly terminated on him according to his law, they are highly pleasing and acceptable to God, yea, sometimes above other sacrifices and holy things given to him; and which, as he commands, he

878 HEBREWS XIII

will at present greatly reward with temporal and spiritual blessings, and with everlasting riches and glory in heaven, Prov. xix. 17; Micah vi. 6—8; Matt. ix. 13; xxv. 34—40; 2 Cor. ix. 12.

17 [a]Obey them that ‖ have the rule over you, and submit yourselves: for [b]they watch for your souls, as they that must give account, that they may do it with joy, and not with grief: for that is unprofitable for you.

a Phil. 2. 29. 1 Thess. 5. 12. 1 Tim. 5. 17. ver. 7. ‖ Or, *guide.* b Ezek. 3. 17. & 33. 2, 7. Acts 20. 26, 28.

Obey them that have the rule over you, and submit yourselves: the further duty required by Christ from the subjects of his kingdom, is their due demeanour to their present pastors, and church guides, or rulers. He chargeth them to esteem and account of them, as they are, and he hath constituted them in his church, to attend on their ministry and teaching, yielding full obedience of faith to the doctrine which they delivered from Christ, and to be subject to the power and authority Christ hath given them over them for their edification, and not for destruction; and that they imitate them in their believing and holy conversation, Acts xx. 18. And this as to all of them, set over them by the Holy Ghost, whether ordinary or extraordinary, as the apostles, evangelists, elders, pastors, teachers, doing all as commissioned by Christ, and in his name exercising their power and authority, according to his express written law about it, Eph. iv. 11, 12; knowing that who receiveth or despiseth them, dealeth so with Christ and God, who sent them, Matt. x. 40; Luke x. 16. *For they watch for your souls, as they that must give account:* good reason have they to perform this duty, because of their concern in and care for their souls. How great, by Christ's law, are the night watchings, and day cares, and tears, studies, exhortations, reproofs, comfortings, their preachings, and prayers with tears, and strong cries to God for their souls! Will you pay duty to those who watch to preserve and protect your natural life, and not unto those spiritual watchers, and God's charge given to them? Acts xx. 28—31; 2 Tim. iv. 5; Rev. iii. 2, 3. And God will exact an account of them for your souls; and they must render it at a dear rate, Ezek. iii. 17—21; xxxiii. 7, 9. It is at their peril, if they are faithless and neglect their duty, and your souls miscarry, Matt. xviii. 23; xxv. 14, 30. *That they may do it with joy, and not with grief;* that they may not only do their work cheerfully and comfortably among you, but that they may give up their account joyfully about you to God, when they have brought you home to him, 1 Thess. ii. 19, 20; and which will be an eternal comfort unto you, 2 Thess. i. 7, 10. If you be disobedient to them, though they will have their reward for their fidelity from their Lord, yet with what sighs, tears, groans, sorrow, and heaviness of heart, must they see their labours and your souls lost, and to charge you before God with it! 2 Cor. iii. 15, 16; xii. 21. *For that is unprofitable for you:* and what damage will both your disobedience to the word of God and them, and their account of it to God, bring on yourselves! Will it then quit the cost to find your punishment more intolerable than that of Sodom and Gomorrah, Matt. x. 15; xi. 22. 24, when he will give you your portion with hypocrites, Matt. xxiv. 51, and punish you with everlasting destruction? 2 Thess. i. 7—9.

18 [c]Pray for us: for we trust we have [d]a good conscience, in all things willing to live honestly.

c Rom. 15. 30. Eph. 6. 19. Col. 4. 3. 1 Thes. 5. 25. 2 Thes. 3. 1. d Acts 23. 1. & 24. 16. 2 Cor. 1. 12.

Pray for us: the closing duty becoming the subjects of the kingdom of Christ, is prayer, upon some special accounts, ver. 18, 19, that they would with their renewed souls, influenced and assisted by the Spirit of grace and supplication, pour forth their desires to God with faith, fervency, and importunity, for his vouchsafing to the apostle himself, and for their spiritual guides and rulers, that the things they need, and God hath promised to them, as to the successful course of their ministry, may be bestowed on them, which the Spirit specifieth elsewhere, 2 Cor. iii. 5, 6; Eph. vi. 18—20; Col. iv. 3, 4; 2 Thess. iii. 1, 2. *For we trust we have a good conscience, in all things willing to live honestly:* he urgeth this on them, for that he was a fit subject to be prayed for, however any might accuse or charge him for rejecting Judaism out of singularity, prejudice, or some evil design; he assures them from the Spirit of God, that he had a rightly informed conscience by God's word, and which testified his innocency and sincerity, and which did dictate and influence him to be communicating and promoting, with all and to all, the truth of the gospel; and that his own life and conversation in the world was agreeable to the gospel rule, in all godliness and honesty, Acts xxiii. 1; xxiv. 14; compare 1 Cor. iv. 4; 2 Cor. i. 12.

19 But I beseech *you* [e]the rather to do this, that I may be restored to you the sooner.

e Philem. 22.

He is the more urging and pressing them to the exercise of this duty more fervently, instantly, and abundantly, at this time, that they might prevail with God to remove hinderances by his enemies, freeing him from his chain and restraint at Rome, and to speed his liberty for a return to them, that it might be in the fulness of the blessing of the gospel. So the church prayed for Peter, and prevailed, Acts xii. 12, and he had hopes that God would hear them for him also, Philem. 22.

20 Now [f]the God of peace, [g]that brought again from the dead our Lord Jesus, [h]that great shepherd of the sheep, [i]through the blood of the everlasting ‖ covenant,

f Rom. 15. 33. 1 Thess. 5. 23. g Acts 2. 24, 32. Rom. 4. 24. & 8. 11. 1 Cor. 6. 14, & 15. 15. 2 Cor. 4. 14. Gal. 1. 1. Col. 2. 12.
1 Thess. 1. 10. 1 Pet. 1. 21. h Is. 40. 11. Ezek. 34. 23. & 37. 24. John 10. 11, 14. 1 Pet. 2. 25. & 5. 4. i Zech. 9. 11. ch. 10. 22. ‖ Or, *testament*.

As the apostle desires the church's prayers for himself, so he poureth out his for them; with the which he introduceth the conclusion of this Epistle, ver. 20, 21. Now God the Father, the God and Author of peace and reconciliation of sinners to himself, the propagator and lover of peace among all the subjects of his kingdom, the dispenser of the fulness of good, blessing, and happiness, Rom. xv. 3; Phil. iv. 9; 1 Thess. v. 23, who gloriously manifested his power by the resurrection of our Lord Jesus from the dead, Eph. i. 19, 20; Rom. i. 4, who is *the great Shepherd of his sheep,* exalted to this office, because he poured out his blood a sacrifice for sins, to purchase them, justify and sanctify them, a peculiar flock for himself, according to the covenant of grace that God made with them, and in him with and for sinners, who should repent and believe in him, John x. 9—30; 1 Cor. vi. 11; Phil. ii. 7, 10; Tit. ii. 14; 1 Pet. i. 18, 19, and to perfect them with himself above, 1 Pet. v. 4, by the same power wherewith he was raised, perfect you, &c. Eph. i. 19.

21 [k]Make you perfect in every good work to do his will, ‖[l]working in you that which is wellpleasing in his sight, through Jesus Christ; [m]to whom *be* glory for ever and ever. Amen.

k 2 Thess. 2. 17. 1 Pet. 5. 10. ‖ Or, *doing*. l Phil. 2. 13.
m Gal. 1. 5. 2 Tim. 4. 18. Rev. 1. 6.

Make you perfect in every good work to do his will: may this God dispose, incline, and fit you for, may he finish and perfect in you, grace to perform all the forementioned duties, and every other good work, which he enjoineth on you towards God, one another, and all men, 2 Cor. xiii. 9; Eph. iv. 12; Tit. iii. 14; 1 Pet. iv. 2; v. 10, according to his written will and law, Eph. ii. 10. *Working in you that which is well-pleasing in his sight, through Jesus Christ:* working in you by his Spirit continually, that all these good works may satisfy his expectation, be a sweet savour in his nostrils, and so pleasing in his sight, that his soul may delight in them, Phil. ii. 13; Col. i. 9, 10; that God's good-will may return unto them, and he may reward them according to their works, chap. xi. 5, 6; while all is rendered by Jesus Christ, sprinkled with his blood, and perfumed with his incense, chap. x. 19—22. As they are to have all done through Christ, so through his merit and intercession the apostle begs all this from the Father for them. *To whom be glory for ever and ever ;* to this God the Father, in the Son, and by the Spirit, working all this good in them and for them, be really, truly, heartily, and perpetually, throughout all ages, ascribed the honour and glory due to him for the glorious manifestation of his perfections in them, Eph. iii. 21; Phil. iv. 20; 2 Pet. iii. 18; Rev. iv. 11; v. 13. The firm seal of this, from his believing heart, is his *Amen*, longing for the addition of God's *Amen*, so be it in heaven, to his on earth.

22 And I beseech you, brethren, suffer the word of exhortation: for ⁿI have written a letter unto you in few words.

ⁿ 1 Pet. 5. 12.

The apostle now drawing to a close, desires them candidly to accept his Epistle; that, considering their relation to him as Christians and Hebrews, he doth affectionately entreat them, that they would fully receive, entertain, and hold fast, as well as bear with, or suffer, all the doctrine, reproof, exhortation, and consolation, even his whole discourse to them in this Epistle, which *the word* implies. He had so comprised, summed up, and delivered the revelation of the doctrine of Christ, testified by Moses and the prophets, in a very few words, and sent them kindly and affectionately, in the form of an epistle or letter to them, that it might not be burdensome, either for its matter or length: though how weary are most professing Christians of the shortest heavenly discourse!

23 Know ye that ᵒ*our* brother Timothy ᵖis set at liberty; with whom, if he come shortly, I will see you.

ᵒ 1 Thes. 3 2.
ᵖ 1 Tim. 6. 12.

He acquaints them with the good news of his dismissing Timothy to them, to acquaint them how it fared with him, as he dismissed and sent Tychicus to the Colossians, Col. iv. 7, 8, Epaphroditus to the Philippians, Phil. ii. 25, 28, as he intended to have sent Timothy with them, ver. 19, 23, 24, but he stopped him to see the issue of his appearance before Nero Cæsar; which being over, he despatched him with an account of it to these Hebrews, and the rest of the churches, and signifieth his purpose, that if he quickly returns from them again, then he would visit them together with him. That the word ἀπολελυμένος noteth, or signifieth, the dismission of a person about business, is seen, Acts xiii. 3. To which interpretation the subscription of the Epistle inclines; and the Scripture is silent of any troubles or restraint of Timothy at all, Phil. ii. 19, 20.

24 Salute all them ᵩthat have the rule over you, and all the saints. They of Italy salute you.

ᵩ ver. 7, 17.

He sends his salutations, which were good wishes and prayers for the peace, prosperity, health, and happiness of their souls and bodies, and success in all their concernments; first unto their excellent guides and rulers, ver. 7, 17, that they may prosper and succeed in their work among the saints; and then unto *the saints* themselves, conveying the gospel peace, according to Christ's command, Matt. x. 12; Luke x. 5. Which *saints* were all those Hebrews dispersed in several places, and there convening, and maintaining church society; and to whose hand the Epistle first came, they were to receive the salutations themselves, and transmit them to others. With his own he transmits the salutations of all that part of the church of Christ which was in Italy to them. Which salutations, though commonly abused, yet are of great weight and worth where communicated and received by the churches in which the Holy Spirit abideth.

25 ʳGrace *be* with you all. Amen.

ʳ Tit. 3. 15.

He closeth all with his wonted gracious valediction, wherewith he shutteth up all his Epistles, as he testifieth, 2 Thess. iii. 17, 18. He, like an apostle influenced by the Divine Spirit, admiring *grace* vouchsafed to himself, and heartily and fervently wishing it down upon all to whom he writeth, even all the spiritual fruits of God's grace and love in Jesus Christ, from election to salvation. And he sealeth up his desire, prayer, and declaration of this, upon them *all* who were the true subjects of it, with his *Amen*. Even so let the whole earth be filled with the glory of thy grace, O Trinity of relations in Unity of essence, from henceforth and for ever. Amen.

¶ Written to the Hebrews from Italy by Timothy.

THE GENERAL EPISTLE

OF

J A M E S

THE ARGUMENT

THAT the authority of this Epistle hath been questioned by some anciently, appears plainly by Eusebius and Jerome, who speak suspiciously of it; and that it hath been denied by some more lately, is no less clear (to say nothing of Cajetan and Erasmus) in Luther, who (though in his after-writings he was more modest) at first spoke slightly of it; and some of his more early followers were of his mind. But as for the ancients, (admitting the two forementioned authors wrote their own sense, and not, as some think, and their words cited by Brochmand and others may well import, the opinion of other men,) why should not this Epistle, being unquestionably received by most of the fathers and primitive Christians before Eusebius or Jerome were born, and many councils, be more effectual to prove its being canonical, than the doubts of a few to persuade us to the contrary? What do we find in it disagreeable to the doctrine of the gospel, unbecoming the style of an apostle, or the Holy Ghost's inditing? Hath it not the same majesty, purity, spirituality, efficacy, and power on men's consciences, that other Scriptures have? To Cajetan and Erasmus we oppose the universality, not only of protestants, but of papists themselves; and to Luther all the modern Lutherans, who now generally receive it. That which drew Luther himself to reject it (to speak a little of that as being of weight) was, partly the seeming difference between James and Paul in the point of justification, which will be spoken to in the 2nd chapter; and partly his speaking nothing (though he wrote to Christians) of the death, or merits, or resurrection of Christ, &c. Whereas, indeed, though he is more sparing in handling evangelical doctrines, yet several he toucheth upon: what doth he mean but the gospel of Christ by *the ingrafted word*, chap. i. 21, and *law of liberty*, ver. 25? And who doth he understand by *the judge*, chap. v. 9, but Christ? and whose coming doth he speak of, ver. 7, but Christ's? And how expressly doth he mention *the faith of our Lord Jesus Christ!* chap. ii. 1. But the truth is, the persons for whom this Epistle seems designed, and the scope of the writer, call for such a way of writing, as here we have. He bends himself mainly against a licentious, sensual sort of professors, who boasted of the name of faith, but wanted the thing, and (being rather libertines than saints) blemished the Christian profession with unsuitable practice. These he takes upon him to correct, and evinceth their faith and religion (being barren of good works) to be vain. It was not therefore necessary he should so largely insist upon the doctrine of faith, when his chief design was to reform manners. Paul having many times to do with men of Pharisaical spirits, or such as were difficultly weaned from Judaism, and an opinion of self-righteousness, makes it his business to settle the doctrine of grace, and justification by faith; and why may not James, having to do with those who (probably, and as Austin thinks, misunderstanding Paul) abused the doctrine of grace, and turned it into an occasion of licentiousness, be allowed to tax that abuse, and insist the more fully on matters of practice, and press them to live up to their faith, and bring forth fruits answerable to that holy truth they had received? Remedies must be suited to diseases: there is as little need to urge a Solifidian to rely on grace of which he already presumes, as to persuade a Pharisee of the necessity of good works, upon which of himself he lays but too much stress.

But as the authority of this Epistle hath been questioned formerly, though with little reason, so the penman of it is still doubted of, perhaps with more. However, this question is less material; we need not be over-solicitous to know what amanuensis the Spirit of God made use of in penning it, so long as we find the impress of God upon it. It is certain that this James was not the son of Zebedee, whom Herod had beheaded (if chronology fail not) before the writing of this Epistle, Acts xii. 1. It is not certain that there were three Jameses, two of them apostles, and the third (called Oblias, and James the Just) one of the seventy disciples; the Scripture mentioning but two, one the son of Zebedee, the other of Alpheus, called *the brother of the Lord*, Gal. i. 19, as being of kin to his family; and said to be a *pillar*, Gal. ii. 9, and joined with Peter and John. And though some have thought the James there mentioned to have been the third James, called Oblias, and one of the seventy; yet it is more probable that he was indeed no other than the son of Alpheus, and one of the twelve: nor is it likely, that one of the disciples should be numbered as one of the three *pillars*, and therein preferred above so many apostles. This James, therefore, upon the whole, I take to be the penman of this Epistle; and his not calling himself an apostle, need not be objected against his being so, when he doth no more in omitting it than Paul doth in four of his Epistles, viz. to the Philippians, both to the Thessalonians, and that to Philemon.

Why this Epistle is called *general* is much questioned, and a satisfactory reason not easily given. Some think, because it is not inscribed to any particular church or person, as Paul's are. But then why are the two latter Epistles of John reckoned among the catholic or general ones, though directed to particular persons, and that to the Hebrews not counted among them, though it have no such particular inscription? Others think, that this and the six other were called catholic, upon their catholic or general reception and approbation among the churches, in opposition to the Epistles of Barnabas, Ignatius, Clemens, &c., which never were received as any part of the canon. These are the best reasons of this title I meet with; which is the more probable, let the reader judge.

The matter of this Epistle is, in a manner, wholly practical, but very various; though chiefly, either corrective of the vices and abuses which had crept into the conversations of professors; or monitory and hortatory, partly to awaken the drowsy among them out of their stupidness and security, and stir them up to the practice of their neglected duty, (to which he points them particularly, by minding them of approaching judgment,) and partly to persuade sincere and humble believers to patience under tribulations and oppressions, by propounding unto them suitable encouragements for their support and consolation in such a condition. Many excellent and useful truths are promiscuously laid down throughout the whole, which cannot easily be reduced to any certain method, but will be severally spoken to in the respective places where they occur.

CHAP. I

The apostle's address to the dispersed Jews, 1. He recommendeth patience and joy in afflictions, 2—4, and prayer with faith, 5—8. He giveth advice to the poor and to the rich, 9—11. The reward of those that are proof under trial, 12. Our own lusts, and not God, tempt us to sin, 13—16. God is the unchangeable author of all good to his creatures, 17, 18. We must receive the word with purity and meekness, and not only hear, but do it, 19—25. The necessity of governing the tongue, 26. The essential duties of true religion, 27.

ᵃJAMES, ᵇa servant of God and of the Lord Jesus Christ, ᶜto the twelve tribes ᵈwhich are scattered abroad, greeting.

James, the son of Alpheus and brother of Jude, called likewise *the brother of the Lord*, Gal. i. 19. *A servant;* not only by creation, as all the creatures are, Psal. cxix. 91, or by redemption, as all believers are, but by special commission in the office of an apostle; see Gal. i. 10; Phil. i. 1; 2 Pet. i. 1; compare likewise Rom. i. 9. *Of God and of the Lord Jesus Christ:* the members of this clause may be taken, either jointly, and then the conjunction *and* hath the power only of an explication, q. d. The servant of God, *even* the Lord Jesus Christ, as Tit. ii. 11; and the sense must be, the servant of Jesus Christ, who is God: or, separately, (which our translation seems to favour,) to let his countrymen know, that in serving Christ he served the God of his fathers; and by the authority both of God and of Christ wrote this to them. *To the twelve tribes which are scattered abroad:* being one of the apostles of the circumcision, Gal. ii. 9, he writes to all his believing countrymen wherever dispersed, as they were upon several occasions, and at several times, into divers countries, Acts ii. 9—11. *Greeting;* a salutation usual, not only among the heathen, but the Jews, Matt. xxvi. 49; xxvii. 29; and used by the Christians, Acts xv. 23. It seems to answer to the Hebrew salutation, *peace*, which was comprehensive of all happiness; and so is this here to be understood.

2 My brethren, ᶜcount it all joy ᶠwhen ye fall into divers temptations;

My brethren; both as being of the same nation and the same religion; so he calls them, that the kindness of his compellation might sweeten his exhortations. *Count it;* esteem it so by a spiritual judgment, though the flesh judge otherwise. *All joy;* matter of the chiefest joy, viz. spiritual. So *all* is taken, 1 Tim. i. 15. *When ye fall into;* when ye are so beset and circumvented by them, that there is no escaping them, but they come upon you, though by the direction of God's providence, yet not by your own seeking. *Divers temptations;* so he calls afflictions, from God's end in them, which is to try and discover what is in men, and whether they will cleave to him or not. The Jews were hated by other nations, and the Christian Jews even by their own, and therefore were exposed to divers afflictions, and of divers kinds, 1 Pet. i. 6.

3 ᵍKnowing *this*, that the trying of your faith worketh patience.

Knowing this; considering. *That the trying of your faith;* the reason why he called afflictions temptations, as well as why believers should count it all joy to fall into them, viz. because they are trials of their faith, and such trials as tend to approbation, as the word (different from that in the former verse) imports. *Of your faith;* both of the truth of the grace itself, and of your constancy in the profession of it. *Worketh patience;* not of itself, but as a means in the hand of God, made effectual to that end. *Object.* Rom. v. 3, it is said, *Tribulation worketh patience, and patience, experience,* or trial; whereas here it is said, that trial works patience. *Answ.* The words used here and Rom v. are different; here it is ἰοκίμιον, which signifies actively, the trying itself, and this works patience; there it is δοκιμὴ, which is taken passively, for the experiment following upon the trial; or, as we read it, the experience, viz. of our sincerity, as well as of God's consolation, which may well be the effect of patience wrought by and under trials. And so both are true, that tribulation, as Paul speaks, and trial, as James, work patience; and patience, not a further trial, but rather discovery, or experiment, or approbation of what we are, which appears by nothing more than by patience under sufferings.

JAMES I

4 But let patience have *her* perfect work, that ye may be perfect and entire, wanting nothing.

But let patience have her perfect work; i. e. effect: q. d. Let it have its full efficacy in you, both in making you absolutely subject to God's will, and constant to the end under all your sufferings. *That ye may be perfect and entire;* that you may grow perfect in this grace, as well as in others, and have the image of Christ (to whom ye are to be conformed) completed in you. *Wanting nothing;* either not failing, not fainting in trials, or not defective in any thing which is a needful part of Christianity.

h 1 Kings 3. 9, 11, 12.
Prov. 2. 3.
i Matt. 7. 7. & 21. 22.
Mark 11. 24.
Luke 11. 9.
John 14. 13. & 15. 7. & 16. 23. k Jer. 29. 12. 1 John 5. 14, 15.

5 [h]If any of you lack wisdom, [i]let him ask of God, that giveth to all *men* liberally, and upbraideth not; and [k]it shall be given him.

If any of you lack wisdom; if, doth not imply a doubt, but supposeth something which they themselves would grant; viz. that they did lack wisdom, either in whole or in part. It is as if he had said, Since, or seeing, ye lack, &c. See the like, Mal. i. 6. Though this hold true of wisdom taken more generally, yet wisdom here is to be restrained, according to the circumstances of the text, and taken for wisdom or skill to bear afflictions so as to rejoice in them. *Let him ask of God;* by believing, fervent prayer. *That giveth to all men;* either to all sorts of men, Jew or Gentile, bond or free, &c., or to all that so ask, as appears by the next verse. *Liberally;* or simply, Rom. xii. 8, i. e. with an open, free, large heart, in opposition to the contracted, narrow spirits of covetous misers. Our translation renders it well *liberally;* and so the word is used, 2 Cor. viii. 2; ix. 13. *And upbraideth not;* doth not twit them with their importunity, or frequency in asking, (as men often do,) however he may upbraid them with their unthankfulness for, or abuse of, what they have received. *And it shall be given him:* see Matt. vii. 7, 8; John xvi. 23. The promise is here added to encourage faith in asking.

l Mark 11. 24. 1 Tim. 2. 8.

6 [l]But let him ask in faith, nothing wavering. For he that wavereth is like a wave of the sea driven with the wind and tossed.

But let him ask in faith; with confidence of God's hearing, grounded on the Divine attributes and promises, Mark xi. 24; 1 John v. 14. *Nothing wavering;* either not disputing God's power or promise; or rather, not doubting, not staggering *through unbelief,* Rom. iv. 20, where the same Greek word is used: so Acts x. 20, *nothing doubting;* and Mark xi. 23, where it is opposed to believing. *For he that wavereth is like a wave of the sea driven with the wind and tossed:* this notes either the emptiness and unprofitableness of faithless prayer, when men's minds are thus at uncertainties, tossed to and fro; the confidence they sometimes seem to have, like waves, falls down and fails, and their prayers come to nothing: or, the disquiet and torment distrust works in the minds of such waverers, which are never settled till faith come and fix them, Isa. lvii. 20.

7 For let not that man think that he shall receive any thing of the Lord.

For let not that man; he that wavers, in opposition to him that asks in faith: all doubting doth not hinder the hearing of prayer, but that which excludes faith, Mark ix. 23, 24. *Think;* vainly conceit, or persuade himself. *That he shall receive any thing of the Lord;* even the least mercy, much less the wisdom mentioned.

m ch. 4. 8.

8 [m]A double minded man *is* unstable in all his ways.

A double minded man; either, 1. A hypocrite, who is said to have a double heart, Psal. xii. 2. Or rather, 2. He that is of a doubtful mind, wavering, and fluctuating with contrary motions, sometimes of one mind, sometimes of another; sometimes hoping, sometimes desponding. *Is unstable;* either unconstant, without any fixedness or consistency of spirit, as ready to depart from God as to cleave to him; or unquiet, troubled, full of inward tumults. *In all his ways;* by a Hebraism, *ways,* for counsels, purposes, actions, &c.

9 Let the brother of low degree ‖ rejoice in that he is exalted:

‖ Or, *glory.*

Let the brother; i. e. the believer, (for to such he writes,) all believers, or saints, being brethren in Christ, 1 Cor. xvi. 20; 1 Thess. v. 26; 1 Tim. vi. 2. *Of low degree;* the Greek word signifies both lowliness of mind and lowness of condition, (as the Hebrew word doth, to which it answers,) but here is to be understood of the latter, (as Luke i. 48,) but especially of such a low estate as a man is brought into for Christ's sake and the gospel's. *Rejoice in that he is exalted;* either exalted to be a brother, a member of Christ, a child of God, and heir of glory, which is the greatest preferment; or exalted to the honour of suffering for Christ: see Acts v. 41; Rom. v. 3.

10 But the rich, in that he is made low: because [n]as the flower of the grass he shall pass away.

n Job 14. 2. Ps. 37. 2. & 90. 5, 6. & 102. 11. & 103. 15. & 40. 6. Is. 1 Cor. 7. 31. ch. 4. 14. 1 Pet. 1. 24. 1 John 2. 17.

But the rich; viz. brother, he that is in a high, honourable, or plentiful condition in the world. *In that he is made low;* supply from the former verse, let him rejoice in that he is made low; not as to his outward state, (for he is supposed to be rich still,) but his inward disposition and frame of mind, God having given him a lowly heart in a high condition, and thereby prepared him for the cross, though as yet he be not under it. *Because as the flower of the grass he shall pass away:* the reason why the rich brother should be humble in his greatest abundance, viz. because of the uncertainty of his enjoying what at present he possesseth; he is neither secure of his life, nor his wealth; he and his enjoyments pass away, and his pomp vanisheth as easily as the flower of the grass, which fades as soon as it flourisheth.

11 For the sun is no sooner risen with a burning heat, but it withereth the grass, and the flower thereof falleth, and the grace of the fashion of it perisheth: so also shall the rich man fade away in his ways.

With a burning heat; or, the scorching east wind, which in those countries was wont to rise with the sun, Jonah iv. 8. *So also shall the rich man fade away;* either *shall* is here put for *may,* the future tense for the potential mood; and then the apostle doth not so much declare what always certainly shall be. as what easily may be, and frequently is, the prosperity of rich men not being always of so short continuance. Or, *shall* may be taken properly, as we read it; and then this is a general proposition, showing the mutable nature and short continuance of rich men and their riches, whose longest life is but short, and death, when it comes, strips them of their enjoyments: and though this frailty be common to all, yet he speaks of the rich especially, because they are so apt to bear themselves high upon their wealth, and put confidence in it, 1 Tim. vi. 17. *In his ways;* either in his journeyings and travels for his riches, or rather in his counsels, purposes, actions, Psal. cxlvi. 4.

12 [o]Blessed *is* the man that endureth temptation: for when he is tried, he shall receive [p]the crown of life, [q]which the Lord hath promised to them that love him.

o Job 5. 17. Prov. 3. 11. 12. Heb. 12. 5. Rev. 3. 19. p 1 Cor. 9. 25. 2 Tim. 4. 8. ch. 2. 5. 1 Pet. 5. 4. Rev. 2. 10. q Matt. 10. 22. & 19. 28, 29. ch. 2. 5.

Blessed is the man that endureth; holds out against the assaults and impressions of temptations with patience and constancy, chap. v. 11; Heb. xii. 5, 7. *Temptations;* afflictions, as ver. 2. *For when he is tried;* approved, and found upon the trial to be sound in the faith: a metaphor taken from metals tried by fire, and found pure. *He shall receive the crown of life;* so the heavenly glory is called, Rev. ii. 10, either because it is not to be had but in eternal life, or because of its duration and not fading away, 1 Pet. v. 4. *Which the Lord hath promised:* this shows on what ground it is to be expected, viz. on the account of the promise, and how sure we may be of it. *To them that love him;* i. e. all true believers, whose faith, and thereby title to the crown, is evidenced by love, which is the fulfilling of the law. *Object.* Why not promised to them that suffer for Christ, of whom he here speaks? *Answ.* That is implied, for none love him more, or evidence their love to him more, than they that suffer for him.

881

13 Let no man say when he is tempted, I am tempted of God: for God cannot be tempted with ‖ evil, neither tempteth he any man:

¹ Or, *evils.*

Let no man say; neither with his mouth, nor so much as in his heart, blasphemously cast the blame of his sins upon God, to clear himself. *When he is tempted;* so stirred up to sin as to be drawn to it. *I am tempted of God;* either solicited by God to sin, or enforced to it. *For God cannot be tempted with evil;* cannot be drawn aside to any thing that is unrighteous, by any motion from within, or impression from without. *Neither tempteth he any man;* doth no way seduce or enforce to sin, so as to be justly chargeable as the author of it. *Object.* God is said to be tempted, Exod. xvii. 2, 7; Deut. vi. 16; Psal. lxxviii. 41; and to tempt, Gen. xxii. 1; Deut. viii. 2; xiii. 3. *Answ.* Both are to be understood of temptations of exploration, or for the discovery of something that was before hidden. Men tempt God, that they may know what he will do; God tempts men, that they (not he, for he knows it already) may know what themselves will do, which then appears, when the temptation draws it out; but neither is to be understood of the temptation here spoken of, viz. of seduction, or drawing into sin. God tempts by giving hard commands, Gen. xxii. 1; by afflicting, as in Job's case; by letting loose Satan or other wicked instruments to tempt, 1 Kings xxii. 22; by withholding his grace and deserting men, 1 Sam. xxviii. 15; by presenting occasions which corruption within improves unto sin, and by ordering and governing the evil wills of men, as that a thief should steal out of this flock rather than that, that Nebuchadnezzar should come against Jerusalem rather than Rabbah, Ezek. xxi. 21, 22. But God doth not tempt by commanding, suggesting, soliciting, or persuading to sin.

14 But every man is tempted, when he is drawn away of his own lust, and enticed.

He shows the great cause of sin; that lust hath a greater hand in it than either the devil or his instruments, who cannot make us sin without ourselves: they sometimes tempt, and do not prevail; but when lust tempts, it always prevails, either in whole or in part, it being a degree of sin to be our own tempters. *Drawn away;* either this notes a degree of sin, the heart's being drawn off from God; or the way whereby lust brings into sin, viz. the impetuousness and violence of its motions in us. *Of his own lust;* original corruption in its whole latitude, though chiefly with respect to the appetitive faculties. *And enticed;* either a further degree of sin, *enticed* by the pleasantness of the object, as represented by our own corruption; or another way of lust's working in us to sin, viz. by the delightfulness and pleasure of its motions: in the former it works by a kind of force, in this by flattery and deceit. It is either a metaphor taken from a fish enticed by a bait, and drawn after it, or rather from a harlot drawing a young man out of the right way, and alluring him with the bait of pleasure to commit folly with her.

^r Job 15. 35. Ps. 7. 14.

15 Then ^r when lust hath conceived, it bringeth forth sin: and sin, when it is finished, ^s bringeth forth death.

^s Rom. 6. 21, 23.

Then when lust hath conceived; lust (compared to a harlot) may be said to conceive, when the heart is pleased with the motion, and yields some consent to it. *It bringeth forth sin;* the birth of sin may be the complete consent of the will to it, or the outward act of it. *And sin;* actual sin, the fruit and product of original. *When it is finished;* sin is finished, when it is not only committed, but continued in, as the way and course of a man's life. *Bringeth forth death;* not only temporal, but eternal. Or we may thus take the order and progress of sin: the first indeliberate motion of lust, is the temptation or bait, which by its pleasantness enticeth, and by its vehemency draws the heart after it (as the harlot, Prov. vii. 21, with the flattering of her lips forced the young man, telling him of the pleasure he should enjoy, ver. 14, 16—18, and then he goes after her, ver. 22); the heart's lingering about and being entangled with the delightful motion of lust, is its committing folly with it; when the full consent is joined, lust hath conceived; when the outward act is performed, sin is brought forth; and when sin is finished in a settled course, it brings forth death; which, though every sin do in the merit of it, yet sin only finished doth in the event. *Object.* Doth not this imply lust, and its first motions, not to be sin? *Answ.* No: for, 1. The least motions of it are forbidden, Matt. v. 28; Rom. vii. 7. 2. It is contrary to the law and Spirit of God, Rom. vii. 23, 25; Gal. v. 16, 17. 3. It is the fountain of impurity, and therefore is itself impure, Job xiv. 4; Matt. vii. 15, 16; James iii. 11. 4. Evil thoughts defile a man, Matt. xv. 19; Acts viii. 22. *Object.* How is lust said here to bring forth sin, when, Rom. vii. 8, sin is said to work lust? *Answ.* James calls the corrupt principle itself *lust,* and the actings of it, *sin;* whereas Paul calls the same principle *sin,* and the actings of it *lust.* And so both are true, lust, as a root, brings forth the acts of sin as its fruits; and sin as a root, brings forth actual lusts, as its fruits.

16 Do not err, my beloved brethren.

Viz. in imputing your sins to God, and saying, that when you are tempted you are tempted of him.

17 ^t Every good gift and every perfect gift is from above, and cometh down from the Father of lights, ^u with whom is no variableness, neither shadow of turning.

^t John 3. 27. 1 Cor. 4. 7.

^u Num. 23. 19. 1 Sam. 15. 29. Mal. 3. 6. Rom. 11. 29.

Every good gift; Greek, giving; and so it may be distinct from *gift* in the next clause; to show, that whereas men sometimes give good gifts in an evil way, and with an evil mind, God's giving, as well as gift, is always good; and therefore when we receive any thing of him, we should look not only to the thing itself, but to his bounty and goodness in giving it. Or, it may be rendered as our translators do, *gift,* and so the word is sometimes used by profane writers themselves; and then, though it may be implied, that all good gifts, and of all kinds, of nature and of grace, are from God, yet the apostle's design in this place being to prove that God is not the author of sin, *good gifts* may most fairly be understood the best gifts, those of grace, (spiritual blessings, Eph. i. 3,) such being contrary to sin, and destructive of it, in one of which he instanceth, viz. regeneration, ver. 18. *And every perfect gift;* the highest degree of good gifts, those that perfect us most; to intimate, that all the parts and steps of spiritual life, from the first beginning of grace in regeneration to the consummation of it in glory, are of God. *Is from above;* i. e. from heaven, John iii. 27, 31; and heaven is put for God that dwells there, Luke xv. 21. *And cometh down from the Father;* the Creator, Author, or First Cause, as Heb. xii. 9; it is spoken after the manner of the Hebrews: see Gen. iv. 20, 21. *Of lights;* God is the author of all perfection, and so of corporeal light; but here we are to understand spiritual light, the light of knowledge, faith, holiness, as opposed to the darkness of ignorance, unbelief, sin; of which he cannot be the author. *With whom is no variableness, neither shadow of turning:* he here sets forth God as essentially and immutably good, and the Father of lights, by allusion to the sun, the fountain of corporeal light, and makes use of terms borrowed from astronomy. The sun, though it scattereth its beams every where, yet is not without its changes, parallaxes, and diversities of aspects, not only sometimes clear and sometimes eclipsed, but one while in the east, another in the south, then in the west; nor without its turnings in its annual course from tropic to tropic, (to which the Greek word here used seems to allude,) its various accesses and recesses, by reason of which it casts different shadows: but God is always the same, like himself, constant in the emanations of his goodness, without casting any dark shadow of evil, which might infer a change in him.

18 ^x Of his own will begat he us with the word of truth, ^y that we should be a kind of ^z firstfruits of his creatures.

^x John 1. 13. & 3. 3. 1 Cor. 4. 1^s. 1 Pet. i. 23. ^y Eph. 1. 12. ^z Jer. 2. 3. Rev. 14. 4.

Of his own will; out of his mere good pleasure, as the original cause, and not moved to it by any dignity or merit in us, Eph. i. 9; 2 Tim. i. 9. *Begat he us;* by a spiritual generation, whereby we are new-born, and are made partakers of a Divine nature, John i. 13; 1 Pet. i. 3, 23. *With the word of truth;* i. e. the word of the gospel, as the instrument or means whereby we are regenerated: why it is called *the word of truth*, see Eph. i. 13. *That we should be a kind of first-fruits*; i. e. most excellent creatures, being singled out and separated from the rest, and consecrated to God, as under the law the first-fruits were, Rev. xiv. 4. *Of his creatures*; viz. reasonable creatures; the word creature being elsewhere restrained to men: see Mark xvi. 15; Col. i. 15.

a Eccles.5.1.
b Prov. 10. 19. & 17. 27. Eccles. 5. 2.
c Prov. 14. 17. & 16. 32. Eccles. 7. 9.

19 Wherefore, my beloved brethren, ᵃ let every man be swift to hear, ᵇ slow to speak, ᶜ slow to wrath:

Let every man be swift to hear; prompt and ready to hear God speaking in *the word of truth*, before mentioned. *Slow to speak*; either silently and submissively hear the word, or speak not rashly and precipitately of the things of faith, but be well furnished yourselves with spiritual knowledge, ere you take upon you to teach others. *Slow to wrath*; either, be not angry at the word, or the dispensers of it, though it come close to your consciences, and discover your secret sins; the word is salt, do not quarrel if it make your sores smart, being it will keep them from festering: or, be not angrily prejudiced against those that dissent from you.

20 For the wrath of man worketh not the righteousness of God.

For the wrath of man: that anger which is merely human, and generally sinful, inordinate passion and carnal zeal. *Worketh not the righteousness of God;* will not accomplish the ends of the word in you, viz. to work that righteousness which in the word God prescribes you. But here is withal a meiosis in the words, less being spoken than is intended; it is implied therefore, that the wrath of man hinders the operation of the word, and disposeth to that unrighteousness which is forbidden by it.

d Col. 3. 8.
1 Pet. 2. 1.
e Acts 13.26. Rom. 1. 16. 1 Cor. 15. 2. Eph. 1. 13. Tit. 2. 11. Heb. 2. 3. 1 Pet. 1. 9.

21 Wherefore ᵈ lay apart all filthiness and superfluity of naughtiness, and receive with meekness the engrafted word, ᵉ which is able to save your souls.

Wherefore lay apart; not only restrain it, and keep it in; but put off, and throw it away as a filthy rag, Isa. xxx. 22: see Eph. iv. 22; Col. iii. 8; 1 Pet. ii. 1. *All*, of every kind. *Filthiness*; or, sordidness; a metaphor borrowed from the filth of the body, 1 Pet. iii. 21, and thence transferred to the soul; and it here seems to imply, not only sensuality or covetousness, but all sorts of lusts, whereby men are defiled, 2 Cor. vii. 1; 2 Pet. ii. 20. *And superfluity of naughtiness;* i. e. that naughtiness which is superfluous. That is said to be superfluous or redundant, which is more than should be in a thing; in which respect all sin is superfluous in the soul, as being that which should not be in it: and so this intimates that we are not only to lay apart more gross pollutions, but all the lusts of the flesh, and relics of old Adam, as being all superfluities which may well be spared, or excrements, (as some render the word, agreeably to the former metaphor,) which should be cast away. *And receive;* not only into your heads by knowledge, but into your hearts by faith. *With meekness;* with humility, modesty, and gentleness, which makes men submissive to the truth of the word, and ready to learn of God even those things which are above their natural capacity, Psal. xxv. 9; Isa. lxvi. 2; Matt. xi. 5, 27: this is opposed to wrath, which makes men unteachable. *The ingrafted word;* either which is ingrafted or implanted, viz. ministerially, by the preachers of the gospel, 1 Cor. iii. 6, 7; principally by the Spirit of God, who writes it in the heart, Jer. xxxi. 33. And thus it may be taken particularly for the word of the gospel, in opposition to the law, which came to men's ears from without, and admonished them of their duty, but was not written in their hearts, or ingrafted thereto from them unto obedience to it. Or, that it may be ingrafted, i. e. intimately united to, or rooted in, the heart by a vital union; or made natural to it, (as some render the word,) the heart being transformed by the power of it, and conformed to the precepts of it, 2 Cor. iii. 18; Rom. vi. 17. *Which,* viz. when received by faith, *is able to save*, instrumentally, as being the means wherein God puts forth his power in saving them, Rom. i. 16. *Your souls;* yourselves; the soul, as the noblest part, is by a synecdoche put for the whole person: see 1 Pet. i. 9.

22 But ᶠ be ye doers of the word, and not hearers only, deceiving your own selves.

f Matt. 7.21. Luke 6. 46. & 11. 28. Rom. 2. 13. 1 John 3. 7.

But be ye doers of the word; the same as doers of *the work*, ver. 25, namely, which the word prescribes; q. d. Receive the word by faith into your hearts, and bring forth the fruit of it in your lives: see Luke xi. 28; John xiii. 17. *And not hearers only;* not contenting yourselves with a bare hearing the word, though it have no influence upon you. *Deceiving your own selves;* playing the sophisters with, or putting a fallacy upon, yourselves; particularly, persuading yourselves into a good opinion of your state, merely because of your being hearers of the word, Matt. vii. 21.

23 For ᵍ if any be a hearer of the word, and not a doer, he is like unto a man beholding his natural face in a glass:

g Luke 6.47, &c. See ch. 2. 14, &c.

He is like unto a man: the Greek word here used, properly signifies the sex, not the species, but is indifferently used by this apostle with the other, as ver. 12, and 20, so that by a man looking at his face in a glass, is meant any man or woman. *Beholding his natural face;* or, the face of his nativity, by a Hebraism, for natural face, as we translate it; i. e. his own face, that which nature gave him, or he was born with. *In a glass;* the word is here compared to a looking-glass: as the glass represents to us the features and complexions of our faces, whether beautiful or deformed; so the word shows us the true face of our souls, the beauty of God's image when restored to them, and the spots of sin which so greatly disfigure them.

24 For he beholdeth himself, and goeth his way, and straightway forgetteth what manner of man he was.

The remembrance of what his face is vanisheth as soon as his eye is off the glass; he remembers not the spots he saw in his face, to wipe them off. So he that sees the blemishes of his soul in the glass of the word, and doth not remember them to do them away, looks in that glass (i. e. hears the word) in vain.

25 But ʰ whoso looketh into the perfect ⁱ law of liberty, and continueth *therein*, he being not a forgetful hearer, but a doer of the work, ᵏ this man shall be blessed in his ‖ deed.

h 2 Cor. 3. 18.
i ch. 2. 12.
k John 13. 17.
‖ Or, *doing*.

But whoso looketh into; viz. intently and earnestly, searching diligently into the mind of God. The word signifies a bowing down of the head to look into a thing; and is used of the disciples' looking into Christ's sepulchre, Luke xxiv. 12; John xx. 5; see 1 Pet. i. 12; and seems to be opposed to looking into a glass, which is more slight, and without such prying and inquisitiveness. *The perfect law of liberty;* the whole doctrine of the Scripture, or especially the gospel, called a *law*, Rom. iii. 27, both as it is a rule, and by reason of the power it hath over the heart; and a *law of liberty*, because it shows the way to the best liberty, freedom from sin, the bondage of the ceremonial law, the rigour of the moral, and from the wrath of God; and likewise the way of serving God freely and ingenuously as children; and because, being received into the heart, it is accompanied with the Spirit of adoption who works this liberty, 2 Cor. iii. 17. It is called a perfect law, not only as being entire and without any defect, but as directing us to the greatest perfection, full conformity to God, and enjoyment of him, 2 Tim. iii. 16, 17. *And continueth therein;* perseveres in the study, belief, and obedience of this doctrine, (Psal. i. 2,) in all conditions, and under all temptations and afflictions. This seems to be opposed to him, who, when he hath looked in a glass, goes away, ver. 24. By which are set forth slight, superficial hearers, who do not continue in Christ's word, John viii. 31. *He being not a forgetful hearer;* Greek, hearer of forgetfulness, by a Hebraism, for a forgetful hearer; it answers to him in the former verse, that *forgetteth what manner of man he was;* and implies, not only not remembering the truths we have heard, but a not practising them, as appears by the next clause. *But a doer of the work;* viz. which the word directs him to do: the singular number is put for the plural; he means, he that reduceth what he hears into practice, Psal. ciii. 18. *This man shall be blessed in his deed;* this is opposed to bare hearing, and the doer of the work is said to be blessed in or by his deed, as the evidence of his present begun blessedness, and the way to his future perfect happiness.

26 If any man among you seem to be religious, and ¹bridleth not his tongue, but deceiveth his own heart, this man's religion *is* vain.

<small>l Ps. 34. 13. & 39. 1.
1 Pet. 3. 10.</small>

If any man among you seem to be religious; seems to others, or rather to himself; thinks himself religious, because of his hearing and outward worship : thus the word rendered *seems* is often taken, 1 Cor. iii. 18; viii. 2; xiv. 37; Gal. vi. 3. Here he shows who are not doers of the work, as in the next verse, who are. *And bridleth not his tongue;* restrains it not from the common vices of the tongue, reviling, railing, censuring, &c. *But deceiveth his own heart;* either deceiveth his own heart in thinking himself religious, when indulging himself in things so contrary to religion, or deceiveth his own heart, being blinded with self-love, and lifted up with self-conceit, which is the cause of his censuring and speaking evil of others. *This man's religion is vain;* empty, and to no purpose, having no reality in itself, and bringing no benefit to him.

27 Pure religion and undefiled before God and the Father is this, ᵐTo visit the fatherless and widows in their affliction, ⁿ*and* to keep himself unspotted from the world.

<small>m Is. 1. 16, 17. & 58. 6, 7.
Matt. 25. 36.

n Rom. 12. 2. ch. 4. 4.
1 John 5. 18.</small>

Pure religion; true, sincere, genuine, Matt. v. 8; John xv. 3. *And undefiled;* this seems to reflect upon the hypocritical Jews, whose religion consisted so much in external observances, and keeping themselves from ceremonial defilements, when yet they were sullied with so many moral ones, ver. 14; Matt. xxiii. 23; John xviii. 28; devoured widows' houses. They thought their religion pure and undefiled; the apostle shows here which is really so *before God;* in the sight of God, and according to his judgment. *God and the Father;* i. e. God who is the Father, *and* being only explicative, as Eph. i. 3; v. 20 : yet this title may be given here to God with respect to what follows, and to show that such acts of charity are acceptable to him that is called *the Judge of widows, and the Father of the fatherless,* Psal. lxviii. 5. *To visit;* this includes all other acts of charity to them, comforting, counselling, relieving them, &c. *The fatherless and widows;* he doth not exclude others from being the objects of our charity and compassion, but instanceth in *fatherless and widows,* as being usually most miserable, because destitute of those relations which might be most helpful to them; and possibly in those times persecution might increase the number of widows and orphans. *In their affliction;* when they had most need; lest any should think it sufficient to visit them that were rich, or in a prosperous condition. *And to keep himself unspotted from the world;* untainted by the evil example of men in the world, and free from the lusts of the world, moral pollutions. The apostle doth not here define religion, but only instanceth in these two things, good works and holiness of conversation, as testimonies and arguments of the truth of it.

CHAP. II

It is not agreeable to the Christian profession to regard the rich, and despise the poor, 1—9. *The guilt of any one breach of the law,* 10—12. *The obligation to mercy,* 13. *Faith without works is dead,* 14—19. *We are justified, as Abraham and Rahab were, by works, and not by faith only,* 20—26.

MY brethren, have not the faith of our Lord Jesus Christ, ᵃ*the Lord* of glory, with ᵇrespect of persons.

<small>a 1 Cor. 2. 8.
b Lev. 19 15.
Deut. 1. 17.
& 16 19.
Prov. 24. 23.
& 28. 21.
Matt. 22. 16. ver. 9. Jude 16.</small>

Have not; profess not yourselves, and regard not, or esteem not in others. *The faith of our Lord Jesus Christ;* i. e. faith in our Lord Jesus Christ; not the author but the object of faith is meant, as Gal. ii. 20; iii. 22; Phil. iii. 9. *The Lord of glory; Lord* not being in the Greek, *glory* may be joined with *faith,* (admitting only a trajection in the words, so frequent in the sacred writers,) and then the words will run thus, the faith of the glory of our Lord Jesus Christ, i. e. the faith of his being glorified, which by a synecdoche may be put for the whole work of redemption wrought by him, which was completed by his glorification, as the last part of it; or, by a Hebraism, the faith of the glory, may be for the glorious faith. But the plainest way of reading the words is (as our translators do) by supplying the word *Lord* just before mentioned; *Lord of glory,* (Christ being elsewhere so called, 1 Cor. ii. 8,) i. e. the glorious Lord; as the Father is called *the Father of glory,* Eph. i. 17, i. e. the glorious Father : and then it may be an argument to second what the apostle is speaking of; Christ being the Lord of glory, a relation to him by faith puts an honour upon believers, though poor and despicable in the world; and therefore they are not to be contemned. *With respect of persons;* the word rendered *persons* signifies the face or countenance, and synecdochically the whole person; and, by consequence, all those parts or qualities we take notice of in the person. To respect a person is sometimes taken in a good sense, Gen. xix. 21; 1 Sam. xxv. 35. Mostly in an evil, when either the person is opposed to the cause, we give more or less to a man upon the account of something we see in him which is altogether foreign to his cause, Lev. xix. 15, or when we accept one with injury to or contempt of another. To have, then, the faith of Christ with respect of persons, is to esteem the professors of religion, not for their faith, or relation to Christ, but according to their worldly condition, their being great or mean, rich or poor; this the apostle taxeth in the Hebrews to whom he wrote, that whereas in the things of God all believers are equal, they respected the greater and richer sort of professors, because great or rich; so as to despise those that were poor or low. The Greek hath the word plurally, respects, which may intimate the several ways of respecting persons, in judgment or out of judgment. This doth not exclude the civil respect we owe to magistrates and superiors upon the account of their places or gifts; but only a respecting men in the things of religion upon such accounts as are extrinsical to religion; or, with prejudice to others as considerable in religion as themselves, though inferior to them in the world.

2 For if there come unto your †assembly a man with a gold ring, in goodly apparel, and there come in also a poor man in vile raiment;

<small>† Gr. *synagogue.*</small>

For if there come unto your assembly; either church assemblies for worship, Heb. x. 25; and in these we find some respect of men's persons, which may here be blamed: see 1 Cor. xi. 20—22. Or their assemblies for disposing church offices, and deciding church controversies, &c.; for he speaks of such respecting men's persons as is condemned by the law, ver. 9, which was especially in judgment. *A man with a gold ring, in goodly apparel;* the usual ensigns of honourable or rich persons, Gen. xxxviii. 18, 25; xli. 42; Luke xv. 22; xvi. 19. *And there come in also a poor man;* the word signifies one very poor, even to beggarliness. *In vile raiment;* filthy and sordid, Zech. iii. 3, 4, the sign of extreme poverty.

3 And ye have respect to him that weareth the gay clothing, and say unto him, Sit thou here ∥ in a good place; and say to the poor, Stand thou there, or sit here under my footstool :

<small>∥ Or, *well,* or, *seemly.*</small>

And ye have respect to him; Greek, look upon, viz. with respect and veneration, or a care and concern to please him. *Sit thou here in a good place;* an honourable place, either contrary to the usual orders of the churches, according to which (as some say) the elder sat in chairs, the next to them on benches; and the novices on the pavement at their feet; the apostle taxing their carnal partiality in disposing these places to the people as rich, not as Christians;

or it may note their disposing church offices to them that were rich, or favouring them in their causes rather than the poor. *Stand thou there, or sit here under my footstool;* the meanest places, and belonging to the youngest disciples: both are expressions of contempt.

4 Are ye not then partial in yourselves, and are become judges of evil thoughts?

Are ye not then partial in yourselves? either, are ye not judged in yourselves, convicted by your own consciences of partiality, and accepting men's persons? or, have ye not made a difference? viz. out of a corrupt affection rather than a right judgment; and then it falls in with our translation, *Are ye not partial?* the Greek word is used in this sense, Acts xv. 9; Jude 22. *And are become judges of evil thoughts;* i. e. judges that have evil thoughts, or are evil affected: q. d. You evidence the corruptness of your affections by your thus perversely judging.

c John 7. 48.
1 Cor. 1. 26, 28.
d Luke 12. 21. 1 Tim. 6. 18. Rev. 2. 9.
‖ Or, *that.*
e Ex. 20. 6.
1 Sam. 2. 30.
Prov. 8. 17.
Matt. 5. 3. Luke 6. 20. & 12. 32. 1 Cor. 2. 9. 2 Tim. 4. 8. ch. 1. 12.

5 Hearken, my beloved brethren, ᶜHath not God chosen the poor of this world ᵈrich in faith, and heirs of ‖the kingdom ᵉ which he hath promised to them that love him?

Hath not God chosen the poor? not that God hath chosen all the poor in the world, but his choice is chiefly of them, 1 Cor. i. 26, 28. Poor he means in the things *of this world,* and in the esteem of worldly men; they are opposed to those that Paul calls *rich in this world,* 1 Tim. vi. 17, 18. *Rich:* some insert the verb substantive to be between this and the former clause, and read, Hath not God chosen the poor of this world to be rich, &c. So Rom. viii. 29, *predestinate to be conformed:* the like defective speeches we find, John xii. 46; 2 Cor. iii. 6. And the verb understood here is expressed, Eph. i. 4, after the same word we have in this text. And yet it we read the words as they stand in our translation, they do not prove that foresight of faith is previous to election, any more than that being heirs of the kingdom is so too. *In faith;* either in the greatness and abundance of their faith, Matt. xv. 28; Rom. iv. 20; or rather, rich in those privileges and hopes to which by faith they have a title. *And heirs of the kingdom;* an instance of their being rich, in that they are to inherit a kingdom. *Which he hath promised to them that love him:* see chap. i. 12, where the same words occur, only that which is here a kingdom, is there a crown.

f 1 Cor. 11. 22.
g Acts 13. 50. & 17. 6. & 18. 12. ch. 5. 6.

6 But ᶠye have despised the poor. Do not rich men oppress you, ᵍand draw you before the judgment seats?

But ye have despised the poor; God's poor, viz. by your respecting persons. *Do not rich men?* either those that were unbelieving Jews or heathen; or such as made a profession of Christianity, but were not cordial friends to it; or, both may be included. *Oppress you;* insolently abuse you, and unrighteously, either usurping a power over you which belongs not to them, or abusing the power they have. *And draw you before the judgment-seats;* especially before unbelieving judges, 1 Cor. vi. 1, 6: they would colour their oppression with a pretence of law, and therefore drew the poor saints before the judgment-seat.

7 Do not they blaspheme that worthy name by the which ye are called?

Do not they blaspheme? if the rich here spoken of were Christians, then they may be said to blaspheme Christ's name, when by their wicked carriage they caused it to be blasphemed by others, unbelievers, among whom they were, Rom. ii. 24; Tit. ii. 5, &c.; 1 Tim. vi. 1: but if rich unbelievers be here meant, the rich men of those times being generally great enemies to Christianity; he would from thence show how mean a consideration riches were, to incline the professors of religion to such partiality as he taxeth them for. *That worthy name;* or, good or honourable (as good place, ver. 3, for honourable) name of Christ; they blaspheme what they should adore. *By the which ye are called;* or, which is called upon you, either, which was called upon over you, when you were baptized into it; or rather it is a Hebrew phrase, and implies no more than (as we read it) their being called by it, as children are after their fathers, and wives after their husbands, Gen. xlviii. 16; Isa. iv. 1; for so God's people are called by his name, Deut. xxviii. 10; Eph. iii. 15.

8 If ye fulfil the royal law according to the Scripture, ʰThou shalt love thy neighbour as thyself, ye do well:

h Lev. 19. 18. Matt. 22. 39. Rom. 13. 8, 9. Gal. 5. 14. & 6. 2.

If ye fulfil; or, perfect; the word signifies to accomplish perfectly, but no more is meant by it than sincerity in observing the duties of the law in an indifferent respect to one as well as another, which he seems to oppose to their partiality in the law, by respecting some and neglecting others. *The royal law;* either the law of God the great King, or Christ the King of saints; or rather, *the royal law* is the king's law, i. e. the great law which is the same to all, rich and poor, the common rule by which all are to act, as, *the king's way,* Numb. xxi. 22, i. e. the great plain way in which all are to travel. Here may likewise be a tacit reflection on the servile disposition of these accepters of men's persons, evil becoming them that pretended to be governed by the royal law, which was to be observed with a more free and king-like spirit. *According to the Scripture:* see Matt. xxii. 39; Gal. v. 14. *Ye do well;* ye are not to be blamed, but commended. The apostle seems here to answer an objection they might make in their own defence; that in the respect they gave to rich men, they did but act according to the law which commands us to love our neighbour as ourselves: to this he replies partly in this verse by way of concession, or on supposition; that if the respect they gave to rich men were indeed in obedience to the law of charity, which commands us to love our neighbour as ourselves, then they did well, and he found no fault with them; but the contrary he shows in the next verse.

9 But ⁱif ye have respect to persons, ye commit sin, and are convinced of the law as transgressors.

i ver. 1.

But if ye have respect to persons, ye commit sin; the second part of the apostle's answer, in which he sets *persons* in opposition to *neighbour:* q. d. If you, instead of loving your neighbour, which excludes no sort of men, poor no more than rich, choose and single out (as ye do) only some few (viz. rich men) to whom ye give respect, despising others, ye are so far from fulfilling the royal law, that ye sin against it. *And are convinced of the law;* either by the particular law against respecting persons, Lev. xix. 15, or rather, by that very law you urge; your thus partially respecting the rich to the excluding of the poor, being so contrary to the command of loving your neighbour, which excludes none. *As transgressors;* i. e. to be transgressors, viz. of the whole law, as follows.

10 For whosoever shall keep the whole law, and yet offend in one *point,* ᵏhe is guilty of all.

k Deut. 27. 26. Matt. 5. 19. Gal. 3. 10.

For whosoever shall keep: this is not an assertion, that any man doth keep the whole law so as to offend but in one point, but a supposition that if, or admitting, such a one were. *The whole law;* all the rest of the law, that one point only of the whole being excepted. *And yet offend in one point;* slip, or trip, or stumble at; it seems to signify the least failing in any point of the law. *He is guilty of all;* guilty of the breach, and obnoxious to the punishment, of all; not distributively, or separately, as if he transgressed every precept distinctly; but, 1. Conjunctively or copulatively; he is guilty of not keeping the whole law, though not of breaking each particular command; he breaks the whole law, though not the whole of the law: as he that wounds a man's arm wounds the whole man, though not the whole of the man; he that breaks one link breaks the whole chain, and he that fails in one musical note spoils the whole harmony. 2. He sins against charity, which is the sum of the law, and upon which all the commands depend; and so though he keep most of them, as to the substance, yet he keeps none of them in a right manner, because none out of love, which should be the principle out of which he observes all of them. 3. He sins against the authority of the whole law, which is the same in every command. 4. He is liable to the same punishment, though not the same degree of it, as if he had broken all the commandments, Gal. iii. 1; and his keeping most, cannot exempt him from the punishment due for the breach of that one. This he speaks either in opposition to the Pharisees among the Jews, who thought themselves righteous if they kept most of the law, though in some things they came short; or rather, against hypocrites among Christians, who would pick and choose duties, obey some commands and neglect others; whereas no obedience to God is right, but that which is impartial, and respects all the commands, Psal. cxix. 6; Matt. v. 19.

|| Or, that law which said.
1 Ex. 20. 13, 14.

11 For || he that said, [1]Do not commit adultery, said also, Do not kill. Now if thou commit no adultery, yet if thou kill, thou art become a transgressor of the law.

All proof of what he laid down in the former verse, by instancing in these two commands, there being the same reason of all the rest, the same sovereignty and righteousness of God appearing in them, and it being the will of God to try our obedience in one as well as another. *Thou art become a transgressor of the law;* viz. by contemning the authority and holiness of God, which appears in the whole law, and every command of it.

m ch. 1. 25.

12 So speak ye, and so do, as they that shall be judged by [m]the law of liberty.

So speak ye, and so do: the apostle concluding his discourse about respecting persons, which consisted both in their words and actions, he directs them how to govern themselves in both. *As they that shall be judged;* viz. for both your words and actions, and that, not only in your own consciences at present, but at God's tribunal hereafter. *By the law of liberty;* the gospel, of the liberty of which it is one branch, that these differences among men, of Jew and Gentile, bond and free, circumcised and uncircumcised, &c., are taken away, Acts x. 28; Gal. iii. 28; Col. iii. 11; against this law of liberty sin if you respect persons, and then may well fear to be judged by it; as it takes away differences of persons now, so it will make none at last, but will be as impartial in its judgment as it is in its commands.

n Job 22. 6, &c. Prov.21. 13. Matt. 6. 15. & 18. 35. & 25. 41, 42. o 1 John 4. 17, 18. || Or, glorieth.

13 For [n]he shall have judgment without mercy, that hath shewed no mercy; and [o] mercy ||rejoiceth against judgment.

For he shall have judgment without mercy; shall be judged according to the rigour of the law, by pure justice without any mixture of mercy. *That hath showed no mercy;* that hath been cruel and unmerciful to his neighbour here. *And mercy rejoiceth against judgment;* either, 1. The mercy of God rejoiceth and glorieth over judgment, being as it were superior and victorious in relation to those that show mercy, to whom the promise of obtaining mercy is made, Matt. v. 7. Or rather, 2. The mercy of men, i. e. of those that deal mercifully with others; their mercy having the mercy and promise of God on its side, need not fear, but rather may rejoice, and as it were glory against judgment, as not being like to go against them. *Object.* Is not this to make some ground of glorying to be in men themselves, contrary to Psal. cxliii. 2; Rom. iv. 2? *Answ.* Mercy in believers is an evidence of their interest in God's mercy, which prevails on their belief against his justice; and so its rejoicing against judgment, is not against it as overcome by itself, but by God's mercy. Thus both senses are included.

p Mat. 7. 26. ch. 1. 23.

14 [p]What *doth it* profit, my brethren, though a man say he hath faith, and have not works? can faith save him?

What doth it profit; viz. as to his eternal salvation? wherein are the ends of religion promoted by it? The apostle had just before declared, that they who are unmerciful to men shall find God severe to themselves, and have judgment without mercy: but hypocritical professors boasted of their faith as sufficient to secure them against that judgment, though they neglected the practice of holiness and righteousness. Hence he seems to take occasion for the following discourse, to beat down their vain boasting of an empty, unfruitful faith, and possibly, lest they should abuse or misunderstand what he had said about *the law of liberty,* as if that inferred a licence of sinning, and living as they pleased. *Though a man say;* whether boastingly with his mouth to others, or flatteringly in his heart to himself. The apostle doth not say, that a man's having faith simply is unprofitable, but either that faith he pretends to without works, or his boasting he hath faith, when the contrary is evident by his not having works. *He hath faith;* such as he pretends to be good, and sound, and saving, but is really empty and dead, ver. 26, and unfruitful. *And have not works;* i. e. good works, such as are not only acts of charity, to which the papists would restrain it, but all the fruits of righteousness and holiness proceeding from faith, and appearing both in heart and life. *Can faith save him?* the interrogation is a vehement negation; q. d. It cannot save him, viz. such a faith as a man may have (as well as boast he hath) without works. This James calls *faith* only by way of concession for the present, though it be but equivocally called faith, and no more really so, than the carcass of a man is a man.

q See Job 31. 19, 20. Luke 3. 11.

15 [q]If a brother or sister be naked, and destitute of daily food,

If a brother or sister; a Christian man or woman, who are frequently thus called: see 1 Cor. vii. 12, 15. *Be naked;* badly clothed, or destitute of such clothing as is fit for them, Job xxii. 6; 1 Cor. iv. 11. *And destitute of daily food:* see Matt. vi. 11; that which is necessary for the sustaining of life a day to an end. Under these two of nakedness and hunger, he comprehends all the calamities of human life, which may be relieved by the help of others; as food and raiment contain all the ordinary supports and comforts of life, Gen. xxviii. 20; Matt. vi. 25; 1 Tim. vi. 8.

r 1 John 3. 18.

16 And [r]one of you say unto them, Depart in peace, be *ye* warmed and filled; notwithstanding ye give them not those things which are needful to the body; what *doth it* profit?

Depart in peace; a usual form of salutation, wherein, under the name of peace, they wished all prosperity and happiness to them they greeted, Mark v. 34; Luke vii. 50; viii. 48. *Be ye warmed;* i. e. be ye clothed; the warmth here mentioned being such as is procured by clothes, Job xxxi. 20. *And be ye filled,* or, satisfied with food; a metaphor from the fatting of cattle with grass or hay. The same word is used, Matt. xiv. 20; Mark vi. 42; Phil. iv. 12. These two good wishes answer the two former great wants. *Notwithstanding ye give them not those things which are needful to the body;* understand, when yet ye are able to relieve them; for he speaks to the rich, or such as were in a capacity of being helpful to others. *What doth it profit?* either, what do your good words and charitable wishes profit them, without charitable deeds? or, what do they profit yourselves? or both may be included: as your fair speeches convey no real good to them, so they bring in no reward to you from God.

† Gr. by itself.

17 Even so faith, if it hath not works, is dead, being †alone.

Even so faith; that which they boasted of, and called faith. *Is dead;* void of that life, in which the very essence of faith consists, and which always discovers itself in vital actings and good fruits, where it is not hindered by some forcible impediment; in allusion to a corpse, which plainly appears to have no vital principle in it, all vital operations being ceased. It resembles a man's body, and is called so, but in reality is not so, but a dead carcass. *Being alone;* margin, by itself, or in itself; be it what it will, it is but dead: or, as we render it, *being alone,* i. e. not in conjunction with works, which always it should be.

|| Some copies read, by thy works. s ch. 3. 13.

18 Yea, a man may say, Thou hast faith, and I have works: shew me thy faith || without thy works, [s]and I will shew thee my faith by my works.

A man; any true believer. *May say;* to any such boasting hypocrite. *Thou hast faith;* thou pretendest to have faith, or admit thou hast faith; an historical faith he might have, as ver. 19. *And I have works:* I do not boast of my faith; or, to say nothing of my faith, yet works

I do profess to have. *Show me thy faith without thy works:* there are two readings of these words, but in both the sense agrees with the rest of the apostle's discourse. If we take the marginal reading, show me thy faith by thy works, the sense is, evidence the faith thou pretendest to by thy works, as the fruits of it; let thy actions vouch for thy profession. But if we take the reading in the text, *without thy works*, it is a kind of ironical expression; q. d. Make it appear by convincing arguments that thou hast true faith, when yet thou wantest works, the only argument of the truth of it. Understand here, but this thou canst not. *And I will show thee my faith by my works;* I will easily prove my faith to be true and genuine, by those good works it brings forth in me. Demonstrate the cause to me without the effect, if thou canst; but I will easily demonstrate the cause by the effect, and prove the root of faith to be in me, by my bringing forth that fruit which is proper to it. It cannot hence be inferred, that wherever such works are, as men count and call good, there must needs be faith: the apostle's meaning only is, that wherever true faith is, there good works will certainly be.

t Matt. 8. 29.
Mark 1. 24.
& 5. 7.
Luke 4. 34.
Acts 16. 17.
& 19. 15.

19 Thou believest that there is one God; thou doest well: ᵗthe devils also believe, and tremble.

Thou believest that there is one God; thou givest thy assent to this truth, that there is one God. This may likewise imply other articles of the creed, to which the like assent may be given. *Thou doest well;* either this kind of faith hath its goodness, though it be not saving; or ironically, q. d. A great matter thou dost, when thou goest almost as high as the devils. *The devils also believe;* yield the like assent to the same truth. *And tremble:* the word signifies extreme fear and horror, viz. such as the thoughts of their Judge strike into them. This shows the faith the apostle speaks of in this place, not to be the faith of God's elect, which begets in believers a holy confidence in God, and frees them from slavish fears; whereas the faith here spoken of, if it have any effect upon men, it is but to fill them with horror.

20 But wilt thou know, O vain man, that faith without works is dead?

But wilt thou know? either this question is in order to teaching, as John xiii. 12; Rom. xiii. 3; and then the sense is, If thou hast a mind to know, I shall instruct thee: or, it is a teaching by way of question, as more emphatical and pressing; and then it is as if he had said, Know, O vain man. *O vain man;* an allusion to an empty vessel, which sounds more than one that is full. The carnal professor to whom he speaks is vain, because empty of true faith and good works, though full of noise and boasting. *Object.* Doth not the apostle sin against Christ's command, Matt. v. 22? *Answ.* 1. He speaks not of any particular man, but to all in general, of such a sort, viz. who boasted of their faith, and yet did not evidence it by their works. 2. It is not spoken in rash anger, or by way of contempt, but by way of correction and just reproof; see the like spoken by Christ himself, Matt. xxiii. 17, 19; Luke xxiv. 25; and by Paul, Gal. iii. 1; 1 Cor. xv. 36. *That faith without works is dead;* a defective speech, *faith without works*, for that faith which is without works, or, faith, if it be without works. He doth not say, faith is dead without works, lest it should be thought that works were the cause of the life of faith; but *faith without works is dead*, as ver. 17, 26; implying, that works are the effects and signs of the life of faith.

21 Was not Abraham our father justified by works, ᵘwhen he had offered Isaac his son upon the altar?

u Gen. 22. 9, 12.

Was not Abraham our father; not only the father of us as Jews, (for to them he wrote,) and according to the flesh, but as believers, and according to the promise; so all believers are called Abraham's children, Rom. iv. 11; Gal. iii. 7. *Justified by works;* found or declared to be justified, not only before God, but in the face of the world; and his faith (by which he had been justified above thirty years before in the sight of God) now approved as a true, lively, justifying faith, by this proof he gave of it, upon God's trying him in the offering up his son, Gen. xxii. 9, 12, *Now I know that thou fearest God,* &c. Abraham did fear God, and believe him before, and was justified before in the sight of God; but by the working of his faith in so eminent an act of obedience, the sincerity of all his graces, and so of his faith, was manifested and made known, and so his faith itself justified, as his person was before, and he obtained this ample testimony from the mouth of God himself. So that Abraham's justification here was not the absolution of a sinner, but the solemn approbation of a believer; not a justifying him as ungodly, but commending him for his godliness. He was by his works justified as a righteous person, but not made righteous, or constituted in a justified state, by his works. The design of the apostle is not to show how sinners are justified in God's court, but only what kind of faith it is whereby they are justified, viz. such a one as purifies the heart, Acts xv. 9, and looks to Christ, not only as made righteousness, but sanctification to them, 1 Cor. i. 30; and consequently not only rests on him for justification, but stirs them up to yield obedience to him. *When he had offered Isaac his son;* viz. in his firm purpose and resolution, and was about to do it actually, had not God hindered him. It was no fault in Abraham that it was not actually done, and therefore it was counted to him as if it had been really done, Gen. xxii. 12; Heb. xi. 17. *Upon the altar;* this shows the settled purpose of Abraham to sacrifice Isaac, when he proceeded so far as to bind him, and lay him upon the altar; for that argues, that he expected and intended nothing but his death, which generally was wont to follow in sacrifices when once laid upon the altar.

22 ‖ Seest thou ˣhow faith wrought with his works, and by works was faith made perfect?

‖ Or, *Thou seest.*
x Heb. 11. 17.

Seest thou how faith wrought with his works? he doth not say, works wrought with his faith, as he should have said, if he had intended their concurrence in justification; but *faith wrought with his works*, i. e. his faith was not idle, but effectual in producing good works, it being the office and business of faith to respect Christ for sanctification, as well as righteousness, Acts xxvi. 18. *And by works was faith made perfect;* either, 1. Faith by producing good works is itself encouraged, heightened, improved; and so not made perfect by any communication of the perfection of works to it, but by being stirred up and exercised as to the internal strength and power of it. Or rather, 2. Faith is made perfect by works declaratively, inasmuch as works evidence and manifest the perfection and strength of faith. Faith is the cause, and works are the effects; but the cause is not perfected by the effect, only its perfection is demonstrated by it, as good fruit doth not make a tree good, but show that it is so. See 2 Cor. xii. 9.

23 And the Scripture was fulfilled which saith, ʸAbraham believed God, and it was imputed unto him for righteousness: and he was called ᶻthe Friend of God.

y Gen. 15. 6.
Rom. 4. 3.
Gal. 3. 6.

z 2 Chron. 20. 7. Is. 41. 8.

And the Scripture was fulfilled; this illustrious instance of Abraham's obedience did so clearly evidence the sincerity of his faith, that it did most plainly appear, that what the Scripture said of him, it spoke most truly, viz. that he did indeed believe God, *and it was counted to him for righteousness.* Things are said to be fulfilled when they are most clearly manifested. As those words, Psal. ii. 7, *This day have I begotten thee*, are said to be fulfilled at Christ's resurrection, Acts xiii. 32, 33; not that he was then first begotten of the Father, but that he was then in a glorious manner declared to be the Son of God by the resurrection from the dead, Rom. i. 4. So here Abraham's offering up his son being the evident discovery of his faith, it did by that appear, that the Scripture report of him was true, that he *believed God*, &c.: he did believe before, and his faith was imputed to him before, but it was never so fully made known, as by this so high an act of obedience. *It was imputed unto him for righteousness;* viz. as apprehending Christ in the promise. Faith is said to be imputed for righteousness, Rom. iv. 3—6, as being the instrument or means of applying Christ's righteousness, by which elsewhere we are said to be justified, Rom. iii. 24, 25; v. 19; 2 Cor. v. 21; Phil. iii. 9. *And he was called the Friend of God;* either he was *the friend of God;* to be called, sometimes implies as much as to be, Isa. xlviii. 8; or properly, *he was called,* 2 Chron. xx. 7; Isa. xli. 8; and that not only on the account of God's frequent appearances to him, conversing with him, revealing secrets to him, Gen. xviii. 17, 18; John xv. 15, and entering into covenant with him; but especially his renewing the covenant with him upon the sacrificing of his son, and confirming it by oath, and thereby, as it were, admitting him into a nearer degree of friendship, Gen. xxii. 16, &c.

24 Ye see then how that by works a man is justified, and not by faith only.

Ye see then; an inference either from the instance of Abraham, or from the whole preceding discourse. *How that by works;* works of new obedience. *A man is justified;* declared to be righteous, or approved as such, and acquitted from the guilt of hypocrisy. *And not by faith only;* not by a mere profession of faith, or a bare assent to the truth, without the fruit of good works. *Quest.* How doth this general conclusion follow from the particular case of Abraham? *Answ.* Abraham's faith and justification, both before God and the world, are set forth as the exemplars of ours, to which the faith and justification of all believers, both Jews and Gentiles, is to be conformed, Rom. iv. 11, 12, 23, 24. *Quest.* Doth not James here contradict Paul's doctrine in the matter of justification, Rom. iv.? *Answ.* The contradiction is but seeming, not real, as will appear, if four things be considered: 1. The occasion of these apostles' writing, and their scope in it. Having to do with different sorts of persons, they had likewise different designs. As Christ speaks one way when he dealt with proud Pharisees, whom he would humble; another way, when with humble hearers, whom he would encourage, and Paul carried it one way when among weak brethren, in condescension to whose infirmities he circumcised Timothy, Acts xvi. 2, 3; and another, when he was among false brethren, and men of contention, who opposed Christian liberty, seeking to bring believers into bondage, and then would not suffer Titus to be circumcised, Gal. ii. 3—5. So in the present affair, Paul's business lay with false apostles and Judaizing Christians, such as did, in the matter of justification, either substitute a self-righteousness instead of God's grace, or set it up in conjunction with it; and therefore his scope is (especially in his Epistles to the Romans and Galatians) to show the true cause and manner of justification, and vindicate the freeness of grace in it, by the exclusion of man's works, of what kind soever; to which purpose he propounds the examples of Abraham and David, in their justification, Rom. iv. Whereas James having to do with carnal professors, and such as abused the doctrine of grace to encourage themselves in sin, and thought it sufficient that they had faith, (such as it was,) though they did not live like believers, resting in an empty profession, with the neglect of holiness; his design plainly is, to show the effects and fruits of justification, viz. holiness and good works; thereby to check the vanity and folly of them who did thus divorce faith from a holy life, (which God hath joined to it,) and fancied themselves safe in the profession of the one, without any respect to, or care of, the other, as appears in this chapter, ver. 14, 17, 26. And because they might bear themselves high in this false confidence by the example of Abraham, their father according to the flesh, and whom Paul had set forth, Rom. iv., as justified by faith, without the concurrence of works to his justification; James makes use of the same example of Abraham, as one eminent for holiness as well as faith, and who made his faith famous by the highest act of obedience that ever a saint did, to show, that faith and holiness ought not to be separated; Abraham's faith being so highly commended, especially as productive of it. To the same purpose he makes use of the instance of Rahab, who, though a young saint, and newly come to the knowledge of God, yet showed the truth of her faith by so considerable an exercise of her love and mercy to God's people, as her receiving the spies in peace was. This therefore helps not a little to reconcile the difference between these two apostles. Paul deals with those that magnified works too much, as if they were justified by them, and slighted faith and grace; and therefore, though he frequently shows the usefulness of faith and good works unto salvation, and presseth men every where to the practice of them, yet he proves that they have no interest in the justification of a sinner before God's tribunal, which he asserts to be wholly and solely of grace, and by faith. But James, in dealing with loose Christians, who magnified faith, and slighted good works, not only as having no influence on justification, but as not necessary at all to salvation; he takes upon him to maintain good works, not as necessary to justification, but as the effects, signs, and evidences of it, and such as without which their faith was vain, and themselves in an unjustified state. 2. Paul and James take faith in different senses: Paul speaks of a true, lively faith, which purifies the heart, and *worketh by love,* Gal. v. 6. Whereas James speaks of a profession, or presumption of faith, barren, and destitute of good fruits, such a faith as is dead, ver. 17, such as the devils may have, ver. 19, which is but historical, and consists only in a belief of God's being, not a consent to his offer, or relying on his promises. What contradiction then is there here between these two apostles, if Paul assert justification to be by faith, viz. a lively, working faith; and James deny it to be by faith, viz. an idle, inactive, barren faith, and which hath only the name, but not the nature of that grace, and is rather the image of faith than faith itself? 3. But because James not only denies justification to the faith he speaks of, but ascribes it to works in this verse; therefore it is to be considered, that justification is taken one way by him, and another by Paul. Paul takes it for the absolution and acceptation of a sinner at God's bar, by the imputation of Christ's righteousness, which is the primary and proper notion of justification. But James takes it for the manifestation and declaration of that justification; and the word is taken in the like sense in other scriptures: Luke vii. 29, the people *justified God,* i. e. owned and declared his righteousness by confession of their sins, and submission to John's baptism; and ver. 35, *Wisdom is justified,* i. e. declared to be just and right. Rom. iii. 4, *justified in thy sayings,* i. e. acknowledged and declared to be true in thy word. And what is Christ's being *justified in the Spirit,* 1 Tim. iii. 16, but his being *declared to be the Son of God?* Rom. i. 4. And that James takes justification in this sense, appears, (1.) By the history of Abraham here mentioned: he was (as hath been said) justified by faith long before his offering up his son, Gen. xv., but here is said to be justified, i. e. declared and proved to be so, by this testimony which he gave to the truth of his faith, and consequently to his justification by it; and the Lord therefore tells him, Gen. xxii. 12, *Now I know that thou fearest God,* &c.; q. d. By this obedience thou hast abundantly showed the sincerity of thy graces. (2.) Because if James doth not here speak of Abraham's being justified declaratively, how can it be true which he speaks, ver. 23, that *the Scripture was fulfilled* (in his sacrificing his son) *which saith, He believed God, and it was imputed unto him for righteousness?* For if James intends justification in the proper sense, how was Abraham's being justified by works a fulfilling of the Scripture, which asserts him to be justified by faith? Here therefore again there is no contradiction between these apostles. For it is true, that Abraham was justified, i. e. accepted of God, and absolved from guilt, by faith only; and it is as true, that he was justified, i. e. manifested and declared to be a believer, and a justified person, by his works. 4. Lastly, we may distinguish of the person that is said to be justified; either he is a sinner, in the state of nature; or a believer, in a state of grace; whence ariseth the two-fold justification here mentioned. The justification of a sinner, in the remission of his sins through the imputation of Christ's righteousness, and acquitting him from the condemnation of the law, is the justification properly so called, and which Paul speaks so much of; and this is by faith only. The justification of a believer, is his absolution from condemnation by the gospel, and the charge of infidelity, or hypocrisy, and is no other than that declarative justification James speaks of, or an asserting and clearing up the truth and reality of the former justification, which is done by good works, as the signs and fruits of the faith, by which that former is obtained: and this is but improperly called justification. The former is an absolution from the general charge of sin, this from the special charge of hypocrisy, or infidelity. A sinner's great fear (when first awakened to a sense of his sin and misery) is of a holy law, and a righteous Judge ready to condemn him for the violation of that law; and so his first business is to look to Christ by faith for righteousness, and remission of sin. But when he is justified by that righteousness, men may charge him with hypocrisy or unbelief, and so may the devil and conscience too, when faith is weak, or a temptation strong; and therefore his next work is to clear himself of this imputation, and to evidence the truth and reality of his faith and justification in God's sight, which must be done by producing his obedience and good works, as the indications of his faith; and hereby he proves that he hath indeed closed with the promise of the gospel, and so is clear of the charge of not believing it, which was false; as well as (by consequence) is justified from the charge of sin against the law, which was true. To conclude, therefore, here is no opposition between Paul and James. Paul speaks of Abraham's being justified as a sinner, and properly, and so by faith only; James speaks of his being justified as a believer, improperly, and so by works; by which not his person was justified, but rather his faith declared to be justifying: nor he constituted righteous, but approved as righteous. In a word, what God hath joined must not be divided, and what he hath divided must not be joined. He hath separated faith and works in the business of justification, and therefore we must not join them in it, as Paul disputes; and he hath joined them in the lives of justified persons, and there we must not separate them, as James teaches. Paul assures us they have not a co-efficiency in justification itself; and James assures us they may, and ought to have, a co-existence in them that are justified. If the reader desire further satisfaction yet, let him consult Turretine de Concordia Pauli et Jacobi, where he may find much more to the same purpose as hath been here said.

a Josh. 2. 1.
Heb. 11. 31.

25 Likewise also ^a was not Rahab the harlot justified by works, when she had received the messengers, and had sent *them* out another way?

This instance of *Rahab* is joined to that of Abraham, either to show, that none of any condition, degree, or nation, was ever numbered among true believers, without good works; or else to prove, that faith, wherever it is sincere and genuine, is likewise operative and fruitful, not only in older disciples and stronger, such as Abraham was, but even proportionally in those that are weaker, and but newly converted to the faith, which was Rahab's case. *The harlot;* really and properly so, Josh. ii. 1; Heb. xi. 31; though possibly she might keep an inn, and that might occasion the spies' going to her house, not knowing her to be one of so scandalous a life; which yet the Holy Ghost takes special notice of, that by the infamousness of her former conversation, the grace of God in her conversion might be more conspicuous. *Justified by works;* in the same sense as Abraham was, i. e. declared to be righteous, and her sincerity approved in the face of the congregation of Israel, when, upon her hiding the spies, God gave a commandment to save her alive, though the rest of her people were to be destroyed. *When she had received the messengers, and had sent them out another way:* her receiving them implies likewise her hiding them; both which, together with her sending them forth another way, were acts of love to the people of God, of mercy to the spies, and of great self-denial in respect of her own safety, which she hazarded by thus exposing herself to the fury of the king of Jericho and her countrymen; but all proceeded from her faith in the God of Israel, of whose great works she had heard, and whom she had now taken to be her God, and under whose wings she was now come to trust.

‖ Or,
breath.

26 For as the body without the ‖ spirit is dead, so faith without works is dead also.

The spirit: this may be understood either, according to the marginal reading, of the breath; and then the sense is, that life and breath being inseparable companions, as the want of breath argues want of life in the body, so, lively faith and works being as inseparable, want of works argues want of life in faith: or, according to the reading in the text, *spirit,* taking it for that substance which animates the body, and is the cause of vital functions in it, which is sometimes called spirit, Psal. xxxi. 5; Eccles. xii. 7; 1 Cor. ii. 11; and then the sense is, that as a body is without a soul, so faith is without works, i. e. both are dead. As a body without the soul hath the shape and lineaments of a man, but nothing that may discover life in it; so faith without works may be like true faith, have some resemblance of it, but hath nothing to discover the truth and life of it. *So faith;* not true faith, for that cannot be dead, but an empty profession of faith, which is rather called faith by way of concession, or because of some likeness it hath to it, than really is so; as a dead body, though called a body, is really but a carcass.

CHAP. III.

We must not rashly take upon ourselves to reprove others, 1. *The importance, difficulty, and duty, of governing the tongue.* 2—12. *True wisdom will show itself in meekness, peaceableness, and charity, in opposition to strife and envying,* 13—18.

MY brethren, ^a be not many masters, ^b knowing that we shall receive the greater ‖ condemnation.

a Matt. 23.
8, 14. Rom.
2. 20, 21.
1 Pet. 5. 3.
b Luke 6. 37.
‖ Or, *judgment.*

Be not many masters; let not every man make himself a master of other men's faith and manners, a censor, or supercilious reprover of their failings and infirmities, Matt. vii. 1. All reproof is not here forbidden, neither authoritative by church officers, nor charitative by private brethren; but that which is irregular, either in the ground of it, when that is false; or the manner of it, when it is masterly and imperious, or preposterous, as when we reprehend others and are no less reprehensible ourselves, Rom. ii. 21; or in the end of it, when we seek to advance our own reputation by observing or aggravating others' faults, &c. *Knowing that we shall receive the greater condemnation;* by how much the more severe and rigid we are in judging others, the greater will be our judgment, not only from men, who will be apt to retaliate, but from God himself, Matt. vii. 1—3; Luke vi. 38; Rom. ii. 2, 3. See the like expression, Matt. xxiii. 8, 14.

2 For ^c in many things we offend all. ^d If any man offend not in word, ^e the same *is* a perfect man, *and* able also to bridle the whole body.

c 1 Kings 8.
46. 2 Chron.
6. 36. Prov.
20. 9.
Eccles. 7. 20.
1 John 1. 8.
d Ps. 34. 13.
Ecclus. 14. 1.
e Matt. 12. 37.
& 19. 16. & 25. 8. ch. 1. 26. 1 Pet. 3. 10.

For in many things we offend all: there is no man absolutely free from sin, 1 Kings viii. 46; Job xiv. 4; Prov. xx. 9; Eccles. vii. 20; 1 John i. 8, 10; and therefore we must be not too critical in other men's actions, having so many failings ourselves, Gal. vi. 1. *If any man offend not in word;* know how to govern his tongue aright, speak what, and when, as he ought. *The same is a perfect man;* either sincere, in opposition to the hypocrisy of those that pretend so great zeal in correcting others, when they are alike or more guilty themselves: or rather, we may understand it comparatively, and with respect to others, of one that hath made good proficiency in religion, and is of greater attainments than others: see 1 Cor. ii. 6. *And able also to bridle the whole body;* to govern all the other parts, (eyes, ears, hands, &c.,) as to those actions which are performed by them. No member of the body being more ready to offend than the tongue, he that can rule that, may rule all else.

3 Behold, ^f we put bits in the horses' mouths, that they may obey us; and we turn about their whole body. f Ps. 32. 9.

He illustrates the former proposition, that he that can rule his tongue may rule his whole body, by two similitudes: the first, of an unruly horse, which yet, as wanton as he is, being curbed in with a bit, may be easily managed; intimating, that even so, if a man's tongue be well governed, the rest of the man will be under command.

4 Behold also the ships, which though *they be* so great, and *are* driven of fierce winds, yet are they turned about with a very small helm, whithersoever the governor listeth.

The other similitude, in which a man is compared to a ship, the tongue to the rudder, the governing the whole body to the turning about the ship. As the rudder is but a small thing, in comparison of the much greater bulk of a ship, and yet, being itself turned, turns the whole ship *(though so great, and driven of so fierce winds)* which way soever the steersman pleaseth: so likewise the tongue, though little to the whole man, (which may withal be driven, and acted by storms of furious passions,) yet if it be itself under government, the rest of the man will be so too.

5 Even so ^g the tongue is a little member, and ^hboasteth great things. Behold, how great ‖ a matter a little fire kindleth!

g Prov. 12. 18. & 15. 2.
h Ps. 12. 3. & 73. 8, 9.
‖ Or, *wood.*

The accommodation of the former similitudes. *The tongue is a little member,* i. e. one of the lesser, in comparison of the body. *And boasteth great things;* the Greek word signifies, according to its derivation, the lifting up of the neck (as horses, mentioned ver. 3, are wont to do in their pride) in a way of bravery and triumph; and hence it is used to express boasting and glorying, but here seems to imply something more, viz. not only the uttering big words, but doing great things, whether good and useful, as in the former similitudes, or evil, as in what follows; or its boasting how great things it can do: q. d. The tongue, though little, is of great force and efficacy, and it will tell you so itself; it not only boasts what its fellow members can do, but especially what itself can. *Behold, how great a matter a little fire kindleth!* another similitude, in which he sets forth the evil the tongue, as little as it is, doth, where it is not well governed, as in the former he had shown the good it may do, when kept under rule. *A matter;* the word signifies either any combustible stuff, or, as in the margin, wood, that being the ordinary fuel then in use. *A little fire kindleth;* even a spark, the smallest quantity or particle, which may do great mischief, when lighting in suitable matter.

6 And ⁱthe tongue *is* a fire, a world of iniquity: so is the tongue among our members, that ^k it defileth the whole body, and setteth on fire the †course of nature; and it is set on fire of hell.

i Prov. 16. 27.
k Matt. 15. 11, 18, 19, 20. Mark 7. 15, 20, 23.
† Gr. *wheel.*

The application of the similitude in the foregoing words. *The tongue is a fire,* i. e. hath the force of fire, and resembles it in the mischief it doth. *A world of iniquity;* a heap or aggregation of evils, (as the natural world is an aggregation of many several beings,) as we say, an ocean, or a world, of troubles, meaning, a great multitude of them. And the words may be understood, either with an ellipsis of the word *matter,* expressed just before, and supplied here; and the pointing a little altered, they may be thus read, And the tongue is a fire, a world of iniquity (or an unrighteous world, viz. which lies in wickedness, 1 John v. 19) is the matter, namely, which it inflames. A wicked world is fit fuel for a wicked tongue, and soon catcheth the fire which it kindles. Or rather, as they stand plainly, without any such defect: The tongue is a world of iniquity, i. e. a heap or mass of various sorts of sins; though it be but a little piece of flesh, yet it contains a whole world of wickedness in it, or is as full of evils as the world is of bodies. *It defileth the whole body;* infecteth the whole man with sin, Eccles. v. 6, as being the cause of sin committed by all the members of the body; for though sin begin in the soul, yet it is executed by the body, which therefore seems here put (as ver. 2) for the man. *And setteth on fire the course of nature;* or, setteth on fire the wheel of geniture, or nativity, (in allusion to a wheel set on fire by a violent, rapid motion,) meaning the course of nativity, i. e. the natural course of life, as the face of nativity or geniture, chap. i. 23, for the *natural face:* the sense is, it inflames with various lusts, wrath, malice, wantonness, pride, &c., the whole course of man's life, so that there is no state nor age free from the evils of it. Whereas other vices either do not extend to the whole man, or are abated with age, or worn away with length of time; the vices of the tongue reach the whole man, and the whole time of his life. *And it is set on fire of hell;* i. e. by the devil, the father of lies and slanders, and other tongue-sins, Job i. 10; John viii. 44; Rev. xii. 10; the tongue being the fire, the devil, by the bellows of temptations, inflames it yet more, and thereby kindles the fire of all mischiefs in the world.

7 For every †kind of beasts, and of birds, and of serpents, and of things in the sea, is tamed, and hath been tamed of †mankind:

† Gr. *nature.*
† Gr. *nature of man.*

Every kind; some of every kind. *Of beasts;* wild beasts, such as are most fierce and untractable. *And of birds;* though so movable and wandering, the very vagabonds of nature. *And of serpents;* which are such enemies to mankind. *And of things in the sea;* the inhabitants, as it were, of another world, really of another element. *Is tamed, and hath been tamed of mankind;* either made gentle, or at least, brought into subjection to man by one means or other. He useth both tenses, the present and the preterperfect, to note that such things not only have been, but still are; and that not as the effects of some miraculous providence, as in the case of Daniel, chap. vi., and Paul, Acts xxviii., but as that which is usually experienced, and in man's power still to do.

8 But the tongue can no man tame; *it is* an unruly evil, ^lfull of deadly poison.   l Ps. 140. 3.

But the tongue; not only other men's tongues, but his own. *Can no man tame;* no man of himself, and without the assistance of Divine grace, can bring his tongue into subjection, and keep it in order; nor can any man, by the assistance of any grace promised in this life, so keep it, as that it shall never at all offend. *It is an unruly evil;* or, which cannot be restrained, and kept within bounds: wild beasts are kept in by grates and bars, but this by no restraint. *Full of deadly poison;* the wickedness of the tongue is compared to poison, in respect of the mischief it doth to others. It seems to allude to those kinds of serpents which have poison under their tongues, Psal. cxl. 3, with which they kill those they bite. The poison of the tongue is no less deadly, it murders men's reputations by the slanders it utters, their souls by the lusts and passions it stirs up in them, and many times their bodies too by the contentions and quarrels it raiseth against men.

9 Therewith bless we God, even the Father; and therewith curse we men, ^mwhich are made after the similitude of God.   m Gen. 1. 26. & 5. 1. & 9. 6.

Therewith bless we God; pray, and speak well of God. *Even the Father;* of Christ, and in him of all true believers. *And therewith curse we men;* rail on, revile, speak evil of, as well as wish evil to. *Which are made after the similitude of God;* either, 1. Saints in whom God's image is anew restored; or rather, 2. Men more generally, who, though they have lost that spiritual knowledge, righteousness, and true holiness, in which that image of God, after which man was created, principally consists; yet still have some relics of his image continuing in them. This is added to aggravate the sin; speaking evil of men made after God's image, is speaking evil of God obliquely, and by reflection.

10 Out of the same mouth proceedeth blessing and cursing. My brethren, these things ought not so to be.

He repeats here, by way of exaggeration, what he had said ver. 9, to show how exceedingly absurd it is that two such contrary actions should proceed from the same agent. *These things ought not so to be;* there is a meiosis in the words; he means, things should be quite contrary. See the like expression, 1 Tim. v. 13; Tit. i. 11.

11 Doth a fountain send forth at the same ‖ place sweet *water* and bitter?   ‖ Or, *hole.*

Ordinarily and naturally; if any such be, it is looked upon as uncouth and prodigious.

12 Can the fig tree, my brethren, bear olive berries? either a vine, figs? so *can* no fountain both yield salt water and fresh.

Can the fig tree, my brethren, bear olive berries? either a vine, figs? the same tree cannot ordinarily bring forth fruit of different kinds, (on the same branch, whatever it may on different, by ingrafting,) much less contrary natures: see Matt. vii. 16—18. *So can no fountain both yield salt water and fresh;* or, neither can a salt fountain yield fresh water; but the scope is still the same as in our reading. The apostle argues from what is impossible, or monstrous, in naturals, to what is absurd in manners: q. d. It is as absurd in religion, for the tongue of a regenerate man, which is used to bless God, to take a liberty at other times to curse man, as it would be strange in nature for the same tree, on the same branch, to bear fruits of different kinds; or the same fountain at the same place to send forth bitter water and sweet.

n Gal. 6. 4.
o ch. 2. 18.
p ch. 1. 21.

13 ⁿWho *is* a wise man and endued with knowledge among you? let him shew out of a good conversation ᵒhis works ᵖwith meekness of wisdom.

Who is a wise man and endued with knowledge among you? i. e. if there be a wise man, &c. See Psal. xxv. 12, and 1 Pet. iii. 10, where what David speaks by way of interrogation, Peter explains by way of assertion. The apostle having shown the disease of the tongue, comes now to remove the cause, viz. men's opinion of their own wisdom; (they censure others, because they take themselves to be wiser than others;) and to point out the remedy, godly meekness, which is the truest wisdom. By wisdom and knowledge the same thing may be meant; or if they be taken for several things, (as sometimes there may be great knowledge where there is but little wisdom,) yet these masterly censors he speaks of pretended to both, and were so rigid toward others because so well conceited of themselves: the sense is, You pretend to be wise and knowing, but if you would approve yourselves as such indeed, *show out of a good conversation,* &c. *His works;* let him show us the testimony of his wisdom, not his words in hard censures, but his works, viz. good ones, and those not done now and then, or on the by, but in the constant course and tenor of his life; or show his works to be good, by their being not casual, but constant, and his ordinary practice in his whole conversation. *With meekness of wisdom;* i. e. meek and gentle wisdom, which can hear, and answer, and teach, and admonish, and rebuke mildly and sweetly, with long-suffering, as well as doctrine, 2 Tim. iv. 2: and then it notes the quality of this wisdom, or such meekness as proceeds from wisdom, or is joined with it, there being some which is foolish, affected, carnal, viz. that which is opposed to zeal; whereas true meekness is only opposed to fierceness and rashness: and thus it notes the cause of meekness.

q Rom. 13. 13.
r Rom. 2. 17. 23.

14 But if ye have ᑫbitter envying and strife in your hearts, ʳglory not, and lie not against the truth.

Bitter envying; Greek, zeal, which he calls bitter, partly to distinguish it from that zeal which is good, whereas this he speaks of is evil, and though it pretends to be zeal, yet is really no other than envy; and partly because it commonly proceeds from an imbittered spirit, and tends to the imbittering it more. *Strife;* the usual effect of bitter zeal, or envy. *In your hearts;* the fountain whence it proceeds; or strife in the heart implies a heart propense and inclined to strife. *Glory not;* glory not of your zeal, or rather of your wisdom, as if you were so well able to reprehend others, but rather be humbled; what you make the matter of your glorying, being really just cause of shame. *And lie not against the truth;* viz. by professing yourselves wise, or zealous, when ye are really neither.

s ch. 1. 17.
Phil. 3. 19.
‖ Or, *natural,* Jude 19.

15 ˢThis wisdom descendeth not from above, but *is* earthly, ‖sensual, devilish.

This wisdom, which they pretended so much to, who so criticized on other men's actions, and inveighed against them, and which was accompanied with strife and envy. *Descendeth not from above;* i. e. from God the author of wisdom, from whom, though every good and perfect gift descends, chap. i. 17, and even knowledge and skill in natural things, Isa. xxviii. 26, 29; yet this wisdom, being sinful, is not from him, because it *is earthly,* of the earth, of no higher original than from the first Adam, who was of the earth, and earthly, 1 Cor. xv. 47; and likewise because it is employed, and fixeth men's minds, on earthly things. *Sensual;* this may be understood either, 1. According to the reading in the text, the word here used being so rendered, Jude 19, agreeable to 1 Thess. v. 23, where *soul,* from whence the word is derived, is opposed to *spirit,* and taken for the sensitive powers, which men have in common with brutes, in distinction from the intellectual, which go under the name of spirit, and are proper to men: mere reason, without the Divine grace, being apt to degenerate into brutishness, and easily brought to serve the ends of sensual appetite, this wisdom may well be called sensual. Or, 2. According to the margin, natural, in opposition to spiritual. The natural man (1 Cor. ii. 14, where the same word, in the Greek, is used as here) is one that lives under the conduct of his own carnal reason, not enlightened, nor regenerated by the Spirit of God; a man of soul, (as the word imports,) or that hath no better, no higher principle in him than his own soul. Accordingly, this wisdom here mentioned, is such as proceeds merely from a man's own soul, in its natural state, destitute of the light and grace of God's Spirit, and therefore may be termed natural. *Devilish;* because it is of the devil, or such as is in him, and makes men like him, who is a proud spirit, and envious, a liar and slanderer, John viii. 44, and who observes men's faults, not to amend them, but accuse them for them.

t 1 Cor. 3. 3.
Gal. 5. 20.
† Gr. *tumult,* or, *unquietness.*

16 For ᵗwhere envying and strife *is,* there *is* †confusion and every evil work.

For where envying and strife is; the usual companions of this devilish wisdom. *There is confusion;* or, inconsistency, viz. both with man's self and others; envy makes him unquiet in himself, and troublesome to others, by causing contentions and seditions among them, and breaking their peace, as well as his own. *And every evil work;* all manner of wickedness is ushered in by this confusion and sedition.

u 1 Cor. 2. 6, 7.
‖ Or, *without wrangling.*
x Rom. 12. 9. 1 Pet. 1. 22. & 2. 1.
1 John 3. 18.

17 But ᵘthe wisdom that is from above is first pure, then peaceable, gentle, *and* easy to be intreated, full of mercy and good fruits, ‖without partiality, ˣand without hypocrisy.

But the wisdom that is from above; true wisdom, which is of God, opposed to that which *descendeth not from above,* ver. 15. *Is first pure;* either excluding mixture, and then it is opposed to hypocritical; or rather excluding filthiness, and then it is opposed to *sensual,* ver. 15, and implies freedom from the defilement of sin and error, it being the property of true wisdom to make men adhere both to truth and holiness. *Then peaceable;* disposeth men to peace, both as to the making and keeping it, in opposition to strife and contention, which is the fruit of the earthly wisdom. Peaceableness, which relates to man, is set after purity, which respects God in the first place, to intimate, that purity must have the preference to peace. Our peace with men must always be with a salvo to our respects to God and holiness. *Gentle;* or equal, or moderate, Phil. iv. 5; 1 Tim. iii. 3; Tit. iii. 2. It implies that gentleness (as we translate it) whereby we bear with others' infirmities, forgive injuries, interpret all things for the best, recede from our own right for peace sake; and is opposed to that austerity and rigidness in our practices and censures, which will bear with nothing in weak, dissenting, or offending brethren. *Easy to be entreated;* easily persuadable. True wisdom makes men yield to good admonitions, good counsel, good reason. This is opposed to implacableness, Rom. i. 31; pride, and obstinacy in evil, Prov. xii. 1; xiii. 1. *Full of mercy;* a grace whereby we pity others that are afflicted, or that offend, and is opposed to inhumanity and inexorableness. *And good fruits;* beneficence, liberality, and all other offices of humanity, which proceed from mercy. *Without partiality;* or, without judging, i. e. either a curious inquiring into the faults of others, to find matter for censures, which many times infers wrangling, as our margin renders it; or a discerning between person and person, upon carnal accounts, which is *partiality,* as it is here translated, and chap. ii. 4. *And without hypocrisy;* or, counterfeiting, as they do that judge others, being guilty of the same things, or as bad, themselves: or *hypocrisy* may be here added, to show that sincerity is the perfection of all the rest before named; purity, peace, and gentleness, &c., may be counterfeit; hypocrisy spoils all; and therefore the wisdom that is from above is sincere, and without hypocrisy.

JAMES III. IV

y Prov. 11.
18. Hos. 10.
12. Matt. 5.
9. Phil. 1. 11
Heb. 12. 11.

18 ʸ And the fruit of righteousness is sown in peace of them that make peace.

And the fruit of righteousness; either the fruit we bring forth, which is righteousness itself, Luke iii. 8, 9; Rom. vi. 22; Phil. i. 11; or the fruit we reap, which is the reward of righteousness, viz. eternal life. *Righteousness;* metonymically here put for the heavenly wisdom before described, whereof it is the inseparable companion, or the effect, Job xxviii. 28. *Is sown;* either righteousness, as the good fruit, is wrought or exercised, Hos. x. 12, (as wickedness is said to be sown when it is acted, Job iv. 8,) or it relates to the reward, which is the fruit, of which righteousness is the seed, Psal. xcvii. 11; and then it implies, either the sureness of that reward, that it is as certain as harvest after seed-time; or the non-enjoyment of it for the present, as they that sow their seed receive not the crop till long after. *In peace;* either in a mild, peaceable, amicable way; or *in peace* is as much as with peace, viz. spiritual peace and comfort of conscience. *Of them that make peace;* that follow after and are studious of peace; and so the words may have a two-fold sense: either the meaning is, 1. That they that exercise righteousness must do it in a sweet and peaceable way: in particular, men may reprehend others, so they do it with moderation and gentleness, not as executioners, to torment them, but as physicians, to heal them; as, on the other side, they that are most peaceably disposed, yet must not make peace without sowing righteousness with it, which includes just reprehension, whereby righteousness is promoted. Or, 2. That they who sow righteousness in peace, i. e. join righteousness with their endeavours after peace, shall reap the reward, not only in comfort here, but in glory hereafter.

CHAP. IV

Our evil lusts and passions tend to breed quarrels among ourselves, and to set us at enmity with God, 1—6. *The way to overcome them, and recover God's favour,* 7—10. *Against detraction and censoriousness,* 11, 12. *We must not presume on the future, but commit ourselves to God's providence,* 13—17.

‖ Or, *brawlings.*
‖ Or, *pleasures.*
So ver. 3.
a Rom. 7. 23.
Gal. 5. 17. 1 Pet. 2. 11.

FROM whence *come* wars and ‖ fightings among you? *come they* not hence, *even* of your ‖ lusts ᵃ that war in your members?

Wars and fightings; either it may be understood properly of insurrections, and tumults, in which, possibly, some carnal professors might be engaged; or rather, strife and contention about outward things, wranglings among themselves, and going to law, especially before unbelieving judges, 1 Cor. vi. 1. *Your lusts;* Greek, pleasures, i. e. those lusts whereof pleasure is the end, which is therefore put for the lusts themselves: he means the over-eager desire of riches, worldly greatness, carnal delights, Tit. iii. 3, where *lusts and pleasures* go together. *That war;* oppose and tumultuate against reason, conscience, grace, Rom. vii. 23; 1 Pet. ii. 11. *In your members;* not only the members of the body, but faculties of the soul, exercised by them; all the parts of man unrenewed, Col. iii. 5, which are used as weapons of unrighteousness, Rom. vi. 13

‖ Or, *envy.*

2 Ye lust, and have not: ye ‖ kill, and desire to have, and cannot obtain: ye fight and war, yet ye have not, because ye ask not.

Ye lust; passionately and greedily desire. *And have not;* either soon lose, or rather cannot get, what ye so lust after. *Ye kill;* some copies have it, ye envy, and many suppose that to be the better reading, as agreeing with the context, and with chap. iii. 14; envy being the cause of strife there, and joined with emulation, or a desire of having, here. We read it according to other copies, *ye kill,* which, if he speaketh of wars in a proper sense, ver. 1, was, no doubt, the effect of them; and if he speak only of strife and contentions, yet they might proceed so far, that the death of some (though not intended) might be the consequent of them, and occasioned by them. Or, he may mean their murderous desires, killing men in their hearts, wishing for and gaping after their death, that they might gain by it; and this agrees with what he speaks of the frustration of their greedy desires, none being more frequently disappointed of their hopes than they that hope to be gainers by other men's deaths. *And desire to have;* or, emulate, i. e. ambitiously affect to have what ye see others have, grieving that they should have more than you. *And cannot obtain;* viz. that which ye envy others' having. *Ye fight and war:* you wrangle and quarrel with your neighbours for what they have, that ye may get it for yourselves. *Yet ye have not;* ye are still needy, though still craving; your lusts are infinite and insatiable in themselves, and no way helpful to you. *Because ye ask not;* viz. of God by prayer, who hath promised to give to them that ask, Matt. vii. 7, not to them that war and fight. Instead of humble seeking to God for what ye want, ye would extort it by force or fraud from one another.

b Job 27. 9.
& 35. 12.
Ps. 18. 41.
Prov. 1. 28.
Is. 1. 15.
Jer. 11. 11.

3 ᵇ Ye ask, and receive not, ᶜ because ye ask amiss, that ye may consume *it* upon your ‖ lusts.

Mic. 3. 4. Zech. 7. 13. c Ps. 66. 18. 1 John 3. 22. & 5. 14. ‖ Or, *pleasures.*

Ye ask; he prevents an objection; q. d. Admit you do pray for the good things you want, or, though you pray for them. *Ye ask amiss;* though you pray for good things, yet you do not pray well, or in a right manner, not according to God's will, 1 John v. 14, and therefore ye are not to complain of not being heard. *That ye may consume it upon your lusts;* you pray for the things of this life only, that you may have wherewith to please the flesh, and gratify your carnal appetites, and so an evil end spoils good means; and while you would have God serve your lusts you lose your prayers.

d Ps. 73. 27.
e 1 John 2. 15.
f John 15. 19. & 17. 14.
Gal. 1. 10.

4 ᵈ Ye adulterers and adulteresses, know ye not that ᵉ the friendship of the world is enmity with God? ᶠ whosoever therefore will be a friend of the world is the enemy of God.

Ye adulterers and adulteresses; he means adulterers and adulteresses in a spiritual sense, i. e. worldly-minded Christians, who being, by profession, married to the Lord, yet gave up those affections to the things of the world which were due to God only. The like expression is used, Matt. xii. 39; xvi. 4. *Know ye not;* ye ought to know, and cannot but know. *That the friendship of the world;* inordinate affection to the world, addictedness or devotedness to the things or men of the world. *Is enmity with God;* alienates the soul from God, and God from it, 1 John ii. 15. *Whosoever therefore will be a friend of the world;* if it be the purpose and resolution of a man's heart to get in with the world, though perhaps he cannot obtain its favour; he courts it, though it be coy to him. *Is the enemy of God;* exerciseth hostility against God, by adhering to an interest so contrary to him.

g See Gen. 6. 5. & 8. 21.
Num. 11. 29.
Prov. 21. 10.
‖ Or, *enviously.*

5 Do ye think that the Scripture saith in vain, ᵍ The spirit that dwelleth in us lusteth ‖ to envy?

Do ye think that the Scripture saith in vain? Greek, emptily, or vainly, i. e. to no purpose. This question hath the force of a negation, q. d. It doth not speak in vain. *Quest.* What is it which the Scripture doth not speak in vain? *Answ.* Either those truths he had been speaking of before, particularly in the former verse, *that the friendship of the world is enmity with God;* or, that which follows in this verse, *the spirit that dwelleth in us,* &c. *The spirit that dwelleth in us;* either the Spirit of God, who is said to dwell in believers, 1 Cor. iii. 16, 17; or the spirit of men, viz. as defiled by sin, and acted by the devil, who works in men while children of disobedience; and then it is the same as corrupt nature. *Lusteth to envy;* either is vehemently carried out to envy, or makes us lust, and carrieth us out to it; or lusteth against envy: so the Greek preposition is often used, as Luke xx. 19; Eph. vi. 11; Heb. xii. 4. Under *envy* he comprehends all other fleshly lusts, but instanceth in this particularly, as having been speaking of it before, chap. iii. 14, 16; and because it hath so near a connexion with other lusts, whereof it is the cause, or concomitant, and so is a principal member of the old man.

This latter clause may either be read interrogatively or affirmatively; and then according as we take *spirit*, either for the Spirit of God, or the human spirit, the sense of the words may be either, 1. Doth the Spirit of God, that dwelleth in us, lust unto envy, i. e. incline and dispose us to so base an affection? The answer is understood, No, and confirmed by the next words, *he giveth more grace*, gives freely, liberally, and therefore doth not make us envy others any good they have. Nothing is more contrary to the Spirit of God, who abounds in his gifts to us, than to make us envy others theirs. Or, 2. We may understand it without any interrogation, taking the preposition to signify, against; and then the sense is, That good Spirit which is in us teacheth us better things than strife and envy, &c., for it lusteth against envy, i. e. makes us lust against it, carries out our hearts to hate and resist it. And this well agrees with what follows; The Spirit, &c., lusts against envy, but he gives more grace, viz. than to envy the good of others. Or, 3. If *spirit* here be understood of the spirit of man, corrupt nature, the sense is plain, as the words lie; man's spirit (especially by the instigation of the devil) lusts, or strongly inclines, to envy, and consequently to other wickednesses, but he (that is, God, ver. 4) gives more grace. *Quest.* Where is any such sentence to be found in the Scripture? *Answ.* No where in so many words; but which soever of these ways we take the words, we find the sense in the Scripture. Joshua's envying Eldad and Medad's prophesying, for Moses' sake, seems to be an instance of this lust, Numb. xi. 29, (compared with Gen. vi. 5; viii. 21, where the general inclination of man's heart by nature is said to be evil.) and Moses's not envying them an instance of the two former.

h Job 22. 29. Ps. 138. 6. Prov. 3. 34. & 29. 23. Matt. 23. 12. Luke 1. 52. & 14. 11. & 18. 14. 1 Pet. 5. 5.

6 But he giveth more grace. Wherefore he saith, ʰGod resisteth the proud, but giveth grace unto the humble.

But he, either the Spirit of God, if *spirit* in the former verse be understood of the Spirit of God; or God, if *spirit* be there taken for the spirit of man. *Giveth more grace*; either, though we, according to our natural inclination, be envious, yet God (or his Spirit) is bountiful and liberal; or God gives to those that are renewed, more grace than to be hurried on by their own old spirit, to envy, strife, and suchlike lusts. *Wherefore he saith*; God saith, viz. in the Scripture: or it may be taken indefinitely, and impersonally, for, it is said. The particular place he refers to, is Prov. iii. 34, according to the translation of the LXX., which not only James, but other New Testament writers, frequently follow. *God resisteth*; it is a military term: God sets himself, as in battle, against the proud, defying, beating down, exposing to contempt, and destroying them; he is so far from giving them more gifts, that he rather spoils them, as sworn enemies, of what they have. *The proud*; those that by reason of the gifts God hath given them, lift themselves above others: Solomon, in the parallel place, calls them *scorners*; it being the usual guise of those that think over-well of themselves, to despise others, and even contemn the warnings and judgments of God himself, which may well draw him out to fight against them. *But giveth grace unto the humble*; not only gives favour and honour in the sight of men to those that are lowly in their own eyes, but especially furnisheth them with grace for the overcoming and mortifying their carnal desires and remaining corruptions.

7 Submit yourselves therefore to God.

i Eph. 4. 27. & 6. 11. 1 Pet. 5. 9.

ⁱResist the devil, and he will flee from you.

Submit yourselves therefore to God; viz. voluntarily and freely, and that not only in a way of obedience to all his commands, but (which is chiefly meant here) in a way of humility, and sense of your weakness, and emptiness, and need of his grace. *Therefore*; both because of the danger of pride, (opposed in the former verse to humility,) he *resisteth the proud*; and because of the benefit that comes by humility, he *giveth grace to the humble*. *Resist*, by faith, and the rest of the spiritual armour, Eph. vi. 13, 14, &c. Or, *resist*, i. e. comply not with his motions and temptations. *The devil*; the head and leader of fleshly lusts. These likewise are military terms. Having spoken before of strife and contention, he directs here with whom we may, and with whom we may not, contend. He had commended modesty toward men, they are our equals, we must not lift ourselves above them, nor envy nor strive with them; here he adviseth to submission to God as our supreme Governor, we must not contend with him; and to open war with the devil as our great enemy, our contention must be with him. *And he will flee from you*; as to that particular assault in which you resist him; and though he return again, and tempt you again, yet you still resisting, he will still be overcome; ye are never conquered so long as you do not consent.

8 ᵏDraw nigh to God, and he will draw nigh to you. ˡCleanse *your* hands, ye sinners; and ᵐpurify *your* hearts, ye ⁿdouble minded.

k 2 Chron. 15. 2. l Is. 1. 16. m 1 Pet. 1. 22. 1 John 3. 3. n ch. 1. 8.

Draw nigh to God; by faith, which is a coming to God, Heb. vii. 25; by true repentance, which is a returning to God, Hos. xiv. 1; Mal. iii. 7; and by fervent prayer to him for the help of his grace, Psal. xxv. 1. *And he will draw nigh to you*; by the manifestation of his grace and favour to you, particularly giving you strength against the devil and your lusts. *Cleanse your hands*; reform your actions, amend your lives. Hands, the principal instruments of bodily actions, being put for the actions themselves; cleanness of hands signifies the innocency of the outward conversation, Job xxii. 30; Psal. xxiv. 4; xxvi. 6; Isa. xxxiii. 15, 16. *Ye sinners*; you that are openly and notoriously vicious, whose wickedness appears in your ordinary practices: so such are called, Matt. xi. 19; Mark ii. 15; Luke vii. 37; xv. 2; John ix. 31. *And purify your hearts*; your thoughts and inward affections, from whence the evils of your outward actions proceed, Isa. lv. 7: see 1 Pet. i. 22; 1 John iii. 3. *Ye double minded*; either by the former he understands the profane, and by these, hypocrites, or the same by both, viz. such as had wicked hearts, and led wicked lives; only he shows wherein true repentance consists, viz. in the reformation both of the inward and outward man.

9 ᵒBe afflicted, and mourn, and weep: let your laughter be turned to mourning, and *your* joy to heaviness.

o Matt. 5. 4.

Be afflicted; humble yourselves for your sins, before mentioned, and in the sense of wrath approaching, if ye do not. *And mourn*, with inward sorrow of heart. *And weep*; show your inward grief by weeping, the usual expression and sign of it. *Let your laughter*; your carnal rejoicing in what you get by sinful courses, ver. 1, 2, lusting, warring, fighting. *Be turned into mourning*; exchange your carnal joy for godly sorrow. *And your joy*; to the same purpose as laughter, before: by it he means their pleasing themselves in the success of their unrighteousness, the gain of their rapine and violence. *Into heaviness*; the same as mourning, or an outward expression of it in the dejection of the countenance, which usually proceeds from shame or sorrow, (and the Greek word signifies both,) whereas joy and confidence make men lift up their heads or faces, Ezra ix. 6; Job x. 15; xi. 15; xxii. 26; Luke xxi. 28.

10 ᵖHumble yourselves in the sight of the Lord, and he shall lift you up.

p Job 22. 29. Matt. 23. 12. Luke 14. 11. & 18. 14. 1 Pet. 5. 6.

Humble yourselves: the same duty pressed again, only with respect to the more internal part of it, the debasement of the heart, lest they should rest too much in the outward exercises before mentioned. They did lift up themselves through pride and emulation, and he shows them the best way to the truest exaltation, viz. humility, Matt. xxiii. 12; Prov. xv. 33; xviii. 12. *In the sight of the Lord*; sincerely, as in the presence of the Searcher of hearts. *And he shall lift you up*; as to your outward state and enjoyments, so far as God sees good for you; but, however, in grace here, and glory hereafter, Luke xiv. 11.

11 ᑫSpeak not evil one of another, brethren. He that speaketh evil of *his* brother, ʳand judgeth his brother, speaketh evil of the law, and judgeth the law: but if thou judge the law, thou art not a doer of the law, but a judge.

q Eph. 4. 31. 1 Pet. 2. 1.

r Matt. 7. 1. Luke 6. 37. Rom. 2. 1. 1 Cor. 4. 5.

Speak not evil one of another; viz. unless in the way of

an ordinance, by reproof, admonition, &c., Lev. v. 1; 1 Cor. i. 11; xi. 18; 2 Cor. xi. 13; 2 Tim. iv. 14, 15. He forbids all detraction, rigid censuring, and rash judging the hearts and lives of others, when men condemn whatever doth not suit with their notions or humours, and make their own moroseness the rule of other men's manners. *Judgeth his brother;* finds fault with and condemns him for those things which the law doth not condemn in him, or forbid in him, Rom. xiv. 3, 4. *Judgeth the law;* viz. either, 1. By his practising and approving what the law condemns, i. e. this very censoriousness and detraction: or, 2. By condemning that which the law allows; he condemns the law for allowing it, taxing it as too short and imperfect. *But if thou judge the law, thou art not a doer of the law, but a judge;* if thou not only judgest thy brother, and therein invadest the law's office, (whose part it is to judge him,) but judgest him for what the law doth not forbid him, and therein judgest the law itself, as insufficient, and not strict enough; thou dost cast off the law's government, disown its superiority, exempt thyself from any subjection to it, and make thyself merely a judge of it.

s Matt. 10. 28.
t Rom. 14. 4, 13.

12 There is one lawgiver, ˢ who is able to save and to destroy: ᵗ who art thou that judgest another?

There is one lawgiver; one absolute, supreme, universal and spiritual Lawgiver, and who can simply and directly bind men's consciences, and make laws for their souls, Prov. viii. 15, 16; Isa. xxxiii. 22; Acts iv. 19. By this he intimates, that they did invade God's right, who took upon them a legislative power in prescribing to other men's consciences, and making their own will the rule of the others' duty. *Who is able to save and to destroy,* both temporally and eternally, Deut. xxxii. 39; 1 Sam. ii. 6; Isa. xliii. 13; whereas other lawgivers cannot save or destroy men's souls, nor so much as their lives, without God's concurrence. *Who art thou;* what a sorry creature, a man, a worm, that thou shouldst lift up thyself into God's place, and make thyself a judge of one not subject to thee! *That judgest another;* the servant of another Master, Rom. xiv. 4. It is a fond thing for thee to take upon thee the power of a judge, when thou hast no power of saving or destroying, rewarding or punishing.

u Prov. 27.1.
Luke 12. 18, &c.

13 ᵘ Go to now, ye that say, To day or to morrow we will go into such a city, and continue there a year, and buy and sell, and get gain:

Go to now; either this is a note of transition, or of command to inferiors, or rather of admonition to such as are stupid or rash, and tends to the awakening their attention, and stirring them up to the consideration of their duty, danger, &c. *Ye that say;* either with your mouths, or in your hearts. *To-day or to-morrow we will go into such a city;* not, let us go, but, *we will go,* in the indicative mood; noting the peremptoriness of their purposes, and their presuming upon future times and things, which were not in their power. *And continue there a year, and buy and sell, and get gain:* he doth not condemn merchants travelling into other countries, nor trading there, nor designing gain by their trade, nor forecasting their business; but their professing themselves the continuance of their life, the accomplishing their designs, and the success of their labours, without respect to God's providence and direction, as if their times and their works were in their own hands, not in his.

14 Whereas ye know not what *shall*

|| Or, *For it is.*
x Job 7. 7. Ps. 102. 3. ch. 1. 10. 1 Pet. 1. 24. 1 John 2. 17.

be on the morrow. For what *is* your life? ||ˣ It is even a vapour, that appeareth for a little time, and then vanisheth away.

Whereas ye know not what shall be on the morrow; whether ye yourselves shall continue till then, or what else shall then be, or not be. In vain do ye boast of whole years, when ye cannot command the events of one day. *For what is your life?* this question implies contempt, as 1 Sam. xxv. 10; Psal. cxliv. 3, 4. *It is even a vapour;* like a vapour, frail, uncertain, and of short continuance; and then how vain are those counsels and purposes that

are built upon no more sure a foundation than your own lives.

15 For that ye *ought* to say, ʸ If the Lord will, we shall live, and do this, or that.

y Acts 18.21. 1 Cor. 4. 19. & 16. 7. Heb. 6. 3.

For that ye ought to say: it is the real acknowledgment of God's providence, and the dependence of all our affairs upon him, which is here required; and this is to be done, either expressly with the mouth in such-like forms of speech as this is, so far as is needful for our glorifying God, and distinguishing ourselves from those that are profane, as hath been customary with the saints in Scripture, Acts xviii. 21; Rom i. 10, and other places, but always inwardly, and in the heart. *If the Lord will;* i. e. with his providential or directive will, which as yet we do not know, and therefore we say, *If the Lord will:* for all our counsels and determinations must be regulated by his preceptive or directive will, which we do know; and therefore, with respect to that will, we are not to say, We will do this, or that, if God will, i. e. commands it, but we must first see that it be commanded, and then resolve to do it if God will, that is, if in his providence he shall permit us. *If the Lord will, we shall live, and do this, or that;* some read the words, If the Lord will, and we shall live, we will do this, or that; and then the latter copulative *and* is redundant, and the sense is, that all our actions depend not only upon our living, but upon God's willing; God may permit us to live, and yet not permit us to do this or that. But if we take the words according to our reading, *If the Lord will, we shall live, and do this, or that,* the meaning is, that both our life and actions depend upon the will of God, nor the one, nor the other, is in our power. And so here is a double check to the vain boasts of those that were so peremptory in their resolutions, without considering the frailty of their own lives, or the dependence of their actions upon God's will, when both the one and the other are at his disposal.

16 But now ye rejoice in your boastings: ᶻ all such rejoicing is evil.

z 1 Cor. 5. 6.

But now ye rejoice, or, glory; ye please yourselves with them. *In your boastings;* viz. of your carnal projects, and hopes of what you intend to do, and expect to get: q. d. You vainly boast of your designs and successes, without taking notice of God's providence, under the government of which you and your affairs all are. *All such rejoicing is evil;* both as being contrary to the word, which assures us so often that it is vain to promise ourselves long life, or prosperity in our worldly business, without God's leave and blessing, Psal. cxxvii. 1; Prov. xvi. 9, 33; and likewise as proceeding from pride and security.

17 Therefore ᵃ to him that knoweth to do good, and doeth *it* not, to him it is sin.

a Luke 12. 47. John 9. 41. & 15. 22. Rom. 1. 20, 21, 32. & 2. 17, 18, 23.

Either this may relate to all that the apostle had been before speaking of; q. d. I have admonished you of your duty, and now ye know what ye are to do, and therefore if you do it not it will be your sin: or, it may refer to what he was immediately before discoursing of, and may be spoken to prevent an objection. They might say, he taught them no more than what they knew already; and that they acknowledged God's providence in all things. To this he replies, that if they knew their duty, they ought to practise it, and so actually submit themselves and their affairs to the conduct of that providence; and their not doing it, now that they knew it, would be rather be their sin. *To him it is sin;* i. e. sin indeed, or (as we say) sin with a witness; a greater sin, and which hath more of the nature of sin in it, or is more highly aggravated, by being against knowledge, and so is punishable with severer vengeance, than if done out of ignorance, Luke xii. 47. See the like expression, John ix. 41; xv. 22, 24.

CHAP. V

Wicked rich men are warned of God's impending judgment, 1—6. *The brethren are exhorted to patience, after the example of the prophets and of Job,* 7—11; *to abstain from swearing,* 12; *to pray in affliction and sickness, and*

JAMES V

sing psalms in prosperity, 13—15; *to acknowledge mutually their faults, and to pray for one another,* 16—18; *and to endeavour to reclaim sinners,* 19, 20.

^{a Prov. 11. 28. Luke 6. 24. 1 Tim. 6. 9.} GO ^ato now, *ye* rich men, weep and howl for your miseries that shall come upon *you*.

Go to now: see chap. iv. 13. *Ye rich men;* he speaks to them not simply as rich, (for riches and grace sometimes may go together,) but as wicked, not only wallowing in wealth, but abusing it to pride, luxury, oppression, and cruelty. Against these, either as looking on them as incurable, or upon supposition of their impenitency, he denounceth God's judgments; and that whether they were unconverted Jews, vexing the believing Jews; or Gentiles, oppressing the Christian Jews; or Christians in profession and name, who yet were so vile in their practice, as to condemn and kill the just; and that they might more speciously do it, to draw them before the judgment-seats, &c. *Weep and howl;* to denote the extremity of the calamities coming upon them, in which they should not only weep like men, but howl like wild beasts: see Jer. iv. 8; Micah i. 8; Joel i. 10, 13. *For your miseries that shall come upon you;* or, are coming upon you, to signify the certainty and nearness of them. The miseries he means may be both temporal and eternal.

^{b Job 13. 28. Matt. 6. 20. ch. 2. 2.} 2 Your riches are corrupted, and ^b your garments are motheaten.

Your riches are corrupted: either by *riches* he means the general, and by *garments*, gold and silver, the particulars in which their riches consisted; and then being corrupted, is to be taken generally, as comprehending the several ways whereby the several kinds of their riches were spoiled: or else, by *riches* he understands such things as were liable to corruption, or putrefaction, as corn, wine, oil, which were a great part of their riches. *And your garments are moth-eaten;* costly garments, in which rich men are wont to pride themselves; and under them may be comprehended all such clothes as may be eaten by worms or moths.

3 Your gold and silver is cankered; and the rust of them shall be a witness against you, and shall eat your flesh as it were fire. ^cYe have heaped treasure together for the last days.

^{c Rom. 2. 5.}

Your gold and silver is cankered; the most precious and lasting metals; yet even they, with long disuse, canker, and go to decay. Under these, other metals in esteem among them may be understood. *And the rust of them shall be a witness against you:* by a prosopopœia, that which properly belongs to living persons is ascribed to dead things, as Hab. ii. 11; Luke xix. 40. It is as much as if he had said, The rust shall be a certain evidence against you, and which will as effectually convict you, as any living witness could do, of your folly in putting your trust in perishing things, your greediness in hoarding them up, your unmercifulness in not supplying the wants of others, and your unreasonableness in denying the use of them to yourselves, when you had rather let them lie by and perish, than enjoy the comfort of them, or do good with them. The like expression we have, Mark vi. 11. *And shall eat your flesh;* the rust (the witness of your covetousness and cruelty) which now eats your money, shall hereafter devour yourselves, soul and body, (which he means by *flesh*,) viz. by procuring and kindling the wrath of God upon you, (compared to fire,) and likewise by galling your consciences with a vexatious remembrance of your sin and folly; and so what in the judgment is a witness against you, in hell will be a tormentor to you. *As it were fire;* as if you had reserved fire in your treasure, as well as treasure in your chests. *Ye have heaped treasure together for the last days:* either this may be understood metaphorically, ye have heaped a treasure of wrath for the last days, Rom. ii. 5; or literally, ye have hoarded up your wealth against the last and fatal days, in which God is bringing those judgments upon you which will consume all.

^{d Lev. 19. 13. Job 24. 10, 11. Jer. 22. 13. Mal. 3. 5.} 4 Behold, ^d the hire of the labourers who have reaped down your fields, which is of you kept back by fraud, crieth: and ^ethe cries of them which have reaped are entered into the ears of the Lord of sabaoth.

^{Ecclus. 34. 21, 22. e Deut. 24. 15.}

Behold; this is either a note of demonstration, as John i. 29; q. d. The case is plain, and cannot be denied; or of excitation; q. d. Seriously consider it; or rather, of confirmation, to intimate, that the threatenings here denounced should certainly be made good upon them: see Jude 14. *The hire of the labourers who have reaped down your fields;* the wages of those by whose labour and sweat ye yourselves live and are nourished. *Which is of you kept back by fraud;* either wholly denied them, or detained from them when due to them, contrary to the law, Lev. xix. 13; Deut. xxiv. 14, 15. Deferring payment is a sort of defrauding, as it bereaves the creditor of the benefit of improvement; and so they are taxed here with injustice, as well as covetousness, in that they lived upon other men's labours, and starved the poor to enrich themselves. *Crieth;* viz. to God for vengeance, as such sins are said to do, which either are so openly and boldly committed, as to dare the justice of God, or so secretly, or securely, that they are like to escape the justice of men, Gen. iv. 10; xviii. 20, 21. Among others, oppression of the poor is a loud crying sin, Exod. ii. 23; Job xxiv. 11, 12; Hab. ii. 9, 11, 12. *The Lord of sabaoth;* i. e. the Lord of hosts, as having all the creatures above and below, of all sorts, ranked under him as their great Commander, whose will they are ready to execute. He mentions God by this title, not only for the encouragement of the poor oppressed, whose Patron and Protector he avows himself to be, Exod. xxii. 23, 24, 27; Prov. xxiii. 11; but for terror to the powerful oppressors, who think themselves out of the reach of men's judgment.

5 ^fYe have lived in pleasure on the earth, and been wanton; ye have nourished your hearts, as in a day of slaughter.

^{f Job 21. 13. Amos 6. 1, 4. Luke 16. 19, 25. 1 Tim. 5. 6.}

Ye have lived in pleasure; luxuriously and deliciously, giving up yourselves to your sensual appetites, Amos vi. 4—6; Luke xvi. 19, 25. *On the earth;* where you place your happiness without looking higher, and from whence you fetch your delights, Phil. iii. 19. *And been wanton:* the same word is used 1 Tim. v. 6; it seems to imply effeminate, lascivious behaviour, as the effect of their riotous living. *Ye have nourished your hearts:* either by a Hebrew phrase, *ye have nourished your hearts,* for ye have nourished yourselves, Esth. vi. 6; Job x. 13; or, ye have cheered up and encouraged your hearts in your luxury by pampering your flesh, (Luke xii. 19,) and feeding not to the satisfaction of nature, but the inflaming of your lusts. *As in a day of slaughter;* either securely, and without fear of the destruction coming upon you, as sheep graze quietly, though by and by to be brought to the shambles; or rather, *in a day of slaughter,* i. e. in a day of solemn feasting, when many beasts were killed in sacrifice, on which they were wont to feast, Prov. vii. 14; xvii. 1. They made every day a feasting day, and that, too, lavishing out other men's dues upon their own flesh, and sparing from their labourers that they might spend upon their lusts. This he brings to aggravate their sin.

6 ^gYe have condemned *and* killed the just; *and* he doth not resist you.

^{g ch. 2. 6.}

Ye have condemned and killed; i. e. procured by your wealth and power the passing unrighteous sentences, and thereby the destruction of the just. *The just;* indefinitely and collectively, *the just* for any just man, viz. such as were innocent and just in comparison of their persecuters. *And he doth not resist you;* this notes not only the patience of such in bearing injuries, but their weakness, and being destitute of human help against their adversaries' power.

7 ‖ Be patient therefore, brethren, unto the coming of the Lord. Behold, the husbandman waiteth for the precious fruit of the earth, and hath long patience for it, until he receive ^hthe early and latter rain.

^{Or, *Be long patient,* or, *Suffer with long patience.* h Deut. 11. 14. Jer. 5. 24. Hos. 6. 3. Joel 2. 23. Zech. 10. 1.}

Be patient therefore, brethren, unto the coming of the

JAMES V.

Lord; viz. to judgment, and that either particular, to avenge the quarrels of innocent sufferers upon their tyrannical persecutors; or rather, to the general judgment, in which a full retribution is to be made both to the just and unjust, Rom. ii. 5, 6, &c. To which judgment the Scripture calls all to look, especially those that are under oppression and persecution, 2 Thess. i. 6, 7, &c. *Behold, the husbandman waiteth for the precious fruit of the earth;* which cost him hard labour, and by which he receives great benefit, the sustentation of his life. *Until he receive the early and latter rain;* the rain soon after the sowing, which caused the corn to spring up; and that before the harvest, which plumped it, and made it fit for reaping, Deut. xi. 14; Jer. v. 24; Hos. vi. 3; Joel ii. 23.

8 Be ye also patient; stablish your hearts: ⁱ for the coming of the Lord draweth nigh.

<small>i Phil. 4. 5.
Heb. 10. 25,
37. 1 Pet.4.7.</small>

Be ye also patient; viz. in expectation of your harvest, and the fruit of your labours, as the husbandman is in looking for his. *Stablish your hearts;* let your hearts be stedfast in faith and constant in holiness, encouraging yourselves to both by the coming of the Lord. *For the coming of the Lord draweth nigh;* as before, his coming to the general judgment, which is said to be nigh, because of the certainty of its coming, and the uncertainty of the time when it will come, and because it is continually drawing on, and the whole time of the world's duration till then is but short in comparison of the eternity following; and likewise because the particular judgment of every man is nigh at hand. See Phil. iv. 5; Heb. x. 37.

<small>k ch. 4. 11.
‖ Or, *Groan,*
or, *grieve*
not.
1 Matt. 24.33.
1 Cor. 4. 5.</small>

9 ^k ‖ Grudge not one against another, brethren, lest ye be condemned: behold, the judge ^l standeth before the door.

Grudge not; Greek. Groan not; the sense may be, either, Envy not one another, (or, as we translate it, *Grudge not,*) it being the nature of envy to groan at other men's good; or, Groan not by way of accusation or complaint to God against others, desiring him to avenge your quarrels, as if you were too good to suffer injuries, or God were unjust or forgetful of righting you. *One against another;* brother against brother, Christian against Christian: they were injured not only by rich worldlings and open oppressors, but by their fellow professors, and gave one another mutual cause of sighing and groaning. *Lest ye be condemned;* lest God punish you all; there being none of you but have given others cause of grief and complaint, as well as others have given you, Matt. vii. 1. *Behold, the Judge standeth before the door;* the Lord Jesus Christ, the Judge of you all, is at hand, (Phil. iv. 5,) in a readiness either to bring those evils upon you which you wish may fall upon others, or to give you your reward, if *through patient continuance in well doing* you seek for it, Rom. ii. 7. The like phrase we have, Matt. xxiv. 33; Mark xiii. 29; or it may allude to Gen. iv. 7.

<small>m Matt. 5.
12. Heb. 11.
35, &c.</small>

10 ^m Take, my brethren, the prophets, who have spoken in the name of the Lord, for an example of suffering affliction, and of patience.

Take, my brethren, the prophets; as being most eminent among God's people, and leaders of them; he intimates that it is an honour to suffer among the best. *Who have spoken in the name of the Lord;* by his command and authority, and so were employed in the highest services in the church, and thereby appeared to be approved of God, and most dear to him. *For an example of suffering affliction:* as much as God honoured and loved them, yet they were not exempted from afflictions, but were maligned, traduced, and persecuted by men, 1 Kings xviii. 13; xix. 14; 2 Kings vi. 31; Amos vii. 10; Heb. xi.; and therefore when they suffered such hard things, it is no shame for you to suffer the like, Matt. v. 12. *And of patience;* as the example of their sufferings should prevent your discouragement, so the example of their patience should provoke your imitation; God having set them forth as examples of both, that if you suffer the same things, you may suffer with the same minds.

<small>n Ps. 94. 12.
Matt. 5. 10,
11. & 10. 22.
o Job 1. 21,
22. & 2. 10.</small>

11 Behold, ⁿ we count them happy which endure. Ye have heard of ^o the patience of Job, and have seen ^p the end of the Lord; that ^q the Lord is very pitiful, and of tender mercy.

<small>p Job 42. 16,
&c.
q Num. 14.
18. Ps. 103.
8.</small>

We count them happy which endure; we ourselves count them happy that endure, and therefore should be patient, and not count ourselves miserable if we endure too. *Which endure;* viz. patiently and constantly, Matt. v. 10, 11. *Ye have heard of the patience of Job;* for which he was as eminent as for his sufferings; and though some signs of impatience be showed, yet his patience and submission to God being prevalent, and most remarkable to him, that only is taken notice of, and his failings overlooked. *And have seen the end of the Lord:* Job's patience is heard of, but God's end seen: seeing being a clearer way of perception than hearing, is put in this latter clause, because God's bounty and recompence was more evident than Job's patience. *The end of the Lord;* the good issue God gave to all Job's sufferings, in restoring him to his former state, and doubling his prosperity. *That the Lord is very pitiful;* full of bowels, Greek; the bowels being the seat of compassion, (in which we feel a stirring when strong affections are working in us,) are frequently put to signify the most tender and movable affections, such as mothers have toward their children, Gen. xliii. 30; 1 Kings iii. 26; Isa. lxiii. 15; Col. iii. 12: this seems to note the affection itself, or God's readiness to show mercy, Luke i. 78. *And of tender mercy:* this may imply acts of mercy suitable to a merciful nature, the former mercy within, and this mercy breaking out.

12 But above all things, my brethren, ^r swear not, neither by heaven, neither by the earth, neither by any other oath: but let your yea be yea; and *your* nay, nay; lest ye fall into condemnation.

<small>r Matt. 5.
34, &c.</small>

Because it is a great sin to swear upon every slight occasion, and it was very usual among the Jews, and it was the more difficult to bring them off from it who were so much accustomed to it; therefore the apostle commands them, that *above all things* they should not swear, i. e. should take special care they did not, and watch diligently against a sin so many were addicted to, and into which they might so easily fall. *Swear not;* all swearing is not forbidden, any more than Matt. v. 34; (for oaths are made use of by holy men both in the Old and New Testament, Gen. xxi. 23, 24; xxiv. 3; xxvi. 28; 1 Kings xvii. 1, 2; 2 Cor. i. 23; Gal. i. 20; and the use of an oath is permitted and approved of by God himself, Psal. xv. 4; Heb. vi. 16;) but such oaths as are false, rash, vain, without just cause, or customary and frequent in ordinary discourse, 1 Kings xix. 2; Jer. v. 2; Matt. v. 37. *Neither by heaven, neither by the earth;* by which the Jews thought they might lawfully swear, as likewise by other creatures, so the name of God were not interposed; not considering that where it is not expressed yet it is implied, Matt. xxiii. 20, 21. *Neither by any other oath;* viz. of the like kind. *But let your yea be yea; and your nay, nay:* either, 1. Let your speech be yea, yea, and nay, nay; i. e. by plain affirmations and negations, without the addition of any oath for confirmation, Matt. v. 37: or, 2. *Let your yea be yea, and your nay, nay,* i. e. let your words be in truth and sincerity, your speech seconded by your actions; accustom yourselves to truth and plainness in speaking, and that will take away the occasion of swearing. See the like, 2 Cor. i. 17—19. *Lest ye fall into condemnation;* viz. for taking the name of God in vain, Exod. xx. 7, which is always done in an unwarrantable oath.

13 Is any among you afflicted? let him pray. Is any merry? ^s let him sing psalms.

<small>s Eph. 5. 19.
Col. 3. 16.</small>

Is any among you afflicted? either troubled or afflicted in mind, as appears by the opposite being *merry,* or more generally afflicted any way. Not that we need not pray at other times, but when under afflictions God calls us more especially to it, and our own necessities put us upon it. *Let him pray;* for support, patience, sanctification of afflictions, &c. *Is any merry? let him sing psalms;* express his mirth in a holy manner, by praising God with psalms or spiritual songs for mercies received from him, 1 Cor.

xiv. 15; Eph. v. 19; and so keep up his spiritual mirth by a spiritual exercise, lest his cheerfulness degenerate into vanity and frothiness.

14 Is any sick among you? let him call for the elders of the church; and let them pray over him, ᵗanointing him with oil in the name of the Lord:

<small>t Mark 6. 13. & 16. 18.</small>

Is any sick? or infirm, though not desperately and incurably. *Let him call for the elders;* especially teaching elders, they being usually best furnished with gifts who labour in the word and doctrine, 1 Tim. v. 17. It is in the plural number, either by an enallage for the singular; q. d. Let him send for some or other of the elders; or, because there were in those times usually several elders (an ecclesiastical senate) in each church. *And let them pray over him;* as it were setting him before God, and presenting him to him, which might be a means to stir up the greater affection and warmth in prayer; see 1 Kings xvii. 21; 2 Kings iv. 33, 34; John xi. 41; Acts xx. 10; ix. 40: or laying on their hands, as Acts xxviii. 8, which yet seems to be for the same end. *Anointing him with oil;* an outward rite used in those times, in miraculous healing sick persons, which might then be kept up, while the gift whereof it was the symbol continued; but the gift ceasing, it is vainly used. These cures were sometimes wrought only with a word, Acts ix. 34; xiv. 10; xvi. 18; sometimes by taking by the hand, or embracing, Acts iii. 7; xx. 10; sometimes by laying on of hands, Mark xvi. 18; Acts ix. 17; sometimes by anointing with oil, Mark vi. 13: and so this is not an institution of a sacrament, but a command, that those elders that had the gift of healing, (as many in those days had,) being called by the sick to come to them, should (the Spirit of the Lord so directing them) exercise that gift, as well as pray over them. *In the name of the Lord;* either, calling upon the Lord, and so joining prayer with their anointing; or, *in the name*, is by the authority of the Lord, from whom they had received that gift.

15 And the prayer of faith shall save the sick, and the Lord shall raise him up; ᵘand if he have committed sins, they shall be forgiven him.

<small>u Is. 33. 24. Matt. 9. 2.</small>

And the prayer of faith; i. e. proceeding from faith; the cure is ascribed to prayer, the moral means, and standing ordinance, not to the anointing, which was but ceremonial and temporary; and to faith in prayer, to show that this remedy was effectual only when faith (requisite to the working of miracles) was active, viz. in a certain persuasion that the sick person should be healed. *Shall save the sick;* restore to health, (if God see it fit, and the health of the body be good for the soul,) Mark x. 52; Luke vii. 50; xviii. 42. *And the Lord shall raise him up;* the elders pray, but the Lord raiseth up, being prayed to in faith. *Raise him up;* the same as saving before, only the word seems to respect the sick man's lying upon his bed, from which he riseth when he is healed, Mark i. 31. *If he have committed sins;* if he have by his sins procured his sickness; or, those sins for which particularly God visits him with sickness; sin being often the cause of sickness, Matt. ix. 2; John v. 14; 1 Cor. xi. 30, though not always, John ix. 2. *They shall be forgiven him;* God will take away the cause as well as the effect, heal the soul as well as the body, and prayer is the means of obtaining both.

16 Confess ˣyour faults one to another, and pray one for another, that ye may be healed. ˣThe effectual fervent prayer of a righteous man availeth much.

<small>x Gen. 20. 17. Num. 11. 2. Deut. 9. 18, 19, 20. Josh. 10. 12. 1 Sam. 12. 18. 1 Kings 13. 6. 2 Kings 4. 33. & 19. 15, 20. & 20. 2, 4, &c. Ps. 10. 17. & 34. 15. & 145. 18. Prov. 15. 29. & 28. 9. John 9. 31. 1 John 3. 22.</small>

Confess your faults; some copies have the illative particle, therefore, in the text, but even without that here seems to be a connexion between this and the former verse: he had said, the sick man's sins should be forgiven upon the elders' praying; and here he adds, that they must be confessed. *One to another;* either, that ye may be reconciled to one another when offended, or rather, confess when admonished or reproved for sin, or wounded in your consciences with the sense of it: and so this is not meant of auricular confession made to a priest, but such as should be made, though especially to ministers, yet, when need is, even to godly, experienced Christians, for the easing and disburdening men's consciences, and getting the help of others' prayers. *And pray one for another;* both in other ordinary cases, and chiefly upon occasion of your mutual confessions, and those soul-troubles that prompted you to them. *That ye may be healed;* not only recover bodily health when sick, but spiritual, when weakened or wounded by sin. Healing is often applied to the soul as well as the body, Matt. xiii. 15; Luke iv. 18; Heb. xii. 13; 1 Pet. ii. 24. *The effectual fervent prayer:* our translators use two words (and little enough) to express the significancy of the Greek word in this place: some translate it inwrought; it seems to be a prayer wrought in the soul by the Holy Spirit, and so may imply both the efficiency of God's Spirit, (the Spirit of supplications, Zech. xii. 10,) and the vehemency of holy affections caused by him in prayer, Rom. viii. 26. *Of a righteous man;* one sincerely righteous, and in a gospel sense; the following instance of Elias shows that it is not to be understood of a man absolutely righteous. *Availeth much;* is very powerful with God for obtaining what is desired, 1 John v. 14; whereas God heareth not sinners, Prov. xv. 8, 29.

17 Elias was a man ʸsubject to like passions as we are, and ᶻhe prayed ‖ earnestly that it might not rain: ᵃand it rained not on the earth by the space of three years and six months.

<small>y Acts 14. 15. z 1 Kings 17. 1. ‖ Or, *in prayer*. a Luke 4. 25.</small>

Elias was a man subject to like passions as we are; both of body and mind, natural and moral; and so, though he were righteous, yet he was not perfect; though an eminent prophet, yet but a man. *And he prayed earnestly;* with that effectual, fervent prayer before mentioned. It is a Hebrew phrase, and notes vehemency, as Luke xxii. 15. *That it might not rain;* this is not expressly mentioned in the history, but this apostle might have it by revelation, or by certain tradition well known in his age. Other passages of the like nature we meet with in the New Testament which are not in the Old: see 1 Tim. iii. 8; Heb. xii. 21; Jude 9. *And it rained not on the earth;* or, the land, viz. of the ten tribes, and the places bordering on them, as Sarepta, 1 Kings xvii. 9; Luke iv. 25, 26. *By the space of three years and six months:* so Luke iv. 25. *Quest.* How doth this agree with 1 Kings xviii. 1, where it is said, *the word of the Lord came to Elijah in the third year? Answ.* Most probably it was in the midst of the third year from his coming to Sarepta; and he was by the brook Cherith a year. 1 Kings xvii. 7, where the margin reads it, according to the Hebrew, at the end of days, i. e. the days of a year, as the phrase is often used, Gen. iv. 3; Judg. xvii. 10; so that his time spent in both places may well make up the *three years and six months.*

18 And ᵇhe prayed again, and the heaven gave rain, and the earth brought forth her fruit.

<small>b 1 Kings 18. 42, 45.</small>

And he prayed again; after the destroying the prophets of Baal. Baal-worship especially gave occasion to his former prayer, which he puts up out of his zeal to God's glory, then laid low by the Israelites' idolatry, and a desire to have them by some exemplary punishment for their sin awakened to repentance. And the destruction of the idolaters, and reformation of the people, who now acknowledged the Lord to be God, might give occasion to this. *And the heaven gave rain;* i. e. the air or clouds, which had not been for three years before.

19 Brethren, ᶜif any of you do err from the truth, and one convert him;

<small>c Mat. 18. 15.</small>

The truth; the truth of God revealed in the gospel as the complete rule of faith and life: see the gospel called *the truth* by way of eminency, chap. i. 18; Gal. ii. 5, 14; iii. 1; v. 7; Eph. i. 13; 1 Pet. i. 22. *And one;* any one, minister or private believer, who may be an instrument in the conversion of others; though one acts by way of authority, the other by way of charity, yet both out of duty. *Convert him;* viz. ministerially or instrumentally, in subordination to God. The work is his, Eph. ii. 10, but often is ascribed to the instruments acting under him, and using means appointed by him, and by which he works, Acts xxvi. 18.

d Rom. 11. 14. 1 Cor. 9. 22. 1 Tim. 4. 16. e Prov. 10. 12. 1 Pet. 4. 8.

20 Let him know, that he which converteth the sinner from the error of his way ᵈ shall save a soul from death, and ᵉ shall hide a multitude of sins.

Of his way; of his life and actions, which is contrary to the way which God hath prescribed. *Shall save;* men are said to save in the same way as to convert, viz. instrumentally. *A soul;* the soul of him that is thus converted,

1 Tim. iv. 16 : *soul* for person, as chap. i. 21. *From death :* eternal death, unto which he was hastening while he continued in the error of his way, which led him toward destruction. *And shall hide a multitude of sins;* in the same sense as before he is said to convert and save his soul, viz. in being instrumental to bring him to faith and repentance, upon which God pardons, i. e. hides his sins, (Psal. xxxii. 1,) though not from the eye of his omniscience, yet from the eye of his vindictive justice, and so as not to bring them forth in judgment against him.

THE FIRST EPISTLE GENERAL

OF

PETER

THE ARGUMENT

Of the penman of this Epistle there is no doubt; and of the time of his writing it, no certainty, whether about the year of our Lord 45, or rather 65. The occasion of it may (not improbably) be thought to be the same that was of James's writing his, viz. the folly and perverseness of some in those times, and among the Jewish Christians to whom he wrote, in separating faith from holiness, and their doubting whether Peter and Paul taught the same doctrine. His scope therefore is, partly to confirm these saints in the belief of the gospel, and to testify that the doctrine of the grace of God through Jesus Christ, which they had embraced and did profess, was indeed infallibly true, chap. v. 12, being the same that had been preached by the prophets to the fathers of the Old Testament, chap. i. 10—12; fairly implying it to be the same that Paul preached, by his sending this Epistle to them that were of the circumcision, by Silvanus, a minister of the uncircumcision, and Paul's ordinary companion in the work of the gospel; as likewise he doth by that ample testimony he gives to Paul and his writings, 2 Pet. iii. 15, 16. And partly to exhort them to the practice of godliness, and a conversation suitable to the gospel : and that he doth, both as to the general duties incumbent on all believers, in the first chapter, from ver. 13, to chap. ii. 12; and as to the particular duties which concerned them in their several relations, subjects to magistrates, servants to masters, husbands and wives mutually to each other, ministers to people, younger people to their elders, and especially sufferers towards their oppressors and persecutors; but withal intermixing several general duties, and of concernment to all, and concluding all with prayer and salutation.

CHAP. I

The apostle's address to the strangers elect in Christ, dispersed throughout the Lesser Asia, 1, 2. *He blesseth God for having raised them to the hope of a blessed immortality,* 3—9. *He showeth that their salvation in Christ had been foretold by the prophets of old,* 10—12; *and exhorteth them to a vigilant and holy conversation, suitable to their calling and redemption by the blood of Christ,* 13—21; *and to mutual love,* 22—25.

A. D. cir. 60.
a John 7. 35. Acts 2. 5. 9. 10. Jam. 1. 1.

PETER, an apostle of Jesus Christ, to the strangers ᵃ scattered throughout Pontus, Galatia, Cappadocia, Asia, and Bithynia,

To the strangers; not only metaphorically strangers, as all believers are in the world, chap. ii. 11; but properly, as being out of their own land, and so really strangers in the places here mentioned. *Scattered;* so James i. 1. *Throughout Pontus;* a country of the Lesser Asia, bordering upon the Euxine sea, and reaching as far as Colchis. *Galatia;* which borders upon Pontus, and lies southward of it. To the Gentile churches inhabiting here, Paul wrote his Epistle inscribed to the Galatians. *Cappadocia;* this likewise borders upon Pontus, and is joined with it, Acts ii. 9. *Asia;* that part of Asia the Less, which was especially called Asia, viz. the whole country of Ionia, which contained in it Troas, Phrygia, Lydia, Caria, &c. See Acts xvi. 6, 9; xix. 10, 31. *And Bithynia;* another province of the Lesser Asia, bordering upon Pontus and Galatia, and opposite to Thracia. *Quest.* Who were the strangers to whom this Epistle was written ? *Answ.* Chiefly the Christian Jews scattered in these countries, as appears by chap. ii. 12, and i. 18, where he mentions the *traditions* of their *fathers,* of which the Jews were so fond, Matt. xv. 2; Gal. i. 14; but secondarily, to the converted Gentiles. As Paul, the apostle of the uncircumcision, wrote principally to the converted Gentiles, at Rome, Corinth, Ephesus, &c., but doth not exclude those Jews that were among them, who, being converted to the faith, were of the same mystical body with them; so Peter, though he firstly wrote to the converted Jews, as being an apostle of the circumcision, yet includes the Gentiles that were mingled among them, and joined in faith and worship with them.

2 ᵇ Elect ᶜ according to the foreknowledge of God the Father, ᵈ through sanctification of the Spirit, unto obedience and ᵉ sprinkling of the blood of Jesus Christ : ᶠ Grace unto you, and peace, be multiplied.

b Eph. 1. 4. ch. 2. 9. c Rom. 8. 29. & 11. 2. d 2 Thess. 2. 13. e Heb. 10. 22. & 12. 24. f Rom. 1. 7. 2 Pet. 1. 2. Jude 2.

By *elect* he means, either, 1. Singled out of the world, and separated unto God in their effectual calling, as 1 Cor. i. 1; those that are said to be called, ver. 26, are said to be chosen, ver. 27, 28; and so the word seems to be taken, James ii. 5 : or, 2. Chosen to salvation, and the means of it, in God's eternal decree, Eph. i. 4; 2 Thess. ii. 13. *According to the foreknowledge;* either, 1. The Divine preordination, or decree of election, as the word is taken, ver. 20, and then we may take *elect* in the first sense ; men are chosen out of the world, or called in time, according as they were chosen from eternity, Rom. viii. 30 : or, 2. *Foreknowledge* here is as much as approbation or love, Matt. vii. 25; Rom. xi. 2; and so signifies the free favour and good will of God, which is the fountain from whence the decree of election proceeds; and then we are to take *elect*

I. PETER I

in the latter sense, and so *elect according to the foreknowledge of God,* is, eternally designed unto life, according to, or out of, that free grace and love God did from eternity bear to them, which was the only motive he had for his choosing them: or, (which comes to the same,) by *foreknowledge* we may understand election itself, as it is in God; and by election, the same, as terminated in the creature, and executed in effectual calling. *Of God the Father;* this doth not exclude the Son or Spirit from their interest in and concurrence to the Divine decree, but only notes the order of working among the three Persons in the affair of man's salvation; election is ascribed to the Father, reconciliation to the Son, and sanctification to the Spirit. *Through sanctification:* sanctification seems to be taken in a large sense, for the whole change of our spiritual state, both as to real grace in regeneration, and relative in justification; so that God may then be said to sanctify us, when in our effectual calling he justifies us from our sins, and renews us unto obedience: so it is taken, Heb. x. 10. *Of the Spirit;* this is to be understood rather of the Spirit of God, the efficient of sanctification, than the spirit or soul of man, the subject of it. *Unto obedience;* either, 1. The obedience of Christ to God; and then the sense is, elect, or ordained to be, by the sanctification of the Spirit, made partakers of the benefits of Christ's obedience: or, 2. The obedience of believers to Christ, and that either in their believing, faith being a giving obedience to the great command of the gospel, John vi. 29, and particularly called *obedience.* Rom. i. 5; and then the sense runs thus, elect unto faith, which was to be wrought in you by the sanctification of the Spirit: or else in the exercise of holiness, which is the fruit of faith; and then it signifies the same as Eph. i. 4, chosen, that you might be made, by the sanctification of the Spirit, holy and unblamable, and might accordingly demean yourselves. *And sprinkling of the blood of Jesus Christ;* an allusion to the sprinkling of the blood of the sacrifices under the law, Heb. ix. 13, 14, 20—22; xii. 24; it signifies the application of the blood of Christ for the purging of the conscience, (which was typified by those legal sprinklings,) especially from the guilt of sin; which sprinkling, or application of the blood of Christ to our consciences, is performed on our part by faith, on God's part by his Spirit working that faith in us (as well as enabling us unto obedience) in our effectual calling, as likewise by God's imputing Christ's righteousness to us; and so the sense of the whole is, Elect according to the foreknowledge of God, to be by the sanctification of the Spirit brought into the participation of all the benefits of Christ's redemption; the sum of which consists in the renovation of your natures unto gospel obedience, and the justification of your persons. *Grace unto you, and peace, be multiplied;* there being several kinds of grace, chap. iv. 10, and several kinds of peace, outward and inward, he wisheth them all kinds of each; and there being several degrees and measures of both, he prays for an increase of these degrees in them, and so a multiplication of all good, both temporal and spiritual, to them.

3 ᵍ Blessed *be* the God and Father of our Lord Jesus Christ, which ʰ according to his †abundant mercy ⁱ hath begotten us again unto a lively hope ᵏ by the resurrection of Jesus Christ from the dead,

g 2 Cor. 1. 3.
Eph. 1. 3.
h Tit. 3. 5.
† Gr. *much.*
i John 3, 3, 5.
Jam. 1. 18.
k 1 Cor. 15.
20. 1 Thes. 4.
14. ch. 3. 21.

Blessed be the God and Father of our Lord Jesus Christ; either the conjunction *and* is here but an explicative particle, and so we render it, 2 Cor. i. 3, *God, even the Father,* &c.; or if we take it for a copulative, as Eph. i. 3, God is called the *God* of Jesus Christ, according to Christ's human nature, and his *Father* according to his Divine. *Which according to his abundant mercy;* this shows the fountain from whence regeneration and all other spiritual blessings flow, and excludes all merit and dignity in us, as the cause of so great benefits. *Abundant mercy* is the same with riches of mercy, Eph. ii. 4. *Hath begotten us again;* translated us out of a state of sin and misery into a state of grace and life; and so begotten again here, is the same as sanctifying in the former verse. *Unto a lively hope;* either a *lively hope,* for hope of life; or rather, a lively hope is a true and effectual hope, such as proceeds from a lively faith, and is itself productive of peace and purity, Rom. v. 2;

1 John iii. 3, in opposition to the vain hope of worldly men, which neither comes from faith nor tends to holiness. *By the resurrection of Jesus Christ from the dead:* this may be referred either, 1. To God's begetting us again, and then it implies the resurrection of Christ to be the cause of our regeneration, we being raised to a spiritual life by the power of Christ's resurrection, and our vivification being often ascribed to it, chap. iii. 21; Rom. iv. 25; vi. 4, 5: see Eph. ii. 5. Or, 2. To the lively hope to which he begets us, which depends upon, and ariseth from, the faith of Christ's resurrection, Rom. viii. 11; 1 Cor. xv. 17, 19; 1 Thess. iv. 13, 14. Christ's resurrection being the cause and pledge of ours, as the certainty of ours depends upon his, so the liveliness of our hope follows upon the faith of it. Possibly the apostle may have in these words some respect to the languishing condition of the hope of him, and the other disciples, Luke xxiv. 21, which was then ready to expire, but was again revived by their being well assured of his resurrection, ver. 33, 34.

4 To an inheritance incorruptible, and undefiled, ¹ and that fadeth not away, ᵐ reserved in heaven ∥ for you,

l ch. 5. 4.
m Col. 1. 5.
2 Tim. 4. 8.
∥ Or, *for us.*

To an inheritance; so eternal life is called, Eph. i. 18, and elsewhere, as being given not as wages to hirelings, but as an inheritance to children born of God, and adopted to him. *Incorruptible;* immortal, everlasting, which being once possessed, cannot be taken away, nor pass over to others. *And undefiled;* both as being pure in itself, and having nothing to offend them that enjoy it; and likewise as being incapable of any pollution or defilement, contrary to what is said of the land of Canaan, the earthly inheritance of the Israelites, Jer. ii. 7; Ezek. xxxvi. 17. *And that fadeth not away;* always retains its vigour and gratefulness, never causes weariness or satiety in them that possess it. It seems to be a metaphor taken from flowers, probably the amaranthus, (the very word here used,) which still keeps its freshness and verdure, without any decay or withering. *Reserved;* laid up, Col. i. 5; 2 Tim. iv. 8; secured for the heirs, though not yet possessed by them. *In heaven;* and therefore safe, and out of the reach of enemies. This is opposed to the uncertain condition of earthly possessions, such as Canaan was. *For you;* margin, for us, viz. whom God hath begotten again: or if we read it, as in the text, *for you,* the apostle may change the person in order to his exhortation.

5 ⁿ Who are kept by the power of God through faith unto salvation ready to be revealed in the last time.

n John 10.
28, 29. & 17.
11, 12, 15.
Jude 1.

Who are kept: lest it should be objected, that though the inheritance be safe in heaven, yet the heirs are in danger here upon earth, by reason of the power and stratagems of enemies, and their own imprudence and weakness; he adds, that not only their inheritance is reserved for them, but they preserved unto it, kept securely and carefully, as with a garrison, (for so the word signifies,) against all the assaults, incursions, and devices of the devil and the world. *By the power of God;* which power is infinite and invincible, and therefore able to keep them, John x. 28, 29; Rom. viii. 31, 38, 39; 2 Tim. i. 12. *Through faith;* which, resting on the power of God, overcomes all their enemies, the flesh, 1 John iii. 9, the devil, chap. v. 9; Eph. vi. 16, and the world, 1 John v. 4. It implies, that not only they themselves are kept through faith, whereby they rely on the power of their Keeper, and his promises of keeping them, but that they and their faith too are kept by the power of God. *Unto salvation;* viz. full and complete in glory, and not only begun and imperfect here. *Ready;* as being already purchased, prepared, and laid up for them; and so he intimates, that their not as yet possessing it, is not because it is not ready for them, but because the time of their being put in possession of it is not yet come. *To be revealed:* it was said to be *reserved in heaven,* ver. 4, kept safe, but close too, as a rich treasure, the greatness of it is not yet known, even to them that are the heirs of it, Col. iii. 3, 4; 1 John iii. 2; here he adds, that it is *to be revealed,* and made known to them, so soon as the time of its manifestation shall come. *In the last time;* simply and absolutely the last, viz. the day of judgment, which is called *the last day,* John vi. 39, 40; xi. 24; xii. 48.

I. PETER I

o Matt. 5.12.
Rom. 12. 12.
2 Cor 6. 10.
ch. 4. 13.
p 2 Cor. 4.
17. ch. 5. 10.
q Jam. 1. 2.

6 °Wherein ye greatly rejoice, though now ᵖfor a season, if need be, ᵍye are in heaviness through manifold temptations:

Wherein; this refers to the whole foregoing sentence; Ye rejoice in your being kept by the power of God unto salvation. *Ye greatly rejoice:* the Greek word signifies something more than a bare rejoicing, and therefore is added to a word that signifies to rejoice, Matt. v. 12, and implies an outward expression of the inward gladness of the heart, by looks, words, gestures, &c. Some read the word in the imperative mood, by way of exhortation; but the indicative, according to our translation, seems most agreeable to the context, in which, as yet, he commends the saints, to whom he writes, for the grace of God in them; descending to his exhortation afterward, ver. 13. *Though now for a season;* viz. while this life lasts, which is but a little time, 2 Cor. iv. 17. *If need be;* if God see it fit, needful for your good, and conducing to his glory; intimating, that God doth not always afflict believers, but when he sees just cause, and never doth it without cause. *Ye are in heaviness:* Quest. How could they be in heaviness, and yet rejoice? *Answ.* Their grief and joy were about different objects; they might be in heaviness by reason of present afflictions, and rejoice in hope of future glory; they might grieve as men, and rejoice as saints; sense of suffering might affect them, and yet the faith of better things coming relieve them. If their heaviness did in any degree abate their joy, yet it did not wholly hinder it; and though their joy did overcome their heaviness, yet it did not wholly exclude it. *Through manifold temptations;* he so calls afflictions, from the end and effect of them, the trial of their faith, Luke xxii. 28; Acts xx. 19; Gal. iv. 14; James i. 2; 2 Pet. ii. 9: he calls them *manifold,* as being not only numerous, but various, and of divers kinds.

r Jam. 1. 3.
12. ch. 4. 12.
s Job 23. 10.
Ps. 66. 10.
Prov. 17. 3.
Is. 48. 10.
Zech. 13. 9.
1 Cor. 3. 13.
t Rom. 2. 7.
10. 1 Cor. 4.
5. 2 Thess. 1. 7.—12.

7 That ʳthe trial of your faith, being much more precious than of gold that perisheth, though ˢit be tried with fire, ᵗmight be found unto praise and honour and glory at the appearing of Jesus Christ:

That the trial of your faith; i. e. your faith when tried. He compares the faith of the saints with gold, and argues from the less to the greater: q. d. If men do so far esteem their gold, that they will make the excellency and preciousness of it appear by trying it in the fire, which purgeth away the dross, and discovers the goodness of the metal; no wonder if God will have the faith of the saints (more precious to him than gold is to men) tried by afflictions, that the excellency of it may more fully be discovered. *Being much more precious than of gold;* i. e. than the trial of gold; or gold tried, compared with faith tried. *That perisheth;* is worn away, and consumed by use, as many particles of it likewise may be in the very trial of it, ver. 18; whereas faith is not consumed nor wasted, but increased by being used, and made more conspicuous by being tried. *Might be found unto praise and honour and glory;* i. e. may be found to be, or to have turned, to praise, &c., the dignity of it being by that means evidenced. These several words show whither present trials tend, and in what they issue; they may be reproachful and ignominious now, Heb. xii. 2, but they end in glory. We need not be critical about the difference of these three words, *praise, honour,* and *glory,* which may be synonymous expressions (by way of amplification) of the same thing, yet they are mentioned distinctly with relation to believers elsewhere; *praise,* 1 Cor. iv. 5, *honour,* 1 Sam. ii. 30; John xii. 26, *glory,* as well as honour, Rom. ii. 10. *At the appearing of Jesus Christ;* i. e. at the day of judgment, frequently so called, as ver. 13; chap. v. 4; Col. iii. 4; 2 Thess. i. 7. Christ's glory is at present hid and obscured, while he is instructing his elect, and training them up unto patience, and defers his judging of his enemies; but at last it will be fully manifested in the face of the world, when *he cometh with clouds, and every eye shall see him,* &c., Rev. i. 7.

u 1 John 4. 20.
x John 20.
29, & Cor. 5.
7. Heb. 11.
1, 27.

8 ᵘWhom having not seen, ye love; ˣin whom, though now ye see *him* not, yet believing, ye rejoice with joy unspeakable and full of glory:

Whom; which Christ. *Having not seen;* with your bodily eyes. Most of these Jews lived out of their own country, and so had not seen Christ in the flesh; and this was the commendation of their love, that they loved him whom they had not seen, though sight doth ordinarily contribute toward the stirring up of affection. *Ye see him not;* neither as others have done in the days of his flesh, nor as you yourselves hereafter shall in his glory; ye *walk by faith,* and *not by sight,* 2 Cor. v. 7. *Ye rejoice,* in hope of seeing and enjoying him. *With joy unspeakable;* which cannot be expressed with words. See the like phrase, Rom. viii. 26; 2 Cor. ix. 15. *And full of glory;* both in respect of the object about which this joy is conversant, the heavenly glory; the degree, it is the highest here in the world; the duration of it, it is most solid; as likewise in comparison of the joy of this world, which is vain and transitory, and whereof many times men are afterward ashamed.

9 Receiving ʸthe end of your faith, *even* the salvation of *your* souls.   y Rom. 6. 22.

Receiving; either this word is to be taken improperly, and by an enallage, the future being put for the present tense; q. d. Being about to receive; or rather properly, in the present tense, and then it intimates the certainty of the thing spoken of. *The end of your faith;* i. e. the scope to which faith tends, or the reward of faith. *The salvation;* either, 1. Salvation more generally taken, which is begun in this life, Eph. ii. 8; Tit. iii. 5; or rather, 2. Complete final salvation in the other, as ver. 5: and then the sense is, either, ye rejoice that ye shall certainly receive the full salvation of your souls, or, ye rejoice that ye do receive that salvation, viz. in the promises of it, in those graces of the Spirit wrought in you, which begin this salvation, and are the pledges of it, and in the certain assurance of it. *Of your souls;* i. e. by a usual synecdoche, the salvation of your persons.

z Gen. 49. 10.
Dan. 2. 44.
Hag. 2. 7.
Zech. 6. 12.
Matt. 13. 17.
Luke 10. 24.
2 Pet. 1. 19,
20, 21.

10 ᶻOf which salvation the prophets have enquired and searched diligently, who prophesied of the grace *that should come* unto you:

Of which salvation; either, 1. The more full and clear manifestation of salvation promised to be at the coming of Christ, when *life and immortality* should be *brought to light through the gospel,* 2 Tim. i. 10; and then this place is parallel to Luke x. 24: or, 2. The salvation of the dispersed Jews, i. e. their public conversion by the gospel, and eternal life following upon it; which (as well as the calling of the Gentiles) was reserved for the times and glory of the Messiah. *The prophets;* viz. those under the Old Testament, out of whose writings the faith of New Testament believers is to be confirmed, John v. 39; Acts xvii. 11; and whom this apostle therefore mentions, that he might strengthen the faith of the Christian Jews, by assuring them that the doctrine he had delivered to them was no new invention, but the very truth of God revealed of old to the prophets. *Have inquired and searched diligently;* the words imply their vehement desire of knowing, as well as great diligence in seeking. *Who prophesied of the grace that should come unto you:* what he called *salvation* before, he calls *grace* here, to intimate their salvation to be merely of grace. This grace revealed under the gospel, the prophets foretold, but in a more dark way; the Sun of righteousness not being yet risen, the shadows were not gone, and the light was but obscure.

a ch. 3. 19.
2 Pet. 1. 21.
b Ps. 22. 6.
Is. 53. 3, &c.
Dan. 9. 26.
Luke 24. 25,
26, 44, 46.
John 12. 41.
Acts 26. 22,
23.

11 Searching what, or what manner of time ᵃthe Spirit of Christ which was in them did signify, when it testified beforehand ᵇthe sufferings of Christ, and the glory that should follow.

Searching what? whether near or farther off, or what particular part of time. This may relate particularly to Daniel's weeks, chap. ix. *What manner of time;* whether peaceable or troublesome, when the people were free or when in bondage; what were the qualities of the time, or signs by which it might be known. Jacob foretells Christ's coming, when the sceptre was departed from Judah. Gen.

xlix. 10; Isaiah, in a time of universal peace, chap. ii. 4; xi. 6. This diligent inquiring after the time of Christ's coming showed their earnest longing for it. *The Spirit of Christ;* so styled, as being of the Son, no less than of the Father, both by eternal procession and temporal mission, John xiv. 16, 26; xv. 26. This shows, that not only Christ had a being under the Old Testament before his coming in the flesh, (for if Christ were not, there could be no Spirit of Christ,) but likewise that Christ is God, because of his inspiring the prophets with the knowledge of future things. which none but God can do. *When it testified beforehand the sufferings of Christ;* what the prophets did foretell concerning Christ, was not their own conjecture, but what the Spirit did dictate to them. *And the glory that should follow;* Greek, glories, in the plural number, i. e. the manifold glory which was to follow upon his many sufferings, the glory of his resurrection, ascension, sitting at the right hand of God, sending the Spirit, &c. Christ's suffering and glory are often joined together, Psal. xxii. 6; cx.; Isa. liii. 3, 10—12; Luke xxiv. 26; Phil. ii. 8, 9; Heb. ii. 9, 10; to show that there is the same way (and no other) for the salvation of the members, as for the glory of the Head, viz. by sufferings.

12 ᶜUnto whom it was revealed, that ᵈnot unto themselves, but unto us they did minister the things, which are now reported unto you by them that have preached the Gospel unto you with ᵉthe Holy Ghost sent down from heaven; ᶠwhich things the angels desire to look into.

c Dan. 9. 24. & 12. 9, 13. c Heb. 11. 13, 39, 40.

e Acts 2. 4.

f Ex. 25. 20. Dan. 8. 13. & 12. 5, 6. Eph. 3. 10.

Unto whom; unto which prophets. *It was revealed;* viz. by the Spirit of Christ that was in them. *That not unto themselves;* who lived before Christ's coming in the flesh. *But unto us;* not only apostles, but believers, who live since Christ came. *They did minister;* declare and foretell. The preaching of the word is called a ministry, Acts vi. 4; 2 Cor. iv. 1; v. 18. *The things;* the whole doctrine of the gospel concerning Christ's person, offices, benefits, kingdom, and the whole New Testament state. *Which are now reported unto you;* viz. as fulfilled, and actually exhibited now, which were only foretold by the prophets. *By them that have preached the gospel unto you;* the apostles, and other gospel ministers assistant to them: the sense is, The prophets under the Old Testament did, by the Spirit, foresee and foretell Christ's passion, resurrection, ascension, the effusion of the Spirit, the enlargement of the church by the calling of the Gentiles, &c.; but did not live to see their own prophecies, and God's promises, fulfilled, Heb. xi. 13, as you now do. They did spread the table that you might feed at it; they had but a taste by faith, and at a distance, of those things you feast upon in their accomplishment; yet they did not grudge to declare these things, being instructed by the Spirit, that what they spake of should not be fulfilled in their time, but in the generations to come; that so ye, by comparing what they said should come to pass with what you have now been assured is come to pass, may be confirmed and established in the belief of the truth, being the same held forth by the prophets formerly, and gospel ministers at present. *With the Holy Ghost sent down from heaven:* Christ promised to send the Spirit, Luke xxiv. 49; John xiv. 26; xv. 26; xvi. 7; and actually sent him, Acts ii.: the apostles, not of themselves, but acted by this Spirit, have declared unto you the fulfilling of those things, which the former prophets, by the instinct and power of the same Spirit, (the Spirit of Christ, which was in them,) did foretell would in their proper season come to pass. *Which things;* the things before said to be reported by them that preached the gospel. *The angels desire to look into:* it seems to be an allusion to the cherubims that stood above the ark, with their faces toward the mercy-seat, which was a type of Christ. The word signifies a bowing down the head, and stooping to look into a thing. Luke xxiv. 12; John xx. 5; and implies a prying, or looking narrowly into it; which argues an earnest desire to know it. The angels thus look into the mysteries of the gospel, as desirous to see the accomplishment of them, admiring the manifold grace and wisdom of God in them, Eph. iii. 10, and rejoicing in the salvation of sinners, which is the end and effect of God's revealing them.

13 Wherefore ᵍgird up the loins of your mind, ʰbe sober, and hope † to the end for the grace that is to be brought unto you ⁱat the revelation of Jesus Christ;

g Luke12 35. Eph. 6. 14. h Luke 21. 34. Rom. 13. 13. 1 Thess. 5. 6, 8. ch. 4. 7. & 5. 8. † Gr. *perfectly.* i Luke 17. 30. 1 Cor. 1. 7. 2 Thess. 1. 7.

Wherefore; the following exhortation may be connected, either with ver. 4, Being so glorious an inheritance is reserved in heaven for you, *gird up,* &c.; or with ver. 12, Seeing ye know those things, which the prophets that foretold them did not fully see, and the angels themselves desire to look into; the grace of God vouchsafed to you is so excellent and admirable, *gird up,* &c. *Gird up the loins of your mind;* i. e. let your minds be attent, prompt, ready, prepared for your spiritual work, restrained from all those thoughts, cares, affections, and lusts. which may entangle, detain, hinder them, or make them unfit for it. It is a metaphor taken from the custom of the Oriental nations, who wearing long loose garments, were wont to gird them up about their loins, that they might not hinder them in their travelling or working, 1 Kings xviii. 46; 2 Kings iv. 29; Luke xvii. 8: see on Luke xii. 35, 37. Perhaps it may have a special respect to the like rite used at the Passover, Exod. xii. 11, when the Israelites were just ready to enter upon their journey, and go out of Egypt. *Be sober:* this may relate, either, 1. To the body; and then the sense agrees with Luke xxi. 34, where *the cares of this life* seem to be opposed to the girding up the loins of the mind, and *surfeiting and drunkenness,* to sobriety here. Or rather, 2. To the soul; and then girding up the loins of the mind, may refer to the understanding, and thoughts, and sobriety, to the will and affections, and may signify that moderation which belongs to them, in opposition to their inordinateness, which is a sort of drunkenness. Or, it may be rendered, be watchful, as it is translated, 2 Tim. iv. 5, and with which it is joined, 1 Thess. v. 6, 8; and so it agrees well with the former clause; they that have the loins of their mind girt up, being of a vigilant, present mind, and ready for any work they are to undertake. *And hope to the end;* Greek, perfectly, as in the margin, i. e. sincerely, entirely, with a firm confidence; but the following words favour our translation, which signifies perseverance in hope. See Heb. iii. 6. *For the grace that is to be brought unto you;* final salvation, which is the gift of grace, Rom. vi. 23, and is called *the grace of life,* chap. iii. 7. *At the revelation of Jesus Christ;* called *the appearing of Jesus Christ,* ver. 7.

14 As obedient children, ᵏnot fashioning yourselves according to the former lusts ˡ in your ignorance:

k Rom. 12. 2. ch. 4. 2.

l Acts 17.30. 1 Thess. 4.5.

As obedient children; Greek, children of obedience, by a usual Hebraism, for obedient children. So *children of disobedience,* Eph. ii. 2; Col. iii. 6. And this we may understand either absolutely, children of obedience for obedient persons; or with relation to God, obedient children of God; and then the apostle persuades them to their duty by an argument taken from their adoption; being the children of God, he would have them behave themselves obediently, as becomes them in that relation. *Not fashioning yourselves;* not accommodating, not conforming yourselves, not shaping or ordering your conversation. See the same word, Rom. xii. 2. *According to the former lusts;* the lusts you formerly indulged yourselves in: see Eph. iv. 22. *In your ignorance;* your ignorance of Christ and the gospel: q. d. Not fashioning yourselves according to those lusts you lived in when you were ignorant of Christ. He distinguisheth between the time of their ignorance, and of their illumination. Another age requires other manners. They formerly lived according to the dictates of their lusts, but now ought to live according to the will of Christ: see ver. 18; Acts xvii. 30; Eph. iv. 17, 18.

15 ᵐBut as he which hath called you is holy, so be ye holy in all manner of conversation;

m Luke 1. 74, 75. 2 Cor. 7. 1. 1 Thess. 4. 3, 4, 7. Heb. 12. 14. 2 Pet. 3. 11.

But as he which hath called you; God the Father, to whom, as the First Cause, our calling is frequently ascribed, Rom. ix. 11, 24; 1 Cor. vii. 15; Gal. i. 6, 15. It may be rendered, According to the Holy One that hath called you,

i. e. according to his example; you are children, and should therefore imitate your Father, Eph. v. 1. *Called you;* viz. effectually, to the knowledge and faith of Christ. *Is holy;* so God is often styled by Isaiah and other penmen of the Scripture, as the fountain and exemplar of holiness. *So be ye holy in all manner of conversation;* either, through the whole course, and in the several parts, of your conversation; or, *in all manner of conversation,* as we read it, i. e. with whomsoever ye converse, believers or infidels, friends or enemies, relations or strangers; and in whatsoever condition ye are in, peace or trouble, prosperity or adversity.

n Lev.11.44. & 19. 2. & 20. 7.
16 Because it is written, [n] Be ye holy; for I am holy.

I your Father, and therefore you ought to imitate and obey me: or, I that have severed you from other people, that you should be mine, Lev. xx. 26, to which place particularly this seems to refer.

o Deut. 10. 17. Acts 10. 34. Rom. 2. 11.
p 2 Cor. 7. 1. Phil. 2. 12.
q 2 Cor. 5. 6. Heb. 12. 28. Heb. 11. 13. ch. 2. 11.

17 And if ye call on the Father, [o] who without respect of persons judgeth according to every man's work, [p] pass the time of your [q] sojourning *here* in fear.

And if; this particle is used here, and frequently elsewhere, not as a note of doubting, but by way of assertion, and supposition of a thing known. *Ye call on the Father;* either this is to be meant of invocation, their calling on God in prayer; and then the sense is, If you be servants and worshippers of the Father; prayer being many times put for the whole worship of God, Isa. xliii. 22; Acts ix. 11: or, of their calling God, Father, as Matt. vi. 9; and then the sense is, If you would be counted God's children, James ii. 7. *Who, without respect of persons;* and so will no more excuse you that are Jews, and descended from Abraham, than those that are born of Gentile parents, Job xxxiv. 19; Acts x. 34; Eph. vi. 9. *Judgeth;* and so is not a Father only, but a Judge, and that a most righteous one. *According to every man's work;* i. e. works, the singular number put for the plural, as James i. 25 : see Rom. ii. 6; Job xxxiv. 11. *Pass the time of your sojourning here;* the word signifies the temporary abode of a man in a place where he was not born, or doth not ordinarily reside; such being the condition of believers in the world, that they are sojourners, not citizens of it; they are travelling through it to their Father's house and heavenly country, Heb. xi. 9, 10, 13, 16. They are here exhorted to a suitable carriage, expressed in the next words. *In fear;* which is due to him as a Father and a Judge. It may imply the greatest reverence, and the deepest humility, Phil. ii. 12; 1 Cor. ii. 3; 1 Pet. iii. 2, 15.

r 1 Cor. 6. 20. & 7. 23.
18 Forasmuch as ye know [r] that ye were not redeemed with corruptible things, *as* silver and gold, from your

s Ezek. 20. 18. ch. 4. 3.
vain conversation [s] *received* by tradition from your fathers;

Forasmuch as ye know; considering that ye were, &c. *That ye were not redeemed with corruptible things:* see Tit. ii. 14. This implies them to have been in a servile condition, and in bondage to their own errors, till they were converted to Christ. *As silver and gold;* the most precious things, of greatest esteem among men. *From your vain,* because unprofitable to, and insufficient for, righteousness and salvation, *conversation,* viz. in your Judaism, wherein you were so much addicted to uncommanded rites and ceremonies, as to have little respect for God's law. *Received by tradition;* and so not only by their example and practice, but by their doctrine and precepts, Matt. xv. 3, &c.; Mark vii. 7, &c. See likewise Gal. i. 14. *From your fathers;* either your ancestors, as Ezek. xx. 18, or doctors and instructors, who are sometimes called *fathers,* 1 Cor. iv. 15.

t Acts 20.28. Eph. 1. 7. Heb. 9. 12, 14. Rev. 5. 9. u Ex. 12. 5. Is. 53. 7. John 1. 29, 36. 1 Cor. 5. 7.

19 But [t] with the precious blood of Christ, [u] as of a lamb without blemish and without spot:

Precious; because the blood not only of an innocent person, but of the Son of God, Acts xx. 28. *As of a lamb;* i. e. who was a Lamb. *A lamb; the Lamb of God, that taketh away the sin of the world,* John i. 29: not only like a lamb, for his innocence and gentleness, Isa. liii. 7, but the Antitype of the lambs which under the law were offered in the daily sacrifices, and more especially of the paschal lamb; whatever was shadowed out in that, and those other sacrifices, having its accomplishment in Christ. *Without blemish;* without fault, without defect, in which nothing was wanting that was requisite to its perfection; or, in which nothing could be blamed. The Greek word seems to be derived from the Hebrew *Mum,* so often used for a blemish; see Lev. xxiv. 19, 20. *And without spot;* without any other deformity. The lamb might have no defect, but yet might have some spot; and it was to be perfect, Exod. xii. 5, which implied its having neither the one nor the other. Christ was such a Lamb, perfect in holiness, and free from all sin, John viii. 29, 46; Heb. vii. 26; 1 Pet. ii. 22.

x Rom. 3.25. & 16. 25, 26. Eph. 3. 9,11. Col. 1. 26. 2 Tim. 1. 9, 10. Tit. 1. 2.
20 [x] Who verily was foreordained before the foundation of the world, but was manifest [y] in these last times for you,

3. Rev. 13. 8. y Gal. 4. 4. Eph. 1. 10. Heb. 1. 2. & 9. 26.

Who verily was fore-ordained; by God's decree appointed to the work of redemption, and to be that Lamb that should take away the sins of the world, Eph. i. 9. *Before the foundation of the world;* from eternity; there being nothing before the world began but what was eternal, John xvii. 24. *But was manifested;* not only by his incarnation, 1 Tim. iii. 16, but by the preaching of the gospel. See the Scriptures in the margin. *In these last times;* last, in comparison of the times of the Old Testament; the same as *the fulness of time,* Gal. iv. 4. *For you;* that you, with other believers, might partake of salvation by him. The fruit of Christ's redemption reacheth all ages, but much more abundantly the times after his coming in the flesh. The sum of the argument is, Christ was ordained from eternity, promised to the fathers, but manifested to you: your privilege therefore being greater than theirs, Matt. xiii. 17; Heb. xi. 39, 40, you should be the more holy.

z Acts 2. 24. a Matt. 28. 18. Acts 2. 33. & 3. 13. Eph. 1. 20. Phil. 2. 9. Heb. 2. 9. ch. 3. 22.

21 Who by him do believe in God, [z] that raised him up from the dead, and [a] gave him glory; that your faith and hope might be in God.

Who by him do believe in God; both as revealing God to you, Matt. xi. 27; John i. 14; and making way for you to God, who, out of Christ, is a consuming fire, so that there is no coming to him but by Christ, John xiv. 6; Eph. ii. 18; iii. 12; Heb. vii. 25. *Gave him glory;* viz. in his resurrection, ascension, sitting at the right hand of God, &c., Phil. ii. 9—11; Heb. ii. 9, 10. *That your faith and hope might be in God;* that seeing Christ raised and glorified, ye might be fully confirmed in the belief of a thorough satisfaction made to Divine justice for sin, and perfect reconciliation wrought (for had not Christ fully paid the price of redemption, his Father would never have let him out of the prison of the grave, in which his justice had shut him up); from which faith ariseth a hope, which looks to the resurrection of Christ your Head, as the certain pledge and earnest of your resurrection to life and glory. Christ's resurrection and glory are the great grounds of faith, chap. iii. 21; Acts ii. 32, 33; v. 31; x. 40; Rom. iv. 24, 25; 1 Cor. xv. 14, 17.

b Acts 15. 9. c Rom. 12. 9, 10. 1 Thess. 4. 9. 1 Tim. 1. 5. Heb. 13. 1. ch. 2. 17. & 3. 8. & 4. 8. 2 Pet. 1. 7. 1 John 3. 18. & 4. 7, 21.

22 Seeing ye [b] have purified your souls in obeying the truth through the Spirit unto unfeigned [c] love of the brethren, *see that ye* love one another with a pure heart fervently:

Your souls; i. e. yourselves; the whole person is implied, the soul being the principal part. *In obeying the truth;* in subjecting yourselves to the truth of the gospel, by faith, to which the purification of the heart is ascribed, Acts xv. 9, not only as to justification, and purging away the guilt of sin, but as to sanctification, and cleansing from the defilement of it: q. d. Seeing ye have begun to purify your hearts by faith in Christ, set forth in the gospel, and made sanctification to them that believe, 1 Cor. i. 30. *Through the Spirit;* by the operation of the Spirit working faith in you. *Unto unfeigned love of the brethren;* without hypocrisy, and which is not in word only, but in deed and in truth, 1 John iii. 18. Love to the brethren in Christ, and for Christ's sake. This notes one great end of our sanctification, viz. the exercise of brotherly love, whereby our love to God is likewise manifested, when we love them upon his account. The whole clause may likewise be understood, as an exhortation to purify themselves more and more by faith, that so they might (being purged from carnal affections) be the better able, and more disposed, to love one another. *Love one another with a pure heart;* as the source and fountain of your love to each other, and from whence it proceeds, 1 Tim. i. 5; 2 Tim. ii. 22. *Fervently;* or, vehemently, and intensely, strongly. The word seems to be a metaphor taken from a bow, which the more it is bent, with the greater force it sends forth the arrow; so love, the more fervent and strong it is, the more abundantly it puts forth itself for the benefit of others.

<small>d John 1. 13. & 3. 5.
e Jam. 1. 18. 1 John 3. 9.</small>

23 ^dBeing born again, not of corruptible seed, but of incorruptible, ^eby the word of God, which liveth and abideth for ever.

Being born again: this may refer either, 1. To the general exhortation to holiness, ver. 14, 15, and then the argument runs thus: Ye are in your regeneration become the children of God, and therefore ought to walk holily as become his children. Or, 2. To the more particular exhortation to brotherly love, ver. 22: q. d. You are by your regeneration become spiritual brethren, and therefore ought to live like brethren. *Not of corruptible seed;* which is itself corrupted ere any thing can be generated out of it, or out of which nothing is begotten but what is corruptible; so that all such generations tend but to a mortal life. *But of incorruptible;* so the word is said to be, because containing still the same, and being immutable in itself, it changes and renews the hearts of those that by faith receive it. Or, it may be understood of its being incorruptible effectively, because it leads, or tends, to an immortal life. *The word of God;* the same which he called incorruptible seed, which is the instrument in regeneration, as is implied in the preposition, *by,* going before it. *Which liveth;* this and the following verb may be joined, either, 1. To God, the word of God, who liveth, &c.; or rather, 2. To *the word,* so our translation reads it, which word liveth, and abideth, &c.; and this agrees best with the testimony of Isaiah in the next verse. The word of God is said to be a living word, because it enliveneth the hearts of those that entertain it.

<small>‖ Or, For that.
f Ps. 103. 15. Is. 40. 6. & 51. 12. Jam. 1. 10.</small>

24 ‖ For ^fall flesh *is* as grass, and all the glory of man as the flower of grass. The grass withereth, and the flower thereof falleth away:

All flesh; all men as born of the flesh, and in their natural state, in opposition to regenerate men, ver. 23. *All the glory of man;* whatever is most excellent in man naturally, and which they are most apt to glory in. *The grass withereth, and the flower thereof falleth away:* see James i. 10.

<small>g Ps. 102. 12, 26. Is. 40. 8. Luke 16. 17.
h John 1. 1. 14. 1 John 1. 1, 3.</small>

25 ^gBut the word of the Lord endureth for ever. ^hAnd this is the word which by the Gospel is preached unto you.

But the word of the Lord endureth for ever; not only absolutely in itself, and in respect of its perpetual verity, Psal. cxix. 160; Matt. xxiv. 35; but relatively, as received by and dwelling in believers, 1 John iii. 9, who always experience the effects of it in themselves in their regeneration, receiving a solid and lasting being from it, (the new nature,) which is likewise preserved by it, in opposition to that flux and mutable being they had by their first birth. *And this is the word which by the gospel is preached unto you;* this word, of which Isaiah speaks, and which he so much magnifies, is the very same word of the gospel, which is preached unto you by us apostles.

CHAP. II

The apostle exhorteth the Christian converts to lay aside all uncharitableness, 1—3. *He showeth their privileges through Christ, the chief corner stone,* 4—10. *He beseecheth them to abstain from fleshly lusts, and by their good conversation to promote God's glory among the Gentiles,* 11, 12. *He enforceth obedience to magistrates,* 13—17; *and teacheth servants to obey their masters, and to suffer patiently for well-doing, after the example of Christ,* 18—25.

WHEREFORE ^alaying aside all malice, and all guile, and hypocrisies, and envies, and all evil speakings, <small>a Eph. 4. 22, 25, 31. Col. 3. 8. Heb. 12. 1. Jam. 1. 21. & 5. 9. ch. 4. 2.</small>

Having in the former chapter mentioned the new birth, ver. 23, and exhorted to brotherly love, as agreeable to it, ver. 22, he begins this chapter with a dehortation, wherein he dissuades them from those vices which are contrary to the state of regenerate men in the general, and brotherly love in particular. *Laying aside;* or, put off; a metaphor from an old over-worn garment, fit only to be thrown away: see Eph. iv. 22; Col. iii. 8, 9; James i. 21. *All malice;* malignity, when men do evil to others voluntarily and industriously, or delight in other men's harms: see Rom. i. 29; Eph. iv. 31. *All guile:* all fraudulence and impostures, and circumventing of others in any kind. *Hypocrisies;* all flattering, and counterfeiting friendship, and showing love in words and outward carriage, when the heart is otherwise affected. So Matt. xxii., Christ calls them hypocrites that flattered him, ver. 16, 18. *Envies;* grieving at other men's welfare. *All evil speakings;* all kind of detraction.

2 ^bAs newborn babes, desire the sincere ^cmilk of the word, that ye may grow thereby: <small>b Mat. 18. 3. Mark 10. 15. Rom. 6. 4. 1 Cor. 14. 20. ch. 1. 23. c 1 Cor. 3. 2. Heb. 5. 12, 13.</small>

Pursuant to his discourse, chap. i. 23, where he speaks of their new birth, he here calls them *new-born babes;* but that not in opposition to those that are adult, or *of full age,* as Heb. v. 14; 1 Cor. iii. 1, but in opposition to their former corrupt and unregenerate state, in which they were destitute of all spiritual life; and so this agrees, not only to young converts, but generally to all regenerate persons. *Desire;* being new-born babes, act as such in earnestly desiring and longing for that spiritual nourishment, which is so needful for you, even as children, as soon as they come into the world, are lingering after the breast. *The sincere milk of the word:* the Greek may be rendered (and is by some) reasonable milk, viz. such as is for the soul, not for the body; that whereby the mind is nourished and strengthened; or, wordy milk, the substantive from which it is derived properly and first signifying word, or speech, and being used for *the word of God,* Heb. iv. 12. But this not being proper English, our translation renders it best, the *milk of the word,* i. e. the word which is milk. The apostle useth an adjective for a substantive, but that adjective doth not signify the quality of the subject, *milk,* as the other, *sincere,* doth, but the subject of itself. The like phrase we have, chap. iii. 7; Greek, female, or wifeish, weaker vessel, which we turn by the substantive, *wife,* who is said there to be *the weaker vessel.* So that the doctrine of the gospel is here to be understood, as Isa. lv. 1, believers are to be nourished by the same word, as their food, by which, as the seed, they are said to be begotten, chap. i. 23. This milk of the word is said to be *sincere,* i. e. pure, without mixture or adulteration, not blended, or diluted, (as vintners do by their wine, to whose practice Paul alludes, when he speaks of men's corrupting the word, 2 Cor. ii. 17; iv. 2,) with human fictions or traditions. Infants love the sweetness of their mothers' milk, and desire it pure, as it is: believers should desire the word pure, as it is in itself, not mixed with any thing that may lessen its sweetness and hinder its efficacy. *That ye may grow thereby;* that by the word, as your spiritual nourishment, ye may grow more in spiritual life and strength, till ye come to be perfect men, Eph. iv. 13.

3 If so be ye have ^dtasted that the Lord *is* gracious. <small>d Ps. 34. 8. Heb. 6. 5.</small>

If so be; this doth not imply a doubting, but a supposition, as was before observed, chap. i. 17. *Ye have tasted;* not lightly tasted by a bare ineffectual knowledge, as Heb. vi. 4; but experienced and perceived by the taste of your spiritual palate; your spiritual sense, and ability to judge of spiritual things, being restored to you, with your new birth. He refers to Psal. xxxiv. 8, and possibly to Isa. lxvi. 11. *The Lord;* the Lord Jesus Christ, as appears by the next verse. *Is gracious;* good, kind, or rather, sweet: the same word is applied to wine, Luke v. 39. The sense of the whole is, If ye have by faith received the gospel as glad tidings, and worthy of all acceptation, 1 Tim. i. 15, and therein perceived and experienced the sweetness of those consolations which are in Christ Jesus, Phil. ii. 1; or, which is the same, how sweet he is, who, in the preaching of the gospel, exhibits himself to your spiritual senses, to be fed upon and tasted by you.

4 To whom coming, *as unto* a living stone, ^edisallowed indeed of men, but chosen of God, *and* precious,

e Ps. 118. 22.
Mat. 21. 42.
Acts 4. 11.

To whom; to which Christ. *Coming;* by faith : q. d. In whom believing, John vi. 35, 44, 45. The word is in the present tense, the apostle describing here not their first conversion to Christ, but their present state, that they, being in Christ, were daily coming to him in the continued exercise of their faith. *As unto a living;* not only having life in himself, but enlivening those that by faith adhere to him. *Stone;* viz. a corner-stone, as ver. 6. Being about to set forth the church as a spiritual building, he first mentions Christ as the foundation, and corner-stone. *Disallowed indeed of men;* rejected, not only by the unbelieving Jews and their rulers formerly, but still by the unbelieving world. *But chosen of God;* either chosen to be the foundation of the building, and then it is the same as foreordained, chap. i. 20; or *chosen* is the same as choice, excellent. *And precious:* a different expression of the same thing. Here seems to be an allusion to those stones which men count precious, and have in great esteem; and Christ's being precious in the sight of God, is set in opposition to his being disallowed of men, to intimate, that their unbelief, and rejecting Christ, doth not make him less valuable in himself, when his Father so much honours him.

5 ^fYe also, as lively stones, ||are built up ^ga spiritual house, ^han holy priesthood, to offer up ⁱspiritual sacrifices, ^kacceptable to God by Jesus Christ.

f Eph. 2. 21, 22.
|| Or, *be ye built.*
g Heb. 3. 6.
h Is. 61. 6.
& 66. 21.
ver. 9.
i Hos. 14. 2. Mal. 1. 11. Rom. 12. 1. Heb. 13. 15, 16. k Phil. 4. 18. ch. 4. 11.

As lively; viz. as being enlivened by Christ. The word here translated *lively,* and *living* in the former verse, is the same; but being there spoken of Christ, it is to be understood actively, and here being applied to believers, who receive their spiritual life from Christ, it must be taken passively. *Stones;* each particular believer is here called a stone, as all together a house or temple, 2 Cor. vi. 16; Eph. ii. 21, and in respect of their union among themselves, and with their foundation; though elsewhere, in respect of God's inhabitation, even particular believers are called his temple, 1 Cor. iii. 16, 17; vi. 19. *Are built up;* viz. upon Christ the principal Corner-stone, Eph. ii. 20. This may be understood, either, 1. Imperatively, q. d. Be ye built up; and then it is an exhortation, and relates not only to their continuing in Christ, but their being further built up on him by faith, and is of the same import as ver. 2, *that ye may grow:* or rather, 2. Indicatively; the apostle as yet being engaged in showing the dignity and privileges of believers, and not entering upon his exhortation till ver. 11. The words being in the present tense, implies the building to be still but going on, and not yet finished. *A spiritual house;* in distinction from the material one, relating to those scriptures where the tabernacle or temple is called God's house, Exod. xxiii. 19; xxxiv. 26; Deut. xxiii. 18. The material house built of dead stones, was but a type of the spiritual house made up of lively stones, and built upon Christ the living Stone; and this he brings (the truth being always more excellent than the type) to heighten the privileges of the gospel church. *An holy priesthood;* either the abstract is put for the concrete, *an holy priesthood* for holy priests; or it may note the whole college or society of evangelical priests, consisting of all particular saints, to whom, in the New Testament, this title is given, but never appropriated to gospel ministers: Christ being a Priest for ever after the order of Melchisedec, had no partner with him in his priesthood, but was himself only to offer a propitiatory sacrifice to God for sin. *To offer up spiritual sacrifices;* the immediate end of gospel priests, to offer, not bodily, but spiritual sacrifices; in general themselves, whom they are to consecrate to God, Rom. xii. 1; particularly prayer, thanksgivings, alms, and other duties of religion, Phil. iv. 18; Heb. xiii. 15, 16. *Acceptable to God by Jesus Christ;* by, and through whom alone, as the persons, so the performances, of believers (though in themselves imperfect) are pleasing to God, Christ presenting them to his Father by his intercession, and covering their defects by his own most perfect righteousness. Some refer this clause, *by Jesus Christ,* to the foregoing verb, *to offer up;* and then the words run thus, to offer up spiritual sacrifices by Jesus Christ, acceptable to God; but the former seems most proper, and includes this latter : we are therefore to offer up spiritual sacrifices to God by Christ, because they are acceptable only by him, Heb. xiii. 21, compared with 15, 16.

6 Wherefore also it is contained in the Scripture, ^lBehold, I lay in Sion a chief corner stone, elect, precious : and he that believeth on him shall not be confounded.

l Is. 28. 16.
Rom. 9. 33.

Wherefore also it is contained in the Scripture: the Greek word being of an active form, makes great difference among expositors about these words; not to trouble the reader with variety, the plainest way of understanding them seems to be, either, 1. That God be understood here, and supplied out of the former verse. Wherefore God contains it in the Scripture : or, 2. That the word, though of an active termination, be yet taken in a passive signification, contains, for is contained ; so our translators do, and this way of speaking is not unusual with other writers. *Behold, I;* I the Lord, not man, Psal. cxviii. 23. *Lay in Sion;* viz. by the preaching of the gospel. wherein Christ was declared to be the only foundation of the church, and whereby faith was wrought in the hearts of men, who were thereby actually built on Christ, as their foundation, and so the spiritual house, ver. 5, erected. *Sion;* either by synecdoche, Jerusalem, (whereof Sion was a part,) where by the preaching of Christ first, and the apostles after his ascension, and sending the Spirit, this foundation stone was first laid, and God's temple began to be built, Psal. cx. 2; Isa. ii. 3; Micah iv. 2; Luke xxiv. 47. Or rather, Sion here is to be understood of the gospel church, whereof Sion was a type. *A chief corner-stone;* or, Head of the corner, Psal. cxviii. 22; that which both supports the building, and unites the parts; Christ being the foundation not of a part only, but of the whole church; all the parts of which, Gentile, as well as Jew, are jointly built on him, and upheld by him, Eph. ii. 20. *Elect, precious:* see ver. 5. *And he that believeth on him shall not be confounded;* shall not be disappointed of his expected salvation, and so shall have no cause to be ashamed of his hope. This is according to the LXX., the Hebrew hath it, shall not make haste, i. e. he that believes in Christ shall not through haste, or distrust, or unwillingness to wait God's time and way, seek after any other way of salvation than by Christ; and so (as before) not being disappointed, shall have no cause to be ashamed ; whereas they that do not believe, but make haste, coming short of their expectation, are at last filled with confusion. See the places in the margin.

7 Unto you therefore which believe *he is* || precious : but unto them which be disobedient, ^mthe stone which the builders disallowed, the same is made the head of the corner,

|| Or, *an honour.*
m Ps. 118. 22.
Matt. 21. 42.
Acts 4. 11.

Precious; the margin reads it, according to the Greek, an honour; either the abstract is put for the concrete, an honour, for honourable, or *precious,* (as the text hath it,) and then the sense is plain, that Christ, as he is precious in himself, and to his Father, so he is to them that believe. Or, honour may be put for the cause of honour, and then it is opposed to shame and confusion before mentioned, and the sense is, Ye that believe, shall be so far from being ashamed, or having your faith frustrated, that ye shall be honoured, and saved by Christ. And this agrees well with what follows in this and ver. 8. *Disobedient;* unbelievers, who were disobedient to the great command of the gospel concerning faith in the Lord Jesus Christ. *The builders;* the high priests, scribes, Pharisees, and rulers of the Jews, whose duty it was to build up the church, as having not only the name, but the power then residing in them. *Disal-*

lowed; rejected him, and would not acknowledge him for the promised Messiah, and the great foundation upon which the church of God was to be built. *The same is made the Head of the corner: Quest.* How is Christ to be made the *Head of the corner* to them that reject him? *Answ.* Either, 1. Something is here to be understood, viz. this is said, or spoken, which follows, the stone which the builders, &c.: q. d. They despised him, but God hath honoured him; they would allow him no place in the building, but God hath given him the best, made him the Head-stone of the corner. Or, 2. Christ may be said to be made to the disobedient, in spite of their rejecting and opposing him, the Head of the corner; i. e. a King and a Judge to restrain and curb them in, seeing they would not be ruled by him.

8 ⁿ And a stone of stumbling, and a rock of offence, ᵒ *even to them* which stumble at the word, being disobedient: ᵖ whereunto also they were appointed.

And a stone of stumbling, and a rock of offence; i. e. a stone at which they stumble, a rock at which they are offended; and so it implies Christ not to be the cause of their stumbling, but the object of it; they of their own accord, and through the pravity of their nature, without any just occasion given by him, being offended, either because they find not that in him which they expected, viz. outward encouragements; or find that in him which they do not like, the holiness of his law, and purity of his doctrine, contrary to their corruptions and lusts, and especially his requiring of them faith in him for the justification of their persons, which was so contrary to the pride of their hearts, and which was one great reason of the Jews stumbling at him, as seeking to establish their own righteousness, and therefore not submitting to the righteousness of God, Rom. ix. 32, 33, compared with x. 3. This stumbling includes not only their falling into sin, but into destruction too, the punishment of sin, Isa. viii. 14, 15; whereof Christ can be no more than the inculpable occasion, but their own unbelief the proper cause. *Which stumble at the word, being disobedient;* these words may have a double reading: one according to our translation; and then the sense is, that stumble at the word of the gospel, i. e. are disobedient to it, in rejecting Christ therein offered to them: or, that stumble, being disobedient to the word; i. e. stumble at Christ preached to them in the word, and therefore will not obey it; they show that they are offended at Christ, by their not receiving his doctrine, nor accepting his offers. *Whereunto also they were appointed;* either this may refer, 1. To ver. 6, where Christ is said to be laid (the same word in the Greek with that which is here translated by *appointed*) in Sion, as *a chief corner-stone, elect* and *precious,* on whom whosoever *believeth, shall not be confounded.* The apostle then adds, that even these unbelievers were *appointed* (viz. in their external vocation, as being taken into covenant with God) to be built on Christ by faith, but they stumbled, by their unbelief, at the word of the gospel, and consequently at this stumbling-stone. And then it is a high aggravating the unbelief of the Jews, that they, being God's peculiar people, should reject that salvation which was sent to them, and to the first offer of which they were designed, Acts xiii. 26, 46, 47. Or, 2. To the words immediately going before, *which stumble at the word, being disobedient;* and then the sense is, (speaking concerning the reprobate Jews.) that God appointed them to this stumbling, in his decreeing not to give them faith in Christ, but to leave them to their unbelief, and to punish them justly for it: see Rom. ix. 17; 1 Thess. v. 9; Jude 4. The scope of the apostle in this whole verse seems to be, to keep weak Christians from being offended at the multitude of unbelievers, and especially at their seeing Christ rejected by the Jewish rulers and doctors; and this he doth by pointing them to the Scripture, where all this was long since foretold, and therefore not to be wondered at now, nor be any occasion of offence to them: see the like, John xvi. 1, 4.

9 But ye *are* ᵠa chosen generation, ʳa royal priesthood, ˢan holy nation, ᵗ ‖ a peculiar people; that ye should shew forth the ‖ praises of him who hath called you out of ᵘdarkness into his marvellous light:

But ye; ye believers, in opposition to those reprobates that are disobedient to the word. He shows that those dignities and privileges, which were mentioned by Moses as belonging to their forefathers, did much more belong to them; and that they had the real exhibition in Christ, of those good things whereof their fathers had but a taste, and which the rest of the Jews had lost by their unbelief. *Are a chosen generation;* a people chosen of God, not only out of the world, but from among the rest of your own nation, and not only to an external adoption, and outward privileges, (as the whole body of the nation was,) but to eternal salvation. *A royal priesthood;* or, kingdom of priests. He called them *an holy priesthood,* ver. 5, now he calls them *a royal priesthood,* to show that they were made not only spiritual priests, but spiritual kings; which privilege they had not as Jews, but as believers, who are all of them as priests in respect of God, to whom they are consecrated, and to whom they offer up spiritual sacrifices; so kings in respect both of their enemies, over whom they are victorious, and of the kingdom they are hereafter to inherit. *An holy nation;* Moses calls your fathers *an holy people,* Deut. vii. 6, in respect of their separation from the impurities of the Gentiles, their dedication to God, and the many laws God gave them, obliging them to external and ceremonial purity, whereby they were admonished of internal and real holiness; but ye are a holy nation in respect of that true and inward holiness itself, whereof that ceremonial holiness was but a signification. He seems particularly to allude to Isa. lxii. 12. *A peculiar people:* Exod. xix. 5, it is *a peculiar treasure;* so the same word is rendered, *a special people,* Deut. vii. 6, and, *a peculiar people,* Deut. xiv. 2; the word used by the LXX. implying as much; but Mal. iii. 17, where we render it *jewels,* the LXX. use the same word which Peter doth here, which is as much as, a people of acquisition, or which God hath acquired to himself for his peculiar possession or treasure. God had rescued the Israelites from their Egyptian bondage, and taken them to be his peculiar people above all others, and claimed a right to them, and counted them precious, as having redeemed them with a strong hand, and got possession of them at the expense of so much power, and so many miracles. This deliverance of theirs was the type of Christ's delivering the church from the tyranny of Satan, the spiritual Pharaoh, and the world, the spiritual Egypt, and a state of sin, the worst bondage; upon the account whereof, God's people are called *a peculiar people,* or a people thus acquired, Tit. ii. 14, and *a purchased possession,* Eph. i. 14, where the same word is likewise used. *That ye should show forth, &c.:* this notes the end of all these privileges vouchsafed them, viz. that they should glorify God in the enjoyment of them. He seems to refer to Isa. xliii. 7, 21, *This people have I formed for myself,* (or acquired, as the LXX. hath it,) *they shall show forth my praise.* *Show forth;* publish and declare, both in words and deeds, that others may be excited to glorify God in the like manner. *The praises of him;* or virtues, that wisdom, power, goodness, righteousness, truth, &c., which God hath manifested in his vouchsafements to you, and in the acknowledgment of which he may be glorified. *Who hath called you;* by an effectual calling, according to his purpose, Rom. viii. 28. *Out of darkness;* the darkness of ignorance, unbelief, sin, and misery. The time before the publication of the gospel, was a time of darkness, Matt. iv. 16; Luke i. 79. *Into his marvellous light;* the light of knowledge, faith, holiness, comfort: see Eph. v. 8. It is called *marvellous,* because men see what they never saw before, wonderful things out of God's law, Psal. cxix. 18; and because it is a marvellous thing, that they who sat in so gross darkness should be translated into so glorious a light.

10 ˣ Which in time past *were* not a people, but *are* now the people of God: which had not obtained mercy, but now have obtained mercy.

Which in time past were not a people; either, *were not a people,* i. e. a formed state, or commonwealth, being dispersed in several countries, among other people, and not worth the name of a people : or, were not the people of God, (supplying *God* out of the opposite clause,) since he had given them a bill of divorce, and said *Lo-ammi* and *Lo-ruhamah* to them, Hos. i. These were the Jews of the dispersion, and such as had not returned out of the Babylonish captivity, together with many of other tribes mixed with them, who, before their conversion to Christ, seemed cut off from the body of that people, had no solemn worship of God among them, and were tainted with the corruptions of the heathen, with whom they conversed. *But are now the people of God ;* really God's people, restored to their old covenant state and church privileges, by their believing in Christ. *Which had not obtained mercy, but now have obtained mercy ;* the mercy of being God's people, and enjoying their privileges, being justified, at peace with God, &c. Lest they might any way abuse what he had said in the former verse concerning their great dignity and privileges, so as to ascribe any thing to themselves, the apostle intimates here, that all they enjoyed was merely out of God's mercy.

y 1 Chr. 29. 15. Ps. 39. 12. & 119. 19. Heb. 11. 13. ch. 1. 17. z Rom. 13. 14. Gal. 5. 16. a Jam. 4. 1.

11 Dearly beloved, I beseech *you* [y] as strangers and pilgrims, [z] abstain from fleshly lusts, [a] which war against the soul ;

Strangers and pilgrims ; not only strangers in the several countries where ye inhabit, (being out of your own land,) but strangers in the world, as all believers are, 1 Chron. xxix. 15 ; Psal. xxxix. 12 ; cxix. 19 ; Heb. xi. 13, 14. *Abstain from fleshly lusts ;* not only sensual desires, but all the works of the flesh, Gal. v. 19—21, the carnal mind itself being enmity against God, Rom. viii. 7. *Which war ;* as enemies, oppose and fight against, Rom. vii. 23 ; James iv. 1. *Against the soul ;* the inner man, or regenerate part, or Spirit, which is opposed to fleshly lusts : see Gal. v. 17.

b Rom. 12. 17. 2 Cor. 8. 21. Phil. 2. 15. Tit. 2. 8. ch. 3. 16. ‖ Or, *wherein.* c Matt. 5. 16. d Luke 19. 44.

12 [b] Having your conversation honest among the Gentiles : that, ‖ whereas they speak against you as evildoers, [c] they may by *your* good works, which they shall behold, glorify God [d] in the day of visitation.

Having your conversation honest ; irreprehensible, fruitful, such as may gain men's love, and commend the religion you profess. *Among the Gentiles ;* who, by reason of their differing from your religion, are the more likely to observe you. This proves this Epistle to be written to the Jews. *They may by your good works, which they shall behold, glorify God ;* not only think more favourably of you, but of your religion ; acknowledge the grace of God in you, and more readily subject themselves to him, (the best way of glorifying him,) it being usual with God to make way for the conversion of sinners by the holy conversation of saints. *In the day of visitation ;* viz. a gracious visitation, when God calls them by the gospel to the knowledge of Christ, Luke i. 68, 78 ; vii. 16 ; xix. 44.

e Mat. 22. 21. Rom. 13. 1. Tit. 3. 1.

13 [e] Submit yourselves to every ordinance of man for the Lord's sake : whether it be to the king, as supreme ;

Every ordinance ; of all kinds, whether supreme or subordinate. *Ordinance of man ;* Greek, human creatures, which may be understood either, as Mark xvi. 15, every human creature for every man, only restraining it to the present subject whereof he treats, viz. magistrates, and the sense is, to every magistrate : or rather, (though to the same effect,) to every human ordinance ; or, as we translate it, *ordinance of man ;* the word creature being taken for an ordinance, or constitution, and creating for ordaining, or appointing : so Œcumenius will have the word to signify, Eph. ii. 15, *to make of twain one new man.* But this creature, or ordinance, here is to be understood of the magistrate, (as appears by the following words,) which is called human, not as if magistracy were not an ordinance of God, (for, Rom. xiii. 1, *the powers that are* are said to be *ordained of God,*) but either because it is only among men, and proper to them ; or because it is of man secondarily and instrumentally, though of God primarily and originally, God making use of the ministry of men in bringing them into the magistracy ; as, though church offices are God's ordinance, yet he makes use of men to put them into office. *For the Lord's sake ;* for God's sake, who commands this obedience, and gave them the authority, and is represented by them, and honoured by that obedience which is yielded to them in all things agreeable to his will. The phrase seems to be of the same import with that of being obedient *in the Lord,* Eph. vi. 1. *To the king ;* to Cæsar, the then supreme magistrate, under whose jurisdiction the Jewish Christians were ; and this being a general command extending to all Christians, it follows, that obedience is due from them to those chief magistrates whose subjects respectively they are. *As supreme ;* not only above the people, but above other magistrates.

14 Or unto governors, as unto them that are sent by him [f] for the punishment of evildoers, and [g] for the praise of them that do well. f Rom. 13. 4. g Rom. 13. 3.

Or unto governors ; he seems immediately to intend the governors of provinces under the Roman emperors, such as Pilate, Felix, Festus were in Judea, Sergius Paulus in Cyprus, Acts xiii. 7 ; and other places ; see Luke iii. 1 ; but so as to imply, under the name of governors, all inferior magistrates, as under the name of king he doth all supreme. *As unto them that are sent by him ;* either, 1. By the king, or supreme magistrate, and then the next words show what should be his end in sending, or appointing officers, or subordinate rulers under him : or rather, 2. Sent by God, from whom all rulers, subordinate as well as supreme, have their authority, and which is the great motive on which they are to be obeyed ; and then the following words show what is God's end in appointing them, and another reason for yielding obedience to them, viz. their being set up for the common good of the societies which they rule. *For the praise of them that do well :* praise is a kind of reward, and is here to be taken by a synecdoche for all sorts of rewards given to those that do well, and are obedient to the laws : see Rom. xiii. 3, 4.

15 For so is the will of God, that [h] with well doing ye may put to silence the ignorance of foolish men : h Tit. 2. 8. ver. 12.

For so is the will of God ; his command. *That with well-doing ;* all manner of offices of humanity, whereof obedience to magistrates is a principal one. *Ye may put to silence ;* Greek, muzzle, stop the mouths, Tit. i. 11 ; viz. by taking away all occasion of evil-speaking. *The ignorance ;* either their ignorance of the state and conversation of believers, which may be the occasion of their speaking evil of them ; or their ignorance of God and his ways, to which Christ imputes the fury of persecuters, John xvi. 3. They that know not God themselves, are most ready to reproach and slander those that do. *Of foolish men ;* true wisdom consisting in the knowledge of God, they that are destitute of that knowledge, as unbelievers are, are called foolish.

16 [i] As free, and not † using *your* liberty for a cloke of maliciousness, but as [k] the servants of God. i Gal. 5.1,13. † Gr. *having.* k 1 Cor. 7.22.

As free ; he prevents an objection ; they might pretend they were a free people, as Jews, and therefore were not to obey strangers, Deut. xvii. 15 ; John viii. 33 ; and made free by Christ. He answers, That they were freed indeed, but it was from sin, and not from righteousness, not from obedience to God's law, which requires subjection to magistrates, for they were still the servants of God. *And not using your liberty for a cloak of maliciousness ;* not using your liberty to cover or palliate your wickedness, excusing yourselves from obedience to your superiors by a pretence of Christian liberty, when, though ye be free from sin, yet ye are not from duty. *But as the servants of God ;* and so still bound to obey him, and your rulers in him.

17 ‖ Honour all *men.* [m] Love the brotherhood. [n] Fear God. Honour the king. 1 Rom. 12. 10. Phil. 2.3. ‖ Or, *Esteem.* m Heb. 13. 1. ch. 1. 22. n Prov. 24. 21. Matt. 22. 21. Rom. 13. 7.

Honour all men ; viz. according as honour is due to them, according to their dignity, power, gifts. &c. : see Rom. xii. 10 ; xiii. 7 ; Phil. ii. 3. *Love the brotherhood ;* though all may challenge suitable respects, yet there is a more special affection owing to believers, chap. i. 22; Gal. vi. 10. *Fear God;* with a filial fear or reverence. This command is interposed, either to show what is the true spring and fountain from which all the duties we perform to men are to proceed, viz. the fear of God, because where that doth not prevail no duty to men can be rightly performed; (they love the brotherhood best, and honour the king most, that truly fear God;) or to show the due bounds of all the offices we perform to men, that nothing is to be done for them which is inconsistent with the fear of God. *Honour the king;* with that honour which is peculiarly due to him above all others.

o Eph. 6. 5.
Col. 3. 22.
1 Tim. 6. 1.
Tit. 2. 9.

18 ° Servants, *be* subject to *your* masters with all fear; not only to the good and gentle, but also to the froward.

Servants; the word is not the same which Paul useth, Col. iii. 22, but may well comprehend the servants he speaks of, as implying not only slaves, but those that were made free, yet continued still in the family; and so signifies servants of whatsoever condition. *Be subject to your masters with all fear;* not only reverence of masters, and fear of offending them, is to be understood, but fear of God, as appears by the parallel place, Col. iii. 22: see Eph. vi. 5—7. *Not only to the good and gentle;* by *good* he means not gracious or holy, but, as the next word explains it, gentle, just, equal. *But also to the froward;* morose, crabbed, unjust, unmerciful.

|| Or, *thank.*
Luke 6. 32.
ver. 20.
p Mat. 5. 10.
Rom. 13. 5.
ch. 3. 14.

19 For this *is* || ᵖ thankworthy, if a man for conscience toward God endure grief, suffering wrongfully.

For this is thank-worthy; in the Greek (as in the margin) the substantive is put for the adjective: the sense is either, this is acceptable to God, and will be graciously rewarded by him; or, this is praise-worthy, and will be your glory, as ver. 20. *For conscience toward God;* out of respect to God, and a desire of pleasing him.

q ch. 3. 14.
& 4. 14, 15.

20 For ᵠ what glory *is it*, if, when ye be buffeted for your faults, ye shall take it patiently? but if, when ye do well, and suffer *for it*, ye take it patiently, this

|| Or, *thank. is* || acceptable with God.

For what glory is it? what praise or glory do you get by it? or, what great matter do you do? This interrogation hath the force of a negation, but is to be understood comparatively; it is worthy of praise to suffer patiently, even when men suffer justly, but worthy of little in comparison of suffering patiently when unjustly. *This is acceptable with God:* this shows what is meant by *thank-worthy*, ver. 19; and the apostle adds what kind of thanks or praise he intends, viz. not that which is of man, (which many times may fail, even when men patiently suffer injuries,) but that which is of God, to which believers should especially have respect.

r Mat. 16.24.
Acts 14. 22.
1 Thess. 3. 3.
2 Tim. 3. 12.
s ch. 3. 18.
|| Some read,
for you.
t John 13. 15.
Phil. 2. 5. 1 John 2. 6.

21 For ʳ even hereunto were ye called: because ˢ Christ also suffered || for us, ᵗ leaving us an example, that ye should follow his steps:

For even hereunto; viz. to patient bearing of sufferings, even for well-doing. *Were ye called;* viz. to Christ and the fellowship of his kingdom; q. d. Your very calling and profession, as Christians, requires this of you. *Also;* there is an emphasis in this particle, it is as much as if he had said, Even Christ our Lord and Head hath suffered for us, and therefore we that are but his servants and members must not think to escape sufferings. *For us;* or, as in the margin, for you, which agrees with the beginning and end of the verse, where the second person is used; but most read it as we do, in the first person, and the sense is still the same; only the apostle from a general proposition draws a particular exhortation: Christ suffered for us, (therein he comprehends the saints to whom he writes,) and left an example for us all; do ye therefore to whom, as well as to others, he left this example, follow his steps, John xiii. 15; 1 John ii. 6. *Leaving us an example,* as of other graces, so especially of patience.

22 ᵘ Who did no sin, neither was guile found in his mouth:

u Is. 53. 9.
Luke 23. 41.
John 8. 46.
2 Cor. 5. 21. Heb. 4. 15.

i. e. There was no guile in his mouth; it is a Hebraism; to be found is the same as to be, and not to be found the same as not to be, Gen. ii. 20; Isa. xxxix. 2: see Rom. vii. 10. This signifies Christ's absolute perfection, in that he did not offend so much as with his mouth, James iii. 2. The sense is, Christ was free from all manner of sin, and yet he suffered patiently; and therefore well may ye be content to suffer too, though wrongfully; seeing, though ye may be innocent in your sufferings, yet you come so far short of Christ's perfection.

23 ˣ Who, when he was reviled, reviled not again; when he suffered, he threatened not; but ʸ || committed *himself* to him that judgeth righteously:

x Is. 53. 7.
Matt. 27. 39.
John 8. 48,
49.
Heb. 12. 3.
y Luke 23.
46.
|| Or,
committed his cause.

By Christ's being *reviled,* we are to understand all those injurious words, reproaches, slanders, blasphemies, which his persecutors cast out against him. *Reviled not again;* therefore when he told the Jews they were of their father the devil, John viii. 44, that was not a reviling them, but a just accusation of them, or reproof of their devilish behaviour. *When he suffered;* when he was affected not only with verbal but real injuries, buffeted, spit upon, crowned with thorns, crucified. *He threatened not;* he was so far from avenging himself, or recompensing evil for evil, that he did not so much as threaten what he would afterward do to them. *But committed himself;* or his cause, as in the margin; neither is in the Greek, but either may be well supplied, and to the same purpose: the sense is, Christ did not retaliate, nor act any thing out of private revenge, but so referred himself, and the judgment of his cause, to his Father's good pleasure, as rather to desire pardon for his persecutors, than vengeance on them, Luke xxiii. 34. *To him that judgeth righteously:* the apostle adds this of God's judging righteously, for the comfort of servants to whom he speaks, as Eph. vi. 8, 9; Col. iii. 24; iv. 1, and for the terror of masters, that the former might learn patience, and the latter moderation.

24 ᶻ Who his own self bare our sins in his own body || on the tree, ᵃ that we, being dead to sins, should live unto righteousness: ᵇ by whose stripes ye were healed.

z Is. 53. 4, 5,
6, 11.
Matt. 8. 17.
Heb. 9. 28.
|| Or, *to.*
a Rom. 6. 2,
11. & 7. 6.
b Is. 53. 5.

Who his own self; not by offering any other sacrifice, (as the Levitical priests did,) but by that of himself. *Bare our sins;* or, took up, or lifted up, in allusion to the sacrifices of the Old Testament. the same word being used of them, Heb. vii. 27; James ii. 21. As the sins of the offerer were typically laid upon the sacrifice, which, being substituted in his place, was likewise slain in his stead; so Christ standing in our room, took upon him the guilt of our sins, and bare their punishment, Isa. liii. 4, &c. The Lord laid on him our iniquities, and he willingly took them up; and by bearing their curse, took away our guilt. Or, it may have respect to the cross, on which Christ being lifted up, (John iii. 14, 15; xii. 32,) took up our sins with him, and expiated their guilt by undergoing that death which was due to us for them. *In his own body;* this doth not exclude his soul, but is rather to be understood, by a synecdoche, of his whole human nature, and we have the sufferings of his soul mentioned, Isa. liii. 10, 12; John xii. 27; but mention is made of his body, because the sufferings of that were most visible. *On the tree;* on the cross. *That we, being dead to sins, should live unto righteousness;* another end of Christ's death, the mortification of sin, and our being freed from the dominion of it, Rom. vi. 2, 6, and being reformed to a life of holiness. *By whose stripes ye were healed;* viz. of the wound made in your souls by sin: this seems to relate to the blows that servants might receive of cruel masters, against which the apostle comforts them, and to the patient bearing of which he exhorts them, because Christ by bearing stripes, (a servile punishment,) under which may be comprehended all the sufferings of his death, had healed them of much worse wounds, and spiritual diseases, the guilt of their consciences, and the defilement of their souls.

I. PETER II, III

^{e Is. 53. 6.}
^{Ezek. 34. 6.}
^{d Ezek. 34.}
^{23. & 37. 24.}
^{John 10. 11,}
^{14, 16. Heb.}
^{13. 20. ch. 5. 4.}

25 For ᵉye were as sheep going astray; but are now returned ᵈunto the Shepherd and Bishop of your souls.

For ye were, while ye continued in your Judaism, and had not yet received the gospel, *as sheep going astray,* from Christ the great Shepherd, and the church of believers his flock, and the way of righteousness in which he leads them. Ye were alienated from the life of God, bewildered and lost in the way of sin, Isa. liii. 6. *But are now returned,* in your conversion to the faith, *to the Shepherd;* Christ the good Shepherd, John x., that takes care of souls, as a shepherd doth of his sheep. *And Bishop of your souls;* superintendent, inspector, or, as the Hebrews phrase it, visitor, i. e. he that with care looks to, inspects, and visits the flock. This he adds for the comfort (as of all believers, so) particularly of servants, that even they, as mean as they were, and as much exposed to injuries, yet were under the care and tuition of Christ.

CHAP. III

The apostle teacheth the duty of wives and husbands, 1—7; *exhorting all men to unity and love, and to return good for evil,* 8—13: *to suffer boldly for righteousness' sake, and to give a reason of their hope with meekness and fear; taking especial care to suffer, as Christ did, for well-doing, and not for evil-doing,* 14—18. *The preaching of Christ by his Spirit to the old world,* 19, 20. *After what manner Christian baptism saveth us,* 21, 22.

^{a 1 Cor. 14.}
^{34. Eph. 5.}
^{22. Col. 3. 18.}
^{Tit. 2. 5.}
^{b 1 Cor. 7. 16.}
^{c Matt. 18.}
^{15. 1 Cor. 9.}
^{19,—22.}

LIKEWISE, ᵃye wives, *be* in subjection to your own husbands; that, if any obey not the word, ᵇ they also may without the word ᶜbe won by the conversation of the wives;

To your own husbands; this he adds both to mitigate the difficulty of the duty, *subjection,* in that they were their *own* husbands to whom they were to be subject, and likewise to bound and circumscribe their obedience, that it was to be only to their own husbands, not to others; and so while he persuades them to subjection, he cautions them against unchastity. *That if any obey not the word;* the word of the gospel. He exhorts not only them that had believing husbands, but unbelieving ones, to be in subjection to them. *They also may without the word:* not that they could be converted to Christ without the knowledge of the word, when faith cometh by hearing, Rom. x. 17, but that they who either would not endure their wives' instructing them, or who had before rejected the word, yet, by seeing the effects and fruits of it in their wives, might be brought to have good thoughts of it, and thereby be the more prepared for the hearing of it, whereby faith might be wrought in them. *Be won;* or gained, viz. to Christ and his church: the same metaphor Paul useth, 1 Cor. ix. 19—21; Phil. iii. 8.

^{d ch. 2. 12.}

2 ᵈWhile they behold your chaste conversation *coupled* with fear.

Chaste conversation; free from all manner of impurities, and any thing contrary to the marriage covenant. *Coupled with fear;* such a fear or reverence of your husbands, whereby out of the fear of God, and conscience of his command, you give them all due respect, and do not willingly displease them. See Eph. v.; subjection is required, ver. 22, and fear, ver. 33.

^{e 1 Tim. 2. 9.}
^{Tit. 2. 3, &c.}

3 ᵉWhose adorning let it not be that outward *adorning* of plaiting the hair, and of wearing of gold, or of putting on of apparel;

Let it not be; let it not be chiefly, or not so much the adorning of the outward man as the inward; the negative here is to be taken as a comparative, as Exod. xvi. 8; Luke xiv. 12. The apostle doth not absolutely condemn all kind of ornaments, or rich attire, which we find used sometimes by the godly themselves in the Scripture, Gen. xxiv. 22, 30; Esth. v. 1; compared with Psal. xlv. 9, 13, where the spiritual ornaments of Christ's spouse are set forth by terms taken from the external ornaments of Solomon's wife; and Ezek. xvi. 12, these things are spoken of as God's gifts. But he taxeth all vanity, levity, immoderate sumptuousness or luxury in apparel, and bodily ornaments in women, (or men,) whatsoever is above their place and condition in the world, or above their estate and ability; such as proceeds from any lust, (pride, wantonness, &c.,) or tends to the provoking or cherishing any, or is accompanied with the neglecting or slighting of inward beauty and spiritual ornaments.

^{f Ps. 45. 13.}
^{Rom. 2. 29.}
^{& 7. 22.}
^{2 Cor. 4. 16.}

4 But *let it be* ᶠthe hidden man of the heart, in that which is not corruptible, *even the ornament* of a meek and quiet spirit, which is in the sight of God of great price.

The hidden man of the heart; the inward man, Rom. vii. 22; 2 Cor. iv. 16; either the soul in opposition to the body, or the image of God, and graces of his Spirit in the soul, called elsewhere *the new man,* and opposed to natural corruption, or the old man, Eph. iv. 24; Col. iii. 9, 10. *In that which is not corruptible:* this relates to what follows, *the ornament of a meek,* &c., and is opposed to those external ornaments before mentioned, which are of a fading, perishing nature, whereas this is constant and durable: and therefore women who are more apt to be overmuch pleased with external dresses, and bodily ornaments, are exhorted rather to enrich and beautify their souls with Divine graces, than their bodies with gaudy clothes. *Even the ornament of a meek and quiet spirit:* this notes the particular grace or graces (parts of the new man) in which the spiritual beauty and adorning of women's souls consists; and either these two words, *meek* and *quiet,* are but indifferent expressions of the same grace; or, by meekness may be meant gentleness, easiness and sweetness of spirit, in opposition to moroseness, frowardness, pride, passion, &c.; and by quietness, a peaceable, still, modest temper, in opposition to pragmaticalness, talkativeness, clamorousness. These two usually go in conjunction together, and the latter is the effect of the former: see 1 Tim. ii. 9—12. *Which:* either this refers to *spirit,* or to the whole sentence, *the ornament of a meek,* &c., but the sense is still the same. *Is in the sight of God;* who can best judge, (as looking to the inner man, which is not obvious to the eyes of others,) and whose judgment is most to be valued: here God's judgment is opposed to the judgment of vain women, who think to commend themselves to others by outward bravery, and of a vain world, which esteems such things. *Of great price:* the excellency of grace and spiritual ornaments is set in opposition to gold and costly apparel: q. d. If women will be fine that they may appear beautiful, let them choose the best ornaments, those of the mind and heart, a meek and quiet spirit, which are precious in the sight of God himself, rather than these external ones, which serve only to draw men's eyes toward them.

5 For after this manner in the old time the holy women also, who trusted in God, adorned themselves, being in subjection unto their own husbands;

Holy women; and therefore worthy of imitation. *Who trusted in God;* whose only hope was in God, and therefore their care to please him. *Adorned themselves;* viz. with a meek and quiet spirit, counting that the best ornament.

^{g Gen. 18. 12.}

6 Even as Sara obeyed Abraham, ᵍcalling him lord: whose †daughters ye are, as long as ye do well, and are not afraid with any amazement.

^{† Gr. children.}

Even as Sara; after her name was changed from Sarai, my lady, to Sarah, simply a lady or princess, because kings were to come of her, Gen. xvii. 15, 16: yet even then she *obeyed Abraham;* and this is spoken in commendation of her obedience. *Calling him lord;* not merely in compliment, but in reality, hereby acknowledging his authority and her own subjection. *Whose daughters ye are;* not only according to the flesh, but spiritually, according to the promise. *Ye are;* either ye are made or become, viz. by imitation of her faith and holiness, as well as ye are by kindred and succession; or, ye are declared and known to be, as the phrase is elsewhere used, John xv. 8. *As long*

I. PETER III

as ye do well; follow her in good works, 1 Tim. ii. 10. *And are not afraid with any amazement;* or, afraid of any amazement, any thing frightful, or which might terrify you, taking *amazement* for the object or cause of fear, as ver. 14; Psal. liii. 5; Prov. iii. 25; and the sense may be, either, so long as ye perform your duty with a resolute mind, and keep from that which is contrary to your faith; or, as long as you subject yourselves to your husbands willingly, cheerfully, and without slavish fear of being losers by your obedience, and faring the worse for your patience and submission.

7 [h] Likewise, ye husbands, dwell with them according to knowledge, giving honour unto the wife, [i] as unto the weaker vessel, and as being heirs together of the grace of life; [k] that your prayers be not hindered.

[h] 1 Cor. 7. 3. Eph. 5. 25. Col. 3. 19.
[i] 1 Cor. 12. 23. 1 Thess. 4. 4.
[k] See Job 42. 8. Matt. 5. 23, 24. & 18. 19.

Dwell with them; perform all matrimonial duties to them; by a synecdoche, all the duties of that relation are contained under this one of cohabitation. *According to knowledge;* either, according to that knowledge of the Divine will, which by the gospel ye have obtained; or, prudently and wisely, and as becomes those that understand their duty. *Giving honour unto the wife;* not despising them because of their weakness, or using them as slaves, but respecting them, caring for them, (as Matt. xv. 6; 1 Tim. v. 3.) using them gently, covering their infirmities. *As unto the weaker vessel;* weaker than the husbands, and that both in body and mind, as women usually are. In Scripture any instrument is called a vessel, and the wife is here called so, as being not only an ornament, but a help to the husband and family, Gen. ii. 18. This he adds as a reason why the husband should give honour to the wife, viz. her being *the weaker vessel;* weak vessels must be gently handled; the infirmities of children bespeak their pardon when they offend; and *those members of the body which we think less honourable, on them we bestow more abundant honour,* 1 Cor. xii. 23. It is a part of that prudence according to which men should dwell with their wives, to have the more regard to them because of their infirmities, (in bearing with them and hiding them,) lest they should be discouraged, if they find their weakness makes them contemptible. *And as being heirs together;* another reason why husbands should give honour to their wives, viz. because though by nature they are weak and unequal to their husbands, yet they are equal to them in respect of their being called to the same grace and glory, there being *neither male nor female* in Christ, Gal. iii. 28. *Of the grace of life;* i. e. eternal life, which is the gift of grace; or, is to be given out of grace. *That your prayers be not hindered;* either, that ye be not diverted and hindered from praying; or, that the efficacy of your prayers be not hindered, viz. by those contentions and differences which are like to arise, if you do not dwell with your own wives according to knowledge, and give them the honour that belongs to them.

8 Finally, [l] be ye all of one mind, having compassion one of another, [m] ‖ love as brethren, [n] be pitiful, be courteous:

[l] Rom. 12. 16. & 15. 5. Phil. 3. 16.
[m] Rom. 12. 10. Heb. 13. 1. ch. 2. 17.
‖ Or, *loving to the brethren.* n Col. 3. 12. Eph. 4. 32.

Be ye all of one mind; either, be of one mind in the things of faith, and then this implies the consent of the understanding, and the next, that of the affections; or, be united both in faith and affection: see Rom. xii. 16; 2 Cor. xiii. 11; Phil. iv. 2. *Having compassion one of another:* mutually affected with each other's good or evil, Rom. xii. 15; Heb. x. 34; xiii. 3. This he joins with the other as the consequent of it; they that are united in faith and love are of the same body; and where one member suffers, the rest suffer, 1 Cor. xii. 26. *Love as brethren;* viz. in Christ: see chap. ii. 17. *Be pitiful;* ready to show mercy, of a merciful disposition, Eph. iv. 32; Col. iii. 12. *Be courteous;* kind, affable, humane, of a sweet conversation, in opposition to sourness and moroseness: the same word is used, Acts xxvii. 3.

9 [o] Not rendering evil for evil, or railing for railing: but contrariwise blessing; knowing that ye are thereunto called, [p] that ye should inherit a blessing.

[o] Prov. 17. 13. & 20. 22. Matt. 5. 39. Rom. 12. 14, 17. 1 Cor. 4. 12. 1 Thess. 5. 15.
[p] Mat. 25. 34.

Not rendering evil for evil, or railing for railing; not recompensing evil either in words or deeds, Prov. xxiv. 29: see on chap. ii. 3, of this Epistle; Rom. xii. 14, 17, 19, 21. *But contrariwise blessing;* praying for, and, as ye can, doing good to, those that do evil to you, or speak evil of you, Matt. v. 39, 44; Luke xvi. 27, 28. *Knowing that ye are thereunto called;* either, 1. To bless those that do evil to you, that so by patient bearing of injuries, forbearing private revenge, &c., ye might obtain a blessing. Or, 2. Ye are called hereunto, viz. to inherit a blessing. *Called;* in your conversion to the faith of Christ. *That ye should inherit a blessing:* this either shows how believers came to partake of the blessing, viz. by way of inheritance: or it implies the perpetuity of it, that, whereas they can exercise their patience in suffering injuries but a little while, their recompence shall be for ever. *A blessing;* either, 1. Eternal life, as the greatest blessing; or, 2. The good things of both lives, temporal, spiritual, and eternal mercies, which are all promised to the godly, 1 Tim. iv. 8, and which they have by right of inheritance, Psal. xxxvii. 11; Matt. v. 5: and this seems to agree with ver. 10—12.

10 For [q] he that will love life, and see good days, [r] let him refrain his tongue from evil, and his lips that they speak no guile:

[q] Ps. 34. 12, &c.
[r] Jam. 1. 26. ch. 2. 1, 22. Rev. 14. 5.

He that will love life; he that earnestly desires to lead a quiet and comfortable life here, and to enjoy eternal life hereafter. *And see good days;* peaceable and prosperous; as evil days are such as are grievous and calamitous, Gen. xlvii. 9. *Let him refrain his tongue from evil:* from evil-speaking, railing, reviling, open detraction. *And his lips that they speak no guile;* tell no lies of his neighbour: or, this may imply whispering, backbiting, or any way secretly and closely speaking evil of him. Under these two, all the vices of the tongue, whereby our neighbour may be wronged, are contained, and the contrary virtues commanded, under the name of *blessing.*

11 Let him [s] eschew evil, and do good; [t] let him seek peace, and ensue it.

[s] Ps. 37. 27. Is. 1. 16, 17. 3 John 11.
[t] Rom. 12. 18. & 14. 19. Heb. 12. 14.

Let him eschew evil, and do good; let him not only in general avoid all sin, and exercise himself in all well-doing, (as the prophet's meaning, cited in the margin, seems to be,) but particularly, let him avoid all sin against his neighbour, not recompensing evil to him, and doing him all the good he can, and overcoming evil with good; and to this the apostle accommodates the prophet's words. *Let him seek peace;* not only with God and his own conscience, but with his neighbours, which is here especially meant. *And ensue it:* either seeking and ensuing signify the same thing, viz. an earnest desire of peace, and use of all lawful means to obtain it; or, ensuing it may signify the difficulty of obtaining it; when we seek it, it may seem to fly from us, men may not let us have peace when we would have peace, Psal. cxx. 7, and therefore we must follow it, Heb. xii. 14.

12 For the eyes of the Lord *are* over the righteous, [u] and his ears *are* open unto their prayers: but the face of the Lord *is* † against them that do evil.

[u] John 9. 31. Jam. 5. 16.
† Gr. *upon.*

For the eyes of the Lord are over the righteous, and his ears are open unto their prayers; God watcheth over them, looks favourably on them, and hears their prayers: see Psal. xxxiv. 15. This he lays down as a motive to patience under injuries, and to keep us from tumultuating passions, and desires of revenge; that God sees all we suffer, hath a care of us, is ready to hear, and in due time to help us. *But the face of the Lord is against them that do evil;* his anger, or indignation; *face* being here taken not for God's favour, (as many times it is,) but in the contrary sense, as Lev. xvii. 10; xx. 5; Psal. lxviii. 1, 2. Men show by their countenances whether they be angry or pleased; and hence it is that God's face is sometimes taken for his favour, sometimes for his displeasure. A further argument to persuade us to patience, that God undertakes to plead our cause against our enemies, and avenge us on them; whereas if we think to secure ourselves against them by undue means, we make God an enemy to us.

13 ˣ And who *is* he that will harm you, if ye be followers of that which is good?

And who is he that will harm you? i. e. none or few will harm you, as being convinced and overcome by your good deeds, whereby even they are many times mollified and melted that are of themselves most wicked and hard-hearted, 1 Sam. xxiv. 16, 17. *If ye be followers of that which is good;* either followers of God, who doth good to the evil and unkind; but then it should be rendered, followers of him who is good, or rather, followers of those things that are good: q. d. If you be diligent in doing good to others, none will have the heart to do you hurt.

14 ʸ But and if ye suffer for righteousness' sake, happy *are ye:* and ᶻ be not afraid of their terror, neither be troubled;

But and if ye suffer for righteousness' sake; if ye suffer unjustly, whether it be for the true profession of the gospel, or in the exercise of righteousness, being followers of that which is good, and walking in the practice of the duties before mentioned. *Happy are ye;* both in the spiritual benefit you gain by sufferings, viz. your edification in faith, patience, humility, &c.; the glory which redounds to God, who supports you under and carries you through them; and the reward you yourselves expect after them, Matt. v. 10, &c. *And be not afraid of their terror;* either be not afraid after the manner of carnal men, (as the prophet's meaning is, Isa. viii.,) or rather, (the apostle accommodating the words of the prophet to his present purpose.) be not afraid of those formidable things wherewith they threaten you; or, be not afraid of themselves and their threatenings, whereby they would strike terror into you: and so here is a metonymy in the words; fear, the effect, being put for the cause; thus fear is taken, Psal. lxiv. 1; xci. 5; Prov. i. 26. *Neither be troubled;* viz. inordinately, with such a fear as is contrary to faith, and hinders you from doing your duty, John xiv. 1.

15 But sanctify the Lord God in your hearts: and ᵃ *be* ready always to *give* an answer to every man that asketh you a reason of the hope that is in you with meekness and ‖ fear:

But sanctify the Lord God in your hearts; exalt him in your hearts, and give him the honour of all his glorious perfections, power, wisdom, goodness, faithfulness, &c., by believing them, and depending upon his promises for defence and assistance against all the evils your enemies may threaten you with. *And be ready always;* prepared to answer when duly called to it. *To give an answer;* or, to make an apology or defence, viz. of the faith ye profess; the word is used, Acts xxii. 1; 1 Cor. ix. 3. *To every man that asketh you;* either that hath authority to examine you, and take an account of your religion; or, that asks with modesty, and a desire to be satisfied, and learn of you. *A reason of the hope that is in you;* i. e. faith, for which hope is frequently used in Scripture, which is built upon faith: the sense is, Whereas unbelievers, your persecutors especially, may scoff at your hope of future glory, as vain and groundless, and at yourselves, as mad or foolish, for venturing the loss of all in this world, and exposing yourselves to so many sufferings, in expectation of ye know not what uncertainties in the other; do ye therefore be always ready to defend and justify your faith against all objectors, and to show how reasonable your hope of salvation is, and on how sure a foundation it is built. *With meekness and fear;* either with meekness in relation to men, in opposition to passion and intemperate zeal, (your confession of the faith must be with courage, but yet with a spirit of meekness and modesty,) and fear or reverence in relation to God, which, where it prevails, overcomes the fierceness of men's spirits, and makes them speak modestly of the things of God, and give due respect to men; or, *fear* may be set in opposition to pride, and presumption of a man's own wisdom or strength; q. d. Make confession of your faith humbly, with fear and trembling, not in confidence of your own strength, or gifts, or abilities.

16 ᵇ Having a good conscience; ᶜ that, whereas they speak evil of you, as of evil doers, they may be ashamed that falsely accuse your good conversation in Christ.

Having a good conscience; this may be read either, 1. Indicatively, and joined (as by some it is) to the former verse; and then the sense is, If ye be always ready to answer every one that asketh you a reason of the hope that is in you, ye shall have a good conscience: or rather, 2. Imperatively (which our translation favours); q. d. Not only be ready to make confession of your faith, but let your life and practice be correspondent to it, in keeping yourselves pure from sin, and exercising yourselves unto godliness, from whence a good conscience proceeds; here therefore the effect is put for the cause, a good conscience for a good life, Acts xxiii. 1. *That whereas they speak evil of you, &c.;* the sense is, that whereas they speak evil of you, as of evil-doers, your good conversation may bear witness for you, confute their calumnies, and make them ashamed, when it appears that their accusations are false, and that they have nothing to charge upon you but your being followers of Christ. *Your good conversation in Christ;* i. e. that good conversation which ye lead as being in Christ; viz. according to his doctrine and example, and by the influence of his Spirit.

17 For *it is* better, if the will of God be so, that ye suffer for well doing, than for evil doing.

If the will of God be so; viz. that ye must suffer; intimating that this is an argument for their patience and submission in their sufferings, and a ground of comfort to them, that they are led into them by the providence of God, (not by their own folly or rashness,) and have him for a witness and judge both of their cause and deportment.

18 For Christ also hath ᵈ once suffered for sins, the just for the unjust, that he might bring us to God, ᵉ being put to death ᶠ in the flesh, but ᵍ quickened by the Spirit:

For Christ also hath once suffered; in opposition to the legal sacrifices which were offered from day to day, and from year to year, Heb. vii. 27; ix. 25; and x. 12: and this shows, as the perfection of Christ's sufferings, (in that they needed not be repeated,) so our conformity to him in deliverance from ours; that as Christ underwent death (the principal part of his sufferings) not often, but once only, and then his glory followed; so likewise, if in this life we suffer for righteousness' sake, according to Christ's example, there remains no more suffering for us, but we shall be glorified with him, 2 Tim. ii. 12. *For sins;* i. e. for the expiation of sin. This is another argument for patience under sufferings, that Christ by his sufferings hath taken away the guilt, and freed us from the punishment, of sin; so that our sufferings, though they may be not only by way of trial, but of correction, yet are not properly penal or vindictive. *The just for the unjust;* and therefore well may we, who are in ourselves unrighteous, be content to suffer, especially for his cause and truth. *That he might bring us to God;* i. e. reconcile us to God, and procure for us access to him with freedom and boldness, Rom. v. 2; Eph. iii. 12. *Being put to death in the flesh;* his human nature, frequently in Scripture called *flesh*, as chap. iv. 8; John i. 14; and though his soul, as being immortal, did not die, yet he suffered most grievous torments in it, and his body died by the real separation of his soul from it. *But quickened by the Spirit;* i. e. his own Godhead, John ii. 19; x. 17, 18. The former member of this sentence speaks of the subject of his death, his *flesh*, which was likewise the subject of his life in his resurrection; this latter speaks of the efficient cause of his life, his own eternal *Spirit*.

19 By which also he went and ʰ preached unto the spirits ⁱ in prison;

By which also; by which Spirit, mentioned in the end of the former verse, i. e. by, or in, his Divine nature, the same by which he was quickened. *He;* Christ. This notes the person that went and preached, as the former doth the nature in which, and so shows that what is here spoken of the person of Christ, is to be understood of him according to his Divine nature. *Went;* or, came, viz.

I. PETER III

from heaven, by an anthropopathy, by which figure God is often in Scripture said to go forth, Isa. xxvi. 21, to *come down*, Micah i. 3, and *go down*, Gen. xviii. 21; Exod. iii. 8; which two latter places are best understood of the Second Person. This therefore here notes in Christ not a change of place, but a special operation, and testification of his presence. *And preached;* viz. by Noah, inspired by him, that he might be a preacher of righteousness, to warn a wicked generation of approaching judgment, and exhort them to repentance. *Unto the spirits;* souls of men departed, which are frequently called spirits, Eccles. xii. 7; Acts vii. 59; Heb. xii. 23. *In prison;* i. e. in hell, so it is taken, Prov. xxvii. 20; compare with Matt. v. 25; Luke xii. 58, where *prison* is mentioned as a type or representation of hell; and the Syriac renders the word by *Sheol*, which signifies sometimes the grave and sometimes hell. See the like expression, 2 Pet. ii. 4, 5; Jude 6.

20 Which sometime were disobedient, [k] when once the longsuffering of God waited in the days of Noah, while [l] the ark was a preparing, [m] wherein few, that is, eight souls were saved by water.

[k Gen. 6. 3, 5, 13.
l Het. 11. 7.
m Gen. 7. 7. & 8. 18.
2 Pet. 2. 5.]

Which; which spirits in prison. *Quest.* When were these spirits, to whom Christ preached by Noah, in prison? *Answ.* Then when Peter wrote this Epistle. The Greek participle of the present tense is here to be supplied, and the word thus read, preached to the spirits which are in prison, viz. now at this time; and so the time of their being in prison is opposed to the time of their being disobedient; their disobedience going before their imprisonment; q. d. They were disobedient then, they are in prison now. *Sometime;* viz. in the days of Noah, when they were upon earth. *Were disobedient;* would not believe what Noah told them in God's name, nor be brought to repentance by his preaching. *When once;* not always, but for a determinate time, viz. one hundred and twenty years; which term being expired, there was no hope left for them that they should be spared. *The long-suffering of God;* i. e. God in his patience and long-suffering. *Waited;* for the repentance and reformation of that rebellious generation. *In the days of Noah;* till the one hundred and twenty years were run out, and the ark, which was preparing for the security of him and his family, were finished. *Eight souls;* i. e. eight persons, Noah, and his wife, his three sons, and their wives. *Were saved by water;* either, 1. *By water* is here put for in, as Rom. iv. 11, *that believe, though they be not circumcised:* the same Greek preposition is used as here, and the words may be read, by, or through, or rather in uncircumcision; for uncircumcision was not the cause or means of their believing. See the like use of this particle, 2 Pet. iii. 5. Thus, saved in the water, is as much as, notwithstanding the water, or the water not hindering; so 1 Tim. ii. 15, *saved in childbearing*, where the same preposition is used. Or, 2. *By water;* the water which drowned the world, lifting up the ark and saving Noah and his household. *Quest.* Doth not this place countenance the papists' limbus, or the place where the souls of the Old Testament fathers were reserved (as they pretend) till Christ's coming in the flesh? *Answ.* No: for, 1. The spirits here mentioned were disobedient, which cannot be said of the fathers of the Old Testament, who were true believers. 2. The spirits here mentioned are not said to be delivered out of prison, but only that Christ by his Spirit preached to them, and to his preaching to them their disobedience is opposed. 3. According to the papists, Noah and his family must be in their limbus, whereas they are opposed to those disobedient spirits to whom Christ is said to preach.

21 [n] The like figure whereunto *even* baptism doth also now save us (not the putting away of [o] the filth of the flesh, [p] but the answer of a good conscience toward God,) [q] by the resurrection of Jesus Christ:

[n Eph. 5. 26.
o Tit. 3. 5.
p Rom. 10. 10.
q ch. 1. 3.]

The like figure; Greek, the antitype. Twice this word occurs in Scripture; once Heb. ix. 24, where it signifies simply a type, or exemplar, or representation; and here, where it implies either the likeness or correspondence of one type with another in signifying the same thing: so that here may be two types, the deliverance of Noah and his household in the flood, and baptism, whereof the former was a type of the latter, yet so as both represent the salvation of the church; in that as the waters of the flood lifting up the ark, and saving Noah's family shut up in it, signified the salvation of the church; so likewise baptism signifies the salvation of those that are in the church (as in an ark) from that common destruction which involves the rest of the world: or, it signifies the truth itself, as answering the type or figure; and thus the temporal salvation of Noah, &c. from the flood, in the ark, was the type, and the eternal salvation of believers by baptism is the antitype, or truth figured by it. Our translation seems to favour the former. *Whereunto;* i. e. the saving eight persons by water; q. d. The salvation of believers now by baptism, answers to the deliverance of Noah then; and so this relative, *whereunto,* answers to the foregoing sentence, as its antecedent. *Even baptism doth also now save us;* viz. with an eternal salvation, in answer to the temporal deliverance of Noah by water; and that not only as it is a sign, but a seal whereby the Spirit of God confirms in the hearts of believers the faith of their justification purchased by Christ's death, and witnessed by his resurrection, Rom. iv. 25. *Not the putting away of the filth of the flesh;* not merely the washing of the body with water, or the external part of baptism, which can of itself have no further effect than other bodily washings have, viz. to cleanse the flesh. And so he answers an objection which might be made, How baptism can be said to save us, when so many perish who are baptized, by declaring, as follows, what it is in baptism which is so effectual. *But the answer of a good conscience:* the Greek word here used is several ways rendered, and so this place differently interpreted: the best translation seems to be, either, 1. The petition of a good conscience, and then it notes the effect of baptism, viz. that holy confidence and security wherewith a conscience, sprinkled with the blood of Christ, addresses itself to God in prayer, as a Father. Thus the word is taken, Matt. xv. 23; xvi. 2; Rom. x. 20. Or rather, 2. The stipulation, which by a metonymy is taken for the answer, promise, or restipulation required; and this agrees with our translation. In baptism there is a solemn covenant, or mutual agreement, between God and the party baptized, wherein God offers, applies, and seals his grace, stipulating or requiring the party's acceptance of that grace, and devoting himself to his service; and when he out of a good conscience doth engage and promise this, which is to come up to the terms of covenant, that may properly be called *the answer of a good conscience.* It seems to be an allusion to the manner of baptizing, where the minister asked the party to be baptized concerning his faith in Christ, and he accordingly answered him; Dost thou believe? I believe. Dost thou renounce the devil, &c.? I renounce. See Acts viii. 37. *A good conscience;* a conscience purified by faith from internal and spiritual defilements, (in opposition to putting away the filth of the flesh,) which only sincerely answers to what God requires in baptism. *Toward God;* i. e. in the presence of God, with whom conscience hath to do in baptism, and who alone is the Judge of conscience, and knows whether it be good and sincere, or not: or, *toward God*, is to God; and then it relates to *answer*, and implies the answer or engagement of conscience to be made to God. *By the resurrection of Jesus Christ:* either these words are to be joined to the verb *save*, and the rest of the verse to be read in a parenthesis, according to our translation; and then the sense is, that baptism saves us by the faith of Christ's resurrection, or by virtue derived from Christ's resurrection, under which is comprehended his death and sufferings: or they are to be joined to *answer*, supplying which is; and then, without a parenthesis, the text runs thus, the answer of a good conscience, which is by the resurrection of Christ; and the meaning is, that the answer of a good conscience toward God is by the resurrection of Christ, as the foundation of our believing the promise of forgiveness and free grace, inasmuch as it testifies God to be fully satisfied for sin, and Christ to have fully overcome sin, the devil, &c. For where this faith is not, there can be no good conscience, nor any sincere answering what God requires of us in baptism: if men do not believe the satisfaction of Divine justice by Christ's death, which is evidenced by his resurrection, they will not close with the offers of his grace, nor engage themselves to be the Lord's. See chap. i. 3; 1 Cor. xv. 17.

r Ps. 110. 1.
Rom. 8. 34.
Eph. 1. 20.
Col. 3. 1.
Heb. 1. 3.
s Rom. 8. 38.
1 Cor. 15. 24.
Eph. 1. 21.

22 Who is gone into heaven, and ʳis on the right hand of God; ˢangels and authorities and powers being made subject unto him.

Who is gone into heaven, and is on the right hand of God: see Rom. viii. 34; Heb. i. 3. This is added as another ground of faith and a good conscience. *Angels and authorities and powers:* see Rom. viii. 38; Eph. i. 20, 21; Col. i. 16; ii. 10. *Being made subject unto him;* viz. by his Father, to whom this subjecting all things to Christ is elsewhere ascribed, 1 Cor. xv. 27; Eph. i. 22; Heb. ii. 8.

CHAP. IV

The apostle exhorteth to cease from sin, in regard of Christ's having suffered for it, and of a future judgment, 1—6. *From the approaching end of all things, he urgeth to sobriety, watchfulness, and prayer,* 7; *to charity,* 8; *hospitality,* 9; *and a right use of spiritual gifts,* 10, 11. *Sundry motives of comfort under persecution,* 12—19.

a ch. 3. 18.

FORASMUCH then ᵃas Christ hath suffered for us in the flesh, arm yourselves likewise with the same mind: for

b Rom. 6. 2, 7. Gal. 5. 24.
Col. 3. 3, 5.

ᵇhe that hath suffered in the flesh hath ceased from sin;

The apostle having in the former chapter exhorted believers to patient bearing of afflictions by the example of Christ, ver. 18, proceeds in this to persuade them to improve the crosses they bore outwardly to inward mortification. Christ's death is proposed to us in Scripture as an exemplar both of external mortification in bearing reproaches, persecutions, &c., (this the apostle prosecutes in the former chapter,) and of internal, in the destroying the body of sin; this he exhorts to in this chapter, and indeed draws his argument from Christ's death, not only as the exemplary, but efficient and meritorious, cause of our mortification, and which hath a real influence upon it, in that Christ by his death did not only merit the pardon of sin, but the giving the Spirit, whereby corruption might be destroyed, and our natures renewed. *Forasmuch then as Christ hath suffered for us;* viz. not only as an exemplar of patience and sometimes to the will of God, but for the taking away of sin, both in the guilt and power of it, and that he might be the procurer as well as pattern of our mortification. *In the flesh;* in his human nature, as chap. iii. 18. *Arm yourselves likewise with the same mind;* strengthen and fortify yourselves against all temptations, and unto the mortification of your lusts, with the consideration of these ends, and the mighty efficacy of Christ's death, he suffering in his flesh, i. e. in his human nature, that you might suffer in your flesh, i. e. in your sinful, corrupt nature; or, (which comes to the same,) *with the same mind* which Christ had, who, in his death, aimed not only at the pardon of your sin, but the destruction of it, and the renovation of your natures: or, *arm yourselves with the same mind,* viz. a purpose of suffering in the flesh, i. e. of dying spiritually with Christ in the mortification of your flesh, Rom. vi. 6, 7; as Christ died, and suffered in the flesh, so reckon that you, by the virtue of his death, must die to sin, and crucify your flesh, with its affections and lusts, Gal. v. 24: or else, what *the same mind* is, he declares in the following clause. *For;* or rather, that, the Greek word here seems rather to be explicative than causal. *He that hath suffered in the flesh;* i. e. the old man, his corrupt flesh, *(flesh* being taken here in a different sense from what it was in the former part of the verse,) he that is spiritually dead with Christ, whose old man is crucified with him. *Hath ceased from sin;* from sinning willingly and delightfully, and yielding himself up to the power of sin; compare Rom. vi., which explains this: what Peter here calls suffering in the flesh, Paul there calls a being dead to sin, ver. 2, 11; and what Peter calls a ceasing from sin, Paul calls a living no longer in sin, ver. 2, and a being freed from it, ver. 7. And this may be the *mind,* or thought,

with which they were to be armed, that they being dead with Christ to sin, should not live any longer in it; having their flesh crucified, should not indulge its affections and lusts.

2 ᶜThat he no longer ᵈshould live the rest of *his* time in the flesh to the lusts of men, ᵉbut to the will of God.

c Rom. 14.7.
ch. 2. 1.
d Gal. 2. 20.
ch. 1. 14.
e John 1. 13.
Rom. 6. 11.
2 Cor. 5. 15. Jam. 1. 18.

In the flesh; i. e. in the body, meaning his natural life: *flesh* is here taken in a third sense, different from the two former: so Gal. ii. 20; Phil. i. 22. By *the lusts of men,* he means the corrupt desires and sinful ways of carnal men, to which they were not to conform themselves, or make them the rule of their living, Rom. xii. 2; 1 Cor. iii. 3; Col. ii. 8; Tit. i. 14. *But to the will of God;* the holy will of God revealed to us in his law, (which is the rule by which we are to walk,) in opposition to the lusts of men; we are to live not as men would have us, but as God commands us.

3 ᶠFor the time past of *our* life may suffice us ᵍto have wrought the will of the Gentiles, when we walked in lasciviousness, lusts, excess of wine, revellings, banquetings, and abominable idolatries:

f Ezek. 44. 6.
& 45. 9.
Acts 17. 30.
g Eph. 2. .2.
& 4. 17.
1 Thes. 4. 5.
Tit. 3. 3.
ch. 1. 14.

For the time past of our life may suffice: the apostle doth not mean by this expression merely that they should forbear their former lusts out of a satiety and weariness, as having had their fill of them, but to stir them up to holiness by minding them of their former sinful life; q. d. Ye are concerned to run well now, when ye have for so great a part of your time run wrong. It is a figure whereby he mitigates and lenifies the sharpness of his reproof for their former sinful life: see the like, Ezek. xliv. 6; xlv. 9; Mark xiv. 41. *Us;* some copies read, ye, and that agrees with the following verse, where the second person is made use of: or if we read, according to our translation, *us,* it is a figure called anacoenosis, whereby Peter assumes to himself in common with them what yet, in his own person, he was never guilty of, as Isa. lxiv. 6, 7; Dan. ix. 5, &c.; or else it may be an analogy of the person, whereby the first is put for the second. *To have wrought the will of the Gentiles;* viz. those that were profane and ignorant of God and Christ, and so it is the same as the lusts of men, ver. 2. *When we walked;* had our conversation, as Eph. ii. 3, walking being taken for the course of man's life; and sometimes in an evil way, as 2 Pet. ii. 10; iii. 3; Jude 16, 18; and sometimes in a good, as Luke i. 6. *In lasciviousness;* especially outward acts, here set in distinction from *lusts,* which implies those inward motions from which those outward defilements proceed. *Excess of wine, revellings;* unseasonable and luxurious feasting, Rom. xiii. 13; Gal. v. 21. *Banquetings:* compotations, or meetings for drinking, Prov. xxiii. 30; Isa. v. 11, 12. *And abominable idolatries: Quest.* Why doth Peter charge the Jews with idolatry, who generally kept themselves from it after the Babylonish captivity? *Answ.* 1. Though most did, yet all might not. 2. It is a sort of idolatry to eat things sacrificed to idols, which many of the Jews, being dispersed among the idolatrous Gentiles, and being invited by them to their idol feasts, might possibly do; and, being under the temptation of poverty, might too far conform themselves to the customs of the nations among which they were. 3. Probably this idolatry might be the worship of angels, frequent among the Gentiles, particularly the Colossians, inhabiting a city of Phrygia, which was a part of Asia where many Jews were, chap. i. 1. 4. The churches to which he wrote might be made up of Jews and Gentiles, and the apostle may, by a synecdoche, ascribe that to all in common, which yet is to be understood only of a part.

4 Wherein they think it strange that ye run not with *them* to the same excess of riot, ʰspeaking evil of *you:*

h Acts 13.
45. & 18. 6.
ch. 3. 16.

Wherein they think it strange: Greek, are strangers, i. e. carry themselves as strangers, wondering (as at some new thing) at the change the gospel hath made in you, and your no more conforming yourselves to their wicked courses; they seem to be in another world when among you. *That ye run not with them:* this seems to signify the eagerness and vehemency of these Gentiles in pursuing their lusts, and may perhaps have some respect to the feasts of Bacchus, to which they were wont madly to run, and there commit the abominations mentioned ver. 3. *To the same excess of riot;* or, profuseness, or confusion, of riot or luxury, and then it suits well with that heap of sins before mentioned, whereof this seems to be comprehensive. *Speaking evil;* Greek, blaspheming, or speaking evil; *of you* is added by the translators: this may therefore be understood not only of their speaking evil of believers, as void of humanity and enemies to civil society, but of God and the Christian religion, as a dull, morose, sour way, and which they could not embrace without renouncing all mirth and cheerfulness.

i Acts 10. 42. & 17. 31. Rom. 14. 10. 12. 1 Cor. 15. 51, 52. 2 Tim. 4. 1. Jam. 5. 9.

5 Who shall give account to him that is ready ⁱ to judge the quick and the dead.

Who shall give account to him; of their evil speaking as well as of other sins, Jude 15; it is a metaphor taken from stewards giving account to their masters, Matt. xviii. 23; Luke xvi. 2. *That is ready;* not only prepared for it, but at hand to do it, James v. 9. *To judge the quick and the dead;* those that shall be alive at Christ's coming, and those that died before, but then shall be raised, and brought to judgment. Hereby he intimates, for their comfort, that though their enemies and ill-willers might outlive them, yet they shall not escape God's judgment.

k ch. 3. 19.

6 For for this cause ᵏ was the Gospel preached also to them that are dead, that they might be judged according to men in the flesh, but live according to God in the spirit.

To them that are dead; either, 1. Spiritually dead, i. e. dead in sin, viz. then when the gospel was preached to them; or, 2. Naturally dead, viz. when the apostle wrote this Epistle. The verb *are* not being in the Greek, the words may be understood either way, by supplying were, according to the former exposition, or are, according to the latter, which our translators favour. See the like, Ruth i. 8. *That they might be judged according to men in the flesh:* either, 1. That they might be judged or condemned in the flesh, i. e. that their old man and carnal conversation, according to men walking in their carnal lusts, might be destroyed and abolished; and then, to be judged in the flesh, is of the same import as to suffer in the flesh, ver. 1; to be dead to sin, Rom. vi. 2: or, 2. That they might be judged or condemned in the flesh, according to men, and so far as they could reach, not only by censures, reproaches, and evil speeches, but even death itself, as it had fallen out already to Stephen, James, &c. *But live according to God in the spirit;* that they might live a spiritual life in their souls according to the will of God, and an eternal life with him. To *live in the spirit, to the will of God,* to *walk in newness of life,* &c., are phrases of a like import in the language of the apostles. According to the latter exposition of the former clause, the apostle seems in the whole to remove the scandal of these Christians, being reproached and condemned by unbelievers for their strictness in religion, and nonconformity to the world, by telling them, that their condition was not singular, but so it had fared with others before them, (though now dead,) to whom the gospel was preached, with the same event as to the judgment of worldly men who censured and condemned them, and yet with the same hope of fruit and benefit, viz. that though they were condemned by men in the flesh, or as to their outward man, yet as to their souls, (meant here by spirits,) they might live a holy, spiritual life, a life to God in this world, ending in a life with him in the other.

l Mat. 24. 13. 14. Rom. 13. 12. Phil. 4. 5. Heb. 10. 25. Jam. 5. 8. 2 Pet. 3. 9. 11. 1 John 2. 18. m Matt. 26. 41. Luke 21. 34. Col. 4. 2. ch. 1. 13. & 5. 8.

7 But ˡ the end of all things is at hand: ᵐ be ye therefore sober, and watch unto prayer.

But the end of all things: the last judgment, which will put an end to all the evils as well as good things of this world. *Is at hand:* see James v. 8, 9. *Be ye therefore sober;* both in mind, prudent, moderate, 2 Cor. v. 13; Tit. ii. 6; and in body, temperate in meats and drinks, &c. *And watch:* the word signifies both sobriety, in opposition to drunkenness, 1 Thess. v. 6, 8, and watchfulness, 2 Tim. iv. 5, and this signification agrees best with this place, the former being implied in the word *sober*. *Unto prayer;* the end for which they should be sober and vigilant, viz. that they might observe every season fit for prayer, and might still keep themselves in a praying frame.

n Heb. 13. 1. Col. 3. 14. o Prov. 10. 12. 1 Cor. 13. 7. Jam. 5. 20. ‖ Or, *will.*

8 ⁿ And above all things have fervent charity among yourselves: for ᵒ charity ‖ shall cover the multitude of sins.

And above all things: see the like expression, James v. 12, and on the same occasion, Col. iii. 14. *Have fervent charity;* not only labour after charity diligently and carefully, but let it be fervent, intense, strong. *For charity shall cover the multitude of sins;* partly by preventing anger, railings, revilings, contentions, that they break not out, and partly by repressing, concealing, pardoning them when they do break out, 1 Cor. xiii. 7: see James v. 20.

p Rom. 12. 13. Heb. 13. 2. q 2 Cor. 9. 7. Phil. 2. 14. Philem. 14.

9 ᵖ Use hospitality one to another ᵠ without grudging.

Use hospitality; Christian hospitality in entertaining strangers, those especially that are brought to need your kindness by suffering for the gospel. *Without grudging;* or murmuring, either at the expense you make, or the carriage of those ye entertain; q. d. Use hospitality willingly, freely, cheerfully, Rom. xii. 8; 2 Cor. ix. 7.

r Rom. 12. 6. 1 Cor. 4. 7. s Matt. 24. 45. & 25. 14. 21. Luke 12. 42. 1 Cor. 4. 1, 2. Tit. 1. 7. t 1 Cor. 12. 4. Eph. 4. 11.

10 ʳ As every man hath received the gift, *even so* minister the same one to another, ˢ as good stewards of ᵗ the manifold grace of God.

As every man hath received the gift; any gift, office, faculty, or ability, whereby he may be serviceable to the good of others, all which are received of God, 1 Cor. xii. 11; Eph. iv. 7. *Minister the same one to another;* dispense and communicate modestly and humbly, not lifting himself up above others upon the account of his gifts, but remembering he hath received them, and is a steward to dispense them. *As good stewards;* and therefore faithful in distributing his Lord's goods. *Of the manifold grace of God:* by grace he means the same as by gift before; and so by manifold grace, the various gifts given to them of God, 1 Cor. xii. 4—6.

u Jer. 23. 22. x Rom. 12. 6, 7, 8. 1 Cor. 3. 10. y Eph. 5. 20. ch. 2. 5. 1 Tim. 6. 16. ch. 5. 11. Rev. 1. 6.

11 ᵘ If any man speak, *let him speak* as the oracles of God; ˣ if any man minister, *let him do it* as of the ability which God giveth: that ʸ God in all things may be glorified through Jesus Christ, ᶻ to whom be praise and dominion for ever and ever. Amen.

If any man speak; viz. authoritatively, and by way of office, as a public teacher in the church; though this may be accommodated to private Christians in their charitative instructions of others, yet it seems especially meant of teaching officers. *Let him speak as the oracles of God:* this relates not only to the manner of speaking, that it be with faith in that word the preacher speaketh, and a due reverence of it, but to the matter likewise, that he preach nothing but the pure word of God, and do not obtrude upon the hearers the fancies, figments, or traditions of men, instead of the oracles of God. *If any man minister:* this may be understood either, 1. More particularly of the work of deacons, Acts vi., who were to *serve tables*, ver. 2, distribute the alms of the church, and take care of the poor; or, 2. More generally of any ministry in the church, distinct from that of teaching, (of which he spake before,) as the dispensing of sacraments, exercise of discipline, &c. *Let him do it as of the ability which God giveth;* i. e. not remissly and coldly, but diligently and strenuously, and with his might, as far as God enables him; this being to do it faithfully, which is especially required in a steward, 1 Cor. iv. 2. *That God in all things may be glorified;* in all your gifts, and the communications of them: q. d. God doth not adorn you with his gifts so as to bereave himself of his glory, but that you should give him the honour of them. *Through Jesus Christ;* from whom ye have received the gifts, Eph. iv. 8, and by whom you are enabled to glorify God; and by whom alone what ye do can be accepted of God. See Eph. iii. 21.

12 Beloved, think it not strange concerning

^athe fiery trial which is to try you, as though some strange thing happened unto you:

a 1 Cor. 3. 13. ch. 1. 7.

Think it not strange ; be not offended or troubled at persecution, as at a thing unusual or never heard of; it implies that they should reckon upon it beforehand, that they might not be surprised with it when it comes. The same word is used, ver. 4. *Concerning the fiery trial;* the heat or burning, whereby he means great afflictions, especially those that are for rightesusness' sake, as appears, ver. 12, which are often compared to fire, as being alike painful and grievous to them as fire is to men's bodies; and because men are tried by them as metals are by fire, Psal. lxvi. 10; Isa. xlviii. 10. *Which is to try you:* this he adds as the reason why they should not think strange of persecutions, viz. because they were sent by God, not for their destruction, but for the trial and exercise of their graces.

13 ^bBut rejoice, inasmuch as ^cye are partakers of Christ's sufferings; ^dthat, when his glory shall be revealed, ye may be glad also with exceeding joy.

b Acts 5. 41. Jam. 1. 2.
c Rom. 8. 17. 2 Cor. 1. 7. & 4. 10. Phil. 3. 10. Col. 1. 24. 2 Tim. 2. 12. ch. 5. 1, 10. Rev. 1. 9. *d* ch. 1. 5, 6.

But rejoice; be so far from being offended at your sufferings, as rather to reckon that there is great matter of rejoicing in them; their being trials makes them tolerable, but your being in them partakers of Christ's sufferings makes them comfortable. *Inasmuch as ye are partakers of Christ's sufferings;* i. e. ye suffer, 1. As Christ did, for the confession of the truth, and so ye are such kind of sufferers as Christ was. 2. As members of Christ, ye suffer those evils which are laid out for those that belong to Christ, 1 Thess. iii. 3. 3. Ye are hereby conformed to Christ your Head. 4. Ye partake of the influence of what Christ suffered, for the sanctification of your sufferings: see Phil. iii. 10. *That, when his glory shall be revealed ;* viz. at his second coming, chap. i. 7; Col. iii. 4; 2 Thess. i. 7. *Ye may be glad also with exceeding joy ;* a joy without any the least mixture of pain or grief. The rejoicing of the saints here is mixed with pain and heaviness, but shall be pure hereafter; they rejoice in hope now, but in enjoyment then.

14 ^eIf ye be reproached for the name of Christ, happy *are ye ;* for the spirit of glory and of God resteth upon you : ^fon their part he is evil spoken of, but on your part he is glorified.

e Mat. 5. 11. 2 Cor. 12. 10. Jam. 1. 12. ch. 2. 19, 20. & 3. 14. *f* ch. 2. 12. & 3. 16.

Happy are ye; viz. because of the Spirit's dwelling in you, which is both the means and evidence of your happiness. *The spirit of glory and of God;* i. e. the glorious Spirit of God, or that Spirit of God which is likewise a Spirit of glory, as being not only glorious in himself, but a glory to them in whom he dwells, and the cause of their future glorification. This he adds in counterbalance to the reproaches they suffered for the name of Christ; q. d. It is a greater glory to you to have the Spirit of Christ dwelling in you, (whereof your patient bearing reproaches and persecutions is an argument,) than all the calumnies and obloquies wherewith your enemies load you can be a shame to you. *Resteth upon you :* in allusion to Isa. xi. 2; dwells in you, and shall *abide with you for ever,* John xiv. 16, not leaving you in your sufferings. *On their part he ;* either Christ, or rather the Spirit. *Is evil spoken of ;* the reproaches your enemies cast upon you, reach that Spirit himself that dwells in you, when they revile that good confession into which the Spirit led you, deride the consolations he gives you, and speak evil of your persons, who are the temples in which he dwells. *But on your part he is glorified ;* viz. by your patience and constancy in your sufferings, which shows forth the power of that Spirit which resteth upon you, in that he works so mightily in you, as to enable you to bear what without the assistance of his grace were intolerable.

15 But ^glet none of you suffer as a murderer, or *as* a thief, or *as* an evildoer, ^hor as a busybody in other men's matters.

g ch. 2. 20.
h 1 Thess. 4. 11. 1 Tim. 5. 13.

But *let none of you suffer as a murderer, or as a thief :* keep clear of those crimes which may expose you to suffering by the hand of justice, and carry yourselves so innocently, that you may never suffer from men but unjustly. *Or as an evil-doer ;* either this is a general term, denoting them that offend against any public law; or, it may signify those that are guilty of any offence against the laws, though less than murder or theft. *Or as a busy-body in other men's matters;* either a covetous person, that looks with an evil eye upon what others have, and is ready to catch it as he can ; or rather, one that goes beyond the bounds of his own calling, and invades the callings of others, pragmatically intruding into their business, and making himself a judge of those things which belong not to him. Some nations are said to have punished those that were busy through idleness, impertinently diligent in other men's matters, and negligent of their own. However, if this pragmaticalness did not expose the Christians to the laws of the Gentiles, yet it might make them odious, and expose them to their reproaches.

16 Yet if *any man suffer* as a Christian, let him not be ashamed; ⁱbut let him glorify God on this behalf.

i Acts 5. 41.

Yet if any man suffer as a Christian ; if his Christianity be his only crime, and the cause of his sufferings. *Let him not be ashamed :* see 2 Tim. ii. 12. *But let him glorify God on this behalf ;* i. e. on the account of his sufferings ; let him bless God for keeping him from suffering as an evildoer, and for counting him worthy to suffer for Christ's sake, Acts v. 41, as well as for giving him patience and courage under sufferings.

17 For the time *is come* ^kthat judgment must begin at the house of God : and ^lif *it* first *begin* at us, ^mwhat shall the end *be* of them that obey not the Gospel of God ?

k Is. 10. 12. Jer. 25. 29. & 49. 12. Ezek. 9. 6.
l Mal. 3. 5. Luke 23.31.
m Luke 10. 12, 14.

For the time is come ; or season, viz. that which is fixed by God : the afflictions that befall God's people come in the time appointed, and so are never unseasonable. Or this may imply, that what the prophets spoke in their time, Isa x. 12; Jer. xxv. 29, doth especially agree to gospel times, viz. that judgment begins at the house of God. *Judgment ;* viz. temporary, and for good, in opposition to the destructive judgment he implies in the latter part of the verse ; he means all those afflictions God brings upon his children for their correction, trial, instruction, mortification, 1 Cor. xi. 31, 32. *Must begin at the house of God ;* the church of God, and the members of it, called here his *house,* as 1 Tim. iii. 15 ; Heb. iii. 6, and typified by the material house or temple of God under the Old Testament. *What shall the end be of them that obey not the gospel of God?* how miserable, how dreadful will be the end of all those that would not obey the gospel ! implying, that they shall be in a much worse condition if God take them in hand. If he spare not his children, much less will he his enemies. If the one sip of the cup of God's wrath, the other *shall wring out the dregs, and drink them,* Psal. lxxv. 8.

18 ⁿAnd if the righteous scarcely be saved, where shall the ungodly and the sinner appear ?

n Prov. 11. 31. Luke 23. 31.

Scarcely be saved ; with much labour and difficulty, through many tribulations, Acts xiv. 22, as going in the narrow way, and entering in at the strait gate, Matt. vii. 13, 14. *The ungodly and the sinner ;* unbelievers and impenitent sinners of all sorts ; both words signify the same, in opposition to *the righteous* before mentioned. *Appear ;* he shall not be able to stand in God's judgment against the sentence of condemnation then to be pronounced, Psal. i. 5 : q. d. If the righteous scarcely be saved, the wicked shall certainly perish.

19 Wherefore let them that suffer according to the will of God ^ocommit the keeping of their souls *to him* in well doing, as unto a faithful Creator.

o Ps. 31. 5. Luke 23. 4 ;. 2 Tim. 1. 12.

Let them that suffer ; viz. any manner of affliction or persecution for righteousness' sake. *According to the will of God ;* according to that will of God, whereby he hath ap-

I. PETER V

pointed them to suffer such things, chap. iii. 17; 1 Thess. iii. 3. *Commit;* commend into his hands, or lay up, or intrust with him as a depositum, Psal. xxxi. 5; 2 Tim. i. 12. *The keeping of their souls;* as the most precious things while they live, and most to be cared for when they die; that they may be kept from sin under afflictions, and from perishing in death: or rather, *their souls* here includes their bodies, and so committing their souls is committing their whole selves to God. *In well-doing;* not being deterred from well-doing by the evils they suffer, but by persevering in holiness notwithstanding their afflictions, making it appear to the last, that they do not suffer as evil-doers. *As unto a faithful Creator;* one who, as Creator, is able to keep what they commit to him; and being faithful to his promises, certainly will do it.

CHAP. V.

The elders are exhorted to feed the flock of Christ conscientiously, looking to the chief Shepherd for a reward, 1—4. *The younger are required to submit to the elder, and all to practise humility toward each other,* 5, *with resignation to God,* 6, 7; *to be sober, watchful, and stedfast in the faith, resisting the devil,* 8, 9. *The Epistle is concluded with a prayer and benediction,* 10—14.

THE elders which are among you I exhort, who am also [a] an elder, and [b] a witness of the sufferings of Christ, and also [c] a partaker of the glory that shall be revealed:

The elders which are among you I exhort; viz. those that were such, not so much by age as by office, as appears by his exhorting them to *feed the flock,* ver. 2; he means the ordinary ministers of the churches among the believing Jews. *Who am also an elder:* elder is a general name, comprehending under it even apostles themselves, who were elders, though every elder were not an apostle. *And a witness;* either, 1. In his doctrine, in which he held forth Christ's sufferings, whereof he had been an eye-witness, in which respect the apostles are often called *witnesses,* Luke xxiv. 48; Acts i. 8, 22; ii. 32. Or, 2. In his example, in that he in suffering so much for Christ, did give an ample testimony to the reality of Christ's sufferings, and that Christ had indeed suffered: or, both may well be comprehended. *The glory that shall be revealed;* viz. at Christ's last coming, chap. i. 5; iv. 13; Rom. viii. 17, 18.

2 [d] Feed the flock of God ∥ which is among you, taking the oversight *thereof,* [e] not by constraint, but willingly; [f] not for filthy lucre, but of a ready mind;

Feed; teach and rule, Matt. ii. 6; John xxi. 15—17; Acts xx. 28. *The flock of God;* the church. *Which is among you;* which is with you, or committed to your charge; intimating that the flock not being their own, they were to give an account of it to him that had set them over it. *Taking the oversight thereof;* or, being bishops, or acting as bishops over it, i. e. superintending, inspecting, and watching over it with all care, Acts xx. 28, 29. *Not by constraint;* not merely because ye must: what men do out of compulsion, they do more slightly and perfunctorily, as those that would not do it if they could help it: see the like expression, 2 Cor. ix. 7. *But willingly;* cheerfully and freely, as Exod. xxxvi. 2; Psal. liv. 6: compare 1 Cor. ix. 17. *Not for filthy lucre;* not out of covetousness, or a design of making a gain of the work; it being a shameful thing for a shepherd to feed the sheep out of love to the fleece: see Tit. i. 7; 1 Tim. iii. 3, 8. *But of a ready mind;* out of a good affection to the welfare of the flock, in opposition to the private gain before mentioned. He doth not do his work freely, and of a ready mind, who is either driven to it by necessity, or drawn by covetousness.

3 Neither as ∥ [g] being lords over [h] *God's* heritage, but [i] being ensamples to the flock.

Neither as being lords; not exercising any such lordship or dominion over the people, as temporal lords and magistrates exercise over their subjects, Matt. xx. 25, 26, &c.; Luke xxii. 25: compare 2 Cor. i. 24. *Over God's heritage;* the Lord's clergy, the same as *flock* before; the Greek word is plural, and so it signifies the several churches or flocks which were under the charge of the several elders or pastors. The church of Israel is often called God's inheritance, which as it were fell to him by lot, (as the Greek word signifies,) and which was as dear to him as men's inheritances are to them: see Deut. iv. 20; ix. 29; xxxii. 9; Psal. xxxiii. 12; lxxiv. 2; lxxviii. 71. Accordingly now the Christian church, succeeding it, is called God's inheritance, and the word *clerus* is no where in the New Testament peculiarly ascribed to ministers of the gospel. This title given here to the Lord's people, implies a reason why the elders should not lord it over them, viz. because they are still the Lord's inheritance, and not their own; God having not given them a kingdom but a care, and still retaining his right to his people. *But being ensamples to the flock;* in holiness of life, practising before their eyes what you preach to their ears, Phil. iii. 17; 2 Thess. iii. 9; Tit. ii. 7.

4 And when [k] the chief Shepherd shall appear, ye shall receive [l] a crown of glory [m] that fadeth not away.

And when the chief Shepherd; the Lord Jesus Christ, the only Prince of pastors, called the *great Shepherd of the sheep,* Heb. xiii. 20, as here *the chief Shepherd,* not only for his supereminent dignity over all other pastors, but because of the power he hath over them, they being all subject to his authority, receiving their charge from him, and exercising their office in his name, and being accountable to him for their administrations. *Shall appear:* see chap. i. 7, 13; iv. 13. *Ye shall receive;* or, carry away, viz. from Christ, who, as the Judge, shall award it to you. *A crown of glory,* either, a glorious crown; or, that glory which shall be as a crown to you. It is called *a crown of righteousness,* 2 Tim. iv. 8; a *crown of life,* James i. 12. *That fadeth not away;* in opposition to those crowns which were given to conquerors in war, and in public games, which were made of perishable flowers or herbs: see chap. i. 4; 1 Cor. ix. 25.

5 Likewise, ye younger, submit yourselves unto the elder. Yea, [n] all *of you* be subject one to another, and be clothed with humility: for [o] God resisteth the proud, and [p] giveth grace to the humble.

Ye younger; either he means those that were inferior to the church officers, and then he here prescribes the people their duty, as he had done the ministers; or rather, those that were younger in years, and then he passeth from the more special to the general. *Submit yourselves:* under subjection, he comprehends all those offices which the younger owe to the elder; as, to reverence them, take their advice, be guided by them, &c. Or, if younger be taken in the former sense, this precept falls in with that of the apostle, Heb. xiii. 17. *To the elder:* either elders by office, who were likewise usually elders in years, the younger sort being more rarely chosen to be officers; or rather, elder in age. *Yea, all of you be subject one to another;* viz. in those mutual duties which they owe to each other, as husbands to wives, parents to children, &c. Those that are superior to others, yet are not so exempt from subjection as not to owe some duty: see Phil. ii. 3. *And be clothed with humility;* or, wrapt up, or covered, with humility, as with a garment which is put on over other garments; q. d. Adorn yourselves with humility as with a beautiful garment or robe. The metaphor of putting on is frequent, where mention is made of any grace or virtue, Rom. xiii. 14; Eph. iv. 24; Col. iii. 10, 12.

6 [q] Humble yourselves therefore under the mighty hand of God, that he may exalt you in due time:

The mighty hand of God; by this he means God's omnipotence, which sometimes is called *a strong hand,* Exod. iii. 19, *a mighty hand,* chap. xxxii. 11; Deut. iii. 24, *the right hand of power,* Matt. xxvi. 64; by which he is able

I. PETER V

to beat down those that are proud and high, and to defend or exalt those that are humble and lowly. *In due time;* Greek, in season, viz. that which God sees most fit and conducing to his own glory and your real welfare.

r Ps. 37. 5. & 55. 22.
Wisd. 12. 13.
Matt. 6. 25.
Luke 12. 11, 22. Phil. 4. 6. Heb. 13. 5.

7 *Casting all your care upon him; for he careth for you.*

Casting, as a burden, *ally our care upon him;* your care for all sorts of things, even which concern this life, this care which will otherwise cut and divide your hearts, (as the Greek word in Matthew imports,) and be grievous and tormenting to you. *For he careth for you;* God concerns himself in the affairs of his servants, and in whatsoever befalls them, and takes diligent care that no good thing be wanting to them, Psal. lxxxiv. 11 ; Phil. iv. 6.

s Luke 21. 34, 36.
1 Thess. 5. 6.
ch. 4. 7.
t Job 1. 7. & 2. 2.
Luke 22. 31.
Rev. 12. 12.

8 *Be sober, be vigilant; because your adversary the devil, as a roaring lion, walketh about, seeking whom he may devour:*

Be sober: see chap. i. 13 ; iv. 7 : q. d. Ye have to do with a mad enemy, a raging devil; ye had need yourselves be sober; not only in meats and drinks, &c., but as to the cares of this life, and whatsoever it is that is apt to intoxicate your minds, and expose you to him. *Be vigilant;* spiritually watchful and circumspect, careful of your salvation, and aware of Satan's snares and temptations, Matt. xxiv. 42 ; xxv. 13 ; xxvi. 41 ; 1 Thess. v. 6. *Because your adversary;* or, that adversary of yours; he that contends with you, is plaintiff against you, Matt. v. 25 ; Luke xii. 58. It answers to the Hebrew word *Satan,* Zech. iii. 1. *The devil;* your accuser, he that maligns you, calumniates you, informs against you: he is so called, Matt. iv. 1 ; xiii. 39, and elsewhere, because of his accusing God to men, Gen. iii. 4, 5, and men to God, Job i. 7 ; ii. 2 ; Rev. xii. 10, as well as each to other, John viii. 44. *As a roaring lion;* i. e. strong, fierce, cruel, especially when hungry, and seeking his prey, and roaring after it. *Walketh about;* is diligent and restless in his attempts, either by circumventing or assaulting you: see Job i. 7. *Seeking whom he may devour;* not lightly hurt, but swallow up and utterly destroy, by himself or his instruments.

u Eph. 6. 11, 13. Jam. 4. 7.
x Acts 14. 22. 1 Thess. 3. 3. 2 Tim. 3. 12. ch. 2. 21.

9 "Whom resist stedfast in the faith, *knowing that the same afflictions are accomplished in your brethren that are in the world.*

Whom resist; by not yielding to his temptations, Eph. iv. 27, and by employing your spiritual armour against him, Eph. vi. 11—13, &c.: see James iv. 7. *Stedfast in the faith;* either, 1. Hold your faith, persevering in it, which the devil would fain bereave you of, (as soldiers used in war to look to their shields, it being dishonourable to lose them,) and without which ye will never be able to stand out against the devil : or, 2. Stedfast or strong by faith ; intimating, that faith is a Christian's greatest strength, it being by faith that he engageth the power of God and grace of Christ on his side, whereby he comes to be victorious over all his enemies, 1 John v. 4. *Knowing that the same afflictions;* either, 1. The devil's temptations, which here he calls *afflictions,* because believers are passive in them, and count them the greatest afflictions ; or rather, 2. Persecutions, which though they come upon them immediately from the men of the world, yet it is by the instigation of the devil, the prince of the world, who hath a principal hand in them, and acts by men as his instruments : so that when men oppress them, they are to resist the devil, who thereby tempts them. They have a spiritual enemy to deal with even in temporal afflictions. *Are accomplished in your brethren;* or, fulfilled, or perfected: either, 1. Others of your brethren are filling up the measure of sufferings God hath allotted them, for the mortifying of the flesh, and conforming them to Christ their Head, as well as you are filling up yours, Col. i. 24 ; or, 2. He speaks of the community of their sufferings : q. d. What afflictions ye endure, others endure too, and therefore ye should not grudge to suffer, when ye have so good company in your sufferings. *That are in the world;* either this notes the sufferings of the saints to be universal, so as to reach them all, wheresoever they are dispersed throughout the world ; or, to be

short, as being confined to the time only of their abode in the world.

10 But the God of all grace, *who hath called us unto his eternal glory by Christ Jesus, after that ye have suffered a while,* *make you perfect,* *stablish, strengthen, settle you.*

y 1 Cor. 1. 9. 1 Tim. 6. 12.
z 2 Cor. 4. 17. ch. 1. 6.
a Heb. 13. 21. Jude 24.
b 2 Thess. 2. 17. & 3. 3.

But the God of all grace; i. e. the author and giver of all grace, from whom ye have received what you have, and expect what you want. *Who hath called us unto his eternal glory;* that eternal glory whereof believers at the last day shall be made partakers, which is called God's glory, because it is that which he hath promised to them, and will at last put them in possession of: see ver. 1 ; Rom. v. 2 ; and because they shall after a sort partake of the Divine glory which they behold. *By Christ Jesus;* for Christ's sake, as the meritorious cause of our effectual calling, and by him as the great Apostle of our profession, Heb. iii. 1. Or, *by Christ Jesus* may refer to *glory,* Christ being the cause of their glorification as well as calling. *After that ye have suffered a while;* this he adds for their encouragement, that whatsoever they suffered would be but short, as chap. i. 6 ; 2 Cor. iv. 17. *Make you perfect, stablish, strengthen, settle you;* either, 1. *Perfect* that which is begun, Heb. xiii. 20, 21, *stablish* that which is right, 2 Thess. ii. 16, *strengthen* that which is weak, *settle* or found (by a firm union and conjunction unto Christ) that which is already built, Eph. iii. 17, 18 ; Col. i. 23 : or, 2. These four words may be but different expressions whereby the apostle sets forth the same thing, viz. God's confirming and establishing those saints unto their final perseverance ; and his using so much variety of expressions may imply, that it is a matter of very great difficulty to hold on our Christian course, without failing or coming short of the goal, and therefore we need singular assistance from God to enable us to it.

11 *To him be glory and dominion for ever and ever. Amen.*

c ch. 4. 11. Rev. 1. 6.

To him; to God. *Be glory and dominion;* see chap. iv. 11. The verb *be* in the text is not in the Greek, and so it may be read with a supply of a verb either of the imperative mood, and then it is a doxology, as we render it ; or of the indicative, he hath glory and dominion ; or, to him belongs glory and dominion, or glorious dominion or power ; and then it tends to encourage these saints, in that he, whom the apostle prays to stablish and strengthen them, is of power sufficient to do it.

12 *By Silvanus, a faithful brother unto you, as I suppose, I have* *written briefly, exhorting, and testifying* *that this is the true grace of God wherein ye stand.*

d 2 Cor. 1. 19.
e Heb. 13. 22.
f Acts 20. 24. 1 Cor. 15. 1. 2 Pet. 1. 12.

By Silvanus; either Silas, Acts xv., xvi., whom Peter therefore here calls *a faithful brother* to them, that they might the more readily receive him, though a minister of the uncircumcision ; or else this *Silvanus* was some other that had preached to them, and is therefore said to be *a faithful brother* to them : the former is more probable. *As I suppose;* this doth not signify any doubt, but rather a firm persuasion, of Silvanus's faithfulness ; q. d. I reckon him faithful, having hitherto found him so : or, it may relate to the briefness of the Epistle ; q. d. I suppose it will seem brief to you, as being from one that loves you, and about matters that so much concern you. *Exhorting;* viz. to constancy in the faith, and diligence in duty. *And testifying;* bearing my testimony to the truth ye have received ; this the apostle witnesseth, that being more fully convinced of it, they might more constantly adhere to it. See the like phrase, Neh. ix. 29, 30 ; xiii. 15. *That this is the true grace of God wherein ye stand;* the true doctrine of God, wherein he sets forth the grace of Christ : q. d. Ye are in the right way ; the doctrine ye have embraced is indeed the truth of God.

13 The *church that is* at Babylon, elected together with *you,* saluteth you ; and *so doth* Marcus my son.

g Acts 12. 12, 25.

The church that is at Babylon; Babylon in Chaldea, where it is most probable the apostle was at the writing of this Epistle ; the Jews being very numerous in those parts, as having settled themselves there ever since the captivity, and Peter being an apostle of the circumcision, his work lay much thereabout. The papists would have Babylon here to be Rome, as Rev. xvii., and that Peter gives it that name rather than its own, because, being escaped out of prison at Jerusalem, Acts xii. 12, 25, he would not have it known where he was. But how comes he, that had been so bold before, to be so timorous now? Did this become the head of the church, the vicar of Christ, and prince of the apostles? And is it probable he should live twenty-five years at Rome, (as they pretend he did,) and yet not be known to be there? Wherever he was, he had Mark now with him, who is said to have died at Alexandria the eighth year of Nero, and Peter not till six years after. If Mark then did first constitute the church of Alexandria, and govern it (as they say he did) for many years, it will be hard to find him and Peter at Rome together. But if they will needs have Rome be meant by Babylon, let them enjoy their zeal, who rather than not find Peter's chair, would go to hell to seek it; and are more concerned to have Rome be the seat of Peter than the church of Christ.

14 ʰGreet ye one another with a kiss of charity. ⁱPeace be with you all that are in Christ Jesus. Amen.

<small>h Rom. 16. 16. 1 Cor. 16. 20. 2 Cor. 13. 12. 1 Thess. 5. 26. i Eph. 6. 23.</small>

Greet ye one another with a kiss of charity: see Rom. xvi. 16; 1 Cor. xvi. 20; 2 Cor. xiii. 12. *In Christ Jesus;* united to him by faith, and members of him.

THE SECOND EPISTLE GENERAL

OF

PETER

THE ARGUMENT

It cannot be denied, but that some question there hath been, both about the penman and the authority of this Epistle. The former hath been questioned, because of the difference of the style of this from that of the former Epistle. But, to say nothing of a great likeness of style in both, observed by some; why might not the same person see fit on different occasions, and according to the different things he wrote about, to change his way of writing? Or why may not the Holy Ghost use his instruments in what way he please, and not only dictate to them the matter they are to write, but the expression and phrase? Why must an infinite and sovereign Agent be bound up, and confined to the parts and qualifications of the men he inspired? And if we set aside the judgment of several councils and fathers, (which yet might go far,) two great arguments may be drawn from the first chapter, to prove Peter to be the penman of this Epistle. One from the inscription of it, where we have both his names, *Simon* and *Peter*, prefixed to it. Another from ver. 16, where he affirms himself to have been present with Christ at his transfiguration; from whence we may well argue, that none having ever ascribed it to John, and James being dead before, (though if he had been alive, it cannot be imagined that he should put Peter's name to any epistle of his own writing,) and there being none but they two present with our Lord at that time besides Peter, Matt. xvii. 1, none but he could be the writer of it. And indeed, as some observe, if this Epistle be not Peter's, when his name is set to it, it is so far from being canonical, that it is not fit so much as to be reckoned among the apocryphal books, having so great a lie in the front of it. As for the authority of it, there can be no doubt of that if Peter were the writer, when nothing concurs in it repugnant to other parts of Scripture, or unbecoming the grace and style of an apostle. And though some of the ancients have questioned it, yet many more have acknowledged it; nor was it ever numbered among apocryphal writings. And its not being found in the first Syriac version, can but argue its being questioned by some, not its being rejected by all. It seems to be written to the Jews of the dispersion, as the former was, which appears by chap. iii. 1, 2, where he mentions the former written to them; and this was written not long before his death, chap. i. 14. The scope of it is, partly to call to their remembrance the truths he had preached among them, that so, when they should be destitute of the apostles' preaching to them, yet they might remember the pure doctrine they had learned of them, chap. i. 12, 15, and might thereby be fortified against the errors of false teachers, chap. ii. 1; and partly to persuade and stir them up to diligence in holiness and constancy in the faith. As in his First Epistle he had exhorted them to patience under the tyranny of persecutors, lest they should yield to them; so in this he exhorts them to perseverance in the truth of the gospel, against the deceptions of heretics, lest they should be seduced by them, chap. ii., and continue in holiness, notwithstanding the profaneness of scoffers, chap. iii.

CHAP. I

The apostle, saluting the Christians, admonisheth them of the gifts and promises of the gospel, and their tendency to promote a godly life, 1—4. He exhorteth them to add to their faith such virtues as would make it fruitful, 5—9; and thereby to make their calling and election sure, 10, 11. He is careful to remind them hereof, knowing his dissolution to be near, 12—15; and urgeth the evidence of what he had seen and heard in the holy mount in confirmation of Christ's second coming, together with the word of prophecy, which he recommendeth to their regard, 16—21.

<small>A. D. 66. ‖ Or, *Symeon.* Acts 15. 14. a Rom. 1. 12. 2 Cor. 4. 13. Eph. 4. 5. Tit. 1. 4.</small>

‖ SIMON Peter, a servant and an apostle of Jesus Christ, to them that have obtained ᵃlike precious faith with us through the righteousness † of God and our Saviour Jesus Christ:

<small>† Gr. of our God and Saviour. Tit. 2. 13.</small>

A servant and an apostle; i. e. such a servant as is likewise an apostle. The former agrees to all gospel ministers generally, the latter is a title of a greater eminency; and so he intimates, that he wrote to them not merely as an ordinary minister, but in the authority of an apostle, an officer of the highest degree in the church. *Like precious faith;* not in respect of the degree or strength of it, but in respect of the object, Christ, and the benefits that come by it, justification, sanctification, adoption, &c., in which respect the faith of the weakest believer is as precious as that of the strongest. *With us;* either with us apostles, or with us Jewish Christians, born or inhabiting in Judea. *Through the righteousness of God;* the Greek preposition which we render *through,* may likewise be rendered *with,* as ver. 5; Acts vii. 38, *in the church,* that is, with the church; and so the sense is either, 1. Through the righteousness, i. e. truth and faithfulness, of Christ in his promises, whereof the faith of the saints was an effect: or, 2. Through the righteousness of Christ, as the meritorious cause of their faith : or, 3. With the righteousness of Christ imputed to them, and made theirs upon their believing. They had obtained like precious faith as the apostles themselves and others had, together with the righteousness of Christ, an interest in which always accompanies faith, Rom. iv. 22. *And our Saviour Jesus Christ:* there being but one article in the Greek, these words are to be understood conjunctly, the particle *and* being but an explicative, and the sense is, Through the righteousness of our God, even our Saviour Jesus Christ, who is God : see the like, ver. 11 ; chap. iii. 18; John xx. 28; Tit. ii. 14.

b Dan. 4. 1. & 6. 25.
1 Pet. 1. 2.
Jude 2.

2 ᵇ Grace and peace be multiplied unto you through the knowledge of God, and of Jesus our Lord,

Through the knowledge of God; or acknowledgment, i. e. faith, whereby we are made partakers of all the saving graces of the Spirit; and whereby being justified, we are at peace with God, Rom. v. 1. *And of Jesus our Lord;* there being no saving knowledge of God, or faith in him, but by Christ.

c John 17. 3.
d 1 Thess. 2. 12. & 4. 7.
2 Thess. 2. 14. 2 Tim. 1. 9. 1 Pet. 2. 9. & 3. 9.
∥ Or, *by.*

3 According as his divine power hath given unto us all things that *pertain* unto life and godliness, ᵉ through the knowledge of him ᵈ that hath called us ∥ to glory and virtue :

According as; this may refer either, 1. To what goes before, *Grace and peace be multiplied unto you,* &c., *according as his divine power hath given unto us,* &c.; and then in these words the apostle shows what reason there was to hope, that grace and peace should be multiplied to them, and perfected in them, viz. because God hath already given them all things pertaining to life and godliness; q. d. He that hath done thus much for you, will do more, and finish his work in you. Or, 2. To what follows; and then the Greek phrase rendered *according as,* is not a note of similitude, but of illation, and may be rendered, since, or seeing that, and so the words are not a part of the salutation, but the beginning of the body of the Epistle, and relate to ver. 5 : Seeing that *his Divine power hath given unto us all things that pertain,* &c., *add to your faith virtue,* &c.; as God hath done his part, so do you yours in the diligent performance of what he hath enabled you unto. *Divine power* may relate either to God, or rather to Christ, immediately going before; and then it tends to the confirming their hope of the multiplication of grace and peace to them, not only from God, but from Christ, in that they had already experienced his Divine power in giving them *all things pertaining to life and godliness,* i. e. whatever may be helpful to it, the Spirit, faith, repentance, &c., John vii. 39; 2 Cor. iv. 6; 2 Tim. ii. 25. *Unto life;* either, 1. Spiritual life, and then *godliness* may be added by way of explication, that life which consists in godliness, or a godly life; or, by *life* may be meant the inward, permanent principle of spiritual acts, and the exercise of them may be called *godliness,* as the perfection of that principle is called *glory.* Or, 2. Eternal life, to which we attain through godliness, as the way; and then likewise they are understood distinctly, *life* as the end, and *godliness* as the means; and so *life* in this verse is the same as *peace* in the former, and *godliness* the same as *grace.* To *glory and virtue:* according to our translation, *glory* may be the same as *life* before, and *virtue* the same with *godliness;* and then the words set forth the end of God's calling us, viz. unto *glory* or *life* hereafter, as well as *virtue* or *godliness* now. But the Greek preposition διὰ is no where (as some observe) in the New Testament found to signify *to;* for in Rom. vi. 4 (which some allege) it is best rendered *by, glory* being there put for God's power; and therefore our margin here reads it *by* glory and virtue; which may either be, by an hendiadis, for glorious virtue, taking virtue for power, that glorious power of God which is put forth in calling us, Eph. i. 18, 19, or his goodness and mercy which appear in the same calling, in which sense the word may be understood; see Tit. iii. 4, 5 ; 1 Pet. ii. 9 ; or, (which comes to the same,) glory being often taken for power, John ii. 11, by *glory and virtue* may be meant God's power and goodness, or mercy.

4 ᵉ Whereby are given unto us exceeding great and precious promises : that by these ye might be ᶠ partakers of the divine nature, ᵍ having escaped the corruption that is in the world through lust.

e 2 Cor. 7. 1.

f 2 Cor. 3. 18.
Eph. 4. 24.
Heb. 12. 10.
1 John 3. 2.
g ch. 2. 18,20.

Whereby: this word may be rendered, in that, for that, inasmuch as, and then this is an explication of the things that pertain to life and godliness, to glory and virtue, all those things being contained in the promises ; or *whereby* may be understood of the glory and virtue last mentioned, taking them in the latter sense explained, ver. 3; q. d. By which glorious goodness and mercy to us. *Are given unto us exceeding great and precious promises :* by *promises* we may understand either the matter of the promises, the things promised, Heb. x. 36, such as redemption by Christ, reconciliation, adoption, &c., and then they are called *exceeding great and precious,* in comparison of all temporal and worldly things; or else the promises themselves, which are called *great* because of the excellency of the things contained in them, and *precious* in relation to us; great things being not only contained in the promises, but by them secured to us. *That by these ye might be partakers of the Divine nature :* we are said to be partakers of the Divine nature, not by any communication of the Divine essence to us, but by God's impressing upon us, and infusing into us, those divine qualities and dispositions (knowledge, righteousness, and true holiness) which do express and resemble the perfections of God, and are called his image, Eph. iv. 24; Col. iii. 10. And we are said to be made partakers of this Divine nature by the promises of the gospel, because they are the effectual means of our regeneration, (in which that Divine nature is communicated to us,) by reason of that quickening Spirit which accompanieth them, 2 Cor. iii. 6, works by them, and forms in us the image of that wisdom, righteousness, and holiness of God, which appear in them; or of that *glory of the Lord,* which when by faith we behold in the glass of gospel promises, we are *changed into the same image, even as by the Spirit of the Lord,* 2 Cor. iii. 18. Or, *the Divine nature* may be understood of the glory and immortality of the other life, wherein we shall be conformed to God, and whereof by the promises we are made partakers. *Having escaped the corruption that is in the world through lust;* either by *corruption* here we are to understand, 1. Destruction, to which the greatest part of the world is obnoxious through lust, and then corruption must be opposed to *life* and *peace* before, and *lust* to *virtue* and *godliness:* or rather, 2. All the pravity or wickedness of human nature, which is here said to be, i. e. to reign and prevail, *in the world,* or worldly men, *through lust,* or habitual concupiscence, which is the spring and root from which it proceeds; and then the sense is the same as Gal. v. 24. This *corruption through lust* is opposed to *the Divine nature* before, and *escaping* this corruption agrees with being *partakers* of that Divine nature : see Eph. iv. 22—24 ; Col. iii. 9, 10.

5 And beside this, ʰ giving all diligence, add to your faith virtue; and to virtue ⁱ knowledge ;

h ch. 3. 18.

i 1 Pet. 3. 7.

And beside this, giving all diligence : here the apostle begins his exhortation, that since God had done so much for them, ver. 3, 4, they would likewise do their duty; and that their care and diligence in improving the grace they had received, might be added to his bounty in giving it them. *Add to;* or, minister unto ; or it may be a metaphor taken from the ancient way of dancing, in which they joined hands one with another, thereby helping and holding up one another. *Faith* is here set forth as the first grace, and which (as it were) leads up, the rest following it, and attending upon it, yet all in conjunction one with another. Faith is set in the first place as the prime grace of a Christian, the foundation and root of all other, as being that without which nothing else can be pleasing to God, Heb. xi. 6. By *virtue* he seems to understand universal righteousness, or a complication of all those graces by which faith is wont to work; and this being more general, he proceeds from it to others that are more special. *Knowledge;* by this may be meant spiritual prudence, which governs and directs other virtues in their actings; and it is called *knowledge,* because it consists in the practical knowledge of the will of God: see 2 Cor. vi. 6; 1 Pet. iii. 7.

6 And to knowledge temperance; and to temperance patience; and to patience godliness;

Temperance; a grace which represseth, and curbs in, not only sensual lusts, but all inordinate appetites, Gal. v. 22; Tit. i. 8. *Patience;* that Christian fortitude whereby we bear afflictions and injuries, so as to persevere in our duty without being moved by the evils that attend us in the doing of it. *Godliness;* which respects our immediate duty to God, and comprehends all the duties of the first table. This is joined to *patience,* as being that which teacheth us, in all we suffer, to acknowledge God's providence, and promises of deliverance and recompence.

7 And to godliness brotherly kindness; and *to brotherly kindness charity.

Brotherly kindness; a love to those that are of the household of faith. This is joined to *godliness,* to show that it is in vain to pretend to true religion and yet be destitute of brotherly love. *Charity;* this is more general than the former, and relates to all men, even our enemies themselves.

8 For if these things be in you, and abound, they make *you that ye shall* neither *be* †barren ¹nor unfruitful in the knowledge of our Lord Jesus Christ.

For if these things be in you, and abound; if ye not only have these graces in you, but abound or grow in them, both as to the inward degree and outward exercise of them. *They make you;* either they make you, or declare you, not to be barren, or both; they will be both the causes and evidences of your not being barren. *Barren;* or, slothful, idle, unactive. *Nor unfruitful;* void of good works, which are frequently compared to fruits, Matt. iii. 10; vii. 17—19; Gal. v. 22. *In the knowledge of our Lord Jesus Christ;* i. e. the faith of Christ. But more is implied here than expressed; q. d. They will make you be active and fruitful in the knowledge of Christ, and declare you to be so, and thereby make it appear that ye have not in vain learned Christ.

9 But he that lacketh these things ᵐis blind, and cannot see afar off, and hath forgotten that he was ⁿpurged from his old sins.

But he that lacketh these things; he that doth not live in the exercise of the forementioned graces. *Is blind;* spiritually blind, as being destitute of saving knowledge. *And cannot see afar off:* the Greek word is variously translated; the most probable account of it is either, 1. That it signifies to feel the way, or grope, as blind men do; and then the meaning is, He that lacketh these things is blind, and, as a blind man, gropes, not knowing which way to go; he is really destitute of the knowledge he pretends to: or, 2. To be purblind, or short-sighted, so as to see things near hand, but not *afar off,* as our translation hath it; and then the sense is, That such a one sees only the things of the world, but cannot look so far as heaven to discern things there, which if he did, he would walk in the way that leads thither, viz. in the practice of the duties before prescribed. *And hath forgotten that he was purged from his old sins:* he is judged in the sight of God to forget a benefit received, that is not effectually mindful of it, in living suitably to it. And so here, he that professeth himself to have been purged from his old sins, in justification and sanctification, by the blood and Spirit of Christ, 1 Cor. vi. 11; Eph. v. 25—27, and yet still lives in sin, and in the neglect of the duty he is engaged to, practically declares his forgetfulness of the mercy he professeth to have been vouchsafed him; and accordingly may be interpreted to have forgotten it, in that he acts like one that had. Or, if this be understood of one that is really purged from his old sins, yet he may be said to forget that so far as he returns again to them, or lives not up to the ends of his purgation, Luke i. 74, 75.

10 Wherefore the rather, brethren, give diligence ᵒto make your calling and election sure: for if ye do these things, ᵖye shall never fall:

Give diligence; viz. in the exercise of the forementioned graces. *To make your calling,* your effectual calling to the faith of Christ, *and election,* your eternal election to grace and glory, *sure,* not in respect of God, whose counsel is in itself sure and stable, Rom. xi. 29; 2 Tim. ii. 19; but in respect of yourselves, who may best discern the cause by its effects, and so your election by your good works to which you were chosen, Eph. i. 4, and which prove your calling, (as being the proper genuine fruits of it, Eph. iv. 1, 2, &c.,) as that doth election, from whence it proceeds, Acts xiii. 48; Rom. viii. 30. *For if ye do these things,* the things prescribed, ver. 5—7, *ye shall never fall;* not wholly apostatize from God's ways, nor so fall through temptation into any sin, as not to recover out of it.

11 For so an entrance shall be ministered unto you abundantly into the everlasting kingdom of our Lord and Saviour Jesus Christ.

Abundantly; or richly: while ye minister, or add one grace to another, one good work to another, ver. 5, &c., God likewise will minister, (the same word is here used as ver. 5,) or add largely or richly, the supplies of the Spirit, in grace, and strength, and consolation, and whatsoever is needful for you in the way, whereby your faith may be increased, your joy promoted, and your perseverance secured, till ye come into the possession of the everlasting kingdom.

12 Wherefore ᑫI will not be negligent to put you always in remembrance of these things, ʳthough ye know *them,* and be established in the present truth.

I will not be negligent; i. e. I will be diligent and careful. *Though ye know them:* he prevents an objection; q. d. Though ye know these things already, yet being things of great moment, and you being beset with temptations, encompassed about with infirmities, and, while you are on the earth, being in a land of forgetfulness, it is necessary to put you in mind of what you know, that ye may remember to do it. See the like, Rom. xv. 14, 15; 1 John ii. 21. *The present truth;* the truth of the gospel now revealed to you; that which was the great subject of the apostles' preaching and writings, that Jesus Christ was the Christ; that redemption was wrought by him; that he was risen from the dead; that whosoever believeth on him, should receive remission of sins, &c.; the promise made to the fathers being now fulfilled, Acts xiii. 32, 33, and what was future under the Old Testament being present under the New.

13 Yea, I think it meet, ˢas long as I am in this tabernacle, ᵗto stir you up by putting *you* in remembrance;

In this tabernacle; in the body; q. d. Having not long to live, I would live to the best purpose, and so as I may do the most good. He calls his body a tabernacle both in respect of its short continuance, its mean structure, and his laborious life in it. *To stir you up;* to awaken and rouse you up, as ye have need, the flesh being slothful; and lest ye should by security and slightness lose the benefit of what ye have learned: where knowledge is not wanting, yet admonitions may be useful.

14 ᵘKnowing that shortly I must put off *this* my tabernacle, even as ˣour Lord Jesus Christ hath shewed me.

I must put off; a metaphor taken from garments; the soul, while in the body, is clothed with flesh, and death to the godly is but the putting off their clothes, and going to bed, Isa. lvii. 2. *This my tabernacle:* see 2 Cor. v. 1. *Even as our Lord Jesus Christ hath showed me:* John xxi., Christ tells Peter of the kind of his death, that it should be violent, but speaks nothing there of the circumstance of the time; and therefore either this apostle had a twofold revelation of his death, the former as to the manner of it, and this latter concerning the time; or, if this here were no other but that, John xxi., it may be said, that, ver. 18, 22, Christ intimates that Peter's death should be before

John's, who should live till he came, viz. in judgment against Jerusalem to destroy it, which Peter now (observing the affairs of the Jews, and considering his Master's words, Matt. xxiv.) perceived to be nigh at hand; and thence infers, that his own death was not far off.

15 Moreover I will endeavour that ye may be able after my decease to have these things always in remembrance.

These things; the doctrine before delivered concerning faith in Christ, the practice of good works, and their continuance in both. *Always;* this may be joined either to *endeavour,* and so relate to the apostle himself; he would always be diligent, and do his part, that they might have these things in remembrance: or rather, (according to our translation,) to having *in remembrance,* Peter being now near his end; and therefore this *always* may better refer to them that were to live after him, than to himself that was so soon to die. *In remembrance;* or, to commemorate them, viz. to the benefit and edification of the church; and this includes their having them in remembrance, but implies something more.

16 For we have not followed [y] **cunningly devised fables, when we made known unto you the power and coming of our Lord Jesus Christ, but** [z] **were eye-witnesses of his majesty.**

[y 1 Cor. 1. 17. & 2. 1. & 2 Cor. 2. 17. & 4. 2. z Matt. 17. 1, 2. Mark 9. 2. John 1. 14. 1 John 1. 1. & 4. 14.]

Cunningly devised fables; human figments artificially contrived, either to please and gratify men's fancies, or to deceive and pervert their judgment: q. d. The things we have preached unto you (the sum of which is the power and coming of our Lord Jesus Christ) are the true sayings of God, not the fictions of men: and so he may have respect both to heathenish and Jewish fables. See 1 Tim. i. 4; iv. 7; 2 Tim. iv. 4; Tit. i. 14. *The power;* this relates to the Divine nature of Christ with its glorious effects, the efficacy of his doctrine, the miracles whereby he confirmed it, and especially his resurrection from the dead, Rom. i. 4. *And coming of our Lord Jesus Christ;* this respects his human nature, his coming in the flesh, in which he manifested the power before mentioned; both together contain the sum of the whole gospel, viz. that Christ, the promised Messiah, is come in the flesh, and that he was furnished with power sufficient and ability to save sinners to the utmost. Or, Christ's coming here may be his second coming, to which the word here used is for the most part applied in the New Testament, and whereof his transfiguration, in the following verse, was a representation and a forerunner; and in the belief of which the apostle would confirm these saints against those that scoffed at it, chap. iii. 3, 4. *But were eye-witnesses of his majesty:* by Christ's majesty may be understood all that glory which did shine out in him during the whole time of his abode upon earth, John i. 14, but especially that more eminent manifestation of it in his transfiguration, in the next verse.

17 For he received from God the Father honour and glory, when there came such a voice to him from the excellent glory, [a] **This is my beloved Son, in whom I am well pleased.**

[a Matt. 3. 17. & 17. 5. Mark 1. 11. & 9. 7. Luke 3. 22. & 9.35.]

Either *honour and glory* for glorious honour; or *glory* may relate to that lustre which appeared in the body of Christ at his transfiguration, Matt. xvii. 2, and *honour* to the voice which came to him from his Father, and the honourable testimony thereby given him. *From the excellent glory;* either from heaven, or from the glorious God, the Father of Christ, who, by this voice, did in a special manner manifest his glorious presence. *This is my beloved Son;* i. e. This is the Messiah so often promised, and therefore all that was spoken of the Messiah in the law and the prophets centres in him. *In whom I am well pleased:* this implies not only that Christ is peculiarly the Beloved of the Father, but that all they that are adopted to God by faith in Christ, are beloved, and graciously accepted, in and through him, Matt. iii. 17; John xvii. 26; Eph. i. 6.

18 And this voice which came from [b] **heaven we heard, when we were with him in** [b] **the holy mount.**

[b See Ex. 3. 5. Josh. 5.15. Matt. 17. 6.]

We; I, and James, and John. *Heard:* the apostle avoucheth himself to have been an ear-witness, as well as eye-witness, of Christ's glory, hereby intimating that there was as much certainty of the gospel, even in a human way, as could possibly be obtained of any thing that is done in the world, seeing men can be humanly certain of nothing more than of what they perceive by their senses: compare 1 John i. 1, 3. *The holy mount;* so called, not because of any inherent holiness in it, but because of the extraordinary manifestation of God's presence there; in the same sense as the *ground* is called *holy* where God appeared to Moses and to Joshua, Exod. iii. 5; Josh. v. 15.

19 We have also a more sure word of prophecy; whereunto ye do well that ye take heed, as unto [c] **a light that shineth in a dark place, until the day dawn, and** [d] **the day star arise in your hearts:**

[c Ps. 119. 105. John 5. 35. d Rev 2. 28. & 22. 16. See 2 Cor. 4. 4, 6.]

Peter having proved the certainty of the evangelical doctrine, by their testimony that had seen Christ's glory in his transfiguration, and heard the Father's testimony of him, now proves the same by the testimony of the prophets under the Old Testament, and calls the *word of prophecy a more sure word,* comparing it either, 1. With the voice from heaven, than which he calls the word of prophecy more firm or sure, not in respect of truth, (which was equal in both,) but in respect of the manner of its revelation; the voice from heaven being transient, and heard only by three apostles; whereas the word of prophecy was not only received by the prophets from God, but by his command committed to writing, confirmed by a succession of their fellow prophets in their several generations, and approved by Christ himself, and by him preferred before miracles themselves, Luke xvi. 29, 31. Or, 2. With the testimony of Peter and the other two apostles concerning that voice which came to Christ, than which testimony the word of prophecy is said to be more sure; not simply and in itself, but in respect of those to whom the apostle wrote; it was more firm in their minds who had received it; or, more sure as to them that were Jews, and had so fully entertained the writings of the prophets, and had them in so great veneration, being confirmed by the consent of so many ages; whereas the testimony of these apostles did not so fully appear to them to be Divine, as not being heretofore expressed in Scripture. *Whereunto ye do well that ye take heed;* i. e. that ye search and study it, subject your consciences to the power of it, and order your conversations according to it. *A light;* or, lamp, to which the word is often compared, Psal. cxix. 105; Prov. vi. 23; because, as a lamp or candle lighted dispels the darkness, and gives light to those that are in the house or room where it is; so the word gives light to all that are in God's house, as the church is called, 1 Tim. iii. 15. *A dark place;* or, dirty, squalid, because places that have no light are usually filthy; the dirt which is not seen is not removed. *Until the day dawn, and the day-star arise in your hearts;* either, 1. The last day, called *the day* by way of excellency, because when it once begins it will never end, and will be all light without any darkness: and then what is said of the word of prophecy is to be understood of the whole Scripture; and the sense is, that whereas the whole time of this life is but a kind of night of error and ignorance, God hath set up his candle, given us the light of the Scripture to guide us and lead us, till we come to the glorious light of the future life, in which we shall have no need of the light of the Scripture to direct us, but shall see God as he is, and face to face, 1 Cor. xiii. 12. According to this exposition, the dawning of the day, and the day-star arising, do not signify different parts of the same day, but rather the whole day, as opposed to that darkness which would totally overspread us, were it not for the light the word affords us: our minds of themselves are dark, in them the light of the word shines, and dispels the darkness by degrees, according as the Spirit gives us more understanding of it; but yet the darkness will not be wholly removed, till the day of eternal life dawn upon us, and the day-star of the perfect knowledge of God in the beatifical vision arise in our hearts. Or, 2. By the day dawning, and the day-star arising, may be understood a more full, clear, and explicit knowledge of Christ, and the mysteries of the gospel; and then this relates particularly to the prophecies of the Old Testament; and, as Paul calls the times of the Old Testament a *night*, Rom. xiii. 12, as being a time of darkness and shadows, in comparison of the light and knowledge of Christ under the New Testament; so Peter here compares the writings of the prophets to a candle, which gives some, but less light, and the preaching of the gospel to the dawning day, and day-star arising; and commends these Christian Jews to whom he wrote, for making use of and attending to even this lesser light, till they attained to greater degrees of illumination, and the day-star of a more full and clear knowledge of Christ, as revealed in the gospel, did arise in their hearts. This exposition is favoured by Acts xvii. 11; they there, and so the Jewish converts here, did search the Scriptures, to see if the things spoken by the apostles did agree with what was before written by the prophets; and as they there, so these here, are commended for their diligence in so doing, and intimation given them, that they must attend to the light of the Old Testament prophecies, till they were thereby led into a greater knowledge and understanding of the gospel revelation.

e Rom. 12. 6.   20 Knowing this first, that ^eno prophecy of the Scripture is of any private interpretation.

Knowing this first; either, principally and above other things, as being most worthy to be known; or, knowing this as the first principle of faith, or the first thing to be believed. *That no prophecy of the Scripture is of any private interpretation:* the Greek word here used may be rendered, either, 1. As our translators do, *interpretation,* or explication; and then the meaning is, not that private men are not to interpret the Scripture, only refer all to the church; but that no man nor company of men, no church nor public officers, are to interpret the Scripture of their own heads, according to their own minds, so as to make their private sense be the sense of the Scripture, but to seek the understanding of it from God, who shows them the meaning of the word in the word itself, (the more obscure places being expounded by the more clear,) and by his Spirit leads believers, in their searching the Scripture, into the understanding of his mind in it: God himself being the author of the word, as ver. 21, is the best interpreter of it. Or, 2. Mission or dismission; a metaphor taken from races, where they that ran were let loose from the stage where the race began, that they might run their course. The prophets in the Old Testament are said to *run,* as being God's messengers, Jer. xxiii. 21, and God is said to *send* them, Ezek. xiii. 6, 7. And then this doth not immediately concern the interpretation of the Scripture, but the first revelation of it, spoken of in the next verse; and the question is not, Who hath authority to interpret the Scripture now written? but, What authority the penmen had to write it? and consequently, what respect is due to it? and why believers are so carefully to take heed to it? And then the meaning is, that it is the first principle of our faith, that the Scripture is not of human invention, but Divine inspiration; that the prophets wrote not their own private sense in it, but the mind of God; and at his command, not their own pleasure.

f 2 Tim. 3. 16. 1 Pet. 1. 11.
‖ Or, *at any time.*
g 2 Sam. 23. 2. Luke 1. 70. Acts 1. 16. & 3. 18.

21 For ^fthe prophecy came not ‖ in old time by the will of man: ^gbut holy men of God spake *as they were* moved by the Holy Ghost.

The prophecy; the prophetical writings, or word of prophecy, ver. 19. *Came not in old time by the will of man;* the prophets spake not of themselves what and when they pleased. *But holy men of God;* prophets, called men of God, 1 Sam. ii. 27; ix. 6; 1 Kings xvii. 18, and elsewhere. They are here called *holy,* not only because of their lives, wherein they were examples to others, but because they were the special instruments of the Holy Ghost, who sanctified them to the work of preaching, and penning what he dictated to them. *Spake as they were moved;* or, carried out, or acted, i. e. elevated above their own natural abilities. This may imply the illumination of their minds with the knowledge of Divine mysteries, the gift of infallibility, that they might not err, of prophecy, to foretell things to come, and a peculiar instinct of *the Holy Ghost,* whereby they were moved to preach or write.

CHAP. II

The apostle foretelleth the appearance of false teachers, the impiety of them and their followers, and the judgments that would overtake them, 1—6. *The godly shall be delivered, as Lot was out of Sodom,* 7—9. *The wicked principles and manners of these seducers described,* 10—19. *The mischief of relapsing into sin,* 20—22.

BUT ^athere were false prophets also among the people, even as ^bthere shall be false teachers among you, who privily shall bring in damnable heresies, even ^cdenying the Lord ^dthat bought them, ^eand bring upon themselves swift destruction.

a Deut. 13.1.
b Mat 24.11. Acts 20. 30. 1 Cor. 11. 19. 1 Tim. 4. 1. 2 Tim. 3 1,5. 1 John 4. 1. Jude 18.
c Jude 4.
d 1 Cor. 6.20. Gal 3. 13. Eph. 1. 7. Heb. 10. 29.
e Phil. 3. 19.
1 Pet. 1. 18. Rev. 5. 9.

But there were false prophets also: the apostle having been exhorting them to continuance and progress in faith, admonishes them here of such as might labour to draw them from it; and having made mention of the Old Testament prophets, holy men of God, he hereby takes occasion to tell them of, and caution them against, false teachers which would be among themselves. This *also* in the text plainly relates to what went before: q. d. Together with those prophets which were sent by God, there were likewise false prophets, such as were not sent of him. *Among the people;* the people of Israel. *Even as there shall be false teachers;* teachers of false doctrine, Matt. vii. 15; Acts xx. 29. *Among you;* among you Jewish, as well as among the Gentile Christians; or, among you as Christians and God's people under the New Testament, in opposition to the people of God under the Old. *Who shall privily bring in:* the Greek word signifies either to bring in slily and craftily, under specious pretences, and without being observed, Gal. ii. 4; Jude 4.; or, to bring in over and above, or beside the doctrine of the gospel, which they did not renounce; or both may be implied. *Damnable heresies;* Greek, heresies of destruction, i. e. destructive, such as lead to destruction, viz. eternal, or damnation. *Even denying;* either in their words or their practices, either directly, or by consequence of their doctrines or actions; they that profess they know God, but contradict that profession in their lives, are said to deny him, Tit. i. 16. *The Lord;* either. 1. God the Father, so called, Luke ii. 29; Acts iv. 24, &c., and probably Rev. vi. 10; nor is there any necessity, but, Jude 4, the word may be understood of God the Father. Or rather, 2. Christ. *That bought them:* if we understand it of God the Father, the sense is, either, 1. Denying God that bought them, or acquired them and made them his, viz. by calling them out of the darkness and gross wickedness of the world, to the knowledge of Christ and the gospel, and the fellowship of his church. In this general sense the word buying is sometimes taken, Isa. lv. 1; Rev. iii. 18. Or, 2. Denying God that bought the people of Israel (whereof these false teachers that should be among the Christian Jews were to be a part) out of Egypt, to make them his peculiar people, whereof they would boast themselves, and yet by their wicked practices deny that God that bought them; the words seem to be taken out of Deut. xxxii. 6, *Is not he thy Father that hath bought thee?* as likewise from ver. 5 of that chapter. Peter calls them *spots,* ver. 13 of this chapter. But if we understand it of Christ, which seems most probable, the sense is, either, 1. That Christ bought or redeemed them, (in which sense the word is sometimes taken,) in that by his death he purchased the continuance of their lives, and the staying of their execution, and rescued them from that present destruction which, without Christ's interposition, had seized on them, as it had likewise on the whole visible creation immediately upon the apostacy of mankind. Or, 2. This is spoken not only of their pretences, that they should profess themselves redeemed by Christ, but in the style of the visible church, which should judge them to be so till they declared the contrary by their wicked actions; and it likewise holds true in a forensical or judicial style, according to which whosoever professeth himself to be redeemed by Christ, and yet denies him in his deeds, is said to deny the Lord that bought him; it being alike as to the greatness of the crime, whether he be really redeemed, or, professing himself to be so, denies his Redeemer. *And bring upon themselves swift destruction;* shall hasten their own destruction, it may be temporal in this world; to be sure, eternal in the other. It may be called *swift,* as coming upon them unawares, and when they think least of it, as 1 Thess. v. 3.

2 And many shall follow their ‖ pernicious ways; by reason of whom the way of truth shall be evil spoken of.

‖ Or, *lascivious ways,* as some copies read.

And many shall follow their pernicious ways; Greek, their destructions, i. e. those ways of error which are attended with destruction (the effect being put for the cause by a metonymy); and the sense is, that as these false teachers shall bring destruction upon themselves by their heresies; so others, running with them into the same errors, shall fall into the same destruction. *By reason of whom;* or, by whom, viz. these false teachers, or their followers, or both. *The way of truth;* the gospel, so called, as being the doctrine of saving truth. It is called the *way,* Acts ix. 2; xix. 9; xxii. 4; *the way of salvation,* Acts xvi. 17; *the way of God,* Acts xviii. 26. *Shall be evil spoken of;* blasphemed, whether by false teachers themselves and their followers, or by others taking occasion by them: see Rom. ii. 24; 1 Tim. vi. 1; Tit. ii. 5.

3 And ᶠthrough covetousness shall they with feigned words ᵍmake merchandise of you: ʰ whose judgment now of a long time lingereth not, and their damnation slumbereth not.

f Rom. 16. 18. 2 Cor. 12. 17, 18. 1 Tim. 6. 5.
Tit. 1. 11.
g 2 Cor. 2. 17 ch. 1. 16.
h Deut. 32. 35.
Jude 4, 15.

With feigned words; deceitful speeches, which have a show of truth to hide their errors. *Make merchandise of you;* as of slaves or beasts: it seems to be a metaphor taken from merchants that speak great things of bad wares, the better to vend them; the sense is, with specious words, and pious pretences, they shall deceive you to make a gain of you. *Whose judgment;* or, condemnation. *Now of a long time;* being of old determined by God, and foretold in the Scripture, and so nearer than they themselves imagine. *Lingereth not;* i. e. goes on apace, and hastens on them. *And their damnation;* or, destruction. *Slumbereth not:* i. e. watcheth, as ready to overtake them in its time: it may be a metaphor taken from a traveller, as Prov. vi. 11; or the apostle alludes to Deut. xxxii. 35, where the like expression is found: see ver. 1 of this chapter.

4 For if God spared not ⁱthe angels ᵏthat sinned, but ˡcast *them* down to hell, and delivered *them* into chains of darkness, to be reserved unto judgment;

i Job 4. 18. Jude 6.
k John 8. 44.
1 John 3. 8.
l Luke 8. 31.
Rev. 20. 2, 3.

For if God spared not the angels that sinned, but cast them down to hell: elsewhere called *the deep,* Luke viii. 31, and *the bottomless pit,* Rev. ix. 1; xi. 7; xvii. 8; xx. 1, 3. This implies a change, 1. Of the state of those sinning angels, that whereas before it was the highest among the creatures, now it is the lowest. 2. Of their place, that whereas they were before the throne of God with the rest of the angels, they are now thrust down into a lower place, agreeable to their sin and misery. What place that is we find not expressed in Scripture, and therefore we are not to be over-curious in our inquiries after it; but may rest satisfied, that they are excluded from the place of their primitive happiness, and are in a place where they are afflicted with the pain both of loss and sense. *And delivered them into chains of darkness:* either to be bound, or held with darkness as with chains; or kept in *chains under darkness,* as Jude 6; where *darkness* may imply the misery and horror of their condition, and *chains,* their obduracy in their wickedness, their despair of deliverance, their expectation of future judgment, Heb. x. 27, together with the providence and power of God, watching over and holding them in that condition, till final vengeance come upon them. It is a metaphor taken from malefactors condemned, who are bound in chains, and kept in the dungeon till execution. *To be reserved;* so kept that they cannot escape. *Unto judgment;* viz. that of the last day, the time of their full torment, in which the wrath of God, which they feel in a great measure now, will come upon them to the utmost.

5 And spared not the old world, but saved ᵐNoah the eighth *person,* ⁿa preacher of righteousness, ᵒbringing in the flood upon the world of the ungodly;

m Gen. 7. 1, 7, 23.
Heb. 11. 7.
n 1 Pet. 3. 20.
n 1 Pet. 3.19.
o ch. 3. 6.

And spared not the old world: the world, for men in the world, viz. those that lived in it before the flood. *But saved Noah the eighth person;* viz. together with the other seven, his wife, three sons, and their wives, 1 Pet. iii. 20. Noah may be particularly named, because God had a special respect to him, and for his sake spared others. *A preacher:* constituted to be so by Divine authority and commission. *Of righteousness:* i. e. not only, 1. Of the righteousness of God, who had threatened to destroy the world for its wickedness; but, 2. Of the righteousness of Christ upon all them that should believe. It is not to be doubted but he preached the same righteousness whereof he himself was heir, and that was the righteousness of faith, Heb. xi. 7; and this he did not in words only, but in his actions; in that he built the ark for the saving himself and his household, which was a type of the salvation of believers by Christ. And, 3. Of the righteousness of sanctification, in his exhorting the men that then were to repentance and holiness, if possibly thereby they might prevent the approaching deluge. *Bringing in the flood upon the world of the ungodly;* the whole multitude of wicked men then living in the world.

6 And ᵖturning the cities of Sodom and Gomorrha into ashes condemned *them* with an overthrow, ᑫmaking *them* an ensample unto those that after should live ungodly;

p Gen. 19.24. Deut. 29. 23. Jude 7.
q Num. 26. 10.

The cities of Sodom and Gomorrha; which being the chief of the five, include Admah and Zeboim, Zoar, the fifth, being spared for Lot's sake, Gen. xiv. 18, compared with xix. 25. *Condemned them with an overthrow;* i. e. punished them with a total subversion, or brought that destruction upon them to which he had condemned them. *Making them an ensample unto those that after should live ungodly;* of his wrath and vengeance ready to be poured out upon others that should live ungodly, to deter them from the imitation of the sins of those that had so miserably perished. The word may be rendered a type, (as it is, Heb. viii. 5, and ix. 23,) viz. of hell-fire, which is to be the punishment of wicked men at the last day: Jude 7 implies as much. As the deliverance of the Israelites out of Egypt was a kind of type of the deliverance of all God's people to the end of the world; so the subversion of these cities was so memorable an instance of Divine vengeance, that the Scripture frequently alludes to it, as a type or pattern, when it speaks of the general destruction of the wicked of the world.

7 And ʳdelivered just Lot, vexed with the filthy conversation of the wicked:

r Gen. 19. 16.

Vexed; grievously afflicted or wearied. *The wicked;* unjust, lawless, (understand men,) such as had no respect to law or justice, in opposition to Lot, whom he calls *just* and *righteous.*

8 (ˢFor that righteous man dwelling among them, ᵗin seeing and hearing, vexed *his* righteous soul from day to day with *their* unlawful deeds;)

s Wisd. 19. 17.
t Ps. 119. 139, 158.
Ezek. 9. 4.

Seeing and hearing: their wickedness was so open and shameless, that he not only heard the report of it, but saw them commit it, Isa. iii. 9. *Vexed;* Greek, tormented, i. e. extremely afflicted and troubled his own soul, provoking himself to godly sorrow at the sight and fame of their unlawful deeds. His grief was voluntary, and he active in it; the like is said of Christ, on occasion of Lazarus's death, John xi. 33, where the margin reads, he troubled himself.

9 ᵘThe Lord knoweth how to deliver the godly out of temptations, and to reserve the unjust unto the day of judgment to be punished:

u Ps. 34. 17 19. 1 Cor. 10. 13.

The Lord knoweth; according to the common rule, that words of knowledge in Scripture connote affections, as Psal. i. 6. God's knowing here implies not only his infinite wisdom, whereby he is never at a loss, but knows all the various ways whereby the godly may be delivered; but likewise his love and good will to them, whereby he is ready to do it, hath a heart for it: so the word is taken, Eccles. iv. 13; Amos iii. 10; the text reads, *will no more be admonished,* the margin, knows not, &c. *How to deliver the godly;* those that walk in the steps of just Lot and Noah, who was perfect in his generation. This concludes what the apostle began, ver. 4: the sum is, If God spared neither wicked angels nor wicked men, destroying the old world and Sodom, but delivered Lot and Noah, righteous persons; he still hath wisdom, power, and will to deliver other godly men, and punish other wicked men. *Out of temptations;* afflictions, James i. 2, 12. *And to reserve the unjust unto the day of judgment to be punished:* the Greek word is in the present tense, which may be understood, either, 1. As put for the future, and then the sense is as in our translation, that though God many times lets the wicked alone in this world, so that they escape present punishment, yet they shall not escape future torment; they are a while spared, but never pardoned; and when free from temporal evils, are reserved for eternal vengeance. Or, 2. It may be understood as in the present tense, which agrees well with the instances of God's vengeance before mentioned, which was executed on wicked men in this world; and then the sense is, The Lord knows how to deliver the godly out of temptations when he sees fit, even in this life, and how to reserve those wicked men, whom he punisheth with temporal judgments here, to a much more severe and dreadful punishment at the day of judgment hereafter.

x Jude 4, 7, 8, 10, 16.

10 But chiefly ˣ them that walk after the flesh in the lust of uncleanness, and

‖ Or, dominion. y Jude 8.

despise ‖ government. ʸ Presumptuous *are they,* selfwilled, they are not afraid to speak evil of dignities.

But chiefly them: the apostle here applies the general doctrine delivered to false teachers, whose character he gives in several particulars; the sense is, that God reserves all wicked men to the day of judgment, but those especially that second their corrupt doctrine with a wicked conversation. The verb *reserve* is to be repeated from the former verse. *That walk after the flesh;* to walk after the flesh is either, 1. To follow the conduct of the sensual appetite, like brute beasts, which are led by sense, not by reason or judgment: or, 2. More especially it implies their giving up themselves to filthy lusts, probably unnatural ones, Jude 7, *going after strange flesh. In the lust of;* i. e. through, or out of, implying the cause or spring from whence their actual uncleanness came, viz. their own lust. *Uncleanness;* or, pollution; q. d. In the lust whereby they are polluted, or in their impure lusts. *And despise government;* i. e. governors, or magistrates; as *brotherhood* for brethren, 1 Pet. ii. 17. *Presumptuous;* Greek, bold, or daring, viz. because *they are not afraid to speak evil of dignities. Selfwilled;* stubborn, refractory, addicted to their own ways, and therefore will not be ruled by others. *Dignities;* or, glories, viz. rulers and magistrates, whom God hath made glorious, or on whom he hath put the honour of being above others, and made them his own lieutenants and vicegerents upon earth.

z Jude 9.

11 Whereas ᶻ angels, which are greater in power and might, bring not railing

‖ Some read, against themselves.

accusation ‖ against them before the Lord.

Angels; good angels, Jude 9. *Greater;* either greater than these audacious false teachers, or else greater than the forementioned dignities. *In power and might;* i. e. greater in their natural strength, and in their dignity. *Bring not railing accusation;* use not reviling, reproachful language; the same with speaking evil in the former verse. *Against them;* either, 1. Against dignities, ver. 10; and then the meaning is, that good angels, great and powerful as they are, yet bring not a railing accusation before the Lord against magistrates and princes, but when they have had any thing against them, yet have carried themselves with modesty, and due respect to that dignity in which God had placed such, having a regard to civil government as God's constitution, and being themselves, at God's appointment, guardians and keepers, even of wicked kingdoms, as Dan. x. and xi. Or, 2. Against themselves, as in the margin; and then the sense is, that angels do not reproach nor revile each other, nay, not the devil himself, as appears, Jude 9, which place may explain this; and therefore it did ill become these false teachers, who were so much below angels, to contemn, revile, or rail on princes and civil magistrates, who were so much above themselves, and had their authority from God.

12 But these, ᵃ as natural brute beasts, made to be taken and destroyed, speak evil of the things that they understand not; and shall utterly perish in their own corruption;

a Jer. 12. 3. Jude 10.

But these; the false teachers before mentioned. *As natural brute beasts;* beasts which are void of reason, and follow only their sensual inclination. *Made to be taken and destroyed;* being made for men's use, and so to be a prey to them; while they hasten after their food, they are taken in nets and snares, and being taken are destroyed. *Speak evil of the things that they understand not;* either the great mysteries of religion, whereof they are stupidly ignorant; or rather, dignities, before mentioned, which they, (not knowing, or not considering, them to be of God, and of so great use to men,) following the inclination of their own corrupt natures, speak against. *And shall utterly perish in their own corruption;* or, shall be corrupted in their own corruption, i. e. shall be utterly destroyed by their own fault and folly; penal corruption (or perdition) following upon sinful. The sum is, That as brute beasts, which have no reason, follow their brutish appetite, till it lead them into destruction, and where they sought their meat they find their death, Prov. vii. 23; so these false teachers, not being guided by reason, much less by the light of the Spirit, but merely by sway of their natural inclinations, in speaking evil of that ordinance which God hath honoured, shall bring upon themselves that destruction they have deserved.

13 ᵇ And shall receive the reward of unrighteousness, *as* they that count it pleasure ᶜ to riot in the day time. ᵈ Spots *they are* and blemishes, sporting themselves with their own deceivings while ᵉ they feast with you;

b Phil. 3 19. c See Rom. 13. 13. d Jude 12. e 1 Cor. 11. 20, 21.

And shall receive the reward of unrighteousness: under this general term, all the several sins they are charged with are comprehended. *As they that count it pleasure to riot in the day time;* this is said to aggravate their sin, and signifies either their impudence in it, that they had cast off all shame, and practised their luxury by day-light, whereas ordinary sinners are wont to choose the night for such works of darkness, Rom. xiii. 12, 13; 1 Thess. v. 7; or their security, that they spent the day of their life in their pleasures, placing their happiness in present enjoyments, unmindful of a future reckoning and an eternal state. *Spots they are and blemishes;* not only altogether polluted themselves, but such as defile others, and are blemishes to the church whereof they profess themselves members. *Sporting themselves with their own deceivings:* some read ἀγαπαῖς instead of ἀπαταῖς, leaving out the pronoun, rendered *their own;* and understand this of the love-feasts, in which they luxuriously gorged themselves. This might well agree with Jude 12, but that the generality of Greek copies read ἀπαταῖς, which we turn *deceivings,* i. e. either errors, taking the word passively; q. d. They do but make a sport of sin, and please themselves with it; and this agrees too with Jude 12, *feeding themselves without fear:* or cheatings, or imposings upon others, taking *deceivings* actively; q. d. They sport themselves while they so finely deceive you, pretending love in their feasting with you, when they do it only to gratify their appetites; or sporting themselves, and making merry, with what they have cheated you of. *While they feast with you;* viz. in your feasts of charity, with the specious pretence of which they covered their naughtiness.

14 Having eyes full of † adultery, and

† Gr. an *adulteress.*

that cannot cease from sin; beguiling unstable souls: [f] an heart they have exercised with covetous practices; cursed children:

[f Jude 11.]

Having eyes; he mentions the eyes, both because they let in the objects of lust into the heart, Job xxxi. 1; Matt. v. 28, and because the signs of lust in the heart appear especially in the eyes, Gen. xxxix. 7; Prov. vi. 25. *Full of adultery;* full of an adulteress, which either may be a Hebraism, the concrete being put for the abstract, as drunken for drunkenness, and thirsty for thirst, Deut. xxix. 19; or it may be a proverbial expression of the wretchedness of such men's hearts, when they still carried an adulteress in their eyes. *That cannot cease from sin;* never satisfied with looking upon, or still looking about for, such objects as might inflame their lusts; or still seeking with wanton looks to entice others to folly. *Beguiling;* either alluring them by their wantonness to embrace their false doctrines, promising them pleasures and carnal liberties, ver. 18; or enticing them to lewdness, by instilling false doctrines into them, which tend to licentiousness. *Unstable souls;* those that were not well grounded in the faith and doctrine of holiness, who might therefore easily be drawn aside. *An heart they have exercised with covetous practices;* a heart wholly intent upon getting gain, accustomed to it, and skilful in it. *Practices;* the word is in the plural number, to show that the seducers had several arts and ways of exercising their covetousness. *Cursed children;* Greek, children of the curse. It may be taken either actively, for such as were causes of a curse, brought a curse with them; or passively, for such as were worthy of a curse, or obnoxious to it; as *children of wrath,* Eph. ii. 3.

15 Which have forsaken the right way, and are gone astray, following the way of [g] Balaam *the son* of Bosor, who loved the wages of unrighteousness;

[g Num. 22. 5, 7, 21, 23, 28. Jude 11.]

The right way; the *way of truth,* ver. 2, i. e. the way of faith and holiness, which is the only right way to happiness. *Are gone astray;* into the by-paths of error. There is but one right way, and many wrong, in which they wander that leave the right. He seems to allude to Balaam, Numb. xxii., who left the way of God, which was, to be obedient to God, and not *go beyond* his *word,* ver. 18, and ran into the way of sin, when he went with Balak's messengers to curse God's people; and therefore his *way* is said to be *perverse,* ver. 32. *Following the way of Balaam;* 1. In respect of their false doctrine: for, as Balaam was disobedient to God, and, against his command, went to Balak; so these men forsook the way of truth prescribed by God in his word. 2. In respect of their wicked lives: Balaam taught Balak to entice the children of Israel to *commit fornication,* and *eat things sacrificed unto idols,* Rev. ii. 14; and these taught men to commit lewdness, and indulge themselves in their sensualities. 3. Chiefly in respect of their covetousness, as follows. *Of Bosor;* either this is the name of his country, called *Pethor,* Numb. xxii. 5, and by change of two letters, *P* into *B,* and *th* into *s,* (frequent in the Syriac language,) *Besor,* or *Bosor:* or, the name of his father, called *Beor,* in Numbers, having two names; unless the apostle call him *Bosor* in allusion to *Basar,* flesh, as being of a fleshly mind, as the false teachers here were. Thus *Beth-el* was called *Beth-aven,* Hos. iv. 15; and *Beelzebub* called *Beelzebul,* the god of dung, Matt. x. 25. *Who loved the wages of unrighteousness;* the reward which Balak offered him for an unrighteous act, viz. the cursing of God's people.

16 But was rebuked for his iniquity: the dumb ass speaking with man's voice forbad the madness of the prophet.

But was rebuked; not only by the angel's speaking to him, but by the ass's, as follows. *The dumb ass speaking with man's voice, forbade;* not in express words, that we read of, but the ass's speaking with human voice, discerning the angel before Balaam did, and going back, when he, carried out by the power of his covetousness, would needs go forward, were so prodigious things as might sufficiently convince him of his sin, in going to Balak contrary to God's command at first given; and it was no small dishonour put upon him, that he who would not hearken to God, should have an ass for his teacher. *The madness;* in going against God's command, and to curse those who, God had told him, were blessed. *Object.* Balaam had leave given him to go with Balak's messengers, Numb. xxii. 20, and refused Balak's offers, ver. 18. *Answ.* Balaam did not contemn the gifts offered, but had a desire after them, as appears by his inquiring of God the second time, ver. 19, though God had fully revealed his will to him before, ver. 12. 2. God bade him go that he might bless the people, ver. 12, compared with ver. 20, whereas he went not out of a respect to God's answer, but out of a covetous mind, and a desire to curse Israel, as appears by Josh. xxiv. 9, 10, and by the cursed counsel he gave, Numb. xxv. 1, compared with xxxi. 16, and Rev. ii. 14. *Of the prophet:* Balaam is called a prophet here, either, 1. Because he pretended to be so: thus the false prophets are sometimes called absolutely *prophets,* Jer. vi. 13; xxvi. 7, 8, 11. Or, 2. Because he really was a prophet, though a wicked and covetous one; for he inquired of God, and had answers from him, Numb. vi. 22; viii. 9, 10, 18, 19; and Moses says expressly, that *the Lord put a word in Balaam's mouth,* Numb. xxiii. 5, 16; and that prophecy concerning the Messiah, Numb. xxiv. 17, could not but be of God, yet it is probable that Balaam, out of covetousness, might sometimes use divination, nay, it is plain in some cases he did, Numb. xxiv. 1.

17 [h] These are wells without water, clouds that are carried with a tempest; to whom the mist of darkness is reserved for ever.

[h Jude 12, 13.]

These are wells without water: he compares seducers, 1. To *wells without water;* because as a well invites a traveller to it in hope of quenching his thirst, but being without water, mocks his expectation; so false teachers, making a show of true wisdom and saving knowledge, draw men to them, but being destitute of it, delude them, and make them no wiser than they were. *Clouds that are carried with a tempest;* 2. To *clouds,* &c.; because as clouds many times, promising rain and refreshment, either are scattered with the wind, or break out into a tempest; so these, when they promise to refresh their hearers' souls with the truth of God, being themselves destitute of it, do them no good, or with their pernicious errors, or corrupt manners, do them much harm. By this comparison he sets forth, (1.) Their inconstancy, that, like clouds driven with the wind, they are tossed to and fro, from one doctrine to another, Eph. iv. 14. And, (2.) Their deceitfulness, that they make a show of what they have not, as clouds do of rain, when yet they are scattered, without yielding any. *The mist of darkness;* i. e. the darkest darkness, called *outer darkness,* Matt. viii. 12; xxii. 13; xxv. 30; by which the torments of hell are sometimes set forth, as well as sometimes by fire.

18 For when [i] they speak great swelling *words* of vanity, they allure through the lusts of the flesh, *through much* wantonness, those that [k] were || clean escaped from them who live in error.

[i Jude 16.]
[k Acts 2. 40. ch. 1. 4. ver. 20.]
[|| Or, *for a little,* or, *a while,* as some read.]

Great swelling words of vanity; i. e. big words, full of sound, and void of sense, at least of truth. He seems to tax the affected, vain speech of seducers, who were wont to clothe their erroneous doctrines (if not disguise the truths of God) with strange, uncouth phrases, which made a show of some rare discoveries, or deep mysteries, whereas indeed they were empty of any thing solid, or tending to edification. *They allure:* as with a bait; a metaphor taken from the manner of taking fish. *Through the lusts of the flesh;* to which they give liberty, as a bait to draw men after them. *Through much wantonness;* this explains the former, and shows what lusts they indulge men in, viz. wantonness and uncleanness. *Those that were clean escaped;* truly, or really, which seems the better reading than that in the margin: and this is said of them, 1. In respect of the profession they made of a real conversion. 2. In respect of the assent they gave to the word by which they were called. 3. In respect of the change that appeared in their outward conversation. *From them who live in error:* whether the error of Judaism, or heathenism, wherein they had been formerly involved, and others still were. This might be the case of some in whom yet there was no saving change wrought; that they might be brought off from those more foul ways of sin and error in which they had walked. and yet might afterward return to the same, or as bad, Matt. xii. 43; xiii. 21.

l Gal. 5. 13.
1 Pet. 2. 16.
m John 8. 34. Rom. 6. 16.

19 While they promise them ¹liberty, they themselves are ᵐthe servants of corruption: for of whom a man is overcome, of the same is he brought in bondage.

While they promise them liberty; liberty for their lusts, and so from the yoke of the Divine law. They abused the name of Christian liberty, and extended it to licentiousness. *They themselves are the servants of corruption;* under the power and dominion of sin. *For of whom a man is overcome, of the same is he brought in bondage:* he alludes to the law of war, according to which, he that is overcome, and taken captive by his enemy, becomes his servant. These false teachers, that talked so much of Christian liberty, yet being overcome by their own lusts, and kept under by them, were the worst of slaves.

n Mat. 12.45. Luke 11. 26. Heb. 6. 4, &c. & 10. 26, 27.
o ch. 1. 4.
ver. 18.
p ch. 1. 2.

20 For ⁿif after they ᵒhave escaped the pollutions of the world ᵖthrough the knowledge of the Lord and Saviour Jesus Christ, they are again entangled therein, and overcome, the latter end is worse with them than the beginning.

The pollutions of the world; those more gross wickednesses in which most of the world still lieth, 1 John v. 19. *Through the knowledge of the Lord and Saviour Jesus Christ;* such a knowledge of Christ as brings with it an outward reformation of life, though it do not purify the heart. For that the apostle doth not here speak of those that were rooted in Christ by a saving and heart-purifying faith, appears by ver. 14, where he calls them *unstable souls*. *They are again entangled therein, and overcome;* return to their old sins, yield up themselves to them, and continue in them.

q Luke 12. 47, 48. John 9. 41. & 15. 22.

21 For ᑫit had been better for them not to have known the way of righteousness, than, after they have known *it*, to turn from the holy commandment delivered unto them.

It had been better for them not to have known; their sin had been less if they had not known the truth, but now they sin against knowledge, and therein their apostasy is much worse than their ignorance would have been. *The way of righteousness;* the way of obtaining righteousness by Christ, and of living godly in Christ, 2 Tim. iii. 12, prescribed in the gospel; the same which is called *the right way,* ver. 15, and *the way of truth,* ver. 2. *The holy commandment;* the same in other words. It is called *holy*, not only as proceeding from God, who is holy, but as teaching nothing but what is holy, and being the means God useth in making men holy, and as being opposed to the pollutions of the world before mentioned.

r Prov. 26. 11.

22 But it is happened unto them according to the true proverb, ʳThe dog *is* turned to his own vomit again; and the sow that was washed to her wallowing in the mire.

But it is happened unto them according to the true proverb: this is added, to prevent the scandal that might arise from their apostasy; q. d. It is not to be wondered at that they are again entangled in and overcome by their former pollutions, when there never was a thorough change wrought in their hearts. Dogs and swine (beasts unclean by the law) they still were, under the greatest appearances of reformation, and such they now show themselves to be by their vile apostasy. *The dog is turned to his own vomit again:* as dogs vomit up what is burdensome to them, but, still being dogs, and not having changed their natures by easing their stomachs, lick up their own vomit again; so these, under a fit of conviction, through the power of the word, disgorge those sins which burdened their consciences, but having thereby gotten some ease, and their old nature and love to their former lusts still remaining, they again return to the same sins they had for a time forsaken.

The sow that was washed to her wallowing in the mire: as swine, that naturally love the dirt and mire, if sometimes they be washed from it, yet, still retaining their former disposition, return again to it; so likewise these here mentioned, however they may be washed from the pollutions of the world, and by the preaching of the gospel brought off from their former ways of sin, and brought into a profession of holiness, yet, still retaining their old nature and corrupt dispositions, they are easily prevailed over by them, and so relapse into their former abominations.

CHAP. III.

The apostle declareth it to be the design of both his Epistles to remind the brethren of Christ's coming to judgment, in opposition to scoffers, 1—7. *No argument can be drawn against it from the delay, which is designed to leave men room for repentance,* 8, 9. *He describeth the day of the Lord, and exhorteth to holiness of life in expectation of it,* 10—14. *He showeth that Paul had taught the like in his Epistles,* 15, 16; *and concludeth with advice to beware of seduction, and to grow in Christian grace and knowledge,* 17, 18.

THIS second epistle, beloved, I now write unto you; in *both* which ᵃI stir up your pure minds by way of remembrance: a ch. 1. 13.

This second epistle: this confirms what has been said, that this Epistle was written by Peter, as well as the former. *I stir up your pure minds;* or, sincere minds: the sense is either, 1. I stir up your minds, that they may be pure and sincere; and then he doth not so much commend them for what they were, as direct and exhort them to what they should be, that they might receive benefit by what he wrote, there being nothing that contributes more to the fruitful entertaining of the word, than sincerity and honesty of heart, when men lay aside those things which are contrary to it, and might hinder its efficacy, 1 Pet. ii. 1, 2. Or, 2. I stir up your minds, though pure and sincere, to continuance and constancy in that pure doctrine ye have received. *By way of remembrance:* see chap. i. 13.

2 That ye may be mindful of the words which were spoken before by the holy prophets, ᵇand of the commandment of us the apostles of the Lord and Saviour: b Jude 17.

The words which were spoken before by the holy prophets; the word of prophecy, chap. i. 19: he joins the prophets and apostles together, as concurring in their doctrine, and so useth it as an argument to persuade them to constancy in the faith of the gospel, that what the apostles preached to them was confirmed by what the prophets under the Old Testament had taught before, Acts xxvi. 22; Eph. ii. 20. *And of the commandment of us;* by this he means the whole doctrine of the gospel preached by him and the other apostles: see chap. ii. 21; 1 John iii. 23. *The apostles of the Lord and Saviour;* who was the author of this commandment, and the principal in giving it, and from whom the apostles received it, who were but ministers and instruments in delivering it to others.

3 ᶜKnowing this first, that there shall come in the last days scoffers, ᵈwalking after their own lusts,   c 1 Tim. 4. 1. 2 Tim. 3. 1. Jude 18. d ch. 2. 10.

Knowing this first; especially, as being very necessary to be known. The apostle having in the former chapter cautioned these saints against the more close enemies of the gospel, seducers and false teachers, here he foretells them of more open enemies, profane scoffers. *In the last days:* see 1 Cor. x. 11; 2 Tim. iii. 1. *Scoffers;* profane contemners of God, and deriders of his truth, Psal. i. 1; cxix. 51; Isa. xxviii. 14, 22. *Walking after their own lusts;* such as are natural to them; lusts of ungodliness, Jude 18.

4 And saying, ᵉWhere is the promise of his coming? for since the fathers fell asleep, all things continue as *they were* from the beginning of the creation.   e Isa. 5. 19. Jer. 17. 15. Ezek. 12. 22, 27. Matt. 24. 48. Luke 12. 45.

VOL. III—30

And saying, Where is the promise? questioning or denying the great truths of the gospel, thereby to encourage themselves in walking after their own lusts. *Of his coming;* viz. Christ's, mentioned ver. 2. Possibly these scoffers might drop the name of Christ by way of contempt, not vouchsafing to mention it, as the Jews did, John ix. 29; q. d. Where is the promise of his coming whom you expect? *His coming,* to judge the world; q. d. His promised coming doth not appear, the promise of it is not fulfilled. *For since the fathers,* who died in the faith of Christ's coming, and had the promise of it, *fell asleep;* i. e. died; the usual phrase of Scripture, which these scoffers seem to speak in derision; q. d. It is so long since the fathers fell asleep, (as you call it,) that it were more than time for them to be awakened, whereas we see the contrary. *All things continue as they were from the beginning of the creation;* i. e. the world continues to be the same it was, and hath the same parts it had; we see nothing changed, nothing abolished, but still nature keeps its old course. Thus they argue, that because there had been no such great change, therefore there should be none; because Christ was not yet come to judgment, therefore he should not come at all; not considering the power of God, who is as able to destroy the world as to make it, nor the will of God revealed in his word concerning the end of it.

f Gen. 1. 6, 9.
Ps. 33. 6.
Heb. 11. 3.
+ Gr. *consisting.*
g Ps. 24. 2.
& 136. 6.
Col. 1. 17.

5 For this they willingly are ignorant of, that ᶠby the word of God the heavens were of old, and the earth †ᵍstanding out of the water and in the water:

For this they willingly are ignorant of; they will not know what they ought to know, and, if they would search the Scripture, might know. *That by the word of God;* the command of God, or *word of his power,* as it is called, Heb. i. 3: see Gen. i. 6, 9; Psal. xxxiii. 6; cxlviii. 5. *The heavens were;* were created, or had a being given them, Gen. i. 6. *Of old;* from the beginning of the world. *And the earth;* the globe of the earth, which comprehends likewise the seas and rivers, as parts of the whole. *Standing out of the water and in the water:* according to our translation, the sense of these words may be plainly this, that the earth, standing partly out of the water, (as all the dry land doth, whose surface is higher than the water,) and partly in the water, (as those parts do which are under it,) or in the midst of the water, as being covered and encompassed by seas and rivers. But most expositors follow the marginal reading, and render the Greek word by consisting; and then the meaning may be, either, 1. That the earth consisting of water, as the matter out of which it was formed, (Moses calling the chaos which was that matter, *waters,* Gen. i. 2,) and by water, from which it hath its compactness and solidity, and without which it would be wholly dry, mere useless dust, unfit for the generation and production of natural things. If we understand the words thus, the argument lies against the scoffers; for the earth thus consists of and by water, yet God made use of the water for the destroying of the world; and so natural causes are not sufficient for its preservation without the power of God sustaining it in its being; and whenever he withdraws that power, in spite of all inferior causes, it must perish. Or, 2. The words may thus be read, the heavens were of old, and the earth (supply from the former clause) was out of the water, and consisting by, or in, the water; and the meaning is, that the earth did emerge, or appear out of, or above, the water, viz. when God gathered the waters together, and made the dry land appear; and doth consist by, or among, or in, the midst of the waters, as was before explained.

h Gen. 7. 11,
21, 22, 23.
ch. 2. 5.

6 ʰ Whereby the world that then was, being overflowed with water, perished:

Whereby; by which heavens and water, mentioned in the former verse, the fountains of the great deep being broken up, and the windows of heaven opened, Gen. vii. 11. Or, by the word of God, as the principal cause, and the water as the instrumental, which, at his command, was poured out upon the earth both from above and below. *The world;* the earth, with all the inhabitants of it, eight persons excepted. This the apostle allegeth against the forementioned scoffers, who said that all things continued as they were, when yet the flood had made so great a change in the face of the lower creation.

7 But ⁱthe heavens and the earth, which are now, by the same word are kept in store, reserved unto ᵏ fire against the day of judgment and perdition of ungodly men.

i ver. 10.
k Mat. 25. 41. 2 Thess. 1. 8.

The heavens; the ethereal, or starry heaven, as well as aerial; for, ver. 10, 12, he distinguisheth the heavens that are to perish by fire, from the elements; and ver. 13, he opposeth a new heaven to that heaven which is to be consumed; but the new heaven is not meant merely of the aerial heaven. And why should not this be meant of the same heavens, which elsewhere in Scripture are said to perish? Job xiv. 12. Psal. cii. 26, *All of them wax old,* &c. *By the same word;* the same as ver. 5. *Are kept in store;* are kept safe as in a treasury, and untouched for a time, that they may be destroyed at last. *Reserved unto fire;* that they may be consumed by it. The destruction of the world by fire at the last day, is opposed to the destruction of it by water in the flood. *Against the day of judgment;* the general judgment. *And perdition of ungodly men;* this the apostle speaks with an emphasis, because they were *ungodly* against whom he here bends his discourse.

8 But, beloved, be not ignorant of this one thing, that one day *is* with the Lord as a thousand years, and ˡa thousand years as one day.

l Ps. 90. 4.

Be not ignorant of this one thing; i. e. be sure of it: the same word is here used as ver. 5; and so he cautions them against the ignorance of scoffers, and to prevent it, would have them certainly know *this one thing,* which is extant in the Scripture, which foretells Christ's coming. *That one day is with the Lord;* the Lord Jesus Christ, of whose coming he speaks. *As a thousand years;* by a synecdoche, *a thousand years* is put for any, even the longest revolution of time; and the sense is, that though there be great difference of time, long and short, with us, who are subject to time, and are measured by it; yet with Him who is eternal, without succession, to whom nothing is past, nothing future, but all things present, there is no difference of time, none long, none short, but a thousand years, nay, all the time that hath run out since the creation of the world, is but as a day; and we are not to judge of the Lord's delay in coming by our own sense, but by God's eternity.

9 ᵐ The Lord is not slack concerning his promise, as some men count slackness; but ⁿ is longsuffering to us-ward, ᵒnot willing that any should perish, but ᵖ that all should come to repentance.

m Hab. 2. 3.
Heb. 10. 37.
n Is. 30. 18.
1 Pet. 3. 20.
ver. 15.
o Ezek. 18. 23, 32. & 33. 11.
p Rom. 2. 4.
1 Tim. 2. 4.

The Lord is not slack concerning his promise; i. e. doth not defer the fulfilling of it beyond the appointed time, Isa. lx. 22. *As some men count slackness;* either the scoffers here mentioned, who, because of Christ's not yet coming, questioned whether he would come at all, as if God had changed his purpose, or would not fulfil it: or believers themselves, who, through the weakness of their faith, and greatness of their sufferings, might grow into some degree of impatience, and think Christ slow in coming to avenge their cause, and give them their reward. So much may be gathered from Rev. vi. 10. *But is long-suffering to us-ward;* to us believers, or us elect. *Not willing that any should perish;* any that he hath ordained to life, though not yet called. *But that all should come to repentance;* all whom he hath elected; he would have the whole number of them filled up, and defers the day of judgment till it be so: or this may be meant not of God's secret and effectual will, but of his revealed will, whereby he calls all to repentance promiscuously that hear the gospel preached, hath made it their duty, approves of it, hath prescribed it as the way of salvation, commanded them to seek salvation in that way, and is ready to receive and save them upon their repenting: see 1 Tim. ii. 4.

10 But ᑫthe day of the Lord will come as a thief in the night; in the which

q Mat. 24. 43.
Luke 12. 39.
1 Thess. 5. 2.
Rev. 3. 3.
& 16. 15.

II. PETER III

[r Ps. 102. 26. Is. 51. 6. Matt. 24. 35. Mark 13. 31. Rom. 8. 20. Heb. 1. 11. Rev. 20. 11. & 21. 1.] **ʳthe heavens shall pass away with a great noise, and the elements shall melt with fervent heat, the earth also and the works that are therein shall be burned up.**

But the day of the Lord; the day of judgment is here called *the day of the Lord* by way of eminence, as *the great day*, Jude 6, and the *great day of God Almighty*, Rev. xvi. 14, and *the day of the Lord Jesus*, 1 Cor. i. 8; v. 5; 2 Cor. i. 14; Phil. i. 6, 10. *Will come as a thief in the night;* as a thief comes suddenly and unexpectedly, when he thinks all in the house are most secure. *In the which the heavens;* viz. those that are visible, in distinction from the empyreal heaven, or place of glorified spirits. *Shall pass away;* either wholly, so as to cease to be; or rather, as to their present being and condition, so as to cease to be what they now are, and to give place to the new heaven, Rev. xxi. 1. The same word is used, Matt. xxiv. 35; Luke xvi. 17. *With a great noise;* either swiftly and violently, or with such a noise as is usually caused by such violent and speedy motions. *The elements*, in a natural sense, as integral parts of the universe, air, water, earth. *Shall melt with fervent heat;* so ver. 12, where another word is used in the Greek, which properly signifies melting, or being on fire, or burning, shall be dissolved or destroyed. So the word signifies, John ii. 19; 1 John iii. 8. *The earth also;* the habitable part of the world. Though the earth, as a part of the world, be included in the elements before mentioned, yet here it may be taken with respect to its inhabitants, and the things contained in it. *And the works that are therein shall be burned up;* not only artificial, men's works, but natural, all that variety of creatures, animate and inanimate, wherewith God hath stored this lower world for the present use of man; and so all those delectable things in which carnal men seek their happiness.

11 Seeing then *that* all these things shall be dissolved, what manner *of per-* [s 1 Pet. 1. 15.] *sons* ought ye to be ˢin *all* holy conversation and godliness,

Seeing then that all these things shall be dissolved; seeing the coming of the Lord will be so terrible, as to bring with it the consumption of the world, and the destruction of these things here below, upon which we are so apt to set our affections. *What manner of persons ought ye to be;* how prudent, accurate, diligent, zealous, and every way excellent persons! The Greek word is often used by way of admiration of some singular excellency in persons or things, Matt. viii. 27; Mark xiii. 1; Luke i. 29. *In all holy conversation and godliness:* the words in the Greek are both in the plural number, and may imply not only a continued course of holy walking throughout our whole time, but likewise diligence in the performance of all sorts of duties, and exercise of all those various graces wherewith the Spirit of God furnisheth believers in order thereto.

[t 1 Cor. 1. 7. Tit. 1. 13. ‖Or, *hasting the coming.* u Ps. 50. 3. Is. 34. 4. x Mic. 1. 4. ver. 10.] **12 ᵗLooking for and ‖ hasting unto the coming of the day of God, wherein the heavens being on fire shall ᵘbe dissolved, and the elements shall ˣmelt with fervent heat?**

Looking for; patiently waiting for, and expecting. *And hasting unto;* by fervent desire of it, and diligent preparation for it. *The coming of the day of God;* the day of the Lord, ver. 10.

[y Is. 65. 17. & 66. 22. Rev. 21. 1, 27.] **13 Nevertheless we, according to his promise, look for ʸ new heavens and a new earth, wherein dwelleth righteousness.**

Nevertheless we, according to his promise: the places cited in the margin, to which this text seems to refer, speak of a new state of the church here in the world, yet by way of allusion to the renovation of the world, which is ultimately there promised, and the perpetuity of the gospel church till then is thereby assured. *Look for new heavens and a new earth;* instead of the present world, which is to be consumed by fire, ver. 10, 12, or the first heaven and earth, which pass away, Rev. xxi. 1. These will be new heavens and a new earth, either as to their substance, or as to their qualities, refined and purified from all defilement, and free from all that vanity to which the creature was made subject by the sin of man, Rom. viii. 20, 21. *Wherein dwelleth;* i. e. perpetually abideth, and not only for a time, Rom. viii. 11; 2 Cor. vi. 16; 2 Tim. i. 14. *Righteousness;* either this may be understood of righteousness in the abstract, that together with the destruction of the world the kingdom of sin shall be destroyed, and God's elect, the inhabitants of the new world, shall be filled with righteousness, whereas before sin had dwelt in them: or else the abstract may be put for the concrete, and by *righteousness* may be meant righteous persons, who only shall be the inhabitants of the new world, the wicked being turned into hell, Rev. xxi. 27; and by this way of expressing it may be implied the perfection of the righteousness of such. Not only the new heaven is mentioned, but the new earth, because the whole world will then be the possession and kingdom of the saints, who follow Christ wherever he goes.

14 Wherefore, beloved, seeing that ye look for such things, be diligent ᶻ that ye may be found of him in peace, without spot, and blameless. [z 1 Cor. 1. 8. & 15. 58. Phil. 1. 10. 1 Thess. 2. 13. & 5. 23.]

Such things; Christ's coming to judgment; the destruction of this world; a new heaven and a new earth, in which dwells righteousness. *Of him;* Christ the Judge. *In peace;* at peace with God, from whence proceeds peace of conscience, and an amicable, peaceable disposition toward others; all which may here be comprehended. *Without spot, and blameless:* either, 1. By these words he means absolute perfection; and then he shows what we are to design and aim at in this life, though we attain it not till we come into the other: or, 2. A thorough sanctification through faith in Christ, a being got above fleshly lusts, and the pollutions of the world, and any such carriage as our hearts may reproach us for, 1 Tim. vi. 14. If it be objected, that such, having sin still in them, cannot be said to be *without spot, and blameless*, in the sight of God; it may be answered, that though they have sin in them, yet being, through the righteousness of Christ imputed to them, justified in the sight of God, and accepted in the Beloved, Eph. i. 6, he overlooks their infirmities, and imputes no sin to them, sees no spot in them, so as to condemn them for it. The apostle seems here to reflect on the seducers before mentioned, whom, chap. ii. 13, he had called *spots and blemishes;* and he persuades these saints to look to themselves, that they might be found of Christ (not such as the other were, but) *without spot, and blameless;* or, as it is translated, Eph. v. 27, *without blemish,* i. e. in a state of sanctification, as well as justification.

15 And account *that* ᵃthe longsuffering of our Lord *is* salvation; even as our beloved brother Paul also according to the wisdom given unto him hath written unto you; [a Rom. 2. 4. 1 Pet. 3. 20. ver. 9.]

And account; reckon with yourselves, and be confidently persuaded; or take for granted. *The longsuffering of our Lord;* viz. in his not yet coming to judgment, and bearing with so much sin in the world without presently punishing it. *Is salvation;* i. e. tends or conduceth to salvation, in that hereby he gives space for repentance to the elect unconverted, and alloweth time for the building up and perfecting those that are converted, ver. 9. *Even as our beloved brother Paul;* not only brother in Christ, as a saint, but in office, as an apostle. *According to the wisdom given unto him;* that eminent and profound knowledge in the mysteries of the gospel in which Paul did excel, 1 Cor. ii. 6, 7; Eph. iii. 3, 4. Peter makes such honourable mention of Paul, 1. That he might commend to the Jewish Christians the doctrine Paul had preached, though a minister of the uncircumcision; 2. To show that he had nothing the worse thoughts of him for being so sharply reproved by him, Gal. ii.; and, 3. That he might arm the saints against those heretics that abused Paul's writings, and wrested them to their own meaning, probably, to patronize their errors. *Hath written unto you;* unto you Jewish believers, viz. either, 1. In his Epistle to the Romans, chap ii. 4, where is a passage very like this: or, 2. In his Epistle to the Hebrews, which, though it were not entitled to the Jews of the dispersion, yet was written to their nation; and in that Epistle several places there are of the same purport with this here; (see Heb. ix. 28; x. 23, 25, 36, 37;) and other Epistle of Paul to the Jews we have none: and in this he shows much of that *wisdom* God gave him in the mystery of the gospel; and in this likewise are many things hard to be understood.

^b Rom. 8.19.
1 Cor. 15. 24.
1 Thess. 4. 15.

16 As also in all *his* epistles, ^bspeaking in them of these things; in which are some things hard to be understood, which they that are unlearned and unstable wrest, as *they do* also the other Scriptures, unto their own destruction.

As also in all his epistles; to make the sense complete, we must supply here from the former verse, *he hath written. Speaking in them of these things;* viz. concerning the second coming of Christ, and end of the world, the patience that should be exercised in waiting for it; about avoiding scoffers that deny these truths, and the other instructions contained in these two Epistles, but especially in the two latter chapters of this Second Epistle. *In which are some things hard to be understood;* in which Epistles, or rather, in which things contained in Paul's Epistles, for the Greek relative is of a different gender, and cannot agree with *Epistles:* q. d. Some of the doctrines delivered by Paul in his Epistles are hard to be understood. And so this doth not prove Paul's Epistles, much less the whole Scripture, to be obscure and dark: the style and expression may be as clear as the nature of the things will bear, and yet the things themselves so expressed may be hard to be understood, either by reason of their own obscurity, as prophecies, the excellency and sublimeness of them, as some mysterious doctrines, or the weakness of men's minds, and their incapacity of apprehending spiritual things, 1 Cor. ii. 14, compared with chap. xiii. 9, 10. *Which they that are unlearned;* they that are ignorant of the Scripture, *unskilful in the word of righteousness,* Heb. v. 13; or indocible, that will not be instructed. *And unstable;* such as are ill-grounded, and therefore unstedfast, and easily deceived,

chap. ii. 14: see Eph. iv. 14. *Wrest;* pervert the Scripture, and offer violence to it, and, as it were, rack and torture it to make it confess what it never meant. *To their own destruction;* eternal destruction, viz. while they use the Scriptures to countenance their errors; or stumble at some things in them, which are obscure, thereby taking occasion to deny the truth of God; and so make the Scripture the instrument of their perdition, which God appointed to be the means of salvation.

17 Ye therefore, beloved, ^cseeing ye know *these things* before, ^dbeware lest ye also, being led away with the error of the wicked, fall from your own stedfastness.

^c Mark 13. 23. ch. 1. 12.
^d Eph. 4. 14. ch. 1. 10, 11. & 2. 18.

Seeing ye know these things, which I have been now writing to you of, viz. That the Judge will certainly come; or, that heretics, deceivers, and scoffers will come; or both may be comprehended. *Beware lest ye also;* as well as others have been. *Fall from your own stedfastness;* the stedfastness of your faith. This admonition he gives them, not to discourage them with fear of apostasy, but to awaken them to that holy care which would be a means to prevent it; and so to keep them from security, and trust in themselves, not to weaken their faith, and reliance on the promise.

18 ^eBut grow in grace, and *in* the knowledge of our Lord and Saviour Jesus Christ. ^fTo him *be* glory both now and for ever. Amen.

^e Eph. 4. 15.
1 Pet. 2. 2.

^f 2 Tim. 4. 18. Rev. 1. 6.

But grow in grace; in all those spiritual gifts ye have received from Christ, especially sanctifying. *And in the knowledge of our Lord and Saviour Jesus Christ;* in faith, whereby ye are sanctified, and made partakers of that grace. *To him be glory both now and for ever;* which belongs only to God; and therefore this proves Christ to be God.

THE FIRST EPISTLE GENERAL

OF

JOHN

THE ARGUMENT

Concerning the penman of the First Epistle, it doth not appear there hath been any doubt, the ancients generally ascribing it to the apostle St. John. The time of his writing it is uncertain, some assigning to it an earlier, others a later date. It is thought to have been written directly to the Christian Jews, not living in Judea, but remote in Parthia, (where it appears great numbers of them resided,) being styled by a noted father, "The Epistle to the Parthians." The design of it is to confirm them in the great fundamental doctrine of Christianity, That our Lord Jesus was the Messiah, against the attempts of divers apostate or degenerate Christians, who (whether this Epistle were of the former or latter date) did in his time deny, or essentially deprave, that most important article. And not only to induce them all most stedfastly to believe it, but to impress it more deeply upon their souls, to reduce the more licentious, to raise and quicken the dead and carnal to a more strict, lively, vigorous Christianity; and (which is greatly inculcated) to excite and inflame mutual Christian love among them, as that which would more strongly fortify them against the endeavours of seducers, and render their communion more pleasant among themselves. The other two Epistles are very much of the same argument, (though the latter hath somewhat of a different and peculiar concernment,) but doubted by some whether by the same penman, upon very insufficient grounds, the matter and style, plainly enough, showing them to be this apostle's.

CHAP. I

The apostle professeth to declare what he had formerly seen and known of the Word of life, to the end that others might have fellowship with him, 1—4. *The substance of his doctrine is, That to have fellowship with God, we must be holy as he is holy; and that if we confess our sins, we shall be forgiven through the blood of Christ,* 5—10.

THAT ^awhich was from the beginning, which we have heard, which we have seen with our eyes, ^bwhich we have looked upon, and ^c our hands have handled, of the Word of life;

After A. D. 90.
^a John 1. 1. ch. 2. 13.
^b John 1. 14. 2 Pet. 1. 16. ch. 4. 14.
^c Luke 24. 39. John 20. 27.

The order of discourse requires we begin with the last thing in this verse, *the Word of life.* This phrase, *the Word,* is by this apostle (not here to inquire in what notion some,

I. JOHN I

both Jews and pagans, before took it) familiarly used, to signify the eternal Son of God : and whereas this is his usual style in speaking of this sacred Person, as in the entrance of his Gospel, (so very like that of this Epistle,) so often over in his Revelation, chap. xix. 13, and that afterwards in this Epistle itself, chap. v. 7, he so readily falls into the mention of him by this name, (as not doubting to be understood,) it is scarce to be supposed, that being so constant to himself herein, he should use the same form of speech without any such intendment in this place, where the circumstances do both allow and invite us so to understand him. Nor doth the addition to it here, the Word *of life*, render it the less fit to be applied to this purpose, but rather the more ; as serving to denote the peculiar excellency of this Word, that he is the living and vivifying Word ; whereupon he also styles him in the following verse, simply, *the life*, and, *that eternal life*, (which is fit to be noted here, viz. that these three expressions, *the Word of life, the life*, and *that eternal life*, do, by the contexture of the discourse, plainly mean the same thing, and seem in their principal intendment to be set down as so many titles of the Son of God,) designing to represent him as the original and radical life, the root of the holy, divine life, to all who partake thereof, agreeably to his own words concerning him in the Gospel, John i. 4, *In him* (viz. the Word) *was life, and the life was the light of men* (i. e. the Word was a vital, enlivening light) ; and chap. v. 20, of this Epistle, He (viz. the Son of God) *is eternal life :* and to our Lord's words of himself, *I am the life*, John xi. 25 ; xiv. 6 ; and that *the Father had given him to have life in himself*, John v. 26, and consequently, to be capable of being to others an original or fountain of life. Yet whereas by *the Word*, and *the Word of life*, is often signified the gospel, (chap. ii. 5 ; Phil. ii. 16 ; and elsewhere,) it seems not incongruous or disagreeable to this context, to understand the apostle, as designing to comprehend both the meanings together in one expression, apt enough to include them both. See Dr. Hammond in loco. Nor are they of so remote an import, considered in their relation to us, as not fitly to admit of being both intended at once. The Son of God being his internal Word, the Word of his mind, his Wisdom, (another appellation of him, frequent in Scripture, Prov. viii. and elsewhere,) comprehending all ideas of things to be created or done ; to us, the immediate original of light and life, and by whose vivifying beams we are especially to be transformed into the Divine likeness : the gospel being his external word, the word of his mouth, the radiation of those beams themselves. As we do ourselves first conceive, and form in our minds, what we afterwards utter and express : only whereas our thought, or the word of our mind, is fluid, and soon vanishes ; God's (in whom is no change) is permanent, consubstantial and coeternal with himself, *The Word was with God, and the Word was God*, John i. 1. Neither are these two senses of *the Word of life* less fitly (or with more impropriety) comprehended together under that one expression, than in common discourse : speaking of the sun in reference to ourselves, we often comprehend together in our meaning, both the body of the sun itself and its beams; as when we say it enlightens us, revives us, shines in at this window, or upon that dial, we do not intend (as reasonably we cannot) to exclude either, but mean the sun doth it by its beams. And now the notion being settled of *the Word of life*, (which was necessary first to be done, and which required a larger discourse,) we may the more easily perceive, how what is here said of it may, in the one sense or the other, be applied thereto. *That which was from the beginning;* so the living Word, in the first sense, was, viz. when all things also began; which is not said itself then to have begun, as John i. 1, *In the beginning was the Word, and the Word was with God, and*, at the next step, *the Word was God*. And with what is said by this Word himself, (then taking another, but an equivalent, name, the Wisdom of God,) Prov. viii. 22—30, *The Lord possessed me in the beginning of his way, before his works of old. I was set up from everlasting, from the beginning, or ever the earth was. When, &c.*—*Then I was by him, as one brought up with him*, &c. : where *from the beginning*, and *from everlasting*, we see is all one. See of this Epistle, chap. ii. 13, 14. *Which we have seen with our eyes, which we have looked upon, and our hands have handled :* these are all expressions indifferently applicable both, 1. To the person of the Son of God, primarily meant by *the Word of life ;* for that same glorious Person who was from the beginning with the Father, viz. being now incarnate, became the object of these their very senses, to this and the other apostles, who had so frequent opportunity to hear, and see, and behold him, and even to handle him with their hands, Luke xxiv. 39 ; John xx. 25. And, 2. To the gospel revelation, a secondary (not unintended) notion of *the Word of life*, and whereof these latter expressions seem more especially meant; they denote the perfect certainty the apostles had (the rest of whom his manner of speaking seems purposely to comprehend with himself) of that truth, which, as he after speaks, they testified ; it being their office and business as apostles so to do; see John xv. 27 ; Acts i. 21, 22 ; iv. 20 ; and it was necessary they should be able to do it with such assurance as these expressions import. Therefore having said, *which we have heard*, which imports a more overly notice, it is added, *which we have seen*, a much more certain way of knowing, as 2 Pet. i. 16, 17 ; and *with our eyes*, a more lively expression of that certainty, as Job expresses his expected sight of his Redeemer, chap. xix. 27 : and to signify it was not a casual, transient glance, it is further said, *which we have looked upon*, ἐθεασάμεθα, i. e. studiously, and of set purpose, bent ourselves to contemplate. Unto all which it is moreover added, *and our hands have handled*, ἐψηλάφησαν, which though literally not otherwise applicable than to the person of our Lord incarnate, yet is a most emphatical metaphor, elegantly representing their most certain knowledge and lively sense of his excellent doctrine ; as the expression is usual of a palpable truth, to signify a most evident one. So is that implied to be a truth that may be felt, that this world hath a mighty and bountiful Sustainer and Lord, Acts xvii. 27 ; ψηλαφήσειαν.

2 (For ᵈthe life ᵉwas manifested, and we have seen *it*, ᶠand bear witness, ᵍand shew unto you that eternal life, ʰwhich was with the Father, and was manifested unto us ;)

d John 1. 4. & 11. 25.
e ch. 4. 6. e Rom. 16. 26. 1 Tim. 3. 16. ch. 3. 5.
f John 21. 24. Acts 2. 32.
g ch. 5. 20. h John 1. 1, 2.

He interrupts the stream of his discourse by this seasonable parenthesis, while he therein gives an account how *the Word of life, the life, that eternal life*, (already noted to be here all one, and chiefly to mean the Son of God,) which being *with the Father* must be to us invisible, came to be so sensibly known to mortal men on earth ; which he doth by telling us he *was manifested;* and that was sufficiently done, both who he was, and what he designed, in his partaking with us of flesh and blood, and *being found in fashion as a man*, whereby he subjected himself to the notice of our senses ; and was hereupon said to have been *manifested in the flesh*, chap. iii. 5 ; 1 Tim. iii. 16 ; the glory of his Divinity also shining forth most conspicuously in his God-like conversation, and wonderful works, through this veil, and confirming the truth of his heavenly doctrine, which more distinctly declared both that it was the Son of God who was come down into this wretched world of ours, and what the kind design was of his descent hither. So that what here the apostle says more briefly, that he was *manifested*, well admits the larger account which he gives of it in his Gospel, chap. i. 14, *And the Word was made flesh, and dwelt among us, (and we beheld his glory, the glory as of the only begotten of the Father,) full of grace and truth*. Whereupon (as he adds) he bears witness, and shows forth what he had seen so manifested, as it belonged to his apostolical office to do.

3 ⁱThat which we have seen and heard declare we unto you, that ye also may have fellowship with us : and truly ᵏour fellowship *is* with the Father, and with his Son Jesus Christ.

i Acts 4. 20.
k John 17. 11. 2 Cor. 1. 9. ch. 2. 24.

He now proceeds with what he intended, not only professing to testify most certainly known things, (which he further with great earnestness inculcates,) but declaring also the end of this testimony ; viz. not merely that they to whom he writes might know them too, (as if the being a Christian did only stand in having some peculiar notions from other men, and that they were only to know for knowing' sake,) but that they might *have fellowship*, i. e. partake and communicate with them (viz. the apostles, and the whole community of living Christians) in all the vital influences, holy practice, the dignities, pleasures, and consolations belonging to the Christian state ; whereupon he adds, *and truly our fellowship is with the Father, and with his Son Jesus Christ:* q. d. Nor are the advantages of that state, in their kind and nature, terrene, sensual, secular, but Divine and heavenly, such as are imparted to us by *the Father, and his Son Jesus Christ;* or, wherein we are truly said to participate, and have a communion with them. That blessed Spirit, who is the immediate author to us of all gracious communication, (whence this is also styled *the communion of the Holy Ghost,* 2 Cor. xiii. 14,) being in reality the Spirit of the Father and the Son.

^{l John 15.}
^{11. & 16. 24.}
^{2 John 12.} 4 And these things write we unto you, ^lthat your joy may be full.

Not insipid, spiritless, empty, as carnal joy is, apt through the deficiency of its cause to admit of intermingled qualms ; but lively and vigorous, 2 John 12, well grounded, John xvi. 24, such as is of the right kind, and will grow up into the perfect plenitude and fulness of joy, Psal. xvi. 11.

^{m ch. 3. 11.} 5 ^mThis then is the message which we have heard of him, and declare unto you, that ⁿGod is light, and in him is no darkness at all.

^{n John 1. 9.}
^{& 8. 12. &}
^{9. 5. & 12.}
^{35, 36.}

It being the professed scope and design of his writing, to draw men to a final participation and communion with God in his own blessedness, he reckons nothing more necessary to it, than to settle in their minds a right notion of God. Which, that it might be the more regarded, he introduces with a solemn preface ; *This then is the message,* &c., (though the word also signifies promise, it here more fitly bears this rendering,) to notify, 1. That this which follows was not an imagination of his own concerning God, but his true representation of himself. 2. That it was given him in charge to be delivered and communicated to others ; a message that man neither hath of himself, nor is to reserve to himself, *we have heard* it *of him, and declare* it *to you,* as (consonantly hereto) he speaks. It is the Divine pleasure he should be published to the world, and that all men should know that as from him, i. e. that he is not a Being of mere power, as some, or of mere mercy, as others, are apt to fancy of him, either whereof were a very maimed and most disagreeable notion of the Deity : power without goodness were apt to run into fury ; goodness without wisdom and righteousness would as naturally turn to a supine indifference, and neglect of distinguishing judicially between good and bad ; things neither suitable to the Governor of the world, nor possible to the absolutely perfect Being. *God is light;* in God all true perfections and excellencies must be understood eminently to concur ; and of them more could not have been comprehended under one word, (especially that belong to him considered relatively to his creatures, of which perfections it concerns us to have more distinct, formed, positive conceptions in all our applications to him,) than are here some way represented or resembled by *light,* viz. that he is a Being of most lively, penetrative vigour, absolute simplicity, immutability, knowledge, wisdom, sincerity, righteousness, serenity, benignity, joy, and felicity, and especially of most bright and glorious holiness and purity; and in whom *is no darkness at all,* nothing contrary or repugnant hereto.

^{o 2 Cor. 6.}
^{14. ch. 2. 4.} 6 ^oIf we say that we have fellowship with him, and walk in darkness, we lie, and do not the truth :

Light and darkness are frequently put for holiness and wickedness, Luke xvi. 8; Rom. xiii. 12; Eph. v. 8; 1 Thess. v. 5. The sum then is, That if any pretend to friendship with God, or to have received holy and gracious influences from him, and do yet lead wicked lives, they are liars, even guilty of a practical lie, doing what makes their profession false and insincere.

^{p 1 Cor. 6.}
^{11. Eph. 1.7.}
^{Heb. 9. 14.}
^{1 Pet. 1. 19.}
^{ch. 2. 2.}
^{Rev. 1. 5.} 7 But if we walk in the light, as he is in the light, we have fellowship one with another, and ^pthe blood of Jesus Christ his Son cleanseth us from all sin.

But if we walk; which is a continued and progressive motion, i. e. do persevere and improve in holiness. *In the light;* being transformed into the holy image and likeness of God, and showing themselves *the children of light,* as he is *light,* and *the Father of lights. We have fellowship one with another ;* have fellowship with him, μετ' αὐτοῦ, as one copy reads : however, *we* must comprehend God, and this the contexture of discourse shows. *And the blood of Jesus Christ his Son cleanseth us from all sin;* καθαρίζει lest our purity and holiness should be thought to have deserved such a privilege, it is cautiously added, *and the blood,* &c. is that which alone expiates, or makes atonement for our sins (the proper notion of cleansing here). Our former sinfulness and present imperfect holiness render it impossible God should admit us to communion with him for our own sakes, or without such an intervening sacrifice ; καθάρματα usually signifying expiations. And if we further extend the notion of cleansing, so as to comprehend internal subjective purification, (which also the word may admit,) the further meaning is, that even that purifying influence, whereby we are qualified for present holy walking with God, and for final blessedness in him, we owe to the merit and procurement of the Redeemer's blood.

8 ^qIf we say that we have no sin, we deceive ourselves, ^r and the truth is not in us.

^{q 1 Kings 8.}
^{46. 2 Chron.}
^{6. 36. Job 9.}
^{2. & 15. 14.}
^{& 25. 4.}
^{Prov. 20. 9. Eccles. 7. 20. Jam. 3. 2. r ch. 2. 4.}

In pursance of which scope, he fitly adds, *If we should say,* i. e. either profess it as a principle, or think in our minds, or not bear in our hearts a penitential, remorseful sense, correspondent to the contrary apprehension ; such as is implied in confessing, ver. 9 ; for saying usually signifies the habitual bent and disposition of the heart and practice, Job xxi. 14; Jer. xxii. 21. *That we have no sin;* viz. that we are so innocent creatures as not to need such an expiatory sacrifice as that above mentioned, and such purifying influence thereupon, but that we may be admitted to communion with God upon our own account, and for our worthiness' sake, without being beholden to the blood of Christ. *We deceive ourselves,* delude our own souls. *And the truth;* i. e. the system and frame of gospel doctrine, as 2 John 1, 2, 4. *Is not in us;* cannot be duly entertained, lies not evenly and agreeably with itself in our minds, or hath no place with effect in us, as John viii. 37.

9 ^sIf we confess our sins, he is faithful and just to forgive us *our* sins, and to ^tcleanse us from all unrighteousness.

^{s Ps. 32. 5.}
^{Prov. 28. 13.}
^{t ver. 7.}
^{Ps. 51. 2.}

But on the contrary, *if we confess our sins,* if we apply ourselves to him suitably to the condition of sinners, confessing ourselves such, with that self-abasing sense of sin which may dispose us to accept and apply his offered remedy, (upon which it is implied we will do it,) *he is faithful,* so true to his promise, *and just,* fidelity being a part of justice ; or there is with him that equity and righteousness, (which sometimes signify goodness, or clemency, 1 Sam. xii. 7 ; Psal. cxii. 9, and which, more strictly taken, permit him not to exact from us the satisfaction which he hath accepted in the atonement made by his Son, in his own way applied, and upon his own terms to be reckoned unto us,) that he will not fail *to forgive us our sins. And to cleanse us from all unrighteousness;* which may either be added as a further expression of the same thing ; or may, moreover, signify his vouchsafing that purifying influence of the Spirit of Christ, (obtained also by his blood,) which shall both purge away, and prevent, the defilements that would render us incapable of his own holy communion.

10 If we say that we have not sinned, we make him a liar, and his word is not in us.

If we say that we have not sinned : see ver. 8, 9. *We make him a liar;* which they make him that believe not his word, chap. v. 10, expressly charging all men with sin, Rom. iii. 19, 23. *And,* consequently, *his word,* or *truth,* as ver. 8, which we contradict, *is not in us.* The sum is, That we are not to be received into God's holy society and communion under the notion of always innocent and unoffending persons, but as pardoned and purified sinners.

CHAP. II

Christ is our advocate with the Father, and a propitiation for the sins of the whole world, 1, 2. *Rightly to know*

God is to keep his commandments, 3—6; *the chief of which is, to love one another,* 7—11. *The apostle addresseth Christians of all ages severally,* 12—14, *and warneth them against an inordinate love of this world,* 15—17; *and against deceivers, who were many,* 18, 19. *He showeth the means they had of knowing the truth, and of distinguishing false teachers; and pointeth out their obligation to abide in the truth which they had been taught,* 20—28. *He that doeth righteousness is born of God,* 29.

^{a Rom. 8. 34.}
^{1 Tim. 2. 5.}
^{Heb. 7. 25.}
^{& 9. 24.}

MY little children, these things write I unto you, that ye sin not. And if any man sin, ^a we have an advocate with the Father, Jesus Christ the righteous:

He endeavours in this to steer them a middle course, that they might neither presume to sin, nor despair if they did; and bespeaks them with a compellation, importing both authority and love; well becoming him as then an aged person, an apostle, their teacher, and who was their most affectionate spiritual father. And lets them know, the first design of what he was now writing (had hitherto written, and was further to write) was, That they might to their uttermost avoid sinning at all: but adds, if, through human frailty, they did sin, *we have an Advocate with the Father, Jesus Christ the righteous;* implying our need of Christ for renewed as well as first pardon; and not of his death only, but continual intercession; and represents the advantages Christ hath for success in his interposing for us, in respect both of his relation to God as his Father, (which is put indefinitely, *the Father,* that the consideration might not be excluded of his being our Father also,) and his righteousness, by which he could not but be acceptable to him.

^{b Rom.3.25.}
^{2 Cor. 5. 18.}
^{ch. 1. 7.}
^{& 4. 10.}
^{c John 1. 29.}
^{& 4. 42. &}
^{11. 51, 52. ch. 4. 14.}

2 And ^b he is the propitiation for our sins: and not for our's only, but ^c also for *the sins of the whole world*.

And he is the propitiation for our sins: the adding of these words, shows that our Lord grounds his intercession for pardon of sin unto penitent believers, upon his having made atonement for them before; and therefore that he doth not herein merely supplicate for favour, but (which is the proper business of an advocate) plead law and right; agreeably to what is said above, chap. i. 9. *And not for ours only, but also for the sins of the whole world;* nor is his undertaking herein limited to any select persons among believers, but he must be understood to be an Advocate for all, for whom he is effectually a Propitiation, i. e. for all that truly believe in him, (Rom. iii. 25,) all the world over.

3 And hereby we do know that we know him, if we keep his commandments.

This faith is often in the Holy Scripture signified by the name of knowledge, Isa. liii. 11; John xvii. 3, viz. an appropriative, transformative knowledge, by which we own and accept God in Christ, as ours, (expressed also by acknowledgment, ἐπίγνωσις, Eph. i. 17; Col. ii. 2,) and are changed into his likeness, 2 Cor. iii. 18. The meaning then is, That we perceive, or discern ourselves to be sincere believers, and consequently that Christ is both our Propitiation and Advocate, when it is become habitual and easy to us to obey his commandments.

^{d ch. 1. 6.}
^{& 4. 20.}
^{e ch. 1. 8.}

4 ^d He that saith, I know him, and keepeth not his commandments, ^e is a liar, and the truth is not in him.

A liar; a false, hypocritical pretender, as chap. i. 6.

^{f John 14.}
^{21, 23.}
^{g ch. 4. 12.}
^{h ch. 4. 13.}

5 But ^f whoso keepeth his word, ^g in him verily is the love of God perfected: ^h hereby know we that we are in him.

His faith *worketh by love,* Gal. v. 6; his love is *perfected,* and attains its end in obedience, whereof it is the vital principle, chap. v. 3; John xiv. 15. Such an efficacious governing knowledge of him, therefore, as, by the power of the love which it produces, subdues our souls to the obedience of him, is a certain proof to us of our union with him, chap. v. 20, and relation to him.

6 ⁱ He that saith he abideth in him ^k ought himself also so to walk, even as he walked.

^{i John 15. 4,}
^{5.}
^{k Mat. 11.29}
^{John 13. 15.}
^{1 Pet. 2. 21.}

And this proof we ought to give. For whereas our Lord Jesus Christ was not only our Lawgiver, but our pattern, and practised himself what he commanded us; if indeed we have an abiding, real union with him, we partake of his Spirit, Rom. viii. 9, which must be understood to work uniformly, and enable us *to walk* (in the main of our course, according to our measure of that Spirit) *as he walked.*

7 Brethren, ^l I write no new commandment unto you, but an old commandment ^m which ye had from the beginning. The old commandment is the word which ye have heard from the beginning.

^{l 2 John 5.}
^{m ch. 3. 11.}
^{2 John 5.}

This commandment must be that which he insists on, ver. 9—11, and which in different respects he calleth both *old* and *new.* Not *new,* he says, in opposition to their Gnostic seducers, to intimate he was not about to entertain them with vain novelties, as they did; all whose peculiar doctrines were no other than innovations upon true Christianity: but *old,* viz. a part of original Christianity, as it came pure first from our Lord Christ himself; the *commandment,* or *word, which* they *had,* or had heard, *from the beginning.* This phrase, *from the beginning,* being here put in conjunction with some act of theirs, *ye had,* or have heard, as also 2 John 5, 6, shows it to intend a much later term of commencement than chap. i. 1. Though also, considering them as Jews, whom he here writes to, it might run up as high as the law given by Moses; or, even as men, to the creation, and the first impression of the law of nature (whereof this was a very noble part) upon the heart of man.

8 Again, ⁿ a new commandment I write unto you, which thing is true in him and in you: ^o because the darkness is past, and ^p the true light now shineth.

^{n John 13.}
^{34. & 15. 12.}
^{o Rom. 13.}
^{12. Eph. 5.8.}
^{1Thes. 5.5,8.}
^{p John 1. 9.}
^{& 8. 12, &}
^{12. 35.}

Yet also he calls it *a new commandment,* as our Saviour did, John xiii. 34, upon the subjoined accounts. *Which thing is true;* i. e. evident, or verified, fulfilled, exemplified. *In him;* viz. in that new and high demonstration he had given of the sincerity and greatness of his own love, laying down his life for us, as John xv. 13. *And in you;* or, us, (as some read,) i. e. the mind of God herein is by a new and fresh light most evidently and gloriously signified in or among you, (the subject being here collective and plural, admits this varied and very usual sense of the particle *in,*) inasmuch as *the darkness is past;* i. e. the heathenish ignorance that made the world barbarous; a darkness in which the furious lusts and passions of men are wont to rage, turning this earth into another hell, Psal. lxxiv. 20, is in a great measure vanished; and also the dark umbrage of the Judaic dispensation, (some read σκιά for σκοτία, not *darkness,* but *shadow,*) in which the love of God to men was more obscurely represented, is past away and gone, *and the true light now shineth;* the love and grace of God towards sinners (the pattern and argument of our mutual love to one another) shines with *true light,* that is evident, in opposition to darkness, or immediately substantial, in opposition to type or shadow, as John i. 9, 14, 17: representing the gracious design of God, and his very nature, who *is love,* chap. iv. 8, 16, with so bright and glorious beams as ought to transform us into his likeness; and which therefore render the mutual hatred of one another the most incongruous thing to us in the world. Whereupon he adds,

9 ^q He that saith he is in the light, and hateth his brother, is in darkness even until now.

^{q 1 Cor.13.2.}
^{2 Pet. 1. 9.}
^{ch. 3. 14, 15.}

To be *in the light,* signifies to be under the transforming, governing power of it, as the phrases import of being *in the flesh,* and *in the Spirit,* Rom. viii. 9, being expounded by walking *after the flesh,* and *after the Spirit,* ver. 1. He therefore that *hateth his brother,* a thing so contrary to the design of the gospel, whatever he pretends, *is* still *in darkness,* under the power of the unregenerate principle of impure and malignant darkness: the gospel hath done him no good, is to him but an impotent and ineffectual light, in the midst whereof, by stiff winking, and an obstinate resistance, an exclusion of that pure and holy light, he creates to himself a dark and a hellish night.

r ch. 3. 14.
s 2 Pet. 1. 10.
+ Gr. *scandal*.

10 ʳ He that loveth his brother abideth in the light, and ˢ there is none †occasion of stumbling in him.

His brother, put indefinitely, must be understood universally, i. e. he that loveth not this or that fellow Christian, upon some personal or private reason, but *all*, upon one and the same common and truly Christian account. *Abideth in the light;* shows or doth demonstrate the settled, constant power, the regenerate, Divine principle hath over him. *And there is none occasion of stumbling in him;* Greek, no scandal; no inconsistent thing, that ought to occasion him to judge otherwise of himself, or others to think otherwise of him.

11 But he that hateth his brother is in darkness, and ᵗ walketh in darkness, and knoweth not whither he goeth, because that darkness hath blinded his eyes.

t John 12. 35.

Hath no principle to guide or govern him, but what is common to the unregenerate world, so that his whole life is a continual error; nor doth he understand or consider the tendency of his course, being still under the power of an affected darkness, that makes his eyes, or understanding, of no more use than if he were quite blind, or had none at all. So weighty and important is the precept which he had to lay down, ver. 15, of not loving the world, &c., that he introduces it with the solemnity of a most pathetic preface, contained in these three following verses, wherein he applies himself severally to the distinct orders and ranks into which Christians were capable of being reduced, the matter being of common and equal concernment to all of them. And he speaks suitably to the condition and state of each, such things as whereby he might most effectually insinuate with them, and oblige them deeply to consider what he had to say; doubling also his application to each of them, out of the earnestness of his intention and endeavour to fasten the exhortation upon them which was to follow.

u Luke 24.
47. Acts 4.
12. & 10. 43.
& 13. 38
ch. 1. 7.

12 I write unto you, little children, because ᵘ your sins are forgiven you for his name's sake.

He here uses an appellation before (ver. 1) applied to all in common, being put alone; but being now set in contradistinction to others, must be understood to intend a distinct rank of Christians, viz. those more newly entered into the Christian state; and to them he suggests the free remission of their sins *for his name's sake*, i. e. for his own sake, as the reason why they should, out of ingenuity, and a new, recent sense of God's mercy towards them, comply with his holy pleasure in the following precept. The remission of their sins being a first and most early privilege with them, that commenced from the beginning of their sincere Christianity, and which was sealed to them in their late baptism, it is the more fitly mentioned to this first rank of Christians.

13 I write unto you, fathers, because ye have known him ˣ *that is* from the beginning. I write unto you, young men, because ye have overcome the wicked one. I write unto you, little children, because ye have known the Father.

x ch. 1. 1.

Unto fathers, because to such belong much experience, and the knowledge of ancient things, he ascribeth the knowledge of *him who is* the Ancient of days, *from the beginning*, and than whom none is more ancient, and whom they should be supposed so well to know by their long-continued course in religion, as fully to understand his good and acceptable will, what would be pleasing and what displeasing to him. *I write unto you, young men, because ye have overcome the wicked one:* to such as were in the flower of their strength and age in Christianity, he attributeth victory; to whom therefore it would be inglorious to slur the honour of that noble conquest they had gained over *the wicked one*, the *god of this world*, as he is elsewhere called, 2 Cor. iv. 4, by suffering themselves again to be entangled in its snares and bands. His method is, we see, to place this order of Christians last, as a middle state, which he would have us conceive afterwards to be interposed between the other two; which method we find he observes in going over them again the second time. *I write unto you, little children, because ye have known the Father:* he again first begins with his *little children*, whom he now bespeaks by another compellation in the Greek, (before τεκνία, now παιδία,) importing no material difference, except this latter signify more capacity of instruction; and he now also gives them another character, which implies so much, that he not only considers them as the passive subjects of a privilege, remission of sins, which they were capable of in the first moment of their being born into the Christian state, (as the word τεκνία, above, seems to intimate,) but as being able to use their understanding, and consider whose children they were, *because ye have known the Father;* before said also of the eldest sort of Christians; but he is there mentioned by a description more suitable to their more aged state; and therefore the knowledge ascribed to the one, and to the other, though the same in kind, must, in respect of degrees, be accommodately understood.

14 I have written unto you, fathers, because ye have known him *that is* from the beginning. I have written unto you, young men, because ʸ ye are strong, and the word of God abideth in you, and ye have overcome the wicked one.

y Eph. 6. 10.

To the former sort he only repeateth what he had said before, supposing their greater wisdom to need no more; (see L. Brugens. Not. in Bibl. Sacr. of the insertion of this clause;) only the repetition importeth his earnest desire they would again and again consider it. The other he also puts in mind of their active strength and vigour, and of the rootedness which the gospel must now be supposed to have in them, whereby they were enabled to *overcome the wicked one*. And by all which endowments they were all both enabled and obliged to comport the better with the following precept, and its enforcements.

15 ᶻ Love not the world, neither the things *that are* in the world. ᵃ If any man love the world, the love of the Father is not in him.

z Rom. 12. 2.
a Mat. 6. 24.
Gal. 1. 10.
Jam. 4. 4.

What he here means by the forbidden object of our love, must be gathered from his own explication, ver. 16. The love itself forbidden, in reference thereto, is that excess thereof, whereby any adhere to terrene things, as their best good; wherewith, as he adds, any sincere love to God is inconsistent, as Matt. vi. 24; Luke xiv. 33: a consideration so awful and tremendous, that it is not strange the precept it enforces should have so solemn and urgent an introduction.

16 For all that *is* in the world, the lust of the flesh, ᵇ and the lust of the eyes, and the pride of life, is not of the Father, but is of the world.

b Eccles. 5. 11.

Here he explains his meaning, what, under the name of *the world*, and *the things* of it, we are not to love, or under what notion we ought not to love it, viz. the world as it contains the objects and nutriment of these mentioned lusts; either more grossly sensual, called *the lust of the flesh*, viz. of gluttony, drunkenness, whoredom, &c. Rom. xiii. 13, 14; or that which is excited more immediately by the fancy, unto which the eye especially ministereth, the excessive appetite of much wealth, and great possessions; which the eye is therefore said to desire, and not to be satisfied with, Eccles. ii. 8—10, and iv. 8; called therefore *the lust of the eyes*. And again, the ambitious affectation of the pomp and glory of the world, vain applause, the unmerited and overvalued praise and observance of other men, with power over them, affected for undue ends, or only with a self-exalting design, meant by *the pride of life*, forbidden by our Saviour to his disciples, Matt. xx. 25, 26. This triple distribution some observe to have been before used by some of the ancient learned Jews, and imitated by certain of the more refined heathens; whence, as being formerly known and understood, the apostle might be induced to make use of it. And these lusts are therefore argued to be inconsistent with the love of the Father, as not being of him, but *of the world;* not from the Divine Spirit, but the spirit of the world.

17 And ^c the world passeth away, and the lust thereof: but he that doeth the will of God abideth for ever.

He sets the difference in view, of living according to the common genius, will, or inclination of the world, (which is lust,) and according to the Divine will, that he who unites himself in his will and desire with the former, which vanishes, (objects and appetite altogether,) must (which is implied) perish therewith; but he that unites himself with the supreme eternal good, by a will that is guided by and conformed to the Divine will, *abideth for ever,* partakes a felicity coeternal with the object and rule upon which his heart was set, and which it was guided by.

18 ^d Little children, ^e it is the last time: and as ye have heard that ^f antichrist shall come, ^g even now are there many antichrists; whereby we know ^h that it is the last time.

The last time; the time here referred to seems to be the destruction of Jerusalem, and the finishing of the Jewish state, both civil and ecclesiastical. In the Greek, the last hour, the approaching period of Daniel's seventy weeks, as Mr. Mede understands it, in his Apostacy of the Later Times. Whereas therefore it was now a known and expected thing among Christians, that the eminent *antichrist,* or antichristian state, (expressly foretold, 2 Thess. ii.,) was to come, or take place; therefore the apostle says, *ye,* i. e. the generality of Christians, *have heard* so much. So he says, *even now,* as the forerunners of the eminent one. *are there many antichrists,* (foretold also by our Saviour, Matt. xxiv.,) viz. noted heretics and seducers then in being: not such falsely assuming vicarious Christs, as only pretended to do that part which the Jews expected from their Messiah, the delivering them from the Roman tyranny, and so set up to be merely civil or secular Christs, having themselves never been Christians, but such as had revolted from Christianity, and now laboured fundamentally to subvert it, denying Christ to be *come in the flesh,* ver. 22; 2 John 7; having been before professed Christians, as appears by the following words.

19 ⁱ They went out from us, but they were not of us; for ^k if they had been of us, they would *no doubt* have continued with us: but *they went out,* ^l that they might be made manifest that they were not all of us.

If they had been of us, they would no doubt have continued with us: sincere and living Christians are so strongly held in with Christ, and the truly Christian community, by a union and bond of life, and by sense of pleasures which thereupon they find in that holy communion, with the expectation which their lively faith gives them of eternal life at last, that there is *no doubt* of their continuance. *But they went out, that they might be made manifest that they were not all of us:* others, that are Christians upon external inducements, alter, as these do, and are permitted to do so, that the difference may appear between true and counterfeit ones, 1 Cor. xi. 19.

20 But ^m ye have an unction ⁿ from the Holy One, and ^o ye know all things.

See note on ver. 27.

21 I have not written unto you because ye know not the truth, but because ye know it, and that no lie is of the truth.

He prudently intimates his confidence concerning them, together with the pleasure he himself took (as any one would) in communicating the sentiments of holy truth to prepared, receptive minds; implying also, that any part of false doctrine doth so ill match and square with the frame of Divine truth, that judicious Christians may discern they are not of a piece.

22 ^p Who is a liar but he that denieth that Jesus is the Christ? He is antichrist, that denieth the Father and the Son.

Especially may the ill accord be discerned between Divine truth and a lie, when the lie is so directly levelled against the foundations upon which the whole fabric is built, as the denying Jesus to be the Christ strikes at all. And though he that doth so, seems not only an *antichrist* as directing his opposition but against Christ, he really as much *denieth the Father,* who testified of him.

23 ^q Whosoever denieth the Son, the same hath not the Father: [*but*] ^r *he that acknowledgeth the Son hath the Father also.*

To have the Father and the Son, is, by faith, love, and obedience, vitally to adhere to the one and the other. The latter part of this verse, though it be not in the ordinary Greek copies, is in some of the versions, and said to be in some Greek manuscripts also, whence it is supplied very agreeably to the apostle's scope, and usual way of writing.

24 Let that therefore abide in you, ^s which ye have heard from the beginning. If that which ye have heard from the beginning shall remain in you, ^t ye also shall continue in the Son, and in the Father.

He only exhorts them to persevere in that faith which they at first received, whereby their union with God in Christ would be preserved entire.

25 ^u And this is the promise that he hath promised us, *even* eternal life.

Which perseverance they are highly encouraged to .>y the promise of so great a thing as eternal life at length.

26 These *things* have I written unto you ^x concerning them that seduce you.

So much he thought requisite to be said, in respect of their danger by seducers, though their safety was principally to depend upon what he next mentions.

27 But ^y the anointing which ye have received of him abideth in you, and ^z ye need not that any man teach you: but as the same anointing ^a teacheth you of all things, and is truth, and is no lie, and even as it hath taught you, ye shall abide in ‖ him.   ‖ *Or, it.*

But the anointing which ye have received: it is evident, that the ancient anointing of persons to some eminent office, was not a mere empty rite of investiture, or authorization, but also a symbol of their qualification by another Spirit then coming upon them. Whereupon our Lord Jesus was eminently *the Christ,* or *anointed One,* not only as denoting his solemn investiture with the sacred offices of King, Priest, and Prophet, which were all wont to be entered into by unction; but as signifying also his receiving the Spirit, *(not by measure,)* by which he was most perfectly qualified for them. And whereas he is also said to have made those that believe on him, in a far inferior sense, *kings and priests to his Father;* to them also he imparts of the same Spirit, Rom. viii. 9, whence they are said to be anointed too, 2 Cor. i. 21, 22. And hence, as is here said, and ver. 27, they do not *need,* &c. *Ye need not that any man teach you;* not as if they had absolutely no need at all of human teaching, for the apostle supposes not himself to be now doing a vain or needless thing; but that they had less need, having the internal principles of light and life in them, they were in a great measure capable of steering their own course. They had in themselves a living, ingrafted word, enabling them to teach and commune with themselves, as Deut. xxx. 11, 12; Rom. x. 7—9. Hereupon their own reins could instruct them, Psal. xvi. 7. Or, they could instruct themselves, ἑαυτοὺς, as that may be read, Col. iii. 16, *the word of Christ* dwelling *richly* in them. Therefore they did not so need to be taught, as those that know not the first principles

I. JOHN II, III

of the oracles of God. *Teacheth you of all things;* i. e. all such necessary and essential things to the life and being of Christianity, of which sort that doctrine concerning the Messiah was, which he was now speaking of; not *all things* simply, for that had been to attribute to them far higher knowledge than he could pretend to himself, even that which was peculiar to God only. Nor was that knowledge which they had of those necessary things to be thought the effect of an immediate inspiration, but such as by ordinary external means they had already learned, but made vital and efficacious by the special sanctifying influence and operation of the Holy Ghost; who having begotten in them a correspondent impress to those great truths which are after godliness, formed the new creature in them, which is begotten of the word of truth, had made them capable of dijudication, or of distinguishing by a spiritual sense, Phil. i. 9, 10, between things that were grateful, suitable, and nutritive to the life of the new creature in them, and such things as were noxious and offensive. Whereas, in reference to things more remote from the vitals of religion and godliness, none can assure themselves of such a privilege. And as to these, they are to expect it in the way of their own sincere and diligent endeavours and prayers, as the effect of the habit of grace, maintained and kept up in life and vigour; and a reward of their sincere resignation and subjection of heart and soul to the governing power of truth, so far as it should be understood and known of them, according to that of our Saviour, John vii. 17, *If any man will do his will, he shall know of the doctrine whether it be of God,* &c. And thus they might certainly keep their station, and *abide in him;* unto which they are therefore exhorted.

28 And now, little children, abide in him; that, [b] when he shall appear, we may have confidence, [c] and not be ashamed before him at his coming.

b ch. 3. 2.
c ch. 4. 17.

He condescendingly includes himself with them, *that we may have confidence;* intimating, for their encouragement, the common mutual joy they should have together at Christ's appearance; he, that he had not been wanting in his endeavours that they might persevere; and they, that they had persevered; which is implied in the menace of the contrary, upon the contrary supposition.

d Acts 22.14.
ǁ Or, *know ye.*
e ch. 3.7, 10.

29 [d] If ye know that he is righteous, ǁ ye know that [e] every one that doeth righteousness is born of him.

Lest he should be thought only solicitous to preserve among them the right notions of the Christian docrine, as if that alone would suffice them for their salvation and blessedness, (which was the conceit of the Gnostics, touching their own notions, that the entertaining of them would save men, whatsoever men they were, or howsoever they lived,) he subjoins this serious monition, *If ye know,* &c., intimating, that whatsoever they had of the knowledge of God would avail them nothing, if, whereas *he is righteous,* they were not transformed by it into his likeness, and enabled thereby to *do righteousness,* which alone would evidence their Divine birth, since God hath no children destitute of his image, or who resemble him not

---

CHAP. III

It is a mark of God's singular love toward us, that we are now called his sons, and designed for further happiness hereafter, 1, 2; *and therefore we must obediently keep his commandments,* 3—10, *and love one another with true brotherly kindness and actual beneficence,* 11—24.

a John 1. 12.
b John 15. 18, 19. & 16. 3. & 17. 25.

BEHOLD, what manner of love the Father hath bestowed upon us, that [a] we should be called the sons of God: therefore the world knoweth us not, [b] because it knew him not.

So late mention having been made of that great thing, in the close of the foregoing chapter, being born of God, the holy apostle is here in a transport, in the contemplation of the glorious consequent privilege, to be *called* his *sons;* and of that admirable love, from whence the whole hath proceeded. *What manner;* ποταπὴν or, how great! *Called,* here, (as often referring to God as the author,) signifies to be made, or to be, Matt. v. 9, 45; John i. 12; Rom. iv. 17. He confers not the name without the thing; the new, even a Divine nature, 2 Pet. i. 4, in regeneration; the real advantages and dignity of the relation by adoption; and all of mere (and the greatest) kindness and good-will, Tit. iii. 5—7. Hence he intimates, it ought not to be counted grievous, that *the world knoweth us not,* i. e. doth not own or acknowledge us for its own, is not kind to us, yea, hates and persecutes us; knowing often (after the Hebrew phrase) signifying affection, 1 Cor. viii. 3; 2 Tim. ii. 19; and accordingly, not knowing, disaffection, and the consequent effects, Matt. vii. 23. Nor should it be thought strange, *because it knew him not:* the Father, and the whole family, are to it an *invisum genus,* hated alike.

2 Beloved, [c] now are we the sons of God, and [d] it doth not yet appear what we shall be: but we know that, when he shall appear, [e] we shall be like him; for [f] we shall see him as he is.

c Is. 56. 5.
Rom. 8. 15.
Gal. 3. 26. & 4. 6.
ch. 5. 1.
d Rom. 8.18.
2 Cor. 4. 17.
e Rom. 8. 29.
1 Cor. 15. 49.
Phil. 3. 21.

Col. 3. 4. 2 Pet. 1. 4. f Job 19. 26. Ps. 16. 11. Matt. 5. 8. 1 Cor. 13. 12. 2 Cor. 5. 7.

Our present state he affirms to be unquestionably that of *sons,* whatsoever hardships from the world, or severer discipline from our Father, we must for a while undergo; but for our future state, it is much above us to comprehend distinctly the glory of it; *it doth not yet appear,* it is yet an unrevealed thing, Rom. viii. 18; a veil is drawn before it, which is to be drawn aside at the appointed season of the manifestation of the sons of God, ver. 19. But so much we in the general know of it, (so certain are the apprehensions of faith,) that *when he shall appear,* or display his own glory in the appearance of his Son, who is there to come *in the glory of his Father,* Matt. xvi. 27; 1 Tim. vi. 14—16, *we shall be like him,* as it befits children to be unto their Father; i. e. his image shall then be perfected in us, which was defaced so greatly in the apostacy, is restored imperfectly in regeneration, Eph. iv. 24; Col. iii. 10, must be daily improved in progressive sanctification: so that as God was above said to be light, Christians are to *shine as lights, as the sons of God, without rebuke,* representing and glorifying their Father, Matt. v. 16; Phil. ii. 15; 1 Pet. ii. 9: but is then to be advanced in us to a far higher pitch than ever, in respect both of holiness and blessedness. *For we shall see him as he is;* i. e. so far as the limited capacity of our natures can admit; and are therefore by that likeness to be qualified for such vision: which eternal, efficacious vision doth also continue that likeness, the causal particle, *for,* admitting both those references: see Psal. xvii. 15.

3 [g] And every man that hath this hope in him purifieth himself, even as he is pure.

g ch. 4. 17.

Purifieth himself; i. e. not only is obliged hereto, but by the efficacious influence of this hope, if it be of the same kind, (that *lively hope,* unto which Christians are said to be *begotten,* 1 Pet. i. 3,) is daily more and more transformed, through a continual intention of mind towards the holy God, upon whom that hope is set, (for it is said to be hope *in him,* or rather upon him, ἐπ' αὐτῷ,) into the image of the Divine purity; knowing also, (which must be a potent inducement to very earnest endeavour this way,) that our future conformity to God in glory and blessedness hereafter, depends upon our present vigorous and effectual pursuit of conformity to him in holiness here, Matt. v. 8; Heb. xii. 14. And it is enforced by what follows.

4 Whosoever committeth sin transgresseth also the law: for [h] sin is the transgression of the law.

h Rom. 4.15. ch. 5. 17.

Which is added, to signify nothing can be more unreasonable, than the expectation of partaking with God in the glory and blessedness of the future state, if we now allow ourselves in a course of sin, or of transgressing his holy law, which is the very notion of sin; and is again further enforced from the design of our Redeemer.

5 And ye know [i] that he was manifest-

i ch. 1. 2.

I. JOHN III

ed ᵏto take away our sins; and ¹in him is no sin.

Implying how great an absurdity it were, to expect salvation and blessedness by our sinless Saviour, and yet indulge ourselves in sin, against his design, not only to expiate our sins, but make us sinless like himself.

6 Whosoever abideth in him sinneth not: ᵐwhosoever sinneth hath not seen him, neither known him.

By *sinneth*, he meaneth the same thing as afterwards by *committeth sin*: see ver. 8, 9. Seeing and knowing intend inward union, acquaintance, and converse; such as abode in him implies: see John v. 37; 3 John 11.

7 Little children, ⁿlet no man deceive you: ᵒhe that doeth righteousness is righteous, even as he is righteous.

This caution implies the zealous endeavour of the seducers of that time, to instil their poisonous doctrine and principles of licentiousness; and his own solicitude, lest these Christians should receive them, and be mischiefed by them. Whereas therefore they were wont to suggest, that a merely notional knowledge was enough to recommend men, and make them acceptable to God, though they lived never so impure lives; he inculcates, that only they that did righteousness, viz. in a continued course, living conformably to the rules of the gospel, were righteous; and that they must aim to be so, *even as he is righteous*; not only making the righteousness and holy life of Christ the object of their trust, but the pattern of their walking and practice.

8 ᵖHe that committeth sin is of the devil; for the devil sinneth from the beginning. For this purpose the Son of God was manifested, ᑫthat he might destroy the works of the devil.

He that committeth sin: the apostle's notion of committing sin may be interpreted by his own phrase, 3 John 11, ὁ κακοποιῶν, *a doer of evil*; and by that, used in both Testaments, *a worker of iniquity*; which is not every one that doth any one single act of sin; as his ὁ ποιῶν δικαιοσύνην, ver. 7, *a doer of righteousness*, and ὁ ἀγαθοποιῶν, 3 John 11, *a doer of good*, is not every one that doth any one righteous or good action; any more than we call him a worker or maker of any thing, (as signifying a manual occupation,) who only makes a single attempt, but him who hath acquired the habitual skill, and doth ordinarily employ himself accordingly. A worker or maker of sin, (as we may fitly render this ὁ ποιῶν τὴν ἁμαρτίαν,) is an habitual or customary sinner; one that sinneth with deliberation, not by surprise, from a prevailing habit, that either continueth him in a course of actual known sin, or that withholds him from repenting sincerely, and turning to God from the sin which he hath committed; by which repentance he should not only refrain from further gross acts of sin, (which an impenitent person upon other inducements may do,) but mortify and prevail against all sinful habits and inclinations. In the same sense he useth the expression of sinning, ver. 6, 9. And such a sinner, he says, *is of the devil*; as if he were born of him, were his child, really conformed to him, and having his sinning nature. As our Saviour tells the Jews, having applied to them the same phrase before of committing sin, John viii. 34, that they were of their father the devil, ver. 44. As also this apostle, 3 John 11, says, *He that doeth good is of God*, i. e. born of God, or his child; as we find he uses the expressions of being *born of God*, and *being of God*, promiscuously, and with indifference, ver. 9, 10; chap. v. 18, 19, the latter being elliptical in reference to the former. Whereas sin was therefore originally the devil's work, he adds, (as a further engagement against it,) that *the Son of God was manifested*, (as ver. 5,) appeared in the flesh, showed himself in this world of ours, on purpose *to destroy*, or (as the word signifies) that he might dissolve the frame of all such works.

9 ʳWhosoever is born of God doth not commit sin; for ˢhis seed remaineth in him: and he cannot sin, because he is born of God.

To be *born of God*, is, (in the words of a very learned annotator, Dr. Hammond,) "to have received some special influence from God, and by the help and power of that, to be raised to a pious life. Agreeably, γεγεννημένος ἐκ τοῦ Θεοῦ, *he that hath been born of God*, is literally, he that hath had such a blessed change wrought in him, by the operation of God's Spirit in his heart, as to be translated from the power of darkness into the kingdom of his own dear Son; transformed in the spirit of his mind, i. e. sincerely changed from all evil to all good; from an obedience to the flesh, &c., to an obedience to God. Only it is here to be noted, that the phrase is not so to be taken, as to denote only the act of this change; the first impression of this virtue on the patient, the single transient act of regeneration, or reformation; and that, in the preter tense, now past, but rather a continued course, a permanent state: so as a regenerate man and a child of God are one, and signify him that lives a pious and godly life, and continues to do so," &c. To the same purpose this author also speaks, note on John i. 13, and in his paraphrase on that verse: "Those which live according to the will of God, and neither the natural, nor carnal, nor bare moral principle." This change, introducing the consequent course, divers texts of Scripture explain, John iii. 3, 5, 6; 2 Cor. 17; Eph. ii. 10; iv. 24; James i. 18, &c. Now of one thus born of God, it is said, he *doth not commit sin*, as ver. 8, and for the reason here alleged. *His seed;* the principles of enlivened holy truth, as 1 Pet. i. 23; James i. 8. *And he cannot sin*: which is not to be understood simply, as if he could not sin at all, which were to contradict what he had said before, chap. i. 8, and supposed, chap. ii. 1; but he cannot commit sin, as ver. 8. And it is plain the apostle intends by these two expressions the same thing. He cannot *sin*, i. e. do an act of known, gross sin, deliberately, easily, remorselessly, maliciously, as Cain, ver. 12, out of a hatred of goodness: or, do not such acts customarily, or not so *unto death*, (as chap. v. 16,) but that through the advantage of inlaid principles, or the remaining seed, by dependence upon the grace, Spirit, and covenant of God in Christ, he may timously recover. *Because he is born of God;* i. e. inasmuch as it belongs to his temper and inclination, in respect of the holy new nature received in regeneration, to abhor from the grosser acts, much more from a course of sin; see Gen. xxxix. 9; Acts iv. 20; 2 Cor. xiii. 8; Gal. v. 17: and to his state, as he is a child of God, to have that interest in the grace of Christ, that he may implore, trust, obtain, and improve it, to his being kept from such destructive sinning. And it being evident, by his deep and thorough change, that he is born of God, and chosen to be an heir of eternal life, (as his children are heirs,) he may and ought (not in a way of presumptuous negligence, but of vigilance and humble dependence) certainly to expect being so kept. Nor is it strange so much should be affirmed, upon so unspeakably better grounds, of the Christian state, when such boasts are to be read concerning some among the pagans, that one might as soon divert the sun from its course, as turn such a one from the course of righteousness. Though we may also suppose this form of speech might be intended by the apostle to be understood by the more superficial professors of Christianity, (who might be generally apt enough to look upon themselves as born of God, and his children,) as parenetical, and more enforcingly hortatory, in pursuance of his former scope, to keep them off from the licentious courses of their seducers; q. d. It cannot be, that you, who avow yourselves born of God, should do like them. So we usually say, that cannot but be, or cannot be, which we apprehend more highly and clearly reasonable should be, or not be. *Non potes avelli*, &c. Such rhetoric the apostle uses with Agrippa, *I know that thou believest*, as if it were impossible he should not.

10 In this the children of God are manifest, and the children of the devil: ᵗwhosoever doeth not righteousness is not of God, ᵘneither he that loveth not his brother.

Upon what was said, he reduces all men each to their

own family and father, concluding it manifest whither they belonged; i. e. he shows, upon the grounds before expressed, who do not belong to God and his family, leaving it thence to be collected, since two fathers and families divide the world, to which they must be reckoned; i. e. they belong not to God, and consequently to that worst of fathers, who first, in the general, do not righteousness; the devil being the first sinner, they are his descendants; and who next, particularly, love not their brethren, which most expressly demonstrates a diabolical nature.

x ch. 1. 5.
& 2. 7.
‖ Or, commandment.
y John 13. 34. & 15. 12.
ver. 23. ch. 4. 7, 21. 2 John 5.

11 For ˣ this is the ‖ message that ye heard from the beginning, ʸ that we should love one another.

From the beginning: see chap. ii. 7, 8: q. d. They cannot be of God, therefore, that cross so fundamental a precept, so expressive of his nature and will.

z Gen. 4. 4.
& Heb. 11.
4. Jude 11.

12 Not as ᶻ Cain, *who* was of that wicked one, and slew his brother. And wherefore slew he him? Because his own works were evil, and his brother's righteous.

And what again, on the other hand, (q. d.) can be more devil-like, than such a temper as Cain's was, whose hatred of his brother brake out into actual murder, upon no other account but because his brother was better than he? Which showed him to be *of that wicked one*, of the serpent's seed: so early was such seed sown, and so ancient the enmity between seed and seed.

a John 15. 18, 19. & 17.
14. 2 Tim. 3 12.

13 Marvel not, my brethren, if ᵃ the world hate you.

This being so devilish a quality, and the world so generally under his power, as *the god* of it, 2 Cor. iv. 4, it is not to be thought strange, that good men should be the marks and designed objects of the world's hatred.

b ch. 2. 10.

14 ᵇ We know that we have passed from death unto life, because we love the brethren. ᶜ He that loveth not *his* brother abideth in death.

c ch. 2. 9, 11.

The notion of *brother* must not be understood so narrowly, as only to signify such as we have particular inclination to, as being of our own party and opinion, or kindred, or who have obliged us by special kindness; for to confine our love within such limits, were no argument of our having *passed from death unto life*, or more than is to be found with the worst of men, Matt. v. 46, 47. Nor must it be understood exclusively, of the regenerate only; but must be taken, first, more generally, in the natural sense, for all mankind, in the same latitude as *neighbour* in that summary of the second table, Thou shalt love thy *neighbour as thyself*; originally intended not to Jews, as such, but men; and therefore excludes not our enemies, by our Saviour's interpretation, Matt. v. 43, 44. Secondly, in a more special (viz. the spiritual) sense, for such as are our brethren by regeneration, so the children with us of the same Father; i. e. whereas the blessed God himself is the *primum amabile*, the first object of love, all others (persons or things) ought to be loved proportionally to what prints or characters of the Divine excellency we find impressed upon them. Human nature hath resemblances in his spiritual, intelligent, immortal nature; regeneracy, of his holiness. And so he loves his creatures himself, severing their malignity, (where that is to be found,) that is of themselves, from what of real good there is in them, which is from him. When therefore a correspondent frame of love is impressed upon us, and inwrought into our temper, his image, who *is love*, is renewed in us, which, in this noble part of it, the devil had so eminently defaced in the world, possessing the souls of men with mutual animosities and enmities against one another, but especially such as should be found to have upon them any impress of the most excellent kind of goodness, i. e. of true piety and holiness. And by this renovation of his image in us, whereby we are enabled to love others for his sake, and proportionably to what characters of him are upon them, we appear to be his children, Matt. v. 45, begotten of him into a state of life, out of that death which is upon the rest of the world, Eph. ii. 1. and wherein every one still abides that thus loves not his brother.

15 ᵈ Whosoever hateth his brother is a murderer: and ye know that ᵉ no murderer hath eternal life abiding in him.

d Matt. 5. 21, 22. ch. 4. 20.
e Gal. 5. 21.
Rev. 21. 8.

That life into which the regenerate are begotten, is nothing else than the beginning or first principle of eternal life, John iv. 14, whereof they cannot but be destitute who hate their brethren; a thing so contrary to the Divine life, nature, and image, and which makes the person affected with it, in the temper and habit of his mind, a very murderer.

16 ᶠ Hereby perceive we the love of God, because he laid down his life for us: and we ought to lay down *our* lives for the brethren.

f John 3. 16.
& 15. 13.
Rom. 5. 8.
Eph. 5. 2, 25.
ch. 4. 9, 11.

He laid down his life for us: the intimate union between the Divine nature and the human in Christ, gives ground for the calling Christ's life as man the life of God; as, Acts xx. 28, his blood is said to be God's *own blood*. And this testimony of God's love to us, his laying down his life for us, ought so to transform us into his likeness, that out of the power of that Divine principle, the love of God in us, (so that implanted love is called, ver. 17, *the love of God*,) we should never hesitate, or make a difficulty, to lay down our lives for the Christian community, or even for the common good and welfare of men, being duly called thereto.

17 But ᵍ whoso hath this world's good, and seeth his brother have need, and shutteth up his bowels *of compassion* from him, ʰ how dwelleth the love of God in him?

g Deut. 15. 7.
Luke 3. 11.

h ch. 4. 20.

i. e. If the love of God in us should make us lay down our lives for the brethren, and we be not willing, in their necessity and our own ability, to relieve them, how plain is the case, that it is not in us!

18 My little children, ⁱ let us not love in word, neither in tongue; but in deed and in truth.

i Ezek. 33. 31. Rom. 12. 9. Eph. 4. 15.
Jam. 2. 15.
1 Pet. 1. 22.

q. d. It is a vain thing to make verbal pretences of love, without any real proof of it.

19 And hereby we know ᵏ that we are of the truth, and shall † assure our hearts before him.

k John 18. 37. ch. 1. 8.
† Gr. *persuade*.

And hereby we know that we are of the truth; i. e. this shall demonstrate to us, that we are the children of the truth, begotten by it, James i. 18, when we resemble it, have the correspondent impress of the gospel (that great representation of the love of God) upon us. *And shall assure our hearts before him*; so shall our hearts be quieted, and well satisfied concerning our states God-ward.

20 ˡ For if our heart condemn us, God is greater than our heart, and knoweth all things.

l 1 Cor. 4. 4.

If our heart, or our conscience, *condemn us*, viz. in plain things, (as this of loving our brother is,) and wherein the mind of God is evidently the same with our own conscience; his superiority, to whom our conscience is but an under-judge, ought much more to awe us, especially considering how much more he knows of us than we do of ourselves; as 1 Cor. iv. 4.

21 ᵐ Beloved, if our heart condemn us not, ⁿ *then* have we confidence toward God.

m Job 22. 26.
n Heb. 10. 22.
ch. 2. 28.
& 4. 17.

But for their not condemning us, though the expression be merely negative, it must imply somewhat positive; for there are many whose hearts condemn them not, through ignorance of their rule, or oscitancy, self-indulgence, or neglect of themselves. But if after thorough search, with sincerity in the sight of God, our hearts do not condemn, but acquit us, as upright towards him, not willing to allow ourselves in any ill temper or practice, (such as, for instance, this of not loving, or neglecting, our brother,) *then we have confidence* (liberty of speech the word literally signifies, which well suits with what follows) *toward God*;

we have nothing to hinder or lie as a bar against us in our recourse to him.

22 And °whatsoever we ask, we receive of him, because we keep his commandments, ᴾand do those things that are pleasing in his sight.

o Ps. 34. 15. & 145. 18, 19. Prov. 15. 29. Jer. 29. 12. Matt. 7. 8. & 21. 22. Mark 11. 24. John 14. 13. & 15. 7. & 16. 23, 24. Jam. 5. 16. ch. 5. 14. p John 8. 29. & 9. 31.

It is supposed, where there is that accord with God, that what was last, and is next after, said implies, there will be no disposition to ask any thing disagreeable to his will, or otherwise than as he hath expressed his will about the matter of prayer. And then, *whatsoever we ask, we receive,* i. e. are as sure to receive it, in the kind or in equivalence, as if we had it, chap. v. 14. *Because we keep his commandments;* i. e. this is the cause of our certainty, being the evidence of our state God-ward, Psal. lxvi. 18, 19; not of our receiving the things prayed for, which we only owe to his free promised mercy in Christ.

23 ᑫAnd this is his commandment, That we should believe on the name of his Son Jesus Christ, ʳand love one another, ˢas he gave us commandment.

q John 6. 29. & 17. 3. r Mat. 22. 39. John 13. 34. & 15. 12. Eph. 5. 2. 1 Thess. 4. 9. 1 Pet. 4. 8. ver. 11. ch. 4. 21. s ch. 2. 8, 10.

Thus briefly is comprehended the whole of our duty towards God in Christ, and one another, in a like summary as that, Eccles. xii. 13.

24 And ᵗhe that keepeth his commandments ᵘdwelleth in him, and he in him. And ˣhereby we know that he abideth in us, by the Spirit which he hath given us.

t John 14. 23, & 15. 10. ch. 4. 12, u John 17. 21, &c. x Rom. 8. 9. ch. 4. 13.

He that keepeth his commandments, i. e. he whose whole soul is thus formed to obediential compliance with the Divine will, *dwelleth in him;* hath most intimate union with God in Christ; which is evident by that *Spirit given to us,* which hath effected both that holy frame, and that union: see John xiv. 23,

---

CHAP. IV

The apostle warneth to try by certain rules the spirits that pretend to come from God, 1—6. *He presseth the obligation of mutual love upon Christians from the example and commandment of God,* 7—21.

BELOVED, ᵃbelieve not every spirit, but ᵇtry the spirits whether they are of God: because ᶜmany false prophets are gone out into the world.

a Jer. 29. 8. Matt. 24. 4. b 1 Cor. 14. 29. 1 Thess. 5. 21. Rev. 2. 2. c Matt. 24. 5, 24. Acts 20. 30. 1 Tim. 4. 1. 2 Pet. 2. 1. ch. 2. 18. 2 John 7.

Believe not every spirit; i. e. not every one pretending to inspiration, or a revelation; *spirit,* whether good or bad, being put for the person acted thereby. *But try the spirits;* there being a judgment of discretion or discerning, common to Christians, *de jure,* and which they ought to endeavour for and to use upon such occasions, Acts xvii. 11; Phil. i. 9, 10; 1 Thess. v. 21; and the attainment and exercise whereof is, in reference to the great essentials of religion, more facile and sure: as when heretofore among the Jews, any should attempt the drawing them off from the true God, as Deut. xiii. 1, 2; and so when with Christians it should be endeavoured to tempt them away from Christ, as the *false prophets* or teachers did, now *gone out into the world.*

2 Hereby know ye the Spirit of God: ᵈEvery spirit that confesseth that Jesus Christ is come in the flesh is of God:

d 1 Cor. 12. 3. ch. 5. 1.

He here gives them the general rule, both affirmative and negative, which would suffice them to judge by in their present case; this being the great controversy of that time with the Jews, Whether Jesus were the Messiah? and whether the Messiah were as yet come or no? and with the Gnostics, Whether he were really come in the flesh, in true human nature? or were not, as to that appearance, a mere phantasm? And he affirms, They that confessed him so come, were of God; i. e. thus far they were in the right, this truth was of God. Of the two litigating parties, this was of God, the other not of God; this took his side, that was against him. Yea, and they that not only made this true confession, but did also truly confess him, i. e. sincerely, cordially, practically, so as accordingly to trust in him, subject and devote themselves to him, were born of God, his very children, acted and influenced hereunto by his own Holy Spirit, as chap. v. 1, 5; Matt. xvi. 16, 17; 1 Cor. xii. 3.

3 And ᵉevery spirit that confesseth not that Jesus Christ is come in the flesh is not of God: and this is that *spirit* of antichrist, whereof ye have heard that it should come; and ᶠeven now already is it in the world.

e ch. 2. 22. 2 John 7. f 2 Thess. 2. 7. ch. 2. 18, 22.

But on the contrary, concerning them who against so plain evidence denied him to be so come, the case was plain; as with the Jews, John viii. 24, and with the present heretics, who denying the true manner, could not but deny the true end of his coming; and who also lived so impure lives, as imported the most open opposition and hostility thereto, and so discovered most evidently that antichristian spirit, which it was foreknown would show itself in the world.

4 ᵍYe are of God, little children, and have overcome them: because greater is he that is in you, than ʰhe that is in the world.

g ch. 5. 4. h John 12. 31. & 14. 30. & 16. 11. 1 Cor. 2. 12. Eph. 2. 2. & 6. 12.

Their being born of God, and their participation of a directive and strengthening influence from him, kept them from being overcome by the plausible notions, the alluring blandishments of the flesh and sense, the terror of persecution used towards them by these antichristian or pseudo-christian tempters; and enabled them to overcome, because the Divine Spirit in them was stronger than the others' lying, impure spirit.

5 ⁱThey are of the world: therefore speak they of the world, and ᵏthe world heareth them.

i John 3. 31. k John 15. 19. & 17. 14.

6 We are of God: ˡhe that knoweth God heareth us; he that is not of God heareth not us. Hereby know we ᵐthe spirit of truth, and the spirit of error.

l John 8. 47. & 10. 27. 1 Cor. 14. 37. 2 Cor. 10. 7. m Is. 8. 20. John 14. 17.

He giveth here a further rule whereby to judge of doctrines and teachers, viz. what they severally savour of, and tend to. The doctrines and teachers whereby these Christians were assaulted and tempted, were of an earthly savour and gust, tending only to gratify worldly lusts and inclinations, and to serve secular interests and designs; and therefore men only of a worldly spirit and temper were apt to listen and give entertainment to them. On the other hand, says he, (in the name of the asserters and followers of true and pure Christianity, comprehended with himself,) *We are of God;* i. e. our doctrine and way proceed from God, and tend only to serve, please, and glorify him, and draw all to him; therefore such as *know God,* i. e. are his friends, and converse much with him, *hear us;* the things we propose and offer are grateful and savoury to them, (as John viii. 37, 47,) having manifestly no other aim than to promote serious godliness. And hereby may *the spirit of truth and the spirit of error* in matters of this nature be distinguished; the one being next of kin to purity, and holiness, and a godly life; the other, to sensuality, and a design only of gratifying the animal life.

7 ⁿBeloved, let us love one another: for love is of God; and every one that loveth is born of God, and knoweth God.

n ch. 3. 10, 11, 23.

Beloved, let us love one another: in opposition to the malice and cruelty of these enemies to true and pure Christianity, he exhorteth to mutual love, not limited to themselves, as undoubtedly he did not intend, see note on chap. iii. 14; but that they should do their part towards all others, letting it lie upon them, if it were not reciprocated and mutual. *For love is of God;* this he presses as a further discrimination; nothing being more evidential of relation and alliance to God, than a duly regulated love, which is of him.

I. JOHN IV, V

8 He that loveth not °knoweth not God; for ᵖGod is love.

Yea, since love is his very nature, and that *God is love*, those that love (upon the account and in the way above expressed) are born of him, partake from him that excellent and most delectable nature, know him by a transformative knowledge : but they that love not, they are mere strangers to him, and never had to do with him.

9 ᑫIn this was manifested the love of God toward us, because that God sent his only begotten Son into the world, ʳthat we might live through him.

There could be no higher demonstration of his love, John iii. 16.

10 Herein is love, ˢnot that we loved God, but that he loved us, and sent his Son ᵗ*to be* the propitiation for our sins.

In comparison of this wonderful love of his, in sending his Son to be a sacrifice for sins, our love to him is not worthy the name of love.

11 Beloved, ᵘif God so loved us, we ought also to love one another.

We discover little sense of this love of his to us, if we do not so.

12 ˣNo man hath seen God at any time. If we love one another, God dwelleth in us, and ʸhis love is perfected in us.

The essence of God is to our eyes invisible, incomprehensible to our minds; but by yielding ourselves to the power of his love, so as to be transformed by it, and habituated to the exercise of mutual love, we come to know him by the most pleasant and most apprehensible effects, experiencing his indwelling, vital, operative presence and influences, whereby he is daily perfecting this his own likeness and image in us. This is the most desirable way of knowing God, when, though we cannot behold him at a distance, we may feelingly apprehend him nigh us, and in us.

13 ᶻHereby know we that we dwell in him, and he in us, because he hath given us of his Spirit.

The near inward union between him and us, is best to be discerned by the operations of his Spirit, which is the Spirit of all love and goodness, chap. iii. 24: Eph. v. 9.

14 And ᵃwe have seen and do testify that ᵇ the Father sent the Son *to be* the Saviour of the world.

He here signifies we are not left at any uncertainties, touching that matter of fact, wherein lies this mighty argument for the exercise of mutual love among Christians, God's having *sent the Son to be the Saviour of the world*; for, as he again inculcates, we testify upon eye-sight, having beheld him, and conversed with him, living and dying.

15 ᶜWhosoever shall confess that Jesus is the Son of God, God dwelleth in him, and he in God.

This discourse is most studiously and observably interwoven, of these two great things, mentioned chap. iii. 23, faith in the Messiah, and the love of one another, as being the principal antidotes against the poisonous insinuations of the apostates. Of confessing, see note on ver. 2.

16 And we have known and believed the love that God hath to us. ᵈGod is love; and ᵉhe that dwelleth in love dwelleth in God, and God in him.

Inasmuch as the transformative efficacy of God's love upon us depends upon our certain apprehension of it, he doubles the expression of that certainty: *We have known and believed*, i. e. we are assured of it, both by experimented effects, and by faith; implying, that by having this conception of God thoroughly settled in our souls, that he *is love*, (as was also said, ver. 8,) we shall be so thoroughly changed into his very nature and image, as to *dwell in love*, as in our own element, or a thing now become wholly con-

natural to us. Which will indeed be (by consequence) to be so intimately united with God, that he and we may truly (though in a sense most remote from identification, or being made the same, a horrid notion ! not only not inferred by what is here said, but inconsistent with it and refused by it, for things united are thereby implied to be distinct) be said to indwell one another.

17 Herein is †our love made perfect, that ᶠwe may have boldness in the day of judgment : ᵍbecause as he is, so are we in this world.

And by this means (viz. of our inwardness with God) doth our love grow to that perfection, that we shall have the most fearless freedom and liberty of spirit in the judgment-day; our hearts no way misgiving to appear before him as a Judge, whose very image we find upon ourselves, he having beforehand made us such even in this world, though in an infinitely inferior degree, as he is, compositions of love and goodness. Or, if *the day of judgment* should mean, as some conceive, of our appearance before human tribunals for his sake, such a temper of spirit must give us the same boldness in that case also.

18 There is no fear in love ; but perfect love casteth out fear : because fear hath torment. He that feareth ʰis not made perfect in love.

That he proveth from the contrary natures of fear and love. The fear which is of the baser kind, viz. that is servile, and depresses the spirit, hath no place with love, but is excluded by it, by the same degrees by which that love grows up to perfection, and shall be quite excluded by that love fully perfected : inasmuch as love is a pleasant, fear a tormenting, passion, which, as such, while it remains, shows the imperfection of love.

19 We love him, because he first loved us.

His is the fountain love, ours but the stream : his love the inducement, the pattern, and the effective cause of ours. He that is first in love, loves freely ; the other therefore loves under obligation.

20 ⁱIf a man say, I love God, and hateth his brother, he is a liar : for he that loveth not his brother whom he hath seen, how can he love God ᵏwhom he hath not seen ?

The greater difficulty here is implied, through our present dependence upon sense, of loving the invisible God, than men that we daily see and converse familiarly with. Hence, considering the comprehensiveness of these two things, the love of God, and of our brother, that they are the roots of all that duty we owe to God and man, the fulfilling of the whole law, Matt. xxii. 37—39, he lets us see the falsehood and absurdity of their pretence to eminent piety and sanctity, who neglect the duties of the second table.

21 And ˡthis commandment have we from him, That he who loveth God love his brother also.

Both ought to be conjoined, being required both by the same authority.

CHAP. V

He that loveth God loveth God's children, and keepeth his commandments, 1—3. *A true faith will enable us to overcome the world,* 4, 5. *The witnesses of our faith,* 6—10. *God hath given to believers eternal life through his Son,* 11—13 ; *and will hear and grant their petitions, made according to his will,* 14—17. *God's children are distinguished from the world by abstaining from sin, and by a right knowledge,* 18—20. *A caution against idolatry,* 21.

WHOSOEVER ᵃbelieveth that ᵇJesus is the Christ is ᶜborn of God : ᵈand every one that loveth him that begat loveth him also that is begotten of him.

Whosoever believeth that Jesus is the Christ ; this is not meant of a mere professed, or of a slight and superficial, but of a lively, efficacious, unitive, soul-transforming, and obediential faith in Jesus as the Christ, which is elsewhere made the effect of the regenerating power and grace of God, John i. 12, 13. And as nothing can be more connatural to such a heaven-born faith, than the loving of him that hath begotten us to it; so nothing can be more certainly consequent and agreeable, than the loving of them too who are begotten also of the same Father, viz. with a correspondent love to the more excellent characters and image of God upon them, than are upon other men.

2 By this we know that we love the children of God, when we love God, and keep his commandments.

It is not otherwise to be known that we truly love the children of God, as such; for if we do, we must love them upon God's account, in conformity to him, and obedience to his commandments; wherefore our true love to them supposes our love to him, and is to be evinced by it.

3 ᵉ For this is the love of God, that we keep his commandments: and ᶠ his commandments are not grievous.

For this is the love of God, i. e. this is the most lively, certain expression and effect of our love to God, our keeping his commandments, which are so little grievous, that true love can make no difficulty of doing so, Matt. xi. 30; Psal. xix. 11.

4 For ᵍ whatsoever is born of God overcometh the world: and this is the victory that overcometh the world, *even* our faith.

He explains himself, viz. that to one who is born of God his commandments are not grievous, because such a one, in that divine birth, hath received a life and nature that makes him far superior to this world, exalts him above it, makes him victorious over the worldly spirit, (as chap. iv. 4.) over all worldly desires, and fears, and hopes, and joys, which are the great hinderances of our obedience to God. *This is the victory;* i. e. the instrument, the weapon, by which they overcome, and which virtually includes in itself this victory over the world, as effects are included in the power of their cause, is their *faith,* that principle which in their regeneration (as above) is implanted in them.

5 Who is he that overcometh the world, but ʰ he that believeth that Jesus is the Son of God?

For that faith, viz. *that Jesus is the Son of God,* (or the Christ, as ver. 1,) fills the soul with so great things concerning him, and the design of his coming among us, and what we are to expect thereupon, as easily turn this world into a contemptible shadow, and deprive it of all its former power over us.

6 This is he that came ⁱ by water and blood, *even* Jesus Christ; not by water only, but by water and blood. ᵏ And it is the Spirit that beareth witness, because the Spirit is truth.

For the explaining of this obscure place we must proceed by degrees. 1. It is evident, that *water and blood* cannot be here meant literally. 2. It is therefore consequent, that they must be intended to signify somewhat or other by way of symbolical representation, or that they must have some mystical meaning. 3. They ought to have such a meaning assigned them, as will both be agreeable to the expressions themselves, and to the apostle's present scope and design. 4. It will be very agreeable to the expressions, to understand by *water* the purity of our blessed Lord, and by *blood* his sufferings. 5. His manifest scope and design is, to show the abundantly sufficient credibility of the witnesses and testimony we have, to assure us that Jesus was the Christ, or the Messiah, and to induce us to believe this of him, with so efficacious and transforming a faith, as should evidence our being born of God, and make us so victorious over the world, as constantly to adhere to this Jesus by trust and obedience, against all the allurements and terrors of it. 6. This being his scope, it supposeth that the mentioned coming of Jesus, as Messiah, was for some known end, unto his accomplishment whereof these two, his purity and his sufferings, were apt and certain means, as that they were to be considered under the notion of means, his being said to have come διὰ, by them, doth intimate. And in pursuance of this scope, he must be understood to signify, that his coming so remarkably by these two, did carry with it some very convictive proof and evidence of his being the Son of God, and the Messiah, sufficient to recommend him as the most deserving object of such a faith, and render it highly reasonable we should hereupon so trust and obey him, and entirely resign ourselves to his mercy and government. Wherefore also, 7. This his coming must here be understood in a sense accommodated hereunto, and is therefore in no reason to be taken for the very act or instant, precisely, of his entrance into this world, but to signify his whole course in it, from first to last, a continued motion and agency, correspondent to the intendment of his mission. To the clearing of which notion of his coming, some light may be gained, by considering the account which is given, 2 Thess. ii. 9, 10, of the coming of antichrist, which is said to be *after Satan,* (as it were by his impulsion, and in pursuance of his ends and purposes,) *with all power, and signs, and lying wonders, and all deceivableness of unrighteousness;* where it is manifest, coming must signify a continued course of doing business. So here, our Lord's coming must signify his continual employment for the despatch of the business about which he was sent. 8. The known business and end for which he was sent, was to reduce and bring back sinners to God. 9. How apt and necessary means these two, his purity and sufferings, were to this end, the whole frame of the gospel shows. His sacrifice of himself, in his sufferings, was necessary to our reconciliation; so he was to come and effect his work *by blood:* his purity was requisite to the acceptableness of his sacrifice; so it was to be done *by water;* without which, as was wont to be proverbially said among the Hebrews, there could be no sacrifice. 10. For the evidence his coming so remarkably by these two carried with it, for the inducing of us to believe him to be the Messiah, with such a faith, as whereby we should imitate his purity, and rely upon the value of his sufferings. We may see it in the note upon ver. 8, where the testimony o these two witnesses, the water and the blood, comes to be given in its own place and order. 11. Nor is it strange the apostle should use these mystical expressions to this purpose, if we consider what might lead him thereto: for we must remember, first, That he was a spectator of our Lord's crucifixion, and then beheld, upon the piercing of his side, the streaming forth of the water and blood; which, it appears, at that time made a very deep impression upon his mind, as his words about it in his writing his Gospel import: *There came out blood and water. And he that saw it bare record, and his record is true: and he knoweth that he saith true, that ye might believe,* John xix. 34, 35. That he there lays so great a weight on it, imports that he apprehended some great mystery, if not intended, yet very apt to be signified by it. And, secondly, That he was a Jew, and (as is probable) wrote this Epistle to Jews, among whom the so frequent ablutions with water, as well as the shedding the blood of sacrifices, were most known things, and intended to typify (what they ought to have understood, and he now intimates) these very things, the purity and dying of the Messiah. Not to insist upon what he had long ere now occasion to observe in the Christian church, baptism, and the supper of our Lord, representing in effect severally the same things. Neither was this way of teaching unusual, nor these expressions less intelligible, than our Lord's calling himself (as this evangelist also records) a *shepherd,* a *door,* a *vine,* &c.

And it is the Spirit that beareth witness: that the Spirit is said to bear witness, see ver. 7, 8.

7 For there are three that bear record in heaven, the Father, ˡ the Word, and the Holy Ghost: ᵐ and these three are one.

Having mentioned the Spirit's testifying in the close of ver. 6, he returns to give us in order, in these two verses, the whole testimony of the truth of Christianity, which he reduces to two ternaries of witnesses. The matter of their testimony is the same with that of their faith who are born of God, *that Jesus is the Son of God*, and the Messiah, as may be collected from what was said before, ver. 1, 5, and what is said afterwards, ver. 9. What they believe, is no other thing than what these testify. For the first three, *in heaven*, that is not said to signify heaven to be the place of their testifying; for though the same thing concerning Jesus be also no doubt testified to the glorious inhabitants of that world, yet that is not the apostle's present scope, but to show what reason we have, who inhabit this world, to believe Jesus to be Christ, and the Son of God. *In heaven* therefore is to be referred to *three*, not to *bear record*, or witness; as if the text were read, which it may as well, There are three in heaven who bear witness; the design being to represent their immediate testifying from thence unto us, or the glorious, heavenly, majestic manner of their testifying. So the Father testified of the man Jesus by immediate voice from heaven, at his baptism and transfiguration, *This is my Son*, &c. The eternal Word owned its union with him, in that glory with which it so eminently clothed his humanity, and which visibly shone through it in the holy mount, whereof this apostle was a spectator, and whereto he seems to refer in his Gospel, chap. i. 14, *We beheld his glory, the glory as of the only begotten of the Father*, i. e. such as sufficiently testified him to be so, even the very Son of God. And the Holy Ghost testified, descending *as a dove* in a visible glorious appearance upon him, at his baptism also. *And these three are one*, viz. not only agreeing in their testimony, as ver. 8, but in unity of nature: an express testimony of the triune Deity, by whatsoever carelessness or ill design left out of some copies, but sufficiently demonstrated by many most ancient ones, to belong to the sacred text: of which L. Brug. Not. in loc., with the other critics, and at large, Dr. Hammond.

8 And there are three that bear witness in earth, the spirit, and the water, and the blood: and these three agree in one.

And for the three that are said to *bear witness on earth;* there is, first, *the Spirit*, who, though the Holy Ghost were in the former triad, needs not here be taken for another Spirit, but may be the same, considered under another notion, and as testifying in another manner; not transiently and immediately from heaven, as there, but statedly, and as inacting instruments here on earth; extraordinarily, the man Christ Jesus, all his apostles and first disciples, in all the wonderful works which they did for the confirmation of the Christian doctrine; and ordinarily, the whole church of true Christians; for it animates the whole living body of Christ, and makes it, though in an imperfect measure, by a uniform course of actions, tending to God and heaven, an extant visible proof to the world of the truth of that religion which obtains in it, and of his Divine power and nature who is the Head of it. Next, *the water;* i. e. the continual untainted, God-like purity of our Lord Jesus, through the whole course of his terrestrial state, manifestly showed him to be the Son of God, an incarnate Deity, inhabiting our world. And lastly, *the blood*, his suffering of death, considered in the circumstances, was a most conspicuous, clear testimony and indication who he was; so exactly according to the predictions of the prophets, attended with wonderful amazing concomitants, ending in so glorious a resurrection. And in and with both these *the Spirit*, complicating his testimony, did bear witness too, as is intimated (after the former mention of them both) in the latter part of ver. 6. It testified all along, both in his clear, immaculate life, and in the bloody death in which it assisted him, which it accompanied with so marvellous effects, and out of which at length it fetched him, Rom. i. 4. And that part it took, as being *the Spirit of truth*, ver. 6, and, as it is there expressed, in the (more emphatical) abstract, truth itself.

9 If we receive ⁿ the witness of men, the witness of God is greater: º for this is the witness of God which he hath testified of his Son.

A testimony above exception, being wholly Divine, as he himself argued, John v. 36, 37; viii. 13, 14, 17, 18.

10 He that believeth on the Son of God ᵖ hath the witness in himself: he that believeth not God ᵠ hath made him a liar; because he believeth not the record that God gave of his Son.

i. e. If he truly believe, he hath the effectual impress of this testimony on his own soul; if not, he gives God the lie, as we do to any one whose testimony we believe not. See John iii. 33.

11 ʳ And this is the record, that God hath given to us eternal life, and ˢ this life is in his Son.

His testimony, that this is his Son and the Christ, imports so much, that eternal life is in him, as the source and fountain of it; so that he gives it to us in no other way than in and by him.

12 ᵗ He that hath the Son hath life; *and* he that hath not the Son of God hath not life.

And therefore, that we partake this life, or partake it not, as by faith we are united with him, or not united.

13 ᵘ These things have I written unto you that believe on the name of the Son of God; ʷ that ye may know that ye have eternal life, and that ye may believe on the name of the Son of God.

That, discerning their own faith, they might be in no doubt concerning their title to eternal life, and might be thereby encouraged to persevere in the same faith.

14 And this is the confidence that we have ∥ in him, that, ˣ if we ask any thing according to his will, he heareth us:

Viz. *according to his will*, not negatively, as it only doth not forbid our praying for, or enjoying, such and such things, but positively, i. e. according to his will signified, 1. By his commands, i. e. when the matter of our prayers is some spiritual good thing, which was before the matter of our duty; as when we pray for grace to enable us to be and to do what he requires us, as far as our present state will admit. 2. By his promises, which are more absolute and particular in reference to things of that nature, Matt. v. 6; Luke xi. 13. In reference to things of an inferior nature, of a conditional tenor; or more general, the things promised coming under the common notion of good things, not in themselves only, but for us, in present circumstances; which, whether they be or no, he reserves to himself the liberty of determining, and doth only promise them, if they be; and so we are only to pray for them; for that is praying, according to what signification he hath given us of his will, in such cases. And so we are always sure to be heard in the former case, in the very particular kind, about which his will is expressly made known beforehand.

15 And if we know that he hear us, whatsoever we ask, we know that we have the petitions that we desired of him.

In the latter, in that, or somewhat equivalent, or better; for if he determine that thing to be best for us, all circumstances considered, we shall have it; if he determine otherwise, (supposing we pray according to his will,) we desire it not: for every one intends good to himself, when he prays for any thing, not hurt. And God answers his children according to that general meaning of their prayers, not always according to the particular (which may be often a much mistaken) meaning. According whereto, supposing the thing would be really and in truth hurtful, (and God's judgment is always according to truth,) they constructively pray to be denied it; and the denial is the equivalent, nay, the better thing than what they particularly prayed for; and so they truly have their petitions: see chap. iii. 22. Nor can any be understood to pray according to God's will as the rule, if it be not to his glory as the end, as the order and connexion of petitions shows in that admirable platform prescribed by our Lord himself. And is it possible to be the sense of any one that hath a sincere heart in prayer, that God would gratify him against himself? Therefore that latitude allowed the apostles, John xiv. 13, 14; xv. 16; xvi. 23, &c., must be understood to respect

I. JOHN V

the service of the Christian interest, and is to be limited thereby, as some of the expressions show.

16 If any man see his brother sin a sin *which is* not unto death, he shall ask, and ʸ he shall give him life for them that sin not unto death. ᶻ There is a sin unto death: ᵃ I do not say that he shall pray for it.

If any man see his brother sin a sin which is not unto death; viz. that appears not obstinate and incurable; *he shall ask,* i. e. with *confidence,* as ver. 14. But *there is a sin unto death,* i. e. which doth not barely deserve death, as all sin doth, nor which argues a person to be probably in a present state of death or unregeneracy, which the sinful ways may do of many that never made profession; but of such as have apostatized from a former specious profession into heresy and debauchery, and continue obstinate therein, against all methods of recovery; that are, as Jude 12, even *twice dead,* &c. *I do not say that he shall pray for it;* i. e. I do not give that encouragement to pray for such, with that hope and expectation of success, as for others; though he doth not simply forbid praying for them neither.

17 ᵇ All unrighteousness is sin: and there is a sin not unto death.

He intimates they should be cautious of all sin, especially more deliberate, (which the word ἀδικία seems to import,) but would not have them account that every sin would make their case so hopeless, as such sin, which he called sinning unto death, would do.

18 We know that ᶜ whosoever is born of God sinneth not; but he that is begotten of God ᵈ keepeth himself, and that wicked one toucheth him not.

The great advantage is here signified of the regenerate, who, by the seed remaining in them, (as chap. iii. 9,) are furnished with a self-preserving principle, with the exercise whereof they may expect that co-operation of a gracious Divine influence by which they shall be kept, so as *that wicked one,* the great destroyer of souls, shall not mortally touch them, to make them sin unto death.

19 *And* we know that we are of God, and ᵉ the whole world lieth in wickedness.

And this he doth not exclusively assume to himself, but expresses his charitable confidence of them to whom he writes, that it was their privilege, in common with him, to be thus *of God,* or born of him; notwithstanding the generality of men were under the power of that beforementioned wicked one, (as that phrase may be read,) or in the midst of all impurity and malignity.

20 And we know that the Son of God is come, and ᶠ hath given us an understanding, ᵍ that we may know him that is true, and we are in him that is true, *even* in his Son Jesus Christ. ʰ This is the true God, ⁱ and eternal life.

It is here signified how satisfying a knowledge and certainty sincere Christians had, that Christ was indeed come, by that blessed effect they found upon themselves, viz. a clear and lively light shining, by his procurement and communication, into their minds, whereby they had other apprehensions, more vivid and powerful than ever before, of *the true God,* as John xvii. 3, so as thereby to be drawn into union with him, and to be *in him:* or, which in effect is the same thing, (so entire is the oneness between the Father and the Son,) *we are in his Son Jesus Christ,* who also *is the true God,* as John i. 1, *and eternal life,* as he is called, chap. i. 2.

21 Little children, ᵏ keep yourselves from idols. Amen.

i. e. From those idolatrous communions with the Gentiles in their worship and festivals in their temples, which these pseudo-christians had latitude enough for, as appears by the apostle St. Paul's discourses, 1 Cor. viii.; x. 14 (especially if any danger did urge); wherein, instead of that communion with the Father and the Son, which (chap. i. 3) he was inviting them to, they should have *fellowship with devils,* as that other apostle tells his Corinthians, 1 Cor. x. 20, 21. And he might also have reference to the peculiar idolatries, which this sort of men are noted to have been guilty of towards their great sect-master.

THE SECOND EPISTLE

OF

JOHN

The apostle testifieth his regard and good wishes for a certain pious matron and her children, and his joy in their good behaviour, 1—4. *He exhorteth them to persevere in Christian love and belief, that they lose not their full reward,* 5—9; *and to have nothing to do with those seducers that bring not the true doctrine of Christ,* 10, 11. *He hopeth to see them shortly, and concludeth with salutations,* 12, 13.

THE elder unto the elect lady and her children, ᵃ whom I love in the truth; and not I only, but also all they that have known ᵇ the truth;

The elder; a general name of office, fitly appropriated with eminency here, he being the only apostle, probably, now surviving on earth. *The elect lady;* this appears to have been some noted person, whom both her singular piety, and rank in the world, made eminent, and capable of having great influence for the support of the Christian interest, which her general value with all that had *known the truth,* (i. e. the Christians in those parts,) shows. The opinion that a church is intended by this appellation, had it greater probability, is of no great importance, and need not here be disputed.

2 For the truth's sake, which dwelleth in us, and shall be with us for ever.

The indwelling of evangelical truth, which is here meant, signifies its deep radication, and powerful transforming efficacy, in the soul, so as to be productive of holiness, as John xvii. 17; than which nothing can be a greater inducement among Christians of mutual love.

3 ᶜ Grace †be with you, mercy, *and* peace, from God the Father, and from the Lord Jesus Christ, the Son of the Father, ᵈ in truth and love.

Such salutations see explained where they have formerly occurred.

4 I rejoiced greatly that I found of thy chil-

dren ᵉwalking in truth, as we have received a commandment from the Father.

Some of her sons, it is probably conjectured, he had met with, upon their occasions, at Ephesus, where, it is thought, he now resided, and found them to have a good savour of religion, and to walk according to rule, which was matter of great joy to him.

5 And now I beseech thee, lady, ᶠnot as though I wrote a new commandment unto thee, but that which we had from the beginning, ᵍthat we love one another.

He inculcates that great precept, of which see 1 John ii. 7, 8.

6 And ʰthis is love, that we walk after his commandments. This is the commandment, That, ⁱas ye have heard from the beginning, ye should walk in it.

From this particular command he passes to what is more general, requiring in all things a strict and unanimous adherence to the pure and primitive doctrine of the gospel, which would be the best expression of love to God, and the true centre and bond of love to one another, as 1 John v. 1, 3.

7 For ᵏmany deceivers are entered into the world, ˡwho confess not that Jesus Christ is come in the flesh. ᵐThis is a deceiver and an antichrist.

See 1 John ii. 18, 22; iv. 3.

8 ⁿLook to yourselves, ᵒthat we lose not those things which we have ‖ wrought, but that we receive a full reward.

Some copies read, which ye have gained, but that ye receive, &c.

Such changes of the person, as we here find, are neither unusual, nor, in exhortation, inelegant; but some copies read in the two latter clauses *ye*. He presses to constancy in the true, incorrupt Christian profession. *That we receive a full reward;* that the expected recompence be not lost in the whole, or in any part, as Gal. iii. 3, 4.

9 ᵖWhosoever transgresseth, and abideth not in the doctrine of Christ, hath not God. He that abideth in the doctrine of Christ, he hath both the Father and the Son.

See 1 John ii. 23.

10 If there come any unto you, and bring not this doctrine, receive him not into *your* house, ᵠneither bid him God speed:

11 For he that biddeth him God speed is partaker of his evil deeds.

Such as bring any contrary doctrine, (as Gal. i. 8,) ought not to be harboured or countenanced by any encouraging salutation, lest we involve ourselves in the participation of their guilt, 1 Tim. v. 22.

12 ʳHaving many things to write unto you, I would not *write* with paper and ink: but I trust to come unto you, and speak †face to face, ˢthat ‖ our joy may be full.

The latter *write* is not in the Greek text; but the words bear this sense, that having many things to write, I would not by *paper and ink* impart them to you, (the expression being elliptical,) but hope to come, &c.

13 ᵗThe children of thy elect sister greet thee. Amen.

They were, it is probable, with him at Ephesus, and took the occasion by him now writing, to transmit their salutations. *Amen;* this concluding *Amen* imports his sincerity in what he had written.

THE THIRD EPISTLE

OF

JOHN

The apostle, after a kind salutation to Gaius, testifieth his joy in his piety, 1—4, commending his hospitality towards the preachers of the gospel, 5—8. He censureth Diotrephes, and threateneth him for his ambitious opposition, 9, 10. The ill example of such is not to be followed, 11. He beareth testimony to the good character of Demetrius, 12. He hopeth to see Gaius shortly, and concludeth with salutations, 13, 14.

THE elder unto the well beloved Gaius, ᵃ whom I love ‖ in the truth.

2 Beloved, I ‖ wish above all things that thou mayest prosper and be in health, even as thy soul prospereth.

This *Gaius* was well known by the apostle, not only to be a stedfast professor of the truly Christian, uncorrupted faith, (which is implied in his avowing his love to him *in the truth,* or upon the Christian account,) but to be so improved and well-grown a Christian, that he reckons he might well make the prosperous state of his soul the measure of all the other prosperity he could wish unto him.

3 For I rejoiced greatly, when the brethren came and testified of the truth that is in thee, even as ᵇthou walkest in the truth.

4 I have no greater joy than to hear that ᶜmy children walk in truth.

The truth is familiarly used to signify the pure doctrine of Christianity, which in its principal design aims at correspondent practice. That his *children,* i. e. such as had been converted to Christ by his ministry, (as 1 Cor. iv. 15,) of whom it appears Gaius was one, did *walk in the truth;* (an apt expression of such correspondent practice;) was greatest matter of joy to this holy apostle, especially when the godly lives of such, to whose conversion he had been instrumental, were so observable, as to gain them a testimony from all others that knew them, as it was in the present instance.

5 Beloved, thou doest faithfully whatsoever thou doest to the brethren, and to strangers;

Charity to Christians is reckoned fidelity to Christ, being shown to them upon the Christian account, which is intimated to have been done by this pious person, who so kindly treated *the brethren, and strangers,* i. e. even though they were strangers.

6 Which have borne witness of thy charity before the church: whom if thou bring forward on their journey †after a godly sort, thou shalt do well:

After a godly sort; i. e. after a manner (as the Greek expression is) worthy of God, viz. as becomes them who bear the name of God, as thou dost, or are intent upon his work, as they are; which latter notion is confirmed by what follows.

7 Because that for his name's sake they went forth, [d] taking nothing of the Gentiles.

8 We therefore ought to receive such, that we might be fellowhelpers to the truth.

They went forth, taking nothing of the Gentiles; it thence appears these were Jews, who went out from their own country to serve the interest of the gospel, which therefore he should serve in helping them.

9 I wrote unto the church: but Diotrephes, who loveth to have the preeminence among them, receiveth us not.

10 Wherefore, if I come, I will remember his deeds which he doeth, prating against us with malicious words: and not content therewith, neither doth he himself receive the brethren, and forbiddeth them that would, and casteth *them* out of the church.

I wrote unto the church; this was probably some church of which Gaius was. *Diotrephes,* one who had received or usurped some office or authority in it, to so ill a purpose, as when he had no inclination to be hospitable himself to fellow Christians, prevented others from being so; and upon pretence of the little differences of these Jewish from the Gentile Christians, excluded them their communion.

11 Beloved, [e] follow not that which is evil, but that which is good. [f] He that doeth good is of God. But he that doeth evil hath not seen God.

[d] 1 Cor. 9. 12, 15.
[e] Ps. 37. 27. Is. 1. 16, 17. 1 Pet. 3. 11.
[f] 1 John 2. 10. ib. 3. 6, 9.

Follow not; Μὴ μιμοῦ· by following here he means imitation, i. e. the deformity of evil appearing in the practice of some, and the beauty of true goodness in others, (examples being given of both sorts, ver. 9, and 12,) he exhorts to decline the former, and imitate the other; and enforces the exhortation by the weightiest arguments. *He that doeth good;* a doer of good, one made up of kindness and benignity (as the context draws the sense to that special kind of goodness); ἀγαθοποιῶν and ὁ κακοποιῶν, signify doing well or ill, from a fixed, prevailing habit, 1 John iii. 7, 8. *Is of God;* is allied to heaven, born of God, his offspring. *But he that doeth evil hath not seen God;* an evil-doer, on the other hand, such a one as is a composition of spite, envy, and malice, is a mere stranger to him, hath not been, or known, or had to do with him.

12 Demetrius [g] hath good report of all men, and of the truth itself: yea, and we *also* bear record; [h] and ye know that our record is true.

Some eminent Christian, whom he could with confidence recommend as a pattern.

13 [i] I had many things to write, but I will not with ink and pen write unto thee:

Having much more to say, as 2 John 12, he resolved on a more immediate, grateful, and effectual way of imparting and even impressing his sense, as the term, writing, is used in a greater latitude, Prov. iii. 3, and elsewhere.

14 But I trust I shall shortly see thee, and we shall speak †face to face. Peace be to thee. Our friends salute thee. Greet the friends by name.

Speak face to face; στόμα πρὸς στόμα, viz. by oral conference, which he hoped ere long to have opportunity for. He concludes with the usual Christian salutations.

[g] 1 Tim. 3. 7.
[h] John 21. 24.
[i] 2 John 12.
† Gr. *mouth to mouth.*

THE GENERAL EPISTLE

OF

JUDE

THE ARGUMENT

Some question there hath been concerning the penman of this Epistle, and some have thought that Jude the apostle was not the man, whoever were; 1. Because he doth not give himself the title of apostle: but that is objected against James too, and hath been already answered. 2. Because the writer of this Epistle speaks of himself as coming after the apostles, ver. 17. But what necessity is there for his coming behind them in office and authority, because he doth in time? 3. Because he mentions the contention about the body of Moses, and the prophecy of Enoch, which are no where to be found in Scripture. But when there were divers traditions among the Jews, (whereof this about Moses's body seems to be one,) why might not the Holy Ghost assert some that were true (though before doubtful) by this apostle, and make them certain, as well as he doth by Paul the names of *Jannes and Jambres,* 2 Tim. iii. 8, which were known only by tradition; and Moses's quaking and fearing at Mount Sinai, Heb. xii. 21, whereof no mention had been made in the Scripture? As for the prophecy of Enoch, it seems to have been a tradition too, (for he mentions no writing,) and then the same may be said as to the other. Yet if it were a book, and an apocryphal one too, his citing of it doth not make it to be canonical; for Jude might as well cite a passage out of an apocryphal writer, as Paul doth several out of heathen authors, Acts xvii. 28; 1 Cor. xv. 33; Tit. i. 12. And, 4. Because much of this Epistle seems to be transcribed out of 2 Pet. ii., and therefore not to be dictated by the Spirit. But to this it may be said, that though many passages in this Epistle agree with what Peter speaks, yet there is so much difference in the whole, that it is plain they are not transcribed thence. And yet why might not the Spirit dictate the same truths to several penmen, either to be published to several persons, or the same persons at different times? Most of Obadiah's prophecy is to be found in Jeremiah's; Psal. lx. is in a great part the same with cviii., and Psal. xiv. the same with liii.; and Paul by the same Spirit wrote many of the same things to the Ephesians, and to the Colossians. And what is alleged of the ancients questioning the authority of this Epistle, it is not so considerable, as it might be alleged, even out of them, for the confirmation of it. Sure we may say, the spirit of an apostle breathes in this as well as in others; the same majesty, purity, and efficacy appear in it, and whatever may evidence its Divine authority. It is written to the Christian Jews. The matter of it agrees very much with 2 Pet. ii., and the scope is mostly the same, viz. to arm them against those who, by their

JUDE

wicked errors and wicked manners, secretly and slily brought in, might infect them, and seduce them into the same wickedness with themselves, whereby they might be exposed to the same judgment, which he pronounceth were like to come upon such.

After a general address, Jude exhorteth Christians to constancy in the received faith, 1—3. He foretelleth the punishment of certain false teachers crept into the church, and describeth their evil doctrine and manners, 4—19. He exhorteth true Christians to persevere in the right faith, and in the love of God, 20, 21; and to seek the reformation of others, 22—23. He concludeth with ascribing glory to God, 24, 25.

A. D. cir. 66.
a Luke 6. 16.
Acts 1. 13.
b John 17. 11, 12, 15.
1 Pet. 1. 5.
c Rom. 1. 7.

JUDE, the servant of Jesus Christ, and ^abrother of James, to them that are sanctified by God the Father, and ^bpreserved in Jesus Christ, and ^ccalled:

Jude; called also *Lebbæus*, and *Thaddæus*, Matt. x. 3. *The servant of Jesus Christ*; not only in the general notion, as a believer, but in a more special, as an apostle. Priests and prophets in the Old Testament are peculiarly called God's servants, Psal. cxxxiv.; Amos iii. 7; and so are ministers in the New, 2 Tim. ii. 24. *And brother of James*; that James who was the son of Alphæus, Matt. x. He mentions his brother to distinguish himself from Judas Iscariot; and his brother rather than his father, because James was most famous in the church, Acts xv. Gal. ii. 9; 1 Cor. ix. 5; as likewise to show his consent with his brother in his doctrine, and to make his Epistle the more acceptable. *To them that are sanctified by God the Father*, viz. as the prime efficient cause of sanctification, which he works in believers by the Son, through the Spirit. *And preserved in Jesus Christ*: their salvation, and perseverance, and deliverance from dangers, not being in their own power; he intimates, that Christ was appointed to be their King, and Head, and Keeper, the *Author and Finisher of their faith*, Heb. xii. 2, and furnished with power for their protection and security, and that by him they were kept unto the salvation purchased for them, viz. by his powerful operation and gracious influence maintaining their faith and union with himself. *And called*, with an effectual calling, the beginning of their sanctification, before mentioned. The copulative, *and*, is not in the Greek; and the words may be read, sanctified by God the Father, preserved in Jesus Christ, as being called; and so *called* may be understood as going before the other two; and then the sense is, to the called, sanctified by God the Father, and preserved in Jesus Christ; or, to them who, being called, are sanctified, &c.

d 1 Pet. 1. 2.
2 Pet. 1. 2.

2 Mercy unto you, and ^dpeace, and love, be multiplied.

Mercy unto you; which is the fountain of reconciliation, and all the grace vouchsafed you: see 1 Tim. i. 2; 2 Tim. i. 2; Tit. i. 4. *Love*; either he means God's love to them, or their love to God and each other. *Be multiplied*; mercy in the effects of it, peace in the sense of it, and either the love of God in the manifestation of it, or their love to God and their neighbours in the degrees and exercise of it.

e Tit. 1. 4.

3 Beloved, I have given all diligence to write unto you ^eof the common salvation, it was needful for me to write unto you, and exhort *you* that ^fye should earnestly contend for the faith which was once delivered unto the saints.

f Phil. 1. 27.
1 Tim. 1. 18.
& 6. 12.
2 Tim. 1. 13.
& 4. 7.

When I gave all diligence to write unto you: the apostle here declares the first cause of his writing to them, viz. his own inclination and readiness, according to the duty of his place, (as an apostle,) so to do: q. d. Being of myself willing, and earnestly desirous to promote your welfare, when absent from you, by writing unto you. *Of the common salvation*; i. e. those things which concern the salvation of us all in common, or that salvation which is common to us all; there being but one salvation for all believers, and one way to it. *It was needful for me to write unto you, and exhort you*; the second reason of his writing, viz. the necessity of it, in respect of the danger they were in, as follows, ver. 4. *That ye should earnestly contend*; by con-

stancy in the faith, zeal for the truth, holiness of life, mutual exhortation, prayer, suffering for the gospel, &c., against those that would pervert the gospel. *For the faith*; the doctrine of the gospel; *faith* is taken for the object of faith. *Which was once*; either, once for all, because it was delivered by all the apostles as the only unchangeable rule of governing their lives, and obtaining salvation, to which nothing is to be added, and from which nothing is to be taken away; or it implies, that it was therefore delivered to them that they might never forsake it, and that if they do, they miss of their salvation, as being never like to have another way made known to them. *Delivered unto the saints*; viz. by God, not invented by men.

4 ^gFor there are certain men crept in unawares, ^hwho were before of old ordained to this condemnation, ungodly men, ⁱturning ^kthe grace of our God into lasciviousness, and ^ldenying the only Lord God, and our Lord Jesus Christ.

g Gal. 2. 4.
2 Pet. 2. 1.
h Rom. 9. 21, 22.
i Pet. 2. 8.
i 2 Pet. 2. 10.
k Tit. 2. 11.
Heb. 12. 15.
l Tit. 1. 16.
2 Pet. 2. 1.
1 John 2. 22.

Who were before of old ordained; Greek, forewritten, i. e. of whom it was formerly written, or foretold, viz. by Christ and his apostles; or rather, it is to be understood according to our translation, before ordained, viz. in the eternal counsel of God; God's decree being compared to a book, in which things to be done are written down. This the apostle adds to prevent any offence that might be taken at the wickedness of these seducers; and therefore lets these saints know, that though such men crept in unawares to them, yet it was not without the providence of God so ordering it. *To this condemnation*; or, judgment; and it may be understood, either of a reprobate sense, to which they who thus perverted the gospel were given up by God, according to his preordination; or of that damnation he decreed should follow upon their wickedness, in making shipwreck of the faith themselves, and subverting others. This seems best to agree with 2 Pet. ii. 3. *Turning the grace of our God into lasciviousness*; abusing the doctrine of the grace of God, and benefits of Christ revealed in the gospel, especially the doctrine of Christian liberty, to the encouraging themselves and others in the vilest lusts, 2 Pet. ii. 1. *And denying the only Lord God*: either this may be understood of the Father distinctly from Christ, expressed in the following clause, and *only* is put in not to exclude either of the other Persons of the Trinity from being God, but to exclude idols and false gods: or it may be understood of Christ, as well as the words following; not only because there is but one article in the Greek relating to the whole sentence, but because it seems best to agree with the parallel place, 2 Pet. ii. 1, which is most generally understood of Christ; and because the heresies of those times, which Jude cautions these saints against, struck especially at the Godhead of Christ, which he therefore the more expressly asserts.

5 I will therefore put you in remembrance, though ye once knew this, how that ^mthe Lord, having saved the people out of the land of Egypt, afterward ⁿdestroyed them that believed not.

m 1 Cor. 10. 9.
n Num. 14. 29, 37. & 26. 64. Ps. 106. 26. Heb. 3. 17, 19.

Though ye once: this may be joined either with the verb following, *knew*, according to our translation, and the sense is, though ye knew this certainly, as the word *once* is taken, Psal. lxxxix. 35, or perfectly and thoroughly, or once for all; or rather, with what goes before, and the words may be read, I will yet once (viz. while I am in this tabernacle) put you in remembrance of this, though you know it; as 2 Pet. i. 12. *Having saved the people*; the people of Israel. *Afterward destroyed them*; viz. in the wilderness, by plague, fiery serpents, &c. *That believed not*; he sets forth the Israelites' unbelief, as the original of all their disobedience and rebellions, and the great cause of their destruction. See Heb. iii. 17—19; iv. 2.

6 And ^othe angels which kept not their

o John 8. 44.

JUDE

1 Or, *principality*.
p 2 Pet. 2. 4.
q Rev. 20. 10.

‖ first estate, but left their own habitation, ᵖhe hath reserved in everlasting chains under darkness ᑫunto the judgment of the great day.

Kept not their first estate; in which they were created, their original excellency, truth, holiness, purity, John viii. 44, as well as dignity. *But left their own habitation;* viz. a heavenly one, from whence, though they were righteously thrust out by God, 2 Pet. ii. 4, yet they may be truly said to have left it themselves, in that they voluntarily rebelled against the law of their creation, and committed that sin which they knew would certainly be punished with such a dejection. *He hath reserved in everlasting chains;* into which, Peter says, they were *delivered*.

r Gen. 19. 24.
Deut. 29. 23.
2 Pet. 2. 6.

7 Even as ʳSodom and Gomorrha, and the cities about them in like manner, giving themselves over to fornication,

† Gr. *other*.

and going after † strange flesh, are set forth for an example, suffering the vengeance of eternal fire.

The cities about them; Admah and Zeboim, Jer. xlix. 18; Hos. xi. 8. *In like manner,* as Sodom and Gomorrah did, likeness of sin inferring likeness of punishment. *Strange flesh;* margin, other flesh; he means male flesh, which is other than what God appointed for that use they made of it; or, as we render it, *strange flesh,* i. e. that which is strange, improper, and unfit for such an end. It is the description of the unnatural filthiness of the Sodomites, Gen. xix. 5: see Rom. i. 26, 27. *Are set forth for an example, suffering the vengeance of eternal fire: eternal fire* may be joined either, 1. With *example,* and the words thus placed, are set forth for an example of eternal fire, suffering vengeance; and the meaning is, that the vengeance they suffered in being destroyed by fire, is an example, or type, of eternal fire, that of hell: or, 2. With *vengeance,* according to our reading; and then the sense is, they *are set forth for an example,* (viz. to those that after should live ungodly, 1 Pet. ii. 6,) *suffering the vengeance of eternal fire;* the vengeance they suffer is an example to deter others from the like wickedness. This fire is called *eternal,* either because of the still continuing effects of it, or rather, because it was a type or representation of the fire of hell, and to those miserable Sodomites the very beginning of it, they being brought by these temporal flames into everlasting burnings.

s 2 Pet. 2. 10.

8 ˢLikewise also these *filthy* dreamers defile the flesh, despise dominion, and

t Ex. 22. 28.

ᵗspeak evil of dignities.

Likewise also; notwithstanding so many judgments of God upon others, which should have kept them from the like sins. *These filthy dreamers:* either this may be taken properly, and joined to the next clause, *defile the flesh;* and then it may note the impurity of these wretches, who dreamed of what they loved, and acted over that filthiness in their sleep, to which they were so much addicted when awake: or metaphorically, and so they are called *dreamers,* as having the sense of their minds overcome and laid asleep by their sensual pleasures; or being like men in a dream, deluded by their absurd, though pleasing imaginations. *Defile the flesh:* this notes all those lascivious practices, to which, like the Sodomites, they had given themselves over; and whereby they defiled themselves and others: *the lust of uncleanness,* as it is in Peter. *Despise dominion;* in their minds, judgments, desires, they reject, make void, and abrogate civil government, as a thing not fit to be. *Dominion;* not only governors, but government itself. *And speak evil of dignities;* either spiritual governors, or rather, civil, called *dignities,* because of the honourable titles given them, and gifts bestowed on them: see 2 Pet. ii. 10.

u Dan. 10. 13. & 12. 1.
Rev. 12. 7.
x 2 Pet. 2. 11.

9 Yet ᵘMichael the archangel, when contending with the devil he disputed about the body of Moses, ˣdurst not bring against him a railing accusation,

y Zech. 3. 2.

but said, ʸThe Lord rebuke thee.

Michael the archangel: either this is understood of Christ the Prince of angels, who is often in Scripture called an Angel, or of a created angel; and that either, 1. One of the archangels: Dan. x. 13, *Michael* is called *one of the chief princes,* which though the word archangel be not found in the plural number in Scripture, may well imply a plurality of them; for what is one of the chief princes among the angels, but an archangel? Or, 2. A principal angel, or one that is chief among others. *When contending with the devil;* it may be meant either of Christ contending with the devil, as Matt. iv., in his temptation, and Zech. iii. 1, 2. and Rev. xii. 7; or rather, of Michael, a created angel. *He disputed about the body of Moses:* 1. If *Michael the archangel* be meant of Christ, then *the body of Moses* may be taken figuratively, for that body whereof the Mosaical ceremonies were shadows, Col. ii. 17, i. e. the truth and accomplishment of the law given by Moses; that accomplishment was to be in Christ, who is represented by Joshua, Zech. iii.: him Satan resists in the execution of his office, and by him strikes at Christ, whose type he was, and whom he afterward opposeth in the execution of his office, when he was come in the flesh. Or, 2. If we take *Michael* for a created angel, which agrees best with the parallel place in Peter, then the body of Moses must be taken properly, (as most take it,) and the dispute seems to be, Whether Moses's body should be so buried as to be concealed from the Israelites? Deut. xxxiv. 6, it is said God *buried him,* (which might be by the ministry of Michael the archangel,) and that *no man knoweth of his sepulchre.* The devil opposeth the angel, desiring to have the place of his burial known, that in after-times it might be a snare to that people, and a means to bring them to idolatry. And this seems very probable, if we consider what work the devil hath made in the world with the bodies of saints and martyrs, and how much idolatry he hath brought in thereby. This passage Jude, most probably, had (as was observed in the argument) from some known tradition among the Jews, the truth of which we are now sure of, because certified here concerning it. *Durst not bring against him;* or, could not endure, (as the Greek word is often taken among profane writers,) or find in his heart, not from fear of punishment, but by reason of the holiness of his own nature, and to give an example to us. And this sense agrees to the scope of the place, whether we understand it of Christ, or of a created angel, Heb. xii. 3; 1 Pet. ii. 23. *A railing accusation:* see 2 Pet. ii. 11. *But said, The Lord rebuke thee;* i. e. put thee to silence, restrain thy insolence, hinder thy design, &c.: hereby the angel refers the cause to God.

z 2 Pet. 2. 12.

10 ᶻBut these speak evil of those things which they know not: but what they know naturally, as brute beasts, in those things they corrupt themselves.

But these speak evil of those things which they know **not**; the same as 2 Pet. ii. 12; unless this be more generally to be understood of all those spiritual things whereof they were ignorant. *But what they know naturally;* without reason or judgment. *In those things they corrupt themselves;* debauch and degrade their natures by extreme sensualities, whereby they bring destruction upon themselves: see 2 Pet. ii. 12.

a Gen. 4. 5. 1 John 3. 12.
b Num. 22. 7, 21. 2 Pet. 2. 15.
c Num. 16. 1, &c.

11 Woe unto them! for they have gone in the way ᵃof Cain, and ᵇran greedily after the error of Balaam for reward, and perished ᶜin the gainsaying of Core.

Woe unto them! this is either a lamenting the misery that was to come upon them, or a foretelling it come, not a wishing that it might: see Matt. xi. 21; 1 Cor. ix. 16. *For they have gone in the way of Cain;* followed his manners, and fallen under his punishment. Their likeness to Cain, both as to their actions and the event of them, seems to be implied in this and the following clause, as well as it is plainly in the last. Cain hated his brother, and slew him; they hate their brethren, and by their pernicious doctrines and deceits, murder their souls, and probably stir up persecution against their persons. *And ran greedily after the error of Balaam for reward;* covetousness, to which being excessively addicted, or, as the Greek implies, poured out, they did for the sake of filthy lucre corrupt the doctrine of Christ: see 2 Pet. ii. 15. *And perished in the gainsaying of Core:* Korah, (whom he here names alone, as being the ringleader of the rebellion, in which others joined with him, Numb.

xvi. 1,) affecting the priesthood, rose up seditiously against Moses and Aaron, and perished in the attempt. These imitate him in their rebellion against Christ himself, the state and order of whose church they seditiously disturb, as well as that of the civil state, in despising dominion, and speaking evil of dignities, and that to their own destruction.

d 2 Pet. 2. 13.
e 1 Cor. 11. 21.
f Prov. 25. 14. 2 Pet. 2. 17.
g Eph. 4. 14.
h Mat. 15.13.

12 ^dThese are spots in your ^efeasts of charity, when they feast with you, feeding themselves without fear: ^fclouds *they are* without water, ^gcarried about of winds; trees whose fruit withereth, without fruit, twice dead, ^hplucked up by the roots;

These are spots: see 2 Pet. ii. 13. *In your feasts of charity*; feasts used among the primitive Christians, to show their unity among themselves, and promote and maintain mutual charity, and for relief of the poor among them. *Feeding themselves without fear;* unreasonably cramming themselves, without respect to God or the church. *Clouds they are without water, carried about of winds;* empty, making a show of what they have not, Prov. xxv. 14 ; and inconstant: see 2 Pet. ii. 17. *Trees whose fruit withereth;* he compares them to trees, which having leaves and blossoms, make a show of fruit, but cast it, or never bring it to maturity, or it rots instead of ripening ; so these here make a show of truth and holiness, but all comes to nothing. *Without fruit;* without any good fruit, (which only deserves to be called fruit,) brought forth by them, either in themselves or followers, who never get any real benefit by them. *Twice dead;* wholly dead ; dead over and over; dead by nature, and dead by that hardness of heart they have contracted, or that reprobate sense to which God hath given them up. *Plucked up by the roots;* and so never like to bear fruit, and fit only for the fire ; it notes the incurableness of their apostacy, and their nearness to destruction.

i Is. 57. 20.
k Phil. 3. 19.

13 ⁱRaging waves of the sea, ^kfoaming out their own shame ; wandering stars,

l 2 Pet. 2. 17.

^lto whom is reserved the blackness of darkness for ever.

Raging waves of the sea; not only inconstant as water, but unquiet, turbulent, restless, that cannot cease from sin. *Foaming out their own shame;* that wickedness whereof they should be ashamed; *like the troubled sea, when it cannot rest, whose waters cast up mire and dirt,* Isa. lvii. 20. *Wandering stars;* either planets properly called, or rather meteors called running stars, inconstant in their motion, uncertain in their shining, making a little show, but presently vanishing; such was the doctrine of these, which had a show of light, but a deceitful and inconstant one. *To whom is reserved the blackness of darkness for ever;* the thickest darkness, viz. that of hell ; they would be counted lights, but are themselves cast into utter darkness, 2 Pet. ii. 17. As blackness of darkness shows the horror of their punishment, so its being reserved for them shows the certainty of it.

m Gen. 5. 18.
n Deut. 33.2.
Dan. 7. 10.
Zech. 14. 5.
Mat. 25. 31.
2 Thes. 1. 7.
Rev. 1. 7.

14 And Enoch also, ^mthe seventh from Adam, prophesied of these, saying, Behold, ⁿthe Lord cometh with ten thousand of his saints,

And Enoch also, the seventh from Adam; either to distinguish him from Enoch the son of Cain, or to show the antiquity of the prophecy. *Prophesied;* he doth not say wrote, and therefore from hence it cannot be proved that there was any such book as Enoch's prophecies, received by the Jews as canonical Scripture ; but rather some prophecy of his delivered to them by tradition, to which here the apostle refers, as a thing known among them ; and so argues against these heretics from their own concession, as ver. 9. So here ; q. d. These men own the prophecy of Enoch, that the Lord comes to judgment, &c., and they themselves are in the number of those ungodly ones, and they to whom the prophecy is to be applied. *Of these;* not that he did directly and expressly prophesy of them in particular ; but that his prophecy of the destruction of the world for the same kind of crimes whereof they were guilty, did reach them, and so he foretold what should befall them as well as others. *With ten thousand;* innumerable multitudes; a definite for an indefinite. *Of his saints;* holy angels, Matt. xvi. 27 ; Dan. vii. 10 ; Zech. xiv. 5 ; 2 Thess. i. 7 ; Rev. v. 11. Believers likewise may be here included, as attendants upon Christ when he comes to judgment.

15 To execute judgment upon all, and to convince all that are ungodly among them of all their ungodly deeds which they have ungodly committed, and of all their ^ohard *speeches* which ungodly sinners have spoken against him.

o 1 Sam. 2. 3. Ps. 31. 18. & 94. 4. Mal. 3. 13.

To execute judgment upon all; either upon all the wicked in general, who afterwards may seem to be distinguished into different sorts, or else the Greek preposition κατὰ is put for περὶ, and the word *all* is to be understood of all universally, good and bad ; and the words may be read, to execute judgment over all, i. e. to judge all. *And to convince all that are ungodly among them*: if we take the words in the latter sense mentioned, then he distinguisheth those that are to be judged into good and bad, and the Lord comes to execute judgment over all, having convinced the wicked among them ; but if in the former, the *ungodly* here may be taken for those that are more notoriously so, those that have obstinately rejected the gospel, or wickedly perverted it, or persecuted the saints, &c. *Which they have ungodly committed;* i. e. with an ungodly mind, willingly, delightfully, perseveringly. *Their hard speeches;* i. e. blasphemous, irreverent, against God, his truth and ways. *Which ungodly sinners have spoken against him;* he executes judgment, though upon all the wicked, yet especially upon these *ungodly sinners,* i. e. that are such both in their words and deeds *against him,* in his truths, ways, ordinances, people, &c., and therefore are the worst of sinners.

16 These are murmurers, complainers, walking after their own lusts ; and ^ptheir mouth speaketh great swelling *words,* ^qhaving men's persons in admiration because of advantage.

p 2 Pet. 2. 18.
q Prov. 28. 21. Jam. 2. 1, 9.

Murmurers, complainers; either these two words signify the same thing ; or *murmurers* may be meant with relation to God's decrees, laws, providences, and his ordinations in the church or state, 1 Cor. x. 10 ; and *complainers,* with respect to their own condition, with which they were discontented. *Walking after their own lusts;* minding neither the law of God nor man, but making their lusts their law, and being wholly subject to them, 2 Pet. ii. 10. *And their mouth speaketh great swelling words*: though they were mere slaves to their own lusts, yet they would speak big, and use high and exotic strains in their language, that they might be applauded and admired : see 2 Pet. ii. 18. *Having men's persons in admiration because of advantage;* flattering and magnifying the greater and richer sort of men, not considering what they were, so they could gain them to their party, or get gain by them.

17 ^rBut, beloved, remember ye the words which were spoken before of the apostles of our Lord Jesus Christ;

r 2 Pet. 3. 2.

Especially Paul and Peter : see Acts xx. 29, besides the places in the margin. From this passage it appears that this Epistle was written late, and, likely, after the other apostles. except John, were dead.

18 How that they told you ^sthere should be mockers in the last time, who should walk after their own ungodly lusts.

s 1 Tim. 4. 1. 2 Tim. 3. 1. & 4. 3. 2 Pet. 2. 1. & 3. 3.

Told you; whether in their preaching or writing. *Ungodly lusts;* Greek, lusts of ungodliness ; a Hebraism ; the vilest lusts.

19 These be they ^twho separate themselves, ^usensual, having not the Spirit.

t Prov. 18. 1. Ezek. 14. 7. Hos. 4. 14. & 9. 10.
Heb. 10. 25. u 1 Cor. 2. 14. Jam. 3. 15.

These be they who separate themselves; viz. from the true doctrine and church of Christ, as being in love with their carnal liberties, and loth to come under the yoke of Christ's discipline. *Sensual;* or carnal, or animal, 1 Cor. ii. 14 ; such as are mere men, and have no higher principle in them than human nature, which, left to itself, and being destitute of the sanctifying Spirit, is generally overpowered by sense, and inclines to fleshly lusts. *Having not the Spirit;* the Spirit of God, by which they should be led, and to which they so much pretend; having neither the light, nor grace, nor comfort of the Spirit.

x Col. 2. 7.
1 Tim. 1. 4.
y Rom. 8.26.
Eph. 6. 18.

20 But ye, beloved, ˣbuilding up yourselves on your most holy faith, ʸpraying in the Holy Ghost,

Building up yourselves; he compares them to a house, which is to be built up, whereof faith is the foundation : the same metaphor is used, 1 Cor. iv. 9; Eph. ii. 20—22; 1 Pet. ii. 5. *Most holy;* so he calls faith, as being the means of purifying their hearts, and working holiness in them; and in opposition to the false faith of the hereties he warns them against, which did consist with so much impurity. *Faith;* this may be understood either, 1. Of the grace of faith; and then that is compared to the foundation, as being the first and principal grace in a Christian, and of greatest necessity and use; and then they are here bid to build themselves up in other graces which follow upon faith, as 2 Pet. i. 5. Or, 2. Of the doctrine of faith, that on which their faith itself is founded; and then the meaning is, that they should not rest satisfied in what measure of faith they had already attained, but still be improving it, and making further progress in it, not only hold fast the truth of the gospel, the right foundation on which they had begun to be built, but get themselves, by the due study and meditation of the word, more and more confirmed in the belief of it. *Praying in the Holy Ghost;* i. e. by the assistance of the Spirit, who teacheth what to pray for, and how; from whom faith, fervency, and all praying graces do proceed. Rom. viii. 26, 27, *The Spirit maketh intercession* (prays) *in us,* to note the excitations of his grace; here we are said to *pray in the Holy Ghost,* to note the concurrence of our faculties.

21 Keep yourselves in the love of God,

z Tit. 2. 13.
2 Pet. 3. 12.

ᶻlooking for the mercy of our Lord Jesus Christ unto eternal life.

Keep yourselves in the love of God; i. e. in love to God, or that love whereby ye love God; this implies love to each other, as the cause doth the effect. *Looking for;* viz. by hope: and so in these two verses we have the three cardinal graces, faith, hope, and charity. *The mercy of our Lord Jesus Christ unto eternal life;* the merciful or gracious sentence of Christ the Judge, whereby he puts believers in possession of eternal life, Matt. xxv. 34. This reward of eternal life is promised, but being promised freely, and out of mercy, it is called *mercy,* 2 Tim. i. 18, the effect being put for the cause.

22 And of some have compassion, making a difference:

And of some have compassion; use them gently, mildly reproving and admonishing them, that thereby ye may gain them. *Making a difference:* he makes two sorts of offenders, or misled brethren, who might be restored; and that they might, they should be dealt with in different ways, and suitably to their respective conditions and circumstances; the former, who might be discouraged with roughness, should be handled with more tenderness and compassion.

23 And others ᵃsave with fear, ᵇpulling *them* out of the fire; hating even ᶜthe garment spotted by the flesh.

a Rom. 11. 14. 1 Tim. 4. 16.
b Amos 4. 11.
1 Cor. 3. 15.
Zech. 3. 2.
c Zech. 3. 4, 5. Rev. 3. 4.

And others; those that are further gone, not so easily reducible, and in great danger. *Save;* i. e. labour to save them, as instruments under God. *With fear;* by more severe courses, sharper reprehensions, setting before them God's judgments against obstinate sinners, 1 Cor. v. 5. *Pulling them out of the fire :* it is a proverbial speech, Zech. iii. 2: the sense is, that as they that are in the fire, and like to be destroyed by it, must not be gently exhorted to come out of it of themselves, but speedily and forcibly pulled out, in consideration of their eminent danger; so they that are more stubborn sinners, being in apparent danger of being destroyed by the fire of their lusts, and being as it were in the mouth of hell, must be more harshly and severely dealt with, by setting the Lord's terrors before them, 2 Cor. v. 11, and inflicting church censures on them. *Hating even the garment spotted by the flesh:* it is an allusion to that ceremonial law, Lev. xv. 4, 17, where he that touched a defiled garment was himself defiled. The sense is, either, 1. That where there is danger of infection from hereties and obstinate sinners, all converse with them, and any thing whereby the contagion of their doctrine or manners may reach us, is to be avoided: or, 2. That when we reprehend others, we should do it with suitable affections, and though we would save themselves, we should hate their vices, and any thing that promotes them or savours of them.

24 ᵈ Now unto him that is able to keep you from falling, and ᵉ to present *you* faultless before the presence of his glory with exceeding joy,

d Rom. 16. 25. Eph. 3. 20.
e Col. 1. 22.

Able to keep you from falling; from stumbling in your spiritual course, and so able to make you persevere to the end. *Before the presence of his glory;* or, his glorious presence, i. e. before himself, Eph. v. 27. Having exhorted these saints to perseverance in the faith, he now tells them in whose strength they must stand, and to whom they are to give the glory of it.

25 ᶠTo the only wise God our Saviour, *be* glory and majesty, dominion and power, both now and ever. Amen.

f Rom. 16. 27. 1 Tim. 1. 17. & 2. 3.

To the only wise; only wise infinitely, and of himself. *God our Saviour;* either God, who is sometimes called by this title, 1 Tim. ii. 3; Tit. i. 3; iii. 4; or rather Christ. *Be glory:* see 1 Pet. iv. 11; v. 11. *And majesty;* or, magnificence, Heb. i. 3; viii. 1: it seems to signify the height and excellency of God's glory. *Dominion and power;* authority, and right to govern, which here is ascribed to God, as well as strength or sufficiency for it.

THE REVELATION

OF

S. JOHN THE DIVINE

THE PREFACE TO THE ANNOTATIONS UPON THE REVELATION

ALTHOUGH some particular heretics, such as Cerdon and Marcyon, have doubted the Divine authority of this mysterious piece of holy writ, and some better men in the primitive times doubted of it, the manuscript copy of it having been at first reserved in few hands, and (as some think) in the fewer because of the affairs and fate of the Roman empire revealed in it; yet, besides its general reception as such by the church in all late ages, there is in it such a harmony, both with Daniel's prophecy in the Old Testament, and with the types made use of by the holy prophets; such manifest allusions to the whole order and economy of the Jewish church; such an agreement of the doctrine contained in it with the doctrine of the Old and New Testament, concerning God and Christ, the resurrection from the dead, and the day of judgment; and of the promises and threatenings contained in it, with the promises and threatenings in other parts of holy writ; that none who hath not a vanity to question the whole canon of Scripture, can reasonably dispute the Divine authority of this part of it.

It appeareth from chap. i. 1, that John was the penman of it; and that this John was the beloved disciple, he that was the penman of one of the Gospels, hath been doubted by very few, and with very little reason, as will appear to him that will but wisely consider the terms and phrases used in it almost peculiar to this apostle, and hardly to be found in Scripture any where but in this book and the Gospel of John, such as calling Christ *the Word*, of which he *bare record*, &c. Nor is their objection of any validity, who object, that in the Gospel he ordinarily concealeth his name, which this author doth not; considering that in that he wrote a relation or history of things past, to be proved by many eye and ear-witnesses; but here a Revelation or prophecy of things to come, to which his name was necessary, that men might judge by what authority he thus wrote.

For the time of his writing it, himself tells us, chap. i. 9, that he received this Revelation from God, while he was in Patmos, *for the word of God, and for the testimony of Jesus Christ;* this was (if we may believe history, and we have nothing else to inform us) in the time of Domitian the Roman emperor, about the 94th or 95th year after the nativity of Christ; so as this book pleads a prescription of near sixteen hundred years, in which very few ever questioned its Divine authority.

For the scope of it, it is plainly told us, chap. i. 1, δεῖξαι τοῖς δούλοις αὐτῦ ἅ δεῖ γενέσθαι ἐν τάχει, *to show unto his servants things which must shortly come to pass.* The like we have repeated, chap. xxii. 6: upon which account it is called a *Revelation*, and a *prophecy*, neither of which terms agree to a narration or history, the object of which is some thing or things that are already past.

I will not undertake to give the certain and infallible sense of the several passages of this mysterious prophecy: *In magnis voluisse sat est*. But I have proceeded upon these few *postulata*:

1. That the whole of this book is no historical relation of things that were past before the year 95 or 96, or at least not long before, but of things to come; which hath made me wholly reject the notions of Grotius and Dr. Hammond, so far as they concerned the siege or destruction of Jerusalem, which was past twenty-six or twenty-seven years before John heard of this Revelation. I cannot understand how this can agree with chap. i. 1, or chap. xxii. 6.

2. That it contains a prophecy of the most remarkable things that happened either to the Roman empire, or to the church (all which was within the latitude of that in St. John's time) during the whole time of that; or which should happen after the decay of that, throughout the church, to the end of the world.

3. That this time is reasonably divided into three periods; the first determining with the Roman empire's, continuing pagan, 310 or 325 years after Christ: the second with the total ruin of antichrist; when that shall be I cannot tell: the third with Christ's coming to the last judgment. The first is by some called *Regnum draconis ethnicum;* the second, *Vicariatus draconis antichristianus;* the third, *Regnum Christi,* or, *Status ecclesiæ tranquillus.*

4. I see no reason to dissent from those eminent men, who think that part of the Revelation which relates to the first period, and is predictive of what happened to the church of God until the time of Constantine the Great, 310 or 325 years after Christ, beginneth with chap. iv. and endeth with chap. vii.; and that the *silence in heaven* for *half an hour*, mentioned chap. viii. 1, relateth to the rest which the church had from Constantine's time till the end of Theodosius's reign, about seventy or seventy-five years.

5. Where to fix the epocha, or beginning, of the one thousand two hundred and sixty years, or forty-two months, I cannot tell. That *the mystery of iniquity* begun to work in the apostles' time, is evident from 1 Thess. ii. 7; and reason will tell us, that Rome, as it now stands, or as it was in the year 1606, was not built up in a day, the great corruptions then in it came in and grew up by degrees; but I cannot tell how to count antichrist's reign, but from the time Phocas humoured the pope with the title and style of "supreme" or "universal bishop;" from which time I should rather reckon the one thousand two hundred and sixty years, than from any time before.

6. I do agree with those who think the first eleven chapters contain the sum of whatsoever is prophesied concerning the two first periods, though many things falling within them are more particularly and fully opened, chap. xii.—xix. The 12th chapter gives us a particular account of the church during the first two periods. The 13th gives us a more particular account of antichrist, both in the secular power and in his ecclesiastical jurisdiction. The 15th and 16th chapters more fully open to us what should be done under the sixth trumpet. In the 17th chapter we have a more full description of the beast with two horns, mentioned chap. xiii. 11, which signified antichrist as sitting in the temple of God. The 18th more fully describes his fall, summarily before mentioned, chap. xiv. The 19th, so far as it concerneth the praise given to God for this, relates to that great dispensation of providence.

7. I take the third state of the church (to which I cannot conceive we are yet come, which I called its serene and quiet state) to be foretold and described, chap. xx; after which shall be the battle with all the wicked of the earth, which shall end in Christ's coming to judge the world, and the general resurrection in order to it.

8. I take the last two chapters to describe a state of the church agreeing to none but the church triumphant, and have accordingly interpreted them.

If any differ from me in any of these things, it will be no wonder if he disagreeth with me in the explication of the chapters and verses relating to them.

I dare not be positive as to the sense I have given, but shall only say it is what appeareth to me most probable. There have been found some in the tents of protestants, that have taken much pains to free the papacy from the imputation of antichrist. This I conceive was Grotius's design, in his interpretation of this book, as if it had been a history rather than a prophecy, and if a prophecy, fulfilled in less than two hundred and fifty years after it was published. As to the papacy being antichrist, I think that great person spake well, who would not be peremptory in the case, but said, it had so many of his marks, that upon a hue and cry for antichrist, he should apprehend him. I shall add, that if he were so apprehended and tried, he could never acquit himself either at the bar of Scripture or reason.

CHAP. I

The preface, 1—3. John's salutation to the seven churches of Asia, 4—6. The coming of Christ, 7; his eternal majesty, 8. John relateth his vision of the Son of man with the seven stars and the seven golden candlesticks, 9—20.

A. D. 96.
a John 3. 32.
& 8. 26.
& 12. 49.

THE Revelation of Jesus Christ, ᵃ which God gave unto him, to shew unto his servants things which ᵇ must shortly come to pass; and ᶜ he sent and signified *it* by his angel unto his servant John:

b ch. 4. 1.
ver. 3.
c ch. 22. 16.

The Revelation of Jesus Christ; the Apocalypse, (as this book is sometimes called,) that is, the discovering or unveiling of some hidden things; so the word *revelation* signifieth. The Greek word is often used in the New Testament, and is ordinarily translated so. It is called *The*

REVELATION I

Revelation of Jesus Christ, because Christ received it from his Father, as the next words show. *Which God gave unto him,* as he was Mediator: by *God,* here, is to be understood the Father, not exclusively to the Son, as if he were not God, but to show the order of working in the Holy Trinity, John vii. 16; xiv. 10. Christ in his state of humiliation is said to learn of the Father; in his state of exaltation, to receive from the Father. *To show unto his servants;* to John, and by him to all saints that will be studious of things revealed. *Things which must shortly come to pass;* ἃ δεῖ γενέσθαι ἐν τάχει. This phrase puts us out of doubt, that this book is not a relation or narrative of things past, but a revelation or prediction of things to come: see also chap. xxii. 6, 16. Which makes me wonder at the confidence of a learned annotator of our own, that all things here relate, either to the siege of Jerusalem, (which was past more than twenty years before this Revelation to St. John,) or to pagan Rome, which, indeed, continued two hundred and odd years after this. But his notion is contrary to the general sense of all interpreters, whether the ancient fathers or modern writers. The phrase, indeed, signifies *shortly,* but never what was past, nor always what shall in a few days come to pass; see Luke xviii. 8; Rom. xvi. 20; though indeed sometimes it signifies the time immediately following a command, as Acts xii. 7; xxii. 18: and considering it is God's phrase, to whom *a thousand years are but as yesterday,* Psal. xc. 4, and who calls the things that are not as if they were, and who manifestly calls all those years betwixt Christ's coming and the end of the world (almost one thousand seven hundred of which are past already) the *last days,* we may allow him to say, those things should be *shortly,* which soon after should begin to be effected, though not finished till Christ's second coming. Though therefore we may allow this verse the key to open the whole Apocalypse, yet we must judge the learned author hath turned it the wrong way. Christ had foretold the ruin of Jerusalem, Matt. xxiv., nor was it now the matter of a prophecy, but history. The first six seals plainly show the state of the Christian church under Rome pagan; what shall we say to all things represented under the seventh seal, &c.? *And he sent and signified it by his angel;* first by one angel, and then by another, or (possibly) constantly by the same. *Unto his servant John:* who this John was, we shall declare further, ver. 2, 4.

d 1 Cor. 1. 6.
ch. 6. 9.
& 12. 17.
ver. 9.
e 1 John 1. 1.

2 ^d Who bare record of the word of God, and of the testimony of Jesus Christ, and of all things ^e that he saw.

Who bare record of the word of God: this phrase determines the controversy about the penman of this part of holy writ, and puts it out of doubt that it was John the apostle and evangelist; the phrase so agrees to John i. 19, 32, 34; xix. 35. The word in the Greek signifies, bare testimony to, or of, the word of God. Some understand Christ, so called, 1 John i. 2. Some would have the gospel meant by it; and if any think this the more probable sense, because, though Christ be elsewhere called the *Word,* yet he is not called *the word of God;* and it is not here in the dative, but the accusative case; I see no reason to contradict them. *And of the testimony of Jesus Christ:* by the testimony of Christ is to be understood the doctrine of Christ, called so, because it is a testimony concerning him; or rather, that which he testified, who is elsewhere called *the true and faithful witness. And of all things that he saw:* this may be understood with reference to what went before; so it agreeth with 1 John i.; or to what followeth in this Revelation, made to him in visions in a great measure.

f Luke 11.28.
ch. 22. 7.

g Rom. 13. 11. Jam. 5. 8. 1 Pet. 4. 7. ch. 10. 22.

3 ^fBlessed *is* he that readeth, and they that hear the words of this prophecy, and keep those things which are written therein: for ^g the time *is* at hand.

Blessed is he that readeth, and they that hear the words of this prophecy: from hence is well concluded, that this is a portion of holy writ to be read publicly and privately, otherwise no blessing would have been pronounced to the readers or the hearers of it. It is also well from hence concluded, that this book is no history of things done, but a prediction of things to come to pass; for though *prophecy* in some scriptures signifieth more largely the revelation of the Divine will, yet here it must signify strictly. *And keep those things which are written therein;* that keep it in memory, and live in view of it, and as persons that believe it; they are *blessed,* as they will from it be comforted, concerning all the sufferings of the church, and people of God. *For the time is at hand;* the season for the accomplishment of these things is nigh, not past, but the time when they shall begin to happen is not very far off.

4 JOHN to the seven churches which are in Asia: Grace *be* unto you, and peace, from him ^hwhich is, and ⁱwhich was, and which is to come; ^kand from the seven Spirits which are before his throne;

h Ex. 3. 14.
ver. 8.
i John 1. 1.
k Zech. 3.
9. & 4. 10.
ch. 3. 1. & 4.
5. & 5. 6.

John to the seven churches which are in Asia: John, the apostle and evangelist, writes either to all the churches of Asia under the notion of seven, (which is the number of perfection,) or to those seven churches mentioned ver. 11, *Ephesus, Smyrna, Pergamos, Thyatira, Sardis, Philadelphia,* and *Laodicea,* seven famous places in Asia the Less, where the gospel was planted; which being the most famous churches in that part of the world, John is commanded to deposit this prophecy in their hands, by them to be communicated unto other churches. These churches were in the most famous cities of the Lesser Asia: some think John was the apostle that preached most in Asia, and founded these churches; others, that though they were founded by Peter and Paul, yet after their death John took upon him the charge of them. It is the opinion of some learned men, that the apostle did not, in the epistles to the churches in Asia, design only to tell them of their error, and prescribe to their cure; but that in writing to them, he assigns both a prophetical instruction of us all concerning the state of the church in all periods from that time to the day of judgment, and also to reprove and counsel all present and succeeding churches; but of this we may possibly speak more afterward. *Grace be unto you, and peace:* grace and peace is the common apostolical salutation, as to the sense of which we have often spoken: the apostle wisheth them the free love of God, that is, *grace,* and the seal of it, Rom. v. 1, *peace* with God and their own consciences, and each with other. *From him which is, and which was, and which is to come:* these words are a description of God, particularly of Jesus Christ in his eternity and immutability: he was from eternity; he is now; and he shall be for ever. Or, (as some,) he was in his promises before his incarnation; he is now God manifested in the flesh; and he is to come as a Judge, to judge the quick and the dead. This was an ancient name of God, Exod. iii. 14, *I am that I am.*—*I AM hath sent me unto you.* These words interpret the name *Jehovah. And from the seven Spirits which are before his throne;* it is very difficult to determine what is meant by *the seven Spirits* here *before the throne:* we read of them also, chap. iii. 1; iv. 5; v. 6. Christ is described, chap. iii. 1, as having *the seven Spirits of God.* It is said, chap. iv. 5, that *the seven lamps of fire burning before the throne, are the seven Spirits of God;* and chap. v. 6, that the Lamb's *seven eyes* were *the seven Spirits of God.* This is all the light we have from Scripture. Some think they are seven angels that are here meant. We read, chap. viii. 2, of *seven angels that stood before God;* and in chap. xv. 16, 17, there is a like mention of *seven angels;* and Zech. iv. 2, 10, Zechariah had a vision of *seven lamps,* and *seven pipes,* which, ver. 10, are said to be *the eyes of the Lord, which run to and fro through the whole earth.* But John saluting the churches with grace and peace from these seven Spirits, and joining them with Christ, they do not seem to be creatures, angels, that are here meant, but such a Being from whom grace and peace cometh. Others therefore understand by them, the seven workings of Divine Providence in his management of the affairs of the world, with relation to the church, of which we shall read after; but this also seems hard. The sense seems to be, and from the Holy Ghost, who, though but one spiritual Being, yet exerteth his influence many ways, and by various manifestations, called here *seven Spirits,* because all flow from the same Spirit. They are therefore called, chap. iv. 5, *burning lamps;* the Holy Ghost descending in the appearance of fire, Acts ii., and being compared to fire, Matt. iii. 11. They are called the Lamb's *seven eyes* and *seven horns*, chap. v. 6. Christ had the Spirit without measure; and the Holy Spirit is oft called the Spirit of Christ. This seemeth the best sense; the reader may find the objections to it answered in Mr. Pool's Synopsis Criticorum upon this verse.

5 And from Jesus Christ, ¹*who is* the faithful witness, *and* the ᵐ first begotten of the dead, and ⁿ the prince of the kings of the earth. Unto him ᵒ that loved us, ᵖ and washed us from our sins in his own blood,

And from Jesus Christ, who is the faithful witness: here is an express mention of Jesus Christ, because he was the procurer of our redemption, and our Mediator, to whom the Father committed all power as to the church. He is called *the faithful* and true *witness;* 1 Tim. vi. 13, he *witnessed a good confession before Pontius Plate;* he bare record of himself, John viii. 13, 14 : see also Isa. xliii. 10; lv. 4 ; John xviii. 37. *And the first begotten of the dead;* that is, who first rose from the dead, viz. by his own power, John x. 18, and to die no more : see Acts xiii. 34 ; 1 Cor. xv. 20. *And the prince of the kings of the earth:* the *King of kings,* chap. xvii. 14; xix. 16; 1 Tim. vi. 15. The first name here given to Christ speaketh his prophetical office, the second his priestly office, this last his kingly office. *Unto him that loved us, and washed us from our sins in his own blood:* here begins a doxology, or giving glory to Christ, (such forms are frequent in the Epistles,) first, as he that *washed us from our sins,* both from the guilt and from the power and dominion of our sins, with *his blood,* paying a price, and satisfying God's justice for, and meriting our sanctification : see Heb. ix. 14 ; 1 John i. 7.

6 And hath ᑫ made us kings and priests unto God and his Father; ʳ to him *be* glory and dominion for ever and ever. Amen.

And hath made us kings and priests unto God and his Father : kings, to rule over our own appetite, and govern ourselves by the law of his word, to fight and conquer the world, the flesh, and the devil. Kings in a spiritual sense, for our kingdom is like his from whom we derive it, *not of this world;* therefore he adds, *unto God,* to the honour and glory of God, for his service, who is the Father of Christ. *Priests, to offer up spiritual sacrifices, acceptable to God* through the Beloved, 1 Pet. ii. 5 ; our *bodies* as *a living sacrifice,* Rom. xii. 1 ; part of our estates, Phil. iv. 18 ; *the sacrifice of praise, the fruit of our lips,* Heb. xiii. 15. So as all the privileges of the Jews, Exod. xix. 6, belong to us, and that in a more eminent manner. Through Christ we also are *a royal priesthood, a peculiar people.* To him be glory and dominion for ever and ever. *Amen:* let all praise, and honour, and acknowledgments be paid, and all power ascribed, to him for ever.

7 ˢ Behold, he cometh with clouds ; and every eye shall see him, and ᵗ they *also* which pierced him : and all kindreds of the earth shall wail because of him. Even so, Amen.

St. John being to speak of the various afflictions of the church of God, which should immediately begin, and hold on during the whole time that Rome should continue heathen, and one thousand two hundred and sixty years after, during the whole reign of the beasts, prepareth Christians for it, by calling them by the eye of faith to see (though at a great distance) Christ coming to judgment, whom he speaks of as already coming, according to the usual style of prophets, who use to speak of those things that shall shortly be done, or certainly, as if they were already done. He describes the manner of Christ's coming to judgment, and saith, *he cometh with clouds,* that is, in a glorious manner ; *in the clouds with power and great glory,* Matt. xxiv. 30 ; *in his glory, and all the holy angels with him,* Matt. xxv. 31 ; *with ten thousand of his saints,* Jude 14 ; *with a shout, the voice of the archangel, and the trump of God,* 1 Thess. iv. 16 ; here, *with clouds,* bright and glorious clouds, not obscuring him, but making his appearance more glorious and terrible. *And every eye shall see him;* he shall come visibly, for, Acts i. 11, he shall so come, as he was seen going up to heaven : see Isa. xl. 5. *And they also which pierced him;* they also which pierced him shall look on him, Zech. xii. 10; yea, not those only which pierced him with their spears, but every sinner who hath pierced him with his sins, Heb. vi. 6. From whence we may observe, that the resurrection will be general ; and those in the Great Mogul's country are like to awake out of their sleep in the grave, as well as others. *And all kindreds of the earth shall wail because of him;* all the nations of the earth, (Greek, the tribes of the earth,) shall wail, not with a mourning of repentance, the time for that will be past, but with a wailing of despair and horror. *Even so, Amen:* these words are either a prophetical assertion, confirming the truth of what he had said, or a pious prayer or desire, or rather both together.

8 ᵘ I am Alpha and Omega, the beginning and the ending, saith the Lord, ˣ which is, and which was, and which is to come, the Almighty.

Alpha and *Omega* are the first and last letters in the Greek alphabet, as *Aleph* and *Tau* are in the Hebrew alphabet : the meaning of these is expounded, *the beginning and the ending ;* he who was before all, and shall continue to exist when all creatures shall cease to be; the first and the last, as the same terms are expounded, chap. xxii. 13 : so Isa. xli. 4 ; xliii. 13. *Which is, and which was, and which is to come, the Almighty:* see ver. 4. He addeth *the Almighty,* to show that he was able to make his words good. Thus in this verse, omnipotency, eternity, and immutability, are all applied to God, and particularly predicated of our Lord and Saviour Jesus Christ.

9 I John, who also am your brother, and ʸ companion in tribulation, and ᶻ in the kingdom and patience of Jesus Christ, was in the isle that is called Patmos, ᵃ for the word of God, and for the testimony of Jesus Christ.

I John, who also am your brother; the same mentioned ver. 4, the apostle of Jesus Christ, yet he disdaineth not to call those his brethren whom his Lord so called. *And companion in tribulation:* the pagan persecutions were now begun. Nero first began them about twenty-three years after Christ was ascended into heaven, but he died within three years' time after he had began that course. Then the Christians had some rest for twelve years, by reason of the short reigns of Galba, Otho, and Vitellius, and the kindness of Flavius and Titus Vespasianus ; but about eighty-two years after Christ began Domitian to reign, and to persecute the Christians about the year 90. He lived not long, for he was slain Anno 97, but in those seven years he put to death, imprisoned, and banished many. John is said to have been banished by him, Anno 91, and to have had this revelation, 94 and 95. Domitian lived but four or five years after this. After his death John is said to have come back to Ephesus, and to have died there three years after, about the year 98. But for five years John was the Christians' *companion in tribulation. And in the kingdom and patience of Jesus Christ;* either the kingdom of grace, a member of the Christian church; or the kingdom of glory, which is to be arrived at both by patient waiting and by patient suffering for Jesus Christ, or waiting for the second appearance of Christ, in order to his glorious kingdom. *Was in the isle that is called Patmos:* this island, geographers tell us, was an island in the Icarian or Ægean Sea, about thirty-five miles in compass, one of those fifty-three islands called the Cyclades. *For the word of God, and for the testimony of Jesus Christ:* he tells us how he came to be in Patmos, viz. for preaching the word of God, and those truths to which Christ had given testimony : he did not voluntarily go thither to preach the gospel, (for those isles have in them few inhabitants,) but he was banished thither by the emperor Domitian's officers. Banishment was a very ordinary punishment amongst the Romans, in case of what they would call sedition. Eusebius tells us,

REVELATION I

that one Flavia Dometilia, though she was niece to the consul, was banished upon the same account at this time.

10 [b]I was in the Spirit on [c]the Lord's day, and heard behind me [d]a great voice, as of a trumpet,

I was in the Spirit; not only in spiritual employment, suppose meditation and prayer, but in an ecstasy; my soul was (as it were) separated from my body, and under the more than ordinary influence and communications of the Spirit, as Acts x. 10; xi. 5; xvi. 9; xviii. 9. *On the Lord's day;* upon the Christian sabbath, called *the Lord's day,* (as the eucharist, or breaking of bread, is called *the Lord's supper,* 1 Cor. xi. 20,) because Christ instituted it; or, because the end of its institution was the remembrance of Christ's resurrection, (as the end of the Lord's supper was the commemoration of Christ's death,) or because it was instituted for the honour of Christ. *And heard behind me a great voice, as of a trumpet:* John in the isle of Patmos was keeping the Christian sabbath in spiritual services, meditation and prayer, and fell into a trance, wherein he had a more immediate communion with the Holy Spirit, which begun with his hearing a loud voice, as it were, behind him, as loud as the sound of a trumpet.

11 Saying, [e]I am Alpha and Omega, [f]the first and the last: and, What thou seest, write in a book, and send *it* unto the seven churches which are in Asia; unto Ephesus, and unto Smyrna, and unto Pergamos, and unto Thyatira, and unto Sardis, and unto Philadelphia, and unto Laodicea.

I am Alpha and Omega, the first and the last; I, who speak unto thee, am the eternal, immutable God. *What thou seest, write in a book;* what thou shalt presently see, write in a book, not in loose papers. Whence we may observe, that this book is not only the revelation of the will of Christ, but written by his direction. *And send it unto the seven churches which are in Asia;* not to all that lived within the jurisdiction or compass of these cities, but only to those Christians who lived in or near these places, which are all cities in the Lesser Asia. *Ephesus* was the most famous, where Paul preached, Acts xix. 10, &c., and stayed three years, chap. xx. 31. It was a noble city in that part of Greece which was called Ionia. *Smyrna* was a sea-port city in the same country. *Pergamos* was a city of Troas, or Phrygia. *Thyatira* was a city in Lydia, or Mysia. *Sardis* also was a city in Lydia, near the mountain Tmolus. *Philadelphia* was a city in Lydia, next Mysia. *Laodicea* was a city in Asia, near the river Lycus. In all these cities there were congregations of Christians formed into churches, to whom God here ordereth St. John to send these visions, when he had written them in a book. Our countryman, Mr. Brightman, asks, Where Rome was all this while? and how it came to pass God directed not these mysteries to be sent, and kept in their archives, especially if (as the papists say) the bishop there be Christ's successive vicar? and considering, too, how great friends Peter and John were wont to be? But the forementioned author tartly replies to his own question, That that church, it seems, could never err, and therefore needed not any correptory or monitory epistle.

12 And I turned to see the voice that spake with me. And being turned, [g]I saw seven golden candlesticks;

And I turned to see the voice that spake with me; that is, to see the person whose voice I heard speaking to me: or else, by seeing is meant understanding; but that he might have done without turning; he therefore turned, hoping to see the person that spake. *And being turned, I saw seven golden candlesticks:* by these seven candlesticks which he saw, are meant the seven churches; so we find it infallibly expounded, ver. 20. We shall find in this book frequent allusions to the Jewish temple: here they begin. In the Jewish tabernacle there was one golden candlestick, and seven lamps, to give light against it; so Numb. viii. 2; Zech. iv. 2. John here seeth seven. God had but one church of the Jews, but many amongst the Gentiles. This notion, or comparison of churches to golden candlesticks, both showeth us the nature and office of the churches of Christ, they do not give light of themselves, only hold lights, and it is their duty to keep in them the pure word of God, which is a light to our feet, and a godly ministry; and it also lets us know, that they ought to keep themselves pure (as beaten gold) from all corruption as to doctrine, and their members from all scandalous conversation.

13 [h]And in the midst of the seven candlesticks [i]*one* like unto the Son of man, [k]clothed with a garment down to the foot, and [l]girt about the paps with a golden girdle.

And in the midst of the seven candlesticks; that is, of the churches, resembled by the golden candlesticks. *One like unto the Son of man:* we say, no like is the same; but Christ, who was the Son of man, and who ordinarily calls himself so throughout the gospel, is undoubtedly here meant, as appeareth by ver. 17, 18, which description can agree to him alone. He is said to have come in the *likeness of sinful flesh,* though he came in true human flesh; and Phil. ii. 7, he *was made in the likeness of men.* John saw one who appeared to him as a man in the midst of seven golden candlesticks, which was Christ in the midst of his churches; placed in the midst, partly to let us know his observation of them all, and partly to let us know his being at hand to them all, to help, protect, and defend them. *Clothed with a garment down to the foot;* ποδήρη· the word signifieth a long garment reaching to the feet, whether of linen or woollen, or what other material, is not expressed; so as it seemeth to me hard to determine, whether it was to signify his priestly or kingly office, or neither. It is a habit of gravity. *And girt about the paps with a golden girdle;* nor dare I determine the significancy of the golden girdle about his loins. It was a habit like that in Daniel's vision, Dan. x. 5. They were both symbols of majesty, authority, and dignity, and the appearance agreed very well to him, who was both a High Priest and a King.

14 His head and [m]*his* hairs *were* white like wool, as white as snow; and [n]his eyes *were* as a flame of fire;

His head and his hairs were white like wool, as white as snow: whiteness signifies purity; whiteness of hair signifies old age ordinarily, which commonly is attended with more prudence, as having most experience: hence this appearance of Christ may denote both his purity and wisdom, and that he is *the Ancient of days;* see Dan. vii. 9, 13, 22; though there the term of *Ancient of days* belongs to God the Father, yet it also agreeth to Christ, who is equal with the Father, as to his Divine nature. *And his eyes were as a flame of fire;* such an appearance is applied to God, Ezek. i. 27; Dan. x. 6; and to Christ, Rev. xix. 12, to denote either Christ's knowledge, wisdom, and omniscience; or his grace in purifying souls, as fire doth metals; or his wrath and anger against his enemies.

15 [o]And his feet like unto fine brass, as if they burned in a furnace; and [p]his voice as the sound of many waters.

And his feet like unto fine brass: there are nice disquisitions what this chalcolibanum (which we translate, *fine brass*) was: vid. Poli Synopsin. I understand not of what profit the determination will be to us. By the feet of Christ (probably) are signified his ways, counsels, and methods, in ordering and governing his church, which are compared to fine brass, for the beauty and glory of them, and for their firmness, strength, and steadiness. *As if they burned in a furnace;* they appeared like brass filled with fire, as if it were burning, and red-hot in a furnace. *And his voice as the sound of many waters;* loud and terrible, like the noise of the sea dashing upon a rock, or the shore.

16 [q]And he had in his right hand seven stars: and [r]out of his mouth went a sharp twoedged sword: [s]and his countenance *was* as the sun shineth in his strength.

And he had in his right hand seven stars: the right hand is the hand of power, Psal. xxi. 8; and of favour, Psal.

951

xliv. 3; and of honour and dignity, Psal. cx. 1.' The *seven stars* are expounded, ver. 20, to be the ministers of the gospel, his messengers to his churches, who having in all times been most exposed to the malice and rage of enemies, Christ is said to hold them in his right hand, as to signify the dignity he hath put upon them and the favour he hath showed them, so also to show his resolution to protect them, according to his promise, Matt. xxviii. 20. *And out of his mouth went a sharp two-edged sword;* either his gospel and word, compared to a two-edged sword, Heb. iv. 12; or a sword of justice, which he will use till he hath perfectly overcome and vanquished his enemies. *And his countenance was as the sun shineth in his strength;* that is, was very glorious, so as the apostle was not able to behold him.

17 And ^twhen I saw him, I fell at his feet as dead. And ^uhe laid his right hand upon me, saying unto me, Fear not; ^xI am the first and the last:

I fell at his feet as dead; astonished at the majesty and glory of the appearance: see Josh. v. 14; Dan. viii. 17, 18; Matt. xvii. 6; Acts ix. 4. *And he laid his right hand upon me, saying unto me, Fear not;* to comfort me, and let me know, that I had no reason to be afraid, he would do me no harm. *I am the first and the last:* see ver. 8, 11.

18 ^y*I am* he that liveth, and was dead; and, behold, ^zI am alive for evermore, Amen; and ^ahave the keys of hell and of death.

I am he that liveth, and was dead; and, behold, I am alive for evermore; the living God, who had life in myself, and gave life to the world, but assumed the human nature, and was made man, and in that nature died; but I rose again from the dead, and shall die no more, but ever live to make intercession for my people. *Amen;* this is a great truth. *And have the keys of hell and of death;* and have a power to kill, and cast into hell; or, I have the power over death, and the state of the dead, so as I can raise those that are dead to life again: I have the command of death, whether temporal or eternal; as he who hath the keys of a house can let in and shut out of it whom he pleaseth, so I bring to heaven and throw to hell whom I please.

19 Write ^bthe things which thou hast seen, ^cand the things which are, ^dand the things which shall be hereafter;

Write the things which thou hast seen; either the things which thou hast seen from the beginning of the gospel; for John, Matt. iv. 21, was a companion of Christ from the time presently following his baptism and temptations: or, the vision of me which thou hast now had; which I judge most probably the sense, not understanding why our Lord should set John to write what (though they were not yet written, yet) Christ knew should be written in another book by John himself, viz. in his Gospel, and by Matthew, Mark, and Luke, in their histories of the Gospel, and in the Acts of the Apostles; especially considering they were to be written plainly, so as he who runs may read them; and what John was to write here, was to be written enigmatically, and darkly represented in visions: and it is against reason to think the same things should be first revealed plainly, and then more darkly, and both by direction from God. *And the things which are;* the present affairs of the church; we have the history till Paul was carried prisoner to Rome, (which was about the 60th year after Christ,) in the Acts of the apostles; so that I conceive the farthest that John looked back was but thirty-five years; for he was in Patmos about the year 93, and is conceived to have written this book, 96. Hence the matter of the Revelation is easily concluded: 1. The things which were the present affairs of the church, Anno 96, or looking back only to 60, which things are supposed to be written by John, in chap. ii. 3. *And the things which shall be hereafter;* to the end of the world, under the reign of the dragon, (the pagan Roman empire,) and the reign of antichrist, or the beast, for one thousand two hundred and sixty years, and from thence until Christ shall come to judgment.

20 The mystery ^eof the seven stars which thou sawest in my right hand, ^fand the seven golden candlesticks. The seven stars are ^gthe angels of the seven churches: and ^hthe seven candlesticks which thou sawest are the seven churches.

The mystery of the seven stars, and the seven golden candlesticks: see ver. 12, 16. *The seven stars are the angels of the seven churches;* that is, they signify the angels of the seven churches. By *angels* he means God's messengers and ambassadors to the seven churches, called *angels*, both in respect of their office, being the ambassadors of Christ, 2 Cor. v. 20, and of that holiness which they should show forth in their doctrine and life. To interpret the term of *angels* by nature, seems not agreeable to what we shall hereafter meet with said to some of them; Christ would never have ordered John to have charged them with a loss of their first love, or to admonish them to be faithful unto death, or to repent. Whether the term *angel* denoteth any particular superior minister or bishop in those churches, or is to be taken collectively for all the ministers in those churches, I shall not dispute. Certain it is, ἄγγελος signifieth no more than is common to all ministers, viz. to be God's messengers, and move upon his errand. *And the seven candlesticks which thou sawest are the seven churches;* the seven churches mentioned ver. 11: or else, seven being the number of perfection, all the churches, which are fitly represented by *candlesticks*, in the same sense as they are called *pillars of truth* in Paul's Epistle to Timothy, because they have not the light they show from themselves, only hold it forth from Christ. But it is the opinion of very learned writers upon this book, that our Lord, by these *seven churches*, signifies all the churches of Christ to the end of the world; and by what he saith to them, designs to show what shall be the state of the churches in all ages, and what their duty is. That by the church of Ephesus, was represented the purest state of all the Christian churches, which determined thirty years before this book was written. By the church of Smyrna, the state of all Christian churches till the year 300. By the church of Pergamos, al. the Christian churches till antichrist got up into the saddle, and the Albigenses and Waldenses were so persecuted. By the church of Thyatira, the state of the churches from that time till our Reformation. By the other three, the state of all churches for one hundred and fifty years last past, and which shall be to the end of the world. See Dr. More, Mr. Mede, Cocceius, and Forbes, as learned and diligent inquirers into the sense of this book as any have been, who give many reasons for this: 1. Because no reason else can be given, why epistles should not be written to other churches as well as these. 2. He doth not call them the seven churches of Asia, but seven churches. 3. The number seven is a number used to signify perfection. 4. What is said of Christ's walking in the midst of the golden candlesticks, having the stars in his right hand, &c., agreeth to him with reference to all churches, not to these seven only. 5. His calling ministers *angels*, speaks this a prophecy, for that is a prophetical style. 6. The mentioning the same number of churches and ministers, as of the seals, speaks this part of the Revelation as comprehensive, with respect to time, as the other. 7. It is not probable that these epistles would have been ushered in with such a vision, if they had been merely historical and didactic, not prophetical also. 8. They argue from ver. 19, where John is bid to write not only what is, but what shall come to pass. 9. They argue from the matter of the epistles.—Let the curious reader see more of this in the authors themselves, as also in Mr. Brightman.

CHAP. II

What John was commanded to write in commendation or reproof to the angels of the churches of Ephesus, 1—7, *Smyrna,* 8—11, *Pergamos,* 12—17, *Thyatira,* 18—29.

Some things are to be observed of all the epistles, before we come to the particular epistles. 1. God's writing in this form, (as a man to his friend,) speaks Christ's love to the church, his spouse. 2. There were not seven books written, but one book in which these seven epistles were, out of which each church, or the church in its several

REVELATION II

periods, might learn what concerned it. 3. These epistles concerning matters of faith and manners, are written plainly, not in mysterious expressions. 4. The scope of them all is to instruct, reprove, commend, and comfort. 5. They are all directed to the ministers of the churches, as their heads, but the matter concerns the whole church. 6. It is also observed, that Christ, in the beginning of every epistle, notifieth himself by some one of those things mentioned in the vision in the former chapter. Chap. ii. 1, *These things saith he that holdeth the seven stars*, chap. i. 16. Ver. 8, *The first and the last, which was dead and is alive*, chap. i. 17, 18. Ver. 12. *These things saith he which hath the sharp sword with two edges*, chap. i. 16. Ver. 18, *The Son of God, who hath his eyes like unto a flame of fire, and his feet like fine brass*, chap. i. 14, 15. Chap. iii. 1. *He that hath the seven Spirits of God, and the seven stars*, chap. i. 4, 16. Ver. 7, *He that hath the key of David, that is holy and true, that openeth*, &c., chap. i. 5, 18. Ver. 14, *The faithful and true witness*, chap. i. 5.

UNTO the angel of the church of Ephesus write; These things saith [a]he that holdeth the seven stars in his right hand, [b]who walketh in the midst of the seven golden candlesticks;

a ch. 1. 16, 20.
b ch. 1. 13.

Ephesus was the principal city of Asia the Less, it lay in the western parts of it, upon the Ionian Sea; a city of great riches and trade, but much given to idolatry and superstition, famous for the temple of Diana. Paul was there twice; at his second coming he stayed thereabouts three years, Acts xviii., xix., xx. He was by a tumult driven thence into Macedonia, and left Timothy there, 1 Tim. i. 3. It appears from Acts xx. 17, that there were more ministers there than one; but they were all angels, and from the oneness of their business are all called an *angel*. *These things saith he that holdeth the seven stars in his right hand;* that is, Christ, chap. i. 16, 20, who hath put an honour on his ministers, showeth special favour to them, and will protect them. *Who walketh in the midst of the seven golden candlesticks;* who hath a special eye to his church, being not an idle spectator, but present with his church, to observe how all in it walk and perform their several parts, and is at hand, either to reward or punish them.

2 [c]I know thy works, and thy labour, and thy patience, and how thou canst not bear them which are evil: and [d]thou hast tried them [e]which say they are apostles, and are not, and hast found them liars:

c Ps. 1. 6. ver. 9, 13, 19. ch. 3. 1, 8, 15.
d 1 John 4. 1.
e 2 Cor. 11.: 13. 2 Pet. 2. 1.

I know thy works: these words being in the front of all the seven epistles, cannot be interpreted as signifying a knowledge of approbation, as Psal. i. 6, but of a comprehension in the understanding, and as signifying Christ's omnisciency; though it be true, that the Lord both understood and approved of some of the works of this church particularly. *And thy labour, and thy patience;* their labour in propagating the knowledge of Christ and doctrine of the gospel, and their patient taking up and bearing the cross. *And how thou canst not bear them which are evil;* and their zeal and warmth, that they would not endure either persons erroneous in judgment, or lewd in their lives, in their communion. *And thou hast tried them which say they are apostles, and are not:* in the primitive church there were some that falsely pretended an immediate call or mission from Christ, to preach what they did, but this church would not endure them. It appears from Paul's Second Epistle to Timothy, that there were then false teachers very busy in that church; possibly Ebion and Cerinthus, (who both lived in this time, and Cerinthus preached in Asia,) or their disciples, might be some of them. They tried them, possibly, by the word of God, according to the rules given in it to try the spirits. *And hast found them liars;* and found that they had no such immediate mission, no authority from Christ.

3 And hast borne, and hast patience, and for my name's sake hast laboured, and hast [f]not fainted.

f Gal. 6. 9. Heb. 12. 3, 5.

And hast borne the contradiction of false teachers, and the persecutions of Jews and pagans; for at this time the second persecution was began by Domitian. *And hast patience;* grace (with quietness and submission) to bear the will of God in any sort of evils. *And for my name's sake hast laboured;* and for me hast laboured actively in propagating the truths of my gospel, as well as passively in the furnace of trials and persecutions. *And hast not fainted;* and hast persevered so as thou hast neither been seduced to other doctrine by false teachers, nor lost thy integrity and holiness of conversation.

4 Nevertheless I have *somewhat* against thee, because thou hast left thy first love.

Nevertheless I have somewhat against thee; something to accuse thee of, and blame thee for. *Because thou hast left thy first love;* of late thou hast not been so warm in the propagation of my gospel, and maintaining my truth. The love of many in this church, both toward God and their brethren, probably was cooled, though not wholly extinguished.

5 Remember therefore from whence thou art fallen, and repent, and do the first works; [g]or else I will come unto thee quickly, and will remove thy candlestick out of his place, except thou repent.

g Matt. 21. 41, 43.

Remember therefore from whence thou art fallen; that is, in what degree thy love was formerly, and compare it with what it is now. *And repent;* repentance in man, signifieth both the change of the heart and of the actions. *And do the first works;* recover thy former warmth of love, and zeal for good works. *Or else I will come unto thee quickly;* if thou do not, I that know thee, and walk in the midst of thee, will show myself an enemy to thee. *And will remove thy candlestick out of his place;* and unchurch thee, and say unto thee, Lo-ammi, You are not my people. Which threatening is long since made good; for where is now the famous church of Ephesus?

6 But this thou hast, that thou hatest the deeds of [h]the Nicolaitanes, which I also hate.

h ver. 15.

But this thou hast; thou hast yet thus much to commend thee. *That thou hatest the deeds of the Nicolaitanes;* thou hatest the deeds of those who teach the lawfulness of a common use of wives, and eat things offered to idols; for these, they say, were the tenets of the Nicolaitanes, so called from one Nicholas; but whether he were one of the first deacons, named Acts vi. 5, (who, they say, to avoid the imputation of jealousy, brought forth his wife, being a beautiful woman, and prostituted her,) or from some other of that name, I cannot determine. *Which I also hate;* God, as a lover of his own order, and of human society, hateth such doctrines and practices as are contrary to the rule of his word, and tend to the confusion of human societies.

7 [i]He that hath an ear, let him hear what the Spirit saith unto the churches; To him that overcometh will I give [k]to eat of [l]the tree of life, which is in the midst of the paradise of God?

i Mat. 11. 15. & 13. 9, 43. ver. 11, 17, 29. ch. 3. 6, 13, 22. & 13. 9.
k ch. 22. 2, 14.
l Gen. 2. 9.

He that hath an ear, let him hear; to whom God hath given an ability and power to understand what I say. It is a form of speech which Christ often used, when he would quicken up people's attention, Matt. xi. 15; xiii. 9, 43; Mark iv. 9, 23; vii. 16: we shall find it again in these two chapters six times; from which some would conclude, that in these epistles there is something mysterious, parabolical, and prophetical, it being a form of speech prefixed to many parables. *What the Spirit saith;* the Holy Spirit of God, from whose inspiration all Scripture is. *Unto the churches;* not only at Ephesus, but elsewhere in Asia, or any other part of the world. *To him that overcometh;* that is, a conqueror in fighting the good fight of faith, against the world, the flesh, and the devil. *Will I give to eat of the tree of life;* I will give him a share in my merits, and eternal life; which blessed enjoyments are set out unto us under the notion of eating, Luke xii. 37; xxii. 28, &c.; John x. 28. *This is the promise that he hath promised us,* 1 John ii. 25. Heaven is expressed to us under this notion, with reference to the tree of life, mentioned Gen. ii. 9, which was in the old Paradise; for it is added, *which is in the midst of the paradise of God;* or, which is the same, Christ himself is here intended, who is the tree of life, mentioned chap. xxii. 2; and the happiness of heaven is thus expressed, 1 Thess. iv. 17, *We shall be ever with the Lord.* This is the sum of the epistle to the first-mentioned church, by which those that judge these epistles prophetical, understand all the primitive churches during the apostles' age, or the most of their ages, for John himself lived under the second persecution.

8 And unto the angel of the church in Smyrna write; These things saith ᵐ the first and the last, which was dead, and is alive;

m ch. 1. 8, 17, 18.

Smyrna was a city in Ionia; we read not when, or by whom, the gospel was first planted and a church gathered there; nor can we tell who are meant by *the angel of* this church: see chap i. 20. That it was no single person is probable, for he speaks plurally, ver. 10, *the devil shall cast some of you,* ἐξ ὑμῶν, *into prison. These things saith the first and the last, which was dead, and is alive:* for the meaning of this phrase, see annotations on chap. i. 8, 17, 18; only it is observable how Christ, speaking to this church under great tribulation and persecution, fits a name proper to comfort them; for he himself *was dead,* and yet now *alive,* and he living, those that believe in him, because he lives, shall live also, John xiv. 19; and as he was *the first,* so he will be *the last,* surviving all his enemies, and be at last a conqueror over them.

9 ⁿI know thy works, and tribulation, and poverty, (but thou art °rich) and *I know* the blasphemy of ᴾ them which say they are Jews, and are not, ᑫ but *are* the synagogue of Satan.

n ver. 2.
o Luke 12. 21. 1 Tim. 6. 18. Jam. 2. 5.
p Rom. 2. 17, 28, 29. & 9. 6.
q ch. 3. 9.

I know thy works, and tribulation: though the term *know* doth not necessarily signify approbation, yet, both as to the church of Ephesus and Smyrna, the particular works mentioned assure us, that God approved their patient suffering affliction for his name. *And poverty;* and the poor condition (as to outward things) into which they had brought themselves, for their owning and profession of the gospel of Christ, having their estates rent from them, &c. *But thou art rich;* but yet they were rich, both really in the love and favour of God, and also in the esteem of God, who accounteth them rich who abound in spiritual habits, and good works, the exercise of those habits. *And I know the blasphemy of them which say they are Jews, and are not:* God also knows the evil speeches of his church's enemies, whether native Jews, glorying in circumcision and the law, and that they were descended from Abraham; or false Christians, who may be here meant (called Jews by a figure; the Jews being once the only church of God). *But are the synagogue of Satan;* but are indeed a collection of devils, or the children of the devil, whose works they do, continually reviling true Christians, and murdering the saints, after the manner of their father, who *was a murderer from the beginning.*

10 ʳ Fear none of those things which thou shalt suffer: behold, the devil shall cast *some* of you into prison, that ye may be tried; and ye shall have tribulation ten days: ˢ be thou faithful unto death, and I will give thee ᵗ a crown of life.

r Mat. 10. 22.
s Mat. 24. 13.
t Jam. 1. 12. ch. 3. 11.

Fear none of those things which thou shalt suffer; thou art like to suffer yet sharper things than thou hast suffered, the persecutions are but begun; but pluck up a good courage, fear not your enemies, Matt. x. 28. *Behold, the devil shall cast some of you into prison;* you shall be cast into prison, by Jews and pagans, who are the devil's instruments, and execute his malice against you; which should both encourage you, that your fight is with the common enemy of mankind, and teach you to pity and pray for your persecutors, who are but the devil's instruments, whose hearts he hath filled with malice against you. *That ye may be tried;* that your faith, love, patience, obedience, may be tried. *And ye shall have tribulation ten days:* interpreters are divided about these *ten days,* what space of time is meant by them; some think the whole time of the ten persecutions, but they lasted above two hundred years; others will have them the ten years of Trajan's persecution, from the year 99 to 109. Others observe, that in ten days are two hundred and forty hours, which make up the number of years from 85, when the second persecution began, (under which John at this time was,) to 325, when all the persecutions ceased. But to let these fancies go: it is either a certain number put for an uncertain; or, it signifies many days; as in Gen. xxxi. 42, *Thou hast changed my wages ten times,* that is, many times; so 2 Sam. xix. 43; Job xix. 3. Or else it signifies a little time, as in Gen. xxiv. 55; Amos v. 3; vi. 9. If we understand this epistle as only concerning the church of Smyrna at that time, it may signify a small time. If we understand it prophetically, describing the state of all churches, till the pagan persecution ceased, (which was more than two hundred and forty years,) ten days signifies a long time. *Be thou faithful unto death,* hold fast to thy profession of faith and holiness to the end of thy life here, *and I will give thee a crown of life,* and I will give thee eternal life and salvation, which shall be a great reward. It is called *a crown of righteousness,* 2 Tim. iv. 8.

11 ᵘ "He that hath an ear, let him hear what the Spirit saith unto the churches; He that overcometh shall not be hurt of ˣ the second death.

u ver. 7. ch. 13. 9.
x ch. 20. 14. & 21. 8.

He that hath an ear, let him hear what the Spirit saith unto the churches; He that overcometh: for the opening of these passages, see the notes on ver. 7. *Shall not be hurt of the second death;* we read of *the second death,* chap. xx. 6, 14: the meaning is, that he shall escape the eternal damnation of soul and body in the day of judgment.

Those that make these epistles prophetical say, that the church of Smyrna was a type of all the churches of Christ to the year 325, (when Constantine overcame Lycinius, and gave rest and peace to the churches of Christ,) which was all a time of severe persecution under the Roman emperors, who to that time were all heathens. It is very observable, that Christ blameth nothing in this church; the church of God keeps always its purity best in the fire; but doubtless there were in this time many apostacies, and other errors, but God allows much to his people's temptations; hence, though Job showed much impatience, yet we are called to behold him as a pattern of patience.

12 And to the angel of the church in Pergamos write; These things saith ʸ he which hath the sharp sword with two edges;

y ch. 1. 16.

Pergamos was a famous city of Troas; we read of Pergamos no where else in Scripture, but of Troas we read of Paul's being there, Acts xvi. 8, 11; xx. 5, 6, and preaching Christ there, 2 Cor. ii. 12. *These things saith he which hath the sharp sword with two edges:* see the notes on chap. i. 16.

13 ᶻ I know thy works, and where thou dwellest, *even* ᵃ where Satan's seat *is:* and thou holdest fast my name, and hast not denied my faith, even in those days wherein Antipas *was* my faithful martyr, who was slain among you, where Satan dwelleth.

z ver. 2.
a ver. 9.

I know thy works, and where thou dwellest; God knows all his people's circumstances, where they dwell, as well as what they do, and how they behave themselves in their habitations. *Even where Satan's seat is;* where the devil rules by his pagan deputies and antichrist's officers. *And thou holdest fast my name;* the word of my truth, by which I am known, as a man by his name. *And hast not denied my faith;* neither by the words of thy mouth, nor by any apostacy from this profession, notwithstanding the temptations thou hast had from seducers and from persecutors, and the sight of those who have been put to death for their profession. *Even in those days wherein Antipas was my faithful martyr:* it is much no ecclesiastical history makes mention of this martyr Antipas, which argueth him to have been a person but of an obscure note in the world; but Christ seeth and taketh notice of those little ones who belong to him, though the world overlooks them. Our being able from no history to give an account of this martyr, hath inclined some to think this epistle wholly prophetical, and that Antipas signifieth not any particular person, but all those that have opposed the pope, as if it were *Antipapa*. But certainly there was such a martyr as Antipas belonging to the church at Smyrna at that time, who suffered for the truth, though we do not allow this church to have been typical of all the gospel churches for many years.

14 But I have a few things against thee, because thou hast there them that hold the doctrine of ᵇBalaam, who taught Balac to cast a stumblingblock before the children of Israel, ᶜto eat things sacrificed unto idols, ᵈand to commit fornication.

b Num. 24. 14. & 25. 1. & 31. 16. 2 Pet. 2. 15. Jude 11.
c ver. 20. Acts 15. 29. 1 Cor. 8. 9, 10. & 10. 19, 20.
d 1 Cor. 6. 13, &c.

But I have a few things against thee; though I have much to commend thee for, yet I have some things to accuse thee of, and to complain of thee for. *Because thou hast there them that hold the doctrine of Balaam:* by the doctrine of Balaam, he means the doctrine of the Nicolaitanes, (as he expounds himself, ver. 15,) which was like the doctrine of Balaam. *Who taught Balac to cast a stumblingblock before the children of Israel;* that Balaam of whom we read, Numb. xxiv., xxv., who being sent for by Balak the king of Moab to come and curse Israel, and finding that God restrained him, and turned his tongue from cursing them to pronounce blessings to them, instructed Balak at last how to lay a stumblingblock before them, to make them to fall, viz. to set the Moabitish women to tempt them to commit uncleanness with them, and so to feast with them in their idols' temples, and eat of their meat first offered unto their idols.

15 So hast thou also them that hold the doctrine ᵉof the Nicolaitanes, which thing I hate.

e ver. 6.

So hast thou also them that hold the doctrine of the Nicolaitanes; so, saith he, thou sufferest in thy communion filthy persons, who maintain fornication lawful, and the lawfulness of eating meat offered to idols, which exactly corresponds with Balaam's doctrine or counsel given to Balak, in order to his weakening the Israelites by separating them from God. His counsel took place, to the destruction of twenty-four thousand Israelites. *Which thing I hate;* I am the same God still, and hate such doctrines, as much as ever I did in the time of Balak.

16 Repent; or else I will come unto thee quickly, and ᶠwill fight against them with the sword of my mouth.

f Is. 11. 4. 2 Thess. 2. 8. ch. 1. 16. & 19. 15, 21.

Repent; thou that art guilty of conniving at such things, change thy mind and practice, and let those who have entertained these opinions, and run into those filthy practices, change their hearts and practices; *or else I will come unto thee quickly;* I will quickly come against thee, and punish thee: see the notes on ver. 5. *And will fight against them with the sword of my mouth;* and fight against them by my word; either convincing them, or pronouncing sentence against them; or, by raising up other teachers, who shall preach my word more faithfully, and whose doctrine shall be like a sword to devour and to destroy them.

17 ᵍHe that hath an ear, let him hear what the Spirit saith unto the churches; To him that overcometh will I give to eat of the hidden manna, and will give him a white stone, and in the stone ʰa new name written, which no man knoweth saving he that receiveth *it*.

g ver. 7, 11.
h ch. 3. 12. & 19. 12.

He that hath an ear, let him hear what the Spirit saith unto the churches; To him that overcometh: see the annotations on ver. 7. *Will I give to eat of the hidden manna;* here is a manifest allusion to that *bread from heaven*, with which God fed his people in the wilderness, called *angels' food*, Psal. lxxviii. 25. The story of it we have, Exod. xvi. 31, 32; a pot of which God ordained to be kept in the ark, for a memorial of God's mercy, Heb. ix. 4. It was a type of Christ, who was the *true bread* that came down *from heaven*, John vi. 32, 33. It here signifies Christ himself, with all the influences of his grace, whether for strength or comfort. As a feast was wont to follow a victory; so Christ promiseth to those that fought, and overcame in the spiritual fight, to feast them with himself and the influences of his Spirit. *And will give him a white stone:* the use of stones anciently was so various, that it hath given a great liberty to interpreters to vary in their senses of the *white stone* here mentioned. They made use of them (as we since of counters) to count; they used them also in judgments, acquitting persons by white stones, on which their names were written, as they condemned others by black stones; they also used them in giving suffrages in elections, &c.; they also used them to mark happy or lucky days, and they used other stones to mark such days as they counted unlucky; and finally, they used them as rewards to those who conquered in their games. Hence interpreters vary in their opinions, whether this be a general promise of a reward, or a more particular promise of pardon and absolution; or, of the assurance of their election to life. It seems most properly to be interpreted of pardon, or the notification of pardon of sins, or more generally of a reward. By the *new name, which no man knoweth saving he that receiveth it*, the same thing seemeth to be signified, the Spirit witnessing with their spirits that they are the children of God. They say, that in those white stones (used in absolutions of persons, or in giving suffrages) the name of the person absolved or chosen was wont to be written, and none knew it but those that had it, unless they imparted it, to which custom this allusion is.

Those that make this church typical, say it typified the churches of the gospel during the times of popery, to the end of the persecutions of the Waldenses and Albigenses, when about one hundred thousand of them were destroyed by eight thousand papists; or, the time when antichrist first sat in the temple of God, as chap. xiii., and the woman fled into the wilderness, chap. xii.

18 And unto the angel of the church in Thyatira write, These things saith the Son of God, ⁱwho hath his eyes like unto a flame of fire, and his feet *are* like fine brass;

i ch. 1. 14, 15

Thyatira was a city of Mysia or Lydia, not far from Philippi, the chief city of Macedonia; for Lydia, who traded in purple, and was of this city, went to Philippi to trade, as we read, Acts xvi. 12, 14. *Eyes like unto a flame of fire:* see chap. i. 14, 15: it signifies either angry eyes, or quick and piercing eyes. The comparing of *his feet to fine brass*, seemeth to signify both the purity and holiness of his ways and methods of providence, and also his firmness and steadiness in them.

19 ᵏI know thy works, and charity, and service, and faith, and thy patience, and thy works; and the last *to be* more than the first.

k ver. 2.

I know thy works; the works of the ministry of this church were such as Christ knew, not only with a knowledge of comprehension, but approbation also. *And charity;* such were his charity to Christians that were in distress. *And service;* his diligence in his ministration. *And faith;* his faith, and adherence to Christ, and the doctrine of the gospel. *And thy patience;* his meek bearing of his crosses and trials. *And thy works;* his other works, the fruit of faith and love. *And the last to be more than the first;* and his proficiency both in spiritual habits, and good works, the fruits of them.

20 Notwithstanding I have a few things against thee, because thou sufferest that woman ˡJezebel, which calleth herself a prophetess, to teach and to seduce my servants ᵐto commit fornication, and to eat things sacrificed unto idols.

l 1 Kings 16. 31. & 21. 25. 2 Kings 9. 7. m Ex. 34. 15. Acts 15. 20, 29. 1 Cor. 10. 19, 20. ver. 14.

Notwithstanding I have a few things against thee: see the notes upon ver. 4, 14. *Because thou sufferest that woman Jezebel:* the doctrine of the Nicolaitanes, mentioned ver. 6, 15, is so plainly expressed in the latter part of the verse, viz. maintaining the lawfulness of eating things offered to idols, and of fornication; that whosoever this woman was, it is plain she was one of that filthy sect. It is also plain, that she is called *Jezebel* with allusion to that wicked woman of that name who was the wife of Ahab, of whom we read, 1 Kings xvi. 31. She was an instrument to bring Ahab her husband to serve and worship Baal. It is also plain, that she was one that pretended to Divine revelations; she *called herself a prophetess;* and that taught in public, which no women but prophetesses might do, 1 Cor. xiv. 34; 1 Tim. ii. 11, 12: and that she taught a community of women, and the lawfulness as of *fornication,* so of eating *things sacrificed to idols,* directly contrary to the apostle's doctrine, 1 Cor. ix. 10. But what she was cannot be determined; for though we allow this church to be typical of the church in the times of popery, and the popish synagogue, which maintaineth both these things to be the antitype; yet certainly there was some famous heretical strumpet in this church, which the governors did not restrain and cast out of their communion; which is the thing Christ had against this church, and the officers in it, who ought to have restrained her extravagancies both in teaching such doctrines, (being contrary to the apostle's doctrine in the places before mentioned,) and from teaching at all, being no prophetess though she pretended to it.

n Rom. 2. 4. ch. 9. 20.   21 And I gave her space ⁿ to repent of her fornication; and she repented not.

I was not quick with her, but gave her a time of patience, and did not cut her off at first; but she was incorrigible, and went on in her sinful courses.

22 Behold, I will cast her into a bed, and them that commit adultery with her into great tribulation, except they repent of their deeds.

I will cast her into a bed; another kind of bed than she hath sinned in and by, not a bed of ease and pleasure, but of pain and torment. Nor shall the seduced escape, they shall also be cast into *great tribulation,* pains and torments of conscience, or afflictions more corporal, either from the more immediate hand of God, or the hands of men. *Except they repent of their deeds;* this is to be supposed to all God's threatenings of judgments, the execution of them ordinarily may be prevented by repentance, and such is the patience of God, that he gives the vilest sinners a space to repent.

o 1 Sam. 16. 7. 1 Chr. 28. 9. & 29. 17. 2 Chr. 6. 30. Ps. 7. 9. Jer. 11. 20. & 17. 10. & 20. 12. John 2. 24, 25. Acts 1. 24. Rom. 8. 27. ch. 20. 12.   23 And I will kill her children with death; and all the churches shall know that ᵒ I am he which searcheth the reins and hearts: and ᵖ I will give unto every one of you according to your works.

p ch. 62. 12. Matt. 16. 27. Rom. 2. 6. & 14. 12. 2 Cor. 5. 10. Gal. 6. 5.

And I will kill her children, those who are seduced by her, *with death;* I will destroy them; unless some special death, such as the plague, be here threatened. So shall all the churches near Thyatira know, that I am a God who do not only take notice of overt, scandalous acts, but of the secret thoughts, motions, counsels, and designs of men's hearts, Psal. vii. 10; Jer. xi. 20; xvii. 10; and that I am a just God, who will deal with all according to their works.

24 But unto you I say, and unto the rest in Thyatira, as many as have not this doctrine, and which have not known the depths of Satan, as they speak; ᵠ I will put upon you none other burden.

q Acts 15. 28.

But unto you I say; you that are the ministers, for they are distinguished from the rest in Thyatira. The word again is plural, which lets us know these epistles were directed to no single persons. *And unto the rest in Thyatira, as many as have not this doctrine;* the rest of the members of the church in Thyatira, who have not embraced this doctrine of the Nicolaitanes published by Jezebel, &c. *As they speak;* those seducers call their doctrine deep things, great mysteries revealed to them; as there are *the deep things of God,* 1 Cor. ii. 10, so these seducers would pretend their doctrines also were deep things: Christ calls them the devil's mysteries, deep things of Satan. *I will put upon you none other burden;* I will lay no other burden of trials and afflictions.

r ch. 3. 11.   25 But ʳ that which ye have *already* hold fast till I come.

But that which ye have already; than you already groan under. Or, no other precepts than what you have had from the apostles: the precepts of God are called burdens, Matt. xi. 30; Acts xv. 28. *Hold fast till I come;* hold fast your profession, your faith and holiness, till I come to judgment.

26 And he that overcometh, and keepeth ˢ my works unto the end, ᵗ to him will I give power over the nations:

s John 6. 29. 1 John 3. 23. t Mat. 19. 28. Luke 22. 29, 30. 1 Cor. 6. 3. ch. 3. 21. & 20. 4.

And he that overcometh, and keepeth my works unto the end: see the notes on ver. 7, 11, 17. Overcoming is here expounded by keeping Christ's works; that is, either the works by him commanded, or walking as he walked, and persevering therein to the end of his or their lives. *To him will I give power over the nations;* either to judge those who live heathenish lives; or to convert nations to the faith; or, which is most probable, he shall sit with me upon a throne in the day of judgment, Matt. xix. 28, and *judge the world,* 1 Cor. vi. 2.

27 ᵘ And he shall rule them with a rod of iron; as the vessels of a potter shall they be broken to shivers: even as I received of my Father.

u Ps. 2. 8, 9. & 49. 14. Dan. 7. 22. ch. 12. 5. & 19. 15.

And he shall rule them with a rod of iron: an iron rod either signifies a right rod, that will not be easily bent and made crooked; or a severe rod, which is most probably the sense: see Psal. ii. 9; chap. xii. 5. The words by the psalmist are applied to Christ, and to the church, Rev. xii. 5: to particular saints here, who rule the nations either in Christ their Head, or with Christ as their Chieftain, with the word of God powerfully convincing the world of sin and righteousness. *As the vessels of a potter shall they be broken to shivers;* and all paganism and heathen idolatries shall be broken in pieces. Or, in the day of judgment, the saints that persevere shall sit with Christ, and judge and condemn the world severely; and then they shall be broken in pieces, never again to be sodered or cemented. *Even as I received of my Father;* for such a power and authority my Father hath given me, and I will give it to all them.

28 And I will give him ˣ the morning star.

x 2 Pet. 1. 19. ch. 22. 16.

Either the light of glory, the blessed vision of God, or a certain hope of eternal life; or the Holy Spirit, called so, 2 Pet. i. 19; or rather, of myself. Christ himself is not called the *Sun of righteousness,* Mal. iv. 2, but the *Morning-star,* chap. xxii. 16, because he excelleth all other stars in glory, and scattereth the darkness of ignorance and error by the light of his gospel: I will make him partaker of myself.

29 ʸ He that hath an ear, let him hear what the Spirit saith unto the churches.

y ver. 7.

Here the same conclusion of this epistle as of all the rest, ver. 7, 11, 17: see the notes on ver. 7.

Those who make this epistle typical and prophetical, make it a type of all the churches of Christ, from about the year 1260, or the end of the persecution of the Waldenses, until the protestant religion so far obtained, that whole nations owned it, which was about 1560, by which time England and Scotland had made it the religion of those nations: it had before this prevailed in Germany, Helvetia, France, and many other places, where it was the religion of whole cities and particular jurisdictions, &c.

CHAP. III

What John was commanded to write in commendation or reproof to the angels of the churches of Sardis, 1—6, Philadelphia, 7—13, and Laodicea, 14—22.

AND unto the angel of the church in Sardis write; These things saith he ᵃ that hath the seven Spirits of God, and the seven stars; ᵇ I know thy works, that thou hast a name that thou livest, ᶜ and art dead.

a ch. 1. 4, 16. & 4. 5. & 5. 6. b ch. 2. 2. c Eph. 2. 1, 5. 1 Tim. 5. 6.

The angel of the church: see the notes on chap. ii. 12.

REVELATION III

Write: see the notes on chap. i. 11. *The seven Spirits of God, and the seven stars:* see the notes on chap. i. 3, and chap. i. 20. *I know thy works:* this phrase here (as appears from what follows) can signify nothing but Christ's comprehension of the works of this church in his understanding, not his approbation of them. *That thou hast a name that thou livest;* the ministry of this church had a name, that is, were reported as famous for their faith, diligence, and holiness; but their faith, without suitable works, was dead, and they were no better than hypocrites. *And art dead;* spiritually dead.

2 Be watchful, and strengthen the things which remain, that are ready to die: for I have not found thy works perfect before God.

Be watchful, against sin, and unto thy duty, to perform it in a better manner than formerly. *And strengthen the things which remain, that are ready to die;* improve those gifts and good habits which are left thee as yet, but are faint and ready to die, if thou dost not look after the improvement and strengthening of them. *For I have not found thy works perfect before God;* for I have not found thy works before God (whether thy works in thy ministry, or in thy conversation) such as they ought to be; thou mightest have done me more service, and thou mightest have done what thou hast done with more uprightness and sincerity.

^d 1 Tim. 6. 20. 2 Tim. 1. 13. ver. 11. e ver. 19. f Mat. 24. 42, 43. & 25. 13. Mark 13. 33. Luke 12. 39, 40. 1 Thess. 5. 2, 6. 2 Pet. 3. 10. ch. 16. 15.

3 ^d Remember therefore how thou hast received and heard, and hold fast, and ^e repent. ^f If therefore thou shalt not watch, I will come on thee as a thief, and thou shalt not know what hour I will come upon thee.

Remember therefore how thou hast received and heard; to wit, from the apostles of the Lord Jesus Christ. All true reformation, either of doctrine or manners, lies in the reduction of it to the doctrine delivered, and the rules of life given by them. *And hold fast, and repent:* wherein our judgment or practice is conformable to theirs, it is to be held fast; wherein it hath varied, it is to be repented of. *If therefore thou shalt not watch, I will come on thee as a thief;* if thou shalt not keep thyself free from gross sins or errors, and give diligence to do it, I will come to thee, not as a friend to comfort and refresh thee, but as a thief to rob and destroy thee, and that suddenly. *And thou shalt not know what hour I will come upon thee;* I will surprise thee with my judgments, and thou shalt not know when my judgments shall overtake thee.

g Acts 1. 15.
h Jude 23.
i ch.4.4.& 6 11.& 7. 9, 13.

4 Thou hast ^g a few names even in Sardis which have not ^h defiled their garments; and they shall walk with me ⁱ in white: for they are worthy.

Thou hast a few names even in Sardis, a few persons even in that polluted place, *which have not defiled their garments;* who have kept their integrity and innocency. There is a garment of Christ's righteousness, which, once put on, is never lost, nor can be defiled; but there are garments of holiness also: hence the apostle calls to Christians to be *clothed with humility.* As sin is expressed under the notion of nakedness, so holiness is expressed under the notion of a garment, Ezek. xvi. 10; 1 Pet. v. 5. Those who have not defiled their garments, are those that have kept a pure conscience. *And they shall walk with me in white:* the Romans used to clothe their nobles, and such as were competitors for honours, in white garments; the priests and Levites also amongst the Jews, when they ministered, were clothed in white, 2 Chron. v. 12. God and his holy angels are in Scripture set out to us as clothed in white, Dan. vii. 9; Matt. xvii. 2; xxviii. 3. Those that triumphed upon victories obtained, were clothed in white amongst the Romans. To these usages, or some of them, the allusion is, and the meaning is, they shall be to me as kings, and priests, and nobles, they shall be made partakers of my glory: *for they are worthy;* though they have not merited it, yet I have judged them worthy; they are worthy, though not with respect to their merit, yet with respect to my promise.

k ch. 19. 8.

5 He that overcometh, ^k the same shall be clothed in white raiment; and

I will not ^l blot out his name out of the ^m book of life, but ⁿ I will confess his name before my Father, and before his angels.

l Ex. 32. 32. Ps. 69. 28. m Phil. 4. 3. ch. 13. 8. & 17. 8. & 20. 12. & 21. 27. n Mat. 10. 32. Luke 12. 8.

He that overcometh, the same shall be clothed in white raiment; he that overcometh in the spiritual fight, shall be honoured as a triumpher. *And I will not blot out his name out of the book of life;* that is, I will give him everlasting life: the phrase is an allusion to men who use to keep books, and in them the names of persons to whom they will show kindness. The *book of life,* applied to God, signifieth his eternal predestination, or purpose to bring some to heaven; out of which book, though none can be blotted out whose name is once wrote in, yet those whose names are in this book may be under some fears and apprehensions to the contrary. Christ assures them to the contrary, that they shall certainly be saved, but lets them know that this assurance depends upon their perseverance; of which also some make this phrase a promise. *But I will confess his name before my Father, and before his angels;* in the day of judgment I will own them, and acknowledge them as mine before my Father and all the angels, Matt. x. 32; Luke xii. 8.

6 ^o He that hath an ear, let him hear what the Spirit saith unto the churches.

o ch. 2. 7.

The common conclusion of all the epistles: see the notes on ver. 7, 11, 17, 29.

Those who make these churches typical, and the epistles prophetical of the complexion of all the churches of Christ which shall be to the end of the world, say the church of Sardis typifieth those reformed churches after the year 1560, that should cast off antichrist, but continue in a more imperfect state, contenting themselves with a bare disclaiming antichrist, but not rising up to a perfect reformation.

7 And to the angel of the church in Philadelphia write; These things saith ^p he that is holy, ^q he that is true, he that hath ^r the key of David, ^s he that openeth, and no man shutteth; and ^t shutteth, and no man openeth;

p Acts 3. 14. q 1 John 5. 20. ver. 14. ch. 1. 5. & 6. 10. & 19. 11. r Is. 22. 22. Luke 1. 32. ch. 1. 18. s Mat. 16 19. t Job 12. 14.

And to the angel of the church in Philadelphia write: see the notes on chap. i. 20; ii. 1. Of this Philadelphia we read no more in holy writ. We are told there were three cities of that name, one in Egypt, one in Syria, another in Phrygia, or in Mysia or Lydia, which is that here intended. *These things saith he that is holy;* that is, the Holy One, Acts iii. 14. *He that is true;* true to his word of promise or threatening. *He that hath the key of David;* that is, the key of the house of David, mentioned Isa. xxii. 22; the key of the church, which answered the temple, the house David designed for God: the use of the key is to open and shut, or make fast. *He that openeth, and no man shutteth; and shutteth, and no man openeth;* who admits into the kingdom of heaven whom he pleaseth, and none can hinder him, and shutteth out of heaven whom he pleaseth. The house of David typified the church, the church containeth the number of those that shall be saved; Christ is here described as he who hath the sole and absolute power of saving and condemning whom he pleaseth.

8 ^u I know thy works: behold, I have set before thee ^x an open door, and no man can shut it: for thou hast a little strength, and hast kept my word, and hast not denied my name.

u ver. 1.
x 1 Cor. 16. 9. 2 Cor. 2. 12.

I know thy works: it is very probable, that our Lord, by these ministers' works, understands the works proper to them in their function, their labour in preaching and propagating the gospel, which Christ did not only know and observe, but also approve of, and promiseth them a liberty to go on, and success in their labours, under the notion of *an open door:* see 1 Cor. xvi. 9; 2 Cor. ii. 12; Col. iv. 3. *And no man can shut it;* so as it should not be in the power of adversaries to hinder his success. *For thou hast a little strength;* both inward strength, and outward helps and advantages. *And hast kept my word;* the doctrine of faith is by thee kept pure, as also my precepts for a holy life. *And hast not denied my name;* and thou hast not been by any temptation prevailed upon to apostatize from the profession of the gospel.

y ch 2 9.

9 Behold, I will make ʸthem of the synagogue of Satan, which say they are Jews, and are not, but do lie ; behold,

z Is. 49. 23. & 60. 14.

ᶻI will make them to come and worship before thy feet, and to know that I have loved thee.

Them of the synagogue of Satan ; so he calleth all Jews that opposed Christianity, or all pretended but not real professors. *Which say they are Jews, and are not, but do lie : For he is not a Jew, which is one outwardly ; neither is that circumcision which is of the flesh ; but he is a Jew, which is one inwardly,* &c., Rom. ii. 28, 29. By this term also he may mean all false and hypocritical professors, who would make themselves the church, the only church of God, but are far enough from it, hating, maligning, and opposing those who would keep stricter to the rule of the gospel. *Behold, I will make them to come and worship before thy feet ;* I will by my providence so order it, that these men shall come and honour thee, paying a civil respect and homage to thee. *And to know that I have loved thee ;* and to know that I have a greater kindness for thee than for them.

10 Because thou hast kept the word of

a 2 Pet. 2. 9.

my patience, ªI also will keep thee from the hour of temptation, which shall come

b Luke 2. 1.

upon ᵇall the world, to try them that

c Is. 24. 17.

dwell ᶜupon the earth.

Because thou hast kept the word of my patience : the doctrine of the gospel is, unquestionably, the word here called the word of the Lord's patience, because it was that word, that doctrine, which (as those times went) could not be adhered to and observed without much patience in those that adhered to it ; both actively, waiting for the promises revealed in it, and passively, enduring all manner of trials and crosses. To keep this word, was to keep close not only to the matters of faith revealed in it, but to the duty imposed by it upon ministers and others in the preaching and propagating of the gospel, and all the duties of a holy life. *I also will keep thee from the hour of temptation, which shall come upon all the world ;* for this faithfulness God promises to keep the ministers of this church from those persecutions which raged elsewhere, and were further, in Trajan's time, to come upon all Christians living under the Roman empire. *To try them that dwell upon the earth ;* to try those Christians that lived within that empire, how well they would adhere to Christ, and the profession of the gospel. This I take to be a more proper sense, than theirs who would interpret this *hour of temptation* of the day of judgment, which is never so called.

d Phil. 4. 5.
ch. 1. 3. &
22. 7, 12, 20.
e ver. 3.
ch. 2. 25.
f ch. 2. 10.

11 Behold, ᵈI come quickly : ᵉhold that fast which thou hast, that no man take ᶠthy crown.

Behold, I come quickly ; ταχύ, which certainly is the same with ἐν τάχει ; and it might be as well concluded, that the day of judgment should come by that time Rome pagan should cease, as that all things written in this book had their accomplishment in that time, because Christ told John they should come to pass ἐν τάχει, chap. i. 1 ; xxii. 6. No other coming of Christ, but his coming to the last judgment, can be here meant. *Hold that fast which thou hast ;* κράτει, hold with a strong hand the doctrine of faith, which thou yet hast, pure, and thy pure worship, and discipline, and a pure conscience. *That no man take thy crown ;* that thou mayest not lose that reward which shall be the portion of those that persevere to the end, and of those only.

12 Him that overcometh will I make

g 1 Kings 7.
21. Gal. 2. 9.
h ch. 2. 17.
& 14. 1. &
22. 4.

ᵍa pillar in the temple of my God, and he shall go no more out: and ʰI will write upon him the name of my God, and the name of the city of my God, *which is*

i Gal. 4. 26.
Heb. 12. 22.
ch. 21, 2, 10.
k ch. 22. 4.

ⁱnew Jerusalem, which cometh down out of heaven from my God : ᵏand *I will write upon him* my new name.

Him that overcometh will I make a pillar in the temple of my God : though by *the temple of God* in this place some understand the church of Christ on earth, where those always were, and are, and always shall be, most famous, who have overcome temptations best, from the world, the flesh, and the devil ; yet, considering that all the promises before made to those who overcome are of another life, it seems best rather to interpret this so, that God would make such a one of fame and renown in heaven, *great in the kingdom of heaven,* Matt. v. 19, to sit upon a throne there, Matt. xix. 28. He shall have a higher degree in glory, (for stars differ from one another in glory, 1 Cor. xv. 41,) pillars being not only for support, but ornament, and principal parts in buildings. *And he shall go no more out ;* he shall have an eternal inheritance, of which he shall not be dispossessed. *And I will write upon him the name of my God ;* as men use, upon pillars and monuments erected for their own use and honour, to write their names ; so I will peculiarly own, and challenge such a one for myself. *And the name of the city of my God, which is new Jerusalem ;* and I will write upon him, This man is an inhabitant of the new Jerusalem. *And I will write upon him my new name ;* I will glorify him with that glory of which myself was made partaker, upon my ascension after my resurrection, John xvii. 22, 24.

13 ¹He that hath an ear, let him hear

1 ch. 2. 7.

what the Spirit saith unto the churches.

This we have met with at the close of every epistle : see the notes on ver. 7.

Those who think these churches were typical, and the matter of the epistles not only didactic and corrective, but prophetical, say, this church of Philadelphia was a type of all gospel churches which were to be in the world upon the Reformation ; which more perfectly cast off antichrist, and would allow no key but that of the house of David, reforming themselves strictly according to the rule of the word, not according to state policy, and prudence.

14 And unto the angel of the church ‖ of the Laodiceans write ; ᵐThese things saith the Amen, ⁿ the faithful and true witness, ᵒthe beginning of the creation of God ;

‖ Or, in Laodicea.
m Is. 65. 16.
n ch. 1. 5. &
19. 11. & 22.
6. ver. 7.
o Col. 1. 15.

We read of this church, Col. iv. 16. *Laodicea* was a city in Lydia, by the river Lycus : see chap. i. 11. *These things saith the Amen :* Amen, as we have oft noted, is a particle used in asserting, and in wishing, or praying ; here it hath the use of a noun, and is assertive, he that is true, as it followeth. He may be conceived thus to preface his epistle, to ascertain to the ministers of this church the truth of what he blames in them ; or of the threatenings or promises contained in it ; to which purpose he also calls himself *the faithful and true witness :* see the notes on chap. i. 5. *The beginning of the creation of God :* those that deny the Divinity of Christ, are deceived in their thoughts that this text will afford them any defence for their error ; for ἀρχή, the word here used, doth not only signify the cause, but principality, or the chief, or prince, Eph. iii. 10 ; Col. i. 16. Hence Christ is said to be ἀρχή, which we translate *the beginning,* because he was the Creator, the efficient cause of the creation, or hath a lordship over the whole creation ; all power both in heaven and earth being committed to him, and all knees both in heaven and earth bowing down to him, Phil. ii. 10. Unless we had rather interpret it of the new creation, either in the world, so he was the beginning of the gospel ; or in particular souls, so he is the beginning of regeneration and sanctification. But though this be a truth, and consistent enough with the Greek phrase, Gal. vi. 15, yet I see no reason why we should fly to it against the Arians, or their spurious offspring ; for taking the creation, as ordinarily it signifies, the giving all creatures their first being, Christ was the efficient cause of it, and so the beginning of it, *without him was nothing made ;* and he hath a lordship and dominion over it.

15 ᵖI know thy works, that thou art

p ver. 1.

neither cold nor hot : I would thou wert cold or hot.

I know thy works ; I know and observe thy behaviour, thy ministerial function. *That thou art neither cold nor hot;* thou art neither openly profane and grossly scandalous, like heathens, or such as make no profession; nor yet hast thou any true zeal or warmth, either for the faith once delivered to the saints, or in love to God, seen in keeping his commandments, having the power and efficacy of godliness, teaching thee to deny *all ungodliness and worldly lusts,* Tit. ii. 12. Thou hast a form of godliness, but deniest the life and power thereof. *I would thou wert cold or hot:* we must not think Christ wisheth any persons cold absolutely, but comparatively, intimating to us, that the condition of a downright atheist, or profane person, is more hopeful than that of a close, formal hypocrite: the latter is in the road to hell as well as the other, and no more pleaseth God than the other. It is better not to have known the truth, than knowing it, to live contrary to it, Luke xii. 48; 2 Pet. ii. 21. Commonly such men also are proud, and self-conceited, having something to stop the mouth of their natural conscience, harder to be convinced of their evil state, Matt. xxi. 32, 33.

16 So then because thou art lukewarm, and neither cold nor hot, I will spue thee out of my mouth.

Neither cold nor hot; partly good, partly bad, having something of profession, nothing of the life and power of religion; contenting thyself that thou art not a Jew, nor a pagan; not a superstitious, idolatrous person; but a Christian, a protestant, a minister, or member of the Reformed church; yet neglecting thy duty both as a minister, and as a Christian, living in a sensual satisfaction of thy lusts. *I will spue thee out of my mouth;* I will cast thee off, as men vomit up lukewarm things.

q Hos. 12. 8.
1 Cor. 4. 8.

17 Because thou sayest, ^q I am rich, and increased with goods, and have need of nothing; and knowest not that thou art wretched, and miserable, and poor, and blind, and naked:

Because thou sayest, I am rich: it was said before, that one reason why the condition of a formalist is worse than that of an atheist, or more openly profane person, is, because the former is ordinarily proud and self-conceited, and hath something to stop the mouth of his natural conscience with, which the other wanteth. This is made good in the instance of this lukewarm angel; he said he was *rich* in a spiritual sense, in his state as a Christian, in spiritual gifts and endowments. *And increased with goods;* and every day increasing and growing richer. *And have need of nothing;* and needed nothing to make him happy and blessed. *And knowest not that thou art wretched, and miserable, and poor, and blind, and naked;* in the mean time he was as miserable as one could be. These words used, are several words signifying persons under various bodily afflictions, and applied to signify this angel's forlorn spiritual state, which, in the general, was wretched and miserable, and such as had need of mercy, wanting the true righteousness, wherein any could appear before God not naked, and wanting all true riches; and to complete his misery, he was spiritually blind, and knew not the sad circumstances he was under.

r Is. 55. 1.
Matt. 13. 44.
& 25. 9.

18 I counsel thee ^r to buy of me gold tried in the fire, that thou mayest be

s 2 Cor. 5. 3.
ch. 7. 13.
& 16. 15.
& 19. 8.

rich; and ^s white raiment, that thou mayest be clothed, and *that* the shame of thy nakedness do not appear; and anoint thine eyes with eyesalve, that thou mayest see.

Buying being the usual way amongst men to procure what they want, it is not to be wondered at, that the procuring of that spiritual blessing here mentioned is expressed under this notion; though our buying of God spiritual good things be (as the prophet expresseth it, Isa. lv. 1) *without money and without price.* It is not to be doubted, but that which is here propounded to be bought (that is, obtained, and procured by such ways and means as God hath directed) is Christ himself, with all his benefits, in whom there is a sufficient spiritual supply for all our spiritual wants; that which to the soul will answer whatever gold serveth the body for; and which to the soul answereth what clothing is to the body, viz. righteousness, wherein a soul may stand before God; and that which will answer what salves are to the body for the cure of its wounds, viz. consolation, and healing of all spiritual wounds and infirmities; in short, whatever thou hast need of, considered either as poor, wretched, and miserable, or as blind and naked.

19 ^t As many as I love, I rebuke and chasten: be zealous therefore, and repent.

t Job 5. 17.
Prov. 3. 11,
12. Heb. 12.
5, 6. Jam. 1.
12.

I rebuke and chasten; ἐλέγχω καὶ παιδεύω· the words may be translated, I convince and instruct, or deal with them as children; but it also signifies to *chasten,* and is so translated, 1 Cor. xi. 32; Heb. xii. 7; we translate it *learn,* 1 Tim. i. 20. By these words Christ lets this angel know, that although he had in this epistle dealt smartly with him, yet he had done it from a principle of love, as a father to a child, Heb. xii. 7. *Be zealous therefore, and repent;* he adviseth him therefore to quit himself of his lukewarmness, and to recover a warmth and zeal for God, repenting of his former coldness and negligence in his duty.

20 Behold, ^u I stand at the door, and knock: ^x if any man hear my voice, and open the door, ^y I will come in to him, and will sup with him, and he with me.

u Cant. 5. 2.

x Luke 12. 37.

y John 14. 23.

There is a double interpretation of this text, each of them claiming under very valuable interpreters; some making it a declaration of Christ's readiness to come in to souls, and to give them a spiritual fellowship and communion with himself; others interpreting it of Christ's readiness to come to the last judgment, and to take his saints into an eternal joyful fellowship and communion with himself: hence there is a different interpretation of every sentence in the text. *I stand at the door;* either, in my gospel dispensations, I stand at the door of sinners' hearts; or, I am ready to come to judge the world. *And knock,* by the inward monitions and impressions of my Spirit, or my ministers more externally; or, I am about to knock, that is, I am ready to have the last trump sounded. *If any man hear my voice, and open the door;* that is, if any man will hearken to the counsels and exhortations of my ministers, and to the monitions of my Spirit, and not resist my Holy Spirit; or, if any man hath heard my voice, and opened his heart to me. *I will come in to him;* I will come in by my Spirit, and all the saving influences of my grace; or, I will come to him as a Judge to acquit him. *And will sup with him, and he with me;* and I will have a communion with him in this life, he shall eat my flesh, and drink my blood; or, I will have an eternal fellowship and communion with him in my glory. The phrase seems rather to favour the first sense; the so frequent mention before of Christ's coming to judgment, and the reward of another life, as arguments to persuade the angels of the churches to their duty, favours the latter sense.

21 To him that overcometh ^z will I grant to sit with me in my throne, even as I also overcame, and am set down with my Father in his throne.

z Mat. 19. 28.
Luke 22. 30.
1 Cor. 6. 2.
2 Tim. 2. 12.
ch. 2. 26, 27.

To him that overcometh will I grant to sit with me in my throne; I will give him great honour, dignity, and power; he shall judge the world in the day of judgment, 1 Cor. vi. 3, the twelve tribes of Israel, Matt. xix. 28; he shall be made partaker of my glory, John xvii. 22, 24. *Even as I also overcame, and am set down with my Father in his throne;* but they must come to my throne as I came to it. I overcame the world, sin, death, the devil, and then ascended, and sat down with my Father in his throne: so they that will sit down with me in my throne of glory, must fight the same fight, and overcome, and then be crowned, sitting with me in my throne.

22 ^a He that hath an ear, let him hear what the Spirit saith unto the churches.

a ch. 2. 7.

We have had this in the conclusion of every epistle before: see chap. ii. 7, 11, 17, 29, and in this chapter, ver. 6, 13.

Those who make these churches typical of all Christian churches, from the time John had this Revelation, and prophetical of the complexion of the Christian churches in all ages, say, that the church of Laodicea typifieth the churches towards the end of the world till Christ cometh; but this necessitateth them to think there shall be no such pure and glorious state of the church just before the end of the world, as many believe there shall be, but that the state thereof shall grow yet worse and worse, of a Laodicean temper, so as when Christ cometh he shall hardly *find faith on the earth.*

For my part, I could allow the seven epistles to be typical and prophetical, but can by no means judge them to be purely prophetical; believing there were such churches when John wrote, and that their complexion is in the first place described in these epistles; though possibly, as face answers face in a glass, so succeeding churches have answered, and shall answer, the face of these churches, even to the last day. This chapter concludes John's first vision. In the following chapters we have a representation in visions of what was to happen in the world more remarkably, with reference to the church of God, from the year 95, to the end of the world.

There are very different opinions about the epocha, or the time, when the visions began to be fulfilled. My opinion is, it began soon after John had the vision; for it is twice said, chap. i. 1; xxii. 6, that the visions were to be about things that shall come to pass, (not that were come to pass,) and that shortly; but we cannot fix the certain year, which maketh the interpretation difficult.

There are also divers opinions how far in this book the revelations go that concern the state of the church under Rome pagan, and where they begin that foretell the state of the church under antichrist. But of these we shall speak more particularly as we go along with the several chapters.

CHAP. IV

John seeth the throne of God in heaven, 1—3, encompassed with four and twenty elders, 4, 5, and four beasts full of eyes before and behind, 6, 7. The continual adoration and worship offered by the beasts and elders before him that sat on the throne, 8—11.

AFTER this I looked, and, behold, a door *was* opened in heaven: and *the first voice which I heard *was* as it were of a trumpet talking with me; which said, ᵇCome up hither, ᶜand I will shew thee things which must be hereafter.

After this; after I had the first vision, mentioned chap. i., and had written what it was the pleasure of God I should write to the churches, in a book, perceiving the way God designed to reveal himself to me by vision. *I looked;* I looked again, hoping and being desirous to see something further as to the mind of God. *And, behold, a door was opened;* I saw the heavens opened, as Matt. iii. 16; Acts vii. 56. *In heaven;* he, doubtless, meaneth the third heavens. Such a vision, as to this particular, John had at Christ's baptism, Matt. iii., and Stephen when he was stoned. He also heard the voice of one speaking aloud to him, like the voice he heard, chap. i. 10; *which said, Come up hither,* into heaven, the new Jerusalem which is above; as the old Jerusalem stood upon a hill, or rising ground, so as they who went thither are constantly said to *go up,* Isa. ii. 3; Acts xi. 2; Gal. i. 17, 18; ii. 1. *And I will show thee things which must be hereafter;* not which have been, (for to what purpose had that been?) but which shall happen hereafter both to my church and to her enemies: from which it appears, that God did not here show his prophet the destruction of Jerusalem, for that was already past, in the time of Titus Vespasian the Roman emperor, about the year 69, or 70, after the incarnation; this (as all confess) was in Domitian's time, about the 11th or 12th year of his reign, about twenty-six or twenty-seven years after that was past, which makes the notion of two late annotators very strange.

2 And immediately ᵈI was in the spirit: and, behold, ᵉa throne was set in heaven, and *one* sat on the throne.

In the spirit; in an ecstasy, as Paul, 2 Cor. xii. 2, and Peter, Acts x. 10, and Ezekiel, chap. iii. 12, and himself was both before and after this, chap. i. 10; xvii. 3; xxi. 10. *A throne was set in heaven, and one sat on the throne:* God is constantly described, in the prophetical visions, as sitting upon a throne, to denote his power and dominion, that he is the King of kings, and Lord of lords. See Dan. vii. 9, &c.

3 And he that sat was to look upon like a jasper and a sardine stone: ᶠand *there was* a rainbow round about the throne, in sight like unto an emerald.

This is all but a description of the glory of God, as he appeared to John in this vision. The *jasper stone* is famous for its transparency, and variety of colours it offereth to the eye, and may signify the various and infinite perfections of God. The *sardine stone* is red, and of a bloody colour, which may signify the power, justice, and terror of God. The *rainbow* was the sign of God's covenant with Noah, signifying his being so far reconciled to the world, as that he would not again destroy it by water, Gen. ix. 13. The *emerald* is green, and pleasant to the eye. So as this vision of God represents God powerful, just, and good, and of various and infinite perfections.

4 ᵍAnd round about the throne *were* four and twenty seats: and upon the seats I saw four and twenty elders sitting, ʰclothed in white raiment; ⁱand they had on their heads crowns of gold.

Some think (and not improbably) that here is an allusion to the twenty-four courses of the priests and Levites, established by God for his service in the sanctuary and temple of old, 1 Chron. xxiv. 18; xxv. 31; and that these twenty-four elders either typified the whole church under the New Testament, the number of the tribes of Israel (which made up the church under the Old Testament) being doubled to show the increase of the church's territories under the gospel, or the heads of the church, either under the Old Testament or New, there being twelve patriarchs and twelve apostles. They are represented *sitting,* to denote their state of rest and ease; and *clothed in white raiment,* to denote their purity and holiness, or being clothed with Christ's righteousness; and having *crowns of gold on their heads,* to denote that state of dignity and glory to which God had advanced them.

5 And out of the throne proceeded ᵏlightnings and thunderings and voices: ˡand *there were* seven lamps of fire burning before the throne, which are ᵐthe seven Spirits of God.

And out of the throne proceeded lightnings and thunderings and voices: these words denote a very glorious and terrible appearance of God, denoting his majesty, and power over his enemies. There is, possibly, an allusion to God's appearance at the giving of the law, Exod. xix. 16; only we read there but of one voice, and that of a trumpet, inarticulate. The *lamps of fire before the throne,* have a correspondence with the seven lamps of the tabernacle, which gave light to the whole house of God, Exod. xxvii. 20; and are here expounded to be *the seven Spirits of God,* that is, the Holy Spirit in his seven-fold (that is, manifold) dispensations of grace, 1 Cor. xii. 4, 5, by which he enlighteneth, quickeneth, healeth, and comforteth the several souls that are the true members of his church. See the notes on chap. i. 4.

6 And before the throne *there was* ⁿa sea of glass like unto crystal: ᵒand in the midst of the throne, and round about the throne, *were* four beasts full of eyes before ᵖand behind.

And before the throne; the throne mentioned before, ver. 2, 3, upon which *one sat,* &c. *A sea of glass like unto crystal;* another allusion to the tabernacle or temple, in which was a sea, that is, a large vessel full of water; it was for Aaron and his sons to wash their hands, and feet, and sacrifices in, Exod. xxx. 19; 1 Kings vii. 23; it was ten cubits broad, five cubits high, and thirty cubits about.

Here it is said to have been *of glass;* this, probably, signified the blood of Christ, in which all those souls and services must be washed which are accepted of and acceptable unto God. Its being represented here as of glass, may signify the purity and spotlessness of him whose blood it was. Other guesses there are many at the significancy of this *sea of glass,* but this seems to me most probable, because the use of the sea in the temple is made good in Christ. John in this vision also saw *four beasts,* which beasts are said, 1. To be *in the midst of, and round about the throne.* 2. To be *full of eyes before and behind.* 3. They are, ver. 7, said to have resembled *a lion, a calf, a man* in the *face,* and *a flying eagle;* ver. 8, *each of them had six wings, and they were full of eyes within,* and incessantly glorified God. *Quest.* Whom did these beasts signify? *Solut.* There are various notions about them. Some judge them the four evangelists; but John himself was one of these, and yet alive. Some will have them four apostles that were mostly at Jerusalem; but I see no ground for that. Some will have them angels; others, glorified saints; but we shall afterwards find them distinguished from both these. Others will have them the whole church. But the most probable sense is, that they represented the ministers of the church, who are living creatures, whose place is betwixt God and his church, as those beasts are placed betwixt the throne and the elders; and who are but four to the twenty-four elders, being but few in comparison with the multitude of believers; and yet have eyes on all sides, being enough to see to the affairs of the whole church of Christ on the earth. In this sense I rest; only here remains a question, how these are said to be *in the midst of the throne,* and yet *round about the throne?* To which various answers are given; that which pleaseth me best is, ἐν μίσῳ, in the middle, is not to be strained to signify a place at equal distance from two extremes, but more largely and proverbially for near the throne, or near him who sat upon the throne. See the several notions about this phrase in Mr. Pool's Latin Synopsis.

q Num. 2. 2, &c. Ezek. 1. 10. & 10. 14.

7 ^q And the first beast *was* like a lion, and the second beast like a calf, and the third beast had a face as a man, and the fourth beast *was* like a flying eagle.

It is observed concerning these four living creatures, (for so they were, not beasts in a strict sense, as it is opposed to flying things, for the fourth was a fowl,) 1. That they were the same mentioned in Ezekiel's vision, Ezek. i. 10; only each one there is said to have had the four faces of these creatures, here each one had a single face proper to it. 2. That these were the four creatures whose portraitures were in the four ensigns of the Israelites as they were marshalled into four companies, allotting the men of three tribes to each company. Judah's standard had a lion in its colours, according to Jacob's prophecy of that tribe, Gen. xlix. 9, Ephraim had an ox, Reuben had a man, Dan an eagle. This the learned Mede proves from the Rabbins, who, though fabulous enough, yet in such a thing may be credited. It is also thought they answered the four cherubims in the temple. *Quest.* But what is signified by these four living creatures? *Solut.* Some say the four evangelists; others, four apostles, &c. But certainly they judge best who say, that by them is signified the various gifts with which God blesseth his ministers, giving to some more courage and fortitude, that they are like lions; to others more mildness and meekness, that they are like oxen or calves; others have more wisdom and prudence, which most adorn a man; others a more piercing insight into the mysteries of God's kingdom, rendering them like eagles.

8 And the four beasts had each of them ^r six wings about *him;* and *they* were full of eyes ^s within: and † they rest not day and night, saying, ^t Holy, holy, holy, ^u Lord God Almighty, ^x which was, and is, and is to come.

r Is. 6. 2.
s ver. 6.
+ Gr. *they have no rest.*
t Is. 6. 3.
u ch. 1. 8.
x ch. 1. 4.

And the four beasts had each of them six wings about him: the seraphims in Isaiah's vision, chap. vi. 2, had so; there their use is declared,—*with twain he covered his face, with twain his feet, and with twain he did fly.* If we understand all the wings here for flight, they signify the readiness of God's ministers to move every way that God will send them: if we understand them as interpreted by Isa. vi. 2, they signify their various graces, their fear, dread, and reverence of God; their humility and modesty; their agility, or readiness to obey all the commands of God. *And they were full of eyes within:* this denotes that large measure of knowledge, and diligence, and watchfulness, which should be in a minister of Christ. *And they rest not day and night, saying, Holy, holy, holy, Lord God Almighty:* this was the song of the seraphims, Isa. vi. 3, and shows how much it should be the care of ministers to make God known in all his attributes, his holiness especially, and his power. *Which was, and is, and is to come;* and his eternity and simplicity, as he is the same yesterday, to-day, and for ever, without variableness or shadow of change.

9 And when those beasts give glory and honour and thanks to him that sat on the throne, ^y who liveth for ever and ever,

y ch. 1. 18. & 5. 14. & 15. 7.

And when those beasts, the living creatures before expressed, signifying the ministers of the gospel, *give glory, &c.;* when they praise God who is eternal.

10 ^z The four and twenty elders fall down before him that sat on the throne, ^a and worship him that liveth for ever and ever, ^b and cast their crowns before the throne, saying,

z ch. 5. 8, 14.
a ver. 9.
b ver. 4.

The whole church also paid an homage of reverence and adoration to the same God; acknowledging all the good done to them, or wrought in them, to proceed from God, and the glory of it to be due unto God alone. The ministers of the gospel are, by their preaching unto people their duty, an occasion, or instruments, of that homage and adoration which he hath from all his people.

11 ^c Thou art worthy, O Lord, to receive glory and honour and power: ^d for thou hast created all things, and for thy pleasure they are and were created.

c ch. 5. 12.
d Gen. 1. 1. Acts 17. 24. Eph. 3. 9. Col. 1. 16. ch. 10. 6.

All the praises, homages, and acknowledgments of all the creatures is thy due; as thou art he who gavest the first being to all creatures, and therefore gavest it them, that they might praise, honour, serve, and obey thee.

CHAP. V.

The book sealed with seven seals, which no man is worthy to open, 1—3. *John weeping thereat is comforted,* 4, 5. *The Lamb that was slain taketh the book to open it,* 6, 7. *The beasts and the elders praise him that had redeemed them with his blood,* 8—10. *The angels join with them in ascribing glory to God and to the Lamb,* 11—14.

The same vision yet proceedeth. Hitherto John had only seen a throne, with a person sitting upon it in a very glorious habit and appearance, twenty-four grave persons, and four living creatures, in the shape of a lion, a calf, a man, and an eagle, each of them with six wings, and full of eyes, about the throne; and heard the twenty-four living creatures constantly giving glory to God, and the twenty-four elders harmonizing with them, and joining likewise in the high praises of God. Now the vision proceedeth.

AND I saw in the right hand of him that sat on the throne ^a a book written within and on the backside, ^b sealed with seven seals.

a Ezek. 2. 9, 10.
b Is. 29. 11. Dan. 12. 4.

The disputes what this *book* was are very idle; for it was certainly the book of which we read hereafter, that it was opened, and to which the seven seals mentioned in the following chapters were annexed, of the opening of all which we read; and this could be no other than *codex fatidicus,* (as Mr. Mede calls it,) the book of the counsels, decrees, and purposes of God relating to his church, as to what more remarkable things should happen to it to the end of the world; which book was in the hand of the Father. *Written within, and on the back-side;* very full of matter, so as it was written on all sides. *Sealed with seven seals;*

REVELATION V

hitherto concealed from the world, and to be revealed by parts, as to the bringing to pass of those things decreed in it; though all at once by God here revealed, in a degree, by visions unto John.

2 And I saw a strong angel proclaiming with a loud voice, Who is worthy to open the book, and to loose the seals thereof?

There were no weak angels, but possibly this angel might, in appearance to John, look as if he were stronger than others; or rather, so judged from the great and *loud voice* he used. *Who is worthy to open the book, and to loose the seals thereof?* not that he thought any was able, or worthy. We can only conclude from hence the impotency of men to search, and find out, and expound the deep things of God, and consequently the unlawfulness of too narrow a prying into his secret mysteries.

c ver. 13.

3 And no man ᶜin heaven, nor in earth, neither under the earth, was able to open the book, neither to look thereon.

None of the angels *in heaven*, nor any man upon the *earth*, nor any of them whose bodies are *under the earth* and their souls in heaven, nor any infernal spirits; none was found sufficient *to open the book*, and *to look on it*. There was none who replied to the angel's question, ver. 2.

4 And I wept much, because no man was found worthy to open and to read the book, neither to look thereon.

As it is the nature of man to desire to know secret and hidden things, especially such as we apprehend of concernment to ourselves, or those whom we love, or are interested it; and to be troubled, if we know they may be known, and are at a loss for due means whereby to come to the knowledge of them.

d Gen. 49. 9, 10. Heb. 7. 14.
e Is. 11. 1,10. Rom. 15. 12. ch. 22. 16.
f ver. 1.
ch. 6. 1.

5 And one of the elders saith unto me, Weep not: behold, ᵈthe Lion of the tribe of Juda, ᵉthe Root of David, hath prevailed to open the book, ᶠand to loose the seven seals thereof.

We must remember that John is here describing a vision, and that part of it which is but introductive to the material parts of it. He had in his vision seen a book in the right hand of God the Father, sitting upon his throne of glory; he had heard an angel proclaiming, If any were worthy, he should open the book, and loose the seals. None appeared to answer that voice; he was troubled; he thought he heard one saying to him, Be not troubled, the book shall be opened. Christ shall open the book, and loose the seals of it, who is here expressed under a double character: 1. *The Lion of the tribe of Judah;* he is so called, undoubtedly, with allusion to Jacob's prophecy, Gen. xlix. 9, 10, wherein Judah was compared to *a lion's whelp*, because he should be victorious. Christ was to be born of this tribe, and was to be a great Conqueror. 2. He is called *the Root of David;* he was a *Branch of David*, as he was man, but *the Root of David*, as he was God; therefore David, Psal. cx. 1, called him *Lord*, though he was his Son. *Hath prevailed* with his Father *to open the book, and to loose the seven seals thereof;* for leave to open the book, and loose the seals thereof, i. e. to reveal those things that are the counsels and purposes of God relating to his church, and the affairs thereof, to the world's end. I do not think we are at all concerned to inquire who is here meant by *one of the* twenty-four *elders*. As in parables there are some things put in merely to complete the feigned history, so in the relation of visions some things of that nature are put in, which need not a particular explication. The sum is, That while John was troubled for fear he should not know what was in the book, he took up one of those who attended the throne, that he need not be troubled, for Christ had obtained a liberty from his Father (in whose power only times and seasons for future things were) to reveal these counsels of God as to things to come.

g Is. 53. 7.
John 1. 29, 36. 1 Pet. 1. 19. ch. 13. 8. ver. 9, 12.

6 And I beheld, and, lo, in the midst of the throne and of the four beasts, and in the midst of the elders, stood ᵍa Lamb as it had been slain, having seven horns

and ʰseven eyes, which are ⁱthe seven Spirits of God sent forth into all the earth.

h Zech. 3. 9. & 4. 10.
i ch. 4. 5.

And I beheld; hearing the mention of a Lion of the tribe of Judah, he looks about wistly to see if he could see any justifying that representation. *And, lo, in the midst of the throne and of the four beasts, and in the midst of the elders, stood a Lamb:* instead of a Lion he seeth a Lamb; Christ Jesus, called a *Lamb* by this apostle, John i. 29, 36, and very often in this book; a Lamb, for whiteness and innocency, 1 Pet. i. 19, for meekness and patience, Acts viii. 32, but here with reference to the paschal lamb. *As it had been slain;* for he appears wounded and pierced, as if he had been slain; and to show that he was equal with the Father, he appears in the midst of the throne; and in the midst of the elders, and of the four living creatures, to show his presence with his church and ministers, Matt. xxviii. 28, and his walking (as was said, chap. ii.) in the midst of his churches, which were the golden candlesticks there mentioned. *Having seven horns;* he appeareth now with seven horns, which are members in which the beasts' strength, power, and beauty is much seen, to denote his glory and beauty, and the power he had now received to offend and conquer all his enemies. *And seven eyes, which are the seven Spirits of God;* and with seven eyes, which were the seven Spirits of God, mentioned chap. i. 4; iv. 5; endued with the Spirit of God, (which is also called his Spirit,) not given to him by measure. *Sent forth into all the earth;* which spiritual gifts and perfections he exerciseth over all the earth, both with relation to his church, and to his church's enemies.

7 And he came and took the book out of the right hand ᵏof him that sat upon the throne.

k ch. 4. 2.

This Lamb with seven horns and seven eyes, having been slain, and having prevailed with his Father to open this book, mentioned ver. 1, of all the secrets, counsels, and purposes of God relating to his church, he came and took it of his Father, in whose right hand it was, as ver. 1.

From hence to the end of this chapter, are nothing but songs sang by the living creatures which John saw, and the twenty-four elders which he saw, and an innumerable company of angels, to the honour and glory of Jesus Christ, as the Redeemer of man, and the Head of the church, upon this taking of the book from the right hand of his Father.

8 And when he had taken the book, ˡthe four beasts and four *and* twenty elders fell down before the Lamb, having every one of them ᵐharps, and golden vials full of ‖ odours, ⁿwhich are the prayers of saints.

l ch. 4. 8, 10.
m ch. 14. 2. & 15. 2.
‖ Or, *incense*.
n Ps. 141. 2. ch 8. 3, 4.

When the Lamb that had been slain had obtained of him that sat on the throne to open the book of God's secret counsels relating to his church, mentioned ver. 1, and had taken it out of his right hand, John saw *the four beasts*, the four living creatures, mentioned chap. iv. 6—8, by which seemed to be represented the ministers of the gospel, or the whole church of Christ; *and the four and twenty elders*, that had on their heads crowns of gold, mentioned chap. iv. 4, by which, we said, were represented either the ministers of the church, or the whole church. *Fell down before the Lamb, having every one of them harps, and golden vials full of odours:* he alludeth to the worship of God under the Old Testament, where in the temple they were wont to praise God with instruments of music, and offering up of frankincense: see 1 Chron. xiii. 8; xv. 16; 2 Chron. v. 12; Neh. xii. 27; Psal. xxxiii. 2; cxli. 2; cl. 3. These *vials of odours*, he tells us, signified *the prayers of the saints*. The whole verse signifies the prayers and praises, even all that adoration which God, under the gospel, should have from his ministers and people, for constituting his Son the Head of his church, and making him their Prophet, Priest, and King.

9 And ᵒthey sung a new song, saying, ᵖThou art worthy to take the book, and to open the seals thereof: ᵠfor thou wast

o Ps. 40. 3. ch. 14. 3.
p ch. 4. 11.
q ver. 6.

REVELATION V

^{r Acts 20. 28.}
^{Rom. 3. 24.}
^{1 Cor. 6. 20.}
^{& 7. 23.}
^{Eph. 1. 7.}
^{Col. 1. 14.}
slain, and ^r hast redeemed us to God by thy blood ^s out of every kindred, and tongue, and people, and nation;
^{Heb. 9. 12. 1 Pet. 1. 18, 19. 2 Pet. 2. 1. 1 John 1. 7. ch. 14. 4.} ^{s Dan. 4. 1. & 6. 25. ch. 7. 9. & 11. 9. & 14. 6.}

And they sung a new song: by a *new song* is either to be understood an excellent song, (for new songs are usually most valued,) or (which pleaseth me best) *new* as to the matter of it; for the servants of God under the Old Testament could not bless God for the actual redemption of man by the blood of Christ, but only rejoice in hope, embracing the promises seen afar off by the eye of faith. *Saying, Thou art worthy to take the book, and to open the seals thereof;* they acknowledge Christ worthy to be intrusted with his church, and the revelations of the counsels of God, with relation to it, to open them. *For thou wast slain, and hast redeemed us, &c.;* because he had redeemed his church, scattered over all the world, from sin, death, and hell, unto God, to serve him, and to live for ever with him, and that with no less price than his own blood; *Wherefore* (as the apostle tells us, Phil. ii. 9) *God hath exalted him.*

^{t Ex. 19. 6.}
^{1 Pet. 2. 5, 9.}
^{ch. 1. 6. & 20. 6. & 22. 5.}
10 ^t And hast made us unto our God kings and priests: and we shall reign on the earth.

The four living creatures and four and twenty elders (by which are represented the ministers and members of the church of Christ) go on in showing why they had reason to proclaim Christ worthy to be the Prophet to his church, to open the counsels of God to them, viz. because of the great love he had showed to them, not only in redeeming them with his blood from the guilt and power of sin, but in making them *kings and priests;* giving them the same privileges that the Jewish church had, who were called a royal priesthood, Exod. xix. 6; giving them a power (as priests) to offer up (not such bloody fleshly sacrifices as they offered, but) *spiritual sacrifices, acceptable to God* through the Beloved, 1 Pet. ii. 5: and also (as kings) to rule over their lusts and sensitive appetite; and to *reign* hereafter *on the earth,* judging the world (1 Cor. vi. 3) at the great day, with the great Judge of the quick and the dead.

11 And I beheld, and I heard the
^{u ch. 4. 4, 6.} voice of many angels ^u round about the throne and the beasts and the elders:
^{x Ps. 68. 17.}
^{Dan. 7. 10.}
^{Heb. 12. 22.}
and the number of them was ^x ten thousand times ten thousand, and thousands of thousands;

And I beheld, I still attended diligently, *and I heard the voice of many angels round about the throne and the beasts and the elders;* and I heard many angels, with the living creatures and the elders; (from whence we gather, that we must not, by the living creatures, or elders, understand angels, for they are mentioned apart by themselves, neither could they say, as ver. 9, 10, that Christ had redeemed them with his blood;) these angels joined in this harmony with the church to give glory to Christ. *And the number of them was ten thousand times ten thousand, and thousands of thousands;* their number was infinite, not to be numbered. See the like, Dan. vii. 10.

^{y ch. 4. 11.} 12 Saying with a loud voice, ^y Worthy is the Lamb that was slain to receive power, and riches, and wisdom, and strength, and honour, and glory, and blessing.

Worthy is the Lamb that was slain; the Lamb mentioned ver. 6, with *seven horns and seven eyes,* viz. Jesus Christ. *To receive power, and riches;* he is worthy of those horns he weareth, emblems of power and strength given unto him; for all power was given him in heaven and earth. *And wisdom;* and of those seven eyes he hath, i. e. of *the spirit of wisdom,* Isa. xi. 2, the riches of grace and wisdom. *And strength, and honour, and glory, and blessing;* and of all the homage, glory, praise, blessing, and obedience, which people can give him. I know not whether there be any thing in the observation made by some, that the number of things here mentioned, of which the Lamb is worthy, answereth the number of the seven Spirits of God, before mentioned.

13 And ^z every creature which is in ^{z Phil. 2. 10.}
^{ver. 3.}
heaven, and on the earth, and under the earth, and such as are in the sea, and all that are in them, heard I saying,
^a Blessing, and honour, and glory, and ^{a 1 Chr. 29. 11. Rom. 9. 5. & 16. 27. 1 Tim. 6. 16. 1 Pet. 4. 11. & 5. 11. ch. 1. 6.}
power, *be* unto him ^b that sitteth upon the throne, and unto the Lamb for ever and ever.

14 ^c And the four beasts said, Amen. ^{b ch. 6. 16.}
^{& 7. 10.}
^{c ch. 19. 4.}
And the four *and* twenty elders fell down and worshipped him ^d that liveth for ^{d ch. 4. 9, 10.} ever and ever.

The meaning of the several phrases here used, is not to be strictly and particularly examined; the sense of them all in general is, to show the consent of all the angels and glorified saints, and of the whole church, in giving praise unto God, and particularly to the Lord Jesus Christ, (the Lamb,) for the work of man's redemption; and their particular consent, that Christ is to be worshipped as the Father; and the consent and acquiescence of the whole creation in the counsel and purpose of God, and in the work of his providence, constituting Christ as the King, Priest, and Prophet of his church. And though inanimate creatures, or sensitive creatures, cannot speak, yet they are also said to join in these praises, as the glory of God shineth in them, and they, by him, shall be freed from that vanity under which they groan, Rom. viii. 19—21, and enjoy something of the liberty of the sons of God; and shall all be subject and obedient unto Christ in their respective stations and orders, Phil. ii. 9, 10, and fulfil his will in the execution of his counsels and purposes in the government of the world, in order to the preservation of his church.

CHAP. VI

The opening of six of the seals in order, and what followed thereupon.

We are now come to the prophetical, and therefore the most difficult, part of this mysterious book; as to which I judge it reasonable, before we come to open the mysterious text, (after Mr. Pool's method in his Latin Synopsis,) to premise some things which may instruct the reader of these notes, both of the things wherein the difficulties lie, and of the fairest way to find out the sense of them. Hitherto we have met with no great difficulties; what have been, have been chiefly, 1. Concerning the seven Spirits of God. 2. Concerning the seven churches, and epistles to them; whether the churches be to be considered typically, and what was written to them be to be understood in a prophetic, as well as a didactic, or a corrective sense? But in what follows we shall find great (if not some inextricable) difficulties. To prepare a way for the explication of which,

I. I shall first take it for granted, that from this chapter to the end of the book, is revealed the most remarkable things which have happened, or shall happen, to the church of God over all the earth, from the time of this Revelation first made to John, to the end of the world.

II. Hence it followeth, that many of the things prophesied are fulfilled; but how many is hard to determine, because the time is not set when these revelations should take place; whether (as some would have it) from the beginning of Christianity, which, to me, seemeth not probable; because at this time ninety-five years were elapsed since that time, and this prophecy was concerning the things that were to be after the time of John's being in Patmos, chap. i. 1; xxii. 6; or from the beginning of the time when the Jewish church and state ceased, which was twenty-six or twenty-seven years before this; or from the time when this Revelation was, which was Anno 95, or thereabouts, in the time when Domitian was the Roman emperor, and had began his persecution of the Christians, which (as historians tell us) was but five years before he was slain, for he was slain in September, 97. And for those that are fulfilled, the things spoken are so applicable to various accidents happening in that period of time, that it is very difficult ofttimes to assert the sense of the prophecy.

III. I take it for granted also, that things happened in the same order as is here described; so as the things under the second seal came not to pass till those prophesied of under the first seal were, in a great measure, accomplished, &c.

IV. I agree with those who think, that what we have, chap. xii., xiii., xvii., xviii., are but a prophecy of other things that happened to the church at the same times spoken of, chap. vi.—x.

V. I do believe the visions of the seals, trumpets, and vials, chap. vi., viii., xv., xvi., the principal prophecies, and contain the revelation of things in order as they were to happen; and of these, that of the seals is the principal.

VI. I agree with those who think, that God, by the first six seals, intends the whole space from the time when the things written in this book began to be fulfilled, unto the time when paganism was rooted out of the Roman empire, which some make the year 310, some, 325. In which time (counting the beginning from the time when John was in Patmos, which was in Domitian's time) the emperors of Rome were Nerva, Trajan, Adrianus, Antoninus Pius, Antoninus Philosophus, Antoninus Verus, Commodus, Severus, Caracalla, Macrinus, Heliogabalus, Alexander Severus, Maximinus, Gordianus, Philippus, Decius, Valerianus, Gallienus, Claudius, Aurelianus, Tacitus, Probus, Carus, Numerianus, Dioclesianus with Maximinianus, Constantius Chlorus with Galerius, Constantius with Galerus, Constantinus; in all, twenty-seven, in about two hundred years: they were all persecutors, and God allowed them short reigns. So as what we have revealed in and under the first six seals, happened within the short space of the three hundred or three hundred and twenty-five first years after Christ; I am apt to think, after ninety-eight or one hundred of them were elapsed. These things being premised, let us now come to consider the text.

AND [a] I saw when the Lamb opened one of the seals, and I heard, as it were the noise of thunder, [b] one of the four beasts saying, Come and see.

John's vision continueth still: by *the Lamb* he means Christ, the Lamb oft mentioned chap. v.; and by *one of the seals*, one of the seven seals mentioned chap. v. 1, that were set upon the book which John saw in the right hand of God the Father, given to Christ, ver. 7. Christ began to discover the counsels of God relating to that first period of his church. And John heard one of the four living creatures speaking to him with a great and terrible voice, like *the noise of thunder*. Inviting him to come near, or to attend and see.

2 And I saw, and behold [c] a white horse: [d] and he that sat on him had a bow; [e] and a crown was given unto him: and he went forth conquering, and to conquer.

Some, by this *white horse*, understand the gospel; others, the Roman empire. And by him that sat thereon with a bow, some understand Christ going forth with power to convert the nations; others (and in my opinion more probably) the Roman emperors, armed with power, and having the imperial crown, carrying all before them. So as that which God intended by this to reveal to St. John, was, that the Roman emperors should yet continue, and use their power against his church. Those that understand by the *white horse*, the gospel, or God's dispensations to his church under the first period, and by the rider, Christ, (amongst whom is our famous Mede,) think, that hereby all the time is signified from Christ's ascension, which was in the thirty-fourth year after his incarnation, till the time that all the apostles were dead, that is, the first hundred years after Christ (for so long histories tell us John lived). It was the age then current, and so may take up part of the vision of things that were to come. The history of all but forty of those years we have in the Acts, till Paul was carried prisoner to Rome. In this period ruled Augustus Cæsar, (in whose time Christ was born, Luke ii. 1,) Tiberius, Claudius, and Nero, Galba, Otho, F. Vespasianus,

Titus, and Domitian, Nerva, and Trajan, ten or eleven in all. They went on *conquering, and to conquer* the world. But till Nero's time, about the year 66, they did not begin to persecute the Christians; nor did Vespasian and Titus much rage, nor Domitian, till he had reigned eight years: so as I leave it indifferent to the reader, whether to understand by the *white horse* and his rider, God's dispensations of providence to his church these first years, causing his gospel to prevail much, and conquering many to the profession of it, or the Roman empire, with those that ruled it: what is said is true of both.

3 And when he had opened the second seal, [f] I heard the second beast say, Come and see.

The second seal; the second of those seven seals with which the book, mentioned chap. v. 1, was sealed. *The second beast;* the beast *like a calf*, chap. iv. 7. *Come and see;* inviting John to attend.

4 [g] And there went out another horse *that was* red: and *power* was given to him that sat thereon to take peace from the earth, and that they should kill one another: and there was given unto him a great sword.

And there went out another horse that was red; signifying blood and slaughter. *And power was given to him that sat thereon to take peace from the earth;* either to Christ, (as some say,) or to those that ruled the affairs of the Roman empire at that time, to disturb the peace of the church. *And that they should kill one another:* this was a time of much blood. *And there was given unto him a great sword;* and therefore a sword is given to him that rode upon the this horse. Some think that this period began with Nero, thirty-four years before the other ended (according to what was said before); others make it to begin with Trajan, and to comprehend eighty years, until the time of Commodus; in which time Trajan, and Hadrian, and the three Antoninuses successively ruled the Roman empire: the reigns of Trajan and Hadrian took up near half the time, in which time this prophecy was most eminently fulfilled; for in Trajan's time the Jews rebelling, and killing many subjects of the Roman empire, to the number of twenty-two thousand in one place, and two hundred and forty thousand in another place, themselves were as miserably handled by the Roman forces sent by Trajan and Hadrian, who slew of them (as histories tell us) five hundred and fourscore thousand: nay, the Jews themselves say, they lost double the number of those who came out of Egypt, and more than they lost by Nebuchadnezzar, or by Titus when their city was taken: on the other side the Romans lost very many. Many Christians also were put to death during this period, during which was the third and fourth persecution.

5 And when he had opened the third seal, [h] I heard the third beast say, Come and see. And I beheld, and lo [i] a black horse; and he that sat on him had a pair of balances in his hand.

The third beast was he who had *the face of a man*, who also inviteth John to *come and see* what came forth upon his opening *the third seal*. He seeth *a black horse*, and a rider upon him, with *a pair of balances*. There is a difference amongst interpreters what should be signified by this *black horse;* some by it understand famine, because a scarcity of victuals bringeth men to a black and swarthy colour; some understand by it justice, because the rider is said to have *a pair of balances in his hand;* others understand by it heresies, and great sufferings of the church by heretics and others. *He that sat on him had a pair of balances in his hand;* either to give men their bread by weight, (as is usual in times of great scarcity,) or to measure out every one their due.

6 And I heard a voice in the midst of the four beasts say, ‖ A measure of wheat for a penny, and three measures of barley for a penny; and [k] *see* thou hurt not the oil and the wine.

‖ The word *chœnix* signifieth a measure containing one wine quart, and the twelfth part of a quart.

A measure of wheat for a penny, and three measures of barley for a penny: interpreters are at so great a loss here to fix the sense, that some think this phrase signifies famine and scarcity ; others think it signifies great plenty. The Greek word here used, signifieth, say some, half a bushel ; others say it signifieth so much bread corn as is sufficient for four loaves ; others say, something more than a quart ; others, so much as was allowed servants for maintenance for a day: let it be which it will, it signifies no great scarcity ; for the word signifying *a penny,* signified but as much in our money as came to seven pence halfpenny. I think therefore Mr. Mede judgeth well, that by the *black horse* was signified not a time of famine and scarcity, but of plenty ; and the rather, because it is added, *hurt not the oil and the wine :* and that the *balances* in the rider's hands signified not scales to give men their bread by weight, (as in a time of scarcity,) but the balance of justice ; nor will the colour of the horse conclude the contrary. The whole therefore of this prophecy seemeth to foretell that this period, from the time of Commodus the Roman emperor, who ruled the empire from the year 180 to 197, and was followed by Severus, Macrinus, Caracalla, Heliogabalus, and Alexander Severus, the son of Mammeas, who came to the empire Anno 222, and reigned to 237, should be a time of great plenty and civil justice. Histories tell us of no famine in that time, but large stories of the great care of two of those emperors especially, for supplying their countries with corn, and for the administering of civil justice. The things foretold by the opening of this seal, our famous Mede makes to have had their accomplishment with the determination of the reign of Alexander Severus.

7 And when he had opened the fourth seal, ¹I heard the voice of the fourth beast say, Come and see.

l ch. 4. 7

The beast mentioned chap. iv. 7, that had the face of *a flying eagle,* inviteth John to attend to the opening of *the fourth seal,* that is, the revelation of the counsels of God, as to what should happen to the church (within the Roman empire) in the fourth period, which is conceived to have begun with Maximinus, about the year 237, and to have ended with the reign of Diocletian, 294.

8 ᵐAnd I looked, and behold a pale horse: and his name that sat on him was Death, and Hell followed with him. And power was given ‖ unto them over the fourth part of the earth, ⁿto kill with sword, and with hunger, °and with death, ᵖand with the beasts of the earth.

m Zech. 6.3.

‖ Or, *to him.*
n Ezek. 14. 21.
o 2 Esd.15.5.
p Lev. 26. 22.

A pale horse ; a horse of the colour of his rider, *Death,* which makes men look pale, and bringeth them into the state of the dead, (here translated *hell,*) whether heaven or hell, as they have lived. *And power was given unto them over the fourth part of the earth ;* over a great part of the earth. *To kill with sword, and with hunger, and with death, and with the beasts of the earth ;* to kill men all manner of ways, with the sword, famine, pestilence, and by throwing them to wild beasts. Interpreters judge that here was prophesied what should happen to the Roman empire, and the church within it, from the time when Maximinus was made emperor, which was about the year 237, to the time of Aurelianus, which was about 271. Some extend it to Diocletian's time, which ended about 294 ; but Mr. Mede rather reserveth that for the fifth seal. If the former time only be taken in, there was within it the seventh, eighth, and ninth persecutions ; Diocletian began the tenth and greatest of all. Within this time this prophecy was eminently fulfilled : Maximinus destroyed all the towns in Germany, for three or four hundred miles. There was a plague lasted fifteen years together in the time of Gallus, who had the empire Anno 255. Three hundred and twenty thousand Goths were slain by Flavius Claudius. Maximinus and Gallienus were both great butchers, both to their own subjects that were heathens, and to Christians. Gallienus is said to have killed three or four thousand every day. Such wars and devastations could not but be followed with famine ; besides that we are confirmed in it, both by the testimony of Eusebius and Cyprian, the latter of whom lived within this period.

9 And when he had opened the fifth seal, I saw under ᑫthe altar ʳthe souls of them that were slain ˢfor the word of God, and for ᵗthe testimony which they held:

q ch. 8. 3. & 9. 13. & 14. 18.
r ch. 20. 4.
s ch. 1. 9.
t 2 Tim. 1. 8. ch. 12. 17. & 19. 10.

And when he had opened the fifth seal : this and the next seal's opening, is not prefaced with any living creature calling to John to *come and see.* We must consider, 1. The number of the beasts was but four, who all had had their courses. 2. Some have thought that it is, because here is no mention of any new persecution, but a consequent of the former. 3. But this vision was so plain, it needed no expositor. *I saw under the altar ;* still he speaks in the dialect of the Old Testament, where in the temple was the altar of burnt-offering and the altar of incense ; the allusion here is judged to be to the latter. *The souls of them that were slain for the word of God, and for the testimony which they held ;* from whence we may not conclude, that the souls of men and women when they die do sleep, as some dreamers have thought. These are said to be the souls of them that were slain *for the word of God,* &c., for preaching the word, and their profession of the gospel, bearing a testimony to Christ and his truths. Mr. Mede thinks that under this seal is comprehended the ten bloody years of Diocletian's persecution, which of all others was most severe ; paganism at that time (as dying things are wont) most struggling to keep itself alive. This tyrant is said, in the beginning of his reign, within thirty days to have slain seventeen thousand, and in Egypt alone, during his ten years, one hundred and forty-four thousand. He thinks that the souls of those which this wretch had slain throughout all his dominions, within his short period of ten years, were those principally which were showed John upon the opening of this seal.

10 And they cried with a loud voice, saying, "How long, O Lord, ˣholy and true, ʸdost thou not judge and avenge our blood on them that dwell on the earth?

u See Zech. 1. 12.
x ch. 3. 7.
y ch. 11. 18. & 19. 2.

And they cried with a loud voice ; their souls cried, or their souls cried to God, *saying, How long, O Lord, holy ;* and therefore thou canst not abide iniquity, and of all iniquity canst least abide innocent blood, which is the blood of thy saints, whose blood is precious in thy sight. *And true ;* and who art true to thy word of threatenings against bloodthirsty men, and to thy promises for the deliverance of thy people. *Dost thou not judge and avenge our blood on them that dwell on the earth ?* dost thou not judge our cause, and avenge us, who have committed vengeance to thee, not daring to avenge ourselves upon wicked men, who dwelling upon the earth are seen, and their practices known to and by thee, and are under thy power, so as thou canst at pleasure do it.

11 And ᶻwhite robes were given unto every one of them; and it was said unto them, ᵃthat they should rest yet for a little season, until their fellowservants also and their brethren, that should be killed as they *were,* should be fulfilled.

z ch. 3. 4, 5. & 7. 9, 14.
a Heb. 11. 40. ch. 14. 13.

And white robes were given unto every one of them ; white robes of glory ; for the white robes of Christ's righteousness, and of a holy life, were by them put on before they were slain. *That they should rest yet for a little season ;* that they should be satisfied, and acquiesce in God's dispensations. *Until their fellow-servants also and their brethren, that should be killed as they were ;* for God had yet more faithful witnesses to be martyred, (though not in such flocks as before,) who should die for the same faith and profession. *Should be fulfilled ;* when the number of those his martyrs should be completed, he would avenge their blood upon their enemies.

12 And I beheld when he had opened the sixth seal, ᵇand, lo, there was a great earthquake ; and ᶜthe sun became black as sackcloth of hair, and the moon became as blood ;

b ch. 16. 18.
c Joel 2. 10, 31. & 3. 15.
Matt. 24. 29.
Acts 2. 20.

And I beheld when he had opened the sixth seal; the sixth of those seals with which the book was sealed, mentioned chap. v. 1 : this signifieth the revelation of some things which should happen in some certain period of time, but what period is the question, as to which interpreters differ. Some think, the time when Jerusalem was taken; but this was a time past twenty-six or twenty-seven years before John was in Patmos, where he had this vision about things that shall be, chap. i. 1 ; xxii. 6. Some think, that period of time which shall be immediately before the day of judgment; but that guess seemeth worse, for after this there was a seventh seal to be opened. Some think, the period of the church's conflict with antichrist. But Mr. Mede's judgment (followed by many other famous men) seems best, that it denotes that period when Constantine, the first Christian emperor, restored peace to the church, by overturning the whole pagan state, and making Christianity the religion of the greatest part of the world. This was about the year 311, and perfected upon his victory over Licinius, 325. In this I acquiesce. Let us now see how what is said in this and the following verses about this period will agree to that time. *And, lo, there was a great earthquake :* the great question is here, what is meant by this great earthquake, the darkening of the sun, the moon becoming as blood, &c. No history recording any such prodigies, hath made many (taking these things in the natural, literal sense) to say the period under the first seal signifies either the time when Jerusalem was taken, or the day of judgment; but there is a metaphorical sense of these expressions, very usual in the prophetical writings, to show great changes in states; and in this sense it is to be taken here. Thus the prophet describeth the great change God would make in Jerusalem, Isa. xxix. 6, *Thou shalt be visited of the Lord of hosts with thunder, and with earthquake, and great noise, with storm and tempest, and the flame of devouring fire :* and Jer. xv. 9, *Her sun is gone down while it was yet day.* And, Ezek. xxxii. 7, the change God would work in the ruin of Egypt, is thus expressed : *When I shall put thee out, I will cover the heaven, and make the stars thereof dark; and the moon shall not give her light. All the bright lights of heaven will I make dark over thee.* So Joel ii. 10, 31, and chap. iii. 15. What is an earthquake, but the shaking of the earth ? And under this notion God expresseth the changes he makes in states and kingdoms, Isa. ii. 19, 21 ; xxiv. 18; Hag. ii. 6, 7. Thus by *earthquake* here is to be understood a great change in the Roman empire. *And the sun became black as sackcloth of hair, and the moon became as blood :* the *sun* signifies those that are in the highest power ; the *moon,* those that are next to them in place and dignity.

d ch. 8. 10. & 9. 1.

|| Or, *green figs.*

13 ᵈ And the stars of heaven fell unto the earth, even as a fig tree casteth her || untimely figs, when she is shaken of a mighty wind.

This is but another phrase signifying a great change : the whole verse is much the same with Isa. xxxiv. 4. Literally these things were never yet fulfilled. It is a phrase signifying the fall of great and mighty men.

e Ps. 102. 26. Is. 34. 4. Heb. 1. 12, 13. f Jer. 3. 23. & 4. 24. ch. 16. 20.

14 ᵉ And the heaven departed as a scrowl when it is rolled together; and ᶠ every mountain and island were moved out of their places.

Two expressions more signifying the same thing. The first is used by the prophet, to signify the change God would make in the state of the Edomites, Isa. xxxiv. 4, as will appear by comparing what that prophet saith, with what Jeremiah, Ezekiel, and Obadiah say, upon the same argument, Jer. xlix. 7—22 ; Ezek. xxxv. *And every mountain and island were moved out of their places;* all sorts of people shall be destroyed, or all the paganish religion shall be rooted out.

15 And the kings of the earth, and the great men, and the rich men, and the chief captains, and the mighty men, and every bondman, and every free man, ᵍ hid themselves in the dens and in the rocks of the mountains ;

g Is. 2. 19.

A terror shall fall upon all sorts of men, high and low; and, like men affrighted, they shall seek for themselves hiding-places, where they can think themselves most secure : see Isa. ii. 19.

h Hos. 10. 8. Luke 23. 30. ch. 9. 6.

16 ʰ And said to the mountains and rocks, Fall on us, and hide us from the face of him that sitteth on the throne, and from the wrath of the Lamb :

And said to the mountains and rocks, Fall on us, and hide us : see Hos. x. 8 ; Luke xxiii. 30. They shall be in a great consternation, and be ready to take any course for security. *From the face of him that sitteth on the throne, and from the wrath of the Lamb ;* from the wrath of God, and of Jesus Christ.

i Is. 13. 6, &c. Zeph. l. 14, &c. ch. 16. 14. k Ps. 76. 7.

17 ⁱ For the great day of his wrath is come ; ᵏ and who shall be able to stand ?

For this judgment that is upon us, is the effect of his wrath for our abusing and persecuting his members; and we, with all our courage, might, and power, are not able to abide his wrath. These words import, that in this great change, as the greatest persons should be at a loss what to do, so they should perish under a conviction that the great vengeance of God was come upon them for their opposing the gospel, and provoking Christ by persecuting of his members.

There are other more particular explications of the *sun, moon, stars, heavens,* &c., but they all centre in this general, that here is prophesied a great and universal change of the religion of the world, which should strike a great terror into the pagan rulers, and issue in the overturning of all their altars and temples, and the ruin of the great men, relating either to their civil or ecclesiastical state ; and that they at last should know that God was God, and that these judgments came upon them for their opposition to Christ. And (which addeth strength to this interpretation) Mr. Durham hath observed, that no so short period of time hath produced so many remarkable judgments, and extorted so many ingenuous confessions from enemies, that what came upon them was for their persecutions ; and a catalogue of which may be found in Mr. Mede, and in Mr. Durham. Mr. Mede reckoneth Galerius, Maximinus, and Licinius. Galerius was eaten up of worms, being before he died sensible of his guilt, ceasing from his persecution, and begging the Christians' prayers. Maximinus, another Roman emperor, (or partner in the empire with the former,) being beaten by Licinius, fled to Tarsus, and there fell upon his pagan priests, who had deceived him by their lying oracles, and made a decree for the Christians' liberty ; but God would not suffer so bloody a wretch to die after the ordinary death of man ; he died miserably through intolerable pain, his eyes dropping out of his head. Licinius was a Christian, and joined a while with Constantine, but apostatized, was overcome in two battles, taken, and by him put to death. All these three were within the space of eighteen years. Mr. Durham to these adds the instances of Dioclesian and Maximinian, little above twenty years before, in the heat of their persecution making a stop, and through a horror of conscience laying down their imperial dignity ; and Maxentius, drowned in the river Tiber ; and he says Licinius, before mentioned, before he died, revenged himself upon his idolatrous priests that had persuaded him to forsake Constantine's God. The change was so great in the empire, upon Constantine the Great's coming to the throne, by the death of some great persons, turning others out of place, destroying the whole frame and practice of the pagans' religion, that it might well be expressed by earthquakes, the sun turning black, the moon as blood, the stars falling from heaven to earth, the heavens departing like a scroll, and the removal of islands and mountains, and by the consternation it would bring all the pagan great men into, &c. And this time, which was a period of about twenty-five or twenty-seven years, is thought to be understood to be the time predicted upon the opening of the sixth seal. Thus we see the dragon's reign at an end in about three hundred and eleven or three hundred and twenty-five years after Christ ; the empire, as pagan, persecuting the church of Christ, and following it with ten successive persecutions, quite overturned, and a Christian emperor, Constantine the Great, ruling it. But we must understand these great things were not perfected in a few months; some relics of paganism remained; for though Constantine shut up the pagan temples, yet all the idols in them were not destroyed until the time of Theodosius, who began to rule in the empire Anno 379, and reigned sixteen years. Betwixt Constantine and him were Constantius and Constans, Julian the Apostate, and Jovianus, Valentinianus, Valens, and Gratian; during some of whose reigns (Julian's especially) the Christians suffered much both from pagans and Arians, so that the Christians had not a full and perfect quiet till after the year 390.

CHAP. VII

John seeth four angels holding the four winds, 1; *and another angel coming to seal the servants of God in their foreheads,* 2, 3. *The number of them that were sealed out of each of the tribes of Israel,* 4—8. *An innumerable multitude out of all other nations stand before the throne in white robes, with palms in their hands, praising God and the Lamb,* 9, 10. *The angels, elders, and beasts, worship and glorify God,* 11, 12. *One of the elders showeth John who they are that are clad in white robes, and what is their blessedness for ever,* 13—17.

AND after these things I saw four angels standing on the four corners of the earth, ^aholding the four winds of the earth, ^bthat the wind should not blow on the earth, nor on the sea, nor on any tree.

a Dan. 7. 2.
b ch. 9. 4.

The first sufferings of the church under the Roman emperors that were pagans, was foretold under the first six seals, as hath been showed; but they had yet more, if not greater, things to suffer, which are discovered to John, as we shall see when we come to the opening of the seventh and last seal in the next chapter; only it pleaseth God by a vision, in this chapter, to comfort his church: so as though this vision relateth to the sixth seal, and was before the opening of the seventh, yet it hath a relation to that, to show the care that God would take of his church under those great evils that should happen upon the opening of the seventh seal, or when the things foretold upon the opening of it should come to be accomplished. *I saw four angels standing on the four corners of the earth;* four good angels; God is called their God, ver. 3. *Holding the four winds of the earth;* that is, to whom God had given it in charge that they should inflict his judgments upon all the parts of the earth; for God often useth, by his prophets, the metaphor of winds, to express stormy, troublesome dispensations, as Jer. xviii. 17; xlix. 36; li. 1. *That the wind should not blow on the earth, nor on the sea, nor on any tree:* this phrase is interpreted variously, God making use of the winds, 1. In a way of judgment, to throw down buildings and trees. 2. In a way of mercy, to purify the air, and by their gentle breathings to cherish things. Some interpret this command to the angels, into a command to these angels to forbear awhile those storms of judgment which were coming, till the servants of God should be sealed. Others interpret them into a command to bring judgments, either corporal or spiritual, which they think is signified by the winds not blowing. The last seemeth to be favoured by the next verse, *to whom it was given to hurt the earth and the sea;* which seemeth to me to interpret the blowing mentioned in this verse of a hurtful blowing. *The earth, the sea,* and *the trees,* seem to signify all the sublunary world, especially the church.

2 And I saw another angel ascending from the east, having the seal of the living God: and he cried with a loud voice to the four angels, to whom it was given to hurt the earth and the sea,

By this other *angel,* some understand an angel by nature; some, a man, Elijah, or Constantine; others, Christ himself, called *an Angel,* Exod. xxiii. 20. It is not much material whether we by this angel understand Christ, or some angel which he made his instrument. He gives a command to those *four angels,* whom God had made the ministers or executioners of his wrath and justice in the world.

3 Saying, ^cHurt not the earth, neither the sea, nor the trees, till we have ^d sealed the servants of our God ^e in their foreheads.

c ch. 6. 6. & 9. 4.
d Ezek. 9. 4. ch. 14. 1.
e ch. 22. 4.

A manifest allusion to Ezek. ix. 4, and, as some think, to the usage of some eastern countries, for masters to set their names upon the forehead of their slaves, by which they were known to be theirs, as we mark our sheep or other beasts. Men as vainly dispute what this seal should be, as what the ת meant in Ezek. ix., the mark set upon those that mourned for the abominations of Jerusalem. The place where they were to be sealed signified the end of their sealing to be not so much for confirmation, for which seals are. used, as notification, to signify to others they belong to God; so as it was of the same use as the blood upon the two side-posts and the upper door-posts of the Israelites in Egypt, Exod. xii. 13.

4 ^fAnd I heard the number of them which were sealed: *and there were* sealed ^g an hundred *and* forty *and* four thousand of all the tribes of the children of Israel.

f ch. 9. 16.
g ch. 14. 1.

5 Of the tribe of Juda *were* sealed twelve thousand. Of the tribe of Reuben *were* sealed twelve thousand. Of the tribe of Gad *were* sealed twelve thousand.

6 Of the tribe of Aser *were* sealed twelve thousand. Of the tribe of Nepthalim *were* sealed twelve thousand. Of the tribe of Manasses *were* sealed twelve thousand.

7 Of the tribe of Simeon *were* sealed twelve thousand. Of the tribe of Levi *were* sealed twelve thousand. Of the tribe of Issachar *were* sealed twelve thousand.

8 Of the tribe of Zabulon *were* sealed twelve thousand. Of the tribe of Joseph *were* sealed twelve thousand. Of the tribe of Benjamin *were* sealed twelve thousand.

For the understanding of these five verses several things are to be noted.

1. That the whole number is one hundred and forty-four thousand, which is the product of twelve, as the original number, (setting aside the ciphers,) for twelve times twelve make one hundred and forty-four. The number of one hundred and forty-four, chap. xxi. 17, was the measure of the wall of the new Jerusalem. Twelve, which is the root of this number one hundred and forty-four, seemeth to be God's number, and used in Scripture about one hundred and forty-four times, and almost generally in things belonging to the church; which had twelve patriarchs, twelve tribes under the Old Testament, twelves apostles (as its head) under the New Testament: and the new Jerusalem from heaven, chap. xxi. 12, is said to have *twelve gates, and at the gates twelve angels;* ver. 14, *the wall had twelve foundations;* the length of it, ver. 16, *twelve thousand furlongs.*

2. That we must not by one hundred and forty-four thousand understand a certain, but an uncertain number, which yet was very great.

3. That by the tribes of Israel mentioned here, are to be understood the several gospel churches of the Gentiles, who are now God's Israel ingrafted into the true olive.

4. That the tribe of Dan is here left out, and Ephraim is not named, though included in Joseph. Of the tribe of Dan there were none sealed. Dan was a great ringleader to idolatry, so was Ephraim; see the 17th and 18th chapters of Judges; and at Dan it was that Jeroboam set up his calves. Levi is put in instead of Dan, and Joseph instead of Ephraim, by which means here are yet twelve tribes; which teacheth us this, That Christians, if idolaters, must not look for any special protection or favour from God in a day of evil.

5. These tribes are not set in order, according to their birthright. *Juda* was Leah's fourth son, Gen. xxix. 35, put first, because Christ descended from him. *Reuben,* her eldest son, is put next, giving place only to the Messiah's

tribe. *Gad,* Jacob's son by Zilpah, Gen. xxx. 11, is put next. *Aser,* Jacob's son by Zilpah, in the fourth place, Gen. xxx. 13. *Nepthalim* is put next, who was Jacob's son by Bilhah, Rachel's maid, Gen. xxx. 8. *Manasses* is put next, who was Joseph's son. *Simeon,* Jacob's second son by Leah, Gen. xxix. 33, is put in the seventh place. *Levi,* Leah's third son, Gen. xxix. 34, in the eighth place. *Issachar,* Leah's fifth son, Gen. xxx. 18, is put in the'ninth place. *Zabulon,* Leah's sixth son, is put in the tenth place, Gen. xxx. 20. *Joseph* is put in the eleventh place, for Ephraim his son. *Benjamin,* Rachel's second son, is put in the last place.

If there be any mystery in this order, differing from all other scriptures where there is a mention made of the twelve patriarchs, it is probable that Mr. Mede hath hit upon it, in regard of the good or ill deserts of these tribes, some of which are mentioned by him; all may be learned from the history of the Jews recorded in holy writ. Hence we may learn, that the summary sense of all these verses is this, That although within that period of time which is signified under the seventh seal, there should be great persecutions of the church, yet God would preserve unto himself a great number in all his churches, which should not apostatize, and who in the persecutions should not be hurt; so as his church should not fail, though the archers should shoot sore at it; for though men raged, yet it was by God's permission; and his angels overruled it, who should take notice of those numbers that he had sealed, and marked in their foreheads.

h Rom. 11. 25.

9 After this I beheld, and, lo, ʰa great multitude, which no man could number,

i ch. 5. 9.

ⁱof all nations, and kindreds, and people, and tongues, stood before the throne,

k ch. 3. 5, 18. & 4. 4. & 6. 11. ver. 14.

and before the Lamb, ᵏclothed with white robes, and palms in their hands;

If we inquire who these were, we are told, ver. 14, by the best Interpreter, *These are they which came out of great tribulation, and have washed their robes,* &c. So that they do not seem to be the one hundred and forty-four thousand mentioned for preservation in and from the evil, ver. 4, but such as had escaped, or were not in or going into tribulation, but come out. The number of the former was determined; it is said of these, it could not be numbered. These were glorified ones, not militant; they *stood before the throne, and the Lamb, clothed with white robes;* clothed in the habits of such as amongst the Romans had fought, and conquered, and triumphed; and to this end they are said to have carried *palms,* the ensigns of victory, *in their hands.*

l Ps. 3. 8. Is. 43. 11. Jer. 3. 23. Hos. 13. 4. ch. 19. 1. m ch. 5. 13.

10 And cried with a loud voice, saying, ˡSalvation to our God ᵐ which sitteth upon the throne, and unto the Lamb.

They acknowledge their temporal, spiritual, and eternal salvation to the gift and free mercy of God, in whom they had trusted, and to the Lord Jesus Christ, by whose merits and Spirit they had got the victory.

n ch. 4. 6.

11 ⁿAnd all the angels stood round about the throne, and *about* the elders and the four beasts, and fell before the throne on their faces, and worshipped God,

And all the angels stood round about the throne; the good angels, who always in heaven behold the face of their and our heavenly Father. *And about the elders;* and about the twenty-four elders, mentioned chap. iv. 4. *And the four beasts;* and the living creatures, mentioned chap. iv. 6. *And fell before the throne on their faces;* the angels, elders, and living creatures, all fall down on their faces, in a reverential sense of the infinite distance between them and their Creator. *And worshipped God;* thus paying an homage to God fitted to their glorified state, in consideration of his excellency.

o ch.5. 13,14.

12 ºSaying, Amen: Blessing, and glory, and wisdom, and thanksgiving, and honour, and power, and might, *be* unto our God for ever and ever. Amen.

These words only signify the union and harmony of the angels and saints in praising God: see the notes on chap. v. 12.

13 And one of the elders answered, saying unto me, What are these which are arrayed in ᵖwhite robes? and whence came they? p ver. 9.

Not that he did not know, but to try whether John knew, or rather to set John upon inquiring.

14 And I said unto him, Sir, thou knowest. And he said to me, ᵠThese are they which came out of great tribulation, and have ʳwashed their robes, and made them white in the blood of the Lamb.

q ch. 6. 9. & 17. 6.
r Is. 1. 18. Heb. 9. 14. 1 John 1. 7. ch. 1. 5. See Zech. 3. 3, 4, 5.

John confessing his own ignorance, applies himself to this elder for instruction, who tells him, These were the souls of them that came out of great sufferings and persecution; but he addeth, that they were such as were washed in the blood of Christ. Suffering will not bring us to heaven, without having our souls washed with the blood of Christ.

15 Therefore are they before the throne of God, and serve him day and night in his temple: and he that sitteth on the throne shall ˢdwell among them.

s Is. 4. 5, 6. ch. 21. 3.

Therefore are they before the throne of God; not that they by their sufferings have merited heaven, but because it pleaseth God of his free grace so to reward them; therefore it was said, not only that they were such as came out of tribulation, but that they had washed their garments in the blood of the Lamb, whose blood had paid the price of their salvation. *And serve him day and night in his temple:* by the *temple,* some understand the church in this life, but it is foreign to the true sense of the text; for John saw only their souls before the throne, their bodies were in their graves. By the *temple* is meant heaven, where God dwelleth, and is worshipped more gloriously and constantly than he was in the Jewish temple, or in any part of the militant church. *And he that sitteth on the throne shall dwell among them;* as God by his gracious presence dwelt in the Jewish temple, so God by his glorious presence shall dwell amongst his glorified saints.

16 ᵗThey shall hunger no more, neither thirst any more; ᵘneither shall the sun light on them, nor any heat.

t Is. 49. 10.
u Ps. 121. 6. ch. 21. 4.

This is taken out of Isa. xlix. 10. They are all metaphorical expressions, all signifying the perfect state of glorified saints; they shall have no wants, nor be exposed to any afflictive providences.

17 For the Lamb which is in the midst of the throne ˣshall feed them, and shall lead them unto living fountains of waters: ʸand God shall wipe away all tears from their eyes.

x Ps. 23. 1.& 36. 8. John 10, 11, 14.
y Is. 25 8. ch. 21. 4.

For the Lamb which is in the midst of the throne; Christ, the Lamb mentioned chap. v. 6. *Shall feed them, &c.;* shall take care of them, to satisfy and to protect them, and give them the best supplies, and both make them to forget their former sorrows, and prevent any further cause of sorrow and affliction to them. A perfect description of the glorious and happy state of saints in heaven. For wherein lieth the happiness of heaven, but in a freedom from all the evils that encumber us in this life, and the enjoyment of all the happiness we are capable of, and being ever with the Lord Jesus Christ, under his influence and conduct? So as I cannot agree with Mr. Mede, or any of those who think this vision and these phrases describe any happy, peaceable state of the church in this life, after the throwing down of antichrist; but do think that John was showed this great reward of martyrs, to encourage the church of God under all those evils they were to suffer under antichrist and the beast, in that period of time which is described mystically upon the opening of the seventh seal, which we now come to in the next chapter.

CHAP. VIII

The seventh seal opened, 1. Seven angels receive seven trumpets, 2. An angel presenteth the prayers of the saints with incense on the golden altar before the throne, 3—5. Four of the angels sound their trumpets, and great plagues severally follow, 6—13.

a ch. 6. 1. AND ^a when he had opened the seventh seal, there was silence in heaven about the space of half an hour.

And when he; that is, the Lamb, mentioned chap. v. 7, who *took the book out of the hand of him that sat upon the throne,* the book of God's counsels, and had now revealed mysteriously to John what should come to pass (under all the pagan emperors) to the church of Christ, until the time of Constantine the Great, who, (as was said,) about the year 325, had settled the Christian religion, and shut up all the idols' temples, having conquered the apostate Licinius. *Had opened the seventh seal;* he cometh now to open the seventh seal, that is, to reveal to John what should be in the succeeding time of the church to the end of the world. *There was silence in heaven about the space of half an hour:* but before the great evils should break out, which were to come to pass in this time, there was in the church a rest for a small time; for from the year 317, when Constantine bare the greatest sway in the empire, or 325, when he had got a full victory over Licinius, the church had a great peace for a little time, till 339, when the empire being divided, and Constantius having the eastern part, and Constans the western, (both sons of Constantine,) Constantius, being an Arian, (who denied the Godhead of Christ,) began again to persecute the Christians; and after him Julian, who apostatized to paganism. But after him they had a little further respite to the year 395, when Theodosius died, and the Christians' quiet died with him. I rather choose to interpret this thus, than with those who understand the *silence in heaven,* of a silence in the third heavens, in allusion to the Jewish order; who, though they sung during the time of the sacrifice, and played upon instruments of music all that time, yet kept silence while the incense was offering. For (as divers have noted) it seemeth hard to judge, that in this Revelation there should be no mention of that short truce which the church had during the reign of Constantine, and for a small time after.

b Tob. 12. 15. Matt. 18. 10. Luke 1. 19. c 2 Chro. 29. 25.—28. 2 ^b And I saw the seven angels which stood before God; ^c and to them were given seven trumpets.

The seven angels which stood before God; the seven mentioned hereafter, which blew with the trumpets; for we presently read, that *seven trumpets* were given to them. Trumpets were used to call the people together, to proclaim festivals, and in war. The use of these trumpets we shall hereafter read, which was to proclaim the will and counsels of God, as to things to come.

3 And another angel came and stood at the altar, having a golden censer; and there was given unto him much incense, that he should ‖ offer *it* with ^d the prayers of all saints upon ^e the golden altar which was before the throne.

‖ Or, *add it to the prayers.* d ch. 5. 8. e Ex. 30. 1. ch. 6. 9.

And another angel came; by this angel I understand Christ, as do many very valuable authors; nor, indeed, can what is said of this angel agree to any other but him, who is called an *Angel,* Gen. xlviii. 16, and the Angel *of the covenant,* Mal. iii. 1. Here is a manifest allusion to the order of the Jewish worship; they had an altar of incense, Exod. xxx. 1, upon which the high priest was to burn incense every morning and evening, ver. 7, 8. Whilst the priest was burning incense, as appears, Luke i. 10, the people were without, praying. Christ is here represented as *having a golden censer.* The high priest's censer amongst the Jews was of brass; but he was a more excellent High Priest. *And there was given unto him much incense;* by which is meant the infinite merit of his death, to be offered up by himself (who is *the golden altar) with the prayers of all his saints.* By all this Christ is represented to us, as interceding for his saints that were to live after this time, during all troubles that were immediately to begin, and to follow on, during the reign of antichrist.

4 And ^f the smoke of the incense, *which came* with the prayers of the saints, ascended up before God out of the angel's hand.

f Ps. 141. 2. Luke 1. 10

This only denotes the acceptableness of Christ's intercession, and God's people's prayers, through the virtue of that intercession, unto God.

5 And the angel took the censer, and filled it with fire of the altar, and cast *it* ‖ into the earth: and ^g there were voices, and thunderings, and lightnings, ^h and an earthquake.

‖ Or, *upon.* g ch. 16. 18. h 2 Sam. 22. 8. 1 Kings 19. 11. Acts 4. 31.

I doubt not but by *fire* here, is to be understood the wrath of God, often in holy writ compared to fire, poured out upon the Roman empire, or the visible church. Upon which followed great judgments, and confusions, and tumults, expressed here, or ushered in, as before, chap. vi. 1, with *thunderings;* which being here more generally mentioned, are by and by more particularly expressed.

6 And the seven angels which had the seven trumpets prepared themselves to sound.

The angels are God's ministers, by which he bringeth his counsels to pass in the world: they hearing the *thunderings* and *voices,* knew the time was come when they were to begin the execution of God's judgments upon the earth; the execution of which was intrusted to them, and they are therefore set out (though they be always ready) after the manner of men, preparing themselves to execute what God had intrusted them with the execution of.

7 The first angel sounded, ⁱ and there followed hail and fire mingled with blood, and they were cast ^k upon the earth: and the third part ^l of trees was burnt up, and all green grass was burnt up.

i Ezek. 38. 22. k ch. 16. 2. l Is. 2. 13. ch. 9. 4.

The first angel sounded; the first of the seven angels to whom the seven trumpets were given, ver. 2, began to execute his commission; the consequents of which were *hail and fire mingled with blood, cast upon the earth:* by which some understand the primitive church's persecutions by the Jews and the heathen emperors; but these were over. Some understand God's revenge upon the Jews; but this also was taken some hundreds of years since. Some understand unseasonable weather in many parts of the world; but we read nothing like this in history. Some understand contests happening in the church; others understand heresies. But I cannot but rather agree with the reverend Mr. Mede, who expounds it of great troubles, and blood, and slaughter which should happen; and thinks that this prophecy began to be fulfilled about the death of Theodosius, Anno 395. For in this very year (saith he) Alaricus the king of the Goths brake into Macedonia, with a great army went into Thessalia, and so into Achaia, Peloponnesus, Corinth, Argos, Sparta, burning, wasting, and ruining all places; and so went on till the year 400; then fell upon the eastern empire, and committed the same outrages in Dalmatia and Hungary; then went into Stiria and Bavaria, thence into Italy and to Venice. After this, in the year 404, these barbarous nations invaded Italy, and took divers places. In the year 406 the Vandals and Alans, with many others, invaded France, Spain, and Africa: all which he proveth from the testimony of Jerome, Ep. 3. 11. This he judgeth the effect of the first angel's sounding, and to have been signified by the *hail and fire mingled with blood,* consonant to other scriptures. Isaiah, chap. xxviii. 2, compareth Shalmaneser to a storm of hail; and, chap. xxx. 30, he so likeneth the ruin to come unto the Assyrians. By the *trees burnt up,* are (saith he) the great and rich men to be understood, ordinarily in Scripture compared to trees, Isa. ii. 13; xiv. 8; Zech. xi. 2; and by the *green grass,* the ordinary common people. Thus he judgeth the effects of this first trumpet's sounding to have been determined in fifteen years, viz. from the year 395 to 410.

REVELATION VIII, IX

m Jer. 51.25.
Amos 7. 4.

n ch. 16. 3.
o Ezek. 14. 19.

8 And the second angel sounded, ^m and as it were a great mountain burning with fire was cast into the sea: ⁿ and the third part of the sea ^obecame blood;

There is a great variety of senses also about this *mountain of fire cast into the sea*. Some by it understand things happening in Judea; but this had been not to have showed John the things which should be, but which had been. Others will have the devil understood; others, the power of the Roman empire; others, some great war stirred up amongst people; others, some notable heresy or heretic; others, some famous persons in the church: but I most like Mr. Mede's notion again here, who understands by this mountain, Rome, the seat of the western empire; great cities being called *mountains* in Scripture phrase, Isa. xxxvii. 24; Jer. li. 25. *And the third part of the sea became blood*: this phrase speaks only the great effusion of blood upon the taking of Rome by its enemies.

p ch. 16. 3.

9 ^pAnd the third part of the creatures which were in the sea, and had life, died; and the third part of the ships were destroyed.

Phrases all signifying the miserable catastrophe that should follow the destruction of this city, by the slaughter of men, the ruin of houses and towns in Italy, &c. History (as Mr. Mede showeth) excellently agreeth with this. In the year 410, Rome was taken by Alaricus; this was followed with great devastations both in France and Spain. Honorius, to recover the empire, was glad to give the Goths a seat and government in France, and the Burgundians and Vandals a place near unto the river Rhone; and, Anno 415, to the Vandals a place in Spain; and, Anno 455, Rome was again taken by Genserieus the Vandal, who divided the whole empire into ten kingdoms: 1. That of the Britons, ruled by Vortimer. 2. The Saxons, ruled by Hengist. 3. The Franks, ruled by Childeric. 4. The Burgundians, ruled by Gundericus. 5. The Visigoths, ruled by Theodoricus II. 6. The Alans and Suevi, ruled by Riciarius. 7. The Vandals, ruled by Genserieus. 8. The Germans, ruled by Sumanus. 9. The Ostrogoths, ruled by Theodemirus. 10. The Grecians, ruled by Marcianus. This is the sum of what Mr. Mede saith, and to this tract of time, betwixt the years 410 and 455, the second trumpet seemeth to relate.

q Is. 14. 12.
ch. 9. 1.

10 And the third angel sounded, ^qand there fell a great star from heaven, burning as it were a lamp, ^rand it fell upon the third part of the rivers, and upon the fountains of waters;

r ch. 16. 4.

There fell a great star from heaven: stars, in their metaphorical notion, signify some eminent persons in the state, or in the church; accordingly interpreters are divided in their senses; some thinking that it is meant of a political star, some eminent civil governor, and apply it to Cæsar Augustulus, who, about the year 480, was forced to give over the empire, by Odoacer; of him Mr. Mede understands this prophecy. Others understand it of some ecclesiastical star, who apostatized, and apply it to Pelagius. I do rather incline to those who apply it to some ecclesiastical star; and Pelagius might be pointed at, as probably as any other in these times, for he was a great professor, and so burned *as a lamp*. *And it fell upon the third part of the rivers, and upon the fountains of waters;* and did corrupt a great part of the church.

s Ruth 1. 20.
t Ex. 15. 23.
Jer. 9. 15.
& 23. 15.

11 ^sAnd the name of the star is called Wormwood: ^tand the third part of the waters became wormwood; and many men died of the waters, because they were made bitter.

His doctrine was as bitter as wormwood; and he was the ruin of many souls. But if any do rather choose to understand it of a political star, Mr. Mede's notion bids as fair for the sense as any, because the western empire determined in Augustulus, and he reigned but a very short time; and he was a prince of many sorrows and afflictions, and many perished with him in those sorrows and afflictions which he underwent. Whether we understand it of some eminent political magistrate, (such was Augustulus,) or some eminent light in the church, (such was Pelagius,) they both fell about this time, the one from his terrene dignity, the other spiritually from the honour he had in the church; and many fell with them, either in a civil or in a spiritual sense.

12 ^uAnd the fourth angel sounded, and the third part of the sun was smitten, and the third part of the moon, and the third part of the stars; so as the third part of them was darkened, and the day shone not for a third part of it, and the night likewise.

u Is. 13. 10.
Amos 8. 9.

Interpreters (setting aside one or two, who conceit the Revelation is nothing but a repetition of things that happened in Judea before John's time) generally agree, that the period of time to which this prophecy relates, is from the year 480, when the western empire ceased. The history of the age next following, both relating to civil and ecclesiastical things, doth so fit this prophecy, that interpreters are much divided about the sense of it, whether it be to be understood of the miseries befalling the Roman empire or the church in that time; for, as great princes in the former, so great lights in the latter, are metaphorically expressed in Scripture under the notions of *the sun, moon,* and *stars,* in regard of the great influence they have upon men, as those luminaries of heaven have upon the earth. Mr. Mede understands it of political magistrates, here expressed (as in Joseph's dream) by *the sun, moon,* and *stars:* and to show us how the event fitted the prophecy, he tells us out of the best authors, that when Odoacer had routed Augustulus, and turned him out of the empire, himself ruled Rome under the title of a king sixteen years, and destroyed all their old magistracy, but after two years restored it. That Theodoricus, following him in the government of Italy, restored all their rights again, which so continued under three kings (all Goths) for near fifty years. But after the year 546, Rome was taken and burnt once and again, and a third part of it demolished by Totilas. Others understand it of Pelagius, or some famous heretic in that time. But to speak freely, the words of the prophecy, and the histories we have, rather agree to Mr. Mede's sense; for (except Pelagius, who began about the year 406) we read of none in this age to whom the words of this prophecy will agree in any good sense.

13 And I beheld, ^xand heard an angel flying through the midst of heaven, saying with a loud voice, ^yWoe, woe, woe, to the inhabiters of the earth by reason of the other voices of the trumpet of the three angels, which are yet to sound!

x ch. 14. 6.
& 19. 17.

y ch. 9. 12.
& 11. 14.

This verse is but an introduction to the other three angels sounding, declaring that the times which were to follow would be much more full of miseries and woes *to the inhabitants of the earth;* by which I understand all those countries which lately were subject to the Roman empire. Others understand the more earthy, unsound, hypocritical part of the church. The *woe* is thrice repeated, either to show the greatness of the calamities, or rather correspondently to the number of the angels yet to sound.

CHAP. IX

At the sounding of the fifth angel a star falleth from heaven, to whom is given the key of the bottomless pit, 1: *he opens the pit, and there come forth locusts like scorpions, who have power to hurt men for a time,* 2—11. *The first woe past,* 12. *At the sounding of the sixth angel four angels which were bound are loosed, and bring great plagues on the earth for a limited time,* 13—21.

AND the fifth angel sounded, ^aand I saw a star fall from heaven unto the earth: and to him was given the key of ^bthe bottomless pit.

a Luke 10. 18. ch. 8. 10.

b Luke 8. 31. ch. 17. 8. & 20. 1. ver. 2, 11.

REVELATION IX

And the fifth angel sounded; the fifth of the seven angels mentioned chap. viii. 2, to whom were given seven trumpets. It denoteth the beginning of a new period of calamities and miseries to the earth, or to the church. *And I saw a star fall from heaven unto the earth:* what this star falling from heaven means, is not easy to resolve. Those who think it the devil, once a star, but fallen, forget that John is not here told a story of what was in the beginning of the world, but what should be, and that five hundred years after Christ's coming. And the same reason holds against those who think those seditious persons are meant, who did so much mischief in and about Jerusalem during the siege; this had been to have revealed to John those things which he knew were done many years before. Amongst those who think some particular eminent minister of the church, who apostatized, is meant, those seem to me to judge better, who think that Boniface the Third is meant, who, in the year 606, obtained the privilege of the pope's supremacy, than those who understand it of Arius or Pelagius, who both of them fell two hundred years before this. It seems very harsh to interpret it of Christ, or any good angel's descending from heaven, because the word πεπτωκότα is rightly by us translated falling, and not to be interpreted so softly as descending. In all probability, therefore, the first apostacy of the bishop of Rome was here prophesied. But how *to him was given the key of the bottomless pit,* (by which hell is meant here, as often in Scripture,) is hard to say; unless we understand it of his instrumentality, to send many thousands to hell by that corrupt doctrine and worship, which by him then began to obtain. But his key was borrowed, (if God had not permitted him he could not have done it,) and it turned but one way; he had only a power to open it, not (as Christ) both to open and shut it.

2 And he opened the bottomless pit; and ^c there arose a smoke out of the pit, as the smoke of a great furnace; and the sun and the air were darkened by reason of the smoke of the pit.

^c Joel 2. 2, 10.

And he opened the bottomless pit; he was a means of hell's breaking loose, by loosing Satan. *And there arose a smoke out of the pit, as the smoke of a great furnace:* I had rather interpret this generally of the great influence upon the world, that the devil, being loosed, had, in filling the world with ignorance, error, and wickedness, (for which this and the following age are infamous in all histories,) and then particularly of the errors this time abounded with. *And the sun and the air were darkened by reason of the smoke of the pit;* this influence of the devil darkened the sun of the gospel, and the whole church of that age, with ignorance, error, and abominable superstition in the worship of God, attended with the lewdness and debauchery of men in their lives, which usually go together.

3 And there came out of the smoke ^d locusts upon the earth: and unto them was given power, ^e as the scorpions of the earth have power.

^d Ex. 10. 4. Judg. 7. 12.
^e ver. 10.

And there came out of the smoke locusts upon the earth; from the influence which the devil thus let loose had upon the world, came forth a generation of men, that in their practices resembled locusts. Who are to be understood by these *locusts,* is not easy to resolve. The locusts were an insect with which God sometimes plagued the Egyptians; they are much in the Eastern countries. It was an east wind which brought them upon Egypt, Exod. x. 12, 13. God often hath punished people with them, they are therefore threatened, or mentioned as a judgment in case of disobedience, Deut. xxviii. 38, 42; 1 Kings viii. 37; Joel i. 4; ii. 25. Two things are to be remarked of them: 1. They were wont to go in infinite numbers: Prov. xxx. 27, *They go forth by bands:* Nah. iii. 15, *Make thyself many as the locusts: without number,* Psal. cv. 34. 2. The mischief they do is expressed there, ver. 35, to *eat up the herbs of the land,* and *to devour the fruit of the ground:* so they did in Egypt. We have a little specimen of them in our caterpillars in times of drought, usually caused from the wind hanging long in the east. The psalmist, Psal. cv. 34, joineth the locusts and the caterpillars together. By the following description of these locusts, and the mischief which they did, ver. 4, 7—10, it appeareth plainly that these were no natural, but metaphorical locusts, men that, for their numbers and the mischief they did in the world, did resemble locusts; but who these were is the question. I find but two opinions that have any probability: the one is of a late learned writer, who judgeth them the popish clergy, to whom, indeed, many things agree. 1. They come *out of the smoke,* that is, the great influence which the devil hath upon the world. 2. They are numerous. 3. Their king is Abaddon; they destroy every green herb, nipping religion, in all places, in the bud. But I cannot see how two or three things can agree to them: 1. That they do no hurt to the Lord's sealed ones, whenas their particular malice is against the purest and strictest profession. 2. That they do not kill, but only torment men, ver. 5. 3 And (which is the greatest) I cannot see how the period of time agreeth to them. For this prophecy seemeth to respect the sixth and seventh age; and though all these things agree to the Romish clergy in later ages, especially since the Jesuits grew numerous, which is not much above one hundred and twenty years since, yet these three did not so agree to the Romish clergy in the sixth and seventh age. Their Benedictine orders began but in the year 530, and their orders of Dominicans, much more mischievous, not till upwards of the year 1200; the Jesuits, after the year 1500. I therefore rather agree with the learned and judicious Mr. Mede, with whom I also find John Napier and others agreeing, that by these locusts are meant the Turks and Saracens. 1. Their time agreeth; for they first appeared formidably to the world about the year 620. 2. They were always very numerous. 3. They came the locusts' road, from Arabia, and the eastern parts. The Arabians (which the Saracens are) are called *the children of the east,* and said to be like *grasshoppers for multitude.* Two things are objected: 1. That these locusts are commanded not to hurt the Lord's sealed ones. 2. That their commission is but for five months. As to the latter, we shall speak to it when we come to that clause. As to the former, why may it not denote the liberty that in their conquests they generally give to all religions, so as they put none to death upon that account? How far other things will agree to them, I leave to be further considered in the next verses. *And unto them was given power, as the scorpions of the earth have power;* that is, such a power as scorpions have. We shall have a more particular account of this, ver. 10.

4 And it was commanded them ^f that they should not hurt ^g the grass of the earth, neither any green thing, neither any tree; but only those men which have not ^h the seal of God in their foreheads.

^f ch. 6. 6. & 7. 3.
^g ch. 8. 7.
^h ch. 7. 3. See Exod. 12. 23. Ezek. 9. 4.

And it was commanded them; that is, these locusts; God so ordered it by his providence. *That they should not hurt, &c.:* this makes it appear, that these locusts were no insects so called, but typical; for natural locusts live upon green things; they were only to hurt profane men, and hypocrites. It is a sure rule, that when things are attributed to living creatures which do not agree to their natures, the terms are to be understood typically, not literally. Locusts use not to kill men; we may therefore be assured, that the locusts here intended, were men, not insects.

5 And to them it was given that they should not kill them, ⁱ but that they should be tormented five months: and their torment was as the torment of a scorpion, when he striketh a man.

ⁱ ch. 11. 7. ver. 10.

Supposing the Saracens and Turks here meant by the locusts, here arise two difficulties: 1. How it can be said of them, that they had no power to *kill,* but only *torment* men. 2. How their time is set for *five months,* whereas they have already tormented the world more than a thousand years; and how long they shall yet continue to do so, God only knows: they are both great difficulties. Alsted tells us, That Mahomet began in the year 622, and the Saracens entered Spain 714, where they were called Moors, and kept possession of that kingdom eight hundred years, and that in the year 719, they besieged Constantinople with a navy of three thousand ships and three hundred thousand land soldiers ; that before this time they had made themselves masters of Arabia, Palestina, Syria, Persia, Egypt, Africa, and Spain ; and in the year 726, carried into France an army consisting of three hundred and seventy-five thousand, where they were beaten by Charles Martell, father to King Pepin. Mr. Mede telleth us, that the Saracens grievously vexed the countries subject to the Roman emperor, but could not take either Rome or Constantinople. The latter was taken by the Turks, in the year 1457, commanded by Sultan Mahomet. This is but a hard interpretation of those words, *that they should not kill them;* which, it may be, hath made some other interpreters choose to interpret these locusts to signify the Roman clergy, who indeed did not kill men for religion, of many years. But both the one and the other tormented the world enough, and that like a scorpion, which pierceth a man with a venomous sting, and puts him to great pain. For the *five months,* we shall again meet with them, ver. 10.

k Job 3. 21.
Is. 2. 19.
Jer. 8. 3.
ch. 6. 16.

6 And in those days [k] shall men seek death, and shall not find it ; and shall desire to die, and death shall flee from them.

The calamities of those days shall be so great, that men shall be weary of their lives.

l Joel 2. 4.

7 And [l] the shapes of the locusts *were* like unto horses prepared unto battle ;

m Nah. 3. 17.

[m] and on their heads *were* as it were

n Dan. 7. 8.

crowns like gold, [n] and their faces *were* as the faces of men.

This whole description of these locusts speaks them no insects, but to be mischievous men ; they were very terrible to look upon, like horses harnessed ready to fight ; so Joel ii. 4. *And upon their heads were as it were crowns like gold;* this signified they should be great and rich conquerors. *And their faces were as the faces of men;* yet these were men.

8 And they had hair as the hair of wo-

o Joel 1. 6.

men, and [o] their teeth were as *the teeth* of lions.

And they had hair as the hair of women; dishevelled, or hanging loose ; the Arabians were wont to go so ; or this may signify, that they were beautiful as well as terrible to look upon. *And their teeth were as the teeth of lions;* sharp and strong : see Joel i. 6.

9 And they had breastplates, as it were breastplates of iron ; and the sound of

p Joel 2. 5, 6, 7.

their wings *was* [p] as the sound of chariots of many horses running to battle.

And they had breastplates, as it were breastplates of iron ; armed with the best armour of defence. *And the sound of their wings was as the sound of chariots of many horses running to battle ;* like locusts, they moved very swiftly. This agreeth to the Saracens, who made such haste in their conquests, that (saith Mr. Mede) in little more than eighty years they had subdued Palestina, Syria, both the Armenias, almost all the Lesser Asia, Persia, India, Egypt, Numidia, all Barbary, Portugal, Spain ; and within a few more, Sicily, Candia, Cyprus, and were come to the very gates of Rome ; so as they had many crowns on their heads, and moved as with wings.

10 And they had tails like unto scorpions, and there were stings in their tails :

q ver. 5.

[q] and their power *was* to hurt men five months.

And they had tails like unto scorpions ; a kind of venomous serpents that have their *stings in their tails,* with which they presently kill both men and beasts. *And their power was to hurt men five months ;* what these *five months* mean is very hard to say ; certainly it is a certain number for an uncertain, and mentioned rather than any other time, because it is (as they say) the usual time of the life of locusts ; though some observe, that five months have in them (counting as the Hebrews, thirty days to the month) one hundred and fifty days, and a day standing for a year, as in prophetical writings, it denoteth the just time the Saracens raged in Italy, from the year 830 to the year 980 ; as to which I refer my reader to search histories.

11 [r] And they had a king over them,

r Eph. 2. 2.

which is [s] the angel of the bottomless pit,

s ver. 1.

whose name in the Hebrew tongue *is* Abaddon, but in the Greek tongue hath

‖ That is to say, *a destroyer.*

his name ‖ Apollyon.

Solomon saith, Prov. xxx. 27, *The locusts have no king, yet go they forth by bands;* according to which these locusts cannot be understood of insects so called ; or, if they have a king, yet it is certain the devil is not their king, who is here called *the angel of the bottomless pit. Abaddon ;* from אבד he hath destroyed. *Apollyon;* that is, a destroyer ; intimating that the whole business of this barbarous enemy should be to ruin and destroy nations.

12 [t] One woe is past ; *and,* behold, there

t ch. 8. 13.

come two woes more hereafter.

One period of time is over, in which God hath plagued the world with a very great judgment ; but there are two more to come, which will be equally, if not more, calamitous.

13 And the sixth angel sounded, and I heard a voice from the four horns of the golden altar which is before God,

That is, from God, I heard him give a command, which voice is said to have proceeded *from the golden altar,* (in allusion to Exod. xxx. 3,) because there God received the prayers of his people ; and this voice proceeding from that place, might signify the following judgment to come, in answer to the prayers of his servants' souls from thence crying to him for vengeance. See chap. vi. 9, 10.

14 Saying to the sixth angel which had the trumpet, Loose the four angels which are bound [u] in the great river Euphrates.

u ch. 16. 12.

By these *four angels,* or instruments of God to execute his vengeance, I find the most valuable interpreters understanding the Turks, considered as distinct from the Saracens, and succeeding to them, whose empire began in Ottoman, Anno 1296, or thereabouts. Mr. Mede saith these four angels denote so many sultanies or kingdoms, into which the Turks were dispersed, having passed the river Euphrates, which river is famous for four things : 1. It was the boundary of David and Solomon's kingdom, Deut. xi. 24 ; Josh. i. 4. 2. It was that river by which Babylon stood, Jer. xiii. 4—6. 3. It was the boundary of the Roman empire, beyond which it could never extend itself. 4. And it also was the seat of the Turks, who having some years before come over the Euphrates, first divided themselves into a tetrarchy ; of which one in Asia, another at Aleppo, another at Damascus, a fourth at Antioch. Mr. Mede gives us a table or diagram of it, Clav. Apoc. 40. p. 102. Here they were bounded for a while, but about the year 1300 they were loosed, and began further to invade Europe ; which is the severe providence of God, conceived to be here foretold as the consequent of this sixth angel's sounding. The Turks who, though come over the river Euphrates, had hitherto by the providence of God been bounded near unto it, not much contending to enlarge their territories, now joined together with the Saracens under Ottoman, and went further into Europe, and could by no means be stopped till they had got the empire of Constantinople.

15 And the four angels were loosed, which were prepared ‖ for an hour, and

‖ Or, *at.*

a day, and a month, and a year, for to slay the third part of men.

For an hour, and a day, and a month, and a year; that is, say some, for any time whatsoever God would have them move ; or for that certain time which God had determined ; but Mr. Mede hath here a peculiar notion ; he observeth that an hour, and a day, and a month, and a year, make just three hundred and ninety-six years. In a year are three hundred and sixty-five days, in a month thirty, which make three hundred and ninety-five, to which add the odd day, they make three hundred and ninety-six. The Turks began their empire under Ottoman, who began his reign Anno 1296 : but their leader, Tangrolipix, upon the taking of Bagdad was inaugurated, and put on the imperial robe, Anno 1057. Constantinople was taken by them Anno 1453, between which are just three hundred and ninety-six years. In which time they slew a numberless number of men, called here *the third part.*

^{x Ps. 68. 17.}
^{Dan. 7. 10.}
^{y Ezek. 38. 4.}
^{z ch. 7. 4.}

16 And ^xthe number of the army ^y of the horsemen *were* two hundred thousand thousand : ^zand I heard the number of them.

He saith nothing of the infantry, but leaves us to conjecture how great that must be, from the number of the horse; we must not think there was precisely this number, but the meaning is, that the armies should be vastly great, as we know all the Turkish armies are. Magog's army is described from the cavalry, Ezek. xxxviii. 4, 15.

17 And thus I saw the horses in the vision, and them that sat on them, having breastplates of fire, and of jacinth, and brimstone : ^a and the heads of the horses *were* as the heads of lions; and out of their mouths issued fire and smoke and brimstone.

^{a 1 Chr. 12. 6. Is. 5. 28, 29.}

We have no such description or representation as this in any other place of holy writ. Some understand it of the several-coloured breastplates that the soldiers wore; some of a red and flaming colour, like fire; others blue, like the jacinth; some pale : all such as wear them look terribly. Mr. Mede hath here again a peculiar notion; thinking that the Holy Ghost doth here signify their fighting with great guns, (not known before the siege of Constantinople,) which throw out fire and smoke, &c., and so alter the air, the medium by which we see, that the opposite party in fighting appear to those that use these arms, as if they were covered with breastplates that were red, and blue, and pale. To confirm this, he tells us of Chalcondylas's report of this siege, who mentioneth great guns used at it of that vast bigness, that one of them required threescore and ten yoke of oxen and two thousand men to draw it, &c. It is at least a very ingenious conjecture, and I could not but mention it in honour to the learned author; leaving it to my reader's liberty, whether he will, with Mr. Mede, judge this literal sense of the text is best, or interpret all these phrases more generally, only of a terrible appearance of those armies.

18 By these three was the third part of men killed, by the fire, and by the smoke, and by the brimstone, which issued out of their mouths.

That is, a great part of men were killed by these numerous armies. No such devastations were ever made by any enemies that ever appeared in the world, as by the Turks have been; nor ever were there such vast great guns made, out of which came *fire, and smoke, and brimstone.*

19 For their power is in their mouth, and in their tails : ^b for their tails *were* like unto serpents, and had heads, and with them they do hurt.

^{b Is. 9. 15.}

By *their tails* some understand their infantry or foot soldiery; others, their serpentine craft and subtlety : as the locusts, ver. 10, are compared to scorpions, whose sting was in their tails, and who were said to hurt with their tails; so the same thing is said of these armies, intimating that the Turks should be mischievous by the same arts and means as their predecessors the Saracens. These are said to have had heads in their tails, which was not said of the locusts; the reason of which interpreters judge to have arisen from the different animals by which they are represented.

20 And the rest of the men which were not killed by these plagues ^cyet repented not of the works of their hands, that they should not worship ^ddevils, ^eand idols of gold, and silver, and brass, and stone, and of wood : which neither can see, nor hear, nor walk :

^{c Deu. 31. 29.}
^{d Lev. 17. 7. Deut. 32. 17. Ps. 106. 37. 1 Cor. 10. 20. e Ps. 115. 4. & 135. 15. Dan. 5. 23.}

And the rest of the men which were not killed by these plagues; the two-thirds of men that should be left, for we read of one-third part destroyed; and this also must be understood of men dwelling in countries subject formerly to the Roman empire on this side of the Euphrates. *Yet repented not of the works of their hands, that they should not worship devils :* this leaves this applicable to none but papists; for there are none else but them who worship demons, Greek, δαιμόνια, or idols of gold and silver. By *devils* are meant demons, that is, persons that are dead, whom the heathens made their petty gods, and worshipped as middle beings betwixt them and the supreme gods, according to their notion; which is the same thing the papists are guilty of, with this only difference, (as Mr. Mede excellently observeth,) that the heathens made many supreme gods, and these modern idolaters own but one in that notion, but as many *deastri* or demons as they did, which are all those saints to whom they pay an adoration, as to those who should present their desires to God, which, as Mr. Mede sufficiently proves from writers, was the very work the pagans allotted for those whom they canonized after death. From whence came the names of Baal and Bel, &c., but from Belus, who is said to have been the first prince, whom, being dead, they made a god, and adored? Which demons God in Scripture calleth devils. Nor do any but they now worship images, the works of men's hands, made of *gold, silver, brass,* and *wood,* who are here described in the same words as by the psalmist, Psal. cxv. 4; cxxxv. 15. Notwithstanding God's great judgment executed upon the Grecian churches, yet they repented not of their idolatry and superstition; so as God hath brought them wholly under the power of those barbarous enemies; and though the Romish party seeth this, yet neither do they repent; which may give them cause to fear that God should make use of the same adversary to destroy them likewise; especially considering that neither to this day do they repent.

21 Neither repented they of their murders, ^fnor of their sorceries, nor of their fornication, nor of their thefts.

^{f ch. 22. 15.}

Neither repented they of their murders; of their murdering the saints of God, but go on in that practice; *nor of their fornication,* which is publicly allowed amongst them; *nor of their theft* and sacrilege, and other wickedness, but are as infamous for their debaucheries as for their superstition and idolatry. How long this great judgment of the Turk shall continue upon Christians we cannot tell; it is Mr. Brightman's opinion that it shall determine in the year 1696; but of that the Scripture hath not informed us, and guessing is a vanity, where we have no sure foundation; and so many have appeared to have been mistaken in such particular determinations, that he lightly exposeth his reputation that will adventure further upon such rocks.

CHAP. X

A mighty angel appeareth with a book open in his hand, 1—4; *and sweareth by him that liveth for ever, that there shall be no more time,* 5—7. *John is commanded to take and eat the book, and to prophesy,* 8—11.

We have had in the former chapters Christ's revelation to St. John of what should happen in the Roman empire under the first six seals, that is, during their pagan state, which determined in Constantine's time, Anno 310, or 325. Under the seventh seal (that is, from chap. viii. 1) he hath revealed to him what should happen after that time to the Roman empire by the Goths and Vandals under the first four trumpets, and by the Saracens under the fifth trumpet, and the Turks under the sixth trumpet, who are yet rampant and going on in their outrages. The seventh trumpet in course should sound next, but we come not to that till chap. xi. 15. In this chapter, and to the 15th verse of the next chapter, seems an interruption of the history, that Christ might reveal to his prophet the main things that should concern his church. About the sense of this interpreters are divided, some thinking this a distinct prophecy relating to the affairs of the church, yet not in a continued story, but made up of several visions, some contemporary with the times before mentioned, some continu-

REVELATION X

ing to the time after the sixth trumpet; which prophecy, as they judge, beginneth at the 11th chapter, to which what we have in this chapter is introductive. Of this mind are our Dr. More, Mr. Mede, and other very valuable interpreters, whose reasons may be read in Mr. Pool's Latin Synopsis upon this chapter, and some of them may be noted by us as we go through this chapter. Others think it is no distinct prophecy.

AND I saw another mighty angel come down from heaven, clothed with a cloud: ᵃand a rainbow *was* upon his head, and ᵇhis face *was* as it were the sun, and ᶜhis feet as pillars of fire:

a Ezek. 1. 28.
b Mat. 17. 2.
ch. 1. 16.
c ch. 1. 15.

And I saw another mighty angel; the most and best interpreters understand by this angel, Christ, formerly represented to us as a *Lamb,* here as an *Angel;* none but he could call the two witnesses, chap. xi. 3, his witnesses; besides, the glorious appearance of this angel speaketh him no ordinary angel. *Come down from heaven;* God being about to do or speak some great thing, is oft thus set out as coming down from heaven. *Clothed with a cloud;* Christ is described as coming with clouds, chap. i. 7. *The Lord hath said that he would dwell in the thick darkness,* 2 Chron. vi. 1. *And a rainbow was upon his head;* which was the sign of the covenant made with Noah, Gen. ix. 16, and fitted Christ's head, as he that brought peace to the world, and to his church in special. *And his face was as it were the sun;* see Matt. xvii. 2. *And his feet as pillars of fire;* signifying the steadiness and efficacy of his actions.

2 And he had in his hand a little book open: ᵈand he set his right foot upon the sea, and *his* left *foot* on the earth,

d Mat. 28.18.

And he had in his hand a little book open; the same book with that mentioned chap. v. 1; though some by it understand the Scriptures. There it was represented to John as *sealed with seven seals;* here *open,* to let us know that all the counsels of God, however sealed as to us, are open to Christ, and that he would open to John what should come to pass in his church to the end of the world. *And he set his right foot upon the sea, and his left foot on the earth;* to let us know the dominion he had over the whole world, as well the more unquiet as quieter parts of it.

3 And cried with a loud voice, as *when* a lion roareth: and when he had cried, ᵉseven thunders uttered their voices.

e ch. 8. 5.

And cried with a loud voice, as when a lion roareth: this voice suited him who is the Lion of the tribe of Judah: the lion's voice is both loud and terrible. *And when he had cried, seven thunders uttered their voices:* interpreters judge these seven thunders to signify those judgments of God which should be executed in the world upon the sounding of the seventh trumpet, and precedaneous to the day of judgment, which we shall find more fully opened under the seventh trumpet by the seven vials poured out, which signify the same thing; yet some understand by these *seven thunders* the powerful preaching the gospel; but the other seemeth more probable.

4 And when the seven thunders had uttered their voices, I was about to write: and I heard a voice from heaven saying unto me, ᶠSeal up those things which the seven thunders uttered, and write them not.

f Dan. 8. 26.
& 12. 4, 9.

I was about to write; to write what he understood of the voices of these thunders. *Seal up those things which the seven thunders uttered, and write them not;* he was forbidden the publication of them, because they concerned things to be fulfilled at some distance of time, and should be afterward more fully revealed.

5 And the angel which I saw stand upon the sea and upon the earth ᵍlifted up his hand to heaven,

g Ex. 6. 8.
Dan. 12. 7.

And the angel which I saw stand upon the sea and upon the earth: see ver. 2; which Angel was Christ. *Lifted up his hand to heaven;* as Dan. xii. 7, with which prophecy this agreeth. It is an ordinary gesture used in swearing.

6 And sware by him that liveth for ever and ever, ʰwho created heaven, and the things that therein'are, and the earth, and the things that therein are, and the sea, and the things which are therein, ⁱthat there should be time no longer:

h Neh. 9. 6.
ch. 4. 11. &
14. 7.

i Dan. 12. 7.
ch. 16. 17.

And sware by him that liveth, &c.; that is, by God; for this description can agree to no other, neither is it lawful to swear by any other: see Dan. xii. 7. *That there should be time no longer;* there shall be an end of the world, so some; but this John knew well enough. It is rather to be understood of the time of the fourth monarchy, the Roman empire should come to an end; or, the time of the afflictions of the church, whether by pagan or antichristian enemies, should be no more.

7 But ᵏin the days of the voice of the seventh angel, when he shall begin to sound, the mystery of God should be finished, as he hath declared to his servants the prophets.

k ch. 11. 15.

But in the days of the voice of the seventh angel; of whom, and his sounding, we shall read, chap. xi. 15. *When he shall begin to sound, the mystery of God should be finished;* from that time that he beginneth to sound shall begin the mystery of God to be finished; either the mystery mentioned chap. xi. 15, when the *kingdoms of this world* shall *become the kingdoms of our Lord, and his Christ;* or, more generally, whatsoever God hath revealed concerning the propagation of the gospel, the ruin of antichrist, and the end of the world. *As he hath declared to his servants the prophets;* whatsoever God hath declared by his servants the prophets about these things, (as to which see Isa. xxiv., xxvi., xxvii., lxvi.; Dan. vii. 11, 12; Zech. xiv.; Mal. iii. 4,) it shall be fulfilled, and begin to be fulfilled when the seventh angel shall begin to blow; within which period of time most interpreters judge we are, as being begun some time since.

8 And ˡthe voice which I heard from heaven spake unto me again, and said, Go *and* take the little book which is open in the hand of the angel which standeth upon the sea and upon the earth.

l ver. 4.

And the voice which I heard from heaven; the voice mentioned ver. 4. *Go and take the little book;* the little book mentioned ver. 2. John is bid to take this book, by which some understand the Scriptures; but it is most probably the book mentioned chap. v. 1, before sealed, now open.'

9 And I went unto the angel, and said unto him, Give me the little book. And he said unto me, ᵐTake *it,* and eat it up; and it shall make thy belly bitter, but it shall be in thy mouth sweet as honey.

m Jer. 15.16.
Ezek. 2. 8.
& 3. 1, 2, 3.

Take it, and eat it up: thus Ezekiel was bidden to eat the roll; and it was in his mouth as sweet as honey, Ezek. ii. 8; iii. 3. The eating of a book signifies the due reading of it, digesting it, and meditating upon the matters in it. *And it shall make thy belly bitter, but it shall be in thy mouth sweet as honey;* it should be sweet in his mouth, as it was the revelation of the mind and will of God, (which is sweet to all pious souls; see Jer. xv. 16,) but in his belly it should be bitter, being the revelation of the Divine will, as to the bringing such terrible judgments upon an impenitent people.

10 And I took the little book out of the angel's hand, and ate it up; ⁿand it was in my mouth sweet as honey: and as soon as I had eaten it, ᵒmy belly was bitter.

n Ezek. 3. 3.

o Ezek. 2. 10.

And I took the little book, and ate it up; according to the command, ver. 9. *And it was in my mouth sweet as honey;* as it was the revelation of God's will. *And as soon as I had eaten it, my belly was bitter;* but when he came to think upon it, it was either so mysterious that he could not comprehend it, or the matter of it was so sad that it gave him great trouble.

11 And he said unto me, Thou must prophesy again before many peoples, and nations, and tongues, and kings.

Thou must prophesy again: these words (as many think) evince this a prophecy distinct from the former; he must *prophesy again. Before many peoples, and nations, and tongues, and kings;* who shall be concerned to hear what shall now be revealed to thee concerning the rise of antichrist, his rule and tyranny, and his fall and ruin, which are things began long before, during the periods of time, when the six before-mentioned trumpets sounded, but were not there clearly revealed; which things I will reveal unto thee, that thou, and after thee the ministers of the gospel, may in their several periods reveal them in the hearing of *many people, and nations,* &c.; so that hereby John (as some think) was constituted a prophet to reveal the state of the church under antichrist, and his tyranny, and finally his ruin, which began at the sounding of the seventh trumpet, chap. xi. 15; but when it shall be finished, God alone must inform the world by the issues of his providence.

CHAP. XI

John is commanded to measure the temple, all but the outer court, 1, 2. *The two witnesses that shall prophesy,* 3, 4; *their power,* 5, 6; *the beast shall fight against them, and kill them,* 7; *they shall lie unburied three days and a half,* 8—10; *and then rise again, and ascend into heaven,* 11, 12. *A great earthquake,* 13. *The second woe past,* 14. *The seventh trumpet sounded : the heavenly choir celebrate the glories of God's kingdom,* 15—19.

a Ezek. 40. 3, &c.
Zech. 2. 1.
ch. 21, 15.
b Num. 23. 18.

AND there was given me [a]a reed like unto a rod; and the angel stood, saying, [b]Rise, and measure the temple of God, and the altar, and them that worship therein.

And there was given me a reed like a rod; the next words tell us the use of this reed. It was a *measuring reed,* such a one as Ezekiel in his vision (Ezek. xl. 3) saw in the man's hand. There, the measuring was in order to a rebuilding; here, in order to preserving. *And the angel stood, saying, Rise, and measure the temple of God :* we cannot well understand what followeth, without understanding the structure of the temple. The Jews, for the place of their worship, had first a tabernacle, then a temple. The tabernacle was a movable house, which they took down and carried about with them in their journeyings, and pitched down when in any place they pitched their tents. We read of it, Exod. xl. We read but of one court in that, into which only the priests and Levites entered; the people were without it, pitching their tents round about it. It had in it an altar of gold for incense, Exod. xl. 5, which stood before the ark, ver. 26, 27; and an altar for burnt-offering, which stood by the door of the tabernacle, ver. 29. The temple was built by Solomon, 1 Kings vi., and afterwards rebuilt by Zerubbabel, upon their return out of captivity. That was built with two courts; an inner court, 1 Kings vi. 36, in which was the altar; and an outward court, which is called *the great court,* 2 Chron. iv. 9, and in Ezekiel, many times, the *outward court.* This is called *the house,* in the First Book of Kings, chap. vi. 17. It was in length forty cubits; the oracle was within it, ver. 19, where stood the ark covered with the cherubims. Into the inward court the priests and Levites only came; into the outward court came any of the Israelites. Herod, upon the additional building to the temple, added another large court, called *the court of the Gentiles;* but that not being of God's direction, nor in Solomon's temple, or Zerubbabel's, is not here mentioned. This *temple* was a type of the church under the New Testament, 1 Cor. iii. 17; 2 Cor. vi. 16, and is so to be interpreted generally in this book : for the material temple at Jerusalem was destroyed by the Romans more than twenty years before this prophecy, never to be built more; not one stone was left upon another; so that John here was bid to measure the church. *And the altar, and them that worship therein;* yet not the whole church, but that part of it which the inner court typified; the altar, and those that worshipped within that space where that was, which of old were only the priests and Levites; and under the New Testament signified those who were to be *a holy priesthood, a spiritual house,* those that should offer up *spiritual sacrifices acceptable to God by Jesus Christ,* 1 Pet. ii. 5, who could endure a measuring by God's reed, the word of God.

2 But [c]the court which is without the temple †leave out, and measure it not; [d]for it is given unto the Gentiles : and the holy city shall they [e]tread under foot [f]forty *and* two months.

c Ezek. 40. 17, 20.
† Gr. *cast out.*
d Ps. 79. 1.
Luke 21. 24.
e Dan. 8. 10.
1 Mac. 3. 51.
f ch. 13. 5.

There is no great doubt, but the same persons are here to be understood by *the court which is without the temple,* (that is, without the inward court,) *and the holy city;* and by them, both the generality of those people who come under the name of the Christian church, who are all of them, in some sense, *a holy people,* 1 Cor. vii. 14, as all the Jews were; yet, for the greatest part of them, John is commanded to omit, or neglect them, as those who would not endure a measure by the reed, and of whose preservation God would take no such care, but give them up to the Gentiles, to be trodden under foot; by which many learned and good men understand God's suffering antichrist to have a power over and against them. I find some understanding by *the altar, and them that worship therein,* the primitive church, that for some hundreds of years after Christ kept close to the Divine rule, whom God preserved, though in the midst of the ten first persecutions : and by the outward *court,* the church after that time, which God suffered to fall under the power of the beast, and antichrist, that is, the papacy; which are well enough called *the Gentiles,* as bringing in Gentilism again into the church, and hardly differing in any thing, saving that the old heathens owned many supreme gods, and these new Gentiles but one. God showeth John here, that he would give up the outward court, or this *holy city,* the generality of Christians, to these Gentiles, that they should rule and domineer over them for *forty and two months,* the meaning of which we shall by and by show. A late pious and learned writer differs a little in his sense, as thinking that God here showeth John something further, viz. that under the sixth trumpet he would give the generality of those called Christians, that will not endure the measure of the reed, so over to antichrist, that they shall turn papists, and help to kill the Lord's witnesses; of which we shall speak, ver. 3. So as this is not a new prophecy, but a continuation of what shall happen after the sounding of the sixth, and before the sounding of the seventh trumpet : if so, I conceive that those words, *shall they tread under foot forty and two months,* must be understood, until the end of the forty-two months; for the forty-two months being the whole time of antichrist, or the beast, must be in a great measure spent before the sounding of the sixth angel. But it seems to be the opinion of this learned man, that a very great part of those who pretend to constitute the Reformed protestant church at this day, but are but as the outward court, not such as worship within the oracle, shall, before the sounding of the seventh trumpet, apostatize, and fall off to popery, until antichrist's one thousand two hundred and sixty days shall expire, and join with papists in the killing of the witnesses. The truth of which we must leave to the providence of God in time to discover; although whoso considereth the face of things this day in Europe, (within which the greatest part of the Christian church is,) will judge there is too great a probability of what this learned man saith; but I dare determine nothing in it.

3 And ‖ I will give *power* unto my two [g]witnesses, [h]and they shall prophesy [i]a thousand two hundred *and* threescore days, clothed in sackcloth.

‖ Or, *I will give unto my two witnesses that they may prophesy.*
g ch. 20. 4.
h ch. 19. 10. i ch. 12. 6.

And I will give power unto my two witnesses: there hath been a great dispute amongst godly and learned men, who these *two witnesses* should be : some have thought them to be Enoch and Elijah, who, though long since glorified, they

REVELATION XI

have thought (with no great probability, as I suppose any indifferent person will judge) shall come again, and be killed on the earth; yet this is the general notion of the popish writers. Others would have them the two sorts of gospel churches, one of which was made up of native Gentiles, the other of Jews proselyted to the Christian faith. Others have interpreted it of the Old Testament and the New: others, of some two eminent divines; and as to them there have been various guesses: others, of the ministers whom God employed upon the Reformation: others, of a Christian magistracy and ministry. For my own part, the name of *witnesses* is so often applied to the first ministers of the gospel, Acts i. 22; ii. 32; iii. 15; iv. 33; v. 32; x. 41; xxii. 15; xxvi. 16; 1 Pet. v. 1; that I cannot but understand it of that faithful part of the ministry, who preach the gospel faithfully during the whole reign of antichrist. Neither do I think that the number *two* at all relates to their number. but to their witness-bearing; *two* being the number which God ordained as sufficient to establish all civil things, Deut. xvii. 6; xix. 15; Matt. xviii. 16; Heb. x. 28; unless there be a regard had to those pairs, which all along the Old Testament bare testimony for God; Moses and Aaron, Caleb and Joshua, Elijah and Elisha; and after the captivity, Zerubbabel and Joshua, and the two olive trees, mentioned Zech. iv. 11, 14, to which plainly this text hath relation, ver. 4. To which some also add Abraham and Lot, Ezra and Nehemiah, Haggai and Zechariah, Paul and Barnabas, Peter and John; and note, that when Christ first sent out his apostles, Matt. x., he sent them out two by two. *And they shall prophesy a thousand two hundred and threescore days, clothed in sackcloth:* we read before, that *the holy city,* that is, the true church, should be trodden under foot by the Gentiles *forty and two months;* we read here, that the witnesses should *prophesy in sackcloth a thousand two hundred and threescore days.* It is apparent, that in the prophetical style a day signifies a year Numb. xiv. 34, *Forty days, each day for a year, shall ye bear your iniquities, even forty years.* So Ezek. iv. 6, *I have appointed thee each day for a year.* So Dan. ix. 24, the *seventy weeks* must signify four hundred and ninety years, (for in seventy weeks there are four hundred and ninety days,) or else the promise as to the coming of the Messiah failed. So the prophetical year contains three hundred and sixty years, and the prophetical month thirty years (for they did count thirty days to each month); so forty-two months are just one thousand two hundred and sixty days, that is, one thousand two hundred and sixty years. We shall find, chap. xii. 6, that the woman (that is, the church) was in the wilderness just this time, one thousand two hundred and sixty days; and in chap. xiii. 5, this was also the time of the beast that rose up out of the sea, having seven heads and ten horns, and upon his horns ten crowns: by which it appeareth, that these four things ran all parallel at the same time; the beast arising, and exercising his power; the new Gentiles trampling upon the church, the holy city; the woman's abiding in the wilderness; and the witnesses prophesying in sackcloth. If we could find out where any one of these began, we should find out the time of all the rest. Those who fix the rise of the beast in or about the year 400, must add to this 1260. Then in 1660 antichrist's reign should have determined, and also the time of the church's persecution, and the time when faithful ministers should prophesy in sackcloth: but if the rise of the beast were in the year 500, the expiration must be in 1760; if it be fixed in 600, all these things will determine in 1860; for the same number of days being assigned to all the four, it is manifest that all four began together, and shall end together, and that at the end of a thousand two hundred and sixty years after the beginning of them. For my own part, I look upon it as very hard to determine: but the difficulty lies in finding out the time when the beast first arose; for that being once found out, it is easy to conclude from Scripture, when both the popedom shall have an end, and the calamitous time for the church, especially the ministry of it, shall cease. That which God showeth John in this verse, is only, that his faithful ministers that should truly reveal his will, (which is here called prophesying,) should have a mournful time for a thousand two hundred and threescore years.

k Ps. 52. 8. Jer. 11. 16. Zech. 4. 3, 11, 14.

4 These are the [k]two olive trees, and the two candlesticks standing before the God of the earth.

Here is a manifest allusion to Zechariah's vision, Zech. iv. 2, 3, 11—14, though with some little difference. He saw *a candlestick all of gold, with a bowl upon the top of it, and his seven lamps thereon, and seven pipes to the seven lamps, which were upon the top thereof: and two olive trees by it, one upon the right side of the bowl, and the other upon the left side thereof.* The angel tells him, that *these two olive branches which through the two golden pipes* did *empty the golden oil out of themselves,* were *the two anointed ones,* or the two sons of oil, *that stood by the Lord of the whole earth.* By which some understand Zerubbabel and Joshua; some, those godly magistrates and priests, which after the captivity the Jewish church should have, and prefigured a gospel ministry, who being filled with knowledge and grace, should feed the Lord's church (as pastors after his own heart) with wisdom and understanding, from the gifts and graces of God's Holy Spirit, which they should receive; which further confirmeth me, that by the *two witnesses,* ver. 3, we are to understand a godly magistracy and ministry, or rather the latter only, to whom prophesying most strictly agreeth, and who have a more special relation to the candlesticks here mentioned, by which churches are meant, chap. i. 20. *And the two candlesticks standing before the God of the earth:* in Zechariah's vision was but one candlestick, how comes here a mention to be made of two? Mr. Mede confesseth himself at a loss here, unless here another candlestick be added to signify the Gentiles' conversion to Christ. Others think that it denoteth the small number of gospel churches that should be left; they were reckoned seven, chap. i. 20; here they are reduced to two. Possibly it may denote the different state of God's church. In the Old Testament God had but one church, viz. that of the Jews; but now he hath many churches, and they are all fed from faithful ministers, as olive branches pouring out their oil of grace and knowledge upon them.

5 And if any man will hurt them, [l]fire proceedeth out of their mouth, and devoureth their enemies: [m]and if any man will hurt them, he must in this manner be killed.

l 2 Kings 1. 10, 12. Jer. 1. 10. & 5. 14. Ezek. 43. 3. Hos. 6. 5. m Num. 16. 29.

And if any man will hurt them; that is, my faithful ministers, the two olive branches before mentioned, which fill the candlesticks with oil. *Fire proceedeth out of their mouth, and devoureth their enemies:* here is a plain allusion to the stories of Moses and Elijah, calling for fire from heaven; but God showeth, that the victory of his ministers under the gospel shall not be by a miraculous fire called for down from heaven, (as Elijah hurt the captains and their bands sent to apprehend him,) but by *fire out of their mouths;* according to that, Jer. v. 14, *Behold, I will make my words in thy mouth fire, and this people wood, and it shall devour them:* see also Jer. i. 9, 10. This also is according to Zechariah's vision before mentioned, and the revelation of the will of God in it, ver. 6, *Not by might, nor by power, but by my Spirit, saith the Lord of hosts.* The meaning is, that they shall be too hard for them, either by their faithful, lively, and powerful preaching, or by their fervent prayers.

6 These [n]have power to shut heaven, that it rain not in the days of their prophecy: and [o]have power over waters to turn them to blood, and to smite the earth with all plagues, as often as they will.

n 1 Kings 17. 1. James 5. 16, 17. o Ex. 7. 19.

It is plain that here is an allusion to Elijah, who *prayed earnestly that it might not rain; and it rained not on the earth by the space of three years and six months,* James v. 17; see the story, 1 Kings xvii. 1: and to Moses, who turned the waters into blood in Egypt; and after was an instrument to smite the land of Egypt with plagues. But what power analogous to this the ministers of the gospel have had, or have, is not easy to determine. It is certain, the apostles had a miraculous power, but they rarely used it, but in doing good to men; Ananias and Sapphira indeed were struck dead upon their word, Acts v.; and

Elymas the sorcerer was struck blind by them; but this power is long since ceased. Mr. Mede understands this power of the keys of doctrine and church censures the ministers of the gospel should be intrusted with; so as they should not preach the gospel unto such as contemned their ministry; by the withholding of which means of grace, also, they would be deprived of the dew of heavenly grace. And, indeed, this seemeth more proper than to understand it of the keys of discipline; for what power of this nature have ministers over those who are without? I take a general explication to be the best. If any hurt them, God shall revenge their cause, not only by spiritual, but by temporal judgments, bringing all manner of evils upon their adversaries. They are said to have power to do it, because God will do it in the revenge of the injuries done unto them.

7 And when they p shall have finished their testimony, q the beast that ascendeth r out of the bottomless pit s shall make war against them, and shall overcome them, and kill them.

p Luke 13. 32.
q ch. 13. 1, 11. & 17. 8.
r ch. 9. 2.
s Dan. 7. 21. Zech. 14. 2.

And when they shall have finished their testimony; ὅταν τελέσωσοι· Mr. Mede notes, that this is ill translated by the preterperfect tense; the true English of it is, when they shall be about to finish their testimony: when they have prophesied in sackcloth the most of their twelve hundred and sixty years, they shall meet with *ultimum conatum antichristi*, the last struggle of the beast for life. *The beast that ascendeth out of the bottomless pit*, that is, the beast mentioned chap. xiii. 1, 4, (by which the papacy is meant, whom they have plagued all the time of their prophecy, though continual sufferers from it,) *shall make war against them;* shall get life again, and make one push more, possibly the sharpest yet made; *and shall overcome them, and kill them;* and be too hard for them, and kill them. It is a great question, whether this be to be understood of taking away their natural lives, or of a civil death relating to them as witnesses. making them as if they were naturally dead. The latter of these seemeth to me much the more probable, for these reasons: 1. Supposing the godly magistracy, or ministry, or the latter alone, to be the *two witnesses*, it doth not seem probable that ever the papacy shall so far prevail, as to kill all such over the face of the whole church. 2. Neither is the Holy Ghost here speaking of them as men, but as *witnesses*. 3. Nor would either friends or enemies suffer dead bodies to be unburied three days and a half, in the street of a great city, as ver. 8, 9. 4. Neither is their resurrection, mentioned ver. 11, to be understood of a corporal resurrection. I take therefore the killing here mentioned, to be understood of a destroying them as witnesses, turning magistrates out of their places, and ministers out of their places; though it be not probable that such a malice and hatred as should cause this, should terminate without the blood of some of them; but that surely is not the thing principally here intended.

8 And their dead bodies *shall lie* in the street of t the great city, which spiritually is called Sodom and Egypt, u where also our Lord was crucified.

t ch. 14. 8. & 17. 1, 5. & 18. 10.
u Heb. 13 12. ch. 18. 24.

Their bodies dead, in the sense before mentioned, shall continue so for three days and a half, of which we shall speak, ver. 11. But what is here meant, 1. By *the great city?* 2. By the *street of the great city?* Some, by *the great city,* would have Jerusalem understood; but that was now far from a great city, nor do the addition of those words in the latter end of the verse prove it; for Christ was not crucified in that city, but without the gates. Most judicious interpreters, by *the great city* here, understand Rome, which is seven or eight times (under the name of Babylon) so called in this book, chap. xiv. 8; xvi. 19; xviii. 10, 16, 18, 19, 21; nor is any other city but that so called. This great city is here said, in a spiritual sense, to be *Sodom and Egypt; Sodom,* for whoredom and filthiness; *Egypt,* for oppression of the Lord's Israel. As to the second question, what is here meant by *the street of the great city?* Mr. Mede hath irrefragably proved, that it cannot be meant of any parish, or such place in this city, as we call a street: 1. Because our Lord was crucified neither in any street, or parish, or any other place within the walls of Jerusalem. 2. Both Jerusalem and Rome had many more than one street. 3. Because the bodies being dead, doubtless lay in the place where they were slain; but men do not use to fight in the streets of cities. 4. Nor was that a place for all people, kindred, tongues, and nations, to see them in. He therefore rightly judgeth, that the Greek word which we translate *street*, signifies the territories and jurisdiction of this city. See what he says to justify this in his Clavis Apocal. 40. p. 138. And this makes the last clause plain; for though our Lord was not crucified within any city, or in the street of any city, yet he was crucified in a place belonging to the jurisdiction of the Roman emperor; and it is very likely that it is in Europe that the witnesses shall be slain, which, in this sense, was all of it a street belonging to the city of Rome.

9 x And they of the people and kindreds and tongues and nations shall see their dead bodies three days and an half, y and shall not suffer their dead bodies to be put in graves.

x ch. 17. 15.
y Ps. 79. 2, 3.

And they of the people and kindreds and tongues and nations; that is, a multitude of people of all sorts shall take notice of this suppression of these two witnesses in their bearing witness for God, and all the cruel dealings with them. *Shall see their dead bodies three days and an half:* there are great disputes what time these *three days and an half* denote: it cannot be understood of three natural, or artificial days; for (as it is noted by the most judicious interpreters) this is much too short a time for all people to *see their dead bodies*, to *rejoice over them*, and to *make merry*, and to *send gifts one to another* in testification of the satisfaction of their lusts, upon the victory got over them. I find some understand these *three days and an half* of the one thousand two hundred and sixty years, wherein they prophesied in sackcloth, ver. 3, which they thus make out; they first conclude, that these are prophetical days, and so signify three years and a half; then they resolve each of those years into days, and count three times three hundred and sixty days (for in those countries they say the year was counted to contain but three hundred and sixty days); to which they add one hundred and eighty, the half of three hundred and sixty, for the half day, which make up one thousand two hundred and sixty days, or forty-two months; which is the just time both of the beast's reign, and of the woman's abode in the wilderness, and of the witnesses' prophesying in sackcloth, and of the Gentiles' treading down the outward court. 1. But it seems very hard, thus first to make the three days three years in a prophetical sense, and then again to resolve those years into days, and make those days so many more years; this looks as much like oppression to the text, as the counting interest upon interest to a debtor. 2. It plainly confounds the time of the prophesying of the witnesses in sackcloth, with the time of their lying dead. Now although the time of their lying dead must be within the one thousand two hundred and sixty days, in the latter end thereof, (for it must be within the beast's forty-two months, mentioned chap. xiii. 5,) yet it seems hard to make it as long as the beast's reign. It certainly signifies a time toward the end of the beast's reign, when there shall be a more eminent and universal suppression of the faithful witnesses of Christ than ever was before: it seemeth therefore rather to be understood more generally for a short time, as much such a phrase or way of speaking is used, Hos. vi. 2, or else for a determinate time of such three years and a half as we ordinarily count. I must confess the half day being added, makes me more incline to the latter; for though it be usual with us to express a short time by, two or three days, and this seems by that text of Hosea to have been an ancient way of speaking, yet we do not use to put in half days when we so speak. I do therefore agree with those who think the time here specified is to be understood of three ordinary years and a half; and the rather, because this is the very time that Christ was under the power of the Pharisees. As three days (that is, part of them) was the time of his being under the power of death, so three years and a half was the just time of all the indignity that he suffered from his manifestation to the world, to his death: and (as we read in 1 Macc.) it was the just time of Antiochus's oppressing of the Jews, whom divines judge that Daniel, in his 11th chapter, makes a type of antichrist. *And shall not suffer their dead bodies to be put in graves:* divines are divided whether these words be to be understood of enemies or friends. If it be to be understood of friends, the death being a civil death principally that was spoken of, it signifieth the providence of God so working for his witnesses, by the adherence of a party to them, that their adversaries the popish party should not wholly extinguish them; which hath been seen all along the story of the church: though their adversaries have been warring against them, overcome and killed them, yet they have not been able to bury them; nor shall they be able to do it at this last pinch, when they shall have a greater victory over them than ever before, and kill them to a further degree. But methinks the phrase rather signifies this an act of enemies, who, to show their further malice to them, and contempt and scorn of them, are said to be so inhuman, as not to suffer their dead bodies to be buried.

z ch. 12. 12. & 13. 8.

10 ^z And they that dwell upon the earth shall rejoice over them, and make merry,

a Esth. 9.19, 22.
b ch. 16. 10.

^a and shall send gifts one to another; ^b because these two prophets tormented them that dwelt on the earth.

It is plain by the repeating of the same words in the close of the verse, that by those that *dwell upon the earth* are meant earthly, carnal men, whether papists or atheists; men that are mad upon their lusts; for these are those in whose consciences faithful and powerful preaching breeds a torment and uneasiness, so as they always count godly ministers their enemies, (as Ahab told Elijah,) and are not able to bear their words (as the Israelites could not bear the words of Amos). *Shall rejoice over them, and make merry, and shall send gifts one to another;* these therefore shall keep holiday, when they see these their enemies conquered, and show all signs and expressions of joy. These preachers were they that hindered them from a quiet sleep in their beds of lust. *Because these two prophets tormented them that dwelt on the earth;* and though they fought against them only with a fire going out of their mouths, as prophets declaring the will of God to be contrary to their lewd practices, and denouncing God's wrath against those that did such things; yet their preaching made their heads ache, partly by alarming their consciences, so as they often flew in their faces; and by it they were exposed to the reproach of people, as living directly contrary to the Divine rule, and in defiance of his law: thus they torment wicked men, who therefore always did, and always will, triumph in their suppression, or in any evil that shall betide them. And as they see their suppression greater than ever before, (as it will be undoubtedly during these three years and a half,) so the triumph of lewd and wicked men will be proportionably more, though it will be but like a widow's joy, for a short time, for it will appear that their dead bodies were not put into the grave.

c ver. 9.
d Ezek. 37. 5, 9, 10, 14.

11 ^c And after three days and an half ^d the Spirit of life from God entered into them, and they stood upon their feet; and great fear fell upon them which saw them.

And after three days and an half; after that short time which God had determined for antichrist, (just before his time should be expired,) or after the precise time of forty-two months, or three years and a half, was expired, when the Gentiles thought they had fully prevailed, and should be no more troubled with Christ's witnesses. *The Spirit of life from God entered into them, and they stood upon their feet;* God, who alone can quicken the dead, reviveth them, and restoreth them again to their employment as his prophets; for it is plain this cannot be understood of a corporal resurrection: for, 1. Their death was not of that nature; nor, 2. Doth the Scripture give us any hints of any such resurrection before the coming of Christ to the last judgment. *And great fear fell upon them which saw them;* this strikes a great fear into all their enemies, amazed to think what God was about to do, and rightly presaging this would be their ruin.

It is a great question now, whether the time here spoken of for slaying the witnesses, and their rising again, be past, or yet to come. I must confess, the papacy had got such a victory over the faithful witnesses of Christ for some ages before the Reformation began in Germany, about the year 1517, and there was so sudden a resurrection of them in the first Reformers, brought to pass and carried on by such a stupendous series of providences, that I cannot wonder that some did think the time past: but we who have outlived that time more than one hundred and fifty years, seeing the Turks (whom all judicious interpreters make the four angels, bound by the river Euphrates, loosed) still so rampant, and the papacy still so predominant, and daily treading down the outward court, have no reason to judge the slaying of the witnesses yet over, at least that they are yet risen, and standing upon their feet; or that the seventh angel hath yet sounded; but that we are as yet under the period of time signified by the sounding of the sixth trumpet; and to expect a further degree of this evening before it will be light over the universal church (for we must not think any particular church intended here): and this appears most probable also from what followeth before the sounding of the seventh angel, ver. 15.

12 And they heard a great voice from heaven saying unto them, Come up hither. ^e And they ascended up to heaven ^f in a cloud; ^g and their enemies beheld them.

e Is. 14. 13.
ch. 12. 5.
f Is. 60. 8.
Acts 1. 9.
g 2 Kings 2. 1, 5, 7.

And they, that is, the two witnesses, so often before spoken of, *heard a great voice from heaven saying unto them, Come up hither;* heard God by a singular providence calling them again to their former work and station in his church; or (as some) to a higher and more famous place in his church than they formerly enjoyed; for by *heaven* the most and best interpreters understand the church, as it often signifies in this book. *And they ascended up to heaven in a cloud; and their enemies beheld them;* and this was done in the face of their enemies. In this sense of this verse I find the generality of judicious interpreters agreed.

13 And the same hour ^h was there a great earthquake, ⁱ and the tenth part of the city fell, and in the earthquake were slain † of men seven thousand: and the remnant were affrighted, ^k and gave glory to the God of heaven.

h ch. 6. 12.
i ch. 16. 19.
† Gr. names of men. ch. 3. 4.
k Josh. 7. 19. ch. 14. 7. & 15. 4.

And the same hour; that is, about the same time, when the Spirit of life from God entered into the witnesses, and they were again restored. *Was there a great earthquake;* by *earthquake* doubtless is here meant a great confusion in the world, and shaking of nations by differences one with another, and wars: see the notes on chap. vi. 12. *And the tenth part of the city fell;* by *the city* is doubtless meant the *great city* before named, *spiritually called Sodom and Egypt;* elsewhere, *Babylon;* by which Rome is to be understood. What is meant by the tenth part of it falling, is not so well agreed; some by it understanding many kingdoms falling off from its jurisdiction; others, a great part of its tribute or dominion. *And in the earthquake were slain of men seven thousand:* these words seem to intimate that the restoration of the witnesses shall not be without opposition, and that the opposition shall not be great; seven thousand is a small number to fall in such a quarrel: but the papal party shall appear to have cheated the world so with their impostures, and so to have imposed upon them, that the world shall grow sick of them, and when the time comes for God to put a final period to them, the number shall be but few that adventure for them. *And the remnant were affrighted;* others shall be *affrighted,* either from their own consciences, or from the stupendous dispensations of Divine Providence in the fall of the great city. *And gave glory to the God of heaven;* and give glory to God, by confessing their errors, and turning to an ingenuous and sincere acknowledgment of the truth. Instead of worshipping saints, and angels, and images, worshipping the true and living God of heaven and earth only.

14 ^l The second woe is past; *and,* behold, the third woe cometh quickly.

l ch. 8. 13. & 9. 12. & 15. 1.

The second woe is past; that is, here endeth the misery that is like to come upon the world in that period of time which shall follow the sounding of the sixth trumpet. *And, behold, the third woe cometh quickly:* the third woe signifies those calamities which should come in that period of time prophesied of by the sounding of the seventh trumpet; this makes a late learned author think that all that which went before, viz. the Gentiles treading down the outward court, the slaying of the witnesses, and their resuscitation, must be under the sixth trumpet; which period endeth not until the church's enemies be ready to be destroyed; whose destruction is afterwards opened to us in the angels pouring out their vials.

15 And ᵐthe seventh angel sounded; ⁿand there were great voices in heaven, saying, °The kingdoms of this world are become *the kingdoms* of our Lord, and of his Christ; ᵖand he shall reign for ever and ever.

m ch. 10. 7.
n Is. 27. 13. ch. 16. 17. & 19. 6.
o ch. 12. 10.
p Dan. 2. 44. & 7. 14, 18, 27.

And the seventh angel sounded; the last of those angels mentioned chap. viii. 2. *And there were great voices in heaven, saying;* St. John in his vision heard great acclamations and shoutings for the victory which Christ and his gospel had got over the beast. *The kingdoms of this world are become the kingdoms of our Lord, and of his Christ; and he shall reign for ever and ever;* so that a great part of the world, casting off the papacy, that new Gentilism, together with all their abominable idolatries and superstitions, embraced the truth of the gospel. Here ariseth a great question, whether the seven vials, of which we shall find the 16th chapter treating, do belong all to the seventh trumpet, or some of them belong to the sixth trumpet, of which mention hath been before made. Great divines are on both sides as to this question. Mr. Pool, in his Latin Synopsis, hath collected together their reasons, of which I shall give a short account, leaving my reader for a fuller satisfaction to the Latin Synopsis.

Those who think that the seven vials do all relate to the seventh trumpet, and contemporize with it, in defence of their opinion say,

1 That the seven seals, and the seven trumpets, and the seven vials, are all mentioned in the same form of speech; and therefore the seven vials are not to be divided, some to one trumpet, some to another.

2. Because the seventh trumpet and the seven vials are one and the same thing, nothing being revealed under the seven vials which doth not belong to the seventh trumpet; they agree in their titles of woes, in the nature of the revelations, in their objects, both the one and the other declaring the ruin of antichrist; both of them are mentioned as the last plagues to come upon the world before the last day.

3. All the vials are of the same nature, declaring but the judgments by which God, setting up the kingdom of Christ, would ruin antichrist; they only differ in the degrees of the plagues, each one rising higher than the other.

4. The seventh trumpet cannot declare the ruin of antichrist, unless the seven vials be poured out under it, for they show the means by which he must be destroyed.

5. The seventh trumpet soundeth immediately upon the slaying of the witnesses, and contemporizeth with the whole course of their renewed liberty, and therefore the period signified by it must be before the fall of antichrist, declared by the sixth vial.

6. The seventh trumpet soundeth immediately after the expiration of the twelve hundred and sixty days; before the end of which none of the vials were poured out.

Those who think that divers of the vials were poured out, or shall be poured out, before the sounding of this seventh trumpet, say, that the beast's kingdom beginning to fall under the sixth trumpet, several of the vials, declaring the degrees of his falling, must belong to that. It appeareth by all we have in this chapter from ver. 7 to 15, that antichrist's kingdom was in a great measure weakened under the sixth trumpet, particularly from ver. 11—13. To which those who think that all the vials related to the seventh trumpet say, that they grant that there were some preparations to the final ruin of antichrist, during the period of the sixth trumpet, but the seven vials signify the further progress and perfection of his ruin, which falls under the period signified by the seventh trumpet. This being premised, I proceed with the text.

It is doubted here whether those words, *are become the kingdoms of our Lord, and of his Christ,* be to be understood as being actually so, or now beginning to be so. Those who make the sense that they now actually were so, must understand the time to be the day of judgment, or some time next to it, and consequently must think that five at least of the seven vials, mentioned chap. xvi., belonged to the sixth trumpet. Those who make the sense, are beginning to become the kingdoms of the Lord, or shall shortly be so, may make all the seven vials to belong to the seventh trumpet. By becoming the kingdoms of the Lord Christ, he means in outward profession; so as antichrist shall reign no more, but they shall be ruled by the officers of the Lord Christ, until they be taken up to reign with him in glory.

16 And ᑫthe four and twenty elders, which sat before God on their seats, fell upon their faces, and worshipped God,

q ch. 4. 4. & 5. 8. & 19. 4.

I take this to signify no more than the triumph of the saints and angels in heaven upon this victory of the Lord over antichrist, and the promoting of Christ's kingdom; and certainly if there be joy in heaven upon the conversion of *one sinner,* as we are told, Luke xv. 7, we must imagine a much greater joy upon the conversion of nations and kingdoms unto Christ.

17 Saying, We give thee thanks, O Lord God Almighty, ʳwhich art, and wast, and art to come; because thou hast taken to thee thy great power, ˢand hast reigned.

r ch. 1. 4, 8. & 4. 8. & 16. 5.
s ch. 19. 6.

Which art, and wast, and art to come; it is a phrase denoting God's eternity and immutability; we met with it before, chap. iv. 8. *Because thou hast taken to thee thy great power, and hast reigned;* those celestial beings bless God for exerting his power, and recovering the kingdom of Christ out of the hands of antichrist, and setting his King upon his holy hill of Zion.

18 ᵗAnd the nations were angry, and thy wrath is come, ᵘand the time of the dead, that they should be judged, and that thou shouldest give reward unto thy servants the prophets, and to the saints, and them that fear thy name, ˣsmall and great; ʸand shouldest destroy them which ‖ destroy the earth.

t ver. 2, 9.
u Dan. 7. 9, 10. ch. 6. 10.
x ch. 19. 5.
y ch. 13. 10. & 18. 6.
‖ Or, *corrupt.*

And the nations were angry; those who have not been of thy true Israel, but old or modern Gentiles, they have been angry long enough. *And thy wrath is come;* now it is time for thee to show thyself angry, and thou hast begun to do it. *And the time of the dead, that they should be judged;* the time is come for thee to judge the cause of thy faithful witnesses, and all those who have died in testimony to thy truth. *And that thou shouldest give reward unto thy servants the prophets;* and for thee to reward such as have faithfully revealed thy will. *And to the saints;* and not only them, but all thy holy ones. *And them that fear thy name, small and great;* without respect to their quality in the world, be they little or great. *And shouldest destroy them which destroy the earth;* the time also is come, when thou hast destroyed, or wilt destroy, that antichristian brood, which so long hath plagued the earth, and destroyed thy people in it.

19 And ᶻthe temple of God was opened in heaven, and there was seen in his temple the ark of his testament: and ᵃthere were lightnings, and voices, and thunderings, and an earthquake, ᵇand great hail.

z ch. 15. 5, 8.
a ch. 8. 5. & 16. 18.
b ch. 16. 21.

And the temple of God: some here, by *the temple of God,* understand the representation of the temple in Jerusalem; others understand the church triumphant; others, the church of Christ militant here upon earth. *Was opened in heaven:* accordingly, by *heaven* they understand either the natural heavens, or the Christian church: it seemeth to be a plain allusion to the Jewish church, whose temple was ordinarily shut up in the time of wicked and idolatrous princes, who regarded not the true worship of God; so as all the time of Saul's reign the ark abode in the private house of Obed-edom; and when Josiah came to reign, he found the temple neglected all the days of his father Amon and grandfather Manasseh, and the book of the law in the rubbish. But when good princes came to the throne, such as Hezekiah and Josiah, they opened the temple, restoring the true worship of God. So under the New Testament, during the whole reign of antichrist, where he prevails, idolatry and superstition obtain, and the true worship of God is suppressed; but his time being now expiring, God showeth John that there shall be a restoring of the true worship of God, and a liberty both to ministers and people to worship God according to his will. For though antichrist was not yet wholly destroyed, nor his party extinguished, yet he had lost his power and dominion, and God was now beginning to reckon with him for the blood of his saints; which was all to be done before all the kingdoms of the world should become the kingdoms of the Lord Christ. *And there was seen in his temple the ark of his testament:* in the temple of old, the ark of the covenant was the great symbol of God's presence; hence God is said to have dwelt betwixt the cherubims. In the ark were the two tables of the law; so as this phrase may either note the pure, free, and ordinary expounding of the law of God, which should be upon the downfal of antichrist; or the presence of God with his church in that more pure and reformed state. But such a work of providence being not like to be effected without the ruin of antichrist, God showeth it shall be ushered in with *lightnings, and voices, and thunderings, and an earthquake, and great hail;* by *terrible things in righteousness,* as the psalmist speaketh. The consequents of which were the seven vials, of which we shall read, chap. xvi., pouring out plagues upon the antichristian party, until they should be wholly rooted out and Christ alone should be exalted in his church, and rule as King upon his holy hill of Zion.

From this mysterious portion of holy writ thus opened, it appeareth that God, in these foregoing chapters, hath (though more summarily) instructed his prophet in what should come to pass to the final ruin of the Roman empire, (considered as pagan, that is, till Constantine's time,) and also of the reign of antichrist. From whence it must needs follow, that whatsoever followeth this chapter, and cannot be applied to the time of Christ's kingdom, must contemporize with something which went before, and belong to some period comprehended under the vision of the seals, or of the trumpets. The next three chapters are judged to relate wholly to things past, God therein representing to his prophet the state of his church (as some think) from the nativity of Christ; however, from his time, during the whole time that Rome continued pagan, or should continue antichristian; the following chapters showing the gradual destruction of antichrist by the seven last plagues.

CHAP. XII

A woman clothed with the sun travaileth, 1, 2. *A great red dragon standeth ready to devour her child,* 3, 4. *She is delivered, and fleeth into the wilderness,* 5, 6. *Michael and his angels fight with the dragon, who is cast out of heaven with his angels,* 7—9. *The victory proclaimed in heaven,* 10—12. *The dragon, cast down to the earth, persecuteth the woman,* 13—17.

‖ Or, *sign.* AND there appeared a great ‖ wonder in heaven; a woman clothed with the sun, and the moon under her feet, and upon her head a crown of twelve stars:

And there appeared a great wonder in heaven: I see no reason to doubt, but that John was all this while in heaven, whither he was taken up, chap. iv. 2, where he saw in a vision *a great wonder,* or a most remarkable thing. *A woman clothed with the sun;* I find all valuable interpreters agreeing, that this woman represented the church, well enough compared to a woman; 1. As she is the spouse of Christ (though here expressed as his mother.) 2. As the woman is the weaker sex, and the church hath always been the weakest part of the world. (I look upon the interpretation of it by popish authors, with reference to the virgin Mary, as very idle; for when did she flee into the wilderness? when was she with child, and pained to be delivered?) Interpreters also are as well agreed, that by *the sun,* with which she is said to be *clothed,* is meant Christ, called *the Sun of righteousness,* Mal. iv. 2, and he who giveth light, Eph. v. 14; and believers (of whom the church consists) are said to have *put on Christ,* Rom. xiii. 14; Gal. iii. 27. *And the moon under her feet:* by *the moon,* most understand the world, by reason of its mutability and uncertainty, which the church of Christ despiseth, and hath under her feet, minding heaven and heavenly things. But Mr. Mede rather understands it of the Jewish worship, which, as to its times, was much directed by the moon; which *hand-writing which was against us* (the apostle tells us, Col. ii. 14) Christ took away, *nailing it to his cross;* so as the gospel church hath it under her feet. The apostle calls them *carnal ordinances,* Heb. ix. 10, and *the rudiments of the world,* Col. ii. 20, yea, *beggarly elements,* Gal. iv. 9. *And upon her head a crown of twelve stars;* the ministry of the gospel, preaching and building upon the true foundation, the doctrine of the prophets, and twelve apostles, which is the honour of any church.

2 And she being with child cried, ^atravailing in birth, and pained to be delivered. a Is. 66. 7. Gal. 4. 19.

Being with child; not with Christ considered personally, who was long before brought forth by the virgin Mary, but with the truth, and gospel of Christ, or with Christ mystical. *Cried;* desiring to bring many children to the kingdom of Christ; or to bring forth Christ in the souls of others: of this burden and labour she desired *to be delivered.* The phrase is judged to signify both the primitive church's desire to propagate the gospel, and also her many sufferings for that endeavour.

3 And there appeared another ‖ wonder in heaven; and behold ^ba great red dragon, ^chaving seven heads and ten horns, ^dand seven crowns upon his heads. ‖ Or, *sign.* b ch. 17. 3. c ch. 17. 9, 10. d ch. 13. 1.

And there appeared another wonder in heaven; there appeared to John, being yet in his vision, another amazing sight, which was a sign or type of something differing from what it appeared like. *And behold a great red dragon:* see ver. 7, 9, 17. Most judicious interpreters, by the *great red dragon,* understand the Roman emperors that first persecuted the Christian church, of which Claudius was the first; yet some understand it of the devil, the old serpent; but the most and best interpreters understand it of the pagan emperors, by whom the devil did this work, called a *great dragon,* because of the vastness of that empire; and a *red dragon,* for their cruelty against the Christians. *Having seven heads;* the Holy Ghost, chap. xvii. 9, hath expounded these *seven heads,* by *seven mountains.* The *ten horns* are thought to signify the ten provinces belonging to that empire, the governors of which ruled like ten kings. It is expounded by *ten kings,* chap. xvii. 12. Strabo tells us, that Augustus Cæsar divided the whole empire into twenty provinces; ten of which, being more quiet, he gave to the people to govern, the other ten he reserved to his own government. The *seven crowns* are expounded by *seven kings,* chap. xvii. 10, of which we shall speak more when we come so far.

4 And ^ehis tail drew the third part ^fof the stars of heaven, ^gand did cast them to the earth: and the dragon stood ^hbefore the woman which was ready to be delivered, ⁱfor to devour her child as soon as it was born. e ch. 9. 10, 19. f ch. 17. 18. g Dan. 8. 10. h ver. 2. i Ex. 1. 16.

The *tail* of the *red dragon* signifies his followers, his civil and military officers, whosoever were by him employed to execute his commands. By *the stars,* here, are either meant the ministers of the Christian church, or the professors of it. *And did cast them to the earth;* turning them out of their places and stations, making them as useless as he could. *And the dragon stood before the woman which was ready to be delivered, for to devour her child as soon as it was born;* that is, before the church that was ready to propagate itself, watching upon her increase to devour them. I take this to be a much more probable sense than theirs who understand it of Constantine; for I know not, with reference to him, who should be understood by the *red dragon*. Mr. Mede hath ingeniously observed, that Pharaoh was a type of this red dragon. He is resembled by a dragon, Psal. lxxiv. 13, 14; Isa. li. 9; Ezek. xxix. 3, and watched upon God's ancient church to destroy it, as the pagan emperors did upon the Christian church.

5 And she brought forth a man child, [k] who was to rule all nations with a rod of iron: and her child was caught up unto God, and *to* his throne.

k Ps. 2. 9. ch. 2. 27. & 19. 15.

By this *man-child* some understand Constantine the Great; others understand Christ mystical, or many children brought forth unto God. As the Jews multiplied, do Pharaoh what he could to destroy them, so the church increased, notwithstanding all the malice and rage of her enemies. Interpreters accordingly are divided concerning the person or persons here spoken of, that should *rule all nations with a rod of iron*. It was prophesied of Christ, Psal. ii. 9, that he should *break* the nations *with a rod of iron*. It is applied to the servants of Christ, who overcome, and keep Christ's words to the end, chap. ii. 27. So as it is here applicable to believers, whom the church should bring forth, who shall *judge the world*, as the apostle tells us; and I had rather thus interpret it, than concerning Constantine the Great. *And her child was caught up unto God, and to his throne:* these words are something hard to be interpreted. To interpret it of Christ's being taken up into heaven, is to turn a mysterious prophecy into a plain relation, or history of things past. To interpret it concerning Constantine the Great, seemeth very hard; for how was he, more than any other Christians, *caught up unto God, and to his throne?* If we say, when he died; so are they: if we say the imperial throne is here understood by God's throne, it seemeth to me very hard; for although of magistrates God saith, *I have said, Ye are gods*, yet their thrones are never called God's throne. I had rather give this phrase a more general interpretation, viz. God took this offspring of the woman into his royal protection, so as the dragon could not devour it, it was out of his reach.

6 And [l]the woman fled into the wilderness, where she hath a place prepared of God, that they should feed her there [m]a thousand two hundred *and* threescore days.

l ver. 4.
m ch. 11. 3.

And the woman fled into the wilderness: as the Israelites, when they fled from Pharaoh, went into the wilderness; and Joseph, watched upon by Herod, fled into Egypt; so the church did hide herself during the antichristian persecutions, every one shifting for themselves as well as they could. *Where she hath a place prepared of God;* God provided for them in some more obscure places.

7 And there was war in heaven: [n]Michael and his angels fought [o]against the dragon; and the dragon fought and his angels,

n Dan. 10. 13, 21. & 12. 1.
o ver. 3.
ch. 20. 2.

And there was war in heaven: by *heaven*, in this place, doubtless is meant the church of God; and supposing that the pagan emperors are to be understood by the *dragon*, (which is pretty generally agreed,) there can be no great doubt, but by this *war in heaven*, is to be understood those persecutions which the primitive church endured betwixt the years 64 and 310. *Michael and his angels fought against the dragon, and the dragon fought and his angels:* the two parties were the pagan emperors, and their officers, and party, and *Michael and his angels*. But who is here meant by *Michael and his angels?* Some, by this *Michael*, understand a principal angel called *the archangel*, Jude 9, *one of the chief princes*, Dan. x. 13. Others, by *Michael* here understand Christ himself, who, they think, is understood by *Michael*, Dan. xii. 1. The matter is not much; it is most certain that the battle is not ours, but Christ's. It is as certain that Christ exerciseth his power by his angels, and that they have a ministration about his church. The meaning is no more than this, that Christ and his party opposed the pagan persecutors and their party.

8 And prevailed not; neither was their place found any more in heaven.

The pagans were at length routed in this battle; the Christians overcame them by the preaching of the gospel, and by their faith and patience; and paganism found no place within the same territories where the church was. This was fulfilled in the time of Constantine the Great, who altered the face of the Roman empire; and more eminently in the time of Theodosius, about the year 380.

9 And [p]the great dragon was cast out, [q]that old serpent, called the Devil, and Satan, [r]which deceiveth the whole world: [s]he was cast out into the earth, and his angels were cast out with him.

p Luke 10. 18. John 12. 31
q Gen. 3. 1, 4. ch. 20. 2.
r ch. 20. 3.
s ch. 9. 1.

And the great dragon was cast out; the dragon mentioned ver. 3, which typified the pagan emperors. In casting them out, *the devil* who influenced them, was cast out, who is here called the *old serpent*, with reference to the form in which he seduced Eve, as well as his malignity to man. *The devil*, that is, the accuser of the brethren, (of which we have an instance in Job i.,) *and Satan*, which name he hath from his opposition to Christ and all Christians. *Which deceiveth the whole world;* by seducing them to idolatry and superstition. *He was cast out into the earth;* cast down from his former state. *And his angels were cast out with him;* the instruments he used in persecuting the church, were put out of power. Mr. Mede understands it of the demons which the heathens worshipped as inferior gods. John, being in his trance still, thought he saw a great red dragon, (which he judged to be the devil,) and Christ, or the good angels, fighting with and overcoming him; and that he saw the devil, and those evil angels assisting him, thrown down to the earth. This prophetically and typically signified, that though the Roman emperors, being pagans, should persecute the church upwards of three hundred years, yet they should be overthrown, and paganism, with all its idolatry and superstition, should be rooted out; which occasioned a great deal of glory to God from the praises and thanksgivings of his people, expressed in the next three verses.

10 And I heard a loud voice saying in heaven, [t]Now is come salvation, and strength, and the kingdom of our God, and the power of his Christ: for the accuser of our brethren is cast down, [u]which accused them before our God day and night.

t ch. 11. 15. & 19. 1.
u Job 1. 9. & 2. 5. Zech. 3. 1.

And I heard a loud voice saying in heaven: John undoubtedly heard this voice as in the third heaven, whither he was caught; but it is not only expressive of the joy and satisfaction which the glorious angels and glorified saints had, upon their knowledge of what was done upon the earth, but prophetical of the great joy which should be over all the church, upon Constantine's stopping the persecution, and restoring peace to the church, by casting out all pagan idolatries and superstitions. *Now is come salvation;* temporal salvation, and deliverance from persecutors. *And strength;* now God hath showed himself a strong and mighty God. *And the kingdom of our God;* and the King of kings, who reigneth over all the earth. *And the power of his Christ;* now Christ hath shown his power. *For the accuser of our brethren is cast down, who accused them before our God day and night;* for the devil, who incessantly accuseth the saints, is overcome. Two things are here observable: 1. That the holy angels call the saints *brethren*. 2. That the accusers of Christians, for their piety towards God, are of their father the devil, for his works they do. Informers show who is their father, by accusing others, by murdering the servants of God; they differ no more than as elder and younger brethren, both are children of the same father.

11 And [x]they overcame him by the blood of the Lamb, and by the word of their testimony; [y]and they loved not their lives unto the death.

x Rom. 8. 33, 34. 37. & 16. 20.
y Luke 14. 26.

And they overcame him; Michael and his angels, mentioned ver. 7, overcame the dragon and his angels: the Christians overcame the pagans. *By the blood of the Lamb:* some translate διὰ here, *propter*, because of, as denoting the meritorious cause, which is true; for Christ's blood was both the meritorious and exemplary cause of their victory. But this will not agree with the usage of the term in the next words. Others therefore rather choose to translate it, *by*, as denoting the efficient cause, whether principal (as was the blood of the Lamb) or instrumental. *And by the word of their testimony;* as was their preaching, and professing the gospel. *And they loved not their lives unto the death;* and by their patient bearing the cross, not shunning the danger of death, that they might preach Christ, and own his truths, and live up to the holy rule of his gospel.

z Ps. 96. 11.
Is. 49. 13.
ch. 18. 20.
a ch. 8. 13.
& 11. 10.

12 Therefore rejoice, *ye* heavens, and ye that dwell in them. ᵃWoe to the inhabiters of the earth and of the sea! for the devil is come down unto you, having

b ch. 10. 6.

great wrath, ᵇbecause he knoweth that he hath but a short time.

Therefore rejoice, ye heavens, and ye that dwell in them: he calls to the angels and saints again to rejoice; some think, to the church also: these tell us, that *the inhabitants of the earth, and of the sea*, in St. John's writings, always signify the enemies of the church, earthly, carnal men. *For the devil is come down unto you, having great wrath;* the devil now being divested of the power he exercised against the church, will fall upon you; for though he principally hateth the saints, as most opposite to him, yet he is the common hater of mankind. *Because he knoweth that he hath but a short time;* and he hath but a little time to execute his malice, he shall shortly be confined to the bottomless pit. It is hard to say whether here be intended all in general, or the worser part of the world only; for great judgments after this came upon the whole Roman empire by the Goths and Vandals, and upon the church by the Arians, and by antichrist, of whose rise we shall read in the next chapter.

13 And when the dragon saw that he was cast unto the earth, he persecuted

c ver. 5.

ᶜ the woman which brought forth the man child.

And when the dragon saw that he was cast unto the earth; when the devil saw that he could not uphold his kingdom by paganism, nor further execute his malice by pagan emperors, but was wholly routed and overcome, as to that power. *He persecuted the woman which brought forth the man-child;* to let us know that he retained his malice, though he had lost his former power, he goes on in pursuing the church of God to its ruin, only doth it in another form; heretofore in the form of a pagan, now under the pretence of a Christian; by heretics, the spawn of Arius and Photinus, (who were before this time,) and by Pelagius, Nestorius, and Eutyches, who all were betwixt the years 400 and 500, and by antichrist, the *beast* we shall read of, chap. xiii. 1, with *seven heads and ten horns*.

d Ex. 19. 4.
1 Mac. 2.
29, 30, 31.
e ver. 6.
f ch. 17. 3.

14 ᵈAnd to the woman were given two wings of a great eagle, ᵉ that she might fly ᶠinto the wilderness, into her

g Dan. 7. 25.
& 12. 7.

place, where she is nourished ᵍ for a time, and times, and half a time, from the face of the serpent.

And to the woman; to the sincerer part of Christians, represented by *the woman*, ver. 1, and by *the temple, and altar, and them that worship therein,* viz. in the oracle where the altar stood, chap. xi. 1. *Were given two wings of a great eagle:* the eagle being the ensign of the Roman empire, and Theodosius having two sons, Honorius and Arcadius, betwixt which he divided the empire, making Honorius the emperor of the west, and Arcadius of the east, leadeth some very judicious interpreters to expound this passage of the providence of God (by this division of the empire about the year 390) in some measure securing his church from the great troubles that presently ensued. For in the year 411, Alaricus king of the Goths took Rome, and continual troubles so ensued, that by the year 480 the western empire was quite extinguished, ending in Augustulus, who, because of his manifold afflictions, is supposed to be the *star* mentioned chap. viii. 10, 11, called *Wormwood*, who fell upon the sounding of the third trumpet. *That she might fly into the wilderness:* by *the wilderness* is here undoubtedly meant some places which were like a wilderness for solitariness, where the church might have some rest. *Into her place;* the place said to be by God prepared for the church, ver. 6. *Where she is nourished;* where God hid, and protected, and provided for his people a certain time, expressed in the next words. I know not whether we need be so critical or no, or whether it be not safer to expound all the foregoing words more generally, viz. that God graciously provided for his people hiding-places against the storm now coming upon the whole Roman empire, bearing them, as it were, *on eagles' wings*, as he did his old Israelites when he brought them out of the land of Egypt. It is the very phrase used by God, Exod. xix. 4. *For a time, and times, and half a time:* it is apparent, that the same space of time is here meant that is mentioned ver. 6, and called *a thousand two hundred and threescore days*. Most interpreters agree, that it signifieth three years and a half, consisting each of them of three hundred and sixty prophetical days, that is, years; for although we count three hundred and sixty-five days to the year, (and there are strictly so many, besides some odd hours,) yet anciently they counted but three hundred and sixty, leaving out the five odd days, as we do now the odd hours and minutes, which in four years make up an odd day, which makes every fourth year leap year. Now three times three hundred and sixty make up a thousand and eighty, to which add one hundred and eighty for the half year, it makes just a thousand two hundred and sixty, the number of days mentioned ver. 6. If any inquire why what was expressed by one thousand two hundred and sixty days there, is thus expressed here? it is answered, To make this comport with the prophecy of Daniel, chap. vii. 25; xii. 7, where it is thus expressed.

15 And the serpent ʰ cast out of his

h Is. 59. 19.

mouth water as a flood after the woman, that he might cause her to be carried away of the flood.

And the serpent; the devil, the old serpent, mentioned ver. 9, being able no longer to execute his malice as a dragon, by the civil power of the heathen emperors, tearing Christians in pieces, but discerning the church secured by the special providence of God, went to work another way. *Cast out of his mouth water as a flood;* corrupting the judgments of several persons, who, out of the abundance of error in their hearts, preached corrupt doctrine. Such were the followers of Arius, Nestorius, Eutyches, Pelagius, &c. *The words of a man's mouth are as deep waters*, Prov. xviii. 4. *The mouth of the wicked poureth out evil things*, Prov. xv. 28. *That he might cause her to be carried away of the flood;* on purpose to ruin the church: and, indeed, such were the ill effects of these heresies, that he who is but meanly versed in the history of the fifth age, will see reason to adore the providence of God, that the Roman emperors, upon the sight of them, did not again turn pagans, and add their force to the malice of these pretended Christians against the sincerer part of the church.

16 And the earth helped the woman, and the earth opened her mouth, and swallowed up the flood which the dragon cast out of his mouth.

And the earth helped the woman: there are divers notions here of *the earth;* to me theirs seemeth most probable, who understand by *the earth* the Goths and Vandals, &c., who, Anno 410, invaded the Roman empire, and gave it continual trouble, till they had put an end to the western empire, Anno 480. By whose continual contests with the subjects of the Roman empire, the church enjoyed some quiet in the exercises of religion; and though all this while they were troubled by the broods of Arians, Pelagians, Nestorians, and Eutychians, yet they could do them no great hurt; and the church had a liberty to condemn them by the second and third general councils; in which, it is probable, there were many too that deserved no better name than *the earth. And the earth opened her mouth, and swallowed up the flood which the dragon cast out of his mouth;* but yet they served, in a great measure, to swallow up that flood of heresies which the devil threw out of his mouth by these heretics.

17 And the dragon was wroth with the woman, ⁱand went to make war with the remnant of her seed, ᵏwhich keep the commandments of God, and have ˡthe testimony of Jesus Christ.

i Gen. 3. 15. ch. 11. 7. & 13. 7.
k ch. 14. 12. 1 1 Cor. 2. 1. 1 John 5. 10.
l ch. 1. 2, 9. & 6. 9. & 20. 4.

And the dragon was wroth with the woman: the devil hath been defeated in two designs against the whole church; he could not wholly root it out by the ten persecutions under the Roman emperors, nor by the water thrown out of his mouth, pestilent doctrines which he influenced some to broach; but he was angry still, his rage was not extinguished. *And went to make war with the remnant of her seed;* he gives over his design to ruin the whole church, as not practicable, but resolves to do all the mischief he could to the remnant of her seed, to particular Christians; those especially, which kept closest to the doctrine of faith, called here *the testimony of Jesus Christ,* and to the rule of a holy life, which is meant by keeping *the commandments of God.* Hence antichrist's rage hath not been against Christians in general, as was the pagans', but only against such Christians as he hath not been able to bring over to him, in a compliance with his corruptions in doctrine, worship, and discipline.

CHAP. XIII.

A beast with seven heads and ten horns riseth out of the sea, to whom the dragon giveth his power, wherewith he blasphemeth God, and vexeth the saints, 1—10. *Another beast cometh up out of the earth, which supporteth the worship of the former beast,* 11—17. *The number of the beast,* 18.

God is now coming to show his prophet that grand enemy of his church, who is emphatically called antichrist; after the determination of whose time of one thousand two hundred and sixty years, the kingdom of Christ shall begin, whether in the day of judgment, or in some period of time before that, and here upon the earth, I dare not determine.

The rise, power, and prevalency of this adversary, is described in this chapter; the opposition made to him by Christ and his followers, chap. xiv.; his fall, chap. xv.—xviii.; for which praise is given to God, chap. xix.

This enemy of the church is showed to John by the symbol or representation of two beasts; the one having the body of a leopard, the feet of a bear, and the mouth of a lion; the other having two horns like a lamb, but speaking like a dragon, ver. 11.

The reader must understand, that the rise of these beasts, their rage, and prevalency, was contemporaneous with some of the six trumpets, mentioned chap. viii. and ix. For, chap. ix. 15, upon the sounding of the seventh trumpet antichrist began to fall; whose gradual fall we shall find more fully described in chap. xvi., by pouring out of the vials; only (as was before said) there is from chap. xii. a more particular description of what should happen to and in the church under the first six trumpets.

The best interpreters, by these two beasts, understand the antichrist, (for in a larger sense there are more antichrists than one,) and by the antichrist they understand the pope, as armed both with a secular and ecclesiastical power; yet I durst not conclude from that notion, the civil magistracy of the Roman empire, who either helped the pope into his chair, or held him there.

The greatest loss we are at, is to determine the time when the papacy began: it could not be before the pagan empire was thrown down, that was about the year 325, nor before the *silence in heaven for half an hour* was over, which (if that by it the rest be meant which the church enjoyed in the time of Constantine and Theodosius) was about the year 390, or 400; but if we fix the rise of the papacy there, I know no ground for it, and it would, besides, have been determined in the year 1660, or thereabouts. I think, therefore, we must distinguish betwixt the rise and reign of antichrist. It doth not seem to me reasonable to make his reign to commence higher than the year 600, or 606, when he arrogated to himself the primacy; and that was confirmed to Boniface the Third by Phocas, in requital of Boniface's kindness to him, who had got the empire by the base murder of Mauritius his master, and of all his children, and stood in need of the pope's help to support him. From that time, I judge, the one thousand two hundred and sixty years should be counted; but *Nemo repente fit pessimus,* we must allow the papacy some time to come to this virile estate from his cradle. And I see no great harm of allowing the two hundred years, from the year 400 to 600, for this. So that I do think that in this chapter is shortly revealed what should happen to the church from about the year 400, or the space of forty-two months, or one thousand two hundred and sixty years, the time of the beast's reign.

AND I stood upon the sand of the sea, and saw ᵃa beast rise up out of the sea, ᵇhaving seven heads and ten horns, and upon his horns ten crowns, and upon his heads the ‖name of blasphemy.

a Dan. 7. 2, 7.
b ch. 12. 3. & 17. 3, 9, 12.
‖ Or, *names.* ch. 17. 3.

And I stood upon the sand of the sea: the place of John's present residence was Patmos, which was an island, chap. i. 9. He was yet in a vision, but thought he was upon the sea-shore, either in Patmos, or elsewhere. *And saw a beast rise up out of the sea;* that is, as I should think, unexpectedly; for who would expect to see a leopard rise from thence? *Having seven heads and ten horns, and upon his horns ten crowns:* this beast is described like the dragon, chap. xii. 3, (only that is described with but seven crowns,) by which we understand the devil in the heathen emperors of Rome; and we shall find it, ver. 2, answering Daniel's vision of the four monarchies, that I cannot but think the Roman emperors, after the time of Theodosius, are meant, several of which were Arians, as also were the Goths and Vandals, (many of them,) who from the year 402 invaded the empire, and were not beaten out till 564, little above forty years before Boniface was confirmed in his primacy. *And upon his heads the name of blasphemy:* the Arians denying the eternal existence of Christ as God, may well be said to have *the name of blasphemy* upon them, or upon their *heads:* but whether by these ten heads be meant the ten sorts of governors made use of in the empire, or the ten governments into which the Goths and Vandals divided the empire, is not easy to determine, nor, possibly, much material. There are other notions about this beast: some would have it to be the devil, but he is plainly distinguished, ver. 2, 4, from the dragon. Some would have it to be the Turk; but we read of the worshipping of this beast, which is what we read not done to the Turkish emperors, who also began not till above the year 1200, (though indeed the Saracens began five hundred years before,) but Rome, which never was the Turk's seat, is made the seat of this beast. Some would have it to be idolatry itself; this was Grotius's notion: see the reasons against it in Mr. Pool's Synopsis Latina. Some would have it the pagan empire of Rome; but John never saw the first rise of that. This is a beast that rose after the dragon was cast down; which must be the Roman empire under the dominion of the papacy, in which respect only it is now one beast again; for otherwise in civil respects it is divided into ten crowned horns, i. e. distinct, independent kingdoms or principalities.

2 ᶜAnd the beast which I saw was like unto a leopard, ᵈand his feet were as *the feet* of a bear, ᵉand his mouth as the mouth of a lion: and ᶠthe dragon gave him his power, ᵍand his seat, ʰand great authority.

c Dan. 7. 6.
d Dan. 7. 5.
e Dan. 7. 4.
f ch. 12. 9.
g ch. 16. 10.
h ch. 12. 4.

Daniel, in his vision of the Chaldaic, Persian, Grecian, and Roman monarchies, by which the world was successively ruled from his time to St. John's, and many years after, had the first represented to him by a lion, for its nobleness and fierceness; the second by a bear, for its cruelty; the third, by a leopard, for the smallness of its bulk, the swiftness of its conquests, its strength, &c.; the fourth, by a beast (not named) strong, and exceedingly terrible, that had great iron teeth, that devoured, and brake in pieces, and stamped the residue under its feet. This beast is certainly here described, which had several forms: John saw it at first under the representation of a red dragon, which signified that empire, while pagan, for three hundred years after Christ; in which time the old serpent could not prevail nothing against the church. Then (after a rest to the church of a few years, which ended with Theodosius about the year 380 or 400) he saw it under the form of *a leopard*, ruled by Arian emperors till near 600. This beast had *the feet of a bear* and *the mouth of a lion*. These emperors, with the Goths and Vandals that were Arians, were as cruel to true Christians as the pagan emperors had been. Gitimer, king of the Vandals, Anno 530, and the Goths under Totilas, 540, made miserable havoc amongst the Christians. *And the dragon gave him his power;* these together inherited both the power of the heathen emperors, *and their seat*, and Rome, which was their seat, or throne, and exercised there *great authority*. All this was done in the form of *a leopard*, not so terrible as that of a dragon; for the Arians disclaimed paganism, and the worship of pagan idols. All this while the papacy was creeping up, but till the year 552, or thereabouts, the Goths and Vandals, and other barbarous nations, were not driven out of Italy. Totilas (who took Rome Anno 547) was then killed, and Thejas succeeded him, who was the last king of the Goths in Italy, who about twenty years after was beaten by Narsetes, and driven out, after the Goths and Vandals had reigned in Italy about seventy-seven years.

i ver. 12, 14.
† Gr. *slain*.
k ch. 17. 8.

3 And I saw one of his heads ¹as it were †wounded to death; and his deadly wound was healed: and ᵏall the world wondered after the beast.

And I saw one of his heads; that is, the leopard's head. *As it were wounded to death:* the seven heads of this beast are interpreted by the Spirit of God himself, to be *seven kings*, chap. xvii. 10, i. e. seven forms of sovereign government in the Roman state, and these successive one to another; for it is said there, *Five are fallen, and one is, and the other is yet to come:* so that this head must be either that then in being, or that to come; it cannot be that to come, because that does not receive its fatal blow and deadly wound till the final dissolution of the Roman (as the fourth metal) monarchy; therefore it must be that head then in being, viz. that of the pagan emperors: and the wounding of this head to death, is the conquering the pagan emperors, and the abolishing of paganism and idolatry, and putting a stop to persecution by the Christian emperors; *and his deadly wound was healed;* and consequently this wound was healed when idolatry (for substance the same with the heathenish, though in a new dress) and persecution was restored (gradually) by the doctrine and practice of the Romish Church.

4 And they worshipped the dragon which gave power unto the beast: and they worshipped the beast, saying, ¹Who is like unto the beast? who is able to make war with him?

l ch. 18. 18.

And they worshipped the dragon: by *the dragon*, here, is to be understood the devil. *Which gave power unto the beast;* who gave power to these emperors; not that they did so directly, but interpretatively; they worshipped idols, which ordinarily in Scripture are called devils. *And they worshipped the beast, saying, Who is like unto the beast?* possibly worshipping in this latter clause is not to be understood of a Divine adoration, but a civil subjection; people, upon the driving out of these their enemies, generally gave themselves up to the obedience of their emperors and the bishops of Rome, commanding them idolatrous worship; and admired these two, as those by whom they had been delivered from these enemies who had plagued them so long.

m Dan. 7. 8, 11, 25. & 11. 36.
‖ Or, *to make war*.
n ch. 11. 2. & 12. 6.

5 And there was given unto him ᵐa mouth speaking great things and blasphemies; and power was given unto him ‖ to continue ⁿforty *and* two months.

And there was given unto him a mouth speaking great things and blasphemies: by *him* here must be meant antichrist, (as appears by the forty-two months, his period, being the same with one thousand two hundred and sixty days,) both the secular power of the emperors of Rome at this time, and the ecclesiastical power of the bishops of Rome concurred to make one antichrist. God permitted, and the devil influenced, this beast to speak *great things*, as Dan. vii. 11, which is interpreted by the term *blasphemies*. Blasphemies against God signifies strictly any reproachful speeches against him, whether attributing to him the creature's imperfections, or denying him the perfection proper to him, or giving to the creature what belongs to God only, which blasphemy must be in all idolatry; for adoration is due unto God alone, and when this is given to any creature, there is both blasphemy in the doctrine which teacheth the lawfulness of it, and idolatry in the practice of it. *And power was given unto him to continue forty and two months:* these forty-two months are (as hath been before showed) the same term of time with one thousand two hundred and sixty days, and must be the term of antichrist, which was given him to tread down the outward court in; so as the beast here spoken of must be the antichrist, who began in the civil power of the Roman empire, but was quickly metamorphosed into the ecclesiastical power of the bishop of Rome; in comparison of whose power (after he had obtained the primacy) indeed the emperor's power was very small.

6 And he opened his mouth in blasphemy against God, to blaspheme his name, °and his tabernacle, and them that dwell in heaven.

o John 1. 14. Col. 2. 9.

That is, antichrist opened his mouth to blaspheme God. Mr. Mede noteth well, that antichrist's time must not be counted from his beginning to persecute, but from his beginning to blaspheme, either by maintaining pernicious doctrine, or setting up idolatrous worship; for till the year 1206, when the Inquisition was set up, (the doctrine of transubstantiation having been about that time decreed by Innocent the Third, and confirmed by the council of Lateran,) the persecution was not great. It is also the observation of the same learned author, that the threefold idolatry of the Church of Rome is here described to us; their blaspheming the Lord's name, by giving Divine adoration to images; their blaspheming the human nature of Christ, (which he thinks is here to be understood by the Lord's *tabernacle*,) by their doctrine of transubstantiation, giving every mass-priest power to make it of a piece of bread; and their putting the glorified saints in the place of the pagan demons, by their invocation of saints. The observation is very ingenious, but whether the sense of this text I doubt; for we are now about the period when antichrist began to reign, which we suppose to be soon after the year 600. The blasphemies here mentioned, were his first-fruits: but the doctrine of transubstantiation, though it might be broached one hundred years before, yet was made no doctrine of their church of six hundred years after the first beginning of the papacy; and therefore cannot well be reckoned amongst antichrist's first blasphemies. But whoso is acquainted with the history of the church after the year 606, will find enough to justify this text, though we do not restrain their blasphemy to these three things.

7 And it was given unto him ᵖto make war with the saints, and to overcome them: ᑫand power was given him over all kindreds, and tongues, and nations.

p Dan. 7. 21. ch. 11. 7. & 12. 17.
q ch. 11. 18. & 17. 15.

God showeth John, that after antichrist had gone on blaspheming the name, and tabernacle, and saints of God, some years, the devil should influence him also *to make war* against God's holy ones, and he would suffer him *to overcome them;* and he should have a *power over all the nations* of that part of the world, where God had his church. This was eminently fulfilled after the year 1200, when the doctrine of transubstantiation was established. The Inquisition was set up in Spain, 1206; the number of those murdered by it was exceeding great. But yet this was too slow a work, the pope quickly raised vast armies against the Albigenses, first under the conduct of his legate, then of Simon de Montford. Perionius (one of their own) saith, that more than a million were slain in these wars of these poor people, merely for not complying with the Church of Rome in her apostacy. But what were these to those slain in the valleys of Piedmont, Provence, Calabria, Alsatia, Bohemia, before the year 1517, when the Reformation began in Germany? What slaughters have been since made in Germany, Hungary, Flanders, Ireland,

&c., every one knows. The latter clause was eminently verified until the year 1517, there being no nation in Europe but was subject to the pope of Rome, so as he had a *power over all kindreds, and tongues, and nations.* The poor Albigenses thought themselves concerned in this prophecy; for when the popish general, Simon de Montford, had made a vast slaughter of them, and the archbishop of Tholouse interceded for those that survived, upon condition that they would embrace the Romish faith, they boldly refused, sending the archbishop word, that they were the overcome servants of Jesus Christ; and all died comforting themselves with the prophecy of this text.

r Ex. 32. 32. Dan. 12. 1. Phil. 4. 3. ch. 3. 5. & 20. 12, 15. & 21. 27. s ch. 17. 8.

8 And all that dwell upon the earth shall worship him, ʳ whose names are not written in the book of life of the Lamb slain ˢ from the foundation of the world.

God here showed his prophet the general subjection that would be of all people to the papacy, except some few, whom he had chosen to eternal life and salvation, whom Christ had redeemed with his blood, and would preserve from this pollution.

t ch. 2. 7.

9 ᵗ If any man have an ear, let him hear.

Either, let him hear what hath been already said, and take heed that he be not one of those that worship the beast; or, let him hear what followeth concerning the ruin of antichrist and his adherents: but from the usage of this phrase in other scriptures, where it is oft made use of to stir up attention to some remarkable thing, it seemeth rather to be applied to what went before. The phrase also further lets us know, that (comparatively) the number of those who should refuse to worship the beast would be very small, as indeed it proved.

u Is. 33. 1. x Gen. 9. 6. Mat. 26. 52.

10 ᵘ He that leadeth into captivity shall go into captivity: ˣ he that killeth with the sword must be killed with the sword.

y ch. 14. 12.

ʸ Here is the patience and the faith of the saints.

As it was God's manner by the prophets of old, when he had denounced judgments against his people, to comfort them by a prediction of the ruin of their enemies; so here, by this his New Testament prophet, he assureth his church, that antichrist also should have his period, and have the same measure meted to him which he had meted out to others, by leading into captivity, and killing with the sword: and indeed, there are no sins which God doth so ordinarily punish by retaliation, as sins against justice and mercy, (of which nature persecutions are the most eminent,) Isa. xxxiii. 1, 2. *Here is the patience and the faith of the saints;* that is, there is a time for God's people to exercise their faith and patience: patience, because they are like to wait for deliverance a long time, and to suffer many sharp things in the mean time; and faith, because their deliverance will be a thing out of sight, of which they will have no security but from the promise of God.

z ch. 11. 7.

11 And I beheld another beast ᶻ coming up out of the earth; and he had two horns like a lamb, and he spake as a dragon.

There are great disputes about this other beast, who is represented or signified by it. The popish writers say it is some eminent impostor, who shall appear in the world before the coming of antichrist. Others would have it to be magic practised by Apollonius Thyaneus, the vanity of which notion Dr. More hath sufficiently demonstrated. The generality of protestant writers agree it to be antichrist himself, the same beast which was before spoken of, only in another form. The design, and time, and power of both is the same; neither hath this other beast any other figure assigned to him; and in the end of this chapter we shall find mention but of one beast, the *mark, name,* and *number* of the beast, mentioned ver. 16—18, is but of one beast; and we shall find the power of both to be the same; only he is called *another,* because appearing in another form. or under another type. The former beast typified the civil power of antichrist; this, his ecclesiastical power. He is said to have come up *out of the earth;* either because he was of a meaner extraction than the other, or because he stole upon the world insensibly. The pope and the clergy are judged by the best interpreters to be here meant. *And he had two horns like a lamb;* he pretends to the power of Christ, as his vicar, and therefore is said to have *horns like a lamb. And he spake as a dragon;* but he should speak terribly; or his doctrines should be such as the apostle calls *doctrines of devils;* or his words and practice should be like those of the great red dragon.

12 And he exerciseth all the power of the first beast before him, and causeth the earth and them which dwell therein to worship the first beast, ᵃ whose deadly wound was healed.

a ver. 3.

The power of the first beast was to speak *great words and blasphemies, and to make war with, and overcome the saints,* ver. 5, 7. This power also should be exercised by the papacy, (according to this prophecy,) and time hath witnessed the truth of it. And as, before he arrived at the height of power, he had persuaded the latter emperors to establish idolatry and superstition; so having now the power in his own hands, and being by the first beast made head of the church, he now vigorously causeth all under his power to obey the edicts, decrees, and commands of that nature, which those emperors had published; choosing rather to do this in the name of others, than from himself; that in case of the non-compliance of any, he might charge them with sedition or disobedience to the imperial laws, or dissenting from antiquity, &c. Hence he *causeth* them *to worship the first beast* rather than himself.

13 And ᵇ he doeth great wonders, ᶜ so that he maketh fire come down from heaven on the earth in the sight of men,

b Deut. 13. 1, 2, 3. Matt. 24. 24. 2 Thess. 2. 9. ch. 16. 14. c 1 Kings 18. 38. 2 Kings 1. 10, 12

And he doeth great wonders, lying wonders, 2 Thess. ii. 9. such as, by God's permission, false prophets might do, Deut. xiii. 1, 2. Prophets were to be judged true or false, not from any signs or wonders which they did, but from the doctrine they taught, and would by those signs establish. *So that he maketh fire come down from heaven on the earth in the sight of men;* wonders as great as those which Elijah wrought.

14 And ᵈ deceiveth them that dwell on the earth ᵉ by *the means of* those miracles which he had power to do in the sight of the beast; saying to them that dwell on the earth, that they should make an image to the beast, which had the wound by a sword, ᶠ and did live.

d ch. 12. 9. & 19. 20. e 2 Thess. 2. 9, 10.

f 2 Kings 20. 7.

The Lord showeth his prophet by what means the papacy should cheat the world, viz. by pretences of miracles, which it had a power to work, (the doctrines of the Church of Rome to this are sufficiently known,) all which are done *in the sight of the beast,* that is, to his honour, and to gain him a reputation. As God gave his prophets and apostles a power to work true miracles for the confirmation of their mission from him, and of the doctrines which they brought; so he permitted others to work *lying wonders* for the confirmation of their false doctrine. The apostle therefore describeth the coming of antichrist to be *with all power and signs and lying wonders, and with all deceivableness of unrighteousness,* 2 Thess. ii. 9, 10. *Saying to them that dwell on the earth, that they should make an image to the beast, which had the wound by a sword, and did live:* these words show the design of this last-mentioned beast, viz. to *make an image to the beast which had the wound by a sword.* Mr. Mede's notion here seemeth best to me, that by *the beast which had the wound by a sword,* is to be understood the dragon, of whose wound we read, chap. vi. He was the type of the pagan emperors, whom God rooted out. Antichrist's design was to make an image of that old beast, in which it might again live; which he did by his setting up the veneration of images, and the invocation of saints; the pagan idolatry lying chiefly in their adoration of persons (who had been famous amongst them) when they were dead, making them their mediators to their supreme gods, and in the veneration of their images and statues. The making the image of this beast, was the restoring of the same idolatry, changing only the names of princes and great soldiers, whom the pagans worshipped after their death, into the names of saints; in which image the dragon lived again: and it is sufficiently known how the Romish clergy deceiveth people into this idolatry by their stories of miracles done by such saints.

† Gr. *breath.*

15 And he had power to give †life unto the image of the beast, that the image of the beast should both speak, ᵍand cause that as many as would not worship the image of the beast should be killed.

g ch. 16. 2. & 19. 20. & 20. 4.

The beast, mentioned ver. 11, *had power to give life* unto this new-formed idolatry, conformable to that of the pagans, in which the old beast again lived: he gave life to it by his decrees and bulls, and canon laws, and by his excommunications and censures of those that would not comply with his idolatry as heretics; after which the persons so adjudged were delivered up to the secular power to be put to death.

16 And he caused all, both small and great, rich and poor, free and bond, ʰ†to receive a mark in their right hand, or in their foreheads:

h ch. 14. 9. & 19. 20. & 20. 4.
† Gr. *to give them.*

No particular character is here to be understood, but only the general imposition of the Romish faith upon all sorts of persons. His *mark* was nothing else but either the profession of his faith and religion, or a vowed subjection to his commands, which we know is the practice of the papacy where it obtaineth in any country.

17 And that no man might buy or sell, save he that had the mark, or ⁱthe name of the beast, ᵏor the number of his name.

i ch. 14. 11.
k ch. 15. 2.

And that no man might buy or sell: this the popish church effects by its excommunications; it was begun in the council of Lateran, anathematizing all who entertained any of the Waldenses, or traded with them; and the late learned bishop of Armagh, in his book De Successione Ecclesiæ, hath given us an account of such a canon of a synod in France, which in express terms forbade any commerce with heretics in buying or selling. Paræus tells us Pope Martin the Fifth hath best interpreted this prophecy, in his bull added to the council of Constance, where he prohibits Roman Catholics to suffer any heretics to have any dwellings in their countries, or to make any bargains, or use any trades, or to perform to them any civil offices. *Save he that had the mark, or the name of the beast, or the number of his name:* there have been great disputes about the *name* and *number of the beast.* I must profess myself not able to distinguish betwixt the *mark*, *name*, and *number* of the beast; they may all signify the same thing, viz. the profession of the Romish religion. Some think the number is contained in the name, and that the name is ΛΑΤΕΙΝΟΣ, in which the number six hundred and sixty-six is contained; of which we shall speak more by and by.

18 ¹Here is wisdom. Let him that hath understanding count ᵐ the number of the beast: ⁿfor it is the number of a man; and his number *is* Six hundred threescore *and* six.

l ch. 17. 9.
m ch. 15. 2.
n ch. 21. 17.

Here is wisdom; that is, Herein is the wisdom, the unsearchable wisdom, of God seen in the trial of his church; or, (which is more probably the sense,) this is a point will exercise the wisdom of men. *Let him that hath understanding count the number of the beast;* let him that is spiritually wise count the number of the beast. *For it is the number of a man;* it is such as may be numbered after the way men use to number. *And his number is Six hundred threescore and six:* what this meaneth hath exercised the wits of the greatest divines in all ages. A late learned and valuable writer thinks that 666 doth not signify a certain definite number, but an indefinite number, and that not of years, but of pernicious errors, by the broaching and upholding of which antichrist may be known. But the most interpreters think a number, and that a definite, certain number, of years is to be understood here: but they are again divided; some thinking them determining the time of the fall of this beast; others judging them to determine or define the year or time of his beginning to reign, the time from whence his period and term of forty-two months, or one thousand two hundred and sixty years, commenceth: most of those who think this number determinative of the time when he should fall, understood by it the year 1666, which raised the expectation of many good and some learned men (though we see in this thing they were deceived) upon that year. A countryman of our own, who hath written an English Dissertation about the Name, Number, and Character of the Beast, hath with much more probability judged this number definitive of the time when he began to reign under the title of "universal bishop," which was about the year 606; but there seemeth to be a want then of sixty years; to answer which objection, the aforesaid author (N. Stephens) undertaketh to make out, that the year which according to our account was 606, was according to Daniel's chronology 666; for it is the six hundred and sixty-sixth year of the Roman monarchy, which, saith he, is to be counted from the time when that empire first invaded the church, which was when Cicero and Antonius were consuls, about sixty years before Christ; for then the Romans first subdued the Jews, the ancient church of God. As to this notion, there is nothing to be proved, but that 666 must be counted from that epocha; for admitting that, the time of the beast's reign, as to the beginning of it, fell much about the year 666. I shall only say of it, that I do not judge it a contemptible notion. This makes this prophecy a prediction of the time when this beast should begin to show his power, and therefore it is called *the number of his name* (*name* in Holy Scripture often signifying dominion and power). But there is yet another notion, which is the most learned Dr. Potter's, in his book called The Interpretation of the Number Six Hundred and Sixty-six; a book justly valuable both for the great wit and learning in it, and much magnified both by Dr. More, and Mr. Mede, whose judgment of it is prefixed to it; in which he saith, It is the happiest tract that ever yet came into the world,—and though at first he read the book with much prejudice, yet when he had done it, it left him possessed with as much admiration. The foundation on which he goeth is, that this number is to be interpreted by the opposite number of 144, chap. xxi. 17, as the measure of the wall of the new Jerusalem; which is to be understood of square measure, as he proveth, chap. 6.; for the wall could not be 144 cubits high, nor 144 cubits broad; but in square measure so much, that is 12 cubits high and 12 cubits broad (for the length cannot be understood); it being impossible that a wall 144 cubits long, should encompass a city 91 furlongs about. In like manner he thinks 666 ought to be counted by the square root of that number, which is $25\frac{25}{31}$. Hence he concludeth, that as 12, the square root of 144, is God's number, so 25 is the square root of antichrist's number 666; and by this enigmatical expression we are taught that antichrist should be a political body, that should as much affect the number of 25, as God seemeth to have in his church affected the number of 12. Under the Old Testament God built his church upon twelve patriarchs, it was made up of twelve tribes: Jerusalem, mentioned by Ezekiel, chap. xlviii. 31, and in this book, chap. xxi. 12, *had twelve gates;* ver. 21, these *were twelve pearls; at the gates,* ver. 12, were *twelve angels; the wall,* ver. 14, *had twelve foundations, and in them the names of the twelve apostles;* ver. 16, the measure of the city was *twelve thousand furlongs;* chap. xxii. 22, *the tree of life* had *twelve manner of fruits:* by all which it appears that 12 was the number God affected to use with reference to his church, and the square root, both of the 144 cubits, which were the measure of the wall, chap. xxi. 17, and likewise of the 144 thousands, mentioned in the next chapter as the number of Christ's retinue. On the contrary, 25 is the square root of 666, (adding the fraction,) which is the beast's number; and that learned author proves, that the pope and his clergy as much affected the number of 25 in their first forming their church, as God did the number of 12. They at first divided Rome into 25 parishes, (instead of the old 35 tribes,) over which they set 25 cardinals, (which were their first number,) who had 25 churches: they made 25 gates to the city; at last they also brought the articles of their creed to 25. This that learned author abundantly proveth, chap. 17—20,

22. He also, chap. 24—26, showeth how in a multitude of things of lesser moment they affected this number of 25. This seemeth a very probable notion. I further refer my reader to the learned author's book, where he enlargeth upon these things with great wit and learning. In this variety I shall positively determine nothing, but have shortly mentioned the senses I think most probable, as to this mysterious number 666.

CHAP. XIV

The Lamb with his company standing on Mount Sion, 1—5, *an angel preacheth the gospel,* 6, 7; *another proclaimeth the fall of Babylon,* 8; *and a third, the punishment of them that worship the beast,* 9—12. *The blessedness of those that die in the Lord,* 13. *The harvest of the world,* 14—16. *The vintage and winepress of God's wrath,* 17—20.

a ch. 5. 5.
b ch. 7. 4.
c ch. 7. 3. & 13. 16.

AND I looked, and, lo, ᵃ a Lamb stood on the mount Sion, and with him ᵇ an hundred forty *and* four thousand, ᶜ having his Father's name written in their foreheads.

God, in this part of the vision, showeth his servant John, that during the whole reign of antichrist, till the voice mentioned ver. 8, *Babylon is fallen,* should be heard, notwithstanding all his rage, he would preserve his church, though it would be but a small number, bearing no better proportion to the whole world than one hundred and forty-four thousand (the number of those sealed of each tribe of Israel, chap. vii.) bare to whole Israel, which were above six hundred thousand upon both their numberings, Numb. i. 26. The *Lamb* here signifieth Christ, chap. v. 6. *Mount Sion* signifieth the church of the gospel, typified by Mount Sion amongst the Jews where the temple stood. *An hundred forty and four thousand* is the same number that was sealed of all the tribes of Israel, chap. vii.: not that there was just so many which made up the church under antichrist's persecution; but it signifies, 1. A small number in comparison of such as should be of another stamp. 2. It is a number made up of twelve times twelve, by which is signified that they were a people that should answer the Israelites indeed of the Old Testament, that remnant of the twelve tribes whom God had chosen, who adhere to the doctrine and precepts of the twelve apostles. *Having his Father's name written in their foreheads;* making an open profession of being the children and servants of God: as those servants and soldiers did that had anciently the names of their masters and generals in their foreheads; it being an ancient custom for masters to brand their servants, and captains their soldiers, as we do our beasts at this day.

2 And I heard a voice from heaven,
d ch. 1. 15. & 19. 6.
ᵈ as the voice of many waters, and as the voice of a great thunder: and I heard
e ch. 5. 8.
the voice of ᵉ harpers harping with their harps:

As the voice of many waters, and as the voice of a great thunder; a loud voice, and terrible also to the followers of antichrist. *The voice of harpers harping with their harps;* a musical, melodious voice, as of persons rejoicing. Mr. Mede rather thinks, that the *voice as of many waters,* signifies no more than *a great multitude,* and indeed it is so expounded, chap. xix. 6.

f ch. 5. 9. & 15. 3.
3 And ᶠ they sung as it were a new song before the throne, and before the four beasts, and the elders: and no man could
g ver. 1.
learn that song ᵍ but the hundred *and* forty *and* four thousand, which were redeemed from the earth.

And they sung as it were a new song before the throne: by *the throne* here is meant the throne of God in glory. The *new song* here spoken of, is probably the same with that we met with before, chap. v. 11, 12, sang by the *voice of many angels round about the throne and the beasts and the elders:* called *new,* either for the excellency of it; or, because sung unto God after Christ was manifested in the flesh; the design of it was to declare the worthiness of Christ to *receive power, and riches, and wisdom, and strength, and honour, and glory, and blessing:* see chap. v. 12. Mr. Mede saith thus of it; "If God shall at any time make me fully to understand it, I will happily more largely explain it, for it is deeply settled in my mind, that the whole mystery of evangelical worship is in it contained." And quite through the Scripture generally, a *new song* signifies a song which praiseth God for some new benefits received from him. *And before the four beasts, and the elders;* the *throne, beasts,* and *elders,* described before, chap. iv. *And no man could learn that song but the hundred and forty and four thousand, which were redeemed from the earth:* during the reign of antichrist none could learn this new song, viz. to give glory to Jesus Christ alone, ascribing to him *power, riches, wisdom, strength, honour, glory, and blessing;* but a small number redeemed through the blood of Christ, from that *vain conversation received by tradition from* their *fathers,* 1 Pet. i. 18. All the other part of the world gave Christ's honour and glory to the virgin Mary, angels, and saints, &c.

4 These are they which were not defiled with women; ʰ for they are virgins.
h 2 Cor. 11. 2.
These are they ⁱ which follow the Lamb whithersoever he goeth. These †ᵏ were redeemed from among men, ˡ *being* the firstfruits unto God and to the Lamb.
i ch. 3. 4. & 7. 15, 17. & 17. 14.
† Gr. *were bought.*
k ch. 5. 9.
l Jam. 1. 18.

These are they which were not defiled with women; for they are virgins; that is, that would not comply with antichristian idolatry and superstition; for idolatry is all along in holy writ compared to whoredom and fornication. *Which follow the Lamb whithersoever he goeth;* that follow the Lord Christ fully, in all things keeping close to the rules of worship and life which he hath given. *These were redeemed from among men;* these show themselves to be redeemed by the blood of Christ from the vain conversation of men, whether towards God, in matters of worship, or towards men. *Being the first-fruits unto God and to the Lamb;* that are consecrated to, and accepted of God, as the first-fruits were, being the only part of the world that are not profane.

5 And ᵐ in their mouth was found no guile: for ⁿ they are without fault before the throne of God.
m Ps. 32. 2. Zeph. 3. 13.
n Eph. 5. 27. Jude 24.

Not that any liveth and sinneth not against God, but it is to be understood comparatively; they are without fault in comparison of the rest of the world, they have not in them the guile of hypocrisy, they are sincere. Or, possibly by *guile* is here understood a lie. All idolaters are liars, Rom. i. 25, and idols are called lies, Jer. xvi. 19; Amos ii. 4. Mr. Mede expoundeth this text by Zeph. iii. 13. The words may either more generally signify the holiness of these persons, in opposition to profaneness and hypocrisy; or more particularly, their freedom and purity from antichristian superstitions and idolatry.

6 And I saw another angel ᵒ fly in the midst of heaven, ᵖ having the everlasting Gospel to preach unto them that dwell on the earth, ᵠ and to every nation, and kindred, and tongue, and people,
o ch. 8. 13.
p Eph. 3. 9, 10, 11. Tit. 1. 2.
q ch. 13. 7.

God having in a vision showed unto his servant John the reign and rage of antichrist, chap. xiii., and in this chapter the care he would extend toward his church for the preservation of a godly seed during his reign, he now cometh by further visions to instruct him in what should be done during antichrist's reign of forty-two months. The gospel should be preached: this I take to be the substance of this verse. This angel seems to me to represent faithful ministers' speed and diligence to preach the gospel in all parts of the world. It is called *the everlasting gospel,* either with reference to the time past, as much as to say, the old gospel; or to the time to come, it being that doctrine of salvation, besides which there neither is, nor ever shall be, revealed any other while the world endureth, Acts iv. 12.

7 Saying with a loud voice, ʳ Fear God, and give glory to him; for the hour of his judgment is come: ˢ and worship him
r ch. 11. 18. & 15. 4.
s Neh. 9. 6. Ps. 33. 6. & 124. 8. & 146. 5, 6. Acts 14. 15. & 17. 24.

that made heaven, and earth, and the sea, and the fountains of waters.

These angels, or ministers of God, whether civil or ecclesiastical witnesses, cried aloud against the papal idolatry, in worshipping saints and images, admonishing all men to give Divine adoration only to the true and living God, who was the Creator of all things. The worshipping of images began soon after antichrist began to reign: we find it decreed in a synod held at London about the year 710, but it was abolished by a synod at Constantinople, 712. In 723, it was again established by a synod at Mentz. By a synod in Syria it was defended, Anno 725, and the emperor Leo Isaurus was excommunicated for opposing it; but in 730, a synod at Constantinople decreed for Leo against it. Another synod, held there Anno 755, under the emperor Constantinus Copronymus, decreed against it; but two other synods held in Bavaria, 765, 766, again decreed for it. In the year 786 the second synod of Nice established it; since which time it hath constantly obtained amongst the papists. But as from the first broaching of this idolatry it was opposed by five emperors of Constantinople, so it hath all along been declaimed against by the faithful ministers of Christ, preaching the everlasting gospel, and calling upon men to perform Divine adoration only to *him who made heaven and earth.*

t Is. 21. 9.
Jer. 51. 8.
ch. 18. 2.
u Jer. 51. 7.
ch. 11. 8. &
16. 19. & 17.
2, 5. & 18. 3.
10, 18, 21. &
19. 2.

8 And there followed another angel, saying, ^tBabylon is fallen, is fallen, ^uthat great city, because she made all nations drink of the wine of the wrath of her fornication.

The apostle is shown, that other messengers of God should come forth, during the reign of antichrist, that should declare his ruin as certainly as if it were already effected. *Babylon is fallen, is fallen, that great city:* these words are taken from Isa. xxi. 9, *Babylon is fallen, is fallen; and all the graven images of her gods he hath broken unto the ground.* So Jer. li. 8, *Babylon is suddenly fallen and destroyed.* There is no doubt but both the prophets spake of that Babylon into which the Jews were carried captive; but that Babylon was typical of another Babylon, called here the *great city,* and *great Babylon,* chap. xvi. 19; xvii. 5; xviii. 10, 21; and *the mother of harlots,* chap. xvii. 5. There neither is, nor ever was, any city in the world to whom these things could agree, but to Rome, rightly enough called *the mother of harlots, and abominations of the earth,* chap. xvii. 5, both in respect of carnal filthiness there tolerated to make the bishop of Rome a revenue, and spiritual whoredom, whi h is idolatry: called also *Sodom and Egypt,* chap. xi. 8, the former of which was famous for beastly lusts, the latter for idolatry, and oppression of God's Israel. The ruin of old Babylon is denounced by the prophet, Isa. xxi. 9, because of her idolatry in image worship, for which the new Babylon is every whit as famous. *Because she made all nations drink of the wine of the wrath of her fornication:* the word translated *wrath,* though it oft so signifies, yet should rather be here translated *poison,* as we translate it, Deut. xxxii. 33; Job xx. 16. The LXX. in those texts use the same word that is here used, Θυμὸς; so the sense is, with the poisonous wine of her idolatry, intimating to us the venomous condition of Romish superstitions and idolatries, to entice ignorant people to be in love with them; as harlots use with their philters, or poisoned cups, to make men in love with them. If we better approve of our translation of the term *wrath, the wine of the wrath of her fornication* signifieth her fornication which brings wrath upon them that join with her in it.

9 And the third angel followed them,

x ch. 13. 14,
15, 16.

saying with a loud voice, ^xIf any man worship the beast and his image, and receive *his* mark in his forehead, or in his hand,

God letteth his servant John know, that during the reign and rage of antichrist, as he would have ministers of the gospel that should preach the truth, and mind men to keep themselves from idols, worshipping God alone; and others that should assure them the papacy should go down, mystical Babylon should fall; so he would have others that should give warning to men and women of those dreadful plagues that should come upon them that entered themselves in this great city, either worshipping the devil after the pagan manner, or the image of the beast, i. e. committing idolatry after the antichristian, popish fashion, or that should either be subject to this idolatrous head, or be a soldier to fight for it. What those judgments should be, God showeth in ver. 10, and possibly there is not a more severe denunciation of judgment in the whole book of God.

10 The same ^yshall drink of the wine of the wrath of God, which is ^zpoured out without mixture into ^athe cup of his indignation; and ^bhe shall be tormented with ^cfire and brimstone in the presence of the holy angels, and in the presence of the Lamb:

y Ps. 75. 8.
Is. 51. 17.
Jer. 25. 15.
z ch. 18. 6.
a ch. 16. 19.
b ch. 20. 10.
c ch. 19. 20.

Those that do yield a subjection to him, and profess his faith, *shall drink of the wine of the wrath of God;* that is, shall feel the severity of God's judicial dispensations, which in Scripture are expressed by *the wine cup of* his *fury,* Jer. xxv. 15; see also Job xxi. 20; Psal. lxxv. 8; Isa. li. 17; either from the intoxicating quality of wine, or the stupifying quality of it, when mixed with myrrh, or other stupifying things. But here it is said *without mixture,* which signifies their sensible feeling of the effects of Divine wrath. *And he shall be tormented with fire and brimstone in the presence of the holy angels, and in the presence of the Lamb;* that is, in short, he shall go to hell at last; the exquisiteness of which torments, as to the pain of sense, is set out by *fire and brimstone;* brimstone being a material in which fire holds longest to torment any flesh put into it.

11 And ^dthe smoke of their torment ascendeth up for ever and ever: and they have no rest day nor night, who worship the beast and his image, and whosoever receiveth the mark of his name.

d Is. 34. 10.
ch. 19. 3.

And the smoke of their torment ascendeth up for ever and ever; that is, their torments shall be everlasting, as well as most exquisite, and causing the most acute pain. *And they have no rest day nor night;* this is but the same thing in other words; their torments shall be such as shall give them no rest at any time. *Who worship the beast and his image, and whosoever receiveth the mark of his name:* the sense of these two verses is no more than this, That all idolaters shall fall under the vengeance of God in this life, and at last shall be thrown to hell; not only such as worship the beast, committing paganish idolatry, worshipping stocks and stones, and devils, as the term of their worship, but such as worship the image of that beast set up by antichrist, worshipping of angels and saints, or their images. From hence an easy answer may be given to that question, Whether a man can be saved in that which at this day is called the Roman Catholic religion? If they either worship the beast, or the image of the beast, they cannot: whether they do or no, let the reader judge from what hath been before said.

12 ^eHere is the patience of the saints: ^fhere *are* they that keep the commandments of God, and the faith of Jesus.

e ch. 13. 10.
f ch. 12 17.

Here is the patience of the saints: God having in the former chapter shown his servant John the reign and rage of antichrist in his time of forty-two months, and in this chapter what shall be the end of him and all his adherents; here concludeth with telling him, This is a period of time wherein the patience of his holy ones will be tried, both in waiting for their deliverance, and also in their patient enduring antichrist's oppression and tyranny. *Here are they that keep the commandments of God, and the faith of Jesus;* and here will be the trial of men, whether they will keep to the faith of Christ, and obedience of God's commandments, by coming out of, or keeping in, this spiritual Babylon: those that come out of her will show both; those that keep in that idolatrous communion will show neither.

13 And I heard a voice from heaven saying unto me, Write, ^gBlessed *are* the dead ^h which die in the Lord ‖ from henceforth: Yea, saith the Spirit, ⁱ that

g Eccles. 4.
1, 2. ch. 20. 6.
h 1Cor. 15. 18.
1 Thes. 4. 16.
‖ Or, *from henceforth saith the Spirit. Yea.*
i 2 Thes. 1. 7. Heb. 4. 9, 10. ch. 6. 11.

REVELATION XIV

they may rest from their labours; and their works do follow them.

And I heard a voice from heaven saying unto me, Write: these words denote the excellency of the following saying; it is *a voice from heaven,* therefore worthy of our attention. John is commanded to *write* it, to be kept in memory for the comfort and encouragement of God's people, who might be discouraged at the hearing of those calamitous times which they were like to meet with during the reign of antichrist, in which many of them were like to be put to death. *Blessed are the dead which die in the Lord:* this phrase of dying in the Lord, is applicable to any persons that die united to Christ by a true and lively faith; all such die in the Lord. But if we consider the Scriptural usage of it, it seems rather to signify martyrs, such as die for the Lord; for ἐν often in Scripture signifieth *for,* Rom. xvi. 2, 8, 12; 1 Pet. iv. 14, &c. If any shall be put to death for adherence to Christ, they shall be no losers; for they shall be blessed, and that not only upon the account of that glory into which they shall pass, but upon the account of that *rest* which their death will give them from the troubles of the calamitous times before or hereafter mentioned. *From henceforth:* there is some little difference amongst interpreters about the sense of this particle: certain it is, it is not to be understood of the time following this revelation exclusively, as to those who before died to Christ; for they also were blessed, they also rested from their labours, &c.; yet the particle seems to refer to the time to come. The emphasis of the particle seems to be, to obviate the doubts of those who should happen to die under antichrist's rage, because they died not by the hands of pagans and avowed enemies of the gospel, but of such as should call themselves Christians; such, saith God, die for the Lord, and are blessed, and shall be blessed. *Yea, saith the Spirit;* the Spirit of truth affirms it. *That they may rest from their labours;* they shall be at rest from the troubles of this life. *And their works do follow them;* and their good deeds and patient sufferings shall follow them, as witnesses for them before the Judge of the quick and the dead.

Here follow two visions, the one of a harvest, the other of a vintage; there is no great difficulty in determining, that they both signify some judicial dispensations of God, that he would bring upon the world, or some part of it, the latter of which should be greater than the former: yet Dr. More and Mr. Mede have another notion of them. But there is some doubt amongst interpreters, whether they signify God's general judgment in the last day, or some particular judgments before that day, mentioned chap. xv. and xvi., and belong to the vials which we there read of. Those who think that the last judgment is here showed to John, are led to it from the representation of the day of judgment, under the notion of a harvest, Matt. iii. 12; xiii. 39. But I rather agree with them who think that the harvest here mentioned, is a representation of some judicial dispensations of God before that time, particularly God's vengeance upon the beast, more fully expressed, chap. xvi. For, 1. The last judgment is fully described afterward, chap. xix., xx. 2. To express that, there needed not two types, the one of a harvest, the other of a vintage. 3. Here is no mention of the resurrection, which must go before the last judgment. Mr. Mede hath noted, that there are three things belonging to a harvest; (1.) Cutting down of corn. (2.) Gathering it into the barn. (3.) Threshing it. Whence, in Scripture, it signifieth either cutting and destroying, or safety and preserving, which is the end of gathering corn into the barn. We have examples of the former, Isa. xvii. 3, 5; Jer. li. 33; but of the latter we have only examples in the New Testament, Luke x. 2. It is his opinion, that the conversion of the Jews, going before the great slaughter mentioned chap. xix., is that which is here meant; but I rather agree with those who think, that by this parable is signified God's judgments upon antichrist, and that the general scope of both the parables is to declare, that God would grievously punish antichrist, first by lesser, then by greater judgments, as is more particularly expressed in the two next chapters, to which this, to me, seemeth prefatory. Let us now come to the text itself.

k Ezek. 1.26. Dan. 7. 13. ch. 1. 13. 14 And I looked, and behold a white cloud, and upon the cloud *one* sat ᵏlike unto the Son of man, ˡhaving on his head a golden crown, and in his hand a sharp sickle. l ch. 6. 2.

The description here can agree to none but Christ, sitting, as it were, upon clouds, and coming out in his judicial dispensations of providence, to execute judgment upon his enemies, to which purpose he is said to have *in his hand a sharp sickle.*

15 And another angel ᵐcame out of the temple, crying with a loud voice to him that sat on the cloud, ⁿThrust in thy sickle, and reap: for the time is come for thee to reap; for the harvest °of the earth is ‖ ripe. m ch. 16. 17. n Joel 3. 13. Matt. 13. 39. o Jer. 51. 33. ch. 13. 12. ‖ Or, *dried.*

Most interpreters understand this of the prayers of God's people, from the church, soliciting the Lord Jesus Christ (say some) to gather in the Jews, or the number of his elect, the fields being now white to that harvest, (as Christ useth the metaphor of the Samaritans, John iv. 35,) or, (as others say, with whom I rather agree,) to execute vengeance on antichrist and his adherents.

16 And he that sat on the cloud thrust in his sickle on the earth; and the earth was reaped.

According to the afore-mentioned different notion of the harvest, there is amongst them a different interpretation of this verse; some interpreting it of God's calling in the Jews, or his elect, by the preaching of the gospel; others, of his vengeance upon antichrist and his adherents, more fully expressed, chap. xv., xvi.

17 And another angel came out of the temple which is in heaven, he also having a sharp sickle.

This angel some will have to be some instrument God would make use of to cut down antichrist: others would have it to be the word of God in the mouth of his ministers, which, Heb. iv. 12, *is sharper than a two-edged sword, piercing to the dividing asunder of soul and spirit;* and thus they judge this angel to be the same with the rider upon the white horse, chap. xix., out of whose mouth went a sharp sword, ver. 15.

18 And another angel came out from the altar, ᵖwhich had power over fire; and cried with a loud cry to him that had the sharp sickle, saying, ᵠThrust in thy sharp sickle, and gather the clusters of the vine of the earth; for her grapes are fully ripe. p ch. 16. 8. q Joel 3. 13.

From the altar; the place of sacrifices and burnt-offerings. *Which had power over fire;* which had commission to execute God's judgments, compared to fire, Psal. xi. 6; xxi. 9; l. 3. *And cried with a loud cry to him that had the sharp sickle, saying:* God's holy ones cry unto him who hath a power to execute vengeance. *Thrust in thy sharp sickle, and gather the clusters of the vine of the earth;* put an end to the rage of antichrist, and gather those clusters which grew upon this vine of Sodom, and were as the clusters of Gomorrah. *For her grapes are fully ripe;* for their iniquities were come to the full, and they were now ripe for judgment. Our learned Dr. More expounds this ripeness, of a readiness for conversion, as well as for destruction, and thinks the first is here rather intended: the last words of the next verse incline me to judge otherwise.

19 And the angel thrust in his sickle into the earth, and gathered the vine of the earth, and cast *it* into ʳthe great winepress of the wrath of God. r ch. 19. 15.

Dr. More thinks the sense of this is, that men were pressed in conscience upon the sharp conviction of Christ's powerful ministers, with sorrow for their sins, and so felt the wrath of God in them. But Mr. Mede, with whom (as to the sense of this text) I rather agree, tells us, that the treading of the vintage, in parabolical Scripture, constantly signifies a cruel, bloody, and deadly slaughter; he thinks that it is the same slaughter mentioned chap. xix. 19 —21, as to which, ver. 15, much the same metaphor is

REVELATION XIV, XV

used, *he treadeth the winepress of the fierceness and wrath of Almighty God.*

20 And *the winepress was trodden without the city, and blood came out of the winepress, even unto the horse bridles, by the space of a thousand *and* six hundred furlongs.

And the winepress was trodden without the city: by *the city,* Dr. More thinks Babylon is here meant, and that the meaning is, that the powerful convictions of the word before mentioned, shall not reach Babylon, the Romish hierarchy and polity, as being hardened against any such thing. But Mr. Mede and others think, that the city of Jerusalem is here meant, or the Holy Land, which comprehends exactly one thousand six hundred furlongs, that is, two hundred Italian miles, or one hundred and sixty Grecian miles. But what that place shall be, where this slaughter shall be, is a great secret. *And blood came out of the winepress, even unto the horse bridles, by the space of a thousand and six hundred furlongs:* it is plain it shall be a great slaughter, by the depth of the blood mentioned, and the length of the ground which it should to that depth overflow. It is very probable, that great battle is meant, mentioned chap. xix. 20, 21, in the place called Armageddon, upon the pouring out of the sixth vial, chap. xvi. 16. In so difficult a business nothing can be positively determined.

CHAP. XV

The seven angels with the seven last plagues, 1. *The song of them which overcome the beast,* 2—4. *The seven angels receive the seven golden vials full of the wrath of God,* 5—8.

AND *I saw another sign in heaven, great and marvellous, *seven angels having the seven last plagues; *for in them is filled up the wrath of God.

And I saw another sign in heaven, great and marvellous; that is, a representation which appeared to John great and wonderful. *Seven angels;* ministers of God, used by him in the dispensations of his providence. *Having the seven last plagues;* having a commission to execute the seven last judgments of God, by which he designed to destroy antichrist. *For in them is filled up the wrath of God;* for by them the wrath of God was to be executed upon him to the uttermost.

2 And I saw as it were ^da sea of glass *mingled with fire: and them that had gotten the victory over the beast, ^fand over his image, and over his mark, *and* over the number of his name, stand on the sea of glass, ^ghaving the harps of God.

This *sea of glass* (as our learned More thinks) hath either an allusion to the *sea of glass like unto crystal,* reflected upon by the *lamps of fire burning before the throne,* chap. iv. 5, 6, or to the waters of the Red Sea congealed (while the Israelites passed over) reflected upon by the pillar of fire. Others make it the church gathered out of all nations, said to be of glass, because of its splendour and glory. Others make it to signify the world, which is said to be *of glass,* to let us understand God seeth through it. It seemeth to me to signify heaven; for it is mentioned as the place of the glorified saints, who had overcome all temptations to idolatry, either from pagans, (which were *the beast,*) or from antichrist and his party, (which are called the *image* of the beast,) and had avoided all kind of compliance with them in profession of the religion which he would endeavour to impose upon them. *Harps of God* signify either the most excellent harps, or holy harps. Mr. Forbes saith well, they signify hearts tempered with joy, and love, and a grateful sense of the mercies of God towards them.

3 And they sing ^hthe song of Moses the servant of God, and the song of the Lamb, saying, ⁱGreat and marvellous *are* thy works, Lord God Almighty; ^kjust and true *are* thy ways, thou King of ‖saints.

And they sing the song of Moses the servant of God; the song which Moses sang upon God's delivery of the Israelites from the danger of Pharaoh, which we have, Exod. xv.; not that they sang those words, but to the same sense. *And the song of the Lamb;* a song to the honour of Christ, to the same sense that Moses sang, and upon a much like occasion. *Saying, Great and marvellous are thy works, Lord God Almighty;* admiring the greatness and marvellousness of what God had done in their deliverance, and giving him the glory of his Almighty power. *Just and true are thy ways, thou King of saints;* acknowledging, that all the acts of his providence were both *just,* God in them giving to every one their due, and *true,* God by them but justifying his promises and threatenings. These words are taken out of Psal. cxlv. 17.

4 ^lWho shall not fear thee, O Lord, and glorify thy name? for *thou* only *art* holy: for ^mall nations shall come and worship before thee; for thy judgments are made manifest.

Acknowledging, that for this God deserved to be worshipped and served by all the world, because of his holiness, much seen in the justice and truth of his ways; declaring their faith and hope, that now all nations should own and acknowledge Christ, and be subject unto him, now that his judgments upon antichrist, and his justice in all his dispensations, was made so evident to the world.

5 And after that I looked, and, behold, ⁿthe temple of the tabernacle of the testimony in heaven was opened:

Here is a plain allusion to the Jewish tabernacle or temple, in which was the holy place, and the holy of holies; into the latter the high priest only entered. There were kept in the ark the two tables of God's law, often called *the testimonies of God.* From this *tabernacle of the testimony* proceeded God's oracles, there God gave answers from the mercy-seat, and therefore in the Book of Kings it is called *the oracle.* The sense some put upon this is, That God here showed unto his prophet the liberty that should be, after the downfal of antichrist, to preach the gospel. But in this sense it must be an anticipation of what orderly should have come in after the pouring out of the vials: I had rather understand it of God's being now about to give out an answer to his people's prayers for a deliverance from the tyranny of antichrist; as the place called *the oracle* in the Jewish temple was opened when the high priest had been inquiring of God, to give an account of the answer he had.

6 ^oAnd the seven angels came out of the temple, having the seven plagues, ^pclothed in pure and white linen, and having their breasts girded with golden girdles.

And the seven angels; the seven ministers of God's vengeance on antichrist, to whom the vials were given. *Came out of the temple;* that is, out of the *tabernacle of the testimony;* for in Moses's tabernacle there was only this inward court for the priests, the people worshipped without. They came (as the high priest was wont) out of the oracle to bring God's answer to all his saints' prayers. *Having the seven plagues:* the answer was *seven plagues,* that is, that God had employed them to bring seven plagues successively upon the antichristian party, and all the enemies of his church, till by them they should be consumed. *Clothed in pure and white linen, and having their breasts girded with golden girdles;* these angels came in the habit of high priests, when they went in to inquire of God, or came out with an answer from God.

7 ^qAnd one of the four beasts gave unto the seven angels seven golden vials full of the wrath of God, ^rwho liveth for ever and ever.

And one of the four beasts; one of those four beasts

round about the throne, chap. iv. 6. *Gave unto the seven angels;* the seven angels mentioned ver. 6. *Seven golden vials:* a vial is a plain pot or glass with a wide mouth, used to drink in: these were *full of the wrath of God, who liveth for ever and ever.* The meaning is no more than that the seven angels, before mentioned, were commissioned from God, by one plague after another, to bring antichrist to his ruin.

8 And [s] the temple was filled with smoke [t] from the glory of God, and from his power; and no man was able to enter into the temple, till the seven plagues of the seven angels were fulfilled.

s Ex. 40. 34.
1 Kings 8.
10. 2 Chron.
5. 14. Is. 6. 4.
t 2 Thess. 1. 9.

And the temple; that is, the church, as *temple* most ordinarily signifieth in this book. *Was filled with smoke:* by *smoke*, doubtless, is meant confusions and troubles. *From the glory of God, and from his power;* caused by God's glorious manifestation of his power, in bringing antichrist to ruin, who had so twisted his interest with that of the civil magistracy in several kingdoms, that there was no rooting him out, without a terrible shaking of all those parts of the earth where he set his foot. *And no man was able to enter into the temple, till the seven plagues of the seven angels were fulfilled;* so as no part of the church could be at rest until God had fulfilled his ruin by these plagues: nor must any quiet state of the church be expected, until this great work be effected.

CHAP. XVI

The seven angels are commanded to pour out their vials on the earth, 1. *Great plagues follow thereupon*, 2—14. *Christ cometh suddenly as a thief: blessed are they that watch*, 15—21.

God having showed unto his servant John in the vision of the first six seals, the fate of the church under the pagan emperors of Rome, chap. v., vi., and its fate under antichrist, in the vision of the six first trumpets, under the seventh seal, chap. viii., ix., and diverted him by the vision of the little book opened, chap. x., and by the contents of it, chap. xii.—xiv., and instructed him concerning the affairs of the church during all the time of the reign of the dragon, and antichrist, who was the image of the dragon, comes now to instruct him particularly how and by what means he would ruin antichrist, and restore peace to his church.

AND I heard a great voice out of the temple saying [a] to the seven angels, Go your ways, and pour out the vials [b] of the wrath of God upon the earth.

a ch. 15. 1.
b ch. 14. 10. & 15. 7.

And I heard a great voice out of the temple; either out of the church triumphant, Christ, the Head of it, commanding the executioners of his justice to go and do their office; or out of the church militant, by their prayers soliciting God to execute vengeance upon the beast. All the beast's territories, or the several parts of his kingdom, are expressed in this chapter, under the notions of *the earth, the sea, the rivers and fountains, the sun,* and *the seat of the beast.* The first command to the executioners of God's justice, is, to pour out his wrath on *the earth.* By the *earth,* Pareus understands some parts of the earth; others, the common people; others, the Roman empire; but others, considering the earth as the firmest part of the universe, say, that by *the earth* is meant the popish clergy, the basis of the papacy; and I am very much inclined to judge that the most probable sense of it, not only because there is little of heaven in them, and their whole frame and model is the product of earthly policy, but because experience hath told us that the pope here received his first wound, in the diminution of their power and authority, and a contempt of them. God hath used many instruments to pour out this vial, even so many (whether princes or ministers) as he hath made use of to root out monasteries and abbeys, and to expose mass priests to scorn and contempt. Mr. Mede seemeth to be of another mind, thinking, that by *earth* is meant the commonalty of the people, whose defection from the pope was his first plague: but that which is to be understood by *the earth*, being the affected part of antichrist, I cannot agree with that learned man; for though the beast suffered by the defection of the commonalty, yet I cannot see how those that made the defection suffered at all by it.

2 And the first went, and poured out his vial [c] upon the earth; and [d] there fell a noisome and grievous sore upon the men [e] which had the mark of the beast, and *upon* them [f] which worshipped his image.

c ch. 8. 7.
d Ex. 9. 9. 10, 11.
e ch. 13. 16, 17.
f ch. 13. 14.

Here is a plain allusion to the plagues which God brought upon Pharaoh king of Egypt for his oppression of his ancient Israel; God hereby showing us, that he would deal by this Romish beast for his persecutions of his gospel churches, as he dealt by Pharaoh: as he turned the Egyptian rivers into blood, so as the fish died, and the waters stunk, Exod. vii. 20, 21, and as he plagued the Egyptians with boils and blains, Exod. ix. 9; so he would plague the papacy by proportionable judgments, until, as Pharaoh with his whole party was at last drowned in the Red Sea, so all the antichristian party shall be rooted out. Here are two of the Egyptian plagues mentioned, but this vision begins with the sixth of the Egyptian plagues, viz. that of boils breaking out in blains. What is meant by this *grievous sore* I must profess myself not to understand, but think Dr. More speaks very probably, interpreting it of trouble and vexation, which the popish party should have upon the first prospect of their kingdom's going down; it being of the nature of sores to vex and disturb those that are affected with them, so as they are very uneasy so long as they are affected with them. And, indeed, I find many interpreters agree in this notion.

3 And the second angel poured out his vial [g] upon the sea; and [h] it became as the blood of a dead *man:* [i] and every living soul died in the sea.

g ch. 8. 8.
h Ex. 7. 17, 20.
i ch. 8. 9.

This answered the first plague upon Pharaoh, Exod. vii. 20, *All the waters that were in the river were turned to blood; and the fish that was in the river died.* By *the sea* here Dr. More understands the jurisdiction and dominion of the papacy, wherein he agrees with Mr. Mede. I rather agree with those who understand the whole system of the popish religion; their rites and ceremonies, their doctrines of indulgences and purgatory, &c. God showeth his prophet, and instructeth us, that he will bring the papacy to ruin, 1. By bringing his clergy (which are *the earth* upon which he stands) into scorn and contempt; discovering their frauds and cheats. 2. By discovering the folly and vanity of their pompous and theatrical religion, consisting only in vain shows, and idle rites and ceremonies, without any regard to that religion which is spiritual, and pure, and undefiled before God; discovering the cheats of their confessions and absolutions, their masses, pardons, and indulgences; making them appear to be not only idle, but pernicious and damnable; so as Christians could not live in the communion of their church, but it must be damnable to those who keep in the communion of it.

4 And the third angel poured out his vial [k] upon the rivers and fountains of waters; [l] and they became blood.

k ch. 8. 10.
l Ex. 7. 20.

Mr. Mede and Dr. More both agree in interpreting this of the Jesuits and other popish emissaries, and the laws made for the execution of them in England in the time of Queen Elizabeth, not excluding those civil powers which are the upholders and maintainers of antichrist, as the Spaniard, who also within these last hundred years hath had blood enough given him to drink, both in 1588, and in the Low Countries. It seemeth a little hard to interpret a prophecy relating to the whole church, by what is done in so small a part of it. We know in what credit these emissaries are at this day, both in the empire, and in Spain, and in France, and Venice, from whence they sometime were expelled. We have, indeed, laws against them in England, but principally relating to those of them who, being native subjects of England, have apostatized.

So as I had rather think this vial is not yet poured out, or that interpreters mistake the meaning of these *rivers and fountains*, than agree with them in that interpretation of this prophecy. I am much disposed to believe that we are not further than the pouring out of the second vial. God, indeed, hath made the Romish clergy contemptible enough, and hath vexed and enraged them sufficiently. He hath also made their scenical religion as contemptible to, and justly abhorred by, a great part of the Christian world; but how far he hath proceeded further to the ruin of antichrist, I do not understand.

5 And I heard the angel of the waters say, ^mThou art righteous, O Lord, ⁿwhich art, and wast, and shalt be, because thou hast judged thus.

m ch. 15. 3.
n ch. 1. 4, 8.
& 4. 8. & 11. 17.

This and the two following verses do but express the honour and glory that shall be given unto God, when he shall have accomplished his great work in destroying those who feed, and uphold, and maintain the beast, partly by those instruments he shall use in that work, expressed here by *the angel of the waters*, partly from others. *Thou art righteous, O Lord, which art, and wast, and shalt be, because thou hast judged thus;* acknowledging the Lord's justice and righteousness in such destruction.

6 For ^othey have shed the blood ^pof saints and prophets, ^qand thou hast given them blood to drink; for they are worthy.

o Matt. 23. 34, 35.
ch. 13. 15.
p ch. 11. 18. & 18. 20.
q Is. 49. 26.

Because of their persecutions of, and cruelty towards, God's faithful ministers and people, which rendered the spilling of their blood but a condign punishment suited to their sin.

7 And I heard another out of the altar say, Even so, ^rLord God Almighty, ^strue and righteous *are* thy judgments.

r ch. 15. 3.
s ch. 13. 10. & 14. 10. & 19. 2.

Others also, either members of the church triumphant or militant, or both, shall in that day give glory to God, as a God of power, able to do such things; of righteousness, thus giving these bloody men their due; and of truth, thus fulfilling both his promises to his people and his threatenings against his enemies. But it is easier to determine who shall thus rejoice, than the time when this joy shall be. This certainly is God's work, but *in fieri*, now doing, but not yet done.

8 And the fourth angel poured out his vial ^tupon the sun; ^uand power was given unto him to scorch men with fire.

t ch. 8. 12.
u ch. 9. 17, 18. & 14. 18.

Here we have no history to guide us in the government of our fancies and judgments, but their opinion seems most probable to me, who, by *the sun*, understand some great prince or potentate, or the whole civil power in the antichristian heaven; suppose the Spaniard, or the emperor. It seems to signify either some destruction of such civil powers, or some defection of them from the papacy, which will vex and enrage antichrist and his party, as if they were scorched with fire. This I look upon as much more probable than theirs who interpret it of the natural sun, or the word of God.

‖ Or, *burned*.

9 And men were ‖ scorched with great heat, and ^xblasphemed the name of God, which hath power over these plagues: ^y and they repented not ^z to give him glory.

x ver. 11, 21.
y Dan. 5. 22, 23. ch. 9. 20.
z ch. 11. 13. & 14. 7.

What the damned do in hell, where the wrath of God is poured out upon men to the utmost, that reprobates do upon earth, they are *scorched with great heat*, the vengeance of God cometh upon them; they are mad and enraged, and speak evil of a just and righteous God, who bringeth such plagues on them; but they have no sense of their sins, nor any thoughts of turning to God, confessing their sins, and giving him glory. This will be the upshot of God's lesser judgments upon the papacy: they will be mad at them, and rage, and reproach God's justice, but prove a hardened generation, given over to ruin, that will never be sensible that these judgments come upon them for their idolatries and superstitions, and for their persecutions, and the shedding the blood of God's holy ones. Not that all adhering to that church will be so, (many, probably, will convert, and be brought to acknowledge the truth,) but there will be a great party of them, whom nothing but the wrath of God come upon them in the bottomless pit to the utmost, will ever make sensible that they have done amiss, being given up to strong delusions, to a blind mind, and a hard heart, and a reprobate judgment.

10 And the fifth angel poured out his vial ^aupon the seat of the beast; ^band his kingdom was full of darkness; ^cand they gnawed their tongues for pain,

a ch. 13. 2.
b ch. 9. 2.
c ch. 11. 10.

And the fifth angel; the fifth of the seven angels mentioned ver. 1, by which, as was said, is to be understood the instruments which God will use gradually to destroy the papacy; the fifth rank of persons, whom God will employ in the execution of this his purpose, by his acts of providence. *Poured out his vial upon the seat of the beast;* shall execute God's wrath upon the city of Rome itself, wholly destroying the papacy in their power. *And his kingdom was full of darkness;* upon which his whole kingdom shall be full of the darkness of misery, trouble, and affliction. (Darkness was one of the plagues of Egypt.) *And they gnawed their tongues for pain;* and they shall be full of calamities, like men in so much pain that they bite their own tongues for pain. When this shall be God alone knows. I think, and experience hath proved, that they were much too hasty in their speculations, that prophesied it should be in the year 1656, or 1660, or 1666. For my own part, I do not believe it will be before 1866, or betwixt that and the year 1900. The determination of it depends upon the right fixing of the epocha, or beginning of the forty-two months, or one thousand two hundred and sixty prophetical days, which I think most probably fixed upon the year 606, or (according to Mr. Stephens's notion) 666, which, according to the Julian account, is the same: see the note on chap. xiii. 18.

11 And ^dblasphemed the God of heaven because of their pains and ^etheir sores, ^fand repented not of their deeds.

d ver. 9, 21.
e ver. 2.
f ver. 9.

This is the same that was said, ver. 9, of a former party belonging to the beast, and doth but signify, that there will be found the same vein of blindness of mind, hardness of heart, and reprobacy of sense, running through that whole party, until they be wholly ruined.

12 And the sixth angel poured out his vial ^gupon the great river Euphrates; ^hand the water thereof was dried up, ⁱthat the way of the kings of the east might be prepared.

g ch. 9. 14.
h See Jer. 50. 38. & 51. 36.
i Is. 41. 2, 25.

Upon the great river Euphrates; upon the Turkish empire: see the notes on chap. ix. 14. *And the water thereof was dried up;* their force, power, and strength shall be destroyed. *That the way of the kings of the east might be prepared;* that a way may be prepared for the conversion of the Jews. This I find to be the sense of the most learned and judicious interpreters of this mysterious book, amongst whom I count Mr. Mede, Dr. More, Pareus, Mr. Durham, &c. But it will be reasonable to say something further to show the probability of this sense. Euphrates was a great river that ran by Babylon, the depth of it was (as historians tell us) about two men's height. When Cyrus and Darius came to conquer Babylon, they diverted this river, Jer. li. 32, 36. Here is an allusion to that history. The Turks first took up their habitation about this great river, as was said in our notes on chap. ix. 14, where the providence of God restrained them for many years, till the sixth trumpet sounded. The Jews, who are observed to be in greatest numbers in the Eastern countries, having had a promise, Exod. xix. 6, to be *a kingdom of priests*, may well be called here *the kings of the east*. Two things hinder their embracing the Christian faith: 1. The image worship and idolatry of the papists. 2. The power of the Turks, with the success they have had against Christians. But both these being taken away, by the fall of Babylon and the ruin of the Turks, the way seems to be prepared for the Jews' receiving of the Christian faith. In a case where nothing can be certainly determined, this seemeth a very probable opinion. To which it contributes a little, that it is probable, that *the sixth vial* answereth *the sixth trumpet;* and that as they were the people first let loose by Euphrates, where they were bound, so they are the people to be destroyed under the notion of drying up the waters of Euphrates: and this seemeth to be a work of Providence brought forth after the ruin of Rome, and the total breaking of the power and dominion of the papacy. Thus we have foretold the breaking both of pope and Turk, and all their upholders; but we must not imagine them so ruined, but that parties of both should be left in the world, which combining, made up the army to fight the devil's last battle in Armageddon, of which we shall read, ver. 16.

k 1 John 4. 1, 2, 3.
l ch. 12. 3, 9.
13 And I saw three unclean ᵏ spirits like frogs *come* out of the mouth of ˡ the dragon,
m ch. 19. 20. & 20. 10.
and out of the mouth of the beast, and out of the mouth of ᵐ the false prophet.

God here showeth John, that after the power and strength both of the pope and Turks should be broken, the devil would yet make one push more; to which purpose he would influence some on the behalf of the antichristian secular power, others on the behalf of *the beast* with two horns, or *the false prophet.*

n 1 Tim. 4. 1. Jam. 3. 15.
o 2 Thess. 2. 9. ch. 13. 13, 14. & 19. 20.
p Luke 2. 1.
q ch. 17. 14. & 19. 19. & 20. 8.
14 ⁿ For they are the spirits of devils, ᵒ working miracles, *which* go forth unto the kings of the earth ᵖ and of the whole world, to gather them to ᑫ the battle of that great day of God Almighty.

Which, from the influence of the devil, should solicit the kings of the earth to join together in a battle against the church. This is, undoubtedly, the battle in Armageddon, ver. 16.

r Mat. 24. 43. 1 Thess. 5. 2. 2 Pet. 3. 10. ch. 3. 3.
s 2 Cor. 5. 3. ch. 3. 4, 18.
15 ʳ Behold, I come as a thief. Blessed *is* he that watcheth, and keepeth his garments, ˢ lest he walk naked, and they see his shame.

I come as a thief; that is, I come suddenly and unexpectedly: see Matt. xxiv. 43, 44; Luke xii. 39; 1 Thess. v. 2; Rev. iii. 3. It may be understood either of Christ's coming to the last judgment, or of his coming in his vindicative providence to be revenged on his enemies. *Blessed is he that watcheth,* he is a happy man that maketh it his business to keep himself from sin, in prospect of any such coming, *and keepeth his garments,* and that persevereth in my ways and truth; *lest he walk naked, and they see his shame;* for if he doth not, he will be found one of those that are not clothed with my righteousness, and his hypocrisy will appear to all men.

t ch. 19. 19.
16 ᵗ And he gathered them together into a place called in the Hebrew tongue Armageddon.

Either the devil brought them together, or God by his providence ordered that they should be gathered together, into the place where God designed to destroy them and their armies, for so the word *Armageddon* signifieth, say some; but others make it to signify the mountain of the gospel, or the mountain of apples, or fruits; but the first etymology in this place seems best. The word doth not signify any particular place; but here is an allusion, as some think, to that *Megiddo,* mentioned Judg. v. 19, where Barak overcame Sisera with his great army, and where Josiah was slain, 2 Kings xxiii. 30. Of the issue of this last battle with the enemies of the church of Christ we shall read more, chap. xix.

17 And the seventh angel poured out his vial into the air; and there came a great voice out of the temple of heaven,
u ch. 21. 6.
from the throne, saying, ᵘ It is done.

And the seventh angel poured out his vial into the air: I take this to be best interpreted (as Mr. Mede doth it) by *the power of the air,* of which Satan is called *the prince,* Eph. ii. 2, that is, upon all the children of the devil, that had so long given disturbance to the church of Christ. *It is done;* that is, the work of God is done, his counsels for the destruction of his enemies, and the deliverance of his people, are brought forth in the issue of his providence, not fully yet brought to an issue, but accomplishing.

18 And ˣ there were voices, and thunders, and lightnings; ʸ and there was a great earthquake, ᶻ such as was not since men were upon the earth, so mighty an earthquake, *and* so great.
x ch. 4. 5. & 8. 5. & 11. 19.
y ch. 11. 13.
z Dan. 12. 1.

See chap. iv. 5; vi. 12; xi. 13, 19. Either declarative of the majesty and power of God. (as Exod. xix. 16, when God came forth to give his law,) the violation of which God here was coming out to punish; or of the great stirs and confusions in that part of the world where the beast's greatest interest lay. Or, the *voices, thunders, and lightnings,* may be understood as declarative of the former, and the *great earthquake* of the latter.

19 And ᵃ the great city was divided into three parts, and the cities of the nations fell: and great Babylon ᵇ came in remembrance before God, ᶜ to give unto her the cup of the wine of the fierceness of his wrath.
a ch. 14. 8. & 17. 18.
b ch. 18. 5.
c Is. 51. 17, 23. Jer. 25. 15, 16. ch. 14. 10.

The great city; Rome, afterwards called *great Babylon* in this verse. *Was divided into three parts;* the pagan part, the evangelical part, and the antichristian part, (saith Dr. More,) the three parties that made up the armies that fought in Armageddon: or else this is added as the effect of the great earthquake. *And great Babylon came in remembrance, &c.;* God now took vengeance on the papacy, and all their adherents, though he had for twelve hundred and sixty years spared them, notwithstanding their idolatries and persecutions, and behaved himself toward them as if he had forgot them.

20 And ᵈ every island fled away, and the mountains were not found.
d ch. 6. 14.

These are the effects of great earthquakes: see chap. vi. 14. Some, by *islands* and *mountains,* understand the inhabitants of both. I know not whether those reverend authors, who by this term understand their idol worship and superstition, or ecclesiastical dignities, (I suppose because the heathens, and Jews, in imitation of them, committed idolatry on mountains and high hills,) be not here too critical.

21 ᵉ And there fell upon men a great hail out of heaven, *every stone* about the weight of a talent: and ᶠ men blasphemed God because of ᵍ the hail; for the plague thereof was exceeding great.
e ch. 11. 19.
f ver. 9, 11.
g See Ex. 9. 23, 24, 25.

The hail was another of the Egyptian plagues, Exod. ix. 22—25. The allusion also may be to the hailstones by which God fought against the five Canaanitish kings, Josh. x. 11. It signifies only further great judgments with which God will pursue the beast and his party, until they all be destroyed. The latter words only show the continued hardness of heart of the beast, and all his party; wherein also they answered Pharaoh and the Egyptians, (their type,) who would relent with no steadiness and certainty, until they were all ruined by the waters of the Red Sea. In all this prediction of the final ruin of the papacy, Pharaoh and the Egyptians are apparently made the type of the pope and all his party: 1. As to their sins, which were idolatry, and the oppression of God's Israel. 2. In the plagues by which they were destroyed gradually; turning waters into blood, boils and blains, darkness, hail. 3. In their impenitency, and hardness of heart; only with these two differences, by which the antitype exceeded the type in wickedness: (1.). We read of Pharaoh oft relenting, though his goodness was like a morning dew, and he returned to his former stubbornness. (2.) We read nothing of the Egyptians blaspheming God, because of their plagues, which is often said of these Egyptians.

CHAP. XVII

John's vision of the great whore, sitting upon the scarlet coloured beast, arrayed in purple and scarlet, with a golden cup in her hand, 1—4. *Her name,* 5. *She is drunken with the blood of saints,* 6. *The interpretation of the mystery of the beast, and of his seven heads and ten horns,* 7—17; *and of the woman,* 18.

REVELATION XVII

^a ch. 21. 9. AND there came ^aone of the seven angels which had the seven vials, and talked with me, saying unto me, Come hither; ^bI will shew unto thee the judgment of ^cthe great whore ^dthat sitteth upon many waters:

^b ch. 16. 19. & 18. 16, 17, 19.
^c Nah. 3. 4.
ch. 19. 2.
^d Jer. 51. 13.
ver. 15.

This whole verse is but a preface to a new vision which John had; not new, as to the matter revealed in it; for it plainly revealeth matters relating to antichrist; and the matter of it contemporizeth with the three last vials, about the final ruin of antichrist, who was before described under the notion of a *beast*, here under the notion of a *great whore*. A whore properly signifies one that is married, and is false to her husband's bed; and so very well suits the Church of Rome, (if they yet deserve that name,) *whose faith* was formerly *spoken of throughout the world*, Rom. i. 8, but is long since turned idolatrous (idolatry, in the prophetic style, being quite through the Scripture called whoredom). She is said to *sit upon many waters*, either because she exerciseth a jurisdiction over much people, or with allusion to old Babylon, (which gave her her name,) which was situated near Euphrates, a river in which there was a great collection of waters. John is called to hear the counsels of God concerning her destruction, which though more generally and shortly revealed before, yet God here designs to reveal to John more fully, particularly, and plainly.

^e ch. 18. 3.
^f Jer. 51, 7. ch. 14. 8. & 18. 3.

2 ^eWith whom the kings of the earth have committed fornication, and ^fthe inhabitants of the earth have been made drunk with the wine of her fornication.

With whom the kings of the earth have committed fornication; with which *great whore* several princes of the world have committed spiritual fornication, receiving her idolatrous worship, yielding to her authority, and following her example. *And the inhabitants of the earth have been made drunk with the wine of her fornication*; and not the kings only of the earth, but the generality of the people, have been influenced with a mad heat, and *with the wine of her fornication*, that is, with that wine by which she enticed them to commit idolatry with her. By this *wine* are meant honours, riches, preferments, pleasure, the gaudery of her worship, the magnificence of the apostolic see, their pretended antiquity, unity; in short, whatsoever specious arguments papists use to entice persons into the idolatrous communion of their church.

^g ch. 12. 6, 14.
^h ch. 12. 3.
ⁱ ch. 13. 1.
^k ver. 9.
^l ver. 12.

3 So he carried me away in the spirit ^ginto the wilderness: and I saw a woman sit ^hupon a scarlet coloured beast, full of ⁱnames of blasphemy, ^khaving seven heads and ^lten horns.

So he carried me away in the spirit; that is, being in an ecstasy; see chap. iv. 2; whether in the body or out of the body he could not tell, as Paul expresseth it, 2 Cor. xii. 2. *Into the wilderness;* a place not, or not much, inhabited, either as fittest for contemplation, or to signify that this *great whore*, which had driven the spouse of Christ into the wilderness, should shortly herself come into her state, according to the fate of old Babylon, Jer. l. 13. *And I saw a woman sit upon a scarlet coloured beast;* the great *whore*, mentioned ver. 1, upheld by the Roman emperors. *Full of names of blasphemy, having seven heads and ten horns;* the same which is mentioned chap. xiii. 1: see the notes there. Here a great question ariseth, who this *woman* is, or, (which is the same, as appeareth by ver. 5,) what city is meant by *Babylon*, mentioned ver. 5; a question (as Mr. Pool noteth) of high concernment; for whoever this *woman* is, or whatsoever this *Babylon* signifieth, the people of God are upon pain of damnation admonished to avoid any communion with her, and to come out of her, chap. xiv. 9, 10. Mr. Pool hath diligently collected into his Latin Synopsis all opinions about it, and showed what is to be said for or against them; I will give my reader the sum of what he saith.

1. Some would have it to be the whole world of wicked men. Against this it is said, (1.) That John speaks here of a certain great city which reigneth over the kings of the earth, ver. 18: this cannot be of the wicked world.

(2.) The world of wicked men are those *inhabitants of the earth*, whom this woman *made drunk with the wine of her fornication:* now she that made them drunk, and those that were made drunk, cannot be the same. (3.) This woman sitteth on seven mountains, ver. 9, and so do not all the wicked of the world. (4.) We are commanded to come out of this Babylon, but we are not obliged to go out of the world.

2. Others would have this *woman*, or this *Babylon*, to be the old Chaldean Babylon. But, (1.) Where then is the *mystery*, mentioned ver. 5? (2.) The Babylon here mentioned, is by all agreed to be the seat of antichrist; so was that never.

3. The generality agree it to be Rome. Amongst the ancients, Tertullian, Jerome, Ambrose, Œcumenius, Augustine, Eusebius: of later writers, Beda, Aquinas, Salmeron, Pererius, Bellarmine, Lapide, Ribera, (all papists,) besides a multitude of protestant writers. (1.) That city is also like old Babylon for power and greatness, for oppression and tyranny of and over God's Israel; besides, the city here mentioned is described by two characters, agreeing to none but Rome, ver. 9, dwelling upon seven hills. (2.) Reigning over the kings of the earth: for the first Rome is the only city in the world founded upon seven hills, and famed for it by its old poets, Ovid, Virgil, Horace, Propertius, &c. It is attested to be so founded by Plutarch, Pliny, Dionysius, Halicarnassæus. The names of these hills are known: Palatinus, Quirinalis, Aventinus, Celius, Veminalis, Esquilinus, Capitolinus. Both papist and protestant writers agree that here by Babylon Rome is meant; but they are divided, whether it be to be understood of Rome in its old pagan state, or in its present state, or in a state yet to come.

4. Some would have it to be Rome in its pagan state; of this mind are Grotius, and Dr. Hammond, and some others. But against this many things are said: (1.) It is manifest that God here describes Rome not as under its sixth head, viz. the pagan emperors, but as it was under its last head, the eighth king, ver. 11, as it should ascend out of the bottomless pit, ver. 8. (2.) What John saw herein mentioned as a secret about the blood of the saints, which he wondered at; now the pagan emperors' spilling the blood of saints was a thing long since done. (3.) The desolation of the Babylon here mentioned was to be final, never to be repaired, as appears by chap. xviii. 21—23; but pagan Rome was never made so desolate. (4.) If Rome pagan be here meant, then, after its fall, Rome Christian was the habitation of devils, chap. xviii. 2. (5.) Rome pagan fell upon our saints with downright blows, not with allurements, making them *drunk with the wine of her fornication*, as ver. 2.

5. The papists, who grant that by *Babylon* Rome is meant, would have it to be Rome toward the end of the world, when, they say, Rome shall apostatize from the pope to paganism again; but for this opinion there is no foundation in Scripture, nor the judgment of the ancients, and some of the papists themselves reject it as improbable and detestable.

6. The generality and best of protestant writers understand by *Babylon*, and by this *woman*, Rome, as it is at this day under the conduct of the pope, for which they give these reasons. (1.) Because it cannot be understood of Rome in either of the other notions, as hath been proved. (2.) Because antichrist is to *sit in the temple of God*, 2 Thess. ii. 4, as God, therefore not in any pagan city. The *mystery of iniquity* was working in the apostle's time, but, ver. 7, the Roman empire hindered the appearance of antichrist till the popes had wrung Rome out of their hands, and were the sole rulers there; then antichrist showed himself. (3.) Because there is nothing said of this *great whore*, or this *Babylon*, but admirably agreeth to Rome in its present state.

^m ch. 18. 12, 16.
ⁿ Dan. 11. 38. † Gr. *gilded*.
^o Jer. 51. 7. ch. 18. 6.
^p ch. 14. 8.

4 And the woman ^mwas arrayed in purple and scarlet colour, ⁿand †decked with gold and precious stones and pearls, ^ohaving a golden cup in her hand ^pfull of abominations and filthiness of her fornication:

And the woman was arrayed in purple and scarlet colour;

REVELATION XVII

purple was the colour of kings and princes: this *woman*, chap. xviii. 7, said she was *queen*. *Scarlet* also was a rich and noble colour, anciently most used in a time of war. How much it is in use with the pope and his cardinals, is sufficiently known. *And decked with gold and precious stones and pearls;* this shows the worldly riches of the papacy. *Having a golden cup in her hand full of abominations and filthiness of her fornication;* alluring and tempting persons to idolatry, as whores use to do with their philters, or enchanted cups, allure and provoke men to sensual satisfactions.

5 And upon her forehead *was* a name written, q MYSTERY, BABYLON r THE GREAT, s THE MOTHER OF ∥ HARLOTS AND ABOMINATIONS OF THE EARTH.

q 2 Thes. 2. 7.
r ch. 11. 8.
& 14. 8. &
16. 19. & 18.
2, 10, 21.
s ch. 18. 9.
& 19. 2.
∥ Or, *fornications*.

And upon her forehead was a name written; as public harlots were wont to write their names, some upon the fronts of their houses, some upon their foreheads: it denotes the open guilt and impudence of this spiritual harlot. *Mystery;* that is, there is a mystery in what follows in her name. *Babylon the great;* not to be understood of the Chaldean Babylon, but of a city or polity under the gospel; as, chap. xi. 8, she was *called spiritually Sodom and Egypt,* so also in a spiritual or mystical sense she is called *Babylon,* because a city like to Babylon for idolatry and persecution of God's Israel. *The mother of harlots;* not a mere harlot, but one that bred up harlots, and nursed up idolatry, communicating it to others. This is the true name of Rome, instead of "holy mother church." *And abominations of the earth;* a place in which not only idolatry reigneth, but all abominable things committed in the world; carnal whoredom tolerated by them, and sodomy, &c.

6 And I saw t the woman drunken u with the blood of the saints, and with the blood of x the martyrs of Jesus: and when I saw her, I wondered with great admiration.

t ch. 18. 24.
u ch. 13. 15.
& 16. 6.
x ch. 6. 9, 10.
& 12. 11.

And I saw the woman, the papacy, *drunken with the blood of the saints, and with the blood of the martyrs of Jesus;* filled with the blood of those holy ones, which she caused to be slain for bearing testimony to Jesus Christ. *And when I saw her, I wondered with great admiration;* which he would not have done had it been a pagan Rome he had seen in this vision. But that any that owned Christ, and called themselves the holy church, should kill men for bearing testimony to Christ, and adherence to his rule of faith and life, this caused in John a just wonderment.

7 And the angel said unto me, Wherefore didst thou marvel? I will tell thee the mystery of the woman, and of the beast that carrieth her, which hath the seven heads and ten horns.

The angel promiseth to open this vision, it being the key of the former vision, and is the only vision expounded throughout this whole book.

8 The beast that thou sawest was, and is not; and y shall ascend out of the bottomless pit, and z go into perdition: and they that dwell on the earth a shall wonder, b whose names were not written in the book of life from the foundation of the world, when they behold the beast that was, and is not, and yet is.

y ch. 11. 7.
& 13. 1.
z ch. 13. 10.
ver. 11.
a ch. 13. 3.
b ch. 13. 8.

The beast that thou sawest; this beast was the Roman empire, the *scarlet coloured beast* which carried the whore, ver. 3. *Was, and is not; was* of old, in Rome's pagan state, and *is not,* not in that form, not now pagan; *and yet is* (as is said in the close of the verse) the same in another form, idolatrous and persecuting. *And shall ascend out of the bottomless pit;* either, out of the sea, which signifies a multitude of people; or, from hell; the word signifies both. *And go into perdition;* and shall certainly be destroyed. *And they that dwell on the earth shall wonder, &c.:* but before he goes into perdition he shall so cheat the world, that the generality of the people shall wonder at the beast, (see chap. xiii. 8,) setting aside those who are chosen of God to eternal salvation; the one hundred and forty-four thousand, mentioned chap. xiv. I conceive that which hath made interpreters so divided in their notions about this beast is, because those words, *and yet is,* are not added in the beginning of the verse, which being understood, there appears no difficulty considerable; for it is certain the Roman empire was from before Christ, and continued pagan till the year 310; then was not pagan, but Christian, yet after some years was again as idolatrous and bloody against Christians, as the old pagan empire was; especially when swallowed up by the pope, *the beast* with *two horns like a lamb.* This is the *beast* with *seven heads and ten horns,* chap. xiii. 1.

9 And c here *is* the mind which hath wisdom. d The seven heads are seven mountains, on which the woman sitteth.

c ch. 13. 18.
d ch. 13. 1.

And here is the mind which hath wisdom; that is, here is that which requireth a mind endued with spiritual wisdom. *The seven heads are seven mountains, on which the woman sitteth;* the *seven heads* which he saw the beast with, signified *seven mountains* or hills upon which Rome is situated; they were named before: see the notes on ver. 3. They tell us now Rome is situated in Campo Martio. *Resp.* Whatever it now is, certain it is, that in St. John's time it was situated upon them, and they are now within the compass of Rome.

10 And there are seven kings · five are fallen, and one is, *and* the other is not yet come; and when he cometh, he must continue a short space.

And there are seven kings; the *seven heads* do not only signify seven hills or mountains, but also *seven kings,* that is, (according to the best interpretation I meet with,) seven forms of government which ruled Rome; the term *kings,* in Scripture, signifying rulers, whether the government was in single persons, or more, as Deut. xxxiii. 5. Rome was governed, 1. By kings. 2. By consuls. 3. Tribunes. 4. Decemvirs. 5. Dictators. 6. Emperors that were pagans. 7. Emperors that were Christians. *Five are fallen;* five of these were fallen, extinguished before John's time, viz. the government by kings, consuls, tribunes, decemvirs, dictators. *And one is;* the government by pagan emperors was at that time in being. *And the other is not yet come;* the government by Christian emperors was not yet in being. *And when he cometh, he must continue a short space;* and when it came, it held but a little time before the bishops of Rome wrested the government of Italy out of their hands. This to me seemeth the most probable interpretation of this difficult text.

11 And the beast that was, and is not, even he is the eighth, and is of the seven, e and goeth into perdition.

e ver. 8.

And the beast that was, and is not, even he is the eighth; this made the eighth succession of governments in the Roman empire. *And is of the seven;* this was of the seventh head; for although this was the eighth government in order as we have counted them, yet one of these, viz. the seventh, (which was that of true Christian emperors,) must not be counted as one of the seven heads, which were all idolatrous: so though this was the eighth government, yet he was one of the seven heads, i. e. idolatrous governments. *And goeth into perdition;* and to be destroyed as they were.

12 And f the ten horns which thou sawest are ten kings, which have received no kingdom as yet; but receive power as kings one hour with the beast.

f Dan. 7. 20.
Zech. 1. 18,
19, 21.
ch. 13. 1.

And the ten horns which thou sawest are ten kings: possibly by *ten kings* here are not meant monarchs, but governments. *Which have received no kingdom as yet;* which were not in being in John's time, nor in many years after. *But receive power as kings one hour with the beast;* but should, during some time of the beast's reign, have power with the papacy, employing their power with his to establish his idolatry. But who these ten monarchs are, or what these ten governments are, I must confess myself at a loss to determine. It is plain they should be, 1. Such as should be contemporaneous with the reign of the beast. 2. Such as employed their power in conjunction with his. 3. Such as should afterwards be instruments to ruin the papacy, ver. 16, 17. The beast's reign being twelve hundred and sixty years, there hath been, and will be, such a variety of princes and governments, as it is very hard to determine who they shall be. But their being contemporaneous with the beast, makes me think it cannot be understood either of any that were in the world before the year 606, when the beast's reign began (though *the mystery of iniquity* was working, and the *image of the beast* was making, long before); as also that the ten barbarous nations that disturbed Italy from the year 410 till near 600 could not be meant, being all before antichrist came to any reign; nor did they ever show any great love or hatred to the pope; sometimes serving, sometimes opposing him, as suited their respective civil interests. I am very inclinable to think the prophecy to concern some kings nearer the end of antichrist's reign, who though for a while they served the papacy, yet shall at last be instruments to ruin him; but who they are shall do this, or when it shall be, I cannot determine.

13 These have one mind, and shall give their power and strength unto the beast.

They shall all be papists, and for a while shall employ all their power and strength to uphold the popish religion.

g ch. 16. 14. & 19. 19.

14 ᵍ These shall make war with the Lamb, and the Lamb shall overcome them: ʰ for he is Lord of lords, and King of kings: ⁱ and they that are with him are called, and chosen, and faithful.

h Deu. 10.17. 1 Tim. 6. 15. ch. 19. 16.
i Jer. 50. 44. 45. ch. 14. 4.

These shall make war with the Lamb; these ten kings shall a while oppose themselves to the gospel, taking part with antichrist. *And the Lamb shall overcome them;* Christ shall overcome them by the power of his gospel, or some of them that way; others, that will not be converted, shall be confounded, some way or other brought to ruin. *For he is Lord of lords and King of kings: and they that are with him are called, and chosen, and faithful;* for he hath a power above others, and knows how to fit instruments for his purpose; so as those whom he shall make use of in this work, shall be chosen persons, and faithful in discharge of the trust committed to them.

k Is. 8. 7. ver. 1.

15 And he saith unto me, ᵏ The waters which thou sawest, where the whore sitteth, are peoples, and multitudes, and nations, and tongues.

l ch. 13. 7.

John saw *the great whore* sitting upon *seven mountains,* ver. 9, and *upon many waters,* ver. 1; these signified her dominion and jurisdiction over many people.

m Jer. 50. 41, 42. ch. 16. 12.
n Ezek. 16. 37,—44. ch. 18 16.
o ch. 18. 8.

16 And the ten horns which thou sawest upon the beast, ᵐ these shall hate the whore, and shall make her desolate ⁿ and naked, and shall eat her flesh, and ᵒ burn her with fire.

And the ten horns which thou sawest upon the beast: see ver. 3, 12. *These shall hate the whore, &c.;* the ten kings shall apostatize from the papacy, and be great instruments of God to ruin it. When we see some other kingdoms, now in vassalage to the pope, do as much as hath been done in England, and Scotland, and Sweden, and some other places, we may possibly understand this prophecy better than we yet do.

p 2 Thes. 2. 11.

17 ᵖ For God hath put in their hearts to fulfil his will, and to agree, and give their kingdom unto the beast, ᵠ until the words of God shall be fulfilled.

q ch. 10. 7.

For God hath put in their hearts to fulfil his will; that is, what he hath determined shall be done; not what he commandeth men to do, or approveth their doing of; his permissive will. *And to agree, and give their kingdom unto the beast;* for God puts malice against himself and his Son into the hearts of none, which is the cause of any persons' assisting the beast. *Until the words of God shall be fulfilled;* nor shall they do this any longer than till the forty-two months be expired, which he by his word hath declared he hath allowed to these mongrel Gentiles, to tread down the outward court: but till that time be expired, these kingdoms will agree to give their power to the beast, whom about the expiration of that time they shall hate, and help to destroy.

18 And the woman which thou sawest ʳ is that great city, ˢ which reigneth over the kings of the earth.

r ch. 16. 19. s ch. 12, 4.

And the woman which thou sawest: see ver. 3. *Is that great city;* that is, signifieth that great city, Babylon the great: see ver. 5. *Which reigneth over the kings of the earth,* commanding and punishing them as she pleaseth. To what person or power that either now is, or ever was, upon the earth, is this applicable, but to the pope, who makes emperors hold his stirrup, sends his edicts to princes to execute, excommunicates them, and interdicts their subjects, and arms them against them if they refuse? So that if the pope sits upon seven hills, or Rome be built upon them; if the papacy hath allured the inhabitants of the earth to idolatry; if in her idolatries she be the image of the old pagan idolaters; if to her many princes have given their power and strength; if she reigneth over the kings of the earth; and these things be applicable to no other person or government; there is no more doubt, whether the pope be antichrist, and Rome mystical Babylon, which shall certainly be destroyed for her idolatries and shedding the blood of God's holy ones, than there is of what we have chap. i. 1, 2. that this book contains *The Revelation of Jesus Christ, to show unto his servants things which must shortly come to pass;* which he sent and signified by his angel unto his servant John; *who bare record of the word of God, and of the testimony of Jesus Christ, and of all things that he saw.*

CHAP. XVIII

A mighty angel declareth the fall of Babylon, 1—3. *God's people commanded to depart out of her,* 4—7. *Her judgment,* 8. *The kings of the earth,* 9, 10, *and the merchants,* 11—16, *and mariners, lament over her,* 17—19. *The saints are excited to rejoice over her,* 20. *A millstone cast into the sea denoteth her irrecoverable fall,* 21—24.

AND ᵃ after these things I saw another angel come down from heaven, having great power; ᵇ and the earth was lightened with his glory.

a ch. 17. 1.
b Ezek. 43.2.

It is a matter of no great moment, whether by this *angel* we understand Christ, or a created angel; the description agreeth to Christ, and may agree to a created angel. *Having great power;* to whom God had given power and authority to declare the ruin of Babylon. *And the earth was lightened with his glory;* and he had communicated to him a great glory, suited to his splendour and greatness whose messenger he was.

2 And he cried mightily with a strong voice, saying, ᶜ Babylon the great is fallen, is fallen, and ᵈ is become the habitation of devils, and the hold of every foul spirit, and ᵉ a cage of every unclean and hateful bird.

c Is. 13. 19. & 21. 9. Jer. 51. 8. ch. 14. 8.
d Is. 13. 21. & 21. 8. & 34. 14. Jer. 50. 39. & 51. 37. e Is. 14. 23. & 34. 11. Mark 5. 2, 3.

And he cried mightily with a strong voice, saying, Babylon the great is fallen, is fallen: whoever was meant by the *angel* whom John saw, ver. 1, his business was to give warning to the whole world, (therefore he crieth *with a strong voice,*) that Rome, the *great city, the mother* of spiritual harlots, should fall. This angel was a prophet, and the messenger of him who calls the things that are not as if they were; and therefore he speaks in a Divine, prophetic style: the prophets (ordinarily) speaking of things to come as past, or present, to denote the certain futurity of them, and doubling their words to assure us of it; for this, *is fallen,* is expounded by *shall be thrown down,* ver. 21. We read of this angel, chap. xiv. 8; but it is ordinary with prophets to repeat the same things, and it is done as to the Chaldean Babylon, the type to this antitype, both Isaiah and Jeremiah declared in more than one sermon its certain approaching ruin. These words are taken from Isa. xxi. 9, where the word *fallen* is doubled, as here. They are found also, Jer. li. 8. God here explaineth what he had said before, chap. xiv. 8. *And is become the habitation of devils, &c.:* the words

REVELATION XVIII

are such as might signify a sinful fall, or apostacy; and what is here, is true of it in that sense; idols in Scripture being ordinarily called *devils:* but they seem rather to be understood of a penal fall, for such is that spoken of Isa. xxi. 9, after which it should become a habitation of devils, and a cage of unclean birds. See the like spoken of literal Babylon, Isa. xiii. 19—21; wild beasts and hateful birds usually frequenting desolate places.

3 For all nations ᶠhave drunk of the wine of the wrath of her fornication, and the kings of the earth have committed fornication with her, ᵍand the merchants of the earth are waxed rich through the ║abundance of her delicacies.

For all nations have drunk of the wine of the wrath of her fornication; that is, her fornications which she brought this wrath upon her. *And the kings of the earth have committed, &c.;* she hath not only herself committed idolatry, but allured others to it, teaching them to break the commandments of God, and hath influenced princes to establish, and propagate, and to uphold, and maintain it; and all sorts of men have been bewitched by her, growing rich by her abundance, and being drenched in her luxury.

4 And I heard another voice from heaven, saying, ʰCome out of her, my people, that ye be not partakers of her sins, and that ye receive not of her plagues.

And I heard another voice from heaven, saying: a command from God. *Come out of her, my people:* they are the words of God by his prophet, Jer. l. 8; li. 6, calling to his people, that the years of their captivity being now expired, and they having a liberty to go back to Jerusalem, they would not linger longer in Babylon, nor partake *of her sins;* for God was about to destroy that place; and if they were found in it, they would be in danger of being destroyed with it, especially if they were found partakers of its sins. But they are also a general warning to all to take heed of any fellowship with idolaters; and so the apostle applieth part of these words, 2 Cor. vi. 17. Here they are applied to mystical Babylon, which is Rome antichristian. God calls to all that either love him, or their own souls, to forsake the communion of it; for while they continue in it, they must partake of its sins, worshipping the beast, by paying, at his command, a Divine homage to saints and angels, to the virgin Mary, to images and statues, nay, to a piece of baker's bread; and doing so, they will be involved in her *plagues.* This text looks terribly upon those who apostatize to that idolatry; and instead of coming out, (in obedience to the command of God,) being come out, go in again, and that not by compulsion, but out of choice, and voluntarily.

5 ⁱFor her sins have reached unto heaven, and ᵏGod hath remembered her iniquities.

For her sins have reached unto heaven; that is, the cry of her sins; according to what is said of Sodom, (one of the types of antichrist,) Gen. xviii. 20, 21. *And God hath remembered her iniquities;* the time is come when God will punish her for her idolatry and persecution, and all the abominable things done and committed by her.

6 ˡReward her even as she rewarded you, and double unto her double according to her works: ᵐin the cup which she hath filled ⁿfill to her double.

This verse soundeth in mine ears, as if God had reserved the ruin of the papacy to be effected by some protestant hands, some of those whom they had persecuted; if not some of their persons, yet some of the same faith.

7 ᵒHow much she hath glorified herself, and lived deliciously, so much torment and sorrow give her: for she saith in her heart, I sit a ᵖqueen, and am no widow, and shall see no sorrow.

How much she hath glorified herself, and lived deliciously, so much torment and sorrow give her: this speaketh thus much; That whenever God's time cometh for the ruin of the papacy, the condition of all that party shall appear as miserable as it appears now splendid and happy. *For she saith in her heart, I sit a queen, and am no widow, and shall see no sorrow;* and one great reason of this so great affliction, will be the pride, presumption, and security of that faction, much after the rate of old Babylon, Isa. xlvii. 8. Old Babylon thought itself impregnable; and new mystical Babylon thinks herself infallible and impregnable too; the only church, (if we will believe her,) against whom the gates of hell shall not prevail.

8 Therefore shall her plagues come ᑫin one day, death, and mourning, and famine; and ʳshe shall be utterly burned with fire: ˢfor strong *is* the Lord God who judgeth her.

Therefore shall her plagues come in one day; as was threatened to old Babylon, Isa. xlvii. 9. *In one day;* that is, in a short time. *Death, and mourning, and famine; and she shall be utterly burned with fire;* all manner of judgments, till she be fully consumed. *For strong is the Lord God who judgeth her;* for she hath to do with a strong Lord: she thinks she hath secured herself from man, by interesting kings and princes in her quarrel; but it is the Lord that judgeth her, and she will find him strong enough to accomplish his word upon her.

9 And ᵗthe kings of the earth, who have committed fornication and lived deliciously with her, ᵘshall bewail her, and lament for her, ˣwhen they shall see the smoke of her burning,

Not all of them, for some of them shall help to burn her, chap. xvii. 16; but such as God had left to their hardness of heart, that they still live in her fellowship and communion: or, if others also, it must proceed from their humanity, not being able to see so splendid a city, as that of Rome, ruined, and so many ruined as will perish by her fall, without the moving of their bowels by some pity and commiseration.

10 Standing afar off for the fear of her torment, saying, ʸAlas, alas that great city Babylon, that mighty city! ᶻfor in one hour is thy judgment come.

As well as they loved her, they will not come nigh her in the time of her torments; the fire will be too hot for them, they will only stand aloof off, and pity her, that so great and brave a city should be so suddenly ruined; such a gay and splendid church, so politicly founded and put together, should be in a sudden so broken to pieces.

11 And ᵃthe merchants of the earth shall weep and mourn over her; for no man buyeth their merchandise any more:

As the merchants, Ezek. xxvii. 27, lamented for Tyre, that they could barter and truck no more there, because all the trade thereof was destroyed; so those ecclesiastical merchants, that were wont to trade with Rome for indulgences, and pardons, and dispensations, and faculties, for cardinals' caps, and bishoprics, and prebendaries, and other church preferments, shall lament when the papacy falls, that there will be no more such merchandise to be bought or sold there.

12 ᵇ The merchandise of gold, and silver, and precious stones, and of pearls, and fine linen, and purple, and silk, and scarlet, and all ║thyine wood, and all manner vessels of ivory, and all manner vessels of most precious wood, and of brass, and iron, and marble,

13 And cinnamon, and odours, and ointments, and frankincense, and wine, and oil, and fine flour, and wheat, and beasts, and sheep, and horses, and chariots, and ║slaves, and ᶜsouls of men.

14 And the fruits that thy soul lusted after are departed from thee, and all things which were dainty and goodly are departed from thee, and thou shalt find them no more at all.

Here is a large enumeration of several sorts of wares, such as were most precious, *gold, silver, precious stones*; such as were most useful for ornament, *fine linen, purple, silk, scarlet* most gratifying the exterior senses, *thyine wood, odours, ointments, &c.*; most necessary, *beasts, sheep, horses, chariots*; all which, as is prophesied, shall depart from Rome: that is, whatsoever she had, which allured men into her idolatrous communion; all their idols and images, cardinals' caps, priests' copes, all their preferments and dignities, whatsoever served the lust of the eye, the lust of the flesh, or the pride of life; whatsoever their own carnal and ambitious minds, or the carnal and ambitious minds of others that courted this whore, thirsted after, which brought them to seek her communion; they should all perish, and she be despoiled of them. It is very remarkable, that here is one piece of merchandise to be had no where but at Rome, viz. the *souls of men;* which lets us know they are no earthly merchants that are here understood. As souls are to be sold a thousand ways, so they are to be bought; by paying for pardons, indulgences, dispensations, so the silly chapmen think they buy their own souls; by purchasing of cardinals' caps, bishoprics, great livings, all manner of ecclesiastical dignities and preferments, so they really buy the souls of others; but when the papacy shall be wholly destroyed, none of these things shall any more be found.

d ver. 3, 11.

15 ᵈThe merchants of these things, which were made rich by her, shall stand afar off for the fear of her torment, weeping and wailing,

Not knowing how to help her, and fearing lest the buyers and sellers should be punished both alike; yet bewailing themselves that their trading is destroyed, and they are like to buy such pennyworths no more.

e ch. 17. 4.

16 And saying, Alas, alas that great city, ᵉthat was clothed in fine linen, and purple, and scarlet, and decked with gold, and precious stones, and pearls!

Alas, alas that great city! the Church of Rome, that was so gay, and splendid, and rich, and glorious.

f ver. 10.
g Is. 23. 14.
Ezek. 27. 29.

17 ᶠFor in one hour so great riches is come to nought. And ᵍevery shipmaster, and all the company in ships, and sailors, and as many as trade by sea, stood afar off,

In one hour; that is, suddenly. The term denotes rather the surprisal of this judgment, than the short space of time within which it should be effected.

h Ezek. 27. 30, 31.
ver. 9.
i ch. 13. 4.

18 ʰAnd cried when they saw the smoke of her burning, saying, ⁱWhat *city is* like unto this great city!

k Josh. 7. 6.
1 Sam. 4. 12.
Job 2. 12.
Ezek. 27. 30.

19 And ᵏthey cast dust on their heads, and cried, weeping and wailing, saying, Alas, alas that great city, wherein were made rich all that had ships in the sea by reason of her costliness! ˡfor in one hour is she made desolate.

l ver. 8.

We all know ship-masters and sailors are persons that live by carrying merchants' goods; and therefore, properly, the terms signify all such persons (of what rank and order soever) who get their livings by serving this mystical Babylon, whether silversmiths that make shrines for Diana, or clerks, or notaries, or any officers in that church, employed in gathering its revenues of annats and first-fruits, selling of offices, gathering of Peter-pence, drawing of pardons and indulgences, or dispensations, or such as in that synagogue hold any offices of profit. All who will be highly concerned in the ruin of the papacy, as that by the upholding of which they live, by reason of the great riches thus coming in, the whole rabble of their ecclesiastical hierarchy, with all their petty officers, seem to be here meant.

m Is. 44. 23. & 49. 13.
Jer. 51. 48.
n Luke 11. 49, 50.
ch. 19. 2.

20 ᵐRejoice over her, *thou* heaven, and *ye* holy apostles and prophets; for ⁿGod hath avenged you on her.

Rejoice over her, thou heaven; that is, over her ruin, which is not a more proper object for the sorrow and mourning of all her adherents and dependants, than of the joy of all spiritual, heavenly persons, which are the true church, who oppose this antichristian synagogue. *And ye holy apostles and prophets; for God hath avenged you on her:* you also that were apostles of our Lord Jesus Christ, and such as have been exercised as prophets in revealing to men God's mind and will, do you rejoice, for God hath revenged you upon her, for your doctrine corrupted by her, your rules of worship violated, and some of your blood that hath been spilt, and for all the indignities you have suffered from her.

21 And a mighty angel took up a stone like a great millstone, and cast *it* into the sea, saying, ᵒThus with violence shall that great city Babylon be thrown down, and ᵖshall be found no more at all.

o Jer. 51. 64.
p ch. 12. 8. & 16. 20.

And a mighty angel took up a stone like a great millstone, and cast it into the sea; for a sign or symbol of the irreparable ruin of Rome, signified by that great millstone which had ground to powder so many of God's holy ones. By this sign God shows his prophet, 1. That Rome shall be ruined. 2. That it shall be done with violence. 3. That it shall be a total, utter ruin, from whence it shall never recover.

22 ᑫAnd the voice of harpers, and musicians, and of pipers, and trumpeters, shall be heard no more at all in thee; and no craftsman, of whatsoever craft *he be,* shall be found any more in thee; and the sound of a millstone shall be heard no more at all in thee;

q Is. 24. 8.
Jer. 7. 34. & 16. 9. & 25. 10.
Ezek. 26. 13.

23 ʳAnd the light of a candle shall shine no more at all in thee; ˢand the voice of the bridegroom and of the bride shall be heard no more at all in thee: for ᵗthy merchants were the great men of the earth; ᵘfor by thy sorceries were all nations deceived.

r Jer. 25. 10.
s Jer. 7. 34. & 16. 9. & 25. 10. & 33. 11.
t Is. 23. 8.
u 2 Kings 9. 22. Nah. 3. 4. ch. 17. 2, 5.

And the voice of harpers, &c., shall be heard no more at all in thee; all those seem to me but the expression of an utter ruin and desolation, by various phrases and expressions; they should have no more occasion of mirth, nor any more business done in their city. If any will understand these expressions, of their organs, and other musical instruments used in worship, and of spiritual craftsmen, I shall not contradict it; but I think it more proper to understand the words more largely. *For thy merchants were the great men of the earth; for by thy sorceries were all nations deceived:* though thou hast had a trade with great men, and by the enchanted cups of the wine of thy fornication hast intoxicated many in all nations, yet thou shalt use that trade no more; the nations shall be deceived no more by thee; here shall be an end of thee. And one thing that brings thee to thy ruin, shall be thy seducing others to idolatry, so as they have seemed to reasonable men to be bewitched by thee.

24 And ˣin her was found the blood of prophets, and of saints, and of all that ʸwere slain upon the earth.

x ch. 17. 6.
y Jer. 51. 49.

In the rubbish of Rome, when destroyed, will be found the blood of all those holy servants of God, whether ministers of the gospel, or professors of it, who ever since the year 606, when the pope came first to his power, have been put to death for the testimony of Christ, and a faithful adherence to the purity of doctrine by him delivered, the purity of worship by him prescribed and directed, or the purity of discipline by his direction set up. As it is storied, that upon the dissolution of abbeys, and monasteries, and nunneries here in England, there were found in holes of walls, and ponds, the skulls and bones of many infants, the supposed bastards of those fathers: so, though men cannot or will not see it now, yet when the papacy shall have its period, men shall understand, that no prophet nor righteous man hath violently been put to death for the truth out of Rome, that is, out of the jurisdiction and influence of Rome; but though it may be they have been no professed papists that have been the cause or instruments of their death, yet they have done it as influenced from that bloody city; and the principles have been perfectly popish and antichristian which madly hurried them on to such cruelties. It was one of Luthers reasons why he would have none put to death for heresy, (as they call it,) because he would have this particular character reserved for that antichristian synagogue.—But ah, Lord Jesus! when shall these things be? or who shall live when the wise providence of God shall effect them, to join with the whole church, both triumphant and militant, in the song which we have prophesied of upon this occasion in the next chapter. *It is not for* us *to know the times or the seasons, which the Father hath put in his own power,* Acts i. 7.

CHAP. XIX

God is praised in heaven for judging the great whore, and avenging the blood of his saints, 1—5. *The triumph because of the marriage of the Lamb,* 6—9. *The angel who showed John these things, refuseth to be worshipped,* 10. *The vision of the Word of God sitting upon a white horse, and followed by his armies,* 11—16. *The fowls called to feast on the flesh of those that took part with the beast,* 17—19. *The beast and false prophet cast into the lake of fire and brimstone; and the rest slain,* 20, 21.

a ch. 11. 15.   AND after these things [a]I heard a great voice of much people in heaven, saying,
b ch. 4. 11 & 7. 10, 12. & 12. 10.   Alleluia; [b]Salvation, and glory, and honour, and power, unto the Lord our God:

And after these things; after the pouring out of the fifth vial *upon the seat of the beast,* chap. xvi. 10; for chap. xvii. and xviii., as we have formerly hinted, is but a parenthesis to the history. God, in this chapter, more fully describes the effects of the pouring out that vial. *I heard a great voice of much people in heaven, saying:* it may be understood either of the third heavens, or the heaven upon earth, the church of God; for the church triumphant and militant both will concur in praising God for the ruin of antichrist's power. *Alleluia* is a Hebrew word, and signifies, Praise ye the Lord. *Salvation, and glory, and honour, and power, unto the Lord our God:* all these are but terms of honour and praise given unto God, acknowledging that the church's salvation is from him, the effect of his power; and that to him, upon that account, all honour and glory imaginable is due, as having shown himself his people's God.

c ch. 15. 3. & 16. 7.   2 For [c]true and righteous *are* his judgments: for he hath judged the great whore, which did corrupt the earth with
d Deut. 32. 43. ch. 6. 10. & 18. 20.   her fornication, and [d]hath avenged the blood of his servants at her hand.

For true and righteous are his judgments: the Lord's *judgments,* in holy writ, sometimes signify his precepts, sometimes his dispensations of providence, either more generally, or more specially; in which last sense it signifies (as here) his punishment of sinners: these are just and righteous, and therefore called *judgments. For he hath judged the great whore,* for he hath punished the papacy, *which did corrupt the earth with her fornication,* which corrupted a great part of the earth with its idolatry. *And hath avenged the blood of his servants at her hand;* and by these judicial dispensations God hath also taken vengeance on them for the blood of his saints shed by them. It is remarkable, that all along this book idolatry and persecution are made the beast's provoking sins.

e Is. 34. 10. ch. 14. 11. & 18. 9, 18.   3 And again they said, Alleluia. And [e]her smoke rose up for ever and ever.

As the church proceeded in her praises, so God proceeded in his judgments upon the great whore, until she was ruined past recovery.

f ch. 4. 4, 6, 10. & 5. 14.   4 And [f]the four and twenty elders and the four beasts fell down and worshipped God that sat on the throne, saying, [g]Amen; Alleluia.
g 1 Chro. 16. 36. Neh. 5. 13. & 8. 6. ch. 5. 14.

See the notes on chap. iv. All the heavenly choir praise God upon this account, desiring that the Lord would fulfil what he had begun.

5 And a voice came out of the throne, saying, [h]Praise our God, all ye his servants, and ye that fear him, [i]both small and great.
h Ps. 134. 1. & 135. 1. i ch. 11. 18. & 20. 12.

And a voice came out of the throne, from Christ, declaring it the will of God, that all holy ones should praise him upon this account.

6 [k]And I heard as it were the voice of a great multitude, and as the voice of many waters, and as the voice of mighty thunderings, saying, Alleluia: for [l]the Lord God omnipotent reigneth.
k Ezek. 1. 24. & 43. 2. ch. 14. 2.
l ch. 11. 15, 17. & 12. 10. & 21. 22.

By this *multitude* most understand the church. Some understand the Jews as well as the Gentiles, supposing that they shall be before this time converted and added to the church. Others think their conversion is the marriage spoken of in the next verse. The saints do not rejoice in the ruin of their adversaries, but in the glory of God advanced by it, and as his kingdom is by it promoted.

7 Let us be glad and rejoice, and give honour to him: for [m]the marriage of the Lamb is come, and his wife hath made herself ready.
m Matt. 22. 2. & 25. 10. 2 Cor. 11. 2. Eph. 5. 32. ch. 21. 2, 9.

A late reverend author tells us, That as there is a threefold resurrection mentioned in Scripture; 1. A rising to a newness of life, Eph. v. 14; 2. The conversion of the Jews, called *life from the dead,* Rom. xi. 15; 3. In the end of the world: so there is a threefold marriage of the Lamb; 1. To particular souls, when by faith they are united to Christ; 2. To his church completed, when the Jews shall be called; 3. When all his elect shall be made one with him in glory, after the general resurrection. He seemeth to understand it of all these. Probably the conversion of the Jews stayeth for the fall of the papacy, whose worship and persecution are great scandals to them. Probably also, upon the fall of it, many will be converted besides the Jews, and the general resurrection will not be far off. The learned Dr. More seems to restrain it to the Jews' conversion; I had rather understand it more generally.

8 And [n]to her was granted that she should be arrayed in fine linen, clean and || white: [o]for the fine linen is the righteousness of saints.
n Ps. 45. 13, 14. Ezek. 16. 10. ch. 3. 18.
|| Or, *bright.*
o Ps. 132. 9.

And to her was granted; that is, to the Lamb's wife, whether Jews or Gentiles, or both. *That she should be arrayed in fine linen, clean and white;* that she should be clothed with the righteousness of Christ, reckoned to her for righteousness. This *is the righteousness of the saints;* called *the righteousness of God,* Rom. i. 17; a righteousness *through the faith of Christ,* Phil. iii. 9: called *righteousness,* in the Greek, because there are many saints to be clothed with it; and because it is imputed both for justification and sanctification, not to excuse us from holiness, but to make up our defects.

9 And he saith unto me, Write, [p]Blessed *are* they which are called unto the marriage supper of the Lamb. And he saith unto me, [q]These are the true sayings of God.
p Matt. 22. 2, 3. Luke 14, 15, 16.
q ch. 21. 5. & 23. 6.

And he saith unto me, Write; write it, as a business of moment, of which a record is fit to be kept. *Blessed are they which are called to the marriage supper of the Lamb;* that is, (say those who understand by *the marriage of the Lamb* the Jews' conversion,) who live in this happy period of time when the Jews shall be converted, and with the Gentiles make one gospel church. But this seems to me not sufficient. The *marriage* is one thing, the *supper* another, and (ordinarily) consequential to the marriage itself.

r ch. 22. 8.
s Acts 10.26.
& 14. 14, 15.
ch. 22. 9.
t 1 John 5.
10. ch. 12.
17.

10 And ʳI fell at his feet to worship him. And he said unto me, ˢSee *thou do it* not: I am thy fellowservant, and of thy brethren ᵗthat have the testimony of Jesus: worship God: for the testimony of Jesus is the spirit of prophecy.

And I fell at his feet to worship him: prostration, or falling at the feet of superiors, to pay them an homage in consideration of their superiority, was ordinarily used in those Eastern countries, Gen. xliv. 14; 1 Sam. xxv. 24; 2 Kings iv. 37; Esth. viii. 3. To *worship him*, therefore, here must be understood of prayer or praise, which are pieces of Divine adoration, which it is not probable this great apostle would have offered, had he not mistaken him, and thought him an uncreated angel. *And he said unto me, See thou do it not;* but the angel doth not only refuse it, but with some indignation; "Ορα μὴ, Have a care you do it not. From whence we may observe, what a fig-leaf they have made to cover the papists' idolatry, in worshipping the bread in the eucharist, who (to show us their great skill in divinity) think they may be excused from idolatry in it, because *they think* the bread is turned into the body of Christ; idolatry is not to be excused by *think so's. I am thy fellow servant, and of thy brethren that have the testimony of Jesus:* the angel gives him a reason why there was no adoration due to him, because he was his equal in office, though not in nature; he was both his and all their brethren's fellow servant, who by preaching the gospel give a testimony to Christ. Well, therefore, chap. ii. and iii., may the ministers of churches be called *angels. Worship God;* there is no prayer, no praise, due but to the Creator. *For the testimony of Jesus is the spirit of prophecy:* there are divers senses given of the last phrase; but of all given, there are two which seem to me most probable: either, 1. *The spirit of* this *prophecy*, by which I have revealed these things to thee, is not mine, it is *the testimony of Jesus;* he therefore is to be adored, not I. Or, 2. Thy preaching the gospel, which is thy testimony to Christ, is as much from the Spirit of God, as my spirit of prophecy: we are therefore equals, and I am not to be worshipped more than thou art. We have the same, chap. xxii. 8, 9, to let us know that even good men may twice run into the same error; and to let us know, that by the mouth of these two witnesses this truth ought to have been established, so that papists should not after this have paid any Divine adoration to angels, much less to saints; and if invocation be no Divine adoration, nothing is. This deserveth the consideration of them, who think it so easy to excuse the popish religion from idolatry.

u ch. 15. 5.
x ch. 6. 2.
y ch. 3. 14.
z Is. 11. 4.

11 ᵘAnd I saw heaven opened, and behold ˣa white horse; and he that sat upon him *was* called ʸFaithful and True, and ᶻin righteousness he doth judge and make war.

The remaining part of this chapter is conceived more fully to open what shall come to pass under the sixth and seventh vials, mentioned chap. xvi. 12, 17, more especially the battle in *Armageddon*, mentioned there, ver. 16. There mention was made only of the armies' being gathered together; here it is more fully described. At the beginning of the gospel, (saith a late learned annotator,) John saw only a door opened, chap. iv. 1. At the resurrection of the witnesses, he saw the temple opened, chap. xi. 19. Here, after the ruin of Babylon, he seeth *heaven opened. And behold a white horse:* John saw such a horse, chap. vi. 2. Dr. More observes, that the horse with his rider signifies rule; and the white colour, prosperity and success. It appears here, that the rider was Christ, because he is called *Faithful and True*, which agrees with chap. i. 5; and by the names in the following verses, 13 and 16, given to him.

a ch. 1. 14.
& 2. 18.
b ch. 6. 2.

12 ᵃHis eyes *were* as a flame of fire, ᵇand on his head *were* many crowns;

c ch. 2. 17.
ver. 16.

ᶜand he had a name written, that no man knew, but he himself.

His eyes were as a flame of fire: see chap. i. 14; ii. 18. This denoted either his piercing knowledge, or his infinite wisdom and understanding. *And on his head were many crowns;* and there needs must be so; for, ver. 16, he is said to be the *King of kings, and Lord of lords. And he had a name written, that no man knew, but he himself;* this denoted the incomprehensibleness of his Divine essence and perfections.

d Is. 63. 2, 3.

13 ᵈAnd he *was* clothed with a vesture dipped in blood: and his name is called ᵉThe Word of God.

e John 1. 1.
1 John 5. 7.

And he was clothed with a vesture dipped in blood; either to denote that he was he who redeemed us by his blood; or rather, to signify that he was now coming forth to shed the blood of his enemies, both in vindication of his own honour and glory, or of his people; in which notion it also agrees with Isaiah's vision of him, chap. lxiii. 1—3: ver. 3, *Their blood shall be sprinkled upon my garments, and I will stain all my raiment. And his name is called The Word of God:* see the notes on John i. 1. He is also called *the Word*, chap. i. 2, a name given him hardly by any except this apostle.

f ch. 14. 20.
g Matt. 28. 3. ch. 4. 4.
& 7. 9.

14 ᶠAnd the armies *which were* in heaven followed him upon white horses, ᵍclothed in fine linen, white and clean.

And the armies which were in heaven followed him; the glorious angels, 2 Thess. i. 7, and ten thousands of his saints, Jude 14, who follow the Lamb whithersoever he goeth. *Upon white horses;* to prophesy success and victory. *Clothed in fine linen, white and clean;* to denote their glory, purity, and holiness.

h Is. 11. 4.
2 Thess. 2. 8.
ch. 1. 16.
ver. 21.
i Ps. 2. 9.
ch. 2. 27. &
12. 5.
k Is. 63. 3.
ch. 14. 19, 20.

15 And ʰout of his mouth goeth a sharp sword, that with it he should smite the nations: and ⁱhe shall rule them with a rod of iron: and ᵏhe treadeth the winepress of the fierceness and wrath of Almighty God.

And out of his mouth goeth a sharp sword: I can easily agree that this two-edged sword is the word of Christ coming out of his mouth, but not the gospel, (the time was past for that, it was the time of the sacrifice in Bozrah,) but his word of command, calling out his people to take vengeance upon the remainder of his enemies. The sword was both the sword of the Lord, commanding it to be drawn, and the sword of his people, whose hands were to wield it. *That with it he should smite the nations: and he shall rule them with a rod of iron:* with this he now smites the remainder of his enemies, and breaks them to pieces. *And he treadeth the winepress of the fierceness and wrath of Almighty God:* his enemies were the grapes, that now were put into the winepress of God's watchful providence; Christ trod them there: see Isa. lxiii. 3.

l ver. 12.
m Dan. 2. 47.
1 Tim. 6. 15.
ch. 17. 14.

16 And ˡhe hath on *his* vesture and on his thigh a name written, ᵐKING OF KINGS, AND LORD OF LORDS.

The same name as in chap. xvii. 14; 1 Tim. vi. 15; see the notes on those two texts; denoting the sovereign power and authority which he had. This he always had, but he now comes forth openly to manifest it; therefore this name is said to be *written on his vesture and on his thigh*, that all might take notice of it.

n ver. 21.
o Ezek. 39. 17.

17 And I saw an angel standing in the sun; and he cried with a loud voice, saying ⁿto all the fowls that fly in the midst of heaven, ᵒCome and gather yourselves together unto the supper of the great God;

The best conjecture I can find at the sense of these words, is, that they signify the preachers' of the gospel bold and clear foretelling the ruin of antichrist. There are divers kinds of fowls; amongst others, some that feed on flesh. These are those fowls here mentioned, such as feed upon dead carcasses. They are invited *to the supper of the great God;* called so, because it is made and prepared by the power of him who is the great God, or because it is a sacrifice to the justice of God: see 1 Sam. xvii. 46; Isa. xviii. 6; Jer. xii. 9; Ezek. xxxix. 17. God's justice upon his enemies is called *a sacrifice,* Isa. xxxiv. 6; Jer. xlvi. 10; Ezek. xxxix. 17. Idolaters were wont upon their sacrificing to have a feast; God hath also a feast upon this his sacrifice, but it is for the fowls and beasts, that feed on dead carcasses.

18 ^p That ye may eat the flesh of kings, and the flesh of captains, and the flesh of mighty men, and the flesh of horses, and of them that sit on them, and the flesh of all *men, both* free and bond, both small and great.

p Ezek. 39. 18, 20.

In the former verse God invited all the ravenous fowls to a supper, he here showeth their cheer. The meaning is no more than this, that in the great battle of Armageddon, which was for the destruction of all the remainder of the enemies of the church, whether papists, or atheists, or Turks; men of all sorts and orders should be slain, and their dead bodies made meat for the fowls of heaven, that feed on dead flesh.

19 ^q And I saw the beast, and the kings of the earth, and their armies, gathered together to make war against him that sat on the horse, and against his army.

q ch. 16. 16. & 17. 13, 14.

The beast, whether by it be understood *the dragon,* or *the beast* with *seven heads and ten horns,* or *the beast* with *two horns,* or all of them, shall before this time be all destroyed, that is, as to their power and dominion; but there will be relics left, both of pagans, and Turks, and papists, of whom it is probable that this is to be understood; viz. that after God, upon the pouring out of the fifth vial, shall have deprived the papacy of their dominion; and by the pouring out of the sixth vial, shall have deprived the Turk of his dominion; that yet such pagans, Turks, and papists, as shall be left, shall be gathered together, and make one or more great armies, with whom the Jews and Gentiles (now united in one church) shall fight under the conduct of Christ, as the Captain-general of his church, by whom they shall be overcome; and that this shall be the great battle in Armageddon, mentioned chap. xvi. 16.

20 ^r And the beast was taken, and with him the false prophet that wrought miracles before him, with which he deceived them that had received the mark of the beast, and ^s them that worshipped his image. ^t These both were cast alive into a lake of fire ^u burning with brimstone.

r ch. 16. 13, 14.
s ch. 13. 12, 15.
t ch. 20. 10. See Dan. 7. 11.
u ch. 14. 10. & 21. 8.

The issue of this great battle will be the total ruin of all the enemies of the church, their bodies being made meat for the fowls of the heaven, their souls cast into the bottomless pit of hell. The secular part of antichrist is here meant by *the beast;* the ecclesiastical antichrist, by *the false prophet,* that had cheated credulous princes and credulous people, with his pretended miracles, into an idolatry, that was but the image of the old idolatry of the heathens, in worshipping demons, and the images of such as were in great estimation amongst them while they were alive. *These both were cast alive into a lake of fire burning with brimstone;* both these, the laic and secular popish party, and all their church party, that should be left to this day, shall all now be destroyed. In a matter of fact, not likely to appear in the world yet of two hundred years or more, and thus darkly foretold, who can be positive and particular? But this seemeth the sense of it, upon the former hypotheses: That *the beast* with the *seven heads and ten horns,* mentioned chap. xiii. 1, and *the beast* with *two horns,* also there mentioned, ver. 11, are antichrist, beginning with those Roman emperors that favoured the idolatry introduced by the bishops of Rome, and ending in the universal bishop, or popes of Rome, and their clergy, who quickly wormed out the emperor's power, and for one thousand two hundred and sixty years reigned, setting up idolatry and superstition, and corrupting the doctrine of faith, and for the latter six hundred years of time, persecuting the true church of Christ more notoriously. After which God will begin to reckon with him, gradually pouring out five vials upon him. I am very inclinable to think, that we in this age are yet under the pouring out of the second of these vials, seeing little yet effected towards the ruin of the papacy, more than the exposing of their idolatries and cheats to several princes and states, and to the generality of thinking people; nor hath the providence of God proceeded far in that as yet. The three other vials are yet to be poured out upon the papacy, besides that upon Euphrates, and then this last upon all the enemies of the church together: and who shall live when God shall do these things?

21 And the remnant ^x were slain with the sword of him that sat upon the horse, which *sword* proceeded out of his mouth: ^y and all the fowls ^z were filled with their flesh.

x ver. 15.
y ver. 17, 18.
z ch. 17. 16.

In all armies there are are common soldiers as well as officers. What the issue of this battle shall be, as to the leaders in it, the former verse told us: this tells us how it shall fare with those under the command of them. It seems they shall not be excused because they followed their leaders, and did only what they bade them; Christ commands that they also should be slain. *And all the fowls were filled with their flesh;* and this bloody day (whenever it comes) will be a day of great slaughter, for the dead bodies will be enough to sup and fill all the fowls of heaven.

CHAP. XX

Satan bound for a thousand years, 1—3. *The first resurrection,* 4—6. *Satan again let loose gathereth Gog and Magog to battle, who are devoured with fire,* 7—9. *The devil cast into the lake of fire and brimstone,* 10. *The general resurrection, and last judgment,* 11—15.

We are now come to the darkest part of the whole revelation. What is meant by the *thousand years,* and *the first* and *second resurrection,* and by *Gog and Magog,* chap. xx., or *the new heavens and new earth,* and the *Jerusalem coming down from heaven,* discoursed on, chap. xxi., xxii., is very hard to say, and possibly much more cannot with any probability be conjectured as to them than hath been already said. I shall only tell my reader that, leaving him to judge what is most probable, and leaving it to the Divine Providence to give us a certain and infallible exposition of what is contained in these last three chapters.

AND I saw an angel come down from heaven, ^a having the key of the bottomless pit and a great chain in his hand.

a ch. 1. 18. & 9. 1.

The description of this angel can agree to none but Christ, or one that exerciseth a power by delegation from him: for, chap. i. 18, it is he who hath the power *of hell and death;* and it is he who alone is stronger than the devil, which must be supposed to him that binds him, or we must think the devil much tamer than he is.

2 And he laid hold on ^b the dragon, that old serpent, which is the Devil, and Satan, ^c and bound him a thousand years,

b ch. 12. 9. See 2 Pet. 2. 4. Jude 6.
c Tobit 8. 3.

There can be no question who is meant by *the dragon* here, and the *old serpent,* for the Holy Ghost interpreteth it, *the devil,* the enemy of mankind. *And bound him:* by binding also is meant the restraint of the devil in the exercise of his natural power, or the power God had before allowed him to exercise for the trial of his saints' faith and patience. The devil is restrained in the restraint of his instruments. It is expounded, ver. 3, *that he should deceive the nations no more. A thousand years:* whether these *thousand years* signify that certain space of time, or a long time, I cannot say; only it is probable, that if it signifies an uncertain, indefinite time, it is much longer time than any other period of time spoken of, (which have all hitherto been expressed by days, or months, or a lesser number of years,) by far. But what the complexion of the world shall be during this long time, or when the epocha or beginning of these *thousand years* shall be, are both of them very hard questions. It was the opinion of the old Chiliasts or Millenaries, that six thousand years of the world should pass, then antichrist with all wicked men should be destroyed; that in the next thousand years Christ should appear, and be upon the earth, ruling it with his saints; after which there would be another time of sharp persecution, according to what is said, ver. 7, to which Christ should put a period by coming to the last judgment. It is plain that (if most men be not mistaken, that have counted the years from the beginning of the world) these men were mistaken; for more than six thousand years are passed, yet there is no such thing come to pass. Divers very good and learned men (leaving out the age of the world when these thousand years should begin) have judged, that after the great battle in Armageddon, (which, as was said before, shall be after the ruin both of Turk and pope,) the church of Christ shall for a thousand years enjoy great quiet under the conduct of Christ, (as some think,) who in these thousand years shall personally be upon the earth; or of such a godly magistracy in all places of the church, as shall do and execute what Christ would have done and executed. After which the enemies of the church (mentioned here, ver. 8, under the notions of *Gog and Magog*) shall rally again, but be destroyed by Christ appearing to the last judgment. This opinion hath had, and hath, many learned and grave patrons. I shall only say this, that I do not understand what these *thousand years* mean, if they do not denote a serene and calm time for the church of God, of long continuance, before the day of judgment. Whether Christ shall be here personally, or none but saints shall be in places of power, or the power of Christ only shall be seen in so ruling and governing all magistrates, that they shall not, as before, impose superstition and idolatry, and kill or ruin men for not complying with them; but the servants of God, that worship him in spirit and truth, shall under magistrates live quiet and peaceable lives in all godliness and honesty; I cannot determine; but do in my own thoughts most incline to the last, that the *thousand years* only denote a large space of time, (as yet at a great distance,) when the church of God shall freely enjoy their liberty, without such temptations to idolatry, superstition, or other wickedness, as they have yet all along had, either from Jews, pagans, or antichrist's party.

3 And cast him into the bottomless pit, and shut him up, and ᵈset a seal upon him, ᵉthat he should deceive the nations no more, till the thousand years should be fulfilled: and after that he must be loosed a little season.

d Dan. 6. 17.
e ch. 16. 14, 16. ver. 8.

And cast him into the bottomless pit; that is, into hell, his proper place: he shall no longer, or at least not till these thousand years be expired, exercise his power, as *prince of the power of the air,* Eph. ii. 2, or compassing the earth, and *walking up and down in it,* as Job i. 7. *And shut him up, and set a seal upon him;* he shall be restrained as much as one shut up in prison, whose doors are sealed up. *That he should deceive the nations no more, till the thousand years should be fulfilled;* that till this time of God's counsel for the quiet of his church be run out, he shall not deceive people by his old arts. *And after that he must be loosed a little season;* and after that he shall have a liberty again (as ver. 7) for a little time.

f Dan. 7. 9, 22, 27. Matt. 19. 28. Luke 22. 30.
g 1 Cor. 6. 2, 3.
h ch. 6. 9.

4 And I saw ᶠthrones, and they sat upon them, and ᵍjudgment was given unto them: and *I saw* ʰthe souls of them that were beheaded for the witness of Jesus, and for the word of God, and ⁱwhich had not worshipped the beast, ᵏneither his image, neither had received *his* mark upon their foreheads, or in their hands; and they lived and ˡreigned with Christ a thousand years.

i ch. 13. 12.
k ch. 13. 15, 16.
l Rom. 8. 17. 2 Tim. 2. 12. ch. 5. 10.

This is a very difficult text. *Thrones* are places of dignity and judicature; they seem here to signify only places of dignity. *And they sat upon them;* those mentioned afterward in this text sat upon them. *And judgment was given unto them;* that is, a power of judgment, 1 Cor. vi. 2, 3, to be executed afterward. The persons sitting upon these thrones are described to be, 1. Such as had kept themselves from idolatry, or any compliance with antichrist, either in the form of the beast, or of the image of the beast. 2. And for that non-compliance had suffered death, and for witnessing to the truths of Christ contained in his word. These are described as living with Christ in honour and dignity, all that space of the church's rest and tranquillity before expressed. Our learned Dr. More interprets the *thrones* and *judgment,* concerning those thrones or places of judicature, upon which the dragon's officers sat to condemn the saints of God, from whence issued the putting to death of many of the saints of God, and thinks that in this vision there is a recourse to the second thunder. Now these saints are said to *live and reign with Christ a thousand years;* that is, say some, in heaven, in a blessed state of glory, while the militant church upon the earth enjoyed great rest and quiet on earth. Others have thought that these should be raised from the dead, and live with Christ on earth these thousand years. Which notion (if true) will solve a great phenomenon, and render it not improbable, that the number of the saints on earth will, during these thousand years, be enough to rule the world, and overbalance the number of all the wicked of the earth. Those who think thus, judge there will be two resurrections; the first, of martyrs, which shall antedate the general resurrection a thousand years: but the Scripture no where else mentions more than one resurrection. For my own part, I shall freely confess that I do not understand this and the two next verses, nor shall I be positive as to any sense of them: for the spiritual resurrection, as to the martyrs, it was long since past, or else they had died in their sins. But of this see more in the next verse.

5 But the rest of the dead lived not again until the thousand years were finished. This *is* the first resurrection.

By the rest of the dead, some understand all except martyrs; others, only that party who adhered to antichrist. Those who by *the rest* understand all the dead, both good and bad, (the martyrs alone excepted,) judge that there will be two resurrections: the first more particular, of those that have suffered death for Christ; the second general, of all the rest of the dead. I must confess I find a difficulty to allow this; it is too great a point to found upon a single text, in a portion of holy writ so clouded with metaphors as this, and I know no suffragan text. Those who understand by *the rest of the dead,* only the wicked, understand by this living again, a politic life, that is, recovered not their former power, continued as dead men, able to do no mischief, till the thousand years of the church's peace and tranquillity were expired. May this sense of living, and living again, be allowed, it will deliver us from almost all our difficulties about the sense of these verses; for then, by living, in the foregoing verse, is signified a political living, not a resurrection from a natural death. But then ariseth a question, If these beheaded saints did not rise from their natural death, how could they be restored to places of dignity with Christ in the church? To which they answer, That those formerly suffering for the name of Christ, and all the saints upon the earth, are to be considered as one church; and so those formerly beheaded, lived and reigned with Christ in their successors in the same faith; that is, those alive at that time, being restored to their peace, and liberty, and reputation in the world, the martyrs, who were members of the same body, are also said to live. This appears to me the most probable sense: for that the glorified saints should leave heaven (as to their souls) to be again clothed with flesh, and in it to live a thousand years, and be concerned in the following troubles the church should meet with after these thousand years, seems to me to be utterly improbable, and to lay a foundation for so many difficult questions, as will pose the wisest man to answer to reasonable satisfaction. But yet there remains a difficulty, how this restoring God's holy ones to a better state can be called *the first resurrection.* That it may be called a *resurrection* is plain, as the conversion of the Jews, and restoring them to their former state as the church of God is called *life from the dead,* Rom. xi. 15; and the restoration of the witnesses, chap. xi. 11, is called so; though neither the one nor the other were naturally dead. Nor is it unusual in Scriptural and prophetical writings, to speak of people recovered to their former and better state,

REVELATION XX

as being risen from the dead. It may be called *the first*, with reference to that far more excellent state which they shall be put in after the last judgment, when they shall live and reign with Christ in a more happy and glorious manner. If this may not be allowed as the sense of these two verses, I must confess this such a δυσνόητον, or difficulty of Scripture, as I do not understand. I shall proceed with the following verses upon this hypothesis, that this is the sense, though I dare not be positive in it.

6 Blessed and holy *is* he that hath part in the first resurrection: on such ᵐthe second death hath no power, but they shall be ⁿpriests of God and of Christ, °and shall reign with him a thousand years.

m ch. 2. 11. & 21. 8.
n Is. 61. 6. 1 Pet. 2. 9. ch. 1. 6. & 5. 10.
o ver. 4.

That is, they only are holy ones that shall be thus restored to share in the church's happiness, and such as shall not perish eternally; but they shall be as priests to God and Christ, glorifying him with the spiritual sacrifices of prayer and praise, and shall enjoy a quiet and honourable station with Christ upon the earth for a long time.

7 And when the thousand years are expired, ᵖSatan shall be loosed out of his prison,

p ver. 2.

When the long time expressed under the notion of a thousand years shall be expired, God shall take off his restraint from the devil, so as he shall influence the wicked of the earth once more to make opposition to his church.

8 And shall go out ᵠto deceive the nations which are in the four quarters of the earth, ʳGog and Magog, ˢto gather them together to battle: the number of whom *is* as the sand of the sea.

q ver. 3, 10.
r Ezek. 38. 2. & 39. 1.
s ch. 16. 14.

And shall go out to deceive the nations which are in the four quarters of the earth; that is, the devil, being got from under the restraint of Divine Providence, shall fall upon his old work, going about to deceive men over all the world, either tempting them to idolatry, or heresy, or lewdness of life, or (which seemeth most probable) stirring them up to one attempt more to ruin the church. These people are called *Gog and Magog*, about the meaning of which there are various opinions. We read of *Magog*, Gen. x. 2; he was one of the sons of Japheth; see also 1 Chron. i. 5; he inhabited that country called Syria, and from thence, his posterity being multiplied, (as some think,) transplanted some colonies into America. We read of *Gog* no where in Scripture but in Ezekiel, chap. xxxviii., xxxix., where both *Gog* and *Magog* are mentioned as the great enemies of God's ancient Israel. *Gog* there, chap. xxxviii. 2, is named as *the chief prince of Meshech and Tubal*. There are disputes who are meant by *Gog and Magog* in those two chapters. The Jewish rabbies apply the terms to some nations whom the Messiah (expected by them) shall encounter and overcome; but if we consider that prophecy as made in Babylon, and to comfort the people in that captivity, we can hardly think the enemies there intended were to appear at such a distance of time as more than two thousand years, for so many, and more, are elapsed already since Ezekiel's prophecy. The best interpreters therefore rather think, that Antiochus, and the race of Seleucus, (a king of Syria, who in those quarters of the world succeeded Alexander, of whom we read in the book of Maccabees,) is there intended, whose ruin is there foretold, as being a great enemy to the Jews after their return from Babylon; yet some think, that in both these chapters Ezekiel prophesied of the same *Gog and Magog* here intended, which should be the last enemies of the church. The papists, who (according to their interest) contend for antichrist as yet to come, make *Gog and Magog* here to signify some king or kings that shall join with antichrist when he appeareth. Others think that *Gog and Magog*, in this place, signifies more generally, a colluvies, or mixed company of all wicked men, a very great multitude, who shall come from all parts, only typified by the *Gog and Magog* in Ezekiel, as being like them, 1. For number; 2. In their design to ruin the church, upon its restoration to a more quiet, peaceable state; 3. And who shall be ruined like them, by the more than ordinary providence of God; for the *Gog and Magog* mentioned in Ezekiel, are described in three texts of that prophecy as coming from the north, but these are described as coming from the four quarters of the world: this seemeth a much more probable opinion than theirs, who will have them some particular nations, whether Americans, Turks, or Indians. *The number of whom is as the sand of the sea:* these enemies shall make a vast number, therefore compared to the sand of the sea; and in this they hold a proportion also with the *Gog and Magog* mentioned in Ezekiel, who were *a great company*, chap. xxxviii. 4, *many people*, ver. 6, *covering the land*, ver. 9.

9 ᵗAnd they went up on the breadth of the earth, and compassed the camp of the saints about, and the beloved city: and fire came down from God out of heaven, and devoured them.

t Is. 8. 8. Ezek. 38. 9, 16.

And they went up on the breadth of the earth; that is, in all parts of it where the church of Christ was. *And compassed the camp of the saints about, and the beloved city;* the church of God (typified by old Jerusalem, which was God's beloved city) they encompassed in a military order and manner, designing to destroy it, or make it subject to their lusts. *And fire came down from God out of heaven, and devoured them:* thus Ezekiel prophesied of the issue of the *Gog and Magog* by him mentioned, Ezek. xxxviii. 18—22: ver. 22, *And I will plead against him with pestilence and with blood; and I will rain upon him, and upon his bands, and upon the many people that are with him, an overflowing rain, and great hailstones, fire, and brimstone*. The meaning is, that God would destroy them with a quick and terrible destruction, such as is that destruction of persons and places which is by fire.

10 ᵘAnd the devil that deceived them was cast into the lake of fire and brimstone, ˣwhere the beast and the false prophet *are*, and ʸshall be tormented day and night for ever and ever.

u ver. 8.
x ch. 19. 20.
y ch. 14. 10, 11.

After this shall be the end of the world, when the devil shall be restrained to hell, the place of torments, where he shall have all heathens, and all the rabble of antichrist, who shall be there tormented constantly and for ever and ever.

11 And I saw a great white throne, and him that sat on it, from whose face ᶻthe earth and the heaven fled away; ᵃand there was found no place for them.

z 2 Pet. 3. 7, 10, 11.
ch. 21. 1.
a Dan. 2. 35.

God now giveth his prophet a vision of the last day, the day of judgment. He seeth *a throne*, a place of judicature; said to be *great*, to denote its gloriousness; *white*, to signify Christ's purity and holiness in his judging the world. And he saw Christ sitting upon it, and all old things passing away. Peter thus describes this flying away of the earth and heavens; *The heavens shall pass away with a great noise, and the elements shall melt with fervent heat, the earth also and the works therein shall be burned up*, 2 Pet. iii. 10. *All these things shall be dissolved*, ver. 11.

12 And I saw the dead, ᵇsmall and great, stand before God; ᶜand the books were opened: and another ᵈbook was opened, which is *the book* of life: and the dead were judged out of those things which were written in the books, ᵉaccording to their works.

b ch. 19. 5.
r Dan. 7. 10.
d Ps. 69. 28.
Dan. 12. 1.
Phil. 4. 3.
ch. 3. 5. & 13. 8. & 21. 27.
e Jer. 17. 10. & 32. 19.
Mat. 16. 27.
Rom. 2. 6.
ch. 2. 23. & 22. 12.
ver. 13.

The former verses gave us an account of Christ, the great Judge of the quick and the dead in the last day; the Lord Jesus Christ sat upon a throne of glory, about to execute his last holy and righteous judgment. Now he describes the persons to be judged, viz. all, both *small and great*. *And the books were opened:* to show the justice and righteousness according to which this Judge would proceed, books are said to be opened. What books? The book of God's law; the book of God's omniscience; the book of men's consciences. In the former is contained what all men should have done; the two latter will discover what they have thought, spake, or done in the flesh. *And an-*

REVELATION XX, XXI

other book was opened, which is the book of life; the book of life, mentioned chap. iii. 5, by which is to be understood the book of God's election, wherein are the names of all those who, being from eternity chosen to life, were redeemed with the blood of Christ, and afterwards effectually called, justified, and sanctified. *And the dead were judged out of those things which were written in the books, according to their works;* according to these books shall the last judgment be, Rom. ii. 16, with respect had unto every one's work.

13 And the sea gave up the dead which were in it; ᶠand death and ‖hell delivered up the dead which were in them: ᵍand they were judged every man according to their works.

f ch. 6. 8.
‖ Or, *the grave.*
g ver. 12.

By *hell* is meant all places where the dead are; whosoever shall be at that day in the state of the dead; the bodies of men, whether buried in the earth or sea; and the souls of men, whether they be in the place of torments or happiness, shall all be re-united to their bodies, that they may both in soul and body receive their final doom of eternal happiness, or eternal misery, accordingly as they have lived in the world; and those who shall be alive at that day, who shall be *changed,* (as the apostle speaks, 1 Cor. xv. 51,) are to be counted dead in the sense of this text, their change being instead of death to them. It is not said they shall be judged for their works, (though that as to the wicked is true,) but *according to their works;* which is true as to the elect, who though their names be written in the book of life, yet must work righteousness; and they shall have judgment of absolution, not according to the perfection, but the sincerity, of their works, done in obedience to the will of God.

14 And ʰdeath and hell were cast into the lake of fire. ⁱThis is the second death.

h 1 Cor. 15. 26, 54, 55.
i ver. 6.
ch. 21. 8.

And death and hell were cast into lake of fire; there shall be no more natural death, nor any more separate state of souls, (so ᾅδης signifies,) they shall all be swallowed up in the issue of the last judgment, where some shall go into life, some into eternal condemnation. Dr. More expoundeth it of the whole region of mortality being set on fire at the last thunder. *This,* as to the wicked of the earth, *is the second death,* mentioned chap. ii. 11.

15 And whosoever was not found written in the book of life ᵏwas cast into the lake of fire.

k ch. 19. 20.

The book of life: see note on ver. 12.

CHAP. XXI.

A new heaven and a new earth, 1. *The new Jerusalem,* 2. *The blessedness of God's people,* 3—7: *the judgment of the wicked,* 8. *A description of the heavenly Jerusalem,* 9—27.

This chapter begins with the vision of *the new heaven and the new earth,* by which all understand a new state of the church, but are divided in their opinions, whether what is spoken be to be understood of the church militant upon the earth, or of the church triumphant in heaven. Those who understand it of the church militant here upon earth, are divided in their opinions as to that period of the church which is here spoken of; some understanding it of the thousand years after the time of Constantine, for which I see no reason (nor, I believe, will any that wisely considers the state of the church in that time); others understanding it of the thousand years mentioned chap. xx., in which (as was said) the church should enjoy great quiet and peace. I must confess I choose much rather to agree with them who judge it signifieth the church triumphant, being overcome with the reasons given by those reverend authors, a summary of which may be found in Mr. Pool's Latin Synopsis. 1. That interpretation carrieth on the history in order; whereas, according to the other, we must say the history, chap. xx. 1—5, was interrupted by the battle with Gog and Magog, and the account of the day of judgment, ver. 7—15. 2. In reason, as the close of the former chapter gave us an account of the issue of the day of judgment, as to wicked men, so this should give us some account how it should fare with the saints. 3. We shall find some things in the *new Jerusalem* here described, which will agree to no state of the church upon earth: see ver. 22, 23.

AND ᵃI saw a new heaven and a new earth: ᵇfor the first heaven and the first earth were passed away; and there was no more sea.

a Is. 65. 17. & 66. 22.
b 2 Pet. 3. 13.
b ch. 20. 11.

A new heaven and a new earth; a new and glorious state of things relating to the church. *For the first heaven and the first earth were passed away; and there was no more sea;* for now there was an end to the world, and all the troubles that the people of God had met with in it, as well as the material earth, heaven, and sea, were passed away. This new heaven was prophesied of of old by Isaiah, and more lately by Peter, 2 Pet. iii. 13.

2 And I John saw ᶜthe holy city, new Jerusalem, coming down from God out of heaven, prepared ᵈas a bride adorned for her husband.

c Is. 52. 1. Gal. 4. 26. Heb. 11. 10. & 12. 22. & 13. 14. ch. 3. 12. ver. 10.
d ch. 54. 5. & 61. 10. 2 Cor. 11. 2.

The holy city, new Jerusalem; that is, the whole chorus or number of the elect of God, answering God's chosen people in Jerusalem. *Coming down from God out of heaven;* not locally coming down, but who had their original from heaven, and were all persons of heavenly minds. *Prepared as a bride adorned for her husband;* in their best robes of glory, such as brides use to wear, when on their wedding-day they adorn themselves for their bridegrooms.

3 And I heard a great voice out of heaven saying, Behold, ᵉthe tabernacle of God *is* with men, and he will dwell with them, and they shall be his people, and God himself shall be with them, *and be* their God.

e Lev. 26. 11, 12.
Ezek. 43. 7.
2 Cor. 6. 16.
ch. 7. 15.

What is said here, is applicable to the church of God in this life, yea, to every true believer, whose body is said to be *the temple of the Lord,* and in whom the Lord *dwells,* according to the phrase of the Holy Ghost in many places of the New Testament; of whom it is also true, that God is *with them, and* will *be their God;* but more especially applicable to the church triumphant, as dwelling signifies a constancy of abode, and more full manifestation of a person. The state of the saints in glory is thus described by a being *ever with the Lord,* 1 Thess. iv. 17.

4 ᶠAnd God shall wipe away all tears from their eyes; and ᵍthere shall be no more death, ʰneither sorrow, nor crying, neither shall there be any more pain: for the former things are passed away.

f Is. 25. 8.
ch. 7. 17.
g 1 Cor. 15. 26, 54.
ch. 20. 14.
h Is. 35. 10. & 61. 3. & 65. 19.

Scarce any of the passages in this verse, taken in the plain, literal sense, are applicable to any state of the church in this life: for though in the thousand years, mentioned chap. xx., the state of the church (as it is presumed) will be very happy comparatively to what it ever was before, and free from its enemies' molestations and persecutions; yet I think none hath asserted that in that time no members of it shall die, or be sick, or have any sorrow or pain. There must be a great allowance of figures, if we will apply this to any state of the militant church; but all will be literally true as to the church in heaven.

5 And ⁱhe that sat upon the throne said, ᵏBehold, I make all things new. And he said unto me, Write: for ˡthese words are true and faithful.

i ch. 4. 2, 9. & 5. 1. & 20. 11.
k Is. 43. 19.
2 Cor. 5. 17.
l ch. 19. 9.

And he that sat upon the throne, that is, Christ, *said, Behold, I make all things new;* behold, I will put a new face upon all things; the state of my people shall not for ever be a troubled and afflicted state. *And he said unto me, Write:* because the vision is to be for an appointed time, and what I now tell thee will not be accomplished of many years, and yet the knowledge and prospect of it, and meditations upon it, are of highest importance to keep up the spirits of my people under all their sufferings, during

REVELATION XXI

that time of the dragon (the Romish heathen emperors) not yet run out, and the twelve hundred and sixty years of antichrist, &c., therefore write it, that all my people in all ages may know it, believe it, and suffer patiently in the hopes of it. *For these words are true and faithful;* for what I tell thee is what comes from the true and faithful Witness, and shall have a certain being in its time.

6 And he said unto me, ᵐ It is done. ⁿ I am Alpha and Omega, the beginning and the end. ᵒ I will give unto him that is athirst of the fountain of the water of life freely.

And he said unto me, It is done; the world is at an end, and all my threatenings against my enemies, and promises to my people, are now fulfilled, in the eternal damnation of the one, and deliverance and salvation of the other. *I am Alpha and Omega, the beginning and the end:* I first made the world, and I have put a period to it. I first gave out those promises and threatenings, and I have now fulfilled them. *I will give unto him that is athirst of the fountain of the water of life freely;* and my people who have thirsted after my righteousness and salvation, now have it freely, and shall drink, and drink abundantly.

7 He that overcometh shall inherit ‖ all things; and ᵖ I will be his God, and he shall be my son.

He that overcometh, shall inherit all things: God revealed this to John almost sixteen hundred years since; and how long it shall be before this glorious time shall come, God alone knows: the most of this time hath been, and will be, a time of fighting with the world, the flesh, and the devil; but whoever he be that shall fight this good fight, and come out of it a conqueror, shall inherit all the joys and happiness of heaven. *I will be his God, and he shall be my son:* I will be to him all in all; I will be his God to love and glorify him, and he shall be with me as my son, to live with me for ever and ever.

8 ᑫ But the fearful, and unbelieving, and the abominable, and murderers, and whoremongers, and sorcerers, and idolaters, and all liars, shall have their part in ʳ the lake which burneth with fire and brimstone: which is the second death.

All those who are without the church invisible, whether profane persons, (such are murderers, whoremongers, sorcerers, liars,) or idolaters, or unbelievers and hypocrites, shall all be cast to hell. *The fearful,* who, through fear of losing their reputation, estates, honours, or lives, deny me, or shall not dare to own me. *And unbelieving;* such as will not agree to the proposition of my gospel, or will not come to me that they might have life. *The abominable;* sodomites, and such as live in beastly lusts. *Murderers;* such as, without any warrant from God, take away men's lives wilfully. *Whoremongers;* such as defile their neighbours' wives. *Sorcerers;* such as exercise witchcraft, consult the devil, and trade with familiar spirits. *Idolaters;* whether they commit the idolatry of Ahab, giving Divine adoration to the creatures, as the term of their worship; or the idolatry of Jeroboam, worshipping the true God by images. *And all liars;* and all such as are liars with their tongues, speaking what they know to be false; or liars in practice, that is, hypocrites, seeming to be what they are not. *Shall have their part in the lake which burneth with fire and brimstone: which is the second death:* all these, and all such like, shall be eternally damned.

9 And there came unto me one of ˢ the seven angels which had the seven vials full of the seven last plagues, and talked with me, saying, Come hither, I will shew thee ᵗ the bride, the Lamb's wife.

One of the seven angels; one of those mentioned chap. xv. 6. *I will show thee the bride, the Lamb's wife;* I will show thee the whole church, (invisible heretofore,) the glorious state of the church triumphant, under the representation of a great city.

10 And he carried me away ᵘ in the spirit to a great and high mountain, and shewed me ˣ that great city, the holy Jerusalem, descending out of heaven from God,

And he carried me away in the spirit; in a trance or ecstasy, as before. *To a great and high mountain;* from whence men use to have the best prospect of cities, or other places. *And showed me that great city, the holy Jerusalem, descending out of heaven from God;* there he caused me to see the whole triumphant church, answering as the antitype to Jerusalem, but more holy; being not of the earth, earthly, but from heaven, heavenly, founded, built up, and adorned by God.

11 ʸ Having the glory of God: and her light *was* like unto a stone most precious, even like a jasper stone, clear as crystal;

Having the glory of God; a most excellent glory, received from God. *And her light,* that is, (as some interpret it,) that which gave her light, (as the sun is called the light of the earth,) or her enlightener, *was like unto a stone most precious,* was Christ himself, who is a stone most precious: ver. 23, *The Lamb is the light thereof. Like a jasper stone:* see chap. iv. 3. God is there compared to a *jasper stone;* here, to a *jasper stone, clear as crystal.* They say of the jasper stone, that it is very glorious to the eye, precious and pure; so it is very fit to resemble in part a pure and glorious God.

12 And had a wall great and high, *and* had ᶻ twelve gates, and at the gates twelve angels, and names written thereon, which are *the names* of the twelve tribes of the children of Israel:

And had a wall, that is, this city, by which is meant the church of God, *had a wall great and high.* Walls are for the protection and defence of a place; the higher and greater they are, the greater defence and protection they give. By this God is meant, who is often called his people's Rock and Defence. *And had twelve gates:* the use of the gates of a city, are to let persons in and out. The church is said to have twelve gates, because of the free liberty of access to the church while it was militant, and to signify that the church in heaven will be made up of persons come into it from all parts; or for the greater state and glory of it. Some think, because of the twelve apostles, who were the first ministers of the gospel who admitted men into this church. *And at the gates twelve angels;* denoting the guard of angels about the church; unless by *angels* ministers be to be understood, proportioned to the several parts of the church. *And names written thereon, which are the names of the twelve tribes of the children of Israel;* because as, of old, only the twelve tribes of God's chosen people Israel made up the church in that period; so only God's elect and peculiar people, typified by that Israel, come in at the gates of this church. It is very observable, how God affects the number of twelve in the affairs of his church.

13 ᵃ On the east three gates; on the north three gates; on the south three gates; and on the west three gates.

To signify it was made up of persons from all parts of the world. This agreeth with Ezekiel's vision, chap. xlviii. 31—34. The triumphant church will be a collection of believers, who from all nations have come into it.

14 And the wall of the city had twelve foundations, and ᵇ in them the names of the twelve apostles of the Lamb.

And the wall of the city had twelve foundations; the ancient church of God was founded in twelve patriarchs, and twelve tribes; the gospel church in twelve apostles; Christ is the only foundation of both, 1 Cor. iii. 11, but he is the foundation upon which the church is built. The twelve apostles are called the foundations *per quæ,* or *per quos,* by which the gospel church had its beginning. *And in them the names of the twelve apostles of the Lamb;* as workmen sometimes set their names upon foundation-stones, by which it is made known who were they that builded the wall.

REVELATION XXI

c Ezek. 40. 3.
Zech. 2. 1.
ch. 11. 1.

15 And he that talked with me ^c had a golden reed to measure the city, and the gates thereof, and the wall thereof.

This seemeth to signify the transcendency of the state of the church now, to what it was before; it was then measured by a man, chap. xi., now by an angel; then by an ordinary reed, now by a golden reed.

16 And the city lieth foursquare, and the length is as large as the breadth: and he measured the city with the reed, twelve thousand furlongs. The length and the breadth and the height of it are equal.

The church militant, measured by the reed of the word, is unequal in its parts; some parts of it are purer than others; but in the new Jerusalem all parts shall be equal in perfection and purity, as all the sides of a thing foursquare are equal.

17 And he measured the wall thereof, an hundred *and* forty *and* four cubits, *according to* the measure of a man, that is, of the angel.

This could not be the measure of the compass, (it was for that much too little,) nor of the height or breadth, (for either of them it was much too great,) from whence Dr. Potter concluded, it must be the square measure; so as the height and breadth of it was twelve cubits, for twelve times twelve make one hundred and forty-four. *According to the measure of a man, that is, of the angel*; as men use to measure, and as this angel measured, who appeared as a man in this action.

18 And the building of the wall of it was *of* jasper: and the city *was* pure gold, like unto clear glass.

And the building of the wall of it was of jasper; strong and impregnable, not subject to impressions from enemies, as it is said of the jasper, that no hammer will break it. *And the city was pure gold*; all that make up this city are perfect and noble. *Like unto clear glass*; pure, without spots.

d Is. 54. 11.

19 ^d And the foundations of the wall of the city *were* garnished with all manner of precious stones. The first foundation *was* jasper; the second, sapphire; the third, a chalcedony; the fourth, an emerald;

And the foundations of the wall of the city, by which, we noted before, are to be understood the apostles, who, building upon the one foundation, Christ Jesus, by their holy doctrine laid the beginnings of the gospel churches, the first stones, (upon the Rock Christ,) which were afterwards multiplied, others being builded upon them, till the whole church was perfected.

20 The fifth, sardonyx; the sixth, sardius; the seventh, chrysolyte; the eighth, beryl; the ninth, a topaz; the tenth, a chrysoprasus; the eleventh, a jacinth; the twelfth, an amethyst.

I cannot tell what to make of these *precious stones*, with which they are said to be *garnished*, unless it be their spiritual gifts and habits of grace; the various manifestations of the Holy Spirit given to the apostles to profit the church withal, with which they adorned the doctrine of the gospel, and won upon the pagan world, making themselves admirable in the eyes of men and women. Nor were it hard to descant upon these several sorts of stones, and to show of what graces they may be types: the *jasper*, of steadiness and constancy; the *sapphire*, of heavenly-mindedness (it being a stone of the colour of the heavens); the *chalcedony*, of zeal; the *emerald*, of vigour and liveliness; the *sardonyx*, (a stone of various colours,) of various gifts and graces; the *sardius*, of courage and fortitude, and a readiness to shed their blood for Christ; the *chrysolyte*, of love, or wisdom, and knowledge; the *beryl*, of a quickness of sight and understanding; the *topaz*, of searching out Divine mysteries; the *chrysoprasus*, of gravity and severity; the *jacinth*, of spiritual joy, calmness, and serenity of mind; the *amethyst*, of sobriety and temperance. But it seemeth to me too great curiosity to philosophize so far upon the nature of these stones; take them together, they probably signify all the gifts and graces of the blessed apostles, by which the religion of the gospel was first commended, and made to appear lovely to the world.

21 And the twelve gates *were* twelve pearls; every several gate was of one pearl: ^e and the street of the city *was* pure gold, as it were transparent glass.

e ch. 22. 2.

I am not willing to descant further in particulars, conjecturing (for it is no more) what each metaphorical term signifies in this unusual description of a city. I do think the scope of the whole is no more, than to let us know that the mansions of heaven will be most glorious places, giving the souls of those to whom God shall give to enter into them, an infinite satisfaction, beyond what the most rich and glorious things in the world can give our outward senses.

22 ^f And I saw no temple therein: for the Lord God Almighty and the Lamb are the temple of it.

f John 4. 23.

And I saw no temple therein: I cannot take *temple* so strictly here, as those who understand all this but as a description of the blessed state of the militant church, during the thousand years; but understand it of all such worship and ordinances as we serve God in, and by, in this life. *For the Lord God Almighty and the Lamb are the temple of it*; the immediate fruition of God shall there supply all, God shall be *all in all*, 1 Cor. xv. 28. Ordinances are but perspectives, of use in this life to see God at a distance; means, whereby we know in part: there we shall see God face to face, and know him as we are known. The saints there shall want nothing, and therefore shall not need a house of prayer; they shall know perfectly, and therefore will not need any to teach them; they shall always see Christ, and so will need no sacraments whereby to remember him.

23 ^g And the city had no need of the sun, neither of the moon, to shine in it: for the glory of God did lighten it, and the Lamb *is* the light thereof.

g Is. 24. 23.
& 60. 19, 20.
ch. 22. 5.
ver. 11.

The sun and *the moon* are the two great luminaries of the world, which God hath made, the one to rule the day, the other to rule the night; in heaven there will be no need of any of these. *Light*, in Scripture, (in its metaphorical notion,) signifies knowledge or comfort; there will in heaven be no need of any created beings, to help us to either of these; God and Christ shall there fill the souls of his saints with knowledge and joy not to be expressed.

24 ^h And the nations of them which are saved shall walk in the light of it: and the kings of the earth do bring their glory and honour into it.

h Is. 60. 3, 5,
11. & 66. 12.
Tob. 13. 11.

And the nations of them which are saved shall walk in the light of it; all that go to heaven shall be thus happy. *And the kings of the earth do bring their glory and honour into it*; and such kings of the earth as shall come into heaven, shall see all their honour and glory swallowed up in the glory and honour of that place and state; and confess that all their crowns are infinitely short of this blessed and glorious crown, all their thrones nothing to these thrones.

25 ⁱ And the gates of it shall not be shut at all by day: for ^k there shall be no night there.

i Is. 60. 11.
k Is. 60. 20.
Zech. 14. 7.
ch. 22. 5.

And the gates of it shall not be shut at all by day: the reason of shutting a city's gates, is either to shut out enemies, or to keep in such as are within: there will be no need of shutting these gates on either of these accounts; there will be no enemies to fear, and those that are within this city will have no need nor desire to go out. *For there shall be no night there*: we do not ordinarily shut our city gates by day, but there shall be nothing but day, no night in a natural or metaphorical sense.

26 ^l And they shall bring the glory and honour of the nations into it.

l ver. 24.

Whatsoever is excellent or desirable in the world, shall

REVELATION XXI. XXII.

be supplied to the souls of those that are in heaven, by good of another make, but which shall be equally (nay, infinitely more) satisfactory to the soul.

27 And ᵐthere shall in no wise enter into it any thing that defileth, neither *whatsoever* worketh abomination, or *maketh* a lie: but they which are written in the Lamb's ⁿbook of life.

And there shall in no wise enter into it: in the Greek there are two negative particles, which though in the Latin they make an affirmative, yet in the Greek make a stronger negative, which we translate *in no wise,* or by no means. *Any thing that defileth:* this strongly denying particle is brought to make the bar excluding all unclean persons from heaven evident. And alas! how often had this need be denied, to make men and women, mad of their lusts, believe it! The word translated, *that defileth,* signifieth, what is common; nothing. no person that hath not by a holy life separated himself from the world, and all sin and wickedness. and dedicated himself to God. *Neither whatsoever worketh abomination;* no profane or lewd person. *Or maketh a lie;* nor any false or lying hypocrites, nor any idolaters, for idols are lies. *But they which are written in the Lamb's book of life;* none but those whose names are written in the book of life, predetermined to salvation, and redeemed with the blood of Christ. Some are not pleased with this sense; but what other thing can be meant? This is, at least, the sixth time we have met with this phrase in this book, chap. iii. 5; xiii. 8; xvii. 8; xx. 12, 15. It is also mentioned, Phil. iv. 3. And what else can be meant in Moses's prayer, Exod. xxxii. 32? It is twice (chap. xiii. 8; xvii. 8) said, that names were written in it *from the foundation of the world.* God hath a particular, certain. infallible knowledge who are his, and had it from eternity; and whence he should know it, without willing of it, is very hard to conceive. It is called *the Lamb's book,* to let us know, that the act of redemption by Christ bears proportion to the counsels of election.

CHAP. XXII

The river and tree of life, 1, 2. *The glorious state of the servants of God,* 3—7. *John is forbidden by the angel to worship him,* 8, 9; *and commanded to seal up the prophecy,* 10, 11. *Christ's coming and eternity,* 12, 13. *The blessedness of them that do God's commandments,* 14—17. *Nothing must be added to or taken from this prophecy,* 18 —20. *The concluding benediction,* 21.

AND he shewed me ᵃa pure river of water of life, clear as crystal, proceeding out of the throne of God and of the Lamb.

And he; the angel, who showed him all before mentioned. *Showed me a pure river of water of life, clear as crystal:* no place can be happy without the accommodation of water; those places have the best accommodation of it that are near a river, especially a pure river. Let us know, that in heaven there shall be no want of any thing that can make the saints happy, it is described as having by it, or running through it, *a pure river,* whose water is clear, and no ordinary water, but such as giveth and preserveth life. What could this signify, but the pure and unmixed joys of heaven? *Proceeding out of the throne of God and of the Lamb;* flowing from the saints there enjoying of God and Jesus Christ.

2 ᵇIn the midst of the street of it, and on either side of the river, *was there* ᶜthe tree of life, which bare twelve *manner of* fruits, *and* yielded her fruit every month: and the leaves of the tree *were* ᵈfor the healing of the nations.

In the midst of the street of it, and on either side of the river, was there the tree of life: trees, especially fruit trees, and those laden with fruit, and variety of fruit, and such as, instead of being prejudicial to life, are wholesome, and give life, are very beautiful, especially in or near a city. The city in Ezekiel's vision, chap. xlvii. 7, is thus described. This expression further shows the infinite pleasure and soul-satisfaction the saints shall have in heaven. But we are further told here, that the tree here was *the tree of life;* a manifest allusion to a tree so called in old Paradise, Gen. ii. 9; and who can this agree to, but Christ? *Which bare twelve manner of fruits;* in whom all fulness dwelt, the fulness of the Godhead, and who was anointed, and received the Spirit without measure. *And yielded her fruit every month;* and is daily distributing of his fulness to his people. *And the leaves of the trees were for the healing of the nations;* and in whom there is nothing useless, but what tends either to the life or healing of his people out of all nations.

3 And ᵉthere shall be no more curse: ᶠbut the throne of God and of the Lamb shall be in it; and his servants shall serve him:

And there shall be no more curse; nothing that is devoted to the devil, κατανάθεμα, no accursed person, or thing. *But the throne of God and of the Lamb shall be in it;* the presence of a holy and pure God will prevent and forbid that. *And his servants shall serve him;* it is a place in which God alone shall be served by his own servants.

4 And ᵍthey shall see his face; and ʰhis name *shall be* in their foreheads.

And they shall see his face; it is a phrase by which the happiness of the glorified saints is oft expressed, Matt. v. 8; 1 Cor. xiii. 12; Heb. xii. 14; 1 John iii. 2; they shall enjoy him immediately. *And his name shall be in their foreheads;* there shall be none that have the name of the beast on their foreheads; they shall have God's name on their foreheads, and be so manifested to be the sons of God.

5 ⁱAnd there shall be no night there; and they need no candle, neither light of the sun; for ᵏthe Lord God giveth them light: ˡand they shall reign for ever and ever.

See the notes on chap. xxi. 23.

6 And he said unto me, ᵐThese sayings *are* faithful and true: and the Lord God of the holy prophets ⁿsent his angel to shew unto his servants the things which must shortly be done.

All the words of this book, particularly the things of the last vision, are such as proceed from him who is *the faithful witness,* chap. i. 5; iii. 14; from him who *was called faithful,* chap. xix. 11; and which God will show himself true and faithful in bringing to pass: and such things as God hath revealed to his prophets under the Old Testament in part, and now to me his prophet, to show to his people the things that shall come to pass, and shall shortly begin to be accomplished: see chap. i. 1.

7 ᵒBehold, I come quickly: ᵖblessed *is* he that keepeth the sayings of the prophecy of this book.

I come quickly to the last judgment. He is a happy man that observeth and keepeth in memory, that understandeth, believeth, and liveth up to *the prophecy of this book.*

8 And I John saw these things, and heard *them.* And when I had heard and seen, ᑫI fell down to worship before the feet of the angel which shewed me these things.

I John saw these things; I saw the vision. *And heard them;* I heard the words spoken to me relating to them.

9 Then saith he unto me, ʳSee *thou do it* not: for I am thy fellowservant, and of thy brethren the prophets, and of them which keep the sayings of this book: worship God.

See thou do it not: see the notes on chap. xix. 10. *For I am thy fellow servant, and of thy brethren the prophets;* whose employment is the same with thine, to reveal the

REVELATION XXII

will of God; *and of them which keep the sayings of this book*; yea, and a brother to all the servants of God. Thou mistakest the object of thine adoration, I am a created being, and can accept no such homage.

10 ^sAnd he saith unto me, Seal not the sayings of the prophecy of this book : ^tfor the time is at hand.

And he saith unto me; this *he* is Christ, as appeareth from ver. 12. 13. *Seal not the sayings of the prophecy of this book;* let these things be open to be promulgated, and published to the whole church. *For the time is at hand;* for it will not be long before they shall begin to be fulfilled.

11 ^uHe that is unjust, let him be unjust still : and he which is filthy, let him be filthy still: and he that is righteous, let him be righteous still : and he that is holy, let him be holy still.

He that is unjust, let him be unjust still: and he which is filthy, let him be filthy still: it may be the keeping of this book open, and the publication of it, will displease wicked and filthy men; but let them be displeased, the truths of God must not be concealed. *And he that is righteous, let him be righteous still: and he that is holy, let him be holy still:* it will, on the other side, confirm the servants of God in their faith, patience, and holiness, and all the fruits of righteousness.

12 ^xAnd, behold, I come quickly; and ^ymy reward *is* with me, ^zto give every man according as his work shall be,

I come quickly, to the last judgment, as before, ver. 7. *And my reward is with me;* I bring with me a power and authority to recompense every man according to what he hath done, chap. xx. 13; Dan. xii. 2; Matt. xxv. 34, 35, &c.; Rom. ii. 6.

13 ^aI am Alpha and Omega, the beginning and the end, the first and the last.

See the notes on chap. i. 8; xxi. 6.

14 ^bBlessed *are* they that do his commandments, that they may have right ^cto the tree of life, ^dand may enter in through the gates into the city.

Blessed are they that do his commandments; that believe in the Lord Jesus Christ, (for that is the great commandment of the gospel,) and live in conformity to the law of God. *That they may have right to the tree of life;* to Christ, called before, *the tree of life,* ver. 2, by virtue of the promise, chap. ii. 7, for no works of ours will give us a right of purchase to it. *And may enter in through the gates into the city;* that they may enter into heaven; the joys and pleasures of which have been described under the metaphor of a great and glorious city.

15 For ^ewithout *are* ^fdogs, and sorcerers, and whoremongers, and murderers, and idolaters, and whosoever loveth and maketh a lie.

Without heaven, that is, in hell, shall be all *dogs* that bark at, and bite, and devour the church of God, all profane persons, idolaters, and hypocrites: see chap. xxi. 8, 27; 1 Cor. vi. 9, 10; and the notes there.

16 ^gI Jesus have sent mine angel to testify unto you these things in the churches. ^hI am the root and the offspring of David, *and* ⁱthe bright and morning star.

I Jesus have sent mine angel to testify unto you these things in the churches: in these words Christ owneth the Revelation as his; the angel did but testify, John did but hear and write it. *I am the root and the offspring of David;* David's Lord, and yet his Son: his Root, as I am God, and gave a being to his family, as to all the families of the earth; and yet his Son, a Branch out of the root of Jesse. *And the bright and morning star;* who, as the morning-star first brings or prognosticates light to the world, so have myself first published my gospel, or this Revelation, to give light to my people, concerning the fate of my people to the last day.

17 And the Spirit and ^kthe bride say, Come. And let him that heareth say, Come. ^lAnd let him that is athirst come. And whosoever will, let him take the water of life freely.

And the Spirit; the spirit in the hearts of believers, or rather, the Holy Spirit. *And the bride say, Come;* because *the bride,* that is, the church, is also mentioned, to desire the second coming of Christ to judgment. *And let him that heareth say, Come;* and every one that heareth of and believeth these things, should also desire the same thing. *And let him that is athirst come;* and in order to that, every one that wanteth, and is sensible of his want of righteousness, or any habit of grace, is also invited unto Christ, under the notion of *the water of life,* to take him *freely,* as Isa. lv. 1.

18 For I testify unto every man that heareth the words of the prophecy of this book, ^mIf any man shall add unto these things, God shall add unto him the plagues that are written in this book:

I Christ, or I John, testify to every one to whose hands or ears the words of this book shall come, That if any man shall invent new prophecies contrary to the prophecies contained in this book, God shall severely punish him, by adding to him the plagues threatened against sinners in this book.

19 And if any man shall take away from the words of the book of this prophecy, ⁿGod shall take away his part ‖ out of the book of life, and out of ^othe holy city, and *from* the things which are written in this book.

Divines generally do further extend the sense of these two verses, considering this as the last portion of holy writ, not only placed last in our Bibles, but revealed and written last. They conceive these verses the seal of all canonical Scripture, and that God here denounces a curse to those who shall pretend any new revelations of his will, other than what are to be found in the books of the Old and New Testament; as also against all those who shall deny, corrupt, or deprave any part of them. God, as to such persons, saith, they shall not have any such part or portion in heaven, as they would pretend a right to, or seemed to have.

20 He which testifieth these things saith, ^pSurely I come quickly; ^qAmen. ^rEven so, come, Lord Jesus.

He which testifieth these things saith, Surely I come quickly; that is, Christ, who publisheth these things by his angel, or by his servant John, saith he is quickly coming to judgment. *Amen;* John replies, Lord, let it be so. *Even so, come, Lord Jesus;* this expounds *Amen* used here as a particle of wishing and desiring, though it may be interpreted as an assertive particle, and joined to the former part of the sentence.

21 ^sThe grace of our Lord Jesus Christ *be* with you all. Amen.

This is a salutation used by the apostles in all their Epistles, containing a desire of the fulness and increase of all grace, very proper here upon the prospect which John in this Revelation had, of the long and great trials the church would meet with before the glorious appearance of our blessed Lord and Saviour.

To God, the Author of this, and all the other books of holy writ, be honour and glory.

THE END.